Paul Lauter
Trinity College
General Editor

Richard Yarborough
University of California at Los Angeles
Associate General Editor

Juan Bruce-Novoa
University of California at Irvine

Jackson Bryer
University of Maryland

Elaine Hedges
Towson State University

Anne Goodwyn Jones
University of Florida

Amy Ling
University of Wisconsin—Madison

Wendy Martin
Claremont Graduate University

Charles Molesworth
Queens College, City University of New York

Carla Mulford
Pennsylvania State University

Raymund Paredes
University of California at Los Angeles

Linda Wagner-Martin
University of North Carolina, Chapel Hill

Andrew O. Wiget
New Mexico State University

John Alberti
Northern Kentucky University
Editor, Instructor's Guide

Randall Bass
Georgetown University
Editor, Electronic Resources

The Heath Anthology of American Literature

THIRD EDITION

Volume 1

Houghton Mifflin Company
Boston New York

For Elaine Hedges (1927–1997), our friend and colleague.

Sponsoring Editor: Jayne M. Fargnoli
Senior Associate Editor: Janet Edmonds
Assistant Editor: Leah Strauss
Senior Project Editor: Rosemary R. Jaffe
Production/Design Coordinator: Jennifer Meyer Dare
Director of Manufacturing: Michael O'Dea
Marketing Manager: Nancy Lyman

Cover design: Rebecca Fagan
Cover photograph: Detail from *Acoma: Mesa Plain,* by Tryntje Van Ness Seymour, from the limited edition portfolio, *Acoma,* published by Lime Rock Press, a small Connecticut press. Copyright © 1979 by Tryntje Van Ness Seymour.

page 1: *An Indian Conjurer,* from a drawing by John White. North Wind Picture Archives.
page 503: *Burning of the Stamp Act,* Library of Congress.
page 1275: *A View in the Rocky Mountains,* North Wind Picture Archives.
page 1964: Historical Pictures/Stock Montage.

Library of Congress Catalog Card Number: 97-72515

Printed in the U.S.A.

ISBN: 0-395-86822-X

1 2 3 4 5 6 7 8 9-DW-01 00 99 98 97

CONTENTS

PREFACE TO THE FIRST EDITION

This anthology has been long in the making. Indeed, some of the readers of this first edition may not have been born when the idea for it was initially discussed in 1968. At that time many literary scholars were becoming aware of the narrowness of what was taught as "American Literature." Many courses—and some textbooks as well—were limited to perhaps a dozen "major" writers; yet it was increasingly clear that any coherent and accurate account of our cultural heritage meant knowing a far wider range of authors. In graduate school during the 1950s, the only minority writers, rarely encountered, were Richard Wright, Ralph Ellison, and James Baldwin; yet, as the Civil Rights movement had begun to make clear, blacks and other people of color in American society had developed rich literary cultures. But where were these writers in American literature courses and anthologies? Similarly, most women authors, except perhaps Emily Dickinson and one or two others, were ignored as marginal; yet as one began to read American women writers, one discovered work of great power and vitality. Where were the women? It was acknowledged that the texts of English colonists, such as John Smith and William Bradford; of Puritan divines, such as Cotton Mather and Jonathan Edwards; and of the Founding Fathers were appropriate to American literature courses. But contemporary works from the half-continent that was then Spanish America and later texts concerned with similar issues of religion and politics were mainly dismissed as outside the bounds of literary study. It seemed inconsistent to relegate Cabeza de Vaca, Frederick Douglass, or Charlotte Perkins Gilman to courses on history or politics.

In short, like many black scholars before them, large numbers of teachers and scholars of all ethnic backgrounds began to question the "canon" of American literature—that is, the list of works and authors believed to be sufficiently important to read, study, write about, teach, and thus transmit to the next generation of readers. This questioning led in a number of directions. First, scholars documented the fact that the canon of American literature had changed substantially over time. In the period after World War I, for example, the "Schoolroom Poets"—Henry Wadsworth Longfellow, Oliver Wendell Holmes, James Russell Lowell, John Greenleaf Whittier—fell from eminence, and Herman Melville, who had been all but forgotten, came to be viewed as one of America's major novelists. Similarly, many of the women writers who had once been widely read and studied—such as Harriet Beecher Stowe, Mary E. Wilkins Freeman, and Edith Wharton—began to receive less attention as compared with Mark Twain and Stephen Crane. As the canon changed, so too did the courses and anthologies. A new anthology would necessarily be different from its predecessors, for as Emerson had put it, "the experience of each new age requires a new confession, and the world seems always waiting for its poet."

Second, scholars in the late 1960s, recognizing the richness and diversity of American culture, began to seek out the large number of lost, forgotten, or suppressed literary texts that had emerged from and illustrated that diversity. That has been a long and slow process, for it entailed not only locating, editing, and publishing such work, but also rethinking traditional ideas about what is of value in literature and about intellectual frameworks for studying it. In the 1970s a whole new scholarship developed that examined the cultural implications of gender, race, and class for our understanding and appreciation of literature. But courses in American literature, and the textbooks on which they depended, were slow to respond to the new scholarship. Many works from the past were reissued briefly, only to disappear from the market; others remained out of print. Anthologies were even slower to change; they continued to focus on a canon little different from that established half a century ago. The problem came to be how to provide teachers and students with a textbook that truly displayed the enormous richness of the cultures of America.

In 1979, in an effort to accelerate the process of change in teaching, my colleagues and I organized a project through The Feminist Press called "Reconstructing American Literature." It was supported by the Fund for the Improvement of Post-Secondary Education, and later by the Rockefeller Foundation and the Lilly Endowment. In 1982, that project convened a summer institute at Yale University designed to explore the implications of minority and feminist scholarship for the teaching of American literature. In the intense and often conflicted weeks of the institute, the forty participants and the resource people—including Elizabeth Ammons, Houston Baker, Juan Bruce-Novoa, Mary Anne Ferguson, Ann Fitzgerald, Phyllis Franklin, Henry Louis Gates, Jr., Carlos Hortas, Annette Kolodny, Amy Ling, Peggy McIntosh, Annette Niemtzow, A. LaVonne Brown Ruoff, Mary Helen Washington, and Ana Zentella—discussed both issues of theory and the practical problems of initiating and institutionalizing change. A number of activities emerged from that institute.

Participants organized and held a series of workshops in different parts of the country on the issues raised at the institute and, more generally, on the problem of reconstructing American literature. These seminars made it plain that the movement for change in scholarship and in curriculum was deep and widespread. To further its momentum, a volume of syllabi, course materials, and commentary—some of it prepared at the institute—was gathered and published under the title *Reconstructing American Literature* (ed. Paul Lauter, Old Westbury: Feminist Press, 1983). That book provided faculty with models for changing their own courses, and it helped scholars who were developing anthologies to determine what was being taught in relatively advanced classrooms. But the book also illustrated how teachers were constrained by the limitations of existing texts: For example, hardly any syllabi included work by Latino or Asian-American writers, largely because no such writings were then included in any anthology. We determined that, in preparing a new anthology—the final objective of the Reconstructing American Literature project—we would break through such limitations.

Most of the ideas that have guided the construction of this anthology were given definition at the Yale institute. Because we want students to be able to gain a sense of the formal and historical cross-currents that helped shape individual works within a given period, we provide a much richer selection of authors from each time frame than is available in any other anthology. Thus, for example, we include substantial selections from the traditionally important antebellum fiction writers, Poe, Hawthorne, and Melville—incorporating eight Poe tales, all of *The Scarlet Letter,* and two Melville novellas, among other works. But we also present a uniquely rich group of other narratives of the period, including material by the most widely read American of the time, Harriet Beecher Stowe, and important prose by William Wells Brown, Alice Cary, Rebecca Harding Davis, Caroline Kirkland, Harriet Prescott Spofford, Elizabeth Drew Stoddard, and Harriet Wilson, among others. These writers produced works of literary excellence and historical significance that are worth studying on their own terms. They also newly illuminate the texts of better-known authors as well as the milieu from which they emerged. We believe that reading this *range* of writers offers opportunities for drawing stimulating comparisons and contrasts between canonical and noncanonical figures, between female and male, between one ethnic writer and another. It allows us to study the diverse and changing cultures of America, not only a narrow group of authors. It is not that heretofore noncanonical texts provide, so to speak, the landscape of "minor" writing from which the great monuments of American literature rise. Rather, studying and comparing these differing works will enlarge our understanding of—even help us fundamentally redefine—the literature that has in fact been produced in the United States. This comparative process may thus play a key role in changing the traditional foci and contexts for the study of American literature and bring into the classroom the energy and excitement generated by the new scholarship on women and minorities.

We have sought to use such mutually illuminating texts throughout. Thus we print fifteenth- and sixteenth-century Spanish and French, as well as English, narratives of discovery and exploration. Additionally, we have included some Native American responses to the arrival and the advances of the Europeans. And later, in the nineteenth century, we present selections from the quite different visions of Indian-White interactions of James Fenimore Cooper and Catharine Maria Sedgwick, as well as the views on that subject of Native American writers like William Apess, Elias Boudinot, and John Rollin Ridge.

A second principle of selection concerns reasonably familiar but undervalued writers. We include several works by authors like Charles Chesnutt, Mary E. Wilkins Freeman, and Edith Wharton, who have often been represented by single well-worn pieces. Thus, instead of limiting students to Freeman's "A New England Nun," for example, or the deservedly popular "The Revolt of 'Mother,'" we also include "A Church Mouse"—her account of a poor woman's application of the ideas of nonviolent action to her own survival—as well as the powerful and disturbing "Old Woman Magoun." Similarly, we include not only the largest selection of Emily Dickinson's poems available in an anthology, but 24 of her letters, mainly because for Dickinson—as for many women—letter and journal writing were significant forms of artistic expression.

Third, in choosing among works of literary accomplishment—both by lesser-known writers and by those in the traditional canon—we have in part been guided by how a text engages concerns central to the period in which it was written as well as to the overall development of American culture. Our goal has not been to turn this literature anthology into a series of historical illustrations nor to organize it according to arbitrary themes. Rather, our selections reflect an effort, which we believe appropriate and important, to reconnect literature and its study with the society and culture of which it is fundamentally a part. For example, the question of gender—the nature of difference, the "proper spheres" of women and men, the character of women's and men's work and sexuality—has been a key concern since the earliest period. Thus, in the eighteenth century, work by Judith Sargent Murray became important; and in the nineteenth century, material by Margaret Fuller, excerpts from Harriet Ann Jacobs's *Incidents in the Life of a Slave Girl,* Charlotte Perkins Gilman's classic "The Yellow Wall-Paper," and Sarah Orne Jewett's "A White Heron" became obvious choices. But this concern also led to selecting from the large corpus of Melville's work "The Paradise of Bachelors and the Tartarus of Maids," a story rich both in symbolism and social commentary. It also led to including texts otherwise unavailable in such an anthology by eighteenth-century women poets, as well as by Sarah Grimké, Elizabeth Cady Stanton, Fanny Fern, Sojourner Truth, and Frances Ellen Watkins Harper, and particular fictional selections from Louisa May Alcott and Elizabeth Stuart Phelps. We believe readers will discover these to be not only of great interest in themselves, but also important to the discussion of gender as a category of contemporary as well as of eighteenth- and nineteenth-century literary discourse. Further, this type of selection enables the kind of illuminating comparisons—between, for example, Melville's "Paradise and Tartarus" story and Rebecca Harding Davis's "Life in the Iron Mills"—to which we alluded above.

Similarly, many of the works we have chosen treat issues and subjects that have often been downplayed, even avoided: such topics include household labor in poems of the colonial period, child abuse in one Alice Cary story, sexuality, including homosexuality, in poetry from Whitman to Rich, the forms of affirmation as well as the experience of racial violence in minority communities, described by writers like Sui-Sin Far (Edith Maud Eaton), Carlos Bulosan, and Paule Marshall. Nor have we confined ourselves to traditional analyses of familiar themes, such as what it means to be "American." This question has been of central concern to writers since the colonial period; Franklin, Emerson, and Henry Adams offer different, though related, responses to it. But their work, vital as it is, by no means exhausts the inquiry. In fact, the question intensifies for those who begin on the margins of American society, as slaves, immigrants, or "native" Americans. Accordingly, we have included in the late nineteenth- and early twentieth-century period an unusual and what we think readers will find to be a moving selection from the writings of Booker T. Washington, Abraham Cahan, Sui-Sin Far, Zitkala-Sa (Gertrude Bonnin), Alexander Posey, and Mary Antin.

As this roster of authors suggests, a major principle of selection has been to represent as fully as possible the varied cultures of the United States. American cultures sometimes overlap, sometimes differ, sometimes develop separately, sometimes in interactive patterns. To convey this diversity, we have included what is by far the widest sampling of the work of minority and white women writers available in any anthology of American literature. This selection includes material by 134 women of all races, more than 30 individual Native American authors, some anonymous (as well as some 20 texts from tribal origins), 62 Africans and African-Americans, 19 Latinos (as well as 13 texts from earlier Spanish originals and 2 from French), and 12 Asian-Americans. We have also included significant selections from Jewish, Italian, and other ethnic traditions. In choosing this varied work, we have *not* limited ourselves to contemporary writers, but have tried to show how the flourishing of ethnic and minority literatures today is deeply rooted in both formal and folk traditions that have developed in this land over centuries. For these reasons and for their inherent interest, we have also printed a number of songs and tales from America's differing cultures.

We have also sought to underline the historical development of particular literary voices in American culture by placing together writers who, in one way or another, constituted a group or "school." In some situations, these writers knew and were influenced by each other. Such was the case, for example, among abolitionists, among many of the later nineteenth-century women writers who make up the first section of Volume 2, or among the writers of the New Negro Renaissance, whom we have placed together. We believe this organizational innovation will offer useful linkages for reading and teaching without imposing a historical artifice on the writers. It could be argued, of course, that placing the artists of the New Negro Renaissance together in a sense ghettoizes them and deemphasizes their impact upon the development of modernism. We are aware of this problem; but having this rich selection of writers together will, we believe, enable students to better comprehend the scope and internal diversity of the Renaissance, the interactions of its participants, as well as the connections between this cultural movement and the wider black community.

We have in general sought to organize the texts in units we believe will be interesting for reading and helpful to teaching. Underlying this organizational strategy is our belief that the paradigms we use to frame the study of literature are as important to how we understand it as the content of our study *per se.* For example, the ideas as well as the institutions of Puritanism are obviously important. But the religious life of what is now America has roots far older and more diverse than those established in the Massachusetts Bay colony. A class on "Puritan Writings" offers significant opportunity for studying essential works, but it leads in different directions from a class on "Early American Religious Cultures," which might incorporate Spanish Catholic works as well as texts from Native American oral origins. Neither approach is "right"—or "wrong." But they foreground different texts and different cultural traditions. Our units are not designed to foreclose other organizational schemes but to make visible the intellectual assumptions always present in any method of structuring an anthology.

In order to accomplish the major broadening of coverage at which we have aimed, we have, especially in the contemporary selection, chosen authors we think of as representing different cultural voices. Of course, no one writer can "represent" the uniqueness of any other writer. In another sense, however, anthologies have always selected at least some writers on this basis—to "represent" the Imagist movement, for example, or social protest literature of the 1930s or "local color" writing of an earlier time. Whatever injustice this procedure may do to individual writers we have omitted, it has virtues over and above that of breadth. It allows readers to emphasize—as is reasonable for a survey text—historical contexts and literary trends rather than to focus primarily on a few prominent authors. As readers will see, we include larger selections of the traditionally canonical writers than are likely to be read in a survey course. But on balance, we have felt it more vital to strive for the kind of range offered here than to provide readers with additional but more peripheral works by writers who are already familiar to most readers.

In addition to helping us develop the conceptual frameworks for this project, the Yale institute provided the organizational strategy for pulling together this distinctive anthology. It was clear from the outset that no small, homogeneous editorial board—of the sort that had up to then characterized *every* anthology—could bring together all the scholarly resources necessary to carry out this effort. Therefore, one of our first decisions was to gather an editorial board unique in its large size and in its diversity: in its initial composition the board had equal numbers of women and men, minority and white participants; members came from every part of the country, taught in virtually every kind of institution, and specialized in most of the periods and varieties of American literature.

In addition, however, an institute participant, Margaret O'Connor, proposed that instead of having even this large editorial board responsible for gathering all the writing to be included in the anthology, we ask the profession at large which authors and works they thought should be considered for a "reconstructed" American literature text. Consequently, we wrote to thousands of faculty members teaching American literature. More than 500 authors were suggested for inclusion. Potential "contributing editors" were then asked to suggest specific texts, and to provide a brief rationale for their selections. The editorial board read through this enormously fascinating—and physically huge—set of recommended texts, made an initial cut, and then in a series of meetings over three years narrowed the selections to what could fit within the covers of two large volumes.

This process, while cumbersome and time-consuming, has had a number of virtues. First, it represented a resurveying of the territory—really, given the changes in what was called "American literature," an initial survey of what was virtually a new literary world. Instead of basing our initial selection on that of previous anthologies or on our graduate school training, and then supplementing or subtracting according to our own principles, we began with the vast range of the literary output of this country and have narrowed from that. We would hardly claim that nothing worthwhile has been omitted; but much that was lost and is excellent has been found.

Furthermore, this process has enabled us to incorporate in the anthology, and thus make available to readers, a great deal of new scholarship developed by leading specialists in their fields. These specialists made the initial suggestions about what should be included, wrote the headnotes for the authors they proposed, prepared notes for the texts finally selected, compiled selected bibliographies, and provided materials for the teaching guide. While editorial board members are responsible for the final versions of the headnotes, we have been able to extend the range of this anthology far beyond the limits of the board as a whole.

Finally, this process offers readers differing approaches to authors and varied writing styles in headnotes and introductions. In a way, these critical differences reflect the very diversity of the literature included here. They may also furnish students with a wider range of models for engaging texts and thus, perhaps, encourage confidence in their own judgments and ways of reading.

Whenever possible, the date of first publication follows each selection. In a few instances of special significance, the date of composition is also given.

We decided that it would be helpful to provide extended introductions to each historical period, as well as to the divisions within those periods. These introductions have been designed to offer readers information about the American society and cultures within which the authors created. Increasingly, literary study has moved away from purely formal scrutiny of isolated texts toward analyses that depend upon an examination of such historical contexts. We ask not only how a poem or story is constructed, about its language and imagery, but also about how it "worked" in its world (and works in ours), and how it was related to other texts of its own and other times. While these introductions do not pretend to be complete accounts of the periods, we believe that, together with the variety of texts themselves, they will provide a basis for informed interpretation of the works included in these volumes.

One member of the editorial board was ultimately in charge of writing each period introduction and the briefer section introductions; many other members contributed materials to one or more of the introductions. Carla Mulford was responsible for the introductions to the Colonial Period: to 1700 and the Eighteenth Century; she used materials provided by Wendy Martin, Juan Bruce-Novoa, Andrew Wiget, and Richard Yarborough. Paul Lauter was responsible for the Early Nineteenth Century: 1800–1865 introduction, using materials provided by Amy Ling, Daniel Littlefield, Raymund Paredes, and Andrew Wiget. Elaine Hedges was responsible for the Late Nineteenth Century: 1865–1910 introduction, using materials provided by Amy Ling, Daniel Littlefield, Raymund Paredes, Andrew Wiget, and Richard Yarborough. Charles Molesworth was responsible for the introduction to the Modern Period: 1910–1945, using materials provided by Elaine Hedges, Paul Lauter, Amy Ling, and Daniel Littlefield; Hortense Spillers was responsible for the introduction to the New Negro Renaissance. Linda Wagner-Martin was responsible for the introduction to the Contemporary Period: 1945 to the Present, using materials provided by Paul Lauter, Amy Ling, Andrew Wiget, and Richard Yarborough.

As for the contributing editors who "sponsored" so many of the writers included, this is very much their anthology too. We appreciate the help of our colleagues included in the following list: Thomas P. Adler (Purdue University); Elizabeth Ammons (Tufts University); William L. Andrews (University of Kansas); Frances R. Aparicio (University of Michigan); Elaine Sargent Apthorp (San Jose State University); Evelyn Avery (Towson State University); Liahna Babener (Montana State University); Barbara A. Bardes (Loyola University of Chicago); Helen Barolini; Marleen Barr (Virginia Polytechnic Institute and State University); Sam S. Baskett (Michigan State University); Rosalie Murphy Baum (University of South Florida); Herman Beavers (University of Pennsylvania); Eileen T. Bender (Indiana University at Bloomington); Carol Marie Bensick (University of California, Riverside); David Bergman (Towson State University); Susan L. Blake (Lafayette College); Michael Boccia (Tufts University); Robert H. Brinkmeyer, Jr. (University of Mississippi); Carol A. Burns (Southern Illinois University Press); John F. Callahan (Lewis and Clark College); Jane Campbell (Purdue University, Calumet); Jean Ferguson Carr (University of Pittsburgh); Allan Chavkin (Southwest Texas State University); King-Kok Cheung (University of California, Los Angeles); Beverly Lyon Clark (Wheaton College); C. B. Clark (Oklahoma City University); Arthur B. Coffin (Montana State University); Constance Coiner (State University of New York at Binghamton); James W. Coleman (University of North Carolina at Chapel Hill); Martha E. Cook (Longwood College); Angelo Costanzo (Shippensburg University); Patti Cowell (Colorado State University); John W.

Crowley (Syracuse University); Sister Martha Curry (Wayne State University); Walter C. Daniel (University of Missouri—Columbia); Cathy N. Davidson (Duke University); Jane Krause DeMouy; Dorothy L. Denniston (Brown University); Kathryn Zabelle Derounian-Stodola (University of Arkansas at Little Rock); Margaret Dickie (University of Georgia); Raymond F. Dolle (Indiana State University); Sheila Hurst Donnelly (Orange County Community College); Carole K. Doreski (Daniel Webster College); Sally Ann Drucker (North Carolina State University); Arlene A. Elder (University of Cincinnati); Everett Emerson (University of North Carolina at Chapel Hill); Bernard F. Engel (Michigan State University); Betsy Erkkila (University of Pennsylvania); Lillian Faderman (California State University—Fresno); Charles Fanning (Southern Illinois University); Robert M. Farnsworth (University of Missouri—Kansas City); Laraine Fergenson (City University of New York, Bronx Community College); Judith Fetterley (State University of New York at Albany); Joseph Fichtelberg (Hofstra University); Lucy M. Freibert (University of Louisville); George S. Friedman (Towson State University); Susan Stanford Friedman (University of Wisconsin—Madison); Albert Furtwangler (Mount Allison University); Diana Hume George (Pennsylvania State University at Erie—Behrend College); Leah Blatt Glasser, (Mount Holyoke College); Wendell P. Glick (University of Minnesota); William Goldhurst (University of Florida); Rita K. Gollin (State University of New York College at Geneseo); Suzanne Gossett (Loyola University of Chicago); Philip Gould (DePaul University); Maryemma Graham (Northeastern University); Theodora Rapp Graham (Pennsylvania State University at Harrisburg); Robert M. Greenberg (Temple University); Barry Gross (Michigan State University); James Guimond (Rider College); Minrose C. Gwin (University of New Mexico); Alfred Habegger (University of Kansas); Joan F. Hallisey (Regis College); Jeffrey A. Hammond (St. Mary's College of Maryland); Earl N. Harbert (Northeastern University); Sharon M. Harris (University of Nebraska); Trudier Harris (Emory University); Ellen Louise Hart (University of California, Santa Cruz); William L. Hedges (Goucher College); Joan D. Hedrick (Trinity College); Allison Heisch (San Jose State University); Robert Hemenway (University of Kentucky); Kristin Herzog; Donald R. Hettinga (Calvin College); Hilary W. Holladay (University of North Carolina at Chapel Hill); Elvin Holt (Southwest Texas State University); Kenneth Alan Hovey (University of Texas at San Antonio); Akasha (Gloria) Hull (University of California, Santa Cruz); James M. Hutchisson (The Citadel); Paul Jones (University of North Carolina at Chapel Hill); Joyce Ann Joyce (Chicago State University); Nancy Carol Joyner (Western Carolina University); Rose Yalow Kamel (Philadelphia College of Pharmacy and Science); Carolyn L. Karcher (Temple University); Janet Kaufman (University of Iowa); Richard S. Kennedy (Temple University); Carol Farley Kessler (Pennsylvania State University); Elizabeth Keyser (Hollins College); Elaine H. Kim (University of California, Berkeley); Michael Kreyling (Vanderbilt University); Him Mark Lai; David M. Larson (Cleveland State University); Estella Lauter (University of Wisconsin—Green Bay); Barry Leeds (Central Connecticut State University); George S. Lensing (University of North Carolina at Chapel Hill); James A. Levernier (University of Arkansas at Little Rock); Cliff Lewis (University of Massachusetts at Lowell); Patricia Liggins-Hill (University of San Francisco); Genny Lim;

Shirley Geok-lin Lim (University of California at Santa Barbara); John Lowe (Louisiana State University); Juanita Luna-Lawhn (San Antonio College); Joseph Mancini, Jr. (George Washington University); Daniel Marder (University of Tulsa); Robert A. Martin (Michigan State University); Deborah E. McDowell (University of Virginia); Joseph R. McElrath (Florida State University); Peggy McIntosh (Wellesley College); Nellie Y. McKay (University of Wisconsin—Madison); D. H. Melhem (Union for Experimenting Colleges and Universities); Michael J. Mendelsohn (University of Tampa); Gabriel Miller (Rutgers University); James A. Miller (Trinity College); Jeanne-Marie A. Miller (Howard University); Keith D. Miller (Arizona State University); Arthenia J. Bates Millican; James S. Moy (University of Wisconsin—Madison); Joel Myerson (University of South Carolina); Cary Nelson (University of Illinois at Urbana—Champaign); Margaret F. Nelson (Oklahoma State University); Charles H. Nichols (Brown University); Vera Norwood (University of New Mexico); Michael O'Brien (Miami University); Margaret Anne O'Connor (University of North Carolina at Chapel Hill); Genaro M. Padilla (University of California, Berkeley); Linda Pannill (Transylvania University); James W. Parins (University of Arkansas at Little Rock); Vivian M. Patraka (Bowling Green State University); John J. Patton (Atlantic Community College); James Robert Payne (New Mexico State University); Richard Pearce (Wheaton College); Michael W. Peplow (Western International University); Ronald Primeau (Central Michigan University); John Purdy (Western Washington University); Jennifer L. Randisi (California State University—San Bernardino); Geoffrey Rans (University of Western Ontario); Julius Rowan Raper (University of North Carolina at Chapel Hill); John M. Reilly (United University Professions); Phillip M. Richards (Colgate University); Marilyn Richardson; Evelyn Hoard Roberts (Saint Louis Community College at Meramec); James A. Robinson (University of Maryland); William H. Robinson (Rhode Island College); Kenneth M. Roemer (University of Texas at Arlington); Judith Roman-Royer (Indiana University East); Nicholas D. Rombes, Jr. (Pennsylvania State University); Lora Romero (Stanford University); Robert C. Rosen (William Paterson College); Deborah S. Rosenfelt (University of Maryland); Karen E. Rowe (University of California, Los Angeles); A. LaVonne Brown Ruoff (University of Illinois at Chicago); Roshni Rustomji-Kerns (Sonoma State University); Doreen Alvarez Saar (Drexel University); Enrique Sacerio-Garí (Bryn Mawr College); Ramón Saldívar (Stanford University); Sonia Saldívar-Hull (University of California, Los Angeles); George J. Searles (Mohawk Valley Community College); Cynthia Secor (HERS, Mid America at the University of Denver); David S. Shields (The Citadel); Thelma J. Shinn (Arizona State University); Frank C. Shuffelton (University of Rochester); Peggy Skaggs (Angelo State University); Beth Helen Stickney (Queens College, City University of New York); Catharine R. Stimpson (Rutgers University); Janis P. Stout (Texas A & M University); Claudia Tate (George Washington University); John Edgar Tidwell (Miami University); Eleanor Q. Tignor (City University of New York, La Guardia Community College); Jane Tompkins (Duke University); Steven C. Tracy; Eleanor W. Traylor (Howard University); Richard Tuerk (East Texas State University); Bonnie TuSmith (Bowling Green State University); Paula Uruburu (Hofstra University); Donald Vanouse (State University of New York College at Oswego); Daniel

Walden (Pennsylvania State University); Arthur E. Waterman (Georgia State University); Sybil Weir (San Jose State University); Judith Wellman (State University of New York College at Oswego); James L. W. West III (Pennsylvania State University); Thomas R. Whitaker (Yale University); Barbara A. White (University of New Hampshire); Margaret B. Wilkerson (University of California, Berkeley); Kenny J. Williams (Duke University); Marcellette G. Williams (Michigan State University); James C. Wilson (University of Cincinnati); Norma Clark Wilson (University of South Dakota); Amy E. Winans (Pennsylvania State University); Kate H. Winter (State University of New York at Albany); Frederick Woodard (University of Iowa); Jean Fagan Yellin (Pace University); Amy Marie Yerkes (University of Pennsylvania); Judith Yung (University of California, Santa Cruz); Sandra A. Zagarell (Oberlin College).

The completion of this complex project owes debts to colleagues other than those who constitute the editorial board and the 205 authorities who have served as contributing editors. Mary Helen Washington, Annette Kolodny, Hortense Spillers, and Paula Gunn Allen served on the editorial board at earlier stages. Staff members at The Feminist Press—particularly Denise Wyatt, Sophie Zimmerman, Helen Schrader, and Peggy Gifford—helped move this effort forward. Members of the advisory board of the Reconstructing American Literature project provided important advice and counsel; they included Warner Berthoff, Barbara Christian, Margarita Cota-Cárdenas, Michael Dorris, Mary Anne Ferguson, Dexter Fisher, Phyllis Franklin, Donna Gerstenberger, Michael Harper, the late George Kent, Marian E. Musgrave, Katharine D. Newman, Marco Portales, the late Warren Sussman, Alan Trachtenberg, Henrietta Whiteman, and Larzer Ziff. The project could not have been completed without the financial support of the federal Fund for the Improvement of Post-Secondary Education (FIPSE), the Lilly Endowment, and the Rockefeller Foundation; we particularly wish to thank the program officers—Richard Hendrix, Ralph Lundgren, and Stephen Lavine, respectively—for their assistance and encouragement. The University of California at Los Angeles provided support for an editorial board meeting, and the University of California at Santa Cruz, the State University of New York/College at Old Westbury, and Trinity College gave help for other aspects of this project; in particular we wish to express our appreciation to William Schaefer of UCLA, Michael Cowan and Byron Wheeler of Santa Cruz, Norman Hostetter and Eudora Pettigrew of Old Westbury, and Jan Cohn of Trinity.

A number of our colleagues were kind enough to comment upon the table of contents or sections of the manuscript. They included Michael Adams; Barry Ahearn (Tulane University); William Hilton Anderson (University of Southern Mississippi); John Anderson (University of Pennsylvania); Robert Armour (Virginia Commonwealth University); Tucker Arnold (Florida International University); Kathleen Ashley (University of Southern Maine); Liahna Babener (Montana State University); Peter Balakian (Colgate University); Veronica Bassil (State University of New York at Geneseo); John Bayer (Saint Louis Community College at Meramec); Robert Bergstrom (University of Nebraska—Lincoln); Susan L. Blake (Lafayette College); James Busskohl (Eastern Washington University); William Cain (Wellesley College); D. Dean Cantrell (Berry College); Robert Con Davis (University of Oklahoma); D. Dean Dunham (William Jewell College); Barbara

Eckstein (Tulane University); Donna Gerstenberger (University of Washington); Sandra Gilbert (University of California at Riverside); Norman Grabo (University of Tulsa); Janet Groth (State University of New York at Plattsburgh); Douglas Haneline (Ferris State College); Robert Hemenway (University of Kentucky); Carol Holly (St. Olaf College); June Howard (University of Michigan), Alan Howell (California Polytechnic University); Marcia Jacobson (Auburn University); Joan Joffe Hall (University of Connecticut); Fran Kaye (University of Nebraska); Bonnie Kime Scott (University of Delaware); Jerome Klinkowitz (Northern Iowa State University); Michael Kreyling (Vanderbilt University); Joann Krieg (Hofstra University); Lewis Lawson (University of Maryland); James Leonard (The Citadel); Kenneth Lincoln (University of California at Los Angeles); Don Makosky (St. Lawrence University); Charlotte McClure (Georgia State University); Charlotte Meyer (Edgewood College); Theodore D. Nostwich (Iowa State University); Linda Panero (Manhattan College); John Parks (Miami University); Betty Reagan (Kutztown University of Pennsylvania); David S. Reynolds (City University of New York, Baruch College); George Sebouhian (State University of New York at Fredonia); John Seelye (University of Florida); Candadai Seshachari (Weber State College); Conrad Shumaker (University of Central Arkansas); Paul Smith (Trinity College); Philip Smith (University of Nebraska); Sherry Sullivan (University of Alabama); William Sutton (Eastern Kentucky University); Frederic Svoboda (University of Michigan—Flint); Mary Helen Washington (University of Massachusetts—Boston); Ray Lewis White (Illinois State University); Glen Wiese (Weber State College); Bonnie Zimmerman (San Diego State University). Anne Fitzgerald read and made suggestions for all of the introductions. We want to thank all for their honest criticisms and for the support they provided.

Paul Lauter's students in English 204 at Trinity College used much of Volume 1 in photocopied form and provided valuable comments and suggestions, as did Wendy Martin's students at The Claremont Graduate School. Cynthia Andrzejczyk, Gary Enke, and Matthew Judd of The Claremont Graduate School gave particular assistance in gathering and helping edit materials for the early period, as did Stephen Cormany, Kathryn Davinroy, Kathleen Healey, Jean Niencamp, and Nicholas Rombes of Pennsylvania State University and Louis A. Cellucci of Temple University. Bill Kelly, Barbara Bowen, and Melvin Dixon of Queens College provided particular help for the introduction to modernism, and the twenties and thirties. We also appreciate the aid of Janice Radway and Philip Leininger.

Finally, we wish to acknowledge the extraordinary work of the editorial staff at D. C. Heath: Holt Johnson, Kim Mrazek Hastings, and particularly Paul Smith, who acted as a full member of the editorial board; without his encouragement, faith, and tenacity, these volumes would never have seen the light of day.

Paul Lauter, Trinity College, for the Editorial Board

PREFACE TO THE THIRD EDITION

The beginning of the preface to the second edition of this book read: "In revising *The Heath Anthology of American Literature*, we have taken as our guide the old adage 'if it ain't broke, don't fix it.' The strongly positive reception of the first edition of this anthology led us to feel that its central principles of selection and organization worked well for both students and teachers. And the adoption of the anthology in every kind of institution of higher education, as well as in some secondary schools, has demonstrated that the opportunities this anthology affords to extend canon and curriculum are welcomed by most of our colleagues."

We see no particular reasons to revise those judgments. The principles of literary value and pedagogy on the basis of which this anthology is constructed have very wide currency today. These include the desire to convey to students a sense of the diversity that has marked this nation's culture together with certain themes and issues that have preoccupied most Americans; the need to understand the ways in which texts and contexts interact and condition one another; the importance of organizational frameworks in shaping how we experience the works of art encountered within structures like anthologies, museums, and curricula; and the reality that what readers esteem changes somewhat over time—the time marked out by eras, by generations, and by individual human lives. These are still the principles which guide our work.

For example, one significant strand in the nation's diverse culture has been the work of writers of Jewish origins. We have in this edition extended the already-strong representation of this strand by adding a play by Mordecai Manuel Noah in Volume I, as well as poetry and fiction focused on the Holocaust by Charles Reznikoff and Cynthia Ozick in Volume II. Or, to illustrate the last principle, we have confronted the assumption that late-nineteenth-century American women poets were necessarily banal and sentimental—a view so hilariously forwarded both by Caroline Kirkland's satire of Miss Fidler in *A New Home—Who'll Follow?* and by Mark Twain's parody of Emmeline Grangerford in *Huckleberry Finn.* But as the sheaf of poems assembled by contributing editor Paula Bennett illustrates, such views, however amusing, can mislead us because, in fact, much poetry of value was being written in that time over 100 years ago—a time that was largely hidden from serious critical scrutiny for much of this century.

Other changes in this edition derive from what our readers urged upon us. For example, we were asked to provide a greater variety of long texts; how to do that within the confines of an already bursting anthology wasn't very clear. We finally decided, after much discussion, to remove *The Scarlet Letter* and *Adventures of Huckleberry Finn* from the pages of the anthology proper and to make them available separately with the main books. That enabled us not only to broaden the inclusiveness of the anthology volumes, but also to offer instructors the opportunity to choose alternative longer complete texts from among those available in the Riverside editions series.

We could not, of course, take all the suggestions for change readers have made; some came late, some seemed impractical, some were too costly, and some we simply did not agree with. There will be in the next few years ample opportunity to discuss, even argue about, these choices, for the two anthology volumes do not stand alone. As most readers will know, a Newsletter related to the anthology is now published twice a year. It contains materials helpful for students and for faculty—for example, on teaching Southern writing, or on gay and lesbian texts. It also provides a forum within which to discuss the issues that shape many classrooms and curricula, as well as an anthology. An even more flexible forum exists in the form of an on-line discussion list, T-AMLIT(t-amlit@list.cren.net), wherein it has been possible for practitioners in American literature, whether or not they use *The Heath Anthology*, to talk about the issues that concern them. And by the time you read this, we will have mounted a World Wide Web site for the anthology as well. These and other "support" mechanisms help realize what we called in the "Preface to the Second Edition" the "wide democratic participation of readers in the book's creation and use." We wish to continue encouraging that democratic spirit, not only in these forums for discussion but through the more informal mechanisms of e-mail and the good old P.O. Readers would, we think, be surprised at how many of the revisions for this edition originated—and will continue to originate—in the proposals of individual teachers of American literature.

Another way of saying this is that—especially in a time of expansion of electronic mechanisms for teaching and research—the covers of an anthology no longer mark its confines, and the publication date no longer terminates the processes of its development. *The Heath Anthology of American Literature* continues to be a participatory adventure, in which we invite all readers to join.

Many readers, friends, and critics did join the editorial board and the large group of contributing editors in strengthening this third edition. We wish to thank particularly the group of reviewers who provided us with very extensive comments on the strengths and limitations of the second edition. They included Ngwarsungu Chiwengo, Maurice Duke, Dale Flynn, B.C. Hall, Hank Lazer, Martha Leighty, Judy Michna, Miles Orvell, Pamela Presser, Michael K. Ritchie, Elizabeth Wheeler, and Marilyn Wyman. Though we considered these commentaries very carefully, we were not always able to follow the advice of our reviewers. For example, Hank Lazer argued eloquently for a selection of the "Language Poets," but we were not persuaded that they would be taught by most users of the anthology. We could be wrong, and we would certainly like to hear from others on that subject, among others.

We wish also to thank the many others who commented upon or otherwise aided us in bringing together this edition. They included Elizabeth Archuleta, Helen Barolini, Janette Bradley, Lawrence Buell, William Cain, Sandi Dahlberg, Sharon L. Dean, Shelley Fisher Fishkin, Fritz Fleischmann, Barbara Foley, John N. Fritz, Thomas S. Gladsky, Gregory Jay, Yiorgos D. Kalogeras, Major Rick Keating, Jeanne Phoenix Laurel, Tillie Olsen, Rhonda Pettit, David Reynolds, Cheri Louise Ross, LaVonne Brown Ruoff, Epifanio S. San Juan, Jr., Catharine Stimpson, Herman Joseph Sutter, Amy Winans, and Magdelena J. Zaborowska. Many of these scholars proposed writers for inclusion in the anthology whom we could not, at least in this edition, accommodate; but such proposals constitute the lifeblood of an ongoing project like the Heath. We thank also Eric Sundquist, who was kind enough to annotate the musical epigraphs in the selections from W.E.B. Du Bois' *The Souls of Black Folk*.

A note of particular thanks to those contributors who composed new entries for this edition of the anthology. They included Elizabeth Ammons, Samuel S. Baskett, Rosalie Murphy Baum, Paula Bennett, Carol A. Burns, John F. Callahan, Jane Campbell, Randolph Chilton, Martha E. Cook, Martha Curry, Sharon L. Dean, Margaret Dickie, Joanne Dobson, Everett Emerson, Judith Fetterley, Joseph Fichtelberg, Rita K. Gollin, Theodora Rapp Graham, Tresa Grauer, Sharon M. Harris, Hyun Yi Kang, Richard S. Kennedy, Karen Kilcup, Craig Kleinman, Thomas W. Krise, Cliff Lewis, Joel Myerson, Cary Nelson, Charles H. Nichols, Margaret Anne O'Connor, Geoffrey Rans, John M. Reilly, Sonia Saldivar-Hull, James C. Wilson, Amy Winans, and Xiaojing Zhou.

Finally, we wish to thank the staff at Houghton Mifflin, which rose magnificently to the difficult undertaking of this enormous project: Alison Zetterquist, Janet Edmonds, Terri Teleen, Nancy Lyman, Paul A. Smith, Margaret Roll, Rosemary Jaffe, Jayne Fargnoli, and particularly Leah Strauss, who shepherded the manuscript—and many of the editors—through. These volumes could not have emerged without the efforts of Kim Mrazek Hastings, who brought the manuscript from gestation to birth.

Paul Lauter, Trinity College, for the Editorial Board

Colonial Period

to 1700

WHEN he was captured in December 1607 by a large band of Algonkians hunting deer, Captain John Smith was taken by the *wero-wance*—the headman, or tribal chief—of the group to be the white werowance of the Jamestown colony that had arrived in the area the year before. According to native custom, it was inappropriate to put werowances to death, so Smith could not be killed. Instead, his fate could only be determined by Powhatan, the hereditary chief of the Algonkians who had pushed north from the present-day Carolinas to expand the Algonkian realm into the tidewater Virginia area. Smith was taken, via a circuitous route, to Powhatan's residence, where he impressed the native chief with his self-confident bravery in the face of possible death and his seemingly supernatural pocket compass. Powhatan evidently invoked an Algonkian custom and in a ceremony of transformation adopted Smith as a subordinate werowance into his group. The ceremony involved his eleven- or twelve-year-old daughter, Pocahontas. As Smith told the story years later in his *Generall Historie of Virginia, New-England, and the Summer Isles* (1624),

having feasted him after their best barbarous manner they could, a long consultation was held, but the conclusion was, two great stones were brought before Powhatan: then as many as could layd hands on him, dragged him to them, and thereon laid his head, and being ready with their clubs, to beate out his braines, Pocahontas the Kings dearest daughter, when no intreaty could prevaile, got his head in her armes, and laid her owne upon his to save him from death: whereat the Emperour was contented he should live to make him hatchets, and her bells, beads, and copper; for they thought him as well of all occupations as themselves.

Smith's story of Pocahontas emerged among English-speaking groups as a story of the charity and bravery of the young woman, Pocahontas, who was willing, it seemed to Smith, to sacrifice her life before her own presumably savage and barbarous people in order to save this man of superior merit. And thus the story remained for centuries, until anthropologists and ethnographers began to dismantle the assumptions behind the tale. These assumptions seem to stem from one key belief—that the explorers who had come to the Americas were much superior to the Native Americans already there. Such ethnocentrism, the attitude that one's own race and culture is superior to any other race and culture, characterized the attitudes held by European settlers—whether Spanish or French or English—who came to the Americas and confronted the different Native Americans in their homelands.

What of those Native Americans? They were, most likely, equally ethnocentric. Captain John Smith might have thought that he was superior to the Indians he met because of his race, his navigational instruments and weaponry, and his Christianity. Yet the people he met were equally as secure in and sure of their own capabilities. We know now, for instance, that the Jamestown colonists arrived at a time when the eastern native groups were in the process of cultural change. When Smith met Powhatan, Powhatan was in the midst of consolidating control over about thirty different groups in the Chesapeake region. This was, for Powhatan, an important time. Tribal populations had suffered devastation from the European diseases brought to the Indians, who had no natural immunities to such diseases, before Jamestown was founded. The groups had disintegrated and scattered in the face of European intrusion upon the lands and peoples. Powhatan, who evidently appeared in immense dignity before his amalgamated peoples, took advantage of the opportunity to consolidate power into his own Algonkian band. In fact, some scholars suggest that had the process of Powhatan's empire-building continued without the further interruption of the Europeans, indigenous states not unlike those of the Aztec, Incan, or Mayan groups of Central and South America might have established themselves over the course of the next several centuries.

Clearly, when Powhatan allowed Smith in this ritual ceremony to become a werowance, he was known at least to his own people to be subjecting Smith to his own power. When Powhatan then used his quasi-alliance with Smith to trade for European goods that appealed to his native allies, he was further creating in his own dominion a center of power. Smith himself observed that everything that was stolen from Jamestown found its way into Powhatan's hands. Smith was illustrating the redistributive function of the chief, to whom all booty was offered and from whom all booty was distributed. Finally, when Powhatan married his daughter Pocahontas to the English settler and tobacco planter John Rolfe in 1614, he was engaging in a guarded peace with the white settlers. Powhatan, then, used Smith and the English (not to mention his own daughter), in part, to demonstrate his power to his own Native American people.

Native American Culture and Traditions

Captain John Smith was ethnocentric in his views; he believed his own race and culture superior to the indigenes. But he was also one of the first to point out the falseness of the common English view that Native Americans lacked the attributes of what in the western hemisphere was considered an organized society: law, inheritance, religion, and systematic agriculture. In fact, the native peoples of the Americas had centuries-old traditions, traditions antedating Christianity and western European social organizations, traditions from which they derived their own cultural stories about the origin of all peoples, the existence of what could be construed as good and evil in the world, the development of different societies, the development of agriculture, and so forth. They did not consider themselves primitive peoples.

Even the term *Indian* was a rather late misnomer Columbus gave the peoples he found in October 1492 in the Bahamas. Columbus thought he had found the Indies (until he died, he persisted in thinking he had found Asia), so he called the Bahaman natives "los Indios," Indians. Most ethnographers today call the people who were here at the time of the Spanish exploration and settlement *Native Americans,* for the migrations of these peoples antedated the arrival of the Spanish in the fifteenth century. Indeed, the migrations of these peoples antedated the settlement of Indo-European speakers in western Europe. According to many anthropologists, the forerunners of the Native American population, often called Paleo-Indians, probably arrived in the Americas more than thirty thousand years ago, having traveled a now submerged land connection between Asia and North America at the site of the Bering Strait. Nomadic peoples, they hunted game and gathered wild fruits and greens for sustenance, and they eventually spread—over the course of many centuries—through

North and South America. Natives living in central Mexico began to cultivate food crops by about 5,500 years ago, when a growing interest in agricultural production brought about a change in their nomadic existence; most then started to live more stationary lives.

In the areas now known as Mexico and Guatemala (Mesoamerica) the most advanced Native American civilizations—the Aztec and the Maya—evolved from great empires characterized by large cities, ceremonial sites with massive pyramid-like temples, hereditary rule by an elite of warrior-priests, and agricultural production of food. The Aztecs, warlike peoples, had consolidated control over central Mexico by the time the Spanish arrived there. The Mayan civilization, already in a decline by the time the Spanish came, had invented systems of writing and mathematics, along with a calendar. Such developments had begun to be lost from historical record even by the time the English arrived in the sixteenth century: the Spanish invaders of the fifteenth century had deliberately destroyed native cities, representationally signifying Spanish domination. On the sites that had once held Aztec and Mayan and Incan temples, the Spanish built cathedrals and monasteries. And, despite the occasional intervention of priests, the Spanish burned or otherwise destroyed the vestiges of any written records they had found. The historical record indicates that the native peoples to the north of these ancient civilizations fared somewhat better in that the English, French, and Dutch, not immediately interested in colonizing the lands they found, did not so fully and systematically interfere with the native populations. This is not to suggest, however, that the changes foisted upon these native groups were any less incontrovertible.

Generally speaking, knowledge of Native American culture as it was *then* has not been available from written records; instead, what little we know about these peoples has been pieced together from various material artifacts, such as stone implements and pottery pieces and shards, that have been laboriously uncovered at myriads of indigenous cultural sites and from oral stories as they have been passed as traditions down through scores of generations of native peoples. What the traditions reveal is that the peoples the Europeans encountered upon their arrival in North America were well-adapted to their environments: those who lived in environments not well-suited to agriculture (like the Paiutes and Shoshonis, who inhabited the part of the Great Basin now known as Nevada and Utah) continued in seasonal movements; those who combined agriculture in varying degrees with fishing, gathering, and hunting (like the Chinooks of present-day Washington and Oregon, the Arikaras of the Missouri River Valley, and the Algonkians of what is now eastern Canada and northeastern United States) tended to remain in relatively defined territories in which they made occasional seasonal movements within a somewhat circumscribed land area. Their languages, social and political structures, and religions differed widely yet were derived from models that had evolved, sometimes patrilineally (along male birth lines) and sometimes matrilineally (through the female line), over the course of centuries. When the Europeans arrived in the fifteenth century, then, they faced a wide variety of cultures—perhaps four to six million people—available in North America. These peoples spoke well over a thousand different languages. No wonder they did not like being grouped together as if they were one people; no wonder, too, that they did not at first consider uniting to repel the European intruders.

As the cultures of the Native American peoples differed, so did their religious practices. For the most part, as we might expect, their religions reflected their cultural practices, and, for the most part, the Native Americans were polytheistic (that is, they believed in a multitude of gods). Their religious rituals often related to their chief means of subsistence. As we have seen, their means of subsistence varied. Native Americans who relied upon agriculture (like the Pueblo peoples of the present-day American Southwest, who began raising squash and beans about 3,000 years ago) tended to evoke major deities associated with cultivation, and their chief festivals centered on planting and harvest. By contrast, those Native Americans whose subsistence was based upon hunting and gathering (like the Siouan-speaking tribes of the Great Plains) associated their religious practices with animals, and their major festivals were related to hunting. Unlike the religious practices of the patriarchally determined European societies (which placed men at the fore of their familial, social, and religious systems), some Native American groups gave prominent religious roles to women. In the East, for instance, the Six Nations or Iroquois peoples gave women the most prominent religious positions; Iroquois women performed most of their societies' agricultural chores. Native Americans varied, then, in their religious practices, and their religious practices often varied according to their means of subsistence and even according to the producers of their foods. If Europeans returned to Europe with conflicting reports about the Native Americans they encountered, it was due in part to the diverse populations they had witnessed.

Given their manner of living, their social and political organizations, and their religions, Native Americans generally had little use for written records. They relied instead upon group traditions and group memory. Their lives in constant flux from seasonal change or tribal intrusion, Native Americans valued highly the oratorical skills by which their traditions could be transmitted to the group. In stories of the development and peopling of the world, of the group's determination of places to live, of the presence of good and evil in the world, Native Americans orally transmitted their cultures for generations. Full of rhythm and repetition, native oral forms—ceremonial or popular songs, prayers, chants or incantations, and historical narratives—thus figure large in the Native American canon. Native American oral transmissions resemble dramatic performances in that, in addition to speaking, a narrator enacts scenes, sometimes adopting different voices and gestures for different characters, sometimes moving around, within a circumscribed area, in order to reflect particular tribally known—and tribally significant—places and times. In Navajo ritual, for instance, a speaker or chanter will work within a sand-painted circle inside a hogan (a consecrated dwelling), selecting symbolic postures and voices so as to invoke, in a ritually correct performance, particular Holy People, the supernatural beings of the Navajos. Thus, an individual speaking voice reinforces communal values, creating or recreating in both the spoken word and physical gesture a culturally significant moment in the tribal formation or belief system.

Early Native American oral forms, individuals speaking of group conditions and beliefs, are known today primarily through their literary transactions, written transmissions that, precisely because they are written, cannot represent the cultural norms and circumstances under which the literature originally emerged. Readers today must read Native American songs or chants or narratives in the absence of a generally well known, accompanying cultural "text"—the narrator, the narrative scene, and the cultural assumptions—from which the forms emerged. And even the words that we today reproduce in anthologies like this one are not the words, not the languages, the Native Americans used. Most North American native works from the early period are transcriptions that were made largely in the late nineteenth and early twentieth centuries, when anthropologists and ethnographers as a group first sought to record native traditions and languages just as the Native Americans who carried on in their own traditions and languages were banished to reservations. Older, written versions of Native American oral traditions are few.

And even those older written forms that we read today—primarily the works of the Mayas group of Central America—are linguistically transformed, in that the Mayas recorded their history and culture in the Spanish language soon after their conquest by the Spanish, in *The Book of Chilam Balam of Chumayel* (as it is called in the twentieth-century English translation). As noted above, the Mayan civilization was in decline when the Spanish found them in the fifteenth century. The Mayan chant "The Beginning of Sickness" speaks of the time before the Spanish arrived, a time when the Mayas felt in harmony with their environment, and it bespeaks the Mayan perception of the result of the Spanish conquest. The words here make a fitting conclusion to our discussion of the earliest Native Americans.

The Beginning of Sickness

Then they adhered to their reason.
There was no sin;
in the holy faith their lives were passed.
There was then no sickness;
they had then no aching bones;
they had then no high fever;
they had then no smallpox;
they had then no burning chest;
they had then no abdominal pains;
they had then no consumption;
they had then no headache.
At that time the course of humanity was
orderly.
The foreigners made it otherwise when
they arrived here.
They brought shameful things when
they came . . .
this was the cause of our sickness also.
There were no more lucky days for us;
we had no sound judgment.
At the end of our loss of vision,
and of our shame,
everything shall be revealed.

The Europeans Arrive

"They came from the east," the Mayas report in *The Book of Chilam Balam of Chumayel:*

They came from the east when they
arrived.
Then Christianity also began.
The fulfillment of its prophecy is
ascribed to the east . . .
Then with the true God, the true *Dios,*
came the beginning of our misery.
It was the beginning of tribute,
the beginning of church dues,
the beginning of strife with purse-
snatching,
the beginning of strife with blow-guns;
the beginning of strife by trampling on
people,
the beginning of robbery with violence,
the beginning of forced debts,
the beginning of debts enforced by false
testimony,
the beginning of individual strife,
a beginning of vexation.

The Mayan version of the Spaniards' arrival offers the Native Americans' view of an intrusion that forced upon their culture a complete transformation. One of only a few contemporary views available, the poem tells of the intrusion from the side of the people whose ways were irreparably altered rather than from the side of the conquerors. It reveals, too, the understood motive for the Spanish exploration: colonization and wealth.

But it also reveals the extent to which, in the absence of the known and written language of the speakers, the written evidence that remains indicates how the native speaker's language transformed to accommodate the language of the conquerer. That is, before the Spanish arrived, the Mayan language would have had no word for "Christianity," nor for the many other factors associated with a money-based economy (e.g., "purse"). With the onslaught of the Christianizing Spanish, the Mayas adapted to and adopted the language—and thus the learned culture—of their intruders. With Spanish as the mediating language, the Mayas would never again record their culture within its own linguistic construct.

This is an interesting point to remember, for the Spanish likewise faced a linguistic barrier: how, in the absence of words available to describe the very different peoples they met, were the Spanish to name the peoples they encountered and attempted to assimilate into their own culture? The Spanish language, too, was constructed from those experiences the Spaniards had garnered in Europe and in world travel. The Spanish language, in other words, was conditioned by a Spanish past that would serve to condition the Spanish in the Americas. Here was a new problem—how to record phenomena they had no language to describe. In some instances, the Spanish adopted native names. More simply, they renamed things, like the land they found, thus accommodating their own colonial expectations. In the language and attitude of the conqueror, Columbus promptly renamed the island he found in the Bahamas *San Salvador,* claiming it for the king and queen of Spain. Absolutely sure that he had reached the Indies, he called the people *los Indios,* Indians.

An odd irony appears in this: the Spanish had come upon a land they didn't want, a land perceived as an obstruction rather than an expectation, a land they were seeking to get around, not inhabit. When Spain sent its fleets westward in the fifteenth century, it was looking for a passage to the east, to Asia, which offered the riches—and the African slaves—that neighboring Portugal had acquired a century earlier. A century after the Spanish, the French likewise sent expeditions through the northeast portion of the present-day United States, searching for a legendary "Northwest Passage" to Asia and the Far East. In the process of exploring and then of naming anew, the Spanish came to realize what they had found. Before long, Europeans generally acknowledged that a significant section of the world, a section about which they had known nothing, was available to them.

The Spanish and French were among the first to dispatch exploratory voyages. Among the leaders of early voyages was the Florentine Amerigo Vespucci (who explored the South American coast in 1499). He was the first to publish the idea among Europeans that a new continent had been found; the lands were thus by name credited to him, as *America.* More than five hundred years earlier, Norse explorers had briefly colonized present-day Newfoundland; before that, according to some accounts, the Chinese had explored the coast of what is now southern California. In addition, recent archaeological work suggests that African ships had visited the Americas by, if not before, the early fourteenth century. Spain controlled the seas in the late medieval and early Renaissance era. The voyages of Columbus were thus the ones that brought the Old World to the New World. Once Spain announced that land was available to the west, across the ocean, all Europe became interested in western exploration. The accounts of explorers like John Cabot (1497), Giovanni da Verrazano (1524), Jacques Cartier (1534), and Henry Hudson (1609–1610)—all of whom searched for a Northwest Passage—held Europe's attention. Each new account seemed more promising and fascinating than the last. The public demanded stories about the intriguing "new" land and its inhabitants; monarchs sought information about the possibilities of enlarging their empires and increasing their treasuries; the Pope saw possibilities of extending the Catholic Church in missionary efforts.

Except for Portugal, a poorer country that had nonetheless effected (in the fifteenth century) the introduction of African slaves into Europe, only Spain was in a position—due to a reinvigorated monarchy that encouraged dominion over the seas—to move immediately into the areas Europeans had discovered in what is now Central and South America, Florida and the southeastern United States, and the southwestern United States (through the West and Pacific Northwest). By the 1520s, the Spanish dreams of wealth and dominion were realized: Cortés conquered the Aztec empire when he gained the capital city, Tenochtitlán, a gain that encouraged the Aztecs to kill their ruler, Moctezuma; the Aztec treasures of gold and silver were claimed for Spain. While the explorations of conquistadores like Juan Rodríguez Cabrillo (who sailed along the California coast), Hernando de Soto (who explored the Mississippi River), and Francisco Vásquez de Coronado (who explored the Southwest) proved less monetarily valuable, those of Francisco Pizarro (who explored western and coastal South America) were fruitful for Spain. Pizarro conquered and enslaved the Incas in 1535, claiming for Spain the richest silver mines in the world. Within half a century after Columbus's voyages, then, Spain controlled—as its own possession—the most extensive empire known since ancient Rome.

The quickly acquired wealth exacted its own demands on Spain, however. The economy of Spain could not easily adapt to the new-found gold and silver; rapid inflation caused Spanish products to become overpriced in international trade, eventually bringing about the collapse of Spain's world-renowned textile manufactures, among scores of other businesses. Eventually, the South American mines showed signs of giving out by the middle of the seventeenth century, and Spain's economy crumbled. In addition, the missionary efforts of the Catholic Church created—from the very start—problems for the wealth-seeking colonizers. A 1493 Papal Bull, expressing an aim to Christianize Native Americans rather than enslave them, prevented open aggression against the native populations. A 1542 Spanish law forbidding the enslavement of the Native Americans temporarily interfered with colonizing efforts. The Spaniards quickly turned instead to the African slave trade for its labor force. The colonists, mostly men, formed relations with native and later black women, which created the racially mixed population of present-day Latin America. Finally, when the Spanish Armada saw defeat in 1588, Spain lost its century-long control of the rich lands and the seas to the west.

England and France watched greedily while Spain extended its empire, and both countries took advantage of Spain's losses as the sixteenth century progressed. France had early established outposts for trade—largely furs from the Native Americans for European metalworks and cloth—in the eastern portions of what is now North America. While searching for a Northwest Passage, the French established control over fur traffic at Quebec (1608) and Montreal (1642) and along the St. Lawrence River. Although the interests of France were largely for trade with the native peoples rather than enslavement of them, the French presence nonetheless influenced native societies, which shifted to some extent from subsistence hunting or agriculture to trapping and trade. Combined with the trading activities of the Swedish (at Fort Christina on the Delaware River, 1638) and the Dutch (at New Amsterdam and Fort Orange, 1624), French activities had a significant impact upon the interests and resources of Native Americans.

But it was finally the English who, though their influence was last, made what has for three centuries been considered the strongest impact on what is now the United States. Seeking wealth and colonization to match Spain's, England began sending exploratory parties to the eastern seaboard in the 1580s. English efforts proved largely unsuccessful until England eventually changed its endeavor from accelerated colonization to agricultural community-making. That is, unlike Spain, France, and the Netherlands, England finally succeeded when it sent large numbers of men—and some women—to set up agriculturally based communities. Efforts at Jamestown would largely have failed (and nearly did fail) had not John Smith, despite the reservations and open hostility of the men who landed with him in 1607, insisted upon a daily regimen of work, planting, and hunting, during the first year of settlement. England's control of the tobacco planting and trade shortly followed the Jamestown settlement. When religious and social changes in England caused the English Separatists to leave Holland and settle at Plymouth in 1620 and the Congregationalists to leave England and settle at Massachusetts Bay in 1630, England's endeavors to dominate the New World systems were fully confirmed.

English Settlements

The Jamestown colony was not the first English attempt to found a permanent settlement in North America (the colonizing expedition led by Ralph Lane in 1585 is considered the first), but the Jamestown settlement was the first *successful* attempt. *Success,* however, is a relative term: of the 144 who originally set sail from England in 1607, only 104 survived the voyage; by January 1608, only 38 of the original colonists still survived. The precariousness of the situation necessitated John Smith's famous "he who does not work shall not eat" policy, a policy of which Smith was justly proud, for it forced the wealthy men with whom he had sailed to work, in order to survive. But as we have seen, cordial relations with the Algonkian confederation held the key to English survival at Jamestown. The colonists learned from the Algonkians how to hunt and fish, and most importantly, how to cultivate corn and tobacco. Furthermore, the colonists learned the importance of trade with the Native Americans.

The Separatists who settled in the area they called Plymouth in 1620 learned the same lesson. They had set sail with a group of adventurers bound for the upper reaches of the Virginia area. Indeed, of the more than 100 who set sail on the crowded *Mayflower,* only 30 were Separatist Puritans. Having gone off course, they arrived at what is now Cape Cod as winter was setting in. Although they were, as a group, more willing than the Virginia colonists to work, they could not plant crops so late in the season. As it was, by spring only half of the *Mayflower*'s passengers were alive. They might have failed entirely, without the aid of the Native Americans. Like the Virginia settlers, the Plymouth settlers benefitted from the circumstances of their native neighbors.

The Pokanokets (or Wampanoags) on Cape Cod had suffered terrible losses in an epidemic (probably of smallpox) in the years 1616–1618. Massasoit, their leader, was in the midst of repairing the group's losses, to protect it from incursions of the powerful Narragansetts of the southern New England coast (who were untouched by the disease). When the colonists made efforts to trade with the Pokanokets, Massasoit quickly signed a protective treaty with them; the Pokanokets supplied the colonists with the foodstuffs essential for survival and showed them how to hunt, fish, and plant crops. Mutual trade benefits—foodstuffs for metalworks and weaponry—kept relations between the colonists and the native population fairly good for several years.

By the end of the 1620s another, larger colonial effort was launched, this time chartered by King Charles I. (The Separatist effort had been privately chartered by the Virginia Company.) The new Massachusetts Bay colony would not have survived without the aid of their Plymouth and Native American neighbors. Their colony thrived after some initial years of hardship, and it succeeded in establishing enough control over the surrounding areas that when New England was rechartered in 1691, the Plymouth colony was subsumed under the dominion of Massachusetts Bay.

English colonizing efforts differed in kind from the efforts of Spain and France and the Netherlands, as we have seen. For a variety of reasons related to its economic and social formation, England recognized the necessity of settling agricultural communities in the North American areas it was claiming. This is not to say, however, that the English efforts at Jamestown and in New England were similar. One significant difference influenced the two respective settlements: Jamestown was settled predominantly by men, men who were of a class that was less willing to work at subsistence living. In addition, the Jamestown settlers had little similarity beyond that evident in their elite class assumptions. Some historians suggest that the New England communities fared somewhat better for a variety of reasons: first, because women were brought *from the start* (thus ensuring essential repopulation at the earliest colonial stage); second, because the "middling" and merchant class background of the people generally made them accept field labor; and third, because many of the settlers had a common ideological goal, the development of, as John Winthrop (borrowing from the biblical book of Matthew) phrased it, a "city upon a hill."

Puritanism

For centuries it has been argued that the motivations that brought the English Puritans to North America were primarily religious motivations. More recently, however, social historians have noted that the rise of Puritanism in England might have been a consequence of distinct social changes that were taking place there. Between the years 1530 and 1680, the population in England doubled; people were living longer; babies were surviving into (at least) young adulthood; childbearing less frequently resulted in the death of the mother. The dramatic demographic shift created tension in an already troubled economy: fewer consumable goods were available for more people, which brought a rising inflation, made worse as the number of workers increased

Rules and Precepts That Are Observed in the College.

1. When any scholar is able to understand Tully, or suchlike classical Latin author extempore, and make and speak true Latin in verse and prose, *suo ut aiunt Marte* [by his own effort, as they say]; and decline perfectly the paradigms of nouns and verbs in the Greek tongue, let him then and not before be capable of admission into the college.

2. Let every student be plainly instructed and earnestly pressed to consider well the main end of his life and studies is *to know God and Jesus Christ which is eternal life* (John 17:3), and therefore to lay Christ in the bottom as the only foundation of all sound knowledge and learning. And seeing the Lord only gives wisdom, let everyone seriously set himself by prayer in secret to seek it of Him (Prov. 2:3).

3. Everyone shall so exercise himself in reading the Scriptures twice a day that he shall be ready to give such an account of his proficiency therein, both in theoretical observations of the language and logic, and in practical and spiritual truths, as his tutor shall require, according to his ability; seeing *the entrance of the word giveth light, it giveth understanding to the simple* (Ps. 119:130).

Anon., "Account of Harvard College," 1643

and real wages dropped. Social tensions added to the problem: the well-to-do, alarmed at the rising population of the lower classes, feared what they considered might be the disappearance of their traditional ways of life. The English Reformation, then, was only a part of the picture.

When, in the Reformation, Henry VIII established the Church of England (1533), he developed a Church that for the most part differed little from the Roman Catholic Church. Some reformers thought Henry VIII had not gone far enough. The Continental Protestant reformers Martin Luther (1483–1546), a German monk, and John Calvin (1509–1564), a French cleric and lawyer who settled in Geneva, argued for less ritual and more individual interpretation of the Bible. Following Calvin, English Protestants, many of whom studied with Calvin in Geneva, sought greater change in the English Church. Some, like the Congregationalists, argued that the Anglican Church could be purified from within the church structure. Some, like the Separatists, considered the church so corrupt that it was not salvageable. The Separatists (whom William Bradford called the Pilgrims) eventually fled England, going first to Holland and then to North America. Nearly a decade later, the Congregationalist Puritans followed the Separatists to the "new" world.

Religion was a daily presence in the lives of the Puritans. Followers of Calvin, they believed that God predestined their souls for heaven or for hell and that even devout believers in Christ could do nothing to alter their predetermined fate. With mere belief not assurance of salvation, constant vigilance and self-examination, on the individual and the communal levels, formed a necessary part of the Puritans' primary duties as Christians. With heaven the destination for only a few—the "elect," the "saints," or (following Old Testament terminology) the "chosen ones"—they believed that only those who felt sure that God was with them should enter into church membership. The interior examination of one's soul thus entered the external arena of social action. Self-questioning was, to some extent, a kind of pre-condition to social place. But even the most pious continually doubted their place with God, and many, like John Winthrop and Samuel Sewall, kept diaries in which they carefully detailed and examined everyday occurrences for signs of God's hand in their endeavors.

Their common purpose surely contributed to their survival. Their later prosperity—although they considered it a sign of their God's hand working favorably among them—brought about their dispersal. The community relied upon the necessary interdependence of its individuals, with the Old Testament model of the patriarch (in New England, the governor) at the head of the state and the church. Modeling their environment upon the one they had left, the Puritans established a patriarchal community: just as God the father directed the endeavors of the elect Church, so did the husband and father direct the activities of the family (which included not just his wife and children, but his servants and slaves as well). The patriarchal hierarchical structure in church and family, a structure founded upon "Christian Charity" (the model of love Winthrop spoke of on board the *Arbella*), was modified by the conception of mutual consent. The covenantal nature of their faith—the belief that God had made an agreement with them by choosing them, of all other people, to come to America—coalesced with the covenantal relationships they established on the familial and church level. Theirs was a community—whether in Plymouth or in Massachusetts Bay—based on mutual consent. The Mayflower Compact (1620), then, like the Fundamental Orders of Connecticut (1639), established social systems that reflected their beliefs in covenanted communities based upon the mutual consent of those so governed. The Puritans signaled their religious and governmental goals by establishing compact towns with churches and common grounds at their centers. Their communal endeavor, their attempt to establish a "city upon a hill," ensured them mutual support in the most trying times of earliest settlement.

But trouble emerged from the start. Encroachments upon the Connecticut River Valley brought a war with the Pequots, who were native to the area (1637). Roger Williams had warned in 1635 that England had no right to be giving away charters to lands held by Native Americans and that the Puritans had no right to impose themselves and their faith on all people. His advocacy threatened disunity, and he was banished from Massachusetts (1635); he founded the town of Providence, known for its tolerance of all faiths, on Narragansett Bay.

Another dissenter, Anne Marbury Hutchinson, brought even greater challenge to Massachusetts Bay authorities. Arguing that the elect could communicate with God directly and get assurance of salvation, Hutchinson threatened the structure of the institutional church, because her religious assumptions denied the necessity for a minister's mediating efforts. As a midwife, she first gained many followers among the women in Massachusetts Bay. When the husbands of her women followers started to join them for Bible study in Hutchinson's home instead of in church, authorities grew uneasy. Hutchinson was brought before the General Court of Massachusetts in 1637, ostensibly because she threatened religious orthodoxy. But she threatened the patriarchal hierarchy as well. Puritans believed all people were equal before God but that women were inferior to men because tainted by Eve's guilt. The magistrates who tried Anne Hutchinson commented upon her "masculine" behavior as much as they commented upon her religious beliefs. John Winthrop accused her of setting wife against husband. Another judge was more indignant: "You have stept out of your place," he adjudged, continuing, "you have rather bine a Husband than a Wife and a preacher than a Hearer; and a Magistrate than a Subject." Anne Hutchinson was expelled from Massachusetts Bay in 1637.

New World Cultures

The Puritans' community-sanctioned ousting of Williams and Hutchinson suggests their consuming hegemonic vision of a community free of trouble and dedicated to the fulfillment of God's vision. That God's vision might differ if one were not a Puritan white man seems finally not to have been a question most Puritans wished to address. Theirs was a community based upon the individual's acceptance of his or her status, and status (including its educational and financial prerogatives), they ethnocentrically thought, was God-granted both in church and state: men above women, whites above all other races, Protestant English above all other cultures.

Such attitudes were peculiar neither to the Puritans nor to the English. We have seen that the Spanish, too, worked largely from the belief that theirs was the one true course for glory, whether that glory was signified by wealth acquired here (as with the conquistadores) or hereafter (as with the missionary priests). The patriarchal assumptions held by Renaissance and late Renaissance European societies both Catholic and Protestant directed actions that held women and other cultures in minority positions, in subjection—to the husband, the governor, and God. The Americas merely offered a new arena for Europe's working out its ages-old rivalries, as Spain, France, the Netherlands, and England vied over souls and resources.

But these cultures did not vie for dominion without resistance from Native Americans. Thirty years after Pedro Menéndez de Avilés, along with a group of soldiers, priests, and settlers, established Spain's first permanent settlement in North America (St. Augustine, Florida, 1565), a similar group led by Juan de Oñate colonized New Mexico. Their mutual goals of finding wealth and Christianizing native peoples spurred them to make ruthless encroachments upon Native Americans. Native laborers were forced to destroy their own religious places and set up monasteries and to work the Spaniards' fields and care for their livestock. Spanish settlers and missionaries, based at Santa Fe (beginning in 1610), saw success meet their efforts for a half-century before the Pueblos revolted. In 1680, under the leadership of Popé, a respected medicine man whom the Pueblos called Tío Pepe, the Pueblos drove the Spanish intruders from New Mexico. Their uprising continued until Spanish authority was restored, at least in name, in 1692, when Spain decided upon a policy of cooperation with rather than coercion of the Pueblo peoples.

Systematic repression of the Native Americans occurred not merely at the hands of the Spanish. The English settlements, in their continued incursions on Native American lands and culture, likewise forced the Native Americans to strike back at the intruders. At the outset the Powhatan confederacy established peaceable enough connections with the English, even to the point where racial intermarriage was encouraged—as it was in New Spain—as an ameliorating and peacekeeping device. But when the continually expanding Virginia tobacco culture took away the best Algonkian lands and threatened encroachment upon additional Algonkian territories, stripping them of trees and fertile planting areas, the Powhatan confederacy attacked the Virginia colony (1622). Not until 1646 did the Powhatans reach an uneasy treaty with the English.

By the early 1670s, however, Virginians wanted the rich lands north of the York River, lands that had been ceded to native groups in earlier treaties. As justification for an attack against the Doegs and Susquehannocks, some Virginia planters pointed to the July 1675 killing of a white servant by a Doeg as a cause demanding white retaliation. The powerful Susquehannock bands responded with raids of their own during the winter of 1676. When white planters rallied behind a recently arrived planter, Nathaniel Bacon, who wanted, he said, "to ruine and extirpate all Indians in generall," the Virginia Burgesses declared their aggression a rebellious act against the state. Alternately fighting the Indians and the Burgesses, Bacon soon died of dysentery. A 1677 treaty, however, opened the disputed lands to white planters and settlers.

Similar problems over lands and peoples occurred in the English settlements to the north. The Pequot War (1637) signaled the end of peaceable relations between whites and natives in the Connecticut River Valley area. When small English raids on their villages continued from 1636 into 1637, the Pequots (having attempted, but failing to gain support from other local bands) attacked the new town of Wethersfield in April 1637; they killed nine and captured two colonists. A retaliatory party of Massachusetts Bay settlers, aided by some of their Narragansett allies, attacked and burned the key Pequot town on the Mystic River. At least four hundred people—many of them women and children—were killed, with the few survivors being captured and enslaved. The Narragansetts learned too late that the Pequots had been right to question the English encroachments. In 1642, the Narragansett leader Miantonomi (or Miantonomo) attempted to forge a pan-Indian alliance, saying, according to one record, that "so are we all Indians as the English are . . . so must we be one as they are, otherwise we shall all be gone shortly." Miantonomi was killed in 1643, at the hands of native persons serving the English.

Another significant (and perhaps the best-known) English and Indian war occurred before the seventeenth century concluded. It was a war fought, again, over the fertile Connecticut River Valley, led by Metacomet, known to the colonists as King Philip, the son of Massasoit. Resenting the geographical and cultural intrusions the English were making on his people, Metacomet (leader, after the death of his father, of the Pokanoket or Wampanoag band) sought the support of the neighboring Nipmucks and Narragansetts. In the fall of 1675, the three native groups made joint attacks upon settlements in the Connecticut River Valley, and in the winter and spring of 1676, they even attacked Plymouth and Providence. Despite lessening food and ammunition stores, the natives were largely successful until the English were aided in their retaliatory efforts by "praying" (converted) Indians. The English regained their control over the valley when Metacomet was killed in ambush in the autumn of 1676; his wife and son were captured and sold to the West Indian slave trade. The New England Indian alliance, thus broken, never gathered force again.

Part of the success of the New England settlers can be attributed to the Puritan ideology that formed the basis of their culture, even though that ideology came to be questioned by the end of the century. Indeed, perhaps the self-questioning especially prevalent by the end of the century was itself a result of the construct of doubt that the Puritans themselves encouraged. Doubt itself formed a part of the salvation process, to most Puritans. Ample cause for an emerging doubt arrived with hordes of new colonists in the 1640s and 1650s. When it was clear that the Massachusetts Bay settlers were surviving the ordeal of colonization, greater numbers of settlers came over in what historians have called the Great Migration. Some of the new colonists were Puritans; others were merchants and artisans simply bent upon making their way in the English colonies. The numbers of people emigrating combined with the increasing population (children born in New England survived in greater proportions than their counterparts in England in the seventeenth century) to require larger Puritan landholdings and a dispersal of the once centralized population. There were societal changes for Puritan and non-Puritan alike.

A key change was that fewer and fewer people wished to attend to the rigor of Puritan church discipline. By 1662, the Half-Way Covenant was established, which offered admission to one of two church sacraments (baptism, but not the taking of the Lord's Supper) to the children of baptized church members. In the earliest days of the Puritan settlement, each applicant for church membership was required to relate to the congregation (or to the minister and church elders, for women) his or her own grace-begetting experience, that moment when God signaled to the applicant that the applicant was "saved." The Half-Way Covenant enabled those who were *born of members* who had expressed a visible sainthood—but who had not themselves experienced God's grace—to attend church sacraments. The breakdown in church rigor, it was believed, might encourage more people to attend to the state of their souls—and to attend church. For those who admired the rigor of Puritanism in its oldest form, the introduction of the Half-Way Covenant was a doleful, tension-producing sign that God's people were failing.

The necessity of the Half-Way Covenant, the dissenting opinions offered by Williams and Hutchinson, the increasing Indian wars, the shifting socio-economic picture—all contributed to an era of self-doubt for the Puritan patriarchy. Although it was part of the functioning of the Puritan faith that the individual continually concern himself or herself with the soul's state, individual self-doubt emerged into a kind of communal self-doubt. Some thought the devil had somehow arisen in the unwary New England community. Some addressed the doubt as if it were the chastisement of a vengeful Lord ready at any moment to strike at the failing community of saints. Others insisted that their self-doubt was a sign from God of their humility before his all-powerful Word. Still others merely awaited the numerically magical year 1666, the time when some felt assured that Christ would come a second time.

But the years passed on, until various crises social and religious culminated in the Salem witch trials of the 1690s. Some historians argue that, considering the demographic trends of the time and the fact that more women than men were tried as witches, the trials at Salem resulted from the growing tensions in a community comprised of an overabundance of unmarried women. Others argue that the trials represent the communal Puritan self-doubt gone awry into self-mutilation. Surely there were many contributing causes for this still unaccountable phenomenon of neighbor accusing neighbor of witchery. By the end of the trials, twenty-seven people were convicted of witchcraft, fifty more had "confessed," and one hundred others were imprisoned and awaiting trial. Twenty people died as accused witches. An additional two hundred had been accused, but they never went to trial, for as quickly as the trials began, they stopped. Public embarrassment, doubt, and communal sorrow brought an end to a very traumatic era for the Puritan commonwealth. Those who had initiated the trial action were publicly discredited. Samuel Sewall, a judge, recanted his role in the proceedings. He was the only one publicly to do so.

One of those earliest accused of witchcraft was Tituba, a black slave and housekeeper in the household of Rev. Samuel Parris. It seems likely now that interracial uncertainty contributed to the growing social tensions felt in New England and in the colonies as a whole. The importation of slaves had grown throughout the colonies, especially in the South, where labor-intensive crops like tobacco, rice, and indigo required daily care. But slavery occurred in the North as well. Samuel Sewall himself wrote a pamphlet, *The Selling of Joseph* (1700), condemning the institution of slavery. The Quakers who were beginning to settle in the Middle Atlantic area denounced as early as 1670 the "traffic in menbody." Despite the occasional opposition to slaveholding, however, by the end of the seventeenth century African or West Indian slaves were increasingly more common in the households of the well-to-do from Massachusetts Bay to Florida, Jamestown to Santa Fe and beyond.

Africans had traveled to the Americas with the earliest exploring parties from Spain, including those directed by Coronado and Cabeza de Vaca. Indeed, a black man named Pedro Alonso Niño is said to have participated in the first expedition of Columbus. Records indicate that the transatlantic slave trade began in 1502, when the Spanish brought the first Africans to work plantations in the West Indies. Balboa's 1513 expedition to the Pacific included thirty slaves, and slaves accompanied Hernando de Soto on his Mississippi exploration in 1539. The best-known (because of written records) of these early slave travelers, Estévan (also called Estevanico and Esteban), explored with Cabeza de Vaca and Fray Marcos de Niza the areas that are now Arizona and New Mexico and lived with Cabeza de Vaca among the Native Americans. Then, in the late 1530s, he served as a guide for Fray Marcos de Niza in his search for the Seven Cities of Cíbola. Blacks also accompanied Alarçon and Coronado and were with Menéndez at the founding of St. Augustine.

Initially, the Spanish attempted to draw their slave labor from the indigenous peoples of the New World. In addition to practical problems encountered in this effort, both the Catholic Church and the Spanish government eventually prohibited the enslavement of the indigenous peoples. In 1517, in protesting the exploitation of natives, the Spanish missionary Bartolomé de Las Casas proposed the use of African slaves instead. Permission to import Africans was soon granted, and by the mid-sixteenth century roughly ten thousand blacks were being brought into the Spanish colonies annually. By the time the English developed their own settlements in the Caribbean and North America, the Spanish had held Africans in slavery for over a century.

Historical evidence seems to suggest that the blacks who arrived during the first two to three decades of English settlement came as indentured servants, which meant that they eventually became free. Such servants arrived at Jamestown on a Dutch vessel in 1619, only twelve years after the founding of the settlement. Precisely because indentured servants could eventually become free and move off the lands they had worked, planters in the South came to rely upon the slave market for laborers. The increasing demand for slaves meant that larger and larger groups of Africans were captured on their homelands and sold into bondage. Some, like those taken to South Carolina, were skilled agricultural laborers, and they taught their owners much about survival and success in environments like that in the Carolina lowlands. The South was not the only place where English acquired slaves, however. Africans were first imported into Connecticut in 1629 and in 1637 to Massachusetts, which became the first colony to mention slaves in its legal code (1641). It was also about this time that New England ships became actively involved in the slave trade.

As the plantation-based economy of the southern colonies expanded, the importation of slaves accelerated rapidly. Not surprisingly, with the swelling black population came greater numbers of slave escapes and revolts. Indeed, in a number of areas, fugitive slaves called "maroons" (from the Spanish *cimarrones*) had established independent communities and were creating trouble for local white settlements. Elsewhere, some blacks found refuge with Native Americans after their flight from slavery. In retaliation for this and other rebellious black behavior, whites enacted increasingly strict slave codes in order to regulate the behavior of their human property. One of the most important legal actions relating to the treatment of blacks was the law—first passed in Virginia in 1662—which stipulated that the status of the child would follow that of his or her mother. In combination with the forbidding of interracial marriage (and also of sexual contact between black males and white women), this legislation insured that the numerous illegitimate slave off-

II. On the Nativity Conditions of Slavery (December 1662)

Whereas some doubts have arisen whether children got by an Englishman upon a Negro woman should be slave or free, *be it therefore enacted and declared by this present Grand Assembly,* that all children born in this country shall be held bond or free only according to the condition of the mother; and that if any Christian shall commit fornication with a Negro man or woman, he or she so offending shall pay double the fines imposed by the former act.

V. On the Killing of Slaves (October 1669)

Whereas the only law in force for the punishment of refractory servants resisting their master, mistress, or overseer cannot be inflicted upon Negroes, nor the obstinacy of many of them be suppressed by other than violent means, *be it enacted and declared by this Grand Assembly* if any slave resists his master (or other by his master's order correcting him) and by the extremity of the correction should chance to die, that his death shall not be accounted a felony, but the master (or that other person appointed by the master to punish him) be acquitted from molestation, since it cannot be presumed that premeditated malice (which alone makes murder a felony) should induce any man to destroy his own estate.

Virginia Slave Laws

spring of white males would have no right to freedom and, in fact, would simply serve to enrich the slaveowner's human stock. The most tragic result of these developments was the rampant sexual abuse of black women.

Gradually, the morality of slavery as an institution began to be called into question by some of the colonists. In 1652, for example, Rhode Island passed the first antislavery law, although the law probably was not strictly enforced. Then, in 1688, Quakers in the Philadelphia area became one of the first organized groups to denounce the enslavement of blacks publicly; and by 1711 the Quaker denomination generally had taken a strong abolitionist position. From this point on, the slavery issue (and the question of racial difference on which it rested) presented America with one of its most vexing dilemmas.

From its start, the "American" community was multi-racial and multi-cultural. The Puritan vision of a single New World community was doomed from the start, as were the idyllic visions of the fabled El Dorado, of the seven cities of Cíbola, or of a Northwest Passage. Visions like these exist in the literatures as seemingly quaint dreams of an improbable future and a past nostalgically longed for, never to be fulfilled. What time and historical record have made clear is that the creation of what has become the United States of America was from the start a multinational competition for dominance and possession rather than an establishment of utopian communities in isolated colonies that eventually clashed (in the nineteenth century) as culture met culture in the farther reaches of the American continent, somewhere along the Nueces River in Texas, or the Arkansas River in Colorado, or at Monterey Bay in California. The Europeans' New World, comprised of defined spheres of influence over territories claimed and counterclaimed by European sovereign powers, early offered signs of the necessary mingling of red, white, and black that remain as both a defining and a contested national vision.

New World Literatures

As we have seen, the discoverers, explorers, and settlers who came to the New World left cultures—whether in Spain or France or England—that were experiencing enormous transformations. The discovery of lands to the west, across the ocean, was only one of a number of important changes Europeans would experience. Discoveries of lands westward only fed imaginations already attuned to wonder because of the invention of moveable type for printing presses, the revival of classical Greek and Roman literature and architecture, and the rise of the arts—painting, sculpture, and architecture. Of course, the Renaissance occurred largely because of and for the privileged classes; with the possibility of a developing printing culture, however, information and knowledge would never again be the sole province of the well-to-do.

The privileged form of writing during the Renaissance was poetry, especially epic poetry. Christian epic poetry, from Tasso to Spenser and later to Milton, informed the imaginations of those who wished to believe that the lands to the west were provided entirely for the working-out of their own Christian journeys. Thus, Anne Bradstreet transformed du Bartas, and Edward Taylor evoked the writings of John Donne, George Herbert, and other English metaphysical writers. But other poetic forms, the pastoral and the lyric, informed the culture, along with comedy and tragedy and pastoral in drama. Late in the sixteenth century, and predictably concomitant with the rise of socio-economic changes, verse satire emerged as a significant poetic form.

But prose, too, saw increased development. Essayists from Sir Philip Sidney to Richard Hooker sought to inform their readers on cultural matters from poetry to theology, while others wrote detailed behavioral guides and character studies. With the European discovery of the westward lands, exploration and travel literature emerged in Europe as the most significant prose form, encouraging narratives ranging from those considered informative (Hakluyt's *Principal Navigations and Discoveries of the English Nation*) to those utopian (Thomas More's *Utopia*). Travel literature dominated the prose forms until it was surpassed in popularity by the most important prose romance of the day, Cervantes's *Don Quixote*.

All of these genres, and many others as well, form the basis for a new world literature that would provide a record of experience according to old world values. As the Spanish language conditioned the Mayan record of their own experiences, so it conditioned Spain's own record of what was new. Cotton Mather's and Roger Williams's attempts to record the Native Americans' words signify what must have been a frustrating attempt to encode a language structured to accommodate a different system entirely, a system oral in origination and glyphic in form. Readers often lament that so little from this period has survived. Perhaps it is more relevant to consider how much did survive (albeit in altered form) in a European world in which linguistic and cultural constructs so fully determined the Europeans' responses to the newly found lands and peoples.

The linguistic construct was predominantly Spanish and English, the cultural construct Christian, ethnocentric, and patriarchal. The new lands were considered to be the province of the Europeans. For instance, when Arthur Barlowe's exploring party reached shoal water off the coast of Virginia in 1584, Barlowe reported that they smelled sweet air, "so strong a smell as if we had been in the midst of some delicate garden, abounding with all kinds of oderiferous flowers." He continued, describing the Native Americans as "most gentle, loving, and faithful, void of all guile, and treason, and such as lived after the manner of the golden age." The natives were, he claimed, "the most kind and loving people of the world." Surely Barlowe's picture of the Virginia coastal area is conditioned by his reading of classical literature, the Bible, and other travel literature. And surely it is designed in part to encourage the crown's funding of other, future expeditions. Barlowe's account, like the accounts of most explorers, presents the new in terms of the familiar, the potentially dangerous in terms comfortable. Like Fray Marcos de Niza, who felt assured he'd seen the seven cities of Cíbola, Barlowe could only imagine his party would meet with success. The writings of Columbus, Casteñeda, Villagrá, Champlain, Hakluyt and Purchas—all work from Europeanized metaphors to encourage interest in the colonies and, more centrally, funding for exploration. As exploration continued, other narratives developed from the explorers' experiences. Cabeza de Vaca, stranded among native peoples, learned to adjust and adapt to a culture he had once deplored. His narrative of captivity heads a long list of such narratives that detail the extent to which the individual comes to accept the other's world. In Cabeza's experience, he finally learned he was fully welcome neither among native people nor among the Spanish, when he was again found. The uneasy journey into the other culture, then, became a kind of otherworldly journey into a new land, a journey that perhaps best signifies what might be called the most American of experiences. Arthur Barlowe wrote of a kind of American dream; Cabeza de Vaca, of a kind of American nightmare.

The explorers' writings are predetermined by their own ideological circumstances and so, in a sense, construct events to conform to their own expectations. The Puritans' settlement narratives, from William Bradford's *Of Plymouth Plantation* to Mary Rowlandson's own captivity narrative, work much in the same way.

That is, the Puritans saw all events as occurring according to providential will, all crises as tests offered by Satan and watched over carefully by God. When Bradford reports that the surveying party found native corn buried, he insists that God was thus providing for the Separatist journey. When Mary Rowlandson speaks of the remarkable providences that enabled her captors to flee from the English army, she is signaling her sense of awe before an all-powerful God who wished to see her mettle tested. Thus, from Puritan histories through the diaries, poems, and sermons of their day, readers find a relentless searching for biblical precedent and for God in all events. To Cotton Mather, John Winthrop was not just a good governor, he was an American Nehemiah. Theirs was to be the last, best world.

Both the poetry (from Villagrá on) and prose that comprise the canon of the earliest American literature offer a paradigm of the ideal enterprise, the search for the ideal state either here or hereafter. Whether the text is a Puritan captivity narrative or a Native American chant, we can witness, in our earliest American literature, artists' attempts to re-create experience in ways that will accommodate the multitude of situations life in America offers.

Throughout these writings, regardless of the circumstances of the writer's or speaker's birth, the resilience of the speaking voice is abundantly clear. The following song from the Teton Sioux is an opening prayer from the sun-dance ceremony, a principal religious celebration of these peoples. Recorded by Frances Densmore during her fieldwork at the Standing Rock Reservation in North and South Dakota between 1911 and 1914, the song resonates with the speaker's power in the world.

Opening Prayer of the Sun Dance

Grandfather,
a voice I am going to send.
Hear me.
All over the universe,
a voice I am going to send.
Hear me,
Grandfather.
I will live.
I have said it.

Perhaps American literature can best be described not as a literature that continually tested itself until it found a voice against the literature of England but as a literature that was multi-vocal from the start. And perhaps its key resides not in any particular interpretation of world events so much as in the necessity of the artist-creator, the speaker of a text, to formulate and thus form experience amid a multitude of possibilities.

Native American Oral Literatures

At the moment when Native Americans first entered the consciousness of the European kingdoms through the Columbian contacts, more than ten million people occupied present-day North America, living in different patterns of settlement, with different economies, different ways of tracing ancestry, and different structures for distributing authority and responsibility. Only the broadest and thinnest generalizations can link these differences under a single title as "Native American." Among them, they spoke more than 350 languages and developed complex genre systems of verbal art within the familiar categories of speech, chant, and song. Today, two million of their descendants live in the United States, and in America, north of Mexico, perhaps as many as 200 languages are still spoken. Far from being the plain and casual utterances the foreign invaders often took them to be, the oral literatures of these Native American communities are distinguishable by form, content, style, and features of performance well-known to the native communities in which they have evolved. These works thus correspond well to the most fundamental notions of literature, however much their themes, forms, and styles may differ from Euro-American traditions.

The principal difference, of course, is the mode of presentation. Oral literatures are performed in the presence of audiences that evaluate the manner of performance as well as the content. Evaluation is not reserved for the conclusion of the performance; it is an ongoing activity reflected in degrees of attention and overt comment. Audiences apprehend the structure of a story through the slightly varied repetitions of incident, respond to characterizations highlighted by changes in the voice volume and pitch, or wait in the full silence of a pause. The canons of aesthetic value for performance differ from community to community and within each community from genre to genre. Oral literature is less a tradition of texts than a tradition of performances. This difference between the joint, contemporary realization of an oral performance and the delayed collaboration between an author and a reader through a text is worth reflecting on. Within the limits imposed by translation and textualizations, contemporary readers can usefully read these texts aloud, weighing line breaks, punctuation and sentence length in an attempt to simulate the experience of an oral literature. Each performance, then, is unique, but its uniqueness is modulated by a framework of expectations. Many works exist in different versions, while others have been rigidly governed by sanctions which restricted variation. This interplay between conservation and innovation is the very life of the oral tradition, and, as the Yuchi story and the Seneca story of "How America Was Discovered" witness, contact with Europeans has been an important element of that dynamic.

In Europe the Age of the Book coincided with the Age of Discovery. For this reason and others, most of the European newcomers were slow to recognize the existence of these Native American literatures. The terrible but transparent irony is that the process of recording them did not begin in earnest until the nineteenth century, when Native American communities themselves were being pressed to the brink of annihilation. While there is little doubt that the long-term effect of the European presence has been to reduce Native American populations and undermine the integrity of their cultures, nevertheless many Indian communities today still sustain viable oral literatures, preserving old forms and evolving new ones, while literacy has enabled the emergence of masterful writing in English by Native American authors.

The transformation of oral literature into literary texts, a process which includes both transcription and translation, is not simply a technical problem of how to write down spoken words. Every act of textualization reflects the nature of the non-Indian audience at which it is aimed and the specific interests motivating it. Differences in audience and interest substantially affect the form of the textualization and the nature of the Euro-American and Indian collaboration required to produce change. Most of the first Europeans understood language as a tool through which one could have access to important cultural information about Native Americans. Acts of textualization always employed the Latin alphabet, which obscured differences in sound and style, and the block or paragraph format (familiar from European conventions for expository writing), which obscured differences in genre forms. Moreover, in the act of textualization, what began as dialogue or first-person direct address was often reduced to depersonalized statements framed in the grammatical third person, thus obscuring the Native American speaker. In this way Indian-authored utterances were re-presented to non-Indian audiences as authoritative Indian texts.

The need for information useful for advancing the aims of religious, economic, or political colonization was not the only reason for textualizing oral literatures. As early as the sixteenth century, some of the Spanish priests and the Nahua converts they had educated began textualizing the oral poetry of the Aztecs. Their interest was in those forms of discourse most closely analogous to categories recognized in the West as literature. Recording of native materials was usually undertaken by individuals interested in representing Native Americans in a light most favorable to Europeans. One result was that such acts of textualization, especially those in English that began in earnest in the nineteenth century, often re-presented native verbal art in forms and styles most closely resembling whatever was the current conventional Western notion of the literary. This was true whether those producing the texts were Indian, as in the case of David Cusick or Arthur Parker, or non-Indian. A comparison of their texts in this volume reveals just how different the models of "literariness" can be; indeed, comparison can open a valuable avenue of inquiry into the social and aesthetic values implicit in textmaking and the agents and audiences involved in that activity.

By and large, the textualizations that have proven most durable are those produced by linguists and anthropologists in this century. Careful transcription and translation has secured texts, such as Ruth Bunzel's Zuni texts in this volume, that closely approximate both the individual voice and cultural aesthetics. In this way, these texts make available a singular instance of a story or song that has been circulating orally for perhaps hundreds of years. Today, newer models of textmaking provide for recording patterns of sound and silence or employ culturally distinctive grammatical markers to structure texts.

These oral works have emerged from a confluence of forces, but we can still usefully ask familiar questions about them. For example, anthropologists interested in recording stories as representative cultural or linguistic documents often ignored the creative role of the individual singer or storyteller and contributed to a misconception about anonymous or communal authorship. Authoring is a cultural role, burdened by many assumptions. In most Indian societies, some stories and songs are considered common property, while others are the property of a particular social or religious group, and still others are said to belong to individuals. These notions of ownership differ from contemporary Western notions that emphasize individual ownership as private property and authorship as Romantic and "inspired." To focus on the role of the individual author, when known, such as in the Aztec or Inuit poetry, is to raise the same kinds of questions we ask of any author's attempt to negotiate a respect for tradition with a desire for innovation within the framework of communal sanctions.

Similarly, we may rightly ask familiar questions about verisimilitude, about the text's representation of the world. Understanding character motivation, image, or theme, however, requires expending some effort to understand cultural values and beliefs about the shape of the world and human nature, often very different from the reader's own, as an appropriate context for interpretation. It is only one's intimate but nevertheless learned familiarity with the cultural values and beliefs of one's own community which makes them seem "natural" or "universal." And the same may be said for aesthetic judgments, which often emerge from a reader's almost instinctive comparison between the work at hand and works judged to be similar in form, theme, or style. But using the appearance of similarity to establish an intertextual context for evaluation often fails to weigh the work justly, because the intertextual tradition against which it is judged is European or American, not Siouan, Zuni, or Seneca. In short, aesthetic values emerge from rather than transcend specific cultural contexts, and we quickly discover the limits of our own assumptions and knowledge in encountering literatures from outside the more familiar Euro-American traditions.

In developing a sample of the oral literatures of Native America for inclusion in this anthology, a number of values had to be weighed and balanced. While it is important to emphasize, for example, that Native American oral literatures not only survive, but in many cases, flourish today alongside contemporary Native American writing, these texts were placed at the beginning of the volume, although most of them were recorded, as the dates appended to them attest, in the nineteenth and twentieth centuries. The placement was meant to highlight the depth of oral traditions, for some of these stories and songs were certainly told for centuries and reflect pre-contact cultural realities. We wish to underscore the fact that humanity's experience on this continent was articulated in complex forms long before the Europeans came. Columbus did not enter a silent world. Also, the wish to offer a number of texts of different genres from within a single culture had to be balanced by an equally important commitment to represent the cultural diversity of Native American peoples. Another difficult challenge was to choose works which were at once complex enough in form, theme, and language to adequately represent the multiplicity of interests, beliefs, and values that shaped them, while not requiring the development of a critical apparatus so extensive and cumbersome that it would overshadow the literature. Individual works were not chosen because they were "masterworks"; indeed, while a Zuni would place a very high value on "Sayatasha's Night Chant" or a Lakota on the story of White Buffalo Calf Pipe Woman, it is doubtful they would single out any one work from their literatures as a "masterwork." Such tendencies toward canonization reflect our interests, not those of native communities. Among the many genres of verbal art actualized by performance at different times and in different settings throughout the year, the stories and songs included in this anthology were valuable for many reasons. And their interest for us as a secondary audience will to some degree be different from their interest for their original audience.

In the end, with each fresh encounter, the reader must struggle, with imagination and understanding, to modulate his or her own individual interests with those of the author, community, and world from which the text emerged.

Andrew O. Wiget
New Mexico State University

Native American Oral Narrative

Native American stories, rich in tradition, are inextricably rooted in the things of tribal experiences; and, because they are oral rather than written, the tales rely upon a performance dimension that is lost to a reader. For instance, Navajo and Iroquois stories are told in complex performances that, for an understanding of their fullest dimensions, require the audience's knowledge of the location of particular places where events occurred and the specific voices in which certain characters are speaking. Ritual dances in both cultures ascribe to certain locations inside the audience circle the geographical places afar off that are mentioned in the stories. Sand paintings, in the Navajo traditions, are ritualistic and sacred, for they symbolize sacred places and sacred acts that inform the Navajo stories being told. The creation story of the Iroquois similarly relies upon the experiences known to the listeners; the long houses of the sky dwellers in the Iroquois creation story resemble the long houses traditional in Iroquois culture. Native American stories, then—whether they are chants, songs, or narratives—rely upon a performance, a dramatic presentation that the written word for the most part cannot convey.

Cycles of stories relate to the Native Americans' subsistence experiences—planting, hunting, and fishing—and to life experiences—birth, puberty, and death. Other stories explain the more distant origin of the world and emergence of the people, the development of the particular Native American population and crucial events in the history of that population, and the uncertain nature of human existence. The latter groups of stories are offered here—stories of origin and emergence, historical narratives, and trickster tales.

Origin and Emergence Stories are complex symbolic tales that typically dramatize the tribal explanation of the origin of the earth and its people; establish the central relationships among people, the cosmos or universe, and the other creatures (flora and fauna) of the earth; distinguish gender roles and social organization for the tribe; account for the distinctive aspects of climate and topography of the tribe's homeland; and tell of the origins of the tribe's most significant social institutions and activities. Given the great numbers of Native American tribes, it can be expected that some of the stories offer interesting similarities while others suggest great differences among tribes.

Several different types of origin tales are prominent in the Native American canon. The two most common are the Emergence story, found throughout the southwestern United States, and the Earth-Diver story, which predominates throughout Canada and the eastern region. The Earth-Diver story tells of a great flood that covered the earth and of beings who are borne upon the water until, after several failed attempts, an animal brings up enough mud from beneath the water to begin the magical creation of the earth. David Cusick, a Tuscarora Indian whose tribe was allied to the Iroquoian Confederacy, began the history of his people with a version of the Earth-Diver story. Because it resembled that of Noah and the flood of the biblical tradition, many Euro-Americans considered the Indians to be descended from the Lost Tribes of Israel, a group of ten tribes that, after the conquest and destruction of ancient Israel, never returned. It is possible that the Biblical stories and the Native Americans' stories have an ancient, common antecedent.

Native American tales more frequently differ, however, from the stories of biblical tradition. For most of the pueblo dwellers and many other Native American groups, people did not originate in a protoworld (like Eden) but rather in the womb of the Earth Mother, from which they were called out into the daylight of their Sun Father. Most widely developed among agricultural peoples, the Emergence story narrates the original passage from darkness to light, from chaos to order, and from undetermined to distinctly human form. The dynamic of evolution—that life evolves from one form to another—serves as a fundamental metaphor for transformations of all kinds. If one is ill, or if the community is without rain or food, restoration can be achieved by a ritual return to the place of Emergence and recovery of the original power from that place.

Both the Emergence and Earth-Diver stories are part of much longer narratives, in which they are followed by migration stories, as in the Zuni search for the Center of the World, or **Culture Hero Stories,** like the Navajo story of Changing Woman and the Hero Twins. Culture Hero Stories dramatize a people's belief about how a remarkable individual altered the original world and social order to its culturally accepted norm. The events in these stories account for the origin of distinctive cultural beliefs, values and practices. So, for example, the Lakota tell how a supernatural woman, White Buffalo Calf Pipe Woman, brought to them the sacred pipe and taught them how to pray with it to the Great Spirit. The Seneca tell of a young man named Gaqka or Crow who went to the south and, listening to the earth, learned all the stories, and brought back storytelling to the Seneca.

The Biblical stories of Genesis, which most Europeans believed, functioned in a similar manner for the colonists. Yet a comparison of Native American origin tales and Biblical stories illuminates profound cultural differences. Generally speaking, Native Americans traditionally did not believe in a single supreme, autonomous, and eternal being who established the conditions under which all beings must exist. Nor did they consider humans as having a radically different nature from the rest of earth's inhabitants, which they conceived of as intelligent, self-willed, and communicative. Given such beliefs, Native Americans found that the proper relation between people and the earth should be one of familial and personal respect, a relation honorable because of a kinship derived from a common beginning.

Perhaps most importantly, no Native American origin myth identifies anything at all analogous to the Christian belief in sin or a fall from the grace of a god. That is, there is no evil pre-condition, no lost harmony and balance, in the Native American interpretation of origin. Thus, there is likewise no story similar to that of the Christian savior. Many Native American tales, by contrast, explain that people and the universe at the same time moved from chaos and disorder to balance and harmony. These stories offer examples of prototypical relationships that show reciprocal and cyclic evolution, an evolution tied to a very particular place. Jews and Christians over the centuries have transported to each new settlement the divine commission given to Adam at the moment of creation. The Zuni, the Navajo, the Iroquois, indeed each Native American people, lived in a particular homeland known to be their own since their beginning, given to them, as the Zuni myth so aptly expresses it, as their Center. For most Native Americans this Center was both a specific life-sustaining environment and a compelling identity-sustaining idea, especially in times of tribal trouble. To move or be moved from their Center was, for these Native Americans, unthinkable.

Historical Narratives explain the movements of the tribe, and thus frequently recount the colonization of the tribe by the Europeans. Some historical narratives feature legendary figures of mythical proportions who move about in recognizably historic settings. In these narratives, the relationship between actual event and tribal belief is not always clear. Other historical narratives serve primarily as tribal record, and are thus extraordinarily accurate. As the Hopi narrative of the coming of the Spanish suggests, in some tribes what has been called "memory culture" might encompass centuries.

Many stories of this vast historical literature are of value for Euro-Americans, for they tell of colonization from the Native American perspective. The Hopi narrative, with its unflattering picture of Franciscan missionizing, a narrative substantiated in large measure by the documentary record, stands in stark contrast to Villagrá's Catholic vision of the conquest as a glorious march of the cross. More importantly, the story highlights the profound differences between the two cultures, differences even centuries of contact would not alter. The Spanish understood native religions as paganism which, for the sake of the Native Americans, the Spanish were bound by their God to eradicate. Pueblo Indians like the Hopi, on the other hand, wondered about a God who commanded them to abandon their kachina religion, knowing that extinction was the logical consequence of suppressing the religion that had secured rain, food, life itself, since their Emergence into the dayworld. The Seneca story of "How America Was Discovered," like the Yuchi story, historicizes elements of origin myths into a critical account of the effects of contact with European invaders.

As the Native Americans' stories of their origin, religious life, and social activity differed markedly from the Europeans', so did their stories explaining life's uncertainties. **Trickster Tales** illustrate a testing of the limits of cultural formation and practice. That is, Native American stories about trickster characters—people in the form of Coyote, Raven, or Rabbit—feature humorous and often scandalous attempts to violate the established customs and values of the tribe. The Trickster figure, stereotyped as alone and wandering on the margins of the social world, frequently engages in socially unacceptable acts to call attention to the arbitrary and tentative nature of established cultural patterns. For instance, when Raven cures a girl in the Tsimshian story by imitating the behavior of the medicine men (in order to gain both material and sexual rewards), Raven's actions cast doubt upon both the motives and methods used by medicine men, thus urging the audience to distinguish between the *role* a person plays in society and the *character* of the person in the role. Both scandalous and instructive, trickster stories ultimately offer cultural lessons. Told with relish, the stories ironically provide useful and necessary correctives to cultural self-satisfaction.

Whether the stories are socially corrective trickster tales or emergence or historical narratives, these and other Native American genres show the people aspiring for harmonious interaction with the earth. Native American communities continually return in prayer and ritual, story and song, to the fundamental relationships established as part of their tribal identity. At the same time, many contemporary Native

American writers, who have never participated in the life of a tribal community, have discovered a new strength in old traditions. The ancient stories endure, despite radical changes in the circumstances of the people who produced them and who tell them today, because they provide a structure of meaning and value at once intellectually satisfying and imaginatively compelling.

Andrew O. Wiget
New Mexico State University

PRIMARY WORKS

Washington Matthews, *Navajo Legends,* 1897; John R. Swanton, *Tlingit Myths and Texts,* Bulletin Thirty-Nine of the Bureau of American Ethnology, 1909; Franz Boas, *Tsimshian Mythology,* Thirty-First Annual Report of the Bureau of American Ethnology, 1916; Stith Thompson, *Tales of the North American Indian,* 1929, 1973; Ruth Bunzel, "Zuni Origin Myths," Forty-Seventh Annual Report of the Bureau of American Ethnology, 1930; Edmund Nequatewa, *Truth of a Hopi,* 1936, 1967; John Bierhorst, *The Red Swan: Myths and Tales of the American Indians,* 1976.

SECONDARY WORKS

Paul Radin, *The Trickster,* 1956; Dell Hymes, *'In Vain I Tried to Tell You': Essays in Native American Ethnopoetics,* 1981; William Sturtevant, ed., *Handbook of North American Indians,* 15 vols., 1981–; Dennis Tedlock, *The Spoken Word and the Work of Interpretation,* 1983; Brian Swann and Arnold Krupat, *Recovering the Word: Essays on Native American Literature,* 1987; David Murray, *Forked Tongues: Speech, Writing, and Representation in North American Indian Texts,* 1991.

Talk Concerning the First Beginning (Zuni)[1]

Yes, indeed. In this world there was no one at all. Always the sun came up; always he went in. No one in the morning gave him sacred meal; no one gave him prayer sticks; it was very lonely.[2] He said to his two children:[3] "You will go into the fourth womb.

[1]The Zuni Indians, inheritors of the ancient Anasazi and Mogollon cultures, live in the Southwest, primarily in New Mexico. Their agricultural subsistence enabled them to develop large pueblos along the Zuni River valley. Visited by the Spanish expedition seeking the fabled Seven Cities of Cibola, they drove off the Spanish in 1539–1540. The Spanish eventually established a mission among the Zuni in 1629, and the Zuni joined in the Pueblo Revolt of 1680. Today the population of their New Mexico reservation exceeds 8,000.

[2]There is a reciprocal gift-giving relationship between the Sun Father and all creatures, including people. According to Zuni tradition, the Sun Father gives corn and breath, the gifts of life. In return, the Zuni offer corn meal and downy feathers, symbolizing clouds and breath, which are attached to ritually painted sticks. Both are deposited at shrines near Zuni.

[3]The two children are the Ahaiyute, the War God Hero Twins.

Your fathers, your mothers, kä-eto·we, tcu-eto·we, mu-eto·we, le-eto·we, all the society priests, society pekwins, society bow priests, you will bring out yonder into the light of your sun father."[4] Thus he said to them. They said, "But how shall we go in?" "That will be all right." Laying their lightning arrow across their rainbow bow, they drew it. Drawing it and shooting down, they entered.

When they entered the fourth womb it was dark inside. They could not distinguish anything. They said, "Which way will it be best to go?" They went toward the west. They met someone face to face. They said, "Whence come you?" "I come from over this way to the west." "What are you doing going around?" "I am going around to look at my crops. Where do you live?" "No, we do not live any place. There above our father the Sun, priest, made us come in. We have come in," they said. "Indeed," the younger brother said. "Come, let us see," he said. They laid down their bow. Putting underneath some dry brush and some dry grass that was lying about, and putting the bow on top, they kindled fire by hand. When they had kindled the fire, light came out from the coals. As it came out, they blew on it and it caught fire. Aglow! It is growing light. "Ouch! What have you there?" he said. He fell down crouching. He had a slimy horn, slimy tail, he was slimy all over, with webbed hands. The elder brother said, "Poor thing! Put out the light." Saying thus, he put out the light. The youth said, "Oh dear, what have you there?" "Why, we have fire," they said. "Well, what (crops) do you have coming up?" "Yes, here are our things coming up." Thus he said. He was going around looking after wild grasses.

He said to them, "Well, now, let us go." They went toward the west, the two leading. There the people were sitting close together. They questioned one another. Thus they said, "Well, now, you two, speak. I think there is something to say. It will not be too long a talk. If you let us know that we shall always remember it." "That is so, that is so," they said. "Yes, indeed, it is true. There above is our father, Sun. No one ever gives him prayer sticks; no one ever gives him sacred meal; no one ever gives him shells. Because it is thus we have come to you, in order that you may go out standing yonder into the daylight of your sun father. Now you will say which way (you decide)." Thus the two said. "Hayi! Yes, indeed. Because it is thus you have passed us on our roads.[5] Now that you have passed us on our roads here where we stay miserably, far be it from us to speak against it. We can not see one another. Here inside where we just trample on one another, where we just spit on one another, where we just urinate on one another, where we just befoul one another, where we just follow one another about, you have passed us on our roads. None of us can speak against it. But rather, as the priest of the north says, so let it be. Now you two call him." Thus they said to the two, and they came up close toward the north side. . . .

[4]Zuni people are organized into religious societies, each responsible for a different aspect of the community's welfare. The *-eto:we* are fetishes, each representing that spirit, originating deep within the womb of the earth, which is the foundational force of each society. The Pekwin is the sun priest who keeps the ritual calendar; the Bow Priests govern warfare and regulate social behavior. In bringing all these from the earth's fourth womb onto the earth's surface, the War God Twins are assisting at the birth of the Zuni tribe, the "daylight people."

[5]A formulaic phrase, suggesting something like destiny. Everyone's life, and indeed the life of the community, can be imagined as a "road"; to "pass another on the road" is to acknowledge converging destinies.

They met the north priest on his road. "You have come," he said. "Yes, we have come. How have you lived these many days?" "Here where I live happily you have passed me on my road. Sit down." When they were seated he questioned them. "Now speak. I think there is something to say. It will not be too long a talk. So now, that you will let me know." "Yes, indeed, it is so. In order that you may go out standing there into the daylight of your sun father we have passed you on your road. However you say, so shall it be." "Yes, indeed, now that you have passed us on our road here where we live thus wretchedly, far be it from me to talk against it. Now that you have come to us here inside where we just trample on one another, where we just spit on one another, where we just urinate on one another, where we just befoul one another, where we just follow one another about, how should I speak against it?" so he said. Then they arose. They came back. Coming to the village where they were sitting in the middle place, there they questioned one another. "Yes, even now we have met on our roads. Indeed there is something to say; it will not be too long a talk. When you let me know that, I shall always remember it," thus they said to one another. When they had spoken thus, "Yes, indeed. In order that you may go out standing into the daylight of your sun father, we have passed you on your road," thus they said. "Hayi! Yes, indeed. Now that you have passed us on our road here where we cannot see one another, where we just trample on one another, where we just urinate on one another, where we just befoul one another, where we just follow one another around, far be it from me to speak against it. But rather let it be as my younger brother, the priest of the west shall say. When he says, 'Let it be thus,' that way it shall be. So now, you two call him." Thus said the priest of the north and they went and stood close against the west side. . . .[6]

"Well, perhaps by means of the thoughts of someone somewhere it may be that we shall go out standing into the daylight of our sun father." Thus he said.

Then the two thought. "Come on, let us summon our grandson," thus they said. They went. They came to where humming bird[7] was staying. "You have come?" "Yes, how have you lived these days?" "Where I live happily these days you have passed me on my road. Sit down." When they had sat down: "Well, now, speak. I think there is something to say; it will not be too long a talk. So now if you let me know that, I shall always remember it." "Yes, indeed, it is so. When our fathers, kä-eto·we, tcu-eto·we, mu-eto·we, le-eto·we, the society priests, go out standing into the daylight of their sun father, you shall be the one to look for their road; for that we have summoned you." "Is that so?" Saying this, they went. When they got there, he questioned them. "Well, even now you summoned me. Surely there is something to say. It will not be too long a talk. So now when you let me know that I shall always remember it." Thus he said. "Yes, indeed, it is so. When our fathers, kä-eto·we, tcu-eto·we, mu-eto·we, le-eto·we, the society priests, go out into the daylight of their sun father, that you shall be the one to look for their road, for that we have

[6]The Twins visit the Priest of the North first, since he is the senior priest. The Zuni order lists according to the cardinal directions, moving "sunwise" (counterclockwise), beginning at the north. In the section omitted, priests for the other three directions are consulted in similar passages. Four is a sacred number, signifying wholeness or completion.

[7]Consistent with the Zuni pattern of fourfold repetition, three other birds had tried to find a way out before the hummingbird succeeded.

summoned you." Thus the two said. He went out toward the south. He went on. Coming back to his starting place, nothing was visible. Farther out he went. Coming back to the same place, nothing was visible. Then for the third time he went. Coming back to the same place, nothing was visible. For the fourth time he went close along the edge of the sky. Coming back to the same place, nothing was visible. He came. Coming where kä-eto·we were staying, "Nothing is visible." "Hayi!" "Yes. Well, I am going now." "Very well, go." He went.

The two said, "What had we better do now? That many different kinds of feathered creatures, the ones who go about without ever touching the ground, have failed." Thus the two said. "Come, let us talk with our grandson, locust. Perhaps that one will have a strong spirit because he is like water."[8] Thus they said. They went. Their grandson, locust, they met. "You have come." "Yes, we have come." "Sit down. How have you lived these days?" "Happily." "Well, even now you have passed me on my road. Surely there is something to say; it will not be too long a talk. So now when you let me know that, that I shall always remember." Thus he said. "Yes, indeed, it is so. In order that our fathers, kä-eto·we, tcu-eto·we, mu-eto·we, le-eto·we, the society priests, may go out standing into the daylight of their sun father, we have come to you." "Is that so?" Saying this, they went. When they arrived they sat down. Where they were sitting, he questioned them. "Well, just now you came to me. Surely there is something to say; it will not be too long a talk. So now if you let me know that, that I shall always remember." "Yes, indeed. In order that our fathers, kä-eto·we, tcu-eto·we, mu-eto·we, le-eto·we, the society priests, may go out standing into the daylight of their sun father, we have summoned you." "Indeed?" Saying this, locust rose right up. He goes up. He went through into another world. And again he goes right up. He went through into another world. And again he goes right up. Again he went through into another world. He goes right up. When he had just gone a little way his strength gave out, he came back to where kä-eto·we were staying and said, "Three times I went through and the fourth time my strength gave out." "Hayi! Indeed?" Saying this, he went.

When he had gone the two thought. "Come, let us speak with our grandson, Reed Youth. For perhaps that one with his strong point will be all right." Saying this, they went. They came to where Reed Youth stayed. "You have come?" "Yes; how have you lived these days." "Where I stay happily you have passed me on my road. Sit down." Thus he said. They sat down. Then he questioned them. "Yes. Well, even now you have passed me on my road. I think there is something to say; it will not be too long a talk. When you let me know that, that I shall always remember." Thus he said. "Yes, indeed, in order that our fathers, kä-eto·we, tcu-eto·we, mu-eto·we, le-eto·we, the society priests, may go out standing into the daylight of their sun father, we have come to you." "Hayi! Is that so?" Having spoken thus, they went. When they arrived they sat down. There he questioned them. "Yes, even now that you have summoned me I have passed you on your roads. Surely there is something to say; it will not be too long a talk. When you let me know that, that I shall always remember." "Yes, indeed, it is so. In order that our fathers, kä-eto·we, tcu-eto·we,

[8]That is, like water, he can go through anything solid. [Bunzel's note]

mu-eto·we, le-eto·we, the society priests, may go forth standing into the daylight of their sun father, we have summoned you." Thus they said. "Hayi! Is that so?" Saying this, he went out. Where Locust had gone out he went out. The first time he passed through, the second time he passed through, the third time he passed through. Having passed through the fourth time and come forth standing into the daylight of his sun father, he went back in. Coming back in he came to where kä-eto·we were staying. "You have come?" Thus they said. "Yes," he said. "Far off to see what road there may be you have gone. How may it be there now?" Thus they said. "Yes, indeed, it is so. There it is as you wanted it. As you wished of me, I went forth standing into the daylight of my sun father now." Thus he said. "Halihi! Thank you!" "Now I am going." "Go." Saying this, he went.

After he had gone they were sitting around. Now as they were sitting around, there the two set up a pine tree for a ladder. They stayed there. For four days they stayed there. Four days, they say, but it was four years. There all the different society priests sang their song sequences for one another. The ones sitting in the first row listened carefully. Those sitting next on the second row heard all but a little. Those sitting on the third row heard here and there. Those sitting last on the fourth row heard just a little bit now and then. It was thus because of the rustling of the dry weeds.

When their days there were at an end, gathering together their sacred things they arose. "Now what shall be the name of this place?" "Well, here it shall be sulphur-smell-inside-world; and furthermore, it shall be raw-dust world." Thus they said. "Very well. Perhaps if we call it thus it will be all right." Saying this, they came forth.

After they had come forth, setting down their sacred things in a row at another place, they stayed there quietly. There the two set up a spruce tree as a ladder. When the ladder was up they stayed there for four days. And there again the society priests sang their song sequences for one another. Those sitting on the first row listened carefully. Those sitting there on the second row heard all but a little. Those sitting there on the third row heard here and there. Those sitting last distinguished a single word now and then. It was thus because of the rustling of some plants. When their days there were at an end, gathering together their sacred things there they arose. "Now what shall it be called here?" "Well, here it shall be called soot-inside-world, because we still can not recognize one another." "Yes, perhaps if it is called thus it will be all right." Saying this to one another, they arose.

Passing through to another place, and putting down their sacred things in a row, they stayed there quietly. There the two set up a piñon tree as a ladder. When the piñon tree was put up, there all the society priests and all the priests went through their song sequences for one another. Those sitting in front listened carefully. Those sitting on the second row heard all but a little. Those sitting behind on the third row heard here and there. Those sitting on the fourth row distinguished only a single word now and then. This was because of the rustling of the weeds.

When their days there were at an end, gathering together their sacred things they arose. Having arisen, "Now what shall it be called here?" "Well, here it shall be fog-inside-world, because here just a little bit is visible." "Very well, perhaps if it is called thus it will be all right." Saying this, rising, they came forth.

Passing through to another place, there the two set down their sacred things in a row, and there they sat down. Having sat down, the two set up a cottonwood tree as a ladder. Then all the society priests and all the priests went through their song sequences for one another. Those sitting first heard everything clearly. Those sitting on the second row heard all but a little. Those sitting on the third row heard here and there. Those sitting last on the fourth row distinguished a single word now and then. It was thus because of the rustling of some plants.

When their days there were at an end, after they had been there, when their four days were passed, gathering together their sacred possessions, they arose. When they arose, "Now what shall it be called here?" "Well, here it shall be wing-inner-world, because we see our sun father's wings."[9] Thus they said. They came forth.

Into the daylight of their sun father they came forth standing. Just at early dawn they came forth. After they had come forth there they set down their sacred possessions in a row. The two said, "Now after a little while when your sun father comes forth standing to his sacred place you will see him face to face. Do not close your eyes." Thus he said to them. After a little while the sun came out. When he came out they looked at him. From their eyes the tears rolled down. After they had looked at him, in a little while their eyes became strong. "Alas!" Thus they said. They were covered all over with slime. With slimy tails and slimy horns, with webbed fingers, they saw one another. "Oh dear! is this what we look like?" Thus they said.

Then they could not tell which was which of their sacred possessions. Meanwhile, nearby an old man of the Dogwood clan[10] lived alone. Spider said to him, "Put on water. When it gets hot, wash your hair." "Why?" "Our father, our mothers, kä-eto·we, tcu-eto·we, mu-eto·we, le-eto·we, all the society priests, into the daylight of their sun father have come forth standing. They can not tell which is which. You will make this plain to them." Thus she said. "Indeed? Impossible. From afar no one can see them. Where they stay quietly no one can recognize them." Thus he said. "Do not say that. Nevertheless it will be all right. You will not be alone. Now we shall go." Thus she said. When the water was warm he washed his hair.

Meanwhile, while he was washing his hair, the two said, "Come let us go to meet our father, the old man of the Dogwood clan. I think he knows in his thoughts; because among our fathers, kä-eto·we, tcu-eto·we, mu-eto·we, le-eto·we, we can not tell which is which." Thus they said. They went. They got there. As they were climbing up, "Now indeed! They are coming." Thus Spider said to him. She climbed up his body from his toe. She clung behind his ear. The two entered. "You have come," thus he said. "Yes. Our father, how have you lived these days?" "As I live happily you pass me on my road. Sit down." They sat down. "Well, now, speak. I think some word that is not too long, your word will be. Now, if you let me know that, remembering it, I shall live." "Indeed it is so. Our fathers, kä-eto·we, tcu-eto·we, mu-eto·we, le-eto·we, all the society priests, into the daylight of their sun father have risen and come out. It is not plain which is which. Therefore we have passed you on your road." "Haiyi, is that so? Impossible! From afar no one can see them. Where they stay quietly no one can recognize them." Thus he said. "Yes, but we have chosen you." Thus the two said. They went. When they came there, "My fathers, my

[9]The "wings" are the rays of sunlight slanting into this world through the Emergence hole in the sky above, which opens onto the earth's surface, the "daylight world." This is the last of the four lower worlds.

[10]The first Pekwin, or Sun Priest, keeper of the ritual calendar, a hereditary responsibility in the Dogwood clan. His hair-washing is an act of spiritual as well as physical purification.

mothers, how have you lived these days?" "Happily, our father, our child. Be seated." Thus they said. He sat down. Then he questioned them. "Yes, now indeed, since you have sent for me, I have passed you on your road. I think some word that is not too long your word will be. Now if you let me know that, remembering it, I shall always live."

Thus he said. "Indeed, it is so. Even though our fathers, our mothers, kä-eto·we, tcu-eto·we, mu-eto·we, le-eto·we, have come out standing into the daylight of their sun father, it is not plain which of these is which. Therefore we have sent for you." Thus they said. "Haiyi, Well, let me try." "Impossible. From afar no one can see them. Where they stay quietly no one can tell which is which." "Well, let me try." Thus he said. Where they lay in a row he stood beside them. Spider said to him, "Here, the one that lies here at the end is kä-eto·we and these next ones touching it are tcu-eto·we, and this next one is le-eto·we, and these next ones touching it are mu-eto·we." Thus she said. He said, "Now this is kä-eto·we, and these all touching it are tcu-eto·we, and this one is le-eto·we, and all these touching it are mu-eto·we." Thus he said. "Halihi! Thank you. How shall be the cycle of the months for them?" Thus he said: "This one Branches-broken-down. This one No-snow-on-the-road. This one Little-sand-storms. This one Great-sand-storms. This the Month-without-a-name. This one Turn-about. This one Branches-broken-down. This one No-snow-on-the-road. This one Little-sand-storms. This one Great-sand-storms. This the Month-without-a-name. This one Turn-about. Thus shall be all the cycle of the months." "Halihi! Thank you. Our father, you shall not be poor. Even though you have no sacred possessions toward which your thoughts bend, whenever Itiwana is revealed to us, because of your thought, the ceremonies of all these shall come around in order. You shall not be a slave." This they said. They gave him the sun. "This shall be your sacred possession." Thus they said. When this had happened thus they lived.

Four days—four days they say, but it was four years—there they stayed. When their days were at an end, the earth rumbled. The two said, "Who was left behind?" "I do not know, but it seems we are all here." Thus they said. Again the earth rumbled. "Well, does it not seem that some one is still left behind?" Thus, the two said. They went. Coming to the place where they had come out, there they stood. To the mischief-maker and the Mexicans[11] they said, "Haiyi! Are you still left behind?" "Yes." "Now what are you still good for?" Thus they said. "Well, it is this way. Even though kä-eto·we have issued forth into the daylight, the people do not live on the living waters of good corn; on wild grasses only they live. Whenever you come to the middle you will do well to have me. When the people are many and the land is all used up, it will not be well. Because this is so I have come out." Thus he said. "Haiyi! Is that so? So that's what you are. Now what are you good for?" Thus they said. "Indeed, it is so. When you come to the middle, it will be well to have my seeds. Because kä-eto·we do not live on the good seeds of the corn, but on wild grasses only. Mine are the seeds of the corn and all the clans of beans." Thus he said. The two took him with them. They came to where kä-eto·we were staying. They sat down. Then they

[11]The mischief-maker is Coyote, the Trickster. The Mexicans have been introduced as emerging later because they were not part of the emerging Zuni people. The linking of Coyote and the Mexicans makes a negative comment about historical Zuni relations with the Spanish.

questioned him. "Now let us see what you are good for." "Well, this is my seed of the yellow corn." Thus he said. He showed an ear of yellow corn. "Now give me one of your people." Thus he said. They gave him a baby. When they gave him the baby it seems he did something to her. She became sick. After a short time she died. When she had died he said, "Now bury her." They dug a hole and buried her. After four days he said to the two, "Come now. Go and see her." The two went to where they had come out. When they got there the little one was playing in the dirt. When they came, she laughed. She was happy. They saw her and went back. They came to where the people were staying. "Listen! Perhaps it will be all right for you to come. She is still alive. She has not really died." "Well, thus it shall always be." Thus he said.[12]

Gathering together all their sacred possessions, they came hither. To the place called since the first beginning, Moss Spring, they came.[13] There they set down their sacred possessions in a row. There they stayed. Four days they say, but it was four years. There the two washed them. They took from all of them their slimy tails, their slimy horns. "Now, behold! Thus you will be sweet." There they stayed.

When their days were at an end they came hither. Gathering together all their sacred possessions, seeking Itiwana, yonder their roads went. To the place called since the first beginning Massed-cloud Spring, they came. There they set down their sacred possessions in a row. There they stayed quietly. Four days they stayed. Four days they say, but it was four years. There they stayed. There they counted up the days. For kä-eto·we, four nights and four days. With fine rain caressing the earth, they passed their days. The days were made for le-eto·we, mu-eto·we. For four days and four nights it snowed. When their days were at an end there they stayed.

When their days were at an end they arose. Gathering together all their sacred possessions, hither their roads went. To the place called since the first beginning Mist Spring their road came. There they sat down quietly. Setting out their sacred possessions in a row, they sat down quietly. There they counted up the days for one another. They watched the world for one another's waters. For kä-eto·we, four days and four nights, with heavy rain caressing the earth they passed their days. When their days were at an end the days were made for le-eto·we and mu-eto·we. Four days and four nights with falling snow the world was filled. When their days were at an end, there they stayed.

When all their days were passed, gathering together all their sacred possessions, hither their road went. To Standing-wood Spring they came. There they sat down quietly. Setting out their sacred possessions in a row, they stayed quietly. There they watched one another's days. For kä-eto·we, four days and four nights with fine rain caressing the earth, they passed their days. When all their days were at an end, the days were made for le-eto·we and mu-eto·we. For four days and four nights, with falling snow, the world was filled. When all their days were at an end, there they stayed.

When all their days were passed, gathering together their sacred possessions, and arising, hither they came. To the place called since the first beginning Upuilima they came. When they came there, setting down their sacred possessions in a row,

[12]This symbolic story of the first death in exchange for corn suggests the reciprocal relationship between life and death.

[13]One of dozens of springs that mark the route of the migration from the Emergence Place to Zuni, the Center of the World.

they stayed quietly. There they strove to outdo one another. There they planted all their seeds. There they watched one another's days for rain. For kä-eto·we, four days with heavy rain caressing the earth. There their corn matured. It was not palatable, it was bitter. Then the two said, "Now by whose will will our corn become fit to eat?" Thus they said. They summoned raven. He came and pecked at their corn, and it became good to eat. "It is fortunate that you have come." With this then, they lived.

When their days were at an end they arose. Gathering together their sacred possessions, they came hither. To the place called since the first beginning, Cornstalk-place they came. There they set down their sacred possessions in a row. There they stayed four days. Four days they say, but it was four years. There they planted all their seeds. There they watched one another's days for rain. During kä-eto·we's four days and four nights, heavy rain fell. During le-eto·we's and mu-eto·we's four days and four nights, the world was filled with falling snow. Their days were at an end. Their corn matured. When it was mature it was hard. Then the two said, "By whose will will our corn become soft? Well, owl." Thus they said. They summoned owl. Owl came. When he came he pecked at their corn and it became soft.

Then, when they were about to rise, the two said, "Come, let us go talk to the corn priest." Thus they said. They went. They came to where the corn priest stayed. "How have you lived these days?" "As we are living happily you have passed us on our road. Sit down." They sat down. There they questioned one another. "Well, speak. I think some word that is not too long, your word will be. Now, if you let me know that, remembering it, I shall always live." "Indeed, it is so. To-morrow, when we arise, we shall set out to seek Itiwana. Nowhere have we found the middle. Our children, our women, are tired. They are crying. Therefore we have come to you. To-morrow your two children will look ahead. Perhaps if they find the middle when our fathers, our mothers, kä-eto·we, tcu-eto·we, mu-eto·we, le-eto·we, all the society priests, come to rest, there our children will rest themselves. Because we have failed to find the middle." "Haiyi! Is that so? With plain words you have passed us on our road. Very well, then, thus it shall be." Thus he said. The two went.

Next morning when they were about to set out they put down a split ear of corn and eggs. They made the corn priest stand up. They said, "Now, my children, some of you will go yonder to the south. You will take these." Thus he said (indicating) the tip of the ear and the macaw egg. And then the ones that were to come this way took the base of the ear and the raven egg. Those that were to go to the south took the tip of the ear and the macaw egg. "Now, my children, yonder to the south you will go. If at any time you come to Itiwana, then some time we shall meet one another."[14] Thus they said. They came hither.

They came to the place that was to be Katcina village. The girl got tired. Her brother said, "Wait, sit down for a while. Let me climb up and look about to see what kind of a place we are going to." Thus he said. His sister sat down. Her brother climbed the hill. When he had climbed up, he stood looking this way. "Eha! Maybe the place where we are going lies in this direction. Maybe it is this kind of a place." Thus he said and came down. Meanwhile his sister had scooped out the sand. She rested against the side of the hill. As she lay sleeping the wind came and raised her

[14]This passage, which represents the first major social division of the emergent community, is understood to establish Zuni's relationship to Indian tribes to the south.

apron of grass. . . . As he came down he saw her. He desired her. He lay down upon his sister and copulated with her. His sister awoke. "Oh, dear, oh, dear," she was about to say (but she said,) "Watsela, watsela." Her brother said, "Ah!" He sat up. With his foot he drew a line. It became a stream of water. The two went about talking. The brother talked like Koyemci. His sister talked like Komakatsik. The people came.

"Oh alas, alas! Our children have become different beings."[15] Thus they said. The brother speaking: "Now it will be all right for you to cross here." Thus he said. They came and went in. They entered the river. Some of their children turned into water snakes. Some of them turned into turtles. Some of them turned into frogs. Some of them turned into lizards. They bit their mothers. Their mothers cried out and dropped them. They fell into the river. Only the old people reached the other side. They sat down on the bank. They were half of the people. The two said, "Now wait. Rest here." Thus they said. Some of them sat down to rest. The two said (to the others), "Now you go in. Your children will turn into some kind of dangerous animals and will bite you. But even though you cry out, do not let them go. If, when you come out on the other side, your children do not again become the kind of creatures they are now, then you will throw them into the water." Thus they said to them. They entered the water. Their children became different creatures and bit them. Even though they cried out, they crossed over. Then their children once more became the kind of creatures they had been. "Alas! Perhaps had we done that it would have been all right." Now all had crossed over.

There setting down their sacred possessions in a row, they stayed quietly. They stayed there quietly for four days. Thus they say but they stayed for four years. There each night they lived gaily with loud singing. When all their time was passed, the two said, "Come, let us go and talk to Ne'we·kwe." Thus they said. They went to where the Ne'we·kwe were staying. They came there. "How have you passed these days?" "Happily. You have come? Be seated." They sat down. Then they questioned them. "Now speak. I think some word that is not too long your word will be. If you let me know that, remembering it I shall always live." "Indeed it is so. To-morrow we shall arise. Our fathers, our mothers, kä-eto·we, tcu-eto·we, mu-eto·we, le-eto·we, all the society priests, are going to seek the middle. But nowhere have we come to the middle. Our children and our women are tired. They are crying now. Therefore we have passed you on your road. To-morrow you will look ahead. If perhaps somewhere you come to Itiwana there our children will rest." Thus they said. "Alas! but we are just foolish people. If we make some mistake it will not be right." Thus he said. "Well,

[15] A very important event in the migration narrative: in breaking the incest taboo, the brother and sister have reversed the process of physical and social evolution, and they suffer the consequences in their own persons; their language is confused, their appearance deformed. Nevertheless, their mistake has useful consequences. The line they draw becomes a river separating the Emergence World into two domains. At this moment on the river, all kinds of transformations are possible. When some of the children return to their preemergence water-creature form, they are dropped by the parents and sink to the bottom of the river, where they become the kachinas whose transformative powers provide an eternal source of renewal for the Zuni. They promise to return to Zuni with rain and moisture when they are called.

that is of no importance. It can't be helped. We have chosen you." Thus they said. "Well indeed?" "Yes. Now we are going." "Go ahead." The two went out.

They came (to where the people were staying). "Come, let us go and speak to our children." Thus they said. They went. They entered the lake. It was full of katcinas. "Now stand still a moment. Our two fathers have come." Thus they said. The katcinas suddenly stopped dancing. When they stopped dancing they said to the two, "Now our two fathers, now indeed you have passed us on our road. I think some word that is not too long your word will be. If you will let us know that we shall always remember it." Thus he said. "Indeed it is so. To-morrow we shall arise. Therefore we have come to speak to you." "Well indeed? May you go happily. You will tell our parents, 'Do not worry.' We have not perished. In order to remain thus forever we stay here. To Itiwana but one day's travel remains. Therefore we stay near by. When our world grows old and the waters are exhausted and the seeds are exhausted, none of you will go back to the place of your first beginning. Whenever the waters are exhausted and the seeds are exhausted you will send us prayer sticks. Yonder at the place of our first beginning with them we shall bend over to speak to them. Thus there will not fail to be waters. Therefore we shall stay quietly near by." Thus they said to them. "Well indeed?" "Yes. You will tell my father, my mother, 'Do not worry.' We have not perished." Thus they said. They sent strong words to their parents. "Now we are going. Our children, may you always live happily." "Even thus may you also go." Thus they said to the two. They went out. They arrived. They told them. "Now our children, here your children have stopped. 'They have perished,' you have said. But no. The male children have become youths, and the females have become maidens. They are happy. They live joyously. They have sent you strong words. 'Do not worry,' they said." "Haiyi! Perhaps it is so."

They stayed overnight. Next morning they arose. Gathering together all their sacred possessions, they came hither. They came to Hanlipinka. Meanwhile the two Ne'we·kwe looked ahead. They came to Rock-in-the-river. There two girls were washing a woolen dress. They killed them. After they had killed them they scalped them. Then someone found them out. When they were found out, because they were raw people, they wrapped themselves in mist. There to where kä-eto·we were staying they came. "Alack, alas! We have done wrong!" Thus they said. Then they set the days for the enemy. There they watched one another's days for rain. Kä-eto·we's four days and four nights passed with the falling of heavy rain. There where a waterfall issued from a cave the foam arose. There the two Ahaiyute appeared. They came to where kä-eto·we were staying. Meanwhile, from the fourth innerworld, Unasinte, Uhepololo, Kailuhtsawaki, Hattunka, Oloma, Catunka, came out to sit down in the daylight. There they gave them the comatowe song cycle.[16] Meanwhile, right there, Coyote was going about hunting. He gave them their pottery drum. They sang comatowe.

After this had happened, the two said, "Now, my younger brother, Itiwana is less than one day distant. We shall gather together our children, all the beast priests, and

[16]The first culpable death provokes the return of the War God Twins who give the people the *comatowe* ceremonial for relieving the guilt associated with killing in war.

the winged creatures, this night." They went.[17] They came yonder to Comkäkwe. There they gathered together all the beasts, mountain lion, bear, wolf, wild cat, badger, coyote, fox, squirrel; eagle, buzzard, cokapiso, chicken hawk, bald-headed eagle, raven, owl. All these they gathered together. Now squirrel was among the winged creatures, and owl was among the beasts. "Now my children, you will contest together for your sun father's daylight. Whichever side has the ball, when the sun rises, they shall win their sun father's daylight." Thus the two said. "Indeed?" They went there. They threw up the ball. It fell on the side of the beasts. They hid it. After they had hidden it, the birds came one by one but they could not take it. Each time they paid four straws. They could not take it.

At this time it was early dawn. Meanwhile Squirrel was lying by the fireplace. Thus they came one by one but they could not take it. Eagle said, "Let that one lying there by the fireplace go." They came to him and said, "Are you asleep?" "No. I am not asleep." "Oh dear! Now you go!" Thus they said. "Oh no, I don't want to go," he said. He came back. "The lazy one does not wish to." Thus they said. Someone else went. Again they could not take it. Now it was growing light. "Let that one lying by the fireplace go." Thus they said. Again Buzzard went. "Alas, my boy, you go." "Oh, no, I don't feel like it." Thus he said. Again he went back. "He does not want to," he said. Again some one else went. Again they did not take it. Now it was growing light. Spider said to him, "Next time they come agree to go." Thus she said. Then again they said, "Let that one lying by the fireplace go." Thus they said; and again someone went. When he came there he said, "Alas, my boy, you go." "All right, I shall go." Thus he said and arose. As he arose Spider said to him, "Take that stick." He took up a stick, so short. Taking it, he went. Now the sun was about to rise. They came there. Spider said to him, "Hit those two sitting on the farther side." Thus she said. Bang! He knocked them down. He laid them down. Then, mountain lion, who was standing right there, said, "Hurry up, go after it. See whether you can take it." Thus he said. Spider said to him, "Say to him, 'Oh, no, I don't want to take it.' So she said." "Oh, no, I don't want to take it. Perhaps there is nothing inside. How should I take it? There is nothing in there." "That is right. There is nothing in there. All my children are gathered together. One of them is holding it. If you touch the right one, you will take it." "All right." Now Spider is speaking: "No one who is sitting here has it. That one who goes about dancing, he is holding it." Thus she said. He went. He hit Owl on the hand. The white ball came out. He went. He took up the hollow sticks and took them away with him. Now the birds hid the ball. Spider came down. Over all the sticks she spun her web. She fastened the ball with her web. Now the animals came one by one. Whenever they touched a stick, she pulled (the ball) away. Each time they paid ten straws. The sun rose. After sunrise, he was sitting high in the sky. Then the two came. They said, "Now, all my children, you have won your sun father's daylight, and you, beasts, have lost your sun father's daylight. All day you will sleep. After sunset, at night, you will go about hunting. But you, owl, you have not stayed

[17]The Contest for Daylight story, which is widespread throughout Native America, is told here to account for the characteristic behaviors of different species. It leads directly to a comment about the deaths of animals. Though it is not mentioned, the killing of animals must also be done in a ritually prescribed way in order not to repudiate the Sun, the Father and gift-giver.

among the winged creatures. Therefore you have lost your sun father's daylight. You have made a mistake. If by daylight, you go about hunting, the one who has his home above will find you out. He will come down on you. He will scrape off the dirt from his earth mother and put it upon you. Then thinking, 'Let it be here,' you will come to the end of your life. This kind of creature you shall be." Thus they said. They stayed there overnight. The animals all scattered.

The two went. They came to where kä-eto·we were staying. Then they arose. Gathering together all their sacred possessions, they arose. Le-eto·we said, "Now, my younger brothers, hither to the north I shall take my road. Whenever I think that Itiwana has been revealed to you, then I shall come to you." Thus he said, and went to the north. Now some woman, seeing them, said, "Oh dear! Whither are these going?" Thus she said:

Naiye heni aiye
Naiye heni aiye.

In white stripes of hail they went.

Meanwhile kä-eto·we came hither. They came to House Mountain. When they came there they would not let them pass through. They fought together. A giant went back and forth before them. Thus they fought together.[18] Thus evening came. In the evening they came back to Hanlipinka. Next day they went again. In heavy rain they fought together. In the evening they went back again. Next morning they went again for the third time. Again they fought together. The giant went back and forth in front. Even though she had arrows sticking in her body she did not die. At sunset they went back again. Next morning they went. They came there, and they fought together. Still they would not surrender. The giant went back and forth in front. Although she was wounded with arrows, she would not surrender. Ahaiyute said, "Alas, why is it that these people will not let us pass? Wherever may her heart be, that one that goes back and forth? Where her heart should be we have struck her, yet she does not surrender. It seems we can not overcome her. So finally go up to where your father stays. Without doubt he knows." Thus he said. His younger brother climbed up to where the sun was.

It was nearly noon when he arrived. "You have come?" "Yes, I have come." "Very well, speak. I think some word that is not too long your word will be. So if you let me know that, I shall always remember it." Thus he said. "Indeed, it is so. Our fathers, our mothers, kä-eto·we, tcu-eto·we, mu-eto·we, le-eto·we, all the society priests, have issued forth into the daylight. Here they go about seeking Itiwana. These people will not let them pass. Where does she have her heart, that one who goes back and forth before them? In vain have we struck her where her heart should be. Even though the arrows stick in her body, she does not surrender." "Haiyi! For nothing are you men! She does not have her heart in her body. In vain have you struck her there. Her heart is in her rattle." Thus he said. "This is for you and this is for your elder brother." Thus he said, and gave him two turquoise rabbit sticks.

[18]The slaying of a giant, who stands in the way of peaceful settlement of the land, is a common theme in southwestern Native literatures. This should be compared with a similar episode in the Navajo story "Changing Woman and the Hero Twins," where the giant is named Yéitso, the "Great Fear." The giant is slain with the help of the Sun.

"Now, when you let these go with my wisdom I shall take back my weapons." "Haiyi! Is that so? Very well, I am going now." "Go ahead. May you go happily." Thus he said. He came down. His elder brother said to him, "Now, what did he tell you?" "Indeed, it is so. In vain do we shoot at her body. Not there is her heart; but in her rattle is her heart. With these shall we destroy her." Thus he said, and gave his brother one of the rabbit sticks. When he had given his brother the rabbit stick, "Now go ahead, you." Thus he said. The younger brother went about to the right. He threw it and missed. Whiz! The rabbit stick went up to the sun. As the rabbit stick came up the sun took it. "Now go ahead, you try." Thus he said. The elder brother went around to the left. He threw it. As he threw it, zip! His rabbit stick struck his rattle. Tu---n! They ran away. As they started to run away, their giant died. Then they all ran away. The others ran after them. They came to a village. They went into the houses. "This is my house;" "This is my house;" and "This is mine." Thus they said. They went shooting arrows into the roof. Wherever they first came, they went in. An old woman and a little boy this big and a little girl were inside.

In the center of their room was standing a jar of urine.[19] They stuffed their nostrils with känaite flowers and with cotton wool. Then they thrust their noses into the jar. The people could see them. "Oh, dear! These are ghosts!" Thus they said. Then the two said to them, "Do not harm them, for I think they know something. So even though it is dangerous they are still alive." Thus they said. The two entered. As they came in they questioned them. "And now do you know something? Therefore, even though it is dangerous, you have not perished." "Well, we have a sacred object." "Indeed! Very well, take them. We shall go. Your fathers, your mothers, kä-eto·we, tcu-eto·we, mu-eto·we, le-eto·we, you will pass on their roads. If your days are the same as theirs you will not be slaves. It does not matter that he is only a little boy. Even so, he will be our father. It does not matter that she is a little girl, she will be our mother." Thus he said. Taking their sacred object they went. They came to where kä-eto·we were staying. There they said to them, "Now make your days." "Oh, no! We shall not be first. When all your days are at an end, then we shall add on our days." Thus they said. Then they worked for kä-eto·we. Kä-eto·we's days were made. Four days and four nights, with fine rain falling, were the days of kä-eto·we. When their days were at an end, the two children and their grandmother worked. Their days were made. Four days and four nights, with heavy rain falling, were their days. Then they removed the evil smell. They made flowing canyons. Then they said, "Halihi! Thank you! Just the same is your ceremony. What may your clan be?" "Well, we are of the Yellow Corn clan." Thus they said. "Haiyi! Even though your eton·e is of the Yellow Corn clan, because of your bad smell, you have become black. Therefore you shall be the Black Corn clan." Thus they said to them.[20]

Then they arose. Gathering together all their sacred possessions, they came hither, to the place called, since the first beginning, Halona-Itiwana, their road came. There they saw the Navaho helper, little red bug. "Here! Wait! All this time we have been searching in vain for Itiwana. Nowhere have we seen anything like this." Thus

[19]The stench of urine is believed to repel ghosts. That the family inside are ghosts suggests that they have a special power. By obtaining the object, the Twins have provided a way for the people to be free from being terrorized by ghosts.

[20]This incident accounts for the origin of Zuni clans.

they said. They summoned their grandchild, water bug. He came. "How have you lived these many days?" "Where we have been living happily you have passed us on our road. Be seated." Thus they said. He sat down. Then he questioned them. "Now, indeed, even now, you have sent for me. I think some word that is not too long your word will be. So now, if you will let me know that, I shall always remember it." "Indeed, it is so. Our fathers, our mothers, kä-eto·we, tcu-eto·we, mu-eto·we, le-eto·we, all the society priests, having issued forth into the daylight, go about seeking the middle. You will look for the middle for them. This is well. Because of your thoughts, at your heart, our fathers, kä-eto·we, tcu-eto·we, mu-eto·we, le-eto·we, will sit down quietly. Following after those, toward whom our thoughts bend, we shall pass our days." Thus they said. He sat down facing the east. To the left he stretched out his arm. To the right he stretched out his arm, but it was a little bent. He sat down facing the north. He stretched out his arms on both sides. They were just the same. Both arms touched the horizon. "Come, let us cross over to the north. For on this side my right arm is a little bent." Thus he said. They crossed (the river). They rested. He sat down. To all directions he stretched out his arms. Everywhere it was the same. "Right here is the middle."[21] Thus he said. There his fathers, his mothers, kä-eto·we, tcu-eto·we, mu-eto·we, le-eto·we, all the society priests, the society pekwins, the society bow priests, and all their children came to rest.

Thus it happened long ago.

1930

Changing Woman and the Hero Twins after the Emergence of the People (Navajo)[1]

The Navajos now removed to White Standing Rock, where, a few days after they arrived, they found on the ground a small turquoise image of a woman; this they preserved. Of late the monsters had been actively pursuing and devouring the people, and at the time this image was found there were only four persons remaining alive; these were an old man and woman and their two children, a young man and a young woman. Two days after the finding of the image, early in the morning, before they rose, they heard the voice of the Talking God, crying his call of "Wu'hu'hu'hú" so faint and far that they could scarcely hear it. After a while the call was repeated a second time, nearer and louder than at first. Again, after a brief silence, the call was

[21]Having completed their physical, religious, and social evolution, the Zuni end their journey in the Middle, the place of achievement and balance, from which no further movement is necessary. The sacred name of Zuni Pueblo is Halona-Itiwana, "The Middle Ant Hill of the World."

[1]The Navajo Indians of the southwest United States migrated from northwestern Canada by about 1200 A.D. They came to the Southwest as a hunting and gathering people; they learned agriculture from the pueblo peoples and in the sixteenth century acquired livestock from the Spanish. Their religious customs are thus somewhat similar to the Hopi people.

heard for the third time, still nearer and still louder. The fourth call was loud and clear, as if sounded near at hand; as soon as it ceased, the shuffling tread of moccasined feet was heard, and a moment later Talking God stood before them.

He told the four people to come up to the top of *Tsolíhi* after twelve nights had passed, bringing with them the turquoise image they had found, and at once he departed. They pondered deeply on his words, and every day they talked among themselves, wondering why Talking God had summoned them to the mountain.

On the morning of the appointed day they ascended the mountain by a holy trail, and on a level spot, near the summit, they met a party that awaited them there. They found there Talking God, Calling God, White Body (who came up from the lower world with the Navajos), the eleven brothers (of Maid Who Becomes a Bear), the Mirage Stone People, the Daylight People standing in the east, the Blue Sky People standing in the south, the Yellow Light People standing in the west, and the Darkness People standing in the north. White Body stood in the east among the Daylight People, bearing in his hand a small image of a woman wrought in white shell, about the same size and shape as the blue image which the Navajos bore.

Talking God laid down a sacred buckskin with its head toward the west. The Mirage Stone People laid on the buckskin, heads west, the two little images,—of turquoise and white shell,—a white and a yellow ear of corn, the Pollen Boy, and the Grasshopper Girl. On top of all these Talking God laid another sacred buckskin with its head to the east, and under this they now put Wind.

Then the assembled crowd stood so as to form a circle, leaving in the east an opening through which Talking God and Calling God might pass in and out, and they sang the sacred song of Blessingway. Four times the gods entered and raised the cover. When they raised it for the fourth time, the images and the ears of corn were found changed to living beings in human form: the turquoise image had become the Woman Who Changes (or rejuvenates herself); the white shell image had become the White Shell Woman; the white ear of corn had become the White Corn Boy and the yellow ear of corn, the Yellow Corn Girl. After the ceremony, White Body took Pollen Boy, Grasshopper Girl, White Corn Boy, and Yellow Corn Girl with him into *Tsolíhi;* the rest of the assembly departed, and the two divine sisters, Changing Woman and White Shell Woman,[2] were left on the mountain alone.

The women remained here four nights; on the fourth morning Changing Woman said: "Younger Sister, why should we remain here? Let us go to yonder high point and look around us." They went to the highest point of the mountain, and when they had been there several days Changing Woman said: "It is lonely here; we have no one to speak to but ourselves; we see nothing but that which rolls over our heads (the sun), and that which drops below us (a small dripping waterfall). I wonder if they can be people. I shall stay here and wait for the one in the morning, while you go down among the rocks and seek the other."

In the morning Changing Woman found a bare, flat rock and lay on it with her feet to the east, and the rising sun shone upon her. White Shell Woman went down

[2]Changing Woman represents Nature as cyclical—the seasons, the parts of a day, the ages of an individual life. White Shell Woman is not a separate individual, but Changing Woman in another form. In this version of the story, each conceives a son; yet, Changing Woman alone has conceived twins.

where the dripping waters descended and allowed them to fall upon her. At noon the women met again on the mountain top and Changing Woman said to her sister: "It is sad to be so lonesome. How can we make people so that we may have others of our kind to talk to?" White Shell Woman answered: "Think, Elder Sister; perhaps after some days you may plan how this is to be done."

Four days after this conversation White Shell Woman said: "Elder Sister, I feel something strange moving within me; what can it be?" and Changing Woman answered: "It is a child. It was for this that you lay under the waterfall. I feel, too, the motions of a child within me. It was for this that I let the sun shine upon me." Soon after the voice of Talking God was heard four times, as usual, and after the last call he and Water Sprinkler[3] appeared. They came to prepare the women for their approaching delivery.

In four days more they felt the commencing throes of labor, and one said to the other: "I think my child is coming." She had scarcely spoken when the voice of the approaching god was heard, and soon Talking God and Water Sprinkler were seen approaching. The former was the accoucheur of Changing Woman, and the latter of White Shell Woman. To one woman a drag-rope of rainbow was given, to the other a drag-rope of sunbeam, and on these they pulled when in pain, as the Navajo woman now pulls on the rope. Changing Woman's child was born first. Talking God took it aside and washed it. He was glad, and laughed and made ironical motions, as if he were cutting the baby in slices and throwing the slices away. They made for the children two baby-baskets, both alike; the foot-rests and the back battens were made of sun-beam, the hoods of rainbow, the side-strings of sheet lightning, and the lacing strings of zigzag lightning. One child they covered with the black cloud, and the other with the female rain.[4] They called the children grandchildren, and they left, promising to return at the end of four days.

When the gods returned at the end of four days, the boys had grown to be the size of ordinary boys of twelve years of age. The gods said to them: "Boys, we have come to have a race with you." So a race was arranged that should go all around a neighboring mountain, and the four started,—two boys and two gods. Before the long race was half done the boys, who ran fast, began to flag, and the gods, who were still fresh, got behind them and scourged the lads with twigs of mountain mahogany. Talking God won the race, and the boys came home rubbing their sore backs. When the gods left they promised to return at the end of another period of four days.

As soon as the gods were gone, the Wind whispered to the boys and told them that the old ones were not such fast runners, after all, and that if the boys would practice during the next four days they might win the coming race. So for four days they ran hard, many times daily around the neighboring mountain, and when the gods came back again the youths had grown to the full stature of manhood. In the second contest the gods began to flag and fall behind when half way round the mountain, where the others had fallen behind in the first race, and here the boys got behind their elders and scourged the latter to increase their speed. The elder of the boys won

[3]A holy being responsible for rain.

[4]The fundamental principle of the Navajo world is complementarity. All things can be termed male or female and are associated with colors and the cardinal directions. Male rain is the dark thunderstorm; female rain is the light shower.

this race, and when it was over the gods laughed and clapped their hands, for they were pleased with the spirit and prowess they witnessed.

The night after the race the boys lay down as usual to sleep; but hearing the women whispering together, they lay awake and listened. They strained their attention, but could not hear a word of what was uttered. At length they rose, approached the women, and said: "Mothers, of what do you speak?" and the women answered: "We speak of nothing." The boys then said: "Grandmothers, of what do you speak?" but the women again replied: "We speak of nothing." The boys then questioned: "Who are our fathers?" "You have no fathers," responded the women; "you are illegitimate." "Who are our fathers?" again demanded the boys, and the women answered: "The round cactus and the sitting cactus are your fathers."[5]

Next day the women made rude bows of juniper wood, and arrows, such as children play with, and they said to the boys: "Go and play around with these, but do not go out of sight from our hut, and do not go to the east." Notwithstanding these warnings the boys went to the east the first day, and when they had travelled a good distance they saw an animal with brownish hair and a sharp nose. They drew their arrows and pointed them toward the sharp-nosed stranger; but before they could shoot he jumped down into a canyon and disappeared. When they returned home they told the women—addressing them as "Mother" and "Grandmother"—what they had seen. The women said: "That is Coyote which you saw. He is a spy for the monster *Téelgĕt.*". . .[6] Alas, our children! What shall we do to make you hear us? What shall we do to save you? You would not listen to us. Now the spies of the *alien gods* in all quarters of the world have seen you. They will tell their chiefs, and soon the monsters will come here to devour you, as they have devoured all your kind before you."

The next morning the women made a corncake and laid it on the ashes to bake. Then White Shell Woman went out of the *hogán,* and, as she did so, she saw *Yéitso,*[7] the tallest and fiercest of the alien gods, approaching. She ran quickly back and gave the warning, and the women hid the boys under bundles and sticks. *Yéitso* came and sat down at the door, just as the women were taking the cake out of the ashes. "That cake is for me," said *Yéitso.* "How nice it smells!" "No," said Changing Woman, "it was not meant for your great maw." "I don't care," said *Yéitso.* "I would rather eat boys. Where are your boys? I have been told you have some here, and I have come to get them." "We have none," said Changing Woman. "All the boys have gone into the paunches of your people long ago." "No boys?" said the giant. "What, then, has made all the tracks around here?" "Oh! these tracks I have made for fun," replied the woman. "I am lonely here, and I make tracks so that I may fancy there are many

[5]The mystery of the boys' paternity is linked to that of the monsters they will slay, for they will discover that the Sun is the father of both the slayers and the slain.

[6]This edition of the story eliminates three repetitions of this episode in which the Twins, who should be hiding from the monsters who are terrorizing the people, play in the open where they are observed by spies for the monsters. *Téelgĕt* is a monstrous, horned quadruped.

[7]The name means "the Great Fear." The monsters were conceived unnaturally in the underworld by women who had turned away from men. Each monster or obstacle the Twins overcome can be understood to represent certain kinds of fears.

people around me." She showed *Yéitso* how she could make similar tracks with her fist. He compared the two sets of tracks, seemed to be satisfied, and went away.

When he was gone, the White Shell Woman went up to the top of a neighboring hill to look around, and she beheld many of the anáye hastening in the direction of her lodge. She returned speedily, and told her sister what she had seen. Changing Woman took four colored hoops, and threw one toward each of the cardinal points,—a white one to the east, a blue one to the south, a yellow one to the west, and a black one to the north. At once a great gale arose, blowing so fiercely in all directions from the *hogán* that none of the enemies could advance against it.

Next morning the boys got up before daybreak and stole away. Soon the women missed them, but could not trace them in the dark. When it was light enough to examine the ground the women went out to look for fresh tracks. They found four footprints of each of the boys, pointing in the direction of the mountain of *Dsilnáotil,* but more than four tracks they could not find. They came to the conclusion that the boys had taken a holy trail, so they gave up further search and returned to the lodge.

The boys travelled rapidly in the holy trail, and soon after sunrise, near *Dsilnáotil,* they saw smoke arising from the ground. They went to the place where the smoke rose, and they found it came from the smoke-hole of a subterranean chamber. A ladder, black from smoke, projected through the hole. Looking down into the chamber they saw an old woman, the Spider Woman,[8] who glanced up at them and said: "Welcome, children. Enter. Who are you, and whence do you two come together walking?" They made no answer, but descended the ladder. When they reached the floor she again spoke to them, asking: "Whither do you two go walking together?" "Nowhere in particular," they answered; "we came here because we had nowhere else to go." She asked this question four times, and each time she received a similar answer. Then she said: "Perhaps you would seek your father?" "Yes," they answered, "if we only knew the way to his dwelling." "Ah!" said the woman, "it is a long and dangerous way to the house of your father, the Sun. There are many of the monsters dwelling between here and there, and perhaps, when you get there, your father may not be glad to see you, and may punish you for coming. You must pass four places of danger,—the rocks that crush the traveller, the reeds that cut him to pieces, the cane cactuses that tear him to pieces, and the boiling sands that overwhelm him. But I shall give you something to subdue your enemies and preserve your lives." She gave them a charm, the feather of the alien gods, which consisted of a hoop with two life-feathers (feathers plucked from a living eagle) attached, and another life-feather to preserve their existence. She taught them also this magic formula, which, if repeated to their enemies, would subdue their anger: "Put your feet down with pollen. Put your hands down with pollen. Put your head down with pollen. Then your feet are pollen; your hands are pollen; your body is pollen; your mind is pollen; your voice is pollen. The trail is beautiful. Be still."[9]

[8]In southwestern Native literatures, Spider Woman is a grandmotherly figure whose great wisdom is often placed at the service of humanity.

[9]This is a prayer for life and peace, symbolized by pollen, which serves to bless their journey.

Soon after leaving the house of Spider Woman, the boys came to the rocks that crush.[10] There was here a narrow chasm between two high cliffs. When a traveller approached, the rocks would open wide apart, apparently to give him easy passage and invite him to enter; but as soon as he was within the cleft they would close like hands clapping and crush him to death. These rocks were really people; they thought like men; they were monsters. When the boys got to the rocks they lifted their feet as if about to enter the chasm, and the rocks opened to let them in. Then the boys put down their feet, but withdrew them quickly. The rocks closed with a snap to crush them; but the boys remained safe on the outside. Thus four times did they deceive the rocks. When they had closed for the fourth time the rocks said: "Who are ye; whence come ye two together, and whither go ye?" "We are children of the Sun," answered the boys. "We come from *Dsilnáotil,* and we go to seek the house of our father." Then they repeated the words the Spider Woman had taught them, and the rocks said: "Pass on to the house of your father." When next they ventured to step into the chasm the rocks did not close, and they passed safely on.

The boys kept on their way and soon came to a great plain covered with reeds that had great leaves on them as sharp as knives. When the boys came to the edge of the field of reeds, the latter opened, showing a clear passage through to the other side. The boys pretended to enter, but retreated, and as they did so the walls of reeds rushed together to kill them. Thus four times did they deceive the reeds. Then the reeds spoke to them, as the rocks had done; they answered and repeated the sacred words. "Pass on to the house of your father," said the reeds, and the boys passed on in safety.

The next danger they encountered was in the country covered with cane cactuses. These cactuses rushed at and tore to pieces whoever attempted to pass through them. When the boys came to the cactuses the latter opened their ranks to let the travellers pass on, as the reeds had done before. But the boys deceived them as they had deceived the reeds, and subdued them as they had subdued the reeds, and passed on in safety.

After they had passed the country of the cactus they came, in time, to the land of the rising sands. Here was a great desert of sands that rose and whirled and boiled like water in a pot, and overwhelmed the traveller who ventured among them. As the boys approached, the sands became still more agitated and the boys did not dare venture among them. "Who are ye?" said the sands, "and whence come ye?" "We are children of the Sun, we came from *Dsilnáotil,* and we go to seek the house of our father." These words were four times said. Then the elder of the boys repeated his sacred formula; the sands subsided, saying: "Pass on to the house of your father," and the boys continued on their journey over the desert of sands.

Soon after this adventure they approached the house of the Sun. As they came near the door they found the way guarded by two bears that crouched, one to the right and one to the left, their noses pointing toward one another. As the boys drew near, the bears rose, growled angrily, and acted as if about to attack the intruders; but the elder boy repeated the sacred words the Spider Woman had taught him, and

[10]These mythical places are also identified with real locales in the Navajo world, so that the story accounts for how the landscape came to assume its present form.

when he came to the last words, "Be still," the bears crouched down again and lay still. The boys walked on. After passing the bears they encountered a pair of sentinel serpents, then a pair of sentinel winds, and, lastly, a pair of sentinel lightnings. As the boys advanced, all these guardians acted as if they would destroy them; but all were appeased with the words of prayer.

The house of the Sun God was built of turquoise; it was square like a pueblo house, and stood on the shore of a great water. When the boys entered they saw, sitting in the west, a woman; in the south, two handsome young men; and in the north, two handsome young women. The women gave a glance at the strangers and then looked down. The young men gazed at them more closely, and then, without speaking, they rose, wrapped the strangers in four coverings of the sky, and laid them on a shelf.

The boys had lain there quietly for some time when a rattle that hung over the door shook and one of the young women said: "Our father is coming." The rattle shook four times, and soon after it shook the fourth time, the Sun Bearer entered his house. He took the sun off his back and hung it up on a peg on the west wall of the room, where it shook and clanged for some time, going "tla, tla, tla, tla," till at last it hung still.

Then the Sun Bearer turned to the woman and said, in an angry tone: "Who are those two who entered here to-day?" The woman made no answer and the young people looked at one another, but each feared to speak. Four times he asked this question, and at length the woman said: "It would be well for you not to say too much. Two young men came hither to-day, seeking their father. When you go abroad, you always tell me that you visit nowhere, and that you have met no woman but me. Whose sons, then, are these?" She pointed to the bundle on the shelf, and the children smiled significantly at one another.

He took the bundle from the shelf. He first unrolled the robe of dawn with which they were covered, then the robe of blue sky, next the robe of yellow evening light, and lastly the robe of darkness. When he unrolled this the boys fell out on the floor. He seized them, and threw them first upon great, sharp spikes of white shell that stood in the east; but they bounded back, unhurt, from these spikes, for they held their life-feathers tightly all the while. He then threw them in turn on spikes of turquoise in the south, on spikes of haliotis in the west, and spikes of black rock in the north; but they came uninjured from all these trials and the Sun Bearer said: "I wish it were indeed true that they were my children."

He said then to the elder children—those who lived with him,—"Go out and prepare the sweat-house and heat for it four of the hardest boulders you can find. Heat a white, a blue, a yellow, and a black boulder." When the Winds heard this they said: "He still seeks to kill his children. How shall we avert the danger?" The sweat-house was built against a bank. Wind dug into the bank a hole behind the sudatory, and concealed the opening with a flat stone. Wind then whispered into the ears of the boys the secret of the hole and said: "Do not hide in the hole until you have answered the questions of your father." The boys went into the sweat-house, the great hot boulders were put in, and the opening of the lodge was covered with the four sky-blankets. Then the Sun Bearer called out to the boys: "Are you hot?" and they answered: "Yes, very hot." Then they crept into the hiding-place and lay there. After a while the Sun Bearer came and poured water through the top of the sweat-house on the stones, making them burst with a loud noise, and a great heat and steam was raised. But in time the stones cooled and the boys crept out of their hiding-place into the sweat-house. The Sun Bearer came and asked again: "Are you hot?" hoping to get no reply; but the boys still answered: "Yes, very hot." Then he took the coverings off the sweat-house and let the boys come out. He greeted them in a friendly way and said: "Yes, these are my children," and yet he was thinking of other ways by which he might destroy them if they were not.

The four sky-blankets were spread on the ground one over another, and the four young men were made to sit on them, one behind another, facing the east. "My daughters, make these boys to look like my other sons," said the Sun Bearer. The young women went to the strangers, pulled their hair out long, and moulded their faces and forms so that they looked just like their brethren. Then Sun bade them all rise and enter the house. They rose and all went, in a procession, the two strangers last.

As they were about to enter the door they heard a voice whispering in their ears: "St! Look at the ground." They looked down and beheld a spiny caterpillar, who, as they looked, spat out two blue spits on the ground. "Take each of you one of these," said Wind, "and put it in your mouth, but do not swallow it. There is one more trial for you,—a trial by smoking." When they entered the house the Sun Bearer took down a pipe of turquoise that hung on the eastern wall and filled it with tobacco. "This is the tobacco he kills with," whispered Wind to the boys. The Sun Bearer held the pipe up to the sun that hung on the wall, lit it, and gave it to the boys to smoke. They smoked it, and passed it from one to another till it was finished. They said it tasted sweet, but it did them no harm.

When the pipe was smoked out and the Sun Bearer saw the boys were not killed by it, he was satisfied and said: "Now, my children, what do you want from me? Why do you seek me?" "Oh, father!" they replied, "the land where we dwell is filled with monsters, who devour the people. There are Yéitso and the Horned Monster, the Giant Eagle, Those-Who-Slay-With-Their-Eyes, and many others. They have eaten nearly all of our kind; there are few left; already they have sought our lives, and we have run away to escape them. Give us, we beg, the weapons with which we may slay our enemies. Help us to destroy them."

"Know," said the Sun Bearer, "that Yéitso who dwells at *Tsótsil* is also my son, yet I will help you to kill him. I shall hurl the first bolt at him, and I will give you those things that will help you in war." He took from pegs where they hung around the room and gave to each a hat, a shirt, leggings, moccasins, all made of flint,[11] a chain-lightning arrow, a sheet-lightning arrow, a sunbeam arrow, a rainbow arrow, and a great stone knife or knife club. "These are what we want," said the boys. They put on the clothes of flint, and streaks of lightning shot from every joint.

Next morning the Sun Bearer led the boys out to the edge of the world, where the sky and the earth came close together, and beyond which there was no world. Here sixteen wands or poles leaned from the earth to the sky; four of these were of

[11]Actually, armor, like arrow points and knife blades, made from flint.

white shell, four of turquoise, four of haliotis shell, and four of red stone. A deep stream flowed between them and the wands. As they approached the stream, the Wind whispered: "This is another trial;" but he blew a great breath and formed a bridge of rainbow, over which the brothers passed in safety. Wind whispered again: "The red wands are for war, the others are for peace;" so when the Sun Bearer asked his sons: "On which wands will ye ascend?" they answered: "On the wands of red stone," for they sought war with their enemies. They climbed up to the sky on the wands of red stone, and their father went with them.

They journeyed on till they came to the sky-hole which is in the centre of the sky. The hole is edged with four smooth, shining cliffs that slope steeply downwards,—cliffs of the same materials as the wands by which they had climbed from the earth to the sky. They sat down on the smooth declivities,—the Sun Bearer on the west side of the hole, the brothers on the east side. The latter would have slipped down had not the Wind blown up and helped them to hold on. The Sun Bearer pointed down and said: "Where do you belong in the world below? Show me your home." The brothers looked down and scanned the land; but they could distinguish nothing; all the land seemed flat; the wooded mountains looked like dark spots on the surface; the lakes gleamed like stars, and the rivers like streaks of lightning. The elder brother said: "I do not recognize the land, I know not where our home is." Now Wind prompted the younger brother, and showed him which were the sacred mountains and which the great rivers, and the younger exclaimed, pointing downwards: "There is the Male Water (San Juan River), and there is the Female Water (Rio Grande); yonder is the mountain of *Tsisnadzini;* below us is *Tsótsil;* there in the west is *Dokoslid;* that white spot beyond the Male Water is *Depentsa;* and there between these mountains is *Dsilnáotil,* near which our home is."[12] "You are right, my child, it is thus that the land lies," said the Sun Bearer. Then, renewing his promises, he spread a streak of lightning; he made his children stand on it,—one on each end,—and he shot them down to the top of *Tsótsil* (Mt. Taylor).

They descended the mountain on its south side and walked toward the warm spring at *Tósato.* As they were walking along under a high bluff, where there is now a white circle, they heard voices hailing them. "Whither are you going? Come hither a while." They went in the direction in which they heard the voices calling and found four holy people,—Holy Man, Holy Young Man, Holy Boy, and Holy Girl. The brothers remained all night in a cave with these people, and the latter told them all about Yéitso. They said that he showed himself every day three times on the mountains before he came down, and when he showed himself for the fourth time he descended from *Tsótsil* to *Tósato* to drink; that, when he stooped down to drink, one hand rested on *Tsótsil* and the other on the high hills on the opposite side of the valley, while his feet stretched as far away as a man could walk between sunrise and noon.

[12]These rivers and the sacred boundary mountains (*Depentsa,* Hesperus Peak, in the north; *Tsisnadzini,* the Sangre de Cristo Mountains in the east; *Tsótsil,* Mt. Taylor, in the south; and *Dokoslid,* the San Francisco Peaks, in the east) mark Navajo land, of which *Dsilnáotil,* or Gobernador Knob, is the Center.

They left the cave at daybreak and went on to *Tósato,* where in ancient days there was a much larger lake than there is now. There was a high, rocky wall in the narrow part of the valley, and the lake stretched back to where Blue Water is to-day. When they came to the edge of the lake, one brother said to the other: "Let us try one of our father's weapons and see what it can do." They shot one of the lightning arrows at *Tsótsil;* it made a great cleft in the mountain, which remains to this day, and one said to the other: "We cannot suffer in combat while we have such weapons as these."

Soon they heard the sound of thunderous footsteps, and they beheld the head of Yéitso peering over a high hill in the east; it was withdrawn in a moment. Soon after, the monster raised his head and chest over a hill in the south, and remained a little longer in sight than when he was in the east. Later he displayed his body to the waist over a hill in the west; and lastly he showed himself, down to the knees, over *Tsótsil* in the north. Then he descended the mountain, came to the edge of the lake, and laid down a basket which he was accustomed to carry.

Yéitso stooped four times to the lake to drink, and, each time he drank, the waters perceptibly diminished; when he had done drinking, the lake was nearly drained. The brothers lost their presence of mind at sight of the giant drinking, and did nothing while he was stooping down. As he took his last drink they advanced to the edge of the lake, and Yéitso saw their reflection in the water. He raised his head, and, looking at them, roared: "What a pretty pair have come in sight! Where have I been hunting?" (*i.e.,* that I never saw them before). "Throw (his words) back in his mouth," said the younger to the elder brother. "What a great thing has come in sight! Where have we been hunting?" shouted the elder brother to the giant. Four times these taunts were repeated by each party. The brothers then heard Wind whispering quickly, "Akó'! Akó'! Beware! Beware!" They were standing on a bent rainbow just then; they straightened the rainbow out, descending to the ground, and at the same instant a lightning bolt, hurled by Yéitso, passed thundering over their heads. He hurled four bolts rapidly; as he hurled the second, they bent their rainbow and rose, while the bolt passed under their feet; as he discharged the third they descended, and let the lightning pass over them. When he threw the fourth bolt they bent the rainbow very high, for this time he aimed higher than before; but his weapon still passed under their feet and did them no harm. He drew a fifth bolt to throw at them; but at this moment the lightning descended from the sky on the head of the giant and he reeled beneath it, but did not fall. Then the elder brother sped a chain-lightning arrow; his enemy tottered toward the east, but straightened himself up again. The second arrow caused him to stumble toward the south (he fell lower and lower each time), but again he stood up and prepared himself to renew the conflict. The third lightning arrow made him topple toward the west, and the fourth to the north. Then he fell to his knees, raised himself partly again, fell flat on his face, stretched out his limbs, and moved no more.

When the arrows struck him, his armor was shivered in pieces and the scales flew in every direction. The elder brother said: "They may be useful to the people in the future."[13] The brothers then approached their fallen enemy and the younger

[13]By providing the Navajo with flint for blades and arrow points.

scalped him. Heretofore the younger brother bore only the name, Child of the Water; but now his brother gave him also the warrior name of He Who Cuts Around. What the elder brother's name was before this we do not know; but ever after he was called Monster Slayer.

They cut off his head and threw it away to the other side of *Tsótsil,* where it may be seen to-day on the eastern side of the mountain.[14] The blood from the body now flowed in a great stream down the valley, so great that it broke down the rocky wall that bounded the old lake and flowed on. Wind whispered to the brothers: "The blood flows toward the dwelling of Those-Who-Slay-With-Their-Eyes; if it reaches them, Yéitso will come to life again." Then Monster Slayer took his flint club, and drew with it across the valley a line. Here the blood stopped flowing and piled itself up in a high wall. But when it had piled up here very high it began to flow off in another direction, and Wind again whispered: "It now flows toward the dwelling of the Bear that Pursues; if it reaches him, Yéitso will come to life again." Hearing this, Monster Slayer again drew a line with his knife on the ground, and again the blood piled up and stopped flowing. The blood of Yéitso fills all the valley to-day, and the high cliffs in the black rock that we see there now are the places where Monster Slayer stopped the flow with his flint club.

They then put the broken arrows of Yéitso and his scalp into his basket and set out for their home near *Dsilnáotil.* When they got near the house, they took off their own suits of armor and hid these, with the basket and its contents, in the bushes. The mothers were rejoiced to see them, for they feared their sons were lost, and they said: "Where have you been since you left here yesterday, and what have you done?" Monster Slayer replied: "We have been to the house of our father, the Sun. We have been to *Tsótsil* and we have slain Yéitso." "Ah, my child," said Changing Woman, "do not speak thus. It is wrong to make fun of such an awful subject." "Do you not believe us?" said Monster Slayer; "come out, then, and see what we have brought back with us." He led the women out to where he had hidden the basket and showed them the trophies of Yéitso. Then they were convinced and they rejoiced, and had a dance to celebrate the victory. . . .[15]

"Surely all the monsters are now killed," said Changing Woman. "This storm must have destroyed them." But Wind whispered into Monster Slayer's ear, "Old Age still lives." The hero said then to his mother: "Where used Old Age to dwell?" His mother would not answer him, though he repeated his question four times. At last Wind again whispered in his ear and said: "She lives in the mountains of *Depentsa.*"

Next morning he set out for the north, and when, after a long journey, he reached *Depentsa,* he saw an old woman who came slowly toward him leaning on a

[14]Forty miles northeast of Mt. Taylor is Cabezon ("The Head") Peak. Yéitso's blood coagulated into The Malpais, an extensive lava flow south of Mt. Taylor.

[15]This is the first Scalp Dance, which celebrates victory over the enemy while it cleanses the warrior from the effects of contact with enemy dead. After this initial victory, the Twins slay many other monsters and return home after a storm, presuming to have made the world safe and habitable for humankind. In the remarkable encounters which follow, people learn that, although they might have power over some things, the use of power might not always be wise.

staff. Her back was bent, her hair was white, and her face was deeply wrinkled. He knew this must be Old Age. When they met he said: "Grandmother, I have come on a cruel errand. I have come to slay you." "Why would you slay me?" she said in a feeble voice, "I have never harmed any one. I hear that you have done great deeds in order that men might increase on the earth, but if you kill me there will be no increase of men; the boys will not grow up to become fathers; the worthless old men will not die; the people will stand still. It is well that people should grow old and pass away and give their places to the young. Let me live, and I shall help you to increase the people." "Grandmother, if you keep this promise I shall spare your life," said Monster Slayer, and he returned to his mother without a trophy.

When he got home Wind whispered to him: "Cold Woman still lives." Monster Slayer said to Changing Woman: "Mother, grandmother, where does Cold Woman dwell?" His mother would not answer him; but Wind again whispered, saying: "Cold Woman lives high on the summits of *Depentsa,* where the snow never melts."

Next day he went again to the north and climbed high among the peaks of *Depentsa,* where no trees grow and where the snow lies white through all the summer. Here he found a lean old woman, sitting on the bare snow, without clothing, food, fire, or shelter. She shivered from head to foot, her teeth chattered, and her eyes streamed water. Among the drifting snows which whirled around her, a multitude of snow-buntings were playing; these were the couriers she sent out to announce the coming of a storm. "Grandmother," he said, "a cruel man I shall be. I am going to kill you, so that men may no more suffer and die by your hand," and he raised his knife-club to smite her. "You may kill me or let me live, as you will. I care not," she said to the hero; "but if you kill me it will always be hot, the land will dry up, the springs will cease to flow, the people will perish. You will do well to let me live. It will be better for your people." He paused and thought upon her words. He lowered the hand he had raised to strike her, saying: "You speak wisely, grandmother; I shall let you live." He turned around and went home.

When Monster Slayer got home from this journey, bearing no trophy, Wind again whispered in his ear and said: "Poverty still lives." He asked his mother where Poverty used to live, but she would not answer him. It was Wind who again informed him. "There are two, and they dwell at *Dsildasdzini."*

He went to *Dsildasdzini* the next day and found there an old man and an old woman, who were filthy, clad in tattered garments, and had no goods in their house. "Grandmother, grandfather," he said, "a cruel man I shall be. I have come to kill you." "Do not kill us, my grandchild," said the old man: "it would not be well for the people, in days to come, if we were dead; then they would always wear the same clothes and never get anything new. If we live, the clothing will wear out and the people will make new and beautiful garments; they will gather goods and look handsome. Let us live and we will pull their old clothes to pieces for them." So he spared them and went home without a trophy.

The next journey was to seek Hunger, who lived, as Wind told him, at White Spot of Grass. At this place he found twelve of the Hunger People. Their chief was a big, fat man, although he had no food to eat but the little brown cactus. "I am going to be cruel," said Monster Slayer, "so that men may suffer no more the pangs of hunger and die no more of hunger." "Do not kill us," said the chief, "if you wish your people to increase and be happy in the days to come. We are your friends. If we die, the people will not care for food; they will never know the pleasure of cooking and eating nice things, and they will never care for the pleasures of the chase." So he spared also Hunger, and went home without a trophy.

When Monster Slayer came back from the home of Hunger, Wind spoke to him no more of enemies that lived. The Monster Slayer said to his mother: "I think all the monsters must be dead, for every one I meet now speaks to me as a relation; they say to me, 'my grandson,' 'my son,' 'my brother.'" Then he took off his armor—his knife, moccasins, leggings, shirt, and cap—and laid them in a pile; he put with them the various weapons which the Sun had given him, and he sang this song:—

Now Monster Slayer arrives
Here from the house made of the dark stone knives.
From where the dark stone knives dangle on high,
You have the treasures, holy one, not I.

The Child of the Water now arrives,
Here from the house made of the serrate knives.

From where the serrate knives dangle on high,
You have the treasures, holy one, not I.

He who was reared beneath the Earth arrives,
Here from the house made of all kinds of knives.
From where all kinds of knives dangle on high,
You have the treasures, holy one, not I.

The hero, Changing Grandchild, now arrives,
Here from the house made of the yellow knives.
From where the yellow knives dangle on high,
You have the treasures, holy one, not I.[16]

1897

[16]In this song, the Twins bring the story full circle by acknowledging that Changing Woman is really the most powerful being, the one for whom the Sun's weapons have been used, the one whose treasures benefit everyone.

Wohpe and the Gift of the Pipe (Lakota)

Finger[1]

In the long ago the Lakotas were in camp and two young men lay upon a hill watching for signs. They saw a long way in the distance a lone person coming, and they ran further toward it and lay on another hill hidden so that if it were an enemy they would be able to intercept it or signal to the camp. When the person came close, they saw that it was a woman and when she came nearer that she was without clothing of any kind except that her hair was very long and fell over her body like a robe. One young man said to the other that he would go and meet the woman and embrace her and if he found her good, he would hold her in his tipi. His companion cautioned him to be careful for this might be a buffalo woman who could enchant him and take him with her to her people and hold him there forever. But the young man would not be persuaded and met the woman on the hill next to where they had watched her. His companion saw him attempt to embrace her and there was a cloud closed about them so that he could not see what happened. In a short time the cloud disappeared and the woman was alone. She beckoned to the other young man and told him to come there and assured him that he would not be harmed. As she spoke in the Lakota language the young man thought she belonged to his people and went to where she stood.

When he got there, she showed him the bare bones of his companion and told him that the Crazy Buffalo had caused his companion to try to do her harm and that she had destroyed him and picked his bones bare. The young man was very much afraid and drew his bow and arrow to shoot the woman, but she told him that if he would do as she directed, no harm would come to him and he should get any girl he wished for his woman, for she was *wakan*[2] and he could not hurt her with his arrows. But if he refused to do as she should direct, or attempt to shoot her, he would be destroyed as his companion had been. Then the young man promised to do as she should bid him.

[1]James R. Walker was a physician to the Oglala at the Pine Ridge (South Dakota) Reservation from 1896 to 1914. Faced with the tremendous medical problems on the reservation, especially tuberculosis, he sought the assistance of the medicine men to help him understand and serve the Lakotas. They began to teach him the stories and ceremonies of the Lakotas, stating, "We will do this so you may know how to be a medicine man for the people. . . . We will tell you of the ceremonies as if you were an Oglala who wished to take part in them."

Finger, an old and very conservative Oglala holy man who was very helpful in enabling Walker to understand some of the most complex Oglala beliefs, told this story on March 25, 1914, in response to Walker's inquiries about how the pipe came to the Lakotas. *Wohpe* is one of the forms of the *wakan tanka,* which is often described singularly as the Great Spirit, but which, according to Oglala holy man George Sword, has sixteen different aspects. *Wohpe* is feminine and the mediator between earth and sky, so she is recognized in nature as the meteor or falling star. She is familiarly personified, though not named in this narrative, as White Buffalo Calf Woman. She is responsible for bringing to the Lakotas the seven principal rites, of which the pipe is one. This text is taken from James R. Walker, *Lakota Belief and Ritual,* 1980.

[2]*Wakan* is customarily translated as "sacred" or "holy," but it more precisely means anything charged with power which can only be approached through ritual.

She then directed him to return to the camp and call all the council together and tell them that in a short time they would see four puffs of smoke under the sun at midday. When they saw this sign they should prepare a feast, and all sit in the customary circle to have the feast served when she would enter the camp, but the men must all sit with their head bowed and look at the ground until she was in their midst. Then she would serve the feast to them and after they had feasted she would tell them what to do: that they must obey her in everything; that if they obeyed her in everything they would have their prayers to the *Wakan Tanka* answered and be prosperous and happy; but that if they disobeyed her or attempted to do her any harm, they would be neglected by *Wakan Tanka* and be punished as the young man who had attempted to embrace her had been.

Then she disappeared as a mist disappears so that the young man knew that she was *wakan.* He returned to the camp and told these things to the people and the council decided to do as she had instructed the young man. They made preparation for the feast and in a few days they saw four puffs of black smoke under the sun at midday, so they prepared for a feast and all dressed in their best clothing and sat in the circle ready to be served and every man bowed his head and looked toward the ground. Suddenly the women began uttering low exclamations of admiration, but all the men steadily kept their eyes toward the ground except one young man and he looked toward the entrance of the camp. He saw a puff of black smoke which blew into his eyes and a voice said, "You have disobeyed me and there will be smoke in your eyes as long as you live." From that time, that young man had very sore eyes and all the time they were as if biting smoke was in them.

Then the woman entered the circle and took the food and served it, first to the little children and then to the women and then she bade the men to look up. They did so and saw a very beautiful woman dressed in the softest deer skin which was ornamented with fringes and colors more beautiful than any woman of the Lakota had ever worked. Then she served the men with food, and when they had feasted she told them that she wished to serve them always; that they had first seen her as smoke and that they should always see her as smoke. Then she took from her pouch a pipe and willow bark and Lakota tobacco and filled the pipe with the bark and tobacco and lighted it with a coal of fire.[3]

She smoked a few whiffs and handed the pipe to the chief and told him to smoke and hand it to another. Thus the pipe was passed until all had smoked. She then instructed the council how to gather the bark and the tobacco and prepare it, and gave the pipe into their keeping, telling them that as long as they preserved this pipe she would serve them. But she would serve them in this way. When the smoke came from the pipe she would be present and hear their prayers and take them to the *Wakan Tanka* and plead for them that their prayers should be answered.

[3]The pipe is used in all rituals and is therefore the central integrating element in Lakota ritual life. In its complex forms of stone, wood, feathers, and animal carvings, it also represents the Lakota cosmos. The smoke offered to the four directions carried prayer to Wakan Tanka. Bonds between groups, vows to *Wakantanka,* and prophecies were validated by means of the pipe, and any transgressions against it would cause the offender or his family to suffer misfortune or even death. Thus the pipe could not be desecrated by word or deed, and it could only be handled by persons properly trained in its protocol.

After this she remained in this camp for many days and all the time she was there everyone was happy for she went from tipi to tipi with good words for all. When the time came for her to go, she called all the people together and bade the women to build a great fire of dried cottonwood, which they did. Then she directed all to sit in a circle about the fire and the shaman to have an abundance of sweetgrass. She stood in the midst of the circle and when the fire had burned to coals she directed the shaman to place on it the sweetgrass. This made a cloud of smoke and the woman entered the smoke and disappeared. Then the shamans knew that it was *Wohpe* who had given the pipe and they appointed a custodian for it with instructions that it was to be kept sacred and used only on the most solemn and important occasions. With due ceremony they made wrappers for the pipe so that it is *wakan.* The shamans instructed the people that they could make other pipes and use them and that *Wohpe* would be in the smoke of any such pipe if smoked with proper solemnity and form.

Thus it was that the Beautiful Woman brought the pipe to the Lakotas.

1980

The Origin of Stories (Seneca)

There was once a boy who had no home. His parents were dead and his uncles would not care for him. In order to live this boy, whose name was Gaqka, or Crow, made a bower of branches for an abiding place and hunted birds and squirrels for food.[1]

He had almost no clothing but was very ragged and dirty. When the people from the village saw him they called him Filth-Covered-One, and laughed as they passed by, holding their noses. No one thought he would ever amount to anything, which made him feel heavy-hearted. He resolved to go away from his tormentors and become a great hunter.

One night Gaqka found a canoe. He had never seen this canoe before, so he took it. Stepping in he grasped the paddle, when the canoe immediately shot into the air, and he paddled above the clouds and under the moon. For a long time he went always southward. Finally the canoe dropped into a river and then Gaqka paddled for shore.

[1]The theme that stories originated in the earth or elsewhere beyond human understanding and are only communicated to humans either through dreams or magical agents (such as this speaking cliff) confirms a deep belief in the seriousness of stories as chartering original relations among all the elements of the universe. The motif of the despised orphan who alone is capable and worthy of receiving sacred knowledge is widespread. This text is taken from Arthur C. Parker, *Seneca Myths and Folk Tales,* 1923.

On the other side of the river was a great cliff that had a face that looked like a man. It was at the forks of the river where this cliff stood. The boy resolved to make his home on the top of the cliff and so climbed it and built a bark cabin.

The first night he sat on the edge of the cliff he heard a voice saying, "Give me some tobacco." Looking around the boy, seeing no one, replied, "Why should I give tobacco?"

There was no answer and the boy began to fix his arrows for the next day's hunt. After a while the voice spoke again, "Give me some tobacco."

Gaqka now took out some tobacco and threw it over the cliff. The voice spoke again: "Now I will tell you a story."

Feeling greatly awed the boy listened to a story that seemed to come directly out of the rock upon which he was sitting. Finally the voice paused, for the story had ended. Then it spoke again saying, "It shall be the custom hereafter to present me with a small gift for my stories." So the boy gave the rock a few bone beads. Then the rock said, "Hereafter when I speak, announcing that I shall tell a story you must say, 'Nio,' and as I speak you must say 'Hĕ'',' that I may know that you are listening. You must never fall asleep but continue to listen until I say 'Dā̆neho nigagā̆is.' (So thus finished is the length of my story). Then you shall give me presents and I shall be satisfied."[2]

The next day the boy hunted and killed a great many birds. These he made into soup and roasts. He skinned the birds and saved the skins, keeping them in a bag.

That evening the boy sat on the rock again and looked westward at the sinking sun. He wondered if his friend would speak again. While waiting he chipped some new arrow-points, and made them very small so that he could use them in a blow gun. Suddenly, as he worked, he heard the voice again. "Give me some tobacco to smoke," it said. Gaqka threw a pinch of tobacco over the cliff and the voice said, "Hau'nio''," and commenced a story. Long into the night one wonderful tale after another flowed from the rock, until it called out, "So thus finished is the length of my story." Gaqka was sorry to have the stories ended but he gave the rock an awl made from a bird's leg and a pinch of tobacco.

The next day the boy hunted far to the east and there found a village. Nobody knew who he was but he soon found many friends. There were some hunters who offered to teach him how to kill big game, and these went with him to his own camp on the high rock. At night he allowed them to listen to the stories that came forth from the rock, but it would speak only when Gaqka was present. He therefore had many friends with whom to hunt.

Now after a time Gaqka made a new suit of clothing from deer skin and desired to obtain a decorated pouch. He, therefore, went to the village and found one house where there were two daughters living with an old mother. He asked that a pouch be

[2]In many oral literatures, stories are marked off from other forms of discourse by opening and closing formulas. Audiences are often required to indicate their attentiveness and imaginative participation by responding with formulaic words. The value and importance of storytelling is further signalled by giving gifts to the storyteller and to the earth.

made and the youngest daughter spoke up and said, "It is now finished. I have been waiting for you to come for it." So she gave him a handsome pouch.

Then the old mother spoke, saying, "I now perceive that my future son-in-law has passed through the door and is here." Soon thereafter, the younger woman brought Gaqka a basket of bread and said, "My mother greatly desires that you should marry me." Gaqka looked at the girl and was satisfied, and ate the bread. The older daughter was greatly displeased and frowned in an evil manner.

That night the bride said to her husband, "We must now go away. My older sister will kill you for she is jealous." So Gaqka arose and took his bride to his own lodge. Soon the rock spoke and began to relate wonder stories of things that happened in the old days. The bride was not surprised, but said, "This standing rock, indeed, is my grandfather. I will now present you with a pouch into which you must put a trophy for every tale related."

All winter long the young couple stayed in the lodge on the great rock and heard all the wonder tales of the old days. Gaqka's bag was full of stories and he knew all the lore of former times.

As springtime came the bride said, "We must now go north to your own people and you shall become a great man." But Gaqka was sad and said, "Alas, in my own country I am an outcast and called by an unpleasant name."

The bride only laughed, saying, "Nevertheless we shall go north."

Taking their pelts and birdskins, the young couple descended the cliff and seated themselves in the canoe. "This is my canoe," said the bride. "I sent it through the air to you."

The bride seated herself in the bow of the canoe and Gaqka in the stern. Grasping a paddle he swept it through the water, but soon the canoe arose and went through the air. Meanwhile the bride was singing all kinds of songs, which Gaqka learned as he paddled.

When they reached the north, the bride said, "Now I shall remove your clothing and take all the scars from your face and body." She then caused him to pass through a hollow log, and when Gaqka emerged from the other end he was dressed in the finest clothing and was a handsome man.

Together the two walked to the village where the people came out to see them. After a while Gaqka said, "I am the boy whom you once were accustomed to call 'Cia''dō dă'.' I have now returned." That night the people of the village gathered around and listened to the tales he told, and he instructed them to give him small presents and tobacco. He would plunge his hand in his pouch and take out a trophy, saying, "Ho ho! So here is another one!" and then looking at his trophy would relate an ancient tale.

Everybody now thought Gaqka a great man and listened to his stories. He was the first man to find out all about the adventures of the old-time people. That is why there are so many legends now.

1923

Iroquois or Confederacy of the Five Nations (Iroquois)[1]

By the tradition of the Five Nations it appears that in their early history, they were frequently engaged in petty wars one with another, as well also with tribes living north of the lakes. The Five Nations, on account of their small numbers, suffered more by these wars than their neighbors, until there sprang up among the Onondagas a man more formidable in war than a whole tribe or nation. He consequently became the terror of all the surrounding nations, especially of the Cayugas and Senecas. This man, so formidable and whose cabin was as impregnable as a tower, is said to have had a head of hair, the ends of each terminating in a living snake; the ends of his fingers, and toes, his ears, nose & lips, eye brows & eye lashes all terminated in living snakes. He required in war, no bow and arrow, no battle axe or war club, for he had but to look upon his enemies, & they fell dead—so great was the power of the snakes that enshrouded him. He was a warrior by birth, and by his great power he had become the military despot of all the surrounding nations. And when he marched against his enemies they fled before his fatal sight.

Among the Onondagas there lived a man renowned for his wisdom, and his great love of peace. For a long time he had watched with great anxiety the increasing power of this military despot who on account of his snakey habilaments, was known by the applicable name Tadodahoh, or Atotahoh, signifying tangled because the snakes seemed to have tangled themselves into his hair; he saw bands of noble warriors fall before his fatal look. He revolved in his mind by what means he could take from the Tadodahoh his power, and also to divest him of his snakey appendages. He well knew that he could not wrest his power from him, unless he could put into his hands some means by which he could still exercise power and influence. He therefore concluded to call a general council, of the Five Nations, and to invite to this council the Tadodahoh, at which council he proposed to lay before the wise men a plan of Union that would secure not only amity and peace among themselves, and a perpetual existence as a confederacy but they would render themselves formidable & superior in power to any nation on the Continent. He accordingly called a council to be held upon the east bank of the Onondaga Lake, and to this council the Tadodahoh was invited, who it is said lived near the shores of Lake Ontario a short distance from Irondequoit Bay. He accepted the invitation and proceeded to the place. He occupied the council grounds alone, for no one would approach near to him, although great numbers had come to attend. The projector of the alliance alone proceeded to the grounds and into the presence of the Tadodahoh. He proceeded to divulge his plan when he was informed that his daughter had died whom he had left

[1]The Iroquois were a confederacy of five nations—the Cayuga, Mohawk, Oneida, Onondaga, and Seneca Indians. These five Indian groups, later joined by the Tuscarora, joined together about 1450 under the legendary leadership of Dekanawida (probably a Huron) and Hiawatha (a Mohawk). Because they lived in what is now the Northeast, largely in present-day New York state, the Iroquois confederacy successfully slowed the westward expansion of the Europeans until nearly the middle of the eighteenth century.

at home sick. He drew his robe about him, covering himself completely, and mourned for her. (His style of mourning was afterwards adopted by the Confederacy as the custom to mourn for sachems just before another was to be installed in his place.) He mourned night and day, and in his mourning which he did in a kind of song, he repeated the whole plan of Union. And when he had finished, no one of the wise men seemed to understand or comprehend his meaning and objects. Daganowedah, the projector of the plan of alliance, being provoked at their dullness of comprehension, which resulted more from their ignorance of civil matters than dullness of comprehension, arose in the night and travelled towards the east. He had not travelled far when he struck a small lake, and anyone could go around it sooner than to cross it in a canoe. Yet he chose to make a canoe of bark and go across it. It seems that he did not wish to deviate from a straight line. While he was crossing the lake, his canoe ran upon what he supposed to be a sand bar; he put his paddle down into the water to ascertain the cause of the stopping of the boat; in taking out his paddle he found a quantity of small shells, he took pains to put a sufficient quantity into his canoe, and after going ashore, he made a pouch of a young deer skin, and put these shells into it, after having first made a number of belts, and put the rest into strings of equal lengths. To this he gave the name of wampum, and the belts and strings he had made of the shells, he converted into the records of his wise sayings & the entire plan of his projcct of alliance.

He then proceeded on his journey, and he had not travelled far when he came to an Indian castle.[2] Without calling a council he began to rehearse his plan of alliance, by means of his belts and strings of wampum. But the people of this castle were unable to comprehend the benefits of his project, and talked of him as crazy. When he heard what they were saying concerning him, he proceeded on his journey, sorrowing that he could not find a people who would listen to the words of wisdom. He at length came to another settlement, which was one of the Mohawk castles. Here again he rehearsed his plan of Union. Still his sayings were incomprehensible to that people. They however listened carefully for the purpose of ascertaining what it was that he could talk so long upon. All that they could understand of it, was the manner in which councils were to be called. A council was accordingly called and he invited to attend. They invited him for the purpose of giving him an opportunity to say in council and before a large number what he had been so long saying in the open fields. But after he had taken his seat in council and nothing was said or done, no exchange of wampum belts (for he had lent them a belt with which to call a council), he arose and again went into the fields and there repeated his speeches. He concluded by saying that they too were ignorant, and knew nothing about transacting civil matters. This was reported to the Grand Chief of the Mohawks and again he called another council and invited Daganowedah. When the council was opened and the wise man had taken his seat, the Mohawk Chief presented to him a belt of wampum, with a request that whatever he should have to say, should be said in open council. If he was a messenger from another tribe, they would hear in open council what were their wishes. He merely replied that he was the messenger of no one; that he had conceived a

[2]A settlement.

noble plan of alliance, but had not found a nation wise enough to comprehend its benefits, and thus he had travelled and should continue so to travel until he found support. He then rehearsed in open council his plan of Union, which though they could not comprehend it, was pronounced by all to be a noble project. Daganowedah the Onondaga wise man was immediately adopted into the Mohawk Nation, nor could the Onondagas afterwards claim him, since they first rejected his project of Alliance. He was also made a chief of the Mohawk Nation, and was to exercise equal power with the original Mohawk chief. They were to live in the same lodge, and to be, in every respect, equals.

But he had lived with the original chief but a short time, when he was ordered about as though he had been a mere servant. To this a free spirit will ever revolt, he therefore left him, and again went into the fields. He was asked why he left the house of his friend. He replied that he had not been treated as a friend or visitor, but as a slave. The original chief begged his pardon, and solicited him to return. He did, and was thenceforth treated with great regard. Daganowedah at length suggested the propriety of sending runners to the west, from whence he had come, to ascertain what may be doing from whence he had come. He wanted runners to go and seek the smoke of the council fire. The chief of the Mohawks at once called upon some runners to go towards the west in search of the smoke of a council fire. The guardian bird of the runners was the heron; they accordingly took upon themselves the form of herons. They went towards the west, but flying too high they did not see the smoke of the council fire of Onondaga. They proceeded as far west as Sandusky in Ohio, where they were unable to transform or change themselves again into men. Another set of runners were then sent out, who took upon them the form or shape of crows. They found the smoke of the council fire at Onondaga and so reported.

Daganowedah then proposed to send a few runners to the council to inform them that they had found a wise man of the Onondaga nation, who had conceived a plan of Union, and to request that he might be heard before the Great Tadodahoh. This was done; and as soon as the council at Onondaga heard where their wise man had gone, they sent a deputation to recall him. Daganowedah had in the mean time made arrangement with the Mohawk Chief to act as his spokesman when they should be in council. He was also to take the lead in the file, and to perform all the duties necessary to the completion of the Alliance, but he was to act as Daganowedah should direct. His reason for choosing a spokesman, was that he had not been heard when the council first opened, and that probably they might listen to a wise man of the Mohawks. To this arrangement the Mohawk agreed. He agreed also to divest Tadodahoh of his snakes, and to make him as other men, except that he should clothe him in civil power as the Head of the Confederacy that should be formed. They then proceeded with a delegation of the Mohawks to the council grounds at Onondaga. When they had arrived they addressed Todadahoh the great military despot. The Mohawk divested him of his snakes, and for this reason he was styled Hayowenthah, or one who takes away or divests.

The plan of alliance was at first simple. It provided for the establishment of a confederacy, enjoying a democratic form of government. The civil and legislative power was to be vested in a certain number of wise men who should be styled civil sachems, and the military and executive power in another set of men who should be styled military sachems. The Union was to be established as a family organization, the Mohawks, Onondagas and Senecas to compose the Fathers and the Cayugas and Oneidas the children. This plan was adopted.[3]

Raven and Marriage (Tlingit)[1]

Next Raven married the daughter of a chief named Fog-over-the-salmon. It was winter, and they were without food, so Raven wanted salmon very much. His wife made a large basket and next morning washed her hands in it. When she got through there was a salmon there. Both were very glad, and cooked and ate it. Every day afterward she did the same thing until their house was full of drying salmon. After that, however, Raven and his wife quarreled, and he hit her on the shoulder with a piece of dried salmon. Then she ran away from him, but, when he ran after her and seized her, his hands passed right through her body. Then she went into the water and disappeared forever, while all of the salmon she had dried followed her. He could not catch her because she was the fog. After that he kept going to his father-in-law to beg him to have his wife come back, but his father-in-law said, "You promised me that you would have respect for her and take care of her. You did not do it, therefore you can not have her back."

Then Raven had to leave this place, and went on to another town where he found a widower. He said to this man, "I am in the same fix as you. My wife also has died." Raven wanted to marry the daughter of the chief in that town, so he said, "Of course I have to marry a woman of as high caste as my first wife. That is the kind I am looking for." But *TsAgwâ'n,* a bird, who was also looking for a high-caste wife, followed Raven about all the time. He said to the people, "That man is telling stories

[3]This text was transcribed about 1850 by Ely S. Parker, a full Seneca born on the Tonawanda Seneca Reservation in New York state. Educated at a mission school and then sent to Canada, Parker eventually returned to New York, learned English, and studied law, only to be denied legal practice because he was Indian. He worked on the Genesee Valley canal as an engineer until he was appointed superintendent of construction of the custom house and marine hospital at Galena, Illinois. Parker entered into Civil War conflict in 1863, serving as secretary to General Grant, whom he had known at Galena. Having remained in the army after the war until 1869, Parker served until 1871 as President Grant's commissioner of Indian affairs. When Parker died in 1895, he was a member of the New York City police department. Parker wrote about this narrative, "I cannot tell how much reliance can be placed upon this tradition, which is more of an allegory than real. The main facts of its origin may be embodied in the allegory, while it has been painted up by the imagination of the Indians."

[1]The Tlingit Indians are a northwest coastal group that occupied the southeastern coast of Alaska from Yakutat Bay to Cape Fox. Their abundant food supply from hunting, fishing, and gathering afforded the Tlingits ample time in winter to develop complex social systems and religious ceremonies. They lived in cedar plank dwellings, and they traded freely with the Russians, Americans, and English.

around here. His first wife left him because he was cruel to her." For this reason they refused to give the girl to him. Then he said to the chief, "If I had married your daughter you would have had a great name in the world. You will presently see your daughter take up with some person who is a nobody, and, when they speak of you in the world, it will always be as Chief-with-no-name. You may listen to this *TsAgwâ'n* if you want to, but you will be sorry for it. He is a man from whom no good comes. Hereafter this *TsAgwâ'n* will live far out at sea. And I will tell you this much, that neither *TsAgwâ'n* nor myself will get this woman." This is why *TsAgwâ'n* is now always alone. Raven also said to the chief, "You will soon hear something of this daughter of yours." All the high-caste men wanted to marry this woman, but she would not have them.

Going on again, Raven came to an old man living alone, named *DAmnā'djî,* and said to him, "Do you know the young daughter of the chief close by here?" "Yes, I know her." "Why don't you try to marry her?" "I can't get her. I know I can't, so I don't want to try." Then Raven said, "I will make a medicine to enable you to get her." "But I have no slave," said the old man; "to get her a man must have slaves." "Oh!" said Raven, "you do not have to have a slave to get her. She will take a liking to you and nobody can help it. She will marry you. Her father will lose half of his property." Then he made the old man look young, got feathers to put into his hair and a marten-skin robe to put over him so that he appeared very handsome. But Raven said to him, "You are not going to look like this all of the time. It is only for a day or so."

After this the rejuvenated man got into his skin canoe, for this was well to the north, and paddled over to where the girl lived. He did not ask her father's consent but went directly to her, and she immediately fell in love with him. Although so many had been after her she now said, "I will marry you. I will go with you even if my father kills me for it."

When the chief's slaves found them in the bedroom at the rear of the house, they said to the chief, "Your daughter is married." So her mother looked in there and found it was true. Then her father said, "Come out from that room, my daughter." He had already told his slaves to lay down valuable furs on the floor for his daughter and her husband to sit on. He thought if she were already married it was of no use for him to be angry with her. So the girl came out with her husband, and, when her father saw him he was very glad, for he liked his looks, and he was dressed like a high-caste person.

Then the chief related to his son-in-law how a fellow came along wanting to marry his daughter, and how *TsAgwâ'n* had come afterward and told him that he had been cruel to his first wife. Said the chief, "This man had a wife. His first wife is living yet. I don't want to hurt his wife's feelings."

After that his son-in-law said, "My father told me to start right out after him today in my canoe." He was in a hurry to depart because he was afraid that all of his good clothing would leave him. He said to his wife, "Take only your blanket to use on the passage, because I have plenty of furs of every description at home." So she took nothing but her marten-skin robe and a fox robe.

As she lay in the canoe, however, with her head resting on his lap she kept feeling drops of water fall upon her face, and she said many times, "What is that dripping on my face?" Then he would say, "It must be the water splashing from my paddle," but it was really the drippings that fall from an old man's eyes when he is very filthy. Her husband had already become an old man again and had lost his fine clothing, but she could not see it because her face was turned the other way. When the woman thought that they were nearly at their destination she raised herself to look out, glanced at her husband's face, and saw that he was an altogether different man. She cried very hard.

After they had arrived at his town the old man went from house to house asking the people to take pity on him and let him bring his wife to one of them, because he knew that his own house was not fit for her. These, however, were some of the people that had wanted to marry this woman, so they said, "Why don't you take her to your own fine house? You wanted her." Meanwhile she sat on the beach by the canoe, weeping. Finally the shabby sister of this old man, who was still older than he, came down to her and said, "See here, you are a high-caste girl. Everybody says this man is your husband, and you know he is your husband, so you better come up to the house with me." Then she saw the place where he lived, and observed that his bed was worse than that of one of her father's slaves. The other people also paid no attention to her, although they knew who she was, because she had married this man. They would eat after everybody else was through, and, while he was eating, the people of the town would make fun of him by shouting out, "*DAmnā'djî's* father-in-law and his brothers-in-law are coming to his grand house to see him." Then he would run out to see whether it were so and find that they were making fun of him. Every morning, while he was breakfasting with his wife, the people fooled him in this way.

Although he had not said so, the father-in-law and the brothers-in-law of *DAmnā'djî* thought that he was a very high-caste person because he was dressed so finely. So they got together all their expensive furs to visit him, and they had one canoe load of slaves, which they intended to give him, all dressed with green feathers from the heads of mallard drakes. One morning the people again shouted, "*DAmnā'djî's* father-in-law and his brothers-in-law are coming to see him." Running out to look this time, he saw canoe after canoe coming, loaded down deep. Then he did not know what to do. He began to sweep out the house and begged some boys to help him clean up, but they said, "You clean up yourself. Those are your people coming." The people of the place also began hiding all of their basket-work pots, and buckets.

As they came in, the people in the canoes sang together and all of them were iridescent with color. They were very proud people. Then the old man begged the boys to carry up the strangers' goods, but they replied as before, "You carry them up yourself. You can do it." So the strangers had to bring up their own things into the house and sit about without anyone telling them where. The old man's sister was crying all the time. Then the strangers understood at once what was the matter and felt very sorry for these old people.

After that the old man kept saying to the boys who came in to look at his visitors, "One of you go after water," but they answered, "Go after water yourself. You can do it." He tried to borrow a basket for his guests to eat off of, but they all said, "Use your own basket. What did you go and get that high-caste girl for? You knew that you couldn't afford it. Why didn't you get a poor person like yourself instead of a chief's daughter? Now you may know that it isn't fun to get a high-caste person when one is poor." His brothers-in-law and his father-in-law felt ashamed at what they heard, and they also felt badly for him. Then the old woman gave her brother a basket that was unfit for the chief's slaves to eat out of, and he ran out to get water for his guests.

When he got there, however, and was stooping down to fill his basket, the creek moved back from him and he followed it. It kept doing this and he kept running after it until he came to the mountain, where it finally vanished into a house. Running into this, he saw a very old woman sitting there who said to him, "What are you after? Is there anything I can do for you?" He said, "There is much that you can do for me, if you can really do it. My friends are very mean to me. My father-in-law and the other relations of my wife have all come to my place to visit me. I married a very high-caste woman, and the people of my place seem to be very mean about it. I am very poor and have nothing with which to entertain them." He told all of his troubles to her from the beginning, and, when he was through, she said, "Is that all?" "Yes, that is all." Then the woman brushed back his hair several times with her hand, and lo! he had a head of beautiful hair, while his ragged clothes changed into valuable ones. He was handsomer and better clothed than at the time when he first obtained his wife. The old basket he had also turned into a very large beautiful basket. Then she said to him, "There is a spring back in the corner. Go there and uncover it and dip that basket as far down as you can reach." He did so and, when he drew it out, it was full of dentalia.

Now *DAmnā'djî* returned home very quickly, but nobody recognized him at first except his wife and those who had seen him when he went to get her. Afterward he gave water to his guests, and they could see dentalia shells at the bottom. The house was now filled with spectators, and those who had made fun of him were very much ashamed of themselves. After he had given them water, he gave them handfuls of dentalia, for which his father-in-law and his brothers-in-law gave him slaves, valuable furs, and other property. So he became very rich and was chief of that town. That is why the Indians do the same now. If a brother-in-law gives them the least thing they return much more than its value.

Now he had a big house built, and everything that he said had to be done. The people that formerly made fun of him were like slaves to him. He also gave great feasts, inviting people from many villages. But, after he had become very great among them, he was too hard upon the people of his town. His wife was prouder than when she was with her father and if boys or anyone else displeased her they were put to death.

As they were now very proud and had plenty of people to work for them, the husband and wife spent much time sitting on the roof of their house looking about. One spring the woman saw a flock of swans coming from the southeast, and said, "Oh! there is a high-caste person among those birds that I was going to marry." Another time they went up, and a flock of geese came along. Then she again said to her husband, "Oh! there is the high-caste person I was going to marry." By and by some sand-hill cranes flew past, and she repeated the same words. But, when the brants came over, and she spoke these words, they at once flew down to her and carried her off with them. Her husband ran after the brants underneath as fast as he could, and every now and then some of her clothing fell down, but he was unable to overtake her.

When the birds finally let this woman drop, she was naked and all of her hair even was gone. Then she got up and walked along the beach crying, and she made a kind of apron for herself out of leaves. Continuing on along the beach, she came upon a red snapper head, which she picked up. She wandered on aimlessly, not knowing what to do, because she was very sad at the thought of her fine home and her husband. Presently she saw smoke ahead of her and arrived at a house where was an old woman. She opened the door, and the old woman said, "Come in." Then she said to the old woman, "Let us cook this red snapper head." "Yes, let us cook it," said the latter. After they had eaten it, the old woman said to her, "Go along the beach and try to find something else." So she went out and found a sculpin. Then she came back to the house and cooked that, but, while they were eating, she heard many boys shouting, and she thought they were laughing at her because she was naked. She looked around but saw no one. Then the old woman said to her, "Take the food out to that hole." She went outside with the tray and saw an underground sweathouse out of which many hands protruded. This was the place from which the shouting came. She handed the tray down and it was soon handed up again with two fine fox skins in it. Then the old woman said to her, "Make your clothing out of these furs," and so she did.

After she had put the skins on, this old woman said, "Your father and mother live a short distance away along this beach. You better go to them. They are living at a salmon creek." So the girl went on and soon saw her father and mother in a canoe far out where her father was catching salmon. But, when she ran down toward the canoe to meet them, her father said to his wife, "Here comes a fox." As he was looking for something with which to kill it, she ran back into the woods.

Then she felt very badly, and returned to the old woman crying. "Did you see your father?" said the latter. "Yes." "What did he say to you?" "He took me for a fox. He was going to kill me." Then the old woman said, "Yes, what else do you think you are? You have already turned into a fox. Now go back to your father and let him kill you."

The woman went to the same place again and saw her father still closer to the shore; and she heard him say, "Here comes that big fox again." Then she ran right up to him, saying to herself, "Let him kill me," and he did so. Years ago all the high-caste people wore bracelets and necklaces, and each family had its own way of fixing them. Now, as this woman was skinning the fox, she felt something around its foreleg. She looked at it and found something like her daughter's bracelet. Afterward she also cut around the neck and found her daughter's necklace. Then she told her husband to come and look saying, "Here on this fox are our daughter's necklace and bracelet." So they cried over the fox and said, "Something must have made her turn into a fox." They knew how this fox ran toward them instead of going away.

Now they took the body of the fox, placed it upon a very nice mat, and laid another over it. They put eagle's down, which was always kept in bags ready for use, on the body, crying above it all the time. They also began fasting, and all of her brothers and relations in that village fasted with them. All cleaned up their houses and talked to their Creator. One midnight, after they had fasted for many days, they felt the house shaking, and they heard a noise in the place where the body lay. Then the father and mother felt very happy. The mother went there with a light and saw that her daughter was in her own proper shape, acting like a shaman. Then the woman named the spirits in her. The first she mentioned was the swan spirit, the next the goose spirit, the next the sand-hill-crane spirit, the next the brant spirit. Another spirit was the red-snapper-head spirit which called itself Spirit-with-a-*labret*-in-its-chin, and another the fox spirit. Now the father and mother of this woman were very happy, but her husband lost all of his wealth and became poor again.[2]

1909

Raven Makes a Girl Sick and Then Cures Her (Tsimshian)[1]

Raven went on, not knowing which way to turn.[2] He was very hungry, staying in a lonely place. After a while he came to the end of a large town. He saw many people walking about, and he was afraid to let himself be seen. Raven sat down there; and on the following day, while he was still sitting there, he saw a large canoe being launched on the beach. Aboard were many young women who went to pick blueberries. Then Raven thought how he could enter the great town. Finally it occurred to him to catch a deer. He went into the woods and caught a deer, skinned it, put on the skin, and then swam in front of the large canoe which was full of young women who were going to pick blueberries.[3] Among them was a young princess, the daughter of the master of that large town. Raven saw that she was among the young women. She was sitting near the middle of the large canoe, between two women. Now, they saw the stag swimming along in front of the canoe. Then the princess said to her com panions, "Let us pursue him!" They did so. They paddled along, and soon they caught and killed the stag, and took him into the canoe. Raven thought, "Let them put me down in front of the princess!" and then they took him into the canoe and placed him in front of the princess, as Raven had wished them to do. Then they paddled along toward the place where the blueberries were. Before they reached the blueberry-patch, the deer moved his hind leg and kicked the princess in the stomach. Then he leaped out of the canoe and ran into the woods. The princess fainted when she received the wound, and therefore the young women turned back and went home. The princess became worse as they went along.

[2]The complex social systems of the Tlingits usually kept young men from marrying women of higher social standing.

[1]The Tsimshian Indians live on the northwest coast, along the Nass and Skeena Rivers and the islands that now form western British Columbia. Their abundant food supply from gathering, fishing, and hunting enabled them to live in stationary cedar plank dwellings and develop arts and crafts related to their complex ceremonial life. They traded with the Russians, Americans, and English.

[2]The Trickster is often figured as a wanderer who lacks foresight and self-consciousness but who is an opportunist in satisfying his appetites.

[3]Women and food are the perpetual objects of Trickster's attention. The references throughout this tale to "princess," "master," and "slaves" reflect the nature of Tsimshian society, which was stratified according to kinship and status. The Tsimshians fostered competition for status and accumulation of wealth.

Finally they reached the beach in front of the house of the head chief. They told the people what had happened to them on their journey. Then they took the princess up to her father's house. A great number of people were following them. The chief was very sorrowful because his only daughter was hurt. He called together all the wise men, and asked them what he should do to cure his daughter. The wise men told him to gather all the shamans, and let them try to cure her wound. There was a wound under her ribs made by the hind leg of the deer. Then the chief ordered his attendants to call all the shamans. The attendants went and called all the shamans. They gathered in the chief's great house. Then the shamans worked over her with their supernatural powers, but they all failed. The wound could not be cured by the supernatural powers of the shamans. The girl became worse and worse, until she was very ill. Still the shamans worked on, day and night. Three days had passed, and the many shamans had been working in vain. On the fourth day, behold! before the evening set in a canoe filled with young men came to town. They came ashore, and some people went down to meet them. Then the people who were going down saw a shaman sitting in the middle of the canoe. They went up quickly and told the chief that a shaman had come to town. Therefore the chief sent to him, asking him to cure his only daughter. (This shaman was Raven and the crew of his canoe were his grandchildren the Crows.)

In the evening, when he came in, he saw the princess lying there very ill, for he had hurt her a few days before; and all the shamans who had failed before were sitting along the wall on one side of the house. Raven pretended to be a shaman. He sat down near the head of the princess, who was lying down; and all the young men followed him, carrying a large box which contained his magic powers. He took charcoal and rubbed it on his face, and rubbed ashes over it. He put on the crown of bears' claws, placed a ring of red-cedar bark around his neck, and put on his shaman's dancing-apron, and took up his large shaman's rattle. He started with beating of the drum; and after the drumming and beating, he began his song; and when they were singing, they pronounced these words:

> "Let the mighty hail fall on the roof of this chief's house,
> On the roof of this chief's house,
> On the roof of this chief's house!"

and as the singers pronounced these words, hail beat on the roof of the chief's house terribly. (Before Raven arrived in the town, he had ordered some of his grandchildren the Crows to take each a small white stone in his mouth, and said, "When we pronounce the words of our song, then drop the stones on the roof of the chief's house." Thus had Raven spoken to his grandchildren the Crows, and they had done so.) When the mighty hail ceased, Raven said, "Bring me a mat of cedar bark." They brought him the mat, and he spread it over the princess to cover her. He himself also went under it with the girl,[4] touched the wound, said, "Be cured, wound under the right ribs!" and so it happened.

Then the chief was very glad because his daughter had been cured of her illness. He gave Raven all kinds of food. Now, the chief spoke to the shaman after he had fed

[4]Trickster's sexual relations with the girl, which are euphemistically glossed over here, are made explicit in other texts. He does, nevertheless, cure her.

him, and said, "Ask me whatever you wish, and I will give it to you." Then he made a promise unto him: "Whatever you may ask me, I will give it to you, my dear, good, and true supernatural man,—you, who are possessed of supernatural powers,—for you have succeeded in restoring my only daughter." Then Raven looked around and smiled. He said, "What I want is that you should move, and leave for me all the provisions you have; for my young men have nothing, because we have no time to obtain our own provisions, for we are going around all the time healing those who need us." Then the chief ordered his slaves to go out, and ordered the people to move on the next day. Then the slaves ran out, crying, "Leave, great tribe, and leave your provisions behind!"[5] The people did so. They left in the morning, and left all their food, according to the order of their master. Raven was very glad, because now he had much food.

On the following day he took a walk; and while he was absent, his grandchildren assembled, opened many boxes of crabapples mixed with grease, and ate them all. When Raven came home from his walk, behold! he saw all the empty boxes, and he knew that his grandchildren had done this.[6]

1916

The Bungling Host (Hitchiti)[1]

Bear and Rabbit were traveling about together. They had become friends. Bear said to Rabbit, "Come and visit me. That red house way off yonder is my home." He went off. At the appointed time Rabbit set out and came to where Bear lived. Bear's home was a hollow tree. At the bottom of the tree was a hole. There was where he lived. When Rabbit came Bear said, "Sit down." So Rabbit sat down and both talked for a while.

Bear went around back of his house while Rabbit sat watching him. He went out of sight. When he came back to where Rabbit was sitting he had a lot of good lard. He put the lard into some beans which were cooking and when the beans were done he set them out for Rabbit, who ate all he could.

[5]Given what the audience knows of Trickster, the chief's assessment of his character and his willingness to move the village reflect a lack of wisdom, which will be charged against him.

[6]Trickster figures seldom realize an enduring benefit from their tricks.

[1]The Hitchiti, mentioned in DeSoto's chronicles, were probably at one time the most important tribe in southern Georgia. In historic times, they affiliated with the invading Creeks as part of the Lower Creek towns. A colonist passing through the region in 1799 described them as "honest and industrious," and remarked that their towns were well-planned and that they had cattle, horses, and hogs. They were removed to Indian Territory west of the Mississippi during the removals of Andrew Jackson's presidency and settled in the center of the Creek Nation and near Okmulgee. This text is taken from G. E. Lankford, *Native American Legends,* 1987.

Now when Rabbit was preparing to go home he said, "Come and visit me, too. I live way over yonder where you see that white house. That is my home." Bear said, "All right." By a white house Rabbit meant white grass.

On the appointed day Bear started to visit Rabbit and reached his place. His house was made of dry grass. When Bear got there Rabbit said, "Sit down." So Bear sat down and they talked. Then Rabbit stood up and went round back of his house. Bear saw him and thought, "He may hurt himself." While Bear was sitting there he heard Rabbit cry out, *"Dowik."* He started out and when he reached Rabbit found he had cut his belly and sat with a little blue hanging out of it. "Oh, I alone can do that. You have hurt yourself," he said. He took Rabbit and laid him down in his house.

Then Bear went out to look for a doctor. Finding Buzzard, he said to him, "My friend, Rabbit has hurt himself badly. I am looking for a man able to treat him." "I make medicine," said Buzzard. So Bear led him back to the place where Rabbit was lying. When Buzzard saw him he said, "Make some hominy and place it near by and I will treat him." The hominy was prepared. "Now shut up the house and make a hole in the roof and I can treat him," he said. So the house was shut up and a hole was made in the roof. Then Buzzard sat in the room where Rabbit lay eating hominy. Presently Rabbit said, *"Dowik."* "What are you doing to him?" they called out. "He is afraid of the medicine," said Buzzard. As he sat there with Rabbit he struck at him, killed him, and ate him. He ate him all up and flew out through the roof. Then he said to the people, "He is lying there waiting for you," and he went away. Bear entered the house and found only Rabbit's bones lying there.

When Bear saw this he was very angry. Just then an orphan with a bow who was traveling around came to the place and Bear said to him, "We asked Buzzard to doctor Rabbit but he devoured him and has flown away. Shoot at him and see if you can hit him." The orphan shot at him and brought him down. Bear beat him and killed him, and hung him up. He lighted a fire under him and smoked him, and Buzzard hung there many days. He came to look yellowish, it is said. Therefore, because the little boy shot him and they hung him in the smoke, he is yellow.

This is how they tell it.

1987

Native American Oral Poetry

In the world's numerous oral literatures, poetry is song, whether the psalms of David, the lyrics of Orpheus, or the meditations of Tecayahuatzin. The movement from recitation to chant and song is often correlated with other factors, such as increasing seriousness, emotional intensity, or complexity of linguistic form. In short, like other poetry song consists of affectively charged, sophisticated language. Ritual poetry, created for communal expression, is widespread in Native America; lyric poetry, which articulates an individual response, is far less common.

Ritual poetry both commemorates and creates. In a wide variety of settings, it transports participants back to the time of origin recalling the prototypical events and persons who gave structure and meaning, life and health, to this world, or it calls them forward to belief in a new world to come. In either case, the symbolic language and narrative form of most ritual poetry aims to re-create the sacred in the present moment. The complex Navajo healing ceremonials transform the patient's home into the world just after the emergence, and heal by identifying the patient with the culture heroes Monster-Slayer and Born-for-Water, who rid the world of monsters. Similarly, whole communities regularly seek to be restored to their original fecundity in cyclic ceremonials, which anthropologists call world-renewal rituals. In some cultures, ritual poetry may be quite brief and imagistic, achieving its impact through repetition which induces in the participants a powerful sense of imaginative transport. In other cultures, it may be quite long and predominantly narrative, drawing heavily upon its mythic subtext. In either case, it is usually marked by conventionalized symbolic expressions called formulae, which may be as short as a phrase or as long as several lines (block formula).

"Sayatasha's Night Chant" is a fine instance of Native American ritual poetry. It is sung as part of the extensive Zuni world-renewal ceremonial commonly called Shalako, after the ten-foot tall masked impersonations of those spirits. The formal name of the ceremony, however, means "The Coming of the Gods," and refers to the fact that the kachinas, who are patron spirits of both the earth's forces and the Zuni ancestral dead, promised at the beginning of time to return every December to the village in the high desert of New Mexico with seeds and moisture to renew life for the coming year. The gods return incarnated in the persons of masked, costumed men, who have spent most of the previous year in arduous preparation for these sacred responsibilities. Thus begins the half-year-long season in which the kachinas are present and visible among men until their going home in late summer. Throughout this season, everyone at Zuni is busy in fulfilling ritual obligations, which are accompanied by complex songs and prayers, rich in agricultural and environmental symbolism, for the aim of Zuni religion is nothing less than to promote the continuance of life.

The poem is chanted in unison by the Shalako priests, a section at a time with breaks in between, over the course of the eighth night of Shalako, the whole performance, with accompanying rituals, taking about six hours. The narrative structure of the poem has two distinct sections. The first is an extended flashback consisting of several elements: the events of the previous New Year when Pautiwa chose and consecrated the present Sayatasha narrator (ll. 1–103); a more limited flashback in which Sayatasha recounts his formal investiture and the immediate preparation for this Shalako which began forty-nine days before (ll. 104–379); and the recounting of his visits during this preparatory period to the sacred shrines where he contacted the rain-making ancestral spirits, while retracing the route of the Zuni aboriginal migration to their present home (ll. 380–520). The second section narrates contemporary occurrences taking place on the eighth night of Shalako, the house consecration and the gift of seed, game and human fertility (ll. 521–758), and the concluding litany of blessings (ll. 759–774).

Looking more closely at the chant, we can describe it as a singular manifestation of a more basic pattern recurrent throughout the world, including Native America: the quest for power. Having assumed the responsibility to be the Sayatasha impersonator, the narrator obliges himself to present the needs of the community to those who can answer them. Especially important here is his visit to Kothluwalawa, the Zuni "Heaven" and Kachina village, to which he comes as a man, but from which he leaves fully invested as Sayatasha the kachina (ll. 178–379). Endowed with the kachina's power to promote life and growth, symbolized by the pouch of all seeds which was given to him, he returns to Zuni to confer these blessings upon his people. His ability as masked impersonator to represent both humans and kachinas enables him to serve as a mediator between the two communities. Not all Native American ritual poetry is as long or as formulaic as "Sayatasha's Night Chant," but however different Native American tribes have been and are from each other, they continue to create the majority of their oral poetry in ritual contexts.

Other forms of ritual poetry, including shorter prayers and dream songs, often compressed speech and imagery in poetic language and form. The two Cherokee formulas included here use a prescribed seven-part form that is rigidly followed and a color symbolism laden with cultural significance as key elements in reconfiguring reality through magical speech. These brief, but socially sanctioned forms contrast with other more private forms. In the Pima deer-hunting song, the hunter enters into the spirit of the hunted, imagining and vocalizing the delirium of the deer in its death throes. In the prayer before going into battle, a Blackfeet man addresses the Sun and asks to be delivered from the fate he dreamed. Other shorter forms are genuine lyrics, individually composed to focus through concentrated language and song an intense emotional response to personal experience. The several songs of love and war included here, though brief, were sung repeatedly to deepen the singer's recovery of the original experience.

Lyric poetry, which articulates a uniquely individualized response, is less common than ritual poetry. This may not have been the reality in the community, however, so much as a bias in the record. Because the anthropologists who recorded texts were often more interested in collecting oral literature that reflected a density of cultural beliefs, especially mythic narratives and ritual material, individualized works were less often recorded. As a result, we have been denied access to those voices who individualized the common experience. Instead of the factions and differences within a community, we are left, as a result of this historical bias, with an artificial sense of a common "cultural" response that contributes to the creation of stereotypes. Yet the insouciance of the Makah woman To'ak's reply to the vain man who was courting her or the plea of Victoria to mothers in his community suggests that every community rings with many voices, not always in harmony, and reminds us again that our concept of other cultures is shaped for us by those who do the recording. Among the early anthropologists, the most diligent recorder of the names and social situations of Indian singers and storytellers was Frances Densmore, who devoted her life to recording the music and sung poetry of Native America.

Nevertheless, among a few Native peoples the creation of lyric poetry was culturally celebrated as an artistic act of the highest order. Among the Aztecs, indeed, it mimed the actions of the Lord of the Close and the Near, the Creator who created himself, for whom invention was the fundamental principle of being and the entire world his mask. The creation of poetry was a task for well-educated Aztec nobles. Individual composers like Tecayhuatzin, Ayocuan, or Nezahualcoyotl earned renown for their poetry, which celebrated the transience of life even as the Aztec empire was at its height, a theme which they articulated repeatedly by subtly manipulating a small but rich poetic vocabulary of flowers and jewels. Life, precious as jade or quetzal feather, could be shattered like the former, crushed like the latter. They thought of themselves as cut flowers, captured for a moment in time, decaying in the very instant their beauty is being contemplated. Life, so solid, so apparently real, was thus an illusion. Only by creating art, by imitating the Lord of the Close and the Near, could they aspire to immortality. So well-known were these songs, that more than seventy-five years after the death of Nezahualcoyotl they were still being sung, this time to Spanish-educated, Christianized Aztecs who recorded them and insured their composers' immortality.

Inuit (Eskimo) lyric poetry, with its often violent imagery, its pained, urgent voice, its short stanzas and simple refrains is very different in content, tone, and structure from the cool, contemplative, and complex Aztec lyrics. Inuit poetry was not, after all, the poetry of an educated and secure elite, but a poetry of the masses, of men and women who struggled to create life and beauty in a brutal environment wrapped for months in darkness. In the silence of the snowy night, abroad on the heaving ice, however, they waited for the words that would name their experience. "Songs are thoughts," Orpingalik said, "sung out with the breath when people are moved by great forces and ordinary speech no longer suffices. Man is moved just like the ice flow sailing here and there out in the current. His thoughts are driven by a flowing force when he feels joy, when he feels sorrow. Thoughts can wash over him like a flood, making his blood come in gasps, and his heart throb. Something like an abatement in the weather will keep him thawed up, and then it will happen that we, who always think we are small, will feel still smaller. And we will fear to use words. But it will happen that the words we need will come of themselves. When the words we want to use shoot up by themselves—we get a new song." Orpingalik's words communicate the origins of Inuit poetry, not unlike Wordsworth's "emotion recollected in tranquility," but many of the songs themselves suggest that a good deal of forethought and anxiety went into composing as well. All of this poetry was for public performance, after all, the equivalent of publication; there were evidently no closet poets among the Inuit. Well-wrought poetry was valued. As one Inuit poet commented, "The most festive thing of all is joy in beautiful, smooth words and our ability to express them."

Andrew O. Wiget
New Mexico State University

PRIMARY WORKS

Ruth Bunzel, "Zuni Ritual Poetry," *Forty-Seventh Annual Report of the Bureau of American Ethnology,* 1930; *Eskimo Poems from Canada and Greenland,* trans. Tom Lowenstein, 1973; John Bierhorst, *Four Masterworks of American Indian Literature,* 1974; John Bierhorst, *Cantares Mexicanos,* 1986.

SECONDARY WORKS

Miguela Leon-Portilla, *Pre-Columbian Literatures of Mexico,* 1969; Ruth Finnegan, *Oral Poetry,* 1977; Andrew Wiget, "Aztec Lyrics: Poetry in a World of Continually Perishing Flowers," *Latin American Indian Literatures* 4 (1980): 1–11; Andrew Wiget, "Sayatasha's Night Chant: A Literary, Textual Analysis of a Zuni Ritual Poem," *American Indian Culture and Research Journal* 4: 1 & 2 (1980): 99–140; Andrew Wiget, *Native American Literature,* 1985; Miguel Leon-Portilla, *Fifteen Poets of the Aztec World,* 1992.

Zuni Poetry

Sayatasha's Night Chant

And now indeed it has come to pass.
When the sun who is our father
Had yet a little ways to go to reach his left-hand altar,[1]

Our daylight father,
Pekwin of the Dogwood clan,
Desired the waters, the seeds
Of his fathers,
Priests of the masked gods.
Then our fathers,
Sharing one another's desire, sat down together
In the rain-filled room
Of those that first came into being.
Yonder following all the springs,
They sought those ordained to bring long life to man,
Those that stand upright,
But (like the waters of the world),
Springing from one root, are joined together fast.
At the feet of some fortunate one
Offering prayer meal,
Turquoise, corn pollen,
Breaking the straight young shoots,
With their warm human hands
They held them fast[2]
Taking the massed cloud robe of their grandfather, turkey man,
Eagle's mist garment,
The thin cloud wings and massed cloud tails
Of all the birds of summer,

[1]"*I.e.,* the south, therefore at the winter solstice," [Bunzel's note]. Most of the poem (ll. 1–520), which is sung on the eighth night of Shalako, is an elaborate flashback recounting the events that have led up to this moment. Thus, the Pekwin or Sun Priest began preparations for this year's Shalako a year ago by gathering the priests, "the fathers," in the kiva, a subterranean room for prayer and planning which is entered through the roof. The kiva is called a "rain-filled room" because its form symbolizes the wet, lower worlds from which the Zuni emerged onto this earth's surface. (See "Talk Concerning the First Beginning.") When they enter the kiva, the priests symbolically enter the lower world of their preemergence, whence all creative transformations originate.

[2]Willow shoots are gathered to be made into prayer sticks. As the block formula which follows (ll. 24–45) indicates, through the prayerful intention of the priests, these prayer sticks are endowed with spirit so that they can communicate man's intentions to the kachinas, the ancestral spirit powers of the world. (cf. ll. 114–20).

With these four times clothing their plume wands,
They made the plume wands into living beings.
With the flesh of their mother,
Cotton woman,
Even a thread badly made,
A soiled cotton thread,
Four times encircling their wand they made their belts;
With rain-bringing prayer feathers
They made them into living beings.
With the flesh of their two mothers,
Black paint woman,
Clay woman,
Clothing their plume wands with flesh,
They made them into living beings.
When they said, "Let it be now,"
The ones who are our fathers
Commissioned with prayers
The prayer wands that they had fashioned.

When the sun who is our father,
Had gone in to sit down at his ancient place,
Then over toward the south,
Whence the earth is clothed anew,
Our father, Kawulia Pautiwa,
Perpetuating what had been since the first beginning
Again assumed human form.[3]
Carrying his fathers' finished plume wands
He made his road come hither.
Wherever he thought, "Let it be here,"
Into his fathers' rain-filled room,
He made his road to enter.
And when our sun father,
Had yet a little ways to go
To go in to sit down at his ancient place,
Yonder from all sides
Rain-bringing birds,
Pekwin, priest
From where he stays quietly,
Made his road come forth.
Making his road come hither,
Into his fathers' rain-filled room,

[3]Pautiwa is pekwin of the Kachinas, who have a social organization in their underwater village, Kothluwala, which parallels that of Zuni. Here he is impersonated by a Zuni, though not wearing Pautiwa's distinctive mask. Of masking, Bunzel notes, "The impersonator dons a mask and becomes the god, and inversely the god assumes human form. As a matter of fact, in the evening the impersonator comes unmasked, the mask having been previously taken to the Kiva."

He made his road to enter.
With his wings,
His fathers' cloud house he fashioned,
Their bed of mist he spread out,
Their life-giving road of meal he sent forth
Their precious spring he prepared.[4]
When all was ready,
Our father, Käwulia Pautiwa
Reaching his house chiefs,
His pekwin
His bow priests,
He made his road to go in.
Following one road,
Sitting down quietly
A blessed night
The divine ones
With us, their children, came to day.

Next day, when our sun father
Had come out standing to his sacred place,
Saying, "Let it be now."
Over there to the south,
Whence the earth is clothed anew,
Our father, Käwulia Pautiwa,
Perpetuating what had been since the first beginning,
Again assumed human form.
Carrying his waters,
Carrying his seeds,
Carrying his fathers' precious plume wands,
He made his road come forth.
He made his road come hither.
The country of the Corn priests,
Four times he made his road encircle.
Yonder wherever all his kiva children's rain-filled roads come out
His precious plume wands
He laid down.
Then turning he went back to his own country.

My father picked up the prayer plume,
And with the precious prayer plume
Me he appointed.
The moon, who is our mother,

[4]As the Zuni pekwin prepares an altar of sand-painted images in the kiva (ll. 69–73), his kachina counterpart, Pautiwa, approaches the pueblo in order to appoint all those who will serve as impersonators of the kachinas for the next year, including the Sayatasha impersonator (ll. 100–107).

Yonder in the west waxed large;
And when standing fully grown against the eastern sky,
She made her days,
For my fathers,
Rain maker priests,
Priests of the masked gods.
I fashioned prayer plumes into living beings.
My own common prayer plume,
I fastened to the precious prayer plume of my fathers.
At the place since the first beginning called "cotton hanging,"
I brought my fathers prayer plumes.
Drawing my prayer plumes toward them,
They spoke to those inside the place of our first beginning.[5]
Yonder following all the springs,
On all the mossy mountains,
In all the wooded places,
At the encircling ocean,
With my prayer plumes,
With my sacred meal,
With my sacred words,
They talked to those within.
Winter,
Summer,
Through the cycle of the months,
Though my prayer plumes were but poor ones,
There toward the south,
Wherever my fathers' roads come out
I continued to give them prayer plumes.

And when the cycle of months was at an end[6]
My fathers made their rain roads come in
To their fathers,
Their mothers,
Those that first came into being.
Sharing one another's desire, they sat down together.
With the flesh of their mother,
Cotton woman,
Even a cord badly made,
A soiled cotton cord,
With this four times

[5]Throughout the year, the Sayatasha impersonator has visited all the sacred springs around Zuni, depositing at these shrines the prayer sticks by means of which the needs of the Zuni people are communicated to the ancestral rain-making spirits in the springs.

[6]*I.e.,* the many months of prayer and ritual obligations which consumed most of the year having been completed, the 49-day preparatory period, starting in mid-October, begins, during which a single knot is untied each day from a knotted day-count cord (l. 147) until the beginning of Shalako in early December.

They made the day counts into living beings.
Saying, "Let it be now,"
They sent for me.
I came to my fathers,
Where they were waiting for me.
With their day count
They took hold of me fast.
Carrying their day count
I came back to my house.
Saying, "Let it be now,"
And carrying the prayer plumes which I had prepared,
Yonder to the south
With prayers, I made my road go forth.
To the place ever since the first beginning called "Ants go in,"
My road reached.[7]
There where my fathers' water-filled roads come out,
I gave them plume wands;
I gave them prayer feathers;
There I asked for light for you.
That you may grow old,
That you may have corn,
That you may have beans,
That you may have squash,
That you may have wheat,
That you may kill game,
That you may be blessed with riches,
For all this I asked.
Then over toward the west
Where the road of my fathers comes in,
I gave them plume wands.

And now, when all of their days were past,[8]
Over toward the west,
Where the gray mountain stands,

[7]The man who has been given the role of the Sayatasha reports that he has indeed fulfilled his obligations by visiting all the springs throughout the year.

[8]The man who is impersonating Sayatasha visits Kothlawalawa, the Kachinas' underwater village, sometimes popularly called "Zuni Heaven," the source of life and renewal. There his "father," the actual kachina Sayatasha (represented by the chief Zuni kachina priest) invests him as Sayatasha. This involves two rites, ritual smoking and baptism with cornmeal, which are part of other Zuni ceremonials, and for which block formulas are used. Smoke is a complex symbol at Zuni, associated with mist and rain, with breath and life, and with thought and intention, all comprehended by the distinctive formulaic phrase: "I added to their hearts (breath)." Smoking is also a sign of peace and marks reciprocal relations as among kin (ll. 230–234). The ritual smoking formula occurs several times (ll. 205–33, 421–47, 597–620). Baptism with prayer meal is an act of physical blessing (ll. 190–200, 401–416, 584–91). The cornmeal, like pollen, fertilizes that upon which it lands.

And the blue mountain,
Where rain always falls,
Where seeds are renewed,
Where life is renewed,
Where no one ever falls down,
At the abiding place
Of those who are our children,
There I met them on their roads.
There where the one who is my father
Had prepared my seat
Four times my father sprinkled prayer meal.
On the crown of my head
Four times he sprinkled prayer meal.
And after he had sprinkled prayer meal on his rain seat,
Following him,
My prayer meal
Four times I sprinkled.
My father's rain seat
I stood beside.
My father took hold of me.
Presenting me to all the directions, he made me sit down.
When I had sat down,
My father
Took his grandson,
Reed youth.
Within his body,
He bored a hole going through him.
Four times drawing toward him his bag of native tobacco,
Into the palm of his hand
He measured out the tobacco.
Within his body
He placed mist.
He took his grandmother by the hand,
And made her sit down in the doorway.
Having made her sit in the doorway,
Four times inhaling, he drew the mist through.
With the mist
He added to the hearts
Of the rain maker priests of all directions.
It is well;
Praying that the rain makers
Might not withhold their misty breath,
With his prayers
He added to their hearts.
He handed it to me.
Four times inhaling,
Into my body

I made the mist pass through.
Then with the mist,
I added to the hearts of my fathers of all the directions.
When this was at an end,
We greeted one another with terms of kinship:
Father,
Son; elder brother, younger brother; uncle, nephew; grandfather, grandson; ancestor, descendant.
With this many words we greeted one another.
When all this was at an end,
My father questioned me:
"Yes, now indeed
You have passed us on our roads.
Surely you will have something to say, some words that are not too long."
Thus he spoke to me.

"Yes, indeed it is so.
Back at the New Year,
All my fathers
Desiring something,
With their precious prayer plume
Appointed me.
Yonder toward the south,
At all the places where the roads of the rain makers come out,
I have continued to offer you prayer plumes.
Now that the cycle of your months is at an end,
Now that the counted number of your days has been told off
Now that this many days
Anxiously we have awaited your day,
Now this day,
We have reached the appointed time.
Now I have passed you on your roads."
Thus I spoke to them.

When I had spoken thus,
Hurriedly, without delay,
My father took hold of me.[9]
From the very soles of my feet
Even to the crown of my head
He clothed me all over with all things needful.
When all this was at an end,

[9]Sayatasha the kachina now invests the man who will impersonate him, not only costuming him for his public ceremonial appearances in the kachina's stead, but more importantly supplying him with all the requisite elements for renewing life at Zuni and empowering him to effectively bless the people with fertility.

Then also with that which is called my belt,
His prayer meal,
He covered my navel.
With his bundle that covered it all over.
He took hold of me,
His bundle reached all around my body.
When all this was at an end,
Then also the different kinds of seeds four times he placed over
my navel.
All different kinds of seeds his bundle contained:
The seeds of the yellow corn,
The seeds of the blue corn,
The seeds of the red corn,
The seeds of the white corn,
The seeds of the speckled corn,
The seeds of the black corn,
And also that by means of which you may have firm flesh,
Namely, the seeds of the sweet corn;
And also those which will be your sweet tasting delicacies,
Namely, all the clans of beans—
The yellow beans,
The blue beans
The red beans,
The white beans,
The spotted beans,
The black beans,
The large beans,
The small beans,
The little gray beans,
The round beans,
The string beans,
Then also those that are called the ancient round things—
The striped squash,
The crooked-neck squash.
The watermelons,
The sweet melons,
And also those which you will use to dip up your clear water,
Namely, the gourds;
And then also the seeds of the piñon tree,
The seeds of the juniper tree,
The seeds of the oak tree,
The seeds of the peach tree,
The seeds of the black wood shrub,
The seeds of the first flowering shrub,
The seeds of the kapuli shrub.
The seeds of the large yucca,
The seeds of the small yucca,

The seeds of the branched cactus,
The seeds of the brown cactus,
The seeds of the small cactus;
And then also the seeds of all the wild grasses—
The evil smelling weeds,
The little grass,
Tecukta,
Kucutsi,
O'co,
Apitalu,
Sutoka,
Mololoka,
Piculiya
Small piculiya,
Hamato
Mitaliko;
And then also the seeds of those that stand in their doorways,
Namely the cat-tails,
The tall flags,
The water weeds,
The water cress,
The round-leafed weed;
Across my navel
His bundle reached.
And then also, the yellow clothing bundle of the priest of the north,
The blue clothing bundle of the priest of the west,
The red clothing bundle of the priest of the south,
The white clothing bundle of the priest of the east,
The many colored bundle of the priest of the above,
The dark colored bundle of the priest of the below;
Across my navel
His bundle reached.

When all this was at an end,
My father spoke to me:[10]
"Thus you will go.
Your daylight fathers,
Your daylight mothers,
Your daylight children
You will pass on their roads.
And wherever you come to rest,
We shall come to you.

[10]The spirit of the ancestral dead, who, clothed with clouds, are partly responsible for bringing rain, promise to come to Zuni when the impersonator of Sayatasha, Rain Priest of the North, calls. The description is a block formula, repeated in ll. 480 ff.

Assuredly none of us shall be left behind—
All the men,
Those with snow upon their heads,
With moss on their faces,
With skinny knees, no longer upright, and leaning on canes,
Even all of these;
And furthermore the women,
Even those who are with child,
Carrying one child on the back,
Holding another on a cradle board,
Leading one by the hand,
With yet another going before,
Even all of us,
Our daylight fathers,
Our daylight mothers,
Our children,
We shall pass on their roads."

Thus my father said.
Having spoken thus,
He took hold of me.
Presenting me to all the directions he made me arise.
With his prayer meal
Four times he sprinkled his water-filled ladder.[11]

After him,
Four times I sprinkled my prayer meal.
Taking four steps,
Four times striding forward,
Standing, I came out.

[Having come out standing,
Yonder to all directions I looked;
I looked toward the north,
I looked toward the west,
I looked toward the south,
I looked toward the east.
Hither, toward the place of dawn,
I saw four roads going side by side.
Along the middle road,
Four times my prayer meal I sprinkled.
There I made the sound of the water-filled breath of the priest of
the north.
Taking four steps,

[11]Because the kiva is meant to represent a spring, "a rain-filled room," the ladder descending into it from the roof is called "water-filled."

Four times striding forward,
To the place known since the first beginning as Great Lake,[12]
My road came.

Where my father's road comes out
I stood in the doorway.
That which formed my belt,
My prayer meal,
Four times sprinkling inside,
I opened their curtain of scum.
After that,
Four times sprinkling prayer meal inside
Standing I came in.
When I came in standing,
My father
Hurrying without delay
Where he had prepared his rain seat,
His prayer meal
Four times he sprinkled.
On the top of my head
His prayer meal
Four times he sprinkled.

After him
Four times sprinkling my prayer meal,
My father's rain seat
I stood beside.
As I stood up beside it
My father took hold of me,
Yonder to all the directions presenting me,
He made me sit down.

Having seated me
The one who is my father
Took the water bringing cigarettes which he had prepared.
Four times drawing it toward him,
He took his grandmother by the hand
And made her sit down in the doorway,
Four times inhaling, he drew the mist through
With the mist
He added to the hearts of fathers,
Rain maker priests.

[12]One of the 29 sacred springs visited by the Zuni during their post-emergence migration in search of their present home. At each spring, the Sayatasha impersonator actually enters the spring, moving aside the algae scum, which is imagined as a curtain serving as a door for the "rain-filled room" (l. 400). At each of the 29 springs, the baptism with corn meal and the ritual smoking occur, inviting the ancestral rain-making spirits residing in the spring to return to Zuni.

Thus it is well;
In order that the rain makers may not withhold their misty breath.
With mist he added to their hearts.
When all this was at an end,
My father handed it to me.
Four times inhaling, I drew the mist through.
Into my body drawing the misty breath,
With the mist
I added to the hearts of my fathers.
This is well;
In order that the rain makers may not withhold their misty breath,
With mist I added to their hearts.
When all this was at an end,
We greeted one another with terms of kinship:
Father,
Son; elder brother, younger brother; uncle, nephew; grandfather, grandson; ancestor, descendant.
With these words we greeted one another.

When all this was at an end
My father questioned me:
"Yes, now at this time
You have passed us on our roads.
Surely you will have something to say, some word that is not too long,
If you let us know that,
I shall know it for all time."
Thus my father spoke.
When he had spoken thus, (I answered)
"Yes, indeed it is so.
Yonder to the south,
Following wherever your roads come out,
I have been bringing you prayer sticks,
I have been bringing you prayer feathers.
Now this day,
Having reached the appointed time,
I have passed you on your roads."
"Is that so. With plain words you have come to us.
We are clothed with your prayer sticks;
We hold your prayer meal;
With your prayer plumes in our hair we are sitting in here waiting.
Here where we are just standing around,
Where we are just sitting on our haunches,
You have come to us.[13]

[13]The relationship between men and spirits is not a compulsive but a generous one. The spirits, it seems, need to feel needed and have been waiting for the Zuni to request their assistance.

When the sun who is our father
Has yet a little ways to go,
Before he goes in to sit down at his sacred place,
Nearby your daylight fathers,
Your daylight mothers,
Your children,
You will pass on their roads.
Wherever you come to rest,
All together we shall come to you.
All the men,
Those with snow upon their heads, with moss upon their faces,
With skinny knees,
No longer upright but leaning on canes;
And the women,
Even those who are with child,
Carrying one upon the back,
Holding another on the cradle board,
Leading one by the hand,
With yet another going before.
Yes, with all of these,
Your daylight fathers,
Your daylight mothers,
Your children,
You will pass on their roads,
And wherever you come to rest
We shall come to you."
Thus my father spoke.

When he had spoke thus,
He took hold of me.
Yonder to all the directions
Presenting me
He made me arise.
After he had made me arise
With his prayer meal
His water-filled ladder
He sprinkled.
After him sprinkling my prayer meal
Standing, I came out.][14]

* * *

[14]The bracketed portion of the text, ll. 380–509, is repeated 29 times, the only change being the substitution in l. 393 of the name of a different one of the 29 springs, which the Zuni visited during their post-emergence migration. By visiting each of these springs in order, the Sayatasha impersonator reenacts that mythic migration search for the Center of the world.

Coming out standing
Yonder to all directions I looked.
I looked to the north,
I looked to the west,
I looked to the south,
I looked to the east,
Hither toward Itiwana I saw four roads going side by side.
Along the middle road,
My prayer meal
Four times I sprinkled before me.
Then I made the sound of the rain-filled breath of the rain maker
    priest of the below.

Taking four steps,
Four times striding forward,
Where descends the watery road.
Of my daylight fathers,
My daylight mothers,
I stood.
Then I consecrated the place
Where my father's watery road descends.[15]
That none of his children might fall from the ladder,
Having still one rung left to go,
Having still two rungs left to go,
Having still three rungs left to go,
Having still four rungs left to go;
In order that none of his children should fall down
I consecrated the place where his watery road descends.
When all this was at an end
The one who is my father
On the crown of my head
Four times sprinkled prayer meal.
Four times he threw prayer meal upward.
Then after him,
My prayer meal
Sprinkling before me,
Where my father's water-filled road ascends
I made my road ascend.
The one who is my father
Four times sprinkled prayer meal before him.

[15]The flashback portion of the chant ends here, as the narration of the Sayatasha impersonator has caught up with events. On this eighth night of Shalako, he has entered into the Shalako house, a home representing the Zuni community as a family. He consecrates the house by rooting it in the earth, like a living plant (ll. 554–68), so that there may be long life (ll. 529, 534) and fertility (ll. 570–82).

After him
Four times sprinkling prayer meal before me,
Standing, I came in.
As standing I came in
I could scarcely see all my fathers,
So full was his house.

Then my father's rain-filled room
I rooted at the north,
I rooted at the west,
I rooted at the south,
I rooted at the east,
I rooted above,
Then in the middle of my father's roof,
With two plume wands joined together,
I consecrated his roof.
This is well;
In order that my father's offspring may increase,
I consecrated the center of his roof.
And then also, the center of my father's floor,
With seeds of all kinds,
I consecrated the center of his floor.
This is well;
In order that my father's fourth room
May be bursting with corn,
That even in his doorway,
The shelled corn may be scattered before the door,
The beans may be scattered before the door,
That his house may be full of little boys,
And little girls,
And people grown to maturity;
That in his house
Children may jostle one another in the doorway,
In order that it may be thus,
I have consecrated the rain-filled room
Of my daylight father,
My daylight mother.

When all this was at an end,
The one who is my father
Four times sprinkled prayer meal
Where he had prepared my seat.
Following him,
Four times sprinkling prayer meal before me,
Where my father had prepared my seat,
I stood beside it.

My father took hold of me.
Presenting me to all the directions, he made me sit down.
After my father had seated me,
The rain invoking cigarette which he had prepared
My father drew toward him.
He took his grandmother by the hand
And made her sit in the doorway.
Having seated her in the doorway,
Four times inhaling he made the mist pass through;
Into his body
He drew the misty breath.
With the mist he added to the hearts of his fathers.
This is well:
That the rain makers may not withhold their misty breath,
With mist
He added to the hearts of his fathers.
He handed it to me.
Four times inhaling I made the mist pass through;
Into my warm body
I drew the misty breath.
With mist I added to the hearts of my fathers.
This is well:
That the rain makers may not withhold their misty breath,
With mist I added to their hearts.
When all this was at an end,
We greeted one another with terms of kinship:
Father,
Son, elder brother, younger brother; uncle, nephew; grandfather,
grandson; ancestor, descendant.
With this many words we greeted one another.

When all this was at an end,
My daylight father questioned me:
"Yes, now indeed
You have passed us on our roads,
The one whom all our fathers,
Desiring something,
Appointed at the New Year.
Yonder to the south
Wherever emerge the precious roads of our fathers,
Rain maker priests,
Rain maker Pekwins,
Rain maker bow priests.
With your prayer plumes—poorly made though they were,
You have asked for light for us.
Now this day, the appointed time has come."

Thus my father said to me.
Now our fathers,[16]
Shola-witsi, pekwin priest,
Sayatasha, bow priest,
Hututu, bow priest,
The two Yamuhakto, bow priests,
Perpetuating their rite,
Have once more assumed human form.
Their seeds,
Their riches,
Their fecundity,
The seeds of the yellow corn,
The seeds of the blue corn,
The seeds of the red corn,
The seeds of the white corn,
The seeds of the speckled corn,
The seeds of the black corn,
The seeds of the sweet corn,
All the clans of beans,
All the ancient round things,
The seeds of all the different trees,
The seeds of all the wild weeds,
I carry over my navel.
Those which we brought,
These seeds we now leave here
In the rain-filled rooms
Of our daylight fathers,
Our daylight mothers.

When in the spring,
Your earth mother is enriched with living waters,
Then in all your water-filled fields,
These, with which you will renew yourselves,
Your mothers,
All the different kinds of corn,
Within your earth mother
You will lay down.
With our earth mother's living waters,
They will once more become living beings.
Into the daylight of our sun father
They will come out standing.
They will stand holding out their hands to all the directions,

[16]Sholawitsi, the little Fire God, represents the Sun and carries a fawn skin full of different seeds. Hututu, the Rain Priest of the South, is the deputy of Sayatasha, Rain Priest of the North. The Yamuhakto are patron spirits of the forests and game animals. All are represented by masked impersonators.

Calling for water.
And from somewhere,
Our fathers with their fresh water
Will come to them.
Their fresh waters
They will drink in.
They will clasp their children in their arms;
Their young will finish their roads.
Into your house,
You will bring them,
To be your beloved ones.
In order that you may live thus,
In the rain-filled rooms
Of our daylight fathers,
Our daylight mothers,
Our daylight children,
The seeds which we brought tied about our waists
We leave here now.
This is well;
That going but a little ways from their house
Our fathers may meet their children;[17]
That going about, as they say,
With your water-filled breath
(You may meet) antelope,
Mountain goats.
Does,
Bucks,
Jack rabbits,
Cottontails,
Wood rats,
Small game—even little bugs;
So that thus going out from your houses,
With the flesh of these
You may satisfy your hunger.

This is well;
In order that my daylight father's rain-filled rooms,
May be filled with all kinds of clothing,
That their house may have a heart,[18]
That even in his doorway

[17]As the parallelism suggests, these are the game animals. The ceremonial of which this chant is a part, while focusing primarily on agricultural imagery, is a world renewal ceremony to promote fertility in all living persons, whether animal, vegetable, or human. Indeed, given the corn-flesh and animal-human transformations that are central to the Zuni creation story, all life is one and all creatures are persons. See "Talk Concerning the First Beginning," [Zuni], above.

[18]"An empty house 'has no heart.' The heart of a house is anything which has been used by human beings." [Bunzel's note]

The shelled corn may be spilled before his door,
That beans may be spilled before his door,
That wheat may be spilled outside the door,
(That the house may be full of) little boys,
And little girls,
And men and women grown to maturity,
That in his house
Children may jostle one another in the doorway,
In order that it may be thus,
With two plume wands joined together,
I have consecrated the center of his roof.
Praying for whatever you wished,
Through the winter,
Through the summer,
Throughout the cycle of the months,
I have prayed for light for you.
Now this day,
I have fulfilled their thoughts.
Perpetuating the rite of our father,
Sayatasha, bow priest,
And giving him human form
I have passed you on your roads.
My divine father's life-giving breath,
His breath of old age,
His breath of waters,
His breath of seeds,
His breath of riches,
His breath of fecundity,
His breath of power,
His breath of strong spirit,
His breath of all good fortune whatsoever,
Asking for his breath,
And into my warm body
Drawing his breath,
I add to your breath now.
Let no one despise the breath of his fathers,
But into your bodies,
Draw their breath.
That yonder to where the road of our sun father comes out,
Your roads may reach;
That clasping hands,
Holding one another fast,
You may finish your roads,[19]

[19]This exhortation captures the purpose of this Zuni ceremonial in which a representative from the human community seeks the life-giving aid ("the breath") of the ancestral spirits ("the fathers") and brings it back to renew the community ("add to our breath"). Only continuity with the past can insure continuance in the future.

To this end, I add to your breath now.
Verily, so long as we enjoy the light of day
May we greet one another with love;[20]
Verily, so long as we enjoy the light of day
May we wish one another well,
Verily may we pray for one another.
To this end, my fathers,
My mothers,
My children:
May you be blessed with light;
May your roads be fulfilled;
May you grow old;
May you be blessed in the chase;
To where the life-giving road of your sun father comes out
May your roads reach;
May your roads all be fulfilled.

1930

Aztec Poetry

The Singer's Art[1]

I polish the jade to brilliance,
I arrange the black-green feathers,
I ponder the roots of the song,
I order in rank the yellow feathers,
  So that a beautiful song I sing.
I strike the jade continuously
To break out light from the flower's blossoming,
  Only to honor the Lord of the Close and the Near.

The yellow plumes of the troupial,
The black-green of the trogon,
The crimson of the rosy spoonbill,
I freshly arrange.
  My noble song, sounding golden tones,
  My song I will sing.
A golden finch my song is proclaimed.

[20]"Literally, 'call one another by terms of relationship,'" [Bunzel note], as in l. 619. A more appropriate translation than "love," which is burdened by Western Romantic notions, may be: "May we greet one another as family."

[1]From Daniel Brinton, *Ancient Nahuatl Poetry* (Philadelphia, 1890). Trans. from the Nahuatl by Andrew Wiget. Composing a poem is compared to fine craftsmanship in other valued materials, precious stones and rare feathers.

I sing it in the place of the raining flowers,[2]
    Before the face of the Lord of the Close and the Near.

A song good in its origins,
From the place whence comes the gold I bring it forth.
To the heavens I uncover the song I sing.
    A golden finch, a glittering jade it is.
I will make blossom a beautiful new song.
I will bring forth the perfume of mixed flowers to sweeten my
        song,
Before the face of the Lord of the Close and the Near.

The rosy spoonbill answers me,
When my bell-toned song reaches
The place of beautiful new songs.
    A polished jewel, a jade precious and brilliant.
    Of deepest green, it is made,
    A spring flower prepared to perfume the heavens.
    To the place of rosy flowers,
    Toward there I sing my song.

I choose the colors,
I mix the flowers,
In the place of beautiful new songs.
    A polished jewel, a jade precious and brilliant.
    Of deepest green, it is made,
    A spring flower prepared to perfume the heavens.
    To the place of rosy flowers,
    Toward there I sing my song.

I am honored, I am made glad,
Chasing the much-prized flower, the aroma of the rose in the place
        of song.
So that with sweetness my heart is filled.
Wave after wave I send to buffet my heart.
I inhale the perfume;
My soul becomes drunk.
I so long for the place of beauty.
The place of flowers, the place of my fulfillment,
That with flowers my soul is made drunk.

1890

[2]A metaphor for the Aztec Paradise, the home of the Sun and of song.

Two Songs[1]

I

We came only to sleep,
We came only to dream.
It is not so, it is not so,
That we came to endure on earth.

II

We become as the verdant spring.
Our hearts are rejuvenated,
Burst forth anew.
But our bodies are as the flowers:
Some blossom; they wither away.

Is it yet true there is living on earth?
Not forever on earth; but a moment here.
If it is jade, it shatters.
If it is gold, it crumbles.
If it is feather, it rends.
Not forever on earth; but a moment here.

1973

Like Flowers Continually Perishing[1]

(by Ayocuan)

Lo! From within the womb of the heavens they come,
The beautiful flower, the beautiful song.
Our eagerness destroys them,
Our diligence destroys them.
Truly perhaps even those of the Prince of the Chichimecs,[2]
    Tecoyahuatzin.
With his flowers, let all enjoy themselves!

The exotic perfume of flowers filters down,
Friendship, a rain of precious flowers,
Plumes of white heron interlaced
With the precious cut flowers.
In the place of the branches,

[1]From the *Cantares Mexicanos.* Trans. by Arthur J.O. Anderson, in his *Grammatical Examples, Exercises and Review, for Use with "Rules of the Aztec Language."* (Salt Lake City: U Utah, 1973).

[1]From Birgitta Leander, *Flor y Canto* (Mexico: Instituto Nacional Indigenista, 1972). Trans. from the Nahuatl by Andrew Wiget.

[2]Another name for the Aztecs.

They go about sipping at the flowers,
The lords and the nobles.

Yet you, O golden, belling bird!
How beautiful our song,
How beautifully you intone it!
There among the wreathed flowers,
There among the branching flowers, there you sing.

Perhaps you are this precious bird, O Giver of Life?[3]
Perhaps thus you have spoken, you, the god?
From the beginning, when you sit viewing the dawn,
You set about singing.

Eagerly my heart desires it,
The shield flowers,
The flowers of the Giver of Life.
  What shall my heart do?
  In vain we come to this place,
  We come to live on earth.

Yet only like these am I to be,
Like flowers continually perishing.
Will my name endure anywhere?
Will my fame end here on earth?
At least the flower, at least the song remains!
  What shall my heart do?
  In vain we come to this place,
  We come to live on earth.

Let us be content, O my friends!
Here there is embracing.
In a world of flowers we are living.
Of these not one will be destroyed,
The flower, the song.
They live in the house of the Giver of Life.

How brief an instant here on earth!
Will it be like this also in the next place of living?
Will there be rejoicing there? Friends?
Is it only here we come to know ourselves,
  On earth?

1972

[3]Another name for the Creator, the Lord of the Close and the Near.

Inuit Poetry

Song[1]

(Copper Eskimo)

And I thought over again
My small adventures
As with a shore wind I drifted out
In my kayak
and thought I was in danger.

My fears,
Those small ones
That I had thought so big
For all the vital things
I had to get and reach.
And yet there is only
One great thing,
The only thing:
To live to see in huts and on journeys
The great day that dawns
And the light that fills the world.

1942

Moved

Uvavnuk[1] *(Iglulik Eskimo)*

The great sea stirs me.
The great sea sets me adrift.
It sways me like a weed
On a river stone.

The sky's height stirs me.
The strong wind blows through my mind.
It carries me away
And moves my inward parts with joy.

1973

[1]From Knud Rasmussen, *The Mackenzie Eskimo.* Ed. H. Ostermann. Report of the Fifth Thule Expedition, 1921–24. 10:2 (Copenhagen, 1942).

[1]From *Eskimo Poetry from Canada and Greenland.* Trans. Tom Lowenstein. (Pittsburgh: U Pittsburgh P, 1973). Uvavnuk entered the hut singing this song. Afterward she explained that she had been looking up at the night sky when a star rushed down, struck her and gave her this song. References to the sea, wind, and sky all allude to *silap inue,* the "Great Weather," the supernatural being who animates the environment.

Improvised Greeting[1]

Takomaq (Iglulik Eskimo)

Ajaja-aja-jaja.
The lands around my dwelling
Are more beautiful
From the day
When it is given me to see
Faces I have never seen before.
All is more beautiful,
All is more beautiful,
And life is thankfulness.
These guests of mine
Make my house grand.
Ajaja-aja-jaja.

1929

Widow's Song[1]

Quernertoq (Copper Eskimo)

Why will people
have no mercy on me?
Sleep comes hard
since Maula's[2] killer
showed no mercy.
Ijaja-ijaja.

Was the agony I felt so strange
when I saw the man I loved
thrown on the earth
with bowed head?
Murdered by enemies,
worms have forever deprived him
of his homecoming.
Ijaja-ijaja.

He was not alone
in leaving me.

[1]From Knud Rasmussen, *Intellectual Culture of the Iglulik Eskimo.* Report of the Fifth Thule Expedition. 7:1 (1929). This woman composed this song spontaneously as she brewed tea to greet Rasmussen.

[1]From *Eskimo Poetry from Canada and Greenland.* Trans. Tom Lowenstein. (Pittsburgh: U Pittsburgh P, 1973).

[2]Maula, her husband.

My little son
has vanished
to the shadow-land.
Ijaja-ijaja.

Now I'm like a beast
caught in the snare
of my hut.
Ijaja-ijaja.

Long will be my journey
on the earth.
It seems as if
I'll never get beyond
the foot-prints that I make.
Ijaja-ijaja.

A worthless amulet[3]
is all my property;
while the northern light
dances its sparkling steps
in the sky.
Ijaja-ijaja.

1973

My Breath[1]

Orpingalik (Netsilik Eskimo)

My breath . . . this is what I call my song, because it is as important for me to sing it as it is to draw breath.

This is my song: a powerful song.
Unaija-unaija.
Since autumn I have lain here,
helpless and ill,
as if I were my own child.

Sorrowfully, I wish my woman
to another hut,

[3]Amulets made of bone, wood, and stone represent the individual's spirit-helper whose protection is essential for survival.

[1]From *Eskimo Poetry from Canada and Greenland.* Trans. Tom Lowenstein. (Pittsburgh: U Pittsburgh P, 1973).

another man for refuge,
firm and safe as the winter-ice.
Unaija-unaija.

And I wish my woman
a more fortunate protector,
now I lack the strength
to raise myself from bed.
Unaija-unaija.

Do you know yourself?
How little of yourself you understand!
Stretched out feebly on my bench,
my only strength is in my memories.
Unaija-unaija.

Game! Big game,
chasing ahead of me!
Allow me to re-live that!
Let me forget my frailty,
by calling up the past.
Unaija-unaija.

I bring to mind that great white one,
the polar bear,
approaching with raised hind-quarters,
his nose in the snow—
convinced, as he rushed at me,
that of the two of us,
he was the only male!
Unaija-unaija.

Again and again he threw me down:
but spent at last,
he settled by a hump of ice,
and rested there,
ignorant that I was going to finish him.
He thought he was the only male around!
But I too was a man!
Unaija-unaija.

Nor will I forget that great blubbery one,
the fjord-seal, that I slaughtered
from an ice-floe before dawn,
while friends at home
were laid out like the dead,
feeble with hunger,

famished with bad luck.
Unaija-unaija.

I hurried home,
laden with meat and blubber,
as though I were just running across the ice
to view a breathing-hole.
Yet this had been an old and cunning bull,
who'd scented me at once—
but before he had drawn breath,
my spear was sinking
through his neck.
Unaija-unaija.

This is how it was.
Now I lie on my bench,
too sick even to fetch
a little seal oil for my woman's lamp.
Time, time scarcely seems to pass,
though dawn follows dawn,
and spring approaches the village.
Unaija-unaija.

How much longer must I lie here?
How long? How long must she go begging
oil for the lamp,
reindeer-skins for her clothes,
and meat for her meal?
I, a feeble wretch:
she, a defenceless woman.
Unaija-unaija.

Do you know yourself?
How little of yourself you understand!
Dawn follows dawn,
and spring is approaching the village.
Unaija-unaija.

1973

A Selection of Poems

Deer Hunting Song

Virsak Vai-i[1] *(O'odham)*

At the time of the White Dawn;
At the time of the White Dawn,
I arose and went away.
        At Blue Nightfall I went away.

I ate the thornapple leaves[2]
        and the leaves made me dizzy.
I drank the thornapple flowers
        and the drink made me stagger.

The hunter, Bow-remaining,
        he overtook and killed me,
cut and threw my horns away.
        The hunter, Reed-remaining,
he overtook me and killed me,
        cut and threw my feet away.

Now the flies become crazy
        and they drop with flapping wings.
The drunken butterflies sit
        with opening and shutting wings.

1985

Love Song[1]

Aleut

I cannot bear it, I cannot bear it at all.
I cannot bear to be where I usually am.

[1]This song was sung by Virsak Vai-i and recorded by Frank Russell on the Gila River Reservation in Arizona in 1902. Vai-i's people, whom Russell and other Americans knew as the Pima, call themselves O'odham, "the people." Historically organized in patrilineages, they live on the Gila River and Salt River Reservations in Arizona. This text is from Frank Russell, *The Pima Indians,* 1985.

[2]A species of Datura with psychochemical properties. The deer speaks in this poem of being sickened by it. This deer-hunting song, like many other hunting songs, was also used by medicine men for curing. This song was used for curing illnesses that had symptoms of dizziness and vomiting.

[1]This is one of many songs recorded among the Aleut people who live on the island chain of Alaska which bears their name, and now part of the Aleutian Manuscript Collection at the New York Public Library. This text is taken from Avram Yarmolinsky's report in the *New York Public Library Bulletin,* 1944.

She is yonder, she moves near me, she is dancing.
I cannot bear it
If I may not smell her breath, the
fragrance of her.

1944

Song of Repulse to a Vain Lover

To'ak[1] *(Makah)*

Keep away
Just a little touch of you
is sufficient.

1939

A Dream Song

Annie Long Tom[1] *(Clayoquot)*

Do not listen to the other singing.
Do not be afraid to sing your own song.

1939

[1]This song was recorded by Frances Densmore from Helen Irving during Densmore's work on the Makah Reservation at Neah Bay, Washington, during the summers of 1923 and 1926. Historically, the Makah were great whalers and lived by hunting sea mammals and fishing. Densmore wrote: "The composer of this song was a blind woman named To'ak. The interpreter remembered her and said that she sat against the wall all day, singing and tapping her knuckles on the wall as an accompaniment. Her name refers to a beach and was thought to mean a pile of valuables on the shore. To'ak belonged to the Ozette band of Makah. There was no one to take care of her and she drifted from one family to another, but people were glad to have her because she was always so happy." This text is from Frances Densmore, *Nootka and Quileute Music,* 1939.

[1]This song was also recorded by Densmore during her Neah Bay fieldwork. Annie Long Tom, a Clayoquot, was the widow of a Makah man who survived by seasonal work and making baskets for sale. She received many of her songs in dreams. According to Densmore, "Annie Long Tom has a drum with which she accompanies her songs as she sits alone in her house. In describing some of her dream songs, she said the melodies came to her at night when she was asleep . . . [she] dreamed this song at the time when the Shaker religion came to Neah Bay. The Shaker religion is now established in the village, having a commodious building and many adherents, but Mrs. Long Tom has never attended the meetings. At first she debated the matter in her own mind, but a crow came to her in a dream and gave her this song, so she held aloof from the new religion." This text is from Frances Densmore, *Nootka and Quileute Music,* 1939.

Woman's Divorce Dance Song

Jane Green[1]

I thought you were good at first,
I thought you were like silver
and I find you are lead.

You see me high up.
I
walk through the sun.
I
am like sunlight itself.

1943

Formula to Secure Love[1]

(Cherokee)

Now! I am as beautiful as the very blossoms themselves

I am a man, you lovely ones, you women of the Seven
Clans![2]

[1]This song was recorded in September, 1926, by Frances Densmore from Jane Green, an Indian woman from the upper Skeena River, who had traveled more than five hours by car to work at a hop-picking camp near Chilliwack, British Columbia. Densmore did not specify Green's tribal affiliation. Of divorce in these patrilineal, patrilocal tribes, Green told Densmore, "If a woman quarreled with her husband and was sent away, she gave a dance in about three days and her husband gave a second dance three days after hers. Both spent much money in their dances and many presents. At the woman's dance about seven women stood in a row, about two arms' lengths apart, and moved their heads as they danced, while the woman who had been sent away by her husband stood still in the middle of the row." This is one of three songs sung during the dance. This text is from Frances Densmore, *Music of the Indians of British Columbia,* 1943.

[1]The Cherokees had many magical formulas, called *i:gawe:sdi,* words which focused or directed thought. Many of these were recorded by medicine men in manuscript books in the Cherokee syllabary. This one was recorded in southeast Adair County, Oklahoma. These magical formulas feature repetition of key words, a structure highlighted by the most sacred number seven, the use of the pronoun "I," and a long pause during which the reciter thinks intently upon the purpose of the ritual. They may be recited, sung or simply thought, and are often used to infuse tobacco with magical power. This is an example of an *ado:du:hiso?di:yi,* a "rebeautifying" formula which through magic surrounds the singer with a spiritual aura which makes him or her irresistible. The root *uhi:so?di* refers to the excruciating longing or lovesickness which the formula produces in the woman to whom it is directed. This text is from J. Frederick and A. G. Kilpatrick, *Walk in Your Soul: Love Incantations of the Oklahoma Cherokee,* 1965.

[2]This formula was accompanied by a note in the manuscript book: "This written is the utmost for young men growing up to help themselves. To be said four times. One is to blow [his breath toward the woman of his choice] upon finishing." Seven is the Cherokee number signifying wholeness and totality. So, the whole Cherokee Nation and, by extension, the whole world.

(Now these are my people, ____________, and this is my name,
____________.)

Now! You women who reside among the Seven Peoples, I
have just come to intrude myself among you.
All of you have just come to gaze upon me alone, the
most beautiful.
Now! You lovely women, already I just took your souls!

I am a man!
You women will live in the very middle of my soul.

Forever I will be as beautiful as the bright red blossoms![3]

1965

Formula to Cause Death

A'yunini, the Swimmer[1] *(Cherokee)*

Listen! Now I have come to step over your soul.

You are of the ____________ clan. Your name is
____________.
Your spittle I have put at rest under the earth.[2]
Your soul I have put at rest under the earth.

I have come to cover you over with the black rock.[3]
I have come to cover you over with the black slabs,
never to reappear.

[3]Red in Cherokee color symbolism referred to victory or power.

[1]This formula was recorded by James Mooney on the North Carolina Cherokee Reservation in the early 1880s from the manuscript book supplied by A'yunini or The Swimmer, a Cherokee medicine man. At first reluctant to cooperate with Mooney, The Swimmer succumbed from what Mooney called "professional pride" to the latter's argument that preservation of these texts would demonstrate to later generations just how much the Cherokees knew. Despite anxieties about his reputation, The Swimmer overcame the objections of other rival Cherokee medicine men and supplied Mooney with the manuscript book. This text is from James Mooney, *Sacred Formulas of the Cherokees,* 1886.

[2]According to ethnologist James Mooney, "When the shaman wishes to destroy the life of another, either for his own purposes or for hire, he conceals himself near the trail along which the victim is likely to pass. When the doomed man appears the shaman waits until he goes by and then follows him secretly until he chances to spit upon the ground. On coming to the spot the shaman collects upon the end of the stick a little of the dust thus moistened with the victim's spittle. The possession of the man's spittle gives him power over the life of the man himself."

[3]In Cherokee color symbolism, black is the color of death and oblivion.

Toward the black coffin in the Darkening Land your
path shall stretch out.
So shall it be for you.

The clay of the upland has come to cover you.
Instantly the black clay has lodged there where it
is at rest at the black houses in the Darkening
Land.
With the black coffin and the black slabs I have
come to cover you.

Now your soul has faded away.
It has become blue.[4]

When darkness comes
Your spirit shall grow less
And dwindle away,
Never to reappear.

Listen!

1886

Song of War

(Blackfeet)[1]

Old man on high [Sun],
help me,
that I may be saved from my dream!
Give me a good day!
I pray you, pity me!

1911

[4]In Cherokee color symbolism, blue is the color of failure, weakness and spiritual depression. Mooney writes of this formula: "If the ceremony has been properly carried out, the victim becomes blue, that is, he feels the effects upon himself at once, and, unless he employs the counter charms of some more powerful shaman, his soul begins to shrivel and dwindle, and within seven days, he is dead."

[1]Historically the Blackfeet were primarily buffalo hunters who lived on high plains in Montana and Alberta, where today they have reservations. Like other Plains peoples, the Blackfeet view the Sun as the giver of life and the being to whom prayer is ultimately directed. The sense of dependence and humility expressed in the plea for "pity" was a deeply felt part of the ethos of many Plains tribes. "Warfare" consisted principally of raiding and retaliation. This warrior sings that he may be saved from a dream which has made him anxious about going into battle. This text is from C. C. Uhlenbeck, *Original Blackfoot Texts,* 1911.

War Song

(Crow)[1]

Eternal are the heavens and the earth.
Old people are poorly off.
Do not be afraid.[2]

1935

Song of War

Odjib'we[1] *(Anishinabe)*[2]

The Sioux women
pass to and fro wailing.
As they gather up their wounded men
the voice of their weeping comes back to me.[3]

1913

[1]Historically the Absaroke, called the Crow by Anglo-Americans, were buffalo hunters, organized in matrilineal clans, who lived on the eastern slopes of the Rockies and the adjacent high plains in northern Wyoming and in southern Montana, where their reservation is located today. The name of the singer of this song has not been recorded. The text is from Robert Lowie, *The Crow Indians,* 1935.

[2]Robert Lowie writes of the Crow that historically "social standing and chieftanship depended on military prowess; and that was the only road to distinction. Value was set on other qualities, such as liberality, aptness at storytelling, success as a doctor. But the property a man distributed was largely the booty he had gained in raids; and any accomplishments, prized as they might be, were merely decorative frills, not substitutes for the substance of a reputation, a man's record as a warrior. . . . There were four types of creditable exploits: leadership of a successful raid; capturing a horse picketed within a hostile camp; being the first to touch an enemy; and snatching a foeman's bow or gun."

[1]Densmore writes, "When Odjib'we was a boy his paternal grandfather, two of the latter's brothers, and two of his own brothers, were killed by the Sioux. Hatred filled his heart and he determined to hunt and kill the Sioux. Thus at an early age he chose the career of a warrior."

[2]The Anishinabe, called Chippewa by Anglo-Americans, historically occupied the wooded lake country of Minnesota and Wisconsin and far western Ontario. Pressures on their land forced them into conflict with the Sioux nations, originally also woodland peoples from the same area, and the two groups became bitter enemies. Frances Densmore recorded this song on the White Earth Reservation in Minnesota in the first decade of this century. She writes, "[Chippewa] War songs are of four kinds: dream songs of individual warriors, songs concerning war charms and medicines, songs of the conduct of war expeditions, and those which commemorate success." Today many war songs are sung as social songs. This text is from Frances Densmore, *Chippewa Music II,* 1913.

[3]This song is one of three Densmore recorded from Odjib'we connected with an expedition against the Sioux, their traditional enemies encamped in a village on the upper waters of the Minnesota River. Densmore notes, "A war party of more than a hundred Chippewa attacked this village and the first man killed was the Sioux Chief. During the fight, the Sioux women rushed out and dragged back the wounded men that they might not be scalped."

War Song

***Young Doctor*[1] *(Makah)*[2]**

The only reason I do not cut off your head[3]
is that your face would have a crying expression
when I carried it.

1939

Song of Famine

Holy-Face Bear*[1] *(Dakota)

The old men now
are so few
that they are not worth counting.
I myself
am
the last
living.
Therefore a hard time I have.

1918

[1]Densmore wrote that Young Doctor was "formerly a medicine man. In the early morning he goes fishing, being able to manage a boat although he is so crippled he cannot stand upright. His store and his work in wood and stone carving occupy his time during the day and he is constantly busy."

[2]This song was recorded during Frances Densmore's fieldwork on the Makah Reservation at Neah Bay, Washington during the summers of 1923 and 1926. This text is from Frances Densmore, *Nootka and Quileute Music,* 1939.

[3]The pointedness of the sarcasm in this song derives from the Makah custom of beheading their enemies, which, Densmore says, they attributed "to the mythical personage Kwati, who stole the box containing the daylight. The owner of the box overtook Kwati, regained the box, and killed him. When Kwati was about to be killed, he said they must not bury him but must cut off his head, take it home and let it lie on a smooth sandy beach for four days, then put it on a pole, stick the pole upright in the sand, and let it remain there until it fell."

[1]Densmore recorded this song from Holy-Face Bear, about whom she says nothing, in 1911 on the Sisseton Reservation. The Dakota are one of three dialectically distinct groups (the others are Lakota and Nakota) known to Anglo-Americans as the Sioux, a French corruption of a Chippewa word. This text is from Frances Densmore, *Teton Sioux Music,* 1918.

Song of War

Two Shields[1] (Lakota)

As the young men go by,
I was looking for him.
It surprises me anew
that he is gone.
It is something
to which I can not
be reconciled.

1918

Song of War

Victoria[1] (Tohona O'odham)

Men shouting "Brother," men shouting "Brother,"—
Among the mountains they have taken
little Apache children
where the sun went down in sorrow.
All women, what shall we do
to realize this.[2]

1929

[1]Densmore recorded this song from Two Shields during her fieldwork on the Standing Rock Reservation in South Dakota, which occupied her from 1911 to 1914. She provides no information on Two Shields. The Lakota are one of three dialectically distinct groups known to Anglo-Americans as the Sioux, a French corruption of a Chippewa word. This text is from Frances Densmore, *Teton Sioux Music,* 1918.

[1]Densmore recorded this song during fieldwork in November and December of 1920 near Sells, Arizona, where the Tohona O'odham, known to ethnographers as the Papago, have a reservation. Densmore described Victoria [sic] as "an aged member of his tribe. . . . His voice is weak but he knows many songs." This text is from Frances Densmore, *Papago Music,* 1929.

[2]Densmore writes, "When the warriors approached the village, the women, especially the relatives of the warriors, went to meet them, to receive the trophies they brought. The warriors danced on their way to the village, and on reaching the village they went to every house and danced. When they were finished, they stopped until evening, when the scalp dance began. Captives, as well as scalps, were brought by the returning warriors, and [this song] is concerning children taken captive among the Apaches." Apaches were ancient tribal enemies of the Tohona O'odham. This song points to the tragic irony of the women among the victors identifying with the mothers among their enemies.

Cultures in Contact: Voices from the Imperial Frontier

In 1897 historian Francis Parkman asserted in *The Jesuits in North America in the Seventeenth Century* that "Spanish civilization crushed the Indian; English civilization scorned and neglected him; [and] French civilization embraced and cherished him." This assessment shows an anti-Spanish bias typical of Parkman's era, and it romanticizes French treatment of Native Americans above that given them at the hands of Spanish and English colonizers. Yet, assuming—and this is a large assumption—that a pacific religious takeover of peoples is less damaging to them than their enslavement or displacement (whether by the *encomienda* system of the Spanish or the township system of the English), the French, at least if one considers their missionary efforts alone, would seem to have treated Native Americans in a more respectful manner than their Spanish and English neighbors.

The movements of the French Empire in North America began with the potentially missionary efforts initiated by Jacques Cartier, who explored for France the North American territories (now Quebec) accessible via the St. Lawrence in the 1530s and 1540s. The French were ostensibly searching for souls to convert to Catholicism, if Francois I's 1540 announcement is to believed. Speaking of his intent to sponsor a permanent French colony in the "new" world, Francois I said he was seeking "to do something pleasing to God our creator and redeemer and which may lead to the augmentation of His Holy sacred name and of our mother Holy Catholic Church of whom we are called and named the first son." Yet Jacques Cartier's 1541 return expedition to North America—though it was intended "to establish the Christian Religion in a country of savages separated from France by all the extent of the earth"—carried only six churchmen in a vessel loaded with men and equipment; indeed, "two goldsmiths and lapidaries (workers in gems)" were much higher up on the list than these churchmen. If Cartier held high hopes for a religious mission, these hopes were nonetheless modified by equal aspirations for material gains.

The French were ultimately searching for a Northwest Passage to Asia, so that they could develop their own trade systems to compete with those already established by Portugal and Spain. In establishing relations with the native peoples of the Northeast, they were hoping to learn of trading and mining opportunities equal to those found by Spain in Mesoamerica. A key factor in French colonizing efforts was learning native languages. Cartier exchanged French boys for native boys, an exchange that Samuel de Champlain half a century later would continue. It seems that the French first sought mastery of native languages for purposes of exploration, then for missionary efforts, and finally for the steady development of a system of fur trade, which ultimately became the economic and inter-societal mainstay of New France.

Unlike their Spanish and English counterparts, the French did not seek the extermination or displacement of native peoples, largely, it seems, because they needed native allies for the fur trade and for raids against their Spanish and English neighbors. French activities in the Northeast nonetheless had a significant impact upon the area's indigenous population. The Abenakis of present-day Maine, for instance, grew to rely upon trade for food with the Massachusetts to the south, because the Abenakis began to devote their energies to trapping fur-bearing animals for trade with the French. Native lives were not in jeopardy, perhaps, but native livelihoods, indeed the entire ways of looking at the material world, would irrevocably change as a result of contact with the French and with Europeans generally.

Samuel de Champlain, a geographer, is often credited with the success of the development of New France, for he played a major role in establishing good relations with native peoples of the Northeast. Indeed, the alliance between the French and natives in the area was so strong that well into the eighteenth century, English settlers in New England and the Middle Atlantic area feared French and Indian encroachment. Some of the fears of the Protestant English related to the Catholicism of the French and the Indians among whom Jesuit missionaries were working. Champlain persistently sought Jesuit missionaries for Quebec; when the Jesuits went to Acadia instead, he asked for "some good friars, with zeal and affection for the glory of God, whom I might persuade to send or come themselves with me to this country to try to plant there the faith." Among the Recollects of Brouage he found some "good friars." A poor order, vowed to poverty, they had no funds to maintain missionaries, but they had no strong fears, as well, of living among natives. The missionary work of the Jesuits and the Recollects was persistent, if ill-funded; their efforts did not always coincide with the efforts of fur traders, but their influence was widespread and well-known.

By the beginning of the eighteenth century, the French controlled—through missionary efforts or trading posts, or both—large portions of present-day Canada down into what is now the state of Illinois, and they occupied the mouth of the Mississippi and asserted a claim to its vast watershed. Occupation of the lower Mississippi enabled wide-ranging exploratory parties to cross westward in the hope of finding gold mines and an overland route to the Pacific. The English feared that the French would form a vast and strong connection along the Mississippi and up to Canada, thus cutting off the possibility of English expansion westward.

The Spanish, a century before the English worried about the French Empire, feared similar French incursions in Spanish territory in Mesoamerica, Florida, and the Carolinas, and the Southwest. Columbus's establishment of a base at Hispaniola (present-day Haiti) provided Spain with the opportunity for wide exploration fanning out along the Caribbean basin. Juan Ponce de León reached Florida in 1513, about the time Vasco Nuñez de Balboa crossed the Isthmus of Panama and found the Pacific Ocean. Less than ten years later, Cortés seized the wealth (and history) of the Aztecs. Other conquistadores went northward: Juan Rodriguez Cabrillo sailed along the California coast; Hernando de Soto discovered the Mississippi River; and Francisco Vásquez de Coronado explored the Southwest. The way was open to Spain to conquer a vast dominion in the Americas, in part because of the riches found by Cortés among the Aztecs and by Francisco Pizarro among the Incas, and in part because of the souls of Native Americans to be gained for the Catholic Church. With Portugal and with Pope Alexander VI, Spain had signed the Treaty of Tordesillas in 1494. This treaty allowed that Spain could have dominion over all of the Americas except Brazil; Brazil and Africa were therein given to Portuguese dominance.

The Spanish system of colonization was under the tight control of the Spanish crown. Wealth in the colonies came from exploitation of the native population and of slaves taken from Africa. Laws adopted in 1542 forbade the taking of native people as slaves but allowed for the system of *encomienda,* whereby native people were required to pay tribute to local conquistadores, later simply to the wealthiest leading officials in the territories. Through the mid-sixteenth century, it was the *encomienda* system which enabled native labor to substitute for slave labor to Europeans. Missionary activity often competed with the activity of the colonizers. Franciscan, Dominican, Augustinian, and later Jesuit missionaries all sought at first to eradicate native faith practices. When these efforts went unfulfilled, missionaries tended to content themselves with sacramental instruction. The task of the missionaries was not simply conversion but the complete education and hispanicization of native society. As a function of this effort, *congregación,* the establishing of nucleated settlements apart from indigenous settlements, was essential. In this, their missionary efforts and methods differed markedly from the Recollects and Jesuits of New France, who established their missions amid the woods of the North.

As this summary of fifteenth- and sixteenth-century colonization by Spain and France should suggest, very few English were early involved in exploring the Americas. They arrived after the Atlantic coast—from Nova Scotia to the Caribbean—had been claimed by both French and Spanish expeditions and named as Spanish territory by the latter group. Despite geographically ambiguous claims resulting from an early sixteenth-century voyage made by Sebastian Cabot, the first permanent English colony (Jamestown, 1607) came nearly a half-century after the French and Spanish had fought over disputed claims in Florida and the Carolinas. And Menéndez de Avilés had already defeated French Huguenots in order to found in 1565 what is now the oldest city of European origin in the United States (St. Augustine, Florida), and to set about establishing missions as far north as Virginia. By the time the English achieved a precarious beachhead, the Spanish had traversed North America from the Atlantic to the Pacific, and the French were moving up the St. Lawrence River toward the Great Lakes. Such competition initiated the tradition of bloody, no-quarter struggles among European claimants to American space which inevitably caught up the native populations, who in the end would suffer the greatest casualties. It also initiated, however, another tradition: the literature of the Americas, whose founding texts offer epic tales in languages not English, but French and Spanish. It was, therefore, in these languages that the unique problems of the textualization of the American Other were first confronted.

Writings of native and European American contact reveal the peculiar dilemmas of the authors, who found that they had no familiar language for the remarkable world they were experiencing. In Europeans' writings, the *new* had to be conveyed in terms of the old (which resulted in the continual comparison and contrast with European materials and images) or else it might have been branded by those who financially supported the trips as insignificant, meaningless, wasteful—and thus too expensive (with too little return) for further funding. When Columbus wrote of the "great affliction" he felt, he spoke of personal frustration: although ignorant of the natural world around him, he was certain of its value for Spain. He knew that unless he could record this "new" world in its full splendor, he might never be given the opportunity to see it again. That is why he collected samples of exploitable natural objects, from aloe trees to natives, as visible proof of the potential financial return on investments. And when later voyages failed to deliver on the promised material gains, he switched to verbal justification, explaining the Europeans' New World as the centuries-sought source of creation, thus marshalling both ancient "science" and the Bible to his defense. When Cabeza de Vaca found himself in the opprobrious position of having to explain the utter failure of an expedition to which he had been assigned as the guardian of the Emperor's investment, he claimed to have seen signs of precious metals, but since he brought back none, he also offered a textual justification for his experience that his Catholic patron could appreciate: his material failure was clear evidence of divine providence's plan for his conversion into a religious healer, a voice crying in the wilderness, a born-again Christian returned with the message of New World man. These precarious overlays of European ideal maps on the American geography started a tradition still not completely played out. The Americas have never ceased being an ideal dream. Like Columbus and Cabeza de Vaca, all the authors of early contact chronicles faced the difficulty of phrasing the unfamiliar in familiar words; yet despite the continual analogies to things European, the *new and unfamiliar* seeped through—Cabeza de Vaca's trek followed the "route of corn," as no European pilgrim before him could have done—imposing itself, forcing adjustments, intercultural accommodations, that have marked Euro-American literature from its beginnings.

From that start, also, the American Dream of success has been a dream primarily of material but also of spiritual domination. The earliest narratives combine stories of strange environments and fantastic beliefs with the potential benefits of immediate exploitation and eventual incorporation of natives into the belief systems of the traveler. The Europeans aimed at acquiring both territory for the home nation and converts for Christianity. Whether searching for the fabled lands of Marco Polo or dreaming of the Terrestrial Paradise of Eden (Columbus), envisioning the fabled Seven Cities of Cíbola (Fray Marcos, Coronado), or tracking routes taken by other, earlier explorers (Champlain), the chroniclers of exploration spoke two messages: one about their inability to decipher, encode, and thus control this strange "new" world, and another about their success in accommodating themselves to the challenge of the new environment. They compensated for their sense of powerlessness by imagining cultural superiority over the native populations they encountered, and they too often tried to prove a cultural superiority through the application of violence.

The interplay of cultural forces produced a tension of accommodation in which the European writer, while preserving a semblance of old world identity, becomes a different self. Over and over the European narrator recalls the sense of being lost in the immensity of the uncharted Americas—as when Columbus faced the strange behavior of basic tools of navigation; Cabeza de Vaca wandered at the whim of Gulf waters or Native American masters; Juan Ortiz was captured and almost put to death until saved by an indigenous woman; Laudonnière was unable to decipher a native ritual of which he somehow conceived himself the guest of honor; Coronado walked through grass lands so vast that an army left no trace of where it had passed; Champlain became lost in the American forest. Each writer sought resolution to experiences that threatened to overwhelm him, from Columbus's plan to learn the secrets of inscrutable native culture by encouraging intermarriage, to Cabeza de Vaca's willingness to perform any task the natives required of him in order to gain stature and mobility among them, to Avilés's pleas for more priests to convert the hostile tribes, to Villagrá's courtly rendering of the Acoma massacre in the best light of noble warfare, to Champlain's matter-of-fact documenting of the first French military intervention in native disputes. From the earliest narratives, dreams of overwhelming whole races and conquering cities of stupendous wealth commingle with dreams of saving souls from eternal perdition. Such aspirations reflect what can be called a multinational competition for dominance and possession, not only of particular isolated spaces but of entire peoples and ways of life.

The selections that follow trace some of the most famous (some might say infamous) European exploring expeditions in the Americas, from Columbus's intensely uncertain account of his discovery of the lands (the Caribbean) he thought the Indies, through Fray Marcos's assurances about the mythical Seven Cities of Cíbola, to Villagrá's epic poem about the Spanish conquest of a brave new world. The accounts trace major exploration patterns in North America. Cabeza de Vaca's narrative of the ill-fated plan of Pánfilo de Narváez to explore the Gulf coast (1528–1529) maps a foreign territory made more familiar by the time Hernando de Soto prepared for a journey along the coast and up the Mississippi River (1539–1543). Both Cabeza de Vaca and the Gentleman of Elvas speak of captivities among the native people and the ingenuities necessitated by life in a strange country. Although he was taken to be a faith healer, like the three other survivors of the shipwrecked Narváez party, Cabeza de Vaca had to perform menial chores, thus becoming a slave and captive. When the Moor Estévan, Cabeza de Vaca, and two others decided to head westward to find their own people, they faced a land that offered little food and less promise. And when they finally reencountered slave-seeking Spanish conquistadores, Cabeza de Vaca had lasting memories of the "kindness and good will" with which the natives had shared their food with him, memories that caused him to distrust his own race. Like that of Juan Ortiz (the Narváez expedition survivor whose recovery from the natives is reported by the Gentleman of Elvas), the life of Cabeza de Vaca provides one of our first records of the liminal experience (a middle-world experience, when one is neither here, nor there) felt by a European in this odd, new land.

With the enterprise of the Floridas and the Spanish conquest (1565–1568), we have a record of a key European battle fought in America. Seeking territories for France, René Goulaine de Laudonnière and Jean Ribault were also seeking new peoples to convert to their Huguenot faith. They were overpowered by the larger fleet and better equipment of Pedro Menéndez de Avilés, who likewise sought territory and souls, this time for Spain and the Catholic faith. Avilés's accounts of fortifications against attacks by the French and later by the Indians form a necessary refrain to his injunction to Philip II that "it is expedient that the religious who may come to these parts be truly religious; otherwise, it were better that they should not come."

"It were better that they should not come" was likely an assessment also made by the men who set out northward from Mexico in 1598 with their governor, Juan de Oñate. In their search to find the famed Seven Cities of Cíbola spoken of by Fray Marcos and to trace territory similar to that first noted by the men who followed Coronado, the men of the Oñate expedition made the desert passage across an area later called Jornada del Muerto (the Dead Man's March). The epic journey of these men was recorded in *The History of New Mexico* by Gaspar Pérez de Villagrá, a former courtier of King Philip II and a scholar with a classical education. Modeled on Virgil's *Aeneid,* Villagrá's epic poem of thirty-four cantos traces a dramatic picture of the triumphant march of the Spanish crown and the Catholic Church. His theme, that the True Faith prevailed amid combat with noble and worthy foes, derives from the high epic style of ancient times, adapted and transformed during the Renaissance into an enduring poetic genre.

At the same time that the Spanish were conquering the southern and western areas of the present-day United States, the French were exploring the eastern regions. Samuel de Champlain's journals trace his own sea and land explorations from Nova

Scotia to Cape Cod and across what became New York state. Neither a member of a large expedition group nor a missionary, Champlain's record of his journey in the wilderness of the Northeast reveals the strength and sheer determination that were necessary to make one's way in an unfriendly terrain.

A Yuchi story, "Creation of the Whites," heads these selections. Although the writings of Europeans dominate historical record, oral narratives like this Yuchi tale bespeak a sense of wonder that might have been experienced by Native Americans. Narratives like the Yuchi narrative suggest, on the part of Native Americans, the sense of wonder Shakespeare's character Miranda registers in *The Tempest* as she exclaims to her father Prospero:

> O wonder!
> How many goodly creatures are there here!
> How beauteous mankind is! O brave new world
> That has such people in't!

Carla Mulford
Pennsylvania State University

Juan Bruce-Novoa
University of California at Irvine

"Creation of the Whites" (Yuchi)

Among some of the Southeast Indians, the origin of the people is ascribed not to emergence (as in the Zuni narrative, for instance), but rather to the sun, sky, moon, sea, ashes, eggs, and plants. The Yuchis call themselves the "Offspring of the Sun." It is not surprising, then, that white people, in Yuchi narrative, are said to come from sea foam.

The Yuchis once inhabited the southern Appalachian mountains, but in the seventeenth and eighteenth centuries, they moved southward and eastward, occupying the lowlands. John Bartram described their villages in 1788 as "thriving, full of youth and young children." He estimated one village's population at 1,500. The Yuchis were removed during the historic and infamous removals in the 1830s to the new territory assigned the Creeks, west of the Mississippi. They settled in the northwest part of this territory, keeping separate from but nevertheless retaining representation in the Creek National Assembly.

A very interesting version of the following story appears among the Hitchitis, another group that originally occupied the Southeast. As told in J. R. Swanton's *Early History of the Creek Indians,* according to the Hitchitis, the whites who came to them brought whiskey: After staying a while at the ocean's shore, "people came across the water to visit them. These were the white people, and the Indians treated them hospitably, and at that time they were on very friendly terms with each other. The white people disappeared, however, and when they did so they left a keg of something which we know was whiskey. A cup was left with this, and the Indians began pouring whiskey into this cup and smelling it, all being much pleased with the odor. Some went so far as to drink a little. They became intoxicated and began to reel and stagger and butt each other with their heads. Then the white people came back and the Indians began trading peltries, etc., for things which the white people had." Stories like these suggest the variety of explanations that Native Americans created to account for the coming of whites to their lands.

Andrew O. Wiget
New Mexico State University

PRIMARY WORK

G. E. Lankford, *Native American Legends,* 1987.

SECONDARY WORKS

J. R. Swanton, *Early History of the Creek Indians,* 1922; C. Vecsey, *Imagine Ourselves Richly: Mythic Narratives of North American Indians,* 1991.

Yuchi Tale

Creation of the Whites

It was out upon the ocean. Some sea-foam formed against a big log floating there. Then a person emerged from the sea-foam and crawled out upon the log. He was seen sitting there. Another person crawled up, on the other side of the log. It was a woman. They were whites. Soon the Indians saw them, and at first thought that they were sea-gulls, and they said among themselves, "Are they not white people?" Then they made a boat and went out to look at the strangers more closely.

Later on the whites were seen in their house-boat. Then they disappeared.

In about a year they returned, and there were a great many of them. The Indians talked to them but they could not understand each other. Then the whites left.

But they came back in another year with a great many ships. They approached the Indians and asked if they could come ashore. They said, "Yes." So the whites landed, but they seemed to be afraid to walk much on the water. They went away again over the sea.

This time they were gone a shorter time; only three months passed and they came again. They had a box with them and asked the Indians for some earth to fill it. It was given to them as they desired. The first time they asked they had a square box, and when that was filled they brought a big shallow box. They filled this one too. Earth was put in them and when they were carried aboard the ship the white men planted seed in them and many things were raised. After they had taken away the shallow box, the whites came back and told the Indians that their land was very strong and fertile. So they asked the Indians to give them a portion of it that they might live on it. The Indians agreed to do it, the whites came to the shore, and they have lived there ever since.

1987

Christopher Columbus 1451–1506

Columbus made four voyages to the Americas, convinced that he had discovered the Indies and then the "Terrestrial Paradise" (the Garden of Eden). On his first journey, he arrived at (October 12, 1492) and named for Spain the island of San Salvador, then proceeded to "discover" the Bahamas, Cuba, and Hispaniola (Haiti). He recorded notes about this voyage in a journal now lost but abstracted at that time by Bartolomé de Las Casas. Columbus's second journey, in September of 1493, took him to Puerto Rico, Jamaica, parts of Cuba, the Virgin Islands, and the Lesser Antilles, but the exploration was yet another unsuccessful attempt to find silver and gold and fabled cities. A record made by Michele de Cuneo is the only source of information about this second voyage. Two later voyages proved equally unsuccessful, although Columbus located Trinidad and the Spanish Main, and landed on the continent of South America.

Until his death, Columbus continued to think he had discovered the Indies and had only to get around the next mountain and over the next river to find the fabled cities of silver and gold made so inviting by the words of Marco Polo. When discovery after discovery did not yield his heart's desire, he established for himself the theory that he had indeed discovered the Garden of Eden.

On the third voyage, a problem with the navigation equipment led him to muse on the *imago mundi* of his European contemporaries. In turn, this led him to claim to have discovered the original location of the biblical paradise, a logical conclusion of his rhetorical argument based on what passed for scientific knowledge and religious "truth" in Europe. We glimpse an epiphany in the Old World-New World dialogue in which the latter's phenomena forces a readjustment in the former's traditional assumptions. The result is a discourse no longer European, yet certainly not native to the Europeans' New World; it could be called an American intercultural, synthetic text.

During his last voyage, Columbus, alone, ill, and lost in a cove off Jamaica, dreamed of Cathay and voices from heaven. He returned to Spain, disillusioned and unhappy.

The accounts that follow are from the first and third voyages, largely in the words of Bartolomé de Las Casas, although we begin with a quotation from Columbus.

Carla Mulford
Pennsylvania State University

Juan Bruce-Novoa
University of California at Irvine

PRIMARY WORKS

Journal of the First Voyage to America by Christopher Columbus, 1825 (first voyage); J. M. Cohen, ed. and trans., *The Four Voyages of Columbus,* 1969 (third voyage).

SECONDARY WORKS

Bartolomé de Las Casas, *History of the Indies* (written 1550–63), 1875; S. E. Morison, *Admiral of the Ocean Sea,* 1942; S. E. Morison, *Journals and Other Documents of the Life and Voyages of Christopher Columbus,* 1963.

from Journal of the First Voyage to America, 1492–1493

Sunday, Oct. 21st [1492]. At 10 o'clock, we arrived at a cape of the island, and anchored, the other vessels in company. After having dispatched a meal, I went ashore, and found no habitation save a single house, and that without an occupant; we had no doubt that the people had fled in terror at our approach, as the house was completely furnished. I suffered nothing to be touched, and went with my captains and some of the crew to view the country. This island even exceeds the others in beauty and fertility. Groves of lofty and flourishing trees are abundant, as also large lakes, surrounded and overhung by the foliage, in a most enchanting manner. Everything looked as green as in April in Andalusia. The melody of the birds was so exquisite that one was never willing to part from the spot, and the flocks of parrots obscured the heavens. The diversity in the appearance of the feathered tribe from those of our country is extremely curious. A thousand different sorts of trees, with their fruit were to be met with, and of a wonderfully delicious odour. It was a great affliction to me to be ignorant of their natures, for I am very certain they are all valuable; specimens of them and of the plants I have preserved. Going round one of these lakes, I saw a snake, which we killed, and I have kept the skin for your Highnesses; upon being discovered he took to the water, whither we followed him, as it was not deep, and dispatched him with our lances; he was seven spans in length; I think there are many more such about here. I discovered also the aloe tree, and am determined to take on board the ship to-morrow, ten quintals of it, as I am told it is valuable. While we were in search of some good water, we came upon a village of the natives about half a league from the place where the ships lay; the inhabitants on discovering us abandoned their houses, and took to flight, carrying off their goods to the mountain. I ordered that nothing which they had left should be taken, not even the value of a pin. Presently we saw several of the natives advancing towards our party, and one of them came up to us, to whom we gave some hawk's bells and glass beads, with which he was delighted. We asked him in return, for water, and after I had gone on board the ship, the natives came down to the shore with their calabashes full, and showed great pleasure in presenting us with it. I ordered more glass beads to be given them, and they promised to return the next day. It is my wish to fill all the water casks of the ships at this place, which being executed, I shall depart immediately, if the weather serve, and sail round the island, till I succeed in meeting with the king, in order to see if I can acquire any of the gold, which I hear he possesses. Afterwards I shall set sail for another very large island which I believe to be *Cipango,* according to the indications I receive from the Indians on board. They call the Island *Colba,*[1] and say there are many large ships, and sailors there. This other island they name *Bosio,* and inform me that it is very large; the others which lie in our course, I shall examine on the passage, and according as I find gold or spices in abundance, I shall determine what to do; at all events I am determined to proceed on to the continent, and visit the city of *Guisay*[2] where I shall deliver the letters of your Highnesses to the *Great Can,* and demand an answer, with which I shall return.

Monday, Oct. 22d. Through the night, and today we remained waiting here to see if the king, or any others would bring us gold or anything valuable. Many of the natives visited us, resembling those of the other islands, naked like them, and painted white, red, black and other colours; they brought javelins and clews of cotton to barter, which they exchanged with the sailors for bits of glass, broken cups, and fragments of earthenware. Some of them wore pieces of gold at their noses; they readily

[1]Cuba.
[2]*Guisay,* or *Quensay, the city of Heaven,* and residence of the Great Khan, according to Marco Polo.

gave them away for hawk's bells and glass beads; the amount collected in this manner, however, was very inconsiderable. Any small matter they received from us, they held in high estimation, believing us to have come from heaven. We took in water for the ships from a lake in the neighbourhood of this cape, which I have named *Cabo del Isleo:* in this lake Martin Alonzo Pinzon, captain of the Pinta, killed a snake similar to that of yesterday, seven spans long. I ordered as much of the aloe to be collected as could be found.

Tuesday, Oct. 23d. It is now my determination to depart for the island of *Cuba,* which I believe to be *Cipango,* from the accounts I have received here, of the multitude and riches of the people. I have abandoned the intention of staying here and sailing round the island in search of the king, as it would be a waste of time, and I perceive there are no gold mines to be found. Moreover it would be necessary to steer many courses in making the circuit, and we cannot expect the wind to be always favourable. And as we are going to places where there is great commerce, I judge it expedient not to linger on the way, but to proceed and survey the lands we met with, till we arrive at that most favourable for our enterprise. It is my opinion that we shall find much profit there in spices; but my want of knowledge in these articles occasions me the most excessive regrets, inasmuch as I see a thousand sorts of trees, each with its own species of fruit, and as flourishing at the present time, as the fields in Spain, during the months of May and June; likewise a thousand kinds of herbs and flowers, of all which I remain in ignorance as to their properties, with the exception of the aloe, which I have directed to-day to be taken on board in large quantities for the use of your Highnesses. I did not set sail to-day for want of wind, a dead calm and heavy rain prevailing. Yesterday it rained much without cold; the days here are hot, and the nights mild like May in Andalusia.

Wednesday, Oct. 24th. At midnight weighed anchor and set sail from *Cabo del Isleo* of the island of *Isabela,* being in the North part, where I had remained preparing to depart for the island of *Cuba,* in which place the Indians tell me I shall find a great trade, with abundance of gold and spices, and large ships, and merchants; they directed me to steer toward the W.S.W., which is the course I am pursuing. If the accounts which the natives of the islands and those on board the ships have communicated to me by signs (for their language I do not understand) may be relied on, this must be the island of *Cipango,* of which we have heard so many wonderful things; according to my geographical knowledge it must be somewhere in this neighbourhood. . . .[3]

The Indians on board told them that the island of *Cuba* was distant from thence a voyage of a day and a half in their canoes, which are small things, made of a log, and carrying no sail. Departed for *Cuba,* which from the Indians signifying to them the abundance of gold and pearls there, as well as the magnitude of the island, they doubted not, was Cipango.[4]

[3]Here the words of Columbus cease for the present, and the narrative continues in the language of Bartolomé de Las Casas.

[4]The belief that Cipango was a part of the newly discovered country continued for some time. In a letter written by Columbus to the Pope in 1502, describing his voyage, he introduces the following remark.—"This island is Tarsis, Cethia, Ophir, Ophaz and Cipango, we h named it Española."

Sunday, Oct. 28th. Continued on S.S.W., in quest of the island of *Cuba,* keeping close to the shore. They entered a fine river, free from shallows and all other obstructions, which in fact is the case with all the coast here, the shore being very bold. The mouth of the river had a depth of water of twelve fathoms, and a breadth sufficient for ships to beat in. They anchored within the river, and the Admiral states that the prospect here exceeded in beauty anything he ever saw, the river being surrounded with trees of the most beautiful and luxuriant foliage of a singular appearance, and covered with flowers and fruits of all sorts. Birds were here in abundance singing most delightfully. Great numbers of palm trees were noticed, different from those of Guinea, and ours, wanting their particular manner of bark; they were of a moderate height, and bore very large leaves, which the natives use for coverings to their houses. The land appeared quite level. The Admiral went ashore in the boat, and found two dwellings, which he supposed to be those of fishermen, and that the owners had fled; he found in one of them a dog unable to bark. Both houses contained nets of palm, lines, horn fish-hooks, harpoons of bone, and other implements for fishing, as also many fire-places, and each seemed to be adapted to the reception of a large number of persons. The Admiral gave orders that nothing should be touched, which directions were adhered to. The grass was as high as it is in Andalusia in April and May, and they found purslain and strawberry-blite in abundance. They returned on board the boat and ascended the river some distance, where the Admiral says it was exceedingly pleasant to behold the delightful verdure and foliage which presented itself, not to mention the birds in the neighbourhood; the whole offered a scene of such enchantment that it was hardly possible to part from it. He declares this to be the most beautiful island ever seen, abounding in good harbours, and deep rivers, with a shore upon which it appears that the sea never breaks high, as the grass grows down to the water's edge, a thing which never happens where the sea is rough. Indeed a high sea they had not as yet experienced among these islands. This isle, he says, is full of pleasant mountains, which are lofty, although not of great extent, the rest of the country is high, after the manner of Sicily, abounding in streams, as they understood from the Indians of *Guanahani,* which were on board the ships, who informed them by signs that it contained ten large rivers, and was of such a size that with their canoes they could not sail round it in twenty days. When the ships were sailing towards the island, some of the natives put off from the shore in two canoes, and perceiving the Spaniards entering into the boat and rowing towards the mouth of the river to sound for an anchorage, they took to flight. The Indians told them there were mines of gold here and pearls, and the Admiral observed muscles and other indications of these articles in the neighbourhood. They further informed him that there came large ships hither from the *Great Can,* and that the main land was distant ten days' voyage. The Admiral named this river and port *San Salvador. . . .*[5]

Thursday, Nov. 1st. At sunrise the Admiral sent the boats to land to visit the houses they saw there; they found the inhabitants all fled, but after some time they espied a man; the Admiral then dispatched one of his Indians on shore, who called out to him from a distance and bade him not be fearful, as the Spaniards were a friendly people, not injuring anyone, nor belonging to the *Great Can,* but on the con-

[5]The Bay of Nipé in the eastern part of Cuba.

trary, had made many presents of their goods among the inhabitants of the islands. The natives having ascertained that no ill was intended them, gathered confidence, and came in above sixteen canoes to the ships, bringing cotton yarn and other things, which the Admiral ordered should not be taken from them, as he wished them to understand that he was in search of nothing but gold, which they call *nucay.* All day the canoes kept passing between the ships and the shore. The Admiral saw no gold among them, but remarks having observed an Indian with a bit of wrought silver at his nostrils, which he conceived to be an indication of the existence of that metal in the country. The Indians informed them by signs that within three days there would come many traders from the interior to purchase the goods of the Spaniards, to whom they would communicate news of the king, who as far as could be learned from the signs of the natives, was about four days' journey distant. They informed the Spaniards also that many persons had been dispatched to inform the king respecting the Admiral. These people were found to be of the same race and manners with those already observed, without any religion that could be discovered; they had never remarked the Indians whom they kept on board the ships to be engaged in any sort of devotion of their own, but they would, upon being directed, make the sign of the cross, and repeat the *Salve* and *Ave Maria* with the hands extended towards heaven. The language is the same throughout these islands, and the people friends to one another, which the Admiral says he believes to be the case in all the neighbouring parts, and that they are at war with the *Great Can,* whom they call *Cavila,* and his country *Bafan.* These people go naked like the rest. The river here he describes as deep, and having a bold shore at the mouth, where ships may lay close to the land; the water of the river salt for a league upwards when it becomes very fresh. It is certain, says the Admiral, that this is the continent, and that we are in the neighbourhood of *Zayto* and *Guinsay,*[6] a hundred leagues more or less distant from the one or the other. . . .

Sunday, Nov. 4th. Early in the morning the Admiral went on shore in the boat to shoot birds, and at his return, Martin Alonzo Pinzon came to him with two pieces of cinnamon, saying that a Portuguese on board his vessel had seen an Indian with two large handfuls of it, but was afraid to purchase it on account of the prohibition of the Admiral, and furthermore that the Indian had some reddish things resembling nutmegs. The boatswain of the Pinta declared he had seen cinnamon trees. The Admiral went to the place but found none. He showed some of the natives pepper and cinnamon which he had brought from Castile, they recognized it as he declares, and intimated to him by signs that much of it was to be found not far from thence to the southeast. He likewise showed them gold and pearls, and was informed by some old men that these existed in great abundance in a place which they called *Bohio,*[7] being worn by the people at their necks, ears, arms and legs. They had, according to the same account, large ships, and carried on traffic, and this was all at the southeast. They further informed him that at a distance there were men with one eye only, and others with faces like dogs, who were man-eaters, and accustomed upon taking a

[6]Columbus was convinced that he had arrived at the continent of India.

[7]*Bohio,* according to Las Casas, was the name the Indians gave to their houses. The Indians may have intended to signify by this name the island of Española which the inhabitants called *Hayti.*

prisoner, to cut his throat, drink his blood, and dismember him. The Admiral then determined to return to his ship and wait for the men whom he had sent into the country, when he was resolved to depart in quest of the regions which had been described to him, unless he should receive such accounts from the interior as would induce him to stay. He says "these people are very mild and timorous, naked as I have described the others, without weapons or laws. The soil is very fertile abounding with *mames,*[8] a root like a carrot, with a taste of chestnuts; beans likewise are here, very dissimilar to ours, also cotton, growing spontaneously among the mountains; I am of opinion that this is gathered at all seasons of the year, as I observed upon a single tree blossoms, pods unripe, and others burst open. A thousand other productions, which are doubtless of great value, I remarked, but find it impossible to describe them. . . ."

Tuesday, Nov. 6th. Last night, says the Admiral, the two men whom I had sent into the country returned, and related as follows. After having travelled a dozen leagues they came to a town containing about fifty houses, where there were probably a thousand inhabitants, every house containing a great number; they were built in the manner of large tents. The inhabitants received them after their fashion with great ceremony; the men and women flocked to behold them, and they were lodged in their best houses. They signified their admiration and reverence of the strangers by touching them, kissing their hands and feet, and making signs of wonder. They imagined them come from heaven, and signified as much to them. They were feasted with such food as the natives had to offer. Upon their arrival at the town they were led by the arms of the principal men of the place, to the chief dwelling, here they gave them seats, and the Indians sat upon the ground in a circle round them. The Indians who accompanied the Spaniards explained to the natives the manner in which their new guests lived, and gave a favourable account of their character. The men then left the place, and the women entered, and seated themselves around them in the same manner, kissing their hands and feet, and examining whether they were flesh and bone like themselves. They entreated them to remain there as long as five days. The Spaniards showed them the cinnamon, pepper and other spices which they had received from the Admiral, and they informed them by signs that there was much of these in the neighbourhood at the southeast, but they knew not of any in this place. The Spaniards not discovering any great number of towns here, resolved to return to the ships, and had they chosen to admit the natives to accompany them, might have been attended back by more than five hundred men and women, who were eager to bear them company, thinking they were returning to heaven. They took none along with them but one of the principal inhabitants with his son; with these the Admiral held some conversation, and showed them great civilities; the Indian described to him by signs many countries and islands in these parts, and the Admiral thought to carry him home to Spain, but says he was unable to find whether the Indian was willing. At night he seemed to grow fearful, and wished to go on shore; the Admiral says that having the ship aground he thought it not advisable to oppose him, and so let him return, requesting him to come back the next morning, but they saw him no more. The Spaniards upon their journey met with great multitudes of people, men

[8]Probably sweet potatoes.

and women with firebrands in their hands and herbs to smoke after their custom.[9] No village was seen upon the road of a larger size than five houses, but all the inhabitants showed them the same respect. Many sorts of trees were observed, and herbs and odoriferous flowers. Great numbers of birds they remarked, all different from those of Spain except the nightingales, who entertained them with their songs, and the partridges and geese, which were found in abundance. Of quadrupeds they described none except dumb dogs. The soil appeared fertile and under good cultivation, producing the *mames* aforementioned and beans very dissimilar to ours, as well as the grain called panic-grass. They saw vast quantities of cotton, spun and manufactured, a single house contained above five hundred *arrobas,*[10] four thousand quintals might be collected here per annum. The Admiral says it appears to him that they do not sow it, but that it is productive the whole year round; it is very fine with an exceeding long staple. Everything which the Indians possessed they were ready to barter at a very low price; a large basket of cotton they would give for a leather thong, or other trifling thing which was offered them. They are an inoffensive, unwarlike people, naked, except that the women wear a very slight covering at the loins; their manners are very decent, and their complexion not very dark, but lighter than that of the inhabitants of the Canary Islands. "I have no doubt, most serene Princes," says the Admiral, "that were proper devout and religious persons to come among them and learn their language, it would be an easy matter to convert them all to Christianity, and I hope in our Lord that your Highnesses will devote yourselves with much diligence to this object, and bring into the church so many multitudes, inasmuch as you have exterminated those who refused to confess the Father, Son and Holy Ghost, so that having ended your days (as we are all mortal) you may leave your dominions in a tranquil condition, free from heresy and wickedness, and meet with a favourable reception before the eternal Creator, whom may it please to grant you a long life and great increase of kingdoms and dominions, with the will and disposition to promote, as you always have done, the holy Christian religion, Amen.

"This day I launched the ship, and made ready to depart in the name of God, next Thursday, for the S.E. in quest of gold and spices, as well as to discover the country." These are the words of the Admiral, who expected to sail on Thursday, but the wind being contrary, detained him till the twelfth day of November.

Monday, Nov. 12th. They sailed from the port and river *de Mares* at daybreak: they directed their course in search of an island which the Indians on board affirmed repeatedly was called *Babeque,*[11] where as they related by signs, the inhabitants

[9]Las Casas in his General History of the Indies gives the following relation of this circumstance: "The two Spaniards met upon their journey great numbers of people of both sexes; the men always with a firebra in their hands and certain herbs for smoking: these are dry, and fixed in a leaf also dry, after the manner of those paper tubes which the boys in Spain use at Whitsuntide: having lighted one end they draw the smoke by sucking at the other, this causes a drowsiness and sort of intoxication, and according to their accounts relieves them from the sensation of fatigue. These tubes they call by the name of *tabacos.* I knew many Spaniards in the island of Española who were addicted to the use of them, and on being reproached with it as a bad habit, replied that they could not bring themselves to give it up. I do not see what relish or benefit they could find in them." Here we see the origin of *cigars.*

[10]An arroba is twenty-five pounds.

[11]This name was given by the natives, to the coast of Tierra Firme, which they also called *Bohio* and *Caritaba.*—Las Casas.

collected gold at night by torchlight upon the shore, and afterwards hammered it into bars. In order to reach this island they directed to steer East by South. Having sailed eight leagues along the coast, they discovered a river, and four leagues further onward, another, very large, exceeding in size all which they had seen. The Admiral was unwilling to remain, and put into either of them, for two reasons, the first and principal one, because the wind and weather were favourable to proceed to the above-mentioned island of *Babeque;* the other was, that were there any large towns near the sea, they might easily be discovered, but in case they were far up the rivers, they could only be reached by ascending the stream in small vessels, which those of his fleet were not. A desire, therefore, not to waste time determined him not to explore these rivers, the last of which was surrounded with a well-peopled country; he named it *Rio del Sol.*[12] He states that the Sunday previous he had thought it would be well to take a few of the natives from the place where the ships lay for the purpose of carrying them to Spain, that they might acquire our language, and inform us what their country contained, besides becoming Christians and serving us at their return as interpreters, "for I have observed," says he, "that these people have no religion, neither are they idolaters, but are a very gentle race, without the knowledge of any iniquity; they neither kill, nor steal, nor carry weapons, and are so timid that one of our men might put a hundred of them to flight, although they will readily sport and play tricks with them. They have a knowledge that there is a God above, and are firmly persuaded that we have come from heaven. They very quickly learn such prayers as we repeat to them, and also to make the sign of the cross. Your Highnesses should therefore adopt the resolution of converting them to Christianity, in which enterprise I am of opinion that a very short space of time would suffice to gain to our holy faith multitudes of people, and to Spain great riches and immense dominions, with all their inhabitants; there being, without doubt, in these countries vast quantities of gold, for the Indians would not without cause give us such descriptions of places where the inhabitants dug it from the earth, and wore it in massy bracelets at their necks, ears, legs, and arms. Here are also pearls and precious stones, and an infinite amount of spices. In the river *de Mares,* which I left last evening, there is undoubtedly a great deal of mastick, and the quantity might be increased, for the trees transplanted easily take root; they are of a lofty size, bearing leaves and fruit like the lentisk; the tree, however, is taller and has a larger leaf than the lentisk, as is mentioned by Pliny, and as I have myself observed in the island of Scio in the Archipelago. I ordered many of these trees to be tapped in order to extract the resin, but as the weather was rainy all the time I was in the river, I was unable to procure more than a very small portion, which I have preserved for your Highnesses. It is possible also that this is not the proper season for collecting it, which, it is likely, may be in the spring, when they begin to put forth their blossoms; at present the fruit upon them is nearly ripe. Great quantities of cotton might be raised here, and sold, as I think, profitably, without being carried to Spain, but to the cities of the *Great Can,* which we shall doubtless discover, as well as many others belonging to other sovereigns; these may become a source of profit to your Highnesses by trading thither with the productions of Spain and the other European countries. Here also is to be found abundance of aloe, which, however, is not a thing of very great value, but the mastick

[12]Puerto del Padre.

assuredly is, being met with nowhere else except in the before-mentioned island of Scio, where, if I remember rightly, it is produced to the amount of fifty thousand ducats' value in a year. The mouth of this river forms the best harbour I have yet seen, being wide, deep and free from shoals, with a fine situation for a town and fortification where ships may lie close along the shore, the land high, with a good air and fine streams of water. Yesterday a canoe came to the ship with six young men; five of them came on board, whom I ordered to be detained, and have them with me; I then sent ashore to one of the houses, and took seven women and three children: this I did that the Indians might tolerate their captivity better with their company, for it has often happened that the Portuguese have carried the natives from Guinea to Portugal for the purpose of learning their language, and when this was done and they returned with them to Guinea, expecting by reason of the good treatment they had showed them, and the presents they had given them, to find great benefit in their use, they have gone among their own people and never appeared more. Others have done differently, and by keeping their wives, have assured themselves of their possession. Besides, these women will be a great help to us in acquiring their language, which is the same throughout all these countries, the inhabitants keeping up a communication among the islands by means of their canoes. This is not the case in Guinea, where there are a thousand different dialects, one tribe not understanding another. This evening came on board the husband of one of the women and father of the three children, which were a boy and two girls; he intreated me to let him accompany them, which I very willingly granted; the natives whom I had taken from here were all so delighted at this as to induce me to think them his relations. He is a person of about forty-five years of age." All this is in the exact words of the Admiral; he also says that he found the weather somewhat cold, and being in the winter, thought it not advisable to prosecute his discoveries any farther towards the north. . .[13]

1825

from Narrative of the Third Voyage, 1498–1500

Each time I sailed from Spain to the Indies I found that when I reached a point a hundred leagues west of the Azores, the heavens, the stars, the temperature of the air and the waters of the sea abruptly changed. I very carefully verified these observations, and found that, on passing this line from north to south, the compass needle, which had previously pointed north-east, turned a whole quarter of the wind to the north-west. It was as if the seas sloped upwards on this line. I also observed that here they were full of a vegetation like pine branches loaded with fruit similar to that of the mastic. This weed is so dense that on my first voyage I thought we had reached shallows, and that the ships might run aground. We had not seen a single strand of weed before we came to that line. I noticed that when we had passed it the sea was

[13]From what he here relates, it appears that had he proceeded northerly he would undoubtedly, in two days, have discovered Florida.—Las Casas.

calm and smooth, never becoming rough even in a strong wind. I found also that westwards of this line the temperature of the air was very mild and did not change from winter to summer. Here the Pole Star describes a circle of five degrees in diameter, and when it is at its lowest the Guards[1] point towards the right. It then rises continuously until they point to the left. It then stands at five degrees, and from there it sinks until they are again on the right.[2]

On this present voyage I sailed from Spain to Madeira, from Madeira to the Canaries, and then to the Cape Verde Islands. From here, as I have already said, I followed a southward course in order to cross the Equator. On reaching a point exactly on the parallel which passes through Sierra Leone in Guinea, I found such heat and such strength in the sun's rays that I was afraid I might be burnt. Although it rained and the sky was overcast, I remained in a state of exhaustion until the Lord gave me a fair wind and the desire to sail westwards, encouraged by the thought that, on reaching the line of which I have spoken, I should find a change in temperature. On coming to this line I immediately found very mild temperatures which became even milder as I sailed on. But I found no corresponding change in the stars. At nightfall the Pole Star stood at five degrees, with the Guards pointing straight overhead, and later, at midnight, it had risen to ten degrees, and at daybreak stood at fifteen degrees, with the Guards pointing downwards. I found the sea as smooth as before, but not the same vegetation. I was greatly surprised by this behaviour of the Pole Star and spent many nights making careful observations with the quadrant, but found that the plumb line always fell to the same point. I regard this as a new discovery, and it may be established that here the heavens undergo a great change in a brief space.

I have always read that the world of land and sea is spherical. All authorities and the recorded experiments of Ptolemy and the rest, based on the eclipses of the moon and other observations made from east to west, and on the height of the Pole Star made from north to south, have constantly drawn and confirmed this picture, which they held to be true. Now, as I said, I have found such great irregularities that I have come to the following conclusions concerning the world: that it is not round as they describe it, but the shape of a pear, which is round everywhere except at the stalk, where it juts out a long way; or that it is like a round ball, on part of which is something like a woman's nipple. This point on which the protuberance stands is the highest and nearest to the sky. It lies below the Equator, and in this ocean, at the farthest point of the east, I mean by the farthest point of the east the place where all land and islands end. . . .

Ptolemy and the other geographers believed that the world was spherical and that the other hemisphere was as round as the one in which they lived, its centre lying on the island of Arin, which is below the Equator between the Arabian and Persian gulfs; and that the boundary passes over Cape St Vincent in Portugal to the west, and eastward to China and the *Seres*.[3] I do not in the least question the roundness of

[1]The pointers.

[2]Conventional sailing manuals had the Pole Star describe a seven-degree diameter, indicat ing that the Pole Star was lowest when the pointers stood between the right arm and the head.

[3]This was the Romans' name for the Chinese, of whom they knew nothing except that they produced the silk which arrived along the caravan trails.

that hemisphere, but I affirm that the other hemisphere resembles the half of a round pear with a raised stalk, as I have said, like a woman's nipple on a round ball. Neither Ptolemy nor any of the other geographers had knowledge of this other hemisphere, which was completely unknown, but based their reasoning on the hemisphere in which they lived, which is a round sphere, as I have said.

Now that your Highnesses have commanded navigation, exploration and discovery, the nature of this other hemisphere is clearly revealed. For on this voyage I was twenty degrees north of the Equator in the latitude of Hargin[4] and the African mainland, where the people are black and the land very parched. I then went to the Cape Verde Islands, whose inhabitants are blacker still, and the farther south I went the greater the extremes. In the latitude in which I was, which is that of Sierra Leone, where the Pole Star stood at five degrees at nightfall, the people are completely black, and when I sailed westwards from there the heats remained excessive. On passing the line of which I have spoken, I found the temperatures growing milder, so that when I came to the island of Trinidad, where the Pole Star also stands at five degrees at nightfall, both there and on the mainland opposite the temperatures were extremely mild. The land and the trees were very green and as lovely as the orchards of Valencia in April, and the inhabitants were lightly built and fairer than most of the other people we had seen in the Indies. Their hair was long and straight and they were quicker, more intelligent and less cowardly. The sun was in Virgo above their heads and ours. All this is attributable to the very mild climate in those regions, and this in its turn to the fact that this land stands highest on the world's surface, being nearest to the sky, as I have said. This confirms my belief that the world has this variation of shape which I have described, and which lies in this hemisphere that contains the Indies and the Ocean Sea, and stretches below the Equator. This argument is greatly supported by the fact that the sun, when Our Lord made it, was at the first point of the east; in other words the first light was here in the east, where the world stands at its highest. Although Aristotle believed that the Antarctic Pole, or the land beneath it, is the highest part of the world and nearest to the sky, other philosophers contest it, saying that the land beneath the Arctic Pole is the highest. This argument shows that they knew one part of the world to be higher and nearer to the sky than the rest. It did not strike them however that, for the reasons of shape that I have set down, this part might lie below the Equator. And no wonder, since they had no certain information about this other hemisphere, only vague knowledge based on deduction. No one had ever entered it or gone in search of it until now when your Highnesses commanded me to explore and discover these seas and lands. . . .

Holy Scripture testifies that Our Lord made the earthly Paradise in which he placed the Tree of Life. From it there flowed four main rivers: the Ganges in India, the Tigris and the Euphrates in Asia, which cut through a mountain range and form Mesopotamia and flow into Persia, and the Nile, which rises in Ethiopia and flows into the sea at Alexandria.

I do not find and have never found any Greek or Latin writings which definitely state the worldly situation of the earthly Paradise, nor have I seen any world map which establishes its position except by deduction. Some place it at the source of the Nile in Ethiopia. But many people have travelled in these lands and found nothing

[4]Arguin, an island off the west coast of Africa.

in the climate or altitude to confirm this theory, or to prove that the waters of the Flood which covered, etc., etc. . . . reached there. Some heathens tried to show by argument that it was in the Fortunate Islands (which are the Canaries); and St Isidore, Bede, Strabo, the Master of Scholastic History,[5] St Ambrose and Scotus and all learned theologians agree that the earthly Paradise is in the East, etc.

I have already told what I have learnt about this hemisphere and its shape, and I believe that, if I pass below the Equator, on reaching these higher regions I shall find a much cooler climate and a greater difference in the stars and waters. Not that I believe it possible to sail to the extreme summit or that it is covered by water, or that it is even possible to go there. For I believe that the earthly Paradise lies here, which no one can enter except by God's leave. I believe that this land which your Highnesses have commanded me to discover is very great, and that there are many other lands in the south of which there have never been reports. I do not hold that the earthly Paradise has the form of a rugged mountain, as it is shown in pictures, but that it lies at the summit of what I have described as the stalk of a pear, and that by gradually approaching it one begins, while still at a great distance, to climb towards it. As I have said, I do not believe that anyone can ascend to the top. I do believe, however, that, distant though it is, these waters may flow from there to this place which I have reached, and form this lake. All this provides great evidence of the earthly Paradise, because the situation agrees with the beliefs of those holy and wise theologians and all the signs strongly accord with this idea.[6] For I have never read or heard of such a quantity of fresh water flowing so close to the salt and flowing into it, and the very temperate climate provides a further confirmation. If this river does not flow out of the earthly Paradise, the marvel is still greater. For I do not believe that there is so great and deep a river anywhere in the world.

1969

Alvar Nuñez Cabeza de Vaca 1490?–1556?

Cabeza de Vaca, a promising young noble, was assigned by Emperor Carlos V as the crown's treasurer to the Pánfilo de Narváez expedition chartered to explore the Gulf coast in 1528. Narváez, who had lost out to Cortés in a power struggle during the conquest of Mexico, was attempting to stake out his own area to exploit. Cabeza de Vaca's official charge was to protect the Emperor's investment, assure compliance with Spanish law, and keep separate books both on expenditures and on everything seen, found, or done. His encyclopedic task of textual absorption reflected well the self-assurance of the Spanish conquistadors, especially after the

[5]Petrus Comestor, author of *Historia Scolastica.*

[6]In Book I of his *Historia de las Indias,* Las Casas refutes this theory on the grounds of Columbus's lack of grounding in Holy Scripture, ancient history, and the teaching of the Holy Fathers and secular writers. He excuses what he considers to be Columbus's poor choice of language and lack of simile by mentioning his humble origins and foreign birth.

incredibly successful experience in Mexico. Yet it also placed on Cabeza de Vaca an enormous responsibility for the fate of the project. When the high expectations floundered in the inhospitable vastness of North America, the result was a chronicle of self-justification under the onus of failure.

Of the hundreds of men Narváez disembarked in Florida, only four survived after seven years. The troops had floated on improvised rafts from Florida to Texas, having lost contact with Narváez somewhere off the mouth of the Mississippi when, as Cabeza de Vaca depicted it, the governor had abandoned them to their fate in order to save himself. Shipwrecked and reduced to a handful of men, they were enslaved by Indians and held for a number of years, during which many died. Cabeza de Vaca and three companions survived by acculturating to the point where they were allowed to move freely among the tribes. They commenced a trek in search of Spanish settlements that led them through the present-day Southwest into northwestern Mexico. Upon his return to Spain, Cabeza de Vaca, faced with the failure of his mission, wrote his memoirs to justify himself and his new petition for the continued support of the Crown.

Failure made it impossible to utilize the discourse of conquest, so Cabeza de Vaca had to reformulate his experience into some alternative code of value. He chose the medieval genre of hagiography, the life of a saint. Thus, his texts became a Christian conversion tale, the first in the U.S. tradition, in which the undeniable losses suffered are interpreted as part of God's plan to reform a chosen representative on earth. The author recounts having been stripped of all signs of European civilization—clothes, status, social context, everything on which his identity was founded—except his faith. As a captive—also the first in the U.S. tradition—he is forced to become a religious practitioner, a healer of the sick with nothing but the word of God, creating a syncretic religious practice from Native American customs and Catholic prayers. His failure thus is repackaged as a spiritual success, a working out of a divine plan; the fact of his survival is translated into the proof of his religious merit; his intimate knowledge of Native American ways, the basis for a petition for a new appointment in the Americas. He received a commission as governor of Paraguay.

Cabeza de Vaca's tale is hagiography, captivity narrative, and immigrant tale. As an immigrant, Cabeza de Vaca voyaged with high expectations and, like many an immigrant after him, arrived to find less than hospitable natives organized into a society not fully comprehensible. He forged a new identity based on improvised service. He learned a new language, deciphered the code of social interaction, worked hard at whatever he was permitted to do, and then exploited all opportunities. All through it, the immigrant's dream was to return to the homeland. However, having acculturated to survive, Cabeza de Vaca was no longer the Spaniard who set out on the voyage, but a hybrid New World man, a state he acknowledged upon finally meeting up with fellow Europeans.

Cabeza de Vaca's is the New World, mestizo voice speaking for the first time from what is now the U.S. literary tradition. His text both narrates and incarnates the process of becoming something new we now call American.

Juan Bruce-Novoa
University of California at Irvine

PRIMARY WORK

Relation of Alvar Nuñez Cabeza de Vaca, trans. Buckingham Smith, 1871; rpt. 1966. (First published in Seville in 1542.)

SECONDARY WORKS

Frederick W. Turner, *Beyond Geography: The Western Spirit Against the Wilderness,* 1980; Tzvetan Todorov, *The Conquest of America: The Question of the Other,* 1984; Nartín A. Favata and José B. Fernández, "Introduction" to *The Account: Alvar Nunez Cabeza de Vaca's Relacion,* 1993; Juan Bruce-Novoa, "Shipwrecked in the Seas of Signification," *Reconstructing Our Past,* ed., Maria Herrera-Sobek, 1993.

from Relation of Alvar Nuñez Cabeza de Vaca

from Chapter VII
The Character of the Country[1]

The country where we came on shore to this town and region of Apalachen, is for the most part level, the ground of sand and stiff earth. Throughout are immense trees and open woods, in which are walnut, laurel and another tree called liquidamber, cedars, savins, evergreen oaks, pines, red-oaks and palmitos like those of Spain. There are many lakes, great and small, over every part of it; some troublesome of fording, on account of depth and the great number of trees lying throughout them. Their beds are sand. The lakes in the country of Apalachen are much larger than those we found before coming there.

In this Province are many maize fields; and the houses are scattered as are those of the Gelves. There are deer of three kinds, rabbits, hares, bears, lions and other wild beasts. Among them we saw an animal with a pocket on its belly, in which it carries its young until they know how to seek food; and if it happen that they should be out feeding and any one come near, the mother will not run until she has gathered them in together. The country is very cold. It has fine pastures for herds. Birds are of various kinds. Geese in great numbers. Ducks, mallards, royal-ducks, fly-catchers, night-herons and partridges abound. We saw many falcons, gerfalcons, sparrow-hawks, merlins, and numerous other fowl.

Two hours after our arrival at Apalachen, the Indians who had fled from there came in peace to us, asking for their women and children, whom we released; but the detention of a cacique by the Governor produced great excitement, in consequence of which they returned for battle early the next day [June 26], and attacked us with such promptness and alacrity that they succeeded in setting fire to the houses in which we were. As we sallied they fled to the lakes near by, because of which and the large maize fields, we could do them no injury, save in the single instance of one Indian, whom we killed. The day following, others came against us from a town on the opposite side of the lake, and attacked us as the first had done, escaping in the same way, except one who was also slain.

[1]We pick up Cabeza de Vaca's journey in June, 1528, in northern Florida.

We were in the town twenty-five days [July 19], in which time we made three incursions, and found the country very thinly peopled and difficult to travel for the bad passages, the woods and lakes. We inquired of the cacique we kept and the natives we brought with us, who were the neighbors and enemies of these Indians, as to the nature of the country, the character and condition of the inhabitants, of the food and all other matters concerning it. Each answered apart from the rest, that the largest town in all that region was Apalachen; the people beyond were less numerous and poorer, the land little occupied, and the inhabitants much scattered; that thenceforward were great lakes, dense forests, immense deserts and solitudes. We then asked touching the region towards the south, as to the towns and subsistence in it. They said that in keeping such a direction, journeying nine days, there was a town called Aute, the inhabitants whereof had much maize, beans and pumpkins, and being near the sea, they had fish, and that those people were their friends.

In view of the poverty of the land, the unfavorable accounts of the population and of everything else we heard, the Indians making continual war upon us, wounding our people and horses at the places where they went to drink, shooting from the lakes with such safety to themselves that we could not retaliate, killing a lord of Tescuco,[2] named Don Pedro,[3] whom the Commissary brought with him, we determined to leave that place and go in quest of the sea, and the town of Aute of which we were told. . . .

The Indians we had so far seen in Florida are all archers. They go naked, are large of body, and appear at a distance like giants. They are of admirable proportions, very spare and of great activity and strength. The bows they use are as thick as the arm, of eleven or twelve palms in length, which they will discharge at two hundred paces with so great precision that they miss nothing.

Having got through this passage, at the end of a league we arrived at another of the same character, but worse, as it was longer, being half a league in extent. This we crossed freely, without interruption from the Indians, who, as they had spent on the former occasion their store of arrows, had nought with which they dared venture to engage us. Going through a similar passage the next day [July 21], I discovered the trail of persons ahead, of which I gave notice to the Governor, who was in the rear guard, so that though the Indians came upon us, as we were prepared they did no harm. After emerging upon the plain they followed us, and we went back on them in two directions. Two we killed, and they wounded me and two or three others. Coming to woods we could do them no more injury, nor make them further trouble. . . .

from Chapter VIII
We Go from Aute

The next morning we left Aute,[4] and traveled all day before coming to the place I had visited. The journey was extremely arduous. There were not horses enough to

[2]Tezcoco, in Mexico City.

[3]Thought to be the brother of an heir to the Aztec throne, Ixtlilxochitl, dispossessed by his own father. The brothers allied themselves with Cortés against the Aztecs, and Don Pedro commanded an army in the final battle for Mexico City.

[4]The party found their way to Aute, yet found no Christians there, as had been hoped, and left the town August 3.

carry the sick, who went on increasing in numbers day by day, and we knew of no cure. It was piteous and painful to witness our perplexity and distress. We saw on our arrival how small were the means for advancing farther. There was not any where to go; and if there had been, the people were unable to move forward, the greater part being ill, and those were few who could be on duty. I cease here to relate more of this, because any one may suppose what would occur in a country so remote and malign, so destitute of all resource, whereby either to live in it or go out of it; but most certain assistance is in God, our Lord, on whom we never failed to place reliance. One thing occurred, more afflicting to us than all the rest, which was, that of the persons mounted, the greater part commenced secretly to plot, hoping to secure a better fate for themselves by abandoning the Governor and the sick, who were in a state of weakness and prostration. But, as among them were many hidalgos and persons of gentle condition, they would not permit this to go on, without informing the Governor and the officers of your Majesty; and as we showed them the deformity of their purpose, and placed before them the moment when they should desert their captain, and those who were ill and feeble, and above all the disobedience to the orders of your Majesty, they determined to remain, and that whatever might happen to one should be the lot of all, without any forsaking the rest.

After the accomplishment of this, the Governor called them all to him, and of each apart he asked advice as to what he should do to get out of a country so miserable, and seek that assistance elsewhere which could not here be found, a third part of the people being very sick, and the number increasing every hour; for we regarded it as certain that we should all become so, and could pass out of it only through death, which from its coming in such a place was to us all the more terrible. These, with many other embarrassments being considered, and entertaining many plans, we coincided in one great project, extremely difficult to put in operation, and that was to build vessels in which we might go away. This appeared impossible to every one: we knew not how to construct, nor were there tools, nor iron, nor forge, nor tow, nor resin, nor rigging; finally, no one thing of so many that are necessary, nor any man who had a knowledge of their manufacture; and, above all, there was nothing to eat, while building, for those who should labor. Reflecting on all this, we agreed to think of the subject with more deliberation, and the conversation dropped from that day, each going his way, commending our course to God, our Lord, that he would direct it as should best serve Him. . . .

During this time some went gathering shell-fish in the coves and creeks of the sea, at which employment the Indians twice attacked them and killed ten men in sight of the camp, without our being able to afford succor.[5] We found their corpses traversed from side to side with arrows; and for all some had on good armor, it did not give adequate protection or security against the nice and powerful archery of which I have spoken. According to the declaration of our pilots under oath, from the entrance to which we had given the name *Bahía de la Cruz* to this place, we had traveled two hundred and eighty leagues or thereabout. Over all that region we had not seen a single mountain, and had no information of any whatsoever.

[5]The group was able to make ready five small boats.

Before we embarked there died more than forty men of disease and hunger, without enumerating those destroyed by the Indians. By the twenty-second of the month of September, the horses had been consumed, one only remaining; and on that day we embarked in the following order: In the boat of the Governor went forty-nine men; in another, which he gave to the Comptroller and the Commissary, went as many others; the third, he gave to Captain Alonzo del Castillo and Andrés Dorantes, with forty-eight men; and another he gave to two captains, Tellez and Peñalosa, with forty-seven men. The last was given to the Assessor and myself, with forty-nine men. After the provisions and clothes had been taken in, not over a span of the gunwales remained above water; and more than this, the boats were so crowded that we could not move: so much can necessity do, which drove us to hazard our lives in this manner, running into a turbulent sea, not a single one who went, having a knowledge of navigation.

from Chapter X
The Assault from the Indians

[November 2] I found myself in thirty fathoms. . . .[6] [The Governor] asked me what I thought we should do. I told him we ought to join the boat which went in advance, and by no means to leave her; and, the three being together, we must keep on our way to where God should be pleased to lead. He answered saying that could not be done, because the boat was far to sea and he wished to reach the shore. . . . [B]ut the Governor having in his boat the healthiest of all the men, we could not by any means hold with or follow her. Seeing this, I asked him to give me a rope from his boat, that I might be enabled to keep up with him; but he answered me that he would do no little, if they, as they were, should be able to reach the land that night. I said to him, that since he saw the feeble strength we had to follow him, and do what he ordered, he must tell me how he would that I should act. He answered that it was no longer a time in which one should command another; but that each should do what he thought best to save his own life; that he so intended to act; and saying this, he departed with his boat. . . .

Near the dawn of day [November 5] . . . a wave took us, that knocked our boat out of the water the distance of the throw of a crowbar, and from the violence with which she struck, nearly all the people who were in her like dead, were roused to consciousness. Finding themselves near the shore, they began to move on hands and feet, crawling to land into some ravines.

from Chapter XI
Of What Befel Lope de Oviedo with the Indians

As it appeared to us [Oviedo] was gone a long time, we sent two men that they should look to see what might have happened. They met him near by, and saw that

[6]The group neared the entrance to the Mississippi River by November 2, 1528.

three Indians with bows and arrows followed and were calling to him, while he, in the same way, was beckoning them on. Thus he arrived where we were, the natives remaining a little way back, seated on the shore. Half an hour after, they were supported by one hundred other Indian bowmen, who if they were not large, our fears made giants of them. . . . We gave them beads and hawk-bells, and each of them gave me an arrow, which is a pledge of friendship. They told us by signs that they would return in the morning and bring us something to eat, as at the time they had nothing.

from Chapter XXI Our Cure of Some of the Afflicted

[September 1528: Cabeza de Vaca and his mates, separated from Narváez, have been shipwrecked off the Louisiana/Texas coast, captured and forced to serve the Indians.]

That same night of our arrival, some Indians came to Castillo and told him that they had great pain in the head, begging him to cure them. After he made over them the sign of the cross, and commended them to God, they instantly said that all the pain had left, and went to their houses bringing us prickly pears, with a piece of venison, a thing to us little known. As the report of Castillo's performances spread, many came to us that night sick, that we should heal them, each bringing a piece of venison, until the quantity became so great we knew not where to dispose of it. We gave many thanks to God, for every day went on increasing his compassion and his gifts. After the sick were attended to, they began to dance and sing, making themselves festive, until sunrise; and because of our arrival, the rejoicing was continued for three days.

When these were ended, we asked the Indians about the country farther on, the people we should find in it, and of the subsistence there. They answered us, that throughout all the region prickly pear[7] plants abounded; but the fruit was now gathered and all the people had gone back to their houses. They said the country was very cold, and there were few skins. Reflecting on this, and that it was already winter, we resolved to pass the season with these Indians.

Five days after our arrival, all the Indians went off, taking us with them to gather more prickly pears, where there were other peoples speaking different tongues. After walking five days in great hunger, since on the way was no manner of fruit, we came to a river and put up our houses. We then went to seek the product of certain trees, which is like peas. As there are no paths in the country, I was detained some time. The others returned, and coming to look for them in the dark, I got lost. Thank God I found a burning tree, and in the warmth of it passed the cold of that night. In the morning, loading myself with sticks, and taking two brands with me, I returned to seek them. In this manner I wandered five days, ever with my fire and load; for if the wood had failed me where none could be found, as many parts are without any, though I might have sought sticks elsewhere, there would have been no fire to kindle them. This was all the protection I had against cold, while walking naked as I was

[7]Fruit of the cactus.

born. Going to the low woods near the rivers, I prepared myself for the night, stopping in them before sunset. I made a hole in the ground and threw in fuel which the trees abundantly afforded, collected in good quantity from those that were fallen and dry. About the whole I made four fires, in the form of a cross, which I watched and made up from time to time. I also gathered some bundles of the coarse straw that there abounds, with which I covered myself in the hole. In this way I was sheltered at night from cold. On one occasion while I slept, the fire fell upon the straw, when it began to blaze so rapidly that notwithstanding the haste I made to get out of it, I carried some marks on my hair of the danger to which I was exposed. All this while I tasted not a mouthful, nor did I find anything I could eat. My feet were bare and bled a good deal. Through the mercy of God, the wind did not blow from the north in all this time, otherwise I should have died.

At the end of the fifth day I arrived on the margin of a river, where I found the Indians, who with the Christians, had considered me dead, supposing that I had been stung by a viper. All were rejoiced to see me, and most so were my companions. They said that up to that time they had struggled with great hunger, which was the cause of their not having sought me. At night, all gave me of their prickly pears, and the next morning we set out for a place where they were in large quantity, with which we satisfied our great craving, the Christians rendering thanks to our Lord that he had ever given us his aid.

from **Chapter XXIV**
Customs of the Indians of That Country

From the Island of Malhado to this land, all the Indians whom we saw have the custom from the time in which their wives find themselves pregnant, of not sleeping with them until two years after they have given birth. The children are suckled until the age of twelve years, when they are old enough to get support for themselves. We asked why they reared them in this manner; and they said because of the great poverty of the land, it happened many times, as we witnessed, that they were two or three days without eating, sometimes four, and consequently, in seasons of scarcity, the children were allowed to suckle, that they might not famish; otherwise those who lived would be delicate having little strength.

If any one chance to fall sick in the desert, and cannot keep up with the rest, the Indians leave him to perish, unless it be a son or a brother; him they will assist, even to carrying on their back. It is common among them all to leave their wives when there is no conformity, and directly they connect themselves with whom they please. This is the course of the men who are childless; those who have children, remain with their wives and never abandon them. When they dispute and quarrel in their towns, they strike each other with the fists, fighting until exhausted, and then separate. Sometimes they are parted by the women going between them; the men never interfere. For no disaffection that arises do they resort to bows and arrows. After they have fought, or had out their dispute, they take their dwellings and go into the woods, living apart from each other until their heat has subsided. When no longer offended and their anger is gone, they return. From that time they are friends as if nothing had happened; nor is it necessary that any one should mend their friendships, as they in this way again unite them. If those that quarrel are single, they go to some neighboring people, and although these should be enemies, they receive them well and welcome them warmly, giving them so largely of what they have, that when their animosity cools, and they return to their town, they go rich.

They are all warlike, and have as much strategy for protecting themselves against enemies as they could have were they reared in Italy in continual feuds. When they are in a part of the country where their enemies may attack them, they place their houses on the skirt of a wood, the thickest and most tangled they can find, and near it make a ditch in which they sleep. The warriors are covered by small pieces of stick through which are loop holes; these hide them and present so false an appearance, that if come upon they are not discovered. They open a very narrow way, entering into the midst of the wood, where a spot is prepared on which the women and children sleep. When night comes they kindle fires in their lodges, that should spies be about, they may think to find them there; and before daybreak they again light those fires. If the enemy comes to assault the houses, they who are in the ditch make a sally; and from their trenches do much injury without those who are outside seeing or being able to find them. When there is no wood in which they can take shelter in this way, and make their ambuscades, they settle on open ground at a place they select, which they invest with trenches covered with broken sticks, having apertures whence to discharge arrows. These arrangements are made for night.

While I was among the Aguenes, their enemies coming suddenly at midnight, fell upon them, killed three and wounded many, so that they ran from their houses to the fields before them. As soon as these ascertained that their assailants had withdrawn, they returned to pick up all the arrows the others had shot, and following after them in the most stealthy manner possible, came that night to their dwellings without their presence being suspected. At four o'clock in the morning the Aguenes attacked them, killed five, and wounded numerous others, and made them flee from their houses, leaving their bows with all they possessed. In a little while came the wives of the Quevenes to them and formed a treaty whereby the parties became friends. The women, however, are sometimes the cause of war. All these nations, when they have personal enmities, and are not of one family, assassinate at night, waylay, and inflict gross barbarities on each other.

from Chapter XXVII
We Moved Away and Were Well Received

. . . At sunset we reached a hundred Indian habitations. Before we arrived, all the people who were in them came out to receive us, with such yells as were terrific, striking the palms of their hands violently against their thighs. They brought us gourds bored with holes and having pebbles in them, an instrument for the most important occasions, produced only at the dance or to effect cures, and which none dare touch but those who own them. They say there is virtue in them, and because they do not grow in that country, they come from heaven: nor do they know where they are to be found, only that the rivers bring them in their floods. So great were the fear and distraction of these people, some to reach us sooner than others, that they might touch us, they pressed us so closely that they lacked little of killing us; and without letting us put our feet to the ground, carried us to their dwellings. We were so crowded upon by numbers, that we went into the houses they had made for us. On no account would we consent that they should rejoice over us any more that night. The night long they passed in singing and dancing among themselves; and the next day they brought us all the people of the town, that we should touch and bless them in the way we had done to others among whom we had been. After this performance they presented many arrows to some women of the other town who had accompanied theirs.

The next day we left, and all the people of the place went with us: and when we came to the other Indians we were as well received as we had been by the last. They gave us of what they had to eat, and the deer they had killed that day. Among them we witnessed another custom, which is this: they who were with us took from him who came to be cured, his bow and arrows, shoes and beads if he wore any, and then brought him before us that we should heal him. After being attended to, he would go away highly pleased, saying that he was well. So we parted from these Indians, and went to others by whom we were welcomed. They brought us their sick, which, we having blessed, they declared were sound; he who was healed, believed we could cure him; and with what the others to whom we had administered would relate, they made great rejoicing and dancing, so that they left us no sleep. . . .

from Chapter XXXII The Indians Give Us the Hearts of Deer

. . . We were in this town three days.[8] A day's journey farther was another town, at which the rain fell heavily while we were there, and the river became so swollen we could not cross it, which detained us fifteen days. In this time Castillo saw the buckle of a sword-belt on the neck of an Indian and stitched to it the nail of a horse shoe. He took them, and we asked the native what they were: he answered that they came from heaven. We questioned him further, as to who had brought them thence: they all responded, that certain men who wore beards like us, had come from heaven and arrived at that river; bringing horses, lances, and swords, and that they had lanced two Indians. In a manner of the utmost indifference we could feign, we asked them what had become of those men: they answered us that they had gone to sea, putting their lances beneath the water, and going themselves also under the water; afterwards that they were seen on the surface going towards the sunset. For this we gave many thanks to God our Lord. We had before despaired of ever hearing more of Christians. Even yet we were left in great doubt and anxiety, thinking those people were merely persons who had come by sea on discoveries. However, as we had now such exact information, we made greater speed, and as we advanced on our way, the news of the Christians continually grew. We told the natives that we were going in search of that people, to order them not to kill nor make slaves of them, nor take them from their lands, nor do other injustice. Of this the Indians were very glad.

[8] At an earlier point in the narrative, the journal reports that "we called the place Pueblo de los Corazones," on the gulf of Cortés.

We passed through many territories and found them all vacant: their inhabitants wandered fleeing among the mountains, without daring to have houses or till the earth for fear of Christians. The sight was one of infinite pain to us, a land very fertile and beautiful, abounding in springs and streams, the hamlets deserted and burned, the people thin and weak, all fleeing or in concealment. As they did not plant, they appeased their keen hunger by eating roots, and the bark of trees. We bore a share in the famine along the whole way; for poorly could these unfortunates provide for us, themselves being so reduced they looked as though they would willingly die. They brought shawls of those they had concealed because of the Christians, presenting them to us; and they related how the Christians, at other times had come through the land destroying and burning the towns, carrying away half the men, and all the women and the boys, while those who had been able to escape were wandering about fugitives. We found them so alarmed they dared not remain anywhere. They would not, nor could they till the earth; but preferred to die rather than live in dread of such cruel usage as they received. Although these showed themselves greatly delighted with us, we feared that on our arrival among those who held the frontier and fought against the Christians, they would treat us badly, and revenge upon us the conduct of their enemies; but when God our Lord was pleased to bring us there, they began to dread and respect us as the others had done, and even somewhat more, at which we no little wondered. Thence it may at once be seen, that to bring all these people to be Christians and to the obedience of the Imperial Majesty, they must be won by kindness, which is a way certain, and no other is. . . .[9]

from Chapter XXXIII
We See Traces of Christians

When we saw sure signs of Christians, and heard how near we were to them, we gave thanks to God our Lord, for having chosen to bring us out of a captivity so melancholy and wretched. The delight we felt let each one conjecture, when he shall remember the length of time we were in that country, the suffering and perils we underwent. That night I entreated my companions that one of them should go back three days' journey after the Christians who were moving about over the country, where we had given assurance of protection. Neither of them received this proposal well, excusing themselves because of weariness and exhaustion; and although either might have done better than I, being more youthful and athletic, yet seeing their unwillingness, the next morning I took the negro[10] with eleven Indians, and following the Christians by their trail, I traveled ten leagues, passing three villages, at which they had slept.

The day after I overtook four of them on horseback, who were astonished at the sight of me, so strangely habited as I was, and in company with Indians. They stood staring at me a length of time, so confounded that they neither hailed me nor drew

[9]As the concluding section here suggests, the advice of Cabeza de Vaca went unheeded, even by the Christians he met. By this time the party had entered northern Mexico.

[10]Estévan, a black member of the Spanish expedition.

near to make an inquiry. I bade them take me to their chief: accordingly we went together half a league to the place where was Diego de Alcaraz, their captain.

After we had conversed, he stated to me that he was completely undone; he had not been able in a long time to take any Indians; he knew not which way to turn, and his men had well begun to experience hunger and fatigue. I told him of Castillo and Dorantes, who were behind, ten leagues off, with a multitude that conducted us. He thereupon sent three cavalry to them, with fifty of the Indians who accompanied him. The negro returned to guide them, while I remained. I asked the Christians to give me a certificate of the year, month and day, I arrived there, and of the manner of my coming, which they accordingly did. From this river to the town of the Christians, named San Miguel, within the government of the province called New Galicia, are thirty leagues.

from Chapter XXXIV
Of Sending for the Christians

Five days having elapsed, Andrés Dorantes and Alonzo del Castillo arrived with those who had been sent after them. They brought more than six hundred persons of that community, whom the Christians had driven into the forests, and who had wandered in concealment over the land. Those who accompanied us so far, had drawn them out, and given them to the Christians, who thereupon dismissed all the others they had brought with them. Upon their coming to where I was, Alcaraz begged that we would summon the people of the towns on the margin of the river, who straggled about under cover of the woods, and order them to fetch us something to eat. This last was unnecessary, the Indians being ever diligent to bring us all they could. Directly we sent our messengers to call them, when there came six hundred souls, bringing us all the maize in their possession. They fetched it in certain pots, closed with clay, which they had concealed in the earth. They brought us whatever else they had; but we, wishing only to have the provision, gave the rest to the Christians, that they might divide among themselves. After this we had many high words with them; for they wished to make slaves of the Indians we brought.

In consequence of the dispute, we left at our departure many bows of Turkish shape we had along with us and many pouches. The five arrows with the points of emerald were forgotten among others, and we lost them. We gave the Christians a store of robes of cowhide and other things we brought. We found it difficult to induce the Indians to return to their dwellings, to feel no apprehension and plant maize. They were willing to do nothing until they had gone with us and delivered us into the hands of other Indians, as had been the custom; for if they returned without doing so, they were afraid they should die, and going with us, they feared neither Christians nor lances. Our countrymen became jealous at this, and caused their interpreter to tell the Indians that we were of them, and for a long time we had been lost; that they were the lords of the land who must be obeyed and served, while we were persons of mean condition and small force. The Indians cared little or nothing for what was told them; and conversing among themselves said the Christians lied: that we had come whence the sun rises, and they whence it goes down: we healed the sick, they killed the sound; that we had come naked and barefooted, while they had arrived in clothing and on horses with lances; that we were not covetous of anything, but all that was given to us, we directly turned to give, remaining with nothing; that the others had the only purpose to rob whomsoever they found, bestowing nothing on any one.

In this way they spoke of all matters respecting us, which they enhanced by contrast with matters concerning the others, delivering their response through the interpreter of the Spaniards. To other Indians they made this known by means of one among them through whom they understood us. Those who speak that tongue we discriminately call Primahaitu, which is like saying Vasconyados.[11] We found it in use over more than four hundred leagues of our travel, without another over that whole extent. Even to the last, I could not convince the Indians that we were of the Christians; and only with great effort and solicitation we got them to go back to their residences. We ordered them to put away apprehension, establish their towns, plant and cultivate the soil. . . .

1542

A Gentleman of Elvas fl. 1537–1557

The Gentleman of Elvas, of Portuguese origin, chronicled Hernando de Soto's expedition of 1539–1543, in which the wealthy veteran of the Peruvian conquest led seven hundred men in search of riches, wandering from Florida to Oklahoma and back to the Mississippi River (which had been first explored by Alonso Alvarez de Piñeda), where de Soto died of fever. Less than half of the men reappeared in Panuco, northern Mexico, in 1543.

This selection, however, picks up the tale of yet another survivor of the Narváez expedition (see Cabeza de Vaca). Juan Ortiz had not disembarked with the main party, but on a subsequent trip to the coast in search of Narváez, he was taken prisoner by a native group. In an anecdote not unlike John Smith's later Pocahontas story (and many more to follow all across the continent), Ortiz is saved by the mediation of a young Indian woman. Like Cabeza de Vaca's, his is another tale of European survival among Native Americans through adaptation and acculturation. Considering the fate of de Soto's expedition, Ortiz may well have wished he had never been rescued.

Juan Bruce-Novoa
University of California at Irvine

PRIMARY WORK

The Discovery and Conquest of Terra Florida, trans. Richard Hakluyt, 1611 (First printing, 1609); rpt. Burt Franklin, n. d. (First published in Evora, Portugal, in 1557).

[11]Basques from northern Spain who speak Basque, not Spanish.

from The Discovery and Conquest of Terra Florida[1]

Chapter VIII
Of some inrodes that were made into the countrie; and how there was a Christian found, which had bin long time in the power of an Indian Lord.

From the towne of Ucita, the Governour sent the alcalde mayor, Baltasar de Gallegos, with 40 horsemen and 80 footemen, into the countrie, to see if they could take any Indians; and the captaine, John Rodriguez Lobillo, another way with 50 footemen; the most of them were swordmen and target-tours, and the rest were shot and crossebowmen. They passed through a countrie full of bogges, where horses could not travell. Halfe a league from the campe, they lighted upon certaine cabins of Indians neere a river; the people that were in them leaped into the river; yet they tooke foure Indian women; and twentie Indians charged us, and so distressed us, that wee were forced to retire to our campe, being, as they are, exceeding readie with their weapons. It is a people so warlike and so nimble, that they care not a whit for any footemen. For if their enemies charge them, they runne away, and if they turne their backs, they are presently upon them. And the thing that they most flee, is the shot of an arrow. They never stand still, but are alwaies running and traversing from one place to another; by reason whereof neither crossebow nor arcubuse can aime at them; and before one crossebowman can make one shot, an Indian will discharge three or foure arrowes; and he seldome misseth what hee shooteth at. An arrow, where it findeth no armour, pierceth as deepely as a crossebow. Their bowes are very long, and their arrowes are made of certain canes like reedes, very heavie, and so strong, that a sharpe cane passeth thorow a target; some they arme in the point with a sharpe bone of a fish like a chisel, and in others they fasten certaine stones like points of diamants. For the most part, when they light upon an armour, they breake in the place where they are bound together. Those of cane do split and pierce a coate of maile, and are more hurtfull then the other. John Rodriguez Lobillo returned to the campe with sixe men wounded, whereof one died, and brought the foure Indian women, which Baltasar Gallegos had taken in the cabins or cotages. Two leagues from the towne, comming into the plaine field, he espied ten or eleven Indians, among whom was a Christian, which was naked, and scorched with the sunne, and had his armes razed after the manner of the Indians, and differed nothing at all from them. And as soone as the horsemen saw them, they ran toward them. The Indians fled, and some of them hid themselves in a wood, and they overtooke two or three of them, which were wounded; and the Christian, seeing an horseman runne upon him with his lance, began to crie out, Sirs, I am a Christian, slay me not, nor these Indians, for they have saved my life. And straightway he called them, and put them out of feare, and they came foorth of the wood unto them. The horsemen tooke both the

[1]The text, taken directly from a translation published by Richard Hakluyt, has not been modernized. Hakluyt anglicized all Spanish first names.

Christian and the Indians up behind them; and toward night came into the campe with much joy; which thing being knowne by the Governour, and them that remained in the campe, they were received with the like.

Chapter IX
How this Christian came to the land of Florida, and who he was; and what conference he had with the Governour.

This Christian's name was John Ortiz, and he was borne in Sivil,[2] in worshipful parentage. He was twelve yeeres in the hands of the Indians. He came into this countrie with Pamphilo de Narvaez,[3] and returned in the ships to the Island of Cuba, where the wife of the Governour, Pamphilo de Narvaez, was: and by his commandement, with twenty or thirty other, in a brigandine, returned backe againe to Florida; and comming to the port in the sight of the towne, on the shore they saw a cane sticking in the ground, and riven at the top, and a letter in it: and they beleeved that the Governour had left it there to give advertisement of himselfe, when he resolved to goe up into the land; and they demanded it of foure or five Indians, which walked along the sea shore; and they bad them, by signes, to come on shore for it, which, against the will of the rest, John Ortiz and another did. And as soone as they were on land, from the houses of the towne issued a great number of Indians, which compassed them about, and tooke them in a place where they could not flee; and the other, which sought to defend himselfe, they presentlie killed upon the place, and tooke John Ortiz alive, and carried him to Ucita their lord. And those of the brigandine sought not to land, but put themselves to sea, and returned to the island of Cuba. Ucita commanded to bind John Ortiz hand and foote upon foure stakes aloft upon a raft, and to make a fire under him, that there he might bee burned. But a daughter of his desired him that he would not put him to death, alleaging that one only Christian could do him neither hurt nor good, telling him, that it was more for his honour to keepe him as a captive. And Ucita granted her request, and commanded him to be cured of his wounds; and as soone as he was whole, he gave him the charge of the keeping of the temple, because that by night the wolves did cary away the dead corpses out of the same; who commended himselfe to God, and tooke upon him the charge of his temple. One night the wolves gate from him the corpes of a little child, the sonne of a principal Indian; and going after them, he threw a darte at one of the wolves, and strooke him that carried away the corps, who, feeling himselfe wounded, left it, and fell downe dead neere the place; and hee not woting[4] what he had done, because it was night, went backe againe to the temple; the morn ing being come, and finding not the bodie of the child, he was very sad. As soone as Ucita knew thereof, he resolved to put him to death; and sent by the tract, which he said the wolves went, and found the bodie of the child, and the wolfe dead a little beyond: whereat Ucita was much contented with the Christian, and with the watch which hee kept in the temple, and from thence forward esteemed him much. Three

[2]Seville in southern Spain.

[3]Pánfilo de Narváez, the leader of Cabeza de Vaca's ill-fated expedition in 1528.

[4]Knowing.

yeeres after hee fell into his hands, there came another lord, called Mocoço, who dwelleth two daies journy from the port, and burned his towne. Ucita fled to another towne that he had in another sea port. Thus John Ortiz lost his office and favour that he had with him. These people being worshippers of the divell, are wont to offer up unto him the lives and blood of their Indians, or of any other people they can come by; and they report, that when he will have them doe that sacrifice unto him, he speaketh with them, and telleth them that he is athirst, and willeth them to sacrifice unto him. John Ortiz had notice by the damsell that had delivered him from the fire, how her father was determined to sacrifice him the day following, who willed him to flee to Mocoço, for shee knew that he would use him well; for she heard say, that he had asked for him, and said he would be glad to see him; and because he knew not the way, she went with him halfe a league out of the towne by night, and set him in the way, and returned, because she would not be discovered. John Ortiz travailed all that night, and by the morning came unto a river, which is in the territorie of Mocoço; and there he saw two Indians fishing; and because they were in war with the people of Ucita, and their languages were different, and hee knew not the language of Mocoço, he was afraid (because he could not tell them who hee was, nor how hee came thither, nor was able to answer any thing for himselfe) that they would kill him, taking him for one of the Indians of Ucita; and before they espied him, he came to the place where they had laid their weapons; and as soone as they saw him, they fled toward the towne; and although he willed them to stay, because he meant to do them no hurt, yet they understood him not, and ran away as fast as ever they could. And as soone as they came to the towne with great outcries, many Indians came forth against him, and began to compasse him to shoote at him: John Ortiz seeing himselfe in so great danger, shielded himselfe with certaine trees, and began to shreeke out, and crie very loud, and to tell them that he was a Christian, and that he was fled from Ucita, and was come to see and serve Mocoço his lord. It pleased God, that at that very instant there came thither an Indian that could speake the language and understood him, and pacified the rest, who told them what hee said. Then ran from thence three or foure Indians to beare the newes to their lord, who came foorth a quarter of a league from the towne to receive him, and was very glad of him. He caused him presently to sweare according to the custome of the Christians, that he would not run away from him to any other lord, and promised him to entreate him very well; and that if at any time there came any Christians into that countrie, he would freely let him goe, and give him leave to goe to them; and likewise tooke his oth to performe the same, according to the Indian custome.

About three yeares after, certaine Indians, which were fishing at sea two leagues from the towne, brought newes to Mocoço that they had seene ships; and hee called John Ortiz, and gave him leave to go his way; who, taking his leave of him, with all the haste he could, came to the sea, and finding no ships, he thought it to be some deceit, and that the cacique had done the same to learne his mind; so he dwelt with Mocoço nine yeeres, with small hope of seeing any Christians. As soone as our Governor arrived in Florida, it was knowne to Mocoço, and straightway he signified to John Ortiz that Christians were lodged in the towne of Ucita: and he thought he had jested with him, as hee had done before, and told him, that by this time he had forgotten the Christians, and thought of nothing else but to serve him. But he assured him that it was so, and gave him licence to goe unto them; saying unto him, that if hee would not doe it, and if the Christians should goe their way, he should not blame him, for he had fulfilled that which hee had promised him. The joy of John Ortiz was so great, that hee could not beleeve that it was true; notwithstanding, he gave him thankes, and tooke his leave of him; and Mocoço gave him tenne or eleven principall Indians to beare him companie; and as they went to the port where the Governour was, they met with Baltasar de Gallêgos, as I have declared before.

As soone as he was come to the campe, the Governour commanded to give him a sute of apparrell, and very good armour, and a faire horse, and enquired of him, whether hee had notice of any countrie, where there was any gold or silver? He answered, No, because he never went ten leagues compasse from the place where he dwelt; but that thirty leagues from thence dwelt an Indian lord, which was called Parocossi, to whom Mocoço and Ucita, with al the rest of that coast, paied tribute, and that hee peradventure[5] might have notice of some good countrie; and that his land was better then that of the sea coast, and more fruitfull and plentifull of maiz; whereof the Governour received great contentment; and said, that he desired no more then to finde victuals, that hee might goe into the maine land, for the land of Florida was so large that in one place or other there could not chuse but bee some rich countrie. The cacique Mocoço came to the port to visit the Governor, and made this speech following:

Right hie and mightie Lord, I being lesser in mine owne conceit for to obey you, then any of those which you have under your command; and greater in desire to doe you greater services, doe appeare before your Lordship with so much confidence of receiving favour, as if in effect this my good will were manifested unto you in workes: not for the small service I did unto you, touching the Christian which I had in my power, in giving him freely his libertie (for I was bound to doe it to preserve mine honour, and that which I had promised him), but because it is the part of great men to use great magnificences: and I am persuaded, that as in bodily perfections, and commanding of good people, you doe exceede all men in the world, so likewise you doe in the parts of the minde, in which you may boast of the bountie of nature. The favour which I hope for of your Lordship is, that you would hold mee for yours, and bethinke your selfe to command me any thing, wherein I may doe you service.

The Governour answered him, that although in freeing and sending him the Christian, he had preserved his honour and promise, yet he thanked him, and held it in such esteeme, as it had no comparison; and that hee would alwaies hold him as his brother, and would favor him in all things to the utmost of his power. Then he commanded a shirt to be given him, and other things, wherewith the cacique being verie well contented, tooke his leave of him, and departed to his owne towne.

1557

[5]Perhaps.

René Goulaine de Laudonnière fl. 1562–1582

The Huguenots, French Protestants, conducted a protracted religious war against the Catholic crown between 1562 and 1598. They were permitted by authorities, however, to participate in colonial ventures, especially where such ventures would disrupt the Spanish colonies. After failing in Brazil, the Huguenots turned to the northern Atlantic coast, claimed by the Spanish. From there they could attack the Spanish Silver Fleets. Jean Ribault's Port Royal, South Carolina, failed in 1562, but René Goulaine de Laudonnière's Fort Caroline colony near the mouth of the St. John's River in Florida proved more promising in 1564. France and Spain were at peace in Europe, but the French crown turned a blind eye to Huguenot attacks and violations of international agreements, since the potential profits were enormous. The king of Spain, however, ordered the colony eliminated by the permanent Spanish colonization of Florida, a name which covered from New Mexico on the west to Newfoundland in the north. Menéndez de Avilés enacted Philip II's policy with deadly skill.

Like the Spanish writers, the French chroniclers functioned as early anthropologists, documenting Native American customs. Yet, as this text demonstrates, they often could not fathom entirely the meaning of what they were witnessing. This brutal event may be understood better as a sacred ritual in a culture that had not replaced the human victim with a symbolic substitute.

Juan Bruce-Novoa
University of California at Irvine

PRIMARY WORK

A Notable History Containing Four Voyages Made By Certain French Captains unto Florida, trans. Richard Hakluyt, 1587; rpt. by H. Stevens, Sons and Stiles, 1964.

SECONDARY WORKS

Henry Folmer, *Franco-Spanish Rivalry in North America, 1524–1763,* 1953; Woodbury Lowery, *The Spanish Settlements Within the Present Limits of the United States,* v. 2, 1959.

from A Notable Historie Containing Foure Voyages Made by Certaine French Captaines unto Florida[1]

The good cheere being done, and the discourses ended, my men embarked themselves againe with intention to bring me those good newes unto the fort *Caroline.* But after they had sayled a very long whyle downe the river, and were come within three leagues of us, the tide was so strong against them, that they were constrayned to goe on land, and to retire themselves because of the night unto the dwelling of a certain *Paracoussy* named *Molona,* which shewed himselfe very glad of their arrival: for he

[1]The text is Hakluyt's, slightly modernized.

desired to know some newes of *Thimogoua,* and thought that the French men went thither for none other occasion but for to invade them. Which captain *Vasseur* perceiving dissembled so wel, that he made him beleeve that he went to *Thimogoua,* with none other intention, but to subdue them, and to destroy them with the edge of the sword without mercy, but that their purpose had not such successe as they desired, because that the people of *Thimogoua* being advertised of this enterprise, retired into the woods, and saved themselves by flight: yet neverthelesse they had taken some as they were flying away which carried to newes thereof unto their fellowes. The *Paracoussy* was so glad of this relation, that he enterrupted him, and asked *Vasseur* of the beginning and maner of his execution, and praied him that he would shew him by signes how all things passed. Immediatly *Frauncis la Caille* the seargeant of my band took his sword in his hand, saying that with the point thereof he had thrust through two Indians which ran into the woods, and that his companions had done no lesse for their parts. And that if fortune had so favoured them, that they had not bin discovered by the men of *Thimogoua,* they had had a victorie most glorious and worthy of eternall memory. Hereupon the *Paracoussy* shewed himselfe so wel satisfied, that he could not devise how to gratifie our men, which he caused to come into his house to feast them more honorably: and having made captaine *Vasseur* to sit next him, and in his own chaire (which the Indians esteeme for the chiefest honour) and then underneath him two of his sonnes, goodly and might fellowes, he commanded al the rest to place themselves as they thought good. This done, the Indians came according to their good custom, to present their drink *Cassine* to the *Paracoussy,* and then to certaine of his chiefest friends, and the Frenchmen. Then he which brought it set the cup aside, and drew out a little dagger which hung stucke up in the roofe of the house, and like a mad man he lift his head aloft, and ran apace, and went and smote an Indian which sate alone in one of the corners of the hall, crying with a loud voyce, *Hyou,* the poore Indian stirring not at al for the blow, which he seemed to endure paciently. He which held the dagger went quickly to put the same in his former place, and began again to give us drink, as he did before: but he had not long continued, and had scarcely given 3. or 4. thereof, but he left his bowle againe, tooke the dagger in his hand, and quickly returned unto him which he had stroken before, to whom he gave a very sore blow on the side, crying *Hyou,* as he had done before: then he went to put the dagger in his place, and set him self down among the rest. A little while after, he that had bin stroken fel down backwards, stretching out his armes and legs as if he had bin ready to yeld up the latter gaspe. And then the younger soone of the *Paracoussy* apparrelled in a long white skin, fel down at the feet of him that was fallen backward, weeping bitterly halfe a quarter of an houre. after two other of his brethren clad in like apparel, came about him that was so stricken, and began to sigh pitifully. Their mother bearing a little infant in her arms came from another part, and going to the place where her sonnes were, at the first she used infinit numbers of outcries, then one while lifting up her eies to heaven, an other while falling down unto the ground, she cried so dolefully, that her lamentable mournings would have moved the most hard and stonie heart in the world with pity. Yet this sufficed not, for there came in a company of young gyrles which did never lyn weeping for a long while in the place where the Indian was fallen down, whom afterward they took, and with the saddest gestures they could devise, caried him away into another house a little way of from the great hal of the *Paracoussy,* and continued their weepings and mournings by the space of two long houres: in which meane while the Indians ceassed not to drink Cassine, but with such silence that one word was not heard in the parler. *Vasseur* beeing grieved that hee understood not these ceremonies, demaunded of the *Paracoussy* what these thinges meant: which answered him slowly, *Thimogoua, Thimogoua,* with out saying any more. Beeing more displeased then he was before with so slight an answeare, he turned unto another Indian the *Paracoussyes* brother, who was a *Paracoussy* as well as his brother, called *Malica,* which made him a like answere as he did at the first, praying him to aske no more of these matters, and to have patience for that time. The subtile old *Paracoussy* praied him within a while after to shew him his sword, which he would not deny him, thinking that hee would have beholde the fashion of his weapons: but he soone perceived that it was to another end: for the old man holding it in his hand, beheld it a long while on every place to see if he could find any blood upon it which might shew that any of their enemies had bin killed: (for the Indians are woont to bring their weapons wherwith their enemies have bin defeated with some blood upon them, for a token of their victories.) But seeing no signe thereof upon it, he was upon the point to say unto him, that he had killed none of the men of *Thimogoua,* when as *Vasseur* preventing that which he might object, declared and shewed to him by signes the maner of his enterprise, adding that by reason of the 2. Indians which he had slaine, his sword was so bloudy, that he was inforced to wash and make it cleane a long while in the river: which the old man beleeved to be like to be true, and made no maner of reply thereunto. *Vasseur, la Caille,* and their other companions went out of the hall to go into the roome whither they had carried the Indian: there they found the *Paracoussy* sitting upon tapistries made of smal reeds, which was at meat after the Indian fashion, and the Indian that was smitten hard by him, lying upon the selfsame tapistry, about whom stood the wife of the *Paracoussy,* with all the young damsels which before bewailed him in the hall: which did nothing els but warme a great deale of mosse in steede of napkins to rub the Indians side. Hereupon our men asked the *Paracoussy* again, for what occasion the Indian was so persecuted in his presence: he answered, that this was nothing els but a kind of ceremony wherby they would cal to mind the death and persecutions of the *Paracoussies* their ancestors executed by their enemy *Thimogoua:* alledging moreover, that as often as he himself, or any of his friends and alies returned from the countrey, without they brought the heads of their enimies, or without bringing home some prisoner, he used for a perpetual memory of al his predecessors, to beate the best beloved of all his children, with the selfsame weapons, wherewith they had bin killed in times past: to the ende that by renewing of the wounde their death should be lamented afresh.

1587

Pedro Menéndez de Avilés 1519–1574

A naval officer of renown, bravery, and skill, Menéndez de Avilés became Captain-General under Philip II, who also commissioned him to colonize Florida, an indefinite area at the time stretching from New Mexico on the west to Newfoundland in the north. The mandate was permanently to colonize the territory and to expel the Huguenots who were threatening the Spanish trade route (see Laudonnière). Arriving at St. John's River in 1565, Menéndez de Avilés surprised the French garrison at Fort Caroline, executed the Protestant prisoners, including Jean Ribault, and rechristened the site Fort Matéo. He also founded St. Augustine, now the oldest permanent city of European origin in the United States.

Unlike the aims of Narváez or de Soto, Menéndez de Avilés's goal was not mineral riches but the settling of as large an area as possible, for his grant was to him and his family in perpetuity. As was the custom at the time, while his venture required official approval, the crown invested only a small percentage of the total funds needed. To outfit a formidable fleet, a military land force, and the colonizers needed to settle the land, Menéndez de Avilés had to organize investors, tapping his family's and his friends' fortunes. Success would bring them prosperity for generations; failure, ruin. So, in addition to soldiers, he recruited craftsmen from thirty-eight trades, over one hundred farmers, and twenty-seven families, including women and children. He had permission to take five hundred black slaves to perform the most difficult work. Determined to expand his holdings, he sent missionaries north into Santa Maria Bay (the Chesapeake), and built blockhouses from the coast of the present Carolinas to the Alleghanys. From St. Augustine the Camino Real would set out toward Tallahassee and points west.

But the desperate tone to his letters, in which he pleaded for equipment to hold the land and priests to christianize the natives, was well-founded. His mistake, perhaps, was to try to occupy too much territory with too few settlers at a time when the king was unwilling to invest more funds, once the immediate French threat had been eliminated. Menéndez de Avilés lacked the personal fortune to keep his lieutenants content in outposts where they were both incredibly uncomfortable and perilously outnumbered by hostile natives. The colonials mutinied continually, until the far-flung outpost had to be abandoned, leaving only the settlement concentrated around St. Augustine, which continued as the emporium of Spanish power in the area for almost three centuries.

Juan Bruce-Novoa
University of California at Irvine

PRIMARY WORK

The Settlement of Florida, ed. Charles E. Bennett, 1968. The letters were translated by Jeannette Thurber Connor.

SECONDARY WORKS

Henry Folmer, *Franco-Spanish Rivalry in North America, 1524–1763,* 1953; Woodbury Lowery, *The Spanish Settlements Within the Present Limits of the United States,* v. 2, 1959; Roger Kennedy, *Rediscovering America,* 1990.

from Letter to Philip II (October 15, 1565)

I wrote to your Majesty by the galleon San Salvador on the tenth of September, the day on which she left from this port; the duplicate of the letter goes with this one; and immediately after, within that very hour, I being on the bar in a shallop, with two boats laden with artillery and munitions, the four French galleons we had pursued came upon us, with two other pinnaces at the poop, to prevent our disembarking here, and to take from us our artillery and supplies; and although the time was unfavorable for crossing the bar, I preferred to fight, at the risk of drowning myself there with one hundred and fifty persons who were with me, and with the bronze artillery and demi-culverins, rather than see myself in their power and thus strengthen them. It was Our Lord's will to save us miraculously, for the tide was low and there was but a scant fathom and a half of water on the bar, while the ship needed a full fathom and a half; and they, seeing I had escaped them, came to talk with me, saying I should surrender and have no fear, and then went off to search for the galleon, for let it be understood that they held she could not escape from them. Within two days a hurricane and very great storm came upon them, and as it seemed to me that they could not have returned to their fort, that they were in danger of shipwreck, and that to come to look for me as they had, they must have brought with them the greater part of the best forces they had; that their fort would remain weakened, and that now was the opportunity to go and attack it. I discussed with the captains the fine undertaking we might carry through, and it appeared so to them likewise; I at once had five hundred men equipped—three hundred arquebusiers, the others with pikes and bucklers, although there were few of these last—and we made up our knapsacks, wherein each man put six pounds of biscuit which he carried on his back; also his wine bottle, containing from three quarts to a gallon of wine, and his arms; for each captain and solider, and I first to set the example, carried this food and the arms on his back. As we did not know the way, we thought we should arrive in two days, and that there would be but six or eight leagues to march, for so two Indians who came with us had told us by signs. Setting out from this Fort of St. Augustine in this order and with this determination, on the eighteenth of September we met with rivers so swollen by the great rainfall, that by the evening of the nineteenth we had walked at least fifteen leagues, when we encamped one league from the fort more or less; more than fifteen leagues, in order to avoid the rivers, all through swamps and wilderness, through a region never before trod. On the twentieth, the eve of the day of the blessed apostle and evangelist San Mateo, at dawn when the day was breaking, we prayed to Our Lord and His Blessed Mother, beseeching them to give us victory over those Lutherans,[1] as we had already agreed to attack openly with twenty ladders which we were carrying; and His Divine Majesty granted us such favor, and guided events in such a manner, that we took the fortress and all that it contained without the slaughter of a single man of ours, and with the wounding of but one, who has already recovered. One hundred and thirty-two men were killed, and next day ten more, who were captured in the woods, and among them many gentlemen; and he who was governor and alcalde, who called himself Monsieur Laudonnière, a relative of the Admiral of France, and who had been his majordomo, fled to the woods; a soldier pursued him and dealt him a blow with his pike; we can not find out what has become of him. About fifty or sixty persons escaped either to the woods, or by swimming, or in two boats of the three ships which they had in front of the fort. I sent at once to their ships a trumpeter to make them surrender, and give up their arms and

[1]The French referred to were actually Huguenots, followers of Calvin, not Luther.

vessels, but they would not. We sent one of the ships to the bottom with artillery which was there in the fort, and the other rescued the people and went down stream, where one league away, there were two other ships with many supplies, which were among the seven that had come from France, and had not yet been unloaded.

As it appeared to me that I ought not to lose this prize, I set out for this Fort of Saint Augustine to prepare three boats that were here, with which to go in search of them, but they were warned by the Indians; and since the French were few in number, they took the two best ships of the three they had, and sank the other; within three days they fled, and being advised of this, I gave up my journey. My men wrote me from the fort that after those ships had departed, there appeared in the woods about twenty Frenchmen, who go about in their shirts, many of them wounded, and it is thought that among them may be Monsieur Laudonnière.[2] I have dispatched orders that they shall try to capture them by every means possible, and work justice upon them. There were found, counting women, girls, and boys under fifteen years, about fifty persons, and very great is my anxiety at seeing them in the company of my people, because of their evil sect, and I feared Our Lord would punish me if I used cruelty towards them, for eight or ten of the boys were born here. These Frenchmen had many friends among the Indians, who have shown much sorrow for their loss, especially for that of two or three teachers of their wicked doctrine who taught the caciques and Indians, who followed around after them as the apostles followed Our Lord, for it is a marvelous thing to see how the Lutherans have bewitched this poor savage people. I shall try everything possible to gain the good will of these Indians who were friends of these Frenchmen, and to have no occasion to break with them; for if one does not resist them by action, they are such great traitors and thieves and so envious, that one cannot well live with them. The caciques and Indians who are their enemies all show me friendship, which I keep and shall keep with them, even if it be not to their liking, for their malicious disposition shall play no part in making me do anything else.

On the twenty-eighth of September the Indians came to inform me that many Frenchmen were six leagues from here by the seashore, who had lost their ships, and had escaped by swimming and in the boats. I took fifty soldiers and arrived with them at break of day; and keeping my people in ambush, I went forth with one companion along a river, as they were on the other side and I on this. I spoke with them and told them I was Spanish, and they told me they were French; they asked me, either with or without my companion, to swim the river to where they were, as it was narrow. I replied that we did not know how to swim; that one of them should cross over, upon assurance of safety. They agreed to do it, and sent over a man of good understanding, a shipmaster.

He related to me in detail that they had sailed from their fort with four galleons and eight pinnaces which each carried twenty-four oars, with four hundred picked soldiers and two hundred sailors; Juan Ribao (Jean Ribault)[3] as General, Monsieur La Grange who was General of the infantry, and other good captains and soldiers

[2]Laudonnière escaped and returned to France.

[3]Ribault was the leader of the failed attempt to establish a French Huguenot settlement at Port Royal, South Carolina. Having gone b to France, Ribault returned to America, intending to attempt yet another fortification (Fort Caroline) in 1565, when he was met Menéndez de Avilés.

and gentlemen, with the intention of seeking and engaging me at sea; and, in case I had landed, of landing their forces in those pinnaces and attacking me. He said that if they had wished to land, they could well have done so, but they had not dared; and that desiring to return to their fort, a hurricane and storm overtook them, so that from twenty to twenty-five leagues from here three of their galleons were destroyed; and they carried about four hundred persons, of whom one hundred and forty only were there alive; as to the rest, some had been drowned, others killed by the Indians, and about fifty of them the Indians had captured and carried away; that Jean Ribault with his flagship was five leagues from them, anchored in three fathoms, aground on some shoals, without any masts, for he had had them cut down, and that there were on board the ship about two hundred people, little less; that they believe he is lost; and that all the bronze artillery, whereof there were many and very good pieces, with the ammunition, were lost in those three vessels; that part of them were on the ship of Jean Ribault, and they considered that he was certainly lost. And he told me that his companions, those captains and soldiers who were safe, prayed that I should give them safe conduct to go to their fort, since they were not at war with Spaniards. I answered him that we had taken their fort and killed those in it, because they had erected it there without Your Majesty's permission, and because they were implanting their evil Lutheran sect in these Your Majesty's provinces; and that I, as Governor and Captain-General of these provinces, would wage a war of fire and blood against all those who should come to people these lands and implant the wicked Lutheran sect; seeing that I had come by Your Majesty's command to spread the Gospel in these parts, to enlighten the natives as to what the Holy Mother Church of Rome says and believes, so that they may save their souls; and that therefore I would not give them safe conduct; rather would I follow them on land and sea, until I had taken their lives. He begged me to let him return with this message, and he promised that he would swim back at night; he asked also that I should grant him his life. I did it because I saw he was dealing truthfully with me, and he could make clear to me many things; and immediately after he had returned to his companions, there came a gentleman to tempt me, Monsieur Laudonnière's lieutenant, who was very crafty in these matters; and having conferred with me, he offered that they should lay down their arms, and give themselves up, provided I spared their lives. I replied to him that they could give up their arms, and place themselves at my mercy, for me to do with them that which Our Lord should command me; and from this he could not move me, nor will he, unless God Our Lord inspire me otherwise. And thus he went back with this answer, and they came over and laid down their arms, and I had their hands tied behind them, and had them put to the knife.[4]

Only sixteen were left, of whom twelve were Breton sailors whom they had kidnapped, the other four being carpenters and calkers, people of whom I had need. It appeared to me that to chastise them in this manner would be serving God Our Lord and Your Majesty, so that henceforth this wicked sect shall leave us more free to im-

[4]The massacre of prisoners must be contextualized historically among contemporary practices. That is, the French massacred Protestants in 1572 (three thousand in one night, in Paris alone); the Dutch massacred the English at Amboyna, 1623; Cromwell massacred the Irish at Drogheda, 1649; and the Puritan colonists massacred 800 Pequots in Connecticut and all the male Narragansetts of Block Island in the early 1600s. Menéndez de Avilés, unfortunately, was not exceptional in this.

plant the Gospel in these parts, enlighten the natives, and bring them to allegiance to Your Majesty; and forasmuch as this land is very large, there will be much to do these fifty years, but good beginnings give hope of good endings, and so I hope in Our Lord that He will give me success in everything, that I and my descendants may give these kingdoms to Your Majesty free and unobstructed, and that the people thereof may become Christians; for this is what particularly interests me, as I have written to Your Majesty; and we shall gain much reputation with the Indians, and shall be feared by them, even though we make them gifts.

Meditating on what Jean Ribault had done, I concluded that within ten leagues of where he was anchored with his ship, the three other ships of his company had been lost; that whether he should be wrecked or whether he abandoned his ship, he would land his forces and entrench himself, landing what provisions he could from his ship, and would occupy himself in getting out what bronze guns he could from the three ships; that if his vessel were not lost he would repair damages as best he could from the masts and rigging of the other three ships, and would come back to the fort, thinking it still his; but that if the ship were lost, getting together all the forces he could, he would march along the shore. If he does this, I am waiting for him, so that, with God's help, he will be destroyed; yet he may go inland to a cacique who is friendly to him and very powerful, who is about thirty leagues distant from him; and if this is the case I shall go there to seek him, for it is not fitting that he or his companions remain alive; and if he comes with his ship to the fort, I have provided at the bar two cannon and two demi-culverins wherewith to send him to the bottom after he shall have entered; a brigantine is kept in readiness to capture the men, and I shall do everything possible to prevent him from escaping.

The articles found in the fort were only four bronze pieces, of from ten to fifteen quintals, because as they had brought their cannons from France dismounted and as ballast, they took all the others, and all the rest of the munitions, on the galleons when they went in search of me. There were found, besides, twenty-five bronze muskets weighing two quintals; about twenty quintals of powder, and all the ammunition for these pieces; one hundred and seventy casks of flour, three to a ton; about twenty pipes of wine, as they had not unloaded the greater part of the supplies. . . . I supplicate Your Majesty that for love of Our Lord, you command that what is due me be delivered to me with great promptness, and that those supplies be provided which are for Your Majesty's account; likewise the men's pay, and the pay to be given over there to the two hundred soldiers, so that all may be here during April, and by the beginning of May I may go to Santa Elena[5] and to the Bay of Santa María,[6] which is the outpost and frontier that Your Majesty must hold to be master of these parts; for unless this be done, we shall have done nothing, and if the French set foot there, much money will be spent, and much time must elapse, before they can be driven out from there; and it is not well to treat this matter lightly. . . .

And because they are Lutherans, and in order that such an evil sect may not survive in these parts, I shall so strive for my part, and induce the Indians my friends to

[5]St. Elena presumably was located in 1970 by excavations at the Parris Island Marine base.

[6]Chesapeake Bay. In 1570 eight Jesuits established a mission on the bay in what is now Virginia, although the exact location is still uncertain. The missionaries were massacred shortly after by Don Carlos, a native of who had been taken to Spain and whom the missionaries had helped return, supposedly to proselytize his brethren.

do so on theirs, that within five or six months very few, if any, will remain alive; and of the thousand French who had landed when I arrived in these provinces, with their fleet of twelve sails, two ships only have escaped, badly damaged, with forty or fifty people on board. As they are ill-provided and equipped, they may not reach France; and if these should arrive, they would not bring news of the death of Jean Ribault and the destruction of his armada; the later they come to know of this in France, the better it will be, because their minds are at rest, thinking they have strong forces here. And now it is more necessary than ever that everything I ask for be provided with great diligence and secrecy, so that it may be here during April, and the coming summer I can gain control of this coast of Florida, and thus Your Majesty will soon be master thereof, without opposition or anxiety; and being master of Florida, you will secure the Indies and the navigation thereto. And I assure Your Majesty that henceforth you can sustain Florida at very little cost, and it will yield Your Majesty much money, and will be worth more to Spain than New Spain, or even Peru. It can be said that this land is a suburb of Spain; for in truth, it took me no more than forty days of sailing to come to it, and ordinarily as many more are necessary to return to those kingdoms. Owing to the burning of the fort, we endure very great hunger, as the flour was burned, and the biscuit that I brought here is becoming stale and giving out. If we are not succored soon, we shall suffer, and many will pass away from this world from starvation; but trusting that Your Majesty is sure that I am serving you with fidelity and love, and that in everything I am dealing truthfully and shall continue to do so, I say no more, except that I shall advise Your Majesty, in every way I can, of all that may occur. May Our Lord keep and cause to prosper the royal Catholic person of Your Majesty with the extension of greater kingdoms and dominions, as Christianity has need thereof, and we, Your Majesty's servants, desire. From these provinces of Florida, on the beach of San Pelayo and Fort of St. Augustine, on the fifteenth of October in the year 1565.

Your Majesty's humble servant, who kisses your royal hands.

P. Menéndez

1968

To a Jesuit Friend[1] (October 15, 1566)

Through letters from Pedro del Castillo[2] I have heard of the many favors done me in all those kingdoms, by the Order of the Society of Jesus: and by means of their prayers, Our Lord has granted me many mercies, and does each day, giving me

[1]The Jesuits were a religious society founded by the Spaniard St. Ignacio Loyola in 1534. In 1571, when the project was beginning to shrink into the narrower confines of the St. Augustine area, they were replaced in the Floridas by Franciscans.

[2]Pedro del Castillo, a Cadiz alderman, sank his entire fortune in Menéndez de Avilés's venture, along with twenty thousand ducats he raised from other investors.

victory and success in all the things to which we have set our hand, I and the Spaniards who are with me, since we arrived in these provinces. And although we have suffered the greatest hunger, hardships, and perils, and there have been some who could not endure them, and who, like weak men, became discouraged; yet others never felt them, and I among them, although the greatest sinner of them all, for I was certain I was undergoing them for Our Lord, and his reward would not fail me; and I went about more hale and hearty, contented, and cheerful than ever I had been, even in the period of greatest need, when each week the Indians came two or three times, killing two or three of our men and wounding others, and we had nothing to eat; nor had those of us in one fort known for two months whether those in the other were dead or alive. On the eve of St. Peter's Day, (on that same day I sailed from Spain with the Armada, bound for this land), seventeen ships appeared off this harbor of St. Augustine, and all entered safely. They brought fifteen hundred soldiers and five hundred sailors, much artillery and munitions, and were all laden with supplies; whereupon everyone received great pleasure and consolation, and those who were in this fort would meet one another, weeping for joy, their eyes and hands raised to heaven, praising Our Lord.

At that time I was not in this fort. I came within eight days: and when I did, I saw all the goods and succor that His Majesty the King Don Philip was sending us, and that Our Lord had brought them in safety.

On the one hand, I received the greatest satisfaction at seeing how well the King Our Lord had aided us; but on the other, I felt distressed and lost, on seeing that no one from the Society had come, nor indeed any learned religious; for on account of the many caciques we have for friends, the good judgment and understanding of the natives of these provinces, and the great desire they have to become Christians and know the Law of Jesus Christ, six such religious could accomplish more in one month than many thousands of men such as we could in many years; we even need them for our own instruction. And it is wasted time to think that the Holy Gospel can be established in this land with the army alone. Your worship may be certain, if I am not mistaken, that the Word of Our Lord will spread in these parts; for the ceremonies of these people consist in great measure in adoring the sun and moon, and dead deer and other animals they hold as idols; and each year they have three or four festivals for their devotions, during which they worship the sun, and remain three days without eating, drinking, or sleeping; these are their fast days. And he who is weak, and cannot endure this, is considered a bad Indian, and therefore looked upon with contempt by their noble caste; and he who comes through these hardships the best is held to be one of the most important men, and treated with utmost courtesy.

They are a people of such strength; very agile and swift, and great swimmers; they carry on many wars against one another, and no powerful cacique is known among them. I have not wanted to be friends with any cacique in order to make war on his enemy, even though he were also mine, because I tell them that Our Lord is in heaven, and is the Cacique of all the caciques of the earth, and of all that which is created; and He is angry with them because they make war and kill one another like beasts. And thus a few have allowed me to make them friends, and have left their idols and asked me to give them crosses before which they may worship; I have already given them some, and they worship them, and I have given them some youths and soldiers to teach them the Christian Doctrine.

They have begged me to let them become Christians like us, and I have replied to them that I am expecting your worships, in order that you may make vocabularies and soon learn their language; and that then you will tell them how to become Christians, and undeceive them as to how, not being so, they serve and hold for their Master the most wicked creature in the world, who is the devil, and that he misleads them; but once they are Christians, they will be undeceived and serve Our Lord, who is the Cacique of heaven and earth; and then, happy and joyful, they will be our brothers in truth and we will give them of what we may have.

And as I had told them that with this expected succor, these religious would come, who would soon be able to talk to them and teach them to be Christians; and they did not come—the Indians held me to be a liar, and some of them have become irritated, saying that I am deceiving them; and the caciques, my enemies, laugh at them and at me.

It has done the greatest harm, that none of your worships, nor any other learned religious, have come to instruct these people; for as they are great traitors and liars, if, with time and labor, peace with them is not confirmed, so as to open the door to the preaching of the Holy Gospel, the caciques confirming what the religious say, later we shall accomplish nothing, they thinking that we deceive them. May Our Lord inspire that good Society of Jesus to send to these parts as many as six of its members—may they be such—for they will certainly reap the greatest reward. . . .

We have not gone inland, because of fortifying ourselves on the coast and trying to make friends with its caciques, so that we can feel secure behind our backs; and therefore we have not seen any large towns, although there are many Indians and boys. There is news that inland there are many people, and a great report of a Salt River which goes to China; wherefore it is expedient that the religious who may come to these parts be truly religious; otherwise, it were better that they should not come. And since your worship understands this better than I can write it, this is enough so that the Society may provide what is fitting in the matter. . . .

Many times I kiss the hands of all those gentlemen of the Society; may they have the reward of Our Lord for the many favors they do me in entreating Our Lord to help and protect me in all things. And I therefore beg them as a mercy, as much as I can, to continue to do so. And if this should reach your worship in Cadiz, tell Pedro del Castillo that I kiss his hands, and he is to consider this letter as his.

May Our Lord keep and increase your worship's most magnificent person and estate, as I desire. From Florida, from this Fort of St. Augustine, on the fifteenth of October, of the year 1566.

Your worship's servant,
Pedro Menéndez

1968

Fray Marcos de Niza 1495?–1542

The party headed by Cabeza de Vaca related tales of a populated area far to the north in which the natives spoke of the fabulously rich "Seven Cities of Cíbola." This stirred hopes of another Mexico awaiting conquest. Antonio de Mendoza, the first viceroy of New Spain, sent the Franciscan Fray Marcos to explore the area, guided by Estévan, Cabeza de Vaca's black companion. Estévan took to breaking the trail, advancing well beyond Fray Marcos and the main party. It was thus that he was killed, under circumstances difficult to confirm, although Fray Marcos would narrate the event as if he had thorough knowledge of it. In the same fashion, Fray Marcos claimed he had seen Cíbola, somewhat as Moses had been allowed to glimpse the promised land he could not enter. His narrative bolstered Cabeza de Vaca's claims, and moved Coronado, the Governor of New Galicia, to organize a massive expedition (see Casteñeda). When it was found, however, that the pueblos, though extraordinary in their construction, were not centers of great wealth, Fray Marcos lost both his reputation and his position with Coronado. Yet his text stands as an example of the rhetoric of promise just over the horizon that would become essential to the American experience, drawing waves of immigrants in search of their fortunes.

Juan Bruce-Novoa
University of California at Irvine

from A Relation of the Reverend Father Fray Marcos de Niza, Touching His Discovery of the Kingdom of Ceuola or Cibola . . .

. . . After the three days were past, many people assembled to go with me, of whom I chose thirty chiefs, who were very well supplied with necklaces of turquoises, some of them wearing as many as five or six strings. With these I took the retinue necessary to carry food for them and me and started on my way. I entered the desert on the ninth day of May. On the first day, by a very wide and well travelled road, we arrived for dinner at a place where there was water, which the Indians showed to me, and in the evening we came again to water, and there I found a shelter which the Indians had just constructed for me and another which had been made for *Stephen*[1] to sleep in when he passed. There were some old huts and many signs of fire, made by people passing to *Cibola*[2] over this road. In this fashion I journeyed twelve days, always very well supplied with victuals of venison, hares, and partridges of the same color and flavor as those of Spain, although rather smaller. . . .

[1]Estévan served as guide and interpreter. As they traveled, Estévan began to be accompanied by an Indian woman. The friars sent him ahead, into Zuni territory. The Zuni, unfamiliar with black races, killed Estévan.

[2]The Spaniard's name for the Zuni pueblos he found.

Continuing our journey, at a day's march from Cibola, we met two other Indians, of those who had gone with Stephen, who appeared bloody and with many wounds. At this meeting, they and those that were with me set up such a crying, that out of pity and fear they also made me cry. So great was the noise that I could not ask about Stephen nor of what had happened to them, so I begged them to be quiet that we might learn what had passed. They said to me: "How can we be quiet, when we know that our fathers, sons and brothers who were with Stephen, to the number of more than three hundred men, are dead? And we no more dare go to Cibola, as we have been accustomed." Nevertheless, as well as I could, I endeavored to pacify them and to put off their fear, although I myself was not without need of someone to calm me. I asked the wounded Indians concerning Stephen and as to what had happened. They remained a short time without speaking a word, weeping along with those of their towns. At last they told me that when Stephen arrived at a day's journey from Cibola, he sent his messengers with his calabash to the lord of Cibola to announce his arrival and that he was coming peacefully and to cure them. When the messengers gave him the calabash and he saw the rattles, he flung it furiously on the floor and said: "I know these people; these rattles are not of our style of workmanship; tell them to go back immediately or not a man of them will remain alive." Thus he remained very angry. The messengers went back sad, and hardly dared to tell Stephen of the reception they had met. Nevertheless they told him and he said that they should not fear, that he desired to go on, because, although they answered him badly, they would receive him well. So he went and arrived at the city of Cibola just before sunset, with all his company, which would be more than three hundred men, besides many women. The inhabitants would not permit them to enter the city, but put them in a large and commodious house outside the city. They at once took away from Stephen all that he carried, telling him that the lord so ordered. "All that night," said the Indians, "they gave us nothing to eat nor drink. The next day, when the sun was a lance-length high, Stephen went out of the house and some of the chiefs with him. Straightway many people came out of the city and, as soon as he saw them, he began to flee and we with him. Then they gave us these arrow-strokes and cuts and we fell and some dead men fell on top of us. Thus we lay till nightfall, without daring to stir. We heard loud voices in the city and we saw many men and women watching on the terraces. We saw no more of Stephen and we concluded that they had shot him with arrows as they had the rest that were with him, of whom there escaped only us."

In view of what the Indians had related and the bad outlook for continuing my journey as I desired, I could not help but feel their loss and mine. God is witness of how much I desired to have someone of whom I could take counsel, for I confess I was at a loss what to do. I told them that Our Lord would chastize Cibola and that when the Emperor knew what had happened he would send many Christians to punish its people. They did not believe me, because they say that no one can withstand the power of Cibola. I begged them to be comforted and not to weep and consoled them with the best words I could muster, which would be too long to set down here. With this I left them and withdrew a stone's throw or two apart, to commend myself to God, and remained thus an hour and a half. When I went back to them, I found one of my Indians, named Mark, who had come from Mexico, and he said to me: "Father, these men have plotted to kill you, because they say that on account of you and Stephen their kinsfolk have been murdered, and that there will not remain a man or woman among them all who will not be killed." I then divided among them all that remained of dry stuffs and other articles, in order to pacify them. I told them to observe that if they killed me they would do me no harm, because I would die a Christian and would go to heaven, and that those who killed me would suffer for it, because the Christians would come in search of me, and against my will would kill them all. With these and many other words I pacified them somewhat, although there was still high feeling on account of the people killed. I asked that some of them should go to Cibola, to see if any other Indian had escaped and to obtain some news of Stephen, but I could not persuade them to do so. Seeing this, I told them that, in any case, I must see the city of Cibola and they said that no one would go with me. Finally, seeing me determined, two chiefs said that they would go with me.

With these and with my own Indians and interpreters, I continued my journey till I came within sight of Cibola. It is situated on a level stretch on the brow of a roundish hill. It appears to be a very beautiful city, the best that I have seen in these parts; the houses are of the type that the Indians described to me, all of stone with their storeys and terraces, as it appeared to me from a hill whence I could see it. The town is bigger than the city of Mexico.[3] At times I was tempted to go to it, because I knew that I risked nothing but my life, which I had offered to God the day I commenced the journey; finally I feared to do so, considering my danger and that if I died, I would not be able to give an account of this country, which seems to me to be the greatest and best of the discoveries. When I said to the chiefs who were with me how beautiful Cibola appeared to me, they told me that it was the least of the seven cities, and that Totonteac is much bigger and better than all the seven, and that it has so many houses and people that there is no end to it. Viewing the situation of the city, it occurred to me to call that country the new kingdom of St. Francis, and there, with the aid of the Indians, I made a big heap of stones and on top of it I placed a small, slender cross, not having the materials to construct a bigger one. I declared that I placed that cross and landmark in the name of Don Antonio de Mendoza, viceroy and governor of New Spain for the Emperor, our lord, in sign of possession, in conformity with my instructions. I declared that I took possession there of all the seven cities and of the kingdoms of Tontonteac and Acus and Marata, and that I did not go to them, in order that I might return to give an account of what I had done and seen.

Then I started back, with more more fear than food, and went to meet the people whom I had left behind, with the greatest haste I could make. I overtook them after two day's march and went with them till we had passed the desert and arrived at their home. Here I was not made welcome as previously, because the men as well as the women indulged in much weeping for the persons killed at Cibola. Without tarrying I hastened in fear from that people and that valley. The first day I went ten leagues, then I went eight and again ten leagues, without stopping till I had passed the second desert.

On my return, although I was not without fear, I determined to approach the open tract, situated at the end of the mountain ranges, of which I said above that I had some account. As I came near, I was informed that it is peopled for many days' journey towards the east, but I dared not enter it, because it seemed to me that we

[3]A clear exaggeration.

must go to colonize and to rule that other country of the seven cities and the kingdoms I have spoken of, and that then one could see it better. So I forebore to risk my person and left it alone to given an account of what I had seen. However, I saw, from the mouth of the tract seven moderate-sized towns at some distance, and further a very fresh valley of very good land, whence rose much smoke. I was informed that there is much gold in it and that the natives of it deal in vessels and jewels for the ears and little plates with which they scrape themselves to relieve themselves of sweat, and that these people will not consent to trade with those of the other part of the valley; but I was not able to learn the cause for this. Here I placed two crosses and took possession of all this plain and valley in the same manner as I had done with the other possessions, according to my instructions. From there I continued my return journey, with all the haste I could, till I arrived at the town of San Miguel, in the province of Culiacan, expecting to find there Francisco Vazquez de Coronado, governor of New Galicia. As I did not find him there, I continued my journey to the city of Compostella, where I found him. From there I immediately wrote word of my coming to the most illustrious lord, the viceroy of New Spain, and to our father provincial, Friar Antonio of Ciudad-Rodrigo, asking him to send me orders what to do.

I omit here many particulars which are not pertinent; I simply tell what I saw and what was told me concerning the countries where I went and those of which I was given information, in order to make a report to our father provincial, that he may show it to the father of our order, who may advise him, or to the council of the order, at whose command I went, that they may give it to the most illustrious lord, the viceroy of New Spain, at whose request they sent me on this journey.—*Fray Marcos de Niza, vice comissarius.*

1539

Pedro de Casteñeda 1510?–1570?

As Fray Marcos de Niza set out to verify Cabeza de Vaca's accounts, Viceroy Mendoza also was preparing for a full-scale exploration to be launched out of the northern province of New Galicia. To secure it as a base, he appointed as governor his protegé Francisco Vásquez de Coronado. When Fray Marcos returned with glowing tales of Cíbola, Coronado was commissioned to lead an expedition of some two thousand people—including at least three women—and almost as many animals moving by land, and a fleet under Hernando de Alarcón proceeding up the Gulf of California. The venture set out with great expectations.

Disappointment soon replaced optimism when the capture of Cíbola (Zuni) revealed Fray Marcos's penchant for hyperbole. The friar was sent back, but Coronado continued farther and farther into the heart of the continent following other voices of exaggerated promises. The most infamous was offered by "the Turk," a Plains Indian, who convinced the Spaniards that Quivira was the city of their dreams. Coronado led a splinter group as far as central Kansas, encountering the Wichita, who were numerous but not rich in gold. He also encountered herds of buffalo and described the ocean-like plains that centuries later would swallow wagon trains from the east. Coronado eventually returned south in failure, the purpose of his mission—gold and the location of another Mexico City—having eluded him.

Little is known of Pedro de Casteñeda, who recorded the account of Coronado's journey over twenty years after the event. A native of Najera in northern Spain, he had established himself at the Spanish outpost at Culiacan, in northwestern Mexico, at the time Coronado formed his expedition.

Juan Bruce-Novoa
University of California at Irvine

PRIMARY WORK

The Journey of Coronado, 1540–1542 [by Pedro de Casteñeda], trans. George Parker Winship, 1904.

from The Narrative of the Expedition of Coronado

Chapter XXI
Of how the army returned to Tiguex[1] and the general reached Quivira.

The general started from the ravine with the guides that the Teyas[2] had given him. He appointed the alderman Diego Lopez his army-master, and took with him the men who seemed to him to be most efficient, and the best horses. The army still had some hope that the general would send for them, and sent two horsemen, lightly equipped and riding post, to repeat their petition.

The general arrived—I mean, the guides ran away during the first few days and Diego Lopez had to return to the army for guides, bringing orders for the army to return to Tiguex to find food and wait there for the general. The Teyas, as before, willingly furnished him with new guides. The army waited for its messengers and spent a fortnight here, preparing jerked beef to take with them. It was estimated that during this fortnight they killed 500 bulls.[3] The number of these that were there without any cows was something incredible. Many fellows were lost at this time who went out hunting and did not get back to the army for two or three days, wandering about the country as if they were crazy, in one direction or another, not knowing how to get back where they started from, although this ravine extended in either direction so that they could find it. Every night they took account of who was missing, fired guns and blew trumpets and beat drums and built great fires, but yet some of them went off so far and wandered about so much that all this did not give them any help, although it helped others. The only way was to go back where they had killed an animal and start from there in one direction and another until they struck the ravine or fell in with somebody who could put them on the right road. It is worth noting that

[1]The region of the New Mexican pueblo settlements.
[2]The Spanish name for the Indians they encountered in Texas. It meant "friend" in the native language.
[3]Buffalo.

the country there is so level that at midday, after one has wandered about in one direction and another in pursuit of game, the only thing to do is to stay near the game quietly until sunset, so as to see where it goes down, and even then they have to be men who are practiced to do it. Those who are not, had to trust themselves to others.

The general followed his guides until he reached Quivira, which took forty-eight days' marching, on account of the great detour they had made toward Florida.[4] He was received peacefully on account of the guides whom he had. They asked the Turk why he had lied and had guided them so far out of their way. He said that his country was in that direction and that, besides this, the people at Cicuye had asked him to lead them off on to the plains and lose them, so that the horses would die when their provisions gave out, and they would be so weak if they ever returned that they would be killed without any trouble, and thus they could take revenge for what had been done to them.[5] This was the reason why he had led them astray, supposing that they did not know how to hunt or to live without corn, while as for the gold, he did not know where there was any of it. He said this like one who had given up hope and who found that he was being persecuted, since they had begun to believe Ysopete[6] who had guided them better than he had, and fearing lest those who were there might give some advice by which some harm would come to him. They garroted him, which pleased Ysopete very much, because he had always said that Ysopete was a rascal and that he did not know what he was talking about and had always hindered his talking with anybody. Neither gold nor silver nor any trace of either was found among these people. Their lord wore a copper plate on his neck and prized it highly.

The messengers whom the army had sent to the general returned, as I said, and then, as they brought no news except what the alderman had delivered, the army left the ravine and returned to the Teyas, where they took guides who led them back by a more direct road. They readily furnished these, because these people are always roaming over this country in pursuit of the animals and so know it thoroughly. They keep their road in this way: In the morning they notice where the sun rises and observe the direction they are going to take, and then shoot an arrow in this direction. Before reaching this they shoot another over it, and in this way they go all day toward the water where they are to end the day. In this way they covered in 25 days what had taken them 37 days going, besides stopping to hunt cows on the way. They found many salt lakes on this road, and there was a great quantity of salt. There were thick pieces of it on top of the water bigger than tables, as thick as four or five fingers. Two or three spans down under water there was salt which tasted better than that in the floating pieces, because this was rather bitter. It was crystalline. All over these plains there were large numbers of animals like squirrels[7] and a great number of their holes.

On its return the army reached the Cicuye river more than 30 leagues below there—I mean below the bridge they had made when they crossed it, and they

[4]Texas was considered part of Florida, and it appeared as such on early maps.

[5]The Spanish used force to subdue the Pueblo Indians.

[6]Another member of the Plains Indian tribe found in captivity with the Pueblos. From the beginning he had tried to alert the Spanish to Turk's lies.

[7]The first report of the extensive prairie dog towns common to the southwestern United States.

followed it up to that place. In general, its banks are covered with a sort of rose bushes, the fruit of which tastes like muscatel grapes.[8] They grow on little twigs about as high up as a man. It has the parsley leaf. There were unripe grapes and currants and wild marjoram. The guides said this river joined that of Tiguex more than 20 days from here, and that its course turned toward the east. It is believed that it flows into the mighty river of the Holy Spirit (Espiritu Santo)[9] which the men with Don Hernando de Soto discovered in Florida. A painted Indian woman ran away from Juan de Saldibar and hid in the ravines about this time, because she recognized the country of Tiguex where she had been a slave. She fell into the hands of some Spaniards who had entered the country from Florida to explore it in this direction. After I got back to New Spain I heard them say that the Indian told them that she had run away from other men like them nine days, and that she gave the names of some captains; from which we ought to believe that we were not far from the region they discovered, although they said they were more than 200 leagues inland. I believe the land at that point is more than *600 leagues*[10] across from sea to sea.

As I said, the army followed the river up as far as Cicuye, which it found ready for war and unwilling to make any advances toward peace or to give any food to the army. From there they went on to Tiguex where several villages had been reinhabited, but the people were afraid and left them again.

1904

Gaspar Pérez de Villagrá 1555–1620

Villagrá was the official chronicler, military outfitter, and missionizer of the Juan de Oñate expedition (1598–1608) that explored and then established permanent Spanish settlements in north central New Mexico. To this expedition also go the honors of having generated the first drama and the first epic poem of European origin, *Historia de la Nueva México* (1610), in the present U.S. territory.

While Oñate, interested in mineral wealth, dispatched his troops in wide-ranging forays into the surrounding areas, the settlers in his party wanted him to concentrate on securing the colony for agriculture and livestock raising. Conflicts were inevitable. To add to Oñate's problems, one of the forays provoked violence at the Acoma pueblo. The ensuing battle set an ominous precedent for European-Native American encounters, repeated from New England to Patagonia by colonizers of different national origins.

The Acoma pueblo, which had received the Coronado expedition in friendship sixty years earlier, submitted peacefully to Oñate. However, when a small band of Spaniards abused their welcome, the Acomas killed thirteen soldiers, including the commanding officer Juan de Saldívar. Oñate sent Vicente de Saldívar on a punitive expedition against the fortress-like city high on a mesa. After days of struggle, in which the Spaniards had to deploy artillery to level the village, the Acomas were decimated, with some 800 killed.

[8]Reports of the lush growth of edible plants encouraged later settlers who came to make permanent agricultural settlements.

[9]The Mississippi.

[10]Approximately 2,400 miles.

Those who surrendered were indentured, many after having one foot severed as punishment.

Villagrá, in the literary fashion of the era, composed his chronicle in epic verse. With one eye on recording events and the other on the demands of his craft and genre, the poet/chronicler filtered facts through a grid of Renaissance literary conventions, juxtaposing brutal genocide and the elegance of classic verse.

Juan Bruce-Novoa
University of California at Irvine

Amy E. Winans
Dickinson College

PRIMARY WORKS

Historia de la Nueva México, 1616; *Historia de la Nueva México, 1610,* trans. and ed. M. Encinias, A. Rodríguez, and J. P. Sánchez, 1992.

from The History of New Mexico[1]

from **Canto I**

Which sets forth the outline of the history and the location of New Mexico, and the reports had of it in the traditions of the Indians, and of the true origin and descent of the Mexicans.

I sing of arms and the heroic man,
The being, courage, care, and high emprise
Of him whose unconquered patience,
Though cast upon a sea of cares,
In spite of envy slanderous,
Is raising to new heights the feats,
The deeds, of those brave Spaniards who,
In the far India of the West,
Discovering in the world that which was hid,
'Plus ultra' go bravely saying
By force of valor and strong arms,
In war and suffering as experienced
As celebrated now by pen unskilled.
I beg of thee, most Christian Philip,[2]
Being the Phoenix of New Mexico
Now newly brought forth from the flames
Of fire and new produced from ashes

[1]This text is taken from M. Encinias, A. Rodríguez, and J. P. Sánchez, trans. and ed., *Historia de la Nueva México, 1610,* 1992.

[2]Philip III, King of Spain, 1598–1621.

Of the most ardent faith, in whose hot coals
Sublime your sainted Father and our lord
We saw all burned and quite undone,
Suspend a moment from your back
The great and heavy weight which bears you down
Of this enormous globe which, in all right,
Is by your arm alone upheld,
And, lending, O great King, attentive ear,
Thou here shalt see the load of toil,
Of calumny, affliction, under which
Did plant the evangel holy and the Faith of Christ
That Christian Achilles whom you wished
To be employed in such heroic work.
And if in fortune good I may succeed
In having you, my Monarch, listener,
Who doubts that, with a wondering fear,
The whole round world shall listen too
To that which holds so high a King intent.
For, being favored thus by you,
It being no less to write of deeds worthy
Of being elevated by the pen
Than to undertake those which are no less
Worthy of being written by this same pen,
'Tis only needed that those same brave men
For whom this task I undertook
Should nourish with their great, heroic valor
The daring flight of this my pen,
Because I think that this time we shall see
The words well equaled by the deeds.
Hear me, great King, for I am witness
Of all that here, my Lord, I say to you.

Beneath the Arctic Pole, in height
Some thirty-three degrees, which the same
Are, we know, of sainted Jerusalem,
Not without mystery and marvel great,
Are spread, extended, sown, and overflow
Some nations barbarous, remote
From the bosom of the Church,[3] where
The longest day of all the year contains and has
Some fourteen hours and a half when it arrives,
The furious sun, at the rising of Cancer,
Through whose zenith he doth usually pass
The image of Andromeda and Perseus,
Whose constellation always influences

[3]Villagrá placed the expedition among those that sought the continued expansion of the Catholic Church, represented in the Acts of the Apostles as moving westward from Jerusalem, to Asia Minor, to Rome, and westward.

The quality of Venus and Mercury.
And shows to us its location in longitude,
According as most modern fixed meridian
Doth teach us and we practice,
Two hundred just degrees and seventy
Into the temperate zone and the fourth clime,
Two hundred long leagues from the place
Where the Sea of the North[4] and Gulf of Mexico
Approach the most and nearest to the coast
On the southeast; and to the side
Toward the rough Californio[5] and Sea of the Pearls[6]
The distance in that direction is about the same
Toward where the southwest wind strikes the coast
And from the frozen zone its distance is
About five hundred full long leagues;
And in a circle round we see it hold,
Beneath the parallel, if we should take
The height of thirty-seven degrees,
Five thousand goodly Spanish leagues,
Whose greatness it is a shame it should be held
By so great sum of people ignorant
About the blood of Christ, whose holiness
It causes pain to think so many souls know not.
From these new regions[7] 'tis notorious,
Of public voice and fame, that there descended
Those oldest folk of Mexico
Who to the famous city, Mexico,
Did give their name, that it might be
Memorial eternal of their name, and lasting,
In imitation of wise Romulus
Who put a measure to the walls of Rome. . . .

Canto XXX[8]

How the new General, having given orders to his soldiers, went to take leave of Luzcoija, and the battle he had with the Spaniards, and the things that happened.

[4]The Atlantic Ocean.

[5]The Colorado River.

[6]The Gulf of California.

[7]That the ancient races came from northern regions is an allusion to the myth of Aztlán, renewed by Chicano literature of the 1960s.

[8]On July 11, 1598, Oñate established temporary headquarters near San Juan Pueblo, north of present-day Santa Fe, before setting out for th west with the main body of the expedition. Near the end of October, 1598, Oñate met wit some leaders at Acoma, a pueblo built atop a high, isolated mesa, and elicited from them what he judged to be promises of cooperation and allegiance. Then he moved west to Zuni and Hopi. The smaller force following Oñate, led by Juan de Saldívar, was attacked on December 4. Villagrá's narrative culminates in the retaliatory attack on Acoma by Vicente de Saldívar, Juan's brother.

When man enkindles himself against right
And forces his desires to bend themselves
To undertake a thing that has no plan,
With what ease he doth mark and note
What is in favor, what against that thing
That he wills to undertake against justice.
Gicombo, then, fearing and foreseeing,
Being prudent, skillful, and cautious,
That Zutacapán and all the people
Together would fail him at any time,
Did make them bind themselves and take an oath
According to their laws, rites, and customs,
As Hannibal once swore upon the fanes
And altars of his gods that he would be
Ever a mortal foe to the Romans,
So that they would keep inviolate,
Subject to penalties, controls, and force,
The conditions made and agreed.
The ceremony done and done also
The vile and superstitious oath taking,
He, with his own hand, did select
Five hundred brave barbarian warriors
And ordered them to go in a body
Unto a great cavern, by nature made,
Near to the two ditches we have mentioned,
Purposing, when your men should pass that place,
That they should sally forth from their ambush and
Deprive them, then and there, of all their lives.
And when he'd posted them and entrusted
To brave Bempol, Chumpo, Zutancalpo,
To Calpo, Buzcoico, and Ezmicaio,[9]
To each of these a squadron well-chosen,
The better to trap us into their hands
He carefully gave us to understand
That all the town was deserted.
And when the shining sun had gone to rest
And the dark bodies had been plunged
Into deep shadows, and in silence deep
All living things remained at rest,
From the sea came forth the night,
Enveloping the earth in a dark veil.

[9]Like Gicombo, these men—whose historical identity is now lost in the Spanish transliterations—were Acoma leaders who had urged peace. After the first violent encounter following the attack on Juan de Saldívar's party, a council is convened in which Gicombo is named war captain. All agree that, despite the reservations about defeating the Spanish, they will unite with the aggressive-minded faction led by Zutacapán, Villagrá's real villain.

And before all the stars had run
The mighty course which they do take,
He went to take leave of Luzcoija,
Who was awaiting him in that same place
Where he had chosen to leave her, wounded
Deeply by that love which did burn in her.
And when she saw him, overcome,
Like a mild turtledove which, lost
From its sweet company, roosts not
Nor takes repose on flowering branches,
But on the dry and leafless trees,
And like a tender mother who carries
Her tender child about with her, hanging
About her lovely neck, and, filled with love,
Yearns over him and grows tender
In loving fire, and wastes away,
So this poor woman, conquered by her love,
Making two fountains of her tears,
Did there raise her discouraged voice:
"If the dear pure love I have had for you,
A thousand times more loving you than my own soul,
Deserveth that you give me some comfort,
I beg of you, my lord, not to permit
A flower so tender to wither
Which you have made me think was e'er
To you more pleasing, sweet, and beautiful
Than the life which you live and do enjoy.
By which dear gift I beg of you
That if you come, lord, but to go,
You take my life, for I cannot
Live without you a single hour."
And she became expectantly quiet,
Awaiting a reply, and then spoke out
The sad barbarian: "Madam, I swear
Now by the beauty of those eyes
Which are the peace and light of mine,
And by those lips with which you hide
Those lovely oriental pearls,
And by those soft, delicate hands
Which hold me in such sweet prison,
That now I cannot make excuse
From going to battle against Spain.
Wherefore you must rouse your courage
And strengthen mine, so this sad soul
May return but to look on you,
For though 'tis true it fears your loss
It has firm hope to enjoy you.

And though I die a thousand times I swear
I shall return to see and console you,
And that, dear love, you may understand this
I leave you as ransom my heart and soul."
And so he took his leave, for now
The morning light was appearing,
And, entering the cavern with his men,
The light came fast and embroidered
All of the sky with bright red clouds.
At this great time and conjuncture
The Father Fray Alonso, saying mass,
Did celebrate the day of his name saint,
And having given communion to us all,
Turned from the altar and addressed us thus:
"Ye valiant cavaliers of Christ
And of our most holy laws defenders,
I have not to exhort you to the Church
For as her noble sons you have always
Taken great pains to serve and respect her.
By Jesus Christ I ask and beg of you,
And by His holy blood, that you restrain
Your keen swords, in so far as possible,
From shedding the blood of the enemy,
For thus the valor of the Spaniards is,
To conquer without blood and death whom they attack.
And since you carry God within your souls,
May He bless all of you and may His powerful hand
Protect you, and I, in His name,
Do bless you all." And having thus
Received the blessing from this holy Father there,
We then climbed to the lofty passageway,
Whence we all saw from afar off
That all the pueblo was deserted quite
And that no living soul was seen.
For this reason thirteen immediately
Did pass both ditches from the passageway
Without the Sergeant's order or his permission,
And hardly had they, all together, occupied
The further side when all at once
There charged from the horrible cave
The valiant Gicombo, roaring loud.
And, like the young whale which, wounded
By keen harpoon and deadly steel,
Projects on high thick clouds of spume
And lashes the sea with his tail and cleaves
The water here and there, rising
His spacious back, and, in anger

Snorting and restless, doth stir up
A thousand whirlpools in the deep, so he,
Enraged, his mighty weapons lifted high,
Attacked with them and struck at all.
Seeing the enemy so near at hand
Our men did, in a volley, fire
Their ready harquebuses and, though many
Were stricken down, they yet were forced,
Unable to load a second time,
To come to swords, and in the hot melee,
Mixed with each other, we could not
Give any aid to them because they had
Taken that beam by which they crossed
Unto the second ditch and did not note
They left the first without means of crossing.
All thus involved in such confusion,
Plunging their daggers and the sharp edges
Of their swift swords into a great slaughter
Of miserable, shattered bodies,
They made a fearful butchery.
And so, proud, brave, and fiery
There the two valorous brothers,
Cristóbal Sánchez and Francisco Sánchez,
Captain Quesada and Juan Piñero,
Francisco Vázquez and Manuel Francisco,
Cordero, Juan Rodríguez, Pedraza,
Like to the fingers of the human hand,
Which, being unequal, yet combine
Each with the others and do form,
When closed, a fist that doth destroy
Some strong substance and crushes it,
All joined together in one band,
Each with the others, and charged in.
And, opening great wounds, they shed
From the barbarian breasts and sides,
Eyes, heads, and legs, and from their throats,
Swift-flowing streams of their fresh blood,
And through these great and fearful mouths
Their fearful souls did take swift flight,
All going thence so not to fall
Into such powerful hands. And then
Carrasco, Isasti, Casas, Montesinos,
Their swords red up to their elbows,
Were plying well their brawny arms
When Zutancalpo and great Buzcoico,
With reinforcements, came and did drive back
Your Spaniards, and with so great a force

That, all cornered upon a slope
Which was a trifle deep and protected,
By rain of rocks which they discharged
Upon them, though they wounded none,
Yet so swift and so overwhelming
They were burying them beyond all help.
The brave youth then, seeing that little ship
So overwhelmed and now about to sink,
Shouted with a great voice that someone should
Immediately go and bring a beam.
Hearing this, then, I did fall back,
For, lord, I thought he spoke to me,
Some nine paces and, like to Curtius,
I was running, near desperate,
Toward the first ditch and the Sergeant,
Thinking that I would be dashed to pieces,
Did grasp me by the shield, and, had he not
Loosed me no doubt that had been
The last test I had made of fortune in my life.
But, as he loosed me quickly, I gathered
Momentum for that leap to such effect
That finally I jumped the ditch and then,
Not free from fear and trembling, I took
The log as best I might and dragged,
And, passage made between the ditches,
Your men did quickly pass over.
And hardly had the trumpet blared aloud
When, from the slope on which they were,
Our friends so dear who were buried
Did all come forth, as needs must be
Upon the trumpet's sound shall rise,
On that day of the ultimate judgment,
All of the dead from out their sepulchers.
And seeing that all the lost ground
Was now regained by our men,
Bursting with shame and with sense of disgrace,
Like fiery coals that were buried
And came from the ashes ablaze,
Fiercer than courageous lions
They all did charge, being aided by
Captain Romero and Juan Velarde,
Carabajal, Bañuelos, and Archuleta,
De Lorenzo, Salado, and de Zubia
And many other noble Castilians
Who to the right and left dispatched
Idolaters most swiftly from this life.
Because of this the strong Zutancalpo,

With brave Gicombo and Buzcoico,
Just as the sea in tumult and tempest
Doth boil all over, raising up
Huge crests of water, high summits
Wetting the high heaven, and haughtily
Swells and increases, moans and roars,
And breaks and foams its wild fury
On mighty rocks, and does not rest
So long as the winds temper not
The force of their blasts nor do show themselves
All temperate in peaceful calm,
So were these brave, ferocious barbarians,
Who, urging on their men, did order them
To speed from their swift ready bows
A flight of arrows full as numerous
As the thick drops of water and hailstones
That the high heaven rains or hails.
By whose sharp force sorely wounded
They left Quesada and the ensign, too,
Carabajal and good Antonio Hernández,
Francisco García, and Lizama.
At this, Asencio de Archuleta
Did set firmly against his breast
The stock of his harquebus and did align
The rear sight with thc front sight in such wise
That, not knowing how 'twas or where he shot,
He shot through, with four heavy balls,
The greatest comrade and the dearest friend
Whom the poor man had ever in his life.
O divine Shepherd, how You stretch
Your most holy crook out and direct it
To that sad, disobedient sheep
Which we have seen of its free will
Departing very far from out the fold.
Their just punishment is well shown
By unhappy Salado, for, seeing
Eight deadly mouths there open wide
In back and breast and in his sides,
Shrugging his shoulders and raising
His eyes unto the lofty Heavens,
The poor wretch thus did raise his voice to God:
"Lord, it is two years since I have confessed
No matter how my friends have begged me to.
I know, my Lord, I have offended Thee
And I beg only that Thou wait for me
'Till I wash off the stains with which I have
Contaminated my sad soul, redeemed

By that most precious blood You shed."
Hearing of this misfortune, then did come
The Sergeant Major in a mighty haste,
And that he might confess he then ordered
That six good soldiers should take him down.
And he, understanding that aid,
Did beg of him with much sincerity
That since he had alone given offense
To God, our Lord, it be allowed to him
To seek his remedy alone.
Seeing how sincerely he begged
He pleased him in this, but, appearing nonchalant,
He ordered that those men should go with him.
Now, as they followed, he came to a cliff
Of a great height, whereon he saw
A fearful demon who did say to him:
"O valorous soldier, if you now desire
To leave this sad life in triumph,
Throw yourself off here, for I, in these hands,
Will hold your body so that it cannot
Receive an injury in any place."
The sad christian one, hearing this,
Though filled with fear and suspicion,
Summoning courage, answered thus:
"Begone from here, accursed! Tempt me not,
For I am God's soldier, and if I have followed
Your vain standards, this is no time
For such calamity." And, turning back
His tired feet, he then followed
The proper road and clambered down
Unto the Father's tent, where, just as soon
As he confessed his faults and was absolved,
He there lay senseless, for his soul had gone.
The Angels praise you, O my God,
That You thus cure our wounds and show to us
That however You afflict and destroy
The miserable body You gave us,
The soul yet lives and is raised up
Unto the highest height and excellence
That doth await and expect us.
And since the storm of battle as it goes
Grows hotter, and since I do feel myself
Without the strength or courage to continue it,
I wish to stop here that I may write it.

1992

Samuel de Champlain 1570?–1635

Champlain first explored North America as Royal Geographer on an expedition in 1603 intended to repeat Jacques Cartier's famous trip up the St. Lawrence in 1534–1535. He returned a year later as part of a Huguenot expedition led by de Monts and participated in exploration, fur trade, and settlement projects for several decades. In addition to discovering the lake that bears his name and founding Quebec, the second permanent European city north of Mexico, he escalated the French alliance with the Hurons into an active role in their war against the Iroquois. This decision, dictated by necessity, turned the Iroquois into relentless enemies of the French. The first selection shows Champlain's curiosity about the landscape through which he is traveling, one oriented towards observations about the exploitable potential of the wilderness. In the context of his affiliation with the fur trade, his comment on the abundance of beaver assumes commercial significance. His introduction of firearms into native warfare, with awesome impact, coincides with Villagrá's description of a similar application of European technology in New Mexico. Around this time the Dutch began supplying their native allies with arms and powder. Native warfare, and thus their societies, were forever altered.

The second selection seems to be simply another story of the European lost in the American landscape which turns out to be familiar home territory to the native. Yet more significant is the ending in which the natives of the area admit, perhaps unknowingly, that they no longer really control their world, for Champlain is its new center. If he dies their mobility would be curtailed, so they must keep him alive, guard, and guide him. The European has assumed central value here. Just as in the first selection, the introduction of the European element changes Native American life.

Juan Bruce-Novoa
University of California at Irvine

Carla Mulford
Pennsylvania State University

PRIMARY WORK

The Voyages of Samuel de Champlain, 1604–1618, ed. W.L. Grant, 1907.

SECONDARY WORKS

Marcel Trudel, *Dictionary of Canadian Biography,* v. 1, 1966; W. J. Eccles, *France in America,* 1990.

from The Voyages of Samuel de Champlain, 1604–1618

from The Voyages to the Great River St. Lawrence, 1608–1612

[An Encounter with the Iroquois]

We set out on the next day,[1] continuing our course in the river as far as the entrance of the lake. There are many pretty islands here, low, and containing very fine woods

[1]July 13, 1609.

and meadows, with abundance of fowl and such animals of the chase as stags, fallow-deer, fawns, roe-bucks, bears, and others, which go from the main land to these islands. We captured a large number of these animals. There are also many beavers, not only in this river, but also in numerous other little ones that flow into it. These regions, although they are pleasant, are not inhabited by any savages, on account of their wars; but they withdraw as far as possible from the rivers into the interior, in order not to be suddenly surprised.

The next day we entered the lake,[2] which is of great extent, say eighty or a hundred leagues long, where I saw four fine islands, ten, twelve, and fifteen leagues long, which were formerly inhabited by the savages, like the River of the Iroquois; but they have been abandoned since the wars of the savages with one another prevail. There are also many rivers falling into the lake, bordered by many fine trees of the same kinds as those we have in France, with many vines finer than any I have seen in any other place; also many chestnut-trees on the border of this lake, which I had not seen before. There is also a great abundance of fish, of many varieties; among others, one called by the savages of the country *Chaousarou,*[3] which varies in length, the largest being, as the people told me, eight or ten feet long. I saw some five feet long, which were as large as my thigh; the head being as big as my two fists, with a snout two feet and a half long, and a double row of very sharp and dangerous teeth. Its body is, in shape, much like that of a pike; but it is armed with scales so strong that a poniard[4] could not pierce them. Its color is silver-gray. The extremity of its snout is like that of swine. This fish makes war upon all others in the lakes and rivers. It also possesses remarkable dexterity, as these people informed me, which is exhibited in the following manner. When it wants to capture birds, it swims in among the rushes, or reeds, which are found on the banks of the lake in several places, where it puts its snout out of water and keeps perfectly still: so that, when the birds come and light on its snout, supposing it to be only the stump of a tree, it adroitly closes it, which it had kept ajar, and pulls the birds by the feet down under water. The savages gave me the head of one of them, of which they make great account, saying that, when they have the headache, they bleed themselves with the teeth of this fish on the spot where they suffer pain, when it suddenly passes away.

Continuing our course over this lake on the western side, I noticed, while observing the country, some very high mountains[5] on the eastern side, on the top of which there was snow. I made inquiry of the savages whether these localities were inhabited, when they told me that the Iroquois dwelt there, and that there were beautiful valleys in these places, with plains productive in grain, such as I had eaten in this country, together with many kinds of fruit without limit. They said also that the lake extended near mountains, some twenty-five leagues distant from us, as I judge. I saw, on the south, other mountains,[6] no less high than the first, but without any snow. The savages told me that these mountains were thickly settled, and that it was there we were to find their enemies; but that it was necessary to pass a fall[7] in order to go there (which I afterwards saw), when we should enter another lake,[8] nine or ten leagues

[2]Lake Champlain.
[3]"Garpike."
[4]Dagger.
[5]The Green Mountains of Vermont.
[6]The Adirondacks.
[7]Ticonderoga.
[8]Lake George.

long. After reaching the end of the lake, we should have to go, they said, two leagues by land, and pass through a river[9] flowing into the sea on the Norumbegue coast, near that of Florida, whither it took them only two days to go by canoe, as I have since ascertained from some prisoners we captured, who gave me minute information in regard to all they had personal knowledge of, through some Algonquin interpreters, who understood the Iroquois language.

Now, as we began to approach within two or three days' journey of the abode of their enemies, we advanced only at night, resting during the day. But they did not fail to practise constantly their accustomed superstitions, in order to ascertain what was to be the result of their undertaking; and they often asked me if I had had a dream, and seen their enemies, to which I replied in the negative. Yet I did not cease to encourage them, and inspire in them hope. When night came, we set out on the journey until the next day, when we withdrew into the interior of the forest, and spent the rest of the day there. About ten or eleven o'clock, after taking a little walk about our encampment, I retired. While sleeping, I dreamed that I saw our enemies, the Iroquois, drowning in the lake near a mountain, within sight. When I expressed a wish to help them, our allies, the savages, told me we must let them all die, and that they were of no importance. When I awoke, they did not fail to ask me, as usual, if I had had a dream. I told them that I had, in fact, had a dream. This, upon being related, gave them so much confidence that they did not doubt any longer that good was to happen to them.

When it was evening, we embarked in our canoes to continue our course; and, as we advanced very quietly and without making any noise, we met on the 29th of the month the Iroquois, about ten o'clock at evening, at the extremity of a cape[10] which extends into the lake on the western bank. They had come to fight. We both began to utter loud cries, all getting their arms in readiness. We withdrew out on the water, and the Iroquois went on shore, where they drew up all their canoes close to each other and began to fell trees with poor axes, which they acquire in war sometimes, using also others of stone. Thus they barricaded themselves very well.

Our forces also passed the entire night, their canoes being drawn up close to each other, and fastened to poles, so that they might not get separated, and that they might be all in readiness to fight, if occasion required. We were out upon the water, within arrow range of their barricades. When they were armed and in array, they despatched two canoes by themselves to the enemy to inquire if they wished to fight, to which the latter replied that they wanted nothing else: but they said that, at present, there was not much light, and that it would be necessary to wait for daylight, so as to be able to recognize each other; and that, as soon as the sun rose, they would offer us battle. This was agreed to by our side. Meanwhile, the entire night was spent in dancing and singing, on both sides, with endless insults and other talk; as, how little courage we had, how feeble a resistance we should make against their arms, and that, when day came, we should realize it to our ruin. Ours also were not slow in retorting, telling them they would see such execution of arms as never before, together with an abundance of such talk as is not unusual in the siege of a town. After this singing, dancing, and bandying words on both sides to the fill, when day came, my companions and myself continued under cover, for fear that the enemy would see us.

[9]The Hudson.

[10]Crown Point.

We arranged our arms in the best manner possible, being, however, separated, each in one of the canoes of the savage Montagnais. After arming ourselves with light armor, we each took an arquebuse,[11] and went on shore. I saw the enemy go out of their barricade, nearly two hundred in number, stout and rugged in appearance. They came at a slow pace towards us, with a dignity and assurance which greatly amused me, having three chiefs at their head. Our men also advanced in the same order, telling me that those who had three large plumes were the chiefs, and that they had only these three, and that they could be distinguished by these plumes, which were much larger than those of their companions, and that I should do what I could to kill them. I promised to do all in my power, and said that I was very sorry they could not understand me, so that I might give order and shape to their mode of attacking their enemies, and then we should, without doubt, defeat them all; but that this could not now be obviated, and that I should be very glad to show them my courage and good-will when we should engage in the fight.

As soon as we had landed, they began to run for some two hundred paces towards their enemies, who stood firmly, not having as yet noticed my companions, who went into the woods with some savages. Our men began to call me with loud cries; and, in order to give me a passage-way, they opened in two parts, and put me at their head, where I marched some twenty paces in advance of the rest, until I was within about thirty paces of the enemy, who at once noticed me, and halting, gazed at me, as I did also at them. When I saw them making a move to fire at us, I rested my musket against my cheek, and aimed directly at one of the three chiefs. With the same shot, two fell to the ground; and one of their men was so wounded that he died some time after. I had loaded my musket with four balls. When our side saw this shot so favorable for them, they began to raise such loud cries that one could not have heard it thunder. Meanwhile, the arrows flew on both sides. The Iroquois were greatly astonished that two men had been so quickly killed, although they were equipped with armor woven from cotton thread, and with wood which was proof against their arrows. This caused great alarm among them. As I was loading again, one of my companions fired a shot from the woods, which astonished them anew to such a degree that, seeing their chiefs dead, they lost courage, and took to flight, abandoning their camp and fort, and fleeing into the woods, whither I pursued them, killing still more of them. Our savages also killed several of them, and took ten or twelve prisoners. The remainder escaped with the wounded. Fifteen or sixteen were wounded on our side with arrow-shots; but they were soon healed.

After gaining the victory, our men amused themselves by taking a great quantity of Indian corn and some meal from their enemies, also their armor, which they had left behind that they might run better. After feasting sumptuously, dancing and singing, we returned three hours after, with the prisoners. The spot where this attack took place is in latitude 43° and some minutes, and the lake was called Lake Champlain.

[11]A portable matchlock gun dating from the fifteenth century.

from The Voyages of 1615

[Champlain, among the Huron, Lost in the Woods]

When they first went out hunting,[1] I lost my way in the woods, having followed a certain bird that seemed to me peculiar. It had a beak like that of a parrot, and was of the size of a hen. It was entirely yellow, except the head which was red, and the wings which were blue, and it flew by intervals like a partridge. The desire to kill it led me to pursue it from tree to tree for a very long time, until it flew away in good earnest. Thus losing all hope, I desired to retrace my steps, but found none of our hunters, who had been constantly getting ahead, and had reached the enclosure. While trying to overtake them, and going, as it seemed to me, straight to where the enclosure was, I found myself lost in the woods, going now on this side now on that, without being able to recognize my position. The night coming on, I was obliged to spend it at the foot of a great tree, and in the morning set out and walked until three o'clock in the afternoon, when I came to a little pond of still water. Here I noticed some game, which I pursued, killing three or four birds, which were very acceptable, since I had had nothing to eat. Unfortunately for me there had been no sunshine for three days, nothing but rain and cloudy weather, which increased my trouble. Tired and exhausted I prepared to rest myself and cook the birds in order to alleviate the hunger which I began painfully to feel, and which by God's favor was appeased.

When I had made my repast I began to consider what I should do, and to pray God to give me the will and courage to sustain patiently my misfortune if I should be obliged to remain abandoned in this forest without counsel or consolation except the Divine goodness and mercy, and at the same time to exert myself to return to our hunters. Thus committing all to His mercy I gathered up renewed courage, going here and there all day, without perceiving any foot-print or path, except those of wild beasts, of which I generally saw a good number. I was obliged to pass here this night also. Unfortunately I had forgotten to bring with me a small compass which would have put me on the right road, or nearly so. At the dawn of day, after a brief repast, I set out in order to find, if possible, some brook and follow it, thinking that it must of necessity flow into the river on the border of which our hunters were encamped. Having resolved upon this plan, I carried it out so well that at noon I found myself on the border of a little lake, about a league and a half in extent, where I killed some game, which was very timely for my wants; I had likewise remaining some eight or ten charges of powder, which was a great satisfaction.

I proceeded along the border of this lake to see where it discharged, and found a large brook, which I followed until five o'clock in the evening, when I heard a great noise, but on carefully listening failed to perceive clearly what it was. On hearing the noise, however, more distinctly, I concluded that it was a fall of water in the river which I was searching for. I proceeded nearer, and saw an opening, approaching which I found myself in a great and far-reaching meadow, where there was a large number of wild beasts, and looking to my right I perceived the river, broad and long.

[1]Champlain was in the company of the Huron Indians in northern Canada in the fall of 1615.

I looked to see if I could not recognize the place, and walking along on the meadow I noticed a little path where the savages carried their canoes. Finally, after careful observation, I recognized it as the same river, and that I had gone that way before.

I passed the night in better spirits than the previous ones, supping on the little I had. In the morning I re-examined the place where I was, and concluded from certain mountains on the border of the river that I had not been deceived, and that our hunters must be lower down by four or five good leagues. This distance I walked at my leisure along the border of the river, until I perceived the smoke of our hunters, where I arrived to the great pleasure not only of myself but of them, who were still searching for me, but had about given up all hopes of seeing me again. They begged me not to stray off from them any more, or never to forget to carry with me my compass, and they added: If you had not come, and we had not succeeded in finding you, we should never have gone again to the French, for fear of their accusing us of having killed you. After this he was very careful of me when I went hunting, always giving me a savage as companion, who knew how to find again the place from which he started so well that it was something very remarkable.

1907

Cultures in Contact: Voices from the Anglo-Americans' "New" World

The European settlers who came to the "new" world in the sixteenth and seventeenth centuries left the old world at the height of a rebirth of interest in the arts and sciences, an interest based upon the Renaissance rediscovery of classical texts about strange lands and pagan gods, about epic wars and superhuman heroes. The new world offered the earliest European explorers and settlers a "pristine" contemporary arena in which they could test themselves and create new texts of life experience. The explorers and settlers produced epic poems (like Villagrá's history of New Mexico) that render the Spaniards' battles according to classical models like Virgil's *Aeneid,* and imposing epic histories (like those of Bradford and Winthrop), histories based upon the biblical past of Israelite heroes who could be reformulated in the context of the new world.

Spain and France and England (along with the Netherlands) were competing for territory, for the domination of the environment and its peoples, surely; but they competed for the language of dominance as well. That is, the Spanish, French, and English settlers who came to America knew that if they could find the language in which they could best promote interest in their colonial efforts, their efforts would be funded and thus secure. The competition was not just among the different nations, however—not just Spain against France and then, after the defeat of the Spanish Armada in 1588, England against Spain and France. The competition was within each group as well.

Englishman fought Englishman in order to have his report be the one favored by patrons. If he did not succeed in keeping the power in the colony, then he wrote his own report. At Jamestown, for instance, John Smith competed for dominance with John Newport and with Edward Maria Wingfield, a man who in old England was his social superior. Smith's and Wingfield's reports, written for those in England who did (or might) fund the colony, stress their own abilities and profess forthrightness while placing blame for failures upon others whom they call recalcitrant, lazy, and unhappy. And the reports of those like Smith and Wingfield who were in power in Virginia show only one side of the conflict of opinion. Smith and Wingfield had their differences, and each wished to air his position precisely because he sought to establish his own power center and remain in the colony. But others who traveled to Jamestown, like Richard Frethorne, an indentured servant, were powerless from the start, and they wished only to return home. The letters from people like Frethorne, in fact, provide an intriguing corrective to the promotional (and self-promotional) efforts of those who had power.

For different reasons, a competition between factions of the settlers likewise emerged in New England. William Bradford's tale of Thomas Morton's activities among peoples native to the Plymouth area could not silence Morton, who told his own version of the story in *New English Canaan,* a discourse devised from a Renaissance rhetoric based upon classical satire.

Telling of his mistreatment at the hands of the too-serious Separatists, Morton offered a version of the Puritan past rarely considered because it was a discourse that lost the battle for power in the new world. The language of the Puritans was the one that prevailed.

The Puritan discourse was one based upon the plainness of the Geneva Bible (which they preferred above the Anglican King James version); the Puritan text was the one established in the Old and New Testaments. Like the Israelites of old, Bradford's pilgrims searching for their holy city were engaged in an epic battle, not just for their own survival but for the hereafter. Winthrop's group of Congregationalist Puritans had a similar purpose. On board the ship *Arbella* Winthrop cautioned his listeners that "we must be knit together in this work as one man," so that they could "find that the God of Israel is among us," making them "a praise and glory, that men shall say of succeeding plantations: the lord make it like that of New England." The Puritans were setting up a new world colony for the chosen people of God, as prophesied in the Bible, so that the kingdom of Israel would be theirs.

This ethnocentric world view caused the Puritans no little trouble. To set up such a colony, whether in Plymouth or in Massachusetts Bay, those in power had to find a way to quell dissident voices. As Bradford banished Morton, so Winthrop and the magistrates banished Roger Williams and Anne Hutchinson. Too interested (the Puritans thought) in the languages of others, like the Native Americans who were being supplanted by the missionizing and messianic Puritans, Williams established his own community in Providence, where Anne Hutchinson eventually landed, after she too had been exiled from Massachusetts Bay. Whatever could not fall within the centered, mainstream ideology so precariously established was considered satanic and was not tolerated.

One way the Puritans implemented their mainstream ideology was by establishing texts that would effect their cultural ends. Michael Wigglesworth's *Day of Doom* (1662), a poem that offered in doleful but easily memorized verse a Puritan catechism, proved a means to the end of Puritan acculturation. *The Bay Psalm Book* (1640) and *The New England Primer* (1683?) likewise served as vehicles for cultural formation. All three texts offered Puritan doctrine and social lessons in linguistic forms that could be readily learned (and, it was hoped, practiced). *The Bay Psalm Book,* which took advantage of colonists' memories of popular songs and ballads from England, proved an especially useful and adaptable means by which church dignitaries could inculcate their messages.

Although the Puritans' world was fairly inflexible, hierarchical in structure, and uncompromising, most of Renaissance culture was similarly devised along rigidly imposed social and religious lines. And the Puritans, though they were in New England, were conversant with that culture, as most notably evidenced by their poetry. Anne Bradstreet's poems, like Edward Taylor's and those of the seventeenth-century wits after her, deploy devices common in European continental literature. (The nightingale Bradstreet mentions in "Contemplations," for instance, is merely a figure of speech; nightingales were not indigenous to New England.) Although there was much prose, poetry, the privileged genre of the Renaissance, was written in the new world as well as in the old. Common Renaissance poetic genres—meditations, lyrics, pastorals, sonnets—all contribute to the canon of the earliest Euro-American literature.

Yet the form of literature most often noted in early Anglo-American literature was the diary. Attuned as they were to their own spiritual quests for salvation, Puritans preoccupied themselves with their inner psychological states so as to assess the states of their souls. By recording their experiences in diaries, they could map their journeys toward salvation. Such inward contemplation is evident in the diary of Samuel Sewall, whose outward social success imperiously competed with the success of his inward soul. Sewall's inner turmoils, his questioning about his motives in the Salem witch trials, and his insistence that slavery was unacceptable before God, provide a record of the signal conflicts of his time, a time when Puritanism began to wane amid a vastly changing world.

The changing world worried Cotton Mather, who sought in vain among those of his generation for signs of the strength of Puritans of old. Earthquakes, hailstorms, attacks against the community by the indigenous people, witches in New England, and his own inability to get the recognition he thought he deserved all evidenced to Mather that God was striking back at his generation for lacking the strength of their forefathers. But the evolution of his society was inevitable. More people were coming safely to the colonies, and more children were surviving to adulthood. Increased population brought a growing economy and trade and contributed to a general breakdown of the tight social order established by the earliest settlers.

Changes in the Puritans' lives meant change in the lives of their Native American neighbors as well. In the 1670s, when Puritans' settlements had overtaken the most desirable portions of the Connecticut River valley and displaced the native populations to less fertile lands, Metacomet (King Philip) struck back. But the pan-Indian alliance (of Wampanoags, Nipmucks, and Narragansetts) was quickly broken by the more stable establishments of the Puritans, who subsequently ransomed captives like those in the Rowlandson family. Like Juan Ortiz and Cabeza de Vaca (who were taken captive by natives after a shipwreck of the Narváez group off the Texas coast), Mary Rowlandson was forced to experience life on the other side, among those whom she had been acculturated to consider beneath her, even to abhor. Rowlandson's Puritan captivity narrative, like that of John Williams, locates the otherness of the Indians in the paganism of the heathen in the Old Testament. That she survived to be redeemed meant for Rowlandson a double gain: redemption back into the Puritan community and redemption into God's hands.

While the Puritans were attempting to forge for England a tightly focused, introspective, and concentrated community in the Northeast, the Spanish were traversing and attaining thousands of miles of territory for Spain and the Catholic Church. Their territorial claims would not be contested for several more years. What has become clear, however, is that both the English and Spanish, testing themselves against the environment and the native populations, created new world texts after their own images.

Carla Mulford
Pennsylvania State University

Handsome Lake (Seneca)

Handsome Lake, who related the original version of this narrative, was a chief in the League of the Iroquois and a half-brother of Cornplanter. He had a vision in the spring on 1799 in which three messengers of the Creator appeared to him in traditional Iroquoian dress and told him that he and the people must abandon alcohol, that witches were corrupting them, and that the people must repent their corruption and ensure that the traditional Strawberry Festival, which celebrated their relationship to the Earth, must be held every year. The other visions that followed apocalyptically predicted the destruction of the world by fire if the return to the old ways was not thorough and immediate. The prophet also rejected any attempts at further ceding of Indian lands to whites. Thus began one of the best-documented responses, which anthropologists call revitalization or nativist movements, to European impacts. Handsome Lake's Longhouse Religion prospered to good effect among Iroquois people; seventy-five years later, another revitalization movement, the Ghost Dance of the Great Basin and Plains Indians, would lead to the tragedy at Wounded Knee.

In its reevaluation of Christian elements and its negative evaluation of the motives and influence of Europeans, this narrative represents an Iroquoian vision of what are today called Columbian consequences. For this reason, the relation is placed in this section of the anthology, which offers materials by writers who explored and settled in Iroquoian territory. The relation might be read in conjunction with the Samuel de Champlain selection, too, just as it would complement well the reading of the works contemporary with the original relation by Samson Occom and Hendrick Aupaumut.

The relation was recorded by Arthur C. Parker, himself a Seneca from a distinguished family, who was among the many Native Americans at the turn of the twentieth century who worked singly or with Anglo-American ethnographers to preserve traditions they felt were disappearing under the reservation and allotment systems.

Andrew O. Wiget
New Mexico State University

PRIMARY WORK

A.C. Parker, *Seneca Myths and Folktales,* ed. W. H. Fenton, 1923, 1989.

SECONDARY WORK

A.F.C. Wallace, *The Death and Rebirth of the Seneca,* 1969.

How America Was Discovered

According to Chief Cornplanter, Handsome Lake taught that America was discovered in the manner here related.

A great queen had among her servants a young minister. Upon a certain occasion she requested him to dust some books that she had hidden in an old chest. Now when the young man reached the bottom of the chest he found a wonderful book which he opened and read. It told that the white men had killed the son of the Creator and it said, moreover, that he had promised to return in three days and then again forty but that he never did. All his followers then began to despair but some said, "He surely will come again some time." When the young preacher read this book he was worried because he had discovered that he had been deceived and that his Lord was not on earth and had not returned when he promised. So he went to some of the chief preachers and asked them about the matter and they answered that he had better seek the Lord himself and find if he were not on the earth now. So he prepared to find the Lord and the next day when he looked out into the river he saw a beautiful island and marveled that he had never noticed it before. As he continued to look he saw a castle built of gold in the midst of the island and he marveled that he had not seen the castle before. Then he thought that so beautiful a palace on so beautiful an isle must surely be the abode of the son of the Creator. Immediately he went to the wise men and told them what he had seen and they wondered greatly and answered that it must indeed be the house of the Lord. So together they went to the river and when they came to it they found that it was spanned by a bridge of gold. Then one of the preachers fell down and prayed a long time and arising to cross the bridge turned back because he was afraid to meet his Lord. Then the other crossed the bridge and knelt down upon the grass and prayed but he became afraid to go near the house. So the young man went boldly over to attend to the business at hand and walking up to the door knocked. A handsome man welcomed him into a room and bade him be of ease. "I wanted you," he said. "You are bright young man; those old fools will not suit me for they would be afraid to listen to me. Listen to me, young man, and you will be rich. Across the ocean there is a great country of which you have never heard. The people there are virtuous, they have no evil habits or appetites but are honest and single-minded. A great reward is yours if you enter into my plans and carry them out. Here are five things. Carry them over to the people across the ocean and never shall you want for wealth, position or power. Take these cards, this money, this fiddle, this whiskey and this blood corruption and give them all to the people across the water. The cards will make them gamble away their goods and idle away their time, the money will make them dishonest and covetous, the fiddle will make them dance with women and their lower natures will command them, the whiskey will excite their minds to evil doing and turn their minds, and the blood corruption will eat their strength and rot their bones."

The young man thought this a good bargain and promised to do as the man had commanded him. He left the palace and when he had stepped over the bridge it was gone, likewise the golden palace and also the island. Now he wondered if he had seen the Lord but he did not tell the great ministers of his bargain because they might try to forstall him. So he looked about and at length found Columbus to whom he told the whole story. So Columbus fitted out some boats and sailed out into the ocean to find the land on the other side. When he had sailed for many days on the water the sailors said that unless Columbus turned about and went home they would behead him but he asked for another day and on that day land was seen and that land was America. Then they turned around and going back reported what they had discovered. Soon a great flock of ships came over the ocean and white men came swarming into the country bringing with them cards, money, fiddles, whiskey and blood corruption.

Now the man who had appeared in the gold palace was the devil and when afterward he saw what his words had done he said that he had made a great mistake and even he lamented that his evil had been so enormous.

1923

John Smith 1580–1631

John Smith has often been described by twentieth-century scholars as a swashbuckling colonial statesman, a self-made man who in his writing proffered the hardworking and enterprising the hope that they too could realize the American dream. Born in Lincolnshire, England, to a yeoman farmer and his wife, Smith completed a grammar school education and was subsequently apprenticed to a merchant in nearby King's Lynn. Soon after his father's death, however, he left his apprenticeship to begin his career as a soldier, and joined the British volunteers fighting in the Dutch war of independence from Spain. He later joined the Austrian forces fighting against the Turks and was soon promoted to captain for his work in Hungary. While battling the Turks he was captured and sold into slavery. In one of his last works, *The True Travels, Adventures, and Observations of Captaine John Smith, in Europe, Asia, Affrica, and America* (1630), Smith would vividly dramatize his daring escape and travels through Russia, Poland, and Transylvannia. Upon his return to England in 1605, Smith grew interested in plans to colonize Virginia. When the Virginia Company's first colonists sailed the following year, Smith sailed with them as one of the seven councillors.

Unlike the Puritan settlements that were later established in Massachusetts, the goals of the Jamestown colony were primarily commercial rather than religious in nature from the outset. The organizers of the Virginia Company and many of the first settlers were inspired by Spain's model of colonization; profit for the company's stockholders was to be accumulated through conquest and the discovery of gold, not agriculture. The Jamestown population, particularly during the colony's early years, was almost entirely composed of men, many of whom were of the elite classes and did not expect to have to grow the food the settlement needed for its survival. Unlike the Puritan settlements which would rely upon strong, hierarchical religious and familial structures and on common goals to unite their members, the Jamestown settlement, troubled by quarreling colonists with competing interests, was in a precarious position from its inception.

Even before becoming president in 1608, Smith worked to make survival, not gold, the settlement's priority. He spent much of his time exploring the region and negotiating with Native Americans for food. As president, Smith organized the building of houses, fortifications, and a church, and he instituted a policy of military discipline. Well-known today as an excellent manager of men in a time of crisis, Smith's policy that "he who does not work shall not eat" was extremely unpopular, particularly among members of the elite classes. But, as Smith clearly surmised, this was the policy that kept the colonists alive: during Smith's administration the survival rate among colonists rose dramatically to more than ninety percent.

Recognizing that the colony's relations with the surrounding Native American populations were crucial to its survival, Smith sent young men to live among the Native Americans to learn their language, customs, and methods of agriculture. Smith, a keen observer of Native Americans, realized that knowledge of the surrounding populations was a prerequisite to establishing strong and vital trade relations. Yet despite the overall success—in survival terms—of Smith's policies, the colony remained unable to produce a profit for its investors. In 1609 the Virginia Company decided to reorganize the colony by sending five hundred new settlers and replacing Smith and his government. Before the new president could arrive, however, a serious wound from a gunpowder explosion forced Smith to return to England.

Despite repeated offers of his services to the colony, Smith was never to return to Virginia. He soon shifted his attention to promoting colonization in the region he would name New England, obtaining valuable information about the region's natural history and geography during his voyage there in 1614. When his further attempts at colonization of New England were blocked by weather, pirates, and lack of funding, he turned his efforts to writing about the cause for which he was no longer wanted as an active participant.

Much of Smith's writing, beginning with his first work, *A True Relation . . . of Virginia* (1608) served the dual purpose of promoting colonization and establishing Smith's own reputation as exemplary colonizer. To this end in his best-known work, *The Generall Historie of Virginia, New-England, and the Summer Isles* (1624), Smith drew on his own earlier writings on Virginia and New England and the writing of others. Although this and other works fall into the genre of travel writing, popularized by Richard Hakluyt's *The Principall Navigations, Voiages and Discoveries of the English Nation* (1589), they differ in that—as Smith was always quick to remind his readers—their writer had first-hand experience with the colonial enterprise. As Smith asserted at the opening of *The Generall Historie,* "I am no Compiler by hearsay, but have beene a real Actor." Indeed, whether he is contending with other writers, the gold-digging settlers, the Virginia Company, or Powhatan, it is the voice of this actor which we hear most consistently throughout his work.

Of the numerous adventures Smith recounts in *The Generall Historie* none is better known than the account of his captivity in the court of Powhatan and Pocahontas's "saving" his life. Because Pocahontas made no appearance in Smith's first account of the story in *A True Relation,* some have doubted its veracity and challenged Smith's reliability as historian. More significant than the issue of the accuracy of this story, however, is the relative positioning of the two cultures within the story itself. Pocahontas's apparent willingness to offer her own life in place of Smith's is a romanticized depiction of a Native American's willingness to yield to the interests of the "superior" civilization. The scene depicts the paradigm which appears throughout many later colonialist writings, that Native Americans are ready to submit to the advance of a European civilization superior to their own.

Smith devoted much of the third book of *The General Historie* to a description of the interaction between the two very different civilizations. Less concerned with the ethics of colonization than the sheer survival of the colony, Smith formulated a controversial policy toward the Native Americans. From their arrival at Jamestown, the colonists had found themselves in a rather embarassing position; not only were they unable to feed themselves, but they were dependent upon "inferior" populations for food. Despite the Virginia Company's continual requests for a gentler policy toward the Native Americans, Smith sought to intimidate and control the Powhatans through shows of force. Even as he negotiated with Powhatan for the food upon which the colony depended for its very survival, Smith continued his ongoing argument with Powhatan regarding the necessity of the English wearing their arms while in his presence.

Smith's final work, *Advertisements for*

the Unexperienced Planters of New England (1631), is a summation of Smith's ideas about colonization based upon his experience with Virginia and his knowledge of New England. The Massachusetts Bay Colony came much closer than the Virginia settlement to epitomizing Smith's ideal; with its emphasis on private property, it drew settlers from the "middling group" of English society who were willing to work hard. Reflecting back, once again, on his Virginia experience, Smith described his accomplishments in the face of the many obstacles he had confronted. To the end Smith lamented the fact that despite his lifelong devotion to the cause of colonization, his expertise and accomplishments had never been sufficiently appreciated.

Amy E. Winans
Dickinson College

PRIMARY WORKS

A True Relation of . . . Virginia, 1608; *A Description of New England,* 1616; *The Generall Historie of Virginia, New-England, and the Summer Isles,* 1624; *The True Travels, Adventures, and Observations of Captaine John Smith,* 1630; *Advertisements for the Unexperienced Planters of New England, or Anywhere,* 1631; *The Complete Works of Captain John Smith (1580–1631),* 3 vols., ed. P.L. Barbour, 1986; Karen Ordahl Kupperman, *Captain John Smith,* 1988.

SECONDARY WORKS

Philip L. Barbour, *The Three Worlds of Captain John Smith,* 1964; Alden T. Vaughan, *American Genesis: Captain John Smith and the Founding of Virginia,* 1975; Kevin J. Hayes, *Captain John Smith,* 1991; J. A. Leo Lemay, *The American Dream of Captain John Smith,* 1991; Everett H. Emerson, *Captain John Smith,* 1993.

from The Generall Historie of Virginia, New-England, and the Summer Isles[1]

from **Book III**
from **Chapter 2**

[Smith as captive at the court of Powhatan in 1608]

At last they brought him[2] to *Meronocomoco* [*5 Jan. 1608*], where was *Powhatan* their Emperor. Here more than two hundred of those grim Courtiers stood wondering at him, as he had beene a monster; till *Powhatan* and his trayne had put themselves in their greatest braveries. Before a fire upon a seat like a bedsted, he sat covered with a great robe, made of *Rarowcun*[3] skinnes, and all the tayles hanging by. On either hand did sit a young wench of 16 or 18 yeares, and along on each side the house, two rowes of men, and behind them as many women, with all their heads and shoulders painted red: many of their heads bedecked with the white downe of Birds; but every

[1]*The Generall Historie* was first published in London in 1624. This text, slightly modified, is taken from *The Complete Works of Captain John Smith,* 3 vols., 1986.

[2]Smith. Smith wrote this version of his captivity entirely in the third person.

[3]Raccoon.

one with something: and a great chayne of white beads about their necks. At his entrance before the King, all the people gave a great shout. The Queene of *Appamatuck* was appointed to bring him water to wash his hands, and another brought him a bunch of feathers, in stead of a Towell to dry them: having feasted him after their best barbarous manner they could, a long consultation was held, but the conclusion was, two great stones were brought before *Powhatan:* then as many as could layd hands on him, dragged him to them, and thereon laid his head, and being ready with their clubs, to beate out his braines, *Pocahontas* the Kings dearest daughter, when no intreaty could prevaile, got his head in her armes, and laid her owne upon his to save him from death: whereat the Emperour was contented he should live to make him hatchets, and her bells, beads, and copper; for they thought him aswell of all occupations as themselves. For the King himselfe will make his owne robes, shooes, bowes, arrowes, pots; plant, hunt, or doe any thing so well as the rest.

They say he bore a pleasant shew,
But sure his heart was sad.
For who can pleasant be, and rest,
That lives in feare and dread:
And having life suspected, doth
It still suspected lead.

Two dayes after [*7 Jan. 1608*], *Powhatan* having disguised himselfe in the most fearefullest manner he could, caused Captain *Smith* to be brought forth to a great house in the woods, and there upon a mat by the fire to be left alone. Not long after from behinde a mat that divided the house, was made the most dolefullest noyse he ever heard; then *Powhatan* more like a devill then a man, with some two hundred more as blacke as himselfe, came unto him and told him now they were friends, and presently he should goe to *James* towne, to send him two great gunnes, and a gryndstone, for which he would give him the Country of *Capahowosick,* and for ever esteeme him as his sonne *Nantaquoud.* So to *James* towne with 12 guides *Powhatan* sent him. That night [*7 Jan. 1608*] they quarterd in the woods, he still expecting (as he had done all this long time of his imprisonment) every houre to be put to one death or other: for all their feasting. But almightie God (by his divine providence) had mollified the hearts of those sterne *Barbarians* with compassion. The next morning [*8 Jan.*] betimes they came to the Fort, where *Smith* having used the Salvages with what kindnesse he could, he shewed *Rawhunt, Powhatans* trusty servant, two demi-Culverings[4] and a millstone to carry *Powhatan:* they found them somewhat too heavie; but when they did see him discharge them, being loaded with stones, among the boughs of a great tree loaded with Isickles, the yce and branches came so tumbling downe, that the poore Salvages ran away halfe dead with feare. But at last we regained some conference with them, and gave them such toyes; and sent to *Powhatan,* his women, and children such presents, as gave them in generall full content. . . . Now ever once in foure or five dayes, *Pocahontas* with her attendants, brought him so much provision, that saved many of their lives, that els for all this had starved with hunger.

Thus from numbe death our good God sent reliefe,
The sweete asswager of all other griefe.

[4]Demi-culverins, small cannons.

His relation of the plenty he had seene, especially at *Werawocomoco,* and of the state and bountie of *Powhatan,* (which till that time was unknowne) so revived their dead spirits (especially the love of *Pocahontas*[5]) as all mens feare was abandoned.

from Chapter 8

[Smith's Journey to Pamaunkee]

The 12 of January we arrived at Werowocomoco, where the river was frozen neare halfe a myle from the shore; but to neglect no time, the President with his Barge so far had approached by breaking the ice, as the ebbe left him amongst those oasie shoules, yet rather then to lye there frozen to death, by his owne example he taught them to march neere middle deepe, a flight shot through this muddy frozen oase. When the Barge floated, he appoynted two or three to returne her aboord the Pinnace. Where for want of water in melting the ice, they made fresh water, for the river there was salt. But in this march Master Russell, (whom none could perswade to stay behinde) being somewhat ill, and exceeding heavie, so overtoyled himselfe as the rest had much adoe (ere he got ashore) to regaine life into his dead benummed spirits. Quartering in the next houses we found, we sent to Powhatan for provision, who sent us plentie of bread, Turkies, and Venison; the next day having feasted us after his ordinary manner, he began to aske us when we would be gone: fayning he sent not for us, neither had he any corne; and his people much lesse: yet for fortie swords he would procure us fortie Baskets. The President shewing him the men there present that brought him the message and conditions, asked Powhatan how it chanced he became so forgetfull; thereat the King concluded the matter with a merry laughter, asking for our Commodities, but none he liked without gunnes and swords, valuing a Basket of Corne more precious then a Basket of Copper; saying he could eate his Corne, but not the Copper.

Captaine Smith seeing the intent of this subtill Salvage began to deale with him after this manner.

> *Powhatan, though I had many courses to have made my provision, yet beleeving your promises to supply my wants, I neglected all to satisfie your desire: and to testifie my love, I send you my men for your building, neglecting mine owne. What your people had you have engrossed, forbidding them our trade: and now you thinke by consuming the time, we shall consume for want, not having to fulfill your strange demands. As for swords and gunnes, I told you long agoe I had none to spare; and you must know those I have can keepe me from want: yet steale or wrong you I will not, nor dissolve that friendship we have mutually promised, except you constraine me by our bad usage.*

[5]Pocahontas married John Rolfe, a tobacco planter, in 1613. Smith maintained that the marriage resulted in "friendly trade and commerce" with the Powhatans. In 1616 Pocahontas traveled to England (with her husband and infant son), where she died the following year.

The King having attentively listned to this Discourse, promised that both he and his Country would spare him what he could, the which within two dayes they should receive. Yet Captaine Smith, sayth the King,

> *some doubt I have of your comming hither, that makes me not so kindly seeke to relieve you as I would: for many doe informe me, your comming hither is not for trade, but to invade my people, and possesse my Country, who dare not come to bring you corne, seeing you thus armed with your men. To free us of this feare, leave aboord your weapons, for here they are needlesse, we being all friends, and for ever Powhatans.*

With many such discourses they spent the day, quartering that night in the Kings houses. The next day he renewed his building, which hee little intended should proceede. For the Dutch-men finding his plentie, and knowing our want, and perceiving his preparations to surprise us, little thinking we could escape both him and famine; (to obtaine his favour) revealed to him so much as they knew of our estates and projects, and how to prevent them. One of them being of so great a spirit, judgement, and resolution, and a hireling that was certaine of his wages for his labour, and ever well used both he and his Countrymen; that the President knew not whom better to trust; and not knowing any fitter for that imployment, had sent him as a spy to discover Powhatans intent, then little doubting his honestie, nor could ever be certaine of his villany till neare halfe a yeare after.

Whilst we expected the comming in of the Country, we wrangled out of the King ten quarters of Corne for a copper Kettell, the which the President perceiving him much to affect, valued it at a much greater rate; but in regard of his scarcity he would accept it, provided we should have as much more the next yeare, or els the Country of Monacan. Wherewith each seemed well contented, and Powhatan began to expostulate the difference of Peace and Warre after this manner.

> *Captaine Smith, you may understand that I having seene the death of all my people thrice, and not any one living of those three generations but my selfe; I know the difference of Peace and Warre better then any in my Country. But now I am old and ere long must die, my brethren, namely Opitchapam, Opechancanough, and Kekataugh, my two sisters, and their two daughters, are distinctly each others successors. I wish their experience no lesse then mine, and your love to them no lesse then mine to you. But this bruit from Nandsamund, that you are come to destroy my Country, so much affrighteth all my people as they dare not visit you. What will it availe you to take that by force you may quickly have by love, or to destroy them that provide you food. What can you get by warre; when we can hide our provisions and fly to the woods? whereby you must famish by wronging us your friends. And why are you thus jealous of our loves seeing us unarmed, and both doe, and are willing still to feede you, with that you cannot get but by our labours? Thinke you I am so simple, not to know it is better to eate good meate, lye well, and sleepe quietly with my women and children, laugh and be merry with you, have copper, hatchets, or what I want being your friend: then be forced to flie from all, to lie cold in the woods, feede upon Acornes, rootes, and such trash, and be so hunted by you, that I can neither rest, eate, nor sleepe; but my tyred men must watch, and if a twig but breake, every one cryeth there commeth Captaine Smith: then must I fly I know not whether: and thus with miserable feare, end my miserable life, leaving my pleasures to such youths as you, which through your rash unadvisednesse may quickly as miserably end, for want*

of that, you never know where to finde. Let this therefore assure you of our loves, and every yeare our friendly trade shall furnish you with Corne; and now also, if you would come in friendly manner to see us, and not thus with your guns and swords as to invade your foes.

To this subtill discourse, the President thus replyed.

Seeing you will not rightly conceive of our words, we strive to make you know our thoughts by our deeds; the vow I made you of my love, both my selfe and my men have kept. As for your promise I find it every day violated by some of your subjects: yet we finding your love and kindnesse, our custome is so far from being ungratefull, that for your sake onely, we have curbed our thirsting desire of revenge; els had they knowne as well the crueltie we use to our enemies, as our true love and courtesie to our friends. And I thinke your judgement sufficient to conceive, as well by the adventures we have undertaken, as by the advantage we have (by our Armes) of yours: that had we intended you any hurt, long ere this we could have effected it. Your people comming to James Towne are entertained with their Bowes and Arrowes without any exceptions; we esteeming it with you as it is with us, to weare our armes as our apparell. As for the danger of our enemies, in such warres consist our chiefest pleasure: for your riches we have no use: as for the hiding your provision, or by your flying to the woods, we shall not so unadvisedly starve as you conclude, your friendly care in that behalfe is needlesse, for we have a rule to finde beyond your knowledge.

Many other discourses they had, till at last they began to trade. But the King seeing his will would not be admitted as a law, our guard dispersed, nor our men disarmed, he (sighing) breathed his minde once more in this manner.

Captaine Smith, I never use any Werowance so kindely as your selfe, yet from you I receive the least kindnesse of any. Captaine Newport gave me swords, copper, cloathes, a bed, tooles, or what I desired; ever taking what I offered him, and would send away his gunnes when I intreated him: none doth deny to lye at my feet, or refuse to doe what I desire, but onely you; of whom I can have nothing but what you regard not, and yet you will have whatsoever you demand. Captaine Newport you call father, and so you call me; but I see for all us both you will doe what you list, and we must both seeke to content you. But if you intend so friendly as you say, send hence your armes, that I may beleeve you; for you see the love I beare you, doth cause me thus nakedly to forget my selfe.

Smith seeing this Salvage but trifle the time to cut his throat, procured the Salvages to breake the ice, that his Boate might come to fetch his corne and him: and gave order for more men to come on shore, to surprise the King, with whom also he but trifled the time till his men were landed: and to keepe him from suspicion, entertained the time with this reply.

Powhatan you must know, as I have but one God, I honour but one King; and I live not here as your subject, but as your friend to pleasure you with what I can. By the gifts you bestow on me, you gaine more then by trade: yet would you visit mee as I doe you, you should know it is not our custome, to sell our curtesies as a vendible commodity. Bring all your countrey with you for your guard, I will not dislike it as being over jealous. But to content you, tomorrow I will leave my Armes, and trust to your promise. I call you father indeed, and as a father you shall see I will love you: but the small care you have of such a childe caused my men perswade me to looke to my selfe.

By this time Powhatan having knowledge his men were ready whilest the ice was a breaking, with his luggage women and children, fled. Yet to avoyd suspicion, left two or three of the women talking with the Captaine, whilest hee secretly ran away, and his men that secretly beset the house. Which being presently discovered to Captaine Smith, with his pistoll, sword, and target hee made such a passage among these naked Divels; that at his first shoot, they next him tumbled one over another, and the rest quickly fled some one way some another: so that without any hurt, onely accompanied with John Russell, hee obtained the *corps du guard.* When they perceived him so well escaped, and with his eighteene men (for he had no more with him a shore) to the uttermost of their skill they sought excuses to dissemble the matter: and Powhatan to excuse his flight and the sudden comming of this multitude, sent our Captaine a great bracelet and a chaine of pearle, by an ancient Oratour that bespoke us to this purpose, perceiving even then from our Pinnace, a Barge and men departing and comming unto us.

> *Captaine Smith, our Werowance is fled, fearing your gunnes, and knowing when the ice was broken there would come more men, sent these numbers but to guard his corne from stealing, that might happen without your knowledge: now though some bee hurt by your misprision, yet Powhatan is your friend and so will for ever continue. Now since the ice is open, he would have you send away your corne, and if you would have his company, send away also your gunnes, which so affright his people, that they dare not come to you as hee promised they should.*

Then having provided baskets for our men to carry our corne to the boats, they kindly offered their service to guard our Armes, that none should steale them. A great many they were of goodly well proportioned fellowes, as grim as Divels; yet the very sight of cocking our matches, and being to let fly, a few wordes caused them to leave their bowes and arrowes to our guard, and beare downe our corne on their backes; wee needed not importune them to make dispatch. But our Barges being left on the oase by the ebbe, caused us stay till the next high-water, so that wee returned againe to our old quarter. Powhatan and his Dutch-men brusting with desire to have the head of Captaine Smith, for if they could but kill him, they thought all was theirs, neglected not any oportunity to effect his purpose. The Indians with all the merry sports they could devise, spent the time till night: then they all returned to Powhatan, who all this time was making ready his forces to surprise the house and him at supper. Notwithstanding the eternall all-seeing God did prevent him, and by a strange meanes. For Pocahontas his dearest jewell and daughter, in that darke night came through the irksome woods, and told our Captaine great cheare should be sent us by and by: but Powhatan and all the power he could make, would after come kill us all, if they that brought it could not kill us with our owne weapons when we were at supper. Therefore if we would live shee wished us presently to bee gone. Such things as shee delighted in, he would have given her: but with the teares running downe her cheekes, shee said shee durst not be seene to have any: for if Powhatan should know it, she were but dead, and so shee ranne away by her selfe as she came. . .

1624

from A Description of New England[1]

[Appeal for settlers to plant a colony in New England]

Who can desire more content, that hath small meanes; or but only his merit to advance his fortune, then to tread, and plant that ground hee hath purchased by the hazard of his life? If he have but the taste of virtue and magnanimitie, what to such a minde can bee more pleasant, then planting and building a foundation for his Posteritie, gotte from the rude earth, by Gods blessing and his owne industrie, without prejudice to any? If hee have any graine of faith or zeale in Religion, what can hee doe lesse hurtfull to any: or more agreeable to God, then to seeke to convert those poore Salvages to know Christ, and humanitie, whose labors with discretion will triple requite thy charge and paines? What so truely su[i]tes with honour and honestie, as the discovering things unknowne? erecting Townes, peopling Countries, informing the ignorant, reforming things unjust, teaching virtue; and gaine to our Native mother-countrie a kingdom to attend her: finde imployment for those that are idle, because they know not what to doe: so farre from wronging any, as to cause Posteritie to remember thee; and remembring thee, ever honour that remembrance with praise? . . .

I have not beene so ill bred, but I have tasted of *Plenty* and *Pleasure,* as well as *Want* and *Miserie:* nor doth necessitie yet, or occasion of discontent, force me to these endeavors: nor am I ignorant what small thanke I shall have for my paines; or that many would have the Worlde imagine them to be of great judgement, that can but blemish these my designes, by their witty objections and detractions: yet (I hope) my reasons with my deeds, will so prevaile with some, that I shall not want imployment in these affaires, to make the most blinde see his owne senselessnesse, and incredulity; Hoping that gaine will make them affect that, which Religion, Charity, and the Common good cannot. It were but a poore device in me, To deceive my selfe; much more the King, State, my Friends and Countrey, with these inducements: which, seeing his Majestie hath given permission, I wish all sorts of worthie, honest, industrious spirits, would understand: and if they desire any further satisfaction, I will doe my best to give it: Not to perswade them to goe onley; but goe with them: Not leave them there; but live with them there. I will not say, but by ill providing and undue managing, such cources may be taken, [that] may make us miserable enough: But if I may have the execution of what I have projected; if they want to eate, let them eate or never digest Me. If I performe what I say, I desire but that reward out of the gaines [which] may su[i]te my paines, quality, and condition. And if I abuse you with my tongue, take my head for satisfaction. If any dislike at the yeares end, defraying their charge, by my consent they should freely returne. I feare not want of companie sufficient, were it but knowne what I know of those Countries; and by the proofe of that wealth I hope yearely to returne, if God please to blesse me from such accidents, as are beyond my power in reason to prevent: For, I am not so simple to thinke, that

[1] *A Description of New England* was first published in London in 1616. This text, slightly modified, is taken from *The Complete Works of Captain John Smith,* 3 vols., 1986.

ever any other motive then wealth, will ever erect there a Commonweale; or draw companie from their ease and humours at home, to stay in *New England* to effect my purposes. And lest any should thinke the toile might be insupportable, though these things may be had by labour, and diligence: I assure my selfe there are who delight extreamly in vaine pleasure, that take much more paines in *England,* to enjoy it, then I should doe heere [*New England*] to gaine wealth sufficient: and yet I thinke they should not have halfe such sweet content: for, our pleasure here is still gaines; in *England* charges and losse. Heer nature and liberty affords us that freely, which in *England* we want, or it costeth us dearely. What pleasure can be more, then (being tired with any occasion a-shore, in planting Vines, Fruits, or Hearbs, in contriving their owne Grounds, to the pleasure of their owne mindes, their Fields, Gardens, Orchards, Buildings, Ships, and other works, &c.) to recreate themselves before their owne doores, in their owne boates upon the Sea; where man, woman and childe, with a small hooke and line, by angling, may take diverse sorts of excellent fish, at their pleasures? And is it not pretty sport, to pull up two pence, six pence, and twelve pence, as fast as you can ha[u]le and veare a line? He is a very bad fisher [that] cannot kill in one day with his hooke and line, one, two, or three hundred Cods: which dressed and dried, if they be sould there for ten shillings the hundred, though in England they will give more than twentie, may not both the servant, the master, and marchant, be well content with this gaine? If a man worke but three dayes in seaven, he may get more then hee can spend, unlesse he will be excessive. Now that Carpenter, Mason, Gardiner, Taylor, Smith, Sailer, Forgers, or what other, may they not make this a pretty recreation though they fish but an houre in a day, to take more then they eate in a weeke? or if they will not eate it, because there is so much better choice; yet sell it, or change it, with the fisher men, or marchants, for any thing they want. And what sport doth yeeld a more pleasing content, and lesse hurt or charge then angling with a hooke; and crossing the sweete ayre from Ile to Ile, over the silent streames of a calme Sea? Wherein the most curious may finde pleasure, profit, and content. Thus, though all men be not fishers: yet all men, whatsoever, may in other matters doe as well. For necessity doth in these cases so rule a Commonwealth, and each in their severall functions, as their labours in their qualities may be as profitable, because there is a necessary mutuall use of all.

For Gentlemen, what exercise should more delight them, then ranging dayly those unknowne parts, using fowling and fishing, for hunting and hawking? and yet you shall see the wilde-haukes give you some pleasure, in seeing them stoope (six or seaven after one another) an houre or two together, at the skuls of fish in the faire harbours, as those a-shore at a foule; and never trouble nor torment yourselves, with watching, mewing, feeding, and attending them: nor kill horse and man with running and crying, *See you not a hawk?* For hunting also: the woods, lakes, and rivers affoord not onely chase sufficient, for any that delights in that kinde of toyle, or pleasure; but such beasts to hunt, that besides the delicacy of their bodies for food, their skins are so rich, as may well recompence thy dayly labour, with a Captains pay.

For labourers, if those that sowe hemp, rape, turnups, parsnips, carrats, cabidge, and such like; give 20, 30, 40, 50 shillings yearely for an acre of ground, and meat drinke and wages to use it, and yet grow rich; when better, or at least as good ground, may be had, and cost nothing but labour; it seems strange to me, any such should there grow poore.

My purpose is not to perswade children from their parents; men from their wives; nor servants from their masters: onely, such as with free consent may be spared: But that each parish, or village, in Citie or Countrey, that will but apparell their fatherlesse children, of thirteene or fourteen years of age, or young mar[r]ied people, that have small wealth to live on; heere by their labour may live exceeding well: provided alwaies that first there bee a sufficient power to command them, houses to receive them, meanes to defend them, and meet provisions for them; for, any place may bee overlain: and it is most necessarie to have a fortresse (ere this grow to practice) and sufficient masters (as, Carpenters, Masons, Fishers, Fowlers, Gardiners, Husbandmen, Sawyers, Smiths, Spinsters, Taylors, Weavers, and such like) to take ten, twelve, or twentie, or as ther is occasion, for Apprentises. The Masters by this may quicklie growe rich; these may learne their trades themselves, to doe the like; to a generall and an incredible benefit, for King, and Countrey, Master, and Servant. . . .

Religion, above all things, should move us (especially the Clergie) if wee were religious, to shewe our faith by our workes; in converting those poore salvages, to the knowledge of God, seeing what paines the *Spanyards* take to bring them to their adulterated faith. Honor might move the Gentrie, the valiant, and industrious; and the hope and assurance of wealth, all; if wee were that we would seeme, and be accounted. Or be we so far inferior to other nations, or our spirits so far dejected, from our auncient predecessors, or our mindes so [set] upon spoile, piracie, and such villany, as to serve the *Portugall, Spanyard, Dutch, French,* or *Turke,* (as to the cost of *Europe,* too many dooe) rather then our God, our King, our Country, and our selves? excusing our idlenesse, and our base complaints, by want of imploiement; when heere is such choise of all sorts, and for all degrees, in the planting and discovering these North parts of *America*. . . .

But, to conclude, *Adam* and *Eve* did first beginne this innocent worke, To plant the earth to remaine to posteritie, but not without labour, trouble, and industrie. *Noe,* and his family, beganne againe the second plantation; and their seede as it still increased, hath still planted new Countries, and one countrie another: and so the world to that estate it is. But not without much hazard, travell, discontents, and many disasters. Had those worthie Fathers, and their memorable off-spring not beene more diligent for us now in these Ages, then wee are to plant that yet unplanted, for the after livers: Had the seede of *Abraham,* our Saviour Christ, and his Apostles, exposed themselves to no more daungers to teach the Gospell, and the will of God then wee; Even wee our selves, had at this present beene as Salvage, and as miserable as the most barbarous Salvage yet uncivilized. . . . Then seeing we are not borne for our selves, but each to helpe other, and our abilities are much alike at the houre of our birth, and the minute of our death: Seeing our good deedes, or our badde, by faith in Christs merits, is all we have to carrie our soules to heaven, or hell: Seeing honour is our lives ambition; and our ambition after death, to have an honourable memorie of our life: and seeing by noe meanes wee would bee abated of the dignities and glories of our Predecessors; let us imitate their vertues to bee worthily their successors.

1616

from Advertisements for the Unexperienced Planters of New-England, or Anywhere, Or the Path-way to Experience to Erect a Plantation[1]

[Review of the colonies planted in New England and Virginia]

from Chapter 1

The Warres in *Europe, Asia,* and *Affrica,* taught me how to subdue the wilde Salvages in *Virginia* and *New-England,* in *America;* which now after many a stormy blast of ignorant contradictors, projectors, and undertakers, both they and I have beene so tossed and tortured into so many extremities, as despaire was the next wee both expected, till it pleased God now at last to stirre up some good mindes, that I hope will produce glory to God, honour to his Majesty, and profit to his Kingdomes: although all our Plantations have beene so foyled and abused, their best good willers have beene for the most part discouraged, and their good intents disgraced, as the generall History of them will at large truly relate [to] you.

Pardon me if I offend in loving that I have cherished truly, by the losse of my prime fortunes, meanes, and youth: If it over-glad me to see Industry her selfe adventure now to make use of my aged ende[a]vours, not by such (I hope) as rumour doth report, a many of discontented Brownists,[2] Anabaptists, Papists, Puritans, Separatists, and such factious Humorists.[3] for no such they will suffer among them, if knowne, as many of the chiefe of them [*John Winthrop &c.*] have assured mee; and the much conferences I have had with many of them, doth confidently perswade me to write thus much in their behalfe.

I meane not the Brownists of *Leyden* and *Amsterdam* at *New-Plimoth,*[4] who although by accident, ignorance, and wilfulnesse, [they] have endured, with a wonderfull patience, many losses and extremities; yet they subsist and prosper so well, not any of them will abandon the Country, but to the utmost of their powers increase their numbers. But of those which are gone within this eighteene moneths [*April 1629–Oct. 1630*] for Cape *Anne,* and the Bay of the *Massachusets.* Those which are their chiefe Undertakers are Gentlemen of good estate, some of 500, some a thousand pound land a yeere, all which they say they will sell for the advancing [of] this harmlesse and pious worke; men of good credit and well-beloved in their Country [*district*], not such as flye for debt, or any scandall at home; and are good Catholike

[1]*Advertisements* was first published in London in 1631. This text, slightly modified, is taken from *The Complete Works of Captain John Smith,* 3 vols., 1986.

[2]Followers of Robert Browne (1550–1633), who formulated the principles of Congregationalism and led a group of Separatists to Holland in 1582.

[3]People driven by a single humor, eccentrics.

[4]The Pilgrims. As Separatists who had fled to Holland, they were commonly referred to as Brownists, the better-known group of Separatists that had done the same thing earlier, though Browne was not their leader.

Protestants according to the reformed Church of *England,* if not, it is well they are gone. The rest of them men of good meanes, or Arts, Occupations, and Qualities, much more fit for such a businesse, and better furnished of all necessaries if they arrive well, than was ever any Plantation went out of *England.* I will not say but some of them may be more precise than needs, nor that they all be so good as they should be; for Christ had but twelve apostles, and one was a traitor: and if there be no dissemblers among them, it is more than a wonder; therefore doe not condemne all for some. But however they have as good authority from his Majesty as they could desire: if they doe ill, the losse is but their owne; if well, a great glory and exceeding good to this Kingdome, to make good at last what all our former conclusions have disgraced. Now they take not that course the *Virginia* company did for the Planters there, their purses and lives were subject to some few here in *London* who were never there, that consumed all in Arguments, Projects, and their owne conceits: every yeare trying new conclusions, altering every thing yearely as they altered opinions, till they had consumed more than two hundred thousand pounds, and neere eight thousand mens lives.

It is true, in the yeere of our Lord 1622. they were, the Company in *England* say 7. or 8. thousand: the Counsell in *Virginia* say but 2200. or thereabouts, English indifferently well furnished with most necessaries, and many of them grew to that height of bravery, living in that plenty and excesse, that went thither not worth any thing, [that] made the Company here thinke all the world was Oatmeale there; and all this proceeded by surviving those that died: nor were they ignorant to use as curious tricks there as here, and out of the juice of Tabacco, which at first they sold at such good rates, they regarded nothing but Tabacco; a commodity then so vendable, it provided them all things. And the loving Salvages their kinde friends, they trained so well up to shoot in a Peece, to hunt and kill them fowle, they became more expert than our owne Country-men; whose labours were more profitable to their Masters in planting Tabacco and other businesse.

This superfluity caused my poore beginnings [to be] scorned, or to be spoken of but with much derision, that never sent Ship from thence fraught, but onely some small quantities of Wainscot, Clap-board, Pitch, Tar, Rosin, Sope-ashes, Glasse, Cedar, Cypresse, Blacke Walnut, Knees for Ships, Ash for Pikes, Iron Ore none better, some Silver Ore but so poore it was not regarded; better there may be, for I was no Mineralist; some Sturgion, but it was too tart of the Vinegar (which was of my owne store, for little came from them which was good); and Wine of the Countries wilde Grapes, but it was too sowre; yet better than they sent us any, [which was] in two or three years but one Hogshead of Claret. . . .

Now because I sent not their ships full fraught home with those commodities; they kindly writ to me, if we failed the next returne, they would leave us there as banished men, as if houses and all those commodities did grow naturally, only for us to take at our pleasure; with such tedious Letters, directions, and instructions, and most contrary to that was fitting, we did admire [*wonder*] how it was possible such wise men could so torment themselves and us with such strange absurdities and impossibilities: making Religion their colour, when all their aime was nothing but present profit, as most plainly appeared, by sending us so many Refiners, Goldsmiths, Jewellers, Lapidaries, Stone-cutters, Tobacco-pipe-makers, Imbroderers, Perfumers, Silkemen, with [not only] all their appurtenances but materialls, and all those had great summes out of the common stocke; and [were] so many spies and super-intendents over us, as if they supposed we would turne Rebels, all striving to suppresse and advance they knew not what. . . . Much they blamed us for not converting the Salvages, when those they sent us were little better, if not worse; nor did they all, convert any of those [*natives*] we sent them to *England* for that purpose. So doating of Mines of gold, and the South Sea; that all the world could not have devised better courses to bring us to ruine than they did themselves, with many more such like strange conceits. . . .

from Chapter 2

For all this, our letters that still signified unto them the plaine truth, would not be beleeved, because they required such things as was most necessary: but their opinion was otherwayes, for they desired but to packe over so many as they could, saying necessity would make them get victuals for themselves, as for good labourers they were more usefull here in *England.* But they found it otherwayes; the charge was all one to send a workman as a roarer; whose clamors to appease, we had much adoe to get fish and corne to maintaine them from one supply till another came with more loyterers without victuals still to make us worse and worse, for the most of them would rather starve than worke: yet had it not beene for some few that were Gentlemen, both by birth, industry, and discretion, we could not possibly have subsisted. . . .

Yet in the yeare 1622. there were about seven or eight thousand *English,* as hath beene said, so well trained, secure, and well furnished, as they reported and conceited. These simple Salvages, their bosome friends, I so much oppressed, had laid their plot how to cut all their throats in a morning: and upon the 22. of March [1622], so innocently attempted it, they slew three hundred forty seven, set their houses on fire, slew their cattell, and brought them to that distraction and confusion [that] within lesse than a yeare, there were not many more than two thousand remaining. . . .

from Chapter 3

Notwithstanding since they have beene left in a manner, as it were, to themselves, they have increased [*by Oct. 1630*] their numbers to foure or five thousand, and neere as many catell, with plenty of Goats: abundance of Swine Poultry and Corne, that as they report, they have sufficient and to spare, to entertaine three or foure hundred people, which is much better than to have many people more than provision. Now having glutted the world with their too much overabounding Tabacco: Reason, or necessity, or both, will cause them, I hope, [to] learne in time better to fortifie themselves, and make better use of the trials of their grosse commodities that I have propounded, and at the first sent over: and were it not a lamentable dishonour so goodly a Countrey after so much cost, losse, and trouble, should now in this estate not bee regarded and supplied. And to those of *New-England* may it not be a great comfort to have so neare a neighbour of their owne Nation, that may furnish them with their spare cattell, swine, poultry, and other roots and fruits, much better than from *England.* But I feare the seed of envy, and the rust of covetousnesse doth grow too fast, for some would have all men advance *Virginia* to the ruine of *New-England;* and others the losse of *Virginia* to sustaine *New-England,* which God of his mercy forbid: for at first it was intended by that most memorable Judge Sir *John Popham,* then Lord chiefe Justice of *England,* and the Lords of his Majesties Privy Councel, with divers others, that two Colonies should be planted, as now they be, for the better strengthening each other against all occurrences; the which to performe, shall ever be my hearty prayers to Almighty God, to increase and continue that mutuall love betwixt them for ever.

By this you may perceive somewhat, what unexpected inconveniences are incident to a planation, especially in such a multitude of voluntary contributers, superfluity of officers, and unexperienced Commissioners. But it is not so, as yet, with those for *New-England;* for they will neither beleeve nor use such officers, in that they are overseers of their owne estates, and so well bred in labour and good husbandry as any in *England:* where as few as I say was sent me to *Virginia,* but those [that] were naught here and worse there.

from **Chapter 9**

Now if you but truly consider how many strange accidents have befallen those plantations and my selfe; how oft up, how oft downe, sometimes neere despaire, and ere long flourishing; how many scandals and Spanolized English[5] have sought to disgrace them, bring them to ruine, or at least hinder them all they could; how many have shaven and couzened both them and me, and their most honourable supporters and well-willers: [you] cannot but conceive Gods infinite mercy both to them and me. Having beene a slave to the Turks, prisoner amongst the most barbarous Salvages, after my deliverance commonly discovering and ranging those large rivers and unknowne Nations with such a handfull of ignorant companions that the wiser sort often gave mee [up] for lost, alwayes in mutinies [*i.e., of others*] wants and miseries, blowne up with gunpowder; A long time [a] prisoner among the French Pyrats, from whom escaping in a little boat by my selfe, and adrift all such a stormy winter night, when their ships were split, more than a hundred thousand pound lost [which] they had taken at sea, and most of them drowned upon the Ile of *Ree,* not farre from whence I was driven on shore in my little boat &c. Any many a score of the worst of winter moneths [have] lived in the fields: yet to have lived neere 37. yeares [1593–1630] in the midst of wars, pestilence and famine, by which many an hundred thousand have died about mee, and scarce five living of them [that] went first with me to *Virginia:* and [yet to] see the fruits of my labours thus well begin to prosper: though I have but my labour for my paines, have I not much reason both privately and publikely to acknowledge it and give God thankes, whose omnipotent power onely delivered me, to doe the utmost of my best to make his name knowne in those remote parts of the world, and his loving mercy to such a miserable sinner.

1631

[5]Englishmen who support Spain or adopt Spanish ways.

Edward Maria Wingfield 1560?–1613?

The early years of the Jamestown colony, established in Virginia in 1607, were fraught with difficulty. The initial group consisted of a fractious company of 104 men and boys, among them effete gentry with few practical skills, adventurers beguiled by visions of the riches to be extracted from the New World, and artisans whose abilities were of little use in the primitive conditions at hand. On the whole, they were ill-equipped for the hard labor needed to sustain the settlement.

Life at Jamestown proved calamitous from the outset. The community was erected on swampy ground where dank air and mosquito infestation made conditions unhealthful. Attention was immediately diverted to the futile search for gold and a water route to the West. Assuming that they would be kept in supplies by the Virginia Company, the men made few attempts to raise food; a fire in the first winter destroyed most of the buildings and wiped out the few remaining food stores not contaminated by rats. The absence of wives and families as well as class tensions contributed to social instability, and much energy was dissipated in drink and idleness. Antagonistic relations with regional tribes resulted in continuing strife. Weakened by the stresses of settlement, the colonists fell victim to a barrage of lethal diseases, and within months of their arrival, fewer than half of the original group were alive.

The turmoil of habitation was augmented by ineffectual governance. The first president of Jamestown was Edward Maria Wingfield, a former military commander and adventurer who was elected according to the provisions of the Virginia Company Charter of 1606. One of the seven original members of the Royal Council appointed to administer the colony, Wingfield was a well meaning but indecisive leader who proved unable to reconcile the divided company. Wingfield's aristocratic lineage estranged him from working-class colonists; his unwillingness to endorse favored status for "gentlemen" lost him the support of fellow Councillors; and his Roman Catholic background was suspect in the primarily Protestant band.

The atmosphere of distrust among officials was heightened by the pressures of sickness, famine, and cold, and within months of his election, Wingfield was under fire from the Council. Charged with pillaging the company stores (a serious accusation in a time of severe deprivation), practicing atheism (it was observed that he neglected to carry a Bible on his person), and assorted other complaints, Wingfield was summarily deposed from the "Presidentship," prompting an administrative crisis that was not quelled until John Smith was elected to that office in 1608.

Following his removal, Wingfield penned *A Discourse of Virginia,* a defense of his own actions and a narrative which provides one of the few eyewitness accounts of the struggle to settle Jamestown. Paired with other early documents such as Bradford's *Of Plymouth Plantation,* Morton's *The New English Canaan,* and especially Winthrop's "Speech to the General Court" recorded in his *Journal,* Wingfield's chronicle illuminates the personal pressures facing colonial leaders and identifies a number of critical political and social issues central to the founding of democratic governments in the New World.

Liahna Babener
Montana State University

PRIMARY WORK

A Discourse of Virginia, 1608.

from A Discourse of Virginia

[Here Followeth What Happened in James Town, in Virginia, after Captain Newport's Departure for England.]

Captain Newport,[1] having always his eyes and ears open to the proceedings of the Colony, three or four days before his departure asked the President[2] how he thought himself settled in the government—whose answer was that no disturbance could endanger him or the Colony but it must be wrought either by Captain Gosnold or Mr. Archer.[3] For the one was strong with friends and followers, and could if he would; and the other was troubled with an ambitious spirit, and would if he could. The Captain gave them both knowledge of this, the President's opinion, and moved them with many entreaties to be mindful of their duties to His Majesty and the Colony.

June, 1607, the 22nd: Captain Newport returned for England, for whose good pasage and safe return we made many prayers to our Almighty God.

June the 25th, an Indian came to us from the great Powhatan[4] with the word of peace—that he desired greatly our friendship, that the werowances[5] Pasyaheigh and Tapahanah should be our friends, that we should sow and reap in peace or else he would make wars upon them with us. This message fell out true; for both those werowances have ever since remained in peace and trade with us. We rewarded the messenger with many trifles which were great wonders to him. This Powhatan dwelleth 10 miles from us, upon the River Pamunkey[6] which lies north from us. . . .

July—the 3rd of July, seven or eight Indians presented the President a deer from Pamaonke, a werowance desiring our friendship. They inquired after our shipping, which the President said was gone to Croutoon.[7] They fear much our ships; and therefore he would not have them think it far from us. Their werowance had a hatchet sent him. They were well contented with trifles. A little after this came a deer to the President from the Great Powhatan. He and his messengers were pleased with the like trifles. The President likewise bought, diverse times, deer of the Indians, beavers and other flesh, which he always caused to be equally divided among the Colony.

About this time diverse of our men fell sick. We missed above forty before September did see us, amongst whom was the worthy and religious gentleman Capt. Bartholomew Gosnold, upon whose life stood a great part of the good success and fortune of our government and Colony. In his sickness time the President did easily foretell his own deposing from his command—so much differed the President and the other councillors in managing the government of the Colony.

July—the 7th of July, Tapahanah, a werowance dweller on Salisbury side,[8] hailed us with the word of peace. The President, with a shallop well manned, went to him.

[1]Commander of the expedition's flagship and one of the original seven Councillors.

[2]Wingfield refers to himself in the third person as "the President" through most of the narrative.

[3]Both members of the original Council.

[4]Chief ruler over the Algonkians in tidewater Virginia.

[5]Local chieftains.

[6]York River.

[7]Indian town thought to be where the survivors of the ill-fated Roanoke settlement might have gone in 1587.

[8]South shore of the James River.

He found him sitting on the ground crosslegged, as is their custom, with one attending on him which did often say, "This is the werowance Tapahanah"; which he did likewise confirm with stroking his breast. He was well enough known, for the President had seen him diverse times before. His countenance was nothing cheerful, for we had not seen him since he was in the field against us; but the President would take no knowledge thereof, and used him kindly, giving him a red waistcoat which he did desire. Tapahanah did inquire after our shipping. He received answer as before. He said his old store was spent, that his new was not at full growth by a foot, [and] that as soon as any was ripe he would bring it; which promise he truly performed.

The —— of ——[9] Mr. Kendall[10] was put off from being of the Council and committed to prison, for that it did manifestly appear he did practice to sow discord between the President and Council. Sickness had not now left us six able men in our town. God's only mercy did now watch and ward for us; but the President hid this our weakness carefully from the savages, never suffering them in all this time to come into our town.

September—the 6th of September, Pasyaheigh sent us a boy that was run from us. This was the first assurance of his peace with us; besides, we found them no cannibals.[11] The boy observed the men and women to spend the most part of the night in singing or howling, and that every morning the women carried all the little children to the river side; but what they did there he did not know. The rest of the werowances do likewise send our men renegades to us home again, using them well during their being with them; so as now, they being well rewarded at home at their return, they take little joy to travel abroad without passports.

The Council demanded some larger allowance for themselves, and from some sick [persons], their favorites—which the President would not yield unto without their warrants. . . . He prayed them further to consider the long time before we expected Capt. Newport's return, the uncertainty of his return (if God did not favor his voyage), the long time before our harvest would be ripe, and the doubtful peace that we had with the Indians (which they would keep no longer than opportunity served to do us mischief).

It was then therefore ordered that every meal of fish or flesh should excuse the allowance for porridge, both against the sick and [against the] whole. The Council, therefore, sitting again upon this proposition, instructed in the former reasons and order, did not think fit to break the former order by enlarging their allowance. . . . Now was the common store of oil, vinegar, sack, and aquavita all spent, saving two gallons of each. The sack [was] reserved for the Communion Table, the rest for such extremities as might fall upon us, which the President had only made known to Capt. Gosnold of which course he liked well. The vessels were, therefore, bunged up.[12] When Mr. Gosnold was dead, the President did acquaint the rest of the Council with the said remnant; but, Lord, how they then longed to sup up that little remnant! For they had now emptied all their own bottles, and all others that they could smell out.

[9]In this and subsequent references, omitted dates are left out of the original manuscript

[10]One of the original seven Councillors.

[11]Rumors and stories had been widely circulated that some of the indigenous tribes were cannibalistic, a belief shared by John Smith. Such fears were the product of European prejudices and anxieties about native peopl and had no basis in fact.

[12]Stopped up with a cork.

A little while after this the Council did again fall upon the President for some better allowance for themselves and some few [of] the sick, their privates. The President protested he would not be partial; but, if one had anything of him, every man should have his portion according to their places. Nevertheless [he said] that, upon [being shown] their warrants, he would deliver what [it] pleased them to demand. If the President had at that time enlarged the proportion according to their request, without doubt in very short time he had starved the whole company. He would not join with them, therefore, in such ignorant murder without their own warrant.

The President, well seeing to what end their impatience would grow, desired them earnestly and oftentimes to bestow the Presidentship among themselves, [and said] that he would obey, [as] a private man, as well as they could command. But they refused to discharge him of the place, saying they might not do it; for that he did His Majesty good service in it. In this meantime the Indians did daily relieve us with corn and flesh, that in three weeks the President had reared up 20 men able to work; for, as his store increased, he mended the common pot, he had laid up, besides, provision for three weeks' wheat beforehand.

By this time the Council had fully plotted to depose Wingfield, their then President, and had drawn certain articles in writing amongst themselves, and took their oaths upon the Evangelists to observe them—the effect whereof was, first: to depose the then President; to make Mr. Ratcliffe[13] the next President; not to depose the one the other; not to take the deposed President into Council again; not to take Mr. Archer into the Council, or any other, without the consent of every one of them. To these [articles] they had subscribed, as out of their own mouths at several times it was easily gathered. Thus had they forsaken His Majesty's government, [as] set us down in the instructions, and made it a triumvirate. It seemeth Mr. Archer was nothing acquainted with these articles. Though all the rest crept out of his notes and commentaries that were preferred against the President, yet it pleased God to cast him into the same disgrace and pit that he prepared for another, as will appear hereafter.

September—the 10th of September, Mr. Ratcliffe, Mr. Smith, and Mr. Martin[14] came to the President's tent, with a warrant subscribed under their hands, to depose the President, saying they thought him very unworthy to be either President or of the Council; and therefore discharged him of both. He answered them that they had eased him of a great deal of care and trouble [and] that, long since, he had diverse times proffered them the place at an easier rate. And [he said] further, that the President ought to be removed (as appeareth in His Majesty's instructions for our government) by the greater number of 13 voices, Councillors, [and] that they were but three;[15] and therefore [he] wished them to proceed advisedly. But they told him if they did him wrong they must answer [for] it. Then said the deposed President, "I am at your pleasure. Dispose of me as you will, without further garboils."[16]

I will now write what followeth in my own name, and give the new President his

[13]Another of the original seven Council members who was later elected to succeed Wingfield; he experienced similar problems of leadership and was also deposed within a year. John Smith then became President.

[14]Members of the original Council.

[15]Of the original seven Councillors, Newport had sailed for England; Gosnold had now died; Kendall had been deposed; leaving—aside from Wingfield—Ratcliff, Smith, and Martin.

[16]Confusion.

title. I shall be the briefer, being thus discharged. I was committed to a sergeant, and sent to the pinnace; but I was answered with, "If they did me wrong, they must answer [for] it."

The 11th of September, I was sent for to come before the President and Council upon their court day. They had now made Mr. Archer recorder of Virginia. The President made a speech to the Colony that he thought it fit to acquaint them why I was deposed. (I am now forced to stuff my paper with frivolous trifles, that our grave and worthy Council may the better strike those veins where the corrupt blood lieth, and that they may see in what manner of government the hope of the Colony now travaileth.) First, Master President said that I had denied him a penny-whistle, a chicken, a spoonful of beer, and served him with foul corn; and with that [he] pulled some grain out of a bag, showing it to the company. Then started up Mr. Smith and said that I had told him plainly how he lied; and that I said though we were equal here, yet, if he were in England, [I] would scorn his name. . . . Mr. Martin followed with, "He reporteth that I do slack the service in the Colony, and do nothing but tend my pot, spit, and oven; but he hath starved my son and denied him a spoonful of beer. I have friends in England shall be revenged on him, if ever he come in London."

I asked Mr. President if I should answer these complaints and whether he had aught else to charge me withal. With that he pulled out a paper book, loaded full with articles against me, and gave them [to] Mr. Archer to read. I told Mr. President and the Council that, by the instructions for our government, our proceeding ought to be verbal, and I was there ready to answer; but they said they would proceed in that order. I desired a copy of the articles and time given me to answer them likewise by writing; but that would not be granted. I bade them then please themselves. Mr. Archer then read some of the articles—when, on the sudden, Mr. President said, "Stay, stay! We know not whether he will abide our judgment, or whether he will appeal to the King." [He said] to me, "How say you: will you appeal to the King, or no?" I apprehended presently that God's mercy had opened me a way, through their ignorance, to escape their malice; for I never knew how I might demand an appeal. Besides, I had secret knowledge how they had forejudged me to pay five-fold for anything that came to my hands, whereof I could not discharge myself by writing; and that I should lie in prison until I had paid it.

The Captain Merchant had delivered me our merchandise, without any note of the particulars, under my hand; for himself had received them in gross. I likewise, as occasion moved me, spent them in trade or by gift amongst the Indians. So likewise did Capt. Newport take of them. . . . And disposed of them as was fit for him. Of these, likewise, I could make no account; only I was well assured I had never bestowed the value of three penny-whistles to my own use nor to the private use of any other; for I never carried any favorite over with me, or entertained any there. I was all [to] one and one to all. Upon these considerations I answered Mr. President and the Council that His Majesty's hands were full of mercy and that I did appeal to His Majesty's mercy. Then they committed me prisoner again to the master of the pinnace, with these words, "Look to him well; he is now the King's prisoner."

Then Mr. Archer pulled out of his bosom another paper book full of articles against me, desiring that he might read them in the name of the Colony. I said I stood there, ready to answer any man's complaint whom I had wronged; but no one man spoke one word against me. Then was he willed to read his book, whereof I complained; but I was still answered, "If they do me wrong, they must answer [for] it." I have forgotten the most of the articles, they were so slight (yet he glorieth much in his penwork). I know well the last—and a speech that he then made savored well of a mutiny—for he desired that by no means I might lie prisoner in the town, lest both he and others of the Colony should not give such obedience to their command as they ought to do; which goodly speech of his they easily swallowed.

But it was usual and natural to this honest gentleman, Mr. Archer, to be always hatching of some mutiny in my time. He might have appeared an author of three several mutinies. And he (as Mr. Pearsy [Percy] sent me word) had bought some witnesses' hands against me to diverse articles, with Indian cakes (which was no great matter to do after my deposal, and considering their hunger), persuasions, and threats. At another time he feared not to say, openly and in the presence of one of the Council, that, if they had not deposed me when they did, he had gotten twenty others to himself which should have deposed me. But this speech of his was likewise easily digested. Mr. Crofts[17] feared not to say that, if others would join with him, he would pull me out of my seat and out of my skin too. Other would say (whose names I spare) that, unless I would amend their allowance, they would be their own carvers. For these mutinous speeches I rebuked them openly, and proceeded no further against them, considering therein of men's lives in the King's service there. One of the Council was very earnest with me to take a guard about me. I answered him I would [have] no guard but God's love and my own innocence. In all these disorders was Mr. Archer a ringleader.

When Mr. President and Mr. Archer had made an end of their articles above mentioned, I was again sent prisoner to the pinnace; and Mr. Kendall, taken from thence, had his liberty, but might not carry arms. All this while the savages brought to the town such corn and flesh as they could spare. Pasyaheigh, by Tapahanah's mediation, was taken into friendship with us. The Councillors, Mr. Smith especially, traded up and down the river with the Indians for corn; which relieved the Colony well.

As I understand by a report, I am much charged with starving the Colony. I did always give every man his allowance faithfully, both of corn, oil, aquavita, etc., as was by the Council proportioned; neither was it bettered after my time, until, towards the end of March, a biscuit was allowed to every working man for his breakfast, by means of the provision brought us by Capt. Newport, as will appear hereafter. It is further said I did much banquet and riot. I never had but one squirrel roasted, whereof I gave part to Mr. Ratcliffe, then sick—yet was that squirrel given me. I did never heat a flesh-pot but when the common pot was so used likewise. Yet how often Mr. President's and the Councillor's spits have night and day been endangered to break their backs—so laden with swans, geese, ducks, etc.! How many times their flesh-pots have swelled, many hungry eyes did behold to their great longing. And what great thieves and thieving there hath been in the common store since my time—I doubt not but it is already made known to his Majesty's Council for Virginia.

The 17th day of September I was sent for to the Court to answer a complaint exhibited against me by Jehu Robinson; for [he charged] when I was President I did say [that] he with others had consented to run away with the shallop to Newfoundland. At

[17]One of the original settlers, classified officially as a "gentleman."

another time I must answer Mr. Smith for [the charge] that I had said he did conceal an intended mutiny. I told Mr. Recorder those words would bear no actions—that one of the causes was done without the limits mentioned in the patent granted to us. And therefore [I] prayed Mr. President that I might not be thus lugged with these disgraces and troubles, but he did wear no other eyes or ears than grew on Mr Archer's head. The jury gave the one of them 100 pounds and the other 200 pounds damages for slander. Then Mr. Recorder did very learnedly comfort me, [saying] that if I had wrong I might bring my writ of error in London; whereat I smiled.

I, seeing their law so speedy and cheap, desired justice for a copper kettle which Mr. Croft did detain from me. He said I had given it him. I did bid him bring his proof for that. He confessed he had no proof. Then Mr. President did ask me if I would be sworn I did not give it him. I said I knew no cause why to swear for mine own [property]. He asked Mr. Croft if he would make oath I did give it him; which oath he took, and won my kettle from me, that was in that place and time worth half his weight in gold. Yet I did understand afterwards that he would have given John Capper the one half of the kettle to have taken the oath for him; but he would [have] no copper on that price. I told Mr. President I had not known the like law, and prayed they would be more sparing of law until we had more wit or wealth. [I said] that laws were good spies in a populous, peaceable, and plentiful country, where they did make the good men better and stayed the bad from being worse; yet we were so poor as they did but rob us of time that might be better employed in service in the Colony.

The —— day of ——the President did beat James Read, the smith. The smith struck him [back] again. For this he was condemned to be hanged; but before he was turned off the ladder he desired to speak with the President in private—to whom he accussed Mr. Kendall of a mutiny, and so escaped himself. What indictment Mr. Recorder framed against the smith I know not; but I know it is familiar for the President, Councillors, and other officers, to beat men at their pleasure. One lieth sick till death, another walketh lame, the third crieth out of all his bones; which miseries they do take upon their consciences to come to them by this their alms of beating. Were this whipping, lawing, beating, and hanging in Virginia known in England, I fear it would drive many well-affected minds from this honorable action of Virginia.

This smith, coming aboard the pinnace . . . two or three days before his arraignment, brought me commendations from Mr. Pearsy [Percy], Mr. Waller, Mr. Kendall, and some others, saying they would be glad to see me on shore. I answered him they were honest gentlemen and had carried themselves very obediently to their governors. I added further that upon Sunday if the weather were fair I would be at the sermon. Lastly, I said that I was so sickly, starved, [and] lame, and did lie so cold and wet in the pinnace, as I would be dragged thither before I would go thither any more. Sunday proved not fair; I went not to the sermon.

The —— day of —— Mr. Kendall was executed, being shot to death for a mutiny. In the arrest of his judgement he alleged to Mr. President that his name was Sicklemore, not Ratcliffe,[18] and so [he] had no authority to pronounce judgement. Then Mr. Martin pronounced judgment.

[18] There was apparently some confusion over Ratcliffe's correct name. His name appeared in the Virginia Charter as "Captain John Sicklemore, alias Ratcliffe."

Somewhat before this time the President and Council had sent for the keys of my coffers, supposing that I had some writings concerning the Colony. I requested that the Clerk of the Council might see what they took out of my coffers; but they would not suffer him or any other. Under color hereof they took my books of accounts and all my notes that concerned the expenses of the Colony, and instructions under the Captain Merchant's hand of the store of provisions, diverse other books, and trifles of my own proper goods, which I could never recover. Thus was I made good prize on all sides.

The —— day of —— the President commanded me to come on shore, which I refused, as not rightfully deposed. And [I] desired that I might speak to him and the Council in the presence of ten of the best sort of the gentlemen. With much entreaty some of them were sent for. Then I told them I was determined to go into England to acquaint our Council there with our weakness. I said further [that] their laws and government were such as I had no joy to live under them any longer, that I did much mislike their triumvirate, having forsaken His Majesty's instructions for our government; and therefore prayed there might be more made of the Council. I said further I desired not to go into England, if either Mr. President or Mr. Archer would go, but was willing to take my fortune with the Colony; and [I] did also proffer to furnish them with £100 towards the fetching home [of] the Colony, if the action was given over. They did like of none of my proffers, but made diverse shot at me in the pinnace. I, seeing their resolutions, went ashore to them—where, after I had stayed a while in conference, they sent me to the pinnace again.

December—the 10th of December Mr. Smith went up the river of the Chickahominy to trade for corn. He was desirous to see the head of that river; and, when it was not possible with the shallop, he hired a canoe and an Indian to carry him up further. The river . . . grew worse and worse. Then he went on shore with his guide and left Robinson and Emmery, two of our men in the canoe—which were presently slain by the Indians, Pamunkey's [Pamaonke's] men. And he himself [was] taken prisoner, and by the means of his guide his life was saved. And Pamunkey [Pamaonke], having him prisoner, carried him to his neighbors' werowances to see if any of them knew him for one of those which had been, some two or three years before us, in a river amongst them northward and [had] taken away some Indians from them by force. At last he brought him to the great Powhatan (of whom before we had no knowledge), who sent him home[19] to our town the 8th of January.

During Mr. Smith's absence the President did swear Mr. Archer one of the Council, contrary to his oath taken in the articles agreed upon between themselves (before spoken of), and contrary to the King's instructions, and without Mr. Martin's consent; whereas there were no more but the President and Mr. Martin then of the Council.

Mr. Archer, being settled in his authority, sought how to call Mr. Smith's life in question, and had indicted him upon a chapter in Leviticus[20] for the death of his two men. He had had his trial the same day of his return and, I believe, his hanging the same or the next day—so speedy is our law there. But it pleased God to send Captain Newport unto us the same evening, to our unspeakable comfort; whose arrival

[19]Powhatan . . . sent him home: An allusion to the famous episode in which Pocahontas was said to have interceded with her father, Powhatan, on John Smith's behalf.

[20]Leviticus 24:19–21.

saved Mr. Smith's life and mine, because he took me out of the pinnace and gave me leave to lie in the town. Also by his coming was prevented a parliament, which the new Councillor, Mr. Recorder, intended there to summon. Thus error begot error.

Captain Newport, having landed, lodged, and refreshed his men, employed some of them about a fair storehouse, others about a stove, and his mariners about a church—all which works they finished cheerfully and in short time.

January—the 7th of January our town was almost quite burnt[21] with all our apparel and provision; but Captain Newport healed our wants, to our great comforts, out of the great plenty sent us by the provident and loving care of our worthy and most worthy Council.

This vigilant Captain, slacking no opportunity that might advance the prosperity of the Colony, having settled the company upon the former works, took Mr. Smith and Mr. Scrivener (another Councillor of Virginia, upon whose discretion liveth a great hope of the action) [and] went to discover the River Pamunkey on the further side whereof dwelleth the Great Powhatan, and to trade with him for corn. This river lieth north from us, and runneth east and west. I have nothing but by relation of that matter, and therefore dare not make any discourse thereof, lest I might wrong the great desert which Captain Newport's love to the action hath deserved—especially himself being present, and best able to give satisfaction thereof. I will hasten, therefore, to his return.

March—the 9th of March he returned to Jamestown with his pinnace well laden with corn, wheat, beans, and peas to our great comfort and his worthy commendations.

By this time the Council and Captain, having attentively looked into the carriage both of the Councillors and other officers, removed some officers out of the store, and Captain Archer, a Councillor whose insolency did look upon that little himself with great-sighted spectacles, derogating from others' merits by spewing out his venomous libels and infamous chronicles upon them, as doth appear in his own handwriting; for which, and other worse tricks, he had not escaped the halter, but that Captain Newport interposed his advice to the contrary.

Captain Newport, having new dispatched all his business and set the clock in a true course (if so the Council will keep it), prepared himself for England upon the 10th of April, and arrived at Blackwall on Sunday, the 21st of May, 1608.

1608

Richard Frethorne fl. 1623

Richard Frethorne was a young Englishman who came over to the New World in 1623 as an indentured servant and settled in Virginia, near the Jamestown colony. Other than the three letters to his parents included here, there is no historical record of his life. The letters, however, provide an illuminating picture of the hardships of

[21]A reference to the fire that had destroyed most of the colony's provisions and buildings in the early winter of 1607–1608.

colonization in the early seventeenth century. Combatting homesickness, disease, hunger, discomfort, and isolation, Frethorne and his fellow settlers struggled to make a success of their fledgling community. As might be expected, many longed to be "redeemed out of Egypt" and return to their former lives across the Atlantic. Frethorne's correspondence reveals the poignancy of the struggle for survival waged by the class of indentured servants in the new world.

Liahna Babener
Montana State University

from Richard Frethorne, to His Parents (Virginia, 1623)

Loving and kind father and mother:

My most humble duty remembered to you, hoping in God of your good health, as I myself am at the making hereof. This is to let you understand that I your child am in a most heavy case by reason of the nature of the country, [which] is such that it causeth much sickness, as the scurvy and the bloody flux and diverse other diseases, which maketh the body very poor and weak. And when we are sick there is nothing to comfort us; for since I came out of the ship I never ate anything but peas, and loblollie (that is, water gruel). As for deer or venison I never saw any since I came into this land. There is indeed some fowl, but we are not allowed to go and get it, but must work hard both early and late for a mess of water gruel and a mouthful of bread and beef. A mouthful of bread for a penny loaf must serve for four men which is most pitiful. . . . People cry out day and night—Oh! that they were in England without their limbs—and would not care to lose any limb to be England again, yea, though they beg from door to door. For we live in fear of the enemy every hour, yet we have had a combat with them on the Sunday before Shrovetide,[1] and we took two alive and made slaves of them. But it was by policy, for we are in great danger; for our plantation is very weak by reason of the death and sickness of our company. For we came but twenty for the merchants, and they are half dead just; and we look every hour when two more should go. Yet there came some four other men yet to live with us, of which there is but one alive; and our Lieutenant is dead, and his father and his brother. And there was some five or six of the last year's twenty, of which there is but three left, so that we are fain to get other men to plant with us; and yet we are but 32 to fight against 3000 if they should come. And the nighest help that we have is ten miles of us, and when the rogues overcame this place last they slew 80 persons. How then shall we do, for we lie even in their teeth? They may easily take us, but that God is merciful and can save with few as well as with many, as he showed to Gilead.[2] . . .

[1]The three days before Ash Wednesday, formerly set aside as a period of confession and a time of festivity preceding Lent in Christian practice.

[2]A region east of the Jordan River settled in biblical times by, among others, Israelites who were successfully defended in battle against vastly superior numbers of invaders by Judas Maccabeus and his warriors.

And I have nothing to comfort me, nor there is nothing to be gotten here but sickness and death, except that one had money to lay out in some things for profit. But I have nothing at all—no, not a shirt to my back but two rags (2), nor no clothes but one poor suit, nor but one pair of shoes, but one pair of stockings, but one cap, but two bands. My cloak is stolen by one of my own fellows, and to his dying hour [he] would not tell me what he did with it; but some of my fellows saw him have butter and beef out of a ship, which my cloak, I doubt [not], paid for. So that I have not a penny, nor a penny worth, to help me to either spice or sugar or strong waters, without the which one cannot live here. For as strong beer in England doth fatten and strengthen them, so water here doth wash and weaken these here [and] only keeps life and soul together. But I am not half a quarter so strong as I was in England, and all is for want of victuals; for I do protest unto you that I have eaten more in [one] day at home than I have allowed me here for a week. You have given more than my day's allowance to a beggar at the door; and if Mr. Jackson had not relieved me, I should be in a poor case. But he like a father and she like a loving mother doth still help me. . . .

Goodman Jackson pitied me and made me a cabin to lie in . . . which comforted me more than peas or water gruel. Oh, they be very godly folks, and love me very well, and will do anything for me. And he much marvelled that you would send me a servant to the Company; he saith I had been better knocked on the head. And indeed so I find it now, to my great grief and misery; and saith that if you love me you will redeem me suddenly, for which I do entreat and beg. And if you cannot get the merchants to redeem me for some little money, then for God's sake get a gathering or entreat some good folks to lay out some little sum of money in meal and cheese and butter and beef. Any eating meat will yield great profit. Oil and vinegar is very good; but, father, there is great loss in leaking. But for God's sake send beef and cheese and butter, or the more of one sort and none of another. But if you send cheese, it must be very old cheese; and at the cheesemonger's you may buy very good cheese for twopence farthing or halfpenny, that will be liked very well. But if you send cheese, you must have a care how you pack it in barrels; and you must put cooper's chips between every cheese, or else the heat of the hold will rot them. And look whatsoever you send me—be it never so much—look, what[ever] I make of it, I will deal truly with you. I will send it over and beg the profit to redeem me; and if I die before it come, I have entreated Goodman Jackson to send you the worth of it, who hath promised he will. . . . Good father, do not forget me, but have mercy and pity my miserable case. I know if you did but see me, you would weep to see me; for I have but one suit. . . . Wherefore, for God's sake, pity me. I pray you to remember my love to all my friends and kindred. I hope all my brothers and sisters are in good health, and as for my part I have set down my resolution that certainly will be; that is, that the answer of this letter will be life or death to me. Therefore, good father, send as soon as you can; and if you send me any thing let this be the mark.

ROT

Richard Frethorne,
Martin's Hundred

The names of them that be dead of the company [that] came over with us to serve under our Lieutenants:

John Flower	George Goulding
John Thomas	Jos. Johnson
Thos. Howes	our lieutenant, his
John Butcher	father and brother
John Sanderford	Thos. Giblin
Rich. Smith	George Banum
John Olive	a little Dutchman
Thos. Peirsman	one woman
William Cerrell	one maid
	one child

All these died out of my master's house, since I came; and we came in but at Christmas, and this is the 20th day of March. And the sailors say that there is two-thirds of the 150 dead already. And thus I end, praying to God to send me good success that I may be redeemed out of Egypt. So *vale in Christo.*

Loving father, I pray you to use this man very exceeding kindly, for he hath done much for me, both on my journey and since. I entreat you not to forget me, but by any means redeem me; for this day we hear that there is 26 of Englishmen slain by the Indians. And they have taken a pinnace[3] of Mr. Pountis, and have gotten pieces, armor, swords, all things fit for war; so that they may now steal upon us and we cannot know them from English till it is too late—that they be upon us—and then there is no mercy. Therefore if you love or respect me as your child, release me from the bondage and save my life. Now you may save me, or let met be slain with infidels. Ask this man—he knoweth that all is true and just that I say here. If you do redeem me, the Company must send for me to my Mr. Harrod; for so is this Master's name. April, the second day,

Your loving son,
Richard Frethorne

Moreover, on the third day of April we heard that after these rogues had gotten the pinnace and had taken all furnitures [such] as pieces, swords, armor, coats of mail, powder, shot and all the things that they had to trade withal, they killed the Captain and cut off his head. And rowing with the tail of the boat foremost, they set up a pole and put the Captain's head upon it, and so rowed home. Then the Devil set them on again, so that they furnished about 200 canoes with above 1000 Indians, and came, and thought to have taken the ship; but she was too quick for them—which thing was very much talked of, for they always feared a ship. But now the rogues grow very bold and can use pieces, some of them, as well or better than an Englishman; for an Indian did shoot with Mr. Charles, my master's kinsman, at a mark of white paper, and he hit it at the first, but Mr. Charles could not hit it. But see the envy of these slaves, for when they could not take the ship, then our men saw them threaten Accomack, that is the next plantation. And now there is no way but starving; . . . For they had no crop last year by reason of these rogues, so that we have no corn but as ships do relieve us, nor we shall hardly have any crop this year; and we are as like to

[3]A small sailing boat, often used as a scout for a larger vessel.

perish first as any plantation. For we have but two hogsheads of meal left to serve us this two months, . . . that is but a halfpennyloaf a day for a man. Is it not strange to me, think you? But what will it be when we shall go a month or two and never see a bit of bread, as my master doth say we must do? And he said he is not able to keep us all. Then we shall be turned up to the land and eat barks of trees or molds of the ground; therefore with weeping tears I beg of you to help me. Oh, that you did see my daily and hourly sighs, groans, and tears, and thumps that I afford mine own breast, and rue and curse the time of my birth, with holy Job. I thought no head had been able to hold so much water as hath and doth daily flow from mine eyes.

But this is certain: I never felt the want of father and mother till now; but now, dear friends, full well I know and rue it, although it were too late before I knew it. . . .

Your loving son,
Richard Frethorne
Virginia, 3rd April, 1623

1881

Thomas Morton 1579?–1647?

Little is known about Morton's early life except that he became a lawyer in the "west countries" of England and married in 1621. In 1622 he first sailed to New England and in 1626 established himself as head of a trading post at Passonagessit, which he renamed "Ma-re Mount" (or, as Bradford spelled it, "Merry-mount"). There he offended the neighboring Separatist Puritan settlement by erecting a maypole and cavorting with the Indians, to whom, according to Bradford, he sold guns. He was arrested by Miles Standish, the military leader at Plymouth, and sent back to England in 1628. He returned, however, acquitted of the charges against him in 1629, but in 1630 his property at Ma-re Mount was seized or burned by Puritan authorities, and he was banished to England again. He then worked with the anti-Puritan Anglican authorities in England to undermine the Massachusetts Bay Company, but his effort did not succeed. He returned to New England in 1643, was imprisoned for slander by the authorities in Boston in the winter of 1644–1645, and died two years later in Maine (then part of the Massachusetts colony), where he had finally settled. His only literary work is *New English Canaan* (1637), best-known for its satire of Puritans in general and the Separatists in particular.

In *New English Canaan* Morton offers a secularized version of many of the same events of 1620–1630 that are recounted from an opposing point of view in Bradford's history. The book is not a history, however, but a promotional tract in three parts. It sets out to prove the thesis that New England is a valuable region inhabited by friendly natives, a region that well deserves British colonization. It avers that the colonial effort is being hampered by religious fanatics, the Separatist Pilgrims and their Puritan allies. The middle section of the three describes the natural wealth of New England, while the first and last offer sharply contrasted portraits of the humane Indians and the inhumane Puritans. The evidence for the panegyric in part one and for the satire in part three is presented in brief essays and loosely related anecdotes rather than in the form of continuous historical narration.

Morton omits much, never mentioning, for instance, the most serious of the

Puritan charges against him: his alleged sale of guns and gunpowder to Indians hostile to the other colonists. And Morton also clearly exaggerates or fictionalizes most of the anecdotes he includes. But although his "facts" are partial and unreliable, his style is so witty and his examples so vivid that he renders the argument of the book appealing and even plausible. The Indians, as he sees them, adhere to a natural religion supported by the virtues of hospitality to strangers and respect for authority. Instead of striving for personal wealth, they prefer to enjoy and share nature's bounty. This core of common humanity Morton shares with them and finds supported by his own Anglicanism, with its traditional celebration of saints' days, like that upon which Morton set up the maypole. He asserts that the Puritans, on the other hand, condemn natural pleasure, are inhospitable, respect neither king nor church tradition, and live only for what they consider the "spirit" but what Morton considers private gain.

Attaching titles like those found in Jacobean comedy to his main characters, especially "the Great Monster" to himself and "Captain Shrimp" to Miles Standish, Morton turns his caricature of the Puritans into a parody of knightly romance in the manner of *Don Quixote*. Standish as mock-hero becomes the real villain, while Morton as mock-villain becomes the real hero, the defender of both Indian and traditional English ways martyred for his humanity by would-be saints. Delightful as fiction though doubtful as fact, New English Canaan sharply defines central conflicts in the early British settlement of New England. Its astonishingly positive portrait of the Indians, no less than its negative one of the Pilgrims, offers a valuable counter-balance to Bradford's pro-Pilgrim and sometimes anti-Indian history, *Of Plymouth Plantation.*

Kenneth Alan Hovey
University of Texas at San Antonio

PRIMARY WORK

New English Canaan, 1637.

SECONDARY WORKS

Charles Francis Adams, "Introduction" to *New English Canaan,* 1883; Donald F. Connors, *Thomas Morton,* 1969.

from New English Canaan

from Book I

Containing the originall of the Natives, their manners & Customes, with their tractable nature and love towards the English.

from Chapter IV
Of their Houses and Habitations.

. . . They use not to winter and summer in one place, for that would be a reason to make fuell scarse; but, after the manner of the gentry of Civilized natives, remoove for their pleasures; some times to their hunting places, where they remaine keeping good hospitality for that season; and sometimes to their fishing places, where they abide for that season likewise: and at the spring, when fish comes in plentifully, they have meetinges from severall places, where they exercise themselves in gaminge and playing of juglinge trickes and all manner of Revelles, which they are deligted in; [so] that it is admirable to behould what pastime they use of severall kindes, every one striving to surpasse each other. After this manner they spend their time.

from Chapter VI
Of the Indians apparrell.

. . . Mantels made of Beares skinnes is an usuall wearinge, among the Natives that live where the Beares doe haunt: they make shooes of Mose skinnes, which is the principall leather used to that purpose; and for want of such lether (which is the strongest) they make shooes of Deeres skinnes, very handsomly and commodious; and, of such deeres skinnes as they dresse bare, they make stockinges that comes within their shooes, like a stirrop stockinge, and is fastned above at their belt, which is about their middell; Every male, after hee attaines unto the age which they call Pubes, wereth a belt about his middell, and a broad peece of lether that goeth betweene his leggs and is tuckt up both before and behinde under that belt; and this they weare to hide their secreats of nature, which by no meanes they will suffer to be seene, so much modesty they use in that particular. . . .

Their women have shoes and stockinges to weare likewise when they please, such as the men have, but the mantle they use to cover their nakednesse with is much longer then that which the men use; for, as the men have one Deeres skinn, the women have two soed together at the full lenght, and it is so lardge that it trailes after them like a great Ladies trane; and in time I thinke they may have their Pages to beare them up; and where the men use but one Beares skinn for a Mantle, the women have two soed together; and if any of their women would at any time shift one, they take that which they intend to make use of, and cast it over them round, before they shifte away the other, for modesty, being unwilling to be seene to discover their nakednesse; and the one being so cast over, they slip the other from under them in a decent manner, which is to be noted in people uncivilized; therein they seeme to have as much modesty as civilized people, and deserve to be applauded for it.

Chapter VIII
Of their Reverence, and respect to age.

It is a thing to be admired, and indeede made a president, that a Nation yet uncivilized should more respect age then some nations civilized, since there are so many precepts both of divine and humane writers extant to instruct more Civill Nations: in that particular, wherein they excell, the younger are allwayes obedient unto the elder people, and at their commaunds in every respect without grummbling; in all councels, (as therein they are circumspect to do their acciones by advise and councell, and not rashly or inconsiderately,) the younger mens opinion shall be heard, but the old mens opinion and councell imbraced and followed: besides, as the elder feede and provide for the younger in infancy, so doe the younger, after being growne to yeares of manhood, provide for those that be aged: and in distribution of Acctes the elder men are first served by their dispensator;[1] and their counsels (especially if they be powahs) are esteemed as oracles amongst the younger Natives.

The consideration of these things, mee thinkes, should reduce some of our irregular young people of civilized Nations, when this story shall come to their knowledge, to better manners, and make them ashamed of their former error in this kinde, and to become hereafter more duetyfull; which I, as a friend, (by observation having found,) have herein recorded for that purpose.

Chapter XVI
Of their acknowledgment of the Creation, and immortality of the Soule.

Although these Salvages are found to be without Religion, Law, and King (as Sir William Alexander[2] hath well observed,) yet are they not altogether without the knowledge of God (historically); for they have it amongst them by tradition that God made one man and one woman, and bad them live together and get children, kill deare, beasts, birds, fish and fowle, and what they would at their pleasure; and that their posterity was full of evill, and made God so angry that hee let in the Sea upon them, and drowned the greatest part of them, that were naughty men, (the Lord destroyed so;) and they went to Sanaconquam, who feeds upon them (pointing to the Center of the Earth, where they imagine is the habitation of the Devill:) the other, (which were not destroyed,) increased the world, and when they died (because they were good) went to the howse of Kytan, pointing to the setting of the sonne; where they eate all manner of dainties, and never take paines (as now) to provide it.

Kytan makes provision (they say) and saves them that laboure; and there they shall live with him forever, voyd of care. And they are perswaded that Kytan is hee that makes corne growe, trees growe, and all manner of fruits.

And that wee that use the booke of Common prayer[3] doo it to declare to them, that cannot reade, what Kytan has commaunded us, and that wee doe pray to him with the helpe of that booke; and doe make so much accompt of it, that a Salvage (who had lived in my howse before hee had taken a wife, by whome hee had children) made this request to mee, (knowing that I allwayes used him with much more respect than others,) that I would let his sonne be brought up in my howse, that hee might be taught to reade in that booke: which request of his I granted; and hee was a very joyfull man to thinke that his sonne should thereby (as hee said) become an Englishman; and then hee would be a good man.

[1]One who dispenses goods, a steward.
[2]Scottish poet and statesman (1567?–1640), who founded and colonized Nova Scotia in the 1620s.
[3]The book containing the liturgical services and prayers of the Church of England.

I asked him who was a good man; his answere was, hee that would not lye, nor steale.

These, with them, are all the capitall crimes that can be imagined; all other are nothing in respect of those; and hee that is free from these must live with Kytan for ever, in all manner of pleasure.

from Chapter XX
That the Salvages live a contended life.

A Gentleman and a traveller, that had bin in the parts of New England for a time, when hee retorned againe, in his discourse of the Country, wondered, (as hee said,) that the natives of the land lived so poorely in so rich a Country, like to our Beggers in England. Surely that Gentleman had not time or leasure whiles hee was there truely to informe himselfe of the state of that Country, and the happy life the Salvages would leade weare they once brought to Christianity.

I must confesse they want the use and benefit of Navigation, (which is the very sinnus[4] of a flourishing Commonwealth,) yet are they supplied with all manner of needefull things for the maintenance of life and lifelyhood. Foode and rayment are the cheife of all that we make true use of; and of these they finde no want, but have, and may have, them in a most plentifull manner. . . .

Now since it is but foode and rayment that men that live needeth, (though not all alike,) why should not the Natives of New England be sayd to live richly, having no want of either? Cloaths are the badge of sinne; and the more variety of fashions is but the greater abuse of the Creature: the beasts of the forrest there doe serve to furnish them at any time when they please: fish and flesh they have in greate abundance, which they both roast and boyle.

They are indeed not served in dishes of plate[5] with variety of Sauces to procure appetite; that needs not there. The rarity of the aire, begot by the medicinable quality of the sweete herbes of the Country, alwayes procures good stomakes to the inhabitants.

I must needs commend them in this particular, that, though they buy many commodities of our Nation, yet they keepe but fewe, and those of speciall use.

They love not to bee cumbered with many utensilles, and although every proprietor knowes his owne, yet all things, (so long as they will last), are used in common amongst them: A bisket cake given to one, that one breakes it equally into so many parts as there be persons in his company, and distributes it. Platoes Commonwealth[6] is so much practised by these people.

According to humane reason, guided onely by the light of nature, these people leades the more happy and freer life, being voyde of care, which torments the mindes of so many Christians: They are not delighted in baubles, but in usefull things.

[4]Sinews.
[5]Gold or silver.
[6]The communal society described in Plato's *Republic.*

from Book III

Containing a description of the People that are planted there, what remarkable Accidents have happened there since they were setled, what Tenents they hould, together with the practise of their Church.

from Chapter I
Of a great League made with the Plimmouth Planters after their arrivall, by the Sachem of those Territories.

The Sachem of the Territories where the Planters of New England are setled, that are the first of the now Inhabitants of New Canaan, not knowing what they were, or whether they would be freindes or foes, and being desirous to purchase their freindship that hee might have the better Assurance of quiet tradinge with them, (which hee conceived would be very advantagious to him,) was desirous to prepare an ambassador, with commission to treat on his behalfe, to that purpose; and having one that had beene in England (taken by a worthlesse man out of other partes, and after left there by accident,) this Salvage[7] hee instructed how to behave himselfe in the treaty of peace; and the more to give him incouragement to adventure his person amongst these new come inhabitants, which was a thinge hee durst not himselfe attempt without security or hostage, promised that Salvage freedome, who had beene detained there as theire Captive: which offer hee accepted, and accordingly came to the Planters, salutinge them with wellcome in the English phrase, which was of them admired to heare a Salvage there speake in their owne language, and used him great courtesie: to whome hee declared the cause of his comminge, and contrived the businesse so that hee brought the Sachem and the English together, betweene whome was a firme league concluded, which yet continueth.

from Chapter V
Of a Massacre made upon the Salvages at Wessaguscus.

[T]he Plimmouth men . . . came in the meane time to Wessaguscus, and there pretended to feast the Salvages of those partes, bringing with them Porke and thinges for the purpose, which they sett before the Salvages. They eate thereof without suspition of any mischeife, who were taken upon a watchword given, and with their owne knives, (hanging about their neckes,) were by the Plimmouth planters stabd and slaine: one of which were hanged up there, after the slaughter. . . .

The Salvages of the Massachusetts, that could not imagine from whence these men should come, or to what end, seeing them performe such unexpected actions;

[7]Morton has apparently conflated Squanto, the Indian who was kidnapped by Captain Thomas Hunt, with Samoset, the Indian who first greeted the Pilgrims.

neither could tell by what name properly to distinguish them; did from that time afterwards call the English Planters Wotawquenange, which in their language signifieth stabbers, or Cutthroates: and this name was received by those that came there after for good, being then unacquainted with the signification of it, for many yeares following.

from Chapter VII
Of Thomas Mortons entertainement at Plimmouth, and castinge away upon an Island.

This man arrived in those parts, and, hearing newes of a Towne that was much praised, he was desirous to goe thither, and see how thinges stood; where his entertainement was their best, I dare be bould to say: for, although they had but 3. Cowes in all, yet had they fresh butter and a sallet of egges in dainty wise, a dish not common in a wildernes. There hee bestowed some time in the survey of this plantation. His new come servants, in the meane time, were tane to taske, to have their zeale appeare, and questioned what preacher was among their company; and finding none, did seeme to condole their estate as if undone, because no man among them had the guift to be in Jonas steade, nor they the meanes to keepe them in that path so hard to keepe.[8]

Our Master, say they, reades the Bible and the word of God, and useth the booke of common prayer: but this is not the meanes, the answere is: the meanes, they crie, alas, poore Soules where is the meanes? you seeme as if betrayed, to be without the meanes: how can you bc stayed from fallinge headlonge to perdition? *Facilis descensus averni:*[9] the booke of common prayer, sayd they, what poore thinge is that, for a man to reade in a booke? No, no, good sirs, I would you were neere us, you might receave comfort by instruction: give me a man hath the guiftes of the spirit, not a booke in hand. I doe professe sayes one, to live without the meanes is dangerous, the Lord doth know.

By these insinuations, like the Serpent, they did creepe and winde into the good opinion of the illiterate multitude, that were desirous to be freed and gone to them, no doubdt, (which some of them after confessed); and little good was to be done one them after this charme was used: now plotts and factions how they might get loose. . . . [B]ut their Master to prevent them caused the sales and oares to be brought a shore, to make a tilt if neede should be, and kindled fire, broched that Hogshed, and caused them fill the can with lusty liqour, Claret sparklinge neate; which was not suffered to grow pale and flatt, but tipled of with quick dexterity: the Master makes a shew of keepinge round,[10] but with close lipps did seeme to make longe draughts, knowinge

[8]According to Morton, the Pilgrims at Plymouth considered themselves to have preachers who had the "gifts of the spirit" and who could dispense "the means of salvation" (the word of God properly preached). Morton's company lacked such a Puritan preacher. Jonah in the Bible was the one worshipper of God in a ship full of pagans.

[9]"The descent to the underworld is easy" (Virgil, *Aeneid* 6.126).

[10]Drinking as much as his companions.

the wine would make them Protestants;[11] and so the plot was then at large disclosed and discovered. . . .

from Chapter XIV
Of the Revells of New Canaan.

The Inhabitants of Pasonagessit, (having translated the name of their habitation from that ancient Salvage name to Ma-re Mount, and being resolved to have the new name confirmed for a memorial to after ages,) did devise amongst themselves to have it performed in a solemne manner, with Revels and merriment after the old English custome; [they] prepared to sett up a Maypole upon the festivall day of Philip and Jacob,[12] and therefore brewed a barrell of excellent beare and provided a case of bottles, to be spent, with other good cheare, for all commers of that day. And because they would have it in a compleat forme, they had prepared a song fitting to the time and present occasion. And upon Mayday they brought the Maypole to the place appointed, with drumes, gunnes, pistols and other fitting instruments, for that purpose; and there erected it with the help of Salvages, that came thether of purpose to see the manner of our Revels. A goodly pine tree of 80. foote longe was reared up, with a peare of buckshorns nayled one somewhat neare unto the top of it: where it stood, as a faire sea marke for directions how to finde out the way to mine Hoste of Ma-re Mount.[13] . . .

The setting up of this Maypole was a lamentable spectacle to the precise seperatists, that lived at new Plimmouth. They termed it an Idoll; yea, they called it the Calfe of Horeb, and stood at defiance with the place, naming it Mount Dagon;[14] threatning to make it a woefull mount and not a merry mount. . . .

There was likewise a merry song made, which, (to make their Revells more fashionable,) was sung with a Corus, every man bearing his part; which they performed in a daunce, hand in hand about the Maypole, whiles one of the Company sung and filled out the good liquor, like gammedes and Jupiter.[15]

The Songe

Cor.

Drinke and be merry, merry, merry boyes;
Let all your delight be in the Hymens[16] joyes;
Iö[17] to Hymen, now the day is come,
About the merry Maypole take a Roome.
Make greene garlons, bring bottles out

[11]Instead of "precise Seperatists" like the Pilgrims.

[12]The feast day of St. Philip and St. James, celebrated on May 1 by the Church of England.

[13]Morton's name for himself. "Host," in this case, suggests hosteler or innkeeper.

[14]The calf of Horeb was the golden figure of a calf destroyed as a false idol by Moses in Exodus 32. Dagon was the false idol of the Philistines (I Samuel 5).

[15]Ganymede is the cup-bearer of Jupiter, the king of the gods in Roman mythology.

[16]Hymen is the Roman god of marriage.

[17]A Latin word meaning "hurrah," generally used in celebrations of Hymen.

And fill sweet Nectar freely about.
Uncover thy head and feare no harme,
For hers good liquor to keepe it warme.
Then drinke and be merry, &c.
Iô to Hymen, &c.
Nectar is a thing assign'd
By the Deities owne minde
To cure the hart opprest with greife,
And of good liquors is the cheife.
Then drinke, &c.
Iô to Hymen, &c.
Give to the Mellancolly man
A cup or two of't now and than;
This physick will soone revive his bloud,
And make him be of a merrier moode.
Then drinke, &c.
Iô to Hymen, &c.
Give to the Nymphe thats free from scorne
No Irish stuff[18] nor Scotch over worne.
Lasses in beaver coats come away,
Yee shall be welcome to us night and day.
To drinke and be merry &c.
Iô to Hymen, &c.

This harmeles mirth made by younge men, (that lived in hope to have wifes brought over to them, that would save them a laboure to make a voyage to fetch any over,) was much distasted of the precise Seperatists, that keepe much a doe about the tyth of Muit and Cummin,[19] troubling their braines more than reason would require about things that are indifferent: and from that time sought occasion against my honest Host of Ma-re Mount, to overthrow his ondertakings and to destroy his plantation quite and cleane. . . .

Some of them affirmed that the first institution [of the Maypole] was in memory of a whore; not knowing that it was a Trophe erected at first in honor of Maja, the Lady of learning which they despise, vilifying the two universities[20] with uncivile termes, accounting what is there obtained by studdy is but unnecessary learning; not considering that learninge does inable mens mindes to converse with eliments of a higher nature then is to be found within the habitation of the Mole.

Chapter XV
Of a great Monster supposed to be at Ma-re-Mount; and the preparation made to destroy it.

The Seperatists, envying the prosperity and hope of the Plantation at Ma-re Mount, (which they perceaved beganne to come forward, and to be in a good way for gaine in the Beaver trade,) conspired together against mine Host especially, (who was the

[18]Cloth.

[19]The Pharisees are accused in Matthew 23:23 of paying "tithe of mint and anise and cummin" while omitting "weightier matters of the law, judgment, mercy, and faith."

[20]Oxford and Cambridge.

owner of that Plantation,) and made up a party against him; and mustred up what aide they could, accounting of him as a great Monster.

Many threatening speeches were given out both against his person and his Habitation, which they divulged should be consumed with fire: And taking advantage of the time when his company, (which seemed little to regard theire threats,) were gone up into the Inlands to trade with the Salvages for Beaver, they set upon my honest host at a place called Wessaguscus, where, by accident, they found him. The inhabitants there were in good hope of the subvertion of the plantation at Mare Mount, (which they principally aymed at;) and the rather because mine host was a man that indeavoured to advaunce the dignity of the Church of England; which they, (on the contrary part,) would laboure to vilifie with uncivile termes: enveying against the sacred booke of common prayer, and mine host that used it in a laudable manner amongst his family, as a practise of piety.

There hee would be a meanes to bringe sacks to their mill, (such is the thirst after Beaver,) and helped the conspiratores to surprise mine host, (who was there all alone;) and they chardged him, (because they would seeme to have some reasonable cause against him to sett a glosse upon their mallice,) with criminall things; which indeede had beene done by such a person, but was of their conspiracy; mine host demaunded of the conspirators who it was that was author of that information, that seemed to be their ground for what they now intended. And because they answered they would not tell him, hee as peremptorily replyed, that hee would not say whether he had, or he had not done as they had bin informed.

The answere made no matter, (as it seemed,) whether it had bin negatively or affirmatively made; for they had resolved what hee should suffer, because, (as they boasted,) they were now become the greater number: they had shaked of their shackles of servitude, and were become Masters, and masterles people.

It appeares they were like beares whelpes in former time, when mine hosts plantation was of as much strength as theirs, but now, (theirs being stronger,) they, (like overgrowne beares,) seemed monsterous. In breife, mine host must indure to be their prisoner untill they could contrive it so that they might send him for England, (as they said,) there to suffer according to the merrit of the fact which they intended to father upon him; supposing, (belike,) it would proove a hainous crime.

Much rejoycing was made that they had gotten their capitall enemy, (as they concluded him;) whome they purposed to hamper in such sort that hee should not be able to uphold his plantation at Ma-re Mount.

The Conspirators sported themselves at my honest host, that meant them no hurt, and were so joccund that they feasted their bodies, and fell to tippeling as if they had obtained a great prize; like the Trojans when they had the custody of Hippeus pinetree horse.[21]

Mine host fained greefe, and could not be perswaded either to eate or drinke; because hee knew emptines would be a meanes to make him as watchfull as the Geese kept in the Roman Cappitall:[22] whereon, the contrary part, the conspirators

[21]The famous wooden horse made by Epeius (incorrectly called Hippeus, "horseman"). The Trojans welcomed it into their city, unaware that it was filled with Greek soldiers, and they lost the Trojan War as a result.

[22]According to the Roman historian Livy, the squawking of geese in the Capitol warned the citizens of Rome that enemies were approaching while they slept and, thereby saved the city.

would be so drowsy that hee might have an opportunity to give them a slip, insteade of a tester.[23] Six persons of the conspiracy were set to watch him at Wessaguscus: But hee kept waking; and in the dead of night, (one lying on the bed for further suerty,) up gets mine Host and got to the second dore that he was to passe, which, notwithstanding the lock, hee got open, and shut it after him with such violence that it affrighted some of the conspirators.

The word, which was given with an alarme, was, ô he's gon, he's gon, what shall wee doe, he's gon! The rest, (halfe a sleepe,) start up in a maze, and, like rames, ran theire heads one at another full butt in the darke.

Theire grande leader, Captaine Shrimp,[24] tooke on most furiously and tore his clothes for anger, to see the empty nest, and their bird gone.

The rest were eager to have torne theire haire from theire heads; but it was so short that it would give them no hold.[25] Now Captaine Shrimp thought in the losse of this prize, (which hee accoumpted his Master peece,) all his honor would be lost for ever.

In the meane time mine Host was got home to Ma-re Mount through the woods, eight miles round about the head of the river Monatoquit that parted the two Plantations, finding his way by the helpe of the lightening, (for it thundered as hee went terribly;) and there hee prepared powther, three pounds dried, for his present imployement, and foure good gunnes for him and the two assistants left at his howse, with bullets of severall sizes, three hounderd or there-abouts, to be used if the conspirators should pursue him thether: and these two persons promised theire aides in the quarrell, and confirmed that promise with health in good rosa solis.[26]

Now Captaine Shrimp, the first Captaine in the Land, (as hee supposed,) must doe some new act to repaire this losse, and, to vindicate his reputation, who had sustained blemish by this oversight, begins now to study, how to repaire or survive his honor: in this manner, callinge of Councell, they conclude.

Hee takes eight persons more to him, and, (like the nine Worthies of New Canaan,) they imbarque with preparation against Ma-re-Mount, where this Monster of a man, as theire phrase was, had his denne; the whole number, had the rest not bin from home, being but seaven, would have given Captaine Shrimpe, (a quondam Drummer,) such a wellcome as would have made him wish for a Drume as bigg as Diogenes tubb,[27] that hee might have crept into it out of sight.

Now the nine Worthies are approached, and mine Host prepared: having intelligence by a Salvage, that hastened in love from Wessaguscus to give him notice of their intent.

One of mine Hosts men prooved a craven: the other had prooved his wits[28] to purchase a little valoure, before mine Host had observed his posture.

The nine worthies comming before the Denne of this supposed Monster, (this seaven headed hydra, as they termed him,) and began, like Don Quixote against the

[23] "The slip, instead of a tip." A tester is a British coin of the sixteenth century.

[24] Miles Standish.

[25] Some Puritans wore their hair short and went without wigs; they were sometimes called "Round-heads."

[26] Cordial made of spirits (usually brandy) with spice and sugar.

[27] Diogenes, the ancient Greek philosopher, is supposed to have made his home in a tub.

[28] Gotten drunk.

Windmill, to beate a parly, and to offer quarter, if mine Host would yeald; for they resolved to send him for England; and bad him lay by his armes.

But hee, (who was the Sonne of a Souldier,) having taken up armes in his just defence, replyed that hee would not lay by those armes, because they were so needefull at Sea, if hee should be sent over. Yet, to save the effusion of so much worty bloud, as would have issued out of the vaynes of these 9. worthies of New Canaan, if mine Host should have played upon them out at his port holes, (for they came within danger like a flocke of wild geese, as if they had bin tayled one to another, as coults to be sold at a faier,) mine Host was content to yeelde upon quarter; and did capitulate with them in what manner it should be for more certainety, because hee knew what Captaine Shrimpe was.

Hee expressed that no violence should be offered to his person, none to his goods, nor any of his Howsehold: but that hee should have his armes, and what els was requisit for the voyage: which theire Herald retornes, it was agreed upon, and should be performed.

But mine Host no sooner had set open the dore, and issued out, but instantly Captaine Shrimpe and the rest of the worties stepped to him, layd hold of his armes, and had him downe: and so eagerly was every man bent against him, (not regarding any agreement made with such a carnall man,) that they fell upon him as if they would have eaten him: some of them were so violent that they would have a slice with scabbert, and all for haste; untill an old Souldier, (of the Queenes, as the Proverbe is,) that was there by accident, clapt his gunne under the weapons, and sharply rebuked these worthies for their unworthy practises. So the matter was taken into more deliberate consideration.

Captaine Shrimpe, and the rest of the nine worthies, made themselves, (by this outragious riot,) Masters of mine Host of Ma-re Mount, and disposed of what hee had at his plantation.

This they knew, (in the eye of the Salvages,) would add to their glory, and diminish the reputation of mine honest Host; whome they practised to be ridd of upon any termes, as willingly as if hee had bin the very Hidra of the time.

Chapter XVI
How the 9. worthies put mine Host of Ma-re-Mount into the inchaunted Castle at Plimmouth, and terrified him with the Monster Briareus.[29]

The nine worthies of New Canaan having now the Law in their owne hands, (there being no generall Governour in the Land; nor none of the Seperation that regarded the duety they owe their Soveraigne, whose naturall borne Subjects they were, though translated out of Holland, from whence they had learned to worke all to their owne ends, and make a great shewe of Religion, but no humanity,) for they were now to sit in Counsell on the cause.

[29] The hundred-armed monster that, according to Roman myth, fought the Titans and guarded hell.

And much it stood mine honest Host upon to be very circumspect, and to take Eacus[30] to taske; for that his voyce was more allowed of then both the other: and had not mine Host confounded all the arguments that Eacus could make in their defence, and confuted him that swaied the rest, they would have made him unable to drinke in such manner of merriment any more. So that following this private counsell, given him by one that knew who ruled the rost, the Hiracano ceased that els would split his pinace.

A conclusion was made and sentence given that mine Host should be sent to England a prisoner. But when hee was brought to the shipps for that purpose, no man durst be so foole hardy as to undertake carry him. So these Worthies set mine Host upon an Island, without gunne, powther, or shot or dogge or so much as a knife to get any thinge to feede upon, or any other cloathes to shelter him with at winter then a thinne suite which hee had one at that time. Home hee could not get to Ma-re-Mount. Upon this Island hee stayed a moneth at least, and was releeved by Salvages that tooke notice that mine Host was a Sachem of Passonagessit, and would bringe bottles of strong liquor to him, and unite themselves into a league of brother hood with mine Host; so full of humanity are these infidels before those Christians.

From this place for England sailed mine Host in a Plimmouth shipp, (that came into the Land to fish upon the Coast,) that landed him safe in England at Plimmouth: and hee stayed in England untill the ordinary time for shipping to set forth for these parts, and then retorned: Noe man being able to taxe him of any thinge.

But the Worthies, (in the meane time,) hoped they had bin ridd of him.

1637

John Winthrop 1588–1649

At the time of John Winthrop's birth in Groton, England, the *Mayflower* had not yet departed for the new world, but the economic and religious upheavals of the coming years would spawn a large emigration of people (not all Puritans) to New England. At the age of fourteen, Winthrop entered Trinity College, and within only two years he married the first of four wives. By eighteen, he was a Justice of the Peace and shortly thereafter a steward for the manor on which he had been raised—a job which provided him with the administrative skills that would serve him well in New England. His "wild and dissolute" boyhood, as he would later describe it, soon gave way to austere self-abasement and "an insatiable thirst" to know God, a thirst that would shape not only his own private life but his conception of civil government. As Governor of the Massachusetts Bay Colony for twelve of the nineteen years during which he lived there, Winthrop was integral in influencing—and recording—the social, political, and religious growth of the colony.

Although he was not personally oppressed by the economic hardships that had befallen England by the 1620s (he was one of a few thousand wealthy men in

[30]One of the three judges of the underworld in Greek mythology, here used to refer to one of the leaders of Plymouth, probably Thomas Fuller.

England), he was, nonetheless, distressed at the economic and religious conditions around him. As early as 1622 Winthrop had referred to England as "this sinfull land," plagued by poverty, unemployment, inequitable taxation, and a bureaucratic legal system. Later he would write that "this Land grows weary of her Inhabitants," and continue with a blistering attack against the religious and educational systems of England. Furthermore, the monarchy in England was becoming increasingly hostile to Puritanism, favoring instead Catholicism, which resulted in the silencing of many ministers who refused to conform.

However, it seems as if Winthrop's decision to depart for the new world was rather sudden. Only in the Cambridge Agreement of 1629, made less than a year before the *Arbella* set sail, did the Congregationalist Puritans officially decide to plant a colony in New England. The charter, which granted the Massachusetts Bay Company the right to settle in New England, is unique in that no provision was made for a designated meeting place for the administration of the Company, thus freeing it to establish a government in New England. The company was lucky to have been granted such a liberal charter, since only six days after it was officially granted, King Charles dissolved Parliament. Winthrop was elected Governor of the Company in 1629, and he left, with nearly 400 other people, for New England aboard the *Arbella* the following year.

Winthrop envisioned "a city of God" as the Utopian foundation for the new society that he and his fellow Puritans would be building, and he fully expected that the hardships they would face in the wilderness would test their sainthood. This new land would be an opportunity for the Puritans, according to Winthrop, to *practice* what had only been *professed* in England. He longed for the transformation of abstract Christian ideals into concrete gestures that would pervade daily living. Yet this new land, however fertile for spiritual rejuvenation, was also a wellspring of new temptations. Although wealth was certainly one indicator of status in the Puritan community, it was also a source of conflict for the Puritans in New England, who struggled to reconcile God, commerce, and individualism. Although the new society would extol charity and strong sense of community, Winthrop did not hesitate to note that God designated that "some must be rich some poor, some high and eminent in power and dignitie; others mean and in subjection." This conflict between the physical and incorporeal reflects the paradoxical Puritan conception of freedom and authority. In 1645, responding to charges that he had exceeded the powers of his office, Winthrop delivered a speech in his defense which epitomizes this struggle in Puritan religious and political thought. In it, he deftly distinguished between natural and civil liberties, designating the former as the ability to do evil as well as good—a trait which he felt the colonists had in common with "the beasts"—and the latter as the liberty to do what is "good, just, and honest." He argued that this second form of liberty cannot exist without authority. Having chosen to live under this authority (of either Christ or the magistrates in the Colony), the colonists must obey.

Perhaps the most formidable challenge that Winthrop, as well as the entire Puritan oligarchy, would face was the threat posed by Anne Hutchinson, whom Winthrop described in his journal as "a woman of ready wit and bold spirit." In what would later become known as the Antinomian controversy, Hutchinson, who had been influenced by John Cotton, argued that good works were no indication of God's favor. And since the elect were guaranteed salvation, the Church's mediating role between God and man was obsolete. In her home she held religious meetings, which were quite popular. Her interpretation of the Covenant of Grace threatened the religious and patriarchal hierarchy since it could have led to the collapse of distinctions of birth, education, and wealth. For a while little was done to stop Hutchinson, and a plurality of openly expressed ideas abounded in Boston. Along with her compatriots, she was soon censured, however, and banished from Boston.

A *Modell of Christian Charity,* a sermon delivered aboard the *Arbella,* is perhaps one of Winthrop's more famous writings—important because it eloquently forwards a spiritual blueprint of sorts for the "city upon a Hill." Written as a series of questions, answers, and objections, a rhetorical maneuver which reflects Winthrop's legal training, the sermon was, in part, a plea for a real *community* in which "the care of the public must oversway all private respects" and in which its inhabitants must "bear one another's burthens." In a more immediate sense, however, it also served to assuage tensions among the tired, water-bound passengers of the *Arbella.* Written about six years later, his "Christian Experience" is representative of the spiritual autobiography, which Puritans perceived as a vital expression of salvation. Typically self-debasing, Winthrop chronicles his spiritual struggles from his "lewdly disposed" boyhood through adulthood, revealing moments of spiritual despair alongside religious epiphanies reflecting his thirst to know God. Written during the Antinomian controversy "Christian Experience" may also be read as Winthrop's reaffirmation of the importance of good works in light of Hutchinson's radical claims about free grace. Although Winthrop's journal, which he began aboard the *Arbella,* is historically significant because it charts the Puritans' progress in the new world, it is perhaps even more significant because it charts Puritan thought. Much of what we know about the colony's social, political, and religious strata comes from Winthrop's journal. And America's first flirtations with democracy, indeed her eventual conception of liberty itself, are rooted in the conflicts and contradictions of Puritan thinking, reflected in the writings of John Winthrop.

Nicholas D. Rombes, Jr.
University of Detroit Mercy

PRIMARY WORKS

James Kendall Hosmer, ed., *Winthrop's Journal: History of New England, 1630–1649,* 1908; A. Forbes, ed., *The Winthrop Papers,* 1929–1945.

SECONDARY WORKS

Edmund Morgan, *The Puritan Dilemma: The Story of John Winthrop,* 1965; D. B. Rutman, *Winthrop's Boston,* 1965; Richard S. Dunn, "John Winthrop Writes His Journal," *William and Mary Quarterly* 41 (1984): 185–212; Lee Schweninger, *John Winthrop,* 1990.

from A Modell of Christian Charity[1]

Christian Charitie

A Modell Hereof

God Almightie in his most holy and wise providence hath soe disposed of the Condicion of mankinde, as in all times some must be rich some poore, some highe and eminent in power and dignitie; others meane and in subjeccion.

The Reason Hereof

1. REAS: *First,* to hold conformity with the rest of his workes, being delighted to shewe forthe the glory of his wisdome in the variety and differance of the Creatures and the glory of his power, in ordering all these differences for the preservacion and good of the whole, and the glory of his greatnes that as it is the glory of princes to have many officers, soe this great King will have many Stewards counting himselfe more honoured in dispenceing his guifts to man by man, then if hee did it by his owne immediate hand.

2. REAS: *Secondly,* That he might have the more occasion to manifest the worke of his Spirit: first, upon the wicked in moderateing and restraineing them: soe that the riche and mighty should not eate upp the poore, nor the poore, and dispised rise upp against theire superiours, and shake off theire yoake; 2ly in the regenerate in exerciseing his graces in them, as in the greate ones, theire love mercy, gentlenes, temperance etc., in the poore and inferiour sorte, theire faithe patience, obedience etc:

3. REAS: Thirdly, That every man might have need of other, and from hence they might be all knitt more nearly together in the Bond of brotherly affeccion: from hence it appeares plainely that noe man is made more honourable then another or more wealthy etc., out of any perticuler and singuler respect to himselfe but for the glory of his Creator and the Common good of the Creature, Man; Therefore God still reserves the propperty of these guifts to himselfe as Ezek: 16. 17. he there calls wealthe his gold and his silver etc.[2] Prov: 3. 9. he claimes theire service as his due honour the Lord with thy riches etc.[3] All men being thus (by divine providence) rancked into two sortes, riche and poore; under the first, are comprehended all such as are able to live comfortably by theire owne meanes duely improved; and all others are poore according to the former distribution. There are two rules whereby wee are to walke one towards another: JUSTICE and MERCY. These are allwayes distinguished in theire Act and in theire object, yet may they both concurre in the same Subject in eache respect; as sometimes there may be an occasion of shewing mercy to a rich

[1]Winthrop preached his lay sermon aboard the *Arbella,* sometime before the colonists set foot on America. The text is taken from *The Winthrop Papers,* ed. A. Forbes. The manuscript of the sermon seems to have been circulated widely during Winthrop's lifetime.

[2]"Thou hast also taken thy fair jewels of my gold and my silver, which I had given thee, and madest to thyself images of men, and didst commit whoredom with them."

[3]"Honor the Lord with thy substance, and with the first fruits of all thine increase: so shall thy barns be filled with plenty, and thy presses burst out with new wine."

man, in some sudden danger of distresse, and allsoe doeing of meere Justice to a poor man in regard of some perticuler contract etc. There is likewise a double Lawe by which wee are regulated in our conversacion one towardes another: in both the former respects, the lawe of nature and the lawe of grace, or the morrall lawe or the lawe of the gospell, to omitt the rule of Justice as not propperly belonging to this purpose otherwise then it may fall into consideracion in some perticuler Cases: By the first of these lawes man as he was enabled soe withall [is] commaunded to love his neighbour as himselfe;[4] upon this ground stands all the precepts of the morrall lawe, which concernes our dealings with men. To apply this to the works of mercy this lawe requires two things first that every man afford his help to another in every want or distresse. Secondly, That hee performe this out of the same affeccion, which makes him carefull of his owne good according to that of our Saviour Math: [7.12] Whatsoever ye would that men should doe to you.[5] This was practised by Abraham and Lott in entertaineing the Angells and the old man of Gibea.[6]

The Lawe of Grace or the Gospell hath some differance from the former as in these respectes, first the lawe of nature was given to man in the estate of innocency; this of the gospell in the estate of regeneracy:[7] 2ly, the former propounds one man to another, as the same fleshe and Image of god, this as a brother in Christ allsoe, and in the Communion of the same spirit and soe teacheth us to put a difference betweene Christians and others. Doe good to all especially to the household of faith; upon this ground the Israelites were to putt a difference betweene the brethren of such as were strangers though not of the Canaanites.[8] 3ly. The Lawe of nature could give noe rules for dealeing with enemies for all are to be considered as freinds in the estate of innocency, but the Gospell commaunds love to an enemy. proofe. If thine Enemie hunger feede him; Love your Enemies doe good to them that hate you Math: 5.44.

This Lawe of the Gospell propoundes likewise a difference of seasons and occasions: there is a time when a christian must sell all and give to the poore as they did in the Apostles times.[9] There is a tyme allsoe when a christian (though they give not all yet) must give beyond theire abillity, as they of Macedonia. Cor:2.6. likewise community of perills calls for extraordinary liberallity and soe doth Community in some speciall service for the Churche. Lastly, when there is noe other meanes whereby our Christian brother may be releived in this distresse, wee must help him beyond our ability, rather then tempt God, in putting him upon help by miraculous or extraordinary meanes.

[4]Matthew 5:43; 19:19.

[5]"All things therefore whatsoever ye would that men should do unto you even so do ye also unto them: for this is the law of the prophets" (Matthew 7:12).

[6]Genesis 18:1–2 tells of Abraham's entertainment of the angels. Lot, Abraham's nephew, defended two angels against a mob and thus escaped the destruction of the city of Sodom (Genesis 19:1–14). In Judges 19:16–21, an old citizen of Gibeah sheltered a Levite or traveling priest, defending him from enemies.

[7]In the Garden of Eden, mankind was naturally innocent; when Adam and Eve fell from innocence, they entered an unregenerate state. Mankind was redeemed from sin when Christ came, offering salvation to those who would believe. Those who believed in Christ became regenerate and were saved.

[8]Canaan was the Israelites' promised land.

[9]Luke 18:22.

This duty of mercy is exercised in the kindes, Giveing, lending, and forgiveing. . . .

Haveing allready sett forth the practise of mercy according to the rule of gods lawe, it will be usefull to lay open the groundes of it allsoe being the other parte of the Commaundement and that is the affeccion from which this exercise of mercy must arise, the Apostle tells us that this love is the fullfilling of the lawe,[10] not that it is enough to love our brother and soe noe further; but in regard of the excellency of his partes giveing any motion to the other as the Soule to the body and the power it hath to sett all the faculties on worke in the outward exercise of this duty as when wee bid one make the clocke strike he doth not lay hand on the hammer which is the immediate instrument of the sound but setts on worke the first mover or maine wheele, knoweing that will certainely produce the sound which hee intends; soe the way to drawe men to the workes of mercy is not by force of Argument from the goodnes or necessity of the worke, for though this course may enforce a rationall minde to some present Act of mercy as is frequent in experience, yet it cannot worke such a habit in a Soule as shall make it prompt upon all occasions to produce the same effect but by frameing these affeccions of love in the hearte which will as natively bring forthe the other, as any cause doth produce the effect.

The diffinition which the Scripture gives us of love is this Love is the bond of perfection.[11] First, it is a bond, or ligament. 2ly, it makes the worke perfect. There is noe body but consistes of partes and that which knitts these partes together gives the body its perfeccion, because it makes eache parte soe contiguous to other as thereby they doe mutually participate with eache other, both in strengthe and infirmity in pleasure and paine, to instance in the most perfect of all bodies, Christ and his church make one body: the severall partes of this body considered aparte before they were united were as disproportionate and as much disordering as soe many contrary quallities or elements but when christ comes and by his spirit and love knitts all these partes to himselfe and each to other, it is become the most perfect and best proportioned body in the world, Eph: 4. 16. "Christ, by whome all the body being knitt together by every joynt for the furniture thereof, according to the effectuall power which is in the measure of every perfeccion of partes; a glorious body without spott or wrinckle the ligaments hereof being Christ or his love for Christ is love, I John: 4. 8." Soe this definition is right; Love is the bond of perfeccion.

From hence wee may frame these Conclusions.

1 first all true Christians are of one body in Christ I. Cor. 12. 12. 13. 17. [27.] Ye are the body of Christ and members of [your] parte.

2ly. The ligamentes of this body which knitt together are love.

3ly. Noe body can be perfect which wants its propper ligamentes.

4ly. All the partes of this body being thus united are made soe contiguous in a speciall relacion as they must needes partake of each others strength and infirmity, joy, and sorrowe, weale and woe. I Cor: 12. 26. If one member suffers, all suffer with it; if one be in honour, all rejoyce with it.

[10]Paul, in Romans 13:10; 9:31.

[11]Colossians 3:14. Winthrop probably used the Geneva version of the Bible, which reads "love, which is the bond of perfectnesse." Quotations in these notes are from the King James version of the Bible, which is more commonly available.

5ly. This sensiblenes and Sympathy of each others Condicions will necessarily infuse into each parte a native desire and endeavour, to strengthen, defend, preserve, and comfort the other.

To insist a little on this Conclusion being the product of all the former the truthe hereof will appeare both by precept and patterne 1. John 3. 10. yee ought to lay downe your lives for the brethren Gal: 6. 2. beare ye one anothers burthens and soe fulfill the lawe of Christ.

For patterns wee have that first of our Saviour whoe out of his good will in obedience to his father, becomeing a parte of this body, and being knitt with it in the bond of love, found such a native sensiblenes of our infirmities and sorrowes as hee willingly yeilded himselfe to deathe to ease the infirmities of the rest of his body and soe heale theire sorrowes: from the like Sympathy of partes did the Apostles and many thousands of the Saintes lay downe theire lives for Christ againe, the like wee may see in the members of this body among themselves. 1 Rom. 9. Paule could have beene contented to have beene seperated from Christ that the Jewes might not be cutt off from the body: It is very observable which hee professeth of his affectionate part[ak]eing with every member: whoe is weake (saith hee) and I am not weake? whoe is offended and I burne not;[12] and againe. 2 Cor: 7. 13. therefore wee are comforted because yee were comforted. of Epaphroditus he speaketh Phil: 2. 30.[13] that he regarded not his owne life to [do] him service soe Phebe. and others are called the servantes of the Churche,[14] now it is apparant that they served not for wages or by Constrainte but out of love, the like wee shall finde in the histories of the churche in all ages: the sweete Sympathie of affeccions which was in the members of this body one towardes another, theire chearfullness in serveing and suffering together, how liberall they were without repineing, harbourers without grudgeing, and helpfull without reproacheing, and all from hence they had fervent love amongst them, which onely make[s] the practise of mercy constant and easie.

The next consideracion is how this love comes to be wrought; Adam in his first estate was a perfect modell of mankinde in all theire generacions, and in him this love was perfected in regard of the habit, but Adam Rent in himselfe from his Creator, rent all his posterity allsoe one from another, whence it comes that every man is borne with this principle in him, to love and seeke himselfe onely and thus a man continueth till Christ comes and takes possession of the soule, and infuseth another principle, love to God and our brother. And this latter haveing continuall supply from Christ, as the head and roote by which hee is united get the predominency in the soule, soe by little and little expells the former I John 4. 7. love cometh of god and every one that loveth is borne of god, soe that this love is the fruite of the new birthe, and none can have it but the new Creature, now when this quallity is thus formed in the soules of men it workes like the Spirit upon the drie bones Ezek. 37. [7] bone came to bone, it gathers together the scattered bones of perfect old man Adam and knitts them into one body againe in Christ whereby a man is become againe a liveing soule.

[12] 2 Corinthians 11:29.

[13] In Philippians 2:25–30, Paul tells the Philippians he will send them Epaphroditus, "my brother and companion in labor."

[14] Romans 16:1.

The third Consideracion is concerning the exercise of this love, which is twofold, inward or outward, the outward hath beene handled in the former preface of this discourse, for unfolding the other wee must take in our way that maxime of philosophy, Simile simili gaudet or like will to like; for as it is things which are carved with disafeccion to eache other, the ground of it is from a dissimilitude or *[blank]* ariseing from the contrary or different nature of the things themselves, soe the ground of love is an apprehension of some resemblance in the things loved to that which affectes it. This is the cause why the Lord loves the Creature, soe farre as it hath any of his Image in it, he loves his elect because they are like himselfe, he beholds them in his beloved sonne: soe a mother loves her childe, because shee throughly conceives a resemblance of herselfe in it. Thus it is betweene the members of Christ, each discernes by the worke of the spirit his owne Image and resemblance in another, and therefore cannot but love him as he loves himselfe: Now when the soule which is of a sociable nature findes any thing like to it selfe, it is like Adam when Eve was brought to him, shee must have it one with herselfe this is fleshe of my fleshe (saith shee) and bone of my bone shee conceives a greate delighte in it, therefore shee desires nearenes and familiarity with it: shee hath a greate propensity to doe it good and receives such content in it, as feareing the miscarriage of her beloved shee bestowes it in the inmost closett of her heart, shee will not endure that it shall want any good which shee can give it, if by occasion shee be withdrawne from the Company of it, shee is still lookeing towardes the place where shee left her beloved, if shee heare it groane shee is with it presently, if shee finde it sadd and disconsolate shee sighes and mournes with it, shee hath noe such joy, as to see her beloved merry and thriveing, if shee see it wronged, shee cannot beare it without passion, she setts noe boundes of her affeccions, nor hath any thought of reward, shee findes recompence enoughe in the exercise of her love towardes it, wee may see this Acted to life in Jonathan and David.[15] Jonathan a valiant man endued with the spirit of Christ, soe soone as hee Discovers the same spirit in David had presently his hearte knitt to him by this linement of love, soe that it is said he loved him as his owne soule, he takes soe great pleasure in him that hee stripps himselfe to adorne his beloved, his fathers kingdome was not soe precious to him as his beloved David, David shall have it with all his hearte, himselfe desires noe more but that hee may be neare to him to rejoyce in his good hee chooseth to converse with him in the wildernesse even to the hazzard of his owne life, rather then with the greate Courtiers in his fathers Pallace; when hee sees danger towards him, hee spares neither care paines, nor perill to divert it, when Injury was offered his beloved David, hee could not beare it, though from his owne father, and when they must parte for a Season onely, they thought theire heartes would have broake for sorrowe, had not theire affeccions found vent by aboundance of Teares: other instances might be brought to shewe the nature of this affeccion as of Ruthe and Naomi[16] and many others, but this truthe is cleared enough. If any shall object that it is not possible that love should be bred or upheld without hope of requitall, it is graunted but that is not our cause, for this love is allwayes under reward it never gives, but it allwayes receives with advantage: first, in regard that among the

[15]David and Jonathan appear in 1 Samuel 19ff.

[16]Ruth refused to leave her mother-in-law, Naomi, during a time of trouble: "For whither thou goest, I will go; and where thou lodgest, I will lodge" (Ruth 1:16).

members of the same body, love and affection are reciprocall in a most equall and sweete kinde of Commerce. 2ly [3ly], in regard of the pleasure and content that the exercise of love carries with it as wee may see in the naturall body the mouth is at all the paines to receive, and mince the foode which serves for the nourishment of all the other partes of the body, yet it hath noe cause to complaine; for first, the other partes send backe by secret passages a due proporcion of the same nourishment in a better forme for the strengthening and comforteing the mouthe. 2ly the labour of the mouthe is accompanied with such pleasure and content as farre exceedes the paines it takes: soe is it in all the labour of love, among christians, the partie loveing, reapes love againe as was shewed before, which the soule covetts more then all the wealthe in the world. 2ly [4ly]. noething yeildes more pleasure and content to the soule then when it findes that which it may love fervently, for to love and live beloved is the soules paradice, both heare and in heaven: In the State of Wedlock there be many comfortes to beare out the troubles of that Condicion; but let such as have tryed the most, say if there be any sweetnes in that Condicion comparable to the exercise of mutuall love.

From the former Consideracions ariseth these Conclusions.

1 First, This love among Christians is a reall thing not Imaginarie.

2ly. This love is as absolutely necessary to the being of the body of Christ, as the sinewes and other ligaments of a naturall body are to the being of that body.

3ly. This love is a divine, spirituall nature, free, active, strong, Couragious, permanent, under valueing all things beneathe its propper object, and of all the graces this makes us nearer to resemble the virtues of our heavenly father.

4ly, It restes in the love and wellfare of its beloved, for the full and certaine knowledge of these truthes concerning the nature use, [and] excellency of this grace, that which the holy ghost hath left recorded 1. Cor. 13. may give full satisfaccion which is needfull for every true member of this lovely body of the Lord Jesus, to worke upon theire heartes, by prayer, meditacion, continuall exercise at least of the speciall [power] of this grace till Christ be formed in them and they in him all in eache other knitt together by this bond of love.

It rests now to make some applicacion of this discourse by the present designe which gave the occasion of writeing of it. Herein are 4 things to be propounded: first the persons, 2ly, the worke, 3ly, the end, 4ly the meanes.

1. For the persons, wee are a Company professing our selves fellow members of Christ, In which respect onely though wee were absent from eache other many miles, and had our imploymentes as farre distant, yet wee ought to account our selves knitt together by this bond of love, and live in the exercise of it, if wee would have comforte of our being in Christ, this was notorious in the practise of the Christians in former times, as is testified of the Waldenses[17] from the mouth of one of the adversaries Aeneas Sylvius,[18] mutuo [solent amare] penè antequam norint, they use to love any of theire owne religion even before they were acquainted with them.

2ly. for the worke wee have in hand, it is by a mutuall consent through a speciall overruleing providence, and a more then an ordinary approbation of the Churches

[17]The Waldenses were followers of Pater Valdes, an early French reformer.

[18]Aeneas Sylvius Piccolomini (1405–1464), Pope Pius II, scholar and historian.

of Christ to seeke out a place of Cohabitation and Consorteshipp under a due forme of Government both civill and ecclesiasticall. In such cases as this the care of the publique must oversway all private respects, by which not onely conscience, but meare Civill pollicy doth binde us; for it is a true rule that perticuler estates cannott subsist in the ruine of the publique.

3ly. The end is to improve our lives to doe more service to the Lord the comforte and encrease of the body of christe whereof wee are members that our selves and posterity may be the better preserved from the Common corrupcions of this evill world to serve the Lord and worke out our Salvation under the power and purity of his holy Ordinances.

4ly for the meanes whereby this must bee effected, they are 2fold, a Conformity with the worke and end wee aime at, these wee see are extraordinary, therefore wee must not content our selves with usuall ordinary meanes; whatsoever wee did or ought to have done when wee lived in England, the same must wee doe and more allsoe where wee goe: That which the most in theire Churches maineteine as a truthe in profession onely, wee must bring into familiar and constant practise, as in this duty of love wee must love, brotherly, without dissimulation; wee must love one another with a pure hearte fervently; wee must beare one anothers burthens; wee must not looke onely on our owne things, but allsoe on the things of our brethren; neither must wee think that the lord will beare with such faileings at our hands as hee dothe from those among whome wee have lived, and that for 3 Reasons.

1. In regard of the more neare bond of mariage, betweene him and us, wherein he hath taken us to be his after a most strickt and peculiar manner which will make him the more Jealous of our love and obedience soe he tells the people of Israell, you onely have I knowne of all the families of the Earthe therefore will I punishe you for your Transgressions.

2ly, because the lord will be sanctified in them that come neare him. Wee know that there were many that corrupted the service of the Lord some setting upp Alters before his owne, others offering both strange fire and strange Sacrifices allsoe; yet there came noe fire from heaven, or other sudden Judgement upon them as did upon Nadab and Abihu[19] whoe yet wee may thinke did not sinne presumptuously.

3ly When God gives a speciall Commission he lookes to have it stricktly observed in every Article, when hee gave Saule a Commission to destroy Amaleck hee indented with him upon certaine Articles and because hee failed in one of the least, and that upon a faire pretence, it lost him the kingdome, which should have beene his reward, if hee had observed his Commission:[20] Thus stands the cause betweene God and us, wee are entered into Covenant with him for this worke,[21] wee have taken out a Commission, the Lord hath given us leave to drawe our owne Articles

[19]"And Nadab and Abihu, the sons of Aaron, took either of them his censer, and put fire therein, and put incense thereon, and offered strange fire before the Lord, which he commanded them not. And there went out fire from the Lord, and devoured them, and they died before the Lord" (Leviticus 10:1–2). To Winthrop, punishment is greater for the chosen people than for unbelievers.

[20]Saul agreed to destroy the Amalekites and their possessions, yet he spared their sheep and oxen. Because Saul disobeyed, he was rejected as king (1 Samuel 15:1–34).

[21]A covenant is like a legal contract. God promised to protect the Israelites if they were faithful and followed His word.

wee have professed to enterprise these Accions upon these and these ends, wee have hereupon besought him of favour and blessing: Now if the Lord shall please to heare us, and bring us in peace to the place wee desire, then hath hee ratified this Covenant and sealed our Commission, [and] will expect a strickt performance of the Articles contained in it, but if wee shall neglect the observacion of these Articles which are the ends wee have propounded, and dissembling with our God, shall fall to embrace this present world and prosecute our carnall intencions, seekeing greate things for our selves and our posterity, the Lord will surely breake out in wrathe against us, be revenged of such a perjured people, and make us knowe the price of the breache of such a Covenant.

Now the onely way to avoyde this shipwracke and to provide for our posterity is to followe the Counsell of Micah, to doe Justly, to love mercy, to walke humbly with our God.[22] For this end, wee must be knitt together in this worke as one man, wee must entertaine each other in brotherly Affeccion, wee must be willing to abridge our selves of our superfluities, for the supply of others necessities, wee must uphold a familiar Commerce together in all meekenes, gentlenes, patience and liberallity, wee must delight in eache other, make others Condicions our owne, rejoyce together, mourne together, labour, and suffer together, allwayes having before our eyes our Commission and Community in the worke, our Community as members of the same body, soe shall wee keepe the unitie of the spirit in the bond of peace,[23] the Lord will be our God and delight to dwell among us, as his owne people and will commaund a blessing upon us in all our wayes, soe that wee shall see much more of his wisdome, power, goodnes, and truthe then formerly wee have beene acquainted with, wee shall finde that the God of Israell is among us, when tenn of us shall be able to resist a thousand of our enemies, when hee shall make us a prayse and glory, that men shall say of succeeding plantacions: the lord make it like that of New England: for wee must Consider that wee shall be as a Citty upon a Hill,[24] the eyes of all people are uppon us; soe that if wee shall deale falsely with our god in this worke wee have undertaken and soe cause him to withdrawe his present help from us, wee shall be made a story and a by-word through the world, wee shall open the mouthes of enemies to speake evill of the ways of god and all professours for Gods sake; wee shall shame the faces of many of gods worthy servants, and cause theire prayers to be turned into Cursses upon us till we be consumed out of the good land whether wee are goeing: And to Shutt upp this discourse with that exhortacion of Moses that faithfull servant of the Lord in his last farewell to Israell Deut. 30.[25] Beloved there is now sett before us life, and good, deathe and evill in that wee are Commaunded this day to love the Lord our God, and to love one another to walke in his wayes and to keepe his

[22]Micah 6:8; 7:9.

[23]Ephesians 4:4.

[24]"Ye are the light of the world. A city that is set on a hill cannot be hid. Neither do men light a candle, and put it under a bushel, but on a candlestick; and it giveth light unto all that are in the house" (Matthew 5:14–15).

[25]"And it shall come to pass, when all these things are come upon thee, the blessing and the curse, which I have set before thee, and thou shalt call them to mind among all the nations, whither the Lord thy God hath driven thee, and shalt return unto the Lord thy God, and shalt obey his voice according to all that I command thee this day, thou and thy children, with all thine heart, and with all thy soul; that then the Lord thy God will turn thy captivity, and have compassion upon thee, and will return and gather thee from all the nations, whither the Lord thy God hath scattered thee" (Deuteronomy 30:1–3).

Commaundements and his Ordinance, and his lawes, and the Articles of our Covenant with him that wee may live and be multiplyed, and that the Lord our God may blesse us in the land whether wee goe to possesse it: But if our heartes shall turne away soe that wee will not obey, but shall be seduced and worshipp other Gods our pleasures, and proffitts, and serve them; it is propounded unto us this day, wee shall surely perishe out of the good Land whether wee passe over this vast Sea to possesse it;

Therefore lett us choose life,
that wee, and our Seede,
may live; by obeyeing his
voyce, and cleaveing to him,
for hee is our life, and
our prosperity.

1838

John Winthrop's Christian Experience[1]

In my youth I was very lewdly disposed, inclining unto and attempting (so far as my yeares enabled mee) all kind of wickednesse, except swearing and scorning religion, which I had no temptation unto in regard of my education. About ten years of age, I had some notions of God, for in some great frighting or danger, I have prayed unto God, and have found manifest answer; the remembrance whereof many yeares after made mee think that God did love mee, but it made mee no whit the better:

After I was 12. yeares old, I began to have some more savour of Religion, and I thought I had more understanding in Divinity then many of my yeares; for in reading of some good books I conceived, that I did know divers of those points before, though I knew not how I should come by such knowledge (but since I perceived it was out of some logicall principles, whereby out of some things I could conclude others) yet I was still very wild, and dissolute, and as years came on my lusts grew stronger, but yet under some restraint of my naturall reason; whereby I had the command of my self that I could turne into any form. I would as occasion required write letters etc. of meer vanity; and if occasion were I could write others of savory and godly counsell.

About 14 years of age, being in Cambridge[2] I fell into a lingring feaver, which took away the comfort of my life. For being there neglected, and despised, I went up and down mourning with myself; and being deprived of my youthfull joyes, I betook my self to God whom I did believe to bee very good and mercifull, and would welcome any that would come to him, especially such a yongue soule, and so well qualifyed as I took my self to bee; so as I took pleasure in drawing neer to him. But how

[1]This spiritual autobiography, which Winthrop wrote in New England in January 1637, treats his boyhood and young adulthood.

[2]Winthrop was admitted to Trinity College at age fourteen, and he evidently attended school there for two years.

my heart was affected with my sins, or what thoughts I had of Christ I remember not. But I was willing to love God, and therefore I thought hee loved mee. But so soon as I recovered my perfect health, and met with somewhat els to take pleasure in, I forgot my former acquaintance with God, and fell to former lusts, and grew worse then before. Yet some good moodes I had now, and then, and sad checks of my naturall Conscience, by which the Lord preserved mee from some foule sins, which otherwise I had fallen into. But my lusts were so masterly as no good could fasten upon mee, otherwise then to hold mee to some task of ordinary dutyes for I cared for nothing but how to satisfy my voluptuous heart.

About 18 yeares of age (being a man in stature, and in understanding as my parents conceived mee) I married into a family under Mr. Culverwell his ministry in Essex; and living there sometimes I first found the ministry of the word to come to my heart with power (for in all before I found onely light) and after that I found the like in the ministry of many others. So as there began to bee some change which I perceived in my self, and others took notice of. Now I began to come under strong exersises of Conscience: (yet by fits only) I could no longer dally with Religion. God put my soule to sad tasks sometimes, which yet the flesh would shake off, and outweare still. I had withall many sweet invitations which I would willingly have intertained, but the flesh would not give up her interest. The mercifull Lord would not thus bee answered, but notwithstanding all my stubbornesse, and unkind rejections of mercy, hee left mee not till hee had overcome my heart to give up itself to him, and to bid farewell to all the world, and untill my heart could answer, Lord what wilt thou have mee to doe?

Now came I to some peace and comfort in God and in his wayes, my cheif delight was therein, I loved a Christian, and the very ground hee went upon. I honoured a faythful minister in my heart and could have kissed his feet: Now I grew full of zeal (which outranne my knowledge and carried mee sometimes beyond my calling) and very liberall to any good work. I had an unsatiable thirst after the word of God and could not misse a good sermon, though many miles off, especially of such as did search deep into the conscience. I had also a great striveing in my heart to draw others to God. It pittyed my heart to see men so little to regard their soules, and to despise that happines which I knew to bee better then all the world besides, which stirred mee up to take any opportunity to draw men to God, and by successe in my endeavors I took much encouragement hereunto. But those affections were not constant but very unsetled. By these occasions I grew to bee of some note for religion (which did not a little puffe mee up) and divers would come to mee for advice in cases of conscience; and if I heard of any that were in trouble of mind I usually went to comfort them; so that upon the bent of my spirit this way and the successe I found of my endeavors, I gave up my selfe to the study of Divinity, and intended to enter into the ministry, if my freinds had not diverted mee.

But as I grew into employment and credit thereby; so I grew also in pride of my guifts, and under temptations which sett mee on work to look to my evidence more narrowly then I had done before (for the great change which God had wrought in mee, and the generall approbation of good ministers and other Christians, kept mee from makeing any great question of my good estate, though my secrett corruptions, and some tremblings of heart (which was greatest when I was among the most Godly persons) put me to some plunges; but especially when I perceived a great decay in my zeale and love, etc.) And hearing sometimes of better assurance by the seale of the spirit, which I also knew by the word of God, but could not, nor durst say that ever I had it; and finding by reading of Mr. Perkins[3] and other books that a reprobate might (in appearance) attaine to as much as I had done: finding withall much hollownes and vaine glory in my heart, I began to grow very sad, and knew not what to doe, I was ashamed to open my case to any minister that knew mee; I feared it would shame my self and religion also, that such a eminent professour as I was accounted, should discover such corruptions as I found in my selfe, and had in all this time attained no better evidence of salvation; and I should prove a hypocrite it was too late to begin anew: I should never repent in truth having repented, so oft as I had done. It was like hell to mee to think of that in Hebr: 6.[4] Yet I should sometimes propound questions afarre off to such of the most Godly ministers as I mett, which gave mee ease for the present, but my heart could not find where to rest; but I grew very sad, and melancholy; and now to hear others applaud mee was a dart through my liver; for still I feared I was not sound at the root, and sometimes I had thoughts of breaking from my profession, and proclaiming myself an Hipocrite. But those troubles came not all at once but by fits, for sometimes I should find refreshing in prayer, and sometimes in the love that I had had to the Saints: which though it were but poor comfort (for I durst not say before the Lord that I did love them in truth) yet the Lord upheld mee, and many times outward occasions put these feares out of my thoughts. And though I had knowne long before the Doctrine of free Justification by Christ and had often urged it upon my owne soul and others, yet I could not close with Christ to my satisfaction. I have many times striven to lay hold upon Christ in some promise and have brought forth all the arguments that I had for my part in it. But insteed of finding it to bee mine, I have lost sometimes the fayth of the very general truth of the promise, sometimes after much striveing by prayer for fayth in Christ, I have thought I had received some power to apply Christ unto my soule: but it was so doubtfull as I could have little comfort in it, and it soon vanished.

Upon these and the like troubles, when I could by no meanes attaine sure and setled peace; and that which I did get was still broken off upon every infirmity; I concluded there was no way to help it, but by walking more close with God and more strict observation of all dutyes; and hereby though I put myself to many a needlesse task, and deprived my self of many lawfull comforts, yet my peace would fayle upon every small occasion, and I was held long under great bondage to the Law (sinne, and humble myself; and sinne, and to humiliation again, and so day after day) yet neither got strength to my Sanctification nor betterd my Evidence, but was brought to such bondage, as I durst not use any recreation, nor meddle with any worldly businesse etc.: for feare of breaking my peace (which even such as it was, was very preteous to mee) but this would not hold neither, for then I grew very melancholy and mine own thoughts wearied mee, and wasted my spirits.

While I wandred up and downe in this sad and doubtful estate (wherein yet I had many intermissions, for the flesh would often shake off this yoake of the law, but

[3]William Perkins (1558–1602), author of *A Declaration of the State of Grace and Condemnation,* was celebrated among the Puritans.

[4]Hebrews 6:4–6. "For it is impossible for those who were once enlightened, and have tasted of the heavenly gift, and were made partakers of the Holy Ghost, and have tasted the good word of God, and the powers of the world to come, if they shall fall away, to renew them again unto repentance; seeing they crucify to themselves the Son of God afresh, and put him to an open shame."

was still forced to come under it again) wherein my greatest troubles were not the sense of Gods wrath or fear of damnation, but want of assurance of salvation, and want of strength against my corruptions; I knew that my greatest want was fayth in Christ, and faine would I have been united to Christ but I thought I was not holy enough. I had many times comfortable thoughts about him in the word prayer, and meditation, but they gave mee no satisfaction but brought mee lower in mine own eyes, and held mee still to a constant use of all meanes, in hope of better thinges to come. Sometimes I was very confident that hee had given mee a hungring and thirsting soule after Christ and therefore would surely satisfy mee in his good time. Sometimes againe I was ready to entertaine secret murmurings that all my paines and prayers etc. should prevayle no more: but such thoughts were soon rebuked: I found my heart still willing to justify God. Yea I was perswaded I should love him though hee should cast mee off.

Being in this condition it pleased the Lord in my family exercise to manifest unto mee the difference between the Covenant of grace, and the Covenant of workes (but I took the foundation of that of workes to have been with man in innocency, and onely held forth in the law of Moses to drive us to Christ).[5] This Covenant of grace began to take great impression in mee and I thought I had now enough: To have Christ freely, and to bee justifyed freely was very sweet to mee; and upon sound warrant (as I conceived) but I could not say with any confidence, it had been sealed to mee, but I rather took occasion to bee more remisse in my spirituall watch, and so more loose in my conversation.

I was now about 30 yeares of age, and now was the time come that the Lord would reveale Christ unto mee whom I had long desired, but not so earnestly as since I came to see more clearely into the covenant of free grace. First therefore hee laid a sore affliction upon mee wherein hee laid mee lower in myne owne eyes then at any time before, and showed mee the emptines of all my guifts, and parts; left mee neither power nor will, so as I became as a weaned child. I could now no more look at what I had been or what I had done nor bee discontented for want of strength or assurance mine eyes were onely upon his free mercy in Jesus Christ. I knew I was worthy of nothing for I knew I could doe nothing for him or for my selfe. I could only mourn, and weep to think of free mercy to such a vile wretch as I was. Though I had no power to apply it yet I felt comfort in it. I did not long continue in this estate, but the good spirit of the Lord breathed upon my soule, and said I should live. Then every promise I thought upon held forth Christ unto me saying I am thy salvation. Now could my soule close with Christ, and rest there with sweet content, so ravished with his love, as I desired nothing nor feared anything, but was filled with joy unspeakable, and glorious and with a spirit of Adoption. Not that I could pray with more fervency or more enlargement of heart than sometimes before, but I could now cry my father with more confidence. Mee thought this condition and that frame of heart which I had after, was in respect of the former like the reigne of Solomon, free, peaceable, prosperous and glorious, the other more like that of Ahaz, full of troubles, feares and abasements. And the more I grew thus acquainted with the spirit of God

[5]The Puritans believed that God made a covenant or contract with mankind in the Garden of Eden. They called this the covenant of works. When mankind broke this covenant, the Puritans argued, God offered Christ for salvation, in a covenant of grace.

the more were my corruptions mortifyed, and the new man quickened: the world, the flesh and Satan were for a time silent, I heard not of them: but they would not leave mee so. This Estate lasted a good time (divers months), but not alwayes alike, but if my comfort, and joy slackened a while, yet my peace continued, and it would returne with advantage. I was now growne familiar with the Lord Jesus Christ, hee would oft tell mee he loved mee, I did not doubt to believe him; If I went abroad hee went with mee, when I returned hee came home with mee. I talked with him upon the way, hee lay down with mee and usually I did awake with him. Now I could goe into any company and not loose him: and so sweet was his love to mee as I desired nothing but him in heaven or earth.

This Estate would not hold neither did it decline suddainly but by degrees. And though I found much spirituall strength in it, yet I could not discerne but my hunger after the word of God, and my love to the Saints had been as great (if not more) in former times. One reason might bee this, I found that many blemishes and much hollow heartednesse which I discerned in many professors, had weakned the esteem of a Christian in my heart. And for my comfort in Christ, as worldly imployments, and the love of temporall things did steal away my heart from him so would his sweet countenance bee withdrawne from mee. But in such a condition hee would not long leave mee, but would still recall mee by some word of affliction or in prayer or meditation, and I should then bee as a man awakened out of a dreame or as if I had been another man. And then my care was (not so much to get pardon for that was sometimes sealed to mee while I was purposing to goe seek it, and yet sometimes I could not obtaine it without seeking and wayteing also but) to mourn for my ingratitude towards my God, and his free, and rich mercy. The consideration whereof would break my heart more, and wring more teares from myne eyes, then ever the fear of Damnation or any affliction had done; so as many times and to this very day a thought of Christ Jesus, and free grace bestowed on mee melts my heart that I cannot refraine.

Since this time I have gone under continuall conflicts between the flesh and the spirit, and sometimes with Satan himself (which I have more discerned of late then I did formerly) many falls I have had, and have lyen long under some, yet never quite forsaken of the Lord. But still when I have been put to it by any suddaine danger or fearefull temptation, the good spirit of the Lord hath not fayled to beare witnesse to mee, giveing mee comfort, and courage in the very pinch, when of my self I have been very fearefull, and dismayed. My usuall falls have been through dead heartedness, and presumptuousnesse, by which Satan hath taken advantage to wind mee into other sinnes. When the flesh prevayles the spirit withdrawes, and is sometimes so greived as hee seemes not to acknowledge his owne work. Yet in my worst times hee hath been pleased to stirre, when hee would not speak, and would yet support mee that my fayth hath not fayled utterly.

1929–45

from The Journal of John Winthrop

[July 5, 1632] At Watertown there was (in the view of divers witnesses) a great combat between a mouse and a snake; and, after a long fight, the mouse prevailed and killed the snake. The pastor of Boston, Mr. Wilson, a very sincere, holy man, hearing of it, gave this interpretation: That the snake was the devil; the mouse was a poor contemptible people, which God had brought hither, which should overcome Satan here, and dispossess him of his kingdom. Upon the same occasion, he told the governor,[1] that, before he was resolved to come into this country, he dreamed he was here, and that he saw a church arise out of the earth, which grew up and became a marvellous goodly church.

[December 27, 1633] The governor and assistants met at Boston, and took into consideration a treatise, which Mr. Williams[2] (then of Salem) had sent to them, and which he had formerly written to the governor and council of Plymouth, wherein, among other things, he disputes their right to the lands they possessed here, and concluded that, claiming by the king's grant, they could have no title, nor otherwise, except they compounded with the natives. For this, taking advice with some of the most judicious ministers, (who much condemned Mr. Williams's error and presumption,) they gave order, that he should be convented[3] at the next court, to be censured, etc. There were three passages chiefly whereat they were much offended: 1, for that he chargeth King James to have told a solemn public lie, because in his patent he blessed God that he was the first Christian prince that had discovered this land; 2, for that he chargeth him and others with blasphemy for calling Europe Christendom, or the Christian world; 3, for that he did personally apply to our present king, Charles, these three places in the Revelations, viz., [*blank*].

Mr. Endicott being absent, the governor wrote to him to let him know what was done, and withal added divers arguments to confute the said errors, wishing him to deal with Mr. Williams to retract the same, etc. Whereto he returned a very modest and discreet answer. Mr. Williams also wrote to the governor,[4] and also to him and the rest of the council, very submissively, professing his intent to have been only to have written for the private satisfaction of the governor, etc., of Plymouth, without any purpose to have stirred any further in it, if the governor here had not required a copy of him; withal offering his book, or any part of it, to be burnt.

At the next court he appeared penitently, and gave satisfaction of his intention and loyalty. So it was left, and nothing done in it.

[January 20, 1634] Hall and the two others, who went to Connecticut November 3, came now home, having lost themselves and endured much misery. They informed us that the small pox was gone as far as any Indian plantation was known to the west, and much people dead of it, by reason whereof they could have no trade.

At Naragansett, by the Indians' report, there died seven hundred; but, beyond Pascataquack, none to the eastward.

[1]Winthrop himself.

[2]Roger Williams (c. 1603–1683) was called to the First Church of Boston but refused the post because the Congregationalist Puritans would not separate from the Anglican Church.

[3]Summoned to appear.

[4]Edward Winslow was governor in 1633.

[January 24, 1634] The governor and council met again at Boston, to consider of Mr. Williams's letter, etc., when, with the advice of Mr. Cotton[5] and Mr. Wilson, and weighing his letter, and further considering of the aforesaid offensive passages in his book, (which, being written in very obscure and implicative phrases, might well admit of doubtful interpretation,) they found the matters not to be so evil as at first they seemed. Whereupon they agreed, that, upon his retraction, etc., or taking an oath of allegiance to the king, etc., it should be passed over.

[January 11, 1636] The governor[6] and assistants met at Boston to consider about Mr. Williams, for that they were credibly informed, that, notwithstanding the injunction laid upon him (upon the liberty granted him to stay till the spring) not to go about to draw others to his opinions, he did use to entertain company in his house, and to preach to them, even of such points as he had been censured for; and it was agreed to send him into England by a ship then ready to depart. The reason was, because he had drawn above twenty persons to his opinion, and they were intended to erect a plantation about the Naragansett Bay, from whence the infection would easily spread into these churches, (the people being, many of them, much taken with the apprehension of his godliness). Whereupon a warrant was sent to him to come presently to Boston, to be shipped, etc. He returned answer, (and divers of Salem came with it,) that he could not come without hazard of his life, etc. Whereupon a pinnace[7] was sent with commission to Capt. Underhill, etc., to apprehend him, and carry him aboard the ship, (which then rode at Natascutt;) but, when they came at his house, they found he had been gone three days before; but whither they could not learn.

He had so far prevailed at Salem, as many there (especially of devout women) did embrace his opinions, and separated from the churches, for this cause, that some of their members, going into England, did hear the ministers there, and when they came home the churches here held [to be in] communion with them.

[October 21, 1636] One Mrs. Hutchinson,[8] a member of the church of Boston, a woman of a ready wit and bold spirit, brought over with her two dangerous errors: 1. That the person of the Holy Ghost dwells in a justified[9] person. 2. That no sanctification can help to evidence to us our justification—From these two grew many branches; as, 1. Our union with the Holy Ghost, so as a Christian remains dead to every spiritual action, and hath no gifts nor graces, other than such as are in hypocrites, nor any other sanctification but the Holy Ghost himself.

There joined with her in these opinions a brother of hers, one Mr. Wheelwright, a silenced minister sometimes in England.

[October 25, 1636] The other ministers in the bay, hearing of these things, came to Boston at the time of a general court, and entered conference in private with them, to the end they might know the certainty of these things; that if need were, they might write to the church of Boston about them, to prevent (if it were possible) the

[5]John Cotton (1584–1652), an influential preacher in the colony, was pastor of the First Church of Boston.

[6]John Hays (1594–1654). Winthrop was re-elected governor in 1637.

[7]A small sailing boat, often used as a scout for a larger vessel.

[8]Anne Hutchinson (1591–1643), like Roger Williams, was cast out of the Massachusetts Bay Colony. With Williams's assistance, she settled on the outskirts of Providence.

[9]One chosen for salvation by God.

dangers, which seemed hereby to hang over that and the rest of the churches. At this conference, Mr. Cotton was present, and gave satisfaction to them, so as he agreed with them all in the point of sanctification, and so did Mr. Wheelwright; so as they all did hold, that sanctification did help to evidence justification. The same he had delivered plainly in public, divers times; but, for the indwelling of the person of the Holy Ghost, he held that still, as some other of the ministers did, but not union with the person of the Holy Ghost, (as Mrs. Hutchinson and others did,) so as to amount to a personal union.

[November 1, 1637] There was great hope that the late general assembly would have had some good effect in pacifying the troubles and dissensions about matters of religion; but it fell out otherwise. For though Mr. Wheelwright and those of his party had been clearly confuted and confounded in the assembly, yet they persisted in their opinions, and were as busy in nourishing contentions (the principal of them) as before.

The court also sent for Mrs. Hutchinson, and charged her with divers matters, as her keeping two public lectures every week in her house, whereto sixty or eighty persons did usually resort, and for reproaching most of the ministers (viz., all except Mr. Cotton) for not preaching a covenant of free grace, and that they had not the seal of the spirit, nor were able ministers of the New Testament; which were clearly proved against her, though she sought to shift it off. And, after many speeches to and fro, at last she was so full as she could not contain, but vented her revelations; amongst which this was one, that she had it revealed to her, that she should come into New England, and should here be persecuted, and that God would ruin us and our posterity, and the whole state, for the same. So the court proceeded and banished her; but, because it was winter, they committed her to a private house, where she was well provided, and her own friends and the elders permitted to go to her, but none else.

The court called also Capt. Underhill, and some five or six more of the principal, whose hands were to the said petition; and because they stood to justify it, they were disfranchised, and such as had public places were put from them.

The court also ordered, that the rest, who had subscribed the petition, (and would not acknowledge their fault, and which near twenty of them did,) and some others, who had been chief stirrers in these contentions, etc., should be disarmed. This troubled some of them very much, especially because they were to bring them in themselves; but at last, when they saw no remedy, they obeyed.

All the proceedings of this court against these persons were set down at large, with the reasons and other observations, and were sent into England to be published there, to the end that all our godly friends might not be discouraged from coming to us, etc.

[March, 1638] While Mrs. Hutchinson continued at Roxbury,[10] divers of the elders and others resorted to her, and finding her to persist in maintaining those gross errors beforementioned, and many others, to the number of thirty or thereabout, some of them wrote to the church at Boston, offering to make proof of the same before the church, etc., 15; whereupon she was called, (the magistrates being desired to give her license to come,) and the lecture was appointed to begin at ten. (The

[10]Near Boston.

general court being then at Newtown, the governor[11] and the treasurer, being members of Boston, were permitted to come down, but the rest of the court continued at Newtown.) When she appeared, the errors were read to her. The first was, that the souls of men are mortal by generation, but, after, made immortal by Christ's purchase. This she maintained a long time; but at length she was so clearly convinced by reason and scripture, and the whole church agreeing that sufficient had been delivered for her conviction, that she yielded she had been in an error. Then they proceeded to three other errors: 1. That there was no resurrection of these bodies, and that these bodies were not united to Christ, but every person united hath a new body, etc. These were also clearly confuted, but yet she held her own; so as the church (all but two of her sons) agreed she should be admonished, and because her sons would not agree to it, they were admonished also.

Mr. Cotton pronounced the sentence of admonition with great solemnity, and with much zeal and detestation of her errors and pride of spirit. The assembly continued till eight at night, and all did acknowledge the special presence of God's spirit therein; and she was appointed to appear again the next lecture day.

[March 22, 1638] Mrs. Hutchinson appeared again; (she had been licensed by the court, in regard she had given hope of her repentance, to be at Mr. Cotton's house, that both he and Mr. Davenport[12] might have the more opportunity to deal with her;) and the articles being again read to her, and her answer required, she delivered it in writing, wherein she made a retractation of near all, but with such explanations and circumstances as gave no satisfaction to the church; so as she was required to speak further to them. Then she declared, that it was just with God to leave her to herself, as He had done, for her slighting His ordinances, both magistracy and ministry; and confessed that what she had spoken against the magistrates at the court (by way of revelation) was rash and ungrounded; and desired the church to pray for her. This gave the church good hope of her repentance; but when she was examined about some particulars, as that she had denied inherent righteousness, etc., she affirmed that it was never her judgment; and though it was proved by many testimonies, that she had been of that judgment, and so had persisted, and maintained it by argument against divers, yet she impudently persisted in her affirmation, to the astonishment of all the assembly. So that, after much time and many arguments had been spent to bring her to see her sin, but all in vain, the church, with one consent, cast her out. Some moved to have her admonished once more; but, it being for manifest evil in matter of conversation, it was agreed otherwise; and for that reason also the sentence was denounced by the pastor, matter of manners belonging properly to his place.

After she was excommunicated, her spirits, which seemed before to be somewhat dejected, revived again, and she gloried in her sufferings, saying, that it was the greatest happiness, next to Christ, that ever befell her. Indeed, it was a happy day to the churches of Christ here, and to many poor souls, who had been seduced by her, who, by what they heard and saw that day, were (through the grace of God) brought off quite from her errors, and settled again in the truth. . . .

[11]Winthrop himself.

[12]John Davenport (1597–1670), a Puritan minister.

After two or three days, the governor sent a warrant to Mrs. Hutchinson to depart this jurisdiction before the last of this month, according to the order of court, and for that end set her at liberty from her former constraint, so as she was not to go forth of her own house till her departure; and upon the 28th she went by water to her farm at the Mount, where she was to take water, with Mr. Wheelwright's wife and family, to go to Pascataquack; but she changed her mind, and went by land to Providence, and so to the island in the Naragansett Bay, which her husband and the rest of that sect had purchased of the Indians.

[September, 1638] . . . Mrs. Hutchinson, being removed to the Isle of Aquiday, in the Naragansett Bay, after her time was fulfilled, that she expected deliverance of a child, was delivered of a monstrous birth, which, being diversely related in the country, (and, in the open assembly at Boston, upon a lecture day, [was] declared by Mr. Cotton to be twenty-seven several lumps of man's seed, without any alteration or mixture of anything from the woman, and thereupon gathered that it might signify her error in denying inherent righteousness, but that all was Christ in us, and nothing of ours in our faith, love, etc.). Hereupon the governor wrote to Mr. Clarke, a physician and a preacher to those of the island, to know the certainty thereof. . . .

[July 3 1645] Then was the deputy governor desired by the court to go up and take his place again upon the bench, which he did accordingly, and the court being about to arise, he desired leave for a little speech, which was to this effect.

> I suppose something may be expected from me, upon this charge that is befallen me, which moves me to speak now to you; yet I intend not to intermeddle in the proceedings of the court, or with any of the persons concerned therein. Only I bless God, that I see an issue of this troublesome business. I also acknowledge the justice of the court, and for mine own part, I am well satisfied, I was publicly charged, and I am publicly and legally acquitted, which is all I did expect or desire. And though this be sufficient for my justification before men, yet not so before the God, who hath seen so much amiss in my dispensations (and even in this affair) as calls me to be humble. For to be publicly and criminally charged in this court, is matter of humiliation, (and I desire to make a right use of it,) notwithstanding I be thus acquitted. If her father had spit in her face, (saith the Lord concerning Miriam,[13]) should she not have been ashamed seven days? Shame had lien upon her, whatever the occasion had been. I am unwilling to stay you from your urgent affairs, yet give me leave (upon this special occasion) to speak a little more to this assembly. It may be of some good use, to inform and rectify the judgments of some of the people, and may prevent such distempers as have arisen amongst us. The great questions that have troubled the country, are about the authority of the magistrates and the liberty of the people. It is yourselves who have called us to this office, and being called by you, we have our authority from God, in way of an ordinance, such as hath the image of God eminently stamped upon it, the contempt and violation whereof hath been vindicated with examples of divine vengeance. I entreat you to consider, that when you choose magistrates, you take them from among yourselves, men subject to like passions as you are. Therefore when you see

[13]Moses' and Aaron's sister. "And the Lord said to Moses, If her father had but spit in her face, should she not be ashamed seven days? Let her be shut out from the camp seven days, and after that let her be received in again" (Numbers 12:14).

infirmities in us, you should reflect upon your own, and that would make you bear the more with us, and not be severe censurers of the failings of your magistrates, when you have continual experience of the like infirmities in yourselves and others. We account him a good servant, who breaks not his covenant. The covenant between you and us is the oath you have taken of us, which is to this purpose, that we shall govern you and judge your causes by the rules of God's laws and our own, according to our best skill. When you agree with a workman to build you a ship or house, etc., he undertakes as well for his skill as for his faithfulness, for it is his profession, and you pay him for both. But when you call one to be a magistrate, he doth not profess nor undertake to have sufficient skill for that office, nor can you furnish him with gifts, etc., therefore you must run the hazard of his skill and ability. But if he fail in faithfulness, which by his oath he is bound unto, that he must answer for. If it fall out that the case be clear to common apprehension, and the rule clear also, if he transgress here, the error is not in the skill, but in the evil of the will: it must be required of him. But if the case be doubtful, or the rule doubtful, to men of such understanding and parts as your magistrates are, if your magistrates should err here, yourselves must bear it.

For the other point concerning liberty, I observe a great mistake in the country about that. There is a twofold liberty, natural (I mean as our nature is now corrupt) and civil or federal. The first is common to man with beasts and other creatures. By this, man, as he stands in relation to man simply, hath liberty to do what he lists; it is a liberty to evil as well as to good. This liberty is incompatible and inconsistent with authority, and cannot endure the least restraint of the most just authority. The exercise and maintaining of this liberty makes men grow more evil, and in time to be worse than brute beasts: *omnes sumus licentia deteriores.*[14] This is that great enemy of truth and peace, that wild beast, which all the ordinances of God are bent against, to restrain and subdue it. The other kind of liberty I call civil or federal, it may also be termed moral, in reference to the covenant between God and man, in the moral law, and the politic covenants and constitutions, amongst men themselves. This liberty is the proper end and object of authority, and cannot subsist without it; and it is a liberty to that only which is good, just, and honest. This liberty you are to stand for, with the hazard (not only of your goods, but) of your lives, if need be. Whatsoever crosseth this, is not authority, but a distemper thereof. This liberty is maintained and exercised in a way of subjection to authority; it is of the same kind of liberty wherewith Christ hath made us free. The woman's own choice makes such a man her husband; yet being so chosen, he is her lord, and she is to be subject to him, yet in a way of liberty, not of bondage; and a true wife accounts her subjection her honor and freedom, and would not think her condition safe and free, but in her subjection to her husband's authority. Such is the liberty of the church under the authority of Christ, her king and husband; his yoke is so easy and sweet to her as a bride's ornaments; and if through forwardness or wantonness, etc., she sake it off, at any time, she is at no rest in her spirit, until she take it up again; and whether her lord smiles upon her, and embraceth her in his arms, or whether he frowns, or rebukes, or smites her, she apprehends the sweetness of his love in all, and is refreshed, supported, and instructed by every such dispensation of his authority over her. On the other side, ye know who they are that com-

[14]We are all the worse for license.

plain of this yoke and say, let us break their bands, etc., we will not have this man to rule over us. Even so, brethren, it will be between you and your magistrates. If you stand for your natural corrupt liberties, and will do what is good in your own eyes, you will not endure the least weight of authority, but will murmur, and oppose, and be always striving to shake off that yoke; but if you will be satisfied to enjoy such civil and lawful liberties, such as Christ allows you, then will you quietly and cheerfully submit unto that authority which is set over you, in all the administrations of it, for your good. Wherein, if we fail at any time, we hope we shall be willing (by God's assistance) to hearken to good advice from any of you, or in any other way of God; so shall your liberties be preserved, in upholding the honor and power of authority amongst you.

The deputy governor having ended his speech, the court arose, and the magistrates and deputies retired to attend their other affairs. . . .

1826

William Bradford 1590–1657

Born into a Yorkshire family of yeoman farmers, William Bradford's early misfortune must have made him more receptive to the religious fervor and sense of community that Puritanism later provided. By the age of seven, Bradford was orphaned of both parents and a grandfather, and soon was sent to live with his uncles, who raised him as a farmer. His fragile health and sense of isolation allowed him plenty of time to read his Bible, and when at the age of twelve he heard the sermons of Richard Clyfton, a nonconformist minister, Bradford felt spiritually moved. Despite the scorn of family and friends, Bradford in 1606 became a member of this group of Separatists who had formed their own congregation in the village of Scrooby under the direction of Clyfton, John Rob-inson, his later successor to the pulpit, and William Brewster, the group's preeminent elder. Because of pressure to conform to the hierarchy of the Anglican Church, the Scrooby group in 1608 fled to Holland and eventually settled in Leyden. After one disastrous business venture, William Bradford became a weaver.

In 1620 part of the Leyden congregation, along with an assortment of less pious emigrants, departed on the Mayflower to establish a settlement where they could maintain a church of "ancient purity" freed from European entanglements. In November they arrived off the shores of what is now Cape Cod, Massachusetts (somewhat farther north than they had intended), and in December disembarked at Plymouth. Since John Robinson had stayed behind in Leyden, William Brewster now became the settlers' spiritual leader, preaching regularly on Sundays; because of the Separatist emphasis upon spontaneity, other members gave short, impromptu sermons as they wished. When Plymouth's first governor, John Carver, died in 1621, Bradford was elected to take his place. The governor wielded extensive powers by contemporary standards: chief judge and jury, superintendant of agriculture and trade, and secretary of state. During his lifetime Bradford was re-elected to the position thirty times, serving almost continuously, for a total term of thirty-three years until his death in 1657.

In 1630 William Bradford wrote the first book of his history, *Of Plymouth Plantation.* Perhaps the settlement that year of a much larger, and potentially overshadowing, Puritan colony at Massachusetts Bay prompted Bradford's beginning of his history. He put aside the manuscript until 1644, when he finished the eleventh chapter, and, between 1646 and 1650, he brought the account of the colony's struggles and achievements through the year 1646. The unfinished manuscript of *Of Plymouth Plantation* is not Bradford's only literary effort—he wrote a journal of Plymouth's first year, some poems, and a series of dialogues—but it constitutes his greatest literary achievement. Moreover, the manuscript significantly influenced a number of later New England historians such as Nathaniel Morton, Cotton Mather, and Thomas Prince.

The way in which Bradford composed *Of Plymouth Plantation* should remind us that his history is not a yearly chronicle of events, but a retrospective attempt to interpret God's design for his "saints," that exclusive group of believers predestined for eternal salvation. Like the Puritan journal, the genre of Puritan history served a distinctly *useful* purpose in enhancing spiritual life. Bradford hoped to demonstrate the workings of divine providence for the edification of future generations, and since all temporal events theoretically conveyed divine meaning, the texture of Bradford's writing is rich in historical detail. Yet a major tension in his narrative involves the difficulty in interpreting the providential will. As Bradford repeatedly encounters human wickedness and duplicity, *Of Plymouth Plantation* increasingly reveals its author's perplexity over the apparent ambiguity of divine providence. Bradford maintains his piety, but he is forced to acknowledge his perception of an infinite gulf between man and God. Such an acknowledgment amplifies the narrative's tone of humility, established at the outset, in Bradford's declaration that he shall write in the Puritan "plain style" of biblical simplicity and concrete image, and tell the "simple truth" as well as his "slender judgment" would permit.

Many readers of *Of Plymouth Plantation* have noted the elegiac note of sadness on which it ends. If Bradford's realization that "so uncertain are the mutable things of this unstable world" dictates his humility throughout, his final entries particularly pronounce a sense of loss. In the eulogy to William Brewster (included below) Bradford lamented, most of all, the disappearance of a communitarian vision embodied by the first-generation founders like Brewster and John Robinson. To Bradford, those first emigrants whom he called "Pilgrims" exemplified the value of community and sense of purpose that were presumably waning in the 1640s as second-generation inhabitants and new immigrants looked for better farmland. *Of Plymouth Plantation* thus speaks a message characteristic of much of the literature of immigration: the paradoxical nature of prosperity and success, the sense that, in this case, the founding of the first successful British settlement in New England led only to fragmentation and dispersal.

Philip Gould
Brown University

PRIMARY WORKS

Mourt's Relation, 1622; *Of Plymouth Plantation,* ed. S. E. Morison, 1952, 1959; "A Dialogue Between Young Men Born in New England and Sundry Ancient Men that Came Out of Holland and Old England," n.d.

SECONDARY WORKS

Bradford Smith, *Bradford of Plymouth,* 1951; Alan B. Howard, "Art and History in Bradford's *Of Plymouth Plantation,*" *William and Mary Quarterly,* 3rd ser., 28, 1971; David Levin,

"William Bradford: The Value of Puritan Historiography," in Everett H. Emerson's *Major Writers of Early American Literature,* 1972; Robert Daly, "William Bradford's Vision of History," *American Literature,* 44, 1973; Walter P. Wenska, "Bradford's Two Histories," *Early American Literature* 8, 1978; David Cressy, *Coming Over,* 1987.

from Of Plymouth Plantation

And first of the occasion and inducements thereunto; the which, that I may truly unfold, I must begin at the very root and rise of the same. The which I shall endeavour to manifest in a plain style, with singular regard unto the simple truth in all things; at least as near as my slender judgment can attain the same.

from **Book I**

from **Chapter I**
The Separatist Interpretation of the Reformation in England 1550–1607

It is well known unto the godly and judicious, how ever since the first breaking out of the light of the gospel in our honourable nation of England,[1] (which was the first of nations whom the Lord adorned therewith after the gross darkness of popery which had covered and overspread the Christian world), what wars and oppositions ever since, Satan hath raised, maintained and continued against the Saints,[2] from time to time, in one sort or other. Sometimes by bloody death and cruel torments; other whiles imprisonments, banishments and other hard usages; as being loath his kingdom should go down, the truth prevail and the churches of God revert to their ancient purity and recover their primitive order, liberty and beauty.

But when he could not prevail by these means against the main truths of the gospel, but that they began to take rooting in many places, being watered with the blood of the martyrs and blessed from Heaven with a gracious increase; he then began to take him to his ancient stratagems, used of old against the first Christians. That when by the bloody and barbarous persecutions of the heathen emperors he could not stop and subvert the course of the gospel, but that it speedily overspread, with a wonderful celerity, the then best known parts of the world; he then began to sow errours, heresies and wonderful dissensions amongst the professors[3] themselves, working upon their pride and ambition, with other corrupt passions incident to all mortal men, yea to the saints themselves in some measure, by which woeful effects

[1]The Protestant Reformation.

[2]Not the canonical saints of the Roman Catholic church, but faithful Christians in general, a term often applied simply to all Puritans.

[3]Those who profess true Christianity, a term often applied simply to all Puritans.

followed. As not only bitter contentions and heartburnings, schisms, with other horrible confusions; but Satan took occasion and advantage thereby to foist in a number of vile ceremonies, with many unprofitable canons and decrees, which have since been as snares to many poor and peaceable souls even to this day. . . .

So many, therefore, of these professors as saw the evil of these things in these parts, and whose hearts the Lord had touched with heavenly zeal for His truth, they shook off this yoke of antichristian bondage, and as the Lord's free people joined themselves (by a covenant of the Lord) into a church estate, in the fellowship of the gospel, to walk in all His ways made known, or to be made known unto them, according to their best endeavours, whatsoever it should cost them, the Lord assisting them.[4] And that it cost them something this ensuing history will declare. . . .

from Chapter IX
Of their Voyage, and how they Passed the Sea; and of their Safe Arrival at Cape Cod[5]

September 6. These troubles being blown over, and now all being compact together in one ship, they put to sea again with a prosperous wind, which continued divers days together, which was some encouragement unto them; yet, according to the usual manner, many were afflicted with seasickness. And I may not omit here a special work of God's providence. There was a proud and very profane young man, one of the seamen, of a lusty, able body, which made him the more haughty; he would alway be contemning the poor people in their sickness and cursing them daily with grievous execrations; and did not let to tell them that he hoped to help to cast half of them overboard before they came to their journey's end, and to make merry with what they had; and if he were by any gently reproved, he would curse and swear most bitterly. But it pleased God before they came half seas over, to smite this young man with a grievous disease, of which he died in a desperate manner, and so was himself the first that was thrown overboard. Thus his curses light on his own head, and it was an astonishment to all his fellows for they noted it to be the just hand of God upon him. . . .

[4]A paraphrase of the words of the covenant that people made when they formed a Separatist (later Congregational) church.

[5]In a previous chapter Bradford offers a number of reasons that compelled a minority of the Leyden group to leave for America. A treaty between Holland and Spain was due to expire in 1621, and some of the Separatists were afraid of a Spanish (and Catholic) invasion of the Low Countries. Some of the Leyden group were also concerned about their children's potential assimilation into Dutch society. Moreover, the Dutch were lax in maintaining the purity of the sabbath day. The Leyden group received two successive patents from the Virginia Company (which were eventually useless because of their accidental arrival in New England, north of the Company's domain), and although King James I did not grant them religious toleration, he did promise not to interfere with them, so long as they maintained themselves peacefully. Some of the economic arrangements with the financial backers in London proved to be difficult as well. Finally, because one of their ships, the Speedwell, was forced to turn back because of a leak, those members still willing to make the voyage joined the Mayflower which then departed for a second time with 101 passengers, about 35 of whom were Separatists.

But to omit other things (that I may be brief) after long beating at sea they fell with that land which is called Cape Cod; the which being made and certainly known to be it, they were not a little joyful. After some deliberation had amongst themselves and with the master of the ship, they tacked about and resolved to stand for the southward (the wind and weather being fair) to find some place about Hudson's River for their habitation. But after they had sailed that course about half the day, they fell amongst dangerous shoals and roaring breakers, and they were so far entangled therewith as they conceived themselves in great danger; and the wind shrinking upon them withal, they resolved to bear up again for the Cape and thought themselves happy to get out of those dangers before night overtook them, as by God's good providence they did. And the next day they got into the Cape Harbor[6] where they rid in safety. . . .

Being thus arrived in a good harbor, and brought safe to land, they fell upon their knees and blessed the God of Heaven who had brought them over the vast and furious ocean, and delivered them from all the perils and miseries thereof, again to set their feet on the firm and stable earth, their proper element. And no marvel if they were thus joyful, seeing wise Seneca[7] was so affected with sailing a few miles on the coast of his own Italy, as he affirmed, that he had rather remain twenty years on his way by land than pass by sea to any place in a short time, so tedious and dreadful was the same unto him.

But here I cannot but stay and make a pause, and stand half amazed at this poor people's present condition; and so I think will the reader, too, when he well considers the same. Being thus passed the vast ocean, and a sea of troubles before in their preparation (as may be remembered by that which went before), they had now no friends to welcome them nor inns to entertain or refresh their weatherbeaten bodies; no houses or much less towns to repair to, to seek for succour. It is recorded in Scripture as a mercy to the Apostle and his shipwrecked company, that the barbarians showed them no small kindness in refreshing them,[8] but these savage barbarians, when they met with them (as after will appear) were readier to fill their sides full of arrows than otherwise. And for the season it was winter, and they that know the winters of that country know them to be sharp and violent, and subject to cruel and fierce storms, dangerous to travel to known places, much more to search an unknown coast. Besides, what could they see but a hideous and desolate wilderness, full of wild beasts and wild men—and what multitudes there might be of them they knew not. Neither could they, as it were, go up to the top of Pisgah to view from this wilderness a more goodly country to feed their hopes,[9] for which way soever they turned their eyes (save upward to the heavens) they could have little solace or content in respect of any outward objects. For summer being done, all things stand upon them with a weather-beaten face, and the whole country, full of woods and thickets, represented a wild and savage hue. If they looked behind them, there was the mighty ocean which they had passed and was now as a main bar and gulf to separate them from all the civil parts of the world. If it be said they had a ship to succour them, it is true; but what heard they daily from the master and company? But that with speed

[6]Now Provincetown harbor.

[7]Roman statesman, playwright, and Stoic philosopher (3? B.C.–A.D. 65?).

[8]Acts 28:2.

[9]As Moses viewed the Promised Land in Numbers 23:14; Deuteronomy 3:27.

they should look out a place (with their shallop) where they would be, at some near distance; for the season was such as he would not stir from thence till a safe harbor was discovered by them, where they would be, and he might go without danger; and that victuals consumed apace but he must and would keep sufficient for themselves and their return. Yea, it was muttered by some that if they got not a place in time, they would turn them and their goods ashore and leave them. Let it also be considered what weak hopes of supply and succour they left behind them, that might bear up their minds in this sad condition and trials they were under; and they could not but be very small. It is true, indeed, the affections and love of their brethren at Leyden was cordial and entire towards them, but they had little power to help them or themselves; and how the case stood between them and the merchants at their coming away hath already been declared.

What could now sustain them but the Spirit of God and His grace? May not and ought not the children of these fathers rightly say: "Our fathers were Englishmen which came over this great ocean, and were ready to perish in this wilderness; but they cried unto the Lord, and He heard their voice and looked on their adversity,"[10] etc. "Let them therefore praise the Lord, because He is good: and His mercies endure forever." "Yea, let them which have been redeemed of the Lord, shew how He hath delivered them from the hand of the oppressor. When they wandered in the desert wilderness out of the way, and found no city to dwell in, both hungry and thirsty, their soul was overwhelmed in them. Let them confess before the Lord His lovingkindness and His wonderful works before the sons of men."[11]

from Book II
Chapter XI
The Remainder of Anno 1620

[The Mayflower Compact]

I shall a little return back, and begin with a combination made by them before they came ashore; being the first foundation of their government in this place.[12] Occasioned partly by the discontented and mutinous speeches that some of the strangers amongst them had let fall from them in the ship: That when they came ashore they would use their own liberty, for none had power to command them, the patent they had being for Virginia and not for New England, which belonged to another government, with which the Virginia Company had nothing to do. And partly that such an act by them done, this their condition considered, might be as firm as any patent, and in some respects more sure.

The form was as followeth

IN THE NAME OF GOD, AMEN.

[10]Bradford's adaptation of Deuteronomy 26:5, 7.
[11]Psalm 107:1–5, 8.
[12]This is commonly referred to as the Mayflower Compact.

We whose names are underwritten, the loyal subjects of our dread Sovereign Lord King James, by the Grace of God of Great Britain, France, and Ireland King, Defender of the Faith, etc.

Having undertaken, for the Glory of God and advancement of the Christian Faith and Honour of our King and Country, a Voyage to plant the First Colony in the Northern Parts of Virginia, do by these presents solemnly and mutually in the presence of God and one of another, Covenant and Combine ourselves together into a Civil Body Politic, for our better ordering and preservation and furtherance of the ends aforesaid; and by virtue hereof to enact, constitute and frame such just and equal Laws, Ordinances, Acts, Constitutions and Offices, from time to time, as shall be thought most meet and convenient for the general good of the Colony, unto which we promise all due submission and obedience. In witness whereof we have hereunder subscribed our names at Cape Cod, the 11th of November, in the year of the reign of our Sovereign Lord King James, of England, France and Ireland the eighteenth, and of Scotland the fifty-fourth. Anno Domini 1620.

After this they chose, or rather confirmed, Mr. John Carver (a man godly and well approved amongst them) their Governor for that year. And after they had provided a place for their goods, or common store (which were long in unlading for want of boats, foulness of the winter weather and sickness of divers) and begun some small cottages for their habitation; as time would admit, they met and consulted of laws and orders, both for their civil and military government as the necessity of their condition did require, still adding thereunto as urgent occasion in several times, and as cases did require.

In these hard and difficult beginnings they found some discontents and murmurings arise amongst some, and mutinous speeches and carriages in other; but they were soon quelled and overcome by the wisdom, patience, and just and equal carriage of things, by the Governor and better part, which clave faithfully together in the main.

[The Starving Time]

But that which was most sad and lamentable was, that in two or three months' time half of their company died, especially in January and February, being the depth of winter, and wanting houses and other comforts; being infected with the scurvy and other diseases which this long voyage and their inaccommodate condition had brought upon them. So as there died some times two or three of a day in the foresaid time, that of 100 and odd persons, scarce fifty remained. And of these, in the time of most distress, there was but six or seven sound persons who to their great commendations, be it spoken, spared no pains night nor day, but with abundance of toil and hazard of their own health, fetched them wood, made them fires, dressed them meat, made their beds, washed their loathsome clothes, clothed and unclothed them. In a word, did all the homely and necessary offices for them which dainty and queasy stomachs cannot endure to hear named; and all this willingly and cheerfully, without any grudging in the least, showing herein their true love unto their friends and brethren; a rare example and worthy to be remembered. Two of these seven were Mr. William Brewster, their reverend Elder, and Myles Standish, their Captain and military commander, unto whom myself and many others were much beholden in our low and sick condition. And yet the Lord so upheld these persons as in this general calamity they were not at all infected either with sickness or lameness. And what I have said of these I may of many others who died in this general visitation, and others yet living; that whilst they had health, yea, or any strength continuing, they were not wanting to any that had need of them. And I doubt not but their recompense is with the Lord.

But I may not here pass by another remarkable passage not to be forgotten. As this calamity fell among the passengers that were to be left here to plant, and were hasted ashore and made to drink water that the seamen might have the more beer, and one[13] in his sickness desiring but a small can of beer, it was answered that if he were their own father he should have none. The disease began to fall amongst them also, so as almost half of their company died before they went away, and many of their officers and lustiest men, as the boatswain, gunner, three quartermasters, the cook and others. At which the Master was something strucken and sent to the sick ashore and told the Governor he should send for beer for them that had need of it, though he drunk water homeward bound.

But now amongst his company there was far another kind of carriage in this misery than amongst the passengers. For they that before had been boon companions in drinking and jollity in the time of their health and welfare, began now to desert one another in this calamity, saying they would not hazard their lives for them, they should be infected by coming to help them in their cabins; and so, after they came to lie by it, would do little or nothing for them but, "if they died, let them die." But such of the passengers as were yet aboard showed them what mercy they could, which made some of their hearts relent, as the boatswain (and some others) who was a proud young man and would often curse and scoff at the passengers. But when he grew weak, they had compassion on him and helped him; then he confessed he did not deserve it at their hands, he had abused them in word and deed. "Oh!" (saith he) "you, I now see, show your love like Christians indeed one to another, but we let one another lie and die like dogs." Another lay cursing his wife, saying if it had not been for her he had never come this unlucky voyage, and anon cursing his fellows, saying he had done this and that for some of them; he had spent so much and so much amongst them, and they were now weary of him and did not help him, having need. Another gave his companion all he had, if he died, to help him in his weakness; he went and got a little spice and made him a mess of meat once or twice. And because he died not so soon as he expected, he went amongst his fellows and swore the rogue would cozen him, he would see him choked before he made him any more meat; and yet the poor fellow died before morning.

[Indian Relations]

All this while the Indians came skulking about them, and would sometimes show themselves aloof off, but when any approached near them, they would run away; and once they stole away their tools where they had been at work and were gone to dinner. But about the 16th of March, a certain Indian came boldly amongst them and

[13]Bradford himself.

spoke to them in broken English, which they could well understand but marveled at it. At length they understood by discourse with him, that he was not of these parts, but belonged to the eastern parts where some English ships came to fish, with whom he was acquainted and could name sundry of them by their names, amongst whom he had got his language. He became profitable to them in acquainting them with many things concerning the state of the country in the east parts where he lived, which was afterwards profitable unto them; as also of the people here, of their names, number and strength, of their situation and distance from this place, and who was chief amongst them. His name was Samoset. He told them also of another Indian whose name was Squanto, a native of this place, who had been in England and could speak better English than himself.

Being, after some time of entertainment and gifts dismissed, a while after he came again, and five more with him, and they brought again all the tools that were stolen away before, and made way for the coming of their great Sachem, called Massasoit. Who, about four or five days after, came with the chief of his friends and other attendance, with the aforesaid Squanto. With whom, after friendly entertainment and some gifts given him, they made a peace with him (which hath now continued this 24 years) in these terms:

1. That neither he nor any of his should injure or do hurt to any of their people.
2. That if any of his did hurt to any of theirs, he should send the offender, that they might punish him.
3. That if anything were taken away from any of theirs, he should cause it to be restored; and they should do the like to his.
4. If any did unjustly war against him, they would aid him; if any did war against them, he should aid them.
5. He should send to his neighbours confederates to certify them of this, that they might not wrong them, but might be likewise comprised in the conditions of peace.
6. That when their men came to them, they should leave their bows and arrows behind them.

After these things he returned to his place called Sowams, some 40 miles from this place, but Squanto continued with them and was their interpreter and was a special instrument sent of God for their good beyond their expectation. He directed them how to set their corn, where to take fish, and to procure other commodities, and was also their pilot to bring them to unknown places for their profit, and never left them till he died. . . .

from Chapter XIV
Anno Domini 1623

[End of the "Common Course and Condition"]

All this while no supply was heard of, neither knew they when they might expect any. So they began to think how they might raise as much corn as they could, and obtain a better crop than they had done, that they might not still thus languish in misery. At length, after much debate of things, the Governor (with the advice of the chiefest amongst them) gave way that they should set corn every man for his own particular, and in that regard trust to themselves; in all other things to go on in the general way as before. And so assigned to every family a parcel of land, according to the proportion of their number, for that end, only for present use (but made no division for inheritance) and ranged all boys and youth under some family. This had very good success, for it made all hands very industrious, so as much more corn was planted than otherwise would have been by any means the Governor or any other could use, and saved him a great deal of trouble, and gave far better content. The women now went willingly into the field, and took their little ones with them to set corn; which before would allege weakness and inability; whom to have compelled would have been thought great tyranny and oppression.

The experience that was had in this common course and condition, tried sundry years and that amongst godly and sober men, may well evince the vanity of that conceit of Plato's[14] and other ancients applauded by some of later times; that the taking away of property and bringing in community into a commonwealth would make them happy and flourishing; as if they were wiser than God. For this community (so far as it was) was found to breed much confusion and discontent and retard much employment that would have been to their benefit and comfort. For the young men, that were most able and fit for labour and service, did repine that they should spend their time and strength to work for other men's wives and children without any recompense. The strong, or man of parts, had no more in division of victuals and clothes than he that was weak and not able to do a quarter the other could; this was thought injustice. The aged and graver men to be ranked and equalized in labours and victuals, clothes, etc., with the meaner and younger sort, thought it some indignity and disrespect unto them. And for men's wives to be commanded to do service for other men, as dressing their meat, washing their clothes, etc., they deemed it a kind of slavery, neither could many husbands well brook it. Upon the point all being to have alike, and all to do alike, they thought themselves in the like condition, and one as good as another; and so, if it did not cut off those relations that God hath set amongst men, yet it did at least much diminish and take off the mutual respects that should be preserved amongst them. And would have been worse if they had been men of another condition. Let none object this is men's corruption, and nothing to the course itself. I answer, seeing all men have this corruption in them, God in His wisdom saw another course fitter for them. . . .

from Chapter XIX Anno Domini 1628

[Thomas Morton of Merrymount]

About some three or four years before this time, there came over one Captain Wollaston (a man of pretty parts[15]) and with him three or four more of some eminency, who brought with them a great many servants, with provisions and other implements

[14] Plato's idea of a communistic society depicted in *The Republic*.

[15] A clever man, intellectually gifted at least in a superficial way.

for to begin a plantation. And pitched themselves in a place within the Massachusetts which they called after their Captain's name, Mount Wollaston. Amongst whom was one Mr. Morton, who it should seem had some small adventure of his own or other men's amongst them, but had little respect amongst them, and was slighted by the meanest servants. Having continued there some time, and not finding things to answer their expectations nor profit to arise as they looked for, Captain Wollaston takes a great part of the servants and transports them to Virginia, where he puts them off at good rates, selling their time to other men; and writes back to one Mr. Rasdall (one of his chief partners and accounted their merchant) to bring another part of them to Virginia likewise, intending to put them off there as he had done the rest. And he, with the consent of the said Rasdall, appointed one Fitcher to be his Lieutenant and govern the remains of the Plantation till he or Rasdall returned to take further order thereabout. But this Morton abovesaid, having more craft than honesty (who had been a kind of pettifogger of Furnival's Inn) in the others' absence watches an opportunity (commons being but hard amongst them) and got some strong drink and other junkets and made them a feast; and after they were merry, he began to tell them he would give them good counsel. "You see," saith he, "that many of your fellows are carried to Virginia, and if you stay till this Rasdall return, you will also be carried away and sold for slaves with the rest. Therefore I would advise you to thrust out this Lieutenant Fitcher, and I, having a part in the Plantation, will receive you as my partners and consociates; so may you be free from service, and we will converse, plant, trade, and live together as equals and support and protect one another," or to like effect. This counsel was easily received, so they took opportunity and thrust Lieutenant Fitcher out o' doors, and would suffer him to come no more amongst them, but forced him to seek bread to eat and other relief from his neighbours till he could get passage for England.

After this they fell to great licentiousness and led a dissolute life, pouring out themselves into all profaneness. And Morton became Lord of Misrule, and maintained (as it were) a School of Atheism. And after they had got some goods into their hands, and got much by trading with the Indians, they spent it as vainly in quaffing and drinking, both wine and strong waters in great excess (and, as some reported) £10 worth in a morning. They also set up a maypole, drinking and dancing about it many days together, inviting the Indian women for their consorts, dancing and frisking together like so many fairies, or furies, rather; and worse practices. As if they had anew revived and celebrated the feasts of the Roman goddess Flora, or the beastly practices of the mad Bacchanalians. Morton likewise, to show his poetry composed sundry rhymes and verses, some tending to lasciviousness, and others to the detraction and scandal of some persons, which he affixed to this idle or idol maypole. They changed also the name of their place, and instead of calling it Mount Wollaston they call it Merry-mount, as if this jollity would have lasted ever. But this continued not long, for after Morton was sent for England (as follows to be declared) shortly after came over that worthy gentleman Mr. John Endecott, who brought over a patent under the broad seal for the government of the Massachusetts. Who, visiting those parts, caused that maypole to be cut down and rebuked them for their profaneness and admonished them to look there should be better walking. So they or others now changed the name of their place again and called it Mount Dagon.[16]

[16]The "false idol" of the Philistines (Judges 16:23).

Now to maintain this riotous prodigality and profuse excess, Morton, thinking himself lawless, and hearing what gain the French and fishermen made by trading of pieces, powder and shot to the Indians, he as the head of this consortship began the practice of the same in these parts. And first he taught them how to use them, to charge and discharge, and what proportion of powder to give the piece, according to the size or bigness of the same; and what shot to use for fowl and what for deer. And having thus instructed them, he employed some of them to hunt and fowl for him, so as they became far more active in that employment than any of the English, by reason of their swiftness of foot and nimbleness of body, being also quicksighted and by continual exercise well knowing the haunts of all sorts of game. So as when they saw the execution that a piece would do, and the benefit that might come by the same, they became mad (as it were) after them and would not stick to give any price they could attain to for them; accounting their bows and arrows but baubles in comparison of them.

And here I may take occasion to bewail the mischief that this wicked man began in these parts, and which since, base covetousness prevailing in men that should know better, has now at length got the upper hand and made this thing common, notwithstanding any laws to the contrary. So as the Indians are full of pieces all over, both fowling pieces, muskets, pistols, etc. They have also their moulds to make shot of all sorts, as musket bullets, pistol bullets, swan and goose shot, and of smaller sorts. Yea some have seen them have their screw-plates to make screw-pins themselves when they want them, with sundry other implements, wherewith they are ordinarily better fitted and furnished than the English themselves. Yea, it is well known that they will have powder and shot when the English want it nor cannot get it; and that in a time of war or danger, as experience hath manifested, that when lead hath been scarce and men for their own defense would gladly have given a groat a pound, which is dear enough, yet hath it been bought up and sent to other places and sold to such as trade it with the Indians at 12*d* the pound. And it is like they give 3*s* or 4*s* the pound, for they will have it at any rate. And these things have been done in the same times when some of their neighbours and friends are daily killed by the Indians, or are in danger thereof and live but at the Indians' mercy. Yea some, as they have acquainted them with all other things, have told them how gunpowder is made, and all the materials in it, and that they are to be had in their own land; and I am confident, could they attain to make saltpeter, they would teach them to make powder.

O, the horribleness of this villainy! How many both Dutch and English have been lately slain by those Indians thus furnished, and no remedy provided; nay, the evil more increased, and the blood of their brethren sold for gain (as is to be feared) and in what danger all these colonies are in is too well known. O that princes and parliaments would take some timely order to prevent this mischief and at length to suppress it by some exemplary punishment upon some of these gain-thirsty murderers, for they deserve no better title, before their colonies in these parts be overthrown by these barbarous savages thus armed with their own weapons, by these evil instruments and traitors to their neighbours and country! But I have forgot myself and have been too long in this digression; but now to return.

This Morton having thus taught them the use of pieces, he sold them all he could spare, and he and his consorts determined to send for many out of England and had by some of the ships sent for above a score. The which being known, and his neighbours meeting the Indians in the woods armed with guns in this sort, it was a terror unto them who lived stragglingly and were of no strength in any place. And other places (though more remote) saw this mischief would quickly spread over all, if not prevented. Besides, they saw they should keep no servants, for Morton would entertain any, how vile soever, and all the scum of the country or any discontents would flock to him from all places, if this nest was not broken. And they should stand in more fear of their lives and goods in short time from this wicked and debased crew than from the savages themselves.

So sundry of the chief of the straggling plantations, meeting together, agreed by mutual consent to solicit those of Plymouth (who were then of more strength than them all) to join with them to prevent the further growth of this mischief, and suppress Morton and his consorts before they grew to further head and strength. Those that joined in this action, and after contributed to the charge of sending him for England, were from Piscataqua, Naumkeag, Winnisimmet, Wessagusset, Nantasket and other places where any English were seated. Those of Plymouth being thus sought to by their messengers and letters, and weighing both their reasons and the common danger, were willing to afford them their help though themselves had least cause of fear or hurt. So, to be short, they first resolved jointly to write to him, and in a friendly and neighbourly way to admonish him to forbear those courses, and sent a messenger with their letters to bring his answer.

But he was so high as he scorned all advice, and asked who had to do with him, he had and would trade pieces with the Indians, in despite of all, with many other scurrilous terms full of disdain. They sent to him a second time and bade him be better advised and more temperate in his terms, for the country could not bear the injury he did. It was against their common safety and against the King's proclamation. He answered in high terms as before; and that the King's proclamation was no law, demanding what penalty was upon it. It was answered, more than he could bear—His Majesty's displeasure. But insolently he persisted and said the King was dead and his displeasure with him, and many the like things. And threatened withal that if any came to molest him, let them look to themselves for he would prepare for them.

Upon which they saw there was no way but to take him by force; and having so far proceeded, now to give over would make him far more haughty and insolent. So they mutually resolved to proceed, and obtained of the Governor of Plymouth to send Captain Standish and some other aid with him, to take Morton by force. The which accordingly was done. But they found him to stand stiffly in his defense, having made fast his doors, armed his consorts, set divers dishes of powder and bullets ready on the table; and if they had not been over-armed with drink, more hurt might have been done. They summoned him to yield, but he kept his house and they could get nothing but scoffs and scorns from him. But at length, fearing they would do some violence to the house, he and some of his crew came out, but not to yield but to shoot; but they were so steeled with drink as their pieces were too heavy for them. Himself with a carbine, overcharged and almost half filled with powder and shot, as was after found, had thought to have shot Captain Standish; but he stepped to him and put by his piece and took him. Neither was there any hurt done to any of either side, save that one was so drunk that he ran his own nose upon the point of a sword that one held before him, as he entered the house; but he lost but a little of his hot blood.

Morton they brought away to Plymouth, where he was kept till a ship went from the Isle of Shoals for England, with which he was sent to the Council of New England, and letters written to give them information of his course and carriage. And also one was sent at their common charge to inform their Honours more particularly and to prosecute against him. But he fooled of the messenger, after he was gone from hence, and though he went for England yet nothing was done to him, not so much as rebuked, for aught was heard, but returned the next year. Some of the worst of the company were dispersed and some of the more modest kept the house till he should be heard from. But I have been too long about so unworthy a person, and bad a cause. . . .

from Chapter XXIII
Anno Domini 1632

[Prosperity Brings Dispersal of Population]

Also the people of the Plantation began to grow in their outward estates, by reason of the flowing of many people into the country, especially into the Bay of the Massachusetts. By which means corn and cattle rose to a great price, by which many were much enriched and commodities grew plentiful. And yet in other regards this benefit turned to their hurt, and this accession of strength to their weakness. For now as their stocks increased and the increase vendible, there was no longer any holding them together, but now they must of necessity go to their great lots. They could not otherwise keep their cattle, and having oxen grown they must have land for plowing and tillage. And no man now thought he could live except he had cattle and a great deal of ground to keep them, all striving to increase their stocks. By which means they were scattered all over the Bay quickly and the town in which they lived compactly till now was left very thin and in a short time almost desolate.

And if this had been all, it had been less, though too much; but the church must also be divided, and those that had lived so long together in Christian and comfortable fellowship must now part and suffer many divisions. First, those that lived on their lots on the other side of the Bay, called Duxbury, they could not long bring their wives and children to the public worship and church meetings here, but with such burthen as, growing to some competent number, they sued to be dismissed and become a body of themselves. And so they were dismissed about this time, though very unwillingly. But to touch this sad matter, and handle things together that fell out afterward; to prevent any further scattering from this place and weakening of the same, it was thought best to give out some good farms to special persons that would promise to live at Plymouth, and likely to be helpful to the church or commonwealth, and so tie the lands to Plymouth as farms for the same; and there they might keep their cattle and tillage by some servants and retain their dwellings here. And so some special lands were granted at a place general called Green's Harbor, where no allotments had been in the former division, a place very well meadowed and fit to keep and rear cattle good store. But alas, this remedy proved worse than the disease; for within a few years those that had thus got footing there rent themselves away, partly by force and partly wearing the rest with importunity and pleas of necessity, so as they must either suffer them to go or live in continual opposition and contention.

And other still, as they conceived themselves straitened or to want accommodation, broke away under one pretence or other, thinking their own conceived necessity and the example of others a warrant sufficient for them. And this I fear will be the ruin of New England, at least of the churches of God there, and will provoke the Lord's displeasure against them.

from Chapter XXVIII Anno Domini 1637

[The Pequot War]

In the fore part of this year, the Pequots fell openly upon the English at Connecticut, in the lower parts of the river, and slew sundry of them as they were at work in the fields, both men and women, to the great terrour of the rest, and went away in great pride and triumph, with many high threats. They also assaulted a fort at the river's mouth, though strong and well defended; and though they did not there prevail, yet it struck them with much fear and astonishment to see their bold attempts in the face of danger.[17] Which made them in all places to stand upon their guard and to prepare for resistance, and earnestly to solicit their friends and confederates in the Bay of Massachusetts to send them speedy aid, for they looked for more forcible assaults. Mr. Vane, being then Governor, writ from their General Court to them here to join with them in this war . . .

In the meantime, the Pequots, especially in the winter before, sought to make peace with the Narragansetts, and used very pernicious arguments to move them thereunto: as that the English were strangers and began to overspread their country, and would deprive them thereof in time, if they were suffered to grow and increase. And if the Narragansetts did assist the English to subdue them, they did but make way for their own overthrow, for if they were rooted out, the English would soon take occasion to subjugate them. And if they would hearken to them they should not need to fear the strength of the English, for they would not come to open battle with them but fire their houses, kill their cattle, and lie in ambush for them as they went abroad upon their occasions; and all this they might easily do without any or little danger to themselves. The which course being held, they well saw the English could not long subsist but they would either be starved with hunger or be forced to forsake the country. With many the like things; insomuch that the Narragansetts were once wavering and were half minded to have made peace with them, and joined against the English. But again, when they considered how much wrong they had received from the Pequots, and what an opportunity they now had by the help of the English to right themselves; revenge was so sweet unto them as it prevailed above all the rest, so as they resolved to join with the English against them, and did.

[17]The English had accused the Pequot of three recent murders and in retaliation had sent a raiding expedition into Connecticut to demand that the murderers be handed over to them. Rebuffed, the English burned and looted Pequot lands, and the violence that Bradford describes here was in response to both that expedition and the construction of the English fort at Old Saybrook at the mouth of the Connecticut River.

The Court here agreed forthwith to send fifty men at their own charge; and with as much speed as possibly they could, got them armed and had made them ready under sufficient leaders, and provided a bark to carry them provisions and tend upon them for all occasions. But when they were ready to march, with a supply from the Bay, they had word to stay; for the enemy was as good as vanquished and there would be no need.

I shall not take upon me exactly to describe their proceedings in these things, because I expect it will be fully done by themselves who best know the carriage and circumstances of things. I shall therefore but touch them in general. From Connecticut, who were most sensible of the hurt sustained and the present danger, they set out a party of men, and another party met them from the Bay, at Narragansetts', who were to join with them. The Narragansetts were earnest to be gone before the English were well rested and refreshed, especially some of them which came last. It should seem their desire was to come upon the enemy suddenly and undiscovered. There was a bark of this place, newly put in there, which was come from Connecticut, who did encourage them to lay hold of the Indians' forwardness, and to show as great forwardness as they, for it would encourage them, and expedition might prove to their great advantage. So they went on, and so ordered their march as the Indians brought them to a fort of the enemy's (in which most of their chief men were) before day. They approached the same with great silence and surrounded it both with English and Indians, that they might not break out; and so assaulted them with great courage, shooting amongst them, and entered the fort with all speed. And those that first entered found sharp resistance from the enemy who both shot at and grappled with them; others ran into their houses and brought out fire and set them on fire, which soon took in their mat; and standing close together, with the wind all was quickly on a flame, and thereby more were burnt to death than was otherwise slain; It burnt their bowstrings and made them unserviceable; those that scaped the fire were slain with the sword, some hewed to pieces, others run through with their rapiers, so as they were quickly dispatched and very few escaped. It was conceived they thus destroyed about 400 at this time. It was a fearful sight to see them thus frying in the fire and the streams of blood quenching the same, and horrible was the stink and scent thereof; but the victory seemed a sweet sacrifice,[18] and they gave the praise thereof to God, who had wrought so wonderfully for them, thus to enclose their enemies in their hands and give them so speedy a victory over so proud and insulting an enemy. . . .

from Chapter XXIX
Anno Domini 1638

[Great and Fearful Earthquake]

This year, about the first or second of June, was a great and fearful earthquake. It was in this place heard before it was felt. It came with a rumbling noise or low murmur,

[18]Leviticus 2:1–2. Bradford thus places the Pequot War in a line of great battles waged by God's chosen people.

like unto remote thunder. It came from the northward and passed southward; as the noise approached nearer, the earth began to shake and came at length with that violence as caused platters, dishes and such-like things as stood upon shelves, to clatter and fall down. Yea, persons were afraid of the houses themselves. It so fell out that at the same time divers of the chief of this town were met together at one house, conferring with some of their friends that were upon their removal from the place, as if the Lord would hereby show the signs of His displeasure, in their shaking a-pieces and removals one from another. However, it was very terrible for the time, and as the men were set talking in the house, some women and others were without the doors, and the earth shook with that violence as they could not stand without catching hold of the posts and pales that stood next them. But the violence lasted not long. And about half an hour, or less came another noise and shaking, but neither so loud nor strong as the former, but quickly passed over and so it ceased. It was not only on the seacoast, but the Indians felt it within land, and some ships that were upon the coast were shaken by it. So powerful is the mighty hand of the Lord, as to make both the earth and sea to shake, and the mountains to tremble before Him, when He pleases. And who can stay His hand?[19]

It was observed that the summers for divers years together after this earthquake were not so hot and seasonable for the ripening of corn and other fruits as formerly, but more cold and moist, and subject to early and untimely frosts by which, many times, much Indian corn came not to maturity. But whether this was any cause I leave it to naturalists to judge.

from Chapter XXXII Anno Domini 1642

[Wickedness Breaks Forth]

Marvelous it may be to see and consider how some kind of wickedness did grow and break forth here, in a land where the same was so much witnessed against and so narrowly looked unto, and severely punished when it was known, as in no place more, or so much, that I have known or heard of; insomuch that they have been somewhat censured even by moderate and good men for their severity in punishments. And yet all this could not suppress the breaking out of sundry notorious sins (as this year, besides other, gives us too many sad precedents and instances), especially drunkenness and uncleanness. Not only incontinency between persons unmarried, for which many both men and women have been punished sharply enough, but some married persons also. But that which is worse, even sodomy and buggery (things fearful to name) have broke forth in this land oftener than once.

I say it may justly be marveled at and cause us to fear and tremble at the consideration of our corrupt natures, which are so hardly bridled, subdued and mortified; nay, cannot by any other means but the powerful work and grace of God's Spirit. But (besides this) one reason may be that the Devil may carry a greater spite against the

[19]Daniel 4:35 and Haggai 2:6.

churches of Christ and the gospel here, by how much the more they endeavour to preserve holiness and purity amongst them and strictly punisheth the contrary when it ariseth either in church or commonwealth; that he might cast a blemish and stain upon them in the eyes of [the] world, who use to be rash in judgment. I would rather think thus, than that Satan hath more power in these heathen lands, as some have thought, than in more Christian nations, especially over God's servants in them.

2. Another reason may be, that it may be in this case as it is with waters when their streams are stopped or dammed up. When they get passage they flow with more violence and make more noise and disturbance than when they are suffered to run quietly in their own channels; so wickedness being here more stopped by strict laws, and the same more nearly looked unto so as it cannot run in a common road of liberty as it would and is inclined, it searches everywhere and at last breaks out where it gets vent.

3. A third reason may be, here (as I am verily persuaded) is not more evils in this kind, nor nothing near so many by proportion as in other places; but they are here more discovered and seen and made public by due search, inquisition and due punishment; for the churches look narrowly to their members, and the magistrates over all, more strictly than in other places. Besides, here the people are but few in comparison of other places which are full and populous and lie hid, as it were, in a wood or thicket and many horrible evils by that means are never seen nor known; whereas here they are, as it were, brought into the light and set in the plain field, or rather on a hill, made conspicuous to the view of all. . . .

But it may be demanded how came it to pass that so many wicked persons and profane people should so quickly come over into this land and mix themselves amongst them? Seeing it was religious men that began the work and they came for religion's sake? I confess this may be marveled at, at least in time to come, when the reasons thereof should not be known; and the more because here was so many hardships and wants met withal. I shall therefore endeavour to give some answer hereunto.

1. And first, according to that in the gospel, it is ever to be remembered that where the Lord begins to sow good seed, there the envious man will endeavour to sow tares.[20]

2. Men being to come over into a wilderness, in which much labour and service was to be done about building and planting, etc., such as wanted help in that respect, when they could not have such as they would, were glad to take such as they could; and so, many untoward servants, sundry of them proved, that were thus brought over, both men and womenkind who, when their times were expired, became families of themselves, which gave increase hereunto.

3. Another and a main reason hereof was that men, finding so many godly disposed persons willing to come into these parts, some began to make a trade of it, to transport passengers and their goods, and hired ships for that end. And then, to make up their freight and advance their profit, cared not who the persons were, so they had money to pay them. And by this means the country became pestered with many unworthy persons who, being come over, crept into one place or other.

4. Again, the Lord's blessing usually following His people as well in outward as spiritual things (though afflictions be mixed withal) do make many to adhere to the

[20]Matthew 13:24–30.

People of God, as many followed Christ for the loaves' sake (John vi.26) and a "mixed multitude" came into the wilderness with the People of God out of Egypt of old (Exodus xii.38). So also there were sent by their friends, some under hope that they would be made better; others that they might be eased of such burthens, and they kept from shame at home, that would necessarily follow their dissolute courses. And thus, by one means or other, in 20 years' time it is a question whether the greater part be not grown the worser? . . .

from Chapter XXXIII
Anno Domini 1643

[The Life and Death of Elder Brewster]

I am to begin this year with that which was a matter of great sadness and mourning unto them all. About the 18th of April died their Reverend Elder and my dear and loving friend Mr. William Brewster, a man that had done and suffered much for the Lord Jesus and the gospel's sake, and had borne his part in weal and woe with this poor persecuted church above 36 years in England, Holland and in this wilderness, and done the Lord and them faithful service in his place and calling. And notwithstanding the many troubles and sorrows he passed through, the Lord upheld him to a great age. He was near fourscore years of age (if not all out) when he died. He had this blessing added by the Lord to all the rest; to die in his bed, in peace, amongst the midst of his friends, who mourned and wept over him and ministered what help and comfort they could unto him, and he again recomforted them whilst he could. His sickness was not long, and till the last day thereof he did not wholly keep his bed. His speech continued till somewhat more than half a day, and then failed him, and about nine or ten a clock that evening he died without any pangs at all. A few hours before, he drew his breath short, and some few minutes before his last, he drew his breath long as a man fallen into a sound sleep without any pangs or gaspings, and so sweetly departed this life unto a better. . . .

I cannot but here take occasion not only to mention but greatly to admire the marvelous providence of God! That notwithstanding the many changes and hardships that these people went through, and the many enemies they had and difficulties they met withal, that so many of them should live to very old age! It was not only this reverend man's condition (for one swallow makes no summer as they say) but many more of them did the like, some dying about and before this time and many still living, who attained to sixty years of age, and to sixty-five, divers to seventy and above, and some near eighty as he did. It must needs be more than ordinary and above natural reason, that so it should be. For it is found in experience that change of air, famine or unwholesome food, much drinking of water, sorrows and troubles, etc., all of them are enemies to health, causes of many diseases, consumers of natural vigour and the bodies of men, and shorteners of life. And yet all of these things they had a large part and suffered deeply in the same. They went from England to Holland, where they found both worse air and diet than that they came from; from thence, enduring a long imprisonment as it were in the ships at sea, into New England; and how it hath been with them here hath already been shown, and what crosses, troubles, fears, wants and sorrows they had been liable unto is easy to conjecture. So as in some sort they may say with the Apostle, 2 Corinthians xi.26, 27, they were "in journeyings often, in perils of waters, in perils of robbers, in perils of their own nation, in perils among the heathen, in perils in the wilderness, in perils in the sea, in perils among false brethren; in weariness and painfulness, in watching often, in hunger and thirst, in fasting often, in cold and nakedness."

What was it then that upheld them? It was God's visitation that preserved their spirits. Job x.12: "Thou hast given me life and grace, and thy visitation hath preserved my spirit." He that upheld the Apostle upheld them. "They were persecuted, but not forsaken, cast down, but perished not."[21] "As unknown, and yet known; as dying, and behold we live; as chastened, and yet not killed"; 2 Corinthians vi.9.

God, it seems, would have all men to behold and observe such mercies and works of His providence as these are towards His people, that they in like cases might be encouraged to depend upon God in their trials, and also to bless His name when they see His goodness towards others. Man lives not by bread only, Deuteronomy viii.3. It is not by good and dainty fare, by peace and rest and heart's ease in enjoying the contentments and good things of this world only that preserves health and prolongs life; God in such examples would have the world see and behold that He can do it without them; and if the world will shut their eyes and take no notice thereof, yet He would have His people to see and consider it. Daniel could be better liking with pulse than others were with the king's dainties.[22] Jacob, though he went from one nation to another people and passed through famine, fears and many afflictions, yet he lived till old age and died sweetly and rested in the Lord,[23] as infinite others of God's servants have done and still shall do, through God's goodness, notwithstanding all the malice of their enemies, "when the branch of the wicked shall be cut off before his day" (Job xv.32) "and the bloody and deceitful men shall not live [out] half their days"; Psalm lv.23.

[The New England Confederation and the Narragansetts]

By reason of the plottings of the Narragansetts ever since the Pequots' War the Indians were drawn into a general conspiracy against the English in all parts, as was in part discovered the year before; and now made more plain and evident by many discoveries and free confessions of sundry Indians upon several occasions from divers places, concurring in one. With such other concurring circumstances as gave them sufficiently to understand the truth thereof. And to think of means how to prevent the same and secure themselves. Which made them enter into this more near union and confederation following.

These were the articles of agreement in the union and confederation which they now first entered into. And in this their first meeting held at Boston the day and year abovesaid, amongst other things they had this matter of great consequence to consider on:

[21]II Corinthians 4:9.
[22]Daniel 1:8–16.
[23]Genesis 47:28; 49:33.

The Narragansetts, after the subduing of the Pequots, thought to have ruled over all the Indians about them. But the English, especially those of Connecticut, holding correspondency and friendship with Uncas, sachem of the Mohegan Indians which lived near them (as the Massachusetts had done with the Narragansetts) and he had been faithful to them in the Pequot War, they were engaged to support him in his just liberties and were contented that such of the surviving Pequots as had submitted to him should remain with him and quietly under his protection. This did much increase his power and augment his greatness, which the Narragansetts could not endure to see. But Miantonomo,[24] their chief sachem, an ambitious and politic man, sought privately and by treachery, according to the Indian manner, to make him away by hiring some to kill him. Sometime they assayed to poison him; that not taking, then in the night time to knock him on the head in his house or secretly to shoot him, and suchlike attempts. But none of these taking effect, he made open war upon him (though it was against the covenants both between the English and them, as also between themselves and a plain breach of the same). He came suddenly upon him with 900 or 1000 men, never denouncing any war before. The other's power at that present was not above half so many, but it pleased God to give Uncas the victory and he slew many of his men and wounded many more; but the chief of all was, he took Miantonomo prisoner.

And seeing he was a great man, and the Narragansetts a potent people and would seek revenge, he would do nothing in the case without the advice of the English, so he, by the help and direction of those of Connecticut, kept him prisoner till this meeting of the Commissioners. The Commissioners weighed the cause and passages as they were clearly represented and sufficiently evidenced betwixt Uncas and Miantonomo; and the things being duly considered, the Commissioners apparently saw that Uncas could not be safe whilst Miantonomo lived; but either by secret treachery or open force, his life would be still in danger. Wherefore they thought he might justly put such a false and blood-thirsty enemy to death; but in his own jurisdiction, not in the English plantations. And they advised in the manner of his death all mercy and moderation should be showed, contrary to the practice of the Indians, who exercise tortures and cruelty. And Uncas having hitherto showed himself a friend to the English, and in this craving their advice, if the Narragansett Indians or others shall unjustly assault Uncas for this execution, upon notice and request the English promise to assist and protect him as far as they may against such violence.

This was the issue of this business. The reasons and passages hereof are more at large to be seen in the acts and records of this meeting of the Commissioners. . . . And Uncas followed this advice and accordingly executed him in a very fair manner according as they advised, with due respect to his honour and greatness.[25]

[24]Miantonomo was attempting to forge a pan-Indian alliance in New England, in an effort to ward the English off Native American lands. To succeed, Miantonomo had to attack Uncas, a faithful ally of the English.

[25]The supposedly "very fair manner" in which Uncas executed Miantonomo was this: Miantonomo was bound and slain by a hatchet wielded by Uncas's brother.

from Chapter XXXIV
Anno Domini 1644

[*Proposal to Remove to Nauset*]

Mr. Edward Winslow was chosen Governor this year.

Many having left this place (as is before noted) by reason of the straitness and barrenness of the same and their finding of better accommodations elsewhere more suitable to their ends and minds; and sundry others still upon every occasion desiring their dismissions, the church began seriously to think whether it were not better jointly to remove to some other place than to be thus weakened and as it were insensibly dissolved.[26] Many meetings and much consultation was held hereabout, and divers were men's minds and opinions. Some were still for staying together in this place, alleging men might here live if they would be content with their condition, and that it was not for want or necessity so much that they removed as for the enriching of themselves. Others were resolute upon removal and so signified that here they could not stay; but if the church did not remove, they must. Insomuch as many were swayed rather than there should be a dissolution, to condescend to a removal if a fit place could be found that might more conveniently and comfortably receive the whole, with such accession of others as might come to them for their better strength and subsistence; and some such-like cautions and limitations.

So as, with the aforesaid provisos, the greater part consented to a removal to a place called Nauset, which had been superficially viewed and the good will of the purchasers to whom it belonged obtained, with some addition thereto from the Court. But now they began to see their errour, that they had given away already the best and most commodious places to others, and now wanted themselves. For this place was about 50 miles from hence, and at an outside of the country remote from all society; also that it would prove so strait as it would not be competent to receive the whole body, much less be capable of any addition or increase; so as, at least in a short time, they should be worse there than they are now here. The which with sundry other like considerations and inconveniences made them change their resolutions. But such as were before resolved upon removal took advantage of this agreement and went on, notwithstanding; neither could the rest hinder them, they having made some beginning.[27]

And thus was this poor church left, like an ancient mother grown old and forsaken of her children, though not in their affections yet in regard of their bodily presence and personal helpfulness; her ancient members being most of them worn away by death, and these of later time being like children translated into other families, and she like a widow left only to trust in God.[28] Thus, she that had made many rich became herself poor.[29] . . .

[26]Bradford and likeminded Pilgrims welcomed the establishment of new towns and churches in the Colony by newcomers, as at Scituate and Taunton, but they wanted the original Plymouth church, including members of the second generation, to stick together.

[27]After looking it over twice, a committee of the Plymouth church reported that there was not enough room for all.

[28]I Timothy 5:5.

[29]II Corinthians 6:10.

Roger Williams 1603?–1683

Banished in his time, beloved in ours, Roger Williams represents a paradoxical early expression of the American ideals of democracy and religious freedom. William Bradford described him as "godly and zealous . . . but very unsettled in judgment" with "strange opinions"; John Winthrop said Williams held "diverse new and dangerous opinions." Cotton Mather vilified him as a kind of Don Quixote, the "first rebel against the divine-church order in the wilderness" with a "windmill" whirling so furiously in his head that "a whole country in America [is] like to be set on fire." Providence, Rhode Island, which prospered under his tolerance, became a notorious haven for heretics, runaways, and malcontents, a "Rogue's Island." Since the nineteenth century, Americans have enshrined Roger Williams as a symbol of liberty of individual conscience and toleration of racial and religious differences, an apostle of civil and spiritual freedom. He was an advocate of the separation of church and state, a friend of the Narragansett Indians and defender of their property rights, a devout Separatist Puritan, whose political ideas were founded on his beliefs that the elect must be free to seek God's truth and that Christianity must be free from secular concerns and the "foul embrace" of civil authority. These positions threatened the theocracy of Massachusetts Bay, and he was forced to flee into the wilderness in January 1636.

He grew up in the Smithfield district of London, a center of Separatist activity. In 1617 his skill at shorthand earned him the patronage of Sir Edward Coke, who enrolled him at Cambridge in 1623, where Williams completed a B.A. in 1627 and began an M.A. Having "forsaken the university" for Puritanism, he became a chaplain in 1629. His religious beliefs grew increasingly radical. He met John Winthrop and John Cotton, who would become his chief adversary. On December 10, 1630, Williams sailed with the Great Migration.

His unorthodoxy started trouble almost as soon as the Puritans arrived in February, 1631. Called to be minister of Boston's First Church, he "durst not officiate to an unseparated people." He insisted that they separate and repent worshipping with the Church of England. Also, he denounced magistrates for punishing violations of the Sabbath, arguing that they had no authority to enforce the first four Commandments, thus beginning a battle with the Puritan leaders over separation of church and state. Moving to Plymouth when charged with subversion and spreading discord, he continued to preach three extreme positions: (1) the Puritans should become Separatists (a position that endangered the charter and the relative freedom it granted); (2) the Massachusetts Bay Company charter was invalid since Christian kings had no right to heathen lands (a position based on separation of spiritual and material prerogatives); and (3) the civil magistrates had no jurisdiction over matters of conscience and soul, only material and social matters (a position that undermined the Puritan oligarchy). After two years as a trader and friend of the Indians, the gifted preacher accepted a call as pastor to Salem, but his political views remained subversive. The Governor and magistrates saw the dangerous implications of Williams's positions, and on July 8, 1635, he was indicted for heresy and divisiveness, then sentenced to banishment on October 9. To avoid deportation, Williams fled south to an Indian settlement.

He purchased land from the Narragansetts and founded Providence, where he devoted himself to creating a heavenly city on earth. Exiles followed him, including Anne Hutchinson, and dissenters of all kinds from Quakers to Jews. This diverse expansion led to disorder, so in 1643

Williams sailed for England to incorporate Providence, Newport, and Portsmouth under a charter that recognized separation of church and state. After the Puritan execution of King Charles I invalidated the charter, he again voyaged to England in 1651 and returned with a second patent in 1654 that assured political stability. As president of the General Assembly, he guided the policies of the colony, such as welcoming Quakers. For most of his life he held offices, continuing to fight for Indian rights and his religious principles. His last major public role was as negotiator for the Narragansetts during King Philip's War. Tragically, he failed to keep them out of the war; consequently, Providence was burned and the tribe was wiped out.

His first and most artistic work is *A Key into the Language of America.* It follows the tradition of the promotional tract in describing the climate, flora, fauna, and natives. In each chapter is a topical vocabulary list of *"Implicite Dialogue,"* Narragansett on the left, English on the right. This section is followed by an "Observation" on the topic, ranging from food, clothing, houses, marriage and family relationships, hunting and fishing, trade and money, and war, to beliefs about nature, the stars, dreams, and religion. Each chapter then presents a "*generall* Observation" that draws cultural and spiritual conclusions and offers moral instruction through meditation and analogy. The chapters end with emblematic poems that satirize English civilized degeneracy and sympathize with Indian barbaric virtue. These poems express Williams's view of the tragic effects of the colonizing process. The massive sociolinguistic project shows sensitivity for their language and admiration for their natural civility and harmony with nature, while at the same time offering a lament that these pagans are damned. A dilemma arises because the Indians had to be civilized before they could be Christianized, but civilizing them often destroyed their natural virtue, which suggested the ironic comparison of civilization with barbarism.

In his other important works, polemical tracts, Williams used his Cambridge training in medieval disputation to compose prolix, rhetorical, erudite arguments, loaded with biblical and classical allusions and quotations. For example, *Mr. Cotton's Letter* presents Williams's version of his banishment, defending his Separatist position, citing intolerance in Massachusetts, and characterizing Cotton as a self-righteous bigot. Williams's most famous work, *The Bloody Tenent of Persecution,* is a refutation of Cotton's tenet justifying persecution for personal beliefs. In a dialogue between Truth and Peace, the first half of *The Bloody Tenent* is a point-by-point rebuttal and a plea for liberty of conscience as a human right. The second half argues that a government is granted power by the people, most of whom are unregenerate. As delegates of the people, therefore, magistrates could not interfere with religion, for the unregenerate have no power in Christ's church. His most famous letter is "To the Town of Providence" (January 1655), written to settle a controversy that divided the town over religious autonomy and civil restraint. While defending a government's right to require civil obedience, he also shows that liberty of conscience does not lead to anarchy. As a septuagenarian he engaged in a vehement debate with the Quakers and wrote a seemingly uncharacteristic denunciation of "the cursed sect" and their leader, George Fox. Although opposed to their fanatic assurance of their infallibility and "inner light," which he felt repudiated the Bible and Christ, he never wanted them subjected to legal persecution. He met their threat to social peace in his heavenly city by arguing against their errors, remaining true to his principles of religious toleration.

Raymond F. Dolle
Indiana State University

PRIMARY WORKS

A Key into the Language of America, 1643; *The Bloody Tenent of Persecution for Cause of Conscience, Discussed in a Conference betweene Truth and Peace,* 1644; *Mr. Cotton's Letter Lately Printed, Examined, and Answered,* 1644; *Queries of the Highest Consideration,* 1644; *Christenings Make Not Christians,* 1645; *The Bloody Tenent Yet More Bloudy by Mr. Cotton's Endeavor to Wash it White in the Blood of the Lambe,* 1652; *Experiments of Spiritual Life and Health,* 1652; *The Fourth Paper Presented by Major Butler,* 1652; *The Hireling Ministry None of Christs,* 1652; *George Fox Digg'd Out of His Burrowes,* 1676; *The Complete Writings of Roger Williams,* 6 vols., ed. J. Hammond Trumball, 1866–1874; rpt. with an additional volume by Perry Miller, 1963; *The Correspondence of Roger Williams,* 2 vols., ed. Glenn LaFantasie, 1988.

SECONDARY WORKS

Perry Miller, *Roger Williams: His Contribution to the American Tradition,* 1953; Ola Elizabeth Winslow, *Master Roger Williams: A Biography,* 1957; Edmund S. Morgan, *Roger Williams: The Church and the State,* 1967; Henry Chupack, *Roger Williams,* 1969; Wallace Coyle, *Roger Williams: A Reference Guide,* 1977; W. Clark Gilpin, *The Millenarian Piety of Roger Williams,* 1979; Hugh Spurgin, *Roger Williams and Puritan Radicalism in the English Separatist Tradition,* 1989; L. Raymond Camp, *Roger Williams, God's Apostle of Advocacy,* 1990.

from A Key into the Language of America[1]

[Preface]
To my Deare and Welbeloved Friends *and* Countreymen, in *old and new* England

I present you with a *Key;* I have not heard of the like, yet framed, since it pleased God to bring that mighty *Continent of America* to light: Others of my Countrey-men have often, and excellently, and lately written of the *Countrey* (and none that I know beyond the goodnesse and worth of it.) This *Key,* respects the *Native Language* of it, and happily may unlocke some *Rarities* concerning the *Natives* themselves, not yet discovered.

I drew the *Materialls* in a rude lumpe at Sea,[2] as a private *helpe* to my owne memory, that I might not by my present absence *lightly lose* what I had so *dearely bought* in some few years *hardship,* and *charges* among the *Barbarians;* yet being reminded by some, what pitie it were to bury those *Materialls* in my *Grave* at land or Sea; and withall, remembring how oft I have been importun'd by *worthy friends,* of all sorts, to afford them some helps this way.

[1]Subtitled *An help to the Language of the Natives in that part of America, called New-England,* the *Key* was first published in London in 1643. This text, slightly modernized, is taken from *The Complete Writings of Roger Williams,* 7 vols., 1963.

[2]Williams composed *A Key* during his two-month transatlantic crossing in 1643.

I resolved (by the assistance of the *most High*) to cast those *Materialls* into this *Key, pleasant* and *profitable* for *All,* but speally for my *friends* residing in those parts:

A little *Key* may open a *Box,* where lies a *bunch* of *Keyes.*

With this I have entred into the secrets of those *Countries,* where ever *English* dwel about two hundred miles, betweene the *French* and *Dutch* Plantations; for want of this, I know what grosse *mis-takes* my selfe and others have run into.

There is a mixture of this *Language North* and *South,* from the place of my abode, about six hundred miles; yet within the two hundred miles (aforementioned) their *Dialects* doe exceedingly differ;[3] yet not so, but (within that compasse) a man may, by this *helpe,* converse with *thousands* of *Natives* all over the *Countrey:* and by such converse it may please the *Father of Mercies* to spread *civilitie,* (and in his owne most holy season) *Christianitie;* for *one Candle* will light *ten thousand,* and it may please *God* to blesse a *little Leaven* to season the *mightie Lump* of those *Peoples* and *Territories.*

It is expected, that having had so much converse with these *natives,* I should write some litle of them.

Concerning them (a little to gratifie expectation) I shall touch upon *foure Heads:*

First, by what *Names* they are distinguished.

Secondly, Their *Originall*[4] and *Descent.*

Thirdly, their *Religion, Manners, Customes,* &c.

Fourthly, That great *Point* of their *Conversion.*

To the first, their *Names* are of two sorts:

First, those of the *English* giving: as *Natives, Salvages, Indians, Wild-men,* (so the *Dutch* call them *Wilden*) *Abergeny*[5] *men, Pagans, Barbarians, Heathen.*

Secondly, their *Names,* which they give themselves.

I cannot observe, that they ever had (before the comming of the *English, French* or *Dutch* amongst them) any *Names* to difference *themselves* from strangers, for they knew none; but two sorts of *names* they had, and have amongst *themselves.*

First, *generall,* belonging to all *Natives,* as *Ninnuock, Ninnimissinnûwock, Eniskeetompaŭwog,* which signifies *Men, Folke,* or *People.*

Secondly, particular *names,* peculiar to severall *Nations,* of them amongst *themselves,* as, *Nanhigganĕuck, Massachusêuck, Cawasumsêuck, Cowwesĕuck, Quintikóock, Quinnipiĕuck, Pequttóog,* &c.

They have often asked mee, why we call them *Indians Natives,* &c. And understanding the reason, they will call themselues *Indians,* in opposition to *English,* &c.

For the second Head proposed, their *Originall* and *Descent.*

From *Adam* and *Noah* that they spring, it is granted on all hands.

But for their later *Descent,* and whence they came into those parts, it seemes as hard to finde, as to finde the *Wellhead* of some fresh *Streame,* which running many miles out of the *Countrey* to the salt *Ocean,* hath met with many mixing *Streames* by the way. They say themselves, that they have *sprung* and *growne* up in that very place, like the very *trees* of the *Wildernesse.*

[3]The Indians in the region spoke dialects of the Algonkian language family, which included Narragansett.

[4]Tribal origin.

[5]Aborigine.

They say that their *Great God Cawtantowwit* created those parts, as I observed in the Chapter of their *Religion.* They have no *Clothes, Bookes,* nor *Letters,* and conceive their *Fathers* never had; and therefore they are easily perswaded that the *God* that made *English* men is a greater *God,* because Hee hath so richly endowed the *English* above *themselves:* But when they heare that about sixteen hundred yeeres agoe, *England* and the *Inhabitants* thereof were like unto *themselves,* and since have received from *God, Clothes, Bookes,* &c. they are greatly affected with a secret hope concerning *themselves.*

Wise and *Judicious* men, with whom I have discoursed, maintaine their *Originall* to be *Northward* from *Tartaria:*[6] and at my now taking ship, at the *Dutch Plantation,* it pleased the *Dutch* Governour, (in some discourse with mee about the *Natives*), to draw their *Line* from *Iceland,* because the name *Sackmakan* (the name for an *Indian* Prince, about the *Dutch*) is the name for a *Prince* in *Iceland.*

Other opinions I could number up: under favour I shall present (not mine opinion, but) my *Observations* to the judgement of the Wise.

First, others (and my selfe) have conceived some of their words to hold affinitie with the *Hebrew.*

Secondly, they constantly *annoint* their *heads* as the *Jewes* did.

Thirdly, they give *Dowries* for their wives, as the *Jewes* did.

Fourthly (and which I have not so observed amongst other *Nations* as amongst the *Jewes,* and *these:*) they constantly separate their Women (during the time of their monthly sicknesse) in a little house along by themselves foure or five dayes, and hold it an *Irreligious thing* for either *Father* or *Husband* or any *Male* to come neere them.

They have often asked me if it bee so with *women* of other *Nations,* and whether they are so *separated:* and for their practice they plead *Nature* and *Tradition.* Yet againe I have found a greater *Affinity* of their Language with the *Greek* Tongue.

2. As the *Greekes* and other *Nations,* and our selves call the seven *Starres* (or Charles Waine the *Beare,*) so doe they *Mosk* or *Paukunnawaw* the Beare.[7]

3. They have many strange Relations of one *Wétucks,* a man that wrought great *Miracles* amongst them, and *walking upon the waters,* &c. with some kind of broken Resemblance to the *Sonne of God.*

Lastly, it is famous that the *Sowwest (Sowaniu)* is the great Subject of their discourse. From thence their *Traditions.* There they say (at the *South-west*) is the Court of their *great God Cautántouwit:* At the *South-west* are their *Forefathers* soules; *to the South-west* they goe themselves when they dye; From the *South-west* came their *Corne,* and Beanes out of their Great *God Cautántowwits* field: and indeed the further *Northward* and *Westward* from us their Corne will not grow, but to the *Southward* better and better. I dare not conjecture in these *Uncertainties,* I believe they are *lost,* and yet hope (in the Lords holy season) some of the wildest of them shall be found to share in the blood of the Son of God. To the third *Head,* concerning their *Religion, Customes, Manners* &c. I shall here say nothing, because in those 32. Chapters of the whole Book,[8] I have briefly touched those of all sorts, from their *Birth* to

[6]Mongolia. If the Indians were human, they had to be descended from Adam and Noah, and thus must have an Old World origin.

[7]The constellation Ursa Major, the Great Bear; also known as Charlemagne's wagon.

[8]*A Key* itself.

their *Burialls,* and have endeavored (as the Nature of the worke would give way) to bring some short *Observations* and *Applications* home to *Europe* from *America.*

Therefore fourthly, to that great Point of their *Conversion* so much to bee longed for, and by all *New-English* so much pretended,[9] and I hope in Truth.

For my selfe I have uprightly laboured to suite my endeavours to my pretences: and of later times (out of desire to attaine their Language) I have run through varieties of *Intercourses*[10] with them Day and Night, Summer and Winter, by Land and Sea, particular passages tending to this, I have related divers, in the Chapter of their Religion.

Many solemne discourses I have had with all *sorts of Nations* of them, from one end of the Countrey to another (so farre as opportunity, and the little Language I have could reach.)

I know there is no small *preparation* in the hearts of Multitudes of them. I know their many solemne *Confessions* to my self, and one to another of their lost *wandring Conditions.*

I know strong *Convictions* upon the *Consciences* of many of them, and their desires uttred that way.

I know not with how little *Knowledge* and *Grace* of Christ the Lord may save, and therefore neither will *despaire,* nor *report* much.

But since it hath pleased some of my Worthy *Country-men* to mention (of late in print) *V Vequash,* the *Pequt Captaine,* I shall be bold so farre to second their *Relations,* as to relate mine owne Hopes of Him (though I dare not be so confident as others.[11]

Two dayes before his Death, as I past up to *Qunnihticut*[12] River, it pleased my worthy friend Mr. *Fenwick* whom I visited at his house in *Say-Brook* Fort at the mouth of that River) to tell me that my old friend *V Vequash* lay very sick: I desired to see him, and Himselfe was pleased to be my Guide two mile where *V Vequash* lay.

Amongst other discourse concerning his *sicknesse* and *Death* (in which hee freely bequeathed his son to Mr. *Fenwick*) I closed with him concerning his *Soule:* Hee told me that some two or three yeare before he had lodged at my House, where I acquainted him with the *Condition* of *all mankind,* & his *Own* in particular, how *God* created *Man* and *All things:* how *Man* fell from *God,* and of his present *Enmity* against *God,* and the *wrath of God* against *Him* untill *Repentance:* said he *your words were never out of my heart to this present;* and said hee *me much pray to Jesus Christ:* I told him so did many *English, French,* and *Dutch,* who had never turned to *God,* nor loved Him: He replyed in broken English: *me so big naughty Heart, me heart all one stone! Savory expressions* using to breath *from compunct and broken Hearts,* and a sence of *inward hardnesse* and *unbrokennesse.* I had many discourses with him in his Life, but this was the summe of our last parting untill our generall meeting.[13]

Now because this is the great Inquiry of all men what *Indians* have been converted? what have the *English* done in those parts? what hopes of the *Indians* receiving the Knowledge of Christ!

[9]Professed.
[10]Discussions, discourses.
[11]Thomas Shepard described the conversion of Wequash in *New England's First Fruits* (1643).
[12]Connecticut.
[13]Judgment Day.

And because to this Question, some put an edge from the boast of the Jesuits in *Canada* and *Maryland,* and especially from the wonderfull conversions made by the Spaniards and Portugalls in the *West-Indies,* besides what I have here written, as also, beside what I have observed in the Chapter of their Religion! I shall further present you with a briefe Additionall discourse concerning this Great Point, being comfortably perswaded that that Father of Spirits, who was graciously pleased to perswade *Japhet*[14] (the Gentiles) to dwell in the Tents of *Shem*[15] (the Jewes) will in his holy season (I hope approaching) perswade, these Gentiles of *America* to partake of the mercies of *Europe,* and then shall bee fulfilled what is written, by the Prophet *Malachi,*[16] from the rising of the Sunne in *(Europe)* to the going down of the same (in *America*) my Name shall be great among the Gentiles.) So I desire to hope and pray,

Your unworthy Country-man
Roger Williams

Directions for the use of the Language

1. A Dictionary *or* Grammer *way* I *had consideration of, but purposely avoided, as not so accommodate to the Benefit of all, as I hope this Forme is.*

2. A Dialogue *also I had thoughts of, but avoided for brevities sake, and yet (with no small paines) I have so framed every Chapter and the matter of it, as I may call it an Implicite Dialogue.*

3. *It is framed chiefly after the* Narrogánset *Dialect, because most spoken in the Countrey, and yet (with attending to the variation of peoples and Dialects) it will be of great use in all parts of the Countrey.*

4. *Whatever your occasion bee either of Travell, Discourse, Trading & c. turne to the Table which will direct you to the Proper Chapter.*

5. *Because the Life of all Language is in the Pronuntiation, I have been at the paines and charges to Cause the Accents, Tones, or sounds to be affixed, (which some understand, according to the* Greeke *Language, Acutes, Graves, Circumflexes) for example, in the second leafe*[17] *in the word* Ewò *He: the sound or Tone must not be put on* E, *but* wò *where the grave Accent is.*

In the same leafe, in the word Ascowequássin, *the sound must not be on any of the Syllables, but on* quáss, *where the Acute or sharp sound is.*

In the same leafe in the word Anspaumpmaûntam, *the sound must not be on any other syllable but* Maûn, *where* the Circumflex *or long sounding Accent is.*

6. *The* English *for every* Indian *word or phrase stands in a straight line directly against the* Indian: *yet sometimes there are two words for the same thing (for their Language is exceeding copious, and they have five or six words sometimes for one thing) and then the* English *stands against them both: for example in the second leafe,*

Cowáunckamish & Cuckquénamish.	*I pray your Favour.*

[14]The third son of Noah, traditionally progenitor of the Medes and Greeks.

[15]The eldest son of Noah, ancestor of the Semitic peoples.

[16]See Malachi 1.11.

[17]On page two.

Chapter XX

Of their nakednesse and *clothing*

Paũskesu.	*Naked.*
Pauskesítchick	*Naked men and women.*
Nippóskiss.	*I am naked.*

They have a two-fold nakednesse:

First ordinary and constant, when although they have a Beasts skin, or an English mantle on, yet that covers ordinarily but their hinder parts and all the foreparts from top to toe, (excep their secret parts, covered with a little Apron, after the patterne of their and our first Parents)[18] I say all else open and naked.

Their male children goe starke naked, and have no Apron untill they come to ten or twelve yeeres of age; their Female they, in a modest blush cover with a little Apron of an hand breadth from their very birth.

Their second nakednesse is when their men often abroad and both men and women within doòres, leave off their beasts skin, or English cloth, and so (excepting their little Apron) are wholly naked; yet but few of the women but will keepe their skin or cloth (though loose) or neare to them ready to gather it up about them.

Custome hath used their minds and bodies to it, and in such a freedom from any wantonnesse, that I have never seen that wantonnesse amongst them, as, (with griefe) I have heard of in *Europe*.

Nippóskenitch	*I am rob'd of my coat.*
Nippóskenick ewò.	*He takes away my Coat.*
Acòh.	*Their Deere skin.*
Tummóckquashunck.	*A Beavers coat.*
Nkéquashunck.	*An Otters coat.*
Mohéwonck.	*A Rakoone-skin coat.*
Natóquashunck.	*A Wolves-skin coat.*
Mishannéquashunck.	*A Squirrill-skin coat.*
Neyhommaûashunck	*A Coat or Mantle,* curiously made of the fairest feathers of their *Neyhommaũog,* or Turkies, which commonly their old men make; and is with them as Velvet with us.
Maũnek: nquittiashíagat.	*An English Coat or Mantell.*
Cáudnish.	*Put off.*
Ocquash.	*Put on.*
Neesashíagat.	*Two coats.*
Shwíshiagat.	*Three Coats.*
Piuckquashíagat.	*Ten coats, &c.*

[18]See Genesis 3:7: "They sewed fig leaves together and made themselves aprons." Williams believed that the Indians were descended from Adam and Eve, and thus were human beings who could be saved.

Obs. Within their skin or coat they creepe contentedly, by day or night, in house, or in the woods, and sleep soundly counting it a felicitie, (as indeed an earthly one it is); *Intra pelliculam quemque tenere suam,* That every man be content with his skin.

Squáus aúhaqut.	*a Womans Mantle.*
Muckis aúhaqut.	*A childs Mantle.*
Pétacaus.	*an English Wastecoat.*
Petaoawsunnèse.	*a little wastecoat.*
Aũtah & aútawhun.	*Their apron.*
Caukóanash.	*Stockins.*
Nquittetiagáttash.	*a paire of stockins.*
Mocússinass, & Mockussínchass.	*Shooes.*

Obs. Both these, Shoes and Stockins they make of their Deere skin worne out, which yet being excellently tann'd by them, is excellent for to travell in wet and snow; for it is so well tempered with oyle, that the water cleane wrings out; and being hang'd up in their chimney, they presently drie without hurt as my selfe hath often proved.

Noonacóminash.	*Too little.*
Taubacóminash.	*Big enough.*
Saunketíppo, *or,* Ashónaquo.	*a Hat* or *Cap.*
Moôse.	*The skin of a great Beast* as big as an Ox, some call it a red Deere
Wussùckhósu.	*Painted.*

They also commonly paint these *Moose* and Deere-skins for their Summer wearing, with varietie of formes and colours.

Petouwàssinug.	*Their Tobacco-bag,* which hangs at their necke, or sticks at their girdle, which is to them in stead of an English pocket.

Obs. Our English clothes are so strange unto them, and their bodies inured so to indure the weather, that when (upon gift &c.) some of them have had *English* cloathes, yet in a showre of raine, I have seen them rather expose their skins to the wet then their cloaths, and therefore pull them off, and keep them drie.

Obs. While they are amongst the *English* they keep on the *English* apparell, but pull of all as soone as they come againe into their owne Houses, and Company.

Generall Observations *of their Garments*

How deep are the purposes and Councells, of God? what should bee the reason of this mighty difference of One mans children that all the Sonnes of men on this side[19]

[19]Williams published *A Key* in London, so he refers to Europe as "this side" and America as "the other side."

the way (in *Europe, Asia* and *Africa,* should have such plenteous clothing for Body, for Soule! and the rest of *Adams* sonnes and Daughters on the other side, or *America* (some thinke as big as the other three,) should neither have nor desire clothing for their naked Soules, or Bodies.

More particular:

O what a Tyrant's Custome long,
How doe men make a tush,[20]
At what's in use, though ne're so fowle:
Without once shame or blush?

Many thousand proper Men and Women,
I have seen met in one place:
Almost all naked, yet not one,
Thought want of clothes disgrace.

Israell was naked, wearing cloathes!
The best clad English-man,
Not cloth'd with Christ, more naked is:
Then naked Indian.

from Chapter XXI

Of Religion, the soule, &c.

Manìt-manittó-wock. — *God, Gods.*

Obs. He that questions whether God made the World, the *Indians* will teach him. I must acknowledge I have received in my converse with them many Confirmations of those two great points, *Heb.* 11. 6. *viz:*

1. That God is.
2. That hee is a rewarder of all them that diligently seek him.

They will generally confesse that God made all: but then in speciall, although they deny not that *English-mans* God made *English* Men, and the Heavens and Earth there! yet their Gods made them and the Heaven, and Earth where they dwell.

Nummusquaunamúckqun manìt. — *God is angry with me?*

Obs. I have heard a poore *Indian* lamenting the losse of a child at break of day, call up his Wife and children, and all about him to Lamentation, and with abundance of teares cry out! O God thou hast taken away my child! thou art angry with me: O turne thine anger from me, and spare the rest of my children.

If they receive any good in hunting, fishing, Harvest &c. they acknowledge God in it.

Yea, if it be but an ordinary accident, a fall, &c. they will say God was angry and did it, *musquántum manit* God is angry. But herein is their Misery.

[20]Fuss.

First they branch their God-head into many Gods.

Secondly, attribute it to Creatures.

First, many Gods: they have given me the Names of thirty seven, which I have, all which in their solemne Worships they invocate: as

Kautántowwit the great South-West God, to whose

House all soules goe, and from whom came their Corne, Beanes, as they say.

Wompanànd.	*The Easterne God.*
Chekesuwànd.	*The Westerne God.*
Wunnanaméanit.	*The Northerne God.*
Sowwanànd.	*The Southerne God.*
Wetuómanit.	*The house God.*

Even as the Papists have their He and Shee Saint Protectors as St. *George,* St. *Patrick,* St. *Denis,* Virgin *Mary,* &c.

Squáuanit.	*The Womans God.*
Muckquachuckquànd.	*The Childrens God.*

Obs. I was once with a *Native* dying of a wound, given him by some murtherous *English* (who rob'd him and run him through with a Rapier, from whom in the heat of his wound, he at present escaped from them, but dying of his wound, they suffered Death at new *Plymouth,* in *New-England,*[21] this *Native* dying call'd much upon *Muckquachuckquànd,* which of other *Natives* I understood (as they believed) had appeared to the dying young man, many yeares before, and bid him when ever he was in distresse call upon him.

Secondly, as they have many of these fained Deities: so worship thcy thc Creatures in whom they conceive doth rest some Deitie:

Keesuckquànd.	*The Sun God.*
Nanepaûshat.	*The Moone God.*
Paumpágussit.	*The Sea.*
Yotáanit.	*The Fire God.*

Supposing that Deities be in these, &c.

When I have argued with them about their Fire-God: can it say they be, but this fire must be a God, or Divine power, that out of a stone will arise in a Sparke, and when a poore naked *Indian* is ready to starve with cold in the House, and especially in the Woods, often saves his life, doth dresse all our Food for us, and if it be angry will burne the House about us, yea if a spark fall into the drie wood, burnes up the Country, (though this burning of the Wood to them they count a Benefit both for destroying of vermin, and keeping downe the Weeds and thickets?)

Præsentem narrat quælibet herba Deum,

Every little Grasse doth tell,
The sons of Men, there God doth dwell.

[21]Four runaway servants from Plymouth murdered a Narragansett in the summer of 1638. Williams demanded justice for the murder in a letter to Winthrop. Bradford described the crime, trial, and execution of the murderers in his *History of Plymouth Plantation.*

Besides there is a generall Custome amongst them, at the apprehension of any Excellency in Men, Women, Birds, Beasts, Fish, &c. to cry out *Manittóo,* that is, it is a God, as thus if they see one man excell others in Wisdome, Valour, strength, Activity &c. they cry out *Manittóo* A God: and therefore when they talke amongst themselves of the *English* ships, and great buildings, of the plowing of their Fields, and especially of Bookes and Letters, they will end thus: *Manittôwock* They are Gods: *Cummanittôo,* you are a God, &c. A strong Conviction naturall in the soule of man, that God is; filling all things, and places, and that all Excellencies dwell in God, and proceed from him, and that they only are blessed who have that Jehovah their portion.

Nickómmo.	*A Feast or Dance.*

Of this Feast they have publike, and private and that of two sorts.

First in sicknesse, or Drouth, or Warre, or Famine.

Secondly, after Harvest, after hunting, when they enjoy a caulme of Peace, Health, Plenty, Prosperity, then *Nickómmo* a Feast, especially in Winter, for then (as the Turke saith of the Christian, rather the Antichristian,) they run mad once a yeare) in their kind of Christmas feasting.

Powwáw.	*A Priest.*
Powwaûog.	*Priests.*

Obs. These doe begin and order their service, and Invocation of their Gods, and all the people follow, and joyne interchangeably in a laborious bodily service, unto sweating, especially of the Priest, who spends himselfe in strange Antick Gestures, and Actions even unto fainting.

In sicknesse the Priest comes close to the sick person, and performes many strange Actions about him, and threaten and conjures out the sicknesse. They conceive that there are many Gods or divine Powers within the body of a man: In his pulse, his heart, his Lungs, &c.

I confesse to have most of these their customes by their owne Relation, for after once being in their Houses and beholding what their Worship was, I durst never bee an eye witnesse, Spectatour, or looker on, least I should have been partaker of Sathans Inventions and Worships, contrary to *Ephes.* 5. 14.[22]

Nanouwétea.	*An over-Seer and Orderer of their Worship.*
Neen nanowwúnnemun.	*I will order or oversee.*

They have an exact forme of King, Priest, and Prophet, as was in Israel typicall of old in that holy Land of *Canaan,* and as the Lord Jesus ordained in his spirituall Land of *Canaan* his Church throughout the whole World: their Kings or Governours called *Sachimaüog,* Kings, and *Atauskowaũg* Rulers doe govern: Their Priests, performe and manage their Worship: Their wise men and old men of which number the Priests are also,) whom they call *Taupowaüog* they make solemne speeches and Orations, or Lectures to them, concerning Religion, Peace, or Warre and all things.

Nowemaúsitteem.	*I give away at the Worship.*

[22]Ephesians 5:11: "Take no part in the unfruitful works of darkness, but instead expose them."

He or she that makes this *Nickòmmo* Feast or Dance, besides the Feasting of sometimes twenty, fifty, an hundreth, yea I have seene neere a thousand persons at one of these Feasts) they give I say a great quantity of money, and all sort of their goods (according to and sometimes beyond their Estate) in severall small parcells of goods, or money, to the value of eighteen pence, two Shillings, or thereabouts to one person: and that person that receives this Gift, upon the receiving of it goes out, and hollowes thrice for the health and prosperity of the Party that gave it, the Mr. or Mistris of the Feast.

Nowemacaũnash.	*Ile give these things.*
Nitteaũguash.	*My money.*
Nummaumachíuwash.	*My goods.*

Obs. By this Feasting and Gifts, the Divell drives on their worships pleasantly (as he doth all false worships, by such plausible Earthly Arguments of uniformities, universalities, Antiquities, Immunities, Dignities, Rewards, unto submitters, and the contrary to Refusers) so that they run farre and neere and aske

Awaun. Nákommit?	*Who makes a Feast?*
Nkekinneawaûmen.	*I goe to the Feast.*
Kekineawaũi.	*He is gone to the Feast.*

They have a modest Religious perswasion not to disturb any man, either themselves *English, Dutch,* or any in their Conscience, and worship, and therefore say:

Aquiewopwaũwash. Aquiewopwaũwock.	*Peace, hold your peace.*
Peeyaúntam.	*He is at Prayer.*
Peeyaúntamwock.	*They are praying.*
Cowwéwonck.	*The Soule,*

Derived from *Cowwene* to sleep, because say they, it workes and operates when the body sleepes. *Míchachunck* the soule, in a higher notion, which is of affinity, with a word signifying a looking glasse, or cleere resemblance, so that it hath its name from a cleere sight or discerning, which indeed seemes very well to suit with the nature of it.

Wuhóck	*The Body.*
Nohòck: cohòck.	*My body, your body.*
Awaunkeesitteoúwincohòck:	*Who made you?*
Tunna-awwa commítchichunck-kitonckquèan?	*Whether goes your soule when you die?*
An. Sowánakitaũwaw.	*It goes to the South-West.*

Obs. They beleive that the soules of Men and Women goe to the Sou-west, their great and good men and Women to *Cautàntouwit* his House, where they have hopes (as the Turkes have of carnall Joyes): Murtherers thieves and Lyers, their Soules (say they) wander restlesse abroad.

Now because this Book (by Gods good providence) may come into the hand of many fearing God, who may also have many an opportunity of occasionall discourse with some of these their wild brethren and Sisters, and may speake a word for their and our glorious Maker, which may also prove some preparatory Mercy to their Soules: I shall propose some proper expressions concerning the Creation of the World, and mans Estate, and in particular theirs also, which from my selfe many hundreths of times, great numbers of them have heard with great delight, and great convictions: which who knowes (in Gods holy season) may rise to the exalting of the Lord Jesus Christ in their conversion, and salvation?

Nétop Kunnatótemous.	*Friend, I will aske you a Question.*
Natótema:	*Speake on.*
Tocketunnántum?	*What thinke you?*
Awaun Keesiteoûwin Kéesuck?	*Who made the Heavens?*
Aûke Wechêkom?	*The Earth, the Sea?*
Mittauke.	*The World.*

Some will answer *Tattá* I cannot tell, some will answer *Manittôwock* the Gods.

Tasuóg, Maníttowock.	*How many Gods bee there?*
Maunaũog Mishaúnawock.	*Many, great many.*
Nétop machàge.	*Friend, not so.*
Pausuck naúnt manìt.	*There is onely one God.*
Cuppíssittone.	*You are mistaken.*
Cowauwaúnemun.	*You are out of the way.*

A phrase which much pleaseth them, being proper for their wandring in the woods, and similitudes greatly please them.

Kukkakótemous, wâchit-quáshouwe.	*I will tell you, presently.*
Kuttaunchemókous.	*I will tell you newes.*
Paûsuck naúnt manít kéesittin keesuck, &c	*One onely God made the Heavens, &c..*
Napannetashèmittan naugecautúmmonab nshque.	*Five thousand yeers agoe and upwards.*
Naũgom naũnt wukkesittínnes wâme teâgun.	*He alone made all things.*
Wuche mateâg	*Out of nothing.*
Quttatashuchuckqúnnacaus-keesitínnes wâme.	*In six dayes he made all things.*
Nquittaqúnne. Wuckéesitin wequâi.	*The first day Hee made the Light.*
Néesqunne. Wuckéesitin Keésuck.	*The Second day Hee made the Firmament.*
Shúckqunne wuckéesitin Aũke kà wechêkom.	*The third day hee made the Earth and Sea.*
Yóqunne wuckkéesitin Nip-paũus kà Nanepaũshat.	*The fourth day he made the Sun and the Moon.*
Neenash-mamockíuwash wêquanantíganash.	*Two great Lights.*

Kà wáme anócksuck.	*And all the Starres.*
Napannetashúckqunne Wuckéesittin pussuckfeésuck wâme.	*The fifth day hee made all the Fowle.*
Keesuckquíuke.	*In the Ayre, or Heavens,*
Ka wame namaũsuck. Wechekommíuke.	*And all the Fish in the Sea.*
Quttatashúkqunne wuckkeésittin penashímwockwamè	*The sixth day hee made all the Beasts of the Field.*
Wuttàke wuchè wuckeesittin. pausuck Enìn, *or,* Enefkéetomp.	*Last of all he made one Man*
Wuche mishquòck.	*Of red Earth,*
Ka wesuonckgonnakaûnes Adam, túppautea mishquòck.	*And call'd him Adam, or red Earth.*
Wuttàke wuchè, Câwit mishquock.	*Then afterward, while Adam, or red Earth slept.*
Wuckaudnúmmenes manìt peetaũgon wuche Adam.	*God tooke a rib from Adam, or red Earth.*
Kà wuchè peteaũgon. Wukkeefitinnes paũsuck squàw.	*And of that rib he made One woman,*
Kà pawtouwúnnes Adâmuck.	*And brought her to Adam.*
Nawônt Adam wuttúnnawaun nuppeteâgon ewò.	*When Adam saw her, he said, This is my bone.*
Enadatashúckqunne, aquêi.	*The seventh day hee rested,*
Nagaû wuchè quttatashúckqune anacaũsuock Englishmánuck.	*And therefore Englishmen worke six dayes.*
Enadatashuckqunnóckat taubataũmwock.	*On the seventh day they praise God.*

Obs. At this Relation they are much satisfied, with a reason why (as they observe) the *English* and *Dutch,* &c. labour six dayes, and rest and worship the seventh.

Besides, they will say, Wee never heard of this before: and then will relate how they have it from their Fathers, that *Kautántowwit* made one man and woman of a stone, which disliking, he broke them in pieces, and made another man and woman of a Tree, which were the Fountaines of all mankind.

They apprehending a vast difference of Knowledge betweene the *English* and themselves, are very observant of the *English* lives: I have heard them say to an Englishman (who being hindred, broke a promise to them) You know God, Will you lie Englishman? . . .

The generall Observation *of* Religion, &c.

The wandring Generations of *Adams* lost posteritie,[23] having lost the true and living God their Maker, have created out of the nothing of their owne inventions many false and fained Gods and Creators.

More particular:

Two forts of men shall naked stand.
Before the burning ire
Of him that shortly shall appeare,
In dreadfull flaming fire.

First, millions know not God, nor for
His *knowledge, care to seeke:*
Millions have knowledge store, but in
Obedience are not meeke.

If woe to Indians, *Where shall* Turk,
Where shall appeare the Jew?
O, where shall stand the Christian false?
O blessed then the True.

Chapter XXIX

Of Their Warre, &c.

A Quène.	*Peace.*
Nanoúeshin, & Awêpu.	*A peaceable calme;* for *Awēpu* signifies a calme.
Chépewess, & Mishittâshin.	*A Northern storme of warre,* as they wittily speake, and which *England* now wofully feeles, untill the Lord Jesus chide the winds, and rebuke the raging seas.
Nummusquântum.	*I am angry.*
Tawhìtch musquawnaméan?	*Why are you angry?*
Aquie musquántash.	*Cease from anger.*
Chachépissu, nishqûetu.	*Fierce.*
Tawhìtch chachepiséttit nishquéhettit?	*Why are they fierce?*
Cummusquáunamuck.	*He is angry with you.*
Matwaûog.	*Souldiers.*
Matwaûonck.	*A Battle.*

[23]A popular theory about the origins of the Indians was that they were descended from the Ten Lost Tribes of Israel, which were carried into captivity by the King of Assyria.

Cummusqnaúnamish	*I am angry with you.*
Cummusquawnamè?	*Are you angry with me?*
Miskisaûwaw.	*A quarrelsome fellow.*
Tawhítch niskqúekean?	*Why are you so fierce?*
Ntatakcómmuckqun ewò.	*He strucke mee.*
Nummokókunitch Ncheckéqunnitch.	*I am robbed.*
Mecaûtea.	*A fighter.*
Mecâuntitea.	*Let us fight.*
Mecaúnteass.	*Fight with him.*
Wepè cummécautch.	*You are a quarreller.*
Jûhettítea.	*Let us fight.*
Jûhetteke.	*Fight,* Which is the word of incouragement which they use when they animate each other in warre; for they use their tongues in stead of drummes and trumpets.
Awaùn necáwni aum píasha?	*Who drew the first bow, or shot the first shot?*
Nippakétatunck.	*He shot first at me.*
Nummeshannántam Nummayaôntam.	*I scorne, or take it indignation.*

Obs. This is a common word, not only in warre, but in peace also (their spirits in naked bodies being as high and proud as men more gallant) from which sparkes of the lusts of pride and passion, begin the flame of their warres.

Whauwháutowaw ánowat.	*There is an Alarum.*
Wopwawnónckquat.	*An hubbub.*
Amaúmuwaw paúdsha.	*A Messenger is come.*
Keénomp / Múckquomp } paûog.	*Captaines,* or *Valiant men.*
Negonshâchick.	*Leaders.*
Kuttówonck.	*A Trumpet.*
Popowuttáhig.	*A Drumme.*

Obs. Not that they have such of their owne making; yet such they have from the *French:* and I have knowne a good Drumme made amongst them in imitation of the *English.*

Quaquawtatatteâug	*They traine.*
Machíppog	*A Quiver.*
Caúquat -tash.	*Arrow, Arrowes.*
Onúttug.	*An halfe Moone in war.*
Péskcunck.	*A Gunne.*
Saûpuck.	*Powder.*
Mátit.	*Unloden.*
Méchimu.	*Loden.*

Mechimúash.	*Lode it.*
Shóttash.	*Shot;* A made word from us, though their Gunnes they have from the *French,* and often sell many a score to the *English,* when they are a little out of frame or Kelter.
Pummenúmmin teáuquash.	*To contribute to the warres.*
Askwhítteass.	*Keep watch.*
Askwhitteâchick.	*The Guard.*
Askwhitteaûg?	*Is it the Guard?*

Obs. I once travelled (in a place conceived dangerous) with a great Prince, and his Queene and Children in company, with a Guard of neere two hundred, twentie, or thirtie fires were made every night for the Guard (the Prince and Queene in the midst) and Sentinells by course, as exact as in *Europe;* and when we travelled through a place where ambushes were suspected to lie, a speciall Guard, like unto a Life-guard, compassed (some neerer, some farther of) the King and Queen, my selfe and some *English* with me.[24]

They are very copious and patheticall in Orations to the people, to kindle a flame of wrath, Valour or revenge from all the Common places which Commanders use to insist on.

Wesássu	*Afraid.*
Cowésass?	*Are you afraid?*
Tawhitch wesásean?	*Why feare you?*
Manowêsass.	*I fear none.*
Kukkúshickquock.	*They feare you.*
Nofemitteúnckquock	*They fly from us.*
Onamatta cowaûta	*Let us pursue.*
Núckqusha.	*I feare him.*
Wussémo-wock.	*He flies, they flie.*
Npauchippowem	*I flie for succour.*
Keesaũname.	*Save me.*
Npúmmuck.	*I am shot.*
Chenawaũsu.	*Churlish.*
Waumaũsu.	*Loving.*
Tawhìtch chenawaûsean?	*Why are you churlish?*
Aumánsk. Waukaunòsint.	*A Fort.*
Cupshitteaûg.	*They lie in the way.*
Aumanskitteaũg.	*They fortifie.*
Kekaũmwaw.	*A scorner or mocker.*
Nkekaũmuck ewò.	*He scornes me.*
Aquìe kekaúmowash.	*Doe not scorne.*

[24]In September 1638 Williams accompanied Miantunnomu (or Miantonomo) to Hartford for a conference with the magistrates of Connecticut, which required them to cross through the territories of the Pequots, Mohegans, and their confederates.

Obs. This mocking (between their great ones) is a great kindling of Warres amongst them: yet I have known some of their chiefest say, what should I hazard the lives of my precious Subjects, them and theirs to kindle a Fire, which no man knowes how farre, and how long it will burne, for the barking of a Dog?

Sekineam.	*I have no mind to it.*
Nisékineug.	*He likes not me.*
Nummánneug.	*He hates me.*
Sekinneauhettùock.	
Maninnewauhettùock.	*They hate each other.*
Nowetompátimmin	*We are Friends.*
Wetompáchick.	*Friends.*
Nowepinnátimin.	*We joyne together.*
Nowepinnâchick.	*My Companions in War. or Associats.*
Nowechusettimmin.	*We are Confederates.*
Néchuse ewò	*This is my Associate.*
Wechusittûock.	*They joyne together.*
Nwéche kokkêwem.	*I will be mad with him.*
Chickaũta wêtu.	*An house fired.*

Once lodging in an Indian house full of people, the whole Company (Women especially) cryed out in apprehension that the Enemy had fired the House, being about midnight: The house was fired but not by an Enemy: the men ran up on the house top, and with their naked hands beat out the Fire: One scorcht his leg, and suddenly after they came into the house againe, undauntedly cut his leg with a knife to let out the burnt blood.

Yo ánawhone	*There I am wounded.*
Missínnege	*A Captive.*
Nummissinnàm ewo.	*This is my Captive.*
Waskeiûhettimmitch.	*At beginning of the fight.*
Nickqueintónckquock	*They come against us.*
Nickqueintouôog.	*I will make Warre upon them.*
Nippauquanaũog.	*I will destroy them.*
Queintauatíttea.	*Let us goe against them.*
Kunnauntatáuchuckqun.	*He comes to kill you.*
Paúquana.	*There is slaughter.*
Pequttôog paúquanan.	*The Pequts are slaine.*
Awaun Wuttúnnene?	*Who have the Victory?*
Tashittáwho?	*How many are slaine?*
Neestáwho.	*Two are slaine.*
Piuckqunneánna.	*Ten are slaine.*

Obs. Their Warres are farre lesse bloudy, and devouring then the cruell Warres of *Europe;* and seldome twenty slaine in a pitcht field: partly because when they fight in a wood every Tree is a Bucklar.

When they fight in a plaine, they fight with leaping and dancing, that seldome an Arrow hits, and when a man is wounded, unless he that shot followes upon the wounded, they soone retire and save the wounded: and yet having no Swords, nor

Guns, all that are slaine are commonly slain with great Valour and Courage: for the Conquerour ventures into the thickest, and brings away the Head of his Enemy.

Niss-nissoke.	*Kill kill.*
Kúnnish	*I will kill you.*
Kunnìshickqun ewò.	*He will kill you.*
Kunníshickquock.	*They will kill you.*
Siuckissûog.	*They are stout men.*
Nickummissuog.	*They are Weake.*
Nnickummaunamaûog.	*I shall easily vanquish them.*
Neene núppamen.	*I am dying?*
Cowaúnckamish.	*Quarter, quarter.*
Kunnanaumpasúmmish.	*Mercy, Mercy*
Kekuttokaũnta,	*Let us parley.*
Aquétuck.	*Let us cease Armes.*
Wunnishaũnta.	*Let us agree.*
Cowammáunsh.	*I love you.*
Wunnêtu ntá.	*My heart is true.*
Tuppaûntash.	*Consider what I say.*
Tuppaúntamoke.	*Doe you all consider.*
Cummequaùnum cummittamussusuck ká cummuckiaûg.	*Remember your Wives, and Children.*
Eatch kèen anawâyean.	*Let all be as you say.*
Cowawwunnaûwem.	*You speake truly.*
Cowauôntam.	*You are a wise man.*
Wetompátitea.	*Let us make Friends.*

Generall Observations *of their Warres*

How dreadfull and yet how righteous is it with the most righteous Judge of the whole World, that all the generations of Men being turn'd Enemies against, and fighting against Him who gives them breath and Being, and all things, (whom yet they cannot reach) should stab, kill, burne, murther and devoure each other?

More particular:

The Indians count of Men as Dogs,
It is no Wonder then:
They teare out one anothers throats!
But now that English *men,*

That boast themselves Gods Children, and
Members of Christ to be,
That they should thus break out in flames.
Sure 'tis a Mystery!
The second sea'ld Mystery or red Horse,
Whose Rider hath power and will,

To take away Peace from Earthly Men,
They must Each *other* kill.[25]

1643

To the Town of Providence[1]

[Providence?]

Loving Friends and Neighbours

It pleaseth GOD, yet to continue this great Liberty of our Town-Meetings, for which, we ought to be humbly thankful, and to improve these Liberties to the Praise of the Giver, and to the Peace and Welfare of the Town and Colony, without our own private Ends.[2]—I thought it my Duty, to present you with this my impartial Testimony, and Answer to a Paper sent you the other Day from my Brother,—*That it is Blood-Guiltiness, and against the Rule of the Gospel, to execute Judgment upon Transgressors, against the private or public Weal.*[3]—That ever I should speak or write a Tittle[4] that tends to such an infinite Liberty of Conscience, is a Mistake; and which I have ever disclaimed and abhorred. To prevent such Mistakes, I at present shall only propose this Case.—There goes many a Ship to Sea, with many a Hundred Souls in one Ship, whose Weal and Woe is common; and is a true Picture of a Common-Wealth, or an human Combination, or Society.[5] It hath fallen out sometimes, that both *Papists* and *Protestants, Jews,* and *Turks,* may be embarqued into one Ship. Upon which Supposal, I do affirm, that all the Liberty of Conscience that ever I pleaded for, turns upon these two Hinges, that none of the *Papists, Protestants, Jews,* or *Turks,* be forced to come to the Ships Prayers or Worship; nor, secondly, compelled from their own particular Prayers or Worship, if they practice any. I further add, that I never denied, that notwithstanding this Liberty, the Commander of this Ship ought to command the Ship's Course; yea, and also to command that Justice, Peace, and Sobriety, be kept and practised, both among the Seamen and all the Passengers. If any Seamen refuse to perform their Service, or Passengers to pay their Freight;—if any refuse to help in Person or Purse, towards the Common Charges, or Defence;—if any refuse to obey the common Laws and Orders of the Ship, concerning their common Peace and Preservation;—if any shall mutiny and rise up against their Commanders, and Officers;—if any shall preach or write, that

[25]In the King James version, Revelation 6:3–4: "When he opened the second seal, I heard the second living creature say 'Come!' And out came another horse, bright red; its rider was permitted to take peace from the earth, so that men should slay one another; and he was given a great sword."

[1]Written ca. January 1654–1655. Undated, but believed to have been written after Williams's return to Providence from England in 1654. This text is taken from *The Correspondence of Roger Williams,* ed. Glenn LaFantasie, 1988.

[2]The controversy that divided the community may have been the issue of compulsory military service and its implications for religious autonomy and civil obedience.

[3]This work is lost and the author unknown.

[4]Dot, least bit.

[5]This analogy is Williams's reply to the argument that a citizen could not be prosecuted for resisting civil law if he claimed that it violated his private conscience. This fallacious idea was based on a misreading of *The Bloody Tenent.*

there ought to be no Commanders, nor Officers, because all are equal in CHRIST, therefore no Masters, nor Officers, no Laws, nor Orders, no Corrections nor Punishments—I say, I never denied, but in such Cases, whatever is pretended, the Commander or Commanders may judge, resist, compel, and punish such Transgressors, according to their Deserts and Merits. This, if seriously and honestly minded, may, if it so please the Father of Lights, let in some Light, to such as willingly shut not their Eyes.—I—remain, studious of our common Peace and Liberty,—

Roger Williams

1874

Testimony of Roger Williams relative to his first coming into the Narragansett country

Narragansett, June 18, 1682.

I testify, as in the presence of the all-making and all-seeing God, that about fifty years since,[1] I coming into this Narragansett country, I found a great contest between three Sachems, two, (to wit, Canonicus and Miantonomo) were against Ousamaquin, on Plymouth side, I was forced to travel between them three, to pacify, to satisfy all their and their dependents' spirits of my honest intentions to live peaceably by them. I testify, that it was the general and constant declaration, that Canonicus his father had three sons, whereof Canonicus was the heir, and his youngest brother's son, Miantonomo, (because of youth,) was his marshal and executioner, and did nothing without his uncle Canonicus' content; and therefore I declare to posterity, that were it not for the favor God gave me with Canonicus, none of these parts, no, not Rhode Island, had been purchased or obtained, for I never got any thing out of Canonicus but by gift.[2] I also profess, that very inquisitive of what the title or denomination Narragansett should come, I heard that Narragansett was so named from a little island between Puttiquomscut and Musquomacuk on the sea and fresh water side. I went on purpose to see it; and about the place called Sugar Loaf Hill, I saw it, and was within a pole of it, but could not learn why it was called Narragansett. I had learned, that the Massachusetts was called so, from the Blue Hills, a little island thereabout; and Canonicus' father and ancestors, living in these southern parts, transferred and brought their authority and name into those northern parts, all along by the sea-side, as appears by the great destruction of wood all along near the sea-side and I desire posterity to see the gracious hand of the Most High, (in whose hands are all hearts) that when the hearts of my countrymen and friends and brethren failed me, his infinite wisdom and merits stirred up the barbarous heart of Canonicus to love me as his son to his last gasp, by which means I had not only Miantonomo and all the lowest Sachems my friends, but Ousamaquin also, who

[1]Williams fled from Salem to Seekonk, Narragansett Bay, in January 1636. This text, slightly modernized, is taken from *The Complete Writings of Roger Williams,* 7 vols., 1963.

[2]On March 24, 1638, Williams obtained a "Town Evidence" deed from the Narragansett sachems.

because of my great friendship with him at Plymouth, and the authority of Canonicus, consented freely, being also well gratified by me, to the Governor Winthrop and my enjoyment of Prudence, yea of Providence itself, and all the other lands I procured of Canonicus which were upon the point, and in effect whatsoever I desired of him; and I never denied him or Miantonomo whatever they desired of me as to goods or gifts or use of my boats or pinnace, and the travels of my own person, day and night, which, though men know not, nor care to know, yet the all-seeing Eye hath seen it, and his all-powerful hand hath helped me. Blessed be his holy name to eternity.

Roger Williams

1963

Anne Bradstreet 1612?–1672

Anne Dudley Bradstreet is among the best known of early North American poets, the first in the British colonies to have a book of poetry published. She was born in England to Dorothy Yorke, whom Cotton Mather described as "a gentlewoman whose extract and estate were considerable" and Thomas Dudley, steward to the Earl of Lincoln at Sempringham. She had access as a child to private tutors and the Earl's library, a circumstance that allowed her educational opportunities unusual for women of her time. Her family was part of the Nonconformist group of Puritans actively planning for the settlement of Massachusetts Bay Colony. In 1628, Anne Dudley married Simon Bradstreet (also Nonconformist), and in 1630 (with Winthrop's group) she arrived with her husband and parents in Massachusetts. Many years later she wrote to her children of her first impressions of North America, where she "found a new world and new manners, at which [her] heart rose. But after [she] was convinced it was the way of God, [she] submitted to it and joined to the church at Boston."

The Bradstreets soon left Boston for Newtown (now Cambridge), then Ipswich, and after 1644 they moved to North Andover, where Bradstreet remained until her death in 1672. While her husband and her father began long careers in public service to the new colony, she raised eight children and wrote poetry. *The Tenth Muse Lately Sprung Up in America* was published in London in 1650 at the insistence of John Woodbridge, Bradstreet's brother-in-law. The poems had evidently circulated among various members of Bradstreet's family. Taking a manuscript copy to London, Woodbridge inserted a preface to assure readers of the book's authenticity:

> *. . . the worst effect of his [the reader's] reading will be unbelief, which will make him question whether it be a woman's work, and ask, is it possible? If any do, take this as an answer from him that dares avow it; it is the work of a woman, honored, and esteemed where she lives, for her gracious demeanor, her eminent parts, her pious conversation, her courteous disposition, her exact diligence in her place, and discreet managing of her family occasions, and more than so, these poems are the fruit but of some few hours, curtailed from her sleep and other refreshments.*

Woodbridge's care to point out that Bradstreet's poems were not written in neglect of family duties says much about Renaissance suspicions regarding literary women.

The 1650 edition of Bradstreet's poems contains her early conventional verse: quaternions, elegies, and dialogues that reveal more about the literary influences upon her writing (Quarles, DuBartas, Sylvester, Sidney, Spenser, Thomas Dudley) than about her responses to a new environment. Despite opposition from "carping tongues" who said her "hand a needle better fits" than a pen, Bradstreet continued to write. A Boston edition of her poems appeared posthumously in 1678, with a substantial quantity of new material, much of it her finest work.

This later work, from which most of the selections included here are taken, develops from the conventional public verse of the first edition to more private themes of family, love, nature, sorrow, faith, and resignation. The assertiveness about women's abilities in public pieces such as "The Prologue" grows into an uninhibited use of images drawn from women's experiences, particularly her own. In her mature poems, as in the prose meditations she left to her children, Bradstreet "avoided encroaching upon other's conceptions, because [she] would leave [them] nothing but [her] own." The poet's voice becomes distinct and individual, revealing tensions between conventional literary subject matter and her own experience, between rebellion against and acquiescence to her frontier circumstances, between her love of this world and her concern for the afterlife of Puritan doctrine. While Bradstreet's didactic motives frequently remain, they become less overt. She intends no moralizing in verse, but simply to react to her own experiences. With those personal reactions, she occasionally makes the Puritan aesthetic within which she worked satisfy a larger aesthetic, one more accessible to modern readers. As the first widely recognized woman poet in a North American literature not known for its attention to women writers, Anne Bradstreet is a model for future generations.

Pattie Cowell
Colorado State University

PRIMARY WORKS

The Tenth Muse Lately Sprung Up in America, 1650; *Several Poems Compiled with Great Variety of Wit and Learning,* 1678, rpt. 1758; *The Works of Anne Bradstreet in Prose and Verse,* ed. John Harvard Ellis, 1867; *The Works of Anne Bradstreet,* ed. Jeannine Hensley, 1967; *The Complete Works of Anne Bradstreet,* ed. Joseph R. McElrath, Jr. and Allan P. Robb, 1981.

SECONDARY WORKS

Elizabeth Wade White, *Anne Bradstreet: The Tenth Muse,* 1971; Ann Stanford, *Anne Bradstreet: The Worldly Puritan,* 1974; Pattie Cowell and Ann Stanford, eds., *Critical Essays on Anne Bradstreet,* 1983; Wendy Martin, *An American Triptych: Anne Bradstreet, Emily Dickinson, Adrienne Rich,* 1984; Rosamond Rosenmeier, *Anne Bradstreet Revisited,* 1991.

The Prologue [To Her Book][1]

1

To sing of wars, of captains, and of kings,
Of cities founded, commonwealths begun,
For my mean[2] pen are too superior things:
Or how they all or each their dates have run,
Let poets and historians set these forth,
My obscure lines shall not so dim their worth.

2

But when my wond'ring eyes and envious heart
Great Bartas'[3] sugar'd lines do but read o'er
Fool I do grudge the Muses[4] did not part
'Twixt him and me that overfluent store;
A Bartas can do what a Bartas will,
But simple I according to my skill.

3

From schoolboy's tongue no rhet'ric we expect,
Nor yet a sweet consort from broken strings,
Nor perfect beauty where's a main defect:
My foolish, broken, blemish'd Muse so sings,
And this to mend, alas, no art is able,
'Cause nature made it so irreparable.

4

Nor can I, like that fluent sweet tongu'd Greek,
Who lisp'd at first,[5] in future times speak plain;
By art he gladly found what he did seek,
A full requital of his striving pain.

[1]It is surmised that this prologue was originally written for "Quaternions," Bradstreet's epic on the history of mankind and the "four monarchies." In *The Tenth Muse* (1650), the poem stood as an introductory address.

[2]Low or humble.

[3]Guillaume de Salluste du Bartas (1544–1590), French writer of religious epics, was admired by the Puritans.

[4]The Greek Muses were nine female deities of the arts and sciences. Calliope, mentioned in stanza 6, was the muse of epic poetry.

[5]The Greek orator Demosthenes (c. 383–322 B.C.) was born with a lisp.

Art can do much, but this maxim's most sure:
A weak or wounded brain admits no cure.

5

I am obnoxious to each carping tongue
Who says my hand a needle better fits,
A poet's pen all scorn I should thus wrong,
For such despite they cast on female wits:
If what I do prove well, it won't advance,
They'll say it's stol'n, or else it was by chance.

6

But sure the antique Greeks were far more mild,
Else of our sex, why feigned they those Nine,
And poesy made Calliope's own child;
So 'mongst the rest they placed the arts divine,
But this weak knot, they will full soon untie,
The Greeks did nought, but play the fools and lie.

7

Let Greeks be Greeks, and women what they are,
Men have precedency and still excel,
It is but vain unjustly to wage war;
Men can do best, and women know it well.
Preeminence in all and each is yours;
Yet grant some small acknowledgment of ours.

8

And oh ye high flown quills[6] that soar the skies,
And ever with your prey still catch your praise,
If e'er you deign these lowly lines your eyes,
Give thyme or parsley wreath, I ask no bays;[7]
This mean and unrefined ore of mine
Will make your glist'ring gold but more to shine.

1650

[6]Quills were used as pens.
[7]Laurels, foliage from a tree in southern Europe used by the ancient Greeks as a crown of honor.

The Author to Her Book[1]

Thou ill-form'd offspring of my feeble brain,
Who after birth did'st by my side remain,
Till snatcht from thence by friends, less wise than true,
Who thee abroad expos'd to public view,
Made thee in rags halting to th' press to trudge,
Where errors were not lessened (all may judge).
At thy return my blushing was not small,
My rambling brat (in print) should mother call;
I cast thee by as one unfit for light,
Thy visage was so irksome in my sight;
Yet being mine own, at length affection would
Thy blemishes amend, if so I could:
I wash'd thy face, but more defects I saw,
And rubbing off a spot, still made a flaw.
I stretcht thy joints to make thee even feet,
Yet still thou run'st more hobbling than is meet;
In better dress to trim thee was my mind,
But nought save homespun cloth i' th' house I find;
In this array, 'mongst vulgars may'st thou roam,
In critic's hands, beware thou dost not come;
And take thy way where yet thou art not known,
If for thy father asked, say thou had'st none:
And for thy mother, she alas is poor,
Which caus'd her thus to send thee out of door.

1678

To Her Father with Some Verses

Most truly honored, and as truly dear,
If worth in me, or ought[1] I do appear,
Who can of right better demand the fame,
Then may your worthy self from whom it came?
The principle might yield a greater sum,[2]
Yet handled ill, amounts but to this crumb;
My stock's so small, I know not how to pay,

[1]Bradstreet's book, *The Tenth Muse,* was published in London in 1650. It is thought that she wrote this poem in 1666, when a second edition seemed to have been considered.

[1]Anything.
[2]Principal, or primary capital, yields interest.

My bond[3] remains in force unto this day;
Yet for part payment take this simple mite,
Where nothing's to be had kings loose their right;
Such is my debt, I may not say forgive,
But as I can, I'll pay it while I live:
Such is my bond, none can discharge but I,
Yet paying is not paid until I die.

1678

Contemplations

Some time now past in the autumnal tide,
When Phoebus[1] wanted but one hour to bed,
The trees all richly clad, yet void of pride,
Were gilded o'er by his rich golden head.
Their leaves and fruits seemed painted, but was true,
Of green, of red, of yellow, mixed hue;
Rapt were my senses at this delectable view.

2

I wist not what to wish, yet sure thought I,
If so much excellence abide below,
How excellent is He that dwells on high,
Whose power and beauty by his works we know?
Sure he is goodness, wisdom, glory, light,
That hath this under world so richly dight;[2]
More heaven than earth was here, no winter and no night.

3

Then on a stately oak I cast mine eye,
Whose ruffling top the clouds seemed to aspire;
How long since thou wast in thine infancy?
Thy strength, and stature, more thy years admire,
Hath hundred winters past since thou wast born?
Or thousand since thou brakest thy shell of horn?
If so, all these as nought, eternity doth scorn.

[3]Contract.
[1]The sun god Apollo in Greek mythology.
[2]Decked, dressed.

4

Then higher on the glistering Sun I gazed,
Whose beams was shaded by the leavie tree;
The more I looked, the more I grew amazed,
And softly said, "What glory's like to thee?"
Soul of this world, this universe's eye,
No wonder some made thee a deity;
Had I not better known, alas, the same had I.

5

Thou as a bridegroom from thy chamber rushes,
And as a strong man, joys to run a race;[3]
The morn doth usher thee with smiles and blushes;
The Earth reflects her glances in thy face.
Birds, insects, animals with vegative,
Thy heat from death and dullness doth revive,
And in the darksome womb of fruitful nature dive.

6

Thy swift annual and diurnal course,
Thy daily straight and yearly oblique path,
Thy pleasing fervor and thy scorching force,
All mortals here the feeling knowledge hath.
Thy presence makes it day, thy absence night,
Quaternal seasons caused by thy might:
Hail creature, full of sweetness, beauty, and delight.

7

Art thou so full of glory that no eye
Hath strength thy shining rays once to behold?
And is thy splendid throne erect so high,
As to approach it, can no earthly mould?
How full of glory then must thy Creator be,
Who gave this bright light luster unto thee?
Admired, adored for ever, be that Majesty.

[3]The sun, as "a bridegroom coming out of his chamber, . . . rejoiceth as a strong man to run a race" (Psalm 19:4–5).

8

Silent alone, where none or saw, or heard,
In pathless paths I lead my wand'ring feet,
My humble eyes to lofty skies I reared
To sing some song, my mazed Muse thought meet.
My great Creator I would magnify,
That nature had thus decked liberally;
But Ah, and Ah, again, my imbecility!

9

I heard the merry grasshopper then sing.
The black-clad cricket bear a second part;
They kept one tune and played on the same string,
Seeming to glory in their little art.
Shall creatures abject thus their voices raise
And in their kind resound their Maker's praise,
Whilst I, as mute, can warble forth no higher lays?

10

When present times look back to ages past,
And men in being fancy those are dead,
It makes things gone perpetually to last,
And calls back months and years that long since fled.
It makes a man more aged in conceit
Than was Methuselah, or's grandsire great,[4]
While of their persons and their acts his mind doth treat.

11

Sometimes in Eden fair he seems to be,
Sees glorious Adam there made lord of all,
Fancies the apple, dangle on the tree,
That turned his sovereign to a naked thrall.[5]
Who like a miscreant's driven from that place,
To get his bread with pain and sweat of face,
A penalty imposed on his backsliding race.

[4]According to Genesis 5:18–27, Methuselah lived 969 years; his grandfather, Jared, 962 years. "Conceit" is thought or conception.

[5]A slave.

12

Here sits our grandame in retired place,
And in her lap her bloody Cain new-born;[6]
The weeping imp oft looks her in the face,
Bewails his unknown hap and fate forlorn;
His mother sighs to think of Paradise,
And how she lost her bliss to be more wise,
Believing him that was, and is, father of lies.

13

Here Cain and Abel come to sacrifice,
Fruits of the earth and fatlings each do bring,
On Abel's gift the fire descends from skies,
But no such sign on false Cain's offering;
With sullen hateful looks he goes his ways,
Hath thousand thoughts to end his brother's days,
Upon whose blood his future good he hopes to raise.

14

There Abel keeps his sheep, no ill he thinks;
His brother comes, then acts his fratricide;
The virgin Earth of blood her first draught drinks,
But since that time she often hath been cloyed.
The wretch with ghastly face and dreadful mind
Thinks each he sees will serve him in his kind,
Though none on earth but kindred near then could he find.

15

Who fancies not his looks now at the bar,
His face like death, his heart with horror fraught,
Nor malefactor ever felt like war,
When deep despair with wish of life hath fought,
Branded with guilt and crushed with treble woes,
A vagabond to Land of Nod he goes.
A city builds, that walls might him secure from foes.

[6]According to Genesis 3–4, Eve believed the "father of lies" and thus lost Paradise. Her son Cain murdered his younger brother Abel (Genesis 4:8), and Cain then went to live in the Land of Nod, an unidentified area east of Eden (Genesis 4:1–16).

16

Who thinks not oft upon the father's ages,
Their long descent, how nephews' sons they saw,
The starry observations of those sages,
And how their precepts to their sons were law,
How Adam sighed to see his progeny,
Clothed all in his black sinful livery,
Who neither guilt nor yet the punishment could fly.

17

Our life compare we with their length of days
Who to the tenth of theirs doth now arrive?
And though thus short, we shorten many ways,
Living so little while we are alive;
In eating, drinking, sleeping, vain delight
So unawares comes on perpetual night,
And puts all pleasures vain unto eternal flight.

18

When I behold the heavens as in their prime,
And then the earth (though old) still clad in green,
The stones and trees, insensible of time,
Nor age nor wrinkle on their front are seen;
If winter come and greenness then do fade,
A spring returns, and they more youthful made;
But man grows old, lies down, remains where once he's laid.

19

By birth more noble than those creatures all,
Yet seems by nature and by custom cursed,
No sooner born, but grief and care makes fall
That state obliterate he had at first;
Nor youth, nor strength, nor wisdom spring again,
Nor habitations long their names retain,
But in oblivion to the final day remain.

20

Shall I then praise the heavens, the trees, the earth
Because their beauty and their strength last longer?

Shall I wish there, or never to had birth,
Because they're bigger, and their bodies stronger?
Nay, they shall darken, perish, fade and die,
And when unmade, so ever shall they lie,
But man was made for endless immortality.

21

Under the cooling shadow of a stately elm
Close sat I by a goodly river's side,
Where gliding streams the rocks did overwhelm,
A lonely place, with pleasures dignified.
I once that loved the shady woods so well,
Now thought the rivers did the trees excel,
And if the sun would ever shine, there would I dwell.

22

While on the stealing stream I fixt mine eye,
Which to the longed-for ocean held its course,
I marked, nor crooks, nor rubs,[7] that there did lie
Could hinder aught, but still augment its force.
"O happy flood," quoth I, "that holds thy race
Till thou arrive at thy beloved place,
Nor is it rocks or shoals that can obstruct thy pace,

23

Nor is't enough, that thou alone mayst slide,
But hundred brooks in thy clear waves do meet,
So hand in hand along with thee they glide
To Thetis' house, where all embrace and greet.[8]
Thou emblem true of what I count the best,
O could I lead my rivulets to rest,
So may we press to that vast mansion, ever blest."

24

Ye fish, which in this liquid region 'bide,
That for each season have your habitation,
Now salt, now fresh where you think best to glide

[7]Neither bends nor obstructions.
[8]Thetis, the mother of Achilles, lived in the sea.

To unknown coasts to give a visitation,
In lakes and ponds you leave your numerous fry;
So nature taught, and yet you know not why,
You wat'ry folk that know not your felicity.

25

Look how the wantons frisk to taste the air,
Then to the colder bottom straight they dive;
Eftsoon to Neptune's glassy hall repair[9]
To see what trade the great ones there do drive,
Who forage o'er the spacious sea-green field,
And take the trembling prey before it yield,
Whose armor is their scales, their spreading fins their shield.

26

While musing thus with contemplation fed,
And thousand fancies buzzing in my brain,
The sweet-tongued Philomel perched o'er my head[10]
And chanted forth a most melodious strain
Which rapt me so with wonder and delight,
I judged my hearing better than my sight,
And wished me wings with her a while to take my flight.

27

"O merry Bird," said I, "that fears no snares,
That neither toils nor hoards up in thy barn,
Feels no sad thoughts nor cruciating cares
To gain more good or shun what might thee harm.
Thy clothes ne'er wear, thy meat is everywhere,
Thy bed a bough, thy drink the water clear,
Reminds not what is past, nor what's to come dost fear."

28

"The dawning morn with songs thou dost prevent,[11]
Sets hundred notes unto thy feathered crew,

[9]Neptune was the Roman god of the ocean.

[10]Philomel is the nightingale, named for Philomela, whose tongue was torn out after she was raped by her brother-in-law; she was transformed into a bird. The allusion is a poetic device only; nightingales were not found in the New England colonies.

[11]Anticipate.

So each one tunes his pretty instrument,
And warbling out the old, begin anew,
And thus they pass their youth in summer season,
Then follow thee into a better region,
Where winter's never felt by that sweet airy legion."

29

Man at the best a creature frail and vain,
In knowledge ignorant, in strength but weak,
Subject to sorrows, losses, sickness, pain,
Each storm his state, his mind, his body break,
From some of these he never finds cessation,
But day or night, within, without, vexation,
Troubles from foes, from friends, from dearest, near'st relation.

30

And yet this sinful creature, frail and vain,
This lump of wretchedness, of sin and sorrow,
This weatherbeaten vessel wracked with pain,
Joys not in hope of an eternal morrow;
Nor all his losses, crosses, and vexation,
In weight, in frequency and long duration
Can make him deeply groan for that divine translation.[12]

31

The mariner that on smooth waves doth glide
Sings merrily and steers his bark with ease,
As if he had command of wind and tide,
And now become great master of the seas:
But suddenly a storm spoils all the sport,
And makes him long for a more quiet port,
Which 'gainst all adverse winds may serve for fort.

32

So he that saileth in this world of pleasure,
Feeding on sweets, that never bit of th' sour,
That's full of friends, of honor, and of treasure,

[12]Transformation.

Fond fool, he takes this earth ev'n for heav'n's bower.
But sad affliction comes and makes him see
Here's neither honour, wealth, nor safety;
Only above is found all with security.

33

O Time the fatal wrack of mortal things,
That draws oblivion's curtains over kings;
Their sumptuous monuments, men know them not,
Their names without a record are forgot,
Their parts, their ports, their pomp's all laid in th' dust[13]
Nor wit nor gold, nor buildings scape times rust;
But he whose name is graved in the white stone[14]
Shall last and shine when all of these are gone.

1678

The Flesh and the Spirit

In secret place where once I stood
Close by by the banks of Lacrim[1] flood,
I heard two sisters reason on
Things that are past and things to come;
One flesh was called, who had her eye
On wordly wealth and vanity;
The other Spirit, who did rear
Her thoughts unto a higher sphere:
Sister, quoth Flesh, what liv'st thou on,
Nothing but meditation?
Doth contemplation feed thee so
Regardlessly to let earth go?
Can speculation satisfy
Notion[2] without reality?
Dost dream of things beyond the moon,
And dost thou hope to dwell there soon?
Hast treasures there laid up in store

[13]That is, the features of former times, vain monuments and places of refuge, are all gone.

[14]"To him that overcometh, will I give to eat of the hidden manna, and will give him a white stone, and in the stone a new name written, which no man knoweth saving him that receiveth it" (Revelation 2:17).

[1]*Lacrima,* in Latin, means "tear."

[2]Knowledge, from the Latin, *notio.*

That all in th' world thou count'st but poor?
Art fancy sick, or turned a sot
To catch at shadows which are not?
Come, come, I'll show unto thy sense,
Industry hath its recompense.
What canst desire, but thou may'st see
True substance in variety?
Dost honor like? Acquire the same,
As some to their immortal fame,
And trophies to thy name erect
Which wearing time shall ne'er deject.
For riches doth thou long full sore?
Behold enough of precious store.
Earth hath more silver, pearls, and gold,
Than eyes can see or hands can hold.
Affect's thou pleasure? Take thy fill,
Earth hath enough of what you will.
Then let not go, what thou may'st find
For things unknown, only in mind.

Spirit: Be still thou unregenerate[3] part,
Disturb no more my settled heart,
For I have vowed (and so will do)
Thee as a foe still to pursue.
And combat with thee will and must,
Until I see thee laid in th' dust.
Sisters we are, yea, twins we be,
Yet deadly feud 'twixt thee and me;
For from one father are we not,
Thou by old Adam wast begot.
But my arise is from above,
Whence my dear Father I do love.
Thou speak'st me fair, but hat'st me sore,
Thy flatt'ring shows I'll trust no more,
How oft thy slave, hast thou me made,
When I believed what thou hast said,
And never had more cause of woe
Than when I did what thou bad'st do.
I'll stop mine ears at these thy charms,
And count them for my deadly harms.
Thy sinful pleasures I do hate,
Thy riches are to me no bait,
Thine honors do, nor will I love;
For my ambition lies above.
My greatest honor it shall be

[3]Not "saved," unrepentant.

When I am victor over thee,
And triumph shall with laurel head,
When thou my captive shalt be led,
How I do live, thou need'st not scoff,
For I have meat thou know'st not of;[4]
The hidden manna[5] I do eat,
The word of life it is my meat.
My thoughts do yield me more content
Than can thy hours in pleasure spent.
Nor are they shadows which I catch,
Nor fancies vain at which I snatch,
But reach at things that are so high,
Beyond thy dull capacity;
Eternal substance I do see,
With which enriched I would be.
Mine eye doth pierce the heavens and see
What is invisible to thee.
My garments are not silk nor gold,
Nor such like trash which earth doth hold,
But royal robes I shall have on,
More glorious than the glist'ring sun;
My crown not diamonds, pearls, and gold,
But such as angels' heads enfold.
The city where I hope to dwell,[6]
There's none on earth can parallel;
The stately walls both high and strong,
Are made of precious jasper stone;
The gates of pearl, both rich and clear,
And angels are for porters there;
The streets thereof transparent gold,
Such as no eye did e'er behold;
A crystal river there doth run,
Which doth proceed from the Lamb's throne.
Of life, there are the waters sure,
Which shall remain forever pure,
Nor sun, nor moon, they have no need,
For glory doth from God proceed.
No candle there, nor yet torchlight,
For there shall be no darksome night.
From sickness and infirmity
For evermore they shall be free;
Nor withering age shall e'er come there,

[4]See John 4:32.

[5]The Israelites miraculously received manna, or food from heaven, when they were in the wilderness (Exodus 16:15). Mystical "hidden manna" is promised in Revelation 2:17.

[6]The heavenly city of the New Jerusalem is described in lines 85 to 106; they are based on Revelation 21:10–27 and 22:1–5.

But beauty shall be bright and clear;
This city pure is not for thee,
For things unclean there shall not be.
If I of heaven may have my fill,
Take thou the world and all that will.

1678

Before the Birth of One of Her Children

All things within this fading world hath end,
Adversity doth still our joys attend;
No ties so strong, no friends so dear and sweet,
But with death's parting blow is sure to meet.
The sentence past is most irrevocable,
A common thing, yet oh inevitable;
How soon, my dear, death may my steps attend,
How soon't may be thy lot to lose thy friend,
We both are ignorant, yet love bids me
These farewell lines to recommend to thee,
That when that knot's untied that made us one,
I may seem thine, who in effect am none.
And if I see not half my days that's due,
What nature would, God grant to yours and you;
The many faults that well you know I have,
Let be interr'd in my oblivion's grave;
If any worth or virtue were in me,
Let that live freshly in thy memory,
And when thou feel'st no grief, as I no harms,
Yet love thy dead, who long lay in thine arms:
And when thy loss shall be repaid with gains,
Look to my little babes, my dear remains.
And if thou love thy self, or loved'st me,
These O protect from step-dame's injury.[1]
And if chance to thine eyes shall bring this verse,
With some sad sighs honor my absent hearse;
And kiss the paper for thy love's dear sake,
Who with salt tears this last farewell did take.

1678

[1]Bradstreet alludes to tales of evil stepmothers.

To My Dear and Loving Husband

If ever two were one, then surely we.
If ever man were loved by wife, then thee;
If ever wife was happy in a man,
Compare with me, ye women, if you can.
I prize thy love more than whole mines of gold
Or all the riches that the East doth hold.
My love is such that rivers cannot quench,
Nor ought but love from thee, give recompense.
Thy love is such I can no way repay,
The heavens reward thee manifold, I pray.
Then while we live, in love let's so persevere
That when we live no more, we may live ever.

1678

A Letter to Her Husband, Absent Upon Public Employment

My head, my heart, mine eyes, my life, nay more,
My joy, my magazine[1] of earthly store,
If two be one, as surely thou and I,
How stayest thou there, whilst I at Ipswich[2] lie?
So many steps, head from the heart to sever,
If but a neck, soon should we be together:
I, like the earth this season, mourn in black,
My sun is gone so far in's zodiac,
Whom whilst I 'joy'd, nor storms, nor frosts I felt,
His warmth such frigid colds did cause to melt.
My chilled limbs now numbed lie forlorn;
Return, return sweet Sol from Capricorn;[3]
In this dead time, alas, what can I more
Then view those fruits which through thy heat I bore?
Which sweet contentment yield me for a space,
True living pictures of their father's face.
O strange effect! now thou art southward gone,
I weary grow, the tedious day so long;
But when thou northward to me shalt return,

[1]Warehouse.
[2]Town north of Boston, Massachusetts.
[3]When Sol (the Sun) is in Capricorn (the tenth zodiacal sign), it is winter.

I wish my sun may never set, but burn
Within the Cancer[4] of my glowing breast,
The welcome house of him my dearest guest.
Where ever, ever stay, and go not thence,
Till nature's sad decree shall call thee hence;
Flesh of thy flesh, bone of thy bone,
I here, thou there, yet both but one.

1678

In Reference to Her Children, 23 June 1659[1]

I had eight birds hatcht in one nest,
Four cocks there were, and hens the rest,
I nurst them up with pain and care,
Nor cost, nor labor did I spare,
Till at the last they felt their wing,
Mounted the trees, and learn'd to sing;
Chief of the brood then took his flight,[2]
To regions far, and left me quite.
My mournful chirps I after send,
Till he return, or I do end:
Leave not thy nest, thy dam and sire,
Fly back and sing amidst this choir.
My second bird[3] did take her flight,
And with her mate flew out of sight;
Southward they both their course did bend,
And seasons twain they there did spend:
Till after blown by southern gales,
They norward steer'd with filled sails.
A prettier bird was no where seen,
Along the beach among the treen.
I have a third of color white,[4]
On whom I plac'd no small delight;

[4]When the sun is in Cancer (the fourth sign of the zodiac), it is summer.

[1]In manuscript this poem is dated 1656, yet Bradstreet's nineteenth-century editor, J. H. Ellis, notes that the poem refers to events that occurred after that date. The Hensley edition of Bradstreet's works places the poem in 1659, the date adopted here.

[2]Bradstreet's oldest son Samuel went to England in 1657 to study medicine and returned to Massachusetts in 1661.

[3]Bradstreet's daughter Dorothy married the Reverend Seaborn Cotton in 1654. They lived for a time in Wethersfield, Connecticut; in 1660 they moved to Hampton, New Hampshire.

[4]Bradstreet's daughter Sarah married Richard Hubbard of Ipswich.

Coupled with mate loving and true,
Hath also bid her dam adieu:
And where Aurora[5] first appears,
She now hath percht to spend her years;
One[6] to the academy flew
To chat among that learned crew:
Ambition moves still in his breast
That he might chant above the rest,
Striving for more than to do well,
That nightingales he might excel.
My fifth,[7] whose down is yet scarce gone,
Is 'mongst the shrubs and bushes flown,
And as his wings increase in strength,
On higher boughs he'll perch at length.
My other three,[8] still with me nest,
Until they're grown, then as the rest,
Or here or there, they'll take their flight,
As is ordain'd, so shall they light.
If birds could weep, then would my tears
Let others know what are my fears
Lest this my brood some harm should catch,
And be surpris'd for want of watch,
Whilst pecking corn, and void of care
They fall un'wares in fowler's[9] snare:
Or whilst on trees they sit and sing,
Some untoward boy at them do fling:
Or whilst allur'd with bell and glass,
The net be spread, and caught, alas.
Or least by lime-twigs they be foil'd,[10]
Or by some greedy hawks be spoil'd.
O would my young, ye saw my breast,
And knew what thoughts there sadly rest,
Great was my pain when I you bred,
Great was my care when I you fed,
Long did I keep you soft and warm,
And with my wings kept off all harm,
My cares are more, and fears than ever,
My throbs such now, as 'fore were never:
Alas my birds, you wisdom want,
Of perils you are ignorant,

[5]The Roman name for the female deity of the dawn.

[6]Bradstreet's son Simon graduated from Harvard College in 1660.

[7]Probably Bradstreet's son Dudley. Although he is the seventh rather than the fifth child, Dudley is the next son after Simon.

[8]Bradstreet's remaining three children were Hannah, Mercy, and John.

[9]Fowler is a term for bird-catcher.

[10]Branches of trees were coated with a sticky substance ("lime") that snared the birds that alighted on the branches.

Oft times in grass, on trees, in flight,
Sore accidents on you may light.
O to your safety have an eye,
So happy may you live and die:
Mean while my days in tunes I'll spend,
Till my weak lays[11] with me shall end.
In shady woods I'll sit and sing,
And things that past, to mind I'll bring.
Once young and pleasant, as are you,
But former toys (no joys) adieu.
My age I will not once lament,
But sing, my time so near is spent.
And from the top bough take my flight,
Into a country beyond sight,
Where old ones instantly grow young,
And there with seraphims[12] set song:
No seasons cold, nor storms they see,
But spring lasts to eternity.
When each of you shall in your nest
Among your young ones take your rest,
In chirping language, oft them tell,
You had a dam that lov'd you well,
That did what could be done for young,
And nurst you up till you were strong,
And 'fore she once would let you fly,
She show'd you joy and misery;
Taught what was good, and what was ill,
What would save life, and what would kill.
Thus gone, amongst you I may live,
And dead, yet speak, and counsel give:
Farewell, my birds, farewell adieu,
I happy am, if well with you.

1678

In Memory of My Dear Grandchild Elizabeth Bradstreet, Who Deceased August, 1665, Being a Year and Half Old

Farewell dear babe, my heart's too much content,
Farewell sweet babe, the pleasure of mine eye,
Farewell fair flower that for a space was lent,

[11]Poems or songs.

[12]Winged angels.

Then ta'en away unto eternity.
Blest babe, why should I once bewail thy fate,
Or sigh thy days so soon were terminate,
Sith thou art settled in an everlasting state.

2

By nature trees do rot when they are grown,
And plums and apples thoroughly ripe do fall,
And corn and grass are in their season mown,
And time brings down what is both strong and tall.
But plants new set to be eradicate,
And buds new blown to have so short a date,
Is by His hand alone that guides nature and fate.

1678

On My Dear Grandchild Simon Bradstreet, Who Died on 16 November, 1669, being but a Month, and One Day Old

No sooner came, but gone, and fall'n asleep,
Acquaintance short, yet parting caused us weep;
Three flowers, two scarcely blown, the last i' th' bud,
Cropt by th' Almighty's hand; yet is He good.
With dreadful awe before Him let's be mute,
Such was His will, but why, let's not dispute,
With humble hearts and mouths put in the dust,
Let's say He's merciful as well as just.
He will return and make up all our losses,
And smile again after our bitter crosses
Go pretty babe, go rest with sisters twain;
Among the blest in endless joys remain.

1678

Upon the Burning of Our House July 10th, 1666

In silent night when rest I took
For sorrow near I did not look
I wakened was with thund'ring noise
And piteous shrieks of dreadful voice.
That fearful sound of "Fire!" and "Fire!"
Let no man know is my desire.
I, starting up, the light did spy,
And to my God my heart did cry
To strengthen me in my distress
And not to leave me succorless.
Then, coming out, beheld a space
The flame consume my dwelling place.
And when I could no longer look,
I blest His name that gave and took,
That laid my goods now in the dust.
Yea, so it was, and so 'twas just.
It was His own, it was not mine,
Far be it that I should repine;
He might of all justly bereft
But yet sufficient for us left.
When by the ruins oft I past
My sorrowing eyes aside did cast,
And here and there the places spy
Where oft I sat and long did lie:
Here stood that trunk, and there that chest,
There lay that store I counted best.
My pleasant things in ashes lie,
And them behold no more shall I.
Under thy roof no guest shall sit,
Nor at thy table eat a bit.
No pleasant tale shall e'er be told,
Nor things recounted done of old.
No candle e'er shall shine in thee,
Nor bridegroom's voice e'er heard shall be.
In silence ever shall thou lie,
Adieu, Adieu, all's vanity.
Then straight I 'gin my heart to chide,
And did thy wealth on earth abide?
Didst fix thy hope on mold'ring dust?
The arm of flesh didst make thy trust?
Raise up thy thoughts above the sky
That dunghill mists away may fly.

Thou hast an house on high erect,
Framed by that mighty Architect,
With glory richly furnished,
Stands permanent though this be fled.
It's purchased and paid for too
By Him who hath enough to do.
A price so vast as is unknown
Yet by His gift is made thine own;
There's wealth enough, I need no more,
Farewell, my pelf, farewell my store.
The world no longer let me love,
My hope and treasure lies above.

1666

To My Dear Children

This book by any yet unread,
I leave for you when I am dead,
That being gone, here you may find
What was your living mother's mind.
Make use of what I leave in love,
And God shall bless you from above.

My dear children,

I, knowing by experience that the exhortations of parents take most effect when the speakers leave to speak, and those especially sink deepest which are spoke latest, and being ignorant whether on my death bed I shall have opportunity to speak to any of you, much less to all, thought it the best, whilst I was able, to compose some short matters (for what else to call them I know not) and bequeath to you, that when I am no more with you, yet I may be daily in your remembrance (although that is the least in my aim in what I now do), but that you may gain some spiritual advantage by my experience. I have not studied in this you read to show my skill, but to declare the truth, not to set forth myself, but the glory of God. If I had minded the former, it had been perhaps better pleasing to you, but seeing the last is the best, let it be best pleasing to you.

The method I will observe shall be this: I will begin with God's dealing with me from my childhood to this day.

In my young years, about 6 or 7 as I take it, I began to make conscience of my ways, and what I knew was sinful, as lying, disobedience to parents, etc., I avoided it. If at any time I was overtaken with the like evils, it was as a great trouble, and I could not be at rest 'till by prayer I had confessed it unto God. I was also troubled at the neglect of private duties though too often tardy that way. I also found much comfort in reading the Scriptures, especially those places I thought most concerned my condition, and as I grew to have more understanding, so the more solace I took in them.

In a long fit of sickness which I had on my bed I often communed with my heart and made my supplication to the most High who set me free from that affliction.

But as I grew up to be about 14 or 15, I found my heart more carnal, and sitting loose from God, vanity and the follies of youth take hold of me.

About 16, the Lord laid His hand sore upon me and smote me with the smallpox. When I was in my affliction, I besought the Lord and confessed my pride and vanity, and He was entreated of me and again restored me. But I rendered not to Him according to the benefit received.

After a short time I changed my condition and was married, and came into this country, where I found a new world and new manners, at which my heart rose. But after I was convinced it was the way of God, I submitted to it and joined to the church at Boston.

After some time I fell into a lingering sickness like a consumption together with a lameness, which correction I saw the Lord sent to humble and try me and do me good, and it was not altogether ineffectual.

It pleased God to keep me a long time without a child, which was a great grief to me and cost me many prayers and tears before I obtained one, and after him gave me many more of whom I now take the care, that as I have brought you into the world, and with great pains, weakness, cares, and fears brought you to this, I now travail in birth again of you till Christ be formed in you.

Among all my experiences of God's gracious dealings with me, I have constantly observed this, that He hath never suffered me long to sit loose from Him, but by one affliction or other hath made me look home, and search what was amiss; so usually thus it hath been with me that I have no sooner felt my heart out of order, but I have expected correction for it, which most commonly hath been upon my own person in sickness, weakness, pains, sometimes on my soul, in doubts and fears of God's displeasure and my sincerity towards Him; sometimes He hath smote a child with a sickness, sometimes chastened by losses in estate, and these times (through His great mercy) have been the times of my greatest getting and advantage; yea, I have found them the times when the Lord hath manifested the most love to me. Then have I gone to searching and have said with David, "Lord, search me and try me, see what ways of wickedness are in me, and lead me in the way everlasting," and seldom or never but I have found either some sin I lay under which God would have reformed, or some duty neglected which He would have performed, and by His help I have laid vows and bonds upon my soul to perform his righteous commands.

If at any time you are chastened of God, take it as thankfully and joyfully as in greatest mercies, for if ye be His, ye shall reap the greatest benefit by it. It hath been no small support to me in times of darkness when the Almighty hath hid His face from me that yet I have had abundance of sweetness and refreshment after affliction and more circumspection in my walking after I have been afflicted. I have been with God like an untoward child, that no longer than the rod has been on my back (or at least in sight) but I have been apt to forget Him and myself, too. Before I was afflicted, I went astray, but now I keep Thy statutes.

I have had great experience of God's hearing my prayers and returning comfortable answers to me, either in granting the thing I prayed for, or else in satisfying my mind without it, and I have been confident it hath been from Him, because I have found my heart through His goodness enlarged in thankfulness to Him.

I have often been perplexed that I have not found that constant joy in my pilgrimage and refreshing which I supposed most of the servants of God have, although He hath not left me altogether without the witness of His holy spirit, who hath oft given me His word and set to His seal that it shall be well with me. I have sometimes tasted of that hidden manna that the world knows not, and have set up my Ebenezer, and have resolved with myself that against such a promise, such tastes of sweetness, the gates of hell shall never prevail; yet have I many times sinkings and droopings, and not enjoyed that felicity that sometimes I have done. But when I have been in darkness and seen no light, yet have I desired to stay myself upon the Lord, and when I have been in sickness and pain, I have thought if the Lord would but lift up the light of His countenance upon me, although He ground me to powder, it would be but light to me; yea, oft have I thought were I in hell itself and could there find the love of God toward me, it would be a heaven. And could I have been in heaven without the love of God, it would have been a hell to me, for in truth it is the absence and presence of God that makes heaven or hell.

Many times hath Satan troubled me concerning the verity of the Scriptures, many times by atheism how I could know whether there was a God; I never saw any miracles to confirm me, and those which I read of, how did I know but they were feigned? That there is a God my reason would soon tell me by the wondrous works that I see, the vast frame of the heaven and the earth, the order of all things, night and day, summer and winter, spring and autumn, the daily providing for this great household upon the earth, the preserving and directing of all to its proper end. The consideration of these things would with amazement certainly resolve me that there is an Eternal Being. But how should I know He is such a God as I worship in Trinity, and such a Saviour as I rely upon? Though this hath thousands of times been suggested to me, yet God hath helped me over. I have argued thus with myself. That there is a God, I see. If ever this God hath revealed himself, it must be in His word, and this must be it or none. Have I not found that operation by it that no human invention can work upon the soul, hath not judgments befallen divers who have scorned and contemned it, hath it not been preserved through all ages maugre all the heathen tyrants and all of the enemies who have opposed it? Is there any story but that which shows the beginnings of times, and how the world came to be as we see? Do we not know the prophecies in it fulfilled which could not have been so long foretold by any but God Himself?

When I have got over this block, then have I another put in my way, that admit this be the true God whom we worship, and that be his word, yet why may not the Popish religion be the right? They have the same God, the same Christ, the same word. They only enterpret it one way, we another.

This hath sometimes stuck with me, and more it would, but the vain fooleries that are in their religion together with their lying miracles and cruel persecutions of the saints, which admit were they as they term them, yet not so to be dealt withal.

The consideration of these things and many the like would soon turn me to my own religion again.

But some new troubles I have had since the world has been filled with blasphemy and sectaries, and some who have been accounted sincere Christians have been carried away with them, that sometimes I have said, "Is there faith upon the earth?" and I have not known what to think; but then I have remembered the works of Christ that so it must be, and if it were possible, the very elect should be deceived. "Behold," saith our Saviour, "I have told you before." That hath stayed my heart, and I can now say, "Return, O my Soul, to thy rest, upon this rock Christ Jesus will I build my faith, and if I perish, I perish"; but I know all the Powers of Hell shall never prevail against it. I know whom I have trusted, and whom I have believed, and that He is able to keep that I have committed to His charge.

Now to the King, immortal, eternal and invisible, the only wise God, be honour, and glory for ever and ever, Amen.

This was written in much sickness and weakness, and is very weakly and imperfectly done, but if you can pick any benefit out of it, it is the mark which I aimed at.

1867

Michael Wigglesworth 1631–1705

Michael Wigglesworth, born in England, emigrated to New England with his family when he was seven. Raised in New Haven, Connecticut, he trained for the ministry at Harvard, graduated in 1651, and stayed on as a tutor. Wigglesworth excelled in the classics and was chosen to deliver one of the Harvard commencement addresses; appropriate to his future as New England's most famous poet, he spoke on the uses of eloquence. Ordained as minister at Malden, Massachusetts, in 1656, he became the very model of the "faithful man," as Cotton Mather would later call him.

For many years chronic ill health kept Wigglesworth from performing his ministerial duties, and he turned to poetry as a means of spreading and defending the Puritan faith. He could hardly have been more successful. *The Day of Doom,* his thundering epic on the Judgment Day, was early America's best-selling poem. It has been estimated that when it first appeared in 1662, one copy existed for every twenty-five to thirty-five New Englanders. Frequently reprinted on both sides of the Atlantic, *The Day of Doom* made the poet a household name among the Puritan faithful. Edward Taylor's first wife, Elizabeth Fitch, memorized portions of it, and Jonathan Mitchell, pastor at Cambridge, praised Wigglesworth for fulfilling the highest goal of Puritan poetry: "To set forth Truth and win men's Souls to bliss." At Wigglesworth's death in 1705, Cotton Mather attested to his skill in providing for "the Edification of such Readers, as are for Truth's dressed up in a *Plaine Meeter.*"

Mather's comment explains the immense popularity of *The Day of Doom.* Its 224 stanzas of ballad meter present, largely through a debate between sinners and Christ, the chief tenets of Puritan theology. Many Puritans used the poem as a verse catechism, reading it to their children and committing it to memory as a vivid guide to the complexities of the faith. Its dramatic confrontations between Christ and the sinners, the unflattering portrayal of sin, the relentless rhythms, and the heavy dependence on scripture (complete with Bible references in the margins), made it ideal for teaching the faith to the uninitiated or for rekindling it in the hearts of more experienced believers. Wigglesworth's other book of verse, *Meat Out of the Eater* (1670), spoke more directly to the afflictions and rewards of the individual soul. The title poem spelled out the value of worldly suffering as a prelude to heavenly joy. A second part of the collection, *Riddles Unriddled,* extended the theme by exploring various paradoxes of the faith. As in *The Day of Doom,* Wigglesworth's message was that such perplexing "riddles" would resolve themselves not through human logic, but through simple, heartfelt belief.

A third work, "God's Controversy with New-England," was written the year *The Day of Doom* appeared but was not published until the nineteenth century. "God's Controversy" applied the themes of the doomsday epic to the here-and-now of New England. Both poems reflect the widespread perception, among the ministers, of a crisis endangering the Puritan mission. Most of the founding settlers had died; New England was rapidly becoming a more diverse and secular society; the Puritan experiment with political rule in Old England had recently ended with the Restoration of the monarchy; and a severe drought had struck New England—all of which seemed to signal God's disfavor. Like Jeremiah weeping for the sins of backsliders, many ministers railed, in sermons as well as in verse, against what they saw as the lukewarm zeal of New England.

The most successful poetic "jeremiads" of early New England, Wigglesworth's poems provide special insight into Puritan popular art. His broad audience and all-encompassing themes resulted in poetry as different from Edward Taylor's *Preparatory Meditations* and Anne Bradstreet's *Tenth Muse* as a fast-paced feature article is from a reflective personal essay. Puritan readers, born into a culture obsessed with theology and Biblical interpretation, found his poetry entertaining as well as instructive: their appreciation of his poems might well compare with our enjoyment of a Gothic novel or a disaster film.

The following selections from *The Day of Doom* include Wigglesworth's opening description of the Second Coming, a portion of the debate, the sinners' reaction to Christ's arguments and their sentencing to hell, and the final joy of the elect. Although the poem derives much of its power from its overall pace and structure, these scenes convey something of Wigglesworth's skill in shaping the nuances of theology into vivid, tightly compressed narratives.

Jeffrey A. Hammond
St. Mary's College of Maryland

PRIMARY WORKS

The Day of Doom, 1662; *Meat Out of the Eater,* 1670, 1717; "God's Controversy with New-England," 1873; *The Diary of Michael Wigglesworth 1653–1657: The Conscience of a Puritan,* ed. Edmund S. Morgan, 1946, rpt. 1965; *The Poems of Michael Wigglesworth,* ed. Ronald A. Bosco, 1989.

SECONDARY WORKS

Richard Crowder, *No Featherbed to Heaven: A Biography of Michael Wigglesworth, 1631–1705,* 1962; Robert Daly, *God's Altar: The World and the Flesh in Puritan Poetry,* 1978; Alan H. Pope, "Petrus Ramus and Michael Wigglesworth: The Logic of Poetic Structure," in *Puritan Poets and Poetics: Seventeenth-Century American Poetry in Theory and Practice,* ed. Peter White, 1985; Jeffrey A. Hammond, *Sinful Self, Saintly Self: The Puritan Experience of Poetry,* 1993.

from The Day of Doom[1]

1

The Security of the World before Christ's coming to Judgment. Luke 12: 19

Still was the night, Serene and Bright,
when all Men sleeping lay;
Calm was the season, and carnal reason
thought so 'twould last for ay.[2]
Soul, take thine ease, let sorrow cease,
much good thou hast in store:
This was their Song, their Cups among,
the Evening before.

2

Wallowing in all kind of sin,
vile wretches lay secure:[3]
The best of men had scarcely then
their Lamps kept in good ure.[4]
Virgins unwise, who through disguise
amongst the best were number'd,
Had clos'd their eyes; yea, and the wise
through sloth and frailty slumber'd.

Matt. 25: 5

3

Like as of old, when Men grow bold
God's threatnings to contemn,
Who stopt their Ear, and would not hear,
when Mercy warned them:
But took their course, without remorse,
till God began to powre
Destruction the World upon
in a tempestuous showre.

Matt. 24: 37, 38

4

They put away the evil day,
and drown'd their care and fears,
Till drown'd were they, and swept away

[1]The text is adapted from Ronald Bosco, ed., *The Poems of Michael Wigglesworth.*
[2]Forever.
[3]Careless, unconcerned.
[4]Use, condition.

by vengeance unawares:
I Thess. 5: 3
So at the last, whilst Men sleep fast
in their security,
Surpriz'd they are in such a snare
as cometh suddenly.

5

The Suddenness, Majesty, and Terror of Christ's appearing. Matt. 25: 6 II Pet. 3: 10

For at midnight brake forth a Light,
which turn'd the night to day,
And speedily an hideous cry
did all the world dismay.
Sinners awake, their hearts do ake,
trembling their loynes suprizeth;
Amaz'd with fear, by what they hear,
each one of them ariseth.

6

They rush from Beds with giddy heads,
and to their windows run,
Viewing this light, which shines more bright
Matt. 24: 29, 30
then doth the Noon-day Sun.
Straightway appears (they see't with tears)
the Son of God most dread;
Who with his Train comes on amain
To Judge both Quick and Dead.

. . .

130

Others plead for Pardon both from God's mercy and justice. Ps. 78: 38

Others Argue, and not a few,
is not God gracious?
His Equity and Clemency
are they not marvellous?
Thus we believ'd; are we deceiv'd?
cannot his mercy great,
(As hath been told to us of old)
asswage his angers heat?

131

II Kings 14: 26
How can it be that God should see
his Creatures endless pain,

Or hear the groans and rueful moans,
   and still his wrath retain?
Can it agree with Equitie?
   can mercy have the heart
To recompence few years offence
   with Everlasting smart?

132

Can God delight in such a sight
   as sinners misery?
Or what great good can this our blood
   bring unto the most High?
Ps. 30: 9
Mic. 7: 18
Oh, thou that dost thy Glory most
   in pard'ning sin display!
Lord, might it please thee to release,
   and pardon us this day?

133

Unto thy Name more glorious fame
   would not such mercy bring?
Would not it raise thine endless praise,
   more than our suffering?
With that they cease, holding their peace,
   but cease not still to weep;
Grief ministers a flood of tears,
   in which their words to steep.

134

But all too late, grief's out of date,
   when life is at an end.
The glorious King thus answering,
   all to his voice attend:
They answered.
God gracious is, quoth he, like his
   no mercy can be found;
His Equity and Clemency
   to sinners do abound.

135

Mercy that now shines forth in the vessels of Mercy.
Mic. 7: 18
Rom. 9: 23

As may appear by those that here
are plac'd at my right hand;[5]
Whose stripes I bore, and clear'd the score,
that they might quitted[6] stand.
For surely none, but God alone,
whose Grace transcends mens thought,
For such as those that were his foes
like wonders would have wrought.

136

Did also long wait upon such as abused it.
Rom. 2: 4
Hos. 11: 4

And none but he such lenitee[7]
and patience would have shown
To you so long, who did him wrong,
and pull'd his judgments down.
How long a space[8] (O stiff neck'd race)
did patience you afford?
How oft did love you gently move,
to turn unto the Lord?

137

Luke 13: 34
The day of Grace now past.

With Cords of love God often strove
your stubborn hearts to tame:
Nevertheless your wickedness,
did still resist the same.
If now at last Mercy be past
from you for evermore,
And Justice come in Mercies room,
yet grudge you not therefore.

138

Luke 19: 42, 43
Jude 4

If into wrath God turned hath
his long long suffering,
And now for love you vengeance prove,[9]
it is an equal[10] thing.

[5]See Matthew 25:33: "And he shall set the sheep on his right hand, but the goats on the left."
[6]Acquitted.
[7]Mercy.
[8]Time.
[9]Feel, experience.
[10]Just, fair.

Your waxing worse, hath stopt the course
 of wonted[11] Clemency:
Mercy refus'd, and Grace misus'd,
 call for severity.

139

Rom. 2: 5, 6
Isa. 1: 24
Amos 2: 13
Gen. 18: 25

It's now high time that ev'ry Crime
 be brought to punishment:
Wrath long contain'd, and oft restrain'd,
 at last must have a vent:
Justice severe cannot forbear
 to plague sin any longer,
But must inflict with hand most strict
 mischief upon the wronger.

140

Matt. 25: 3, 11, 12
Prov. 1: 28, 29, 30

In vain do they for Mercy pray,
 the season being past,
Who had no care to get a share
 therein, while time did last.
The man whose ear refus'd to hear
 the voice of Wisdoms cry,
Earn'd this reward, that none regard
 him in his misery.

141

Isa. 5: 18, 19
Gen. 2: 17
Rom. 2: 8, 9

It doth agree with equity,
 and with Gods holy Law,
That those should dye eternally
 that death upon them draw.
The Soul that sins damnation wins,
 for so the Law ordains;
Which Law is just, and therefore must
 such suffer endless pain.

[11]Customary, usual.

142

Rom. 6: 23
II Thess. 1: 8, 9

Eternal smart[12] is the desert,[13]
  ev'n of the least offence;
Then wonder not if I allot
  to you this Recompence:
But wonder more, that since so sore
  and lasting plagues are due
To every sin, you liv'd therein,
  who well the danger knew.

143

Ezek. 33: 11
Exod. 34: 7
and 14: 17
Rom. 9: 22

God hath no joy to crush or 'stroy,
  and ruine wretched wights,[14]
But to display the glorious Ray
  of Justice he delights.
To manifest he doth detest,
  and throughly hate all sin,
By plaguing it as is most fit,
  this shall him glory win.

. . .

187

Matt. 22: 12
Rom. 2: 5, 6
Luke 19: 42

Their mouths are shut, each man is put
  to silence and to shame:
Nor have they ought within their thought,
  Christ's Justice for to blame.
The Judge is just, and plague them must,
  nor will he mercy shew
(For Mercies day is past away)
  to any of this Crew.

188

Matt. 28: 18
Ps. 139: 7

The Judge is strong, doers of wrong
  cannot his power withstand:
None can by flight run out of sight,
  nor scape out of his hand.

[12]Pain.
[13]Reward.
[14]Souls.

Sad is their state: for Advocate
to plead their Cause there's none:
None to prevent their punishment,
or misery bemone.

189

Isa. 33: 14
Ps. 11: 6
Num. 23: 19

O dismal day! wither shall they
for help and succour flee?
To God above, with hopes to move
their greatest Enemee:
His wrath is great, whose burning heat
no floods of tears can slake:
His word stands fast, that they be cast
into the burning Lake.

. . .

201

The Judge pronounceth the Sentence of condemnation. Matt. 25: 41

Ye sinful wights, and cursed sprights,[15]
that work Iniquity,
Depart together from me for ever
to endless Misery;
Your portion take in yonder Lake,
where Fire and Brimstone flameth:
Suffer the smart, which your desert
as its due wages claimeth.

202

The terrour of it.

Oh piercing words more sharp than swords!
what, to depart from *Thee,*
Whose face before for evermore
the best of Pleasures be!
What? to depart (unto our smart)
from thee *Eternally:*
To be for aye banish'd away,
with *Devils* company!

[15]Spirits.

203

What? to be sent to *Punishment,*
and flames of *Burning Fire,*
To be surrounded, and eke confounded
with Gods *Revengful ire.*
What? to abide, not for a tide
these Torments, but for *Ever:*
To be released, or to be eased,
not after years, but *Never.*

204

Oh, *fearful Doom!* now there's no room
for hope or help at all:
Sentence is past which aye shall last,
Christ will not it recall.
There might you hear them rent and tear
the Air with their out-cries:
The hideous noise of their sad voice
ascendeth to the Skies.

205

Luke 13: 28

They wring their hands, their caitiff[16]-hands
and gnash their teeth for terrour;
They cry, they roar for anguish sore,
and gnaw their tongues for horrour.
But get away without delay,
Christ pitties not your cry:
Depart to Hell, there may you yell,
and roar Eternally.

Prov. 1: 26

. . .

219

The Saints rejoyce to see Judgment executed upon the wicked World. Ps. 58: 10 Rev. 19: 1, 2, 3

The Saints behold with courage bold,
and thankful wonderment,
To see all those that were their foes
thus sent to punishment:
Then do they sing unto their King
a Song of endless Praise:

[16]Captive, wretched.

They praise his Name, and do proclaim
that just are all his ways.

220

They ascend with Christ into Heaven triumphing. Matt. 25: 46 I John 3: 2 I Cor. 13: 12

Thus with great joy and melody
to Heav'n they all ascend,
Him there to praise with sweetest layes,[17]
and Hymns that never end:
Where with long Rest they shall be blest,
and nought shall them annoy:
Where they shall see as seen they be,
and whom they love enjoy.

221

Their Eternal happiness and incomparable Glory there.

O glorious Place! where face to face
Jehovah may be seen,
By such as were sinners whilere[18]
and no dark vail between.
Where the Sun shine, and light Divine,
of Gods bright Countenance,
Doth rest upon them every one,
with sweetest influence.

222

O blessed state of the Renate![19]
O wondrous Happiness,
To which they're brought, beyond what thought
can reach, or words express!
Rev. 21: 4
Griefs water-course, and sorrows sourse,
are turn'd to joyful streams,
Their old distress and heaviness
are vanished like dreams.

223

For God above in arms of love
doth dearly them embrace,

[17]Songs.
[18]Before.
[19]Reborn, elect.

Ps. 16: 11 And fills their sprights with such delights,
  and pleasures in his grace;
As shall not fail, nor yet grow stale
  through frequency of use:
Nor do they fear Gods favour there,
  to forfeit by abuse.

224

Heb. 12: 23 For there the Saints are perfect Saints,
  and holy ones indeed,
From all the sin that dwelt within
  their mortal bodies freed:
Made Kings and Priests to God through Christs
Rev. 1: 6 and 22: 5 dear loves transcendency,
There to remain, and there to reign
  with him Eternally.

1662

The Bay Psalm Book (1640)
The New England Primer (1683?)

The Bay Psalm Book and *The New England Primer* were, next to the Bible, the most commonly owned books in seventeenth-century New England. Together, they served to disseminate Puritan values for over a hundred years. Designed as inexpensive and easily portable, they addressed the Puritan concern for having personal faith reconfirmed in daily activity. They established the basic texts of Puritan culture, setting them to familiar hymn tunes and pictured alphabets, thus enabling singing, recitation, and memorization. These books made possible individual participation in the culture, but they also represent the authoritative disciplining of that individuality through culturally sanctioned texts and behavior.

In 1647, the Massachusetts courts warned against that "old deluder, Satan," who strove "to keep men from the knowledge of the Scriptures, . . . by keeping them in an unknown tongue." *The Bay Psalm Book* addressed this warning by translating the Hebrew psalms of David into idiomatic, metrical English to be sung by the entire congregation both in church and at home. *The New England Primer* offered every child ("and apprentice") the chance to learn to read the catechism and a set of moral precepts. Both books insisted on the cultural and religious importance of reading in the vernacular instead of in a language available only to university-trained clergy. The 1647 court hoped that "learning may not be buried in the grave of the fathers in the church and commonwealth."

The Bay Psalm Book was the collaborative project of over twelve leading Puritan divines and the first publishing venture of the Massachusetts colony. The 1700 copies of the first edition provided Puritans with "a plain and familiar translation" designed to represent more "faithfully" the

Hebrew psalms than did the version used by the Pilgrims of neighboring Plymouth. As John Cotton wrote in 1643, the translation was "as near the original as we could express it in our English tongue." In his preface, Cotton defended the Puritans' version as attending to "Conscience rather than Elegance, fidelity rather than poetry": "If therefore the verses are not always so smooth and elegant as some may desire or expect; let them consider that God's Altar needs not our polishings." Often printed in England and Scotland as well as in the colonies, the psalter went through over fifty editions in the next century. Revised by Richard Lyon and Henry Dunster (the first president of Harvard) in 1651, and three more times in the 1700s (once by Cotton Mather), *The Bay Psalm Book* was widely used until it was supplanted in the eighteenth century by psalters written by Nahum Tate and Nicholas Brady (1696), by Isaac Watts (1719), and by John and Charles Wesley (1737). Psalm singing continued to be considered an important means by which the general population could learn the cultural text through the eighteenth century and into the nineteenth century. Emerson, describing the singing of the psalms during the 1835 bicentennial celebration of Concord, spoke with a kind of reverence about the psalm singing: "It was a noble ancient strain, & had the more effect from being 'deaconed' out, a line at a time, after the fashion of our grandfathers, & sung by the whole congregation."

The New England Primer, which is estimated to have sold five million copies of its various versions from 1683 to 1830, offered the Puritan child literacy and religious training combined. By means of an illustrated alphabet, moral sentences, poems, and a formal catechism (either the Westminster Assembly's "Shorter Catechism" or John Cotton's "Spiritual Milk for Babes"), the child was to be "both instructed in his Duty, and encouraged in his Learning." The book was the practical outgrowth of the colony's insistence on the importance of widespread literacy as a means for salvation and civic order. A 1642 law required town leaders to inquire into the training of children, "especially their ability to read and understand the principles of Religion and the Capital laws of the country." The Primer's exemplary poem by the martyred John Rogers exhorts children to treasure the "little Book" of their father's words, to "Lay up [God's] Laws within your heart, and print them in your thought." The young readers of the Primer, like Rogers's children, were not just the "Heirs of earthly Things"; they were expected to inherit and preserve the cultural and religious values of the community, to be responsible for "that part,/ which never shall decay" as long as each generation learned the words and creeds, the promises and definitions upon which Puritan culture was based.

Both the *Psalm Book* and the *Primer* are evolving texts, whose frequent revisions show their valued yet contested status as cultural transmissions. They are the product neither of a single author nor of one historical period, but embody the changing values of a changing society and show the influence of new events and situations, of variation in language and literary taste. Although both books clearly advance a dominant ideology, insisting on specific religious beliefs and moral precepts, they also show concern for making creeds responsive to the particular historical circumstances of the colonists. The preface to the *Psalm Book* warns against mere imitation of ancient poetry, advocating instead that "every nation without scruple might follow . . . their own country poetry." The *Psalm Book* was revised to satisfy the desire for "a little more Art," in reaction to changing practices of church singing and under the influence of neoclassical and Latin poetry. The introduction to the 1752 revision justified changes because "the Flux of Languages has rendered several Phrases in it obsolete, and the Mode of Expression in various Places less acceptable." The 1758 revision sought to elevate "diminutive Terms" into "more grand and noble Words" (changing, for example, "Hills" to "Mountains," "Floods" to "Seas") and to match diction more closely with mood ("for *grand Ideas,* I seek the *most majestick Words;* for *tender Sentiments,* the *softest Words*").

The *Primer* proved even more chameleon, as it was adapted to different geographical areas (e.g., *The Albany Primer, The Pennsylvania Primer*) and to different ethnic groups (an Indian Primer of 1781 was a dual-language text, designed for Mohawk children "to acquire the spelling and reading of their own: As well as to get acquainted with the English Tongue, which for that purpose is put on the opposite page"). Although certain sections of the primer were regularly retained (especially the catechism, the pictured alphabet, and John Rogers's poem), revisions over time show the influence of events (the American Revolution, the evangelical movement of the 1800s) and changes in attitudes (the softening of attitudes toward punishment and sin, the move toward more secularized moral education), as well as changes in children's literature. In later, more secularized versions, naughty children are threatened not with tempests and the consuming fire, but with losing "Oranges, Apples, Cakes, or Nuts," and the grim poem of the martyr is printed in uneasy conjunction with Isaac Watts's soothing "Cradle Song." The value of literacy as a route to eternal salvation becomes, in a 1790 English revision, the promise of economic advancement. An 1800 version even replaces the trademark illustrated alphabet with a milder verse, "A was an apple-pie." Thus the *Psalm Book* and the *Primer,* in their multiple versions, both chronicle and foster historical change. They are central texts of Puritan culture, and they mark the subsequent transformations and uses of that culture.

Jean Ferguson Carr
University of Pittsburgh

PRIMARY WORKS

John Cotton, John Wilson, Peter Bulkely, and others, *The Whole Booke of Psalms Faithfully Translated into English Metre,* known as *The Bay Psalm Book,* 1640; revised 1651, 1718, 1752, 1758; reprint 1862; facsimile reprint 1903, 1956. *The New England Primer* or *Milk for Babes,* 1683?; *The New England Primer Enlarged,* 1687; facsimile reprint of the earliest extant edition (1727) 1897, 1962; Denise D. Knight, ed. *Cotton Mather's Verse in English,* 1989.

SECONDARY WORKS

Paul Ford, ed., *The New England Primer,* facsimile of 1727 edition with historical essay, 1897, rpt., 1962; Clifton Johnson, *Old-Time Schools and School-Books,* 1904, rpt. 1963; C. Heartman, *The New England Primer,* 1914, Second edition, R.R. Bowker, 1934; Zoltan Haraszti, *The Enigma of the Bay Psalm Book,* 1956; Maxine T. Turner, *A History of the Bay Psalm Book,* Diss., 1970.

from The Bay Psalm Book

from "The Preface" by John Cotton

The singing of Psalms, though it breathe forth nothing but holy harmony, and melody: yet such is the subtlety of the enemy, and the enmity of our nature against the Lord, and his wayes, that our hearts can find matter of discord in this harmony, and crotchets of division in this holy melody. . . . There have been three questions especially stirring concerning singing. First, what psalms are to be sung in churches? whether David's and other scripture psalms, or the psalms invented by the gifts of godly men in every age of the church. Secondly, if scripture psalms, whether in their own words, or in such meter as English poetry is wont to run in? Thirdly, by whom are they to be sung? whether by the whole churches together with their voices? or by one man singing alone and the rest joining in silence and in the close saying amen.

Touching the first, certainly the singing of David's psalms was an acceptable worship of God, not only in his own, but in succeeding times. . . . So that if the singing David's psalms be a moral duty and therefore perpetual; then we under the New Testament are bound to sing them as well as they under the Old; . . . [y]et we read that they are commanded to sing in the words of David and Asaph,[1] which were ordinarily to be used in the public worship of God: and we doubt not but those that are wise will easily see; that those set forms of psalms of God's own appointment not of man's conceived gift or humane imposition were sung in the Spirit by those holy Levites, as well as their prayers were in the spirit which themselves conceived, the Lord not then binding them therin to any set forms; and shall set forms of psalms appointed of God not be sung in the spirit now, which others did then?. . .

As for the scruple that some take at the translation of the book of psalms into meter, because David's psalms were sung in his own words without meter, we answer—First, there are many verses together in several psalms of David which run in rhythms . . . which shews at least the lawfulness of singing psalms in English rhythms.

Secondly, the psalms are penned in such verses as are suitable to the poetry of the Hebrew language, and not in the common style of such other books of the Old Testament as are not poetical; now no Protestant doubteth but that all the books of the scripture should by Gods ordinance be extant in the mother tongue of each nation, that they may be understood of all, hence the psalms are to be translated into our English tongue; and if in our English tongue we are to sing them, then as all our English songs (according to the course of our English poetry) do run in metre, so ought David's psalms to be translated into meter, that so we may sing the Lord's songs, as in our English tongue so in such verses as are familiar to an English ear. . . . [B]ut the truth is, as the Lord hath hid from us the Hebrew tunes, lest we should think our selves bound to imitate them, so also the course and frame (for the most

[1]Asaph, who composed several of the psalms, was the chief of the Levites, whom David appointed "to minister before the ark of the Lord, and to record, and to thank and praise the Lord God of Israel" (I Chronicles 16:4).

part) of their Hebrew poetry, that we might not think our selves bound to imitate that, but that every nation without scruple might follow as the graver sort of tunes of their own country songs, so the graver sort of verses of their own country poetry.

Neither let any think, that for the metre sake we have taken liberty or poetical license to depart from the true and proper sense of David's words in the Hebrew verses, no; but it hath been one part of our religious care and faithful endeavour, to keep close to the original text.

As for other objections taken from the difficulty of *Ainsworth's* tunes,[2] and the corruptions in our common psalm books,[3] we hope they are answered in this new edition of psalms which we here present to God and his Churches. For although we have cause to bless God in many respects for the religious endeavours of the translators of the psalms into metre usually annexed to our Bibles, yet it is not unknown to the godly learned that they have rather presented a paraphrase than the words of David translated according to the rule 2 *Chron.* 29, 30,[4] and that their addition to the words, detractions from the words are not seldom and rare, but very frequent and many times needless (which we suppose would not be approved of if the psalms were so translated into prose) and that their variations of the sense, and alterations of the sacred text too frequently, may justly minister matter of offence to them that are able to compare the translation with the text; of which failings, some judicious have oft complained, others have been grieved, whereupon it hath been generally desired, that as we do enjoy other, so (if it were the Lords will) we might enjoy this ordinance also in its native purity: we have therefore done our endeavour to make a plain and familiar translation of the psalms and words of David into English metre, and have not so much as presumed to paraphrase to give the sense of his meaning in other words; we have therefore attended herein as our chief guide the original, shunning all additions, except such as even the best translators of them in prose supply, avoiding all material detractions from words or sense. . . .

As for our translations, we have with our English Bibles[5] (to which next to the Original we have had respect) used the Idioms of our own tongue in stead of Hebraisms, lest they might seem English barbarisms. . .

If therefore the verses are not always so smoothe and elegant as some may desire or expect, let them consider that God's Altar needs not our polishings: Ex. 20.[6] for we have respected rather a plain translation, than to smooth our verses with the sweetnes of any paraphrase, and so have attended Conscience rather than Elegance, fidelity rather than poetry, in translating the Hebrew words into English language, and David's poetry into English metre; that so we may sing in Sion the Lord's songs of praise according to his own will; until he take us from hence, and wipe away all our tears, and bid us enter into our master's joy to sing eternal Hallelujahs.

1640

[2]Henry Ainsworth, minister of the English Church in Amsterdam, translated the psalms in 1612 and included "singing notes" in his book. His version of the psalms was used by the Plymouth Pilgrims.

[3]The Puritans objected to the influential Sternhold-Hopkins translation of 1562, which was attached to the Book of Common Prayer.

[4]"Moreover Hezekiah the king and the princes commanded the Levites to sing praise unto the Lord with the words of David, and of Asaph the seer" (II Chronicles 29:30).

[5]The Puritans used primarily the Geneva Bible (1560), although they made occasional reference to the King James version (1611).

[6]"An altar of earth thou shalt make unto me. . . . And if thou wilt make me an altar of stone, thou shalt not build it of hewn stone: for if thou lift up thy tool upon it, thou hast polluted it" (Exodus 20:24–25).

Psalm 1

O Blessed man, that in th'advice
  Of wicked doeth not walk:
Nor stand in sinners way, nor sit
  In chair of scornful folk.

But in the law of Jehovah
  Is his longing delight:
And in his law doth meditate,
  By day and eke by night.

And he shall be like to a tree
  Planted by water-rivers:
That in his season yields his fruit,
  And his leaf never withers.

And all he doth, shall prosper well,
  The wicked are not so:
But they are like unto the chaff,
  Which wind drives to and fro.

Therefore shall not ungodly men,
  Rise to stand in the doom,
Nor shall the sinners with the just,
  In their assembly come.

For of the righteous men, the Lord
  Acknowledgeth the way:
But the way of ungodly men,
  Shall utterly decay.

1640

Psalm 6

To the chief musician on Neginoth upon Sheminith, a psalm of David

Lord in thy wrath rebuke me not,
  nor in thy hot wrath chasten me.
Pity me Lord, for I am weak,
  Lord heal me, for my bones vexed be.
Also my soul is troubled sore:

how long Lord wilt thou me forsake?
Return O Lord, my soul release:
O save me for thy mercy's sake.
In death no mem'ry is of thee,
and who shall praise thee in the grave?
I faint with groans; all night my bed
swims; I with tears my couch washed have.
Mine eye with grief is dim and old:
because of all mine enemies.
But now depart away from me,
all ye that work iniquities:
For Jehovah ev'n now hath heard
the voice of these my weeping tears.
Jehovah hear my humble suit,
Jehovah doth receive my prayers,
Let all mine enemies be asham'd
and greatly troubled let them be;
Yea let them be returned back,
and be ashamed suddenly.

1640

Psalm 8

To the chief Musician upon Gittith, a psalm of David

O Lord our God in all the earth
How's thy name wondrous great—
Who hast thy glorious majesty
Above the heavens set.

Out of the mouth of sucking babes,
Thy strength thou didst ordain,
That thou mightst still the enemy,
And them that thee disdain.

When I thy fingers' work, thy Heav'ns,
The moon and stars consider
Which thou hast set: What's wretched man
That thou dost him remember?

Or what's the Son of man, that thus
Him visited thou hast?
For next to Angels, thou hast him
A little lower plac't,

And hast with glory crowned him,
And comely majesty:
And on thy works hast given him
Lordly authority.

All hast thou put under his feet,
All sheep and oxen, yea
And beasts of field. Fowls of the air,
And fishes of the sea,

And all that pass through paths of seas.
O Jehovah our Lord,
How wondrously magnificent
Is thy name through the world?

1640

Psalm 19

To the chief musician, a psalm of David

The heavens do declare
The majesty of God:
Also the firmament shows forth
His handiwork abroad.

Day speaks to day, knowledge
Night hath to night declar'd.
There neither speech nor language is,
Where their voice is not heard.

Through all the earth their line
Is gone forth, and unto
The utmost end of all the world,
Their speeches reach also:

A Tabernacle he
In them pitched for the Sun,
Who Bridegroom-like from 's chamber goes,
Glad Giant's-race to run.

The Lord's law perfect is,
The soul converting back:
God's testimony faithful is,
Makes wise who wisdom lack.

The statutes of the Lord
 Are right, and glad the heart:
The Lord's commandment is pure,
 Light doth to eyes impart.

Jehovah's fear is clean,
 And doth endure forever:
The judgments of the Lord are true,
 And righteous altogether.

Than gold, than much fine gold.
 More to be prized are,
Than honey, and the honeycomb,
 Sweeter they are by far.

Also thy servant is
 Admonished from hence:
And in the keeping of the same
 Is a full recompense.

Who can his errors know?
 From secret faults cleanse me.
And from presumptuous sins, let thou
 kept back thy servant be:

Let them not bear the rule
 In me, and then shall I
Be perfect, and shall cleansed be
 From much iniquity.

Let the words of my mouth,
 And the thoughts of my heart,
Be pleasing with thee, Lord, my Rock,
 Who my redeemer art.

1640

Psalm 23

A Psalm of David

The Lord to me a shepherd is,
 Want therefore shall not I.

He in the folds of tender grass
Doth cause me down to lie:

To waters calm me gently leads,
Restore my soul doth he,
He doth in paths of righteousness
For his name's sake lead me.

Yea though in valley of death's shade
I walk, none ill I'll fear:
Because thou art with me, thy rod
And staff my comfort are.

For me a table thou hast spread,
In presence of my foes:
Thou dost anoint my head with oil,
My cup it overflows.

Goodness and mercy surely shall
All my days follow me:
And in the Lord's house I shall dwell
So long as days shall be.

1640

Psalm 100[1]

A Psalm of Praise

Make ye a joyful sounding noise
Unto Jehovah, all the earth:
Serve ye Jehovah with gladness:
before his presence come with mirth.
Know, that Jehovah he is God,
who hath us formed it is he,
And not ourselves: his own people
and sheep of his pasture are we.

[1]Following Psalm 100 in the *Bay Psalm Book* is "Another of the Same," which offers slightly different wordings. The last lines, for example, read: "Because Jehovah He is good, /his bounteous mercy/Is everlasting: and his truth/is to eternity."

Enter into his gates with praise,
into his courts with thankfulness:
Make ye confession unto him,
and his name reverently bless.
Because Jehovah he is good,
for evermore is his mercy:
And unto generations all
continue doth his verity.

1640

Psalm 137

The rivers on of Babylon
there when we did sit down:
Yea even then we mourned, when
we remembered Sion.
Our harps we did hang it amid,
upon the willow tree.
Because there they that us away
led in captivity,
Requir'd of us a song, and thus
asked mirth, us waste who laid,
Sing us among a Sion's song,
unto us then they said.
The Lord's song sing can we? being
in stranger's land. Then let
Loose her skill my right hand, if I
Jerusalem forget.
Let cleave my tongue my palate on,
if mind thee do not I:
If chief joys o'er I prize not more
Jerusalem my joy.
Remember Lord, Edom's sons' word,
unto the ground said they,
It raze, it raze, when as it was
Jerusalem her day.
Blesst shall he be, that payeth thee,
daughter of Babylon,
Who must be waste: that which thou hast
rewarded us upon.
O happy he shall surely be
that taketh up, that eke
Thy little ones against the stones
doth into pieces break.

1640

from The New England Primer[1]

Alphabet

A In *Adam's* Fall
We Sinned all.

B Thy Life to Mend
This *Book* Attend.

C The *Cat* doth play
And after slay.

D A *Dog* will bite
A Thief at night.

E An *Eagle's* flight
Is out of sight.

F The Idle *Fool*
Is whipt at School.

G As runs the *Glass*
Man's life doth pass.

H My *Book* and *Heart*
Shall never part.

J *Job* feels the Rod
Yet blesses GOD.

K Our KING the
good
No man of blood.

L The *Lion* bold
The *Lamb* doth hold.

M The *Moon* gives light
In time of night.

N *Nightengales* sing
In Time of Spring.

O The Royal Oak
it was the Tree
That sav'd His
Royal Majestie.

P *Peter* denies
His Lord and cries

Q *Queen Esther* comes
in Royal State
To Save the JEWS
from dismal Fate

R *Rachel* doth mourn
For her first born.

S *Samuel* anoints
Whom God appoints.

T *Time* cuts down all
Both great and small.

U Uriah's beauteous Wife
Made David seek his
Life.

W *Whales* in the Sea
God's Voice obey.

X *Xerxes* the great did
die,
And so must you & I.

Y *Youth* forward slips
Death soonest nips.

Z *Zacheus* he
Did climb the Tree
His Lord to see,

[1]The pictured alphabet and "The Death of John Rogers" probably appeared in the earliest versions of the *Primer.* Later versions revised these items and added new material. Items are dated by their first inclusion in the *Primer.*

Now the Child being entred in his Letters and Spelling, let him learn these and such like Sentences by Heart, whereby he will be both instructed in his Duty, and encouraged in his Learning.

1683?

The Dutiful Child's Promises

I Will fear GOD, and honour the KING.
I will honour my Father & Mother.
I will Obey my Superiours.
I will Submit to my Elders,
I will Love my Friends.
I will hate no Man.
I will forgive my Enemies, and pray to God for them.
I will as much as in me lies keep all God's Holy Commandments.
I will learn my Catechism.
I will keep the Lord's Day Holy.
I will Reverence God's Sanctuary,
  For our GOD is a consuming Fire.

1727

Verses

I in the Burying Place may see
  Graves shorter there than I;
From Death's Arrest no Age is free,
  Young Children too may die;
My God, may such an awful Sight,
  Awakening be to me!
Oh! that by early Grace I might
  For Death prepared be.

[1727][2]

* * *

[2]This poem, originally titled "The Child Seeing the Funeral of Another Child," was Part VI of Cotton Mather's "Instructions for Children," first printed in his *The A.B.C. of Religion* (Boston, 1713). In Mather's version, the Graves are "not so long as I." The poem appeared in the 1727 edition on pages that no longer exist. The text used here appeared in later editions of the *Primer.*

Good Children must,

Fear God all Day,	Love Christ alway,
Parents obey,	In Secret Pray,
No false thing say,	Mind little Play,
By no Sin stray,	Make no delay,

In doing Good.

1727

* * *

Awake, arise, behold thou hast
Thy Life a Leaf, thy Breath a Blast;
At Night lye down prepar'd to have
Thy sleep, thy death, thy bed, thy grave.

1727

The Death of John Rogers[3]

Mr. *John Rogers,* Minister of the Gospel in *London,* was the first Martyr in Q *Mary's* Reign, and was burnt at *Smithfield, February* the fourteenth, 1554 His Wife, with nine small Children, and one at her Breast, following him to the Stake, with which sorrowful sight he was not in the least daunted, but with wonderful Patience died couragiously for the Gospel of Jesus Christ.

Some few Days before his Death, he writ the following Exhortation to his Children.

Give ear my Children to my words,
  whom God hath dearly bought,
Lay up his Laws within your heart,
  and print them in your thought,
I leave you here a little Book,
  for you to look upon;
That you may see your Fathers face,
  when he is dead and gone.
Who for the hope of heavenly things,
  while he did here remain,
Gave over all his golden Years
  to Prison and to Pain.
Where I among my Iron Bands,
  inclosed in the dark,
Not many days before my Death

[3]This popular English poem was first printed in 1559. It appears in the various versions of the *Primer* with illustrations of Rogers's family watching the scene of his martyrdom.

I did compose this Work.
And for Example to your Youth,
to whom I wish all good;
I send you here God's perfect Truth,
and seel it with my Blood
To you my Heirs of earthly Things,
which I do leave behind,
That you may read and understand,
and keep it in your mind.
That as you have been Heirs of thet
which once shall wear away,
you also may possess that part,
which never shall decay.
. . .

1683?

Mary White Rowlandson [Talcott] 1637?–1711

Mary White Rowlandson's narrative of her three-month captivity by Algonkian Indians during King Philip's War (1675–1678) was one of the first best-sellers in American literature. Four editions of the *The Soveraignty and Goodness of GOD, Together With the Faithfulness of His Promises Displayed; Being a Narrative of the Captivity and Restauration of Mrs. Mary Rowlandson* appeared in 1682, and it remained a popular success into the early nineteenth century. In moments of national crisis such as the American Revolution, new editions of Rowlandson's text figured prominently in the discourse of national rights and of God's challenges to the nation. More than thirty editions have been published to date, and the *Narrative* is acknowledged as a major contribution to an early American genre, the captivity narrative, which extends back to the period of European exploration. (See, for instance, the Hopi account, "The Coming of the Spanish.") The genre was explored by many other early writers, including John Gyles and Elizabeth Meader Hanson, who experienced real-life captivities. Early novels (most notably, Ann Eliza Schuyler Bleecker's *The History of Maria Kittle* and James Fenimore Cooper's *The Last of the Mohicans*) again expanded the genre when their authors crafted fictionalized versions of captivity narratives. It was thus that one woman's trauma-ridden experience of captivity became an icon of a national ideology.

Mary White was born in Somerset, England, probably in 1637. With her parents, Joan and John White, she and her nine siblings emigrated to New England, settling first in Salem, Massachusetts, and finally in the frontier town of Lancaster, Massachusetts. Little is known of Mary White's early years in New England, but around 1656 she married the Rev. Joseph Rowlandson of Lancaster. Their first child, Mary, died just after her third birthday; three other children were born to the Rowlandsons.

When the events that led to King Philip's War began to emerge in New England, a forty-year period of relative tranquility between the colonists and the indigenous people of the region was destroyed, and Rowlandson's comfortable life in Lancaster was shattered. Intercolonial and intertribal differences—between the governments of Plymouth, Massachusetts Bay, and Rhode Island on the one hand, and between Algonkian tribes such as the Wampanoags, Narragansetts, and the Mohegans on the other—created an atmosphere of strained relations that abetted the outbreak of war. The major impetus for King Philip's War, however, was the continuing encroachment by Euro-American settlers onto lands occupied by the Algonkians.

In 1664, the leaders of Plymouth Colony seized Wamsutta, a Wampanoag chief, even though the Wampanoags had maintained peaceful relations with the colonists since the rule of Massasoit, father of Wamsutta and Metacom. The leadership of Plymouth Colony had hoped to convince Wamsutta to relinquish the early pact with England, which granted his people full rights to their land, in favor of an agreement that would give Plymouth Colony the right to purchase the land. While in captivity, Wamsutta died, and Metacom became chief and agreed to the colonists' demands. Still not content with their gains, the colonists continued their unprecedented encroachment; when conflicts between Native Americans and the settlers broke out in various communities, the Plymouth colonists placed the blame on Metacom and were supported in their efforts by their once contentious neighbors in Massachusetts Bay. In 1671 the leadership of Plymouth Colony demanded that Metacom (or "Philip," as the white settlers referred to him) appear before them to answer charges of aggression. Then, in 1674 events escalated into a series of retributive acts, the facts of which are blurred by charges and countercharges: a "praying Indian," John Sassamon, was murdered; the colonists assumed Metacom's people were responsible, and they executed three Wampanoags in retaliation; on June 20, 1675, Metacom counter-retaliated by leading an attack on the village of Swansea, Massachusetts. At this point, the colonies of Massachusetts Bay and Rhode Island joined with Plymouth and sent combined troops in pursuit of Metacom. War was officially declared on September 9, 1675. King Philip's War lasted for almost three years; it devastated the New England region and decimated the Algonkians.

The war completely altered Mary Rowlandson's life as well. On February 10, 1676, a group of Narragansett Indians attacked the village of Lancaster. Joseph Rowlandson was in Boston where he was attempting to raise aid for the defense of Lancaster. Mary Rowlandson and their three children—Joseph (age 14), Mary (age 10), and Sarah (age 6)—were taken captive, and many of her relatives and neighbors were killed or also taken captive. The events of Rowlandson's captivity are related in her autobiographical narrative, as she closely details the twenty "removes" that she and her captors underwent. Sarah died within a week of the attack, and, although she could occasionally see her son while held captive, Rowlandson was immediately separated from the other two children. She herself was ransomed on May 2, 1676, but it was several weeks later before Rowlandson and her husband were able to effect the release of their two remaining children.

For a year after their reunion, the Rowlandsons remained in Boston; in 1677 they sought to reestablish their lives when Joseph Rowlandson accepted a position in Wethersfield, Connecticut, and the family resettled in that community. He died less than two years later, however. Following seventeenth-century expectations, Mary remarried on August 6, 1679. Her second husband was Capt. Samuel Talcott, a Harvard-educated farmer and community leader. As a member of the War Council during the years of King Philip's War, Talcott undoubtedly empathized with the trauma Rowlandson had endured at that time. Mary Rowlandson Talcott lived for a decade after her second husband's death in 1691, but she did not marry again. At the age of seventy-three, she died in Wethersfield on January 5, 1711.

Although thirty years eclipsed the 1682 publication of Rowlandson's narrative and her death, the *Narrative* remains her only known comment on her months of captivity. The narrative was written in the years between her ransom and Joseph's death; she asserted that her purpose in writing about her experiences was simply for the edification of her children and friends. With graphic realism, she recounted the exterior events of her captivity: the initial raid; the hardships of her captivity; and most poignantly, the death of her daughter Sarah and the necessity of leaving her daughter in an unmarked grave in the "wilderness."

In the Puritan culture, which repressed women's public speaking and writing, the decision to publish her account was almost as exceptional as the experience itself. Several reasons may be considered for the encouragement of the publication of this text. Attesting to her experiences as God's means of testing her faith, Rowlandson's text appeared at a time when Congregationalist church membership had declined in New England. The decision to publish her narrative, therefore, had the support of the leading Congregationalist clergymen, including Increase Mather, who is assumed to be the author of a preface that accompanied the first editions. In a broader sense, the text also supported the colonists' negative representations of Native Americans as "savages" who inhabited Satan's domain. Although Rowlandson occasionally acknowledges an act of kindness from one of her captors, her representations most often depict her captors as "barbarians," an attitude that supported the colonists' belief in the "correctness" of the removal of Native Americans from regions that the colonists were increasingly interested in settling. The dominant culture could thus argue that the removal of the Algonkians and other native peoples was in the "national" interest.

On the other hand, the *Narrative* explores the interior consequences of Rowlandson's experiences. If the text begins with her sense of the Narragansetts as an alien people, it ends with her own sense of alienation from the comfort that her community once offered. It is a powerful account of one woman's endurance in captivity and of the psychological means and behavioral adaptations she used to survive. If she composed her account in alliance with her religious beliefs and prejudices, she also honestly expressed her opinions about the personal, psychological consequences of her experiences. No longer can she "sleep quietly without workings in my thoughts, whole nights together," for "when others are sleeping mine eyes are weeping."

Sharon M. Harris
University of Nebraska

PRIMARY WORK

"The Soveraignty and the Goodness of GOD, Together With the Faithfulness of His Promises Displayed; Being a Narrative of the Captivity and Restauration of Mrs. Mary Rowlandson . . . ," 1682.

SECONDARY WORKS

Alden T. Vaughan and Edward C. Clark, eds., *Puritans Among the Indians: Accounts of Captivity and Redemption 1676–1724,* 1981; David L. Greene, "New Light on Mary Rowlandson," *Early American Literature* 20:1 (1985); Kathryn Zabelle Derounian, "The Publication, Promotion, and Distribution of Mary Rowlandson's Indian Captivity Narrative in the Seventeenth Century," *Early American Literature* 23 (1988); Mitchell Robert Breitwieser, *American Puritanism and the Defense of Mourning: Religion, Grief, and Ethnology in Mary Rowlandson's Captivity Narrative,* 1990; Amy Schrager Lang, Introduction to "A True History of the Captivity and Restoration of Mrs. Mary Rowlandson," *Journeys in New Worlds: Early American Women's Narratives,* ed. William Andrews, et al., 1990.

from A Narrative of the Captivity and Restauration of Mrs. Mary Rowlandson

On the tenth of February 1675, Came the Indians with great numbers upon Lancaster;[1] Their first coming was about Sun-rising; hearing the noise of some Guns, we looked out; several Houses were burning, and the Smoke ascending to Heaven. There were five persons taken in one house, the Father, and the Mother and a sucking Child, they knockt on the head; the other two they took and carried away alive. There were two others, who being out of their Garison[2] upon some occasion were set upon; one was knockt on the head, the other escaped: Another their was who running along was shot and wounded, and fell down; he begged of them his life, promising them Money (as they told me) but they would not hearken to him but knockt him in head, and stript him naked, and split open his Bowels. Another seeing many of the Indians about his Barn, ventured and went out, but was quickly shot down. There were three others belonging to the same Garison who were killed; the Indians getting up upon the roof of the Barn, had advantage to shoot down upon them over their Fortification. Thus these murtherous wretches went on, burning, and destroying before them.

At length they came and beset our own house, and quickly it was the dolefullest day that ever mine eyes saw. The House stood upon the edg of a hill; some of the Indians got behind the hill, others into the Barn, and others behind any thing that could shelter them; from all which places they shot against the House, so that the Bullets seemed to fly like hail; and quickly they wounded one man among us, then another, and then a third, About two hours (according to my observation, in that amazing time) they had been about the house before they prevailed to fire it (which they did with Flax and Hemp, which they brought out of the Barn, and there being no defence about the House, only two Flankers[3] at two opposite corners and one of them not finished) they fired it once and one ventured out and quenched it, but they quickly fired it again, and that took. Now is the dreadfull hour come, that I have often heard of (in time of War, as it was the case of others) but now mine eyes see it. Some in our house were fighting for their lives, others wallowing in their blood, the House on fire over our heads, and the bloody Heathen ready to knock us on the head, if we stirred out. Now might we hear Mothers and Children crying out for themselves, and one another, Lord, What shall we do? Then I took my Children[4] (and one of my sisters, hers) to go forth and leave the house: but as soon as we came to the dore and appeared, the Indians shot so thick that the bullets rattled against the House, as if one had taken an handfull of stones and threw them, so that we were fain to give back. We had six stout Dogs belonging to our Garrison, but none of them would stir, though another time, if any Indian had come to the door, they were ready

[1]Lancaster, Massachusetts. A frontier village 30 miles west of Boston, one of many attacked during King Philip's War (1675–1678).

[2]One of six fortified houses in Lancaster. Only the Rowlandson house fell to the Indians upon attack.

[3]Projections or bastions of fortified houses from which defenders could position themselves against their attackers.

[4]Joseph, Mary, and Sarah Rowlandson.

to fly upon him and tear him down. The Lord hereby would make us the more acknowledge his hand, and to see that our help is always in him. But out we must go, the fire increasing, and coming along behind us, roaring, and the Indians gaping before us with their Guns, Spears and Hatchets to devour us. No sooner were we out of the House, but my Brother in Law[5] (being before wounded, in defending the house, in or near the throat) fell down dead, wherat the Indians scornfully shouted, and hallowed, and were presently upon him, stripping off his cloaths, the bulletts flying thick, one went through my side, and the same (as would seem) through the bowels and hand of dear Child in my arms.[6] One of my elder Sisters Children, named William, had then his Leg broken, which the Indians perceiving, they knockt him on head. Thus were we butchered by those merciless Heathen, standing amazed, with the blood running down to our heels. My eldest Sister being yet in the House, and seeing those wofull sights, the Infidels haling Mothers one way, and Children another, and some wallowing in their blood: and her elder Son telling her that her Son William was dead, and my self was wounded, she said, And, Lord, let me dy with them; which was no sooner said, but she was struck with a Bullet, and fell down dead over the threshold. I hope she is reaping the fruit of her good labours, being faithfull to the service of God in her place. In her younger years she lay under much trouble upon spiritual accounts, till it pleased God to make that precious Scripture take hold of her heart, 2 Cor. 12. 9. *And he said unto me, my Grace is sufficient for thee.* More then twenty years after I have heard her tell how sweet and comfortable that place was to her. But to return: The Indians laid hold of us, pulling me one way, and the Children another, and said, Come go along with us; I told them they would kill me: they answered, If I were willing to go along with them, they would not hurt me.

Oh the dolefull sight that now was to behold at this House! *Come, behold the works of the Lord, what dissolations he had made in the Earth.* Of thirty seven persons who were in this one House, none escaped either present death, or a bitter captivity, save only one,[7] who might say as he, Job 1. 15, *And I only am escaped alone to tell the News.* There were twelve killed, some shot, some stab'd with their Spears, some knock'd down with their Hatchets. When we are in prosperity, Oh the little that we think of such dreadfull sights, and to see our dear Friends, and Relations ly bleeding out their heart-blood upon the ground. There was one who was chopt into the head with a Hatchet, and stript naked, and yet was crawling up and down. It is a solemn sight to see so many Christians lying in their blood, some here, and some there, like a company of Sheep torn by Wolves, All of them stript naked by a company of hell-hounds, roaring, singing, ranting and insulting, as if they would have torn our very hearts out; yet the Lord by his Almighty power preserved a number of us from death, for there were twenty-four of us taken alive and carried Captive.

I had often before this said, that if the Indians should come, I should chuse rather to be killed by them then taken alive but when it came to the tryal my mind changed; their glittering weapons so daunted my spirit, that I chose rather to go along with those (as I may say) ravenous Beasts, then that moment to end my dayes; and that I may the better declare what happened to me during that grievous

[5]John Divoll, husband of Rowlandson's younger sister, Hannah.

[6]Rowlandson's younger daughter, Sarah.

[7]Ephraim Roper. Rowlandson was unaware that three children had also escaped.

Captivity, I shall particularly speak of the severall Removes we had up and down the Wilderness.

The First Remove[8]

Now away we must go with those Barbarous Creatures, with our bodies wounded and bleeding, and our hearts no less than our bodies. About a mile we went that night, up upon a hill within sight of the Town, where they intended to lodge. There was hard by a vacant house (deserted by the English before, for fear of the Indians). I asked them whither I might not lodge in the house that night to which they answered, what will you love English men still? this was the dolefullest night that ever my eyes saw. Oh the roaring, and singing and danceing, and yelling of those black creatures in the night, which made the place a lively resemblance of hell. And as miserable was the wast that was there made, of Horses, Cattle, Sheep, Swine, Calves, Lambs, Roasting Pigs, and Fowl (which they had plundered in the Town) some roasting, some lying and burning, and some boyling to feed our merciless Enemies; who were joyful enough though we were disconsolate. To add to the dolefulness of the former day, and the dismalness of the present night: my thoughts ran upon my losses and sad bereaved condition. All was gone, my Husband gone (at least separated from me, he being in the Bay,[9] and to add to my grief, the Indians told me they would kill him as he came homeward) my Children gone, my Relations and Friends gone, our House and home and all our comforts within door, and without, all was gone, (except my life) and I knew not but the next moment that might go too. There remained nothing to me but one poor wounded Babe, and it seemed at present worse than death that it was in such a pitiful condition, bespeaking Compassion, and I had no refreshing for it, nor suitable things to revive it. Little do many think what is the savageness and bruitishness of this barbarous Enemy, I[10] even those that seem to profess more than others among them, when the English have fallen into their hands.

Those seven that were killed at Lancaster the summer before upon a Sabbath day, and the one that was afterward killed upon a week day, were slain and mangled in a barbarous manner, by one-ey'd John[11] and Marlborough's Praying Indians,[12] which Capt. Mosely brought to Boston, as the Indians told me.

The Second Remove

But now, the next morning, I must turn my back upon the Town, and travel with them into the vast and desolate Wilderness, I knew not whither. It is not my tongue, or pen can express the sorrows of my heart, and bitterness of my spirit, that I had at this departure: but God was with me, in a wonderfull manner, carrying me along, and bearing up my spirit, that it did not quite fail. One of the Indians carried my poor

[8]After each move, the group remained encamped for several days.

[9]*I.e.,* in or near Boston.

[10]Ay.

[11]One-eyed John, also known as Monoco and Apequinsah.

[12]"Praying Indians" refers to a settlement of Christianized Indians at Marlborough, Massachusetts.

wounded Babe upon a horse, I went moaning all along, I shall dy, I shall dy. I went on foot after it, with sorrow that cannot be exprest. At length I took it off the horse, and carried it in my armes till my strength failed, and I fell down with it: Then they set me upon a horse with my wounded Child in my lap, and there being no furniture upon the horse back, as we were going down a steep hill, we both fell over the horses head, at which they like inhumane creatures laught, and rejoyced to see it, though I thought we should there have ended our dayes, as overcome with so many difficulties. But the Lord renewed my strength still, and carried me along, that I might see more of his Power; yea, so much that I could never have thought of, had I not experienced it.

After this it quickly began to snow, and when night came on, they stopt: and now down I must sit in the snow, by a little fire, and a few boughs behind me, with my sick Child in my lap; and calling much for water, being now (through the wound) fallen into a violent Fever. My own wound also growing so stiff, that I could scarce sit down or rise up; yet so it must be, that I must sit all this cold winter night upon the cold snowy ground, with my sick Child in my armes, looking that every hour would be the last of its life; and having no Christian friend near me, either to comfort or help me. Oh, I may see the wonderfull power of God, that my Spirit did not utterly sink under my affliction: still the Lord upheld me with his gracious and mercifull Spirit, and we were both alive to see the light of the next morning.

The Third Remove[13]

The morning being come, they prepared to go on their way. One of the Indians got up upon a horse, and they set me up behind him, with my poor sick Babe in my lap. A very wearisome and tedious day I had of it; what with my own wound, and my Childs being so exceeding sick, and in a lamentable condition with her wound. It may be easily judged what a poor feeble condition we were in, there being not the least crumb of refreshing that came within either of our mouths, from Wednesday night to Saturday night, except only a little cold water. This day in the afternoon, about an hour by Sun, we came to the place where they intended, *viz*[14] an Indian Town, called Wenimesset, Norward of Quabaug[15] When we were come, Oh the number of Pagans (now merciless enemies) that there came about me, that I may say as David, Psal. 27. 13, *I had fainted, unless I had believed,* etc.[16] The next day was the Sabbath: I then remembered how careless I had been of Gods holy time, how many Sabbaths I had lost and mispent, and how evily I had walked in Gods sight; which lay so close unto my spirit, that it was easie for me to see how righteous it was with God to cut off the thread of my life, and cast me out of his presence for ever. Yet the Lord still shewed mercy to me, and upheld me; and as he wounded me with one hand, so he healed me with the other. This day there came to me one Robbert Pepper (a man belonging to Roxbury) who was taken in Captain Beers his Fight, and had been now a considerable time with the Indians; and up with them almost as far as

[13]The third remove ended at an Indian village, Menameset, on the Ware River; this is now New Braintree, Massachusetts.

[14]Latin: namely.

[15]Now Brookfield, Massachusetts.

[16]". . . to see the goodness of the Lord in the land of the living."

Albany, to see king Philip,[17] as he told me, and was now very lately come into these parts. Hearing, I say, that I was in this Indian Town, he obtained leave to come and see me. He told me, he himself was wounded in the leg at Captain Beers his Fight; and was not able some time to go, but as they carried him, and as he took Oaken leaves and laid to his wound, and through the blessing of God he was able to travel again. Then I took Oaken leaves and laid to my side, and with the blessing of God it cured me also; yet before the cure was wrought, I may say, as it is in Psal. 38. 5, 6. *My wounds stink and are corrupt, I am troubled, I am bowed down greatly, I go mourning all the day long.* I sat much alone with a poor wounded Child in my lap, which moaned night and day, having nothing to revive the body, or cheer the spirits of her, but in stead of that, sometimes one Indian would come and tell me one hour, that your Master will knock your Child in the head, and then a second, and then a third, your Master[18] will quickly knock your Child in the head.

This was the comfort I had from them, miserable comforters are ye all, as he said.[19] Thus nine dayes I sat upon my knees, with my Babe in my lap, till my flesh was raw again; my Child being even ready to depart this sorrowfull world, they bade me carry it out to another Wigwam (I suppose because they would not be troubled with such spectacles) Whither I went with a very heavy heart, and down I sat with the picture of death in my lap. About two houres in the night, my sweet Babe like a Lambe departed this life, on Feb. 18, 1675. It being about six yeares, and five months old. It was nine dayes from the first wounding, in this miserable condition, without any refreshing of one nature or other, except a little cold water. I cannot, but take notice, how at another time I could not bear to be in the room where any dead person was, but now the case is changed; I must and could ly down by my dead Babe, side by side all the night after. I have thought since of the wonderfull goodness of God to me, in preserving me in the use of my reason and senses, in that distressed time, that I did not use wicked and violent means to end my own miserable life. In the morning, when they understood that my child was dead they sent for me home to my Masters Wigwam: (by my Master in this writing, must be understood Quanopin, who was a Saggamore, and married King Phillips wives Sister; not that he first took me, but I was sold to him by another Narrhaganset Indian, who took me when first I came out of the Garison). I went to take up my dead child in my arms to carry it with me, but they bid me let it alone: there was no resisting, but goe I must and leave it. When I had been at my masters wigwam, I took the first opportunity I could get, to go look after my dead child: when I came I askt them what they had done with it? then they told me it was upon the hill: then they went and shewed me where it was, where I saw the ground was newly digged, and there they told me they had buried it: There I left that Child in the Wilderness, and must commit it, and my self also in this Wilderness-condition, to him who is above all. God having taken away this dear Child, I went to see my daughter Mary, who was at this same Indian town, at a Wigwam not very far off, though we had little liberty or opportunity to see one another. She was about ten years old, and taken from the door at first by a Praying Ind and afterward sold for a gun. When I came in sight, she would fall a weeping; at which

[17]The Wampanoag leader, Metacom, also known as Metacomet.

[18]Rowlandson's Indian captor and owner.

[19]Job 16:1–2.

they were provoked, and would not let me come near her, but bade me be gone; which was a heart-cutting word to me. I had one Child dead, another in the Wilderness, I knew nor where, the third they would not let me come near to: *Me* (as he said) *have ye bereaved of my Children, Joseph is not, and Simeon is not, and ye will take Benjamin also, all these things are against me.* I could not sit still in this condition, but kept walking from one place to another. And as I was going along, my heart was even overwhelm'd with the thoughts of my condition, and that I should have Children, and a Nation which I knew not ruled over them. Whereupon I earnestly entreated the Lord, that he would consider my low estate, and shew me a token for good, and if it were his blessed will, some sign and hope of some relief. And indeed quickly the Lord answered, in some measure, my poor prayers: for as I was going up and down mourning and lamenting my condition, my Son came to me, and asked me how I did; I had not seen him before, since the destruction of the Town, and I knew not where he was, till I was informed by himself, that he was amongst a smaller percel of Indians, whose place was about six miles off; with tears in his eyes, he asked me whether his Sister Sarah was dead; and told me he had seen his Sister Mary; and prayed me, that I would not be troubled in reference to himself. The occasion of his coming to see me at this time, was this: There was, as I said, about six miles from us, a smal Plantation of Indians, where it seems he had been during his Captivity: and at this time, there were some Forces of the Ind. gathered out of our company, and some also from them (among whom was my Sons master) to go to assault and burn Medfield: In this time of the absence of his master, his dame brought him to see me. I took this to be some gracious answer to my earnest and unfeigned desire. The next day, *viz.* to this, the Indians returned from Medfield, all the company, for those that belonged to the other smal company, came thorough the Town that now we were at. But before they came to us, Oh! the outragious roaring and hooping that there was: They began their din about a mile before they came to us. By their noise and hooping they signified how many they had destroyed (which was at that time twenty three.)[20] Those that were with us at home, were gathered together as soon as they heard the hooping, and every time that the other went over their number, these at home gave a shout, that the very Earth rung again: And thus they continued till those that had been upon the expedition were come up to the Sagamores Wigwam; and then, Oh, the hideous insulting and triumphing that there was over some Englishmens scalps that they had taken (as their manner is) and brought with them, I cannot but take notice of the wonderfull mercy of God to me in those afflictions, in sending me a Bible. One of the Indians that came from Medfield fight, had brought some plunder, came to me, and asked me, if I would have a Bible, he had got one in his Basket. I was glad of it, and asked him, whether he thought the Indians would let me read? he answered, yes: So I took the Bible, and in that melancholy time, it came into my mind to read first the 28. Chap. of Deut.,[21] which I did, and when I had read it, my dark heart wrought on this manner, That there was no mercy for me, that the blessing were gone, and the curses come in their room, and that I had lost my opportunity. But the Lord helped me still to go on reading till I came to Chap. 30 the seven first verses, where I found,

[20]The Indian custom of whooping signaled the number of enemy killed and captured in the battle.

[21]Recital of blessings for obedience to God and curses for disobedience.

there was mercy promised again, if we would return to him by repentance; and though we were scatered from one end of the Earth to the other, yet the Lord would gather us together, and turn all those curses upon our Enemies. I do not desire to live to forget this Scripture, and what comfort it was to me. . . .

The Fourth Remove

. . . Heart-aking thoughts here I had about my poor Children, who were scattered up and down among the wild beasts of the forrest: My head was light and dissey (either through hunger or hard lodging, or trouble or altogether) my knees feeble, my body raw by sitting double night and day, that I cannot express to man the affliction that lay upon my Spirit, but the Lord helped me at that time to express it to himself. I opened my Bible to read, and the Lord brought that precious Scripture to me, Jer. 31. 16. *Thus saith the Lord, refrain thy voice from weeping, and thine eyes from tears, for thy work shall be rewarded, and they shall come again from the land of the Enemy.* This was a sweet Cordial to me, when I was ready to faint, many and many a time have I sat down, and weept sweetly over this Scripture. At this place we continued about four dayes.

The Fifth Remove[22]

The occasion (as I thought) of their moving at this time, was, the English Army,[23] it being near and following them: For they went, as if they had gone for their lives, for some considerable way, and then they made a stop, and chose some of their stoutest men, and sent them back to hold the English Army in play whilst the rest escaped: And then, like Jehu,[24] they marched on furiously, with their old, and with their young: some carried their old decrepit mothers, some carried one, and some another. Four of them carried a great Indian upon a Bier; but going through a thick Wood with him, they were hindered, and could make no hast; whereupon they took him upon their backs, and carried him, one at a time, till they came to Bacquaug River. Upon a Friday, a little after noon we came to this River. When all the company was come up, and were gathered together, I thought to count the number of them, but they were so many, and being somewhat in motion, it was beyond my skil. In this travel, because of my wound, I was somewhat favoured in my load; I carried only my knitting work and two quarts of parched meal:[25] Being very faint I asked my mistriss to give me one spoonfull of the meal, but she would not give me a taste. They quickly fell to cutting dry trees, to make Rafts to carry them over the river: and soon my turn came to go over: By the advantage of some brush which they had laid upon the Raft to sit upon, I did not wet my foot (which many of themselves at the other end were mid-leg deep) which cannot but be acknowledged as a favour of God to my weakned body, it being a very cold time. I was not before acquainted with such kind of doings

[22]This remove included crossing the Baquag River in Orange.

[23]The colonial militia, consisting of Massachusetts and Connecticut forces under Captain Thomas Savage.

[24]King of Israel (c. 843–816 B.C.).

[25]A favorite traveling food.

or dangers. *When thou passeth through the waters I will be with thee, and through the Rivers they shall not overflow thee,* Isai. 43.2. A certain number of us got over the River that night, but it was the night after the Sabbath before all the company was got over. On the Saturday they boyled an old Horses leg which they had got, and so we drank of the broth, as soon as they thought it was ready, and when it was almost all gone, they filled it up again.

The first week of my being among them, I hardly ate any thing; the second week, I found my stomach grow very faint for want of something; and yet it was very hard to get down their filthy trash: but the third week, though I could think how formerly my stomach would turn against this or that, and I could starve and dy before I could eat such things, yet they were sweet and savoury to my taste. I was at this time knitting a pair of white cotton stockins for my mistriss; and had not yet wrought upon a Sabbath day; when the Sabbath came they bade me go to work; I told them it was the Sabbath day, and desired them to let me rest, and told them I would do as much more to morrow; to which they answered me, they would break my face. And here I cannot but take notice of the strange providence of God in preserving the heathen: They were many hundreds, old and young, some sick, and some lame, many had Papooses at their backs, the greatest number at this time with us, were Squaws, and they travelled with all they had, bag and baggage, and yet they got over this River aforesaid; and on Munday they set their Wigwams on fire, and away they went: On that very day came the English Army after them to this River, and saw the smoak of their Wigwams, and yet this River put a stop to them. God did not give them courage or activity to go over after us; we were not ready for so great a mercy as victory and deliverance; if we had been, God would have found out a way for the English to have passed this River, as well as for the Indians with their Squaws and Children, and all their Luggage. *Oh that my People had hearkened to me, and Israel had walked in my ways, I should soon have subdued their Enemies, and turned my hand against their Adversaries,* Psal. 81: 13.14.

The Eighth Remove[26]

On the morrow morning we must go over the River, *i.e.* Connecticot, to meet with King Philip; two Cannoos ful, they had carried over, the next Turn I my self was to go; but as my foot was upon the Cannoo to step in, there was a sudden out-cry among them, and I must step back; and instead of going over the River, I must go four or five miles up the River farther Northward. Some of the Indians ran one way, and some another. The cause of this rout was, as I thought, their espying some English Scouts, who were thereabout. In this travel up the River, about noon the Company made a stop, and sate down; some to eat, and others to rest them. As I sate amongst them, musing of things past, my Son Joseph unexpectedly came to me: we asked of each others welfare, bemoaning our dolefull condition, and the change that had come upon uss. We had Husband and Father, and Children, and Sisters, and Friends, and Relations, and House, and Home, and many Comforts of this Life: but now we may say, as Job, *Naked came I out of my Mothers Womb, and naked shall I*

[26]To Coasset in South Vernon, Vermont.

return: The Lord gave, and the Lord hath taken away, Blessed be the Name of the Lord.[27] I asked him whither he would read; he told me, he earnestly desired it, I gave him my Bible, and he lighted upon that comfortable Scripture, Psal. 118. 17, 18. *I shall not dy but live, and declare the works of the Lord: the Lord hath chastened me sore, yet he hath not given me over to death.* Look here, Mother (sayes he) did you read this? And here I may take occasion to mention one principall ground of my setting forth these Lines: even as the Psalmist sayes, To declare the Works of the Lord, and his wonderfull Power in carrying us along, preserving us in the Wilderness, while under the Enemies hand, and returning of us in safety again, And His goodness in bringing to my hand so many comfortable and suitable Scriptures in my distress.[28] But to Return, We travelled on till night; and in the morning, we must go over the River to Philip's Crew. When I was in the Cannoo, I could not but be amazed at the numerous crew of Pagans that were on the Bank on the other side. When I came ashore, they gathered all about me, I sitting alone in the midst: I observed they asked one another questions, and laughed, and rejoyced over their Gains and Victories. Then my heart began to fail: and I fell a weeping which was the first time to my remembrance, that I wept before them. Although I had met with so much Affliction, and my heart was many times ready to break, yet could I not shed one tear in their sight: but rather had been all this while in a maze, and like one astonished: but now I may say as, Psal. 137. 1. *By the Rivers of Babylon, there we sate down: yea, we wept when we remembered Zion.* There one of them asked me, why I wept, I could hardly tell what to say: yet I answered, they would kill me: No, said he, none will hurt you. Then came one of them and gave me two spoon-fulls of Meal to comfort me, and another gave me half a pint of Pease; which was more worth than many Bushels at another time. Then I went to see King Philip, he bade me come in and sit down, and asked me whether I woold smoke it (a usual Complement nowadayes amongst Saints and Sinners)[29] but this no way suited me. For though I had formerly used Tobacco, yet I had left it ever since I was first taken. It seems to be a Bait, the Devil layes to make men loose their precious time: I remember with shame, how formerly, when I had taken two or three pipes, I was presently ready for another, such a bewitching thing it is: But I thank God, he has now given me power over it; surely there are many who may be better imployed than to ly sucking a stinking Tobacco-pipe.

Now the Indians gather their Forces to go against North-Hampton: over-night one went about yelling and hooting to give notice of the design. Whereupon they fell to boyling of Ground-nuts, and parching of Corn (as many as had it) for their Provision: and in the morning away they went. During my abode in this place, Philip spake to me to make a shirt for his boy, which I did, for which he gave me a shilling: I offered the mony to my master, but he bade me keep it: and with it I bought a piece of Horse flesh. Afterwards he asked me to make a Cap for his boy, for which he invited me to Dinner. I went, and he gave me a Pancake, about as big as two fingers; it was made of parched wheat, beaten, and fryed in Bears grease, but I thought I never tasted pleasanter meat in my life. . . .

[27]Job 1:21.

[28]Rowlandson probably had Psalm 145:4 in mind: "One generation shall praise thy works to another and shall declare thy mighty acts."

[29]*I.e.,* among believers (saints) as well as the unregenerate.

The Twelfth Remove

It was upon a Sabbath-day-morning, that they prepared for their Travel. This morning I asked my master whither he would sell me to my Husband; he answered me *Nux,*[30] which did much rejoyce my spirit. My mistriss, before we went, was gone to the burial of a Papoos, and returning, she found me sitting and reading in my Bible; she snatched it hastily out of my hand, and threw it out of doors; I ran out and catcht it up, and put it into my pocket, and never let her see it afterward. Then they packed up their things to be gone, and gave me my load: I complained it was too heavy, whereupon she gave me a slap in the face, and bade me go; I lifted up my heart to God, hoping the Redemption was not far off: and the rather because their insolency grew worse and worse.

But the thoughts of my going homeward (for so we bent our course) much cheared my Spirit, and made my burden seem light, and almost nothing at all. But (to my amazement and great perplexity) the scale was soon turned: for when we had gone a little way, on a sudden my mistriss gives out, she would go no further, but turn back again, and said, I must go back again with her, and she called her *Sannup,* and would have had him gone back also, but he would not, but said, He would go on, and come to us again in three dayes. My Spirit was upon this, I confess, very impatient, and almost outragious. I thought I could as well have dyed as went back: I cannot declare the trouble that I was in about it; but yet back again I must go. As soon as I had an opportunity, I took my Bible to read, and that quieting Scripture came to my hand, Psal. 46. 10. *Be still, and know that I am God.* Which stilled my spirit for the present: But a sore time of tryal, I concluded, I had to go through, My master being gone, who seemed to me the best friend that I had of an Indian, both in cold and hunger, and quickly so it proved. Down I sat, with my heart as full as it could hold, and yet so hungry that I could not sit neither: but going out to see what I could find, and walking among the Trees, I found six Acorns, and two Ches-nuts, which were some refreshment to me. Towards Night I gathered me some sticks for my own comfort, that I might not ly a-cold: but when we came to ly down they bade me go out, and ly some-where-else, for they had company (they said) come in more than their own: I told them, I could not tell where to go, they bade me go look; I told them, if I went to another Wigwam they would be angry, and send me home again. Then one of the Company drew his sword, and told me he would run me thorough if I did not go presently. Then was I fain to stoop to this rude fellow, and to go out in the night, I knew not whither. Mine eyes have seen that fellow afterwards walking up and down Boston, under the appearance of a Friend-Indian, and severall others of the like Cut. I went to one Wigwam, and they told me they had no room. Then I went to another, and they said the same; at last an old Indian bade me come to him, and his Squaw gave me some Ground-nuts; she gave me also something to lay under my head, and a good fire we had: and through the good providence of God, I had a comfortable lodging that night. In the morning, another Indian bade me come at night, and he would give me six Ground-nuts, which I did. We were at this place and time about two miles from Connecticut River. We went in the morning to gather Ground-nuts, to the River, and went back again that night. I went with a good load at my back (for

[30]Yes.

they when they went, though but a little way, would carry all their trumpery with them) I told them the skin was off my back, but I had no other comforting answer from them than this, That it would be no matter if my head were off too.

The Thirteenth Remove[31]

Instead of going toward the Bay, which was that I desired, I must go with them five or six miles down the River into a mighty Thicket of Brush: where we abode almost a fortnight. Here one asked me to make a shirt for her Papoos, for which she gave me a mess of Broth, which was thickened with meal made of the Bark of a Tree, and to make it the better, she had put into it about a handful of Pease, and a few roasted Ground-nuts. I had not seen my son a pritty while, and here was an Indian of whom I made inquiry after him, and asked him when he saw him: he answered me, that such a time his master roasted him, and that himself did eat of piece of him, as big as his two fingers, and that he was very good meat: But the Lord upheld my Spirit, under this discouragement; and I considered their horrible addictedness to lying, and that there is not one of them that makes the least conscience of speaking of truth. In this place, on a cold night, as I lay by the fire, I removed a stick that kept the heat from me, a Squaw moved it down again, at which I lookt up, and she threw a handfull of ashes in mine eyes; I thought I should have been quite blinded, and have never seen more: but lying down, the water run out of my eyes, and carried the dirt with it, that by the morning, I recovered my sight again. Yet upon this, and the like occasions, I hope it is not too much to say with Job, *Have pitty upon me, have pitty upon me, O ye my Friends, for the Hand of the Lord has touched me.*[32] And here I cannot but remember how many times sitting in their Wigwams, and musing on things past, I should suddenly leap up and run out, as if I had been at home, forgetting where I was, and what my condition was: But when I was without, and saw nothing but Wilderness, and Woods, and a company of barbarous heathens, my mind quickly returned to me, which made me think of that, spoken concerning Sampson, who said, *I will go out and shake my self as at other times, but he wist not that the Lord was departed from him.*[33] About this time I began to think that all my hopes of Restoration would come to nothing. I thought of the English Army, and hoped for their coming, and being taken by them, but that failed. I hoped to be carried to Albany, as the Indians had discoursed before, but that failed also. I thought of being sold to my Husband, as my master spake, but in stead of that, my master himself was gone, and left behind, so that my Spirit was now quite ready to sink. I asked them to let me go out and pick up some sticks, that I might get alone, And poure out my heart unto the Lord. Then also I took my Bible to read, but I found no comfort here neither, which many times I was wont to find: So easie a thing it is with God to dry up the Streames of Scripture-comfort from us. Yet I can say, that in all my sorrows and afflictions, God did not leave me to have my impatience work towards himself, as if his wayes were unrighteous. But I knew that he laid upon me less then I deserved. Afterward, before this dolefull time ended with me, I was turning the leaves of my Bible, and the Lord brought to me some Scriptures, which did a little revive me, as that Isai. 55. 8,

[31]The encampment shifted to Hindsdale, New Hampshire, near the Connecticut River.

[32]Job 19:21.

[33]Judges 16:20.

For my thoughts are not your thoughts, neither are your wayes my ways, saith the Lord. And also that, Psal. 37. 5, *Commit thy way unto the Lord, trust also in him, and he shal bring it to pass.* About this time they came yelping from Hadly, where they had killed three English men, and brought one Captive with them, *viz.* Thomas Read. They all gathered about the poor Man, asking him many Questions. I desired also to go and see him; and when I came, he was crying bitterly, supposing they would quickly kill him. Whereupon I asked one of them, whether they intended to kill him; he answered me, they would not: He being a little cheared with that, I asked him about the wel-fare of my Husband, he told me he saw him such a time in the Bay, and he was well, but very melancholly. By which I certainly understood (though I suspected it before) that whatsoever the Indians told me respecting him was vanity and lies. Some of them told me, he was dead, and they had killed him: some said he was Married again, and that the Governour wished him to Marry; and told him he should have his choice, and that all perswaded I was dead. So like were these barbarous creatures to him who was a lyer from the beginning.[34]

As I was sitting once in the Wigwam here, Phillips Maid came in with the Child in her arms, and asked me to give her a piece of my Apron, to make a flap for it, I told her I would not: then my Mistriss bad me give it, but still I said no: the maid told me if I would not give her a piece, she would tear a piece off it: I told her I would tear her Coat then, with that my Mistriss rises up, and takes up a stick big enough to have killed me, and struck at me with it, but I stept out, and she struck the stick into the Mat of the Wigwam. But while she was pulling of it out, I ran to the Maid and gave her all my Apron, and so that storm went over.

Hearing that my Son was come to this place, I went to see him, and told him his Father was well, but melancholly: he told me he was as much grieved for his Father as for himself; I wondered at his speech, for I thought I had enough upon my spirit in reference to my self, to make me mindless of my Husband and every one else: they being safe among their Friends. He told me also, that a while before, his Master (together with other Indians) where[35] going to the French for Powder; but by the way the Mohawks met with them, and killed four of their Company which made the rest turn back again, for it might have been worse with him, had he been sold to the French, than it proved to be in his remaining with the Indians.

I went to see an English Youth in this place, one John Gillberd of Springfield. I found him lying without dores, upon the ground; I asked him how he did? he told me he was very sick of a flux,[36] with eating so much blood: They had turned him out of the Wigwam, and with him an Indian Papoos, almost dead, (whose Parents had been killed) in a bitter cold day, without fire or clothes: the young man himself had nothing on, but his shirt and wastcoat. This sight was enough to melt a heart of flint. There they lay quivering in the Cold, the youth round like a dog; the Papoos stretcht out, with his eyes and nose and mouth full of dirt, and yet alive, and groaning. I advised John to go and get to some fire: he told me he could not stand, but I perswaded him still, lest he should ly there and die: and with much adoe I got him to a fire, and went my self home. As soon as I was got home, his Masters Daughter came after me,

[34]Satan.
[35]Were.
[36]Dysentery.

to know what I had done with the English man, I told her I had got him to a fire in such a place. Now had I need to pray Pauls Prayer, 2 Thess. 3. 2. *That we may be delivered from unreasonable and wicked men.* For her satisfaction I went along with her, and brought her to him; but before I got home again, it was noised about, that I was running away and getting the English youth, along with me, that as soon as I came in, they began to rant and domineer: asking me Where I had been, and what I had been doing? and saying they would knock him on the head: I told them, I had been seeing the English Youth, and that I would not run away, they told me I lyed, and taking up a Hatchet, they came to me, and said they would knock me down if I stirred out again; and so confined me to the Wigwam. Now may I say with David, 2 Sam. 24. 14. *I am in a great strait.* If I keep in, I must dy with hunger, and if I go out, I must be knockt in head. This distressed condition held that day, and half the next; And then the Lord remembred me, whose mercyes are great. Then came an Indian to me with a pair of stockings that were too big for him, and he would have me ravel them out, and knit them fit for him. I shewed my self willing, and bid him ask my mistriss if I might go along with him a little way; she said yes, I might, but I was not a little refresht with that news, that I had my liberty again. Then I went along with him, and he gave me some roasted Ground-nuts, which did again revive my feeble stomach.

Being got out of her sight, I had time and liberty again to look into my Bible: Which was my Guid by day, and my Pillow by night. Now that comfortable Scripture presented it self to me, Isa. 54. 7. *For a smal moment have I forsaken thee, but with great mercies will I gather thee.* Thus the Lord carried me along from one time to another, and made good to me this precious promise, and many others. Then my Son came to see me, and I asked his master to let him stay a while with me, that I might comb his head, and look over him, for he was almost overcome with lice. He told me, when I had done, that he was very hungry, but I had nothing to relieve him; but bid him go into the Wigwams as he went along, and see if he could get any thing among them. Which he did, and it seems tarried a little too long; for his Master was angry with him, and beat him, and then sold him. Then he came running to tell me he had a new Master, and that he had given him some Groundnuts already. Then I went along with him to his new Master who told me he loved him: and he should not want. So his Master carried him away, and I never saw him afterward, till I saw him at Pascataqua in Portsmouth.

That night they bade me go out of the Wigwam again: my Mistrisses Papoos was sick, and it died that night, and there was one benefit in it, that there was more room. I went to a Wigwam, and they bade me come in, and gave me a skin to ly upon, and a mess of Venson and Ground-nuts, which was a choice Dish among them. On the morrow they buried the Papoos, and afterward, both morning and evening, there came a company to mourn and howle with her: though I confess, I could not much condole with them. Many sorrowfull dayes I had in this place: often getting alone; *like a Crane, or a Swallow, so did I chatter: I did mourn as a Dove, mine eyes ail with looking upward. Oh, Lord, I am oppressed; undertake for me,* Isa. 38. 14. I could tell the Lord as Hezeckiah, ver. 3. *Remember now O Lord, I beseech thee, how I have walked before thee in truth.*[37] Now had I time to examine all my wayes: my

[37]Isaiah 38:3.

Conscience did not accuse me of un-righteousness toward one or other: yet I saw how in my walk with God, I had been a careless creature. As David said, *Against thee, thee only have I sinned:*[38] and I might say with the poor Publican, *God be merciful unto me a sinner.*[39] On the Sabbath-dayes, I could look upon the Sun and think how People were going to the house of God, to have their Souls refresht; and then home, and their bodies also: but I was destitute of both; and might say as the poor Prodigal, *he would fain have filled his belly with the husks that the Swine did eat, and no man gave unto him.* Luke 15. 16. For I must say with him, *Father I have sinned against Heaven, and in thy sight,*[40] ver. 21. I remembred how on the night before and after the Sabbath, when my Family was about me, and Relations and Neighbours with us, we would pray and sing, and then have a comfortable Bed to ly down on: but in stead of all this, I had only a little Swill for the body, and then like a Swine, must ly down on the ground. I cannot express to man the sorrow that lay upon my Spirit, the Lord knows it. Yet that comfortable Scripture would often come to my mind, *For a small moment have I forsaken thee, but with great mercies will I gather thee.*[41]

The Nineteenth Remove

They said, when we went out, that we must travel to Wachuset this day. But a bitter weary day I had of it, travelling now three dayes together, without resting any day between. At last, after many weary steps, I saw Wachuset hills, but many miles off. Then we came to a great Swamp, through which we travelled, up to the knees in mud and water, which was heavy going to one tyred before. Being almost spent, I thought I should have sunk down at last, and never gat out; but I may say, as in Psal. 94. 18, *When my foot slipped, thy mercy, O Lord, held me up.* Going along, having indeed my life, but little spirit, Philip, who was in the Company, came up and took me by the hand, and said, Two weeks more and you shal be Mistress again. I asked him, if he spake true? he answered, Yes, and quickly you shal come to your master again; who had been gone from us three weeks. After many weary steps we came to Wachuset, where he was: and glad I was to see him. He asked me, When I washt me? I told him not this month, then he fetcht me some water himself, and bid me wash, and gave me the Glass to see how I lookt; and bid his Squaw give me something to eat: so she gave me a mess of Beans and meat, and a little Ground-nut Cake. I was wonderfully revived with this favour shewed me, Psal. 106. 46, *He made them also to be pittied, of all those that carried them Captives.*

My master had three Squaws, living sometimes with one, and sometimes with another one, this old Squaw, at whose Wigwam I was, and with whom my Master had been those three weeks. Another was Wattimore, with whom I had lived and served all this while: A severe and proud Dame she was, bestowing every day in dressing her self neat as much time as any of the Gentry of the land: powdering her hair, and painting her face, going with Neck-laces, with Jewels in her ears, and Bracelets upon her hands: When she had dressed her self, her work was to make Girdles of Wampom and Beads. The third Squaw was a younger one, by whom he had two

[38]Psalm 51:4.
[39]Luke 6:36.
[40]Luke 15:21.
[41]Isaiah 54:7.

Papooses. By that time I was refresht by the old Squaw, with whom my master was, Wettimores Maid came to call me home, at which I fell a weeping. Then the old Squaw told me, to encourage me, that if I wanted victuals, I should come to her, and that I should ly there in her Wigwam. Then I went with the maid, and quickly came again and lodged there. The Squaw laid a Mat under me, and a good Rugg over me, the first time I had any such kindness shewed me. I understood that Wettimore thought, that if she should let me go and serve with the old Squaw, she would be in danger to loose, not only my service, but the redemption-pay also. And I was not a little glad to hear this; being by it raised in my hopes, that in Gods due time there would be an end of this sorrowfull hour. Then came an Indian, and asked me to knit him three pair of Stockins, for which I had a Hat, and a silk Handkerchief. Then another asked me to make her a shift, for which she gave me an Apron.

Then came Tom and Peter,[42] with the second Letter from the Council, about the Captives. Though they were Indians, I gat them by the hand, and burst out into tears; my heart was so full that I could not speak to them; but recovering my self, I asked them how my husband did, and all my friends and acquaintance? they said, They are all very well but melancholy. They brought me two Biskets, and a pound of Tobacco. The Tobacco I quickly gave away; when it was all gone, one asked me to give him a pipe of Tobacco, I told him it was all gone; then began he to rant and threaten. I told him when my Husband came I would give him some: Hang him Rogue (sayes he) I will knock out his brains, if he comes here. And then again, in the same breath they would say, That if there should come an hundred without Guns, they would do them no hurt. So unstable and like mad men they were. So that fearing the worst, I durst not send to my Husband, though there were some thoughts of his coming to Redeem and fetch me, not knowing what might follow. For there was little more trust to them then to the master they served. When the Letter was come, the Saggamores met to consult about the Captives, and called me to them to enquire how much my husband would give to redeem me, when I came I sate down among them, as I was wont to do, as their manner is: Then they bade me stand up, and said, they were the General Court.[43] They bid me speak what I thought he would give. Now knowing that all we had was destroyed by the Indians, I was in a great strait: I thought if I should speak of but a little, it would be slighted, and hinder the matter; if of a great sum, I knew not where it would be procured: yet at a venture, I said Twenty pounds, yet desired them to take less; but they would not hear of that, but sent that message to Boston, that for Twenty pounds I should be redeemed. It was a Praying-Indian that wrote their Letter for them. There was another Praying Indian, who told me, that he had a brother, that would not eat Horse; his conscience was so tender and scrupulous (though as large as hell, for the destruction of poor Christians). Then he said, he read that Scripture to him, 2 Kings, 6. 25. *There was a famine in Samaria, and behold they beseiged it, untill an Asses head was sold for fourscore pieces of silver, and the fourth part of a Kab of Doves dung, for five pieces of silver.* He expounded this place to his brother, and shewed him that it was lawfull to eat that in a Famine which is not at another time. And now, sayes he, he will eat Horse with any Indian of them all. There was another Praying-Indian, who when he had done all the mischief that he could,

[42]Christian Indians Tom Dublet and Peter Conway, who were negotiating for ransom.

[43]In imitation of the Colonial Assembly of Massachusetts.

betrayed his own Father into the English hands, thereby to purchase his own life. Another Praying-Indian was at Sudbury-fight,[44] though, as he deserved, he was afterward hanged for it. There was another Praying Indian, so wicked and cruel, and he said, it was too true, for they had made sad work at Sudbury, as indeed it proved. Yet they came home without that rejoycing and triumphing over their victory, which they were wont to shew at other times, but rather like Dogs (as they say) which have lost their ears. Yet I could not perceive that it was for their own loss of men: They said, they had not lost above five or six: and I missed none, except in one Wigwam. When they went, they acted as if the Devil had told them that they should gain the victory: and now they acted, as if the Devil had told them they should have a fall. Whither it were so or no, I cannot tell, but so it proved, for quickly they began to fall, and so held on that Summer, till they came to utter ruine. . . .

The Twentieth Remove[45]

It was their usual manner to remove, when they had done any mischief, lest they should be found out: and so they did at this time. We went about three or four miles, and there they built a great Wigwam, big enough to hold an hundred Indians, which they did in preparation to a great day of Dancing. They would say now amongest themselves, that the Governour would be so angry for his loss at Sudbury, that he would send no more about the Captives, which made me grieve and tremble. My Sister being not far from the place where we now were, and hearing that I was here, desired her master to let her come and see me, and he was willing to it, and would go with her: but she being ready before him, told him she would go before, and was come within a Mile or two of the place; Then he overtook her, and began to rant as if he had been mad; and made her go back again in the Rain; so that I never saw her till I saw her in Charlestown. But the Lord requited many of their ill doings, for this Indian her Master, was hanged afterward at Boston. The Indians now began to come from all quarters, against their merry dancing day. Among some of them came one Goodwife Kettle. I told her my heart was so heavy that it was ready to break: so is mine too said she, but yet said, I hope we shall hear some good news shortly. I could hear how earnestly my Sister desired to see me, and I as earnestly desired to see her: and yet neither of us could get an opportunity. My Daughter was also now about a mile off, and I had not seen her in nine or ten weeks, as I had not seen my Sister since our first taking. I earnestly desired them to let me go and see them: yea, I intreated, begged, and perswaded them, but to let me see my Daughter; and yet so hard hearted were they, that they would not suffer it. They made use of their tyrannical power whilst they had it: but through the Lords wonderfull mercy, their time was now but short.

On a Sabbath day, the Sun being about an hour high in the afternoon, came Mr. John Hoar[46] (the Council permitting him, and his own foreward spirit inclining him)

[44]An April 18 attack on Sudbury, Massachusetts.

[45]This remove, from April 28–May 2, was to an encampment near the southern end of Wachusett Lake, Princeton, Massachusetts.

[46]Delegated by Rowlandson's husband to represent him at the Council for the Sagamore Indians and to bargain for Mrs. Rowlandson's redemption.

together with the two fore-mentioned Indians, Tom and Peter, with their third Letter from the Council. When they came near, I was abroad: though I saw them not, they presently called me in, and bade me sit down and not stir. Then they catched up their Guns, and away they ran, as if an Enemy had been at hand; and the Guns went off apace. I manifested some great trouble, and they asked me what was the matter? I told them, I thought they had killed the English-man (for they had in the mean time informed me that an English-man was come) they said, No; They shot over his Horse and under, and before his Horse; and they pusht him this way and that way, at their pleasure: shewing what they could do: Then they let them come to their Wigwams. I begged of them to let me see the English-man, but they would not. But there was I fain to sit their pleasure. When they had talked their fill with him, they suffered me to go to him. We asked each other of our welfare, and how my Husband did, and all my Friends? He told me they were all well, and would be glad to see me. Amongst other things which my Husband sent me, there came a pound of Tobacco: which I sold for nine shillings in Money: for many of the Indians for want of Tobacco, smoaked Hemlock, and Ground-Ivy. It was a great mistake in any, who thought I sent for Tobacco: for through the favour of God, that desire was overcome. I now asked them, whither I should go home with Mr. Hoar? They answered No, one and another of them: and it being night, we lay down with that answer; in the morning, Mr. Hoar invited the Saggamores to Dinner; but when we went to get it ready, we found that they had stollen the greatest part of the Provision Mr. Hoar had brought, out of his Bags, in the night. And we may see the wonderfull power of God, in that one passage, in that when there was such a great number of the Indians together, and so greedy of a little good food; and no English there, but Mr. Hoar and my self: that there they did not knock us in the head, and take what we had: there being not only some Provision, but also Trading cloth,[47] a part of the twenty pounds agreed upon: But instead of doing us any mischief, they seemed to be ashamed of the fact, and said, it were some Matchit Indian[48] that did it. Oh, that we could believe that there is no thing too hard for God! God shewed his Power over the Heathen in this, as he did over the hungry Lyons when Daniel was cast into the Den.[49] Mr. Hoar called them betime to Dinner, but they ate very little, they being so busie in dressing themselves, and getting ready for their Dance: which was carried on by eight of them, four Men and four Squaws: My master and mistress being two. He was dressed in his Holland shirt,[50] with great Laces sewed at the tail of it, he had his silver Buttons, his white Stockins, his Garters were hung round with Shillings, and he had Girdles of Wampom[51] upon his head and shoulders. She had a Kersey Coat,[52] and covered with Girdles of Wampom from the Loins upward: her armes from her elbows to her hands were covered with Bracelets; there were handfulls of Necklaces about her neck, and severall sorts of Jewels in her ears. She had fine red Stokins and white Shoos, her hair powdered and face painted Red, that was alwayes before Black. And all the Dancers were after the same manner. There were two other singing and knocking on a Kettle for their musick. They keept hopping up and down one after

[47]Cloth used for barter.

[48]A bad Indian.

[49]See Daniel 6:1–29.

[50]Linen.

[51]Polished shell beads used by the Indians as currency.

[52]Coarse cloth, ribbed and woven from long wool.

another, with a Kettle of water in the midst, standing warm upon some Embers, to drink of when they were dry. They held on till it was almost night, throwing out Wampom to the standers by. At night I asked them again, if I should go home? They all as one said No, except[53] my Husband would come for me. When we were lain down, my Master went out of the Wigwam, and by and by sent in an Indian called James the Printer[54] who told Mr. Hoar, that my Master would let me go home to morrow, if he would let him have one pint of Liquors. Then Mr. Hoar called his own Indians, Tom and Peter, and bid them go and see whither he would promise it before them three: and if he would, he should have it; which he did, and he had it. Then Philip[55] smelling the business cal'd me to him, and asked me what I would give him, to tell me some good news, and speak a good word for me. I told him, I could not tell what to give him, I would any thing I had, and asked him what he would have? He said, two Coats and twenty shillings in Mony, and half a bushel of seed Corn, and some Tobacco. I thanked him for his love: but I knew the good news as well as the crafty Fox. My Master after he had had his drink, quickly came ranting into the Wigwam again, and called for Mr. Hoar, drinking to him, and saying, He was a good man: and then again he would say, Hang him Rogue: Being almost drunk, he would drink to him, and yet presently say he should be hanged. Then he called for me. I trembled to hear him, yet I was fain to go to him, and he drank to me, shewing no incivility. He was the first Indian I saw drunk all the while that I was amongst them. At last his Squaw ran out, and he after her, round the Wigwam, with his mony jingling at his knees: But she escaped him: But having an old Squaw he ran to her: and so through the Lords mercy, we were no more troubled that night. Yet I had not a comfortable nights rest: for I think I can say, I did not sleep for three nights together. The night before the Letter came from the Council, I could not rest, I was so full of feares and troubles, God many times leaving us most in the dark, when deliverance is nearest: yea, at this time I could not rest night nor day. The next night I was overjoyed, Mr. Hoar being come, and that with such good tidings. The third night I was even swallowed up with the thoughts of things, *viz.* that ever I should go home again; and that I must go, leaving my Children behind me in the Wilderness; so that sleep was now almost departed from mine eyes.

On Tuesday morning they called their General Court (as they call it) to consult and determine, whether I should go home or no: And they all as one man did seemingly consent to it, that I should go home; except Philip, who would not come among them.

But before I go any further, I would take leave to mention a few remarkable passages of providence, which I took special notice of in my afflicted time.

1. Of the fair opportunity lost in the long March, a little after the Fort-fight, when our English Army was so numerous, and in pursuit of the Enemy, and so near as to take several and destroy them: and the Enemy in such distress for food, that our men might track them by their rooting in the earth for Ground-nuts, whilest they were flying for their lives. I say, that then our Army should want Provision, and be forced to leave their pursuit and return homeward: and the very next week the

[53]Unless.

[54]Indian who assisted Reverend John Eliot in his printing of the Bible.

[55]An Indian who aided Rowlandson earlier in the journey.

Enemy came upon our Town, like Bears bereft of their whelps, or so many ravenous Wolves, rending us and our Lambs to death. But what shall I say? God seemed to leave his People to themselves, and order all things for his own holy ends. *Shal there be evil in the City and the Lord hath not done it?*[56] *They are not grieved for the affliction of Joseph, therefore shal they go Captive, with the first that go Captive.*[57] It is the Lords doing, and it should be marvelous in our eyes.

2. I cannot but remember how the Indians derided the slowness, and dulness of the English Army, in its setting out. For after the desolations at Lancaster and Medfield, as I went along with them, they asked me when I thought the English Army would come after them? I told them I could not tell: It may be they will come in May, said they. Thus did they scoffe at us, as if the English would be a quarter of a year getting ready.

3. Which also I have hinted before, when the English Army with new supplies were sent forth to pursue after the enemy, and they understanding it, fled before them till they came to Baquaug River, where they forthwith went over safely; that that River should be impassable to the English. I can but admire to see the wonderfull providence of God in preserving the heathen for farther affliction to our poor Countrey. They could go in great numbers over, but the English must stop: God had an over-ruling hand in all those things.

4. It was thought, if their Corn were cut down, they would starve and dy with hunger: and all their Corn that could be found, was destroyed, and they driven from that little they had in store, into the Woods in the midst of Winter; and yet how to admiration did the Lord preserve them for his holy ends, and the destruction of many still amongst the English! strangely did the Lord provide for them; that I did not see (all the time I was among them) one Man, Woman, or Child, die with hunger.

Though many times they would eat that, that a Hog or a Dog would hardly touch; yet by that God strengthned them to be a scourge to his People.

The chief and commonest food was Ground-nuts: They eat also Nuts and Acorns, Harty-choaks,[58] Lilly roots, Ground-beans, and several other weeds and roots, that I know not.

They would pick up old bones, and cut them to pieces at the joynts, and if they were full of wormes and magots, they would scald them over the fire to make the vermine come out, and then boile them, and drink up the Liquor, and then beat the great ends of them in a Morter, and so eat them. They would eat Horses guts, and ears, and all sorts of wild Birds which they could catch: also Bear, Vennison, Beaver, Tortois, Frogs, Squirrels, Dogs, Skunks, Rattle-snakes; yea, the very Bark of Trees; besides all sorts of creatures, and provision which they plundered from the English. I can but stand in admiration to see the wonderful power of God, in providing for such a vast number of our Enemies in the Wilderness, where there was nothing to be seen, but from hand to mouth. Many times in a morning, the generality of them would eat up all they had, and yet have some forther supply against they wanted. It is said, Psal. 81. 13, 14. *Oh, that my People had hearkned to me, and Israel had walked in my wayes, I should soon have subdued their Enemies, and turned my hand against their Adversaries.* But now our perverse and evil carriages in the sight of the Lord,

[56] Amos 3:6.
[57] Amos 6:6–7.
[58] The Jerusalem artichoke which grows wild in North America.

have so offended him, that instead of turning his hand against them, the Lord feeds and nourishes them up to be a scourge to the whole Land.

5. Another thing that I would observe is, the strange providence of God, in turning things about when the Indians was at the highest, and the English at the lowest. I was with the Enemy eleven weeks and five dayes, and not one Week passed without the fury of the Enemy, and some desolation by fire and sword upon one place or other. They mourned (with their black faces) for their own lossess, yet triumphed and rejoyced in their inhumane, and many times devilish cruelty to the English. They would boast much of their Victories; saying, that in two hours time they had destroyed such a Captain, and his Company at such a place; and such a Captain and his Company in such a place; and such a Captain and his Company in such a place: and boast how many Towns they had destroyed, and then scoffe, and say, They had done them a good turn, to send them to Heaven so soon. Again, they would say, This Summer that they would knock all the Rogues in the head, or drive them into the Sea, or make them flie the Countrey: thinking surely, Agag-like,[59] *The bitterness of Death is past.*[60] Now the Heathen begins to think all is their own, and the poor Christians hopes to fail (as to man) and now their eyes are more to God, and their hearts sigh heaven-ward: and to say in good earnest, *Help Lord, or we perish:* When the Lord had brought his people to this, that they saw no help in any thing but himself: then he takes the quarrel into his own hand: and though they had made a pit, in their own imaginations, as deep as hell for the Christians that Summer, yet the Lord hurll'd them selves into it. And the Lord had not so many wayes before to preserve them, but now he hath as many to destroy them.

But to return again to my going home, where we may see a remarkable change of Providence: At first they were all against it, except my Husband would come for me; but afterwards they assented to it, and seemed much to rejoyce in it; some askt me to send them some Bread, others some Tobacco, others shaking me by the hand, offering me a Hood and Scarfe to ride in; not one moving hand or tongue against it. Thus hath the Lord answered my poor desire, and the many earnest requests of others put up unto God for me. In my travels an Indian came to me, and told me, if I were willing, he and his Squaw would run away, and go home along with me: I told him No: I was not willing to run away, but desired to wait Gods time, that I might go home quietly, and without fear. And now God hath granted me my desire. O the wonderfull power of God that I have seen, and the experience that I have had: I have been in the midst of those roaring Lyons, and Salvage Bears, that feared neither God, nor Man, nor the Devil, by night and day, alone and in company: sleeping all sorts together, and yet not one of them ever offered me the least abuse of unchastity to me, in word or action. Though some are ready to say, I speak it for my own credit; But I speak it in the presence of God, and to his Glory. Gods Power is as great now, and as sufficient to save, as when he preserved Daniel in the Lions Den: or the three Children in the fiery Furnace. I may well say as his Psal. 107. 12, *Oh give thanks unto the Lord for he is good, for his mercy endureth for ever.*[61] Let the Redeemed of the Lord say so, whom he hath redeemed from the hand of the Enemy, especially that I should come away in the midst of so many hundreds of Enemies quietly and peacably, and

[59] King of Amalek; defeated by Saul and thought himself spared but was slain instead by Samuel.

[60] I Samuel 15:32.

[61] Daniel 3:13–30.

not a Dog moving his tongue. So I took my leave of them, and in coming along my heart melted into tears, more then all the while I was with them, and I was almost swallowed up with the thoughts that ever I should go home again. About the Sun going down, Mr. Hoar, and my self, and the two Indians came to Lancaster, and a solemn sight it was to me. There had I lived many comfortable years amongst my Relations and Neighbours, and now not one Christian to be seen, nor one house left standing. We went on to a Farm house that was yet standing, where we lay all night: and a comfortable lodging we had, though nothing but straw to ly on. The Lord preserved us in safety that night, and raised us up again in the morning, and carried us along, that before noon, we came to Concord. Now was I full of joy, and yet not without sorrow: joy to see such a lovely sight, so many Christians together, and some of them my Neighbours: There I met with my Brother, and my Brother in Law, who asked me, if I knew where his Wife was? Poor heart! he had helped to bury her, and knew it not; she being shot down by the house was partly burnt: so that those who were at Boston at the desolation of the Town, and came back afterward, and buried the dead, did not know her. Yet I was not without sorrow, to think how many were looking and longing, and my own Children amongst the rest, to enjoy that deliverance that I had now received, and I did not know whither ever I should see them again. Being recruited with food and raiment we went to Boston that day, where I met with my dear Husband, but the thoughts of our dear Children, one being dead, and the other we could not tell where, abated our comfort each to other. I was not before so much hem'd in with the merciless and cruel Heathen, but now as much with pittiful, tender-hearted and compassionate Christians. In that poor, and destressed, and beggerly condition I was received in, I was kindly entertained in severall Houses: so much love I received from several (some of whom I knew, and others I knew not) that I am not capable to declare it. But the Lord knows them all by name: The Lord reward them seven fold into their bosoms of his spirituals, for their temporals. The twenty pounds the price of my redemption was raised by some Boston Gentlemen, and Mrs. Usher, whose bounty and religious charity, I would not forget to make mention of. Then Mr. Thomas Shepard of Charlstown received us into his House, where we continued eleven weeks; and a Father and Mother they were to us. And many more tender-hearted Friends we met with in that place. We were now in the midst of love, yet not without much and frequent heaviness of heart for our poor Children, and other Relations, who were still in affliction. The week following, after my coming in, the Governour and Council sent forth to the Indians again; and that not without success; for they brought in my Sister, and Good-wife Kettle: Their not knowing where our Children were, was a sore tryal to us still, and yet we were not without secret hopes that we should see them again. That which was dead lay heavier upon my spirit, than those which were alive and amongst the Heathen; thinking how it suffered with its wounds, and I was no way able to relieve it; and how it was buried by the Heathen in the Wilderness from among all Christians. We were hurried up and down in our thoughts, sometime we should hear a report that they were gone this way, and sometimes that; and that they were come in, in this place or that: We kept enquiring and listning to hear concerning them, but no certain news as yet. About this time the Council had ordered a day a publick Thanks-giving:[62] though I thought I had still cause of mourning, and being unsettled in our minds, we thought

[62]Thanksgiving, June 29, 1676.

we would ride toward the Eastward, to see if we could hear any thing concerning our Children. And as we were riding along (God is the wise disposer of all things) between Ipswich and Rowly we met with Mr. William Hubbard, who told us that our Son Joseph was come in to Major Waldrens, and another with him, which was my Sisters Son. I asked him how he knew it? He said, the Major himself told him so. So along we went till we came to Newbury; and their Minister being absent, they desired my Husband to Preach the Thanks giving for them; but he was not willing to stay there that night, but would go over to Salisbury, to hear further, and come again in the morning; which he did, and Preached there that day. At night, when he had done, one came and told him that his Daughter was come in at Providence: Here was mercy on both hands: Now hath God fulfiled that precious Scripture which was such a comfort to me in my distressed condition. When my heart was ready to sink into the Earth (my Children being gone I could not tell whither) and my knees trembled under me, And I was walking through the valley of the shadow of Death: Then the Lord brought, and now has fulfilled that reviving word unto me: *Thus saith the Lord, Refrain thy voice from weeping, and thine eyes from tears, for thy Work shall be rewarded, saith the Lord, and they sall come again from the Land of the Enemy.*[63] Now we were between them, the one on the East, and the other on the West: Our Son being nearest, we went to him first, to Portsmouth, where we met with him, and with the Major also: who told us he had done what he could, but could not redeem him under seven pounds; which the good People thereabouts were pleased to pay. The Lord reward the Major, and all the rest, though unknown to me, for their labour of Love. My Sisters Son was redeemed for four pounds, which the Council gave order for the payment of. Having now received one of our Children, we hastened toward the other; going back through Newbury, my Husband preached there on the Sabbath-day: for which they rewarded him many fold.

On Munday we came to Charlstown, where we heard that the Governour of Road-Island had sent over for our Daughter, to take care of her, being now within his Jurisdiction: which should not pass without our acknowledgments. But she being nearer Rehoboth than Road-Island, Mr. Newman went over, and took care of her, and brought her to his own House. And the goodness of God was admirable to us in our low estate, in that he raised up passionate[64] Friends on every side to us, when we had nothing to recompance any for their love. The Indians were now gone that way, that it was apprehended dangerous to go to her: But the Carts which carried Provision to the English Army, being guarded, brought her with them to Dorchester, where we received her safe: blessed be the Lord for it, For great is his Power, and he can do whatsoever seemeth him good. Her coming in was after this manner: She was travelling one day with the Indians, with her basket at her back; the company of Indians were got before her, and gone out of sight, all except one Squaw; she followed the Squaw till night, and then both of them lay down, having nothing over them but the heavens, and under them but the earth. Thus she travelled three dayes together, not knowing whither she was going: having nothing to eat or drink but water, and green Hirtle-berries.[65] At last they came into Providence, where she was kindly en-

[63]Jeremiah 31:16.
[64]Compassionate.
[65]Huckleberries.

tertained by several of that Town. The Indians often said, that I should never have her under twenty pounds: But now the Lord hath brought her in upon free-cost, and given her to me the second time. The Lord make us a blessing indeed, each to others. Now have I seen that Scripture also fulfilled, Deut. 30:4, 7. *If any of thine be driven out to the outmost parts of heaven, from thence will the Lord thy God gather thee, and from thence will he fetch thee. And the Lord thy God will put all these curses upon thine enemies, and on them which hate thee, which persecuted thee.* Thus hath the Lord brought me and mine out of that horrible pit, and hath set us in the midst of tender-hearted and compassionate Christians. It is the desire of my soul, that we may walk worthy of the mercies received, and which we are receiving.

Our Family being now gathered together (those of us that were living) the South Church in Boston hired an House for us: Then we removed from Mr. Shepards, those cordial Friends, and went to Boston, where we continued about three quarters of a year: Still the Lord went along with us, and provided graciously for us. I thought it somewhat strange to set up House-keeping with bare walls; but as Solomon sayes, *Mony answers all things,*[66] and that we had through the benevolence of Christian-friends, some in this Town, and some in that, and others: And some from England, that in a little time we might look, and see the House furnished with love. The Lord hath been exceeding good to us in our low estate, in that when we had neither house nor home, nor other necessaries; the Lord so moved the hearts of these and those towards us, that we wanted neither food, nor raiment for our selves or ours, Prov. 18. 24. *There is a Friend which sticketh closer than a Brother.* And how many such Friends have we found, and now living amongst? And truly such a Friend have we found him to be unto us, in whose house we lived, *viz.* Mr. James Whitcomb, a Friend unto us near hand, and afar off.

I can remember the time, when I used to sleep quietly without workings in my thoughts, whole nights together, but now it is other wayes with me. When all are fast about me, and no eye open, but his who ever waketh, my thoughts are upon things past, upon the awfull dispensation of the Lord towards us; upon his wonderfull power and might, in carrying of us through so many difficulties, in returning us in safety, and suffering none to hurt us. I remember in the night season, how the other day I was in the midst of thousands of enemies, and nothing but death before me: It is then hard work to perswade my self, that ever I should be satisfied with bread again. But now we are fed with the finest of the Wheat, and, as I may say, With honey out of the rock:[67] In stead of the Husk, we have the fatted Calf.[68] The thoughts of these things in the particulars of them, and of the love and goodness of God towards us, make it true of me, what David said of himself, Psal. 6. 5.[69] *I watered my Couch with my tears.* Oh! the wonderfull power of God that mine eyes have seen, affording matter enough for my thoughts to run in, that when others are sleeping mine eyes are weeping.

I have seen the extrem vanity of this World: One hour I have been in health, and wealth, wanting nothing: But the next hour in sickness and wounds, and death, having nothing but sorrow and affliction.

[66]Ecclesiastes 10:19.
[67]Psalm 81:16.
[68]Luke 15:23.
[69]Psalm 6:6.

Before I knew what affliction meant, I was ready sometimes to wish for it. When I lived in prosperity, having the comforts of the World about me, my relations by me, my Heart chearfull, and taking little care for any thing; and yet seeing many, whom I preferred before my self, under many tryals and afflictions, in sickness, weakness, poverty, losses, crosses, and cares of the World, I should be sometimes jealous least I should have my portion in this life, and that Scripture would come to my mind. Heb. 12. 6 *For whom the Lord loveth he chasteneth, and scourgeth every Son whom he receiveth.* But now I see the Lord had his time to scourge and chasten me. The portion of some is to have their afflictions by drops, now one drop and then another; but the dregs of the Cup, the Wine of astonishment, like a sweeping rain that leaveth no food, did the Lord prepare to be my portion. Affliction I wanted, and affliction I had, full measure (I thought) pressed down and running over; yet I see, when God calls a Person to any thing, and through never so many difficulties, yet he is fully able to carry them through and make them see, and say they have been gainers thereby. And I hope I can say in some measure, As David did, *It is good for me that I have been afflicted.*[70] The Lord hath shewed me the vanity of these outward things. That they are the Vanity of vanities, and vexation of spirit; that they are but a shadow, a blast, a bubble, and things of no continuance. That we must rely on God himself, and our whole dependance must be upon him. If trouble from smaller matters begin to arise in me, I have something at hand to check my self with, and say, why am I troubled? It was but the other day that if I had had the world, I would have given it for my freedom, or to have been a Servant to a Christian. I have learned to look beyond present and smaller troubles, and to be quieted under them, as Moses said, Exod. 14. 13. *Stand still and see the salvation of the Lord.*

1682

Edward Taylor 1642?–1729

Celebrated today as colonial America's most prolific and inventive poet, Edward Taylor was virtually unpublished in his lifetime. Not until the twentieth century did Thomas Johnson unearth Taylor's long-buried manuscripts at the Yale University Library and in 1937 publish the first selections from Taylor's *Preparatory Meditations* (wr. 1682–1725) and *Gods Determinations touching his Elect* (c. 1680). These collections revealed Taylor to be a frontier parson with a secret passion for the confessional meditative lyrics and versified theological allegories popular among seventeenth-century English poets and clerics. Despite Taylor's prominence as minister of the Congregational Church in the fortified town of Westfield for fifty-eight years until his death on June 24, 1729, details of his life remain rudimentary, recounted only in laconic notes from an 1848 family memoir, the Westfield *Church Rec-ords,* and Taylor's all too brief *Diary* (wr. 1668–1671).

Most likely born in 1642 in Sketchley, Leicestershire, England, the son of a yeo-

[70]Psalm 119:71.

man farmer, Taylor often adopts quaint colloquialisms and the imagery of provincial farming and weaving in his later poems. According to great-grandson Henry Wyllys Taylor's genealogical journal, Taylor studied for either four or seven years at Cambridge University, although certain proof is lacking. As a Protestant dissenter, he was buoyed by Oliver Cromwell's Puritan Commonwealth (1649–1660), then buffeted during the 1660 monarchical Restoration under Charles II, and finally exiled by choice in 1668. His refusal to sign the 1662 Act of Uniformity probably prevented Taylor from teaching school (as he may have done earlier in Bagworth), worshiping, or pursuing a licensed clerical career. His earliest extant verse and later sermons virulently satirize "Popish" and Anglican worship as well as other heresies (such as Quakerism) that threatened an orthodox Calvinist theology and congregational polity.

Brimming with nautical observations of shifting winds, stormy delays, treacherous shoals, and whale sightings, Taylor's *Diary* catalogues his Atlantic crossing, from the April 26, 1668, departure to his safe deliverance on July 5 in the Massachusetts Bay Colony, where he received cordial welcomes and lodging from notables Reverend Increase Mather and the mintmaster, merchant John Hull. After conferring with President Charles Chauncy, he entered Harvard University July 23 as an upperclassman, where he served two years as college butler, collecting food and drink payments, and was chamber-fellow with diarist Samuel Sewall, a lifelong friend and correspondent. When he departed on November 27, 1671, for Westfield, Taylor records that it was "not without much apprehension of a tedious and hazzardous journey"—one hundred miles in dead winter through the Connecticut Valley's rugged wilderness forests. Despite his fears, Taylor settled energetically into his multiple roles as farmer, rural physician, and minister to a small, frequently endangered band of the pioneering Elect, who were called to Sabbath worship by "beat of drum." After delays occasioned by King Philip's War against the Indians and early hardships, the first church at Westfield was formally organized on August 27, 1679. The gathering of local elders and neighboring clergy included Northampton's Solomon Stoddard, with whom Taylor would later split bitterly over differences in administering the Lord's Supper. Delivered on this occasion, Taylor's spiritual "Relation" and his "Foundation Day Sermon," now in the Westfield *Church Records,* are among his earliest extant prose writings. They reveal Taylor in his dual position as penitent sinner, who movingly recounts his personal conversion and acceptance of God's grace, and as community preacher, leading his congregation to the founding of a "Particular Church" which "is an Habitation of God through the Spirit" and over which he would preside for another fifty years as spiritual guide, disciplinary statesman, and piously learned theologian.

Although Taylor wrote several *pro forma* funeral elegies for Harvard dignitaries and public figures and a verse declamation defending the English language, these early literary efforts (1668–1671) were somberly pedantic exercises in heroic couplets. But in his next attempts at occasional verse (1674–1683), he sought for more varied lyrical forms and styles, whether through acrostics and love poems to his wife-to-be ("Were but my Muse an Huswife Good"), miniature allegories on insects or domestic objects, as in "Upon a Spider Catching a Fly" and "Huswifery," or spiritualized contemplations of natural "occurants," such as "The Ebb & Flow" or "Upon the Sweeping Flood." Among the most moving poems is the anguished pathos of "Upon Wedlock, & Death of Children" (1682?). On November 5, 1674, Taylor had married Elizabeth Fitch, who bore him eight children, five of whom died in infancy; his second wife (1692), Ruth

Wyllys, produced six children. With its heart-wrenching personal grief, "Upon Wedlock, & Death of Children" resembles the elegies of Anne Bradstreet, whose 1678 second edition of poems Taylor owned. The premature death of infants tested Taylor's faithful submission, as a loving father and husband, to God's will and strengthened the "True-Love Knot" binding him to both wife and Deity. His 1689 funeral elegy for Elizabeth Fitch, "My Onely Dove," echoes, though not without "Gust of Sorrows groan," the customary eulogistic praise for a Puritan woman as "Mistriss, Mother, Wife." During this early period, Taylor also inaugurated his first version (1674–1675) of metrical paraphrases of the Psalms (1–9, 18). He transcribed a second version, of virtually all different Psalms (11–39, 48–49), during the early 1680s. The paraphrases are a self-conscious tutorial in versification, imitative of the English Sternhold-Hopkins psalter and the Massachusetts *Bay Psalm Book.* In the occasional poems as well as Psalm paraphrases, Taylor's distinctive meditative voice begins to emerge, perhaps as a result of the discipline itself, his identification with David's gift of hymn-like poesy, or the inspiration of "occurant" contemplations.

During the late 1670s and early 1680s, Taylor also brought together his vision of Christian salvation history with varied verse experiments to create his first major poem, *Gods Determinations touching his Elect: and The Elects Combat in their Conversion, and Coming up to God in Christ together with the Comfortable Effects thereof.* Having imaginatively reenacted God's "Glorious Handywork" of cosmic creation and the debate between Justice and Mercy over mankind's destiny, the collection of thirty-five poems then traces Christ's ensuing combat with Satan for three ranks of Elect human souls. Taylor's own ministerial "warfare" to rescue his Westfield flock from Indian attacks and second-generation backsliding would have been a likely stimulus, as well as a need to maintain doctrinal purity by admitting only regenerate converts to the Church and Lord's Supper. Hence, the poems, as in "Satans Sophestry," focus on the Devil's insidious stratagems to tempt the Elect to doubt their inward worthiness and God's assurances of saving grace. While critics today often praise Taylor's occasional lyrics, because they appeal to modern, post-romantic sensibilities, the formally didactic history of spiritual combat was commonplace in an age that valued plain-style rationality and in which Taylor might turn for models to John Milton's *Paradise Lost,* Paul Bunyan's *The Holy War,* Michael Wigglesworth's *The Day of Doom,* or countless sermons and tracts. *Gods Determinations* captures the dynamic *psychomachia* of both providential history and the individual soul that arches dramatically from the perfect promise of Creation, through the sinful downfall and soul's constant battle against Satan's renewed temptations, to the final joyful acceptance of "Church Fellowship rightly attended."

Whether inspired by his occasional verse or the patterned deliberateness of the Psalm paraphrases and *Gods Determinations,* Taylor inaugurated in 1682 the *Preparatory Meditations before my Approach to the Lords Supper,* two extended series of 217 poems—and his greatest artistic achievement. Generally composed after he had drafted a sermon or preaching notes, the poems are private meditations "Chiefly upon the Doctrin preached upon the Day of administration," in which Taylor applies to his own soul lessons gleaned from the Sacrament day's biblical text, which doubles as the poem's title. Like *The Temple* (1633) by Anglican George Herbert, with whom Taylor is most often compared, the *Preparatory Meditations* belongs to a tradition of meditative writing in verse and prose. As Louis Martz has argued, treatises, such as Richard Baxter's *The Saints Everlasting Rest* (1650), articulated a process which utilized the soul's three faculties: the Memory draws forth scriptural doctrines, which the Judgment (or understanding) considers, thereby rousing the soul to feel the affections of the Will, particularly love and desire that lead to hope and joy. Taylor's meditations seem both to recapitulate reasoned doctrinal analysis and to elicit emotionally affecting responses or, as he declares, they "force my Will, and Reason to thee [God] so," that "my Soule, rid of their Sophistry/In rapid flames of Love to thee may fly." Each meditation disciplines the mind by formally squeezing theological complexities into an inflexible iambic pentameter *ababcc* stanza, yet each also releases spiritual affections through cumulative floods of ingenious images and metaphors. Taylor's purpose is self-examination, to root out sins that infect his soul and to cultivate instead a heart receptive to God's sweet grace and readied to hymn "New Psalms on Davids Harpe to thee."

As a preacher and Puritan, wracked with the debilitating leprosy of original sin and debased by his human condition, Taylor felt spiritually unworthy of God's grace. His poetic petitions to God and Christ serve as ritualized cathartic cleansings and as twofold preparations of the soul: first, for the imminent preaching of God's Word to his Westfield congregation and administering of the Lord's Supper; second, as a saint's lifelong preparation for the eternal heavenly union with Christ. As the 1693–94 *Treatise Concerning the Lord's Supper* indicates, Taylor reacted vehemently against Solomon Stoddard's liberalizing doctrine that permitted all Church members to partake of the Lord's Supper as a "converting ordinance." By contrast, Taylor demanded an "Evangelicall Preparation"; those desiring to partake of the Lord's Supper were expected to give witness by making a prior spiritual relation of conversion and by practicing "prayer, meditation, and self-examination," leading to a proper "festival frame of spirit." Meditation, therefore, provided a means for examining the heart and for contemplating the feast's benefits, mainly its nature as a covenant seal and commemoration of Christ's sacrifice.

But these poems also became Taylor's private spiritual diary, a preparation not merely for his own earthly Supper, but for the eternal feast at which Taylor, like the heavenly angels, would be wed as a "Loving Spouse" to the Bridegroom Christ forever. Not surprisingly, the second series Meditations evolve thematically from the Old Testament types (1–30) which foreshadow Christ, then focus on the New Testament Christology (2.42–56) and the Supper (2.102–111), and culminate finally with a twelve-year study of Canticles (2.115–165). The Song of Solomon was regarded as one of the Bible's most poetic books and a clearly predictive allegory of Christ's promised marriage with the redeemed Church and saints. With its lavishly sensuous metaphors of feasts, gardens, lovers' wooing, anatomized beauties, and marital union, it might also have been Taylor's own visionary preparation for death. After suffering a severe illness in 1720, he also composed three versions of "A Valediction to all the World preparatory for Death 3^{d} of the 11^{m} 1720" (January 1721) and two variants of "A Fig for thee Oh! Death," which in their renouncing of earth's splendors and defying of death's terrors complement the heavenly visions of the final Canticles poems.

Although Taylor's reputation will undoubtedly rest upon the *Preparatory Meditations,* these poems account for a mere twenty-five percent of the output from an immensely imaginative mind that also produced 20,000 lines of *A Metrical History of Christianity.* But the plethora of Psalm and Job paraphrases, elegies, acrostics, love poems, allegorical histories, meditations, and occasional lyrics, written during a lifetime spent in New England, give ample proof that the wilderness frontier did not deaden, but instead fructified Taylor's latent poetic talent. Taylor's themes are sin (inherited from Adam's fall) and salvation (Christ's curative grace); Christ's mediation for mankind, so that God's justice might be tempered with mercy; the Son's sacrifice through His incarnation as God made man; God's providential design that makes all history an ordained script for redemption; the Old Testament's predictive typology that is fulfilled in the New Testament; the Lord's Supper as a spiritual commemoration of Christ's body and blood; and the Supper as a mere shadow of the eternal marriage feast to come.

Taylor inherited an exegetical and poetic tradition that was rooted in the Calvinist belief in the literal text and sole authority of Scripture as God's Word, from which spiritual meanings might be drawn only within strict frameworks of prudent interpretation. He struggles rebelliously against the limits of a fallen language and "Goose quill-slabbred draughts," so inadequate to the divine subject that demands a "Transcendent style." But, through the repeated task of poetic composition and soul-searching examination, he underscores his desire to perfect both faith and art, so that "when dresst up in glory and bright glee," he will "sing together fore his blessed face/Our Weddin Songs with Angells mild * * * * */In ravishing notes throughout Eternity." Even though they were not published, the care with which Taylor transcribed the minor poems, *Gods Determinations,* and the *Preparatory Meditations* into 400 manuscript pages of the leatherbound "Poetical Works" suggests his intent to preserve these poetic offerings. For the modern reader, they are a truly rare find, from a man described by his grandson Ezra Stiles as "of quick passions, yet serious and grave. Exemplary in piety, and for a very sacred observance of the Lord's day," but only long after his death known as New England's premier poet.

Karen E. Rowe
University of California at Los Angeles

PRIMARY WORKS

The Poetical Works of Edward Taylor, ed. Thomas H. Johnson, 1939; *The Poems of Edward Taylor,* ed. Donald E. Stanford, 1960, abridged edition 1963, rpt. 1989; *Edward Taylor's Christographia,* ed. Norman S. Grabo, 1962; *A Transcript of Edward Taylor's Metrical History of Christianity,* ed. Donald E. Stanford, 1962, rpt. 1977; *The Diary of Edward Taylor,* ed. Francis Murphy, 1964; *Edward Taylor's Treatise Concerning the Lord's Supper,* ed. Norman S. Grabo, 1965; *The Unpublished Writings of Edward Taylor;* vol. 1, *Edward Taylor's "Church Records" and Related Sermons;* vol. 2, *Edward Taylor vs. Solomon Stoddard: The Nature of the Lord's Supper;* vol. 3, *Edward Taylor's Minor Poetry,* ed. Thomas M. and Virginia L. Davis, 1981; *Harmony of the Gospels,* 4 vols., ed. Thomas M. and Virginia L. Davis, 1983; *Upon the Types of the Old Testament,* 2 vols., ed. Charles W. Mignon, 1989.

SECONDARY WORKS

Norman S. Grabo, *Edward Taylor,* 1961, revised edition, 1988; *Early American Literature,* special Taylor issue, 4 (Winter 1969–1970); William J. Scheick, *The Will and the Word: The Poetry of Edward Taylor,* 1974; Karl Keller, *The Example of Edward Taylor,* 1975; Karen E. Rowe, *Saint and Singer: Edward Taylor's Typology and the Poetics of Meditation,* 1986; John Gatta, *Gracious Laughter: The Meditative Wit of Edward Taylor,* 1989; Thomas M. Davis, *A Reading of Edward Taylor,* 1992; Jeffrey A. Hammond, *Sinful Self, Saintly Self: The Puritan Experience of Poetry,* 1993; Jeffrey A. Hammond, *Edward Taylor: Fifty Years of Scholarship and Criticism,* 1993; *The Tayloring Shop: Essays in Honor of Thomas M. and Virginia L. Davis,* ed. Michael Schuldiner, 1997.

from The Psalm Paraphrases[1]

Version 1

Ps. 1[2]

1 Blesst is the man that walks not in
Th' ungodly's Counsell here,
Nor standeth in the Sinners way,
Nor sits in Scorners Chaire:
2 But in the Law of the Lord[3]
Is onely his delight;
And in his Law doth meditate
Aright both day, & night.

3 He shall be like a planted tree
By water Course: tall,
That brings his fruit in season forth,
His leafe nere wither shall;
What e're he doth shall prosper well.
4 Th' ungodly are not so:
But they are like the Chafe the which
The winde away doth blow.

5 Therefore th' ungodly shall not stand
In judgment when in hand;
Nor in the Congregation of
The just shall Sinners Stand.
6 Because the Lord knoweth the way
Of Righteous persons all;
Whereas the way of those that be
Ungodly perish shall.

c. 1674–75
1977

[1]Version 1 dates from 1674–75 and includes extant Psalms 1–9 and 18; Version 2, transcribed in the early to mid-eighties, includes Psalms 11–39 and 48–49. Seventy-three of the 150 Psalms are assigned to David, and all, except 48 and 49, of Taylor's known paraphrases are of David's Psalms and use the common meter (alternating lines of eight and six syllables) for singing hymns. Text is from Davis and Davis, eds., *Minor Poetry.*

[2]From the Greek *psalmos,* a poem sung to the accompaniment of musical instruments.

[3]The Old Testament Law transmitted by Jehovah to Moses and the Israelites. Although the "Law of the Lord" is summarized in the Ten Commandments, the term also signifies all of God's truth revealed in the Bible.

Version 2

Ps. 19
To the Chief Musician: A Psalm of David

1 The Heavens do declare (in truth)
The Glory of our God
Also the firmament doth shew
His handy works abroad.
2 Day unto day vents Speech: & night
To night tells knowledge (choice)
3 There is no Speech nor language quite
Where's not heard their voice.

4 Their line doth thro' the whole earth's trace
Their words to th' worlds end (run)
He doth a tabernacle place
Fast in them for the Sun.[1]
5 Which as a Bridesgroom coming forth
Out of his Chamber('s place)
Rejoyceth as a Strong man doth
(Swiftly) to run a race.

6 His going out is from the end
O[f] heaven, his circuit (greate)
Is to its ends, & nought (here bend)
Is hidden from its heat.
7 Jehovahs law is perfect, (pure)
Converts the Soule, likewise
Jehovahs testimonie's sure
Making the Simple wise.

8 The Statues of the Lord are right
Rejoycing of the heart.
The Lords command is pure, doth light
Unto your [w]ayes impart.
9 Jehovah's (Fear is cleane in truth)
Enduring fast for ever.
The judgments of the Lord are truth,
They're righteous altogether.

[1]"Sun" may refer to the concept of man "under the sun," who needs to be taught spiritually or by law how to live life within the realm of nature.

10 They're more to be desired than
Gold, yea than a vast Sum
Of [pure]st gold. & Sweeter than
[Hon]y, & hony combe.
11 More o're thy Servants warnd thereby
In keeping them's greate gain.
12 Who doth his errours throughly spy?
Cleanse me from Secret (stains.)

13 Thy Servant keep from proude Sins free
O're me dominion
Ne're grant them, then intire Ist bee
And cleare great vileness from.
14 Let Lord, the words my mouth doth [speak]
And my hearts musing fre[e]
Accepted in thy Sight my Rock,[2]
And my Redeemer, bee.

copied 1680–85?

1981

from Gods Determinations[1]

The Preface

Infinity, when all things it beheld
In Nothing, and of Nothing all did build,
Upon what Base was fixt the Lath, wherein
He turn'd this Globe, and riggalld[2] it so trim?
Who blew the Bellows of his Furnace Vast?
Or held the Mould wherein the world was Cast?
Who laid its Corner Stone?[3] Or whose Command?

[2]See Exodus 17:6, Luke 6:48, and Matthew 16:18 for the biblical origins of Christ as the Rock.

[1]Taylor's "debate" sequence of thirty-five poems explores the human soul's progress from the world's creation and fall of man to the redemption of Christian souls through Christ's crucifixion. Christ's mercy triumphs over justice—the punishment that man deserves for his disobedience—and the soul is finally carried to heaven to share in the joys of the Resurrection. The complete title of the sequence is *Gods Determinations touching his Elect: and The Elects Combat in their Conversion, and Coming up to God in Christ together with the Comfortable Effects thereof* (probably completed about 1680; transcribed in final form in 1681–1682). Text is from Stanford, ed., *Poems.*

[2]Verb from the noun *riggal,* a ring-like mark, or a groove in wood or stone.

[3]See Job 38:4–11.

Where stand the Pillars upon which it stands?
Who Lac'de and Fillitted[4] the earth so fine,
With Rivers like green Ribbons Smaragdine?[5]
Who made the Sea's its Selvedge,[6] and it locks
Like a Quilt Ball[7] within a Silver Box?
Who Spread its Canopy? Or Curtains Spun?
Who in this Bowling Alley bowld the Sun?
Who made it always when it rises set
To go at once both down, and up to get?
Who th'Curtain rods made for this Tapistry?
Who hung the twinckling Lanthorns in the Sky?
Who? who did this? or who is he? Why, know
Its Onely Might Almighty this did doe.
His hand hath made this noble worke which Stands
His Glorious Handywork not made by hands.
Who spake all things from nothing; and with ease
Can speake all things to nothing, if he please.
Whose Little finger at his pleasure Can
Out mete[8] ten thousand worlds with halfe a Span:
Whose Might Almighty can by half a looks
Root up the rocks and rock the hills by th'roots.
Can take this mighty World up in his hande,
And shake it like a Squitchen[9] or a Wand.[10]
Whose single Frown will make the Heavens shake
Like as an aspen leafe the Winde makes quake.
Oh! what a might is this Whose single frown
Doth shake the world as it would shake it down?[11]
Which All from Nothing fet,[12] from Nothing, All:
Hath All on Nothing set, lets Nothing fall.
Gave All to nothing Man indeed, whereby
Through nothing man all might him Glorify.
In Nothing then imbosst the brightest Gem
More pretious than all pretiousness in them.

[4]Filleted, bound, or girded as with an ornamental band or material strip.

[5]Consisting of a smaragd (precious bright green stone); of an emerald green.

[6]Border of woven material to prevent unraveling.

[7]Treasured pincushions, exquisitely decorated with needlework, even laced with silver thread and green silk, were kept in boxes; stuffed ball cushions covered with salvaged embroidered fabric could be suspended from the girdle.

[8]To measure out; apportion; the noun means a boundary mark or line, a limit.

[9]Altered form of quitch, a species of couch-grass or weed, or a variant of scutcheon and escutcheon, a shield depicting a coat of arms.

[10]A walking cane, young sapling, switch, sceptre, or ceremonial staff.

[11]Earthquakes rocked England in 1661, April 3, 1668 (twenty-three days before Taylor's departure), 1678, and 1680, and were often read as providential signs of God's power and judgment.

[12]Fetch, to bring from a distance, in a sweeping movement; to summon by force.

But Nothing man did throw down all by Sin:
And darkened that lightsom Gem in him.
That now his Brightest Diamond is grown
Darker by far than any Coalpit Stone.

c. 1680

1939

The Souls Groan to Christ for Succour

Good Lord, behold this Dreadfull Enemy
Who makes me tremble with his fierce assaults,
I dare not trust, yet feare to give the ly,
For in my soul, my soul finds many faults.
And though I justify myselfe to's face:
I do Condemn myselfe before thy Grace.

He strives to mount my sins, and them advance
Above thy Merits, Pardons, or Good Will
Thy Grace to lessen, and thy Wrath t'inhance
As if thou couldst not pay the sinners bill.
He Chiefly injures thy rich Grace, I finde
Though I confess my heart to sin inclin'de.

Those Graces which thy Grace enwrought in mee,
He makes as nothing but a pack of Sins.
He maketh Grace no grace, but Crueltie,
Is Graces Honey Comb, a Comb of Stings?
This makes me ready leave thy Grace and run.
Which if I do, I finde I am undone.

I know he is thy Cur,[1] therefore I bee
Perplexed lest I from thy Pasture stray.
He bayghs, and barks so veh'mently at mee.
Come rate[2] this Cur, Lord, breake his teeth I pray.
Remember me I humbly pray thee first.
Then halter up this Cur that is so Curst.

c. 1680

1939

[1]A worthless, low-bred, or snappish dog.
[2]To scold or rebuke angrily or violently.

Christs Reply

Peace, Peace, my Hony, do not Cry,
My Little Darling, wipe thine eye,
Oh Cheer, Cheer up, come see.
Is anything too deare, my Dove,[1]
Is anything too good, my Love
To get or give for thee?

If in the severall[2] thou art
This Yelper fierce will at thee bark:
That thou art mine this shows.
As Spot barks back the sheep again
Before they to the Pound[3] are ta'ne,
So he and hence 'way goes.

But yet this Cur that bayghs so sore
Is broken tootht, and muzzled sure,
Fear not, my Pritty Heart.
His barking is to make thee Cling
Close underneath thy Saviours Wing.
Why did my sweeten start?

And if he run an inch too far,
I'le Check his Chain, and rate the Cur.
My Chick, keep clost to mee.
The Poles shall sooner kiss, and greet[4]
And Paralells shall sooner meet
Than thou shalt harmed bee.

He seeks to aggrivate thy sin
And screw[5] them to the highest pin,[6]
To make thy faith to quaile.
Yet mountain Sins like mites should show
And then these mites for naught should goe
Could he but once prevaile.

[1]See Song of Solomon 2:10–14, 5:2, 6:9, where Solomon's love for the Shulamite maiden, his bride and Dove, serves as a figure for God's love of Israel and an allegory of Christ's love for His heavenly Bride, the individual soul, and the Church.

[2]Privately owned land, especially enclosed pastures not held in common; divided, existing apart, hence the soul is torn between Christ and the Devil.

[3]Enclosure to shelter sheep or cattle.

[4]See George Herbert's "The Search," lines 41–44.

[5]To torture by means of a thumbscrew; figuratively, to extort by moral or physical pressure.

[6]A tuning peg for regulating the tension of a stringed musical instrument; a figure applied also to the torture rack.

I smote thy sins upon the Head.[7]
They Dead'ned are, though not quite dead:
And shall not rise again.
I'l put away the Guilt thereof,
And purge its Filthiness cleare off:
My Blood doth out the stain.

And though thy judgment was remiss
Thy Headstrong Will too Wilfull is.
I will Renew the same.
And though thou do too frequently
Offend as heretofore hereby
I'l not severly blaim.

And though thy senses do inveagle
Thy Noble Soul to tend the Beagle,
That t'hunt her games forth go.
I'le Lure her back to me, and Change
Those fond[8] Affections that do range
As yelping beagles doe.

Although thy sins increase their race,
And though when thou hast sought for Grace,
Thou fallst more than before
If thou by true Repentence Rise,
And Faith makes me thy Sacrifice,
I'l pardon all, though more.

Though Satan strive to block thy way
By all his Stratagems he may:
Come, come though through the fire.
For Hell that Gulph of fire for sins,
Is not so hot as t'burn thy Shins.
Then Credit not the Lyar.

Those Cursed Vermin Sins that Crawle
All ore thy Soul, both Greate, and small
Are onely Satans own:
Which he in his Malignity
Unto thy Souls true Sanctity
In at the doors hath thrown.

[7]See Genesis 3:15. After Adam and Eve commit the original sin, God curses their tempter, the serpent (Satan or the Devil), and prophesies that the seed of woman, Christ through his death and resurrection, will bruise the serpent's head, thereby vanquishing sin, death, and Satan forever (Revelation 12:9).

[8]Foolish.

And though they be Rebellion high,
Ath'ism[9] or Apostacy:[10]
Though blasphemy it bee:
Unto what Quality, or Sise
Excepting one, so e're it rise.
Repent, I'le pardon thee.

Although thy Soule was once a Stall
Rich hung with Satans nicknacks all;
If thou Repent thy Sin,
A Tabernacle in't I'le place
Fild with Gods Spirit, and his Grace.
Oh Comfortable thing!

I dare the World therefore to show
A God like me, to anger slow:
Whose wrath is full of Grace.
Doth hate all Sins both Greate, and small:
Yet when Repented, pardons all.
Frowns with a Smiling Face.

As for thy outward Postures each,
Thy Gestures, Actions, and thy Speech,
I Eye and Eying spare,
If thou repent. My Grace is more
Ten thousand times still tribled ore
Than thou canst want, or ware.

As for the Wicked Charge he makes,
That he of Every Dish first takes
Of all thy holy things.
Its false, deny the same, and say,
That which he had he stool away
Out of thy Offerings.[11]

[9]Disbelief in the existence of deity and rejection of all religious faith and practice.

[10]Apostasy, or renouncing of a religious faith. Though the term essentially implies total abandonment of what one has religiously professed (*i.e.,* faith in Christ) as opposed to mere heresy or schism, for the Puritan it meant mankind's rebellion against God's decrees and, consequently, his fall and ruin.

[11]The Israelites made sacrificial offerings to God of the first fruits of their labor (grain or animals) as a holy gift of worship and an expiation for sins, expressing the desire for God's purification and forgiveness. Christ here accuses Satan of having taken from Adam and Eve, hence all mankind, the bounty of Eden out of which our first parents might provide offerings of praise and thanksgiving to God.

Though to thy Griefe, poor Heart, thou finde
In Pray're too oft a wandring minde,
In Sermons Spirits dull.
Though faith in firy furnace[12] flags,
And Zeale in Chilly Seasons lags.
Temptations powerfull.

These faults are his, and none of thine
So far as thou dost them decline.
Come then receive my Grace.
And when he buffits thee therefore
If thou my aid, and Grace implore
I'le shew a pleasant face.

But still look for Temptations Deep,
Whilst that thy Noble Sparke doth keep
Within a Mudwald Cote.
These White Frosts and the Showers that fall
Are but to whiten thee withall.
Not rot the Web they smote.

If in the fire where Gold is tride
Thy Soule is put, and purifide
Wilt thou lament thy loss?
If silver-like this fire refine
Thy Soul and make it brighter shine:
Wilt thou bewaile the Dross?

Oh! fight my Field: no Colours fear:
I'l be thy Front, I'l be thy reare.
Fail not: my Battells fight.
Defy the Tempter, and his Mock.
Anchor thy heart on mee thy Rock.[13]
I do in thee Delight.

c. 1680

1939

[12]See Daniel 3 for the account of Shadrach, Meshach, and Abednego in the fiery furnace.

[13]See Exodus 17:6. The Rock of Horeb becomes a type of Christ the Rock (I Corinthians 10:4), smitten so that the spirit of life flows from Him to all who drink. In Matthew 16:18 and I Peter 2:4–8, Christ is also referred to as the rock (*petra,* or massive rock) or cornerstone upon which the Church is built.

Some of Satans Sophestry

The Tempter greatly seeks, though secretly,
With an Ath'istick Hoodwinke man to blinde,
That so the Footsteps of the Deity
Might stand no longer stampt upon his minde.
Which when he can't blot out, by blinding quite,
He strives to turn him from the Purer Light.

With Wiles enough, he on his thoughts intrudes,
That God's a Heape of Contradictions high,
But when these thoughts man from his thoughts excludes
Thou knowst not then (saith he) this Mystery.
And when the first String breaks, he strives to bring
Into sins brambles by the other string.

When God Calls out a Soule,[1] he subtilly
Saith God is kinde: you need not yet forsake
Your Sins: but if he doth, he doth reply,
Thou'st outstood Grace. Justice will vengeance take.
He'l tell you you Presume on Grace, to fright
You to despare, beholding Justice bright.

Though just before mans mountain sins were mites,
His mites were nothing. Now the scales are turn'd.
His mites are mountains now, of mighty height
And must with Vengeance-Lightening be burn'd.
Greate Sins are Small, till men repent of Sin:
Then Small are far too big to be forgi'n.

While man thinks slightly, that he will repent,
There's time enough (saith he), it's easly done.
But when repent he doth, the time is spent,
Saith he, it is too late to be begun.
To keep man from't, it's easly done, saith he,
To dant him in't, he saith, it Cannot bee.

[1]The Puritan morphology of conversion maps out five stages in man's progress toward God: election, vocation, justification, sanctification, and glorification. Having been "called" (vocation) by the Spirit's offer of grace, working through prayer, sermons, reading of Scripture, and self-examination, man seeks to turn toward God in faith. He must experience a conviction of and repentance for sin that acknowledges his dependent need of God's grace before justification, in which the election (pre-ordained by God) is made effectual and the soul redeemed. Through saving faith, usually signified by a public profession and admittance to the Church fellowship and Lord's Supper, the soul is brought to sanctification, a state sustained by moral actions, worship, and the Supper. At any stage, would-be saints can be besieged by doubts, lest the devil lead them to a false assurance. Glorification removes all doubts of one's election, but was commonly believed to be achieved only in the afterlife.

So Faith is easy till the Soule resolves
To Live to Christ and upon Christ rely.
Then Saving Faith[2] he bold presumption Calls.
Hast thou (saith he) in Christ propriety?
The Faithfulls Faith, he stiles Presumption great,
But the Presumptuous, theirs is Faith Compleat.

Nay though the Faith be true he acts so sly,
As to raise doubts: and then it must not do:
Unless Assurance[3] do it Certify:
Which if it do, it douts of it also.
Faith is without Assurance shuffled out,
And if Assurance be, that's still a Doubt.

But should the Soule assured once, once Doubt,
Then his Assurance no Assurance is:
Assurance doth assure the Soul right out
Leave not a single Doubt to do amiss.
But Satan still will seeke to Pick an hole
In thy Assurance to unsure thy Soul.

Should any Soule once an Assurance get,
Into his hands, soon Satans Pick-Lock key
With Sinfull Wards[4] Unlocks his Cabinet
To Steal the Jewell in it thence away.
The Soul thus pillag'de, droops unto the grave.
It's greater grief to lose than not to have.

He doth molest the Soule, it cannot see
Without Assurance Extraordinary
Which should it have, it would soon take to bee
A Mere Delusion of the Adversary.
Assurance would not serve, should God Convay
It in an Usuall or Unusuall way.

Thus I might search, Poor Soul, the Magazeen
Of Gospell Graces over: I might paint

[2]Saving faith, the first principle of Puritan theology, required a belief in Christ and resting in God for life and salvation, because of Christ's righteousness, under a deep sense that men have none of their own.

[3]Individual assurance of salvation is a preliminary step to regeneration. It comes about only by way of the Covenant of Grace, under which God promises redemption from sin and the hope of eternal life, if mankind believes in Christ's willing sacrifice through His death and resurrection.

[4]The ridges projecting from a lock's inside plate to prevent passage of any key not provided with bits of corresponding form and size. In literary use, the application is sometimes reversed, the ward denoting the lock's cavities or the key's solid parts.

Out Satan sculking each side each unseen
To Hoodwinck Sinners, and to hopple[5] Saints.
For he to dim their Grace, and slick up sin
Calls Brass bright Gold, bright Golde but brass or tin.

He tempts to bring the soul too low or high,
To have it e're in this or that extream:
To see no want or want alone to eye:
To keep on either side the golden mean.
If it was in't to get it out he'l 'ledge,
Thou on the wrong side art the Pale[6] or Hedge.

When God awakes a Soule he'l seeke to thrust
It on Despare for want of Grace or get
And puff't with Pride, or in Securety hush't
Or Couzen[7] it with Graces Counterfet.
Which if he can't he'l Carp at Grace, and raile
And say, this is not Grace, it thus doth faile.

And thus he strives with Spite, Spleen, bitter Gall
That Sinners might Dishonour God Most high:
That Saints might never honour God at all.
That those in Sin, Those not in Grace might dy.
And that the Righteous, Gracious, Pious, Grave,
Might have no Comfort of the Grace they have.

Lest you be foild herewith, watch well unto
Your Soul, that thrice Ennobled noble Gem:
For Sins are flaws therein, and double woe
Belongs thereto if it be found in them.
Are Flaws in Venice Glasses bad? What in
Bright Diamonds? What then in man is Sin?

c. 1680
1939

[5]Earlier form of *to hobble;* to fasten together an animal's legs to prevent it from straying.
[6]A stake, pointed piece of wood, or upright bar, driven into the ground to form a fence.
[7]Cozen, to cheat or defraud by deceit.

The Joy of Church Fellowship rightly attended[1]

In Heaven soaring up, I dropt an Eare
  On Earth: and oh! sweet Melody:
And listening, found it was the Saints[2] who were
  Encoacht for Heaven that sang for Joy.
  For in Christs Coach they sweetly sing;
  As they to Glory ride therein.

Oh! joyous hearts! Enfir'de with holy Flame!
  Is speech thus tassled[3] with praise?
Will not your inward fire of Joy contain;
  That it in open flames doth blaze?
  For in Christ's Coach Saints sweetly sing,
  As they to Glory ride therein.

And if a string do slip, by Chance, they soon
  Do screw it up[4] again: whereby
They set it in a more melodious Tune
  And a Diviner Harmony.
  For in Christs Coach they sweetly sing
  As they to Glory ride therein.

In all their Acts, publick, and private, nay
  And secret too, they praise impart.
But in their Acts Divine and Worship, they
  With Hymns do offer up their Heart.
  Thus in Christs Coach they sweetly sing
  As they to Glory ride therein.

Some few not in; and some whose Time, and Place
  Block up this Coaches way doe goe
As Travellers afoot, and so do trace
  The Road that gives them right thereto
  While in this Coach these sweetly sing
  As they to Glory ride therein.

c. 1680

1937

[1]This is the final poem in *Gods Determinations,* in which Taylor visualizes the redeemed saints entering into Church fellowship, meaning the Church on earth (the coach) which also foreshadows the saints' journey after death and the eternal fellowship after Christ's Second Coming and the Final Judgment.

[2]The "visible Saints," who were church members when alive.

[3]Tasselled, or adorned with a tassel.

[4]To tighten or adjust tuning pegs regulating the tension or pitch of a string on a musical instrument.

from Occasional Poems[1]

2. *Upon a Spider Catching a Fly*

Thou Sorrow, venom Elfe.
Is this thy ploy,
To Spin a web out of thyselfe
To Catch a Fly?
For Why?

I saw a pettish wasp
Fall foule therein.
Whom yet thy whorlepins[2] did not [clasp]
Lest he should fling
His Sting.

But as affraid, remote
Didst Stand hereat
And with thy little fingers stroke
And gently tap
His back.

Thus gently him didst treate
Lest he Should pet,[3]
And in a froppish,[4] waspish heate
Should greatly fret
Thy net.

Whereas the Silly Fly,
Caught by its leg
Thou by the throate tookst hastily
And 'hinde the head
Bite Dead.

This goes to pot,[5] that not
Nature doth call.

[1]What remains in the "Poetical Works" manuscript is a torn fragment of the heading "*** occurrants occasioning what follow" that introduces a section of eight numbered poems, probably copied in the early 1680s. Allegorizations of natural events, or what Taylor calls "occurants," was common among Puritan theologians and writers. Texts are from Davis and Davis, eds., *Minor Poetry.*

[2]A whorle is a small fly-wheel on the spindle of a spinning wheel that regulates speed. A whorlepin is a pin fastening together the whorl and spindle. Something that whirls, coils, or spirals, such as a spider spinning a web to entrap its victim.

[3]To stroke gently or to pamper; also to take offense or sulk, as in a fit of peevishness or anger.

[4]Fretful, peevish.

[5]Perhaps an obsolete form of "put," meaning to propose to put before a person for consideration; or of "pote," to push or thrust, as with a stick. Taylor seems to mean to show, to point toward, or to illustrate.

Strive not above what strength hath got
Lest in the brawle
Thou fall.

This Frey seems thus to us
Hells Spider gets
His intrails Spun to whip Cords[6] thus
And wove to nets
And sets.

To tangle Adams race
In's Stratigems
To their Destructions, Spoil'd made base
By venom things
Damn'd Sins.

But mighty, Gracious Lord
Communicate
Thy Grace to breake the Cord afford
Us Glorys Gate
And State.

We'l Nightingaile Sing like
When pearcht on high
In Glories Cage, thy glory, bright,
[And] thankfully,
For joy.

c. 1680–82
1939

4. *Huswifery*[1]

Make mee, O Lord, thy Spining Wheele compleat.
Thy Holy Words my Distaff make for mee.
Make mine Affections thy Swift Flyers neate
And make my Soule thy holy Spoole to bee.
My Conversation make to be thy Reele
And reele the yarn there on Spun of thy Wheele.[2]

[6]A thin tough cord of braided hemp or catgut, of which whip-lashes are made.

[1]The function or province of a woman (usually married) who manages household affairs, often with skill and thrift. Taylor's "huswifery," or housekeeping, here means weaving more particularly and alludes to a linen cloth between fine and coarse for family uses.

[2]In this stanza Taylor refers to the parts of a spinning wheel: the distaff holds the flax or raw wool; flyers control the spinning; the spool or spindle twists the yarn; and the reel takes up the finished thread.

Make me thy Loome then, knit therein this Twine:
And make thy Holy Spirit, Lord, winde quills:[3]
Then weave the Web thyselfe. The yarn is fine.
Thine Ordinances make my Fulling Mills.[4]
Then dy the same in Heavenly Colours Choice,
All pinkt[5] with Varnisht Flowers of Paradise.

Then cloath therewith mine Understanding, Will,
Affections, Judgment, Conscience, Memory
My Words, & Actions, that their Shine may fill
My wayes with glory and thee glorify.
Then mine apparell shall display before yee
That I am Cloathd in Holy robes for glory.

c. 1682–83
1937

6. *Upon Wedlock, & Death of Children*[1]

A Curious Knot[2] God made in Paradise,
And drew it out inamled neatly Fresh.
It was the True-Love Knot, more Sweet than spice
And Set with all the flowres of Graces dress.
Its Weddens Knot, that ne're can be unti'de.
No Alexanders Sword[3] can it divide.

The Slips[4] here planted, gay & glorious grow:
Unless an Hellish breath do sindge their Plumes.
Here Primrose, Cowslips, Roses, Lilies blow,[5]
With Violets & Pinkes that voide perfumes.
Whose beautious leaves ore lai'd with Hony Dew.

[3]To wind thread or yarn on a quill, *i.e.,* a bobbin, spool, or spindle.

[4]A mill in which cloth is beaten with wooden mallets and cleansed with fuller's earth or soap. To "full" also means to shrink and thicken woolen cloth by moistening, heating, and pressing.

[5]Ornamented by cutting or punching eyelet-holes, figures, or letters; said of flounces, frills, ribbons, which have raw edges cut into scallops, jags, or narrow points.

[1]Stanzas 5 and 7 were originally printed in Cotton Mather's *Right Thoughts in Sad Hours* (London, 1689) and are among Taylor's only poetry known to have been published in his lifetime. Taylor married Elizabeth Fitch of Norwich in November 1674. Stanford dates this poem to 1682, based upon references to the first four of Taylor's fourteen children.

[2]A flower or garden bed. Figuratively, it refers to the "True-Love Knot" or intimate bond of union (as between Adam and Eve) in marriage, to the original Covenant of Works uniting God and man, which was broken and superseded by the Covenant of Grace, and to the wedding knot, that spiritually joins the saint or "Bride" to the beloved "Bridegroom," Christ.

[3]Alexander the Great (356–323 B.C.), King of Macedonia, famous for his military conquests, cut the Gordian knot, devised by the King of Phrygia, when he learned that anyone who could undo it would rule Asia.

[4]Cuttings (stems, roots, twigs) of a plant used for replanting or grafting.

[5]Bloom.

And Chanting birds Cherp out sweet Musick true.

When in this Knot I planted was, my Stock
Soon knotted, & a manly flower out brake.[6]
And after it my branch again did knot
Brought out another Flowre its Sweet breathd mate.[7]
One knot gave one tother the tothers place.
Whence Checkling[8] Smiles fought in each others face.

But oh! a glorious hand from glory came
Guarded with Angells, soon did Crop this flowre
Which almost tore the root up of the same
At that unlookt for, Dolesom, darksome houre.
In Pray're to Christ perfum'de[9] it did ascend,
And Angells bright did it to heaven tend.

But pausing on't, this Sweet perfum'd my thought,
Christ would in Glory have a Flowre, Choice, Prime,
And having Choice, chose this my branch forth brought;
Lord take't. I thanke thee, thou takst ought of mine,
It is my pledg in glory, part of mee
Is now in it, Lord, glorifi'de with thee.

But praying ore my branch, my branch did Sprout
And bore another manly flower, & gay[10]
And after that another, Sweet brake out,[11]
The which the former hand soon got away.
But oh! the tortures, Vomit, Screechings, groans,
And Six weeks Fever would pierce hearts like Stones.

Griefe o're doth flow: & nature fault would finde
Were not thy Will, my Spell Charm, Joy, & Gem:
That as I said, I say, take, Lord, they're thine.
I piecemeale pass to Glory bright in them.
I joy, may I sweet Flowers for Glory breed,
Whether thou getst them green, or lets them Seed.

c. 1682
1937

[6]Samuel Taylor, born August 27, 1675, survived to maturity.

[7]Elizabeth Taylor, born December 27, 1676, died on December 25, 1677 (see line 20).

[8]From an obsolete verb, to checkle, meaning to laugh violently or giddily; closely related to chuckling. Taylor commonly creates puns, perhaps here from "cheek."

[9]In the Old Testament, incense offerings (types of prayer and praise) were regularly given up to God by the High Priests, and perfumed oils were used for cleansing and anointing (see Exodus 30). But Taylor may also have in mind the continuing analogy with flowers and possibly the preparation of the body for burial.

[10]James Taylor, born on October 12, 1678, lived to maturity.

[11]Abigail, born August 6, 1681, died August 22, 1682.

7. *The Ebb & Flow*

When first thou on me Lord, wrought'st thy Sweet Print,
My heart was made thy tinder box.[1]
My 'ffections were thy tinder in't.
Where fell thy Sparkes by drops.
Those holy Sparks of Heavenly Fire that came
Did ever catch & often out would flame.

But now my Heart is made thy Censar[2] trim,
Full of thy golden Altars[3] fire,
To offer up Sweet Incense in
Unto thyselfe intire:
I finde my tinder scarce thy Sparks can feel
That drop out from thy Holy flint & Steel.[4]

Hence doubts out bud for feare thy fire in mee
'S a mocking Ignis Fatuus,[5]
Or lest thine Altars fire out bee,
Its hid in ashes thus.
Yet when the bellows of thy Spirit blow
Away mine ashes, then thy fire doth glow.

c. 1682–83
1937

from Preparatory Meditations[1]

First Series

Prologue

Lord, Can a Crumb of Dust the Earth outweigh,
Outmatch all mountains, nay the Chrystall Sky?

[1]A metal box for holding tinder (a very flammable substance used as kindling) and usually a flint and steel for striking a spark.

[2]A vessel for burning incense. Leviticus 16:12 describes Aaron's use of burning coals in the censer during the annual Feast of Atonement.

[3]Located within the tabernacle's holy place before the veil, the golden altar was used for daily and special incense offerings. See Exodus 30.

[4]Flint is a hard stone, commonly steely gray in color, which gives off sparks when struck with iron or steel. "Flint and steel" is an apparatus used to provide fire by igniting tinder.

[5]A phosphorescent light that hovers over marshy ground, supposedly due to the spontaneous combustion of an inflammable gas from decaying organic matter. Popularly called "Will-o-the-wisp" or "Jack-a-lantern," it was superstitiously believed to be mischievous spirits, intentionally leading benighted travelers astray. It comes to signify a deceptive goal, delusive guiding principles, or foolish hope.

[1]Composed as self-examinations preparatory to the Lord's Supper, 217 meditations, dated from 1682 to 1725, survive in the manuscript "Poetical Works." The dates suggest that Taylor ad-

Imbosom in't designs that shall Display
And trace into the Boundless Deity?
Yea hand a Pen whose moysture doth guild ore
Eternall Glory with a glorious glore.

If it its Pen had of an Angels Quill,[2]
And Sharpend on a Pretious Stone ground tite,
And dipt in Liquid Gold, and mov'de by Skill
In Christall leaves should golden Letters write
It would but blot and blur yea jag, and jar
Unless thou mak'st the Pen, and Scribener.

I am this Crumb of Dust which is design'd
To make my Pen unto thy Praise alone,
And my dull Phancy[3] *I would gladly grinde*
Unto an Edge on Zions Pretious Stone.[4]
And Write in Liquid Gold upon thy Name
My Letters till thy glory forth doth flame.

Let not th'attempts breake down my Dust I pray
Nor laugh thou them to scorn but pardon give.
Inspire this Crumb of Dust till it display
Thy Glory through't: and then thy dust shall live.
Its failings then thou'lt overlook I trust,
They being Slips slipt from thy Crumb of Dust.

Thy Crumb of Dust breaths two words from its breast,
That thou wilt guide its pen to write aright
To Prove thou art, and that thou art the best
And shew thy Properties to shine most bright.

ministered the Supper at irregular intervals, but the frequent clusters on a single text and lengthy series on biblical themes indicate that he composed sermon series and the accompanying poems over extended periods of time. His topics included Old Testament types (2.1–18, 20–30, 58–61, 70–71), Christ's nature and qualifications (2.42–56), the Lord's Supper (2.102–111), and the Song of Solomon (2.115–153, 156–157B, 160–165). Extant sermons have been published in *Upon the Types of the Old Testament* and *Edward Taylor's Christographia.* Taylor dates his sermons and poems according to an ecclesiastical calendar with the first month being March and the twelfth being February. Both Taylor's and, as needed, the commonly accepted Gregorian year [in brackets] are given below. The complete title of the text is *Preparatory Meditations before my Approach to the Lords Supper. Chiefly upon the Doctrin preached upon the Day of administration* from Stanford, ed., *Poems.*

[2]The tube or barrel of a feather from a large bird (often a goose) formed into a pen by pointing and slitting the lower end; loosely used for a feather, poetically for a wing.

[3]Fancy, a mental image or representation; imagination, especially of a delusive sort, but used during the Renaissance to refer to the power of conception and representation in art and poetry.

[4]See Revelation 21:11, 19–21, describing the heavenly city, the New Jerusalem, garnished with precious stones, streets of gold, and transparent glass. Throughout Revelation (14:3, 19:9, 21:5) a heavenly voice instructs John to "write."

And then thy Works will shine as flowers on Stems
Or as in Jewellary Shops, do jems.

Undated [1682?]
1937

[6.] *Another Meditation at the same time.*[1]

Am I thy Gold? Or Purse, Lord, for thy Wealth;
Whether in mine, or mint refinde for thee?
Ime counted so, but count me o're thyselfe,
Lest gold washt face, and brass in Heart I bee.
I Feare my Touchstone[2] touches when I try
Mee, and my Counted Gold too overly.

Am I new minted by thy Stamp indeed?
Mine Eyes are dim; I cannot clearly see.
Be thou my Spectacles that I may read
Thine Image, and Inscription stampt on mee.
If thy bright Image do upon me stand
I am a Golden Angell[3] in thy hand.

Lord, make my Soule thy Plate: thine Image bright
Within the Circle of the same enfoile.
And on its brims in golden Letters write
Thy Superscription in an Holy style.
Then I shall be thy Money, thou my Hord:
Let me thy Angell bee, bee thou my Lord.

Undated [1683?]
1939

[1]Unlike most of the meditations, this one lacks a date and a biblical verse, but the manuscript positions it between Meditation 1.5 (September 1683) and Meditation 1.7 (February 1684).

[2]A smooth, fine-grained, black or dark-colored variety of quartz or jasper, used for testing the quality of gold and silver alloys; that which serves to test the genuineness or value of anything.

[3]An English coin (1470–1634) showing the archangel Michael slaying the dragon. See also Revelation 8–11 for the seven archangels heralding Christ's Second Coming and the New Jerusalem.

8. *Meditation. Joh. 6.51. I am the Living Bread.*[1]

I kening[2] through Astronomy Divine
    The Worlds bright Battlement,[3] wherein I spy
A Golden Path my Pensill cannot line,
    From that bright Throne unto my Threshold ly.
    And while my puzzled thoughts about it pore
    I finde the Bread of Life in't at my doore.

When that this Bird of Paradise[4] put in
    This Wicker Cage (my Corps) to tweedle praise
Had peckt the Fruite forbad: and so did fling
    Away its Food; and lost its golden dayes;
    It fell into Celestiall Famine sore:
    And never could attain a morsell more.

Alas! alas! Poore Bird, what wilt thou doe?
    The Creatures field no food for Souls e're gave.
And if thou knock at Angells dores they show
    An Empty Barrell: they no soul bread have.
    Alas! Poore Bird, the Worlds White[5] Loafe is done.
    And cannot yield thee here the smallest Crumb.

In this sad state, Gods Tender Bowells[6] run
    Out streams of Grace: And he to end all strife
The Purest Wheate in Heaven, his deare-dear Son
    Grinds, and kneads up into this Bread of Life.
    Which Bread of Life from Heaven down came and stands
    Disht on thy Table up by Angells Hands.[7]

[1]See John 6:22–59. As elsewhere in the *Preparatory Meditations,* Taylor here composes a short series of Meditations (1:8–10) on linked biblical texts and themes focusing upon Christ's flesh and blood as elements of the Lord's Supper. Fulfilling the Old Testament type of the manna which God provided daily for the Israelites (Exodus 16), Christ offers his body, the "living bread that came down from heaven," as a token or sign, which is "given for the life of the world."

[2]To discover by sight or signs and derive knowledge through instruction, here of divine astronomy. A kenning also denotes the distance bounding the range of ordinary vision, especially a marine measure of twenty miles; a dry measure of a half bushel; or a vessel containing that quantity of meal or grain. A kenning-glass is a spy-glass or small telescope.

[3]"Like a jasper stone, clear as crystal," bright light radiates from the New Jerusalem, whose parapets (battlements) mark the outer reaches of the new heavenly city of "pure gold, like clear glass," prophesied in Revelation 21–22. Enclosed within are God Almighty's white throne and the eternal paradise promised to redeemed saints after the Final Judgment.

[4]The soul is analogous to a "Bird of Paradise" housed within the body's cage.

[5]Israel's manna is "like coriander seed, white; and the taste of it was like wafers made with honey" (Exodus 16:31).

[6]Intestines or interior of the body; seat of tenderness, pity, and grace; the heart.

[7]See also John 6:1–14 for Christ's miracle of feeding the five thousand with barley loaves and fishes, which is linked with the Passover (a type also of the Lord's Supper) and which precedes His declaration as the living bread.

Did God mould up this Bread in Heaven, and bake,
Which from his Table came, and to thine goeth?
Doth he bespeake thee thus, This Soule Bread take.
Come Eate thy fill of this thy Gods White Loafe?[8]
Its Food too fine for Angells, yet come, take
And Eate thy fill. Its Heavens Sugar Cake.

What Grace is this knead in this Loafe? This thing
Souls are but petty things it to admire.
Yee Angells, help: This fill would to the brim
Heav'ns whelm'd-down[9] Chrystall meele Bowle, yea and higher.
This Bread of Life dropt in thy mouth, doth Cry.
Eate, Eate me, Soul, and thou shalt never dy.

June 8, 1684

1937

Second Series

1. Meditation. Col. 2.17. Which are Shaddows of things to come and the body is Christs.

Oh Leaden heeld. Lord, give, forgive I pray.
Infire my Heart: it bedded is in Snow.
I Chide myselfe seing myselfe decay.
In heate and Zeale to thee, I frozen grow.
File my dull Spirits: make them sharp and bright:
Them firbush[1] for thyselfe, and thy delight.

My Stains are such, and sinke so deep, that all
The Excellency in Created Shells
Too low, and little is to make it fall
Out of my leather Coate wherein it dwells.
This Excellence is but a Shade to that
Which is enough to make my Stains go back.

[8]In the sacrament of the Lord's Supper, instituted by Christ (Luke 22:19), the bread spiritually signifies Christ's body "broken" during the crucifixion, His incarnate sacrifice to expiate mankind's sins, and God's grace and promise of eternal life to faithful communicants who are invited to come and eat.

[9]Turned upside down, as a dish or vessel to cover something. The *Oxford English Dictionary* quotes an illuminating passage from Dryden: "That the earth is like a trencher [wooden platter] and the Heavens a dish whelmed over it." In Revelation 15:7 seven angels carry "seven golden bowls [vials]" of God's wrath, but Taylor here envisions the new heavens as an inverted crystal bowl beaming forth eternally radiant light.

[1]Set on fire, using a fuel (firebrush, or firbrush, the needle foliage of fir trees) to ignite flames; sharpen, as a needle from the fir bush; a play on words with "firebrand," meaning one who inflames the passions.

The glory of the world slickt up in types
   In all Choise things chosen to typify,
His glory upon whom the worke doth light,
   To thine's a Shaddow, or a butterfly.
   How glorious then, my Lord, art thou to mee
   Seing to cleanse me, 's worke alone for thee.

The glory of all Types[2] doth meet in thee.
   Thy glory doth their glory quite excell:
More than the Sun excells in its bright glee
   A nat, an Earewig, Weevill, Snaile, or Shell.
   Wonders in Crowds start up; your eyes may strut
   Viewing his Excellence, and's bleeding cut.

Oh! that I had but halfe an eye to view
   This excellence of thine, undazled: so
Therewith to give my heart a touch anew
   Untill I quickned am, and made to glow.
   All is too little for thee: but alass
   Most of my little all hath other pass.

Then Pardon, Lord, my fault: and let thy beams
   Of Holiness pierce through this Heart of mine.
Ope to thy Blood a passage through my veans.
   Let thy pure blood my impure blood refine.
   Then with new blood and spirits I will dub
   My tunes upon thy Excellency good.

1693
1960

Meditation 26. Heb. 9.13.14. How much more shall the blood of Christ, etc.

Unclean, Unclean:[1] My Lord, Undone, all vile
   Yea all Defild: What shall thy Servant doe?
Unfit for thee: not fit for holy Soile,
   Nor for Communion of Saints below.

[2]In *Upon the Types of the Old Testament,* Taylor defines a type as "a Certain thing Standing with a Sacred impression set upon it by God to Signify Some good to come as Christ, or the Gospell Concerns in this Life." He composes 36 Sermons and corresponding Meditations 2.1–18, 20–30, 58–61, and 70–71, between 1693 and 1706, to illustrate how Old Testament persons, ceremonies, providences, and seals, foreshadow New Testament fulfillments through Christ and His Church.

[1]See Leviticus 13:44–46, instructing lepers to cry "Unclean, unclean," and to be put outside Israel's camp. Leviticus 13 and 14:1–32 record the priest's duty of identifying and ceremonially cleansing leprous persons, using sacrificial rites that Taylor traces more minutely in Meditation 2.27.

A bag of botches, Lump of Loathsomeness:
Defild by Touch, by Issue: Leproust flesh.[2]

Thou wilt have all that enter do thy fold
Pure, Cleane, and bright, Whiter than whitest Snow
Better refin'd than most refined Gold:
I am not so: but fowle: What shall I doe?
Shall thy Church Doors be shut, and shut out mee?
Shall not Church fellowship my portion bee?[3]

How can it be? Thy Churches do require
Pure Holiness: I am all filth, alas!
Shall I defile them, tumbled thus in mire?
Or they mee cleanse before I current pass?
If thus they do, Where is the Niter bright
And Sope they offer mee to wash me White?

The Brisk Red heifer's Ashes,[4] when calcin'd,
Mixt all in running Water, is too Weake
To wash away my Filth: The Dooves assign'd
Burnt, and Sin Offerings[5] neer do the feate
But as they Emblemize the Fountain Spring
Thy Blood, my Lord, set ope to wash off Sin.

Oh! richest Grace! Are thy Rich Veans then tapt
To ope this Holy Fountain (boundless Sea)
For Sinners here to lavor off (all sapt
With Sin) their Sins and Sinfulness away?
In this bright Chrystall Crimson Fountain flows
What washeth whiter, than the Swan or Rose.

Oh! wash mee, Lord, in this Choice Fountain, White
That I may enter, and not sully here
Thy Church, whose floore is pav'de with Graces bright
And hold Church fellowship with Saints most cleare.

[2]In *Upon the Types of the Old Testament* and corresponding Meditations, Taylor categorizes Old Testament types of ceremonial uncleanness by touching (2.26), issues and leprosy (2.27), and moral impurity (2.28).

[3]In Sermons and Meditations 2.26–28, Taylor typologically interprets Old Testament priestly purifications, since "the Discipline enacted by God to fit Such as were Ceremonially unclean, for Church Fellowship under the Legall Dispensation, was typicall of Christ's Evangelicall preparing Such as are Spiritually unclean, for Church Fellowship in the Gospell day."

[4]See Numbers 19 for the purification of those unclean by touching (of a corpse) by the sacrifice of a red heifer.

[5]See Leviticus 15; unclean issues require the sacrifice of two turtledoves as sin and burnt offerings, by which the priest makes atonement.

My Voice all sweet, with their melodious layes
Shall make sweet Musick blossom'd with thy praise.

June 26, 1698
1957

Meditation 43. Rom. 9.5. God blessed forever.[1]

When, Lord, I seeke to shew thy praises, then
Thy shining Majesty doth stund my minde,
Encramps my tongue and tongue ties fast my Pen,
That all my doings, do not what's designd.
My Speeche's Organs are so trancifide[2]
My words stand startld, can't thy praises stride.

Nay Speeches Bloomery can't from the Ore
Of Reasons mine, melt words for to define
Thy Deity, nor t'deck the reechs[3] that sore[4]
From Loves rich Vales, sweeter than hony rhimes.
Words though the finest twine of reason, are
Too Course a web for Deity to ware.

Words Mentall are syllabicated thoughts:
Words Orall but thoughts Whiffld[5] in the Winde.
Words Writ, are incky, Goose quill-slabbred[6] draughts,[7]
Although the fairest blossoms of the minde.
Then can such glasses cleare enough descry
My Love to thee, or thy rich Deity?

Words are befould, Thoughts filthy fumes that smoake,
From Smutty Huts, like Will-a-Wisps[8] that rise

[1]Meditations 2.42–56, composed between August 1701 and October 1703, are linked with fourteen corresponding sermons which focus on Christ's nature and qualifications. See the *Christographia.*

[2]Entranced, as in a swoon; to be cast into a state of extreme dread, doubt, or suspense; stupified.

[3]Reek, as in smoke, vapors, or perfume; a stench; applies also to whirls of fine particles.

[4]Soar.

[5]Blown or puffed about by slight gusts of air.

[6]Slobbered or drooled, as with saliva or ink; sloppy; clumsy.

[7]Drafts; preliminary sketches or outlines of a writing or document from which the fair or finished copy is made.

[8]Popular name for an *ignis fatuus,* a phosphorescent light hovering over marshy ground, due supposedly to the spontaneous combustion of an inflammable gas from decaying organic matter. Superstitiously believed to be mischievous spirits intentionally leading benighted travelers astray, it comes to signify a deceptive goal, delusive guiding principle, or foolish hope.

From Quaugmires, run ore bogs where frogs do Croake,
Lead all astray led by them by the eyes.
My muddy Words so dark thy Deity,
And cloude thy Sun-Shine, and its Shining Sky.

Yet spare mee, Lord, to use this hurden ware.[9]
I have no finer Stuff[10] to use, and I
Will use it now my Creed but to declare
And not thy Glorious Selfe to beautify.
Thou art all-God: all Godhead then is thine
Although the manhood there unto doth joyne.

Thou art all Godhead bright, although there bee
Something beside the Godhead in thee bright.
Thou art all Infinite although in thee
There is a nature pure, not infinite.
Thou art Almighty, though thy Humane tent
Of Humane frailty upon earth did sent.

He needs must be the Deity most High,
To whom all properties essensiall to
The Godhead do belong Essentially
And not to others: nor from Godhead go
And thou art thus, my Lord, to Godhead joynd.
We finde thee thus in Holy Writ definde.

Thou art Eternall; Infinite thou art;
Omnipotent, Omniscient, Erywhere,
All Holy, Just, Good, Gracious, True, in heart,
Immortal, though with mortall nature here.
Religious worship hence belongs to thee
From men and angells: all, of each degree.

Be thou my God, and make mee thine Elect
To kiss thy feet, and worship give to thee:
Accept of mee, and make mee thee accept.
So I'st be safe, and thou shalt served bee.
I'le bring thee praise, buskt[11] up in Songs perfum'de,
When thou with grace my Soule hast sweetly tun'de.

October 26, 1701

1954

[9]A coarse fabric made from flax or hemp.

[10]Textile suitable for clothing, especially wool or worsted fabric; in literary or artistic production, writing, discourse, or ideas of little value.

[11]Dressed, decked out.

50. Meditation. Joh. 1.14. Full of Truth.

The Artists Hand more gloriously bright,
Than is the Sun itselfe, in'ts shining glory
Wrought with a stone axe made of Pearle, as light
As light itselfe, out of a Rock all flory[1]
Of Precious Pearle,[2] a Box most lively made
More rich than gold Brimfull of Truth enlaid.

Which Box should forth a race of boxes send
Teemd from its Womb such as itselfe, to run
Down from the Worlds beginning to its end.
But, o! this box of Pearle Fell, Broke, undone.
Truth from it flew: It lost Smaragdine[3] Glory:
Was filld with Falshood: Boxes teemd of Sory.

The Artist puts his glorious hand again
Out to the Worke: His Skill out flames more bright
Now than before. The worke he goes to gain,
He did portray in flaming Rayes of light.
A Box of Pearle shall from this Sory, pass
More rich than that Smaragdine Truth-Box was.

Which Box, four thousand yeares, o'r ere 'twas made,
In golden Scutchons[4] lay'd[5] in inke Divine
Of Promises, of a Prophetick Shade,
And in embellishments of Types that shine.
Whose Beames in this Choice pearle-made-Box all meet
And bedded in't their glorious Truth to keep.

But now, my Lord, thy Humane Nature, I
Doe by the Rayes this Scutcheon sends out, finde
Is this Smaragdine Box where Truth doth ly
Of Types, and Promises, that thee out lin'de.
Their Truth they finde in thee: this makes them shine.
Their Shine on thee makes thee appeare Divine.

Thou givst thy Truth to them, thus true they bee.
They bring their Witness out for thee. Hereby

[1]Flowery, showy.
[2]Taylor apparently draws upon Revelation 21:18–21, which describes the New Jerusalem's pearly gates, and upon Matthew 13:45–46, which identifies the pearl of great price with the true Church and as a metaphor for Christ.
[3]Consisting of a smaragd (precious bright green stone), or of an emerald green.
[4]Escutcheon, as in heraldry, a shield depicting a coat of arms.
[5]From inlayed, to embed a substance of a different kind in a surface.

Their Truth appeares emboxt indeed in thee:
And thou the true Messiah shin'st thereby.
Hence Thou, and They make One another true
And They, and Thou each others Glory shew.

Hence thou art full of Truth, and full dost stand,
Of Promises, of Prophesies, and Types.
But that's not all: All truth is in thy hand,
Thy lips drop onely Truth, give Falshood gripes.
Leade through the World to glory, that ne'er ends
By Truth's bright Hand all such as Grace befriends.

O! Box of Truth! tenent[6] my Credence in
The mortase[7] of thy Truth: and Thou in Mee.
These Mortases, and Tenents make so trim,
That They and Thou, and I ne'er severd bee.
Embox my Faith, Lord, in thy Truth a part
And I'st by Faith embox thee in my heart.

December 27, 1702

1960

60[B]. Meditation. Cor. 10.4. And all drunk the same spirituall drinke.[1]

Ye Angells bright, pluck from your Wings a Quill.[2]
Make me a pen thereof that best will write.
Lende me your fancy, and Angellick skill
To treate this Theme, more rich than Rubies bright.
My muddy Inke, and Cloudy fancy dark,
Will dull its glory, lacking highest Art.

An Eye at Centre righter may describe
The Worlds Circumferentiall glory vast

[6]In carpentry, to join together by fitting a tenon, or projection on a piece of wood, into a mortice, so as to form a secure joint; possibly in the double sense of tenet, to hold firmly a doctrine, dogma, or opinion in religion or philosophy.

[7]Mortise, or mortice, the cavity or hole cut in a piece of timber to receive the shaped end (tenon); mortise and tenon are the component parts of a joint, but it also refers collectively to the method of joining.

[1]This meditation is part of a five-poem sequence, offering Taylor's interpretation of Israel's journey out of Egypt (2.58), the pillar of cloud and fire (2.59), the manna (2.60A), Rock of Horeb (2.60B), and serpent in the wilderness (2.61) as types of extraordinary deliverances and providential seals of faith. See Exodus 12–17 and Numbers 21:5–9.

[2]The tube or barrel of a feather from a large bird (often a goose), formed into a pen by pointing and slitting the lower end; a hollow stem or reed made into a small water or musical pipe.

As in its nutshell bed it snugs fast tide,
Than any angells pen can glory Cast
Upon this Drink Drawn from the Rock,[3] tapt by
The Rod of God, in Horeb, typickly.

Sea water straind through Mineralls, Rocks, and Sands
Well Clarifi'de by Sunbeams, Dulcifi'de,
Insipid, Sordid, Swill, Dishwater stands.
But here's a Rock of Aqua-Vitae[4] tride.
When once God broacht it, out a River came
To bath and bibble[5] in, for Israels train.

Some Rocks have sweat. Some Pillars bled out tears.
But here's a River in a Rock up tun'd
Not of Sea Water nor of Swill. Its beere.
No Nectar like it. Yet it once Unbund
A River down out runs through ages all.
A Fountain opte, to wash off Sin and Fall.

Christ is this Horebs Rock, the streames that slide
A River is of Aqua Vitae Deare
Yet costs us nothing, gushing from his side.
Celestiall Wine our Sinsunk souls to cheare.
This Rock and Water, Sacramentall Cup
Are made, Lords Supper Wine for us to sup.

This Rock's the Grape that Zions Vineyard[6] bore
Which Moses Rod did smiting pound, and press[7]
Untill its blood, the brooke of Life, run ore.
All Glorious Grace, and Gracious Righteousness.
We in this brook must bath: and with faiths quill
Suck Grace, and Life out of this Rock our fill.

Lord, oynt me with this Petro[8] oyle. I'm sick.
Make mee drinke Water of the Rock. I'm dry.

[3]See Exodus 17:1–7, for the account of Moses smiting the Rock of Horeb, which becomes a type of Christ the Rock, whose death releases new life through the Holy Spirit, and of the Lord's Supper wine, which commemorates Christ's sacrifice and seals the New Testament Covenant of Grace and redemption.

[4]Literally "water of life"; any brandy or spiritous liquor; originally applied by alchemists to ardent spirits. Taylor draws upon references to the waters of Paradise from Revelation 7:17; 21:6; 22:1, 17.

[5]Dabble with the bill like a duck; to drink.

[6]See John 15:1–8, in which Christ is the Vine. The parable of the vineyard in Matthew 21:33–46 identifies Christ with the slain son and as a risen cornerstone of the Church.

[7]Christ (and his crucifixion) is metaphorically identified with the winepress, which gives forth the "blood" and "wine" from the grape, but in Revelation 14:18–20 and 19–15, the winepress also becomes an instrument of God's wrath against his enemies.

[8]Possibly Peter's oil; Greek for stone or rock, with particular reference perhaps to Matthew 16:18.

Me in this fountain wash. My filth is thick.
I'm faint, give Aqua Vitae or I dy.
If in this stream thou cleanse and Chearish mee
My Heart thy Hallelujahs Pipe shall bee.

July 30, 1704
1939

115. *Meditation. Cant. 5:10. My Beloved.*[1]

What art thou mine? Am I espousd to thee?
What honour's this? It is more bright Renown.
I ought to glory more in this sweet glee
Than if I'd wore greate Alexanders[2] Crown.
Oh! make my Heart loaded with Love ascend
Up to thyselfe, its bridegroom, bright, and Friend.

Her whole delight, and her Belov'de thou art.
Oh! Lovely thou: Oh! grudg my Soule, I say,
Thou straitend standst, lockt up to Earths fine parts
Course matter truly, yellow earth, Hard Clay.
Why should these Clayey faces be the keyes
T'lock, and unlock thy love up as they please?

Lord, make thy Holy Word, the golden Key
My Soule to lock and make its bolt to trig[3]
Before the same, and Oyle the same to play
As thou dost move them off and On to jig[4]
The ripest Fruits that my affections beare
I offer, thee. Oh! my Beloved faire.

Thou standst the brightest object in bright glory
More shining than the shining sun to 'lure.

[1]Between September 4, 1713, and October 1725, Taylor culminated his *Preparatory Meditations* with an extended series on the Canticles, or Song of Solomon. Forty-nine of his final fifty-three Meditations poetically explicate consecutive verses from Canticles 5:10–16; 6:1–13; 7:1–6; 5:1; and 2:1, 3–5. Written during a period of severe illness and declining health (1722–1725), the final seven poems (161A–165) are part of Taylor's poignant epithalamium and *ars moriendi,* expressing his desire (as the Bride) for a heavenly, eternal union with Christ the Bridegroom. Regarded as a premier poetic book of the Bible with the most clearly erotic imagery, Solomon's lyrical celebration of his love for the Shulamite maiden was interpreted by Puritan expositors as a figurative revelation of God's love for His covenant people (Israel) and as a spiritual allegory of Christ's love for His heavenly Bride, the Church, and the individual Elect soul. Canticles signifies a lyric, little song, or hymn.

[2]Alexander the Great (356–323 B.C.), King of Macedonia, was famous for his military conquests of Greece, the Persian Empire, and northwestern India.

[3]Hold firm or fast; make faithful, trim, or tidy.

[4]To move up and down, to and fro with a rapid, jerky motion, as in jiggle.

Unto thyselfe the purest Love. The Stories
Within my Soul can hold refinde most pure
In flaming bundles polishd all with Grace
Most sparklingly about thyselfe t'imbrace.

The most refined Love in Graces mint
In rapid flames is best bestowd on thee
The brightest: metall with Divinest print
Thy tribute is, and ever more shall bee.
The Loving Spouse and thou her Loved Sweet
Make Lovely Joy when she and thee do meet:

Thou art so lovely, pitty 'tis indeed
That any drop of love the Heart can hold
Should be held back from thee, or should proceed
To drop on other Objects, young, or old.
Best things go best together: best agree:
But best are badly usd, by bad that bee.

Thou all o're Lovely art, Most lovely Thou:
Thy Spouse, the best of Loving Ones: Her Love,
The Best of Love: and this she doth avow
Thyselfe. And thus she doth thyself approve.
That object robs thee of thy due that wares
Thy Spouses Love. With thee none in it shares.

Lord fill my heart with Grace refining Love.
Be thou my onely Well-Belov'd I pray.
And make my Heart with all its Love right move
Unto thyselfe, and all her Love display.
My Love is then right well bestow'd, alone
When it obtains thyselfe her Lovely One.

My Best love then shall on Shoshannim[5] play,
Like David[6] her Sweet Musick, and thy praise

[5]The Hebrew titles of Psalms 45, 60, 69, and 80 suggest that shoshannim refers to lilies, thought to indicate (a) the popular melody to which these psalms were sung; (b) a lily-shaped long silver trumpet used by priests to announce festivals or assemble the congregation; or (c) an old rite in which revelations, testimony, or omens were taken from lilies, which were also (in Canticles) an emblem of love.

[6]David (Hebrew, beloved; also meaning chieftain) was a shepherd, son of Jesse, who became Israel's second King, of such heroic aspect that he was regarded not only as a lineal ancestor but also as a type of the Messiah. Considered the sweet singer of Israel, he was designated author in the Hebrew titles of seventy-three Psalms, of a song of deliverance, and of a lamentation for Saul and Jonathan, the latter of which Taylor also paraphrased in the "Poetical Works." See I Samuel 16:12 through I Kings 2:11, I Chronicles 11–29, and the Psalms.

Inspire her Songs, that Glory ever may
In Sweetest tunes thy Excellency Glaze.
And thou shalt be that burden of her Song
Loaded with Praise that to thyselfe belong.

September 4, 1713
1960

from A Valediction to all the World preparatory for Death 3d of the 11m 1720[1]

from Version 1[2]

Cant. 3. Valediction, to the Terraqueous[3] *Globe*

Thou Realm of Senses, Sensuality
Enchanting e'ry Sense to take its fill,
Cooking up to the Tast Cocksbowl[4] full high.
Unto the Eare's enchanting Melodies Skill,
Unto the Eyes enticing Beauteous Sights
And to the Touch silk downy soft delights;
While in this Earthly Paradise that brings
Things to entice to Sensualities.
Most Sparkling Sights of various sorts of things
Delicious dishes Spic'de Varieties,
Melodies Sounds, & Aromatick Smells
And downy Soft delight enchanting Spells.
While in the Senses markets, Souls, beware
That in their truck[5] thou do not erre nor miss,
Oh never make thy Choicest food & fare

[1]Nearly eighty and after a severe illness in December 1720, Taylor composed this poem as a farewell to earthly things in anticipation of death, which did not come until June 24, 1729. When dating his poems, Taylor used March as the first month of the year; hence, the "Valediction" was written in January 1721. Text is from Davis and Davis, eds., *Minor Poetry.*

[2]The Canticles excerpted here are two of eight in Version 1 from the "Poetical Works" manuscript. The "Valediction" exists in three versions and provides an opportunity to observe Taylor's practice of composing in several stages.

[3]Terraqueous, consisting of land and water.

[4]Cock may refer to (a) the male domestic fowl; (b) a spout to channel liquids and, therefore, a "cocksbowl" or vessel to hold liquids; or (c) a short form of "cockle," a shellfish, oyster, or plant grown in cornfields.

[5]Bartering or exchanging commodities, especially in an underhanded way; short for "truckle," to act subserviently, bend obsequiously.

A mess of butterd Cocks crumbs in a Dish.[6]
If I should you hold & ne'er so hard & fast,
You sure would leave me in the lurch at last.
Will I or will I. Hence you Cheats adjue[7]
You will but Gull mee, if I leave not you.

My Cloaths farewell: no more by mee to be worn
You'l no more warm me, no nor me adorn.
My Bed farewell, my Coverlids & Rug[8]
A Coffin, Grave, or Green turffe I now hug;
My Meat, my Drink & Physick all adjue,
I'me got within Gods Paradise its trew.
Where's my best life & no Physickal here
Is ever needed: Here's the Best best Cheere.
The Tree of Life[9] doth bear mee. Oh food Choice
That is within the pale of Paradise.
And of the pure pure water of the River
Of Gods Stilld Aqua Vitae,[10] I'st drink ever.

. . .

My House & lands, my Stock & State I finde
Can't ease my tooth's nor Head ach nor my minde;
My Friends & mine acquaintances very deare,
My Deare-Deare Wife & little twigs that peare
Out of my Stock, Bits of myself, I finde
Exceeding dear whom now I leave behinde.
Tho' attending me with pickled Eyes,
Dropping their brine upon my Cask that lies
Gasping for Breath & panting. Oh! I could
My Pickle mix with yours, which if I could
All would not keep me Sweet. My Vessell soon
Would tainte, tho' all your Love & Skill should bloom.
I now do wish you well & say adjue
You'l leave me helpless, if I leave not you.

[6]A delicacy or "pretty dish" of stewed (or preserved) cocks-combs, i.e. rooster's crests (or shellfish?), sometimes stuffed with crumbled meats and spices; possibly the reddish-purple or yellow-orange flowering plant called cockscomb.

[7]Variant of (a) adieu, French meaning "I commend you to God," and commonly to bid farewell, with regret at a loss, or a formal leavetaking; or (b) adjure, to charge or entreat solemnly or earnestly, as if under oath or the penalty of a curse; to exorcise an evil spirit by adjuration in God's name.

[8]A coarse woolen material or coverlet; a heavy bed covering handmade of sturdy linen or wool backing densely set with raised loops of yarn.

[9]See Genesis 2:9, 3:22; Revelation 2:7, 22:2, 14, for the Tree of Life.

[10]Literally, "water of life;" any brandy or spiritous liquor; originally applied by alchemists to ardent spirits. Taylor draws upon references to the waters of Paradise from Revelation 7:17; 21:6; 22:1, 17. Thirty-four lines of the poem, which would normally follow this line, have been omitted in this edition.

I leave you all biding you all adjue
You'l soon leave me if I do not leave you.
My study, Books, Pen, Inke, & Paper all
My Office implements off from me fall.
My People, aye & Pulpet leave be hinde
Unto a Voice thence uttering Gods minde
For some more richly laid in, for Christs work
Bringing a richer blessing, & no Shirk
To fill Christs warehous full of Spirituall Trades
And not an empty Sound of Some Vain blades.

But yet my Lord I give thee hearty thanks
Thou'st let me these to tend me to the banks
Of thy high & Eternall glorious Throne
And now do leave them here tho' calld mine Own.
Untill the last day dawns & up then springs
At whose good morrow when the last Trump[11] rings
I do expect these Organs, once again
To Sing thy praises then in Sweeter Strain.
And drest up all in glorious robes Rich Grace
Deckt if it be appeare before the judgments place.
When Angells bright shall bid me then good morrow
Wholy acquitted of all Sin & Sorrow.
And in these Organs with Angellick Phrase
Sing out Gods glory in Ceremoniall Praise,
Which now I laying down tho' ne'er so bright
Till then & therefore bid them all good night.

Cant. 4. A Suite[12] to Christ here upon

Empty, my Lord, my very heart doth, and
Its Leantoe Tent[13] Affections, empty stand.
I banisht have, those mundine things mine ile
Ev'n All except some handfull yet a while.
And earnestly do pray their empty places
That thou wouldst fill & furnish with thy graces.

[11] I Corinthians 15:52, signifying the trumpet that heralds the resurrection of the redeemed dead at Christ's Second Coming and the ascension into the New Jerusalem after the millennium and Last Judgment. This passage is just before the well-known I Corinthians 15:55, "O death, where is thy sting? O grave, where is thy victory?" See also Revelation 8, 9, 11.

[12] An appeal for justice or redress by way of petition or entreaty; may have the secondary undertone of an orchestral concert or instrumental musical arrangement, although Puritan practice forbade music in church worship.

[13] During one of the three Passover feasts, the Feast of Tabernacles (Sukkoth), families lived in tents or booths made of boughs in remembrance of the forty years' wandering in the wilderness. See Leviticus 23:33–44; Nehemiah 8:13–18. "Leanto" may also mean a rough shed or shelter.

Give Spirituall Sight unto myne Eyes delight,
An Holys Beauty Spirituall rich sweet Light.
My Spirituall fare grant Spirituall Melodies;
Oh fill top full with Heavens Sweet Musicks joys
The Stoppill[14] of my Spirituall Narin[15] Roomes,
Let by thy Spirits Aromatick fumes
My Spirituall Palate please with Holy Fare
The Heavenly Mannah, that Grace doth prepare.
My Spirituall Touch with Spirituall Satin pure
Furnish my Soule with Graces furniture,
And Cloath my life with Gods brave holy dress,
The Holy Ghosts fine Lawn,[16] Christs Righteousness.
Let the Master of thy Ceremonies all
Teach me the mode & Gestures of thy Hall,
That I may fitted bee well to behave
Myselfe when there with Spirituall manners brave.
When thou shall me there in thy work imploy,
And in thy Sweet Work thee to glorify.
When I've skipt ore the purling Stile[17] with joy
Twixt Swift wing'd Time & Fixt Eternity
And am got in the heavenly strand on High
My Harp shall sing thy praise melodiously.
But who am I that I should with my Quill
Ere any joy into thine ears distill.
The present world I finde 's filld to its brim
With bitter griefs, smart sorrows, & black sin.
That is the Realm of joy and blessed praise
Wherein my Musick * * * in measured phrase.
I hence do crave thy leave to borrow
What Melody I meet with in my Sorrow.

And first I'de borrow of all birds within
The Woods where they their bagpipes blow make sing
And thence I run to sweet fine flowers whose tune
Is silent given in beauty & perfume.
Then at the Angells doore, those happy Friends,
And 'treat them me their melodie to lend,
And mix their tunes with mine heapt in a lump
A greater melody might sweetly jump
Off from my Cimball strings, yet thou'rt too high

[14]Stopple, something that closes an aperture, as a plug.

[15]From naris, referring to the opening of the nose.

[16]A fine, sheer, plain-woven linen or cotton fabric.

[17]Steps or rungs allowing passage over or through a fence to one person, while barring sheep or cattle; often referred to in records of and directions for funeral services. Taylor creates a likely turn of phrase on "purling stream."

For this to touch thee with a fresh new joy.
But yet my Tunes enlinde with holy praise
Keep table to thee in richest phrase
And will thy Saints & Angells bright make to Sing
And with Sweet Melody thy palace t' ring.

January 3, 1720 [21]

1972

A Fig for thee Oh! Death

Version 2[1]

Thou King of Terrours with thy Gastly Eyes
With Butter teeth, bare bones Grim looks likewise.
And Grizzly Hide, & clawing Tallons, fell,[2]
Opning to Sinners Vile, Trap Door of Hell,
That on in Sin impenitently trip
The Down fall art of the infernall Pit,
Thou struckst thy teeth deep in my Lord's blest Side:
Who dasht it out, & all its venom 'Stroyde.
That now thy Poundrill[3] shall onely dash
My Flesh & bones to bits, & Cask shall clash.[4]
Thou'rt not so frightful now to me, thy knocks
Do crack my shell, its Heavenly kernells box
Abides most safe. Thy blows do breake its Shell,
Thy Teeth its Nut. Cracks are that on it fell
Thence out its kirnell fair & not by worms.
Once Viciated out, new formd forth turns
And on the wings of some bright Angell flies,
Out to bright glory of Gods blissful joyes.
Hence thou to mee with all thy Gastly face
Art not so dreadfull unto mee thro' Grace.
I am resolvde to fight thee, & ne'er yield
Blood up to th' Ears; & in the battle field.
Chassing thee hence: But not for this my flesh,

[1]Version 1 appears in the "Manuscript Book," probably copied in 1723–1724, while the second—and final—version appears in the "Poetical Works," in which Taylor usually transcribed his finished poems. Text is from Davis and Davis, eds., *Minor Poetry.*

[2]Deadly.

[3]A pounder or instrument for crushing by heavy blows into small fragments or powder, such as a pestle or heavy wooden hammer.

[4]His body will feel the resounding blow.

My Body, my vile harlot, its thy Mess.[5]
Labouring to drown me into Sin's disguise
By Eating & by drinking such evill joyes
Tho' Grace preserv'd mee that I nere have
Surprised been nor tumbled in Such grave [6]
Hence for my Strumpet I'le ne'er draw my Sword
Nor thee restrain at all by Iron Curb
Nor for her Safty will I 'gainst thee Strive
But let thy frozen grips take her Captive
And her imprison in thy dungeon Cave
And grinde to powder in thy Mill the grave,
[W]hich powder in thy Van[7] thou'st safely keep
[T]ill She hath slept out quite her fatall Sleep.
[W]hen the last Cock shall Crow the last day in
And the Arch Angells Trumpets sound shall ring[8]
Then th' Eye Omniscient seek shall all there round
Each dust death's mill had very findly ground,
Which in death's Smoky furnace well refinde
And each to'ts fellow hath exactly joyn'd,
[I]s raised up anew & made all bright
And Christalized; & top full of delight.
And entertains its Soule again in bliss
And Holy Angells waiting all on this.
The Soule & Body now, as two true Lovers
[E]ry night how do they hug & kiss each other.
[A]nd going hand in hand thus thro' the Skies
[U]p to Eternall glory glorious rise.
[I]s this the Worse thy terrours then can? why
Then Should this grimace at me terrify?
Why comst thou then so slowly? mend thy pace
Thy Slowness me detains from Christ's bright face.
Altho' thy terrours rise to th' highst degree,
[I] still am where I was, a Fig[9] for thee.

Copied 1723–25?

1960

[5]Dinner.

[6]In the first version Taylor's sense in lines 24–28 becomes clearer: "My harlot body, make thou it, thy Mess,/ That oft ensnared mee with its Strumpets guise/ Of Meats and drinks dainty Sensualities./ Yet Grace ne'er suffer me to turn aside/ As Sinners oft fall in & do abide."

[7]Winnowing basket.

[8]Revelation 8, 9, 11 presents the seven archangels and trumpets that announce Christ's new reign on earth, when the redeemed will be resurrected from the dead. After the millennium and Final Judgment (of the damned), a second resurrection will take place, into the New Jerusalem where the saints will dwell throughout eternity. See also I Corinthians 15.

[9]Fig may refer to (a) a poisoned fig used secretly to destroy an obnoxious person; or (b) the *Fica,* a contemptuous gesture created by thrusting the thumb between two closed fingers into the mouth, thereby offering an obscene insult or crude dismissal. See Micah 4:4; Isaiah 34:4; Revelation 6:12–14.

Samuel Sewall 1652–1730

In his own day, Samuel Sewall was probably best known for his immense guilt over his actions as a judge during the Salem witch trials and for his anti-slavery pamphlet, *The Selling of Joseph* (1700), the first anti-slavery statement to be published by a Puritan. From the late nineteenth century on, however, Sewall's private life, especially his courtship of the widow Katherine Winthrop, has come under the interest of most readers of his journal. But Sewall's two-volume journal, which dates from 1673 to 1728, offers much more than a glimpse of a Puritan who searched his conscience about right conduct in this world and who calculated the costs of an embarrassing and mismanaged courtship. *The Diary of Samuel Sewall* signals the key shifts emergent in American culture as the seventeenth century gave way to the eighteenth century.

Born in England, Samuel Sewall traveled to Boston with his mother when he was nine, arriving July 6, 1661. The family had followed to America Sewall's father, Henry Sewall, a Puritan minister whose forte in business dealings brought him to New England to manage inherited family estates. Samuel Sewall was devout in both private and public life, and he early felt called to religious duty. As a member of the class of 1671, Sewall attended Harvard College, where he became both "chum and bedfellow" to a lifelong friend, Edward Taylor. Although most of his classmates became ministers and he himself had been called to a pulpit in Woodbridge, New Jersey, Sewall evidently experienced stronger callings into the world of public dealings among men. He married Hannah Hull in 1676, and assisted with the very successful mercantile business of her father, John Hull, Master of the Mint and one of the wealthiest men in Massachusetts. When his father-in-law died in 1684, Sewall's activities became more and more central to affairs in Boston.

He had entered public service in his twenties, managing the printing press of the colony while he acted as deputy of the General Court (1683) and later on the Council (1684–86); under the new Massachusetts Charter of 1692, Sewall remained a member of the General Court for thirty-three years. He was appointed Justice of the Superior Court in 1692, and from 1718 to 1728, he was Chief Justice of Massachusetts. His glowing record of public service seems at times to suggest that the man had few private concerns, yet, as his guilt-ridden retraction (posted January 14, 1697, a fast day) of his actions as a Salem judge attests, Samuel Sewall was an intensely thoughtful and conservative Puritan. He was the only "hanging judge" to offer publicly a statement of his guilt and his regret. And he was the first Puritan to publish an anti-slavery tract.

The selections offered below reveal a man who throughout his life sought assurance that he did not—as he once admonished young Timothy Dwight—"make the convictions wrought by God's spirit a stalking horse to any other thing." Whether he was seeking church membership, or considering whether or not the Puritans were dealing justly with the local Indians, or retracing his thoughts about the witch trials and the deaths the trials countenanced, or engaging in heated controversy the most celebrated of local townsmen in his denouncement of slavery as un-Christian, Samuel Sewall seems constantly to have sought the counsel of his God and his own clearness of thought before acting upon his beliefs. Such was the man's inner turmoil and his inner strength. Perhaps more than any other text from the era, the diary of Samuel Sewall offers readers a very revealing portrait of an intense Puritan who was a man of public affairs in a world that was fast changing from colony to province.

Sewall wrote *The Selling of Joseph* during a heated controversy about the holding of slaves. The Puritan-enacted Body of Liberties had established slavery in New England in 1641. By 1700, the slave trade was an institution. Indeed, in 1708, in Boston alone, about 400 slaves were concentrated within a population of about 7,000 whites. By the year 1720, the colony had about 2,000 slaves.

Sewall's diary reveals that his concerns about slavery began as early as 1673. The immediate impulse behind Sewall's pamphlet, however, was Belknap's petition brought before the General Court to free a slave and his wife. The slave probably was Adam, a slave owned by John Saffin (see the seventeenth-century poetry selection), who had spent some time in Virginia before settling in Boston. Among other more respectable posts, Saffin was a slave-trader who, after promising Adam his freedom after a certain duration of time, then hired him out for work beyond the promised date of freedom. Sewall's pamphlet so enraged Saffin that Saffin replied to it with *A Brief and Candid Answer to a late Printed Sheet, Entitled The Selling of Joseph* in 1701. Adam was finally freed, with Sewall's assistance, in 1703.

In part as a result of the controversy that was brewing between Sewall and Saffin, Cotton Mather wrote and published *The Negro Christianized* (1706), a pamphlet that employed one of the lines of argument prominent in pro-slavery rhetoric prior to the Civil War—that a black Christian would make a happier slave than a black non-Christian, and that baptising slaves was freeing them.

Sewall's actions against slavery came at a time when white Puritans were beginning to grow wealthy through a three-way trade route which included the taking and selling of slaves. In such a climate of activity, Sewall's publication of *The Selling of Joseph* and his continued dispersal of the pamphlet wherever he thought it might do good has to be interpreted as a courageous act. This seems, at least, to have been the opinion of John Greenleaf Whittier, who in the nineteenth century wrote of Sewall:

Green forever the memory be
Of the Judge of the old Theocracy,
Whom even his errors glorified . . .
Honor and praise to this Puritan
Who the halting step of his age outran.

Carla Mulford
Pennsylvania State University

PRIMARY WORKS

S. Kaplan, ed., *The Selling of Joseph: A Memorial,* 1969; M. Halsey Thomas, ed., *The Diary of Samuel Sewall,* 2 vols., 1973.

SECONDARY WORKS

L. W. Towner, "The Sewall-Saffin Dialogue on Slavery," *William and Mary Quarterly,* 21, 1964:40–52; Ola E. Winslow, *Samuel Sewall of Boston,* 1964; T.B. Strandness, *Samuel Sewall: A Puritan Portrait,* 1967; David D. Hall, "The Mental World of Samuel Sewall," *Proc., Massachusetts Historical Society,* 92, 1980:21–44.

from The Diary of Samuel Sewall[1]

Augt. 25. [1692] Fast at the old [First] Church, respecting the Witchcraft, Drought, &c.

Monday, Sept. 19, 1692. About noon, at Salem, Giles Corey[2] was press'd to death for standing Mute; much pains was used with him two days, one after another, by the Court and Capt. Gardner of Nantucket who had been of his acquaintance: but all in vain.

Sept. 20. [1692] Now I hear from Salem that about 18 years agoe, he was suspected to have stamped and press'd a man to death, but was cleared. Twas not remembered till Anne Putnam was told of it by said Corey's Spectre the Sabbath-day night before Execution.[3]

Sept. 20, 1692. The Swan brings in a rich French Prize of about 300 Tuns, laden with Claret, White Wine, Brandy, Salt, Linnen Paper, &c.

Sept. 21. [1692] A petition is sent to Town in behalf of Dorcas Hoar, who now confesses: Accordingly an order is sent to the Sheriff to forbear her Execution, notwithstanding her being in the Warrant to die to morrow. This is the first condemned person who has confess'd.

Nov. 6. [1692] Joseph threw a knop of Brass and hit his Sister Betty on the forhead so as to make it bleed and swell; upon which, and for his playing at Prayertime, and eating when Return Thanks, I whipd him pretty smartly. When I first went in (call'd by his Grandmother) he sought to shadow and hide himself from me behind the head of the Cradle: which gave me the sorrowfull remembrance of Adam's carriage.

Monday, April 29, 1695. The morning is very warm and Sunshiny; in the Afternoon there is Thunder and Lightening, and about 2 P.M. a very extraordinary Storm of Hail, so that the ground was made white with it, as with the blossoms when fallen; 'twas as bigg as pistoll and Musquet Bullets; It broke of the Glass of the new House about 480 Quarrels [squares] of the Front; of Mr. Sergeant's about as much; Col. Shrimpton, Major General, Govr Bradstreet, New Meetinghouse, Mr. Willard, &c. Mr. Cotton Mather dined with us, and was with me in the new Kitchen when this was; He had just been mentioning that more Minister Houses than others proportionably had been smitten with Lightening; enquiring what the meaning of God should be in it. Many Hail-Stones broke throw the Glass and flew to the middle of the Room, or farther: People afterward Gazed upon the House to see its Ruins. I got Mr. Mather to pray with us after this awfull Providence; He told God He had broken the brittle part of our house, and prayd that we might be ready for the time when our Clay-Tabernacles should be broken. Twas a sorrowfull thing to me to see the house so far undon again before twas finish'd. It seems at Milton [near Boston] on the one hand, and at Lewis's [the tavern at Lynn] on the other, there was no Hail.

[1]Sewall's diary begins on December 3, 1673, and ends on December 25, 1728. This slightly modernized text is taken from *The Diary of Samuel Sewall,* ed. M. Halsey Thomas, 1973.

[2]Giles Corey was eighty in 1692.

[3]Anne Putnam was twelve when she became a witness against witches.

Jany 15. [1697] . . . Copy of the Bill I put up on the Fast day [January 14]; giving it to Mr. Willard as he pass'd by, and standing up at the reading of it, and bowing when finished; in the Afternoon.[4]

Samuel Sewall, sensible of the reiterated strokes of God upon himself and family, and being sensible, that as to the Guilt contracted, upon the opening of the late Commission of Oyer and Terminer at Salem (to which the order for this Day relates) he is, upon many accounts, more concerned than any that he knows of, Desires to take the Blame and Shame of it, Asking pardon of Men, And especially desiring prayers that God, who has an Unlimited Authority, would pardon that Sin and all other his Sins; personal and Relative: And according to his infinite Benignity, and Soveraignty, Not Visit the Sin of him, or of any other, upon himself or any of his, nor upon the Land: But that He would powerfully defend him against all Temptations to Sin, for the future; and vouchsafe him the Efficacious, Saving Conduct of his Word and Spirit.

July, 15. 1698. Mr. Edward Taylor comes to our house from Westfield. *Monday July 18. [1698]* I walk'd with Mr. Edward Taylor upon Cotton Hill, thence to Becon Hill, the Pasture, along the Stone-wall: As came back, we sat down on the great Rock, and Mr. Taylor told me his courting his first wife,[5] and Mr. Fitch his story of Mr. Dod's prayer to God to bring his Affection to close with a person pious, but hard-favoured. Has God answered me in finding out one Godly and fit for me, and shall I part for fancy? When came home, my wife gave me Mr. Tappan's Letter concerning Eliza,[6] which caus'd me to reflect on Mr. Taylor's Discourse. And his Prayer was for pardon of error in our ways—which made me think whether it were not best to overlook all, and go on. This day John Ive, fishing in great Spiepond, is arrested with mortal sickness which renders him in a manner speechless and senseless; dies next day; buried at Charlestown on the Wednesday. Was a very debauched, atheistical man. I was not at his Funeral. Had Gloves sent me, but the knowledge of his notoriously wicked life made me sick of going; and Mr. Mather, the president, came in just as I was ready to step out, and so I staid at home, and by that means lost a Ring: but hope had no loss.[7] Follow thou Me, was I suppose more complied with, than if had left Mr. Mather's company to go to such a Funeral.

Fourth-day, June 19, 1700 . . . Having been long and much dissatisfied with the Trade of fetching Negros from Guinea; at last I had a strong Inclination to Write something about it; but it wore off. At last reading Bayne, Ephes. about servants, who mentions Blackamoors; I began to be uneasy that I had so long neglected doing any thing.[8] When I was thus thinking, in come Bror Belknap to shew me a Petition he intended to present to the Genl Court for the freeing a Negro and his wife, who were unjustly held in Bondage. And there is a Motion by a Boston Comittee to get a Law that all Importers of Negros shall pay 40s *per* head, to discourage the bringing

[4]Sewall was the only witchcraft judge to make a public statement about his guilt over the Salem witch trials. He had lost two children in 1696, one child born dead and another, a daughter, who died December 23.

[5]Elizabeth Fitch, who died July 7, 1689.

[6]Elizabeth Tappan, Sewall's niece.

[7]The ring was a memorial token. Invitations to funerals were made by the presentation of gloves.

[8]Sewall evidently read Paul Baynes, *A Commentary upon the First Chapter of the Epistle of St. Paul. Written to the Ephesians* (London, 1618), and decided to write *The Selling of Joseph,* which was published June 24, 1700.

of them. And Mr. C. Mather resolves to publish a sheet to exhort Masters to labour their Conversion. Which makes me hope that I was call'd of God to Write this Apology for them; Let his Blessing accompany the same.

Lord's Day, June, 10. 1705. The Learned and pious Mr. Michael Wigglesworth dies at Malden about 9. m. Had been sick about 10. days of a Fever; 73 years and 8 moneths old. He was the Author of the Poem entituled The Day of Doom, which has been so often printed: and was very useful as a Physician.

Febr. 6. [1718] This morning wandering in my mind whether to live a Single or a Married Life;[9] I had a sweet and very affectionat Meditation Concerning the Lord Jesus; Nothing was to be objected against his Person, Parentage, Relations, Estate, House, Home! Why did I not resolutely, presently close with Him! And I cry'd mightily to God that He would help me so to doe! . . .

March, 14. [1718] Deacon Marion comes to me, sits with me a great while in the evening; after a great deal of Discourse about his Courtship—He told [me] the Olivers said they wish'd I would Court their Aunt.[10] I said little, but said twas not five Moneths since I buried my dear Wife. Had said before 'twas hard to know whether best to marry again or no; whom to marry. Gave him a book of the Berlin Jewish Converts.

Sept 5. [1720] Mary Hirst goes to Board with Madam Oliver and her Mother Loyd, Going to Son Sewall's I there meet with Madam Winthrop, told her I was glad to meet her there, had not seen her a great while; gave her Mr. Homes's Sermon.

Sept. 30. [1720] Mr. Colman's Lecture: Daughter Sewall acquaints Madam Winthrop that if she pleas'd to be within at 3. P.M. I would wait on her. She answer'd she would be at home.

October 1. [1720] Satterday, I dine at Mr. Stoddard's: from thence I went to Madam Winthrop's just at 3. Spake to her, saying, my loving wife died so soon and suddenly, 'twas hardly convenient for me to think of Marrying again; however I came to this Resolution, that I would not make my Court to any person without first Consulting with her. Had a pleasant discourse about 7 Single persons sitting in the Foreseat [September] 29th, viz. Madm Rebekah Dudley, Catharine Winthrop, Bridget Usher, Deliverance Legg, Rebekah Loyd, Lydia Colman, Elizabeth Bellingham. She propounded one and another for me; but none would do, said Mrs. Loyd was about her Age.[11]

Octobr 3. 2. [1720] Waited on Madam Winthrop again; 'twas a little while before she came in. Her daughter Noyes being there alone with me, I said, I hoped my Waiting on her Mother would not be disagreeable to her.[12] She answer'd she should not be against that that might be for her Comfort. I Saluted her, and told her I perceiv'd I must shortly wish her a good Time; (her mother had told me, she was with

[9]Hannah Hull Sewall died October 19, 1717. Sewall married Abigail Tilley, October 29, 1719; she died within a year. In the fall of 1720, a few months after the death of his second wife, Sewall started courting Katherine Winthrop.

[10]Katherine Brattle Winthrop, widow of Chief Justice Wait Still Winthrop, a friend of Sewall.

[11]The front pews of churches were usually reserved for the widows in the congregation.

[12]Katherine Winthrop Jeffries Noyes, the first child of Katherine Brattle Winthrop. Madame Winthrop was fifty-six years old at this time; of the children she bore, three lived to maturity. "Saluted" means kissed.

Child, and within a Moneth or two of her Time). By and by in came Mr. Airs, Chaplain of the Castle,[13] and hang'd up his Hat, which I was a little startled at, it seeming as if he was to lodge there. At last Madam Winthrop came in. After a considerable time, I went up to her and said, if it might not be inconvenient I desired to speak with her. She assented, and spake of going into another Room; but Mr. Airs and Mrs. Noyes presently rose up, and went out, leaving us there alone. Then I usher'd in Discourse from the names in the Fore-seat; at last I pray'd that Katharine [Mrs. Winthrop] might be the person assign'd for me. She instantly took it up in way of Denyal, as if she had catch'd at an Opportunity to do it, saying she could not do it before she was asked. Said that was her mind unless she should Change it, which she believed she should not; could not leave her Children. I express'd my Sorrow that she should do it so Speedily; pray'd her Consideration, and ask'd her when I should wait on her agen. She setting no time, I mention'd that day Sennight.[14] Gave her Mr. Willard's Fountain open'd with the little print and verses; saying I hop'd if we did well read that book,[15] we should meet together hereafter if we did not now. She took the Book, and put it in her Pocket. Took Leave.[16]

1878–82

The Selling of Joseph, A Memorial[1]

Forasmuch as Liberty *is in real value next unto* Life:[2] *None ought to part with it themselves, or deprive others of it, but upon most mature Consideration.*

The Numerousness of Slaves at this day in the Province, and the Uneasiness of them under their Slavery, hath put many upon thinking whether the Foundation of it be firmly and well laid; so as to sustain the Vast Weight that is built upon it. It is most certain that all Men, as they are the Sons of *Adam,* are Coheirs; and have equal Right unto Liberty, and all other outward Comforts of Life. *God hath given the Earth* [with all its Commodities] *unto the Sons of Adam, Psal* 115. 16. *And hath made of One Blood, all Nations of Men, for to dwell on all the face of the Earth, and hath determined the Times before appointed, and the bounds of their habitation: That they should seek the Lord. Forasmuch then as we are the Offspring of GOD* &c. *Act* 17. 26,

[13]Obadiah Ayers, chaplain of Castle William in Boston Harbor.

[14]"That day seven-night," or, a week later.

[15]He gave her Samuel Willard's *The Fountain Opened, or the Great Gospel Privilege of Having Christ Exhibited to Sinful Men* (Boston, 1700).

[16]After many negotiations, Sewall and Winthrop could not come to terms about marrying. He married a widow, Mary Gibbs, on March 29, 1722; she survived him.

[1]With slight modernization, the text printed here was published in Boston by Green and Allen, June 24, 1700.

[2]Sewall's translation of William Ames's "quia Libertas ex naturali aestimatione proxime accedit ad vitam ipsam," cited in the final sentence of this tract; quoted from Ames's *De conscientia, et eius iure, vel casibus* (London, 1623). Dr. William Ames (1576–1633), celebrated English Puritan, fled to Holland in 1610 but died before his hoped-for migration to New England.

27, 29. Now although the Title given by the last ADAM, doth infinitely better Mens Estates, respecting GOD and themselves; and grants them a most beneficial and inviolable Lease under the Broad Seal of Heaven, who were before only Tenants at Will: Yet through the Indulgence of GOD to our First Parents after the Fall, the outward Estate of all and every of their Children, remains the same, as to one another. So that Originally, and Naturally, there is no such thing as Slavery. *Joseph* was rightfully no more a Slave to his Brethren, than they were to him: and they had no more Authority to *Sell* him, than they had to *Slay* him. And if *they* had nothing to do to Sell him; the *Ishmaelites* bargaining with them, and paying down Twenty pieces of Silver could not make a Title. Neither could *Potiphar* have any better Interest in him than the *Ishmaelites* had. *Gen.* 37. 20, 27, 28.[3] For he that shall in this case plead *Alteration of Property,* seems to have forfeited a great part of his own claim to Humanity. There is no proportion between Twenty Pieces of Silver, and LIBERTY. The Commodity it self is the Claimer. If *Arabian* Gold be imported in any quantities, most are afraid to meddle with it, though they might have it at easy rates; lest if it should have been wrongfully taken from the Owners, it should kindle a fire to the Consumption of their whole Estate. 'Tis pity there should be more Caution used in buying a Horse, or a little lifeless dust; than there is in purchasing Men and Women: Whenas they are the Offspring of GOD, and their Liberty is,

. . . . *Auro pretiosior Omni.*[4]

And seeing GOD hath said, *He that Stealeth a Man and Selleth him, or if he be found in his hand, he shall surely be put to Death.* Exod. 21. 16. This Law being of Everlasting Equity, wherein Man Stealing is ranked amongst the most atrocious of Capital Crimes: What louder Cry can there be made of that Celebrated Warning,

Caveat Emptor![5]

And all things considered, it would conduce more to the Welfare of the Province, to have White Servants for a Term of Years, than to have Slaves for Life. Few can endure to hear of a Negro's being made free; and indeed they can seldom use their freedom well; yet their continual aspiring after their forbidden Liberty, renders them Unwilling Servants. And there is such a disparity in their Conditions, Colour & Hair, that they can never embody with us, and grow up into orderly Families, to the Peopling of the Land: but still remain in our Body Politick as a kind of extravasat Blood.[6] As many Negro men as there are among us, so many empty places there are in our Train Bands, and the places taken up of Men that might make Hus-

[3]Genesis 37:20, "Come now therefore, and let us slay him, and cast him into some pit, and we will say, Some evil beast hath devoured him: and we shall see what will become of his dreams"; 37:27–28, "Come, let us sell him to the Ishmeelites, and let not our hand be upon him; for he is our brother and our flesh. And his brethren were content. Then there passed by Midianites merchantmen; and they drew and lifted up Joseph out of the pit, and sold Joseph to the Ishmeelites for twenty pieces of silver: and they brought Joseph into Egypt."

[4]"More precious than all gold." Isaiah 13:12 reads: "I will make a man more precious then fine gold, even a man above the wedge of gold of Ophir."

[5]"Let the buyer beware!"

[6]Blood forced out of its proper vessels, thus indicating Sewall's worries, despite his anti-slavery stance, about miscegenation.

bands for our Daughters. And the Sons and Daughters of *New England* would become more like *Jacob,* and *Rachel,* if this Slavery were thrust quite out of doors. Moreover it is too well known what Temptations Masters are under, to connive at the Fornication of their Slaves; lest they should be obliged to find them Wives, or pay their Fines. It seems to be practically pleaded that they might be Lawless, 'tis thought much of, that the Law should have Satisfaction for their Thefts, and other Immoralities; by which means, *Holiness to the Lord,* is more rarely engraven upon this sort of Servitude. It is likewise most lamentable to think, how in taking Negros out of *Africa,* and Selling of them here, That which GOD ha's joyned together men do boldly rend asunder; Men from their Country, Husbands from their Wives, Parents from their Children. How horrible is the Uncleanness, Mortality, if not Murder, that the Ships are guilty of that bring great Crouds of these miserable Men, and Women. Methinks, when we are bemoaning the barbarous Usage of our Friends and Kinsfolk in *Africa:* it might not be unseasonable to enquire whether we are not culpable in forcing the *Africans* to become Slaves amongst our selves. And it may be a question whether all the Benefit received by *Negro* Slaves, will balance the Accompt of Cash laid out upon them; and for the Redemption of our own enslaved Friends out of *Africa.* Besides all the Persons and Estates that have perished there.

Obj. 1. *These Blackamores are of the Posterity of* Cham, *and therefore are under the Curse of Slavery.* Gen. 9. 25, 26, 27.[7]

Answ. Of all Offices, one would not begg this; *viz.* Uncall'd for, to be an Executioner of the Vindictive Wrath of God; the extent and duration of which is to us uncertain. If this ever was a Commission; How do we know but that it is long since out of Date? Many have found it to their Cost, that a Prophetical Denunciation of Judgment against a Person or People, would not warrant them to inflict that evil. If it would, *Hazael* might justify himself in all he did against his Master, and the *Israelites,* from 2 *Kings* 8. 10, 12.[8]

But it is possbile that by cursory reading, this Text may have been mistaken. For *Canaan* is the Person Cursed three times over, without the mentioning of *Cham.* Good Expositors suppose the Curse entaild on him, and that this Prophesie was accomplished in the Extirpation of the *Canaanites,* and in the Servitude of the *Gibeonites. Vide Pareum.*[9] Whereas the Blackmores are not descended of *Canaan,* but of *Cush.* Psal. 68. 31. *Princes shall come out of Egypt* [Mizraim], *Ethiopia* [Cush] *shall soon stretch out her hands unto God.* Under which Names, all *Africa* may be comprehended; and their Promised Conversion ought to be prayed for. *Jer.* 13. 23. *Can the Ethiopian change his skin?* This shows that Black Men are the Posterity of

[7]Genesis 9:25–27, "And he said, Cursed be Canaan; a servant of servants shall he be unto his brethren. And he said, Blessed be the Lord God of Shem; and Canaan shall be his servant. God shall enlarge Japheth, and he shall dwell in the tents of Shem; and Canaan shall be his servant."

[8]II Kings 8:10, "And Elisha said unto him, Go, say unto him, Thou mayest certainly recover: howbeit the Lord hath shewed me that he shall surely die"; 12, "And Hazael said, Why weepeth my lord? And he answered, Because I know the evil that thou wilt do unto the children of Israel: their strong holds wilt thou set on fire, and their young men wilt thou slay with the sword, and wilt dash their children, and rip up their women with child."

[9]"See Pareus," David Pareus (1548–1635), a well-known Protestant theologian of Heidelberg.

Cush: Who time out of mind have been distinguished by their Colour. And for want of the true, *Ovid* assigns a fabulous cause of it.

Sanguine tum credunt in corpora summa vocato
Æthiopum populus nigrum traxisse colorem.

Metamorph. lib. 2.[10]

Obj. 2. *The* Nigers *are brought out of a Pagan Country, into places where the Gospel is Preached.*

Answ. Evil must not be done, that good may come of it. The extraordinary and comprehensive Benefit accruing to the Church of God, and to *Joseph* personally, did not rectify his brethrens Sale of him.

Obj. 3. *The* Africans *have Wars one with another: Our Ships bring lawful Captives taken in those Wars.*

Answ. For ought is known, their Wars are much such as were between *Jacob's* Sons and their Brother *Joseph.* If they be between Town and Town; Provincial, or National: Every War is upon one side Unjust. An Unlawful War can't make lawful Captives. And by Receiving, we are in danger to promote, and partake in their Barbarous Cruelties. I am sure, if some Gentlemen should go down to the *Brewsters* to take the Air, and Fish: And a stronger party from *Hull* should Surprise them, and Sell them for Slaves to a Ship outward bound: they would think themselves unjustly dealt with; both by Sellers and Buyers. And yet 'tis to be feared, we have no other kind of Title to our *Nigers. Therefore all things whatsoever ye would that men should do to you, do ye even so to them: for this is the Law and the Prophets.* Matt. 7. 12.

Obj. 4. Abraham *had Servants bought with his Money, and born in his House.*

Answ. Until the Circumstances of *Abraham's* purchase be recorded, no Argument can be drawn from it. In the mean time, Charity obliges us to conclude, that He knew it was lawful and good.

It is Observable that the *Israelites* were strictly forbidden the buying, or selling one another for Slaves. *Levit.* 25. 39. 46.[11] *Jer.* 34 8. . . . . . . 22.[12] And GOD gaged

[10]In a passage from the myth of Phaeton, Ovid's *Metamorphoses,* Book 2, reads, "It was then, as men think, that the peoples of Ethiopia became black-skinned, since the blood was drawn to the surface of their bodies by the heat."

[11]Leviticus 25:39, "And if thy brother that dwelleth by thee be waxen poor, and be sold unto thee; thou shalt not compel him to serve as a bondservant"; 46, "And ye shall take them as an inheritance for your children after you, to inherit them for a possession; they shall be your bondmen for ever: but over your brethren the children of Israel, ye shall not rule one over another with rigour."

[12]Jeremiah 34:8–22: "This is the word that came unto Jeremiah from the Lord, after that the king Zedekiah had made a covenant with all the people which were at Jerusalem, to proclaim liberty unto them; That every man should let his manservant, and every man his maidservant, being an Hebrew or an Hebrewess, go free; that none should serve himself of them, to wit, of a Jew his brother. Now when all princes, and all the people, which had entered into the covenant, heard that every one should let his manservant, and every one his maidservant, go free, that none should serve themselves of them any more, then they obeyed, and let them go. But afterward they turned, and caused the servants and the handmaids, whom they had let go free, to return, and brought them into subjection for servants and for handmaids. Therefore the word of the Lord came to Jeremiah from the Lord, saying, Thus saith the Lord, the God of Israel: I made a covenant with your fathers in the day that I brought them forth out of the land of Egypt, out of the house of bondmen, saying, At the end of

His Blessing in lieu of any loss they might conceipt they suffered thereby. *Deut.* 15. 18.[13] And since the partition Wall is broken down, inordinate Self love should likewise be demolished. GOD expects that Christians should be of a more Ingenuous and benign frame of spirit. Christians should carry it to all the World, as the *Israelites* were to carry it one towards another. And for men obstinately to persist in holding their Neighbours and Brethren under the Rigor of perpetual Bondage, seems to be no proper way of gaining Assurance that God ha's given them Spiritual Freedom. Our Blessed Saviour ha's altered the Measures of the ancient Love-Song, and set it to a most Excellent New Tune, which all ought to be ambitious of Learning. *Matt.* 5. 43, 44.[14] *John* 13. 34.[15] These *Ethiopians,* as black as they are; seeing they are the Sons and Daughters of the First *Adam,* the Brethren and Sisters of the Last ADAM, and the Offspring of GOD; They ought to be treated with a Respect agreeable.

Servitus perfecta voluntaria, inter Christianum & Christianum, ex parte servi patientis sæpe est licita, quia est necessaria: sed ex parte domini agentis, & procurando & exercendo, vix potest esse licita: quia non convenit regulæ illi generali: Quæcunque volueritis ut faciant vobis homines, ita & vos facite eis. Matt. 7. 12.

seven years let ye go every man his brother an Hebrew, which hath been sold unto thee; and when he hath served thee six years, thou shalt let him go free from thee: but your fathers hearkened not unto me, neither inclined their ear. And ye were now turned, and had done right in my sight, in proclaiming liberty every man to his neighbour; and ye had made a covenant before me in the house which is called by my name: But ye turned and polluted my name, and caused every man his servant, and every man his handmaid, whom he had set at liberty at their pleasure, to return, and brought them into subjection, to be unto you for servants and for handmaids. Therefore saith the Lord: Ye have not hearkened unto me, in proclaiming liberty, every one to his brother, and every man to his neighbour: behold, I proclaim a liberty for you, saith the Lord, to the sword, to the pestilence, and to the famine: and I will make you to be removed into all the kingdoms of the earth. And I will give the men that have transgressed my covenant, which have not performed the words of the covenant which they had made before me, when they cut the calf in twain, and passed between the parts thereof, The princes of Judah, and the princes of Jerusalem, the eunuchs, and the priests, and all the people of the land, which passed between the parts of the calf; I will even give them into the hand of their enemies, and into the hand of them that seek their life: and their dead bodies shall be for meat unto the fowls of the heaven, and to the beasts of the earth. And Zedekiah king of Judah and his princes will I give into the hand of their enemies, and into the hand of them that seek their life, and into the hand of the king of Babylon's army, which are gone up from you. Behold I will command, saith the Lord, and cause them to return to this city; and they shall fight against it, and take it, and burn it with fire: and I will make the cities of Judah a desolation without an inhabitant."

[13]Deuteronomy 15:18, "It shall not seem hard unto thee, when thou sendest him away free from thee; for he hath been worth a double hired servant to thee, in serving thee six years: and the Lord thy God shall bless thee in all that thou doest."

[14]Matthew 5:43–44, "Ye have heard that it hath been said, Thou shalt love thy neighbour, and hate thine enemy. But I say unto you, Love your enemies, bless them that curse you, do good to them that hate you, and pray for them which despitefully use you, and persecute you."

[15]John 13:34, "A new commandment I give unto you, That ye love one another; as I have loved you, that ye also love one another."

Perfecta servitus pœnæ, non potest jure locum habere, nisi ex delicto gravi quod ultimum supplicium aliquo modo meretur: quia Libertas ex naturali æstimatione proxime accedit ad vitam ipsam, & eidem a multis præferri solet.

Ames. Cas. Consc. Lib. 5. Cap. 23. Thes. 2, 3.[16]

1700

My Verses upon the New Century [Jan. 1, 1701][1]

Once more! Our GOD, vouchsafe to Shine:
Tame Thou the Rigour of our Clime.
Make haste with thy Impartial Light,
And terminate this long dark Night.

Let the transplanted *English* Vine
Spread further still: still Call it Thine.
Prune it wtih Skill: for yield it can
More Fruit to Thee the Husbandman.

Give the poor *Indians* Eyes to see
The Light of Life: and set them free;
That they Religion may profess,
Denying all Ungodliness.

From hard'ned *Jews* the Vail remove,
Let them their Martyr'd JESUS love;
And Homage unto Him afford,
Because He is their Rightfull LORD.

[16]This passage, taken from William Ames's *De conscientia, et eius iure, vel casibus,* Book 5, Chapter 23, Theses 2, 3, reads, in a translation called *Conscience with the Power and Cases thereof* (London, 1643), "2.2 Perfect servitude, so it be voluntary, is on the patients part often lawfull betweene Christian and Christian, because indeed it is necessary: but on the Masters part who is the agent, in procuring and exercising the authority, it is scarce lawfull; in respect, it thwarts that generall Canon, *What you would have men doe unto you, even so doe unto them; Matth.* 17.12. 3.3, Perfect servitude, by way of punishment, can have no place by right, unlesse for some hainous offence, which might deserve the severest punishment, to wit, death: because our liberty in the naturall account, is the very next thing to life it selfe, yea by many is preferred before it." The passage is taken from "The Fift Booke of the Duties of Man Towards his Neighbour."

[1]Printed as a broadside, these verses were written to ring in the new year, 1701. On January 1, several trumpeters met on Boston common and, Sewall wrote in his diary, "sounded there till about sunrise." The text, with slight modernization, is taken from the broadside, which is headed: "Wednesday, January 1. 1701. A little before Break-a-Day, at Boston of the Massachusets."

So false Religions shall decay,
And Darkness fly before bright Day:
So Men shall GOD in CHRIST adore;
And worship Idols vain, no more.

As *Asia*, and *Africa*,
Europa, with *America*;
All Four, in Consort join'd, shall Sing
New Songs of Praise to CHRIST our KING.

1701

Cotton Mather 1663–1728

Cotton Mather was the grandson of two important religious leaders of the first generation of Puritans in Massachusetts: John Cotton, after whom he was named, and Richard Mather. His father, Increase Mather, rose during the first half of Cotton's life to become pastor of the Old North Church, president of Harvard College, and the man who won a new charter for Massachusetts from the king of England and selected the first governor and council to serve under it. Cotton, as eldest son, intended to follow in Increase's footsteps. A child prodigy who stuttered, Cotton Mather graduated from Harvard at age sixteen. At age twenty-one, he married the first of the two women who eventually bore him fifteen children.

In 1685 he matched the first accomplishment of his father by being ordained pastor of the Old North Church, a position he held until his death. He never became president of Harvard, although he was offered (and refused) the presidency of Yale. He wished to match his father's achievements, yet his political influence never approached that of Increase Mather. In fact, Cotton Mather's influence, like his father's, declined from 1694 on, largely as a result of political changes brought on by the new Massachusetts charter. A more serious embarrassment was the Salem witch trials of 1692, opposed by Increase but reluctantly supported by his son. But Cotton's reaction to the witches, while pronounced, was not unusual in an age still absorbed by providences. Although Mather would continue to find momentous importance in common incidents, never again would he do so with such abandon.

Despite Cotton's failure to match Increase's public career, the son far surpassed the father as a writer. Well over four hundred separate publications marked his literary career, and when he died he left a substantial body of still unpublished manuscripts, including one he considered his masterwork, the *Biblia Americana*. Of the topics upon which he wrote, one of the most important was science. He was elected to the preeminent scientific body, the Royal Society, in 1713; he was an early proponent of vaccination; and he published such influential scientific works as *The Christian Philosopher* (1720). Careful scientific observation is to be found in his sermons, papers, and personal letters. But the invisible world intrigued him as much as the visible world, and it is his *Wonders of the Invisible World* (1692) that has given him more lasting, if dubious, fame than his scientific works. This highly homiletical report of the witchcraft trials, written at the instance of the judges, was the "bible" of Irving's Ichabod Crane and has made Mather's name a symbol of Puritan superstition rather than science.

Neither the natural nor the supernatural world, however, interested Mather as much as the lives of men, especially the men of God who had founded New England and made it great. Mather's longest and most admired work is the *Magnalia Christi Americana: or, the Ecclesiastical History of New England.* At once an encyclopedic account of New England's history and a gallery of its eminent lives, the *Magnalia* broadly attempts to preserve a sense of the colony's sacred mission. To that end, most of Mather's biographies are quite similar, for each New England hero is made to fit a common, saintly pattern from early conversion experience to oracular deathbed scene, and each is highly eulogized. But in each life distinctive features are emphasized, and many of these clearly reflect the author's own reforming interests. For instance, in the life of John Eliot, the "apostle to the Indians" whom Nathaniel Hawthorne was later to admire, Mather's notable discussion of Eliot's would-be mission to black slaves as well as the successful mission to the Indians points the way to Mather's own later advocacy of both missions in *The Negro Christianized* (1706) and *India Christiana* (1721). Although the former work does not condemn slaveowning itself, as did Samuel Sewall's *The Selling of Joseph* (1700), Mather does advocate Christian instruction by the masters themselves, and on large plantations, by teachers appointed for the purpose. Mather praised past models to stimulate present action, whether by individuals or by "reforming societies" like those described in *Bonifacius or Essays to Do Good* (1710). Inspired by *Bonifacius,* men like Benjamin Franklin went on to do good singly or form groups devoted to improvement in secular and religious life.

One of the most striking features of all Mather's works is their distinctive means of expression. Full of ingenious turns of phrase and adorned with many allusions, often in Latin, Greek, or Hebrew, this style was aptly described by Mather himself as "cloth of gold . . . stuck with as many jewels as the gown of a Russian ambassador." Such sheer delight in verbal play seems a strange accompaniment to serious Puritan content, but both the style and the religion are deeply rooted in early seventeenth-century models. Mather, however, clearly outdid his models and at a time when Baroque ornamentation and orthodox theology were on their way out. Thus his florid verbosity was attacked by rationalist critics in his own day, and it continues to alienate readers today. The verbal clothing of his biographies, for instance, is so thick that it is often difficult to see the men within. Nevertheless, their very gorgeousness often has a deeper sense, linking these lives with the patterns of sacred history. If Mather did not live up to his father and forefathers in action, he surpassed them in the words with which he honored them.

Kenneth Alan Hovey
University of Texas at San Antonio

Joseph Fichtelberg
Hofstra University

PRIMARY WORKS

Wonders of the Invisible World, 1692; *Magnalia Christi Americana,* 1702; *The Negro Christianized,* 1706; *Bonifacius,* 1710; *The Christian Philosopher,* 1720; *Manductio ad Ministerium,* 1726.

SECONDARY WORKS

Robert Middlekauff, *The Mathers: Three Generations of Puritan Intellectuals, 1596–1728,* 1971; Sacvan Bercovitch, "Cotton Mather," in *Major Writers of Early American Literature,* ed. Everett Emerson, 1972; Sacvan Bercovitch, *The Puritan Origins of the American Self,* 1975; Mitchell Breitwieser, *Cotton Mather and Benjamin Franklin: The Price of Representative Personality,* 1984; Kenneth Silverman, *The Life and Times of Cotton Mather,* 1984.

from The Wonders of the Invisible World[1]

[The Devil Attacks the People of God]

The New Englanders are a people of God settled in those, which were once the devil's territories; and it may easily be supposed that the devil was exceedingly disturbed, when he perceived such a people here accomplishing the promise of old made unto our blessed Jesus, that He should have the utmost parts of the earth for His possession.[2] There was not a greater uproar among the Ephesians, when the Gospel was first brought among them,[3] than there was among the powers of the air (after whom those Ephesians walked) when first the silver trumpets of the Gospel here made the joyful sound. The devil thus irritated, immediately tried all sorts of methods to overturn this poor plantation: and so much of the church, as was fled into this wilderness, immediately found the serpent cast out of his mouth a flood for the carrying of it away.[4] I believe that never were more satanical devices used for the unsettling of any people under the sun, than what have been employed for the extirpation of the vine which God has here planted, casting out the heathen, and preparing a room before it, and causing it to take deep root, and fill the land, so that it sent its boughs unto the Atlantic Sea eastward, and its branches unto the Connecticut River westward, and the hills were covered with a shadow thereof.[5] But all those attempts of hell have hitherto been abortive, many an Ebenezer[6] has been erected unto the praise of God, by his poor people here; and having obtained help from God, we continue to this day.[7] Wherefore the devil is now making one attempt more upon us; an attempt more difficult, more surprising, more snarled with unintelligible circumstances than any that we have hitherto encountered; an attempt so critical, that if we get well through, we shall soon enjoy halcyon days with all the vultures of hell trodden under our feet.[8] He has wanted his incarnate legions to persecute us, as the people of God have in the other hemisphere been persecuted: he has therefore drawn forth his more spiritual ones to make an attack upon us. We have been advised by some credible Christians yet alive, that a malefactor, accused of witchcraft as well as murder, and executed in this place more than forty years ago, did then give notice of an horrible plot against the country by witchcraft, and a foundation of witchcraft then laid, which if it were not seasonably discovered, would probably blow up, and pull down all the churches in the country. And we have now with horror seen the discovery of such a witchcraft! An army of devils is horribly broke in upon the place which is the center, and after a sort, the firstborn of our English settlements: and the houses of the good people there are filled with doleful shrieks of their children and servants, tormented by invisible hands, with tortures altogether preternatural. After the mischiefs there endeavored, and since in part conquered, the terrible plague of evil angels hath made its progress into some other places, where other persons have

[1]First published in 1693; this slightly modernized text is taken from the reprint by John Russell Smith (London, 1862).

[2]Psalm 2:2.

[3]Acts 19:22–41.

[4]Revelation 12:6, 15.

[5]Psalm 80:8–12.

[6]Stone of help (I Samuel 7:12).

[7]Acts 26:22.

[8]Isaiah 28:3.

been in like manner diabolically handled. These our poor afflicted neighbors, quickly after they become infected and infested with these demons, arrive to a capacity of discerning those which they conceive the shapes of their troublers; and notwithstanding the great and just suspicion that the demons might impose the shapes of innocent persons in their spectral exhibitions upon the sufferers (which may perhaps prove no small part of the witch-plot in the issue), yet many of the persons thus represented, being examined, several of them have been convicted of a very damnable witchcraft: yea, more than one twenty have confessed, that they have signed unto a book, which the devil showed them, and engaged in his hellish design of bewitching and ruining our land. We know not, at least I know not, how far the delusions of Satan may be interwoven into some circumstances of the confessions; but one would think all the rules of understanding human affairs are at an end, if after so many most voluntary harmonious confessions, made by intelligent persons of all ages, in sundry towns, at several times, we must not believe the main strokes wherein those confessions all agree: especially when we have a thousand preternatural things every day before our eyes, wherein the confessors do acknowledge their concernment, and give demonstration of their being so concerned. If the devils now can strike the minds of men with any poisons of so fine a composition and operation, that scores of innocent people shall unite, in confessions of a crime, which we see actually committed, it is a thing prodigious, beyond the wonders of the former ages, and it threatens no less than a sort of a dissolution upon the world. Now, by these confessions 'tis agreed that the Devil has made a dreadful knot of witches in the country, and by the help of witches has dreadfully increased that knot: that these witches have driven a trade of commissioning their confederate spirits to do all sorts of mischiefs to the neighbors, whereupon there have ensued such mischievous consequences upon the bodies and estates of the neighborhood, as could not otherwise be accounted for: yea, that at prodigious witch-meetings, the wretches have proceeded so far as to concert and consult the methods of rooting out the Christian religion from this country, and setting up instead of it perhaps a more gross diabolism than ever the world saw before. And yet it will be a thing little short of miracle, if in so spread a business as this, the Devil should not get in some of his juggles, to confound the discovery of all the rest.

* * *

But I shall no longer detain my reader from his expected entertainment, in a brief account of the trials which have passed upon some of the malefactors lately executed at Salem, for the witchcrafts whereof they stood convicted. For my own part, I was not present at any of them; nor ever had I any personal prejudice at the persons thus brought upon the stage; much less at the surviving relations of those persons, with and for whom I would be as hearty a mourner as any man living in the world: The Lord comfort them! But having received a command so to do, I can do no other than shortly relate the chief matters of fact, which occurred in the trials of some that were executed, in an abridgment collected out of the court papers on this occasion put into my hands. You are to take the truth, just as it was; and the truth will hurt no good man. There might have been more of these, if my book would not thereby have swollen too big; and if some other worthy hands did not perhaps intend something further in these collections; for which cause I have only singled out four or five, which may serve to illustrate the way of dealing, wherein witchcrafts use to be concerned; and I report matters not as an advocate, but as an historian.

* * *

V. The Trial of Martha Carrier at The Court of Oyer and Terminer,[9] Held by Adjournment at Salem, August 2, 1692.

I. Martha Carrier was indicted for the bewitching certain persons, according to the form usual in such cases, pleading not guilty to her indictment; there were first brought in a considerable number of the bewitched persons who not only made the court sensible of an horrid witchcraft committed upon them, but also deposed that it was Martha Carrier, or her shape, that grievously tormented them, by biting, pricking, pinching and choking of them. It was further deposed that while this Carrier was on her examination before the magistrates, the poor people were so tortured that every one expected their death upon the very spot, but that upon the binding of Carrier they were eased. Moreover the look of Carrier then laid the afflicted people for dead; and her touch, if her eye at the same time were off them, raised them again: which things were also now seen upon her trial. And it was testified that upon the mention of some having their necks twisted almost round, by the shape of this Carrier, she replied, "It's no matter though their necks had been twisted quite off."

II. Before the trial of this prisoner, several of her own children had frankly and fully confessed not only that they were witches themselves, but that this their mother had made them so. This confession they made with great shows of repentance, and with much demonstration of truth. They related place, time, occasion; they gave an account of journeys, meetings and mischiefs by them performed, and were very credible in what they said. Nevertheless, this evidence was not produced against the prisoner at the bar,[10] inasmuch as there was other evidence enough to proceed upon.

III. Benjamin Abbot gave his testimony that last March was a twelvemonth, this Carrier was very angry with him, upon laying out some land near her husband's: her expressions in this anger were that she would stick as close to Abbot as the bark stuck to the tree; and that he should repent of it afore seven years came to an end, so as Doctor Prescot should never cure him. These words were heard by others besides Abbot himself; who also heard her say, she would hold his nose as close to the grindstone as ever it was held since his name was Abbot. Presently after this, he was taken with a swelling in his foot, and then with a pain in his side, and exceedingly tormented. It bred into a sore, which was lanced by Doctor Prescot, and several gallons of corruption[11] ran out of it. For six weeks it continued very bad, and then another sore bred in the groin, which was also lanced by Doctor Prescot. Another sore then

[9]"To hear and determine."
[10]Before the court.
[11]The sore, cut open, produced much pus.

bred in his groin, which was likewise cut, and put him to very great misery: he was brought unto death's door, and so remained until Carrier was taken, and carried away by the constable, from which very day he began to mend, and so grew better every day, and is well ever since.

Sarah Abbot also, his wife, testified that her husband was not only all this while afflicted in his body, but also that strange, extraordinary and unaccountable calamities befell his cattle; their death being such as they could guess at no natural reason for.

IV. Allin Toothaker testified that Richard, the son of Martha Carrier, having some difference with him, pulled him down by the hair of the head. When he rose again he was going to strike at Richard Carrier but fell down flat on his back to the ground, and had not power to stir hand or foot, until he told Carrier he yielded; and then he saw the shape of Martha Carrier go off his breast.

This Toothaker had received a wound in the wars; and he now testified that Martha Carrier told him he should never be cured. Just afore the apprehending of Carrier, he could thrust a knitting needle into his wound four inches deep; but presently after her being seized, he was thoroughly healed.

He further testified that when Carrier and he some times were at variance, she would clap her hands at him, and say he should get nothing by it; whereupon he several times lost his cattle, by strange deaths, whereof no natural causes could be given.

V. John Rogger also testified that upon the threatening words of this malicious Carrier, his cattle would be strangely bewitched; as was more particularly then described.

VI. Samuel Preston testified that about two years ago, having some difference with Martha Carrier, he lost a cow in a strange, preternatural, unusual manner; and about a month after this, the said Carrier, having again some difference with him, she told him he had lately lost a cow, and it should not be long before he lost another; which accordingly came to pass; for he had a thriving and well-kept cow, which without any known cause quickly fell down and died.

VII. Phebe Chandler testified that about a fortnight before the apprehension of Martha Carrier, on a Lordsday, while the Psalm was singing in the Church, this Carrier then took her by the shoulder and shaking her, asked her, where she lived: she made her no answer, although as Carrier, who lived next door to her father's house, could not in reason but know who she was. Quickly after this, as she was at several times crossing the fields, she heard a voice, that she took to be Martha Carrier's, and it seemed as if it was over her head. The voice told her she should within two or three days be poisoned. Accordingly, within such a little time, one half of her right hand became greatly swollen and very painful; as also part of her face: whereof she can give no account how it came. It continued very bad for some days; and several times since she has had a great pain in her breast; and been so seized on her legs that she has hardly been able to go. She added that lately, going well to the house of God, Richard, the son of Martha Carrier, looked very earnestly upon her, and immediately her hand, which had formerly been poisoned, as is abovesaid, began to pain her greatly, and she had a strange burning at her stomach; but was then struck deaf, so that she could not hear any of the prayer, or singing, till the two or three last words of the Psalm.

VIII. One Foster, who confessed her own share in the witchcraft for which the prisoner stood indicted, affirmed that she had seen the prisoner at some of their witch-meetings, and that it was this Carrier, who persuaded her to be a witch. She confessed that the Devil carried them on a pole to a witch-meeting; but the pole broke, and she hanging about Carrier's neck, they both fell down, and she then received an hurt by the fall, whereof she was not at this very time recovered.

IX. One Lacy, who likewise confessed her share in this witchcraft, now testified, that she and the prisoner were once bodily present at a witch-meeting in Salem Village; and that she knew the prisoner to be a witch, and to have been at a diabolical sacrament, and that the prisoner was the undoing of her and her children by enticing them into the snare of the devil.

X. Another Lacy, who also confessed her share in this witchcraft, now testified, that the prisoner was at the witch-meeting, in Salem Village, where they had bread and wine administered unto them.

XI. In the time of this prisoner's trial, one Susanna Sheldon in open court had her hands unaccountably tied together with a wheel-band[12] so fast that without cutting it, it could not be loosed: it was done by a specter; and the sufferer affirmed it was the prisoner's.

Memorandum. This rampant hag, Martha Carrier, was a person of whom the confessions of the witches, and of her own children among the rest, agreed that the devil had promised her she should be Queen of Hebrews.

from Magnalia Christi Americana; or, The Ecclesiastical History of New-England[1]

from ***A General Introduction***

Dicam hoc propter utilitatem eorum qui Lecturi sunt hoc opus.
Theodoret[2]

I. I WRITE the *Wonders* of the CHRISTIAN RELIGION, flying from the Depravations of *Europe,* to the *American Strand.*[3] And, assisted by the Holy Author of that *Religion,* I do, with all Conscience of *Truth,* required therein by Him, who is the

[12]A band or strap, usually of metal or leather, that goes around a wheel.

[1]"A History of Christ's Wonderful Works in America." The full subtitle is *The Ecclesiastical History of New-England from its First Planting, in the Year 1620, unto the Year of Our Lord, 1698.* First published in London in 1702; this slightly modernized text is taken from the edition by Thomas Robbins (Hartford, Conn., 1855).

[2]"This I say for the benefit of those who may happen to read the book." This quotation, printed in the original text in Greek as well as Latin, is by Theodoret (393?–457), a Greek bishop and church historian.

[3]See George Herbert, "The Church Militant," 235–36.

Truth itself, Report the *Wonderful Displays* of His Infinite Power, Wisdom, Goodness, and Faithfulness, wherewith His Divine Providence hath *Irradiated* an *Indian Wilderness.*

I Relate the *Considerable Matters,* that produced and attended the First Settlement of COLONIES, which have been Renowned for the Degree of REFORMATION, Professed and Attained by *Evangelical Churches,* erected in those *Ends of the Earth:*[4] And a *field* being thus prepared, I proceed unto a Relation of the *Considerable Matters* which have been acted thereupon.

I first introduce the *Actors,* that have, in a more exemplary manner served those *Colonies;* and give *Remarkable Occurrences,* in the exemplary LIVES of many *Magistrates,* and of more *Ministers,* who so *Lived,* as to leave unto Posterity, *Examples* worthy of *Everlasting Remembrance.*[5]

I add hereunto, the *Notables* of the only *Protestant Univeristy,*[6] that ever *shone* in that Hemisphere of the *New World;* with particular Instances of *Criolians,*[7] in our *Biography,* provoking the *whole World,* with vertuous Objects of Emulation.

I introduce then, the *Actions* of a more Eminent Importance, that have signalized those *Colonies;* Whether the *Establishments,* directed by their *Synods;* with a Rich Variety of *Synodical* and *Ecclesiastical* Determinations;[8] or, the *Disturbances,* with which they have been from all sorts of *Temptations* and *Enemies* Tempestuated; and the *Methods* by which they have still weathered out each *Horrible Tempest.*[9]

And into the midst of these *Actions,* I interpose an entire *Book,* wherein there is, with all possible Veracity, a *Collection* made, of *Memorable Occurrences,* and amazing *Judgments* and *Mercies,* befalling many *particular Persons* among the People of *New-England.*[10]

Let my Readers expect all that I have promised them, in this *Bill of Fare;* and it may be they will find themselves entertained with yet many other Passages, above and beyond their Expectation, deserving likewise a room in *History:* In all which, there will be nothing, but the *Author's* too mean way of preparing so great Entertainments, to Reproach the Invitation . . .

3. It is the History of these PROTESTANTS, that is here attempted: PROTESTANTS that highly honoured and affected *The Church of* ENGLAND, and humbly Petition to be a *Part* of it: But by the Mistake of a few powerful *Brethren,* driven to seek a place for the Exercise of the *Protestant Religion,* according to the Light of their Consciences, in the Desarts of *America.* And in this Attempt I have proposed, not only to preserve and secure the Interest of *Religion,* in the Churches of that little Country *NEW-ENGLAND,* so far as the Lord Jesus Christ may please to Bless it for that End, but also to offer unto the Churches of the *Reformation,* abroad in the World, some small *Memorials,* that may be serviceable unto the Designs of *Reformation,* whereto, I believe, they are quickly to be awakened . . . Tho' the *Reformed Churches* in the *American Regions,* have, by very Injurious Representations of their Brethren (all which they desire to Forget and Forgive!) been many times thrown into a *Dung-Cart;* yet, as they have been a *precious Odour to God in Christ,* so, I hope, they

[4]The topic of the first book of the *Magnalia.*

[5]The second book of the *Magnalia* consists of biographies of magistrates, the third of biographies of ministers.

[6]The fourth book describes Harvard and its best students.

[7]Creoles, people of European or African descent naturalized in America.

[8]The topic of the fifth book.

[9]The topic of the seventh and last book.

[10]The topic of the sixth book.

will be a *precious Odour* unto *His People;* and not only *Precious,* but *Useful* also, when the *History* of them shall come to be considered. A *Reformation of the Church* is coming on, and I cannot but thereupon say, with the dying *Cyrus* to his Children in *Xenophon*[11] . . . *Learn from the things that have been done already, for this is the best way of Learning.* The Reader hath here an Account of *The Things that have been done already. Bernard*[12] upon that Clause in the *Canticles,* [*O thou fairest among Women*] has this ingenious Gloss, *Pulchram, non omnimodo quidem, sed pulchram inter mulieres cam dicit, videlicet cum Distinctione, quatenus et ex hoc amplius reprimatur, & sciat quid desit sibi.*[13] Thus I do not say, That the Churches of *New-England* are the most *Regular* that can be; yet I do say, and am sure, That they are very like unto those that were in the *First Ages* of Christianity. And if I assert, That in the *Reformation* of the Church, the State of it in those *First Ages,* is to be not a little considered, the Great *Peter Ramus,*[14] among others, has emboldened me. . . . In short, The *First Age* was the *Golden Age:* To return unto *That,* will make a Man a *Protestant,* and I may add, a *Puritan.* 'Tis possible, That our Lord Jesus Christ carried some Thousands of *Reformers* into the Retirements of an *American Desart,* on purpose, that, with an opportunity granted unto many of his Faithful Servants, to enjoy the precious *Liberty* of their *Ministry,* tho' in the midst of many *Temptations* all their days, He might there, *To* them first, and then *By* them, give a *Specimen* of many Good Things, which He would have His Churches elsewhere aspire and arise unto: And *This* being done, He knows whether there be not *All done,* that *New-England* was planted for; and whether the Plantation may not, soon after this, *Come to Nothing.* Upon that Expression in the Sacred Scripture, *Cast the unprofitable Servant into Outer Darkness,*[15] it hath been imagined by some, That the *Regiones Exteræ*[16] of *America,* are the *Tenebræ Exteriores,*[17] which the *Unprofitable* are there condemned unto. No doubt, the Authors of those Ecclesiastical Impositions and Severities, which drove the English Christians into the *Dark Regions* of *America,* esteemed those *Christians* to be a very *unprofitable* sort of Creatures. But behold, ye *European* Churches, There are *Golden Candlesticks* [more than *twice Seven times Seven!*][18] in the midst of this *Outer Darkness:* Unto the *upright* Children of *Abraham,* here hath arisen *Light in Darkness.* And let us humbly speak it, it shall be *Profitable* for you to consider the *Light,* which from the midst of this *Outer Darkness,* is now to be Darted over unto the other side of the *Atlantick Ocean.* But we must therewithal ask your Prayers, that these *Golden Candlesticks* may not *quickly* be *Removed out of their place!*

4. But whether *New England* may *Live* any where else or no, it must *Live* in our *History!* . . .

1702

[11]Ancient Greek author (430?–355? B.C.), whose *Anabasis* recounts the accomplishments of the Persian prince, Cyrus the Younger.

[12]St. Bernard of Clairvaux (1090–1153) commenting on Song of Solomon 1:8 ("Canticles" is an alternative name for Song of Solomon).

[13]"He says that she is fair, not in a universal sense, but fair among women, plainly with a distinction, to which extent his praise is qualified and she may know what she lacks."

[14]Pierre de la Ramée (1515–1572), French philosopher and educational reformer who converted to Protestantism.

[15]Matthew 25:30.

[16]Outer regions.

[17]Outer shadows (or darkness).

[18]Revelations 1:12–13, 20; 2:5.

Galeacius Secundus:[1] *The Life of William Bradford, Esq., Governor of Plymouth Colony*

Omnium Somnos illius vigilantia defendit; omnium otium, illius Labor; omnium Delitias, illius Industria; omnium vacationem, illius occupatio.[2]

I. It has been a matter of some observation, that although Yorkshire be one of the largest shires in England; yet, for all the *fires* of martyrdom which were kindled in the days of Queen Mary, it afforded no more *fuel* than one poor *Leaf;* namely, John Leaf, an apprentice, who suffered for the doctrine of the Reformation at the same time and stake with the famous John Bradford.[3] But when the reign of Queen Elizabeth would not admit the Reformation of worship to proceed unto those degrees, which were proposed and pursued by no small number of the faithful in those days, Yorkshire was not the least of the shires in England that afforded suffering *witnesses* thereunto. The Churches there gathered were quickly molested with such a raging persecution, that if the spirit of separation in them did carry them unto a further *extream* than it should have done, one blameable cause thereof will be found in the *extremity* of that persecution. Their troubles made that *cold* country too *hot* for them, so that they were under a necessity to *seek* a retreat in the Low Countries;[4] and yet the watchful malice and fury of their adversaries rendred it almost impossible for them to *find* what they sought. For them to leave their native soil, their lands and their friends, and go into a strange place, where they must hear foreign language, and live meanly and hardly, and in other imployments than that of husbandry, wherein they had been educated, *these* must needs have been such discouragements as could have been conquered by none, save those who "sought first the kingdom of God, and the righteousness thereof."[5] But that which would have made these discouragements the more unconquerable unto an ordinary faith, was the terrible zeal of their enemies to guard all ports, and search all ships, that none of them should be carried off. I will not relate the sad things of this kind then *seen* and *felt* by this people of God; but only exemplifie those trials with one short story. Divers of this people having hired a Dutchman, then lying at Hull, to carry them over to Holland, he promised faithfully to take them in between Grimsly[6] and Hill; but they coming to the place a day or two too soon, the appearance of such a multitude alarmed the officers of the town adjoining, who came with a great body of soldiers to seize upon them. Now it happened that one boat full of men had been carried aboard, while the women were yet in a bark that lay aground in a creek at low water. The Dutchman perceiving the storm that was thus beginning ashore, swore by the sacrament that he would stay no longer

[1]"The second shield-bearer"; Bradford was elected governor of Plymouth colony when the first governor, John Carver, died.

[2]"His vigilance defends others' sleep; his labor, their rest; his diligence, their pleasures; his constancy, their leisure."

[3]John Bradford (1510?–1555), an English theologian, was burned at the stake with Leaf on July 1, 1555. Under the reign of Mary Tudor (1553–1558), a number of clergy who would not practice Roman Catholicism were executed.

[4]The Dutch provinces of Holland and Zeeland.

[5]Matthew 6:33.

[6]In Bradford's *History of Plymouth Plantation,* Grimsby and Hull, on the Lincolnshire coast, near the Humber River. Mather here follows Bradford's account.

for any of them; and so taking the advantage of a fair wind then blowing, he put out to sea for Zealand. The women thus left near Grimsly-common, bereaved of their husbands, who had been hurried from them, and forsaken of their neighbours, of whom none durst in this fright stay with them, were a very rueful spectacle; some crying for *fear,* some shaking for *cold,* all dragged by troops of armed and angry men from one Justice to another, till not knowing what to do with them, they even dismissed them to shift as well as they could for themselves. But by their singular *afflictions,* and by their Christian *behaviours,* the *cause* for which they exposed themselves did gain considerably. In the mean time, the men at sea found reason to be glad that their families were not with them, for they were surprized with an horrible tempest, which held them for fourteen days together, in seven whereof they saw not sun, moon or star, but were driven upon the coast of Norway. The mariners often despaired of life, and once with doleful shrieks gave over all, as thinking the vessel was foundred: but the vessel rose again, and when the mariners with sunk hearts often cried out, "We sink! we sink!" the passengers, without such distraction of mind, even while the water was running into their mouths and ears, would cheerfully shout, "Yet, Lord, thou canst save! Yet, Lord, thou canst save!" And the Lord accordingly brought them at last safe unto their desired haven: and not long after helped their distressed relations thither after them, where indeed they found upon almost all accounts a *new world,* but a world in which they found that they must live like strangers and pilgrims.

2. Among those devout people was our William Bradford, who was born *Anno 1588,* in an obscure village called Ansterfield, where the people were as unacquainted with the Bible, as the Jews do seem to have been with *part* of it in the days of Josiah;[7] a most ignorant and licentious *people,* and *like unto their priest.* Here, and in some other places, he had a comfortable inheritance left him of his honest parents, who died while he was yet a child, and cast him on the education, first of his grand parents, and then of his uncles, who devoted him, like his ancestors, unto the affairs of husbandry. Soon a long sickness kept him, as he would afterwards thankfully say, from the *vanities of youth,* and made him the fitter for what he was afterwards to undergo. When he was about a dozen years old, the reading of the Scriptures began to cause great impressions upon him; and those impressions were much assisted and improved, when he came to enjoy Mr. Richard Clifton's[8] illuminating ministry, not far from his abode; he was then also further befriended, by being brought into the company and fellowship of such as were then called professors; though the young man that brought him into it did after become a prophane and wicked *apostate.* Nor could the wrath of his uncles, nor the scoff of his neighbours, now turned upon him, as one of the *Puritans,* divert him from his pious inclinations.

3. At last, beholding how fearfully the evangelical and apostolical *church-form* whereinto the churches of the primitive times were cast by the good spirit of God, had been *deformed* by the apostacy of the succeeding times; and what little progress the Reformation had yet made in many parts of Christendom towards its recovery, he set himself by reading, by discourse, by prayer, to learn whether it was not his duty

[7]Josiah, King of Judah (638?–608? B.C.), rediscovered the Book of the Law (Bible) forsaken by his predecessors. See II Kings 22:10 ff.

[8]A Puritan minister in the town of Scrooby, Clifton settled with the Scrooby Separatists in Amsterdam.

to withdraw from the communion of the parish-assemblies, and engage with some society of the faithful, that should keep close unto the *written word* of God, as the *rule* of their worship. And after many distresses of mind concerning it, he took up a very deliberate and understanding resolution, of doing so; which resolution he chearfully prosecuted, although the provoked rage of his friends tried all the ways imaginable to reclaim him from it, unto all whom his answer was:

"Were I like to endanger my life, or consume my estate by any ungodly courses, your counsels to me were very seasonable; but you know that I have been diligent and provident in my calling, and not only desirous to augment what I have, but also to enjoy it in your company; to part from which will be as great a cross as can befal me. Nevertheless, to keep a good conscience, and walk in such a way as God has prescribed in his Word, is a thing which I must prefer before you all, and above life it self. Wherefore, since 'tis for a good cause that I am like to suffer the disasters which you lay before me, you have no cause to be either angry with me, or sorry for me; yea, I am not only willing to part with every thing that is dear to me in this world for this cause, but I am also thankful that God has given me an heart to do, and will accept me so to suffer for him."

Some lamented him, some derided him, *all* disswaded him: nevertheless, the more they did it, the more fixed he was in his purpose to seek the ordinances of the gospel, where they should be dispensed with most of the *commanded purity;* and the sudden deaths of the chief relations which thus lay at him, quickly after convinced him what a folly it had been to have quitted his profession, in expectation of any satisfaction from them. So to Holland he attempted a removal.

4. Having with a great company of Christians hired a ship to transport them for Holland, the master perfidiously betrayed them into the hands of those persecutors, who rifled and ransacked their goods, and clapped their persons into prison at Boston,[9] where they lay for a month together. But Mr. Bradford being a young man of about eighteen, was dismissed sooner than the rest, so that within a while he had opportunity with some others to get over to Zealand, through *perils,* both by *land* and *sea* not inconsiderable; where he was not long ashore ere a viper seized on his hand—that is, an officer—who carried him unto the magistrates, unto whom an envious passenger had accused him as having *fled* out of England. When the magistrates understood the true cause of his coming thither, they were well satisfied with him; and so he repaired joyfully unto his brethren at Amsterdam, where the difficulties to which he afterwards stooped in learning and serving of a Frenchman at the working of silks, were abundantly compensated by the delight wherewith he sat under the shadow of our Lord, in his purely dispensed ordinances. At the end of two years, he did, being of age to do it, convert his estate in England into money; but setting up for himself, he found some of his designs by the *providence* of God frowned upon, which he judged a *correction* bestowed by God upon him for certain decays of *internal piety,* whereinto he had fallen; the consumption of his *estate* he thought came to prevent a consumption in his *virtue.* But after he had resided in Holland about half a score years, he was one of those who bore a part in that hazardous and

[9]Boston, England.

generous enterprise of removing into New-England, with part of the English church at Leyden, where, at their first landing, his dearest consort[10] accidentally falling overboard, was drowned in the harbour; and the rest of his days were spent in the services, and the temptations, of that American wilderness.

5. Here was Mr. Bradford, in the year 1621, unanimously chosen the governour of the plantation: the difficulties whereof were such, that if he had not been a person of more than ordinary piety, wisdom and courage, he must have sunk under them. He had, with a laudable industry, been laying up a treasure of experiences, and he had now occasion to use it: indeed, nothing but an *experienced* man could have been suitable to the necessities of the people. The potent nations of the Indians, into whose country they were come, would have cut them off, if the blessing of God upon *his* conduct had not quelled them; and if his prudence, justice and moderation had not over-ruled them, they had been ruined by their own distempers. One specimen of his demeanour is to this day particularly spoken of.[11] A company of young fellows that were newly arrived, were very unwilling to comply with the governour's order for working abroad on the publick account; and therefore on Christmas-day, when he had called upon them, they excused themselves, with a pretence that it was against their conscience to *work* such a day. The governour gave them no answer, only that he would spare them till they were better informed; but by and by he found them all at *play* in the street, sporting themselves with various diversions; whereupon commanding the instruments of their games to be taken from them, he effectually gave them to understand. "*That it was against his conscience that they should play whilst others were at work:* and that if they had any devotion to the day, they should show it at home in the exercises of religion, and not in the streets with pastime and frolicks," and this gentle reproof put a final stop to all such disorders for the future.

6. For two years together after the beginning of the colony, whereof he was now governour, the poor people had a great experiment of "man's not living by bread alone;"[12] for when they were left all together without one morsel of bread for many months one after another, still the good providence of God relieved them, and supplied them, and this for the most part out of the *sea.* In this low condition of affairs, there was no little exercise for the prudence and patience of the governour, who chearfully bore his part in all: and, that industry might not flag, he quickly set himself to settle *propriety* among the new-planters;[13] foreseeing that while the whole country laboured upon a common stock, the husbandry and business of the plantation could not flourish, as Plato and others long since dreamed that it would, if a *community* were established. Certainly, if the spirit which dwelt in the old puritans, had not inspired these new-planters, they had sunk under the burden of these difficulties; but our Bradford had a double portion of that spirit.

7. The plantation was quickly thrown into a storm that almost overwhelmed it, by the unhappy actions of a minister sent over from England by the adventurers[14]

[10]His wife.

[11]Following Bradford's account of the incident in his *History* for 1621. Puritans did not consider Christmas day a holiday.

[12]Luke 4:4.

[13]Common property.

[14]In 1624 John Lyford and John Oldham arrived at Plymouth, and soon attracted a "faction" opposing the colonists' separatism, charging them in England with a variety of offenses. Although both men were convicted and expelled, Lyford's continued agitation ended in the breakup of the investors (adventurers), who stopped sending provisions to the colony.

concerned for the plantation; but by the blessing of Heaven on the conduct of the governour, they weathered out that storm. Only the adventurers hereupon breaking to pieces, threw up all their concealments with the infant-colony; whereof they gave this as one reason, "That the planters dissembled with his Majesty and their friends in their petition, wherein they declared for a church-discipline, agreeing with the French and others of the reforming churches in Europe."[15] Whereas 'twas now urged, that they had admitted into their communion a person who at his admission utterly renounced the Churches of England, (which person, by the way, was *that* very man who had made the complaints against them,) and therefore, though they denied the *name* of Brownists,[16] yet they were the thing. In answer hereunto, the very words written by the governour were these:

"Whereas you tax us with dissembling about the *French discipline,* you do us wrong, for we both hold and practice the *discipline* of the French and other Reformed Churches (as they have published the same in the Harmony of Confessions) according to our means, in effect and substance. But whereas you would tie us up to the French *discipline* in every circumstance, you derogate from the *liberty* we have in Christ Jesus. The Apostle Paul would have none to *follow him* in any thing, but wherein he *follows* Christ; much less ought any Christian or church in the world to do it. The French may err, we may err, and other churches may err, and doubtless do in many *circumstances.* That honour therefore belongs only to the *infallible Word of God,* and *pure Testament of Christ,* to be propounded and followed as the only rule and pattern for direction herein to all churches and Christians. And it is too great arrogancy for any man or church to think that he or they have so sounded the Word of God unto the bottom, as precisely to set down the church's discipline without error in substance or circumstances, that no other without blame may digress or differ in any thing from the same. And it is not difficult to shew that the Reformed Churches differ in many *circumstances* among themselves."

By which words it appears how far he was free from that rigid spirit of separation, which broke to pieces the Separatists themselves in the Low Countries, unto the great scandal of the reforming churches. He was indeed a person of a well-tempered spirit, or else it had been scarce possible for him to have kept the affairs of Plymouth in so good a temper for thirty-seven years together; in every one of which he was chosen their governour, except the three years wherein Mr. Winslow, and the two years wherein Mr. Prince, at the choice of the people, took a turn with him.[17]

8. The leader of a people in a wilderness had need be a Moses; and if a Moses had not led the people of Plymouth Colony, when this worthy person was their governour, the people had never with so much unanimity and importunity still called him to lead them.[18] Among many instances thereof, let this one piece of self-denial be told for a memorial of him, wheresoever this History shall be considered: The Patent of the Colony was taken in his name, running in these terms: "To William

[15]The Edict of Nantes (1598) enabled freedom of worship while it retained the authority of the Crown in France.

[16]Robert Browne (c. 1550–1663) advocated separation from the Church of England on the grounds that it did not exclude the corrupt. He called instead for independent congregations.

[17]Edward Winslow (1595–1655) and Thomas Prince (1600–1673).

[18]Moses was the lawgiver who led the Israelites from Egypt.

Bradford his heirs, associates, and assigns." But when the number of the freemen[19] was much increased, and many new townships erected, the General Court there desired of Mr. Bradford, that he would make a surrender of the same into their hands, which he willingly and presently assented unto, and confirmed it according to their desire by his hand and seal, reserving no more for himself than was his proportion, with others, by agreement. But as he found the providence of Heaven many ways recompensing his many acts of self-denial, so he gave this testimony to the faithfulness of the divine promises: "That he had forsaken friends, houses and lands for the sake of the gospel, and the Lord gave them him again." Here he prospered in his estate; and besides a worthy son which he had by a former wife, he had also two sons and a daughter by another, whom he married in this land.

9. He was a person for study as well as action; and hence, notwithstanding the difficulties through which he passed in his youth, he attained unto a notable skill in languages: the Dutch tongue was become almost as vernacular to him as the English; the French tongue he could also manage; the Latin and the Greek he had mastered; but the Hebrew he most of all studied, "Because," he said, "he would see with his own eyes the ancient oracles of God in their native beauty." He was also well skilled in History, in Antiquity, and in Philosophy; and for Theology he became so versed in it, that he was an irrefragable disputant against the *errors,* especially those of Anabaptism,[20] which with trouble he saw rising in his colony; wherefore he wrote some significant things for the confutation of those errors. But the *crown* of all was his holy, prayerful, watchful, and fruitful walk with God, wherein he was very exemplary.

10. At length he fell into an indisposition of body, which rendred him unhealthy for a whole winter; and as the spring advanced, his health yet more declined; yet he felt himself not what he counted sick, till one day; in the night after which, the God of heaven so filled his mind with ineffable consolations, that he seemed little short of Paul, rapt up unto the unutterable entertainments of Paradise.[21] The next morning he told his friends, "That the good Spirit of God had given him a pledge of his happiness in another world, and the first-fruits of his eternal glory;" and on the day following he died, May 9, 1657, in the 69th year of his age—lamented by all the colonies of New-England, as a common blessing and father to them all.

O mihi si Similis Contingat Clausula Vitæ![22]

Plato's brief description of a governour, is all that I will now leave as his character, in an

EPITAPH.[23]

MEN are but FLOCKS: BRADFORD beheld their need,
And long did them at once both rule and feed.

1702

[19]Those who worked on their own, for themselves, rather than as indentured servants.

[20]Anabaptists did not believe in the baptism of children, and they sought to separate church affairs from those of the state.

[21]In II Corinthians 12:1–4, Paul describes the divine revelations that helped him through his sufferings.

[22]"Oh, that I might reach a similar end of life."

[23]The Greek philosopher Plato (427?–347 B.C.) wrote about republican states. In the original publication, Mather provided the Greek for the following: "The shepherd, the provider of the human flock." His verse epitaph carries the same effect.

from The Triumphs of the Reformed Religion in America: Or, The Life of the Renowned John Eliot

Preliminary I The Birth, Age, and Family of Mr Eliot.

The inspired Moses, relating the lives of those Ante-Diluvian Patriarchs in whom the Church of God and line of Christ was continued, through the first sixteen hundred years of time, recites little but their *birth,* and their *age,* and their *death,* and their *sons* and *daughters.* If those articles would satisfie the appetites and enquiries of such as come to read the life of our Eliot, we shall soon have dispatched the work now upon our hands.

The *age,* with the *death* of this worthy man, has been already terminated, in the ninetieth year of the present century, and the eighty-sixth year of his own pilgrimage. And for his *birth,* it was at a town in England, the name whereof I cannot presently recover; nor is it necessary for me to look back so far as the place of his nativity; any more than it is for me to recite the vertues of his parentage, of which he said, *Vix ea nostru voco;*[1] though indeed the pious education which they gave him, caused him in his age to write these words: "I do see that it was a great favour of God unto me, to season my first times with the fear of God, the word, and prayer."

The Atlantick Ocean, like a river of Lethe[2] may easily cause us to forget many of the things that happened on the other side. Indeed, the *nativity* of such a man were an honour worthy the contention of as many places as laid their claims unto the famous Homer's: but whatever places may challenge a share in the reputation of having enjoyed the *first breath* of our Eliot, it is New-England that with most right can call him her's; his *best breath,* and afterwards his *last breath* was here; and here 'twas that God bestowed upon him sons and daughters.

He came to New-England in the month of November, A.D. 1631, among those blessed old planters which laid the foundations of a remarkable country, devoted unto the exercise of the Protestant religion, in its purest and highest reformation. He left behind him in England a vertuous young gentlewoman, whom he had pursued and purposed a marriage unto; and she coming hither the year following, that marriage was consummated in the month of October, A.D. 1632. . . .

Part III Or, Eliot as an Evangelist

The titles of a *Christian* and of a *minister* have rendred our Eliot considerable; but there is one memorable title more, by which he has been signalized unto us. An honourable person did once in print put the name of an evangelist upon him; whereupon, in a letter of his to that person, aftwards printed, his expressions were, "There is a *redundancy* where you put the title of Evangelist upon me; I beseech you suppress all such things; let us do and speak and carry all things with humility; it is the Lord

[1] "I can hardly call them mine."
[2] In classical myth, the river of forgetfulness.

who hath done what is done; and it is most becoming the spirit of Jesus Christ to lift up him, and lay our selves low; I wish that word could be obliterated." My reader sees what a caution Mr. Eliot long since entred against our giving him the title of an evangelist; but his *death* has now made it safe, and his *life* had long made it just, for us to acknowledge him with such a title. I know not whither that of an evangelist, or one separated for the employment of preaching the gospel in such places whereunto churches have hitherto been gathered, be not an office that should be continued in our days; but this I know, that our Eliot very notably did the *service* and *business* of such an officer.

Cambden[3] could not reach the height of his conceit[4] who bore in his shield a salvage of America, with his hand pointing to the sun, and this motto: *Mihi Accessu, Tibi Recessu.*[5] Reader, prepare to behold this *device* illustrated!

The natives of the country now possessed by the New-Englanders had been forlorn and wretched heathen ever since their first herding here; and though we know not *when* or *how* those Indians first became inhabitants of this mighty continent, yet we may guess that probably the devil decoyed those miserable salvages hither, in hopes that the gospel of the Lord Jesus Christ would never come here to destroy or disturb his *absolute empire* over them. But our Eliot was in such ill terms with the devil, as to alarm him with sounding the silver trumpets of Heaven in his territories, and make some noble and zealous attempts towards ousting him of ancient possessions here. There were, I think twenty several *nations* (if I may call them so) of Indians upon that spot of ground which fell under the influence of our Three United Colonies;[6] and our Eliot was willing to rescue as many of them as he could from that old usurping *landlord* of America, who is, "by the wrath of God, the prince of this world."

The exemplary charity of this excellent person in this important affair, will not be seen in its due lustres, unless we make some reflections upon several circumstances which he beheld these forlorn Indians in. Know, then, that these doleful creatures are the veriest *ruines of mankind* which are to be found any where upon the face of the earth. No such *estates* are to be expected among them, as have been the *baits* which the pretended converters in other countries have snapped at. One might see among them what an hard master the devil is to the most devoted of his vassals! These abject creatures live in a country full of mines; we have already made entrance upon our *iron;* and in the very surface of the ground among us, it is thought there lies *copper* enough to supply all this world; besides other mines hereafter to be exposed; but our shiftless Indians were never owners of so much as a knife till we come among them; their name for an English man was a *Knife-man;* stone was instead of metal for their tools; and for their coins, they have only little beads with holes in them to string them upon a bracelet, whereof some are white; and of these there go six for a penny; some are black or blue; and of these, go three for a penny: this wampam, as they call it, is made of the shell-fish which lies upon the sea-coast continually.

They live in a country where *we* now have all the conveniences of human life: but as for *them,* their *housing* is nothing but a few mats tyed about poles fastened in the earth, where a good *fire* is their *bed-clothes* in the coldest seasons; their *clothing*

[3]William Camden (1551–1623), English antiquary and historian.

[4]Conception, idea.

[5]"As I rise, you set."

[6]Massachusetts, Connecticut, and Rhode Island.

is but skin of a beast, covering their hind-parts, their fore-parts having but a little apron, where nature calls for secrecy; their *diet* has not a greater dainty than their *Nokehick*—that is, a spoonful of their parched meal, with a spoonful of water, which will strengthen them to travel a day together; except we should mention the flesh of deers, bears, mose, rakoons, and the like, which they have when they can *catch* them; as also a little fish, which, if they would preserve, it was by drying, not by salting; for they had not a grain of salt in the world, I think, till we bestowed it on them. Their *physick*[7] is, excepting a few odd specificks,[8] which some of them encounter certain cases with, nothing hardly but an hot-house or a powaw; their *hot-house* is a little cave, about eight foot over, where, after they have terribly heated it, a crew of them go sit and sweat and smoke for an hour together, and then immediately run into some very cold adjacent brook, without the least mischief to them; it is this way they recover themselves from some diseases, particularly from the French;[9] but in most of their dangerous distempers, it is a *powaw* that must be sent for; that is, a priest, who has more familiarity with Satan than his neighbours; this conjurer comes and roars, and howls, and uses magical ceremonies over the sick man, and will be well paid for it when he has done; if this don't effect the cure, the "man's time is come, and there's an end."

They live in a country full of the best ship-timber under heaven: but never saw a ship till some came from Europe hither; and then they were scared out of their wits to see the *monster* come sailing in, and spitting fire with a mighty noise out of her floating side; they cross the water in canoes, made sometimes of trees, which they burn and hew, till they have hollowed them; and sometimes of barks, which they stitch into a light sort of a vessel, to be easily carried over land; if they overset, it is but a little paddling like a dog, and they are soon where they were.

Their way of living is infinitely barbarous: the men are most abominably slothful; making their poor squaws, or wives, to plant and dress, and barn and beat their corn, and build their wigwams for them: which perhaps may be the reason of their extraordinary ease in childbirth. In the mean time, their chief employment, when they'll *condescend* unto any, is that of *hunting;* wherein they'll go out some scores, if not hundreds of them in a company, driving all before them.

They continue in a place till they have burnt up all the wood thereabouts, and then they pluck up stakes; to follow the *wood,* which they cannot fetch home unto themselves; hence when they enquire about the English, "Why come they hither?" they have themselves very learnedly determined the case, " 'Twas because we wanted firing." No *arts* are understood among them, except just so far as to maintain their brutish conversation, which is little more than is to be found among the very bevers upon our streams.

Their division of time is by *sleeps,* and *moons,* and *winters;* and, by lodging abroad, they have somewhat observed the motions of the *stars;* among which it has been surprising unto me to find that they have always called "Charles's Wain" by the name of *Paukunnawaw,* or *the Bear,* which is the name whereby Europeans also have distinguished it.[10] Moreover, they have little, if any, traditions among them worthy of

[7]Medical practice.
[8]Medicines.
[9]Syphilis.
[10]Ursus Major ("The Great Bear"), known commonly today as the Big Dipper.

our notice: and reading and writing is altogether unknown to them, though there is a rock or two in the country that has unaccountable characters engraved upon it. All the religion they have amounts unto thus much: they believe that there are many gods, who made and own the several nations of the world; of which a certain *great God* in the south-west regions of heaven bears the greatest figure. They believe that every remarkable creature has a peculiar god within it or about it: there is with them a *Sun God,* a *Moon God,* and the like; and they cannot conceive but that the fire must be a kind of a god, inasmuch as a *spark* of it will soon produce very strange effects. They believe that when any good or ill happens to them, there is the favour or the anger of a god expressed in it; and hence, as in a time of calamity, they keep a *dance,* or a day of extravagant ridiculous devotions to their god; so in a time of prosperity they likewise have a *feast,* wherein they also make presents one unto another. Finally, they believe that their chief god *(Kautantowit)* made a man and a woman of a *stone;* which, upon dislike, he broke to pieces, and made another man and woman of a *tree,* which were the fountains of mankind; and that we all have in us immortal *souls,* which, if we were godly, shall go to a splendid entertainment with Kautantowit, but otherwise must wander about in restless horror for ever. But if you say to them any thing of a *resurrection,* they will reply upon you, "I shall never believe it!" And when they have any weighty undertaking before them, it is an usual thing for them to have their assemblies, wherein, after the usage of some diabolical rites, a devil appears unto them, to inform them and advise them about their circumstances; and sometimes there are odd events of their making these applications to the devil. For instance, it is particularly affirmed that the Indians, in their wars with us, finding a sore inconvenience by our dogs, which would make a sad yelling if in the night they scented the approaches of them, they sacrificed a dog to the devil; after which no English dog would bark at an Indian for divers months ensuing. This was the miserable people which our Eliot propounded unto himself to teach and save! And he had a double work incumbent on him; he was to make men of them, ere he could hope to see them saints; they must be *civilized* ere they could be *Christianized;* he could not, as Gregory once of our nation,[11] see any thing *angelical* to bespeak his labours for their eternal welfare: all among them was *diabolical.* To think on raising a number of these hedious creatures unto the elevations of our holy religion, must argue more than common or little sentiments in the undertaker; but the faith of an Eliot could encounter it!

I confess that was one—I cannot call it so much *guess* as wish—wherein he was willing a little to indulge himself; and that was, "that our *Indians* are the posterity of the dispersed and rejected *Israelites,* concerning whom our God has promised, that they shall yet be saved by the deliverer coming to turn away ungodliness from them." He saw the Indians using many *parables* in their discourses; much given to anointing of their *heads;* much delighted in *dancing,* especially after victories; computing their times by *nights* and *months;* giving *dowries* for wives, and causing their women to "dwell by themselves," at certain seasons, for secret causes; and accustoming themselves to grievous *mournings* and *yellings* for the dead; all which were usual things

[11]Pope Gregory I (d. 604), who first sent Christian missionaries to England, is reported to have exclaimed when he first saw some of the native Angles of Britain, "Not Angles, but angels!"

among the Israelites. They have, too, a great unkindness for our *swine;* but I suppose that is because our hogs devour the clams which are a dainty[12] with them. He also saw some learned men looking for the lost Israelites among the Indians in America, and counting that they had *thorow-good* reasons for doing so. And a few small *arguments,* or indeed but *conjectures,* meeting with a favourable disposition in the hearer, will carry some conviction with them; especially if a report of a *Menasseh ben Israel*[13] be to back them. He saw likewise the *judgments* threatened unto the Israelites of old, strangely fulfilled upon our Indians; particularly that "Ye shall eat the flesh of your sons,"[14] which is done with exquisite cruelties upon the prisoners that they take from one another in their battles. Moreover, it is a prophesy in Deuteronomy xxviii. 68, "The Lord shall bring thee into Egypt again with ships, by the way whereof I spake unto thee, thou shalt see it no more again; and there shall be sold unto your enemies, and no man shall buy you." This did our Eliot imagine accomplished, when the captives taken by us in our late wars upon them, were sent to be sold in the coasts lying not very remote from Egypt on the Mediterranean sea, and scarce any chapmen[15] would offer to take them off. Being upon such as these accounts not unwilling, if it were possible, to have the Indians found Israelites, they were, you may be sure, not a whit the less "beloved for their (supposed) father's sake;" and the fatigues of his travails went on the more *cheerfully,* or at least the more *hopefully,* because of such possibilities.

The first step which he judged necessary now to be taken by him, was to learn the Indian language; for he saw them so stupid and senseless, that they would never do so much as enquire after the religion of the strangers now come into their country, much less would they so far imitate us as to leave off their beastly way of living, that they might be partakers of any spiritual advantage by us: unless we could first address them in a language of their own. Behold, new difficulties to be surmounted by our indefatigable Eliot! He hires a native to teach him this exotick language, and with a laborious care and skill reduces it into a grammar, which afterwards he published. There is a letter or two of our alphabet, which the Indians never had in theirs; though there were enough of the *dog* in their *temper,* there can scarce be found an *R* in their language, (any more than in the language of the Chinese or of the Greenlanders) save that the Indians to the northward, who have a peculiar dialect, pronounce an *R* where an *N* is pronounced by our Indians; but if their alphabet be short, I am sure the words composed of it are long enough to tire the patience of any scholar in the world; they are *Sesquipedalia Verba,*[16] of which their *linquo*[17] is composed; one would think they had been growing ever since Babel unto the dimensions to which they are now extended. For instance, if my reader will count how many letters there are in this word, *Nummatchekodtantamooonganunnonash,* when he has done, for his reward, I'll tell him it signifies no more in English than *our lusts;* and if I were to translate, *our loves,* it must be nothing shorter than *Noowomantammooonkanunonnash.* Or, to give my reader a longer word than either of these, *Kummogkodonattoottummooetiteaongannunnonash* is in English *our question:* but I pray, sir, count the letters! Nor do we find in all this language the least affinity to, or derivation from any European speech that we are acquainted with. I know not what

[12]Delicacy.
[13]Jewish theologian and founder of the Jewish community in England (1604–1657).
[14]In Leviticus 26:29, God promises this punishment for idolaters.
[15]Traders.
[16]Long words.
[17]Language, lingo.

thoughts it will produce in my reader, when I inform him that once, finding that the *Dæmons* in a possessed young woman understood the Latin, and Greek, and Hebrew languages my curiosity led me to make trial of this Indian language, and the Daemons did seem as if they did not understand it.[18] This tedious language our Eliot (the anagram of whose name was TOILE) quickly became a master of; he employed a pregnant[19] and witty Indian, who also spoke English well, for his assistance in it; and compiling some discourses by his help, he would single out a word, a noun, a verb, and pursue it through all its variations: having finished his grammar, at the close he writes, "Prayers and pains through faith in Christ Jesus will do any thing!" and being by his *prayers* and *pains* thus furnished, he set himself in the year 1646 to preach the gospel of our Lord Jesus Christ among these desolate outcasts.

The Conclusion; Or, Eliot Expiring

By this time, I have doubtless made my reader loth to have me tell what now remains of this little history; doubtless they are wishing that this John might have "tarried unto the second coming of our Lord."[20] But, alas! all-devouring death at last snatched him from us, and slighted all those lamentations of ours, "My father, my father, the chariots of Israel, and the horsemen thereof!"[21]

When he was become a sort of Miles Emeritus,[22] and began to draw near his *end,* he grew still more heavenly, more savoury,[23] more divine, and scented more of the spicy country at which he was ready to put ashore. As the historian observes of Tiberius,[24] that when his *life* and *strength* were going from him, his *vice* yet remained with him; on the contrary, the *grace* of this excellent man rather increased than abated, when every thing else was dying with him. It is too usual with old men, that when they are past *work,* they are least sensible of their inabilities and incapacities, and can scarce endure to see another succeeding them in any part of their office. But our Eliot was of a temper quite contrary thereunto; for finding, many months before his expiration, that he had not strength enough to edify his congregation with publick prayers and sermons, he importuned his people with some impatience to call another minister; professing himself unable to die with comfort until he could see a good successor ordained, settled, fixed among them.

But although he thus dismissed himself, as one so near to the age of ninety might well have done, from his publick labours, yet he would not give over his endeavours, in a more private sphere, to "do good unto all." He had always been an enemy to idleness; any one that should look into the little diary that he kept in his Almanacks, would see that there was with him, "no day without a line;" and he was troubled particularly when he saw how much *time* was devoured by that slavery to tobacco, which too many debase themselves unto; and now he grew old, he was desirous that his *works* should hold pace with his *life;* the less *time* he saw *left,* the less was he willing to have *lost.* He imagined

[18]In *Memorable Providences, Relating to Witchcrafts and Possessions* (1689), Mather describes performing this "experiment" on the possessed Martha Goodwin.

[19]Intelligent.

[20]John 21:22.

[21]In II Kings 2:12, Elisha utters this lament upon witnessing the prophet Elijah taken up to heaven in a whirlwind.

[22]Retired soldier (of Christ).

[23]See II Corinthians 2:15, "We are unto God a sweet savour of Christ."

[24]Roman emperor (42 B.C.–A.D. 37), as described by Suetonius.

that he could now do nothing to any purpose in any service for God; and sometimes he would say, with an air peculiar to himself, "I wonder for what the Lord Jesus Christ lets me live; he knows that now I can do nothing for him!" And yet he could not forbear essaying to *do something* for his Lord; he conceived that though the English could not be benefited by any gifts which he now fancied himself to have only the ruins of, yet who can tell but the *negroes* might! He had long lamented it, with a bleeding and a burning passion, that the English used their *negroes* but as their *horses* or their *oxen,* and that so little care was taken about their immortal souls; he looked upon it as a prodigy that any wearing the *name* of *Christians,* should so much have the *heart* of *devils* in them, as to prevent and hinder the instructions of the poor blackamores, and confine the souls of their miserable slaves to a destroying ignorance, meerly for fear of thereby losing the benefit of their vassalage; but now he made a motion to the English within two or three miles of him, that at such a time and place they would send their negroes once a week unto him: for he would then catechise them, and enlighten them, to the utmost of his power in the things of their everlasting peace. However, he did not live to make much progress in this undertaking.

He fell into some languishments attended with a fever, which in a few days brought him into the *pangs* (may I say? or *joys*) of death; and while he lay in these, Mr. Walter coming to him, he said unto him, "Brother, thou art welcome to my very soul. Pray retire to thy study for me, and give me leave to be gone;" meaning that he should not, by petitions to Heaven for his life, detain him here. It was in these languishments that, speaking about the work of the gospel among the Indians, he did after this heavenly manner express himself: "There is a cloud, (said he) a dark cloud upon the work of the gospel among the poor Indians. The Lord revive and prosper that work, and grant it may live when I am dead. It is a work which I have been doing much and long about.—But what was the word I spoke last? I recall that word, *my doings!* Alas, they have been poor and small, and lean doing, and I'll be the man that shall throw the first stone at them all."

It has been observed that they who have spoke many considerable things in their *lives,* usually speak few at their *deaths.* But it was otherwise with our Eliot, who, after much speech of and for God in his lifetime, uttered some things little short of *oracles* on his death-bed, his last breath smelt strong of heaven, and was articled into none but very gracious notes; one of the last whereof was, "Welcome joy!" and at last it went away, calling upon the standers by to "Pray, pray, pray!" which was the thing in which so vast a portion of it had been before employed.

This was the peace in the end of this "perfect and upright man;" thus was there another *star* fetched away to be placed among the rest that the third heaven is now enriched with. He had once, I think a pleasant fear that the old saints of his acquaintance, especially those two dearest neighbours of his, Cotton of Boston, and Mather of Dorchester,[25] which were got safe to heaven before him, would suspect him to be gone the wrong way, because he staid so long behind them. But they are now together with a blessed Jesus, "beholding of his glory," and celebrating the high praises of him that has "called them into his marvellous light."[26]

1702

[25]John Cotton (1584–1652) and Richard Mather (1596–1669), leading Puritan ministers of early Massachusetts and grandfathers to Cotton Mather.

[26]I Peter 2:9.

from The Negro Christianized[1]

It is a *Golden Sentence,* that has been sometimes quoted from *Chrysostom;* That *for a man to know the Art of Alms, is more than for a man to be Crowned with the Diadem of Kings: But to Convert one Soul unto God, is more than to pour out Ten Thousand Talents into the Baskets of the Poor.*[2] Truly, to Raise a *Soul,* from a dark State of Ignorance and Wickedness, to the Knowledge of GOD, and the Belief of CHRIST, and the practice of our Holy and Lovely RELIGION; 'Tis the noblest Work, that ever was undertaken among the Children of men. An Opportunity to Endeavour the CONVERSION of a Soul, from a Life of *Sin,* which is indeed a woeful *Death,* to Fear God, and Love CHRIST, and by a Religious Life to Escape the *Paths of the Destroyer;* it cannot but be Acceptable to all that have themselves had in themselves Experience of such a *Conversion.* And such an Opportunity there is in your Hands, O all you that have any **Negroes** in your Houses; an Opportunity to try, Whether you may not be the Happy *Instruments,* of Converting, the *Blackest* Instances of *Blindness* and *Baseness,* into admirable *Candidates* of Eternal Blessedness. Let not this Opportunity be Lost; if you have any concern for *Souls,* your Own or Others; but, make a Trial, Whether by your Means, the most *Bruitish* of Creatures upon Earth may not come to be disposed, in some Degree, like the *Angels* of Heaven; and the *Vassals* of Satan, become the *Children* of God. Suppose these Wretched *Negroes,* to be the Offspring of *Cham*[3] (which yet is not so very certain,) yet let us make a Trial, Whether the CHRIST who *dwelt in the Tents of Shem,*[4] have not some of His Chosen among them; Let us make a Trial, Whether they that have been Scorched and Blacken'd by the Sun of *Africa,* may not come to have their Minds Healed by the more Benign Beams of the *Sun of Righteousness.*

It is come to pass by the *Providence* of God, without which there comes nothing to pass, that Poor **Negroes** are cast under your Government and Protection. You take them into your *Families;* you look on them as part of your *Possessions;* and you Expect from their Service, a Support, and perhaps an Increase, of your other *Possessions.* How agreeable would it be, if a Religious Master or Mistress thus attended, would now think with themselves! *Who can tell but that this Poor Creature may belong to the Election of God! Who can tell, but that God may have sent this Poor Creature into my Hands, that so One of the Elect may by my means be Called; & by my Instruction be made Wise unto Salvation! The glorious God will put an unspeakable Glory upon me, if it may be so!* The Considerations that would move you, To Teach your *Negroes* the *Truths* of the Glorious Gospel, as far as you can, and bring them, if

[1]The complete title is *The Negro Christianized. An Essay to Excite and Assist that Good Work, The Instruction of Negro-Servants in Christianity.* This text was first published in 1706.

[2]In his *Homilies on First Corinthians,* Homily III, John Chrysostom (c. 347–407) argues that "although thou give countless treasure unto the poor, thou wilt do no such work as he who converteth one soul."

[3]In Genesis 9:22–27, Ham (or Cham), Noah's second son, has the temerity to observe his father as he lies drunk and naked. For that offense Noah curses Ham, the progenitor of Canaan, condemning him to be a "servant of servants" (v. 25). The passage was often used by apologists for slavery, who saw Africans as Ham's descendants.

[4]In Genesis 9:27, Noah declares that God shall "dwell in the tents of Shem," his oldest son. Since "Canaan shall be his servant," Mather argues that cursed servants may nevertheless be redeemed in godly households.

it may be, to Live according to those *Truths,* a *Sober,* and a *Righteous,* and a *Godly* Life; They are *Innumerable;* And, if you would after a *Reasonable* manner consider, the Pleas which we have to make on the behalf of *God,* and of the *Souls* which He has made, one would wonder that they should not be *Irresistible. Show your selves Men,* and let *Rational Arguments* have their Force upon you, to make you treat, not as *Bruits* but as *Men,* those *Rational Creatures* whom God has made your *Servants.*

For,

First; The Great GOD *Commands* it, and *Requires* it of you; to do what you can that *Your Servants,* may also be *His.* It was an Admonition once given; Eph. 5.9.[5] *Masters, Know that your Master is in Heaven.* You will confess, That the God of Heaven is your *Master.* If your *Negroes* do not comply with your *Commands,* into what Anger, what Language, Perhaps into a misbecoming *Fury,* are you transported? But you are now to attend unto the *Commands* of your more Absolute *Master;* and they are His *Commands* concerning your *Negroes* too. What can be more Expressive; than those words of the Christian Law? Col. 4.1. *Masters, give unto your Servants, that which is Just & Equal, knowing that ye also have a Master in Heaven.* Of what *Servants* is this Injunction to be understood? Verily, of *Slaves.* For *Servants* were generally such, at the time of Writing the New Testament. Wherefore, *Masters,* As it is *Just & Equal,* that your *Servants* be not *Over-wrought,* and that while they *Work* for you, you should *Feed* them, and *Cloath* them, and afford convenient *Rest* unto them, and make their Lives comfortable; So it is *Just* and *Equal,* that you should Acquaint them, as far as you can, with the way to Salvation by JESUS CHRIST. You deny your *Master in Heaven,* if you do nothing to bring your *Servants* unto the Knowledge and Service of that glorious *Master.* One Table of the *Ten Commandments,* has this for the Sum of it; *Thou shalt Love thy Neighbour as thy self.* Man, Thy *Negro* is thy *Neighbour.* T'were an Ignorance, unworthy of a *Man,* to imagine otherwise. Yea, if thou dost grant, *That God hath made of one Blood, all Nations of men,* he is thy *Brother* too. Now canst thou *Love* thy *Negro,* and be willing to see him ly under the Rage of Sin, and the Wrath of God? Canst thou *Love* him, and yet refuse to do any thing, that his miserable Soul may be rescued from Eternal miseries? Oh! Let thy *Love* to that Poor *Soul,* appear in thy concern, to make it, if thou canst, as happy as thy own! We are Commanded, Gal. 6.10. *As we have opportunity let us Do Good unto all men, especially unto them, who are of the Houshold of Faith.* Certainly, we have *Opportunity,* to *Do Good* unto our *Servants,* who are of our *own Houshold;* certainly, we may do something to *make them Good,* and bring them to be of the *Houshold of Faith.* In a word, All the Commandments in the Bible, which bespeak our *Charity* to the *Souls* of others, and our *Endeavour* that the *Souls* of others may be delivered from the Snares of Death; every one of these do oblige us, to do what we can, for the *Souls* of our *Negroes.* They are more nearly *Related* unto us, than many others are; we are more fully *capable* to do for them, than for many others. . . .

Yea, the pious *Masters,* that have instituted their *Servants* in Christian Piety, will even in this Life have a sensible *Recompence.* The more *Serviceable,* and Obedient

[5]Actually, Ephesians 6:9.

and obliging Behaviour of their *Servants* unto them, will be a sensible & a notable *Recompence.* Be assured, Syrs; Your *Servants* will be the *Better Servants,* for being made *Christian Servants.* To *Christianize* them aright, will be to *fill them with all Goodness. Christianity* is nothing but a very Mass of Universal *Goodness.* Were your *Servants* well tinged with the Spirit of *Christianity,* it would render them exceeding *Dutiful* unto their *Masters,* exceeding *Patient* under their *Masters,* exceeding faithful in their Business, and afraid of speaking or doing any thing that may justly displease you. It has been observed, that those *Masters* who have used their *Negroes* with most of *Humanity,* in allowing them all the Comforts of Life, that are necessary and *Convenient* for them, (Who have remembered, that by the Law of God, even an *Ass* was to be relieved, When *Sinking under his Burden,*[6] and an *Ox* might not be *Muzzled* when *Treading out the Corn;*[7] and that if a *Just man will regard the Life of his Beast,* he will much more allow the comforts of life to and not hide himself *from his own Flesh:*) have been better *Serv'd,* had more work done for them, and better done, than those *Inhumane Masters,* who have used their *Negroes* worse than their *Horses.* And those *Masters* doubtless, who use their *Negroes* with most of *Christianity,* and use most pains to inform them in, and conform them to, *Christianity,* will find themselves no losers by it. *Onesimus*[8] was doubtless a *Slave:* but this poor *Slave,* on whose behalf a great Apostle of God was more than a little concerned; yea, one Book in our Bible was Written on his behalf! When he was *Christianized,* it was presently said unto his *Master,* Philem. 11. *In time past he was unprofitable to thee, but now he will be profitable.* But many *Masters* whose *Negroes* have greatly vexed them, with miscarriages, may do well to examine, Whether Heaven be not chastising of them, for their failing in their Duty about their *Negroes.* Had they done more, to make their *Negroes* the knowing and willing *Servants* of God, it may be, God would have made their *Negroes* better *Servants* to them. Syrs, you may Read your *Sin* in the *Punishment.*

And now, what *Objection* can any Man Living have, to refund the force of these *Considerations*? Produce the *cause,* O Impiety, *Bring forth thy strong reasons,* and let all men see what Idle and silly cavils, are thy best *Reasons* against this Work of God.

It has been cavilled, by some, that it is questionable Whether the *Negroes* have *Rational Souls,* or no. But let that *Bruitish* insinuation be never Whispered any more. Certainly, their *Discourse,* will abundantly prove, that they have *Reason. Reason* showes it self in the *Design* which they daily act upon. The vast improvement that *Education* has made upon *some* of them, argues that there is a *Reasonable Soul* in *all* of them. An old Roman, and Pagan, would call upon the Owner of such Servants, *Homines tamen esse memento.*[9] They are *Men,* and not *Beasts* that you have bought,

[6]A reference to Exodus 23:5.

[7]See Deuteronomy 25:4. In 1 Corinthians 9:9, Paul, referring to this Mosaic protection of draught animals, asks rhetorically, "Doth God take care for oxen?" Cf. also 1 Timothy 5:18, where the protection of oxen prompts Paul to claim that one who labors "in the word and doctrine . . . is worthy of his reward."

[8]In his Epistle to Philemon, Paul asks pardon for the slave boy Onesimus, who has been his companion in prison and whom he has converted. "Onesimus" means "useful" or "profitable."

[9]"But remember that they are men."

and they must be used accordingly. 'Tis true; They are *Barbarous.* But so were our own *Ancestors.* The *Britons* were in many things as *Barbarous,* but a little before our Saviours Nativity, as the *Negroes* are at this day if there be any Credit in *Cæsars Commentaries. Christianity* will be the best cure for this *Barbarity.* Their *Complexion* sometimes is made an Argument, why nothing should be done for them. A *Gay* sort of argument! As if the great God went by the *Complexion* of Men, in His Favours to them! As if none but *Whites* might hope to be Favoured and Accepted with God! Whereas it is well known, That the *Whites,* are the least part of Mankind. The biggest part of Mankind, perhaps, are *Copper-Coloured;* a sort of *Tawnies.* And our *English* that inhabit some Climates, do seem growing apace to be not much unlike unto them. As if, because a people, from the long force of the African *Sun* & *Soil* upon them, (improved perhaps, to further Degrees by maternal imaginations, and other accidents,) are come at length to have the small *Fibres* of their *Veins,* and the Blood in them, a little more Interspersed thro their Skin than other People, this must render them less valuable to Heaven then the rest of Mankind? Away with such Trifles. The God who *looks on the Heart,* is not moved by the colour of the *Skin;* is not more propitious to one *Colour* than another. Say rather, with the Apostle; Acts 10.34, 35. *Of a truth I perceive, that God is no respector of persons; but in every Nation, he that feareth Him and worketh Righteousness, is accepted with Him.* Indeed their *Stupidity* is a *Discouragement.* It may seem, unto as little purpose, to *Teach,* as to *wash an Æthopian.* But the greater their *Stupidity,* the greater must be our *Application.* If we can't learn them so much as we *Would,* let us learn them as much as we *Can.* A little divine *Light* and *Grace* infused into them, will be of great account. And the more *Difficult* it is, to fetch such *forlorn things* up out of the perdition whereinto they are fallen, the more *Laudable* is the undertaking: There will be the more of a *Triumph,* if we prosper in the undertaking. Let us encourage our selves from that word; Mat. 3.9 *God is able of these Stones, to raise up Children unto Abraham.*

Well; But if the *Negroes* are *Christianized,* they will be *Baptized;* and their *Baptism* will presently entitle them to their *Freedom;* so our *Money* is thrown away.

Man, If this were true; that a *Slave* bought with thy *Money,* were by thy means brought unto the *Things that accompany Salvation,* and thou shouldest from this time have no more Service from him, yet thy *Money* were not thrown away. That Man's *Money will perish with him,* yet he had rather the *Souls* in his Family should *Perish,* than that he should lose a little *Money.* And suppose it were so, that *Baptism* gave a legal Title to *Freedom.*[10] Is there no guarding against this Inconvenience? You may by sufficient *Indentures,* keep off the things, which you reckon so Inconvenient. But it is all a Mistake. There is no such thing. What *Law* is it, that Sets the *Baptized Slave* at *Liberty?* Not the *Law of Christianity:* that allows of *Slavery;* Only it wonderfully Dulcifies, and Mollifies, and Moderates the Circumstances of it. *Christianity* directs a *Slave,* upon his embracing the *Law of the Redeemer,* to satisfy himself, *That he is the Lords Free-man,* tho' he continues a *Slave.* It supposes, (Col. 3.11.) That there are *Bond* as well as *Free,* among those that have been *Renewed in the Knowledge and Im-*

[10]Popular belief, stimulated by such English works as Morgan Godwin's *The Negro's & Indians Advocate* (1680), held that baptism conferred manumission. The 1729 Yorke-Talbot decision confirmed Mather's claim that baptism was irrelevant.

age of Jesus Christ. Will the *Canon-law* do it? No; The *Canons* of Numberless *Councils,* mention, the *Slaves* of *Christians,* without any contradiction. Will the *Civil Law* do it? No: Tell, if you can, any part of *Christendom,* wherein *Slaves* are not frequently to be met withal. But is not *Freedom* to be claim'd for a *Baptised Slave,* by the *English* Constitution? The English *Laws,* about *Villains,*[11] or, *Slaves,* will not say so; for by those *Laws,* they may be granted *for Life,* like a *Lease,* and passed over with a *Mannor,* like other *Goods or Chattels.* And by those *Laws,* the Lords may sieze the Bodies of their *Slaves* even while a Writt, *De libertate probanda,*[12] is depending. These English *Laws* were made when the *Lords* & the *Slaves,* were both of them *Christians;* and they stand still unrepealed. If there are not now such *Slaves* in *England* as formerly, it is from the *Lords,* more than from the *Laws.* The *Baptised* then are not thereby entitled unto their *Liberty.* Howbeit, if they have arrived unto such a measure of *Christianity,* that *some are forbid Water for the Baptising of them,* it is fit, that they should enjoy those *comfortable circumstances* with us, which are due to them, not only as the *Children* of *Adam,* but also as our *Brethren,* on the same level with us in the expectations of a blessed Immortality, thro' the *Second Adam.* Whatever Slaughter the Assertion may make among the pretensions which are made unto *Christianity,* yet while the *sixteenth* Chapter of *Matthew* is in the Bible,[13] it must be asserted; the *Christian,* who cannot so far *Deny himself,* can be no *Disciple* of the Lord JESUS CHRIST. But, O Christian, thy *Slave* will not Serve thee one jot the worse for that *Self denial.*

The way is now cleared, for the work that is proposed: that excellent **WORK, The Instruction of the** Negroes **in the Christian Religion.**

A CATECHISM shall be got ready for them; first a *Shorter,* then a *Larger;* Suited unto their poor Capacities.

They who cannot themselves *Personally* so well attend the *Instruction* of the *Negroes,* may employ and reward those that shall do it for them. In many *Families,* the *Children* may help the *Negroes,* to Learn the *Catechism,* or their well-instructed and well-disposed *English Servants* may do it: And they should be *Rewarded* by the *Masters,* when they do it.

In a Plantation of many *Negroes,* why should not a *Teacher* be hired on purpose, to instil into them the principles of the *Catechism?*

Or, if the *Overseers* are once *Catechised* themselves, they may soon do the Office of *Catechisers* unto those that are under them.

However, Tis fit for the *Master* also *Personally* to enquire into the progress which his *Negroes* make in *Christianity,* and not leave it *Entierly* to the management of others.

There must be *Time* allow'd for the *Work.* And why not **The Lords-Day**? The precept of God concerning the *Sabbath,* is very positive; *Remember the SABBATH-DAY, to keep it Holy. Thou shalt not then do any work, thou nor thy Son, nor thy Daughter, thy Man-Servant, nor thy Maid-Servant.*[14] By virtue of this precept, we do

[11]The term for a feudal serf. In *Chamberline* v. *Marley* (1696–97), villeinage was used to claim that English law supported absolute ownership of persons and property.

[12]"Proving freedom."

[13]In Matthew 16:24, Jesus exhorts his followers, "If any man will come after me, let him deny himself, and take up his cross, and follow me."

[14]Exodus 20:8, 10.

even demand, **The Lords-Day,** for the *Negroes:* that they may be permitted the Freedom of **The Lords-Day,** and not be then unnecessarily diverted from attending on such *means of Instruction,* as may be afforded unto them.

To quicken them unto the learning of the *Catechism,* it would be very well to propose unto the *Negroes, Agreeable Recompences, & Priviledges,* to be receiv'd and enjoy'd by them, when they shall have made a good progress in it. Syrs, A *Mahometan* will do as much as this comes to, for any one that will embrace his *Alcoran.* Oh, Christians, will not you do more for *your Generation,* than the *Children of this World* for theirs. And it is to be desired, that the *Negroes* may not learn to say their *Catechism* only by rote, like *Parrots;* but that their Instructors, may put unto them such other *Questions* relating to the points of the *Catechism,* that by their *Answers,* (at least of YES, or, NO,) it may be perceived, that they *Know* what they *Say.*

But it will be also needful and useful, to uphold a more particular *Conference* often with the *Negroes;* and in conferring with them, to inculcate on them such *Admonitions of Piety;* as may have a special tendency to *Form* & *Mould* their Souls for the Kingdom of God.

Having told them, *Who Made* them, and *Why* He made them, and that they have *Souls,* which will be *Wretched* or *Happy* forever, according as they mind *Religion;* then tell them;

That by their sin against God, they are fallen into a dreadful condition.

Show them, That the Almighty *God is Angry* with them, and that, if they Dy under the *Anger of God,* they will after *Death,* be cast among *Devils;* and that all the *Stripes,* and all the *Wants,* and all the sad things they ever suffered in this World, are nothing, to the *many Sorrows,* which they shall suffer among the Damned, in the *Dungeon of Hell.*

Tell them; *That JESUS CHRIST is a Saviour for them as well as others, and as willing to save them out of their dreadful condition, as any others.*

Show them, That JESUS CHRIST, who is both *God* and *Man* in One Person, came, and Kept the *Law* of God, and then Offer'd up His *Life* to God, on the *Cross,* to make amends for our Sin; and that JESUS CHRIST invites *Them* as well as others, to *Look* to Him, and *Hope* in Him, for Everlasting Life; and that if they come to JESUS CHRIST, they shall be as Welcome to Him, as any People; Tho' He be the *King of Kings,* and *Lord of Lords,* yet He will cast a Kind Look upon Sorry *Slaves* and *Blacks* that Believe on Him, and will prepare a *Mansion* in *Heaven* for them.

Tell them; *That if they Serve God patiently and cheerfully in the Condition which he orders for them, their condition will very quickly be infinitely mended, in Eternal Happiness.*

Show them, That it is GOD who has caused them to be *Servants;* and that they Serve JESUS CHRIST, while they are at work for their *Masters,* if they are *Faithful* and *Honest Servants,* and if they do cheerfully what they do, because the Lord JESUS CHRIST has bid them to do it; and that, if they give themselves up to JESUS CHRIST, and keep always afraid of Sinning against Him, it won't be *Long* before they shall be in a most *Glorious Condition;* It can't be *Long* before they Dy, and *then!* they shall *Rest* from all their Labours, and all their Troubles, and they shall be Companions of *Angels* in the Glories of a *Paradise.*

Discourse with them, on these things, till their *Hearts burn within them.* In Discourse with them, at length put it unto them;

Well; Do you desire to Know the Only true God, and Jesus Christ, whom He hath sent?

Is it your Desire, that JESUS CHRIST may Save you from the Guilt of Sin, and the Curse of God?

Are you willing to put your self into the Gracious Hands of JESUS CHRIST, and be Ruled by all His Holy Laws?

Do you wish that the Blessed Spirit of the Lord, may Enter your Hearts, and make you Know and Love and Chuse the things that please Him?

Who can tell, but that while you are propounding such things to the poor *Negroes,* their conquered *Souls* may Consent unto them, and by that *Consent* open a *Well* that shall Spring up, & Spread out, unto *Everlasting Life?*

But in a Special manner Teach them to **Pray.** Teach them and Charge them every Day to fall down on their Knees before the Lord; with Supplications of this Importance.

Heavenly Father; Give me thy CHRIST; Give me thy SPIRIT; Pardon my Sins; Make me thy Servant; Bring me to Heaven. **Amen.**

Or, as they get further on, they may

Pray after this Manner.

O *Great GOD; Thou hast made me, and all the World.*

Make me truly Sorry for my Sinning against my Maker.

Let thy Glorious CHRIST Save me: and help me to Know, and to Take His Great Salvation.

Teach me to Serve Thee, O Lord. And make me a Blessing unto those that have me for their Servant.

Bring me to a part in Heaven among thy Children for ever more.

Amen.

1706

from Bonifacius. . . . With Humble Proposals . . . *to Do Good in the World*[1]

[Proposal concerning reforming societies]

Reforming Societies, or *Societies for the Supression of Disorders,* have begun to grow somewhat into fashion; and it is one of the best *omens* that the world has upon it. *Behold, how great a matter a little* of this heavenly *fire* may kindle! Five or six gentlemen in *London,* began with an heroic resolution, and association, to encounter the torrent of wickedness, which was carrying all before it in the nation. More were soon

[1]The complete title is *Bonifacius. An Essay upon the Good, that is to be Devised and Designed, by Those Who Desire to Answer the Great End of Life, and to Do Good while They Live.* This text was first published in 1710.

added unto them; and though they met with great opposition, from *wicked spirits,* and these *incarnate* as well as *invisible,* and some in *high places* too, yet they proceeded with a most honorable and invincible courage. Their *success,* if not proportionable to their *courage,* yet was far from *contemptible.* In the *punishments* inflicted on them who transgressed the laws of *good morality,* there were soon offered many thousands of *sacrifices,* unto the holiness of GOD. Hundreds of *houses* which were the *chambers* of Hell, and the *scandals* of earth, were soon extinguished. There was a remarkable check soon given to raging *profanity;* and the Lord's Day was not openly and horribly profaned as formerly. And among other *essays to do good,* they scattered thousands of *good books,* that had a tendency to reform the evil manners of the people. It was not long before this excellent example was followed in other parts of the *British* Empire. Virtuous men of diverse qualities and persuasions, became the members of the *societies:* persons high and low, Con[forming] and Noncon[forming],[2] united; the union became formidable to the Kingdom of Darkness. The report of the *societies* flew over the seas; the pattern was followed in other countries; men of wisdom in remote parts of *Europe* have made their joyful remark upon them, *that they cause unspeakable good, and annunciate a more illustrious state of the Church of God, which is to be expected,*

The repetition of these passages, is enough to make way for the Proposal:

That a fit number in a neighborhood, whose hearts God has touched with a *zeal to do good,* would combine into a *society,* to meet, when and where they shall agree, and consider that case, "What are the DISORDERS that we may see rising among us? And what may be done, either by ourselves immediately, or by others through our advice, to suppress those disorders?" That they would obtain if they can, the presence of a *minister* with them, and every time they meet, have a *prayer* wherein the glorious Lord shall be called upon, to bless the design, direct and prosper it. That they would also have a *justice of peace,* if it may be, to be a member of the Society. That they once in half a year choose two *stewards,* to dispatch the *business* and *messages* of the *Society,* and manage the *votes* in it; who shall nominate unto the *Society,* their successors, when their term is expired. That they would have a faithful *treasurer,* in whose hands their *stock of charity* may be deposited: and a *clerk,* to keep a convenient *record* of *transactions* and *purposes.* And, finally, that they do with as *modest* and *silent* a conduct as may be, carry on all their undertakings.

I will finish the PROPOSAL, by reciting the POINTS OF CONSIDERATION which the SOCIETIES may have read unto them from time to time at their meetings, with a due *pause* upon each of them, for anyone to offer what he please upon it.

I. Is there any REMARKABLE DISORDER in the place that requires our endeavor for the suppression of it? And in what good, fair, likely way may we endeavor it?

II. "Is there any PARTICULAR PERSON, whose *disorderly behaviors* may be so scandalous and so notorious, that we may do well to send unto the said person our charitable *admonitions?* Or, are there any *contending persons,* whom we should admonish, to quench their *contentions?*

[2]Members of the Church of England and other Protestants.

III. "Is there any *special service* to the interest of religion, which we may conveniently desire our MINISTERS, to take notice of?

IV. "Is there anything, which we may do well to mention and recommend unto the JUSTICES, for the further promoting of *good order?*

V. "Is there any sort of OFFICERS among us, to such a degree unmindful of their duty, that we may do well to mind them of it?

VI. "Can any further methods be devised, that *ignorance* and *wickedness* may be more chased from our people in general? And that HOUSEHOLD-PIETY in particular, may flourish among them?

VII. "Does there appear any instance of OPPRESSION or FRAUDULENCE, in the *dealings* of any sort of people, that may call for our essays, to get it rectified?

VIII. "Is there any matter to be humbly moved unto the LESISLATIVE POWER to be enacted into a LAW for public benefit?

IX. "Do we know of any person languishing under sad and sore AFFLICTION; and is there anything that we may do, for the succor of such an afflicted neighbor?

X. "Has any person any PROPOSAL to make, for our own further advantage and assistance, that we ourselves may be in a probable and regular capacity, to pursue the INTENTIONS before us?"

1710

John Williams 1664–1729

John Williams's life uniquely prepared him for writing *The Redeemed Captive Returning to Zion.* He lived among many of the most influential New England Puritans of the day, such as Samuel Danforth, Joseph Dudley, John Eliot, Increase Mather, Samuel Sewall, and John Wise. He was familiar with Indians employed on the farms and in domestic work as well as the converts of John Eliot, often called the "Apostle to the Indians." And he experienced years of threatened or actual warfare, involving the English and Dutch, the Indians, and the English and French. It is not surprising, then, that *The Redeemed Captive* is remarkable as captivity narrative, jeremiad, and account of the theological struggle between the French and the English during the French and Indian Wars.

Williams was the grandson of Robert Williams, who emigrated from Norwich to Roxbury in 1637, and the son of Samuel Williams, a shoemaker and large landholder, who became deacon and later Ruling Elder in the Roxbury church of John Eliot. He attended Roxbury Latin School; graduated from Harvard in 1683; became Congregational minister of Deerfield in 1686; and married Eunice Mather, niece of Increase Mather and stepdaughter of Solomon Stoddard, in 1687.

The sporadic skirmishes between Indians and settlers, even after King Philip's War and before the beginning of the Great War for Empire (also known as the French and Indian Wars), made Deerfield, in the Connecticut River Valley (with only Northfield closer to Canada) a potentially dangerous place to be. During King William's War, the village had built a palisade for defense and successfully repulsed a Canadian attack in 1694. In February, 1704, however, during Queen Anne's War, an attack by Hertel de Rouville and more than 300 French-Canadians and Abnakis and Caughnawaga Mohawks resulted in the destruction of the village. Many of the inhabitants were killed, including two of Williams's children, John Williams, Jr., six, and Jerusha Williams, six weeks. More than a hundred villagers—including Williams, his wife, and five of his children (Samuel, 15; Esther, 13; Stephen, 10; Eunice, 7; and Warham, 4)—were marched to Canada.

Williams's narrative describes the long march through the snow; the death of his wife, who, having given birth only a few weeks earlier, could not keep up with the prisoners and was killed by the Indians; the cruelties and kindnesses of the Indians; Williams's attempts to obtain news about his children, who had been separated from him; his efforts to serve members of his congregation who were scattered among Indian and French settlements; his purchase by the French and the Jesuit efforts to convert him; his correspondence with his son Samuel, who briefly converted to Catholicism; and Williams's return home after more than two years of bondage, with all of his children except Eunice, then ten, who preferred to remain with the Indians.

The narrative has long been recognized as one of the best New England captivity narratives. It is also clearly a jeremiad. John Williams suggests from the beginning of his "history" that the events he will describe show "the anger of God" toward his "professing people" and the patience of Christians who are suffering "the will of God in very trying public calamities!" Of at least equal significance, however, is the narrative's importance as history, both for an understanding of the relationship between the Indians, French, and English during the Great War for Empire and as an account of Jesuit efforts to convert the Puritans to Catholicism. It is often forgotten that Williams was a captive of the Indians for only eight weeks. From April 25, 1704, to May 16, 1706, he was a captive of the French, struggling against Jesuits, who, he recounts, used all means possible "to seduce poor souls" from their Puritan faith.

Although negotiations for Williams's return were begun by John Sheldon of Deerfield in 1704, final arrangements were made by Governor Joseph Dudley's son William, a fact acknowledged in Williams's Dedication of *The Redeemed Captive* to Governor Dudley. The final terms of the arrangement were that the notorious French pirate Baptiste be released in exchange for Williams and other New Englanders. In 1706, Williams returned to Deerfield; he later married his wife's cousin Abigal Allen Bissell and became involved in negotiations for release of English prisoners. Among his other writings are essays on matter, the earth, water, wind, fire, insects, fishes, birds, beasts, Mars, Mercury, and Vulcan.

Rosalie Murphy Baum
University of South Florida

PRIMARY WORKS

The Redeemed Captive Returning to Zion, 1707, facsimile, 1966; critical, modernized text, ed. Edward W. Clark, 1976.

SECONDARY WORKS

Stephen W. Williams, *A Biographical Memoir of the Rev. John Williams,* 1837; George Sheldon, *A History of Deerfield, Massachusetts,* 1895; George Sheldon, *Heredity and Early Environment of John Williams,* 1905; Richard Slotkin, *Regeneration Through Violence,* 1973; Richard Van Der Beets, *Held Captive by Indians: Selected Narratives 1642–1836,* 1973; James A. Levernier and Hennig Cohen, eds., *The Indians and Their Captives,* 1977; Alden T. Vaughan and Edward W. Clark, *Puritans Among the Indians: Accounts of Captivity and Redemption, 1676–1724,* 1981; Alden T. Vaughan, *Narratives of North American Indian Captivity: A Selective Bibliog-*

raphy, 1983; Richard Van Der Beets, *The Indian Captivity Narrative: An American Genre,* 1984; June Namias, *White Captives,* 1993; Kathryn Zabelle Derounian-Stodola and James A. Levernier, *The Indian Captivity Narrative 1550–1900,* 1993; Rosalie Murphy Baum, "John Williams's Captivity Narrative: A Consideration of Normative Ethnicity," in *A Mixed Race,* ed. Frank Shuffelton, 1993.

from The Redeemed Captive Returning to Zion[1]

[The Attack]

On the twenty-ninth of February 1704, not long before break of day, the enemy came in like a flood upon us, our watch being unfaithful: an evil, whose awful effects in a surprisal of our fort, should bespeak all watchmen to avoid, as they would not bring the charge of blood upon themselves. They came to my house in the beginning of the onset and, by their violent endeavors to break open doors and windows with axes and hatchets, awakened me out of sleep; on which I leaped out of bed, and running toward the door, perceived the enemy making their entrance into the house. I called to awaken two soldiers in the chamber and returned towards my bedside for my arms. The enemy immediately broke into the room, I judge to the number of twenty, with painted faces and hideous acclamations. I reached up my hands to the bedtester for my pistol, uttering a short petition to God for everlasting mercies for me and mine on the account of the merits of our glorified redeemer, expecting a present passage through the Valley of the Shadow of Death, saying in myself as Isaiah 38:10–11: "I said in the cutting off my days, 'I shall go to the gates of the grave. I am deprived of the residue of my years.' I said, 'I shall not see the Lord, even the Lord, in the land of the living. I shall behold man no more with the inhabitants of the world.'" Taking down my pistol, I cocked it and put it to the breast of the first Indian who came up, but my pistol missing fire, I was seized by three Indians who disarmed me and bound me naked, as I was in my shirt, and so I stood for near the space of an hour. Binding me, they told me they would carry me to Quebec. My pistol missing fire was an occasion of my life's being preserved, since which I have also found it profitable to be crossed in my own will. The judgment of God did not long slumber against one of the three which took me, who was a captain, for by sunrising he received a mortal shot from my neighbor's house, who opposed so great a number of French and Indians as three hundred and yet were no more than seven men in an ungarrisoned house.

I cannot relate the distressing care I had for my dear wife, who had lain-in but a few weeks before, and for my poor children, family, and Christian neighbors. The enemy fell to rifling the house and entered in great numbers into the house. I begged

[1]The complete title of Williams's narrative is *The Redeemed Captive Returning to Zion. A Faithful History of Remarkable Occurrences in the Captivity and the Deliverance of Mr. John Williams, Minister of the Gospel.* Zion is a city of God, the ideal nation envisaged by the Israelites.

of God to remember mercy in the midst of judgment, that He would so far restrain their wrath as to prevent their murdering of us, that we might have grace to glorify His name, whether in life or death, and, as I was able, committed our state to God. The enemies who entered the house were all of them Indians and Mohawks, insulted over me awhile, holding hatchets over my head threatening to burn all I had. But yet God beyond expectation made us in a great measure to be pitied, for though some were so cruel and barbarous as to take and carry to the door two of my children and murder them, as also a Negro woman, yet they gave me liberty to put on my clothes, keeping me bound with a cord on one arm, till I put on my clothes to the other, and then changing my cord, they let me dress myself and then pinioned me again. [They] gave liberty to my dear wife to dress herself and our children.

About sun an hour high we were all carried out of the house for a march and saw many of the houses of my neighbors in flames, perceiving the whole fort, one excepted, to be taken. Who can tell what sorrows pierced our souls when we saw ourselves carried away from God's sanctuary to go into a strange land exposed to so many trials, the journey being at least three hundred miles we were to travel, the snow up to the knees, and we never inured to such hardships and fatigues, the place we were to be carried to a popish country? . . .

[The Journey Northward]

After this we went up the mountain and saw the smoke of the fires in the town and beheld the awful desolations of our town, and, before we marched any farther, they killed a sucking child of the English. There were slain by the enemy of the inhabitants of our town to the number of thirty-eight besides nine of the neighboring towns. We traveled not far the first day; God made the heathen so to pity our children that, though they had several wounded persons of their own to carry upon their shoulders for thirty miles before they came to the river, yet they carried our children, incapable of traveling, upon their shoulders and in their arms.

When we came to our lodging-place the first night,[2] they dug away the snow and made some wigwams, cut down some of the small branches of spruce trees to lie down on, and gave the prisoners somewhat to eat, but we had but little appetite. I was pinioned and bound down that night, and so I was every night while I was with the army. Some of the enemy who brought drink with them from the town fell to drinking, and in their drunken fit they killed my Negro man, the only dead person I either saw at the town or on the way. In the night an Englishman made his escape; in the morning I was called for and ordered by the general[3] to tell the English that, if any more made their escape, they would burn the rest of the prisoners.

He that took me was unwilling to let me speak with any of the prisoners as we marched; but on the morning of the second day, he being appointed to guard the rear, I was put into the hands of my other master who permitted me to speak to my wife when I overtook her and to walk with her to help her in her journey. On the way

[2]Greenfield Meadows, five miles north of Deerfield.

[3]François Hertel de Rouville.

we discoursed of the happiness of them who had a right to a house not made with hands, eternal in the heavens and God for a father and a friend; as also that it was our reasonable duty quietly to submit to the will of God and to say the will of the Lord be done. My wife told me her strength of body began to fail and that I must expect to part with her, saying she hoped God would preserve my life and the lives of some, if not all of our children with us, and commended to me, under God, the care of them. She never spoke any discontented word as to what had befallen us, but with suitable expressions justified God in what had befallen us.

We soon made a halt in which time my chief surviving master came up, upon which I was put upon marching with the foremost, and so made to take my last farewell of my dear wife, the desire of my eyes, and companion in many mercies and afflictions. . . .

[The Jesuits at St. Francis Fort]

That night we arrived at the fort called St. Francis, where we found several poor children who had been taken from the Eastward the summer before, a sight very affecting, they being in habit very much like Indians and in manner very much symbolizing with them.[4] At this fort lived two Jesuits, one of which was made Superior of the Jesuits at Quebec. One of these Jesuits met me at the fort gate and asked me to go into the church and give God thanks for preserving my life; I told him I would do that in some other place. When the bell rang for evening prayers, he that took me bid me go, but I refused.

The Jesuits came to our wigwam and prayed a short prayer and invited me to sup with them and justified the Indians in what they did against us, rehearsing some things done by Major Walden[5] above thirty years ago, and how justly God retaliated them in the last war, and inveighed against us for beginning this war with the Indians. And [then they] said we had before the last winter, and in the winter, been very barbarous and cruel in burning and killing Indians. I told them that the Indians in a very perfidious manner had committed murders on many of our inhabitants after the signing articles of peace, and, as to what they spoke of cruelties, they were undoubtedly falsehoods, for I well knew the English were not approvers of inhumanity or barbarity towards enemies.

They said that an Englishman had killed one of St. Castin's relations, which occasioned this war;[6] for, say they, the nations in a general counsel had concluded not to engage in the war, on any side, till they themselves were first molested, and then all of them as one would engage against them that began a war with them; and that upon the killing of [St.] Castin's kinsman, a post was dispatched to Canada to advertise the Mohawks and Indians that the English had begun a war. On which they

[4]Taking on the symbols or trappings of Indian life, for example, dress, language, customs. For Williams, most disturbing would be the adopting of the symbols of Catholicism, such as wearing a cross, carrying a rosary, or praying before statues.

[5]Edward W. Clark speculates this may be Major Waldron of Dover, Maine.

[6]Baron Vincent de Saint Castin, former French army officer living in Canada; Queen Anne's War.

gathered up their forces, and the French joined with them to come down on the Eastern parts; and, when they came near New England, several of the Eastern Indians told them of the peace made with the English, and the satisfaction given them from the English for that murder. But the Mohawks told them it was now too late, for they were sent for and were now come and would fall on them if without their consent they made a peace with the English. [They] said also that a letter was shown them sent from the governor of Port Royal,[7] which he said was taken in an English ship, being a letter from the queen of England to our governor writing how she approved his designs to ensnare and deceitfully to seize on the Indians; so that being enraged from that letter and being forced as it were, they began the present war. I told them the letter was a lie forged by the French.

The next morning the bell rang for Mass. My master bid me to go to church. I refused. He threatened me and went away in a rage. At noon the Jesuits sent for me to dine with them, for I ate at their table all the time I was at the fort. And after dinner they told me the Indians would not allow of any of their captives staying in their wigwams while they were at church and were resolved by force and violence to bring us all to church if we would not go without. I told them it was highly unreasonable so to impose upon those who were of a contrary religion, and to force us to be present at such service as we abhorred was nothing becoming Christianity. They replied they were savages and would not hearken to reason but would have their wills; [they] said also [that] if they were in New England themselves, they would go into the churches to see their ways of worship.

I answered the case was far different, for there was nothing (themselves being the judges) as to matter or manner of worship but what was according to the word of God in our churches; and therefore it could not be an offense to any man's conscience. But among them there were idolatrous superstitions in worship; they said, "Come and see and offer us conviction of what is superstitious in [our] worship." To which I answered that I was not to do evil that good might come on it, and that forcing in matters of religion was hateful. They answered the Indians were resolved to have it so, and they could not pacify them without my coming; and they would engage they should offer no force or violence to cause any compliance with their ceremonies.

The next Mass my master bid me go to church. I objected; he arose and forcibly pulled me out by head and shoulders out of the wigwam to the church that was nigh the door. So I went in and sat down behind the door, and there saw a great confusion instead of gospel order. For one of the Jesuits was at the altar saying Mass in a tongue unknown to the savages, and the other between the altar and the door saying and singing prayers among the Indians at the same time saying over their Pater Nosters and Ave Marias by tale from their chaplets, or beads on a string. At our going out, we smiled at their devotion so managed, which was offensive to them, for they said we made a derision of their worship. When I was here, a certain savagess died; one of the Jesuits told me she was a very holy woman who had not committed one sin in twelve years.

After a day or two the Jesuits asked me what I thought of their way now [that] I saw it? I told them I thought Christ said of it as Mark 7:7–9: "Howbeit in vain do they worship me, teaching for doctrines the commandments of man. For laying aside the

[7]Nova Scotia.

commandment of God, ye hold the tradition of men as the washing of pots and cups and many such like things ye do. And he said unto them, 'Full well ye reject the commandment of God that ye may keep your own tradition.'" They told me they were not the commandments of men but apostolical traditions of equal authority with the holy Scriptures. And that after my death I would bewail my not praying to the Virgin Mary, and that I should find the want of intercession for me with her Son, judging me to Hell for asserting the Scriptures to be perfect rule of faith, and said I abounded in my own sense, entertaining explications contrary to the sense of the pope regularly sitting with a general council explaining Scripture and making articles of faith. I told them [that] it was my comfort that Christ was to be my judge and not they at the Great Day, and, as for their censuring and judging of me, I was not moved by it. . . .

My master took hold of my hand to force me to cross myself, but I struggled with him and would not suffer him to guide my hand; upon this he pulled off a crucifix from his own neck and bade me kiss it, but I refused once again. He told me he would dash out my brains with his hatchet if I refused. I told him I should sooner choose death than to sin against God; then he ran and caught up his hatchet and acted as though he would have dashed out my brains. Seeing I was not moved, he threw down his hatchet, saying he would first bite off all my nails if I still refused; I gave him my hand and told him I was ready to suffer. He set his teeth in my thumbnails and gave a grip with his teeth, and then said, "No good minister, no love God, as bad as the devil," and so left off.

I have reason to bless God who strengthened me to withstand; by this he was so discouraged as nevermore to meddle with me about my religion. I asked leave of the Jesuits to pray with those English of our town that were with me, but they absolutely refused to give us any permission to pray one with another and did what they could to prevent our having any discourse together. . . .

[At Montreal]

When I came to Montreal, which was eight weeks after my captivity, the Governor de Vaudreuil redeemed me out of the hands of the Indians, gave me good clothing, took me to his table, gave me the use of a very good chamber, and was in all respects relating to my outward man courteous and charitable to admiration. At my first entering into his house, he sent for my two children who were in the city that I might see them and promised to do what he could to get all my children and neighbors out of the hands of the savages. My change of diet after the difficulties of my journeys caused an alteration of my body; I was physicked, blooded, and very tenderly taken care of in my sickness. . . .

[At Chateau Richer]

Not many days after and a few days before Governor de Vaudreuil coming down, I was sent away fifteen miles down the river that I might not have opportunity of converse with the English. I was courteously treated by the French and the priest of that parish; they told me he was one of the most learned men in the country; he was a very ingenious man, zealous in their way but yet very familiar. I had many disputes with the priests who came there, and, when I used their own authors to confute some of their positions, my books borrowed of them were taken away from me, for they said I made an ill use of them. They, many of them having boasted of their unity in doctrine and profession, were loath I should show them from their own best approved authors as many different opinions as they could charge against us.

Here again a gentleman in the presence of the old bishop and a priest offered me his house and whole living with assurance of honor, wealth, and employment if I would embrace their ways. I told them I had an indignation of soul against such offers on such terms as parting with what was more valuable than all the world, alleging, "What is a man profited if he gain the whole world and lose his own soul? Or what shall a man give in exchange for his soul?"

I was sometimes told I might have all my children if I would comply and must never expect to have them on any other terms; I told them my children were dearer to me than all the world, but I would not deny Christ and his truths for the having of them with me; I would still put my trust in God who could perform all things for me.

I am persuaded that the priest of that parish where I [was] kept abhorred their sending down the heathen to commit outrages against the English, saying [that] it was more like committing murders than managing a war. In my confinement in this parish I had many undisturbed opportunities to be humbly imploring grace for ourselves, for soul and body, for His protecting presence with New England, and His disappointing the bloody designs of enemies, that God would be a little sanctuary to us in a Land of Captivity, and that our friends in New England might have grace to make a more thankful and fruitful improvement of means of grace than we had done, who by our neglects found ourselves out of God's sanctuary.

[Aid and Comfort from New England]

ON THE TWENTY-FIRST of October 1704, I received some letters from New England with an account that many of our neighbors escaped out of the desolations in the fort, and that my dear wife was recarried and decently buried. And that my eldest son who was absent in our desolation was sent to college[8] and provided for, which occasioned thanksgiving to God in the midst of afflictions and caused prayers even in Canada to be going daily up to heaven for a blessing upon benefactors showing such kindness to the desolate and afflicted.

The consideration of such crafty designs to ensnare young ones and to turn them from the simplicity of the gospel to Romish superstition was very exercising; sometimes they would tell me my children, sometimes my neighbors, were turned to be of their religion. Some made it their work to allure poor souls by flatteries and great promises, some threatened, some offered abusive carriages to such as refused to go to church and be present at Mass; for some they industriously contrived to get married among them. A priest drew up a compendium of the Romish Catholic faith and pretended to prove it by the Scriptures, telling the English that all they required was contained in the Scriptures, which they acknowledged to be the rule of faith and manners, but it was by Scriptures horribly perverted and abused. I could never come

[8] Eleazar Williams received his B.A. from Harvard in 1708.

to the sight of it, though I often earnestly entreated a copy of it, until I was aboard ship for our voyage for New England, but hearing of it I endeavored to possess the English with their danger of being cheated with such a pretense. I understood they would tell the English that I was turned that they might gain them to change their religion; these their endeavors to seduce to popery were very exercising to me.

And in my solitariness I drew up these following sorrowful, mournful considerations (though unused to and unskillful in poetry) yet in a plain style for the use of some of the captives who would sometimes make their secret visits to me, which at the desire of some of them are here made public.

Some Contemplations of the Poor and Desolate State of the Church at Deerfield

The sorrows of my heart enlarged are,
While I my present state with past compare,
I frequently unto God's house did go,
With Christian friends, his praises forth to show,
But now I solitary sit, both sigh and cry,
While my flock's misery think on do I.
Many, both old and young, were slain outright,
Some in a bitter season take their flight.
Some burned to death, and others stifled were,
The enemy no sex or age would spare.
The tender children with their parents sad
Are carried forth as captives, some unclad.
Some murdered in the way unburied left,
And some through famine were of life bereft.
After a tedious journey some are sold,
Some kept in heathen hands; all from Christ's fold
By popish rage and heathenish cruelty
Are banished. Yea, some compelled to be
Present at Mass. Young children parted are
From parents and such as instructors were.
Crafty designs are used by papists all
In ignorance of truth them to enthrall.
Some threatened are unless they comply
In heathen hands again be made to lie.
To some large promises are made if they
Will truths renounce and choose their popish way.
Oh Lord! mine eyes on Thee shall waiting be
Till Thou again turn our captivity.
Their Romish plots Thou canst confound, and save
This little flock, this mercy I do crave.
Save us from all our sins and yet again
Deliver us from them who truth disdain.
Lord! for Thy mercy sake thy covenant mind,
And in thy house again rest let us find.
So we thy praises forth will show and speak
Of all thy wondrous works, yea we will seek

The advancement of thy great and glorious name,
Thy rich and sovereign grace we will proclaim.

The hearts of some were ready to be discouraged and sink, saying [that] they were "out of sight and so out of mind." I endeavored to persuade them we were not forgotten, that undoubtedly many prayers were continually going up to heaven for us. Not long after came Capt. Livingston and Mr. Sheldon with letters from his excellency our governor to the governor of Canada about the exchange of prisoners, which gave a revival to many and raised expectations of a return. These visits from New England to Canada so often greatly strengthened many who were ready to faint and gave some check to the designs of the papists to gain proselytes.

But God's time of deliverance was not yet come; as to some particular persons their temptations and trials were increased, and some abused because they refused a compliance with their superstitions. A young woman of our town met with a new trial. For on a day a Frenchman came into the room where she was and showed her his beads and boasted of them, putting them near to her; she knocked them out of his hands on the floor, for which she was beaten and threatened with death and for some days imprisoned. I pleaded with God His overruling this first essay for the deliverance of some as a pledge of the rest being delivered in due time.

I improved Capt. de Beauville,[9] who had always been very friendly, to intercede with the governor for the return of my eldest daughter, and for his purchasing my son Stephen from the Indians at St. Francis Fort, and for liberty to go up and see my children and neighbors at Montreal. Divine Providence appeared to a moderating [of] my affliction in that five English persons of our town were permitted to return with Capt. Livingston, among whom went my eldest daughter.[10] And my son Stephen was redeemed and sent to live with me. He was almost quite naked and very poor; he had suffered much among the Indians. One of the Jesuits took upon him to come to the wigwam and whip him on some complaint that the squaws had made that he did not work enough for them.

As to my petition for going up to Montreal to see my children and neighbors, it was denied, as [was] my former desire of coming up to the city before Capt. Livingston's coming. God granted me favor as to two of my petitions, but yet brought me by His grace to be willing that He should glorify Himself in disposing of me and mine as He pleased and knew to be most for His glory. And almost always before any remarkable favor I was brought to lie down at the foot of God and made to be willing that God should govern the world so as might be most for His own honor and brought to resign all to His holy sovereignty. A frame of spirit when wrought in me by the grace of God giving the greatest content and satisfaction, and very often a forerunner of the mercy asked of God or a plain demonstration that the not obtaining my request was best for me. I had no small refreshing in having one of my children with me for four months. And the English were many of them strengthened with hopes that the treaty between the governments would issue in opening a door of escape for all.

[9]Capt. de Beauville negotiated exchanges of English captives held by the Indians (including Esther and Stephen Williams) for French prisoners held by the English.

[10]Esther.

In August Mr. Dudley and Capt. Vetch arrived, and great encouragements were given as to an exchange of all in the spring of the year; and some few again were sent home, among whom I obtained leave to send my son Stephen. Upon Mr. Dudley's and Capt. Vetch's petitioning, I was again permitted to go up to Quebec. But disputing with a [Récollet] Friar who said he was an Englishman sent from France to endeavor the conversion of the English at Quebec, who arrived at Canada while our gentlemen were there, I was by the priests' means ordered again to return to Chateau Richer, and no other reason given but because I discoursed with that priest and their fear I should prevent his success among the captives.

But God showed His dislike of such a persecuting spirit: for the very next day, which was September 20, Old Style, October 1, New Style,[11] the Seminary, a very famous building, was most of it burned down, occasioned by a joiner's letting a coal of fire drop down among the shavings. The chapel in the priests' garden and the great cross were burned down; the library of the priests burned up. This Seminary and another library had been burned but about three years before. The day after my first being sent away by the priests' means from Quebec, there was a thunderstorm and the lightning struck the Seminary in the very place where the fire now began.

A little before Mr. Dudley's arrival came a soldier into my landlord's house barefoot and barelegged, going on a pilgrimage to Saint Anne.[12] For, said he, "My captain, who died some years ago, appeared to me and told me he was in Purgatory, and told me I must go a pilgrimage to Saint Anne doing penance, and get a Mass said for him, and then he should be delivered." And many believed him and were much affected with it, came and told me of it to gain my credit of their devised Purgatory. The soldier told me [that] the priests had counseled him to undertake this pilgrimage. And I am apt to think [they] ordered his calling in at my lordlord's that I might see and speak with him. I laughed at the conceit that a soldier must be pitched upon to be sent on this errand, but they were much displeased and lamented my obstinacy in that I would not be reclaimed from a denial of Purgatory by such a "miraculous Providence."

As I was able, I spread the case before God, beseeching of him to disappoint them of their expectations to proselyte any of the captives by this stratagem, and by the goodness of God it was not very serviceable, for the soldier's conversation was such that several among the French themselves judged it to be a forgery. And though the captain spoken of was the governor's lady's brother, I never more heard any concernment or care to get him out of Purgatory.

One of the parish where I lived told me that on the twenty-second of July 1705, he was at Quebec at the [Récollet] Friars' Church on one of their feast days in honor of a great saint of their order and that at five o'clock Mass in the morning, near two hundred persons present, a great grey cat broke or pushed aside some glass, and entered into the church, and passed along it near the altar, and put out five or six candles that were burning, and that no one could tell which way the cat went out; and he thought it was the devil.

1707

[11]The new year opens with March 25 in the old or Julian calendar, January 1 in the new or Gregorian. In addition, in the eighteenth century there is an eleven-day difference between calendar dates.

[12]Mission on Île de Montreal.

A Selection of Seventeenth-Century Poetry

Despite the distance from London literary circles and the rigorous demands of colonial life, colonists read and wrote a great deal of poetry in seventeenth-century America during their spare moments. Heirs of the Renaissance, educated colonists, like their English contemporaries, read classical poets as well as the chief "moderns": Sidney, Jonson, Donne, Herbert, Quarles, and later, Milton and Dryden. Many colonists considered themselves heirs of the Reformation as well, and they cherished the poetry of the Bible, especially David's Psalms and Solomon's Song. Finally, British Americans were avid readers of each other's verse. Poems were circulated in manuscript, exchanged in letters, read aloud in families, copied into diaries and commonplace books, and sometimes published.

Considered the most stately and moving form of language, poetry offered a popular vehicle for commemorating important events in personal and public life. Such New World occasions as the death of a local political or religious leader, conflicts with the Native Americans, a bountiful harvest, or a crippling drought were addressed in adaptations of Old World poetic forms: the elegy, the epic, the ballad, the verse satire. Private lyrics commemorated personal and domestic events: spiritual episodes, courtship, family love, deliverance from illness, the death of a loved one. Whether public or private, poetry helped reveal the preordained order presumed to govern human lives—a goal especially important to settlers facing the illegibility of a strange new world. Poetic wit, defined far more broadly than today, offered a means of connecting the particular with the general, of discovering one's place on the cosmic and cultural map. For many New Englanders, that map was biblical and religious; in the more secular middle and southern colonies, it was often English, patriotic, and mercantile. Puns, conceits, emblems, anagrams, and acrostics served as verbal tools for confirming harmony beneath a chaotic surface. This baroque or metaphysical tendency, as much a habit of mind as a literary style, often joined seemingly disparate and even contradictory elements: classical mythology with biblical literalism, a sensitivity to nature with a celebration of commerce, a lament for societal corruption with extreme pride of place, verbal play with earnest piety, sensory imagery with otherworldly devotion. Such juxtapositions reflected post-Elizabethan verbal exuberance and an unremitting drive to make sense of things—especially to reconcile Old World culture with New World realities. Seeking to celebrate and internalize pre-existent truths rather than to create new truths, most poets wrote for specific purposes: to teach, to preach, to warn, to inspire, to console, and to entertain. To read their work is to rediscover an important early role of poetry in confirming cultural values and identity.

The era's major poets—Anne Bradstreet, Michael Wigglesworth, Edward Taylor, and Ebenezer Cook—appear elsewhere in the anthology. Poems can also be found in the selections from John Smith, Thomas Morton, Roger Williams, Cotton Mather, Samuel Sewall, and Sarah Kemble Knight. The poets gathered in this section, arranged by date of birth, further underscore the range and diversity of early Anglo-American poetry.

Jeffrey A. Hammond
St. Mary's College of Maryland

PRIMARY WORKS

Harrison T. Meserole, ed., *American Poetry of the Seventeenth Century,* 1968, 1985; Kenneth Silverman, ed., *Colonial American Poetry,* 1968; Pattie Cowell, ed., *Women Poets in Pre-Revolutionary America 1650–1775,* 1981.

SECONDARY WORKS

Harold S. Jantz, *The First Century of New England Verse,* 1944, 1966; J. A. Leo Lemay, *Men of Letters in Colonial Maryland,* 1972; William J. Scheick and JoElla Doggett, *Seventeenth-Century American Poetry: A Reference Guide,* 1977; Donald P. Wharton, *Richard Steere: Colonial Merchant Poet,* 1979; Catherine Rainwater and William J. Scheick, "Seventeenth-Century American Poetry: A Reference Guide Updated," *Resources for American Literary Study* 10, 1980, pp. 121–45; Peter White, *Benjamin Tompson, Colonial Bard,* 1980; Peter White, ed., *Puritan Poets and Poetics: Seventeenth-Century American Poetry in Theory and Practice,* 1985; William J. Scheick, "The Poetry of Colonial America," in *Columbia Literary History of the United States,* ed. Emory Elliott, 1988.

Edward Johnson 1599–1672

Edward Johnson was a militia captain, town clerk of Woburn (Massachusetts), printer of the 1648 Massachusetts Laws, surveyor, and historian. His most popular work, *A History of New England from the English Planting in the Yeere 1628, untill the Yeere 1652* (1653), is better known as *Wonder-Working Providence of Sion's Saviour in New England.* Interspersed in Johnson's *Wonder-Working Providence,* a history of God's support of the Puritan Church in New England, are many verse commemorations of people, places, and events that relate to Johnson's program of revealing God's triumphs amid the "chosen people" of New England.

Poem for Thomas Hooker[1]

Come, *Hooker,* come forth of thy native soile:
  Christ, I will run, sayes *Hooker,* thou hast set
My feet at large, here spend thy last dayes toile;
  Thy Rhetorick shall peoples affections whet.
Thy Golden Tongue, and Pen Christ caus'd to be
  The blazing of his golden truths profound,
Thou sorry worme its Christ wrought this in thee;
  What Christ hath wrought must needs be very sound.
Then looke on *Hookers* workes, they follow him
  To Grave, this worthy resteth there a while:
Die shall he not that hath Christs warrier bin;
  Much lesse Christs Truth, cleer'd by his peoples toile.
Thou Angell bright, by Christ for light now made,
  Throughout the World as seasoning salt to be,
Although in dust thy body mouldering fade;
  Thy Head's in Heaven, and hath a crown for thee.

1653

[1]Text is from H. T. Meserole, ed., *American Poetry of the Seventeenth Century.* Hooker (1586–1647), Puritan preacher and theologian, helped found Hartford, Connecticut.

John Saffin 1626–1710

Born in Devonshire, England, Saffin was brought to Scituate (Massachusetts) when he was about eight years old. He trained as a lawyer and became a leader in colonial affairs, in addition to amassing a large fortune from commercial ventures, including trading in slaves. Saffin supported slavery; he argued in prose and verse that manumission was impractical and potentially dangerous. His refusal to assist his slave Adam brought him public distress when Samuel Sewall wrote the pamphlet *The Selling of Joseph* (1700), denouncing as unChristian the keeping of slaves. Saffin's poems appear primarily in his commonplace book (a private journal). He was well-known as a versifier, and he wrote in the standard genres of his day—elegies, epitaphs, love poems, verse letters, and occasional pieces.

Acrostic on Mrs. Winifret Griffin[1]

*W*ithin the casket of thy coelic[2] breast,
*I*nclosed is virtue like the phoenix nest.
*N*or can the merits of a noble mind,
*I*nvested be, with one more true and kind.
*F*air Venus, and Minerva,[3] both combine:
*R*esplendently, to make their graces thine:
*E*ach in her proper station; Wit, and Beauty
*T*ake thee for mistress out of bounden duty.

*G*reat are Jove's favors on thee passing sense,
*R*are masterpiece of Nature's excellence.
*I*uno[4] confer on thee out of her treasure,
*F*resh new supplies of riches, honor, pleasure:
*F*irm to abide, may Hymen[5] give consent,
*I*n nuptial state, to crown thee with content,
*N*e'er may those joys abate, and then endeavor
In your own Cupidons[6] to live forever.

1928

[1]Text is adapted from C. Hazard, ed., *John Saffin, His Book.*
[2]Heavenly.
[3]Roman goddesses of love and wisdom.
[4]Juno, queen of the gods and wife of Jove (Jupiter).
[5]Roman god of marriage.
[6]Little cupids; a reference to Griffin's children.

George Alsop 1636?–1673?

Alsop was baptized at St. Martin in the Fields in June, 1636. Despite his wide reading, evident in his book, *A Character of the Province of Mary-Land* (1666), Alsop was probably born into humble circumstances. As a Royalist (a loyal follower of King Charles I), Alsop seems to have feared unhappy political recriminations when Oliver Cromwell rose to power, so he signed an indenture that brought him to Maryland in 1658. He spent four years of his indenture near Baltimore before returning to England, where he wrote *A Character,* a lively promotional tract that blended pastoral and commercial themes.

Trafique is Earth's Great Atlas[1]

Trafique[2] is Earth's great *Atlas,* that supports
The pay of Armies, and the height of Courts,
And makes Mechanicks[3] live, that else would die
Meer starving Martyrs to their penury:[4]
None but the Merchant of this thing can boast,
He, like the Bee, comes loaden from each Coast,
And to all Kingdoms, as within a Hive,
Stows up those Riches that doth make them thrive:
Be thrifty, *Mary-Land,* keep what thou hast in store,
And each years Trafique to thy self get more.

1666

Sarah Whipple Goodhue 1641–1681

Of the poets collected in this group, Sarah Whipple Goodhue was the first native-born writer. She was born into a middle-class family of merchants; she married Joseph Goodhue (1639–1697), who was to become a leader of Ipswich, her native town. Her volume, *The Copy of a Valedictory* (1681), a religious and monitory book written in anticipation of her death, was published after she died giving birth to twins.

[1]Text is from H. T. Meserole, ed., *American Poetry of the Seventeenth Century.*
[2]Commerce, trade.
[3]Tradesmen, laborers.
[4]Poverty.

Lines to Her Family[1]

My first, as thy name is Joseph, labor so in knowledge to increase,
As to be freed from the guilt of thy sins, and enjoy eternal peace.

Mary, labor so to be arrayed with the hidden man of the heart,
That with Mary thou mayst find thou hast chosen the better part.[2]

William, thou hast that name for thy grandfather's sake,
Labor so to tread in his steps, as over sin conquest thou mayst make.

Sarah, Sarah's daughter thou shalt be, if thou continuest in doing well,
Labor so in holiness among the daughters to walk, as that thou may
excel.
So my children all, if I must be gone, I with tears bid you all farewell.
The Lord bless you all.

Now, dear husband, I can do no less than turn unto thee,
And if I could, I would naturally mourn with thee:

. . .

O dear heart, if I must leave thee and thine here behind,
Of my natural affection here is my heart and hand.

1681

Benjamin Tompson 1642–1714

Among the first native-born Anglo-American poets, Tompson was born into a family of zealous Puritans. He became a schoolmaster for several towns around Boston, his most famous pupil being Cotton Mather. Tompson's fame as a poet arose from his volume *New Englands Crisis* (1676) and its revision *New Englands Tears* (London, 1676), a verse epic treating the war with the Algonquin Confederation during the 1670s as a test of the faith of the elect in New England.

[1]Text is from P. Cowell, ed., *Women Poets in Pre-Revolutionary America.*

[2]See Romans 7:22: "For I delight in the law of God after the inward man." Martha and Mary represented the active and the contemplative life (Luke 10:41–42).

Chelmsfords *Fate*[1]

Ere famous *Winthrops* bones are laid to rest
The pagans *Chelmsford* with sad flames arrest,[2]
Making an artificial day of night
By that plantations formidable light.
Here's midnight shrieks and Soul-amazing moanes,
Enough to melt the very marble stones:
Fire-brands and bullets, darts and deaths and wounds
Confusive outcryes every where resounds:
The natives shooting with the mixed cryes,
With all the crueltyes the foes devise
Might fill a volume, but I leave a space
For mercyes still successive in there place
Not doubting but the foes have done their worst,
And shall by heaven suddenly be curst.

Let this dear Lord the sad Conclusion be
Of poor New-Englands *dismal tragedy.*
Let not the glory of thy former work
Blasphemed be by pagan Jew or Turk:
But in its funeral ashes write thy Name
So fair all Nations may expound the same:
Out of her ashes let a Phoenix rise
That may outshine the first and be more wise.

1676

Richard Steere 1643?–1721

Steere was born to a clothworker at Chertsey, Surrey (about twenty miles north of London), and educated at a local singing school and then at a Latin grammar school. Apprenticed to the cordwainer's trade in London, Steere became a staunch Whig and avoided Charles II's suppression of Whigs by taking ship to New England in 1683. He settled in New London, Connecticut, where he became a merchant, but soon moved to Southold, Long Island, to protest local persecution of Quakers. His major work, *The Daniel Catcher* (1713), was an anti-Catholic answer to John Dryden's *Absalom and Achitophel.* Steere's verse has an unusual range and quality among early Anglo-American poets.

[1]Text is from H. T. Meserole, ed., *American Poetry of the Seventeenth Century.*

[2]Chelmsford, Massachusetts, was then in the colony of Connecticut. Connecticut Governor John Winthrop, Jr., died in 1676.

On a Sea-Storm nigh the Coast[1]

All round the Horizon black Clouds appear;
A Storm is near:
Darkness Eclipseth the Sereener Sky,
The Winds are high,
Making the Surface of the Ocean Show
Like mountains Lofty, and like Vallies Low.

The weighty Seas are rowled from the Deeps
In mighty heaps,
And from the Rocks Foundations do arise
To Kiss the Skies
Wave after Wave in Hills each other Crowds,
As if the Deeps resolv'd to Storm the Clouds.

How did the Surging Billows Fome and Rore
Against the Shore
Threatning to bring the Land under their power
And it Devour:
Those Liquid Mountains on the Clifts were hurld
As to a Chaos they would shake the World.

The Earth did Interpose the Prince of Light,
'Twas Sable night:
All Darkness was but when the Lightnings fly
And Light the Sky,
Night, Thunder, Lightning, Rain, and *raging* Wind,
To make a Storm had all their forces joyn'd.

c. 1700

Anna Tompson Hayden 1648–1720

Anna Tompson Hayden was half-sister to Benjamin Tompson and Joseph Tompson, in whose journal all of her known poems have been preserved. She married Ebenezer Hayden of Boston and had one child, born in 1679. Hayden's two extant poems are elegiac; they reveal an acceptance of death in humble accord with God's plan.

[1]Text is from H. T. Meserole, ed., *American Poetry of the Seventeenth Century.*

Upon the Death of Elizabeth Tompson[1]

A lovely flow'r cropt in its prime
By Death's cold fatal hand;
A warning here is left for all
Ready prepar'd to stand.
For none can tell who shall be next,
Yet all may it expect;
Then surely it concerneth all,
Their time not to neglect.
How many awful warnings that
Before us oft are set,
That as a flaming sword to mind
Our youth hath often met,
To stop them in their course
And mind them of their end,
To make them to consider
Whither their ways to tend.
We see one suddenly taken hence
That might have lived as long
For the few years she'd lived here
As any she lived among.
Her harmless blameless life
Will stand for her defence,
And be an honor to her name
Now she is gone from hence.

A Supplement

Charity bids us hope that she'll among those virgins be,
When Christ shall come to reign,[2]
Whom he will own among the wise,
And for his entertain.

1712

[1]Text is from P. Cowell, ed., *Women Poets in Pre-Revolutionary America.* The complete title of the poem in manuscript in Joseph Tompson's copybook is: "Upon the Death of that Desirable Young Virgin, Elizabeth Tompson, Daughter of Joseph and Mary Tompson of Bilerika, Who Deceased in Boston Out of the House of Mr. Legg, 24 August, 1712, Aged 22 Years."

[2]A reference to the parable of the wise virgins, whose lamps were trimmed and filled with oil in preparation for the bridegroom (Matt. 25:1–13).

Elizabeth Sowle Bradford 1663?–1731

Elizabeth Bradford was born to a Quaker printer in London, and she married her father's apprentice, William Bradford, in 1685, the same year the couple set off for Philadelphia. She eventually settled with William in New York, where they established a thriving printing business. When they printed an edition of *War with the Devil* (1707) by Baptist minister Benjamin Keach, both Bradfords contributed poems to the volume. Elizabeth Bradford's poem follows.

To the Reader, in Vindication of this Book[1]

One or two lines to thee I'll here commend,
This honest poem to defend
From calumny, because at this day,
All poetry there's many do gain-say,
And very much condemn, as if the same
Did worthily deserve reproach and blame.
If any book in verse, they chance to spy,
Away profane, they presently do cry:
But though this kind of writing some dispraise,
Sith men so captious are in these our days,
Yet I dare say, how e'er the scruple rose,
Verse hath express'd as secret things as prose.
Though some there be that poetry abuse,
Must we therefore, not the same method use?
Yea, sure, for of my conscience 'tis the best,
And doth deserve more honor than the rest.
For 'tis no humane knowledge gain'd by art,
But rather 'tis inspir'd into the heart
By divine means; for true divinity
Hath with this science great affinity:
Though some through ignorance, do it oppose,
Many do it esteem, far more than prose:
And find also that unto them it brings
Content, and hath been the delight of kings.
David, although a king, yet was a poet,
And Solomon, also, the Scriptures show it.
Then what if for all this some should abuse it?
I'm apt to think that angels do embrace it,
And though God giv't here but in part to some,
Saints shall hav't perfect in the world to come.[2]

1707

[1]Text is from P. Cowell, ed., *Women Poets in Pre-Revolutionary America.*

[2]The Book of Revelation foretold that saints in heaven would sing "a new song before the throne" (Rev. 14:3).

Bathsheba Bowers 1672?–1718

Bowers was born in Charlestown (Massachusetts) into a family of Quakers that was persecuted by Puritans in the area. While she was still young, Bowers was sent with three of her sisters to Philadelphia, where Quakers were welcomed. As an adult, Bowers led a reclusive life, preferring not to marry. She practiced vegetarianism and conducted religious debates at her home, which she called "Bathsheba's Bower." When she was about thirty-five, she moved to South Carolina, where she died in 1718. Her spiritual autobiography, *An Alarm Sounded to Prepare . . . the World to Meet the Lord* (1709), was published in New York, probably by William Bradford (see Elizabeth Sowle Bradford).

Lines from the Spiritual Autobiography[1]

Who can know Heaven's blest continent,
Till they, with me,
Be made to set,
That 'tis in Love's sweet cement.
Or who can tell the depth of Hell,
Whilst they, as I,
Be made to cry,
Where raging [horrors?] dwell.

1709

Roger Wolcott 1679–1767

Wolcott began what would become a very public life in humble circumstances. After being trained by his mother to read and write, he was apprenticed to a clothier. When he was twenty, he left that business and set up his own successful trade, but after his marriage, Wolcott moved to South Windsor, Connecticut, to enter farming. He became a selectman at Windsor in 1707 and thereafter developed a very successful public life as town magistrate, lawyer, and military leader, eventually becoming governor of Connecticut in 1750. His volume of poems, *Poetical Meditations, Being the Improvement of Some Vacant Hours,* was published in 1725; it seems to have been the first book of poetry published in Connecticut.

[1]Text is from P. Cowell, ed., *Women Poets in Pre-Revolutionary America.*

Psalm 64:6—"The heart is deep"[1]

He that can trace a ship making her way
Amidst the threatening surges on the sea,
Or track a tow'ring eagle in the air,
Or on a rock find the impressions there
Made by a serpent's footsteps. Who surveys
The subtle intrigues that a young man lays
In his sly courtship of an harmless maid,
Whereby his wanton amours are conveyed
Into her breast—'tis he alone that can
Find out cursed policies of man.

1725

Mary French 1687?–?

Mary French has survived in literary history because her 104-line poem to her sister, upon a captivity among Indians, was printed by Cotton Mather in his volume, *Good Fetch'd Out of Evil* (Boston, 1706). French had been captured at age sixteen during a 1703 Indian raid on Deerfield, Massachusetts. Forbidden to meet together for worship in their own Puritan faith, the captives were evidently pushed by their captors to accept Catholicism.

from A Poem Written by a Captive Damsel[1]

Dear sister, Jesus does you call
    To walk on in his ways.
I pray make no delay at all,
    Now in your youthful days.
O turn to him, who has you made,
    While in your tender years,
For as the withering grass we fade,
    Which never more appears.
But if that God should you afford
    A longer life to live,

[1]Text is adapted from H. T. Meserole, ed., *American Poetry of the Seventeenth Century*.

[1]Text is from P. Cowell, *Women Poets in Pre-Revolutionary America.* The complete title of the poem was "A Poem Written By a Captive Damsel, About Sixteen or Seventeen Years of Age, Who Being [Told?] That Her Younger Sister at a Distance From Her [Would?] Be Led Away by the Popish [Demons?], Address'd Her in these Lines."

Remember that unto the Lord
The praises you do give.

. . .

That earthly things are fading flow'rs
We by experience see;
And of our years and days and hours
We as observers be.
Of all degrees, and every age,
Among the dead we find;
Many there fell by bloody rage,
When we were left behind.
Let us be silent then this day
Under our smarting rod.
Let us with patience meekly say,
It is the will of God.
Of friends and parents we're bereaved,
Distresst and left alone;
Lord, we thy spirit oft have grieved:
And now as doves we moan.

. . .

Dear sister, bear me in your mind;
Learn these few lines by heart;
Alas, an aching heart I find,
Since we're so long to part.
But to the care of God on high
Our cause we will commend.
For your soul sake these lines now I
Your loving sister send.

1706

Tales of Incorporation, Resistance, and Reconquest in New Spain

The purpose of European missionaries, whether Catholic or Protestant, was the religious conversion of Native Americans. That their proselytizing directly related to the success of colonization was obvious to civil authorities like Menéndez de Avilés, who pleaded for more priests. The primary obstacle was Native Americans' resistance to new beliefs that required their abandoning their own belief systems. The Virgin of Guadalupe can be seen as a syncretic figure that bridged the cultures instead of serving their opposition. She represents a merging of old and new world religions as symbolized by the Catholic Virgin Mary and the Nahuatl Tonantzin. Her image could mediate between the races. Yet despite the potential mediative function of the Virgin of Guadalupe, native resistance continued, and it erupted into numerous rebellions over the centuries, revolts often waged under the banner of the Virgin of Guadalupe.

English settlements, especially in the Northeast, tended to drive Native Americans out of their ancestral homelands. Spanish settlements were located—by order of King Philip II of Spain in the Royal Ordinances of 1573—alongside, but not in place of, native settlements. This did not prevent, however, attempts by missionaries to eradicate Native Americans' beliefs and rituals (which the missionaries considered "pagan" or demonic). In New Mexico, Franciscan friars burned Pueblo religious symbols and places of worship. Yet, just as Native Americans managed to keep their own farms going until the seventeenth century—despite their forced labor for both civil and religious authorities—many of them continued to practice their religions in secret. The figure of the missionary, who persistently sought to convert the native population, became the object of violent retaliation, as the Hopi narrative and Governor Otermín's letter amply demonstrate.

A number of factors converged from the 1640s on to make the lives of Southwest Pueblo peoples increasingly intolerable. Friars competed with civil officials for Native Americans' loyalty and work, thus enslaving the natives and confusing them with a sense of divided loyalties. While the Church upheld the equality of those who had converted to Catholicism, in practice such supposed equalization competed with the Spaniards' need for a free labor force and their sense of racial superiority. Severe droughts in 1640 and through the 1660s caused crop failure and famine, especially among the Pueblos, whose own crops suffered because their toils and their water went to support the farms of governors and missionaries. In addition, nearby Apaches, interpreting the mere submission of the Pueblo peoples as willing compliance with Spanish dominion, attacked them, raiding and burning villages and churches. Finally, due to Apache attacks, starvation, and flight from the troubled homeland, the Pueblo populations were diminishing. Many pueblos were abandoned, and survivors consolidated in the larger villages among the Jemez, Zunis, and other groups.

Conditions continued to worsen until August 1680, when Popé, a Tewa whom the Pueblos called Tío Pepe and a religious leader from San Juan Pueblo (located along the Rio Grande), sent word that the Pueblos should revolt against the Spanish on August 10–11, 1680. Although the Pueblo peoples differed in culture and interests, they were nonetheless ready to unite. Tewa, Tiwa, Keres, Hopi, and Zuni Pueblo peoples joined forces over several days; pueblo after pueblo rebelled—Taos (where Popé centered his operations), San Juan, Tesuque, Santa Cruz, Santa Clara, Picuris, Pecos, Galisteo, and others. By the end of the initial part of the rebellion, twenty-one missionaries and 400 colonists were killed, and Santa Fe (the location of the governor's *villa*) was under siege for nine days. Governor Antonio de Otermín willingly accepted the blame for what he called the "lamentable tragedy, such as never before happened in the world," yet clearly the misguided (or unguided) actions of Spanish colonists for over half a century had led to the Revolt. On August 21, the surviving Spanish, accompanied by some loyal followers like those from the Senecú or Socorro pueblos, left Santa Fe, heading toward El Paso in a long march during which they saw many dead countrymen. In El Paso the colonists found refuge, while their native allies, following the colonial pattern, founded new pueblos nearby, named after the ones from which they had fled. There they awaited the outcome of the campaign to retake the Kingdom of New Mexico.

Meanwhile, back in the north, after the rebellion, Popé consolidated his forces and imposed strict Native American rules. Any people who showed the slightest deviation from the Indian way—even if they were merely employing useful Spanish tools—were summarily punished, some executed. The alliance slowly crumbled under Popé's strict regime, controlled from the Spanish colonists' places of power in Santa Fe. The alliance dissolved with Popé's death several years after the Revolt, when continued drought and Apache raids weakened their native unity.

The first pueblo to fall again into Spanish dominion was Zía Pueblo, which offered no real resistance to the Spanish troops marching northward from El Paso in 1689. Spanish officials continued to make claim after claim of dominion, until troops under the new governor Don Diego de Vargas occupied Santa Fe in 1692. Although Vargas faced a continued power struggle with the Pueblo peoples for nearly the next decade, the Spanish, with the aid of friendly native villages that sought Spanish protection from the occasionally marauding Apaches and Navajos, were victorious.

The most serious Native American revolt against Spanish occupation came to an end with Vargas's reconquest. However, the threat of another rebellion had the effect of forcing some reforms. While the church would continue its efforts to convert the Indians, the missionaries no longer were given free reign. Vargas's policy was to pardon those Indians who would pledge to cooperate. The surge of new missionary efforts would focus on Texas and California in the next century.

Carla Mulford
Pennsylvania State University

Juan Bruce-Novoa
University of California at Irvine

History of the Miraculous Apparition of the Virgin of Guadalupe in 1531

Tradition has it that a miraculous apparition of the Virgin Mary took place near Mexico City in 1531, as the following text relates. The Virgin of Guadalupe is a syncretic religious figure. She represents a particular form of the Virgin Mary, mother of Jesus Christ, and as such she mediates between humans and God the Father. She is the symbolic mother of all Catholics. At the same time, her brown skin and Indian features make her a Native American Virgin Mother. In addition, she appeared to a poor Indian. Finally, her apparition was on a sacred site traditionally associated with a female Indian god of fertility, Tonantzin. For centuries she has been the image of miscegenation incarnate, the blending of Spanish and Indian worlds.

In the eighteenth century, when American independence movements were stirring throughout the colonies, Mexican nationalists turned the Virgin of Guadalupe into an image of cultural and political nationalism. Her image became the standard of a war of independence, and the miscegenation of Spanish and Indian was deemphasized in favor of an image of New World hybridity, the *mestizo.* While she competes regionally with other forms of the Virgin, like Our Lady of Conquest in New Mexico or La Virgin de San Juan in Texas, Guadalupe has become a central icon of Mexican American culture. Her image appears in statues on home altars, painted in murals on the side of buildings, tattooed on biceps and etched into windows of lowrider, customized automobiles. Her image serves many different functions, from religious to political, turning up in churches, picket lines, and Chicano literature. She is generally associated with the struggle for civil rights, although her symbol cannot be divorced from traditional values of Catholicism, women, and the family.

Juan Bruce-Novoa
University of California at Irvine

PRIMARY WORK

Donald Demarest and Coley Taylor, eds., *The Dark Virgin: The Book of Our Lady of Guadalupe,* 1956.

SECONDARY WORKS

Eric Wolf, "The Virgin of Guadelupe: A Mexican National Symbol," *Journal of American Folklore,* 71 (1958): pp. 34–39; Richard Dorson, "Foreword," *Folktales of Mexico,* ed. & trans. Americo Paredes, 1970; Ramón Gutiérrez, *When Jesus Came, the Corn Mother Went Away,* 1991.

History of the Miraculous Apparition of the Virgin of Guadalupe in 1531[1]

Herein is told, in all truth, how by a great miracle the illustrious Virgin, Blessed Mary, Mother of God, Our Lady, appeared anew, in the place known as Tepeyacac.

She appeared first to an Indian named Juan Diego; and later her divine Image appeared in the presence of the first Bishop of Mexico, Don Fray Juan de Zumárraga; also there are told various miracles which have been done. It was ten years after the beginning of bringing water from the mountain of Mexico, when the arrow and the shield had been put away, when in all parts of the country there was tranquillity which was beginning to show its light, and faith and knowledge of Him was being taught through Whose favor we have our being, Who is the only true God.

In the year 1531, early in the month of December, it happened that an humble Indian, called Juan Diego, whose dwelling, it is said, was in Quahutítlan, although for divine worship he pertained to Tlatilolco, one Saturday very early in the morning, while he was on his way to divine worship according to his custom, when he had arrived near the top of the hill called Tepeyacac, as it was near dawn, he heard above the hill a singing like that when many choice birds sing together, their voices resounding as if echoing throughout the hills; he was greatly rejoiced; their song gave him rapture exceeding that of the bell-bird and other rare birds of song.

Juan Diego stopped to wonder and said to himself: *Is it I who have this good fortune to hear what I hear? Or am I perhaps only dreaming? Where am I? Perhaps this is the place the ancients, our forefathers, used to tell about—our grandfathers—the flowery land, the fruitful land? Is it perchance the earthly paradise?*

And while he was looking towards the hilltop, facing the east, from which came the celestial song, suddenly the singing stopped and he heard someone calling as if from the top of the hill, saying: *Juan.* Juan Diego did not dare to go there where he was being called; he did not move, perhaps in some way marvelling; yet he was filled with great joy and delight, and then, presently, he began to climb to the summit where he was called.

And, when he was nearing it, on the top of the peak he saw a lady who was standing there who had called him from a distance, and, having come into her presence, he was struck with wonder at the radiance of her exceeding great beauty, her garments shining like the sun; and the stones of the hill, and the caves, reflecting the brightness of her light were like precious gold; and he saw how the rainbow clothed the land so that the cactus and other things that grew there seemed like celestial plants, their leaves and thorns shining like gold in her presence. He made obeisance and heard her voice, her words, which rejoiced him utterly when she asked, very tenderly, as if she loved him:

[1]The original version of this text was published in Náhuatl, the language of the Aztecs, by Bachiller Luis Lazo de Vega, Chaplain of the Sanctuary of Our Lady of Guadalupe, in 1649, over a century after the event. The text is believed to be the work of Antonio Valeriano, a contemporary of Juan Diego and Bishop Zumárraga. The story of the Virgin's appearance is essentially an oral tradition, however, and to this day it is maintained as such among Mexican-Americans.

Listen, xocoyote[2] *mio, Juan, where are you going?*

And he replied: *My Holy One, my Lady, my Damsel, I am on my way to your house at Mexico-Tlatilulco; I go in pursuit of the holy things which our priests teach us.*

Whereupon She told him, and made him aware of her divine will, saying: *You must know, and be very certain in your heart, my son, that I am truly the eternal Virgin, holy Mother of the True God, through Whose favor we live, the Creator, Lord of Heaven, and the Lord of the Earth. I very much desire that they build me a church here, so that in it I may show and may make known and give all my love, my mercy and my help and my protection—I am in truth your merciful mother—to you and to all the other people dear to me who call upon me, who search for me, who confide in me; here I will hear their sorrow, their words, so that I may make perfect and cure their illnesses, their labors, and their calamities. And so that my intention may be made known, and my mercy, go now to the episcopal palace of the Bishop of Mexico and tell him that I send you to tell him how much I desire to have a church built here, and tell him very well all that you have seen and all that you have heard; and be sure in your heart that I will pay you with glory and you will deserve much that I will repay you for your weariness, your work, which you will bear diligently doing what I send you to do. Now hear my words, my dear son, and go and do everything carefully and quickly.*

Then he humbled himself before her and said: *My Holy One, my Lady, I will go now and fulfill your commandment.*

And straightway he went down to accomplish that with which he was charged, and took the road that leads straight to Mexico.

And when he had arrived within the city, he went at once to the episcopal palace of the Lord Bishop, who was the first [Bishop] to come, whose name was Don Fray Juan de Zumárraga, a religious of St. Francis. And having arrived there, he made haste to ask to see the Lord Bishop, asking his servants to give notice of him. After a good while they came to call him, and the Bishop advised them that he should come in; and when he had come into his presence, he knelt and made obeisance, and then after this he related the words of the Queen of Heaven, and told besides all that he had seen and all that he had heard. And [the Bishop] having heard all his words and the commandment as if he were not perfectly persuaded, said in response:

My son, come again another time when we can be more leisurely; and I will hear more from you about the origin of this; I will look into this about which you have come, your will, your desire.

And he departed with much sorrow because he had not been able to convince him of the truth of his mission.

Thereupon he returned that same day and went straightway to the hill where he had seen the Queen of Heaven, who was even then standing there where he had first seen Her, waiting for him, and he, having seen Her, made obeisance, kneeling upon the ground, and said:

My Holy One, most noble of persons, My Lady, my Xocoyota, my Damsel, I went there where You sent me; although it was most difficult to enter the house of the Lord

[2]*Xocoyote:* This Náhuatl word is variously translated into Spanish as if it were "my little son" or "my dear son." *Xocoyota* is the form for "daughter."

Bishop, I saw him at last, and in his presence I gave him your message in the way You instructed me; he received me very courteously, and listened with attention; but he answered as if he could not be certain and did not believe; he told me: Come again another time when we can be at leisure, and I will hear you from beginning to end; I will look into that about which you come, what it is you want and ask me for. He seemed to me, when he answered, to be thinking perhaps that the church You desire to have made here was perchance not Your will, but a fancy of mine. I pray You, my Holy One, my Lady, my Daughter, that any one of the noble lords who are well known, reverenced and respected be the one to undertake this so that Your words will be believed. For it is true that I am only a poor man; I am not worthy of being there where You send me; pardon me, my Xocoyota, I do not wish to make your noble heart sad; I do not want to fall into your displeasure.

Then the always noble Virgin answered him, saying: *Hear me, my son, it is true that I do not lack for servants or ambassadors to whom I could entrust my message so that my will could be verified, but it is important that you speak for me in this matter, weary as you are; in your hands you have the means of verifying, of making plain my desire, my will; I pray you, my xocoyote, and advise you with much care, that you go again tomorrow to see the Bishop and represent me; give him an understanding of my desire, my will, that he build the church that I ask; and tell him once again that it is the eternal Virgin, Holy Mary, the Mother of God, who sends you to him.*

And Juan Diego answered her, saying: *Queen of Heaven, my Holy One, my Damsel, do not trouble your heart, for I will go with all my heart and make plain Your voice, Your words. It is not because I did not want to go, or because the road is stony, but only because perhaps I would not be heard, and if I were heard I would not be believed. I will go and do your bidding and tomorrow in the afternoon about sunset I will return to give the answer to your words the Lord Bishop will make; and now I leave You, my Xocoyota, my Damsel, my Lady; meanwhile, rest You.*

With this, he went to his house to rest. The next day being Sunday, he left his house in the morning and went straightway to Tlatilulco, to attend Mass and the sermon. Then, being determined to see the Bishop, when Mass and the sermon were finished, at ten o'clock, with all the other Indians he came out of the church; but Juan Diego left them and went to the palace of the Lord Bishop. And having arrived there, he spared no effort in order to see him and when, after great difficulty, he did see him again, he fell to his knees and implored him to the point of weeping, much moved, in an effort to make plain the words of the Queen of Heaven, and that the message and the will of the most resplendent Virgin would be believed; that the church be built as She asked, where She wished it.

But the Lord Bishop asked Juan Diego many things, to know for certain what had taken place, questioning him: Where did he see Her? What did the Lady look like whom he saw? And he told the Lord Bishop all that he had seen. But although he told him everything exactly, so that it seemed in all likelihood that She was the Immaculate Virgin, Mary most pure, the beloved Mother of Our Lord Jesus Christ, the Bishop said he could not be certain. He said: It is not only with her words that we have to do, but also to obtain that for which she asks. It is very necessary to have some sign by which we may believe that it is really the Queen of Heaven who sends you.

And Juan Diego, having heard him, said to the Lord Bishop: *My Lord, wait for whatever sign it is that you ask for, and I will go at once to ask the Queen of Heaven, who sent me.* And the Lord Bishop, seeing that he had agreed, and so that he should not be confused or worried, in any way, urged him to go; and then, calling some of his servants in whom he had much confidence, he asked them to follow and to watch where he went and see whomsoever it was that he went to see, and with whom he might speak. And this was done accordingly, and when Juan Diego reached the place where a bridge over the river, near the hill, met the royal highway, they lost him, and although they searched for him everywhere they could not find him in any part of that land. And so they returned, and not only were they weary, but extremely annoyed with him, and upon their return they abused him much with the Lord Bishop, over all that had happened, for they did not believe in him; they said that he had been deceiving him, and had imagined all that he had come to relate to him, or perhaps he had dreamed it, and they agreed and said that if he should come again they would seize him and chastise him severely so that he would not lie another time.

The next day, Monday, when Juan Diego was to bring some sign by which he might be believed, he did not return, since, when he arrived at his house, an uncle of his who was staying there, named Juan Bernardino, was very ill of a burning fever; Juan Diego went at once to bring a doctor and then he procured medicine; but there still was no time because the man was very ill. Early in the morning his uncle begged him to go out to bring one of the priests from Tlatilulco so that he might be confessed, for he was very certain that his time had come to die, now that he was too weak to rise, and could not get well.

And on Tuesday, very early in the morning, Juan Diego left his house to go to Tlatilulco to call a priest, and as he was nearing the hill on the road which lies at the foot of the hill towards the west, which was his usual way, he said to himself: *If I go straight on, without doubt I will see Our Lady and She will persuade me to take the sign to the Lord Bishop; let us first do our duty; I will go first to call the priest for my poor uncle; will he not be waiting for him?*

With this he turned to another road at the foot of the slope and was coming down the other side towards the east to take a short cut to Mexico; he thought that by turning that way the Queen of Heaven would not see him, but She was watching for him, and he saw Her on the hilltop where he had always seen Her before, coming down that side of the slope, by the shortest way, and She said to him:

Xocoyote mio, where are you going? What road is this you are taking?

And he was frightened; it is not known whether he was disgusted with himself, or was ashamed, or perhaps he was struck with wonder; he prostrated himself before Her and greeted her, saying: *My Daughter, my Xocoyota, God keep You, Lady. How did You waken? And is your most pure body well, perchance? My Holy One, I will bring pain to your heart—for I must tell You, my Virgin, that an uncle of mine, who is Your servant, is very sick, with an illness so strong that without doubt he will die of it; I am hastening to Your house in Mexico to call one of Our Lord's dear ones, our priests, to come to confess him, and when I have done that, then I will come back to carry out Your commandment. My Virgin, my Lady, forgive me, be patient with me until I do my duty, and then tomorrow I will come back to You.*

And having heard Juan Diego's explanation, the most holy and immaculate Virgin replied to him:

Listen, and be sure, my dear son, that I will protect you; do not be frightened or grieve, or let your heart be dismayed; however great the illness may be that you speak of, am I not here, I who am your mother, and is not my help a refuge? Am I not of your kind?[3] *Do not be concerned about your uncle's illness, for he is not now going to die; be assured that he is now already well. Is there anything else needful?* (And in that same hour his uncle was healed, as later he learned.)

And Juan Diego, having heard the words of the Queen of Heaven, greatly rejoiced and was convinced, and besought Her that She would send him again to see the Lord Bishop, to carry him some sign by which he could believe, as he had asked.

Whereupon the Queen of Heaven commanded him to climb up to the top of the hill where he had always seen her, saying: *Climb up to the top of the hill, my xocoyote, where you have seen me stand, and there you will find many flowers; pluck them and gather them together, and then bring them down here in my presence.*

Then Juan Diego climbed up the hill and when he had reached the top he marvelled to see blooming there many kinds of beautiful flowers of Castile, for it was then very cold, and he marvelled at their fragrance and odor. Then he began to pluck them, and gathered them together carefully, and wrapped them in his mantle, and when he had finished he descended and carried to the Queen of Heaven all the flowers he had plucked. She, when she had seen them, took them into her immaculate hands, gathered them together again, and laid them in his cloak once more and said to him:

My xocoyote, all these flowers are the sign that you must take to the Bishop; in my name tell him that with this he will see and recognize my will and that he must do what I ask; and you who are my ambassador worthy of confidence, I counsel you to take every care that you open your mantle only in the presence of the Bishop, and you must make it known to him what is that you carry, and tell him how I asked you to climb to the top of the hill to gather the flowers. Tell him also all that you have seen, so that you will persuade the Lord Bishop and he will see that the church is built for which I ask.

And the Queen of Heaven having acquainted him with this, he departed, following the royal highway which leads directly to Mexico; he traveled content, because he was persuaded that now he would succeed; he walked carefully, taking great pains not to injure what he was carrying in his mantle; he went glorying in the fragrance of the beautiful flowers. When he arrived at the Bishop's palace, he encountered his majordomo and other servants and asked them to tell the Bishop that he would like to see him; but none of them would, perhaps because it was still very early in the morning or, perhaps recognizing him, they were vexed or, because they knew how others of their household had lost him on the road when they were following him. They kept him waiting there a long time; he waited very humbly to see if they would call him, and when it was getting very late, they came to him to see what it was he was carrying as a proof of what he had related. And Juan Diego, seeing that he

[3]The Virgin identifies herself as an Indian.

could not hide from them what he was carrying, when they had tormented him and jostled him and knocked him about, let them glimpse that he had roses, to deliver himself from them; and they, when they saw that they were roses of Castile, very fragrant and fresh, and not at all in their season, marvelled and wanted to take some of them. Three times they made bold to take them, but they could not because, when they tried to take them, they were not roses that they touched, but were as if painted or embroidered. Upon this, they went to the Lord Bishop to tell him what they had seen, and that the Indian who was there often before had come again and wanted to see him, and that they had kept him waiting there a long time.

The Lord Bishop, having heard this, knew that now this was the sign that should persuade him whether what the Indian had told him was true. He straightway asked that he be brought in to see him.

Having come into his presence, Juan Diego fell to his knees (as he had always done) and again related fully all that he had seen, and full of satisfaction and wonder he said: *My Lord, I have done that which you asked me; I went to tell my Holy One, the Queen of Heaven, the beloved Virgin Mary, Mother of God, how you asked me for some sign that you might believe that it was She who desired you to build Her the church for which She asked. And also I told Her how I had given my word that I would bring you some sign so that you could believe in what She had put in my care, and She heard with pleasure your suggestion and found it good, and just now, early this morning, She told me to come again to see you and I asked Her for the sign that I had asked Her to give me, and then She sent me to the hilltop where I have always seen Her, to pluck the flowers that I should see there. And when I had plucked them, I took them to the foot of the mountain where She had remained, and She gathered them into her immaculate hands and then put them again into my mantle for me to bring them to you. Although I knew very well that the hilltop was not a place for flowers, since it is a place of thorns, cactuses, caves and mezquites, I was not confused and did not doubt Her. When I reached the summit I saw there was a garden there of flowers with quantities of the fragrant flowers which are found in Castile; I took them and carried them to the Queen of Heaven and She told me that I must bring them to you, and now I have done it, so that you may see the sign that you ask for in order to do Her bidding, and so that you will see that my word is true. And here they are.*

Whereupon he opened his white cloak, in which he was carrying the flowers, and as the roses of Castile dropped out to the floor, suddenly there appeared the most pure image of the most noble Virgin Mary, Mother of God, just exactly as it is, even now, in Her holy house, in Her church which is named Guadalupe;[4] and the Lord Bishop, having seen this, and all those who were with him, knelt down and gazed with wonder; and then they grew sad, and were sorrowful, and were aghast,

[4]The original significance of this word is unclear. It is probably a Hispanic form of a compound derived from the Náhuatl (Aztec) word for "snake," *coatl,* and the Spanish word for "crush, trample," *llope.* Thus, *coatl-llope,* "she crushes the serpent." Interestingly, the image described here is clearly modelled on traditional Catholic figures of Immaculate Mary, Queen of Heaven, statues of whom (based on Genesis 3:15) feature the Virgin standing on a half-moon, crushing with her foot the Devil, represented as a snake. In addition, the Aztec culture hero is Quetzalcoatl, the Plumed Serpent, and the Virgin is requesting that her Cathedral be built over the site of an Aztec place of worship, which, in fact, it was.

and the Lord Bishop with tenderness and weeping begged Her forgiveness for not having done Her bidding at once. And when he had finished, he untied from Juan Diego's neck the cloak on which was printed the figure of the Queen of Heaven. And then he carried it into his chapel; and Juan Diego remained all that day in the house of the Bishop, who did not want him to go. And the following day the Bishop said to him: *Come, show us where it is the Queen of Heaven wishes us to build Her church.* And when he had shown them where it was, he told them that he wanted to go to his house to see his uncle Juan Bernardino who had been very ill and he had set out for Tlatilulco to get a priest to confess him, but the Queen of Heaven had told him that he was already cured.

They did not let him go alone, but went with him to his house, and when they arrived there, they saw that his uncle was well and that nothing was now the matter with him; and the uncle wondered much when he saw such a company with his nephew, and all treating him with great courtesy, and he asked him: *How is it they treat you this way? And why do they reverence you so much?*

And Juan Diego told him that when he had gone from the house to call a confessor for him, he saw the Queen of Heaven on the hill called Tepeyacac and She had sent him to Mexico to see the Lord Bishop to have a church built for Her. And that She had also told him not to worry about his uncle, that he was now well.

Whereupon his uncle showed great joy and told him that it was true that at that very hour he had been healed, and that he himself had seen exactly that same Person, and that She had told him how She had sent him to Mexico to see the Bishop, and also that when he saw him again, to tell him all that he had seen also, and how, miraculously, he had been restored to health, and that the most holy Image of the Immaculate Virgin should be called Santa María de Guadalupe.

And after this they brought Juan Bernardino into the Lord Bishop's presence so that he might tell him under oath all that he had just related; and the Bishop kept the two men (that is, Juan Diego and Juan Bernardino) as his guests in his own house several days until the church for the Queen of Heaven was built where Juan Diego had shown them. And the Lord Bishop moved the sacred Image of the Queen of Heaven, which he had in his chapel, to the cathedral so that all the people could see it.

All the city was in a turmoil upon seeing Her most holy portrait; they saw that it had appeared miraculously, that no one in the world had painted it on Juan Diego's mantle; for this, on which the miraculous Image of the Queen of Heaven appeared, was *ayate,* a coarse fabric made of cactus fibre, rather like homespun, and well woven, for at that time all the Indian people covered themselves with *ayate,* except the nobles, the gentlemen and the captains of war, who dressed themselves in cloaks of cotton, or in cloaks made of wool.

The esteemed *ayate* upon which the Immaculate Virgin, Our Sovereign Queen, appeared unexpectedly is made of two pieces sewn together with threads of cotton; the height of Her sacred Image from the sole of Her foot to the top of Her head measures six hands, and one woman's hand. Her sacred face is very beautiful, grave, and somewhat dark; her precious body, according to this, is small; her hands are held at her breast; the girdle at her waist is violet; her right foot only shows, a very little, and her slipper is earthen in color; her robe is rose-colored; in the shadows it appears deeper red, and it is embroidered with various flowers outlined in gold; pendant at her throat is a little gold circlet which is outlined with a black line around it; in the middle it has a cross; and one discovers glimpses of another, inner vestment of white cotton, daintily gathered at her wrists. The outer mantle which covers her from her head almost to her feet is of heavenly blue; half-way down its fullness hangs in folds, and it is bordered with gold, a rather wide band of gold thread, and all over it there are golden stars which are in number forty-six. Her most holy head is turned towards the right and is bending down; and on her head above her mantle she wears a shining gold crown, and at her feet there is the new moon with its horns pointed upward; and exactly in the middle of it the Immaculate Virgin is standing, and, it would seem also, in the middle of the sun, since its rays surround her everywhere. These rays number a hundred; some are large and others are small; those on each side of her sacred face and those above her head number twelve, in all they number fifty on each side. And outside the edges of this and her robes She is encircled with white clouds. This divine Image as it is described stands above an angel, half of whose body only appears, since he is in the midst of clouds. The angel's outstretched arms hold the edges of her outer robes as they hang in folds near her sacred feet. His garment is of rosy color with a gold ornament at his neck; his wings are made or composed of various sizes of feathers, and it seems as if he were very happy to be accompanying the Queen of Heaven.

1649

Don Antonio de Otermín fl. 1680

At the end of the seventeenth century, the Kingdom of New Mexico, as it was called, was the jewel of the northern frontier of Spain's American empire. It was also the central cog in the defensive line that held that frontier. To be governor of such a province was both a great honor and a tremendous responsibility. From 1678 to 1683 the honor fell to Don Antonio de Otermín, but it was his fate that that honor turned to shame when he became the first governor forced to surrender his province to native rebels.

In 1680 about 2,800 Spanish settlers lived in New Mexico, with many more Indians interacting with them in the colonial system. The settlements were located in the north-central area of the present state, in the upper valley of the Rio Grande. For a century, since the arrival of Oñate, the colony had been evolving a culture of its own, already distinct from that of New Spain far to the south. Agriculture, sheep herding, buffalo hunting, and some mining were staples of the economy. Franciscan missionaries still staffed the churches, although the long-standing settlement could no longer be considered a recently opened territory.

Yet the native population had not been incorporated well into the church, and the Franciscans continually pressured them to convert. As long as that pressure respected certain limits, the missionaries were tolerated, but toward the second half of the 1600s the missionaries' zeal led them to interfere with the Indians' private practices. They preached against the use of kiva ceremonies, and they attempted to destroy native symbolic objects, such as masks and kachina dolls. At the same time, the demands for forced labor from both the state and the church were leaving almost no time for the natives to cultivate their own lands. The situation was intolerable. As a result, the Indians, under the leadership of Popé, a Tewa religious leader known among his people as Tío Pepe, united in a well-organized, surprise attack that swept the Spaniards out of northern New Mexico. In the process, twenty-one of the thirty-two Franciscans were killed; many churches were destroyed (like the enormous structure at Pecos, the largest church built in the U.S. territory until St. Patrick's Cathedral in New York City, centuries later); and the governor's palace was taken over by the ruler of the coalition.

Otermín's letter, like Cabeza de Vaca's a century and a half before, is an attempt to justify failure. The governor had lost an entire province, miles of territory, a century of accumulated investments in land and livestock and buildings. Even more, he had allowed the "lowly" natives to defeat the representatives of the royal crown. In 1681 his attempt to retake the territory was beaten back, only proving the seriousness of the rebellion and the need for a large and concerted campaign of reconquest. The disgrace echoed throughout the empire, causing deep preoccupation lest the story spread and lead to more uprisings. Otermín's tale of the irresistible forces allied against him, the confusion into which the Spaniards were thrown, and the flight for their lives might easily have been read as a judgment on the state of the empire itself, and the consequences could have been disastrous. Latin America in general was not that much different from New Mexico; the façade of control was precarious. Otermín's defeat was the equivalent of Custer's last stand two centuries later, a revelation of defeat which temporarily shocked the Spanish colonizers.

Juan Bruce-Novoa
University of California at Irvine

PRIMARY WORK

C. W. Hackett, ed., *Historical Documents Relating to New Mexico, Nueva Vizcaya, and Approaches Thereto, to 1773,* 3 vols., 1937.

SECONDARY WORK

David J. Weber, *New Spain's Far Northern Frontier: Essays on Spain in the American West, 1540–1821,* 1979.

Letter on the Pueblo Revolt of 1680

My very reverend father, Sir, and friend, most beloved Fray Francisco de Ayeta: The time has come when, with tears in my eyes and deep sorrow in my heart, I commence to give an account of the lamentable tragedy, such as has never before happened in the world, which has occurred in this miserable kingdom and holy *custodia,*[1] His Divine Majesty having thus permitted it because of my grievous sins. Before beginning my narration I desire, as one obligated and grateful, to give your reverence the thanks due for the demonstrations of affection and kindness which you have given in your solicitude in ascertaining and inquiring for definite notices about both my life and those of the rest in this miserable kingdom, in the midst of persistent reports which

[1]Guardianship.

had been circulated of the deaths of myself and the others, and for sparing neither any kind of effort nor large expenditures. For this only Heaven can reward your reverence, though I do not doubt that his Majesty (may God keep him) will do so.

After I sent my last letter to your reverence by the *maese de campo,*[2] Pedro de Leyba, while the necessary things were being made ready alike for the escort and in the way of provisions, for the most expeditious despatch of the returning carts and their guards, as your reverence had enjoined me, I received information that a plot for a general uprising of the Christian Indians was being formed and was spreading rapidly. This was wholly contrary to the existing peace and tranquillity in this miserable kingdom, not only among the Spaniards and natives, but even on the part of the heathen enemy, for it had been a long time since they had done us any considerable damage. It was my misfortune that I learned of it on the eve of the day set for the beginning of the said uprising, and though I immediately, at that instant, notified the lieutenant-general on the lower river and all the other *alcaldes mayores*[3]—so that they could take every care and precaution against whatever might occur, and so that they could make every effort to guard and protect the religious ministers and the temples—the cunning and cleverness of the rebels were such, and so great, that my efforts were of little avail. To this was added a certain degree of negligence by reason of the [report of the] uprising not having been given entire credence, as is apparent from the ease with which they captured and killed both those who were escorting some of the religious, as well as some citizens in their houses, and, particularly, in the efforts that they made to prevent my orders to the lieutenant-general passing through. This was the place where most of the forces of the kingdom were, and from which I could expect some help, but of three orders which I sent to the said lieutenant-general, not one reached his hands. The first messenger was killed and the others did not pass beyond Santo Domingo, because of their having encountered on the road the certain notice of the deaths of the religious[4] who were in that convent, and of the *alcalde mayor,* some other guards, and six more Spaniards whom they captured on that road. Added to this is the situation of this kingdom which, as your reverence is aware, makes it so easy for the said [Indian] alcaldes to carry out their evil designs, for it is entirely composed of *estancias,*[5] quite distant from one another.

On the eve [of the day] of the glorious San Lorenzo, having received notice of the said rebellion from the governors of Pecos and Tanos, [who said] that two Indians had left the Theguas, and particularly the pueblo of Thesuque,[6] to which they belonged, to notify them to come and join the revolt, and that they [the governors] came to tell me of it and of how they were unwilling to participate in such wickedness and treason, saying that they now regarded the Spaniards as their brothers, I thanked them for their kindness in giving the notice, and told them to go to their pueblos and remain quiet. I busied myself immediately in giving the said orders which I mentioned

[2]A military officer.

[3]A category of civil official combining the functions of mayor and judge. The reference here includes Native American officials.

[4]The uprising was aimed specifically at the missionaries who threatened the Native American religious and political hegemony.

[5]Farms.

[6]Native American villages in the upper Rio Grande valley, between present-day Santa Fe and Taos.

to your reverence, and on the following morning as I was about to go to mass there arrived Pedro Hidalgo, who had gone to the pueblo of Thesuque, accompanying Father Fray Juan Pio, who went there to say mass. He told me that the Indians of the said pueblo had killed the said Father Fray Pio and that he himself had escaped miraculously. [He told me also] that the said Indians had retreated to the sierra with all the cattle and horses belonging to the convent, and with their own.

The receipt of this news left us all in the state that may be imagined. I immediately and instantly sent the *maese de campo,* Francisco Gómez, with a squadron of soldiers sufficient to investigate this case and also to attempt to extinguish the flame of the ruin already begun. He returned here on the same day, telling me that [the report] of the death of the said Fray Juan Pio was true. He said also that there had been killed that same morning Father Fray Tomás de Torres, *guardián* of Nambé, and his brother, with the latter's wife and a child, and another resident of Thaos, and also Father Fray Luis de Morales, *guardián* of San Ildefonso, and the family of Francisco de Anaya; and in Poxuaque Don Joseph de Goitia, Francisco Ximénez, his wife and family, and Doña Petronila de Salas with ten sons and daughters; and that they had robbed and profaned the convents and [had robbed] all the haciendas of those murdered and also all the horses and cattle of that jurisdiction and La Cañada.

Upon receiving this news I immediately notified the *alcalde mayor* of that district to assemble all the people in his house in a body, and told him to advise at once the *alcalde mayor* of Los Taos to do the same. On this same day I received notice that two members of a convoy had been killed in the pueblo of Santa Clara, six others having escaped by flight. Also at the same time the *sargento mayor,*[7] Bernabe Márquez, sent to ask me for assistance, saying that he was surrounded and hard pressed by the Indians of the Queres and Tanos nations. Having sent the aid for which he asked me, and an order for those families of Los Cerrillos to come to the villa, I instantly arranged for all the people in it and its environs to retire to the *casas reales.*[8] Believing that the uprising of the Tanos and Pecos might endanger the person of the reverend father custodian, I wrote him to set out at once for the villa, not feeling reassured even with the escort which the lieutenant took, at my orders, but when they arrived with the letter they found that the Indians had already killed the said father custodian; Father Fray Domingo de Vera; Father Fray Manuel Tinoco, the minister *guardián* of San Marcos, who was there; and Father Fray Fernando de Velasco, *guardián* of Los Pecos, near the pueblo of Galisteo, he having escaped that far from the fury of the Pecos. The latter killed in that pueblo Fray Juan de la Pedrosa, two Spanish women, and three children. There died also at the hands of the said enemies in Galisteo Joseph Nieto, two sons of *Maestre de Campo* Leiba, Francisco de Anaya, the younger, who was with the escort, and the wives of *Maestre de Campo* Lieba and Joseph Nieto, with all their daughters and families. I also learned definitely on this day that there had died in the pueblo of Santo Domingo fathers Fray Juan de Talabán, Fray Francisco Antonio Lorenzana, and Fray Joseph de Montesdoca, and the *alcalde mayor,* Andrés de Peralta, together with the rest of the men who went as escort.

[7]Sergeant-major.
[8]Central public buildings; governor's palace.

Seeing myself with notices of so many and such untimely deaths, and that not having received any word from the lieutenant-general was probably due to the fact that he was in the same exigency and confusion, or that the Indians had killed most of those on the lower river, and considering also that in the pueblo of Los Taos the fathers *guardianes* of that place and of the pueblo of Pecuries might be in danger, as well as the *alcalde mayor* and the residents of that valley, and that at all events it was the only place from which I could obtain any horses and cattle—for all these reasons I endeavored to send a relief of soldiers. Marching out for that purpose, they learned that in La Cañada, as in Los Taos and Pecuries, the Indians had risen in rebellion, joining the Apaches of the Achos nation.[9] In Pecuries they had killed Francisco Blanco de la Vega, a *mulata* belonging to the *maese de campo,* Francisco Xavier, and a son of the said *mulata.*[10] Shortly thereafter I learned that they also killed in the pueblo of Taos the father *guardián,* Fray Francisco de Mora, and Father Fray Mathías Rendón, the *guardián* of Pecuries, and Fray Antonio de Pro, and the *alcalde mayor,* as well as another fourteen or fifteen soldiers, along with all the families of the inhabitants of that valley, all of whom were together in the convent. Thereupon I sent an order to the *alcalde mayor,* Luis de Quintana, to come at once to the villa with all the people whom he had assembled in his house, so that, joined with those of us who were in the *casa reales,* we might endeavor to defend ourselves against the enemy's invasions. It was necessarily supposed that they would join all their forces to take our lives, as was seen later by experience.

On Tuesday, the thirteenth of the said month, at about nine o'clock in the morning, there came in sight of us in the suburb of Analco, in the cultivated field of the hermitage of San Miguel, and on the other side of the river of the villa, all the Indians of the Tanos and Pecos nations and the Querez of San Marcos, armed and giving war-whoops. As I learned that one of the Indians who was leading them was from the villa and had gone to join them shortly before, I sent some soldiers to summon him and tell him on my behalf that he could come to see me in entire safety, so that I might ascertain from him the purpose for which they were coming. Upon receiving this message he came to where I was, and, since he was known, as I say, I asked him how it was that he had gone crazy too—being an Indian who spoke our language, was so intelligent, and had lived all his life in the villa among the Spaniards, where I had placed such confidence in him—and was now coming as a leader of the Indian rebels. He replied to me that they had elected him as their captain, and that they were carrying two banners, one white and the other red, and that the white one signified peace and the red one war. Thus if we wished to choose the white it must be [upon our agreeing] to leave the country, and if we chose the red, we must perish, because the rebels were numerous and we were very few; there was no alternative, inasmuch as they had killed so many religious and Spaniards.

[9]The Pueblos and Apaches were enemies, so this comment indicates the extreme danger represented by pan-Indianism spurred by the common opposition to European colonialism.

[10]Woman of black and white racial mixture. The fact that she "belonged to" an official alludes to the presence of slavery in the colonies, although she could have been a servant.

On hearing his reply, I spoke to him very persuasively, to the effect that he and the rest of his followers were Catholic Christians, [asking] how they expected to live without the religious; and said that even though they had committed so many atrocities, still there was a remedy, for if they would return to the obedience of his Majesty they would be pardoned; and that thus he should go back to his people and tell them in my name all that had been said to him, and persuade them to [agree to] it and to withdraw from where they were; and that he was to advise me of what they might reply. He came back from there after a short time, saying that his people asked that all classes of Indians who were in our power be given up to them, both those in the service of the Spaniards and those of the Mexican nation of that suburb of Analco. He demanded also that his wife and children be given up to him, and likewise that all the Apache men and women whom the Spaniards had captured in war [be turned over to them], inasmuch as some Apaches who were among them were asking for them. If these things were not done they would declare war immediately, and they were unwilling to leave the place where they were because they were awaiting the Taos, Pecuries, and Theguas nations, with whose aid they would destroy us.

Seeing his determination, and what they demanded of us, and especially the fact that it was untrue that there were any Apaches among them, because they were at war with all of them, and that these parleys were intended solely to obtain his wife and children and to gain time for the arrival of the other rebellious nations to join them and besiege us, and that during this time they were robbing and sacking what was in the said hermitage and the houses of the Mexicans, I told him (having given him all the preceding admonitions as a Christian and a Catholic) to return to his people and say to them that unless they immediately desisted from sacking the houses and dispersed, I would send to drive them away from there. Whereupon he went back, and his people received him with peals of bells and trumpets, giving loud shouts in sign of war.

With this, seeing after a short time that they not only did not cease the pillage but were advancing toward the villa with shamelessness and mockery, I ordered all the soldiers to go out and attack them until they succeeded in dislodging them from that place. Advancing for this purpose, they joined battle, killing some at the first encounter. Finding themselves repulsed, they took shelter and fortified themselves in the said hermitage and the houses of the Mexicans, from which they defended themselves a part of the day with the firearms that they had and with arrows. Having set fire to some of the houses in which they were, thus having them surrounded and at the point of perishing, there appeared on the road from Thesuque a band of the people whom they were awaiting, who were all the Teguas. Thus it was necessary to go to prevent these latter from passing on to the villa, because the *casas reales* were poorly defended; whereupon the said Tanos and Pecos fled to the mountains and the two parties joined together, sleeping that night in the sierra of the villa. Many of the rebels remained dead and wounded, and our men retired to the *casas reales* with one soldier killed and the *maese de campo,* Francisco Gómez, and some fourteen or fifteen soldiers wounded, to attend them and entrench and fortify ourselves as best we could.

On the morning of the following day, Wednesday, I saw the enemy come down all together from the sierra where they had slept, toward the villa. Mounting my horse, I went out with the few forces that I had to meet them, above the convent. The enemy saw me and halted, making ready to resist the attack. They took up a better position, gaining the eminence of some ravines and thick timber, and began to give war-whoops, as if daring me to attack them.

I paused thus for a short time, in battle formation, and the enemy turned aside from the eminence and went nearer the sierras, to gain the one which comes down behind the house of the *maese de campo,* Francisco Gómez. There they took up their position, and this day passed without our having any further engagements or skirmishes than had already occurred, we taking care that they should not throw themselves upon us and burn the church and the houses of the villa.

The next day, Thursday, the enemy obliged us to take the same step as on the day before of mounting on horseback in fighting formation. There were only some light skirmishes to prevent their burning and sacking some of the houses which were at a distance from the main part of the villa. I knew well enough that these dilatory tactics were to give time for the people of the other nations who were missing to join them in order to besiege and attempt to destroy us, but the height of the places in which they were, so favorable to them and on the contrary so unfavorable to us, made it impossible for us to go and drive them out before they should all be joined together.

On the next day, Friday, the nations of the Taos, Pecuries, Hemes, and Querez having assembled during the past night, when dawn came more than 2,500 Indians fell upon us in the villa, fortifying and entrenching themselves in all its houses and at the entrances of all the streets, and cutting off our water, which comes through the *arroyo*[11] and the irrigation canal in front of the *casas reales.* They burned the holy temple and many houses in the villa. We had several skirmishes over possession of the water, but seeing that it was impossible to hold even this against them, and almost all the soldiers of the post being already wounded, I endeavored to fortify myself in the *casas reales* and to make a defense without leaving their walls. [The Indians were] so dexterous and so bold that they came to set fire to the doors of the fortified tower of Nuestra Señora de las Casas Reales, and, seeing such audacity, and the manifest risk that we ran of having the *casas reales* set on fire, I resolved to make a sally into the plaza of the said *casas reales* with all my available force of soldiers, without any protection, to attempt to prevent the fire which the enemy was trying to set. With this endeavor we fought the whole afternoon, and, since the enemy, as I said above, had fortified themselves and made embrasures in all the houses, and had plenty of arquebuses, powder, and balls. They did us much damage. Night overtook us thus and God was pleased that they should desist somewhat from shooting us with arquebuses and arrows. We passed this night, like the rest, with much care and watchfulness, and suffered greatly from thirst because of the scarcity of water.

On the next day, Saturday, they began at dawn to press us harder and more closely with gunshots, arrows, and stones, saying to us that now we should not escape them, and that besides their own numbers, they were expecting help from the Apaches whom they had already summoned. They fatigued us greatly on this day, because all was fighting, and above all we suffered from thirst, as we were already oppressed by it. At nightfall, because of the evident peril in which we found ourselves by their gaining the two stations where cannon were mounted, which we had at the

[11]*Arroyos* are great cuts in the land where rain water collects and forms streams.

doors of the *casas reales,* aimed at the entrances of the streets, in order to bring them inside it was necessary to assemble all the forces that I had with me, because we realized that this was their [the Indians'] intention. Instantly all the said Indian rebels began a chant of victory and raised war-whoops, burning all the houses of the villa, and they kept us in this position the entire night, which I assure your reverence was the most horrible that could be thought of or imagined, because the whole villa was a torch and everywhere were war chants and shouts. What grieved us most were the dreadful flames from the church and the scoffing and ridicule which the wretched and miserable Indian rebels made of the sacred things, intoning the *alabado*[12] and the other prayers of the church with jeers.

Finding myself in this state, with the church and the villa burned, and with the few horses, sheep, goats, and cattle which we had without feed or water for so long that many had already died, and the rest were about to do so, and with such a multitude of people, most of them children and women, so that our numbers in all came to about a thousand persons, perishing with thirst—for we had nothing to drink during these two days except what had been kept in some jars and pitchers that were in the *casas reales*—surrounded by such a wailing of women and children, with confusion everywhere, I determined to take the resolution of going out in the morning to fight with the enemy until dying or conquering. Considering that the best strength and armor were prayers to appease the Divine wrath, though on the preceding days the poor women had made them with fervor, that night I charged them to do so increasingly, and told the father *guardián* and the other two religious to say mass for us at dawn, and exhort all alike to repentance for their sins and to conformance with the Divine will, and to absolve us from guilt and punishment. These things being done, all of us who could mounted our horses, and the rest [went] on foot with their arquebuses, and some Indians who were in our service with their bows and arrows, and in the best order possible we directed our course toward the house of the *maese de campo,* Francisco Xavier, which was the place where (apparently) there were the most people and where they had been most active and boldest. On coming out of the entrance to the street it was seen that there was a great number of Indians. They were attacked in force, and though they resisted the first charge bravely, finally they were put to flight, many of them being overtaken and killed. Then turning at once upon those who were in the streets leading to the convent, they also were put to flight with little resistance. The houses in the direction of the house of the said *maestre de campo,* Francisco Xavier, being still full of Indians who had taken refuge in them, and seeing that the enemy with the punishment and deaths that we had inflicted upon them in the first and second assaults were withdrawing toward the hills, giving us a little room, we laid siege to those who remained fortified in the said houses. Though they endeavored to defend themselves, and did so, seeing that they were being set afire and that they would be burned to death, those who remained alive surrendered and much was made of them. The deaths of both parties in this and the other encounters exceeded three hundred Indians.

[12]Hymn in praise of the sacrament of the Holy Eucharist.

Finding myself a little relieved by this miraculous event, though I had lost much blood from two arrow wounds which I had received in the face and from a remarkable gunshot wound in the chest on the day before, I immediately had water given to the cattle, the horses, and the people. Because we now found ourselves with very few provisions for so many people, and without hope of human aid, considering that our not having heard in so many days from the people on the lower river would be because of their all having been killed, like the others in the kingdom, or at least of their being or having been in dire straits, with the view of aiding them and joining with them into one body, so as to make the decisions most conducive to his Majesty's service, on the morning of the next day, Monday, I set out for La Isleta,[13] where I judged the said comrades on the lower river would be. I trusted in Divine Providence, for I left without a crust of bread or a grain of wheat or maize, and with no other provisions for the convoy of so many people except four hundred animals and two carts belonging to private persons, and, for food, a few sheep, goats, and cows.

In this manner, and with this fine provision, besides a few small ears of maize that we found in the fields, we went as far as the pueblo of La Alameda, where we learned from an old Indian whom we found in a maize-field that the lieutenant-general with all the residents of his jurisdictions had left some fourteen or fifteen days before to return to El Paso to meet the carts. This news made me very uneasy, alike because I could not be persuaded that he would have left without having news of me as well as of all the others in the kingdom, and because I feared that from his absence there would necessarily follow the abandonment of this kingdom. On hearing this news I acted at once, sending four soldiers to overtake the said lieutenant-general and the others who were following him, with orders that they were to halt wherever they should come up with them. Going in pursuit of them, they overtook them at the place of Fray Cristóbal. The lieutenant-general, Alonso Garcia, overtook me at the place of Las Nutrias, and a few days' march thereafter I encountered the *maese de campo,* Pedro de Leiba, with all the people under his command, who were escorting these carts and who came to ascertain whether or not we were dead, as your reverence had charged him to do, and to find me, ahead of the supply train. I was so short of provisions and of everything else that at best I should have had a little maize for six days or so.

Thus, after God, the only succor and relief that we have rests with your reverence and in your diligence. Wherefore, and in order that your reverence may come immediately, because of the great importance to the service of God and the king of your reverence's presence here, I am sending the said *maese de campo,* Pedro de Leyba, with the rest of the men whom he brought so that he may come as escort for your reverence and the carts or mule-train in which we hope you will bring us some assistance of provisions. Because of the haste which the case demands I do not write at more length, and for the same reason I cannot make a report at present concerning the above to the señor viceroy, because the *autos*[14] are not verified and there has

[13]The Native Americans from Isleta were taken south by Otermín, when he retreated after the failed campaign of 1681, and they resettled in Isleta Sur southeast of El Paso, Texas.

[14]Official reports.

been no opportunity to conclude them. I shall leave it until your reverence's arrival here. For the rest I refer to the account which will be given to your reverence by the father secretary, Fray Buene Ventura de Berganza. I am slowly overtaking the other party, which is sixteen leagues from here, with the view of joining them and discussing whether or not this miserable kingdom can be recovered. For this purpose I shall not spare any means in the service of God and of his Majesty, losing a thousand lives if I had them, as I have lost my estate and part of my health, and shedding my blood for God. May He protect me and permit me to see your reverence in this place at the head of the relief. September 8, 1680. Your servant, countryman, and friend kisses your reverence's hand. DON ANTONIO DE OTERMIN.

1937

The Coming of the Spanish and the Pueblo Revolt (Hopi)

Among Native American tales, historical narratives frequently relate the encounter with European colonizers and efforts to resist their domination. In this Hopi narrative of the coming of the Spanish, we find what some native groups call "memory culture" embracing centuries of time as if it existed on one chronological level. The story relates events in the absence of a linear historical sense which would locate events according to their relationship in real time. In other words, the story collapses chronology, telling centuries of happenings within one time-reference.

Many stories of this vast historical literature are of value for Euro-Americans, for they tell of colonization and its rejection from the Native American perspective. The Hopi narrative, with its unflattering picture of Franciscan missionizing—substantiated in large measure by documentary records—stands in stark contrast to Villagrá's Catholic vision of the conquest as a glorious march of the cross. More importantly, the story highlights the profound differences between the two cultures, differences even centuries of contact have not altered. The Spanish understood native religions as paganism and felt duty-bound to eradicate them, for the good of the individual native as well as for the larger community. Indians, on the other hand, questioned a God who commanded them to abandon their kachina religion, knowing that extinction was the logical consequence of suppressing a traditional religion that had secured rain, food, and life itself, since their emergence into the day-world. While some tribes would forge a close working relationship with the colonizers—Spanish and Anglo-Americans—the Hopis pride themselves on never having given in or up.

Juan Bruce-Novoa
University of California at Irvine

PRIMARY WORK

Edmund Nequatewa, *Truth of a Hopi,* 1936, 1967.

SECONDARY WORKS

Denis Tedlock, *The Spoken Word and the Work of Interpretation,* 1983; Ramón Gutiérrez, *When Jesus Came, the Corn Mothers Went Away,* 1991.

The Coming of the Spanish and the Pueblo Revolt (Hopi)[1]

It may have taken quite a long time for these villages to be established. Anyway, every place was pretty well settled down when the Spanish came.[2] The Spanish were first heard of at Zuni and then at Awatovi. They came on to Shung-opovi, passing Walpi. At First Mesa, Siky-atki was the largest village then, and they were called Si-kyatki, not Walpi. The Walpi people were living below the present village on the west side. When the Spaniards came, the Hopi thought that they were the ones they were looking for—their white brother, the Bahana, their savior.[3]

The Spaniards visited Shung-opovi several times before the missions were established. The people of Mishongovi welcomed them so the priest who was with the white men built the first Hopi mission at Mishongovi. The people of Shung-opovi were at first afraid of the priests but later they decided he was really the Bahana, the savior, and let him build a mission at Shung-opovi.

Well, about this time the Strap Clan were ruling at Shung-opovi and they were the ones that gave permission to establish the mission. The Spaniards, whom they called Castilla, told the people that they had much more power than all their chiefs and a whole lot more power than the witches. The people were very much afraid of them, particularly if they had much more power than the witches. They were so scared that they could do nothing but allow themselves to be made slaves. Whatever they wanted done must be done. Any man in power that was in this position the Hopi called *Tota-achi,* which means a grouchy person that will not do anything himself, like a child. They couldn't refuse, or they would be slashed to death or punished in some way. There were two *Tota-achi.*

The missionary did not like the ceremonies. He did not like the Kachinas and he destroyed the altars and the customs. He called it idol worship and burned up all the ceremonial things in the plaza.

When the Priests started to build the mission, the men were sent away over near the San Francisco peaks to get the pine or spruce beams. These beams were cut and put into shape roughly and were then left till the next year when they had dried out. Beams of that size were hard to carry and the first few times they tried to carry these

[1]The Hopi Indians, descendants of the Anasazi who had occupied cliff dwellings, occupy a number of pueblos in northeastern Arizona. Agricultural in their culture and economy, they had their own complex social and religious customs when they were subjected to the missionary efforts of the Spanish in 1629; Coronado had visited them in 1540. They joined the Pueblo Revolt of 1680.

[2]The first Spaniard to visit the Hopi was Coronado in 1540. Other expeditions followed. The Catholic missions, staffed by Franciscan priests, were established there in the beginning of the seventeenth century.

[3]The Hopis, like the Aztecs, believed that a fair-skinned culture hero would return from exile in the East to establish peace and prosperity. This belief in the *Bahana* had been greatly influenced by Christianity by the time the present narrative was published in 1936, but it is clear from available evidence that both Cortez in Mexico and the Spanish priests at Hopi used it as a means of entrance into the community.

beams on their backs, twenty to thirty men walking side by side under the beam. But this was rather hard in rough places and one end had to swing around. So finally they figured out a way of carrying the beam in between them. They lined up two by two with the beam between the lines. In doing this, some of the Hopis were given authority by the missionary to look after these men and to see if they all did their duty If any man gave out on the way he was simply left to die. There was great suffering. Some died for lack of food and water, while others developed scabs and sores on their bodies.

It took a good many years for them to get enough beams to Shung-opovi to build the mission. When this mission was finally built, all the people in the village had to come there to worship, and those that did not come were punished severely. In that way their own religion was altogether wiped out, because they were not allowed to worship in their own way. All this trouble was a heavy burden on them and they thought it was on account of this that they were having a heavy drought at this time. They thought their gods had given them up because they weren't worshiping the way they should.[4]

Now during this time the men would go out pretending they were going on a hunting trip and they would go to some hiding place, to make their prayer offerings. So to-day, a good many of these places are still to be found where they left their little stone bowls in which they ground their copper ore to paint the prayer sticks. These places are called *Puwa-kiki,* cave places. If these men were caught they were severely punished.

Now this man, Tota-achi (the Priest)[5] was going from bad to worse. He was not doing the people any good and he was always figuring what he could do to harm them. So he thought out how the water from different springs or rivers would taste and he was always sending some man to these springs to get water for him to drink, but it was noticed that he always chose the men who had pretty wives. He tried to send them far away so that they would be gone two or three days, so it was not very long until they began to see what he was doing. The men were even sent to the Little Colorado River to get water for him, or to Moencopi. Finally, when a man was sent out he'd go out into the rocks and hide, and when the night came he would come home. Then, the priest, thinking the man was away, would come to visit his wife, but instead the man would be there when he came. Many men were punished for this.

All this time the priest, who had great power, wanted all the young girls to be brought to him when they were about thirteen or fourteen years old. They had to live

[4]The Hopi religion, like that of the Zunis and other pueblos, uses mask dancing to invoke the assistance of the ancestral dead and the kachinas in securing life-giving rain for the crops. Spanish missionary policy was to destroy native religion by disrupting ceremonies and by destroying all ritual objects, especially masks, which they identified with the Devil.

[5]The precise identity of this priest is unclear. Several priests served at Shungopovi prior to the Pueblo Revolt. Fr. José Trujillo, who came to the Hopi from service in the Philippines, was a charismatic, intense, religious zealot. Fr. Salvador de Guerra, who preceded him, was transferred from Shungopovi to Jemez, much farther east, as discipline for having tortured the Indians in his charge. It is likely that this Tota-achi is a corporate figure, whose image conflates the memory of the misdeeds of several individuals.

with the priest. He told the people they would become better women if they lived with him for about three years. Now one of these girls told what the Tota-achi were doing and a brother of the girl heard of this and he asked his sister about it, and he was very angry. This brother went to the mission and wanted to kill the priest that very day, but the priest scared him and he did nothing. So the Shung-opovi people sent this boy, who was a good runner, to Awatovi to see if they were doing the same thing over there, which they were. So that was how they got all the evidence against the priest.

Then the chief at Awatovi sent word by this boy that all the priests would be killed on the fourth day after the full moon. They had no calendar and that was the best way they had of setting the date. In order to make sure that everyone would rise up and do this thing on the fourth day the boy was given a cotton string with knots in it and each day he was to untie one of these knots until they were all out and that would be the day for the attack.[6]

Things were getting worse and worse so the chief of Shung-opovi went over to Mishongnovi and the two chiefs discussed their troubles. "He is not the savior and it is your duty to kill him," said the chief of Shung-opovi. The chief of Mishongnovi replied, "If I end his life, my own life is ended."

Now the priest would not let the people manufacture prayer offerings, so they had to make them among the rocks in the cliffs out of sight, so again one day the chief of Shung-opovi went to Mishongnovi with tobacco and materials to make prayer offerings. He was joined by the chief of Mishongnovi and the two went a mile north to a cave. For four days they lived there heartbroken in the cave, making *pahos.* Then the chief of Mishongnovi took the prayer offerings and climbed to the top of the Corn Rock and deposited them in the shrine, for according to the ancient agreement with the Mishongnovi people it was their duty to do away with the enemy.

He then, with some of his best men, went to Shung-opovi, but he carried no weapons. He placed his men at every door of the priest's house. Then he knocked on the door and walked in. He asked the priest to come out but the priest was suspicious and would not come out. The chief asked the priest four times and each time the priest refused. Finally, the priest said, "I think you are up to something."

The chief said, "I have come to kill you." "You can't kill me," cried the priest, "you have no power to kill me. If you do, I will come to life and wipe out your whole tribe."

The chief returned, "If you have this power, then blow me out into the air; my gods have more power than you have.[7] My gods have put a heart into me to enter

[6]The Pueblo Revolt of August 13, 1680, was a concerted, successful effort of the Pueblo Indian communities to throw off Spanish military and religious oppression. Many soldiers and perhaps as many as 28 priests were killed in the uprising. The remaining colonists retreated south to El Paso del Norte and did not re-establish control over the northern frontier until Vargas's reconquest in 1692. The present narrative views the events at Hopi as a solution to a particular problem and not as part of a larger action.

[7]The debate between the Mishongnovi and Shungopovi chiefs indicates that the core of the Hopi interest in this narrative is religious, not military, conflict. Christianity fails because a drought follows the suppression of the kiva religion and because the priest fails to live up to his own culture's Christ-like ideal and the Hopi's ideal of the *Bahana.*

your home. I have no weapons. You have your weapons handy, hanging on the wall. My gods have prevented you from getting your weapons."

The old priest made a rush and grabbed his sword from the wall. The chief of Mishongnovi yelled and the doors were broken open. The priest cut down the chief and fought right and left but was soon overpowered, and his sword taken from him

They tied his hands behind his back. Out of the big beams outside they made a tripod. They hung him on the beams, kindled a fire and burned him.

1936

Don Diego de Vargas ?–1704

Diego de Vargas Zapata y Luján Ponce de León y Contreras was appointed captain-general and governor of New Mexico in 1691, charged with a territorial reconquest that was already in progress, as Vargas's comments on his predecessor's violent battles indicate. Eleven years before, the Indians had organized under the Tewa religious leader Popé to drive out the Spaniards. For a decade, the colonists and some loyal natives waited in northern Mexico for the territory to be reclaimed. The project, however, was slow in advancing, for the Indians held the fortress-like mesa and resisted fiercely. By the time Vargas took command, few Christian colonists remained in El Paso. Fewer still wanted to return; they required forceful convincing by Vargas.

Meanwhile, however, the French had designs on the northern provinces of the Spanish empire. In 1681, Count de Peñalosa, a Peruvian-born ex-governor of New Mexico, had presented to the French government a project for the conquest of territory lying east of New Mexico and another proposal to conquer the Mexican province of New Biscaya with its rich mineral wealth. Peñalosa's plan proposed the taking of the territory from the mouth of the Rio Grande to San Diego on the Pacific coast, and including the Mines in Parral and the city of Durango. At the same time, the French were cultivating alliances with Plains Indians, especially the Pawnees, and moving into the heartland from their bases in the Great Lakes area. All of this made it imperative to Spain that New Mexico be retaken and settled as part of the defense of the empire. The Conde de Galve, viceroy of New Spain, meant to fortify the entire northern frontier. To carry out this plan, New Mexico was essential.

Vargas achieved his assignment with deliberate professionalism. On September 14, 1692, with the theatricality of European ceremony, he officially reclaimed the Plaza of Santa Fe. By 1693 he could compose the report that follows. His discourse is that of the panoptic ruler, viewing his kingdom as a great circle fanning out from the center, which he occupies with the authority of his royal commission. At the same time, his projection of settlements and numbers of colonizers are veiled pleas for support, reprising a tradition initiated by Menéndez de Avilés a century earlier. Yet there is a security, even a calmness in his tone—perhaps the arrogance his countrymen would accuse him of when he stood trial a few years later for allegedly abusing his authority. There are no flights of literary fancy here, just the description of the lay of the land. Vargas, having carried out his charge, surveyed his holdings, apparently secure in the power of his government to reclaim all they saw, although in truth unconquered tribes surrounded him. The reconquest was so important to the empire that the viceroy commissioned one of Mexico's best writers, Carlos Sigüenza y Góngora, to write a tract celebrating the victory. *Mercurio Volante* recounted in stirring literary style Vargas's success. The empire had been restored.

Yet, by 1695, Vargas ordered a careful questioning of a band of Apaches who had arrived to trade of stories about the large number of French who were moving into the plains of Cíbola. The menace was so convincing that Vargas wrote the central government in Mexico to request artillery to prepare his defenses before the French arrived. In 1696, the Pueblos rebelled again, killing priests and settlers, but not all of the tribes joined, and Vargas, with great personal bravery, was able to quell the rebellion. Next he faced accusations of abuse, house arrest, and a bitter power struggle—yet once again he survived to regain authority.

The French never reached New Mexico in Vargas's lifetime, but no governor of New Mexico would ever again be able to write a letter as calm and secure as the letter that appears below. The reconquest was more than the end of an Indian revolt, it was the beginning of the end of New Mexico's isolation at the edge of the Spanish empire. New Mexico would not fall to a foreign power for another century and a half, but its position at the end of the seventeenth century was already shifting to that of an international crossroads. Vargas's letter can be read as a calm before the storm.

Juan Bruce-Novoa
University of California at Irvine

PRIMARY WORK

Coronado Cuarto Centennial Publications, 1540–1940; vol. 4, 1940.

SECONDARY WORKS

Jessie B. Bailey, *Diego Vargas and the Reconquest of New Mexico,* 1940; J. Manuel Espinosa, *Crusaders of the Río Grande: The Story of Don Diego de Varagas and the Reconquest and Refounding of New Mexico,* 1942; Henry Folmer, *Franco-Spanish Rivalry in North America, 1524–1763,* 1953; David J. Weber, *New Spain's Far Northern Frontier: Essays on Spain in the American West, 1540–1821,* 1979; John L. Kessell, *Remote Beyond Compare, Letters of Don Diego de Vargas to His Family,* 1989.

from Letter on The Reconquest of New Mexico, 1692

Excellent Sir:

I scarcely arrived from my happy conquest, on the twentieth of December last, when two hours later the courier arrived with the answer to that which, with testimony of the records, I sent to your Excellency from the villa of Santa Fe, notifying your Highness through them and the letter of transmittal of what had been conquered up to the said day. A happy day, luck, and good fortune were attained, your Excellency, through the impulse which, fervently, spurred by the faith and as a loyal vassal of his Majesty, led me to undertake the said enterprise, considering that it is a region so large as to be a kingdom, all of which was in rebel hands for the past twelve years, and only on the confines of which was it known that they had been visited. For their safety, they were living on the mesas, the approaches to which made it difficult to invade them without their being assured of victory. All these conditions could have justly embarrassed me, but, realizing that the defense of my faith and my king were of greater importance, I scorned them and put into execution the said enterprise. . . .

I acknowledge the command and order of your Excellency, made in agreement with the real junta de hacienda,[1] in which you say, order, and command that I should continue in the region. I wrote your Excellency, telling you that upon my return from subduing and conquering the Pecos, the Keres tribes living on various mesas, and the Jémez, I would make entry to the rock of Acoma and the provinces of Zuñi and Moqui, should I consider it possible for the horses to travel two hundred leagues. I answer that despite great obstacles, as attested in the records, I made the said entry which I had previously proposed to your Excellency with doubt; having also succeeded in obtaining some *almagre* earth, or vermilion,[2] which is believed to contain quicksilver ore, and having made known the new route which might be used for transit from the said kingdom, for his Majesty, should it contain quicksilver. With great interest I embarked upon the discovery of the said route and crossing, and, having come out at the pueblo of Socorro on the tenth of December last, there was such continuous snow and ice that on the following day we found the river frozen over. And we found that to return to the said villa and its surrounding pueblos by this route would be a waste of time and unfruitful, for it entailed the danger of the enemy Apaches as well as their partisans in this region of El Paso. I decided to hasten there so that the inhabitants would have the defense and garrison of the arms of their presidio and in order that the horses might gain strength and recuperate in order that I might carry out your Excellency's orders.

With regard to the transportation of the families which may be found at this pueblo of El Paso, I decided to visit them in order to make a census list, which I am sending to your Excellency so that your Highness may have record of the exact number of children and other persons who are under the care of each family. Those who can be taken unburdened will go, trusting that your Excellency will take into consideration my report which I referred to in the letter of remission adjoined to the said census. As for the return of the inhabitants who have withdrawn and who live in the kingdoms of [New] Vizcaya and [New] Galicia, I have decided to go in person in order effectively to persuade them, for I shall endeavor to find those who are living in haciendas and known localities, and in the settlements, announcing your Excellency's order and command to the royal authorities, and with their assistance they also will be made known by the proclamation which I will have published. And I shall make known therein that all those who desire to come and colonize the said kingdom will be promised all that which is contained in your Excellency's order. I will enlist them all with their privileges, paying the expenses of those who are to be transported, not only to this pueblo of El Paso, but as far as the villa of Santa Fe. In order that your Excellency may be entirely without anxiety

[1]The royal administration.

[2]Vermillion indicates the presence of cinnabar, the prime source of mercury, which is indispensable for refining silver. The mention of vermillion held out the possibility of an important mineral resource which could justify expenditures on the colony of New Mexico.

with regard to the said colonization, I shall at all costs set out from this pueblo of El Paso with both groups of settlers upon my return from the said kingdoms, providing that your Excellency, in view of this, will send me the necessary sum, in response to the same and with the same courier. He will find me at the camp of Sombrerete collecting the twelve thousand pesos which your Excellency has placed to my account, if it is not obtainable at Guadiana. For I shall also visit that place for the purpose of enlisting some people, as those obtained for these parts must be of good quality, campaigners and persons agile in the pursuit of this war. . . .

As for the settlement of the region, the soldiers needed for its presidio, its defense and safety, and that of the lives of the religious, I repeat to your Excellency my opinion that five hundred families are necessary for the settlement of the villa and the following districts, not counting the one hundred soldiers necessary for the presidio at the villa of Santa Fe.

While I was there I examined and appraised the land. And, nine days after its conquest, having taken the road to the pueblo of Galisteo, which is the wagon road, and having entered the pueblo of the Pecos tribe, I returned to the said villa by way of the short road through the mountains, which the said tribes travel on foot and on horseback. I then went to the pueblos of the Tegua and Tano tribes, continued to that of Picuríes, and from there to that of Taos. Having seen the said thirteen pueblos and inspected the character of their lands, pastures, water supply, and wood, I find that the only place adequate for the founding of the said villa is its existing site, setting it up and establishing it on this side [*sic*] of the arroyo where it overlooks and dominates the pueblo and stronghold occupied there by the Tegua and Tano tribes, which comprises what was formerly the major portion of the palace and royal houses of the governor, and those of the inhabitants of the said villa who left as a result of their rebellion. They have extended and raised the walls, and fortified them, so that the said pueblo is walled. Besides, in La Ciénega and its lowland, the waters gather from the surrounding mountains and mesas, and the said stronghold being near by, it is in the shade, and for that reason it is hidden from the sun in the morning, and in the afternoon it also is without the sun's rays. And, due to the climate and temperature of the said kingdom, which is extremely cold, cloudy, and abounding in water, with heavy frosts and ice, and due to its shade and thick fog and mists of known and evident detriment, the said place is unsatisfactory.

The favor granted to the said natives, which I promised them at the time of their conquest, is not prejudicial to the said colonists, rather it is to their interest to settle at the place where I established my encampment on the day of my entry there. It is located a musket shot distance away. Its land dominates and overlooks the said stronghold, the place having sufficient height so that the artillery may control and cause much respect from the enemy. Also the surrounding country is well supplied with wood, farm lands, and pastures. These can be reserved, setting aside and reserving from the entrance at Las Bocas along the road to Santo Domingo, a distance of seven leagues. And as for the pueblo of La Ciénega, which I found abandoned, if some Keres Indians should repopulate it, it will be with the *tasación*[3]

[3]Measurement.

of five hundred varas, from the door of the church to the four cardinal points, and no more. Also with regard to the abandoned hacienda of El Alamo, to whomsoever lays claim to it will be given the lands with limits, but without liability claims with regard to the said horses.

With regard to the abandoned hacienda which is located a distance of two leagues from there, beyond the arroyo or river called the Seco, also to its owner [*sic*], in the same manner, if he wishes to settle it, and the aforesaid length and distance, with its entrances and exits, will be reserved as the common land not only for the horses and mules of the inhabitants who settle there, but also for those of the soldiers of the presidio. And also, the said place should be settled because it has dry land, with very little gravel, and is clear, getting the sun all day, and enjoying the winds from every direction.

With regard to its settlers, as many as one hundred and fifty families may enter and settle the said villa, as well as the one hundred presidial soldiers, who may cover the land with their arms by being established at this central point which controls a distance of ninety leagues in the following manner: thirty-two long leagues to the pueblo of Taos, to the north, thirty leagues to the pueblos of the Jémez and the Keres of Sia, which are between the south and west, and thirty leagues to the pueblo of Isleta, which is to the west. At the said place they will be assured of having provisions, whether or not the weather is good, and should the population be augmented such that they will need additional sources of supply, the one hundred and fifty families may settle part of the land; for, the said kingdom having the protection of the arms of the presidio, many will decide to settle on the haciendas which they formerly had and which they abandoned at the time of the uprising. The number of those which are occupied will be shared with the families hailing from other parts.

It is my wish, with those with whom I enter, including the soldiers, that they should, first and foremost, personally build the church and holy temple, setting up in it before all else the patroness of the said kingdom and villa, who is the one that was saved from the ferocity of the savages, her title being Our Lady of the Conquest. And so, with the aid of the soldiers and settlers, the foundations will be laid and the walls of the holy temple raised, bringing at the same time, by means of the oxen that will be taken, the timber necessary. At the same time the said construction will be hastened, so that by our example the conquered will be moved to build gladly their churches in their pueblos, which I hope will be accomplished. . . .

With regard to the settlement at the pueblo of Taos, which is on the frontier, and the most distant one of the kingdom, where the Apaches continually make their entry, it will be necessary to place one hundred settlers there. This pueblo has a site even more favorable for settlement, because its valleys are very broad, and it has many arroyos, wood, and pastures, and the land is very fertile and will yield good crops and is very suitable for the raising of all types of livestock, large and small. The said number of settlers, backed by the strength of the arms of the presidio of the said villa, will make it impossible for the enemy easily to swoop down on the pueblos of the said tribes; and also those who rebuild and resettle their haciendas may live in safety, for on the way to this pueblo there are many abandoned sites which were pointed out to me and named by their previous owners.

At the pueblo of Pecos, a distance of eight leagues from Santa Fe, fifty families may be settled, for it is also an Apache frontier and is surrounded by very mountainous country, very adaptable to ambush. And so, if it is settled, and with the said arms at the said villa, it will be possible to prevent the thefts and deaths otherwise facilitated by easy entry. It is very fertile land, which responds with great abundance to all the types of seeds that are planted.

Between the pueblos of Santo Domingo and Cochití, the original inhabitants of this kingdom who so desire may settle, should the Indians of the Keres tribe not come down to occupy the said pueblos. Those of Cochití are living on the mesa and mountain of La Cieneguilla, a distance of four leagues away; and those of Santo Domingo are living on the mesa of the Cerro Colorado with the Keres Indians of Captain Malacate who were absent from their pueblo of Sia at the time General Don Domingo Jironza, my predecessor, burned it and captured those who escaped from fire and arms. And so the people of this Keres tribe are living on the said mesas, which are those of the said two pueblos and the one of Sia. From what they told me on the mesa of the Cerro Colorado, where they again have their pueblo, it is doubtful that they will return to resettle the one of Sia, which was burned by General Don Domingo. They said that they would not return to the pueblo for the additional reason that the land is nitrous, lacks sufficient water, is without wood, and is very sterile, and that if they should descend they would settle in the canyon between the pueblo of Sia and that of abandoned Santa Ana.

In the vicinity of this pueblo of Santa Ana, another fifty settlers may be established, because it has good lands and also because they are necessary to close the way to the enemy Apache; and so that the fathers who minister to the Keres Indians, and those of the Jémez tribe, may have the said settlers near by for their protection, and may, without fear of risking their lives, minister to them, punish them, and reprehend them as the case might be.

In the abandoned pueblo of Jémez, the walls of the church and most of the houses of the dwellings are standing, in which pueblo, should the Indians who are living on the mesa of the canyon remain there, one hundred residents can be settled. It has plenty of lands for planting and pastures, with water and very fertile, and the settlement of the said place would be very important because the Apaches make entry there, by virtue of which some of the Indians are rebellious in spirit and are our enemies.

From the hacienda of "La Angostura," two leagues from the pueblo of "La Angostura," that is, San Felipe, to the abandoned pueblo of Sandía, and one league from the abandoned pueblo of Puaray, at the said first one of Sandía Spaniards also may be settled. The walls of the church and some houses, although badly damaged, may be repaired. The lands are good, with their irrigation ditches. The said pueblos are on the camino real, and it would be very desirable to settle the region with another one hundred colonists, who will be able to live very comfortably and prosperously. It is a distance of twenty leagues from the said villa and will be of great value for the protection of the haciendas which extend from "Las Huertas."

At a distance of ten leagues, on the said camino real, on the other side of the river, there is situated the pueblo of Isleta, which is abandoned. The walls of the church are in good condition, as are most of the houses of the Indians of the Tegua nation who were withdrawn by General Don Antonio de Otermín when he made the entry in the year of 'eighty-one, at the expense of his Majesty, in the time of his

Excellency, the viceroy, Conde de Paredes. The natives of the said tribe now live in some miserable huts in the pueblo of Isleta, in this district of El Paso, and so it will be desirable to restore them to their pueblo. They will be assured success in cultivating the fields which they plant at the pueblo, because the lands are extensive, in a good climate, and can be easily irrigated. And they will be protected if the said intervening haciendas called "Las Huertas" are settled, along with those extending from Las Barrancas, and those toward the abandoned pueblos of Alamillo and Sevilleta, whose natives are scattered and restless, and with the settlement of the said haciendas and the pueblo referred to, it will be possible to restore them to their pueblos.

Continuing a distance of ten leagues, Socorro is found, which may be settled with the Indians who at present occupy this one of Socorro in this district of El Paso, and they may be joined by the Piros, who are few, and who live in the pueblo of Senecú in this district, for it is a vast and fertile land; it has its irrigation ditches, and some of the walls of the convent are in good condition. Senecú, which the Piros occupied previously, a distance of ten leagues away, should not be settled because the river has damaged the land, and furthermore it is on a frontier infested with many Apaches. If it is the wish of some to settle the abandoned haciendas, it will be useful for the protection of the said Indians, and it will also prepare the way for the filling in and occupying of the land. The above is only the form in which the settlement should be made, in order that the natives of the said tribes, aware of the neighboring settlers and of the armed strength of the presidio, may be kept in submission, and so that our holy faith may be spread among them, and their children may join it with full obedience, and the missionaries, their teachers of Christian doctrine, may not find themselves alone and afraid to teach them, as I repeat, the doctrines of our holy faith.

As for the natives of the rock of Acoma, since they are a distance of twenty-four leagues from Isleta, and also those of the province of Zuñi, they may be left as they are. But as for those of the province of Moqui, in case the said vermilion earth is found not to contain quicksilver ore, it is my opinion that they should be removed from their pueblos to the abandoned ones of Alamillo and Sevilleta and the region between them, for in this way they will be safe and their missionaries will have control over them, for otherwise they would undergo great risk.

1693

Eighteenth Century

I appeal to any white to say, if ever he entered Logan's cabin hungry, and he gave him not meat: if ever he came cold and naked and he clothed him not.

During the course of the last long bloody war, Logan remained idle in his cabin, an advocate for peace. Such was my love for the whites, that my countrymen pointed as they passed, and said, "Logan is the friend of the white man."

I had even thought to have lived with you, but for the injuries of one man. Col. Cresap the last spring, in cold blood, and unprovoked, murdered all the relations of Logan; not even sparing my women and children.

There runs not a drop of my blood in the veins of any living creature. This called on me for revenge. I have sought it. I have killed many. I have fully glutted my vengeance. For my country, I rejoice at the beams of peace. But do not harbor a thought that mine is the joy of fear. Logan never felt fear. He will not turn on his heel to save his life. Who is there to mourn for Logan?—Not one!

So, it is said, spoke Tachnechdorus—whom the colonists called John Logan—a Mingo leader whose frontier family was killed, even as the Revolutionary War was beginning, in a scramble for land and power in the far northwestern territory of the Virginia colony. During the eighteenth century, English colonists in both the North and the South continued to move westward on the continent, pushing Native Americans ever farther from their homelands, killing them in intercultural warfare, wresting from them the most arable lands, the most useful waterways. The English takeover was felt especially in the Chesapeake and Virginia areas, where the large plantation culture forced the displacement of many native people, not all of them from the same groups.

Logan's family, Shawnees or Mingoes, had once formed part of the extended Six Nations Iroquois confederacy, but the dispersal of the several confederacy nations after the French and Indian War (the "last long bloody war" Logan mentioned, when the Iroquois had joined with the French, who lost the war) reduced their once-central power base into isolated settlements. Indeed, the Great War for Empire, as the French and Indian War has been called, was in reality a series of continuous skirmishes among French and English and native populations caught up in European imperial rivalries.

Logan testified that his family was murdered near the mouth of Yellow Creek, below Wheeling on the Ohio River, in April, 1774. Some historians have questioned whether Logan's family was actually attacked in the fight, but none doubt that the incident helped precipitate Logan's retaliatory raids in what has been called Lord Dunmore's (or Cresap's) War, fought between the Shawnees and the Virginia militia. Conflict between natives and whites lasted through the summer of 1774, but ended when the Virginia militia won a decisive battle at Point Pleasant. When the Native Americans capitulated to the militia, a "treaty" between native groups and the English resulted in the opening of Shawnee lands (in present-day Kentucky) to white settlement, with mere hunting and fishing rights being granted the Shawnees.

To mark his acceptance of defeat, Logan delivered the speech in his native tongue in October, 1774. The speech was translated for Lord Dunmore (the royal governor of Virginia) by General John Gibson, Logan's brother-in-law and Dunmore's envoy to the peace conference following Logan's defeat. According to Thomas Jefferson over a decade later, the speech evidenced the nobility of Native Americans in both peace and war, a nobility resembling that found in ancient Athens and Rome. In *Notes on the State of Virginia* (1787), Jefferson used the translation of Logan's speech to evidence the native honor and simplicity—in action and word—of native peoples, whom Europeans often considered to be degenerated savages. Alluding to the classic republican times Europeans admired, Jefferson insisted that Logan's speech could "challenge the whole orations of Demosthenes and Cicero, and of any more eminent orator." Printed in the *Virginia Gazette* and then widely in other newspapers in the colonies and Europe, printed again in Washington Irving's *Sketch Book* and in nineteenth-century editions of the popular schoolbook *McGuffey's Reader,* the speech enjoyed a wide readership, especially among white readers.

Jefferson had introduced Logan's speech into *Notes on the State of Virginia* to argue against the prevailing tendency of European philosophers to consider the American colonial experience as one of degeneration. The best-known proponent of the theory about American degeneration was the Frenchman George Louis Leclerc, the Comte du Buffon. Buffon considered the American environment cool and moist and thus less suited for human improvement than that of Europe. Living conditions in America, he wrote, would work against the nobility of the human race, forcing Europeans to deteriorate in both physical and civic life. By locating Logan's speech among those of the most illustrious of classical orators, Demosthenes and Cicero, Jefferson hoped to confer, ostensibly for Native Americans but in effect for all white Americans, a status of natural nobility. Jefferson's was both a pro- and a proto-American argument.

Yet the argument was made from the side of the dominant white writer who was in a position of accepted intellectual superiority, which enabled him to condescend to make this point. Jefferson made his point not in behalf of Native Americans, but primarily to support his claim in behalf of the quality of life for Euro-Americans—that white people in America could regenerate and progress rather than degenerate. If the American environment could produce such "noble savages," surely it would provide the opportunity for engendering even finer white Euro-Americans. To some extent, then, the popularity of the speech attests to the position of power, after the Revolutionary War, that whites held over other cultures in America. Precisely because theirs became the dominant culture, whites could comfortably label native people as simple and honorably noble like the Greeks and Romans of old—especially if such a characterization might improve their own position with those Europeans who still considered themselves superior to Americans. That the whites were elevating themselves by using precisely those people—the Indians—whom they subjected to their own dominion seems not to have been, for most whites, a problem. Logan's speech, translated, transcribed, and disseminated as it was by whites, might have provided evidence of an honorable race of people who resembled the classical republicans so admired by the Europeans. Yet the speech, noble as it might have seemed, could not prevent the encroachment of whites on lands held since ancient times by Native Americans. The whites would dominate both the land and the language of the native peoples of America. Thus, poignantly, the speech represents today not only Logan's private loss but the Europeans' sense of the potential loss of a whole people, an entire culture, as a structure of power was forged by the Euro-American population.

In many ways, the historical moment the speech describes is a paradigm for key eighteenth-century events. It suggests the early potential for peaceable relations between whites and natives, relations that became less and less tenable as more whites (especially from different ethnic groups) either arrived in America from Europe or, if born in America, survived to adulthood. The speech reveals as well the extent to which relations—between whites and natives, and among the native groups themselves—broke down amid the battle over native lands waged by the French against the English during the French and Indian Wars of the 1740s and 1750s. With the mid-century defeat of the Six Nations Iroquois and French, English groups advanced upon territory once held by French traders and Native Americans. Under English dominion, European settlers acquired ever more power over the native groups whom most whites considered inferior because different.

Perhaps the most telling irony of Logan's speech and its use over the years is that it was delivered by a native headman before an English delegation representing royal authority that would itself crumble within a decade to the growing forces of American colonists. At the moment that Logan bespoke an acceptance of his own subjected role to the English royal governor, the power of that royal governor was itself being questioned by colonists who would soon rebel against King George III. Later, after the American "patriots" won the Revolutionary War against the English, Jefferson would (still subjecting the Native Americans) use Logan's speech to place Americans in the elevated positions of ancient republican states. Patriot Americans had won the Revolutionary War, but, having won by the sword, they needed yet to win by the pen. To gain respectability and retain their newly gained international power, they had to find the language that would convince Europeans of their superior position. Providing the most favorable rhetorical figure to the events became central to patriot writers, especially after those events—Lord Dunmore's War and the Revolutionary War—receded into the past. That these wars finally became linguistically transcribed and honored by Americans suggests the extent to which events in the eighteenth century fulfill what one anthropologist calls the key human stages, from plough to sword to book.

A World of Change

Eighteenth-century Americans witnessed significant changes in their lives, changes demographic, economic, and, of course, political. In many ways, the alterations in the colonial demography and economy that took place in the first half of the century contributed to the key political event—the Revolutionary War—that took place in the latter part of the century. Eighteenth-century Americans indeed faced a world of change.

One of the most striking shifts was demographic. Compared to life in Europe, where population was dense and more urban, life in the colonies was more healthful, especially in the colonies north of Virginia. The population grew by natural increase as more children survived to adulthood and as women married at more youthful ages. If a woman married at a younger age, she would likely bear between five and eight children. More healthful than formerly in the colonies and in Europe, life in early eighteenth-century America exemplified the immense possibilities John Smith had announced a century earlier—hard work and a little property could bring prosperity to (white) colonists.

For hard work, primarily at the plough, many Europeans (whether as independent farmers or as indentured workers) ventured across the Atlantic. Migration was massive. Unlike the earlier migrations, those of the eighteenth century were marked by increasing numbers of non-English settlers. Indeed, by 1775, half the population south of New England was of non-English origin. The institution of slavery and the vast Spanish territory in Florida both account in part for this figure. About 275,000 black slaves were brought to the colonies during the century. And Spanish missionaries continued their movement into both Florida and the Southwest, where Franciscans set up chains of missions. By the late eighteenth century, Spain had dominion over a vast territory extending from California (initially colonized in 1769) through Texas (settled largely after 1700) to the Gulf Coast. Yet the largest immigration movement in the English colonies occurred along the eastern seaboard, where non-English settlers—Scotch-Irish, German, and Scottish, and, to a lesser extent, Dutch, French Hugenots, and Jews (usually coming from the Netherlands)—began to arrive in increasing numbers as the century progressed.

Ethnic diversity, combined with the healthful circumstances of life in eighteenth-century America, strengthened the population and helped bring about a rising standard of living. Benjamin Franklin was among the first to note the possibilities, precisely because of demographic circumstances, for the English empire and improved economy. In his 1751 pamphlet *Observations Concerning the Increase of Mankind,* Franklin predicted that in another century "the greatest Number of Englishmen will be on this [the American] side the water." He appealed to English imperialism: "What an Accession of Power to the British Empire by Sea as well as Land! . . . What Increase of Trade and Navigation!" In light of population statistics, Franklin was probably correct in his assessment: In the year 1650, the overall Euro-American population had been 52,000, the size of a small city today. By the year 1700, the Euro- and African-American population had grown to 250,000, and by 1730, that figure had more than doubled. By 1775, this population had expanded to 2.5 million; by the 1790s, to 3,500,000. According to some historians, such a rate of population growth—doubled nearly every twenty years—is unparalleled in recorded history.

Franklin's allusions to the economic and trade gains resulting from "the increase of mankind" in America were not unfounded. Generally speaking, the standard of living was on the rise for all property-owning Americans. Household inventories show the acquisition of amenities, such as earthenware and a variety of metal utensils

On American White Women

They are cold and without passion, however, and—a thing that is unpermissible except in an uncontrollable delirium—they endure the company of their lovers for whole hours without being sufficiently moved to change their expression. They always act as though everything they do is done for a purpose.

When one considers the unlimited liberty which young ladies enjoy, one is astonished by their universal eagerness to be married, to become wives who will for the most part be nothing but housekeepers of their husbands' homes. But this eagerness is just another exhibition of self-love, inspired by the fear that she who does not marry will be thought to have some fault that disgusted her suitors.

Moreau de St. Méry, *American Journey, 1793–1798*

to replace the wooden items previously used. Indeed, after 1750, the presence of luxury items like silver and silver plate in homes of the wealthy and English ceramics and teapots in homes of the "middling" sort suggests that colonial Americans were quickly realizing an upward trend in class mobility. Yet the rise of the standard of living was not evenly distributed. By mid-century, signs of an increasingly poorer urban population indicate that those already having property were gaining, those who had no property were not. There was very little available land in areas already settled by white colonists, making land more expensive for everyone. In addition, the greater number of children surviving in each family brought about a pressure on cities, for the children of country people would seek increasingly scarce work in the cities nearby. Surely, Benjamin Franklin was not the only young man in Boston who, in search of a trade, "had an Inclination for the Sea," as he reports in his *Autobiography*.

The New England economy was driven by its sea trade, which had grown as the seventeenth century reached its close. But the local American economies were, as colonies subject to a European power that waged its own political warfare, subject to fluctuations caused by the impact of European wars and by variations in overseas demands for American products. Not surprisingly, wars and trade differences brought separate results for the different colonies. The New England area, marked by rocky terrain and great pine forests, could be farmed for subsistence but not for crops for exportation; thus, merchant sea trade and shipbuilding understandably predominated. Significantly, New England traders benefited financially from the slave trade, as the South made increasing demands for slave importation. New Englanders were dependent upon the seas for their livelihoods. Thus, the imperial wars between England and other European nations had a distinct effect upon the New England economy, for they disrupted trade patterns and work opportunities.

The most significant European war to affect the colonies was King George's War (known in Europe as the War of the Austrian Succession), 1739–1748. England had, in 1739, declared war on Spain. New England initially gained from increased shipbuilding and the need for sailors, but the region suffered heavy losses after 1744, when France joined Spain against England and England started losing to the combined power of its two neighboring antagonists. The war took a great toll on New England men and supplies both at sea and on land. New Englanders were taxed heavily for their own militia's capture of the French fortress of Louisbourg at the mouth of the St. Lawrence River in 1745, and they resented the 1748 treaty of Aix-la-Chapelle, which gave Louisbourg back to the French.

On the other hand, the Middle Colonies prospered during this period. The greater fertility of the soil provided larger and richer farms for the dominant white population that could afford lands. The farms required tenant farmers, and they provided work for those in the area. The Middle Colonies gained from the greater wartime demand for foodstuffs. By mid-century, the economy in Philadelphia and New York surpassed that of Boston, which had deteriorated under the wartime situation. The Chesapeake area and the Lower South also benefited from the European wartime demand for food and supplies. After 1745, some Chesapeake planters began to convert tobacco fields to wheat and corn to meet the demand; yet most planters kept their fields in tobacco, thus taking advantage of a world trade market that brought for tobacco nearly double the price of grain produce. To handle the labor-intensive work of tobacco planting and curing, planters during this time escalated their acquisition of a slave force whose size was surpassed only by that in the areas to the south.

The Lower South—the Carolinas and Georgia—depended upon staple crops and slave labor. In mid-century, tobacco and rice crops climbed in value, despite some minor setbacks in trade caused by King George's War, so that the South generally became, as a region, richer than the North. South Carolina, for instance, had the highest average wealth per freeholder in Anglo-America by the time of the Revolutionary War. Its large slave force, which grew larger by natural increase, brought the dominant whites in the area a vast affluence, unparalleled in the colonies.

But the land seemed too small to fulfill the dreams and expectations of all immigrants, and many coveted the territory westward, where Native Americans in increasing numbers were forced to resettle. Westward movement, with its consequent displacement of native populations, seemed the only recourse to the dominant white culture. As they had from the earliest days of exploration, the Europeans viewed the Native Americans as formidable but ultimately subduable foes. English domination over the Indians resulted in part from their superior military weaponry during the earliest days and in part from the native peoples' unwillingness to form alliances with hereditary native foes against their newest, common enemy, the English. Yet the indigenous people evidently determined that they could use antagonisms among European powers to forestall European encroachment: they could remain neutral as the Europeans—Spanish, English, and French, primarily—attacked one another, or they could threaten alliance with one European power against another.

The natives' policies of neutrality, with the added threat of potentially antagonistic alliance, worked well in the East, until the time of the Great War for Empire, the French and Indian War, in the middle of the eighteenth century. The early sixteenth-century Six Nations Iroquois confederacy had dominated the Northeast territory from the earliest days of European exploration until the first half of the eighteenth century. Composed of five Indian nations, the Mohawks, Oneidas, Onondagas, Cayugas, Senecas—and, in 1722, the Tuscaroras—the Six Nations confederacy had, until the early 1750s, managed to remain relatively free of territorial agitation. In 1701, the confederacy officially adopted a policy of neutrality toward the Europeans. At the same time, the confederacy maintained power against their hereditary enemies, the Catawbas (who had allied with the English), and dominated the Shawnees and Delawares (in present-day western Pennsylvania and Ohio) as well. The group remained neutral toward the Europeans, and they engaged in trade relations with the French, thus enabling the latter to locate strategically placed trading posts along the Ohio River. Real trouble for the Iroquois began when English fur traders pushed into the Ohio country in 1752, causing the French traders there to fortify existing outposts along the rivers and to build new ones southward from Lake Erie.

Fearing French intrusion in lands potentially English, a delegation from seven northern and middle colonies met at Albany, New York, in June 1754. At this meeting, later called the Albany Congress, the colonial delegates adopted a plan of union for mutual legislation and support, and agreed to seek an English-Iroquois alliance and thus create a coordinated defense of the English colonies. The plan came too late, however. Gov. Robert Dinwiddie of Virginia had already pushed Virginia militia into present-day western Pennsylvania, where the French had established a stronghold at the juncture of the Allegheny and Monangahela Rivers (now Pittsburgh). Dinwiddie's inexperienced troops suffered a serious defeat against the French. Taking the English failure as a sign of ineptitude and future losses, the Six Nations peoples joined forces with the French.

For a time, the Indians' decision seemed appropriate, as suggested by the

July 1755 defeat—memorably recorded later in Franklin's *Autobiography*—of General Braddock near Fort Duquesne. English and colonial losses continued until July 1758, when the fort at Louisbourg was recaptured. A year later, French defenses were broken at Quebec. The English eventually won the war, and England gained—at the Treaty of Paris, signed in 1763—the major North American holdings of the French. In addition, England obtained Spanish Florida; Spain, having joined France against England toward the end of the war, ceded Florida to the English in return for its gain of French holdings in Louisiana.

Inter-group neutrality among eastern natives had worked well while France and Spain were still competing for territory against England. But with France no longer contending for the lands, and with Spain in territory west of the Mississippi, a strategy of neutrality was not useful. All along the eastern seaboard natives found themselves forced ever farther westward into central North America, away from their homelands. Similar developments occurred in the South, where English inroads against the Creeks and Cherokees provoked a Cherokee attack in 1760. The combined forces of British regulars and colonial militia forced the Native Americans in 1761 to submit to English dominion.

In the Northwest Territory (extending from present-day western Pennsylvania to western Michigan), the British monopoly over land and trade made life increasingly difficult for the native peoples. English encroachments reached crisis proportions finally in 1763, when in an unprecedented move, Pontiac, an Ottawa war chief, brought about an alliance among the Ottawas, Chippewas, Hurons, Potawatomis, Delawares, Shawnees, and even a portion of the Mingoes (Pennsylvania Iroquois). During the spring of 1763, the Indians beseiged a number of forts in the territory and raided the Pennsylvania and Virginia frontiers unimpeded, until Pontiac, in late October, suspended the attacks for the winter. Although Pontiac's alliance had dissolved, Scotch-Irish settlers from Paxton township in southwestern Pennsylvania retaliated against the only Native Americans in the area, a peaceful band of Christianized Conestoga Indians. After killing twenty people, the "Paxton Boys" marched toward Philadelphia to demand military protection against future Indian attack. As Benjamin Franklin movingly noted in his *Narrative of the Late Massacres,* "The only crime of these poor wretches [the Conestoga Indians] seems to have been that they had reddish-brown skin and black hair; and some people of that sort, it seems, had murdered some of our relations." Fearing violence from the Paxton Boys, city officials mustered a militia, but the Paxton protesters made their requests in an orderly fashion, and violence in Philadelphia was averted.

English response to the frontier situation was ineffectual for the most part. In a Proclamation of 1763, for example, the English government declared that the source waters of rivers flowing eastward to the Atlantic from the Appalachian Mountains should be the colonists' western boundary. This was a futile effort from a London government that had little knowledge of the frontier contest being waged. English settlers had already passed the boundary by the time the Proclamation of 1763 was enacted.

The march of the Paxton Boys to Philadelphia in order to make their claims known reveals the evolving hierarchy of authority at the time. Native Americans were increasingly dominated by white settlers who themselves were under the dominion of governments located largely in the East, from Savannah and Charleston to Philadelphia, New York, and Boston. Yet those centers of power were themselves theoretically directed by an overseas authority, the English king and parliament. But the overseas government consistently seemed to know less and less about the colonies, even as the colonists themselves became more and more aware of their potential for superiority over their English counterparts in fields ranging from political to scientific and philosophical inquiry. Ethnic diversity and economic ability led American colonists into a broader questioning of values than the Puritans a century earlier would ever have imagined. With the constantly shifting demographic and economic balances, it seems only logical to conclude that the colonists would begin to worry more about relations among themselves than about their relations to God or king, both of whom seemed far away to the many diverse Americans. American intellectuals were in a prime position to test the political, scientific, and philosophical "truths" about which their Puritan forebears and their European counterparts could only theorize.

The Enlightenment and the Great Awakening

Like their European counterparts, educated colonists were well aware of the scientific findings of Sir Isaac Newton (1642–1727) and the political, scientific, and philosophical theorizing of Thomas Hobbes (1588–1679) and John Locke (1632–1704). Most intellectuals would readily have concurred with Alexander Pope's pronouncement in the *Essay on Man* (1733–1734):

> Know then Thy-self, presume not God to scan;
> The proper Study of Mankind is *Man.*

And they would have agreed with his assertion that Newton showed the superiority of mankind in his ability to "unfold all Nature's Laws." Interest in science, given credence by the 1660 founding of the Royal Society, was promulgated in the eighteenth century in both poetry and prose. Some writers, like Cotton Mather, followed Newton's thinking and considered that the study of man and nature would add to the progress of human knowledge and thus to the greater glory of God. Others worked from Newton's scientific discoveries—the laws of gravitation and the refraction of light—and dispensed with his insistence that these discoveries evidenced God's hand in a harmonious universe and the natural world.

As Isaac Newton was influential in the areas of science and theology, so Newton's contemporaries Thomas Hobbes and John Locke were influential in psychological, political, and philosophical inquiry. Both Hobbes and Locke sought ways to argue against medieval scholasticism and the Renaissance neo-Platonists' intuitional philosophy, which was based upon the assumption that mankind was given, *a priori,* innate knowledge by God. Hobbes, insisting upon the absolute power of the state, studied human psychology and averred that mankind in the state of nature formed social groups out of fear and the need for mutual protection. Locke, born two generations later, took a different approach. He argued that each person was born with a "tabula rasa," a blank slate, upon which experience inscribed knowledge. Human knowledge was thus, for Locke and his followers, accrued according to experience, not divinely parcelled out at birth and given the sanction of intuition. Locke's view of human nature was more favorable than Hobbes's, and his conception of government—for mutual benefit—more readily adaptable to life in the colonies during the eighteenth century.

Except perhaps in the case of Jonathan Edwards, who studied Newton and Locke very closely, many colonists (especially of the "middling" group but also those of the politically influential elite) by mid-century seem generally to have followed popularized versions of the philosophy of enlightenment promoted by what has come to be called the Scottish Common Sense "school," a consequence of the Scottish Enlightenment. The writers and philosophers of the Scottish Enlightenment—including, among others, Francis Hutcheson (1694–1746), Henry Home, Lord Kames (1696–1782), Thomas Reid (1710–1796), David Hume (1711–1776), William Robertson (1721–1793), Adam Ferguson (1723–1816), James Beattie (1735–1803), Dugald Stewart (1753–1828), and even Adam Smith (1723–1790)—were responding to the theories of Newton, Hobbes, and Locke, even as they were responding to the intellectual, economic, social, and political turmoil in Europe. The philosophy of the Scottish Enlightenment is a rich and various body of thought that is difficult to characterize. Colonists seem to have been attracted to Adam Ferguson, whose social theories called into question the prevailing assumptions about the state of nature; they admired Henry Home, Lord Kames, for his theories of jurisprudence, which held to views of historical relativism; for history, they read David Hume and William Robertson and enjoyed the comparative views of the latter; for moral philosophy, Francis Hutcheson and Adam Smith provided bases for progressive views of human nature. Even in medicine, intellectuals in the colonies tended to look to Edinburgh until well after the Revolution.

Part of the explanation for the influence of the Common Sense philosophers upon American colonists might arise from the originally Calvinist base of this philosophy (which might have appealed to New Englanders), though the philosophy can hardly be said to evidence orthodox Calvinism. In addition, however, because many of the original settlers in the southern colonies were Scots or Scotch-Irish, the traditions of dissent and moral philosophy represented by the Scottish philosophers would have been brought with the colonists as they emigrated. For colonists in the eighteenth century, the central philosopher of common sense was Thomas Reid, whose appeal was democratic and utilitarian. Rather than arguing the particulars of what can or cannot be proved by reasoning, Reid insisted, philosophers should, on the grounds of experience, consensus, and necessity, assume that the human mind can know actual objects and that "a wise and good Author of nature" will "continue the same laws of nature, and the same connections of things, for a long time." A reasonable and predictable God is close to the deity of Jefferson and Paine. And the practical philosophy of reliance upon moral and sensory impressions ap-

> Among the natural rights of the colonists are these: first, a right to life; second, to liberty; third, to property; together with the right to support and defend them in the best manner they can. These are evident branches of, rather than deductions from, the duty of self-preservation, commonly called the first law of nature.
>
> All men have a right to remain in a state of nature as long as they please; and in case of intolerable oppression, civil or religious, to leave the society they belong to, and enter into another.
>
> When men enter into society, it is by voluntary consent; and they have a right to demand and insist upon the performance of such conditions and previous limitations as form an equitable original compact.
>
> Every natural right not expressly given up, or, from the nature of a social compact, necessarily ceded, remains.
>
> Samuel Adams, "The Rights of the Colonists," 1772

pealed to these men who were about to create what they argued could be a rational and predictable future.

The rise of empirical science (the inquiry into natural phenomena) in the late seventeenth and early eighteenth centuries made the colonies a good testing-place for scientific, political, and philosophical beliefs. There, as never before, European assumptions about nature and human nature could be tested. Some intellectuals, like Jonathan Edwards, found in the American testing-place ample demonstration of the theological certainties of Newton, that evidence of God's hand was everywhere apparent in the natural world. Others, like Franklin and Jefferson, found political and social evidence of Locke's and the Common Sense philosophers' positions on government, and they developed arguments insisting upon the necessary and infallible progress of human affairs.

Given the paradisiacal expectations associated with the colonies from the times of earliest exploration, it is no wonder that some people took comfort in the Newtonian position that scientific inquiry could help demonstrate God's presence in their world. And, given the immense changes both demographic and economic in the eighteenth century, it is also no wonder that these same people wanted reassurance of God's steadying presence. One of the strongest American supporters of Newtonian and Lockean philosophy was Jonathan Edwards (1703–1758), a quiet and introspective minister whose preaching and writing assisted one of America's largest evangelical movements.

At a time when strict Puritan practice was giving way to a more ecumenical protestant approach to salvation, Jonathan Edwards used the most recent scientific and philosophical treatises to insist upon his own devout belief in the necessity for each person to have a felt experience of God's grace in order to be assured of salvation. His maternal grandfather, Solomon Stoddard, had helped introduce the Half-Way Covenant in New England, permitting a liberal, more ecumenical Puritanism in keeping with the aspiring congregation he served in Northampton. Edwards held, contrary to Stoddard and others, that such a liberalizing transformation of strict Puritan doctrine was "repugnant to the design and tenor of the gospel." His reading in the works of Newton, Locke, and their followers suggested to him, first, that God's hand was evident in all the natural creation, and second, that careful inquiry into one's relationship with God could create the psychological state necessary for one to achieve a felt presence of the godhead. For Edwards, it was insufficient to comprehend God mentally; one had to experience the truth of the gospel. His reading in Locke convinced him that sense impressions could convey signs of God's presence, and he sought to create in the members of the Northampton congregation, which he took over upon the death of his grandfather, the sensate impressions of God's presence among them.

He was successful for a time. In 1735, his congregation seemed to be "seized," he later said, "with a deep concern about their eternal salvation," and many members related their experiences of God's grace. A revival began to spread to other congregations in the neighboring communities. News of the awakening in western Massachusetts spread to Boston, where it was publicized and debated. The publicity led to renewed spiritual questionings in many New England communities. With only minor setbacks, the awakening continued to flourish in New England settlements, only to become more widespread by the late 1730s. The years 1738 and 1739 brought reports of a wide evangelical movement in England, then in the southern and middle colonies, under the work of English evangelist George Whitefield (1714–1770). Whitefield reached New England in 1740, where congregation after congregation was moved into evangelical fervor and spiritual concern. Insisting that God had touched them and given them conversion experiences, hundreds of people flocked to their churches for spiritual outpouring and renewal. The Great Awakening, as it was called, was at its height. With its emphasis on individual experience above time-honored authority, the Great Awakening was, in effect, a large and democratic movement in the colonies. Anyone, it seemed—rich or poor, black or Native American or white—could awaken and so join, on an equal footing, in a national movement toward salvation. A key factor of the Great Awakening was the extent to which it drew people from nonelite and rural culture into a communal bond, a communal identity. Edwards's work, central to the Great Awakening, had helped to disseminate broadly the philosophical trends of European intellectuals.

Other Americans took the same intellectual tradition Edwards followed and began to suggest, like the Europeans they read, that salvation for mankind was not in the hands of God but in the hands of men. Philosophers of the Enlightenment, these intellectuals considered that Newton's scientific discoveries would light the way of mankind into a more perfect human community. To them, the ecclesiastical insistence upon revealed "truth" only produced sectarian differences. Known as Deists, these intellectuals argued that the structure of the universe, not the Bible, attested to God. Enlightenment thinkers believed the universe to be governed by rational laws that could be uncovered and understood through scientific inquiry. In their view, mankind's ability to reason and make deductions about the world would enable them to define and categorize the natural world and to design systems of government that would enable humankind to further its necessary progress in that world. Whereas Christian theologians believed that God intervened directly and immediately in human life, Enlightenment philosophers like Franklin considered God a kind of supreme architect or watchmaker who designed the world, set it in motion, and then left it to operate on its own. It was up to people, not God, to see that the world functioned for the good of all, not just those who happened to belong to one religious sect or another. Religious fanaticism was an object worthy only of satire—as Franklin's "A Witch Trial at Mount Holly" (1730) suggests. Outside of religious belief, people should inquire into doing good in the world. The best endeavors, Enlightenment thinkers argued, concerned benefits to all people.

One religious society that concerned itself with benefits to all people, regardless of creed, race, or class, increased its numbers during the eighteenth century. The Society of Friends, or Quakers as they were commonly called, early implemented their theories of equality and toleration in their social practice. Welsh, Irish, Dutch, and German Quakers had in the late seventeenth century established themselves in Pennsylvania, where Quaker William Penn had formed a colony, in part from lands granted him by Charles II and in part from lands he purchased from the Delawares (or Lenni Lenapes) in the area. Pacifist and egalitarian in principles, the Quakers became known for their tolerance of all peoples, which brought Pennsylvania a number of Native American groups from western Maryland, Virginia, and North Carolina along with many European immigrants. Quakers believed that all the creation was God's, whether one were black, red, or white, and that the individual's experience of God's love could manifest itself as an inner light of harmony expressed outwardly as love for all in God's world. Their egalitarian practice was evident in meetinghouse (where both men and women could pray or speak if they felt moved to do so) and countinghouse. The Quakers were the first group to work in behalf of freedom of worship for black slaves, the first to seek, in a Yearly Meeting notice from the 1680s, the abolition of slavery, the institution they called "the traffic in menbody." Franklin might have fallen asleep in a Quaker meeting upon his first entrance into Philadelphia, as he jokingly reports in his *Autobiography,* but he evidently did not fail to note the attractive democratic egalitarianism of Quaker principles when he went to Paris for peace negotiations at the time of the American Revolution. He there donned a fur cap and let the French celebrate him as a new-world Quaker, a representative of toleration and democratic principles.

Daily Life and the Woman's Sphere

Quakers, known for their egalitarianism, were the first group of Euro-Americans to allow women full voice in religious meeting and in the home. For the most part, the Euro-American community continued in the well-established patriarchal social tradition that allocated to men certain social privileges outside the home, privileges associated with church and state affairs, that were not available to women. With the exception of the Quaker household, then, gender roles were fairly well established. Men would have the public speaking voices. And, for the most part and with the exception of popular evangelism in more rural areas, it was the men of the elite culture who established themselves as public spokesmen.

White men and women who could afford the leisure time required for writing lived primarily in the plantation South and in northern cities. Such leisure time was a luxury in the colonies, where an overwhelming majority—more than ninety percent of the population—lived in rural areas. Given the abundance of literature that has survived, we tend easily to forget that nearly all adult white men and women lived and worked on farms. Whether a man were a miller or blacksmith and whether his wife ran a small business selling the family's surplus produce, both engaged in these activities in addition to their central tasks of farming.

Rural women typically worked on household affairs—food preparation (milking cows and making butter, planting and harvesting of gardens, in addition to cooking and canning), clothing manufacture (from spinning the thread for the cloth to cutting and sewing garments), and cleaning (making the soap, then washing clothes in a nearby water source or carrying the water home). Life was not easy for such women, and their chores were performed in addition to training the five to eight children they bore. It is no wonder, then, that the diaries of women frequently contain entries made up entirely of statements about chores they accomplished or complaints about personal weakness and sickness. Men in eighteenth-century households also experienced heavy workloads. Their wives' gardens were for the family; their own pastures were usually cultivated for market. Thus, they planted and cultivated large fields, ran herds of cattle into pastures, and slaughtered animals for home and city markets. In households governed largely by the seasons and by available light, the accomplishment of such arduous chores necessitated the help of children or, in wealthier households, servants or slaves.

For the small percentage of the population that lived in cities, life took on a different character. Mercantile in nature and usually coastal or riverside in location, city life was dominated by the market, which brought in foodstuffs and wares from rural areas and goods imported from abroad. The cities thus offered more opportunity for socializing, and wealthier urbanites were afforded the leisure time for reading, walking or riding, card-playing, dancing, and attending plays or concerts.

City dwellers, not isolated on vast farm acres but living in the middle of crowds, had opportunities to learn more about the world than their farmer counterparts. News from London and the rest of Europe, along with that from other colonies, appeared in local newspapers.

Printers and presses increased in number as the century wore on: by the middle of the eighteenth century, every major city had at least one newspaper, and some cities had two or three. Twenty-six newspapers were published weekly by the year 1765. Competing for a relatively small readership, newspapers regularly announced the "latest news" and "newest imported goods."

City life and work opportunities tended to attract rural workers, single women, and widows. Women, whether unmarried or widowed with children, could rarely run farmsteads without the aid of adult males, so they tended to seek work in the cities for their own livelihoods, as nurses or midwives, seamstresses, servants, or prostitutes. Only unmarried women or widows could legally run independent businesses, and very few had the capital necessary to open up their own businesses (shops, inns, or boardinghouses). The common-law system of coverture, in which a married woman became one person with her husband (who was given all legal rights to her personal property), prevented married women from seeking work or social activity outside the domestic sphere. For the eleven or twelve women before 1776 who managed the presses after their printer-husbands died, life must indeed have been interesting, for they could not only break the implied social barrier against their working, but engage in trades that brought them positions of power—the dissemination of knowledge—within the community.

At least in some situations, women could work outside the home for their own livelihoods. Slaves rarely had such opportunity. More than ninety-five percent of black families were held as slaves. The majority of South Carolina's population was black; in Georgia, about half the population and, in the Chesapeake, forty percent was black. In these areas, the average household held about ten workers as slaves. And, given the size of such plantation households, workers' labors were specialized. Men typically worked as blacksmiths, woodworkers, and field workers, while women worked the dairies or made clothing or food. But only about twenty percent of the slaves engaged in specialized labor. By far the majority—especially on the larger plantations—were assigned to the fields. As James Grainger's long poem *The Sugar Cane* (1764) makes clear, the situation of the South was like—though less intense than—that in the West Indies. Anxiety about controlling the slave population functioned as a repression revealing a curiosity about "the other"—African and African-descended slaves—but a curiosity born of fear and desire for "mastery" over the black slave body.

Because most slaves were prevented from learning to read and write, stories by blacks tended to be passed down in an oral tradition. Autobiographical accounts like *The Interesting Narrative of the Life of Olaudah Equiano, or Gustavus Vassa, the African* (1789) provide rare glimpses into the lives of slaves. The importance of oral expression in African culture encouraged slaves to maintain the vitality of similar expression in their new American surroundings, a vitality lost to white masters who did not understand the symbolic resilience of their slaves' oral transmissions.

Literacy and Education

Colonial life, especially in the first half of the eighteenth century, was hierarchically structured, men over women, and whites over blacks and Native Americans. Power was in the hands of the dominant white men, typically those educated, and, as the century wore on, those educated and engaged in city or colonial government. The abundance of the literature from this era might lead readers falsely to conclude that most British Americans could both read and write. Yet most—almost all blacks, half the white women, and one-fifth the white men—could do neither. Colonial culture was—at least in the first half of the eighteenth century, before the market economy started to develop and printing presses became fully established—an oral culture, one that depended upon the person-to-person transmission of information.

By mid-century, this situation began to shift. The newer elite culture, made up of merchants and tradesmen in cities and northern farmers and southern rural plantation-holders, was oriented toward the printed medium, toward individual rather than communal accomplishment, and toward the city. Literacy, less essential in a rurally based and orally established society like that of early eighteenth-century America, became a sign of status and thus an accomplishment. Parents who held property wanted to distinguish themselves from their neighbors, so they sent their male children to study, usually with the local minister, in preparation for collegiate training in one of the newly founded universities—schools now known as the College of William and Mary (chartered, 1693; established, 1726); Princeton (1747); Columbia (1754); Brown (1765); Rutgers (1766)—or to Harvard (1636) or Yale (1701). Except for the first students, native students, at Princeton and Dartmouth (Moor's Indian School), education was for the propertied elite. Indeed, the wealthiest families, to set themselves apart from their colonial peers, sent their children to Europe—usually London or Edinburgh (the center of Enlightenment thought in Scotland)—for college.

Very few families sent women to study at the minister's home, much less to college. Yet public (or dame) schools were established on an increasingly frequent basis in the eastern seaboard cities and even in more urban areas in the countryside. Consequently, by mid-century, more and more children—male and female—were being trained in reading and writing. Along with a rudimentary intellectual education, usually in reading but not in writing, girls from elite families might also have received instruction in music, dancing, and fancy needlework, these three abilities signifying genteel status.

In contrast, the vast majority of slaves received only such formal education as their white masters deemed necessary for them to perform their duties. For the average slave, this meant no training whatsoever. Furthermore, most slaveholders—especially in the South—believed that literacy ill-suited a slave to accept his or her place and thus was detrimental to local security. As a result, many governments passed laws making it illegal to teach slaves to read and write. The relatively small number of free blacks in the English colonies had only slightly better educational opportunities, for most schools did not enroll black students. By comparison, Native Americans might seem to have fared somewhat better. Between the 1730s and 1760s, a flurry of Indian education experiments were made, in the Middle Colonies especially. As a result, a number of Native Americans received formal educations. Yet in terms of the total population of Native Americans, only a small proportion of native people were selected for training, which itself was determined by the Christianizing attitudes of the whites who ran the schools.

Revolution and Confederation

Demographic differences in the colonies generally affected Americans' attitudes toward revolution against England. For example, in the South, where the population was most racially mixed, the white colonists' zeal for revolution was countered by their interest in keeping their slave territory free of intrusion and slave revolts. The Revolution confronted non-whites with the complex dilemma of determining allegiance. For the majority of African-Americans, the choices were especially stark: possible emancipation versus continued enslavement. At the outset of the war, the willingness of free northern blacks to support the rebellion was dramatized most memorably by the case of Crispus Attucks, an ex-slave who was one of the first people killed in the revolutionary cause when he was shot by British troops in the Boston Massacre in 1770. Then, in 1775, African-Americans played active roles in the engagements at Lexington, Concord, and Bunker Hill (where the black Peter Salem is said to have been responsible for killing the British Major Pitcairn) and in the efforts of the Green Mountain Boys in Vermont. However, in late 1775, blacks were officially barred from the American military, partially because of fear among slaveholders that arming them would prove disruptive. Moving to take advantage of the colonists' paranoia, in November of 1775 the British attempted to destabilize the colonial workforce in the South by offering freedom to male slaves and indentured servants who joined their side. This action forced George Washington and the Continental Congress to reverse their decision on the enlistment of blacks. In addition, it served to consolidate support for the Revolution—especially in the South, where many whites had initially remained loyal to England. With the British attempt to undermine the slave system, however, "patriot" American propagandists were able to argue successfully that any serious division among whites could render the southern colonies, where blacks often made up one-half or more of the population, vulnerable to slave insurrections.

Likewise, fear of attack by Native Americans brought those on the western frontier into the Revolution in behalf of the rebel Americans. The Indians, frustrated and displaced by whites' pressures on their homelands, might have been willing to use a British alliance to retaliate against the colonists, who seemed increasingly uninterested in the rights of Native Americans. Indeed, although the Proclamation of 1763 did not finally protect Native Americans from incursions, it did suggest to them that British officials in London respected their claims to lands more fully than the colonists who had overrun their territories. When Lord Dunmore's War erupted in western Virginia in 1774, the way seemed clear for an Indian alliance with the British. Out of self-defense and their awareness that colonial relations with the Indians were very poor, revolutionaries sought Native Americans' neutrality in the conflict. The Cherokees were the only large group to attack Americans—the western borders of settlements in the Carolinas and Virginia, in the summer of 1776—during the Revolutionary War. Other groups seem to have paid attention to the message of the Second Continental Congress that the war was "a family quarrel between us and Old England," that "you Indians are not concerned in it."

Problems in the "family," between the colonies and England, had emerged at least as early as the 1750s. As a result of the French and Indian War (often called the Great War for Empire or the Seven Years War), which concluded with the 1763 Treaty of Paris, the British treasury was depleted. Convinced that the colonists should contribute to the cost of their own defense, members of Parliament passed a series of taxes designed to enhance the English treasury at the Americans' expense. The first of these, the Sugar Act of 1764, led to a colonial boycott of English goods. The Stamp Act of 1765 brought a similar response, along with more direct action: the Stamp Act Congress drafted a "Declaration of Rights and Grievances" for presentation to King and Parliament. As tempers flared on both sides of the Atlantic, conciliatory voices grew silent. Evidently seeking to affirm its authority, Parliament passed a series of measures—the Declaratory Act, the Townshend Acts, the Tea Act, the Coercive Acts—that proved inimical to Americans. Although some of these measures were repealed, the colonists were ready for open revolt by 1776.

Even before the *Declaration of Independence,* however, the Boston Massacre

(1770) and the Boston Tea Party (1773) had mobilized anti-British resistance, which erupted into armed skirmishes at Lexington and Concord in 1775. Significant open warfare, after the *Declaration* was made, occurred in New York City, where George Washington's patriot forces lost to the British regulars and Hessian mercenaries in June, 1776. The British expected a brief campaign of decisive victories. They planned for the war to be over in 1776. George Washington, commander-in-chief of the American army, considered winning battles less important than preventing major losses. He lacked regular troops—the Continental Army never numbered more than 18,500 men—but he nonetheless found the necessary militia at crucial times. Washington lost his first battle, that over New York City in 1776; his retreat across New Jersey allowed the British to occupy New York and New Jersey. Wintering at Valley Forge, Washington's troops faced what Thomas Paine in *The American Crisis* called "the times that try men's souls." The colonial militia rallied and struck back—during Christmastime, 1776, and the early part of 1777—at the battles of Trenton and Princeton. In the meantime, the British general William Howe, having plotted with Joseph Galloway and other Tories (pro-British sympathizers) in Philadelphia, left New York City and took over Philadelphia in 1777. But the Americans had a victory in upper New York, where the militia under the command of General Horatio Gates surrounded British general Burgoyne late in the year. As a result, officials in London decided that a shift in command and in strategy was necessary. They sent Sir Henry Clinton to replace Howe in Philadelphia. In the meantime, in 1778, the French joined the American colonists against the English.

The British set about attacking the South in 1779 and 1780. Charleston, the most important city in the American South, fell to British forces in May, 1780; South Carolina was under attack throughout the year. American retaliation in South Carolina began in October, 1780, in the west Appalachians, where a group of "over-mountain men" defeated a large party of loyalists and redcoats. In 1781, American generals Nathanael Greene and Daniel Morgan confronted British regiments under Tarleton and Cornwallis in the Carolinas. When Cornwallis withdrew his troops to the tip of the Virginia peninsula between the York and James Rivers, Washington quickly advanced over seven thousand troops southward and, with the aid of the Comte de Grasse, who brought a French fleet from the West Indies, forced a British surrender there in October, 1781. By November, 1782, a preliminary peace agreement was reached at Paris; it was formally signed in September, 1783.

The years immediately following the end of the Revolution were extremely difficult for the new nation. A post-war economic depression created restlessness among farmers, and the government under the Articles of Confederation (1781) failed to establish control over the divided states. Cries for a more effective national government became more frequent. As a result, the men who gathered in Philadelphia in 1787 to work out a revision of the Articles dismantled the old system in favor of a new form of government. They wrote a Constitution that based its authority on neither God nor a king but on the people, from whom all power would emanate. Reprinted in all newspapers in the colonies, the constitutional articles produced a controversy over ratification that led to a bitter debate between federalists (those interested in strong central government) and anti-federalists (who preferred regional interests to rule over national ones). Sectional differences emerged as southerners feared the loss of power due to their agriculturally based economy in the face of northern merchant and industrial enterprise. With the public dissemination of the constitutional articles, the will of the people—diverse as that will was—was consulted for the first time in America. The Constitution was ratified in 1788, and George Washington was inaugurated as first President of the United States in 1789.

The ratification of the Constitution signaled a shift in political ideology, a shift best reflected in the phrase, "We, the People," which began the document and created a basis for common identity while being sufficiently vague to permit a range of complex interpretations. The Constitution set up a system designed to prevent any one faction from gaining absolute control by providing for checks and balances among the executive, the legislative, and the judicial branches of the government. Committed to the efficacy of compromise, the men who devised the Constitution hoped to unify conflicting sections of American society.

A Nation of Disparate Peoples

Underlying the constitutional debate about power was an ideological debate about the basis of human nature: Were humans innately depraved and did they thus need strong, centralized governmental control to prevent them from pursuing unrestrained self-interest? Or, was human nature basically good—or, if not basically good, improvable—and thus deserving of the freedom necessary for progressive achievement? It was a vexing issue, one that in many ways resembled the religious controversies of earlier centuries, in which Puritans argued that mankind deserved the constraints and chastisement given by an angry God while Catholics and Anglicans argued that mankind could, through good works, achieve salvation. Yet the constitutional debate of the eighteenth century took its premises not so much from religious beliefs as from seventeenth- and eighteenth-century philosophical positions. Some American political theorists—John Adams most prominently—looked with skepticism upon liberal conceptions of progress, and they argued that governmental restraints were necessary because mankind could not be trusted to behave well. Other political theorists—Jefferson, most notably—favored the notion that scientific rationalism could free people for personal and civic betterment. The debate about the nature of the American government was officially over once the Constitution was ratified, yet the debate about human nature has not ceased to exist, as Americans still attempt to establish just who "We, the People" are and how extensive our rights might be.

With the ratification of the Constitution, a new era was at hand. In the year 1775, about half the population, white and black, was under sixteen years of age. This is a significant figure. Americans tend to consider the men who devised the Constitution, honorifically called the Founding Fathers, as sage, elder statesmen. Except for Franklin, however, most of them were just reaching the height of their legal careers. Their Constitution was for their children, and for the Americans, red, white, and black, who had been squabbling among themselves for years. Once the Constitution was devised and ratified, the real challenge emerged: leaders would have to make such a youthful and diverse population accept the radically new form of government.

The youthful age of Americans at the time of the Revolution perhaps contributed to the greater impetus, after the Revolution, to establish an educational system for most Americans. As we have seen, education during most of the century had been available for the well-to-do, a personal benefit obtainable through private means. After the Revolution, however, education was needed to serve a public purpose. Two very important changes in educational practice occurred in America during the late 1780s and the 1790s: states became willing to fund public elementary schools from tax monies, and schooling was improved for girls. At this key time, demographics worked in the favor of women's education: the new generation of mothers would have to be instructed, leaders publicly argued, if the new nation were to run smoothly. Some of these public leaders were women. Judith Sargent Murray, for instance, argued in behalf of women's education on the grounds that women were as intellectually capable as men.

But mere education was not enough for some women who sought equality on all social issues. One female "Matrimonial Republican" argued, contrary to the patriarchal social assumptions of her day, "marriage ought never to be considered as a contract between a superior and an inferior, but a reciprocal union of interest." In New Jersey, unmarried women, widows, and free blacks even seized voting rights in 1776. Yet most eighteenth-century Americans, regardless of gender, considered women's place to be in the home, as wives and mothers subject to the authority of husbands and fathers. Free blacks and women were disenfranchised by the New Jersey state legislature in 1807. Deeply held attitudes would not be overturned so quickly.

But social changes were imminent. A great deal of internal migration occurred in post-Revolutionary America: between five and ten percent of the population moved each year, usually westward. When poor white southern farmers moved westward into Kentucky and Tennessee, then to the rich lands in western Georgia or to the Gulf Coast, they displaced their entire households, including their slaves. Amid the social upheaval, evangelical religion offered to many the only sense of social cohesion they could muster. A Second Great Awakening began about 1800 in the western areas, this time evoked among Baptist, Presbyterian, and Methodist groups. Both women and blacks formed significant portions of those spiritually awakened, and they preached as well, exhorting both white and black listeners to universal salvation. This awakening, in line with the Constitutional disestablishment of a state religion and in line as well with increased racial ferment in the Upper South, produced the first signs of the collective empowering of blacks and women at the level of nonelite culture. In this regard, the work of ministers like Lemuel Haynes stands as a significant achievement.

Members of minority groups felt empowered locally, perhaps, but they had little voice in the larger, public debate about their status in the new world they had a major part in creating. Slaves, free blacks, Mexicans, and Native Americans had almost no part in the process of establishing norms, scant opportunity to voice their objections to the established practices of the dominant white culture. Discrimination against these groups was already entrenched—in both law and custom—and white Americans were well on the way to developing a coherent racist theory that would justify the oppression of non-whites. Some groups—for example, white slaveholders—even began to call into question the very humanity of non-white peoples (specifically, blacks) as a way to maintain their power in a nation that had just proclaimed that "*all* men are created equal."

Blacks did not let such racism remain unnoticed. Benjamin Banneker set about directly challenging Jefferson's assumption—as expressed in his influential *Notes on the State of Virginia* (1787)—of blacks' intellectual inferiority. Banneker—a free black surveyor, astronomer, mathematician, and almanac-maker—sent Thomas Jefferson a copy of his latest almanac in 1791. Jefferson complimented Banneker on his ability but suggested to him that he was an exception among blacks.

Other blacks attacked whites for their hypocritical imposition of slavery in a supposedly free society. In 1789, Olaudah Equiano attacked the institution of slavery, denouncing it as an arbitrary value system that, where the rights of African-Americans were concerned, promoted

You say that you are sent to instruct us how to worship the Great Spirit agreeably to His mind, and, if we do not take hold of the religion which you white people teach, we shall be unhappy hereafter. You say that you are right and we are lost. How do we know this to be true? We understand that your religion is written in a book. If it was intended for us as well as you, why has not the Great Spirit given to us, and not only to us, but why did He not give to our forefathers the knowledge of that book, with the means of understanding it rightly? We only know what you tell us about it. How shall we know when to believe, being so often deceived by the white people?

Brother, you say there is but one way to worship and serve the Great Spirit. If there is but one religion, why do you white people differ so much about it? Why not all agreed, as you can all read the book?

Brother, we do not understand these things. We are told that your religion was given to your forefathers and has been handed down from father to son. We also have a religion which was given to our forefathers and has been handed down to us, their children. We worship in that way. It teaches us to be thankful for all the favors we receive, to love each other, and to be united. We never quarrel about religion.

Brother, the Great Spirit has made us all, but He has made a great difference between His white and red children. He has given us different complexions and different customs. To you He has given the arts. To these He has not opened our eyes. We know these things to be true. Since He has made so great a difference between us in other things, why may we not conclude that He has given us a different religion according to our understanding? The Great Spirit does right. He knows what is best for His children; we are satisfied.

Sagoyewatha (Red Lion), 1805

Christianity in principle but not in practice. Because white churches often refused to minister to black parishioners, two black ministers, Absalom Jones and Richard Allen, founded the Free African Society in 1787, an organization that eventually developed into the African Methodist Episcopal Church. In response to the wide evangelical success of several black ministers during the Second Great Awakening, other writers, supported by members of the clergy, spoke of slavery as a social imbalance "unbecoming the excellence of true religion."

Blacks struggled with the question of how they could participate in American society. Some, like Prince Hall, who brought together the first black Masonic order in 1775, developed separate social institutions for blacks. In 1777, Hall, with the assistance of a contingent of free blacks in Boston, petitioned the Massachusetts House of Representatives to abolish slavery, arguing that freedom was "the natural right of all men—and their children who were born in this land of liberty." To disregard the cause of freedom was to be in violation of the "law of nature and of a nation." In behalf of free blacks, Hall petitioned for public education for children of tax-paying blacks. The petition was denied.

Whites, from their own vantage-point, faced similar questions about integration. Some whites, like Ezra Stiles, president of Yale, advocated the colonization of free blacks in West Africa. In January, 1787, Prince Hall, with seventy-three other blacks, petitioned the Massachusetts General Court for financial or other assistance for blacks to emigrate to Africa. Emigration westward seemed another answer to disempowered blacks. Around the year 1779, the black Jean Baptiste Point du Sable established a trading post on the southern shore of Lake Michigan, an area that eventually became the city of Chicago. In 1781, a small group of *pobladores,* or settlers, established the *Pueblo de Nuestra Senora la Reina de los Angeles de Porciuncula* in California. Of the forty-four *pobladores,* twenty-six were either of black or a mixture of black and hispanic ancestry. These Afro-Mexicans created the founding location of present-day Los Angeles.

But the emigration of free blacks was hardly a workable solution to an overwhelming cultural problem, the institution of slavery. In the decades following the Revolution, the northern states chose to address the issue by abolishing slavery—either immediately or over a predetermined number of years. In 1777 Vermont became the first state to ban slavery within its borders; by 1783, Massachusetts had done likewise. In 1780, Pennsylvania set up a plan for gradual emancipation, as did Connecticut and Rhode Island in 1784. Other northern states devised similar legislation. The possibility of this trend spreading to the South grew dimmer with each passing year, however, for the southern economic system was far more directly dependent upon slave labor than was that of the North. Furthermore, with Eli Whitney's invention of the cotton gin in 1793, the South became even more economically dependent upon cotton and, in turn, upon slave labor.

The sectional differences between North and South over the slave question were officially evident at least as far back as 1776, when Thomas Jefferson removed a statement attacking Great Britain for its support of the slave trade from the *Declaration of Independence* he had drafted. Considering that twenty-five of the fifty-five delegates to the Constitutional Convention in 1787 were slaveholders, it is hardly surprising that the Constitution itself bespoke an uneasy compromise on an issue over which, Americans painfully learned, there could be no compromise. The strategy adopted at the time was to appease the southern interests by allowing three-fifths of the total number of slaves to be included in the population totals for each state in determining taxation and the apportionment of votes in the House of Representatives. In return, the South permitted the inclusion of a clause stipulating that the importation of slaves would be illegal after twenty years. Thus, not only did the Constitution have no effect whatsoever upon the internal slave trade, but it forbade states to harbor fugitive slaves, and it left unaddressed the rights of free blacks.

These concessions also led to further concessions to proslavery interests. For example, in 1803, Congress allowed slavery in the newly purchased Louisiana territory. At the close of 1819 twenty-two states had been admitted to statehood, eleven slave (Virginia, Maryland, Delaware, Kentucky, Tennessee, North Carolina, South Carolina, Georgia, Alabama, Mississippi, and Louisiana) and eleven free (Massachusetts, Connecticut, Rhode Island, Vermont, New Hampshire, New York, New Jersey, Pennsylvania, Ohio, Indiana, and Illinois). The political balance had been maintained by an alternating pattern of admission of slave and free states. When Missouri and Maine petitioned Congress for statehood at the close of 1819, northern fears arose that, through the vehicle of Missouri statehood, slavery would ultimately extend northward to the Canadian border. In 1820, Congress passed the Missouri Compromise, which decreed that free and slave states would be admitted into the Union in equal numbers and drew a line limiting the expansion of slavery.

Yet these steps did little to address the fundamental issue of whether the United States, having just successfully waged a war of liberation, was ready to confront the extent to which large groups of Americans were not free. In retrospect, we now see that the Revolution and the first decades of the new republic marked but one stage in this nation's ongoing struggle to reconcile its extraordinary idealism with a social reality that so clearly ran counter to the principles upon which it was founded.

From the Plough, to the Sword, to the Book

As we have seen, eighteenth-century Americans witnessed immense changes in their lives, changes that affected all races and all classes of people. The colonies progressed from largely independent, rural regions to putatively unified political bodies strong enough to win the Revolutionary War and then again to states that, with written legislation, would remain inextricably interdependent political entities. Given the regional differences and the diverse population, continually shifting because of its youth and its dispersal, the forging of a single national identity would be difficult. The situation provided an unusual opportunity for writers. A great number of increasingly educated readers would require reading material, and the presses that became fully established in Revolutionary and post-Revolutionary Anglo-America would have to suit the demands of a wide readership.

Yet writers were in a quandary. Many continued to write patriotic songs and ballads, along with political treatises favoring the latest laws enacted by Congress and by the states. The writing of other types of works, especially fiction, was more difficult. There was one key problem: writers and their readers were used to looking to Europe, especially to England, for cultural and artistic models. Yet part of the propaganda message of the Revolutionary era had been that Americans were more virtuous than their luxury-loving European counterparts, because Americans, sober, industrious, and frugal, did not favor the vain display of crafts and fine arts that the European elite classes afforded for their own hedonistic satisfaction. Writers wishing to produce anything not specifically and openly patriotic would face the dilemma of convincing their audience that their works offered instruction in virtue.

The most popular writers, whether they wrote plays, poems, or novels, evidently did manage to persuade their audience that their texts would inculcate virtue and dispel vice. Thus, Royall Tyler's *The Contrast* (1787) offers a "manly" view of sobriety, honesty, and industry in contrast with the foppishness of Billy Dimple's Europeanized actions. Other authors, like novelist William Hill Brown (*The Power of Sympathy,* 1789), chose to detail the actions of seductive Europeans in order to warn young women away from them. Such a ploy was popular: novelists provided sensational and lurid details of just the behavior they wished readers to find reprehensible, and they gained a readership thereby. Other novelists, Susanna Rowson and Hannah Webster Foster among them, used the same means, delineating Europeanized social practices while ostensibly extolling virtue. Like the legal and social institutions that were fostered during the era, literature was considered a means by which American cultural norms, those behaviors considered suitable for the welfare of the society, could be reinforced.

When the French Revolution of 1789 turned into the French bloodbath of 1793, Americans took an increasingly negative look at their European neighbors, fearing that mob action might become popular in America. In the face of farmers' uprisings and skirmishes with native peoples in frontier areas, politicians argued that strong central government was needed to forestall excessive and irrational behavior in America. Writers vehemently attacked the excess emotionalism that might lead to anarchy. The rise in Europe of gothicism—with its emphasis upon darkness and secrecy, psychological confusion, and amorality—was taken by Americans to be evidence of yet another sign of European degeneracy. Notably, Charles Brockden Brown, who experimented with gothicism in his novels, found that in America, novels about ventriloquism and sleepwalking, fratricide and revenge, would not sell to the troubled populace of the 1790s. The revolutionary generation ultimately was seeking conformity; cultural norms were being established to keep the body politic under control.

The cultural norms were politically conservative, patriarchal, and white-dominant. Yet, if minority cultures would be held in subjection, they would nonetheless show signs of having learned an important lesson from the dominant culture: the power of the word to move masses of people. During the 1780s and 1790s, white women, African-Americans, and Native Americans were finding voice for their positions as never before. The elite might control the government, and by extension most social practices—including that of "literature"—but it could not very easily control the voices of those who for the first time in America were—at least in theory—offered rights to free speech.

To Native Americans, the right to free speech was a small freedom in the face of the near-total loss of homelands. In addition to the soldiers from the Revolution who had been granted lands in the Ohio territory in lieu of payment for their wartime services, thousands of new settlers were migrating westward, onto lands held by the natives, many of whom preferred hunting to agriculture. Native Americans, some of them age-old enemies, were forced to share lands over which they had for centuries had full and independent control. Eastern native groups, the relative newcomers to the western territories, were displaced not only in terms of the land itself but in terms of modes of subsistence. Where formerly they had pursued agriculture, they found themselves amid unfriendly hunting groups. Rights to lands westward were granted to white settlers, at the expense of the varied population and cultures of Native Americans.

With Thomas Jefferson in office for two terms as third president, the American government ineffectually sought solution after solution to the land rights question. Jefferson, knowing primarily the agricultural groups of the East, considered that all Native Americans should become farmers rather than remain hunters. Such a change, he argued, would free the large territory necessitated by a hunting culture to the new settlers, both red and white, that he wanted to farm the area. Insisting in 1808 to the Native Americans of central North America that "Nothing is so easy as to learn to cultivate the earth; all your women understand it; and . . . we are always ready to teach you how to make plows, hoes, and other necessary utensils," Jefferson totally misunderstood the people to whom he was speaking.

They found their own leader in Tecumseh, a Shawnee whose Algonkian family had settled in the Ohio area a century before his birth in 1768. The Constitution had spoken of "We, the People," but Tecumseh quickly realized that the "we" of that document did not freely include Native Americans. Watching both the English and the French maneuvers as the War of 1812 was developing, Tecumseh decided that the time was opportune for Native Americans to attempt against the Americans one last struggle. "We all belong to one family," Tecumseh insisted to the peoples of the Great Lakes region, to the Creeks, Cherokees, and Choctaws in the South, and to the Osages across the Mississippi. In a speech to the Osages, after one of his long horseback journeys across the vast territory of the Midwest, Tecumseh announced, "The whites are not friends to the Indians. At first, they only asked for land sufficient for a wigwam; now nothing will satisfy them but the whole of our hunting grounds, from the rising to the setting sun." By 1811, the white encroachment, aided by the institution of forts in the area whites called Indian Country and raids planned by government agents like William Henry Harrison, proved a real threat to native ways of life.

Tecumseh spoke more directly, then. Adopting some of the phraseology of the white leaders whose activities he deplored, Tecumseh delivered a series of speeches that made him famous as an Indian orator. He sought a massive Indian alliance with the English, against the Americans. In an oration reported to have been given before the Choctaws, Tecumseh—whose name in Shawnee, prophetically, means Falling Star or Meteor—spoke of former times and present distresses.

. . . But what need is there to speak of the past? It speaks for itself and asks, Where today are the Pequot? Where are the Narraganset, the Mohican, the Pocanoket and many other once powerful tribes of our people? They have vanished before the avarice and oppression of the white man, as snow before a summer sun. In the vain hope of defending alone their ancient possessions, they have fallen in wars. . . . Look abroad over their once beautiful country, and what see you now? Nought but the ravages of the paleface destroyers. So it will be with you Choctaw and Chickasaw! . . .

The annihilation of our race is at hand, unless we unite in one common cause against the common foe. Think not, brave Choctaw, that you can remain passive and indifferent to the common danger and thus escape the common fate. Your people, too, will soon be as falling leaves and scattering clouds before the blighting wind. You too will be driven away from your native land and ancient domains as leaves are driven in the wintry storms . . .

Before the palefaces came among us, we enjoyed the happiness of unbounded freedom and were acquainted with neither wants nor oppression. How is it now? Need and oppression are our lot—for are we not controlled in everything, and dare we move without asking by your leave? Are we not being stripped day by day of the little that remains of our ancient liberty? . . . Then let us by unity of action destroy them all, which we now can do, or drive them back whence they came. To fight or to be exterminated is now our only choice . . .

That people will continue longest in the enjoyment of peace who timely prepare to vindicate themselves and manifest a determination to protect themselves whenever they are wronged.

Tecumseh joined the British during the War of 1812, and he died on Canadian soil in the Battle of the Thames (Ontario). Tecumseh's oration to the Choctaws, the conclusion of which resembles Washington's presidential *Farewell Address,* provides a telling reminder that "We, the People" would continue through succeeding centuries to speak and to fight for the right of self-determination.

Tradition and Change in Anglo-America

The lives and writings of Sarah Kemble Knight, William Byrd II, Jonathan Edwards, Elizabeth Ashbridge, John Woolman, and selected poets offer readers today signs of the extraordinary cultural change that took place during the eighteenth century. As a group, the writings suggest the immense social and religious transformations that resulted from the increased peopling of the colonies and the new economic and political patterns. On another level, these writings, particularly the autobiographical ones, also reveal the extent to which writers found their places in the world by writing out their experiences of it. While ostensibly recording the events of their day, these writers spoke about themselves, thus making themselves the subjects of their narratives. From the almost fictionalized diaries of Knight and Byrd to the spiritual autobiographies of Edwards, Woolman, and Ashbridge to the variety of poetic voices, we learn as much about how these writers wished themselves to be seen as we do about the changing life of the eighteenth century.

From the time of colonial contact, travel journals formed a significant literary genre in America. To a much greater extent than earlier travel journals, those from the eighteenth century offer social critiques of manners and institutions. Writers were often traversing territory already covered by other travel writers, so they wrote less about compass measurements and flora and fauna than about the people they met along the way. The travel diaries of Sarah Kemble Knight and William Byrd II were likely intended for their circles of friends and acquaintances. Neither author sought publication of the diary, yet both writers' manuscripts were circulated privately and thus "published" in the way that many manuscripts were published in the early part of the century.

William Byrd had been sent on a public expedition to settle the placement of the dividing line between Virginia and North Carolina. His travel diaries, both the history of the dividing line expedition and the "secret" history, evoke the secular literature of the day: published travel journals, scientific and philosophical treatises, and fictional tales. In the public history, Byrd functions as a learned man whose account of the journey is ostensibly free, Byrd no doubt contended, of political bias. From his disquisitions on intermarriage with Native Americans to those on the Edenic opportunities available to the industrious, Byrd constantly reminded his readers of the place of English settlers, especially those in Virginia, in world history. In the "secret" history, Byrd figures large as "Steddy," the model leader, a kind of "natural aristocrat" whose steady presence kept chaos (especially among the supposedly less reliable North Carolinians) at bay. In both diaries, Byrd records a journey that places himself—and by extension all moderate, good Virginia men—at the center of the texts and the center of Virginia political life.

Although she was on an entirely different kind of mission, one to settle a private estate rather than a public trust, Sarah Kemble Knight, like William Byrd, centered her commentary upon her own actions, even as she recorded the events of the world about her. Knight's allusions to published literature both classic and contemporary show the extent to which she was learned in both public and domestic matters. Knight might on occasion defer to providence or a "great benefactor" and to the men who served as her guides, yet the journal continually pictures Knight in control of her life (and thus her text), whether she is precariously crossing a river in an unsteady "canoo," arguing with an innkeeper about the price of a travel guide, or reporting on customs in strange cities. Like the travel diaries of William Byrd, the travel journal of Sarah Kemble Knight signals the increasingly secular tendencies of the age.

The writings of Jonathan Edwards, Elizabeth Ashbridge, and John Woolman suggest the countervailing spiritual tendencies of the age. As a Puritan minister, Jonathan Edwards might have felt distinctly opposed to the theology of Quakers Ashbridge and Woolman, yet his evangelical leanings and his emphasis upon the felt experience of God's grace are not in effect different from the Quaker conception of the inner light. This is not to say that Puritanism was in any way similar to Quakerism. Puritan doctrine, based upon a belief in original sin and predestined grace for God's elect church of saints, clearly differed from Quaker theology, which held that God loved all creatures and thus extended salvation to all who might experience inwardly a light of spiritual truth. Yet Edwards and Woolman and Ashbridge all wrote during a time when spiritual questions seemed to many people less important than secular ones. Their evangelical callings to write of their religious experiences suggest that they wished to offer models of spiritual reformation to a backsliding people.

Like the journals of Woolman and Ashbridge, Edwards's "Personal Narrative" falls into the tradition of spiritual autobiography, a tradition that dates back to the classical Christian epoch and that was, in the seventeenth century, popularized in John Bunyan's *Pilgrim's Progress* (1678). In America, the tradition of spiritual autobiographical writing informed the works of John Winthrop, Edward Taylor, and Anne Bradstreet. Spiritual autobiographies detail their authors' journeys toward salvation, offering evidence that true faith can become stronger through moments of illness and uncertainty. Puritan spiritual autobiographies differ from Quaker texts in their centering upon the Puritan conversion experience; Quaker spiritual autobiographies tend to emphasize less the subtleties of the conversion experience than the life-evidence, or witness, of the converted believer. Whether they were Puritan or Quaker in theological orientation, spiritual autobiographies modeled for readers the journeys of Christians in a world fraught with trials. Both the Puritan and Quaker spiritual autobiographies of the eighteenth century signal their writers' awareness of the immense social, economic, and political changes that Americans faced.

These changes were likewise addressed in the less explicitly autobiographical writings of Edwards and Woolman. Woolman addressed the social issues of poverty and slavery, pointing to the inequities among mankind despite what he considered to be God's free and equal gift of love for all human beings. For Woolman, worldly concerns kept one fettered, making God's love inaccessible. Curing economic inequity would free all people so that they could experience the inward light of God's love, he argued, and thus assist in the amelioration of the human condition. Edwards seems to have considered that such amelioration lay in the understanding that life on earth was entirely dependent upon God's will. Perplexed by social inequities, Edwards searched the writings of key philosophers and scientists of his day for a means of understanding the individual's social responsibility. Throughout his life, Edwards attempted to construct a theology that insisted upon man's dependence on an all-powerful God while proffering hope of salvation for those who might believe. Whether writing upon his own life or upon the larger philosophical questions regarding virtue and social betterment, Edwards pursued his writing career with the same evangelical fervor with which he sought assurance of salvation. His writings, like those of the other authors with whom he is grouped here, speak clearly of himself as subject as much as they bespeak the issues they ostensibly address.

The varieties—and vagaries—of eighteenth-century colonial life are clearly registered in the poetic writings that conclude this section of the anthology. As these poets' writings suggest, concerns about one's place in the world were foremost on the minds of many North American colonists. The variety of concerns expressed by these poets attests to the changing social, economic, and political situations that these writers faced. Their remarkable productivity evidences their resilience in the face of uncertainty. Finally these poets' contributions, whether public or private, evince (along with the writings of other poets—Jupiter Hammon, Phillis Wheatley, Judith Sargent Murray, Philip Freneau, and Joel Barlow—located elsewhere among the eighteenth-century selections) the tremendous attraction that the formal poetic medium held for many writers.

Carla Mulford
Pennsylvania State University

Sarah Kemble Knight 1666–1727

Since its publication in 1825, Sarah Kemble Knight's journal, composed as an account of her roundtrip journey from Boston to New York in 1704–1705, has remained a literary landmark of the colonial era, in part because of the larger-than-life character it reveals and in part because it records an arduous journey not usually undertaken by women. In addition to providing a funny, often racy, account of the people and places she encounters along the way, Knight's journal paints a vivid verbal picture of New England backwoods settlements. Typical of the picaro, she views the wilderness as romantic and literary, colonized and domesticated, dangerous yet comic and amoral. Unlike many other latter-day Puritans who considered the frontier "a hideous and desolate wilderness," Knight considered it a challenge for her to conquer.

The first daughter of Thomas Kemble and Elizabeth Trerice Kemble, Sarah was born in Boston. Sometime between 1688 and 1689, she married Richard Knight, who was apparently much older than she. Tradition holds that Richard Knight was a shipmaster and agent in London for an American company, zand that Sarah Kemble was his second wife, but neither claim can be confirmed. Their one child, Elizabeth, was born in Boston on May 8, 1689. Even before Richard Knight died (probably in 1706), his wife seems to have taken over many of his business responsibilities. She evidently attained some degree of business and legal acumen, skills she used in settling estates. In fact, the journey her journal documents was made so that she could settle, in the absence of her husband, the estate of her cousin Caleb Trowbridge, who left a young widow. Sarah Kemble Knight kept a shop and house on Moon Street in Boston. That she also ran a writing school attended by Benjamin Franklin is more likely rumor than fact. When her daughter married John Livingston of New London, Connecticut, Knight moved, when widowed, to be near her. Knight seems to have continued some business activities in Connecticut; when she died, her estate was valued at £1800.

Given the era in which she grew up, Knight's work might be expected to fall into the tradition of Puritan journal-keeping, yet its content, style, and tone seem very un-Puritan indeed. First, Knight's journal is primarily a story, not a history, whose heroine is more like Chaucer's Wife of Bath than the self-effacing stereotype of Puritan womanhood. Second, Knight's style is worldly and literary. And third, her tone encompasses several different types of humor.

In many ways, Knight's journal serves well as a mock- and folk-epic, yet it also uses many devices common in picaresque fiction. In this travel journal, Knight dashes from place to place, intent on her goal of reaching the city and transacting her business, only pausing to jot down people and places of interest. Structured episodically, the journal is dominated by the narrator, an unusually resourceful, independent, intrepid, and shrewd middle-class woman. Like a picaro, whose activities take him outside the center of typically upperclass society, Knight retains the capacity for precise observation. But unlike most picaros she is no rogue; her journal merely takes her outside conventional society and brings her into contact with lower-class people. Much of the humor of the journal results precisely because of Knight's sarcastic comments about the people she meets. Yet, like Moll Flanders—also a picaresque character—Knight is an overwhelming figure in her story, a teller of tales about others—but especially about herself.

Kathryn Zabelle Derounian-Stodola
University of Arkansas at Little Rock

PRIMARY WORK

The Journals of Madam Knight, and Rev. Mr. Buckingham, from the Original Manuscripts, written in 1704 and 1710, 1825.

SECONDARY WORKS

Alan Margolies, "The Editing and Publication of 'The Journal of Madam Knight,'" *Papers of the Bibliographical Society of America* 58, 1964:25–32; R.O. Stephens, "The Odyssey of Sarah Kemble Knight," *College Language Association Journal* 7, 1964:247–55; Peter Thorpe, "Sarah Kemble Knight and the Picaresque Tradition," *College Language Association Journal* 10, 1966:114–21; Faye Vowell, "A Commentary on *The Journal of Sarah Kemble Knight,*" *The Emporia State Research Studies* 24, 1976:44–52; Robert D. Arner, "Sarah Kemble Knight," *American Literature Before 1800,* eds. James A. Levernier and Douglas R. Wilmes, 1983:857–59; Sargent Bush, introduction, *The Journal of Madam Knight, Journeys in New Worlds, Early American Women's Narratives,* ed. William L. Andrews, 1990:69–83; Kathryn Zabelle Derounian-Stodola, "The New England Frontier and the Picaresque in Sarah Kemble Knight's Journal," *Early American Literature and Culture: Essays Honoring Harrison T. Meserole,* 1992:122–31; Julia Stern, "To Relish and to Spew: Disgust as Cultural Critique in *The Journal of Madam Knight,*" *Legacy: A Journal of American Women Writers* 14, 1997: 1–12.

The Journal of Madam Knight[1]

Monday, Octb'r. ye second, 1704.—About three o'clock afternoon, I begun my Journey from Boston to New-Haven; being about two Hundred Mile. My Kinsman, Capt. Robert Luist, waited on me as farr as Dedham, where I was to meet ye Western post.[2]

I vissitted the Reverd. Mr. Belcher,[3] ye Minister of ye town, and tarried there till evening, in hopes ye post would come along. But he not coming, I resolved to go to Billingses where he used to lodg, being 12 miles further. But being ignorant of the way, Madm Billings,[4] seing no persuasions of her good spouses or hers could prevail with me to Lodg there that night, Very kindly went wyth me to ye Tavern, where I hoped to get my guide, And desired the Hostess to inquire of her guests whether any of them would go with mee. But they being tyed by the Lipps to a pewter engine, scarcely allowed themselves time to say what clownish * * *.

***Peices of eight, I told her no, I would not be accessary to such extortion.

Then John shan't go, sais shee. No, indeed, shan't hee; And held forth at that rate a long time, that I began to fear I was got among the Quaking tribe, beleeving not a Limbertong'd sister among them could out do Madm. Hostes.

Upon this, to my no small surprise, son John arrose, and gravely demanded what I would give him to go with me? Give you, sais I, are you John? Yes, says he, for want of a Better; And behold! this John look't as old as my Host, and perhaps had bin a man in the last Century. Well, Mr. John, sais I, make your demands. Why, half a pss. of eight and a dram, sais John. I agreed, and gave him a Dram (now) in hand to bind the bargain.

My hostess catechis'd John for going so cheep, saying his poor wife would break her heart***His shade on his Hors resembled a Globe on a Gate post. His habitt, Hors and furniture, its looks and goings Incomparably answered the rest.

Thus Jogging on with an easy pace, my Guide telling mee it was dangero's to Ride hard in the Night, (whch his horse had the sence to avoid,) Hee entertained me with the Adventurs he had passed by late Rideing, and eminent Dangers he had escaped, so that, Remembring the Hero's in Parismus and the Knight of the Oracle,[5] I didn't know but I had mett wth a Prince disguis'd.

When we had Ridd about an how'r, wee come into a thick swamp, wch. by Reason of a great fogg, very much startled mee, it being now very Dark. But nothing

[1]Knight's *Journal* was first published, along with that of Reverend Thomas Buckingham of Hartford, in New York, 1825, by Theodore Dwight. Since then, the journal has gone through a number of editions, among them one by Perry Miller and Thomas Johnson (1938), the source of the present text. This edition places superscript letters on the line; for the most part, Miller's and Johnson's notes are printed below.

The original manuscript, now lost, was evidently torn in two places, and a few manuscript sheets were lost. In the present text, these places where manuscript has been lost are marked by asterisks. We print the journal in its entirety.

[2]Dispatch messenger who carried mail from stage to stage.

[3]The Reverend Joseph Belcher (1669–1723).

[4]Mrs. Belcher, wife of the pastor.

[5]References to the romances *The History of Parismus* (1598), by Emmanuel Ford, and *The Famous History of Montelion, Knight of the Oracle* (earliest surviving edition 1633).

dismay'd John: Hee had encountered a thousand and a thousand such Swamps, having a Universall Knowledge in the woods; and readily Answered all my inquiries wch. were not a few.

In about an how'r, or something more, after we left the Swamp, we come to Billinges, where I was to Lodg. My Guide dismounted and very Complasantly help't me down and shewd the door, signing to me wth his hand to Go in; wch I Gladly did—But had not gone many steps into the Room, ere I was Interogated by a young Lady I understood afterwards was the Eldest daughter of the family, with these, or words to this purpose, (viz.) Law for mee—what in the world brings You here at this time a night?—I never see a woman on the Rode so Dreadfull late, in all the days of my versall life. Who are You? Where are You going? I'me scar'd out of my witts—with much now of the same Kind. I stood aghast, Prepareing to reply, when in comes my Guide—to him Madam turn'd, Roreing out: Lawfull heart, John, is it You?—how de do! Where in the world are you going with this woman? Who is she? John made no Ansr. but sat down in the corner, fumbled out his black Junk,[6] and saluted that instead of Debb; she then turned agen to mee and fell anew into her silly questions, without asking me to sitt down.

I told her shee treated me very Rudely, and I did not think it my duty to answer her unmannerly Questions. But to get ridd of them, I told her I come there to have the post's company with me to-morrow on my Journey, &c. Miss star'd awhile, drew a chair, bid me sitt, And then run up stairs and putts on two or three Rings, (or else I had not seen them before,) and returning, sett herself just before me, showing the way to Reding, that I might see her Ornaments, perhaps to gain the more respect. But her Granam's new Rung[7] sow, had it appeared, would affected me as much. I paid honest John wth money and dram according to contract, and Dismist him, and pray'd Miss to shew me where I must Lodg. Shee conducted me to a parlour in a little back Lento,[8] wch was almost fill'd wth the bedsted, wch was so high that I was forced to climb on a chair to gitt up to ye wretched bed that lay on it; on wch having Stretcht my tired Limbs, and lay'd my head on a Sad-colourd pillow, I began to think on the transactions of ye past day.

Tuesday, October ye third, about 8 in the morning, I with the Post proceeded forward without observing any thing remarkable; And about two, afternoon, Arrived at the Post's second stage, where the western Post mett him and exchanged Letters. Here, having called for something to eat, ye woman bro't in a Twisted thing like a cable, but something whiter; and laying it on the bord, tugg'd for life to bring it into a capacity to spread; wch having wth great pains accomplished, shee serv'd in a dish of Pork and Cabage, I suppose the remains of Dinner. The sause was of a deep Purple, wch I tho't was boil'd in her dye Kettle; the bread was Indian, and every thing on the Table service Agreeable to these. I, being hungry, gott a little down; but my stomach was soon cloy'd, and what cabbage I swallowed serv'd me for a Cudd the whole day after.

Having here discharged the Ordnary[9] for self and Guide, (as I understood was the custom,) About Three afternoon went on with my Third Guide, who Rode very

[6]A pipe for smoking.

[7]*I.e.,* having a ring through the snout.

[8]A lean-to room.

[9]An ordinary was an eating house or tavern providing meals at a fixed price.

hard; and having crossed Providence Ferry, we come to a River wch they Generally Ride thro'. But I dare not venture; so the Post got a Ladd and Cannoo to carry me to tother side, and hee rid thro' and Led my hors. The Cannoo was very small and shallow, so that when we were in she seem'd redy to take in water, which greatly terrified mee, and caused me to be very circumspect, sitting with my hands fast on each side, my eyes stedy, not daring so much as to lodg my tongue a hair's breadth more on one side of my mouth then tother, nor so much as think on Lott's wife, for a wry thought would have oversett our wherey:[10] But was soon put out of this pain, by feeling the Cannoo on shore, wch I as soon almost saluted with my feet; and Rewarding my sculler, again mounted and made the best of our way forwards. The Rode here was very even and ye day pleasant, it being now near Sunsett. But the Post told mee we had neer 14 miles to Ride to the next Stage, (where we were to Lodg.) I askt him of the rest of the Rode, foreseeing wee must travail in the night. Hee told mee there was a bad River we were to Ride thro', wch was so very firce a hors could sometimes hardly stem it: But it was but narrow, and wee should soon be over. I cannot express The concern of mind this relation sett me in: no thoughts but those of the dang'ros River could entertain my Imagination, and they were as formidable as varios, still Tormenting me with blackest Ideas of my Approaching fate—Sometimes seing my self drowning, otherwhiles drowned, and at the best like a holy Sister Just come out of a Spiritual Bath in dripping Garments.

Now was the Glorious Luminary,[11] wth his swift Coursers arrived at his Stage, leaving poor me wth the rest of this part of the lower world in darkness, with which *wee* were soon Surrounded. The only Glimering we now had was from the spangled Skies, Whose Imperfect Reflections rendered every Object formidable. Each lifeless Trunk, with its shatter'd Limbs, appear'd an Armed Enymie; and every little stump like a Ravenous devourer. Nor could I so much as discern my Guide, when at any distance, which added to the terror.

Thus, absolutely lost in Thought, and dying with the very thoughts of drowning, I come up wth the post, who I did not see till even with his Hors: he told mee he stopt for mee; and wee Rode on Very deliberatly a few paces, when we entred a Thickett of Trees and Shrubbs, and I perceived by the Hors's going, we were on the descent of a Hill, wch, as wee come neerer the bottom, 'twas totaly dark wth the Trees that surrounded it. But I knew by the Going of the Hors wee had entred the water, wch my Guide told mee was the hazzardos River he had told me off; and hee, Riding up close to my Side, Bid me not fear—we should be over Imediatly. I now ralyed all the Courage I was mistriss of, Knowing that I must either Venture my fate of drowning, or be left like ye Children in the wood. So, as the Post bid me, I gave Reins to my Nagg; and sitting as Stedy as Just before in the Cannoo, in a few minutes got safe to the other side, which hee told mee was the Narragansett country.

Here We found great difficulty in Travailing, the way being very narrow, and on each side the Trees and bushes gave us very unpleasant welcomes wth their Branches and bow's, wch wee could not avoid, it being so exceeding dark. My Guide, as before so now, putt on harder than I, wth my weary bones, could follow; so left mee and the way beehind him. Now Returned my distressed aprehensions of the place

[10]A wherry was a light rowing boat for transporting river passengers.

[11]The moon.

where I was: the dolesome woods, my Company next to none, Going I knew not whither, and encompased wth Terrifying darkness; The least of which was enough to startle a more Masculine courage. Added to which the Reflections, as in the afternoon of ye day that my Call was very Questionable, wch till then I had not so Prudently as I ought considered. Now, coming to ye foot of a hill, I found great difficulty in ascending; But being got to the Top, was there amply recompenced with the friendly Appearance of the Kind Conductress of the night, Just then Advancing above the Horisontall Line. The Raptures wch the Sight of that fair Planett produced in mee, caus'd mee, for the Moment, to forgett my present wearyness and past toils; and Inspir'd me for most of the remaining way with very divirting tho'ts, some of which, with the other Occurances of the day, I reserved to note down when I should come to my Stage. My tho'ts on the sight of the moon were to this purpose:

> Fair Cynthia,[12] all the Homage that I may
> Unto a Creature, unto thee I pay;
> In Lonesome woods to meet so kind a guide,
> To Mee's more worth than all the world beside.
> Some Joy I felt just now, when safe got or'e
> Yon Surly River to this Rugged shore,
> Deeming Rough welcomes from these clownish Trees,
> Better than Lodgings wth Nereidees.[13]
> Yet swelling fears surprise; all dark appears—
> Nothing but Light can disipate those fears.
> My fainting vitals can't lend strength to say,
> But softly whisper, O I wish 'twere day.
> The murmur hardly warm'd the Ambient air,
> E're thy Bright Aspect rescues from dispair:
> Makes the old Hagg her sable mantle loose,
> And a Bright Joy do's through my Soul diffuse.
> The Boistero's Trees now Lend a Passage Free,
> And pleasent prospects thou giv'st light to see.

From hence wee kept on, with more ease than before: the way being smooth and even, the night warm and serene, and the Tall and thick Trees at a distance, especially when the moon glar'd light through the branches, fill'd my Imagination wth the pleasent delusion of a Sumpteous citty, fill'd wth famous Buildings and churches, wth their spiring steeples, Balconies, Galleries and I know not what: Granduers wch I had heard of, and wch the stories of foreign countries had given me the Idea of.

> Here stood a Lofty church—there is a steeple,
> And there the Grand Parade—O see the people!
> That Famous Castle there, were I but nigh,
> To see the mote and Bridg and walls so high—
> They'r very fine! sais my deluded eye.

Being thus agreably entertain'd without a thou't of any thing but thoughts themselves, I on a suden was Rous'd from these pleasing Imaginations, by the Post's

[12]Poetic name for the moon personified as a goddess.

[13]The Nereides were sea nymphs.

sounding his horn, which assured mee hee was arrived at the Stage, where we were to Lodg: and that musick was then most musickall and agreeable to mee.

Being come to mr. Havens', I was very civilly Received, and courteously entertained, in a clean comfortable House; and the Good woman was very active in helping off my Riding clothes, and then ask't what I would eat. I told her I had some Chocolett, if shee would prepare it; which with the help of some Milk, and a little clean brass Kettle, she soon effected to my satisfaction. I then betook me to my Apartment, wch was a little Room parted from the Kitchen by a single bord partition; where, after I had noted the Occurrances of the past day, I went to bed, which, tho' pretty hard, Yet neet and handsome. But I could get no sleep, because of the Clamor of some of the Town tope-ers in next Room, Who were entred into a strong debate concerning ye Signifycation of the name of their Country, (viz.) *Narraganset.* One said it was named so by ye Indians, because there grew a Brier there, of a prodigious Highth and bigness, the like hardly ever known, called by the Indians Narragansett; And quotes an Indian of so Barberous a name for his Author; that I could not write it. His Antagonist Replyed no—It was from a Spring it had its name, wch hee well knew where it was, which was extreem cold in summer, and as Hott as could be imagined in the winter, which was much resorted too by the natives, and by them called Narragansett, (Hott and Cold,) and that was the originall of their places name—with a thousand Impertinances not worth notice, wch He utter'd with such a Roreing voice and Thundering blows with the fist of wickedness on the Table, that it peirced my very head. I heartily fretted, and wish't 'um tongue tyed; but wth as little succes as a freind of mine once, who was (as shee said) kept a whole night awake, on a Jorny, by a country Left.[14] and a Sergent, Insigne and a Deacon, contriving how to bring a triangle into a Square. They kept calling for tother Gill,[15] wch while they were swallowing, was some Intermission; But presently, like Oyle to fire, encreased the flame. I set my Candle on a Chest by the bed side, and setting up, fell to my old way of composing my Resentments, in the following manner:

I ask thy Aid, O Potent Rum!
To Charm these wrangling Topers Dum.
Thou hast their Giddy Brains possest—
The man confounded wth the Beast—
And I, poor I, can get no rest.
Intoxicate them with thy fumes:
O still their Tongues till morning comes!

And I know not but my wishes took effect, for the dispute soon ended wth 'tother Dram; and so Good night!

Wedensday, Octobr 4th. About four in the morning, we set out for Kingston (for so was the Town called) with a french Docter in our company. Hee and ye Post put on very furiously, so that I could not keep up with them, only as now and then they'd stop till they see mee. This Rode was poorly furnished wth accommodations for Travellers, so that we were forced to ride 22 miles by the post's account, but neerer thirty by mine, before wee could bait so much as our Horses, wch I exceedingly complained

[14]Lieutenant. Sometimes still pronounced, and formerly spelled, *leftenant.*

[15]Measure used for wine.

of. But the post encourag'd mee, by saying wee should be well accommodated anon at mr. Devills, a few miles further. But I questioned whether we ought to go to the Devil to be helpt out of affliction. However, like the rest of Deluded souls that post to ye Infernal denn, Wee made all possible speed to this Devil's Habitation; where alliting, in full assurance of good accommodation, wee were going in. But meeting his two daughters, as I suposed twins, they so neerly resembled each other, both in features and habit, and look't as old as the Divel himselfe, and quite as Ugly, We desired entertainm't, but could hardly get a word out of 'um, till with our Importunity, telling them our necesity, &c. they call'd the old Sophister, who was as sparing of his words as his daughters had bin, and no, or none, was the reply's hee made us to our demands. Hee differed only in this from the old fellow in to'ther Country: hee let us depart. However, I thought it proper to warn poor Travailers to endeavour to Avoid falling into circumstances like ours, wch at our next Stage I sat down and did as followeth:

May all that dread the cruel feind of night
Keep on, and not at this curs't Mansion light.
'Tis Hell; 'tis Hell! and Devills here do dwell:
Here dwells the Devill—surely this's Hell.
Nothing but Wants: a drop to cool yo'r Tongue
Cant be procur'd these cruel Feinds among.
Plenty of horrid Grins and looks sevear,
Hunger and thirst, But pitty's bannish'd here—
The Right hand keep, if Hell on Earth you fear!

Thus leaving this habitation of cruelty, we went forward; and arriving at an Ordinary about two mile further, found tollerable accommodation. But our Hostes, being a pretty full mouth'd old creature, entertain'd our fellow travailer, ye french Docter, wth Inumirable complaints of her bodily infirmities; and whispered to him so lou'd, that all ye House had as full a hearing as hee: which was very divirting to ye company, (of which there was a great many,) as one might see by their sneering. But poor weary I slipt out to enter my mind in my Jornal, and left my Great Landly with her Talkative Guests to themselves.

From hence we proceeded (about ten forenoon) through the Narragansett country, pretty Leisurely; and about one afternoon come to Paukataug River, wch was about two hundred paces over, and now very high, and no way over to to'ther side but this. I darid not venture to Ride thro, my courage at best in such cases but small, And now at the Lowest Ebb, by reason of my weary, very weary, hungry and uneasy Circumstances. So takeing leave of my company, tho' wth no little Reluctance, that I could not proceed wth them on my Jorny, Stop at a little cottage Just by the River, to wait the Waters falling, wch the old man that lived there said would be in a little time, and he would conduct me safe over. This little Hutt was one of the wretchedest I ever saw a habitation for human creatures. It was suported with shores enclosed with Clapbords, laid on Lengthways, and so much asunder, that the Light come throu' every where; the doore tyed on wth a cord in ye place of hinges; The floor the bear earth; no windows but such as the thin covering afforded, nor any furniture but a Bedd wth a glass Bottle hanging at ye head on't; an earthan cupp, a small pewter Bason, A Bord wth sticks to stand on, instead of a table, and a block or two in ye corner instead of chairs. The family were the old man, his wife and two Children; all and every part being the picture of poverty. Notwithstanding both the Hutt and its Inhabitance were very clean and tydee: to the crossing the Old Proverb, that bare walls make giddy hows-wifes.

I Blest myselfe that I was not one of this misserable crew; and the Impressions their wretchedness formed in me caused mee on ye very Spott to say:

Tho' Ill at ease, A stranger and alone,
All my fatigu's shall not extort a grone.
These Indigents have hunger with their ease;
Their best is wors behalfe then my disease.
Their Misirable hutt wch Heat and Cold
Alternately without Repulse do hold;
Their Lodgings thyn and hard, their Indian fare,
The mean Apparel which the wretches wear,
And their ten thousand ills wch can't be told,
Makes nature er'e 'tis midle age'd look old.
When I reflect, my late fatigues do seem
Only a notion or forgotten Dreem.

I had scarce done thinking, when an Indian like Animal come to the door, on a creature very much like himselfe, in mien and feature, as well as Ragged cloathing; and having 'litt, makes an Awkerd Scratch wth his Indian shoo, and a Nodd, sitts on ye block, fumbles out his black Junk, dipps it in ye Ashes, and presents it piping hott to his muscheeto's, and fell to sucking like a calf, without speaking, for near a quarter of an hower. At length the old man said how do's Sarah do? who I understood was the wretches wife, and Daughter to ye old man: he Replyed—as well as can be expected, &c. So I remembred the old say, and suposed I knew Sarah's case. Butt hee being, as I understood, going over the River, as ugly as hee was, I was glad to ask him to show me ye way to Saxtons, at Stoningtown; wch he promising, I ventur'd over wth the old mans assistance; who having rewarded to content, with my Tattertailed guide, I Ridd on very slowly thro' Stoningtown, where the Rode was very Stony and uneven. I asked the fellow, as we went, divers questions of the place and way, &c. I being arrived at my country Saxtons, at Stonington, was very well accommodated both as to victuals and Lodging, the only Good of both I had found since my setting out. Here I heard there was an old man and his Daughter to come that way, bound to N. London; and being now destitute of a Guide, gladly waited for them, being in so good a harbour, and accordingly, Thirsday, Octobr ye 5th, about 3 in the afternoon, I sat forward with neighbour Polly and Jemima, a Girl about 18 Years old, who hee said he had been to fetch out of the Narragansetts, and said they had Rode thirty miles that day, on a sory lean Jade, wth only a Bagg under her for a pillion, which the poor Girl often complain'd was very uneasy.

Wee made Good speed along, wch made poor Jemima make many a sow'r face, the mare being a very hard trotter; and after many a hearty and bitter Oh, she at length Low'd out: Lawful Heart father! this bare mare hurts mee Dingeely,[16] I'me

[16]Apparently Knight's own coined intensifier meaning "extremely."

direfull sore I vow; with many words to that purpose: poor Child sais Gaffer—she us't to serve your mother so. I don't care how mother us't to do, quoth Jemima, in a pasionate tone. At which the old man Laught, and kik't his Jade[17] o' the side, which made her Jolt ten times harder.

About seven that Evening, we come to New London Ferry: here, by reason of a very high wind, we mett with great difficulty in getting over—the Boat tos't exceedingly, and our Horses capper'd at a very surprizing Rate, and set us all in a fright; especially poor Jemima, who desired her father to say so jack to the Jade, to make her stand. But the careless parent, taking no notice of her repeated desires, She Rored out in a Passionate manner: Pray suth father, Are you deaf? Say so Jack to the Jade, I tell you. The Dutiful Parent obey's; saying so Jack, so Jack, as gravely as if hee'd bin to saying Catechise after Young Miss, who with her fright look't of all coullers in ye Rain Bow.

Being safely arrived at the house of Mrs. Prentices in N. London, I treated neighbour Polly and daughter for their divirting company, and bid them farewell; and between nine and ten at night waited on the Revd Mr. Gurdon Saltonstall,[18] minister of the town, who kindly Invited me to Stay that night at his house, where I was very handsomely and plentifully treated and Lodg'd; and made good the Great Character I had before heard concerning him: viz. that hee was the most affable, courteous, Genero's and best of men.

Friday, Octor 6th. I got up very early, in Order to hire somebody to go with mee to New Haven, being in Great parplexity at the thoughts of proceeding alone; which my most hospitable entertainer observing, himselfe went, and soon return'd wth a young Gentleman of the town, who he could confide in to Go with mee; and about eight this morning, wth Mr. Joshua Wheeler my new Guide, takeing leave of this worthy Gentleman, Wee advanced on towards Seabrook. The Rodes all along this way are very bad, Incumbred wth Rocks and mountainos passages, wch were very disagreeable to my tired carcass; but we went on with a moderate pace wch made ye Journy more pleasent. But after about eight miles Rideing, in going over a Bridge under wch the River Run very swift, my hors stumbled, and very narrowly 'scaped falling over into the water; wch extreemly frightened mee. But through God's Goodness I met with no harm, and mounting agen, in about half a miles Rideing, come to an ordinary, were well entertained by a woman of about seventy and vantage, but of as Sound Intellectuals as one of seventeen. Shee entertain'd Mr. Wheeler wth some passages of a Wedding awhile ago at a place hard by, the Brides-Groom being about her Age or something above, Saying his Children was dredfully against their fathers marrying, wch shee condemned them extreemly for.

From hence wee went pretty briskly forward, and arriv'd at Saybrook ferry about two of the Clock afternoon; and crossing it, wee call'd at an Inn to Bait, (foreseeing we should not have such another Opportunity till we come to Killingsworth.) Landlady come in, with her hair about her ears, and hands at full pay scratching. Shee told us shee had some mutton wch shee would broil, wch I was glad to hear;

[17]Contemptuous name for an inferior, vicious, or worn-out horse.

[18]Gurdon Saltonstall (1666–1724), minister at New London, was a celebrated preacher. He sat at one time as Chief Justice of the Supreme Court of the Connecticut Colony.

But I supose forgot to wash her scratchers; in a little time shee brot it in; but it being pickled, and my Guide said it smelt strong of head sause, we left it, and pd sixpence a piece for our Dinners, wch was only smell.

So wee putt forward with all speed, and about seven at night come to Killingsworth, and were tollerably well with Travillers fare, and Lodgd there that night.

Saturday, Oct. 7th, we sett out early in the Morning, and being something unaquainted wth the way, having ask't it of some wee mett, they told us wee must Ride a mile or two and turne down a Lane on the Right hand; and by their Direction wee Rode on but not Yet comeing to ye turning, we mett a Young fellow and ask't him how farr it was to the Lane which turn'd down towards Guilford. Hee said wee must Ride a little further, and turn down by the Corner of uncle Sams Lott. My Guide vented his Spleen at the Lubber; and we soon after came into the Rhode, and keeping still on, without any thing further Remarkabell, about two a clock afternoon we arrived at New Haven, where I was received with all Posible Respects and civility. Here I discharged Mr. Wheeler with a reward to his satisfaction, and took some time to rest after so long and toilsome a Journey; And I Inform'd myselfe of the manners and customs of the place, and at the same time employed myselfe in the afair I went there upon.

They are Govern'd by the same Laws as wee in Boston, (or little differing,) thr'out this whole Colony of Connecticot, And much the same way of Church Government, and many of them good, Sociable people, and I hope Religious too: but a little too much Independant in their principalls, and, as I have been told, were formerly in their Zeal very Riggid in their Administrations towards such as their Lawes made Offenders, even to a harmless Kiss or Innocent merriment among Young people. Whipping being a frequent and counted an easy Punishment, about wch as other Crimes, the Judges were absolute in their Sentances. They told mee a pleasant story about a pair of Justices in those parts, wch I may not omit the relation of.

A negro Slave belonging to a man in ye Town, stole a hogs head from his master, and gave or sold it to an Indian, native of the place. The Indian sold it in the neighbourhood, and so the theft was found out. Thereupon the Heathen was Seized, and carried to the Justices House to be Examined. But his worship (it seems) was gone into the feild, with a Brother in office, to gather in his Pompions.[19] Whither the malefactor is hurried, And Complaint made, and satisfaction in the name of Justice demanded. Their Worships cann't proceed in form without a Bench: whereupon they Order one to be Imediately erected, which, for want of fitter materials, they made with pompions—which being finished, down setts their Worships, and the Malefactor call'd, and by the Senior Justice Interrogated after the following manner. You Indian why did You steal from this man? You sho'dn't do so—it's a Grandy wicked thing to steal. Hol't Hol't, cryes Justice Junr, Brother, You speak negro to him. I'le ask him. You sirrah, why did You steal this man's Hoggshead? Hoggshead? (replys the Indian,) me no stomany. No? says his Worship; and pulling off his hatt, Patted his own head with his hand, sais, Tatapa—You, Tatapa—you; all one this. Hoggs-head all one this. Hah! says Netop, now me stomany that. Whereupon the Company fell into a great fitt of Laughter, even to Roreing. Silence is comanded, but to no

[19]Pumpkins.

effect: for they continued perfectly Shouting. Nay, sais his worship, in an angry tone, if it be so, *take mee off the Bench.*

Their Diversions in this part of the Country are on Lecture days and Training days mostly:[20] on the former there is Riding from town to town.

And on training dayes The Youth divert themselves by Shooting at the Target, as they call it, (but it very much resembles a pillory,) where hee that hitts neerest the white has some yards of Red Ribbin presented him, wch being tied to his hattband, the two ends streeming down his back, he is Led away in Triumph, wth great applause, as the winners of the Olympiack Games. They generally marry very young: the males oftener as I am told under twentie than above; they generally make public wedings, and have a way something singular (as they say) in some of them, viz. Just before Joyning hands the Bridegroom quitts the place, who is soon followed by the Bridesmen, and as it were, dragg'd back to duty—being the reverse to ye former practice among us, to steal ms Pride.

There are great plenty of Oysters all along by the sea side, as farr as I Rode in the Collony, and those very good. And they Generally lived very well and comfortably in their famelies. But too Indulgent (especially ye farmers) to their slaves: sufering too great familiarity from them, permitting them to sit at Table and eat with them, (as they say to save time,) and into the dish goes the black hoof as freely as the white hand. They told me that there was a farmer lived nere the Town where I lodgd who had some difference wth his slave, concerning something the master had promised him and did not punctualy perform; wch caused some hard words between them; But at length they put the matter to Arbitration and Bound themselves to stand to the award of such as they named—wch done, the Arbitrators Having heard the Allegations of both parties, Order the master to pay 40s to black face, and acknowledge his fault. And so the matter ended: the poor master very honestly standing to the award.

There are every where in the Towns as I passed, a Number of Indians the Natives of the Country, and are the most salvage of all the salvages of that kind that I had ever Seen: little or no care taken (as I heard upon enquiry) to make them otherwise. They have in some places Landes of their owne, and Govern'd by Law's of their own making;—they marry many wives and at pleasure put them away, and on the ye least dislike or fickle humour, on either side, saying *stand away* to one another is a sufficient Divorce. And indeed those uncomely *Stand aways* are too much in Vougue among the English in this (Indulgent Colony) as their Records plentifully prove, and that on very trivial matters, of which some have been told me, but are not proper to be Related by a Female pen, tho some of that foolish sex have had too large a share in the story.

If the natives committ any crime on their own precincts among themselves, ye English takes no Cognezens of. But if on the English ground, they are punishable by our Laws. They mourn for their Dead by blacking their faces, and cutting their hair, after an Awkerd and frightfull manner; But can't bear You should mention the names of their dead Relations to them: they trade most for Rum, for wch theyd hazzard their

[20] Lecture days, when the weekly religious lecture took place, were on Thursdays. Training days were specifically appointed for militia drill.

very lives; and the English fit them Generally as well, by seasoning it plentifully with water.

They give the title of merchant to every trader; who Rate their Goods according to the time and spetia they pay in: viz. Pay, mony, Pay as mony, and trusting. *Pay* is Grain, Pork, Beef, &c. at the prices sett by the General Court that Year; *mony* is pieces of Eight, Ryalls, or Boston or Bay shillings (as they call them,) or Good hard money, as sometimes silver coin is termed by them; also Wampom, vizt. Indian beads wch serves for change. *Pay as mony* is provisions, as aforesd one Third cheaper then as the Assembly or Genel Court sets it; and *Trust* as they and the mercht agree for time.

Now, when the buyer comes to ask for a comodity, sometimes before the merchant answers that he has it, he sais, *is Your pay redy?* Perhaps the Chap Reply's Yes: what do You pay in? say's the merchant. The buyer having answered, then the price is set; as suppose he wants a sixpenny knife, in pay it is 12d—in pay as money eight pence, and hard money its own price, viz. 6d. It seems a very Intricate way of trade and what Lex Mercatoria[21] had not thought of.

Being at a merchants house, in comes a tall country fellow, wth his alfogeos[22] full of Tobacco; for they seldom Loose their Cudd, but keep Chewing and Spitting as long as they'r eyes are open,—he advanc't to the midle of the Room, makes an Awkward Nodd, and spitting a Large deal of Aromatick Tincture, he gave a scrape with his shovel like shoo, leaving a small shovel full of dirt on the floor, made a full stop, Hugging his own pretty Body with his hands under his arms, Stood staring rown'd him, like a Catt let out of a Baskett. At last, like the creature Balaam Rode on, he opened his mouth and said: have You any Ribinen for Hatbands to sell I pray? The Questions and Answers about the pay being past, the Ribin is bro't and opened. Bumpkin Simpers, cryes its confounded Gay I vow; and beckning to the door, in comes Jone Tawdry, dropping about 50 curtsees, and stands by him: hee shows her the Ribin. *Law, You,* sais shee, *its right Gent,*[23] do You, take it, *tis dreadfull pretty.* Then she enquires, *have You any hood silk I pray?* wch being brought and bought, Have You any *thred silk to sew it wth* says shee, wch being accomodated wth they Departed. They Generaly stand after they come in a great while speachless, and sometimes dont say a word till they are askt what they want, which I Impute to the Awe they stand in of the merchants, who they are constantly almost Indebted too; and must take what they bring without Liberty to choose for themselves; but they serve them as well, making the merchants stay long enough for their pay.

We may Observe here the great necessity and bennifitt both of Education and Conversation; for these people have as Large a portion of mother witt, and sometimes a Larger, than those who have bin brought up in Citties; But for want of emprovements, Render themselves almost Ridiculos, as above. I should be glad if they would leave such follies, and am sure all that Love Clean Houses (at least) would be glad on't too.

[21]Latin for "the law of merchants," that is, the legally recognized commercial system.

[22]Alfogeos, or Spanish saddlebags, also referred to a baboon's cheeks. Thus Knight uses this word in a humorously derogatory way.

[23]Genteel.

They are generaly very plain in their dress, throuout all ye Colony, as I saw, and follow one another in their modes; that You may know where they belong, especially the women, meet them where you will.

Their Cheif Red Letter day is St. Election,[24] wch is annualy Observed according to Charter, to choose their Govenr: a blessing they can never be thankfull enough for, as they will find, if ever it be their hard fortune to loose it. The present Govenor in Conecticott is the Honlbe John Winthrop Esq.[25] A Gentleman of an Ancient and Honourable Family, whose Father was Govenor here sometime before, and his Grand father has bin Govr of the Massachusetts. This gentleman is a very curteous and afable person, much Given to Hospitality, and has by his Good services Gain'd the affections of the people as much as any who had bin before him in that post.

Decr 6th. Being by this time well Recruited and rested after my Journy, my business lying unfinished by some concerns at New York depending thereupon, my Kinsman, Mr. Thomas Trowbridge of New Haven, must needs take a Journy there before it could be accomplished, I resolved to go there in company wth him, and a man of the town wch I engaged to wait on me there. Accordingly, Dec. 6th we set out from New Haven, and about 11 same morning came to Stratford ferry; wch crossing, about two miles on the other side Baited our horses and would have eat a morsell ourselves, But the Pumpkin and Indian mixt Bred had such an Aspect, and the Barelegg'd Punch so awkerd or rather Awfull a sound, that we left both, and proceeded forward, and about seven at night come to Fairfield, where we met with good entertainment and Lodg'd; and early next morning set forward to Norowalk, from its halfe Indian name *North-walk,* when about 12 at noon we arrived, and Had a Dinner of Fryed Venison, very savoury. Landlady wanting some pepper in the seasoning, bid the Girl hand her the spice in the little *Gay* cupp on ye shelfe. From hence we Hasted towards Rye, walking and Leading our Horses neer a mile together, up a prodigios high Hill; and so Riding till about nine at night, and there arrived and took up our Lodgings at an ordinary, wch a French family kept. Here being very hungry, I desired a fricasee, wch the Frenchman undertakeing, mannaged so contrary to my notion of Cookery, that I hastned to Bed superless; And being shewd the way up a pair of stairs wch had such a narrow passage that I had almost stopt by the Bulk of my Body; But arriving at my apartment found it to be a little Lento Chamber furnisht amongst other Rubbish with a High Bedd and a Low one, a Long Table, a Bench and a Bottomless chair,—Little Miss went to scratch up my Kennell wch Russelled as if shee'd bin in the Barn amongst the Husks, and supose such was the contents of the tickin—nevertheless being exceeding weary, down I laid my poor Carkes (never more tired) and found my Covering as scanty as my Bed was hard. Annon I heard another Russelling noise in Ye Room—called to know the matter—Little miss said shee was making a bed for the men; who, when they were in Bed, complained their leggs lay out of it by reason of its shortness—my poor bones complained bitterly not being used to such Lodgings, and so did the man who was with us; and poor I made but one Grone, which was from the time I went to bed to the time I Riss, which was about three in the morning, Setting up by the Fire till Light, and having discharged

[24]Knight's colloquial manner of indicating that Election Days were officially observed.

[25]Fitz-John Winthrop (1638–1707), eldest son of Governor John Winthrop, was Governor of Connecticut from 1698 to 1707.

our ordinary wch was as dear as if we had had far Better fare—wee took our leave of Monsier and about seven in the morn come to New Rochell a french town, where we had a good Breakfast. And in the strength of that about an how'r before sunsett got to York. Here I applyd myself to Mr. Burroughs, a merchant to whom I was recommended by my Kinsman Capt. Prout, and received great Civilities from him and his spouse, who were now both Deaf but very agreeable in their Conversation, Diverting me with pleasant stories of their knowledge in Brittan from whence they both come, one of which was above the rest very pleasant to me viz. my Lord Darcy had a very extravagant Brother who had mortgaged what Estate hee could not sell, and in good time dyed leaving only one son. Him his Lordship (having none of his own) took and made him Heir of his whole Estate, which he was to receive at the death of his Aunt. He and his Aunt in her widowhood held a right understanding and lived as become such Relations, shee being a discreat Gentlewoman and he an Ingenios Young man. One day Hee fell into some Company though far his inferiors, very freely told him of the Ill circumstances his fathers Estate lay under, and the many Debts he left unpaid to the wrong of poor people with whom he had dealt. The Young gentleman was put out of countenance—no way hee could think of to Redress himself—his whole dependance being on the Lady his Aunt, and how to speak to her he knew not—Hee went home, sat down to dinner and as usual sometimes with her when the Chaplain was absent, she desired him to say Grace, wch he did after this manner:

Pray God in Mercy take my Lady Darcy
Unto his Heavenly Throne,
That little John may live like a man,
And pay every man his own.

The prudent Lady took no present notice, But finishd dinner, after wch having sat and talk't awhile (as Customary) He Riss, took his Hatt and Going out she desired him to give her leave to speak to him in her Clossett, Where being come she desired to know why hee prayed for her Death in the manner aforesaid, and what part of her deportment towards him merritted such desires. Hee Reply'd, none at all, But he was under such disadvantages that nothing but that could do him service, and told her how he had been affronted as above, and what Impressions it had made upon him. The Lady made him a gentle reprimand that he had not informed her after another manner, Bid him see what his father owed and he should have money to pay it to a penny, And always to lett her know his wants and he should have a redy supply. The Young Gentleman charm'd with his Aunts Discrete management, Beggd her pardon and accepted her kind offer and retrieved his fathers Estate, &c. and said Hee hoped his Aunt would never dye, for shee had done better by him than hee could have done for himself.—Mr. Burroughs went with me to Vendue[26] where I bought about 100 Rheem of paper wch was retaken in a flyboat from Holland and sold very Reasonably here—some ten, some Eight shillings per Rheem by the Lott wch was ten Rheem in a Lott. And at the Vendue I made a great many acquaintances amongst the good women of the town, who curteosly invited me to their houses and generously entertained me.

[26]Place of public sale or auction.

The Cittie of New York is a pleasant, well compacted place, situated on a Commodius River wch is a fine harbour for shipping. The Buildings Brick Generaly, very stately and high, though not altogether like ours in Boston. The Bricks in some of the Houses are of divers Coullers and laid in Checkers, being glazed look very agreeable. The inside of them are neat to admiration, the wooden work, for only the walls are plasterd, and the Sumers and Gist[27] are plained and kept very white scowr'd as so is all the partitions if made of Bords. The fire places have no Jambs (as ours have) But the Backs run flush with the walls, and the Hearth is of Tyles and is as farr out into the Room at the Ends as before the fire, wch is Generally Five foot in the Low'r rooms, and the peice over where the mantle tree should be is made as ours with Joyners work, and as I supose is fasten'd to iron rodds inside. The House where the Vendue was, had Chimney Corners like ours, and they and the hearths were laid wth the finest tile that I ever see, and the stair cases laid all with white tile which is ever clean, and so are the walls of the Kitchen wch had a Brick floor. They were making Great preparations to Receive their Govenor, Lord Cornbury[28] from the Jerseys, and for that End raised the militia to Gard him on shore to the fort.

They are Generaly of the Church of England and have a New England Gentleman for their minister, and a very fine church set out with all Customary requisites. There are also a Dutch and Divers Conventicles as they call them, viz. Baptist, Quakers, &c. They are not strict in keeping the Sabbath as in Boston and other places where I had bin, But seem to deal with great exactness as farr as I see or Deall with. They are sociable to one another and Curteos and Civill to strangers and fare well in their houses. The English go very fasheonable in their dress. But the Dutch, especially the middling sort, differ from our women, in their habitt go loose, were French muches wch are like a Capp and a head band in one, leaving their ears bare, which are sett out wth Jewells of a large size and many in number. And their fingers hoop't with Rings, some with large stones in them of many Coullers as were their pendants in their ears, which You should see very old women wear as well as Young.

They have Vendues very frequently and make their Earnings very well by them, for they treat with good Liquor Liberally, and the Customers Drink as Liberally and Generally pay for't as well, by paying for that which they Bidd up Briskly for, after the sack has gone plentifully about, tho' sometimes good penny worths are got there. Their Diversions in the Winter is Riding Sleys about three or four Miles out of Town, where they have Houses of entertainment at a place called the Bowery, and some go to friends Houses who handsomely treat them. Mr. Burroughs cary'd his spouse and Daughter and myself out to one Madame Dowes, a Gentlewoman that lived at a farm House, who gave us a handsome Entertainment of five or six Dishes and choice Beer and metheglin,[29] Cyder, &c. all which she said was the produce of her farm. I believe we mett 50 or 60 slays that day—they fly with great swiftness and some are so furious that they'le turn out of the path for none except a Loaden Cart. Nor do they spare for any diversion the place affords, and sociable to a degree, they'r Tables being as free to their Naybours as to themselves.

[27]Beams and joints.

[28]Edward Hyde, Lord Cornbury, governor of New York, 1702–1708.

[29]Alcoholic drink made with fermented honey; spiced mead.

Having here transacted the affair I went upon and some other that fell in the way, after about a fortnight's stay there I left New-York with no Little regrett, and Thursday, Dec. 21, set out for New Haven wth my Kinsman Trowbridge, and the man that waited on me about one afternoon, and about three come to half-way house about ten miles out of town, where we Baited and went forward, and about 5 come to Spiting Devil, Else Kings bridge,[30] where they pay three pence for passing over with a horse, which the man that keeps the Gate set up at the end of the Bridge receives.

We hoped to reach the french town and Lodg there that night, but unhapily lost our way about four miles short, and being overtaken by a great storm of wind and snow which set full in our faces about dark, we were very uneasy. But meeting one Gardner who lived in a Cottage thereabout, offered us his fire to set by, having but one poor Bedd, and his wife not well, &c. or he would go to a House with us, where he thought we might be better accommodated—thither we went, But a surly old shee Creature, not worthy the name of woman, who would hardly let us go into her Door, though the weather was so stormy none but shee would have turnd out a Dogg. But her son whose name was gallop, who lived Just by Invited us to his house and shewed me two pair of stairs, viz. one up the loft and tother up the Bedd, wch was as hard as it was high, and warmed it with a hott stone at the feet. I lay very uncomfortably, insomuch that I was so very cold and sick I was forced to call them up to give me something to warm me. They had nothing but milk in the house, wch they Boild, and to make it better sweetened wth molasses, which I not knowing or thinking oft till it was down and coming up agen wch it did in so plentifull a manner that my host was soon paid double for his portion, and that in specia. But I believe it did me service in Cleering my stomach. So after this sick and weary night at East Chester, (a very miserable poor place,) the weather being now fair, Friday the 22d Dec. we set out for New Rochell, where being come we had good Entertainment and Recruited ourselves very well. This is a very pretty place well compact, and good handsome houses, Clean, good and passable Rodes, and situated on a Navigable River, abundance of land well fined and Cleerd all along as wee passed, which caused in me a Love to the place, wch I could have been content to live in it. Here wee Ridd over a Bridge made of one entire stone of such a Breadth that a cart might pass with safety, and to spare—it lay over a passage cutt through a Rock to convey water to a mill not farr off. Here are three fine Taverns within call of each other, very good provision for Travailers.

Thence we travailed through Merrinak, a neet, though little place, wth a navigable River before it, one of the pleasantest I ever see—Here were good Buildings, Especialy one, a very fine seat, wch they told me was Col. Hethcoats, who I had heard was a very fine Gentleman. From hence we come to Hors Neck, where wee Baited,[31] and they told me that one Church of England parson officiated in all these three towns once every Sunday in turns throughout the Year; and that they all could but poorly maintaine him, which they grudg'd to do, being a poor and quarelsome crew as I understand by our Host; their Quarelling about their choice of Minister, they chose to have none—But caused the Government to send this Gentleman to them.

[30]Spuyten Duyvil Creek, at Kingsbridge. The creek divides Manhattan Island from the mainland.

[31]Stopped at an inn to feed the horses and refresh the passengers.

Here wee took leave of York Government, and Descending the Mountainos passage that almost broke my heart in ascending before, we come to Stamford, a well compact Town, but miserable meeting house, wch we passed, and thro' many and great difficulties, as Bridges which were exceeding high and very tottering and of vast Length, steep and Rocky Hills and precipices, (Buggbears to a fearful female travailer.) About nine at night we come to Norrwalk, having crept over a timber of a Broken Bridge about thirty foot long, and perhaps fifty to ye water. I was exceeding tired and cold when we come to our Inn, and could get nothing there but poor entertainment, and the impertinant Bable of one of the worst of men, among many others of which our Host made one, who, had he bin one degree Impudenter, would have outdone his Grandfather. And this I think is the most perplexed night I have yet had. From hence, Saturday, Dec. 23, a very cold and windy day, after an Intolerable night's Lodging, wee hasted forward only observing in our way the Town to be situated on a Navigable river wth indiferent Buildings and people more refind than in some of the Country towns wee had passed, tho' vicious enough, the Church and Tavern being next neighbours. Having Ridd thro a difficult River wee come to Fairfield where wee Baited and were much refreshed as well with the Good things wch gratified our appetites as the time took to rest our wearied Limbs, wch Latter I employed in enquiring concerning the Town and manners of the people, &c. This is a considerable town, and filled as they say with wealthy people—have a spacious meeting house and good Buildings. But the Inhabitants are Litigious, nor do they well agree with their minister, who (they say) is a very worthy Gentleman.[32]

They have aboundance of sheep, whose very Dung brings them great gain, with part of which they pay their Parsons sallery, And they Grudg that, prefering their Dung before their minister. They Lett out their sheep at so much as they agree upon for a night; the highest Bidder always caries them, And they will sufficiently Dung a Large quantity of Land before morning. But were once Bitt by a sharper who had them a night and sheared them all before morning—From hence we went to Stratford, the next Town, in which I observed but few houses, and those not very good ones. But the people that I conversed with were civill and good natured. Here we staid till late at night, being to cross a Dangerous River ferry, the River at that time full of Ice; but after about four hours waiting with great difficulty wee got over. My fears and fatigues prevented my here taking any particular observation. Being got to Milford, it being late in the night, I could go no further; my fellow travailer going forward, I was invited to Lodg at Mrs.——, a very kind and civill Gentlewoman, by whom I was handsomely and kindly entertained till the next night. The people here go very plain in their apparel (more plain than I had observed in the towns I had passed) and seem to be very grave and serious. They told me there was a singing Quaker living there, or at least had a strong inclination to be so, His Spouse not at all affected that way. Some of the singing Crew come there one day to visit him, who being then abroad, they sat down (to the woman's no small vexation) Humming and singing and groneing after their conjuring way—Says the woman are you singing quakers? Yea says They—Then take my squalling Brat of a child here and sing to it

[32]Joseph Webb (1666–1732), minister in Fairfield, Connecticut, from 1694 to 1732.

says she for I have almost split my throat wth singing to him and cant get the Rogue to sleep. They took this as a great Indignity, and mediately departed. Shaking the dust from their Heels left the good woman and her Child among the number of the wicked.

This is a Seaport place and accomodated with a Good Harbour, But I had not opportunity to make particular observations because it was Sabbath day—This Evening.

December 24. I set out with the Gentlewomans son who she very civilly offered to go with me when she see no parswasions would cause me to stay which she pressingly desired, and crossing a ferry having but nine miles to New Haven, in a short time arrived there and was Kindly received and well accommodated amongst my Friends and Relations.

The Government of Connecticut Collony begins westward towards York at Stanford (as I am told) and so runs Eastward towards Boston (I mean in my range, because I dont intend to extend my description beyond my own travails) and ends that way at Stonington—And has a great many Large towns lying more northerly. It is a plentiful Country for provisions of all sorts and its Generally Healthy. No one that can and will be dilligent in this place need fear poverty nor the want of food and Rayment.

January 6th. Being now well Recruited and fitt for business I discoursed the persons I was concerned with, that we might finnish in order to my return to Boston. They delayd as they had hitherto done hoping to tire my Patience. But I was resolute to stay and see an End of the matter let it be never so much to my disadvantage—So January 9th they come again and promise the Wednesday following to go through with the distribution of the Estate which they delayed till Thursday and then come with new amusements. But at length by the mediation of that holy good Gentleman, the Rev. Mr. James Pierpont, the minister of New Haven, and with the advice and assistance of other our Good friends we come to an accommodation and distribution, which having finished though not till February, the man that waited on me to York taking the charge of me I sit out for Boston. We went from New Haven upon the ice (the ferry being not passable thereby) and the Rev. Mr. Pierpont wth Madam Prout Cuzin Trowbridge and divers others were taking leave wee went onward without any thing Remarkabl till wee come to New London and Lodged again at Mr. Saltonstalls—and here I dismist my Guide, and my Generos entertainer provided me Mr. Samuel Rogers of that place to go home with me—I stayed a day here Longer than I intended by the Commands of the Honble Govenor Winthrop to stay and take a supper with him whose wonderful civility I may not omitt. The next morning I Crossed ye Ferry to Groton, having had the Honor of the Company, of Madam Livingston (who is the Govenors Daughter) and Mary Christophers and divers others to the boat—And that night Lodgd at Stonington and had Rost Beef and pumpkin sause for supper. The next night at Haven's and had Rost fowle, and the next day wee come to a river which by Reason of Ye Freshetts coming down was swell'd so high wee feard it impassable and the rapid stream was very terryfying—However we must over and that in a small Cannoo. Mr. Rogers assuring me of his good Conduct, I after a stay of near an how'r on the shore for consultation went into the Cannoo, and Mr. Rogers paddled about 100 yards up the Creek by the shore side, turned into the swift stream and dexterously steering her in a moment wee come to the other side as swiftly passing as an arrow shott out of the Bow by a strong arm. I staid on ye shore till Hee returned to fetch our horses, which he caused to swim over himself bringing the furniture in the Cannoo. But it is past my skill to express the Exceeding fright all their transactions formed in me. Wee were now in the colony of the Massachusetts and taking Lodgings at the first Inn we come too had a pretty difficult passage the next day which was the second of March by reason of the sloughy ways then thawed by the Sunn. Here I mett Capt. John Richards of Boston who was going home, So being very glad of his Company we Rode something harder than hitherto, and missing my way in going up a very steep Hill, my horse dropt down under me as Dead; this new surprize no little hurt me meeting it Just at the Entrance into Dedham from whence we intended to reach home that night. But was now obliged to gett another Hors there and leave my own, resolving for Boston that night if possible. But in going over the Causeway at Dedham the Bridge being overflowed by the high waters comming down I very narrowly escaped falling over into the river Hors and all wch twas almost a miracle I did not—now it grew late in the afternoon and the people having very much discouraged us about the sloughy way wch they said wee should find very difficult and hazardous it so wrought on mee being tired and dispirited and disapointed of my desires of going home that I agreed to Lodg there that night wch wee did at the house of one Draper, and the next day being March 3d wee got safe home to Boston, where I found my aged and tender mother and my Dear and only Child in good health with open arms redy to receive me, and my Kind relations and friends flocking in to welcome mee and hear the story of my transactions and travails I having this day bin five months from home and now I cannot fully express my Joy and Satisfaction. But desire sincearly to adore my Great Benefactor for thus graciously carying forth and returning in safety his unworthy handmaid.

1825

William Byrd II 1674–1744

William Byrd II was born the heir to a large Virginia estate acquired in the 1630s by his great-grandfather and made larger by his great uncle and father. At age seven he was sent to England to be educated, and he remained there, with only one brief visit home, for twenty-four years. During those years he became a lawyer, joined the Royal Society (the leading association of scientists), mingled with prominent "wits" and men of letters in London, and was welcomed into the highest circles of British society. Upon the death of his father, he returned to Virginia in 1705, married an heiress, and took over his father's public offices, the receiver-generalship of the colony and membership in the House of Burgesses. He retained the latter office until his death; he was eventually elected president of the House. In 1715, however, he returned to London and lived there for ten more years (coming back to Virginia in 1720–21), serving as agent for the House, largely in opposition to its rival for colonial power, the governor, Alexander Spotswood.

Following the death of his wife in 1716, Byrd indulged liberally in all the pleasures of London high life, but in 1724 remarried and two years later returned permanently to his hereditary estate. There he rebuilt his father's mansion at Westover and stored it with a valuable collection of portraits and a library larger than any other in the colonies but that owned by Cotton Mather. Byrd also went on several expeditions away from his plantation, founding the cities of Richmond and Petersburg, purchasing large tracts of western land, and participating in the 1728 survey of the southern border of Virginia, an expedition memorialized in *The History of the Dividing Line betwixt Virginia and North Carolina.*

Throughout his life Byrd was an avid writer, but most of his writings are brief and occasional: descriptions of personality types, letters, diaries, travel journals, and a few poems. Some he wrote only for himself (notably the diaries, written in shorthand code, which detail his sexual escapades), some for a small circle of friends. Even the one work evidently written for the public, *The History of the Dividing Line,* he never sought to publish. Clearly Byrd regarded himself as a literate gentleman, not a professional author. Yet the richly visualized satire and ironic style distinguishable even in his familiar letters show William Byrd II to be one of the most important men of letters from Virginia prior to the Revolutionary War.

It is only after Byrd made Virginia his permanent home at age fifty-two that he devoted his writing to American subjects and produced his most important work. His letters from that date are addressed chiefly to correspondents in England, and they vividly depict the contrast between England and America. For Byrd, England is a cold and overpopulated land of decadent private extravagance and cynical public thievery. Although Byrd longs for England's sophisticated city life, he glorifies America as a warm country of extraordinary fertility, where private pleasure and public good meet. Even the lack of city socializing is good, for it forces Byrd's highly erotic imagination to invent its own amusements. Still, the country living in America has some dangers of its own. A warm sun seconded by easy access to rum and increasing dependence on slave labor make Virginia the land of ignoble sloth as well as thoughtful ease.

Byrd's major work, *The History of the Dividing Line* (written in 1729 but not published until 1841), develops a number of contrasts within America rather than between America and England. The differences between the origin of the northern colonies and the origin of the southern ones, between Virginians and North Carolinians, between the pious and the religiously indifferent, between whites and Indians, between women and men, and between men and bears reflect the central contrast between industry and idleness that runs through the work. Byrd clearly favors industry as he takes us further and further from all signs of it into the South and West, while offering us brilliant satirical portraits of indolence. Yet Byrd also favors nature, especially its fertility, and shows how that increases as industry, the product of civilization, declines. Thus he paradoxically admires what he satirizes, creating panegyrics, not without a tongue in cheek, of the value of bear meat as an aphrodisiac, of intermarriage as a means of converting and pacifying the Indians, and of men's "industry" in the getting of children as a key to North Carolina's future glory.

A further contrast is provided by Byrd's companion volume, *The Secret History of the Dividing Line* (not published until 1929). This work describes the same surveying expedition covered in *The History of the Dividing Line,* but instead of depicting public events, *The Secret History* narrates the private exploits of the surveyors. While the public history offers "an account of the good" the team did, this history offers what one "smart lass" they meet suggests be told as well, "an account of the evil." In their idle hours, the surveyors drank, joked, gambled, squabbled, hunted, and chased a variety of women. Much like Morton's *New English Canaan,* Byrd's narration of these activities turns the survey into a quixotic journey, filled with "noble captains," "truss damsels," and "romantic adventure." This frivolous comedy of the type-cast surveyors provides the perfect counterpart to the serious satire of the inhabitants surveyed in the public history. Through both histories and through the letters as well moves "Steddy," Byrd's name for himself, a character as comic as anyone else but peculiarly able to walk the dividing line between all contrasts and conflicts without ever losing his balance.

Kenneth Alan Hovey
University of Texas at San Antonio

PRIMARY WORKS

The Prose Works of William Byrd, ed. Louis B. Wright, 1966; *The Correspondence of the Three William Byrds,* ed. Marion Tingling, 1977.

from The History of the Dividing Line betwixt Virginia and North Carolina *and* The Secret History of the Line[1]

Before I enter upon the Journal of the Line between Virginia and North Carolina, it will be necessary to clear the way to it, by shewing how the other British Colonies on the Main have, one after the other, been carved out of Virginia, by Grants from his Majesty's Royal Predecessors. All that part of the Northern American Continent now under the Dominion of the King of Great Britain, and Stretching quite as far as the Cape of Florida, went *at first under the General Name of Virginia.*

The only Distinction, in those early Days, was, that all the Coast to the Southward of Chesapeake Bay was called South Virginia, and all to the Northward of it, North Virginia.

The first Settlement of this fine Country was owing to that great Ornament of the British Nation, Sir Walter Raleigh, who obtained a Grant thereof from Queen Elizabeth of ever-glorious Memory, by Letters Patent, dated March the 25th, 1584. . . .

As it happen'd some Ages before to be the fashion to Santer to the Holy Land,[2] and go upon other Quixot Adventures, so it was now grown the Humour to take a Trip to America. The Spaniards had lately discovered Rich Mines in their Part of the West Indies, which made their Maritime Neighbours eager to do so too. This Modish Frenzy being still more Inflam'd by the Charming Account given of Virginia, by the first Adventurers, made many fond of removeing to such a Paradise.

Happy was he, and still happier She, that cou'd get themselves transported, fondly expecting their Coarsest Utensils, in that happy place, would be of Massy Silver.

[1]The texts of *The History of the Dividing Line betwixt Virginia and North Carolina* and *The Secret History* are taken from *The Prose Works of William Byrd,* ed. Louis B. Wright (Cambridge, 1966). Byrd began the official history within two years after the dividing line expedition, yet he never published it. For the convenience of the reader, we are providing, in sequence, both the texts of the official history and the secret history. The secret history appears in italics.

[2]The Crusades of the Middle Ages.

This made it easy for the Company to procure as many Volunteers as they wanted for their new Colony. . . .

These Wretches were set Ashoar not far from Roanoak Inlet, but by some fatal disagreement, or Laziness, were either Starved or cut to Pieces by the Indians.

Several repeated Misadventures of this kind did, for some time, allay the Itch of Sailing to this New World; but the Distemper broke out again about the Year 1606. Then it happened that the Earl of Southampton and several other Persons, eminent for their Quality and Estates, were invited into the Company, who apply'd themselves once more to People the then almost abandon'd Colony. For this purpose they embarkt about an Hundred men, most of them Riprobates of good Familys, and related to some of the company, who were men of Quality and Fortune.

The Ships that carried them made a Shift to find a more direct way to Virginia, and ventured thro the Capes into the Bay of Chesapeak. The same Night they came to an Anchor at the Mouth of Powatan, the same as James River, where they built a Small Fort at a Place call'd Point Comfort.

This Settlement stood its ground from that time forward in spite of all the Blunders and Disagreement of the first Adventurers, and the many Calamitys that befel the Colony afterwards.

The six gentlemen who were first named of the company by the crown, and who were empowered to choose an annual President from among themselves, were always engaged in Factions and Quarrels, while the rest detested Work more than Famine. At this rate the Colony must have come to nothing, had it not been for the vigilance and Bravery of Capt. Smith, who struck a Terrour into all the Indians round about. This Gentleman took some pains to perswade the men to plant Indian corn, but they look upon all Labor as a Curse. They chose rather to depend upon the Musty Provisions that were sent from England: and when they fail'd they were forct to take more pains to Seek for Wild Fruits in the Woods, than they would have taken in tilling the Ground. Besides, this Exposed them to be knockt on the head by the Indians, and gave them Fluxes into the Bargain, which thind the Plantation very much. To Supply this mortality, they were reinforct the year following with a greater number of People, amongst which were fewer Gentlemen and more Labourers, who, however, took care not to kill themselves with Work.

These found the First Adventurers in a very starving condition, but relieved their wants with the fresh Supply they brought with them. From Kiquotan they extended themselves as far as James-Town, where like true Englishmen, they built a Church that cost no more than Fifty Pounds, and a Tavern that cost Five hundred.

They had now made peace with the Indians, but there was one thing wanting to make that peace lasting. The Natives coud, by no means, perswade themselves that the English were heartily their Friends, so long as they disdained to intermarry with them. And, in earnest, had the English consulted their own Security and the good of the Colony—Had they intended either to Civilize or Convert these Gentiles, they would have brought their Stomachs to embrace this prudent Alliance.

The Indians are generally tall and well-proportion'd, which may make full Amends for the Darkness of their Complexions. Add to this, that they are healthy & Strong, with Constitutions untainted by Lewdness, and not enfeebled by Luxury. Besides, Morals and all considered, I cant think the Indians were much greater Heathens than the first Adventurers, who, had they been good Christians, would have had the Charity to take this only method of converting the Natives to Christianity. For, after all that can be said, a sprightly Lover is the most prevailing Missionary that can be sent amongst these, or any other Infidels.

Besides, the poor Indians would have had less reason to Complain that the English took away their Land, if they had received it by way of Portion with their Daughters. Had such Affinities been contracted in the Beginning, how much Bloodshed had been prevented, and how populous would the Country have been, and, consequently, how considerable? Nor wou'd the Shade of the Skin have been any reproach at this day; for if a Moor may be washt white in 3 Generations, Surely an Indian might have been blancht in two. . . .

About the same time New England was pared off from Virginia by Letters Patent, bearing date April the 10th, 1608. Several Gentlemen of the Town and Neighbourhood of Plymouth obtain'd this Grant, with the Ld Chief Justice Popham at their Head.

Their Bounds were Specified to Extend from 38 to 45 Degrees of Northern Latitude, with a Breadth of one Hundred Miles from the Sea Shore. The first 14 Years, this Company encounter'd many Difficulties, and lost many men, tho' far from being discouraged, they sent over Numerous Recruits of Presbyterians, every year, who for all that, had much ado to stand their Ground, with all their Fighting and Praying.

But about the year 1620, a Large Swarm of Dissenters fled thither from the Severities of their Stepmother, the Church. These Saints conceiving the same Aversion to the Copper Complexion of the Natives, with that of the first Adventurers to Virginia, would, on no Terms, contract Alliances with them, afraid perhaps, like the Jews of Old, lest they might be drawn into Idolatry by those Strange Women.

Whatever disgusted them I cant say, but this false delicacy creating in the Indians a Jealousy that the English were ill affected towards them, was the Cause that many of them were cut off, and the rest Exposed to various Distresses.

This Reinforcement was landed not far from Cape Codd, where, for their greater Security they built a Fort, and near it a Small Town, which in Honour of the Proprietors, was call'd New Plymouth. But they Still had many discouragements to Struggle with, tho' by being well Supported from Home, they by Degrees Triumph't over them all.

Their Bretheren, after this, flockt over so fast, that in a few Years they extended the Settlement one hundred Miles along the Coast, including Rhode Island and Martha's Vineyard.

Thus the Colony throve apace, and was throng'd with large Detachments of Independents and Presbyterians, who thought themselves persecuted at home.

Tho' these People may be ridiculd for some Pharisaical Particularitys in their Worship and Behaviour, yet they were very useful Subjects, as being Frugal and Industrious, giving no Scandal or bad Example, at least by any Open and Public Vices. By which excellent Qualities they had much the Advantage of the Southern Colony, who thought their being Members of the Establish't Church sufficient to Sanctifie very loose and Profligate Morals. For this Reason New England improved much faster than Virginia, and in Seven or Eight Years New Plimouth, like Switzerland, seemed too Narrow a Territory for its Inhabitants. . . .

Both the French and the Spaniards had, in the Name of their Respective Monarchs, long ago taken Possession of that Part of the Northern Continent that now goes by the Name of Carolina; but finding it Produced neither Gold nor Silver, as they greedily expected, and meeting such returns from the Indians as their own Cruelty and Treachery deserved, they totally abandond it. In this deserted Condition that country lay for the Space of 90 Years, till King Charles the 2d, finding it a DERELICT, granted it away to the Earl of Clarendon and others, by His Royal Charter, dated March the 24th, 1663. The Boundary of that Grant towards Virginia was a due West Line from Luck-Island, (the same as Colleton Island), lying in 36 degrees N. Latitude, quite to the South Sea.

But afterwards Sir William Berkeley, who was one of the Grantees and at that time Governour of Virginia, finding a Territory of 31 Miles in Breadth between the Inhabited Part of Virginia and the above-mentioned Boundary of Carolina, advisd the Lord Clarendon of it. And His Lordp had Interest enough with the King to obtain a Second Patent to include it, dated June the 30th, 1665.

In the mean time, the People on the Frontiers Entered for Land, & took out Patents by Guess, either from the King or the Lords Proprietors. But the Crown was like to be the loser by this Incertainty, because the Terms both of taking up and seating Land were easier much in Carolina. The Yearly Taxes to the Public were likewise there less burdensom, which laid Virginia under a Plain disadvantage.

This Consideration put that Government upon entering into Measures with North Carolina, to terminate the Dispute, and settle a Certain Boundary between the two colonies.

The Governor and Council of Virginia in the year 1727 received an express order from His Majesty to appoint commissioners who, in conjunction with others to be named by the government of North Carolina, should run the line betwixt the two colonies. The rule these gentlemen were directed to go by was a paper of proposals formerly agreed on between the two governors, at that time Spotswood and Eden.[3] *It would be a hard thing to say of so wise a man as Mr. Spotswood thought himself that he was overreached, but it has appeared upon trial that Mr. Eden was much better informed how the land lay than he. However, since the King was pleased to agree to these unequal proposals, the government of Virginia was too dutiful to dispute them. They therefore appointed Steddy*[4] *and Merryman commissioners on the part of Virginia to execute that order and Astrolabe and Capricorn to be the surveyors. But Merryman dying, Firebrand and Meanwell made interest to fill his place. Most of the Council inclined to favor the last, because he had offered his services before he knew that any pay would belong to the place. But Burly, one of the honorable board, perceiving his friend Firebrand would lose it if it came to the vote, proposed the expedient of sending three commissioners upon so difficult and hazardous an expedition. To this a majority agreed, being unwilling to be thought too frugal of the public money. Accordingly, they were both joined with Steddy in this commission. When this was over, Steddy proposed that a chaplain might be allowed to attend the commissioners, by reason they should have a number of men with them sufficient for a small congregation and were to pass through an ungodly country where they should find neither church nor minister; that, besides, it would be an act of great charity to give the gentiles of that part of the world an opportunity to christen both them*

[3]Colonel Alexander Spotswood, Lieutenant-Governor of Virginia, and Sir Charles Eden, Governor of North Carolina.

[4]Byrd's name for himself. The other names of members of the surveying party given in the *Secret History* are imaginary, too, though they represent real people.

and their children. This being unanimously consented to, Dr. Humdrum was named upon Steddy's recommendation.

Of all these proceedings notice was dispatched to Sir Richard Everard, Governor of North Carolina, desiring him to name commissioners on the part of that province to meet those of Virginia the spring following. In consequence whereof that government named Jumble, Shoebrush, Plausible, and Puzzlecause, being the flower and cream of the Council of that province. The next step necessary to be taken was for the commissioners on both sides to agree upon a day of meeting at Currituck Inlet in order to proceed on this business, and the fifth of March was thought a proper time, because then Mercury and the moon were to be in conjunction. . . .

[March] 8 . . . [W]e rowed up an arm of the sound called the Back Bay till we came to the head of it. There we were stopped by a miry pocosin[5] full half a mile in breadth, through which we were obliged to daggle on foot, plunging now and then, though we picked our way, up to the knees in mud. At the end of this charming walk we gained the terra firma of Princess Anne County. In that dirty condition we were afterwards obliged to foot it two miles as far as John Heath's plantation, where we expected to meet the surveyors and the men who waited upon them. . . .

All the people in the neighborhood flocked to John Heath's to behold such rarities as they fancied us to be. The men left their beloved chimney corners, the good women their spinning wheels, and some, of more curiosity than ordinary, rose out of their sick beds to come and stare at us. They looked upon us as a troop of knights-errant who were running this great risk of our lives, as they imagined, for the public weal: and some of the gravest of them questioned much whether we were not all criminals condemned to this dirty work for offenses against the state.

8. . . . Amongst other spectators came two girls to see us, one of which was very handsome and the other very willing. However, we only saluted them, and if we committed any sin at all, it was only in our hearts.

9. In the morning we walked with the surveyors to the line, which cut through Eyland's plantation, and came to the banks of North River. Hither the girls abovementioned attended us, but an old woman came along with them for the security of their virtue. . . .

10. The Sabbath happened very opportunely, to give some ease to our jaded people, who rested religiously from every work but that of cooking the kettle. We observed very few cornfields in our walks and those very small, which seemed the stranger to us because we could see no other tokens of husbandry or improvement. But upon further inquiry we were given to understand people only made corn for themselves and not for their stocks, which know very well how to get their own living. Both cattle and hogs ramble into the neighboring marshes and swamps, where they maintain themselves the whole winter long and are not fetched home till the spring. Thus these indolent wretches during one half of the year lose the advantage of the milk of their cattle, as well as their dung, and many of the poor creatures perish in the mire, into the bargain, by this ill management. Some who pique themselves more upon industry than their neighbors will now and then, in compliment to their cattle, cut down a tree whose limbs are loaded with the moss aforementioned. The

[5]A low, flat, swampy region.

trouble would be too great to climb the tree in order to gather this provender, but the shortest way (which in this country is always counted the best) is to fell it, just like the lazy Indians, who do the same by such trees as bear fruit and so make one harvest for all. By this bad husbandry milk is so scarce in the winter season that were a big-bellied woman to long for it she would tax her longing. And, in truth, I believe this is often the case, and at the same time a very good reason why so many people in this province are marked with a custard complexion.

The only business here is raising of hogs, which is managed with the least trouble and affords the diet they are most fond of. The truth of it is, the inhabitants of North Carolina devour so much swine's flesh that it fills them full of gross humors. For want, too, of a constant supply of salt, they are commonly obliged to eat it fresh, and that begets the highest taint of scurvy. Thus, whenever a severe cold happens to constitutions thus vitiated, 'tis apt to improve into the yaws, called there very justly the country distemper. This has all the symptoms of the pox, with this aggravation, that no preparation of mercury will touch it. First it seizes the throat, next the palate, and lastly shows its spite to the poor nose, of which 'tis apt in a small time treacherously to undermine the foundation. This calamity is so common and familiar here that it ceases to be a scandal, and in the disputes that happen about beauty the noses have in some companies much ado to carry it. Nay, tis said that once, after three good pork years, a motion had like to have been made in the House of Burgesses, that a man with a nose should be incapable of holding any place of profit in the province; which extraordinary motion could never have been intended without some hopes of a majority.

Thus, considering the foul and pernicious effects of eating swine's flesh in a hot country, it was wisely forbid and made an abomination to the Jews, who lived much in the same latitude with Carolina.

11. . . . We had encamped so early that we found time in the evening to walk near half a mile into the woods. There we came upon a family of mulattoes that called themselves free, though by the shyness of the master of the house, who took care to keep least in sight, their freedom seemed a little doubtful. It is certain many slaves shelter themselves in this obscure part of the world, nor will any of their righteous neighbors discover them. On the contrary, they find their account in settling such fugitives on some out-of-the way corner of their land to raise stocks for a mean and inconsiderable share, well knowing their condition makes it necessary for them to submit to any terms. Nor were these worthy borderers content to shelter runaway slaves, but debtors and criminals have often met with the like indulgence. But if the government of North Carolina have encouraged this unneighborly policy in order to increase their people, it is no more than what ancient Rome did before them, which was made a city of refuge for all debtors and fugitives and from that wretched beginning grew up in time to be mistress of great part of the world. And, considering how Fortune delights in bringing great things out of small, who knows but Carolina may, one time or other, come to be the seat of some other great empire?

11. . . . In the meanwhile, Shoebrush and I took a walk into the woods and called at a cottage where a dark angel surprised us with her charms. Her complexion was a deep copper, so that her fine shape and regular features made her appear like a statue en bronze *done by a masterly hand. Shoebrush was smitten at the first glance and examined all her neat proportions with a critical exactness. She struggled just enough to make her admirer more eager, so that if I had not been there, he would have been in danger of carrying his joke a little too far.*

12. . . . *I retired early to our camp at some distance from the house, while my colleagues tarried withindoors and refreshed themselves with a cheerful bowl. In the gaiety of their hearts, they invited a tallow-faced wench that had sprained her wrist to drink with them, and when they had raised her in good humor they examined all her hidden charms and played a great many gay pranks. While Firebrand, who had the most curiosity, was ranging over her sweet person, he picked off several scaps as big as nipples, the consequence of eating too much pork. The poor damsel was disabled from making any resistance by the lameness of her hand; all she could do was to sit still and make the fashionable exclamation of the country, "Flesh alive and tear it!" and, by what I can understand, she never spake so properly in her life.*

One of the representatives of North Carolina made a midnight visit to our camp, and his curiosity was so very clamorous that it waked me, for which I wished his nose as flat as any of his porcivorous countrymen.

15. . . . At the end of eighteen miles we reached Timothy Ivy's plantation, where we pitched our tent for the first time and were furnished with everything the place afforded. We perceived the happy effects of industry in this family, in which every one looked tidy and clean and carried in their countenances the cheerful marks of plenty. We saw no drones there, which are but too common, alas, in that part of the world. Though, in truth, the distemper of laziness seizes the men oftener much than the women. These last spin, weave, and knit, all with their own hands, while their husbands, depending on the bounty of the climate, are slothful in everything but getting of children, and in that only instance make themselves useful members of an infant colony.

15. . . . Timothy Ives . . . supplied us with everything that was necessary. He had a tall, straight daughter of a yielding, sandy complexion, who having the curiosity to see the tent, Puzzlecause gallanted her thither, and might have made her free of it had not we come seasonably to save the damsel's chastity. Here both our cookery and bedding were more cleanly than ordinary. The parson lay with Puzzlecause in the tent to keep him honest or, peradventure, to partake of his diversion if he should be otherwise.

16. . . . We passed by no less than two Quaker meetinghouses, one of which had an awkward ornament on the west end of it that seemed to ape a steeple. I must own I expected no such piece of foppery from a sect of so much outside simplicity. That persuasion prevails much in the lower end of Nansemond County, for want of ministers to pilot the people a decenter way to Heaven. The ill reputation of tobacco planted in those lower parishes makes the clergy unwilling to accept of them, unless it be such whose abilities are as mean as their pay. Thus, whether the churches be quite void or but indifferently filled, the Quakers will have an opportunity of gaining proselytes. 'Tis a wonder no popish missionaries are sent from Maryland to labor in this neglected vineyard, who we know have zeal enough to traverse sea and land on the meritorious errand of making converts. Nor is it less strange that some wolf in sheep's clothing arrives not from New England to lead astray a flock that has no shepherd. People uninstructed in any religion are ready to embrace the first that offers. 'Tis natural for helpless man to adore his Maker in some form or other, and were there any exception to this rule, I should suspect it to be among the Hottentots of the Cape of Good Hope and of North Carolina.

17. . . . One thing may be said for the inhabitants of that province, that they are not troubled with any religious fumes and have the least superstition of any people living. They do not know Sunday from any other day, any more than Robinson Crusoe did, which would give them a great advantage were they given to be industrious. But they keep so many Sabbaths every week that their disregard of the seventh day has no manner of cruelty in it, either to servants or cattle.

18. . . . We made the best of our way to Mr. Thomas Speight's, who appeared to be a grandee of North Carolina. There we arrived about four, though the distance could not be less than twenty-five miles. Upon our arrival our poor landlord made a shift to crawl out upon his crutches, having the gout in both his knees. He bid us welcome, and a great bustle was made in the family about our entertainment. We saw two truss[6] *damsels stump about very industriously, that were handsome enough upon a march.*

19. . . . My landlord's daughter, Rachel, offered her service to wash my linen and regaled me with a mess of hominy, tossed up with rank butter and glyster sugar. This I was forced to eat to show that nothing from so fair a hand could be disagreeable. She was a smart lass, and, when I desired the parson to make a memorandum of his christenings that we might keep an account of the good we did, she asked me very pertly who was to keep an account of the evil? I told her she should be my secretary for that if she would go along with me.

20. . . . Judge Jumble, who left us at Currituck, returned now from Edenton and brought three cormorants along with him. One was his own brother, the second was brother to Shoebrush, and the third, Captain Genneau, who had sold his commission and spent the money. These honest gentlemen had no business but to help drink out our liquor, having very little at home. . . .

At night the noble captain retired before the rest of the company and was stepping without ceremony into our bed, but I arrived just time enough to prevent it. We could not possibly be so civil to this free gentleman as to make him so great a compliment, much less let him take possession, according to the Carolina breeding, without invitation. Had Ruth or Rachel, my landlord's daughters, taken this liberty, we should perhaps have made no words, but in truth the captain had no charms that merited so particular an indulgence.

25. . . . Our landlord had not the good fortune to please Firebrand with our dinner, but, surely, when people do their best, a reasonable man would be satisfied. But he endeavored to mend his entertainment by making hot love to honest Ruth, who would by no means be charmed either with his persuasion or his person. While the master was employed in making love to one sister, the man made his passion known to the other; only he was more boisterous and employed force when he could not succeed by fair means. Though one of the men rescued the poor girl from this violent lover but was so much his friend as to keep the shameful secret from those whose duty it would have been to punish such violations of hospitality. . . .

[25] . . . Surely there is no place in the world where the inhabitants live with less labor than in North Carolina. It approaches nearer to the description of Lubberland[7] than any other, by the great felicity of the climate, the easiness of raising provisions,

[6]Compact, shapely.
[7]Imaginary land of plenty without labor.

and the slothfulness of the people. Indian corn is of so great increase that a little pains will subsist a very large family with bread, and then they may have meat without any pains at all, by the help of the low grounds and the great variety of mast that grows on the high land. The men, for their parts, just like the Indians, impose all the work upon the poor women. They make their wives rise out of their beds early in the morning, at the same time that they lie and snore till the sun has risen one-third of his course and dispersed all the unwholesome damps. Then, after stretching and yawning for half an hour, they light their pipes, and, under the protection of a cloud of smoke, venture out into the open air; though if it happen to be never so little cold they quickly return shivering into the chimney corner. When the weather is mild, they stand leaning with both their arms upon the cornfield fence and gravely consider whether they had best go and take a small heat at the hoe but generally find reasons to put it off till another time. Thus they loiter away their lives, like Solomon's sluggard,[8] with their arms across, and at the winding up of the year scarcely have bread to eat. To speak the truth, 'tis a thorough aversion to labor that makes people file off to North Carolina, where plenty and a warm sun confirm them in their disposition to laziness for their whole lives. . . .

27. . . . Within three or four miles of Edenton[9] the soil appears to be a little more fertile, though it is much cut with slashes, which seem all to have a tendency toward the Dismal. This town is situate on the north side of Albemarle Sound, which is there about five miles over. A dirty slash runs all along the back of it, which in the summer is a foul annoyance and furnishes abundance of that Carolina plague, mosquitoes. There may be forty or fifty houses, most of them small and built without expense. A citizen here is counted extravagant if he has ambition enough to aspire to a brick chimney. Justice herself is but indifferently lodged, the courthouse having much of the air of a common tobacco house. I believe this is the only metropolis in the Christian or Mahometan world where there is neither church, chapel, mosque, synagogue, or any other place of public worship of any sect or religion whatsoever. What little devotion there may happen to be is much more private than their vices. The people seem easy without a minister as long as they are exempted from paying him. Sometimes the Society for Propagating the Gospel has had the charity to send over missionaries to this country; but, unfortunately, the priest has been too lewd for the people, or, which oftener happens, they too lewd for the priest. For these reasons these reverend gentlemen have always left their flocks as arrant heathen as they found them. Thus much, however, may be said for the inhabitants of Edenton, that not a soul has the least taint of hypocrisy or superstition, acting very frankly and aboveboard in all their exercises.

Provisions here are extremely cheap and extremely good, so that people may live plentifully at a trifling expense. Nothing is dear but law, physic, and strong drink, which are all bad in their kind, and the last they get with so much difficulty that they are never guilty of the sin of suffering it to sour upon their hands. Their vanity generally lies not so much in having a handsome dining room as a handsome house of

[8]Proverbs 6:6–11.

[9]Then the unofficial capital of North Carolina, an important commercial center named after Governor Eden.

office:[10] in this kind of structure they are really extravagant. They are rarely guilty of flattering or making any court to their governors but treat them with all the excesses of freedom and familiarity. They are of opinion their rulers would be apt to grow insolent if they grew rich, and for that reason take care to keep them poorer and more dependent, if possible, than the saints in New England used to do their governors. They have very little coin, so they are forced to carry on their home traffic with paper money. This is the only cash that will tarry in the country, and for that reason the discount goes on increasing between that and real money and will do so to the end of the chapter.

April 1. . . . Wherever we passed we constantly found the borderers laid it to heart if their land was taken into Virginia; they chose much rather to belong to Carolina, where they pay no tribute, either to God or to Caesar. Another reason was that the government there is so loose and the laws are so feebly executed that, like those in the neighborhood of Sidon formerly, everyone does just what seems good in his own eyes.[11] If the Governor's hands have been weak in that province, under the authority of the Lords Proprietors, much weaker, then, were the hands of the magistrate, who, though he might have had virtue enough to endeavor to punish offenders, which very rarely happened, yet that virtue had been quite impotent for want of ability to put it in execution. Besides, there might have been some danger, perhaps, in venturing to be so rigorous, for fear of undergoing the fate of an honest justice in Currituck precinct. This bold magistrate, it seems, taking upon him to order a fellow to the stocks for being disorderly in his drink, was for his intemperate zeal carried thither himself and narrowly escaped being whipped by the rabble into the bargain.

5. Our surveyors made an elegant plat of our line from Currituck Inlet to the place where they left off, containing the distance of seventy-three miles and thirteen poles.[12] *Of this exact copies were made and, being carefully examined, were both signed by the commissioners of each colony. . . . The poor chaplain was the common butt at which all our company aimed their profane wit and gave him the title of "Dean Pip," because instead of a pricked line he had been so maidenly as to call it a pipped line. I left the company in good time, taking as little pleasure in their low wit as in their low liquor, which was rum punch. . . .*

7. . . . In the morning we dispatched a runner to the Nottoway town to let the Indians know we intended them a visit that evening, and our honest landlord was so kind as to be our pilot thither, being about four miles from his house. Accordingly, in the afternoon we marched in good order to the town, where the female scouts, stationed on an eminence for that purpose, had no sooner spied us but they gave notice of our approach to their fellow citizens by continual whoops and cries, which could not possibly have been more dismal at the sight of their most implacable enemies. This signal assembled all their great men, who received us in a body and conducted us into the fort.

This fort was a square piece of ground, enclosed with substantial puncheons or strong palisades about ten feet high and leaning a little outwards to make a scalade

[10]Outbuilding.
[11]Judges 21:25; Matthew 11:21–22.
[12]A pole is a unit of measure equal to a rod, 16½ feet.

more difficult. Each side of the square might be about a hundred yards long, with loopholes at proper distances through which they may fire upon the enemy. Within this enclosure we found bark cabins sufficient to lodge all their people in case they should be obliged to retire thither. These cabins are no other but close arbors made of saplings, arched at the top and covered so well with bark as to be proof against all weather. The fire is made in the middle, according to the Hibernian[13] fashion, the smoke whereof finds no other vent but at the door and so keeps the whole family warm, at the expense both of their eyes and complexion. The Indians have no standing furniture in their cabins but hurdles[14] to repose their persons upon which they cover with mats or deerskins. We were conducted to the best apartments in the fort, which just before had been made ready for our reception and adorned with new mats that were very sweet and clean.

The young men had painted themselves in a hideous manner, not so much for ornament as terror. In that frightful equipage they entertained us with sundry war dances, wherein they endeavored to look as formidable as possible. The instrument they danced to was an Indian drum, that is, a large gourd with a skin braced taut over the mouth of it. The dancers all sang to this music, keeping exact time with their feet while their head and arms were screwed into a thousand menacing postures.

Upon this occasion the ladies had arrayed themselves in all their finery. They were wrapped in their red and blue matchcoats, thrown so negligently about them that their mahogany skins appeared in several parts, like the Lacedaemonian damsels of old. Their hair was braided with white and blue peak and hung gracefully in a large roll upon their shoulders.

This peak consists of small cylinders cut out of a conch shell, drilled through and strung like beads. It serves them both for money and jewels, the blue being of much greater value than the white for the same reason that Ethiopian mistresses in France are dearer than French, because they are more scarce. The women wear necklaces and bracelets of these precious materials when they have a mind to appear lovely. Though their complexions be a little sad-colored, yet their shapes are very straight and well proportioned. Their faces are seldom handsome, yet they have an air of innocence and bashfulness that with a little less dirt would not fail to make them desirable. Such charms might have had their full effect upon men who had been so long deprived of female conversation but that the whole winter's soil was so crusted on the skins of those dark angels that it required a very strong appetite to approach them. The bear's oil with which they anoint their persons all over makes their skins soft and at the same time protects them from every species of vermin that use to be troublesome to other uncleanly people.

We were unluckily so many that they could not well make us the compliment of bedfellows according to the Indian rules of hospitality, though a grave matron whispered one of the commissioners very civilly in the ear that if her daughter had been but one year older she should have been at his devotion. It is by no means a loss of reputation among the Indians for damsels that are single to have intrigues with the men; on the contrary, they account it an argument of superior merit to be liked by a

[13]Irish.
[14]Wattles, frames interwoven with branches.

great number of gallants. However, like the ladies that game, they are a little mercenary in their amours and seldom bestow their favors out of stark love and kindness. But after these women have once appropriated their charms by marriage, they are from thenceforth faithful to their vows and will hardly ever be tempted by an agreeable gallant or be provoked by a brutal or even by a fumbling husband to go astray.

The little work that is done among the Indians is done by the poor women, while the men are quite idle or at most employed only in the gentlemanly diversions of hunting and fishing. In this, as well as in their wars, they now use nothing but firearms, which they purchase of the English for skins. Bows and arrows are grown into disuse, except only amongst their boys. Nor is it ill policy, but on the contrary very prudent, thus to furnish the Indians with firearms, because it makes them depend entirely upon the English, not only for their trade but even for their subsistence. Besides, they were really able to do more mischief while they made use of arrows, of which they would let silently fly several in a minute with wonderful dexterity, whereas now they hardly ever discharge their firelocks more than once, which they insidiously do from behind a tree and then retire as nimbly as the Dutch horse used to do now and then formerly in Flanders.

We put the Indians to no expense but only of a little corn for our horses, for which in gratitude we cheered their hearts with what rum we had left, which they love better than they do their wives and children. Though these Indians dwell among the English and see in what plenty a little industry enables them to live, yet they choose to continue in their stupid idleness and to suffer all the inconveniences of dirt, cold, and want rather than disturb their heads with care or defile their hands with labor.

The whole number of people belonging to the Nottoway town, if you include women and children, amount to about two hundred. These are the only Indians of any consequence now remaining within the limits of Virginia. The rest are either removed or dwindled to a very inconsiderable number, either by destroying one another or else by the smallpox and other diseases. Though nothing has been so fatal to them as their ungovernable passion for rum, with which, I am sorry to say it, they have been but too liberally supplied by the English that live near them.

And here I must lament the bad success Mr. Boyle's charity has hitherto had toward converting any of these poor heathens to Christianity.[15] Many children of our neighboring Indians have been brought up in the College of William and Mary. They have been taught to read and write and been carefully instructed in the principles of the Christian religion till they came to be men. Yet after they returned home, instead of civilizing and converting the rest, they have immediately relapsed into infidelity and barbarism themselves. . . .

I am sorry I can't give a better account of the state of the poor Indians with respect to Christianity, although a great deal of pains has been and still continues to be taken with them. For my part, I must be of opinion, as I hinted before, that there is

[15]Robert Boyle (1627–1691), the famous English scientist, bequeathed £4000 from his estate to go to "pious and charitable uses." £45 per annum went to William and Mary College for the education of Indians.

but one way of converting these poor infidels and reclaiming them from barbarity, and that is charitably to intermarry with them, according to the modern policy of the Most Christian King in Canada and Louisiana. Had the English done this at the first settlement of the colony, the infidelity of the Indians had been worn out at this day with their dark complexions, and the country had swarmed with people more than it does with insects. It was certainly an unreasonable nicety that prevented their entering into so good-natured an alliance. All nations of men have the same natural dignity, and we all know that very bright talents may be lodged under a very dark skin. The principal difference between one people and another proceeds only from the different opportunities of improvement. The Indians by no means want understanding and are in their figure tall and well proportioned. Even their copper-colored complexion would admit of blanching, if not in the first, at the farthest in the second, generation. I may safely venture to say, the Indian women would have made altogether as honest wives for the first planters as the damsels they used to purchase from aboard the ships. 'Tis strange, therefore, that any good Christian should have refused a wholesome, straight bedfellow, when he might have had so fair a portion with her as the merit of saving her soul.

8. When we were dressed, Meanwell and I visited most of the princesses at their own apartments, but the smoke was so great there, the fire being made in the middle of the cabins, that we were not able to see their charms. Prince James's princess sent my wife a fine basket of her own making, with the expectation of receiving from her some present of ten times its value. An Indian present, like those made to princes, is only a liberality put out to interest and a bribe placed to the greatest advantage.

I could discern by some of our gentlemen's linen, discolored by the soil of the Indian ladies, that they had been convincing themselves in the point of their having no fur.[16] . . .

October 13. . . . In the afternoon our hunters went forth and returned triumphantly with three brace of wild turkeys. They told us they could see the mountains distinctly from every eminence, though the atmosphere was so thick with smoke that they appeared at a greater distance than they really were.

In the evening we examined our friend Bearskin[17] concerning the religion of his country, and he explained it to us without any of that reserve to which his nation is subject. He told us he believed there was one supreme god, who had several subaltern deities under him. And that this master god made the world a long time ago. That he told the sun, the moon, and stars their business in the beginning, which they, with good looking-after, have faithfully performed ever since. That the same power that made all things at first has taken care to keep them in the same method and motion ever since. He believed that God had formed many worlds before he formed this, but that those worlds either grew old and ruinous or were destroyed for the dishonesty of the inhabitants. That God is very just and very good, ever well pleased

[16]Because of the summer heat and the seasonal crops, from April to September the survey was discontinued, as Byrd explains in his letter of May 20, 1729.

[17]An Indian who had joined them to help hunt game.

with those men who possess those godlike qualities. That he takes good people into his safe protection, makes them very rich, fills their bellies plentifully, preserves them from sickness and from being surprised or overcome by their enemies. But all such as tell lies and cheat those they have dealings with he never fails to punish with sickness, poverty, and hunger and, after all that, suffers them to be knocked on the head and scalped by those that fight against them.

He believed that after death both good and bad people are conducted by a strong guard into a great road, in which departed souls travel together for some time till at a certain distance this road forks into two paths, the one extremely level and the other stony and mountainous. Here the good are parted from the bad by a flash of lightning, the first being hurried away to the right, the other to the left. The right-hand road leads to a charming, warm country, where the spring is everlasting and every month is May; and as the year is always in its youth, so are the people, and particularly the women are bright as stars and never scold. That in this happy climate there are deer, turkeys, elks, and buffaloes innumerable, perpetually fat and gentle, while the trees are loaded with delicious fruit quite throughout the four seasons. That the soil brings forth corn spontaneously, without the curse of labor, and so very wholesome that none who have the happiness to eat of it are ever sick, grow old, or die. Near the entrance into this blessed land sits a venerable old man on a mat richly woven, who examines strictly all that are brought before him, and if they have behaved well, the guards are ordered to open the crystal gate and let them enter into the land of delight. The left-hand path is very rugged and uneven, leading to a dark and barren country where it is always winter. The ground is the whole year round covered with snow, and nothing is to be seen upon the trees but icicles. All the people are hungry yet have not a morsel of anything to eat except a bitter kind of potato, that gives them the dry gripes and fills their whole body with loathsome ulcers that stink and are insupportably painful. Here all the women are old and ugly, having claws like a panther with which they fly upon the men that slight their passion. For it seems these haggard old furies are intolerably fond and expect a vast deal of cherishing. They talk much and exceedingly shrill, giving exquisite pain to the drum of the ear, which in that place of the torment is so tender that every sharp note wounds it to the quick. At the end of this path sits a dreadful old woman on a monstrous toadstool, whose head is covered with rattlesnakes instead of tresses, with glaring white eyes that strike a terror unspeakable into all that behold her. This hag pronounces sentence of woe upon all the miserable wretches that hold up their hands at her tribunal. After this they are delivered over to huge turkey buzzards, like harpies, that fly away with them to the place above-mentioned. Here, after they have been tormented a certain number of years according to their several degrees of guilt, they are again driven back into this world to try if they will mend their manners and merit a place the next time in the regions of bliss.

This was the substance of Bearskin's religion and was as much to the purpose as could be expected from a mere state of nature, without one glimpse of revelation or philosophy. It contained, however, the three great articles of natural religion: the belief of a god, the moral distinction betwixt good and evil, and the expectation of rewards and punishments in another world. Indeed, the Indian notion of a future happiness is a little gross and sensual, like Mahomet's Paradise. But how can it be otherwise in a people that are contented with Nature as they find her and have no other lights but what they receive from pur-blind tradition?

14. *It began to rain about three o'clock this morning, but so gently that we had leisure to secure the bread from damage. It continued raining all night and till near noon, when it held up; the clouds looked very heavy and frightened us from all thoughts of decamping. Meanwell and I lay abed all the morning, believing that the most agreeable situation in wet weather. The wind, blowing hard at north-east, made the air very raw and uncomfortable. However, several of the men went hunting in the afternoon and killed three deer and four turkeys, so that the frying pan was not cool till next morning. The chaplain, disdaining to be useful in one capacity only, condescended to darn my stockings; he acquired that with his other university learning at the College of Dublin. At six it began to rain again and held not up till nine, when the clouds seemed to break away and give us a sight of the stars. I dreamt the three Graces appeared to me in all their naked charms; I singled out Charity from the rest, with whom I had an intrigue.*

14. . . . This was the first time we had ever been detained a whole day in our camp by the rain and therefore had reason to bear it with the more patience.

As I sat in the tent, I overheard a learned conversation between one of our men and the Indian. He ask[ed] the Englishman what it was that made that rumbling noise when it thundered. The man told him merrily that the god of the English was firing his great guns upon the god of the Indians, which made all that roaring in the clouds, and that the lightning was only the flash of those guns. The Indian, carrying on the humor, replied very gravely he believed that might be the case indeed, and that the rain which followed upon the thunder must be occasioned by the Indian god's being so scared he could not hold his water. . . .

17. . . . *About a mile southwest from our camp was a high mount that commanded a full prospect of the mountains and a very extensive view of all the flat country, but being with respect to the mountains no more than a pimple, we called it by that name.*

20. . . . And now I mention the northern Indians, it may not be improper to take notice of their implacable hatred to those of the south. Their wars are everlasting, without any peace, enmity being the only inheritance among them that descends from father to son, and either party will march a thousand miles to take their revenge upon such hereditary enemies . . . 'Tis amazing to see their sagacity in discerning the track of a human foot, even amongst dry leaves, which to our shorter sight is quite undiscoverable. If by one or more of those signs they be able to find out the camp of any southern Indians, they squat down in some thicket and keep themselves hush and snug till it is dark: then, creeping up softly, they approach near enough to observe all the motions of the enemy. And about two o'clock in the morning, when they conceive them to be in a profound sleep, for they never keep watch and ward, pour in a volley upon them, each singling out his man. The moment they have discharged their pieces they rush in with their tomahawks and make sure work of all that are disabled. Sometime, when they find the enemy asleep round their little fire, they first pelt them with little stones to wake them, and when they get up, fire in upon them, being in that posture a better mark than when prostrate on the ground.

They that are killed of the enemy or disabled, they scalp: that is, they cut the skin all round the head just below the hair, and then, clapping their feet to the poor mortal's shoulders, pull the scalp off clean and carry it home in triumph, being as proud of those trophies as the Jews used to be of the foreskins of the Philistines.[18] This way of scalping was practiced by the ancient Scythians, who used these hairy scalps as towels at home and trappings for their horses when they went abroad. They also made cups of their enemies' skulls, in which they drank prosperity to their country and confusion to all their foes.

The prisoners they happen to take alive in these expeditions generally pass their time very scurvily. They put them to all the tortures that ingenious malice and cruelty can invent. And (what shows the baseness of the Indian temper in perfection) they never fail to treat those with greatest inhumanity that have distinguished themselves most by their bravery, and if he be a war captain, they do him the honor to roast him alive and distribute a collop to all that had a share in stealing the victory. Though who can reproach the poor Indians for this, when Homer makes his celebrated hero, Achilles, drag the body of Hector at the tail of his chariot for having fought gallantly in defense of his country? Nor was Alexander the Great, with all his famed generosity, less inhuman to the brave Tyrians, two thousand of which he ordered to be crucified in cold blood for no other fault but for having defended their city most courageously against him during a siege of seven months. And what was still more brutal, he dragged——alive at the tail of his chariot through all the streets, for defending the town with so much vigor.

They are very cunning in finding out new ways to torment their unhappy captives, though, like those of hell, their usual method is by fire. Sometimes they barbecue them over live coals, taking them off every now and then to prolong their misery; at other times they will stick sharp pieces of lightwood all over their bodies and, setting them on fire, let them burn down into the flesh to the very bone. And when they take a stout fellow that they believe able to endure a great deal, they will tear all the flesh off his bones with red-hot pincers. While these and suchlike barbarities are practicing, the victors are so far from being touched with tenderness and compassion that they dance and sing round these wretched mortals, showing all the marks of pleasure and jollity. And if such cruelties happen to be executed in their towns, they employ their children in tormenting the prisoners, in order to extinguish in them betimes all sentiments of humanity. In the meantime, while these poor wretches are under the anguish of all this inhuman treatment, they disdain so much as to groan, sigh, or show the least sign of dismay or concern so much as in their looks: on the contrary, they make it a point of honor all the time to soften their features and look as pleased as if they were in the actual enjoyment of some delight; and if they never sang before in their lives, they will be sure to be melodious on this sad and dismal occasion. So prodigious a degree of passive valor in the Indians is the more to be wondered at, because in all articles of danger they are apt to behave like cowards. And what is still more surprising, the very women discover on such occasions as great fortitude and contempt, both of pain and death, as the gallantest of their men can do.

30. . . . I gave order that four men should set off early and clear the way, that the baggage horses might travel with less difficulty and more expedition. We followed them about eleven, and, the air being clear, we had a fair prospect of the mountains both to

[18]I Samuel 18:25–27.

the north and south. That very high one to the south with the precipice at the west end we called the Lover's Cure, because one leap from thence would put a sudden period both to his passion and his pain. On the highest ledge, that stretched away to the northeast, rose a mount in the shape of a maiden's breast, which for that reason we called by that innocent name. . . .

This being His Majesty's birthday, we drank his health in a dram of excellent cherry brandy but could not afford one drop for the Queen and the royal issue. We therefore remembered them in water as clear as our wishes. And because all loyal rejoicings should be a little noisy, we fired canes instead of guns, which made a report as loud as a pistol, the heat expanding the air shut up within the joints of this vegetable and making an explosion. . . .

30. . . . In the evening we pitched our tent near Miry Creek, though an uncomfortable place to lodge in, purely for the advantage of the canes. Our hunters killed a large doe and two bears, which made all other misfortunes easy. Certainly no Tartar ever loved horseflesh or Hottentot guts and garbage better than woodsmen do bear. The truth of it is, it may be proper food perhaps for such as work or ride it off, but, with our chaplain's leave, who loved it much, I think it not a very proper diet for saints, because 'tis apt to make them a little too rampant. And, now, for the good of mankind and for the better peopling an infant colony, which has no want but that of inhabitants, I will venture to publish a secret of importance which our Indian disclosed to me. I asked him the reason why few or none of his countrywomen were barren. To which curious question he answered, with a broad grin upon his face, they had an infallible secret for that. Upon my being importunate to know what the secret might be, he informed me that if any Indian woman did not prove with child at a decent time after marriage, the husband, to save his reputation with the women, forthwith entered into a bear diet for six weeks, which in that time makes him so vigorous that he grows exceedingly impertinent to his poor wife, and 'tis great odds but he makes her a mother in nine months. And thus much I am able to say besides for the reputation of the bear diet, that all the married men of our company were joyful fathers within forty weeks after they got home, and most of the single men had children sworn to them within the same time, our chaplain always excepted, who, with much ado, made a shift to cast out that importunate kind of devil by dint of fasting and prayer.

31. . . . We took up our camp at Miry Creek and regaled ourselves with one buck and two bears, which our men killed in their march. Here we promoted our chaplain from the deanery of Pip to the bishopric of Beardom. For as those countries where Christians inhabit are called Christendom, so those where bears take up their residence may not improperly go by the name of Beardom. And I wish other bishops loved their flock as entirely as our Doctor loves his.

November 4. . . . John Ellis, who was one of the men we had sent to bring up the tired horses, told us a romantic adventure which he had with a bear on Saturday last. He had straggled from his company and treed a young cub. While he was new priming his gun to shoot at it, the old gentlewoman appeared, who, seeing her heir apparent in distress, came up to his relief. The bear advanced very near to her enemy, reared up on her posteriors, and put herself in guard. The man presented his piece at her, but, unfortunately, it only snapped, the powder being moist. Missing his fire in this manner, he offered to punch her with the muzzle of his gun, which Mother Bruin, being aware of, seized the weapon with her paws and by main strength wrenched it out of his hand. Being thus fairly disarmed and not knowing in the fright but the bear might turn his own cannon upon him, he thought it prudent to retire as fast as his legs could carry him. The brute, being grown more bold by the flight of her adversary, immediately pursued, and for some time it was doubtful whether fear made one run faster or fury the other. But after a fair course of forty yards, the poor man had the mishap to stumble over a stump and fell down at his full length. He now would have sold his life a pennyworth, but the bear, apprehending there might be some trick in this fall, instantly halted and looked very earnestly to observe what the man could mean. In the meantime, he had with much presence of mind resolved to make the bear believe he was dead by lying breathless on the ground, upon the hopes that the bear would be too generous to kill him over again. He acted a corpse in this manner for some time, till he was raised from the dead by the barking of a dog belonging to one of his companions. Cur came up seasonably to his rescue and drove the bear from her pursuit of the man to go and take care of her innocent cub, which she now apprehended might fall into a second distress.

12. . . . Here was very scanty fare for the horses, who could pick only here and there a sprig of wild rosemary, which they are fond of, the misfortune was there was not enough of it. John Ellis killed a bear in revenge for the fright one of that species had lately put him into. Nor was this revenge sweeter to him than a griskin of it was to the Doctor, who of all worldly food conceives this to be the best. Though, in truth, 'tis too rich for a single man and inclines the eater of it strongly to the flesh, insomuch that whoever makes a supper of it will certainly dream of a woman or the devil, or both.

15. . . . I drew out the men after dinner and harangued them on the subject of our safe return in the following terms:

"Friends and fellow travelers, it is with abundance of pleasure that I now have it in my power to congratulate your happy arrival among the inhabitants. You will give me leave to put you in mind how manifestly Heaven has engaged in our preservation. No distress, no disaster, no sickness of any consequence has befallen any one of us in so long and so dangerous a journey. We have subsisted plentifully on the bounty of Providence and been day by day supplied in the barren wilderness with food convenient for us. This is surely an instance of divine goodness never to be forgotten, and, that it may still be more complete, I heartily wish that the same protection may have been extended to our families during our absence." . . .

22. . . . We arrived at Coggins Point about four, where my servants attended with boats in order to transport us to Westover. I had the happiness to find all the family well. This crowned all my other blessings and made the journey truly prosperous, of which I hope I shall ever retain a grateful remembrance. Nor was it all that my people were in good health, but my business was likewise in good order. Everyone seemed to have done their duty, by the joy they expressed at my return. My neighbors had been kind to my wife, when she was threatened with the loss of her son and heir. Their assistance was kind as well as seasonable, when her child was threatened with fatal symptoms and her husband upon a long journey exposed to great variety of perils. Thus, surrounded with the most fearful apprehensions, Heaven was pleased to support her spirits and bring back her child from the grave and her husband from the mountains, for which blessings may we be all sincerely thankful.

1841, 1929

Letter to Mrs. Jane Pratt Taylor[1]

Virginia, the 10th of October, 1735

If my dear cousen Taylor be not a little indulgent, she will be apt to think me a troublesome correspondent this year. It's now the fourth time I have broke in upon her meditations, which is pretty fair for one who lives quite out of the latitude of news, and adventures, nor can pick up one dash of scandal to season a letter withall. 'Tis a mighty misfortune for an epistolizer not to live near some great city like London or Paris, where people play the fool in a well-bred way, & furnish their neighbours with discourse. In such places stories rowle about like snow balls, & gather variety of pretty circumstances in their way, til at last they tell very well, & serve as a good entertainment for a country cousen.

But alas what can we poor hermits do, who know of no intrigues, but such as are carry'd on by the amorous turtles, or some such innocent lovers? Our vices & disorders want all that wit & refinement, which make them palatable to the fine world. We are unskild in the arts of makeing our follys agreable, nor can we dress up the D——so much to advantage, as to make him pass for an angel of light. Therefore without a little invention, it would not be possible for one of us anchorites to carry on a tolerable correspondence, but like French historians, where we don't meet with pretty incidents, we must e'en make them, & lard a little truth with a great deal of fiction.

Perhaps you'll think the story I am going to tell you of this poetical sort. We have here an Italian bona roba,[2] whose whole study is to make her person charming, which to be sure will sound very strangely in the ears of an English lady. Those who understand physognomy suspect this dear creature has been a Venetian cortezan, because her whole mien & every motion proves she has been traind up in the art of pleaseing. She does not only practice graces at her glass, but by her skill in opticks, has instructed her eyes to reflect their rays in a very mischeivous manner. In a word she knows how to make the most of every part that composes her lovely frame, as you will see by the harmless adventure that follows.

You must know the two little hillucks in her bosome have lost a pretty deal of their natural firmness & elasticity. This is reacond a disadvantage to a fine neck not easy to be repaird, but she has an invention to brace them up again to a maiden protuberancy. She has a silver pipe made so exceedingly small at one end, that 'twill enter the narrow orifice of the nipple. At the other end of the tube her fille de chambre[3] blows with all her might, til the breast swells & struts like any blown bladder. This is no sooner performd, but a composition of wax, rosin & Spanish brown is nimbly applyd to hinder the imprisond wind from escapeing. Thus she preserves all the charms of the horizontal chest, without the German artifice of bolstering it up with a douzen of napkins. And 'tis moreover so hard and thrummy, that if any of the monsters with eight legs and no eyelids shoud presume to stray that way, she may fairly crack them upon it.

[1]Widow of Thomas Taylor, the brother of Byrd's second wife.

[2]Wench.

[3]Maid.

But as no human skil is ever so perfect, as to be secure from misadventures, so you will be sorry for what befell this gentlewoman one day at a ball. It happend she had deckt herself with all her artificial ornaments, but the warmth of the weather, joind with the agility of her motion, occasiond so copious a perspiration, that it softend & dissolvd the cement smeard upon her mammels. By this accident the doors being set open, the wind unluckily rusht forth, as fast as it well coud do, thro' so narrow a channel, & produced a sound that was a little unseemly. And that too not in seperate notes, but with a long winded blast, which a genius to musick might have modulated into a tune. It is not easy to tell you, whether the company was more diverted, or the seignora more confounded at this accident: but so much is certain, that we were all surprizd at the unusual length of the noise, & the quarter from whence it sallyd out. We vertuosos[4] took, her immediately for one of those bellyspeaker's[5] whose gift it is to make a voice seem to issue out of any part of their body. The religious part of the company which consisted chiefly of old women, concluded her to be a demonaique, in the power of some evil spirit who chose to play his gambols in so fair an habitation. While we were taken up in debating upon this uncommon event, the unfortunate person slunk away thro' the crowd, & has never appeard out of her doors since.

Heaven be praisd I am able to tell my dear cousen Taylor that we are all in chearfull good health. We often discourse you in effigie, and call the painter a bungler for falling so short of the original. I hope you are not grown so thin as he has made you, because a lady can't loose her enbonpoint, without haveing some of her health go along with it. May you keep that jewel intire, 'til Time himself grow sick with age & all his iron teeth drop out of his head. I am without one word of a lye my dear cousen Taylors most &c.

1901

Jonathan Edwards 1703–1758

Nearly a century after the landing of the *Mayflower* at Plymouth, the writer who, according to novelist William Dean Howells "first gave our poor American provinciality world standing," was born in East Windsor, a new settlement in the Connecticut River valley. Edwards's father Timothy was a well-read Harvard graduate who held the sole pastorship of the small town's Congregationalist church. Edwards's maternal grandfather, Solomon Stoddard, pastor of a much larger and more influential congregation upriver in Northampton, Massachusetts, was, like Edwards, a significant theologian. Opposing his more conservative peers, Stoddard had devised a policy of relaxing the requirements for full membership in the established church.

Edwards was prepared for college by his father and matriculated in 1716 to the recently opened Collegiate School (later Yale University), which Cotton Mather had helped to found in hopes of counteracting

[4]Amateur scientists or collectors of curiosities.
[5]Ventriloquists.

the "liberal" drift of the younger generation of faculty at Harvard. During Edwards's junior year, the College received a major gift of recent books in science and philosophy, a gift which introduced Edwards and his classmates to such famous recent authors as Sir Isaac Newton and John Locke. Valedictorian of his class, Edwards received his B.A. in 1720. He remained in New Haven for postgraduate study until 1722, when he accepted a job as pastor of a Presbyterian church (identical in theology but more formal and hierarchical in governance than the Congregationalist churches of his father and grandfather) in New York City.

After nine months, Edwards left the New York pastorate to complete a master's thesis in theology in New Haven in the summer of 1722. From the year 1720, Edwards had made sporadic entries in a conventional personal diary, but returning home after taking his graduate degree, Edwards began making voluminous notes on his original inquiries in physical science, theology, and philosophy. At the urging of his father, Edwards prepared a scientific paper on the so-called "flying spider," and his father sent it to a member of the British Royal Society. In 1724 Edwards accepted an appointment as a tutor at Yale.

Edwards left the College in 1726 to return to the ministry, settling down to the duties first as assistant to his grandfather Stoddard at Northampton, and then, on Stoddard's death in 1729, as sole pastor of the Northampton congregation. He married Sarah Pierrepont, a daughter of a New Haven minister whom he had known since college. In response to influential colleagues who were laying stress upon the powers of the soul to affect its own conversion, Edwards preached in 1734 a series of corrective sermons emphasizing the Calvinist (but in fact traditionally Augustinian and Pauline) tenet of the passivity of the convert before God's all-powerful offer of grace.

In 1735, Edwards's more "evangelical" emphasis brought about a number of conversions in the Northampton congregation. Hearing of the revival in Northampton that quickly outstripped any of Stoddard's "harvests," the Reverend Benjamin Colman, pastor of the "liberal" Brattle Street Church (founded in Edwards's childhood to open a pulpit to theological opponents of the Mathers), asked Edwards to prepare an authoritative account of the awakening. Published by Colman in pamphlet form, Edwards's letter had a wide circulation, spreading his fame among Protestants on both sides of the Atlantic. While the pamphlet remained in circulation, Edwards expanded and rewrote it for book publication as *A Faithful Narrative of the Surprising Work of God* (published in America in 1737 and later in England the same year).

Northampton's small revival seemed temperate compared to the sensation attending the 1739–1740 colonial preaching tour by a young English preacher, George Whitefield, who had established a reputation in Britain in the "methodist" or evangelical Anglican movement associated with John and Charles Wesley at Oxford University. Whitefield traveled throughout the provinces of British North America from Georgia to Massachusetts. Barred from speaking by local ministers and universities, Whitefield evoked thousands of conversions among audiences. Meanwhile, within the native anti-Anglican establishment, Presbyterian and Congregationalist alike, homebred American awakeners like Gilbert Tennent and Joseph Davenport achieved effects similar to Whitefield's.

Particularly in scholarly New England, the so-called "Great Awakening" drove American ministers to their pens. Some defended, some denounced as heresy the conversions and the itinerant evangelical preaching that had produced them. Edwards, who was at one with his contemporary Benjamin Franklin in finding Whitefield personally likeable, nevertheless perceived the statements of both parties as confused. On the premise that ministers could not meaningfully celebrate or condemn the particular emotional experiences of converts without having a clear theory of the place of emotion in religion, and trusting that clarification of the terms and points at issue would be welcome in the debate, Edwards devoted himself to producing a systematic study. Edwards's *Treatise Concerning Religious Affections* attempted to transcend the politicized issues by lifting the discussion to a philosophical plane. While too subtle to have much direct practical effect on the passions of the time, the book survived to become indispensable to such major modern philosophers and psychologists of religion as William James.

For Edwards as author, the results of the Awakening were happy; for Edwards as pastor, they ultimately were not. Emboldened by the increase in parishioners testifying to grace-begetting experiences, in 1748 Edwards attempted to abolish Stoddard's practice of admitting anyone who had been baptized to the Lord's Supper, returning instead to the original "New England Way" of first requiring a formal profession of a saving experience. Although a considerable number of the seriously devout in Northampton were prepared to accept Edwards's reform, many—reflecting the decreased respect for local ministerial authority that was turning out everywhere to be the legacy of the Awakening's itinerant revivalists—were not. In a climate of accumulated family rivalries exacerbated by the military threat of French and Indian soldiers on the nearby colonial borders, ancient disputes over salaries (a problem endemic to the New England congregations), and new disputes over methods of disciplining parish children, took on new importance in Edwards's church. In 1750, Edwards's attempted return to pre-Stoddard membership requirements became the formal issue over which his congregation ultimately voted in sufficient numbers to dismiss him.

With his family of eleven surviving children, Edwards remained in Northampton, working on various writing projects. In spite of financial hardship and accepting none of the pastorships offered from the American South to as far away as Scotland, Edwards refused to return to ministry, after a year opting instead for an administrative position at a Congregational mission to the Housatonic Indians at Stockbridge, on the western border of Massachusetts. Compared to his pastoral responsibilities, administrative duties posed no intellectual competition for Edwards's primary work as an author.

The fourth year after he moved to Stockbridge, Edwards brought out a book that was accepted instantly as a major contribution to an international debate going back at least to St. Augustine. Edwards's *Careful and Strict Enquiry into the modern prevailing Notions of that Freedom of Will Which is supposed to be essential to . . . Praise and Blame* (familiarly called *The Freedom of the Will*) would be used as a standard textbook at Yale and other colleges for decades. As the *Treatise Concerning Religious Affections* had done regarding conversion, Edwards's *Freedom of the Will* made a painstaking attempt to rescue philosophers from their own confusion about human self-determination. Edwards averred that people entered the world in a state of total depravity and that they carried no disposition to good or bad action. The sole liberty people possess, in Edwards's view, was the liberty that "I *can* do, if I *will*." Yet the will, Edwards concluded in this treatise, is not free; it is determined by motives toward "apparent *good*" or "that which is agreeable." So long as people could do what they willed to do, Edwards argued, they were free. No higher liberty was conceivable, even though people were not necessarily able to choose their choices. *Freedom of the Will* was a complicated treatise for complicated philosophical times.

In 1757 Edwards was called to another post, again in administration, this time as President of the College of New Jersey at Nassau Hall (now Princeton).

Edwards was at first disposed to resist the offer, but he finally agreed to take the post. Ahead of his family, Edwards traveled alone to Princeton. He had barely arrived when, in the aftermath of a failed inoculation for smallpox, he died at the age of fifty-five years. Before his death, publishers in Northampton, Boston, New York, and London had published twenty-four original titles by Edwards, making him indisputably one of the few major figures in colonial American literary history.

Edwards's literary career seems to fall into three phases. In the first, Edwards primarily wrote speculatively on original topics in science and philosophy, producing works appropriate to an international lay audience; in the second, he wrote "applied" studies in a variety of subjects common to pastoral Christianity, addressing a comparatively local (Anglo-American) professional audience. The work of the third phase is speculative and aimed at a wide audience. Edwards seems to have early dedicated himself to speculative thought, laid speculation aside for the practical purposes of marriage and child-rearing, then turned again to speculative writing just before he died. Edwards clearly pursued his writing with the expectation of eventual publication, yet, as he got further and further behind on his projects, he evidently at some point accepted that the audience he was addressing was one of the future.

Carol M. Bensick
University of California at Riverside

PRIMARY WORKS

A Faithful Narrative of the Surprising Work of God in the Conversions of Many Hundred Souls . . ., 1737; *A Treatise Concerning Religious Affections,* 1746; *A Careful and Strict Enquiry into the modern prevailing Notions of that Freedom of Will, Which is supposed to be essential to . . . Praise and Blame,* 1754; *The Great Christian Doctrine of Original Sin defended; Evidences of it's Truth produced and Arguments to the Contrary answered,* 1758.

SECONDARY WORKS

Ola Winslow, *Jonathan Edwards,* 1940; Perry Miller, *Jonathan Edwards,* 1949, rpt. 1981; A.O. Aldridge, *Jonathan Edwards,* 1964; Norman Fiering, *Jonathan Edwards's Moral Thought and Its British Context,* 1981; R.C. de Prospo, *Theism in the Discourse of Jonathan Edwards,* 1985; N. Hatch and H. E. Stout, *Jonathan Edwards and the American Experience,* 1988; M.X. Lesser, *Jonathan Edwards,* 1988; Gerald McDermott, *One Holy and Happy Society: The Public Theology of Jonathan Edwards,* 1992.

Resolutions[1]

Being sensible that I am unable to do anything without God's help, I do humbly entreat him by his grace, to enable me to keep these Resolutions, so far as they are agreeable to his will, for Christ's sake.

[1]Edwards wrote these resolutions before his twenty-first year. Of the seventy resolutions he wrote, the first thirty-four were written before Dec. 18, 1722; the last resolution, before the end of August, 1723. They were written, then, during his last period of study for the ministry at Yale, his eight months preaching in New York, and his summer in Connecticut. He began writing a diary shortly after he had begun this series of resolutions.

The text is from Sereno Dwight's 1829–1830 edition, *The Works of President Edwards.*

Remember to read over these Resolutions once a week.

1. *Resolved,* That *I will do whatsoever* I think to be most to the glory of God and my own good, profit and pleasure, in the whole of my duration; without any consideration of the time whether now, or never so many myriads of ages hence. Resolved to do whatever I think to be my *duty,* and most for the good and advantage of mankind in general. Resolved, so to do, whatever *difficulties* I meet with, how many soever, and how great soever.

2. *Resolved,* To be continually endeavouring to find out some *new contrivance,* and invention, to promote the forementioned things.

3. *Resolved,* If ever I shall fall and grow dull, so as to neglect to keep any part of these Resolutions, to repent of all I can remember, when I come to myself again.

4. *Resolved,* Never *to do* any manner of thing, whether in soul or body, less or more, but what tends to the glory of God, nor *be,* nor *suffer* it, if I can possibly avoid it.

5. *Resolved,* Never to lose one moment of time, but to improve it in the most profitable way I possibly can.

6. *Resolved,* To live with all my might, while I do live.

7. *Resolved,* Never to do any thing, which I should be afraid to do, if it were the last hour of my life.

8. *Resolved,* To act, in all respects, both speaking and doing, as if nobody had been so vile as I, and as if I had committed the same sins, or had the same infirmities or failings as others; and that I will let the knowledge of their failings promote nothing but shame in myself, and prove only an occasion of my confessing my own sins and misery to God.

9. *Resolved,* To think much, on all occasions, of my own dying, and of the common circumstances which attend death.

10. *Resolved,* When I feel pain, to think of the pains of Martyrdom, and of Hell.

11. *Resolved,* When I think of any Theorem in divinity to be solved, immediately to do what I can towards solving it, if circumstances do not hinder.

12. *Resolved,* If I take delight in it as a gratification of pride, or vanity, or on any such account, immediately to throw it by.

13. *Resolved,* To be endeavouring to find out fit objects of charity and liberality.

14. *Resolved,* Never to do any thing out of Revenge.

15. *Resolved,* Never to suffer the least motions of anger towards irrational beings.

16. *Resolved,* Never to speak evil of any one, so that it shall tend to his dishonour, more or less, upon no account except for some real good.

17. *Resolved,* That I will live so, as I shall wish I had done when I come to die.

18. *Resolved,* To live so, at all times, as I think is best in my most devout frames, and when I have the clearest notions of the things of the Gospel, and another world.

19. *Resolved,* Never to do any thing, which I should be afraid to do, if I expected it would not be above an hour, before I should hear the last trump.

20. *Resolved,* To maintain the strictest temperance, in eating and drinking.

21. *Resolved,* Never to do any thing, which, if I should see in another, I should count a just occasion to despise him for, or to think any way the more meanly of him.

22. *Resolved,* To endeavour to obtain for myself as much happiness, in the other world, as I possibly can, with all the power, might, vigour, and vehemence, yea violence, I am capable of, or can bring myself to exert, in any way that can be thought of.

23. *Resolved,* Frequently to take some deliberate action, which seems most unlikely to be done, for the glory of God, and trace it back to the original intention, designs and ends of it; and if I find it not to be for God's glory, to repute it as a breach of the fourth Resolution.

24. *Resolved,* Whenever I do any conspicuously evil action, to trace it back, till I come to the original cause; and then, both carefully endeavour to do so no more, and to fight and pray with all my might against the original of it.

25. *Resolved,* To examine carefully, and constantly, what that one thing in me is, which causes me in the least to doubt of the love of God; and to direct all my forces against it.

26. *Resolved,* To cast away such things, as I find do abate my assurance.

27. *Resolved,* Never wilfully to omit any thing, except the omission be for the glory of God; and frequently to examine my omissions.

28. *Resolved,* To study the Scriptures so steadily, constantly and frequently, as that I may find, and plainly perceive myself to grow in the knowledge of the same.

29. *Resolved,* Never to count that a prayer, nor to let that pass as a prayer, nor that as a petition of a prayer, which is so made, that I cannot hope that God will answer it; nor that as a confession, which I cannot hope God will accept.

30. *Resolved,* To strive, every week, to be brought higher in Religion, and to a higher exercise of grace, than I was the week before.

31. *Resolved,* Never to say any thing at all against any body, but when it is perfectly agreeable to the highest degree of christian honour, and of love to mankind, agreeable to the lowest humility, and sense of my own faults and failings, and agreeable to the Golden Rule; often, when I have said any thing against any one, to bring it to, and try it strictly by the test of this Resolution.

32. *Resolved,* To be strictly and firmly faithful to my trust, that that, in Prov. xx, 6, *A faithful man, who can find?* may not be partly fulfilled in me.

33. *Resolved,* To do, always, what I can towards making, maintaining and preserving peace, when it can be done without an over-balancing detriment in other respects. *Dec.* 26, 1722.

34. *Resolved,* In narrations, never to speak any thing but the pure and simple verity.

35. *Resolved,* Whenever I so much question whether I have done my duty, as that my quiet and calm is thereby disturbed, to set it down, and also how the question was resolved. *Dec.* 18, 1722.

36. *Resolved,* Never to speak evil of any, except I have some particular good call to it. *Dec.* 19, 1722.

37. *Resolved,* To enquire every night, as I am going to bed, Wherein I have been negligent,—What sin I have committed,—and wherein I have denied myself;—also, at the end of every week, month and year. *Dec.* 22 *and* 26, 1722.

38. *Resolved,* Never to utter any thing that is sportive, or matter of laughter, on a Lord's day. *Sabbath evening, Dec.* 23, 1722.

39. *Resolved,* Never to do any thing, of which I so much question the lawfulness, as that I intend, at the same time, to consider and examine afterwards, whether it be lawful or not; unless I as much question the lawfulness of the omission.

40. *Resolved,* To enquire every night, before I go to bed, whether I have acted in the best way I possibly could, with respect to eating and drinking. *Jan.* 7, 1723.

41. *Resolved,* To ask myself, at the end of every day, week, month and year, wherein I could possibly, in any respect, have done better. *Jan.* 11, 1723.

42. *Resolved,* Frequently to renew the dedication of myself to God, which was made at my baptism, which I solemnly renewed, when I was received into the communion of the church, and which I have solemnly re-made this 12th day of January, 1723.

43. *Resolved,* Never, henceforward, till I die, to act as if I were any way my own, but entirely and altogether God's; agreeably to what is to be found in Saturday, Jan. 12th. *Jan.* 12th, 1723.

44. *Resolved,* That no other end but religion, shall have any influence at all on any of my actions; and that no action shall be, in the least circumstance, any otherwise than the religious end will carry it. *Jan.* 12, 1723.

45. *Resolved,* Never to allow any pleasure or grief, joy or sorrow, nor any affection at all, nor any degree of affection, nor any circumstance relating to it, but what helps Religion. *Jan.* 12 *and* 13, 1723.

46. *Resolved,* Never to allow the least measure of any fretting or uneasiness at my father or mother. *Resolved,* To suffer no effects of it, so much as in the least alteration of speech, or motion of my eye; and to be especially careful of it with respect to any of our family.

47. *Resolved,* To endeavour, to my utmost, to deny whatever is not most agreeable to a good and universally sweet and benevolent, quiet, peaceable, contented and easy, compassionate and generous, humble and meek, submissive and obliging, diligent and industrious, charitable and even, patient, moderate, forgiving and sincere, temper; and to do, at all times, what such a temper would lead me to; and to examine strictly, at the end of every week, whether I have so done. *Sabbath Morning, May* 5, 1723.

48. *Resolved,* Constantly, with the utmost niceness and diligence, and the strictest scrutiny, to be looking into the state of my soul, that I may know whether I have truly an interest in Christ or not; that when I come to die, I may not have any negligence respecting this, to repent of. *May* 26, 1723.

49. *Resolved,* That this never shall be, if I can help it.

50. *Resolved,* That I will act so, as I think I shall judge would have been best, and most prudent, when I come into the future world. *July* 5, 1723.

51. *Resolved,* That I will act so, in every respect, as I think I shall wish I had done, if I should at last be damned. *July* 8, 1723.

52. I frequently hear persons in old age, say how they would live, if they were to live their lives over again: *Resolved,* That I will live just so as I can think I shall wish I had done, supposing I live to old age. *July* 8, 1723.

53. *Resolved,* To improve every opportunity, when I am in the best and happiest frame of mind, to cast and venture my soul on the Lord Jesus Christ, to trust and confide in him, and consecrate myself wholly to him; that from this I may have assurance of my safety, knowing that I confide in my Redeemer. *July* 8, 1723.

54. *Resolved,* Whenever I hear any thing spoken in commendation of any person, if I think it would be praiseworthy in me, that I will endeavour to imitate it. *July* 8, 1723.

55. *Resolved,* To endeavour, to my utmost, so to act, as I can think I should do, if I had already seen the happiness of Heaven, and Hell torments. *July* 8, 1723.

56. *Resolved,* Never to give over, nor in the least to slacken, my fight with my corruptions, however unsuccessful I may be.

57. *Resolved,* When I fear misfortunes and adversity, to examine whether I have done my duty, and resolve to do it, and let the event be just as Providence orders it. I will, as far as I can, be concerned about nothing but my duty, and my sin. *June* 9, *and July* 13, 1723.

58. *Resolved,* Not only to refrain from an air of dislike, fretfulness, and anger in conversation, but to exhibit an air of love, cheerfulness and benignity. *May* 27, *and July* 13, 1723.

59. *Resolved,* When I am most conscious of provocations to ill-nature and anger, that I will strive most to feel and act good-naturedly; yea, at such times, to manifest good-nature, though I think that in other respects it would be disadvantageous, and so as would be imprudent at other times. *May* 12, *July* 11, *and July* 13.

60. *Resolved,* Whenever my feelings begin to appear in the least out of order, when I am conscious of the least uneasiness within, or the least irregularity without, I will then subject myself to the strictest examination. *July* 4, *and* 13, 1723.

61. *Resolved,* That I will not give way to that listlessness which I find unbends and relaxes my mind from being fully and fixedly set on religion, whatever excuse I may have for it—that what my listlessness inclines me to do, is best to be done, &c. *May* 21, *and July* 13, 1723.

62. *Resolved,* Never to do any thing but my duty, and then according to Eph. vi, 6–8, to do it willingly and cheerfully, as unto the Lord, and not to man: knowing that whatever good thing any man doth, the same shall he receive of the Lord. *June* 25, *and July* 13, 1723.

63. On the supposition, that there never was to be but one individual in the world, at any one time, who was properly a complete christian, in all respects of a right stamp, having christianity always shining in its true lustre, and appearing excellent and lovely, from whatever part and under whatever character viewed: *Resolved,* To act just as I would do, if I strove with all my might to be that one, who should live in my time. *Jan.* 14, *and July* 13, 1723.

64. *Resolved,* When I find those *"groanings which cannot be uttered,"* of which the Apostle speaks, and those "*breakings of soul* for the longing it hath," of which the Psalmist speaks, Psalm cxix, 20, That I will promote them to the utmost of my power, and that I will not be weary of earnestly endeavouring to vent my desires, nor of the repetitions of such earnestness. *July* 23, *and August* 10, 1723.

65. *Resolved,* Very much to exercise myself in this, all my life long, viz. With the greatest openness, of which I am capable, to declare my ways to God, and lay open my soul to him, all my sins, temptations, difficulties, sorrows, fears, hopes, desires, and every thing, and every circumstance, according to Dr. Manton's Sermon on the 119th Psalm. *July* 26, *and Aug.* 10, 1723.

66. *Resolved,* That I will endeavour always to keep a benign aspect, and air of acting and speaking in all places, and in all companies, except it should so happen that duty requires otherwise.

67. *Resolved,* After afflictions, to enquire, What I am the better for them; What good I have got by them; and, What I might have got by them.

68. *Resolved,* To confess frankly to myself all that which I find in myself, either

infirmity or sin; and, if it be what concerns religion, also to confess the whole case to God, and implore needed help. *July* 23, *and August* 10, 1723.

69. *Resolved,* Always to do that, which I shall wish I had done when I see others do it. *Aug.* 11, 1723.

70. Let there be something of benevolence, in all that I speak. *Aug.* 17, 1723.

1829–30

from A Faithful Narrative of the Surprising Work of God[1]

. . . There is a vast difference, as has been observed, in the degree, and also in the particular manner of persons' experiences, both at and after conversion; some have grace working more sensibly in one way, others in another. Some speak more fully of a conviction of the justice of God in their condemnation; others more of their consenting to the way of salvation by Christ; some more of the actings of love to God and Christ: some more of acts of affiance, in a sweet and assured conviction of the truth and faithfulness of God in his promises; others more of their choosing and resting in God as their whole and everlasting portion, and of their ardent and longing desires after God, to have communion with him; others more of their abhorrence of themselves for their past sins, and earnest longings to live to God's glory for their time to come: some have their minds fixed more on God; others on Christ, as I have observed before, but it seems evidently to be the same work, the same thing done, the same habitual change wrought in the heart; it all tends the same way, and to the same end; and 'tis plainly the same spirit that breathes and acts in various persons. There is an endless variety in the particular manner and circumstances in which persons are wrought on, and an opportunity of seeing so much of such a work of God will shew that God is further from confining himself to certain steps, and a particular method, in his work on souls, than it may be some do imagine. I believe it has occasioned some good people amongst us, that were before too ready to make their

[1]When Reverend Benjamin Colman (1673–1747) of Boston's Brattle Street Church learned of Edwards's remarkable conversions of parishioners in western Massachusetts, he wrote to Edwards requesting an account of the "great awakening." Edwards replied in a letter dated May 30, 1735, telling of a number of conversions at Northampton and in neighboring communities. Impressed, Colman published Edwards's letter in 1736. The published letter was then sent to some clergymen in London. Its popularity there induced Edwards to expand his account of the Great Awakening; he offered additional examples of conversions and distinguished types of conversion experiences. The revised account was published in London late in 1737 as *A Faithful Narrative of the Surprising Work of God in the Conversion of Many Hundred Souls in Northampton and the Neighboring Towns . . . in the Province of Massachusetts Bay in New England. A Faithful Narrative* was so popular that it went through three editions and twenty printings between 1737 and 1739.

This selection has been taken from Edwards's *Works,* ed. S. Austin (1808).

own experiences a rule to others, to be less censorious and more extended in their charity. The work of God has been glorious in its variety, it has the more displayed the manifoldness and unsearchableness of the wisdom of God, and wrought more charity among its people.

There is a great difference among those that are converted as to the degree of hope and satisfaction that they have concerning their own state. Some have a high degree of satisfaction in this matter almost constantly: and yet it is rare that any do enjoy so full an assurance of their interest in Christ, that self-examination should seem needless to them; unless it be at particular seasons, while in the actual enjoyment of some great discovery, that God gives of his glory and rich grace in Christ, to the drawing forth of extraordinary acts of grace. But the greater part, as they sometimes fall into dead frames of spirit, are frequently exercised with scruples and fears concerning their condition.

They generally have an awful apprehension of the dreadfulness and undoing nature of a false hope; and there has been observable in most a great caution, lest in giving an account of their experiences, they should say too much, and use too strong terms. And many after they have related their experiences, have been greatly afflicted with fears, lest they have played the hypocrite, and used stronger terms than their case would fairly allow of; and yet could not find how they could correct themselves.

I think that the main ground of the doubts and fears that persons, after their conversion, have been exercised with about their own state, has been that they have found so much corruption remaining in their hearts. At first their souls seem to be all alive, their hearts are fixed, and their affections flowing; they seem to live quite above the world, and meet with but little difficulty in religious exercises; and they are ready to think it will always be so. Though they are truly abased under a sense of their vileness by reason of former acts of sin, yet they are not then sufficiently sensible what corruption still remains in their hearts; and therefore are surprised when they find that they begin to be in dull and dead frames, to be troubled with wandering thoughts in the time of public and private worship, and to be utterly unable to keep themselves from 'em; also when they find themselves unaffected at seasons in which, they think, there is the greatest occasion to be affected; and when they feel worldly dispositions working in them, and it may be pride and envy, and stirrings of revenge, or some ill spirit towards some person that has injured them, as well as other workings of indwelling sin: their hearts are almost sunk with the disappointment; and they are ready presently to think that all this they have met with is nothing, and that they are mere hypocrites.

They are ready to argue, that if God had indeed done such great things for them, as they hoped, such ingratitude would be inconsistent with it. They cry out of the hardness and wickedness of their hearts; and say there is so much corruption, that it seems to them impossible that there should be any goodness there: and many of them seem to be much more sensible how corrupt their hearts are, than ever they were before they were converted; and some have been too ready to be impressed with fear, that instead of becoming better, they are grown much worse, and make it an argument against the goodness of their state. But in truth, the case seems plainly to be, that now they feel the pain of their own wounds; they have a watchful eye upon their hearts, that they don't use to have: they take more notice what sin is there, and sin is now more burdensome to 'em, they strive more against it, and feel more of the strength of it.

They are somewhat surprised that they should in this respect find themselves so different from the idea that they generally had entertained of godly persons; for though grace be indeed of a far more excellent nature than they imagined, yet those that are godly have much less of it, and much more remaining corruption, than they thought. They never realized it, that persons were wont to meet with such difficulties, after they were once converted. When they are thus exercised with doubts about their state, through the deadness of their frames of spirit, as long as these frames last, they are commonly unable to satisfy themselves of the truth of their grace, by all their self-examination. When they hear of the signs of grace laid down for 'em to try themselves by, they are often so clouded that they don't know how to apply them: they hardly know whether they have such and such things in them or no, and whether they have experienced them or not: that which was sweetest, and best and most distinguishing in their experiences, they can't recover a sense or idea of. But on a return of the influences of the Spirit of God, to revive the lively actings of grace, the light breaks through the cloud, and doubting and darkness soon vanish away.

Persons are often revived out of their dead and dark frames by religious conversation: while they are talking of divine things, or ever they are aware, their souls are carried away into holy exercises with abundant pleasure. And oftentimes, while they are relating their past experiences to their Christian brethren, they have a fresh sense of them revived, and the same experiences in a degree again renewed. Sometimes while persons are exercised in mind with several objections against the goodness of their state, they have Scriptures, one after another, coming to their minds, to answer their scruples and unravel their difficulties, exceeding apposite and proper to their circumstances; by which means their darkness is scattered; and often before the bestowment of any new remarkable comforts, especially after long continued deadness and ill frames, there are renewed humblings, in a great sense of their own exceeding vileness and unworthiness, as before their first comforts were bestowed.

Many in the country have entertained a mean thought of this great work that there has been amongst us, from what they have heard of impressions that have been made on persons' imaginations. But there have been exceeding great misrepresentations and innumerable false reports concerning that matter. 'Tis not, that I know of, the profession or opinion of any one person in the town, that any weight is to be laid on anything seen with the bodily eyes: I know the contrary to be a received and established principle amongst us. I cannot say that there have been no instances of persons that have been ready to give too much heed to vain and useless imaginations; but they have been easily corrected, and I conclude it will not be wondered at, that a congregation should need a guide in such cases, to assist them in distinguishing wheat from chaff. But such impressions on the imagination as have been more usual, seem to me to be plainly no other than what is to be expected in human nature in such circumstances, and what is the natural result of the strong exercise of the mind, and impressions on the heart.

I do not suppose that they themselves imagined that they saw anything with their bodily eyes; but only have had within them ideas strongly impressed, and as it were, lively pictures in their minds: as for instance, some when in great terrors, through fear of hell, have had lively ideas of a dreadful furnace. Some, when their hearts have been strongly impressed, and their affections greatly moved with a sense of the beauty and excellency of Christ, it has wrought on their imaginations so, that together with a sense of his glorious spiritual perfections, there has arisen in the mind an idea of one of glorious majesty, and of a sweet and a gracious aspect. So some, when they have been greatly affected with Christ's death, have at the same time a lively idea of Christ hanging upon the cross, and of his blood running from his wounds; which things won't be wondered at by them that have observed how strong affections about temporal matters will excite lively ideas and pictures of different things in the mind.

. . . There have indeed been some few instances of impressions on persons' imaginations, that have been something mysterious to me, and I have been at a loss about them; for though it has been exceeding evident to me by many things that appeared in them, both then (when they related them) and afterwards, that they indeed had a great sense of the spiritual excellency of divine things accompanying them; yet I have not been able well to satisfy myself, whether their imaginary ideas have been more than could naturally arise from their spiritual sense of things. However, I have used the utmost caution in such cases; great care has been taken both in public and in private to teach persons the difference between what is spiritual and what is merely imaginary. I have often warned persons not to lay the stress of their hope on any ideas of any outward glory, or any external thing whatsoever, and have met with no opposition in such instructions. But 'tis not strange if some weaker persons, in giving an account of their experiences, have not so prudently distinguished between the spiritual and imaginary part; which some that have not been well affected to religion, might take advantage of.

There has been much talk in many parts of the country, as though the people have symbolized with the Quakers,[2] and the Quakers themselves have been moved with such reports; and came here, once and again, hoping to find good waters to fish in; but without the least success, and seemed to be discouraged and have left off coming. There have also been reports spread about the country, as though the first occasion of so remarkable a concern on people's minds here, was an apprehension that the world was near to an end, which was altogether a false report. Indeed, after this stirring and concern became so general and extraordinary, as has been related, the minds of some were filled with speculation, what so great a dispensation of divine providence might forebode: and some reports were heard from abroad, as though certain divines and others thought the conflagration was nigh; but such reports were never generally looked upon [as] worthy of notice.

The work that has now been wrought on souls is evidently the same that was wrought in my venerable predecessor's days;[3] as I have had abundant opportunity to know, having been in the ministry here two years with him, and so conversed with a

[2]Those who heard about the Great Awakening sometimes compared the Puritans' conversion experiences to those of the Quakers. Yet Quaker experience of the inward light differed, like their theology, from Puritan conversion.

[3]Edwards became a colleague of his grandfather, Reverend Solomon Stoddard, in Northampton in 1726.

considerable number that my grandfather thought to be savingly converted in that time; and having been particularly acquainted with the experiences of many that were converted under his ministry before. And I know no one of them, that in the least doubts of its being the same spirit and the same work. Persons have now no otherwise been subject to impressions on their imaginations than formerly: the work is of the same nature, and has not been attended with any extraordinary circumstances, excepting such as are analogous to the extraordinary degree of it before described. And God's people that were formerly converted, have now partook of the same shower of divine blessing in the renewing, strengthening, edifying influences of the Spirit of God, that others have, in his converting influences; and the work here has also been plainly the same with that which has been wrought in those of other places that have been mentioned, as partaking of the same blessing. I have particularly conversed with persons about their experiences that belong to all parts of the county, and in various parts of Connecticut, where a religious concern has lately appeared; and have been informed of the experiences of many others by their own pastors.

'Tis easily perceived by the foregoing account that 'tis very much the practice of the people here to converse freely one with another of their spiritual experiences; which is a thing that many have been disgusted at. But however our people may have, in some respects, gone to extremes in it, yet 'tis doubtless a practice that the circumstances of this town, and [of] neighboring towns, has naturally led them into. Whatsoever people are in such circumstances, where all have their minds engaged to such a degree in the same affair, that 'tis ever uppermost in their thoughts; they will naturally make it the subject of conversation one with another when they get together, in which they will grow more and more free: restraints will soon vanish; and they will not conceal from one another what they meet with. And it has been a practice which, in the general, has been attended with many good effects, and what God has greatly blessed amongst us. But it must be confessed, there may have been some ill consequences of it; which yet are rather to be laid to the indiscreet management of it than to the practice itself: and none can wonder, if among such a multitude some fail of exercising so much prudence in choosing the time, manner, and occasion of such discourse, as is desirable.

1736

Personal Narrative[1]

I had a variety of concerns and exercises about my soul from my childhood; but had two more remarkable seasons of awakening, before I met with that change, by which I was brought to those new dispositions, and that new sense of things, that I have

[1]Written during or after January 1739, Edwards's account of his spiritual life was not published until after his death, when his friend Samuel Hopkins published it as "An Account of His Conversion, Experiences, and Religious Exercises," in *The Life and Character of the Late Rev. Mr. Jonathan Edwards* (1765).

since had. The first time was when I was a boy, some years before I went to college, at a time of remarkable awakening in my father's congregation. I was then very much affected for many months, and concerned about the things of religion, and my soul's salvation; and was abundant in duties. I used to pray five times a day in secret, and to spend much time in religious talk with other boys; and used to meet with them to pray together. I experienced I know not what kind of delight in religion. My mind was much engaged in it, and had much self-righteous pleasure; and it was my delight to abound in religious duties. I, with some of my school-mates joined together, and built a booth in a swamp, in a very secret and retired place, for a place of prayer. And besides, I had particular secret places of my own in the woods, where I used to retire by myself; and used to be from time to time much affected. My affections seemed to be lively and easily moved, and I seemed to be in my element, when engaged in religious duties. And I am ready to think, many are deceived with such affections, and such a kind of delight, as I then had in religion, and mistake it for grace.

But in process of time, my convictions and affections wore off; and I entirely lost all those affections and delights, and left off secret prayer, at least as to any constant performance of it; and returned like a dog to his vomit, and went on in ways of sin.[2]

Indeed, I was at some times very uneasy, especially towards the latter part of the time of my being at college. 'Till it pleas'd God, in my last year at college, at a time when I was in the midst of many uneasy thoughts about the state of my soul, to seize me with a pleurisy;[3] in which he brought me nigh to the grave, and shook me over the pit of hell.

But yet, it was not long after my recovery, before I fell again into my old ways of sin. But God would not suffer me to go on with any quietness; but I had great and violent inward struggles: 'till after many conflicts with wicked inclinations, and repeated resolutions, and bonds that I laid myself under by a kind of vows to God, I was brought wholly to break off all former wicked ways, and all ways of known outward sin; and to apply myself to seek my salvation, and practice the duties of religion: But without that kind of affection and delight, that I had formerly experienced. My concern now wrought more by inward struggles and conflicts, and self-reflections. I made seeking my salvation the main business of my life. But yet it seems to me, I sought after a miserable manner: Which has made me some times since to question, whether ever it issued in that which was saving; being ready to doubt, whether such miserable seeking was ever succeeded. But yet I was brought to seek salvation, in a manner that I never was before. I felt a spirit to part with all things in the world, for an interest in Christ. My concern continued and prevailed, with many exercising thoughts and inward struggles; but yet it never seemed to be proper to express my concern that I had, by the name of terror.

From my childhood up, my mind has been wont to be full of objections against the doctrine of God's sovereignty, in choosing whom he would to eternal life, and rejecting whom he pleased; leaving them eternally to perish, and be everlastingly tormented in hell. It used to appear like a horrible doctrine to me. But I remember the time very well, when I seemed to be convinced, and fully satisfied, as to this sover-

[2]"As a dog returneth to his vomit, so a fool returneth to his folly" (Proverbs 26:11).

[3]An illness in the respiratory system.

eignty of God, and his justice in thus eternally disposing of men, according to his sovereign pleasure. But never could give an account, how, or by what means, I was thus convinced; not in the least imagining, in the time of it, nor a long time after, that there was any extraordinary influence of God's spirit in it; but only that now I saw further, and my reason apprehended the justice and reasonableness of it. However, my mind rested in it; and it put an end to all those cavils and objections, that had 'till then abode with me, all the preceding part of my life. And there has been a wonderful alteration in my mind, with respect to the doctrine of God's sovereignty, from that day to this; so that I scarce ever have found so much as the rising of an objection against God's sovereignty, in the most absolute sense, in showing mercy to whom he will show mercy, and hardening and eternally damning whom he will.[4] God's absolute sovereignty, and justice, with respect to salvation and damnation, is what my mind seems to rest assured of, as much as of any thing that I see with my eyes; at least it is so at times. But I have often times since that first conviction, had quite another kind of sense of God's sovereignty, than I had then. I have often since, not only had a conviction, but a *delightful* conviction. The doctrine of God's sovereignty has very often appeared, an exceeding pleasant, bright and sweet doctrine to me: and absolute sovereignty is what I love to ascribe to God. But my first conviction was not with this.

The first that I remember that ever I found any thing of that sort of inward, sweet delight in God and divine things, that I have lived much in since, was on reading those words, I Tim. i. 17. "Now unto the king eternal, immortal, invisible, the only wise God, be honor and glory for ever and ever, Amen." As I read the words, there came into my soul, and was as it were diffused thro' it, a sense of the glory of the Divine Being; a new sense, quite different from any thing I ever experienced before. Never any words of scripture seemed to me as these words did. I thought with myself, how excellent a being that was; and how happy I should be, if I might enjoy that God, and be wrapt up to God in Heaven, and be as it were swallowed up in Him. I kept saying, and as it were singing over these words of scripture to myself; and went to prayer, to pray to God that I might enjoy him; and prayed in a manner quite different from what I used to do; with a new sort of affection. But it never came into my thought, that there was any thing spiritual, or of a saving nature in this.

From about that time, I began to have a new kind of apprehensions and ideas of Christ, and the work of redemption, and the glorious way of salvation by Him. I had an inward, sweet sense of these things, that at times came into my heart; and my soul was led away in pleasant views and contemplations of them. And my mind was greatly engaged, to spend my time in reading and meditating on Christ; and the beauty and excellency of His person, and the lovely way of salvation, by free grace in Him. I found no books so delightful to me, as those that treated of these subjects. Those words Cant. ii. I. used to be abundantly with me: *I am the Rose of Sharon, the lily of the valleys.* The words seemed to me, sweetly to represent, the loveliness and beauty of Jesus Christ. And the whole Book of Canticles[5] used to be pleasant to me;

[4]"Therefore hath he mercy on whom he will have mercy, and whom he will he hardeneth" (Romans 9:18).

[5]Canticles is another name for the Song of Solomon.

and I used to be much in reading it, about that time. And found, from time to time, an inward sweetness, that used, as it were, to carry me away in my contemplations; in what I know not how to express otherwise, than by a calm, sweet abstraction of soul from all the concerns of this world; and a kind of vision, or fix'd ideas and imaginations, of being alone in the mountains, or some solitary wilderness, far from all mankind, sweetly conversing with Christ, and wrapt and swallowed up in God. The sense I had of divine things, would often of a sudden as it were, kindle up a sweet burning in my heart; an ardor of my soul, that I know not how to express.

Not long after I first began to experience these things, I gave an account to my father, of some things that had pass'd in my mind. I was pretty much affected by the discourse we had together. And when the discourse was ended, I walked abroad alone, in a solitary place in my father's pasture, for contemplation. And as I was walking there, and looked up on the sky and clouds; there came into my mind, a sweet sense of the glorious majesty and grace of God, that I know not how to express. I seemed to see them both in a sweet conjunction: majesty and meekness join'd together: it was a sweet and gentle, and holy majesty; and also a majestic meekness; an awful sweetness; a high, and great, and holy gentleness.

After this my sense of divine things gradually increased, and became more and more lively, and had more of that inward sweetness. The appearance of every thing was altered: there seem'd to be, as it were, a calm, sweet cast, or appearance of divine glory, in almost every thing. God's excellency, his wisdom, his purity and love, seemed to appear in every thing; in the sun, moon and stars; in the clouds, and blue sky; in the grass, flowers, trees; in the water, and all nature; which used greatly to fix my mind. I often used to sit and view the moon, for a long time; and so in the day time, spent much time in viewing the clouds and sky, to behold the sweet glory of God in these things: in the mean time, singing forth with a low voice, my contemplations of the Creator and Redeemer. And scarce any thing, among all the works of nature, was so sweet to me as thunder and lightning. Formerly, nothing had been so terrible to me. I used to be a person uncommonly terrified with thunder: and it used to strike me with terror, when I saw a thunder-storm rising. But now, on the contrary, it rejoiced me. I felt God at the first appearance of a thunder-storm. And used to take the opportunity at such times to fix myself to view the clouds, and see the lightnings play, and hear the majestic and awful voice of God's thunder: which often times was exceeding entertaining, leading me to sweet contemplations of my great and glorious God. And while I viewed, used to spend my time, as it always seem'd natural to me, to sing or chant forth my meditations; to speak my thoughts in soliloquies, and speak with a singing voice.

I felt then a great satisfaction as to my good estate. But that did not content me.[6] I had vehement longings of soul after God and Christ, and after more holiness; wherewith my heart seemed to be full, and ready to break: which often brought to my mind, the words of the psalmist, Psal. cxix. 28. *My soul breaketh for the longing it hath.* I often felt a mourning and lamenting in my heart, that I had not turned to God sooner, that I might have had more time to grow in grace. My mind was greatly fix'd on divine things; I was almost perpetually in the contemplation of them. Spent

[6]Edwards here speaks of his spiritual state.

most of my time in thinking of divine things, year after year. And used to spend abundance of my time, in walking alone in the woods, and solitary places, for meditation, soliloquy and prayer, and converse with God. And it was always my manner, at such times, to sing forth my contemplations. And was almost constantly in ejaculatory prayer, wherever I was. Prayer seem'd to be natural to me, as the breath, by which the inward burnings of my heart had vent.

The delights which I now felt in things of religion, were of an exceeding different kind, from those forementioned, that I had when I was a boy. They were totally of another kind; and what I then had no more notion or idea of, than one born blind has of pleasant and beautiful colors. They were of a more inward, pure, soul-animating and refreshing nature. Those former delights, never reached the heart; and did not arise from any sight of the divine excellency of the things of God; or any taste of the soul-satisfying, and life-giving good, there is in them.

My sense of divine things seemed gradually to increase, 'till I went to preach at New York;[7] which was about a year and a half after they began. While I was there, I felt them, very sensibly, in a much higher degree, than I had done before. My longings after God and holiness, were much increased. Pure and humble, holy and heavenly Christianity, appeared exceeding amiable to me. I felt in me a burning desire to be in every thing a complete Christian; and conformed to the blessed image of Christ: and that I might live in all things, according to the pure, sweet and blessed rules of the gospel. I had an eager thirsting after progress in these things. My longings after it, put me upon pursuing and pressing after them. It was my continual strife day and night, and constant inquiry, How I should be more holy, and live more holily, and more becoming a child of God, and disciple of Christ. I sought an increase of grace and holiness, and that I might live an holy life, with vastly more earnestness, than ever I sought grace, before I had it. I used to be continually examining myself, and studying and contriving for likely ways and means, how I should live holily, with far greater diligence and earnestness, than ever I pursued any thing in my life: But with too great a dependence on my own strength; which afterwards proved a great damage to me. My experience had not then taught me, as it has done since, my extreme feebleness and impotence, every manner of way; and the innumerable and bottomless depths of secret corruption and deceit, that there was in my heart. However, I went on with my eager pursuit after more holiness; and sweet conformity to Christ.

The Heaven I desired was a heaven of holiness; to be with God, and to spend my eternity in divine love, and holy communion with Christ. My mind was very much taken up with contemplations on heaven, and the enjoyments of those there; and living there in perfect holiness, humility and love. And it used at that time to appear a great part of the happiness of heaven, that there the saints could express their love to Christ. It appear'd to me a great clog and hindrance and burden to me, that what I felt within, I could not express to God, and give vent to, as I desired. The inward ardor of my soul, seem'd to be hindered and pent up, and could not freely flame out as it would. I used often to think, how in heaven, this sweet principle should freely and fully vent and express itself. Heaven appeared to me exceeding delightful as a

[7]Edwards assisted as a pastor in New York at a Presbyterian Church from 1722 until April, 1723. He speaks in this passage of the felt presence he had of Christ.

world of love. It appeared to me, that all happiness consisted in living in pure, humble, heavenly, divine love.

I remember the thoughts I used then to have of holiness. I remember I then said sometimes to myself, I do certainly know that I love holiness, such as the gospel prescribes. It appeared to me, there was nothing in it but what was ravishingly lovely. It appeared to me, to be the highest beauty and amiableness, above all other beauties: that it was a *divine* beauty; far purer than any thing here upon earth; and that every thing else, was like mire, filth and defilement, in comparison of it.

Holiness, as I then wrote down some of my contemplations on it, appeared to me to be of a sweet, pleasant, charming, serene, calm nature. It seemed to me, it brought an inexpressible purity, brightness, peacefulness and ravishment to the soul: and that it made the soul like a field or garden of God, with all manner of pleasant flowers; that is all pleasant, delightful and undisturbed; enjoying a sweet calm, and the gently vivifying beams of the sun. The soul of a true Christian, as I then wrote my meditations, appear'd like such a little white flower, as we see in the spring of the year; low and humble on the ground, opening its bosom, to receive the pleasant beams of the sun's glory; rejoicing as it were, in a calm rapture; diffusing around a sweet fragrancy; standing peacefully and lovingly, in the midst of other flowers round about; all in like manner opening their bosoms, to drink in the light of the sun.

There was no part of creature-holiness, that I then, and at other times, had so great a sense of the loveliness of, as humility, brokenness of heart and poverty of spirit: and there was nothing that I had such a spirit to long for. My heart as it were panted after this, to lie low before God, and in the dust; that I might be nothing, and that God might be all; that I might become as a little child.[8]

While I was there at New York, I sometimes was much affected with reflections on my past life, considering how late it was, before I began to be truly religious; and how wickedly I had lived 'till then: and once so as to weep abundantly, and for a considerable time together.

On January 12, 1722–3. I made a solemn dedication of myself to God, and wrote it down; giving up myself, and all that I had to God; to be for the future in no respect my own; to act as one that had no right to himself, in any respect. And solemnly vowed to take God for my whole portion and felicity; looking on nothing else as any part of my happiness, nor acting as if it were: and his law for the constant rule of my obedience: engaging to fight with all my might, against the world, the flesh and the devil, to the end of my life. But have reason to be infinitely humbled, when I consider, how much I have fail'd of answering my obligation.

I had then abundance of sweet religious conversation in the family where I lived, with Mr. John Smith, and his pious mother. My heart was knit in affection to those, in whom were appearances of true piety; and I could bear the thoughts of no other companions, but such as were holy, and the disciples of the blessed Jesus.

I had great longings for the advancement of Christ's kingdom in the world. My secret prayer used to be in great part taken up in praying for it. If I heard the least

[8]"Verily, I say unto you, Whosoever shall not receive the kingdom of God as a little child, he shall not enter therein" (Mark 10:15).

hint of any thing that happened in any part of the world, that appear'd to me, in some respect or other, to have a favorable aspect on the interest of Christ's kingdom, my soul eagerly catch'd at it; and it would much animate and refresh me. I used to be earnest to read public news-letters, mainly for that end; to see if I could not find some news favorable to the interest of religion in the world.

I very frequently used to retire into a solitary place, on the banks of Hudson's river, at some distance from the city, for contemplation on divine things, and secret converse with God; and had many sweet hours there. Sometimes Mr. Smith and I walked there together, to converse of the things of God; and our conversation used much to turn on the advancement of Christ's kingdom in the world, and the glorious things that God would accomplish for his church in the latter days.

I had then, and at other times, the greatest delight in the holy Scriptures, of any book whatsoever. Often-times in reading it, every word seemed to touch my heart. I felt an harmony between something in my heart, and those sweet and powerful words. I seem'd often to see so much light, exhibited by every sentence, and such a refreshing ravishing food communicated, that I could not get along in reading. Used often-times to dwell long on one sentence, to see the wonders contained in it; and yet almost every sentence seemed to be full of wonders.

I came away from New York in the month of April, 1723, and had a most bitter parting with Madam Smith and her son. My heart seemed to sink within me, at leaving the family and city, where I had enjoyed so many sweet and pleasant days. I went from New York to Weathersfield[9] by water. As I sail'd away, I kept sight of the city as long as I could; and when I was out of sight of it, it would affect me much to look that way, with a kind of melancholy mixed with sweetness. However, that night after this sorrowful parting, I was greatly comforted in God at Westchester, where we went ashore to lodge: and had a pleasant time of it all the voyage to Saybrook.[10] It was sweet to me to think of meeting dear Christians in heaven, where we should never part more. At Saybrook we went ashore to lodge on Saturday, and there kept sabbath; where I had a sweet and refreshing season, walking alone in the fields.

After I came home to Windsor, remained much in a like frame of my mind, as I had been in at New York, but only sometimes felt my heart ready to sink, with the thoughts of my friends at New York. And my refuge and support was in contemplations on the heavenly state; as I find in my diary of May 1, 1723. It was my comfort to think of that state, where there is fulness of joy; where reigns heavenly, sweet, calm and delightful love, without alloy; where there are continually the dearest expressions of this love; where is the enjoyment of the persons loved, without ever parting; where these persons that appear so lovely in this world, will really be inexpressibly more lovely, and full of love to us. And how sweetly will the mutual lovers join together to sing the praises of God and the Lamb![11] How full will it fill us with joy, to think, that this enjoyment, these sweet exercises will never cease or come to an end; but will last to all eternity!

[9]Wethersfield, Connecticut.

[10]Westchester, New York, and Saybrook, Connecticut.

[11]In Revelation, the Lamb is the symbol of Christ.

Continued much in the same frame in the general, that I had been in at New York, till I went to New Haven, to live there as tutor of the college; having some special seasons of uncommon sweetness: particularly once at Boston, in a journey from Boston, walking out alone in the fields. After I went to New Haven, I sunk in religion; my mind being diverted from my eager and violent pursuits after holiness, by some affairs that greatly perplexed and distracted my mind.

In September, 1725, was taken ill at New Haven; and endeavoring to go home to Windsor, was so ill at the North Village, that I could go no further: where I lay sick for about a quarter of a year. And in this sickness, God was pleased to visit me again with the sweet influences of His spirit. My mind was greatly engaged there on divine, pleasant contemplations, and longings of soul. I observed that those who watched with me, would often be looking out for the morning, and seemed to wish for it. Which brought to my mind those words of the psalmist, which my soul with sweetness made its own language. *My soul waitest for the Lord, more than they that watch for the morning, I say, more than they that watch for the morning.*[12] And when the light of the morning came, and the beams of the sun came in at the windows, it refreshed my soul from one morning to another. It seemed to me to be some image of the sweet light of God's glory.

I remember, about that time, I used greatly to long for the conversion of some that I was concerned with. It seem'd to me, I could gladly honor them, and with delight be a servant to them, and lie at their feet, if they were but truly holy.

But some time after this, I was again greatly diverted in my mind, with some temporal concerns, that exceedingly took up my thoughts, greatly to the wounding of my soul: and went on through various exercises, that it would be tedious to relate, that gave me much more experience of my own heart, than ever I had before.

Since I came to this town,[13] I have often had sweet complacency in God, in views of his glorious perfections, and the excellency of Jesus Christ. God has appeared to me, a glorious and lovely being, chiefly on the account of His holiness. The holiness of God has always appeared to me the most lovely of all His attributes. The doctrines of God's absolute sovereignty, and free grace, in showing mercy to whom He would show mercy; and man's absolute dependence on the operations of God's Holy Spirit, have very often appeared to me as sweet and glorious doctrines. These doctrines have been much my delight. God's sovereignty has ever appeared to me, as great part of His glory. It has often been sweet to me to go to God, and adore Him as a sovereign God, and ask sovereign mercy of Him.

I have loved the doctrines of the gospel: They have been to my soul like green pastures. The gospel has seem'd to me to be the richest treasure; the treasure that I have most desired, and longed that it might dwell richly in me. The way of salvation by Christ, has appeared in a general way, glorious and excellent, and most pleasant and beautiful. It has often seem'd to me, that it would in a great measure spoil heaven, to receive it in any other way. That Text has often been affecting and delightful to me, Isai. xxxii. 2. *A man shall be an hiding place from the wind, and a covert from the tempest etc.*

[12]Psalm 130:6.

[13]Edwards went to Northampton, Massachusetts, to assist his grandfather in parish duties, in 1726.

It has often appear'd sweet to me, to be united to Christ; to have Him for my head, and to be a member of His body: and also to have Christ for my teacher and prophet. I very often think with sweetness and longings and pantings of soul, of being a little child, taking hold of Christ, to be led by Him through the wilderness of this world. That text, Matth. xviii. at the beginning, has often been sweet to me, *Except ye be converted, and become as little children etc.* I love to think of coming to Christ, to receive salvation of Him, poor in spirit, and quite empty of self; humbly exalting Him alone; cut entirely off from my own root, and to grow into, and out of Christ: to have God in Christ to be all in all; and to live by faith on the Son of God, a life of humble, unfeigned confidence in Him. That Scripture has often been sweet to me, Psal. cxv. I. *Not unto us, O Lord, not unto us, but unto Thy name give glory, for Thy mercy, and for Thy truth's sake.* And those words of Christ, *Luk. x. 21. In that hour Jesus rejoiced in spirit, and said, I thank thee, O Father, Lord of heaven and earth, that Thou hast hid these things from the wise and prudent, and hast revealed them unto babes: Even so Father, for so it seemed good in Thy sight.* That sovereignty of God that Christ rejoiced in, seemed to me to be worthy to be rejoiced in; and that rejoicing of Christ, seemed to me to show the excellency of Christ, and the spirit that He was of.

Sometimes only mentioning a single word, causes my heart to burn within me: or only seeing the Name of Christ, or the name of some attribute of God. And God has appeared glorious to me, on account of the Trinity. It has made me have exalting thoughts of God, that he subsists in three persons; Father, Son, and Holy Ghost.

The sweetest joys and delights I have experienced, have not been those that have arisen from a hope of my own good estate; but in a direct view of the glorious things of the gospel. When I enjoy this sweetness, it seems to carry me above the thoughts of my own safe estate. It seems at such times a loss that I cannot bear, to take off my eye from the glorious, pleasant object I behold without me, to turn my eye in upon myself, and my own good estate.

My heart has been much on the advancement of Christ's kingdom in the world. The histories of the past advancement of Christ's kingdom, have been sweet to me. When I have read histories of past ages, the pleasantest thing in all my reading has been, to read of the kingdom of Christ being promoted. And when I have expected in my reading, to come to any such thing, I have lotted upon it all the way as I read. And my mind has been much entertained and delighted, with the Scripture promises and prophecies, of the future glorious advancement of Christ's kingdom on earth.

I have sometimes had a sense of the excellent fulness of Christ, and His meetness and suitableness as a Saviour; whereby He has appeared to me, far above all, the chief of ten thousands.[14] And His blood and atonement has appeared sweet, and His righteousness sweet; which is always accompanied with an ardency of spirit, and inward strugglings and breathings and groanings, that cannot be uttered, to be emptied of myself, and swallowed up in Christ.

Once, as I rid out into the woods for my health, *Anno*[15] 1737; and having lit from my horse in a retired place, as my manner commonly has been, to walk for di-

[14]"My beloved is white and ruddy, the chiefest among ten thousand" (Song of Solomon 5:10).

[15]The year.

vine contemplation and prayer; I had a view, that for me was extraordinary, of the glory of the Son of God; as mediator between God and man; and his wonderful, great, full, pure and sweet grace and love, and meek and gentle condescension. This grace, that appear'd to me so calm and sweet, appear'd great above the heavens. The person of Christ appear'd ineffably excellent, with an excellency great enough to swallow up all thought and conception, which continued, as near as I can judge, about an hour; which kept me, the bigger part of the time, in a flood of tears, and weeping aloud. I felt withal, an ardency of soul to be, what I know not otherwise how to express, than to be emptied and annihilated; to lie in the dust, and to be full of Christ alone; to love Him with a holy and pure love; to trust in Him; to live upon Him; to serve and follow Him, and to be totally wrapt up in the fullness of Christ; and to be perfectly sanctified and made pure, with a divine and heavenly purity. I have several other times, had views very much of the same nature, and that have had the same effects.

I have many times had a sense of the glory of the third person in the Trinity, in His office of sanctifier; in His holy operations communicating divine light and life to the soul. God in the communications of His Holy Spirit, has appear'd as an infinite fountain of divine glory and sweetness; being full and sufficient to fill and satisfy the soul: pouring forth itself in sweet communications, like the sun in its glory, sweetly and pleasantly diffusing light and life.

I have sometimes had an affecting sense of the excellency of the word of God, as a word of life; as the light of life; a sweet, excellent, life-giving word: accompanied with a thirsting after that word, that it might dwell richly in my heart.

I have often since I lived in this town, had very affecting views of my own sinfulness and vileness; very frequently so as to hold me in a kind of loud weeping, sometimes for a considerable time together: so that I have often been forced to shut myself up.[16] I have had a vastly greater sense of my own wickedness, and the badness of my heart, since my conversion, than ever I had before. It has often appeared to me, that if God should mark iniquity against me, I should appear the very worst of all mankind; of all that have been since the beginning of the world to this time: and that I should have by far the lowest place in hell. When others that have come to talk with me about their soul concerns, have expressed the sense they have had of their own wickedness, by saying that it seem'd to them, that they were as bad as the devil himself; I thought their expressions seemed exceeding faint and feeble, to represent my wickedness. I thought I should wonder, that they should content themselves with such expressions as these, if I had any reason to imagine, that their sin bore any proportion to mine. It seemed to me, I should wonder at myself, if I should express *my* wickedness in such feeble terms as they did.

My wickedness, as I am in myself, has long appear'd to me perfectly ineffable, and infinitely swallowing up all thought and imagination; like an infinite deluge, or infinite mountains over my head. I know not how to express better, what my sins appear to me to be, than by heaping infinite upon infinite, and multiplying infinite by infinite. I go about very often, for this many years, with these expressions in my mind, and in my mouth, "Infinite upon infinite. Infinite upon infinite!" When I look into

[16]Take to meditation alone in my room.

my heart, and take a view of my wickedness, it looks like an abyss infinitely deeper than hell. And it appears to me, that were it not for free grace, exalted and raised up to the infinite height of all the fulness and glory of the great Jehovah,[17] and the arm of His power and grace stretched forth, in all the majesty of His power, and in all the glory of His sovereignty; I should appear sunk down in my sins infinitely below hell itself, far beyond sight of every thing, but the piercing eye of God's grace, that can pierce even down to such a depth, and to the bottom of such an abyss.

And yet, I ben't in the least inclined to think, that I have a greater conviction of sin than ordinary. It seems to me, my conviction of sin is exceeding small, and faint. It appears to me enough to amaze me, that I have no more sense of my sin. I know certainly, that I have very little sense of my sinfulness. That my sins appear to me so great, don't seem to me to be, because I have so much more conviction of sin than other Christians, but because I am so much worse, and have so much more wickedness to be convinced of. When I have had these turns of weeping and crying for my sins, I thought I knew in the time of it, that my repentance was nothing to my sin.

I have greatly longed of late, for a broken heart, and to lie low before God. And when I ask for humility of God, I can't bear the thoughts of being no more humble, than other Christians. It seems to me, that tho' their degrees of humility may be suitable for them; yet it would be a vile self-exaltation in me, not to be the lowest in humility of all mankind. Others speak of their longing to be humbled to the dust. Tho' that may be a proper expression for them, I always think for myself, that I ought to be humbled down below hell. 'Tis an expression that it has long been natural for me to use in prayer to God. I ought to lie infinitely low before God.

It is affecting to me to think, how ignorant I was, when I was a young Christian, of the bottomless, infinite depths of wickedness, pride, hypocrisy and deceit left in my heart.

I have vastly a greater sense, of my universal, exceeding dependence on God's grace and strength, and mere good pleasure, of late, than I used formerly to have; and have experienced more of an abhorrence of my own righteousness. The thought of any comfort or joy, arising in me, on any consideration, or reflection on my own amiableness, or any of my performances or experiences, or any goodness of heart or life, is nauseous and detestable to me. And yet I am greatly afflicted with a proud and self-righteous spirit; much more sensibly, than I used to be formerly. I see that serpent rising and putting forth it's head, continually, everywhere, all around me.

Tho' it seems to me, that in some respects I was a far better Christian, for two or three years after my first conversion, than I am now; and lived in a more constant delight and pleasure: yet of late years, I have had a more full and constant sense of the absolute sovereignty of God, and a delight in that sovereignty; and have had more of a sense of the glory of Christ, as a mediator, as revealed in the gospel. On one Saturday night in particular, had a particular discovery of the excellency of the gospel of Christ, above all other doctrines; so that I could not but say to myself; "This is my chosen light, my chosen doctrine": and of Christ, "This is my chosen prophet." It appear'd to me to be sweet beyond all expression, to follow Christ, and to be taught and enlighten'd and instructed by Him; to learn of Him, and live to Him.

[17]God, in the Old Testament.

Another Saturday night, January, 1738–9, had such a sense, how sweet and blessed a thing it was, to walk in the way of duty, to do that which was right and meet to be done, and agreeable to the holy mind of God; that it caused me to break forth into a kind of a loud weeping, which held me some time; so that I was forced to shut myself up, and fasten the doors. I could not but as it were cry out, "How happy are they which do that which is right in the sight of God! They are blessed indeed, they are the happy ones!" I had at the same time, a very affecting sense, how meet and suitable it was that God should govern the world, and order all things according to his own pleasure; and I rejoiced in it, that God reigned, and that his will was done.

1765

Sinners in the Hands of an Angry God[1]

Deuteronomy 32.35

Their foot shall slide in due time.[2]

In this verse is threatened the vengeance of God on the wicked unbelieving Israelites, who were God's visible people, and who lived under the means of grace,[3] but who, notwithstanding all God's wonderful works towards them, remained (as in verse 28.) void of counsel, having no understanding in them.[4] Under all the cultivations of heaven, they brought forth bitter and poisonous fruit, as in the two verses next preceding the text.[5] The expression I have chosen for my text, "Their foot shall slide in due time," seems to imply the following things, relating to the punishment and destruction to which these wicked Israelites were exposed.

[1]Edwards delivered this sermon before the congregation at Enfield on Sunday, July 8, 1741. Said to have been one of the quietest, least spectacular of preachers in his own day, Edwards used this sermon during the Great Awakening, when his audiences often broke out in hysteria. According to Reverend Eleazer Wheelock, future president of Dartmouth College, "There was such a breathing of distress, and weeping, that the preacher was obliged to speak to the people and desire silence, that he might be heard" (reported by Benjamin Trumbull in *A Complete History of Connecticut,* 1797).

The text of the sermon is from Sereno Dwight, ed., *The Works of Jonathan Edwards,* vol. 7 (1829–30).

[2]"To me belongeth vengeance, and recompense; their foot shall slide in due time: for the day of their calamity is at hand, and the things that shall come upon them make haste."

[3]The Israelites were given the Ten Commandments. For most Puritans, "means of grace" were the preaching of the word of God and the administration of the two sacraments, baptism and the Lord's Supper.

[4]"They are a nation void of counsel, neither is there any understanding in them" (Deuteronomy 32:28).

[5]"For their vine is of the vine of Sodom, and the fields of Gomorrah: their grapes are grapes of gall, their clusters are bitter: their wine is the poison of dragons, and the cruel venom of asps" (Deuteronomy 32:32–33). Sodom and Gomorrah, cities of wickedness, were destroyed by a rain of fire and sulphur (Genesis 19:28).

1. That they were always exposed to destruction; as one that stands or walks in slippery places is always exposed to fall. This is implied in the manner of their destruction coming upon them, being represented by their foot sliding. The same is expressed, Psalm 73.18: "Surely thou didst set them in slippery places; thou castedst them down into destruction."

2. It implies that they were always exposed to sudden unexpected destruction. As he that walks in slippery places is every moment liable to fall, he cannot foresee one moment whether he shall stand or fall the next; and when he does fall, he falls at once without warning. Which is also expressed in Psalm 73. 18–19: "Surely thou didst set them in slippery places; thou castedst them down into destruction: How are they brought into desolation as in a moment!"

3. Another thing implied is, that they are liable to fall of themselves, without being thrown down by the hand of another; as he that stands or walks on slippery ground needs nothing but his own weight to throw him down.

4. That the reason why they are not fallen already, and do not fall now, is only that God's appointed time is not come. For it is said, that when that due time or appointed times comes, their foot shall slide. Then they shall be left to fall, as they are inclined by their own weight. God will not hold them up in these slippery places any longer, but will let them go; and then, at that very instant, they shall fall into destruction; as he that stands on such slippery declining ground, on the edge of a pit, he cannot stand alone, when he is let go he immediately falls and is lost.

The observation from the words that I would now insist upon is this. "There is nothing that keeps wicked men at any one moment out of hell, but the mere pleasure of God." By the mere pleasure of God, I mean His sovereign pleasure, His arbitrary will, restrained by no obligation, hindered by no manner of difficulty, any more than if nothing else but God's mere will had in the least degree, or in any respect whatsoever, any hand in the preservation of wicked men one moment. The truth of this observation may appear by the following considerations.

1. There is no want of power in God to cast wicked men into hell at any moment. Men's hands cannot be strong when God rises up. The strongest have no power to resist Him, nor can any deliver out of His hands. He is not only able to cast wicked men into hell, but He can most easily do it. Sometimes an earthly prince meets with a great deal of difficulty to subdue a rebel, who has found means to fortify himself, and has made himself strong by the numbers of his followers. But it is not so with God. There is no fortress that is any defense from the power of God. Though hand join in hand, and vast multitudes of God's enemies combine and associate themselves, they are easily broken in pieces. They are as great heaps of light chaff before the whirlwind; or large quantities of dry stubble before devouring flames. We find it easy to tread on and crush a worm that we see crawling on the earth; so it is easy for us to cut or singe a slender thread that any thing hangs by: thus easy is it for God, when he pleases, to cast His enemies down to hell. What are we, that we should think to stand before him, at whose rebuke the earth trembles, and before whom the rocks are thrown down?

2. They deserve to be cast into hell; so that divine justice never stands in the way, it makes no objection against God's using His power at any moment to destroy them. Yea, on the contrary, justice calls aloud for an infinite punishment of their sins. Divine justice says of the tree that brings forth such grapes of Sodom, "Cut it down,

why cumbereth it the ground?" Luke 13.7. The sword of divine justice is every moment brandished over their heads, and it is nothing but the hand of arbitrary mercy, and God's will, that holds it back.

3. They are already under a sentence of condemnation to hell. They do not only justly deserve to be cast down thither, but the sentence of the law of God, that eternal and immutable rule of righteousness that God has fixed between Him and mankind, is gone out against them, and stands against them; so that they are bound over already to hell. John 3.18: "He that believeth not is condemned already." So that every unconverted man properly belongs to hell; that is his place; from thence he is, John 8.23: "Ye are from beneath." And thither he is bound; it is the place that justice, and God's word, and the sentence of his unchangeable law assign to him.

4. They are now the objects of that very same anger and wrath of God that is expressed in the torments of hell. And the reason why they do not go down to hell at each moment is not because God, in whose power they are, is not then very angry with them as He is with many miserable creatures now tormented in hell, who there feel and bear the fierceness of His wrath. Yea, God is a great deal more angry with great numbers that are now on earth: yea, doubtless, with many that are now in this congregation, who it may be are at ease, than He is with many of those who are now in the flames of hell.

So that it is not because God is unmindful of their wickedness, and does not resent it, that He does not let loose His hand and cut them off. God is not altogether such an one as themselves, though they may imagine Him to be so. The wrath of God burns against them, their damnation does not slumber; the pit is prepared, the fire is made ready, the furnace is now hot, ready to receive them; the flames do now rage and glow. The glittering sword is whet, and held over them, and the pit hath opened its mouth under them.

5. The devil stands ready to fall upon them, and seize them as his own, at what moment God shall permit him. They belong to him; he has their souls in his possession, and under his dominion. The scripture represents them as his goods, Luke 11.12. The devils watch them; they are ever by them at their right hand; they stand waiting for them, like greedy hungry lions that see their prey, and expect to have it, but are for the present kept back. If God should withdraw His hand, by which they are restrained, they would in one moment fly upon their poor souls. The old serpent is gaping for them; hell opens it mouth wide to receive them; and if God should permit it, they would be hastily swallowed up and lost.

6. There are in the souls of wicked men those hellish principles reigning that would presently kindle and flame out into hell fire, if it were not for God's restraints. There is laid in the very nature of carnal men a foundation for the torments of hell. There are those corrupt principles, in reigning power in them, and in full possession of them, that are seeds of hell fire. These principles are active and powerful, exceeding violent in their nature, and if it were not for the restraining hand of God upon them, they would soon break out, they would flame out after the same manner as the same corruptions, the same enmity does in the hearts of damned souls, and would beget the same torments as they do in them. The souls of the wicked are in scripture compared to the troubled sea, Isaiah 57.20. For the present, God restrains their wickedness by His mighty power, as He does the raging waves of the troubled sea,

saying, "Hitherto shalt thou come, but no further;"[6] but if God should withdraw that restraining power, it would soon carry all before it. Sin is the ruin and misery of the soul; it is destructive in its nature; and if God should leave it without restraint, there would need nothing else to make the soul perfectly miserable. The corruption of the heart of man is immoderate and boundless in its fury; and while wicked men live here, it is like fire pent up by God's restraints, whereas if it were let loose, it would set on fire the course of nature; and as the heart is now a sink of sin, so if sin was not restrained, it would immediately turn the soul into a fiery oven, or a furnace of fire and brimstone.

7. It is no security to wicked men for one moment that there are no visible means of death at hand. It is no security to a natural man that he is now in health and that he does not see which way he should now immediately go out of the world by any accident, and that there is no visible danger in any respect in his circumstances. The manifold and continual experience of the world in all ages, shows this is no evidence that a man is not on the very brink of eternity, and that the next step will not be into another world. The unseen, unthought-of ways and means of persons going suddenly out of the world are innumerable and inconceivable. Unconverted men walk over the pit of hell on a rotten covering, and there are innumerable places in this covering so weak that they will not bear their weight, and these places are not seen. The arrows of death fly unseen at noonday;[7] the sharpest sight cannot discern them. God has so many different unsearchable ways of taking wicked men out of the world and sending them to hell, that there is nothing to make it appear that God had need to be at the expense of a miracle, or go out of the ordinary course of His providence, to destroy any wicked man at any moment. All the means that there are of sinners going out of the world are so in God's hands, and so universally and absolutely subject to His power and determination, that it does not depend at all the less on the mere will of God whether sinners shall at any moment go to hell than if means were never made use of or at all concerned in the case.

8. Natural men's prudence and care to preserve their own lives, or the care of others to preserve them, do not secure them a moment. To this, divine providence and universal experience do also bear testimony. There is this clear evidence that men's own wisdom is no security to them from death; that if it were otherwise we should see some difference between the wise and politic men of the world, and others, with regard to their liableness to early and unexpected death: but how is it in fact? Ecclesiastes 2.16: "How dieth the wise man? even as the fool."

9. All wicked men's pains and contrivance which they use to escape hell, while they continue to reject Christ, and so remain wicked men, do not secure them from hell one moment. Almost every natural man[8] that hears of hell, flatters himself that he shall escape it; he depends upon himself for his own security; he flatters himself in what he has done, in what he is now doing, or what he intends to do. Every one

[6]Job 38:11.

[7]"Thou shalt not be afraid for the terror by night; nor for the arrow that flieth by day" (Psalm 91:5).

[8]One unsaved, not having experienced God's grace.

lays out matters in his own mind how he shall avoid damnation, and flatters himself that he contrives well for himself, and that his schemes will not fail. They hear indeed that there are but few saved, and that the greater part of men that have died heretofore are gone to hell; but each one imagines that he lays out matters better for his own escape than others have done. He does not intend to come to that place of torment; he says within himself that he intends to take effectual care, and to order matters so for himself as not to fail.

But the foolish children of men miserably delude themselves in their own schemes, and in confidence in their own strength and wisdom; they trust to nothing but a shadow. The greater part of those who heretofore have lived under the same means of grace, and are now dead, are undoubtedly gone to hell; and it was not because they were not as wise as those who are now alive: it was not because they did not lay out matters as well for themselves to secure their own escape. If we could speak with them, and inquire of them, one by one, whether they expected, when alive, and when they used to hear about hell, ever to be the subjects of that misery, we doubtless, should hear one and another reply, "No, I never intended to come here: I had laid out matters otherwise in my mind; I thought I should contrive well for myself: I thought my scheme good. I intended to take effectual care; but it came upon me unexpected; I did not look for it at that time, and in that manner; it came as a thief: Death outwitted me: God's wrath was too quick for me. Oh, my cursed foolishness! I was flattering myself, and pleasing myself with vain dreams of what I would do hereafter; and when I was saying, peace and safety, then suddenly destruction came upon me."

10. God has laid Himself under no obligation by any promise to keep any natural man out of hell one moment. God certainly has made no promises either of eternal life or of any deliverance or preservation from eternal death but what are contained in the covenant of grace,[9] the promises that are given in Christ, in whom all the promises are yea and amen. But surely they have no interest in the promises of the covenant of grace who are not the children of the covenant, who do not believe in any of the promises, and have no interest in the Mediator of the covenant.

So that, whatever some have imagined and pretended about promises made to natural men's earnest seeking and knocking, it is plain and manifest that whatever pains a natural man takes in religion, whatever prayers he makes, till he believes in Christ, God is under no manner of obligation to keep him a moment from eternal destruction.

So that, thus it is that natural men are held in the hand of God, over the pit of hell; they have deserved the fiery pit, and are already sentenced to it; and God is dreadfully provoked, His anger is as great towards them as to those that are actually suffering the executions of the fierceness of His wrath in hell, and they have done nothing in the least to appease or abate that anger, neither is God in the least bound by any promise to hold them up one moment; the devil is waiting for them, hell is

[9]The Covenant of Works was the original covenant God made with Adam; the Covenant of Grace is a second covenant, made through the intercession of Christ, that if mankind would believe in Christ, mankind would be saved. Christ is thus the mediator for mankind.

gaping for them, the flames gather and flash about them, and would fain lay hold on them, and swallow them up; the fire pent up in their own hearts is struggling to break out: and they have no interest in any Mediator, there are no means within reach that can be any security to them. In short, they have no refuge, nothing to take hold of; all that preserves them every moment is the mere arbitrary will, and uncovenanted, unobliged forbearance of an incensed God.

Application

The use of this awful subject may be for awakening unconverted persons in this congregation. This that you have heard is the case of every one of you that are out of Christ. That world of misery, that lake of burning brimstone is extended abroad under you. There is the dreadful pit of the glowing flames of the wrath of God; there is hell's wide-gaping mouth open; and you have nothing to stand upon, nor any thing to take hold of; there is nothing between you and hell but the air; it is only the power and mere pleasure of God that holds you up.

You probably are not sensible of this; you find you are kept out of hell, but do not see the hand of God in it; but look at other things, as the good state of your bodily constitution, your care of your own life, and the means you use for your own preservation. But indeed these things are nothing; if God should withdraw His hand, they would avail no more to keep you from falling, than the thin air to hold up a person that is suspended in it.

Your wickedness makes you as it were heavy as lead, and to tend downwards with great weight and pressure towards hell; and if God should let you go, you would immediately sink and swiftly descend and plunge into the bottomless gulf, and your healthy constitution, and your own care and prudence, and best contrivance, and all your righteousness, would have no more influence to uphold you and keep you out of hell, than a spider's web would have to stop a fallen rock. Were it not for the sovereign pleasure of God, the earth would not bear you one moment; for you are a burden to it; the creation groans with you; the creature is made subject to the bondage of your corruption, not willingly; the sun does not willingly shine upon you to give you light to serve sin and Satan; the earth does not willingly yield her increase to satisfy your lusts; nor is it willingly a stage for your wickedness to be acted upon; the air does not willingly serve you for breath to maintain the flame of life in your vitals, while you spend your life in the service of God's enemies. God's creatures are good, and were made for men to serve God with, and do not willingly subserve to any other purpose, and groan when they are abused to purposes so directly contrary to their nature and end. And the world would spew you out, were it not for the sovereign hand of Him who hath subjected it in hope. There are black clouds of God's wrath now hanging directly over your heads, full of the dreadful storm, and big with thunder; and were it not for the restraining hand of God, it would immediately burst forth upon you. The sovereign pleasure of God, for the present, stays His rough wind; otherwise it would come with fury, and your destruction would come like a whirlwind, and you would be like the chaff of the summer threshing floor.

The wrath of God is like great waters that are dammed for the present; they increase more and more, and rise higher and higher, till an outlet is given; and the longer the stream is stopped, the more rapid and mighty is its course when once it is let loose. It is true that judgment against your evil works has not been executed hitherto; the floods of God's vengeance have been withheld; but your guilt in the meantime is constantly increasing, and you are every day treasuring up more wrath; the waters are constantly rising, and waxing more and more mighty; and there is nothing but the mere pleasure of God that holds the waters back, that are unwilling to be stopped, and press hard to go forward. If God should only withdraw His hand from the floodgate, it would immediately fly open, and the fiery floods of the fierceness and wrath of God, would rush forth with inconceivable fury, and would come upon you with omnipotent power; and if your strength were ten thousand times greater than it is, yea, ten thousand times greater than the strength of the stoutest, sturdiest devil in hell, it would be nothing to withstand or endure it.

The bow of God's wrath is bent, and the arrow made ready on the string, and justice bends the arrow at your heart, and strains the bow, and it is nothing but the mere pleasure of God, and that of an angry God, without any promise or obligation at all, that keeps the arrow one moment from being made drunk with your blood. Thus all you that never passed under a great change of heart, by the mighty power of the Spirit of God upon your souls, all you that were never born again, and made new creatures, and raised from being dead in sin, to a state of new, and before altogether unexperienced light and life, are in the hands of an angry God. However you may have reformed your life in many things, and may have had religious affections, and may keep up a form of religion in your families and closets,[10] and in the house of God, it is nothing but His mere pleasure that keeps you from being this moment swallowed up in everlasting destruction. However unconvinced you may now be of the truth of what you hear, by and by you will be fully convinced of it. Those that are gone from being in the like circumstances with you see that it was so with them; for destruction came suddenly upon most of them; when they expected nothing of it and while they were saying, peace and safety: now they see that those things on which they depended for peace and safety, were nothing but thin air and empty shadows.

The God that holds you over the pit of hell, much as one holds a spider or some loathsome insect over the fire, abhors you, and is dreadfully provoked: His wrath towards you burns like fire; He looks upon you as worthy of nothing else but to be cast into the fire; He is of purer eyes than to bear to have you in His sight; you are ten thousand times more abominable in His eyes than the most hateful venomous serpent is in ours. You have offended Him infinitely more than ever a stubborn rebel did his prince; and yet it is nothing but His hand that holds you from falling into the fire every moment. It is to be ascribed to nothing else, that you did not go to hell the last night; that you was suffered to awake again in this world, after you closed your eyes to sleep. And there is no other reason to be given, why you have not dropped into hell since you arose in the morning, but that God's hand has held you up. There is no other reason to be given why you have not gone to hell, since you have sat here in the house of God, provoking His pure eyes by your sinful wicked manner of attending His solemn worship. Yea, there is nothing else that is to be given as a reason why you do not this very moment drop down into hell.

[10]Places of meditation.

O sinner! Consider the fearful danger you are in: it is a great furnace of wrath, a wide and bottomless pit, full of the fire of wrath, that you are held over in the hand of that God, whose wrath is provoked and incensed as much against you, as against many of the damned in hell. You hang by a slender thread, with the flames of divine wrath flashing about it, and ready every moment to singe it, and burn it asunder; and you have no interest in any Mediator, and nothing to lay hold of to save yourself, nothing to keep off the flames of wrath, nothing of your own, nothing that you ever have done, nothing that you can do, to induce God to spare you one moment. And consider here more particularly,

1. Whose wrath it is? It is the wrath of the infinite God. If it were only the wrath of man, though it were of the most potent prince, it would be comparatively little to be regarded. The wrath of kings is very much dreaded, especially of absolute monarchs, who have the possessions and lives of their subjects wholly in their power, to be disposed of at their mere will. Proverbs 20.2: "The fear of a king is as the roaring of a lion: Whoso provoketh him to anger, sinneth against his own soul." The subject that very much enrages an arbitrary prince, is liable to suffer the most extreme torments that human art can invent, or human power can inflict. But the greatest earthly potentates in their greatest majesty and strength, and when clothed in their greatest terrors, are but feeble, despicable worms of the dust, in comparison of the great and almighty Creator and King of heaven and earth. It is but little that they can do, when most enraged, and when they have exerted the utmost of their fury. All the kings of the earth, before God, are as grasshoppers; they are nothing, and less than nothing: both their love and their hatred is to be despised. The wrath of the great King of kings, is as much more terrible than theirs, as His majesty is greater. Luke 12.4–5: "And I say unto you, my friends, Be not afraid of them that kill the body, and after that, have no more that they can do. But I will forewarn you whom you shall fear: fear him, which after he hath killed, hath power to cast into hell: yea, I say unto you, Fear him."

2. It is the fierceness of His wrath that you are exposed to. We often read of the fury of God; as in Isaiah 59.18: "According to their deeds, accordingly he will repay fury to his adversaries." So Isaiah 66.15: "For behold, the Lord will come with fire, and with his chariots like a whirlwind, to render his anger with fury, and his rebuke with flames of fire." And in many other places. So, Revelation 19.15: we read of "the wine press of the fierceness and wrath of Almighty God." The words are exceeding terrible. If it had only been said, "the wrath of God," the words would have implied that which is infinitely dreadful: but it is "the fierceness and wrath of God." The fury of God! the fierceness of Jehovah![11] Oh, how dreadful must that be! Who can utter or conceive what such expressions carry in them! But it is also "the fierceness and wrath of Almighty God." As though there would be a very great manifestation of His almighty power in what the fierceness of His wrath should inflict, as though omnipotence should be as it were enraged, and exerted, as men are wont to exert their strength in the fierceness of their wrath. Oh! then, what will be the consequence! What will become of the poor worms that shall suffer it! Whose hands can be

[11]The God of the Old Testament.

strong? And whose heart can endure? To what a dreadful, inexpressible, inconceivable depth of misery must the poor creature be sunk who shall be the subject of this!

Consider this, you that are here present that yet remain in an unregenerate state. That God will execute the fierceness of His anger implies that He will inflict wrath without any pity. When God beholds the ineffable extremity of your case, and sees your torment to be so vastly disproportioned to your strength, and sees how your poor soul is crushed, and sinks down, as it were, into an infinite gloom; He will have no compassion upon you, He will not forbear the executions of His wrath, or in the least lighten His hand; there shall be no moderation or mercy, nor will God then at all stay His rough wind; He will have no regard to your welfare, nor be at all careful lest you should suffer too much in any other sense, than only that you shall not suffer beyond what strict justice requires. Nothing shall be withheld because it is so hard for you to bear. Ezekiel 8.18: "Therefore will I also deal in fury: mine eye shall not spare, neither will I have pity; and though they cry in mine ears with a loud voice, yet I will not hear them." Now God stands ready to pity you; this is a day of mercy; you may cry now with some encouragement of obtaining mercy. But when once the day of mercy is past, your most lamentable and dolorous cries and shrieks will be in vain; you will be wholly lost and thrown away of God as to any regard to your welfare. God will have no other use to put you to, but to suffer misery; you shall be continued in being to no other end; for you will be a vessel of wrath fitted to destruction; and there will be no other use of this vessel, but to be filled full of wrath. God will be so far from pitying you when you cry to Him, that it is said He will only "laugh and mock." Proverbs 1.25–26, etc.[12]

How awful are those words, Isaiah 63.3, which are the words of the great God: "I will tread them in mine anger, and will trample them in my fury, and their blood shall be sprinkled upon my garments, and I will stain all my raiment." It is perhaps impossible to conceive of words that carry in them greater manifestations of these three things, viz., contempt, and hatred, and fierceness of indignation. If you cry to God to pity you, He will be so far from pitying you in your doleful case, or showing you the least regard or favor, that instead of that, He will only tread you under foot. And though He will know that you cannot bear the weight of omnipotence treading upon you, yet He will not regard that, but He will crush you under His feet without mercy; He will crush out your blood, and make it fly and it shall be sprinkled on His garments, so as to stain all His raiment. He will not only hate you, but He will have you in the utmost contempt: no place shall be thought fit for you, but under His feet to be trodden down as the mire of the streets.

3. The misery you are exposed to is that which God will inflict to that end, that He might show what that wrath of Jehovah is. God hath had it on His heart to show to angels and men both how excellent His love is, and also how terrible His wrath is. Sometimes earthly kings have a mind to show how terrible their wrath is, by the extreme punishments they would execute on those that would provoke them. Nebuchadnezzar, that mighty and haughty monarch of the Chaldean empire, was willing

[12]"But ye have set at nought all my counsel, and would none of my reproof: I also will laugh at your calamity; I will mock you when your fear cometh."

to show his wrath when enraged with Shadrach, Meshech, and Abednego; and accordingly gave orders that the burning fiery furnace should be heated seven times hotter than it was before; doubtless, it was raised to the utmost degree of fierceness that human art could raise it.[13] But the great God is also willing to show His wrath, and magnify His awful majesty and mighty power in the extreme sufferings of His enemies. Romans 9.22: "What if God, willing to show his wrath, and to make his power known, endure with much long-suffering the vessels of wrath fitted to destruction?" And seeing this in His design, and what He has determined, even to show how terrible the restrained wrath, the fury and fierceness of Jehovah is, He will do it to effect. There will be something accomplished and brought to pass that will be dreadful with a witness. When the great and angry God hath risen up and executed His awful vengeance on the poor sinner, and the wretch is actually suffering the infinite weight and power of His indignation, then will God call upon the whole universe to behold that awful majesty and mighty power that is to be seen in it. Isaiah 33.12–14: "And the people shall be as the burnings of lime, as thorns cut up shall they be burnt in the fire. Hear ye that are far off, what I have done; yet that are near, acknowledge my might. The sinners in Zion are afraid; fearfulness hath surprised the hypocrites," etc.

Thus it will be with you that are in an unconverted state, if you continue in it; the infinite might, and majesty, and terribleness of the omnipotent God shall be magnified upon you, in the ineffable strength of your torments. You shall be tormented in the presence of the holy angels, and in the presence of the Lamb; and when you shall be in this state of suffering, the glorious inhabitants of heaven shall go forth and look on the awful spectacle, that they may see what the wrath and fierceness of the Almighty is; and when they have seen it, they will fall down and adore that great power and majesty. Isaiah 66.23–24: "And it shall come to pass, that from one new moon to another, and from one sabbath to another, shall flesh come to worship before me, saith the Lord. And they shall go forth and look upon the carcasses of the men that have transgressed against me; for their worm shall not die, neither shall their fire be quenched, and they shall be an abhorring unto all flesh."

4. It is everlasting wrath. It would be dreadful to suffer this fierceness and wrath of Almighty God one moment; but you must suffer it to all eternity. There will be no end to this exquisite horrible misery. When you look forward, you shall see a long forever, a boundless duration before you, which will swallow up your thoughts, and amaze your soul; and you will absolutely despair of ever having any deliverance, and end, any mitigation, any rest at all. You will know certainly that you must wear out long ages, millions of millions of ages, in wrestling and conflicting with this almighty merciless vengeance; and then when you have so done, when so many ages have actually been spent by you in this manner, you will know that all is but a point to what remains. So that your punishment will indeed be infinite. Oh, who can express what the state of a soul in such circumstances is! All that we can possibly say about it gives but a very feeble, faint representation of it; it is inexpressible and inconceivable: For "who knows the power of God's anger?"[14]

[13]Daniel 3:1–30.
[14]Psalm 90:11.

How dreadful is the state of those that are daily and hourly in the danger of this great wrath and infinite misery! But this is the dismal case of every soul in this congregation that has not been born again, however moral and strict, sober and religious, they may otherwise be. Oh that you would consider it, whether you be young or old! There is reason to think that there are many in this congregation now hearing this discourse that will actually be the subjects of this very misery to all eternity. We know not who they are, or in what seats they sit, or what thoughts they now have. It may be they are now at ease, and hear all these things without much disturbance, and are now flattering themselves that they are not the persons, promising themselves that they shall escape. If they knew that there was one person, and but one, in the whole congregation, that was to be the subject of this misery, what an awful thing would it be to think of! If we knew who it was, what an awful sight would it be to see such a person! How might all the rest of the congregation lift up a lamentable and bitter cry over him! But, alas! instead of one, how many is it likely will remember this discourse in hell? And it would be a wonder, if some that are now present should not be in hell in a very short time, even before this year is out. And it would be no wonder, if some persons, that now sit here, in some seats of this meetinghouse, in health, quiet and secure, should be there before tomorrow morning. Those of you that finally continue in a natural condition, that shall keep out of hell longest will be there in a little time! your damnation does not slumber; it will come swiftly, and, in all probability, very suddenly upon many of you. You have reason to wonder that you are not already in hell. It is doubtless the case of some whom you have seen and known, that never deserved hell more than you, and that heretofore appeared likely to have been now alive as you. Their case is past all hope; they are crying in extreme misery and perfect despair; but here you are in the land of the living and in the house of God, and have an opportunity to obtain salvation. What would not those poor damned hopeless souls give for one day's opportunity such as you now enjoy!

And now you have an extraordinary opportunity, a day wherein Christ has thrown the door of mercy wide open, and stands in calling and crying with a loud voice to poor sinners; a day wherein many are flocking to Him, and pressing into the kingdom of God. Many are daily coming from the east, west, north and south; many that were very lately in the same miserable condition that you are in are now in a happy state, with their hearts filled with love to Him who has loved them, and washed them from their sins in His own blood, and rejoicing in hope of the glory of God. How awful is it to be left behind at such a day! To see so many others feasting, while you are pining and perishing! To see so many rejoicing and singing for joy of heart, while you have cause to mourn for sorrow of heart, and howl for vexation of spirit! How can you rest one moment in such a condition? Are not your souls as precious as the souls of the people at Suffield,[15] where they are flocking from day to day to Christ?

Are there not many here who have lived long in the world, and are not to this day born again? and so are aliens from the commonwealth of Israel, and have done nothing ever since they have lived, but treasure up wrath against the day of wrath?

[15]"A town in the neighborhood" [Edwards's note].

Oh, sirs, your case, in an especial manner, is extremely dangerous. Your guilt and hardness of heart is extremely great. Do you not see how generally persons of your years are passed over and left, in the present remarkable and wonderful dispensation of God's mercy? You had need to consider yourselves, and awake thoroughly out of sleep. You cannot bear the fierceness and wrath of the infinite God. And you, young men, and young women, will you neglect this precious season which you now enjoy, when so many others of your age are renouncing all youthful vanities, and flocking to Christ? You especially have now an extraordinary opportunity; but if you neglect it, it will soon be with you as with those persons who spent all the precious days in youth in sin, and are now come to such a dreadful pass in blindness and hardness. And you, children, who are unconverted, do not you know that you are going down to hell, to bear the dreadful wrath of that God, who is now angry with you every day and every night? Will you be content to be the children of the devil, when so many other children in the land are converted, and are become the holy and happy children of the King of kings?

And let every one that is yet of Christ, and hanging over the pit of hell, whether they be old men and women, or middle-aged, or young people, or little children, now hearken to the loud calls of God's word and providence. This acceptable year of the Lord, a day of such great favors to some, will doubtless be a day of as remarkable vengeance to others. Men's hearts harden, and their guilt increases apace at such a day as this, if they neglect their souls; and never was there so great danger of such person being given up to hardness of heart and blindness of mind. God seems now to be hastily gathering in His elect in all parts of the land; and probably the greater part of adult persons that ever shall be saved, will be brought in now in a little time, and that it will be as it was on the great outpouring of the Spirit upon the Jews in the apostles' days;[16] the election will obtain, and the rest will be blinded. If this should be the case with you, you will eternally curse this day, and will curse the day that ever you was born, to see such a season of the pouring out of God's Spirit, and will wish that you had died and gone to hell before you had seen it. Now undoubtedly it is, as it was in the days of John the Baptist, the axe is in an extraordinary manner laid at the root of the trees,[17] that every tree which brings not forth good fruit, may be hewn down and cast into the fire.

Therefore, let everyone that is out of Christ, now awake and fly from the wrath to come. The wrath of Almighty God is now undoubtedly hanging over a great part of this congregation: Let everyone fly out of Sodom: "Haste and escape for your lives, look not behind you, escape to the mountain, lest you be consumed."[18]

1829–30

[16]Peter urged people to conversion, saying, "Save yourselves from this untoward generation. Then they that gladly received his word were baptized: and the same day there were added unto them about three thousand souls" (Acts 2:40–41).

[17]"And now also the axe is laid unto the root of the trees: therefore every tree which brings not forth good fruit is hewn down, and cast into the fire" (Matthew 3:10).

[18]Genesis 19:17.

Elizabeth Ashbridge 1713–1755

Although little is known about Elizabeth Ashbridge beyond what is recorded in her brief autobiography, *Some Account of the Fore Part of the Life of Elizabeth Ashbridge . . . Written by her own Hand many years ago* (1755), the narrative itself provides a portrait of a remarkable woman whose spiritual questing and marital trials reveal much about religious imperatives and gender roles in eighteenth-century American culture.

Born to Anglican parents in England, Ashbridge lived a rather adventurous adolescence. Eloping at fourteen, an act which prompted permanent estrangement from her authoritarian father, she became a widow within months of her marriage. Banished from her parents' home, she spent several years in Ireland, where she became a seeker after religious enlightenment. At nineteen she emigrated to the colonies as an indentured servant, hoping to begin a new life. The first part of the *Account* records these experiences and presents a protagonist who even as a young girl showed signs of the fervent independence and spiritual predilection which would mark her adult life as a convinced (that is, converted) Quaker.

Lamenting that the Anglican ministry was closed to women, she turned to other denominations but found little consolation among the Baptists, Presbyterians, and Catholics with whom she worshipped in search of spiritual truth. Her appeals to the priestly patriarchy of various churches were met with imperious indifference. Ashbridge's indenture to a cruel master whom she had taken for "a very religious man" augmented her sense of the hypocrisy of much that passed for piety; it also impelled her to buy her freedom and marry a worldly suitor named Sullivan who "fell in love with me for my dancing." Not long after, visiting Quaker relations in Pennsylvania, she embraced their religion, a commitment which profoundly changed her.

Despite her initial distaste for the practices of the Society of Friends who sanctioned—against her early ecclesiastical and social tradition—the preaching of women, Ashbridge was drawn to the beauty and eloquence of the faith, and her conversion is told with simple power. Her newfound spiritual mission made her a more somber and self-directed woman, alienating the husband who had loved her for her mirthful nature. The remainder of the narrative is a poignant account of Ashbridge's struggle to observe her new faith against the growing anger and abuse of her husband. It was not until the death of Sullivan, retold in the *Account,* and her eventual union with Aaron Ashbridge, himself a Quaker, that she found the marital and spiritual harmony she had for so long sought.

Elizabeth Ashbridge's *Account* underscores the importance of life-writing as a tool of female vindication in a patriarchal culture. For its candor and emotional power, for the integrity of the religious sensibility which it conveys, and for its illuminating portrayal of domestic relations in colonial America, the narrative merits a significant place in our literary history.

Liahna Babener
Montana State University

PRIMARY WORKS

Some Account of the Fore-Part of the Life of Elizabeth Ashridge, . . . Wrote by Herself, 1774; *Some Account of the Fore Part of the Life of Elizabeth Ashbridge, . . . Written by her own Hand many years ago,* ed. by Daniel B. Shea, 1990.

SECONDARY WORKS

Cristine M. Levenduski, *Elizabeth Ashbridge's "Remarkable Experiences": Creating the Self in a Quaker Personal Narrative,* 1989 (dissertation); Daniel B. Shea, ed., "Elizabeth Ashbridge and the Voice Within," in *Journeys in New Worlds: Early American Women's Narratives,* ed., William L. Andrews, et al., 1990.

from Some Account of the Fore Part of the Life of Elizabeth Ashbridge, . . . Written by her own Hand many years ago[1]

I now began to think of my Relations in Pennsylvania whom I had not yet seen; and having a great Desire that way, Got Leave of my Husband to go & also a Certificate from the Priest on Long Island in order that if I made any stay, I might be receiv'd as a Member wherever I came; Then Setting out, my husband bore me Company to the Blazing Star Ferry, saw me Safe over & then returned. On the way near a place called Maidenhead [New Jersey] I fell from my horse & I was Disabled from Traveling for some time: In the interval I abode at the house of an Honest Like Dutchman, who with his wife were very kind to me, & tho' they had much trouble going to the Doctor and waiting upon me, (for I was Several Days unable to help my self) yet would have nothing for it (which I thought Exceeding kind) but Charged me if ever I came that way again to call and Lodge there.—I mention this because by and by I shall have occasion to remark this Place again.

Hence I came to Trenton [New Jersey] Ferry, where I met with no small Mortification upon hearing that my Relations were Quakers, & what was the worst of all my Aunt a Preacher. I was Sorry to hear it, for I was Exceedingly prejudiced against these People & have often wondered with what face they Could Call them Selves Christians. I Repented my Coming and had a mind to have turned back. At Last I Concluded to go & see them since I was so far on my journey, but Expected little Comfort from my Visit. But see how God brings unforeseen things to Pass, for by my going there I was brought to my Knowledge of his Truth.—I went from Trenton to Philadelphia by Water, thence to my Uncle's on Horseback, where I met with very kind reception; for tho' my Uncle was dead and my Aunt married again, yet both her husband and She received me in a very kind manner.

I had not been there three Hours before I met with a Shock, & my opinion began to alter with respect to these People.—For seeing a Book lying on the Table (& being much for reading) I took it up: My Aunt Observing said, "Cousin that is a Quakers' Book," for Perceiving I was not a Quaker, I suppose she thought I would not like it: I made her no answer but revolving in my mind, "what can these People write about, for I have heard that they Deny the Scriptures & have no other bible but

[1]This text of the *Account* has been edited by Daniel B. Shea, in *Journeys in New Worlds: Early American Women's Narratives,* ed. W.L. Andrews, 1990.

George Fox's Journal,[2] & Deny all the holy Ordinances?" So resolved to read, but had not read two Pages before my very heart burned within me and Tears Issued from my Eyes, which I was Afraid would be seen; . . . I walked into the garden, sat Down, and the piece being Small, read it through before I went in; but Some Times was forced to Stop to Vent my Tears, my heart as it were uttering these involuntary Expressions; "my God must I (if ever I come to the true knowledge of thy Truth) be of this man's Opinion, who has sought thee as I have done & join with these People that a few hours ago I preferred the Papists before? O thou, the God of my Salvation & of my Life, who hast in an abundant manner manifested thy Long Suffering & tender Mercy, Redeeming me as from the Lowest Hell, a Monument of thy grace: Lord, my soul beseecheth thee to Direct me in the right way & keep me from Error, & then According to thy Covenant, I'll think nothing too near to Part with for thy name's Sake. If these things be so, Oh! happy People thus beloved of God."

After I came a little to my Self again I washed my face least any in the House should perceive I had been weeping. But this night got but Little Sleep, for the old Enemy began to Suggest that I was one of those that wavered & was not Steadfast in the faith, advancing several Texts of Scripture against me & them, as, in the Latter Days there should be those that would deceive the very Elect: & these were they, & that I was in danger of being deluded. Here the Subtile Serpent transformed himself so hiddenly that I verily believed this to be a timely Caution from a good Angel—so resolved to beware of the Deceiver, & for Some weeks Did not touch any of their Books.

The next Day being the first of the week I wanted to have gone to Church, which was Distant about four Miles, but being a Stranger and having nobody to go along with me, was forced to Give it out, & as most of the Family was going to Meeting, I went with them, but with a resolution not to like them, & so it was fully Suffered: for as they sat in silence I looked over the Meeting, thinking with my self, "how like fools these People sit, how much better would it be to stay at home & read the Bible or some good Book, than to come here and go to Sleep." For my Part I was very Sleepy & thought they were no better than my Self. Indeed at Length I fell a sleep, and had like to fallen Down, but this was the last time I ever fell asleep in a Meeting, Tho' often Assaulted with it.

Now I began to be lifted up with Spiritual Pride & thought my Self better than they, but thro' Mercy this did not Last Long, for in a Little time I was brought Low & saw that these were the People to whom I must join.—It may seem strange that I who had Lived so long with one of this Society in Dublin, should yet be so great a Stranger to them. In answer let it be Considered that During the time I was there I never read one of their Books nor went to one Meeting, & besides I had heard such ridiculous stories of them as made me Esteem them the worst of any Society of Peo-

[2]Englishman George Fox (1624–1691) was the founder of the Society of Friends and the initiator of the Quaker belief in "inner light" theology. Fox's *Journal,* originally published in 1694, recounted the many persecutions and incarcerations he endured as a result of his belief. It served as a sort of manifesto for Quakers and other religious dissenters who sought freedom of conscience.

ple; but God that knew the Sincerity of my heart looked with Pity on my Weakness & soon Let me see my Error.

In a few weeks there was an afternoon's Meeting held at my Uncle's to which came that Servant of the Lord Wm. Hammans who was made then Instrumental to the Convincing me of the truth more Perfectly, & helping me over Some great Doubts: tho' I believe no one did ever sit in Greater opposition than I did when he first stood up; but I was soon brought Down for he preached the Gospel with such Power I was forced to give up & Confess it was the truth. As soon as meeting Ended I Endeavoured to get alone, for I was not fit to be seen, I being So broken; yet afterward the Restless adversary assaulted me again, on this wise. In the morning before this meeting, I had been Disputing with my Uncle about Baptism, which was the subject this good Man[3] Dwelt upon, which was handled so Clearly as to answer all my Scruples beyond all objection: yet the Crooked Serpent alleged that the Sermon that I had heard did not proceed from divine Revelation but that my Uncle and Aunt had acquainted the Friend of me; which being Strongly Suggested, I fell to Accusing them with it, of which they both cleared themselves, saying they had not seen him Since my Coming into these Parts until he came into the meeting. I then Concluded he was a messenger sent of God to me, & with fervent Cryes Desired I might be Directed a right and now Laid aside all Prejudice & set my heart open to receive the truth in the Love of it. And the Lord in his own good time revealed to my Soul not only the Beauty there is in truth, & how those should shine that continue faithful to it, but also the Emptiness of all shadows, which in the day were Gloryous, but now he the Son of Glory was come to put an end to them all, & to Establish Everlasting Righteousness in the room thereof, which is a work in the Soul. He likewise let me see that all I had gone through was to prepare me for this Day & that the time was near that he would require me to go forth & declare to others what he the God of Mercy had done for my Soul; at which I was Surprized & begged to be Excused for fear I should bring dishonour to the truth, and cause his Holy name to be Evil spoken of.

All the while, I never Let any know the Condition I was in, nor did I appear like a Friend, & fear'd a Discovery. I now began to think of returning to my husband but found a restraint to stay where I was. I then Hired to keep School & hearing of a place for him, wrote desiring him to come to me, but Let him know nothing how it was with me. I loved to go to meetings, but did not like to be seen to go on week days, & therefore to Shun it used to go from my school through the Woods, but notwithstanding all my care the Neighbours that were not friends began to revile me, calling me Quaker, saying they supposed I intended to be a fool and turn Preacher; I then receiv'd the same censure that I (a little above a year before) had Passed on one of the handmaids of the Lord at Boston, & so weak was I, alas! I could not bear the reproach, & in order to Change their Opinions got into greater Excess in Apparel than I had freedom to Wear for some time before I came Acquainted with Friends.

In this Condition I continued till my Husband came, & then began the Tryal of my Faith. Before he reached me he heard I was turned Quaker, at which he stampt, saying, "I'd rather heard She had been dead as well as I Love her, for if so, all my

[3]The minister William Hammans.

comfort is gone." He then came to me & had not seen me before for four Months. I got up & met him saying, "My Dear, I am glad to see thee," at which he flew in a Passion of anger & said, "the Divel thee thee, don't thee me."[4] I used all the mild means I could to pacify him, & at Length got him fit to go & Speak to my Relations, but he was Alarmed, and as soon as we got alone said, "so I see your Quaker relations have made you one." I told him they had not, which was true, nor had I ever told him how it was with me: But he would have it that I was one, & therefore would not let me stay among them; & having found a place to his mind, hired and came Directly back to fetch me hence, & in one afternoon walked near thirty Miles to keep me from Meeting, the next Day being first Day;[5] & on the Morrow took me to the Afforesaid Place & hired Lodgings at a churchman's house; who was one of the Wardens, & a bitter Enemy to Friends & used to Do all he could to irritate my Husband against them, & would tell me abundance of Ridiculous Stuff; but my Judgement was too Clearly convinced to believe it.

I still did not appear like a Friend, but they all believed I was one. When my Husband and he Used to be making their Diversion & reviling, I used to sit in Silence, but now and then an involuntary Sigh would break from me: at which he would tell my husband: "there, did not I tell you that your wife was a Quaker; & She will be a preacher." Upon which My Husband once in a Great rage came up to me, & Shaking his hand over me, said, "you had better be hanged in that Day." I then, Peter like, in a panick denied my being a Quaker, at which great horror seized upon me, which Continued near three Months: so that I again feared that by Denying the Lord that Bought me, the heavens were Shut against me; for great Darkness Surrounded, & I was again plunged into Despair. I used to Walk much alone in the Wood, where no Eye saw nor Ear heard, & there Lament my miserable Condition, & have often gone from Morning till Night and have not broke my Fast.

Thus I was brought so Low that my Life was a burden to me; the Devil seem'd to Vaunt that tho' the Sins of my youth were forgiven, yet now he was sure of Me, for that I had Committed the unpardonable Sin & Hell inevitable would be my portion, & my Torment would be greater than if I had hanged my Self at first. In this Doleful State I had none to bewail my Doleful Condition; & Even in the Night when I Could not Sleep under the painful Distress of mind, if my husband perceived me weeping he would revile me for it. At Length when he and his Friends thought themselves too weak to over Set me (tho' I feared it was all ready done) he went to the Priest at Chester [Pennsylvania] to Advise what to Do with me. This man knew I was a member of the Church,[6] for I had Shewn him my Certificate: his advice was to take me out of Pennsylvania, and find some place where there was no Quakers; and then it would wear off. To this my Husband Agreed saying he did not Care where he went,

[4]In Ashbridge's day, Quakers employed the familiar "thee" and "thou," rather than "you," in everyday speech. Her use of the pronoun in her interchanges with her husband confirmed for him her following of Quaker belief and practice. Non-believers often disparaged Quakers for this linguistic practice.

[5]Quakers traditionally refer to the days of the week and the months of the year by numbers rather than the conventional names, associated with pagan deities.

[6]The Anglican Church.

if he Could but restore me to that Livelyness of Temper I was naturally of, & to that Church of which I was a member. I on my Part had no Spirit to oppose the Proposal, neither much cared where I was, For I seemed to have nothing to hope for, but Dayly Expected to be made a Spectacle of Divine Wrath, & was Possessed with a Thought that it would be by Thunder ere long.

The time of Removal came, & I must go. I was not Suffered to go to bid my Relations farewell; my husband was Poor & kept no horse, so I must travel on foot; we came to Wilmington [Delaware] (fifteen Miles) thence to Philadelphia by Water; here he took me to a Tavern where I soon became the Spectacle & discourse of the Company. My Husband told them, "my wife is a Quaker," & that he Designed if Possible to find out some Place where there was none. "O," thought I, "I was once in a Condition deserving that name, but now it is over with me. O! that I might from a true hope once more have an Opportunity to Confess to the truth;" tho' I was Sure of Suffering all manner of Crueltys, I would not Regard it.

These were my Concerns while he was Entertaining the Company with my Story, in which he told them that I had been a good Dancer, but now he Could get me neither to Dance nor Sing, upon which one of the Company stands up saying, "I'll go fetch my Fiddle, & we'll have a Dance," at which my husband was much pleased. The fiddle came, the sight of which put me in a sad Condition for fear if I Refused my husband would be in a great Passion: however I took up this resolution, not to Comply whatever be the Consequence. He comes to me, takes me by the hand saying, "come my Dear, shake off that Gloom, & let's have a civil Dance; you would now and then when you was a good Churchwoman, & that's better than a Stiff Quaker." I trembling desired to be Excused; but he Insisted on it, and knowing his Temper to be exceeding Cholerick, durst not say much, yet did not Consent. He then pluck'd me round the Room till Tears affected my Eyes, at Sight whereof the Musician Stopt and said, "I'll play no more, Let your wife alone," of which I was Glad.

There was also a man in Company who came from Freehold in East Jersey: he said, "I see your Wife is a Quaker, but if you will take my advice you need not go so far (for my husband's design was for Staten Island); come & live amongst us, we'll soon cure her of her Quakerism, for we want a School Master & Mistress Too" (I followed the Same Business); to which he agreed, & a happy turn it was for me, as will be seen by and by: and the Wonderfull turn of Providence, who had not yet Abandoned me, but raised a glimmering hope, affording the Answer of peace in refusing to Dance, for which I was more rejoyced than to be made Mistress of much Riches; & in floods of Tears said, "Lord, I dread to ask and yet without thy gracious Pardon I'm Miserable; I therefore fall Down before thy Throne, imploring Mercy at thine hand. O Lord once more I beseech thee, try my Obedience, & then what soever thou Commands, I will Obey, & not fear to Confess thee before men."

Thus was my Soul Engaged before God in Sincerity & he in tender Mercy heard my cries, & in me has Shewn that he Delights not in the Death of a Sinner, for he again set my mind at Liberty to praise him & I longed for an Opportunity to Confess to his Truth, which he shewed me should come, but in what manner I did not see, but believed the word that I had heard, which in a little time was fulfilled to me.—My Husband as afforesaid agreed to go to Freehold, & in our way thither we came to Maidenhead, where I went to see the kind Dutchman before mentioned, who made us welcome & Invited us to stay a day or Two.

While we were here, there was held a great Meeting of the Presbyterians, not only for Worship but Business also: for one of their preachers being Charged with Drunkenness, was this day to have his Trial before a great number of their Priests, &c. We went to it, of which I was afterwards glad. Here I perceived great Divisions among the People about who Should be their Shepherd: I greatly Pitied their Condition, for I now saw beyond the Men made Ministers, & What they Preached for: and which those at this Meeting might have done had not the prejudice of Education, which is very prevalent, blinded their Eyes. Some Insisted to have the old Offender restored, some to have a young man they had upon trial some weeks, a third Party was for sending for one from New England. At length stood up one & Directing himself to the Chief Speaker said "Sir, when we have been at the Expence (which will be no Small Matter) of fetching this Gentleman from New England, may be he'll not stay with us." *Answer,* "don't you know how to make him stay?" *Reply,* "no Sir." "I'll tell you then," said he (to which I gave good attention), "give him a good Salary & I'll Engage he'll Stay." "O" thought I, "these Mercenary creatures: they are all Actuated by one & the same thing, even the Love of Money, & not the regard of Souls." This (Called Reverend) Gentleman, whom these People almost adored, to my knowledge had left his flock on Long Island & moved to Philadelphia where he could get more money. I my self have heard some of them on the Island say that they almost Impoverished themselves to keep him, but not being able to Equal Philadelphia's Invitation he left them without a Shepherd. This man therefore, knowing their Ministry all proceeded from one Cause, might be purchased with the Same thing; surely these and Such like are the Shepherd that regards the fleece more than the flock, in whose mouths are Lies; saying the Lord had sent them, & that they were Christ's Ambassadors, whose Command to those he sent was, "Freely ye have receiv'd, freely give; & Blessed be his holy Name;" so they do to this day.

I durst not say any Thing to my Husband of the Remarks I had made, but laid them up in my heart, & they Served to Strengthen me in my Resolution. Hence we set forward to Freehold, & Coming through Stony Brook [New Jersey] my Husband turned towards me tauntingly & Said, "Here's one of Satan's Synagogues, don't you want to be in it? O I hope to See you Cured of this New Religion." I made no answer but went on, and in a little time, we came to a large run of Water over which was no Bridge, & being Strangers knew no way to escape it, but thro' we must go: he Carried over our Clothes, which we had in Bundles. I took off my Shoes and waded over in my Stockings, which Served some what to prevent the Chill of the Water, being Very Cold & a fall of Snow in the 12 Mo. My heart was Concerned in Prayer that the Lord would Sanctify all my Afflictions to me & give me Patience to bear whatsoever should be suffered to come upon me. We Walked the most part of a mile before we came to the first house, which was a sort of a Tavern. My husband Called for Some Spiritous Liquors, but I got some weakened Cider Mull'd, which when I had Drank of (the Cold being struck to my heart) made me Extremely sick, in so much that when we were a Little past the house I expected I should have Fainted, & not being able to stand, fell Down under a Fence. My husband Observing, tauntingly said, "What's the Matter now; what, are you Drunk; where is your Religion now?" He knew better & at that time I believe he Pitied me, yet was Suffered grievously to Afflict me. In a Little time I grew Better, & going on We came to another Tavern, where we Lodged: the next Day I was Indifferent well, so proceeded, and as we Journeyed a young man Driving an Empty Cart overtook us. I desired my husband to ask the young man to Let us Ride; he did, twas readily granted.

I now thought my Self well off, & took it as a great favour, for my Proud heart was humbled, & I did not regard the Looks of it, tho' the time had been that I would not have been seen in one; this Cart belonged to a man at Shrewsbury [New Jersey] & was to go thro' the place we Designed for, so we rode on (but soon had the Care of the team to our Selves from a failure in the Driver) to the place where I was Intended to be made a prey of; but see how unforeseen things are brought to Pass, by a Providential hand. Tis said and answered, "shall we do Evil that good may Come?" God forbid, yet hence good came to me. Here my husband would have had me Stay while we went to see the Team Safe at home: I Told him, no, since he had led me thro' the Country like a Vagabond, I would not stay behind him, so went on, & Lodged that Night at the man's house who owned the Team. Next morning in our Return to Freehold, we met a man riding on full Speed, who Stopping said to my Husband, "Sir, are you a School Master?" *Answer,* "Yes." "I came to tell you," replied the Stranger, "of Two new School Houses, & want a Master in Each, & are two miles apart." How this Stranger came to hear of us, who Came but the night before, I never knew, but I was glad he was not one Called a Quaker, Least my husband might have thought it had been a Plot; and then turning to my husband I said, "my Dear, look on me with Pity; if thou has any Affections left for me, which I hope thou hast, for I am not Conscious of having Done anything to Alienate them; here is (continued I) an Opportunity to Settle us both, for I am willing to do all in my Power towards getting an Honest Livelihood."

My Expressions took place, & after a Little Pause he consented, took the young man's Directions, & made towards the place, & in our way came to the house of a Worthy Friend, Whose wife was a Preacher, tho' we did not know it. I was Surprized to see the People so kind to us that were Strangers; we had not been long in the house till we were Invited to Lodge there that night, being the Last in the Week.—I said nothing but waited to hear my Master Speak; he soon Consented saying, "My wife has had a Tedious Travel & I pity her"; at which kind Expression I was Affected, for they Were now very Seldom Used to me. The friends' kindness could not proceed from my appearing in the Garb of a Quaker, for I had not yet altered my dress: The Woman of the house, after we had Concluded to Stay, fixed her Eyes upon me & Said, "I believe thou hast met with a deal of Trouble," to which I made but Little Answer. My husband, Observing they were of that sort of people he had so much Endeavoured to shun, would give us no Opportunity for any discourse that night, but the next morning I let the friend know a Little how it was with me. Meeting time came, to which I longed to go, but durst not ask my husband leave for fear of Disturbing him, till we were Settled, & then thought I, "if ever I am favoured to be in this Place, come Life or Death, I'll fight through, for my Salvation is at Stake." The Friend getting ready for Meeting, asked my husband if he would go, saying they knew who were to be his Employers, & if they were at Meeting would Speak to them. He then consented to go; then said the Woman Friend, "& wilt thou Let thy Wife go?," which he denied, making Several Objections, all which She answered so prudently that he Could not be angry, & at Last Consented; & with Joy I went, for I had not been at one for near four Months, & an Heavenly Meeting This was: I now renewed my Covenant & Saw the Word of the Lord made Good, that I should have another Opportunity to Confess his Name, for which my Spirit did rejoice in the God of my Salvation, who had brought Strange things to Pass: May I ever be preserved in Humility, never forgetting his tender Mercies to me.

Here According to my Desire we Settled; my husband got one School & I the Other, & took a Room at a Friend's house a Mile from Each School and Eight Miles from the Meeting House:—before next first day we were got to our new Settlement: & now Concluded to Let my husband to see I was determined to joyn with friends. When first day Came I directed my Self to him in this manner, "My Dear, art thou willing to let me go to a Meeting?," at which he flew into a rage, saying, "No you shan't." I then Drew up my resolution & told him as a Dutyfull Wife ought, So I was ready to obey all his Lawfull Commands, but where they Imposed upon my Conscience, I no longer Durst: For I had already done it too Long, & wronged my Self by it, & tho' he was near & I loved him as a Wife ought, yet God was nearer than all the World to me, & had made me sensible this was the way I ought to go, the which I Assured him was no Small Cross to my own will, yet had Given up My heart, & hoped that he that Called for it would Enable me the residue of my Life to keep it steadyly devoted to him, whatever I Suffered for it, adding I hoped not to make him any the worse Wife for it. But all I could Say was in vain; he was Inflexible & Would not Consent.

I had now put my hand to the Plough, & resolved not to Look back, so went without Leave; but Expected to be immediately followed & forced back, but he did not: I went to one of the neighbours & got a Girl to Show me the way, then went on rejoicing & Praising God in my heart, who had thus far given me Power & another Opportunity to Confess to his Truth. Thus for some time I had to go Eight Miles on foot to Meetings, which I never thought hard; My Husband soon bought a Horse, but would not Let me ride him, neither when my Shoes were worn out would he Let me have a new Pair, thinking by that means to keep me from going to meetings, but this did not hinder me, for I have taken Strings & tyed round to keep them on.

He finding no hard Usage could alter my resolution, neither threatening to beat me, nor doing it, for he several times Struck me with sore Blows, which I Endeavoured to bear with Patience, believing the time would Come when he would see I was in the right (which he Accordingly Did), he once came up to me & took out his pen knife saying, "if you offer to go to Meeting tomorrow, with this knife I'll cripple you, for you shall not be a Quaker." I made him no Answer, but when Morning came, set out as Usual & he was not Suffered to hurt me. In Despair of recovering me himself, he now flew to the Priest for help and told him I had been a very Religious Woman in the way of the Church of England, was a member of it, & had a good Certificate from Long Island, but now was bewitched and turn'd Quaker, which almost broke his heart. He therefore Desired as he was one who had the Care of souls, he would Come and pay me a Visit and use his Endeavours to reclaim me & hoped by the Blessing of God it would be done. The Priest Consented to Come, the time was Set, which was to be that Day two Weeks, for he said he could not come Sooner. My Husband Came home extremely Pleased, & told me of it, at which I smiled Saying, "I hope to be Enabled to give him a reason for the hope that is in me," at the same time believing the Priest would never Trouble me (nor ever did).

Before his Appointed time came it was required of me in a more Publick manner to Confess to the world what I was and to give up in Prayer in a Meeting, the sight of which & the power that attended it made me Tremble, & I could not hold my Self still. I now again desired Death & would have freely given up my Natural Life a Ransom; & what made it harder to me I was not yet taken under the care of Friends, & what kept me from requesting it was for fear I might be overcome & bring a Scandal on the Society. I begged to be Excused till I was joyned to Friends & then I would give up freely, to which I receiv'd this Answer, as tho' I had heard a Distinct Voice: "I am a Covenant keeping God, and the word that I spoke to thee when I found thee In Distress, even that I would never leave thee nor forsake thee If thou would be obedient to what I should make known to thee, I will Assuredly make good: but if thou refuse, my Spirit shall not always strive; fear not, I will make way for thee through all thy difficulties, which shall be many for my name's Sake, but be thou faithfull & I will give thee a Crown of Life." I being then Sure it was God that Spoke said, "thy will O God, be done, I am in thy hand; do with me according to thy Word," & gave up. But after it was over the Enemy came in like a flood, telling me I had done what I ought not, & Should now bring Dishonour to this People. This gave me a Little Shock, but it did not at this time Last Long.

This Day as Usual I had gone on foot. My Husband (as he afterwards told me) lying on the Bed at home, these Words ran thro' him, "Lord where shall I fly to shun thee &c." upon which he arose and seeing it Rain got his horse and Came to fetch me; and Coming just as the Meeting broke up, I got on horseback as quick as possible, least he Should hear what had happened. Nevertheless he heard of it, and as soon as we were got into the woods he began, saying, "What do you mean thus to make my Life unhappy? What, could you not be a Quaker without turning fool after this manner?" I Answered in Tears saying, "my Dear, look on me with Pity, if thou hast any. Canst thou think, that I in the Bloom of my Days, would bear all that thou knowest of & a great deal more than thou knowest not of if I did not believe it to be my Duty?" This took hold of him, & taking my hand he said, "Well, I'll E'en give you up, for I see it don't avail to Strive. If it be of God I can't over throw it, & if it be of your self it will soon fall." I saw tears stand in his Eyes, at which my heart was overcome with Joy, and I would not have Changed Conditions with a Queen.

I already began to reap the fruits of my Obedience, but my Tryal Ended not here, the time being up that the Priest was to come; but no Priest Appeared. My Husband went to fetch him, but he would not come, saying he was busy; which so Displeased my husband, that he'd never go to hear him more, & for Some time went to no place of Worship.—Now the Unwearied adversary found out another Scheme, and with it wrought so Strong that I thought all I had gone through but a little to this: It came upon me in such an unexpected manner, in hearing a Woman relate a book she had read in which it was Asserted that Christ was not the son of God. As soon as She had Spoke these words, if a man had spoke I could not have more distinctly heard these words, "no more he is, it's all a fancy & the Contrivance of men," & an horrour of Great Darkness fell upon me, which Continued for three weeks.

The Exercise I was under I am not Able to Express, neither durst I let any know how it was with me. I again sought Desolate Places where I might make my moan, & have Lain whole nights, & don't know that my Eyes were Shut to Sleep. I again thought my self alone, but would not let go my Faith in him, often saying in my heart, "I'll believe till I Die," & kept a hope that he that had Delivered me out of the Paw of the Bear & out of the jaws of the Devouring Lion, would in his own time Deliver me out of his temptation also; which he in Mercy Did, and let me see that this was for my good, in order to Prepare me for future Service which he had for me to Do & that it was Necessary his Ministers should be dipt into all States, that thereby they might be able to Speak to all Conditions, for which my Soul was thankfull to him, the God of Mercies, who had at Several times redeemed me from great distress, & I found the truth of his Words, that all things should work together for good to those that Loved & feared him, which I did with my whole heart & hope ever shall while I have a being. This happened just after my first appearance, & Friends had not been to talk with me, nor did they know well what to do till I had appeared again, which was not for some time, when the Monthly Meeting appointed four Friends to give me a Visit, which I was Glad of; and gave them Such Satisfaction, that they left me well Satisfy'd. I then joyned with Friends.

My Husband still went to no place of Worship. One day he said, "I'd go to Meeting, only I am afraid I shall hear you Clack, which I cannot bear." I used no persuasions, yet when Meeting time Came, he got the horse, took me behind him & went to Meeting: but for several months if he saw me offer to rise, he would go out, till once I got up before he was aware and then (as he afterwards said) he was ashamed to go, & from that time never did, nor hindered me from going to Meetings. And tho' he (poor man) did not take up the Cross, yet his judgement was Convinced: & sometimes in a flood of tears would say, "My Dear, I have seen the Beauty there is in the Truth, & that thou art in the Right, and I Pray God Preserve thee in it. But as for me the Cross is too heavy, I cannot Bear it." I told him, I hoped he that had given me strength Would also favour him: "O!" said he, "I can't bear the Reproach thou Doest, to be Called turncoat & to become a Laughing Stock to the World; but I'll no Longer hinder thee," which I looked on as a great favour, that my way was thus far made easy, and a little hope remained that my Prayers would be heard on his account.

In this Place he had got linked in with some, that he was afraid would make game of him, which Indeed they already Did, asking him when he Designed to Commence Preacher, for that they saw he Intended to turn Quaker, & seemed to Love his Wife better since she did than before (we were now got to a little house by our Selves which tho' Mean, & little to put in it, our Bed no better than Chaff, yet I was truly Content & did not Envy the Rich their Riches; the only Desire I had now was my own preservation, & to be Bless'd with the Reformation of my husband). These men used to Come to our house & there Provoke my husband to Sit up and Drink, some times till near day, while I have been sorrowing in a Stable. As I once sat in this Condition I heard my husband say to his Company, "I can't bear any Longer to Afflict my Poor Wife in this manner, for whatever you may think of her, I do believe she is a good Woman," upon which he came to me and said, "Come in, my Dear; God has Given thee a Deal of Patience. I'll put an End to this Practice;" and so he did, for this was the Last time they sat up at Night.

My Husband now thought that if he was in any Place where it was not known that he'd been so bitter against Friends, he Could do better than here. But I was much against his Moving; fearing it would tend to his hurt, having been for some months much Altered for the Better, & would often in a broken and Affectionate Manner condemn his bad Usage to me: I told him I hoped it had been for my Good, even to the Better Establishing me in the Truth, & therefore would not have him to be Afflicted about it, & According to the Measure of Grace received did what I could both by Example and advice for his good: & my Advice was for him to fight thro' here, fearing he would Grow Weaker and the Enemy Gain advantage over him, if he thus fled: but All I could say did not prevail against his Moving; & hearing of a place at Bordentown [New Jersey] went there, but that did not suit; he then Moved to Mount Holly [New Jersey] & there we Settled. He got a good School & So Did I.

Here we might have Done very well; we soon got our house Prettily furnished for Poor folks; I now began to think I wanted but one thing to complete my Happiness, Viz. the Reformation of my husband, which Alas! I had too much reason to Doubt; for it fell out according to my Fears, & he grew worse here, & took much to Drinking, so that it Seem'd as if my Life was to be a Continual scene of Sorrows & most Earnestly I Pray'd to Almighty God to Endure me with Patience to bear my Afflictions & submit to his Providence, which I can say in Truth I did without murmuring or ever uttering an unsavoury expression to the Best of my Knowledge; except once, my husband Coming home a little in drink (in which frame he was very fractious) & finding me at Work by a Candle, came to me, put it out & fetching me a box on the Ear said, "you don't Earn your light;" on which unkind Usage (for he had not struck me for Two Years so it went hard with me) I utter'd these Rash Expressions, "thou art a Vile Man," & was a little angry, but soon recovered & was Sorry for it; he struck me again, which I received without so much as a word in return, & that likewise Displeased him: so he went on in a Distracted like manner uttering Several Expressions that bespoke Despair, as that he now believed that he was predestinated to damnation, & he did not care how soon God would Strike him Dead, & the like. I durst say but Little; at Length in the Bitterness of my Soul, I Broke out in these Words, "Lord look Down on mine Afflictions and deliver me by some means or Other." I was answered, I Should Soon be, & so I was, but in such a manner, as I Verily thought It would have killed me.—In a little time he went to Burlington where he got in Drink, & Enlisted him Self to go a Common soldier to Cuba anno 1740.

I had drank many bitter Cups—but this Seemed to Exceed them all for indeed my very Senses Seemed Shaken; I now a Thousand times blamed my Self for making Such an unadvised request, fearing I had Displeased God in it, & tho' he had Granted it, it was in Displeasure, & Suffered to be in this manner to Punish me; Tho' I can truly say I never Desired his Death, no more than my own, nay not so much. I have since had cause to believe his mind was benefitted by the Undertaking, (which hope makes up for all I have Suffered from him) being Informed he did in the army what he Could not Do at home (Viz) Suffered for the Testimony of Truth. When they Came to prepare for an Engagement, he refused to fight; for which he was whipt and brought before the General, who asked him why he Enlisted if he would not fight; "I did it," said he, "in a drunken frolick, when the Divel had the Better of me, but my judgment is convinced that I ought not, neither will I whatever I Suffer; I have but one Life, & you may take that if you Please, but I'll never take up Arms."—They used him with much Cruelty to make him yield but Could not, by means whereof he was So Disabled that the General sent him to the Hospital at Chelsea,[7] where in Nine Months time he Died & I hope made a Good End, for which I prayed both night & Day, till I heard of his Death.

[7]In what is now London, England.

Thus I thought it my duty to say what I could in his Favour, as I have been obliged to say so much of his hard usage to me, all which I hope Did me good, & altho' he was so bad, yet had Several Good Properties, & I never thought him the Worst of Men. He was one I Lov'd & had he let Religion have its Perfect work, I should have thought my Self Happy in the Lowest State of Life; & I've Cause to bless God, who Enabled me in the Station of a Wife to Do my Duty & now a Widow to Submit to his Will, always believing everything he doeth to be right. May he in all Stations of Life so Preserve me by the arm of Divine Power, that I may never forget his tender mercies to me, the Rememberance whereof doth often Bow my Soul, in Humility before his Throne, saying, "Lord, what was I; that thou should have reveal'd to me the Knowledge of thy Truth, & do so much for me, who Deserved thy Displeasure rather, But in me hast thou shewn thy Long Suffering & tender Mercy; may thou O God be Glorifyed and I abased for it is thy own Works that praise thee, and of a Truth to the humble Soul thou Makest every bitter thing Sweet.—The End.—

1755

John Woolman 1720–1772

John Woolman, sometimes referred to as the "Quaker Saint," was born near the Rancocas River in Burlington County, New Jersey (then West Jersey). His family on both sides had strong roots in the Quaker colony they had helped to settle and then to shape. One of thirteen children, Woolman grew up surrounded by a large and supportive family, and he early displayed a sensitivity for spiritual matters and a love for nature and Quaker traditions. Like many eighteenth-century Quakers, Woolman had a limited formal education, but he nonetheless valued learning, and evidence suggests that his reading extended far beyond the list of books normally prescribed to members of the Society of Friends, as Quakers are officially called.

In 1749, Woolman married Sarah Ellis, from neighboring Chesterfield. Little is known about Ellis except Woolman's famous description of her in his *Journal* as "a well inclined damsel," but there is no information to suggest that their marriage was anything but an extremely felicitous one. The couple eventually had two children, but only one, a daughter, survived into adulthood. Prior to his marriage, Woolman had assisted a local tailor. His success in that endeavor led him to establish a business of his own in Mount Holly, New Jersey, where he also managed a large farm and tended to occasional jobs such as writing legal documents and, for a time, even teaching. Because of his well-deserved reputation for honesty and industry, Woolman found himself becoming wealthy, and his business expanded at a rate that gave him cause for reflection. Fearing that inordinate wealth and excessive involvement in business endangered his soul by drawing his attention too much into worldly matters, Woolman decided early in his marriage to curtail his business activities, limiting them to what was essential for the support of his family. Eventually Woolman gave up mercantile trade altogether and devoted his energies almost exclusively to his family, his farm, and his work as a Quaker spokesperson.

While it may indeed appear radical by modern standards and while his action certainly did not conform with the values extolled by his contemporary Benjamin Franklin in such works as *Poor Richard's Almanac* or the *Autobiography,* Woolman's deliberate withdrawal from the world of commerce is consistent with Quaker beliefs that life should be conducted in a simple and direct manner and that the internal world of things spiritual should always take precedence over the external world of things material. Above all, Quakers, whose beginnings can be traced back to the Reformation teachings of George Fox during the seventeenth century, believe that all individuals harbor within themselves an innate sense of right and wrong which they term the "Inner Light." It is the responsibility of the individual, Quakers believe, to cultivate the workings of the "Inner Light" by removing oneself from all unnecessary distractions and encumbrances. In line with this reasoning, Quakers of Woolman's day, like Quakers of today, attempted to practice a simple lifestyle based on hard work, frugality, and contemplation. When politics or business entanglements encroach on their quest for inner harmony, Quakers are simply encouraged to withdraw from the source of conflict. Such was the case, for example, in 1756, when, at the outbreak of the French and Indian War, a tax imposed by the Pennsylvania legislature for purposes of military defence conflicted with Quaker commitments to pacifism, causing Quaker leaders throughout the colony to resign from their government positions.

Even Quaker worship is designed so as to minimize external distractions. Unlike their Puritan, Presbyterian, and Anglican neighbors to the north and south, the Quakers of the Middle Colonies shunned traditional rituals. The typical Quaker meeting, as it was called, consisted simply of a quiet gathering, with men and boys seated on one side of the room and women and girls on the other. If during the meeting a member of the group should feel an inner urging or "prompting" to address the assembly, that person would stand and speak. Sometimes, however, Quaker meetings passed in total silence. Quakers also distance themselves from the concept of an organized clergy. If after several meetings a particular individual is recognized for having spoken frequently and wisely on behalf of the spirit, that person, whether male or female, is accorded local recognition as a minister but is not required to undergo ordination or even for that matter any formalized process of theological instruction.

While he was yet in his early twenties, Woolman showed signs of a special ministerial calling and was acknowledged a minister by the community of Quakers where he lived. In the years to follow, Woolman pursued his calling to wherever his "Inner Light" led him, traveling thousands of miles, often on foot, throughout the colonies and eventually to England. The main focus of his ministry was the abolition of slavery, which he denounced as a "dark gloominess hanging over the land" and an unspeakable injustice. Woolman's abhorrence of slavery began early in life when the man to whom he was apprenticed asked him to write a bill of sale for a slave belonging to a senior member of the Quakers. His dislike of slavery continued to grow, especially after he had labored in the South and seen at first hand the degradation that slavery brought to both slave and slaveholder alike. Always quiet and persistent in his determination to convince the world that slavery and Christianity were totally incompatible, Woolman illustrated through his own conduct the principles of compassion and goodwill that formed the central message of his itinerant ministry. He refused, for example, to use sugar products or dyes because these items were obtained largely through a reliance on slave labor, and during his travels he insisted on paying a remuneration to any slaves who worked in homes where he lodged. Such behavior was his special way of drawing attention to his convictions, and it was apparently not without effect, for he records in the *Journal* instances where he was successful in altering the hearts of slaveholders he encountered.

In addition to his work on behalf of abolition, Woolman championed the rights of the Indians and the poor. On the eve of Pontiac's war with the colonies, Woolman journeyed on a mission of peace to the Wyalusing Indians of western Pennsylvania. Woolman was never in good health, and throughout this trip he was frequently in danger of his life from both the hostilities that surrounded him and the primitive living conditions he of necessity endured. Nonetheless, he persisted in his mission and was well received by the Indians. After observing the situation of the Indians and listening to their grievances, Woolman returned home with a severe indictment of frontier traders, on whose greed in selling rum to the Indians he blamed the war then taking place. Eventually Woolman's compassion for the downtrodden led him to England, where he died of smallpox on October 7, 1772, just a few months after his arrival.

As a writer, Woolman is best remembered today for the *Journal* that he kept intermittently between 1756 and his death. Published posthumously by the Society of Friends in 1774, Woolman's *Journal* is but one of many first-person accounts of the lives of pious eighteenth-century American Quakers; indeed, it participates in a tradition of journal-writing begun by George Fox himself and continues to the present. It is generally acknowledged, however, that Woolman's *Journal* stands out among others in the genre for its remarkable sense of clarity and conviction; for this reason alone, popular interest in the *Journal* has never slackened.

Woolman's *Journal* is much more than a cultural document about the life and wisdom of a truly remarkable man who labored untiringly and unselfishly to rectify injustices and establish social tranquility. The lasting appeal of the *Journal* ultimately rests in the fact that its self-effacing humility and genuine expression of love transcend the limitations of time and space and speak, as few works do, to every generation about the potential and the failures of the human condition. Furthermore, the *Journal* aptly articulates the essential elements of Quaker humanism. Because Woolman's love for humanity crossed over barriers of sex, race, and religion, few people can read his *Journal* without being moved by the simple life of conviction and compassion it records.

James A. Levernier
University of Arkansas at Little Rock

PRIMARY WORKS

Considerations on the Keeping of Negroes, 1754; *Journal,* 1774; *A Plea for the Poor,* 1793; *The Journal and Major Essays of John Woolman,* ed. Phillips Moulton, 1971.

SECONDARY WORKS

Janet Whitney, *John Woolman: American Quaker,* 1942; Phillips P. Moulton, "John Woolman: Exemplar of Ethics," *Quaker History,* 54, 1965:81–93; Edwin H. Cady, *John Woolman,* 1966; Paul Rosenblatt, *John Woolman,* 1969; Phillips P. Moulton, ed., "Introduction," *The Journal and Major Essays of John Woolman,* 1971.

from The Journal of John Woolman[1]

[Early Life and Vocation]

I have often felt a motion of love to leave some hints in writing of my experience of the goodness of God, and now, in the thirty-sixth year of my age, I begin this work. I was born in Northampton, in Burlington County in West Jersey, A.D. 1720, and before I was seven years old I began to be acquainted with the operations of divine love. Through the care of my parents, I was taught to read near as soon as I was capable of it, and as I went from school one Seventh Day,[2] I remember, while my companions went to play by the way, I went forward out of sight; and sitting down, I read the twenty-second chapter of the Revelations: "He showed me a river of water, clear as crystal, proceeding out of the throne of God and the Lamb, etc." And in reading it my mind was drawn to seek after that pure habitation which I then believed God had prepared for His servants. The place where I sat and the sweetness that attended my mind remains fresh in my memory.

This and the like gracious visitations[3] had that effect upon me, that when boys used ill language it troubled me, and through the continued mercies of God I was preserved from it. The pious instructions of my parents were often fresh in my mind when I happened amongst wicked children, and was of use to me. My parents, having a large family of children, used frequently on First Days after meeting[4] to put to read in the Holy Scriptures or some religious books, one after another, the rest sitting by without much conversation, which I have since often thought was a good practice. From what I had read and heard, I believed there had been in past ages people who walked in uprightness before God in a degree exceeding any that I knew, or heard of, now living; and the apprehension of there being less steadiness and firmness amongst people in this age than in past ages often troubled me while I was a child.

I had a dream about the ninth year of my age as follows: I saw the moon rise near the west and run a regular course eastward, so swift that in about a quarter of an hour she reached our meridian, when there descended from her a small cloud on a direct line to the earth, which lighted on a pleasant green about twenty yards from the door of my father's house (in which I thought I stood) and was immediately turned into a beautiful green tree. The moon appeared to run on with equal swiftness and soon set in the east, at which time the sun arose at the place where it commonly does in the summer, and shining with full radiance in a serene air, it appeared as pleasant a morning as ever I saw.

[1]Woolman's journal was first published in 1774. The source of this text is Phillips Moulton's edition, *The Journal and Major Essays of John Woolman,* 1971.

[2]Saturday. During Woolman's day, Quakers, or members of the Society of Friends, did not use the seven weekday names, which derive from the names of pagan gods.

[3]Moments when he experienced the felt presence of God.

[4]Quakers worship at "meeting," when they gather together for common prayer, but not for actual church service. Typically, those gathered together remain silent until a motion to speak emerges in a worshiper.

All this time I stood still in the door in an awful frame of mind, and I observed that as heat increased by the rising sun, it wrought so powerfully on the little green tree that the leaves gradually withered; and before noon it appeared dry and dead. There then appeared a being, small of size, full of strength and resolution, moving swift from the north, southward, called a sun worm.[5]

Another thing remarkable in my childhood was that once, going to a neighbor's house, I saw on the way a robin sitting on her nest; and as I came near she went off, but having young ones, flew about and with many cries expressed her concern for them. I stood and threw stones at her, till one striking her, she fell down dead. At first I was pleased with the exploit, but after a few minutes was seized with horror, as having in a sportive way killed an innocent creature while she was careful for her young. I beheld her lying dead and thought those young ones for which she was so careful must now perish for want of their dam to nourish them; and after some painful considerations on the subject, I climbed up the tree, took all the young birds and killed them, supposing that better than to leave them to pine away and die miserably, and believed in this case that Scripture proverb was fulfilled, "The tender mercies of the wicked are cruel."[6] I then went on my errand, but for some hours could think of little else but the cruelties I had committed, and was much troubled.

Thus He whose tender mercies are over all His works hath placed a principle in the human mind which incites to exercise goodness toward every living creature; and this being singly attended to, people become tender-hearted and sympathizing, but being frequently and totally rejected, the mind shuts itself up in a contrary disposition.

About the twelfth year of my age, my father being abroad, my mother reproved me for some misconduct, to which I made an undutiful reply; and the next First Day as I was with my father returning from meeting, he told me he understood I had behaved amiss to my mother and advised me to be more careful in future. I knew myself blameable, and in shame and confusion remained silent. Being thus awakened to a sense of my wickedness, I felt remorse in my mind, and getting home I retired and prayed to the Lord to forgive me, and do not remember that I ever after that spoke unhandsomely to either of my parents, however foolish in other things.

Having attained the age of sixteen years, I began to love wanton company, and though I was preserved from profane language or scandalous conduct, still I perceived a plant in me which produced much wild grapes. Yet my merciful Father forsook me not utterly, but at times through His grace I was brought seriously to consider my ways, and the sight of my backsliding affected me with sorrow. But for want of rightly attending to the reproofs of instruction, vanity was added to vanity, and repentance to repentance; upon the whole my mind was more and more alienated from the Truth, and I hastened toward destruction. While I meditate on the gulf toward which I travelled and reflect on my youthful disobedience, for these things I weep; mine eye runneth down with water.

Advancing in age the number of my acquaintance increased, and thereby my way grew more difficult. Though I had heretofore found comfort in reading the Holy

[5]This is an imagined event.
[6]Proverbs 12:10.

Scriptures and thinking on heavenly things, I was now estranged therefrom. I knew I was going from the flock of Christ and had no resolution to return; hence serious reflections were uneasy to me and youthful vanities and diversions my greatest pleasure. Running in this road I found many like myself, and we associated in that which is reverse to true friendship.

But in this swift race it pleased God to visit me with sickness, so that I doubted of recovering. And then did darkness, horror, and amazement with full force seize me, even when my pain and distress of body was very great. I thought it would have been better for me never to have had a being than to see the day which I now saw. I was filled with confusion, and in great affliction both of mind and body I lay and bewailed myself. I had not confidence to lift up my cries to God, whom I had thus offended, but in a deep sense of my great folly I was humbled before Him, and at length that Word which is as a fire and a hammer broke and dissolved my rebellious heart. And then my cries were put up in contrition, and in the multitude of His mercies I found inward relief, and felt a close engagement that if He was pleased to restore my health, I might walk humbly before Him.

After my recovery this exercise[7] remained with me a considerable time; but by degrees giving way to youthful vanities, they gained strength, and getting with wanton[8] young people I lost ground. The Lord had been very gracious and spoke peace to me in the time of my distress, and I now most ungratefully turned again to folly, on which account at times I felt sharp reproof but did not get low enough to cry for help. I was not so hardy as to commit things scandalous, but to exceed in vanity and promote mirth was my chief study. Still I retained a love and esteem for pious people, and their company brought an awe upon me.

My dear parents several times admonished me in the fear of the Lord, and their admonition entered into my heart and had a good effect for a season, but not getting deep enough to pray rightly, the tempter when he came found entrance. I remember once, having spent a part of the day in wantonness, as I went to bed at night there lay in a window near my bed a Bible, which I opened, and first cast my eye on the text, "We lie down in our shame, and our confusion covers us."[9] This I knew to be my case, and meeting with so unexpected a reproof, I was somewhat affected with it and went to bed under remorse of conscience, which I soon cast off again.

Thus time passed on; my heart was replenished with mirth and wantonness, while pleasing scenes of vanity were presented to my imagination till I attained the age of eighteen years, near which time I felt the judgments of God in my soul like a consuming fire, and looking over my past life the prospect was moving. I was often sad and longed to be delivered from those vanities; then again my heart was strongly inclined to them, and there was in me a sore conflict. At times I turned to folly, and then again sorrow and confusion took hold of me. In a while I resolved totally to leave off some of my vanities, but there was a secret reserve in my heart of the more refined part of them, and I was not low enough to find true peace. Thus for some months I had great trouble, there remaining in me an unsubjected will which rendered my labours fruitless, till at length through the merciful continuance of heavenly visitations I was made to bow down in spirit before the Lord.

[7]Religious outpouring.
[8]Shallow, frivolous.
[9]Jeremiah 3:25.

I remember one evening I had spent some time in reading a pious author, and walking out alone I humbly prayed to the Lord for His help, that I might be delivered from all those vanities which so ensnared me. Thus being brought low, He helped me; and as I learned to bear the cross I felt refreshment to come from His presence; but not keeping in that strength which gave victory, I lost ground again, the sense of which greatly affected me; and I sought deserts and lonely places and there with tears did confess my sins to God and humbly craved help of Him. And I may say with reverence He was near to me in my troubles, and in those times of humiliation opened my ear to discipline.

I was now led to look seriously at the means by which I was drawn from the pure Truth, and learned this: that if I would live in the life which the faithful servants of God lived in, I must not go into company as heretofore in my own will, but all the cravings of sense must be governed by a divine principle. In times of sorrow and abasement these instructions were sealed upon me, and I felt the power of Christ prevail over selfish desires, so that I was preserved in a good degree of steadiness. And being young and believing at that time that a single life was best for me, I was strengthened to keep from such company as had often been a snare to me.

I kept steady to meetings, spent First Days after noon chiefly in reading the Scriptures and other good books, and was early convinced in my mind that true religion consisted in an inward life, wherein the heart doth love and reverence God the Creator and learn to exercise true justice and goodness, not only toward all men but also toward the brute creatures; that as the mind was moved on an inward principle to love God as an invisible, incomprehensible being, on the same principle it was moved to love Him in all His manifestations in the visible world; that as by His breath the flame of life was kindled in all animal and sensitive creatures, to say we love God as unseen and at the same time exercise cruelty toward the least creature moving by His life, or by life derived from Him, was a contradiction in itself.

I found no narrowness respecting sects and opinions, but believed that sincere, upright-hearted people in every Society who truly loved God were accepted of Him.

As I lived under the cross and simply followed the openings of Truth,[10] my mind from day to day was more enlightened; my former acquaintance was left to judge of me as they would, for I found it safest for me to live in private and keep these things sealed up in my own breast.

While I silently ponder on that change wrought in me, I find no language equal to it nor any means to convey to another a clear idea of it. I looked upon the works of God in this visible creation and an awfulness covered me; my heart was tender and often contrite, and a universal love to my fellow creatures increased in me. This will be understood by such who have trodden in the same path. Some glances of real beauty may be seen in their faces who swell in true meekness. There is a harmony in the sound of that voice to which divine love gives utterance, and some appearance of right order in their temper and conduct whose passions are fully regulated. Yet all

[10]That is, as he remained mindful of Christ's humble sacrifice and awaited the felt experience of God. Quakers called their perceived messages from God "openings."

these do not fully show forth that inward life to such who have not felt it, but this white stone and new name is known rightly to such only who have it.[11]

Now though I had been thus strengthened to bear the cross, I still found myself in great danger, having many weaknesses attending me and strong temptations to wrestle with, in the feelings whereof I frequently withdrew into private places and often with tears besought the Lord to help me, whose gracious ear was open to my cry.

All this time I lived with my parents and wrought on the plantation, and having had schooling pretty well for a planter, I used to improve in winter evenings and other leisure times. And being now in the twenty-first year of my age, a man in much business shopkeeping and baking asked me if I would hire with him to tend shop and keep books. I acquainted my father with the proposal, and after some deliberation it was agreed for me to go.

At home I had lived retired, and now having a prospect of being much in the way of company, I felt frequent and fervent cries in my heart to God, the Father of Mercies, that He would preserve me from all taint and corruption, that in this more public employ I might serve Him, my gracious Redeemer, in that humility and self-denial with which I had been in a small degree exercised in a very private life.

The man who employed me furnished a shop in Mount Holly, about five miles from my father's house and six from his own, and there I lived alone and tended his shop. Shortly after my settlement here I was visited by several young people, my former acquaintance, who knew not but vanities would be as agreeable to me now as ever; and at these times I cried to the Lord in secret for wisdom and strength, for I felt myself encompassed with difficulties and had fresh occasion to bewail the follies of time past in contracting a familiarity with a libertine people. And as I had now left my father's house outwardly, I found my Heavenly Father to be merciful to me beyond what I can express.

By day I was much amongst people and had many trials to go through, but in evenings I was mostly alone and may with thankfulness acknowledge that in those times the spirit of supplication was often poured upon me, under which I was frequently exercised and felt my strength renewed.

In a few months after I came here, my master bought several Scotch menservants from on board a vessel and brought them to Mount Holly to sell,[12] one of which was taken sick and died. The latter part of his sickness he, being delirious, used to curse and swear most sorrowfully, and after he was buried I was left to sleep alone the next night in the same chamber where he died. I perceived in me a timorousness. I knew, however, I had not injured the man but assisted in taking care of him according to my capacity, and was not free to ask anyone on that occasion to sleep with me. Nature was feeble, but every trial was a fresh incitement to give myself up wholly to the service of God, for I found no helper like Him in times of trouble.

[11]"To him that overcometh will I give to eat of the hidden manna, and will I give him a white stone, and in the stone a new name written, which no man knoweth saving he that receiveth it": Revelation 2:17.

[12]That is, the man for whom Woolman worked bought the indentures of some Scottish men. Laborers commonly contracted to work for a negotiated amount of years, in order to "pay" for their passage to America. The contracts, often taken by shipmasters, would be re-negotiated upon arrival in America.

After a while my former acquaintance gave over expecting me as one of their company, and I began to be known to some whose conversation was helpful to me. And now, I had experienced the love of God through Jesus Christ to redeem me from many pollutions and to be a succour to me through a sea of conflicts, with which no person was fully acquainted, and as my heart was often enlarged in this heavenly principle, I felt a tender compassion for the youth who remained entangled in snares like those which had entangled me. From one month to another this love and tenderness increased, and my mind was more strongly engaged for the good of my fellow creatures.

I went to meetings in an awful frame of mind and endeavoured to be inwardly acquainted with the language of the True Shepherd. And one day being under a strong exercise of spirit, I stood up and said some words in a meeting, but not keeping close to the divine opening, I said more than was required of me; and being soon sensible of my error, I was afflicted in mind some weeks without any light or comfort, even to that degree that I could take satisfaction in nothing. I remembered God and was troubled, and in the depth of my distress He had pity upon me and sent the Comforter. I then felt forgiveness for my offense, and my mind became calm and quiet, being truly thankful to my gracious Redeemer for His mercies.[13] And after this, feeling the spring of divine love opened and a concern to speak, I said a few words in a meeting, in which I found peace. This I believe was about six weeks from the first time, and as I was thus humbled and disciplined under the cross, my understanding became more strengthened to distinguish the language of the pure Spirit which inwardly moves upon the heart and taught [me] to wait in silence sometimes many weeks together, until I felt that rise which prepares the creature to stand like a trumpet through which the Lord speaks to His flock.

From an inward purifying, and steadfast abiding under it, springs a lively operative desire for the good of others. All faithful people are not called to the public ministry, but whoever are, are called to minister of that which they have tasted and handled spiritually. The outward modes of worship are various, but wherever men are true ministers of Jesus Christ it is from the operation of His spirit upon their hearts, first purifying them and thus giving them a feeling sense of the conditions of others. This truth was early fixed in my mind, and I was taught to watch the pure opening and to take heed lest while I was standing to speak, my own will should get uppermost and cause me to utter words from worldly wisdom and depart from the channel of the true gospel ministry.

In the management of my outward affairs I may say with thankfulness I found Truth to be my support, and I was respected in my master's family, who came to live in Mount Holly within two year after my going there.

About the twenty-third year of my age, I had many fresh and heavenly openings in respect to the care and providence of the Almighty over his creatures in general, and over man as the most noble amongst those which are visible. And being clearly convinced in my judgment that to place my whole trust in God was best for me, I felt

[13]That is, Woolman believed he had not remained close to the original "concern" or divinely inspired motion to speak. He felt as if he had spoken from a selfish or worldly desire, rather than from an understanding disciplined by God's love.

renewed engagements that in all things I might act on an inward principle of virtue and pursue worldly business no further than as Truth opened my way therein.

About the time called Christmas I observed many people from the country and dwellers in town who, resorting to the public houses, spent their time in drinking and vain sports, tending to corrupt one another, on which account I was much troubled. At one house in particular there was much disorder, and I believed it was a duty laid on me to go and speak to the master of that house. I considered I was young and that several elderly Friends in town had opportunity to see these things, and though I would gladly have been excused, yet I could not feel my mind clear.

The exercise was heavy, and as I was reading what the Almighty said to Ezekiel[14] respecting his duty as a watchman, the matter was set home more clearly; and then with prayer and tears I besought the Lord for His assistance, who in lovingkindness gave me a resigned heart. Then at a suitable opportunity I went to the public house, and seeing the man amongst a company, I went to him and told him I wanted to speak with him; so we went aside, and there in the fear and the dread of the Almighty I expressed to him what rested on my mind, which he took kindly, and afterward showed more regard to me than before. In a few years after, he died middle-aged, and I often thought that had I neglected my duty in that case it would have given me great trouble, and I was humbly thankful to my gracious Father, who had supported me herein.

My employer, having a Negro woman, sold her and directed me to write a bill of sale, the man being waiting who bought her. The thing was sudden, and though the thoughts of writing an instrument of slavery for one of my fellow creatures felt uneasy, yet I remembered I was hired by the year, that it was my master who directed me to do it, and that it was an elderly man, a member of our Society, who bought her; so through weakness I gave way and wrote it, but at the executing it, I was so afflicted in my mind that I said before my master and the Friend that I believed slavekeeping to be a practice inconsistent with the Christian religion. This in some degree abated my uneasiness, yet as often as I reflected seriously upon it I thought I should have been clearer if I had desired to be excused from it as a thing against my conscience, for such it was. And some time after this a young man of our Society spake to me to write an instrument of slavery, he having lately taken a Negro into his house. I told him I was not easy to write it, for though many kept slaves in our Society, as in others, I still believed the practice was not right, and desired to be excused from writing [it]. I spoke to him in good will, and he told me that keeping slaves was not altogether agreeable to his mind, but that the slave being a gift made to his wife, he had accepted of her.

* * *

[Travels through North Carolina]

About this time believing it good for me to settle, and thinking seriously about a companion, my heart was turned to the Lord with desires that He would give me wis-

[14]The prophet Ezekiel was a watchman for the Israelites, sent to deliver warnings from God; Ezekiel 3:17.

dom to proceed therein agreeable to His will; and He was pleased to give me a well-inclined damsel, Sarah Ellis, to whom I was married the 18th day, 8th month, 1749.[15]

In the fall of the year 1750 died my father Samuel Woolman with a fever, aged about sixty years.[16] In his lifetime he manifested much care for us his children, that in our youth we might learn to fear the Lord, often endeavouring to imprint in our minds the true principles of virtue, and particularly to cherish in us a spirit of tenderness, not only toward poor people, but also towards all creatures of which we had the command.

After my return from Carolina I made some observations on keeping slaves, which I had some time before showed him, and he perused the manuscript, proposed a few alterations, and appeared well satisfied that I found a concern on that account. And in his last sickness as I was watching with him one night, he being so far spent that there was no expectation of his recovery, but had the perfect use of his understanding, he asked me concerning the manuscript, whether I expected soon to offer it to the Overseers of the Press, and after some conversation thereon said, "I have all along been deeply affected with the oppression of the poor Negroes, and now at last my concern for them is as great as ever."[17]

By his direction I had wrote his will in a time of health, and that night he desired me to read it to him, which I did, and he said it was agreeable to his mind. He then made mention of his end, which he believed was now near, and signified that though he was sensible of many imperfections in the course of his life, yet his experience of the power of Truth and of the love and goodness of God from time to time, even till now, was such that he had no doubt but that in leaving this life he should enter into one more happy.

The next day his sister Elizabeth came to see him and told him of the decease of their sister Anne, who died a few days before. He then said, "I reckon sister Anne was free to leave this world." Elizabeth said she was. He then said, "I also am free to leave it," and being in great weakness of body said, "I hope I shall shortly go to rest." He continued in a weighty frame of mind and was sensible till near the last.

2nd day, 9th month, 1751. Feeling drawings in my mind to visit Friends at the Great Meadows, in the upper part of West Jersey, with the unity of our Monthly Meeting I went there and had some searching laborious exercise amongst Friends in those parts, and found inward peace therein.

In the 9th month, 1753, in company with my well-esteemed friend John Sykes,[18] and with unity of Friends, we traveled about two weeks visiting Friends in Bucks County.[19] We laboured in the love of the gospel according to the measure received, and through the mercies of Him who is strength to the poor who trust in Him, we found satisfaction in our visit. And in the next winter, way opening to visit Friends' families within the compass of our Monthly Meeting, partly by the labors of two

[15]Sarah Ellis (1721–1787), raised near Mount Holly, was a childhood friend of Woolman.

[16]Samuel Woolman (1690–1750) had spent his lifetime on the farm on Rancocas River, Burlington County, New Jersey.

[17]Woolman's *Some Considerations on the Keeping of Negroes* was published in 1754.

[18]John Sykes (1682–1771), a Quaker missionary, often accompanied Woolman on his journeys through the middle colonies.

[19]Pennsylvania.

friends from Pennsylvania, I joined some in it, having had a desire some time that it might go forward amongst us.

About this time a person at some distance lying sick, his brother came to me to write his will. I knew he had slaves, and asking his brother, was told he intended to leave them slaves to his children. As writing is a profitable employ, as offending sober people is disagreeable to my inclination, I was straitened in my mind; but as I looked to the Lord, He inclined my heart to His testimony, and I told the man that I believed the practice of continuing slavery to this people was not right and had a scruple in mind against doing writings of that kind: that though many in our Society kept them as slaves, still I was not easy to be concerned in it and desired to be excused from going to write the will. I spake to him in the fear of the Lord, and he made no reply to what I said, but went away; he also had some concerns in the practice, and I thought he was displeased with me.

In this case I had a fresh confirmation that acting contrary to present outward interest from a motive of divine love and in regard to truth and righteousness, and thereby incurring the resentments of people, opens the way to a treasure better than silver and to a friendship exceeding the friendship of men.

On the 7th day, 2nd month, 1754, at night, I dreamed that I was walking in an orchard, it appeared to be about the middle of the afternoon; when on a sudden I saw two lights in the east resembling two suns, but of a dull and gloomy aspect. The one appeared about the height of the sun at three hours high, and the other more northward and one-third lower. In a few minutes the air in the east appeared to be mingled with fire, and like a terrible storm coming westward the streams of fire reached the orchard where I stood, but I felt no harm. I then found one of my acquaintance standing near me, who was greatly distressed in mind at this unusual appearance. My mind felt calm, and I said to my friend, "We must all once die, and if it please the Lord that our death be in this way, it is good for us to be resigned." Then I walked to a house hard by, and going upstairs, saw people with sad and troubled aspects, amongst whom I passed into another room where the floor was only some loose boards. There I sat down alone by a window, and looking out I saw in the south three great red streams standing at equal distance from each other, the bottom of which appeared to stand on the earth and the top to reach above the region of the clouds. Across those three streams went less ones, and from each end of such small stream others extended in regular lines to the earth, all red and appeared to extend through the whole southern firmament. There then appeared on a green plain a great multitude of men in a military posture, some of whom I knew. They came near the house, and passing on westward some of them, looking up at me, expressed themselves in a scoffing, taunting way, to which I made no reply; soon after, an old captain of the militia came to me, and I was told these men were assembled to improve in the discipline of war. . . .

Until the year 1756 I continued to retail goods, besides following my trade as a tailor, about which time I grew uneasy on account of my business growing too cumbersome. I began with selling trimmings for garments and from thence proceeded to sell clothes and linens, and at length having got a considerable shop of goods, my trade increased every year and the road to large business appeared open; but I felt a stop in my mind.

Through the mercies of the Almighty I had in a good degree learned to be content with a plain way of living. I had but a small family, that on serious consideration I believed Truth did not require me to engage in much cumbrous affairs. It had been my general practice to buy and sell things really useful. Things that served chiefly to please the vain mind in people I was not easy to trade in, seldom did it, and whenever I did I found it weaken me as a Christian.

The increase of business became my burden, for though my natural inclination was toward merchandise, yet I believed Truth required me to live more free from outward cumbers and there was now a strife in my mind between the two; and in this exercise my prayers were put up to the Lord, who graciously heard me and gave me a heart resigned to His holy will. Then I lessened my outward business, and as I had opportunity told my customers of my intentions that they might consider what shop to turn to, and so in a while wholly laid down merchandise, following my trade as a tailor, myself only, having no apprentice. I also had a nursery of apple trees, in which I employed some of my time—hoeing, grafting, trimming, and inoculating.

In merchandise it is the custom where I lived to sell chiefly on credit, and poor people often get in debt, and when payment is expected, not having wherewith to pay, their creditors often sue for it at law. Having often observed occurrences of this kind, I found it good for me to advise poor people to take such goods as were most useful and not costly.

In the time of trading, I had an opportunity of seeing that too liberal a use of spirituous liquors and the custom of wearing too costly apparel lead some people into great inconveniences, and these two things appear to be often connected one with the other. For by not attending to that use of things which is consistent with universal righteousness, there is an increase of labor which extends beyond what our Heavenly Father intends for us. And by great labor, and often by much sweating in the heat, there is even amongst such who are not drunkards a craving of some liquors to revive the spirits: that partly by the wanton, luxurious drinking of some, and partly by the drinkings of others led to it through immoderate labor, very great quantities of rum are every year expended in our colonies, the greater part of which we should have no need did we steadily attend to pure wisdom.

Where men take pleasure in feeling their minds elevated with strong drink and so indulge their appetite as to disorder their understandings, neglect their duty as members in a family or civil society, and cast off all pretense to religion, their case is much to be pitied. And where such whose lives are for the most part regular, and whose examples have a strong influence on the minds of others, adhere to some customs which strongly draw toward the use of more strong liquor than pure wisdom directs to the use of, this also, as it hinders the spreading of the spirit of meekness and strengthens the hands of the more excessive drinkers, is a case to be lamented.

As the least degree of luxury hath some connection with evil, for those who profess to be disciples of Christ and are looked upon as leaders of the people, to have that mind in them which was also in Him, and so stand separate from every wrong way, is a means of help to the weaker. As I have sometimes been much spent in the heat and taken spirits to revive me, I have found by experience that in such circumstance the mind is not so calm nor so fitly disposed for divine meditation as when all such extremes are avoided, and have felt an increasing care to attend to that Holy Spirit which sets right bounds to our desires and leads those who faithfully follow it to apply all the gifts of divine providence to the purposes for which they were intended. Did such who have the care of great estates attend with singleness of heart to this Heavenly Instructor, which so opens and enlarges the mind that men love their neighbors as themselves, they would have wisdom given them to manage without finding occasion to employ some people in the luxuries of life or to make it necessary for others to labor too hard. But for want of steadily regarding this principle of divine love, a selfish spirit takes place in the minds of people, which is attended with darkness and manifold confusions in the world. . . .

When I was at Newbegun Creek,[20] a Friend was there who labored for his living, having no Negroes, and had been a minister many years. He came to me the next day, and as we rode together he signified that he wanted to talk with me concerning a difficulty he had been under, and related it near as follows, to wit: That as monies had of late years been raised by a tax to carry on the wars, he had a scruple in his mind in regard to paying it and chose rather to suffer distraint of goods than pay it. And as he was the only person who refused it in them parts and knew not that anyone else was in the like circumstance, he signified that it had been a heavy trial upon him, and the more so for that some of his brethren had been uneasy with his conduct in that case, and added that from a sympathy he felt with me yesterday in meeting, he found a freedom thus to open the matter in the way of querying concerning Friends in our parts; whereupon I told him the state of Friends amongst us as well as I was able, and also that I had for some time been under the like scruple. I believed him to be one who was concerned to walk uprightly before the Lord and esteemed it my duty to preserve this memorandum.

From hence I went back into Virginia and had a meeting near James Copeland's; it was a time of inward suffering, but through the goodness of the Lord I was made content. Then to another meeting where through the renewings of pure love we had a very comfortable meeting.

Traveling up and down of late, I have renewed evidences that to be faithful to the Lord and content with his will concerning me is a most necessary and useful lesson for me to be learning, looking less at the effects of my labor than at the pure motion and reality of the concern as it arises from heavenly love. In the Lord Jehovah is everlasting strength, and as the mind by a humble resignation is united to Him and we utter words from an inward knowledge that they arise from the heavenly spring, though our way may be difficult and require close attention to keep in it, and though the manner in which we may be led may tend to our own abasement, yet if we continue in patience and meekness, heavenly peace is the reward of our labors.

From hence I went to Curles Meeting, which, though small, was reviving to the honest-hearted. Thence to Black Creek and Caroline Meetings, from whence, accompanied by William Stanley[21] before-mentioned, we rode to Goose Creek, being much through the woods and about one hundred miles. We lodged the first night at a public house, the second in the woods, and the next day we reached a Friend's house at Goose Creek. In the woods we lay under some disadvantage, having no fireworks, nor bells for our horses, but we stopped some before night and let them feed on wild grass, which was plenty, we the meantime cutting with our knives a store

[20]North Carolina.

[21]William Stanley (1729–1807), of Cedar Creek, Virginia.

against night, and then tied them; and gathering some bushes under an oak we lay down, but the mosquitoes being plenty and the ground damp, I slept but little.

Thus lying in the wilderness and looking at the stars, I was led to contemplate the condition of our first parents when they were sent forth from the garden, and considered that they had no house, no tools for business, no garments but what their Creator gave them, no vessels for use, nor any fire to cook roots or herbs. But the Almighty, though they had been disobedient, was a father to them; way opened in process of time for all the conveniences of life. And He who by the gracious influence of His spirit illuminated their understand and showed them what was acceptable to Him and tended to their felicity as intelligent creatures, did also provide means for their happy living in this world as they attended to the manifestations of His wisdom. . . .

1774

from Some Considerations on the Keeping of Negroes[1]

Recommended to the Professors of Christianity of Every Denomination

Introduction

Customs generally approved and opinions received by youth from their superiors become like the natural produce of a soil, especially when they are suited to favourite inclinations. But as the judgments of God are without partiality, by which the state of the soul must be tried, it would be the highest wisdom to forego customs and popular opinions, and try the treasures of the soul by the infallible standard: Truth.

Natural affection needs a careful examination. Operating upon us in a soft manner, it kindles desires of love and tenderness, and there is danger of taking it for something higher. To me it appears an instinct like that which inferior creatures have; each of them, we see, by the ties of nature love self best. That which is a part of self they love by the same tie or instinct. In them it in some measure does the offices of reason, by which, among other things, they watchfully keep and orderly feed their helpless offspring. Thus natural affection appears to be a branch of self-love, good in the animal race, in us likewise with proper limitations, but otherwise is productive of evil by exciting desires to promote some by means prejudicial to others.

Our blessed Saviour seems to give a check to this irregular fondness in nature and, at the same time, a precedent for us: "Who is my mother, and who are my

[1]First published in 1754, Woolman's *Considerations* argues in behalf of the abolition of slavery. The source of the present text is Phillips Moulton's edition, *The Journal and Major Essays of John Woolman,* 1971.

brethren?"—thereby intimating that the earthly ties of relationship are, comparatively, inconsiderable to such who, through a steady course of obedience, have come to the happy experience of the Spirit of God bearing witness with their spirits that they are his children: "And he stretched forth his hands towards his disciples and said, 'Behold my mother and my brethren; for whosoever shall do the will of my Father which is in heaven (arrives at the more noble part of true relationship) the same is my brother, and sister, and mother.'" Mt. 12:48 [–50].

This doctrine agrees well with a state truly complete, where love necessarily operates according to the agreeableness of things or principles unalterable and in themselves perfect. If endeavouring to have my children eminent amongst men after my death be that which no reasons grounded on those principles can be brought to support, then to be temperate in my pursuit after gain and to keep always within the bounds of those principles is an indispensable duty, and to depart from it a dark unfruitful toil.

In our present condition, to love our children is needful; but except this love proceeds from the true heavenly principle which sees beyond earthly treasures, it will rather be injurious than of any real advantage to them. Where the fountain is corrupt, the streams must necessarily be impure.

That important injunction of our Saviour (Mt. 6:33), with the promise annexed, contains a short but comprehensive view of our duty and happiness. If then the business of mankind in this life is to first seek another, if this cannot be done but by attending to the means, if a summary of the means is not to do that to another which (in like circumstances) we would not have done unto us, then these are points of moment and worthy of our most serious consideration.

What I write on this subject is with reluctance, and the hints given are in as general terms as my concern would allow. I know it is a point about which in all its branches men that appear to aim well are not generally agreed, and for that reason I chose to avoid being very particular. If I may happily have let drop anything that may excite such as are concerned in the practice to a close thinking on the subject treated of, the candid amongst them may easily do the subject such further justice as, on an impartial enquiry, it may appear to deserve; and such an enquiry I would earnestly recommend.

Some Consideration on the Keeping of Negroes

"Forasmuch as ye did it to the least of these my brethren, ye did it unto me." Mt. 25:40.

As many times there are different motives to the same actions, and one does that from a generous heart which another does for selfish ends, the like may be said in this case.

There are various circumstances amongst them that keep Negroes, and different ways by which they fall under their care; and, I doubt not, there are many well-disposed persons amongst them who desire rather to manage wisely and justly in this difficult matter than to make gain of it. But the general disadvantage which these poor Africans lie under in an enlightened Christian country having often filled me with real sadness, and been like undigested matter on my mind, I now think it my duty, through divine aid, to offer some thoughts thereon to the consideration of others.

When we remember that all nations are of one blood (Gen. 3:20); that in this world we are but sojourners; that we are subject to the like afflictions and infirmities of body, the like disorders and frailties in mind, the like temptations, the same death and the same judgment; and that the All-wise Being is judge and Lord over us all, it seems to raise an idea of a general brotherhood and a disposition easy to be touched with a feeling of each other's afflictions. But when we forget those things and look chiefly at our outward circumstances, in this and some ages past, constantly retaining in our minds the distinction betwixt us and them with respect to our knowledge and improvement in things divine, natural, and artificial, our breasts being apt to be filled with fond notions of superiority, there is danger of erring in our conduct toward them.

We allow them to be of the same species with ourselves; the odds is we are in a higher station and enjoy greater favours than they. And when it is thus that our Heavenly Father endoweth some of his children with distinguished gifts, they are intended for good ends. But if those thus gifted are thereby lifted up above their brethren, not considering themselves as debtors to the weak nor behaving themselves as faithful stewards, none who judge impartially can suppose them free from ingratitude. When a people dwell under the liberal distribution of favours from heaven, it behooves them carefully to inspect their ways and consider the purposes for which those favours were bestowed, lest through forgetfulness of God and misusing his gifts they incur his heavy displeasure, whose judgments are just and equal, who exalteth and humbleth to the dust as he seeth meet.

It appears by Holy Record that men under high favours have been apt to err in their opinions concerning others. Thus Israel, according to the description of the prophet (Is. 65:5), when exceedingly corrupted and degenerated, yet remembered they were the chosen people of God and could say, "Stand by thyself, come not near me, for I am holier than thou." That this was no chance language, but their common opinion of other people, more fully appears by considering the circumstances which attended when God was beginning to fulfil his precious promises concerning the gathering of the Gentiles.

The Most High, in a vision, undeceived Peter, first prepared his heart to believe, and at the house of Cornelius showed him of a certainty that God was no respecter of persons. The effusion of the Holy Ghost upon a people with whom they, the Jewish Christians, would not so much as eat was strange to them. All they of the circumcision were astonished to see it, and the apostles and brethren of Judea contended with Peter about it, till he having rehearsed the whole matter and fully shown that the Father's love was unlimited, they are thereat struck with admiration and cry out, "Then hath God also to the Gentiles granted repentance unto life!" [Acts 11:18].

The opinion of peculiar favours being confined to them was deeply rooted, or else the above instance had been less strange to them, for these reasons: First, they were generally acquainted with the writings of the prophets, by whom this time was repeatedly spoken of and pointed at. Secondly, our blessed Lord shortly before expressly said, "I have other sheep, not of this fold; them also must I bring," etc. [Jn. 10:16]. Lastly, his words to them after his resurrection, at the very time of his ascension, "Ye shall be witnesses to me not only in Jerusalem, Judea, and Samaria, but to the uttermost parts of the earth" [Acts 1:8].

Those concurring circumstances, one would think, might have raised a strong expectation of seeing such a time. Yet when it came, it proved matter of offense and astonishment.

To consider mankind otherwise than brethren, to think favours are peculiar to one nation and exclude others, plainly supposes a darkness in the understanding. For as God's love is universal, so where the mind is sufficiently influenced by it, it begets a likeness of itself and the heart is enlarged towards all men. Again, to conclude a people froward, perverse, and worse by nature than others (who ungratefully receive favours and apply them to bad ends), this will excite a behavior toward them unbecoming the excellence of true religion.

To prevent such error let us calmly consider their circumstances, and, the better to do it, make their case ours. Suppose, then, that our ancestors and we have been exposed to constant servitude in the more servile and inferior employments of life; that we had been destitute of the help of reading and good company; that amongst ourselves we had had few wise and pious instructors; that the religious amongst our superiors seldom took notice of us; that while others in ease have plentifully heaped up the fruit of our labour, we had received barely enough to relieve nature, and being wholly at the command of others had generally been treated as a contemptible, ignorant part of mankind. Should we, in that case, be less abject than they now are? Again, if oppression be so hard to bear that a wise man is made mad by it (Eccles. 7:7), then a series of those things altering the behaviour and manners of a people is what may reasonably be expected.

When our property is taken contrary to our mind by means appearing to us unjust, it is only through divine influence and the enlargement of heart from thence proceeding that we can love our reputed oppressors. If the Negroes fall short in this, an uneasy, if not a disconsolate, disposition will be awakened and remain like seeds in their minds, producing sloth and many other habits appearing odious to us, with which being free men they perhaps had not been chargeable. These and other circumstances, rightly considered, will lessen that too great disparity which some make between us and them.

Integrity of heart hath appeared in some of them, so that if we continue in the world of Christ (previous to discipleship, Jn. 8:31) and our conduct towards them be seasoned with his love, we may hope to see the good effect of it, the which, in a good degree, is the case with some into whose hands they have fallen. But that too many treat them otherwise, not seeming conscious of any neglect, is, alas! too evident.

When self-love presides in our minds our opinions are biased in our own favour. In this condition, being concerned with a people so situated that they have no voice to plead their own cause, there's danger of using ourselves to an undisturbed partiality till, by long custom, the mind becomes reconciled with it and the judgment itself infected.

To humbly apply to God for wisdom, that we may thereby be enabled to see things as they are and ought to be, is very needful; hereby the hidden things of darkness may be brought to light and the judgment made clear. We shall then consider mankind as brethren. Though different degrees and a variety of qualifications and abilities, one dependent on another, be admitted, yet high thoughts will be laid aside, and all men treated as becometh the sons of one Father, agreeable to the doctrine of Christ Jesus.

He hath laid down the best criterion by which mankind ought to judge of their own conduct, and others judge for them of theirs, one towards another—viz., "Whatsoever ye would that men should do unto you, do ye even so to them." I take it that all men by nature are equally entitled to the equality of this rule and under the indispensable obligations of it. One man ought not to look upon another man or society of men as so far beneath him but that he should put himself in their place in all his actions towards them, and bring all to this test—viz., How should I approve of this conduct were I in their circumstances and they in mine?—Arscott's Considerations, *Part III, Fol. 107.*[2]

This doctrine, being of a moral unchangeable nature, hath been likewise inculcated in the former dispensation: "If a stranger sojourn with thee in your land, ye shall not vex him; but the stranger that dwelleth with you shall be as one born amongst you, and thou shalt love him as thyself." Lev. 19:33, 34. Had these people come voluntarily and dwelt amongst us, to have called them strangers would be proper. And their being brought by force, with regret and a languishing mind, may well raise compassion in a heart rightly disposed. But there is nothing in such treatment which upon a wise and judicious consideration will any ways lessen their right of being treated as strangers. If the treatment which many of them meet with be rightly examined and compared with those precepts, "Thou shalt not vex him nor oppress him; he shall be as one born amongst you, and thou shalt love him as thyself" (Lev. 19:33; Deut. 27:19), there will appear an important difference betwixt them.

It may be objected there is cost of purchase and risk of their lives to them who possess 'em, and therefore needful that they make the best use of their time. In a practice just and reasonable such objections may have weight; but if the work be wrong from the beginning, there's little or no force in them. If I purchase a man who hath never forfeited his liberty, the natural right of freedom is in him. And shall I keep him and his posterity in servitude and ignorance? How should I approve of this conduct were I in his circumstances and he in mine? It may be thought that to treat them as we would willingly be treated, our gain by them would be inconsiderable; and it were, in diverse respects, better that there were none in our country.

We may further consider that they are now amongst us, and those of our nation the cause of their being here, that whatsoever difficulty accrues thereon we are justly chargeable with, and to bear all inconveniences attending it with a serious and weighty concern of mind to do our duty by them is the best we can do. To seek a remedy by continuing the oppression because we have power to do it and see others do it, will, I apprehend, not be doing as we would be done by.

[2]This quotation, slightly altered, is found in Alexander Arscott, *Some Considerations Relating to the Present State of the Christian Religion, wherein the Nature, End, and Design of Christianity, as well as the Principle Evidence of the Truth of it, are Explained and Recommended out of the Holy Scriptures; with a General Appeal to the Experience of all Men for Confirmation thereof,* Part III (London, 1734), 78. Arscott (1676–1737), an Oxford graduate, was a schoolmaster. About 1700, to the great dismay of his parents, he became a Quaker. He served many years as clerk of the London Yearly Meeting. He intended this volume as an apologetic for Christianity based on both Scripture and reason, apart from the special point of view of the Friends. All three parts were reprinted in Philadelphia, the first two by Benjamin Franklin in 1732, the third by A. Bradford in 1738 [Moulton's note].

How deeply soever men are involved in the most exquisite difficulties, sincerity of heart and upright walking before God, freely submitting to his providence, is the most sure remedy. He only is able to relieve not only persons but nations in their greatest calamities. David, in a great strait when the sense of his past error and the full expectation of an impending calamity as the reward of it were united to the aggravating his distress, after some deliberation saith, "Let me fall now into the hands of the Lord, for very great are his mercies; let me not fall into the hand of man." I Chron. 21:13.

To act continually with integrity of heart above all narrow or selfish motives is a sure token of our being partakers of that salvation which God hath appointed for walls and bulwarks (Is. 5:26; Rom. 15:8), and is, beyond all contradiction, a more happy situation than can ever be promised by the utmost reach of art and power united, not proceeding from heavenly wisdom.

A supply to nature's lawful wants, joined with a peaceful, humble mind, is the truest happiness in this life. And if here we arrive to this and remain to walk in the path of the just, our case will be truly happy. And though herein we may part with or miss of some glaring shows of riches and leave our children little else but wise instructions, a good example, and the knowledge of some honest employment, these, with the blessing of providence, are sufficient for their happiness, and are more likely to prove so than laying up treasures for them which are often rather a snare than any real benefit, especially to them who, instead of being exampled to temperance, are in all things taught to prefer the getting of riches and to eye the temporal distinctions they give as the principal business of this life. These readily overlook the true happiness of man as it results from the enjoyment of all things in the fear of God, and miserably substituting an inferior good, dangerous in the acquiring and uncertain in the fruition, they are subject to many disappointments; and every sweet carries its sting.

It is the conclusion of our blessed Lord and his apostles, as appears by their lives and doctrines, that the highest delights of sense or most pleasing objects visible ought ever to be accounted infinitely inferior to that real intellectual happiness suited to man in his primitive innocence and now to be found in true renovation of mind, and that the comforts of our present life, the things most grateful to us, ought always to be received with temperance and never made the chief objects of our desire, hope, or love, but that our whole heart and affections be principally looking to that city "which hath foundations, whose maker and builder is God" [Heb. 11:10].

Did we so improve the gifts bestowed on us that our children might have an education suited to these doctrines, and our example to confirm it, we might rejoice in hopes of their being heirs of an inheritance incorruptible. This inheritance, as Christians, we esteem the most valuable; and how then can we fail to desire it for our children? Oh, that we were consistent with ourselves in pursuing means necessary to obtain it!

It appears by experience that where children are educated in fullness, ease, and idleness, evil habits are more prevalent than is common amongst such who are prudently employed in the necessary affairs of life. And if children are not only educated in the way of so great temptation, but have also the opportunity of lording it over their fellow creatures and being masters of men in their childhood, how can we hope otherwise than that their tender minds will be possessed with thoughts too high for them?—which by continuance, gaining strength, will prove like a slow current, gradually separating them from (or keeping from acquaintance with) that humility and meekness in which alone lasting happiness can be enjoyed. . . .

1754

A Selection of Eighteenth-Century Poetry

Before the Revolution, the English comfortably tended to consider that the course of empire would lead to the progressive betterment of the new colonies. George Berkeley wrote of the westward translation of English empire and the arts when he attempted in 1725 to found a college in Bermuda. Published in 1752, Berkeley's poem "On the Prospect of Planting Arts and Learning in America" speaks of the "Seat of Innocence" in "Happy Climes," "Where Nature guides and Virtue rules":

There shall be sung another golden Age,
The rise of Empire and of Arts,
The Good and Great inspiring epic Rage,
The wisest Heads and noblest Hearts.

Not such as *Europe* breeds in her decay;
Such as she bred when fresh and young,
When heav'nly Flame did animate her Clay,
By future Poets shall be sung.

Westward the Course of Empire takes its Way;
The first four Acts already past,
A fifth shall close the Drama with the Day;
Time's noblest Offspring is the last.

For Berkeley and his early eighteenth-century contemporaries, poetry was still, as it had been in the Renaissance, the privileged literary genre and epic the privileged form. Yet the epic era of European colonization was fast waning, and the demographic changes the colonies were experiencing brought a wider readership that would find prose works, from almanacs to travel journals and fictional vignettes to novels, more appealing and accessible. Poetry—especially epic poetry, based upon the precondition of high social class—became the province of intellectuals and, to some extent, of pietists.

Even as the colonies engaged in a Revolution that would break down the hierarchic social and political structure that epic poetry had privileged, knowledge of and ability to write poetry was advanced by some as a mark of intellectual excellence. Philip Freneau and Hugh Henry Brackenridge (in their 1771 Princeton commencement poem "On the Rising Glory of America") and Joel Barlow (in his 1787 *Vision of Columbus,* an attempt to write an American epic), along with many lesser-known poets, would speak of the country's promise and of necessary American progress. That both promise and progress would require less privilege and a more democratic ideology seems to have escaped most of the 1770s writers who sought for Americans a place in epic literature like those places held by ancient Greeks and Romans.

Poetry was a signal literary genre of the dominant class, and the dominant poetic voice was public and male. This is not to suggest that men wrote poems only on public issues and that women wrote only on private ones. Nor is it to imply that men did not write on friendship or concerns typically considered "domestic." Yet it is true that men controlled the printing presses, and men's writings more frequently reached print than women's writings. Thus published poems on topics of political, social, or literary importance were usually written and published by men through the first half of the century.

Writers generally used the same neoclassical poetic models and methods as their English contemporaries. English neoclassicism had reached its height with the works of Dryden, Pope, and Swift. These poets' interest in the classics was a response to the social chaos caused by the civil wars in seventeenth-century England. The disruptions in language and meter, the multitudinous poetic conceits of seventeenth-century writers were replaced by what eighteenth-century neoclassicists considered to be precision and control, "correctness" and regularity, in their poetic lines and themes. They labelled as "false wit" the linguistic turns and the use of astonishing conceits and rhythms of seventeenth-century writings; they sought instead what they called "true wit," a comfortable degree of predictability and clarity. The marked regularities of eighteenth-century poetic lines were thought to model for readers the regular and harmonious attitudes that writers sought to inculcate in society. Literature, they argued, should be didactic; it should teach those less informed about manners and morals in a refined society. What emerged, in the neoclassic era, was a highly public and social poetry, where satire flourished and the lyric nearly disappeared. Writing on themes ranging from the battle of the books (whether the classic writings were "better" than contemporary texts), to the battle between the sexes, to nature poems, poets continually sifted and tested both language and meter to find what they considered to be the best poetic expression.

Like the poetry of the seventeenth-century, then, eighteenth-century poetry is marked by its use and transformation of poetic styles common in eighteenth-century England. Anglo-American poets, writing for an audience in England as well as in the colonies, wrote of colonial experiences in forms common to English readers—pastorals, odes, elegies, satires, and others. The writers thus evidenced to their European counterparts their familiarity with the accepted modes of the elite groups that held, as they did during the Renaissance, that poetry was the highest form of written art. By displaying a knowledge of "high" forms—by displaying their intellectual and educational equivalence with their English contemporaries, that is—Anglo-American writers could claim for themselves a position in the New World that counterbalanced the tendency of those in English elite society to view all Americans as hardscrabble hicks trapped in a wilderness.

Two of the most common forms of early eighteenth-century English poetry are satire and the pastoral, both of which had roots in classical Greek and Roman writing. In fact, the classicism of early eighteenth-century England is often called Augustan, so named after the times of Augustus Caesar, the first Roman emperor. English writers, seeking ways to address the cultural transformations at hand, found the recourse to classical forms a welcome solution to social and political troubles in England. Life's complications and uncertainties could be made more palatable if mocked in satire or transformed into pastoral allegory. American writers, in a world witnessing change not only in England but in the colonies, found these English models useful.

Although the privileged form was public and male-dominated in the earlier part of the eighteenth century, there remained a distinct tradition of pietistic writing, both public and private, as well. Christian epic poetry had reached its height during the Renaissance, as we have seen. But the Christian epic formed only one poetic genre. Ministers had long been accustomed to writing devotional poems, as the work of Edward Taylor in the seventeenth century amply demonstrates. Indeed, a large devotional poetic literature evolved during the middle of the eighteenth century, at the same time that the Great Awakening was taking hold. Evangelistic ministers played upon the millennial expectations of their listeners and readers, exhorting them in sermon and in poem to believe in Christ and their own so-called manifest American destiny.

At the same time that social and political shifts were emerging mid-century, more and more young men and women were needing guidance. Education was on the rise, and many more women than ever before were able to read. Some women were trained in writing, as well. Their reading, like that of the men, no doubt related to political, social, and literary issues. Often, their writing likewise addressed these public concerns. Yet most women, if they published their writings, more frequently spoke publicly upon those matters that society considered within their province, issues domestic and devotional. Whether or not women freely chose to publish on these subjects or merely acquiesced in public expectation is difficult to determine. What is clear is that as the century wore on, the increased public interest in women's education combined with a widespread evangelical movement (beginning with the first Great Awakening and enhanced by the Second Great Awakening) which enabled women in greater numbers to find voice for their concerns—both on private and public issues—as they had never done before.

Hundreds of poems by colonial women have been preserved over the centuries in print and manuscript, yet few have been readily available to interested readers. Most remain in manuscript or have been out of print for many decades. Written largely by white women from well-to-do families—Lucy Terry, North America's first black poet, is a significant exception—the poems provide an important addition to our understanding of colonial life. Colonial women poets shared the concerns of their male contemporaries: religion, politics, social events, important public figures, death, love, marriage, war, family. And they wrote in the many poetic forms available to the literate populace of their day: verse letters and plays, elegies and odes to friends of prominent figures, religious meditations, love poems, historical narratives, hymns, social and political satires, translations and paraphrases of the classics and the Bible, poetic dialogues. But these women poets frequently brought a new perspective to familiar themes and forms. They wrote of conflicts between internalized gender roles and competing aspirations. They wrote of child-bearing and rearing, the deaths of children, loving (and not-so-loving) husbands, parents, domestic duties, and home life. In the process, they adapted a range of image and metaphor less available to their male contemporaries.

The frequency with which colonial women wrote poetry should not suggest that writing, for women, had no risk. Hampered by rigid role definitions and social expectations, most colonial women were neither expected nor encouraged to develop artistic or literary talents. The individual toll of their gender-defined work roles and of continuous child-bearing must have kept many a would-be writer from pursuing her craft. If lack of leisure did not suffice to keep women writers from developing their skills, the social stigma attached to stepping outside of conventional gender roles would have offered an additional restraining force. In 1650, Thomas Parker, minister of Newbury, Massachusetts, forcefully clarified colonial attitudes in an open letter to his sister, Elizabeth Avery, in England: "your printing of a book, beyond the custom of your sex, doth rankly smell." Nearly a century later, an anonymous writer in the *Boston Weekly Magazine* for March 2, 1743, explained "to a poetical lady" the social consequences of a woman's insistence upon writing poetry:

What's beauty, wealth and wit beside?
Nor God, nor man will love her.

The attitudes of a colonial patriarchy provided more subtle obstacles than damaged reputations to women poets. Living among such male leaders as Edward Johnson and Nathaniel Ward who spoke of "silly women laden with diverse lusts," "phantastical madness," and "squirrel's brains" inevitably influenced women's perceptions of themselves and their abilities. The condescension of Benjamin Tompson's "On a Fortification at Boston begun by Women" or Nathaniel Ward's poem on Anne Bradstreet's *Tenth Muse* was representative:

It half revives my chill frost-bitten
blood,
To see a woman once do ought that's
good.

How many self-fulfilling prophecies of failure women writers accepted is impossible to determine.

Though colonial society at large seldom supported their work, colonial women poets encouraged one another. They read the published works of a few well-known women, British and American—Anne Bradstreet, Elizabeth Carter, Lady Mary Wortley Montagu, Elizabeth Singer Rowe, Katherine Philips, Anne Finch, Margaret of Newcastle, Mary Astell, Anne Killigrew, Catherine Macauley, and Elizabeth Montagu among them. In addition, many colonial women poets knew one another personally, corresponded and exchanged their poems. For instance, one of Elizabeth Graeme Fergusson's extant commonplace books was evidently prepared for the New Jersey poet Annis Stockton. Anna Young Smith, Fergusson's niece and ward, occasionally wrote verse. Ann Bleecker's verse was published posthumously by her daughter, Margaretta Faugères, herself a poet. Abigail Dennie almost certainly read the verse of her sister Jane Turell, and her only extant piece is a verse letter to Turell. Other occasions for intellectual and literary contact were fostered when Fergusson followed the tradition of the European salon by initiating regular gatherings of talented women and men at Graeme Park, north of Philadelphia. Annis Stockton held similar salons at "Morven," the Stockton estate.

Further evidence of this direct contact among women poets lies in their frequent verses, one poet to another. Sarah Morton's ode to Mercy Warren, included here, is representative. Judith Sargent Murray and Sarah Morton exchanged poems in the *Massachusetts Magazine.* Even those women who did not seek publication of their verse circulated their manuscripts among friends. Such networks allowed women to encourage one another in an activity generally unsupported by society at large. Put another way, women found that the mutual support of their networks assisted both their poetic inspiration and their sense of an audience for their works. Men's networks were more typically those made available through their college or work experiences, or both.

In the selections that follow, we have attempted to offer a sampling (arranged chronologically according to date of the poets' births) of the variety and versatility of poetic writings by men and women of the northern, middle, and southern colonies in British North America. An examination of the poems by Nathaniel Evans and Thomas Godfrey will show that men, just as much as women (such as Annis Stockton and Elizabeth Fergusson), versified their thoughts on friendly associations. Likewise by looking at the poems by Moore and Bleecker, readers can see the extent to which women wrote on "public," Revolutionary issues. All of the poets reveal an Anglo-American consciousness of poetic norms established in Europe, and many poets—Cook, Lewis, Dawson, and Godfrey, especially—suggest the extent to which Anglo-American writers sought to test the formal conventions typical of European writings. Readers interested in the poetry of the eighteenth century will want to consult additional readings—by Jupiter Hammon, Phillis Wheatley, Judith Sargent Murray, Philip Freneau, Timothy Dwight, Joel Barlow—in this anthology.

Carla Mulford
Pennsylvania State University

Pattie Cowell
Colorado State University

SECONDARY WORKS

J.A. Leo Lemay, *Men of Letters in Colonial Maryland,* 1972; Emily Stipes Watts, *The Poetry of American Women from 1632 to 1945,* 1977; Kenneth N. Requa, ed., *Poems of Jane Turell and Martha Brewster,* 1979; Pattie Cowell, ed., *Women Poets in Pre-Revolutionary America, 1650–1775,* 1981; Cheryl Walker, *The Nightingale's Burden: Women Poets and American Culture,* 1982; David S. Shields, *Oracles of Empire: Poetry, Politics, and Commerce in British America, 1690–1750,* 1990; Carla Mulford, ed., *Only for the Eye of a Friend: The Poetry of Annis Boudinot Stockton,* 1995; Jeffrey H. Richards, *Mercy Otis Warren,* 1995.

Ebenezer Cook 1667–1733

Ebenezer Cook was a tobacco factor (merchant) and plantation owner in Maryland. A prolific writer, he spent much time in London as well as in Maryland. Cook's *The Sot-weed Factor,* first published in London in 1708, is a satire of elitist English expectations about America. The satire is written in the form of Hudibrastic verse, named for Samuel Butler's hilarious satire of Puritans, *Hudibras* (1653–1680). Hudibrastic verse has a Juvenalian (*i.e.,* biting, after the classical writer, Juvenal) satirical stance offered in a form that is jarring to read because of the galloping and potentially monotonous tetrameter lines that end in odd-sounding rhymes. In fact, the incongruity created by "sing-song" lines that might be monotonous except for the unexpected rhymes and odd syntax fosters much of the humor of Hudibrastic verse.

Cook's use of the verse form is doubly satirical. The speaker of *The Sot-weed Factor* speaks as though he were a member of the English elite; he denigrates and mocks Americans as hard-drinking, impious, backwater rogues. Thus, the poem's satire seems on one level to be directed against Americans. Yet the poem really satirizes precisely the English elitist notions about Americans that the speaker holds. The first evidence lies in the fact that the sot-weed factor (tobacco merchant) stands "Erect, with Legs stretch'd wide" (line 67) in a canoe. An American would know that people would not stand in canoes. Other examples repeatedly show the ignorance of the speaker of the poem, who thinks himself superior to the Americans he finds. The last laugh, then, is on the speaker, who thinks himself superior when it is the Americans who really are so.

The text is taken from the original London, 1708, publication of the poem. Unless otherwise noted, annotations are Cook's, from the original publication.

The Sot-weed Factor; or, a Voyage to Maryland, &c.[1]

Condemn'd by Fate to way-ward Curse,
Of Friends unkind, and empty Purse;
Plagues worse than fill'd *Pandora*'s Box,
I took my leave of *Albion*'s Rocks:
With heavy Heart, concern'd that I
Was forc'd my Native Soil to fly,
And the *Old World* must bid good-buy.
But Heav'n ordain'd it should be so,
And to repine is vain we know:
Freighted with Fools, from *Plymouth* sound,
To *Mary-Land* our Ship was bound;
Where we arriv'd in dreadful Pain,
Shock'd by the Terrours of the Main;
For full three Months, our wavering Boat,
Did thro' the surley Ocean float,
And furious Storms and threat'ning Blasts,
Both tore our Sails and sprung our Masts:
Wearied, yet pleas'd, we did escape
Such Ills, we anchor'd at the *Cape,*[2]
But weighing soon, we plough'd the *Bay,*
To Cove[3] it in *Piscato-way,*[4]
Intending there to open Store,
I put myself and Goods a-shore:
Where soon repair'd a numerous Crew,
In Shirts and Drawers of *Scotch-cloth* Blue.[5]
With neither Stockings, Hat, nor Shooe.
These *Sot-weed* Planters Crowd the Shoar,
In Hue as tawny as a Moor:
Figure so strange, no God design'd,
To be a part of Humane Kind:
But wanton Nature, void of Rest,
Moulded the brittle Clay in Jest,
At last a Fancy very odd
Took me, this was the Land of *Nod;*
Planted at first, when Vagrant *Cain,*
His Brother had unjustly slain:

[1]Weed that makes one drunk, *i.e.,* tobacco [Ed.].

[2]By the *Cape,* is meant the *Capes of Virginia,* the first Land on the Coast of *Virginia* and *Mary-Land.* [Cape Henry, Virginia; Ed.].

[3]To *Cove* is to lie at Anchor safe in Harbour.

[4]The Bay of *Piscato-way,* the usual place where our Ships come to an Anchor in *Mary-Land* [Evidently, up the Chesapeake Bay and Potomac River to Piscataway Creek; Ed.].

[5]The Planters generally wear Blue *Linnen.*

Then conscious of the Crime he'd done,
From Vengeance dire, he hither run;
And in a Hut supinely dwelt,
The first in *Furs* and *Sot-weed* dealt.
And ever since his Time, the Place,
Has harbour'd a detested Race;
Who when they cou'd not live at Home,
For Refuge to these Worlds did roam;
In hopes by Flight they might prevent,
The Devil and his fell intent;
Obtain from Tripple Tree[6] reprieve,
And Heav'n and Hell alike deceive:
But e're their Manners I display,
I think it fit I open lay
My Entertainment by the way;
That Strangers well may be aware on,
What homely Diet they must fare on.
To touch that Shoar, where no good Sense is found,
But Conversation's lost, and Maners drown'd.
I crost unto the other side,
A River whose impetuous Tide,
The Savage Borders does divide;
In such a shining odd invention,
I scarce can give its due Dimention.
The *Indians* call this watry Waggon
Canoo, a Vessel none can brag on;[7]
Cut from a *Popular-Tree,* or *Pine,*
And fashion'd like a Trough for Swine:
In this most noble Fishing-Boat,
I boldly put myself a-float;
Standing Erect, with Legs stretch'd wide,
We paddled to the other side:
Where being Landed safe by hap,
As *Sol* fell into *Thetis* Lap.
A ravenous Gang bent on the stroul,
Of Wolves for Prey, began to howl;[8]
This put me in a pannick Fright,
Least I should be devoured quite:
But as I there a musing stood,
And quite benighted in a Wood,
A Female Voice pierc'd thro' my Ears,
Crying, *You Rogue drive home the Steers.*
I listen'd to th' attractive sound,

[6]The gallows [Ed.].

[7]A *Canoo* is an *Indian* Boat, cut out of the body of a Popler-Tree.

[8]Wolves are very numerous in *Mary-Land.*

And straight a Herd of Cattel found
Drove by a Youth, and homewards bound:
Cheer'd with the sight, I straight thought fit,
To ask where I a Bed might get.
The surley Peasant bid me stay,
And ask'd from whom I'de run away.[9]
Surprized at such a saucy Word,
I instantly lugg'd out my Sword;
Swearing I was no Fugitive,
But from *Great-Britain* did arrive,
In hopes I better there might Thrive.
To which he mildly made reply,
I beg your Pardon, Sir, *that I*
Should talk to you Unmannerly;
But if you please to go with me,
To yonder House, you'll welcome be.
Encountering soon the smoaky Seat,
The Planter old did thus me greet:
"Whether you come from Gaol or Colledge,
"You're welcome to my certain Knowledge;
"And if you please all Night to stay,
"My Son shall put you in the way.
Which offer I most kindly took,
And for a Seat did round me look;
When presently amongst the rest,
He plac'd his unknown *English* Guest,
Who found them drinking for a whet,
A Cask of Syder on the Fret,[10]
Till Supper came upon the Table,
On which I fed whilst I was able.
So after hearty Entertainment,
Of Drink and Victuals without Payment;
For Planters Tables, you must know,
Are free for all that come and go.
While Pon and Milk,[11] with Mush[12] well stoar'd,
In wooden Dishes grac'd the Board;
With Homine and Syder-pap,[13]
(Which scarce a hungry Dog wou'd lap)
Well stuff'd with Fat, from Bacon fry'd,
Or with *Molossus* dulcify'd.

[9]'Tis supposed by the Planters, that all unknown Persons are run away from some Master.

[10]Syder-pap is a sort of Food made of Syder and small Homine, like our Oatmeal [*on the Fret:* fermenting; Ed.].

[11]Pon is Bread made of *Indian Corn.*

[12]Mush is a sort of Hasty-Pudding made with Water and *Indian* Flower.

[13]Homine is a Dish that is made of boiled *Indian* Wheat, eaten with Molossus, or Bacon-Fat.

Then out our Landlord pulls a Pouch
As greasy as the Leather Couch
On which he sat, and straight begun,
To load with Weed his *Indian* Gun;[14]
In length, scarce longer than ones Finger,
Or that for which the Ladies linger.
His Pipe smoak'd out with aweful Grace,
With aspect grave and solemn pace;
The reverend Sire walks to a Chest,
Of all his Furniture the best,
Closely confin'd within a Room,
Which seldom felt the weight of Broom;
From thence he lugs a Cag of Rum,
And nodding to me, thus begun:
I find, says he, you don't much care,
For this our *Indian* Country Fare;
But let me tell you, Friend of mine,
You may be glad of it in time,
Tho' now your Stomach is so fine;
And if within this Land you stay,
You'll find it true what I do say.
This said, the Rundlet up he threw,
And bending backwards strongly drew:
I pluck'd as stoutly for my part,
Altho' it made me sick at Heart,
And got so soon into my Head
I scarce cou'd find my way to Bed;
Where I was instantly convey'd
By one who pass'd for Chamber-Maid;
Tho' by her loose and sluttish Dress,
She rather seem'd a *Bedlam-Bess:*[15]
Curious to know from whence she came,
I prest her to declare her Name.
She Blushing, seem'd to hide her Eyes,
And thus in Civil Terms replies;
In better Times, e'er to this Land,
I was unhappily Trapann'd;
Perchance as well I did appear,
As any Lord or Lady here,
Not then a Slave for twice two Year.[16]
My Cloaths were fashionably new,
Nor were my Shifts of Linnen Blue;
But things are changed now at the Hoe,

[14]Tobacco Pipe [Ed.].

[15]Bedlam was an insane asylum in England [Ed.].

[16]'Tis the Custom for Servants to be obliged for four Years to very servile Work; after which time they have their Freedom.

I daily work, and Bare-foot go,
In weeding Corn or feeding Swine,
I spend my melancholy Time.
Kidnap'd and Fool'd, I hither fled,
To shun a hated Nuptial Bed,[17]
And to my cost already find,
Worse Plagues than those I left behind.
Whate'er the Wanderer did profess,
Good-faith I cou'd not choose but guess
The Cause which brought her to this place,
Was supping e'er the Priest said Grace.
Quick as my Thoughts, the Slave was fled,
(Her Candle left to shew my Bed)
Which made of Feathers soft and good,
Close in the Chimney-corner stood;[18]
I threw me down expecting Rest,
To be in golden Slumbers blest:
But soon a noise disturb'd my quiet,
And plagu'd me with nocturnal Riot;
A Puss which in the ashes lay,
With grunting Pig began a Fray;
And prudent Dog, that Feuds might cease,
Most strongly bark'd to keep the Peace.
This Quarrel scarcely was decided,
By stick that ready lay provided;
But *Reynard* arch and cunning Loon,
Broke into my Appartment soon;
In hot pursuit of Ducks and Geese,
With fell intent the same to seize:
Their Cackling Plaints with strange surprize,
Chac'd Sleeps thick Vapours from my Eyes:
Raging I jump'd upon the Floar,
And like a Drunken Saylor Swore;
With Sword I fiercly laid about,
And soon dispers'd the Feather'd Rout:
The Poultry out of Window flew,
And *Reynard* cautiously withdrew:
The Dogs who this Encounter heard,
Fiercely themselves to aid me rear'd,
And to the Place of Combat run,
Exactly as the Field was won.
Fretting and hot as roasting Capon,

[17]These are the general Excuses made by *English* Women, which are sold, or sell themselves to *Mary-Land.*

[18]Beds stand in the Chimney-corner in this Country.

And greasy as a Flitch of Bacon;
I to the Orchard did repair,
To Breathe the cool and open Air;
Expecting there the rising Day,
Extended on a Bank I lay;
But Fortune here, that saucy Whore,
Disturb'd me worse and plagu'd me more,
Than she had done the night before.
Hoarse croaking Frogs did 'bout me ring,[19]
Such Peals the Dead to Life wou'd bring,
A Noise might move their Wooden King.[20]
I stuff'd my Ears with Cotten white
For fear of being deaf out-right,
And curst the melancholy Night:
But soon my Vows I did recant,
And Hearing as a Blessing grant;
When a confounded Rattle-Snake,
With hissing made my Heart to ake:
Not knowing how to fly the Foe,
Or whether in the Dark to go;
By strange good Luck, I took a Tree,
Prepar'd by Fate to set me free;
Where riding on a Limb astride,
Night and the Branches did me hide,
And I the Devil and Snake defy'd.
Not yet from Plagues exempted quite,
The curst Muskitoes did me bite;
Till rising Morn' and blushing Day,
Drove both my Fears and Ills away;
And from Night's Errors set me free.
Discharg'd from hospitable Tree;
I did to Planters Booth repair,
And there at Breakfast nobly Fare,
On rashier broil'd of infant Bear:
I thought the Cub delicious Meat,
Which ne'er did ought but Chesnuts eat;
Nor was young Orsin's flesh the worse,
Because he suck'd a Pagan Nurse.[21]

[19]Frogs are called *Virginea* Bells, and make, (both in that Country and *Mary-Land*) during the Night, a very hoarse ungrateful Noise.

[20]A reference to a fable by Aesop in which frogs, dissatisfied with the log they have been given for their king, ask for another king. They are given a crane, which devours them [Ed.].

[21]A reference to the tale *Valentine and Orson,* in which two abandoned infants are saved; one (Valentine) is taken to the court, and the other (Orson) is nursed by a bear [Ed.].

Our Breakfast done, my Landlord stout,
Handed a Glass of Rum about;
Pleas'd with the Treatment I did find,
I took my leave of Oast so kind;
Who to oblige me, did provide,
His eldest Son to be my Guide,
And lent me Horses of his own,
A skittish Colt, and aged Rhoan,
The four-leg'd prop of his Wife *Joan*.
Steering our Barks in Trot or Pace,
We sail'd directly for a place
In *Mary-Land* of high renown,
Known by the Name of *Battle-Town*.
To view the Crowds did there resort,
Which Justice made, and Law their sport,
In that sagacious County Court:
Scarce had we enter'd on the way,
Which thro' thick Woods and Marshes lay;
But *Indians* strange did soon appear,
In hot persuit of wounded Deer;
No mortal Creature can express,
His wild fantastick Air and Dress;
His painted Skin in colours dy'd,
His sable Hair in Satchel ty'd,
Shew'd Savages not free from Pride:
His tawny Thighs, and Bosom bare,
Disdain'd a useless Coat to wear,
Scorn'd Summer's Heat, and Winters Air;
His manly Shoulders such as please,
Widows and Wives, were bath'd in Grease
Of Cub and Bear, whose supple Oil,
Prepar'd his Limbs 'gainst Heat or Toil.
Thus naked Pict in Battel faught,
Or undisguis'd his Mistress sought;
And knowing well his Ware was good,
Refus'd to screen it with a Hood;
His Visage dun, and chin that ne'er
Did Raizor feel or Scissers bear,
Or knew the Ornament of Hair,
Look'd sternly Grim, surpriz'd with Fear,
I spur'd my Horse, as he drew near:
But Rhoan who better knew than I,
The little Cause I had to fly;
Seem'd by his solemn steps and pace,
Resolv'd I shou'd the Specter face,
Nor faster mov'd, tho' spur'd and lick'd,

Than *Balaam's* Ass by Prophet kick'd.[22]
Kekicknitop[23] the Heathen cry'd;
How is it *Tom.* my Friend reply'd:
Judging from thence the Brute was civel,
I boldly fac'd the Courteous Devil;
And lugging out a Dram of Rum,
I gave his Tawny worship some:
Who in his language as I guess,
(My Guide informing me no less,)
Implored the Devil, me to bless.[24]
I thank'd him for his good Intent,
And forwards on my Journey went,
Discoursing as along I rode,
Whether this Race was framed by God
Or whether some Malignant pow'r,
Contriv'd them in an evil hour
And from his own Infernal Look,
Their Dusky form and Image took:
From hence we fell to Argument
Whence Peopled was this Continent.
My Friend suppos'd *Tartarians* wild,
Or *Chinese* from their Home exiled;
Wandering thro' Mountains hid with Snow,
And Rills did in the Vallies flow,
Far to the South of *Mexico:*
Broke thro' the Barrs which Nature cast,
And wide unbeaten Regions past,
Till near those Streams the humane deludge roll'd,
Which sparkling shin'd with glittering Sands of Gold,
And fetch *Pizarro*[25] from the *Iberian* Shoar,[26]
To Rob the Natives of their fatal Stoar.
I Smil'd to hear my young Logician,
Thus Reason like a Politician;
Who ne're by Fathers Pains and Earning

[22]Numbers 22 [Ed.].

[23]*Kekicknitop* is an *Indian* Expression, and signifies no more than this, *How do you do?*

[24]These *Indians* worship the Devil, and pray to him as we do to God Almighty. 'Tis suppos'd, That *America* was peopl'd from *Scythia* or *Tartaria,* which Borders on *China,* by reason the Tartarians and *Americans* very much agree in their Manners, Arms, and Government. Other Persons are of Opinion, that the *Chinese* first peopled the *West Indies;* Imagining *China* and the Southern part of *America* to be contiguous. Others believe that the *Phoenicians* who were very skilful Mariners, first planted a Colony in the Isles of *America,* and supply'd the Persons left to inhabit there with Women and all other Necessaries; till either the Death or Shipwreck of the first Discoverers, or some other Misfortune occasioned the loss of the Discovery, which had been purchased by the Peril of the first Adventurers.

[25]*Pizarro* was the Person that conquer'd *Peru;* a Man of a most bloody Disposition, base, treacherous, covetous, and revengeful.

[26]*Spanish* Shoar.

Had got at Mother *Cambridge* Learning;
Where Lubber youth just free from birch
Most stoutly drink to prop the Church;
Nor with *Grey Groat* had taken Pains
To purge his Head and Cleanse his Reines:[27]
And in obedience to the Colledge,
Had pleas'd himself with carnal Knowlege:
And tho' I lik'd the youngester's Wit,
I judg'd the Truth he had not hit;
And could not choose but smile to think
What they could do for Meat and Drink,
Who o'er so many Desarts ran,
With Brats and Wives in *Caravan;*
Unless perchance they'd got the Trick
To eat no more than Porker sick;
Or could with well contented Maws,
Quarter like Bears upon their Paws.[28]
Thinking his Reasons to confute,
I gravely thus commenc'd Dispute,
And urg'd that tho' a *Chinese* Host,
Might penetrate this *Indian* Coast;
Yet this was certainly most true,
They never cou'd the Isles subdue;
For knowing not to steer a Boat,
They could not on the Ocean float,
Or plant their Sunburnt Colonies,
In Regions parted by the Seas:
I thence inferr'd *Phoenicians* bol,[29]
Discover'd first with Vessels bold
These Western Shoars, and planted here,
Returning once or twice a Year,
With *Naval Stoars* and Lasses kind,
To comfort those were left behind;
Till by the Winds and Tempest toar,
From their intended Golden Shoar;
They suffer'd Ship-wreck, or were drown'd,
And lost the World so newly found.
But after long and learn'd Contention,
We could not finish our dissention;

[27]There is a very bad Custom in some Colledges, of giving the Students *A Groat ad purgandus Rhenes,* which is usually employ'd to the use of the *Donor.*

[28]Bears are said to live by sucking of their *Paws,* according to the Notion of some Learned Authors.

[29]The *Phoenicians* were the best and boldest Saylors of Antiquity, and indeed the only *Persons,* in former Ages, who durst venture themselves on the Main Sea.

And when that both had talk'd their fill,
We had the self same Notion still.
Thus Parson grave well read and Sage,
Does in dispute with Priest engage;
The one protests they are not Wise,
Who judge by Sense and trust their Eyes;[30]
And vows he'd burn for it at Stake,
That Man may God his Maker make;
The other smiles at his Religion,
And vows he's but a learned Widgeon:
And when they have empty'd all their stoar
From Books and Fathers, are not more
Convinc'd or wiser than before.
Scarce had we finish'd serious Story,
But I espy'd the Town before me,
And roaring Planters on the ground,
Drinking of Healths in Circle round:
Dismounting Steed with friendly Guide,
Our Horses to a Tree we ty'd,
And forwards pass'd amongst the Rout,
To chuse convenient *Quarters* out:
But being none were to be found,
We sat like others on the ground
Carousing Punch in open Air
Till Cryer did the Court declare;
The planting Rabble being met,
Their Drunken Worships likewise set:
Cryer proclaims that Noise shou'd cease,
And streight the Lawyers broke the Peace:
Wrangling for Plaintiff and Defendant,
I thought they ne'er would make an end on't:
With nonsense, stuff and false quotations,
With brazen Lyes and Allegations;
And in the splitting of the Cause,
They us'd such Motions with their Paws,
As shew'd their Zeal was strongly bent,
In Blows to end the Argument.
A reverend Judge, who to the shame
Of all the Bench, cou'd write his Name;[31]
At Petty-fogger took offence,
And wonder'd at his Impudence.

[30]The *Priests* argue, That our Senses in the point of *Transubstantiation* ought not to be believed, for tho' the Consecrated Bread has all the accidents of Bread, yet they affirm, 'tis the Body of Christ, and not Bread but Flesh and Bones.

[31]In the County-Court of *Maryland,* very few of the Justices of the *Peace* can write or read.

My Neighbour *Dash* with scorn replies,
And in the Face of Justice flies:
The Bench in fury streight divide,
And Scribbles take, or Judges side;
The Jury, Lawyers, and their Clyents,
Contending, fight like earth-born Gyants:
But Sheriff wily lay perdue,
Hoping Indictments wou'd ensue,
And when ______________________
A Hat or Wig fell in the way,
He seiz'd them for the *Queen* as stray:
The Court adjourn'd in usual manner,
In Battle Blood, and fractious Clamour:
I thought it proper to provide,
A Lodging for myself and Guide,
So to our Inn we march'd away,
Which at a little distance lay;
Where all things were in such Confusion,
I thought the World at its conclusion:
A Herd of Planters on the ground,
O'er-whelm'd with Punch, dead drunk we found:
Others were fighting and contending,
Some burnt their Cloaths to save the mending.
A few whose Heads by frequent use,
Could better bare the potent Juice,
Gravely debated State Affairs.
Whilst I most nimbly trip'd up Stairs;
Leaving my Friend discoursing oddly,
And mixing things Prophane and Godly:
Just then beginning to be Drunk,
As from the Company I slunk,
To every Room and Nook I crept,
In hopes I might have somewhere slept;
But all the bedding was possest
By one or other drunken Guest:
But after looking long about,
I found an antient Corn-loft out,
Glad that I might in quiet sleep,
And there my bones unfractur'd keep.
I lay'd me down secure from Fray,
And soundly snoar'd till break of Day;
When waking fresh I sat upright,
And found my Shoes were vanish'd quite,
Hat, Wig, and Stockings, all were fled
From this extended *Indian* Bed:
Vext at the Loss of Goods and Chattel,
I swore I'd give the Rascal battel,

Who had abus'd me in this sort,
And Merchant Stranger made his Sport.
I furiously descended Ladder;
No Hare in *March* was ever madder;
In vain I search'd for my Apparel,
And did with Oast and Servants Quarrel;
For one whose Mind did much aspire
To Mischief, threw them in the Fire;[32]
Equipt with neither Hat nor Shooe,
I did my coming hither rue,
And doubtful thought what I should do:
Then looking round, I saw my Friend
Lie naked on a Tables end;
A Sight so dismal to behold,
One wou'd have judg'ed him dead and cold;
When wringing of his bloody Nose,
By fighting got we may suppose;
I found him not so fast asleep,
Might give his Friends a cause to weep:
Rise *Oronooko,* rise, said I,[33]
And from this *Hell* and *Bedlam* fly.
My Guide starts up, and in amaze,
With blood-shot Eyes did round him gaze;
At length with many a sigh and groan,
He went in search of aged Rhoan;
But Rhoan, tho' seldom us'd to faulter,
Had fairly this time slipt his Halter;
And not content all Night to stay
Ty'd up from Fodder, ran away:
After my Guide to ketch him ran,
And so I lost both Horse and Man;
Which Disappointment, tho' so great,
Did only Mirth and Jests create:
Till one more Civil than the rest,
In Conversation for the best,
Observing that for want of Rhoan,
I should be left to walk alone;
Most readily did me intreat,
To take a Bottle at his Seat;
A Favour at that time so great,
I blest my kind propitious Fate;
And finding soon a fresh supply,

[32]'Tis the Custom of the Planters, to throw their own, or any other Persons Hat, Wig, Shooes, or Stockings in the Fire.

[33]Planters are usually call'd by the Name *Oronooko,* from their Planting *Oronooko-Tobacco.*

Of Cloaths from Stoar-house kept hard by,
I mounted streight on such a Steed,
Did rather curb, than whipping need;
And straining at the usual rate,
With spur of Punch which lay in Pate,[34]
E'er long we lighted at the Gate:
Where in an antient *Cedar* House,
Dwelt my new Friend, a Cokerouse;[35]
Whose Fabrick, tho' 'twas built of Wood,
Had many Springs and Winters stood;
When sturdy Oaks, and lofty Pines
Were level'd with Musmelion Vines,[36]
And Plants eradicated were,
By Hurricanes into the air;
There with good Punch and apple Juice,
We spent our Hours without abuse:
Till Midnight in her sable Vest,
Persuaded Gods and Men to rest;
And with a pleasing kind surprize,
Indulg'd soft Slumbers to my Eyes.
Fierce *Ælthon* courser of the Sun.[37]
Had half his Race exactly run;
And breath'd on me a fiery Ray,
Darting hot Beams the following Day,
When snug in Blanket white I lay:
But Heat and *Chinces*[38] rais'd the Sinner,
Most opportunely to his Dinner;
Wild Fowl and Fish delicious Meats,
As good as *Neptune's* Doxy[39] eats,
Began our Hospitable Treat;
Fat Venson follow'd in the Rear,
And Turkies[40] wild Luxurious Chear:
But what the Feast did most commend,
Was hearty welcom from my Friend.
Thus having made a noble Feast,
And eat as well as pamper'd Priest,
Madera strong in flowing Bowls,
Fill'd with extream, delight our Souls;
Till wearied with a purple Flood,

[34]That is, drunk [Ed.].

[35]Cockerouse, is a Man of Quality.

[36]Musmilleon Vines are what we call Muskmilleon Plants.

[37]*Ælthon* is one of the Poetical Horses of the Sun.

[38]*Chinces* are a sort of Vermin like our *Bugs* in *England.*

[39]Sweetheart [Ed.].

[40]Wild Turkies are very good Meat, and prodigiously large in *Maryland.*

Of generous Wine (the Giant's blood,
As Poets feign) away I made,
For some refreshing verdant Shade;
Where musing on my Rambles strange,
And Fortune which so oft did change;
In midst of various Contemplations
Of Fancies odd, and Meditations,
I slumber'd long ________________
Till hazy Night with noxious Dews,
Did Sleep's unwholsom Fetters lose:
With Vapours chil'd, and misty air,
To fire-side I did repair:
Near which a jolly Female Crew,
Were deep engag'ed at *Lanctre-Looe*;[41]
In Nightrails[42] white, with dirty Mein,
Such Sights are scarce in *England* seen:
I thought them first some Witches bent,
On Black Designs in dire Convent.
Till one who with affected air,
Had nicely learn'd to Curse and Swear:
Cry'd Dealing's lost is but a Flam,
And vow'd by G—d she'd keep her *Pam*.[43]
When dealing through the board had run,
They ask'd me kindly to make one;
Not staying often to be bid,
I sat me down as others did:
We scarce had play'd a Round about,
But that these *Indian* Froes[44] fell out.
D—m you, says one, tho' now so brave,
I knew you late a Four-Years Slave;
What if for Planters Wife you go,
Nature design'd you for the Hoe.
Rot you replies the other streight,
The Captain kiss'd you for his Freight;
And if the Truth was known aright,
And how you walk'd the Streets by night,
You'd blush (if one cou'd blush) for shame,
Who from *Bridewell* or *Newgate* came.
From Words they fairly fell to Blows,
And being loath to interpose,
Or meddle in the Wars of Punk,[45]
Away to Bed in hast I slunk.
Waking next day, with aking Head,

[41] A card game [Ed.].
[42] Nightgowns [Ed.].
[43] The highest card [Ed.].
[44] Mean-spirited women [Ed.].
[45] Prostitution [Ed.].

And Thirst, that made me quit my Bed;
I rigg'd myself, and soon got up.
To cool my Liver with a Cup
Of *Succahana* fresh and clear,[46]
Not half so good as *English* Beer;
Which ready stood in Kitchin Pail,
And was in fact but *Adam's* Ale;
For Planters Cellars you must know,
Seldom with good *October* flow,[47]
But Perry Quince and Apple Juice,
Spout from the Tap like any Sluce;
Untill the Cask's grown low and stale,
They're forc'd again to Goad and Pail:[48]
The soathing drought scarce down my Throat,
Enough to put a Ship a float,
With Cockerouse as I was sitting,
I felt a Feaver Intermitting;
A fiery Pulse beat in my Veins,
From Cold I felt resembling Pains:
This cursed seasoning I remember,
Lasted from *March* to cold *December;*
Nor would it then its *Quarters* shift
Until by *Cardus*[49] turn'd a drift,
And had my Doctress wanted skill,
Or Kitchin Physick at her will,
My Father's Son had lost his Lands,
And never seen the *Goodwin-Sands:*
But thanks to Fortune and a Nurse
Whosc Carc depended on my Purse,
I saw myself in good Condition,
Without the help of a Physitian:
At length the shivering ill relieved,
Which long my Head and Heart have grieved;
I then began to think with Care,
How I might sell my *British* Ware,
That with my Freight I might comply,
Did on my Charter party lie:
To this intent, with Guide before,
I tript it to the Eastern Shoar;
While riding near a Sandy Bay,
I met a *Quaker, Yea* and *Nay;*
A Pious Conscientious Rogue,
As e'er woar Bonnet or a Brogue,

[46]*Succahana* is Water.
[47]That is, the best (October-brewed) ale [Ed.].
[48]A *Goad* grows upon as *Indian* Vine, resembling a Bottle, when ripe it is hollow; this the Planters make use of to drink water out of.
[49]A medicine [Ed.].

Who neither Swore nor kept his Word,
But cheated in the Fear of God;
And when his Debts he would not pay,
By Light within he ran away.
With this sly Zealot soon I struck
A Bargain for my *English* Truck,
Agreeing for ten thousand weight,
Of *Sot-weed* good and fit for freight,
Broad *Oronooko* bright and sound,
The growth and product of his ground;
In Cask that should contain compleat,
Five hundred of Tobacco neat.
The Contract thus betwixt us made,
Not well acquainted with the Trade,
My Goods I trusted to the Cheat,
Whose crop was then aboard the Fleet;
And going to receive my own,
I found the Bird was newly flown:
Cursing this execrable Slave,
This damn'd pretended Godly Knave;
On due Revenge and Justice bent,
I instantly to Counsel went,
Unto an ambodexter *Quack,*[50]
Who learnedly had got the knack,
Of giving Glisters, making Pills,
Of filling Bonds, and forging Wills;
And with a stock of Impudence,
Supply'd his want of Wit and Sense;
With Looks demure, amazing People,
No wiser than a Daw in Steeple;
My Anger flushing in my Face,
I stated the preceeding Case:
And of my Money was so lavish,
That he'd have poyson'd half the Parish,
And hang'd his Father on a Tree,
For such another tempting Fee;
Smiling, said he, the Cause is clear,
I'll manage him you need not fear;
The Case is judg'd, good Sir, but look
In *Galen,* No—in my Lord *Cook,*[51]
I vow to God I was mistook:
I'll take out a Provincial Writ,
And Trounce him for his Knavish Wit;

[50]This Fellow was an Apothecary, and turn'd an Attorney at Law.

[51]Galen, the most famous physician of ancient Greece, prepared a handbook on medicine; Sir Edward Coke wrote the *Institutes,* a commentary on the laws [Ed.].

Upon my life we'll win the Cause,
With all the ease I cure the *Yaws*:[52]
Resolv'd to plague the holy Brother,
I set one Rogue to catch another;
To try the Cause then fully bent,
Up to *Annapolis*[53] I went,
A City Situate on a Plain,
Where scarce a House will keep out Rain;
The Buildings fram'd with Cyprus rare,
Resembles much our *Southwark* Fair:[54]
But Stranger here will scarcely meet
With Market-place, Exchange, or Street;
And if the Truth I may report,
'Tis not so large as *Tottenham Court*.[55]
St. Mary's[56] once was in repute,
Now here the Judges try the Suit,
And lawyers twice a Year dispute.
As oft the Bench most gravely meet,
Some to get Drunk, and some to eat
A swinging share of Country Treat.
But as for Justice right or wrong,
Not one amongst the numerous throng,
Knows what they mean, or has the Heart,
To give his Verdict on a Stranger's part:
Now Court being call'd by beat of Drum,
The Judges left their Punch and Rum,
When Pettifogger Doctor draws,
His Paper forth, and opens Cause:
And least I shou'd the better get,
Brib'd *Quack* suppress his Knavish Wit.
So Maid upon the downy Field,
Pretends a Force, and Fights to yield:
The Byast Court without delay,
Adjudg'd my Debt in Country Pay;
In Pipe staves, Corn, or Flesh of Boar,[57]
Rare Cargo for the *English* Shoar:
Raging with Grief, full speed I ran,
To joyn the Fleet at *Kicketan*;[58]
Embarqu'd and waiting for a Wind,
I left this dreadful Curse behind.

[52]The *Yaws* is the *Pox*.

[53]The chief [city] of *Mary-land* containing about twenty four *Houses*.

[54]A London fair [Ed.].

[55]A London district [Ed.].

[56]Annapolis became the Maryland capital in 1694 [Ed.].

[57]There is a Law in this Country, the Plaintiff may pay his Debt in Country pay, which consists in the produce of his Plantation.

[58]The homeward bound Fleet meets here. [*Kicketan* is Hampton, Virginia; Ed.].

May Canniballs transported o'er the Sea
Prey on these Slaves, as they have done on me;
May never Merchant's, trading Sails explore
This Cruel, this Inhospitable Shoar;
But left abandon'd by the World to starve,
May they sustain the Fate they well deserve:
May they turn Savage, or as *Indians* Wild,
From Trade, Converse, and Happiness exil'd;
Recreant to Heaven, may they adore the Sun,
And into Pagan Superstitions run
For Vengence ripe ______________
May Wrath Divine then lay those Regions wast
Where no Man's[59] Faithful, nor a Woman Chast.

1708

Richard Lewis 1700?–1734

Richard Lewis, a prolific writer, probably came to America from Wales in 1718. He became a schoolmaster and member of the Assembly in Maryland. According to his biographer, J.A. Leo Lemay, no other American poet of the early eighteenth century was so widely reprinted.

Like Ebenezer Cook, Richard Lewis creates a peculiarly American poem using an English poetic model. English pastorals, based upon classical models replete with nymphs and shepherds, idealized rural life and rural scenery, in a verse form that emulated the order and harmony of nature. At the hands of English writers like Pope and Philips, the pastoral increasingly began to show the influence of the eighteenth-century realities of English rural life. With its emphasis upon the rural life and its allegorical impulse, the pastoral would have been a welcome form to adapt in America, the place fast turning from a wilderness into a garden. At the hands of Richard Lewis, the pastoral form was transformed into a mode offering a central critique of English poetry because of its pro-American stance. In applying the pastoral tradition to American poetry, Lewis implicitly claimed that American nature was superior to English or European nature as subject, indeed that English and classical poets might have written better had they had America as their topic.

This text is taken from the London *Weekly Register* of January 1, 1732. Unless otherwise noted, annotations are from that publication.

[59]The Author does not intend by this, any of the *English* Gentlemen resident there.

A Journey from Patapsko to Annapolis, April 4, 1730[1]

Me vero primum dulces ante omnia Musae,
Quarum sacra fero ingenti perculsus amore,
Accipiant; Coelique vias & Sydera *monstrent;——*
Sin has ne possim Naturae accedere partes
Frigidus obstiterit circum praecordia Sanguis,
Rura *mihi, &* rigui *placeant in Vallibus* Amnes,
Flumina *amem,* Sylvasque *inglorius.*

VIRG. *Geor.* 2[2]

At length the *wintry* Horrors disappear,
And *April* views with Smiles the infant Year;
The grateful Earth from frosty Chains unbound,
Pours out its *vernal* Treasures all around,
Her Face bedeckt with Grass, with Buds the Trees are crown'd.
In this soft Season, 'ere the Dawn of Day,
I mount my Horse, and lonely take my Way,
From woody Hills that shade *Patapsko's* Head,
(In whose deep Vales he makes his stony Bed,
From whence he rushes with resistless Force,
Tho' huge rough Rocks retard his rapid Course,)
Down to *Annapolis,* on that smooth Stream[3]
Which took from fair *Anne-Arundel* its Name.
And now the *Star* that ushers in the Day,[4]
Begins to pale her ineffectual Ray.
The *Moon,* with blunted Horns, now shines less bright,
Her fading Face eclips'd with growing Light;
The fleecy Clouds with streaky Lustre glow,
And Day quits Heav'n to view the Earth below.
Oe'r yon tall *Pines* the *Sun* shews half his Face,
And fires their floating Foliage with his Rays;
Now sheds aslant on Earth his lightsome Beams,
That trembling shine in many-colour'd Streams:
Slow-rising from the Marsh, the Mist recedes,
The Trees, emerging, rear their dewy Heads;
Their dewy Heads the *Sun* with Pleasure views,
And brightens into Pearls the pendent Dews.

[1]The Patapsko River meets the Chesapeake Bay at Baltimore, which, in its earliest years, took its name from the river [Ed.].

[2]Vergil, *Georgics,* 2:47, 5–77, 483–86: "But as for me—first above all, may the sweet Muses whose holy emblems, under the spell of a mighty love, I bear, take me to themselves, and show me heaven's pathways, [and] the stars . . . But if the chill blood about my heart bar me from reaching those realms of nature, let my delight be the country, and the running streams amid the dells—may I love the waters and the woods, though fame be lost" (Loeb Classical Library translation, 1950) [Ed.].

[3]The Severn River meets the Chesapeake Bay at Annapolis [Ed.].

[4]Venus.

The *Beasts* uprising, quit their leafy Beds,
And to the cheerful *Sun* erect their Heads;
All joyful rise, except the filthy *Swine,*
On obscene Litter stretch'd they snore supine:
In vain the Day awakes, Sleep seals their Eyes,
Till Hunger breaks the Bond and bids them rise.
Mean while the *Sun* with more exalted Ray,
From cloudless Skies distributes riper Day;
Thro' sylvan Scenes my Journey I pursue,
Ten thousand Beauties rising to my View;
Which kindle in my Breast poetic Flame,
And bid me my CREATOR's praise proclaim;
Tho' my low Verse ill-suits the noble Theme.
Here various Flourets grace the teeming Plains,[5]
Adorn'd by Nature's Hand with beauteous Stains;
First-born of *Spring,* here the *Pacone* appears,
Whose golden Root a silver Blossom rears.
In spreading Tufts, see there the *Crowfoot* blue,
On whose green Leaves still shines a globous Dew;
Behold the *Cinque-foil,* with its dazling Dye
Of flaming Yellow, wounds the tender Eye:
But there, enclos'd the grassy *Wheat* is seen,
To heal the aching Sight with cheerful Green.
Safe in yon Cottage dwells the *Monarch-Swain,*
His *Subject-Flocks,* close-grazing, hide the Plain;
For him they live;——and die t'uphold his Reign.
Viands unbought his well-till'd Lands afford,
And smiling *Plenty* waits upon his Board;
Health shines with sprightly Beams around his Head,
And *Sleep,* with downy Wings, o'er-shades his Bed;
His *Sons* robust his daily Labours share,
Patient of Toil, Companions of his Care:
And all their Toils with sweet Success are crown'd.
In graceful Ranks there *Trees* adorn the Ground,
The *Peach,* the *Plum,* the *Apple,* here are found;
Delicious Fruits!——Which from their Kernels rise,
So fruitful is the Soil—so mild the Skies.
The lowly *Quince* yon sloping Hill o'er-shades.
Here lofty *Cherry-Trees* erect their Heads;
High in the Air each spiry Summer waves,
Whose Blooms thick-springing yield no Space for Leaves;
Evolving Odours fill the ambient Air,

[5]Pacone, or Tumeric root, produces a greenish-white flower in April. Crowfoot is a plant that thrives in water; it has a white flower. Cinquefoil, or Potentilla, blooms with a yellow flower [Ed.].

The *Birds* delighted to the Grove repair:
On ev'ry Tree behold a tuneful Throng,
The vocal Vallies echo to their Song.
  But what is *He,*[6] who perch'd above the rest,
Pours out such various Musick from his Breast!
His Breast, whose Plumes a cheerful White display,
His quiv'ring Wings are dress'd in sober Grey.
Sure, all the *Muses,* this their Bird inspire!
And *He,* alone, is equal to the Choir
Of warbling Songsters who around him play,
While, Echo like, *He* answers ev'ry Lay.
The chirping *Lark* now sings with sprightly Note,
Responsive to her Strain *He* shapes his Throat:
Now the poor widow'd *Turtle* wails her Mate,
While in soft Sounds *He* cooes to mourn his Fate.
Oh, sweet Musician, thou dost far excel
The soothing Song of pleasing *Philomel!*
Sweet is her Song, but in few Notes confin'd;
But thine, thou *Mimic* of the feath'ry Kind,
Runs thro' all Notes!——*Thou* only know'st them *All,*
At once the *Copy,——and th'Original.*
  My *Ear* thus charm'd, mine *Eye* with Pleasure sees,
Hov'ring about the Flow'rs, th'industrious *Bees.*
Like them in Size, the *Humming-Bird* I view,
Like them, *He* sucks his Food, the Honey-Dew,
With nimble Tongue, and Beak of jetty Hue.
He takes with rapid Whirl his noisy Flight,
His gemmy Plumage strikes the Gazer's Sight;
And as he moves his ever-flutt'ring Wings,
Ten thousand Colours he around him flings.
Now I behold the Em'rald's vivid Green,
Now scarlet, now a purple Die is seen;
In brightest Blue, his Breast *He* now arrays,
Then strait his Plumes emit a golden Blaze.
Thus whirring round he flies, and varying still,
He mocks the *Poet's* and the *Painter's* Skill;
Who may forever strive with fruitless Pains,
To catch and fix those beauteous changeful Stains;
While Scarlet now, and now the Purple shines,
And Gold, to Blue its transient Gloss resigns.
Each quits, and quickly each resumes its Place,
And ever-varying Dies each other chase.
Smallest of Birds, what Beauties shine in thee!
A living *Rainbow* on thy Breast I see.
  Oh had that *Bard*[7] in whose heart-pleasing Lines,

[6]The Mock Bird.

[7]*Claudian.*

The *Phoenix* in a Blaze of Glory shines,
Beheld those Wonders which are shewn in Thee,
That *Bird* had lost his Immortality!
Thou in His Verse hadst stretch'd thy flutt'ring Wing
Above all other Birds,—their beauteous King.
    But now th'enclos'd Plantation I forsake
And onwards thro' the Woods my Journey take;
The level Road, the longsome Way beguiles,
A blooming Wilderness around me smiles;
Here hardy *Oak,* there fragment *Hick'ry* grows,
Their bursting Buds the tender Leaves disclose;
The tender Leaves in downy Robes appear,
Trembling, they seem to move with cautious Fear,
Yet new to Life, and Strangers to the Air.
Here stately *Pines* unite their whisp'ring Heads,
And with a solemn Gloom embrown the Glades.
See there a green *Savane* opens wide,
Thro' which smooth Streams in wanton Mazes glide;
Thick-branching Shrubs o'er-hang the silver Streams,
Which scarcely deign t'admit the solar Beams.
    While with Delight on this soft Scene I gaze,
The *Cattle* upward look, and cease to graze,
But into covert run thro' various Ways.
And now the Clouds in black Assemblage rise,
And dreary Darkness overspreads the Skies,
Thro' which the Sun strives to transmit his Beams,
"But sheds his sickly light in straggling Streams."[8]
Hush'd is the Musick of the wood-land Choir,
Fore-knowing of the Storm, the Birds retire
For Shelter, and forsake the shrubby Plains,
And dumb Horror thro' the Forest reigns;
In that lone House which opens wide its Door,
Safe may I tarry till the Storm is o'er.
    Hark how the *Thunder* rolls with solemn Sound!
And see the forceful *Lightning* dart a Wound,
On yon toll Oak!——Behold its Top laid bare!
Its Body rent, and scatter'd thro' the Air
The Splinters fly!——Now—now the *Winds* arise,
From different Quarters of the lowring Skies;
Forth-issuing fierce, the *West* and *South* engage,
The waving Forest bends beneath their Rage:
But where the winding Valley checks their Course,
They roar and ravage with redoubled Force;
With circling Sweep in dreadful Whirlwinds move

[8]An allusion to a Dryden translation of Vergil's *Georgics* I: "Or if thro' mists he shoots his sullen beams, / Frugal of light, in loose and straggling streams" [Ed.].

And from its Roots tear up the gloomy Grove,
Down-rushing fall the Trees, and beat the Ground,
In Fragments flie the shatter'd Limbs around;
Tremble the Under-woods, the Vales resound.
  Follows, with patt'ring Noise, the icy *Hail,*
And *Rain,* fast falling, floods the lowly Vale.
Again the *Thunders* roll, the *Lightnings* fly,
And as they first disturb'd, now clear the Sky;
For lo, the *Gust* decreases by Degrees,
The dying *Winds* but sob amidst the Trees;
With pleasing Softness falls the silver Rain,
Thro' which at first faint-gleaming o'er the Plain,
The Orb of Light scarce darts a watry Ray
To gild the Drops that fall from ev'ry Spray;
But soon the dusky Vapours are dispell'd,
And thro' the Mist that late his Face conceal'd,
Bursts the broad *Sun,* triumphant in a Blaze
Too keen for Sight—Yon Cloud refracts his Rays,
The mingling Beams compose th'*ethereal Bow,*
How sweet, how soft, its melting Colours glow!
Gaily they shine, by heav'nly Pencils laid,
Yet vanish swift,——How soon does *Beauty* fade!
  The *Storm* is past, my Journey I renew,
And a new Scene of Pleasure greets my View:
Wash'd by the copious Rain the gummy *Pine,*
Does cheerful, with unsully'd Verdure shine;
The *Dogwood* Flow'rs assume a snowy white,
The *Maple* blushing gratifies the Sight:
No verdant leaves the lovely *Red-Bud* grace,
Cornation blossoms now supply their Place.
The *Sassafras* unfolds its fragrant Bloom,
The *Vine* affords an exquisite Perfume;
These grateful Scents wide-wafting thro' the Air
The smelling Sense with balmy Odours cheer.
And now the *Birds,* sweet singing, stretch their Throats,
And in one Choir unite their various Notes,
Nor yet unpleasing is the *Turtle's* Voice,
Tho' he complains while other Birds rejoice.
  These vernal Joys, all restless Thoughts controul,
And gently-soothing calm the troubled Soul.
  While such Delights my Senses entertain,
I scarce perceive that I have left the *Plain;*
'Till now the Summit of a *Mount* I gain:
Low at whose sandy Base the *River* glides,
Slow-rolling near their Height his languid Tides;
Shade above Shade, the Trees in rising Ranks,
Cloath with eternal Green his steepy Banks:

The Flood, well pleas'd, reflects their verdant Gleam
From the smooth Mirror of his limpid Stream.
But see the *Hawk,* who with acute Survey,
Towring in Air predestinates his Prey
Amid the Floods!——Down dropping from on high,
He strikes the *Fish,* and bears him thro' the Sky.
The Stream disturb'd, no longer shews the Scene
That lately stain'd its silver Waves with green;
In spreading Circles roll the troubled Floods,
And to the Shores bear off the pictur'd Woods.
Now looking round I view the out-stretch'd *Land,*
O'er which the Sight exerts a wide Command;
The fertile Vallies, and the naked Hills,
The Cattle feeding near the chrystal Rills;
The Lawns wide-op'ning to the sunny Ray,
And mazy Thickets that exclude the Day.
A-while the Eye is pleas'd these Scenes to trace,
Then hurrying o'er the intermediate Space,
Far distant Mountains drest in Blue appear,
And all their Woods are lost in empty Air.
The *Sun* near setting now arrays his Head
In milder Beams and lengthens ev'ry Shade.
The rising Clouds usurping on the Day
A bright Variety of Dies display;
About the wide Horizon swift they fly,
"And chase a Change of Colours round the Sky:[9]
And now I view but half the *flaming Sphere,*
Now one faint Glimmer shoots along the Air,
And all his golden Glories disappear.
Onwards the *Ev'ning* moves in Habit grey,
And for her Sister *Night* prepares the Way.
The plumy People seek their secret Nests,
To Rest repair the ruminating Beasts.
Now deep'ning Shades confess th' Approach of Night,
Imperfect Images elude the Sight:
From earthly Objects I remove mine Eye,
And view with Look erect the vaulted Sky;
Where dimly-shining now the Stars appear,
At first thin-scatt'ring thro' the misty Air;
Till Night confirm'd, her jetty Throne ascends,
On her the *Moon* in clouded State attends,
But soon unveil'd her lovely Face is seen,
And *Stars* unnumber'd wait around their Queen;

[9]An allusion to James Thomson on Summer, in the *Seasons:* "See, how at once the bright effulgent sun, / Rising direct, swift chases from the sky / The short-lived Twilight . . ." [Ed.].

Rang'd by their MAKER's Hand in just Array,
They march majestic thro' th'ethereal Way.
Are these bright Luminaries hung on high
Only to please with twinkling Rays our Eye?
Or may we rather count each *Star* a *Sun,*
Round which *full peopled Worlds* their Courses run?
Orb above Orb harmoniously they steer
Their various voyages thro' Seas of Air.
Snatch me some *Angel* to those high Abodes,
The Seats perhaps of *Saints* and *Demigods!*
Where such as bravely scorn'd the galling Yoke
Of *vulgar Error,* and her Fetters broke;
Where *Patriots* who fix the publick Good,
In Fields of Battle sacrific'd their Blood;
Where *pious Priests* who Charity proclaim'd,
And *Poets* whom a *virtuous Muse* enflam'd;
Philosophers who strove to mend our Hearts,
And such as polish'd Life with *useful Arts,*
Obtain a Place; when by the Hand of Death
Touch'd, they retire from this poor Speck of Earth;
Their *Spirits* freed from bodily Alloy
Perceive a Fore-taste of that endless Joy,
Which from Eternity hath been prepar'd,
To crown their labours with a vast Reward.
While to these Orbs my wand'ring Thoughts aspire,
A falling *Meteor* shoots his lambent Fire;
Thrown from the heav'nly Space he seeks the Earth,
From whence he first deriv'd his humble Birth.
The *Mind* advis'd by this instructive Sight,
Descending sudden from th'aerial Height,
Obliges me to view a different Scene,
Of more importance to myself, tho' mean.
These distant Objects I no more pursue,
But turning inward my reflective View,
My working Fancy helps me to survey,
In the just Picture of this *April Day,*
My life o'er past,——a Course of thirty *Years*
Blest with few Joys, perplex'd with num'rous Cares.
In the dim Twilight of our *Infancy,*
Scarce can the Eye surrounding Objects see;
Then thoughtless *Childhood* leads us pleas'd and gay,
In Life's fair Morning thro' a flow'ry Way:
The *Youth* in Schools inquisitive of Good,
Science pursues thro' *Learning's* mazy Wood;
Whose lofty Trees, he, to his Grief perceives,
Are often bare of *Fruit,* and only fill'd with *Leaves:*
Thro' lonely Wilds his tedious Journey lies,

At last a brighter Prospect cheers his Eyes;
Now the gay Fields of *Poetry* he views,
And joyous listens to the *tuneful Muse;*
Now *History* affords him vast Delight,
And opens lovely Landscapes to his Sight:
But ah too soon this Scene of Pleasure flies!
And o'er his Head tempestous Troubles rise.
He hears the Thunders roll, he feels the Rains,
Before a friendly Shelter he obtains;
And thence beholds with Grief the furious Storm
The *noon-tide* Beauties of his *Life* deform:
He views the *painted Bow* in distant Skies;
Hence, in his Heart some Gleams of Comfort rise;
He hopes the *Gust* has almost spent its Force,
And that he safely may pursue his Course.
Thus far *my Life* does with the *Day* agree,
Oh may its coming Stage from Storms be free!
While passing thro' the World's most private Way,
With Pleasure I my MAKER'S Works survey;
Within my Heart let *Peace* a Dwelling find,
Let my *Goodwill* extend to *all Mankind:*
Freed from *Necessity,* and blest with *Health;*
Give me *Content,* let others toil for *Wealth:*
In *busy* Scenes of Life let me exert
A *careful Hand,* and wear an *honest Heart;*
And suffer me my *leisure* Hours to spend,
With chosen *Books,* or a well-natur'd *Friend.*
Thus journeying on, as I advance in Age
May I look back with Pleasure on my Stage;
And as the setting *Sun* withdrew his Light
To rise on other Worlds serene and bright,
Cheerful may I resign my vital Breath,
Nor anxious tremble at th' Approach of *Death;*
Which shall (I hope) but strip me of *my Clay,*
And to a better World my Soul convey.
Thus musing, I my silent Moments spend,
Till to the *River's* margin I descend,
From whence I may discern my *Journey's* End:
Annapolis adorns its further Shore,
To which the *Boat* attends to bear me o'er.
And now the moving *Boat* the Flood divides,
While the *Stars* "tremble on the floating Tides;"[10]
Pleas'd with the Sight, again I raise mine Eye
To the Bright Glories of the azure Sky;

[10]Pope's *Rape of the Lock,* II:48, reads: "The sunbeams trembling on the floating tide" [Ed.].

And while these Works of God's creative Hand,
The *Moon* and *Stars,* that move at his Command,
Obedient thro' their circling Course on high,
Employ my Sight,——struck with amaze I cry,
ALMIGHTY LORD! whom Heav'n and Earth proclaim,
The *Author* of their universal Frame,
Wilt thou vouchsafe to view the *Son of Man,*
Thy Creature, who but *Yesterday* began,
Thro' animated Clay to draw his Breath,
To-morrow doom'd a Prey to ruthless Death!
   TREMENDOUS GOD! May I not justly fear,
That I, unworthy Object of thy Care,
Into this World from thy bright Presence tost,
Am in th'Immensity of *Nature* lost!
And that my Notions of the *World above,*
Are but Creations of my own *Self-Love;*
To feed my coward Heart, afraid to die,
With *fancied* Feasts of *Immortality!*
   These Thoughts, which thy amazing Works suggest,
Oh glorious FATHER, rack my troubled Breast.
   Yet, GRACIOUS GOD, reflecting that my Frame
From *Thee* deriv'd in animating Flame,
And that what e'er I am, however mean,
By thy Command I enter'd on this Scene
Of Life,——thy wretched *Creature of a Day,*
Condemn'd to travel thro' a tiresome Way;
Upon whose Banks (perhaps to cheer my Toil)
I see thin Verdures rise, and *Daisies* smile:
Poor Comforts these, my Pains t'alleviate!
While on my Head tempestuous Troubles beat.
And must I, when I quit this earthly Scene,
Sink total into *Death,* and never rise again?
   No sure,——These *Thoughts* which in my Bosom roll
Must issue from a *never-dying Soul;*
These active *Thoughts* that penetrate the Sky,
Excursive into dark Futurity;
Which hope eternal Happiness to gain,
Could never be bestow'd on *Man* in vain.
To *Thee,* OH FATHER, fill'd with fervent Zeal,
And sunk in humble Silence I appeal;
Take me, my great CREATOR to *Thy Care,*
And gracious listen to my ardent Prayer!
   SUPREME OF BEINGS, omnipresent Power!
My great Preserver from my natal Hour,
Fountain of Wisdom, boundless Deity,
OMNISCIENT GOD, my Wants are known to THEE,
With Mercy look on mine Infirmity!
Whatever State thou shalt for me ordain,

Whether my Lot in Life be *Joy* or *Pain;*
Patient let me sustain thy wise Decree,
And learn to *know myself,* and *honour Thee.*

1732

William Dawson 1704–1752

Dawson's *Poems on Several Occasions* (1736) was first published anonymously as written "by a Gentleman of Virginia." The second president of the College of William and Mary, Dawson called his poems, in the preface to the volume, "the casual productions of youth."

To Sylvia, on Approach of Winter

Come, my Sylvia, come away;
Youth and Beauty will not stay;
Let's enjoy the present now.
Hear, tempestuous Winter's Roar,
How it blusters at the Door,
Charg'd with Frosts, and Storms, and Snow.

Seated near the crackling Fire,
Let's indulge our fond Desire,
Careless of rough Borea's Blast:
Let us teach the blooming Youth,
What Joys attend on Love and Truth;
How much they please, how long they last.

The am'rous Warblers of the Grove,
That in sweet Carols chant their Love,
Can only sing, whilst Spring inspires;
But let us show, no Age, no Time,
No warring Seasons, frozen Clime,
Can damp the Warmth of our Desires.

1736

Anacreontic[1]

Old Poets sing the Dame, to Stone
Converted by Jove's radiant Son:[2]
How Progne[3] builds her clayey Cell
In Chimneys, where she once did dwell.
For me, (did Fate permit to use,
Whatever Form our Fancies choose)
I'd be my lovely Sylvia's Glass,
Still to reflect her beauteous Face;
I'd be the pure and limpid Wave,
In which my Fair delights to lave;
I'd be her Garment, still to hide
Her snowy Limbs, with decent Pride;
I'd be the Girdle, to embrace
The gradual Taper of her Waist;
I'd be her Tippet, still to press
The snowy Velvet of her Breast;
But if the rigid Fates denied
Such Ornaments of Grace and Pride,
I'd be her very Shoe, that she
With scornful Tread might Trample me.

1736

Jane Colman Turell 1708–1735

Jane Colman Turell, a prolific Massachusetts poet, wrote of eighteenth-century rural life, local affairs, childbirth, and death. Her biblical paraphrases and hymns were collected by her husband Ebenezer in *Some Memoirs of the Life and Death of Mrs. Jane Turell* (1741).

[1]This poem is a variation on the standard stanzaic patterns established by Anacreon (6th c. B.C.). *Anacreontics* are short poems, usually on wine, love, and song. Poets of Italy and France, from the Renaissance through the eighteenth century, frequently wrote in this form. Anacreontics were also popular in Germany. This form seems to have been introduced in England by Abraham Cowley, whose writings Dawson no doubt knew.

[2]Refers to the story of Niobe, daughter of Tantalus, King of Lydia, who married Amphion, King of Thebes, and bore him many children. In her pride she boasted of her superiority to Leto, mother of Apollo and Artemis, who to avenge the insult sent Apollo to kill Niobe's sons and Artemis Niobe's daughters. In grief, Niobe prayed to the gods, who took pity on her and changed her into a stone image on the slopes of Mt. Sipylus in Lydia.

[3]In Greek mythology, Progne, sister of Philomela, was changed into a swallow.

[Lines on Childbirth]

Phoebus[1] has thrice his yearly circuit run,
The winter's over, and the summer's done;
Since that bright day on which our hands were join'd,
And to Philander[2] I my all resign'd.

Thrice in my womb I've found the pleasing strife,
In the first struggles of my infant's life:
But O how soon by Heaven I'm call'd to mourn,
While from my womb a lifeless babe is torn?
Born to the grave ere it had seen the light,
Or with one smile had cheer'd my longing sight.

Again in travail pains my nerves are wreck'd,
My eye balls start, my heart strings almost crack'd;
Now I forget my pains, and now I press
Philander's image to my panting breast.
Ten days I hold him in my joyful arms,
And feast my eyes upon his infant charms.
But then the King of Terrors does advance
To pierce its bosom with his iron lance.
Its soul releas'd, upward it takes its flight,
Oh never more below to bless my sight!
Farewell sweet babes I hope to meet above,
And there with you sing the Redeemer's love.

And now O gracious Savior lend thine ear,
To this my earnest cry and humble prayer,
That when the hour arrives with painful throes,
Which shall my burden to the world disclose;
I may deliverance have, and joy to see
A living child, to dedicate to Thee.

1741

Bridget Richardson Fletcher 1726–1770

Bridget Richardson Fletcher, mainly a poet of religious topics, wrote also of women, marriage, and proper conduct. Her work was published posthumously in *Hymns and Spiritual Songs* (1773).

[1]Phoebus Apollo, god of sunlight in Greek mythology.

[2]Pseudonym for Turell's husband, Ebenezer.

Hymn XXXVI. The Greatest Dignity of a Woman, Christ Being Born of One

1

God's only son by woman came,
To take away our shame;
And so thereby, to dignify,
Also to raise our fame.

2

Did Christ our friend, thus condescend,
Of woman to be born;
Did one so high, so dignify,
Those that you treat with scorn?

3

What man is there, that shall thus dare
Woman to treat with scorn,
Since God's own son, from heav'n did come,
Of such an one was born.

4

Did one so high, thus dignify,
And here do such a thing;
Shall we now fear, those that live here,
Although it was a king.

1773

Hymn LXX. The Duty of Man and Wife

1

You gentlemen and who are friend
To your own happiness,
Come now and hear or stop your ear,
As it shall please you best.

2

To every head that is married,
  This song is now entail'd;
If any hiss, I say at this,
  Then let him be expell'd.

3

The matter here, which I'll declare
  I hope will end much strife;
I wish it might, each man invite,
  To love and prize his wife.

4

Let women fair, also take care
  And see they do submit,
As reason there, shall say is fair,
  And as it shall seem fit.

5

Would man and wife, live free from strife,
  How happy might they be,
If they would try, in harmony
  To live in unity.

6

As bone of bone, they should be one
  In heart so in pretence;
For 'tis a shame, if they are twain,
  Since join'd by providence.

7

Their hands and hearts, their skill and arts,
  Should combine together,
Thus join they must, and so one purse
  Hold all they do gather.

8

The poor that come you must give some,
With kindness treat each friend;
And all your store, will be bless'd the more,
Likewise the better spend.

9

Strict care pray take, least you do break,
The bond of unity,
For if that's broke it makes sad work,
Soon ends prosperity.

1773

Mercy Otis Warren 1728–1814

Mercy Otis Warren, historian, dramatist, poet, circulated her philosophical, political, and religious verse among her friends, including prominent citizens of revolutionary America. Though most of her work was published anonymously, in 1790 she signed her name to the published collection *Poems, Dramatic and Miscellaneous.* The text of these poems has been taken from that collection.

To a Young Lady

On shewing an excellent Piece of P*AINTING, much faded.*

Come, and attend, my charming maid;
See how the gayest colours fade;
As beauteous paintings lose their dye,
Age sinks the lustre of your eye.

Then seize the minutes as they pass;
Behold! how swift runs down the glass;
The hasty sands that measure time,
Point you to pleasures more sublime;
And bid you shun the flow'ry path,
That cheats the millions into death.

Snatch every moment time shall give,
And uniformly virtuous live;
Let no vain cares retard thy soul,
But strive to reach the happy goal;
When pale, when unrelenting Death,
Shall say, resign life's vital breath!
May you, swift as the morning lark
That stems her course to heav'n's high arch,
Leave every earthly care, and soar,
Where numerous seraphims adore;
Thy pinions spread and wafted high,
Beyond the blue etherial sky,
May you there chant the glorious lays,
The carols of eternal praise,
To that exhaustless source of light,
Who rules the shadows of the night,
Who lends each orb its splendid ray,
And points the glorious beams of day.

Time and eternity he holds;
Nor all eternity unfolds,
The glories of Jehovah's name;
Nor highest angels can proclaim,
The wonders of his boundless grace,
They bow, and veil before his face.

What then shall mortals of an hour,
But bend submissive to his power;
And learn at wisdom's happy lore,
Nature's great author to adore.

1790

To Mrs. Montague,[1] Author of "Observations on the Genius and Writings of Shakespeare"

Will Montague, whose critic pen adds praise,
Ev'n to a Shakespeare's bold exalted lays;
Who points the faults in sweet Corneille's[2] page,

[1]Elizabeth Robinson Montagu (1720–1800). Though she opposed independence for the North American colonies, Montagu responded favorably to Warren's patriotic plays.

[2]Pierre Corneille (1606–1684), French dramatist.

Sees all the errors of the Gallic stage—
Corrects Voltaire[3] with a superior hand,
Or traces genius in each distant land?
Will she across the Atlantic stretch her eye,
Look o'er the main, and view the western sky;
And there Columbia's[4] infant drama see—
Reflect that Britain taught us to be free;
Survey with candor what she can't approve;
Let local fondness yield to gen'rous love;
And, if fair truth forbids her to commend,
Then let the critic soften to the friend.

The bard of Avon justly bears the meed
Of fond applause, from Tyber to the Tweed;[5]
Each humbler muse at distance may admire,
But none to Shakespeare's fame e'er dare aspire.
And if your isle, where he so long has charm'd,
If Britain's sons, when by his mantle warm'd,
Have soar'd in vain to reach his lofty quill,
Nature to paint with true Shakespearean skill—
A sister's hand may wrest a female pen,
From the bold outrage of imperious men.

If gentle Montague my chaplet[6] raise,
Critics may frown, or mild good nature praise;
Secure I'll walk, and placid move along,
And heed alike their censure or their song;
I'll take my stand by fam'd Parnassus' side,
And for a moment feel a poet's pride.

Plymouth, July 10, 1790

Lucy Terry 1730–1821

Lucy Terry, taken from Africa as a slave, eventually settled in Vermont with her husband, Abijah Prince, a free black from Vermont who bought her freedom. Her only known extant poem, "Bars Fight," was handed down orally for nearly 100 years before being printed in Josiah Holland's *History of Western Massachusetts* in 1855.

[3]François Marie Arouet (1694–1778), French writer and philosopher.
[4]The United States.
[5]Literally, from the Tiber, a river in central Italy flowing through Rome, to the Tweed, a river in southeast Scotland and northeast England flowing into the North Sea. Figuratively, Warren suggests that Shakespeare's fame extends from one end of the Roman empire to the other.
[6]A wreath or garland for the head.

Bars Fight[1]

August, 'twas the twenty-fifth,
Seventeen hundred forty-six;
The Indians did in ambush lay,
Some very valiant men to slay,
The names of whom I'll not leave out.
Samuel Allen like a hero fout,[2]
And though he was so brave and bold,
His face no more shall we behold.
Eleazer Hawks was killed outright,
Before he had time to fight,—
Before he did the Indians see,
Was shot and killed immediately.
Oliver Amsden he was slain,
Which caused his friends much grief and pain.
Simeon Amsden they found dead,
Not many rods distant from his head.
Adonijah Gillett, we do hear,
Did lose his life which was so dear.
John Sadler fled across the water,
And thus escaped the dreadful slaughter.
Eunice Allen see the Indians coming,
And hopes to save herself by running,
And had not her petticoats stopped her,
The awful creatures had not catched her,
Nor tommy hawked her on her head,
And left her on the ground for dead.
Young Samuel Allen, Oh lackaday!
Was taken and carried to Canada.

1885

Thomas Godfrey 1736–1763

Philadelphian Thomas Godfrey was well-known in polite circles and at the College of Philadelphia. Although he published a long poem, *The Court of Fancy* in 1762, Godfrey is perhaps best remembered for his blank verse tragedy, *The Prince of Parthia* (first staged in 1767), though the play was never performed during his lifetime. In 1758 Godfrey left his close friends—including College Provost William Smith, Nathaniel Evans, and Francis Hopkinson—and moved to Wilmington,

[1] *Bars* is a colonial term for "meadow."
[2] Probably "fought."

North Carolina, to become a factor. Evans published Godfrey's *Juvenile Poems on Various Subjects, with the Prince of Parthia, A Tragedy* in Philadelphia in 1765.

A Dithyrambic on Wine[1]

1

COME! let Mirth our hours employ,
The jolly God inspircs;
The rosy juice our bosom fires,
And tunes our souls to joy.
See, great *Bacchus* now descending,
Gay, with blushing honours crown'd;
Sprightly *Mirth* and *Love* attending,
Around him wait,
In smiling state—
Let *Echo* resound,
Let *Echo* resound
The joyful news all around.

2

Fond Mortals come, if love perplex,
In *Wine* relief you'll find;
Who'd whine for womens giddy sex
More fickle than the wind?
If beauty's bloom thy fancy warms,
Here, see her shine,
Cloath'd in superior charms;
More lovely than the blushing morn,
When first the op'ning day
Bedecks the thorn,
And makes the meadows gay.
Here see her in her crystal shrine;
See and adore; confess her all divine,
The Queen of Love and Joy.

[1]In ancient Greece, the *dithyramb* was a hymn to the god Dionysus (or to Bacchus, god of wine, associated with Dionysus). Its form was a choral lyric, with sung exchanges between a leader and a chorus. Godfrey freely adapts the form, loosening the formality of its meter and development.

Heed not thy Chloe's scorn—
This sparkling glass,
With winning grace,
Shall ever meet thy fond embrace,
And never, never, never cloy,
No never, never cloy.

3

Here, POET! see, *Castalia's spring*—[2]
Come, give me a bumper, I'll mount to the skies,
Another, another— 'Tis done! I arise;
On fancy's wing,
I mount, I sing,
And now, sublime,
Parnassus' lofty top I climb—
But hark! what sounds are these I hear,
Soft as the dream of her in love,
Or *Zephyr's* whisp'ring thro' the Grove?
And now, more solemn far than fun'ral woe,
The heavy numbers flow!
And now again,
The varied strain,
Grown louder and bolder, strikes quick on the ear,
And thrills thro' ev'ry vein.

4

'Tis *Pindar's* song![3]
His softer notes the fanning gales
Waft across the spicy vales,
While, thro' the air,
Loud whirlwinds bear
The harsher notes along.
Inspir'd by *Wine,*
He leaves the lazy croud below,
Who never dar'd to peep abroad,
And mounting to his native sky,
For ever there shall shine.
No more I'll plod
The beaten road;

[2]On the slopes of Mt. Parnassus, Castalia's spring is sacred to Apollo and the muses.

[3]Pindar (518–483 B.C.) is often regarded as the greatest Greek lyric poet. He was famous for triumphal odes.

Like him inspir'd, like him I'll moun[t] on high;
Like his my strain shall flow.

5

Haste, ye Mortals! leave your sorrow;
Let pleasure crown to-day — to-morrow
Yield to fate.
Join the universal chorus,
Bacchus reigns,
Ever great;
Bacchus reigns,
Ever glorious—
Hark! the joyful groves rebound,
Sporting breezes catch the sound,
And tell to hill and dale around—
"*Bacchus* reigns"—
While far away,
The busy *Echoes* die away.—

1765

A Night-Piece

1

How awful is the Night! beneath whose shade,
Calm mournful silence e'er serenely reigns;
And musing Meditation, heav'nly Maid!
Unbends the mind, and sooth[e]s the heart-felt pains!

2

What pleasing terrors strike upon the soul
While hills and vales around dusk swims away;
While murmuring streams in plaintive numbers roll,
And with their soft complainings close the day!

3

While silver Cynthia with her pallid beams,
Does clouded nature faintly re-illume,

Tips tops of trees, and dancing on the streams,
Adds livelier horror to the rising gloom!

4

What hand can picture forth the solemn scene,
The deepning shade and the faint glimm'ring light!
How much above th' expressive art of G____n[1]
Are the dim beauties of [a] dewy night!

5

How much this hour does noisy day excel
To those who heav'nly contemplation love!—
Now nought is heard but pensive *Philomel,*[2]
The wat'ry fall, or *Zephyr* in the grove.

6

Now searching thought unlimited may rove,
And into nature's deep recesses pry;
Spread her fleet wings to mount the realms above,
And gain the glowing glories of the sky.

7

Rich in expression, how sublimely bright,
Those lucent arguments above us shine!
Now, Atheist! now lift up thy wondring sight,
And own the great creating pow'r divine.

8

Heav'ns! what a throng, what a dread endless train,
Of complicated wonders yield surprize!
Systems on systems, systems yet again,
And suns on suns, continually arise!

[1]John Griffin, a portrait painter, was Godfrey's close friend. He wrote an elegy on Godfrey's death which prefaces the posthumously published *Juvenile Poems.*

[2]The nightingale.

9

Too daring thought! give o'er thy vain emprize,[3]
Nor rashly pry— at humble distance gaze!
Should heav'n unveil those beauties to our eyes
The dazzled sense would sink beneath the blaze.

10

But leave the glories of heavn's spangl'd dome,
And thy slow-steps to dreary church-yards lead;
The[n] [l]ean attentive on yon marble tomb,
And learn instruction from the silent dead.

11

How dismal is this place! whilst round I gaze,
What chilling fears my thoughtful soul invade!
Exaggerating Fancy shrubs doth raise,
To dreadful spectres gliding cross the shade.

12

Pale sleep! thou emblem of eternal rest,
When lock'd in thy coercive strong embrace,
Those of all-bounteous Nature's gifts possest,
Are but as those whose gloomy haunts I trace.

13

No objects now wide-straining eyes admit;
Deaf is the ear, mute the persuasive tongue,
Discerning judgment, and keen piercing wit
Are lost in thee, and warriors nerves unstrung!

14

Still led by thee imagination roves,
On tow'ring pinion seeks some distant world;

[3]Emprise, or daring enterprise.

Or wanders pleas'd thro' soft enamel'd groves,
Or down the dreadful precipice is hurl'd.

15

While sad reclining on this silent tomb,
Surrounded with promiscuous dead I rest;
Thee, I invoke! sweet friendly sleep, O come!
Lock up my sense, and lull my troubl'd breast!

1765

Annis Boudinot Stockton 1736–1801

Annis Boudinot Stockton, prolific and well-known New Jersey poet, circulated her verse mainly among friends and other women poets. She was well-known to the cultural elite of her day, and she wrote several poems to her friend George Washington, among other statesmen. From childhood, Stockton was a close friend of Elizabeth Graeme Fergusson, and, like Fergusson, she held literary salons for an elite Princeton circle. Publications of her pastoral and sentimental verse appeared under her pseudonym, "Amelia" (or Emelia), while other publications, twenty-one in number, appeared under her initials, "A. S.," or anonymously.

To Laura[1]

Permit a sister muse to soar
To heights she never tried before,
And then look up to thee;

For sure each female virtue join'd,
Conspire to make thy lovely mind
The seat of harmony.

Thy fame has reach'd the calm retreat,
Where I secluded from the great,
Have leisure for my lays;

[1] *Laura* is the pen-name of Elizabeth Graeme Fergusson (1737–1801), the friend to whom Stockton sent this verse epistle.

It rais'd ambition in my breast,
Not such as envious souls possess,
Who hate another's praise.

But that which makes me strive to gain,
And ever grateful to retain,
Thy friendship as a prize;

For friendship soars above low rules,
The formal fetters of the schools
She wisely can despise;

So may fair Laura kindly condescend,
And to her bosom take another friend.

1757

Epistle, To Lucius[1]

When lions in the deserts quit their prey
And tuneful birds forsake the leafy spray
When fish for land shall leave the watery main
And rivers to their fountains flow again
When spring shall cease the flow'ry bud to shoot
And autumn mild refuse the blushing fruit
Then and then only could my heart refrain
To vent to thee its pleasure and its pain
But even then thou dearest of thy kind
Thy lov'd Idea would engross my mind
Oh Could my anxious heart but once believe
What my vain thought would tempt me to receive
When thy sweet voice with fascinating grace
Almost persuades me I have power to please
But ah so conscious of my own demerit
In contemplating thee I lose my spirit
When I the treasures of thy mind survey
Like Sheba's queen[2] I shrink and dye away.
But if the powers of genius ever heard

[1]Lucius is Stockton's pseudonym for her husband Richard.

[2]According to the biblical story, when she heard reports of the immensity of Solomon's wisdom, the Queen of Sheba traveled to see him and test him. She tested his wits with energy, said his wisdom exceeded the reports she had heard, and bestowed him with gifts before sailing away.

A votaries prayer and e'er that prayer prefer'd
On me may wit and elegance bestow
Some emanation bright some softer glow
Some sweet atractive that thy heart may twine
(Stronger than beauty) with each nerve of mine
For oh I find on earth no charms for me
But whats Connected with the thought of thee.

1766

A Poetical Epistle, Addressed by a Lady of New Jersey, to Her Niece, upon Her Marriage[1]

Well! my lov'd Niece, I hear the bustle's o'er,
The wedding cake and visits are no more;
The gay ones buzzing round some other bride,
'While you with grave ones grace the fire's side.
Now with your usual sweetness deign to hear,
What from a heart most friendly flows sincere:
Nor do I fear a supercilious Smile—
To pay with gay contempt the muse's toil.
For be assur'd, I never will presume,
Superior sense or judgment to assume;
But barely that which long experience brings,
To men and women, those capricious things,
Nor do I once forget how very sage
Th'advice of Aunts has been in ev'ry age:
On matrimonial themes they all debate—
Wiseacres too who never try'd the state.
And 'twould, I own, appear as truly vain
For me, but to suppose I could attain
New light, upon a subject worn out quite;
And which both Aunts and Authors deem so trite.
But all the nuptial virtues in the class
Of spirit meek, and prudence, I shall pass;
Good nature—sense—of these you've ample store,
And Oeconomicks you have learnt before.
But there are lurking evils that do prove

[1]This poem, written in 1784, probably for Susan Boudinot Bradford, was published in *The Columbian Magazine,* November, 1786.

Under the name of trifles—death to love.—
And from these trifles, all the jarring springs,
And trust me, child, they're formidable things.
First then—with rev'rence treat in ev'ry place,
The chosen patron of your future days;
For when you shew him but the least neglect,
Yourself you rifle of your due respect.—
But never let your fondness for him rise,
In words or actions to the prying eyes
Of witnesses—who claim a right to sneer
At all the honey'd words, "My life,—my love,—my dear."
    Nor from your husband should you e'er require
Those epithets, which little minds admire—
Such short restraints will constantly maintain
That pow'r which fondness strives to reach in vain.
And give new joy to the returning hour,
When sweet retirement bars the op'ning door.
Nor do nor say, before the man you love,—
What in its nature must offensive prove;
However closely drawn the mystic ties,
Yet men have always microscopic eyes;
And easily advert to former time,
When nice reserve made females all divine.
"Would she to Damon or Alexis say,
"A thing so rude? and am I less than they?"
    Whene'er your husband means to stay at home,
Whate'er th'occasion—dont consent to roam;
For home's a solitary place to one
Who loves his wife, and finds her always gone.
At least consult the temper of his mind,
If vex'd abroad, he finds himself inclin'd
From public business to relax awhile;
How pleasing then the solace of a smile—
A soft companion to relieve his care,
His joy to heighten—or his grief to share?
    Unbend his thoughts and from the world retire,
Within his sacred home and round his chearful fire;
Nor let him know you've made a sacrifice,
He'll find it out himself: And then he'll prize
Your kind endeavours to promote his ease,
And make the study of your life to please.
    Another rule you'll find of equal weight,
When jars subside, never recriminate;
And when the cloud is breaking from his brow,
Repeat not *what* he said—nor *when* nor *how.*
If he's tenacious, gently give him way—
And tho' 'tis night, if he should say, 'tis day—

Dispute it not—but pass it with a smile;
He'll recollect himself—and pay your toil—
And shew he views it in a proper light;
And no Confusion seek—to do you right:
Just in his humour meet him—no debate,
And let it be your pleasure to forget.
His friends with kindness always entertain,
And tho' by chance he brings them, ne'er complain;
Whate'er's provided for himself and you,
With neatness serv'd, will surely please them too.
Nor e'er restrict him, when he would invite
His friends in form, to spend a day or night:
Some ladies think the trouble is so great,
That all such motions cause a high debate;
And madam pouts and says, I would not mind
How much to company you were inclin'd,
If I had things to entertain genteel;
And could but make my table look as well
As Mrs. A. and Mrs. B. can do;
I'd be as fond of company as you.—
And oft a richer service bribes the feast,
Than suits his purse, and makes himself a jest:
And tho' the good man gains his point at last,
It damps convivial mirth, and poisons the repast.
But you, my dear—if you would wish to shine,
Must always say, *your* friends are also *mine:*
The house is your's, and I will do the best,
To give a chearful welcome to each guest.
    Nor are those maxims difficult to cope
When stimulated by so fair a hope,
To reach the summit of domestic bliss;
And crown each day with ever smiling peace.
    Now if these lines one caution should contain,
To gain that end, my labour's not in vain;
And be assur'd, my dear, while life endures
With every tender sentiment, I'm your's.

1786

The Vision, an Ode to Washington[1]

'TWAS in a beauteous verdant shade,
Deck'd by the genius of the glade,
With Nature's fragrant stores;
Where Fairy Elves light trip'd the green—
Where Silvan Nymphs were often seen
To strew the sweetest flowers.

Lethean air from tempes vale,
Wafted an aromatic gale,
And lull'd my soul to rest:
I saw, or musing seem'd to see,
The future years of Destiny
That brighten'd all the West.

The Muse array'd in heavenly grace,
Call'd up each actor in his place
Before my wondering eyes,
The magic of the Aonian Maid
The world of Vision wide display'd,
And bid the scenes arise.

I saw great FABIUS[2] come in state,
I saw the British Lion's fate,
The Unicorns dispair;
Conven'd in Secrecy's Divan,
The Chiefs contriv'd the fav'rite plan,
And *York-Town* clos'd the war.

Nor could the dazzling triumph charm
The friends of faction, or its rage disarm—
Fierce to divide, to weaken and subvert:
I saw the Imps of Discord rise—
Intrigue, with little arts, surprise,
Delude—alarm—and then the State desert.

My soul grew sick of human things—
I took my Harp, and touch'd the strings,
Full often set to woe;
Conjur'd the gentle Muse to take

[1]When this poem was published in the *Gazette of the United States,* May 16, 1789, it appeared under this heading: "The following ode was written and inscribed to General Washington, a short time after the surrender of York-Town."

[2]Fabius is Stockton's pseudonym for General Washington.

The power of future knowledge back—
No more I wish'd to know.

Rash Mortal stop! She cried with zeal,
One secret more I must reveal,
That will renew your prime:
These storms will work the wish'd for cure,
And put the *State* in health so pure,
As to resist old *Time.*

The free born mind will feel the force,
That Justice is the only source
Of Laws concise and clear;
Their native rights, they will resign
To *Men,* who can those rights define,
And every burthen bear.

The SACRED COMPACT, in a band
Of brothers, shall unite the land,
And Envy's self be dead;
The Body one, and one the soul,
Virtue shall animate the whole,
And FABIUS be the head.

Rous'd from the enthusiastic dream,
By the soft murmur of a stream,
That glided thro' the meads,
I tun'd my lyre to themes refin'd,
While Nature's gentle voices join'd,
To sing the glorious deeds.

When lo! HIMSELF, the CHIEF rever'd,
In native elegance appear'd,
And all things smil'd around
Adorn'd with every pleasing art,
Enthron'd the Sov'reign of each heart,
I saw the HERO crown'd.

1789

Elizabeth Graeme Fergusson 1737–1801

Philadelphian Elizabeth Graeme Fergusson was among the best-known of the middle-colony poets of the eighteenth century, despite the fact that a collected edition of her poems has yet to be published. Her celebrity came from the variety and interest of her poetry and from her prolific and lively correspondence with such notable contemporaries as Benjamin Rush, William Smith, Annis Stockton, and Elias Boudinot. It comes as well from her reputation as a leading salon hostess during the years prior to the Revolution.

Originally engaged to Benjamin Franklin's son, William, Fergusson eventually married Henry Hugh Fergusson in 1772. When her husband remained loyal to the British during the Revolution, Fergusson nearly lost her family estate, Graeme Park, to confiscation. Richard Stockton, Benjamin Rush, Francis Hopkinson, and other prominent leaders intervened on her behalf to secure the property, but Fergusson lived the remainder of her life separated from her husband and in financial difficulty.

An Ode Written on the Birthday of Mr. Henry Fergusson[1]

Birth day odes to lords and kings,
Oft are strain'd and stupid things!
Poet laureate's golden lays,
Fulsome hireling's hackney'd praise!

Yet that heart which glows sincere,
Sure may hail the passing year,
Which reminds of the birth
Of a friend of genuine worth,

A friend, that is too cool a name
For the tender ardent flame
Which I feel for Henry's bliss,
All that woman's heart can wish.

What shall I say: the pen is dull
And languid though the heart is full?
Expression is in feeling lost,
For shallow strains oft babble most.

And selfish too I find is all
My love I would to Henry call;
For sure I rise but in the scale,
One prosperous wind expands each sail.

[1]The complete title of this poem in the manuscript is "An Ode Written on the Birthday of Mr. H[enry] F[e]r[gusson] By His Wife When They Had Been Married Two Years, He Aged 26 Years, March 12, 1774."

With him I sink, with him ascend,
My little bark doth his attend!
As through the sham of life we glide,
Upon one ebb or flowing tide.

Then as below we share one fate,
May death at once our souls translate,
Descend one moment to the tomb,
And fall at once near mercy's throne;

Be veil'd at once our [illegible] there,
That thought shall shield us from despair,
And blunt the sting which death prepares
For man and all his short liv'd heirs.

But till that serious hour is come near,
Let us dispell each gloomy fear;
Support and comfort each shall prove,
Till earthly yield to Heavenly love.

1774

On a Beautiful Damask Rose, Emblematical of Love and Wedlock[1]

Queen of the garden! O how oft
  Thy praises have been sung!
In numbers eloquent and soft,
  To please the fair and young.

O! sure thou wast the first form'd flow'r
  Which hail'd young Eden's grove,
The darling of the nuptial bow'r,
  And emblem fit for love.

A transient, rich, and balmy sweet
  Is in thy fragrance found;
But soon the flow'r and scent retreat—
  Thorns left alone to wound.

1789

[1]This poem was published in the *Columbian Magazine,* 3 (May 1789), 312.

On the Mind's Being Engrossed by One Subject[1]

When one fond object occupies the mind,
In nature's scenes we still that object find;
And trees, and meads, and sweetly purling rill,
By us made mirrors with ingenious skill,
Reflect the constant subject of our thought;
We view that image in their substance wrought.
The common peasant treads the fresh turn'd soil,
And hopes of future crops his steps beguiles.
The nat'ralist observes each simple's use,
Where lodg'd the healthy, where the baneful juice.
The lover sees his mistress all around
And her sweet voice in vocal birds is found;
He views the brilliant glories of the skies,
But to remind him of her sparkling eyes.
Th' alchemist still anxious seeks the gold,
For this he pierces every cavern's fold:
Trembling to try the magic hazel's pow'r,
Which points attractive to the darling show'r.
While pious Hervey in each plant and tree
Can nought but God and his redeemer see.
When zephyrs play, or when fierce Boreas roars,
The merchant only for his bark implores.
The beau and belle attentive dread the sky,
Lest angry clouds the sprightly scene deny.
But if a coach's procur'd, torrents may pour,
And winds, and tempests, shattered fleets devour.
Thus over all, self-love presides supreme,
It cheers the morn, and gives the ev'ning dream.
Though oft we change through life's swift gliding stage,
And seek fresh objects at each varying age,
Here we are constant, faithful to one cause,
Our own indulgence as a center draws.
That faithful inmate makes our breast its home,
From the soft cradle, to the silent tomb.

1789

[1]This poem was published in the *Columbian Magazine,* 3 (July 1789), 437–38.

Milcah Martha Moore 1740–1829

Milcah Martha Moore, a Philadelphia Quaker, wrote moral and instructive poetry. Her compilation, *Miscellanies, Moral and Instructive* (1787), published in London and Dublin as well as in America, enlarged her reputation as a teacher and writer.

The Female Patriots. Address'd to the Daughters of Liberty in America, 1768[1]

Since the men, from a party or fear of a frown,
Are kept by a sugar-plum quietly down,
Supinely asleep—and depriv'd of their sight,
Are stripp'd of their freedom, and robb'd of their right;
If the sons, so degenerate! the blessings despise,
Let the Daughters of Liberty nobly arise;
And though we've no voice but a negative here,
The use of the taxables, let us forbear:—
(Then merchants import till your stores are all full,
May the buyers be few, and your traffic be dull!)
Stand firmly resolv'd, and bid Grenville[2] to see,
That rather than freedom we part with our tea,
And well as we love the dear draught when a-dry,
As American Patriots our taste we deny—
Pennsylvania's gay meadows can richly afford
To pamper our fancy or furnish our board;
And paper sufficient at home still we have,
To assure the wiseacre, we will not sign slave;
When this homespun shall fail, to remonstrate our grief,
We can speak viva voce, or scratch on a leaf;
Refuse all their colors, though richest of dye,
When the juice of a berry our paint can supply,
To humor our fancy—and as for our houses,
They'll do without painting as well as our spouses;
While to keep out the cold of a keen winter morn,

[1]A brief letter to the editors of the *Pennsylvania Chronicle* introduces "The Female Patriots": "Gentlemen, I send you the inclosed female performance for a place in your paper, if you think it may contribute any thing to the entertainment or reformation of your male readers, and am, Yours, &c. Q.R."

[2]George Grenville (1712–1770), English statesman whose tax policies in the American colonies (e.g., the Revenue Act of 1764 and the Stamp Act of 1765) became one of the causes of the American Revolution.

We can screen the north-west with a well polished horn;
And trust me a woman, by honest invention,
Might give this state-doctor a dose of prevention.
Join mutual in this—and but small as it seems,
We may jostle a Grenville, and puzzle his schemes;
But a motive more worthy our patriot pen,
Thus acting—we point out their duty to men;
And should the bound-pensioners tell us to hush,
We can throw back the satire, by biding them blush.

1787

Nathaniel Evans 1742–1767

Evans was born in Philadelphia to a merchant who wished his son to follow in his footsteps. Yet Evans followed the encouragement of Provost William Smith at the College of Philadelphia instead. After completing an M.A. at the College, Evans traveled to London and was ordained a minister in the Church of England. He took a post as a missionary for the Church, with the Society for the Propagation of the Bible in Foreign Parts, situated in Haddonfield, New Jersey, across the Delaware River from Philadelphia. Although he himself lamented the early death of his friend, Thomas Godfrey, Evans died of tuberculosis at age twenty-five; William Smith gathered his poems and published them, titled *Poems on Several Occasions* (1772).

Hymn to May

Now had the beam of Titan gay[1]
Usher'd in the blissful May,
Scattering from his pearly bed,
Fresh dew on every mountain's head;
Nature mild and debonair,
To thee, fair maid, yields up her care.
May, with gentle plastic hand,
Clothes in flowery robe the land;
O'er the vales the cowslips spreads,
And eglantine beneath the shades;
Violets blue befringe each fountain,
Woodbines lace each steepy mountain;
Hyacinths their sweets diffuse,

[1]Apollo, god of the sun, later in the poem called "Sol."

And the rose its blush renews;
With the rest of Flora's train,
Decking lowly dale or plain.

Through creation's range, sweet May!
Nature's children own thy sway—
Whether in the crystal flood,
Amorous, sport the finny brood;
Or the feather'd tribes declare,
That they breathe thy genial air,
While they warble in each grove
Sweetest notes of artless love;
Or their wound the beasts proclaim,
Smitten with a fiercer flame;
Or the passions higher rise,
Sparing none beneath the skies,
But swaying soft the human mind
With feelings of ecstatic kind—
Through wide creation's range, sweet May!
All Nature's children own thy sway.

Oft will I, (e'er Phosphor's light
Quits the glimmering skirts of night)
Meet thee in the clover field,
Where thy beauties thou shalt yield
To my fancy, quick and warm,
Listening to the dawn's alarm,
Sounded loud by Chanticleer,
In peals that sharply pierce the ear.
And, as Sol his flaming car
Urges up the vaulted air,
Shunning quick the scorching ray,
I will to some covert stray,
Coolly bowers or latent dells,
Where light-footed silence dwells,
And whispers to my heaven-born dream,
Fair Schuylkill, by thy winding stream![2]
There I'll devote full many an hour,
To the still-finger'd Morphean power,
And entertain my thirsty soul
With draughts from Fancy's fairy bowl;
Or mount her orb of varied hue,
And scenes of heaven and earth review.

[2]The Schuylkill River winds through the city of Philadelphia.

Nor in milder Eve's decline,
As the sun forgets to shine,
And sloping down the ethereal plain,
Plunges in the western main,
Will I forbear due strain to pay
To the song-inspiring May;
But as Hesper[3] 'gins to move
Round the radiant court of Jove,
(Leading through the azure sky
All the starry progeny,
Emitting prone their silver light,
To re-illume the shades of night)
Then, the dewy lawn along,
I'll carol forth my grateful song,
Viewing with transported eye
The blazing orbs that roll on high,
Beaming luster, bright and clear,
O'er the glowing hemisphere.
Thus from the early blushing morn,
Till the dappled eve's return,
Will I, in free unlabor'd lay,
Sweetly sing the charming May!

1772

Ode to My Ingenious Friend[1]

While you, dear Tom, are forced to roam,
In search of fortune, far from home,
  O'er bogs, o'er seas and mountains;
I too, debarr'd the soft retreat
Of shady groves, and murmur sweet
  Of silver prattling fountains,

Must mingle with the bustling throng,
And bear my load of cares along,
  Like any other sinner:
For, where's the ecstasy in this,
To loiter in poetic bliss,
  And go without a dinner?

[3]Hesperus, the planet Venus, as the evening star.

[1]Evans's friend, Thomas Godfrey, left Philadelphia to take a post in North Carolina as a factor.

Flaccus,[2] we know, immortal bard!
With mighty kings and statesmen fared,
And lived in cheerful plenty:
But now, in these degenerate days,
The slight reward of empty praise,
Scarce one receives in twenty.

Well might the Roman swan, along
The pleasing Tiber pour his song,
When bless'd with ease and quiet;
Oft did he grace Mæcenas'[3] board,
Who would for him throw by the lord,
And in Falernian riot.

But, dearest Tom! these days are past,
And we are in a climate cast
Where few the muse can relish;
Where all the doctrine now that's told,
Is that a shining heap of gold
Alone can man embellish.

Then since 'tis thus, my honest friend,
If you be wise, my strain attend,
And counsel sage adhere to;
With me, henceforward, join the crowd,
And like the rest proclaim aloud,
That money is all virtue!

Then may we both, in time, retreat
To some fair villa, sweetly neat,
To entertain the muses;
And then life's noise and trouble leave—
Supremely blest, we'll never grieve
At what the world refuses.

1772

[2]Horatius Flaccus, or Horace (65–8 B.C.), was born to "low" estate but achieved fame as a Roman poet. He was admired by Varius and Virgil, and he became close friend of the aristocrat and statesman, Maecenas, who later became his patron.

[3]Maecenas (70?–8 B.C.), Roman statesman, was well-known as a literary patron.

Ode to the Memory of Mr. Thomas Godfrey

O Death! thou victor of the human frame!
The soul's poor fabric trembles at thy name!
How long shall man be urged to dread thy sway,
For those whom thou untimely tak'st away?
Life's blooming spring just opens to our eyes,
And strikes the senses with a sweet surprise,
When thy fierce arm uplifts the fatal blow
That hurls us breathless to the earth below.

Sudden, as darts the lightning through the sky,
Around the globe thy various weapons fly.
Here war's red engines heap the field with slain,
And pallid sickness there extends thy reign;
Here the soft virgin weeps her lover dead,
There maiden beauty sinks the graceful head;
Here infants grieve their parents are no more,
There reverend sires their children's deaths deplore;
Here the sad friend—O! save the sacred name,
Yields half his soul to thy relentless claim;
O pardon, pardon the descending tear!
Friendship commands, and not the muses, here.
O say, thou much loved dear departed shade,
To what celestial region hast thou stray'd?
Where is that vein of thought, that noble fire
Which fed thy soul, and bade the world admire?
That manly strife with fortune to be just,
That love of praise? an honorable thirst!
The Soul, alas! has fled to endless day,
And left its house a mouldering mass of clay.

There, where no fears invade, nor ills molest,
Thy soul shall dwell immortal with the blest;
In that bright realm, where dearest friends no more
Shall from each other's throbbing breasts be tore,
Where all those glorious spirits sit enshrined,
The just, the good, the virtuous of mankind.
There shall fair angels in a radiant ring,
And the great Son of heaven's eternal King,
Proclaim thee welcome to the blissful skies,
And wipe the tears forever from thine eyes.

How did we hope—alas! the hope how vain!
To hear thy future more enripen'd strain;
When fancy's fire with judgment had combined

To guide each effort of the enraptured mind.
Yet are those youthful glowing lays of thine
The emanations of a soul divine;
Who heard thee sing, but felt sweet music's dart
In thrilling transports pierce his captiv'd heart?
Whether soft melting airs attuned thy song,
Or pleased to pour the thundering verse along,
Still nobly great, true offspring of the Nine,
Alas! how blasted in thy glorious prime!
So when first ope the eyelids of the morn,
A radiant purple does the heavens adorn,
Fresh smiling glory streaks the skies around,
And gaily silvers each enamel'd mound,
Till some black storm o'erclouds the ether fair,
And all its beauties vanish into air.

Stranger, whoe'er thou art, by fortune's hand
Toss'd on the baleful Carolinian strand,
Oh! if thou seest perchance the Poet's grave,
The sacred spot with tears of sorrow lave;
Oh! shade it, shade it with ne'er fading bays.
Hallow'd's the place where gentle Godfrey lays.
(So may no sudden dart from death's dread bow,
Far from the friends thou lov'st, e'er lay thee low,)
There may the weeping morn its tribute bring,
And angels shield it with their golden wing,
Till the last trump shall burst the womb of night,
And the purged atoms to their soul unite!

1765

To Benjamin Franklin, Occasioned by Hearing Him Play on the *Harmonica*

In grateful wonder lost, long had we view'd
Each gen'rous act thy patriot-soul pursu'd;
Our Little State resounds thy just applause,
And, pleas'd, from thee new fame and honour draws:
In thee those various virtues are combin'd,
That form the true pre-eminence of mind.

What wonder struck us when we did survey
The lambent lightnings innocently play,

And down thy rods[1] beheld the dreaded fire
In a swift flame descend—and then expire;
While the red thunders, roaring loud around,
Burst the black clouds, and harmless smite the ground.

Blest use of art! apply'd to serve mankind,
The noble province of the sapient mind!
For this the soul's best faculties were giv'n,
To trace great nature's laws from earth to heav'n!

Yet not these themes alone thy thoughts command,
Each softer *Science* owns thy fostering hand;
Aided by thee, Urania's[2] heav'nly art,
With finer raptures charms the feeling heart;
Th' *Harmonica* shall join the sacred choir,
Fresh transports kindle, and new joys inspire—

Hark! the soft warblings, sounding smooth and clear,
Strike with celestial ravishment the ear,
Conveying inward, as they sweetly roll,
A tide of melting music to the soul;
And sure if aught of mortal-moving strain,
Can touch with joy the high angelic train,
'Tis this enchanting instrument of thine,
Which speaks in accents more than half divine!

1772

Ann Eliza Bleecker 1752–1783

The move that Ann Eliza Bleecker made from the bustle of New York City to the loneliness of frontier Tomhanik contributed greatly to her romantic and sentimental verse. Much of her poetry records the effects of the Revolution on rural women and the honest fear and dismay it inspired.

[1]Alluding to his noble discovery of the use of Pointed Rods of metal for saving houses from damage by lightning [Evans's note].

[2]Urania was the muse of astronomy.

Written in the Retreat from Burgoyne[1]

Was it for this, with thee a pleasing load,
I sadly wander'd through the hostile wood;
When I thought fortune's spite could do no more,
To see thee perish on a foreign shore?
Oh my lov'd babe! my treasures left behind
Ne'er sunk a cloud of grief upon my mind;
Rich in my children—on my arms I bore
My living treasures from the scalper's pow'r:

When I sat down to rest beneath some shade,
On the soft grass how innocent she play'd,
While her sweet sister, from the fragrant wild,
Collects the flow'rs to please my precious child;
Unconscious of her danger, laughing roves,
Nor dreads the painted savage in the groves.
Soon as the spires of Albany appear'd,
With fallacies my rising grief I cheer'd;
"Resign'd I bear," said I, "heaven's just reproof,
"Content to dwell beneath a stranger's roof;
"Content my babes should eat dependent bread,
"Or by the labor of my hands be fed:
"What though my houses, lands, and goods are gone,
"My babes remain—these I can call my own."
But soon my lov'd Abella hung her head,
From her soft cheek the bright carnation fled;
Her smooth transparent skin too plainly shew'd
How fierce through every vein the fever glow'd.
—In bitter anguish o'er her limbs I hung,
I wept and sigh'd, but sorrow chain'd my tongue;
At length her languid eyes clos'd from the day,
The idol of my soul was torn away;
Her spirit fled and left me ghastly clay!
Then—then my soul rejected all relief,
Comfort I wish'd not for, I lov'd my grief:
"Hear my Abella!" cried I, "hear me mourn,
"For one short moment, oh! my child return;
"Let my complaint detain thee from the skies,

[1]John Burgoyne (1722–1792) led 6400 British soldiers from Canada into New York in 1777. Bleecker was forced to flee from her home in Tomhanick before Burgoyne's sudden invasion. Traveling on foot with her two small daughters, she headed south to Albany. Her husband John, away from home at the time of the invasion, joined them a day later. The youngest child, Abella, died of dysentery along the way. The family returned to Tomhanick after Burgoyne's defeat on October 17, 1777.

"Though troops of angels urge thee on to rise."
All night I mourn'd—and when the rising day
Gilt her sad chest with his benignest ray,
My friends press round me with officious care,
Bid me suppress my sighs, nor drop a tear,
Of resignation talk'd—passions subdu'd,
Of souls serene and christian fortitude;
Bade me be calm, nor murmur at my loss,
But unrepining bear each heavy cross.
"Go!" cried I raging, "stoic bosoms go!
"Whose hearts vibrate not to the sound of woe;
"Go from the sweet society of men,
"Seek some unfeeling tiger's savage den,
"There calm—alone—of resignation preach,
"My Christ's examples better precepts teach."
Where the cold limbs of gentle Laz'rus[2] lay
I find him weeping o'er the humid clay;
His spirit groan'd, while the beholders said
(With gushing eyes) "see how he lov'd the dead!"
And when his thoughts on great Jerus'lem turn'd,
Oh! how pathetic o'er her fall he mourn'd!
And sad Gethsemene's nocturnal shade
The anguish of my weeping Lord survey'd:
Yes, 'tis my boast to harbor in my breast
The sensibilities by God exprest;
Nor shall the mollifying hand of time,
Which wipes off common sorrows, cancel mine.

October 29, 1777

On the Immensity of Creation

Oh! could I borrow some celestial plume,
This narrow globe should not confine me long
In its contracted sphere—the vast expanse,
Beyond where thought can reach, or eye can glance,
My curious spirit, charm'd should traverse o'er,
New worlds to find, new systems to explore:
When these appear'd, again I'd urge my flight
Till all creation open'd to my sight.

[2]See John 11 for the account of Christ's raising Lazarus from the dead.

Ah! unavailing wish, absurd and vain,
Fancy return and drop thy wing again;
Could'st thou more swift than light move steady on,
Thy sight as broad, and piercing as the sun,
And Gabriel's years too added to thy own;
Nor Gabriel's sight, nor thought, nor rapid wing,
Can pass the immense domains of th' eternal King;
The greatest seraph in his bright abode
Can't comprehend the labors of a God.
Proud reason fails, and is confounded here;
—Man how contemptible thou dost appear!
What art thou in this scene?—Alas! no more
Than a small atom to the sandy shore,
A drop of water to a boundless sea,
A single moment to eternity.

1773

Anna Young Smith 1756–1780

Anna Young Smith, a Philadelphia poet, was encouraged in her poetic endeavors by her aunt, poet Elizabeth Fergusson. Smith wrote frequently on politics and feminism as well as on the more conventional subjects of courtship, sensibility, and grief. Several poems were published posthumously under her pseudonym, "Sylvia."

An Elegy to the Memory of the American Volunteers, who Fell in the Engagement Between the Massachusetts-Bay Militia, and the British Troops. April 19, 1775.

Let joy be dumb, let mirth's gay carol cease,
See plaintive sorrow comes bedew'd with tears;
With mournful steps retires the cherub peace,
And horrid war with all his train appears.

He comes, and crimson slaughter marks his way,
Stern famine follows in his vengeful tread;
Before him pleasure, hope, and love decay,
And meek-eye'd mercy hangs the drooping head.

Fled like a dream are those delightful hours,
When here with innocence and peace we rov'd

Secure and happy in our native bowers,
Blest in the presence of the youths we lov'd.

The blow is struck, which through each future age
Shall call from pity's eye the frequent tear,
Which gives the brother to the brother's rage,
And dyes with British blood, the British spear.

Where e'er the barb'rous story shall be told,
The British cheek shall glow with conscious shame;
This deed in bloody characters enroll'd,
Shall stain the luster of their former name.

But you, ye brave defenders of our cause,
The first in this dire contest call'd to bleed,
Your names hereafter crown'd with just applause,
Each manly breast with joy-mixt woe shall read;

Your memories, dear to every free-born mind,
Shall need no monument your fame to raise,
Forever in our grateful hearts enshrin'd,
And blest by your united country's praise.

But O permit the muse with grief sincere,
The widow's heart-felt anguish to bemoan,
To join the sisters, and the orphans tear,
Whom this sad day from all they lov'd has torn:

Blest be this humble strain if it imparts
The dawn of peace to but one pensive breast,
If it can hush one sigh that rends your hearts,
Or lull your sorrows to a short liv'd rest.

But vain the hope, too well this bosom knows
How faint is glory's voice to nature's calls:
How weak the balm the laurel wreath bestows,
To heal our breasts, when love or friendship falls.

Yet think, they in their country's cause expir'd,
While guardian angels watch'd their parting sighs,
Their dying breasts with constancy inspir'd,
And bade them welcome to their native skies.

Our future fate is wrapt in darkest gloom
And threat'ning clouds, from which their souls are freed;
Ere the big tempest burst they press the tomb,
Not doom'd to see their much-lov'd country bleed.

O let such thoughts as these assuage your grief,
And stop the tear of sorrow as it flows,
Till Time's all powerful hand shall yield relief,
And shed a kind oblivion o'er your woes.

But oh thou Being infinitely just,
Whose boundless eye with mercy looks on all,
On thee alone thy humbled people trust,
On thee alone for their deliverance call.

Long did thy hand unnumber'd blessings shower,
And crown our land with liberty and peace;
Extend, O lord, again thy saving power,
And bid the horrors of invasion cease.

But if thy awful wisdom has decreed
That we severer evils yet shall know,
By thy Almighty justice doom'd to bleed,
And deeper drink the bitter draughts of woe,

O grant us, Heaven, that constancy of mind
Which over adverse fortune rises still,
Unshaken faith, calm fortitude resign'd,
And full submission to thy holy will.

To Thee, Eternal Parent, we resign
Our bleeding cause and on thy wisdom rest;
With grateful hearts we bless thy power divine,
And own resign'd "Whatever is, is best."

May 2, 1775

1981

Sarah Wentworth Morton 1759–1846

Sarah Wentworth Morton, prolific poet and essayist, enjoyed a prominent place in Boston literary society. Regular publication under her pseudonym "Philenia" included *My Mind and Its Thoughts* (1823). Addressing political and social issues as well as personal and family themes, her poem "The African Chief" received much attention for its anti-slavery sentiments.

Stanzas to a Husband Recently United

In vain upon that hand reclined,
I call each plighted worth my own,
Or rising to thy sovereign mind
Say that it reigns for me alone.

Since, subject to its ardent sway,
How many hearts were left to weep,
To find the granted wish decay,
And the triumphant passion sleep!

Such were of love the transient flame,
Which by the kindling senses led,
To every new attraction came,
And from the known allurement fled.

Unlike the generous care that flows,
With all the rich affections give,
Unlike the mutual hope that knows
But for a dearer self to live.

Was theirs the tender glance to speak
Timid, through many a sparkling tear,
The ever changing hue of cheek,
Its flush of joy, its chill of fear?

Or theirs the full expanded thought,
By taste and moral sense refined,
Each moment with instruction fraught,
The tutor'd elegance of mind?

Be mine the sacred truth that dwells
On One by kindred virtues known,
And mine the chastened glance which tells
That sacred truth to Him alone.

No sordid hope's insidious guise,
No venal pleasure's serpent twine
Invites those soul-illumined eyes,
And blends this feeling heart with thine.

1981

The African Chief

See how the black ship cleaves the main,
High bounding o'er the dark blue wave,
Remurmuring with the groans of pain,
Deep freighted with the princely slave!

Did all the Gods of Afric sleep,
Forgetful of their guardian love,
When the white tyrants of the deep
Betrayed him in the palmy grove?

A chief of Gambia's[1] golden shore,
Whose arm the band of warriors led,
Or more—the lord of generous power,
By whom the foodless poor were fed.

Does not the voice of reason cry,
Claim the first right that nature gave,
From the red scourge of bondage fly,
Nor deign to live a burdened slave?

Has not his suffering offspring clung,
Desponding round his fettered knee;
On his worn shoulder, weeping hung,
And urged one effort to be free?

His wife by nameless wrongs subdued,
His bosom's friend to death resigned;
The flinty path-way drenched in blood,
He saw with cold and frenzied mind.

Strong in despair, then sought the plain,
To heaven was raised his steadfast eye,
Resolved to burst the crushing chain,
Or mid the battle's blast to die.

First of his race, he led the band,
Guardless of danger, hurling round,
Till by his red avenging hand,
Full many a despot stained the ground.

[1]West African country.

When erst Messenia's[2] sons oppressed
Flew desperate to the sanguine field,
With iron clothed each injured breast,
And saw the cruel Spartan yield,

Did not the soul to heaven allied,
With the proud heart as greatly swell,
As when the Roman Decius[3] died,
Or when the Grecian victim fell?[4]

Do later deeds quick rapture raise,
The boon Batavia's[5] William won,
Paoli's[6] time-enduring praise,
Or the yet greater Washington?

If these exalt thy sacred zeal,
To hate oppression's mad control,
For bleeding Afric learn to feel,
Whose Chieftain claimed a kindred soul.

Ah, mourn the last disastrous hour,
Lift the full eye of bootless grief,
While victory treads the sultry shore,
And tears from hope the captive chief.

While the hard race of pallid hue,
Unpracticed in the power to feel,
Resign him to the murderous crew,
The horrors of the quivering wheel,

Let sorrow bathe each blushing cheek,
Bend piteous o'er the tortured slave,
Whose wrongs compassion cannot speak,
Whose only refuge was the grave.

1823

[2]Region in the southwestern Peloponnesus ruled by Polycaon and Messene after Polycaon's exile from Sparta.
[3]Gaius Messius Quintus Traianus Decius (c. 201–251), Roman emperor (249–251). He was the first Roman emperor to institute an organized, empire-wide persecution of the Christians.
[4]"Leonidas." [Morton's note]
[5]City in western New York settled by the Dutch late in the eighteenth century. Batavia became well-known in 1826 when William Morgan, who had written an exposé of the secrets of the Order of the Masons, mysteriously disappeared there.
[6]Pasquale di Paoli (1725–1807), Corsican patriot.

Ode Inscribed to Mrs. M. Warren[1]

Amid the splendor of that fame
Immortal genius rais'd,
With all the love thy virtues claim,
Virtues by envy prais'd,
The least of bright Apollo's[2] choir
Awakes the willing lyre;
And at thy feet the grateful tribute pays,
Due to thy matchless worth, thy fame-embellish'd lays.

Though o'er Columbia's[3] plain,
Fair science smil'd;
And many a muse-enraptur'd swain
Lent music to the wild;
No fair one by Minerva[4] led,
Approach'd Pieria's spring,[5]
Or dar'd the flow'ry paths to tread,
Or tune the golden string.
But timid genius from herself retires,
Conceals her darting rays, and damps her kindling fires.

Till bursting through the veil of night,
Bright as the floating beams of light,
Thy glowing strains appear;
To lead the envied way is thine—
Since only distant praise is mine,
Ah! deign that praise to hear.
While o'er Parnassian[6] heights thy muse ascends,
Low in the vale my humble genius bends.
Not that round thy hallow'd brow,
Fairest wreaths of laurel flow;
That the graces of the Nine,[7]
Every power of song is thine;
That Minerva leads the way,
And thy ready steps obey:
Not from these, alone, I raise
All thy glory, all thy praise;

[1]Mercy Otis Warren (1728–1814), U.S. historian, playwright, poet.
[2]Greek god of sunlight, prophecy, music, and poetry.
[3]The United States.
[4]Roman goddess of wisdom.
[5]Fountain sacred to the Muses, considered a source of poetic inspiration.
[6]Parnassus is a mountain in Greece, considered in mythology to be sacred to Apollo and the Muses.
[7]Nine sister goddesses in Greek mythology who preside over the arts and sciences.

Though to genius much is due,
Brighter plaudits shine on you;

The heart, that melts at every woe,
Which rends another's breast;
The mind, that feels th' enraptured glow,
Whene'er another's blest;
That o'er dejected virtue's sigh,
Can pour the balm of care,
And from the magic of the eye,
Lend patience to despair:
These are thy boast, and these shall grace thy name,
Beyond the glories of a deathless fame.

1790

Memento, for My Infant Who Lived But Eighteen Hours

As the pure snow-drop, child of April tears,
Shook by the rough wind's desolating breath—
Scarce o'er the chilly sod its low head rears,
And trembling dies upon the parent heath,

So my lost boy, arrayed in fancy's charms,
Just born to mourn—with premature decay
To the cold tyrant stretched his feeble arms,
And struggling sighed his little life away.

As not in vain the early snow-drop rose,
Though short its date, and hard the withering gale;
Since its pale bloom ethereal balm bestows,
And cheers with vernal hope the wasted vale.

My perished child, dear pledge of many a pain!
Torn from this ruffian world, in yon bright sphere,
Joins with awakened voice the cherub train,
And pours his sweet breath on a mother's ear.

Kind dreams of morn his fairy phantom bring,
And floating tones of ecstacy impart,
Soft as when seraphs strike the heavenly string
To charm the settled sorrow of the heart.

1823

Poems Published Anonymously

Colonial newspapers and magazines were full of poetry. Given the absence of copyright laws, editors were free to pirate materials from whatever publications came to hand or to print verses sent to them by readers. Many poems were published anonymously or pseudonymously. As a consequence, there is no guarantee that the following pieces are by the people described or implied as having written them. What we do know is that they were widely read in the British North American colonies and articulated a gendered topic of lively public interest.

The Lady's Complaint[1]

Custom, alas! doth partial prove,
Nor gives us equal measure;
A pain for us it is to love,
But is to men a pleasure.

They plainly can their thoughts disclose,
Whilst ours must burn within:
We have got tongues, and eyes, in vain,
And truth from us is sin.

Men to new joys and conquests fly,
And yet no hazard run:
Poor we are left, if we deny,
And if we yield, undone.

Then equal laws let custom find,
And neither sex oppress;
More freedom give to womankind,
Or give to mankind less.

1736

Verses Written by a Young Lady, on Women Born to Be Controll'd![1]

How wretched is a woman's fate,
No happy change her fortune knows,

[1]First published in the *Virginia Gazette* (ed. Parks), October 22, 1736, p. 3, and reprinted several times.

[1]First published in the *South-Carolina Gazette,* Nov. 21, 1743, p. 3, and reprinted several times.

Subject to man in every state.
How can she then be free from woes?

In youth a father's stern command,
And jealous eyes control her will;
A lordly brother watchful stands,
To keep her closer captive still.

The tyrant husband next appears,
With awful and contracted brow;
No more a lover's form he wears,
Her slave's become her sov'reign now.

If from this fatal bondage free,
And not by marriage chains confin'd;
But blest with single life can see,
A parent fond, a brother kind;

Yet love usurps her tender breast,
And paints a Phoenix to her eyes,
Some darling youth disturbs her rest,
And painful sighs in secret rise.

Oh, cruel pow'rs! since you've design'd,
That man, vain man! should bear the sway;
To a slave's fetters add a slavish mind,
That I may cheerfully your will obey.

1743

The Maid's Soliloquy[1]

It must be so—Milton, thou reas'nest well,
Else why this pleasing hope, this fond desire,
This longing after something unpossess'd?
Or whence this secret dread and inward horror

[1]Although it was published anonymously, this poem has recently been attributed to Lewis Morris. J. A. Leo Lemay has reported to the editors that the poem appears among the papers of Robert Morris at Rutgers University Library. In manuscript, the poem is titled "Act V. Scene I of Cato Imitated." John T. Shawcross has identified what is so far the earliest known printing in the *Gentleman's Magazine* 17 (January 1747), p. 42, and the poem was frequently reprinted in English periodicals. The earliest North American printing was in the *New York Evening Post,* December 21, 1747, p. 1. At least two other American printings followed, in the *South Carolina Gazette,* March 4, 1751, and the *Newport Mercury,* May 2, 1763.

Of dying unespous'd? Why shrinks the soul
Back on itself, and startles at the thought?
'Tis instinct! faithful instinct stirs within us,
'Tis nature's self that points out an alliance,
And intimates an husband to the sex.
 Marriage! thou pleasing and yet anxious thought!
Through what variety of hopes and fears,
Through what new scenes, and changes, must we pass:
Th' important state in prospect lies before me,
But shadows, clouds and darkness, rest upon it.
Here will I hold—if Nature prompts the wish,
(And that she does is plain, from all her works)
Our duty and our interest, bid indulge it:
For the great end of nature's law, is bliss.
But yet—in wedlock—women must obey:
I'm weary of these doubts—the priest must end them.
 Thus, rashly do I venture loss and gain,
Bondage and pleasure, meet my thoughts at once;
I wed—my liberty is gone for ever:
If happy—then I'm still secure in life.
Love, will then recompense my loss of freedom;
And when my charms shall fade away, my eyes
Themselves grow dim, my stature bend with years,
Then virtuous friendship, shall succeed to love.
Then pleas'd, I'll scorn infirmities, and death,
Renew'd immortal, in a filial race.

1751

Impromptu, on Reading an Essay on Education. By a Lady[1]

Yes, women, if they dar'd, would nobly soar,
And every art and science would explore;
Though weak their sex, their notions are refin'd,
And e'er would prove a blessing to mankind.
If they our free-born minds would not enslave,
No other boon of Heaven they need to crave;
But while our minds in fetters are enchain'd,
On it rely your hearts will e'er be pain'd:

[1]From the *Virginia Gazette* (eds. Purdie and Dixon), Feb. 11, 1773, p. 4.

While dissipation fondly we pursue,
Believe we small regard can have for you.
Be it your task our intellects to aid,
And you with tenfold interest shall be paid;
Improve our morals, us to honor guide,
And teach us vice from virtue to divide,
And, far as our weak geniuses can go,
Let us each useful theme of learning know:
'Tis then, and then alone, you'll surely prove
There is no blessing like conjugal love.
Thus form'd, the humble friend you'll find, for life,
The faithful comforter, and loving wife.
Should sickness come, she will attend you still,
And ever be obedient to you will.
Should cares attend (as who from cares are free)
A faithful counselor she'll prove to thee;
Though every friend thy sufferings should desert,
In her thou'lt find a true and honest heart,
Who all thy woes will cheerfully partake,
And suffer all for thy beloved sake.
Be generous then, and us to knowledge lead,
And happiness to you will sure succeed;
Then sacred Hymen shall in triumph reign,
And all be proud to wear his pleasing chain.

1773

Enlightenment Voices, Revolutionary Visions

From the perspective of the twentieth century, we tend too readily to assume that the American Revolution was the result of a consensus of American opinion about open revolt against English rule. Yet, as the selections below suggest, several attitudes from the Enlightenment about rebellious agitation emerged during the decades prior to the Revolutionary War. In philosophical terms, the contradictory ideas expressed during the revolutionary era seem to have arisen from conflicting opinions about human nature and the extent to which mankind could progress. Conservatives tended to hold a fairly negative view of human nature. They seem to have feared social change, some arguing (along the lines of Thomas Hobbes and later philosophers who followed him) that beastly mobs would result, others (those who followed Calvinist belief) insisting that social disruption would enable Satan to enter the body politic. Those who held more progressive views of human nature and action tended to follow John Locke, Jean-Jacques Rousseau, the Scottish "Common Sense" school, and other philosophers who suggested that social betterment might result from individual freedom, in both inquiry and action. The natural world, they insisted, was harmonious; if men could freely enquire into natural science, they could design systems of government based upon natural principles of harmony. Combined with the social and economic issues that divided the colonies, these philosophical concerns led to a wide ideological debate about armed revolt and confederation.

The ideological debate is represented in the well-known correspondence, late in their lives, between John Adams and Thomas Jefferson. In June, 1813, Jefferson assessed his past differences with the conservative Adams in this way:

One of those questions you know on which our parties took different sides, was on the improvability of the human mind, in science, in ethics, in government etc. Those who advocated reformation of institutions, pari passu, with the progress of science, maintained that no definite limits could be assigned to that progress. The enemies of reform, on the other hand, denied improvement, and advocated steady adherence to the principles, practices and institutions of our fathers, which they represented as the consummation of wisdom, and akmé of excellence, beyond which the human mind could never advance. Altho' . . . you expressly disclaim the wish to influence the freedom of enquiry, you predict that that will produce nothing more worthy of transmission to posterity, than the principles, institutions, and systems of education received from their ancestors. I do not consider this as your deliberate opinion. You possess, yourself, too much science, not to see how much is still ahead of you, unexplained and unexplored.

Given his unfailing interest in natural science and the improvement of government for the betterment of society, Jefferson seems to have been a member of what Ralph Waldo Emerson later called "a party of hope." He wanted Adams to leave behind what Emerson labelled "a party of memory."

Yet Adams held to his earlier conservative stance that, on the basis of past experience, the present situation, whatever it was, required constraint and control. Indeed, Adams's 1813 response to Jefferson's opinions on human progress was a series of rhetorical questions:

> *Let me now ask you, very seriously my Friend, Where are now in 1813, the Perfection and perfectability of human Nature? Where is now, the progress of the human Mind? Where is the Amelioration of Society? Where the Augmentations of human Comforts? Where the diminutions of human Pains and miseries? . . .*
>
> *When? Where? and how? is the present Chaos to be arranged into Order?*

Order could not result, conservatives like Adams argued, if all people—whites *and* non-whites, men *and* women, elite *and* nonelite—were given the power that would permit them to unleash their wills upon the world.

For those who thought like James Grainger, a plantation owner in the West Indies, order (for colonial whites) could only be obtained with the regulation of the slave body. Grainger's poem *The Sugar Cane* (1764) suggests the remarkably complicated stance an "enlightened" man might take toward the people who made his living possible. Grainger's responses to slave bodies—responses suggesting both attraction and revulsion at the same time—reveal the cultural anxieties of whites in his day, surely, but they also indicate one of the key cultural backdrops for whites' Revolutionary-era rhetoric about being "slaves" to England. Grainger's obsession with observing, recording, and regulating his slaves shows with stark intensity whites' preoccupation with their own freedom from European controls.

To a greater extent than many Americans have been taught to expect, the literature of the era of revolution and confederation suggests ambiguous stances toward political change and culture. Crèvecoeur's Quaker farmer James is perhaps the best-known fictional example of such cultural ambivalence. James celebrates the economic stability and possibility that "America" represents for white immigrants and Americans, yet he deplores the civil degradation of slavery in the South. He suggests that life among native people would be a natural and beneficial corrective to the present social sterility of "civilized" nations, yet he clearly abhors the idea of life alongside natives as one of the "distresses of the frontiersman." James hardly considers life among the indigenous people a suitable alternative for white colonists who do not wish to participate in the Revolutionary War. Progressive ideals were at odds, many writers suggested, with colonial experience. Mere sobriety, industry, and frugality—values honored by Crèvecoeur and many writers from his era—could not a commonwealth make.

Despite the evident differences among those in the revolutionary generation, the literature that has informed the American literary tradition has, by and large, been "patriot" literature promoting Enlightenment ideals and American independence. Thus, Benjamin Franklin has come down through the centuries—despite caveats against a self-satisfied egotism and a doctrine of conformity offered by critics ranging from John Adams to Max Weber to D. H. Lawrence—as the preeminent American patriot statesman, a Renaissance man whose scientific, philosophical, and political inquiry (along with his diplomacy in all three areas) made life better for all Americans. Like John Smith and Cotton Mather before him, Franklin embraced the ideals of industry and frugality, offering in his autobiography the life of a model American who through his own hard work freed himself of financial worry and, spirit renewed, recreated in himself a new man. This pro-American view of Franklin has dominated the tradition to such an extent that few recognize Franklin's hard-headed realism. Perhaps Franklin was not so much an optimist as one who saw no use in pessimism: why be like the croaking Samuel Mickle, perpetually expecting the downfall of Philadelphia, he jovially mocks in the

Autobiography. Skepticism, he believed, made one "half-melancholy" and without will. Individual improvement could lead to changes in manners, morals, and laws that might better society as a whole. Such was the "message" Franklin wittily offered again and again in his voluminous writings.

Anglo-American literature of this era played upon a long tradition of writings about human nature, liberty, and the law. The educated elite, in both progressive and conservative camps, sought precedents for their actions in the literature of the past. Looking to John Locke (whose 1690 *Second Treatise on Civil Government* proved highly influential) and Enlightenment rationalist thinkers, to a multitude of British Commonwealth writers on ancient British liberties, to Common Sense philosophers, and to ancient and continental sources on human nature, American writers constructed an intriguing argument in behalf of freedom from English domination. They considered that in ancient Brittany the people freely chose to constitute themselves together into one body for their own better protection and governance. The officials of the commonwealth—kings, lords, and commons, all acting together—represented the body of the people and determined laws and enacted statutes for the whole. Yet more recent kings, they insisted, took away the colonists' rights as citizens, forcing them into subjection without offering a suitable position of representation in the English common body. This argument developed force among the colonists as Britain continued to attempt to impose legal measures, especially tax laws, without providing the colonists the right to parliamentary representation. Policies that implemented an unequal distribution of wealth and power, they argued—employing a strong, Whig Commonwealth position—would necessitate the breakdown of the British family.

The "family" argument worked especially well for those writers who sought to negate the assumptions about social hierarchy and political power they found in British politics and propaganda. In the arguments of pro-Independence writers, all Britons were alike given ancient liberties. The colonists who came here, whether they were farmers or aristocrats, were of the same family. Family members, they avowed, incurred mutual obligations and so deserved the same rights. According to the rhetorical position these "patriots" took, the British family (England and the colonies) was broken up by the bad behavior of those in power in England. The Americans' parents (the British royal family and by patriarchal extension the government), were not willing to treat all the children (the colonists and mainland England residents) in similar ways. In *Poor Richard's Almanac,* Franklin frequently printed aphorisms that pointedly undermined British pretensions to superior status. To Richard Saunders, "The Monarch, when his Table's spread/To th' Farmer is obliged for bread." Other writers chose more explicit images. In his influential *Common Sense* (1776), Thomas Paine (a recent English immigrant) argued that England could not properly be called the "mother country," for she had forfeited that right by acting like a "monster" who devoured her young rather than like a nurturing, protective mother. Only a few months after *Common Sense* appeared, Jefferson used the appeal of family and kinship in his draft of the *Declaration of Independence* to attack King George III as a bad father figure to a nation desperate for paternal protection. The *Declaration* itself suggested that the King, and not the colonies, was responsible for the break-up of the family: "We have reminded them [Americans' "British Brethren"] of the Circumstances of our Emigration and Settlement here. We have appealed to their native Justice and Magnanimity, and we have conjured them by the Ties of our common Kindred to disavow these Usurpations." Rhetorical appeals like these provided rallying cries for the patriot agitators and helped to effect colonial unity among the disparate colonies.

Carla Mulford
Pennsylvania State University

Benjamin Franklin 1706–1790

On learning of Benjamin Franklin's death in the spring of 1790, the French National Assembly, the "temporary" French government established after the initial stages of the French Revolution, decreed three days of mourning, a fitting tribute for the man who was for most eighteenth-century European intellectuals the quintessential American. Franklin's rise from obscurity to international fame, his transcendence of the bounds of class and rank, represented for Europe the promise and the threat of the newly formed United States. At his death Franklin ranked with Voltaire and Rousseau as a "philosophe," one of those multifaceted geniuses whose writings helped inspire the wave of intellectual and political freedom which swept Western Europe in the closing years of the eighteenth century. Unlike most philosophers, however, Franklin had the chance to put his ideas into practice in the founding of a new nation: "He seized the lightening from the sky and the scepter from the hand of tyrants," proclaimed the philosopher-scientist Turgot.

Franklin's life has become so much the stuff of legend that it is necessary to try to separate fact from myth. The youngest son in a family of eleven living children, Franklin was born in Boston in 1706. After one year of education at the Boston Grammar School and one year at George Brownell's English school, he was apprenticed at age twelve to his brother James, a printer. The precocious and rebellious Franklin rejected his parents' pious congregationalism in favor of free-thinking deism before he turned sixteen. He reluctantly settled to a trade, threatening his parents with his desire to run off to sea, and his adolescent satire of Harvard College suggests that he resented those whose wealth enabled them to escape the drudgery of a tradesman's life despite their inferior intellectual talents. Franklin also joined vigorously in his brother's attacks on Massachusetts worthies such as Increase and Cotton Mather and Samuel Sewall, but after quarreling with his brother he broke his indentures at age seventeen and sailed secretly for New York and then Philadelphia.

Franklin's start in Philadelphia was uncertain, but gradually his hard work, business sense, social talents, community service, political abilities, and literary skill gained him prosperity and public favor. With the free time provided by his growing wealth, Franklin experimented with electricity, making discoveries which earned him international acclaim. His reputation in Philadelphia as a philanthropic leader prompted his entrance into politics, and his local political success led to his appointment as agent for Pennsylvania in England. As dissatisfaction with Britain spread in the colonies, Franklin's growing international reputation led to his appointment as agent for other colonies with grievances against England.

Franklin's achievements in politics and diplomacy during his middle and old age distinguish him as a founder of the new American republic. He served as a delegate to the Second Continental Congress, as American minister to France (America's major ally during the Revolutionary War), as one of the negotiators of the Peace Treaty which ended the Revolutionary War, and as a delegate to the Constitutional Convention. To the chagrin of such ambitious younger rivals as John Adams, Franklin's reputation as a leader of the Revolution was rivalled in his own time only by that of George Washington.

Franklin's talent as a writer served as the foundation for much of his success in philanthropy, politics, and diplomacy. Franklin's literary career began at age sixteen with a series of pseudononymous essays for his brother's newspaper, *The New England Courant.* Known as the "Silence Dogood" papers (1722), after the name of the *persona* or invented spokesperson Franklin employed, these essays display Franklin's precocious mastery of the conventions of the eighteenth-century periodical essay and his adaptation of them to colonial conditions. Inspired by Joseph Addison's and Richard Steele's *Spectator* essays and by local writers, Franklin created a fictitious speaker, the busy-body widow Silence Dogood, and used this *persona* to satirize the follies and vices of Boston, attacking everything from bad poetry to prostitution. To Franklin's delight, his anonymous first attempt at satire was attributed by his brother and his friends to the wittiest young men of Boston.

In Philadelphia, Franklin further honed his literary skills during his struggles to succeed in business, to advance philanthropic projects, and to forward his views on political and controversial issues. During these years (1724–1757) Franklin developed the control of style, voice, tone, and argument that marks his mature work. In his most popular work, *Poor Richard's Almanac* (1733–1738), Franklin created the *persona* of Richard Saunders, a stargazer driven by poverty and a shrewish wife to compose almanacs. Franklin filled his almanacs with wit, bawdiness, moral saws, and prudential advice borrowed from a host of sources. Whatever Franklin borrowed, he improved. His almanacs became the most popular in the colonies, helping to spread his fame as a printer and to develop the pithy wit which became a hallmark of Franklin's writing.

Equally important in developing Franklin's mastery of English prose were the pamphlets he wrote in Philadelphia to further philanthropic and political projects. In the philanthropic pieces, most notably *A Proposal for Promoting Useful Knowledge* (1743), *Proposals Relating to the Education of Youth in Pennsilvania* (1749), and the "Appeal for the Hospital" (1751), Franklin developed his characteristic public *persona,* "the friend of all good men," and his characteristic argumentative strategy, the seamless blending of altruistic and self-interested motives. In his persuasive writings, Franklin usually spoke as the voice of reason and tolerance. In situations which demanded passion, however, Franklin subtly shifted his *persona;* he transformed the fair-minded lover of humanity into an outraged citizen who demanded that the leadings of common sense, justice, and compassion—each of which his opponents had abandoned—be followed. Such openly polemic works as *Plain Truth* (1747) and *A Narrative of the Late Massacres* (1764) exhibit Franklin's ability to unite passionate outrage with reason and common sense.

Still more sophisticated are the occasional satires that Franklin wrote in Philadelphia. For example, in "A Witch Trial at Mount Holly," Franklin posed as a reporter and used the contrast between reportorial style and sensationalistic content to satirize superstition and uncover the sexual hypocrisy underlying popular tests for witchcraft. In "The Speech of Miss Polly Baker" Franklin created a woman whose speech of self-vindication so subtly blends reason and rationalization that many contemporary reformers were taken in, and Polly Baker's speech was praised by the Abbé Raynal as a proof of the power of uneducated reason to distinguish natural truth from artificial law.

During his almost twenty years as a colonial agent in London, Franklin used his persuasive and satiric talents to fight English prejudice against colonists and to defend colonial rights. The satires written there display the range of his talent. In "The Grand Leap of the Whale" (1765) Franklin created an early tall tale featuring a gullible English *persona* whose acceptance of the most absurd stories about America satirizes British fears of American competition; in "Rules by Which a Great Empire May Be Reduced to a Small One" (1773), Franklin ironically gave instructions for reducing the burden of empire by dismembering it, setting forth precisely the policies used by the British administration; and in "An Edict By the King of Prussia" Franklin used an elaborate hoax to place his British readers in the situation of the American colonists, thus making them feel the injustice of British treatment of America.

Although Franklin served as minister to France during the American Revolution and was enmeshed in diplomatic intrigue and consular duties, he found time to write a few pieces in response to the suffering caused by the war. "The Sale of the Hessians" is designed to pillory mercenary aristocrats, expose the falsity of heroic rhetoric, and destroy the traditional metaphoric view of the ruler as father of his subjects. Writing in the voice and mask of the Count De Schaumberg, the Hessian ruler who sold his troops to the British for duty in America, Franklin manipulated the Count's voice to reveal his indifference to his people's death and suffering, luxury and decadence, and hypocrisy. In this work and the similarly bitter "Supplement to the Boston Independent Chronicle, April, 1782," Franklin unleashed a Swiftian fury in the face of human baseness.

The tone of these two satires contrasts sharply with that of the sophisticated short pieces, known as "bagatelles," written during these same years. In the bagatelles Franklin used delicate irony to expose his and humanity's pretenses and self-deception, but because Franklin's wisely tolerant *persona* accepts even as he laughs at human imperfection, the final effect is humorous rather than bitter. To remove misconceptions about America, Franklin also wrote two informative essays designed to counter the wild tales floating about Europe. "Remarks Concerning the Savages of North America" (1783) and "Information to Those Who Would Remove to America" (1784) extended Franklin's reputation as an expert on all things American.

After his return to America (1785) until his death in 1790 Franklin remained as active as his health allowed. In his most famous speech, delivered by proxy on the final day of the Constitutional Convention, September 17, 1787, he employed all of his rhetorical skills in an effort to unite the delegates. Adopting his now-established pose as worldly wise sage, Franklin candidly admitted that he had expressed reservations about the Constitution, and he then suggested that if he could doubt his infallibility and support the Constitution, so should others. In this speech Franklin made one last attempt to preserve the nation that he had helped to create.

The capstone of Franklin's achievement as a writer is his *Autobiography.* Although Franklin worked on the *Autobiography* at four different times (1771, 1784, 1788, and 1788–1789) and revised the completed portions extensively, it remained unfinished at his death. Still Franklin gave the work a rough structural unity, dividing it into three sections. The first section tells the story of Franklin's youth and young manhood in Boston and Philadelphia, viewing the protagonist, the young Franklin, as though he were a character in a novel. Through the eyes of a tolerant elderly narrator, the reader watches the young Franklin learn through experience the necessity of virtue, work, and shrewdness in dealing with the world. The young Franklin possesses numerous faults, but he eventually succeeds because of his talent, industry, and capacity for learning from error. This protagonist is contrasted with foil characters who fail to learn from experience, and his arrogance is softened by the narrator's ironic humor.

The second section of the *Autobiography,* the controversial "art of virtue" section, recounts Franklin's youthful attempt to achieve moral perfection. The ambiguous irony here creates uncertainty about its targets, but the structural significance of the section is clear. A bridge between Franklin's youth and his adulthood, the section codifies the principles that Franklin learned through experience were necessary for happiness and success, but it also satirizes the young Franklin's naive arrogance and rationalization.

The third and last section portrays the adult Franklin's use of the principles of conduct that he discovered in the first section and enumerated in the second. Franklin focuses on his rise to prosperity, his scientific studies, and especially on his work as philanthropist and politician. Franklin occasionally steps back to view his behavior with an ironic eye, reminding his reader that human folly is never eradicated, but for the most part the gap between the narrator and protagonist has vanished, as the naive protagonist has become the experienced narrator.

Benjamin Franklin's *Autobiography* is the most frequently translated literary work of non-fiction that has come from the United States. For readers of many nations it defines the American self and culture. For those who live in the nation that its author helped create and in the culture that his writings helped shape, it is an inescapable text.

David M. Larson
Cleveland State University

PRIMARY WORKS

The Writings of Benjamin Franklin, ed. Albert Henry Smyth, 10 vols., 1905–1907; *The Papers of Benjamin Franklin,* ed. Leonard Labaree, et al., 1959; *The Autobiography of Benjamin Franklin: A Genetic Text,* eds. J. A. Leo Lemay and P. M. Zall, 1981; *Benjamin Franklin's Autobiography,* eds. J. A. Leo Lemay and P. M. Zall, 1986; *Benjamin Franklin,* ed. J. A. Leo Lemay, 1987.

SECONDARY WORKS

Carl Van Doren, *Benjamin Franklin,* 1938; Bruce Granger, *Benjamin Franklin: An American Man of Letters,* 1964; James A. Sappenfield, *A Sweet Instruction: Franklin's Journalism as a Literary Apprenticeship,* 1973; J. A. Leo Lemay, ed., *The Oldest Revolutionary,* 1976; Ormond Seavey, *Becoming Benjamin Franklin: The Autobiography and the Life,* 1988.

from Poor Richard's Almanacks[1]

from March

My Love and I for Kisses play'd,
She would keep stakes, I was content,
But when I won she would be paid;
This made me ask her what she meant:
  Quoth she, since you are in this wrangling vein,
  Here take your Kisses, give me mine again.

[1]The *Almanacs* first appeared in 1733 under the fictitious editorship of "Richard Saunders."

from **June**

After 3 days men grow weary, of a wench, a guest, & weather rainy.

To lengthen thy Life, lessen thy Meals.

The proof of gold is fire, the proof of woman, gold; the proof of man, a woman.

from **July**

Many estates are spent in the getting,
Since women for tea forsook spinning & knitting.

He that lies down with Dogs, shall rise up with fleas.

from **August**

Take counsel in wine, but resolve afterwards in water.

He that drinks fast, pays slow.

He is ill cloth'd, who is bare of Virtue.

Tongue double, brings trouble.

from **September**

Death is a Fisherman, the world we see
His Fish-pond is, and we the Fishes be:
His Net some general Sickness; howe'er he
Is not so kind as other Fishers be;
For if they take one of the smaller Fry,
They throw him in again, he shall not die:
But Death is sure to kill all he can get,
And all is Fish with him that comes to Net.

Men & Melons are hard to know.

from **January**

From a cross Neighbour, and a sullen Wife,
A pointless Needle, and a broken Knife;
From Suretyship, and from an empty Purse,

A Smoaky Chimney and a jolting Horse;
From a dull Razor, and an aking Head,
From a bad Conscience and a buggy Bed;
A Blow upon the Elbow and the Knee,
From each of these, *Good L—d deliver me.*

You cannot pluck roses without fear of thorns,
Nor enjoy a fair wife without danger of horns.

Without justice, courage is weak.

Would you live with ease,
Do what you ought, and not what you please.

1734

from June

The King's cheese is half wasted in parings;
but no matter, 'tis made of the peoples milk.

Nothing but Money,
Is sweeter than Honey.

Humility makes great men twice honourable.

from October

Early to bed and early to rise, makes a man healthy wealthy and wise.

To be humble to Superiors is Duty, to Equals Courtesy, to Inferiors Nobleness.

Here comes the Orator! with his Flood of Words, and his Drop of Reason.

1735

from June

Now I've a sheep and a cow, every body bids me good morrow.

God helps them that help themselves.

from **July**

The rotten Apple spoils his Companion.

from **August**

Don't throw stones at your neighbours, if your own windows are glass.

The excellency of hogs is fatness, of men virtue.

1736

from **October**

Time is an herb that cures all Diseases.

Reading makes a full Man, Meditation a profound Man, discourse a clear Man.

If any man flatters me, I'll flatter him again; tho' he were my best Friend.

1738

from **September**

Up, Sluggard, and waste not life; in the grave will be sleeping enough.

Well done, is twice done.

1741

from **January**

He that hath a Trade, hath an Estate.

Have you somewhat to do to-morrow; do it to-day.

1742

from **May**

Make haste slowly.

1744

from **January**

Strive to be the *greatest* Man in your Country, and you may be disappointed; Strive to be the *best,* and you may succeed: He may well win the race that runs by himself.

1747

The Way to Wealth[1]

Preface to Poor Richard Improved

Courteous Reader,

I have heard that nothing gives an Author so great Pleasure, as to find his Works respectfully quoted by other learned Authors. This Pleasure I have seldom enjoyed; for tho' I have been, if I may say it without Vanity, an *eminent Author* of Almanacks annually now a full Quarter of a Century, my Brother Authors in the same Way, for what Reason I know not, have ever been very sparing in their Applauses; and no other Author has taken the least Notice of me, so that did not my Writings produce me some solid *Pudding,* the great Deficiency of *Praise* would have quite discouraged me.

I concluded at length, that the People were the best Judges of my Merit; for they buy my Works; and besides, in my Rambles, where I am not personally known, I have frequently heard one or other of my Adages repeated, with, *as Poor Richard says,* at the End on't; this gave me some Satisfaction, as it showed not only that my Instructions were regarded, but discovered likewise some Respect for my Authority; and I own, that to encourage the Practice of remembering and repeating those wise Sentences, I have sometimes *quoted myself* with great Gravity.

Judge then how much I must have been gratified by an Incident I am going to relate to you. I stopt my Horse lately where a great Number of People were collected at a Vendue of Merchant Goods. The Hour of Sale not being come, they were conversing on the Badness of the Times, and one of the Company call'd to a plain clean old Man, with white Locks, *Pray, Father* Abraham, *what think you of the Times? Won't these heavy Taxes quite ruin the Country? How shall we be ever able to pay them? What would you advise us to?*—Father *Abraham* stood up, and reply'd, If you'd have my Advice, I'll give it you in short, for a *Word to the Wise is enough,* and *many Words won't fill a Bushel,* as *Poor Richard says.* They join'd in desiring him to speak his Mind, and gathering round him, he proceeded as follows;

"Friends, says he, and Neighbours, the Taxes are indeed very heavy, and if those laid on by the Government were the only Ones we had to pay, we might more easily discharge them; but we have many others, and much more grievous to some of us.

[1]Franklin prepared this essay, in Father Abraham's voice, for the twenty-fifth anniversary issue of the *Almanac.*

We are taxed twice as much by our *Idleness,* three times as much by our *Pride,* and four times as much by our *Folly,* and from these Taxes the Commissioners cannot ease or deliver us by allowing an Abatement. However let us hearken to good Advice, and something may be done for us; *God helps them that help themselves,* as *Poor Richard* says, in his Almanack of 1733.

It would be thought a hard Government that should tax its People one tenth Part of their *Time,* to be employed in its Service. But *Idleness* taxes many of us much more, if we reckon all that is spent in absolute *Sloth,* or doing of nothing, with that which is spent in idle Employments or Amusements, that amount to nothing. *Sloth,* by bringing on Diseases, absolutely shortens Life. *Sloth, like Rust, consumes faster than Labour wears, while the used Key is always bright,* as *Poor Richard* says. But *dost thou love Life, then do not squander Time, for that's the Stuff Life is made of,* as *Poor Richard* says.—How much more than is necessary do we spend in Sleep! forgetting that *The sleeping Fox catches no Poultry,* and that *there will be sleeping enough in the Grave,* as *Poor Richard* says. If Time be of all Things the most precious, *wasting Time* must be, as *Poor Richard* says, *the greatest Prodigality,* since, as he elsewhere tells us, *Lost Time is never found again;* and what we call *Time-enough, always proves little enough.* Let us then up and be doing, and doing to the Purpose; so by Diligence shall we do more with less Perplexity. *Sloth makes all Things difficult, but Industry all easy,* as *Poor Richard* says; and *He that riseth late, must trot all Day, and shall scarce overtake his Business at Night.* While *Laziness travels so slowly, that Poverty soon overtakes him,* as we read in *Poor Richard,* who adds, *Drive thy Business, let not that drive thee;* and *Early to Bed, and early to rise, makes a Man healthy, wealthy, and wise.*

So what signifies *wishing* and *hoping* for better Times. We may make these Times better if we bestir ourselves. *Industry need not wish,* as *Poor Richard* says, and *He that lives upon Hope will die fasting. There are no Gains, without Pains;* then *Help Hands, for I have no Lands,* or if I have, they are smartly taxed. And, as *Poor Richard* likewise observes, *He that hath a Trade hath an Estate,* and *He that hath a Calling hath an Office of Profit and Honour;* but then the *Trade* must be worked at, and the *Calling* well followed, or neither the *Estate,* nor the *Office,* will enable us to pay our Taxes.—If we are industrious we shall never starve; for, as *Poor Richard* says, *At the working Man's House* Hunger *looks in, but dares not enter.* Nor will the Bailiff or the Constable enter, for *Industry pays Debts, while Despair encreaseth them,* says *Poor Richard.*—What though you have found no Treasure, nor has any rich Relation left you a Legacy, *Diligence is the Mother of Good-luck,* as *Poor Richard* says, *and God gives all Things to Industry.* Then *plough deep, while Sluggards sleep, and you shall have Corn to sell and to keep,* says *Poor Dick.* Work while it is called To-day, for you know not how much you may be hindered To-morrow, which makes *Poor Richard* say, *One To-day is worth two To-morrows;* and farther, *Have you somewhat to do To-morrow, do it To-day.* If you were a Servant, would you not be ashamed that a good Master should catch you idle? Are you then your own Master, *be ashamed to catch yourself idle,* as *Poor Dick* says. When there is so much to be done for yourself, your Family, your Country, and your gracious King, be up by Peep of Day; *Let not the Sun look down and say, Inglorious here he lies.* Handle your Tools without Mittens; remember that *the Cat in Gloves catches no Mice,* as *Poor Richard* says. 'Tis true there is much to be done, and perhaps you are weak handed, but stick to it steadily, and you will see great Effects, for *constant Dropping wears away Stones,* and by *Diligence and Patience the Mouse ate in two the Cable;* and *little Strokes fell great Oaks,* as *Poor Richard* says in his Almanack, the Year I cannot just now remember.

Methinks I hear some of you say, *Must a Man afford himself no Leisure?*—I will tell thee, my Friend, what *Poor Richard* says, *Employ thy Time well if thou meanest to gain Leisure;* and, *since thou art not sure of a Minute, throw not away an Hour.* Leisure, is Time for doing something useful; this Leisure the diligent Man will obtain, but the lazy Man never; so that, as *Poor Richard* says, a *Life of Leisure and a Life of Laziness are two Things.* Do you imagine that Sloth will afford you more Comfort than Labour? No, for as *Poor Richard* says, *Trouble springs from Idleness, and grievous Toil from needless Ease. Many without Labour, would live by their* WITS *only, but they break for want of Stock.* Whereas Industry gives Comfort, and Plenty, and Respect: *Fly Pleasures, and they'll follow you. The diligent Spinner has a large Shift,* and *now I have a Sheep and a Cow, every Body bids me Good morrow;* all which is well said by *Poor Richard.*

But with our Industry, we must likewise be *steady, settled* and *careful,* and oversee our own Affairs *with our own Eyes,* and not trust too much to others; for, as *Poor Richard* says,

I never saw an oft removed Tree,
Nor yet an oft removed Family,
That throve so well as those that settled be.

And again, *Three Removes is as bad as a Fire;* and again, *Keep thy Shop, and thy Shop will keep thee;* and again, *If you would have your Business done, go; If not, send.* And again,

He that by the Plough would thrive,
Himself must either hold or drive.

And again, *The Eye of a Master will do more Work than both his Hands;* and again, *Want of Care does us more Damage than Want of Knowledge;* and again, *Not to oversee Workmen, is to leave them your Purse open.* Trusting too much to others Care is the Ruin of many; for, as the *Almanack* says, *In the Affairs of this World, Men are saved, not by Faith, but by the Want of it;* but a Man's own Care is profitable; for, saith *Poor Dick, Learning is to the Studious,* and *Riches to the Careful,* as well as *Power to the Bold,* and *Heaven to the Virtuous.* And farther, *If you would have a faithful Servant, and one that you like, serve yourself.* And again, he adviseth to Circumspection and Care, even in the smallest Matters, because sometimes *a little Neglect may breed great Mischief;* adding, *For want of a Nail the Shoe was lost; for want of a Shoe the Horse was lost; and for want of a Horse the Rider was lost,* being overtaken and slain by the Enemy, all for want of Care about a Horseshoe Nail.

So much for Industry, my Friends, and Attention to one's own Business; but to these we must add *Frugality,* if we would make our *Industry* more certainly successful. A Man may, if he knows not how to save as he gets, *keep his Nose all his Life to the Grindstone,* and die not worth a *Groat* at last. *A fat Kitchen makes a lean Will,* as *Poor Richard* says; and,

Many Estates are spent in the Getting,
Since Women for Tea forsook Spinning and Knitting,
And Men for Punch forsook Hewing and Splitting.

If you would be wealthy, says he, in another Almanack, *think of Saving as well as of Getting: The* Indies *have not made* Spain *rich, because her* Outgoes *are greater than her* Incomes. Away then with your expensive Follies, and you will not have so much Cause to complain of hard Times, heavy Taxes, and chargeable Families; for, as *Poor Dick* says,

> *Women and Wine, Game and Deceit,*
> *Make the Wealth small, and the Wants great.*

And farther, *What maintains one Vice, would bring up two Children.* You may think perhaps, That a *little* Tea, or a *little* Punch now and then, Diet a *little* more costly, Clothes a *little* finer, and a *little* Entertainment now and then, can be no *great* Matter; but remember what *Poor Richard* says, *Many a* Little *makes a Mickle;* and farther, *Beware of* little *Expences; a small Leak will sink a great Ship;* and again, *Who Dainties love, shall Beggars prove;* and moreover, *Fools make Feasts, and wise Men eat them.*

Here you are all got together at this Vendue of *Fineries* and *Knicknacks.* You call them *Goods,* but if you do not take Care, they will prove *Evils* to some of you. You expect they will be sold *cheap,* and perhaps they may for less than they cost; but if you have no Occasion for them, they must be *dear* to you. Remember what *Poor Richard* says, *Buy what thou hast no Need of, and ere long thou shalt sell thy Necessaries.* And again, *At a great Pennyworth pause a while:* He means, that perhaps the Cheapness is *apparent* only, and not *real;* or the Bargain, by straitning thee in thy Business, may do thee more Harm than Good. For in another Place he says, *Many have been ruined by buying good Pennyworths.* Again, *Poor Richard* says, *'Tis foolish to lay out Money in a Purchase of Repentance;* and yet this Folly is practised every Day at Vendues, for want of minding the Almanack. *Wise Men,* as *Poor Dick* says, *learn by others Harms, Fools scarcely by their own;* but, *Felix quem faciunt aliena Pericula cautum.* Many a one, for the Sake of Finery on the Back, have gone with a hungry Belly, and half starved their Families; *Silks and Sattins, Scarlet and Velvets,* as *Poor Richard* says, *put out the Kitchen Fire.* These are not the *Necessaries* of Life; they can scarcely be called the *Conveniencies,* and yet only because they look pretty, how many *want* to *have* them. The *artificial* Wants of Mankind thus become more numerous than the *natural;* and, as *Poor Dick* says, *For one poor Person, there are an hundred* indigent. By these, and other Extravagancies, the Genteel are reduced to Poverty, and forced to borrow of those whom they formerly despised, but who through *Industry* and *Frugality* have maintained their Standing; in which Case it appears plainly, that a *Ploughman on his Legs is higher than a Gentleman on his Knees,* as *Poor Richard* says. Perhaps they have had a small Estate left them, which they knew not the Getting of; they think *'tis Day, and will never be Night;* that a little to be spent out of *so much,* is not worth minding; (*a Child and a Fool,* as *Poor Richard* says, *imagine* Twenty Shillings *and Twenty Years can never be spent*) but, *always taking out of the Meal-tub, and never putting in, soon comes to the Bottom;* then, as *Poor Dick* says, *When the Well's dry, they know the Worth of Water.* But this they might have known before, if they had taken his Advice; *If you would know the Value of Money, go and try to borrow some;* for, *he that goes a borrowing goes a sorrowing;* and indeed so does he that lends to such People, when he goes *to get it in again.*—*Poor Dick* farther advises, and says,

Fond Pride of Dress, *is sure a very Curse;*
E'er Fancy *you consult, consult your Purse.*

And again, *Pride is as loud a Beggar as Want, and a great deal more saucy.* When you have bought one fine Thing you must buy ten more, that your Appearance may be all of a Piece; but *Poor Dick* says, *'Tis easier to* suppress *the first Desire, than to* satisfy *all that follow it.* And 'tis as truly Folly for the Poor to ape the Rich, as for the Frog to swell, in order to equal the Ox.

Great Estates may venture more,
But little Boats should keep near Shore.

'Tis however a Folly soon punished; for *Pride that dines on Vanity sups on Contempt,* as *Poor Richard* says. And in another Place, *Pride breakfasted with Plenty, dined with Poverty, and supped with Infamy.* And after all, of what Use is this *Pride of Appearance,* for which so much is risked, so much is suffered? It cannot promote Health, or ease Pain; it makes no Increase of Merit in the Person, it creates Envy, it hastens Misfortune.

What is a Butterfly? At best
He's but a Caterpillar drest.
The gaudy Fop's his Picture just,

as *Poor Richard* says.

But what Madness must it be to *run in Debt* for these Superfluities! We are offered, by the Terms of this Vendue, *Six Months Credit;* and that perhaps has induced some of us to attend it, because we cannot spare the ready Money, and hope now to be fine without it. But, ah, think what you do when you run in Debt; *You give to another Power over your Liberty.* If you cannot pay at the Time, you will be ashamed to see your Creditor; you will be in Fear when you speak to him; you will make poor pitiful sneaking Excuses, and by Degrees come to lose your Veracity, and sink into base downright lying; for, as *Poor Richard* says, *The second Vice is Lying, the first is running in Debt.* And again, to the same Purpose, *Lying rides upon Debt's Back.* Whereas a freeborn *Englishman* ought not to be ashamed or afraid to see or speak to any Man living. But Poverty often deprives a Man of all Spirit and Virtue: *'Tis hard for an empty Bag to stand upright,* as *Poor Richard* truly says. What would you think of that Prince, or that Government, who should issue an Edict forbidding you to dress like a Gentleman or a Gentlewoman, on Pain of Imprisonment or Servitude? Would you not say, that you are free, have a Right to dress as you please, and that such an Edict would be a Breach of your Privileges, and such a Government tyrannical? And yet you are about to put yourself under that Tyranny when you run in Debt for such Dress! Your Creditor has Authority at his Pleasure to deprive you of your Liberty, by confining you in Gaol for Life, or to sell you for a Servant, if you should not be able to pay him! When you have got your Bargain, you may, perhaps, think little of Payment; but *Creditors, Poor Richard* tells us, *have better Memories than Debtors;* and in another Place says, *Creditors are a superstitious Sect, great Observers of set Days and Times.* The Day comes round before you are aware, and the Demand is made before you are prepared to satisfy it. Or if you bear your Debt in Mind, the Term which at first seemed so long, will, as it lessens, appear extreamly short. *Time* will seem to have added Wings to his Heels as well as Shoulders. *Those have a short Lent,* saith *Poor Richard, who owe Money to be paid at Easter.* Then since, as he says, *The Borrower is a Slave to the Lender, and the Debtor to the Creditor,* disdain the Chain, preserve your Freedom; and maintain your Independency: Be *industrious* and *free;* be *frugal* and *free.* At present, perhaps, you may think yourself in thriving Circumstances, and that you can bear a little Extravagance without Injury; but,

For Age and Want, save while you may;
No Morning Sun lasts a whole Day,

As *Poor Richard* says.—Gain may be temporary and uncertain, but ever while you live, Expence is constant and certain; and *'tis easier to build two Chimnies than to keep one in Fuel,* as *Poor Richard* says. So *rather go to Bed supperless than rise in Debt.*

Get what you can, and what you get hold;
'Tis the Stone that will turn all your Lead into Gold,

as *Poor Richard* says. And when you have got the Philosopher's Stone, sure you will no longer complain of bad Times, or the Difficulty of paying Taxes.

This Doctrine, my Friends, is *Reason* and *Wisdom;* but after all, do not depend too much upon your own *Industry,* and *Frugality,* and *Prudence,* though excellent Things, for they may all be blasted without the Blessing of Heaven; and therefore ask that Blessing humbly, and be not uncharitable to those that at present seem to want it, but comfort and help them. Remember *Job* suffered, and was afterwards prosperous.

And now to conclude, *Experience keeps a dear School, but Fools will learn in no other, and scarce in that;* for it is true, *we may give Advice, but we cannot give Conduct,* as *Poor Richard* says: However, remember this, *They that won't be counselled, can't be helped,* as *Poor Richard* says: And farther, That *if you will not hear Reason, she'll surely rap your Knuckles.*

Thus the old Gentleman ended his Harangue. The People heard it, and approved the Doctrine, and immediately practised the contrary, just as if it had been a common Sermon; for the Vendue opened, and they began to buy extravagantly, notwithstanding all his Cautions, and their own Fear of Taxes.—I found the good Man had thoroughly studied my Almanacks, and digested all I had dropt on those Topicks during the Course of Five-and-twenty Years. The frequent Mention he made of me must have tired any one else, but my Vanity was wonderfully delighted with it, though I was conscious that not a tenth Part of this Wisdom was my own which he ascribed to me, but rather the *Gleanings* I had made of the Sense of all Ages and Nations. However, I resolved to be the better for the Echo of it; and though I had at first determined to buy Stuff for a new Coat, I went away resolved to wear my old One a little longer. *Reader,* if thou wilt do the same, thy Profit will be as great as mine.

I am, as ever,
Thine to serve thee,
RICHARD SAUNDERS.

July 7, 1757

1958

A Witch Trial at Mount Holly[1]

Burlington, Oct. 12. Saturday last at Mount-Holly, about 8 Miles from this Place, near 300 People were gathered together to see an Experiment or two tried on some Persons accused of Witchcraft. It seems the Accused had been charged with making their Neighbours Sheep dance in an uncommon Manner, and with causing Hogs to speak, and sing Psalms, &c. to the great Terror and Amazement of the King's good and peaceable Subjects in this Province; and the Accusers being very positive that if the Accused were weighed in Scales against a Bible, the Bible would prove too heavy for them; or that, if they were bound and put into the River, they would swim; the said Accused desirous to make their Innocence appear, voluntarily offered to undergo the said Trials, if 2 of the most violent of their Accusers would be tried with them. Accordingly the Time and Place was agreed on, and advertised about the Country; The Accusers were 1 Man and 1 Woman; and the Accused the same. The Parties being met, and the People got together, a grand Consultation was held, before they proceeded to Trial; in which it was agreed to use the Scales first; and a Committee of Men were appointed to search the Men, and a Committee of Women to search the Women, to see if they had any Thing of Weight about them, particularly Pins. After the Scrutiny was over, a huge great Bible belonging to the Justice of the Place was provided, and a Lane through the Populace was made from the Justices House to the Scales, which were fixed on a Gallows erected for that Purpose opposite to the House, that the Justice's Wife and the rest of the Ladies might see the Trial, without coming amongst the Mob; and after the Manner of Moorfields, a large Ring was also made. Then came out of the House a grave tall Man carrying the Holy Writ before the supposed Wizard, &c. (as solemnly as the Sword-bearer of London before the Lord Mayor) the Wizard was first put in the Scale, and over him was read a Chapter out of the Books of Moses, and then the Bible was put in the other Scale, (which being kept down before) was immediately let go; but to the great Surprize of the Spectators, Flesh and Bones came down plump, and outweighed that great good Book by abundance. After the same Manner, the others were served, and their Lumps of Mortality severally were too heavy for Moses and all the Prophets and Apostles. This being over, the Accusers and the rest of the Mob, not satisfied with this Experiment, would have the Trial by Water; accordingly a most solemn Procession was made to the Mill-pond; where both Accused and Accusers being stripp'd (saving only to the Women their Shifts) were bound Hand and Foot, and severally placed in the Water, lengthways, from the Side of a Barge or Flat, having for Security only a Rope about the Middle of each, which was held by some in the Flat. The Accuser Man being thin and spare, with some Difficulty began to sink at last; but the rest every one of them swam very light upon the Water. A Sailor in the Flat jump'd out upon the Back of the Man accused, thinking to drive him down to the Bottom, but the Person bound, without any Help, came up some time before the other. The Woman Accuser, being told that she did not sink, would be duck'd a second Time; when she swam again as light as before. Upon which she declared, That she believed

[1]First printed in *The Pennsylvania Gazette,* October 22, 1730.

the Accused had bewitched her to make her so light, and that she would be duck'd again a Hundred Times, but she would duck the Devil out of her. The accused Man, being surpriz'd at his own Swimming, was not so confident of his Innocence as before, but said, *If I am a Witch, it is more than I know.* The more thinking Part of the Spectators were of Opinion, that any Person so bound and plac'd in the Water (unless they were mere Skin and Bones) would swim till their Breath was gone, and their Lungs fill'd with Water. But it being the general Belief of the Populace, that the Womens Shifts, and the Garters with which they were bound help'd to support them; it is said they are to be tried again the next warm Weather, naked.

1730

The Speech of Polly Baker[1]

[The Speech of Miss Polly Baker, before a Court of Judicature, at Connecticut near Boston in New-England; where she was prosecuted the Fifth Time, for having a Bastard Child: Which influenced the Court to dispense with her Punishment, and induced one of her Judges to marry her the next Day.]

May it please the Honourable Bench to indulge me in a few Words: I am a poor unhappy Woman, who have no Money to fee Lawyers to plead for me, being hard put to it to get a tolerable Living. I shall not trouble your Honours with long Speeches; for I have not the Presumption to expect, that you may, by any Means, be prevailed on to deviate in your Sentence from the Law, in my Favour. All I humbly hope is, That your Honours would charitably move the Governor's Goodness on my Behalf, that my Fine may be remitted. This is the Fifth Time, Gentlemen, that I have been dragg'd before your Court on the same Account; twice I have paid heavy Fines, and twice have been brought to Publick Punishment, for want of Money to pay those Fines. This may have been agreeable to the Laws, and I don't dispute it; but since Laws are sometimes unreasonable in themselves, and therefore repealed, and others bear too hard on the Subject in particular Circumstances; and therefore there is left a Power somewhat to dispense with the Execution of them; I take the Liberty to say, That I think this Law, by which I am punished, is both unreasonable in itself, and particularly severe with regard to me, who have always lived an inoffensive Life in the Neighbourhood where I was born, and defy my Enemies (if I have any) to say I ever wrong'd Man, Woman, or Child. Abstracted from the Law, I cannot conceive (may it please your Honours) what the Nature of my Offence is. I have brought Five fine Children into the World, at the Risque of my Life; I have maintain'd them well by my own Industry, without burthening the Township, and would have done it better, if it had not been for the heavy Charges and Fines I have paid. Can it be a Crime (in the Nature of Things I mean) to add to the Number of the King's Subjects, in a

[1] First printed in *The Gentleman's Magazine,* April, 1747.

new Country that really wants People? I own it, I should think it a Praise-worthy, rather than a punishable Action. I have debauched no other Woman's Husband, nor enticed any Youth; these Things I never was charg'd with, nor has any one the least Cause of Complaint against me, unless, perhaps, the Minister, or Justice, because I have had Children without being married, by which they have missed a Wedding Fee. But, can ever this be a Fault of mine? I appeal to your Honours. You are pleased to allow I don't want Sense; but I must be stupified to the last Degree, not to prefer the Honourable State of Wedlock, to the Condition I have lived in. I always was, and still am willing to enter into it; and doubt not my behaving well in it, having all the Industry, Frugality, Fertility, and Skill in Oeconomy, appertaining to a good Wife's Character. I defy any Person to say, I ever refused an Offer of that Sort: On the contrary, I readily consented to the only Proposal of Marriage that ever was made me, which was when I was a Virgin; but too easily confiding in the Person's Sincerity that made it, I unhappily lost my own Honour, by trusting to his; for he got me with Child, and then forsook me: That very Person you all know; he is now become a Magistrate of this Country; and I had Hopes he would have appeared this Day on the Bench, and have endeavoured to moderate the Court in my Favour; then I should have scorn'd to have mention'd it; but I must now complain of it, as unjust and unequal, That my Betrayer and Undoer, the first Cause of all my Faults and Miscarriages (if they must be deemed such) should be advanc'd to Honour and Power in the Government, that punishes my Misfortunes with Stripes and Infamy. I should be told, 'tis like, That were there no Act of Assembly in the Case, the Precepts of Religion are violated by my Transgressions. If mine, then, is a religious Offence, leave it to religious Punishments. You have already excluded me from the Comforts of your Church-Communion. Is not that sufficient? You believe I have offended Heaven, and must suffer eternal Fire: Will not that be sufficient? What Need is there, then, of your additional Fines and Whipping? I own, I do not think as you do; for, if I thought what you call a Sin, was really such, I could not presumptuously commit it. But, how can it be believed, that Heaven is angry at my having Children, when to the little done by me towards it, God has been pleased to add his Divine Skill and admirable Workmanship in the Formation of their Bodies, and crown'd it, by furnishing them with rational and immortal Souls. Forgive me, Gentlemen, if I talk a little extravagantly on these Matters; I am no Divine, but if you, Gentlemen, must be making Laws, do not turn natural and useful Actions into Crimes, by your Prohibitions. But take into your wise Consideration, the great and growing Number of Batchelors in the Country, many of whom from the mean Fear of the Expences of a Family, have never sincerely and honourably courted a Woman in their Lives; and by their Manner of Living, leave unproduced (which is little better than Murder) Hundreds of their Posterity to the Thousandth Generation. Is not this a greater Offence against the Publick Good, than mine? Compel them, then, by Law, either to Marriage, or to pay double the Fine of Fornication every Year. What must poor young Women do, whom Custom have forbid to solicit the Men, and who cannot force themselves upon Husbands, when the Laws take no Care to provide them any; and yet severely punish them if they do their Duty without them; the Duty of the first and great Command of Nature, and of Nature's God, *Encrease and Multiply.* A Duty, from the steady Performance of which, nothing has been able to deter me; but for its Sake, I have hazarded the Loss of the Publick Esteem, and have frequently endured Publick

Disgrace and Punishment; and therefore ought, in my humble Opinion, instead of a Whipping, to have a Statue erected to my Memory.

1747

A Narrative of the Late Massacres

[January 30?, 1764]

These Indians were the Remains of a Tribe of the Six Nations, settled at Conestogoe, and thence called Conestogoe Indians. On the first Arrival of the English in Pennsylvania, Messengers from this Tribe came to welcome them, with Presents of Venison, Corn and Skins; and the whole Tribe entered into a Treaty of Friendship with the first Proprietor, WILLIAM PENN, which was to last "as long as the Sun should shine, or the Waters run in the Rivers."

This Treaty has been since frequently renewed, and the *Chain brightened,* as they express it, from time to time. It has never been violated, on their Part or ours, till now. As their Lands by Degrees were mostly purchased, and the Settlements of the White People began to surround them, the Proprietor assigned them Lands on the Manor of Conestogoe, which they might not part with; there they have lived many Years in Friendship with their White Neighbours, who loved them for their peaceable inoffensive Behaviour.

It has always been observed, that Indians, settled in the Neighbourhood of White People, do not increase, but diminish continually. This Tribe accordingly went on diminishing, till there remained in their Town on the Manor, but 20 Persons, *viz.* 7 Men, 5 Women, and 8 Children, Boys and Girls.

Of these, Shehaes was a very old Man, having assisted at the second Treaty held with them, by Mr. PENN, in 1701, and ever since continued a faithful and affectionate Friend to the English; he is said to have been an exceeding good Man, considering his Education, being naturally of a most kind benevolent Temper.

Peggy was Shehaes's Daughter; she worked for her aged Father, continuing to live with him, though married, and attended him with filial Duty and Tenderness.

John was another good old Man; his Son Harry helped to support him.

George and Will Soc were two Brothers, both young Men.

John Smith, a valuable young Man, of the Cayuga Nation, who became acquainted with Peggy, Shehaes's Daughter, some few Years since, married her, and settled in that Family. They had one Child, about three Years old.

Betty, a harmless old Woman; and her Son Peter, a likely young Lad.

Sally, whose Indian Name was Wyanjoy, a Woman much esteemed by all that knew her, for her prudent and good Behaviour in some very trying Situations of Life. She was a truly good and an amiable Woman, had no Children of her own, but a distant Relation dying, she had taken a Child of that Relation's, to bring up as her own, and performed towards it all the Duties of an affectionate Parent.

The Reader will observe, that many of their Names are English. It is common with the Indians that have an Affection for the English, to give themselves, and their Children, the Names of such English Persons as they particularly esteem.

This little Society continued the Custom they had begun, when more numerous, of addressing every new Governor, and every Descendant of the first Proprietor, welcoming him to the Province, assuring him of their Fidelity, and praying a Continuance of that Favour and Protection they had hitherto experienced. They had accordingly sent up an Address of this Kind to our present Governor, on his Arrival; but the same was scarce delivered, when the unfortunate Catastrophe happened, which we are about to relate.

On Wednesday, the 14th of December, 1763, Fifty-seven Men, from some of our Frontier Townships, who had projected the Destruction of this little Commonwealth, came, all well-mounted, and armed with Firelocks, Hangers and Hatchets, having travelled through the Country in the Night, to Conestogoe Manor. There they surrounded the small Village of Indian Huts, and just at Break of Day broke into them all at once. Only three Men, two Women, and a young Boy, were found at home, the rest being out among the neighbouring White People, some to sell the Baskets, Brooms and Bowls they manufactured, and others on other Occasions. These poor defenceless Creatures were immediately fired upon, stabbed and hatcheted to Death! The good Shehaes, among the rest, cut to Pieces in his Bed. All of them were scalped, and otherwise horribly mangled. Then their Huts were set on Fire, and most of them burnt down. When the Troop, pleased with their own Conduct and Bravery, but enraged that any of the poor Indians had escaped the Massacre, rode off, and in small Parties, by different Roads, went home.

The universal Concern of the neighbouring White People on hearing of this Event, and the Lamentations of the younger Indians, when they returned and saw the Desolation, and the butchered half-burnt Bodies of their murdered Parents, and other Relations, cannot well be expressed.

The Magistrates of Lancaster sent out to collect the remaining Indians, brought them into the Town for their better Security against any further Attempt, and it is said condoled with them on the Misfortune that had happened, took them by the Hand, comforted and *promised them Protection.* They were all put into the Workhouse, a strong Building, as the Place of greatest Safety.

When the shocking News arrived in Town, a Proclamation was issued by the Governor, in the following Terms, *viz.*

"Whereas I have received Information, That on Wednesday, the Fourteenth Day of this Month, a Number of People, armed, and mounted on Horseback, unlawfully assembled together, and went to the Indian Town in the Conestogoe Manor, in Lancaster County, and without the least Reason or Provocation, in cool Blood, barbarously killed six of the Indians settled there, and burnt and destroyed all their Houses and Effects: And whereas so cruel and inhuman an Act, committed in the Heart of this Province on the said Indians, who have lived peaceably and inoffensively among us, during all our late Troubles, and for many Years before, and were justly considered as under the Protection of this Government and its Laws, calls loudly for the vigorous Exertion of the civil Authority, to detect the Offenders, and bring them to condign Punishment; I have therefore, by and with the Advice and Consent of the Council, thought fit to issue this Proclamation, and do hereby strictly charge and enjoin all Judges, Justices, Sheriffs, Constables, Officers Civil and Military, and all other His Majesty's liege Subjects within this Province, to make diligent Search and Enquiry after the Authors and Perpetrators of the said Crime, their Abettors and Accomplices, and to use all possible Means to apprehend and secure them in some of the publick Goals of this Province, that they may be brought to their Trials, and be proceeded against according to Law.

"And whereas a Number of other Indians, who lately lived on or near the Frontiers of this Province, being willing and desirous to preserve and continue the ancient Friendship which heretofore subsisted between them and the good People of this Province, have, at their own earnest Request, been removed from their Habitations, and brought into the County of Philadelphia, and seated, for the present, for their better Security, on the Province-Island, and in other Places in the Neighbourhood of the City of Philadelphia, where Provision is made for them at the public Expence; I do therefore hereby strictly forbid all Persons whatsoever, to molest or injure any of the said Indians, as they will answer the contrary at their Peril.

"Given under my Hand, and the Great Seal of the said Province, at Philadelphia, the Twenty-second Day of December, Anno Domini One Thousand Seven Hundred and Sixty-three, and in the Fourth Year of His Majesty's Reign.

JOHN PENN.

"By His Honour's Command, Joseph Shippen, *jun. Secretary.* "God Save the King."

Notwithstanding this Proclamation, those cruel Men again assembled themselves, and hearing that the remaining fourteen Indians were in the Work-house at Lancaster, they suddenly appeared in that Town, on the 27th of December. Fifty of them, armed as before, dismounting, went directly to the Work-house, and by Violence broke open the Door, and entered with the utmost Fury in their Countenances. When the poor Wretches saw they had *no Protection* nigh, nor could possibly escape, and being without the least Weapon for Defence, they divided into their little Families, the Children clinging to the Parents; they fell on their Knees, protested their Innocence, declared their Love to the English, and that, in their whole Lives, they had never done them Injury; and in this Posture they all received the Hatchet! Men, Women and little Children—were every one inhumanly murdered!—in cold Blood!

The barbarous Men who committed the atrocious Fact, in Defiance of Government, of all Laws human and divine, and to the eternal Disgrace of their Country and Colour, then mounted their Horses, huzza'd in Triumph, as if they had gained a Victory, and rode off—*unmolested!*

The Bodies of the Murdered were then brought out and exposed in the Street, till a Hole could be made in the Earth, to receive and cover them.

But the Wickedness cannot be covered, the Guilt will lie on the whole Land, till Justice is done on the Murderers. THE BLOOD OF THE INNOCENT WILL CRY TO HEAVEN FOR VENGEANCE.

It is said that Shehaes, being before told, that it was to be feared some English might come from the Frontier into the Country, and murder him and his People; he replied, "It is impossible: There are Indians, indeed, in the Woods, who would kill me and mine, if they could get at us, for my Friendship to the English; but the English will wrap me in their Matchcoat, and secure me from all Danger." How unfortunately was he mistaken!

Another Proclamation has been issued, offering a great Reward for apprehending the Murderers, in the following Terms, *viz.*

"Whereas on the Twenty-second Day of December last, I issued a Proclamation for the apprehending and bringing to Justice, a Number of Persons, who, in Violation of the Public Faith; and in Defiance of all Law, had inhumanly killed six of the Indians, who had lived in Conestogoe Manor, for the Course of many Years, peaceably and inoffensively, under the Protection of this Government, on Lands assigned to them for their Habitation; notwithstanding which, I have received Information, that on the Twenty-seventh of the same Month, a large Party of armed Men again assembled and met together in a riotous and tumultuous Manner, in the County of Lancaster, and proceeded to the Town of Lancaster, where they violently broke open the Work-house, and butchered and put to Death fourteen of the said Conestogoe Indians, Men, Women and Children, who had been taken under the immediate Care and Protection of the Magistrates of the said County, and lodged for their better Security in the said Work-house, till they should be more effectually provided for by Order of the Government. And whereas common Justice loudly demands, and the Laws of the Land (upon the Preservation of which not only the Liberty and Security of every Individual, but the Being of the Government itself depend) require that the above Offenders should be brought to condign Punishment; I have therefore, by and with the Advice of the Council, published this Proclamation, and do hereby strictly charge and command all Judges, Justices, Sheriffs, Constables, Officers Civil and Military, and all other His Majesty's faithful and liege Subjects within this Province, to make diligent Search and Enquiry after the Authors and Perpetrators of the said last mentioned Offence, their Abettors and Accomplices, and that they use all possible Means to apprehend and secure them in some of the public Goals of this Province, to be dealt with according to Law.

"And I do hereby further promise and engage, that any Person or Persons, who shall apprehend and secure, or cause to be apprehended and secured, any Three of the Ringleaders of the said Party, and prosecute them to Conviction, shall have and receive for each, the public Reward of Two Hundred Pounds; and any Accomplice, not concerned in the immediate shedding the Blood of the said Indians, who shall make Discovery of any or either of the said Ringleaders, and apprehend and prosecute them to Conviction, shall, over and above the said Reward, have all the Weight and Influence of the Government, for obtaining His Majesty's Pardon for his Offence.

"Given under my Hand, and the Great Seal of the said Province, at Philadelphia, the Second Day of January, in the Fourth Year of His Majesty's Reign, and in the Year of our Lord One Thousand Seven Hundred and Sixty-four.

JOHN PENN.

By His Honour's Command, Joseph Shippen, *jun. Secretary.* "God Save the King."

These Proclamations have as yet produced no Discovery; the Murderers having given out such Threatenings against those that disapprove their Proceedings, that the whole County seems to be in Terror, and no one durst speak what he knows; even the Letters from thence are unsigned, in which any Dislike is expressed of the Rioters.

There are some (I am ashamed to hear it) who would extenuate the enormous Wickedness of these Actions, by saying, "The Inhabitants of the Frontiers are exasperated with the Murder of their Relations, by the Enemy Indians, in the present War." It is possible; but though this might justify their going out into the Woods, to seek for those Enemies, and avenge upon them those Murders; it can never justify their turning in to the Heart of the Country, to murder their Friends.

If an Indian injures me, does it follow that I may revenge that Injury on all Indians? It is well known that Indians are of different Tribes, Nations and Languages, as well as the White People. In Europe, if the French, who are White-People, should injure the Dutch, are they to revenge it on the English, because they too are White People? The only Crime of these poor Wretches seems to have been, that they had a reddish brown Skin, and black Hair; and some People of that Sort, it seems, had murdered some of our Relations. If it be right to kill Men for such a Reason, then, should any Man, with a freckled Face and red Hair, kill a Wife or Child of mine, it would be right for me to revenge it, by killing all the freckled red-haired Men, Women and Children, I could afterwards any where meet with.

But it seems these People think they have a better Justification; nothing less than the *Word of God.* With the Scriptures in their Hands and Mouths, they can set at nought that express Command, *Thou shalt do no Murder;* and justify their Wickedness, by the Command given Joshua to destroy the Heathen. Horrid Perversion of Scripture and of Religion! to father the worst of Crimes on the God of Peace and Love! Even the Jews, to whom that particular Commission was directed, spared the Gibeonites, on Account of their Faith once given. The Faith of this Government has been frequently given to those Indians; but that did not avail them with People who despise Government.

We pretend to be Christians, and, from the superior Light we enjoy, ought to exceed Heathens, Turks, Saracens, Moors, Negroes, and Indians, in the Knowledge and Practice of what is right. I will endeavour to show, by a few Examples from Books and History, the Sense those People have had of such Actions.

HOMER wrote his Poem, called the *Odyssey,* some Hundred Years before the Birth of Christ. He frequently speaks of what he calls not only *the Duties,* but *the sacred Rites of Hospitality,* (exercised towards Strangers, while in our House or Territory) as including, besides all the common Circumstances of Entertainment, full Safety and Protection of Person, from all Danger of Life, from all Injuries, and even Insults. The Rites of Hospitality were called *sacred,* because the Stranger, the Poor and the Weak, when they applied for Protection and Relief, were, from the Religion of those Times, supposed to be sent by the Deity to try the Goodness of Men, and that he would avenge the Injuries they might receive, where they ought to have been protected. These Sentiments therefore influenced the Manners of all Ranks of People, even the meanest; for we find that when Ulysses came, as a poor Stranger, to the Hut of Eumaeus, the Swineherd, and his great Dogs ran out to tear the ragged Man, Eumaeus drave them away with Stones; and

Unhappy Stranger! (thus the faithful Swain
Began, with Accent gracious and humane)
What Sorrow had been mine, if at *my* Gate
Thy rev'rend Age had met a shameful Fate?
—But enter this my homely Roof, and see
Our Woods not void of Hospitality.
He said, and seconding the kind Request,

With friendly Step precedes the unknown Guest.
A shaggy Goat's soft Hide beneath him spread,
And with fresh Rushes heap'd an ample Bed.
Joy touch'd the Hero's tender Soul, to find
So *just* Reception from a Heart so kind:
And oh, ye Gods! with all your Blessings grace
(He thus broke forth) this Friend of human Race!
  The Swain reply'd. It never was our guise
To slight the Poor, or aught humane despise.
For Jove unfolds the hospitable Door,
Tis Jove that sends the Stranger and the Poor.

These Heathen People thought, that after a Breach of the Rites of Hospitality, a Curse from Heaven would attend them in every thing they did, and even their honest Industry in their Callings would fail of Success. Thus when Ulysses tells Eumaeus, who doubted the Truth of what he related, *If I deceive you in this, I should deserve Death, and I consent that you should put me to Death;* Eumaeus rejects the Proposal as what would be attended with both Infamy and Misfortune, saying ironically,

Doubtless, oh Guest! great Laud and Praise were mine,
If, after social Rites and Gifts bestow'd,
I stain'd my Hospitable Hearth with Blood.
How would the Gods my righteous Toils succeed,
And bless the Hand that made a Stranger bleed?
No more.—

Even an open Enemy, in the Heat of Battle, throwing down his Arms, submitting to his Foe, and asking Life and Protection, was supposed to acquire an immediate Right to that Protection. Thus one describes his being saved, when his Party was defeated.

We turn'd to Flight; the gath'ring Vengeance spread
On all Parts round, and Heaps on Heaps lie dead.
—The radiant Helmet from my Brows unlac'd,
And lo on Earth my Shield and Jav'lin cast,
I meet the Monarch with a Suppliant's Face,
Approach his Chariat, and his Knees embrace.
He heard, he sav'd he plac'd me at his Side;
My State he pity'd, and my Tears he dry'd;
Restrain'd the Rage the vengeful Foe express'd,
And turn'd the deadly Weapons from my Breast.
Pious *to guard the Hospitable Rite,*
And *fearing Jove,* whom Mercy's Works delight.

The Suitors of Penelope are by the same ancient Poet described as a Sett of Lawless Men, who were *regardless of the sacred Rites of Hospitality.* And therefore when the Queen was informed they were slain, and that by Ulysses, she, not believing that Ulysses was returned, says,

Ah no!—some God the Suitors Deaths decreed,
Some God descends, and by his Hand they bleed:

Blind, to contemn the Stranger's righteous Cause,
And violate all hospitable Laws!
——The Powers they defy'd;
But Heav'n is just, and by a God they dy'd.

Thus much for the Sentiments of the ancient Heathens. As for the Turks, it is recorded in the Life of Mahomet, the Founder of their Religion, That Khaled, one of his Captains, having divided a Number of Prisoners between himself and those that were with him, he commanded the Hands of his own Prisoners to be tied behind them, and then, in a most cruel and brutal Manner, put them to the Sword; but he could not prevail on his Men to massacre *their* Captives, because in Fight they had laid down their Arms, submitted, and demanded Protection. Mahomet, when the Account was brought to him, applauded the Men for their Humanity; but said to Khaled, with great Indignation, *Oh Khaled, thou Butcher, cease to molest me with thy Wickedness. If thou possessedst a Heap of Gold as large as Mount Obod, and shouldst expend it all in God's Cause, thy Merit would not efface the Guilt incurred by the Murder of the meanest of those poor Captives.*

Among the Arabs or Saracens, though it was lawful to put to Death a Prisoner taken in Battle, if he had made himself obnoxious by his former Wickedness, yet this could not be done after he had once eaten Bread, or drank Water, while in their Hands. Hence we read in the History of the Wars of the Holy Land, that when the Franks had suffered a great Defeat from Saladin, and among the Prisoners were the King of Jerusalem, and Arnold, a famous Christian Captain, who had been very cruel to the Saracens; these two being brought before the Soltan, he placed the King on his right hand, and Arnold on his left; and then presented the King with a Cup of Water, who immediately drank to Arnold; but when Arnold was about to receive the Cup, the Soltan interrupted, saying, *I will not suffer this wicked Man to drink, as that, according to the laudable and generous Custom of the Arabs, would secure him his Life.*

That same laudable and generous Custom still prevails among the Mahometans, appears from the Account but last Year published of his Travels by Mr. Bell of Antermony, who accompanied the Czar Peter the Great, in his Journey to Derbent through Dagestan. "The Religion of the Daggestans, says he, is generally Mahometan, some following the Sect of Osman, others that of Haly. Their Language for the most Part is Turkish, or rather a Dialect of the Arabic, though many of them speak also the Persian Language. One Article I cannot omit concerning their Laws of Hospitality, which is, if their greatest Enemy comes under their Roof for Protection, the Landlord, of what Condition soever, is obliged to keep him safe, from all Manner of Harm or Violence, during his Abode with him, and even to conduct him safely through his Territories to a Place of Security."

From the Saracens this same Custom obtained among the Moors of Africa; was by them brought into Spain, and there long sacredly observed. The Spanish Historians record with Applause one famous Instance of it. While the Moors governed there, and the Spaniards were mixed with them, a Spanish Cavalier, in a sudden Quarrel, slew a young Moorish Gentleman, and fled. His Pursuers soon lost Sight of him, for he had, unperceived, thrown himself over a Garden Wall. The Owner, a Moor, happening to be in his Garden, was addressed by the Spaniard on his Knees, who acquainted him with his Case, and implored Concealment. *Eat this,* said the

Moor, giving him Half a Peach; *you now know that you may confide in my Protection.* He then locked him up in his Garden Apartment, telling him, that as soon as it was Night he would provide for his Escape to a Place of more Safety. The Moor then went into his House, where he had scarce seated himself, when a great Croud, with loud Lamentations, came to his Gate, bringing the Corps of his Son, that had just been killed by a Spaniard. When the first Shock of Surprize was a little over, he learnt, from the Description given, that the fatal Deed was done by the Person then in his Power. He mentioned this to no One; but as soon as it was dark, retired to his Garden Apartment, as if to grieve alone, giving Orders that none should follow him. There accosting the Spaniard, he said, *Christian, the Person you have killed, is my Son: His Body is now in my House. You ought to suffer; but you have eaten with me, and I have given you my Faith, which must not be broken. Follow me.* He then led the astonished Spaniard to his Stables, mounted him on one of his fleetest Horses, and said, *Fly far while the Night can cover you. You will be safe in the Morning. You are indeed guilty of my Son's Blood, but God is just and good, and I thank him that I am innocent of yours, and that my Faith given is preserved.*

The Spaniards caught from the Moors this *Punto* of Honour, the Effects of which remain, in a great Degree, to this Day. So that when there is Fear of a War about to break out between England and Spain, an English Merchant there, who apprehends the Confiscation of his Goods as the Goods of an Enemy, thinks them safe, if he can get a Spaniard to take Charge of them; for the Spaniard secures them as his own, and faithfully redelivers them, or pays the Value, whenever the Englishman can safely demand it.

Justice to that Nation, though lately our Enemies, and hardly yet our cordial Friends, obliges me, on this Occasion, not to omit mentioning an Instance of Spanish Honour, which cannot but be still fresh in the Memory of many yet living. In 1746, when we were in hot War with Spain, the *Elizabeth,* of London, Captain William Edwards, coming through the Gulph from Jamaica, richly laden, met with a most violent Storm, in which the Ship sprung a Leak, that obliged them, for the Saving of their Lives, to run her into the Havannah. The Captain went on Shore, directly waited on the Governor, told the Occasion of his putting in, and that he surrendered his Ship as a Prize, and himself and his Men as Prisoners of War, only requesting good Quarter. *No, Sir,* replied the Spanish Governor, *If we had taken you in fair War at Sea, or approaching our Coast with hostile Intentions, your Ship would then have been a Prize, and your People Prisoners. But when distressed by a Tempest, you come into our Ports for the Safety of your Lives, we, though Enemies, being Men, are bound as such, by the Laws of Humanity, to afford Relief to distressed Men, who ask it of us. We cannot, even against our Enemies, take Advantage of an Act of God. You have Leave therefore to unload your Ship, if that be necessary, to stop the Leak; you may refit here, and traffick so far as shall be necessary to pay the Charges; you may then depart, and I will give you a Pass, to be in Force till you are beyond Bermuda. If after that you are taken, you will then be a Prize, but now you are only a Stranger, and have a Stranger's Right to Safety and Protection.* The Ship accordingly departed, and arrived safe in London.

Will it be permitted me to adduce, on this Occasion, an Instance of the like Honour in a poor unenlightened African Negroe. I find it in Capt. Seagrave's Account of his Voyage to Guinea. He relates that a New-England Sloop, trading there in 1752, left their second Mate, William Murray, sick on Shore, and sailed without him. Murray was at the House of a Black, named Cudjoe, with whom he had contracted an Acquaintance during their Trade. He recovered, and the Sloop being gone, he continued with his black Friend, till some other Opportunity should offer of his getting home. In the mean while, a Dutch Ship came into the Road, and some of the Blacks going on board her, were treacherously seized, and carried off as Slaves. Their Relations and Friends, transported with sudden Rage, ran to the House of Cudjoe to take Revenge, by killing Murray. Cudjoe stopt them at the Door, and demanded what they wanted? The White Men, said they, have carried away our Brothers and Sons, and we will kill all White Men; give us the White Man that you keep in your House, for we will kill him. *Nay,* said Cudjoe; *the White Men that carried away your Brothers are bad Men, kill them when you can catch them; but this White Man is a good Man, and you must not kill him.* But he is a White Man, they cried; the White Men are all bad; we will kill them all. *Nay,* says he, *you must not kill a Man, that had done no Harm, only for being white. This Man is my Friend, my House is his Fort, and I am his Soldier. I must fight for him. You must kill me, before you can kill him. What good Man will ever come again under my Roof, if I let my Floor be stained with a good Man's Blood!* The Negroes seeing his Resolution, and being convinced by his Discourse that they were wrong, went away ashamed. In a few Days Murray ventured abroad again with Cudjoe, when several of them took him by the Hand, and told him they were glad they had not killed him; for as he was a good (meaning an innocent) Man, *their God would have been angry, and would have spoiled their Fishing.* I relate this, says Captain Seagrave, to show, that some among these dark People have a strong Sense of Justice and Honour, and that even the most brutal among them are capable of feeling the Force of Reason, and of being influenced by a Fear of God (if the Knowledge of the true God could be introduced among them) since even the Fear of a false God, when their Rage subsided, was not without its good Effect.

Now I am about to mention something of Indians, I beg that I may not be understood as framing Apologies for *all* Indians. I am far from desiring to lessen the laudable Spirit of Resentment in my Countrymen against those now at War with us, so far as it is justified by their Perfidy and Inhumanity. I would only observe that the Six Nations, as a Body, have kept Faith with the English ever since we knew them, now near an Hundred Years; and that the governing Part of those People have had Notions of Honour, whatever may be the Case with the Rum-debauched, Trader-corrupted Vagabonds and Thieves on Sasquehannah and the Ohio, at present in Arms against us. As a Proof of that Honour, I shall only mention one well-known recent Fact. When six Catawba Deputies, under the Care of Colonel Bull, of Charlestown, went by Permission into the Mohawks Country, to sue for and treat of Peace for their Nation, they soon found the Six Nations highly exasperated, and the Peace at that Time impracticable: They were therefore in Fear for their own Persons, and apprehended that they should be killed in their Way back to New-York; which being made known to the Mohawk Chiefs, by Colonel Bull, one of them, by Order of the Council, made this Speech to the Catawbas:

"Strangers and Enemies,

"While you are in this Country, blow away all Fear out of your Breasts; change the black Streak of Pain on your Cheek for a red One, and let your Faces shine with Bear's-Grease: You are safer here than if you were at home. The Six Nations will not defile their own Land with the Blood of Men that come unarmed to ask for Peace. We shall send a Guard with you, to see you safe out of our Territories. So far you shall have Peace, but no farther. Get home to your own Country, and there take Care of yourselves, for there we intend to come and kill you."

The Catawbas came away unhurt accordingly.

It is also well known, that just before the late War broke out, when our Traders first went among the Piankeshaw Indians, a Tribe of the Twightwees, they found the Principle of *giving Protection to Strangers* in full Force; for the French coming with their Indians to the Piankeshaw Town, and demanding that those Traders and their Goods should be delivered up; the Piankeshaws replied, the English were come there upon their Invitation, and they could not do so base a Thing. But the French insisting on it, the Piankeshaws took Arms in Defence of their Guests, and a Number of them, with their old Chief, lost their Lives in the Cause; the French at last prevailing by superior Force only.

I will not dissemble that numberless Stories have been raised and spread abroad, against not only the poor Wretches that are murdered, but also against the Hundred and Forty christianized Indians, still threatned to be murdered; all which Stories are well known, by those who know the Indians best, to be pure Inventions, contrived by bad People, either to excite each other to join in the Murder, or since it was committed, to justify it; and believed only by the Weak and Credulous. I call thus publickly on the Makers and Venders of these Accusations to produce their Evidence. Let them satisfy the Public that even Will Soc, the most obnoxious of all that Tribe, was really guilty of those Offences against us which they lay to his Charge. But if he was, ought he not to have been fairly tried? He lived under our Laws, and was subject to them; he was in our Hands, and might easily have been prosecuted; was it *English Justice* to condemn and execute him unheard? Conscious of his own Innocence, he did not endeavour to hide himself when the Door of the Work-house, his Sanctuary, was breaking open; *I will meet them,* says he, *for they are my Brothers.* These Brothers of his shot him down at the Door, while the Word Brothers was still between his Teeth! But if Will Soc was a bad Man, what had poor old Shehaes done? what could he or the other poor old Men and Women do? What had little Boys and Girls done; what could Children of a Year old, Babes at the Breast, what could they do, that they too must be shot and hatcheted? Horrid to relate! and in their Parents Arms! This is done by no civilized Nation in Europe. Do we come to America to learn and practise the Manners of *Barbarians?* But this, *Barbarians* as they are, they practise against their Enemies only, not against their Friends.

These poor People have been always our Friends. Their Fathers received ours, when Strangers here, with Kindness and Hospitality. Behold the Return we have made them! When we grew more numerous and powerful, they put themselves under our *Protection.* See, in the mangled Corpses of the last Remains of the Tribe, how effectually we have afforded it to them!

Unhappy People! to have lived in such Times, and by such Neighbours! We have seen, that they would have been safer among the ancient Heathens, with whom the Rites of Hospitality were *sacred.* They would have been considered as *Guests* of the Publick, and the Religion of the Country would have operated in their Favour. But our Frontier People call themselves Christians! They would have been safer, if they had submitted to the Turks; for ever since Mahomet's Reproof to Khaled, even the *cruel Turks,* never kill Prisoners in cold Blood. These were not even Prisoners: But what is the Example of Turks to Scripture Christians? They would have been safer, though they had been taken in actual War against the Saracens, if they had once drank Water with them. These were not taken in War against us, and have drank with us, and we with them, for Fourscore Years. But shall we compare Saracens to Christians? They would have been safer among the Moors in Spain, though they had been *Murderers of Sons;* if Faith had once been pledged to them, and a Promise of Protection given. But these have had the Faith of the English given to them many Times by the Government, and, in Reliance on that Faith, they lived among us, and gave us the Opportunity of murdering them. However, what was honourable in Moors, may not be a Rule to us; for we are Christians! They would have been safer it seems among Popish Spaniards, even if Enemies, and delivered into their Hands by a Tempest. These were not Enemies; they were born among us, and yet we have killed them all. But shall we imitate *idolatrous Papists,* we that are *enlightened Protestants?* They would even have been safer among the Negroes of Africa, where at least one manly Soul would have been found, with Sense, Spirit and Humanity enough, to stand in their Defence: But shall *Whitemen* and *Christians* act like a *Pagan Negroe?* In short it appears, that they would have been safe in any Part of the known World, except in the Neighbourhood of the CHRISTIANS WHITE SAVAGES of Peckstang and Donegall!

O ye unhappy Perpetrators of this horrid Wickedness! Reflect a Moment on the Mischief ye have done, the Disgrace ye have brought on your Country, on your Religion, and your Bible, on your Families and Children! Think on the Destruction of your captivated Country-folks (now among the wild Indians) which probably may follow, in Resentment of your Barbarity! Think on the Wrath of the United Five Nations, hitherto our Friends, but now provoked by your murdering one of their Tribes, in Danger of becoming our bitter Enemies. Think of the mild and good Government you have so audaciously insulted; the Laws of your King, your Country, and your GOD, that you have broken; the infamous Death that hangs over your Heads: For JUSTICE, though slow, will come at last. All good People every where detest your Actions. You have imbrued your Hands in innocent Blood; how will you make them clean? The dying Shrieks and Groans of the Murdered, will often sound in your Ears: Their Spectres will sometimes attend you, and affright even your innocent Children! Fly where you will, your Consciences will go with you: Talking in your Sleep shall betray you, in the Delirium of a Fever you yourselves shall make your own Wickedness known.

One Hundred and Forty peaceable Indians yet remain in this Government. They have, by Christian Missionaries, been brought over to a *Liking,* at least, of our Religion; some of them lately left their Nation which is now at War with us, because they did not chuse to join with them in their Depredations; and to shew their Confidence in us, and to give us an equal Confidence in them, they have brought and put into our Hands their Wives and Children. Others have lived long among us in Northampton County, and most of their Children have been born there. These are all now trembling for their Lives. They have been hurried from Place to Place for Safety, now concealed in Corners, then sent out of the Province, refused a Passage through a neighbouring Colony, and returned, not unkindly perhaps, but disgracefully, on our Hands. O Pennsylvania! once renowned for Kindness to Strangers, shall the Clamours of a few mean Niggards about the Expence of this *Publick Hospitality,* an Expence that will not cost the noisy Wretches *Sixpence* a Piece (and what is the Expence of the poor Maintenance we afford them, compared to the Expence they might occasion if in Arms against us) shall so senseless a Clamour, I say, force you to turn out of your Doors these unhappy Guests, who have offended their own Country-folks by their Affection for you, who, confiding in your Goodness, have put themselves under your Protection? Those whom you have disarmed to satisfy groundless Suspicions, will you leave them exposed to the armed Madmen of your Country? Unmanly Men! who are not ashamed to come with Weapons against the Unarmed, to use the Sword against Women, and the Bayonet against young Children; and who have already given such bloody Proofs of their Inhumanity and Cruelty. Let us rouze ourselves, for Shame, and redeem the Honour of our Province from the Contempt of its Neighbours; let all good Men join heartily and unanimously in Support of the Laws, and in strengthening the Hands of Government; that JUSTICE may be done, the Wicked punished, and the Innocent protected; otherwise we can, as a People, expect no Blessing from Heaven, there will be no Security for our Persons or Properties; Anarchy and Confusion will prevail over all, and Violence, without Judgment, dispose of every Thing.

When I mention the Baseness of the Murderers, in the Use they made of Arms, I cannot, I ought not to forget, the very different Behaviour of *brave Men* and *true Soldiers,* of which this melancholy Occasion has afforded us fresh Instances. The Royal Highlanders have, in the Course of this War, suffered as much as any other Corps, and have frequently had their Ranks thinn'd by an Indian Enemy; yet they did not for this retain a brutal undistinguishing Resentment against *all* Indians, Friends as well as Foes. But a Company of them happening to be here, when the 140 poor Indians above mentioned were thought in too much Danger to stay longer in the Province, chearfully undertook to protect and escort them to New-York, which they executed (as far as that Government would permit the Indians to come) with Fidelity and Honour; and their Captain Robinson, is justly applauded and honoured by all sensible and good People, for the Care, Tenderness and Humanity, with which he treated those unhappy Fugitives, during their March in this severe Season. General Gage, too, has approved of his Officer's Conduct, and, as I hear, ordered him to remain with the Indians at Amboy, and continue his Protection to them, till another Body of the King's Forces could be sent to relieve his Company, and escort their Charge back in Safety to Philadelphia, where his Excellency has had the Goodness to direct those Forces to remain for some Time, under the Orders of our Governor, for the Security of the Indians; the Troops of this Province being at present necessarily posted on the Frontier. Such just and generous Actions endear the Military to the Civil Power, and impress the Minds of all the Discerning with a still greater Respect for our national Government. I shall conclude with observing, that *Cowards* can handle Arms, can strike where they are sure to meet with no Return, can wound, mangle and murder; but it belongs to *brave* Men to spare, and to protect; for, as the Poet says,

Mercy still sways the Brave.

1764

An Edict by the King of Prussia[1]

Dantzick, September 5.

We have long wondered here at the Supineness of the English Nation, under the Prussian Impositions upon its Trade entering our Port. We did not till lately know the *Claims,* antient and modern, that hang over that Nation, and therefore could not suspect that it might submit to those Impositions from a Sense of *Duty,* or from Principles of *Equity.* The following *Edict,* just made public, may, if serious, throw some Light upon this Matter.

"FREDERICK, by the Grace of God, King of Prussia, &c. &c. &c. to all present and to come, HEALTH. The Peace now enjoyed throughout our Dominions, having afforded us Leisure to apply ourselves to the Regulation of Commerce, the Improvement of our Finances, and at the same Time the easing our *Domestic Subjects* in their Taxes: For these Causes, and other good Considerations us thereunto moving, We hereby make known, that after having deliberated these Affairs in our Council, present our dear Brothers, and other great Officers of the State, Members of the same, WE, of our certain Knowledge, full Power and Authority Royal, have made and issued this present Edict, viz.

WHEREAS it is well known to all the World, that the first German Settlements made in the Island of Britain, were by Colonies of People, Subjects to our renowned Ducal Ancestors, and drawn from *their* Dominions, under the Conduct of Hengist, Horsa, Hella, Uffa, Cerdicus, Ida, and others; and that the said Colonies have flourished under the Protection of our august House, for Ages past, have never been *emancipated* therefrom, and yet have hitherto yielded little Profit to the same. And whereas We Ourself have in the last War fought for and defended the said Colonies against the Power of France, and thereby enabled them to make Conquests from the said Power in America, for which we have not yet received adequate Compensation. And whereas it is just and expedient that a Revenue should be raised from the said Colonies in Britain towards our Indemnification; and that those who are Descendants of our antient Subjects, and thence still owe us due Obedience, should contribute to the replenishing of our Royal Coffers, as they must have done had their Ancestors remained in the Territories now to us appertaining: WE do therefore hereby ordain and command, That from and after the Date of these Presents, there shall be levied and paid to our Officers of the Customs, on all Goods, Wares and Merchandizes, and on all Grain and other Produce of the Earth exported from the said Island of Britain, and on all Goods of whatever Kind imported into the same, a *Duty* of *Four and an Half* per Cent. *ad Valorem,* for the Use of us and our Successors. And that the said Duty may more effectually be collected, We do hereby ordain, that all Ships or Vessels bound from Great Britain to any other Part of the World, or from any other Part of the World to Great Britain, shall in their respective Voyages touch at our Port of KONINGSBERG, there to be unladen, searched, and charged with the said Duties.

[1]First printed in *The Public Advertiser,* September 2, 1773.

And whereas there have been from Time to Time discovered in the said Island of Great Britain by our Colonists there, many Mines or Beds of Iron Stone; and sundry Subjects of our antient Dominion, skilful in converting the said Stone into Metal, have in Times past transported themselves thither, carrying with them and communicating that Art; and the Inhabitants of the said Island, *presuming* that they had a natural Right to make the best Use they could of the natural Productions of their Country for their own Benefit, have not only built Furnaces for smelting the said Stone into Iron, but have erected Plating Forges, Slitting Mills, and Steel Furnaces, for the more convenient manufacturing of the same, thereby endangering a Diminution of the said Manufacture in our antient Dominion. We *do therefore* hereby farther ordain, that from and after the Date hereof, no Mill or other Engine for Slitting or Rolling of Iron, or any Plating Forge to work with a Tilt-Hammer, or any Furnace for making Steel, shall be erected or continued in the said Island of Great Britain: And the Lord Lieutenant of every County in the said Island is hereby commanded, on Information of any such Erection within his County, to order and by Force to cause the same to be abated and destroyed, as he shall answer the Neglect thereof to Us at his Peril. But We are nevertheless graciously pleased to permit the Inhabitants of the said Island to transport their Iron into Prussia, there to be manufactured, and to them returned, they paying our Prussian Subjects for the Workmanship, with all the Costs of Commission, Freight and Risque coming and returning, any Thing herein contained to the contrary notwithstanding.

We do not however think fit to extend this our Indulgence to the Article of *Wool,* but meaning to encourage not only the manufacturing of woollen Cloth, but also the raising of Wool in our antient Dominions, and to prevent *both,* as much as may be, in our said Island, We do hereby absolutely forbid the Transportation of Wool from thence even to the Mother Country Prussia; and that those Islanders may be farther and more effectually restrained in making any Advantage of their own Wool in the Way of Manufacture, We command that none shall be carried *out of one County into another,* nor shall any Worsted-Bay, or Woollen-Yarn, Cloth, Says, Bays, Kerseys, Serges, Frizes, Druggets, Cloth-Serges, Shalloons, or any other Drapery Stuffs, or Woollen Manufactures whatsoever, made up or mixt with Wool in any of the said Counties, be carried into any other County, or be Waterborne even across the smallest River or Creek, on Penalty of Forfeiture of the same, together with the Boats, Carriages, Horses, &c. that shall be employed in removing them. *Nevertheless* Our loving Subjects there are hereby permitted, (if they think proper) to use all their Wool as *Manure for the Improvement of their Lands.*

And whereas the Art and Mystery of making *Hats* hath arrived at great Perfection in Prussia, and the Making of Hats by our remote Subjects ought to be as much as possible restrained. And forasmuch as the Islanders before-mentioned, being in Possession of Wool, Beaver, and other Furs, have *presumptuously* conceived they had a Right to make some Advantage thereof, by manufacturing the same into Hats, to the Prejudice of our domestic Manufacture, We do therefore hereby strictly command and ordain, that no Hats or Felts whatsoever, dyed or undyed, finished or unfinished, shall be loaden or put into or upon any Vessel, Cart, Carriage or Horse, to be transported or conveyed *out of one County* in the said Island *into another County,* or to *any other Place whatsoever,* by any Person or Persons whatsoever, on Pain of forfeiting the same, with a Penalty of *Five Hundred Pounds* Sterling for every

Offence. Nor shall any Hat-maker in any of the said Counties employ more than two Apprentices, on Penalty of *Five Pounds* Sterling per Month: We intending hereby that such Hat-makers, being so restrained both in the Production and Sale of their Commodity, may find no Advantage in continuing their Business. But lest the said Islanders should suffer Inconveniency by the Want of Hats, We are farther graciously pleased to permit them to send their Beaver Furs to Prussia; and We also permit Hats made thereof to be exported from Prussia to Britain, the People thus favoured to pay all Costs and Charges of Manufacturing, Interest, Commission to Our Merchants, Insurance and Freight going and returning, as in the Case of Iron.

And lastly, Being willing farther to favour Our said Colonies in Britain, We do hereby also ordain and command, that all the Thieves, Highway and Street-Robbers, House-breakers, Forgerers, Murderers, So[domi]tes, and Villains of every Denomination, who have forfeited their Lives to the Law in Prussia, but whom We, in Our great Clemency, do not think fit here to hang, shall be emptied out of our Gaols into the said Island of Great Britain *for the* BETTER PEOPLING *of that Country.*

We flatter Ourselves that these Our Royal Regulations and Commands will be thought *just* and *reasonable* by Our much-favoured Colonists in England, the said Regulations being copied from their own Statutes of 10 and 11 Will. III. C. 10, 5 Geo. II. C. 22, 23 Geo. II. C. 29, 4 Geo. I. C. 11, and from other equitable Laws made by their Parliaments, or from Instructions given by their Princes, or from Resolutions of both Houses entered into for the GOOD *Government* of their own Colonies in Ireland and America.

And all Persons in the said Island are hereby cautioned not to oppose in any wise the Execution of this Our Edict, or any Part thereof, such Opposition being HIGH TREASON, of which all who are *suspected* shall be transported in Fetters from Britain to Prussia, there to be tried and executed according to the *Prussian Law.*

Such is our Pleasure.

Given at Potsdam this twenty-fifth Day of the Month of August, One Thousand Seven Hundred and Seventy-three, and in the Thirty-third Year of our Reign.

By the KING in his Council

RECHTMAESSIG, *Secr.*"

Some take this Edict to be merely one of the King's *Jeux d'Esprit:* Others suppose it serious, and that he means a Quarrel with England: But all here think the Assertion it concludes with, "that these Regulations are copied from Acts of the English Parliament respecting their Colonies," a very *injurious* one: it being impossible to believe, that a People distinguish'd for their *Love of Liberty,* a Nation so *wise,* so *liberal in its Sentiments,* so *just and equitable* towards its *Neighbours,* should, from mean and *injudicious* Views of *petty immediate Profit,* treat *its own Children* in a Manner so *arbitrary* and TYRANNICAL!

1773

The Ephemera, an Emblem of Human Life

YOU may remember, my dear friend, that when we lately spent that happy day in the delightful garden and sweet society of the Moulin Joly, I stopt a little in one of our walks, and staid some time behind the company. We had been shown numberless skeletons of a kind of little fly, called an ephemera, whose successive generations, we were told, were bred and expired within the day. I happened to see a living company of them on a leaf, who appeared to be engaged in conversation. You know I understand all the inferior animal tongues: my too great application to the study of them is the best excuse I can give for the little progress I have made in your charming language. I listened through curiosity to the discourse of these little creatures; but as they, in their national vivacity, spoke three or four together, I could make but little of their conversation. I found, however, by some broken expressions that I heard now and then, they were disputing warmly on the merit of two foreign musicians, one a *cousin,* the other a *moscheto;* in which dispute they spent their time, seemingly as regardless of the shortness of life as if they had been sure of living a month. Happy people! thought I, you live certainly under a wise, just, and mild government, since you have no public grievances to complain of, nor any subject of contention but the perfections and imperfections of foreign music. I turned my head from them to an old grey-headed one, who was single on another leaf, and talking to himself. Being amused with his soliloquy, I put it down in writing, in hopes it will likewise amuse her to whom I am so much indebted for the most pleasing of all amusements, her delicious company and heavenly harmony.

"It was," said he, "the opinion of learned philosophers of our race, who lived and flourished long before my time, that this vast world, the Moulin Joly, could not itself subsist more than eighteen hours; and I think there was some foundation for that opinion, since, by the apparent motion of the great luminary that gives life to all nature, and which in my time has evidently declined considerably towards the ocean at the end of our earth, it must then finish its course, be extinguished in the waters that surround us, and leave the world in cold and darkness, necessarily producing universal death and destruction. I have lived seven of those hours, a great age, being no less than four hundred and twenty minutes of time. How very few of us continue so long! I have seen generations born, flourish, and expire. My present friends are the children and grandchildren of the friends of my youth, who are now, alas, no more! And I must soon follow them; for, by the course of nature, though still in health, I cannot expect to live above seven or eight minutes longer. What now avails all my toil and labor, in amassing honey-dew on this leaf, which I cannot live to enjoy! What the political struggles I have been engaged in, for the good of my compatriot inhabitants of this bush, or my philosophical studies for the benefit of our race in general! for, in politics, what can laws do without morals? Our present race of ephemeræ will in a course of minutes become corrupt, like those of other and older bushes, and consequently as wretched. And in philosophy how small our progress! Alas! art is long, and life is short! My friends would comfort me with the idea of a name, they say, I shall leave behind me; and they tell me I have lived long enough to nature and to glory. But what will fame be to an ephemera who no longer exists? And what will become of all history in the eighteenth hour, when the world itself, even the whole Moulin Joly, shall come to its end, and be buried in universal ruin?"

To me, after all my eager pursuits, no solid pleasures now remain, but the reflection of a long life spent in meaning well, the sensible conversation of a few good lady ephemeræ, and now and then a kind smile and a tune from the ever amiable *Brillante*.

1778

Information to Those Who Would Remove to America

Many Persons in Europe, having directly or by Letters, express'd to the Writer of this, who is well acquainted with North America, their Desire of transporting and establishing themselves in that Country; but who appear to have formed, thro' Ignorance, mistaken Ideas and Expectations of what is to be obtained there; he thinks it may be useful, and prevent inconvenient, expensive, and fruitless Removals and Voyages of improper Persons, if he gives some clearer and truer Notions of that part of the World, than appear to have hitherto prevailed.

He finds it is imagined by Numbers, that the Inhabitants of North America are rich, capable of rewarding, and dispos'd to reward, all sorts of Ingenuity; that they are at the same time ignorant of all the Sciences, and, consequently, that Strangers, possessing Talents in the Belles-Lettres, fine Arts, &c., must be highly esteemed, and so well paid, as to become easily rich themselves; that there are also abundance of profitable Offices to be disposed of, which the Natives are not qualified to fill; and that, having few Persons of Family among them, Strangers of Birth must be greatly respected, and of course easily obtain the best of those Offices, which will make all their Fortunes; that the Governments too, to encourage Emigrations from Europe, not only pay the Expence of personal Transportation, but give Lands gratis to Strangers, with Negroes to work for them, Utensils of Husbandry, and Stocks of Cattle. These are all wild Imaginations; and those who go to America with Expectations founded upon them will surely find themselves disappointed.

The Truth is, that though there are in that Country few People so miserable as the Poor of Europe, there are also very few that in Europe would be called rich; it is rather a general happy Mediocrity that prevails. There are few great Proprietors of the Soil, and few Tenants; most People cultivate their own Lands, or follow some Handicraft or Merchandise; very few rich enough to live idly upon their Rents or Incomes, or to pay the high Prices given in Europe for Paintings, Statues, Architecture, and the other Works of Art, that are more curious than useful. Hence the natural Geniuses, that have arisen in America with such Talents, have uniformly quitted that Country for Europe, where they can be more suitably rewarded. It is true, that Letters and Mathematical Knowledge are in Esteem there, but they are at the same time more common than is apprehended; there being already existing nine Colleges or Universities, viz. four in New England, and one in each of the Provinces of New York, New Jersey, Pensilvania, Maryland, and Virginia, all furnish'd with learned

Professors; besides a number of smaller Academies; these educate many of their Youth in the Languages, and those Sciences that qualify men for the Professions of Divinity, Law, or Physick. Strangers indeed are by no means excluded from exercising those Professions; and the quick Increase of Inhabitants everywhere gives them a Chance of Employ, which they have in common with the Natives. Of civil Offices, or Employments, there are few; no superfluous Ones, as in Europe; and it is a Rule establish'd in some of the States, that no Office should be so profitable as to make it desirable. The 36th Article of the Constitution of Pennsilvania, runs expressly in these Words; "As every Freeman, to preserve his Independence, (if he has not a sufficient Estate) ought to have some Profession, Calling, Trade, or Farm, whereby he may honestly subsist, there can be no Necessity for, nor Use in, establishing Offices of Profit; the usual Effects of which are Dependence and Servility, unbecoming Freemen, in the Possessors and Expectants; Faction, Contention, Corruption, and Disorder among the People. Wherefore, whenever an Office, thro' Increase of Fees or otherwise, becomes so profitable, as to occasion many to apply for it, the Profits ought to be lessened by the Legislature."

These Ideas prevailing more or less in all the United States, it cannot be worth any Man's while, who has a means of Living at home, to expatriate himself, in hopes of obtaining a profitable civil Office in America; and, as to military Offices, they are at an End with the War, the Armies being disbanded. Much less is it adviseable for a Person to go thither, who has no other Quality to recommend him but his Birth. In Europe it has indeed its Value; but it is a Commodity that cannot be carried to a worse Market than that of America, where people do not inquire concerning a Stranger, *What is he?* but, *What can he do?* If he has any useful Art, he is welcome; and if he exercises it, and behaves well, he will be respected by all that know him; but a mere Man of Quality, who, on that Account, wants to live upon the Public, by some Office or Salary, will be despis'd and disregarded. The Husbandman is in honor there, and even the Mechanic, because their Employments are useful. The People have a saying, that God Almighty is himself a Mechanic, the greatest in the Univers; and he is respected and admired more for the Variety, Ingenuity, and Utility of his Handyworks, than for the Antiquity of his Family. They are pleas'd with the Observation of a Negro, and frequently mention it, that *Boccarorra* (meaning the White men) *make de black man workee, make de Horse workee, make de Ox workee, make ebery ting workee; only de Hog. He, de hog, no workee; he eat, he drink, he walk about, he go to sleep when he please, he libb like a Gentleman.* According to these Opinions of the Americans, one of them would think himself more oblig'd to a Genealogist, who could prove for him that his Ancestors and Relations for ten Generations had been Ploughmen, Smiths, Carpenters, Turners, Weavers, Tanners, or even Shoemakers, and consequently that they were useful Members of Society; than if he could only prove that they were Gentlemen, doing nothing of Value, but living idly on the Labour of others, mere *fruges consumere nati,*[1] and otherwise *good for nothing,* till by their Death their Estates, like the Carcass of the Negro's Gentleman-Hog, come to be *cut up.*

[1] ". . . . . . born
Merely to eat up the corn."—WATTS.
[Franklin's note].

With regard to Encouragements for Strangers from Government, they are really only what are derived from good Laws and Liberty. Strangers are welcome, because there is room enough for them all, and therefore the old Inhabitants are not jealous of them; the Laws protect them sufficiently, so that they have no need of the Patronage of Great Men; and every one will enjoy securely the Profits of his Industry. But, if he does not bring a Fortune with him, he must work and be industrious to live. One or two Years' residence gives him all the Rights of a Citizen; but the government does not at present, whatever it may have done in former times, hire People to become Settlers, by Paying their Passages, giving Land, Negroes, Utensils, Stock, or any other kind of Emolument whatsoever. In short, America is the Land of Labour, and by no means what the English call *Lubberland,* and the French *Pays de Cocagne,* where the streets are said to be pav'd with half-peck Loaves, the Houses til'd with Pancakes, and where the Fowls fly about ready roasted, crying, *Come eat me!*

Who then are the kind of Persons to whom an Emigration to America may be advantageous? And what are the Advantages they may reasonably expect?

Land being cheap in that Country, from the vast Forests still void of Inhabitants, and not likely to be occupied in an Age to come, insomuch that the Propriety of an hundred Acres of fertile Soil full of Wood may be obtained near the Frontiers, in many Places, for Eight or Ten Guineas, hearty young Labouring Men, who understand the Husbandry of Corn and Cattle, which is nearly the same in that Country as in Europe, may easily establish themselves there. A little Money sav'd of the good Wages they receive there, while they work for others, enables them to buy the Land and begin their Plantation, in which they are assisted by the Good-Will of their Neighbours, and some Credit. Multitudes of poor People from England, Ireland, Scotland, and Germany, have by this means in a few years become wealthy Farmers, who, in their own Countries, where all the Lands are fully occupied, and the Wages of Labour low, could never have emerged from the poor Condition wherein they were born.

From the salubrity of the Air, the healthiness of the Climate, the plenty of good Provisions, and the Encouragement to early Marriages by the certainty of Subsistence in cultivating the Earth, the Increase of Inhabitants by natural Generation is very rapid in America, and becomes still more so by the Accession of Strangers; hence there is a continual Demand for more Artisans of all the necessary and useful kinds, to supply those Cultivators of the Earth with Houses, and with Furniture and Utensils of the grosser sorts, which cannot so well be brought from Europe. Tolerably good Workmen in any of those mechanic Arts are sure to find Employ, and to be well paid for their Work, there being no Restraints preventing Strangers from exercising any Art they understand, nor any Permission necessary. If they are poor, they begin first as Servants or Journeymen; and if they are sober, industrious, and frugal, they soon become Masters, establish themselves in Business, marry, raise Families, and become respectable Citizens.

Also, Persons of moderate Fortunes and Capitals, who, having a Number of Children to provide for, are desirous of bringing them up to Industry, and to secure Estates for their Posterity, have Opportunities of doing it in America, which Europe does not afford. There they may be taught and practise profitable mechanic Arts, without incurring Disgrace on that Account, but on the contrary acquiring Respect by such Abilities. There small Capitals laid out in Lands, which daily become more valuable by the Increase of People, afford a solid Prospect of ample Fortunes thereafter for those Children. The Writer of this has known several Instances of large Tracts of Land, bought, on what was then the Frontier of Pensilvania, for Ten Pounds per hundred Acres, which after 20 years, when the Settlements had been extended far beyond them, sold readily, without any Improvement made upon them, for three Pounds per Acre. The Acre in America is the same with the English Acre, or the Acre of Normandy.

Those, who desire to understand the State of Government in America, would do well to read the Constitutions of the several States, and the Articles of Confederation that bind the whole together for general Purposes, under the Direction of one Assembly, called the Congress. These Constitutions have been printed, by order of Congress, in America; two Editions of them have also been printed in London; and a good Translation of them into French has lately been published at Paris.

Several of the Princes of Europe having of late years, from an Opinion of Advantage to arise by producing all Commodities and Manufactures within their own Dominions, so as to diminish or render useless their Importations, have endeavoured to entice Workmen from other Countries by high Salaries, Privileges, &c. Many Persons, pretending to be skilled in various great Manufactures, imagining that America must be in Want of them, and that the Congress would probably be dispos'd to imitate the Princes above mentioned, have proposed to go over, on Condition of having their Passages paid, Lands given, Salaries appointed, exclusive Privileges for Terms of years, &c. Such Persons, on reading the Articles of Confederation, will find, that the Congress have no Power committed to them, or Money put into their Hands, for such purposes; and that if any such Encouragement is given, it must be by the Government of some separate State. This, however, has rarely been done in America; and, when it has been done, it has rarely succeeded, so as to establish a Manufacture, which the Country was not yet so ripe for as to encourage private Persons to set it up; Labour being generally too dear there, and Hands difficult to be kept together, every one desiring to be a Master, and the Cheapness of Lands inclining many to leave Trades for Agriculture. Some indeed have met with Success, and are carried on to Advantage; but they are generally such as require only a few Hands, or wherein great Part of the Work is performed by Machines. Things that are bulky, and of so small Value as not well to bear the Expence of Freight, may often be made cheaper in the Country than they can be imported; and the Manufacture of such Things will be profitable wherever there is a sufficient Demand. The Farmers in America produce indeed a good deal of Wool and Flax; and none is exported, it is all work'd up; but it is in the Way of domestic Manufacture, for the Use of the Family. The buying up Quantities of Wool and Flax, with the Design to employ Spinners, Weavers, &c., and form great Establishments, producing Quantities of Linen and Woollen Goods for Sale, has been several times attempted in different Provinces; but those Projects have generally failed, goods of equal Value being imported cheaper. And when the Governments have been solicited to support such Schemes by Encouragements, in Money, or by imposing Duties on Importation of such Goods, it has been generally refused, on this Principle, that, if the Country is ripe for the Manufacture, it may be carried on by private Persons to Advantage; and if not, it is a Folly to think of forcing Nature. Great Establishments of Manufacture require great Numbers of Poor to do the Work for small Wages; these Poor are to be found in Europe, but will not be found in America, till the Lands are all taken up and cultivated, and the Excess of People, who cannot get Land, want Employment. The Manufacture of Silk, they say, is natural in France, as that of Cloth in England, because each Country produces in Plenty the first Material; but if England will have a Manufacture of Silk as well as that of Cloth, and France one of Cloth as well as that of Silk, these unnatural Operations must be supported by mutual Prohibitions, or high Duties on the Importation of each other's Goods; by which means the Workmen are enabled to tax the home Consumer by greater Prices, while the higher Wages they receive makes them neither happier nor richer, since they only drink more and work less. Therefore the Governments in America do nothing to encourage such Projects. The People, by this Means, are not impos'd on, either by the Merchant or Mechanic. If the Merchant demands too much Profit on imported Shoes, they buy of the Shoemaker; and if he asks too high a Price, they take them of the Merchant; thus the two Professions are checks on each other. The Shoemaker, however, has, on the whole, a considerable Profit upon his Labour in America, beyond what he had in Europe, as he can add to his Price a Sum nearly equal to all the Expences of Freight and Commission, Risque or Insurance, &c., necessarily charged by the Merchant. And the Case is the same with the Workmen in every other Mechanic Art. Hence it is, that Artisans generally live better and more easily in America than in Europe; and such as are good Œconomists make a comfortable Provision for Age, and for their Children. Such may, therefore, remove with Advantage to America.

In the long-settled Countries of Europe, all Arts, Trades, Professions, Farms, &c., are so full, that it is difficult for a poor Man, who has Children, to place them where they may gain, or learn to gain, a decent Livelihood. The Artisans, who fear creating future Rivals in Business, refuse to take Apprentices, but upon Conditions of Money, Maintenance, or the like, which the Parents are unable to comply with. Hence the Youth are dragg'd up in Ignorance of every gainful Art, and oblig'd to become Soldiers, or Servants, or Thieves, for a Subsistence. In America, the rapid Increase of Inhabitants takes away that Fear of Rivalship, and Artisans willingly receive Apprentices from the hope of Profit by their Labour, during the Remainder of the Time stipulated, after they shall be instructed. Hence it is easy for poor Families to get their Children instructed; for the Artisans are so desirous of Apprentices, that many of them will even give Money to the Parents, to have Boys from Ten to Fifteen Years of Age bound Apprentices to them till the Age of Twenty-one; and many poor Parents have, by that means, on their Arrival in the Country, raised Money enough to buy Land sufficient to establish themselves, and to subsist the rest of their Family by Agriculture. These Contracts for Apprentices are made before a Magistrate, who regulates the Agreement according to Reason and Justice, and, having in view the Formation of a future useful Citizen, obliges the Master to engage by a written Indenture, not only that, during the time of Service stipulated, the Apprentice shall be duly provided with Meat, Drink, Apparel, washing, and Lodging, and, at its Expiration, with a compleat new Suit of Cloaths, but also that he shall be taught to read, write, and cast Accompts; and that he shall be well instructed in the Art or Profession of his Master, or some other, by which he may afterwards gain a Livelihood, and be able in his turn to raise a Family. A Copy of this Indenture is given to the Apprentice or his Friends, and the Magistrate keeps a Record of it, to which recourse may be had, in case of Failure by the Master in any Point of Performance. This desire among the Masters, to have more Hands employ'd in working for them, induces them to pay the Passages of young Persons, of both Sexes, who, on their Arrival, agree to serve them one, two, three, or four Years; those, who have already learnt a Trade, agreeing for a shorter Term, in proportion to their Skill, and the consequent immediate Value of their Service; and those, who have none, agreeing for a longer Term, in consideration of being taught an Art their Poverty would not permit them to acquire in their own Country.

The almost general Mediocrity of Fortune that prevails in America obliging its People to follow some Business for subsistence, those Vices, that arise usually from Idleness, are in a great measure prevented. Industry and constant Employment are great preservatives of the Morals and Virtue of a Nation. Hence bad Examples of Youth are more rare in America, which must be a comfortable Consideration to Parents. To this may be truly added, that serious Religion, under its various Denominations, is not only tolerated, but respected and practised. Atheism is unknown there; Infidelity rare and secret; so that persons may live to a great Age in that Country, without having their Piety shocked by meeting with either an Atheist or an Infidel. And the Divine Being seems to have manifested his Approbation of the mutual Forbearance and Kindness with which the different Sects treat each other, by the remarkable Prosperity with which He has been pleased to favour the whole Country.

1784

Remarks Concerning the Savages of North America

Savages we call them, because their Manners differ from ours, which we think the Perfection of Civility; they think the same of theirs.

Perhaps, if we could examine the Manners of different Nations with Impartiality, we should find no People so rude, as to be without any Rules of Politeness; nor any so polite, as not to have some Remains of Rudeness.

The Indian Men, when young, are Hunters and Warriors; when old, Counsellors; for all their Government is by Counsel of the Sages; there is no Force, there are no Prisons, no Officers to compel Obedience, or inflict Punishment. Hence they generally study Oratory, the best Speaker having the most Influence. The Indian Women till the Ground, dress the Food, nurse and bring up the Children, and preserve and hand down to Posterity the Memory of public Transactions. These Employments of Men and Women are accounted natural and honourable. Having few artifical Wants, they have abundance of Leisure for Improvement by Conversation. Our laborious Manner of Life, compared with theirs, they esteem slavish and base; and the Learning, on which we value ourselves, they regard as frivolous and useless. An Instance of this occurred at the Treaty of Lancaster, in Pennsylvania, *anno* 1744, between the Government of Virginia and the Six Nations. After the principal Business was settled, the Commissioners from Virginia acquainted the Indians by a

Speech, that there was at Williamsburg a College, with a Fund for Educating Indian youth; and that, if the Six Nations would send down half a dozen of their young Lads to that College, the Government would take care that they should be well provided for, and instructed in all the Learning of the White People. It is one of the Indian Rules of Politeness not to answer a public Proposition the same day that it is made; they think it would be treating it as a light matter, and that they show it Respect by taking time to consider it, as of a Matter important. They therefore deferr'd their Answer till the Day following; when their Speaker began, by expressing their deep Sense of the kindness of the Virginia Government, in making them that Offer; "for we know," says he, "that you highly esteem the kind of Learning taught in those Colleges, and that the Maintenance of our young Men, while with you, would be very expensive to you. We are convinc'd, therefore, that you mean to do us Good by your Proposal; and we thank you heartily. But you, who are wise, must know that different Nations have different Conceptions of things; and you will therefore not take it amiss, if our Ideas of this kind of Education happen not to be the same with yours. We have had some Experience of it; Several of our young People were formerly brought up at the Colleges of the Northern Provinces; they were instructed in all your Sciences; but, when they came back to us, they were bad Runners, ignorant of every means of living in the Woods, unable to bear either Cold or Hunger, knew neither how to build a Cabin, take a Deer, or kill an Enemy, spoke our Language imperfectly, were therefore neither fit for Hunters, Warriors, nor Counsellors; they were totally good for nothing. We are however not the less oblig'd by your kind Offer, tho' we decline accepting it; and, to show our grateful Sense of it, if the Gentlemen of Virginia will send us a Dozen of their Sons, we will take great Care of their Education, instruct them in all we know, and make *Men* of them."

Having frequent Occasions to hold public Councils, they have acquired great Order and Decency in conducting them. The old Men sit in the foremost Ranks, the Warriors in the next, and the Women and Children in the hindmost. The Business of the Women is to take exact Notice of what passes, imprint it in their Memories (for they have no Writing), and communicate it to their Children. They are the Records of the Council, and they preserve Traditions of the Stipulations in Treaties 100 Years back; which, when we compare with our Writings, we always find exact. He that would speak, rises. The rest observe a profound Silence. When he has finish'd and sits down, they leave him 5 to 6 Minutes to recollect, that, if he has omitted anything he intended to say, or has any thing to add, he may rise again and deliver it. To interrupt another, even in common Conversation, is reckon'd highly indecent. How different this is from the conduct of a polite British House of Commons, where scarce a day passes without some Confusion, that makes the Speaker hoarse in calling *to Order;* and how different from the Mode of Conversation in many polite Companies of Europe, where, if you do not deliver your Sentence with great Rapidity, you are cut off in the middle of it by the Impatient Loquacity of those you converse with, and never suffer'd to finish it!

The Politeness of these Savages in Conversation is indeed carried to Excess, since it does not permit them to contradict or deny the Truth of what is asserted in their Presence. By this means they indeed avoid Disputes; but then it becomes difficult to know their Minds, or what Impression you make upon them. The Missionaries who have attempted to convert them to Christianity, all complain of this as one of the great Difficulties of their Mission. The Indians hear with Patience the Truths of the Gospel explain'd to them, and give their usual Tokens of Assent and Approbation; you would think they were convinc'd. No such matter. It is mere Civility.

A Swedish Minister, having assembled the chiefs of the Susquehanah Indians, made a Sermon to them, acquainting them with the principal historical Facts on which our Religion is founded; such as the Fall of our first Parents by eating an Apple, the coming of Christ to repair the Mischief, his Miracles and Suffering, &c. When he had finished, an Indian Orator stood up to thank him. "What you have told us," says he, "is all very good. It is indeed bad to eat Apples. It is better to make them all into Cyder. We are much oblig'd by your kindness in coming so far, to tell us these Things which you have heard from your Mothers. In return, I will tell you some of those we had heard from ours. In the Beginning, our Fathers had only the Flesh of Animals to subsist on; and if their Hunting was unsuccessful, they were starving. Two of our young Hunters, having kill'd a Deer, made a Fire in the Woods to broil some Part of it. When they were about to satisfy their Hunger, they beheld a beautiful young Woman descend from the Clouds, and seat herself on that Hill, which you see yonder among the blue Mountains. They said to each other, it is a Spirit that has smelt our broiling Venison, and wishes to eat of it; let us offer some to her. They presented her with the Tongue; she was pleas'd with the Taste of it, and said, 'Your kindness shall be rewarded; come to this Place after thirteen Moons, and you shall find something that will be of great Benefit in nourishing you and your Children to the latest Generations.' They did so, and, to their Surprise, found Plants they had never seen before; but which, from that ancient time, have been constantly cultivated among us, to our great Advantage. Where her right Hand had touched the Ground, they found Maize; where her left hand had touch'd it, they found Kidney-Beans; and where her Backside had sat on it, they found Tobacco." The good Missionary, disgusted with this idle Tale, said, "What I delivered to you were sacred Truths; but what you tell me is mere Fable, Fiction, and Falshood." The Indian, offended, reply'd, "My brother, it seems your Friends have not done you Justice in your Education; they have not well instructed you in the Rules of common Civility. You saw that we, who understand and practise those Rules, believ'd all your stories; why do you refuse to believe ours?"

When any of them come into our Towns, our People are apt to crowd round them, gaze upon them, and incommode them, where they desire to be private; this they esteem great Rudeness, and the Effect of the Want of Instruction in the Rules of Civility and good Manners. "We have," say they, "as much Curiosity as you, and when you come into our Towns, we wish for Opportunities of looking at you; but for this purpose we hide ourselves behind Bushes, where you are to pass, and never intrude ourselves into your Company."

Their Manner of entring one another's village has likewise its Rules. It is reckon'd uncivil in travelling Strangers to enter a Village abruptly, without giving Notice of their Approach. Therefore, as soon as they arrive within hearing, they stop and hollow, remaining there till invited to enter. Two old Men usually come out to them, and lead them in. There is in every Village a vacant Dwelling, called *the Strangers' House.* Here they are plac'd, while the old Men go round from Hut to Hut, acquainting the Inhabitants, that Strangers are arriv'd, who are probably hungry and weary; and every one sends them what he can spare of Victuals, and Skins to repose on. When the Strangers are refresh'd, Pipes and Tobacco are brought; and then, but not before, Conversation begins, with Enquiries who they are, whither bound, what News, &c.; and it usually ends with offers of Service, if the Strangers have occasion of Guides, or any Necessaries for continuing their Journey; and nothing is exacted for the Entertainment.

The same Hospitality, esteem'd among them as a principal Virtue, is practis'd by private Persons; of which Conrad Weiser, our Interpreter, gave me the following Instance. He had been naturaliz'd among the Six Nations, and spoke well the Mohock Language. In going thro' the Indian Country, to carry a Message from our Governor to the Council at Onondaga, he call'd at the Habitation of Canassatego, an old Acquaintance, who embrac'd him, spread Furs for him to sit on, plac'd before him some boil'd Beans and Venison, and mix'd some Rum and Water for his Drink. When he was well refresh'd, and had lit his Pipe, Canassatego began to converse with him; ask'd how he had far'd the many Years since they had seen each other; whence he then came; what occasion'd the Journey, &c. Conrad answered all his Questions; and when the Discourse began to flag, the Indian, to continue it, said, "Conrad, you have lived long among the white People, and know something of their Customs; I have been sometimes at Albany, and have observed, that once in Seven Days they shut up their Shops, and assemble all in the great House; tell me what it is for? What do they do there?" "They meet there," says Conrad, "to hear and learn *good Things.*" "I do not doubt," says the Indian, "that they tell you so; they have told me the same; but I doubt the Truth of what they say, and I will tell you my Reasons. I went lately to Albany to sell my Skins and buy Blankets, Knives, Powder, Rum, &c. You know I us'd generally to deal with Hans Hanson; but I was a little inclin'd this time to try some other Merchant. However, I call'd first upon Hans, and asked him what he would give for Beaver. He said he could not give any more than four Shillings a Pound; 'but,' says he, 'I cannot talk on Business now; this is the Day when we meet together to learn *Good Things,* and I am going to the Meeting.' So I thought to myself, 'Since we cannot do any Business to-day, I may as well go to the meeting too,' and I went with him. There stood up a Man in Black, and began to talk to the People very angrily. I did not understand what he said; but, perceiving that he look'd much at me and at Hanson, I imagin'd he was angry at seeing me there; so I went out, sat down near the House, struck Fire, and lit my Pipe, waiting till the Meeting should break up. I thought too, that the Man had mention'd something of Beaver, and I suspected it might be the Subject of their Meeting. So, when they came out, I accosted my Merchant. 'Well, Hans,' says I, 'I hope you have agreed to give more than four Shillings a Pound.' 'No,' says he, 'I cannot give so much; I cannot give more than three shillings and sixpence.' I then spoke to several other Dealers, but they all sung the same song,—Three and sixpence,—Three and sixpence. This made it clear to me, that my Suspicion was right; and, that whatever they pretended of meeting to learn *good Things,* the real purpose was to consult how to cheat Indians in the Price of Beaver. Consider but a little, Conrad, and you must be of my Opinion. If they met so often to learn *good Things,* they would certainly have learnt some before this time. But they are still ignorant. You know our Practice. If a white Man, in travelling thro' our Country, enters one of our Cabins, we all treat him as I treat you; we dry him if he is wet, we warm him if he is cold, we give him Meat and Drink, that he may allay his Thirst and Hunger; and we spread soft Furs for him to rest and sleep on; we demand nothing in return. But, if I go into a white Man's House at Albany, and ask for Victuals and Drink, they say, 'Where is your Money?' and if I have none, they say, 'Get out, you Indian Dog.' You see they have not yet learned those little *Good Things,* that we need no Meetings to be instructed in, because our Mothers taught them to us when we were Children; and therefore it is impossible their Meetings should be, as they say, for any such purpose, or have any such Effect; they are only to contrive *the Cheating of Indians in the Price of Beaver.*"[1]

1784

On the Slave-Trade

To the Editor of the Federal Gazette

March 23d, 1790.

Sir,

Reading last night in your excellent Paper the speech of Mr. Jackson in Congress against their meddling with the Affair of Slavery, or attempting to mend the Condition of the Slaves, it put me in mind of a similar One made about 100 Years since by Sidi Mehemet Ibrahim, a member of the Divan of Algiers, which may be seen in Martin's Account of his Consulship, anno 1687. It was against granting the Petition of the Sect called *Erika,* or Purists, who pray'd for the Abolition of Piracy and Slavery as being unjust. Mr. Jackson does not quote it; perhaps he has not seen it. If, therefore, some of its Reasonings are to be found in his eloquent Speech, it may only show that men's Interests and Intellects operate and are operated on with surprising similarity in all Countries and Climates, when under similar Circumstances. The African's Speech, as translated, is as follows.

"Allah Bismillah, &c. God is great, and Mahomet is his Prophet.

"Have these *Erika* considered the Consequences of granting their Petition? If we cease our Cruises against the Christians, how shall we be furnished with the Commodities their Countries produce, and which are so necessary for us? If we forbear to make Slaves of their People, who in this hot Climate are to cultivate our Lands? Who are to perform the common Labours of our City, and in our Families? Must we not then be our own Slaves? And is there not more Compassion and more Favour due to us as Mussulmen, than to these Christian Dogs? We have now above

[1]It is remarkable that in all Ages and Countries Hospitality has been allow'd as the Virtue of those whom the civiliz'd were pleas'd to call Barbarians. The Greeks celebrated the Scythians for it. The Saracens possess'd it eminently, and it is to this day the reigning Virtue of the wild Arabs. St. Paul, too, in the Relation of his Voyage and Shipwreck on the Island of Melita says the Barbarous People shewed us no little kindness; for they kindled a fire, and received us every one, because of the present Rain, and because of the Cold.—[Franklin's note].

50,000 Slaves in and near Algiers. This Number, if not kept up by fresh Supplies, will soon diminish, and be gradually annihilated. If we then cease taking and plundering the Infidel Ships, and making Slaves of the Seamen and Passengers, our Lands will become of no Value for want of Cultivation; the Rents of Houses in the City will sink one half; and the Revenues of Government arising from its Share of Prizes be totally destroy'd! And for what? To gratify the whims of a whimsical Sect, who would have us, not only forbear making more Slaves, but even to manumit those we have.

"But who is to indemnify their Masters for the Loss? Will the State do it? Is our Treasury sufficient? Will the *Erika* do it? Can they do it? Or would they, to do what they think Justice to the Slaves, do a greater Injustice to the Owners? And if we set our Slaves free, what is to be done with them? Few of them will return to their Countries; they know too well the greater Hardships they must there be subject to; they will not embrace our holy Religion; they will not adopt our Manners; our People will not pollute themselves by intermarrying with them. Must we maintain them as Beggars in our Streets, or suffer our Properties to be the Prey of their Pillage? For Men long accustom'd to Slavery will not work for a Livelihood when not compell'd. And what is there so pitiable in their present Condition? Were they not Slaves in their own Countries?

"Are not Spain, Portugal, France, and the Italian states govern'd by Despots, who hold all their Subjects in Slavery, without Exception? Even England treats its Sailors as Slaves; for they are, whenever the Government pleases, seiz'd, and confin'd in Ships of War, condemn'd not only to work, but to fight, for small Wages, or a mere Subsistence, not better than our Slaves are allow'd by us. Is their Condition then made worse by their falling into our Hands? No; they have only exchanged one Slavery for another, and I may say a better; for here they are brought into a Land where the Sun of Islamism gives forth its Light, and shines in full Splendor, and they have an Opportunity of making themselves acquainted with the true Doctrine, and thereby saving their immortal Souls. Those who remain at home have not that Happiness. Sending the Slaves home then would be sending them out of Light into Darkness.

"I repeat the Question, What is to be done with them? I have heard it suggested, that they may be planted in the Wilderness, where there is plenty of Land for them to subsist on, and where they may flourish as a free State; but they are, I doubt, too little dispos'd to labour without Compulsion, as well as too ignorant to establish a good government, and the wild Arabs would soon molest and destroy or again enslave them. While serving us, we take care to provide them with every thing, and they are treated with Humanity. The Labourers in their own Country are, as I am well informed, worse fed, lodged, and cloathed. The Condition of most of them is therefore already mended, and requires no further Improvement. Here their Livers are in Safety. They are not liable to be impress'd for Soldiers, and forc'd to cut one another's Christian Throats, as in the Wars of their own Countries. If some of the religious mad Bigots, who now teaze us with their silly Petitions, have in a Fit of blind Zeal freed their Slaves, it was not Generosity, it was not Humanity, that mov'd them to the Action; it was from the conscious Burthen of a Load of Sins, and Hope, from the supposed Merits of so good a Work, to be excus'd Damnation.

"How grossly are they mistaken in imagining Slavery to be disallow'd by the Alcoran! Are not the two Precepts, to quote no more, *'Masters, treat your Slaves with kindness; Slaves, serve your Masters with Cheerfulness and Fidelity,'* clear Proofs to the contrary? Nor can the Plundering of Infidels be in that sacred Book forbidden, since it is well known from it, that God has given the World, and all that it contains, to his faithful Mussulmen, who are to enjoy it of Right as fast as they conquer it. Let us then hear no more of this detestable Proposition, the Manumission of Christian Slaves, the Adoption of which would, be depreciating our Lands and Houses, and thereby depriving so many good Citizens of their Properties, create universal Discontent, and provoke Insurrections, to the endangering of Government and producing general Confusion. I have therefore no doubt, but this wise Council will prefer the Comfort and Happiness of a whole Nation of true Believers to the Whim of a few *Erika,* and dismiss their Petition."

The Result was, as Martin tells us, that the Divan came to this Resolution; "The Doctrine, that Plundering and Enslaving the Christians is unjust, is at best *problematical;* but that it is the Interest of this State to continue the Practice, is clear; therefore let the Petition be rejected."

And it was rejected accordingly.

And since like Motives are apt to produce in the Minds of Men like Opinions and Resolutions, may we not, Mr. Brown, venture to predict, from this Account, that the Petitions to the Parliament of England for abolishing the Slave-Trade, to say nothing of other Legislatures, and the Debates upon them, will have a similar Conclusion? I am, Sir, your constant Reader and humble Servant,

HISTORICUS.

1790

Speech in the Convention

At the Conclusion of Its Deliberations[1]

Mr. President,

I confess, that I do not entirely approve of this Constitution at present; but, Sir, I am not sure I shall never approve it; for, having lived long, I have experienced many instances of being obliged, by better information or fuller consideration, to change my opinions even on important subjects, which I once thought right, but found to be otherwise. It is therefore that, the older I grow, the more apt I am to doubt my own

[1]The date of the speech is September 17, 1787, the final day of the Constitutional Convention.

judgment of others. Most men, indeed, as well as most sects in religion, think themselves in possession of all truth, and that wherever others differ from them, it is so far error. Steele, a Protestant, in a dedication, tells the Pope, that the only difference between our two churches in their opinions of the certainty of their doctrine, is, the Romish Church is *infallible,* and the Church of England is *never in the wrong.* But, though many private Persons think almost as highly of their own infallibility as of that of their Sect, few express it so naturally as a certain French Lady, who, in a little dispute with her sister, said, "But I meet with nobody but myself that is *always* in the right." *"Je ne trouve que moi qui aie toujours raison."*

In these sentiments, Sir, I agree to this Constitution, with all its faults,—if they are such; because I think a general Government necessary for us, and there is no *form* of government but what may be a blessing to the people, if well administered; and I believe, farther, that this is likely to be well administered for a course of years, and can only end in despotism, as other forms have done before it, when the people shall become so corrupted as to need despotic government, being incapable of any other. I doubt, too, whether any other Convention we can obtain, may be able to make a better constitution; for, when you assemble a number of men, to have the advantage of their joint wisdom, you inevitably assemble with those men all their prejudices, their passions, their errors of opinion, their local interests, and their selfish views. From such an assembly can a *perfect* production be expected? It therefore astonishes me, Sir, to find this system approaching so near to perfection as it does; and I think it will astonish our enemies, who are waiting with confidence to hear, that our councils are confounded like those of the builders of Babel, and that our States are on the point of separation, only to meet hereafter for the purpose of cutting one another's throats. Thus I consent, Sir, to this Constitution, because I expect no better, and because I am not sure that it is not the best. The opinions I have had of its *errors* I sacrifice to the public good. I have never whispered a syllable of them abroad. Within these walls they were born, and here they shall die. If every one of us, in returning to our Constituents, were to report the objections he has had to it, and endeavour to gain Partisans in support of them, we might prevent its being generally received, and thereby lose all the salutary effects and great advantages resulting naturally in our favour among foreign nations, as well as among ourselves, from our real or apparent unanimity. Much of the strength and efficiency of any government, in procuring and securing happiness to the people, depends on *opinion,* on the general opinion of the goodness of that government, as well as of the wisdom and integrity of its governors. I hope, therefore, for our own sakes, as a part of the people, and for the sake of our posterity, that we shall act heartily and unanimously in recommending this Constitution, wherever our Influence may extend, and turn our future thoughts and endeavours to the means of having it *well administered.*

On the whole, Sir, I cannot help expressing a wish, that every member of the Convention who may still have objections to it, would with me on this occasion doubt a little of his own infallibility, and, to make *manifest* our *unanimity,* put his name to this Instrument.

1837

from The Autobiography, Parts One and Two

Part One

Twyford, at the Bishop of St. Asaph's, 1771.

Dear Son,

I have ever had a Pleasure in obtaining any little Anecdotes of my Ancestors. You may remember the Enquiries I made among the Remains of my Relations when you were with me in England; and the Journey I took for that purpose. Now imagining it may be equally agreeable to you to know the Circumstances of *my* Life, many of which you are yet unacquainted with; and expecting a Week's uninterrupted Leisure in my present Country Retirement, I sit down to write them for you. To which I have besides some other Inducements. Having emerg'd from the Poverty and Obscurity in which I was born and bred, to a State of Affluence and some Degree of Reputation in the World, and having gone so far thro' Life with a considerable Share of Felicity, the conducing Means I made use of, which, with the Blessing of God, so well succeeded, my Posterity may like to know, as they may find some of them suitable to their own Situations, and therefore fit to be imitated. That Felicity, when I reflected on it, has induc'd me sometimes to say, that were it offer'd to my Choice, I should have no Objection to a Repetition of the same Life from its Beginning, only asking the Advantage Authors have in a second Edition to correct some Faults of the first. So would I if I might, besides corr[ectin]g the Faults, change some sinister Accidents and Events of it for others more favourable, but tho' this were deny'd, I should still accept the Offer. However, since such a Repetition is not to be expected, the next Thing most like living one's Life over again, seems to be a *Recollection* of that Life; and to make that Recollection as durable as possible, the putting it down in Writing. Hereby, too, I shall indulge the Inclination so natural in old Men, to be talking of themselves and their own past Actions, and I shall indulge it, without being troublesome to others who thro' respect to Age might think themselves oblig'd to give me a Hearing, since this may be read or not as any one pleases. And lastly, (I may as well confess it, since my Denial of it will be believ'd by no body) perhaps I shall a good deal gratify my own *Vanity.* Indeed I scarce ever heard or saw the introductory Worlds, *Without Vanity I may say,* &c. but some vain thing immediately follow'd. Most People dislike Vanity in others whatever share they have of it themselves, but I give it fair Quarter wherever I meet with it, being pursuaded that it is often productive of Good to the Possessor and to others that are within his Sphere of Action: And therefore in many Cases it would not be quite absurd if a Man were to thank God for his Vanity among the other Comforts of Life.

And now I speak of thanking God, I desire with all Humility to acknowledge, that I owe the mention'd Happiness of my past Life to his kind Providence, which led me to the Means I us'd and gave them Success. My Belief of this, induces me to *hope,* tho' I must not *presume,* that the same Goodness will still be exercis'd towards me in continuing that Happiness, or in enabling me to bear a fatal Reverse, which I may experience as others have done, the Complexion of my future Fortune being known to him only: and in whose Power it is to bless to us even our Afflictions.

The Notes one of my Uncles (who had the same kind of Curiosity in collecting Family Anecdotes) once put into my Hands, furnish'd me with several Particulars relating to our Ancestors. From these Notes I learnt that the Family had liv'd in the same Village, Ecton in Northamptonshire, for 300 Years, and how much longer he knew not (perhaps from the Time when the Name *Franklin* that before was the Name of an Order of People,[1] was assum'd by them for a Surname, when others took Surnames all over the Kingdom). (Here a Note)[2] on a Freehold of about 30 Acres, aided by the Smith's Business which had continued in the Family till his Time, the eldest Son being always bred to that Business. A Custom which he and my Father both followed as to their eldest Sons. When I search'd the Register at Ecton, I found an Account of their Births, Marriages and Burials, from the Year 1555 only, there being no Register kept in that Parish at any time preceding. By that Register I perceiv'd that I was the youngest Son of the youngest Son for 5 Generations back.

My Grandfather Thomas, who was born in 1598, lived at Ecton till he grew too old to follow Business longer, when he went to live with his Son John, a Dyer at Banbury in Oxfordshire, with whom my Father serv'd an Apprenticeship. There my Grandfather died and lies buried. We saw his Gravestone in 1758. His eldest Son Thomas liv'd in the House of Ecton, and left it with the Land to his only Child, a Daughter, who with her Husband, one Fisher of Wellingborough sold it to Mr. Isted, now Lord of the Manor there. My Grandfather had 4 Sons that grew up, viz. Thomas, John, Benjamin and Josiah. I will give you what Account I can of them at this distance from my Papers, and if they are not lost in my Absence, you will among them find many more Particulars. Thomas was bred a Smith under his Father, but being ingenious, and encourag'd in Learning (as all his Brothers like wise were) by an Esquire Palmer then the principal Gentlemen in that Parish, he qualify'd for the Business of Scrivener, became a considerable Man in the County Affairs, was a chief Mover of all publick Spirited Undertakings, for the County, or Town of Northampton and his own Village, of which many Instances were told us at Ecton and he was much taken Notice of and patroniz'd by the then Lord Halifax. He died in 1702, Jan. 6, old Stile, just 4 Years a Day before I was born.[3] The Account we receiv'd of his Life and Character from some old People at Ecton, I remember struck you as something extraordinary from its Similarity to what you knew of mine. Had he died on the same Day, you said one might have suppos'd a Transmigration.

John was bred a Dyer, I believe of Woollens. Benjamin, was bred a Silk Dyer, serving an Apprenticeship at London. He was an ingenious Man, I remember him well, for when I was a Boy he came over to my Father in Boston, and lived in the House with us some Years. He lived to a great Age. His Grandson Samuel Franklin now lives in Boston. He left behind him two Quarto Volumes, M.S. of his own Poetry, consisting of little occasional Pieces address'd to his Friends and Relations, of which the following sent to me, is a Specimen. (Here insert it.)[4] He had form'd a Shorthand of his own, which he taught me, but never practising it I have now forgot it. I was nam'd after this Uncle, there being a particular Affection between him and my Father. He was very pious, a great Attender of Sermons of the best Preachers,

[1]In medieval England a *franklin* was a middle-class landowner.

[2]Franklin omitted the note he intended to insert here.

[3]In 1752 the Julian (or "Old Style") calendar replaced the Gregorian (or "New Style") calendar. Franklin's birthday (January 6, Old Style) thus advanced eleven days to January 17 (New Style).

[4]No sample was included.

which he took down in his Shorthand and had with him many Volumes of them. He was also much of a Politician, too much perhaps for his Station. There fell lately into my Hands in London a Collection he had made of all the principal Pamphlets relating to Publick affairs from 1641 to 1717. Many of the Volumes are wanting, as appears by the Numbering, but there still remains 8 Vols. Folio, and 24 in 4to and 8vo.[5] A Dealer in old Books met with them, and knowing me by my sometimes buying of him, he brought them to me. It seems my Uncle must have left them here when he went to America, which was above 50 Years since. There are many of his Notes in the Margins.

This obscure Family of ours was early in the Reformation, and continu'd Protestants thro' the Reign of Queen Mary, when they were sometimes in Danger of Trouble on Account of their Zeal against Popery.[6] They had got an English Bible, and to conceal and secure it, it was fastned open with Tapes under and within the Frame of a Joint Stool. When my Great Great Grandfather read in it to his Family, he turn'd up the Joint Stool upon his Knees, turning over the Leaves then under the Tapes. One of the Children stood at the Door to give Notice if he saw the Apparitor coming, who was an Officer of the Spiritual Court.[7] In that Case the Stool was turn'd down again upon its feet, when the Bible remain'd conceal'd under it as before. This Anecdote I had from my Uncle Benjamin. The Family continu'd all of the Church of England till about the End of Charles the 2ds Reign,[8] when some of the Ministers that had been outed for Nonconformity, holding Conventicles[9] in Northamptonshire, Benjamin and Josiah adher'd to them, and so continu'd all their Lives. The rest of the Family remain'd with the Episcopal Church.

Josiah, my Father, married young, and carried his Wife with three Children unto New England, about 1682. The Conventicles having been forbidden by Law, and frequently disturbed, induced some considerable Men of his Acquaintance to remove to that Country, and he was prevail'd with to accompany them thither, where they expected to enjoy their Mode of Religion with Freedom. By the same Wife he had 4 Children more born there, and by a second Wife ten more, in all 17, of which I remember 13 sitting at one time at his Table, who all grew up to be Men and Women, and married. I was the youngest Son and the youngest Child but two, and was born in Boston, N. England.

My Mother the 2d Wife was Abiah Folger, a Daughter of Peter Folger, one of the first Settlers of New England, of whom honourable mention is made by Cotton Mather, in his Church History of that Country, (entitled Magnalia Christi Americana) as a *godly learned Englishman,* if I remember the words rightly. I have heard that he wrote sundry small occasional Pieces, but only one of them was printed which I saw now many Years since. It was written in 1675, in the homespun Verse of that Time and People, and address'd to those then concern'd in the Government

[5] "Folio," "quarto," and "octavo" refer to book sizes made from sheets with two, four, or eight pages printed on each side.

[6] Queen Mary, who reigned from 1553–1558, attempted to restore Roman Catholicism in Protestant England.

[7] An ecclesiastical court established to eliminate heresy.

[8] Charles II reigned from 1660–1685.

[9] The secret and illegal meetings of religious nonconformists.

there. It was in favour of Liberty of Conscience, and in behalf of the Baptists, Quakers, and other Sectaries, that had been under Persecution; ascribing the Indian Wars and other Distresses, that had befallen the Country to that Persecution, as so many Judgments of God, to punish so heinous an Offence; and exhorting a Repeal of those uncharitable Laws. The whole appear'd to me as written with a good deal of Decent Plainness and manly Freedom. The six last concluding Lines I remember, tho' I have forgotten the two first of the Stanza, but the Purport of them was that his Censures proceeded from *Goodwill,* and there he would be known as the Author,

because to be a Libeller, (says he)
I hate it with my Heart.
From Sherburne Town[10] where now I dwell,
My Name I do put here,
Without Offence, your real Friend,
It is Peter Folgier.

My elder Brothers were all put Apprentices to different Trades. I was put to the Grammar School at Eight Years of Age, my Father intending to devote me as the Tithe[11] of his Sons to the Service of the Church. My early Readiness in learning to read (which must have been very early, as I do not remember when I could not read) and the Opinion of all his Friends that I should certainly make a good Scholar, encourag'd him in this Purpose of his. My Uncle Benjamin too approv'd of it, and propos'd to give me all his Shorthand Volumes of Sermons I suppose as a Stock to set up with, if I would learn his Character.[12] I continu'd however at the Grammar School not quite one Year, tho' in that time I had risen gradually from the Middle of the Class of that Year to be the Head of it, and farther was remov'd into the next Class above it, in order to go with that into the third at the End of the Year. But my Father in the mean time, from a View of the Expence of a College Education which, having so large a Family, he could not well afford, and the mean Living many so educated were afterwards able to obtain, Reasons that he gave to his Friends in my Hearing, altered his first Intention, took me from the Grammar School, and set me to a School for Writing and Arithmetic kept by a then famous Man, Mr. Geo. Brownell, very successful in his Profession generally, and that by mild encouraging Methods. Under him I acquired fair Writing pretty soon, but I fail'd in the Arithmetic, and made no Progress in it.

At Ten Years old, I was taken home to assist my Father in his Business, which was that of a Tallow Chandler and Sope-Boiler.[13] A Business he was not bred to, but had assumed on his Arrival in New England and on finding his Dying Trade would not maintain his Family, being in little Request. Accordingly I was employed in cutting Wick for the Candles, filling the Dipping Mold, and the Molds for cast Candles, attending the Shop, going of Errands, &c. I dislik'd the Trade and had a strong Inclination for the Sea; but my Father declar'd against it; however, living near the Water, I was much in and about it, learnt early to swim well, and to manage Boats, and when in a Boat or Canoe with other Boys I was commonly allow'd to govern,

[10]"In the Island of Nantucket."—[Franklin's note].

[11]Tenth.

[12]Shorthand system.

[13]A maker of candles and soap.

especially in any case of Difficulty; and upon other Occasions I was generally a Leader among the Boys, and sometimes led them into Scrapes, of which I will mention one Instance, as it shows an early projecting public Spirit, tho' not then justly conducted. There was a Salt Marsh that bounded part of the Mill Pond, on the Edge of which at Highwater, we us'd to stand to fish for Minews. By much Trampling, we had made it a mere Quagmire. My Proposal was to build a Wharf there fit for us to stand upon, and I show'd my Comrades a large Heap of Stones which were intended for a new House near the Marsh, and which would very well suit our Purpose. Accordingly in the Evening when the Workmen were gone, I assembled a Number of my Playfellows, and working with them diligently like so many Emmets,[14] sometimes two or three to a Stone, we brought them all away and built our little Wharff. The next Morning the Workmen were surpriz'd at Missing the Stones; which were found in our Wharff; Enquiry was made after the Removers; we were discovered and complain'd of; several of us were corrected by our Fathers; and tho' I pleaded the Usefulness of the Work, mine convinc'd me that nothing was useful which was not honest.

I think you may like to know Something of his Person and Character. He had an excellent Constitution of Body, was of middle Stature, but well set and very strong. He was ingenious, could draw prettily, was skill'd a little in Music and had a clear pleasing Voice, so that when he play'd Psalm Tunes on his Violin and sung withal as he sometimes did in an Evening after the Business of the Day was over, it was extreamly agreable to hear. He had a mechanical Genius too, and on occasion was very handy in the Use of other Tradesmen's Tools. But his great Excellence lay in a sound Understanding, and solid Judgment in prudential Matters, both in private and publick Affairs. In the latter indeed he was never employed, the numerous Family he had to educate and the straitness of his Circumstances, keeping him close to his Trade, but I remember well his being frequently visited by leading People, who consulted him for his Opinion in Affairs of the Town or of the Church he belong'd to and show'd a good deal of Respect for his Judgment and Advice. He was also much consulted by private Persons about their Affairs when any Difficulty occur'd, and frequently chosen an Arbitrator between contending Parties. At his Table he lik'd to have as often as he could, some sensible Friend or Neighbour, to converse with, and always took care to start some ingenious or useful Topic for Discourse, which might tend to improve the Minds of his Children. By this means he turn'd our Attention to what was good, just, and prudent in the Conduct of Life; and little or no Notice was ever taken of what related to the Victuals on the Table, whether it was well or ill drest, in or out of season, of good or bad flavour, preferable or inferior to this or that other thing of the kind; so that I was bro't up in such a perfect Inattention to those Matters as to be quite Indifferent what kind of Food was set before me; and so unobservant of it, that to this Day, if I am ask'd I can scarce tell, a few Hours after Dinner, what I din'd upon. This has been a Convenience to me in travelling, where my Companions have been sometimes very unhappy for want of a suitable Gratification of their more delicate because better instructed Tastes and Appetites.

My Mother had likewise an excellent Constitution. She suckled all her 10 Children. I never knew either my Father or Mother to have any Sickness but that of

[14]Ants.

which they dy'd, he at 89 and she at 85 Years of age. They lie buried together at Boston, where I some Years since plac'd a Marble stone over their Grave with this Inscription

Josiah Franklin
And Abiah his Wife
Lie here interred.
They lived lovingly together in Wedlock
Fifty-five Years.
Without an Estate or any gainful Employment,
By constant labour and Industry,
With God's Blessing,
They maintained a large Family
Comfortably,
And brought up thirteen Children,
And seven Grand Children
Reputably.
From this Instance, Reader,
Be encouraged to Diligence in thy Calling,
And distrust not Providence.
He was a pious & prudent Man,
She a discreet and virtuous Woman.
Their youngest Son,
In filial Regard to their Memory,
Places this Stone.
J.F. born 1655—Died 1744. Ætat[15] 89
A.F. born 1667—died 1752—85

By my rambling Digressions I perceive my self to be grown old. I us'd to write more methodically. But one does not dress for private Company as for a publick Ball. 'Tis perhaps only Negligence.

To return, I continu'd thus employ'd in my Father's Business for two Years, that is till I was 12 Years old; and my Brother John, who was bred to that Business having left my Father, married and set up for himself at Rhodeisland, there was all Appearance that I was destin'd to supply his Place and be a Tallow Chandler. But my Dislike to the Trade continuing, my Father was under Apprehensions that if he did not find one for me more agreable, I should break away and get to Sea, as his Son Josiah had done to his great Vexation. He therefore sometimes took me to walk with him, and see Joiners, Bricklayers, Turners, Braziers,[16] &c. at their Work, that he might observe my Inclination, and endeavour to fix it on some Trade or other on Land. It has ever since been a Pleasure to me to see good Workmen handle their Tools; and it has been useful to me, having learnt so much by it, as to be able to do little Jobs my self in my House, when a Workman could not readily be got; and to construct little Machines for my Experiments while the Intention of making the Experiment was fresh and warm in my Mind. My Father at last fix'd upon the Cutler's

[15]Latin: aged.

[16]Woodworkers, bricklayers, latheworkers, brassworkers.

Trade, and my Uncle Benjamin's Son Samuel who was bred to that Business in London being about that time establish'd in Boston, I was sent to be with him some time on liking. But his Expectations of a Fee with me displeasing my Father, I was taken home again.

From a Child I was fond of Reading, and all the little Money that came into my Hands was ever laid out in Books. Pleas'd with the Pilgrim's Progress, my first Collection was of John Bunyan's Works, in separate little Volumes.[17] I afterwards sold them to enable me to buy R. Burton's Historical Collections; they were small Chapmen's books and cheap 40 or 50 in all. My Father's little Library consisted chiefly of Books in polemic Divinity, most of which I read, and have since often regretted, that at a time when I had such a Thirst for Knowledge, more proper Books had not fallen in my Way, since it was now resolv'd I should not be a Clergyman. Plutarch's Lives[18] there was, in which I read abundantly, and I still think that time spent to great Advantage. There was also a Book of Defoe's, called an Essay on Projects, and another of Dr. Mather's, call'd Essays to do Good which perhaps gave me a Turn of Thinking that had an Influence on some of the principal future Events of my Life.[19]

This Bookish Inclination at length determin'd my Father to make me a Printer, tho' he had already one Son, (James) of that Profession. In 1717 my Brother James return'd from England with a Press and Letters[20] to set up his Business in Boston. I lik'd it much better than that of my Father, but still had a Hankering for the Sea. To prevent the apprehended Effect of such an Inclination, my Father was impatient to have me bound to my Brother. I stood out some time, but at last was persuaded and signed the Indentures, when I was yet but 12 Years old. I was to serve as an Apprentice till I was 21 Years of Age, only I was to be allow'd Journeyman's Wages[21] during the last Year. In a little time I made great Proficiency in the Business, and became a useful Hand to my Brother. I now had Access to better Books. An Acquaintance with the Apprentices of Booksellers, enabled me sometimes to borrow a small one, which I was careful to return soon and clean. Often I sat up in my Room reading the greatest Part of the Night, when the Book was borrow'd in the Evening and to be return'd early in the Morning lest it should be miss'd or wanted. And after some time an ingenious Tradesman Mr. Matthew Adams who had a pretty Collection of Books, and who frequented our Printing House, took Notice of me, invited me to his Library, and very kindly lent me such Books as I chose to read. I now took a Fancy to Poetry, and made some little Pieces. My Brother, thinking it might turn to account encourag'd me, and put me on composing two occasional Ballads. One was called the *Light House Tragedy,* and contain'd an Account of the drowning of Capt. Worthilake with his Two Daughters; the other was a Sailor Song on the Taking of *Teach* or Blackbeard the Pirate. They were wretched Stuff, in the Grubstreet Ballad Stile,[22] and when they were printed he sent me about the Town to sell them. The first sold wonderfully, the Event being recent, having made a great Noise. This flatter'd my

[17]John Bunyan (1628–1688) wrote *The Pilgrim's Progress* (1678).

[18]Plutarch (A.D. 46?–120?) was a Greek biographer; *Parallel Lives* presents the biographies of forty-six noted Greek and Roman figures.

[19]Daniel Defoe's *Essay Upon Projects* (1697) proposed remedies for economic improvement; Cotton Mather's *Bonafacius* was published in 1710.

[20]Type.

[21]Daily wages.

[22]London's Grub Street was populated with literary hacks.

Vanity. But my Father discourag'd me, by ridiculing my Performances, and telling me Versemakers were generally Beggars; so I escap'd being a Poet, most probably a very bad one. But as Prose Writing has been of great Use to me in the Course of my Life, and was a principal Means of my Advancement, I shall tell you how in such a Situation I acquir'd what little Ability I have in that Way.

There was another Bookish Lad in Town, John Collins by Name, with whom I was intimately acquainted. We sometimes disputed, and very fond we were of Argument, and very desirous of confuting one another. Which disputacious Turn, by the way, is apt to become a very bad Habit, making People often extreamly disagreable in Company, by the Contradiction that is necessary to bring it into Practice, and thence, besides souring and spoiling the Conversation, is productive of Disgusts and perhaps Enmities where you may have occasion for Friendship. I had caught it by reading my Father's Books of Dispute about Religion. Persons of good Sense, I have since observ'd, seldom fall into it, except Lawyers, University Men, and Men of all Sorts that have been bred at Edinborough. A Question was once some how or other started between Collins and me, of the Propriety of educating the Female Sex in Learning, and their Abilities for Study. He was of Opinion that it was improper; and that they were naturally unequal to it. I took the contrary Side, perhaps a little for Dispute sake. He was naturally more eloquent, had a ready Plenty of Words, and sometimes as I thought bore me down more by his Fluency than by the Strength of his Reasons. As we parted without settling the Point, and were not to see one another again for some time, I sat down to put my Arguments in Writing, which I copied fair and sent to him. He answer'd and I reply'd. Three or four Letters of a Side had pass'd, when my Father happen'd to find my Papers, and read them. Without entering into the Discussion, he took occasion to talk to me about the Manner of my Writing, observ'd that tho' I had the Advantage of my Antagonist in correct Spelling and pointing[23] (which I ow'd to the Printing House) I fell far short in elegance of Expression, in Method and in Perspicuity, of which he convinc'd me by several Instances. I saw the Justice of his Remarks, and thence grew more attentive to the *Manner* in Writing, and determin'd to endeavour at Improvement.

About this time I met with an odd Volume of the Spectator.[24] It was the third. I had never before seen any of them. I bought it, read it over and over, and was much delighted with it. I thought the Writing excellent, and wish'd if possible to imitate it. With that View, I took some of the Papers, and making short Hints of the Sentiment in each Sentence, laid them by a few Days, and then without looking at the Book, try'd to compleat the Papers again, by expressing each hinted Sentiment at length and as fully as it had been express'd before, in any suitable Words, that should come to hand.

Then I compar'd my Spectator with the Original, discover'd some of my Faults and corrected them. But I found I wanted a Stock of Words or a Readiness in recollecting and using them, which I thought I should have acquir'd before that time, if I had gone on making Verses, since the continual Occasion for Words of the same Import but of different Length, to suit the Measure,[25] or of different Sound for the

[23]Punctuation.

[24]A daily periodical published between 1711–1712 containing essays on literature and morality.

[25]Meter.

Rhyme, would have laid me under a constant Necessity of searching for Variety, and also have tended to fix that Variety in my Mind, and make me Master of it. Therefore I took some of the Tales and turn'd them into Verse: And after a time, when I had pretty well forgotten the Prose, turn'd them back again. I also sometimes jumbled my Collections of Hints into Confusion, and after some Weeks, endeavour'd to reduce them into the best Order, before I began to form the full Sentences, and compleat the Paper. This was to teach me Method in the Arrangement of Thoughts. By comparing my work afterwards with the original, I discover'd many faults and amended them; but I sometimes had the Pleasure of Fancying that in certain Particulars of small Import, I had been lucky enough to improve the Method or the Language and this encourag'd me to think I might possibly in time come to be a tolerable English Writer, of which I was extreamly ambitious.

My Time for these Exercises and for Reading, was at Night, after Work or before Work began in the Morning; or on Sundays, when I contrived to be in the Printing house alone, evading as much as I could the common Attendance on publick Worship, which my Father used to exact of me when I was under his Care: And which indeed I still thought a Duty; tho' I could not, as it seemed to me, afford the Time to practise it.

When about 16 Years of Age, I happen'd to meet with a Book, written by one Tryon,[26] recommending a Vegetable Diet. I determined to go into it. My Brother being yet unmarried, did not keep House, but boarded himself and his Apprentices in another Family. My refusing to eat Flesh occasioned an Inconveniency, and I was frequently chid for my singularity. I made my self acquainted with Tryon's Manner of preparing some of his Dishes, such as Boiling Potatoes or Rice, making Hasty Pudding, and a few others, and then propos'd to my Brother, that if he would give me Weekly half the Money he paid for my Board I would board my self. He instantly agreed to it, and I presently found that I could save half what he paid me. This was an additional Fund for buying Books: But I had another Advantage in it. My Brother and the rest going from the Printing House to their Meals, I remain'd there alone, and dispatching presently my light Repast, (which often was no more than a Bisket or a Slice of Bread, a Handful of Raisins or a Tart from the Pastry Cook's, and a Glass of Water) had the rest of the Time till their Return, for Study, in which I made the greater Progress from that greater Clearness of Head and quicker Apprehension which usually attend Temperance in Eating and Drinking. And now it was that being on some Occasion made asham'd of my Ignorance in Figures, which I had twice failed in learning when at School, I took Cocker's Book of Arithmetick,[27] and went thro' the whole by my self with great Ease. I also read Seller's and Sturmy's Books of Navigation,[28] and became acquainted with the little Geometry they contain, but never proceeded far in that Science. And I read about this Time Locke on Human Understanding, and the Art of Thinking by Messrs. du Port Royal.[29]

[26]Thomas Tryon, *The Way to Health, Long Life and Happiness, or a Discourse of Temperance* (1683).

[27]Edward Cocker, *Arithmetic* (1677).

[28]John Seller, *An Epitome of the Art of Navigation* (1681), and Samuel Sturmy, *The Mariner's Magazine; or Sturmy's Mathematical and Practical Arts* (1669).

[29]John Locke, *Essays Concerning Human Understanding* (1690); Antoine Arnauld and Pierre Nicole of Port-Royal translated *Logic: or the Art of Thinking* (1662) from Latin into English (1685).

While I was intent on improving my Language, I met with an English Grammar (I think it was Greenwood's)[30] at the End of which there were two little Sketches of the Arts of Rhetoric and Logic, the latter finishing with a Specimen of a Dispute in the Socratic Method. And soon after I procur'd Xenophon's Memorable Things of Socrates,[31] wherein there are many Instances of the same Method. I was charm'd with it, adopted it, dropt my abrupt Contradiction, and positive Argumentation, and put on the humble Enquirer and Doubter. And being then, from reading Shaftsbury and Collins,[32] become a real Doubter in many Points of our Religious Doctrine, I found this Method safest for my self and very embarassing to those against whom I used it, therefore I took a Delight in it, practis'd it continually and grew very artful and expert in drawing People even of superior Knowledge into concessions the Consequences of which they did not foresee, entangling them in Difficulties out of which they could not extricate themselves, and so obtaining Victories that neither my self nor my Cause always deserved.

I continu'd this Method some few Years, but gradually left it, retaining only the Habit of expressing my self in Terms of modest Diffidence, never using when I advance any thing that may possibly be disputed, the Words, *Certainly, undoubtedly,* or any others that give the Air of Positiveness to an Opinion; but rather say, I conceive, or I apprehend a Thing to be so or so, It appears to me, or I should think it so or so for such and such Reasons, or I imagine it to be so, or it is so if I am not mistaken. This Habit I believe has been of great Advantage to me, when I have had occasion to indicate my Opinions and persuade Men into Measures that I have been from time to time engag'd in promoting. And as the chief Ends of Conversation are to *inform,* or to be *informed,* to *please* or to *persuade,* I wish wellmeaning sensible Men would not lessen their Power of doing Good by a Positive assuming Manner that seldom fails to disgust, tends to create Opposition, and to defeat every one of those Purposes for which Speech was given us, to wit, giving or receiving Information, or Pleasure: For if you would *inform,* a positive dogmatical Manner in advancing your Sentiments, may provoke Contradiction and prevent a candid Attention. If you wish Information and Improvement from the Knowledge of others and yet at the same time express your self as firmly fix'd in your present Opinions, modest sensible Men, who do not love Disputation, will probably leave you undisturb'd in the Possession of your Error; and by such a Manner you can seldom hope to recommend your self in *pleasing* your Hearers, or to persuade those whose Concurrence you desire. Pope says, judiciously,

> Men should be taught as if you taught them not,
> And things unknown propos'd as things forgot,

farther recommending it to us,

To speak tho' sure, with seeming Diffidence.[33]

[30]James Greenwood, *An Essay towards a Practical English Grammar* (1711).

[31]Xenophon, *The Memorable Things of Socrates,* translated by Edward Bysshe (1712).

[32]Anthony Ashley Cooper, third Earl of Shaftesbury (1671–1713), was a religious skeptic, and Anthony Collins (1676–1729), a deist.

[33]Alexander Pope, *An Essay on Criticism* (1711), lines 574–575, 567. Franklin is quoting from memory. The first line should read, "Men must be taught as if you taught them not," and the third "And speak, tho' sure, with seeming diffidence."

And he might have coupled with this Line that which he has coupled with another, I think less properly,

For Want of Modesty is Want of Sense.

If you ask why, *less properly,* I must repeat the Lines;

Immodest Words admit of *no* Defence;
For Want of Modesty is Want of Sense.[34]

Now is not *Want of Sense* (where a Man is so unfortunate as to want it) some Apology for his *Want of Modesty?* and would not the Lines stand more justly thus?

Immodest Words admit *but this* Defence,
That Want of Modesty is Want of Sense.

This however I should submit to better Judgments.

My Brother had in 1720 or 21, begun to print a Newspaper. It was the second that appear'd in America,[35] and was called *The New England Courant.* The only one before it, was *the Boston News Letter.* I remember his being dissuaded by some of his Friends from the Undertaking, as not likely to succeed, one newspaper being in their Judgment enough for America. At this time 1771 there are not less than five and twenty. He went on however with the Undertaking, and after having work'd in composing the Types and printing off the Sheets I was employ'd to carry the Papers thro' the Street to the Customers. He had some ingenious Men among his Friends who amus'd themselves by writing little Pieces for this Paper, which gain'd it Credit, and made it more in Demand; and these Gentlemen often visited us. Hearing their Conversations, and their Accounts of the Approbation their Papers were receiv'd with, I was excited to try my Hand among them. But being still a Boy, and suspecting that my Brother would object to printing any Thing of mine in his Paper if he knew it to be mine, I contriv'd to disguise my Hand, and writing an anonymous Paper[36] I put it in at Night under the Door of the Printing House. It was found in the Morning and communicated to his Writing Friends when they call'd in as usual. They read it, commented on it in my Hearing, and I had the exquisite Pleasure, of finding it met with their Approbation, and that in their different Guesses at the Author none were named but Men of some Character among us for Learning and Ingenuity.

I suppose now that I was rather lucky in my Judges: And that perhaps they were not really so very good ones as I then esteem'd them. Encourag'd however by this, I wrote and convey'd in the same Way to the Press several more Papers, which were equally approv'd, and I kept my Secret till my small Fund of Sense for such Performances was pretty well exhausted, and then I discovered[37] it; when I began to be considered a little more by my Brother's Acquaintance, and in a manner that did not quite please him, as he thought, probably with reason, that it tended to make me too

[34]Often attributed to Pope, the couplet is actually from Wentworth Dillon's *Essay on Translated Verse* (1684), lines 113–114. The second line should read, "For want of decency is want of sense."

[35]Actually the fifth.

[36]The first of the "Silence Dogwood" letters, published in the *Courant* from April 12–October 8, 1722.

[37]Revealed.

vain. And perhaps this might be one Occasion of the Differences that we frequently had about this Time. Tho' a Brother, he considered himself as my Master, and me as his Apprentice; and accordingly expected the same Services from me as he would from another; while I thought he demean'd me too much in some he requir'd of me, who from a Brother expected more Indulgence. Our Disputes were often brought before our Father, and I fancy I was either generally in the right, or else a better Pleader, because the Judgment was generally in my favour: But my Brother was passionate and had often beaten me, which I took extreamly amiss; and thinking my Apprenticeship very tedious, I was continually wishing for some Opportunity of shortening it, which at length offered in a manner unexpected.[38]

One of the Pieces in our News-Paper, on some political Point which I have now forgotten, gave Offence to the Assembly.[39] He was taken up, censur'd and imprison'd for a Month by the Speaker's Warrant, I suppose because he would not discover his Author. I too was taken up and examin'd before the Council; but tho' I did not give them any Satisfaction, they contented themselves with admonishing me, and dismiss'd me; considering me perhaps as an Apprentice who was bound to keep his Master's Secrets. During my Brother's Confinement, which I resented a good deal, notwithstanding our private Differences, I had the Management of the Paper, and I made bold to give our Rulers some Rubs in it, which my Brother took very kindly, while others began to consider me in an unfavourable Light, as a young Genius that had a Turn for Libelling and Satyr. My Brother's Discharge was accompany'd with an Order of the House, (a very odd one) *that James Franklin should no longer print the Paper called the New England Courant.* There was a Consultation held in our Printing House among his Friends what he should do in this Case. Some propos'd to evade the Order by changing the Name of the paper; but my Brother seeing Inconveniences in that, it was finally concluded on as a better Way, to let it be printed for the future under the Name of *Benjamin Franklin.* And to avoid the Censure of the Assembly that might fall on him, as still printing it by his Apprentice, the Contrivance was, that my old Indenture should be return'd to me with a full Discharge on the Back of it, to be shown on Occasion; but to secure to him the Benefit of my Service I was to sign new Indentures for the Remainder of the Term, which were to be kept private. A very flimsy Scheme it was, but however it was immediately executed, and the Paper went on accordingly under my Name for several Months. At length a fresh Difference arising between my Brother and me, I took upon me to assert my Freedom, presuming that he would not venture to produce the new Indentures. It was not fair in me to take this Advantage, and this I therefore reckon one of the first Errata of my Life: But the Unfairness of it weigh'd little with me, when under the Impression of Resentment, for the Blows his Passion too often urg'd him to bestow upon me. Tho' he was otherwise not an ill-natur'd Man: Perhaps I was too saucy and provoking.

[38]"I fancy his harsh and tyrannical Treatment of me, might be a means of impressing me with that Aversion to arbitrary Power that has stuck to me thro' my whole Life." [Franklin's note].

[39]One of the two Houses of the Massachusetts legislature.

When he found I would leave him, he took care to prevent my getting Employment in any other Printing-House of the Town, by going round and speaking to every Master, who accordingly refus'd to give me Work. I then thought of going to New York as the nearest Place where there was a Printer: and I was the rather inclin'd to leave Boston, when I reflected that I had already made myself a little obnoxious to the governing Party; and from the arbitrary Proceedings of the Assembly in my Brother's Case it was likely I might if I stay'd soon bring myself into Scrapes; and farther that my indiscrete Disputations about Religion began to make me pointed at with Horror by good People, as an Infidel or Atheist. I determin'd on the Point: but my Father now siding with my Brother, I was sensible that If I attempted to go openly, Means would be used to prevent me. My Friend Collins therefore undertook to manage a little for me. He agreed with the Captain of a New York Sloop for my Passage, under the Notion of my being a young Acquaintance of his that had got a naughty Girl with Child, whose Friends would compel me to marry her, and therefore I could not appear or come away publickly. So I sold some of my Books to raise a little Money, Was taken on board privately, and as we had a fair Wind in three Days I found my self in New York near 300 Miles from home, a Boy of but 17, without the least Recommendation to or Knowledge of any Person in the Place, and with very little Money in my Pocket.

My Inclinations for the Sea, were by this time worne out, or I might now have gratify'd them. But having a Trade, and supposing my self a pretty good Workman, I offer'd my Service to the Printer of the Place, old Mr. Wm. Bradford,[40] (who had been the first Printer in Pensilvania, but remov'd from thence upon the Quarrel of Geo. Keith). He could give me no Employment, having little to do, and Help enough already. But, says he, my Son at Philadelphia has lately lost his principal Hand, Aquila Rose, by Death. If you got thither I believe he may employ you. Philadelphia was 100 Miles farther. I set out, however, in a Boat for Amboy,[41] leaving my Chest and Things to follow me round by Sea. In crossing the Bay we met with a Squall that tore our rotten Sails to pieces, prevented our getting into the Kill,[42] and drove us upon Long Island. In our Way a drunken Dutchman, who was a Passenger too, fell over board; when he was sinking I reach'd thro' the Water to his shock Pate[43] and drew him up so that we got him in again. His Ducking sober'd him a little, and he went to sleep, taking first out of his Pocket a Book which he desir'd I would dry for him. It prov'd to be my old favourite Author Bunyan's Pilgrim's Progress in Dutch, finely printed on good Paper with copper Cuts,[44] a Dress better than I had ever seen it wear in its own Language. I have since found that it has been translated into most of the Languages of Europe, and suppose it has been more generally read than any other Book except perhaps the Bible. Honest John was the first that I know of who mix'd Narration and Dialogue, a Method of Writing very engaging to the Reader, who in the most interesting Parts finds himself as it were brought into the Company; and present at the Discourse. Defoe in his Cruso, his Moll Flanders, Religious

[40]William Bradford (1663–1752), an American printer and father of Franklin's competitor, Andrew Bradford (1686–1742).

[41]Perth Amboy, New Jersey.

[42]Narrow channel separating Staten Island, New York, from New Jersey.

[43]Bushy hair.

[44]Engravings.

Courtship, Family Instructor, and other Pieces, has imitated it with Success. And Richardson has done the same in his Pamela, &c.[45]

When we drew near the Island we found it was at a Place where there could be no Landing, there being a great Surf on the stony Beach. So we dropt Anchor and swung round towards the Shore. Some People came down to the Water Edge and hallow'd to us, as we did to them. But the Wind was so high and the Surf so loud, that we could not hear so as to understand each other. There were Canoes on the Shore, and we made Signs and hallow'd that they should fetch us, but they either did not understand us, or thought it impracticable. So they went away, and Night coming on, we had no Remedy but to wait till the Wind should abate, and in the mean time the Boatman and I concluded to sleep if we could, and so crouded into the Scuttle with the Dutchman who was still wet, and the Spray beating over the Head of our Boat, leak'd thro' to us, so that we were soon almost as wet as he. In this Manner we lay all Night with very little Rest. But the Wind abating the next Day, we made a Shift to reach Amboy before Night, having been 30 Hours on the Water without Victuals, or any Drink but a Bottle of filthy Rum: The Water we sail'd on being salt.

In the evening I found my self very feverish, and went in to Bed. But having read somewhere that cold Water drank plentifully was good for a Fever, I follow'd the prescription, sweat plentifully most of the Night, my Fever left me, and in the Morning crossing the Ferry, I proceeded on my Journey, on foot, having 50 Miles to Burlington,[46] where I was told I should find Boats that would carry me the rest of the Way to Philadelphia.

It rain'd very hard all the Day, I was thoroughly soak'd and by Noon a good deal tir'd, so I stopt at a poor Inn, where I staid all Night, beginning now to wish I had never left home. I cut so miserable a Figure too, that I found by the Questions ask'd me I was suspected to be some runaway Servant, and in danger of being taken up on that Suspicion. However I proceeded the next Day, and got in the Evening to an Inn within 8 or 10 Miles of Burlington, kept by one Dr. Brown.[47]

He entered into Conversation with me while I took some Refreshment, and finding I had read a little, became very sociable and friendly. Our Acquaintance continu'd as long as he liv'd. He had been, I imagine, an itinerant Doctor, for there was no Town in England, or Country in Europe, of which he could not give a very particular Account. He had some Letters,[48] and was ingenious, but much of an Unbeliever, and wickedly undertook some Years after to travesty the Bible in doggrel Verse as Cotton had done Virgil.[49] By this means he set many of the Facts in a very ridiculous Light, and might have hurt weak minds if his Work had been publish'd: but it never was. At his House I lay that Night, and the next Morning reach'd Burlington. But had the Mortification to find that the regular Boats were gone, a lit-

[45]Daniel Defoe wrote *Robinson Crusoe* (1719), *Moll Flanders* (1722), *Religious Courtship* (1722), *The Family Instructor* (1715–18). Samuel Richardson wrote *Pamela, or Virtue Rewarded* (1740). Franklin reprinted *Pamela* in 1744, thereby publishing the first novel in the colonies.

[46]In western New Jersey, about eighteen miles from Philadelphia.

[47]John Browne (c. 1667–1737), a religious skeptic, physician, and innkeeper in Burlington.

[48]Education.

[49]Charles Cotton (1630–1687) wrote the parody, *Scarronides, or the First Book of Virgil Travestied* (1664).

tle before my coming, and no other expected to go till Tuesday, this being Saturday. Wherefore I return'd to an old Woman in the Town of whom I had bought Gingerbread to eat on the Water, and ask'd her Advice; she invited me to lodge at her House till a Passage by Water should offer: and being tired with my foot Travelling, I accepted the Invitation. She understanding I was a Printer, would have had me stay at that Town and follow my Business, being ignorant of the Stock necessary to begin with. She was very hospitable, gave me a Dinner of Ox Cheek with great Goodwill, accepting only of a Pot of Ale in return. And I tho't my self fix'd till Tuesday should come. However walking in the Evening by the Side of the River a Boat came by, which I found was going towards Philadelphia, with several People in her. They took me in, and as there was no Wind, we row'd all the Way; and about Midnight not having yet seen the City, some of the Company were confident we must have pass'd it, and would row no farther, the others knew not where we were, so we put towards the Shore, got into a Creek, landed near an old Fence with the Rails of which we made a Fire, the Night being cold, in October, and there we remain'd till Daylight. Then one of the Company knew the Place to be Cooper's Creek a little above Philadelphia, which we saw as soon as we got out of the Creek, and arriv'd there about 8 or 9 a Clock, on the Sunday morning, and landed at the Market street Wharff.

I have been the more particular in this Description of my Journey, and shall be so of my first Entry into that City, that you may in your Mind compare such unlikely Beginnings with the Figure I have since made there. I was in my Working Dress, my best Cloaths being to come round by Sea. I was dirty from my Journey; my Pockets were stuff'd out with Shirts and Stockings; I knew no Soul, nor where to look for Lodging. I was fatigu'd with Traveling, Rowing and Want of Rest. I was very hungry, and my whole Stock of Cash consisted of a Dutch Dollar and about a Shilling in Copper. The latter I gave the People of the Boat for my Passage, who at first refus'd it on Account of my Rowing; but I insisted on their taking it, a Man being sometimes more generous when he has but a little Money than when he has plenty, perhaps thro' Fear of being thought to have but little.

Then I walk'd up the Street, gazing about, till near the Market House I met a Boy with Bread. I had made many a Meal on Bread, and inquiring where he got it, I went immediately to the Baker's he directed me to in second Street; and ask'd for Bisket, intending such as we had in Boston, but they it seems were not made in Philadelphia, then I ask'd for a threepenny Loaf, and was told they had none such: so not considering or knowing the Difference of Money and the greater Cheapness nor the Names of his Bread, I bad him give me three penny worth of any sort. He gave me accordingly three great Puffy Rolls. I was surpriz'd at the Quantity, but took it, and having no room in my Pockets, walk'd off, with a Roll under each Arm, and eating the other. Thus I went up Market Street as far as fourth Street, passing by the Door of Mr. Read, my future Wife's Father, when she standing at the Door saw me, and thought I made as I certainly did a most awkward ridiculous Appearance. Then I turn'd and went down Chestnut Street and part of Walnut Street, eating my Roll all the Way, and coming round found my self again at Market Street Wharff, near the Boat I came in, to which I went for a Draught of the River Water, and being fill'd with one of my Rolls, gave the other two to a Woman and her Child that came down the River in the Boat with us and were waiting to go farther. Thus refresh'd I walk'd again up the Street, which by this time had many clean dress'd People in it who were all walking the same Way; I join'd them, and thereby was led into the great Meeting house of the Quakers near the Market. I sat down among them, and after looking round a while and hearing nothing said, being very drowsy thro' Labour and want of Rest the preceding Night, I fell fast asleep, and continu'd so till the Meeting broke up, when one was kind enough to rouse me. This was therefore the first House I was in or slept in, in Philadelphia.

Walking again down towards the River, and looking in the Faces of People, I met a young Quaker Man whose Countenance I lik'd, and accosting him requested he would tell me where a Stranger could get Lodging. We were then near the Sign of the Three Mariners. Here, says he, is one Place that entertains Strangers, but it is not a reputable House; if thee wilt walk with me, I'll show thee a better. He brought me to the Crooked Billet in Water-Street. Here I got a Dinner. And while I was eating it, several sly Questions were ask'd me, as it seem'd to be suspected from my youth and Appearance, that I might be some Runaway. After Dinner my Sleepiness return'd: and being shown to a Bed, I lay down without undressing, and slept till Six in the Evening; was call'd to Supper; went to Bed again very early and slept soundly till the next Morning. Then I made my self as tidy as I could, and went to Andrew Bradford the Printer's. I found in the Shop the old Man his Father, whom I had seen at New York, and who travelling on horse back had got to Philadelphia before me. He introduc'd me to his Son, who receiv'd me civilly, gave me a Breakfast, but told me he did not at present want a Hand, being lately supply'd with one. But there was another Printer in town lately set up, one Keimer,[50] who perhaps might employ me; if not, I should be welcome to lodge at his House, and he would give me a little Work to do now and then till fuller Business should offer.

The old Gentleman said, he would go with me to the new Printer: And when we found him, Neighbour, says Bradford, I have brought to see you a young Man of your Business, perhaps you may want such a One. He ask'd me a few Questions, put a Composing Stick in my Hand to see how I work'd, and then said he would employ me soon, tho' he had just then nothing for me to do. And taking old Bradford whom he had never seen before, to be one of the Towns People that had a Good Will for him, enter'd into a Conversation on his present Undertaking and Prospects; while Bradford not discovering that he was the other Printer's Father, on Keimer's saying he expected soon to get the greatest Part of the Business into his own Hands, drew him on by artful Questions and starting little Doubts, to explain all his Views, what Interest he rely'd on, and in what manner he intended to proceed. I who stood by and heard all, saw immediately that one of them was a crafty old Sophister, and the other a mere Novice. Bradford left me with Keimer, who was greatly surpriz'd when I told him who the old Man was.

Keimer's Printing House I found, consisted of an old shatter'd Press, and one small worn-out Fount of English,[51] which he was then using himself, composing in it an Elegy on Aquila Rose before-mentioned, an ingenious young Man of excellent Character much respected in the Town, Clerk of the Assembly, and a pretty Poet. Keimer made Verses, too, but very indifferently. He could not be said to write them,

[50]Samuel Keimer (c. 1688–1742). Unsuccessful as a printer, he left Philadelphia in 1730.

[51]Oversized type.

for his Manner was to compose them in the Types directly out of his Head; so there being no Copy, but one Pair of Cases,[52] and the Elegy likely to require all the Letter, no one could help him. I endeavour'd to put his Press (which he had not yet us'd, and of which he understood nothing) into Order fit to be work'd with; and promising to come and print off his Elegy as soon as he should have got it ready, I return'd to Bradford's who gave me a little Job to do for the present, and there I lodged and dieted. A few Days after Keimer sent for me to print off the Elegy. And now he had got another Pair of Cases, and a Pamphlet to reprint, on which he set me to work.

These two Printers I found poorly qualified for their Business. Bradford had not been bred to it, and was very illiterate; and Keimer tho' something of a Scholar, was a mere Compositor, knowing nothing of Presswork. He had been one of the French Prophets[53] and could act their enthusiastic Agitations. At this time he did not profess any particular Religion, but something of all on occasion; was very ignorant of the World, and had, as I afterwards found, a good deal of the Knave in his Composition. He did not like my Lodging at Bradford's while I work'd with him. He had a House indeed, but without Furniture, so he could not lodge me: But he got me a Lodging at Mr. Read's before-mentioned, who was the Owner of his House. And my Chest and Clothes being come by this time, I made rather a more respectable Appearance in the Eyes of Miss Read, than I had done when she first happen'd to see me eating my Roll in the Street.

I began now to have some Acquaintance among the young People of the Town, that were Lovers of Reading with whom I spent my Evenings very pleasantly and gaining Money by my Industry and Frugality, I lived very agreably, forgetting Boston as much as I could, and not desiring that any there should know where I resided, except my Friend Collins who was in my Secret, and kept it when I wrote to him. At length an Incident happended that sent me back again much sooner than I had intended.

I had a Brother-in-law, Robert Holmes,[54] Master of a Sloop, that traded between Boston and Delaware. He being at New Castle 40 Miles below Philadelphia, heard there of me, and wrote me a Letter, mentioning the Concern of my Friends in Boston at my abrupt Departure, assuring me of their Goodwill to me, and that every thing would be accommodated to my Mind if I would return, to which he exhorted me very earnestly. I wrote an Answer to his Letter, thank'd him for his Advice, but stated my Reasons for quitting Boston fully, and in such a Light as to convince him I was not so wrong as he had apprehended.

Sir William Keith[55] Governor of the Province, was then at New Castle, and Capt. Holmes happening to be in Company with him when my Letter came to hand, spoke to him of me, and show'd him the Letter. The Governor read it, and seem'd surpriz'd when he was told my Age. He said I appear'd a young Man of promising Parts, and therefore should be encouraged: The Printers of Philadelphia were wretched ones, and if I would set up there, he made no doubt I should succeed; for

[52]Trays of type containing uppercase and lowercase letters.

[53]Religious sect given to trances.

[54]Robert Holmes (d. before 1743), husband of Franklin's sister Mary, and a ship's captain.

[55]Sir William Keith (1680–1749), governor of Pennsylvania 1717–1726.

his Part, he would procure me the publick Business, and do me every other Service in his Power. This my Brother-in-Law afterwards told me in Boston. But I knew as yet nothing of it; when one Day Keimer and I being at Work together near the Window, we saw the Governor and another Gentleman (which prov'd to be Col. French, of New Castle) finely dress'd, come directly across the Street to our House, and heard them at the Door. Keimer ran down immediately, thinking it a Visit to him. But the Governor enquir'd for me, came up, and with a Condescension and Politeness I had been quite unus'd to, made me many Compliments, desired to be acquainted with me, blam'd me kindly for not having made my self known to him when I first came to the Place, and would have me away with him to the Tavern where he was going with Col. French to taste as he said some excellent Madeira. I was not a little surpriz'd, and Keimer star'd like a Pig poison'd. I went however with the Governor and Col. French, to a Tavern the Corner of Third Street, and over the Madeira he propos'd my Setting up my Business, laid before me the Probabilities of Success, and both he and Col. French assur'd me I should have their Interest and Influence in procuring the Publick Business of both Governments. On my doubting whether my Father would assist me in it, Sir William said he would give me a Letter to him, in which he would state the Advantages, and he did not doubt of prevailing with him. So it was concluded I should return to Boston in the first Vessel with the Governor's Letter recommending me to my Father. In the mean time the Intention was to be kept secret, and I went on working with Keimer as usual, the Governor sending for me now and then to dine with him, a very great Honour I thought it, and conversing with me in the most affable, familiar, and friendly manner imaginable.

About the End of April 1724, a little Vessel offer'd for Boston. I took Leave of Keimer as going to see my Friends. The Governor gave me an ample Letter, saying many flattering things of me to my Father, and strongly recommending the Project of my setting up at Philadelphia, as a Thing that must make my Fortune. We struck on a Shoal in going down the Bay and sprung a Leak, we had a blustering time at Sea, and were oblig'd to pump almost continually, at which I took my Turn. We arriv'd safe however at Boston in about a Fortnight. I had been absent Seven Months and my Friends had heard nothing of me; for my Br. Holmes was not yet return'd; and had not written about me. My unexpected Appearance surpriz'd the Family; all were however very glad to see me and made me Welcome, except my Brother. I went to see him at his Printing-House: I was better dress'd than ever while in his Service, having a genteel new Suit from Head to foot, a Watch, and my Pockets lin'd with near Five Pounds Sterling in Silver. He receiv'd me not very frankly, look'd me all over, and turn'd to his Work again. The Journey-Men were inquisitive where I had been, what sort of a Country it was, and how I lik'd it? I prais'd it much, and the happy Life I led in it; expressing strongly my Intention of returning to it; and one of them asking what kind of Money we had there, I produc'd a handful of Silver and spread it before them, which was a kind of Raree-Show[56] they had not been us'd to, Paper being the Money of Boston. Then I took an Opportunity of letting them see my Watch: and lastly, (my Brother still grum and sullen) I gave them a Piece of Eight to drink[57] and took my Leave. This visit of mine offended him extreamly. For when my

[56]A sidewalk peepshow.

[57]He gave them a Spanish dollar for drinks.

Mother some time after spoke to him of a Reconciliation, and of her Wishes to see us on good Terms together, and that we might live for the future as Brothers, he said, I had insulted him in such a Manner before his People that he could never forget or forgive it. In this however he was mistaken.

My Father receiv'd the Governor's Letter with some apparent Surprize; but said little of it to me for some Days; when Capt. Holmes returning, he show'd it to him, ask'd if he knew Keith, and What kind of a Man he was: Adding his Opinion that he must be of small Direction, to think of setting a Boy up in Business who wanted yet 3 Years of Being at Man's Estate. Holmes said what he could in favour of the Project; but my Father was clear in the Impropriety of it; and at last gave a flat Denial to it. Then he wrote a civil Letter to Sir William thanking him for the Patronage he had so kindly offered me, but declining to assist me as yet in Setting up, I being in his Opinion too young to be trusted with the Management of a Business so important, and for which the Preparation must be so expensive.

My Friend and Companion Collins, who was a Clerk at the Post-Office, pleas'd with the Account I gave him of my new Country, determin'd to go thither also: And while I waited for my Fathers Determination, he set out before me by Land to Rhodeisland, leaving his Books which were a pretty Collection of Mathematicks and Natural Philosophy,[58] to come with mine and me to New York where he propos'd to wait for me. My Father, tho' he did not approve Sir William's Proposition was yet pleas'd that I had been able to obtain so advantageous a Character from a Person of such Note where I had resided, and that I had been so industrious and careful as to equip my self so handsomely in so short a time: therefore seeing no Prospect of an Accommodation between my Brother and me, he gave his Consent to my Returning again to Philadelphia, advis'd me to behave respectfully to the People there, endeavour to obtain the general Esteem, and avoid lampooning and libelling to which he thought I had too much Inclination; telling me, that by steady Industry and a prudent Parsimony, I might save enough by the time I was One and Twenty to set me up, and that if I came near the Matter he would help me out with the rest. This was all I could obtain, except some small Gifts as Tokens of his and my Mother's Love, when I embark'd again for New York, now with their Approbation and their Blessing.

The Sloop putting in at Newport, Rhodeisland, I visited my Brother John, who had been married and settled there some Years. He received me very affectionately, for he always lov'd me. A Friend of his, one Vernon, having some Money due to him in Pensilvania, about 35 Pounds Currency, desired I would receive it for him, and keep it till I had his Directions what to remit it in. Accordingly he gave me an Order. This afterwards occasion'd me a good deal of Uneasiness. At Newport we took in a Number of Passengers for New York: Among which were two young Women, Companions, and a grave, sensible Matron-like Quaker-Woman with her Attendants. I had shown an obliging readiness to do her some little Services which impress'd her I suppose with a degree of Good-will towards me. Therefore when she saw a daily growing Familiarity between me and the two Young Women, which they appear'd to encourage, she took me aside and said, Young Man, I am concern'd for thee, as thou has no Friend with thee, and seems not to know much of the World, or of the Snares Youth is expos'd to; depend upon it those are very bad Women, I can see it in all their

[58]Natural science.

Actions, and if thee art not upon thy Guard, they will draw thee into some Danger: they are Strangers to thee, and I advise thee in a friendly Concern for thy Welfare, to have no Acquaintance with them. As I seem'd at first not to think so ill of them as she did, she mention'd some Things she had observ'd and heard that had escap'd my Notice; but not convinc'd me she was right. I thank'd her for her kind Advice, and promis'd to follow it. When we arriv'd at New York, they told me where they liv'd, and invited me to come and see them: but I avoided it. And it was well I did: For the next Day, the Captain miss'd a Silver Spoon and some other Things that had been taken out of his Cabbin, and knowing that these were a Couple of Strumpets, he got a Warrant to search their Lodgings, found the stolen Goods, and had the Thieves punish'd. So tho' we had escap'd a sunken Rock which we scrap'd upon in the Passage, I thought this Escape of rather more Importance to me.

At New York I found my Friend Collins, who had arriv'd there some Time before me. We had been intimate from Children, and had read the same Books together. But he had the Advantage of more time for reading, and Studying and a wonderful Genius for Mathematical Learning in which he far outstript me. While I liv'd in Boston most of my Hours of Leisure for Conversation were spent with him, and he continu'd a sober as well as an industrious Lad; was much respected for his Learning by several of the Clergy and other Gentlemen, and seem'd to promise making a good Figure in Life: but during my Absence he had acquir'd a Habit of Sotting[59] with Brandy; and I found by his own Account and what I heard from others, that he had been drunk every day since his Arrival at New York, and behav'd very oddly. He had gam'd too and lost his Money, so that I was oblig'd to discharge[60] his Lodgings, and defray his Expenses to and at Philadelphia: Which prov'd extreamly inconvenient to me. The then Governor of N[ew] York, Burnet,[61] Son of Bishop Burnet hearing from the Captain that a young Man, one of his Passengers, had a great many Books, desired he would bring me to see him. I waited upon him accordingly, and should have taken Collins with me but that he was not sober. The Governor treated me with great Civility, show'd me his Library, which was a very large one, and we had a good deal of Conversation about Books and Authors. This was the second Governor who had done me the Honor to take Notice of me, which to a poor Boy like me was very pleasing.

We proceeded to Philadelphia. I received on the Way Vernon's Money, without which we could hardly have finish'd our Journey. Collins wish'd to be employ'd in some Counting House; but whether they discover'd his Dramming by his Breath, or by his Behaviour, tho' he had some Recommendations, he met with no Success in any Application, and continu'd Lodging and Boarding at the same House with me and at my Expense. Knowing I had the Money of Vernon's he was continually borrowing of me, still promising Repayment as soon as he should be in Business. At length he had got so much of it, that I was distress'd to think what I should do, in case of being call'd on to remit it. His Drinking continu'd about which we sometimes quarrel'd, for when a little intoxicated he was very fractious. Once in a Boat on the Delaware with some other young Men, he refused to row in his Turn: I will be row'd

[59]Getting drunk.
[60]Pay for.
[61]William Burnet (1688–1729), governor of New York and New Jersey (1720–1728).

home, says he. We will not row you, says I. You must or stay all Night on the Water, says he, just as you please. The others said, Let us row; what signifies it? But my Mind being soured with his other Conduct, I continu'd to refuse. So he swore he would make me row, or throw me overboard; and coming along stepping on the Thwarts towards me, when he came up and struck at me and I clapt my Hand under his Crutch, and rising pitch'd him head-foremost into the River. I knew he was a good Swimmer, and so was under little Concern about him; but before he could get round to lay hold of the Boat, we had with a few Strokes pull'd her out of his Reach. And ever when he drew near the Boat, we ask'd if he would row, striking a few Strokes to slide her away from him. He was ready to die with Vexation, and obstinately would not promise to row; however seeing him at last beginning to tire, we lifted him in; and brought him home dripping wet in the Evening. We hardly exchang'd a civil Word afterwards; and a West India Captain who had a Commission to procure a Tutor for the Sons of a Gentleman at Barbadoes, happening to meet with him, agreed to carry him thither. He left me then, promising to remit me the first Money he should receive in order to discharge the Debt. But I never heard of him after.

The Breaking into this Money of Vernon's was one of the first great Errata of my Life. And this Affair show'd that my Father was not much out in his Judgment when he suppos'd me too young to manage Business of Importance. But Sir William, on reading his Letter, said he was too prudent. There was great Difference in Persons, and Discretion did not always accompany Years, nor was Youth always without it. And since he will not set you up, says he, I will do it myself. Give me an Inventory of the Things necessary to be had from England, and I will send for them. You shall repay me when you are able; I am resolv'd to have a good Printer here, and I am sure you must succeed. This was spoken with such an Appearance of Cordiality, that I had not the least doubt of his meaning what he said. I had hitherto kept the Proposition of my Setting up a Secret in Philadelphia, and I still kept it. Had it been known that I depended on the Governor, probably some Friend that knew him better would have advis'd me not to rely on him, as I afterwards heard it as his known Character to be liberal of Promises which he never meant to keep. Yet unsolicited as he was by me, how could I think his generous Offers insincere? I believ'd him one of the best Men in the World.

I presented him an Inventory of a little Printing House, amounting by my Computation to about £100 Sterling. He lik'd it, but ask'd me if my being on the Spot in England to chuse the Types and see that every thing was good of the kind, might not be of some Advantage. Then, says he, when there, you may make Acquaintances and establish Correspondencies in the Bookselling and Stationary Way. I agreed that this might be advantageous. Then says he, get yourself ready to go with Annis;[62] which was the annual Ship, and the only one at that Time usually passing between London and Philadelphia. But it would be some Months before Annis sail'd, so I continu'd working with Keimer, fretting about the Money Collins had got from me, and in daily Apprehensions of being call'd upon by Vernon, which however did not happen for some Years after.

I believe I have omitted mentioning that in my first Voyage from Boston, being becalm'd off Block Island,[63] our People set about catching Cod and hawl'd up a

[62]Thomas Annis, captain of the ship that sailed between England and Philadelphia.

[63]Off the coast of Rhode Island.

great many. Hitherto I had stuck to my Resolution of not eating animal Food; and on this Occasion, I consider'd with my Master Tryon, the taking every Fish as a kind of unprovok'd Murder, since none of them had or ever could do us any Injury that might justify the Slaughter. All this seem'd very reasonable. But I had formerly been a great Lover of Fish, and when this came hot out of the Frying Pan, it smelt admirably well. I balanc'd some time between Principle and Inclination: till I recollected, that when the Fish were opened, I saw smaller Fish taken out of their Stomachs: Then thought I, if you eat one another, I don't see why we mayn't eat you. So I din'd upon Cod very heartily and continu'd to eat with other People, returning only now and then occasionally to a vegetable Diet. So convenient a thing it is to be a *reasonable Creature,* since it enables one to find or make a Reason for every thing one has a mind to do.

Keimer and I liv'd on a pretty good familiar Footing and agreed tolerably well: for he suspected nothing of my Setting up. He retain'd a great deal of his old Enthusiasms, and lov'd Argumentation. We therefore had many Disputations. I us'd to work him so with my Socratic Method, and had trapann'd him so often by Questions apparently so distant from any Point we had in hand, and yet by degrees led to the Point, and brought him into Difficulties and Contradictions that at last he grew ridiculously cautious, and would hardly answer me the most common Question, without asking first, *What do you intend to infer from that?* However it gave him so high an Opinion of my Abilities in the Confuting Way, that he seriously propos'd my being his Colleague in a Project he had of setting up a new Sect. He was to preach the Doctrines, and I was to confound all Opponents. When he came to explain with me upon the Doctrines, I found several Conundrums[64] which I objected to unless I might have my Way a little too, and introduce some of mine. Keimer wore his Beard at full Length, because somewhere in the Mosaic Law it is said, *thou shalt not mar the Corners of thy Beard.*[65] He likewise kept the seventh day Sabbath; and these two Points were Essentials with him. I dislik'd both, but agreed to admit them upon Condition of his adopting the Doctrine of using no animal Food. I doubt, says he, my Constitution will not bear that. I assur'd him it would, and that he would be the better for it. He was usually a great Glutton, and I promised my self some Diversion in half-starving him. He agreed to try the Practice if I would keep him Company. I did so and we held it for three Months. We had our Victuals dress'd and brought to us regularly by a Woman in the Neighbourhood, who had from me a List of 40 Dishes to be prepar'd for us at different times, in all which there was neither Fish Flesh nor Fowl, and the whim suited me the better at this time from the Cheapness of it, not costing us about 18*d.* Sterling each, per Week. I have since kept several Lents most strictly, Leaving the common Diet for that, and that for the common, abruptly, without the least Inconvenience: So that I think there is little in the Advice of making those Changes by easy Gradations, I went on pleasantly, but poor Keimer suffer'd grievously, tir'd of the Project, long'd for the Flesh Pots of Egypt,[66] and order'd a

[64]Puzzling questions.

[65]"Ye shall not round the corners of your heads, neither shall thou mar the corners of thy beard" (Leviticus 19:27).

[66]"And the whole congregation of the children of Israel murmured against Moses and Aaron in the wilderness: and the children of Israel said unto them, Would to God that we had died by the hands of the Lord in the land of Egypt, when we sat by the flesh pots, and when we did eat bread to the full" (Exodus 16:2,3).

roast Pig. He invited me and two Women Friends to dine with him, but it being brought too soon upon table, he could not resist the Temptation, and ate it all up before we came.

I had made some Courtship during this time to Miss Read. I had a great Respect and Affection for her, and had some Reason to believe she had the same for me: but as I was about to take a long Voyage, and we were both very young, only a little above 18. it was thought most prudent by her Mother to prevent our going too far at present, as a Marriage if it was to take place would be more convenient after my Return, when I should be as I expected set up in my Business. Perhaps too she thought my Expectations not so wellfounded as I imagined them to be.

My chief Acquaintances at this time were, Charles Osborne, Joseph Watson, and James Ralph; All Lovers of Reading. The two first were Clerks to an eminent Scrivener or Conveyancer[67] in the Town, Charles Brogden;[68] the other was Clerk to a Merchant. Watson was a pious sensible young Man, of great Integrity. The others rather more lax in their Principles of Religion, particularly Ralph, who as well as Collins had been unsettled by me, for which they both made me suffer. Osborne was sensible, candid, frank, sincere, and affectionate to his Friends; but in litterary Matters too fond of Criticising. Ralph, was ingenious, genteel in his Manners, and extremely eloquent; I think I never knew a prettier Talker. Both of them great Admirers of Poetry, and began to try their Hands in little Pieces. Many pleasant Walks we four had together on Sundays into the Woods near Skuylkill,[69] where we read to one another and conferr'd on what we read.

Ralph was inclin'd to pursue the Study of Poetry, not doubting but he might become eminent in it and make his Fortune by it, alledging that the best Poets must when they first begin to write, make as many Faults as he did. Osborne dissuaded him, assur'd him he had no Genius for Poetry, and advis'd him to think of nothing beyond the Business he was bred to; that in the mercantile way tho' he had no Stock, he might by his Diligence and Punctuality recommend himself to Employment as a Factor,[70] and in time acquire wherewith to trade on his own Account. I approv'd the amusing one's self with Poetry now and then, so far as to improve one's Language, but no farther. On this it was propos'd that we should each of us at our next Meeting produce a Piece of our own Composing, in order to improve by our mutual Observations, Criticisms and Corrections. As Language and Expression was what we had in View, we excluded all Considerations of Invention, by agreeing that the Task should be a version of the 18th Psalm, which describes the Descent of a Deity. When the Time of our Meeting drew nigh, Ralph call'd on me first, and let me know his Piece was ready. I told him I had been busy, and having little Inclination had done nothing. He then show'd me his Piece for my Opinion; and I much approv'd it, as it appear'd to me to have great Merit. Now, says he, Osborne never will allow the least Merit in any thing of mine, but makes 1000 Criticisms out of mere Envy. He is not so jealous of you. I wish therefore you would take this Piece, and produce it as yours. I will pretend not to have had time, and so produce nothing: We shall then see what he will say to it. It was agreed, and I immediately transcib'd it that it might appear in

[67]One who draws up leases and deeds to property.

[68]Chalres Brockden (1683–1769).

[69]Schuylkill River in Philadelphia.

[70]Business agent.

my own hand. We met. Watson's Performance was read: there were some Beauties in it: but many Defects. Osborne's was read: It was much better. Ralph did it Justice, remark'd some Faults, but applauded the Beauties. He himself had nothing to produce. I was backward, seem'd desirous of being excus'd, had not had sufficient Time to correct; &c. but no Excuse could be admitted, produce I must. It was read and repeated; Watson and Osborne gave up the Contest; and join'd in applauding it immoderately. Ralph only made some Criticisms and propos'd some Amendments, but I defended my Text. Osborne was against Ralph, and told him he was no better a Critic than Poet; so he dropt the Argument. As they two went home together, Osborne express'd himself still more strongly in favour of what he thought my Production, having restrain'd himself before as he said, lest I should think it Flattery. But who would have imagin'd, says he, that Franklin had been capable of such a Performance; such Painting, such Force! such Fire! he has even improv'd the Original! In his common Conversation, he seems to have no Choice of Words; he hesitates and blunders; and yet, good God, how he writes! When we next met, Ralph discover'd the Trick, we had plaid him, and Osborne was a little laught at. This Transaction fix'd Ralph in his Resolution of becoming a Poet. I did all I could to dissuade him from it, but He continued scribbling Verses, till Pope cur'd him.[71] He became however a pretty good Prose Writer. More of him hereafter.

But as I may not have occasion again to mention the other two, I shall just remark here, that Watson died in my Arms a few Years after, much lamented, being the best of our Set. Osborne went to the West Indies, where he became an eminent Lawyer and made Money, but died young. He and I had made a serious Agreement, that the one who happen'd first to die, should if possible make a friendly Visit to the other, and acquaint him how he found things in that Separate State. But he never fulfill'd his Promise.

The Governor, seeming to like my Company, had me frequently to his House; and his Setting me up was always mention'd as a fix'd thing. I was to take with me Letters recommendatory to a Number of his Friends, besides the Letter of Credit to furnish me with the necessary Money for purchasing the Press and Types, Paper, &c. For these Letters I was appointed to call at different times, when they were to be ready, but a future time was still named. Thus we went on till the Ship whose Departure too had been several times postponed was on the Point of sailing. Then when I call'd to take my Leave and Receive the Letters, his Secretary, Dr. Bard,[72] came out to me and said the Governor was extreamly busy, in writing, but would be down at Newcastle[73] before the Ship, and there the Letters would be delivered to me.

Ralph, tho' married and having one Child, had determined to accompany me in this Voyage. It was thought he intended to establish a Correspondence, and obtain Goods to sell on Commission. But I found afterwards, that thro' some Discontent with his Wifes Relations, he purposed to leave her on their Hands, and never return again. Having taken leave of my Friends, and interchang'd some Promises with Miss Read, I left Philadelphia in the Ship, which anchor'd at Newcastle. The Governor

[71]Ralph defended some writers attacked by Alexander Pope in the first edition of the *Dunciad* (1728). Pope responded in *Sawney* with the couplet: "Silence, ye Wolves! while Ralph to Cynthia howls,/And makes Night hideous—Answer him ye Owls." III, 159–60.

[72]Patrick Baird, a surgeon.

[73]Delaware.

was there. But when I went to his Lodging, the Secretary came to me from him with the civillest Message in the World, that he could not then see me being engag'd in Business of the utmost Importance; but should send the Letters to me on board, wish'd me heartily a good Voyage and a speedy Return, &c. I return'd on board, a little puzzled, but still not doubting.

Mr. Andrew Hamilton,[74] a famous Lawyer of Philadelphia, had taken Passage in the same Ship for himself and Son: and with Mr. Denham a Quaker Merchant, and Messrs. Onion and Russel Masters of an Iron Work in Maryland, had engag'd the Great Cabin; so that Ralph and I were forc'd to take up with a Birth in the Steerage: And none on board knowing us, were considered as ordinary Persons. But Mr. Hamilton and his Son (it was James, since Governor[75]) return'd from New Castle to Philadelphia, the Father being recall'd by a great Fee to plead for a seized Ship. And just before we sail'd Col. French coming on board, and showing me great Respect, I was more taken Notice of, and with my Friend Ralph invited by the other Gentlemen to come into the Cabin, there being now Room. Accordingly we remov'd thither.

Understanding that Col. French had brought on board the Governor's Dispatches, I ask'd the Captain for those Letters that were to be under my Care. He said all were put into the Bag together; and he could not then come at them; but before we landed in England, I should have an Opportunity of picking them out. So I was satisfy'd for the present, and we proceeded on our Voyage. We had a sociable Company in the Cabin, and lived uncommonly well, having the Addition of all Mr. Hamilton's Stores, who had laid in plentifully. In this Passage Mr. Denham[76] contracted a Friendship for me that continued during his life. The Voyage was otherwise not a pleasant one, as we had a great deal of bad Weather.

When we came into the Channel, the Captain kept his Word with me, and gave me an Opportunity of examining the Bag for the Governor's Letters. I found none upon which my Name was put, as under my Care; I pick'd out 6 or 7 that by the Hand writing I thought might be the promis'd Letters, especially as one of them was directed to Basket the King's Printer,[77] and another to some Stationer. We arriv'd in London the 24th of December, 1724. I waited upon the stationer who came first in my Way, delivering the Letter as from Gov. Keith. I don't know such a Person, says he: but opening the Letter, O, this is from Riddlesden;[78] I have lately found him to be a compleat Rascal, and I will have nothing to do with him, nor receive any Letters from him. So putting the Letter into my Hand, he turn'd on his Heel and left me to serve some Customer. I was surprized to find these were not the Governor's Letters. And after recollecting and comparing Circumstances, I began to doubt his Sincerity. I found my Friend Denham, and opened the whole Affair to him. He let me into Keith's Character, told me there was not the least Probability that he had written any Letters for me, that no one who knew him had the smallest Dependance on him, and he laught at the Notion of the Governor's giving me a Letter of Credit, having as he

[74]Andrew Hamilton (c. 1678–1741).

[75]James Hamilton (c. 1710–1783), governor of Pennsylvania four times between 1748 and 1773.

[76]Thomas Denham (d. 1728), Philadelphia merchant and Franklin's benefactor.

[77]John Baskett (d. 1742).

[78]William Riddlesden (d. before 1733), a swindler known in Maryland as "a Person of matchless Character in Infamy."

said no Credit to give. On my expressing some Concern about what I should do: He advis'd me to endeavour getting some Employment in the Way of my Business. Among the Printers here, says he, you will improve yourself; and when you return to America, you will set up to greater Advantage.

We both of us happen'd to know, as well as the Stationer, that Riddlesden the Attorney, was a very Knave. He had half ruin'd Miss Read's Father by drawing him in to be bound for him. By his Letter it appear'd, there was a secret Scheme on the foot to the Prejudice of Hamilton, (Suppos'd to be then coming over with us,) and that Keith was concern'd in it with Riddlesden. Denham, who was a Friend of Hamilton's, thought he ought to be acquainted with it. So when he arriv'd in England, which was soon after, partly from Resentment and Ill-Will to Keith and Riddlesden, and partly from Good Will to him: I waited on him, and gave him the Letter. He thank'd me cordially, the Information being of Importance to him. And from that time he became my Friend, greatly to my Advantage afterwards on many Occasions.

But what shall we think of a Governor's playing such pitiful Tricks, and imposing so grossly on a poor ignorant Boy! It was a Habit he had acquired. He wish'd to please every body; and having little to give, he gave Expectations. He was otherwise an ingenious sensible Man, a pretty good Writer, and a good Governor for the People, tho' not for his Constituents the Proprietaries,[79] whose Instructions he sometimes disregarded. Several of our best Laws were of his Planning, and pass'd during his Administration.

Ralph and I were inseparable Companions. We took Lodgings together in Little Britain[80] at 3*s.* 6*d.* per Week, as much as we could then afford. He found some Relations, but they were poor and unable to assist him. He now let me know his Intentions of remaining in London, and that he never meant to return to Philadelphia. He had brought no Money with him, the whole he could muster having been expended in paying his Passage. I had 15 Pistoles:[81] So he borrowed occasionally of me, to subsist while he was looking out for Business. He first endeavoured to get into the Playhouse, believing himself qualify'd for an Actor; but Wilkes,[82] to whom he apply'd, advis'd him candidly not to think of that Employment, as it was impossible he should succeed in it. Then he propos'd to Roberts, a Publisher in Pasternoster Row,[83] to write for him a Weekly Paper like the Spectator, on certain Conditions, which Roberts did not approve. Then he endeavour'd to get Employment as a Hackney Writer[84] to copy for the Stationers and Lawyers about the Temple:[85] but could find no Vacancy.

I immediately got into Work at Palmer's then a famous Printing House in Bartholomew Close;[86] and here I continu'd near a Year. I was pretty diligent; but spent with Ralph a good deal of my Earnings in going to Plays and other Places of Amusement. We had together consum'd all my Pistoles, and now just rubb'd on from hand to mouth. He seem'd quite to forget his Wife and Child, and I by degrees

[79]The Penn family, proprietors of Pennsylvania.
[80]A London street near St. Paul's Cathedral.
[81]Spanish gold coins, each worth eighteen English shillings.
[82]Robert Wilks (1665?–1732), London actor.
[83]Center of the printing business.
[84]A copyist.
[85]The Inner and the Middle Temples were two of the four sets of buildings that were London's center for the legal profession.
[86]A small square in London, a center for printers.

my Engagements with Miss Read, to whom I never wrote more than one Letter, and that was to let her know I was not likely soon to return. This was another of the great Errata of my Life, which I should wish to correct if I were to live it over again. In fact, by our Expences, I was constantly kept unable to pay my Passage.

At Palmer's I was employ'd in composing for the second Edition of Woollaston's Religion of Nature.[87] Some of his Reasonings not appearing to me well-founded, I wrote a little metaphysical Piece, in which I made Remarks on them, It was entitled, *A Dissertation on Liberty and Necessity, Pleasure and Pain.* I inscrib'd it to my Friend Ralph. I printed a small Number. It occasion'd my being more consider'd by Mr. Palmer, as a young Man of some Ingenuity, tho' he seriously expostulated with me upon the Principles of my Pamphlet which to him appear'd abominable. My printing this Pamphlet was another Erratum.[88]

While I lodg'd in Little Britain I made an Acquaintance with one Wilcox a Bookseller, whose Shop was at the next Door. He had an immense Collection of second-hand Books. Circulating Libraries were not then in Use; but we agreed that on certain reasonable Terms which I have now forgotten, I might take, read and return any of his Books. This I esteem'd a great Advantage, and I made as much use of it as I could.

My Pamphlet by some means falling into the Hands of one Lyons, a Surgeon, Author of a Book intituled *The Infallibility of Human Judgment,* it occasioned an Acquaintance between us; he took great Notice of me, call'd on me often, to converse on those Subjects, carried me to the Horns a pale Ale-House in [blank] Lane, Cheapside, and introduc'd me to Dr. Mandevile, Author of the Fable of the Bees[89] who had a Club there, of which he was the Soul, being a most facetious entertaining Companion. Lyons too introduc'd me, to Dr. Pemberton, at Batson's Coffee House, who promis'd to give me an Opportunity some time or other of seeing Sir Isaac Newton, of which I was extremely desirous; but this never happened.

I had brought over a few Curiosities among which the principal was a Purse made of the Asbestos, which purifies by Fire. Sir Hans Sloane[90] heard of it, came to see me, and invited me to his House in Bloomsbury Square, where he show'd me all his Curiosities, and persuaded me to let him add to the Number, for which he paid me handsomely.

In our House there lodg'd a young Woman; a Millener, who I think had a Shop in the Cloisters.[91] She had been genteelly bred, was sensible and lively, and of most pleasing Conversation. Ralph read Plays to her in the Evenings, they grew intimate, she took another Lodging, and he follow'd her. They liv'd together some time, but he being still out of Business, and her Income not sufficient to maintain them with her Child, he took a Resolution of going from London, to try for a Country School, which he thought himself well qualify'd to undertake, as he wrote an excellent Hand, and was a Master of Arithmetic and Accounts. This however he deem'd a Business

[87]Actually the third edition (1725) of *The Religion of Nature Delineated* (1722) by William Wollaston.

[88]The pamphlet (1725) denied the existence of vice and virtue, laying Franklin open to charges of atheism.

[89]Bernard Mandeville's *The Fable of the Bees, or Private Vices Public Benefits* was published in 1714.

[90]Hans Sloane (1660–1753) succeeded Newton as president of the Royal Society.

[91]Near St. Bartholomew's Church.

below him, and confident of future better Fortune when he should be unwilling to have it known that he once was so meanly employ'd, he chang'd his Name, and did me the Honour to assume mine. For I soon after had a Letter from him, acquainting me, that he was settled in a small Village in Berkshire, I think it was, where he taught reading and writing to 10 or a dozen Boys at 6 pence each per Week, recommending Mrs. T. to my Care, and desiring me to write to him directing for Mr. Franklin Schoolmaster at such a Place. He continu'd to write frequently, sending me large Specimens of an Epic Poem, which he was then composing, and desiring my Remarks and Corrections. These I gave him from time to time, but endeavour'd rather to discourage his Proceeding. One of Young's Satires was then just publish'd. I copy'd and sent him a great Part of it, which set in a strong Light the Folly of pursuing the Muses with any Hope of Advancement by them. All was in vain. Sheets of the Poem continu'd to come by every Post. In the mean time Mrs. T. having on his Account lost her Friends and Business, was often in Distress, and us'd to send for me, and borrow what I could spare to help her out of them. I grew fond of her Company, and being at this time under no Religious Restraints, and presuming on my Importance to her, I attempted Familiarities (another Erratum) which she repuls'd with a proper Resentment, and acquainted him with my Behaviour. This made a Breach between us, and when he return'd again to London, he let me know he thought I had cancel'd all the Obligations he had been under to me. So I found I was never to expect his Repaying me what I lent to him or advance'd for him. This was however not then of much Consequence, as he was totally unable. And in the Loss of his Friendship I found my self reliev'd from a Burthen. I now began to think of getting a little Money beforehand; and expecting better Work, I left Palmer's to work at Watt's[92] near Lincoln's Inn Fields, a still greater Printing House. Here I continu'd all the rest of my Stay in London.

At my first Admission into this Printing House, I took to working at Press, imagining I felt a Want of the Bodily Exercise I had been us'd to in America, where Presswork is mix'd with Composing. I drank only Water; the other Workmen, nearly 50 in Number, were great Guzzlers of Beer. On occasion I carried up and down Stairs a large Form of Types in each hand, when others carried but one in both Hands. They wonder'd to see from this and several Instances that the Water-American as they call'd me was *stronger* than themselves who drank *strong* Beer. We had an Alehouse Boy who attended always in the House to supply the Workmen. My Companion at the Press, drank every day a Pint before Breakfast, a Pint at Breakfast with his Bread and Cheese; a Pint between Breakfast and Dinner; a Pint at Dinner; a Pint in the Afternoon about Six o'Clock, and another when he had done his Day's-Work. I thought it a detestable Custom. But it was necessary, he suppos'd, to drink *strong* Beer that he might be *strong* to labour. I endeavour'd to convince him that the Bodily Strength afforded by Beer could only be in proportion to the Grain or Flour of the Barley dissolved in the Water of which it was made; that there was more Flour in a Penny-worth of Bread, and therefore if he would eat that with a Pint of Water, it would give him more Strength than a Quart of Beer. He drank on however, and had 4 or 5 Shillings to pay out of his Wages every Saturday Night for that muddling

[92]John Watts (c. 1678–1763).

Liquor; an Expence I was free from. And thus these poor Devils keep themselves always under.

Watts after some Weeks desiring to have me in the Composing Room, I left the Pressmen. A new *Bienvenu*[93] or sum for drink being 5*s.,* was demanded of me by the Compositors. I thought it an Imposition, as I had paid below. The Master thought so too, and forbad my Paying it. I stood out two or three Weeks, was accordingly considered as an Excommunicate, and had so many little Pieces of private Mischief done me, by mixing my Sorts,[94] transposing my Pages, breaking my Matter,[95] &c. &c. if I were ever so little out of the Room, and all ascrib'd to the Chapel Ghost, which they said ever hunted those not regularly admitted, that notwithstanding the Master's Protection, I found myself oblig'd to comply and pay the Money; convinc'd of the Folly of being on ill Terms with those one is to live with continually. I was now on a fair Footing with them, and soon acquir'd considerable influence. I propos'd some reasonable Alterations in their Chapel[96] Laws, and carried them against all Opposition. From my Example a great Part of them, left their muddling Breakfast of Beer and Bread and Cheese, finding they could with me be supply'd from a neighbouring House with a large Porringer of hot Water-gruel, sprinkled with Pepper, crumb'd with Bread, and a Bit of Butter in it, for the Price of a Pint of Beer, viz, three halfpence. This was a more confortable as well as cheaper Breakfast, and kept their Heads clearer. Those who continu'd sotting with Beer all day, were often, by not paying, out of Credit at the Alehouse, and us'd to make Interest with me to get Beer, *their Light,* as they phras'd it, *being out.* I watch'd the Pay table on Saturday Night, and collected what I stood engag'd for them, having to pay some times near Thirty Shillings a Week on their Accounts. This, and my being esteem'd a pretty good Riggite, that is a jocular verbal Satyrist, supported my Consequence in the Society. My constant Attendance, (I never making a St. Monday),[97] recommended me to the Master; and my uncommon Quickness at Composing, occasion'd my being put upon all Work of Dispatch which was generally better paid. So I went on now very agreably.

My Lodging in Little Britain being too remote, I found another in Dukestreet opposite to the Romish Chapel. It was two pair of Stairs backwards at an Italian Warehouse. A Widow Lady kept the House; she had a Daughter and a Maid Servant, and a Journeyman who attended the Warehouse, but lodg'd abroad. After sending to enquire my Character at the House where I last lodg'd, she agreed to take me in at the same Rate, 3*s.* 6*d.* per Week, cheaper as she said from the Protection she expected in having a Man lodge in the House. She was a Widow, an elderly Woman, had been bred a Protestant, being a Clergyman's Daughter, but was converted to the Catholic Religion by her Husband, whose Memory she much revered, had lived much among People of Distinction, and knew a 1000 Anecdotes of them as far back as the Times of Charles the Second. She was lame in her Knees with the Gout, and therefore seldom stirr'd out of her Room, so sometimes wanted Company; and hers

[93]French: Welcome.
[94]Type characters or letters.
[95]Type set up for printing.
[96]"A Printing House is always called a Chappel by the Workmen." [Franklin's note].
[97]*I.e.,* never taking off Monday as a day of religious observance.

was so highly amusing to me; that I was sure to spend an Evening with her whenever she desired it. Our Supper was only half an Anchovy each, on a very little Strip of Bread and Butter, and half a Pint of Ale between us. But the Entertainment was in her Conversation. My always keeping good Hours, and giving little Trouble in the Family, made her unwilling to part with me; so that when I talk'd of a lodging I had heard of, nearer my Business, for 2*s.* a Week, which intent as I now was on saving Money, made some Difference; she bid me not think of it, for she would abate me two Shillings a Week for the future, so I remain'd with her at 1*s.* 6*d.* as long as I staid in London.

In a Garret of her House there lived a Maiden Lady of 70 in the most retired Manner, of whom my Landlady gave me this Account, that she was a Roman Catholic, had been sent abroad when young and lodg'd in a Nunnery with an Intent of becoming a Nun: but the Country not agreeing with her, she return'd to England, where there being no Nunnery, she had vow'd to lead the Life of a Nun as near as might be done in those Circumstances: Accordingly she had given all her Estate to charitable uses, reserving only Twelve Pounds a Year to live on, and out of this Sum she still gave a great deal in Charity, living her self on Water-gruel only, and using no Fire but to boil it. She had lived many Years in that Garret, being permitted to remain there gratis by successive Catholic Tenants of the House below, as they deem'd it a Blessing to have her there. A Priest visited her, to confess her every Day. I have ask'd her, says my Landlady, how she, as she liv'd, could possibly find so much Employment for a Confessor? O, says she, it is impossible to avoid *vain Thoughts*. I was permitted once to visit her: She was chearful and polite, and convers'd pleasantly. The Room was clean, but had no other Furniture than a Matras, a Table with a Crucifix and Book, a Stool which she gave me to sit on, and a Picture over the Chimney of St. Veronica, displaying her Handkerchief with the miraculous Figure of Christ's bleeding Face on it, which she explain'd to me with great Seriousness. She look'd pale, but was never sick, and I give it as another Instance on how small an Income Life and Health may be supported.

At Watts's Printinghouse I contracted an Acquaintance with an ingenious young Man, one Wygate, who having wealthy Relations, had been better educated than most Printers, was a tolerable Latinist, spoke French, and lov'd Reading. I taught him, and a Friend of his, to swim, at twice going into the River, and they soon became good Swimmers. They introduc'd me to some Gentlemen from the Country who went to Chelsea by Water to see the College[98] and Don Saltero's Curiosities.[99] In our Return, at the Request of the Company, whose Curiosity Wygate had excited, I stript and leapt into the River, and swam from near Chelsea to Blackfryars,[100] performing on the Way many Feats of Activity both upon and under Water, that surpriz'd and pleas'd those to whom they were Novelties. I had from a Child been ever delighted with this Exercise, had studied and practis'd all Thevenot's Motions and Positions,[101] added some of my own, aiming at the graceful and easy, as well as the

[98]Chelsea Hospital, erected on the site of the former Chelsea College.

[99]James Salter exhibited various curiosities of doubtful authenticity, including the sword of William the Conqueror and the tears of Job.

[100]Three and one half miles.

[101]Melchisédec de Thévenot, *The Art of Swimming* (1699).

Useful. All these I took this Occasion of exhibiting to the Company, and was much flatter'd by their Admiration. And Wygate, who was desirous of becoming a Master, grew more and more attach'd to me, on that account, as well as from the Similarity of our Studies. He at length propos'd to me travelling all over Europe together, supporting ourselves everywhere by working at our Business. I was once inclin'd to it. But mentioning it to my good Friend Mr. Denham, with whom I often spent an Hour, when I had Leisure. He dissuaded me from it, advising me to think only of returning to Pensilvania, which he was now about to do.

I must record one Trait of this good Man's Character. He had formerly been in Business at Bristol, but fail'd in Debt to a Number of People, compounded[102] and went to America. There, by a close Application to Business as a Merchant, he acquir'd a plentiful Fortune in a few Years. Returning to England in the Ship with me, He invited his old Creditors to an Entertainment, at which he thank'd them for the easy Composition they had favor'd him with, and when they expected nothing but the Treat, every Man at the first Remove,[103] found under his Plate an Order on a Banker for the full Amount of the unpaid Remainder with Interest.

He now told me he was about to return to Philadelphia, and should carry over a great Quantity of Goods in order to open a Store there: He propos'd to take me over as his Clerk, to keep his Books (in which he would instruct me) copy his Letters, and attend the Store. He added, that as soon as I should be acquainted with mercantile Business he would promote me by sending me with a Cargo of Flour and Bread &c. to the West Indies, and procure me Commissions from others; which would be profitable, and if I manag'd well, would establish me handsomely. The Thing pleas'd me, for I was grown tired of London, remember'd with Pleasure the happy Months I had spent in Pennsylvania, and wish'd again to see it. Therefore I immediately agreed, on the Terms of Fifty Pounds a Year, Pennsylvania Money; less indeed than my present Gettings as a Compostor, but affording a better Prospect.

I now took Leave of Printing, as I thought for ever, and was daily employ'd in my new Business; going about with Mr. Denham among the Tradesmen, to purchase various Articles, and seeing them pack'd up, doing Errands, calling upon Workmen to dispatch, &c. and when all was on board, I had a few Days Leisure. On one of these Days I was to my Surprize sent for by a great Man I knew only by Name, a Sir William Wyndham[104] and I waited upon him. He had heard by some means or other of my Swimming from Chelsey to Blackfryars, and of my teaching Wygate and another young Man to swim in a few Hours. He had two Sons about to set out on their Travels; he wish'd to have them first taught Swimming; and propos'd to gratify me handsomely if I would teach them. They were not yet come to Town and my Stay was uncertain, so I could not undertake it. But from this Incident I thought it likely, that if I were to remain in England and open a Swimming School, I might get a good deal of Money. And it struck me so strongly, that had the Overture been sooner made me, probably I should not so soon have returned to America. After many Years, you and I had something of more Importance to do with one of these Sons of Sir William Wyndham, become Earl of Egremont, which I shall mention in its Place.

[102]Partially settled his debts.
[103]First clearing of the plates.
[104]Sir William Wyndham (1687–1740), English politician.

Thus I spent about 18 months in London. Most Part of the Time, I work'd hard at my Business, and spent but little upon my self except in seeing Plays and in Books. My friend Ralph had kept me poor. He owed me about 27 Pounds; which I was now never likely to receive; a great Sum out of my small Earnings. I lov'd him notwithstanding, for he had many amiable Qualities. Tho' I had by no means improv'd my Fortune. But I had pick'd up some very ingenious Acquaintance whose Conversation was of great Advantage to me, and I had read considerably.

We sail'd from Gravesend on the 23rd of July 1726. For the Incidents of the Voyage, I refer you to my Journal, where you will find them all minutely related. Perhaps the most important Part of that Journal is the *Plan*[105] to be found in it which I formed at Sea, for regulating my future Conduct in Life. It is the more remarkable, as being form'd when I was so young, and yet being pretty faithfully adhered to quite thro' to old Age. We landed in Philadelphia the 11th of October, where I found sundry Alterations. Keith was no longer Governor, being superceded by Major Gordon:[106] I met him walking the Streets as a common Citizen. He seem'd a little asham'd at seeing me, but pass'd without saying any thing. I should have been as much asham'd at seeing Miss Read, had not her Friends, despairing with Reason of my Return, after the Receipt of my Letter, persuaded her to marry another, one Rogers, a Potter, which was done in my Absence. With him however she was never happy, and soon parted from him, refusing to cohabit with him, or bear his Name It being now said that he had another Wife. He was a worthless Fellow tho' an excellent Workman which was the Temptation to her Friends. He got into Debt, and ran away in 1727 or 28. Went to the West Indies, and died there. Keimer had got a better House, a Shop well supply'd with Stationary, plenty of new Types, a number of Hands tho' none good, and seem'd to have a great deal of Business.

Mr. Denham took a Store in Water Street, where we open'd our Goods. I attended the Business diligently, studied Accounts, and grew in a little Time expert at selling. We lodg'd and boarded together, he counsell'd me as a Father, having a sincere Regard for me: I respected and lov'd him: and we might have gone on together very happily: But in the Beginning of Feby. 1726/7 when I had just pass'd my 21st Year, we both were taken ill. My Distemper was a Pleurisy, which very nearly carried me off: I suffered a good deal, gave up the Point[107] in my own mind, and was rather disappointed when I found my Self recovering; regretting in some degree that I must now some time or other have all that disagreable Work to do over again. I forget what his Distemper was. It held him a long time, and at length carried him off. He left me a small Legacy in a nuncupative Will,[108] as a Token of his Kindness for me, and he left me once more to the wide World. For the Store was taken into the Care of his Executors, and my Employment under him ended: My Brother-in-law Holmes, being now at Philadelphia, advis'd my Return to my Business. And Keimer tempted me with an Offer of large Wages by the Year to come and take the Management of his Printing-House, that he might better attend his Stationer's Shop. I had heard a bad Character of him in London, from his Wife and her Friends, and was not fond of

[105]The full text of the "Plan" is lost.
[106]Patrick Gordon (1644–1736), Governor of Pennsylvania, 1726–1736.
[107]Will to live.
[108]An oral will.

having any more to do with him. I try'd for farther Employment as a Merchant's Clerk; but not readily meeting with any, I clos'd again with Keimer.

I found in *his* House these Hands; Hugh Meredith[109] a Welsh-Pensilvanian, 30 Years of Age, bred to Country Work: honest, sensible, had a great deal of solid Observation, was something of a Reader, but given to drink: Stephen Potts,[110] a young Country Man of full Age, bred to the Same: of uncommon natural Parts, and great Wit and Humour, but a little idle. These he had agreed with at extream low Wages, per Week, to be rais'd a Shilling every 3 Months, as they would deserve by improving in their Business, and the Expectation of these high Wages to come on hereafter was what he had drawn them in with. Meredith was to work at Press, Potts at Bookbinding, which he by Agreement, was to teach them, tho' he knew neither one nor t'other. John—a wild Irishman brought up to no Business, whose Service for 4 Years Keimer had purchas'd from the Captain of a Ship. He too was to be made a Pressman. George Webb,[111] an Oxford Scholar, whose Time for 4 Years he had likewise bought intending him for a Compositor: of whom more presently. And David Harry,[112] a Country Boy, whom he had taken Apprentice. I soon perceiv'd that the Intention of engaging me at Wages so much higher than he had been us'd to give, was to have these raw cheap Hands form'd thro' me, and as soon as I had instructed them, then, they being all articled to him, he should be able to do without me. I went on however, very chearfully; put his Printing House in Order, which had been in great Confusion, and brought his Hands by degrees to mind their Business and to do it better.

It was an odd Thing to find an Oxford Scholar in the Situation of a bought Servant. He was not more than 18 Years of Age, and gave me this Account of himself; that he was born in Gloucester, educated at a Grammar School there, had been distinguish'd among the Scholars for some apparent Superiority in performing his Part when they exhibited Plays; belong'd to the Witty Club there, and had written some Pieces in Prose and Verse which were printed in the Gloucester Newspapers. Thence he was sent to Oxford; there he continu'd about a Year, but not well-satisfy'd, wishing of all things to see London and become a Player. At length receiving his Quarterly allowance of 15 Guineas, instead of discharging his Debts, he walk'd out of Town, hid his Gown in a Furz Bush,[113] and footed it to London, where having no Friend to advise him, he fell into bad Company, soon spent his Guineas, found no means of being introduc'd among the Players, grew necessitous, pawn'd his Cloaths and wanted Bread. Walking the Street very hungry, and not knowing what to do with himself, a Crimp's Bill[114] was put into his Hand, offering immediate Entertainment and Encouragement to such as would bind themselves to serve in America. He went directly, sign'd the Indentures, was put into the Ship and came over; never writing a Line to acquaint his Friends what was become of him. He was lively, witty,

[109]Hugh Meredith (c. 1696–c. 1749), later Franklin's business partner.

[110]Stephen Potts (d. 1758), bookseller and tavern keeper.

[111]George Webb (b. c. 1709), a printer.

[112]David Harry (1708–1760), later first printer in Barbados.

[113]He hid his academic robe in an evergreen bush.

[114]An advertisement for free passage to the colonies in exchange for labor.

goodnatur'd, and a pleasant Companion, but idle, thoughtless and imprudent to the last Degree.

John the Irishman soon ran away. With the rest I began to live very agreeably; for they all respected me, the more as they found Keimer incapable of instructing them, and that from me they learnt something daily. We never work'd on a Saturday, that being Keimer's Sabbath. So I had two Days for Reading. My Acquaintance with Ingenious People in the Town, increased. Keimer himself treated me with great Civility, and apparent Regard; and nothing now made me uneasy but my Debt to Vernon, which I was yet unable to pay being hitherto but a poor Oeconomist. He however kindly made no Demand of it.

Our Printing-House often wanted Sorts, and there was no Letter Founder in America. I had seen Types cast at James's in London,[115] but without much Attention to the Manner: However I now contriv'd a Mould, made use of the Letters we had, as Puncheons,[116] struck the Matrices[117] in Lead, and thus supply'd in a pretty tolerable way all Deficiencies. I also engrav'd several Things on occasion. I made the Ink, I was Warehouse-man and every thing, in short quite a Factotum.[118]

But however serviceable I might be, I found that my Services became every Day of less Importance, as the other Hands improv'd in the Business. And when Keimer paid my second Quarter's Wages, he let me know that he felt them too heavy, and thought I should make an Abatement. He grew by degrees less civil, put on more of the Master, frequently found Fault, was captious and seem'd ready for an Outbreaking. I went on nevertheless with a good deal of Patience, thinking that his incumber'd Circumstances were partly the Cause. At length a Trifle snapt our Connexion. For a great Noise happening near the Courthouse, I put my Head out of the Window to see what was the Matter. Keimer being in the Street look'd up and saw me, call'd out to me in a loud Voice and angry Tone to mind my Business, adding some reproachful Words, that nettled me the more for their Publicity, all the Neighbours who were looking out on the same Occasion being Witnesses how I was treated. He came up immediately into the Printing-House, continu'd the Quarrel, high Words pass'd on both Sides, he gave me the Quarter's Warning we had stipulated, expressing a Wish that he had not been oblig'd to so long a Warning: I told him his Wish was unnecessary for I would leave him that Instant; and so taking my Hat walk'd out of Doors; desiring Meredith[119] whom I saw below to take care of some Things I left, and bring them to my Lodging.

Meredith came accordingly in the Evening, when we talk'd my Affair over. He had conceiv'd a great Regard for me, and was very unwilling that I should leave the House while he remain'd in it. He dissuaded me from returning to my native Country which I began to think of. He reminded me that Keimer was in debt for all he possess'd, that his Creditors began to be uneasy, that he kept his Shop miserably, sold often without Profit for ready Money, and often trusted without keeping Accounts. That he must therefore fail; which would make a Vacancy I might profit of. I objected my Want of Money. He then let me know, that his Father had a high Opinion of me, and from some Discourse that had pass'd between them, he was sure would advance

[115]Thomas James's foundry, the largest in London.

[116]Stamping tools.

[117]Molds for casting type.

[118]Jack-of-all-trades.

[119]Simon Meredith (d. 1745?).

Money to set us up, if I would enter into Partnership with him. My Time, says he, will be out with Keimer in the Spring. By that time we may have our Press and Types in from London: I am sensible I am no Workman. If you like it, Your Skill in the Business shall be set against the Stock I furnish; and we will share the Profits equally. The Proposal was agreeable, and I consented. His Father was in Town, and approv'd of it, the more as he saw I had great Influence with his Son, had prevail'd on him to abstain long from Dramdrinking,[120] and he hop'd might break him of that wretched Habit entirely, when we came to be so closely connected. I gave an Inventory to the Father, who carry'd it to a Merchant; the Things were sent for; the Secret was to be kept till they should arrive, and in the mean time I was to get work if I could at the other Printing House. But I found no Vacancy there, and so remain'd idle a few Days, when Keimer, on a Prospect of being employ'd to print some Paper-money, in New Jersey, which would require Cuts and various Types that I only could supply, and apprehending Bradford might engage me and get the Jobb from him, sent me a very civil Message, that old Friends should not part for a few Words, the Effect of sudden Passion, and wishing me to return. Meredith persuaded me to comply, as it would give more Opportunity for his Improvement under my daily Instructions. So I return'd, and we went on more smoothly than from some time before. The New Jersey Jobb was obtain'd. I contriv'd a Copper-Plate Press for it, the first that had been seen in the Country. I cut several Ornaments and Checks for the Bills. We went together to Burlington, where I executed the Whole to Satisfaction, and he received so large a Sum for the Work, as to be enabled thereby to keep his Head much longer above Water.

At Burlington I made an Acquaintance with many principal People of the Province. Several of them had been appointed by the Assembly a Committee to attend the Press, and take Care that no more Bills were printed than the Law directed. They were therefore by Turns constantly with us, and generally he who attended brought with him a Friend or two for company. My Mind having been much more improv'd by Reading than Keimer's, I suppose it was for that Reason my Conversation seem'd to be more valu'd. They had me to their Houses, introduc'd me to their Friends and show'd me much Civility, while he, tho' the Master, was a little neglected. In truth he was an odd Fish, ignorant of common Life, fond of rudely opposing receiv'd Opinions, slovenly to extream dirtiness, enthusiastic in some Points of Religion, and a little Knavish withal. We continu'd there near 3 Months, and by that time I could reckon among my acquired Friends, Judge Allen, Samuel Bustill, the Secretary of the Province, Isaac Pearson, Joseph Cooper and several of the Smiths, Members of Assembly, and Isaac Decow the Surveyor General. The latter was a shrewd sagacious old Man, who told me that he began for himself when young by wheeling Clay for the Brickmakers, learnt to write after he was of Age, carry'd the Chain for Surveyors, who taught him Surveying, and he had now by his Industry acquir'd a good Estate; and says he, I foresee, that you will soon work this Man out of his Business and make a Fortune in it at Philadelphia. He had not then the least Intimation of my Intention to set up there or any where. These Friends were afterwards

[120] Drinking small measures of alcoholic beverages.

of great Use to me, as I occasionally was to some of them. They all continued their Regard for me as long as they lived.

Before I enter upon my public Appearance in Business it may be well to let you know the then State of my Mind, with regard to my Principles and Morals, that you may see how far those influenc'd the future Events of my Life. My Parents had early given me religious Impressions, and brought me through my Childhood piously in the Dissenting Way.[121] But I was scarce 15 when, after doubting by turns of several Points as I found them disputed in the different Books I read, I began to doubt of Revelation it self. Some Books against Deism fell into my Hands; they were said to be the Substance of Sermons preached at Boyle's Lectures.[122] It happened that they wrought an Effect on me quite contrary to what was intended by them: For the Arguments of the Deists which were quoted to be refuted, appeared to me much stronger than the Refutations. In short I soon became a thorough Deist. My Arguments perverted some others, particularly Collins and Ralph: but each of them having afterwards wrong'd me greatly without the least Compunction and recollecting Keith's Conduct towards me, (who was another Freethinker) and my own towards Vernon and Miss Read which at Times gave me great Trouble, I began to suspect that this Doctrine tho' it might be true, was not very useful. My London Pamphlet, which had for its Motto those Lines of Dryden

—Whatever is, is right.—
Tho' purblind Man.
Sees but a Part of the Chain, the nearest Link,
His Eyes not carrying to the equal Beam,
That poizes all, above.[123]

And from the Attributes of God, his infinite Wisdom, Goodness and Power concluded that nothing could possibly be wrong in the World, and that Vice and Virtue were empty Distinctions, no such Things existing: appear'd now not so clever a Performance as I once thought it; and I doubted whether some Error had not insinuated itself unperceiv'd into my Argument, so as to infect all that follow'd, as is common in metaphysical Reasonings. I grew convinc'd that *Truth, Sincerity and Integrity* in Dealings between Man and Man, were of the utmost Importance to the Felicity of Life, and I form'd written Resolutions, (which still remain in my Journal Book) to practice them ever while I lived. Revelation had indeed no weight with me as such; but I entertain'd an Opinion, that tho' certain Actions might not be bad *because* they were forbidden by it, or good *because* it commanded them; yet probably those Actions might be forbidden *because* they were bad for us, or commanded *because* they were beneficial to us, in their own Natures, all the Circumstances of things considered. And this Persuasion, with the kind hand of Providence, or some guardian Angel, or accidental favourable Circumstances and Situations, or all together, preserved me (thro' this dangerous Time of Youth and the hazardous

[121] As a Congregationalist, who dissents from the doctrines of the Church of England.

[122] Robert Boyle (1627–1691) established a series of lectures to defend Christianity against skeptics.

[123] The first line is not from John Dryden but from Pope's *Essay on Man* (1733), Epistle I, line 294. The rest is from Dryden's *Oedipus,* Act III, Scene i, lines 244–248.

Situations I was sometimes in among Strangers, remote from the Eye and Advice of my Father) without any *wilful* gross Immorality or Injustice that might have been expected from my Want of Religion. I say *wilful,* because the Instances I have mentioned, had something of *Necessity* in them, from my Youth, Inexperience, and the Knavery of others. I had therefore a tolerable Character to begin the World with, I valued it properly, and determin'd to preserve it.

We had not been long return'd to Philadelphia, before the New Types arriv'd from London. We settled with Keimer, and left him by his Consent before he heard of it. We found a House to hire near the Market, and took it. To lessen the Rent, (which was then but £24 a Year tho' I have since known it let for 70) We took in Tho' Godfrey a Glazier[124] and his Family, who were to pay a considerable Part of it to us, and we to board with them. We had scarce opened our Letters and put our Press in Order, before George House, an Acquaintance of Mine, brought a Country-man to us; whom he had met in the Street enquiring for a Printer. All our Cash was now expended in the Variety of Particulars we had been obliged to procure and this Countryman's Five Shillings being our first Fruits, and coming so seasonably, gave me more Pleasure than any Crown I have since earn'd; and from the Gratitude I felt towards House, has made me often more ready than perhaps I should otherwise have been to assist young Beginners.

There are Croakers in every Country always boding its Ruin. Such a one then lived in Philadelphia, a Person of Note, an elderly Man, with a wise Look, and very grave Manner of speaking. His Name was Samuel Mickle. This Gentleman, a Stranger to me, stopt one Day at my Door, and asked me if I was the young Man who had lately opened a new Printing House: Being answer'd in the Affirmative; he said he was sorry for me, because it was an expensive Undertaking and the Expence would be lost; for Philadelphia was a sinking Place, the People already half Bankrupts or near being so; all Appearances of the contrary, such as new Buildings and the Rise of Rents being to his certain Knowledge fallacious, for they were in fact among the Things that would soon ruin us. And he gave me such a Detail of Misfortunes, now existing or that were soon to exist, that he left me half-melancholy. Had I known him before I engag'd in this Business, probably I never should have done it. This Man continu'd to live in this decaying Place; and to declaim in the same Strain, refusing for many Years to buy a House there, because all was going to Destruction, and at last I had the Pleasure of seeing him give five times as much for one as he might have bought it for when he first began his Croaking.

I should have mention'd before, that in the Autumn of the preceding Year I had form'd most of my ingenious Acquaintance into a Club for mutual Improvement, which we call'd the Junto.[125] We met on Friday Evenings. The Rules I drew up requir'd that every Member in his Turn should produce one or more Queries on any Point of Morals, Politics or Natural Philosophy, to be discuss'd by the Company, and once in three Months produce and read an Essay of his own Writing on any Subject he pleased. Our Debates were to be under the Direction of a President, and to be conducted in the sincere Spirit of Enquiry after Truth, without Fondness for

[124]One who sets glass for windowpanes.

[125]A small, private, or secret group, from the Spanish word for "joined."

Dispute, or Desire of Victory; and to prevent Warmth all Expressions of Positiveness in Opinion, or of direct Contradiction, were after some time made contraband and prohibited under small pecuniary Penalties. The first Members were Joseph Brientnal, A Copyer of Deeds for the Scriveners; a good-natur'd friendly middle-ag'd Man, a great Lover of Poetry, reading all he could meet with, and writing some that was tolerable; very ingenious in many little Nicknackeries, and of sensible Conversation. Thomas Godfrey, a self-taught Mathematician, great in his Way, and afterwards Inventor of what is now call'd Hadley's Quadrant. But he knew little out of his way, and was not a pleasing Companion, as like most Great Mathematicians I have met with, he expected unusual Precision in every thing said, or was forever denying or distinguishing upon Trifles, to the Disturbance of all Conversation. He soon left us. Nicholas Scull, a Surveyor, afterwards Surveyor-General, Who lov'd Books, and sometimes made a few Verses. William Parsons, bred a Shoemaker, but loving Reading, had acquir'd a considerable Share of Mathematics, which he first studied with a View to Astrology that he afterwards laught at. He also became Surveyor General. William Maugridge, a Joiner, a most exquisite Mechanic and a solid sensible Man. Hugh Meredith, Stephen Potts, and George Webb, I have Characteris'd before. Robert Grace, a young Gentleman of some Fortune, generous, lively and witty, a Lover of Punning and of his Friends. And William Coleman, then a Merchant's Clerk, about my Age, who had the coolest clearest Head, the best Heart, and the exactest Morals, of almost any Man I ever met with. He became afterwards a Merchant of Great Note, and one of our Provincial Judges: Our Friendship continued without Interruption to his Death upwards of 40 Years.

And the club continu'd almost as long and was the best School of Philosophy, Morals and Politics that then existed in the Province; for our Queries which were read the Week preceding their Discussion, put us on Reading with Attention upon the several Subjects, that we might speak more to the purpose: and here too we acquired better Habits of Conversation, every thing being studied in our Rules which might prevent our disgusting each other. From hence the long Continuance of the Club, which I shall have frequent Occasion to speak farther of hereafter; But my giving this Account of it here, is to show something of the Interest I had, every one of these exerting themselves in recommending Business to us. Brientnal particularly procur'd us from the Quakers, the Printing 40 Sheets of their History, the rest being to be done by Keimer: and upon this we work'd exceeding hard, for the Price was low. It was a Folio, Pro Patria Size, in Pica[126] with Long Primer[127] Notes. I compos'd of it a Sheet a Day, and Meredith work'd it off at Press. It was often 11 at Night and sometimes later, before I had finish'd my Distribution for the next days Work: For the little Jobbs sent in by our other Friends now and then put us back. But so determin'd I was to continue doing a Sheet a Day of the Folio, that one Night when having impos'd my Forms, I thought my Days Work over, one of them by accident was broken and two Pages reduc'd to Pie,[128] I immediately distributed and compos'd it over again before I went to bed. And this Industry visible to our Neighbours began to give us Character and Credit; particularly I was told, that mention being made of the new Printing Office at the Merchants every-night-Club, the general Opinion was

[126]A large volume, set in 12-point type.
[127]10-point type.
[128]A messy pile.

that it must fail, there being already two Printers in the Place, Keimer and Bradford; but Doctor Baird (whom you and I saw many Years after at his native Place, St. Andrews in Scotland) gave a contrary Opinion; for the Industry of that Franklin, says he, is superior to any thing I ever saw of the kind: I see him still at work when I go home from Club; and he is at Work again before his Neighbours are out of bed. This struck the rest, and we soon after had Offers from one of them to Supply us with Stationary. But as yet we did not chuse to engage in Shop Business.

I mention this Industry the more particularly and the more freely, tho' it seems to be talking in my own Praise, that those of my Posterity who shall read it, may know the Use of that Virtue, when they see its Effects in my Favour throughout this Relation.

George Webb, who had found a Female Friend that lent him wherewith to purchase his Time of Keimer, now came to offer himself as a Journeyman to us. We could not then imploy him, but I foolishly let him know, as a Secret, that I soon intended to begin a Newspaper, and might then have Work for him. My Hopes of Success as I told him were founded on this, that the then only Newspaper,[129] printed by Bradford was a paltry thing, wretchedly manag'd, and no way entertaining; and yet was profitable to him. I therefore thought a good Paper could scarcely fail of good Encouragement. I requested Webb not to mention it, but he told it to Keimer, who immediately, to be beforehand with me, published Proposals for Printing one himself, on which Webb was to be employ'd. I resented this, and to counteract them, as I could not yet begin our Paper, I wrote several Pieces of Entertainment for Bradford's Paper, under the Title of the Busy Body which Brientnal continu'd some Months. By this means the Attention of the Publick was fix'd on that Paper, and Keimers Proposals which we burlesqu'd and ridicul'd, were disregarded. He began his Paper however, and after carrying it on three Quarters of a Year, with at most only 90 Subscribers, he offer'd it to me for a Trifle, and I having been ready some time to go on with it, took it in hand directly, and it prov'd in a few Years extreamly profitable to me.[130]

I perceive that I am apt to speak in the singular Number, though our Partnership still continu'd. The Reason may be, that in fact the whole Management of the Business lay upon me. Meredith was no Compositor, a poor Pressman, and seldom sober. My friends lamented my Connection with him, but I was to make the best of it.

Our first Papers made a quite different Appearance from any before in the Province, a better Type and better printed: but some spirited Remarks of my Writing on the Dispute then going on between Govr. Burnet[131] and the Massachusetts Assembly, struck the principal People, occasion'd by the Paper and the Manager of it to be much talk'd of, and in a few Weeks brought them all to be our Subscribers. Their Example was follow'd by many, and our Number went on growing continually. This was one of the first good Effects of my having learnt a little to scribble. Another was, that the leading Men, seeing a News Paper now in the hands of one who could

[129] *The American Weekly Mercury,* established December 22, 1719.

[130] Franklin took over *The Universal Instructor in All Arts and Sciences: and Pennsylvania Gazette* in October 1729, shortened the title to *The Pennsylvania Gazette,* and made it one of the best papers in the Colonies.

[131] William Burnet (1688–1729), Governor of Massachusetts.

also handle a Pen, thought it convenient to oblige and encourage me. Bradford still printed the Votes and Laws and other Publick Business. He had printed an Address of the House to the Governor in a coarse blundering manner; We reprinted it elegantly and correctly, and sent one to every Member. They were sensible of the Difference, it strengthen'd the Hands of our Friends in the House, and they voted us their Printers for the Year ensuing.

Among my Friends in the House I must not forget Mr. Hamilton before mentioned, who was now returned from England and had a Seat in it. He interested himself[132] for me strongly in that Instance, as he did in many others afterwards, continuing his Patronage till his Death. Mr. Vernon about this time put me in mind of the Debt I ow'd him: but did not press me. I wrote him an ingenuous Letter of Acknowledgments, crav'd his Forbearance a little longer which he allow'd me, and as soon as I was able I paid the Principal with Interest and many Thanks. So that *Erratum* was in some degree corrected.

But now another Difficulty came upon me, which I had never the least Reason to expect. Mr. Meredith's Father, who was to have paid for our Printing House according to the Expectations given me, was able to advance only one Hundred Pounds, Currency, which had been paid, and a Hundred more was due to the Merchant; who grew impatient and su'd us all. We gave Bail, but saw that if the Money could not be rais'd in time, the Suit must come to a Judgment and Execution, and our hopeful Prospects must with us be ruined, as the Press and Letters must be sold for Payment, perhaps at half Price. In this Distress two true Friends whose Kindness I have never forgotten nor ever shall forget while I can remember any thing, came to me separately unknown to each other, and without any Application from me, offering each of them to advance me all the Money that should be necessary to enable me to take the whole Business upon my self if that should be practicable, but they did not like my continuing the Partnership with Meredith, who as they said was often seen drunk in the Streets, and playing at low Games in Alehouses, much to our Discredit. These two Friends were William Coleman and Robert Grace.[133] I told them I could not propose a Separation while any Prospect remain'd of the Merediths fulfilling their Part of our Agreement. Because I thought myself under great Obligations to them for what they had done and would do if they could. But if they finally fail'd in their Performance, and our Partnership must be dissolv'd, I should then think myself at Liberty to accept the Assistance of my Friends.

Thus the matter rested for some time. When I said to my Partner, perhaps your Father is dissatisfied at the Part you have undertaken in this Affair of ours, and is unwilling to advance for you and me what he would for you alone: If that is the Case, tell me, and I will resign the whole to you and go about my Business. No says he, my Father has really been disappointed and is really unable; and I am unwilling to distress him farther. I see this is a Business I am not fit for. I was bred a Farmer, and it was a Folly in me to come to Town and put my Self at 30 Years of Age an Apprentice to learn a new Trade. Many of our Welsh People are going to settle in North Carolina where Land is cheap: I am inclin'd to go with them, and follow my old Employment. You may find Friends to assist you. If you will take the Debts of the

132"I got his Son once £500."—[Franklin's note].

133William Coleman (1704–1769), Robert Grace (1709–1766), original members of Franklin's Junto.

Company upon you, return to my Father the hundred Pound he has advanc'd, pay my little personal Debts, and give me Thirty Pounds and a new Saddle, I will relinquish the Partnership and leave the whole in your Hands. I agreed to this Proposal. It was drawn up in Writing, sign'd and seal'd immediately. I gave him what he demanded and he went soon after to Carolina; from whence he sent me next Year two long Letters, containing the best Account that had been given of that Country, the Climate, Soil, Husbandry, &c. for in those Matters he was very judicious. I printed them in the Papers, and they gave grate Satisfaction to the Publick.

As soon as he was gone, I recurr'd to my two Friends; and because I would not give an unkind Preference to either, I took half what each had offered and I wanted, of one, and half of the other; paid off the Company Debts, and went on with the Business in my own Name, advertising that the Partnership was dissolved. I think this was in or about the Year 1729.[134]

About this Time there was a Cry among the People for more Paper-Money, only £15,000, being extant in the Province and that soon to be sunk. The wealthy Inhabitants oppos'd any Addition, being against all Paper Currency, from an Apprehension that it would depreciate as it had done in New England to the Prejudice of all Creditors. We had discuss'd this Point in our Junto, where I was on the Side of Addition, being persuaded that the first small Sum struck in 1723 had done much good, by increasing the Trade Employment, and Number of Inhabitants in the Province, since I now saw all the old Houses inhabited, and many new ones building, where as I remember'd well, that when I first walk'd about the Streets of Philadelphia, eating my Roll, I saw most of the House in Walnut street between Second and Front streets with Bills on their Doors, to be let; and many likewise in Chestnut Street, and other Streets; which made me then think the Inhabitants of the City were one after another deserting it. Our Debates possess'd me so fully of the Subject, that I wrote and printed an anonymous Pamphlet on it, entituled, *The Nature and Necessity of a Paper Currency.* It was well receiv'd by the common People in general; but the Rich Men dislik'd it; for it increas'd and strengthen'd the Clamour for more Money; and they happening to have no Writers among them that were able to answer it, their Opposition slacken'd, and the Point was carried by a Majority in the House. My Friends there, who conceiv'd I had been of some Service, thought fit to reward me, by employing me in printing the Money, a very profitable Jobb, and a great Help to me. This was another Advantage gain'd by my being able to write. The Utility of this Currency became by Time and Experience so evident, as never afterwards to be much disputed, so that it grew soon to £55,000, and in 1739 to £80,000 since which it arose during War to upwards of £350,000. Trade, Building and Inhabitants all the while increasing. Tho' I now think there are Limits beyond which the Quantity may be hurtful.

I soon after obtain'd, thro' my Friend Hamilton, the Printing of the New Castle Paper Money,[135] another profitable Jobb, as I then thought it; small Things appearing great to those in small Circumstances. And these to me were really great Advantages, as they were great Encouragements. He procured me also the Printing of the

[134]Actually July 14, 1730.

[135]The counties of New-Castle, Kent, and Sussex had the same governor as Pennsylvania but a separate legislature.

Laws and Votes of the Government which continu'd in my Hands as long as I follow'd the Business.

I now open'd a little Stationer's Shop. I had in it Blanks of all Sorts the correctest that ever appear'd among us, being assisted in that by my Friend Brientnal; I had also Paper, Parchment, Chapmen's Books, &c. One Whitemash a Compositor I had known in London, an excellent Workman now came to me and work'd with me constantly and diligently, and I took an Apprentice the Son of Aquila Rose. I began now gradually to pay off the Debt I was under for the Printing House. In order to secure my Credit and Character as a Tradesman, I took care not only to be in *Reality* Industrious and frugal, but to avoid all *Appearances* of the Contrary. I drest plainly; I was seen a no Places of idle Diversion; I never went out a-fishing or shooting; a Book, indeed, sometimes debauch'd me from my Work; but that was seldom, snug, and gave no Scandal: and to show that I was not above my Business, I sometimes brought home the Paper I purchas'd at the Stores, thro' the Streets on a Wheelbarrow. Thus being esteem'd an industrious thriving young Man, and paying duly for what I bought, the Merchants who imported Stationary solicited my Custom, others propos'd supplying me with Books, and I went on swimmingly. In the mean time Keimer's Credit and Business declining daily, he was at last forc'd to sell his Printinghouse to satisfy his Creditors. He went to Barbadoes, and there lived some Years, in very poor Circumstances.

His Apprentice David Harry, whom I had instructed while I work'd with him, set up in his Place at Philadelphia, having bought his Materials. I was at first apprehensive of a powerful Rival in Harry, as his Friends were very able, and had a good deal of Interest. I therefore propos'd a Partnership to him; which he, fortunately for me, rejected with Scorn. He was very proud, dress'd like a Gentleman, liv'd expensively, took much Diversion and Pleasure abroad, ran in debt, and neglected his Business, upon which all Business left him; and finding nothing to do, he follow'd Keimer to Barbadoes; taking the Printinghouse with him. There this Apprentice employ'd his former Master as a Journeyman. They quarrel'd often. Harry went continually behindhand, and at length was forc'd to sell his Types, and return to his Country Work in Pensilvania. The Person that bought them, employ'd Keimer to use them, but in a few years he died. Their remain'd now no Competitor with me at Philadelphia, but the old one, Bradford, who was rich and easy, did a little Printing now and then by straggling Hands, but was not very anxious about the Business. However, as he kept the Post Office, it was imagined he had better Opportunities of obtaining News, his Paper was thought a better Distributer of Advertisements than mine, and therefore had many more, which was a profitable thing to him and a Disadvantage to me. For tho' I did indeed receive and send Papers by Post, yet the publick Opinion was otherwise; for what I did send was by Bribing the Riders who took them privately: Bradford being unkind enough to forbid it: which ocasion'd some Resentment on my Part; and I thought so meanly of him for it, that when I afterwards came into his Situation,[136] I took care never to imitate it.

[136]Franklin became the Deputy Postmaster-General for the Colonies in 1753.

I had hitherto continu'd to board with Godfrey who lived in Part of my House with his Wife and Children, and had one Side of the Shop for his Glazier's Business, tho' he work'd little, being always absorb'd in his Mathematics. Mrs. Godfrey projected a Match for me with a Relation's Daughter, took Opportunities of bringing us often together, till a serious Courtship on my Part ensu'd, the Girl being in herself very deserving. The old Folks encourag'd me by continual Invitations to Supper, and by leaving us together, till at length it was time to explain. Mrs. Godfrey manag'd our little Treaty. I let her know that I expected as much Money with their Daughter as would pay off my Remaining Debt for the Printing-house, which I believe was not then above a Hundred Pounds. She brought me Word they had no such Sum to spare. I said they might mortgage their House in the Loan Office. The Answer to this after some Days was that they did not approve the Match; that on Enquiry of Bradford they had been inform'd the Printing Business was not a profitable one, the Types would soon be worn out and more wanted, that S. Keimer and D. Harry had fail'd one after the other, and I should probably soon follow them; and therefore I was forbidden the House, and the Daughter shut up. Whether this was a real Change of Sentiment, or only Artifice, on a Supposition of our being too far engag'd in Affection to retract, and therefore that we should steal a Marriage, which would leave them at Liberty to give or withold what they pleas'd, I know not: But I suspected the latter, resented it, and went no more. Mrs. Godfrey brought me afterwards some more favourable Accounts of their Disposition, and would have drawn me on again: but I declared absolutely my Resolution to have nothing more to do with that Family. This was resented by the Godfreys, we differ'd, and they removed, leaving me the whole House, and I resolved to take no more Inmates.

But this Affair having turn'd my Thoughts to Marriage, I look'd round me, and made Overtures of Acquaintance in other Places; but soon found that the Business of a Printer being generally thought a poor one, I was not to expect Money with a Wife unless with such a one, as I should not otherwise think agreable. In the mean time, that hard-to-be-govern'd Passion of Youth, had hurried me frequently into Intrigues with low Women that fell in my Way, which were attended with some Expence and great Inconvenience, besides a continual Risque to my Health by a Distemper which of all Things I dreaded, tho' by Great good Luck I escaped it.

A friendly Correspondence as Neighbours and old Acquaintances, had continued between me and Mrs. Read's Family, who all had a Regard for me from the time of my first Lodging in their House. I was often invited there and consulted in their Affairs, wherein I sometimes was of service. I pity'd poor Miss Read's unfortunate Situation, who was generally dejected, seldom chearful, and avoided Company. I consider'd my Giddiness and Inconstancy when in London as in a great degree the Cause of her Unhappiness; tho' the Mother was good enough to think the Fault more her own than mine, as she had prevented our Marrying before I went thither, and persuaded the other Match in my Absence. Our mutual Affection was revived, but there were now great Objections to our Union. That Match was indeed look'd upon as invalid, a preceding Wife being said to be living in England; but this could not easily be prov'd, because of the Distance. And tho' there was a Report of his Death, it was not certain. Then tho' it should be true, he had left many Debts which his Successor might be call'd on to pay. We ventured however, over all these Difficulties, and

I [took] her to Wife Sept. 1, 1730.[137] None of the Inconveniencies happened that we had apprehended, she prov'd a good and faithful Helpmate, assisted me much by attending the Shop, we throve together, and have ever mutually endeavour'd to make each other happy. Thus I corrected that great *Erratum* as well as I could.

About this Time our Club meeting, not at a Tavern, but in a little Room of Mr. Grace's set apart for that Purpose; a Proposition was made by me that since our Books were often referr'd to in our Disquisitions upon the Queries, it might be convenient to us to have them all together where we met, that upon Occasion they might be consulted; and by thus clubbing our Books to a common Library, we should, while we lik'd to keep them together, have each of us the Advantage of using the Books of all the other Members, which would be nearly as beneficial as if each owned the whole. It was lik'd and agreed to, and we fill'd one End of the Room with such Books as we could best spare. The Number was not so great as we expected; and tho' they had been of great Use, yet some Inconveniencies occurring for want of due Care of them, the Collection after about a Year was separated, and each took his Books home again.

And now I set on foot my first Project of a public Nature, that for a Subscription Library. I drew up the Proposals, got them put into Form by our great Scrivener Brockden, and by the help of my Friends in the Junto, procur'd Fifty Subscribers of 40*s.* each to begin with and 10*s.* a Year for 50 Years, the Term our Company was to continue. We afterwards obtain'd a Charter, the Company being increas'd to 100. This was the Mother of all the N American Subscription Libraries now so numerous. It is become a great thing itself, and continually increasing. These Libraries have improv'd the general Conversation of the Americans, made the common Tradesmen and Farmers as intelligent as most Gentlemen from other Countries, and perhaps have contributed in some degree to the Stand so generally made throughout the Colonies in Defence of their Privileges.

Memo.

Thus far was written with the Intention express'd in the Beginning and therefore contains several little family Anecdotes of no Importance to others. What follows was written many Years after in compliance with the Advice contain'd in these Letters, and accordingly intended for the Publick. The Affairs of the Revolution occasion'd the Interruption.

Letter from Mr. Abel James[138] *with Notes of my Life, to be here inserted. Also Letter from Mr. Vaughan*[139] *to the same purpose*

My Dear and honored Friend.

I have often been desirous of writing to thee, but could not be reconciled to the Thoughts that the Letter might fall into the Hands of the British,[140] lest some

[137]Without proof that Deborah's first husband, John Rogers, was dead, Deborah could not officially remarry. Franklin and Deborah entered into "common law" marriage without a civil or church ceremony.

[138]Abel James (c. 1726–1790), Philadelphia Quaker merchant.

[139]Benjamin Vaughan (1751–1835), English diplomat. He edited the first general collection of Franklin's works, 1779.

[140]The letter was written to Franklin in Paris in 1782 while Britain was still at war with the Colonies.

Printer or busy Body should publish some Part of the Contents and give our Friends Pain and myself Censure.

Some Time since there fell into my Hands to my great Joy about 23 Sheets in thy own hand-writing containing an Account of the Parentage and Life of thyself, directed to thy Son ending in the Year 1730 with which there were Notes[141] likewise in thy writing, a Copy of which I inclose in Hopes it may be a means if thou continuedst it up to a later period, that the first and latter part may be put together, and if it is not yet continued, I hope thou wilt not delay it, Life is uncertain as the Preacher tells us, and what will the World say if kind, humane and benevolent Ben Franklin should leave his Friends and the World deprived of so pleasing and profitable a Work, a Work which would be useful and entertaining not only to a few, but to millions.

The Influence Writings under that Class have on the Minds of Youth is very great, and has no where appeared so plain as in our public Friend's Journal. It almost insensibly leads the Youth into the Resolution of endeavouring to become as good and as eminent as the Journalist. Should thine for Instance when published, and I think it could not fail of it, lead the Youth to equal the Industry and Temperance of thy early Youth, what a Blessing with that Class would such a Work be. I know of no Character living nor many of them put together, who has so much in his Power as Thyself to promote a greater Spirit of Industry and early Attention to Business, Frugality and Temperance with the American Youth. Not that I think the Work would have no other Merit and Use in the World, far from it, but the first is of such vast Importance, that I know nothing that can equal it. . . .

Abel James

The foregoing letter and the minutes accompanying it being shewn to a friend, I received from him the following:

Paris, January 31, 1783.

My dearest sir,

When I had read over your sheets of minutes of the principal incidents of your life, recovered for you by your Quaker acquaintance; I told you I would send you a letter expressing my reasons why I thought it would be useful to complete and publish it as he desired. Various concerns have for some time past prevented this letter being written, and I do not know whether it was worth any expectation: happening to be at leisure however at present, I shall be writing at least interest and instruct myself; but as the terms I am inclined to use may tend to offend a person of your manners, I shall only tell you how I would address any other person, who was as good and as great as yourself, but less diffident. I would say to him, Sir, I *solicit* the history of your life from the following motives.

Your history is so remarkable, that if you do not give it, somebody else will certainly give it; and perhaps so as nearly to do as much harm, as your own management of the thing might do good.

[141]Franklin drew up an outline for his autobiography soon after he began to write in 1771.

It will moreover present a table of the internal circumstances of your country, which will very much tend to invite to it settlers of virtuous and manly minds. And considering the eagerness with which such information is sought by them, and the extent of your reputation, I do not know of a more efficacious advertisement than your Biography would give.

All that has happened to you is also connected with the detail of the manners and situation of a *rising* people; and in this respect I do not think that the writings of Caesar and Tacitus can be more interesting to a true judge of human nature and society.

But these, Sir, are small reasons in my opinion, compared with the chance which your life will give for the forming of future great men; and in conjunction with your Art of Virtue, (which you design to publish) of improving the features of private character, and consequently of aiding all happiness both public and domestic.

The two works I allude to, Sir, will in particular give a noble rule and example of *self-education*. School and other education constantly proceed upon false principles, and shew a clumsy apparatus pointed at a false mark; but your apparatus is simple, and the mark a true one; and while parents and young persons are left destitute of other just means of estimating and becoming prepared for a reasonable course in life, your discovery that the thing is in many a man's private power, will be invaluable!

Influence upon the private character late in life, is not only an influence late in life, but a weak influence. It is in youth that we plant our chief habits and prejudices; it is in youth that we take our party as to profession, pursuits, and matrimony. In youth therefore the turn is given; in youth the education even of the next generation is given; in youth the private and public character is determined; and the term of life extending but from youth to age, life ought to begin well from youth; and more especially before we take our party as to our principal objects.

But your Biography will not merely teach self-education, but the education of a wise man; and the wisest man will receive lights and improve his progress, by seeing detailed the conduct of another wise man. And why are weaker men to be deprived of such helps, when we see our race has been blundering on in the dark, almost without a guide in this particular, from the farthest trace of time? Shew then, Sir, how much is to be done, *both to sons and fathers;* and invite all wise men to become like yourself; and other men to become wise.

When we see how cruel statesmen and warriors can be to the humble race, and how absurd distinguished men can be to their acquaintance, it will be instructive to observe the instances multiply of pacific acquiescing manners; and to find how compatible it is to be great and *domestic,* enviable and yet *good-humored.*

The little private incidents which you will also have to relate, will have considerable use, as we want above all things, *rules of prudence in ordinary affairs;* and it will be curious to see how you have acted in these. It will be so far a sort of key to life, and explain many things that all men ought to have once explained to them, to give them a chance of becoming wise by foresight.

The nearest thing to having experience of one's own, is to have other people's affairs brought before us in a shape that is interesting; this is sure to happen from your pen. Your affairs and management will have an air of simplicity or importance that will not fail to strike; and I am convinced you have conducted them with as much originality as if you had been conducting discussions in politics or philosophy; and what more worthy of experiments and system, (its importance and its error considered) than human life!

Some men have been virtuous blindly, others have speculated fantastically, and others have been shrewd to bad purposes; but you, Sir, I am sure, will give under your hand, nothing but what is at the same moment, wise, practical, and good.

Your account of yourself (for I suppose the parallel I am drawing for Dr. Franklin, will hold not only in point of character but of private history), will shew that you are ashamed of no origin; a thing the more important, as you prove how little necessary all origin is to happiness, virtue, or greatness.

As no end likewise happens without a means, so we shall find, Sir, that even you yourself framed a plan by which you became considerable; but at the same time we may see that though the event is flattering, the means are as simple as wisdom could make them; that is, depending upon nature, virtue, thought, and habit.

Another thing demonstrated will be the propriety of every man's waiting for his time for appearing upon the stage of the world. Our sensations being very much fixed to the moment, we are apt to forget that more moments are to follow the first, and consequently that man should arrange his conduct so as to suit the *whole* of a life. Your attribution appears to have been applied to your *life,* and the passing moments of it have been enlivened with content and enjoyment, instead of being tormented with foolish impatience or regrets. Such a conduct is easy for those who make virtue and themselves their standard, and who try to keep themselves in countenance by examples of other truly great men, of whom patience is so often the characteristic.

Your Quaker correspondent, Sir, (for here again I will suppose the subject of my letter resembling Dr. Franklin,) praised your frugality, diligence, and temperance, which he considered as a pattern for all youth; but it is singular that he should have forgotten your modesty, and your disinterestedness, without which you never could have waited for your advancement, or found your situation in the mean time comfortable; which is a strong lesson to shew the poverty of glory, and the importance of regulating our minds.

If this correspondent had known the nature of your reputation as well as I do, he would have said; your former writings and measures would secure attention to your Biography and Art of Virtue; and your Biography and Art of Virtue, in return, would secure attention to them. This is an advantage attendant upon a various character, and which brings all that belongs to it into greater play; and it is the more useful, as perhaps more persons are at a loss for the *means* of improving their minds and characters, than they are for the time or the inclination to do it.

But there is one concluding reflection, Sir, that will shew the use of your life as a mere piece of biography. This style of writing seems a little gone out of vogue, and yet it is a very useful one; and your specimen of it may be particularly serviceable, as it will make a subject of comparison with the lives of various public cutthroats and intriguers, and with absurd monastic self-tormentors, or vain literary triflers. If it encourages more writings of the same kind with your own, and induces more men to spend lives fit to be written; it will be worth all Plutarch's Lives put together.

But being tired of figuring to myself a character of which every feature suits only one man in the world, without giving him the praise of it; I shall end my letter, my dear Dr. Franklin, with a personal application to your proper self.

I am earnestly desirous then, my dear Sir, that you should let the world into the traits of your genuine character, as civil broils may otherwise tend to disguise or traduce it. Considering your great age, the caution of your character, and your peculiar style of thinking, it is not likely that any one besides yourself can be sufficiently master of the facts of your life, or the intentions of your mind.

Besides all this, the immense revolution of the present period, will necessarily turn our attention towards the author of it; and when virtuous principles have been pretended in it, it will be highly important to shew that such have really influenced; and, as your own character will be the principal one to receive a scrutiny, it is proper (even for its effects upon your vast and rising country, as well as upon England and upon Europe), that it should stand respectable and eternal. For the furtherance of human happiness, I have always maintained that it is necessary to prove that man is not even at present a vicious and detestable animal; and still more to prove that good management may greatly amend him; and it is for much the same reason, that I am anxious to see the opinion established, that there are fair characters existing among the individuals of the race; for the moment that all men, without exception, shall be conceived abandoned, good people will cease efforts deemed to be hopeless, and perhaps think of taking their share in the scramble of life, or at least of making it comfortable principally for themselves.

Take then, my dear Sir, this work most speedily into hand: shew yourself good as you are good, temperate as you are temperate; and above all things, prove yourself as one who from your infancy have loved justice, liberty, and concord, in a way that has made it natural and consistent for you to have acted, as we have seen you act in the last seventeen years of your life. Let Englishmen be made not only to respect, but even to love you. When they think well of individuals in your native country, they will go nearer to thinking well of your country; and when your countrymen see themselves well thought of by Englishmen, they will go nearer to thinking well of England. Extend your views even further; do not stop at those who speak the English tongue, but after having settled so many points in nature and politics, think of bettering the whole race of men.

As I have not read any part of the life in question, but know only the character that lived it, I write somewhat at hazard. I am sure however, that the life, and the treatise I allude to (on the Art of Virtue), will necessarily fulfil the chief of my expectations; and still more so if you take up the measure of suiting these performances to the several views above stated. Should they even prove unsuccessful in all that a sanguine admirer of yours hopes from them, you will at least have framed pieces to interest the human mind; and whoever gives a feeling of pleasure that is innocent to man, has added so much to the fair side of a life otherwise too much darkened by anxiety, and too much injured by pain.

In the hope therefore that you will listen to the prayer addressed to you in this letter, I beg to subscribe myself, my dearest Sir, &c. &c.

BENJ. VAUGHAN.

Part Two Continuation of the Account of My Life Begun at Passy[142] 1784

It is some time since I receiv'd the above Letters, but I have been too busy till now to think of complying with the Request they contain. It might too be much better done if I were at home among my Papers, which would aid my Memory and help to ascertain Dates. But my Return being uncertain, and having just now a little Leisure, I will endeavour to recollect and write what I can; if I live to get home, it may there be corrected and improv'd.

Not having any Copy here of what is already written, I know not whether an Account is given of the means I used to establish the Philadelphia publick Library, which from a small Beginning is now become so considerable, though I remember to have come down to near the Time of that Transaction, 1730. I will therefore begin here, with an Account of it, which may be struck out if found to have been already given.

At the time I establish'd my self in Pensylvania, there was not a good Bookseller's Shop in any of the Colonies to the Southward of Boston. In New-York and Philadelphia the Printers were indeed Stationers, they sold only Paper, &c., Almanacks, Ballads, and a few common School Books. Those who lov'd Reading were oblig'd to send for their Books from England. The Members of the Junto had each a few. We had left the Alehouse where we first met, and hired a Room to hold our Club in. I propos'd that we should all of us bring our Books to that Room, where they would not only be ready to consult in our Conferences, but become a common Benefit, each of us being at Liberty to borrow such as he wish'd to read at home. This was accordingly done, and for some time contented us. Finding the Advantage of this little Collection, I propos'd to render the Benefit from Books more common by commencing a Public Subscription Library. I drew a Sketch of the Plan and Rules that would be necessary, and got a skillful Conveyancer, Mr. Charles Brockden to put the whole in Form of Articles of Agreement to be subscribed; by which each Subscriber engag'd to pay a certain Sum down for the first Purchase of Books and an annual Contribution for encreasing them. So few were the Readers at that time in Philadelphia, and the Majority of us so poor, that I was not able with great Industry to find more than Fifty Persons, mostly young Tradesmen, willing to pay down for this purpose Forty shillings each, and Ten Shillings per Annum. On this little Fund we began. The Books were imported. The Library was open one Day in the Week for lending them to the Subscribers, on their Promisory Notes to pay Double the Value if not duly returned. The Institution soon manifested its Utility, was imitated by other Towns and in other Provinces, the Librarys were augmented by Donations, Reading became fashionable, and our People having no publick Amusements to divert their Attention from Study became better acquainted with Books, and in a few Years were observ'd by Strangers to be better instructed and more intelligent than People of the same Rank generally are in other Countries.

When we were about to sign the above-mentioned Articles, which were to be binding on us, our Heirs, &c. for fifty Years, Mr. Brockden, the Scrivener, said to us, "You are young Men, but it is scare probable that any of you will live to see the Ex-

[142]A suburb of Paris, France, where Franklin lived while negotiating the Treaty of Paris (1783).

piration of the Term fix'd in this Instrument." A Number of us, however, are yet living: But the Instrument was after a few Years rendered null by a Charter that incorporated and gave Perpetuity to the Company.

The Objections, and Reluctances I met with in Soliciting the Subscriptions, made me soon feel the Impropriety of presenting one's self as the Proposer of any useful Project that might be suppos'd to raise one's Reputation in the smallest degree above that of one's Neighbours, when one has need of their Assistance to accomplish that Project. I therefore put my self as much as I could out of sight, and stated it as a Scheme of a *Number of Friends,* who had requested me to go about and propose it to such as they thought Lovers of Reading. In this way my Affair went on more smoothly, and I ever after practis'd it on such Occasions; and from my frequent Successes, can heartily recommend it. The present little Sacrifice of your Vanity will afterwards be amply repaid. If it remains a while uncertain to whom the Merit belongs, some one more vain than yourself will be encourag'd to claim it, and then even Envy will be dispos'd to do you Justice, by plucking those assum'd Feathers, and restoring them to their right Owner.

This Library afforded me the means of Improvement by constant Study, for which I set apart an Hour or two each Day; and thus repair'd in some Degree the Loss of the Learned Education my Father once intended for me. Reading was the only Amusement I allow'd my self. I spent no time in Taverns, Games, or Frolicks of any kind. And my Industry in my Business continu'd as indefatigable as it was necessary. I was in debt for my Printing-house, I had a young Family coming on to be educated,[143] and I had to contend with for Business two Printers who were establish'd in the Place before me. My Circumstances however grew daily easier: my original Habits of Frugality continuing. And my Father having among his Instructions to me when a Boy, frequently repeated a Proverb of Solomon, *"Seest thou a Man diligent in his Calling, he shall stand before Kings, he shall not stand before mean Men."*[144] I from thence consider'd Industry as a Means of obtaining Wealth and Distinction, which encourag'd me, tho' I did not think that I should ever literally stand before Kings, which however has since happened.—for I have stood before five,[145] and even had the honor of sitting down with one, the King of Denmark, to Dinner.

We have an English Proverb that says,

He that would thrive
Must ask his Wife;

it was lucky for me that I had one as much dispos'd to Industry and Frugality as my self. She assisted me chearfully in my Business, folding and stitching Pamphlets, tending Shop, purchasing old Linen Rags for the Paper-makers, &c. &c. We kept no idle Servants, our Table was plain and simple, our furniture of the cheapest. For instance my Breakfast was a long time Bread and Milk, (no Tea) and I ate it out of a twopenny earthen Porringer with a Pewter Spoon. But mark how Luxury will enter Families, and make a Progress, in Spite of Principle. Being call'd one Morning to Breakfast, I found it in a China Bowl with a Spoon of Silver. They had been bought

143 William, born about 1731; Francis, born 1732; and Sarah, born 1743.

144 Proverbs 22:29.

145 Louis XV and Louis XVI of France, George II and George III of England, and Christian VI of Denmark.

for me without my Knowledge my Wife, and had cost her the enormous Sum of three and twenty Shillings, for which she had no other Excuse of Apology to make, but that she thought *her* Husband deserv'd a Silver Spoon and China Bowl as well as any of his Neighbours. This was the first Appearance of Plate and China in our House, which afterwards in a Course of Years as our Wealth encreas'd augmented gradually to several Hundred Pounds in Value.

I had been religiously educated as a Presbyterian; and tho' some of the Dogmas of that Persuasion, such as the Eternal Decrees of God, Election, Reprobation, &c. appear'd to me unintelligible, others doubtful, I early absented myself from the Public Assemblies of the Sect, Sunday being my Studying-Day, I never was without some religious Principles; I never doubted, for instance, the Existance of the Deity, that he made the World, and govern'd it by his Providence; that the most acceptable Service of God was the doing Good to man; that our Souls are immortal; and that all Crime will be punished and Virtue rewarded either here or hereafter; these I esteem'd the Essentials of every Religion, and being to be found in all the Religions we had in our Country I respected them all, tho' with different degrees of Respect as I found them more or less mix'd with other Articles which without any Tendency to inspire, promote or confirm Morality, serv'd principally to divide us and make us unfriendly to one another. This Respect to all, with an Opinion that the worst had some good Effects, induc'd me to avoid all Discourse that might tend to lessen the good Opinion another might have of his own Religion; and as our Province increas'd in People and new Places of worship were continually wanted, and generally erected by voluntary Contribution, my Mite for such purpose, whatever might be the Sect, was never refused.

Tho' I seldom attended any Public Worship, I had still an Opinion of its Propriety, and of its Utility when rightly conducted, and I regularly paid my annual Subscription for the Support of the only Presbyterian Minister or Meeting we had in Philadelphia. He us'd to visit me sometimes as a Friend, and admonish me to attend his Administrations, and I was now and then prevail'd on to do so, once for five Sundays successively. Had he been, *in my Opinion,* a good Preacher perhaps I might have continued, notwithstanding the occasion I had for the Sunday's Leisure in my Course of Study: But his Discourses were chiefly either polemic Arguments, or Explications of the peculiar Doctrines of our Sect, and were all to me very dry, uninteresting and unedifying, since not a single moral Principle was inculcated or enforc'd their Aim seeming to be rather to make us Presbyterians than good Citizens. At length he took for his Text that Verse on the 4th Chapter of Philippians, *Finally, Brethren, Whatsoever Things are true, honest, just, pure, lovely, or of good report, if there be any virtue, or any praise, think on these Things;*[146] and I imagin'd in a Sermon on such a Text, we could not miss of having some Morality: But he confin'd himself to five Points only as meant by the Apostle, viz. 1. Keeping holy the Sabbath Day. 2. Being diligent in Reading the Holy Scriptures. 3. Attending duly the Publick Worship. 4. Partaking of the Sacrament. 5. Paying a due Respect to God's Ministers. These might be all good Things, but as they were not the kind of good Things that I expected from that Text, I despaired of ever meeting with them from any other, was disgusted, and attended his Preaching no more. I had some Years before compos'd a little Liturgy or Form of Prayer for my own private Use, viz, in 1728. entitled, *Articles of Belief and Acts of Religion.* I return'd to the Use of this, and went no more

[146]Philippians 4:8.

to the public Assemblies. My Conduct might be blameable, but I leave it without attempting farther to excuse it, my present purpose being to relate Facts, and not to make Apologies for them.

It was about this time that I conceiv'd the bold and arduous Project of arriving at moral Perfection. I wish'd to live without committing any Fault at any time; I would conquer all that either Natural Inclination, Custom, or Company might lead me into. As I knew, or thought I knew, what was right and wrong, I did not see why I might not *always* do the one and avoid the other. But I soon found I had undertaken a Task of more Difficulty than I had imagined. While my *Attention was taken up* in guarding against one Fault, I was often surpriz'd by another. Habit took the Advantage of Inattention. Inclination was sometimes too strong for Reason. I concluded at length, that the mere speculative Conviction that it was our Interest to be compleatly virtuous, was not sufficient to prevent our Slipping, and that the contrary Habits must be broken and good ones acquired and established, before we can have any Dependance on a steady uniform Rectitude of Conduct. For this purpose I therefore contriv'd the following Method.

In the various Enumerations of the moral Virtues I had met with in my Reading, I found the Catalogue more or less numerous, as different Writers included more or fewer Ideas under the same Name. Temperance, for Example, was by some confin'd to Eating and Drinking, while by others it was extended to mean the moderating every other Pleasure, Appetite, Inclination or Passion, bodily or mental, even to our Avarice and Ambition. I propos'd to myself, for the sake of Clearness, to use rather more Names with fewer Ideas annex'd to each, than a few Names with more Ideas; and I included under Thirteen Names of Virtues all that at that time occurr'd to me as necessary or desirable, and annex'd to each a short Precept, which fully express'd the Extent I gave to its Meaning.

These Names of Virtues with their Precepts were

1. TEMPERANCE.

Eat not to Dulness.
Drink not to Elevation.

2. SILENCE.

Speak not but what may benefit others or yourself. Avoid trifling Conversation.

3. ORDER.

Let all your Things have their Places. Let each Part of your Business have its Time.

4. RESOLUTION.

Resolve to perform what you ought. Perform without fail what you resolve.

5. FRUGALITY.

Make no Expence but to do good to others or yourself: i.e., Waste nothing.

6. INDUSTRY.

Lose no Time. Be always employ'd in something useful. Cut off all unnecessary Actions.

7. SINCERITY.

Use no hurtful Deceit.
Think innocently and justly; and, if you speak, speak accordingly.

8. Justice.

Wrong none, by doing Injuries or omitting the Benefits that are your Duty.

9. Moderation.

Avoid Extreams. Forbear resenting Injuries so much as you think they deserve.

10. Cleanliness.

Tolerate no Uncleanness in Body, Cloaths or Habitation.

11. Tranquility.

Be not disturbed at Trifles, or at Accidents common or unavoidable.

12. Chastity.

Rarely use Venery but for Health or Offspring: Never to Dulness, Weakness, or the Injury of your own or another's Peace or Reputation.

13. Humility.

Imitate Jesus and Socrates.

My Intention being to acquire the *Habitude* of all these Virtues, I judg'd it would be well not to distract my Attention by attempting the whole at once, but to fix it on one of them at a time, and when I should be Master of that, then to proceed to another, and so on till I should have gone thro' the thirteen. And as the previous Acquisition of some might facilitate the Acquisition of certain others, I arrang'd them with that View as they stand above. *Temperance* first, as it tends to produce that Coolness and Clearness of Head, which is so necessary where constant Vigilance was to be kept up, and Guard maintained, against the unremitting Attraction of ancient Habits, and the Force of perpetual Temptations. This being acquir'd and establish'd, *Silence* would be more easy, and my Desire being to gain Knowledge at the same time that I improv'd in Virtue, and considering that in Conversation it was obtain'd rather by use of the Ears than of the Tongue, and therefore wishing to break a Habit I was getting into of Prattling, Punning and Joking, which only made me acceptable to trifling Company, I gave *Silence* the second Place. This, and the next, *Order,* I expected would allow me more Time for attending to my Project and my Studies; Resolution, once become habitual, would keep me firm in my Endeavours to obtain all the subsequent Virtues; *Frugality* and *Industry,* by freeing me from my remaining Debt, and producing Affluence and Independance, would make more easy the Practice of *Sincerity* and *Justice,* &c. &c. Conceiving then that agreable to the Advice of Pythagoras[147] in his Golden Verses daily Examination would be necessary, I contriv'd the following Method for conducting that Examination.

I made a little Book in which I allotted a Page for each of the Virtues. I rul'd each Page with red Ink, so as to have seven Columns, one for each Day of the Week, marking each Column with a Letter for the Day. I cross'd these Columns with thirteen red Lines, marking the Beginning of each Line with the first Letter of one of the Virtues, on which Line and in its proper Column I might mark by a little black Spot every Fault I found upon Examination to have been committed respecting that Virtue upon that Day.

[147]Pythagoras (b. 580 B.C.?), Greek philosopher and mathematician. A note in Franklin's manuscript indicated that he intended to include translated verses: "Let sleep not close your eyes till you have thrice examined the transactions of the day: where have I strayed, what have I done, what good have I omitted?"

I determined to give a Week's strict Attention to each of the Virtues successively. Thus in the first Week my great Guard was to avoid every the least Offence against Temperance, leaving the other Virtues to their ordinary Chance, only marking every Evening the Faults of the Day. Thus if in the first Week I could keep my first Line marked T clear of Spots, I suppos'd the Habit of that Virtue so much strengthen'd and its opposite weaken'd, that I might venture extending my Attention to include the next, and for the following Week keep both Lines clear of Spots. Proceeding thus to the last, I could go thro' a Course compleat in Thirteen Weeks, and four Courses in a year. And like him who having a Garden to weed, does not attempt to eradicate all the bad Herbs at once, which would exceed his Reach and his Strength, but works on one of the Beds at a time, and having accomplish'd the first proceeds to a Second; so I should have, (I hoped) the encouraging Pleasure of seeing on my Pages the Progress I made in Virtue, by clearing successively my Lines of their Spots, till in the End by a Number of Courses, I should be happy in viewing a clean Book after a thirteen Weeks daily Examination.

Form of the Pages

Temperance.

Eat not to Dulness.
Drink not to Elevation.

	S	M	T	W	T	F	S
T							
S	••	•		•		•	
O	•	•	•		•	•	•
R			•			•	
F		•			•		
I			•	•			
S							
I							
M							
Cl.							
T							
Ch.							
H							

This my little Book had for its Motto these Lines from Addison's *Cato;*

Here will I hold: If there is a Pow'r above us,
(And that there is, all Nature cries aloud
Thro' all her Works) he must delight in Virtue,
And that which he delights in must be happy.[148]

Another from Cicero.

O Vitæ Philosophia dux! O Virtulum indagatrix, expultrixque vitiorum! Unus dies bene, et ex preceptis tuis actus, peccanti immortalitati est anteponendus.[149]

[148]Joseph Addison, *Cato, A Tragedy* (1713), Act V, Scene i, lines 15–18.

[149]Marcus Tullius Cicero (106–43 B.C.), Roman philosopher and orator. The quotation is from *Tusculan Disputations,* Act V, Scene ii, line 5. Several lines are omitted after *vitiorum.* "Oh philosophy, guide of life! Oh searcher out of virtues and expeller of vices! . . . One day lived well and according to thy precepts is to be preferred to an eternity of sin."

Another from the Proverbs of Solomon speaking of Wisdom or Virtue;

Length of Days is in her right hand, and in her Left Hand Riches and Honours; Her Ways are Ways of Pleasantness, and all her Paths are Peace. III, 16, 17.

And conceiving God to be the Fountain of Wisdom, I thought it right and necessary to solicit his Assistance for obtaining it; to this End I form'd the following little Prayer, which was prefix'd to my Tables of Examination; for daily Use.

O Powerful Goodness! bountiful Father! merciful Guide! Increase in me that Wisdom which discovers my truest Interests; Strengthen my Resolutions to perform what that Wisdom dictates. Accept my kind Offices to thy other Children, as the only Return in my Prayer for thy continual Favours to me.

I us'd also sometimes a little Prayer which I took from Thomson's Poems. viz

Father of Light and Life, thou Good supreme,
O teach me what is good, teach me thy self!
Save me from Folly, Vanity and Vice,
From every low Pursuit, and fill my Soul
With Knowledge, conscious Peace, and Virtue pure,
Sacred, substantial, neverfading Bliss![150]

The Precept of *Order* requiring that every *Part of my Business should have its allotted Time,* one Page in my little Book contain'd the following Scheme on Employment for the Twenty-four Hours of a natural Day.

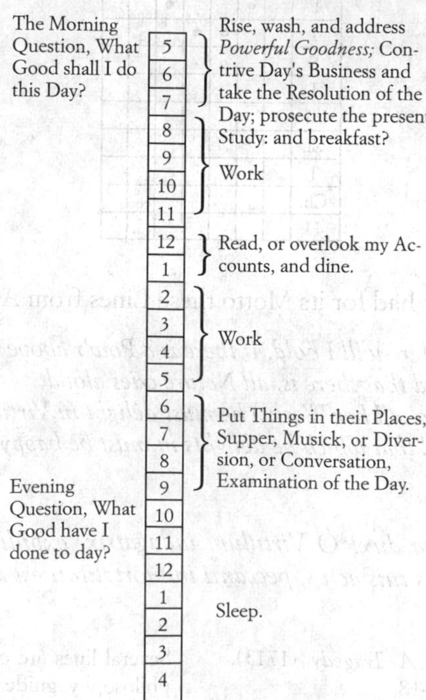

The Morning Question, What Good shall I do this Day?
5
6
7
Rise, wash, and address *Powerful Goodness;* Contrive Day's Business and take the Resolution of the Day; prosecute the present Study: and breakfast?
8
9
10
11
Work
12
1
Read, or overlook my Accounts, and dine.
2
3
4
5
Work
6
7
8
9
Put Things in their Places, Supper, Musick, or Diversion, or Conversation, Examination of the Day.
Evening Question, What Good have I done to day?
10
11
12
1
2
3
4
Sleep.

[150]From James Thomson (1700–1748), *The Seasons,* "Winter" (1726), lines 218–23.

I enter'd upon the Execution of this Plan for Self-Examination, and continu'd it with occasional Intermissions for some time. I was surpriz'd to find myself so much fuller of Faults than I had imagined, but I had the Satisfaction of seeing them diminish. To avoid the Trouble of renewing now and then my little Book, which by scraping out the Marks on the Paper of old Faults to make room for new Ones in a new Course, became full of Holes: I transferr'd my Tables and Precepts to the Ivory Leaves of a Memorandum Book, on which the Lines were drawn with red Ink that made a durable Stain, and on those Lines I mark'd my Faults with a black Lead Pencil, which Marks I could easily wipe out with a wet Sponge. After a while I went thro' one Course only in a Year, and afterwards only one in several years, till at length I omitted them entirely, being employ'd in Voyages and Business abroad with a Multiplicity of Affairs, that interfered, but I always carried my little Book with me.

My scheme of ORDER, gave me the most Trouble, and I found, that tho' it might be practicable where a Man's Business was such as to leave him the Disposition of his Time, that of a Journey-man Printer for instance, it was not possible to be exactly observ'd by a Master, who must mix with the World, and often receive People of Business at their own Hours. *Order* too, with regard to Places for Things, Papers, &c. I found extreamly difficult to acquire. I had not been early accustomed to *Method,* and having an exceeding good Memory, I was not so sensible of the Inconvenience attending Want of Method. This Article therefore cost me so much painful Attention and my Faults in it vex'd me so much, and I made so little Progress in Amendment, and had such frequent Relapses, that I was almost ready to give up the Attempt, and content my self with a faulty Character in that respect. Like the Man who in buying an Ax of a Smith my neighbour, desired to have the whole of its Surface as bright as the Edge; The Smith consented to grind it bright for him if he would turn the Wheel. He turn'd while the Smith press'd the broad Face of the Ax hard and heavily on the Stone, which made the Turning of it very fatiguing. The Man came every now and then from the Wheel to see how the Work went on; and at length would take his Ax as it was without farther Grinding. No, says the Smith, Turn on, turn on; we shall have it bright by and by; as yet 'tis only speckled. Yes, says the Man; but — *I think I like a speckled Ax best.* And I believe this may have been the Case with many who having for want of some such Means as I employ'd found the Difficulty of obtaining good, and breaking bad Habits, in other Points of Vice and Virtue, have given up the Struggle, and concluded that *a speckled Ax was best.* For something that pretended to be Reason was every now and then suggesting to me, that such extream nicety as I exacted of my self might be a kind of Foppery in Morals, which if it were known would make me ridiculous; that a perfect Character might be attended with the Inconvenience of being envied and hated; and that a benevolent Man should allow a few Faults in himself, to keep his Friends in Countenance.

In Truth I found myself incorrigible with respect to *Order;* and now I am grown old, and my Memory bad, I feel very sensibly the want of it. But on the whole, tho' I never arrived at the Perfection I had been so ambitious of obtaining, but fell far short of it, yet I was by the Endeavour a better and a happier Man than I otherwise should have been, if I had not attempted it; As those who aim at perfect Writing by imitating the engraved Copies, tho' they never reach the wish'd for Excellence of those Copies, their Hand is mended by the Endeavour, and is tolerable while it continues fair and legible.

And it may be well my Posterity should be informed, that to this little Artifice, with the Blessing of God, their Ancestor ow'd the constant Felicity of his Life down to his 79th Year in which this is written. What Reserves may attend the Remainder is in the Hand of Providence: But if they arrive the Reflection on past Happiness enjoy'd ought to help his Bearing them with more Resignation. To *Temperance* he ascribes his long-continu'd Health, and what is still left to him of a good Constitution. To *Industry* and *Frugality* the early Easiness of his Circumstances, and Acquisition of his Fortune, with all that Knowledge which enabled him to be an useful Citizen, and obtain'd for him some Degree of Reputation among the Learned. To *Sincerity* and *Justice* the Confidence of his Country, and the honourable Employs it conferr'd upon him. And to the joint Influence of the whole Mass of the Virtues, even in the imperfect State he was able to acquire them, all that Evenness of Temper, and that Chearfulness in Conversation which makes his Company still sought for, and agreable even to his younger Acquaintance. I hope therefore that some of my Descendants may follow the Example and reap the Benefit.

It will be remark'd that, tho' my Scheme was not wholly without Religion there was in it no Mark of any of the distinguishing Tenets of any particular Sect. I had purposely avoided them; for being fully persuaded of the Utility and Excellency of my Method, and that it might be serviceable to People in all Religions, and intending some time or other to publish it, I would not have any thing in it that should prejudice any one of any Sect against it. I purposed writing a little Comment on each Virtue, in which I would have shown the Advantages of possessing it, and the Mischiefs attending its opposite Vice; and I should have called my Book the ART of *Virtue,* because it would have shown the *Means and Manner* of obtaining Virtue, which would have distinguish'd it from the mere Exhortation to be good, that does not instruct and indicate the Means; but is like the Apostle's Man of verbal Charity, who only, without showing to the Naked and the Hungry *how* or where they might get Cloaths or Victuals, exhorted them to be fed and clothed. *James* II, 15, 16.[151]

But it so happened that my Intention of writing and publishing this Comment was never fulfilled. I did indeed, from time to time put down short Hints of the Sentiments, Reasonings, &c. to be made use of in it; some of which I have still by me: But the necessary close Attention to private Business in the earlier part of Life, and public Business since, have occasioned my postponing it. For it being connected in my Mind with a *great and extensive Project* that required the whole Man to execute, and which an unforeseen Succession of Employs prevented my attending to, it has hitherto remain'd unfinish'd.

In this Piece it was my Design to explain and enforce this Doctrine, that vicious Actions are not hurtful because they are forbidden, but forbidden because they are hurtful, the Nature of Man alone consider'd: That it was therefore every one's Interest to be virtuous, who wish'd to be happy even in this World. And I should from this Circumstance, there being always in the World a Number of rich Merchants, Nobility, States and Princes, who have need of honest Instruments for the Management of their Affairs, and such being so rare have endeavoured to convince young

[151]"If a brother or sister be naked, and destitute of daily food. And one of you say unto them, Depart in peace, be ye warmed and filled: notwithstanding ye give them not those things which are needful to the body; what doth it profit?"

Persons, that no Qualities were so likely to make a poor Man's Fortune as those of Probity and Integrity.

My List of Virtues contain'd at first but twelve: But a Quaker Friend having kindly inform'd me that I was generally thought proud; that my Pride show'd itself frequently in Conversation; that I was not content with being in the right when discussing any Point, but was overbearing and rather insolent; of which he convinc'd me by mentioning several Instances; I determined endeavouring to cure myself if I could of this Vice or Folly among the rest, and I added *Humility* to my List, giving an extensive Meaning to the Word. I cannot boast of much Success in acquiring the *Reality* of this Virtue; but I had a good deal with regard to the *Appearance* of it. I made it a Rule to forbear all direct Contradiction to the Sentiments of others, and all positive Assertion of my own. I even forbid myself agreable to the old Laws of our Junto, the Use of every Word or Expression in the Language that imported a fix'd Opinion; such as *certainly, undoubtedly,* &c. and I adopted instead of them, *I conceive, I apprehend,* or *I imagine* a thing to be so or so, or it so appears to me at present. When another asserted something, that I thought an Error, I deny'd my self the Pleasure of contradicting him abruptly, and of showing immediately some Absurdity in his Proposition; and in answering I began by observing that in certain Cases or Circumstances his Opinion would be right, but that in the present case there *appear'd* or *seem'd* to me some Difference, &c. I soon found the Advantage of this Change in my Manners. The Conversations I engag'd in went on more pleasantly. The modest way in which I propos'd my Opinions, procur'd them a readier Reception and less Contradiction; I had less Mortification when I was found to be in the wrong, and I more easily prevail'd with others to give up their Mistakes and join with me when I happen'd to be in the right. And this Mode, which I at first put on, with some violence to natural Inclination, became at length so easy and so habitual to me, that perhaps for these Fifty Years past no one has ever heard a dogmatical Expression escape me. And to this Habit (after my Character of Integrity) I think it principally owing, that I had early so much Weight with my Fellow Citizens, when I proposed new Institutions, or Alterations in the old; and so much Influence in public Councils when I became a Member. For I was but a sad Speaker, never eloquent, subject to much Hesitation in my choice of Words, hardly correct in Language, and yet I generally carried my Points.

In reality there is perhaps no one of our natural Passions so hard to subdue as *Pride.* Disguise it, struggle with it, beat it down, stifle it, mortify it as much as one pleases, it is still alive, and will every now and then peep out and show itself. You will see it perhaps often in this History. For even if I could conceive that I had compleatly overcome it, I should probably by [be] proud of my Humility.

Thus far written at Passy 1784

1791

James Grainger 1721?–1766

James Grainger's major poetical work, *The Sugar Cane,* combines elements of writing that were very popular during the eighteenth century. Grainger incorporated into *The Sugar Cane* elements of New World exploration narratives, imperial topographical poetry (as in such poems as Denham's "Cooper's Hill" and Pope's "Windsor Forest"), and the encyclopedia writing inspired by Diderot's *Encyclopédie.* Yet the poem, highly contemporary in its own day, also drew upon a "georgic" tradition stretching back to Virgil. Poetically, then, Grainger's *Sugar Cane* had antecedents in classical writings; topically, the poem created innovations on its classical model. Moving beyond the georgic tradition of providing instruction to an idealized farmer, Grainger also aimed to give the reader specific, practical information. Indeed, Grainger's poem remains one of the best descriptions of work life on an eighteenth-century sugar plantation. In extensive footnotes, *The Sugar Cane* provides minute details on the history and topography of the various islands of the Antilles, the plant and animal life, the various diseases and their cures.

The fourth and final book of *The Sugar Cane,* included here, details the management of the labor force—enslaved Africans—that makes the sugar plantation possible. Grainger's own difficulty in justifying the slave system is evident throughout: he shifts awkwardly between advice of a practical nature offered to the slave buyer and invocations and prayers for amelioration of slave conditions, marked by a sense of hope for eventual abolition of slavery. Grainger puts a difficult and sometimes anguished description of the management of slaves in place of the georgic's usual culminating celebration of the perfect farm. Along the way, Grainger also provides a poetical version of the standard British defense of slavery (the Spanish started it; Scottish miners are worse off than African slaves) and intriguing insights into the various cultures and manners of the Africans who peopled the West Indian islands.

James Grainger was born about 1721 in Berwickshire in southeast Scotland, the son of a tax collector. He studied medicine at the University of Edinburgh, spent three years as an army surgeon in Scotland and Holland, and made a Grand Tour of Europe before receiving his M.D. degree in 1753. Moving on to London, Grainger joined the Royal College of Physicians, but he met with difficulty in making a living as a physician. He supplemented his income by writing for various magazines on medical and literary topics and by publishing poetry of his own. A self-taught Latinist, Grainger published translations of classical Latin poems, the most notable being the *Elegies of Tibullus,* which was scathingly reviewed by his one-time friend Tobias Smollett, prompting a bitter exchange of insults in print between the two. His later works include what became the standard reference work on West Indian diseases and a ballad included in Percy's *Reliques of Ancient English Poetry.* His literary interests led to friendships with the key figures in London's cultural world at mid-century: Robert Dodsley, Oliver Goldsmith, Samuel Johnson, Thomas Percy, Sir Joshua Reynolds, William Shenstone. In his *Life of Johnson,* James Boswell recorded Bishop Percy's opinion of Grainger: "He was not only a man of genius and learning, but had many excellent virtues; being one of the most generous, friendly, and benevolent men I ever knew."

In hopes of improving his fortune, Grainger set out in 1759 to the West Indies as a paid companion to John Bourryau, a wealthy friend who owned plantations on the island of St. Christopher (now St. Kitts). Shortly after arriving, Grainger met and married a local heiress, whose family made him manager of their estates. Grainger continued his medical practice on the side, hoping one day to be able to buy his own sugar plantation. His authorship of *The Sugar Cane* represents his education in the cultivation and manufacture of sugar, combined with his growing interest in the history, geography, and natural history of the islands. Interestingly, the poem also suggests Grainger's continuing interest in medicine. After four years in the Caribbean, Grainger traveled back to London, where he presented his long georgic poem to his circle of literary friends for their opinion. According to Boswell, the manuscript of the poem was read at Sir Joshua Reynolds's house, where the company was amused by Grainger's account of the ravages caused in the sugarcane fields by rats. The amusement caused among this literary group by the explicit descriptions of the conditions of sugarcane plantations demonstrates how unusual was Grainger's innovation of including specific technical and medical terminology in the neoclassical form of the georgic poem. One of the ways Grainger managed to maintain the high tone of the blank verse while also providing accurate and useful information was to use extensive footnotes detailing the various names and uses of local flora and fauna. The effect of reading the complete poem with all its footnotes is to take a sort of grand tour of the West Indies while the islands were at the height of a sugar-and-slavery system that produced more wealth for Great Britain than all the North American colonies combined.

Thomas W. Krise
U.S. Air Force Academy

PRIMARY WORK

The Sugar-Cane: A Poem. In Four Books. With Notes. 1764.

SECONDARY WORK

David S. Shields, *Oracles of Empire: Poetry, Politics, and Commerce in British America, 1690–1750,* 1990.

from The Sugar Cane. A Poem. In Four Books.

Book IV: The Genius of Africa[1]

ARGUMENT

Invocation to the Genius of Africa.[2] *Address. Negroes when bought should be young, and strong. The Congo-negroes*[3] *are fitter for the house and trades, than for the field. The Gold-Coast,*[4] *but especially the Papaw-negroes, make the best field-negroes: but even these, if advanced in years, should not be purchased. The marks of a sound negroe at a negroe sale. Where the men do nothing but hunt,*

[1]Printed here is a slightly modernized version of *The Sugar Cane,* Book IV, originally published in 1764.

[2]The spirit or personification of Africa [Ed.].

[3]People from the region around the Congo River in modern Zaire [Ed.].

[4]The coast of the Gulf of Guinea, in modern Ghana, West Africa [Ed.].

fish or fight, and all field drudgery is left to the women; these are to be preferred to their husbands. The Minnahs[5] *make good tradesmen, but addicted to suicide. The Mundingos,*[6] *in particular, subject to worms; and the Congas, to dropsical disorders. How salt-water, or new negroes should be seasoned. Some negroes eat dirt. Negroes should be habituated by gentle degrees to field labour. This labour, when compared to that in lead-mines, or of those who work in the gold and silver mines of South America, is not only less toilsome, but far more healthy. Negroes should always be treated with humanity. Praise of freedom. Of the dracunculus, or dragon-worm. Of chigres. Of the yaws. Might not this disease be imparted by inoculation? Of worms, and their multiform appearance. Praise of commerce. Of the imaginary disorders of negroes, especially those caused by their conjurers or Obia-men.*[7] *The composition and supposed virtues of a magic-phiol. Field-negroes should not begin to work before six in the morning, and should leave off between eleven and twelve; and beginning again at two, should finish before sun-set. Of the weekly allowance of negroes. The young, the old, the sickly, and even the lazy, must have their victuals prepared for them. Of negroe-ground, and its various productions. To be fenced in, and watched. Of an American garden. Of the situation of the negroe-huts. How best defended from fire. The great negroe-dance described. Drumming, and intoxicating spirits not to be allowed. Negroes should be made to marry in their masters plantation. Inconveniences arising from the contrary practice. Negroes to be cloathed once a year, and before Christmas. Praise of Lewis XIV,*[8] *for the Code Noir. A body of laws of this kind recommended to the English sugar colonies. Praise of the river Thames. A moon-light landscape and vision.*

Genius of Africk! whether thou bestrid'st
The castled elephants or at the source,
(While howls the desart fearfully around,)
Of thine own Niger,[9] sadly thou reclin'st
Thy temples shaded by the tremulous palm,
Or quick papaw,[10] whose top is necklac'd round
With numerous rows of party-colour'd fruit:
Or hear'st thou rather from the rocky banks
Of Rio Grandê,[11] or black Sanaga?[12]
Where dauntless thou the headlong torrent brav'st
In search of gold, to brede thy wooly locks,
On with bright ringlets ornament thine ears,

[5]People from the region around Minna, a city in central Nigeria, north of the Niger river in West Africa [Ed.].

[6]The Mandingo, or Mande, people of West Africa, a predominantly Muslim tribe, known for their widespread trading activities [Ed.].

[7]Obia, or Obeah, is the traditional magic of West African polytheistic religion; related to vodun (voodoo) in Haiti [Ed.].

[8]King Louis XIV of France (1638–1715; reigned 1643–1715), called the Sun King, promulgated the *Code Noir* in 1685, which placed some restrictions upon the power of slave-owners over their slaves [Ed.].

[9]Major river in West Africa [Ed.].

[10]The fast-growing papaya tree [Ed.].

[11]Now called the Corubal River, in Guinea and Guinea-Bissau in West Africa [Ed.].

[12]River in Cameroon, West Africa [Ed.].

Thine arms, and ankles: O attend my song.
A muse that pities thy distressful state;
Who sees, with grief, thy sons in fetters bound;
Who wished freedom to the race of man;
Thy nod assenting craves: dread Genius, come!

Yet vain thy presence, vain thy favouring nod;
Unless once more the muses; that erewhile
Upheld me fainting in my past career,
Through Caribbe's cane-isles; kind condescend
To guide my footsteps, through parch'd Libya's wilds;
And bind my sun-burnt brow with other bays,
Than ever deck'd the Sylvan bard before.

Say, will my Melvil,[13] from the public care,
Withdraw one moment, to the muses shrine?
Who smit with thy fair fame, industrious cull
An Indian wreath to mingle with thy bays,
And deck the hero, and the scholar's brow!
Wilt thou, whose mildness smooths the face of war,
Who round the victor-blade the myrtle twin'st,
And mak'st subjection loyal and sincere;
O wilt thou gracious hear the unartful strain,
Whose mild instructions teach, no trivial theme,
What care the jetty African requires?
Yes, thou wilt deign to hear; a man thou art
Who deem'st nought foreign that belongs to man.

In mind, and aptitute for useful toil,
The negroes differ: muse that difference sing.

Whether to wield the hoe, or guide the plane;[14]
Or for domestic uses thou intend'st
The sunny Libyan: from what clime they spring,
It not imports; if strength and youth be theirs.

Yet those from Congo's wide-extended plains,
Through which the long Zaire winds with chrystal stream,
Where lavish Nature sends indulgent forth
Fruits of high favour, and spontaneous seeds
Of bland nutritious quality, ill bear
The toilsome field; but boast a docile mind,
And happiness of features. These, with care,

[13]Count de Melvil, a virtuous character in Tobias Smollett's novel *The Adventures of Ferdinand Count Fathom* (1753); he is the benefactor of the dissolute title character, who is, like Grainger, a physician [Ed.].

[14]Or plough [Ed.].

Be taught each nice mechanic art: or train'd
To houshold offices: their ductile souls
Will all thy care, and all thy gold repay.

But, of the labours of the field demand
Thy chief attention; and the ambrosial cane
Thou long'st to see, with spiry frequence, shade
Many an acre: planter, chuse the slave,
Who sails from barren climes; where art alone,
Offspring of rude necessity, compells
The sturdy native, or to plant the soil,
Or stem vast rivers, for his daily food.

Such are the children of the Golden Coast;
Such the Papaws, of negroes far the best:
And such the numerous tribes, that skirt the shore,
From rapid Volta to the distant Rey.[15]

But, planter, from what coast soe'er they sail,
Buy not the old: they ever sullen prove;
With heart-felt anguish, they lament their home;
They will not, cannot work; they never learn
Thy native language; they are prone to ails;
And oft by suicide their being end.—

Must thou from Africk reinforce thy gang?—
Let health and youth their every sinew firm;
Clear roll their ample eye; their tongue be red;
Broad swell their chest; their shoulders wide expand;
Not prominent their belly; clean and strong
Their thighs and legs, in just proportion rise.
Such soon will brave the fervours of the clime;
And free from ails, that kill thy negroe-train.
A useful servitude will long support.

Yet, if thine own, thy childrens life, be dear;
Buy not a Cormantee,[16] tho' healthy, young.
Of breed too generous for the servile field;
They, born to freedom in their native land,
Chuse death before dishonourable bonds:
Or, fir'd with vengeance, at the midnight hour,

[15]Rivers in modern Ghana, West Africa [Ed.].

[16]An African from the region around Cormantyne (or Kormantine), site of a Dutch slaving station in modern Ghana [Ed.].

Sudden they seize thine unsuspecting watch,
And thine own poinard[17] bury in thy breast.

At home, the men, in many a sylvan realm,
Their rank tobacco, charm of sauntering minds,
From clayey tubes inhale; or, vacant, beat
For prey the forest; or, in war's dread ranks,
Their country's foes affront: while, in the field,
Their wives plant rice, or yams, or lofty maize,
Fell hunger to repel. Be these thy choice:
They, hardy, with the labours of the Cane
Soon grow familiar; while unusual toil,
And new severities their husbands kill.

The slaves from Minnah[18] are of stubborn breed:
But, when the bill, or hammer, they affect;
They soon perfection reach. But fly, with care,
The Moco-nation;[19] they themselves destroy.

Worms lurk in all: yet, pronest they to worms,
Who from Mundingo[20] sail. When therefore such
Thou buy'st, for sturdy and laborious they,
Straight let some learned leach[21] strong medicines give,
Till food and climate both familiar grow.
Thus, tho' from rise to set, in Phoebus' eye,[22]
They toil, unceasing; yet, at night, they'll sleep,
Lap'd in Elysium;[23] and, each day, at dawn,
Spring from their couch, as blythsome as the sun.

One precept more, it much imports to know.—
The Blacks, who drink the Quanza's[24] lucid stream,
Fed by ten thousand springs, are prone to bloat,
Whether at home or in these ocean-isles;
And tho' nice art the water may subdue,
Yet many die; and few, for many a year,
Just strength attain to labour for their lord.

[17]A poniard, or dagger [Ed.].

[18]See footnote 5 [Ed.].

[19]Apparently peoples originating in East Africa, who were associated with, or transported from, the Arab port of Mocha on the Red Sea [Ed.].

[20]See footnote 6 [Ed.].

[21]A physician, so called because of the physician's former use of leeches to let blood as a cure [Ed.].

[22]The sun; Phoebus being the title of Apollo as god of the sun [Ed.].

[23]In classical mythology, the place in the Underworld where virtuous souls rest [Ed.].

[24]The River Cuanza or Kwanza, in Angola in southwestern Africa [Ed.].

Would'st thou secure thine Ethiop[25] from those ails,
Which change of climate, change of waters breed,
And food unusual? let Machaon[26] draw
From each some blood, as age and sex require;
And well with vervain,[27] well with sempre-vive,[28]
Unload their bowels.—These, in every hedge,
Spontaneous grow.—Nor will it not conduce
To give what chemists, in mysterious phrase,
Term the white eagle; deadly foe to worms.
But chief do thou, my friend, with hearty food,
Yet easy of digestion, likest that
Which they at home regal'd on; renovate
Their sea-worn appetites. Let gentle work,
Or rather playful exercise, amuse
The novel gang: and far be angry words;
Far ponderous chains; and far disheartening blows.—
From fruits restrain their eagerness; yet if
The acajou, haply, in thy garden bloom,
With cherries,[29] or of white or purple hue,
Thrice wholesome fruit in this relaxing clime!
Safely thou may'st their appetite indulge.
Their arid skins will plump, their features shine:
No rheums, no dysenteric ails torment:
The thirsty hydrops[30] flies.—'Tis even averr'd,
(Ah, did experience sanctify the fact;
How many Lybians[31] now would dig the soil,
Who pine in hourly agonies away!)
This pleasing fruit, if turtle join its aid,
Removes that worst of ails, disgrace of art,
The loathsome leprosy's infectious bane.

There are, the muse hath oft abhorrent seen,
Who swallow dirt; (so the chlorotic fair
Oft chalk prefer to the most poignant cates.[32])
Such, dropsy bloats, and to sure death consigns;

[25]An inhabitant of Ethiopia, in East Africa, here representing Africans generally [Ed.].

[26]Physician to the Greeks in the Trojan War, and son of the god of medicine, Aescalapius [Ed.].

[27]An herbaceous plant, native to Europe [Ed.].

[28]The houseleek, a succulent European plant with reddish flowers [Ed.].

[29]The tree which produces this wholesome fruit is tall, shady, and of quick growth. Its Indian name is *Acajou;* hence corruptly called *Cashew* by the English. . . .

[30]Former name for edema, the build-up of fluid in the cavities of the body, often due to kidney failure [Ed.].

[31]Inhabitants of Libya, in North Africa, here signifying Africans generally [Ed.].

[32]Dainty foods [Ed.].

Unless restrain'd from this unwholesome food,
By soothing words, by menaces, by blows:
Nor yet will threats, or blows, or soothing words,
Perfect their cure; unless thou, Paean,[33] design'st
By medicine's power their cravings to subdue.

To easy labour first inure thy slaves;
Extremes are dangerous. With industrious search,
Let them fit grassy provender[34] collect
For thy keen stomach'd herds.—But when the earth
Hath made her annual progress round the sun,
What time the conch[35] or bell resounds, they may
All to the Cane-ground, with thy gang, repair.

Nor, Negroe, at thy destiny repine,
Tho' doom'd to toil from dawn to setting sun.
How far more pleasant is thy rural task,
Than theirs who sweat, sequester'd from the day,
In dark tartarean caves, sunk far beneath
The earth's dark surface, where sulphureous flames,
Oft from their vapoury prisons bursting wild,
To dire explosion give the cavern'd deep,
And in dread ruin all its inmates whelm?—
Nor fateful only is the bursting flame;
The exhalations of the deep-dug mine,
Tho' slow, shake from their wings as sure a death.
With what intense severity of pain
Hath the afflicted muse, in Scotia, seen
The miners rack'd, who toil for fatal lead?
What cramps, what palsies shake their feeble limbs,
Who, on the margin of the rocky Drave,[36]
Trace silver's fluent ore? Yet white men these!

How far more happy ye, than those poor slaves,
Who, whilom,[37] under native, gracious chiefs,
Incas and emperors, long time enjoy'd
Mild government, with every sweet of life,
In blissful climates? See them dragg'd in chains,
By proud insulting tyrants, to the mines
Which once they call'd their own, and then despis'd!

[33]A surname or title for Apollo, the Greek god of medicine, music, archery, prophecy, and light [Ed.].

[34]Food for livestock [Ed.].

[35]Plantations that have no bells assemble their Negroes by sounding a conch-shell.

[36]A river in Hungary, on whose banks are found mines of quicksilver [i.e., mercury, Ed.].

[37]Formerly [Ed.].

See, in the mineral bosom of their land,
How hard they toil! how soon their youthful limbs
Feel the decrepitude of age! how soon
Their teeth desert their sockets! and how soon
Shaking paralysis unstrings their frame!
Yet scarce, even then, are they allow'd to view
The glorious God of day, of whom they beg,
With earnest hourly supplications, death;
Yet death slow comes, to torture them the more!

With these compar'd, ye sons of Afric, say,
How far more happy is your lot? Bland health,
Of ardent eye, and limb robust, attends
Your custom'd labour: and, should sickness seize,
With what solicitude are ye not nurs'd!—
Ye Negroes, then, your pleasing task pursue;
And, by your toil, deserve your master's care.

When first your Blacks are novel to the hoe;
Study their humours: Some, soft-soothing words;
Some, presents; and some, menaces subdue;
And some I've known, so stubborn is their kind,
Whom blows, alas! could win alone to toil.

Yet, planter, let humanity prevail.—
Perhaps thy Negroe, in his native land,
Possest large fertile plains, and slaves, and herds:
Perhaps, whene'er he deign'd to walk abroad,
The richest silks, from where the Indus rolls,
His limbs invested in their gorgeous pleats:
Perhaps he wails his wife, his children, left
To struggle with adversity: Perhaps
Fortune, in battle for his country fought,
Gave him a captive to his deadliest foe:
Perhaps, incautious, in his native fields,
(On pleasurable scenes his mind intent)
All as he wandered; from the neighbouring grove,
Fell ambush dragg'd him to the hated main.—
Were they even sold for crimes; ye polish'd, say!
Ye, to whom Learning opes her amplest page!
Ye, whom the knowledge of a living God
Should lead to virtue! Are ye free from crimes?
Ah pity, then, these uninstructed swains;
And still let mercy soften the decrees
Of rigid justice, with her lenient hand.
Oh, did the tender muse possess the power;
Which monarchs have, and monarchs oft abuse:

'Twould be the fond ambition of her soul,
To quell tyrannic sway; knock off the chains
Of heart-debasing slavery; give to man,
Of every colour and of every clime,
Freedom, which stamps him image of his God.
Then laws, Oppression's scourge, fair Virtue's prop,
Offspring of Wisdom! should impartial reign,
To knit the whole in well-accorded strife:
Servants, not slaves; of choice, and not compell'd;
The Blacks should cultivate the Cane-land isles.

Say, shall the muse the various ills recount,
Which Negroe-nations feel? Shall she describe
The worm that subtly winds into their flesh,
All as they bathe them in their native streams?
There, with fell increment, it soon attains
A direful length of harm. Yet, if due skill,
And proper circumspection are employed,
It may be won its volumes to wind round
A leaden cylinder: But, O, beware,
No rashness practise; else 'twill surely snap,
And suddenly, retreating, dire produce
An annual lameness to the tortured Moor.

Nor only is the dragon worm to dread:
Fell, winged insects,[38] which the visual ray
Scarcely discerns, their sable feet and hands
Oft penetrate: and, in the fleshy nest,
Myriads of young produce; which soon destroy
The parts they breed in; if assiduous care,
With art, extract not the prolific foe.

Or, shall she sing, and not debase her lay,
The pest peculiar to the Aethiop-kind.
The yaw's[39] infectious bane?—The infected far
In huts, to leeward, lodge; or near the main.
With heartening food, with turtle, and with conchs;
The flowers of sulphur, and hard niccars[40] burnt,
The lurking evil from the blood expel,
And throw it on the surface: There in spots
Which cause no pain, and scanty ichor[41] yield,

[38]These, by the English, are called *Chigoes* or *Chigres* [chiggers, Ed.]. . . .

[39]Yaws, or frambesia, is an infectious tropical disease of the skin [Ed.].

[40]The botanical name of this medicinal shrub is Guilandina. . . .

[41]Watery discharge from a wound or sore [Ed.].

It chiefly breaks about the arms and hips,
A virulent contagion!—When no more
Round knobby spots deform, but the disease
Seems at a pause: then let the learned leach
Give, in due dose, live-silver[42] from the mine;
Till copious spitting the whole taint exhaust—
Nor thou repine, tho' half-way round the sun,
This globe, her annual progress shall absolve;
Ere, clera'd, thy slave from all infection shine.
Nor then be confident; successive crops
Of defoedations[43] oft will spot the skin:
These thou, with turpentine and guaiac pods,
Reduc'd by coction to a wholesome draught,
Total remove, and give the blood its balm.

Say, as this malady but once infests
The sons of Guinea, might not skill ingraft
(Thus, the small-pox are happily convey'd;)
This ailment early to thy Negroe-train?

Yet, of the ills which torture Libya's sons,
Worms tyrannize the worst. They, Proteus-like,[44]
Each symptom of each malady assume;
And, under every mask, the assassins kill.
Now, in the guise of horrid spasms, they writhe
The tortured body, and all sense o'er-power.
Sometimes, like Mania,[45] with her head downcast,
They cause the wretch in solitude to pine;
Or frantic, bursting from the strongest chains,
To frown with look terrific, not his own.
Sometimes like Ague,[46] with a shivering mien,
The teeth gnash fearful, and the blood runs chill:
Anon the ferment maddens in the veins,
And a false vigour animates the frame.
Again, the dropsy's bloated mask they steal;
Or, "melt with minings of the hectic fire."[47]

Say, to such various mimic forms of death;
What remedies shall puzzled art oppose?—
Thanks to the Almighty, in each path-way hedge,

[42]Quicksilver, or mercury [Ed.].
[43]Pollutions, defilements [Ed.].
[44]Classical sea deity, able to prophesy, known for assuming various shapes to avoid answering humans' questions about the future [Ed.].
[45]Personification of mania, or madness [Ed.].
[46]Personification of ague, or acute fever [Ed.].
[47]From John Armstrong, *The Art of Preserving Health, A Poem* (1744), III. 202 [Ed.].

Rank cow-itch[48] grows, whose sharp unnumber'd stings,
Sheath'd in Melasses, from their dens expell,
Fell dens of death, the reptile lurking foe.—
A powerful vermifuge, in skilful hands,
The worm-grass proves; yet, even in hands of skill,
Sudden, I've known it dim the visual ray
For a whole day and night. There are who use
(And sage Experience justifies the use)
The mineral product of the Cornish mine;[49]
Which in old times, ere Britain laws enjoyed,
The polish'd Tyrians,[50] monarchs of the main,
In their swift ships convey'd to foreign realms:
The sun by day, by night the northern star,
Their course conducted.—Mighty commerce, hail!
By thee the sons of Attic's sterile land,
A scanty number, laws impos'd on Greece:
Nor aw'd they Greece alone; vast Asia's King,
Tho' girt by rich arm'd myriads, at their frown
Felt his heart whither on his farthest throne.
Perennial source of population thou!
While scanty peasants plough the flowery plains
Of purple Enna; from the Belgian fens,
What swarms of useful citizens spring up,
Hatch'd by thy fostering wing. Ah where is flown
That dauntless free-born spirit, which of old,
Taught them to shake off the tyrannic yoke
Of Spains insulting King;[51] on whose wide realms,
The sun still shone with undiminished beam?
Parent of wealth! in vain, coy nature hoards
Her gold and diamonds; toil, thy firm compeer,
And industry of unremitting nerve,
Scale the cleft mountain, the loud torrent brave,
Plunge to the center, and thro' Nature's wiles,
(Led on by skill of penetrative soul)
Her following close, her secret treasures find,
To pour them plenteous on the laughing world.
On thee Sylvanus,[52] thee each rural god,

[48]This extraordinary vine should not be permitted to grow in a Cane-piece; for Negroes have been known to fire the Canes, to save themselves from the torture which attends working in grounds where it has abounded. . . .

[49]Tin-filings are a better vermifuge than tin in powder. The western parts of Britain, and the neighbouring isles, have been famous for this useful metal from the remotest antiquity . . . .

[50]The ancient Phoenicians, from Tyre in the Levant [Ed.].

[51]Referring to the long struggle by the Low Countries (modern Belgium and the Netherlands) to secure independence from the Spanish empire [Ed.].

[52]Roman god of the woods (*silva*) [Ed.].

On thee chief Ceres,[53] with unfailing love
And fond distinction, emulously gaze.
In vain hath nature pour'd vast seas between
Far-distant kingdoms; endless storms in vain
With double night brood o'er them; thou dost throw,
O'er far-divided nature's realms, a chain
To bind in sweet society mankind.
By thee white Albion,[54] once a barbarous clime,
Grew fam'd for arms, for wisdom, and for laws;
By thee she holds the balance of the world,
Acknowledged now sole empress of the main.[55]
Coy though thou art, and mutable of love,
There may'st thou ever fix thy wandering steps;
While Eurus[56] rules the wide atlantic foam!
By thee, thy favorite, great Columbus found
That world, where now thy praises I rehearse
To the resounding main and palmy shore;
And Lusitania's[57] chiefs those realms explor'd,
Whence negroes spring, the subject of my song.

Nor pine the Blacks, alone, with real ills,
That baffle oft the wisest rules of art:
They likewise feel imaginary woes;
Woes no less deadly. Luckless he who owns
The slave, who thinks himself bewitch'd; and whom,
In wrath, a conjuror's snake-mark'd[58] staff hath struck!
They mope, love silence, every friend avoid;
They inly pine; all aliment reject;
Or insufficient for nutrition take:
Their features droop: a sickly yellowish hue
Their skin deforms; their strength and beauty fly.
Then comes the feverish fiend, with firy eyes,
Whom drowth, convulsions, and whom death surround,

[53]Roman goddess of grain and harvests [Ed.].
[54]Poetic name for England, called white (*alba*) for the white cliffs of Dover [Ed.].
[55]Britain as ruler of the seas through naval and mercantile power [Ed.].
[56]Roman name for the east wind; here referring to the easterly Trade Winds [Ed.].
[57]Ancient and poetic name for Portugal; Portuguese navigators explored the coast of Africa, opening trade (including the slave trade) between Europeans and Africans [Ed.].
[58]The negroe-conjurors, or Obia-men, as they are called, carry about them a staff, which is marked with frogs, snakes, &c. The blacks imagine that its blow, if not mortal, will at least occasion long and troublesome disorders. A belief in magic is inseparable from human nature, but those nations are most addicted thereto, among whom learning, and of course, philosophy have least obtained. As in all other countries, so in Guinea, the conjurors, as they have more understanding, so are they almost always more wicked than the common herd of their deluded countrymen; and as the negroe-magicians can do mischief, so they can also do good on a plantation, provided they are kept by the white people in proper subordination. [Obia, or Obeah, related to Voodoo, or Vodun, is the traditional belief system of many West African peoples. Ed.]

Fatal attendants! if some subtle slave
(Such, Obia-men are stil'd) do not engage,
To save the wretch by antidote or spell.

In magic spells, in Obia, all the sons
Of sable Africk trust:—Ye, sacred nine!
(For ye each hidden preparation know)
Transpierce the gloom, which ignorance and fraud
Have render'd awful; tell the laughing world
Of what these wonder-working charms are made.

Fern root cut small, and tied with many a knot;
Old teeth extracted from a white man's skull;
A lizard's skeleton; a serpent's head:
These mix'd with salt, and water from the spring,
Are in a phial pour'd; o'er these the leach
Mutters strange jargon, and wild circles forms.

Of this possest, each negroe deems himself
Secure from poison; for to poison they
Are infamously prone: and arm'd with this,
Their sable country daemons they defy,
Who fearful haunt them at the midnight hour,
To work them mischief. This, diseases fly;
Diseases follow: such its wonderous power!
This o'er the threshold of their cottage hung,
No thieves break in; or, if they dare to steal,
Their feet in blotches, which admit no cure,
Burst loathsome out: but should its owner filch,
As slaves were ever of the pilfering kind,
This from detection screens;—so conjurors swear.

'Till morning dawn, and Lucifer withdraw
His beamy chariot; let not the loud bell
Call forth thy negroes from their rushy couch:
And ere the sun with mid-day fervour glow,
When every broom-bush[59] opes her yellow flower;
Let thy black labourers from their toil desist:
Nor till the broom her every petal lock,
Let the loud bell recall them to the hoe.
But when the jalap her bright tint displays,
When the solanum[60] fills her cup with dew,

[59]This small plant, which grows in every pasture, may, with propriety, be termed an American clock; for it begins every forenoon at eleven to open its yellow flowers, which about one are fully expanded, and at two closed. . . .

[60]So some authors name the fire-weed . . . .

And crickets, snakes, and lizards 'gin their coil;
Let them find shelter in their cane-thatch'd huts;
Or, if constrain'd unusual hours to toil,
(For even the best must sometimes urge their gang)
With double nutriment reward their pains.

Howe'er insensate some may deem their slaves,
Nor 'bove the bestial rank; far other thoughts
The muse, soft daughter of humanity!
Will ever entertain.—The Ethiop knows,
The Ethiop feels, when treated like a man;
Nor grudges, should necessity compell,
By day, by night, to labour for his lord.

Not less inhuman, than unthrifty those;
Who, half the year's rotation round the sun,
Deny subsistence to their labouring slaves.
But would'st thou see thy negroe-train encrease,
Free from disorders; and thine acres clad
With groves of sugar: every week dispense
Or English beans, or Carolinian rice;
Iërne's[61] beef, or Pensilvanian flour;
Newfoundland cod, or herrings from the main
That howls tempestuous round the Scotian isles!

Yet some there are so lazily inclin'd,
And so neglectful of their food, that thou,
Would'st thou preserve them from the jaws of death;
Daily, their wholesome viands must prepare:
With these let all the young, and childless old,
And all the morbid share;—so heaven will bless,
With manifold encrease, thy costly care.

Suffice not this; to every slave assign
Some mountain-ground: or, if waste broken land
To thee belong, that broken land divide.
This let them cultivate, one day, each week;
And there raise yams, and there cassada's root:[62]
From a good daemon's staff cassada sprang,
Tradition says, and Caribbees[63] believe;

[61]Ireland's [Ed.].

[62]To an ancient Caribbean, bemoaning the savage uncomfortable life of his countrymen, a deity clad in white apparel appeared, and told him, he would have come sooner to have taught him the ways of civil life, had he been addressed before. He then showed him sharp-cutting stones to fell trees and build houses; and bade him cover them with the palm leaves. Then he broke his staff in three; which, being planted, soon after produced cassada. . . .

[63]Carib Indians, native inhabitants of the Lesser Antilles of the Caribbean [Ed.].

Which into three the white-rob'd genius broke,
And bade them plant, their hunger to repel.
There let angola's bloomy bush supply,[64]
For many a year, with wholesome pulse their board.
There let the bonavist,[65] his fringed pods
Throw liberal o'er the prop; while ochra[66] bears
Aloft his slimy pulp, and help disdains.
There let potatos[67] mantle o'er the ground;
Sweet as the cane-juice is the root they bear.
There too let eddas[68] spring in order meet,
With Indian cale,[69] and foodful calaloo:[70]
While mint, thyme, balm, and Europe's coyer herbs,
Shoot gladsome forth, not reprobate the clime.

This tract secure, with hedges or of limes,
Or bushy citrons, or the shapely tree[71]
That glows at once with aromatic blooms,
And golden fruit mature. To these be join'd,
In comely neighbourhood, the cotton shrub;
In this delicious clime the cotton bursts
On rocky soils.—The coffee also plant;
White as the skin of Albion's lovely fair,
Are the thick snowy fragrant blooms it boasts:
Nor wilt thou, cocô, thy rich pods refuse;
Tho' years, and heat, and moisture they require,
Ere the stone grind them to the food of health.
Of thee, perhaps, and of thy various sorts,
And that kind sheltering tree, thy mother nam'd,[72]
With crimson flowerets prodigally grac'd;
In future times, the enraptur'd muse may sing:
If public favour crown her present lay.

But let some antient, faithful slave erect
His sheltered mansion near; and with his dog,

[64]This is called *Pidgeon-pea* . . . .

[65]This is the Spanish name of a plant, which produces an excellent bean. . . .

[66]Or *Ockro*. . . .

[67]I cannot positively say, whether these vines are of Indian original or not; but as in their fructification, they differ from potatos at home, they probably are not European. They are sweet. There are four kinds, the red, the white, the long, and round. The juice of each may be made into a pleasant cool drink; and, being distilled, yield an excellent spirit.

[68]. . . This wholesome root, in some of the islands, is called *Edda*: . . .

[69]This green, which is a native of the New World, equals any of the greens in the Old.

[70]Another species of Indian pot herb, no less wholesome than the preceding. These, with mezamby, and the Jamaica pickle-weed, yield to no esculent plants in Europe. This is an Indian name.

[71]The orange tree.

[72]. . . It is also called *Cocao* and *Cocô*. . . . those who plant cacao-walks, sometimes screen them by a hardier tree, which the Spaniards aptly term *Madre de Cacao*. . . .

His loaded gun, and cutlass, guard the whole:
Else negroe-fugitives, who skulk 'mid rocks
And shrubby wilds, in bands will soon destroy
Thy labourer's honest wealth; their loss and yours.

Perhaps, of Indian gardens I could sing,
Beyond what bloom'd on blest Phaeacia's isle,[73]
Or eastern climes admir'd in days of yore:
How Europe's foodful, culinary plants;
How gay Pomona's[74] ruby-tinctured births;
And gawdy Flora's[75] various-vested train;
Might be instructed to unlearn their clime,
And by due discipline adopt the sun.
The muse might tell what culture will entice
The ripened melon, to perfume each month;
And with the anana[76] load the fragrant board.
The muse might tell, what trees will best exclude
("Insuperable height of airiest shade")[77]
With their vast umbrage the noon's fervent ray.
Thee, verdant mammey,[78] first, her song should praise:
Thee, the first natives of these Ocean-isles,
Fell anthropophagi,[79] still sacred held;
And from thy large high-flavour'd fruit abstain'd,
With pious awe; for thine high-flavour'd fruit,
The airy phantoms of their friends deceas'd
Joy'd to regale on.—Such their simple creed.
The tamarind[80] likewise should adorn her theme,
With whose tart fruit the sweltering fever loves
To quench his thirst, whose breezy umbrage soon
Shades the pleas'd planter, shades his children long.
Nor, lofty cassia,[81] should she not recount
Thy woodland honours! See, what yellow flowers
Dance in the gale, and scent the ambient air;
While thy long pods, full-fraught with nectared sweets,
Relieve the bowels from their lagging load.
Nor chirimoia,[82] though these torrid isles

[73]The Phaeacians are the luxurious people of the island of Scheria in the Ionian Sea of Greece, whose king, Alcinous, harbors Odysseus in the *Odyssey*, and Jason in the *Argonautica* [Ed.].
[74]Roman goddess of fruit [Ed.].
[75]Roman goddess of flowers [Ed.].
[76]The pineapple (French, *ananas*) [Ed.].
[77]Milton, *Paradise Lost* IV.138 [Ed.].
[78]This is a lofty, shady, and beautiful tree. . . .
[79]Cannibals, which the native Carib Indians were purported to be [Ed.].
[80]. . . This large, shady, and beautiful tree grows fast even in the driest soils, and lasts long; and yet its wood is hard, and very fit for mechanical uses. . . .
[81]Both this tree and its mild purgative pulp are sufficiently known.
[82]Cherimoya, a fruit-bearing tree of Central and South America [Ed.].

Boast not thy fruit, to which the anana yields
In taste and flavour, wilt thou coy refuse
Thy fragrant shade to beautify the scene.
But, chief of palms, and pride of Indian-groves,
Thee, fair palmeto,[83] should her song resound:
What swelling columns, form'd by Jones or Wren,[84]
Or great Palladio,[85] may with thee compare?
Not nice-proportion'd, but of size immense,
Swells the wild fig-tree, and should claim her lay:
For, from its numerous bearded twigs proceed
A filial train, stupendous as their fire,
In quick succession; and, o'er many a rood,
Extend their uncouth limbs; which not the bolt
Of heaven can scathe; nor yet the all-wasting rage
Of Typhon, or of hurricane, destroy.
Nor should, tho' small, the anata[86] not be sung:
Thy purple dye, the silk and cotton fleece
Delighted drink; thy purple dye the tribes
Of Northern-Ind,[87] a fierce and wily race,
Carouse, assembled; and with it they paint
Their manly make in many a horrid form,
To add new terrors to the face of war.
The muse might teach to twine the verdant arch,
And the cool alcove's lofty room adorn,
With ponderous granadillas,[88] and the fruit
Call'd water-lemon; grateful to the taste:
Nor should she not pursue the mountain-streams,
But pleas'd decoy them from their shady haunts,
In rills, to visit every tree and herb;
Or fall o'er fern-clad cliffs, with foaming rage;
Or in huge basons float, a fair expanse;
Or, bound in chains of artificial force,
Arise thro' sculptured stone, or breathing brass.—
But I'm in haste to furl my wind-worn sails,
And anchor my tir'd vessel on the shore.

[83]This being the most beautiful of palms, nay, perhaps, superior to any other known tree in the world, has with propriety obtained the name of *Royal.* . . . I never ride past the charming vista of royal palms on the Cayon-estate of Daniel Mathew, Esq; in St. Christopher, without being put in mind of the pillars of the Temple of the Sun at Palmyra. . . .

[84]Inigo Jones (1573–1652), architect of the Queen's House, Greenwich, and the Banqueting House, Whitehall, London. Sir Christopher Wren (1632–1723), architect of the plan of London and of St. Paul's Cathedral following the Great Fire of 1666 [Ed.].

[85]Andrea Palladio (1508–1580), influential Italian architect [Ed.].

[86]Or *Anotto,* or *Arnotta*; thence corruptly called Indian Otter, by the English. . . . [Now known as *annatto.* Ed.]

[87]Indians of North America [Ed.].

[88]This is the Spanish name, and is a species of the *passiflora,* or passion-flower . . . .

It much imports to build thy Negroe-huts,
Or on the sounding margin of the main,
Or on some dry hill's gently-sloping sides,
In streets, at distance due.—When near the beach,
Let frequent coco cast its wavy shade;
'Tis Neptune's tree; and, nourish'd by the spray,
Soon round the bending stem's aerial height,
Clusters of mighty nuts, with milk and fruit
Delicious fraught, hang clattering in the sky.
There let the bay-grape,[89] too, its crooked limbs
Project enormous; of impurpled hue
Its frequent clusters grow. And there, if thou
Woud'st make the sand yield salutary food,
Let Indian millet[90] rear its corny reed,
Like arm'd battalions in array of war.
But, round the upland huts, bananas plant;
A wholesome nutriment bananas yield,
And sun-burnt labour loves its breezy shade.
Their graceful screen let kindred plantanes join,
And with their broad vans shiver in the breeze;
So flames design'd, or by imprudence caught,
Shall spread no ruin to the neighbouring roof.

Yet nor the sounding margin of the main,
Nor gently sloping side of breezy hill,
Nor streets, at distance due, imbower'd in trees;
Will half the health, or half the pleasure yield,
Unless some pitying naiad deign to lave,
With an unceasing stream, thy thirsty bounds.

On festal days; or when their work is done;
Permit thy slaves to lead the choral dance,
To the wild banshaw's[91] melancholy sound.
Responsive to the sound, head feet and frame
Move aukwardly harmonious; hand in hand
Now lock'd, the gay troop circularly wheels,
And frisks and capers with intemperate joy.
Halts the vast circle, all clap hands and sing;

[89]Or sea side grape, as it is more commonly called.

[90]Or maise. This is commonly called Guinea-corn, to distinguish it from the great or Indian-corn, that grows in the southern parts of North-America. . . . The Indians, Negroes, and poor white people, make many (not unsavoury) dishes with them. It is also called *Turkey wheat.* The turpentine tree will also grow in the sand, and is most useful upon a plantation.

[91]This is a sort of rude guitar, invented by the Negroes. It produces a wild pleasing melancholy sound. [The banjo. Ed.]

While those distinguish'd for their heels and air,
Bound in the center, and fantastic twine.
Meanwhile some stripling, from the choral ring,
Trips forth; and, not ungallantly, bestows
On her who nimblest hath the greensward beat,
And whose flush'd beauties have inthrall'd his soul,
A silver token of his fond applause.
Anon they form in ranks; nor inexpert
A thousand tuneful intricacies weave,
Shaking their sable limbs; and oft a kiss
Steal from their partners; who, with neck reclin'd,
And semblant scorn, resent the ravish'd bliss.
But let not thou the drum their mirth inspire;
Nor vinous spirits: else, to madness fir'd,
(What will not bacchanalian frenzy dare?)
Fell acts of blood, and vengeance they pursue.

Compel by threats, or win by soothing arts,
Thy slaves to wed their fellow slaves at home;
So shall they not their vigorous prime destroy,
By distant journeys, at untimely hours,
When muffled midnight decks her raven-hair
With the white plumage of the prickly vine.[92]

Would'st thou from countless ails preserve thy gang;
To every Negroe, as the candle-weed[93]
Expands his blossoms to the cloudy sky,
And moist Aquarius melts in daily showers;
A woolly vestment give, (this Wiltshire weaves)
Warm to repel chill Night's unwholesome dews:
While strong coarse linen, from the Scotian loom,
Wards off the fervours of the burning day.

The truly great, tho' from a hostile clime,
The sacred Nine embalm; then, Muses, chant,
In grateful numbers, Gallic Lewis'[94] praise:
For private murder quell'd; for laurel'd arts,
Invented, cherish'd in his native realm;
For rapine punish'd; for grim famine fed:
For sly chicane expell'd the wrangling bar;
And rightful Themis[95] seated on her throne:

[92]This beautiful white rosaceous flower is as large as the crown of one's hat, and only blows at midnight. . . .

[93]This shrub, which produces a yellow flower somewhat resembling a narcissus, makes a beautiful hedge, and blows about November. . . .

[94]King Louis XIV of France; see note 8 [Ed.].

[95]Greek goddess, mother of the Seasons, the Fates, and Prometheus; personification of Justice [Ed.].

But, chief, for those mild laws his wisdom fram'd,
To guard the Aethiop from tyrannic sway!

Did such, in these green isles which Albion claims,
Did such obtain; the muse, at midnight-hour,
This last brain-racking study had not ply'd:
But, sunk in slumbers of immortal bliss,
To bards had listned on a fancied Thames!

All hail, old father Thames! tho' not from far
Thy springing waters roll; nor countless streams,
Of name conspicuous, swell thy watery store;
Tho' thou, no Plata,[96] to the sea devolve
Vast humid offerings; thou art king of streams:
Delighted Commerce broods upon thy wave;
And every quarter of this sea-girt globe
To thee due tribute pays; but chief the world
By great Columbus found, where now the muse
Beholds, transported, slow vast fleecy clouds,
Alps pil'd on Alps romantically high,
Which charm the sight with many a pleasing form.
The moon, in virgin-glory, gilds the pole,
And tips yon tamarinds, tips yon Cane-crown'd vale,
With fluent silver; while unnumbered stars
Gild the vast concave with their lively beams.
The main, a moving burnish'd mirror, shines;
No noise is heard, save when the distant surge
With drouzy murmurings breaks upon the shore!—

Ah me, what thunders roll! the sky's on fire!
Now sudden darkness muffles up the pole!
Heavens! what wild scenes, before the affrighted sense,
Imperfect swim!—See! in that flaming scroll,
Which Time unfolds, the future germs bud forth,
Of mighty empires! independent realms!—
And must Britannia, Neptune's favorite queen,
Protect'ress of true science, freedom, arts;
Must she, ah! must she, to her offspring crouch?
Ah, must my Thames, old Ocean's favourite son,
Resign his trident to barbaric streams;
His banks neglected, and his waves unsought,
No bards to sing them, and no fleets to grace?—
Again the fleecy clouds amuse the eye,
And sparkling stars the vast horizon gild—
She shall not crouch; if Wisdom guide the helm,

[96]One of the largest rivers of South America.

Wisdom that bade loud Fame, with justest praise,
Record her triumphs! bade the lacquaying winds
Transport, to every quarter of the globe,
Her winged navies! bade the scepter'd sons
Of earth acknowledge her pre-eminence!—
She shall not crouch; if these Cane ocean-isles,
Isles which on Britain for their all depend,
And must for ever; still indulgent share
Her fostering smile: and other isles be given,
From vanquish'd foes.—And, see, another race!
A golden aera dazzles my fond sight!
That other race, that long'd-for aera, hail!
The British George[97] now reigns, the Patriot King!
Britain shall ever triumph o'er the main.

1764

John Leacock 1729–1802

John Leacock—a prominent merchant, gold- and silversmith, and pro-colonial agitator during the decade prior to the American Revolution—is among the many authors "lost" to traditional American literary scholarship because their writings emerged as much from propagandist motives as from a traditionally valued "literary" aesthetic or impulse. It took nearly two centuries for Leacock to be recognized by scholars as an interesting playwright, and only in recent years has his authorship of a patriot song and biblical parodic satire been established. That Leacock was a merchant and a craftsman of precious metals along with being a writer is not very surprising. Most white, elite "gentlemen" of the eighteenth century practiced writing as an avocation while pursuing more worldly concerns. But that Leacock was a merchant, metalworker, *and* a patriot agitator is surprising—and very significant. Merchants—especially those in America's then-foremost "capital" of Philadelphia, the "Athens of America"—stood to lose their livelihoods with the coming of the Revolution, which would close harbors (and thus mercantile houses) to trade. Nonetheless, at least as early as 1765, when he signed the Philadelphia Non-Importation Agreement, John Leacock was active in American patriot endeavors.

John Leacock was born into a prosperous Philadelphia family. His father (also named John Leacock), was a well-known pewtersmith and shopkeeper, who evidently apprenticed John and his two brothers to Philadelphia craftsmen of precious metals. By the early 1750s, the young John Leacock owned his own gold- and silversmithing business. His interests in business and a variety of scientific and cultural concerns—from engraving and printing to the establishment of a public vineyard—complemented those of relatives: printer brother-in-law David Hall, lawyer brother-

[97]King George III (1738–1820; reigned 1760–1820) [Ed.].

in-law James Read, and cousin-in-law Benjamin Franklin. (Leacock was second cousin to Franklin's wife, Deborah Read.) Family wealth and prominence assured Leacock a successful business and public life. In fact, Leacock was so successful that he gave over his business to family members in the late 1760s and retired to the then-rural area of Lower Merion (just west of Philadelphia) to pursue farming and experiments in agriculture. His first wife, Hannah McCally, died after fifteen years of marriage, in 1767. Leacock was married again in 1770, to Martha Ogilby.

From the 1760s on, Leacock devoted his leisure time to scientific experiments—and to revolutionary agitation. By signing the Philadelphia Non-Importation Agreement of 1765 and by writing *A New Song, On the Repeal of the Stamp-Act* (1766), Leacock established himself as a Revolutionary agitator. In May, 1772, Leacock joined the radical Philadelphia Sons of Liberty and a related, "native" patriot organization for men, The Society of the Sons of Saint Tammany (named for a local Indian hero). In 1779, Leacock was signing bills of credit for revolutionary officers in Easton and Reading. Indeed, his political activity during the Revolution gained for Leacock the coveted post of Coroner of Philadelphia in 1785. Leacock spent most of his life in social, political, and literary prominence. He died November 16, 1802, and he was buried in Christ Church Cemetery near his relative, Benjamin Franklin.

The selections below are from two of Leacock's known works, the first from his biblical parodic satire, *The First Book of the American Chronicles of the Times* (1774–1775), and the second from his play *The Fall of British Tyranny* (1776). Both selections evidence Leacock's interest in and propagandist use of an American ideology represented by the folk heroes of his day: Oliver Cromwell (the militant seventeenth-century English Puritan), Israel Putnam (famed hero of the French and Indian Wars in the colonies), and Tamanend (the legendary chief of the Delawares). Leacock's interest in native and folk heroism, as evidenced by his song to Tammany (Tamanend) and his use of a generalized Indian chief, Occunneocogeecococachee-cacheecadungo, represent the emerging impulses of white Americans to identify themselves with the Native American population in order to propagandize republicanism as a peculiarly American right. All of Leacock's writings show his ability to use material (native, religious, and military heroes) that appealed to both the elite and nonelite cultures while creating sophisticated propagandist messages in behalf of revolution.

The First Book of the American Chronicles of the Times is written after the manner of the Old Testament in a non-chronological narration of the events that preceded the American Revolution. Its six pamphlet chapters cover events in Boston prior to the Revolution, from the Boston Tea Party to the return to Boston of the Massachusetts delegates to the First Continental Congress. In the opening scene of the *American Chronicles,* Mordecai the Benjamite (Benjamin Franklin) addresses King Rehoboam (George III) with letters from the Massachusetts representatives. Rehoboam's response is to send Thomas the Gageite (Thomas Gage) to hold the military command in Boston. Thomas the Gageite and his troops rebuke and insult the Bostonites, who are led in large measure by Jedediah the Priest (Rev. Samuel Cooper) and Obadiah (John Hancock). Two selections from *The First Book of the American Chronicles of the Times* are reproduced here. The first selection is Obadiah's "epic" catalogue, after the manner of Deuteronomy 8, of the riches that the New Englanders argued were their birthright as the New Israelites in the New Canaan. The second selection offers the scene in which Jedediah the Priest consults, with the aid of the witch Mother Carey, the ghost of the great Puritan hero, Oliver Cromwell.

The second selection, the mid-play *Song to St. Tammany* in *The Fall of British Tyranny,* reveals Leacock's interest in and ability to use Native American materials as appeals to both elite and nonelite cultures alike. In the play, the British are continually depicted as backbiting fools, the Americans as virtuous sufferers of British atrocities. The mid-play song to Tammany not only breaks the pace of the oratorical, dramatic action, but it confirms the entire play's affirmation that the patriots will succeed because republicanism (as best represented by the Native American culture) is indigenous and so is clearly an American right.

Carla Mulford
Pennsylvania State University

PRIMARY WORKS

A New Song, On the Repeal of the Stamp-Act, 1766; *The First Book of the American Chronicles of the Times,* 1774–1775; *The Fall of British Tyranny; Or, American Liberty Triumphant,* 1776.

SECONDARY WORKS

Francis James Dallett, Jr., "John Leacock and *The Fall of British Tyranny," Pennsylvania Magazine of History and Biography* 78, 1954:456–75; Carla Mulford, *John Leacock's The First Book of the American Chronicles of the Times, 1774–1775,* 1987.

from The First Book of the American Chronicles of the Times[1]

from Chapter 3: Obadiah (John Hancock) challenges Thomas the Gageite (Thomas Gage)

15. Wherefore should the names of our fathers be taken away from among his family? We have a possession, an inheritance among the brethren of our fathers.

16. Forty years was Moses and the children of Israel in the wilderness of Zin; our fathers and brethren have been in possession of this wilderness of America fourscore and forty years.[2]

17. The Lord our God brought us into this land to shun the persecutions of thy people, and yet thou art come to persecute us; yea, more and more, did he not root out many of the Indian nations before us that were greater and mightier than we?

18. A land in which are rivers of water, and fountains that spring out of the vallies, rocks and hills.

19. A land of wheat and barley, of vineyards and fig trees, pomegranates and pompions, a land of fish and oil, olive and honey, a land wherein we eat bread without scarcity.

[1]The text is from the first pamphlet edition in Philadelphia by Benjamin Towne, 1774–1775.
[2]See Numbers 14:33; Psalms 95:10.

20. Neither do we lack any thing therein; a land whose stones are iron, out of whose mountains are dug gold, and whose pebbles are diamonds.[3]

from Chapters 3 and 4: Jedediah the Priest (Rev. Samuel Cooper), with Mother Carey's aid, speaks with the ghost of Oliver Cromwell

from Chapter 3

. . . 52. And Jedediah said unto her, Now know I of a truth, indeed, that thou art a charmer, and hast a kind familiar spirit, that thou art a regarder of the times, a marker of the flying of fowls, a witch, and converseth with the dead, that thou art highly favoured, that thou canst divine, canst do and tell of things that are mystical, obscure, abstruse and remote from conception.

53. Now therefore I pray thee conjecture unto me by the familiar spirit, and bring me him up whom I shall name unto thee.

54. But the woman, whose name was Carey, was amazed and afraid, and she said unto him, How is it that ye ask such things of me, seeing I have not practised them these fourscore years, behold thou knowest that Matherius Cottonius hath done, how that he hath destroyed the sorcerers, the soothsayers, and the witches out of the land, wherefore then seekest thou to take me in a snare to tell of me, and cause me to die?[4]

55. Then Jedediah, the priest, said unto her, Knowest thou not, sister Carey, old things are done away, and all things are become new, that without thy help we may be all lost.

56. And she said, If thou wilt keep it secret, and sware unto me, then will I satisfy all thy desires.

57. And it came to pass that Jedediah did so, and Mother Carey was therewith content; but Obadiah grumbled within himself, yet nevertheless spake he not a word.

58. Now Mother Carey said, Whom shall I bring up unto thee?

59. Then Jedediah answered and said, Bring me up OLIVER CROMWELL.[5]

60. And when the woman saw Oliver, she cried with a loud voice, and spake unto Jedediah, saying, Why hast thou deceived me; I took thee for Obadiah, but thou art Jedediah, the priest, that hath done this thing, and why hast thou constrained me to call up such a monster?

[3]Verses 17–20 are a parodic rendering of Deuteronomy 8:7–9.

[4]An allusion to the Salem witch trials and Cotton Mather's *Wonders of the Invisible World* (1693). Elizabeth Cary was convicted as a witch but, escaping execution, sought asylum in New York. See I Samuel 28 and II Corinthians 5 for the biblical texts Leacock parodies here.

[5]Cromwell (1599–1658) was the great Puritan hero who was a driving force behind the English Civil War of the seventeenth century. He ruled England at the time Charles I was captured and executed.

61. And he said unto her, Sister Carey, my charmer, be not afraid, the necessity of the times maketh it necessary; what seest thou, what fashion is he of?

62. And she answered, An old man, with a high crowned hat, cometh up, with whiskers, having on a brigandine or coat of mail, a breast plate of boldness, a two edged sword in his hand, half boots on his legs, his belt stuck round with pistols, like the devil in a thorn bush, and a face like unto the face of a rhinoceros.

63. Then Jedediah knew that it was Oliver, and he inclined his face to the ground, and bowed himself, likewise did Aminadab and Obadiah.

64. And Cromwell saluted them and said, GRACE BE UNTO YOU, wherefore have you disquieted me to bring me up?

from Chapter 4

12. Then spake Jedediah, and lifted up his hands and eyes, and said, O how highly favoured are we thy sons, that it be permitted that thou, our great Lord and mighty Protector, regardest his children, who hatest hypocrisy and dissimulation, whose conscience is always void of offence, who refused an earthly crown that thou mightest be rewarded with a crown of glory, who art ambitious only for the glory of the King of Kings; thou whose consummate fortitude, magnanimity and prudence, whose great and divine talents were bestowed from above, to answer wise purposes and happy events, how didst thou raise the fading glory and dying reputation of the British nation, beyond the highest pitch of Roman greatness; the heads of kings and princes were but as snow balls in thine hands, and thou hustled powers, principalities, and kingdoms as in a cap; thou became the dread and terror of the nations round about; thou swayed the sceptre of this terrestrial universe, and held the balance of power in thine own hands, thou broughtest true religion to the highest pitch, and banished enthusiasm, fanaticism, high church bigotry, popish superstition, and pretenders to saintship, out of the land; thou shook his Holiness's hair, made the tripple crown of the great dragon to totter, thou madest the papal cap to fall off from his hoary pate, thou pulled the purple robe from off his shoulders, and made thereof a carpet for the soles of thy shoes, and left him as bare as an unfledged woodpecker; thou suffered not the haughty king of France to enjoy his boasted vain title, but permitted him to be called only the simple French king; the invincible proud Spaniard thou humbled in the dust, and made their Donships, Don Falsey Benabio, and Don Diego Surly Phiz, their ministers, as submissive as spaniels; thou despised their treasure, their silver and their gold, and sunk their galleons in the depths of the sea; the sly Hogan Mogans of the United Provinces trembled at thy nod, they besought thy friendship, and their High Mightynesses became the poor and distressed states; the strong holds and impenetrable castles of the piratical Algerines became but as sport and pastime in thine hands, and the ships of all nations thou made to lower their pride, pay homage, and bow down to thy all conquering flag; thou settest up whatsoever thou pleasest, and pullest down whomsoever thou wilt.

13. Now behold, while Jedediah was speaking, CROMWELL smiled on him, and it pleased him, insomuch that it made his heart glad and leap for joy, for he was not proof against flattery, but rejoiced to hear his own actions and great atcheivements praised and extolled, even unto the skies.

14. And it came to pass, when he had twirled his whiskers, and stroked his beard, he said unto him, He that is not for us is against us, what meaneth Thomas the Usurper.

15. Behold I will shortly let him know to his sorrow, what it is to disturb the pious ashes of them that sleepeth, to threaten my beloved people, and to affront the majesty of OLIVER; for in seven nights will I appear in a vision before him, face to face.

16. Hearken therefore, Jedediah, to what I shall speak in thine ear, take counsel of me, and suffer not your spirits to flag, be thou and our people resolute, give back not one inch, and, if so be ye are constrained to fight with them, behold I will be in the midst of you, you shall find me in the centre, in the wings, and in the fore front of the battle, and when you find me flinch, then execrate the name and memory of OLIVER.

17. For I will break those chains in sunder which have been prepared to shackle you, and they shall moulder away like clay, and you shalt surely prove victorious, and triumph over your enemies; am not I your Lord Protector; for history cannot point out, neither can the Chronicles tell wherein a true born Oliverian ever flinched or forsook his cause; witness my prowess at the memorable battle of Marsdon Moor.

18. Moreover I will cause the heads of Johnny the Butetite, and Haman the Northite,[6] to be lopped from off their shoulders, even as the limb of a tree is lopped off, and they shall be hanged on a gallows fifty cubits high, and they shall remain on the walls of the gates of Britain as a memorial, even as I was ofttimes wont to serve traitors of old and as rebels are served.

19. Then were the hearts of Jedediah and Aminadab and Obadiah glad, and they bowed seven times unto OLIVER, and fell with their faces to the ground.

20. And OLIVER said unto them, Rise and stand up on your feet like men, and go ye into the city and tell my people, you have this night seen the face of Cromwell their Lord Protector, which no man hath seen these six score years.

21. Moreover tell Phineas, the captain of the host, the son of Eleazer, be strong and whet up his plow shares into swords, and his pruning hooks into spears.[7]

22. Tell Occunneocogeecococacheecacheecadungo, my brother, fill up his quiver, and stand up and tarry till I come, and take ye this in thine hand and proclaim it through the city, and throughout all the land of New England; farewel, while I make an excursion to the mansions of them that sleepeth, and awake and rouse up my faithful Fairfax, Lambert, and the rest of my brave warriors: THE LORD PROSPER YOU; GRACE BE UNTO YOU.

23. And he departed out of their sight in a terrible whirlwind, and they saw him no more that time, neither knew they where or which way he went.

1774–75

[6]Allusions to John Stuart, third Earl of Bute, and Frederick North, both of whom advised King George III to pursue repressive measures against the colonies.

[7]Leacock has adapted his texts to the following biblical verses: Matthew 12:30; Mark 9:40; Psalms 2:3; Acts 26:10; Micah 4:3.

from The Fall of British Tyranny; Or, American Liberty Triumphant: Song, The First of May, to St. Tammany

SONG
[Tune. The hounds are all out, etc.]

Of St. George, or St. Bute,[1] let the poet laureate sing,
Of Pharaoh or Pluto of old,
While he rhymes forth their praise, in false, flattering lays,
I'll sing of St. Tamm'ny the bold, my brave boys.

Let Hibernia's sons boast, make Patrick their toast;
And Scots Andrew's fame spread abroad.
Potatoes and oats, and Welch leeks for Welch goats,
Was never St. Tammany's food, my brave boys.

In freedom's bright cause, Tamm'ny pled with applause,
And reason'd most justly from nature;
For this, this was his song, all, all the day long:
Liberty's the right of each creature, brave boys.

Whilst under an oak his great parliament sat,
His throne was the crotch of the tree;[2]
With Solomon's look, without statutes or book,
He widely sent forth his decree, my brave boys.

His subjects stood round, not the least noise or sound,
Whilst freedom blaz'd full in each face:
So plain were the laws, and each pleaded his cause;
That might BUTE, NORTH, and MANSFIELD[3] disgrace, my brave boys.

No duties, nor stamps, their blest liberty cramps,
A king, tho' no tyrant, was he;
He did oft 'times declare, nay sometimes wou'd swear,
The least of his subjects were free, my brave boys.

He, as king of the woods, of the rivers and floods,
Had a right all beasts to controul;

[1]The reference is to the loyalist Society of St. George; Bute is an example of the use of topical satire against England.

[2]Tammany, it is said, was present at the conciliation between Penn and the Indian tribes that took place "under the elm tree at Sachamaxou" in 1682.

[3]Advisers to George III.

Yet, content with a few, to give nature her due:
So gen'rous was Tammany's soul, my brave boys.

In the morn he arose, and a-hunting he goes,
Bold Nimrod[4] his second was he.
For his breakfast he'd take a large venison stake,
And despis'd your flip-flops and tea, my brave boys.

While all in a row, with squaw, dog and bow,
Vermilion adorning his face,
With feathery head he rang'd the woods wide:
St. George sure had never such grace, my brave boys.

His jetty black hair, such as Buckskin saints wear,
Perfumed with bear's grease well smear'd,
Which illum'd the saints face, and ran down apace.
Like the oil from Aaron's old beard,[5] my brave boys.

The strong nervous deer, with amazing career,
In swiftness he'd fairly run down:
And, like Sampson, wou'd tear wolf, lion or bear.
Ne're was such a saint as our own, my brave boys.

When he'd run down a stag, he behind him wou'd lag;
For, so noble a soul had he!
He'd stop, tho' he lost it, tradition reports it,
To give him fresh chance to get free, my brave boys.

With a mighty strong arm, and a masculine bow,
His arrow he drew to the head,
And as sure as he shot, it was ever his lot,
His prey it fell instantly dead, my brave boys.

His table he spread where the venison bled,
Be thankful, he used to say;
He'd laugh and he'd sing, tho' a saint and a king,
And sumptuously dine on his prey, my brave boys.

Then over the hills, o'er the mountains and rills
He'd caper, such was his delight;
And ne'er in his days, Indian history says,
Did lack a good supper at night, my brave boys.

[4]Nimrod, son of Cush, a mighty hunter, Genesis 10:8–9.

[5]Oil was poured upon Aaron's head and ran down his beard. Psalm 113:2.

On an old stump he sat, without cap or hat,
When supper was ready to eat,
Snap, his dog, he stood by, and cast a sheep's eye;
For ven'son, the king of all meat, my brave boys.

Like Isaac of old, and both cast in one mould,
Tho' a wigwam was Tamm'ny's cottage,
He lov'd sav'ry meat, such that patriarch eat,
Of ven'son and squirrel made pottage, brave boys.

When fourscore years old, as I've oft'times been told,
To doubt it, sure, would not be right,
With a pipe in his jaw, he'd buss his old squaw,
And get a young saint ev'ry night, my brave boys.

As old age came on, he grew blind, deaf and dumb.
Tho' his sport, 'twere hard to keep from it,
Quite tired of life, bid adieu to his wife,
And blaz'd like the tail of a comet, brave boys.

What country on earth, then, did ever give birth
To such a magnanimous saint?
His acts far excel all that history tell,
And language too feeble to paint, my brave boys.
Now, to finish my song, a full flowing bowl
I'll quaff, and sing all the long day,
And with punch and wine paint my cheeks for my saint,
And hail ev'ry First of sweet May, my brave boys.

1776

J. Hector St. John de Crèvecoeur 1735–1813

Written from the point of view of an ordinary man, a happy American farmer, Crèvecoeur's *Letters from an American Farmer* is the first American text to ask and answer the question, "What is an American?" Although Crèvecoeur was describing life in the British colonies in America, he used his character, James, to comment on the principles of social organization that were making American society different from any that had gone before and to portray, for the first time, the new consciousness of emerging American society.

Born in Caen, Normandy, Michel-Guilluame-Jean de Crèvecoeur was the child of Norman landowners. He was educated at the Jesuit Collège Royal de Bourbon. Some time after he left school in 1750, he was sent to England, where he became engaged to an English woman. The untimely death of his fiancée is believed to be the reason that Crèvecoeur left England to begin a new life in Canada in 1755. He worked as a surveyor and cartographer in the French militia during the French and Indian War, and he was wounded during the battle of Quebec in 1759. On December 16, 1759, Crèvecoeur disembarked in New York harbor from a British vessel carrying the defeated French troops back to France and began afresh in the British colonies.

For the next ten years, Crèvecoeur worked as a surveyor and trader and traveled extensively. In 1765, he became a naturalized citizen of New York, calling himself J. Hector St. John. Four years later, he married the daughter of a Westchester landowner, settled in Orange county, and began to farm. The outbreak of the Revolution and the desire to see his children's inheritance secured were the likely reasons that Crèvecoeur decided, in 1778, to return to France. The ordinarily long and dangerous trip was further complicated by the war; Crèvecoeur's loyalty was disputed by both the British and the Revolutionaries, so both sides made his departure difficult. After being imprisoned as a spy by the British, he was allowed to leave the colonies in 1780. After his arrival in England, he sold the manuscript of *Letters from an American Farmer* in 1781 to Davis and Davies (the London publishers) and proceeded to France. When *Letters* was published in 1782, its success catapulted Crèvecoeur into French literary and intellectual circles, where he became associated with the *philosophes,* a group of progressive French intellectuals. Encouraged by the support of the *philosophes,* he wrote a French version of *Letters,* which was published in 1784. The influence of Marquis de Turgot and Madame d'Houdetot enabled Crèvecoeur to return to America in 1783 as French consul to New York, New Jersey, and Connecticut. He returned to find his wife dead, his farm burned, and his children resettled in Boston. In America, Crèvecoeur continued his scientific studies and worked closely with Thomas Jefferson in efforts to unite French and American interests. He was made a member of the American Philosophical Society in 1789. In 1790, Crèvecoeur left America for the last time. The confusion of the French Revolution affected his own life: his consulship was revoked by the new French government in 1792, and during the last years of his life, the uncertain political situation in France led him to seek obscurity. In 1801, he published *Voyage dans la Haute Pennsylvanie et dans l'état de New York,* which had little commercial success. He died on November 12, 1813.

The twelve letters which comprise *Letters from an American Farmer* are held together by the movement of the fictional Quaker narrator of the text, James, the American farmer, from happiness to despair as he records his life as a farmer and his travels to Martha's Vineyard, Nantucket, and Charlestown. In the opening letters, James celebrates America as a place where the oppressed masses of Europe are able to pursue their own self-interest as independent landowners, free from the shackles of feudal society, monarchy, and the church. In the later letters, he deals with problems already causing divisions within the new society—slavery, and the Revolution. *Letters* is a form of epistolary, philosophical travel narrative like Montesquieu's *Persian Letters,* a form more common in the eighteenth century than today. Crèvecoeur's readers would have noticed that the ideas of the important philosophical, political, and economic theories of the Enlightenment were integrated into Crèvecoeur's descriptions of ordinary American life. *Letters* was widely read in the late eighteenth century and frequently translated and reprinted. It had some influence on the ideas of the Romantics, particularly Southey and Coleridge.

Doreen Alvarez Saar
Drexel University

PRIMARY WORKS

Letters from an American Farmer, 1782, 1793; *Lettres d'un Cultivateur Américain,* 1784; *Voyage dans la Haute Pennsylvanie et dans l'état de New York,* 1801; *Sketches of Eighteenth Century America,* ed. Bourdin, Gabriel, and Williams, 1925.

SECONDARY WORKS

Thomas Philbrick, *St. John de Crevecoeur,* 1970; Gay Wilson and Roger Asserlineau, *St. John de Crevecoeur: The Life of an American Farmer,* 1987.

from Letters from an American Farmer

from **Letter II On the Situation, Feelings, and Pleasures of an American Farmer**

As you are the first enlightened European[1] I had ever the pleasure of being acquainted with, you will not be surprised that I should, according to your earnest desire and my promise, appear anxious of preserving your friendship and correspondence. By your accounts, I observe a material difference subsists between your husbandry, modes, and customs and ours; everything is local; could we enjoy the advantages of the English farmer, we should be much happier, indeed, but this wish, like many others, implies a contradiction; and could the English farmer have some of those privileges we possess, they would be the first of their class in the world. Good and evil, I see, are to be found in all societies, and it is in vain to seek for any spot where those ingredients are not mixed. I therefore rest satisfied and thank God that my lot is to be an American farmer instead of a Russian boor or an Hungarian peasant. I thank you kindly for the idea, however dreadful, which you have given me of their lot and condition; your observations have confirmed me in the justness of my ideas, and I am happier now than I thought myself before. It is strange that misery, when viewed in others, should become to us a sort of real good, though I am far from rejoicing to hear that there are in the world men so thoroughly wretched; they are no doubt as harmless, industrious, and willing to work as we are. Hard is their fate to be thus condemned to a slavery worse than that of our Negroes. Yet when young, I entertained some thoughts of selling my farm. I thought it afforded but a dull repetition of the same labours and pleasures. I thought the former tedious and heavy, the latter few and insipid; but when I came to consider myself as divested of my farm, I then found the world so wide, and every place so full, that I began to fear lest there would be no room for me. My farm, my house, my barn, presented to my imagina-

[1]James addresses Mr. F. B., the fictional recipient of the letters.

tion objects from which I adduced quite new ideas; they were more forcible than before. Why should not I find myself happy, said I, where my father was before? He left me no good books, it is true; he gave me no other education than the art of reading and writing; but he left me a good farm and his experience; he left me free from debts, and no kind of difficulties to struggle with. I married, and this perfectly reconciled me to my situation; my wife rendered my house all at once cheerful and pleasing; it no longer appeared gloomy and solitary as before; when I went to work in my fields, I worked with more alacrity and sprightliness; I felt that I did not work for myself alone, and this encouraged me much. My wife would often come with her knitting in her hand and sit under the shady tree, praising the straightness of my furrows and the docility of my horses; this swelled my heart and made everything light and pleasant, and I regretted that I had not married before.

I felt myself happy in my new situation, and where is that station which can confer a more substantial system of felicity than that of an American farmer possessing freedom of action, freedom of thoughts, ruled by a mode of government which requires but little from us? I owe nothing but a peppercorn to my country,[2] a small tribute to my king, with loyalty and due respect; I know no other landlord than the lord of all land, to whom I owe the most sincere gratitude. My father left me three hundred and seventy-one acres of land, forty-seven of which are good timothy meadow; an excellent orchard; a good house; and a substantial barn. It is my duty to think how happy I am that he lived to build and to pay for all these improvements; what are the labours which I have to undergo, what are my fatigues, when compared to his, who had everything to do, from the first tree he felled to the finishing of his house? Every year I kill from 1,500 to 2,000 weight of pork, 1,200 of beef, half a dozen of good wethers in harvest; of fowls my wife has always a great stock; what can I wish more? My Negroes are tolerably faithful and healthy; by a long series of industry and honest dealings, my father left behind him the name of a good man; I have but to tread his paths to be happy and a good man like him. I know enough of the law to regulate my little concerns with propriety, nor do I dread its power; these are the grand outlines of my situation, but as I can feel much more than I am able to express, I hardly know how to proceed.

When my first son was born, the whole train of my ideas was suddenly altered; never was there a charm that acted so quickly and powerfully; I ceased to ramble in imagination through the wide world; my excursions since have not exceeded the bounds of my farm, and all my principal pleasures are now centred within its scanty limits; but at the same time, there is not an operation belonging to it in which I do not find some food for useful reflections. This is the reason, I suppose, that when you were here, you used, in your refined style, to denominate me the farmer of feelings; how rude must those feelings be in him who daily holds the axe or the plough, how much more refined on the contrary those of the European, whose mind is improved by education, example, books, and by every acquired advantage! Those feelings, however, I will delineate as well as I can, agreeably to your earnest request.

When I contemplate my wife, by my fireside, while she either spins, knits, darns, or suckles our child, I cannot describe the various emotions of love, of gratitude, of

[2]Traditional offering.

conscious pride, which thrill in my heart and often overflow in involuntary tears. I feel the necessity, the sweet pleasure, of acting my part, the part of an husband and father, with an attention and propriety which may entitle me to my good fortune. It is true these pleasing images vanish with the smoke of my pipe, but though they disappear from my mind, the impression they have made on my heart is indelible. When I play with the infant, my warm imagination runs forward and eagerly anticipates his future temper and constitution. I would willingly open the book of fate and know in which page his destiny is delineated. Alas! Where is the father who in those moments of paternal ecstasy can delineate one half of the thoughts which dilate his heart? I am sure I cannot; then again, I fear for the health of those who are become so dear to me, and in their sicknesses I severely pay for the joys I experienced while they were well. Whenever I go abroad, it is always involuntary. I never return home without feeling some pleasing emotion, which I often suppress as useless and foolish. The instant I enter on my own land, the bright idea of property, of exclusive right, of independence, exalt my mind. Precious soil, I say to myself, by what singular custom of law is it that thou wast made to constitute the riches of the freeholder? What should we American farmers be without the distinct possession of that soil? It feeds, it clothes us; from it we draw even a great exuberancy, our best meat, our richest drink; the very honey of our bees comes from this privileged spot. No wonder we should thus cherish its possession; no wonder that so many Europeans who have never been able to say that such portion of land was theirs cross the Atlantic to realize that happiness. This formerly rude soil has been converted by my father into a pleasant farm, and in return, it has established all our rights; on it is founded our rank, our freedom, our power as citizens, our importance as inhabitants of such a district. These images, I must confess, I always behold with pleasure and extend them as far as my imagination can reach; for this is what may be called the true and the only philosophy of an American farmer.

Pray do not laugh in thus seeing an artless countryman tracing himself through the simple modifications of his life; remember that you have required it; therefore, with candour, though with diffidence, I endeavour to follow the thread of my feelings, but I cannot tell you all. Often when I plough my low ground, I place my little boy on a chair which screws to the beam of the plough—its motion and that of the horses please him; he is perfectly happy and begins to chat. As I lean over the handle, various are the thoughts which crowd into my mind. I am now doing for him, I say, what my father formerly did for me; may God enable him to live that he may perform the same operations for the same purposes when I am worn out and old! I relieve his mother of some trouble while I have him with me; the odoriferous furrow exhilarates his spirits and seems to do the child a great deal of good, for he looks more blooming since I have adopted that practice; can more pleasure, more dignity, be added to that primary occupation? The father thus ploughing with his child, and to feed his family, is inferior only to the emperor of China ploughing as an example to his kingdom. In the evening, when I return home through my low grounds, I am astonished at the myriads of insects which I perceive dancing in the beams of the setting sun. I was before scarcely acquainted with their existence; they are so small that it is difficult to distinguish them; they are carefully improving this short evening space, not daring to expose themselves to the blaze of our meridian sun. I never see an egg brought on my table but I feel penetrated with the wonderful change it would have undergone but for my gluttony; it might have been a gentle, useful hen leading her chicken with a care and vigilance which speaks shame to many women. A cock perhaps, arrayed with the most majestic plumes, tender to its mate, bold, courageous, endowed with an astonishing instinct, with thoughts, with memory, and every distinguishing characteristic of the reason of man. I never see my trees drop their leaves and their fruit in the autumn, and bud again in the spring, without wonder; the sagacity of those animals which have long been the tenants of my farm astonish me; some of them seem to surpass even men in memory and sagacity. I could tell you singular instances of that kind. What, then, is this instinct which we so debase, and of which we are taught to entertain so diminutive an idea? My bees, above any other tenants of my farm, attract my attention and respect; I am astonished to see that nothing exists but what has its enemy; one species pursues and lives upon the other: unfortunately, our king-birds are the destroyers of those industrious insects, but on the other hand, these birds preserve our fields from the depredation of crows, which they pursue on the wing with great vigilance and astonishing dexterity. . . .

from **Letter III**
What Is an American?

I wish I could be acquainted with the feelings and thoughts which must agitate the heart and present themselves to the mind of an enlightened Englishman when he first lands on this continent. He must greatly rejoice that he lived at a time to see this fair country discovered and settled; he must necessarily feel a share of national pride when he views the chain of settlements which embellish these extended shores. When he says to himself, "This is the work of my countrymen, who, when convulsed by factions, afflicted by a variety of miseries and wants, restless and impatient, took refuge here. They brought along with them their national genius,[3] to which they principally owe what liberty they enjoy and what substance they possess." Here he sees the industry of his native country displayed in a new manner and traces in their works the embryos of all the arts, sciences, and ingenuity which flourish in Europe. Here he beholds fair cities, substantial villages, extensive fields, an immense country filled with decent houses, good roads, orchards, meadows, and bridges where an hundred years ago all was wild, woody, and uncultivated! What a train of pleasing ideas this fair spectacle must suggest; it is a prospect which must inspire a good citizen with the most heart-felt pleasure. The difficulty consists in the manner of viewing so extensive a scene. He is arrived on a new continent; a modern society offers itself to his contemplation, different from what he had hitherto seen. It is not composed, as in Europe, of great lords who possess everything and of a herd of people who have nothing. Here are no aristocratical families, no courts, no kings, no bishops, no ecclesiastical dominion, no invisible power giving to a few a very visible one, no great manufactures employing thousands, no great refinements of luxury. The rich and the poor are not so far removed from each other as they are in Europe.

[3]Characteristic national spirit.

Some few towns excepted, we are all tillers of the earth, from Nova Scotia to West Florida. We are a people of cultivators scattered over an immense territory, communicating with each other by means of good roads and navigable rivers, united by the silken bands of mild government, all respecting the laws without dreading their power, because they are equitable. We are all animated with the spirit of an industry which is unfettered and unrestrained, because each person works for himself. If he travels through our rural districts, he views not the hostile castle and the haughty mansion, contrasted with the clay-built hut and miserable cabin, where cattle and men help to keep each other warm and dwell in meanness, smoke, and indigence. A pleasing uniformity of decent competence appears throughout our habitations. The meanest of our log-houses is a dry and comfortable habitation. Lawyer or merchant are the fairest titles our towns afford; that of a farmer is the only appellation of the rural inhabitants of our country. It must take some time ere he can reconcile himself to our dictionary, which is but short in words of dignity and names of honour. There, on a Sunday, he sees a congregation of respectable farmers and their wives, all clad in neat homespun, well mounted, or riding in their own humble waggons. There is not among them an esquire, saving the unlettered magistrate. There he sees a parson as simple as his flock, a farmer who does not riot[4] on the labour of others. We have no princes for whom we toil, starve, and bleed; we are the most perfect society now existing in the world. Here man is free as he ought to be, nor is this pleasing equality so transitory as many others are. Many ages will not see the shores of our great lakes replenished with inland nations, nor the unknown bounds of North America entirely peopled. Who can tell how far it extends? Who can tell the millions of men whom it will feed and contain? For no European foot has as yet travelled half the extent of this mighty continent!

The next wish of this traveller will be to know whence came all these people. They are a mixture of English, Scotch, Irish, French, Dutch, Germans, and Swedes. From this promiscuous breed, that race now called Americans have arisen. The eastern provinces must indeed be excepted as being the unmixed descendants of Englishmen. I have heard many wish that they had been more intermixed also; for my part, I am no wisher and think it much better as it has happened. They exhibit a most conspicuous figure in this great and variegated picture; they too enter for a great share in the pleasing perspective displayed in these thirteen provinces. I know it is fashionable to reflect on them, but I respect them for what they have done; for the accuracy and wisdom with which they have settled their territory; for the decency of their manners; for their early love of letters; their ancient college, the first in this hemisphere; for their industry, which to me who am but a farmer is the criterion of everything. There never was a people, situated as they are, who with so ungrateful a soil have done more in so short a time. Do you think that the monarchical ingredients which are more prevalent in other governments have purged them from all foul stains? Their histories assert the contrary.

[4]To waste or spend recklessly.

In this great American asylum, the poor of Europe have by some means met together, and in consequence of various causes; to what purpose should they ask one another what countrymen they are? Alas, two thirds of them had no country. Can a wretch who wanders about, who works and starves, whose life is a continual scene of sore affliction or pinching penury—can that man call England or any other kingdom his country? A country that had no bread for him, whose fields procured him no harvest, who met with nothing but the frowns of the rich, the severity of the laws, with jails and punishments, who owned not a single foot of the extensive surface of this planet? No! Urged by a variety of motives, here they came. Everything has tended to regenerate them: new laws, a new mode of living, a new social system; here they are become men: in Europe they were as so many useless plants, wanting vegetative mould[5] and refreshing showers; they withered, and were mowed down by want, hunger, and war; but now, by the power of transplantation, like all other plants they have taken root and flourished! Formerly they were not numbered in any civil lists of their country, except in those of the poor; here they rank as citizens. By what invisible power hath this surprising metamorphosis been performed? By that of the laws and that of their industry. The laws, the indulgent laws, protect them as they arrive, stamping on them the symbol of adoption; they receive ample rewards for their labours; these accumulated rewards procure them lands; those lands confer on them the title of freemen, and to that title every benefit is affixed which men can possibly require. This is the great operation daily performed by our laws. Whence proceed these laws? From our government. Whence that government? It is derived from the original genius and strong desire of the people ratified and confirmed by the crown. This is the great chain which links us all, this is the picture which every province exhibits, Nova Scotia excepted.[6] There the crown has done all; either there were no people who had genius or it was not much attended to; the consequence is that the province is very thinly inhabited indeed; the power of the crown in conjunction with the musketos[7] has prevented men from settling there. Yet some parts of it flourished once, and it contained a mild, harmless set of people. But for the fault of a few leaders, the whole was banished. The greatest political error the crown ever committed in America was to cut off men from a country which wanted nothing but men!

What attachment can a poor European emigrant have for a country where he had nothing? The knowledge of the language, the love of a few kindred as poor as himself, were the only cords that tied him; his country is now that which gives him his land, bread, protection, and consequence; *Ubi panis ibi patria*[8] is the motto of all emigrants. What, then, is the American, this new man? He is either an European or the descendant of an European; hence that strange mixture of blood, which you will

[5]Nutrient-rich earth which promotes growth.

[6]Crèvecoeur refers to the British removal of French settlers in 1755. In *Journey into Northern Pennsylvania,* Crèvecoeur says, "About the year 1745, Great Britain, to whom France had just ceded Acadia (today New Scotland-Nova Scotia), instead of keeping it for its former inhabitants, in accordance with the capitulation, snatched from its native land, under some frivolous religious pretext and without compensation . . . this gentle and hard-working people."

[7]Mosquitoes.

[8]Where there is bread, there is one's fatherland.

find in no other country. I could point out to you a family whose grandfather was an Englishman, whose wife was Dutch, whose son married a French woman, and whose present four sons have now four wives of different nations. *He* is an American, who, leaving behind him all his ancient prejudices and manners, receives new ones from the new mode of life he has embraced, the new government he obeys, and the new rank he holds. He becomes an American by being received in the broad lap of our great Alma Mater.[9] Here individuals of all nations are melted into a new race of men, whose labours and posterity will one day cause great changes in the world. Americans are the western pilgrims who are carrying along with them that great mass of arts, sciences, vigour, and industry which began long since in the East; they will finish the great circle. The Americans were once scattered all over Europe; here they are incorporated into one of the finest systems of population which has ever appeared, and which will hereafter become distinct by the power of the different climates they inhabit. The American ought therefore to love this country much better than that wherein either he or his forefathers were born. Here the rewards of his industry follow with equal steps the progress of his labour; his labour is founded on the basis of nature, self-interest; can it want a stronger allurement? Wives and children, who before in vain demanded of him a morsel of bread, now, fat and frolicsome, gladly help their father to clear those fields whence exuberant crops are to arise to feed and to clothe them all, without any part being claimed, either by a despotic prince, a rich abbot, or a mighty lord. Here religion demands but little of him: a small voluntary salary to the minister and gratitude to God; can he refuse these? The American is a new man, who acts upon new principles; he must therefore entertain new ideas and form new opinions. From involuntary idleness, servile dependence, penury, and useless labour, he has passed to toils of a very different nature, rewarded by ample subsistence. This is an American. . . .

Andrew[10] arrived at my house a week before I did, and I found my wife, agreeably to my instructions, had placed the axe in his hands as his first task. For some time, he was very awkward, but he was so docile, so willing, and grateful, as well as his wife, that I foresaw he would succeed. Agreeably to my promise, I put them all with different families, where they were well liked, and all parties were pleased. Andrew worked hard, lived well, grew fat, and every Sunday came to pay me a visit on a good horse, which Mr. P.R. lent him. Poor man, it took him a long time ere he could sit on the saddle and hold the bridle properly. I believe he had never before mounted such a beast, though I did not choose to ask him that question, for fear it might suggest some mortifying ideas. After having been twelve months at Mr. P.R.'s and having received his own and his family's wages, which amounted to eighty-four dollars, he came to see me on a weekday and told me that he was a man of middle age and would willingly have land of his own in order to procure him a home as a shelter against old age, that whenever this period should come, his son, to whom he would give his land, would then maintain him, and thus live altogether; he therefore required my advice and assistance. I thought his desire very natural and praiseworthy,

[9]Fostering mother.
[10]A recent arrival from Scotland whose situation illustrates the success of the new emigrants.

and told him that I should think of it, but that he must remain one month longer with Mr. P.R., who had 3,000 rails to split. He immediately consented. The spring was not far advanced enough yet for Andrew to begin clearing any land, even supposing that he had made a purchase, as it is always necessary that the leaves should be out in order that this additional combustible may serve to burn the heaps of brush more readily.

A few days after, it happened that the whole family of Mr. P.R. went to meeting, and left Andrew to take care of the house. While he was at the door, attentively reading the Bible, nine Indians just come from the mountains suddenly made their appearance and unloaded their packs of furs on the floor of the piazza. Conceive, if you can, what was Andrew's consternation at this extraordinary sight! From the singular appearance of these people, the honest Hebridean[11] took them for a lawless band come to rob his master's house. He therefore, like a faithful guardian, precipitately withdrew and shut the doors; but as most of our houses are without locks, he was reduced to the necessity of fixing his knife over the latch, and then flew upstairs in quest of a broadsword he had brought from Scotland. The Indians, who were Mr. P.R.'s particular friends, guessed at his suspicions and fears; they forcibly lifted the door and suddenly took possession of the house, got all the bread and meat they wanted, and sat themselves down by the fire. At this instant, Andrew, with his broadsword in his hand, entered the room, the Indians earnestly looking at him and attentively watching his motions. After a very few reflections, Andrew found that his weapon was useless when opposed to nine tomahawks, but this did not diminish his anger; on the contrary, it grew greater on observing the calm impudence with which they were devouring the family provisions. Unable to resist, he called them names in broad Scotch and ordered them to desist and be gone, to which the Indians (as they told me afterwards) replied in their equally broad idiom. It must have been a most unintelligible altercation between this honest Barra[12] man and nine Indians who did not much care for anything he could say. At last he ventured to lay his hands on one of them in order to turn him out of the house. Here Andrew's fidelity got the better of his prudence, for the Indian, by his motions, threatened to scalp him, while the rest gave the war whoop. This horrid noise so effectually frightened poor Andrew that, unmindful of his courage, of his broadsword, and his intentions, he rushed out, left them masters of the house, and disappeared. I have heard one of the Indians say since that he never laughed so heartily in his life. Andrew, at a distance, soon recovered from the fears which had been inspired by this infernal yell and thought of no other remedy than to go to the meeting-house, which was about two miles distant. In the eagerness of his honest intentions, with looks of affright still marked on his countenance, he called Mr. P.R. out and told him with great vehemence of style that nine monsters were come to his house—some blue, some red, and some black; that they had little axes in their hands out of which they smoked; and that like highlanders, they had no breeches; that they were devouring all his victuals; and that God only knew what they would do more. "Pacify yourself," said Mr. P.R.; "my house is as safe with these people as if I was there myself; as for the victuals, they are heartily welcome, honest Andrew; they are not people of much ceremony; they help themselves

[11]From the Hebrides Islands of West Scotland. [12]An island of the Hebrides.

thus whenever they are among their friends; I do so too in their wigwams, whenever I go to their village; you had better therefore step in and hear the remainder of the sermon, and when the meeting is over, we will all go back in the waggon together."

At their return, Mr. P.R., who speaks the Indian language very well, explained the whole matter; the Indians renewed their laugh and shook hands with honest Andrew, whom they made to smoke out of their pipes; and thus peace was made and ratified according to the Indian custom, by the calumet.[13] . . .

from Letter IX
Description of Charles Town; Thoughts on Slavery; on Physical Evil; a Melancholy Scene

Charles Town is, in the north, what Lima is in the south; both are capitals of the richest provinces of their respective hemispheres; you may therefore conjecture that both cities must exhibit the appearances necessarily resulting from riches. Peru abounding in gold, Lima is filled with inhabitants who enjoy all those gradations of pleasure, refinement, and luxury which proceed from wealth. Carolina produces commodities more valuable perhaps than gold because they are gained by greater industry; it exhibits also on our northern stage a display of riches and luxury, inferior indeed to the former, but far superior to what are to be seen in our northern towns. Its situation is admirable, being built at the confluence of two large rivers, which receive in their course a great number of inferior streams, all navigable in the spring for flat boats. Here the produce of this extensive territory concentres; here therefore is the seat of the most valuable exportation; their wharfs, their docks, their magazines,[14] are extremely convenient to facilitate this great commercial business. The inhabitants are the gayest in America; it is called the centre of our beau monde[15] and is always filled with the richest planters in the province, who resort hither in quest of health and pleasure. . . .

The three principal classes of inhabitants are lawyers, planters, and merchants; this is the province which has afforded to the first the richest spoils, for nothing can exceed their wealth, their power, and their influence. They have reached the *ne plus ultra*[16] of worldly felicity; no plantation is secured, no title is good, no will is valid, but what they dictate, regulate, and approve. The whole mass of provincial property is become tributary to this society, which, far above priests and bishops, disdain to be satisfied with the poor Mosaical portion of the tenth.[17] I appeal to the many inhabitants who, while contending perhaps for their right to a few hundred acres, have lost by the mazes of the law their whole patrimony. These men are more properly lawgivers than interpreters of the law and have united here, as well as in most other provinces, the skill and dexterity of the scribe with the power and ambition of the prince; who can tell where this may lead in a future day? The nature of our laws and

[13] Ceremonial Indian pipe.
[14] Warehouses.
[15] The world of fashion.
[16] The utmost point one can achieve or reach.
[17] Tithe; the Old Testament law that each person should give one-tenth of his possessions to God.

the spirit of freedom, which often tends to make us litigious, must necessarily throw the greatest part of the property of the colonies into the hands of these gentlemen. In another century, the law will possess in the north what now the church possesses in Peru and Mexico.

While all is joy, festivity, and happiness in Charles Town, would you imagine that scenes of misery overspread in the country? Their ears by habit are become deaf, their hearts are hardened; they neither see, hear, nor feel for the woes of their poor slaves, from whose painful labours all their wealth proceeds. Here the horrors of slavery, the hardship of incessant toils, are unseen; and no one thinks with compassion of those showers of sweat and tears which from the bodies of Africans daily drop and moisten the ground they till. The cracks of the whip urging these miserable beings to excessive labour are far too distant from the gay capital to be heard. The chosen race eat, drink, and live happy, while the unfortunate one grubs up the ground, raises indigo, or husks the rice, exposed to a sun full as scorching as their native one, without the support of good food, without the cordials of any cheering liquor. This great contrast has often afforded me subjects of the most afflicting meditations. On the one side, behold a people enjoying all that life affords most bewitching and pleasurable, without labour, without fatigue, hardly subjected to the trouble of wishing. With gold, dug from Peruvian mountains, they order vessels to the coasts of Guinea; by virtue of that gold, wars, murders, and devastations are committed in some harmless, peaceable African neighbourhood where dwelt innocent people who even knew not but that all men were black. The daughter torn from her weeping mother, the child from the wretched parents, the wife from the loving husband; whole families swept away and brought through storms and tempests to this rich metropolis! There, arranged like horses at a fair, they are branded like cattle and then driven to toil, to starve, and to languish for a few years on the different plantations of these citizens. And for whom must they work? For persons they know not, and who have no other power over them than that of violence, no other right than what this accursed metal has given them! Strange order of things! Oh, Nature, where art thou? Are not these blacks thy children as well as we? On the other side, nothing is to be seen but the most diffusive misery and wretchedness, unrelieved even in thought or wish! Day after day they drudge on without any prospect of ever reaping for themselves; they are obliged to devote their lives, their limbs, their will, and every vital exertion to swell the wealth of masters who look not upon them with half the kindness and affection with which they consider their dogs and horses. Kindness and affection are not the portion of those who till the earth, who carry burthens, who convert the logs into useful boards. This reward, simple and natural as one would conceive it, would border on humanity; and planters must have none of it!

If Negroes are permitted to become fathers, this fatal indulgence only tends to increase their misery; the poor companions of their scanty pleasures are likewise the companions of their labours; and when at some critical seasons they could wish to see them relieved, with tears in their eyes they behold them perhaps doubly oppressed, obliged to bear the burden of Nature—a fatal present—as well as that of unabated tasks. How many have I seen cursing the irresistible propensity and regretting that by having tasted of those harmless joys they had become the authors of double misery to their wives. Like their masters, they are not permitted to partake of those ineffable sensations with which Nature inspires the hearts of fathers and mothers; they must repel them all and become callous and passive. This unnatural state often occasions the most acute, the most pungent of their afflictions; they have no time, like us, tenderly to rear their helpless offspring, to nurse them on their knees, to enjoy the delight of being parents. Their paternal fondness is embittered by considering that if their children live, they must live to be slaves like themselves; no time is allowed them to exercise their pious office; the mothers must fasten them on their backs and, with this double load, follow their husbands in the fields, where they too often hear no other sound than that of the voice or whip of the taskmaster and the cries of their infants, broiling in the sun. These unfortunate creatures cry and weep like their parents, without a possibility of relief; the very instinct of the brute, so laudable, so irresistible, runs counter here to their master's interest; and to that god, all the laws of Nature must give way. Thus planters get rich; so raw, so inexperienced am I in this mode of life that were I to be possessed of a plantation, and my slaves treated as in general they are here, never could I rest in peace; my sleep would be perpetually disturbed by a retrospect of the frauds committed in Africa in order to entrap them, frauds surpassing in enormity everything which a common mind can possibly conceive. I should be thinking of the barbarous treatment they meet with on shipboard, of their anguish, of the despair necessarily inspired by their situation, when torn from their friends and relations, when delivered into the hands of a people differently coloured, whom they cannot understand, carried in a strange machine over an ever agitated element, which they had never seen before, and finally delivered over to the severities of the whippers and the excessive labours of the field. Can it be possible that the force of custom should ever make me deaf to all these reflections and as insensible to the injustice of that trade and to their miseries as the rich inhabitants of this town seem to be? What, then, is man, this being who boasts so much of the excellence and dignity of his nature among that variety of unscrutable mysteries, of unsolvable problems, with which he is surrounded? The reason why man has been thus created is not the least astonishing! It is said, I know, that they are much happier here than in the West Indies because, land being cheaper upon this continent than in those islands, the fields allowed them to raise their subsistence from are in general more extensive. The only possible chance of any alleviation depends on the humour of the planters, who, bred in the midst of slaves, learn from the example of their parents to despise them and seldom conceive either from religion or philosophy any ideas that tend to make their fate less calamitous, except some strong native tenderness of heart, some rays of philanthropy, overcome the obduracy contracted by habit.

I have not resided here long enough to become insensible of pain for the objects which I every day behold. In the choice of my friends and acquaintance, I always endeavour to find out those whose dispositions are somewhat congenial with my own. We have slaves likewise in our northern provinces; I hope the time draws near when they will be all emancipated, but how different their lot, how different their situation, in every possible respect! They enjoy as much liberty as their masters; they are as well clad and as well fed, in health and sickness, they are tenderly taken care of; they live under the same roof and are, truly speaking, a part of our families. Many of them are taught to read and write, and are well instructed in the principles of religion; they are the companions of our labours, and treated as such; they enjoy many perquisites, many established holidays, and are not obliged to work more than white people.

They marry where inclination leads them, visit their wives every week, are as decently clad as the common people; they are indulged in educating, cherishing, and chastising their children, who are taught subordination to them as to their lawful parents: in short, they participate in many of the benefits of our society without being obliged to bear any of its burthens. They are fat, healthy, and hearty; and far from repining at their fate, they think themselves happier than many of the lower class of whites; they share with their masters the wheat and meat provision they help to raise; many of those whom the good Quakers have emancipated have received that great benefit with tears of regret and have never quitted, though free, their former masters and benefactors.

But is it really true, as I have heard it asserted here, that those blacks are incapable of feeling the spurs of emulation and the cheerful sound of encouragement? By no means; there are a thousand proofs existing of their gratitude and fidelity: those hearts in which such noble dispositions can grow are then like ours; they are susceptible of every generous sentiment, of every useful motive of action; they are capable of receiving lights, of imbibing ideas that would greatly alleviate the weight of their miseries. But what methods have in general been made use of to obtain so desirable an end? None; the day in which they arrive and are sold is the first of their labours, labours which from that hour admit of no respite; for though indulged by law with relaxation on Sundays, they are obliged to employ that time which is intended for rest to till their little plantations. What can be expected from wretches in such circumstances? Forced from their native country, cruelly treated when on board, and not less so on the plantations to which they are driven, is there anything in this treatment but what must kindle all the passions, sow the seeds of inveterate resentment, and nourish a wish of perpetual revenge? They are left to the irresistible effects of those strong and natural propensities; the blows they receive, are they conducive to extinguish them or to win their affections? They are neither soothed by the hopes that their slavery will ever terminate but with their lives or yet encouraged by the goodness of their food or the mildness of their treatment. The very hopes held out to mankind by religion, that consolatory system, so useful to the miserable, are never presented to them; neither moral nor physical means are made use of to soften their chains; they are left in their original and untutored state, that very state wherein the natural propensities of revenge and warm passions are so soon kindled. Cheered by no one single motive that can impel the will or excite their efforts, nothing but terrors and punishments are presented to them; death is denounced if they run away; horrid delaceration if they speak with their native freedom; perpetually awed by the terrible cracks of whips or by the fear of capital punishments, while even those punishments often fail of their purpose.

A clergyman settled a few years ago at George Town, and feeling as I do now, warmly recommended to the planters, from the pulpit, a relaxation of severity; he introduced the benignity of Christianity and pathetically made use of the admirable precepts of that system to melt the hearts of his congregation into a greater degree of compassion toward their slaves than had been hitherto customary. "Sir," said one of his hearers, "we pay you a genteel salary to read to us the prayers of the liturgy and to explain to us such parts of the Gospel as the rule of the church directs, but we do not want you to teach us what we are to do with our blacks." The clergyman found it prudent to withhold any farther admonition. Whence this astonishing right, or rather this barbarous custom, for most certainly we have no kind of right beyond that of force? We are told, it is true, that slavery cannot be so repugnant to human nature as we at first imagine because it has been practised in all ages and in all nations; the Lacedaemonians[18] themselves, those great asserters of liberty, conquered the Helotes[19] with the design of making them their slaves; the Romans, whom we consider as our masters in civil and military policy, lived in the exercise of the most horrid oppression; they conquered to plunder and to enslave.[20] What a hideous aspect the face of the earth must then have exhibited! Provinces, towns, districts, often depopulated! Their inhabitants driven to Rome, the greatest market in the world, and there sold by thousands! The Roman dominions were tilled by the hands of unfortunate people who had once been, like their victors, free, rich, and possessed of every benefit society can confer, until they became subject to the cruel right of war and to lawless force. Is there, then, no superintending power who conducts the moral operations of the world, as well as the physical? The same sublime hand which guides the planets round the sun with so much exactness, which preserves the arrangement of the whole with such exalted wisdom and paternal care, and prevents the vast system from falling into confusion—doth it abandon mankind to all the errors, the follies, and the miseries, which their most frantic rage and their most dangerous vices and passions can produce?

The history of the earth! Doth it present anything but crimes of the most heinous nature, committed from one end of the world to the other? We observe avarice, rapine, and murder, equally prevailing in all parts. History perpetually tells us of millions of people abandoned to the caprice of the maddest princes, and of whole nations devoted to the blind fury of tyrants. Countries destroyed, nations alternately buried in ruins by other nations, some parts of the world beautifully cultivated, returned again into their pristine state, the fruits of ages of industry, the toil of thousands in a short time destroyed by few! If one corner breathes in peace for a few years, it is, in turn subjected, torn, and levelled; one would almost believe the principles of action in man, considered as the first agent of this planet, to be poisoned in their most essential parts. We certainly are not that class of beings which we vainly think ourselves to be; man, an animal of prey, seems to have rapine and the love of bloodshed implanted in his heart, nay, to hold it the most honourable occupation in society; we never speak of a hero of mathematics, a hero of knowledge or humanity, no, this illustrious appellation is reserved for the most successful butchers of the world. If Nature has given us a fruitful soil to inhabit, she has refused us such inclinations and propensities as would afford us the full enjoyment of it. Extensive as the surface of this planet is, not one half of it is yet cultivated, not half replenished; she created man and placed him either in the woods or plains and provided him with passions which must forever oppose his happiness; everything is submitted to the power of the strongest; men, like the elements, are always at war; the weakest yield

[18]Another name for the inhabitants of the Greek city-state of Sparta.

[19]Inhabitants of Helos in Laconia, an ancient country in southern Greece. Their name became synonymous with slave.

[20]Reference to eighteenth-century political theories which treat Rome as a paradigm of the republican state.

to the most potent; force, subtlety, and malice always triumph over unguarded honesty and simplicity. Benignity, moderation, and justice are virtues adapted only to the humble paths of life; we love to talk of virtue and to admire its beauty while in the shade of solitude and retirement, but when we step forth into active life, if it happen to be in competition with any passion or desire, do we observe it to prevail? Hence so many religious impostors have triumphed over the credulity of mankind and have rendered their frauds the creeds of succeeding generations during the course of many ages until, worn away by time, they have been replaced by new ones. Hence the most unjust war, if supported by the greatest force, always succeeds; hence the most just ones, when supported only by their justice, as often fail. Such is the ascendancy of power, the supreme arbiter of all the revolutions which we observe in this planet; so irresistible is power that it often thwarts the tendency of the most forcible causes and prevents their subsequent salutary effects, though ordained for the good of man by the Governor of the universe. Such is the perverseness of human nature; who can describe it in all its latitude? . . .

. . . Even under those mild climates which seem to breathe peace and happiness, the poison of slavery, the fury of despotism, and the rage of superstition are all combined against man! There only the few live and rule whilst the many starve and utter ineffectual complaints; there human nature appears more debased, perhaps, than in the less favoured climates. The fertile plains of Asia, the rich lowlands of Egypt and of Diarbeck, the fruitful fields bordering on the Tigris and the Euphrates, the extensive country of the East Indies in all its separate districts—all these must to the geographical eye seem as if intended for terrestrial paradises; but though surrounded with the spontaneous riches of nature, though her kindest favours seem to be shed on those beautiful regions with the most profuse hand, yet there in general we find the most wretched people in the world. Almost everywhere, liberty so natural to mankind is refused, or rather enjoyed but by their tyrants; the word slave is the appellation of every rank who adore as a divinity a being worse than themselves, subject to every caprice and to every lawless rage which unrestrained power can give. Tears are shed, perpetual groans are heard, where only the accents of peace, alacrity, and gratitude should resound. There the very delirium of tyranny tramples on the best gifts of nature and sports with the fate, the happiness, the lives of millions; there the extreme fertility of the ground always indicates the extreme misery of the inhabitants!

Everywhere one part of the human species is taught the art of shedding the blood of the other, of setting fire to their dwellings, of levelling the works of their industry: half of the existence of nations regularly employed in destroying other nations. What little political felicity is to be met with here and there has cost oceans of blood to purchase, as if good was never to be the portion of unhappy man. Republics, kingdoms, monarchies, founded either on fraud or successful violence, increase by pursuing the steps of the same policy until they are destroyed in their turn, either by the influence of their own crimes or by more successful but equally criminal enemies.

If from this general review of human nature we descend to the examination of what is called civilized society, there the combination of every natural and artificial want makes us pay very dear for what little share of political felicity we enjoy. It is a strange heterogeneous assemblage of vices and virtues and of a variety of other principles, forever at war, forever jarring, forever producing some dangerous, some distressing extreme. Where do you conceive, then, that nature intended we should be happy? Would you prefer the state of men in the woods to that of men in a more improved situation? Evil preponderates in both; in the first they often eat each other for want of food, and in the other they often starve each other for want of room. For my part, I think the vices and miseries to be found in the latter exceed those of the former, in which real evil is more scarce, more supportable, and less enormous. Yet we wish to see the earth peopled, to accomplish the happiness of kingdoms, which is said to consist in numbers. Gracious God! To what end is the introduction of so many beings into a mode of existence in which they must grope amidst as many errors, commit as many crimes, and meet with as many diseases, wants, and sufferings!

The following scene will, I hope, account for these melancholy reflections and apologize for the gloomy thoughts with which I have filled this letter: my mind is, and always has been, oppressed since I became a witness to it. I was not long since invited to dine with a planter who lived three miles from ——, where he then resided. In order to avoid the heat of the sun, I resolved to go on foot, sheltered in a small path leading through a pleasant wood. I was leisurely travelling along, attentively examining some peculiar plants which I had collected, when all at once I felt the air strongly agitated, though the day was perfectly calm and sultry. I immediately cast my eyes toward the cleared ground, from which I was but a small distance, in order to see whether it was not occasioned by a sudden shower, when at that instant a sound resembling a deep rough voice, uttered, as I thought, a few inarticulate monosyllables. Alarmed and surprised, I precipitately looked all round, when I perceived at about six rods distance something resembling a cage, suspended to the limbs of a tree, all the branches of which appeared covered with large birds of prey, fluttering about and anxiously endeavouring to perch on the cage. Actuated by an involuntary motion of my hands more than by any design of my mind, I fired at them; they all flew to a short distance, with a most hideous noise, when, horrid to think and painful to repeat, I perceived a Negro, suspended in the cage and left there to expire! I shudder when I recollect that the birds had already picked out his eyes; his cheek-bones were bare; his arms had been attacked in several places; and his body seemed covered with a multitude of wounds. From the edges of the hollow sockets and from the lacerations with which he was disfigured, the blood slowly dropped and tinged the ground beneath. No sooner were the birds flown than swarms of insects covered the whole body of this unfortunate wretch, eager to feed on his mangled flesh and to drink his blood. I found myself suddenly arrested by the power of affright and terror; my nerves were convulsed; I trembled; I stood motionless, involuntarily contemplating the fate of this Negro in all its dismal latitude. The living spectre, though deprived of his eyes, could still distinctly hear, and in his uncouth dialect begged me to give him some water to allay his thirst. Humanity herself would have recoiled back with horror; she would have balanced whether to lessen such reliefless distress or mercifully with one blow to end this dreadful scene of agonizing torture! Had I had a ball in my gun, I certainly should have dispatched him, but finding myself unable to perform so kind an office, I sought, though trembling, to relieve him as well as I could. A shell ready fixed to a pole, which had been used by some Negroes, presented itself to me; filled it with water, and with trembling hands I guided it to the quivering lips of the wretched sufferer. Urged by the irresistible power of thirst, he endeavoured to meet it, as he instinctively guessed its approach by the noise it made in passing through the bars of the cage. "Tanky you, white man; tanky you; puta some poison and give me." "How long have you been hanging there?" I asked him. "Two days, and me no die; the birds, the birds; aaah me!" Oppressed with the reflections which this shocking spectacle afforded me, I mustered strength enough to walk away and soon reached the house at which I intended to dine. There I heard that the reason for this slave's being thus punished was on account of his having killed the overseer of the plantation. They told me that the laws of self-preservation rendered such executions necessary, and supported the doctrine of slavery with the arguments generally made use of to justify the practice, with the repetition of which I shall not trouble you at present. Adieu.

from Letter XII
Distresses of a Frontier Man

I wish for a change of place; the hour is come at last that I must fly from my house and abandon my farm! But what course shall I steer, inclosed as I am? The climate best adapted to my present situation and humour would be the polar regions, where six months' day and six months' night divide the dull year; nay, a simple aurora borealis would suffice me and greatly refresh my eyes, fatigued now by so many disagreeable objects. The severity of those climates, that great gloom where melancholy dwells, would be perfectly analogous to the turn of my mind. Oh, could I remove my plantation to the shores of the Obi,[21] willingly would I dwell in the hut of a Samoyed;[22] with cheerfulness would I go and bury myself in the cavern of a Laplander. Could I but carry my family along with me, I would winter at Pello, or Tobolsk,[23] in order to enjoy the peace and innocence of that country. But let me arrive under the pole, or reach the antipodes, I never can leave behind me the remembrance of the dreadful scenes to which I have been witness; therefore, never can I be happy! Happy—why would I mention that sweet, that enchanting word? Once happiness was our portion; now it is gone from us, and I am afraid not to be enjoyed again by the present generation! Whichever way I look, nothing but the most frightful precipices present themselves to my view, in which hundreds of my friends and acquaintances have already perished; of all animals that live on the surface of this planet, what is man when no longer connected with society, or when he finds himself surrounded by a convulsed and a half-dissolved one? He cannot live in solitude; he must belong to some community bound by some ties, however imperfect. Men mutually support and add to the boldness and confidence of each other; the weakness of each is strengthened by the force of the whole. I had never before these calamitous times formed any such ideas; I lived on, laboured and prospered, without having ever studied on what the security of my life and the foundation of my prosperity were established; I perceived them just as they left me. Never was a situation so singularly terrible as mine, in every possible respect, as a member of an extensive soci-

[21]River in Siberia.
[22]A member of a Siberian nomadic tribe.
[23]Places in Siberia.

ety, as a citizen of an inferior division of the same society, as a husband, as a father, as a man who exquisitely feels for the miseries of others as well as for his own! But alas! So much is everything now subverted among us that the very word *misery,* with which we were hardly acquainted before, no longer conveys the same ideas, or, rather, tired with feeling for the miseries of others, every one feels now for himself alone. When I consider myself as connected in all these characters, as bound by so many cords, all uniting in my heart, I am seized with a fever of the mind, I am transported beyond that degree of calmness which is necessary to delineate our thoughts. I feel as if my reason wanted to leave me, as if it would burst its poor weak tenement; again, I try to compose myself, I grow cool, and preconceiving the dreadful loss, I endeavour to retain the useful guest.

You know the position of our settlement; I need not therefore describe it. To the west it is inclosed by a chain of mountains, reaching to ——; to the east, the country is as yet but thinly inhabited; we are almost insulated, and the houses are at a considerable distance from each other. From the mountains we have but too much reason to expect our dreadful enemy; the wilderness is a harbour where it is impossible to find them. It is a door through which they can enter our country whenever they please; and, as they seem determined to destroy the whole chain of frontiers, our fate cannot be far distant: from Lake Champlain, almost all has been conflagrated one after another. What renders these incursions still more terrible is that they most commonly take place in the dead of the night; we never go to our fields but we are seized with an involuntary fear, which lessens our strength and weakens our labour. No other subject of conversation intervenes between the different accounts, which spread through the country, of successive acts of devastation, and these, told in chimney-corners, swell themselves in our affrighted imaginations into the most terrific ideas! We never sit down either to dinner or supper but the least noise immediately spreads a general alarm and prevents us from enjoying the comfort of our meals. The very appetite proceeding from labour and peace of mind is gone; we eat just enough to keep us alive; our sleep is disturbed by the most frightful dreams; sometimes I start awake, as if the great hour of danger was come; at other times the howling of our dogs seems to announce the arrival of our enemy; we leap out of bed and run to arms; my poor wife, with panting bosom and silent tears, takes leave of me, as if we were to see each other no more; she snatches the youngest children from their beds, who, suddenly awakened, increase by their innocent questions the horror of the dreadful moment. She tries to hide them in the cellar, as if our cellar was inaccessible to the fire. I place all my servants at the windows and myself at the door, where I am determined to perish. Fear industriously increases every sound; we all listen; each communicates to the other his ideas and conjectures. We remain thus sometimes for whole hours, our hearts and our minds racked by the most anxious suspense: what a dreadful situation, a thousand times worse than that of a soldier engaged in the midst of the most severe conflict! Sometimes feeling the spontaneous courage of a man, I seem to wish for the decisive minute; the next instant a message from my wife, sent by one of the children, puzzling me beside with their little questions, unmans me; away goes my courage, and I descend again into the deepest despondency. At last, finding that it was a false alarm, we return once more to our beds; but what good can the kind of sleep of Nature do to us when interrupted by such scenes! Securely placed as you are, you can have no idea of our agitations, but by hearsay; no relation can be equal to what we suffer and to what we feel. Every morning my youngest children are sure to have frightful dreams to relate; in vain I exert my authority to keep them silent; it is not in my power; and these images of their disturbed imagination, instead of being frivolously looked upon as in the days of our happiness, are on the contrary considered as warnings and sure prognostics of our future fate. I am not a superstitious man, but since our misfortunes, I am grown more timid and less disposed to treat the doctrine of omens with contempt.

Though these evils have been gradual, yet they do not become habitual like other incidental evils. The nearer I view the end of this catastrophe, the more I shudder. But why should I trouble you with such unconnected accounts; men secure and out of danger are soon fatigued with mournful details: can you enter with me into fellowship with all these afflictive sensations; have you a tear ready to shed over the approaching ruin of a once opulent and substantial family? Read this, I pray, with the eyes of sympathy, with a tender sorrow; pity the lot of those whom you once called your friends, who were once surrounded with plenty, ease, and perfect security, but who now expect every night to be their last, and who are as wretched as criminals under an impending sentence of the law.

As a member of a large society which extends to many parts of the world, my connexion with it is too distant to be as strong as that which binds me to the inferior division in the midst of which I live. I am told that the great nation of which we are a part is just, wise, and free beyond any other on earth, within its own insular boundaries, but not always so to its distant conquests; I shall not repeat all I have heard because I cannot believe half of it. As a citizen of a smaller society, I find that any kind of opposition to its now prevailing sentiments immediately begets hatred; how easily do men pass from loving to hating and cursing one another! I am a lover of peace; what must I do? I am divided between the respect I feel for the ancient connexion and the fear of innovations, with the consequence of which I am not well acquainted, as they are embraced by my own countrymen. I am conscious that I was happy before this unfortunate revolution. I feel that I am no longer so; therefore I regret the change. This is the only mode of reasoning adapted to persons in my situation. If I attach myself to the mother country, which is 3,000 miles from me, I become what is called an enemy to my own region; if I follow the rest of my countrymen, I become opposed to our ancient masters: both extremes appear equally dangerous to a person of so little weight and consequence as I am, whose energy and example are of no avail. As to the argument on which the dispute is founded, I know little about it. Much has been said and written on both sides, but who has a judgement capacious and clear enough to decide? The great moving principles which actuate both parties are much hid from vulgar eyes, like mine; nothing but the plausible and the probable are offered to our contemplation. The innocent class are always the victims of the few; they are in all countries and at all times the inferior agents on which the popular phantom is erected; they clamour and must toil and bleed, and are always sure of meeting with oppression and rebuke. It is for the sake of the great leaders on both sides that so much blood must be spilt; that of the people is counted as nothing. Great events are not achieved for us, though it is *by* us that they are principally accomplished, by the arms, the sweat, the lives of the people. Books tell me so much that they inform me of nothing. Sophistry, the bane of freemen, launches forth in all her deceiving attire! After all, most men reason from passions; and shall such an ignorant individual as I am decide and say this side is right, that side is wrong? Sentiment and feeling are the only guides I know. Alas, how should I unravel an argument in which Reason herself has given way to brutality and bloodshed! What then must I do? I ask the wisest lawyers, the ablest casuists, the warmest patriots; for I mean honestly. Great Source of wisdom! Inspire me with light sufficient to guide my benighted steps out of this intricate maze! Shall I discard all my ancient principles, shall I renounce that name, that nation which I held once so respectable? I feel the powerful attraction; the sentiments they inspired grew with my earliest knowledge and were grafted upon the first rudiments of my education. On the other hand, shall I arm myself against that country where I first drew breath, against the playmates of my youth, my bosom friends, my acquaintance? The idea makes me shudder! Must I be called a parricide, a traitor, a villain, lose the esteem of all those whom I love to preserve my own, be shunned like a rattlesnake, or be pointed at like a bear? I have neither heroism not magnanimity enough to make so great a sacrifice. Here I am tied, I am fastened by numerous strings, nor do I repine at the pressure they cause; ignorant as I am, I can pervade the utmost extent of the calamities which have already overtaken our poor afflicted country. I can see the great and accumulated ruin yet extending itself as far as the theatre of war has reached; I hear the groans of thousands of families now ruined and desolated by our aggressors. I cannot count the multitude of orphans this war has made nor ascertain the immensity of blood we have lost. Some have asked whether it was a crime to resist, to repel some parts of this evil. Others have asserted that a resistance so general makes pardon unattainable and repentance useless, and dividing the crime among so many renders it imperceptible. What one party calls meritorious, the other denominates flagitious. These opinions vary, contract, or expand, like the events of the war on which they are founded. What can an insignificant man do in the midst of these jarring contradictory parties, equally hostile to persons situated as I am? And after all, who will be the really guilty? Those most certainly who fail of success. Our fate, the fate of thousands, is, then, necessarily involved in the dark wheel of fortune. Why, then, so many useless reasonings; we are the sport of fate. Farewell education, principles, love of our country, farewell; all are become useless to the generality of us: he who governs himself according to what he calls his principles may be punished either by one party or the other for those very principles. He who proceeds without principle, as chance, timidity, or self-preservation directs, will not perhaps fare better, but he will be less blamed. What are *we* in the great scale of events, we poor defenceless frontier inhabitants? What is it to the gazing world whether we breathe or whether we die? Whatever virtue, whatever merit and disinterestedness we may exhibit in our secluded retreats, of what avail? We are like the pismires destroyed by the plough, whose destruction prevents not the future crop. Self-preservation, therefore, the rule of Nature, seems to be the best rule of conduct; what good can we do by vain resistance, by useless efforts? The cool, the distant spectator, placed in safety, may arraign me for ingratitude, may bring forth the principles of Solon or Montesquieu;[24] he may look on me as wilfully

[24]Solon (638?–559? B.C.), a statesman and poet of ancient Athens; Montesquieu (1689–1755), an eighteenth-century French lawyer and philosopher, author of *The Spirit of the Laws.*

guilty; he may call me by the most opprobrious names. Secure from personal danger, his warm imagination, undisturbed by the least agitation of the heart, will expatiate freely on this grand question and will consider this extended field but as exhibiting the double scene of attack and defence. To him the object becomes abstracted; the intermediate glares; the perspective distance and a variety of opinions, unimpaired by affections, present to his mind but one set of ideas. Here he proclaims the high guilt of the one, and there the right of the other. But let him come and reside with us one single month; let him pass with us through all the successive hours of necessary toil, terror, and affright; let him watch with us, his musket in his hand, through tedious, sleepless nights, his imagination furrowed by the keen chisel of every passion; let his wife and his children become exposed to the most dreadful hazards of death; let the existence of his property depend on a single spark, blown by the breath of an enemy; let him tremble with us in our fields, shudder at the rustling of every leaf; let his heart, the seat of the most affecting passions, be powerfully wrung by hearing the melancholy end of his relations and friends; let him trace on the map the progress of these desolations; let his alarmed imagination predict to him the night, the dreadful night when it may be his turn to perish, as so many have perished before. Observe, then, whether the man will not get the better of the citizen, whether his political maxims will not vanish! Yes, he will cease to glow so warmly with the glory of the metropolis; all his wishes will be turned toward the preservation of his family! Oh, were he situated where I am, were his house perpetually filled, as mine is, with miserable victims just escaped from the flames and the scalping knife, telling of barbarities and murders that make human nature tremble, his situation would suspend every political reflection and expel every abstract idea. My heart is full and involuntarily takes hold of any notion from whence it can receive ideal ease or relief. I am informed that the king has the most numerous, as well as the fairest, progeny of children of any potentate now in the world; he may be a great king, but he must feel as we common mortals do in the good wishes he forms for their lives and prosperity. His mind no doubt often springs forward on the wings of anticipation and contemplates us as happily settled in the world. If a poor frontier inhabitant may be allowed to suppose this great personage the first in our system to be exposed but for one hour to the exquisite pangs we so often feel, would not the preservation of so numerous a family engross all his thoughts; would not the ideas of dominion and other felicities attendant on royalty all vanish in the hour of danger? The regal character, however sacred, would be superseded by the stronger, because more natural one of man and father. Oh! Did he but know the circumstances of this horrid war, I am sure he would put a stop to that long destruction of parents and children. I am sure that while he turned his ears to state policy, he would attentively listen also to the dictates of Nature, that great parent; for, as a good king, he no doubt wishes to create, to spare, and to protect, as she does. Must I then, in order to be called a faithful subject, coolly and philosophically say it is necessary for the good of Britain that my children's brains should be dashed against the walls of the house in which they were reared; that my wife should be stabbed and scalped before my face; that I should be either murthered or captivated; or that for greater expedition we should all be locked up and burnt to ashes as the family of the B——n was? Must I with meekness wait for that last pitch of desolation and receive with perfect resignation so hard a fate from ruffians acting at such a distance from the eyes of any superior, monsters left to the wild impulses of the wildest nature? Could the lions of Africa be transported here and let loose, they would no doubt kill us in order to prey upon our carcasses! But their appetites would not require so many victims. Shall I wait to be punished with death, or else to be stripped of all food and raiment, reduced to despair without redress and without hope? Shall those who may escape see everything they hold dear destroyed and gone? Shall those few survivors, lurking in some obscure corner, deplore in vain the fate of their families, mourn over parents either captivated, butchered, or burnt; roam among our wilds and wait for death at the foot of some tree, without a murmur or without a sigh, for the good of the cause? No, it is impossible! So astonishing a sacrifice is not be to expected from human nature; it must belong to beings of an inferior or superior order, actuated by less or by more refined principles. Even those great personages who are so far elevated above the common ranks of men, those, I mean, who wield and direct so many thunders, those who have let loose against us these demons of war, could they be transported here and metamorphosed into simple planters as we are—they would, from being the arbiters of human destiny, sink into miserable victims; they would feel and exclaim as we do, and be as much at a loss what line of conduct to prosecute. Do you well comprehend the difficulties of our situation? If we stay we are sure to perish at one time or another; no vigilance on our part can save us; if we retire, we know not where to go; every house is filled with refugees as wretched as ourselves; and if we remove, we become beggars. The property of farmers is not like that of merchants, and absolute poverty is worse than death. If we take up arms to defend ourselves, we are denominated rebels; should we not be rebels against Nature, could we be shamefully passive? Shall we, then, like martyrs, glory in an allegiance now become useless, and voluntarily expose ourselves to a species of desolation which, though it ruin us entirely, yet enriches not our ancient masters. By this inflexible and sullen attachment, we shall be despised by our countrymen and destroyed by our ancient friends; whatever we may say, whatever merit we may claim, will not shelter us from those indiscriminate blows, given by hired banditti, animated by all those passions which urge men to shed the blood of others; how bitter the thought! On the contrary, blows received by the hands of those from whom we expected protection extinguish ancient respect and urge us to self defence—perhaps to revenge; this is the path which Nature herself points out, as well to the civilized as to the uncivilized. The Creator of hearts has himself stamped on them those propensities at their first formation; and must we then daily receive this treatment from a power once so loved? The fox flies or deceives the hounds that pursue him; the bear, when overtaken, boldly resists and attacks them; the hen, the very timid hen, fights for the preservation of her chicken, nor does she decline to attack and to meet on the wing even the swift kite. Shall man, then, provided both with instinct and reason, unmoved, unconcerned, and passive see his subsistence consumed and his progeny either ravished from him or murdered? Shall fictitious reason extinguish the unerring impulse of instinct? No; my former respect, my former attachment, vanishes with my safety; that respect and attachment were purchased by protection, and it has ceased. Could not the great nation we belong to have accomplished her designs by means of her numerous armies, by means of those fleets which cover the ocean? Must those who are masters of two thirds of the trade of the world, who have in their hands the power which almighty gold can give, who possess a species of wealth that increases with their desires—must they establish their conquest with our insignificant, innocent blood!

Must I, then, bid farewell to Britain, to that renowned country? Must I renounce a name so ancient and so venerable? Alas, she herself, that once indulgent parent, forces me to take up arms against her. She herself first inspired the most unhappy citizens of our remote districts with the thoughts of shedding the blood of those whom they used to call by the name of friends and brethren. That great nation which now convulses the world, which hardly knows the extent of her Indian kingdoms, which looks toward the universal monarchy of trade, of industry, of riches, of power: why must she strew our poor frontiers with the carcasses of her friends, with the wrecks of our insignificant villages, in which there is no gold? When, oppressed by painful recollection, I revolve all these scattered ideas in my mind, when I contemplate my situation and the thousand streams of evil with which I am surrounded, when I descend into the particular tendency even of the remedy I have proposed, I am convulsed—convulsed sometimes to that degree as to be tempted to exclaim, "Why has the Master of the world permitted so much indiscriminate evil throughout every part of this poor planet, at all times, and among all kinds of people?" It ought surely to be the punishment of the wicked only. I bring that cup to my lips, of which I must soon taste, and shudder at its bitterness. What, then, is life, I ask myself; is it a gracious gift? No, it is too bitter; a gift means something valuable conferred, but life appears to be a mere accident, and of the worst kind: we are born to be victims of diseases and passions, of mischances and death; better not to be than to be miserable. Thus, impiously I roam, I fly from one erratic thought to another, and my mind, irritated by these acrimonious reflections, is ready sometimes to lead me to dangerous extremes of violence. When I recollect that I am a father and a husband, the return of these endearing ideas strikes deep into my heart. Alas! They once made it glow with pleasure and with every ravishing exultation; but now they fill it with sorrow. At other times, my wife industriously rouses me out of these dreadful meditations and soothes me by all the reasoning she is mistress of; but her endeavours only serve to make me more miserable by reflecting that she must share with me all these calamities the bare apprehensions of which I am afraid will subvert her reason. Nor can I with patience think that a beloved wife, my faithful helpmate, throughout all my rural schemes the principal hand which has assisted me in rearing the prosperous fabric of ease and independence I lately possessed, as well as my children, those tenants of my heart, should daily and nightly be exposed to such a cruel fate. Self-preservation is above all political precepts and rules, and even superior to the dearest opinions of our minds; a reasonable accommodation of ourselves to the various exigencies of the times in which we live is the most irresistible precept. To this great evil I must seek some sort of remedy adapted to remove or to palliate it; situated as I am, what steps should I take that will neither injure nor insult any of the parties, and at the same time save my family from that certain destruction which awaits it if I remain here much longer. Could I ensure them bread, safety, and subsistence, not the bread of idleness, but that earned by proper labour as heretofore; could this be accomplished by the sacrifice of my life, I would willingly give it up. I attest before heaven that it is only for these I would wish to live and toil, for these whom I have brought into this miserable existence. I resemble, methinks, one of the stones of a ruined arch, still retaining that pristine form which anciently fitted the place I occupied, but the centre is tumbled down; I can be nothing until I am replaced, either in the former circle or in some stronger one. I see one on a smaller scale, and at a considerable distance, but it is within my power to reach it; and since I have ceased to consider myself as a member of the ancient state now convulsed, I willingly descend into an inferior one. I will revert into a state approaching nearer to that of nature, unencumbered either with voluminous laws or contradictory codes, often galling the very necks of those whom they protect, and at the same time sufficiently remote from the brutality of unconnected savage nature. Do you, my friend, perceive the path I have found out? It is that which leads to the tenants of the great —— village of ——, where, far removed from the accursed neighbourhood of Europeans, its inhabitants live with more ease, decency, and peace than you imagine; who, though governed by no laws, yet find in uncontaminated simple manners all that laws can afford. Their system is sufficiently complete to answer all the primary wants of man and to constitute him a social being such as he ought to be in the great forest of Nature. There it is that I have resolved at any rate to transport myself and family: an eccentric thought, you may say, thus to cut asunder all former connexions and to form new ones with a people whom Nature has stamped with such different characteristics! But as the happiness of my family is the only object of my wishes, I care very little where we are or where we go, provided that we are safe and all united together. . . .

Yes, I will cheerfully embrace that resource; it is a holy inspiration; by night and by day, it presents itself to my mind; I have carefully revolved the scheme; I have considered in all its future effects and tendencies the new mode of living we must pursue, without salt, without spices, without linen, and with little other clothing; the art of hunting we must acquire, the new manners we must adopt, the new language we must speak; the dangers attending the education of my children we must endure. These changes may appear more terrific at a distance perhaps than when grown familiar by practice; what is it to us whether we eat well-made pastry or pounded álagrichés,[25] well-roasted beef or smoked venison, cabbages or squashes? Whether we wear neat homespun or good beaver, whether we sleep on feather-beds or on bearskins? The difference is not worth attending to. The difficulty of the language, the fear of some great intoxication among the Indians, finally the apprehension lest my younger children should be caught by that singular charm, so dangerous at their tender years, are the only considerations that startle me. By what power does it come to pass that children who have been adopted when young among these people can never be prevailed on to readopt European manners? Many an anxious parent have I seen last war who at the return of the peace went to the Indian villages where they knew their children had been carried in captivity, when to their inexpressible sorrow they found them so perfectly Indianized that many knew them no longer, and those whose more advanced ages permitted them to recollect their fathers and mothers absolutely refused to follow them and ran to their adoptive parents for protection against the effusions of love their unhappy real parents lavished on them! Incredible as this may appear, I have heard it asserted in a thousand instances, among persons of credit. In the village of ——, where I purpose to go, there lived, about fifteen years

[25]Corn kernels used in making a kind of mush.

ago, an Englishman and a Swede, whose history would appear moving had I time to relate it. They were grown to the age of men when they were taken; they happily escaped the great punishment of war captives and were obliged to marry the squaws who had saved their lives by adoption. By the force of habit, they became at last thoroughly naturalized to this wild course of life. While I was there, their friends sent them a considerable sum of money to ransom themselves with. The Indians, their old masters, gave them their choice, and without requiring any consideration, told them that they had been long as free as themselves. They chose to remain, and the reasons they gave me would greatly surprise you: the most perfect freedom, the ease of living, the absence of those cares and corroding solicitudes which so often prevail with us, the peculiar goodness of the soil they cultivated, for they did not trust altogether to hunting—all these and many more motives which I have forgot made them prefer that life of which we entertain such dreadful opinions. It cannot be, therefore, so bad as we generally conceive it to be; there must be in their social bond something singularly captivating and far superior to anything to be boasted of among us; for thousands of Europeans are Indians, and we have no examples of even one of those aborigines having from choice become Europeans! There must be something more congenial to our native dispositions than the fictitious society in which we live; or else why should children, and even grown persons, become in a short time so invincibly attached to it? There must be something very bewitching in their manners, something very indelible and marked by the very hands of Nature. For, take a young Indian lad, give him the best education you possibly can, load him with your bounty, with presents, nay with riches, yet he would secretly long for his native woods, which you would imagine he must have long since forgot; and on the first opportunity he can possibly find, you will see him voluntarily leave behind all you have given him and return with inexpressible joy to lie on the mats of his fathers. Mr. —— some years ago received from a good old Indian, who died in his house, a young lad of nine years of age, his grandson. He kindly educated him with his children and bestowed on him the same care and attention in respect to the memory of his venerable grandfather, who was a worthy man. He intended to give him a genteel trade, but in the spring season when all the family went to the woods to make their maple sugar, he suddenly disappeared, and it was not until seventeen months after that his benefactor heard he had reached the village of Bald Eagle, where he still dwelt. Let us say what we will of them, of their inferior organs, of their want of bread, etc., they are as stout and well made as the Europeans. Without temples, without priests, without kings, and without laws, they are in many instances superior to us; and the proofs of what I advance are that they live without care, sleep without inquietude, take life as it comes, bearing all its asperities with unparalleled patience, and die without any kind of apprehension for what they have done or for what they expect to meet with hereafter. What system of philosophy can give us so many necessary qualifications for happiness? They most certainly are much more closely connected with Nature than we are; they are her immediate children: the inhabitants of the woods are her undefiled offspring; those of the plains are her degenerated breed, far, very far removed from her primitive laws, from her original design. It is therefore resolved on. I will either die in the attempt or succeed; better perish all together in one fatal hour than to suffer what we daily endure. I do not expect to enjoy in the village of —— an uninterrupted happiness; it cannot be our lot, let us live where we will; I am not founding my future prosperity on golden dreams. Place mankind where you will, they must always have adverse circumstances to struggle with; from nature, accidents, constitution; from seasons, from that great combination of mischances which perpetually leads us to diseases, to poverty, etc. Who knows but I may meet in this new situation some accident whence may spring up new sources of unexpected prosperity? Who can be presumptuous enough to predict all the good? Who can foresee all the evils which strew the paths of our lives? But after all, I cannot but recollect what sacrifice I am going to make, what amputation I am going to suffer, what transition I am going to experience. Pardon my repetitions, my wild, my trifling reflections; they proceed from the agitations of my mind and the fulness of my heart; the action of thus retracing them seems to lighten the burthen and to exhilarate my spirits; this is, besides, the last letter you will receive from me; I would fain tell you all, though I hardly know how. Oh! In the hours, in the moments of my greatest anguish, could I intuitively represent to you that variety of thought which crowds on my mind, you would have reason to be surprised and to doubt of their possibility. Shall we ever meet again? If we should, where will it be? On the wild shores of ——. If it be my doom to end my days there, I will greatly improve them and perhaps make room for a few more families who will choose to retire from the fury of a storm, the agitated billows of which will yet roar for many years on our extended shores. Perhaps I may repossess my house, if it be not burnt down; but how will my improvements look? Why, half defaced, bearing the strong marks of abandonment and of the ravages of war. However, at present I give everything over for lost; I will bid a long farewell to what I leave behind. If ever I repossess it, I shall receive it as a gift, as a reward for my conduct and fortitude. Do not imagine, however, that I am a stoic—by no means I must, on the contrary, confess to you that I feel the keenest regret at abandoning a house which I have in some measure reared with my own hands. Yes, perhaps I may never revisit those fields which I have cleared, those trees which I have planted, those meadows which, in my youth were a hideous wilderness, now converted by my industry into rich pastures and pleasant lawns. If in Europe it is praiseworthy to be attached to paternal inheritances, how much more natural, how much more powerful must the tie be with us, who, if I may be permitted the expression, are the founders, the creators, of our own farms! When I see my table surrounded with my blooming offspring, all united in the bonds of the strongest affection, it kindles in my paternal heart a variety of tumultuous sentiments which none but a father and a husband in my situation can feel or describe. Perhaps I may see my wife, my children, often distressed, involuntarily recalling to their minds the ease and abundance which they enjoyed under the paternal roof. Perhaps I may see them want that bread which I now leave behind, overtaken by diseases and penury, rendered more bitter by the recollection of former days of opulence and plenty. Perhaps I may be assailed on every side by unforeseen accidents which I shall not be able to prevent or to alleviate. Can I contemplate such images without the most unutterable emotions? My fate is determined; but I have not determined it, you may assure yourself, without having undergone the most painful conflicts of a variety of passions—interest, love of ease, disappointed views, and pleasing expectations frustrated—I shuddered at the review. Would to God I was master of the stoical tranquillity of that magnanimous sect; oh, that I were possessed of those sublime lessons which Appollonius of Chalcis gave to the Emperor Antoninus! I could then with much more propriety guide the helm of my little bark, which is soon to be freighted with all that I possess most dear on earth, through this stormy passage to a safe harbour, and when there, become to my fellow-passengers a surer guide, a brighter example, a pattern more worthy of imitation, throughout all the new scenes they must pass and the new career they must traverse. I have observed, notwithstanding, the means hitherto made use of to arm the principal nations against our frontiers. Yet they have not, they will not take up the hatchet against a people who have done them no harm. The passions necessary to urge these people to war cannot be roused; they cannot feel the stings of vengeance, the thirst of which alone can impel them to shed blood: far superior in their motives of action to the Europeans who, for sixpence per day, may be engaged to shed that of any people on earth. They know nothing of the nature of our disputes; they have no ideas of such revolutions as this; a civil division of a village or tribe are events which have never been recorded in their traditions; many of them know very well that they have too long been the dupes and the victims of both parties, foolishly arming for our sakes, sometimes against each other, sometimes against our white enemies. They consider us as born on the same land, and, though they have no reasons to love us, yet they seem carefully to avoid entering into this quarrel, from whatever motives. I am speaking of those nations with which I am best acquainted; a few hundreds of the worst kind mixed with whites worse than themselves are now hired by Great Britain to perpetuate those dreadful incursions. In my youth I traded with the ——, under the conduct of my uncle, and always traded justly and equitably; some of them remember it to this day. Happily their village is far removed from the dangerous neighbourhood of the whites; I sent a man last spring to it who understands the woods extremely well and who speaks their language; he is just returned, after several weeks' absence, and has brought me, as I had flattered myself, a string of thirty purple wampum[26] as a token that their honest chief will spare us half of his wigwam until we have time to erect one. He has sent me word that they have land in plenty, of which they are not so covetous as the whites; that we may plant for ourselves, and that in the meantime he will procure us some corn and meat; that fish is plenty in the waters of ——, and that the village to which he had laid open my proposals have no objection to our becoming dwellers with them. I have not yet communicated these glad tidings to my wife, nor do I know how to do it; I tremble lest she should refuse to follow me, lest the sudden idea of this removal rushing on her mind might be too powerful. I flatter myself I shall be able to accomplish it and to prevail on her; I fear nothing but the effects of her strong attachment to her relations. I would willingly let you know how I purpose to remove my family to so great a distance, but it would become unintelligible to you because you are not acquainted with the geographical situation of this part of the country. Suffice it for you to know that with about twenty-three miles land carriage, I am enabled to perform the rest by water; and when once afloat, I care not whether it be two or three hundred miles. I propose to send all our provisions, furniture, and clothes to my wife's father, who approves of the scheme, and to reserve nothing but a few necessary articles of covering, trusting to the furs of the chase for our future apparel. Were we imprudently to encumber ourselves too

[26]Shells used as money and ornament.

much with baggage, we should never reach to the waters of ——, which is the most dangerous as well as the most difficult part of our journey, and yet but a trifle in point of distance. I intend to say to my Negroes, "In the name of God, be free, my honest lads; I thank you for your past services; go, from henceforth, and work for yourselves; look on me as your old friend and fellow-labourer; be sober, frugal, and industrious, and you need not fear earning a comfortable subsistence." Lest my countrymen should think that I am gone to join the incendiaries of our frontiers, I intend to write a letter to Mr. —— to inform him of our retreat and of the reasons that have urged me to it. The man whom I sent to —— village is to accompany us also, and a very useful companion he will be on every account.

You may therefore, by means of anticipation, behold me under the wigwam; I am so well acquainted with the principal manners of these people that I entertain not the least apprehension from them. I rely more securely on their strong hospitality than on the witnessed compacts of many Europeans. As soon as possible after my arrival, I design to build myself a wigwam, after the same manner and size with the rest in order to avoid being thought singular or giving occasion for any railleries, though these people are seldom guilty of such European follies. I shall erect it hard by the lands which they propose to allot me, and will endeavour that my wife, my children, and myself may be adopted soon after our arrival. Thus becoming truly inhabitants of their village, we shall immediately occupy that rank within the pale of their society, which will afford us all the amends we can possibly expect for the loss we have met with by the convulsions of our own. According to their customs, we shall likewise receive names from them, by which we shall always be known. My youngest children shall learn to swim and to shoot with the bow, that they may acquire such talents as will necessarily raise them into some degree of esteem among the Indian lads of their own age; the rest of us must hunt with the hunter. I have been for several years an expert marksman; but I dread lest the imperceptible charm of Indian education may seize my younger children and give them such a propensity to that mode of life as may preclude their returning to the manners and customs of their parents. I have but one remedy to prevent this great evil, and that is to employ them in the labour of the fields as much as I can; I have even resolved to make their daily subsistence depend altogether on it. As long as we keep ourselves busy in tilling the earth, there is no fear of any of us becoming wild; it is the chase and the food it procures that have this strange effect. Excuse a simile—those hogs which range in the woods, and to whom grain is given once a week, preserve their former degree of tameness, but if, on the contrary, they are reduced to live on ground nuts and on what they can get, they soon become wild and fierce. For my part, I can plough, sow, and hunt as occasion may require; but my wife, deprived of wool and flax, will have no room for industry; what is she then to do? Like the other squaws, she must cook for us the nasaump, the ninchickè,[27] and such other preparations of corn as are customary among these people. She must learn to bake squashes and pompions under the ashes, to slice and smoke the meat of our own killing in order to preserve it; she must cheerfully adopt the manners and customs of her neighbours, in their dress, de-

[27]Types of corn porridge.

portment, conduct, and internal economy, in all respects. Surely if we can have fortitude enough to quit all we have, to remove so far, and to associate with people so different from us, these necessary compliances are but subordinate parts of the scheme. The change of garments, when those they carry with them are worn out, will not be the least of my wife's and daughter's concerns, though I am in hopes that self-love will invent some sort of reparation. Perhaps you would not believe that there are in the woods looking-glasses and paint of every colour; and that the inhabitants take as much pains to adorn their faces and their bodies, to fix their bracelets of silver, and plait their hair as our forefathers the Picts[28] used to do in the time of the Romans. Not that I would wish to see either my wife or daughter adopt those savage customs; we can live in great peace and harmony with them without descending to every article; the interruption of trade hath, I hope, suspended this mode of dress. My wife understands inoculation perfectly well; she inoculated all our children one after another and has successfully performed the operation on several scores of people, who, scattered here and there through our woods, were too far removed from all medical assistance. If we can persuade but one family to submit to it, and it succeeds, we shall then be as happy as our situation will admit of; it will raise her into some degree of consideration, for whoever is useful in any society will always be respected. If we are so fortunate as to carry one family through a disorder, which is the plague among these people, I trust to the force of example we shall then become truly necessary, valued, and beloved; we indeed owe every kind office to a society of men who so readily offer to admit us into their social partnership and to extend to my family the shelter of their village, the strength of their adoption, and even the dignity of their names. God grant us a prosperous beginning; we may then hope to be of more service to them than even missionaries who have been sent to preach to them a Gospel they cannot understand.

As to religion, our mode of worship will not suffer much by this removal from a cultivated country into the bosom of the woods; for it cannot be much simpler than that which we have followed here these many years, and I will with as much care as I can redouble my attention and twice a week retrace to them the great outlines of their duty to God and to man. I will read and expound to them some part of the decalogue, which is the method I have pursued ever since I married.

Half a dozen of acres on the shores of ——, the soil of which I know well, will yield us a great abundance of all we want; I will make it a point to give the overplus to such Indians as shall be most unfortunate in their huntings; I will persuade them, if I can, to till a little more land than they do and not to trust so much to the produce of the chase. To encourage them still farther, I will give a quirn[29] to every six families; I have built many for our poor back-settlers, it being often the want of mills which prevents them from raising grain. As I am a carpenter, I can build my own plough and can be of great service to many of them; my example alone may rouse the industry of some and serve to direct others in their labours. The difficulties of the language will soon be removed; in my evening conversations, I will endeavour to make them regulate the trade of their village in such a manner as that those pests of

[28]Non-Celtic peoples who inhabited ancient Great Britain.

[29]Corn mill.

the continent, those Indian-traders, may not come within a certain distance; and there they shall be obliged to transact their business before the old people. I am in hopes that the constant respect which is paid to the elders, and shame, may prevent the young hunters from infringing this regulation. The son of —— will soon be made acquainted with our schemes, and I trust that the power of love and the strong attachment he professes for my daughter may bring him along with us; he will make an excellent hunter; young and vigorous, he will equal in dexterity the stoutest man in the village. Had it not been for this fortunate circumstance, there would have been the greatest danger; for however I respect the simple, the inoffensive society of these people in their villages, the strongest prejudices would make me abhor any alliance with them in blood, disagreeable no doubt to Nature's intentions, which have strongly divided us by so many indelible characters. In the days of our sickness, we shall have recourse to their medical knowledge, which is well calculated for the simple diseases to which they are subject. Thus shall we metamorphose ourselves from neat, decent, opulent planters, surrounded with every conveniency which our external labour and internal industry could give, into a still simpler people divested of everything beside hope, food, and the raiment of the woods: abandoning the large framed house to dwell under the wigwam, and the featherbed to lie on the mat or bear's skin. There shall we sleep undisturbed by frightful dreams and apprehensions; rest and peace of mind will make us the most ample amends for what we shall leave behind. These blessings cannot be purchased too dear; too long have we been deprived of them. I would cheerfully go even to the Mississippi to find that repose to which we have been so long strangers. My heart sometimes seems tired with beating; it wants rest like my eyelids, which fell oppressed with so many watchings.

These are the component parts of my scheme, the success of each of which appears feasible, whence I flatter myself with the probable success of the whole. Still, the danger of Indian education returns to my mind and alarms me much; then again, I contrast it with the education of the times; both appear to be equally pregnant with evils. . . . Whatever success they may meet with in hunting or fishing shall be only considered as recreation and pastime; I shall thereby prevent them from estimating their skill in the chase as an important and necessary accomplishment. I mean to say to them: "You shall hunt and fish merely to show your new companions that you are not inferior to them in point of sagacity and dexterity." Were I to send them to such schools as the interior parts of our settlements afford at present, what can they learn there? How could I support them there? What must become of me; am I to proceed on my voyage and leave them? That I never could submit to. Instead of the perpetual discordant noise of disputes so common among us, instead of those scolding scenes, frequent in every house, they will observe nothing but silence at home and abroad: a singular appearance of peace and concord are the first characteristics which strike you in the villages of these people. Nothing can be more pleasing, nothing surprises an European so much, as the silence and harmony which prevail among them, and in each family, except when disturbed by that accursed spirit given them by the wood rangers in exchange for their furs. If my children learn nothing of geometrical rules, the use of the compass, or of the Latin tongue, they will learn and practise sobriety, for rum can no longer be sent to these people; they will learn that modesty and diffidence for which the young Indians are so remarkable; they will consider labour as the most essential qualification, hunting as the second. They will prepare themselves in the prosecution of our small rural schemes, carried on for the benefit of our little community, to extend them farther when each shall receive his inheritance. Their tender minds will cease to be agitated by perpetual alarms, to be made cowards by continual terrors; if they acquire in the village of —— such an awkwardness of deportment and appearance as would render them ridiculous in our gay capitals, they will imbibe, I hope, a confirmed taste for that simplicity which so well becomes the cultivators of the land. If I cannot teach them any of those professions which sometimes embellish and support our society, I will show them how to hew wood, how to construct their own ploughs, and with a few tools how to supply themselves with every necessary implement, both in the house and in the field. If they are hereafter obliged to confess that they belong to no one particular church, I shall have the consolation of teaching them that great, that primary worship which is the foundation of all others. If they do not fear God according to the tenets of any one seminary, they shall learn to worship Him upon the broad scale of nature. The Supreme Being does not reside in peculiar churches or communities, He is equally the great Manitou[30] of the woods and of the plains; and even in the gloom, the obscurity of those very woods, His justice may be as well understood and felt as in the most sumptuous temples. Each worship with us hath, you know, its peculiar political tendency; there it has none but to inspire gratitude and truth: their tender minds shall receive no other idea of the Supreme Being than that of the Father of all men, who requires nothing more of us than what tends to make each other happy. We shall say with them: "Soungwanèha, èsa caurounkyawga, nughwonshauza neattèwek, nèsalanga." Our Father, be thy will done in earth as it is in great heaven.

Perhaps my imagination gilds too strongly this distant prospect; yet it appears founded on so few and simple principles that there is not the same probability of adverse incidents as in more complex schemes. These vague rambling contemplations which I here faithfully retrace carry me sometimes to a great distance; I am lost in the anticipation of the various circumstances attending this proposed metamorphosis! Many unforeseen accidents may doubtless arise. Alas! It is easier for me in all the glow of paternal anxiety, reclined on my bed, to form the theory of my future conduct than to reduce my schemes into practice. But when once secluded from the great society to which we now belong, we shall unite closer together, and there will be less room for jealousies or contentions. As I intend my children neither for the law nor the church, but for the cultivation of the land, I wish them no literary accomplishments; I pray heaven that they may be one day nothing more than expert scholars in husbandry: this is the science which made our continent to flourish more rapidly than any other. Were they to grow up where I am now situated, even admitting that we were in safety; two of them are verging toward that period of their lives when they must necessarily take up the musket and learn, in that new school, all the vices which are so common in armies. Great God! Close my eyes forever rather than I should live to see this calamity! May they rather become inhabitants of the woods.

Thus then in the village of ——, in the bosom of that peace it has enjoyed ever since I have known it, connected with mild, hospitable people, strangers to *our* po-

[30]Algonquian "Great Spirit."

litical disputes and having none among themselves; on the shores of a fine river, surrounded with woods, abounding with game, our little society, united in perfect harmony with the new adoptive one, in which we shall be incorporated, shall rest, I hope, from all fatigues, from all apprehensions, from our present terrors, and from our long watchings. Not a word of politics shall cloud our simple conversation; tired either with the chase or the labours of the field, we shall sleep on our mats without any distressing want, having learnt to retrench every superfluous one; we shall have but two prayers to make to the Supreme Being, that He may shed His fertilizing dew on our little crops and that He will be pleased to restore peace to our unhappy country. These shall be the only subject of our nightly prayers and of our daily ejaculations; and if the labour, the industry, the frugality, the union of men, can be an agreeable offering to Him, we shall not fail to receive His paternal blessings. . . .

O Supreme Being! If among the immense variety of planets, inhabited by thy creative power, thy paternal and omnipotent care deigns to extend to all the individuals they contain, if it be not beneath thy infinite dignity to cast thy eye on us wretched mortals, if my future felicity is not contrary to the necessary effects of those secret causes which thou hast appointed, receive the supplications of a man to whom in thy kindness thou hast given a wife and an offspring; view us all with benignity, sanctify this strong conflict of regrets, wishes, and other natural passions; guide our steps through these unknown paths and bless our future mode of life. If it is good and well meant, it must proceed from thee; thou knowest, O Lord, our enterprise contains neither fraud nor malice nor revenge. Bestow on me that energy of conduct now become so necessary that it may be in my power to carry the young family thou hast given me through this great trial with safety and in thy peace. Inspire me with such intentions and such rules of conduct as may be most acceptable to thee. Preserve, O God, preserve the companion of my bosom, the best gift thou hast given me; endue her with courage and strength sufficient to accomplish this perilous journey. Bless the children of our love, those portions of our hearts; I implore thy divine assistance, speak to their tender minds and inspire them with the love of that virtue which alone can serve as the basis of their conduct in this world and of their happiness with thee. Restore peace and concord to our poor afflicted country; assuage the fierce storm which has so long ravaged it. Permit, I beseech thee, O Father of nature, that our ancient virtues and our industry may not be totally lost and that as a reward for the great toils we have made on this new land, we may be restored to our ancient tranquillity and enabled to fill it with successive generations that will constantly thank thee for the ample subsistence thou hast given them.

The unreserved manner in which I have written must give you a convincing proof of that friendship and esteem of which I am sure you never yet doubted. As members of the same society, as mutually bound by the ties of affection and old acquaintance, you certainly cannot avoid feeling for my distresses; you cannot avoid mourning with me over that load of physical and moral evil with which we are all oppressed. My own share of it I often overlook when I minutely contemplate all that hath befallen our native country.

1782

Thomas Paine 1737–1809

Thomas Paine was a renowned pro-American writer and author of some of the most persuasive texts of the American Revolution. In these texts, he used "plain" language in an attempt to engage people of all classes in the struggle for American independence and for a rejection of government based on hereditary monarchy.

Born in 1737 in the English village of Thetford, Paine attended grammar school and apprenticed to his father's trade, becoming a master staymaker. He was unsatisfied with the life of a tradesman, however, and briefly went to sea but soon returned to England. In 1759 he opened his own staymaking business and married Mary Lambert, a household servant. When Mary died less than a year later, Paine again sought to improve his status. In 1762 he became a collector of excise taxes, but was fired in 1765 for falsifying a report. He taught English at a London academy, but was eventually reinstated as a tax collector. In Lewes, Sussex, Paine lodged with the prominent Samuel Ollive family. When Ollive died in 1771, Paine married his daughter and took over Ollive's tobacco shop; but soon thereafter he again lost his position as collector, the tobacco shop failed, and in 1774 he separated from his wife. Paine resolved to start again, but this time in the colonies. During the years that Paine had resided in London and Lewes, he had attended several meetings of radical underground political movements. He had also attended scientific lectures in London, where he had become acquainted with the mathematician George Lewis Scott, who introduced him to Benjamin Franklin.

When Paine arrived in Philadelphia in 1774, he came with letters of introduction from Franklin. He resided in America for only thirteen years, returning to England in 1787, but his impact on the developing nation's political philosophy was immeasurable. As the son of a Quaker, Paine rejected hierarchies in church and state, and as a student of Newtonian science he viewed the universe as governed by harmony, order, and natural laws. Paine brought these social and political philosophies to bear upon his experiences in America, where old local aristocracies (like those in Philadelphia) were being challenged by the rising artisan class. Paine used his extraordinary rhetorical powers to argue for American independence and to suggest the creation of a harmonious social order, with reason as its guiding influence.

At Franklin's recommendation, Paine became editor of the *Pennsylvania Magazine.* He would become best-known, however, for his major works on the rights of independence and studies of the era in which he lived; these included *Common Sense* (1776), the *Crisis* papers (beginning in December 1776 and ending in April 1783), *The Rights of Man* (1791–1792), and *The Age of Reason* (1794–1796). The increasing tensions between England and America—rooted in England's proclaiming the American colonies to be in a state of rebellion, and emerging in the battles at Lexington and Bunker Hill—led in May 1775 to the convening of the Second Continental Congress in Philadelphia.

On January 9, 1776, Paine published *Common Sense,* which argued for American independence from Great Britain and for a republican form of government as superior to hereditary monarchy. Its impact was extraordinary; an unprecedented twenty-five editions appeared in 1776 alone, and the text was circulated hand-to-hand and read to many others who could not read. Later in his life, Paine claimed that it had sold at least 150,000 copies. The text also represents an important rhetorical shift in political commentaries from an ideology rooted in religion to one centered in secular arguments. *Common Sense* was instrumental in spreading a national spirit that led, six months later, to the creation of the *Declaration of Independence.* Perhaps the greatest impact of *Common Sense* was its call for a halt to attempts at reconciliation and for an immediate separation from England, but Paine himself always asserted that his main purpose was to "bring forward and establish the representative system of government."

Paine enlisted and served as an aide-de-camp during several battles. It seems that his writings far exceeded any military contribution he might have made. In December 1776, after Washington had been defeated in New York and was retreating from New Jersey into Pennsylvania, Paine began publishing the *Crisis* papers. Fifteen more installments would appear over a seven-year period, but the rousing spirit of the opening lines of the first paper—"These are the times that try men's souls"—would remain a hallmark of Revolutionary writings. Like Benjamin Franklin, Paine understood the powerful impact of a discursive style that relied upon maxims as an impetus to emotional, patriotic responses; he realized that these impetuses could, in turn, be converted into actions in support of American independence. In the first *Crisis* paper, for instance, he linked three maxims to create one of the text's most powerful passages calling for a commitment to the hardships of a war for independence: "Tyranny, like hell, is not easily conquered; yet we have this consolation with us, that the harder the conflict, the more glorious the triumph. What we obtain too cheap, we esteem too lightly: it is dearness only that gives everything its value." Paine's literary accomplishments earned him a controversial, salaried position from Congress that enabled him to continue writing propaganda to serve the colonial forces.

The last *Crisis* paper appeared in 1783, at the conclusion of the Revolution, and it marked a major transition in Paine's personal life. He was a man of sweeping ideas of political reform and of rhetorical powers, but he seems not to have been patient enough for the establishment of a new government of disparate peoples. In 1787 he returned to England with the intention of raising money to build an iron bridge. When this plan failed, he wrote his second extraordinarily successful work, *The Rights of Man* (1791–1792), intended as a response to Edmund Burke's *Reflections on the Revolution in France* (1790). Paine's argument in *The Rights of Man* against a hereditary monarchy resulted in a charge of sedition, forcing him to flee to France to avoid trial. In France, his second adopted country, his arguments garnered him not only citizenship and a seat in the National Assembly but renown as an advocate of revolution. His status was not long-lived, however. A protest against the execution of Louis XVI, which Paine deemed an act of barbarism rather than of the enlightenment that should result from revolution, led to his imprisonment for ten months as a sympathizer with royalty. The American ambassador James Madison eventually arranged for Paine's release on the grounds of his earlier citizenship in America.

Under Madison's aegis, Paine returned to New York City. He did not, however, regain the status he had acquired during the American Revolution, in large part because of his last major work, *The Age of Reason.* Part I of *The Age of Reason* was published in France; the manuscript was surreptitiously brought to the United States by Joel Barlow. *The Age of Reason* was intended as an exploration of the irrationality of religion and as an advocacy of deism. But in the years since Paine's departure from the colonies, the citizens of the new republic had become far more conservative. *The Age of Reason* was viewed by many Americans as an attack on Christianity and an assertion of atheism. In America and in England, from the pulpit and in newspapers, Thomas Paine was ridiculed and depicted as a threat to Christianity and to democracy.

Paine lived his last years in obscurity in New Rochelle, New York; when he died in 1809, he was buried on his farm after interment in a Quaker graveyard was denied. A decade later, an admirer, William Cobbett, exhumed his remains with the intention of giving Paine a proper burial in England, but it is believed that Paine's remains were lost after Cobbett's death. His contributions to American literature endure, however. Noted most for his "plain style," Paine insisted on the need to reach all classes of citizens, even those "who can scarcely read." As one of America's foremost pamphleteers, his writings were passionate in their demands for political reform based on republican values.

Sharon M. Harris
University of Nebraska

PRIMARY WORKS

The Writings of Thomas Paine, Moncure D. Conway, ed., 4 vols., 1894–1896.

SECONDARY WORKS

Moncure D. Conway, *The Life of Thomas Paine,* 2 vols., 1892; Eric Foner, *Tom Paine and Revolutionary America,* 1976; J. Wilson and W. Ricketson, *Thomas Paine,* 1978; A. Owen Aldridge, *Thomas Paine's American Ideology,* 1984; Larzer Ziff, *Writing in the New Nation: Prose, Print, and Politics in the Early United States,* 1991.

from Common Sense

Thoughts on the Present State of American Affairs[1]

In the following pages I offer nothing more than simple facts, plain arguments, and common sense: and have no other preliminaries to settle with the reader, than that he will divest himself of prejudice and prepossession, and suffer his reason and his feelings to determine for themselves: that he will put on, or rather that he will not put off, the true character of a man, and generously enlarge his views beyond the present day.

Volumes have been written on the subject of the struggle between England and America. Men of all ranks have embarked in the controversy, from different motives, and with various designs; but all have been ineffectual, and the period of debate is closed. Arms as the last resource decide the contest; the appeal was the choice of the King, and the Continent has accepted the challenge.

It hath been reported of the late Mr. Pelham (who tho' an able minister was not without his faults)[2] that on his being attacked in the House of Commons on the score

[1]First published in 1776, *Common Sense* sold nearly a half million copies. Its full title was: *Common Sense: Addressed to the Inhabitants of America, on the following Interesting Subjects: I. Of the Origin and Design of Government in General, with Concise Remarks on the English Constitution. II. Of Monarchy and Hereditary Succession. III. Thoughts on the Present State of American Affairs. IV. Of the Present Ability of America, with Some Miscellaneous Reflections.*

[2]Thomas Pelham (1693–1768), prime minister of England, 1743 to 1754.

that his measures were only of a temporary kind, replied, *"they will last my time."* Should a thought so fatal and unmanly possess the Colonies in the present contest, the name of ancestors will be remembered by future generations with detestation.

The Sun never shined on a cause of greater worth. 'Tis not the affair of a City, a County, a Province, or a Kingdom; but of a Continent—of at least one eighth part of the habitable Globe. 'Tis not the concern of a day, a year, or an age: posterity are virtually involved in the contest, and will be more or less affected even to the end of time, by the proceedings now. Now is the seed-time of Continental union, faith and honour. The least fracture now will be like a name engraved with the point of a pin on the tender rind of a young oak; the wound would enlarge with the tree, and posterity read it in full grown characters.

By referring the matter from argument to arms, a new æra for politics is struck—a new method of thinking hath arisen. All plans, proposals, &c. prior to the nineteenth of April, *i. e.* to the commencement of hostilities,[3] are like the almanacks of the last year; which tho' proper then, are superceded and useless now. Whatever was advanced by the advocates on either side of the question then, terminated in one and the same point, viz. a union with Great Britain; the only difference between the parties was the method of effecting it; the one proposing force, the other friendship; but it hath so far happened that the first hath failed, and the second hath withdrawn her influence.

As much hath been said of the advantages of reconciliation, which, like an agreeable dream, hath passed away and left us as we were, it is but right that we should examine the contrary side of the argument, and enquire into some of the many material injuries which these Colonies sustain, and always will sustain, by being connected with and dependant on Great-Britain. To examine that connection and dependance, on the principles of nature and common sense, to see what we have to trust to, if separated, and what we are to expect, if dependant.

I have heard it asserted by some, that as America has flourished under her former connection with Great-Britain, the same connection is necessary towards her future happiness, and will always have the same effect. Nothing can be more fallacious than this kind of argument. We may as well assert that because a child has thrived upon milk, that it is never to have meat, or that the first twenty years of our lives is to become a precedent for the next twenty. But even this is admitting more than is true; for I answer roundly, that America would have flourished as much, and probably much more, had no European power taken any notice of her. The commerce by which she hath enriched herself are the necessaries of life, and will always have a market while eating is the custom of Europe.

But she has protected us, say some. That she hath engrossed us is true, and defended the Continent at our expense as well as her own, is admitted; and she would have defended Turkey from the same motive, *viz.* for the sake of trade and dominion.

Alas! we have been long led away by ancient prejudices and made large sacrifices to superstition. We have boasted the protection of Great Britain, without considering, that her motive was *interest* not *attachment;* and that she did not protect us

[3]The Battle of Lexington, in Massachusetts, April 19, 1775.

from *our enemies* on *our account;* but from *her enemies* on *her own account,* from those who had no quarrel with us on any *other account,* and who will always be our enemies on the *same account.* Let Britain waive her pretensions to the Continent, or the Continent throw off the dependance, and we should be at peace with France and Spain, were they at war with Britain. The miseries of Hanover last war ought to warn us against connections.[4]

It hath lately been asserted in parliament, that the Colonies have no relation to each other but through the Parent Country, *i. e.* that Pennsylvania and the Jerseys, and so on for the rest, are sister Colonies by the way of England; this is certainly a very roundabout way of proving relationship, but it is the nearest and only true way of proving enmity (or enemyship, if I may so call it.) France and Spain never were, nor perhaps ever will be, our enemies as *Americans,* but as our being the *subjects of Great Britain.*

But Britain is the parent country, say some. Then the more shame upon her conduct. Even brutes do not devour their young, nor savages make war upon their families; Wherefore, the assertion, if true, turns to her reproach; but it happens not to be true, or only partly so, and the phrase *parent* or *mother country* hath been jesuitically adopted by the King and his parasites, with a low papistical design of gaining an unfair bias on the credulous weakness of our minds. Europe, and not England, is the parent country of America. This new World hath been the asylum for the persecuted lovers of civil and religious liberty from *every part* of Europe. Hither have they fled, not from the tender embraces of the mother, but from the cruelty of the monster; and it is so far true of England, that the same tyranny which drove the first emigrants from home, pursues their descendants still.

In this extensive quarter of the globe, we forget the narrow limits of three hundred and sixty miles (the extent of England) and carry our friendship on a larger scale; we claim brotherhood with every European Christian, and triumph in the generosity of the sentiment.

It is pleasant to observe by what regular gradations we surmount the force of local prejudices, as we enlarge our acquaintance with the World. A man born in any town in England divided into parishes, will naturally associate most with his fellow parishioners (because their interests in many cases will be common) and distinguish him by the name of *neighbour;* if he meet him but a few miles from home, he drops the narrow idea of a street, and salutes him by the nature of *townsman;* if he travel out of the county and meet him in any other, he forgets the minor divisions of street and town, and calls him *countryman, i. e. countyman:* but if in their foreign excursions they should associate in France, or any other part of *Europe,* their local remembrance would be enlarged into that of *Englishmen.* And by a just parity of reasoning, all Europeans meeting in America, or any other quarter of the globe, are *countrymen;* for England, Holland, Germany, or Sweden, when compared with the whole, stand in the same places on the larger scale, which the divisions of street,

[4] A kingdom that would become a province of Germany; the scene of heavy fighting during the Seven Years' War, particularly the campaigns of 1757. Also the royal house that occupied the British throne from 1714 to 1901.

town, and county do on the smaller ones; Distinctions too limited for Continental minds. Not one third of the inhabitants, even of this province, [Pennsylvania], are of English descent. Wherefore, I reprobate the phrase of Parent or Mother Country applied to England only, as being false, selfish, narrow and ungenerous.

But, admitting that we were all of English descent, what does it amount to? Nothing. Britain, being now an open enemy, extinguishes every other name and title: and to say that reconciliation is our duty, is truly farcical. The first king of England, of the present line (William the Conqueror) was a Frenchman, and half the peers of England are descendants from the same country; wherefore, by the same method of reasoning, England ought to be governed by France.

Much hath been said of the united strength of Britain and the Colonies, that in conjunction they might bid defiance to the world: But this is mere presumption; the fate of war is uncertain, neither do the expressions mean any thing; for this continent would never suffer itself to be drained of inhabitants, to support the British arms in either Asia, Africa, or Europe.

Besides, what have we to do with setting the world at defiance? Our plan is commerce, and that, well attended to, will secure us the peace and friendship of all Europe; because it is the interest of all Europe to have America a free port. Her trade will always be a protection, and her barrenness of gold and silver secure her from invaders.

I challenge the warmest advocate for reconciliation to show a single advantage that this continent can reap by being connected with Great Britain. I repeat the challenge; not a single advantage is derived. Our corn will fetch its price in any market in Europe, and our imported goods must be paid for buy them where we will.

But the injuries and disadvantages which we sustain by that connection, are without number; and our duty to mankind at large, as well as to ourselves, instruct us to renounce the alliance: because, any submission to, or dependance on, Great Britain, tends directly to involve this Continent in European wars and quarrels, and set us at variance with nations who would otherwise seek our friendship, and against whom we have neither anger nor complaint. As Europe is our market for trade, we ought to form no partial connection with any part of it. It is the true interest of America to steer clear of European contentions, which she never can do, while, by her dependance on Britain, she is made the make-weight in the scale of British politics.

Europe is too thickly planted with Kingdoms to be long at peace, and whenever a war breaks out between England and any foreign power, the trade of America goes to ruin, *because of her connection with Britain.* The next war may not turn out like the last, and should it not, the advocates for reconciliation now will be wishing for separation then, because neutrality in that case would be a safer convoy than a man of war. Everything that is right or reasonable pleads for separation. The blood of the slain, the weeping voice of nature cries, 'TIS TIME TO PART. Even the distance at which the Almighty hath placed England and America is a strong and natural proof that the authority of the one over the other, was never the design of Heaven. The time likewise at which the Continent was discovered, adds weight to the argument, and the manner in which it was peopled, encreases the force of it. The Reformation was preceded by the discovery of America: As if the Almighty graciously meant to open a sanctuary to the persecuted in future years, when home should afford neither friendship nor safety.

The authority of Great Britain over this continent, is a form of government, which sooner or later must have an end: And a serious mind can draw no true pleasure by looking forward, under the painful and positive conviction that what he calls "the present constitution" is merely temporary. As parents, we can have no joy, knowing that this government is not sufficiently lasting to ensure any thing which we may bequeath to posterity: And by a plain method of argument, as we are running the next generation into debt, we ought to do the work of it, otherwise we use them meanly and pitifully. In order to discover the line of our duty rightly, we should take our children in our hand, and fix our station a few years farther into life; that eminence will present a prospect which a few present fears and prejudices conceal from our sight.

Though I would carefully avoid giving unnecessary offence, yet I am inclined to believe, that all those who espouse the doctrine of reconciliation, may be included within the following descriptions.

Interested men, who are not to be trusted, weak men who *cannot* see, prejudiced men who will not see, and a certain set of moderate men who think better of the European world than it deserves; and this last class, by an ill-judged deliberation, will be the cause of more calamities to this Continent than all the other three.

It is the good fortune of many to live distant from the scene of present sorrow; the evil is not sufficiently brought to their doors to make them feel the precariousness with which all American property is possessed. But let our imaginations transport us a few moments to Boston;[5] that seat of wretchedness will teach us wisdom, and instruct us for ever to renounce a power in whom we can have no trust. The inhabitants of that unfortunate city who but a few months ago were in ease and affluence, have now no other alternative than to stay and starve, or turn out to beg. Endangered by the fire of their friends if they continue within the city, and plundered by the soldiery if they leave it, in their present situation they are prisoners without the hope of redemption, and in a general attack for their relief they would be exposed to the fury of both armies.

Men of passive tempers look somewhat lightly over the offences of Great Britain, and, still hoping for the best, are apt to call out, *Come, come, we shall be friends again for all this.* But examine the passions and feelings of mankind: bring the doctrine of reconciliation to the touchstone of nature, and then tell me whether you can hereafter love, honour, and faithfully serve the power that hath carried fire and sword into your land? If you cannot do all these, then are you only deceiving yourselves, and by your delay bringing ruin upon posterity. Your future connection with Britain, whom you can neither love nor honour, will be forced and unnatural, and being formed only on the plan of present convenience, will in a little time fall into a relapse more wretched than the first. But if you say, you can still pass the violations over, then I ask, hath your house been burnt? Hath your property been destroyed before your face? Are your wife and children destitute of a bed to lie on, or bread to live on? Have you lost a parent or a child by their hands, and yourself the ruined and wretched survivor? If you have not, then are you not a judge of those who have. But

[5]Under siege by the Americans from July 1775 to March 1776.

if you have, and can still shake hands with the murderers, then are you unworthy the name of husband, father, friend, or lover, and whatever may be your rank or title in life, you have the heart of a coward, and the spirit of a sycophant.

This is not inflaming or exaggerating matters, but trying them by those feelings and affections which nature justifies, and without which we should be incapable of discharging the social duties of life, or enjoying the felicities of it. I mean not to exhibit horror for the purpose of provoking revenge, but to awaken us from fatal and unmanly slumbers, that we may pursue determinately some fixed object. 'Tis not in the power of Britain or of Europe to conquer America, if she doth not conquer herself by delay and timidity. The present winter is worth an age if rightly employed, but if lost or neglected the whole Continent will partake of the misfortune; and there is no punishment which that man doth not deserve, be he who, or what, or where he will, that may be the means of sacrificing a season so precious and useful.

'Tis repugnant to reason, to the universal order of things, to all examples from former ages, to suppose that this Continent can long remain subject to any external power. The most sanguine in Britain doth not think so. The utmost stretch of human wisdom cannot, at this time, compass a plan, short of separation, which can promise the continent even a year's security. Reconciliation is *now* a fallacious dream. Nature hath deserted the connection, and art cannot supply her place. For, as Milton wisely expresses, "never can true reconcilement grow where wounds of deadly hate have pierced so deep." . . .[6]

A government of our own is our natural right: and when a man seriously reflects on the precariousness of human affairs, he will become convinced, that it is infinitely wiser and safer, to form a constitution of our own in a cool deliberate manner, while we have it in our power, than to trust such an interesting event to time and chance. If we omit it now, some Massanello[7] may hereafter arise, who, laying hold of popular disquietudes, may collect together the desperate and the discontented, and by assuming to themselves the powers of government, finally sweep away the liberties of the Continent like a deluge. Should the government of America return again into the hands of Britain, the tottering situation of things will be a temptation for some desperate adventurer to try his fortune; and in such a case, what relief can Britain give? Ere she could hear the news, the fatal business might be done; and ourselves suffering like the wretched Britons under the oppression of the Conqueror. Ye that oppose independance now, ye know not what ye do: ye are opening a door to eternal tyranny, by keeping vacant the seat of government. There are thousands and tens of thousands, who would think it glorious to expel from the Continent, that barbarous and hellish power, which hath stirred up the Indians and the Negroes to destroy us; the cruelty hath a double guilt, it is dealing brutally by us, and treacherously by them.

To talk of friendship with those in whom our reason forbids us to have faith, and our affections wounded thro' a thousand pores instruct us to detest, is madness and folly. Every day wears out the little remains of kindred between us and them; and can there be any reason to hope, that as the relationship expires, the affection will en-

[6]From *Paradise Lost,* IV, ll. 98–99.

[7]Thomas Anello, also called Massanello, a fisherman of Naples who aroused his countrymen against Spanish oppression, stirred them to revolt, and became king—all in one day.

crease, or that we shall agree better when we have ten times more and greater concerns to quarrel over than ever?

Ye that tell us of harmony and reconciliation, can ye restore to us the time that is past? Can ye give to prostitution its former innocence? neither can ye reconcile Britain and America. The last cord now is broken, the people of England are presenting addresses against us. There are injuries which nature cannot forgive; she would cease to be nature if she did. As well can the lover forgive the ravisher of his mistress, as the Continent forgive the murders of Britain. The Almighty hath implanted in us these unextinguishable feelings for good and wise purposes. They are the Guardians of his Image in our hearts. They distinguish us from the herd of common animals. The social compact would dissolve, and justice be extirpated from the earth, or have only a casual existence were we callous to the touches of affection. The robber and the murderer would often escape unpunished, did not the injuries which our tempers sustain, provoke us into justice.

O! ye that love mankind! Ye that dare oppose not only the tyranny but the tyrant, stand forth! Every spot of the old world is overrun with oppression. Freedom hath been hunted round the Globe. Asia and Africa have long expelled her. Europe regards her like a stranger, and England hath given her warning to depart. O! receive the fugitive, and prepare in time an asylum for mankind.

1776

from The American Crisis[1]

Number 1

These are the times that try men's souls. The summer soldier and the sunshine patriot will, in this crisis, shrink from the service of their country; but he that stands it *now,* deserves the love and thanks of man and woman. Tyranny, like hell, is not easily conquered; yet we have this consolation with us, that the harder the conflict, the more glorious the triumph. What we obtain too cheap, we esteem too lightly: it is dearness only that gives every thing its value. Heaven knows how to put a proper price upon its goods; and it would be strange indeed if so celestial an article as FREEDOM should not be highly rated. Britain, with an army to enforce her tyranny, has declared that she has a right (*not only to TAX*) but "TO BIND *us in* ALL CASES WHATSOEVER,"[2] and if being *bound in that manner,* is not slavery, then is there not such a thing as slavery upon earth. Even the expression is impious; for so unlimited a power can belong only to God.

[1]*The American Crisis* was originally published in the *Pennsylvania Journal,* December 19, 1776.

[2]Paine quotes the Declaratory Act of Parliament (February 1766).

Whether the independence of the continent was declared too soon, or delayed too long, I will not now enter into as an argument; my own simple opinion is, that had it been eight months earlier, it would have been much better. We did not make a proper use of last winter, neither could we, while we were in a dependent state. However, the fault, if it were one, was all our own, we have none to blame but ourselves. But no great deal is lost yet. All that Howe[3] has been doing for this month past, is rather a ravage than a conquest, which the spirit of the Jerseys,[4] a year ago, would have quickly repulsed, and which time and a little resolution will soon recover.

I have as little superstition in me as any man living, but my secret opinion has ever been, and still is, that God Almighty will not give up a people to military destruction, or leave them unsupportedly to perish, who have so earnestly and so repeatedly sought to avoid the calamities of war, by every decent method which wisdom could invent. Neither have I so much of the infidel in me, as to suppose that He has relinquished the government of the world, and given us up to the care of devils; and as I do not, I cannot see on what grounds the king of Britain can look up to heaven for help against us: a common murderer, a highwayman, or a housebreaker, has as good a pretense as he.

'Tis surprising to see how rapidly a panic will sometimes run through a country. All nations and ages have been subject to them: Britain has trembled like an ague at the report of a French fleet of flat bottomed boats; and in the fourteenth century[5] the whole English army, after ravaging the kingdom of France, was driven back like men petrified with fear; and this brave exploit was performed by a few broken forces collected and headed by a woman, Joan of Arc. Would that heaven might inspire some Jersey maid to spirit up her countrymen, and save her fair fellow sufferers from ravage and ravishment! Yet panics, in some cases, have their uses; they produce as much good as hurt. Their duration is always short; the mind soon grows through them; and acquires a firmer habit than before. But their peculiar advantage is, that they are the touchstones of sincerity and hypocrisy, and bring things and men to light, which might otherwise have lain forever undiscovered. In fact, they have the same effect on secret traitors, which an imaginary apparition would have upon a private murderer. They sift out the hidden thoughts of man, and hold them up in public to the world. Many a disguised Tory[6] has lately shown his head, that shall penitentially solemnize with curses the day on which Howe arrived upon the Delaware.

As I was with the troops at Fort Lee, and marched with them to the edge of Pennsylvania, I am well acquainted with many circumstances, which those who live at a distance know but little or nothing of. Our situation there was exceedingly cramped, the place being a narrow neck of land between the North River and the Hackensack. Our force was inconsiderable, being not one fourth so great as Howe could bring against us. We had no army at hand to have relieved the garrison, had we shut ourselves up and stood on our defence. Our ammunition, light artillery, and

[3]Lord William Howe (1729–1814), commander of British forces in America from 1775–1778.

[4]Colonial New Jersey was divided into East Jersey and West Jersey until 1702.

[5]Joan of Arc (1412–1431) in fact lived during the fifteenth century.

[6]American who supported continued allegiance to Great Britain during the American Revolution.

the best part of our stores, had been removed, on the apprehension that Howe would endeavor to penetrate the Jerseys, in which case Fort Lee could be of no use to us; for it must occur to every thinking man, whether in the army or not, that these kinds of field forts are only for temporary purposes, and last in use no longer than the enemy directs his force against the particular object, which such forts are raised to defend. Such was our situation and condition at Fort Lee on the morning of the 20th of November, when an officer arrived with information that the enemy with 200 boats had landed about seven miles above: Major General Green,[7] who commanded the garrison, immediately ordered them under arms, and sent express to General Washington at the town of Hackensack, distant by the way of the ferry, six miles. Our first object was to secure the bridge over the Hackensack, which laid up the river between the enemy and us, about six miles from us, and three from them. General Washington arrived in about three quarters of an hour, and marched at the head of the troops towards the bridge, which place I expected we should have a brush for; however, they did not choose to dispute it with us, and the greatest part of our troops went over the bridge, the rest over the ferry, except some which passed at a mill on a small creek, between the bridge and the ferry, and made their way through some marshy grounds up to the town of Hackensack, and there passed the river. We brought off as much baggage as the wagons could contain, the rest was lost. The simple object was to bring off the garrison, and march them on till they could be strengthened by the Jersey or Pennsylvania militia, so as to be enabled to make a stand. We stayed four days at Newark, collected our out-posts with some of the Jersey militia, and marched out twice to meet the enemy, on being informed that they were advancing, though our numbers were greatly inferior to theirs. Howe, in my little opinion, committed a great error in generalship in not throwing a body of forces off from Staten Island through Amboy, by which means he might have seized all our stores at Brunswick, and intercepted our march into Pennsylvania; but if we believe the power of hell to be limited, we must likewise believe that their agents are under some providential control.

I shall not now attempt to give all the particulars of our retreat to the Delaware; suffice it for the present to say, that both officers and men, though greatly harassed and fatigued, frequently without rest, covering, or provision, the inevitable consequences of a long retreat, bore it with a manly and martial spirit. All their wishes centered in one, which was, that the country would turn out and help them to drive the enemy back. Voltaire has remarked that king William[8] never appeared to full advantage but in difficulties and in action; the same remark may be made on General Washington, for the character fits him. There is a natural firmness in some minds which cannot be unlocked by trifles, but which, when unlocked, discovers a cabinet of fortitude; and I reckon it among those kinds of public blessings, which we do not immediately see, that God hath blessed him with uninterrupted health, and given him a mind that can even flourish upon care.

I shall conclude this paper with some miscellaneous remarks on the state of our affairs; and shall begin with asking the following question, Why is it that the enemy

[7]Nathaniel Green (1742–1786).
[8]Voltaire (1694–1778), French philosopher and writer; William III (1650–1702), King of England, 1689–1702.

have left the New-England provinces, and made these middle ones the seat of war? The answer is easy: New-England is not infested with Tories, and we are. I have been tender in raising the cry against these men, and used numberless arguments to show them their danger, but it will not do to sacrifice a world either to their folly or their baseness. The period is now arrived, in which either they or we must change our sentiments, or one or both must fall. And what is a Tory? Good God! what is he? I should not be afraid to go with a hundred Whigs[9] against a thousand Tories, were they to attempt to get into arms. Every Tory is a coward; for servile, slavish, self-interested fear is the foundation of Toryism; and a man under such influence, though he may be cruel, never can be brave.

But, before the line of irrecoverable separation be drawn between us, let us reason the matter together: Your conduct is an invitation to the enemy, yet not one in a thousand of you has heart enough to join him. Howe is as much deceived by you as the American cause is injured by you. He expects you will all take up arms, and flock to his standard, with muskets on your shoulders. Your opinions are of no use to him, unless you support him personally, for 'tis soldiers, and not Tories, that he wants.

I once felt all that kind of anger, which a man ought to feel, against the mean principles that are held by the Tories: a noted one, who kept a tavern at Amboy, was standing at his door, with as pretty a child in his hand, about eight or nine years old, as I ever saw, and after speaking his mind as freely as he thought was prudent, finished with this unfatherly expression, *"Well! give me peace in my day."*[10] Not a man lives on the continent but fully believes that a separation must some time or other finally take place, and a generous parent should have said, *"If there must be trouble, let it be in my day, that my child may have peace"*; and this single reflection, well applied, is sufficient to awaken every man to duty. Not a place upon earth might be so happy as America. Her situation is remote from all the wrangling world, and she has nothing to do but to trade with them. A man can distinguish himself between temper and principle, and I am as confident, as I am that God governs the world, that America will never be happy till she gets clear of foreign dominion. Wars, without ceasing, will break out till that period arrives, and the continent must in the end be conqueror; for though the flame of liberty may sometimes cease to shine, the coal can never expire.

America did not, nor does not want force; but she wanted a proper application of that force. Wisdom is not the purchase of a day, and it is no wonder that we should err at the first setting off. From an excess of tenderness, we were unwilling to raise an army, and trusted our cause to the temporary defence of a well-meaning militia. A summer's experience has now taught us better; yet with those troops, while they were collected, we were able to set bounds to the progress of the enemy, and, thank God! they are again assembling. I always considered militia as the best troops in the world for a sudden exertion, but they will not do for a long campaign. Howe, it is probable, will make an attempt on this city, should he fail on this side the Delaware, he is ruined: if he succeeds, our cause is not ruined. He stakes all on his side against a part

[9]Americans who opposed continued allegiance to Great Britain and supported the Revolution.

[10]"There shall be peace and truth in my days." Isaiah 39:8.

on ours; admitting he succeeds, the consequence will be, that armies from both ends of the continent will march to assist their suffering friends in the middle states; for he cannot go everywhere, it is impossible. I consider Howe as the greatest enemy the Tories have; he is bringing a war into their country, which, had it not been for him and partly for themselves, they had been clear of. Should he now be expelled, I wish with all the devotion of a Christian, that the names of Whig and Tory may never more be mentioned; but should the Tories give him encouragement to come, or assistance if he come, I as sincerely wish that our next year's arms may expel them from the continent, and the congress appropriate their possessions to the relief of those who have suffered in well-doing. A single successful battle next year will settle the whole. America could carry on a two years war by the confiscation of the property of disaffected persons, and be made happy by their expulsion. Say not that this is revenge, call it rather the soft resentment of a suffering people, who, having no object in view but the *good* of *all,* have staked their *own all* upon a seemingly doubtful event. Yet it is folly to argue against determined hardness; eloquence may strike the ear, and the language of sorrow draw forth the tear of compassion, but nothing can reach the heart that is steeled with prejudice.

Quitting this class of men, I turn with the warm ardor of a friend to those who have nobly stood, and are yet determined to stand the matter out: I call not upon a few, but upon all: not on *this* state, but on *every* state: up and help us; lay your shoulders to the wheel; better have too much force than too little, when so great an object is at stake. Let it be told to the future world, that in the depth of winter, when nothing but hope and virtue could survive, that the city and the country, alarmed at one common danger, came forth to meet and to repulse it. Say not that thousands are gone, turn out your tens of thousands;[11] throw not the burden of the day upon Providence, but *"show your faith by your works,"*[12] that God may bless you. It matters not where you live, or what rank of life you hold, the evil or the blessing will reach you all. The far and the near, the home counties and the back, the rich and the poor, will suffer or rejoice alike. The heart that feels not now, is dead: the blood of his children will curse his cowardice, who shrinks back at a time when a little might have saved the whole, and made *them* happy. I love the man that can smile in trouble, that can gather strength from distress, and grow brave by reflection. 'Tis the business of little minds to shrink; but he whose heart is firm, and whose conscience approves his conduct, will pursue his principles unto death. My own line of reasoning is to myself as straight and clear as a ray of light. Not all the treasures of the world, so far as I believe, could have induced me to support an offensive war, for I think it murder; but if a thief breaks into my house, burns and destroys my property, and kills or threatens to kill me, or those that are in it, and to *"bind me in all cases whatsoever"*[13] to his absolute will, am I to suffer it? What signifies it to me, whether he who does it is a king or a common man; my countryman or not my countryman; whether it be done by an individual villain, or an army of them? If we reason to the root of things we shall find no difference; neither can any just cause be assigned why we should pun-

[11]"Saul hath slain his thousands, and David his ten thousands." I Samuel 18:7.

[12]James 2:18.

[13]Paine quotes the British Declaratory Act of 1766.

ish in the one case and pardon in the other. Let them call me rebel, and welcome, I feel no concern from it; but I should suffer the misery of devils, were I to make a whore of my soul by swearing allegiance to one whose character is that of a sottish, stupid, stubborn, worthless brutish man. I conceive likewise a horrid idea in receiving mercy from a being, who at the last day shall be shrieking to the rocks and mountains to cover him, and fleeing with terror from the orphan, the widow, and the slain of America.

There are cases which cannot be overdone by language, and this is one. There are persons, too, who see not the full extent of the evil which threatens them; they solace themselves with hopes that the enemy, if he succeed, will be merciful. It is the madness of folly, to expect mercy from those who have refused to do justice; and even mercy, where conquest is the object, is only a trick of war; the cunning of the fox is as murderous as the violence of the wolf, and we ought to guard equally against both. Howe's first object is, partly by threats and partly by promises, to terrify or seduce the people to deliver up their arms and receive mercy. The ministry[14] recommended the same plan to Gage,[15] and this is what the Tories will call making their peace, *"a peace which passeth all understanding" indeed!*[16] A peace which would be the immediate forerunner of a worse ruin than any we have yet thought of. Ye men of Pennsylvania, do reason upon these things! Were the back counties to give up their arms, they would fall an easy prey to the Indians, who are all armed: this perhaps is what some Tories would not be sorry for. Were the home counties to deliver up their arms, they would be exposed to the resentment of the back counties, who would then have it in their power to chastise their defection at pleasure. And were any one state to give up its arms, *that* state must be garrisoned by all Howe's army of Britons and Hessians[17] to preserve it from the anger of the rest. Mutual fear is the principal link in the chain of mutual love, and woe be to that state that breaks the compact. Howe is mercifully inviting you to barbarous destruction, and men must be either rogues or fools that will not see it. I dwell not upon the vapors of imagination; I bring reason to your ears, and, in language as plain as A, B, C, hold up truth to your eyes.

I thank God, that I fear not. I see no real cause for fear. I know our situation well, and can see the way out of it. While our army was collected, Howe dared not risk a battle; and it is no credit to him that he decamped from the White Plains, and waited a mean opportunity to ravage the defenceless Jerseys; but it is great credit to us, that, with a handful of men, we sustained an orderly retreat for near an hundred miles, brought off our ammunition, all our field pieces, the greatest part of our stores, and had four rivers to pass. None can say that our retreat was precipitate, for we were near three weeks in performing it, that the country might have time to come in. Twice we marched back to meet the enemy, and remained out till dark. The sign of fear was not seen in our camp, and had not some of the cowardly and disaffected inhabitants

[14]The British government.

[15]General Thomas Gage, commander of British forces in America, 1763–1775.

[16]"And the peace of God, which passeth all understanding, shall keep your hearts and minds through Christ Jesus." Philippians 4:7.

[17]Inhabitants of Hesse, mercenaries who fought for the British in the Revolutionary War.

spread false alarms through the country, the Jerseys had never been ravaged. Once more we are again collected and collecting; our new army at both ends of the continent is recruiting fast, and we shall be able to open the next campaign with sixty thousand men, well armed and clothed. This is our situation, and who will may know it. By perseverance and fortitude we have the prospect of a glorious issue; by cowardice and submission, the sad choice of a variety of evils—a ravaged country—a depopulated city—habitations without safety, and slavery without hope—our homes turned into barracks and bawdyhouses for Hessians, and a future race to provide for, whose fathers we shall doubt of. Look on this picture and weep over it! and if there yet remains one thoughtless wretch who believes it not, let him suffer it unlamented.

1776

from The Age of Reason[1]

Chapter I
The Author's Profession of Faith

It has been my intention, for several years past, to publish my thoughts upon religion; I am well aware of the difficulties that attend the subject, and from that consideration, had reserved it to a more advanced period of life. I intended it to be the last offering I should make to my fellow-citizens of all nations, and that at a time when the purity of the motive that induced me to it could not admit of a question, even by those who might disapprove the work.

The circumstance that has now taken place in France, of the total abolition of the whole national order of priesthood, and of everything appertaining to compulsive systems of religion, and compulsive articles of faith, has not only precipitated my intention, but rendered a work of this kind exceedingly necessary, lest, in the general wreck of superstition, of false systems of government, and false theology, we lose sight of morality, of humanity, and of the theology that is true.

As several of my colleagues, and others of my fellow-citizens of France, have given me the example of making their voluntary and individual profession of faith, I also will make mine; and I do this with all that sincerity and frankness with which the mind of man communicates with itself.

I believe in one God, and no more; and I hope for happiness beyond this life.

I believe in the equality of man, and I believe that religious duties consist in doing justice, loving mercy, and endeavouring to make our fellow-creatures happy.

[1]The first part of the *Age of Reason* was published in 1794; the second part, in 1795 in France and in 1796 in England.

But, lest it should be supposed that I believe many other things in addition to these, I shall, in the progress of this work, declare the things I do not believe, and my reasons for not believing them.

I do not believe in the creed professed by the Jewish church, by the Roman church, by the Greek church, by the Turkish church, by the Protestant church, nor by any church that I know of. My own mind is my own church.

All national institutions of churches, whether Jewish, Christian, or Turkish, appear to me no other than human inventions set up to terrify and enslave mankind, and monopolize power and profit.

I do not mean by this declaration to condemn those who believe otherwise; they have the same right to their belief as I have to mine. But it is necessary to the happiness of man, that he be mentally faithful to himself. Infidelity does not consist in believing, or in disbelieving; it consists in professing to believe what he does not believe.

It is impossible to calculate the moral mischief, if I may so express it, that mental lying has produced in society. When a man has so far corrupted and prostituted the chastity of his mind, as to subscribe his professional belief to things he does not believe, he has prepared himself for the commission of every other crime. He takes up the trade of a priest for the sake of gain, and, in order to qualify himself for that trade, he begins with a perjury. Can we conceive anything more destructive to morality than this?

Soon after I had published the pamphlet COMMON SENSE, in America, I saw the exceeding probability that a revolution in the system of government would be followed by a revolution in the system of religion. The adulterous connection of church and state, wherever it had taken place, whether Jewish, Christian, or Turkish, had so effectually prohibited, by pains and penalties, every discussion upon established creeds, and upon first principles of religion, that until the system of government should be changed, those subjects could not be brought fairly and openly before the world; but that whenever this should be done, a revolution in the system of religion would follow. Human inventions and priest-craft would be detected; and man would return to the pure, unmixed, and unadulterated belief of one God, and no more.

from Chapter II
Of Missions and Revelations

Every national church or religion has established itself by pretending some special mission from God, communicated to certain individuals. The Jews have their Moses; the Christians their Jesus Christ, their apostles and saints; and the Turks their Mahomet; as if the way to God was not open to every man alike.

Each of those churches shows certain books, which they call *revelation,* or the Word of God. The Jews say that their Word of God was given by God to Moses face to face; the Christians say, that their Word of God came by divine inspiration; and the Turks say, that their Word of God (the Koran) was brought by an angel from heaven. Each of those churches accuses the other of unbelief; and, for my own part, I disbelieve them all.

As it is necessary to affix right ideas to words, I will, before I proceed further into the subject, offer some observations on the word *revelation.* Revelation when applied to religion, means something communicated *immediately* from God to man.

No one will deny or dispute the power of the Almighty to make such a communication if he pleases. But admitting, for the sake of a case, that something has been revealed to a certain person, and not revealed to any other person, it is revelation to that person only. When he tells it to a second person, a second to a third, a third to a fourth, and so on, it ceases to be a revelation to all those persons. It is revelation to the first person only, and *hearsay* to every other, and, consequently, they are not obliged to believe it.

It is a contradiction in terms and ideas to call anything a revelation that comes to us at second hand, either verbally or in writing. Revelation is necessarily limited to the first communication. After this, it is only an account of some thing which that person says was a revelation made to him and though he may find himself obliged to believe it, it cannot be incumbent on me to believe it in the same manner, for it was not a revelation made to *me,* and I have only his word for it that it was made to *him.*

When Moses told the children of Israel that he received the two tables of the commandments from the hand of God they were not obliged to believe him, because they had no other authority for it than his telling them so; and I have no other authority for it than some historian telling me so, the commandments carrying no internal evidence of divinity with them. They contain some good moral precepts such as any man qualified to be a lawgiver or a legislator could produce himself, without having recourse to supernatural intervention. . . .

When also I am told that a woman, called the Virgin Mary, said, or gave out, that she was with child without any cohabitation with a man, and that her betrothed husband Joseph, said that an angel told him so, I have a right to believe them or not: such a circumstance required a much stronger evidence than their bare word for it: but we have not even this; for neither Joseph nor Mary wrote any such matter themselves. It is only reported by others that *they said so.* It is hearsay upon hearsay, and I do not chuse to rest my belief upon such evidence.

It is, however, not difficult to account for the credit that was given to the story of Jesus Christ being the Son of God. He was born when the heathen mythology had still some fashion and repute in the world, and that mythology had prepared the people for the belief of such a story. Almost all the extraordinary men that lived under the heathen mythology were reputed to be the sons of some of their gods. It was not a new thing at that time to believe a man to have been celestially begotten; the intercourse of gods with women was then a matter of familiar opinion. Their Jupiter, according to their accounts, had cohabited with hundreds; the story therefore had nothing in it either new, wonderful, or obscene; it was conformable to the opinions that then prevailed among the people called Gentiles, or mythologists, and it was those people only that believed it. The Jews, who had kept strictly to the belief of one God, and no more, and who had always rejected the heathen mythology, never credited the story.

It is curious to observe how the theory of what is called the Christian Church, sprung out of the tail of the heathen mythology. A direct incorporation took place in the first instance, by making the reputed founder to be celestially begotten. The trinity of gods that then followed was no other than a reduction of the former plurality, which was about twenty or thirty thousand. The statue of Mary succeeded the statue of Diana of Ephesus.[2] The deification of heroes changed into the canonization of saints. The Mythologists had gods for everything; the Christian Mythologists had saints for everything. The church became as crouded with the one, as the pantheon had been with the other; and Rome was the place of both. The Christian theory is little else than the idolatry of the ancient mythologists, accommodated to the purposes of power and revenue; and it yet remains to reason and philosophy to abolish the amphibious fraud.

from Chapter III
Concerning the Character of Jesus Christ, and His History

Nothing that is here said can apply, even with the most distant disrespect, to the *real* character of Jesus Christ. He was a virtuous and an amiable man. The morality that he preached and practised was of the most benevolent kind; and though similar systems of morality had been preached by Confucius,[3] and by some of the Greek philosophers, many years before, by the Quakers since, and by many good men in all ages, it had not been exceeded by any.

Jesus Christ wrote no account of himself, of his birth, parentage, or anything else. Not a line of what is called the New Testament is of his writing. The history of him is altogether the work of other people; and as to the account given of his resurrection and ascension, it was the necessary counterpart to the story of his birth. His historians, having brought him into the world in a supernatural manner, were obliged to take him out again in the same manner, or the first part of the story must have fallen to the ground.

The wretched contrivance with which this latter part is told, exceeds everything that went before it. . . .

But the resurrection of a dead person from the grave, and his ascension through the air, is a thing very different, as to the evidence it admits of, to the invisible conception of a child in the womb. The resurrection and ascension, supposing them to have taken place, admitted of public and ocular demonstration, like that of the ascension of a balloon, or the sun at noon day, to all Jerusalem at least. A thing which everybody is required to believe, requires that the proof and evidence of it should be equal to all, and universal; and as the public visibility of this last related act was the only evidence that could give sanction to the former part, the whole of it falls to the ground, because that evidence never was given. . .

The Christian mythologists, after having confined Satan in a pit, were obliged to let him out again to bring on the sequel of the fable. He is then introduced into the garden of Eden in the shape of a snake, or a serpent, and in that shape he enters into familiar conversation with Eve, who is no ways surprised to hear a snake talk; and the

[2]A roman goddess whose main temple was at Ephesus in Asia Minor—one of the seven wonders of the ancient world. Ephesus later became a center of Christianity.

[3]Chinese philosopher, 551?–478 B.C.

issue of this tête-à-tête is, that he persuades her to eat an apple, and the eating of that apple damns all mankind.

After giving Satan this triumph over the whole creation, one would have supposed that the church mythologists would have been kind enough to send him back again to the pit, or, if they had not done this, that they would have put a mountain upon him, (for they say that their faith can remove a mountain) or have put him under a mountain, as the former mythologists had done, to prevent his getting again among the women, and doing more mischief. But instead of this, they leave him at large, without even obliging him to give his parole. The secret of which is, that they could not do without him; and after being at the trouble of making him, they bribed him to stay. They promised him ALL the Jews, ALL the Turks by anticipation, nine-tenths of the world beside, and Mahomet into the bargain. After this, who can doubt the bountifulness of the Christian Mythology? . . .

That many good men have believed this strange fable, and lived very good lives under that belief (for credulity is not a crime) is what I have no doubt of. In the first place, they were educated to believe it, and they would have believed anything else in the same manner. There are also many who have been so enthusiastically enraptured by what they conceived to be the infinite love of God to man; in making a sacrifice of himself, that the vehemence of the idea has forbidden and deterred them from examining into the absurdity and profaneness of the story. The more unnatural anything is, the more is it capable of becoming the object of dismal admiration.

from Chapter VI
Of the True Theology

But if objects for gratitude and admiration are our desire, do they not present themselves every hour to our eyes? Do we not see a fair creation prepared to receive us the instant we are born—a world furnished to our hands, that cost us nothing? Is it we that light up the sun; that pour down the rain; and fill the earth with abundance? Whether we sleep or wake, the vast machinery of the universe still goes on. Are these things, and the blessings they indicate in future, nothing to us? Can our gross feelings be excited by no other subjects than tragedy and suicide? Or is the gloomy pride of man become so intolerable, that nothing can flatter it but a sacrifice of the Creator?

I know that this bold investigation will alarm many, but it would be paying too great a compliment to their credulity to forbear it on that account. The times and the subject demand it to be done. The suspicion that the theory of what is called the Christian church is fabulous, is becoming very extensive in all countries; and it will be a consolation to men staggering under that suspicion, and doubting what to believe and what to disbelieve, to see the subject freely investigated.

* * * * * * * *

It is only in the CREATION that all our ideas and conceptions of a *word of God* can unite. The Creation speaketh an universal language, independently of human speech or human language, multiplied and various as they be. It is an ever existing original, which every man can read. It cannot be forged; it cannot be counterfeited; it cannot be lost; it cannot be altered; it cannot be suppressed. It does not depend upon the will of man whether it shall be published or not; it publishes itself from one end of the earth to the other. It preaches to all nations and to all worlds; and this *word of God* reveals to man all that is necessary for man to know of God.

Do we want to contemplate his power? We see it in the immensity of the creation. Do we want to contemplate his wisdom? We see it in the unchangeable order by which the incomprehensible Whole is governed. Do we want to contemplate his munificence? We see it in the abundance with which he fills the earth. Do we want to contemplate his mercy? We see it in his not withholding that abundance even from the unthankful. In fine, do we want to know what God is? Search not the book called the scripture, which any human hand might make, but the scripture called the Creation. . . .

Any person, who has made observations on the state and progress of the human mind, by observing his own, cannot but have observed, that there are two distinct classes of what are called Thoughts; those that we produce in ourselves by reflection and the act of thinking, and those that bolt into the mind of their own accord. I have always made it a rule to treat those voluntary visitors with civility, taking care to examine, as well as I was able, if they were worth entertaining; and it is from them I have acquired almost all the knowledge that I have. As to the learning that any person gains from school education, it serves only, like a small capital, to put him in the way of beginning learning for himself afterwards. Every person of learning is finally his own teacher; the reason of which is, that principles, being of a distinct quality to circumstances, cannot be impressed upon the memory; their place of mental residence is the understanding, and they are never so lasting as when they begin by conception. Thus much for the introductory part.

From the time I was capable of conceiving an idea, and acting upon it by reflection, I either doubted the truth of the christian system, or thought it to be a strange affair; I scarcely knew which it was; but I well remember, when about seven or eight years of age, hearing a sermon read by a relation of mine, who was a great devotee of the church, upon the subject of what is called *Redemption by the death of the Son of God.* After the sermon was ended, I went into the garden, and as I was going down the garden steps (for I perfectly recollect the spot) I revolted at the recollection of what I had heard, and thought to myself that it was making God Almighty act like a passionate man, that killed his son, when he could not revenge himself any other way; and as I was sure a man would be hanged that did such a thing, I could not see for what purpose they preached such sermons. This was not one of those kind of thoughts that had any thing in it of childish levity; it was to me a serious reflection, arising from the idea I had that God was too good to do such an action, and also too almighty to be under any necessity of doing it. I believe in the same manner to this moment; and I moreover believe, that any system of religion that has any thing in it that shocks the mind of a child, cannot be a true system. . . .

Of all the systems of religion that ever were invented, there is none more derogatory to the Almighty, more unedifying to man, more repugnant to reason, and more contradictory in itself, than this thing called Christianity. Too absurd for belief, too impossible to convince, and too inconsistent for practice, it renders the heart torpid, or produces only atheists and fanatics. As an engine of power, it serves the purpose of despotism; and as a means of wealth, the avarice of priests; but so far as respects the good of man in general, it leads to nothing here or hereafter. . . .

It has been the scheme of the Christian church, and of all the other invented systems of religion, to hold man in ignorance of the Creator, as it is of government to hold him in ignorance of his rights. The systems of the one are as false as those of the other, and are calculated for mutual support. The study of theology as it stands in Christian churches, is the study of nothing; it is founded on nothing; it rests on no principles; it proceeds by no authorities; it has no data; it can demonstrate nothing; and admits of no conclusion. Not any thing can be studied as a science without our being in possession of the principles upon which it is founded; and as this is not the case with Christian theology, it is therefore the study of nothing. . . .

It has been by wandering from the immutable laws of science, and the light of reason, and setting up an invented thing called "revealed religion," that so many wild and blasphemous conceits have been formed of the Almighty. The Jews have made him the assassin of the human species, to make room for the religion of the Jews. The Christians have made him the murderer of himself, and the founder of a new religion to supersede and expel the Jewish religion. And to find pretence and admission for these things, they must have supposed his power or his wisdom imperfect, or his will changeable; and the changeableness of the will is the imperfection of the judgement. The philosopher knows that the laws of the Creator have never changed, with respect either to the principles of science, or the properties of matter. Why then is it to be supposed they have changed with respect to man?

I here close the subject. I have shewn in all the foregoing parts of this work that the Bible and Testament are impositions and forgeries; and I leave the evidence I have produced in proof of it to be refuted, if any one can do it; and I leave the ideas that are suggested in the conclusion of the work to rest on the mind of the reader; certain as I am that when opinions are free, either in matters of government or religion, truth will finally and powerfully prevail.

1794

John Adams 1735–1826
Abigail Adams 1744–1818

John Adams was the first vice president of the United States and the second president (1797–1801). He was also a lively intellectual leader in Revolutionary Boston and in Congress, an able negotiator abroad, the author of many tracts and essays about government, and a reflective correspondent and philosopher in the decades between his retirement from office and his death at the age of ninety. With his wife Abigail Smith Adams he founded a family that would remain distinguished in the United States well into the twentieth century. Their son, John Quincy Adams, was president; their grandson, Charles Francis Adams, was minister to Britain during the Civil War; their great-grandson, Henry Adams, was the famous historian, novelist, and autobiographer.

Adams graduated from Harvard, taught school in Worcester, and prepared there to become an able lawyer. Throughout his life he was a wide-ranging, perceptive, and retentive reader—peppering his letters and papers with fresh and apt allusions to scores of challenging books. He was also a constant writer—of diary entries, legal notes and records, marginal jottings, ample letters, forceful replies to adversaries, letters to the press, and formal reports and state papers. His major writings contribute to the ideological formation of the new American republic and are products of legal scholarship and argument which are perhaps more interesting to students of political theory and history than to general readers today. His *Dissertation on the Canon and the Feudal Law* (1765) and the *Novanglus* papers (1774–1775) warned against British attempts to impose English law on the colonies as part of an effort to subvert American liberties. *A Defence of the Constitutions of Government of the United States of America* (1787–1788) argued the cause of republican and federal government at a time crucial for both European and American history. Adams's diaries and letters, however, show him to be a shrewd and witty judge of character; they provide bright sketches of living people in exciting moments of American politics and provocative insights into American society.

The marriage of John and Abigail Adams in 1764 was an alliance of two strong minds. Abigail's letters reflect an alert American woman pressing for a real change of consciousness during the revolution. Her suggestions seem high-spirited and teasing, in part; John's replies seem equally playful, if not patronizing. But his further letters show that he conceded the force of her ideas.

These partners combined intellectual and moral questioning through long years of revolution, separation, and public life. They also shared a long decline of fame. John Adams lost the election of 1800, and the couple left Washington early on the morning of Jefferson's inauguration—to remain at home in Massachusetts for the rest of their lives. Disgruntled by his rough treatment by the press and by what he perceived as a general public failure to credit his personal contributions to American political life, Adams began a rambling and defensive autobiography in his retirement, but some of his best writing of this period appears in the letters he exchanged after 1812 with Thomas Jefferson.

Repairing the breach in their friendship that stemmed from the election of 1800, Adams and Jefferson carried on a lively discussion about literature, history, and social ideals until both died on the same day, July 4, 1826. Adams balanced Jefferson's idealism with a playful but unrelenting and sometimes acid wit. The correspondence between the two was first published as a single text in the twentieth century, when it captured renewed attention for both men. Their discussion about an aristocracy of talent and virtue, for example, raised important questions about individuals in a democratic society and was noticed by Ezra Pound as he was writing his *Cantos.*

Albert Furtwangler
Mount Allison University

Frank Shuffelton
University of Rochester

PRIMARY WORKS

The Adams-Jefferson Letters, ed. Lester J. Cappon, 2 vols., 1959; *Diary and Autobiography of John Adams,* ed. L.H. Butterfield, 4 vols., 1961; *Adams Family Correspondence,* 1963; *The Book of Abigail and John: Selected Letters of the Adams Family 1762–1784,* ed. L.H. Butterfield, Marc Friedlaender and Mary-Jo Kline, 1975.

SECONDARY WORKS

Merrill D. Peterson, *Adams and Jefferson,* 1976; Edith Gelles, *Portia: The World of Abigail Adams,* 1992; Joseph Ellis, *Passionate Sage: John Adams and America's Original Intentions,* 1993.

from Autobiography of John Adams

[John Adams shares a bed with Benjamin Franklin, 1776]

The Taverns were so full We could with difficulty obtain Entertainment. At Brunswick, but one bed could be procured for Dr. Franklin and me, in a Chamber little larger than the bed, without a Chimney and with only one small Window. The Window was open, and I, who was an invalid and afraid of the Air in the night, shut it close. Oh! says Franklin dont shut the Window. We shall be suffocated. I answered I was afraid of the Evening Air, Dr. Franklin replied, the Air within this Chamber will soon be, and indeed is now worse than that without Doors: come! open the Window and come to bed, and I will convince you: I believe you are not acquainted with my Theory of Colds. Opening the Window and leaping into Bed, I said I had read his Letters to Dr. Cooper in which he had advanced, that Nobody ever got cold by going into a cold Church, or any other cold Air: but the Theory was so little consistent with my experience, that I thought it a Paradox: However I had so much curiosity to hear his reasons, that I would run the risque of a cold. The Doctor then began an harrangue, upon Air and cold and Respiration and Perspiration, with which I was so much amused that I soon fell asleep, and left him and his Philosophy together: but I believe they were equally sound and insensible, within a few minutes after me, for the last Words I heard were pronounced as if he was more than half asleep.

[John Adams arrives in Bordeaux in 1778]

The Company their dresses, Equipages, and the furniture were splendid and the Supper very sumptuous. The Conversation at and after Supper was very gay, animated, chearfull and good humoured as it appeared to my Eyes and Ears and feelings but my Understanding had no Share in it. The Language was altogether incomprehensible. The Company were more attentive to me, then I desired; for they often addressed Observations and questions to me, which I could only understand by the Interpretation of Mr. Bond [Bondfield], and the returns of civility on my part could only be communicated [to] me through the same Channel, a kind of conviviality so tædious and irksome, that I had much rather have remained in silent Observation and Reflection. One Anecdote I will relate, because among many others I heard in Bourdeaux it was Characteristic of the manners at that time. One of the most elegant Ladies at Table, young and handsome, tho married to a Gentleman in the Company, was pleased to Address her discourse to me. Mr. Bondfield must interpret the Speech which he did in these Words "Mr. Adams, by your Name I conclude you are descended from the first Man and Woman, and probably in your family may be preserved the tradition which may resolve a difficulty which I could never explain. I never could understand how the first Couple found out the Art of lying together?" Whether her phrase was L'Art de se coucher ensemble, or any other more energetic, I know not, but Mr. Bondfield rendered it by that I have mentioned. To me, whose Acquaintance with Women had been confined to America, where the manners of the Ladies were universally characterised at that time by Modesty, Delicacy and Dignity, this question was surprizing and shocking: but although I believe at first I blushed,

I was determined not to be disconcerted. I thought it would be as well for once to set a brazen face against a brazen face and answer a fool according to her folly, and accordingly composing my countenance into an Ironical Gravity I answered her "Madame My Family resembles the first Couple both in the name and in their frailties so much that I have no doubt We are descended from that in Paradise. But the Subject was perfectly understood by Us, whether by tradition I could not tell: I rather thought it was by Instinct, for there was a Physical quality in Us resembling the Power of Electricity or of the Magnet, by which when a Pair approached within a striking distance they flew together like the Needle to the Pole or like two Objects in electric Experiments." When this Answer was explained to her, she replied "Well I know not how it was, but this I know it is a very happy Shock." I should have added "in a lawfull Way" after "a striking distance," but if I had her Ladyship and all the Company would only have thought it Pedantry and Bigottry. This is a decent Story in comparison with many which I heard in Bourdeaux, in the short time I remained there, concerning married Ladies of Fashion and reputation. The decided Advances made by married Women, which I heard related, gave rise to many reflections in my mind which may perhaps be detailed hereafter on some similar Occasions. The first was if such a[re] the manners of Women of Rank, Fashion and Reputation [in] France, they can never support a Republican Government nor be reconciled with it. We must therefore take great care not to import them into America.

1961

Letter from Abigail Adams to John Adams, March 31, 1776

I long to hear that you have declared an independancy—and by the way in the new Code of Laws which I suppose it will be necessary for you to make I desire you would Remember the Ladies, and be more generous and favourable to them than your ancestors. Do not put such unlimited power into the hands of the Husbands. Remember all Men would be tyrants if they could. If perticuliar care and attention is not paid to the Laidies we are determined to foment a Rebelion, and will not hold ourselves bound by any Laws in which we have no voice, or Representation.

That your Sex are Naturally Tyrannical is a Truth so thoroughly established as to admit of no dispute, but such of you as wish to be happy willingly give up the harsh title of Master for the more tender and endearing one of Friend. Why then, not put it out of the power of the vicious and the Lawless to use us with cruelty and indignity with impunity. Men of Sense in all Ages abhor those customs which treat us only as the vassals of your Sex. Regard us then as Beings placed by providence under your protection and in immitation of the Supreem Being make use of that power only for our happiness.

1975

Letter from John Adams to Abigail Adams, April 14, 1776

As to Declarations of Independency, be patient. Read our Privateering Laws, and our Commercial Laws. What signifies a Word.

As to your extraordinary Code of Laws, I cannot but laugh. We have been told that our Struggle has loosened the bands of Government every where. That Children and Apprentices were disobedient—that schools and Colledges were grown turbulent—that Indians slighted their Guardians and Negroes grew insolent to their Masters. But your Letter was the first Intimation that another Tribe more numerous and powerfull than all the rest were grown discontented.—This is rather too coarse a Compliment but you are so saucy, I wont blot it out.

Depend upon it, We know better than to repeal our Masculine systems. Altho they are in full Force, you know they are little more than Theory. We dare not exert our Power in its full Latitude. We are obliged to go fair, and softly, and in Practice you know We are the subjects. We have only the Name of Masters, and rather than give up this, which would compleatly subject Us to the Despotism of the Peticoat, I hope General Washington, and all our brave Heroes would fight. I am sure every good Politician would plot, as long as he would against Despotism, Empire, Monarchy, Aristocracy, Oligarchy, or Ochlocracy.—A fine Story indeed. I begin to think the Ministry as deep as they are wicked. After stirring up Tories, Landjobbers, Trimmers, Bigots, Canadians, Indians, Negroes, Hanoverians, Hessians, Russians, Irish Roman Catholicks, Scotch Renegadoes, at last they have stimulated the [ ] to demand new Priviledges and threaten to rebell.

1975

from Letter from John Adams to Mercy Otis Warren, April 16, 1776

. . . The Ladies I think are the greatest Politicians that I have the Honour to be acquainted with, not only because they act upon the Sublimest of all the Principles of Policy, viz., that Honesty is the best Policy, but because they consider Questions more coolly than those who are heated with Party Zeal and inflamed with the bitter Contentions of active public Life. . . .

The Form of Government, which you admire, when its Principles are pure is admirable, indeed, it is productive of every Thing, which is great and excellent among Men. But its Principles are as easily destroyed, as human Nature is corrupted. Such a Government is only to be supported by pure Religion or Austere Morals. Public Virtue cannot exist in a Nation without private, and public Virtue is the only Foundation of Republics. There must be a positive Passion for the public good, the public Interest, Honour, Power and Glory, established in the Minds of the People, or there can be no Republican Government, nor any real Liberty: and this public Passion must be Superiour to all private Passions. Men must be ready, they must pride themselves, and be happy to sacrifice their private Pleasures, Passions and Interests, nay, their private Friendships and dearest Connections, when they stand in Competition with the Rights of Society.

Is there in the World a Nation, which deserves this Character? There have been several, but they are no more. Our dear Americans perhaps have as much of it as any Nation now existing, and New England perhaps has more than the rest of America. But I have seen all along my Life Such Selfishness and Littleness even in New England, that I sometimes tremble to think that, altho We are engaged in the best Cause that ever employed the Human Heart yet the Prospect of success is doubtful not for Want of Power or of Wisdom but of Virtue.

The Spirit of Commerce, Madam, which even insinuates itself into Families, and influences holy Matrimony, and thereby corrupts the morals of families as well as destroys their Happiness, it is much to be feared is incompatible with that purity of Heart and Greatness of soul which is necessary for an happy Republic.

This Same Spirit of Commerce is as rampant in New England as in any Part of the World. Trade is as well understood and as passionately loved there as any where.

Even the Farmers and Tradesmen are addicted to Commerce; and it is too true that Property is generally the standard of Respect there as much as anywhere. While this is the Case there is great Danger that a Republican Government would be very factious and turbulent there. Divisions in Elections are much to be dreaded. Every man must seriously set himself to root out his Passions, Prejudices and Attachments, and to get the better of his private Interest. The only reputable Principle and Doctrine must be that all Things must give Way to the public.

This is very grave and solemn Discourse to a Lady. True, and I thank God, that his Providence has made me Acquainted with two Ladies at least who can bear it. I think Madam, that the Union of the Colonies, will continue and be more firmly cemented. But We must move slowly. Patience, Patience, Patience! I am obliged to invoke this every Morning of my Life, every Noon and every Evening.

1917

from Letters from John Adams to Abigail Adams, July 3, 1776[1]

[1] . . . Yesterday the greatest Question was decided, which ever was debated in America, and a greater perhaps, never was or will be decided among Men. A Resolution was passed without one dissenting Colony "that these united Colonies, are,

[1]John Adams wrote two letters to Abigail Adams on July 3; the passages here come from the first and second, respectively, with the first letter identified as [1] and the second letter identified as [2].

and of right ought to be free and independent States, and as such, they have, and of Right ought to have full Power to make War, conclude Peace, establish Commerce, and to do all the other Acts and Things, which other States may rightfully do." You will see in a few days a Declaration setting forth the Causes, which have impell'd Us to this mighty Revolution, and the Reasons which will justify it, in the Sight of God and Man. A Plan of Confederation will be taken up in a few days.

When I look back to the Year 1761, and recollect the Argument concerning Writs of Assistance, in the Superiour Court, which I have hitherto considered as the Commencement of the Controversy, between Great Britain and America, and run through the whole Period from that Time to this, and recollect the series of political Events, the Chain of Causes and Effects, I am surprized at the Suddenness, as well as Greatness of this Revolution. Britain has been fill'd with Folly, and America with Wisdom, at least this is my Judgment.—Time must determine. It is the Will of Heaven, that the two Countries should be sundered forever. It may be the Will of Heaven that America shall suffer Calamities still more wasting and Distresses yet more dreadfull. If this is to be the Case, it will have this good Effect, at least: it will inspire Us with many Virtues, which We have not, and correct many Errors, Follies, and Vices, which threaten to disturb, dishonour, and destroy Us.—The Furnace of Affliction produces Refinement, in States as well as Individuals. And the new Governments we are assuming, in every Part, will require a Purification from our Vices, and an Augmentation of our Virtues or they will be no Blessings. The People will have unbounded Power. And the People are extreamly addicted to Corruption and Venality, as well as the Great.—I am not without Apprehensions from this Quarter. But I must submit all my Hopes and Fears, to an overruling Providence, in which, unfashionable as the Faith may be, I firmly believe.

[2] Had a Declaration of Independency been made seven Months ago, it would have been attended with many great and glorious Effects. . . . We might before this Hour, have formed Alliances with foreign States.—We should have mastered Quebec and been in Possession of Canada. . . .

But on the other Hand, the Delay of this Declaration to this Time, has many great Advantages attending it.—The Hopes of Reconciliation, which were fondly entertained by Multitudes of honest and well meaning tho weak and mistaken People, have been gradually and at last totally extinguished.—Time has been given for the whole People, maturely to consider the great Question of Independence and to ripen their Judgments, dissipate their Fears, and allure their Hopes, by discussing it in News Papers and Pamphletts, by debating it, in Assemblies, Conventions, Committees of Safety and Inspection, in Town and County Meetings, as well as in private Conversations, so that the whole People in every Colony of the 13, have now adopted it, as their own Act.—This will cement the Union, and avoid those Heats and perhaps Convulsions which might have been occasioned, by such a Declaration Six Months ago.

But the Day is past. The Second Day of July 1776, will be the most memorable Epocha, in the History of America.—I am apt to believe that it will be celebrated, by succeeding Generations, as the great anniversary Festival. It ought to be commemorated, as the Day of Deliverance by solemn Acts of Devotion to God

Almighty. It ought to be solemnized with Pomp and Parade, with Shews, Games, Sports, Guns, Bells, Bonfires and Illuminations from one End of this Continent to the other from this Time forward forever more.

You will think me transported with Enthusiasm but I am not.—I am well aware of the Toil and Blood and Treasure, that it will cost Us to maintain this Declaration, and support and defend these States.—Yet through all the Gloom I can see the Rays of ravishing Light and Glory. I can see that the End is more than worth all the Means. And that Posterity will tryumph in that Days Transaction, even altho We should rue it, which I trust in God We shall not.

1963

Letter from Abigail Adams to John Adams, June 30, 1778

Now I know you are Safe [in France] I wish myself with you. Whenever you entertain such a wish recollect that I would have willingly hazarded all dangers to have been your companion, but as that was not permitted you must console me in your absence by a Recital of all your adventures, tho methinks I would not have them in all respects too similar to those related of your venerable Colleigue [i.e., Franklin], Whose Mentor like appearence, age and philosiphy must certainly lead the polite scientifick Ladies of France to suppose they are embraceing the God of Wisdom, in a Humane Form, but I who own that I never yet wish'd an Angle whom I loved a Man,[1] shall be full as content if those divine Honours are omitted. The whole Heart of my Friend is in the Bosom of his partner, more than half a score of years has so riveted [it] there that the fabrick which contains it must crumble into Dust e'er the particles can be seperated. I can hear of the Brilliant accomplishment[s] of any of my Sex with pleasure and rejoice in that Liberality of Sentiment which acknowledges them. At the same time I regret the trifling narrow contracted Education of the Females of my own country. I have entertaind a superiour opinion of the accomplishments of the French Ladies ever since I read the Letters of Dr. Sherbear,[2] who professes that he had rather take the opinion of an accomplished Lady in matters of polite writing than the first wits of Itally and should think himself safer with her approbation than of a long List of Literati, and he give[s] this reason for it that Women have in general more delicate Sensations than Men, what touches them is for the most part true in Nature, whereas men warpt by Education, judge amiss from previous prejudice and refering all things to the model of the ancients, condemn that by comparison where no true Similitud ought to be expected.

[1] "Back thro' the paths of pleasing sense I ran, / Nor wish'd an Angel whom I lov'd a Man." Alexander Pope, *Eloisa to Abelard,* lines 69–70.

[2] John Shebbeare, notorious English satirist. Both John and Abigail had read his novel, *Letters on the English Nation* (1755).

But in this country you need not be told how much female Education is neglected, nor how fashonable it has been to ridicule Female learning, tho I acknowled[ge] it my happiness to be connected with a person of a more generous mind and liberal Sentiments.

1975

Abigail Adams's Diary of her Return Voyage to America, March 30–May 1, 1788

Sunday London March 30. We took our departure from the Bath Hotell where I had been a Fortnight, and sat out for Portsmouth, which we reachd on Monday Evening. We put up at the Fountain Inn. Here we continued a week waiting for the Ship which was detaind by contrary winds in the River. The wind changing we past over to the Isle of Wight and landed at a place call'd Ryed, where we took post Chaises and proceeded to Newport to dine. From thence to Cows where our Ship was to call for us. Here Mr. Adams, myself and two Servants took up our abode at the Fountain Inn kept by a widow woman whose Name is Symes. Our Lodging room very small, and the drawing room Confind and unpleasent. I found myself on the first Night much disposed to be uneasy and discontented. On the next day I requested the Land Lady to let me have a very large Room from whence we had a fine view of the Harbour, vessels, east Cowes and surrounding Hills. I found my Spirits much relieved. Never before experienced how much pleasure was to be derived from a prospect, but I had been long used to a large House, a large Family and many and various cares. I had now got into an unpleasent place without any occupation for mind or Body. Haveing staid at Portsmouth untill I had read all our Books and done all the Work I had left out, I never before experienced to such a degree what the French term enui.[1] Monday took a walk to the Castle and upon a Hill behind it which commanded a pleasent view of the Harbour and Town which is a small villiage subsisting chiefly by fishing and piloting Vessels. Cowes is a safe and commodious Harbour. Here many Boats ply to take up the oyster which is always found in an Infant State. Small Vessels calld Smacks receive them and carry them to Colchester where they throw them again into water where the Sea only flows up by tides, and there they fatten and are again taken up and carried [to] the London market. The Isle of Wight is taken all together a very fertile agreable place 24 miles Long and 12 Broad. Produces great plenty of Grain, Sheep and Cattle, is a hilly country and a very Healthy Situation. On tuesday we went to Newport in order to visit Carisbrook Castle. This is a very ancient Ruins. The first account of it in English History is in the year 1513. This is the castle where Charles the first was kept a prisoner and they shew you the window from whence he attempted to escape. In this castle is a well of such a depth that the water is drawn from it by an ass walking in a wheel like a turn spit dog. The woman

[1]Boredom.

who shew it to us told us it was 300 feet deep. It is Beautifully stoned and in as good order as if finishd but yesterday. She lighted paper and threw [it] down to shew us its depth and dropping in a pin, it resounded as tho a large stone had been thrown in. We went to the Top of the citidal which commands a most extensive prospect. We returnd to Newport to dine. After dinner a Gentleman introduced himself to us by the Name of Sharp. Professed himself a warm and zealous Friend to America. After some little conversation in which it was easy to discover that he was a curious Character he requested that we would do him the Honour to go to his House and drink Tea. We endeavourd [to] excuse ourselves, but he would insist upon it, and we accordingly accepted. He carried us home and introduced to us an aged Father of 90 Years, a very surprizing old Gentleman who tho deaf appeard to retain his understanding perfectly. Mrs. Sharp his Lady appeard to be an amiable woman tho not greatly accustomed to company. The two young Ladies soon made their appearence, the Youngest about 17 very Beautifull. The eldest might have been thought Handsome, if she had not quite spoild herself by affectation. By aiming at politeness she overshot her mark, and faild in that Symplicity of manners which is the principal ornament of a Female Character.

This Family were very civil, polite and Friendly to us during our stay at Cowes. We drank Tea with them on the Sunday following and by their most pressing invitation we dined with them the tuesday following. Mr. Sharp is a poet, a man of reading and appears to possess a good mind and Heart and [is] enthusiastick in favor of America. He collected a number of his Friends to dine with us all of whom were equally well disposed to our Country and had always Reprobated the war against us. During our stay at Cowes we made one excursion to Yarmouth about 15 miles distant from Cowes, but the road being Bad it scarcly repaid us for the trouble as we did not meet with any thing curious. After spending a whole fortnight at Cowes the Ship came round and on Sunday the 20 of April we embarked on Board the ship Lucretia Captain Callihan with three Gentlemen passengers viz. Mr. Murry a Clergyman, Mr. Stewart a grandson of old Captain Erwin of Boston who is going out to Bermudas collector of the Customs in that Island, His parents being British subjects, Mr. Boyd of Portsmouth a young Gentleman who received His Education in this Country.

The wind with which we saild scarcly lasted us 5 hours, but we continued our course untill Monday Evening when it blew such a gale that we were driven back and very glad to get into Portland Harbour. Here we have lain ever since, now 8 days, a Situation not to be desired, yet better far than we should have been either at Sea or in the downs. Whenever I am disposed to be uneasy I reflect a moment upon my preferable Situation to the poor Girl my maid, who is very near her Time,[2] in poor Health and distressingly Sea sick, and I am then silent. I Hush every murmer, and tho much of my anxiety is on her account, I think that God will suit the wind to the shorn Lamb, that we may be carried through our difficulties better than my apprehensions. Trust in the Lord, and do good. I will endeavour to practise this precept. My own Health is better than it has been. We fortunately have a Doctor on Board, and I have taken an old woman out of kindness and given her a passage who seems kind, active and cleaver, is not Sea sick and I hope will be usefull to me. I am much better ac-

[2]*I.e.,* for giving birth.

commodated than when I came and have not sufferd so much by Sea Sickness. Want of Sleep is the greatest inconvenience I have yet sufferd but I shall not escape so. This day 3 weeks Mr. and Mrs. Smith saild and my dear Grandson just one Year old for New York in the Thyne packet. I fear they will have a bad time as the Westerly Winds have been so strong. God protect them and give us all a happy meeting in our Native Land. We Lie Here near the Town of Weymouth, and our Gentlemen go on shore almost every day which is an amusement to them and really some to me, as they collect something or other to bring Back with them either Mental or Bodily food. This is Sunday 27 April. Mr. Murry preachd us a Sermon. The Sailors made themselves clean and were admitted into the Cabbin, attended with great decency to His discourse from these words, "Thou shalt not take the Name of the Lord thy God in vain, for the Lord will not hold him Guiltless that taketh His Name in vain." He preachd without Notes and in the same Stile which all the Clergymen I ever heard make use of who practise this method, a sort of familiar talking without any kind of dignity yet perhaps better calculated to do good to such an audience, than a more polishd or elegant Stile, but in general I cannot approve of this method. I like to hear a discourse that would read well. If I live to return to America, how much shall I regreet the loss of good Dr. Prices Sermons. They were always a delightfull entertainment to me. I revered the Character and Loved the Man. Tho far from being an orator, his words came from the Heart and reached the Heart. So Humble, so diffident, so liberal and Benevolent a Character does honour to that Religion which he both professes and practises.

On Sunday Eve the wind changed in our favour, so much as to induce the Captain to come to sail. This is Thursday the first of May, but we have made very small progress, the winds have been so light; yesterday we past Sylla and are now out of sight of Land. The weather is very fine and we only want fresher winds. The confinement of a Ship is tedious and I am fully of the mind I was when I came over that I will never again try the Sea. I provided then for my return in the Resolution I took, but now it is absolute. Indeed I have seen enough of the world, small as [it?] has been, and shall be content to learn what is further to be known from the page of History. I do not think the four years I have past abroad the pleasentest part of my Life. Tis Domestick happiness and Rural felicity in the Bosom of my Native Land, that has charms for me. Yet I do not regreet that I made this excursion since it has only more attached me to America.

1961

from Letter from John Adams to Thomas Jefferson, September 2, 1813

. . . Now, my Friend, who are the αριστοι ["aristocrats"]? Philosophy may Answer "The Wise and Good." But the World, Mankind, have by their practice always answered, "the rich the beautiful and well born." And Philosophers themselves in marrying their Children prefer the rich the handsome and the well descended to the wise and good.

What chance have Talents and Virtues in competition, with Wealth and Birth? and Beauty?

Haud facile emergunt, quorum Virtutibus obstant [i.e., obstat]
Res Angusta Domi.

One truth is clear,; by all the World confess'd
Slow rises worth, by Poverty oppress'd.

The five Pillars of Aristocracy, are Beauty Wealth, Birth, Genius and Virtues. Any one of the three first, can at any time over bear any one or both of the two last.

Let me ask again, what a Wave of publick Opinion, in favour of Birth has been spread over the Globe, by Abraham, by Hercules, by Mahomet, by Guelphs, Ghibellines, Bourbons, and a miserable Scottish Chief Steuart? By Zingis by, by, by, a million others? And what a Wave will be spread by Napoleon and by Washington? Their remotest Cousins will be sought and will be proud, and will avail themselves of their descent. Call this Principle, Prejudice, Folly Ignorance, Baseness, Slavery, Stupidity, Adulation, Superstition or what you will. I will not contradict you. But the Fact, in natural, moral, political and domestic History I cannot deny or dispute or question.

And is this great Fact in the natural History of Man? This unalterable Principle of Morals, Philosophy, Policy domestic felicity, and dayly Experience from the Creation; to be overlooked, forgotten neglected, or hypocritically waived out of Sight; by a Legislator? By a professed Writer upon civil Government, and upon Constitutions of civil Government?

Thus far I had written, when your favour of Aug. 22 was laid on my table, from the Post Office. I can only say at present that I can pursue this idle Speculation no farther, at least till I have replied to this fresh proof of your friendship and Confidence. Mrs. A. joins in cordial Thanks, with

John Adams

You may laugh at the introduction of Beauty, among the Pillars of Aristocracy. But Madame Barry says Le veritable Royauté est la B[e]autee ["true royalty is beauty"], and there is not a more certain Truth. Beauty, Grace, Figure, Attitude, Movement, have in innumerable Instances prevailed over Wealth, Birth, Talents Virtues and every thing else, in Men of the highest rank, greatest Power, and sometimes, the most exalted Genius, greatest Fame, and highest Merit.

1963

from Letter from Thomas Jefferson to John Adams, October 28, 1813

. . . I agree with you that there is a natural aristocracy among men. The grounds of this are virtue and talents. Formerly bodily powers gave place among the aristoi. But since the invention of gunpowder has armed the weak as well as the strong with missile death, bodily strength, like beauty, good humor, politeness and other accomplishments, has become but an auxiliary ground of distinction. There is also an artificial aristocracy founded on wealth and birth, without either virtue or talents; for with these it would belong to the first class. The natural aristocracy I consider as the most precious gift of nature for the instruction, the trusts, and government of society. And indeed it would have been inconsistent in creation to have formed man for the social state, and not to have provided virtue and wisdom enough to manage the concerns of the society. May we not even say that that form of government is the best which provides the most effectually for a pure selection of these natural aristoi into the offices of government? The artificial aristocracy is a mischievous ingredient in government, and provision should be made to prevent it's ascendancy. On the question, What is the best provision, you and I differ; but we differ as rational friends, using the free exercise of our own reason, and mutually indulging it's errors. *You* think it best to put the Pseudo-aristoi into a separate chamber of legislation where they may be hindered from doing mischief by their coordinate branches, and where also they may be a protection to wealth against the Agrarian and plundering enterprises of the Majority of the people. I think that to give them power in order to prevent them from doing mischief, is arming them for it, and increasing instead of remedying the evil. For if the coordinate branches can arrest their action, so may they that of the coordinates. Mischief may be done negatively as well as positively. Of this a cabal in the Senate of the U. S. has furnished many proofs. Nor do I believe them necessary to protect the wealthy; because enough of these will find their way into every branch of the legislation to protect themselves. From 15. to 20. legislatures of our own, in action for 30. years past, have proved that no fears of an equalisation of property are to be apprehended from them.

I think the best remedy is exactly that provided by all our constitutions, to leave to the citizens the free election and separation of the aristoi from the pseudo-aristoi, of the wheat from the chaff. In general they will elect the real good and wise. In some instances, wealth may corrupt, and birth blind them; but not in sufficient degree to endanger the society.

1963

from Letter from John Adams to Thomas Jefferson, November 15, 1813

. . . We are now explicitly agreed, in one important point, vizt. That "there is a natural Aristocracy among men; the grounds of which are Virtue and Talents."

You very justly indulge a little merriment upon this solemn subject of Aristocracy. I often laugh at it too, for there is nothing in this laughable world more ridiculous than the management of it by almost all the nations of the Earth. But while We smile, Mankind have reason to say to Us, as the froggs said to the Boys, What is Sport to you is Wounds and death to Us. When I consider the weakness, the folly, the Pride, the Vanity, the Selfishness, the Artifice, the low craft and meaning cunning, the want of Principle, the Avarice the unbounded Ambition, the unfeeling Cruelty of a majority of those (in all Nations) who are allowed an aristocratical influence; and on the other hand, the Stupidity with which the more numerous multitude, not only become their Dupes, but even love to be Taken in by their Tricks: I feel a stronger disposition to weep at their destiny, than to laugh at their Folly.

But tho' We have agreed in one point, in Words, it is not yet certain that We are perfectly agreed in Sense. Fashion has introduced an indeterminate Use of the Word "Talents." Education, Wealth, Strength, Beauty, Stature, Birth, Marriage, graceful Attitudes and Motions, Gait, Air, Complexion, Physiognomy, are Talents, as well as Genius and Science and learning. Any one of these Talents, that in fact commands or influences true Votes in Society, gives to the Man who possesses it, the Character of an Aristocrat, in my Sense of the Word.

Pick up, the first 100 men you meet, and make a Republick. Every Man will have an equal Vote. But when deliberations and discussions are opened it will be found that 25, by their Talents, Virtues being equal, will be able to carry 50 Votes. Every one of these 25, is an Aristocrat, in my Sense of the Word; whether he obtains his one Vote in Addition to his own, by his Birth Fortune, Figure, Eloquence, Science, learning, Craft Cunning, or even his Character for good fellowship and a bon vivant. . . .

A daughter of a green Grocer, walks the Streets in London dayly with a baskett of Cabbage, Sprouts, Dandlions and Spinage on her head. She is observed by the Painters to have a beautiful Face, an elegant figure, a graceful Step and a debonair. They hire her to Sitt. She complies, and is painted by forty Artists in a Circle around her. The scientific Sir William Hamilton outbids the Painters, sends her to Schools for a genteel Education and Marries her. This Lady not only causes the Tryumphs of the Nile of Copinhagen and Trafalgar, but seperates Naples from France and finally banishes the King and Queen from Sicilly. Such is the Aristocracy of the natural Talent of Beauty. Millions of Examples might be quoted from History sacred and profane, from Eve, Hannah, Deborah Susanna Abigail, Judith, Ruth, down to Hellen Madame de Maintenon and Mrs. Fitzherbert. For mercy's sake do not compell me to look to our chaste States and Territories, to find Women, one of whom lett go, would, in the Words of Holopherne's Guards "deceive the whole Earth."[1] . . .

Your distinction between natural and artificial Aristocracy does not appear to me well founded. Birth and Wealth are conferred on some Men, as imperiously by Nature, as Genius, Strength or Beauty. The Heir is honours and Riches, and power has often no more merit in procuring these Advantages, than he has in obtaining an handsome face or an elegant figure. When Aristocracies, are established by human Laws and honour Wealth and Power are made hereditary by municipal Laws and political Institutions, then I acknowledge artificial Aristocracy to commence: but this never commences, till Corruption in Elections becomes dominant and uncontroulable. But this artificial Aristocracy can never last. The everlasting Envys,

[1]The reference here is to Emma, Lady Hamilton, whose lover was Admiral, Lord Nelson.

jealousies, Rivalries and quarrells among them, their cruel rapacities upon the poor ignorant People their followers, compell these to sett up Caesar, a Demagogue to be a Monarch and Master, pour mettre chacun a sa place ["to put each one in his place"]. Here you have the origin of all artificial Aristocracy, which is the origin of all Monarchy. And both artificial Aristocracy, and Monarchy, and civil, military, political and hierarchical Despotism, have all grown out of the natural Aristocracy of "Virtues and Talents." We, to be sure, are far remote from this. Many hundred years must roll away before We shall be corrupted. Our pure, virtuous, public spirited federative Republick will last for ever, govern the Globe and introduce the perfection of Man, his perfectability being already proved by Price Priestly, Condorcet Rousseau Diderot and Godwin.[2] . . .

Your distinction between the aristoi and pseudo aristoi, will not help the matter. I would trust one as soon as the other with unlimited Power. The Law wisely refuses an Oath as a witness in his own cause to the Saint as well as to the Sinner.

1963

Thomas Jefferson 1743–1826

The fluctuations in Thomas Jefferson's reputation since his death in 1826 have paralleled the most vigorously debated controversies over how people in the United States are to understand themselves as a nation and as individuals. As the author of the Declaration of Independence, Jefferson has been praised as a champion of democracy, equality, and human rights, but he has also been criticized for supposed betrayals of his own ideals or outright failures of character. Most recently such criticism has tended to focus on the tension between his claim that all men have inalienable natural rights, with liberty chief among them, and his continuing ownership of slaves. Raised as an issue in his own lifetime by those who wished to discredit his egalitarianism, the contradiction between Jefferson's affirmation of human rights and his practice of slavery demands thoughtful attention in a society still struggling with egalitarian ideology and racist practice.

Born at Shadwell, a family farm near the present-day Monticello but at that time near the western frontier of Virginia, Jefferson was the son of Jane Randolph and Peter Jefferson, the former a member of one of Virginia's most prominent and influential families and the latter a landowner, magistrate, surveyor, and mapmaker. After his father's death, Jefferson attended William and Mary College and subsequently studied law with George Wythe, one of the best legal scholars of colonial America. After admission to the bar, he practiced law, played a part in Virginia colonial politics, and became increasingly critical of England's attempts to exert authority in the American colonies. His 1774 pamphlet, *A Summary View of the Rights of British America,* caught the attention of readers outside of Virginia with its bold argument that Americans had effectually freed themselves from royal and parliamentary authority by exercizing "a right which nature has given to all men, of de-

[2]Adams's appeal here to American incorruptibility is ironic and satiric.

parting from the country in which chance, not choice has placed them." In all likelihood his insistence here that "Kings are the servants, not the proprietors of the people" and that "The God who gave us life gave us liberty at the same time" led to his appointment in 1776 to the committee charged with drafting the Declaration of Independence.

Jefferson's Declaration has become, along with the Constitution and the Bill of Rights, a founding document of the United States; not law itself, it is a fundamental expression of the moral and political ideals of American society. Its claims that all people are created equal and possess inalienable rights to life, liberty, and the pursuit of happiness have too seldom been fully realized in American practice, but at the same time the Declaration's claims are the standards against which American social practice has been measured and criticized. As Abraham Lincoln put it in 1861, "It was [the Declaration] which gave promise that in due time the weights should be lifted from the shoulders of all men, and that *all* should have an equal chance."

While serving as governor of Virginia, Jefferson received a questionnaire from François Marbois, secretary to the French legation in Philadelphia, asking for information on the state. His answers eventually appeared as his only full-length book, *Notes on the State of Virginia* (1787), which was both a pioneering attempt at a scientific study of a community and an effort to direct the culture and political formation of the post-Revolutionary state. As he gathered information for *Notes,* Jefferson realized he had an occasion to address the claims of the Abbé Reynal and the Count de Buffon, the most famous naturalist of the time, that animals and people in the New World were smaller, less vigorous, and generally degenerate when compared to similar organisms in the Old World. The argument was seemingly biological, but its implications were political and cultural. If people dwindled in physical vigor, what sort of society could they be expected to maintain? Jefferson's refutation of Buffon's theory in Query VI on natural productions such as minerals, trees, plants, and animals vindicated Native American virtues in order to defend American character. His version of Logan's speech became a popular representation of Native American oratory, an icon of "natural" culture in America. In Query XIX, "Manufactures," Jefferson offered a more implicit defense of the American environment that was also a classic statement of his agrarian ideal: "Those who labour in the earth are the chosen people of God, if ever he had a chosen people, whose breasts he has made his peculiar deposit for substantial and genuine virtue. . . . Corruption of morals in the mass of cultivators is a phaenomenon of which no age nor nation has furnished the example."

Jefferson used the occasion of *Notes* to pursue his republican political agenda, but here his comments became more problematic. He used chapters on "Laws" and "Manners," among others, to criticize the failings of Virginia's legal system, particularly its failure to remedy the evil of slavery. Queries XIV and XVIII strongly condemned the institution of slavery, but in the former chapter he argued that emancipation should be linked to removal of blacks to a separate colony where they could be "a free and independent people." In explaining the necessity of colonization, he revealed a strain of racialist thinking that was all too common both in his time and later—even though some of his friends who read *Notes* singled out these passages for criticism—but extremely disturbing in ours. He advanced "as a suspicion only" the argument that blacks were inferior to whites "in the endowments both of body and mind," and a basically skeptical turn of mind allowed him to consider evidence for the error of his beliefs. However, despite the examples of black achievement presented to him, such as the almanac of Benjamin Banneker, he never retreated from his belief in the desireability of the eventual separation of the races.

Like many later white abolitionists, Jefferson was able to simultaneously maintain an opposition to slavery with what we would regard as a basically racist attitude. Critics have charged that his racist feelings explain his apparent reluctance to do more to oppose slavery, but the problem is more complex. The rejection in 1776 of his clause in the Declaration about slavery and the subsequent unwillingness of the Virginia legislature to take up emancipation—when he was one of the committee revising its laws—would have made him realize the enormous difficulties in changing the opinions of his Virginian contemporaries. A poor debater, Jefferson spoke seldom in legislative bodies, and he was reluctant to engage in controversy. Giving his grandson "prudential rules for our government in society," he advised "never entering into dispute or argument with another. I never yet saw an instance of one of two disputants convincing the other by argument. . . . Conviction is the effect of our own dispassionate reasoning, either in solitude or weighing within ourselves dispassionately what we hear from others." Holding no political office in Virginia after 1781, Jefferson thought he could offer only "dispassionate reasoning," which increasingly was expressed in his private letters rather than in public statements. In addition, Jefferson was unwilling to ostracize himself from his neighbors when he thought that there was more he could do in Virginia to secure a free society. Immediately after his discussion of slavery and blacks in Query XIV on "Laws," he set out his proposals for a system of public education. Indeed, in the last quarter of his life, faced with what he felt was the impossibility of arguing Virginians into abolition, Jefferson concentrated on the coming generation. Slavery would have to be abolished, he told Edward Coles in 1814, by "the young . . . who can follow it up, and bear it through to its consummation." His own contribution, he thought, would be to found the University of Virginia as a means to encourage progress toward a republican future. He wanted to be remembered on his grave marker as the author of the Declaration and of the Virginia Statute for Religious Freedom and as the father of the University of Virginia. Jefferson's primary commitment was to intellectual freedom; he believed that liberated reason would ultimately purge the world of its tyranny and oppression, but his optimism also seemed to many to ignore the real suffering of the world.

Jefferson's own ideas were, finally, more complex than was his reputation at any given moment. Feminists from Abigail Adams on, for example, have been unhappy with the statement in the Declaration of Independence that "all *men* are created equal," but the egalitarian force of that statement was so powerful that the women of the Seneca Falls Woman's Rights Convention shaped their *Declaration of Sentiments* in terms of Jefferson's rhetoric. Confident that the original Declaration supported their own rights, they made explicit what was implicit, asserting, "We hold these truths to be self-evident: that all men *and* women are created equal." It remains a central irony of our society that the patriarchalism and racism of Jefferson's discourse is perhaps most successfully refuted by his discourse on freedom and equality.

Frank Shuffelton
University of Rochester

PRIMARY WORKS

The Writings of Thomas Jefferson, ed. Lipscomb and Bergh, 1903–1904; *The Papers of Thomas Jefferson,* 1950–; *Notes on the State of Virginia,* ed. William Peden, 1954; *Thomas Jefferson: Writings,* Library of America, ed. Merrill Peterson, 1984.

SECONDARY WORKS

Dumas Malone, *Thomas Jefferson and His Times,* 6 vols., 1951–81; John Chester Miller, *The Wolf by the Ears: Thomas Jefferson and Slavery,* 1977; Noble E. Cunningham, *In Pursuit of Reason: The Life of Thomas Jefferson,* 1978; Frank Shuffelton, *Thomas Jefferson, 1981–1990: An Annotated Bibliography,* 1992; Peter Onuf, ed., *Jeffersonian Legacies,* 1993.

from Autobiography of Thomas Jefferson

Congress proceeded the same day to consider the declaration of Independance which had been reported & lain on the table the Friday preceding, and on Monday referred to a commee of the whole. The pusillanimous idea that we had friends in England worth keeping terms with, still haunted the minds of many. For this reason those passages which conveyed censures on the people of England were struck out, lest they should give them offence. The clause too, reprobating the enslaving the inhabitants of Africa, was struck out in complaisance to South Carolina and Georgia, who had never attempted to restrain the importation of slaves, and who on the contrary still wished to continue it. Our northern brethren also I believe felt a little tender under those censures; for tho' their people have very few slaves themselves yet they had been pretty considerable carriers of them to others. The debates having taken up the greater parts of the 2d 3d & 4th days of July were, in the evening of the last, closed the declaration was reported by the commee, agreed to by the house and signed by every member present except Mr. Dickinson. As the sentiments of men are known not only by what they receive, but what they reject also, I will state the form of the declaration as originally reported. The parts struck out by Congress shall be distinguished by a black line drawn under them; & those inserted by them shall be placed in the margin or in a concurrent column.[1]

A Declaration by the Representatives of the United States of America, in General Congress Assembled

When, in the course of human events, it becomes necessary for one people to dissolve the political bands which have connected them with another, and to assume among the powers of the earth the separate and equal station to which the laws of nature and of nature's God entitle them, a decent respect to the opinions of mankind requires that they should declare the causes which impel them to the separation.

We hold these truths to be self evident: that all men are created equal; that they are endowed by their Creator with CERTAIN [*inherent and*] inalienable rights; that among these are life, liberty, and the pursuit of happiness; that to secure these rights, governments are instituted among men, deriving their just powers from the consent

[1]Here the parts struck out by Congress are italicized and in brackets; the words added by Congress are in large capitals.

of the governed; that whenever any form of government becomes destructive of these ends, it is the right of the people to alter or to abolish it, and to institute new government, laying its foundation on such principles, and organizing its powers in such form, as to them shall seem most likely to effect their safety and happiness. Prudence, indeed, will dictate that governments long established should not be changed for light and transient causes; and accordingly all experience hath shown that mankind are more disposed to suffer while evils are sufferable, than to right themselves by abolishing the forms to which they are accustomed. But when a long train of abuses and usurpations, [*begun at a distinguished period and*] pursuing invariably the same object, evinces a design to reduce them under absolute despotism, it is their right, it is their duty to throw off such government, and to provide new guards for their future security. Such has been the patient sufferance of these colonies; and such is now the necessity which constrains them to ALTER [*expunge*] their former systems of government. The history of the present king of Great Britain is a history of REPEATED [*unremitting*] injuries and usurpations, ALL HAVING [*among which appears no solitary fact to contradict the uniform tenor of the rest, but all have*] in direct object the establishment of an absolute tyranny over these states. To prove this, let facts be submitted to a candid world [*for the truth of which we pledge a faith yet unsullied by falsehood*].

He has refused his assent to laws the most wholesome and necessary for the public good.

He has forbidden his governors to pass laws of immediate and pressing importance, unless suspended in their operation till his assent should be obtained; and, when so suspended, he has utterly neglected to attend to them.

He has refused to pass other laws for the accommodation of large districts of people, unless those people would relinquish the right of representation in the legislature, a right inestimable to them, and formidable to tyrants only.

He has called together legislative bodies at places unusual, uncomfortable, and distant from the depository of their public records, for the sole purpose of fatiguing them into compliance with his measures.

He has dissolved representative houses repeatedly [*and continually*] for opposing with manly firmness his invasions on the rights of the people.

He has refused for a long time after such dissolutions to cause others to be elected, whereby the legislative powers, incapable of annihilation, have returned to the people at large for their exercise, the state remaining, in the meantime, exposed to all the dangers of invasion from without and convulsions within.

He has endeavored to prevent the population of these states; for that purpose obstructing the laws for naturalization of foreigners, refusing to pass others to encourage their migrations hither, and raising the conditions of new appropriations of lands.

He has OBSTRUCTED [*suffered*] the administration of justice BY [*totally to cease in some of these states*] refusing his assent to laws for establishing judiciary powers.

He has made [*our*] judges dependent on his will alone for the tenure of their offices, and the amount and payment of their salaries.

He has erected a multitude of new offices, [*by a self-assumed power*] and sent hither swarms of new officers to harass our people and eat out their substance.

He has kept among us in times of peace standing armies [*and ships of war*] without the consent of our legislatures.

He has affected to render the military independent of, and superior to, the civil power.

He has combined with others to subject us to a jurisdiction foreign to our constitutions and unacknowledged by our laws, giving his assent to their acts of pretended legislation for quartering large bodies of armed troops among us; for protecting them by a mock trial from punishment for any murders which they should commit on the inhabitants of these states; for cutting off our trade with all parts of the world; for imposing taxes on us without our consent; for depriving us IN MANY CASES of the benefits of trial by jury; for transporting us beyond seas to be tried for pretended offences; for abolishing the free system of English laws in a neighboring province, establishing therein an arbitrary government, and enlarging its boundaries, so as to render it at once an example and fit instrument for introducing the same absolute rule into these COLONIES [*states*]; for taking away our charters, abolishing our most valuable laws, and altering fundamentally the forms of our governments; for suspending our own legislatures, and declaring themselves invested with power to legislate for us in all cases whatsoever.

He has abdicated government here BY DECLARING US OUT OF HIS PROTECTION, AND WAGING WAR AGAINST US [*withdrawing his governors, and declaring us out of his allegiance and protection*].

He has plundered our seas, ravaged our coasts, burnt our towns, and destroyed the lives of our people.

He is at this time transporting large armies of foreign mercenaries to complete the works of death, desolation and tyranny already begun with circumstances of cruelty and perfidy SCARCELY PARALLELED IN THE MOST BARBAROUS AGES, AND TOTALLY unworthy the head of a civilized nation.

He has constrained our fellow citizens taken captive on the high seas, to bear arms against their country, to become the executioners of their friends and brethren, or to fall themselves by their hands.

He has EXCITED DOMESTIC INSURRECTION AMONG US, AND HAS endeavored to bring on the inhabitants of our frontiers, the merciless Indian savages, whose known rule of warfare is an undistinguished destruction of all ages, sexes and conditions [*of existence*].

[*He has incited treasonable insurrections of our fellow citizens, with the allurements of forfeiture and confiscation of our property.*

He has waged cruel war against human nature itself, violating its most sacred rights of life and liberty in the persons of a distant people who never offended him, captivating and carrying them into slavery in another hemisphere, or to incur miserable death in their transportation hither. This piratical warfare, the opprobrium of INFIDEL powers, is the warfare of the CHRISTIAN king of Great Britain. Determined to keep open a market where MEN should be bought and sold, he has prostituted his negative for suppressing every legislative attempt to prohibit or to restrain this execrable commerce. And that this assemblage of horrors might want no fact of distinguished die, he is now exciting those very people to rise in arms among us, and to purchase that liberty of which he has deprived them, by murdering the people on whom he also obtruded them: thus paying off former crimes committed against the LIBERTIES of one people, with crimes which he urges them to commit against the LIVES of another.]

In every stage of these oppressions we have petitioned for redress in the most humble terms: our repeated petitions have been answered only by repeated injuries.

A prince whose character is thus marked by every act which may define a tyrant is unfit to be the ruler of a FREE people [*who mean to be free. Future ages will scarcely believe that the hardiness of one man adventured, within the short compass of twelve years only, to lay a foundation so broad and so undisguised for tyranny over a people fostered and fixed in principles of freedom.*]

Nor have we been wanting in attentions to our British brethren. We have warned them from time to time of attempts by their legislature to extend AN UNWARRANTABLE [*a*] jurisdiction over US [*these our states*]. We have reminded them of the circumstances of our emigration and settlement here, [*no one of which could warrant so strange a pretension: that these were effected at the expense of our own blood and treasure, unassisted by the wealth or the strength of Great Britain: that in constituting indeed our several forms of government, we had adopted one common king, thereby laying a foundation for perpetual league and amity with them: but that submission to their parliament was no part of our constitution, nor ever in idea, if history may be credited: and,*] we HAVE appealed to their native justice and magnanimity AND WE HAVE CONJURED THEM BY [*as well as to*] the ties of our common kindred to disavow these usurpations which WOULD INEVITABLY [*were likely to*] interrupt our connection and correspondence. They too have been deaf to the voice of justice and of consanguinity. WE MUST THEREFORE [*and when occasions have been given them, by the regular course of their laws, of removing from their councils the disturbers of our harmony, they have, by their free election, re-established them in power. At this very time too, they are permitting their chief magistrate to send over not only soldiers of our common blood, but Scotch and foreign mercenaries to invade and destroy us. These facts have given the last stab to agonizing affection, and manly spirit bids us to renounce forever these unfeeling brethren. We must endeavor to forget our former love for them, and hold them as we hold the rest of mankind, enemies in war, in peace friends. We might have a free and a great people together; but a communication of grandeur and of freedom, it seems, is below their dignity. Be it so, since they will have it. The road to happiness and to glory is open to us, too. We will tread it apart from them, and*] acquiesce in the necessity which denounces our [*eternal*] separation AND HOLD THEM AS WE HOLD THE REST OF MANKIND, ENEMIES IN WAR, IN PEACE FRIENDS!

[2]We therefore the representatives of the United States of America in General Congress assembled, do in the name, and by the authority of the good people of these [*states reject and renounce all allegiance and subjection to the kings of*

We, therefore, the representatives of the United States of America in General Congress assembled, appealing to the supreme judge of the world for the rectitude of our intentions, do in the name, and by the authority of the good people

[2]In this closing section, where additions and deletions have been lengthy, the editors follow Jefferson's device of printing his version in the left column, and the final adopted text in the right column.

Great Britain and all others who may hereafter claim by, through or under them; we utterly dissolve all political connection which may heretofore have subsisted between us and the people or parliament of Great Britain: and finally we do assert and declare these colonies to be free and independent states,] and that as free and independent states, they have full power to levy war, conclude peace, contract alliances, establish commerce, and to do all other acts and things which independent states may of right do.

And for the support of this declaration, we mutually pledge to each other our lives, our fortunes, and our sacred honor.

of these colonies, solemnly publish and declare, that these united colonies are, and of right ought to be free and independent states; that they are absolved from all allegiance to the British crown, and that all political connection between them and the state of Great Britain is, and ought to be, totally dissolved; and that as free and independent states, they have full power to levy war, conclude peace, contract alliances, establish commerce, and to do all other acts and things which independent states may of right do.

And for the support of this declaration, with a firm reliance on the protection of divine providence, we mutually pledge to each other our lives, our fortunes, and our sacred honor.

The Declaration thus signed on the 4th, on paper, was engrossed on parchment, and signed again on the 2d of August.

from Notes on the State of Virginia

from Query VI **Productions, Mineral, Vegetable, and Animal, Buffon and the Theory of Degeneracy**

It is the opinion of Mons. de Buffon[1] that [humankind in America] furnishes no exception to [the theory of the degeneracy of species in the New World]: "Although the savage of the new world is about the same height as man in our world, this does not suffice for him to constitute an exception to the general fact that all living nature has become smaller on that continent. The savage is feeble, and has small organs of generation; he has neither hair nor beard, and no ardor whatever for his female; although swifter than the European because he is better accustomed to running, he is, on the other hand, less strong in body; he is also less sensitive, and yet more timid and cowardly; he has no vivacity, no activity of mind; the activity of his body is less an exercise, a voluntary motion, than a necessary action caused by want; relieve him of hunger and thirst, and you deprive him of the active principle of all his movements; he will rest stupidly upon his legs or lying down entire days. There is no need for seeking further the cause of the isolated mode of life of these savages and their repugnance for society: the most precious spark of the fire of nature has been refused

[1]Georges Louis Leclerc, Count de Buffon (1707–1788), most eminent natural historian of the age who had argued for the inferior stature and strength of New World life forms.

to them; they lack ardor for their females, and consequently have no love for their fellow men: not knowing this strongest and most tender of all affections, their other feelings are also cold and languid; they love their parents and children but little; the most intimate of all ties, the family connection, binds them therefore but loosely together; between family and family there is no tie at all; hence they have no communion, no commonwealth, no state of society. Physical love constitutes their only morality; their heart is icy, their society cold, and their rule harsh. They look upon their wives only as servants for all work, or as beasts of burden, which they load without consideration with the burden of their hunting, and which they compel without mercy, without gratitude, to perform tasks which are often beyond their strength. They have only few children, and they take little care of them. Everywhere the original defect appears: they are indifferent because they have little sexual capacity, and this indifference to the other sex is the fundamental defect which weakens their nature, prevents its development, and—destroying the very germs of life—uproots society at the same time. Man is here no exception to the general rule. Nature, by refusing him the power of love, has treated him worse and lowered him deeper than any animal."[2] An afflicting picture indeed, which, for the honor of human nature, I am glad to believe has no original. Of the Indian of South America I know nothing; for I would not honor with the appellation of knowledge, what I derive from the fables published of them. These I believe to be just as true as the fables of Æsop. This belief is founded on what I have seen of man, white, red, and black, and what has been written of him by authors, enlightened themselves, and writing amidst an enlightened people. The Indian of North America being more within our reach, I can speak of him somewhat from my own knowledge, but more from the information of others better acquainted with him, and on whose truth and judgment I can rely. From these sources I am able to say, in contradiction to this representation, that he is neither more defective in ardor, nor more impotent with his female, than the white reduced to the same diet and exercise: that he is brave, when an enterprize depends on bravery; education with him making the point of honor consist in the destruction of an enemy by stratagem, and in the preservation of his own person free from injury; or perhaps this is nature; while it is education which teaches us to honor force more than finesse: that he will defend himself against an host of enemies, always chusing to be killed, rather than to surrender, though it be to the whites, who he knows will treat him well: that in other situations also he meets death with more deliberation, and endures tortures with a firmness unknown almost to religious enthusiasm with us: that he is affectionate to his children, careful of them, and indulgent in the extreme: that his affections comprehend his other connections, weakening, as with us, from circle to circle, as they recede from the center: that his friendships are strong and faithful to the uttermost extremity: that his sensibility is keen, even the warriors weeping most bitterly on the loss of their children, though in general they endeavour to appear superior to human events: that his vivacity and activity of mind is equal to ours in the same situation; hence his eagerness for hunting, and for games of chance. The women are submitted to unjust drudgery. This I believe is the case with every

[2]The quotation from Buffon was originally published in French.

barbarous people. With such, force is law. The stronger sex therefore imposes on the weaker. It is civilization alone which replaces women in the enjoyment of their natural equality. That first teaches us to subdue the selfish passions, and to respect those rights in others which we value in ourselves. Were we in equal barbarism, our females would be equal drudges. The man with them is less strong than with us, but their woman stronger than ours; and both for the same obvious reason; because our man and their woman is habituated to labour, and formed by it. With both races the sex which is indulged with ease is least athletic. An Indian man is small in the hand and wrist for the same reason for which a sailor is large and strong in the arms and shoulders, and a porter in the legs and thighs.—They raise fewer children than we do. The causes of this are to be found, not in a difference of nature, but of circumstance. The women very frequently attending the men in their parties of war and of hunting, child-bearing becomes extremely inconvenient to them. It is said, therefore, that they have learnt the practice of procuring abortion by the use of some vegetable; and that it even extends to prevent conception for a considerable time after. During these parties they are exposed to numerous hazards, to excessive exertions, to the greatest extremities of hunger. Even at their homes the nation depends for food, through a certain part of every year, on the gleanings of the forest: that is, they experience a famine once in every year. With all animals, if the female be badly fed, or not fed at all, her young perish: and if both male and female be reduced to like want, generation becomes less active, less productive. To the obstacles then of want and hazard, which nature has opposed to the multiplication of wild animals, for the purpose of restraining their numbers within certain bounds, those of labour and of voluntary abortion are added with the Indian. No wonder then if they multiply less than we do. Where food is regularly supplied, a single farm will shew more of cattle, than a whole country of forests can of buffaloes. The same Indian women, when married to white traders, who feed them and their children plentifully and regularly, who exempt them from excessive drudgery, who keep them stationary and unexposed to accident, produce and raise as many children as the white women. Instances are known, under these circumstances, of their rearing a dozen children. An inhuman practice once prevailed in this country of making slaves of the Indians. It is a fact well known with us, that the Indian women so enslaved produced and raised as numerous families as either the whites or blacks among whom they lived.—It has been said, that Indians have less hair than the whites, except on the head. But this is a fact of which fair proof can scarcely be had. With them it is disgraceful to be hairy on the body. They say it likens them to hogs. They therefore pluck the hair as fast as it appears. But the traders who marry their women, and prevail on them to discontinue this practice, say, that nature is the same with them as with the whites. Nor, if the fact be true, is the consequence necessary which has been drawn from it. Negroes have notoriously less hair than the whites; yet they are more ardent. But if cold and moisture be the agents of nature for diminishing the races of animals, how comes she all at once to suspend their operation as to the physical man of the new world, whom the Count acknowledges to be 'à peu près de même stature que l'homme de notre monde,'[3] and to let loose their influence on his moral faculties? How has this 'com-

[3]". . . nearly the same size as men of our world."

bination of the elements and other physical causes, so contrary to the enlargement of animal nature in this new world, these obstacles to the development and formation of great germs,' been arrested and suspended, so as to permit the human body to acquire its just dimensions, and by what inconceivable process has their action been directed on his mind alone? To judge of the truth of this, to form a just estimate of their genius and mental powers, more facts are wanting, and great allowance to be made for those circumstances of their situation which call for a display of particular talents only. This done, we shall probably find that they are formed in mind as well as in body, on the same module with the 'Homo sapiens Europæus'."[4] The principles of their society forbidding all compulsion, they are to be led to duty and to enterprize by personal influence and persuasion. Hence eloquence in council, bravery and address in war, become the foundations of all consequence with them. To these acquirements all their faculties are directed. Of their bravery and address in war we have multiplied proofs, because we have been the subjects on which they were exercised. Of their eminence in oratory we have fewer examples, because it is displayed chiefly in their own councils. Some, however, we have of very superior lustre. I may challenge the whole orations of Demosthenes and Cicero, and of any more eminent orator, if Europe has furnished more eminent, to produce a single passage, superior to the speech of Logan, a Mingo chief, to Lord Dunmore, when governor of this state. And, as a testimony of their talents in this line, I beg leave to introduce it, first stating the incidents necessary for understanding it. In the spring of the year 1774, a robbery and murder were committed on an inhabitant of the frontiers of Virginia, by two Indians of the Shawanee tribe. The neighbouring whites, according to their custom, undertook to punish this outrage in a summary way. Col. Cresap,[5] a man infamous for the many murders he had committed on those much-injured people, collected a party, and proceeded down the Kanhaway in quest of vengeance. Unfortunately a canoe of women and children, with one man only, was seen coming from the opposite shore, unarmed, and unsuspecting an hostile attack from the whites. Cresap and his party concealed themselves on the bank of the river, and the moment the canoe reached the shore, singled out their objects, and, at one fire, killed every person in it. This happened to be the family of Logan, who had long been distinguished as a friend of the whites. This unworthy return provoked his vengeance. He accordingly signalized himself in the war which ensued. In the autumn of the same year, a decisive battle was fought at the mouth of the Great Kanhaway, between

[4]European man.

[5]Michael Cresap (1742–1775), Maryland frontiersman and soldier. When the accuracy of this account was questioned, particularly Cresap's role, Jefferson made further inquiries and in an appendix to the 1800 Philadelphia edition of *Notes* requested that in later editions the section between the words "In the spring of the year 1774 . . ." and ". . . distinguished as a friend of the whites," be changed to read "In the spring of the year 1774, a robbery was committed by some Indians on certain land-adventurers on the river Ohio. The whites in that quarter, according to their custom, undertook to punish this outrage in a summary way. Captain Michael Cresap, and a certain Daniel Great-house, leading on these parties, surprized, at different times, travelling and hunting parties of the Indians, having their women and children with them, and murdered many. Among these were unfortunately the family of Logan, a chief celebrated in peace and war, and long distinguished as the friend of the whites."

the collected forces of the Shawanees, Mingoes, and Delawares, and a detachment of the Virginia militia. The Indians were defeated, and sued for peace. Logan however disdained to be seen among the suppliants. But, lest the sincerity of a treaty should be distrusted, from which so distinguished a chief absented himself, he sent by a messenger the following speech to be delivered to Lord Dunmore.

'I appeal to any white man to say, if ever he entered Logan's cabin hungry, and he gave him not meat; if ever he came cold and naked, and he clothed him not. During the course of the last long and bloody war, Logan remained idle in his cabin, an advocate for peace. Such was my love for the whites, that my countrymen pointed as they passed, and said, 'Logan is the friend of white men.' I had even thought to have lived with you, but for the injuries of one man. Col. Cresap, the last spring, in cold blood, and unprovoked, murdered all the relations of Logan, not sparing even my women and children. There runs not a drop of my blood in the veins of any living creature. This called on me for revenge. I have sought it: I have killed many: I have fully glutted my vengeance. For my country, I rejoice at the beams of peace. But do not harbour a thought that mine is the joy of fear. Logan never felt fear. He will not turn on his heel to save his life. Who is there to mourn for Logan?—Not one.'

Before we condemn the Indians of this continent as wanting genius, we must consider that letters have not yet been introduced among them. Were we to compare them in their present state with the Europeans North of the Alps, when the Roman arms and arts first crossed those mountains, the comparison would be unequal, because, at that time, those parts of Europe were swarming with numbers; because numbers produce emulation, and multiply the chances of improvement, and one improvement begets another. Yet I may safely ask, How many good poets, how many able mathematicians, how many great inventors in arts or sciences, had Europe North of the Alps then produced? And it was sixteen centuries after this before a Newton could be formed. I do not mean to deny, that there are varieties in the race of man, distinguished by their powers both of body and mind. I believe there are, as I see to be the case in the races of other animals. I only mean to suggest a doubt, whether the bulk and faculties of animals depend on the side of the Atlantic on which their food happens to grow, or which furnishes the elements of which they are compounded? Whether nature has enlisted herself as a Cis or Trans-Atlantic partisan? I am induced to suspect, there has been more eloquence than sound reasoning displayed in support of this theory; that it is one of those cases where the judgment has been seduced by a glowing pen: and whilst I render every tribute of honor and esteem to the celebrated Zoologist, who has added, and is still adding, so many precious things to the treasures of science, I must doubt whether in this instance he has not cherished error also, by lending her for a moment his vivid imagination and bewitching language.

So far the Count de Buffon has carried this new theory of the tendency of nature to belittle her productions on this side the Atlantic. Its application to the race of whites, transplanted from Europe, remained for the Abbé Raynal.[6] 'On doit etre etonné (he says) que l'Amerique n'ait pas encore produit un bon poëte, un habile

[6]Guillaume Thomas François Raynal (1713–1796), French historian and *philosophe*.

mathematicien, un homme de genie dans un seul art, ou une seule science.[7] 'America has not yet produced one good poet.' When we shall have existed as a people as long as the Greeks did before they produced a Homer, the Romans a Virgil, the French a Racine and Voltaire, the English a Shakespeare and Milton, should this reproach be still true, we will enquire from what unfriendly causes it has proceeded, that the other countries of Europe and quarters of the earth shall not have inscribed any name in the roll of poets.[8] But neither has America produced 'one able mathematician, one man of genius in a single art or a single science.' In war we have produced a Washington, whose memory will be adored while liberty shall have votaries, whose name will triumph over time, and will in future ages assume its just station among the most celebrated worthies of the world, when that wretched philosophy shall be forgotten which would have arranged him among the degeneracies of nature. In physics we have produced a Franklin, than whom no one of the present age has made more important discoveries, nor has enriched philosophy with more, or more ingenious solutions of the phænomena of nature. We have supposed Mr. Rittenhouse[9] second to no astronomer living: that in genius he must be the first, because he is self-taught. As an artist he has exhibited as great a proof of mechanical genius as the world has ever produced. He has not indeed made a world; but he has by imitation approached nearer its Maker than any man who has lived from the creation to this day.[10] As in philosophy and war, so in government, in oratory, in painting, in the plastic art, we might shew that America, though but a child of yesterday, has already given hopeful proofs of genius, as well of the nobler kinds, which arouse the best feelings of man, which call him into action, which substantiate his freedom, and conduct him to happiness, as of the subordinate, which serve to amuse him only. We therefore suppose, that this reproach is as unjust as it is unkind; and that, of the geniuses which adorn the present age, America contributes its full share. For comparing it with those countries, where genius is most cultivated, where are the most excellent models for art, and scaffoldings for the attainment of science, as France and England for instance, we calculate thus. The United States contain three millions of inhabitants; France twenty millions; and the British islands ten. We produce a Washington, a Franklin, a Rittenhouse. France then should have half a dozen in each of these lines, and Great-Britain half that number, equally eminent. It may be true, that France has: we are but just becoming acquainted with her, and our acquaintance so

[7]"One must be astonished that America has yet to produce one good poet, an able mathematician, or a man of genius in a single art or a single science."

[8]Has the world as yet produced more than two poets, acknowledged to be such by all nations? An Englishman, only, reads Milton with delight, an Italian Tasso, a Frenchman the Henriade, a Portuguese Camouens: but Homer and Virgil have been the rapture of every age and nation: they are read with enthusiasm in their originals by those who can read the originals, and in translations by those who cannot. [Jefferson's note]

[9]David Rittenhouse (1732–1796), Philadelphia mathematician and astronomer.

[10]There are various ways of keeping truth out of sight. Mr. Rittenhouse's model of the planetary system has the plagiary appellation of an Orrery; and the quadrant invented by Godfrey, an American also, and with the aid of which the European nations traverse the globe, is called Hadley's quadrant. [Jefferson's note. Thomas Godfrey (1704–1749), a Philadelphia glazier, was a member of Franklin's Junto. See the selection of poetry.]

far gives us high ideas of the genius of her inhabitants. It would be injuring too many of them to name particularly a Voltaire, a Buffon, the constellation of Encyclopedists, the Abbé Raynal himself, &c. &c. We therefore have reason to believe she can produce her full quota of genius. The present war having so long cut off all communication with Great-Britain, we are not able to make a fair estimate of the state of science in that country. The spirit in which she wages war is the only sample before our eyes, and that does not seem the legitimate offspring either of science or of civilization. The sun of her glory is fast descending to the horizon. Her philosophy has crossed the Channel, her freedom the Atlantic, and herself seems passing to that awful dissolution, whose issue is not given human foresight to scan.

from Query XI
Aborigines, Original Condition and Origin

When the first effectual settlement of our colony was made, which was in 1607, the country from the sea-coast to the mountains, and from Patowmac to the most southern waters of James river, was occupied by upwards of forty different tribes of Indians. Of these the *Powhatans,* the *Mannahoacs,* and *Monacans,* were the most powerful. Those between the sea-coast and falls of the rivers, were in amity with one another, and attached to the *Powhatans* as their link of union. Those between the falls of the rivers and the mountains, were divided into two confederacies; the tribes inhabiting the head waters of Patowmac and Rappahanoc being attached to the *Mannahoacs;* and those on the upper parts of James river to the *Monacans.* But the *Monacans* and their friends were in amity with the *Mannahoacs* and their friends, and waged joint and perpetual war against the *Powhatans.* We are told that the *Powhatans, Mannahoacs,* and *Monacans,* spoke languages so radically different, that interpreters were necessary when they transacted business. Hence we may conjecture, that this was not the case between all the tribes, and probably that each spoke the language of the nation to which it was attached; which we know to have been the case in many particular instances. Very possibly there may have been antiently three different stocks, each of which multiplying in a long course of time, had separated into so many little societies. This practice results from the circumstance of their having never submitted themselves to any laws, any coercive power, any shadow of government. Their only controuls are their manners, and that moral sense of right and wrong, which, like the sense of tasting and feeling, in every man makes a part of his nature. An offence against these is punished by contempt, by exclusion from society, or, where the case is serious, as that of murder, by the individuals whom it concerns. Imperfect as this species of coercion may seem, crimes are very rare among them: insomuch that were it made a question, whether no law, as among the savage Americans, or too much law, as among the civilized Europeans, submits man to the greatest evil, one who has seen both conditions of existence would pronounce it to be the last: and that the sheep are happier of themselves, than under care of the wolves. It will be said, that great societies cannot exist without government. The Savages therefore break them into small ones. . . .

I know of no such thing existing as an Indian monument: for I would not honour with that name arrow points, stone hatchets, stone pipes, and half-shapen images. Of labour on the large scale, I think there is no remain as respectable as would be a common ditch for the draining of lands: unless indeed it be the Barrows, of which many are to be found all over this country. These are of different sizes, some of them constructed of earth, and some of loose stones. That they were repositories of the dead, has been obvious to all: but on what particular occasion constructed, was matter of doubt. Some have thought they covered the bones of those who have fallen in battles fought on the spot of interment. Some ascribed them to the custom, said to prevail among the Indians, of collecting, at certain periods, the bones of all their dead, wheresoever deposited at the time of death. Others again supposed them the general sepulchres for towns, conjectured to have been on or near these grounds; and this opinion was supported by the quality of the lands in which they are found, (those constructed of earth being generally in the softest and most fertile meadow-grounds on river sides) and by a tradition, said to be handed down from the Aboriginal Indians, that, when they settled in a town, the first person who died was placed erect, and earth put about him, so as to cover and support him; that, when another died, a narrow passage was dug to the first, the second reclined against him, and the cover of earth replaced, and so on. There being one of these in my neighbourhood, I wished to satisfy myself whether any, and which of these opinions were just. For this purpose I determined to open and examine it thoroughly. It was situated on the low grounds of the Rivanna, about two miles above its principle fork, and opposite to some hills, on which had been an Indian town. It was of a spheroidical form, of about 40 feet diameter at the base, and had been of about twelve feet altitude, though now reduced by the plough to seven and a half, having been under cultivation about a dozen years. Before this it was covered with trees of twelve inches diameter, and round the base was an excavation of five feet depth and width, from whence the earth had been taken of which the hillock was formed. I first dug superficially in several parts of it, and came to collections of human bones, at different depths, from six inches to three feet below the surface. These were lying in the utmost confusion, some vertical, some oblique, some horizontal, and directed to every point of the compass, entangled, and held together in clusters by the earth. Bones of the most distant parts were found together, as, for instance, the small bones of the foot in the hollow of a scull, many sculls would sometimes be in contact, lying on the face, on the side, on the back, top or bottom, so as, on the whole to give the idea of bones emptied promiscuously from a bag or basket, and covered over with earth, without any attention to their order. The bones of which the greatest numbers remained, were sculls, jaw-bones, teeth, the bones of the arms, thighs, legs, feet, and hands. A few ribs remained, some vertebræ of the neck and spine, without their processes, and one instance only of the bone[1] which serves as a base to the vertebral column. The sculls were so tender, that they generally fell to pieces on being touched. The other bones were stronger. There were some teeth which were judged to be smaller than those of an adult; a scull, which, on a slight view, appeared to be that of an infant, but it fell to pieces on being taken out, so as to prevent satisfactory examination; a rib, and a fragment of the under-jaw of a person about half grown; another rib of an infant; and part of the jaw of a child, which had not yet cut its teeth. This last furnishing the most decisive proof of the burial of children here, I was particular in my attention to it. It was part of the right-half of the under-jaw. The

[1]The os sacrum.

processes, by which it was articulated to the temporal bones, were entire; and the bone itself firm to where it had been broken off, which, as nearly as I could judge, was about the place of the eye-tooth. Its upper edge, wherein would have been the sockets of the teeth, was perfectly smooth. Measuring it with that of an adult, by placing their hinder processes together, its broken end extended to the penultimate grinder of the adult. This bone was white, all the others of a sand colour. The bones of infants being soft, they probably decay sooner, which might be the cause so few were found here. I proceeded then to make a perpendicular cut through the body of the barrow, that I might examine its internal structure. This passed about three feet from its center, was opened to the former surface of the earth, and was wide enough for a man to walk through and examine its sides. At the bottom, that is, on the level of the circumjacent plain, I found bones; above these a few stones, brought from a cliff a quarter of a mile off, and from the river one-eighth of a mile off; then a large interval of earth, then a stratum of bones, and so on. At one end of the section were four strata of bones plainly distinguishable; at the other, three; the strata in one part not ranging with those in another. The bones nearest the surface were least decayed. No holes were discovered in any of them, as if made with bullets, arrows, or other weapons. I conjectured that in this barrow might have been a thousand skeletons. Every one will readily seize the circumstances above related, which militate against the opinion, that it covered the bones only of persons fallen in battle; and against the tradition also, which would make it the common sepulchre of a town, in which the bodies were placed upright, and touching each other. Appearances certainly indicate that it has derived both origin and growth from the accustomary collection of bones, and deposition of them together; that the first collection had been deposited on the common surface of the earth, a few stones put over it, and then a covering of earth, that the second had been laid on this, had covered more or less of it in proportion to the number of bones, and was then also covered with earth; and so on. The following are the particular circumstances which give it this aspect. 1. The number of bones. 2. Their confused position. 3. Their being in different strata. 4. The strata in one part having no correspondence with those in another. 5. The different states of decay in these strata, which seem to indicate a difference in the time of inhumation. 6. The existence of infant bones among them.

But on whatever occasion they may have been made, they are of considerable notoriety among the Indians: for a party passing, about thirty years ago, through the part of the country where this barrow is, went through the woods directly to it, without any instructions or enquiry, and having staid about it some time, with expressions which were construed to be those of sorrow, they returned to the high road, which they had left about half a dozen miles to pay this visit, and pursued their journey. There is another barrow, much resembling this in the low grounds of the South branch of Shenandoah, where it is crossed by the road leading from the Rock-fish gap to Staunton. Both of these have, within these dozen years, been cleared of their trees and put under cultivation, are much reduced in their height, and spread in width, by the plough, and will probably disappear in time. There is another on a hill in the Blue ridge of mountains, a few miles North of Wood's gap, which is made up of small stones thrown together. This has been opened and found to contain human bones, as the others do. There are also many others in other parts of the country.

Great question has arisen from whence came those aboriginal inhabitants of

America? Discoveries, long ago made, were sufficient to shew that a passage from Europe to America was always practicable, even to the imperfect navigation of ancient times. In going from Norway to Iceland, from Iceland to Groenland, from Groenland to Labrador, the first traject is the widest: and this having been practised from the earliest times of which we have any account of that part of the earth, it is not difficult to suppose that the subsequent trajects may have been sometimes passed. Again, the late discoveries of Captain Cook, coasting from Kamschatka to California, have proved that, if the two continents of Asia and America be separated at all, it is only by a narrow streight. So that from this side also, inhabitants may have passed into America: and the resemblance between the Indians of America and the Eastern inhabitants of Asia, would induce us to conjecture, that the former are the descendants of the latter, or the latter of the former: excepting indeed the Eskimaux, who, from the same circumstance of resemblance, and from identity of language, must be derived from the Groenlanders, and these probably from some of the northern parts of the old continent. A knowledge of their several languages would be the most certain evidence of their derivation which could be produced. In fact, it is the best proof of the affinity of nations which ever can be referred to. How many ages have elapsed since the English, the Dutch, the Germans, the Swiss, the Norwegians, Danes and Swedes have separated from their common stock? Yet how many more must elapse before the proofs of their common origin, which exist in their several languages, will disappear? It is to be lamented then, very much to be lamented, that we have suffered so many of the Indian tribes already to extinguish, without our having previously collected and deposited in the records of literature, the general rudiments at least of the languages they spoke. Were vocabularies formed of all the languages spoken in North and South America, preserving their appellations of the most common objects in nature, of those which must be present to every nation barbarous or civilised, with the inflections of their nouns and verbs, their principles of regimen and concord, and these deposited in all the public libraries, it would furnish opportunities to those skilled in the languages of the old world to compare them with these, now, or at any future time, and hence to construct the best evidence of the derivation of this part of the human race. . . .

from Query XIV
Laws

. . . Many of the laws which were in force during the monarchy being relative merely to that form of government, or inculcating principles inconsistent with republicanism, the first assembly which met after the establishment of the commonwealth appointed a committee to revise the whole code, to reduce it into proper form and volume, and report it to the assembly.[1] . . . The following are the most remarkable alterations proposed:

To change the rules of descent, so as that the lands of any person dying intestate shall be divisible equally among all his children, or other representatives, in equal degree.

[1]Jefferson was one of three members of the Committee of Revisors [Ed.].

To make slaves distributable among the next of kin, as other moveables.

To have all public expences, whether of the general treasury, or of a parish or county, (as for the maintenance of the poor, building bridges, court-houses, &c.) supplied by assessments on the citizens, in proportion to their property.

To hire undertakers for keeping the public roads in repair, and indemnify individuals through whose lands new roads shall be opened.

To define with precision the rules whereby aliens should become citizens, and citizens make themselves aliens.

To establish religious freedom on the broadest bottom.

To emancipate all slaves born after passing the act. The bill reported by the revisors does not itself contain this proposition; but an amendment containing it was prepared, to be offered to the legislature whenever the bill should be taken up, and further directing, that they should continue with their parents to a certain age, then be brought up, at the public expence, to tillage, arts or sciences, according to their geniusses, till the females should be eighteen, and the males twenty-one years of age, when they should be colonized to such place as the circumstances of the time should render most proper, sending them out with arms, implements of houshold and of the handicraft arts, feeds, pairs of the useful domestic animals, &c. to declare them a free and independant people, and extend to them our alliance and protection, till they shall have acquired strength; and to send vessels at the same time to other parts of the world for an equal number of white inhabitants; to induce whom to migrate hither, proper encouragements were to be proposed. It will probably be asked, Why not retain and incorporate the blacks into the state, and thus save the expence of supplying, by importation of white settlers, the vacancies they will leave? Deep rooted prejudices entertained by the whites; ten thousand recollections, by the blacks, of the injuries they have sustained; new provocations; the real distinctions which nature has made; and many other circumstances, will divide us into parties, and produce convulsions which will probably never end but in the extermination of the one or the other race.—To these objections, which are political, may be added others, which are physical and moral. The first difference which strikes us is that of colour. Whether the black of the negro resides in the reticular membrane between the skin and scarf-skin, or in the scarf-skin itself; whether it proceeds from the colour of the blood, the colour of the bile, or from that of some other secretion, the difference is fixed in nature, and is as real as if its seat and cause were better known to us. And is this difference of no importance? Is it not the foundation of a greater or less share of beauty in the two races? Are not the fine mixtures of red and white, the expressions of every passion by greater or less suffusions of colour in the one, preferable to that eternal monotony, which reigns in the countenances, that immoveable veil of black which covers all the emotions of the other race? Add to these, flowing hair, a more elegant symmetry of form, their own judgment in favour of the whites, declared by their preference of them, as uniformly as is the preference of the Oranootan for the black women over those of his own species. The circumstance of superior beauty, is thought worthy attention in the propagation of our horses, dogs, and other domestic animals; why not in that of man? Besides those of colour, figure, and hair, there are other physical distinctions proving a difference of race. They have less hair on the face and body. They secrete less by the kidnies, and more by the glands of the skin, which gives them a very strong and disagreeable odour. This greater degree of transpiration renders them more tolerant of heat, and less so of cold, than the whites. Perhaps too a difference of structure in the pulmonary apparatus, which a late ingenious experimentalist has discovered to be the principal regulator of animal heat, may have disabled them from extricating, in the act of inspiration, so much of that fluid from the outer air, or obliged them in expiration, to part with more of it. They seem to require less sleep. A black, after hard labour through the day, will be induced by the slightest amusements to sit up till midnight, or later, though knowing he must be out with the first dawn of the morning. They are at least as brave, and more adventuresome. But this may perhaps proceed from a want of forethought, which prevents their seeing a danger till it be present. When present, they do not go through it with more coolness or steadiness than the whites. They are more ardent after their female: but love seems with them to be more an eager desire, than a tender delicate mixture of sentiment and sensation. Their griefs are transient. Those numberless afflictions, which render it doubtful whether heaven has given life to us in mercy or in wrath, are less felt, and sooner forgotten with them. In general, their existence appears to participate more of sensation than reflection. To this must be ascribed their disposition to sleep when abstracted from their diversions, and unemployed in labour. An animal whose body is at rest, and who does not reflect, must be disposed to sleep of course. Comparing them by their faculties of memory, reason, and imagination, it appears to me, that in memory they are equal to the whites; in reason much inferior, as I think one could scarcely be found capable of tracing and comprehending the investigations of Euclid; and that in imagination they are dull, tasteless, and anomalous. It would be unfair to follow them to Africa for this investigation. We will consider them here, on the same stage with the whites, and where the facts are not apocryphal on which a judgment is to be formed. It will be right to make great allowances for the difference of condition, of education, of conversation, of the sphere in which they move. Many millions of them have been brought to, and born in America. Most of them indeed have been confined to tillage, to their own homes, and their own society: yet many have been so situated, that they might have availed themselves of the conversation of their masters; many have been brought up to the handicraft arts, and from that circumstance have always been associated with the whites. Some have been liberally educated, and all have lived in countries where the arts and sciences are cultivated to a considerable degree, and have had before their eyes samples of the best works from abroad. The Indians, with no advantages of this kind, will often carve figures on their pipes not destitute of design and merit. They will crayon out an animal, a plant, or a country, so as to prove the existence of a germ in their minds which only wants cultivation. They astonish you with strokes of the most sublime oratory; such as prove their reason and sentiment strong, their imagination glowing and elevated. But never yet could I find that a black had uttered a thought above the level of plain narration; never see even an elementary trait of painting or sculpture. In music they are more generally gifted than the whites with accurate ears for tune and time, and they have been found capable of imagining a small catch.[2]

[2]The instrument proper to them is the Banjar, which they brought hither from Africa, and which is the original of the guitar, its chords being precisely the four lower chords of the guitar.

Whether they will be equal to the composition of a more extensive run of melody, or of complicated harmony, is yet to be proved. Misery is often the parent of the most affecting touches in poetry.—Among the blacks is misery enough, God knows, but no poetry. Love is the peculiar œstrum of the poet. Their love is ardent, but it kindles the senses only, not the imagination. Religion indeed has produced a Phyllis Whately; but it could not produce a poet.[3] The compositions published under her name are below the dignity of criticism. The heroes of the Dunciad are to her, as Hercules to the author of that poem. Ignatius Sancho has approached nearer to merit in composition; yet his letters do more honour to the heart than the head. They breathe the purest effusions of friendship and general philanthropy, and shew how great a degree of the latter may be compounded with strong religious zeal. He is often happy in the turn of his compliments, and his stile is easy and familiar, except when he affects a Shandean fabrication of words. But his imagination is wild and extravagant, escapes incessantly from every restraint of reason and taste, and, in the course of its vagaries, leaves a tract of thought as incoherent and eccentric, as is the course of a meteor through the sky. His subjects should often have led him to a process of sober reasoning: yet we find him always substituting sentiment for demonstration. Upon the whole, though we admit him to the first place among those of his own colour who have presented themselves to the public judgment, yet when we compare him with the writers of the race among whom he lived, and particularly with the epistolary class, in which he has taken his own stand, we are compelled to enroll him at the bottom of the column. This criticism supposes the letters published under his name to be genuine, and to have received amendment from no other hand; points which would not be of easy investigation. The improvement of the blacks in body and mind, in the first instance of their mixture with the whites, has been observed by every one, and proves that their inferiority is not the effect merely of their condition of life. We know that among the Romans, about the Augustan age especially, the condition of their slaves was much more deplorable than that of the blacks on the continent of America. The two sexes were confined in separate apartments, because to raise a child cost the master more than to buy one. Cato, for a very restricted indulgence to his slaves in this particular, took from them a certain price. But in this country the slaves multiply as fast as the free inhabitants. Their situation and manners place the commerce between the two sexes almost without restraint.—The same Cato, on a principle of œconomy, always sold his sick and superannuated slaves. He gives it as a standing precept to a master visiting his farm, to sell his old oxen, old waggons, old tools, old and diseased servants, and every thing else become useless. 'Vendat boves vetulos, plaustrum vetus, ferramenta vetera, servum senem, servum morbosum, & si quid aliud supersit vendat.' Cato de re rusticâ. c. 2. The American slaves cannot enumerate this among the injuries and insults they receive. It was the common practice to expose in the island of Æsculapius, in the Tyber, diseased slaves, whose cure was like to become tedious. The Emperor Claudius, by an edict, gave freedom to such of them as should recover, and first declared, that if any person

[3]Jefferson is speaking of Phillis Wheatley (1753–1784), a distinguished poet whose writings appear elsewhere in this anthology [Ed.].

chose to kill rather than to expose them, it should be deemed homicide. The exposing them is a crime of which no instance has existed with us; and were it to be followed by death, it would be punished capitally. We are told of a certain Vedius Pollio, who, in the presence of Augustus, would have given a slave as food to his fish, for having broken a glass. With the Romans, the regular method of taking the evidence of their slaves was under torture. Here it has been thought better never to resort to their evidence. When a master was murdered, all his slaves, in the same house, or within hearing, were condemned to death. Here punishment falls on the guilty only, and as precise proof is required against him as against a freeman. Yet notwithstanding these and other discouraging circumstances among the Romans, their slaves were often their rarest artists. They excelled too in science, insomuch as to be usually employed as tutors to their master's children. Epictetus, Terence, and Phædrus, were slaves. But they were of the race of whites. It is not their condition then, but nature, which has produced the distinction.—Whether further observation will or will not verify the conjecture, that nature has been less bountiful to them in the endowments of the head, I believe that in those of the heart she will be found to have done them justice. That disposition to theft with which they have been branded, must be ascribed to their situation, and not to any depravity of the moral sense. The man, in whose favour no laws of property exist, probably feels himself less bound to respect those made in favour of others. When arguing for ourselves, we lay it down as a fundamental, that laws, to be just, must give a reciprocation of right: that, without this, they are mere arbitrary rules of conduct, founded in force, and not in conscience: and it is a problem which I give to the master to solve, whether the religious precepts against the violation of property were not framed for him as well as his slave? And whether the slave may not as justifiably take a little from one, who has taken all from him, as he may slay one who would slay him? That a change in the relations in which a man is placed should change his ideas of moral right and wrong, is neither new, nor peculiar to the colour of the blacks. Homer tells us it was so 2600 years ago.

> ʽΗμισυ, γαζ τ' ἀρετῆς ἀποαίνυ|αι εὐρύθπα Ζεὺς
> ʽΑνερος, ευτ' ἄν μιν κατὰ δὁλιον ἥμαζ ἔλησιν.
>
> *Od.* 17.323.

> Jove fix'd it certain, that whatever day
> Makes man a slave, takes half his worth away.

But the slaves of which Homer speaks were whites. Notwithstanding these considerations which must weaken their respect for the laws of property, we find among them numerous instances of the most rigid integrity, and as many as among their better instructed masters, of benevolence, gratitude, and unshaken fidelity.—The opinion, that they are inferior in the faculties of reason and imagination, must be hazarded with great diffidence. To justify a general conclusion, requires many observations, even where the subject may be submitted to the Anatomical knife, to Optical glasses, to analysis by fire, or by solvents. How much more then where it is a faculty, not a substance, we are examining; where it eludes the research of all the senses; where the conditions of its existence are various and variously combined; where the effects of those which are present or absent bid defiance to calculation; let me add too, as a circumstance of great tenderness, where our conclusion would degrade a whole race of men from the rank in the scale of beings which their Creator may perhaps have given them. To our reproach it must be said, that though for a century and a half we have had under our eyes the races of black and of red men, they have never yet been viewed by us as subjects of natural history. I advance it therefore as a suspicion only, that the blacks, whether originally a distinct race, or made distinct by time and circumstances, are inferior to the whites in the endowments both of body and mind. It is not against experience to suppose, that different species of the same genus, or varieties of the same species, may possess different qualifications. Will not a lover of natural history then, one who views the gradations in all the races of animals with the eye of philosophy, excuse an effort to keep those in the department of man as distinct as nature has formed them? This unfortunate difference of colour, and perhaps of faculty, is a powerful obstacle to the emancipation of these people. Many of their advocates, while they wish to vindicate the liberty of human nature, are anxious also to preserve its dignity and beauty. Some of these, embarrassed by the question 'What further is to be done with them?' join themselves in opposition with those who are actuated by sordid avarice only. Among the Romans emancipation required but one effort. The slave, when made free, might mix with, without staining the blood of his master. But with us a second is necessary, unknown to history. When freed, he is to be removed beyond the reach of mixture.

from Query XVII
Religion

. . . The error seems not sufficiently eradicated, that the operations of the mind, as well as the acts of the body, are subject to the coercion of the laws. But our rulers can have authority over such natural rights only as we have submitted to them. The rights of conscience we never submitted, we could not submit. We are answerable for them to our God. The legitimate powers of government extend to such acts only as are injurious to others. But it does me no injury for my neighbour to say there are twenty gods, or no god. It neither picks my pocket nor breaks my leg. If it be said, his testimony in a court of justice cannot be relied on, reject it then, and be the stigma on him. Constraint may make him worse by making him a hypocrite, but it will never make him a truer man. It may fix him obstinately in his errors, but will not cure them. Reason and free enquiry are the only effectual agents against error. Give a loose to them, they will support the true religion, by bringing every false one to their tribunal, to the test of their investigation. They are the natural enemies of error, and of error only. Had not the Roman government permitted free enquiry, Christianity could never have been introduced. Had not free enquiry been indulged, at the æra of the reformation, the corruptions of Christianity could not have been purged away. If it be restrained now, the present corruptions will be protected, and new ones encouraged. Was the government to prescribe to us our medicine and diet, our bodies would be in such keeping as our souls are now. Thus in France the emetic was once forbidden as a medicine, and the potatoe as an article of food. Government is just as infallible too when it fixes systems in physics. Galileo was sent to the inquisition for affirming that the earth was a sphere: the government had declared it to be as flat as a trencher, and Galileo was obliged to abjure his error. This error however at length prevailed, the earth became a globe, and Descartes declared it was whirled round its axis by a vortex. The government in which he lived was wise enough to see that this was no question of civil jurisdiction, or we should all have been involved by authority in vortices. In fact, the vortices have been exploded, and the Newtonian principle of gravitation is now more firmly established, on the basis of reason, than it would be were the government to step in, and to make it an article of necessary faith. Reason and experiment have been indulged, and error has fled before them. It is error alone which needs the support of government. Truth can stand by itself. Subject opinion to coercion: whom will you make your inquisitors? Fallible men; men governed by bad passions, by private as well as public reasons. And why subject it to coercion? To produce uniformity. But is uniformity of opinion desireable? No more than of face and stature. Introduce the bed of Procrustes then, and as there is danger that the large men may beat the small, make us all of a size, by lopping the former and stretching the latter. Difference of opinion is advantageous in religion. The several sects perform the office of a Censor morum over each other. Is uniformity attainable? Millions of innocent men, women, and children, since the introduction of Christianity, have been burnt, tortured, fined, imprisoned; yet we have not advanced one inch towards uniformity. What has been the effect of coercion? To make one half the world fools, and the other half hypocrites. To support roguery and error all over the earth. Let us reflect that it is inhabited by a thousand millions of people. That these profess probably a thousand different systems of religion. That ours is but one of that thousand. That if there be but one right, and ours that one, we should wish to see the 999 wandering sects gathered into the fold of truth. But against such a majority we cannot effect this by force. Reason and persuasion are the only practicable instruments. To make way for these, free enquiry must be indulged; and how can we wish others to indulge it while we refuse it ourselves. But every state, says an inquisitor, has established some religion. No two, say I, have established the same. Is this a proof of the infallibility of establishments? Our sister states of Pennsylvania and New York, however, have long subsisted without any establishment at all. The experiment was new and doubtful when they made it. It has answered beyond conception. They flourish infinitely. Religion is well supported; of various kinds, indeed, but all good enough; all sufficient to preserve peace and order: or if a sect arises, whose tenets would subvert morals, good sense has fair play, and reasons and laughs it out of doors, without suffering the state to be troubled with it. They do not hang more malefactors than we do. They are not more disturbed with religious dissensions. On the contrary, their harmony is unparalleled, and can be ascribed to nothing but their unbounded tolerance, because there is no other circumstance in which they differ from every nation on earth. They have made the happy discovery, that the way to silence religious disputes, is to take no notice of them. Let us too give this experiment fair play, and get rid, while we may, of those tyrannical laws. It is true, we are as yet secured against them by the spirit of the times. I doubt whether the people of this country would suffer an execution for heresy, or a three years imprisonment for not comprehending the mysteries of the Trinity. But is the spirit of the people an infallible, a permanent reliance? Is it government? Is this the kind of protection we receive in return for the rights we give up? Besides, the spirit of the times may alter, will alter. Our rulers will become corrupt, our people careless. A single zealot may commence persecutor, and better men be his victims. It can never be too often repeated, that the time for fixing every essential right on a legal basis is while our rulers are honest, and ourselves united. From the conclusion of this war we shall be going down hill. It will not then be necessary to resort every moment to the people for support. They will be forgotten, therefore, and their rights disregarded. They will forget themselves, but in the sole faculty of making money, and will never think of uniting to effect a due respect for their rights. The shackles, therefore, which shall not be knocked off at the conclusion of this war, will remain on us long, will be made heavier and heavier, till our rights shall revive or expire in a convulsion.

from Query XVIII
Manners . . . Effect of Slavery

It is difficult to determine on the standard by which the manners of a nation may be tried, whether *catholic,*[1] or *particular.* It is more difficult for a native to bring to that standard the manners of his own nation, familiarized to him by habit. There must doubtless be an unhappy influence on the manners of our people produced by the existence of slavery among us. The whole commerce between master and slave is a perpetual exercise of the most boisterous passions, the most unremitting despotism on the one part, and degrading submissions on the other. Our children see this, and learn to imitate it; for man is an imitative animal. This quality is the germ of all education in him. From his cradle to his grave he is learning to do what he sees others do. If a parent could find no motive either in his philanthropy or his self-love, for restraining the intemperance of passion towards his slave, it should always be a sufficient one that his child is present. But generally it is not sufficient. The parent storms, the child looks on, catches the lineaments of wrath, puts on the same airs in the circle of smaller slaves, gives a loose to his worst of passions, and thus nursed, educated, and daily exercised in tyranny, cannot but be stamped by it with odious peculiarities. The man must be a prodigy who can retain his manners and morals undepraved by such circumstances. And with what execration should the statesman be loaded, who permitting one half the citizens thus to trample on the rights of the other, transforms those into despots, and these into enemies, destroys the morals of the one part, and the amor patriæ of the other. For if a slave can have a country in this world, it must be any other in preference to that in which he is born to live and labour for another: in which he must lock up the faculties of his nature, contribute as far as depends on his individual endeavours to the evanishment of the human race, or entail his own miserable condition on the endless generations proceeding from him. With the morals of the people, their industry also is destroyed. For in a warm climate, no man will labour for himself who can make another labour for him. This is so true, that of the proprietors of slaves a very small proportion indeed are ever seen to labour. And can the liberties of a nation be thought secure when we have removed their only firm basis, a conviction in the minds of the people that these liberties are of the gift of God? That they are not to be violated but with his wrath? Indeed I tremble for my country when I reflect that God is just: that his justice cannot sleep for ever: that con-

[1]Universal.

sidering numbers, nature and natural means only, a revolution of the wheel of fortune, an exchange of situation, is among possible events: that it may become probable by supernatural interference! The Almighty has no attribute which can take side with us in such a contest.—But it is impossible to be temperate and to pursue this subject through the various considerations of policy, of morals, of history natural and civil. We must be contended to hope they will force their way into every one's mind. I think a change already perceptible, since the origin of the present revolution. The spirit of the master is abating, that of the slave rising from the dust, his condition mollifying, the way I hope preparing, under the auspices of heaven, for a total emancipation, and that this is disposed, in the order of events, to be with the consent of the masters, rather than by their extirpation.

1785

from Letter to James Madison

Oct. 28, 1785

DEAR SIR,—Seven o'clock, and retired to my fireside, I have determined to enter into conversation with you. This is a village of about 15,000 inhabitants when the court is not here, and 20,000 when they are, occupying a valley through which runs a brook and on each side of it a ridge of small mountains, most of which are naked rock. The King comes here, in the fall always, to hunt. His court attend him, as do also the foreign diplomatic corps; but as this is not indispensably required and my finances do not admit the expense of a continued residence here, I propose to come occasionally to attend the King's levees, returning again to Paris, distant forty miles. This being the first trip, I set out yesterday morning to take a view of the place. For this purpose I shaped my course towards the highest of the mountains in sight, to the top of which was about a league.

As soon as I had got clear of the town I fell in with a poor woman walking at the same rate with myself and going the same course. Wishing to know the condition of the laboring poor I entered into conversation with her, which I began by enquiries for the path which would lead me into the mountain: and thence proceeded to enquiries into her vocation, condition and circumstances. She told me she was a day laborer at 8 sous or 4d. sterling the day: that she had two children to maintain, and to pay a rent of 30 livres for her house (which would consume the hire of 75 days), that often she could get no employment and of course was without bread. As we had walked together near a mile and she had so far served me as a guide, I gave her, on parting, 24 sous. She burst into tears of a gratitude which I could perceive was unfeigned because she was unable to utter a word. She had probably never before received so great an aid. This little *attendrissement,*[1] with the solitude of my

[1]Softening of the heart.

walk, led me into a train of reflections on that unequal division of property which occasions the numberless instances of wretchedness which I had observed in this country and is to be observed all over Europe.

The property of this country is absolutely concentred in a very few hands, having revenues of from half a million of guineas a year downwards. These employ the flower of the country as servants, some of them having as many as 200 domestics, not laboring. They employ also a great number of manufacturers and tradesmen, and lastly the class of laboring husbandmen. But after all there comes the most numerous of all classes, that is, the poor who cannot find work. I asked myself what could be the reason so many should be permitted to beg who are willing to work, in a country where there is a very considerable proportion of uncultivated lands? These lands are undisturbed only for the sake of game. It should seem then that it must be because of the enormous wealth of the proprietors which places them above attention to the increase of their revenues by permitting these lands to be labored. I am conscious that an equal division of property is impracticable, but the consequences of this enormous inequality producing so much misery to the bulk of mankind, legislators cannot invent too many devices for subdividing property, only taking care to let their subdivisions go hand in hand with the natural affections of the human mind. The descent of property of every kind therefore to all the children, or to all the brothers and sisters, or other relations in equal degree, is a politic measure and a practicable one. Another means of silently lessening the inequality of property is to exempt all from taxation below a certain point, and to tax the higher portions or property in geometrical progression as they rise. Whenever there are in any country uncultivated lands and unemployed poor, it is clear that the laws of property have been so far extended as to violate natural right. The earth is given as a common stock for man to labor and live on. If for the encouragement of industry we allow it to be appropriated, we must take care that other employment be provided to those excluded from the appropriation. If we do not, the fundamental right to labor the earth returns to the unemployed. It is too soon yet in our country to say that every man who cannot find employment, but who can find uncultivated land, shall be at liberty to cultivate it, paying a moderate rent. But it is not too soon to provide by every possible means that as few as possible shall be without a little portion of land. The small landholders are the most precious part of a state. . . .

from Letter to James Madison

Dec. 20, 1787

. . . I like much the general idea of framing a government, which should go on of itself, peaceably, without needing continual recurrence to the State legislatures. I like the organization of the government into legislative judiciary and executive. I like the power given the legislature to levy taxes, and for that reason solely, I approve of the greater House being chosen by the people directly. For though I think a House so chosen, will be very far inferior to the present Congress, will be very illy qualified to legislate for the Union, for foreign nations, etc., yet this evil does not weigh against the good, of preserving inviolate the fundamental principle, that the people are not to be taxed but by representatives chosen immediately by themselves. I am captivated by the compromise of the opposite claims of the great and little States, of the latter to equal, and the former to proportional influence. I am much pleased, too, with the substitution of the method of voting by person, instead of that of voting by States; and I like the negative given to the Executive, conjointly with a third of either House; though I should have liked it better, had the judiciary been associated for that purpose, or invested separately with a similar power. There are other good things of less moment. I will now tell you what I do not like. First, the omission of a bill of rights, providing clearly, and without the aid of sophism, for freedom of religion, freedom of the press, protection against standing armies, restriction of monopolies, the eternal and unremitting force of the habeas corpus laws, and trials by jury in all matters of fact triable by the laws of the land, and not by the laws of nations. To say, as Mr. Wilson does, that a bill of rights was not necessary, because all is reserved in the case of the general government which is not given, while in the particular ones, all is given which is not reserved, might do for the audience to which it was addressed; but it is surely a *gratis dictum,* the reverse of which might just as well be said; and it is opposed by strong inferences from the body of the instrument, as well as from the omission of the cause of our present Confederation, which had made the reservation in express terms. It was hard to conclude, because there has been a want of uniformity among the States as to the cases triable by jury, because some have been so incautious as to dispense with this mode of trial in certain cases, therefore, the more prudent States shall be reduced to the same level of calamity. It would have been much more just and wise to have concluded the other way, that as most of the States had preserved with jealousy this sacred palladium of liberty, those who had wandered, should be brought back to it; and to have established general right rather than general wrong. For I consider all the ill as established, which may be established. I have a right to nothing, which another has a right to take away; and Congress will have a right to take away trials by jury in all civil cases. Let me add, that a bill of rights is what the people are entitled to against every government on earth, general or particular; and what no just government should refuse, or rest on inference.

The second feature I dislike, and strongly dislike, is the abandonment, in every instance, of the principle of rotation in office, and most particularly in the case of the President. Reason and experience tell us, that the first magistrate will always be re-elected if he may be re-elected. He is then an officer for life. This once observed, it becomes of so much consequence to certain nations to have a friend or a foe at the head of our affairs, that they will interfere with money and with arms. A Galloman, or an Angloman, will be supported by the nation he befriends. If once elected, and at a second or third election out-voted by one or two votes, he will pretend false votes, foul play, hold possession of the reins of government, be supported by the States voting for him, especially if they be the central ones, lying in a compact body themselves, and separating their opponents; and they will be aided by one nation in Europe, while the majority are aided by another. The election of a President of America, some years hence, will be much more interesting to certain nations of Europe, than ever the election of a King of Poland was. Reflect on all the instances in history, ancient and modern, of elective monarchies, and say if they do not give foundation for my fears; the Roman Emperors, the Popes while they were of any importance, the German Emperors till they became hereditary in practice, the Kings of Poland, the Deys of the Ottoman dependencies. It may be said, that if elections are to be attended with these disorders, the less frequently they are repeated the better. But experience says, that to free them from disorder, they must be rendered less interesting by a necessity of change. No foreign power, nor domestic party, will waste their blood and money to elect a person, who must go out at the end of a short period. The power of removing every fourth year by the vote of the people, is a power which they will not exercise, and if they were disposed to exercise it, they would not be permitted. The King of Poland is removable every day by the diet. But they never remove him. Nor would Russia, the Emperor, etc., permit them to do it. Smaller objections are, the appeals on matters of fact as well as laws; and the binding all persons, legislative, executive, and judiciary by oath, to maintain that constitution. I do not pretend to decide, what would be the best method of procuring the establishment of the manifold good things in this constitution, and of getting rid of the bad. Whether by adopting it, in hopes of future amendment; or after it shall have been duly weighed and canvassed by the people, after seeing the parts they generally dislike, and those they generally approve, to say to them, "We see now what you wish. You are willing to give to your federal government such and such powers; but you wish, at the same time, to have such and such fundamental rights secured to you, and certain sources of convulsion taken away. Be it so. Send together deputies again. Let them establish your fundamental rights by a sacrosanct declaration, and let them pass the parts of the Constitution you have approved. These will give powers to your federal government sufficient for your happiness."

This is what might be said, and would probably produce a speedy, more perfect and more permanent form of government. At all events, I hope you will not be discouraged from making other trials, if the present one should fail. We are never permitted to despair of the commonwealth. I have thus told you freely what I like, and what I dislike, merely as a matter of curiosity; for I know it is not in my power to offer matter of information to your judgment, which has been formed after hearing and weighing everything which the wisdom of man could offer on these subjects. I own, I am not a friend to a very energetic government. It is always oppressive. It places the governors indeed more at their ease, at the expense of the people. The late rebellion in Massachusetts[1] has given more alarm, than I think it should have done. Calculate that one rebellion in thirteen States in the course of eleven years, is but one for each State in a century and a half. No country should be so long without one. Nor will any degree of power in the hands of government, prevent insurrections. In England, where the hand of power is heavier than with us, there are seldom half a dozen years without an insurrection. In France, where it is still heavier, but less despotic, as Montesquieu supposes, than in some other countries, and where there are always two or three hundred thousand men ready to

[1]Shays's Rebellion.

crush insurrections, there have been three in the course of the three years I have been here, in every one of which greater numbers were engaged than in Massachusetts, and a great deal more blood was spilt. In Turkey, where the sole nod of the despot is death, insurrections are the events of every day. Compare again the ferocious depredations of their insurgents, with the order, the moderation and the almost self-extinguishment of ours. And say, finally, whether peace is best preserved by giving energy to the government, or information to the people. This last is the most certain, and the most legitimate engine of government. Educate and inform the whole mass of the people. Enable them to see that it is their interest to preserve peace and order, and they will preserve them. And it requires no very high degree of education to convince them of this. They are the only sure reliance for the preservation of our liberty. After all, it is my principle that the will of the majority should prevail. If they approve the proposed constitution in all its parts, I shall concur in it cheerfully, in hopes they will amend it, whenever they shall find it works wrong. This reliance cannot deceive us, as long as we remain virtuous; and I think we shall be so, as long as agriculture is our principal object, which will be the case, while there remains vacant lands in any part of America. When we get piled upon one another in large cities, as in Europe, we shall become corrupt as in Europe, and go to eating one another as they do there. I have tired you by this time with disquisitions which you have already heard repeated by others a thousand and a thousand times; and therefore, shall only add assurances of the esteem and attachment with which I have the honor to be, dear Sir, your affectionate friend and servant.

P.S. The instability of our laws is really an immense evil. I think it would be well to provide in our constitutions, that there shall always be a twelvemonth between the engrossing a bill and passing it; that it should then be offered to its passage without changing a word; and that if circumstances should be thought to require a speedier passage, it should take two-thirds of both Houses, instead of a bare majority.

1829

Letter to Benjamin Banneker[1]

Aug. 30, 1791

SIR

I thank you sincerely for your letter of the 19th instant and for the Almanac it contained. No body wishes more than I do to see such proofs as you exhibit, that nature has given to our black brethren, talents equal to those of the other colors of men, and that the appearance of a want of them is owing merely to the degraded

[1]Banneker was a free-born black, a mathematician, astronomer, and almanac maker. Jefferson was responsible for his appointment to survey the District of Columbia.

condition of their existence, both in Africa & America. I can add with truth, that no body wishes more ardently to see a good system commenced for raising the condition both of their body & mind to what it ought to be, as fast as the imbecility of their present existence, and other circumstances which cannot be neglected, will admit. I have taken the liberty of sending your Almanac to Monsieur de Condorcet, Secretary of the Academy of Sciences at Paris, and member of the Philanthropic society, because I considered it as a document to which your whole colour had a right for their justification against the doubts which have been entertained of them. I am with great esteem, Sir Your most obed[t] humble servt.

1829

Letter to the Marquis de Condorcet[1]

Aug. 30, 1791

Dear Sir

I am to acknolege the receipt of your favor on the subject of the element of measure adopted by France. Candor obliges me to confess that it is not what I would have approved. It is liable to the inexactitude of mensuration as to that part of the quadrant of the earth which is to be measured, that is to say as to one tenth of the quadrant, and as to the remaining nine tenths they are to be calculated on conjectural data, presuming the figure of the earth which has not yet been proved. It is liable too to the objection that no nation but your own can come at it; because yours is the only nation within which a meridian can be found of such extent crossing the 45th. degree and terminating at both ends in a level. We may certainly say then that this measure is uncatholic, and I would rather have seen you depart from Catholicism in your religion than in your Philosophy.

I am happy to be able to inform you that we have now in the United States a negro, the son of a black man born in Africa, and of a black woman born in the United States, who is a very respectable Mathematician. I procured him to be employed under one of our chief directors in laying out the new federal city on the Patowmac, and in the intervals of his leisure, while on that work, he made an Almanac for the next year, which he sent me in his own handwriting, and which I inclose to you. I have seen very elegant solutions of Geometrical problems by him. Add to this that he is a very worthy and respectable member of society. He is a free man. I shall be delighted to see these instances of moral eminence so multiplied as to prove that the want of talents observed in them is merely the effect of their degraded condition, and not proceeding from any difference in the structure of the parts on which intellect depends.

[1]The Marquis de Condorcet (1743–1794) was a mathematician and *philosophe,* an acquaintance of Jefferson in Paris, and the author of *Progress of the Human Spirit* (1794).

I am looking ardently to the completion of the glorious work in which your country is engaged. I view the general condition of Europe as hanging on the success or failure of France. Having set such an example of philosophical arrangement within, I hope it will be extended without your limits also, to your dependants and to your friends in every part of the earth.—Present my affectionate respects to Madame de Condorcet, and accept yourself assurance of the sentiments of esteem & attachment with which I have the honour to be Dear Sir Your most obedt & most humble servt,

TH: JEFFERSON

1986

Letter to Edward Coles[1]

Aug. 25, 1814

Dear Sir,—Your favour of July 31, was duly received, and was read with peculiar pleasure. The sentiments breathed through the whole do honor to both the head and heart of the writer. Mine on the subject of slavery of negroes have long since been in possession of the public, and time has only served to give them stronger root. The love of justice and the love of country plead equally the cause of these people, and it is a moral reproach to us that they should have pleaded it so long in vain, and should have produced not a single effort, nay I fear not much serious willingness to relieve them & ourselves from our present condition of moral & political reprobation. From those of the former generation who were in the fulness of age when I came into public life, which was while our controversy with England was on paper only, I soon saw that nothing was to be hoped. Nursed and educated in the daily habit of seeing the degraded condition, both bodily and mental, of those unfortunate beings, not reflecting that that degradation was very much the work of themselves & their fathers, few minds have yet doubted but that they were as legitimate subjects of property as their horses and cattle. The quiet and monotonous course of colonial life has been disturbed by no alarm, and little reflection on the value of liberty. And when alarm was taken at an enterprize on their own, it was not easy to carry them to the whole length of the principles which they invoked for themselves. In the first or second session of the Legislature after I became a member, I drew to this subject the attention of Col. Bland, one of the oldest, ablest, & most respected members, and he undertook to move for certain moderate extensions of the protection of the laws to these people. I seconded his motion, and, as a younger member, was more spared in the debate; but he was denounced as an enemy of his country, & was treated with the grossest indecorum. From an early stage

[1]Coles, a former neighbor of Jefferson, opposed slavery, so he removed to Illinois with his slaves, where he freed them.

of our revolution other & more distant duties were assigned to me, so that from that time till my return from Europe in 1789, and I may say till I returned to reside at home in 1809, I had little opportunity of knowing the progress of public sentiment here on this subject. I had always hoped that the younger generation receiving their early impressions after the flame of liberty had been kindled in every breast, & had become as it were the vital spirit of every American, that the generous temperament of youth, analogous to the motion of their blood, and above the suggestions of avarice, would have sympathized with oppression wherever found, and proved their love of liberty beyond their own share of it. But my intercourse with them, since my return has not been sufficient to ascertain that they had made towards this point the progress I had hoped. Your solitary but welcome voice is the first which has brought this sound to my ear; and I have considered the general silence which prevails on this subject as indicating an apathy unfavorable to every hope. Yet the hour of emancipation is advancing, in the march of time. It will come; and whether brought on by the generous energy of our own minds; or by the bloody process of St Domingo, excited and conducted by the power of our present enemy, if once stationed permanently within our Country, and offering asylum & arms to the oppressed, is a leaf of our history not yet turned over. As to the method by which this difficult work is to be effected, if permitted to be done by ourselves, I have seen no proposition so expedient on the whole, as that as emancipation of those born after a given day, and of their education and expatriation after a given age. This would give time for a gradual extinction of that species of labour & substitution of another, and lessen the severity of the shock which an operation so fundamental cannot fail to produce. For men probably of any color, but of this color we know, brought from their infancy without necessity for thought or forecast, are by their habits rendered as incapable as children of taking care of themselves, and are extinguished promptly wherever industry is necessary for raising young. In the mean time they are pests in society by their idleness, and the depredations to which this leads them. Their amalgamation with the other color produces a degradation to which no lover of his country, no lover of excellence in the human character can innocently consent. I am sensible of the partialities with which you have looked towards me as the person who should undertake this salutary but arduous work. But this, my dear sir, is like bidding old Priam to buckle the armour of Hector "trementibus æquo humeris et inutile ferruncingi." No, I have overlived the generation with which mutual labors & perils begat mutual confidence and influence. This enterprise is for the young; for those who can follow it up, and bear it through to its consummation. It shall have all my prayers, & these are the only weapons of an old man. But in the mean time are you right in abandoning this property, and your country with it? I think not. My opinion has ever been that, until more can be done for them, we should endeavor, with those whom fortune has thrown on our hands, to feed and clothe them well, protect them from all ill usage, require such reasonable labor only as is performed voluntarily by freemen, & be led by no repugnancies to abdicate them, and our duties to them. The laws do not permit us to turn them loose, if that were for their good: and to commute them for other property is to commit them to those whose usage of them we cannot control. I hope then, my dear sir, you will reconcile yourself to your country and its unfortunate condition; that you will not lessen its stock of sound disposition by withdrawing your portion from the mass. That, on the contrary you will come forward in the public councils, become the missionary of this doctrine truly christian; insinuate & inculcate it softly but steadily, through the medium of writing and conversation; associate others in your labors, and when the phalanx is formed, bring on and press the proposition perseveringly until its accomplishment. It is an encouraging observation that no good measure was ever proposed, which, if duly pursued, failed to prevail in the end. We have proof of this in the history of the endeavors in the English parliament to suppress that very trade which brought this evil on us. And you will be supported by the religious precept, "be not weary in well-doing." That your success may be as speedy & complete, as it will be of honorable & immortal consolation to yourself, I shall as fervently and sincerely pray as I assure you of my great friendship and respect.

1899

Patriot and Loyalist Songs and Ballads

The stirrings of men's hearts, the expression of their hopes, desires, and motives, inspired many songs and ballads during one of the most emotional periods in American history, the years of the Revolutionary War. The quality of such works is clearly uneven, sometimes because the verses were produced in haste, sometimes because they were conceived by men and women who never before had channeled their feelings into poetic form. A number of songs and ballads, however, were written by well-known literary or political figures, including Benjamin Franklin, John Dickinson, Francis Hopkinson, Thomas Paine, Jonathan Odell, Joseph Stansbury, David Humphreys, Philip Freneau, and Joel Barlow.

Such expressions, especially the most popular ones, remain invaluable for us today because their repetition and survival suggest that they successfully captured—and thus reflect for us—the hearts and the minds of the people. As the poet Joel Barlow commented, upon entering the Army, "I do not know, whether I shall do more for the cause in the capacity of chaplain, than I could in that of poet; I have great faith in the influence of songs; and shall continue, while fulfilling the duties of my appointment, to write one now and then, and to encourage the taste for them which I find in the camp. One good song is worth a dozen addresses or proclamations."

Although contemporary estimates suggest that the American public was fairly evenly divided—one-third in favor of rebellion, one-third opposed, and one-third indifferent—there appear to be considerably more extant patriot (pro-American) songs and ballads than loyalist (pro-English). Several factors could account for this difference: the efforts of loyalist writers began later than that of the patriots; the loyalist response was less appealing and exciting, because it was largely defensive and based in traditional values and structures; and the defeat of the loyalists and the extensive destruction of loyalist property may have affected the amount of loyalist material preserved.

Generally, both the patriot and loyalist poets and versifiers seized upon opportunities to persuade the American public that their side was winning while their opponents' victories were spurious, that their military leaders were brilliant while their opponents' military leaders were fools, that they were fighting fairly and courageously while their opponents were savage and cruel. The loyalists also emphasized the illegality of the Revolution; the loss of

English honor, truth, and loyalty; the strength of the British forces; the advantages of union with England; the dangers of an alliance with France; and the generally disreputable nature of Congress and of the Continental army and its leaders. The patriots emphasized specific recent grievances against England (e.g., the Stamp Act and the Townshend Acts, seen as unfair tax measures); the tyranny and corruption of the English Parliament and King; the need to preserve the accomplishments of America's forefathers; the obligation to protect wives and children; pride in the accomplishments of Congress and in the alliance with France; the willingness to die bravely in a good cause; and the urgency of obtaining liberty and independence. Songs and ballads were also written in honor of heroes and traitors, such as George Washington, Nathan Hale, John André, John Champe, and Benedict Arnold.

These songs and ballads became known through broadsides, pamphlets, newspapers, or word-of-mouth among citizens and soldiers, and they were usually written to songs already familiar to Americans. This section does not, of course, reflect the richly diverse poetic heritage of the Revolutionary period, including, for example, odes, elegies, hymns, dialogues, narratives, epistles, satires, parodies, burlesques, and epigrams.

Rosalie Murphy Baum
University of South Florida

PRIMARY WORKS

Frank Moore, ed., *Songs and Ballads of the American Revolution,* 1855, rpt. 1964; Frederick C. Prescott and John H. Nelson, eds., *Prose and Poetry of the Revolution,* 1925, 1969; James H. Pickering, ed., *The World Turned Upside Down: Prose and Poetry of the American Revolution,* 1975.

SECONDARY WORKS

Moses Coit Tyler, *The Literary History of the American Revolution 1763–1783,* 2 vols., 1957.

"PATRIOT" VOICES

The Liberty Song[1]

Come join hand in hand, brave Americans all,
And rouse your bold hearts at fair Liberty's call;
No tyrannous acts, shall suppress your just claim,
Or stain with dishonor America's name.

[1]Very popular song with patriots, sung to tune of "Hearts of Oak' (composed by William Boyce). Unknown if this is the original or corrected (less "bold") version by John Dickinson (1732–1808), Philadelphia lawyer, member of both Continental Congresses, author of *Letters from a Farmer in Pennsylvania* (1768). Eight lines contributed to original version by Arthur Lee (1740–92), diplomat, member of Continental Congress, 1781–85. Parody by Henry Hulton was, in turn, parodied by Benjamin Church.

In freedom we're born, and in freedom we'll live;
    Our purses are ready,
    Steady, Friends, steady,
Not as *slaves,* but as *freemen* our money we'll give.

Our worthy forefathers—let's give them a cheer—
To climates unknown did courageously steer;
Thro' oceans to deserts, for freedom they came,
And, dying, bequeath'd us their freedom and fame.

Their generous bosoms all dangers despis'd,
So highly, so wisely, their birthrights they priz'd;
We'll keep what they gave, we will piously keep,
Nor frustrate their toils on the land or the deep.

The Tree, their own hands had to Liberty rear'd,
They lived to behold growing strong and rever'd;
With transport then cried,—"Now our wishes we gain,
For our children shall gather the fruits of our pain."

How sweet are the labors that freemen endure,
That they shall enjoy all the profit, secure,—
No more such sweet labors Americans know,
If Britons shall reap what Americans sow.

Swarms of placemen and pensioners soon will appear,
Like locusts deforming the charms of the year:
Suns vainly will rise, showers vainly descend,
If we are to drudge for what others shall spend.

Then join hand in hand brave Americans all,
By uniting we stand, by dividing we fall;
In so righteous a cause let us hope to succeed,
For Heaven approves of each generous deed.

All ages shall speak with amaze and applause,
Of the courage we'll show in support of our laws;
To die we can bear,—but to serve we disdain,
For shame is to freemen more dreadful than pain.

This bumper I crown for our sovereign's health,
And this for Britannia's glory and wealth:
That wealth, and that glory immortal may be,
If she is but just, and we are but free.
    In freedom we're born, &c.

1768

Alphabet[1]

A, stands for Americans, who scorn to be slaves;
B, for Boston, where fortitude their freedom saves;
C, stands for Congress, which, though loyal, will be free;
D, stands for defence, 'gainst force and tyranny.
Stand firmly, A and Z,
We swear for ever to be free!

E, stands for evils, which a civil war must bring;
F, stands for fate, dreadful to both people and king;
G, stands for George,[2] may God give him wisdom and grace;
H, stands for hypocrite, who wears a double face.

J, stands for justice, which traitors in power defy,
K, stands for king, who should to such the axe apply;
L, stands for London, to its country ever true,
M, stands for Mansfield,[3] who hath another view.

N, stands for North,[4] who to the House the mandate brings,
O, stands for oaths, binding on subjects not on kings:
P, stands for people, who their freedom should defend,
Q, stands for *quere,*[5] when will England's troubles end?

R, stands for rebels, not at Boston but at home,
S, stands for Stuart,[6] sent by Whigs abroad to roam,
T, stands for Tories, who may try to bring them back,
V, stands for villains, who have well deserved the rack.

W, stands for Wilkes,[7] who us from warrants saved,
Y, for York, the New, half corrupted, half enslaved,
Z, stands for Zero, but means the Tory minions,
Who threatens us with fire and sword, to bias our opinions.
Stand firmly A and Z,
We swear for ever to be free!

1775

[1]Ballad for children.
[2]George III, King of Great Britain and Ireland during Revolutionary War.
[3]William Murray, Earl of Mansfield; favored coercion of the Colonies.
[4]Frederick North, Earl of Guilford (known as Lord North); Prime Minister under George III.
[5]Question.
[6]Charles Edward Stuart, English prince known as the Young Pretender; son of James Francis Edward Stuart, the Old Pretender.
[7]John Wilkes, English political reformer; champion of patriots in American Revolution.

The King's own REGULARS; And their Triumphs over the *Irregulars.* A New SONG, To the Tune of, *An old Courtier of the Queen's, and the Queen's old Courtier.*[1]

Since you all will have singing, and won't be said, nay,
I cannot refuse where you so beg and pray;
So I'll sing you a song—as a body may say.
'Tis of the King's Regulars, who ne'er run way.
O the old Soldiers of the King, and the King's own Regulars.

At Preston Pans[2] we met with some Rebels one day,
We marshall'd ourselves all in comely array:
Our hearts were all stout, and bid our legs stray,
But our feet were wrong headed and took us away.
O the old soldiers, &c.

At Falkirk we resolv'd to be braver,
And recover some credit by better behaviour;
We would not acknowledge feet had done us a favour;
So feet swore they would stand, but—legs ran however.
O the old soldiers, &c.

No troops perform better than we at reviews;
We march and we wheel, and whatever you chuse.
George would see how we fight, and we never refuse;
There we all fight with courage—you may see it in the news.
O the old soldiers, &c.

To Monongehela with fifes and with drums
We march'd in fine order, with cannon and bombs:
That great expedition cost infinite sums;
But a few irregulars cut us all into crumbs.
O the old soldiers, &c.

[1]Song by Benjamin Franklin (1706–1790); text from William B. Willcox, ed., *The Papers of Benjamin Franklin,* vol. 22, 1982.

[2]The poem lists battle after battle in which the British regulars were defeated: at Prestonpans and Falkirk, near Edinburgh, Scotland, where they were defeated by Highlanders in 1746; at the Monongahela River near Fort Duquesne, where the French and Indians defeated General Edward Braddock in 1755; at Fort William Henry on Lake George ("Fort George") and at Fort Oswego on Lake Ontario, where they were defeated by General Louis Joseph de Montcalm in 1757; and at Ticonderoga, where General Montcalm defeated General James Abercrombie in 1758.

It was not fair to shoot at us from behind trees:
If they had stood open as they ought before our great Guns we should have beat them with ease.
They may fight with one another that way if they please;
But it is not regular to stand and fight with such rascals as these.
O the old soldiers, &c.

At Fort George and Oswego, to our great reputation,
We shew'd our vast skill in fortification;
The French fired three guns, of the fourth they had no occasion;
For we gave up those forts, not thro' fear—but mere persuasion.
O the old soldiers, &c.

To Ticonderoga we went in a passion,
Swearing to be revenged on the whole French nation.
But we soon turned tail, without hesitation
Because they fought behind trees, which is not the fashion.
O the old soldiers, &c.

Lord Loudon[3] he was a fine regular General, they say;
With a great regular army he went his way
Against Louisbourg, to make it his prey;
But return'd without seeing it, for he did not feel bold that day.
O the old soldiers, &c.

Grown proud at reviews, great George had no rest,
Each grandsire, he had heard a rebellion suppress.
He wish'd a rebellion, look'd round and saw none,
So resolv'd a rebellion to make of his own—
With the old soldiers, &c.

The Yankees he bravely pitch'd on, because he thought they would not fight,
And so he sent us over to take away their right,
But least they should spoil our review clothes, he cried braver and louder,
"For God's sake, brother kings, don't sell the cowards any powder."
O the old soldiers, &c.

Our General with his council of war did advise,
How at Lexington we might the Yankees surprise.
We march'd—and we march'd—all surpriz'd at being beat;
And so our wise General's plan of surprise was complete.
O the old soldiers, &c.

[3]John Campbell, 4th Earl of Loudoun, failed to attack Louisbourg in 1757.

For fifteen miles they follow'd and pelted us, we scarce had time to
pull a trigger;
But did you ever know a retreat perform'd with more vigour?
For we did it in two hours, which sav'd us from perdition,
'Twas not in *going out* but in *returning* consisted our *expedition.*
O the old soldiers, &c.

Says our General, we were forced to take to our arms in our own
defence:
(For *arms* read *legs,* and it will be both truth and sense.)
Lord Percy[4] (says He) I must say something of him in civility,
And that is, I can never enough praise him for his great—agility.
O the old soldiers, &c.

Of their firing from behind fences, he makes a great pother,
Ev'ry fence has two sides; they made use of one, and we only forgot to
use the other.
That we turn'd our backs and ran away so fast, don't let that disgrace
us;
'Twas only to make good what Sandwich[5] said, "that the Yankees
would not face us."
O the old soldiers, &c.

As they could not get before us, how could they look us in the face?
We took care they should not, by scampering away apace;
That they had not much to brag of, is a very plain case.
For if they beat us in the fight, we beat them in the race.
O the old soldiers of the King, and the King's own Regulars.

1775

The Irishman's Epistle to the Officers and Troops at Boston[1]

By my faith, but I think ye're all makers of bulls,
With your brains in your breeches, your——in your skulls,
Get home with your muskets, and put up your swords,

[4]General Thomas Gage sent Sir Hugh Percy to the relief of the wounded Lieutenant-Colonel Francis Smith and his men in the British retreat from Lexington. J. A. Leo Lemay reports that the English troops under Lord Percy played "Yankee Doodle"—to ridicule the Americans—as they marched out of Boston April 19, 1775, on their way to Lexington.

[5]John Montagu, 3rd Earl of Sandwich, was first Lord of Admiralty, 1771–82.

[1]Song especially popular with patriots.

And look in your books for the meaning of words.
You see now, my honies, how much your mistaken.
For Concord by discord[2] can never be beaten.

How brave ye went out with your muskets all bright,
And thought to be-frighten the folks with the sight;
But when you got there how they powder'd your pums,
And all the way home how they pepper'd your——,
And it is not, honeys, a comical crack,
To be proud in the face, and be shot in the back.

How come ye to think, now, they did not know how.
To be after their firelocks as smartly as you?
Why, you see now, my honies, 'tis nothing at all,
But to pull at the trigger, and pop goes the ball.

And what have you got now with all your designing,
But a town[3] without victuals to sit down and dine in;
And to look on the ground like a parcel of noodles,
And sing, how the Yankees have beaten the Doodles.
I'm sure if you're wise you'll make peace for a dinner,
For fighting and fasting will soon make ye thinner.

Paddy.[4] 1775

The Yankee's Return from Camp[1]

Father and I went down to camp,
  Along with Captain Gooding,
And there we see the men and boys,
  As thick as hasty pudding.
    Chorus—Yankee Doodle, keep it up,
      Yankee Doodle, dandy,
    Mind the music and the step,
      And with the girls be handy.

[2]Pun upon the word "Concord."
[3]Boston.
[4]Slang for an Irishman.
[1]J. A. Leo Lemay identifies "Yankee Doodle" as "an American folk song," probably dating from the late 1740s. Used occasionally in the pre-Revolutionary period by the English to ridicule the Americans, many variants are extant, some of which were very popular with the patriots.

For the origins and significance of the song, see especially Oscar George Theodore Sonneck, compiler, Library of Congress *Report on "The Star-Spangled Banner," "Hail Columbia," "America," "Yankee Doodle"* (Washington, 1909) and J. A. Leo Lemay, "The American Origins of 'Yankee Doodle'" (*William and Mary Quarterly,* July 1976).

And there we see a thousand men,
  As rich as 'Squire David;
And what they wasted every day,
  I wish it could be saved.

The 'lasses they eat every day,
  Would keep an house a winter;
They have as much that, I'll be bound,
  They eat it when they're a mind to.

And there we see a swamping gun,
  Large as a log of maple,
Upon a deuced little cart,
  A load for father's cattle.

And every time they shoot it off,
  It takes a horn of powder,
And makes a noise like father's gun,
  Only a nation louder.

I went as nigh to one myself,
  As Siah's underpinning;
And father when as nigh again,
  I thought the deuce was in him.

Cousin Simon grew so bold,
  I thought he would have cock'd it;
It scar'd me so, I shrink'd it off,
  And hung by father's pocket.

And Captain Davis had a gun,
  He kind of clapt his hand on't,
And stuck a crooked stabbing iron
  Upon the little end on't.

And there I see a pumpkin shell
  As big as mother's bason;
And every time they touch'd it off,
  They scamper'd like the nation.

I see a little barrel too,
  The heads were made of leather,
They knock'd upon't with little clubs,
  And call'd the folks together.

And there was Captain Washington,
And gentlefolks about him,
They say he's grown so tarnal proud,
He will not ride without 'em.

He got him on his meeting clothes,
Upon a slapping stallion,
He set the world along in rows,
In hundreds and in millions.

The flaming ribbons in his hat,
They look'd so taring fine ah,
I wanted pockily to get,
To give to my Jemimah.

I see another snarl of men
A digging graves, they told me,
So tarnal long, so tarnal deep,
They 'tended they should hold me.

It scar'd me so, I hook'd it off,
Nor stop'd, as I remember,
Nor turn'd about, 'till I got home,
Lock'd up in mother's chamber.

1775

Nathan Hale[1]

The breezes went steadily thro' the tall pines,
A saying "oh! hu-ush!" a saying "oh! hu-ush!"
As stilly stole by a bold legion of horse,
For Hale in the bush, for Hale in the bush.

"Keep still!" said the thrush as she nestled her young,
In a nest by the road; in a nest by the road.
"For the tyrants are near, and with them appear,
What bodes us no good, what bodes us no good."

[1]Nathan Hale, captain in the Continental Army, was captured while on a spying mission by British troops under Sir William Howe. Just before his death, he is purported to have said, "I only regret that I have but one life to lose for my country."

The brave captain heard it, and thought of his home,
In a cot by the brook; in a cot by the brook.
With mother and sister and memories dear,
He so gaily forsook; he so gaily forsook.

Cooling shades of the night were coming apace,
The tattoo had beat; the tattoo had beat.
The noble one sprang from his dark lurking place,
To make his retreat; to make his retreat.

He warily trod on the dry rustling leaves,
As he pass'd thro' the wood; as he pass'd thro' the wood;
And silently gain'd his rude launch on the shore,
As she play'd with the flood; as she play'd with the flood.

The guards of the camp, on that dark, dreary night,
Had a murderous will; had a murderous will.
They took him and bore him afar from the shore,
To a hut on the hill; to a hut on the hill.

No mother was there, nor a friend who could cheer,
In that little stone cell; in that little stone cell.
But he trusted in love, from his father above.
In his heart, all was well; in his heart, all was well.

An ominous owl with his solemn base voice,
Sat moaning hard by; sat moaning hard by.
"The tyrant's proud minions most gladly rejoice,
"For he must soon die; for he must soon die."

The brave fellow told them, no thing he restrain'd,
The cruel gen'ral; the cruel gen'ral.
His errand from camp, of the ends to be gain'd,
And said that was all; and said that was all.

They took him and bound him and bore him away,
Down the hill's grassy side; down the hill's grassy side.
'Twas there the base hirelings, in royal array,
His cause did deride; his cause did deride.

Five minutes were given, short moments, no more,
For him to repent; for him to repent;
He pray'd for his mother, he ask'd not another,
To Heaven he went; to Heaven he went.

The faith of a martyr, the tragedy shew'd,
As he trod the last stage; as he trod the last stage.

And Britons will shudder at gallant Hale's blood,
   As his words do presage, as his words do presage.

"Thou pale king of terrors, thou life's gloomy foe,
   Go frighten the slave, go frighten the slave;
Tell tyrants, to you, their allegiance they owe.
   No fears for the brave; no fears for the brave."

1776

Sir Harry's Invitation[1]

Come, gentlemen Tories, firm, loyal, and true,
Here are axes and shovels, and something to do!
      For the sake of our king,
      Come, labour and sing;
You left all you had for his honour and glory,
And he will remember the suffering Tory:
      We have, it is true,
      Some small work to do;
      But here's for your pay
      Twelve coppers a day,
And never regard what the rebels may say,
But throw off your jerkins and labour away.

To raise up the rampart, and pile up the wall,
To pull down old houses and dig the canal,
      To build and destroy—
      Be this your employ,
In the day time to work at our fortifications,
And steal in the night from the rebels your rations:
      The king wants your aid,
      Not empty parade;
      Advance to your places
      Ye men of long faces,
Nor ponder too much on your former disgraces,
This year, I presume, will quite alter your cases.

[1]Ballad by Philip Freneau (1752–1832), often called the "Poet of the Revolution."

The American-born Sir Henry Clinton was left in command of the garrison in New York in 1779 when Sir William Howe embarked on his expedition to conquer Pennsylvania. He was criticized for his treatment of Tory refugees.

Attend at the call of the fifer and drummer,
The French and the Rebels are coming next summer,
And forts we must build
Though Tories are kill'd—
Then courage, my jockies, and work for your king,
For if you are taken no doubt you will swing—
If York we can hold
I'll have you enroll'd;
And after you're dead
Your names shall be read
As who for their monarch both labour'd and bled,
And ventur'd their necks for their beef and their bread.

'Tis an honour to serve the bravest of nations,
And be left to be hang'd in their capitulations—
Then scour up your mortars
And stand to your quarters,
'Tis nonsense for Tories in battle to run,
They never need fear sword, halberd, or gun;
Their hearts should not fail 'em,
No balls will assail 'em,
Forget your disgraces
And shorten your faces,
For 'tis true as the gospel, believe it or not,
Who are born to be hang'd, will never be shot.

1779

Volunteer Boys[1]

Hence with the lover who sighs o'er his wine,
Cloes and Phillises[2] toasting,
Hence with the slave who will whimper and whine,
Of ardor and constancy boasting.
Hence with love's joys,
Follies and noise,
The toast that I give is the Volunteer Boys.

[1]Frank Moore calls this verse "the best convivial" song of the Revolutionary War and attributes its authorship to Henry Archer, a Scotsman who emigrated to America in 1778 and supported the patriot cause.

[2]Names traditionally used for shepherdesses or rustic maids in pastoral poetry.

Nobles and beauties and such common toasts,
Those who admire may drink, sir;
Fill up the glass to the volunteer hosts,
Who never from danger will shrink, sir.
Let mirth appear,
Every heart cheer,
The toast that I give is the brave volunteer.

Here's to the squire who goes to parade
Here's to the citizen soldier;
Here's to the merchant who fights for his trade,
Whom danger increasing makes bolder,
Let mirth appear,
Union is here,
The toast that I give is the brave volunteer.

Here's to the lawyer, who, leaving the bar,
Hastens where honor doth lead, sir,
Changing the gown for the ensigns of war,
The cause of his country to plead, sir.
Freedom appears,
Every heart cheers,
And calls for the health of the law volunteers.

Here's to the soldier, though batter'd in wars,
And safe to his farm-house retir'd:
When called by his country, ne'er thinks of his scars,
With ardor to join us inspir'd.
Bright fame appears,
Trophies uprear,
To veteran chiefs who became volunteers.

Here's to the farmer who dares to advance
To harvests of honor with pleasure;
Who with a slave the most skilful in France,
A sword for his country would measure.
Hence with cold fear,
Heroes rise here;
The ploughman is chang'd to the stout volunteer.

Here's to the peer, first in senate and field,
Whose actions to titles add grace, sir;
Whose spirit undaunted would never yet yield
To a foe, to a pension or place, sir.
Gratitude here,
Toasts to the peer,
Who adds to his titles, "the brave volunteer."

Thus the bold bands for old Jersey's defence,
The muse hath with rapture review'd, sir;
With our volunteer boys, as our verses commence,
With our volunteer boys they conclude, sir.
Discord or noise,
Ne'er damp our joys,
But health and success to the volunteer boys.

1780

"LOYALIST" VOICES

When Good Queen Elizabeth Governed the Realm[1]

When good Queen Elizabeth govern'd the realm,
And Burleigh's[2] sage counsels directed the helm,
In vain Spain and France our conquests oppos'd;
For Valor conducted what Wisdom propos'd.
Beef and beer was their food;
Love and Truth arm'd their band;
Their courage was ready—
Steady, boys, steady—
To fight and to conquer by sea and by land.

But since tea and coffee, so much to our grief,
Have taken the place of strong beer and roast beef,
Our laurels have wither'd, our trophies been torn;
And the lions of England French triumphs adorn.
Tea and slops are their food;
They unnerve every hand—
Their courage unsteady
And not always ready—
They often are conquer'd by sea and by land.

St. George views with transport our generous flame:
"My sons, rise to glory, and rival my fame.
Ancient manners again in my sons I behold

[1]Song by Joseph Stansbury (1742–1809), with Dr. Jonathan Odell (1737–1818), one of the two best-known loyalist poets. Probably composed for a meeting of the Sons of St. George in New York in 1774 or 1775, to the tune of "Hearts of Oak."

[2]William Cecil, 1st Baron Burleigh (1520–98), advisor to Queen Elizabeth.

And this age must eclipse all the ages of gold."
Beef and beer are our food;
Love and Truth arm our band;
Our courage is steady
And always is ready
To fight and to conquer by sea and by land.

While thus we regale as our fathers of old,
Our manners as simple, our courage as bold,
May Vigor and Prudence our freedom secure
Long as rivers, or ocean, or stars shall endure.
Beef and beer are our food;
Love and Truth arm our band;
Our courage is steady,
And always is ready
To fight and to conquer by sea and by land.

1774 or 1775

Song for a Fishing Party near Burlington, on the Delaware, in 1776[1]

How sweet is the season, the sky how serene;
On Delaware's banks how delightful the scene;
The Prince of the Rivers, his waves all asleep,
In silence majestic glides on to the deep.

Away from the noise of the fife and the drum,
And all the rude din of Bellona we come;
And a plentiful store of good humor we bring
To season our feast in the shade of Cold Spring.

A truce then to all whig and tory debate;
True lovers of freedom, contention we hate:
For the demon of discord in vain tries his art
To possess or inflame a true *Protestant*[2] heart.

True Protestant friends to fair Liberty's cause,
To decorum, good order, religion and laws,

[1]Song by Dr. Jonathan Odell, described by Moses Coit Tyler as "the most powerful and unrelenting of the Tory satirists."

[2]Dr. Odell appended a note to the third verse: "*Protestant* was a term adopted by a circle of Loyalists."

From avarice, jealousy, perfidy, free;
We wish all the world were as happy as we.

We have wants, we confess, but are free from the care
Of those that abound, yet have nothing to spare:
Serene as the sky, as the river serene,
We are happy to want envy, malice, and spleen.

While thousands around us, misled by a few,
The phantoms of pride and ambition pursue,
With pity their fatal delusion we see;
And wish all the world were as happy as we!

1776

Burrowing Yankees[1]

Ye Yankees who, mole-like, still throw up the earth,
And like them, to your follies are blind from your birth;
Attempt not to hold British troops at defiance,
True Britons, with whom you pretend an alliance.

Mistake not; such blood ne'er run in your veins,
'Tis no more than the dregs, the lees, or the drains:
Ye affect to talk big of your hourly attacks;
Come on! and I'll warrant, we'll soon see your backs.

Such threats of bravadoes serve only to warm
The true British hearts, you ne'er can alarm;
The Lion once rous'd, will strike such a terror,
Shall show you, poor fools, your presumption and error.

And the time will soon come when your whole rebel race
Will be drove from the lands, nor dare show your face:
Here's a health to great *George,* may he fully determine,
To root from the earth all such insolent vermin.

1776

[1]Song especially popular with loyalists.

A Birthday Song for the King's Birthday, June 4, 1777[1]

Time was when America hallow'd the morn
On which the lov'd monarch of Britain was born,
Hallow'd the day, and joyfully chanted
        God save the King!
Then flourish'd the blessings of freedom and peace,
And plenty flow'd in with a yearly increase.
Proud of our lot we chanted merrily
        Glory and joy crown the King!

With envy beheld by the nations around,
We rapidly grew, nor was anything found
Able to check our growth while we chanted
        God save the King!
O bless'd beyond measure, had honor and truth
Still nurs'd in our hearts what they planted in youth!
Loyalty still had chanted merrily
        Glory and joy crown the King!

But see! how rebellion has lifted her head!
How honor and truth are with loyalty fled!
Few are there now who join us in chanting
        God save the King!
And see! how deluded the multitude fly
To arm in a cause that is built on a lie!
Yet are we proud to chant thus merrily
        Glory and joy crown the King!

Though faction by falsehood awhile may prevail,
And loyalty suffers a captive in jail,
Britain is rous'd, rebellion is falling:
        God save the King!
The captive shall soon be releas'd from his chain;
And conquest restore us to Britain again,
Ever to join in chanting merrily
        Glory and joy crown the King!

1777

[1]Song by Dr. Jonathan Odell. Dr. Odell also wrote a birthday ode for the King's birthday in 1776.

A Song[1]

Here's a bumper, brave boys, to the health of our king,
Long may he live, and long may we sing,
In praise of a monarch who boldly defends
The laws of the realm, and the cause of his friends.
Then cheer up, my lads, we have nothing to fear,
While we remain steady,
And always keep ready,
To add to the trophies of this happy year.

The Congress did boast of their mighty ally,
But George does both France and the Congress defy;
And when Britons unite, there's no force can withstand
Their fleets and their armies, by sea and on land.

Thus supported, our cause we will ever maintain,
And all treaties with rebels will ever disdain;
Till reduc'd by our arms, they are forc'd to confess,
While ruled by Great Britain they ne'er knew distress.

Then let us, my boys, Britain's right e'er defend,
Who regards not her rights, we esteem not our friend;
Then, brave boys, we both France and the Congress defy,
And we'll fight for Great Britain and George till we die.
Then cheer up, my lads, we have nothing to fear,
While we remain steady,
And always keep ready,
To add to the trophies of this happy year.

1779

An Appeal[1]

The old English cause knocks at every man's door,
And bids him stand up for religion and right;
It addresses the rich as well as the poor;
And fair liberty, bids them, like Englishmen fight.
And suffer no wrong,
From a rebel throng,
Who, if they're not quelled, will enslave us ere long;

[1]Song sung to the tune of "Hearts of Oak."
[1]Song sung to the tune of "The Cat Purse"; very popular with Loyalists.

Most bravely then let us our liberty prize,
Nor suffer the Congress to blind all our eyes;
Or each rebel cut-purse, will soon give us law,
For they are as bad as a Tyler or Straw.[2]
From France, D'Estaing[3] to America has come.
The French banditti will rob our estates;
These robbers are all protected by Rome,[4]
Consult but their annals, record but their dates,
It's their politics
To burn heretics,
Or poison by water that's fetch'd from the Styx.[5]
Let Frenchified rebels, in vain then attempt
To bring our own church, or our king to contempt;
For no rebel cut-purse shall e'er give us law,
Should they prove as daring as Tyler or Straw.

The farces of Rome, with carrying her hosts,
Are laugh'd at and jeer'd by the learned and wise,
And all her thin tinsels apparently lost,
Her stories of relics, and sanctified lies.
Each ignorant joke
Believe, or you smoke,
And if we are conquer'd we receive the Pope's yoke;
But despising the counsels of Adams and Lee,[6]
As loyal Americans, we'll die or be free.
For no rebel cut-throat shall e'er give us law.
Should they prove as daring as Tyler or Straw.

Let curses most vile, and anathemas roar,
Let half-ruin'd France, to the Pope tribute pay;
Britain's thundering cannon, shall guard safe our shore;
Great George shall defend us, none else we'll obey.
Then France, join'd by Spain,
May labor in vain,
For soon the Havana[7] shall be ours again.
The French then will scamper and quit every state,
And find themselves bubbled, when *morbleu*[8] it's too late.
For no Frenchman, or rebel imp of the law,
In our old constitution can point out a flaw.

1780

[2]Walter Tyler, English leader of Peasants' Revolt (1381); Jack Straw, one of the leaders of Tyler's rebellion.

[3]Comte Jean Baptiste Charles Henri Hector d'Estaing, naval commander of French squadron aiding the Patriots.

[4]The loyalists used the colonists' fear of the Roman Catholic Church to suggest the dangers of the patriots' accepting military assistance from the French.

[5]River in Hades.

[6]Richard Henry Lee of Virginia, Samuel Adams of Massachusetts Bay, both prominent defenders of colonial rights.

[7]Country.

[8]The devil!

Contested Boundaries, National Visions: Writings on "Race," Identity, and "Nation"

Half-humorously but with the seriousness of one socially and legally disempowered, Abigail Adams added a "by the way" in her letter (March 31, 1776) to her husband John Adams, who was in Philadelphia attending the emergency sessions of the Continental Congress. "[B]y the way," she wrote, "in the new Code of Laws which I suppose it will be necessary for you to make I desire you would Remember the Ladies, and be more generous and favourable to them than your ancestors." Adams's plea here, for equal rights and equal justice under the law, went unheeded. John Adams remarked—in a tone which he probably considered jocular—in his return letter (April 14, 1776), "As to your extraordinary Code of Laws, I cannot but laugh. We have been told that our Struggle has loosened the bands of Government every where. That Children and Apprentices were disobedient—that schools and Colledges were grown turbulent—that Indians slighted their Guardians and Negroes grew insolent to their Masters. But your Letter was the first Intimation that another Tribe more numerous and powerfull than all the rest were grown discontented."

This remarkable exchange between two remarkable people is perhaps the best-known exchange of the era, but it is by no means the only spoken or written evidence available to us about the extent to which people in non-dominant social and legal circumstances—particularly women, African-Americans, and Native Americans in Anglo-America—willingly spoke about and thus openly confronted the boundaries set for them by the white, elite group of men whose visions of what they considered "just" and "good" constructed the social formation that all citizens, whether or not they could vote, would inhabit. The men in the Continental Congress and later, at the Constitutional Convention, expressed their concerns about equality and laws, rights and obligations. And as the Federalist and Anti-Federalist writings attest, these issues were not, even for the dominant group, easily agreed upon. For the non-dominant group, finding opportunity to speak at all about these issues was difficult. What is clear is that for both dominant and socially subjected groups, what to make of issues of "race," identity, and "nation"—and whose race, identity, and nation would dominate—was hotly contested.

When Prince Hall, speaking of the "chequered world we live in," called upon his fellow masons of his African Lodge (June 24, 1797) for forbearance and patience under their trials, he insisted nonetheless that they should "worship no man" but that they should "Worship God," instead. The Mohegan Samson Occom wrote in his autobiography that he "found Serenity and Pleasure of Soul, in Serving God" and that he thereafter felt "an uncommon Pity and Compassion to my Poor Brethren According to the Flesh." Yet he nonetheless concluded his comments in anguished testimony—"I speak like a fool, but I am Constrained"—about the "difference" the whites made "between me and other missionaries" when paying them and giving credit for missionary work. African-American Lemuel Haynes, having learned from an early age the Calvinist teachings of the whites in his locale, followed their evangelical faith practice. But he also contested the congressional assertion, "We hold these truths to be self-evident, that all men are created Equal," by pointing to what he considered, given a purported "equality," the illegality of the slave trade and the hypocrisy of the white men who quarreled with Britain's oppression while retaining blacks in bondage. There were not *many* voices that spoke out against the dominant group, but the voices clearly represent lines of argument made by feminists, evangelicals, African-Americans, and Native Americans that have, through the years since, continued the critique of what became the established culture. These speakers and writers, self-conscious about their own "low" status, found useful ways—through the vehicles of logical argumentation, legal contest, and an evangelical religion which provided many women and blacks especially a strong sense of identity and community—to call into question the constructions of "race," "nation," and identity that were being established as a founding ideology while the colonies were becoming the so-called "united" states.

Given the population they represented, the number of women, African-Americans, and Native Americans who participated in print culture was, though growing, still very small at the end of the eighteenth and beginning of the nineteenth centuries. Indeed few surviving texts from the era reveal what life was like for these groups from what can be called the "inside" vantage-point. This should come as no surprise, given the fact that the very few blacks and Native Americans who could read and write English at all did so largely at the discretion of the whites who had trained them. Whites would not likely have permitted writings blatantly critical of the dominant culture to reach print.

For many women, Native Americans, and African-Americans, the oral tradition constituted the primary mode of artistic expression, as it had for centuries. The centrality of oral expression in African society, for example, encouraged the continued vitality of such forms among African-American slaves. In fact, that whites were generally deaf to the subtle complexity of black oral expression permitted African-American culture to maintain a resilience, integrity, and subversive thrust that played an important role in the spiritual survival of the slaves.

Those members of non-dominant cultures who did write adopted, consciously or unconsciously, a variety of techniques that enabled their works to be published. For example, Jupiter Hammon, Phillis Wheatley, and Samson Occom—all of whom seem to have been truly pious—found religious narratives, poems, and sermons to be acceptable to white readers. Yet even these writers were forced into accepting a "lower" status for their races. Wheatley's constant self-reference as an "Ethiop" and Occom's allusions to the Indian Moses Paul as a "despised Creature" served to reinforce the dominant whites' views, as if these non-whites accepted their supposed inferior status. On the other hand, Wheatley managed to use her position as a Christianized "Ethiop" to speak to the Cambridge students about a Christianity that offered equality to all who embraced belief. The forthright declaration of religious faith that often entailed these writers' apparent admission of the superiority of white Christian culture ironically provided them with the confidence to call white society to task for not living up to its own ideals. The problem such writers faced was finding the means to assert the worthiness of those for whom they stood without flatly contradicting the notions, almost universally held among whites, that people of color were inferior and thus their writings were not worth reading.

Thomas Jefferson, though he seems to have supported abolition, was fairly typical in his comments about the lack of imagination he attributed to blacks. Of the writings of Phillis Wheatley he commented in *Notes on the State of Virginia* (1787) that "Religion . . . has produced a Phyllis Whately; but it could not produce a poet. The compositions published under her name are below the dignity of criticism." Even Jefferson's comments about abolition register his white-centered thinking. Supporting abolition in 1780, Jefferson wrote, "The whole commerce between master and slave is a perpetual exercise of the most boisterous passions. . . . The man must be a prodigy who can retain his manners and morals undepraved by such circumstances." Jefferson favored abolition, yet his phrasing here, as elsewhere in his writings (most notably in his *Notes on the State of Virginia*), suggests a racism ethnocentrically based and patriarchally established. To be sure, Jefferson was speaking of slavery's harmful effects, but he was concerned with its effects *upon whites* rather than upon the blacks held in subjection. Like Jefferson, most whites who addressed the experiences of non-whites spoke from their own limited viewpoints. The few exceptions, like John Woolman or Fray Carlos José Delgado, seem to point up more dramatically the ignorance and insensitivity of most white commentators.

This is not to suggest that print culture of the era represented solely the concerns of race and identity to the exclusion of imaginative writings. The American Revolution produced significant changes in print culture in the colonies, not only in the increase in printing presses the colonists supported but in the readership and the authorship of works printed. Featuring fiction, advice columns, literary criticism, and poems, literary magazines by the dozens saw print for the first time during the last decade and a half of the eighteenth century. Some folded quickly; others began to flourish as printers and authors searched for the right formula that would attract the ever-growing readership. To a greater extent than we might expect, these magazines were supported by nonelite groups—artisans, servants, and other laborers—as much as they were by members of the elite classes. Late eighteenth-century Americans, representatives of a new and nominally democratic republic, were in the midst of witnessing a change in literary culture, from one of literary patronage to one of the literary marketplace.

For those who sought a livelihood by the pen, the change was both good and bad. A writer might no longer have to seek a literary patron for financial support, both for personal costs and the costs of printing the works dedicated to the patron. A writer might no longer have to dedicate his—and occasionally her—work to a duke or an earl with the hope that the patron liked the work enough to continue financial assistance. That is, the means of literary production—the author's support and press costs—were no longer solely in the hands of the elite class of people. Thus, an author could perhaps more freely express his or her views to the reading public. Yet the author was, in the absence of the system of patronage, forced continually to meet the pleasure of a diverse reading public. No longer was the goodwill of one or two people sought. Instead, the goodwill of all "good, courteous readers" (as the dedication formula often went) would condition the success or failure of the literary venture. To enter the republic of letters, authors had to accept the right of choice expected by an increasing, financially mobile readership. The marketplace would determine the literary text. And the marketplace itself was subject to change as the political and economic climate shifted.

Most writers, men and women, seem to have promoted the values held by government leaders. Their writings, they often openly insisted, reflected the conception that an educated citizenry, free of the vices of luxury and corruption, would seek to read fine literature. In appreciating "good" literature, the citizenry would improve in its general level of taste, manners, and mores. The last quality was key: most writers of imaginative literature attempted to convince their readers that their works would assist in moral improvement. Several means were used to accomplish this end, one of the most popular being the insistence upon showing Europeanized depravity in order to warn others—especially, writers argued, young women—away from European vice. For instance, Susanna Rowson insisted in the preface to *Charlotte Temple* (American edition, 1794), a novel about a seduction, that the book was designed for "the perusal of the young and thoughtless of the fair sex." The preface continues "I wrote with a mind anxious for the happiness of that sex whose morals and conduct have so powerful an influence on mankind in general." This prefatory formula—with its emphasis upon moral edification, especially in young women—was used again and again in novels and poems throughout the era.

The formula was an American transformation of that used in English fiction, in which dedications asserted the instructive value of the fiction (often called "the history," or "tale of truth") that followed. The insistence that the reading of fiction could inculcate virtuous action and a "high" moral sense complemented the neoclassical aesthetic, a very pragmatic theory of art, established by poets earlier in the century. Poets and fiction-writers alike asserted that their works could reform the manners and morals of their age. Readers of fiction, they insisted, could learn about virtue by watching characters struggle to attain—or retain—their own. British novelist Henry Fielding had phrased it this way, in the prefatory chapter "Containing the exordium" in his last novel, *Amelia* (1751):

To retrieve the ill consequences of a foolish conduct, and by struggling manfully with distress to subdue it, is one of the noblest efforts of wisdom and virtue. . . . By examining carefully the several gradations which conduce to bring every model to perfection, we learn truly to know that science in which the model is formed: as histories of this kind, therefore, may properly be called models of HUMAN LIFE, so, by observing minutely the several incidents which tend to the catastrophe or completion of the whole, and minute causes whence those incidents are produced, we shall best be instructed in this most useful of all arts, which I call the ART of LIFE.

Whether or not authors believed in this didactic mimetic (imitative) theory is difficult to determine. What is apparent, however, is that American and English writers alike found the formula successful for attracting and keeping a wide readership, so most tended to assert in one way or another this neoclassic aesthetic. Those writers who did not do so in America, like Charles Brockden Brown, did not succeed.

Brown became interested in the European theoretical inquiry about human psychology and the unconscious that emerged as followers of John Locke (such as Anthony Ashley Cooper, third Earl of Shaftesbury, and Francis Hutcheson) began to develop their own theories about human nature. These theorists argued in behalf of a moral faculty in man. Human emotions were common to all people, they insisted, so artists should seek to instruct this moral sense or faculty. Emotions did not need to be suppressed so much as "improved" for the sake of the social fabric. Mankind could gain refinement in judgment and taste if authors would work to develop what they called the moral sentiment. By the end of the eighteenth century, this theory was transformed into an argument in behalf of the exploration of the interior rather than the "correcting" of the exterior of the human being. English and continental writers were taking up the cause of sentiment, creating works that might excite the passions and emotions of their readers. For some writers, the exploration of human sensibility led to gothicism, an aesthetic movement that favored the natural and primitive, the wild and uncontrolled, in mankind and nature. It was this newer tradition that intrigued Charles Brockden Brown.

Brown could never, while he lived, find a readership in the United States, for he refused to acquiesce to what he considered "the censorious eye of the world" that would always seek to condemn a literature that explored human psychology rather than corrected citizens' behavior. Brown's constant frustrations with the literary marketplace found vent in the essays he published in his own literary magazines. In one entitled "Desultory Observations On The Sensibilities and Eccentricities of Men of Genius: With Remarks on Poets" published in his *Literary Magazine and American Register* (1807), Brown averred that "To be in constant terror of exceeding the cold bounds of propriety, to be perpetually on the watch against any transient extravagance of mind, is not to be a poet. . . . That chilly philosophy which demands the reconcilement of qualities nearly incompatible has always appeared to me far from true wisdom." Like many an author after him, Charles Brockden Brown would not submit to the notion that art should always attempt to instruct the populace. He would not acquiesce to a fiction conditioned by the marketplace. For Brown, identity was not a national issue but a personal one.

What becomes clear from an examination of the writings of the latter part of the eighteenth and early nineteenth centuries is that, even as the states, as political entities, were testing the extent to which they could be "united," the peoples of the United States—red, white, and black—were themselves questioning the constructions of identity, "race," and nationhood that were emerging from the necessity to found a government quickly and securely, before the new system could collapse. We can only speculate about the kind of "nation" the United States might have been had African-Americans, Native Americans, and women been given the franchise from the start. The writings of the era attest to the resilience, vitality, and imaginative power of those writers whose works were, through the vehicle of a growing print culture, reaching an increasingly diverse audience.

Carla Mulford
Pennsylvania State University

Jupiter Hammon 1711–1806?

With the important exception of Lucy Terry, whose "Bars Fight" (included in this anthology) seems to have been well-known, Jupiter Hammon was probably the first known, published black American versifier. His *Evening Thought: Salvation by Christ, With Penetential Cries,* a series of twenty-two quatrains, appeared as a broadside in 1760.

Hammon was born a slave on the Manor House estate of Henry Lloyd at Lloyd's Neck (or Queen's Village) on Long Island, New York, where he and other slave children were offered a rudimentary education at a school built on the premises. Biographical facts about him are most scarce, but it seems clear enough that, at an early age, Hammon became religiously oriented, and, as has been suspected, may well have done some Christian exhorting to whatever black and white audiences he could gather. When he was 22 years old, he purchased a Bible from his master for seven shillings and sixpence. All of his known writings in prose and verse are exclusively pietist.

When Henry Lloyd died in 1763, Hammon became the property of Joseph Lloyd, a patriot who was obliged to flee encircling British troops and race with his family and slaves to Stamford and later Hartford, Connecticut. There Hammon published three more verses, two of them appended to prose sermonizings. At Hartford, too, he published "An Essay on Ten Virgins," advertised in *The Connecticut Courant* for December 14, 1779; as no text has yet been found, it is not known if this piece is prose or verse. Composed originally at "Queen's Village, 24th. Sept. 1786," while he was a slave to John Lloyd, Junior, Hammon's prose *Address to the Negroe: In the State of New-York* was printed in 1787 in New York and reprinted the same year in Philadelphia and again in 1806 in New York. He is also thought to have written a set of verses that celebrated the 1782 visit of Prince William Henry (King William IV of England, 1830–1837) to the Lloyd Manor on Long Island. These verses are not known to exist today in manuscript.

Hammon's sermons, written in the Revolutionary and post-Revolutionary eras, retain an acute consciousness of the gathering political significance of blacks in the period. He mentions the deaths of blacks in the War for Independence, draws upon the jeremiad in order to call for a virtuous black nation within the American nation, and speaks of petitions for freedom on the part of black slaves. Despite the seemingly acquiescent tone of much of his writing, his sermons mount a firm appeal for black moral and social autonomy.

On every single one of Hammon's nine published pieces of prose and verse, acknowledgement—hardly incidental—is made of his being a servant to three generations of the Lloyd family. Indeed, on several of his pieces it is noted that his verse or his prose was printed "with the assistance of his friends," presumably, white friends. Thus receiving the approbation of whites and repeatedly urging a resigned black reconciliation of slavery with unthreatening Christianity, it is not at all surprising that Hammon was permitted to publish as much as he did.

Our sense that Hammon's sermons, directed primarily towards blacks, are overheard and even managed by white patrons indicates an important problem in early African-American writing. Most writing by blacks in the Revolutionary period was published under headnotes that indicated white sanction. Within this context, the reader must decide carefully how to weigh the frequent appeals for liberty and freedom which appear even in such a writer as Hammon. The complex weighing of meanings that such terms assume in the revolutionary rhetoric of white political writers becomes even more complicated in the discourse of blacks.

William H. Robinson
Rhode Island College

Phillip M. Richards
Colgate University

PRIMARY WORK

Stanley Ransom, Jr., *America's First Negro Poet. The Complete Works of Jupiter Hammon,* 1970.

SECONDARY WORKS

Oscar Wegelin, *Jupiter Hammon, American Negro Poet,* 1915; Jacqueline Overton, *Long Island's Story,* 2nd ed., 1961; Gary Nash, *Race and Revolution,* 1990; Phillip M. Richards, "Nationalist Themes in the Preaching of Jupiter Hammon," *Early American Literature* 25, 1990.

An Evening Thought: *Salvation by Christ,* with Penetential Cries

[Composed by Jupiter Hammon, a Negro belonging to Mr. Lloyd of Queen's Village, on Long Island, the 25th of December, 1760.[1]]

Salvation comes by Jesus Christ alone,
The only Son of God;
Redemption now to every one,
That love his holy Word.
Dear Jesus we would fly to Thee,
And leave off every Sin,
Thy tender Mercy well agree;
Salvation from our King.
Salvation comes now from the Lord,
Our victorious King;
His holy Name be well ador'd,
Salvation surely bring.
Dear Jesus give thy Spirit now,
Thy Grace to every Nation,
That han't the Lord to whom we bow,
The Author of Salvation.
Dear Jesus unto Thee we cry,
Give us thy Preparation;
Turn not away thy tender Eye;
We seek thy true Salvation.
Salvation comes from God we know,
The true and only One;
It's well agreed and certain true,
He gave his only Son.
Lord hear our penetential Cry:
Salvation from above;
It is the Lord that doth supply,
With his Redeeming Love,
Dear Jesus by thy precious Blood,
The World Redemption have:
Salvation comes now from the Lord,
He being thy captive Slave.
Dear Jesus let the Nations cry,
And all the People say,
Salvation comes from Christ on high,

[1]This broadside is in the New York Historical Society. There are extant several mistakenly variant printings of this broadside, which appears, in facsimile, in Sidney Kaplan's *The Black Presence in the Era of the American Revolution 1770–1800,* 1973: p. 172.

Haste on Tribunal Day.
We cry as Sinners to the Lord,
Salvation to obtain;
It is firmly fixt his holy Word,
Ye shall not cry in vain.
Dear Jesus unto Thee we cry,
And make our Lamentation:
O let our Prayers ascend on high;
We felt thy Salvation.
Lord turn our dark benighted Souls;
Give us a true Motion,
And let the Hearts of all the World,
Make Christ their Salvation.
Ten Thousand Angels cry to Thee,
Yea louder than the Ocean.
Thou are the Lord, we plainly see;
Thou art the true Salvation.
Now is the Day, excepted Time;
The Day of Salvation;
Increase your Faith, do not repine:
Awake ye every Nation.
Lord unto whom now shall we go,
Or seek a safe Abode;
Thou hast the Word Salvation too
The only Son of God.
Ho! every one that hunger hath,
Or pineth after me,
Salvation be thy leading Staff,
To set the Sinner free.
Dear Jesus unto Thee we fly;
Depart, depart from Sin,
Salvation doth at length supply,
The Glory of our King.
Come ye Blessed of the Lord,
Salvation gently given;
O turn your Hearts, accept the Word,
Your Souls are fit for Heaven.
Dear Jesus we now turn to Thee,
Salvation to obtain;
Our Hearts and Souls do meet again,
To magnify thy Name.
Come holy Spirit, Heavenly Dove,
The Object of our Care;
Salvation doth increase our Love;
Our Hearts hath felt thy fear.
Now Glory be to God on High,
Salvation high and low;

And thus the Soul on Christ rely,
  To Heaven surely go.
Come Blessed Jesus, Heavenly Dove,
  Accept Repentance here;
Salvation give, with tender Love;
  Let us with Angels share.

1760

An Address to Miss Phillis Wheatly *[sic]*, Ethiopian Poetess, in Boston, who came from Africa at eight years of age, and soon became acquainted with the gospel of Jesus Christ.

Miss Wheatly; pray give me leave to express as follows:

1

O Come you pious youth: adore — Eccles. xil. 1.
  The wisdom of thy God,
In bringing thee from distant shore,
  To learn his holy word.

2

Thou mightst been left behind, — Psal. cxxxvi. 1,2,3.
  Amidst a dark abode;
God's tender mercy still combin'd,
  Thou hast the holy word.

3

Fair wisdom's ways are paths of peace, — Psal. i 1,2,3.
  And they that walk therein, — Prov. iii. 7.
Shall reap the joys that never cease,
  And Christ shall be their king.

4

God's tender mercy brought thee here, — Psal. ciii. 1,2,3,4.
  Tost o'er the raging main;
In Christian faith thou hast a share,
  Worth all the gold of Spain.

5

While thousands tossed by the sea, — Death.
  And others settled down,

God's tender mercy set thee free,
From dangers still unknown.

6

That thou a pattern still might be, 2 Cor. v. 10.
To youth of Boston town,
The blessed Jesus set thee free,
From every sinful wound.

7

The blessed Jesus, who came down, Rom. v. 21.
Unvail'd his sacred face,
To cleanse the soul of every wound,
And give repenting grace.

8

That we poor sinners may obtain Psal. xxxiv. 6,7,8.
The pardon of our sin;
Dear blessed Jesus now constrain,
And bring us flocking in.

9

Come you, Phillis, now aspire, Mat. vii. 7,8.
And seek the living God,
So step by step thou mayst go higher,
Till perfect in the word.

10

While thousands mov'd to distant shore, Psal. 1xxxiv. 1.
And others left behind,
The blessed Jesus still adore,
Implant this in thy mind.

11

Thou hast left the heathen shore, Psal. xxxiv. 1,2,3.
Thro' mercy of the Lord,
Among the heathen live no more,
Come magnify thy God.

12

I pray the living God may be, Psal. 1xxx. 1,2,3.
The shepherd of thy soul;
His tender mercies still are free,
His mysteries to unfold.

13

Thou, Phillis, when thou hunger hast, Psal. x1ii. 1,2,3.
Or pantest for thy God;

Jesus Christ is thy relief,
  Thou hast the holy word.

14

The bounteous mercies of the Lord, Psal. xvi. 10,11.
  Are hid beyond the sky,
And holy souls that love his word,
  Shall taste them when they die.

15

These bounteous mercies are from God, Psal. xxxiv. 15.
  The merits of his Son;
The humble soul that loves his word,
  He chooses for his own.

16

Come, dear Phillis, be advis'd, John iv. 13,14.
  To drink Samaria's flood:
There nothing is that shall suffice,
  But Christ's redeeming blood.

17

While thousands muse with earthly toys, Matth. vi. 33.
  And range about the street,
Dear Phillis, seek for heaven's joys,
  Where we do hope to meet.

18

When God shall send his summons down, Psal. cxvi. 15.
  And number saints together,
Blest angel chant, (triumphant sound)
  Come live with me forever.

19

The humble soul shall fly to God, Mat. v. 3,8.
  And leave the things of time,
Start forth as 'twere at the first word,
  To taste things more divine.

20

Behold! the soul shall waft away, Cor. xv. 51,52,53.
  Whene'er we come to die,
And leave its cottage made of clay,
  In twinkling of an eye.

21

Now glory be to the Most High, Psal. cl. 6.
United praises given,

By all on earth, incessantly,
And all the host of heav'n.

Composed by JUPITER HAMMON, a
Negro Man belonging to Mr. Joseph
Lloyd, of Queen's Village, / on Long
Island, now in Hartford.

***The above lines are published by the Author, and a number of his friends, who desire to join with him in their best / regards to Miss Wheatly.

Hartford, August 4, 1778

Samson Occom (Mohegan) 1723–1792

Born in a wigwam in 1723, Samson Occom was the son of Joshua Tomacham and Sarah, reputed to be a descendant of the famous Mohegan chief Uncas. Joshua's father, "Tomockham alias Ashneon," had settled near Uncas Hill (later Mohegan, Connecticut) late in the seventeenth century. In an autobiographical sketch, dated September 17, 1768, Occom described the nomadic life led by his parents and their fellow Mohegans during his youth.

At sixteen, Samson was aroused to religious fervor by the missionaries to the Indians, and he began to study English in order to read the scriptures. His conversion to Christianity a year later increased his desire to read. In 1743, at the age of twenty, Occom went to study for four years with the Reverend Eleazar Wheelock at Lebanon, Connecticut. Ill health and eye strain prevented him from studying longer. He accepted in 1749 the invitation of the Montauk Indians of Long Island to become their schoolmaster. In 1751, he married Mary Fowler (a Montauk), who subsequently bore him ten children. The desperate financial circumstances in which Occom found himself soon after his marriage haunted him for the rest of his life. To support himself and his rapidly growing family, Occom supplemented his stipend by working as a farmer, fisherman, cooper, and bookbinder.

Following his ordination in 1759, Occom spent the next year as an itinerant minister in southern New England. In 1761, he became a missionary to the Oneida Indians. Determined to work among his own people, Occom moved his family in 1764 to Mohegan and assisted the Reverend George Whitefield in raising money for Wheelock's Indian Charity School. (This Indian Charity School became the present-day Dartmouth College.) Occom's effectiveness as a preacher and fund-raiser led to his greatest career opportunity: in 1765, he was selected to journey to Great Britain, accompanied by the Reverend Nathaniel Whitaker of Norwich, to raise money for the school. Supported by Whitefield and his followers, such as the second Earl of Dartmouth, Occom's mission was a great success. Occom preached over 300 sermons during his two-year stay in Great Britain and raised over £12,000.

Occom had difficulty reconciling his dependence upon Wheelock for sustaining his family with his growing pride in being a Native American. His achievements in England could not be reconciled with his financial duress. After his return home in

1768, Occom was less willing to follow Wheelock's direction or to accept the humiliations his lack of money thrust upon him. He was annoyed by Wheelock's removal of the Indian Charity School from Lebanon, Connecticut, to Hanover, New Hampshire, and he was angered by reports that the school's Indian enrollment had shrunk to three. He wrote to Wheelock, reminding his mentor of the school's original purpose. Thereafter, relations between the two men were strained.

Occom devoted his energies to preaching and working on behalf of Indian people. Prior to his tour of England, he had helped the Mohegans try to settle their land claims. Now he became an enthusiastic supporter of the plan formulated by his son-in-law Joseph Johnson (a Mohegan) to remove the Christian Indians of New England to lands offered by the Oneida in western New York. The Revolutionary War halted this move. In an address, Occom urged Indians to maintain neutrality because he felt the war was the work of the devil. Although he pointed out that the English sought to enslave the colonists, nevertheless he urged Indians not to become embroiled in the quarrels of white people.

Occom traveled throughout New England in 1784 to preach and raise funds for resettlement of the Christian Indians on Oneida lands, an activity that absorbed him for the next six years. In 1789, he moved his own family there. His last years were spent in continued service to his people now beset by controversies over land claims. Through his efforts, the Christian Indians withstood Oneida efforts to reclaim their land and white plots to lease the Christian Indians' land for far less than its worth. He died in 1792 at age 69; his funeral was attended by more than 300 Indians. His dream of a secure settlement for New England Indians was destined to fail—as were all subsequent resettlements of Indians. After the War of 1812, white encroachment caused the Brothertown and Stockbridge Indians to purchase land from the Winnebago and Menominee Indians in the Green Bay area of what is now Wisconsin. They and some of the Oneidas subsequently made the long trek to resettlement in that area.

Occom published only two works: *A Sermon Preached by Samson Occom, . . . at the Execution of Moses Paul* (1772), the first Indian best-seller, and *Collection of Hymns and Spiritual Songs* (1774). Undoubtedly the success of the sermon inspired Occom, a fine singer, to publish the collection.

In 1771, Occom had stepped into the public limelight for the first time since his English tour, when he preached the execution sermon for Moses Paul, a fellow Christian Mohegan. Ejected from a Bethany tavern for drunkenness, Paul vowed revenge. He waited outside the tavern and killed the first person to leave—Moses Cook, a prominent citizen of Waterbury, Connecticut. Granted a three-month reprieve by the General Assembly of Connecticut, Paul wrote Occom on July 16, 1771, to ask that he preach at the execution.

The execution, held on September 2, 1771, drew a large crowd both because it was New Haven's first hanging in twenty years and because it was a unique opportunity to hear a famous Indian minister preach at the execution of a fellow tribesman. Whites and Indians flocked to the event. Occom's forceful and emotional sermon so moved his audience that he was immediately urged to publish it. One of the few temperance sermons published during that period, it achieved particular popularity because of its application to Indians whose drunkenness whites feared. Following its publication on October 31, 1772, by Thomas and Samuel Green of New Haven, the sermon went through at least nineteen editions, including a translation into Welsh published in 1827 in Caernarvon, Wales.

Occom was strongly influenced by the

spiritual innovations of the Great Awakening of the 1740s, which had been led by Jonathan Edwards. One of these innovations was the development of itinerant evangelizers, popularized by Occom's friends George Whitefield in New England and Eleazar Wheelock in Connecticut and practiced by the Indian preacher himself. Two other innovative practices are reflected in Occom's sermon: dramatic, conscious conversion as the only way to salvation and emotionally extravagant style. Especially noteworthy is Occom's use of a variety of rhetorical stances and approaches to appeal to the diverse audience of whites, Moses Paul, and other Native Americans.

Although the sermon derives its theology from the Great Awakening, it derives its form from the execution sermon, a genre which originated in Old England and achieved great popularity in New England. Its popularity is based on its relationship to the religious practices of the early colonial period, when probing the depths of one's soul and confessing one's sins were part of private and church ritual. These confessions became an essential part of American conversion literature that flourished in the eighteenth and early nineteenth centuries. One of the most prolific writers of American execution sermons was Increase Mather, whose son Cotton also wrote such sermons. The purpose of execution sermons was to make criminal acts detestable and to induce proper behavior in society as a whole. Whereas in the seventeenth and early eighteenth centuries, the confessors were usually members from *within* society, in the eighteenth century they were more likely to be blacks, Indians, Irishmen, or foreign pirates.

A. LaVonne Brown Ruoff
University of Illinois at Chicago

PRIMARY WORKS

A Sermon Preached by Samson Occom, Minister of the Gospel, and Missionary to the Indians; at the Execution of Moses Paul an Indian, 1772; *Collection of Hymns and Spiritual Songs,* 1774.

SECONDARY WORKS

W. Deloss Love, *Samson Occom and the Christian Indians of New England,* 1899; Leon Burr Richardson, *An Indian Preacher in England,* Dartmouth College Manuscript Series, No. 2, 1933; Harold Blodgett, *Samson Occom,* Dartmouth College Manuscript Series, No. 3, 1935; David Murray, *Forked Tongues: Speech, Writing, and Representation in North American Indian Texts,* 1991; Margaret Connell Szasz, "Samson Occom: Mohegan as Spiritual Intermediary," *Between Indian and White Worlds*, ed. Szasz, 60–78.

A Short Narrative of My Life[1]

From my Birth till I received the Christian Religion

I was Born a Heathen and Brought up In Heathenism, till I was between 16 & 17 years of age, at a Place Calld Mohegan, in New London, Connecticut, in New England. My Parents Livd a wandering life, for did all the Indians at Mohegan, they

[1]The text is transcribed from Occom's manuscript in the Dartmouth College Library. Conjectural readings appear in brackets. Occom's spelling, capitalization, and punctuation have generally been followed.

Chiefly Depended upon Hunting, Fishing, & Fowling for their Living and had no Connection with the English, excepting to Traffic with them in their small Trifles; and they Strictly maintained and followed their Heathenish Ways, Customs & Religion, though there was Some Preaching among them. Once a Fortnight, in ye Summer Season, a Minister from New London used to come up, and the Indians to attend; not that they regarded the Christian Religion, but they had Blankets given to them every Fall of the Year and for these things they would attend and there was a Sort of School kept, when I was quite young, but I believe there never was one that ever Learnt to read any thing,—and when I was about 10 Years of age there was a man who went about among the Indian Wigwams, and wherever he Could find the Indian Children, would make them read; but the Children Used to take Care to keep out of his way;—and he used to Catch me Some times and make me Say over my Letters; and I believe I learnt Some of them. But this was Soon over too; and all this Time there was not one amongst us, that made a Profession of Christianity——Neither did we Cultivate our Land, nor kept any Sort of Creatures except Dogs, which we used in Hunting; and we Dwelt in Wigwams. These are a Sort of Tents, Covered with Matts, made of Flags. And to this Time we were unaquainted with the English Tongue in general though there were a few, who understood a little of it.

From the Time of our Reformation till I left Mr. Wheelocks

When I was 16 years of age, we heard a Strange Rumor among the English, that there were Extraordinary Ministers Preaching from Place to Place and a Strange Concern among the White People. This was in the Spring of the Year. But we Saw nothing of these things, till Some Time in the Summer, when Some Ministers began to visit us and Preach the Word of God; and the Common People all Came frequently and exhorted us to the things of God, which it pleased the Lord, as I humbly hope, to Bless and accompany with Divine Influences to the Conviction and Saving Conversion of a Number of us; amongst whom I was one that was Imprest with the things we had heard. These Preachers did not only come to us, but we frequently went to their meetings and Churches. After I was awakened & converted, I went to all the meetings, I could come at; & Continued under Trouble of Mind about 6 months; at which time I began to Learn the English Letters; got me a Primer, and used to go to my English Neighbours frequently for Assistance in Reading, but went to no School. And when I was 17 years of age, I had, as I trust, a Discovery of the way of Salvation through Jesus Christ, and was enabl'd to put my trust in him alone for Life & Salvation. From this Time the Distress and Burden of my mind was removed, and I found Serenity and Pleasure of Soul, in Serving God. By this time I just began to Read in the New Testament without Spelling,—and I had a Stronger Desire Still to Learn to read the Word of God, and at the Same Time had an uncommon Pity and Compassion to my Poor Brethren According to the Flesh. I used to wish I was capable of Instructing my poor Kindred. I used to think, if I Could once Learn to Read I would Instruct the poor Children in Reading,—and used frequently to talk with our Indians Concerning Religion. This continued till I was in my 19th year: by this Time I Could Read a bit in the Bible. At this Time my Poor Mother was going to Lebanon, and having had Some Knowledge of Mr. Wheelock and hearing he had a Number of English youth under his Tuition, I had a great Inclination to go to him and be with him a week or a Fortnight, and Desired my Mother to Ask Mr. Wheelock, Whether he would take me a little while to Instruct me in Reading. Mother did so; and when She Came Back, She Said Mr. Wheelock wanted to See me as Soon as possible. So I went up, thinking I Should be back again in a few Days; when I got up there, he received me With kindness and Compassion and in Stead of Staying a Forthnight or 3 Weeks, I Spent 4 Years with him.—After I had been with him Some Time, he began to acquaint his Friends of my being with him, and of his Intentions of Educating me, and my Circumstances. And the good People began to give Some Assistance to Mr. Wheelock, and gave me Some old and Some New Clothes. Then he represented the Case to the Honorable Commissioners at Boston, who were Commission'd by the Honourable Society in London for Propagating the gospel among the Indians in New England and parts adjacent. and they allowed him 60 £ in old Tenor, which was about 6 £ Sterling, and they Continu'd it 2 or 3 years, I can't tell exactly.—While I was at Mr. Wheelock's, I was very weakly and my Health much impaired, and at the End of 4 Years, I over Strained my Eyes to such a Degree, I Could not persue my Studies any Longer; and out of these 4 years I Lost Just about one year;—And was obliged to quit my Studies.

From the Time I left Mr. Wheelock till I went to Europe

As soon as I left Mr. Wheelock, I endeavored to find Some Employ among the Indians; went to Nahantuck, thinking they may want a School Master, but they had one; then went to Narraganset, and they were Indifferent about a School, and went back to Mohegan, and heard a number of our Indians were going to *Montauk,* on Long Island,—and I went with them, and the Indians there were very desirous to have me keep a School amongst them, and I Consented, and went back a while to Mohegan and Some time in November I went on the Island, I think it is 17 years ago last November. I agreed to keep School with them Half a Year, and left it with them to give me what they Pleased; and they took turns to Provide Food for me. I had near 30 Scholars this winter; I had an evening School too for those that could not attend the Day School—and began to Carry on their meetings, they had a Minister, one Mr. *Horton,* the Scotch Society's Missionary; but he Spent, I think two thirds of his Time at Sheenecock, 30 Miles from Montauk.[2] We met together 3 times for Divine Worship every Sabbath and once on every Wednesday evening. I [used] to read the Scriptures to them and used to expound upon Some particular Passages in my own Tongue. Visited the Sick and attended their Burials.—When the half year expired, they Desired me to Continue with them, which I complied with, for another half

[2]Both the Shinnecock and Montauk Indians were located on present-day Long Island. Many from both tribes left after 1775 to join Occom at the new Christian Indian town of Brotherton.

year, when I had fulfilled that, they were urgent to have me Stay Longer, So I continued amongst them till I was Married, which was about 2 years after I went there.

And Continued to Instruct them in the Same manner as I did before After I was married a while, I found there was need of a Support more than I needed while I was Single,—and I made my Case Known to Mr. *Buell* and to Mr. *Wheelock,* and also the Needy Circumstances and the Desires of these Indians of my Continuence amongst them and Mr. *Wheelock* and other gentlemen Represented my Circumstances and the Desires of these Indians of my Continuence amongst them, and the Commissioners were so good as to grant £ 15 a year Sterling——And I kept on in my Service as usual, yea I had additional Service; I kept School as I did before and Carried on the Religious Meetings as often as ever, and attended the Sick and their Funerals, and did what Writings they wanted, and often Sat as a Judge to reconcile and Decide their Matters Between them, and had visitors of Indians from all Quarters; and, as our Custom is, we freely Entertain all Visitors. And was fetched often from my Tribe and from others to see into their Affairs Both Religious, Temporal,—Besides my Domestick Concerns. And it Pleased the Lord to Increase my Family fast—and Soon after I was Married, Mr. *Horton* left these Indians and the Shenecock & after this I was [licensed to preach?] and then I had the whole care of these Indians at Montauk, and visited the Shenecock Indians often. Used to Set out Saturdays towards Night and come back again Mondays. I have been obliged to Set out from Home after Sun Set, and Ride 30 Miles in the Night, to Preach to these Indians.—And Some Indians at Shenecock Sent their Children to my School at Montauk; I kept one of them Some Time, and had a Young Man a half year from Mohegan, a Lad from Nahantuck, who was with me almost a year; and had little or nothing for keeping them.

My Method in the School was, as Soon as the Children got together, and took their proper Seats, I Prayed with them, then began to hear them. I generally began (after some of them Could Spell and Read,) With those that were yet in their Alphabets, So around, as they were properly Seated till I got through and I obliged them to Study their Books, and to help one another. When they could not make out a hard word they Brought it to me—and I usually heard them, in the Summer Season 8 Times a Day 4 in the morning, and in ye after Noon.—In the Winter Season 6 Times a Day, As Soon as they could Spell, they were obliged to Spell when ever they wanted to go out. I concluded with Prayer; I generally heard my Evening Scholars 3 Times Round, And as they go out the School, every one, that Can Spell, is obliged to Spell a Word, and to go out Leisurely one after another. I Catechised 3 or 4 Times a Week according to the Assembly's Shorter Catechism, and many Times Proposed Questions of my own, and in my own Tongue. I found Difficulty with Some Children, who were Some what Dull, most of these can soon learn to Say over their Letters, they Distinguish the Sounds by the Ear, but their Eyes can't Distinguish the Letters, and the way I took to cure them was by making an Alphabet on Small bits of paper, and glued them on Small Chips of Cedar after this manner A B & C. I put these on Letters in order on a Bench then point to one Letter and bid a Child to take notice of it, and then I order the Child to fetch me the Letter from the Bench; if he Brings the Letter, it is well, if not he must go again and again till he brings ye right Letter. When they can bring any Letters this way, then I just Jumble them together, and bid them to set them in Alphabetical order, and it is a Pleasure to them; and they soon

Learn their Letters this way.—I frequently Discussed or Exhorted my Scholars, in Religious matters.—My Method in our Religious Meetings was this; Sabbath Morning we Assemble together about 10 o'C and begin with Singing; we generally Sung Dr. Watt's Psalms or Hymns. I distinctly read the Psalm or Hymn first, and then gave the meaning of it to them, after that Sing, then Pray, and Sing again after Prayer. Then proceed to Read from Suitable portion of Scripture, and so Just give the plain Sense of it in Familiar Discourse and apply it to them. So continued with Prayer and Singing. In the after Noon and Evening we Proceed in the Same Manner, and so in Wednesday Evening. Some Time after Mr. Horton left these Indians, there was a remarkable revival of religion among these Indians and many were hopefully converted to the Saving knowledge of God in Jesus. It is to be observed before Mr. Horton left these Indians they had Some Prejudices infused in their minds, by Some Enthusiastical Exhorters from New England, against Mr. Horton, and many of them had left him; by this means he was Discouraged; and Sued a Dismission and was disposed from these Indians. And being acquainted with the Enthusiasts in New England: & the make and the Disposition of the Indians I took a mild way to reclaim them. I opposed them not openly but let them go on in their way, and whenever I had an opportunity, I would read Such pages of the Scriptures, and I thought would confound their Notions, and I would come to them with all Authority, Saying, "thus Saith the Lord"; and by this means, the Lord was pleased to Bless my poor Endeavours, and they were reclaimed, and Brought to hear almost any of the ministers.—I am now to give an Account of my Circumstances and manner of Living. I Dwelt in a Wigwam, a Small Hut with Small Poles and Covered with Matts made of Flags, and I was obligd to remove twice a Year, about 2 miles Distance, by reason of the Scarcity of wood, for in one Neck of Land they Planted their Corn, and in another, they had their wood, and I was obligd to have my Corn carted and my Hay also,—and I got my Ground Plow'd every year, which Cost me about 12 shillings an acre; and I kept a Cow and a Horse, for which I paid 21 shillings every year York currency, and went 18 miles to Mill for every Dust of meal we used in my family. I Hired or Joined with my Neighbours to go to Mill, with a Horse or ox Cart, or on Horse Back, and Some time went myself. My Family Increasing fast, and my Visitors also. I was obligd to contrive every way to Support my Family; I took all opportunities, to get Some thing to feed my Family Daily. I Planted my own Corn, Potatoes, and Beans; I used to be out hoeing my Corn Some times before Sun Rise and after my School is Dismist, and by this means I was able to raise my own Pork, for I was allowed to keep 5 Swine. Some mornings & Evenings I would be out with my Hook and Line to Catch fish, and in the Fall of Year and in the Spring, I used my gun, and fed my Family with Fowls. I Could more than pay for my Powder & Shot with Feathers.[3] At other Times I Bound old Books for Easthampton People, made wooden Spoons and Ladles, Stocked Guns, & worked on Cedar to make Pails, Piggins[4] and Churns & C. Besides all these Difficulties I met with adverse Providence. I bought a Mare, had it but a little while, and she fell into the Quick Sand and Died. After a while Bought another,

[3]Feathers were prized as decorations by white Americans and Europeans and were thus an important exchange item.

[4]A small, wooden pail with a stave for a handle.

I kept her about half year, and she was gone, and I never have heard of nor Seen her from that Day to this; it was Supposed Some Rogue Stole her. I got another and Died with a Distemper, and last of all I Bought a Young Mare, and kept her till She had one Colt, and She broke her Leg and Died, and Presently after the Colt Died also. In the whole I Lost 5 Horse Kind; all these Losses helped to pull me down; and by this Time I got greatly in Debt, and acquainted my Circumstances to Some of my Friends, and they Represented my Case to the Commissioners of Boston, and Interceded with them for me, and they were pleased to vote 15 £ for my Help, and Soon after Sent a Letter to my good Friend at New London, acquainting him that they had Superseded their Vote; and my Friends were so good as to represent my Needy Circumstances Still to them, and they were so good at Last, as to Vote £ 15 and Sent it, for which I am very thankful; and the Revd Mr. Buell was so kind as to write in my behalf to the gentlemen of Boston; and he told me they were much Displeased with him, and heard also once again that they blamed me for being Extravagant; I Can't Conceive how these gentlemen would have me Live. I am ready to impute it to their Ignorance, and I would wish they had Changed Circumstances with me but one month, that they may know, by experience what my Case really was; but I am now fully convinced, that it was not Ignorance, For I believe it can be proved to the world that these Same Gentlemen gave a young Missionary a Single man, *one Hundred Pounds* for one year, and fifty Pounds for an Interpreter, and thirty Pounds for an Introducer; so it Cost them one Hundred & Eighty Pounds in one Single Year, and they Sent too where there was no Need of a Missionary.

Now you See what difference they made between me and other missionaries; they gave me 180 Pounds for 12 years Service, which they gave for one years Services in another Mission.—In my Service (I speak like a fool, but I am Constrained) I was my own Interpreter. I was both a School master and Minister to the Indians, yea I was their Ear, Eye & Hand, as Well as Mouth. I leave it with the World, as wicked as it is, to Judge, whether I ought not to have had half as much, they gave a young man Just mentioned which would have been but £ 50 a year; and if they ought to have given me that, I am not under obligations to them, I owe them nothing at all; what can be the Reason that they used me after this manner? I can't think of any thing, but this as a Poor Indian Boy Said, Who was Bound out to an English Family, and he used to Drive Plow for a young man, and he whipt and Beat him allmost every Day, and the young man found fault with him, and Complained of him to his master and the poor Boy was Called to answer for himself before his master, and he was asked, what it was he did, that he was So Complained of and beat almost every Day. He Said, he did not know, but he Supposed it was because he could not drive any better; but says he, I Drive as well as I know how; and at other Times he Beats me, because he is of a mind to beat me; but says he believes he Beats me for the most of the Time "because I am an Indian".

So I am *ready* to Say, they have used me thus, because I Can't Influence the Indians so well as other missionaries; but I can *assure them* I have endeavoured to teach them as well as I know how;—but I *must Say,* "I believe it is because I am a poor Indian". I Can't help that God has made me So; I did not make my self so.—

1768

A Sermon Preached by Samson Occom[1]

The sacred words that I have chosen to speak from, upon this undesirable occasion are found written in the Epistle of St. Paul to the ROMANS, VI. 23. For the Wages of Sin is Death, but the Gift of God is Eternal Life through Jesus Christ our Lord.

Death is called the king of terrors, and it ought to be the subject of every man and woman's thoughts daily; because it is that unto which they are liable every moment of their lives: And therefore it cannot be unreasonable to think, speak and hear of it at any time, and especially on this mournful occasion; for we must all come to it, how soon we cannot tell; whether we are prepared or not prepared, ready or not ready, whether death is welcome or not welcome, we must feel the force of it: Whether we concern ourselves with death or not, it will concern itself with us. Seeing that this is the case with every one of us, what manner of persons ought we to be in all holy conversation and godliness; how ought men to exert themselves in preparation for death, continually; for they know not what a day or an hour may bring forth, with respect to them. But alas! according to the appearance of mankind in general; death is the least thought of. They go on from day to day as if they were to live here forever, as if this was the only life. They contrive, rack their inventions, disturb their rest, and even hazard their lives in all manner of dangers, both by sea and land; yea, they leave no stone unturned that they may live in the world, and at the same time have little or no contrivance to die well. God and their souls are neglected, and heaven and eternal happiness are disregarded; Christ and his religion are despised—yet most of these very men intend to be happy when they come to die, not considering that there must be great preparation in order to die well. Yea there is none so fit to live as those that are fit to die; those that are not fit to die are not fit to live. Life and death are nearly connected; we generally own that it is a great and solemn thing to die. If this be true, then it is a great and solemn thing to live, for as we live so we shall die. But I say again, how do mankind realize these things? They are busy about the things of this world as if there was no death before them. Dr. *Watts* pictures them out to the life in his psalms.[2]

[1]Moses Paul, a Christian Mohegan, was convicted in 1771 of the murder of Moses Cook, a prominent citizen of Waterbury, Connecticut, and he asked Occom to preach his execution sermon. The execution, held on September 2 at New Haven, drew a large crowd of Indians and whites. Occom's forceful and emotional sermon so moved his audience that he was immediately urged to publish it. The sermon became popular, as much from the novelty of the topic as from the fervor of the language. One of the few temperance sermons published during that period, it achieved particular popularity because of its application to Indians whose drunkenness whites feared. First published at New Haven in 1772, the sermon appeared in at least nineteen editions, including a translation into Welsh in 1827. The version reprinted here is the tenth edition, published at Bennington, Vermont.

[2]Isaac Watts (1674–1748), English hymn writer, published *The Psalms of David Imitated in the Language of the New Testament* in 1719. Occom quotes number 613.

See the vain race of mortals move,
Like shadows o'er the plain,
They rage and strive, desire and love,
But all the noise is vain.

Some walk in honour's gaudy show,
Some dig for golden ore,
They toil for heirs they know not who,
And strait are seen no more.

But on the other hand, life is the most precious thing, and ought to be the most desired by all rational creatures. It ought to be prized above all things; yet there is nothing so abused and despised as life, and nothing so neglected: I mean eternal life is shamefully disregarded by men in general, and eternal death is chosen rather than life. This is the general complaint of the Bible from the beginning to the end. As long as Christ is neglected, life is refused, as long as sin is cherished, death is chosen. And this seems to be the woful case of mankind of all nations, according to their appearance in these days: For it is too plain to be denied, that vice and immorality, and floods of iniquity are abounding every where amongst all nations, and all orders and ranks of men, and in every sect of people. Yea there is a great agreement and harmony among all nations, and from the highest to the lowest to practice sin and iniquity; and the pure religion of Jesus Christ is turned out of doors, and is dying without; or, in other words, the Lord Jesus Christ is turned out of doors by men in general, and even by his professed people. "He Came to his own, and his own received him not."[3] But the devil is admitted, he has free access to the houses and hearts of the children of men: Thus life is refused and death is chosen.

But in further speaking upon our text by divine assistance, I shall consider these two general propositions.

I. That sin is the cause of all the miseries that befall the children of men, both as to their bodies and souls, for time and eternity.

II. That eternal life and happiness is the gift of God through Jesus Christ our Lord.

In speaking to the first proposition, I shall first consider the nature of sin; and secondly I shall consider the consequences of sin or the wages of sin, which is death. First then, we are to describe the nature of sin.

Sin is the transgression of the law:—This is the scripture definition of sin.—Now the law of God being holy, just and good; sin must be altogether unholy, unjust and evil. If I was to define sin, I should call it a contrariety to God; and as such it must be the vilest thing in the world; it is full of all evil; it is the evil of evils; the only evil in which dwells no good thing; and it is most destructive to God's creation, wherever it takes effect. It was sin that transformed the very angels in heaven, into devils; and it was sin that caused hell to be made. If it had not been for sin, there never would have been such a thing as hell or devil, death or misery.

And if sin is such a thing as we have just described, it must be worse than the devils in hell itself.—Sin is full of deadly poison; it is full of malignity and hatred

[3]John 1:11.

against God; against all his divine perfections and attributes, against his wisdom, against his power, against his holiness and goodness, against his mercy and justice, against his law and gospel; yea against his very being and existence. Were it in the power of sin, it would even dethrone God, and set itself on the throne.

When Christ the Son of the Most High came down from the glorious world above, into this wretched world of sin and sorrow, to seek and to save that which was lost, sin or sinners rose up against him, as soon as he entered our world, and pursued him with hellish malice, night and day, for above thirty years together, till they killed him.

Further, sin is against the Holy Ghost; it opposes all its good and holy operations upon the children of men. When, and wherever there is the out pouring of the Spirit of God, upon the children of men, in a way of conviction and conversion; sin will immediately prompt the devil and his children to rise up against it, and they will oppose the work with all their power, and in every shape. And if open opposition will not do, the devil will mimic the work and thus prevent the good effect.

Thus we find by the scripture accounts, that whenever God raises up men, and uses them as instruments of conviction and conversion, the devil and his instruments will rise up to destroy both the reformers and the reformed. Thus it has been from the early days of christianity to this day. We have found it so in our day. In the time of the outpouring of the Spirit of God in these colonies, to the conviction and reformation of many; immediately sin and the devil influenced numbers to rise up against the good work of God, calling it a delusion, and work of the devil. And thus sin also opposes every motion of the Spirit of God, in the heart of every christian; this makes a warfare in the soul.

2. I shall endeavor to show the sad consequences or effects of sin upon the children of men.

Sin has poisoned them, and made them distracted or fools. The psalmist says, The fool hath said in his heart, there is no God.[4] And Solomon, through his proverbs, calls ungodly sinners fools; and their sin he calls their folly and foolishness.[5] The apostle James says, But the tongue can no man tame, it is an unruly evil, full of deadly poison.[6] It is the heart that is in the first place full of deadly poison. The tongue is only an interpreter of the heart. Sin has vitiated the whole man, both soul and body; all the powers are corrupted; it has turned the minds of men against all good, towards all evil. So poisoned are they according to the prophet, Isa. v. 20. "Wo unto them that call evil good and good evil; that put darkness for light, and light for darkness; that put bitter for sweet, and sweet for bitter." And Christ Jesus saith in John iii. 19, 20. "And this is the condemnation, that light has come into the world, and men have loved darkness rather than light, because their deeds were evil. For every one that doeth evil, hateth the light, neither cometh to the light lest his deeds should be reproved." Sin hath stupified mankind, they are now ignorant of God their Maker; neither do they enquire after him. And they are ignorant of themselves, they know not what is good for them, neither do they understand their danger; and they have no fear of God before their eyes.

[4]Psalms 14.1.
[5]See Proverbs 12:23, 14:8, 14:24, 15:2.
[6]James 3:8.

Further, sin hath blinded their eyes, so that they cannot discern spiritual things: neither do they see the way that they should go, and they are as deaf as adders, so that they cannot hear the joyful sound of the gospel that brings glad tidings of peace and pardon to sinners of mankind. Neither do they regard the charmer charming never so wisely.—Not only so, but sin has made man proud, though he has nothing to be proud of; for he has lost his excellency, his beauty and happiness; he is a bankrupt and is excommunicated from God; he was turned out of paradise by God himself, and became a vagabond in God's world, and as such he has no right or title to the least crumb of mercy, in the world: Yet he is proud, he is haughty, and exalts himself above God, though he is wretched and miserable, and poor and blind and naked. He glories in his shame. Sin has made him beastly and devilish; yea, he is sunk beneath the beasts, and is worse than the ravenous beasts of the wilderness. He is become ill-natured, cruel and murderous; he is contentious and quarrelsome. I said he is worse than the ravenous beasts, for wolves and bears don't devour their own kind, but man does; yea, we have numberless instances of women killing their own children; such women I think are worse than she-tygers.

Sin has made man dishonest, and deceitful, so that he goes about cheating and defrauding and deceiving his fellow-men in the world: Yea, he has become a cheat himself, he goes about in vain shew; we do not know where to find man.—Sometimes we find as an angel of God; and at other times we find as a devil, even one and the same man. Sin has made a man a liar even from the womb; so there is no believing nor trusting him. The royal psalmist says, "The wicked are estranged from the womb, they go astray as soon as they are born, speaking lies."[7] His language is also corrupted. Whereas he had a pure and holy language, in his innocency, to adore and praise God his Maker, he now curses and swears, and profanes, the holy name of God, and curses and damns his fellow creatures. In a word, man is a most unruly and ungovernable creature, and is become as the wild ass's colt, and is harder to tame than any of God's creatures in this world.—In short, man is worse than all the creatures in this lower world, his propensity is to evil and that continually; he is more like the devil than any creature we can think of: And I think it is not going beyond the word of God, to say man is the most devilish creature in the world. Christ said to his disciples, One of you is a devil; to the Jews he said, Ye are of your father the devil, and the lusts of your father ye will do.[8] Thus every unconverted soul is a child of the devil, sin has made them so.

We have given some few hints of the nature of sin, and the effects of sin on mankind.

We shall in the next place consider the wages or the reward of sin, which is death.

Sin is the cause of all the miseries that attend poor sinful man, which will finally bring him to death, death temporal and eternal. I shall first consider his temporal death.

His temporal death then begins as soon as he is born. Though it seems to us that he is just beginning to live, yet in fact he is just entered into a state of death: St. Paul

[7]Psalms 58:3.
[8]Psalms 58:3.

says, "W[h]erefore, as by one man sin entered into the world, and death by sin; and so death passed upon all men, for that all have sinned."[9] Man is surrounded with ten thousand instruments of death, and is liable to death every moment of his life; a thousand diseases await him on every side continually; the sentence of death has pass'd upon them as soon as they are born; yea they are struck with death as soon as they breathe. And it seems all the enjoyments of men in this world are also poisoned with sin; for God said to Adam after he had sinned, "Cursed is the ground for thy sake, in sorrow shalt thou eat of it all the days of thy life."[10] By this we plainly see that every thing that grows out of the ground is cursed, and all creatures that God hath made for man are cursed also; and whatever God curses is a cursed thing indeed. Thus death and destruction is in all the enjoyments of men in this life, every enjoyment in this world is liable to misfortune in a thousand ways, both by sea and land.

How many ships, that have been loaded with the choicest treasures of the earth have been swallowed up in the ocean, many times just before they enter their desired haven. And vast treasures have been consumed by fire on the land, &c.—And the fruits of the earth are liable to many judgments. And the dearest and nearest enjoyments of men are generally balanced with equal sorrow and grief.—A man and his wife who have lived together in happiness for many years; that have comforted each other in various changes of life, must at last be separated; one or the other must be taken away first by death, and then the poor survivor is drowned in tears, in sorrow, mourning and grief. And when a child or children are taken away by death, the bereaved parents are bowed down with sorrow and deep mourning. When Joseph was sold by his brethren unto the Ishmaelites, they took his coat and rolled it in blood, and carried it to their father, and the good old patriarch knew it to be Joseph's coat, and he concluded that his dear Joseph was devoured by evil beasts; and he was plunged all over in sorrow and bitter mourning, and he refused to be comforted. And so when tender parents are taken away by death, the children are left comfortless. All this is the sad effects of sin—These are the wages of sin.

And secondly we are to consider man's spiritual death, while he is here in this world. We find it thus written in the word of God, "And the Lord God commanded the man, saying of every tree of the garden thou mayst freely eat: but of the tree of knowledge of good and evil, thou shalt not eat of it, for in the day thou eatest thereof thou shalt surely die."[11] And yet he did eat of it, and so he and all his posterity are but dead men. And St. Paul to the Ephesians saith, "You hath he quickened who were dead in trespasses and sins."[12] The great Mr. Henry says, in this place, that unregenerate souls are dead in trespasses and sins.[13] All those who are in their sins, are dead in sins; yea, in trespasses and sins; and which may signify all sorts of sins, habitual and actual; sins of heart and life. Sin is the death of the soul. Wherever that prevails, there is a privation of all spiritual life. Sinners are dead in state, being destitute of the principles and powers of spiritual life; and cut off from God, the foun-

[9]Romans 5:12.
[10]Genesis 3:17.
[11]Genesis 2:16–17.
[12]Ephesians 2:1.
[13]Mathew Henry (1662–1714), a British nonconformist divine and commentator, is best known for his *Exposition of the Old and New Testament* (1710). Occom cites his commentary on Ephesians 2:1.

tain of life: and they are dead in law, as a condemned malefactor is said to be a dead man. Now a dead man, in a natural sense, is unactive, and is of no service to the living; there is no correspondence between the dead and the living: There is no agreement or union between them, no fellowship at all between the dead and the living. A dead man is altogether ignorant of the intercourse among the living:—Just so it is with men that are spiritually dead; they have no agreeable activity. Their activity in sin, is their deadness and inactivity towards God. They are of no service to God; and they have no correspondence with heaven; and there is no agreement or fellowship between them and the living God; and they are totally ignorant of the agreeable and sweet intercourse there is between God and his children here below: and they are ignorant, and know nothing of that blessed fellowship and union there is among the saints here below. They are ready to say indeed, behold how they love one another! But they know nothing of that love, that the children of God enjoy. As sin is in opposition to God; so sinners are at enmity against God; there is no manner of agreement between them.

Let us consider further. God is a living God, he is all life, the fountain of life; and a sinner is a dead soul; there is nothing but death in him. And now judge ye, what agreement can there be between them! God is a holy and pure God, and a sinner is an unholy and filthy creature;—God is a righteous Being, and a sinner is an unrighteous creature; God is light, and a sinner is darkness itself, &c. Further, what agreement can there be between God and a liar, a thief, a drunkard, a swearer, a profane creature, a whoremonger, an adulterer, an idolater, &c. No one that has any sense, dare say that there is any agreement. Further, as sinners are dead to God, as such, they have no delight in God, and godliness; they have no taste for the religion of Jesus Christ: they have no pleasure in the holy exercise of religion. Prayer is no pleasant work with them; or if they have any pleasure in it, it is not out of love to God, but out of self-love, like the Pharisees of old; they loved to pray in open view of men, that they might have praise from them. And perhaps, they were not careful to pray in secret. These were dead souls, they were unholy, rotten hypocrites, and so all their prayers and religious exercises were cold, dead, and abominable services to God. Indeed they are dead to all the duties that God requires of them: they are dead to the holy bible; to all the laws, commands, and precepts thereof; and to the ordinances of the gospel of the Lord Jesus Christ. When they read the book of God, it is like an old almanack to them, a dead book. But it is because they are dead, and as such, all their services are against God, even their best services are an abomination unto God; yea, sinners are so dead in sin, that the threatenings of God don't move them. All the thunderings and lightnings of Mount-Sinai don't stir them. All the curses of the law are out against them; yea, every time they read these curses in the bible, they are cursing them to their faces, and to their very eyes; yet they are unconcern'd, and go on in sin without fear. And lastly here, sin has so stupified the sinner, that he will not believe his own senses, he won't believe his own eyes, nor his own ears, he reads the book of God, but he does not believe what he reads. And he hears of God, and heaven, and eternal happiness, and of hell and eternal misery; but he believes none of these things; he goes on, as if there were no God, nor heaven and happiness; neither has he any fear of hell and eternal torments; and he sees his fellow-men dropping away daily on every side, yet he goes on carelessly in sin, as if he never was to die. And if he at any time thinks of dying, he hardly believes his own thoughts.——Death is at a great distance, so far off, that he dont concern himself about it, so as to prepare for it. God mournfully complains of his people, that they dont consider;—O that they were wise, that they understood this, that they would consider their latter end.

The next thing I shall consider, is the actual death of the body, or separation between soul and body. At the cessation of natural life, there is no more joy or sorrow; no more hope nor fear, as to the body; no more contrivance and carrying on of business; no more merchandizing and trading; no more farming; no more buying and selling; no more building of any kind, no more contrivance at all to live in the world; no more honor nor reproach; no more praise; no more good report, nor evil report; no more learning of any trades, arts or sciences in the world; no more sinful pleasures, they are all at an end; recreations, visiting, tavern-hunting, musick and dancing, chambering and carousing, playing at dice and cards, or any game whatsoever; cursing and swearing, and profaning the holy name of God, drunkeness, fighting, debauchery, lying and cheating, in this world must cease forever. Not only so, but they must bid an eternal farewell to all the world; bid farewell to all their beloved sins and pleasures; and the places and possessions that knew them once, shall know them no more forever. And further, they must bid adieu to all sacred and divine things. They are obliged to leave the bible, and all the ordinances thereof; and to bid farewell to preachers, and all sermons, and all christian people, and christian conversation; they must bid a long farewell to sabbaths and seasons, and opportunities of worship; yea an eternal farewell to all mercy and all hope; an eternal farewell to God the Father, Son and Holy Ghost, and adieu to heaven and all happiness, to saints and all the inhabitants of the upper world. At your leisure please to read the destruction of Babylon; you will find it written in the 18th of the Revelations.

On the other hand, the poor departed soul must take up its lodging in sorrow, wo and misery, in the lake that burns with fire and brimstone, were the worm dieth not and the fire is not quenched; where a multitude of frightful deformed devils dwell, and the damned ghosts of Adam's race; where darkness, horror and despair reigns, or where hope never comes, and where poor guilty naked souls will be tormented with exquisite torments, even the wrath of the Almighty poured out upon the damned souls; the smoke of their torments ascending up forever and ever; their mouths and nostrils streaming forth with living fire; and hellish groans, cries and shrieks all around them, and merciless devils upbraiding them for their folly and madness, and tormenting them incessantly. And there they must endure the most unsatiable, fruitless desire, and the most overwhelming shame and confusion and the most horrible fear, and the most doleful sorrow, and the most racking despair. When they cast their flaming eyes to heaven, with Dives in torments, they behold an angry GOD, whose eyes are as a flaming fire, and they are struck with ten thousand darts of pain; and the sight of the happiness of the saints above, adds to their pains and aggravates their misery. And when they reflect upon their past folly and madness in neglecting the great salvation in their day, it will pierce them with ten thousand inconceivable torments; it will as it were enkindle their hell afresh; and it will cause them to curse themselves bitterly, and curse the day in which they were born, and curse their parents that were the instruments of their being in the world; yea, they will curse, bitterly curse, and wish that very GOD that gave them their being to be in the same condition with them in hell torments. This is what is called the second death and it is the last death, and an eternal death to a guilty soul.

And O eternity, eternity, eternity! Who can measure it? Who can count the years thereof? Arithmetic must fail, the thoughts of men and angels are drowned in it; how shall we describe eternity? To what shall we compare it? Were it possible to employ a fly to carry off this globe by the small particles thereof, and to carry them to such a distance that it would return once in *ten thousand* years for another particle, and so continue till it has carried off all this globe, and framed them together in some unknown space, till it has made just such a world as this is: After all, eternity would remain the same unexhausted duration. This must be the unavoidable portion of all impenitent sinners, let them be who they will, great or small, honorable or ignoble, rich or poor, bond or free. Negroes, Indians, English, or of what nation soever; all that die in their sins must go to hell together; for the wages of sin is death.

The next thing that I was to consider is this:

That eternal life and happiness is the free gift of God through Jesus Christ our Lord.

Under this proposition I shall now endeavour to show that this life and happiness is.

The life that is mentioned in our text is a spiritual life, it is the life of the soul; from sin to holiness, from darkness to light, a translation from the kingdom and dominion of satan, to the kingdom of God's grace. In other words, it is being restored to the image of God and delivered from the image of satan. And this life consists in union of the soul to God, and communion with God; a real participation of the divine nature, or in the Apostle's words, is a Christ formed within us; I live says he, yet not I but Christ liveth in me.[14] And the Apostle John saith God is love and he that dwelleth in love, dwelleth in God, and God in him.[15] This is the life of the soul. It is called emphatically life, because it is a life that shall never have a period, a stable, a permanent, and unchangeable life, called in the scriptures everlasting life, or life eternal. And the happiness of this life consists in communion with God, or in the spiritual enjoyment of God. As much as a soul enjoys of God in this life, just so much of life and happiness he enjoys or possesses; yea, just so much of heaven he enjoys. A true christian, desires no other heaven but the enjoyment of God; a full and perfect enjoyment of God, is a full and perfect heaven and happiness to a gracious soul.— Further, this life is called eternal life because God has planted a living principle in the soul; and whereas he was dead before, now he is made alive unto God; there is an active principle within him towards God, he now moves towards God in his religious devotions and exercises; is daily comfortably and sweetly walking with God, in all his ordinances and commands; his delight is in the ways of God; he breathes towards God, a living breath, in praises, prayers, adorations and thanksgivings; his prayers are now heard in the heavens, and his praises delight the ears of the Almighty, and his thanksgiving are accepted, so alive is he now to God, that it is his meat and drink, yea more than his meat and drink, to do the will of his heavenly Father. It is his delight, his happiness and pleasure to serve God. He does not drag himself to his duties now, but he does them out of choice, and with alacrity of soul. Yea, so alive is he to God, that he gives up himself and all that he has entirely to God, to be for him

[14]Galatians 2:20.
[15]Occom paraphrases I John 4:8, 12–13.

and no other; his whole aim is to glorify God, in all things, whether by life or death, all the same to him.

We have a bright example of this in St. Paul. After he was converted, he was all alive to God; he regarded not his life but was willing to spend and be spent in the service of his God; he was hated, revil'd, despised, laughed at, and called all manner of evil names; was scourged, stoned and imprisoned; and all could not stop his activity towards God. He would boldly and courageously go on in preaching the gospel of the Lord Jesus Christ, to poor lost and undone sinners; he would do the work God set him about, in spite of all opposition he met with either from men or devils, earth or hell; come death or come life, none of these things moved him, because he was alive unto God. Though he suffered hunger and thirst, cold and heat, poverty and nakedness by day and by night, by sea, and by land, and was in danger always; yet he would serve God amidst all these dangers. Read his amazing account in 2 Cor. 11. 23, and on.

Another instance of marvellous love towards God, we have in Daniel. When there was a proclamation of prohibition, sent by the king to all his subjects forbidding them to call upon their gods for 30 days; which was done by envious men, that they might find occasion against Daniel the servant of the most high God; yet he having the life of God in his soul regarded not the king's decree, but made his petition to his God, as often as he used to do though death was threatened to the disobedient. But he feared not the hell they had prepared; for it seems, the den resembled hell, and the lions represented the devils. And when he was actually cast into the lions den, the ravenous beasts became meek and innocent as lambs, before the prophet, because he was alive unto God; the spirit of the Most High was in him, and the lions were afraid before him. Thus it was with Daniel and Paul; they went through fire and water, as the common saying is, because they had eternal life in their souls in an eminent manner; and they regarded not this life for the cause and glory of God. And thus it has been in all ages with true Christians. Many of the fore-fathers of the English, in this country, had this life and are gone the same way, that the holy Prophets and Apostles went. Many of them went through all manner of sufferings for God; and a great number of them are gone home to heaven, in chariots of fire. I have seen the place in London, called Smithfield, where numbers were burnt to death for the religion of Jesus Christ.[16] And there is the same life in true christians now in these days; and if there should persecutions arise in our day, I verily believe, true christians would suffer with the same spirit and temper of mind, as those did, who suffered in days past.—This is the life which our text speaks of.

We proceed in the next place to show, that this life, which we have described, is the free gift of God, through Jesus Christ our Lord.

Sinners have forfeited all mercy into the hands of divine justice and have merited hell and damnation to themselves; for the wages of sin is everlasting death, but heaven and happiness is a free gift; it comes by favor; and all merit is excluded; and especially if we consider that we are fallen sinful creatures, and there is nothing in us

[16]Smithfield, a market until 1855, was a popular spot for burnings. The last for heresy occurred in 1612 during the reign of James I.

that can recommend us to the favour of God; and we can do nothing that is agreeable and acceptable to God; and the mercies we enjoy in this life are altogether from the pure mercy of God; we are unequal to them. Good old Jacob cried out, under the sense of his unworthiness, "I am less than the least of all thy mercies,"[17] and we have nothing to give unto God if we essay to give all the service that we are capable of, we should give him nothing but what was his own, and when we give up ourselves unto God, both soul and body, we give him nothing; for we were his before; he had a right to do with us as he pleased, either to throw us into hell, or to save us.—There is nothing that we can call our own, but our sins; and who is he that dares to say, I expect to have heaven for my sins? for our text says, that the wages of sin is death. If we are thus unequal and unworthy of the least mercy in this life, how much more are we unworthy of eternal life? Yet God can find it in his heart to give it. And it is altogether unmerited; it is a free gift to undeserving and hell deserving sinners of mankind: it is altogether of God's sovereign good pleasure to give it. It is of free grace and sovereign mercy, and from the unbounded goodness of God; he was self-moved to it. And it is said that this life is given in and through our Lord Jesus Christ. It could not be given in any other way, but in and through the death and suffering of the Lord Jesus Christ; Christ himself is the gift, and he is the christian's life. "For God so loved the world that he gave his only begotten Son, that whosoever believed in him should not perish but have everlasting life."[18] The word says further, "For by grace ye are saved, through faith, and that not of yourselves it is the gift of God."[19] This is given through Jesus Christ our Lord; it is Christ that purchased it with his own blood; he prepared it with his divine and almighty power; and by the same power, and by the influence of his spirit, he prepares us for it; and by his divine grace preserves us to it. In a word, he is all in all in our eternal salvation; all this is the free gift of God.

I have now gone through what I proposed from my text. And I shall now make some application of the whole.

First to the criminal in particular; and then to the auditory in general.

My poor unhappy Brother MOSES,

As it was your own desire that I should preach to you this last discourse, so I shall speak plainly to you.—You are the bone of my bone, and flesh of my flesh. You are an Indian, a despised creature, but you have despised yourself; yea you have despised God more; you have trodden under foot his authority; you have despised his commands and precepts; And now as God says, be sure your sins will find you out. And now, poor Moses, your sins have found you out, and they have overtaken you this day; the day of your death is now come; the king of terrors is at hand; you have but a very few moments to breathe in this world.—The just law of man, and the holy laws of Jehovah, call aloud for the destruction of your mortal life; God says, "Whoso sheddeth man's blood by man shall his blood be shed."[20] This is the ancient decree of heaven, and it is to be executed by man; nor have you the least gleam of hope of escape, for the unalterable sentence is past: The terrible day of execution is come; the unwelcome guard is about you; and the fatal instruments of death are now made ready; your coffin and your grave, your last lodging are open ready to receive you.

[17]Genesis 32:10.
[18]John 3:16.
[19]Ephesians 2:8.
[20]Genesis 9:6.

Alas! poor Moses, now you know by sad, by woful experience, the living truth of our text, that the wages of sin is death. You have been already dead; yea, twice dead: By nature spiritually dead. And since the awful sentence of death has been passed upon you, you have been dead to all the pleasures of this life; or all the pleasures, lawful or unlawful, have been dead to you: And death, which is the wages of sin, is standing even on this side of your grave ready to put a final period to your mortal life; and just beyond the grave, eternal death awaits your poor soul, and devils are ready to drag your miserable soul down to their bottomless den, where everlasting wo and horror reigns; the place is filled with doleful shrieks, howls and groans of the damned. Oh! to what a miserable, folorn, and wretched condition has your extravagance folly and wickedness brought you! i.e. if you die in your sins. And O! what manner of repentance ought you to manifest! How ought your heart to bleed for what you have done! How ought you to prostrate your soul before a bleeding God! And under self-condemnation, cry out ah Lord, ah Lord, what have I done?—Whatever partiality, injustice and error there may be among the judges of the earth, remember that you have deserved a thousand deaths, and a thousand hells, by reason of your sins, at the hands of a holy God. Should God come out against you in strict justice, alas! what could you say for yourself; for you have been brought up under the bright sunshine, and plain, and loud sound of the gospel; and you have had a good education; you can read and write well; and God has given you a good natural understanding: And therefore your sins are so much more aggravated. You have not sinned in such an ignorant manner as others have done; but you have sinned with both your eyes open as it were, under the light even the glorious light of the gospel of the Lord Jesus Christ.—You have sinned against the light of your own conscience, against your knowledge and understanding; you have sinned against the pure and holy laws of God, the just laws of men; you have sinned against heaven and earth; you have sinned against all the mercies and goodness of God; you have sinned against the whole bible, against the Old and New-Testament; you have sinned against the blood of Christ, which is the blood of the everlasting covenant. O poor Moses, see what you have done! And now repent, repent, I say again repent; see how the blood you shed cries against you, and the avenger of blood is at your heels. O fly, fly, to the blood of the Lamb of God for the pardon of all your aggravated sins.

But let us now turn to a more pleasant theme.—Though you have been a great sinner, a heaven-daring sinner; yet hark and hear the joyful sound from heaven, even from the King of kings, and Lord of lords; that the gift of God is eternal life, through Jesus Christ our Lord. It is the free gift offered to the greatest sinners, and upon their true repentance towards God and faith in the Lord Jesus Christ they shall be welcome to the life they have spoken of: it is offered upon free terms. He that hath no money may come; he that hath no righteousness, no goodness may come, the call is to poor undone sinners; the call is not to the righteous, but sinners calling them to repentance. Hear the voice of the Son of the Most High God, Come unto me all ye that labor and are heavy laden, and I will give you rest.[21] This is a call, a gracious call to you poor Moses, under your present burden and distresses. And Christ alone has

[21]Matthew 11:28.

a right to call sinners to himself. It would be presumption for a mighty angel to call a poor sinner in this manner; and were it possible for you to apply to all God's creatures, they would with one voice tell you, that it was not in them to help you. Go to all the means of grace, they would prove miserable helps without Christ himself. Yea, apply to all the ministers of the gospel in the world, they would all say, that it was not in them, but would only prove as indexes, to point out to you, the Lord Jesus Christ, the only Saviour of sinners of mankind. Yea, go to all the angels in heaven they would do the same. Yea, go to God the Father himself without Christ, he could not help you, to speak after the manner of men, he would also point to the Lord Jesus Christ, and say this is my beloved Son, in whom I am well pleased hear ye him. Thus you see, poor Moses, that there is none in heaven, or earth, that can help you, but Christ; he alone has power to save, and to give life.—God the eternal Father appointed him, chose him, authorized and fully commissioned him to save sinners. He came down from heaven into this lower world, and became as one of us, and stood in our room. He was the second Adam. And as God demanded correct obedience of the first Adam; the second fulfil'd it; and as the first sinned and incurred the wrath and anger of God, the second endured it; he suffered in our room. As he became sin for us, he was a man of sorrows, and acquainted with grief; all our stripes were laid upon him; yea, he was finally condemned, because we were under condemnation; and at last was executed and put to death, for our sins; was lifted up between the heavens and the earth, and was crucified on the accursed tree; his blessed hands and feet were fastened there; there he died a shameful and ignominious death; There he finished the great work of our redemption: There his hearts blood was shed for our cleansing: There he fully satisfied the divine justice of God, for penitent, believing sinners, though they have been the chief of sinners.—O Moses! this is good news to you in this last day of your life; here is a crucified Saviour at hand for your sins; his blessed hands are outstretched, all in a gore of blood for you. This is the only Saviour, an Almighty Saviour, just such as you stand in infinite and perishing need of. O, poor Moses! hear the dying prayer of a gracious Saviour on the accursed tree. Father forgive them for they know not what they do. This was a prayer for his enemies and murderers; and it is for you, if you will now only repent and believe in him. O, why will you die eternally, poor Moses, since Christ has died for sinners? Why will you go to hell from beneath a bleeding Saviour as it were? This is the day of your execution, yet it is the accepted time, it is the day of salvation if you will now believe in the Lord Jesus Christ. Must Christ follow you into the prison by his servants and there intreat you to accept of eternal life, and will you refuse it? Must he follow you even to the gallows, and there beseech of you to accept of him, and will you refuse him? Shall he be crucified hard by your gallows, as it were, and will you regard him not. O poor Moses, now believe on the Lord Jesus Christ with all your heart, and thou shalt be saved eternally. Come just as you are, with all your sins and abominations, with all your filthiness, with all your blood-guiltiness, with all your condemnation, and lay hold of the hope set before you this day. This is the last day of salvation with your soul; you will be beyond the bounds of mercy in a few minutes more. O what a joyful day would it be if you would now openly believe in and receive the Lord Jesus Christ; it would be the beginning of heavenly days with your poor soul; instead of a melancholy day, it would be a wedding day to your soul: It would cause the very angels in heaven to rejoice, and the saints on earth to be glad; it would cause the angels to come down from the realms above, and wait hovering about your gallows, ready to convey your soul to the heavenly mansions. There to taste the possession of eternal glory and happiness, and join the heavenly choirs in singing the songs of Moses and the Lamb: There to set down forever with Abraham, Isaac and Jacob in the kingdom of God's glory; and your shame and guilt shall be forever banished from the place, and all sorrow and fear forever fly away, and tears be wiped from your face; and there shall you forever admire the astonishing and amazing and infinite mercy of God in Christ Jesus, in pardoning such a monstrous sinner as you have been; there you will claim the highest note of praise, for the riches of free grace in Christ Jesus. But if you will not except of a Saviour so freely offered to you in this last day of your life, you must this very day bid a farewell to God the Father Son and holy Ghost, to heaven and all the saints and angels that are there; and you must bid all the saints in this lower world an eternal farewell, and even the whole world. And so I must leave you in the hands of God; and I must turn to the whole auditory.

Sirs.—We may plainly see, from what we have heard, and from the miserable object before us, into what a doleful condition sin has brought mankind, even into a state of death and misery. We are by nature as certainly under the sentence of death from God, as this miserable man is by the just determination of man; for we are all dying creatures, and we are, or ought to be sensible of it; and this is the dreadful fruit of sin. O let us then fly from all appearance of sin; let us fight againgst it with all our might; let us repent and turn to God, and believe on the Lord Jesus Christ, that we may live for ever: Let us all prepare for death, for we know not how soon, nor how suddenly we may be called out of the world.

Permit me in particular, reverend gentlemen and fathers in Israel, to speak a few words to you, though I am very sensible that I need to be taught the first principles of the oracles of God, by the least of you. But since the Providence of God has so ordered it, that I must speak here on this occasion, I beg that you would not be offended nor be angry with me.

God has raised you up from among your brethren, and has qualified and authorized you to do his great work; and you are the servants of the Most High God, and ministers of the Lord Jesus Christ; you are Christ's ambassadors; you are called shepherds, watchmen overseers, or bishops, and you are rulers of the temples of God, or of the assemblies of God's people; you are God's angels, and as such you have nothing to do but to wait on God, and to do the work the Lord Jesus Christ your blessed Lord and Master has set you about, not fearing the face of any man, nor seeking to please men, but your Master. You are to declare the whole counsel of God, and to give a portion to every soul in due season; as a physician gives a portion to his patients, according to their diseases, so you are to give a portion to every soul in due season according to their spiritual maladies: Whether it be agreeable or not agreeable to them, you must give it to them; whether they will love you or hate you for it, you must do your work. Your work is to encounter sin and satan; this was the very end of the coming of Christ into the world, and the end of his death and sufferings; it was to make an end of sin and to destroy the works of the devil. And this is your work still, you are to fight the battles of the Lord. Therefore combine together, and be as terrible as an army with banners; attack this monster sin in all its shapes and windings, and lift up your voices as trumpets and not spare, call aloud, call your people to arms against this common enemy of mankind, that sin may not be their ruin. Call upon all orders ranks and degrees of people, to rise up against sin and satan. Arm your selves with fervent prayer continually, this is a terrible weapon against the kingdom of satan. And preach the death and sufferings, and the resurrection of Jesus Christ; for nothing is so destructive to the kingdom of the devil as this is. But what need I speak any more! Let us all attend, and hear the great Apostle of the Gentiles speak unto us in Eph. 6 ch. from the tenth verse and onward. Finally my bretheren, be strong in the Lord, and in the power of his might; put on the whole armour of God, that ye may be able to stand against the wiles of the devil. For we wrestle not against flesh and blood, but against principalities, against powers, against the rulers of darkness of this world, against spiritual wickedness in high places. Wherefore take unto you the whole armour of God, that ye may be able to stand in the evil day, and having done all, to stand. Stand therefore, having your loins girt about with truth, and having on the breast-plate of righteousness; And your feet shod with the preparation of the gospel of peace: Above all, taking the shield of faith, wherewith ye shall be able to quench all the fiery darts of the wicked: And take the helmet of salvation, and the sword of the spirit, which is the word of God: Praying always with all prayer and supplication in the spirit, and watching therunto with all perseverance, and supplication for all saints.

I shall now address myself to the Indians, my bretheren and kindred according to the flesh.

My poor Kindred,

You see the woful consequences of sin, by seeing this our poor miserable countryman now before us, who is to die this day for his sins and great wickedness. And it was the sin of drunkenness that has brought this destruction and untimely death upon him. There is a dreadful wo denounced from the Almighty against drunkards; and it is this sin, this abominable, this beastly and accursed sin of drunkenness, that has stript us of every desirable comfort in this life; by this we are poor miserable and wretched; by this sin we have no name nor credit in the world among polite nations; for this sin we are despised in the world, and it is all right and just, for we despise ourselves more; and if we don't regard ourselves, who will regard us? And it is for our sins and especially for that accursed, that most devilish sin of drunkenness that we suffer every day. For the love of strong drink we spend all that we have, and every thing we can get. By this sin we can't have comfortable houses, nor any thing comfortable in our houses; neither food nor raiment, nor decent utensils. We are obliged to put up with any sort of shelter just to screen us from the severity of the weather, and we go about with very mean, ragged and dirty clothes, almost naked. And we are half-starved, for the most of the time obliged to pick up any thing to eat. And our poor children are suffering every day for want of the necessaries of life; they are very often crying for want of food, and we have nothing to give them; and in the cold weather they are shivering and crying, being pinched with cold. All this for the love of strong drink. And this is not all the misery and evil we bring on ourselves in this world; but when we are intoxicated with strong drink we drown our rational powers, by which we are distinguished from the brutal creation we unman ourselves, and bring ourselves not only level with the beasts of the field, but seven degrees beneath them; yea we bring ourselves level with the devils; I don't know but we make ourselves worse than devils, for I never heard of drunken devils.

My poor kindred, do consider what a dreadful abominable sin drunkenness is. God made us men, and we chuse to be beasts and devils, God made us rational creatures, and we chuse to be fools. Do consider further, and behold a drunkard and see how he looks when he has drowned his reason; how deformed and shameful does he appear? He disfigures every part of him, both soul and body, which was made after the Image of God. He appears with awful deformity, and his whole visage is disfigured; if he attempts to speak he cannot bring out his words distinct, so as to be understood; if he walks he reels and staggers to and fro, and tumbles down. And see how he behaves, he is now laughing, and then he is crying, he is singing, and the next minute he is mourning, and is all love with every one, and anon he is raging and for fighting, and killing all before him, even the nearest and dearest relations and friends: Yea, nothing it too bad for a drunken man to do. He will do that which he would not do for the world, in his right mind; he may lie with his own sister or daughter as Lot did.

Further, when a person is drunk, he is just good for nothing in the world; he is of no service to himself, to his family, to his neighbours, or his country; and how much more unfit is he to serve God: Yet we are just fit for the service of the devil.

Again, a man in drunkenness is in all manner of dangers, he may be killed by his fellow-men, by wild beasts, and tame beasts; he may fall into the fire, into the water, or into a ditch; or he may fall down as he walks along, and break his bones or his neck; and he may cut him-self with edge-tools. Further if he has any money or any thing valuable, he may lose it all, or may be robbed, or he may make a foolish bargain and be cheated out of all he has.

I believe you know the truth of what I have just now said, many of you by sad experience; yet you will go on still in your drunkenness. Though you have been cheated over and over again, and you have lost your substance by drunkenness, yet you will venture to go on in this most destructive sin. O fools, when will ye be wise?—We all know the truth of what I have been saying, by what we have seen and heard of drunken deaths. How many have been drowned in our rivers, and how many frozen to death in the winter season! yet drunkards go on without fear and consideration: Alas, alas! What will become of all such drunkards? Without doubt they must all go to hell, except they truly repent and turn to God. Drunkenness is so common amongst us, that even our young men, (and what is still more shocking) *young women* are not ashamed to get drunk. Our young men will get drunk as soon as they will eat when they are hungry.—It is generally esteemed among men more abominable for a woman to be drunk than a man; and yet there is nothing more common amongst us than female drunkards. Women ought to be more modest than men; the holy scriptures recommend modesty to women in particular;—But drunken women have no modesty at all. It is more intolerable for a woman to get drunk, if we consider further, that she is in great danger of falling into the hands of the sons of Belial, or wicked men and being shamefully treated by them.

And here I cannot but observe, we find in sacred writ, a wo denounced against men who put their bottles to their neighbours mouth to make them drunk, that they may see their nakedness: And no doubt there are such devilish men now in our days, as there were in the days of old.

And to conclude, Consider my poor kindred, you that are drunkards, into what a miserable condition you have brought yourselves. There is a dreadful wo thundering against you every day, and the Lord says, That drunkards shall not inherit the kingdom of heaven.

And now let me exhort you all to break off from your drunkenness, by a gospel repentance, and believe on the Lord Jesus and you shall be saved. Take warning by this doleful sight before us, and by all the dreadful judgments that have befallen poor drunkards. O let us all reform our lives, and live as becomes dying creatures, in time to come. Let us be persuaded that we are accountable creatures to God, and we must be called to an account in a few days. You that have been careless all your days, now awake to righteousness, and be concerned for your poor never-dying souls. Fight against all sins, and especially the sin that easily besets you, and behave in time to come as becomes rational creatures; and above all things receive and believe on the Lord Jesus Christ, and you shall have eternal life; and when you come to die, your souls will be received into heaven, there to be with the Lord Jesus in eternal happiness, with all the saints in glory: Which God of his infinite mercy grant, through Jesus Christ our Lord.—AMEN.

1772

Briton Hammon fl. 1760

Briton Hammon's captivity narrative is widely recognized as the first African-American prose text published in North America. Unfortunately, the historical record of Hammon's life is limited to the information contained within his narrative, from which Hammon explains he has "omitted a great many things." Thus we do not know for certain whether he was a servant or a slave, whether he wrote the narrative in its entirety, or what his life was like after his return to Massachusetts. Yet Hammon's narrative still raises intriguing questions about how a man of African descent who was in servitude gained access to the public sphere and how he made use of the conventions of one of the era's most popular genres, the captivity narrative.

With his master's permission, Hammon departed from Massachusetts in 1747 on a ship bound for Jamaica. After picking up its cargo, the ship foundered off the Florida coast and was attacked by sixty Native Americans. Hammon, the only survivor, was quickly taken into captivity. Although he soon escaped aboard a Spanish schooner, he was later imprisoned for more than four years in a dungeon in Spanish Cuba because he refused to serve on a Spanish ship. After escaping from his Spanish captors, Hammon worked in Cuba before signing on board a ship bound for London. In London, Hammon was happily reunited with his master, General Winslow, after almost thirteen years. Soon after returning to Boston with his master, he published the narrative of his "uncommon sufferings."

Although Hammon is believed to be the author of his narrative, some critics have suggested that the narrative's opening and closing (and perhaps even the narrative itself) might have been authored by a white editor or writer. Ironically, the very characteristic that has caused some to question his authorship—the narrative's rather formulaic opening and closing—was a characteristic shared by numerous other eighteenth-century texts presumably written by *white* men and women, whose authorship remains unquestioned. The questioning of Hammon's authorship is revealing, given that eighteenth-century notions about authorship and about the importance of originality differed from our own century's privileging of authorial status. Many early American literary genres relied on a strict adherence to convention rather than on originality to achieve their didactic aims. That the authorship of Hammon's narrative is unconfirmed is thus unremarkable.

Contemporary readers might find it surprising that Briton Hammon made little reference to his race in his work; indeed, only one phrase in his lengthy title identified him as "A Negro Man,—Servant to General Winslow." In fact, Hammon's class position was undoubtedly much more important than his race from the perspective of his readers, and it is his subordinate position that is emphasized within the text. As a young servant or slave returning to Boston in 1760 during the middle of the Seven Years' War, Hammon would have been welcomed into a city whose male population was significantly depleted. Like young Thomas Brown, whose narrative was also published in Boston in 1760, Hammon represented a whole class of servants whose otherwise marginal status was transformed within the wartime economy. Furthermore, it was during conflicts like the Seven Years' War that the popularity and political importance of captivity narratives increased.

Yet for figures like Hammon, the experience of captivity did not fit neatly into the conventions of his chosen genre. Hammon's initial escape from captivity among Native Americans did not restore him to his community but instead to a second captivity among the Spanish. And although Hammon, like Mary Rowlandson and John Williams before him, describes his captors as barbarians and savages, his description of his eventual return to Boston—his final redemption—is contradictory, for Hammon is redeemed into servitude rather than freedom. The nature of Hammon's redemption is further complicated by the fact that he may well have been more free—at least in terms of receiving wages for his labor—during the intervals surrounding his captivities among Native Americans and the Spanish than he was after returning to Boston with his "good Master." Hammon's narrative, one of only two eighteenth-century African-American captivity narratives, thus adds a significant dimension to the study of an important early American literary genre.

Amy Winans
Dickinson College

PRIMARY WORK

Narrative of the Uncommon Sufferings and Surprizing Deliverance of Briton Hammon, 1760.

SECONDARY WORK

John Sekora, "Red, White, and Black: Indian Captivities, Colonial Printers, and the Early African-American Narrative," in *A Mixed Race: Ethnicity in Early America,* ed. Frank Shuffelton, 1993.

Narrative of the Uncommon Sufferings and Surprizing Deliverance of Briton Hammon[1]

To the Reader,

AS my Capacities and Condition of Life are very low, it cannot be expected that I should make those Remarks on the Sufferings I have met with, or the kind Providence of a good GOD for my Preservation, as one in a higher Station; but shall leave that to the Reader as he goes along, and so I shall only relate Matters of Fact as they occur to my Mind—

On Monday, 25th Day of *December,* 1747, with the leave of my Master, I went from *Marshfield,* with an Intention to go a Voyage to Sea, and the next Day, the 26th, got to *Plymouth,* where I immediately ship'd myself on board of a Sloop, Capt. *John Howland,* Master, bound to *Jamaica* and the *Bay*[2]—We sailed from *Plymouth* in a short Time, and after a pleasant Passage of about 30 Days, arrived at *Jamaica*; we was detain'd at *Jamaica* only 5 Days, from whence we sailed for the *Bay,* where we arrived safe in 10 Days. We loaded our Vessel with Logwood, and sailed from the *Bay* the 25th Day of May following, and the 15th Day of *June,* we were cast away on *Cape Florida,* about 5 Leagues from the Shore; being now destitute of every Help,[3] we knew not what to do or what Course to take in this our sad Condition:—The Captain was advised, intreated, and beg'd on, by every Person on board, to heave over but only 20 Ton of the *Wood,* and we should get clear, which if he had done, might have sav'd his Vessel and Cargo, and not only so, but his own Life, as well as the Lives of the Mate and Nine Hands, as I shall presently relate.

After being upon this Reef two Days, the Captain order'd the Boat to be hoisted out, and then ask'd who were willing to tarry on board? The whole Crew was for going on Shore at this Time, but as the Boat would not carry 12 persons at once, and to prevent any Uneasiness, the Captain, a Passenger, and one Hand tarry'd on board, while the Mate, with Seven Hands besides myself, were order'd to go on Shore in the

[1]The complete title of the Narrative was *NARRATIVE of the UNCOMMON SUFFERINGS AND Surprizing DELIVERANCE OF* BRITON HAMMON, *A Negro Man,—Servant to GENERAL WINSLOW, of Marshfield, in NEW-ENGLAND; Who returned to* Boston, *after having been absent almost Thirteen Years. CONTAINING An Account of the many Hardships he underwent from the Time he left his Master's House, in the Year 1747, to the Time of his Return to* Boston.—*How he was Cast away in the Capes of* Florida;—*the horrid Cruelty and inhuman Barbarity of the* Indians *in murdering the whole Ship's Crew;—the Manner of his being carry'd by them into Captivity. Also, An Account of his being Confined Four Years and Seven Months in a close Dungeon,—And the remarkable Manner in which he met with his* good old Master *in* London; *who returned to* New-England, *a Passenger, in the same Ship.*

[2]John Howland was captain of the ship, not "master" to Hammon. Hammon was probably a free man, despite his having just mentioned a "master" who let him set sail with Howland, but probably someone with whom Hammon had agreed to work. The "bay" destination remains unclear.

[3]Florida was held by Spain at this time.

Boat, which as soon as we had reached, one half were to be Landed, and the other four to return to the Sloop, to fetch the Captain and the others on Shore. The Captain order'd us to take with us our Arms, Ammunition, Provisions and Necessaries for Cooking, as also a Sail to make a Tent of, to shelter us from the Weather; after having left the Sloop we stood towards the Shore, and being within Two Leagues of the same, we espy'd a Number of Canoes, which we at first took to be Rocks, but soon found our Mistake, for we perceiv'd they moved towards us; we presently saw an English Colour hoisted in one of the Canoes, at the Sight of which we were not a little rejoiced, but on our advancing yet nearer, we found them, to our very great Surprize, to be *Indians* of which there were Sixty; being now so near them we could not possibly make our Escape; they soon came up with and boarded us, took away all our Arms, Ammunition, and Provision. The whole Number of Canoes (being about Twenty,) then made for the Sloop, except Two which they left to guard us, who order'd us to follow on with them; the Eighteen which made for the Sloop, went so much faster than we that they got on board above Three Hours before we came along side, and had kill'd Captain *Howland,* the Passenger and the other hand; we came to the Larboard side of the Sloop, and they order'd us round to the Starboard, and as we were passing round the Bow,[4] we saw the whole Number of *Indians,* advancing forward and loading their Guns, upon which the Mate said, *"my Lads we are all dead Men,"* and before we had got round, they discharged their Small Arms upon us, and kill'd Three of our hands, viz. *Reuben Young* of *Cape-Cod,* Mate; *Joseph Little* and *Lemuel Doty* of *Plymouth,* upon which I immediately jump'd overboard, chusing rather to be drowned, than to be kill'd by those barbarous and inhuman Savages. In three or four Minutes after, I heard another Volley which dispatched the other five, viz. *John Nowland,* and *Nathaniel Rich,* both belonging to *Plymouth,* and *Elkanah Collymore,* and *James Webb,* Strangers, and *Moses Newmock,* Molatto. As soon as they had kill'd the whole of the People, one of the Canoes padled after me, and soon came up with me, hawled me into the Canoe, and beat me most terribly with a Cutlass, after that they ty'd me down, then this Canoe stood for the Sloop again and as soon as she came along side, the *Indians* on board the Sloop betook themselves to their Canoes, then set the Vessel on Fire, making a prodigious shouting and hallowing like so many Devils. As soon as the Vessel was burnt down to the Water's edge, the *Indians* stood for the Shore, together with our Boat, on board of which they put 5 hands. After we came to the Shore, they led me to their Hutts, where I expected nothing but immediate Death, and as they spoke broken English, were often telling me, while coming from the Sloop to the Shore, that they intended to roast me alive. But the Providence of God order'd it other ways, for He appeared for my Help, *in this Mount of Difficulty,* and they were better to me then my Fears, and soon unbound me, but set a Guard over me every Night. They kept me with them about five Weeks, during which Time they us'd me pretty well, and gave me boil'd Corn, which was what they often eat themselves. The Way I made my Escape from these Villains was this; A Spanish Schooner arriving there from *St. Augustine,* the Master of which, whose Name was *Romond,* asked the

[4]Evidently, they were on the left side (larboard) and were ordered to remove to the right side (starboard) of the ship, to which side they passed by moving around the ship by way of its front (bow).

Indians to let me go on board his Vessel, which they granted, and the Captain[5] knowing me very well, weigh'd Anchor and carry'd me off to the *Havanna,*[6] and after being there four Days the *Indians* came after me, and insisted on having me again, as I was their Prisoner;—They made Application to the Governor, and demanded me again from him; in answer to which the Governor told them, that as they had put the whole Crew to Death, they should not have me again, and so paid them Ten Dollars for me, adding, that he would not have them kill any Person hereafter, but take as many of them as they could, of those that should be cast away, and bring them to him for which he would pay them Ten Dollars a-head. At the *Havanna* I lived with the Governor in the Castle about a Twelve-month, where I was walking thro' the Street, I met with a Press-Gang who immediately prest me, and put me into Goal, and with a Number of others I was confin'd till next Morning,[7] when we were all brought out, and ask'd who would go on board the King's Ships, four of which having been lately built, were bound to *Old-Spain,* and on my refusing to serve on board, they put me in a close Dungeon, where I was confin'd *Four years and seven months,* during which time I often made application to the Governor, by Persons who came to see the Prisoners, but they never acquainted him with it, nor did he know all this Time what became of me, which was the means of my being confin'd there so long. But kind Providence so order'd it, that after I had been in this Place so long as the Time mention'd above the Captain of a Merchantman, belonging to *Boston,* having sprung a Leak was obliged to put into the *Havanna* to rest, and while he was at Dinner at Mrs. *Betty Howard's,* she told the Captain of my deplorable Condition, and said she would be glad, if he could by some means or other relieve me; The Captain told Mrs. *Howard* he would use his best Endeavours for my Relief and Enlargement.

Accordingly, after Dinner, [the Captain] came to the Prison, and ask'd the Keeper if he might see me; upon his Request I was brought out of the Dungeon, and after the Captain had Interrogated me, told me, he would intercede with the Governor for my Relief out of that miserable Place, which he did, and the next Day the Governor sent an order to release me; I lived with the Governor about a Year after I was delivered from the Dungeon, in which Time I endeavour'd three Times to make my Escape, the last of which proved effectual; the first Time I got on board of Captain *Marsh,* an *English* Twenty Gun Ship, with a Number of others, and lay on board conceal'd that Night; and the next Day the Ship being under sail, I thought myself safe, and so made my Appearance upon Deck, but as soon as we were discovered the Captain ordered the Boat out, and sent us all on Shore—I intreated the Captain to let me, in particular, tarry on board, begging, and crying to him, to commiserate my unhappy Condition, and added, that I had been confin'd almost five Years in a close Dungeon, but the Captain would not hearken to any Intreaties, for fear of having the Governor's Displeasure, and so I was obliged to go on Shore.

After being on Shore another Twelvemonth, I endeavour'd to make my Escape

[5]Hammon's note reads: "The Way I came to know this Gentleman was, by his being taken last War by an *English* Privateer, and brought into *Jamaica,* while I was there."

[6]That is, Hammon boarded a Spanish ship from St. Augustine, Florida, which took him to Havanna, capital of the Spanish colony in present-day Cuba. Francisco Antonio Cagigal de la Vega (1695–1777) was governor of Cuba.

[7]Hammon was seized by an impressment crew, usually supported by the government, and held in jail (goal) for possible service (pressment).

the second Time, by trying to get on board of a Sloop bound to *Jamaica,* and as I was going from the City to the Sloop, was unhappily taken by the Guard, and ordered back to the Castle, and there confined.—However, in a short Time I was set at Liberty, and order'd with a Number of others to carry the Bishop[8] from the Castle, thro' the Country, to confirm the old People, baptize Children, &c. for which he receives large Sums of Money.—I was employ'd in this Service about Seven Months, during which Time I lived very well, and then returned to the Castle again, where I had my Liberty to walk about the City, and do Work for my self;—The *Beaver,* an *English* Man of War then lay in the Harbour, and having been informed by some of the Ship's Crew that she was to sail in a few Days, I had nothing now to do, but to seek an Opportunity how I should make my Escape.

Accordingly one Sunday Night the Lieutenant of the Ship with a Number of the Barge Crew were in a Tavern, and Mrs. *Howard* who had before been a Friend to me, interceded with the Lieutenant to carry me on board: the Lieutenant said he would with all his Heart, and immediately I went on board in the Barge. The next Day the *Spaniards* came along side the *Beaver,* and demanded me again, with a Number of others who had made their Escape from them, and got on board the Ship, but just before I did; but the Captain, who was a true *Englishman,* refus'd them, and said he could not answer it, to deliver up any *Englishman* under *English* Colours.—In a few Days we set Sail for *Jamaica,* where we arrived safe, after a short and pleasant Passage.

After being at *Jamaica* a short Time we sail'd for *London,* as convoy to a Fleet of Merchantmen, who all arrived safe in the *Downs,* I was turned over to another Ship, the *Arcenceil,* and there remained about a Month. From this Ship I went on board the *Sandwich* of 90 Guns; on board the *Sandwich,* I tarry'd 6 Weeks, and then was order'd on board the *Hercules,* Capt. *John Porter,* a 74 Gun Ship, we sail'd on a Cruize, and met with a *French* 84 Gun Ship, and had a very smart Engagement, in which about 70 of our Hands were Kill'd and Wounded, the Captain lost his Leg in the Engagement, and I was Wounded in the Head by a small Shot.[9] We should have taken this Ship, if they had not cut away the most of our Rigging; however, in about three Hours after, a 64 Gun Ship, came up with and took her—I was discharged from the *Hercules* the 12th Day of *May* 1759 (having been on board of that Ship 3 Months) on account of my being disabled in the Arm, and render'd incapable of Service, after being honourably paid the Wages due to me. I was put into the *Greenwich* Hospital where I stay'd and soon recovered.—I then ship'd myself a Cook on board Captain *Martyn,* an arm'd Ship in the King's Service. I was on board this Ship almost Two Months, and after being paid my Wages, was discharg'd in the Month of *October.*—After my discharge from Captain *Martyn,* I was taken sick in *London* of a Fever, and was confin'd about 6 Weeks, where I expended all my Money, and left in very poor Circumstances; and unhappy for me I knew nothing of my *good Master's* being in *London* at this my very difficult Time. After I got well of my sickness, I

[8]The bishop at this time was Pedro Augustín Morell de Santa Cruz (1694–1768). Hammon's note at this point reads: "He is carried (by Way of Respect) in a large Two-arm Chair; the Chair is lin'd with crimson Velvet, and supported by eight Persons."

[9]It remains unclear which French ship is described here. Hammon's note about the "engagement" reads: "A particular Account of this Engagement, has been Publish'd in the *Boston* News-Papers."

ship'd myself on board of a large Ship bound to *Guinea,*[10] and being in a publick House one Evening, I overheard a Number of Persons talking about Rigging a Vessel bound to *New-England,* I ask'd them to what Part of *New-England* this Vessel was bound? They told me, to *Boston;* and having ask'd them who was Commander? they told me, Capt. *Watt;* in a few Minutes after this the Mate of the Ship came in, and I ask'd him if Captain Watt did not want a Cook, who told me he did, and that the Captain would be in, in a few Minutes; and in about half an Hour the Captain came in, and then I ship'd myself at once, after begging off from the Ship bound to *Guinea*; I work'd on board Captain *Watt's* Ship almost Three Months, before she sail'd, and one Day being at Work in the Hold, I overheard some Persons on board mention the Name of *Winslow,* at the Name of which I was very inquisitive, and having ask'd what *Winslow* they were talking about? They told me it was *General Winslow;* and that he was one of the Passengers, I ask'd them what *General Winslow*? For I never knew *my good Master,* by that Title before; but after enquiring more particularly I found it must be *Master,* and in a few Days Time the Truth was joyfully verify'd by a happy Sight of his Person, which so overcome me, that I could not speak to him for some Time—*My good Master* was exceeding glad to see me, telling me that I was like one arose from the Dead, for he thought I had been Dead a great many Years, having heard nothing of me for almost Thirteen Years.

I think I have not deviated from Truth, in any particular of this my Narrative, and tho' I have omitted a great many Things, yet what is wrote may suffice to convince the Reader, that I have been most grievously afflicted, and yet thro' the Divine Goodness, as miraculously preserved, and delivered out of many Dangers; of which I desire to retain a *grateful Remembrance,* as long as I live in the World.

And now, That in the Providence of that GOD, who delivered his Servant David out of the Paw of the Lion and out of the Paw of the Bear,[11] *I am freed from a* long *and* dreadful Captivity, among worse Savages than they; *And am return'd to my* own Native Land, to Shew how Great Things the Lord hath done for Me; *I would call upon all Men, and Say,* O Magnifie the Lord with Me, and let us Exalt his Name together![12]—O that Men would Praise the Lord for His Goodness, and for his Wonderful Works to the Children of Men!

1760

Prince Hall 1735?–1807

Prince Hall's organizational efforts took place at a propitious time in early African-American political and social history. Following the upsurge of the black slave population in the mid-eighteenth century, the Revolutionary and post-Revolutionary period saw an increase in the founding of black benevolent societies, churches, schools, and mutual aid groups. Drawing upon a new sense of African identity, derived possibly from the presence of newly arrived countrymen, African-American ac-

[10]A ship bound for Guinea would have been a ship heading to Africa to acquire a load of slaves.

[11]See I Samuel 17:37.

[12]See Psalm 34:4.

tivists frequently denominated their institutions as "African." This racial self-consciousness was enhanced by the increasing formation of black households and kinship groups in New England, New York, and New Jersey, as slaves were freed.

If Prince Hall had not actually lived, he most certainly would have been invented—which is to say that the pioneering socialization he achieved for and among early black Americans would have been realized sooner or later by some colonial black American. Whether in seemingly passive enslavement or as modestly protesting free persons, blacks were clearly too vital, too fundamentally hardy, to have long been excluded from dignified social groupings, and, thereafter, from variously finding their own American way.

Hall organized some fourteen free black Bostonians in 1775 into a society that eventually became an official, degree-granting Masonic order, "African Lodge No. 459" (later No. 370) on May 6, 1787. As Master of this first lodge, Hall continued his work and brought together an association of black Masonic Grand Lodges that would proliferate into what is today a flourishing, worldwide fraternal society. (In 1977 there were more than 500,000 members of such lodges.) Hall is also remembered as one of the more prolific writers of early black America.

Born sometime between 1735 and 1738 at a place still unknown, Hall seems to have been a slave or indentured servant in the Boston household of leather-dresser William Hall from 1749 until 1770, when he was freed. Thereafter he made a decent living as a leather-dresser, caterer, and perhaps as a shop owner. From the year 1762, Hall was a member of the Reverend Andrew Crosswell's Congregational church on School Street, and "in full communication therewith, for a number of years," he may well have functioned as an unordained preacher to fellow Masons and other interested blacks on the premises of the School Street church, which was abandoned in 1764, when an epidemic of smallpox struck Boston.

From 1777 until four months before his death in December 1807, Prince Hall engaged in activities that were central to the development of a vital African-American identity. He composed and published a group of writings, including letters to London Masonic officials, the Countess of Huntingdon, Boston newspapers, and prominent blacks in Providence and Philadelphia, but most notably he published a series of petitions on behalf of his Masons and free blacks in general. He solicited the abolition of Massachusetts slavery (1777). He petitioned for the proffered but rejected military assistance of some 700 blacks for use by Governor James Bowdoin (who was trying to put down Shays's Rebellion in the western part of the state, 1786). In January of 1787, with 73 other blacks, Hall petitioned the General Court for financial or other assistance in support of plans for blacks to emigrate to Africa. In October of that year, he petitioned, unsuccessfully, for public education for children of taxpaying Boston blacks.

In his own home for most of 1789, Hall housed the Reverend John Marrant (1755–1791), then enroute back to his chosen home in London from a lengthy preaching tour of Eastern Canada. In London in 1785, Marrant had become the first black American ordained minister. Hall also made Marrant a chaplain for his Lodge; for the Lodge Marrant preached at Fanueil Hall an inspirational sermon published later that year.

Hall himself is on record in the "Taxing Books" as having paid both real estate and poll taxes from 1780 onwards. He also petitioned, this time successfully, on behalf of three Boston blacks who were kidnapped into slavery but quickly released (1788). In 1792 he published a racially stimulating Charge to fellow Lodge members; in 1797 he published another such Charge. On May 6, 1806, Hall and a white man, John Vinal of Boston, once a member of Hall's School Street church, gave a deposition acknowledging joint receipt of three thousand dollars for the sale of the church property. Finally, on August 31, 1807, Hall signed another deposition, in effect a testimony of Vinal's character; both of these depositions remain in manuscript.

Prince Hall was much concerned with the organization and dignifying of his fellow Masons, to be sure, but he was just as concerned with the future of the enslaved black American: because black slavery was primarily a white American issue, he was necessarily concerned with the future of America and Americans.

William H. Robinson
Rhode Island College

Philip M. Richards
Colgate University

SECONDARY WORKS

Sidney Kaplan, "Prince Hall: Organizer," in *The Black Presence in the Era of The American Revolution 1770–1800,* 1973; Charles H. Wesley, *Prince Hall: Life and Legacy,* 1977; Joseph A. Walker, *Black Squares & Compass/200 Years of Prince Hall/Freemasonry,* 1979.

To the Honorable Council & House of Representatives for the State of Massachusetts-Bay in General Court assembled January 13th 1777.[1]

The Petition of a great number of Negroes who are detained in a state of Slavery in the Bowels of a free & Christian Country Humbly Shewing

That your Petitioners apprehend that they have, in common with all other Men, a natural & unalienable right to that freedom, which the great Parent of the Universe hath bestowed equally on all Mankind, & which they have never forfeited by any compact or agreement whatever—But they were unjustly dragged, by the cruel hand of Power, from their dearest friends, & some of them even torn from the embraces of their tender Parents. From a populous, pleasant and plentiful Country—& in Violation of the Laws of Nature & of Nation & in defiance of all the tender feelings of humanity, brought hither to be sold like Beasts of Burden, & like them condemned to slavery for Life—Among a People professing the mild Religion of Jesus—A People not insensible of the sweets of rational freedom—Nor without spirit to resent the unjust endeavours of others to reduce them to a State of Bondage & Subjection—Your Honors need not to be informed that a Life of Slavery, like that of your peti-

[1]This is from a typescript of an "improved" version, on file at the Massachusetts Archives, volume 212, p. 132; an original, semi-complete version was published by Jeremy Belknap in the *Massachusetts Historical Collections. Fifth Series,* No. 3 (Boston, 1788).

tioners, deprived of every social privilege, of every thing requisite to render Life even tolerable, is far worse than Non-Existence—In imitation of the laudable example of the good People of these States, your Petitioners have long & patiently waited the event of Petition after Petition by them presented to the legislative Body of this State, & can not but with grief reflect that their success has been but too similar—They can not but express their astonishment, that it has never been considered, that every principle from which America has acted in the course of her unhappy difficulties with Great-Britain, pleads stronger than a thousand arguments in favor of your Petitioners. They therefore humbly beseech your Honors, to give this Petition its due weight & consideration, & cause an Act of the Legislature to be passed, whereby they may be restored to the enjoyment of that freedom which is the natural right of all Men—& their Children (who were born in this Land of Liberty) may not be held as Slaves after they arrive at the age of twenty one years—So may the Inhabitants of this State (no longer chargeable with the inconsistency of acting, themselves, the part which they condemn & oppose in others) be prospered in their present glorious struggles for Liberty; & have those blessings secured to them by Heaven, of which benevolent minds can not wish to deprive their fellow Men.

And your Petitioners, as in Duty Bound shall ever pray.

Lancaster Hill
Peter Bess
Brister Slenten
Prince Hall
Jack Purpont *his mark*
Nero Suneto *his mark*
Newport Symner *his mark*
Job Lock

Negroes Petition to the Honble
Genl Assembly—Mass.
March 18
Judge Sargeant
M. Balton
M. Appleton
Coll. Brooks
M. Stony
W. Lowell
Matter Atlege
W. Davis

1788

A Charge, Delivered to the African Lodge, June 24, 1797, at Menotomy

By the Right Worshipful Prince Hall. Published by the Desire of the Members of Said Lodge. 1797.

Beloved Brethren of the African Lodge,

'Tis now five years since I deliver'd a Charge to you on some parts and points of Masonry. As one branch or superstructure on the foundation; when I endeavoured to shew you the duty of a Mason to a Mason, and charity or love to all mankind, as the mark and image of the great God, and the Father of the human race.[1]

I shall now attempt to shew you that it is our duty to sympathise with our fellow men under their troubles, the families of our brethren who are gone: we hope to the Grand Lodge above, here to return no more. But the cheerfulness that you have ever had to relieve them, and ease their burdens, under their forrows, will never be forgotten by them; and in this manner you will never be weary in doing good.

But my brethren, although we are to begin here, we must not end here; for only look around you and you will see and hear of numbers of our fellow men crying out with holy Job, Have pity on me, O my friends, for the hand of the Lord hath touched me. And this is not to be confined to parties or colours; not to towns or states; not to a kingdom, but to the kingdoms of the whole earth, over whom Christ the king is head and grand master.

Among these numerous sons and daughters of distress, I shall begin with our friends and brethren; and first, let us see them dragg'd from their native country by the iron hand of tyranny and oppression, from their dear friends and connections, with weeping eyes and aching hearts, to a strange land and strange people, whose tender mercies are cruel; and there to bear the iron yoke of slavery & cruelty till death as a friend shall relieve them. And must not the unhappy condition of these our fellow men draw forth our hearty prayer and wishes for their deliverance from these merchants and traders, whose characters you have in the xviii chap. of the Revelations 11, 12, & 13 verses, and who knows but these same sort of traders may in a short time, in the like manner, bewail the loss of the African traffick, to their shame and confusion: and if I mistake not, it now begins to dawn in some of the West-India islands; which puts me in mind of a nation (that I have somewhere read of) called Ethiopeans, that cannot change their skin: But God can and will change their conditions, and their hearts too; and let Boston and the world know, that He hath no respect of persons; and that that bulwark of envy, pride, scorn and contempt, which is so visible to be seen in some and felt, shall fall, to rise no more.

When we hear of the bloody wars which are now in the world, and thousands of our fellow men slain; fathers and mothers bewailing the loss of their sons; wives for the loss of their husbands; towns and cities burnt and destroy'd; what must be the heart-felt sorrow and distress of these poor and unhappy people! Though we cannot help them, the distance being so great, yet we may sympathize with them in their

[1]In 1792, Hall's Masons paid for the printing of *A/CHARGE/Delivered to the Brethren of the/AFRICAN LODGE/ on the 25th of June, 1792./ At the Hall of Brother William Smith,/ In Charlestown./ By the Right Worshipful Master/ PRINCE HALL./ Printed at the Request of the Lodge./ Printed and Sold at the Bible and Heart, Cornhill, Boston.* The printing of both the 1792 and the 1797 Charges was paid for by Hall's Masons, thereby documenting the earliest instance of cooperative black American publishing efforts. As published in William C. Nell's *The Colored Patriots of The American Revolution* (1855), and reprinted in Benjamin Brawley's *Early Negro American Writers* (1935), and in Philip Foner's *Voice of Black America* (1972), the 1797 Charge is hardly verbatim, but is rather an excerpted, variantly rewritten rendition of the original printing, which appears more faithfully in first spellings and syntax and punctuations and paragraphings in Dorothy's Porter's *Early Negro Writing 1760–1837* (1971).

troubles, and mingle a tear of sorrow with them, and do as we are exhorted to—weep with those that weep.

Thus my brethren we see what a chequered world we live in. Sometimes happy in having our wives and children like olive-branches about our tables; receiving the bounties of our great Benefactor. The next year, or month, or week we may be deprived of some of them, and we go mourning about the streets, so in societies; we are this day to celebrate this Feast of St. John's, and the next week we might be called upon to attend a funeral of some one here, as we have experienced since our last in this Lodge. So in the common affairs of life we sometimes enjoy health and prosperity; at another time sickness and adversity, crosses and disappointments.

So in states and kingdoms; sometimes in tranquility, then wars and tumults; rich today, and poor tomorrow; which shews that there is not an independent mortal on earth, but dependent one upon the other, from the king to the beggar.

The great law-giver, Moses, who instructed by his father-in-law, Jethro, an Ethiopean, how to regulate his courts of justice and what sort of men to choose for the different offices; hear now my words, said he, I will give you counsel, and God shall be with you; be thou for the people to Godward, that thou mayest bring the causes unto God, and thou shall teach them ordinances and laws, and shall shew the way wherein they must walk, and the work that they must do: moreover thou shall provide out of all the people, able men, such as fear God, men of truth, hating covetousness, and place such over them, to be rulers of thousands, of hundreds and of tens.

So Moses hearkened to the voice of his father-in-law, and did all that he said. Exodus xviii. 22–24.

This is the first and grandest lecture that Moses ever received from the mouth of man; for Jethro understood geometry as well as laws, *that* a Mason may plainly see: so a little captive servant maid by whose advice Nomen, the great general of Syria's army, was healed of his leprosy; and by a servant his proud spirit was brought down: 2 Kings v. 3–14. The feelings of this little captive for this great man, her captor, was so great, that she forgot her state of captivity, and felt for the distress of her enemy. Would to God (said she to her mistress) my lord were with the prophets in Samaria, he should be healed of his leprosy: So after he went to the prophet, his proud host was so haughty that he not only disdain'd the prophet's direction, but derided the good old prophet; and had it not been for his servant he would have gone to his grave with a double leprosy, the outward and the inward, in the heart, which is the worst of leprosies; a black heart is worse than a white leprosy.

How unlike was this great general's behaviour to that of as grand a character, and as well beloved by his prince as he was; I mean Obadiah, to a like prophet. See for this 1st Kings xviii. from 7 to the 16th.

And as Obadiah was in the way, behold Elijah met him, and he knew him, and fell on his face, and said, Art not thou, my Lord, Elijah, and he told him, Yea, go and tell thy Lord, behold Elijah is here: and so on to the 16th verse. Thus we see that great and good men have, and always will have, a respect for ministers and servants of God. Another instance of this is in Acts viii. 27 to 31, of the Ethiopian Eunuch, a man of great authority, to Philip, the apostle: here is mutual love and friendship between them. This minister of Jesus Christ did not think himself too good to receive the hand, and ride in a chariot with a black man in the face of day; neither did this great monarch (for so he was) think it beneath him to take a poor servant of the Lord by the hand, and invite him into his carriage, though but with a staff, one coat, and no money in his pocket. So our Grand Master, Solomon, was not asham'd to take the Queen of Sheba by the hand, and lead her into his court, at the hour of high twelve, and there converse with her on points of masonry (for if ever there was a female mason in the world she was one) and other curious matters; and gratified her, by shewing her all his riches and curious pieces of architecture in the temple, and in his house: After some time staying with her, he loaded her with much rich presents: he gave her the right hand of affection and parted in love.

I hope that no one will dare openly (tho' in fact the behaviour of some implies as much) to say, as our Lord said on another occasion, Behold a greater than Solomon is here. But yet let them consider that our Grand Master Solomon did not divide the living child, whatever he might do with the dead one, neither did he pretend to make a law to forbid the parties from having free intercourse with one another without the fear of censure, or be turned out of the synagogue.

Now my brethren, as we see and experience that all things here are frail and changeable and nothing here to be depended upon: Let us seek those things which are above, which are sure, and stedfast, and unchangeable, and at the same time let us pray to Almighty God, while we remain in the tabernacle, that he would give us the grace of patience and strength to bear up under all our troubles, which at this day God knows we have our share. Patience I say, for were we not possess'd of a great measure of it you could not bear up under the daily insults you meet with in the streets of Boston; much more on public days of recreation, how are you shamefully abus'd, and that at such a degree that you may truly be said to carry your lives in your hands, and the arrows of death are flying about your heads; helpless old women have their clothes torn off their backs, even to the exposing of their nakedness; and by whom are these disgraceful and abusive actions committed, not by the men born and bred in Boston, for they are better bred; but by a mob or horde of shameless, low-lived, envious, spiteful persons, some of them not long since, servants in gentlemen's kitchens, scouring knives, tending horses, and driving chaise. 'Twas said by a gentleman who saw that filthy behaviour in the common, that in all the places he had been in, he never saw so cruel behaviour in all his life, and that a slave in the West-Indies, on Sunday or holidays enjoys himself and friends without any molestation. Not only this man, but many in town who hath seen their behaviour to you, and that without any provocation—twenty or thirty cowards fall upon one man—have wonder'd at the patience of the Blacks: 'tis not for want of courage in you, for they know that they dare not face you man for man, but in a mob, which we despise, and had rather suffer wrong than to do wrong, to the disturbance of the community and the disgrace of our reputation: for every good citizen doth honor to the laws of the State where he resides.

My brethren, let us not be cast down under these and many other abuses we at present labour under: for the darkest is before the break of day. My brethren, let us remember what a dark day it was with our African brethren six years ago,[2] in the

[2]In 1791, slave insurrections were mounted in Saint Domingue which led eventually to the bloodily established Republic of Haiti in 1804.

French West-Indies. Nothing but the snap of the whip was heard from morning to evening; hanging, broken on the wheel, burning, and all manner of tortures inflicted on those unhappy people for nothing else but to gratify their masters pride, wantonness, and cruelty: but blessed be God, the scene is changed; they now confess that God hath no respect of persons, and therefore receive them as their friends, and treat them as brothers. Thus doth Ethiopia begin to stretch forth her hand, from a sink of slavery to freedom and equality.

Although you are deprived of the means of education,[3] yet you are not deprived of the means of meditation; by which I mean thinking, hearing and weighing matters, men, and things in your own mind, and making that judgment of them as you think reasonable to satisfy your minds and give an answer to those who may ask you a question. This nature hath furnished you with, without letter learning; and some have made great progress therein, some of those I have heard repeat psalms and hymns, and a great part of a sermon, only by hearing it read or preached and why not in other things in nature: how many of this class of our brethren that follow the seas can foretell a storm some days before it comes; whether it will be a heavy or light, a long or short one; foretell a hurricane, whether it will be destructive or moderate, without any other means than observation and consideration.

So in the observation of the heavenly bodies, this same class without a telescope or other apparatus have through a smoak'd glass observed the eclipse of the sun: One being ask'd what he saw through his smoaked glass, said, Saw, saw, de clipsey, or de clipseys.[4] And what do you think of it?—Stop, dere be two. Right, and what do they look like?—Look like, why if I tell you, they look like two ships sailing one bigger than tother; so they sail by one another, and make no noise. As simple as the answers are they have a meaning, and shew that God can out of the mouth of babes and Africans shew forth his glory; let us then love and adore him as the God who defends us and supports us and will support us under our pressures, let them be ever so heavy and pressing. Let us by the blessing of God, in whatsoever state we are, or may be in, to be content; for clouds and darkness are about him; but justice and truth is his habitation; who hath said. Vengeance is mine and I will repay it, therefore let us kiss the rod and be still, and see the works of the Lord.

Another thing I would warn you against, is the slavish fear of man, which bringest a snare, saith Solomon. This passion of fear, like pride and envy, hath slain its thousands.—What but this makes so many perjure themselves; for fear of offending them at home they are a little depending on for some trifles: A man that is under a panic of fear, is afraid to be alone; you cannot hear of a robbery or house broke open or set on fire, but he hath an accomplice with him, who must share the spoil with him; whereas if he was truly bold, and void of fear, he would keep the whole plunder to himself: so when either of them is detected and not the other, he may be call'd to oath to keep it secret, but through fear, (and that passion is so strong)

[3]Obliged to pay poll and real estate taxes, black Bostonians who were financially able were denied a city-wide, tax-supported school system until after the turn of the nineteenth century.

[4]This is the first recorded instance of black American written expression of black dialect.

he will not confess, till the fatal cord is put on his neck; then death will deliver him from the fear of man, and he will confess the truth when it will not be of any good to himself or the community: nor is this passion of fear only to be found in this class of men, but among the great.

What was the reason that our African kings and princes have plunged themselves and their peaceable kingdoms into bloody wars, to the destroying of towns and kingdoms, but the fear of the report of a great gun or the glittering of arms and swords, which struck these kings near the seaports with such a panic of fear, as not only to destroy the peace and happiness of their inland brethren, but plung'd millions of their fellow countrymen into slavery and cruel bondage.

So in other countries; see Felix trembling on his throne. How many Emperors and kings have left their kingdoms and best friends at the sight of a handful of men in arms: how many have we seen that have left their estates and their friends and ran over to the stronger side as they thought; all through the fear of men, who is but a worm, and hath no more power to hurt his fellow worm, without the permission of God, than a real worm.

Thus we see, my brethren, what a miserable condition it is to be under the slavish fear of men; it is of such a destructive nature to mankind, that the scriptures every where from Genesis to the Revelations warns us against it; and even our blessed Saviour himself forbids us from this slavish fear of man, in his sermon on the mount; and the only way to avoid it is to be in the fear of God: let a man consider the greatness of his power, as the maker and upholder of all things here below, and that in Him we live, and move, and have our being, the giver of the mercies we enjoy here from day to day, and that our lives are in his hands, and that he made the heavens, the sun, moon and stars to move in their various orders; let us thus view the greatness of God, and then turn our eyes on mortal man, a worm, a shade, a wafer, and see whether he is an object of fear or not; on the contrary, you will think him in his best estate to be but vanity, feeble and a dependent mortal, and stands in need of your help, and cannot do without your assistance, in some way or other; and yet some of these poor mortals will try to make you believe they are Gods, but worship them not. My brethren, let us pay all due respect to all whom God hath put in places of honor over us: do justly and be faithful to them that hire you, and treat them with that respect they may deserve; but worship no man. Worship God, this much is your duty as christians and as masons.

We see then how becoming and necessary it is to have a fellow feeling for our distres'd brethren of the human race, in their troubles, both spiritual and temporal—How refreshing it is to a sick man, to see his sympathising friends around his bed, ready to administer all the relief in their power; although they can't relieve his bodily pain yet they may ease his mind by good instructions and cheer his heart by their company.

How doth it cheer up the heart of a man when his house is on fire, to see a number of friends coming to his relief; he is so transported that he almost forgets his loss and his danger, and fills him with love and gratitude; and their joys and sorrows are mutual.

So a man wreck'd at sea, how must it revive his drooping heart to see a ship bearing down for his relief.

How doth it rejoice the heart of a stranger in a strange land to see the people cheerful and pleasant and are ready to help him.

How did it, think you, cheer the heart of those our poor unhappy African brethren, to see a ship commissioned from God, and from a nation that without flattery faith, that all men are free and are brethren; I say to see them in an instant deliver such a number from their cruel bolts and galling chains, and to be fed like men and treated like brethren. Where is the man that has the least spark of humanity, that will not rejoice with them; and bless a righteous God who knows how and when to relieve the oppressed, as we see he did in the deliverance of the captives among the Algerines; how sudden were they delivered by the sympathising members of the Congress of the United States, who now enjoy the free air of peace and liberty, to their great joy and surprize, to them and their friends. Here we see the hand of God in various ways bringing about his own glory for the good of mankind, by the mutual help of their fellow men; which ought to teach us in all our straits, be they what they may, to put our trust in Him, firmly believing that he is able and will deliver us and defend us against all our enemies; and that no weapon form'd against us shall prosper; only let us be steady and uniform in our walks, speech and behaviour; always doing to all men as we wish and desire they would do to us in the like cases and circumstances.

Live and act as Masons, that you may die as Masons; let those despisers see, altho' many of us cannot read, yet by our searches and researches into men and things, we have supplied that defect; and if they will let us we shall call ourselves a charter'd lodge of just and lawful Masons; be always ready to give an answer to those that ask you a question; give the right hand of affection and fellowship to whom it justly belongs; let their colour and complexion be what it will, let their nation be what it may, for they are your brethren, and it is your indispensable duty so to do; let them as Masons deny this, and we & the world know what to think of them be they ever so grand: for we know this was Solomon's creed, Solomon's creed did I say, it is the decree of the Almighty, and all Masons have learnt it: tis plain market language, and plain and true facts need no apologies.

I shall now conclude with an old poem which I found among some papers:

Let blind admirers handsome faces praise,
And graceful features to great honor raise,
The glories of the red and white express,
I know no beauty but in holiness;
If God of beauty be the uncreate
Perfect idea, in this lower state,
The greatest beauties of an human mould
Who most resemble Him we justly hold;
Whom we resemble not in flesh and blood,
But being pure and holy, just and good:
May such a beauty fall but to my share,
For curious shape or face I'll never care.

1797

Olaudah Equiano 1745–1797

Olaudah Equiano and his sister were kidnapped in Africa, in what is present-day Nigeria. The eleven-year-old Equiano was later separated from his sister and placed aboard a slave ship headed for the West Indies. After experiencing the horrors of the Middle Passage, Equiano arrived in Barbados and was soon transported to Virginia, where he was purchased by a British captain for service aboard his ship; thus Equiano was spared the harsh plantation life most slaves were sentenced to upon their arrival in the New World.

Eventually, Equiano was given the name of Gustavus Vassa, which was, ironically, the name of a Swedish freedom fighter. Equiano remained a slave for almost ten years, serving on various vessels engaged in commerce and sometimes in naval warfare along the coast of Europe and in the Mediterranean. He crossed the Atlantic many times on voyages to the American colonies and the Caribbean islands. All the while, the young slave worked on his own at profit-making ventures, in order to accumulate enough money to buy his freedom—which he was able to do despite many troubles and false hopes. Equiano became a free man on July 10, 1766. He continued his life at sea for many years, sailing on exploratory expeditions to the Arctic and to Central America and on numerous seagoing business enterprises, including the transporting of slaves. During this time, Equiano witnessed the deepest cruelties of slavery and its dire effects on men and women in several areas of the world. He became a kind of Gulliver, traveling to distant places and observing the strange and awful practices of people in many lands.

Equiano's friends in England and on the sailing vessels taught him to read and write and introduced him to Christianity. In his later years, Equiano settled in England, where his Christian faith deepened and where he furthered his education. Equiano was involved in the controversial and disastrous undertaking in 1787 to send poor blacks to Sierra Leone. His objections to the mismanagement of the project caused his dismissal from his commissary role and drew criticism from many quarters. He recovered from this debacle, however, and later, when the abolition of the slave trade became a fiery issue in Parliament, Equiano dedicated himself to the anti-slavery cause by visiting abolitionist leaders and writing letters to newspapers and important officials, including a lengthy letter to Queen Charlotte. His most important contribution was the publication in England and the United States of his well-written and fascinating two-volume autobiography, *The Interesting Narrative of Olaudah Equiano,* subscribed to by many of the key men and women in the abolitionist crusade. The work was widely read, translated into several languages, and published well into the nineteenth century on both sides of the Atlantic. Several editions were printed, some of them including poems by Phillis Wheatley. The Methodist founder, John Wesley, had high regard for Equiano's work: on his deathbed, Wesley requested that Equiano's autobiography be read to him. In 1792, a news item appeared in the *Gentleman's Magazine* announcing the marriage of Englishwoman Susanna Cullen and Olaudah Equiano. Two daughters were born to the couple in the next few years. Equiano died on March 31, 1797.

Equiano's autobiography was the prototype of the slave narratives of the nineteenth century. It set the pattern for the countless narratives—both nonfictional and fictional—that have influenced American literature down to the present day. Equiano followed the spiritual autobiographical tradition of his day derived from Augustine and Bunyan and adopted by

Puritans and later by his Quaker contemporaries. Yet Equiano added to the genre a new dimension—that of social protest. In addition, his use of irony in the depiction of himself as an enterprising character places his work in the secular autobiographical tradition established by Benjamin Franklin.

Angelo Costanzo
Shippensburg University

PRIMARY WORK

The Interesting Narrative of the Life of Olaudah Equiano, or Gustavus Vassa, the African, 1789.

SECONDARY WORKS

Paul Edwards, *The Life of Olaudah Equiano,* 1969; Angelo Costanzo, *Surprizing Narrative: Olaudah Equiano and the Beginnings of Black Autobiography,* 1987.

from The Interesting Narrative of the Life of Olaudah Equiano, or Gustavus Vassa, the African. Written by Himself.

from Chapter 1

I believe it is difficult for those who publish their own memoirs to escape the imputation of vanity; nor is this the only disadvantage under which they labor: it is also their misfortune that what is uncommon is rarely, if ever, believed, and what is obvious we are apt to turn from with disgust, and to charge the writer with impertinence. People generally think those memoirs only worthy to be read or remembered which abound in great or striking events, those, in short, which in a high degree excite either admiration or pity; all others they consign to contempt and oblivion. It is therefore, I confess, not a little hazardous in a private and obscure individual, and a stranger too, thus to solicit the indulgent attention of the public, especially when I own I offer here the history of neither a saint, a hero, nor a tyrant. I believe there are few events in my life which have not happened to many; it is true the incidents of it are numerous, and, did I consider myself an European, I might say my sufferings were great; but when I compare my lot with that of most of my countrymen, I regard myself as a *particular favorite of heaven,* and acknowledge the mercies of Providence in every occurrence of my life. If, then, the following narrative does not appear sufficiently interesting to engage general attention, let my motive be some excuse for its publication. I am not so foolishly vain as to expect from it either immortality or literary reputation. If it affords any satisfaction to my numerous friends, at whose request it has been written, or in the smallest degree promotes the interests of humanity, the ends for which it was undertaken will be fully attained, and every wish of my heart gratified. Let it therefore be remembered, that, in wishing to avoid censure, I do not aspire to praise.

That part of Africa, known by the name of Guinea, to which the trade for slaves is carried on, extends along the coast above 3400 miles, from Senegal to Angola, and includes a variety of kingdoms. Of these the most considerable is the kingdom of Benin, both as to extent and wealth, the richness and cultivation of the soil, the power of its king, and the number and warlike disposition of the inhabitants. It is situated nearly under the line, and extends along the coast about 170 miles, but runs back into the interior part of Africa to a distance hitherto, I believe, unexplored by any traveller, and seems only terminated at length by the empire of Abyssinia, near 1500 miles from its beginning. This kingdom is divided into many provinces or districts, in one of the most remote and fertile of which, I was born, in the year 1745, situated in a charming fruitful vale, named Essaka.[1] The distance of this province from the capital of Benin and the sea coast must be very considerable, for I had never heard of white men or Europeans, nor of the sea; and our subjection to the king of Benin was little more than nominal, for every transaction of the government, as far as my slender observation extended, was conducted by the chief or elders of the place. The manners and government of a people who have little commerce with other countries are generally very simple, and the history of what passes in one family or village may serve as a specimen of the whole nation. My father was one of those elders or chiefs I have spoken of, and was styled Embrenche, a term, as I remember, importing the highest distinction, and signifying in our language a *mark* of grandeur. This mark is conferred on the person entitled to it, by cutting the skin across at the top of the forehead, and drawing it down to the eyebrows; and while it is in this situation applying a warm hand, and rubbing it until it shrinks up into a thick *weal* across the lower part of the forehead. Most of the judges and senators were thus marked; my father had long borne it; I had seen it conferred on one of my brothers, and I also was *destined* to receive it by my parents. Those Embrenche, or chief men, decided disputes and punished crimes, for which purpose they always assembled together. The proceedings were generally short, and in most cases the law of retaliation prevailed. I remember a man was brought before my father, and the other judges, for kidnapping a boy; and, although he was the son of a chief or senator, he was condemned to make recompense by a man or woman slave. Adultery, however, was sometimes punished with slavery or death, a punishment which I believe is inflicted on it throughout most of the nations of Africa,[2] so sacred among them is the honor of the marriage bed, and so jealous are they of the fidelity of their wives. Of this I recollect an instance—a woman was convicted before the judges of adultery, and delivered over, as the custom was, to her husband, to be punished. Accordingly he determined to put her to death; but it being found, just before her execution, that she had an infant at her breast, and no woman being prevailed on to perform the part of a nurse, she was spared on account of the child. The men, however, do not preserve the same constancy to their wives which they expect from them; for they indulge in a plurality, though seldom in more than two. Their mode of marriage is thus—both parties are usually betrothed when young by their parents (though I have known the males to betroth themselves). On this occasion a feast is prepared, and the

[1]Equiano was born in the country that is now known as Nigeria. He claimed Benim because he was borrowing from books on Africa by Anthony Benezet, the Quaker anti-slavery writer [Ed.].

[2]See Benezet's "Account of Guinea," throughout.

bride and bridegroom stand up in the midst of all their friends, who are assembled for the purpose, while he declares she is henceforth to be looked upon as his wife, and that no other person is to pay any addresses to her. This is also immediately proclaimed in the vicinity, on which the bride retires from the assembly. Some time after, she is brought home to her husband, and then another feast is made, to which the relations of both parties are invited; her parents then deliver her to the bridegroom, accompanied with a number of blessings, and at the same time they tie round her waist a cotton string of the thickness of a goosequill, which none but married women are permitted to wear; she is now considered as completely his wife; and at this time the dowry is given to the new married pair, which generally consists of portions of land, slaves, and cattle, household goods, and implements of husbandry. These are offered by the friends of both parties; besides which the parents of the bridegroom present gifts to those of the bride, whose property she is looked upon before marriage; but after it she is esteemed the sole property of her husband. The ceremony being now ended, the festival begins, which is celebrated with bonfires and loud acclamations of joy, accompanied with music and dancing.

We are almost a nation of dancers, musicians, and poets. Thus every great event, such as a triumphant return from battle or other cause of public rejoicing, is celebrated in public dances, which are accompanied with songs and music suited to the occasion. The assembly is separated into four divisions, which dance either apart or in succession, and each with a character peculiar to itself. The first division contains the married men, who in their dances frequently exhibit feats of arms and the representation of a battle. To these succeed the married women, who dance in the second division. The young men occupy the third, and the maidens the fourth. Each represents some interesting scene of real life, such as a great achievement, domestic employment, a pathetic story, or some rural sport; and as the subject is generally founded on some recent event, it is therefore ever new. This gives our dances a spirit and variety which I have scarcely seen elsewhere.[3] We have many musical instruments, particularly drums of different kinds, a piece of music which resembles a guitar, and another much like a stickado. These last are chiefly used by betrothed virgins, who play on them on all grand festivals.

As our manners are simple, our luxuries are few. The dress of both sexes is nearly the same. It generally consists of a long piece of calico, or muslin, wrapped loosely round the body, somewhat in the form of a highland plaid. This is usually dyed blue, which is our favorite color. It is extracted from a berry, and is brighter and richer than any I have seen in Europe. Besides this, our women of distinction wear golden ornaments, which they dispose with some profusion on their arms and legs. When our women are not employed with the men in tillage, their usual occupation is spinning and weaving cotton, which they afterwards dye, and make into garments. They also manufacture earthen vessels, of which we have many kinds. Among the rest, tobacco pipes, made after the same fashion, and used in the same manner, as those in Turkey.[4]

[3]When I was in Smyrna I have frequently seen the Greeks dance after this manner.

[4]The bowl is earthen, curiously figured, to which a long reed is fixed as a tube. This tube is sometimes so long as to be borne by one, and frequently out of grandeur, two boys.

Our manner of living is entirely plain; for as yet the natives are unacquainted with those refinements in cookery which debauch the taste; bullocks, goats, and poultry supply the greatest part of their food. (These constitute likewise the principal wealth of the country, and the chief articles of its commerce.) The flesh is usually stewed in a pan; to make it savory we sometimes use pepper, and other spices, and we have salt made of wood ashes. Our vegetables are mostly plantains, eadas, yams, beans, and Indian corn. The head of the family usually eats alone; his wives and slaves have also their separate tables. Before we taste food we always wash our hands; indeed, our cleanliness on all occasions is extreme, but on this it is an indispensable ceremony. After washing, libation is made, by pouring out a small portion of the drink on the floor, and tossing a small quantity of the food in a certain place, for the spirits of departed relations, which the natives suppose to preside over their conduct and guard them from evil. They are totally unacquainted with strong or spirituous liquors; and their principal beverage is palm wine. This is got from a tree of that name, by tapping it at the top and fastening a large gourd to it; and sometimes one tree will yield three or four gallons in a night. When just drawn it is of a most delicious sweetness; but in a few days it acquires a tartish and more spirituous flavor, though I never saw anyone intoxicated by it. The same tree also produces nuts and oil. Our principal luxury is in perfumes: one sort of these is an odoriferous wood of delicious fragrance, the other a kind of earth, a small portion of which thrown into the fire diffuses a most powerful odor.[5] We beat this wood into powder, and mix it with palm oil, with which both men and women perfume themselves.

In our buildings we study convenience rather than ornament. Each master of a family has a large square piece of ground, surrounded with a moat or fence, or enclosed with a wall made of red earth tempered, which, when dry, is as hard as brick. Within this, are his houses to accommodate his family and slaves, which, if numerous, frequently present the appearance of a village. In the middle, stands the principal building, appropriated to the sole use of the master and consisting of two apartments; in one of which he sits in the day with his family, the other is left apart for the reception of his friends. He has besides these a distinct apartment in which he sleeps, together with his male children. On each side are the apartments of his wives, who have also their separate day and night houses. The habitations of the slaves and their families are distributed throughout the rest of the enclosure. These houses never exceed one story in height; they are always built of wood, or stakes driven into the ground, crossed with wattles, and neatly plastered within and without. The roof is thatched with reeds. Our day houses are left open at the sides; but those in which we sleep are always covered, and plastered in the inside, with a composition mixed with cow-dung, to keep off the different insects, which annoy us during the night. The walls and floors also of these are generally covered with mats. Our beds consist of a platform, raised three or four feet from the ground, on which are laid skins, and different parts of a spongy tree, called plantain. Our covering is calico or muslin, the

[5]When I was in Smyrna I saw the same kind of earth, and brought some of it with me to England; it resembles musk in strength, but is more delicious in scent, and is not unlike the smell of a rose.

same as our dress. The usual seats are a few logs of wood, but we have benches, which are generally perfumed to accommodate strangers: these compose the greater part of our household furniture. Houses so constructed and furnished require but little skill to erect them. Every man is a sufficient architect for the purpose. The whole neighborhood afford their unanimous assistance in building them, and in return receive and expect no other recompense than a feast.

As we live in a country where nature is prodigal of her favors, our wants are few and easily supplied; of course we have few manufactures. They consist for the most part of calicoes, earthen ware, ornaments, and instruments of war and husbandry. But these make no part of our commerce, the principal articles of which, as I have observed, are provisions. In such a state, money is of little use; however, we have some small pieces of coin, if I may call them such. They are made something like an anchor, but I do not remember either their value or denomination. We have also markets, at which I have been frequently with my mother. These are sometimes visited by stout mahogany-colored men from the south-west of us: we call them *Oye-Eboe,* which term signifies red men living at a distance. They generally bring us firearms, gun-powder, hats, beads, and dried fish. The last we esteemed a great rarity, as our waters were only brooks and springs. These articles they barter with us for odoriferous woods and earth, and our salt of wood ashes. They always carry slaves through our land; but the strictest account is exacted of their manner of procuring them before they are suffered to pass. Sometimes, indeed, we sold slaves to them, but they were only prisoners of war, or such among us as had been convicted of kidnapping, or adultery, and some other crimes, which we esteemed heinous. This practice of kidnapping induces me to think, that, notwithstanding all our strictness, their principal business among us was to trepan our people. I remember too, they carried great sacks along with them, which not long after, I had an opportunity of fatally seeing applied to that infamous purpose.

Our land is uncommonly rich and fruitful, and produces all kinds of vegetables in great abundance. We have plenty of Indian corn, and vast quantities of cotton and tobacco. Our pineapples grow without culture; they are about the size of the largest sugar-loaf, and finely flavored. We have also spices of different kinds, particularly pepper, and a variety of delicious fruits which I have never seen in Europe, together with gums of various kinds, and honey in abundance. All our industry is exerted to improve these blessings of nature. Agriculture is our chief employment; and everyone, even the children and women, are engaged in it. Thus we are all habituated to labor from our earliest years. Everyone contributes something to the common stock; and, as we are unacquainted with idleness, we have no beggars. The benefits of such a mode of living are obvious. The West India planters prefer the slaves of Benin or Eboe to those of any other part of Guinea, for their hardiness, intelligence, integrity, and zeal. Those benefits are felt by us in the general healthiness of the people, and in their vigor and activity; I might have added, too, in their comeliness. Deformity is indeed unknown amongst us, I mean that of shape. Numbers of the natives of Eboe now in London might be brought in support of this assertion: for, in regard to complexion, ideas of beauty are wholly relative. I remember while in Africa to have seen three Negro children who were tawny, and another quite white, who were universally regarded by myself, and the natives in general, as far as related to their complexions, as deformed. Our women, too, were, in my eye at least, uncommonly graceful, alert, and modest to a degree of bashfulness; nor do I remember to have heard of an instance of incontinence amongst them before marriage. They are also remarkably cheerful. Indeed, cheerfulness and affability are two of the leading characteristics of our nation.

Our tillage is exercised in a large plain or common, some hour's walk from our dwellings, and all the neighbors resort thither in a body. They use no beasts of husbandry; and their only instruments are hoes, axes, shovels, and beaks, or pointed iron, to dig with. Sometimes we are visited by locusts, which come in large clouds, so as to darken the air, and destroy our harvest. This, however, happens rarely, but when it does, a famine is produced by it. I remember an instance or two wherein this happened. This common is often the theatre of war; and therefore when our people go out to till their land, they not only go in a body, but generally take their arms with them for fear of a surprise; and when they apprehend an invasion, they guard the avenues to their dwellings, by driving sticks into the ground, which are so sharp at one end as to pierce the foot, and are generally dipt in poison. From what I can recollect of these battles, they appear to have been irruptions of one little state or district on the other, to obtain prisoners or booty. Perhaps they were incited to this by those traders who brought the European goods I mentioned, amongst us. Such a mode of obtaining slaves in Africa is common; and I believe more are procured this way, and by kidnapping, than any other.[6] When a trader wants slaves, he applies to a chief for them, and tempts him with his wares. It is not extraordinary, if on this occasion he yields to the temptation with as little firmness, and accepts the price of his fellow creature's liberty, with as little reluctance as the enlightened merchant. Accordingly he falls on his neighbors, and a desperate battle ensues. If he prevails and takes prisoners, he gratifies his avarice by selling them; but, if his party be vanquished, and he falls into the hands of the enemy, he is put to death; for, as he has been known to foment their quarrels, it is thought dangerous to let him survive, and no ransom can save him, though all other prisoners may be redeemed. We have fire-arms, bows and arrows, broad two-edged swords and javelins; we have shields also which cover a man from head to foot. All are taught the use of these weapons; even our women are warriors, and march boldly out to fight along with the men. Our whole district is a kind of militia: on a certain signal given, such as the firing of a gun at night, they all rise in arms and rush upon their enemy. It is perhaps something remarkable, that when our people march to the field a red flag or banner is borne before them. I was once a witness to a battle in our common. We had been all at work in it one day as usual, when our people were suddenly attacked. I climbed a tree at some distance, from which I beheld the fight. There were many women as well as men on both sides; among others my mother was there, and armed with a broad sword. After fighting for a considerable time with great fury, and many had been killed, our people obtained the victory, and took their enemy's Chief a prisoner. He was carried off in great triumph, and, though he offered a large ransom for his life, he was put to death. A virgin of note among our enemies had been slain in the battle, and her arm was exposed in our marketplace, where our trophies were always exhibited. The spoils

[6]See Benezet's "Account of Africa," throughout.

were divided according to the merit of the warriors. Those prisoners which were not sold or redeemed, we kept as slaves; but how different was their condition from that of the slaves in the West Indies! With us, they do no more work than other members of the community, even their master; their food, clothing, and lodging were nearly the same as theirs (except that they were not permitted to eat with those who were free-born); and there was scarce any other difference between them, than a superior degree of importance which the head of a family possesses in our state, and that authority which, as such, he exercises over every part of his household. Some of these slaves have even slaves under them as their own property, and for their own use.

As to religion, the natives believe that there is one Creator of all things, and that he lives in the sun, and is girted round with a belt; that he may never eat or drink, but, according to some, he smokes a pipe, which is our own favorite luxury. They believe he governs events, especially our deaths or captivity; but, as for the doctrine of eternity, I do not remember to have ever heard of it; some, however, believe in the transmigration of souls in a certain degree. Those spirits which were not transmigrated, such as their dear friends or relations, they believe always attend them, and guard them from the bad spirits or their foes. For this reason they always, before eating, as I have observed, put some small portion of the meat, and pour some of their drink, on the ground for them; and they often make oblations of the blood of beasts or fowls at their graves. I was very fond of my mother, and almost constantly with her. When she went to make these oblations at her mother's tomb, which was a kind of small solitary thatched house, I sometimes attended her. There she made her libations, and spent most of the night in cries and lamentations. I have been often extremely terrified on these occasions. The loneliness of the place, the darkness of the night, and the ceremony of libation, naturally awful and gloomy, were heightened by my mother's lamentations; and these concurring with the doleful cries of birds, by which these places were frequented, gave an inexpressible terror to the scene.

We compute the year, from the day on which the sun crosses the line, and on its setting that evening, there is a general shout throughout the land; at least, I can speak from my own knowledge, throughout our vicinity. The people at the same time make a great noise with rattles, not unlike the basket rattles used by children here, though much larger, and hold up their hands to heaven for a blessing. It is then the greatest offerings are made; and those children whom our wise men foretell will be fortunate are then presented to different people. I remember many used to come to see me, and I was carried about to others for that purpose. They have many offerings, particularly at full moons; generally two, at harvest, before the fruits are taken out of the ground; and when any young animals are killed, sometimes they offer up part of them as a sacrifice. These offerings, when made by one of the heads of a family, serve for the whole. I remember we often had them at my father's and my uncle's, and their families have been present. Some of our offerings are eaten with bitter herbs. We had a saying among us to anyone of a cross temper, "That if they were to be eaten, they should be eaten with bitter herbs."

We practised circumcision like the Jews, and made offerings and feasts on that occasion, in the same manner as they did. Like them also, our children were named from some event, some circumstance, or fancied foreboding, at the time of their birth. I was named *Olaudah,* which in our language signifies vicissitude, or fortunate; also, one favored, and having a loud voice and well spoken. I remember we never polluted the name of the object of our adoration; on the contrary, it was always mentioned with the greatest reverence; and we were totally unacquainted with swearing, and all those terms of abuse and reproach which find their way so readily and copiously into the language of more civilized people. The only expressions of that kind I remember were, "May you rot, or may you swell, or may a beast take you."

I have before remarked that the natives of this part of Africa are extremely cleanly. This necessary habit of decency was with us a part of religion, and therefore we had many purifications and washings; indeed almost as many, and used on the same occasions, if my recollection does not fail me, as the Jews. Those that touched the dead at any time were obliged to wash and purify themselves before they could enter a dwelling-house. Every woman, too, at certain times was forbidden to come into a dwelling-house, or touch any person, or anything we eat. I was so fond of my mother I could not keep from her, or avoid touching her at some of those periods, in consequence of which I was obliged to be kept out with her, in a little house made for that purpose, till offering was made, and then we were purified. . . .

Such is the imperfect sketch my memory has furnished me with, of the manners and customs of a people among whom I first drew my breath. And here I cannot forbear suggesting what has long struck me very forcibly, namely, the strong analogy which even by this sketch, imperfect as it is, appears to prevail in the manners and customs of my countrymen and those of the Jews, before they reached the land of promise, and particularly the patriarchs while they were yet in that pastoral state which is described in Genesis—an analogy, which alone would induce me to think that the one people had sprung from the other. Indeed, this is the opinion of Dr. Gill, who, in his commentary on Genesis, very ably deduces the pedigree of the Africans from Afer and Afra, the descendents of Abraham by Keturah his wife and concubine (for both these titles are applied to her). It is also conformable to the sentiments of Dr. John Clarke, formerly Dean of Sarum, in his truth of the Christian religion; both these authors concur in ascribing to us this original. The reasonings of those gentlemen are still further confirmed by the scripture chronology; and if any further corroboration were required, this resemblance in so many respects, is a strong evidence in support of the opinion. Like the Israelites in their primitive state, our government was conducted by our chiefs or judges, our wise men and elders; and the head of a family with us enjoyed a similar authority over his household, with that which is ascribed to Abraham and the other patriarchs. The law of retaliation obtained almost universally with us as with them: and even their religion appeared to have shed upon us a ray of its glory, though broken and spent in its passage, or eclipsed by the cloud with which time, tradition, and ignorance might have enveloped it; for we had our circumcision (a rule, I believe, peculiar to that people), we had also our sacrifices and burnt-offerings, our washings and purifications, and on the same occasions as they did.

As to the difference of color between the Eboan Africans and the modern Jews, I shall not presume to account for it. It is a subject which has engaged the pens of men of both genius and learning, and is far above my strength. The most able and Reverend Mr. T. Clarkson, however, in his much admired essay on the Slavery and Commerce of the Human Species, has ascertained the cause in a manner that at once solves every objection on that account, and, on my mind at least, has produced the fullest conviction. I shall therefore refer to that performance for the theory,[7] contenting myself with extracting a fact as related by Dr. Mitchel.[8] "The Spaniards, who have inhabited America, under the torrid zone, for any time, are become as dark colored as our native Indians of Virginia; of which *I myself have been a witness.*" There is also another instance[9] of a Portuguese settlement at Mitomba, a river in Sierra Leone, where the inhabitants are bred from a mixture of the first Portuguese discoverers with the natives, and are now become in their complexion, and in the woolly quality of their hair, *perfect Negroes,* retaining however a smattering of the Portuguese language.

These instances, and a great many more which might be adduced, while they show how the complexions of the same persons vary in different climates, it is hoped may tend also to remove the prejudice that some conceive against the natives of Africa on account of their color. Surely the minds of the Spaniards did not change with their complexions! Are there not causes enough to which the apparent inferiority of an African may be ascribed, without limiting the goodness of God, and supposing he forebore to stamp understanding on certainly his own image, because "carved in ebony." Might it not naturally be ascribed to their situation? When they come among Europeans, they are ignorant of their language, religion, manners, and customs. Are any pains taken to teach them these? Are they treated as men? Does not slavery itself depress the mind, and extinguish all its fire and every noble sentiment? But, above all, what advantages do not a refined people possess, over those who are rude and uncultivated? Let the polished and haughty European recollect that his ancestors were once, like the Africans, uncivilized, and even barbarous. Did Nature make *them* inferior to their sons? and should *they too* have been made slaves? Every rational mind answers, No. Let such reflections as these melt the pride of their superiority into sympathy for the wants and miseries of their sable brethren, and compel them to acknowledge that understanding is not confined to feature or color. If, when they look round the world, they feel exultation, let it be tempered with benevolence to others, and gratitude to God, "who hath made of one blood all nations of men for to dwell on all the face of the earth";[10] "and whose wisdom is not our wisdom, neither are our ways his ways."

Chapter 2

I hope the reader will not think I have trespassed on his patience in introducing myself to him, with some account of the manners and customs of my country. They had been implanted in me with great care, and made an impression on my mind, which time could not erase, and which all the adversity and variety of fortune I have since experienced, served only to rivet and record: for, whether the love of one's country be real or imaginary, or a lesson of reason, or an instinct of nature, I still look back

[7]Pages 178 to 216.

[8]Philos. Trans. No. 476, Sec. 4, cited by Mr. Clarkson, p. 205.

[9]Same page.

[10]Acts 17:26.

with pleasure on the first scenes of my life, though that pleasure has been for the most part mingled with sorrow.

I have already acquainted the reader with the time and place of my birth. My father, besides many slaves, had a numerous family, of which seven lived to grow up, including myself and sister, who was the only daughter. As I was the youngest of the sons, I became, of course, the greatest favorite with my mother, and was always with her; and she used to take particular pains to form my mind. I was trained up from my earliest years in the art of war: my daily exercise was shooting and throwing javelins, and my mother adorned me with emblems, after the manner of our greatest warriors. In this way I grew up till I had turned the age of eleven, when an end was put to my happiness in the following manner: Generally, when the grown people in the neighborhood were gone far in the fields to labor, the children assembled together in some of the neighboring premises to play; and commonly some of us used to get up a tree to look out for any assailant, or kidnapper, that might come upon us—for they sometimes took those opportunities of our parents' absence, to attack and carry off as many as they could seize. One day as I was watching at the top of a tree in our yard, I saw one of those people come into the yard of our next neighbor but one, to kidnap, there being many stout young people in it. Immediately on this I gave the alarm of the rogue, and he was surrounded by the stoutest of them, who entangled him with cords, so that he could not escape, till some of the grown people came and secured him. But, alas! ere long it was my fate to be thus attacked, and to be carried off, when none of the grown people were nigh. One day, when all our people were gone out to their works as usual, and only I and my dear sister were left to mind the house, two men and a woman got over our walls, and in a moment seized us both, and, without giving us time to cry out, or make resistance, they stopped our mouths, and ran off with us into the nearest wood. Here they tied our hands, and continued to carry us as far as they could, till night came on, when we reached a small house, where the robbers halted for refreshment, and spent the night. We were then unbound, but were unable to take any food; and, being quite overpowered by fatigue and grief, our only relief was some sleep, which allayed our misfortune for a short time. The next morning we left the house, and continued travelling all the day. For a long time we had kept the woods, but at last we came into a road which I believed I knew. I had now some hopes of being delivered; for we had advanced but a little way before I discovered some people at a distance, on which I began to cry out for their assistance; but my cries had no other effect than to make them tie me faster and stop my mouth, and then they put me into a large sack. They also stopped my sister's mouth, and tied her hands; and in this manner we proceeded till we were out of sight of these people. When we went to rest the following night, they offered us some victuals, but we refused it and the only comfort we had was in being in one another's arms all that night, and bathing each other with our tears. But alas we were soon deprived of even the small comfort of weeping together. The next day proved a day of greater sorrow than I had yet experienced; for my sister and I were then separated, while we lay clasped in each other's arms. It was in vain that we had sought them not to part us; she was torn from me, and immediately carried away, while I was left in a state of distraction not to be described. I cried and grieved continually; and for several days did not eat anything but what they forced into my mouth. At length, after many days' travelling, during which I had often changed masters, I got into the hands of a chieftain, in a very pleasant country. This man had two wives and some children, and they all used me extremely well, and did all they could do to comfort me; particularly the first wife, who was something like my mother. Although I was a great many days' journey from my father's house, yet these people spoke exactly the same language with us. This first master of mine, as I may call him, was a smith, and my principal employment was working his bellows, which were the same kind as I had seen in my vicinity. They were in some respects not unlike the stoves here in gentlemen's kitchens, and were covered over with leather; and in the middle of that leather a stick was fixed, and a person stood up, and worked it in the same manner as is done to pump water out of a cask with a hand pump. I believe it was gold he worked, for it was of a lovely bright yellow color, and was worn by the women on their wrists and ankles. I was there I suppose about a month, and they at last used to trust me some little distance from the house. This liberty I used in embracing every opportunity to inquire the way to my own home; and I also sometimes, for the same purpose, went with the maidens, in the cool of the evenings, to bring pitchers of water from the springs for the use of the house. I had also remarked where the sun rose in the morning, and set in the evening, as I had travelled along; and I had observed that my father's house was towards the rising of the sun. I therefore determined to seize the first opportunity of making my escape, and to shape my course for that quarter; for I was quite oppressed and weighed down by grief after my mother and friends; and my love of liberty, ever great, was strengthened by the mortifying circumstance of not daring to eat with the free-born children, although I was mostly their companion. While I was projecting my escape one day, an unlucky event happened, which quite disconcerted my plan, and put an end to my hopes. I used to be sometimes employed in assisting an elderly slave to cook and take care of the poultry; and one morning, while I was feeding some chickens, I happened to toss a small pebble at one of them, which hit it on the middle, and directly killed it. The old slave, having soon after missed the chicken, inquired after it; and on my relating the accident (for I told her the truth, for my mother would never suffer me to tell a lie), she flew into a violent passion, and threatened that I should suffer for it; and, my master being out, she immediately went and told her mistress what I had done. This alarmed me very much, and I expected an instant flogging, which to me was uncommonly dreadful, for I had seldom been beaten at home. I therefore resolved to fly; and accordingly I ran into a thicket that was hard by, and hid myself in the bushes. Soon afterwards my mistress and the slave returned, and, not seeing me, they searched all the house, but not finding me, and I not making answer when they called to me, they thought I had run away, and the whole neighborhood was raised in the pursuit of me. In that part of the country, as in ours, the houses and villages were skirted with woods, or shrubberies, and the bushes were so thick that a man could readily conceal himself in them, so as to elude the strictest search. The neighbors continued the whole day looking for me, and several times many of them came within a few yards of the place where I lay hid. I expected every moment, when I heard a rustling among the trees, to be found out, and punished by my master; but they never discovered me, though they were often so near that I even heard their conjectures as they were looking about for me; and I now learned from them that any attempts to return home would be hopeless. Most of them supposed I had fled towards home; but the distance was so great, and the way so intricate, that they thought I could never reach it, and that I should be lost in the woods. When I heard this I was seized with a violent panic, and abandoned myself to despair. Night, too, began to approach, and aggravated all my fears. I had before entertained hopes of getting home, and had determined when it should be dark to make the attempt; but I was now convinced it was fruitless, and began to consider that, if possibly I could escape all other animals, I could not those of the human kind; and that, not knowing the way, I must perish in the woods. Thus was I like the hunted deer—

——Every leaf and every whisp'ring breath,
Convey'd a foe, and every foe a death.

I heard frequent rustlings among the leaves, and being pretty sure they were snakes, I expected every instant to be stung by them. This increased my anguish, and the horror of my situation became now quite insupportable. I at length quitted the thicket, very faint and hungry, for I had not eaten or drank anything all the day, and crept to my master's kitchen, from whence I set out at first, which was an open shed, and laid myself down in the ashes with an anxious wish for death, to relieve me from all my pains. I was scarcely awake in the morning, when the old woman slave, who was the first up, came to light the fire, and saw me in the fireplace. She was very much surprised to see me, and could scarcely believe her own eyes. She now promised to intercede for me, and went for her master, who soon after came, and, having slightly reprimanded me, ordered me to be taken care of, and not ill treated.

Soon after this, my master's only daughter, and child by his first wife, sickened and died, which affected him so much that for sometime he was almost frantic, and really would have killed himself, had he not been watched and prevented. However, in a short time afterwards he recovered, and I was again sold. I was now carried to the left of the sun's rising, through many dreary wastes and dismal woods, amidst the hideous roarings of wild beasts. The people I was sold to used to carry me very often, when I was tired, either on their shoulders or on their backs. I saw many convenient well-built sheds along the road, at proper distances, to accommodate the merchants and travellers, who lay in those buildings along with their wives, who often accompany them; and they always go well armed.

From the time I left my own nation, I always found somebody that understood me till I came to the sea coast. The languages of different nations did not totally differ, nor were they so copious as those of the Europeans, particularly the English. They were therefore, easily learned; and, while I was journeying thus through Africa, I acquired two or three different tongues. In this manner I had been travelling for a considerable time, when, one evening, to my great surprise, whom should I see brought to the house where I was but my dear sister! As soon as she saw me, she gave a loud shriek, and ran into my arms—I was quite overpowered; neither of us could speak, but, for a considerable time, clung to each other in mutual embraces, unable to do anything but weep. Our meeting affected all who saw us; and, indeed, I must acknowledge, in honor of those sable destroyers of human rights, that I never met with any ill treatment, or saw any offered to their slaves, except tying them, when necessary, to keep them from running away. When these people knew we were brother and sister, they indulged us to be together; and the man, to whom I supposed we belonged, lay with us, he in the middle, while she and I held one another by the hands across his breast all night; and thus for a while we forgot our misfortunes, in the joy of being together; but even this small comfort was soon to have an end; for scarcely had the fatal morning appeared when she was again torn from me forever! I was now more miserable, if possible, than before. The small relief which her presence gave me from pain, was gone, and the wretchedness of my situation was redoubled by my anxiety after her fate, and my apprehensions lest her sufferings should be greater than mine, when I could not be with her to alleviate them. Yes, thou dear partner of all my childish sports! thou sharer of my joys and sorrows! happy should I have ever esteemed myself to encounter every misery for you and to procure your freedom by the sacrifice of my own. Though you were early forced from my arms, your image has been always riveted in my heart, from which neither time nor fortune have been able to remove it; so that, while the thoughts of your sufferings have damped my prosperity, they have mingled with adversity and increased its bitterness. To that Heaven which protects the weak from the strong, I commit the care of your innocence and virtues, if they have not already received their full reward, and if your youth and delicacy have not long since fallen victims to the violence of the African trader, the pestilential stench of a Guinea ship, the seasoning in the European colonies or the lash and lust of a brutal and unrelenting overseer.

I did not long remain after my sister. I was again sold, and carried through a number of places, till after travelling a considerable time, I came to a town called Tinmah, in the most beautiful country I had yet seen in Africa. It was extremely rich, and there were many rivulets which flowed through it, and supplied a large pond in the centre of the town, where the people washed. Here I first saw and tasted cocoanuts, which I thought superior to any nuts I had ever tasted before; and the trees, which were loaded, were also interspersed among the houses, which had commodious shades adjoining, and were in the same manner as ours, the insides being neatly plastered and whitewashed. Here I also saw and tasted for the first time, sugar-cane. Their money consisted of little white shells, the size of the finger nail. I was sold here for one hundred and seventy-two of them, by a merchant who lived and brought me there. I had been about two or three days at his house, when a wealthy widow, a neighbor of his, came there one evening, and brought with her an only son, a young gentleman about my own age and size. Here they saw me; and, having taken a fancy to me, I was bought of the merchant, and went home with them. Her house and premises were situated close to one of those rivulets I have mentioned, and were the finest I ever saw in Africa: they were very extensive, and she had a number of slaves to attend her. The next day I was washed and perfumed, and when meal time came, I was led into the presence of my mistress, and ate and drank before her with her son. This filled me with astonishment; and I could scarce help expressing my surprise that the young gentleman should suffer me, who was bound, to eat with him who was free; and not only so, but that he would not at any time either eat or drink till I had taken first, because I was the eldest, which was agreeable to our custom. Indeed, every thing here, and all their treatment of me, made me forget that I was a slave. The language of these people resembled ours so nearly, that we understood each other perfectly. They had also the very same customs as we. There were likewise slaves daily to attend us, while my young master and I, with other boys, sported with our darts and bows and arrows, as I had been used to do at home. In this resemblance to my former happy state, I passed about two months; and I now began to think I was to be adopted into the family, and was beginning to be reconciled to my situation, and to forget by degrees my misfortunes, when all at once the delusion vanished; for, without the least previous knowledge, one morning early, while my dear master and companion was still asleep, I was awakened out of my reverie to fresh sorrow, and hurried away even amongst the uncircumcised.

Thus, at the very moment I dreamed of the greatest happiness, I found myself most miserable; and it seemed as if fortune wished to give me this taste of joy only to render the reverse more poignant. The change I now experienced was as painful as it was sudden and unexpected. It was a change indeed, from a state of bliss to a scene which is inexpressible by me, as it discovered to me an element I had never before beheld, and till then had no idea of, and wherein such instances of hardship and cruelty continually occurred, as I can never reflect on but with horror.

All the nations and people I had hitherto passed through, resembled our own in their manners, customs, and language; but I came at length to a country, the inhabitants of which differed from us in all those particulars. I was very much struck with this difference, especially when I came among a people who did not circumcise, and ate without washing their hands. They cooked also in iron pots, and had European cutlasses and cross bows, which were unknown to us, and fought with their fists among themselves. Their women were not so modest as ours, for they ate, and drank, and slept with their men. But above all, I was amazed to see no sacrifices or offerings among them. In some of those places the people ornamented themselves with scars, and likewise filed their teeth very sharp. They wanted sometimes to ornament me in the same manner, but I would not suffer them; hoping that I might some time be among a people who did not thus disfigure themselves, as I thought they did. At last I came to the banks of a large river which was covered with canoes, in which the people appeared to live with their household utensils and provisions of all kinds. I was beyond measure astonished at this, as I had never before seen any water larger than a pond or a rivulet; and my surprise was mingled with no small fear when I was put into one of these canoes, and we began to paddle and move along the river. We continued going on thus till night, and when we came to land, and made fires on the banks, each family by themselves; some dragged their canoes on shore, others stayed and cooked in theirs, and laid in them all night. Those on the land had mats, of which they made tents, some in the shape of little houses; in these we slept; and after the morning meal, we embarked again and proceeded as before. I was often very much astonished to see some of the women, as well as the men, jump into the water, dive to the bottom, come up again, and swim about. Thus I continued to travel, sometimes by land, sometimes by water, through different countries and various nations, till the end of six or seven months after I had been kidnapped, I arrived at the sea coast. It would be tedious and uninteresting to relate all the incidents which befell me during this journey, and which I have not yet forgotten; of the various hands I passed through, and the manners and customs of all the different people among whom I lived—I shall therefore only observe, that in all the places where I was, the soil was exceedingly rich; the pumpkins, eadas, plantains, yams, &c. &c., were in great abundance, and of incredible size. There were also vast quantities of different gums, though not used for any purpose, and everywhere a great deal of tobacco. The cotton even grew quite wild, and there was plenty of red-wood. I saw no mechanics whatever in all the way, except such as I have mentioned. The chief employment in all these countries was agriculture, and both the males and females, as with us, were brought up to it, and trained in the arts of war.

The first object which saluted my eyes when I arrived on the coast, was the sea, and a slave ship, which was then riding at anchor, and waiting for its cargo. These filled me with astonishment, which was soon converted into terror, when I was carried on board. I was immediately handled, and tossed up to see if I were sound, by some of the crew; and I was now persuaded that I had gotten into a world of bad spirits, and that they were going to kill me. Their complexions, too, differing so much from ours, their long hair, and the language they spoke (which was very different from any I had ever heard), united to confirm me in this belief. Indeed, such were the horrors of my views and fears at the moment, that, if ten thousand worlds had been my own, I would have freely parted with them all to have exchanged my condition with that of the meanest slave in my own country. When I looked round the ship too, and saw a large furnace of copper boiling, and a multitude of black people of every description chained together, every one of their countenances expressing dejection and sorrow, I no longer doubted of my fate; and, quite overpowered with horror and anguish, I fell motionless on the deck and fainted. When I recovered a little, I found some black people about me, who I believed were some of those who had brought me on board, and had been receiving their pay; they talked to me in order to cheer me, but all in vain. I asked them if we were not to be eaten by those white men with horrible looks, red faces, and long hair. They told me I was not, and one of the crew brought me a small portion of spirituous liquor in a wine glass; but, being afraid of him, I would not take it out of his hand. One of the blacks, therefore, took it from him and gave it to me, and I took a little down my palate, which, instead of reviving me, as they thought it would, threw me into the greatest consternation at the strange feeling it produced, having never tasted any such liquor before. Soon after this, the blacks who brought me on board went off, and left me abandoned to despair.

I now saw myself deprived of all chance of returning to my native country, or even the least glimpse of hope of gaining the shore, which I now considered as friendly; and I even wished for my former slavery in preference to my present situation, which was filled with horrors of every kind, still heightened by my ignorance of what I was to undergo. I was not long suffered to indulge my grief; I was soon put down under the decks, and there I received such a salutation in my nostrils as I had never experienced in my life: so that, with the loathsomeness of the stench, and crying together, I became so sick and low that I was not able to eat, nor had I the least desire to taste anything. I now wished for the last friend, death, to relieve me; but soon, to my grief, two of the white men offered me eatables; and, on my refusing to eat, one of them held me fast by the hands, and laid me across, I think, the windlass, and tied my feet, while the other flogged me severely. I had never experienced anything of this kind before, and, although not being used to the water, I naturally feared that element the first time I saw it, yet, nevertheless, could I have got over the nettings, I would have jumped over the side, but I could not; and besides, the crew used to watch us very closely who were not chained down to the decks, lest we should leap into the water; and I have seen some of these poor African prisoners most severely cut, for attempting to do so, and hourly whipped for not eating. This indeed was often the case with myself. In a little time after, amongst the poor chained men, I found some of my own nation, which in a small degree gave ease to my mind. I inquired of these what was to be done with us? They gave me to understand, we were to be carried to these white people's country to work for them. I then was a little revived, and thought, if it were no worse than working, my situation was not so desperate; but still I feared I should be put to death, the white people looked and acted, as I thought, in so savage a manner; for I had never seen among any people such instances of brutal cruelty; and this not only shown towards us blacks, but also to some of the whites themselves. One white man in particular I saw, when we were permitted to be on deck, flogged so unmercifully with a large rope near the foremast, that he died in consequence of it; and they tossed him over the side as they would have done a brute. This made me fear these people the more; and I expected nothing less than to be treated in the same manner. I could not help expressing my fears and apprehensions to some of my countrymen; I asked them if these people had no country, but lived in this hollow place (the ship)? They told me they did not, but came from a distant one. "Then," said I, "how comes it in all our country we never heard of them?" They told me because they lived so very far off. I then asked where were their women? had they any like themselves? I was told they had. "And why," said I, "do we not see them?" They answered, because they were left behind. I asked how the vessel could go? They told me they could not tell; but that there was cloth put upon the masts by the help of the ropes I saw, and then the vessel went on; and the white men had some spell or magic they put in the water when they liked, in order to stop the vessel. I was exceedingly amazed at this account, and really thought they were spirits. I therefore wished much to be from amongst them, for I expected they would sacrifice me; but my wishes were vain—for we were so quartered that it was impossible for any of us to make our escape.

While we stayed on the coast I was mostly on deck; and one day, to my great astonishment, I saw one of these vessels coming in with the sails up. As soon as the whites saw it, they gave a great shout, at which we were amazed; and the more so, as the vessel appeared larger by approaching nearer. At last, she came to an anchor in my sight, and when the anchor was let go, I and my countrymen who saw it, were lost in astonishment to observe the vessel stop—and were now convinced it was done by magic. Soon after this the other ship got her boats out, and they came on board of us, and the people of both ships seemed very glad to see each other. Several of the strangers also shook hands with us black people, and made motions with their hands, signifying I suppose, we were to go to their country, but we did not understand them.

At last when the ship we were in, had got in all her cargo, they made ready with many fearful noises, and we were all put under deck, so that we could not see how they managed the vessel. But this disappointment was the least of my sorrow. The stench of the hold while we were on the coast was so intolerably loathsome, that it was dangerous to remain there for any time, and some of us had been permitted to stay on the deck for the fresh air; but now that the whole ship's cargo were confined together, it became absolutely pestilential. The closeness of the place, and the heat of the climate, added to the number in the ship, which was so crowded that each had scarcely room to turn himself, almost suffocated us. This produced copious perspirations, so that the air soon became unfit for respiration, from a variety of loathsome smells, and brought on a sickness among the slaves, of which many died—thus falling victims to the improvident avarice, as I may call it, of their purchasers. This wretched situation was again aggravated by the galling of the chains, now became insupportable, and the filth of the necessary tubs, into which the children often fell, and were almost suffocated. The shrieks of the women, and the groans of the dying, rendered the whole a scene of horror almost inconceivable. Happily perhaps, for myself, I was soon reduced so low here that it was thought necessary to keep me almost always on deck; and from my extreme youth I was not put in fetters. In this situation I expected every hour to share the fate of my companions, some of whom were almost daily brought upon deck at the point of death, which I began to hope would soon put an end to my miseries. Often did I think many of the inhabitants of the deep much more happy than myself. I envied them the freedom they enjoyed, and as often wished I could change my condition for theirs. Every circumstance I met with, served only to render my state more painful, and heightened my apprehensions, and my opinion of the cruelty of the whites.

One day they had taken a number of fishes; and when they had killed and satisfied themselves with as many as they thought fit, to our astonishment who were on deck, rather than give any of them to us to eat, as we expected, they tossed the remaining fish into the sea again, although we begged and prayed for some as well as we could, but in vain; and some of my country men, being pressed by hunger, took an opportunity, when they thought no one saw them, of trying to get a little privately; but they were discovered, and the attempt procured them some very severe floggings. One day, when we had a smooth sea and moderate wind, two of my wearied countrymen who were chained together (I was near them at the time), preferring death to such a life of misery, somehow made through the nettings and jumped into the sea; immediately, another quite dejected fellow, who, on account of his illness, was suffered to be out of irons, also followed their example; and I believe many more would very soon have done the same, if they had not been prevented by the ship's crew, who were instantly alarmed. Those of us that were the most active, were in a moment put down under the deck; and there was such a noise and confusion amongst the people of the ship as I never heard before, to stop her, and get the boat out to go after the slaves. However, two of the wretches were drowned, but they got the other, and afterwards flogged him unmercifully, for thus attempting to prefer death to slavery. In this manner we continued to undergo more hardships than I can now relate, hardships which are inseparable from this accursed trade. Many a time we were near suffocation from the want of fresh air, which we were often without for whole days together. This, and the stench of the necessary tubs, carried off many.

During our passage, I first saw flying fishes, which surprised me very much; they used frequently to fly across the ship, and many of them fell on the deck. I also now first saw the use of the quadrant; I had often with astonishment seen the mariners make observations with it, and I could not think what it meant. They at last took notice of my surprise; and one of them, willing to increase it, as well as to gratify my curiosity, made me one day look through it. The clouds appeared to me to be land, which disappeared as they passed along. This heightened my wonder; and I was now more persuaded than ever, that I was in another world, and that every thing about me was magic. At last, we came in sight of the island of Barbadoes, at which the whites on board gave a great shout, and made many signs of joy to us. We did not know what to think of this;

but as the vessel drew nearer, we plainly saw the harbor, and other ships of different kinds and sizes, and we soon anchored amongst them, off Bridgetown. Many merchants and planters now came on board, though it was in the evening. They put us in separate parcels, and examined us attentively. They also made us jump, and pointed to the land, signifying we were to go there. We thought by this, we should be eaten by these ugly men, as they appeared to us; and, when soon after we were all put down under the deck again, there was much dread and trembling among us, and nothing but bitter cries to be heard all the night from these apprehensions, insomuch, that at last the white people got some old slaves from the land to pacify us. They told us we were not to be eaten, but to work, and were soon to go on land, where we should see many of our country people. This report eased us much. And sure enough, soon after we were landed, there came to us Africans of all languages.

We were conducted immediately to the merchant's yard, where we were all pent up together, like so many sheep in a fold, without regard to sex or age. As every object was new to me, everything I saw filled me with surprise. What struck me first, was, that the houses were built with bricks and stories, and in every other respect different from those I had seen in Africa; but I was still more astonished on seeing people on horseback. I did not know what this could mean; and, indeed, I thought these people were full of nothing but magical arts. While I was in this astonishment, one of my fellow prisoners spoke to a countryman of his, about the horses, who said they were the same kind they had in their country. I understood them, though they were from a distant part of Africa; and I thought it odd I had not seen any horses there; but afterwards, when I came to converse with different Africans, I found they had many horses amongst them, and much larger than those I then saw.

We were not many days in the merchant's custody, before we were sold after their usual manner, which is this: On a signal given (as the beat of a drum), the buyers rush at once into the yard where the slaves are confined, and make choice of that parcel they like best. The noise and clamor with which this is attended and the eagerness visible in the countenances of the buyers, serve not a little to increase the apprehension of terrified Africans, who may well be supposed to consider them as the ministers of the destruction to which they think themselves devoted. In this manner, without scruple, are relations and friends separated, most of them never to see each other again. I remember, in the vessel in which I was brought over, in the men's apartment, there were several brothers, who, in the sale, were sold in different lots; and it was very moving on this occasion, to see and hear their cries at parting. O, ye nominal Christians! might not an African ask you—Learned you this from your God, who says unto you, Do unto all men as you would men should do unto you? Is it not enough that we are torn from our country and friends, to toil for your luxury and lust of gain? Must every tender feeling be likewise sacrificed to your avarice? Are the dearest friends and relations, now rendered more dear by their separation from their kindred, still to be parted from each other, and thus prevented from cheering the gloom of slavery, with the small comfort of being together, and mingling their sufferings and sorrows? Why are parents to lose their children, brothers their sisters, or husbands their wives? Surely, this is a new refinement in cruelty, which, while it has no advantage to atone for it, thus aggravates distress, and adds fresh horrors even to the wretchedness of slavery.

from Chapter 3

I now totally lost the small remains of comfort I had enjoyed in conversing with my countrymen; the women too, who used to wash and take care of me were all gone different ways, and I never saw one of them afterwards.

I stayed in this island for a few days, I believe it could not be above a fortnight, when I, and some few more slaves, that were not saleable amongst the rest, from very much fretting, were shipped off in a sloop for North America. On the passage we were better treated than when we were coming from Africa, and we had plenty of rice and fat pork. We were landed up a river a good way from the sea, about Virginia county, where we saw few or none of our native Africans, and not one soul who could talk to me. I was a few weeks weeding grass and gathering stones in a plantation; and at last all my companions were distributed different ways, and only myself was left. I was now exceedingly miserable, and thought myself worse off than any of the rest of my companions, for they could talk to each other, but I had no person to speak to that I could understand. In this state, I was constantly grieving and pining, and wishing for death rather than anything else. While I was in this plantation, the gentleman, to whom I suppose the estate belonged, being unwell, I was one day sent for to his dwelling-house to fan him; when I came into the room where he was I was very much affrighted at some things I saw, and the more so as I had seen a black woman slave as I came through the house, who was cooking the dinner, and the poor creature was cruelly loaded with various kinds of iron machines; she had one particularly on her head, which locked her mouth so fast that she could scarcely speak; and could not eat nor drink. I was much astonished and shocked at this contrivance, which I afterwards learned was called the iron muzzle. Soon after I had a fan put in my hand, to fan the gentleman while he slept; and so I did indeed with great fear. While he was fast asleep I indulged myself a great deal in looking about the room, which to me appeared very fine and curious. The first object that engaged my attention was a watch which hung on the chimney, and was going. I was quite surprised at the noise it made, and was afraid it would tell the gentleman anything I might do amiss; and when I immediately after observed a picture hanging in the room, which appeared constantly to look at me, I was still more affrighted, having never seen such things as these before. At one time I thought it was something relative to magic; and not seeing it move, I thought it might be some way the whites had to keep their great men when they died, and offer them libations as we used to do our friendly spirits. In this state of anxiety I remained till my master awoke, when I was dismissed out of the room, to my no small satisfaction and relief; for I thought that these people were all made up of wonders. In this place I was called Jacob; but on board the *African Snow,* I was called Michael. I had been some time in this miserable, forlorn, and much dejected state, without having anyone to talk to, which made my life a burden, when the kind and unknown hand of the Creator (who in very deed leads the blind in a way they know not) now began to appear, to my comfort; for one day the captain of a merchant ship, called the *Industrious Bee,* came on some business to my master's house. This gentleman, whose name was Michael Henry Pascal, was a lieutenant in the royal navy, but now commanded this trading ship, which was somewhere in the confines of the county many miles off. While he was at my master's house, it happened that he saw me, and liked me so well that he made a purchase of me. I think I have often heard him say he gave thirty or forty pounds sterling for me; but I do not remember which. However, he meant me for a present to some of his friends in England: and as I was sent accordingly from the house of my then master (one Mr. Campbell) to the place where the ship lay; I was conducted on horseback by an elderly black man (a mode of travelling which appeared very odd to me). When I arrived I was carried on board a fine large ship, loaded with tobacco, &c., and just ready to sail for England. I now thought my condition much mended; I had sails to lie on, and plenty of good victuals to eat; and everybody on board used me very kindly, quite contrary to what I had seen of any white people before; I therefore began to think that they were not all of the same disposition. A few days after I was on board we sailed for England. I was still at a loss to conjecture my destiny. By this time, however, I could smatter a little imperfect English; and I wanted to know as well as I could where we were going. Some of the people of the ship used to tell me they were going to carry me back to my own country, and this made me very happy. I was quite rejoiced at the idea of going back, and thought if I could get home what wonders I should have to tell. But I was reserved for another fate, and was soon undeceived when we came within sight of the English coast. While I was on board this ship, my captain and master named me *Gustavus Vassa.* I at that time began to understand him a little, and refused to be called so, and told him as well as I could that I would be called Jacob; but he said I should not, and still called me Gustavus: and when I refused to answer to my new name, which I at first did, it gained me many a cuff; so at length I submitted, and by which I have been known ever since. The ship had a very long passage, and on that account we had very short allowance of provisions. Towards the last, we had only one pound and a half of bread per week, and about the same quantity of meat, and one quart of water a day. We spoke with only one vessel the whole time we were at sea, and but once we caught a few fishes. In our extremities the captain and people told me in jest they would kill and eat me; but I thought them in earnest, and was depressed beyond measure, expecting every moment to be my last. While I was in this situation, one evening they caught, with a good deal of trouble, a large shark, and got it on board. This gladdened my poor heart exceedingly, as I thought it would serve the people to eat instead of their eating me; but very soon, to my astonishment, they cut off a small part of the tail, and tossed the rest over the side. This renewed my consternation; and I did not know what to think of these white people, though I very much feared they would kill and eat me. There was on board the ship a young lad who had never been at sea before, about four or five years older than myself: his name was Richard Baker. He was a native of America, had received an excellent education, and was of the most amiable temper. Soon after I went on board, he showed me a great deal of partiality and attention, and in return I grew extremely fond of him. We at length became inseparable; and, for the space of two years, he was of very great use to me, and was my constant companion and instructor. Although this dear youth had many slaves of his own, yet he and I have gone through many sufferings together on shipboard; and we have many nights lain in each other's bosoms when we were in great distress. Thus such a friendship was cemented between us as we cherished till his death, which, to my very great sorrow, happened in the year 1759, when he was up the Archipelago, on board his Majesty's ship the *Preston:* an event which I have never ceased to regret, as I lost at once a kind interpreter, an agreeable companion, and a faithful friend; who, at the age of fifteen, discovered a mind superior to prejudice; and who was not ashamed to notice, to associate with, and to be the friend and instructor of one who was ignorant, a stranger, of a different complexion, and a slave! My master had lodged in his mother's house in America; he respected him very much, and made him always eat with him in the cabin. He used often to tell him jocularly that he would kill and eat me. Sometimes he would say to me—the black people were not good to eat, and would ask me if we did not eat people in my country. I said, No; then he said he would kill Dick (as he always called him) first, and afterwards me. Though this hearing relieved my mind a little as to myself, I was alarmed for Dick, and whenever he was called I used to be very much afraid he was to be killed; and I would peep and watch to see if they were going to kill him; nor was I free from this consternation till we made the land. One night we lost a man overboard; and the cries and noise were so great and confused, in stopping the ship, that I, who did not know what was the matter, began, as usual, to be very much afraid, and to think they were going to make an offering with me, and perform some magic; which I still believed they dealt in. As the waves were very high, I thought the Ruler of the seas was angry, and I expected to be offered up to appease him. This filled my mind with agony, and I could not any more, that night, close my eyes again to rest. However, when daylight appeared, I was a little eased in my mind; but still, every time I was called, I used to think it was to be killed. Some time after this, we saw some very large fish, which I afterwards found were called grampusses. They looked to me exceedingly terrible, and made their appearance just at dusk, and were so near as to blow the water on the ship's deck. I believed them to be the rulers of the sea; and as the white people did not make any offerings at any time, I thought they were angry with them; and at last, what confirmed my belief was, the wind just then died away, and a calm ensued, and in consequence of it the ship stopped going. I supposed that the fish had performed this, and I hid myself in the fore part of the ship, through fear of being offered up to appease them, every minute peeping and quaking; but my good friend Dick came shortly towards me, and I took an opportunity to ask him, as well as I could, what these fish were. Not being able to talk much English, I could but just make him understand my question; and not at all, when I asked him if any offerings were to be made to them; however, he told me these fish would swallow anybody which sufficiently alarmed me. Here he was called away by the captain, who was leaning over the quarter-deck railing, and looking at the fish; and most of the people were busied in getting a barrel of pitch to light for them to play with. The captain now called me to him, having learned some of my apprehensions from Dick; and having diverted himself and others for some time with my fears, which appeared ludicrous enough in my crying and trembling, he dismissed me. The barrel of pitch was now lighted and put over the side into the water. By this time it was just dark, and the fish went after it; and to my great joy, I saw them no more.

However, all my alarms began to subside when we got sight of land; and at last the ship arrived at Falmouth, after a passage of thirteen weeks. Every heart on board seemed gladdened on our reaching the shore, and none more than mine. The captain immediately went on shore, and sent on board some fresh provisions, which we wanted very much. We made good use of them, and our famine was soon turned into feasting, almost without ending. It was about the beginning of the spring 1757, when I arrived in England and I was near twelve years of age at that time. I was very much struck with the buildings and the pavement of the streets in Falmouth; and, indeed, every object I saw, filled me with new surprise. One morning, when I got upon deck, I saw it covered all over with the snow that fell over night. As I had never seen anything of the kind before, I thought it was salt: so I immediately ran down to the mate, and desired him, as well as I could, to come and see how somebody in the night had thrown salt all over the deck. He, knowing what it was, desired me to bring some of it down to him. Accordingly I took up a handful of it, which I found very cold indeed; and when I brought it to him he desired me to taste it. I did so, and I was surprised beyond measure. I then asked him what it was; he told me it was snow, but I could not in anywise understand him. He asked me, if we had no such thing in my country; I told him, No. I then asked him the use of it, and who made it; he told me a great man in the heavens, called God. But here again I was to all intents and purposes at a loss to understand him; and the more so, when a little after I saw the air filled with it, in a heavy shower, which fell down on the same day. After this I went to church; and having never been at such a place before, I was again amazed at seeing and hearing the service. I asked all I could about it, and they gave me to understand it was worshipping God, who made us and all things. I was still at a great loss, and soon got into an endless field of inquiries, as well as I was able to speak and ask about things. However, my little friend Dick used to be my best interpreter; for I could make free with him, and he always instructed me with pleasure. And from what I could understand by him of this God, and in seeing these white people did not sell one another as we did, I was much pleased; and in this I thought they were much happier than we Africans. I was astonished at the wisdom of the white people in all things I saw; but was amazed at their not sacrificing, or making any offerings, and eating with unwashed hands, and touching the dead. I likewise could not help remarking the particular slenderness of their women, which I did not at first like; and I thought they were not so modest and shame-faced as the African women.

I had often seen my master and Dick employed in reading: and I had a great curiosity to talk to the books as I thought they did, and so to learn how all things had a beginning. For that purpose I have often taken up a book, and have talked to it, and then put my ears to it, when alone, in hopes it would answer me; and I have been very much concerned when I found it remained silent.

My master lodged at the house of a gentleman in Falmouth, who had a fine little daughter about six or seven years of age, and she grew prodigiously fond of me, insomuch that we used to eat together, and had servants to wait on us. I was so much caressed by this family that it often reminded me of the treatment I had received from my little noble African master. After I had been here a few days, I was sent on board of the ship; but the child cried so much after me that nothing could pacify her till I was sent for again. It is ludicrous enough, that I began to fear I should be betrothed to this young lady; and when my master asked me if I would stay there with her behind him, as he was going away with the ship, which had taken in the tobacco again, I cried immediately, and said I would not leave him. At last, by stealth, one night I was sent on board the ship again; and in a little time we sailed for Guernsey, where she was in part owned by a merchant, one Nicholas Doberry. As I was now amongst a people who had not their faces scarred, like some of the African nation where I had been, I was very glad I did not let them ornament me in that manner when I was with them. When we arrived at Guernsey, my master placed me to board and lodge with one of his mates, who had a wife and family there; and some months afterwards he went to England, and left me in care of this mate, together with my friend Dick. This mate had a little daughter, aged about five or six years, with whom I used to be much delighted. I had often observed that when her mother washed her face it looked very rosy, but when she washed mine it did not look so. I therefore tried oftentimes myself if I could not by washing make my face of the same color as my little play-mate, Mary, but it was all in vain; and I now began to be mortified at the difference in our complexions. This woman behaved to me with great kindness and attention, and taught me everything in the same manner as she did her own child, and, indeed, in every respect treated me as such. I remained here till the summer of the year 1757, when my master, being appointed first lieutenant of his Majesty's ship the *Roebuck,* sent for Dick and me, and his old mate. On this we all left Guernsey, and set out for England in a sloop, bound for London. As we were coming up towards the Nore, where the *Roebuck* lay, a man-of-war's boat came along side to press our people, on which each man ran to hide himself. I was very much frightened at this, though I did not know what it meant, or what to think or do. However I went and hid myself also under a hencoop. Immediately afterwards, the press-gang came on board with their swords drawn, and searched all about, pulled the people out by force, and put them into the boat. At last I was found out also; the man that found me held me up by the heels while they all made their sport of me, I roaring and crying out all the time most lustily; but at last the mate, who was my conductor, seeing this, came to my assistance, and did all he could to pacify me; but all to very little purpose, till I had seen the boat go off. Soon afterwards we came to the Nore, where the *Roebuck* lay; and, to our great joy, my master came on board to us, and brought us to the ship. When I went on board this large ship, I was amazed indeed to see the quantity of men and the guns. However, my surprise began to diminish as my knowledge increased; and I ceased to feel those apprehensions and alarms which had taken such strong possession of me when I first came among the Europeans, and for some time after. I began now to pass to an opposite extreme; I was so far from being afraid of anything new which I saw, that after I had been some time in this ship, I even began to long for an engagement. My griefs, too, which in young minds are not perpetual, were now wearing away; and I soon enjoyed myself pretty well, and felt tolerably easy in my present situation. There was a number of boys on board, which still made it more agreeable; for we were always together, and a great part of our time was spent in play. I remained in this ship a considerable time, during which we made several cruises, and visited a variety of places; among others we were twice in Holland, and brought over several persons of distinction from it, whose names I do not now remember. On the passage, one day, for the diversion of those gentlemen, all the boys were called on the quarter-deck, and were paired proportionably, and then made to fight; after which the gentlemen gave the combatants from five to nine shillings each. This was the first time I ever fought with a white boy; and I never knew what it was to have a bloody nose before. This made me fight most desperately, I suppose considerably more than an hour; and at last, both of us being weary, we were parted. I had a great deal of this kind of sport afterwards, in which the captain and the ship's company used very much to encourage me. . . .

from Chapter 7

Every day now brought me nearer my freedom, and I was impatient till we proceeded again to sea, that I might have an opportunity of getting a sum large enough to purchase it. I was not long ungratified; for, in the beginning of the year 1766, my master bought another sloop, named the *Nancy,* the largest I had ever seen. She was partly laden, and was to proceed to Philadelphia; our captain had his choice of three, and I was well pleased he chose this, which was the largest; for, from his having a large vessel, I had more room, and could carry a larger quantity of goods with me. Accordingly, when we had delivered our old vessel, the *Prudence,* and completed the lading of the *Nancy,* having made near three hundred per cent, by four barrels of pork I brought from Charleston, I laid in as large a cargo as I could, trusting to God's providence to prosper my undertaking. . . .

When we had unladen the vessel, and I had sold my venture, finding myself master of about forty-seven pounds—I consulted my true friend, the captain, how I should proceed in offering my master the money for my freedom. He told me to come on a certain morning, when he and my master would be at breakfast together. Accordingly, on that morning I went, and met the captain there, as he had appointed. When I went in I made my obeisance to my master, and with my money in my hand, and many fears in my heart, I prayed him to be as good as his offer to me, when he was pleased to promise me my freedom as soon as I could purchase it. This speech seemed to confound him, he began to recoil, and my heart that instant sunk within me. "What," said he, "give you your freedom? Why, where did you get the money? Have you got forty pounds sterling?" "Yes, sir," I answered. "How did you get it?" replied he. I told him, very honestly. The captain then said he knew I got the money honestly, and with much industry, and that I was particularly careful. On which my master replied, I got money much faster than he did; and said he would not have made me the promise he did if he had thought I should have got the money so soon. "Come, come," said my worthy captain, clapping my master on the back, "Come, Robert (which was his name), I think you must let him have his freedom; you have laid your money out very well; you have received a very good interest for it all this time, and here is now the principal at last. I know Gustavus has earned you more than a hundred a year, and he will save you money, as he will not leave you. Come, Robert, take the money." My master then said he would not be worse than his promise; and, taking the money, told me to go to the Secretary at the Register Office, and get my manumission drawn up. These words of my master were like a voice from heaven to me. In an instant all my trepidation was turned into unutterable bliss; and I most reverently bowed myself with gratitude, unable to express my feelings, but by the overflowing of my eyes, and a heart replete with thanks to God, while my true and worthy friend, the captain congratulated us both with a peculiar degree of heart-felt pleasure. As soon as the first transports of my joy were over, and that I had expressed my thanks to these my worthy friends, in the best manner I was able, I rose with a heart full of affection and reverence, and left the room, in order to obey my master's joyful mandate of going to the Register Office. As I was leaving the house I called to mind the words of the Psalmist, in the 126th Psalm, and like him, "I glorified God in my heart, in whom I trusted." These words had been impressed on my mind from the very day I was forced from Deptford to the present hour, and I now saw them, as I thought, fulfilled and verified. My imagination was all rapture as I flew to the Register Office; and, in this respect, like the apostle Peter[11] (whose deliverance from prison was so sudden and extraordinary that he thought he was in a vision), I could scarcely believe I was awake. Heavens! who could do justice to my feelings at this moment! Not conquering heroes themselves, in the midst of a triumph—Not the tender mother who has just regained her long lost infant, and presses it to her heart—Not the weary hungry mariner, at the sight of the desired friendly port—Not the lover, when he once more embraces his beloved mistress, after she has been ravished from his arms! All within my breast was tumult, wildness, and delirium! My feet scarcely touched the ground, for they were winged with joy; and, like Elijah, as he rose to Heaven, they "were with lightning sped as I went on." Everyone I met I told of my happiness, and blazed about the virtue of my amiable master and captain.

When I got to the office and acquainted the Register with my errand, he congratulated me on the occasion, and told me he would draw up my manumission for half price, which was a guinea. I thanked him for his kindness; and, having received it, and paid him, I hastened to my master to get him to sign it, that I might be fully released. Accordingly he signed the manumission that day; so that, before night, I, who had been a slave in the morning, trembling at the will of another, was become my own master, and completely free. I thought this was the happiest day I had ever experienced; and my joy was still heightened by the blessings and prayers of many of the sable race, particularly the aged, to whom my heart had ever been attached with reverence.

As the form of my manumission has something peculiar in it, and expresses the absolute power and dominion one man claims over his fellow, I shall beg leave to present it before my readers at full length.

Montserrat.

To all men unto whom these presents shall come: I, Robert King, of the parish of St. Anthony, in the said island, merchant, send greeting. Know ye, that I, the aforesaid Robert King, for and in consideration of the sum of seventy pounds current money of the said island, to me in hand paid, and to the intent that a Negro man slave, named Gustavus Vassa, shall and may become free, having manumitted, emancipated, enfranchised, and set free, and by these presents do manumit, emancipate, enfranchise, and set free, the aforesaid Negro man slave, named Gustavus Vassa, for ever; hereby giving, granting and releasing unto him, the said Gustavus Vassa, all right, title, dominion, sovereignty, and property, which, as lord and master over the aforesaid Gustavus Vassa, I had, or now have, or by any means whatsoever I may or can hereafter possibly have over him, the aforesaid Negro, for ever. In witness whereof, I, the above said Robert King, have unto these presents set my hand and seal, this tenth day of July, in the year of our Lord one thousand seven hundred and sixty-six.

ROBERT KING

Signed, sealed, and delivered in the presence of Terry Legay, Montserrat.

Registered the within manumission at full length, this eleventh day of July 1766, in liber. D.

TERRY LEGAY, Register

[11]Acts 12:9.

In short, the fair as well as the black people immediately styled me by a new appellation, to me the most desirable in the world, which was freeman; and at the dances I gave, my Georgia superfine blue clothes made no indifferent appearance, as I thought. Some of the sable females, who formerly stood aloof, now began to relax and appear less coy; but my heart was still fixed on London, where I hoped to be ere long. So that my worthy captain and his owner, my late master, finding that the bent of my mind was towards London, said to me, "We hope you won't leave us, but that you will still be with the vessels." Here gratitude bowed me down; and none but the generous mind can judge of my feelings, struggling between inclination and duty. However, notwithstanding my wish to be in London, I obediently answered my benefactors, that I would go in the vessel, and not leave them; and from the day I was entered on board as an able-bodied sailor, at thirty-six shillings per month, besides what perquisites I could make. My intention was to make a voyage or two, entirely to please these my honored patrons; but I determined that the year following, if it pleased God, I would see old England once more, and surprise my old master, Captain Pascal, who was hourly in my mind; for I still loved him, notwithstanding his usage of me, and pleased myself with thinking what he would say, when he saw what the Lord had done for me in so short a time, instead of being, as he might perhaps suppose, under the cruel yoke of some planter. With these kind of reveries I used often to entertain myself, and shorten the time till my return; and now, being as in my original free African state, I embarked on board the *Nancy,* after having got all things ready for our voyage. In this state of serenity, we sailed for St. Eustatius; and having smooth seas and calm weather, we soon arrived there. After taking our cargo on board, we proceeded to Savannah, in Georgia, in August, 1766. While we were there, as usual, I used to go for the cargo up the rivers in boats; and on this business have been frequently beset by alligators, which were very numerous on that coast; and shot many of them when they have been near getting into our boats, which we have with great difficulty sometimes prevented, and have been very much frightened at them. I have seen a young one sold in Georgia alive for six pence. . . .

from Chapter 10

Our voyage to the north pole being ended, I returned to London with Doctor Irving, with whom I continued for some time, during which I began seriously to reflect on the dangers I had escaped, particularly those of my last voyage, which made a lasting impression on my mind, and, by the grace of God, proved afterwards a mercy to me; it caused me to reflect deeply on my eternal state, and to seek the Lord with full purpose of heart, ere it was too late. I rejoiced greatly; and heartily thanked the Lord for directing me to London, where I was determined to work out my own salvation, and, in so doing, procure a title to heaven; being the result of a mind blinded by ignorance and sin.

In process of time I left my master, Doctor Irving, the purifier of waters. I lodged in Coventry court, Haymarket, where I was continually oppressed and much concerned about the salvation of my soul, and was determined (in my own strength) to be a first-rate Christian. I used every means for this purpose; and, not being able to find any person amongst those with whom I was then acquainted that acquiesced with me in point of religion, or, in scripture language, that would show me any good, I was much dejected, and knew not where to seek relief; however, I first frequented the neighboring churches, St. James' and others, two or three times a day, for many weeks; still I came away dissatisfied: something was wanting that I could not obtain, and I really found more heart-felt relief in reading my Bible at home than in attending the church; and, being resolved to be saved, I pursued other methods. First I went among the Quakers, where the word of God was neither read or preached, so that I remained as much in the dark as ever. I then searched into the Roman Catholic principles, but was not in the least edified. I at length had recourse to the Jews, which availed me nothing, as the fear of eternity daily harassed my mind, and I knew not where to seek shelter from the wrath to come. However, this was my conclusion, at all events, to read the four evangelists, and whatever sect or party I found adhering thereto, such I would join. . . . Thus I continued to travel in much heaviness, and frequently murmured against the Almighty, particularly in his providential dealings; and, awful to think! I began to blaspheme, and wished often to be anything but a human being. In these severe conflicts the Lord answered me by awful "visions of the night, when deep sleep falleth upon men, in slumberings upon the bed" (Job 33:15). He was pleased, in much mercy, to give me to see, and in some measure understand, the great and awful scene of the judgment day, that "no unclean person, no unholy thing, can enter into the kingdom of God" (Eph. 5:5). I would then, if it had been possible, have changed my nature with the meanest worm on the earth; and was ready to say to the mountains and rocks "fall on me" (Rev. 6:16), but all in vain. I then, in the greatest agony, requested the divine Creator, that he would grant me a small space of time to repent of my follies and vile iniquities, which I felt were grievous. The Lord, in his manifold mercies, was pleased to grant my request, and, being yet in a state of time, the sense of God's mercies were so great on my mind when I awoke that my strength entirely failed me for many minutes, and I was exceedingly weak. This was the first spiritual mercy I ever was sensible of, and being on praying ground, as soon as I recovered a little strength, and got out of bed and dressed myself, I invoked heaven, from my inmost soul, and fervently begged that God would never again permit me to blaspheme his most holy name. The Lord, who is long-suffering and full of compassion to such poor rebels as we are, condescended to hear and answer. I felt that I was altogether unholy, and saw clearly what a bad use I had made of the faculties I was endowed with: they were given me to glorify God with; I thought, therefore, I had better want them here, and enter into life eternal, than abuse them and be cast into hell fire. I prayed to be directed, if there were any holier than those with whom I was acquainted, that the Lord would point them out to me. I appealed to the Searcher of hearts, whether I did not wish to love him more, and serve him better. Notwithstanding all this, the reader may easily discern, if a believer, that I was still in nature's darkness. At length I hated the house in which I lodged, because God's most holy name was blasphemed in it; then I saw the word of God verified, *viz.,* "Before they call, I will answer; and while they are yet speaking, I will hear."

I had a great desire to read the Bible the whole day at home; but not having a convenient place for retirement, I left the house in the day, rather than stay amongst the wicked ones; and that day, as I was walking, it pleased God to direct me to a house where there was an old sea-faring man, who experienced much of the love of

God shed abroad in his heart. He began to discourse with me; and, as I desired to love the Lord, his conversation rejoiced me greatly; and, indeed, I had never heard before the love of Christ to believers set forth in such a manner, and in so clear a point of view. Here I had more questions to put to the man than his time would permit him to answer; and in that memorable hour there came in a dissenting minister; he joined our discourse, and asked me some few questions; among others, where I heard the gospel preached? I knew not what he meant by hearing the gospel; I told him I had read the gospel; and he asked where I went to church, or whether I went at all or not? To which I replied, "I attended St. James's, St. Martin's, and St. Ann's Soho." "So," said he, "you are a churchman?" I answered, I was. He then invited me to a love-feast at his chapel that evening. I accepted the offer, and thanked him; and soon after he went away, I had some further discourse with the old Christian, added to some profitable reading, which made me exceedingly happy. When I left him he reminded me of coming to the feast; I assured him I would be there. Thus we parted, and I weighed over the heavenly conversation that passed between these two men, which cheered my then heavy and drooping spirit more than anything I had met with for many months. However, I thought the time long in going to my supposed banquet. I also wished much for the company of these friendly men; their company pleased me much; and I thought the gentleman very kind in asking me, a stranger, to a feast; but how singular did it appear to me, to have it in a chapel! When the wished-for hour came I went, and happily the old man was there, who kindly seated me, as he belonged to the place. I was much astonished to see the place filled with people, and no signs of eating and drinking. There were many ministers in the company. At last they began by giving out hymns, and between the singing, the ministers engaged in prayer; in short, I knew not what to make of this sight, having never seen anything of the kind in my life before now. Some of the guests began to speak their experience, agreeable to what I read in the Scriptures; much was said by every speaker of the providence of God, and his unspeakable mercies, to each of them. This I knew in a great measure and could most heartily join them. But when they spoke of a future state, they seemed to be altogether certain of their calling and election of God; and that no one could ever separate them from the love of Christ, or pluck them out of his hands. This filled me with utter consternation, intermingled with admiration. I was so amazed as not to know what to think of the company; my heart was attracted, and my affections were enlarged. I wished to be as happy as them, and was persuaded in my mind that they were different from the world "that lieth in wickedness" (I John 5:19). Their language and singing, &c., did well harmonize; I was entirely overcome, and wished to live and die thus. Lastly, some persons in the place produced some neat baskets full of buns, which they distributed about; and each person communicated with his neighbor, and sipped water out of different mugs, which they handed about to all who were present. This kind of Christian fellowship I had never seen, nor ever thought of seeing on earth; it fully reminded me of what I had read in the Holy Scriptures, of the primitive Christians, who loved each other and broke bread, in partaking of it, even from house to house. This entertainment (which lasted about four hours) ended in singing and prayer. It was the first soul feast I ever was present at. This last twenty-four hours produced me things, spiritual and temporal, sleeping and waking, judgment and mercy, that I could not but admire the goodness of God, in directing the blind, blasphemous sinner in the path that he knew not of, even among the just; and, instead of judgment, he has shewed mercy, and will hear and answer the prayers and supplications of every returning prodigal:

O! to grace how great a debtor
Daily I'm constrained to be!

After this I was resolved to win Heaven if possible; and if I perished I thought it should be at the feet of Jesus, in praying to him for salvation. After having been an eye-witness to some of the happiness which attended those who feared God, I knew not how, with any kind of propriety, to return to my lodgings, where the name of God was continually profaned, at which I felt the greatest horror; I paused in my mind for some time, not knowing what to do; whether to hire a bed elsewhere, or go home again. At last fearing an evil report might arise, I went home, with a farewell to card playing and vain jesting, &c. I saw that time was very short, eternity long, and very near; and I viewed those persons alone blessed who were found ready at midnight call, or when the judge of all, both quick and dead, cometh. . . . During this time I was out of employ, nor was I likely to get a situation for me, which obliged me to go once more to sea. I engaged as steward of a ship called the *Hope,* Captain Richard Strange, bound from London to Cadiz in Spain. In a short time after I was on board, I heard the name of God much blasphemed, and I feared greatly lest I should catch the horrible infection. I thought if I sinned again after having life and death set evidently before me, I should certainly go to hell. My mind was uncommonly chagrined, and I murmured much at God's providential dealings with me, and was discontented with the commandments, that I could not be saved by what I had done; I hated all things, and wished I had never been born; confusion seized me, and I wished to be annihilated. One day I was standing on the very edge of the stern of the ship, thinking to drown myself; but this scripture was instantly impressed on my mind—"That no murderer hath eternal life abiding in him" (I John 3:15). Then I paused and thought myself the unhappiest man living. Again I was convinced that the Lord was better to me than I deserved, and I was better off in the world than many. After this I began to fear death; I fretted, mourned, and prayed, till I became a burden to others, but more so to myself. At length I concluded to beg my bread on shore rather than go again to sea amongst a people who feared not God, and I entreated the captain three different times to discharge me; he would not, but each time gave me greater and greater encouragement to continue with him, and all on board shewed me very great civility: notwithstanding all this I was unwilling to embark again. At last some of my religious friends advised me, by saying it was my lawful calling, consequently it was my duty to obey, and that God was not confined to place, &c., &c. particularly Mr. G——— S———, the governor of Tothil-fields, Bridewell, who pitied my case, and read the eleventh chapter of the Hebrews to me, with exhortations. He prayed for me, and I believed that he prevailed on my behalf, as my burden was then greatly removed, and I found a heartfelt resignation to the will of God. The good man gave me a pocket Bible and Alleine's *Alarm to the Unconverted.* We parted, and the next day I went on board again. We sailed for Spain, and I found favor with the captain. It was the fourth of the month of September when we sailed from London; we had a delightful voyage to Cadiz, where we arrived the twenty-third of the same month. The place is strong, commands a fine prospect, and is very rich. The Spanish galleons frequent that port, and some arrived whilst we were there. I had many opportunities of reading the scriptures. I wrestled hard with God in fervent prayer, who had declared in his word that he would hear the groanings and deep sighs of the poor in spirit. I found this verified to my utter astonishment and comfort in the following manner.

On the morning of the 6th of October (I pray you to attend), all that day, I thought I should either see or hear something supernatural. I had a secret impulse on my mind of something that was to take place, which drove me continually for that time to a Throne of Grace. It pleased God to enable me to wrestle with him, as Jacob did: I prayed that if sudden death were to happen, and I perished, it might be at Christ's feet.

In the evening of the same day, as I was reading and meditating on the fourth chapter of Acts, twelfth verse, under the solemn apprehensions of eternity, and reflecting on my past actions, I began to think I had lived a moral life, and that I had a proper ground to believe I had an interest in the divine favor; but still meditating on the subject, not knowing whether salvation was to be had partly for our own good deeds or solely as the sovereign gift of God; in this deep consternation the Lord was pleased to break in upon my soul with his bright beams of heavenly light; and in an instant, as it were, removing the veil, and letting light into a dark place, I saw clearly with an eye of faith, the crucified Saviour bleeding on the cross on mount Calvary; the scriptures became an unsealed book; I saw myself a condemned criminal under the law, which came with its full force to my conscience, and when "the commandment came sin revived, and I died." I saw the Lord Jesus Christ in his humiliation, loaded and bearing my reproach, sin, and shame. I then clearly perceived that by the deeds of the law no flesh living could be justified. I was then convinced that by the first Adam sin came, and by the second Adam (the Lord Jesus Christ) all that are saved must be made alive. It was given me at that time to know what it was to be born again (John 3:5). I saw the eighth chapter to the Romans, and the doctrines of God's decrees, verified agreeable to his eternal, everlasting, and unchangeable purposes. The word of God was sweet to my taste, yea, sweeter than honey and the honeycomb. Christ was revealed to my soul as the chiefest among ten thousand. These heavenly moments were really as life to the dead, and what John calls an earnest of the Spirit.[12] This was indeed unspeakable, and I firmly believe undeniable by many. Now every leading providential circumstance that happened to me, from the day I was taken from my parents to that hour, was then in my view, as if it had but just then occurred. I was sensible of the invisible hand of God, which guided and protected me, when in truth I knew it not: still the Lord pursued me, although I slighted and disregarded it; this mercy melted me down. When I considered my poor wretched state I wept, seeing what a great debtor I was to sovereign free grace. Now the Ethiopian was willing to be saved by Jesus Christ, the sinner's only surety, and also to rely on none other person or thing for salvation. Self was obnoxious, and good works he had none, for it is God that worketh in us both to will and to do. Oh! the amazing things of that hour can never be told—it was joy in the Holy Ghost! I felt an astonishing change; the burden of sin, the gaping jaws of hell, and the fears of death, that weighed me down before, now lost their horror; indeed I thought death would now be the best earthly friend I ever had. Such were my grief and joy as I believe are seldom experienced. I was bathed in tears, and said, What am I that God should thus look on me, the vilest of sinners? I felt a deep

[12]John 16:13, 14, &c.

concern for my mother and friends, which occasioned me to pray with fresh ardor; and in the abyss of thought, I viewed the unconverted people of the world in a very awful state, being without God and without hope.

It pleased God to pour out on me the spirit of prayer and the grace of supplication, so that in loud acclamations I was enabled to praise and glorify his most holy name. When I got out of the cabin, and told some of the people what the Lord had done for me, alas! who could understand me or believe my report! None but to whom the arm of the Lord was revealed. I became a barbarian to them in talking of the love of Christ: his name was to me as ointment poured forth, indeed it was sweet to my soul, but to them a rock of offense. I thought my case singular, and every hour a day until I came to London, for I much longed to be with some to whom I could tell of the wonders of God's love towards me, and join in prayer to him whom my soul loved and thirsted after. I had uncommon commotions within, such as few can tell aught about. Now the Bible was my only companion and comfort; I prized it much, with many thanks to God that I could read it for myself, and was not left to be tossed about or led by man's devices and notions. The worth of a soul cannot be told. May the Lord give the reader an understanding in this. Whenever I looked in the Bible I saw things new, and many texts were immediately applied to me with great comfort, for I knew that to me was the word of salvation sent. Sure I was that the Spirit which indited the word opened my heart to receive the truth of it as it is in Jesus—that the same Spirit enabled me to act faith upon the promises that were precious to me, and enabled me to believe to the salvation of my soul. By free grace I was persuaded that I had a part in the first resurrection, and was enlightened with the "light of the living" (Job 33:30). I wished for a man of God with whom I might converse: my soul was like the chariots of Amminadib (Canticles 6:12). These, among others, were the precious promises that were so powerfully applied to me. "All things whatsoever ye shall ask in prayer, believing, ye shall receive" (Mat. 21:22). "Peace I leave with you, my peace I give unto you" (John 14:27). I saw the blessed Redeemer to be the fountain of life, and the well of salvation. I experienced him to be all in all; he had brought me by a way that I knew not, and he had made crooked paths straight. Then in his name I set up my Ebenezer, saying, Hitherto he hath helped me: and could say to the sinners about me, Behold what a Saviour I have! Thus I was, by the teaching of that all-glorious Deity, the great One in Three, and Three in One, confirmed in the truths of the Bible, those oracles of everlasting truth, on which every soul living must stand or fall eternally, agreeable to Acts 4:12. "Neither is there salvation in any other, for there is none other name under heaven given among men whereby we must be saved, but only Christ Jesus." May God give the reader a right understanding in these facts! "To him that believeth, all things are possible, but to them that are unbelieving nothing is pure" (Titus 1:15).

During this period we remained at Cadiz until our ship got laden. We sailed about the fourth of November; and, having a good passage, we arrived in London the month following, to my comfort, with heartfelt gratitude to God for his rich and unspeakable mercies.

On my return I had but one text which puzzled me, or that the devil endeavored to buffet me with, *viz.,* Rom. 11:6, and, as I had heard of the Rev. Mr. Romaine, and his great knowledge in the scriptures, I wished much to hear him preach. One day I went to Blackfriars church, and, to my great satisfaction and surprise, he preached from that very text. He very clearly shewed the difference between human works and free election, which is according to God's sovereign will and pleasure. These glad tidings set me entirely at liberty, and I went out of the church rejoicing, seeing my spots were those of God's children. I went to Westminster Chapel, and saw some of my old friends, who were glad when they perceived the wonderful change that the Lord had wrought in me, particularly Mr. G—— S——, my worthy acquaintance, who was a man of a choice spirit and had great zeal for the Lord's service. I enjoyed his correspondence till he died, in the year 1784. I was again examined at that same chapel, and was received into church fellowship amongst them. I rejoiced in spirit, making melody in my heart to the God of all my mercies. Now my whole wish was to be dissolved, and to be with Christ—but, alas! I must wait mine appointed time.

1789

Judith Sargent Murray 1751–1820

Judith Sargent Murray's literary career flourished during the 1790s, a time when America was struggling to define itself as independent—politically and aesthetically—from Great Britain. Murray was engaged in this period of change, voicing her opinions on literary nationalism, the federalist system of government, the equality of women, and religious universalism. The seeds of these interests were planted early in Murray's life. She was born in Gloucester, Massachusetts, the eldest child of Captain Winthrop Sargent and Judith Saunders. A socially prominent family, the Sargents were distinguished by their political activity: Winthrop Sargent had served in the provisional government during the Revolutionary War, and his son Winthrop was honored by Washington for his military activities. At an early age Judith Sargent exhibited so high a degree of intelligence that her parents encouraged her to study with her brother, who was preparing with a local Gloucester minister for entrance to Harvard. She thus gained an education far superior to that given most women: she studied the Latin and Greek languages and literatures and was introduced to the sciences, including mathematics and astronomy. The Sargent family became strong supporters of John Murray, who visited Gloucester in his mission to establish Universalism in America. By aligning themselves with this liberal branch of Protestantism, the Sargents elicited scorn from their religiously conservative neighbors.

At age eighteen, Judith Sargent married John Stevens, a prosperous sea captain and trader; the large Stevens house in Gloucester thereafter became a popular meeting-place in the town. Dating from this period are the author's earliest known writings, including several poems and an important essay in which she introduces her ideas on the equality of women, "Desultory Thoughts upon the Utility of encouraging a degree of Self-Complacency, especially in Female Bosoms" (1784). She signed her early work "Constantia," one of the many pseudonyms she would use throughout her career.

When her husband died in 1786, Stevens became a closer friend of John Murray, and they married in 1788. The couple shared both religious beliefs and intellectual interests. The Murrays' move to Boston in 1793 widened the author's literary involvement, and her career flourished. She wrote two plays for the newly reopened Federal Street Theatre, thereby aligning herself with such writers as Royall Tyler. With regular contributions to the *Massachusetts Magazine*—one of the most prestigious journals of the late eighteenth century—Murray established herself as a prominent essayist and poet. Her writings reflect the firm ideas she held on education, the equality of the sexes, literary nationalism, federalism, and Universalism. The three-volume edition of her *Gleaner* essays, published in 1798, attracted over 700 subscribers, among them President Adams and George Washington.

After 1800, Murray turned her attention to editing John Murray's biography and religious writings. Following the death of her husband in 1815, Murray moved to Natchez, Mississippi, to live with her only child, Julia, who had married a wealthy planter. Murray died in 1820.

An assessment of Murray's literary career must consider the fervor with which she addressed the most important issues of her day. The major outlet for these ideas were her two concurrent essay series—*The Repository* (largely religious in nature) and *The Gleaner*—which ran in the *Massachusetts Magazine* from 1792 to 1794. The imaginary author of the *Gleaner* essays, Mr. Vigillius, discussed such varied topics as the new Constitution, the dangers of political factionalism, and the progressive nature of history. Most of the essays are prefaced with poems. Within *The Gleaner* series Murray included critical essays on drama at a time when many writers were concerned about the future of American literature. According to Murray's federalist agenda, the new American drama should reflect the virtues of the new republic: liberty, patriotism, and equality. By focusing on American virtues and scenes, Murray argued, national drama would be revitalized and could break away from the British tradition. Her two plays, *The Medium, or Virtue Triumphant* and *The Traveller Returned,* although not commercially successful, sparked an interest in literary nationalism.

Murray also turned her attention toward a reconsideration of fiction with her brief novel, *The Story of Margaretta,* included within the framework of *The Gleaner.* Unlike most heroines of sentimental fiction, Margaretta is able to escape the cycle of seduction and destruction because of her superior education: she proves herself to be wise and virtuous (by upholding filial duty over passion's inclinations) and is rewarded with a loving husband. This link between education, virtuous filial conduct, and reward is an important aspect of Murray's philosophy about the status of women. She argued that if women were given equal opportunity to develop their rational capacities, they would be able to exercise good judgment and right reason, thus escaping their supposedly female susceptibility to passion and sentimental emotionalism (both considered bad conduct). Murray predicts that advancements in education and thus in social place would allow young women to form "a new era in female history."

"On the Equality of the Sexes" (reportedly drafted in 1779; printed in the *Massachusetts Magazine* in April/May 1790, and signed "Constantia") is perhaps Murray's most influential essay. Here she radically questioned the system that held women subservient to men. She argued that the capacities of imagination and memory are verifiably equal in men and women, and the apparent inequalities in reason and judgment arise only from a difference in education. Murray argued that housework and needlework are mindless activities, ones that deny women any exercise of their intellectual faculties. If women were given the same education as men, Murray maintained, their reason and judgment would develop equally. Murray herself used this system to her advantage; she felt successful in her endeavor "of being considered *independent as a writer.*" It is interesting to note that Murray predicated the need for women's education not only on the equality of their rational capabilities but also on the equality of their souls. Women were equal in the eyes of God, invigorated by the same divine breath. Feminist reform was linked, in Murray's theory, to the egalitarian promise of the new republic. If America were to achieve its destined level of greatness, it would have to develop and cherish the achievements, intellect, and virtue of all citizens.

Amy M. Yerkes
University of Pennsylvania

PRIMARY WORKS

The Gleaner, Massachusetts Magazine, 1792–1794, later published as *The Gleaner; A Miscellaneous Production,* 3 vols., 1798; *The Repository, Massachusetts Magazine,* 1792–1794; *The Medium, or Virtue Triumphant,* 1795; *The Traveller Returned,* 1796; "Desultory Thoughts upon the Utility of encouraging A degree of Self-Complacency, especially in Female Bosoms," *Gentleman and Lady's Town and Country Magazine,* 1784; "On the Domestic Education of Children," *Massachusetts Magazine,* May, 1790; "On the Equality of the Sexes," *Massachusetts Magazine,* March, April, 1790.

SECONDARY WORKS

Vena B. Field, *Constantia: A Study of the Life and Works of Judith Sargent Murray, 1751–1820,* 1930; Bruce Granger, *American Essay Serials from Franklin to Irving,* 1978; Mary Beth Norton, *Liberty's Daughters: The Revolutionary Experience of American Women 1750–1800,* 1980; Pattie Cowell, *Women Poets in Pre-revolutionary America, 1650–1775,* 1981; Cathy Davidson, *Revolution and the Word: The Rise of the Novel in America,* 1986; Nina Baym, Introduction, *The Gleaner,* 1992.

Desultory Thoughts upon the Utility of encouraging a degree of Self-Complacency, especially in Female Bosoms[1]

Self estimation, kept within due bounds,
However oddly the assertion sounds,
May, of the fairest efforts be the root,
May yield the embow'ring shade—the mellow fruit;
May stimulate to most exalted deeds,
Direct the soul where blooming honor leads;
May give her there, to act a noble part,
To virtuous pleasures yield the willing heart.
Self-estimation will debasement shun,
And, in the path of wisdom, joy to run;
An unbecoming act in fears to do,

[1]Published in *Gentleman and Lady's Magazine,* October 22, 1784.

And still, its exaltation keeps in view.
"To rev'rence self," a Bard long since directed,
And, on each moral truth HE well reflected;
But, lost to conscious worth, to decent pride,
Compass nor helm there is, our course to guide:
Nor may we anchor cast, for rudely tost
In an unfathom'd sea, each motive's lost.
Wildly amid contending waves we're beat,
And rocks and quick sands, shoals and depths we meet;
'Till, dash'd in pieces, or, till found'ring, we
One common wreck of all our prospects see!
Nor, do we mourn, for we were lost to fame,
And never hap'd to reach a tow'ring name;
Ne'er taught to "rev'rence self," or to aspire;
Our bosoms never caught ambition's fire;
An indolence of virtue still prevail'd,
Nor the sweet gale of praise was e'er inhal'd;
Rous'd by a new stimulus, no kindling glow.
No soothing emulations gentle flow,
We judg'd that nature, not to us inclin'd,
In narrow bounds our progress had confin'd,
And, that our forms, to say the very best,
Only, not frightful, were by all confest.

I think, to teach young minds to aspire, ought to be the ground work of education: many a laudable achievement is lost, from a persuasion that our efforts are unequal to the arduous attainment. Ambition is a noble principle, which properly directed, may be productive of the most valuable consequences. It is amazing to what heights the mind by exertion may tow'r: I would, therefore, have my pupils believe, that every thing in the compass of mortality, was placed within their grasp, and that, the avidity of application, the intenseness of study, were only requisite to endow them with every external grace; and mental accomplishment. Thus I should impel them to progress on, if I could not lead them to the heights I would wish them to attain. It is too common with parents to expatiate in their hearing, upon all the foibles of their children, and to let their virtues pass, in appearance, unregarded: this they do, least they should, (were they to commend) swell their little hearts to pride, and implant in their tender minds, undue conceptions of their own importance. Those, for example, who have the care of a beautiful female, they assiduously guard every avenue, they arrest the stream of due admiration, and endeavour to divest her of all idea of the bounties of nature: what is the consequence? She grows up, and of course mixes with those who are self interested: strangers will be sincere; she encounters the tongue of the flatterer, he will exaggerate, she finds herself possessed of accomplishments which have been studiously concealed from her, she throws the reins upon the neck of fancy, and gives every encomiast full credit for his most extravagant eulogy. Her natural connections, her home is rendered disagreeable, and she hastes to the scenes, whence arise the sweet perfume of adulation, and when she can obtain the regard due to a merit, which she supposes altogether uncommon. Those who have made her acquainted with the dear secret, she considers as her best friends; and it is more than probable, that she will soon fall a sacrifice to some worthless character, whose interest may lead him to the most hyperbolical lengths in the round of flattery. Now, I should be solicitous that my daughter should possess for me the fondest love, as well as that respect which gives birth to duty; in order to promote this wish of my soul, from my lips she should be accustomed to hear the most pleasing truths, and, as in the course of my instructions, I should doubtless find myself but too often impelled to wound the delicacy of youthful sensibility. I would therefore, be careful to avail myself of this exuberating balance: I would, from the early dawn of reason, address her as a rational being; hence, I apprehend, the most valuable consequences would result in some such language as this, she might from time to time be accosted. A pleasing form is undoubtedly advantageous. Nature, my dear, hath furnished you with an agreeable person, your glass, was I to be silent, would inform you that you are pretty, your appearance will sufficiently recommend you to a stranger, the flatterer will give a more than mortal finishing to every feature; but, it must be your part, my sweet girl, to render yourself worthy respect from higher motives: you must learn "to reverence yourself," that is, your intellectual existance; you must join my efforts, in endeavouring to adorn your mind, for, it is from the proper furnishing of that, you will become indeed a valuable person, you will, as I said, give birth to the most favorable impressions at first sight: but, how mortifying should this be all, if, upon a more extensive knowledge you should be discovered to possess no one mental charm, to be fit only at best, to be hung up as a pleasing picture among the paintings of some spacious hall. The FLATTERER, indeed, will still pursue you, but it will be from interested views, and he will smile at your undoing! Now, then, my best Love, is the time for you to lay in such a fund of useful knowledge as shall continue, and augment every kind sentiment in regard to you, as shall set you above the snares of the artful betrayer.

Thus, that sweet form, shall serve but as a polished casket, which will contain a most beautiful gem, highly finished, and calculated for advantage, as well as ornament. Was she, I say, habituated thus to reflect, she would be taught to aspire; she would learn to estimate every accomplishment, according to its proper value; and, when the voice of adulation should assail her ear, as she had early been initiated into its true meaning, and from youth been accustomed to the language of praise; her attention would not be captivated, the Siren's song would not borrow the aid of novelty, her young mind would not be enervated or intoxicated, by a delicious surprise, she would possess her soul in serenity, and by that means, rise superior to the deep laid schemes which, too commonly, encompass the steps of beauty.

Neither should those to whom nature had been parsimonious, be tortured by me with degrading comparisons; every advantage I would expatiate upon, and there are few who possess not some personal charms. I would teach them to gloss over their imperfections, inasmuch as, I do think, an agreeable form, a very necessary introduction to society, and of course it behoves us to render our appearance as pleasing as possible: I would, I must repeat, by all means guard them against a low estimation of self. I would leave no charm undiscovered or unmarked, for the penetrating eye of the pretended admirer, to make unto himself a merit by holding up to her view; thus, I would destroy the weapons of flattery, or render them useless, by leaving not the least room for their operation.

A young lady, growing up with the idea, that she possesses few, or no personal attractions, and that her mental abilities are of an inferior kind, imbibing at the same time, a most melancholly idea of a female, descending down the vale of life in an unprotected state; taught also to regard her character ridiculously contemptible, will, too probably, throw herself away upon the first who approaches her with tenders of love, however indifferent may be her chance of happiness, least if she omits the present day of grace, she may never be so happy as to meet a second offer, and must then inevitably be stigmatized with that dreaded title, an Old Maid, must rank with a class whom she has been accustomed to regard as burthens upon society, and objects whom she might with impunity turn into ridicule! Certainly love, friendship and esteem, ought to take place of marriage, but, the woman thus circumstanced, will seldom regard these previous requisites to felicity, if she can but insure the honors, which she, in idea, associates with a matrimonial connection—to prevent which great evil, I would early impress under proper regulations, a reverence of self; I would endeavour to rear to worth, and a consciousness thereof: I would be solicitous to inspire the glow of virtue, with that elevation of soul, that dignity, which is ever attendant upon self-approbation, arising from the genuine source of innate rectitude. I must be excused for thus insisting upon my hypothesis, as I am, from observation, persuaded, that many have suffered materially all their life long, from a depression of soul, early inculcated, in compliance to a false maxim, which hath supposed pride would thereby be eradicated. I know there is a contrary extreme, and I would, in almost all cases, prefer the happy medium. However, if these fugitive hints may induce some abler pen to improve thereon, the exemplification will give pleasure to the heart of CONSTANTIA.

October 22, 1784

On the Domestic Education of Children[1]

I hate severity to trembling youth,
Mildness should designate each useful truth;
My soul detests the rude unmanly part,
Which swells with bursting sighs the little heart.
What can an infant do to merit blows?
See, from his eyes a briny torrent flows.
Behold the pretty mourner! pale his cheek,
His tears are fruitless, and he dare not speak.
Lowly he bends beneath yon tyrant's rod;
Unfeeling pedagogue—who like some god
Fabled of old, of bloody savage mind,
To scourge, and not to mend the human race, design'd.

[1]Published in *Massachusetts Magazine,* May 1790.

It would be well if every gentle method to form the young untutored mind, was essayed, previous to a harsher mode of procedure. Do blows ever produce a salutary effect upon a gentle or a generous disposition? It can hardly be presumed that they do; and if not upon the bosom, the feelings of which urbanity hath arranged, is it not more than probable that they tend to make an obstinate being still more perverse? Yet the reins of government I would not consign to children; the young idea I would direct; nor would I permit the dawn of life to pass uncultured by; nevertheless, to barbarous hands I would not yield the tender plant. Behind the pallid countenance of the little culprit, the tender sorrow, the imploring tear, the beseeching eye, the knee bent for forgiveness—and can the offences of a child be other than venial? But it is in vain—the inhuman preceptor continues obdurate—he retains his purpose, and the wretched sufferer receives those blows which only the malefactor can merit! Is there not some reason to suppose, that by a repetition of ignominious punishments, we shall eradicate from the young mind all sense of shame, thus throwing down a very essential barrier, and finally opening the floodgates of vice.

But what shall we substitute instead of those violent and coercive measures? I proceed to give an example. Martesia is blessed with a numerous offspring of both sexes—some of her young folks have discovered dispositions not a little refractory—caprice hath shown its head, and a number of little petulances early displayed themselves; yet, that weapon known by the name of a rod was never so much as heard of among them, nor do they know the meaning of a blow. How then doth Martesia manage, for it is certain that her salutary efforts have well nigh eradicated from her little circle every perverse humour. Her family is a well regulated Commonwealth, the moving spring of which is emulation, *a laudable kind of emulation, which never partakes of envy, save when virtue acknowledgeth the hue of vice.* She hath in her gift various posts of honour; these she distributes according to the merit of the pretender; they are conferred upon those who have made any improvement, and the whole company join to invest the distinguished candidate with his new dignity. Martesia makes it a rule never to appear ruffled before her children, and she is particularly careful to keep every irregular passion from their observation. That she is tenderly concerned for them, and takes a very deep interest in their happiness, is a truth which she daily inculcates. She wishes also to implant in their young minds the most elevated opinion of her understanding; and she conceives that they cannot be too early impressed with an idea of her possessing superiour abilities. The advantages which she will derive from this plan are obvious; her authority will be the more readily acknowledged, and her decisions will obtain the requisite weight. By reiterated petitions she is seldom persecuted, for as the little claimants are sensible of her attachment, and cannot call her judgment in question, they are not accustomed to repeat their requests. Yet, notwithstanding they are taught to believe Martesia ever under the government of reason, should a persevering spirit be found clamourously urgent, the pursuit, however, cannot be long continued, since but one answer will be given; which answer, though mild, is always peremptory and conclusive. To render prevalent in the minds of her children, sentiments of humanity and benevolence, is with Martesia an essential object. A *dignified* condescension to inferiority she also inculcates, and she early endeavours, by judicious advances, to bring them acquainted with that part of the economy of the Deity which hath made our obligations to each other reciprocal: Thus solicitous to enforce the idea of their dependence, even upon the meanest domestick, she exacts from her servants no extraordinary marks of humility toward them, for her view is to choke, if possible, the first buddings of unbecoming pride.

Doth she discover the smallest disposition to cruelty, or are her children deficient in divine sensibility, she is anxiously studious to exterminate the unhappy propensity, and to awaken, or to *create,* the finer feelings of the soul. To this end she hath ever at hand a number of well chosen tales, calculated to promote the interests of virtue, to excite commiseration, and suited to their tender years. Meantime she is sparing of reproaches, and would, if possible, avoid imparting to them a consciousness of the discovery which she hath made. Her rewards are always exactly and impartially proportioned—*the degree of merit she critically examines*—and as this is her invariable rule, a murmur in the little society can never arise, and they are constantly convinced of the propriety of her decisions. The highest honour by which they can be distinguished, is the investiture of a commission to convey to some worthy, but destitute family, a dinner, a garment, or a piece of money; and this office being always adjudged according to the magnitude of any particular action, it often happens that the most insensible are found in this department. Thus they are accustomed to acts of benevolence—they learn to feel, and become humane by habit.

The greatest felicity which our little family can experience, is in the presence of Martesia. They are free from every restraint—pursue, unmolested, their amusements—and of their innocent mirth she not seldom partakes. It is in the pleasure which they derive from her smiles, her approbation, and her society, that she sounds the basis of all her punishments.—When coercive measures are judged indispensable, if the fault is trivial, it remains a profound secret to all but Martesia and the little aggressor: But on the maternal countenance hands a cloud—cold and distant looks take place of benign complacency; nor doth returning tenderness manifest tokens of reconciliation, until full atonement is made for the errour. If the offence is of a more heinous die, it is immediately published throughout the house; from Martesia the culprit receiveth not the smallest attention; not a look, nor a word; while he or she is regarded by every one with studied indifference. Should the transgression be considered as capital, the criminal is forthwith excluded the parental presence—not even a domestick conceives him worthy of notice—and it is with difficulty that he can obtain the assistance of which he stands in need. At length his little heart is almost broke—he petitions for favour, he sueth for forgiveness. No mediator presents, for Martesia reserves to herself the merit of obliging. Well, the concessions of the pretty offender are sufficiently humble—it is judged that his sufferings are adequate to his fault—Martesia is appeased and the offense is cancelled. And it is to be observed, that when once the penitent is admitted into favour, his crime is entirely obliterated—it can no more be held up to view. Martesia, however, seldom hath occasion to exercise the last mentioned severity. Perverseness she hath at length well nigh subdued—and among her little flock a refractory spirit is now hardly known. To behold her in the midst of the sweetly smiling circle is truly charming.

When, for the completion of their education, she is obliged to part with her boys, with a firmness becoming her character she will submit; and should their preceptor pursue her plan, they will undoubtedly be rendered useful members of society; while her girls, continuing under such auspices, cannot be other than worthy and amiable women.

CONSTANTIA.

1790

On the Equality of the Sexes[1]

That minds are not alike, full well I know,
This truth each day's experience will show;
To heights surprising some great spirits soar,
With inborn strength mysterious depths explore;
Their eager gaze surveys the path of light,
Confest it stood to Newton's piercing sight.
  Deep science, like a bashful maid retires,
And but the *ardent* breast her worth inspires;
By perserverance the coy fair is won.
And Genius, led by Study, wears the crown.
  But some there are who wish not to improve,
Who never can the path of knowledge love,
Whose souls almost with the dull body one,
With anxious care each mental pleasure shun;
Weak is the level'd, enervated mind,
And but while here to vegetate design'd.
The torpid spirit mingling with its clod,
Can scarcely boast its origin from God;
Stupidly dull—they move progressing on—
They eat, and drink, and all their work is done.
While others, emulous of sweet applause,
Industrious seek for each event a cause,
Tracing the hidden springs whence knowledge flows,
Which nature all in beauteous order shows.
  Yet cannot I their sentiments imbibe,
Who this distinction to the sex ascribe,
As if a woman's form must needs enrol,
A weak, servile, an inferiour soul;
And that the guise of man must still proclaim,
Greatness of mind, and him, to be the same:
Yet as the hours revolve fair proofs arise,
Which the bright wreath of growing fame supplies;
And in past times some men have *sunk so low,*
That female records nothing *less* can show.
But imbecility is still confin'd,
And by the lordly sex to us consign'd;
They rob us of the power t' improve,
And then declare we only trifles love;
Yet haste the era, when the world shall know,

[1]Published in the *Massachusetts Magazine,* April and May, 1790.

That such distinctions only dwell below;
The soul unfetter'd, to no sex confin'd,
Was for the abodes of cloudless day design'd.
    Mean time we emulate their manly fires,
Though erudition all their thoughts inspires,
Yet nature with *equality* imparts,
And *noble passions,* swell e'en *female hearts.*

Is it upon mature consideration we adopt the idea, that nature is thus partial in her distributions? Is it indeed a fact, that she hath yielded to one half of the human species so unquestionable a mental superiority? I know that to both sexes elevated understandings, and the reverse, are common. But, suffer me to ask, in what the minds of females are so notoriously deficient, or unequal. May not the intellectual powers be ranged under these four heads—imagination, reason, memory and judgment. The province of imagination hath long since been surrendered up to us, and we have been crowned undoubted sovereigns of the regions of fancy. Invention is perhaps the most arduous effort of the mind; this branch of imagination hath been particularly ceded to us, and we have been time out of mind invested with that creative faculty. Observe the variety of fashions (here I bar the contemptuous smile) which distinguish and adorn the female world; how continually are they changing, insomuch that they almost render the wise man's assertion problematical, and we are ready to say, *there is something new under the sun.* Now what a playfulness, what an exuberance of fancy, what strength of inventive imagination, doth this continual variation discover? Again, it hath been observed, that if the turpitude of the conduct of our sex, hath been ever so enormous, so extremely ready are we, that the very first thought presents us with an apology, so plausible, as to produce our actions even in an amiable light. Another instance of our creative powers, is our talent for slander; how ingenious are we at inventive scandal? what a formidable story can we in a moment fabricate merely from the force of a prolifick imagination? how many reputations, in the fertile brain of a female, have been utterly despoiled? how industrious are we at improving a hint? suspicion how easily do we convert into conviction, and conviction, embellished by the power of eloquence, stalks abroad to the surprise and confusion of unsuspecting innocence. Perhaps it will be asked if I furnish these facts as instances of excellency in our sex. Certainly not; but as proofs of a creative faculty, of a lively imagination. Assuredly great activity of mind is thereby discovered, and was this activity properly directed, what beneficial effects would follow. Is the needle and kitchen sufficient to employ the operations of a soul thus organized? I should conceive not. Nay, it is a truth that those very departments leave the intelligent principle vacant, and at liberty for speculation. Are we deficient in reason? we can only reason from what we know, and if an opportunity of acquiring knowledge hath been denied us, the inferiority of our sex cannot fairly be deduced from thence. Memory, I believe, will be allowed us in common, since every one's experience must testify, that a loquacious old woman is as frequently met with, as a communicative old man; their subjects are alike drawn from the fund of other times, and the transactions of their youth, or of maturer life, entertain, or perhaps fatigue you, in the evening of their lives. "But our judgment is not so strong—we do not distinguish so well."—Yet it may be questioned, from what doth this superiority, in this determining faculty of the soul, proceed. May we not trace its source in the difference of education, and continued advantages? Will it be said that the judgment of a male of two years old, is more sage than that of a female's of the same age? I believe the reverse is generally observed to be true. But from that period what partiality! how is the one exalted, and the other depressed, by the contrary modes of education which are adopted! the one is taught to aspire, and the other is early confined and limitted. As their years increase, the sister must be wholly domesticated, while the brother is led by the hand through all the flowery paths of science. Grant that their minds are by nature equal, yet who shall wonder at the *apparent* superiority, if indeed custom becomes *second nature;* nay if it taketh place of nature, and that it doth the experience of each day will evince. At length arrived at womanhood, the uncultivated fair one feels a void, which the employments allotted her are by no means capable of filling. What can she do? to books she may not apply; or if she doth, *to those only of the novel kind,* lest she merit the appellation of a *learned lady;* and what ideas have been affixed to this term, the observation of many can testify. Fashion, scandal, and sometimes what is still more reprehensible, are then called in to her relief; and who can say to what lengths the liberties she takes may proceed. Meantime she herself is most unhappy; she feels the want of a cultivated mind. Is she single, she in vain seeks to fill up time from sexual employments or amusements. Is she united to a person whose soul nature made equal to her own, education hath set him so far above her, that in those entertainments which are productive of such rational felicity, she is not qualified to accompany him. She experiences a mortifying consciousness of inferiority, which embitters every enjoyment. Doth the person to whom her adverse fate hath consigned her, posses a mind incapable of improvement, she is equally wretched, in being so closely connected with an individual whom she cannot but despise. Now, was she permitted the same instructors as her brother, (with an eye however to their particular departments) for the employment of a rational mind an ample field would be opened. In astronomy she might catch a glimpse of the immensity of the Deity, and thence she would form amazing conceptions of the august and supreme Intelligence. In geography she would admire Jehovah in the midst of his benevolence; thus adapting this globe to the various wants and amusements of its inhabitants. In natural philosophy she would adore the infinite majesty of heaven, clothed in condescension; and as she traversed the reptile world, she would hail the goodness of a creating God. A mind, thus filled, would have little room for the trifles with which our sex are, with too much justice, accused of amusing themselves, and they would thus be rendered fit companions for those, who should one day wear them as their crown. Fashions, in their variety, would then give place to conjectures, which might perhaps conduce to the improvement of the literary world; and there would be no leisure for slander or detraction. Reputation would not then be blasted, but serious speculations would occupy the lively imaginations of the sex. Unnecessary visits would be precluded, and that custom would only be indulged by way of relaxation, or to answer the demands of consanguinity and friendship. Females would become discreet, their judgments would be invigorated, and their partners for life being circumspectly chosen, an unhappy Hymen would then be as rare, as is now the reverse.

Will it be urged that those acquirements would supersede our domestick duties. I answer that every requisite in female economy is easily attained; and, with truth I can add, that when once attained, they require no further *mental attention.* Nay, while we are pursuing the needle, or the superintendency of the family, I repeat, that our minds are at full liberty for reflection; that imagination may exert itself in full vigor; and that if a just foundation is early laid, our ideas will then be worthy of rational beings. If we were industrious we might easily find time to arrange them upon paper, or should avocations press too hard for such an indulgence, the hours allotted for conversation would at least become more refined and rational. Should it still be vociferated, "Your domestick employments are sufficient"—I would calmly ask, is it reasonable, that a candidate for immortality, for the joys of heaven, an intelligent being, who is to spend an eternity in contemplating the works of Deity, should at present be so degraded, as to be allowed no other ideas, than those which are suggested by the mechanism of a pudding, or the sewing the seams of a garment? Pity that all such censurers of female improvement do not go one step further, and deny their future existence; to be consistent they surely ought.

Yes, ye lordly, ye haughty sex, our souls are by nature *equal* to yours; the same breath of God animates, enlivens, and invigorates us; and that we are not fallen lower than yourselves, let those witness who have greatly towered above the various discouragements by which they have been so heavily oppressed; and though I am unacquainted with the list of celebrated characters on either side, yet from the observations I have made in the contracted circle in which I have moved I dare confidently believe, that from the commencement of time to the present day, there hath been as many females, as males, who, by the *mere force of natural powers,* have merited the crown of applause; who, *thus unassisted,* have seized the wreath of fame. I know there are who assert, that as the animal powers of the one sex are superiour, of course their mental faculties also must be stronger; thus attributing strength of mind to the transient organization of this earth born tenement. But if this reasoning is just, man must be content to yield the palm to many of the brute creation since by not a few of his brethren of the field, he is far surpassed in bodily strength. Moreover, was this argument admitted, it would prove too much, for occular demonstration evinceth, that there are many robust masculine ladies, and effeminate gentlemen. Yet I fancy that Mr. Pope, though clogged with an enervated body, and distinguished by a diminutive stature, could nevertheless lay claim to greatness of soul; and perhaps there are many other instances which might be adduced to combat so unphilosophical an opinion. Do we not often see, that when the clay built tabernacle is well nigh dissolved, when it is just ready to mingle with the parent soil, the immortal inhabitant aspires to, and even attaineth heights the most sublime, and which were before wholly unexplored. Besides, were we to grant that animal strength proved any thing, taking into consideration the accustomed impartiality of nature, we should be induced to imagine, that she had invested the female mind with superiour strength as an equivalent for the bodily powers of man. But waving this however palpable advantage, for *equality only,* we wish to contend.

I am aware that there are many passages in the sacred oracles which seem to give the advantage to the other sex; but I consider all these as wholly metaphorical. Thus David was a man after God's own heart, yet see him enervated by his licentious passions! behold him following Uriah to the death, and shew me wherein could consist the immaculate Being's complacency. Listen to the curses which Job bestoweth upon the day of his nativity, and tell me where is his perfection, where his patience—*literally* it existed not. David and Job were types of him who was to come; and the superiority of man, as exhibited in scripture, being also emblematical, all arguments deduced from thence, of course fall to the ground. The exquisite delicacy of the female mind proclaimeth the exactness of its texture, while its nice sense of honour announceth its innate, its native grandeur. And indeed, in one respect, the preeminence seems to be tacitly allowed us, for after an education which limits and confines, and employments and recreations which naturally tend to enervate the body, and debilitate the mind; after we have from early youth been adorned with ribbons, and other gewgaws, dressed out like the ancient victims previous to a sacrifice, being taught by the care of our parents in collecting the most showy materials that the ornamenting our exteriour ought to be the principal object of our attention; after, I say, fifteen years thus spent, we are introduced into the world, amid the united adulation of every beholder. Praise is sweet to the soul; we are immediately intoxicated by large draughts of flattery, which being plentifully administered, is to the pride of our hearts the most acceptable incense. It is expected that with the other sex we should commence immediate war, and that we should triumph over the machinations of the most artful. We must be constantly upon our guard; prudence and discretion must be our characteristicks; and we must rise superiour to, and obtain a complete victory over those who have been long adding to the native strength of their minds, by an unremitted study of men and books, and who have, moreover, conceived from the loose characters which they have been portrayed in the extensive variety of their reading, a most contemptible opinion of the sex. Thus unequal, we are, notwithstanding, forced to the combat, and the infamy which is consequent upon the smallest deviation in our conduct, proclaims the high idea which was formed of our native strength; and thus, indirectly at least, is the preference acknowledged to be our due. And if we are allowed an equality of acquirement, let serious studies equally employ our minds, and we will bid our souls arise to equal strength. We will meet upon even ground, the despot man; we will rush with alacrity to the combat, and, crowned by success, we shall then answer the exalted expectations which are formed. Though sensibility, soft compassion, and gentle commiseration, are inmates in the female bosom, yet against every deep laid art, altogether fearless of the event, we will set them in array; for assuredly the wreath of victory will encircle the spotless brow. If we meet an equal, a sensible friend, we will reward him with the hand of amity, and through life we will be assiduous to promote his happiness; but from every deep laid scheme for our ruin, retiring into ourselves, amid the flowery paths of science, we will indulge in all the refined and sentimental pleasures of contemplation. And should it still be urged, that the studies thus inlisted upon would interfere with our more peculiar department, I must further reply, that *early hours,* and close application, will do wonders; and to her who is from the first dawn of reason taught to fill up time rationally, both the requisites will be easy. I grant that niggard fortune is too generally unfriendly to the mind; and that much of that valuable treasure, time, is necessarily expended upon the wants of the body; but it should be remembered, that in embarrassed circumstances our companions have as little leisure for literary improvement, as is afforded to us; for most certainly their provident care is at least as requisite as our exertions. Nay, we have even more leisure for sedentary pleasures, as our avocations are more retired, much less laborious, and, as hath been observed, by no means require that avidity of attention which is proper to the employments of the other sex.

In high life, or, in other words, where the parties are in possession of affluence, the objection respecting time is wholly obviated, and of course falls to the ground; and it may also be repeated, that many of those hours which are at present swallowed up in fashion and scandal, might be redeemed, were we habituated to useful reflections. But in one respect, O ye arbiters of our fate! we confess that the superiority is indubitably yours; you are by nature formed for our protectors; we pretend not to vie with you in bodily strength; upon this point we will never contend for victory. Shield us then, we beseech you, from external evils, and in return we will transact *your* domestick affairs. Yes, *your,* for are you not equally interested in those matters with ourselves? Is not the elegancy of neatness as agreeable to your sight as to ours; is not the well favoured viand equally delightful to your taste; and doth not your sense of hearing suffer as much, from the discordant sounds prevalent in an ill regulated family, produced by the voices of children and many *et ceteras?*

CONSTANTIA.

By way of supplement to the foregoing pages, I subjoin the following extract from a letter, wrote to a friend in the December of 1780.

And now assist me, O thou genius of my sex, while I undertake the arduous task of endeavouring to combat that vulgar, that almost universal errour, which hath, it seems, enlisted even Mr. P—— under its banners. The superiority of your sex hath, I grant, been time out of mind esteemed a truth incontrovertible; in consequence of which persuasion, every plan of education hath been calculated to establish this favourite tenet. Not long since; weak and presuming as I was, I amused myself with selecting some arguments from nature, reason, and experience, against this so generally received idea. I confess that to sacred testimonies I had not recourse. I held them to be merely metaphorical, and thus regarding them, I could not persuade myself that there was any propriety in bringing them to decide in this *very important debate.* However, as you, sir, confine yourself entirely to the sacred oracles, I mean to bend the whole of my artillery against those supposed proofs, which you have from thence provided, and from which you have formed an intrenchment *apparently* so invulnerable. And first, to begin with our great progenitors; but here, suffer me to premise, that it is for mental strength I mean to contend, for with respect to animal powers, I yield them undisputed to that sex, which enjoys them in common with the lion, the tyger, and many other beasts of prey; therefore your observations respecting the *rib under the arm, at a distance from the head, &c. &c.* in no sort militate against my view. Well, but the woman was first in the transgression. Strange how blind *self love* renders you men; were you not wholly absorbed in a partial admiration of your own abilities, you would long since have acknowledged the force of what I am now going to urge. It is true some ignoramuses have absurdly enough informed us, that the beauteous fair of paradise, was seduced from her obedience, by a malignant demon, *in the guise of a baleful serpent;* but we, who are better informed, know that the fallen spirit presented himself to her view, *a shining angel still;* for thus, saith the criticks in the Hebrew tongue, ought the word to be rendered. Let us examine her motive—Hark! the seraph declares that she shall attain a perfection of knowledge; for is there aught which is not comprehended under one or other of the terms *good* and *evil.* It doth not appear that she was governed by any one sensual appetite; but merely by a desire of adorning her mind; a laudable ambition fired her soul, and a thirst for knowledge impelled the predilection so fatal in its consequences. Adam could not plead the same deception; assuredly he was not deceived; nor ought we to admire his superiour strength, or wonder at his sagacity, when we so often confess that example is much more influential than precept. His gentle partner stood before him, a melancholy instance of the direful effects of disobedience; he saw her not possessed of that wisdom which she had fondly hoped to obtain, but he beheld the once blooming female, disrobed of that innocence, which had heretofore rendered her so lovely. To him then deception became impossible, as he had proof positive of the fallacy of the argument, which the deceiver had suggested. What then could be his inducement to burst the barriers, and to fly directly in the face of that command, which *immediately* from the mouth of deity *he* had received, since, I say, he could not plead that fascinating stimulous, the accumulation of knowledge, as indisputable conviction was so visibly portrayed before him. What mighty cause impelled him to sacrifice myriads of beings yet unborn, and by one impious act, which *he saw* would be productive of such fatal effects, entail undistinguished ruin upon a race of beings, which he was yet to produce. Blush, ye vaunters of fortitude; ye boasters of resolution; ye haughty lords of the creation; blush when ye remember, that he was influenced by no other motive than a bare pusillanimous attachment to a woman! by sentiments so exquisitely soft, that all his sons have, from that period, when they have designed to degrade them, described as highly feminine. Thus it should seem, that all the arts of the grand deceiver (since means adequate to the purpose are, I conceive, invariably pursued) were requisite to mislead our general mother, while the father of mankind forfeited his own, and relinquished the happines of posterity, merely in compliance with the blandishments of a female. The subsequent subjection the apostle Paul explains as a figure; after enlarging upon the subject, he adds, *"This is a great mystery; but I speak concerning Christ and the church."* Now we know with what consummate wisdom the unerring father of eternity hath formed his plans; all the types which he hath displayed, he hath permitted *materially* to fail, in the very virtue for which *they* were famed. The reason for this is obvious, we might otherwise mistake his economy, and render that honour to the creature, which is due only to the creator. I know that Adam was a figure of him who was to come. The grace contained in his figure, is the reason of my rejoicing, and while I am very far from prostrating before the shadow, I yield joyfully in all things the preeminence to the second federal head. Confiding faith is prefigured by Abraham, yet he exhibits a contrast to affiance, when he says of his fair companion, she is my sister. Gentleness was the characteristick of Moses, yet he hesitated not to reply to Jehovah himself, with unsaintlike tongue he murmured at the waters of strife, and with rash hands he break the tables, which were inscribed by the finger of divinity. David, dignified with the title of the man after God's own heart, and yet how stained was his life. Solomon was celebrated for wisdom, but folly is wrote in legible characters upon his almost every action. Lastly, let us turn our eyes to man in the aggregate. He is manifested as the figure of strength, but that we may not regard him as any thing more than a figure, his soul is formed in no sort superiour, but every way equal to the mind of her, who is the emblem of weakness, and whom he hails the gentle companion of his better days.

1790

Occasional Epilogue to *The Contrast;* a Comedy, Written by Royal Tyler, Esq.[1]

O Lud, O Lud, O Lud, what a farrago;
These poets do delight their parts to show.
Says I, pray give us something new and pithy,
Ideas fit for frolic, and for me.
An Epilogue, you know, should still be funny,
I like of all things this New England Johnny.

Not but a verse, or two, may point the time,
And as I know you love to scribble rhyme;
Touching once more the panegyric string,
With countless bays, a fragrant sprig to fling,
Upon the close of this returning day,
You may contrive some pretty thing to say.

'Twas thus I chatter'd, reason'd, laugh'd, and talk'd,
As for the muse the destin'd path I chalk'd;
But—heaven bless us—had you seen the look,
The very blood my honest cheeks forsook,
So grave, so cool, unbending, and severe,
We love to fill with dignity our sphere.—

"Madam," and then a reprehending glance,
"If right I understand what you advance,
"You ask an Epilogue for Tyler's play!
"You ask a Garland for this golden day!
"You ask a jest, with humour, sense, and wit!
"On which the critics will in judgment sit.

"Madam, my Pegasus I never spur,
"If he resists an inch I cannot stir,
"But, buoyant on the feathery steed I'll float,
"And as he points—the ready line I'll note—
"Further I cannot promise—or design—
"For, madam—to command, was never mine."

She mounted, sure enough—and such a canter,
Upon my faith it is a downright ranter;

[1]Published in the *Massachusetts Magazine,* March 1794. The editor's preface to the publication announced: "The Epilogue was composed at the request of a friend, and spoken at Gloucester, by Mrs. Solomon, upon the close of the President's *birth day*—1794."

No features of an Epilogue appear,
But listen, beaus and belles, and you shall hear.

"Columbia, blest Columbia—thee I hail,
"Borne gently onward by the *peaceful* gale,
"Fleet are thy footsteps up the hill of fame,
"Vast are the honours of thy brightening name:

"The arts and sciences around thee press,
"While bards, recording bards, thy efforts bless;
"Thy Tyler's bosom, nerv'd by attic fire,
"Whom taste, and sense, and reason must admire;
"The Contrast who, in all its parts conceiv'd,
"Whatever virtuous firmness hath achiev'd;

"Who knew so well to paint the soldier's part
"Whose pen hath sketch'd the wily coxcomb's heart;
"Who could the soul of dauntless valour give,
"And bid a fluttering Billy Dimple live;
"Smiling like Jessamy, and simple too,
"As ever yet an unform'd Yankee grew:
"Coarse as Vanrough—skill'd in the plodding page,
"No Smithfield bargainer could be more sage.

"With nicer touch portraying female worth,
"Or fashion's wild, and most eccentric growth.
"This universal genius, soaring still,
"Ascends with eclat the eventful hill.

"But fainter gems must all unmark'd remain,
"When this day's Hero sweeps along the plain.
"Bright gleam'd the hour, which usher'd in the morn,
"On seraphs wings it was revolving borne.
"Twas then, America; thy genius rose,
"Around thy world augmenting light she throws;
"And when she gave a Washington to thee,
"She gave thee empire, arms, and liberty.
"Again thy weal no treacherous league shall stand,
"Discord in vain employs her murderous band;
"Thy patriot, warrior, statesman, yet remains,
"And all the weight of government sustains.
"Through dark arcanas his pervading ken,
"Unfolds the secrets of designing men;
"No foreign influence, with haughty stride,
"Shall sway thy councils, or thy chiefs divide;
"With native splendor, like the star of day,
"Thy Hero still pursues his radiant way;

"Nor shall he ever set in shades of night,
"Naught can diminish *heaven impressed* light,
"But when he faces from this our hemisphere,
"With added lustre, he shall then appear,
"Where stars, and suns, in floods of brightness rise,
"And where no opaque globe the veil supplies.
"Then shall ascend"—and then—and then—and then—

Oh, memory, confusion wraps my soul!
Of what remain'd I have forgot the whole!
I said, so many lines 'twas hard to con;
I did not get them till the day was done!

But, Candour, if that *you* my cause will plead,
I promise, on my faith, in very deed—
Whene'er our friends shall grace these walls again,
With studious care I will my part retain:
Meantime I bend, in meek obeisance low,
And for your patience all my thanks bestow.

CONSTANTIA.

1794

Philip Freneau 1752–1832

Philip Morin Freneau, the most versatile and vitriolic of the patriot poets, was born in New York, the son of Pierre Fresneau, a tradesman, and Agnes Watson. His father's Huguenot (French Protestant) faith and his mother's Presbyterianism influenced Philip to enroll at the College at Nassau (Princeton), the bastion of New Light Christianity in America. Yet Freneau's mind ran more to speculation than Calvinist orthodoxy. President John Witherspoon, while unable to inspire the student with evangelical zeal, did teach him to embrace republican politics. Freneau joined the American Whig Society, the more libertarian of the college's two student clubs. There Freneau taught himself to be a poet, mastering the techniques of satire in the paper wars against the other club, the Cliosophical Society, and the devices of polite literature in verse prepared for the commencement exercises. With fellow Whigs James Madison and Hugh Henry Brackenridge, he composed a farcical romance, *Father Bombo's Pilgrimmage to Mecca,* a work some scholars have been tempted to designate the first American novel. Of more lasting consequence were "The Power of Fancy," a personal testament to his devotion to imagination, and his commencement poem, a collaboration with Brackenridge, *A Poem on the Rising Glory of America,* which explored the myth of the westward course of empire and arts from the old world to the new world.

Freneau graduated in 1771 when the American market for literature was so undeveloped that no one could make a living from writing. Consequently, he conducted his career as a man of letters as an adjunct to other occupations—schoolmaster, captain of a merchant vessel, government bureaucrat, farmer, and newspaper editor. He advanced his literary reputation by substituting productivity and topicality for exquisiteness and finish in his work. Immersing himself in the print culture (the world of magazines, newspapers, and cheap books then coming into being)—Freneau turned his back on the older belletristic world of private clubs and salons. Every product of his adult pen found its way into print, and every issue of the day prompted him to write. He often worked a poem into final form in public, revising and republishing pieces frequently until a suitable version evolved. Thus Freneau was not only the most prolific poet of early America in terms of numbers of poems, but the most voluble in terms of numbers of versions of individual poems.

Freneau won an audience for his poetry in 1775 with a series of verse satires of British officials and Tories, of which "A Political Litany," has proved the most enduring. Having made himself anathema to the New York Tories, the poet embarked for the West Indies, where he lived for two years until joining the colonial forces as a blockade runner. In 1780 he was captured and incarcerated on a British prison vessel, an experience he memorialized bitterly in *The Prison Ship.* He attached himself to the *Freeman's Journal* in Philadelphia, and lambasted the British and the Tories with a fusillade of verse. The patriotic zeal and sardonic humor of these pieces won Freneau his reputation as "The Poet of the Revolution."

Despite his fame as a political poet, Freneau never restricted his literary concerns to affairs of state—not even when serving as the chief propagandist for Jeffersonian democracy as editor of the *National Gazette* (1790–1793). An encyclopedic curiosity led him to inquire into natural philosophy, speculative theology, history, aesthetics, and social manners. The quality of his work in these areas varies. As a poet of nature Freneau has earned lasting fame, his lyric on "The Wild Honey Suckle" being generally reckoned the inaugural poem in the romantic tradition furthered by William Cullen Bryant and the Transcendentalists. "On Observing a Large Redstreak Apple" is a quintessential high romantic lyric, manifesting the simplicity of language, the mood of intimate engagement with nature, and the mythology of regeneration characteristic of the form. Freneau was less successful, though no less serious, as a theological poet. Freneau's susceptibility to ingenious theological speculation may be seen in the change of his beliefs from decade to decade. He espoused at various times deism, Swedenborgianism, and a Neo-Epicurianism. "On the Universality and other Attributes of the God of Nature" marks the resolution of his lifetime of mental struggle in an affirmation of the divine reasonableness of nature.

Despite Freneau's unique breadth of experience, historians of American literature have yet to come to terms with his talent as a critic of American culture. No other early American writer had Freneau's first-hand knowledge of life and manners in all quarters of North America: he had resided in the West Indies, Charleston, Philadelphia, New Jersey, and New York, and visited myriad other locations. Only his criticisms of the West Indies slave system in "To Sir Toby" have been accorded respect, though he commented insightfully on the spread of commercialism, western land speculation, the cult of fashion, the violence of southern tavern life, and political patronage peddling.

Freneau's importance as a poet is evident in his work in creating a language and a subject matter adjusted to the increasingly democratic ideology of newspapers and magazines. He was America's first public poet in the popular mold.

David S. Shields
The Citadel

PRIMARY WORKS

The Poems of Philip Freneau, Poet of the American Revolution, 3 vols., ed. Fred Lewis Pattee, 1902; *Poems of Freneau,* ed. Harry Hayden Clark, 1929; *The Last Poems of Philip Freneau,* ed. Lewis Leary, 1945; *The Newspaper Verse of Philip Freneau,* ed. Judith R. Hiltner, 1986.

SECONDARY WORK

William D. Andrews, "Philip Freneau and Francis Hopkinson," *American Literature, 1764–1789, The Revolutionary Years,* 1977.

The Power of Fancy[1]

Wakeful, vagrant, restless thing,
Ever wandering on the wing,
Who thy wondrous source can find,
Fancy, regent of the mind;
A spark from Jove's[2] resplendent throne,
But thy nature all unknown.
This spark of bright, celestial flame,
From Jove's seraphic altar came,
And hence alone in man we trace,
Resemblance to the immortal race.
Ah! what is all this mighty whole,
These suns and stars that round us roll!
What are they all, where'er they shine,
But Fancies of the Power Divine!
What is this globe, these lands, and seas,
And heat, and cold, and flowers, and trees,
And life, and death, and beast, and man,
And time—that with the sun began—
But thoughts on reason's scale combin'd,
Ideas of the Almighty mind!
On the surface of the brain
Night after night she walks unseen,
Noble fabrics doth she raise
In the woods or on the seas,
On some high, steep, pointed rock,
Where the billows loudly knock
And the dreary tempests sweep
Clouds along the uncivil deep.
Lo! she walks upon the moon,

[1]Publication of Mark Akenside's *The Pleasures of Imagination* (1744) inspired many meditations on the power of fancy. Freneau composed his while an undergraduate at the College of New Jersey (Princeton).

[2]Chief god in the Roman pantheon.

Listens to the chimy tune
Of the bright, harmonious spheres,[3]
And the song of angels hears;
Sees this earth a distant star,[4]
Pendant, floating in the air;
Leads me to some lonely dome,
Where Religion loves to come,
Where the bride of Jesus[5] dwells,
And the deep ton'd organ swells
In notes with lofty anthems join'd,
Notes that half distract the mind.
Now like lightning she descends
To the prison of the fiends,
Hears the rattling of their chains,
Feels their never ceasing pains—
But, O never may she tell
Half the frightfulness of hell.
Now she views Arcadian[6] rocks,
Where the shepherds guard their flocks,
And, while yet her wings she spreads,
Sees chrystal streams and coral beds,
Wanders to some desert deep,
Or some dark, enchanted steep,
By the full moonlight doth shew
Forests of a dusky blue,
Where, upon some mossy bed,
Innocence reclines her head.
Swift, she stretches o'er the seas
To the far off Hebrides,
Canvas on the lofty mast
Could not travel half so fast—
Swifter than the eagle's flight
Or instantaneous rays of light!
Lo! contemplative she stands
On Norwegia's[7] rocky lands—
Fickle Goddess, set me down
Where the rugged winters frown
Upon Orca's[8] howling steep,

[3]In ancient cosmology the heavens were envisioned as a layered stack of concentric, transparent spheres whose motion produced music.

[4]"Milton's *Paradise Lost,* B. II. v. 1052." [Freneau's note.]

[5]Revelation 21:2. The bride of Jesus is a metaphor for the New Jerusalem of Christian apocalyptic.

[6]The realm of rural contentment which poets identified with a mountainous region of ancient Greece.

[7]Norway's.

[8]The Orkney Islands off the Scottish coast.

Nodding o'er the northern deep,
Where the winds tumultuous roar,
Vext that Ossian[9] sings no more.
Fancy, to that land repair,
Sweetest Ossian slumbers there;
Waft me far to southern isles
Where the soften'd winter smiles,
To Bermuda's orange shades,
Or Demarara's[10] lovely glades;
Bear me o'er the sounding cape,
Painting death in every shape,
Where daring Anson[11] spread the sail
Shatter'd by the stormy gale—
Lo! she leads me wild and far,
Sense can never follow her—
Shape thy course o'er land and sea,
Help me to keep pace with thee,
Lead me to yon' chalky cliff,
Over rock and over reef,
Into Britain's fertile land,
Stretching far her proud command.
Look back and view, thro' many a year,
Cæsar, Julius Cæsar, there.[12]
    Now to Tempe's[13] verdant wood,
Over the mid-ocean flood
Lo! the islands of the sea—
Sappho,[14] Lesbos mourns for thee:
Greece, arouse thy humbled head,[15]
Where are all thy mighty dead,
Who states to endless ruin hurl'd
And carried vengeance through the world?—
Troy, thy vanish'd pomp resume,
Or, weeping at thy Hector's[16] tomb,
Yet those faded scenes renew,
Whose memory is to Homer due.
Fancy, lead me wandering still
Up to Ida's[17] cloud-topt hill;

[9]Gaelic hero of ancient lore popularized during the eighteenth century by a fantasy retelling of his tales by James Macpherson.

[10]Territory in British Guiana famed for sugar.

[11]Admiral George Anson circumnavigated the globe with a British fleet during the 1740s.

[12]Caesar came to Britain in 55 B.C.

[13]A vale in ancient Greece sacred to Apollo.

[14]Sappho of the island of Lesbos was the greatest of Greek women poets; she wrote during the seventh century, B.C.

[15]At the time of Freneau's writing Greece was under Turkish rule; the country would win independence in 1829.

[16]Prince of Troy killed by Achilles in Homer's *Iliad*.

[17]The mountain from which Zeus witnessed the siege of Troy.

Not a laurel there doth grow
But in vision thou shalt show,—
Every sprig on Virgil's[18] tomb
Shall in livelier colours bloom,
And every triumph Rome has seen
Flourish on the years between.
Now she bears me far away
In the east to meet the day,
Leads me over Ganges'[19] streams,
Mother of the morning beams—
O'er the ocean hath she ran,
Places me on Tinian;[20]
Farther, farther in the east,
Till it almost meets the west,
Let us wandering both be lost
On Tahiti's sea-beat coast,
Bear me from that distant strand,
Over ocean, over land,
To California's golden shore—
Fancy, stop, and rove no more.
Now, tho' late, returning home,
Lead me to Belinda's tomb;
Let me glide as well as you
Through the shroud and coffin too,
And behold, a moment, there,
All that once was good and fair—
Who doth here so soundly sleep?
Shall we break this prison deep?—
Thunders cannot wake the maid,
Lightnings cannot pierce the shade,
And tho' wintry tempests roar,
Tempests shall disturb no more.
Yet must those eyes in darkness stay,
That once were rivals to the day?—
Like heaven's bright lamp beneath the main
They are but set to rise again.
Fancy, thou the muses' pride,
In thy painted realms reside
Endless images of things,
Fluttering each on golden wings,
Ideal objects, such a store,
The universe could hold no more:
Fancy, to thy power I owe

[18]The greatest Roman poet, author of the *Georgics, Eclogues,* and the *Aeneid;* lived from 70 to 19 B.C.

[19]The sacred river of the Hindu faith located in India.

[20]Pacific island.

Half my happiness below;
By thee Elysian[21] groves were made,
Thine were the notes that Orpheus play'd;
By thee was Pluto[22] charm'd so well
While rapture seiz'd the sons of hell—
Come, O come—perceiv'd by none,
You and I will walk alone.

1770, 1786

A Political Litany[1]

Libera Nos, Domine.—DELIVER US O LORD, *not only from British Dependence, but also,*

From a junto[2] that labour with absolute power,
Whose schemes disappointed have made them look sour,
From the lords of the council, who fight against freedom,
Who still follow on where delusion shall lead them.

From the group at St. James's,[3] who slight our petitions,
And fools that are waiting for further submissions—
From a nation whose manners are rough and severe,
From scoundrels and rascals,—do keep us all clear.

From pirates sent out by command of the king
To murder and plunder, but never to swing;
From *Wallace* and *Greaves,* and *Vipers* and *Roses,*[4]
Who, if heaven pleases, we'll give bloody noses.

From the valiant *Dunmore,*[5] with his crew of banditti,
Who plunder Virginians at *Williamsburg* city,
From hot-headed *Montague,*[6] mighty to swear,
The little fat man, with his pretty white hair.

[21]In the Greek underworld, the home of the virtuous dead.

[22]In Greek myth the poet Orpheus won release of his wife, Eurydice, from Pluto, overlord of Hades, by the power of his music.

[1]Published in New York, June 1775.

[2]A political circle.

[3]The location of the royal court in London.

[4]"Captains and ships in the British navy, then employed on the American coast." [Freneau's note.]

[5]Royal Governor of Virginia (1732–1809) whose troops (characterized by Freneau as bandits) seized the colony's gunpowder in April, 1775.

[6]British Admiral John Montagu (1719–1795).

From bishops in Britain, who butchers are grown,
From slaves, that would die for a smile from the throne,
From assemblies that vote against *Congress proceedings,*
(Who now see the fruit of their stupid misleadings.)

From *Tryon* the mighty,[7] who flies from our city,
And swelled with importance disdains the committee:[8]
(But since he is pleased to proclaim us his foes,
What the devil care we where the devil he goes.)

From the caitiff,[9] lord *North,*[10] who would bind us in chains,
From a royal king Log,[11] with his tooth-full of brains,
Who dreams, and is certain (when taking a nap)
He has conquered our lands, as they lay on his map.

From a kingdom that bullies, and hectors, and swears,
We send up to heaven our wishes and prayers
That we, disunited, may freemen be still,
And Britain go on—to be damned if she will.

1775

To Sir Toby[1]

A Sugar Planter in the interior parts of Jamaica, near the City of San Jago de la Vega, (Spanish Town) 1784

"The motions of his spirit are black as night,
And his affections dark as Erebus."

—SHAKESPEARE[2]

If there exists a hell—the case is clear—
Sir Toby's slaves enjoy that portion here:
Here are no blazing brimstone lakes—'tis true;
But kindled Rum too often burns as blue;

[7]William Tryon (1725–1788), Royal Governor of New York, who fled the city at the outbreak of the Revolution.

[8]The Committee of Safety, the patriot circle directing the revolutionary effort in New York.

[9]Coward.

[10]Frederick North (1732–1792), Prime Minister of Great Britain during the revolutionary era.

[11]In Aesop's fable the frogs ask for a king. The king of the gods give them a log for a ruler. The allusion is applied to George III.

[1]Titled in some versions "The ISLAND FIELD NEGRO." In its sentiments the poem resembles the anti-slavery verses of Bryan Edwards, Jamaica's foremost poet at the time of Freneau's visit in 1784.

[2]"The Merchant of Venice," V, i, 79. Freneau quotes a corrupt text: "black as night" should be "dull as night."

In which some fiend, whom nature must detest,
Steeps Toby's brand, and marks poor Cudjoe's breast.[3]
  Here whips on whips excite perpetual fears,
And mingled howlings vibrate on my ears:
Here nature's plagues abound, to fret and tease,
Snakes, scorpions, despots, lizards, centipees—
No art, no care escapes the busy lash;
All have their dues—and all are paid in cash—
The eternal driver keeps a steady eye
On a black herd, who would his vengeance fly.
But chained, imprisoned, on a burning soil,
For the mean avarice of a tyrant, toil!
The lengthy cart-whip guards this monster's reign—
And cracks, like pistols, from the fields of cane.
  Ye powers! who formed these wretched tribes, relate,
What had they done, to merit such a fate!
Why were they brought from Eboe's[4] sultry waste,
To see that plenty which they must not taste—
Food, which they cannot buy, and dare not steal;
Yams and potatoes—many a scanty meal!—
  One, with a gibbet[5] wakes his Negro's fears,
One to the windmill nails him by the ears;
One keeps his slave in darkened dens, unfed,
One puts the wretch in pickle ere he's dead:
This, from a tree suspends him by the thumbs,
That, from his table grudges even the crumbs!
  O'er yond' rough hills a tribe of females go,
Each with her gourd, her infant, and her hoe;
Scorched by a sun that has no mercy here,
Driven by a devil, whom men call overseer—
In chains, twelve wretches to their labors haste;
Twice twelve I saw, with iron collars graced!—
  Are such the fruits that spring from vast domains?
Is wealth, thus got, Sir Toby, worth your pains!—
Who would your wealth on terms, like these, possess,
Where all we see is pregnant with distress—
Angola's[6] natives scourged by ruffian hands,
And toil's hard product shipp'd to foreign lands.
  Talk not of blossoms, and your endless spring;
What joy, what smile, can scenes of misery bring?—

[3]"This passage has a reference to the West India custom (sanctioned by law) of branding a newly imported slave on the breast, with a red-hot iron, as evidence of the purchaser's property." [Freneau's note.]

[4]"A small Negro kingdom near the river Senegal." [Freneau's note.]

[5]Gallows.

[6]West African colony whence the Portuguese outshipped slaves.

Though Nature, here, has every blessing spread,
Poor is the laborer—and how meanly fed!—
  Here Stygian[7] paintings light and shade renew,
Pictures of hell, that Virgil's[8] pencil drew:
Here, surly Charons[9] make their annual trip,
And ghosts arrive in every Guinea ship,[10]
To find what beasts these western isles afford,
Plutonian[11] scourges, and despotic lords:—
  Here, they, of stuff determined to be free,
Must climb the rude cliffs of the Liguanee;[12]
Beyond the clouds, in skulking haste repair,
And hardly safe from brother traitors[13] there.—

1792

The Hurricane[1]

Happy the man who, safe on shore,
  Now trims, at home, his evening fire;
Unmov'd, he hears the tempests roar,
  That on the tufted groves expire:
Alas! on us they doubly fall,
Our feeble barque[2] must bear them all.

Now to their haunts the birds retreat,
  The squirrel seeks his hollow tree,
Wolves in their shaded caverns meet,
  All, all are blest but wretched we—
Foredoomed a stranger to repose,
No rest the unsettled ocean knows.

[7]Black and hellish.
[8]Alluding to the Roman poet's description of Hades, *Aeneid,* VI.
[9]In classical myth the boatman who ferried souls over the river Styx to the netherworld.
[10]Slave ship.
[11]Hellish; Pluto was lord of the underworld.
[12]"The mountains northward of Kingston." [Freneau's note.]
[13]"Alluding to the *Independent* Negroes in the blue mountains, who for a stipulated reward, deliver up every fugitive that falls into their hands to the English Government." [Freneau's note.]

[1]Also titled, "VERSES, made at Sea, in a Heavy Gale." Composed in 1784 when Freneau was a ship captain plying the West Indian trade. Freneau's poem belongs to a tradition of sublime poetry depicting Caribbean storms dating back to Edmund Waller's famous poem on Bermuda, "The Battle of the Summer Islands" (1645).
[2]A three-masted vessel.

While o'er the dark abyss[3] we roam,
   Perhaps, with last departing gleam,
We saw the sun descend in gloom,
   No more to see his morning beam;
But buried low, by far too deep,
On coral beds, unpitied, sleep!

But what a strange, uncoasted strand
   Is that, where fate permits no day—
No charts have we to mark that land,
   No compass to direct that way—
What Pilot shall explore that realm,
What new Columbus take the helm!

While death and darkness both surround,
   And tempests rage with lawless power,
Of friendship's voice I hear no sound,
   No comfort in this dreadful hour—
What friendship can in tempests be,
   What comfort on this raging sea?

The barque, accustomed to obey,
   No more the trembling pilots guide:
Alone she gropes her trackless way,
   While mountains burst on either side—
Thus, skill and science both must fall;
And ruin is the lot of all.

1785

The Wild Honey Suckle

Fair flower, that dost so comely grow,
Hid in this silent, dull retreat,
Untouched thy honied blossoms blow,
Unseen thy little branches greet:
      No roving foot shall crush thee here,
      No busy hand provoke a tear.

[3]"Near the east end of Jamaica. July 30, 1784." [Freneau's note.]

By Nature's self in white arrayed,
She bade thee shun the vulgar eye,
And planted here the guardian shade,
And sent soft waters murmuring by;
Thus quietly thy summer goes,
Thy days declining to repose.

Smit with those charms, that must decay,
I grieve to see your future doom;
They died—nor were those flowers more gay,
The flowers that did in Eden bloom;
Unpitying frosts, and Autumn's power
Shall leave no vestige of this flower.

From morning suns and evening dews
At first thy little being came:
If nothing once, you nothing lose,
For when you die you are the same;
The space between, is but an hour,
The frail duration of a flower.

1786

To An Author[1]

Your leaves bound up compact and fair,
In neat array at length prepare,
To pass their hour on learning's stage,
To meet the surly critic's rage;
The statesman's slight, the smatterer's sneer—
Were these, indeed, your only fear,
You might be tranquil and resigned:
What most should touch your fluttering mind;
Is that, few critics will be found
To sift your works, and deal the wound.

Thus, when one fleeting year is past
On some bye-shelf your book is cast—
Another comes, with something new,
And drives you fairly out of view:

[1]The poem is best understood as a remonstrance to Freneau himself not to put great faith in any hope for fame, or critical approval, as rewards for publishing a collection of works.

With some to praise, but more to blame,
The mind returns to—whence it came;
And some alive, who scarce could read
Will publish satires on the dead.
Thrice happy Dryden,[2] who could meet
Some rival bard in every street!

When all were bent on writing well
It was some credit to excel:—

Thrice happy Dryden, who could find
A Milbourne[3] for his sport designed—
And Pope,[4] who saw the harmless rage
Of Dennis[5] bursting o'er his page
Might justly spurn the critic's aim,
Who only helped to swell his fame.

On these bleak climes by Fortune thrown,
Where rigid Reason reigns alone,
Where lovely Fancy has no sway,
Nor magic forms about us play—
Nor nature takes her summer hue
Tell me, what has the muse to do?—

An age employed in edging steel
Can no poetic raptures feel;
No solitude's attracting power,
No leisure of the noon day hour,
No shaded stream, no quiet grove
Can this fantastic century move;

The muse of love in no request—
Go—try your fortune with the rest,
One of the nine you should engage,
To meet the follies of the age:—

On one, we fear, your choice must fall—
The least engaging of them all—
Her visage stern—an angry style—
A clouded brow—malicious smile—
A mind on murdered victims placed—
She, only she, can please the taste!

1788

[2]"See Johnson's lives of the English Poets." [Freneau's note.]

[3]A minor poet (1649–1720) whom Dryden believed to have been the worst of his era.

[4]Alexander Pope (1688–1744), English poet.

[5]John Dennis (1657–1734), a critic, who promoted the poetry of the sublime; Pope considered Dennis's school of poetry bombastic.

On the Universality and Other Attributes of the God of Nature

All that we see, about, abroad,
What is it all, but nature's God?
In meaner works discover'd here
No less than in the starry sphere.

In seas, on earth, this God is seen;
All that exist, upon him lean;
He lives in all, and never stray'd
A moment from the works he made:

His system fix'd on general laws
Bespeaks a wise creating cause;
Impartially he rules mankind
And all that on this globe we find.

Unchanged in all that seems to change,
Unbounded space is his great range;
To one vast purpose always true,
No time, with him, is old or new.

In all the attributes divine
Unlimited perfectings shine;
In these enwrapt, in these complete,
All virtues in that centre meet.

This power who doth all powers transcend,
To all intelligence a friend,
Exists, the *greatest and the best*[1]
Throughout all worlds, to make them blest.

All that he did he first approved
He all things into *being* loved;
O'er all he made he still presides,
For them in life, or death provides.

1815

[1] "Jupiter, optimus, maximus.—Cicero." [Freneau's note.]

On Observing a Large Red-streak Apple

In spite of ice, in spite of snow,
In spite of all the winds that blow,
In spite of hail and biting frost,
Suspended here I see you toss'd;
You still retain your wonted hold
Though days are short and nights are cold.

Amidst this system of decay
How could you have one wish to stay?
If fate or fancy kept you there
They meant you for a *Solitaire*.[1]
Were it not better to descend,
Or in the cider mill to end
Than thus to shiver in the storm
And not a leaf to keep you warm—
A moment, then, had buried all,
Nor you have doomed so late a fall.

But should the stem to which you cling
Uphold you to another spring,
Another race would round you rise
And view the *stranger* with surprize,
And, peeping from the blossoms say
Away, old dotard, get away!

Alas! small pleasure can there be
To dwell, a hermit, on the tree—
Your old companions, all, are gone,
Have dropt, and perished, every one;
You only stay to face the blast,
A sad memento of the past.

Would fate or nature hear my prayer,
I would your bloom of youth repair
I would the wrongs of time restrain
And bring your blossom state again:
But fate and nature both say no;
And you, though late must perish too.

[1]A gem whose ornamental effect depends on being set by itself.

What can we say, what can we hope?
Ere from the branch I see you drop,
All I can do, all in my power
Will be to watch your parting hour:
When from the branch I see you fall,
A grave we dig a-south the wall.
There you shall sleep 'till from your core,
Of youngsters rises three or four;
These shall salute the coming spring
And Red streaks to perfection bring
When years have brought them to their prime
And they shall have their summers time:
This, this is all you can attain,
And thus, I bid you, live again!

1822

The Indian Burying Ground[1]

In spite of all the learned have said,
  I still my old opinion keep;
The posture, that we give the dead,
  Points out the soul's eternal sleep.

Not so the ancients of these lands—
  The Indian, when from life released,
Again is seated with his friends,
  And shares again the joyous feast.[2]

His imaged birds, and painted bowl,
  And venison, for a journey dressed,
Bespeak the nature of the soul,
  Activity, that knows no rest.

His bow, for action ready bent,
  And arrows, with a head of stone,
Can only mean that life is spent,
  And not the old ideas gone.

[1]Originally titled, "Lines occasioned by a visit to an old Indian burying ground" (1787). William Collins's "Pensive Ode, on the death of the poet Thomson," which contains a meditation on the grave of a druid, provided Freneau with a model for this popular poem.

[2]"The North American Indians bury their dead in a sitting posture; decorating the corpse with wampum, the images of birds, quadrupeds, &c: And (if that of a warrior) with bows, arrows, tomahawks, and other military weapons." [Freneau's note.]

Thou, stranger, that shalt come this way,
No fraud upon the dead commit—
Observe the swelling turf, and say
They do not lie, but here they sit.

Here still a lofty rock remains,
On which the curious eye may trace
(Now wasted, half, by wearing rains)
The fancies of a ruder race.

Here still an aged elm aspires,
Beneath whose far-projecting shade
(And which the shepherd still admires)
The children of the forest played!

There oft a restless Indian queen
(Pale Shebah,[3] with her braided hair)
And many a barbarous form is seen
To chide the man that lingers there.

By midnight moons, o'er moistening dews;
In habit for the chase arrayed,
The hunter still the deer pursues,
The hunter and the deer, a shade![4]

And long shall timorous fancy see
The painted chief, and pointed spear,
And Reason's self shall bow the knee
To shadows and delusions here.

1787

On the Causes of Political Degeneracy[1]

Oh! fatal day, when to this peaceful shore,
European despots sent this doctrine o'er,[2]
That man's vast race was born to lick the dust,
Feed on the winds, or toil thro' life accurst;

[3]1 Kings 10: the beautiful Queen of Sheba.

[4]A spirit. The Indian netherworld was popularly known as the "land of shades."

[1]Also titled "Reflections on the Gradual Progress of Nations from Democratical States to Despotic Empires."

[2]Absolute monarchy. The doctrine, associated with Louis XIV of France, in the New World was associated with the imperial programs of France in Canada and Spain in Latin America.

Poor and despis'd, that others might be great,
And swoln to Monarchs to devour the State.

Whence came these ills, or from what causes grew,
This vortex vast, that only spares the few;
Despotic sway, whose very plague combin'd,
Distracts, degrades, and swallows up mankind?
Accuse not nature for the dreadful scene
That glooms her stage, or hides her sky serene;
She, equal she, in all her varying ways,
Her equal blessings through the world displays:
The Suns that now on northern climates glow,
Will soon retire, to melt Antarctic Snow;
The seas she robb'd, to make her clouds and rain,
Return in rivers to their breast again;
But man, wrong'd man, borne down, deceiv'd and vext,

Groans on thro' life, bewilder'd and perplext,
Few suns on him but suns of slavery shine,
Now starv'd in camps, now grovelling in the mine,
Chain'd fetter'd, tortur'd, sent from earth a slave,
To seek rewards in worlds beyond the grave.

If in her general system just to all,
We nature, our impartial parent call,
Why did she not on man's whole race bestow,
Those fine sensations spirits only know,
That, born with reason's uncorruptive mind,
Their proper bliss in common blessings find,
Which, shed o'er all, would all our race pervade,
In streams not niggard[3] by the tyrant made?

Leave this a secret in great Nature's breast;
Confess that all her works tend to the best,
Yet own that man's neglected reason here,
Breeds all the mischiefs that we feel or fear,
In all beside the skill to ride his race,
Man, wise and skillful, gives each part its place,
Each nice machine he plans, to reason true,
Adapting all things to the end in view;
But turn to this, the art himself to rule,
His sense is folly, and himself a fool.
Where the prime strength resides, there rests, 'tis plain,
The power mankind to govern and restrain—

[3]Stingy.

Where lies this strength but in the social plan,
Design'd for all, the common good of man:
The power concentered by the general voice,
In honest men, an honest people's choice,
With constant change, to keep the patriot pure,
And vain from views of power the heart secure;
There lies the secret, hid from Rome and Greece,
That holds the world in awe, and holds in peace.

See through this earth, in ages now retir'd,
Man foe to man, as policy requir'd:
At some proud tyrant's nod what millions rose,
To crush mankind, or make the world their foes.
View Asia ravaged, Europe drench'd in blood,

From feuds, whose cause no nation understood—
The cause, alas! of so much misery sown,
Known at the helm of state, and truly known.
Left to themselves, where'er mankind is found,
In peace they wish to walk life's little round,
In peace to sleep, in peace to till the soil,
Nor gain subsistence from a brother's toil.
All but the base, designing, cunning few,
Who seize on nations with a robber's view.
With crowns and sceptres awe the dazzled eye,
And priests, that hold the artillery of the sky;
These, these with armies, navies, potent grown,
Impoverish man, and bid the nations groan;
These, with pretended balance of free States,
Keep worlds at variance, breed eternal hates,
Make man the poor base slave of low design,
Degrade his nature and his tribes disjoin,
Shed hell's foul plagues o'er his exalted race,
And filch the hard earned mite, to make them base.

Shall views like these involve our happy land,
Where embrio monarchs thirst for wide command,[4]
Shall our young nation's strength and fair renown,
Be sacrified to prop a falling throne,
That ages past the world's great curse has stood,
To thrive on rapine, and to feed on blood—
Americans! will you controul such views
Speak—for you must—you have no time to lose.

1798

[4]Freneau fears the federalist merchants in particular of setting up frontier fiefdoms.

Timothy Dwight 1752–1817

Born in Massachusetts to a merchant family, Dwight was educated at Yale College, which he entered at age thirteen, earning the B.A. (1769) and M.A. (1772) degrees. A grandson of Jonathan Edwards (Dwight's mother was Edwards's daughter), Dwight tended to follow the conservative Congregationalist practices of his forebears. He studied law for a time, but he gave that up to become a tutor at Yale until 1777, when he resigned his post to serve as a chaplain at West Point. From 1779 to 1783 he preached at Northampton, Massachusetts, his birthplace, and he then took a twelve-year post as pastor of the Congregational Church at Greenfield Hill, Connecticut. He then became President of Yale College and served until his death in 1817.

With Joel Barlow and other Yale friends, Dwight spent his early years writing pro-Federalist verse and becoming known as one of the "Connecticut Wits." His poem "African Address" and his 1794 antislavery speech before the Connecticut Society for the Promotion of Freedom are both suggestive of the sympathy Dwight felt for non-dominant groups whose lives were inalterably interrupted by whites. This sympathy is apparent as well in Part IV of *Greenfield Hill: A Poem in Seven Parts* (published in New York in 1794), where Dwight attempts to address Anglo-American guilt over the murder of the Pequot Indians during the Pequot War, 1635–1636. Although Dwight's position today seems a rationalization about the fate of Native Americans, his comments are interesting for their implication of a motif typical among Anglo-Americans of his (and later) generations—that the Native Americans are, by necessity, vanishing before more energetic and organized forces. Indeed, the trope of the "vanishing American" is one that found immense popularity in the early nineteenth century, perhaps spurred by the success of writers like Dwight.

In *Greenfield Hill,* Dwight adopts the pastoral and elegiac modes of Augustan writers such as John Denham (*Cooper's Hill*), Alexander Pope (*Windsor Forest*), and Oliver Goldsmith (*The Deserted Village*) to speak of the problems faced by the Anglo-American colonists in the past and to proffer the example of Connecticut as the ideal society that the new nation should everywhere imitate.

Carla Mulford
Pennsylvania State University

PRIMARY WORK

Greenfield Hill: A Poem in Seven Parts, 1794.

SECONDARY WORKS

Leon Howard, *The Connecticut Wits,* 1943; N. O. Hatch, *The Sacred Cause of Liberty: Republican Thought and the Millenium in Revolutionary New England,* 1977; E. Elliott, *Revolutionary Writers: Literature and Authority in the New Republic, 1725–1810,* 1982; W. C. Dowling, *Poetry and Ideology in Revolutionary Connecticut,* 1990.

from Greenfield Hill

Part II
The Flourishing Village

Fair Verna! loveliest village of the west;
Of every joy, and every charm, possess'd;
How pleas'd amid thy varied walks I rove,
Sweet, cheerful walks of innocence, and love,
And o'er thy smiling prospects cast my eyes,
And see the seats of peace, and pleasure, rise,
And hear the voice of Industry resound,
And mark the smile of Competence, around!
Hail, happy village! O'er the cheerful lawns,
With earliest beauty, spring delighted dawns;
The northward sun begins his vernal smile;
The spring-bird carols o'er the cressy rill:
The shower, that patters in the ruffled stream,
The ploughboy's voice, that chides the lingering team,
The bee, industrious, with his busy song,
The woodman's axe, the distant groves among,
The wagon, rattling down the rugged steep,
The light wind, lulling every care to sleep,
All these, with mingled music, from below,
Deceive intruding sorrow, as I go.

How pleas'd, fond Recollection, with a smile,
Surveys the varied round of wintery toil!
How pleas'd, amid the flowers, that scent the plain,
Recalls the vanish'd frost, and sleeted rain;
The chilling damp, the ice-endangering street,
And treacherous earth that slump'd beneath the feet.

Yet even stern winter's glooms could joy inspire:
Then social circles grac'd the nutwood fire;
The axe resounded, at the sunny door;
The swain, industrious, trimm'd his flaxen store;
Or thresh'd, with vigorous flail, the bounding wheat,
His poultry round him pilfering for their meat;
Or slid his firewood on the creaking snow;
Or bore his produce to the main below;
Or o'er his rich returns exulting laugh'd;
Or pledg'd the healthful orchard's sparkling draught:
While, on his board, for friends and neighbors spread,
The turkey smok'd, his busy housewife fed;
And Hospitality look'd smiling round,
And Leisure told his tale, with gleeful sound.

Then too, the rough road hid beneath the sleigh,
The distant friend despis'd a length of way,
And join'd the warm embrace, and mingling smile,
And told of all his bliss, and all his toil;
And, many a month elaps'd, was pleas'd to view
How well the household far'd, the children grew;
While tales of sympathy deceiv'd the hour,
And Sleep, amus'd, resign'd his wonted power.

Yes! let the proud despise, the rich deride,
These humble joys, to Competence allied:
To me, they bloom, all fragrant to my heart,
Nor ask the pomp of wealth, nor gloss of art.
And as a bird, in prison long confin'd,
Springs from his open'd cage, and mounts the wind,
Thro' fields of flowers, and fragrance, gaily flies,
Or reassumes his birth-right, in the skies:
Unprison'd thus from artificial joys,
Where pomp fatigues, and fussful fashion cloys,
The soul, reviving, loves to wander free
Thro' native scenes of sweet simplicity;
Thro' Peace' low vale, where Pleasure lingers long,
And every songster tunes his sweetest song,
And Zephyr hastes, to breathe his first perfume,
And Autumn stays, to drop his latest bloom:
'Till grown mature, and gathering strength to roam,
She lifts her lengthen'd wings, and seeks her home.

But now the wintery glooms are vanish'd all;
The lingering drift behind the shady wall;
The dark-brown spots, that patch'd the snowy field;
The surly frost, that every bud conceal'd;
The russet veil, the way with slime o'erspread,
And all the saddening scenes of March are fled.

Sweet-smiling village! loveliest of the hills!
How green thy groves! How pure thy glassy rills!
With what new joy, I walk thy verdant streets!
How often pause, to breathe thy gale of sweets;
To mark thy well-built walls! thy budding fields!
And every charm, that rural nature yields;
And every joy, to Competence allied,
And every good, that Virtue gains from Pride!

No griping landlord here alarms the door,
To halve, for rent, the poor man's little store.
No haughty owner drives the humble swain
To some far refuge from his dread domain;

Nor wastes, upon his robe of useless pride,
The wealth, which shivering thousands want beside;
Nor in one palace sinks a hundred cots;
Nor in one manor drowns a thousand lots;
Nor, on one table, spread for death and pain,
Devours what would a village well sustain.

O Competence, thou bless'd by Heaven's decree,
How well exchang'd is empty pride for thee!
Oft to thy cot my feet delighted turn,
To meet thy cheerful smile, at peep of morn;
To join thy toils, that bid the earth look gay;
To mark thy sports, that hail the eve of May;
To see thy ruddy children, at thy board,
And share thy temperate meal, and frugal hoard;
And every joy, by winning prattlers giv'n,
And every earnest of a future Heaven.

There the poor wanderer finds a table spread,
The fireside welcome, and the peaceful bed.
The needy neighbor, oft by wealth denied,
There finds the little aids of life supplied;
The horse, that bears to mill the hard-earn'd grain;
The day's work given, to reap the ripen'd plain;
The useful team, to house the precious food,
And all the offices of real good.

There too, divine Religion is a guest,
And all the Virtues join the daily feast.
Kind Hospitality attends the door,
To welcome in the stranger and the poor;
Sweet Chastity, still blushing as she goes;
And Patience smiling at her train of woes;
And meek-eyed Innocence, and Truth refin'd,
And Fortitude, of bold, but gentle mind.

Thou pay'st the tax, the rich man will not pay;
Thou feed'st the poor, the rich man drives away.
Thy sons, for freedom, hazard limbs, and life,
While pride applauds, but shuns the manly strife:
Thou prop'st religion's cause, the world around,
And show'st thy faith in works, and not in sound.

Say, child of passion! while, with idiot stare,
Thou seest proud grandeur wheel her sunny car;
While kings, and nobles, roll bespangled by,
And the tall palace lessens in the sky;
Say, while with pomp thy giddy brain runs round,

What joys, like these, in splendor can be found?
Ah, yonder turn thy wealth-enchanted eyes,
Where that poor, friendless wretch expiring lies!
Hear his sad partner shriek, beside his bed,
And call down curses on her landlord's head,
Who drove, from yon small cot, her household sweet,
To pine with want, and perish in the street.
See the pale tradesman toil, the livelong day,
To deck imperious lords, who never pay!
Who waste, at dice, their boundless breadth of soil,
But grudge the scanty meed of honest toil.
See hounds and horses riot on the store,
By Heaven created for the hapless poor!
See half a realm one tyrant scarce sustain,
While meager thousands round him glean the plain!
See, for his mistress' robe, a village sold,
Whose matrons shrink from nakedness and cold!
See too the Farmer prowl around the shed,
To rob the starving household of their bread;
And seize, with cruel fangs, the helpless swain,
While wives, and daughters, plead, and weep, in vain;
Or yield to infamy themselves, to save
Their sire from prison, famine, and the grave.

There too foul luxury taints the putrid mind,
And slavery there imbrutes the reasoning kind:
There humble worth, in damps of deep despair,
Is bound by poverty's eternal bar:
No motives bright the ethereal aim impart,
Nor one fair ray of hope allures the heart.

But, O sweet Competence! how chang'd the scene,
Where thy soft footsteps lightly print the green!
Where Freedom walks erect, with manly port,
And all the blessings to his side resort,
In every hamlet, Learning builds her schools,
And beggars, children gain her arts, and rules;
And mild Simplicity o'er manners reigns,
And blameless morals Purity sustains.

From thee the rich enjoyments round me spring,
Where every farmer reigns a little king;
Where all to comfort, none to danger, rise;
Where pride finds few, but nature all supplies;
Where peace and sweet civility are seen,
And meek good-neighborhood endears the green.
Here every class (if classes those we call,
Where one extended class embraces all,

All mingling, as the rainbow's beauty blends,
Unknown where every hue begins or ends)
Each following, each, with uninvidious strife,
Wears every feature of improving life.
Each gains from other comeliness of dress,
And learns, with gentle mein to win and bless,
With welcome mild the stranger to receive,
And with plain, pleasing decency to live.
Refinement hence even humblest life improves;
Not the loose fair, that form and frippery loves;
But she, whose mansion is the gentle mind,
In thought, and action, virtuously refin'd.
Hence, wives and husbands act a lovelier part,
More just the conduct, and more kind the heart;
Hence brother, sister, parent, child, and friend,
The harmony of life more sweetly blend;
Hence labor brightens every rural scene;
Hence cheerful plenty lives along the green;
Still Prudence eyes her hoard, with watchful care,
And robes of thrift and neatness, all things wear.

from Part IV
The Destruction of the Pequods

. . . When pride and wrath awake the world to arms,[1]
How heaves thy snowy breast with fainting throe!
While lust and rapine trumpet death's alarms,
And men 'gainst men with fiery vengeance glow.
In Europe oft, that land of war, and woe,
As her sad steps the lingering mourner draws,
How slowly did thy feet entangled go,
Chain'd by vile tests, and prison'd round by laws;
While bigotry and rage in blood insteep'd thy cause!

When o'er th' Atlantic wild, by Angels borne,
Thy pilgrim barque explor'd it's western way,
With spring and beauty bloom'd the waste forlorn,
And night and chaos shrunk from new-born day.
Dumb was the savage howl; th' instinctive lay
Wav'd, with strange warblings, thro' the woodland's bound;
The village smil'd; the temple's golden ray
Shot high to heaven; fair culture clothed the ground;
Art blossom'd; cities sprang; and sails the ocean crown'd.

[1]This stanza picks up at line 271 of the fourth part of *Greenfield Hill.* In this latter section of Part IV, the poet is tracing the colonization of the Americas, but particularly of New England, as a result of European wars. The persecution of the Puritans is implicated at the end of this stanza and in the next one.

As on heaven's sacred hill, of hills the queen,
At thy command, contention foul shall cease,
Thy solar aspect, every storm serene,
And smooth the rugged wild of man to peace;
So here thy voice (fair earnest of the bliss!)
Transform'd the savage to the meekly child.
Hell saw, with pangs, her hideous realm decrease;
Wolves play'd with lambs; the tyger's heart grew mild;
And on his own bright work the GODHEAD, look'd and smil'd.

Hail Elliot![2] Mayhew[3] hail! by HEAVEN inform'd
With that pure love, which clasps the human kind;
To virtue's path even Indian feet you charm'd,
And lit, with wisdom's beam, the dusky mind:
From torture, blood, and treachery, refin'd,
The new-born convert lisp'd MESSIAH's name.
Mid Choirs complacent, in pure rapture join'd,
Your praise resounds, on yonder starry frame,
While souls, redeem'd from death, their earthly saviours claim.

Oh had the same bright spirit ever reign'd;
Nor trader villains foul'd the Savage mind;
Nor Avarice pin'd for boundless breadth of land;
Nor, with slow death, the wretches been consign'd
To India's curse, that poisons half mankind!
Then, O divine Religion! torture's blaze
Less frequent round thy tender heart had twin'd;
On the wild wigwam peace had cast it's rays,
And the tremendous whoop had chang'd to hymns of praise.

Fierce, dark, and jealous, is the exotic soul,
That, cell'd in secret, rules the savage breast.
There treacherous thoughts of gloomy vengeance roll,
And deadly deeds of malice unconfess'd;
The viper's poison rankling in it's nest.
Behind his tree, each Indian aims unseen:
No sweet oblivion soothes the hate impress'd:
Years fleet in vain: in vain realms intervene:
The victim's blood alone can quench the flames within.

[2]John Eliot (1604–1690), who came to be called "Apostle to the Indians" by the Puritans, established missionary towns in rural areas of Massachusetts. During King Philip's War, he evidently did what he could to protect Christianized Indians from the depredations of retaliatory whites, but his success was at best limited.

[3]Thomas Mayhew (c. 1621–1657) served as a missionary to the Wampanoag Indians in the 1640s and early 1650s. With John Eliot, he was one of the earliest Puritan missionaries to the Indians of New England.

Their knives the tawny tribes in slaughter steep,
When men, mistrustless, think them distant far;
And, when blank midnight shrouds the world in sleep,
The murderous yell announces first the war.
In vain sweet smiles compel the fiends to spare;
Th' unpitied victim screams, in tortures dire;
The life-blood stains the virgin's bosom bare;
Cherubic infants, limb by limb expire;
And silver'd Age sinks down in slowly-curling fire.

Yet savages are men. With glowing heat,
Fix'd as their hatred, friendship fills their mind;
By acts with justice, and with truth, replete,
Their iron breasts to softness are inclin'd.
But when could War of converts boast refin'd?
Or when Revenge to peace and sweetness move?
His heart, man yields alone to actions kind;
His faith, to creeds, whose soundness virtues prove,
Thawn in the April sun, and opening still to love.

Senate august! that sway'st Columbian climes,
Form'd of the wise, the noble, and humane,
Cast back the glance through long-ascending times,
And think what nations fill'd the western plain.
Where are they now? What thoughts the bosom pain,
From mild Religion's eye how streams the tear,
To see so far outspread the waste of man,
And ask "How fell the myriads, HEAVEN plac'd here!"
Reflect, be just, and feel for Indian woes severe.[4]

But cease, foul Calumny! with sooty tongue,
No more the glory of our sires belie.
They felt, and they redress'd, each nation's wrong;
Even Pequod foes they view'd with generous eye,
And, pierc'd with injuries keen, that Virtue try,
The savage faith, and friendship, strove to gain:
And, had no base Canadian fiends been nigh,
Even now soft Peace had smil'd on every plain,
And tawny nations liv'd, and own'd MESSIAH'S reign.

[4]These lines probably refer to Little Turtle's War, which took place from 1786 to 1794, between the Shawnees, Miamis, and Ottawas of the Ohio Territory and the U.S. Government. President Washington eventually sent "Mad Anthony" Wayne into battle with the Indians. In 1793 the Shawnees rejected newly offered U.S. peace terms; they eventually succumbed at the Battle of Fallen Timbers in August 1794. In August of 1795 the Treaty of (Fort) Greenville, securing white settlement on lands northwest of the Ohio River, established another so-called "permanent" boundary for whites.

Amid a circling marsh, expanded wide,
To a lone hill the Pequods wound their way;
And none, but Heaven, the mansion had descried,
Close-tangled, wild, impervious to the day;
But one poor wanderer, loitering long astray.
Wilder'd in labyrinths of pathless wood,
In a tall tree embower'd, obscurely lay:
Strait summon'd down, the trembling suppliant show'd
Where lurk'd his vanish'd friends, within their drear abode.

To death, the murderers were anew requir'd,
A pardon proffer'd, and a peace assur'd;
And, though with vengeful heat their foes were fir'd,
Their lives, their freedom, and their lands, secur'd.
Some yielding heard. In fastness strong immur'd,
The rest the terms refus'd, with brave disdain,
Near, and more near, the peaceful Herald lur'd;
Then bade a shower of arrows round him rain,
And wing'd him swift, from danger, to the distant plain.

Through the sole, narrow way, to vengeance led,
To final fight our generous heroes drew;
And Stoughton[5] now had pass'd the moor's black shade,
When hell's terrific region scream'd anew.
Undaunted, on their foes they fiercely flew;
As fierce, the dusky warriors crowd the fight;
Despair inspires; to combat's face they glue;
With groans, and shouts, they rage, unknowing slight,
And close their sullen eyes, in shades of endless night.

Indulge, my native land! indulge the tear,
That steals, impassion'd, o'er a nation's doom:
To me each twig, from Adam's stock, is dear,
And sorrows fall upon an Indian's tomb.
And, O ye Chiefs! in yonder starry home,
Accept the humble tribute of this rhyme.
Your gallant deeds, in Greece, or haughty Rome,
By Maro[6] sung, or Homer's harp sublime,
Had charm'd the world's wide round, and triumph'd over time.

1794

[5]Israel Stoughton, who led 120 Massachusetts troops after the Pequots who were fleeing eastward toward New York.

[6]Virgil.

Phillis Wheatley 1753–1784

Known best for her Christian verses reflecting orthodox piety, Phillis Wheatley (Peters) in fact wrote on a wide variety of topics. A kidnapped African slave child, aged about seven years old, she was sold from the South Market in Boston to well-to-do Susanna Wheatley. She was raised in a pious Christian household, and the precocious child evidently experienced special, much-indulged comfort and only token slavery. (Phillis Wheatley was manumitted by October 18, 1773.) Tutored by family members, she quickly learned English, Latin, and the Bible, and she began writing in 1765, four years after her landing in Boston harbor.

She wrote to Reverend Samson Occom, a converted Christian Mohican Indian minister, and she sent a poem to Reverend Joseph Sewall of Boston's Old South Church. Both this letter and poem are not extant, but a poem from this early period remains: in 1767, when she was about thirteen or fourteen years old, Phillis Wheatley published her first verses in a Newport, Rhode Island, newspaper. By 1772 she had composed enough poems that she could advertise twenty-eight of them in *The Boston Censor* for February 29, March 14, and April 11. She hoped to publish a volume of her poems that year in Boston.

The range of her topical concerns was already evident in these twenty-eight titles. Along with poems on morality and piety, the volume offered patriotic American pieces, an epithalamium, and a short, racially self-conscious poem, "Thoughts on Being Brought from Africa to America." Had enough subscribers for this volume come forward, it would have been printed. But advertisements brought no subscribers, for reasons in part racially motivated. Wheatley was encouraged by her doting and undaunted mistress to revise her manuscripts, in preparation for a volume that Susanna Wheatley had arranged, with the prestigious cooperation of the Countess of Huntingdon, to have published in London in 1773, complete with an engraved likeness of the poet as a frontispiece. This was the first volume known to have been published by a black American, man or woman.

In the fall of 1779, she ran (six times) proposals for a projected third volume, of thirty-three poems and thirteen letters. The work was to be dedicated to Benjamin Franklin. But again, as in 1772 and 1773, these 1779 proposals were rejected by Bostonians. In the *Boston Magazine* for September, 1784, there would be printed a final solicitation for subscribers to this third volume, but there would be no such book in print by the time Phillis Wheatley died three months later on December 5. She was buried obscurely on December 8, along with the body of the last of three infant children.

Wheatley's poems ably and imaginatively suit the neoclassical poetic norms of her day, yet she was not accepted by whites of her generation. Indeed her life evidences the effects of racial injustice. Her first volume, the projected 1772 Boston publication, was advertised by printers, who although they knew better, claimed that they could not credit "ye performances to be by a Negro." But it was no secret that Wheatley was a black poet. In the half-dozen poems she published in America and London before and during the time she solicited Boston subscribers for her 1772 book, she was almost always identified as a black poet. While her second collection, published as *Poems,* went through at least four London printings for a run of about 1200 copies, in America the same volume fared poorly early on. Wheatley received a second lot of 300 copies of her *Poems* from London in May of 1774, but as late as 1778 she could write to a friend in New Haven and ask for return to her of copies of her "books that remain unsold," announcing with unfounded bravado that she "could easily dispose of them here for 12/Lm°" (that is, twelve pounds Legal money). Her book was never reprinted in America during her lifetime; the first American reprinting appeared in Philadelphia in 1786, two years after she had died.

But if her early rejection seems peculiarly American, so too was her gradual conscious tags, reminding readers that she was African. In more than thirty posthumously published letters and variants, and in several poems published after her 1773 volume, Phillis Wheatley would continue to register her racial awareness, but nowhere more bitingly than in her 1774 letter to Samson Occom.

Phillis Wheatley's poetry, like that of many of her American contemporaries, represents a deeply self-conscious art. Her sense of herself as an African and an American makes her in some ways a dual provincial in relationship to the eighteenth-century Anglo-Atlantic cosmopolitan center. The art of her poetry resides in her capacity to make her political, cultural, and poetic self-consciousness a literary subject in and of itself. That is, her poetic endeavour often resides in her careful exploration of her relationship to her poetic sources and to the socially complex contexts in which her poetry takes place. In her acutely self-aware occasional poetry, she gives us one of the most searching portraits available of the American colonial consciousness as provincial consciousness.

The array of poems included in Wheatley's London-published volume indicates the breadth of the poet's accomplishment. It included not only Christian elegies, but also a highly original English translation from the Latin of Ovid, biblical paraphrases, and poems about nature, imagination, and memory. Like any good poet who sought patrons, Wheatley also included flattering salutes to an English captain and the Earl of Dartmouth, two happy pieces on the good fortunes of two ladies, and even a playful rebus to James Bowdoin. She included as well her poem on being brought from Africa to America, a metrical salute to a local black Boston artist, and several poems that spoke to the issues of racial self-acceptance leading to success here and hereafter. *Poems* was eventually reprinted more than two dozen times in America and Europe, and selections appear with regularity in American textbooks. An autographed copy of her book sells today for several thousands of dollars.

William H. Robinson
Rhode Island College
Phillip M. Richards
Colgate University

PRIMARY WORKS

Poems, 1773; Anonymous, *Memoir and Poems of Phillis Wheatley, A Native African and a Slave,* 1834; Charles Deane, *Letters of Phillis Wheatley, the Negro Slave Poet of Boston,* 1864; Charles F. Heartman, *Phillis Wheatley (Phillis Peters). Poems and Letters. First Collected Edition,* 1915; Julian D. Mason, ed., *The Poems of Phillis Wheatley,* 1966.

SECONDARY WORKS

William H. Robinson, ed., *Critical Essays on Phillis Wheatley,* 1982; William H. Robinson, *Phillis Wheatley and Her Writings,* 1984; John Shields, ed., *The Collected Works of Phillis Wheatley,* 1988; Julian D. Mason, *The Poems of Phillis Wheatley,* 1989; Phillip M. Richards, "Phillis Wheatley and Literary Americanization," *American Quarterly,* 44 June 1992.

To Mæcenas[1]

Mæcenas, you, beneath the myrtle shade,
Read o'er what poets sung, and shepherds play'd.
What felt those poets but you feel the same?
Does not your soul possess the sacred flame?
Their noble strains your equal genius shares
In softer language, and diviner airs.

While *Homer* paints lo! circumfus'd in air,
Celestial Gods in mortal forms appear;
Swift as they move hear each recess rebound,
Heav'n quakes, earth trembles, and the shores resound.
Great Sire of verse, before my mortal eyes,
The lightnings blaze across the vaulted skies,
And, as the thunder shakes the heav'nly plains,
A deep-felt horror thrills through all my veins.
When gentler strains demand thy graceful song,
The length'ning line moves languishing along.
When great *Patroclus* courts *Achilles'* aid,
The grateful tribute of my tears is paid;
Prone on the shore he feels the pangs of love,
And stern *Pelides* tend'rest passions move.

Great *Maro's* strain in heav'nly numbers flows,
The *Nine* inspire, and all the bosom glows.
O could I rival thine and *Virgil's* page,
Or claim the *Muses* with the *Mantuan* Sage;
Soon the same beauties should my mind adorn,
And the same ardors in my soul should burn:
Then should my song in bolder notes arise,
And all my numbers pleasingly surprize;
But here I sit, and mourn a grov'ling mind,
That fain would mount, and ride upon the wind.

Not you, my friend, these plaintive strains become,
Not you, whose bosom is the *Muses* home;
When they from tow'ring *Helicon* retire,
They fan in you the bright immortal fire,
But I less happy, cannot raise the song,
The fault'ring music dies upon my tongue.

[1]The Roman Gaius Cilnius Mæcenas was the special friend and patron of Horace and Virgil. This poem was not listed in the 1772 Proposals.

The happier *Terence*[2] all the choir inspir'd,
His soul replenish'd, and his bosom fir'd;
But say, ye *Muses,* why this partial grace,
To one alone of *Afric's* sable race;
From age to age transmitting thus his name
With the first glory in the rolls of fame?

Thy virtues, great *Mæcenas*! shall be sung
In praise of him, from whom those virtues sprung:
While blooming wreaths around thy temples spread,
I'll snatch a laurel from thine honour'd head,
While you indulgent smile upon the deed.

As long as *Thames* in streams majestic flows,
Or *Naiads* in their oozy beds repose,
While Phœbus reigns above the starry train,
While bright *Aurora* purples o'er the main,
So long, great Sir, the muse thy praise shall sing,
So long thy praise shall make *Parnassus* ring:
Then grant, *Mæcenas,* thy paternal rays,
Hear me propitious, and defend my lays.

Letter to the Right Hon'ble The Earl of Dartmouth per favour of Mr. Wooldridge,[1]

Oct. 10,1772

My Lord,

The Joyful occasion which has given me this Confidence in addressing your Lordship in the enclose'd, will, I hope, sufficiently apologize for this freedom from an African, who with the (now) happy America, exults with equal transport in the view of one of its greatest advocates Presiding, with the Special tenderness of a Fatherly heart, over the American department.

[2]He was an *African* by birth. [Wheatley's note.]

[1]William Legge (1753–1801), third Earl of Dartmouth, appointed Secretary for the North American colonies in August, 1772, to the measured approval of some colonists who recognized Dartmouth's sympathetic ear for colonial grievances.

Thomas Wooldridge (d. 1794), a minor English functionary traveling throughout the colonies in the employ of Lord Dartmouth. Wooldridge visited and interviewed Phillis in Boston, promising that he would deliver the above poem and its cover letter, and he did so, the manuscripts of both being located among the Earl of Dartmouth's papers in the County Record Office, Stafford, England. Also located there is Wooldridge's letter in manuscript, dated "New York Nov. 24th 1772," which describes his interview with Phillis Wheatley.

Nor can they, my Lord, be insensible of the Friendship so much exemplified in your endeavors in their behalf, during the late unhappy disturbances.[2] I sincerely wish your Lordship all Possible success, in your undertakings for the Interest of North America.

That the united Blessings of Heaven and Earth may attend you here, and the endless Felicity of the invisible state, in the presence of the Divine Benefactor may be your portion hereafter, is the hearty desire of, My Lord,

Your Lordship's most Ob^{t}. &
devoted Hum^{e}. Servt.
Phillis Wheatley
Boston, N.E. Oct 10, 1772

To the Right Honourable William, Earl of Dartmouth, His Majesty's Principal Secretary of State for North-America, &c[1]

Hail, happy day, when, smiling like the morn,
Fair *Freedom* rose *New-England* to adorn:
The northern clime beneath her genial ray,
Dartmouth, congratulates thy blissful sway:
Elate with hope her race no longer mourns,
Each soul expands, each grateful bosom burns,
While in thine hand with pleasure we behold
The silken reins, and *Freedom's* charms unfold.
Long lost to realms beneath the northern skies
She shines supreme, while hated *faction* dies:
Soon as appear'd the *Goddess* long desir'd,
Sick at the view, she lanquish'd and expir'd;
Thus from the splendors of the morning light
The owl in sadness seeks the caves of night.

No more, *America,* in mournful strain
Of wrongs, and grievance unredress'd complain,
No longer shalt thou dread the iron chain,
Which wanton *Tyranny* with lawless hand
Had made, and with it meant t' enslave the land.

[2]Wheatley refers to several riotous reactions to various British financial and legal impositions on the colonies.

[1]Dartmouth, sympathetic to Methodists in England, was a friend of the Countess of Huntingdon.

Should you, my lord, while you peruse my song,
Wonder from whence my love of *Freedom* sprung,
Whence flow these wishes for the common good,
By feeling hearts alone best understood,
I, young in life, by seeming cruel fate
Was snatch'd from *Afric's* fancy'd happy seat:
What pangs excruciating must molest,
What sorrows labour in my parent's breast?
Steel'd was that soul and by no misery mov'd
That from a father seiz'd his babe belov'd:
Such, such my case. And can I then but pray
Others may never feel tyrannic sway?

For favours past, great Sir, our thanks are due,
And thee we ask thy favours to renew,
Since in thy pow'r, as in thy will before,
To sooth the griefs, which thou did'st once deplore.
May heav'nly grace the sacred sanction give
To all thy works, and thou for ever live
Not only on the wings of fleeting *Fame,*
Though praise immortal crowns the patriot's name,
But to conduct to heav'ns refulgent fane,
May fiery coursers sweep th' ethereal plain,
And bear thee upwards to that blest abode,
Where, like the prophet, thou shalt find thy God.

Letter to the Rt. Hon'ble the Countess of Huntingdon[1]

Oct. 25, 1770

Most noble Lady,

The occasion of my addressing your Ladiship will, I hope, apologize for this my boldness in doing it. it (sic) is to enclose a few lines on the decease of your worthy chaplain, the Rev'd Mr. Whitefield, in the loss of whom, I sincerely sympathize

[1]The Countess of Huntingdon, Selina Hastings (1702–1791), religious zealot, expended most of her considerable fortune for the support of her dissident form of English Methodism. It was the countess who acted as Wheatley's English patron when she allowed the poet to dedicate *Poems on Various Subjects, Religious and Moral* (London, 1773) to herself; and it was at the countess's insistence that Wheatley's portrait was painted and then engraved as a frontispiece for the collection of poems, the first known published volume by a black American. The text of this letter is from one of two manuscript versions, both housed among the Countess's papers in the Cheshunt Foundation at Cambridge University in England.

with your Ladiship: but your great loss which is his Greater gain, will, I hope, meet with infinite reparation, in the presence of God, the Divine Benefactor whose image you bear by filial imitation.

The Tongues of the learned are insufficient, much less the pen of an untutor'd African, to paint in lively characters, the excellencies of this Citizen of Zion! I beg an Interest in your Ladiship's Prayers, and am

With great humility
Your Ladiship's most Obedient
Humble Servant

Phillis Wheatley

Boston Oct. 25th 1770

On the Death of the Rev. Mr. George Whitefield 1770[1]

Hail, happy saint, on thine immortal throne,
Possest of glory, life, and bliss unknown;
We hear no more the music of thy tongue,
Thy wonted auditories cease to throng.
Thy sermons in unequall'd accents flow'd,
And ev'ry bosom with devotion glow'd;
Thou didst in strains of eloquence refin'd
Inflame the heart, and captivate the mind.
Unhappy we the setting sun deplore,
So glorious once, but ah! it shines no more.

Behold the prophet in his tow'ring flight!
He leaves the earth for heav'n's unmeasur'd height,
And worlds unknown receive him from our sight.
There *Whitefield* wings with rapid course his way,
And sails to *Zion* through vast seas of day.

[1]From Phillis Wheatley, *Poems on Various Subjects, Religious and Moral,* (1773). Personal chaplain to Lady Huntingdon since 1749, the Reverend George Whitefield (1714–1770) was a fiery and enormously popular English evangelist who conducted frequent prayer visits to America, preaching in the Boston area at least six times between 1750 and 1770. His favorite American undertaking was the establishment of Bethesda, an orphanage outside of Savannah, Georgia, which he built in 1764 with rationalized slave labor. The text, above, is a revision of the poem which first appeared as a 62-line broadside in Boston in October, 1770, and was widely reprinted in Boston, Newport, New York, Philadelphia, and London. Another revised version, in 64 lines, was published in London in 1771. The poem established Phillis Wheatley's international reputation.

Thy pray'rs, great saint, and thine incessant cries
Have pierc'd the bosom of thy native skies.
Thou moon hast seen, and all the stars of light,
How he has wrestled with his God by night.
He pray'd that grace in ev'ry heart might dwell,
He long'd to see *America* excel;
He charg'd its youth that ev'ry grace divine
Should with full lustre in their conduct shine;
That Saviour, which his soul did first receive,
The greatest gift that ev'n a God can give,
He freely offer'd to the num'rous throng,
That on his lips with list'ning pleasure hung.

"Take him, ye wretched, for your only good,
"Take him[,] ye starving sinners, for your food;
"Ye thirsty, come to this life-giving stream,
"Ye preachers, take him for your joyful theme;
"Take him[,] my dear *Americans,* ["] he said,
"Be your complaints on his kind bosom laid:
"Take him, ye *Africans,* he longs for you,
"*Impartial Saviour* is his title due:
"Wash'd in the fountain of redeeming blood,
"You shall be son, and kings, and priests to God."

Great *Countess,*[2] we *Americans* revere
Thy name, and mingle in thy grief sincere;
New England deeply feels, the *Orphans* mourn,
Their more than father will no more return.

But, though arrested by the hand of death,
Whitefield no more exerts his lab'ring breath,
Yet let us view him in th'eternal skies,
Let ev'ry heart to this bright vision rise;
While the tomb safe retains its sacred trust,
Till life divine re-animates his dust.

1770

[2]The Countess of *Huntingdon,* to whom Mr. *Whitefield* was Chaplain. [Wheatley's note.]

On the Death of Dr. Samuel Marshall 1771[1]

Through thickest glooms look back, immortal shade,
On that confusion which thy death has made;
Or from *Olympus'* height look down and see
A *Town* involv'd in grief bereft of thee.
Thy *Lucy* sees thee mingle with the dead,
And rends the graceful tresses from her head,
Wild in her woe, with grief unknown opprest[,]
Sigh follows sigh[,] deep heaving from her breast.

Too quickly fled, ah! whither art thou gone?
Ah! lost for ever to thy wife and son!
The hapless child, thine only hope and heir,
Clings round his mother's neck, and weeps his sorrows there.
The loss of thee on *Tyler's* soul returns,
And *Boston* for her dear physician mourns.

When sickness call'd for *Marshall's* healing hand,
With what compassion did his soul expand?
In him we found the father and the friend:
In life how lov'd! how honour'd in his end!

And must not then our *Aesculapius*[2] stay
To bring his ling'ring infant into day?
The babe unborn in the dark womb is tost,
And seems in anguish for its father lost.

Gone is *Apollo* from his house of earth,
But leaves the sweet memorials of his worth:
The common parent, whom we all deplore,
From yonder world unseen must come no more,
Yet 'midst our woes immortal hopes attend
The spouse, the sire, the universal friend.

1773

[1]From Phillis Wheatley's *Poems* (1773), revised from the first appearance of the poem, also in 28 lines, in *The Boston Evening Post* (7 October, 1771), p. 3. Dr. Samuel Marshall (1735–1771) graduated from Harvard College in 1754, and prepared for a medical career in London hospitals, qualifying as an M.D. in 1761. He returned to Boston in 1765, married Lucy Tyler and purchased a newer home on Congress Street, not far from Phillis Wheatley's King Street (today's State Street) home. Marshall fathered one son who died on September 29, 1771. Widely respected, he was described in his obituary in *The Boston Evening Post* (30 September) as "highly esteemed . . . a very skillful Physician, Surgeon and Man Midwife . . . ; his death therefore is to be lamented as a public loss to the community. . . ." A relative of Wheatley's mistress, Marshall likely attended the poet in her chronic medical problems.

[2]Aesculapius, the son of Phoebus Apollo and the princess Coronis, was regarded as "the father of medicine."

On Being Brought from Africa to America[1]

'Twas mercy brought me from my *Pagan* land,
Taught my benighted soul to understand
That there's a God, that there's a *Saviour* too:
Once I redemption neither sought nor knew.
Some view our sable race with scornful eye,
"Their colour is a diabolic die."
Remember, *Christians, Negros,* black as *Cain,*
May be refin'd, and join th'angelic train.

1773

On Imagination

Thy various works, imperial queen, we see,
How bright their forms! how deck'd with pomp by thee!
Thy wond'rous acts in beauteous order stand,
And all attest how potent is thine hand.

From *Helicon's*[1] refulgent heights attend,
Ye sacred choir, and my attempts befriend:
To tell her glories with a faithful tongue,
Ye blooming graces, triumph in my song.

Now here, now there, the roving *Fancy* flies,
Till some lov'd object strikes her wand'ring eyes,
Whose silken fetters all the senses bind,
And soft captivity involves the mind.

Imagination! who can sing thy force?
Or who describe the swiftness of thy course?
Soaring through air to find the bright abode,

[1]This much-reprinted piece has been often cited as an instance of Phillis Wheatley's denigration of things black. Instead, it is a measuredly defiant refutation of the racist notions held by some white Christians, who argue that, by virtue of biblical dictate, black humanity has been forever removed from any hope of Christian membership. The poet defames Africa not because most of its peoples are black, but because she understood it to be a land of "pagans," i.e., non-Christians. The notion that pagan Africa was in critical need of Christianity was repeated by other literate, eighteenth-century blacks, and has persisted to this day. This printing is from Wheatley's 1773 volume of *Poems.*

[1]Helicon, one of several earthly mountain homes of the Greek muses.

Th' empyreal palace of the thund'ring God,
We on thy pinions[2] can surpass the wind,
And leave the rolling universe behind:
From star to star the mental optics rove,
Measure the skies, and range the realms above.
There in one view we grasp the mighty whole,
Or with new worlds amaze th'unbounded soul.

Though *Winter* frowns to *Fancy's* raptur'd eyes
The fields may flourish, and gay scenes arise;
The frozen deeps may break their iron bands,
And bid their waters murmur o'er the sands.
Fair *Flora*[3] may resume her fragrant reign,
And with her flow'ry riches deck the plain;
Sylvanus[4] may diffuse his honours round,
And all the forest may with leaves be crown'd:
Show'rs may descend, and dews their gems disclose,
And nectar sparkle on the blooming rose.

Such is thy pow'r, nor are thine orders vain,
O thou the leader of the mental train:
In full perfection all thy works are wrought,
And thine the sceptre o'er the realms of thought.
Before thy throne the subject-passions bow,
Of subject-passions sov'reign ruler Thou;
At thy command joy rushes on the heart,
And through the glowing veins the spirits dart.

Fancy might now her silken pinions try
To rise from earth, and sweep th'expanse on high;
From *Tithon's*[5] bed now might *Aurora* rise,
Her cheeks all glowing with celestial dies,
While a pure stream of light o'erflows the skies.
The monarch of the day I might behold,
And all the mountains tipt with radiant gold,
But I reluctant leave the pleasing views,
Which *Fancy* dresses to delight the *Muse:*
Winter austere forbids me to aspire,
And northern tempests damp the rising fire;
They chill the tides of *Fancy's* flowing sea,
Cease then, my song, cease the unequal lay.

1773

[2]Pinions are "wings."
[3]Flora, Roman goddess of flowers.
[4]Sylvanus, in Greek mythology, helper of woodsmen.
[5]Tithon (i.e., Tithonus), husband to Aurora, goddess of the dawn, father of her black Ethiopian son, Memnon, whose death in battle is told in *The Iliad*.

To the University of Cambridge, in New England[1]

While an intrinsic ardor prompts to write,
The muses promise to assist my pen;
'Twas not long since I left my native shore
The land of errors, and *Egyptian* gloom:
Father of mercy, 'twas thy gracious hand
Brought me in safety from those dark abodes.

Students, to you 'tis giv'n to scan the heights
Above, to traverse the ethereal space,
And mark the systems of revolving worlds.
Still more, ye sons of science ye receive
The blissful news by messengers from heav'n,
How *Jesus'* blood for your redemption flows.
See him with hands out-strecht upon the cross;
Immense compassion in his bosom glows;
He hears revilers, nor resents their scorn:
What matchless mercy in the Son of God!
When the whole human race by sin has fall'n,
He deign'd to die that they might rise again,
And share with him in the sublimest skies,
Life without death, and glory without end.

Improve your privileges while they stay,
Ye pupils, and each hour redeem, that bears
Or good or bad report of you to heav'n.
Let sin, that baneful evil to the soul,
By you be shunn'd, nor once remit your guard;
Suppress the deadly serpent in its egg.
Ye blooming plants of human race divine,
An *Ethiop*[2] tells you 'tis your greatest foe;
Its transient sweetness turns to endless pain,
And in immense perdition sinks the soul.

1773

[1]The University of Cambridge, in New England, i.e., Harvard College in Cambridge, Massachusetts. The text is from Wheatley's *Poems* (1773).

[2]In several poems, both in her volume and in separately published pieces and variants, Wheatley variously registered her racial self-consciousness.

Philis's [*sic*] Reply to the Answer in our Last by the Gentleman in the Navy.[1]

For one bright moment, heavenly goddess! shine,
Inspire my song and form the lays divine.
Rochford,[2] attend. Beloved of Phoebus! hear,
A truer sentence never reach'd thine ear;
Struck with thy song, each vain conceit resign'd
A soft affection seiz'd my grateful mind,
While I each golden sentiment admire;
In thee, the muse's bright celestial fire.
The generous plaudit 'tis not mine to claim,
A muse untutor'd, an unknown to fame.

The heavenly sisters[3] pour thy notes along
And crown their bard with every grace of song.
My pen, least favour'd by the tuneful nine,
Can never rival, never equal thine;
Then fix the humble Afric muse's seat
At British Homer's[4] and Sir Isaac's[5] feet.
Those bards whose fame in deathless strains arise
Creation's boast, and fav'rites of the skies.
In fair description are thy powers display'd
In artless grottos, and the sylvan shade;
Charm'd with thy painting,[6] how my bosom burns!
And pleasing Gambia on my soul returns,[7]
With native grace in spring's luxuriant reign,
Smiles the gay mead, and Eden blooms again,

[1]This headnote was presumably written by Joseph Greenleaf, editor of *The Royal American Magazine,* in whose December, 1774, issue Wheatley had published a poem, "To A Gentleman in the Navy"; in that same issue was also printed an anonymous poem, "The Answer," written by "the gentleman in the navy," a response to the poem. In the January, 1775, issue of *The Royal American Magazine,* Wheatley published this poem.

[2]This name cannot be found among rosters of Royal Naval officers in Boston in 1774. Presumably, "Rochford" was a verse-writing Royal Naval officer who had served off the coast of Africa, and in 1774 was based in Boston, possibly billeted in the Wheatley household on King Street, where the poet may still have been living. She may be referring to William Henry Zuylestein, fourth Earl of Rochford (1723–1781), who, although not in Boston, had much to do with royal fleet actions abroad.

[3]The Greek muses.

[4]John Milton (1608–1674), poet, author of "Paradise Lost."

[5]Sir Isaac Newton (1642–1727), English natural philosopher and mathematician.

[6]In the anonymous poem, "The Answer," the writer was complimentary to Africa, which he calls ". . . the guilded shore, the happy land,/ Where spring and autumn gentle hand in hand."

[7]The poet may be remembering her African birthplace. Whether or not she is being autobiographical in her extended praises for things African (lines 21–34), she is the first black American poet to so rhapsodize about Africa.

The various bower, the tuneful flowing stream,
The soft retreats, the lovers['] golden dream.
Her soil spontaneous, yields exhaustless stores;
For phoebus revels on her verdant shores.
Whose flowery births, a fragrant train appear,
And crown the youth throughout the smiling year.
There, as in Britain's favour'd isle, behold
The bending harvest ripen into gold!
Just are thy views of Afric's blissful plain,
On the warm limits of the land and main.
   Pleas'd with the theme, see sportive fancy play,
In realms devoted to the God of day!
Europa's bard, who with great depth explor'd,
Of nature, and thro' boundless systems soar'd,
Thro' earth, thro' heaven, and hell's profound domain,
Where night eternal holds her awful reign.
But, lo! in him Britania's prophet dies,
And whence, ah! whence, shall other *Newtons* rise?
Muse, bid thy Rochford's matchless pen display
The charms of friendship in the sprightly lay:
Queen of his song, thro' all his numbers shine,
And plausive glories, goddess; shall be thine!
With partial grace thou mak'st his verse excel,
And *his* the glory to describe so well.
Cerulean bard![8] to thee these strains belong,
The Muse's darling and the prince of song.

December 5th, 1774

To His Excellency General Washington

SIR.

I Have taken the freedom to address your Excellency in the enclosed poem, and entreat your acceptance, though I am not insensible of its inaccuracies. Your being appointed by the Grand Continental Congress to be Generalissimo of the armies of North America, together with the fame of your virtues, excite sensations not easy to suppress. Your generosity, therefore, I presume, will pardon the attempt. Wishing your Excellency all possible success in the great cause you are so generously engaged in. I am,

Your Excellency's most obedient humble servant,
PHILLIS WHEATLEY.

[8]Rochford, whom Wheatley is poetically thanking for his complimentary poem, "The Answer." Uniforms of the Royal Naval officers were "cerulean," or sky-blue.

Providence, Oct. 26, 1775.
His Excellency Gen. Washington.

Celestial choir! enthron'd in realms of light,
  Columbia's[1] scenes of glorious toils I write.
While freedom's cause her anxious breast alarms,
She flashes dreadful in refulgent arms.
See mother earth her offspring's fate bemoan,
And nations gaze at scenes before unknown!
See the bright beams of heaven's revolving light
Involved in sorrows and the veil of night!
  The goddess comes, she moves divinely fair,
Olive and laurel binds her golden hair:
Wherever shines this native of the skies,
Unnumber'd charms and recent graces rise.
  Muse! bow propitious while my pen relates
How pour her armies through a thousand gates,
As when Eolus[2] heaven's fair face deforms,
Enwrapp'd in tempest and a night of storms;
Astonish'd ocean feels the wild uproar,
The refluent surges beat the sounding shore;
Or thick as leaves in Autumn's golden reign,
Such, and so many, moves the warrior's train.
In bright array they seek the work of war,
Where high unfurl'd the ensign waves in air.
Shall I to Washington their praise recite?
Enough thou know'st them in the fields of fight.
Thee, first in peace and honours,—we demand
The grace and glory of thy martial band.
Fam'd for thy valour, for thy virtues more,
Hear every tongue thy guardian aid implore!
  One century scarce perform'd its destined round,
When Gallic powers Columbia's fury found;[3]
And so may you, whoever dares disgrace
The land of freedom's heaven-defended race!
Fix'd are the eyes of nations on the scales,
For in their hopes Columbia's arm prevails.
Anon Britannia droops the pensive head,
While round increase the rising hills of dead.
Ah! cruel blindness to Columbia's state!
Lament thy thirst of boundless power too late.
  Proceed, great chief, with virtue on thy side,

[1]America.
[2]God of the winds.
[3]A reference to the French and Indian War (or the Seven Years War) 1756–1763, from which the colonists emerged triumphant over the French.

Thy ev'ry action let the goddess guide.
A crown, a mansion, and a throne that shine,
With gold unfading, WASHINGTON! be thine.

1776

Liberty and Peace,

A Poem by Phillis Peters[1]

Lo! Freedom comes. Th'prescient Muse foretold,
All Eyes th'accomplish'd Prophecy behold:
Her Port describ'd, *"She moves divinely fair,*
"Olive and Laurel bind her golden Hair."
She, the bright Progeny of Heaven, descends,
And every grace her sovereign Step attends;
For now kind Heaven, indulgent to our Prayer,
In smiling *Peace* resolves the Din of *War.*
Fix'd in *Columbia* her illustrious Line,
And bids in thee her future Councils shine.
To every Realm her Portals open'd wide,
Receives from each the full commercial Tide.
Each Art and Science now with rising Charms,
Th' expanding Heart with Emulation warms.
E'en great *Britannia* sees with dread Surprize,
And from the dazzling Splendors turns her Eyes!
Britain, whose Navies swept th'*Atlantic* o'er,
And Thunder sent to every distant Shore:
E'en thou, in Manners cruel as thou art,
The Sword resign'd, resume the friendly Part!
For *Galia*'s Power espous'd *Columbia*'s Cause,
And new-born *Rome* shall give *Britannia* Law,
Nor unremember'd in the grateful Strain,
Shall princely *Louis'* friendly Deeds remain;
The generous Prince[2] th'impending Vengeance eye's,
Sees the fierce Wrong, and to the rescue flies.
Perish that Thirst of boundless Power, that drew
On *Albion*'s Head the Curse to Tyrants due.
But thou appeas'd submit to Heaven's decree,

[1]Wheatley married John Peters, a free, literate, and ambitious black shopkeeper of Boston in April of 1778, the two of them becoming parents to three children who all died in infancy.

[2]"The generous Prince": France joined the Americans as allies in June, 1778.

That bids this Realm of Freedom rival thee!
Now sheathe the Sword that bade the Brave attone
With guiltless Blood for Madness not their own.
Sent from th'Enjoyment of their native Shore
Ill-fated—never to behold her more!
From every Kingdom on *Europa*'s Coast
Throng'd various Troops, their Glory, Strength and Boast.
With heart-felt pity fair *Hibernia* saw
Columbia menac'd by the Tyrant's Law:
On hostile Fields fraternal Arms engage,
And mutual Deaths, all dealt with mutual Rage;
The Muse's Ear hears mother Earth deplore
Her ample Surface smoak with kindred Gore:
The hostile Field destroys the social Ties,
And ever-lasting Slumber seals their Eyes.
Columbia mourns, the haughty Foes deride,
Her Treasures plunder'd, and her Towns destroy'd:
Witness how *Charlestown's* curling Smoaks arise,
In sable Columns to the clouded Skies!
The ample Dome, high-wrought with curious Toil,
In one sad Hour[3] the savage Troops despoil.
Descending *Peace* the Power of War confounds;
From every Tongue coelestial *Peace* resounds:
As from the East th'illustrious King of Day,
With rising Radiance drives the Shades away,
So Freedom comes array'd with Charms divine,
And in her Train Commerce and Plenty shine.
Britannia owns her Independent Reign,
Hibernia, Scotia, and the Realms of *Spain;*
And great *Germania*'s ample Coast admires
The generous Spirit that *Columbia* fires.
Auspicious Heaven shall fill with fav'ring Gales,
Where e'er *Columbia* spreads her swelling Sails:
To every Realm shall *Peace* her Charms display,
And Heavenly *Freedom* spreads her golden Ray.

1785

[3]From three until four p.m. on June 17, 1776, the Battle of Bunker Hill, on the Charlestown peninsula, just across the bay from North Boston, was fought between outnumbered Americans and British troops, who finally achieved a costly victory, losing over 1000 of their own, while Americans suffered the losses of 450 men. Once ashore, the British troops vindictively burned down the town of Charlestown, then home for some 3000 persons, the flames burning all that afternoon and into that night, the rising smoke blackening the skies, or, as Wheatley puts it, "The ample Dome" was "high wrought with curious Toil."

Letter to Samson Occom

Feb. 11, 1774[1]

Reverend and honoured Sir,

"I have this day received your obliging kind epistle, and am greatly satisfied with your reasons respecting the negroes, and think highly reasonable what you offer in vindication of their natural rights: Those that invade them cannot be insensible that the divine light is chasing away the thick darkness which broods over the land of Africa; and the chaos which has reigned so long, is converting into beautiful order, and reveals more and more clearly the glorious dispensation of civil and religious liberty, which are so inseparably united, that there is little or no enjoyment of one without the other: Otherwise, perhaps, the Israelites had been less solicitous for their freedom from Egyptian slavery; I do not say they would have been contented without it, by no means; for in every human breast God has implanted a principle, which we call love of freedom; it is impatient of oppression, and pants for deliverance; and by the leave of our modern Egyptians I will assert, that the same principle lives in us. God grant deliverance in his own way and time, and get him honour upon all those whose avarice impels them to countenance and help forward the calamities of their fellow creatures. This I desire not for their hurt, but to convince them of the strange absurdity of their conduct, whose words and actions are so diametrically opposite. How well the cry for liberty, and the reverse disposition for the exercise of oppressive power over others agree—I humbly think it does not require the penetration of a philosopher to determine."—

1774

Lemuel Haynes 1753–1833

A significant black writer of the late eighteenth and early nineteenth centuries, Lemuel Haynes engaged in a sustained elaboration of the issues of freedom and autonomy so central to African-American writing in his era. As a New Light minister—one of the few professions to which a black man in his social status might aspire—Haynes fully extended the meanings that evangelical Protestantism might have had to the blacks who so frequently absorbed it.

[1]First printed in the *Connecticut Gazette* for March 11, 1774, probably at the behest of the converted Mohegan Indian minister, the Reverend Samson Occom (1723–1792), the poet's longtime friend, who lived near New London where the *Gazette* was printed. This Wheatley letter was widely reprinted in almost a dozen other New England newspapers, of both Whig and Tory persuasions. The text above is from the printing in the *Newport (R.I.) Mercury* for April 11. This is Phillis Wheatley's strongest anti-slavery statement in print.

When it appeared on April 11, 1774, the letter had the following heading: "The following is an extract of a letter from Phillis, a Negro girl of Mr. Wheatley's, of this town; to the Rev. Samson Occom, dated the 11th of February, 1774."

Paradoxically Haynes's early life and intellectual experience is typical of that of his black contemporaries in the same way that his later life typifies the experiences of his white contemporaries of the conservative Calvinist Protestant ministry. Born July 18, 1753, in West Hartford, Connecticut, Haynes was raised by the evangelical family of David Rose in Middle Granville, Massachusetts. Although Haynes received cursory schooling, it appears that the bulk of his literary, theological, and spiritual instruction occurred within the Rose household. In this context, Haynes was immersed in the Bible as well as in the writings of Isaac Watts, Edward Young, and George Whitefield. In an era when few blacks achieved the literacy demanded for serious literary activity, Haynes developed extensive and informed intellectual interests.

Haynes was one of several African-Americans—including Jupiter Hammon and Phillis Wheatley—who generated the first significant body of African-American writing that emerged from the confluence of revivalist awakening discourse and the Whig rhetoric of the Revolution. He joined the Continental Army in 1775 and fought during the Revolutionary War. Not surprisingly, the Revolution seems to have provided the young Lemuel Haynes with opportunities for some of his first literary initiatives. One of his first verses, which celebrates a battle, was partially entitled "A Poem on the inhuman Tragedy perpetuated on the 19th of April 1778 by a Number of the British Troops under the Command of Thomas Gage." Shortly afterward, Haynes wrote a sustained attack on human bondage, which—borrowing from Revolutionary political formulations and Calvinist theology—called for the immediate emancipation of blacks.

After the Civil War, Haynes declined the chance for schooling at Dartmouth College in order to study classical languages under Daniel Farrand and William Bradford while working on the Rose farm. He was licensed to preach, and with the approval of local ministers, he accepted a proposal of marriage from a white woman, Elizabeth Babbitt, who eventually had ten children with him. Haynes served as a preacher in the Granville church for five years before the church applied for his ordination by the conservative New Light Association of Ministers in Litchfield County, Connecticut. After ordination, he continued preaching in Torrington, Vermont, where he had supplied the pulpit since 1784. He preached there until he received a call from the West Parish of Rutland, Vermont, which provided him with his longest pulpit stay, from 1778 to 1818. He then preached in Manchester, Vermont, for four years, and finally in Granville, New York, for eleven years (until shortly before his death).

Haynes's adult life was atypical of many of his black contemporaries. At Rutland alone, he wrote 5,500 sermons, of which 400 were funeral sermons. In another sense, however, Haynes was very much a typical New Light evangelical Calvinist preacher. The social composition of the ministry changed in the late eighteenth century as a large number of lower- and middle-class men (many of them from rural families) entered the pastorate and got caught up in the revivalism of the period. Once in the profession, they faced difficult parish lives. The number of church separations increased sharply during this turbulent period as a result of theological and ecclesiastical divisions and geographical displacement from communal centers in eastern cities. Ministers often had short-lived pastorates and frequently found themselves preaching beyond the "frontiers" of New England. Within this context, Haynes's ministry was altogether typical. He took over the pastorship of a separate congregation in the Torrington church, one that rejected the Half-Way covenant. The church in West Rutland, Vermont, where he was a successful revivalist, was also a New Light congregation that rejected the the Half-Way measures.

Haynes's commitment to the New Light principles, which led him to like-minded congregations and the frontier, decisively shaped his preaching. One sees not only New Light but also traditional New Divinity theological stances taken in his sermons on divine decrees, a voluntarist psychology locating sinfulness purely in the will and insisting at once upon natural ability and moral inability. Although Haynes's preaching was doctrinally grounded, it drew upon his own idiosyncratic system of New Light and New Divinity principles to create a powerful rhetoric that stressed the sinner's absolute voluntary resistance to godliness and correct doctrine as well as his or her obligation to transform immediately. This rhetoric formed the core of a revivalist message that stressed natural liberty, moral inability, and the obligation of immediate repentance. Significantly, these theological principles led him to a commitment with New Light ministerial groups as well as to involvement in a Federalism that was quite traditional for New Light and New Divinity ministers in the early nineteenth century.

Within the context of Haynes's theological discourse, we see a full elaboration of the isolated elements of Calvinism found in earlier writers such as Wheatley, Hammon, and Equiano. Most important to this elaboration is that liberty is essential for man's spiritual being to realize his moral and spiritual obligations. In other words, the moral obligations defined by Edwardsean theology implied moral right. Haynes's early commitment to Edwardsean theology, traditional Calvinism, and anti-slavery principles in his earliest writing "Liberty Further Extended" was an important point of departure for an altogether typical New Light career. And, in this sense, the much more famous discourse, "Universal Salvation" that provocatively links the doctrine of universalism with the devil's assault upon godliness is part of a sustained characterization of the sinful will, a characterization that shapes much of Haynes's preaching. This career, with its careful elaboration of principle, suggests the nexus of thought that grounded the evangelical Protestant and libertarian principles of early black writers in the late eighteenth and the early nineteenth century.

Phillip M. Richards
Colgate University

PRIMARY WORK

Black Preacher to White America: The Collected Writings of Lemuel Haynes, 1774–1833, ed. Richard Newman, 1990.

SECONDARY WORKS

Timothy Mather Cooley, *Sketches of the Life and Character of the Rev. Lemuel Haynes, A.M., for Many Years Pastor of a Church in Rutland, Vt., and Late in Granville, New York . . . ,* 1837; Richard Newman, ed., *Black Preacher to White America: The Collected Writings of Lemuel Haynes, 1774–1833,* 1990.

Liberty Further Extended: Or Free Thoughts on the Illegality of Slave-keeping[1]

We hold these truths to be self-Evident, that all men are created Equal, that they are Endowed By their Creator with Ceartain unalienable rights, that among these are Life, Liberty, and the pursuit of happyness.

Congress

The Preface. As *Tyrony* had its Origin from the infernal regions: so it is the Deuty, and honner of Every son of freedom to repel her first motions. But while we are Engaged in the important struggle, it cannot Be tho't impertinent for us to turn one Eye into our own Breast, for a little moment, and See, whether thro' some inadvertency, or a self-contracted Spirit, we Do not find the monster Lurking in our own Bosom; that now while we are inspir'd with so noble a Spirit and Becoming Zeal, we may Be Disposed to tear her from us. If the following would produce such an Effect the auther should rejoice.

It is Evident, by ocular demonstration, that man by his Depravety, hath procured many Courupt habits which are detrimental to society; And altho' there is a way pre[s]crib'd Whereby man may be re-instated into the favour of god, yet these courupt habits are Not Extirpated, nor can the subject of renovation Bost of perfection, 'till he Leaps into a state of immortal Existance. yet it hath pleas'd the majesty of Heaven to Exhibet his will to men, and Endow them With an intulect Which is susceptible of speculation; yet, as I observ'd before, man, in consequence of the fall is Liable to digressions. But to proceed,

Liberty, & freedom, is an innate principle, which is unmovebly placed in the human Species; and to see a man aspire after it, is not Enigmatical, seeing he acts no ways incompatible with his own Nature; consequently, he that would infring upon a mans Liberty may reasonably Expect to meet with oposision, seeing the Defendant cannot Comply to Non-resistance, unless he Counter-acts the very Laws of nature.

Liberty is a Jewel which was handed Down to man from the cabinet of heaven, and is Coaeval with his Existance. And as it proceed from the Supreme Legislature of the univers, so it is he which hath a sole right to take away; therefore, he that would take away a mans Liberty assumes a prerogative that Belongs to another, and acts out of his own domain.

One man may bost a superorety above another in point of Natural previledg; yet if he can produse no convincive arguments in vindication of this preheminence his hypothesis is to Be Suspected. To affirm, that an Englishman has a right to his

[1]The full title of the text in manuscript reads: "Liberty Further Extended: Or Free thoughts on the illegality of Slave-keeping; Wherein those arguments that Are useed in its vindication Are plainly confuted. Together with an humble Address to such as are Concearned in the practise. By Lemuel Haynes."

This manuscript was first published in 1983, in *The William and Mary Quarterly.* We reproduce here the text as it was printed in *Black Preacher to White America,* ed. Richard Newman, 1990. Newman preserved all original spellings, structure, and punctuation.

Liberty, is a truth which has Been so clearly Evinced, Especially of Late, that to spend time in illustrating this, would be But Superfluous tautology. But I query, whether Liberty is so contracted a principle as to be Confin'd to any nation under Heaven; nay, I think it not hyperbolical to affirm, that Even an affrican, has Equally as good a right to his Liberty in common with Englishmen.

I know that those that are concerned in the Slave-trade, Do pretend to Bring arguments in vindication of their practise; yet if we give them a candid Examination, we shall find them (Even those of the most cogent kind) to be Essencially Deficient. We live in a day wherein *Liberty* & *freedom* is the subject of many millions Concern; and the important Struggle hath alread caused great Effusion of Blood; men seem to manifest the most sanguine resolution not to Let their natural rights go without their Lives go with them; a resolution, one would think Every one that has the Least Love to his country, or futer posterity, would fully confide in, yet while we are so zelous to maintain, and foster our own invaded rights, it cannot be tho't impertinent for us Candidly to reflect on our own conduct, and I doubt not But that we shall find that subsisting in the midst of us, that may with propriety be stiled *Opression,* nay, much greater opression, than that which Englishmen seem so much to spurn at. I mean an oppression which they, themselves, impose upon others.

It is not my Business to Enquire into Every particular practise, that is practised in this Land, that may come under this Odeus Character; But, what I have in view, is humbly to offer som free thoughts, on the practise of *Slave-keeping.* Opression, is not spoken of, nor ranked in the sacred oracles, among the Least of those sins, that are the procureing Caus of those signal Judgments, which god is pleas'd to bring upon the Children of men. Therefore let us attend. I mean to white [write] with freedom, yet with the greatest Submission.

And the main proposition, which I intend for some Breif illustration is this, Namely, That an *African,* or, in other terms, *that a Negro may Justly Chalenge, and has an undeniable right to his* ["freed(om)" is blotted out] *Liberty: Consequently, the practise of Slave-keeping, which so much abounds in this Land is illicit.*

Every privilege that mankind Enjoy have their Origen from god; and whatever acts are passed in any Earthly Court, which are Derogatory to those Edicts that are passed in the Court of Heaven, the act is *void.* If I have a perticular previledg granted to me by god, and the act is not revoked nor the power that granted the benefit vacated, (as it is imposable but that god should Ever remain immutable) then he that would infringe upon my Benifit, assumes an unreasonable, and tyrannic power.

It hath pleased god to *make of one Blood all nations of men, for to dwell upon the face of the Earth.* Acts 17, 26. And as all are of one Species, so there are the same Laws, and aspiring principles placed in all nations; and the Effect that these Laws will produce, are Similar to Each other. Consequently we may suppose, that what is precious to one man, is precious to another, and what is irksom, or intolarable to one man, is so to another, consider'd in a Law of Nature. Therefore we may reasonably Conclude, that Liberty is Equally as pre[c]ious to a *Black man,* as it is to a *white one,* and Bondage Equally as intollarable to the one as it is to the other: Seeing it Effects the Laws of nature Equally as much in the one as it Does in the other. But, as I observed Before, those privileges that are granted to us By the Divine Being, no one has the Least right to take them from us without our consen[t]; and there is Not the Least precept, or practise, in the Sacred Scriptures, that constitutes a Black man a Slave, any more than a white one.

Shall a mans Couler Be the Decisive Criterion whereby to Judg of his natural right? or Becaus a man is not of the same couler with his Neighbour, shall he Be Deprived of those things that Distuingsheth [Distinguisheth] him from the Beasts of the field?

I would ask, whence is it that an Englishman is so far Distinguished from an African in point of Natural privilege? Did he recieve it in his origenal constitution? or By Some Subsequent grant? Or Does he Bost of some hygher Descent that gives him this pre-heminance? for my part I can find no such revelation. It is a Lamantable consequence of the fall, that mankind, have an insatiable thurst after Superorety one over another: So that however common or prevalent the practise may be, it Does not amount, Even to a Surcomstance, that the practise is warrentable.

God has been pleas'd to distiungs [distinguish] some men from others, as to natural abilitys, But not as to natural *right,* as they came out of his hands.

But sometimes men by their flagitious practise forfeit their Liberty into the hands of men, By Becomeing unfit for society; But have the *affricans* Ever as a Nation, forfited their Liberty in this manner? What Ever individuals have done; yet, I Believe, no such Chaleng can be made upon them, as a Body. As there should be Some rule whereby to govern the conduct of men; so it is the Deuty, and intrest of a community, to form a system of *Law,* that is calculated to promote the commercial intrest of Each other: and so Long as it produses so Blessed an Effect, it should be maintained. But when, instead of contributing to the well Being of the community, it proves bancfull to its subjects over whome it Extends, then it is hygh time to call it in question. Should any ask, where shall we find any system of Law whereby to regulate our moral Conduct? I think their is none so Explicit and indeffinite, as that which was given By the Blessed Saviour of the world. *As you would that men should do unto you, do you Even so to them.* One would think, that the mention of the precept, would strike conviction to the heart of these Slavetraders; unless an aviricious Disposision, governs the Laws of humanity.

If we strictly adhear to the rule, we shall not impose anything upon Others, But what we should Be willing should Be imposed upon us were we in their Condision.

I shall now go on to consider the manner in which the Slave-trade is carried on, By which it will plainly appear, that the practise is vile and atrocious, as well as the most inhuman. it is undoubtedly true that those that Emigrate slaves from *Africa* Do Endevour to rais mutanies among them in order to procure slaves. here I would make some Extracts from a pamphlet printed in Philadelphia, a few years ago: the varacity of which need not be scrupled, seeing it agrees with many other accounts.

N. *Brue,* Directory of the *French* factory at *Senegal,* who Lived twenty-seven years in that country says, "that the *Europeans* are far from desiring to act as peacemakers among the *Negros,* which would Be acting contrary to their intrest, since the greater the wars, the more slaves are procured." *William Boseman,* factor for the Duch at *Delmina,* where he resided sixteen years, relates, "that one of the former Comma[n]ders hired an army of the Negros, of *Jefferia,* and *Cabesteria,* for a Large Sum of money, to fight the Negros of *Commanry* [?], which occasioned a Battle, which was more Bloody than the wars of the Negros usually are: And that another Commander gave at one time five *hundred* pounds, and at another time Eight hundred pounds, to two other Negro nations, to induce them to take up arms against their Country people." This is confirmed by *Barbot,* agent general of the french African company, who says, "The *Hollanders,* a people very zelous for their

Commerce at the Coasts, were very studious to have the war carried on amongst the Blacks, to distract, as Long as possible, the trade of the other Europeans and to that Effect, were very ready to assist upon all occasions, the Blacks, their allies, that they mite Beat their Enemies, and so the Commerce fall into their hands." And one *William Smith,* who was sent By the *African* company, to visit their settlements in the year 1726, from the information he reciev'd from one, who had resided ten years, viz. "that the Discerning Natives accounted it their greatest unhappyness that they were Ever visited by the *Europeans*:—that we Christians introduced the traffick of Slaves, and that Before our comeing they Lived in peace; But, say they, it is observable, that Wherever Christianity comes, there comes with it a Sword, a gun, powder, and Ball." And thus it Brings ignominy upon our holy religion, and mak[e]s the Name of Christians sound Odious in the Ears of the heathen. O Christianity, how art thou Disgraced, how art thou reproached, By the vicious practises of those upon whome thou dost smile! Let us go on to consider the great hardships, and sufferings, those Slaves are put to, in order to be transported into these plantations. There are generally many hundred slaves put on board a vessel, and they are Shackkled together, two by two, wors than Crimanals going to the place of Execution; and they are Crouded together as close as posable, and almost naked; and their sufferings are so great, as I have Been Credibly informed, that it often Carries off one third of them on their passage; yea, many have put an End to their own Lives for very anguish; And as some have manifested a Disposision to rise in their Defence, they have Been put to the most Cruel torters, and Deaths as human art could inflict. And O! the Sorrows, the Greif the Distress, and anguish which attends them! and not onely them But their frinds also in their Own Country, when they must forever part with Each Other? What must be the plaintive noats that the tend[er] parents must assume for the Loss of their Exiled *Child*? Or the husband for his Departed wife? and how Do the Crys of their Departed friends Eccho from the watry Deep! Do not I really hear the fond mother Expressing her Sorrows, in accents that mite well peirce the most obdurate heart? "O! my Child, why why was thy Destiny hung on so precarious a theread! unhappy fate! O that I were a captive with thee or for thee! [About seventy-five words are crossed out and utterly illegible. The mother's words continue:] Cursed Be the Day wherein I Bare thee, and Let that inauspicious Night be remembered no more. Come, O King of terrors. Dissipate my greif, and send my woes into oblivion."

But I need Not stand painting the Dreery Sene. Let me rather appeal to tender parents, whether this is Exaggarating matters? Let me ask them what would be their Distress. Should one of their Dearest *Children* Be snach'd from them, in a Clendestine manner, and carried to *Africa,* or some othe forreign Land, to be under the most abject Slavery for Life, among a strang people? would it not imbitter all your Domestic Comforts? would he not Be Ever upon your mind? nay, Doth not nature Even recoil at the reflection?

And is not their many ready to say, (unless void of natural Effections) that it would not fail to Bring them Down with sorrow to the grave? And surely, this has Been the awfull fate of some of those *Negros* that have been Brought into these plantations; which is not to be wondered at, unless we suppose them to be without natural Effections: which is to rank them Below the very Beasts of the field.

O! what an Emens Deal of Affrican-Blood hath Been Shed by the inhuman Cruelty of Englishmen! that reside in a Christian Land! Both at home, and in their own

Country? they being the fomenters of those wars, that is absolutely necessary, in order to carry on this cursed trade; and in their Emigration into these colonys? and By their merciless masters, in some parts at Least? O ye that have made yourselves Drunk with human Blood! altho' you may go with impunity here in this Life, yet God will hear the Crys of that innocent Blood, which crys from the Sea, and from the ground against you, Like the Blood of Abel, more pealfull [?] than thunder, *vengence! vengence!* What will you Do in that Day when God shall make inquisision for Blood? he will make you Drink the phials of his indignation which Like a potable Stream shall Be poured out without the Least mixture of mercy; Believe it, Sirs, their shall not a Drop of Blood, which you have Spilt unjustly, Be Lost in forgetfullness. But it Shall Bleed affresh, and testify against you, in the Day when God shall Deal with Sinners.

We know that under the Levitical Oeconomy, *man-stealing* was to Be punished with Death; so [?] we Esteem those that Steal any of our Earthy Commadety gilty of a very heinous Crime:

What then must Be an adiquate punishment to Be inflicted on those that Seal [steal] men?

Men were made for more noble Ends than to be Drove to market, like Sheep and oxen. "Our being Christians, (says one) Does not give us the Least Liberty to trample on heathen, nor Does it give us the Least Superiority over them." And not only are they gilty of *man-stealing* that are the immediate actors in this trade, But those in these colonys that Buy them at their hands, ar far from Being guiltless: for when they saw the theif they consented with him. if men would forbear to Buy Slaves off the hands of the Slave-merchants, then the trade would of necessaty cease; if I buy a man, whether I am told he was stole, or not, yet I have no right to Enslave him, Because he is a human Being: and the immutable Laws of God, and indefeasible Laws of nature, pronounced him free.

Is it not exceeding strang that mankind should Become such mere vassals to their own carnal avarice as Even to imbrue their hands in inocent Blood? and to Bring such intollerable opressiones upon others, that were they themselves to feel them, perhaps they would Esteem Death preferable—pray consider the miserys of a Slave, Being under the absolute controul of another, subject to continual Embarisments, fatiuges, and corections at the will of a master; it is as much impossable for us to bring a man heartely to acquiesce in a passive obedience in this case, as it would be to stop a man's Breath, and yet have it caus no convulsion in nature. those negros amongst us that have Children, they, viz. their *Children* are brought up under a partial Disapilne: their white masters haveing but Little, or no Effection for them. So that we may suppose, that the abuses that they recieve from the hands of their masters are often very considerable; their parents Being placed in such a Situation as not being able to perform relative Deutys. Such are those restrictions they are kept under By their task-masters that they are render'd incapable of performing those moral Deutys Either to God or man that are infinitely binding on all the human race; how often are they Seperated from Each other, here in this Land at many hundred miles Distance, Children from parents, and parents from Children, Husbands from wives, and wives from Husbands? those whom God hath Joined together, and pronounced one flesh, man assumes a prerogative to put asunder. What can be more abject than their condission? in short, if I may so speak 'tis a hell upon Earth; and all this for filthy Lucres sake: Be astonished, O ye Heavens, at this! I believe it would Be much Better for these Colonys if their was never a Slave Brought into this Land; theirby our poor are put to great Extremitys, by reason of the plentifullness of Labour, which otherwise would fall into their hands.

I shall now go on to take under Consideration some of those *arguments* which those that are Concern'd in the Slave-trade Do use in vindication of their practise; which arguments, I shall Endevour to Shew, are Lame, and Defective.

The first argument that I shall take notice of is this viz. *that in all probability the Negros are of Canaans posterity, which ware Destined by the almighty to Slavery; theirfore the practise is warrantable.* To which I answer, Whethear the Negros are of Canaans posterity or not, perhaps is not known By any mortal under Heaven. But allowing they were actually of Canaans posterity, yet we have no reason to think that this Curs Lasted any Longer than the comeing of Christ: when that Sun of riteousness arose this wall of partition was Broken Down. Under the *Law,* their were many External Cerimonies that were tipecal of Spiritual things; or which Shadowed forth the purity, & perfection of the Gospel: as Corporeal *blemishes,* Spurious *Birth,* flagicious *practises,* debar'd them from the congregation of the Lord: theirby Shewing, the intrinsick purity of heart that a Conceal'd Gospel requir'd as the pre-requisite for heaven, and as *Ham* uncovered his fathers nakedness, that is, Did not Endevour to Conceal it, but gaz'd perhaps with a Lascivious Eye, which was repugnant to the Law which was afterwards given to the Children of Isarel [Israel]: So it was most [?] Necessary that god Should manifest his Signal Disapprobation of this hainous Sin, By makeing him and his posterity a publick Example to the world, that theirby they mite be set apart, and Seperated from the people of God as unclean. And we find it was a previlege Granted to God's people of old, that they mite Enslave the *heathen, and the Stranger that were in the Land*; theirby to Shew the Superior previleges God's people Enjoy'd above the rest of the world: So that we, Gentiles were then Subject to Slavery, Being then heathen; [illegible] So that if they will keep Close to the Letter they must own themselves yet Subject to the yoak; unless we Suppose them *free* By Being Brought into the same place, or haveing the same previleges with the Jews; then it follows, that we may inslave all Nations, be they White or Black, that are heathens, which they themselves will not allow. We find, under that Dispensation, God Declareing that he would *visit the iniquity of the fathers upon the Children, unto the third, and fourth generation, &c.* And we find it so in the case of *Ham,* as well as many others; their posterity Being Extrinsically unclean.

But now our glorious hygh preist hath visably appear'd in the flesh, and hath Establish'd a more glorious Oeconomy. he hath not only visably Broken Down that wall of partision that interposed Between the ofended majesty of Heaven and rebellious Sinners and removed those tedeous forms under the Law, which savoured so much of servitude, and which *could never make the comers thereunto perfect,* By rendering them obselete: But he has removed those many Embarisments, and Distinctions, that they were incident to, under so contracted a Dispensation. So that whatever *Bodily imperfections,* or whatever *Birth* we sustain, it Does not in the Least Debar us from Gospel previlege's. Or whatever hainous practise any may be gilty of, yet if they manifest a gospel [?] repentance, we have no right to Debar them from our Communion. and it is plain Beyond all Doubt, that at the comeing of Christ, this curse that was upon *Canaan,* was taken off; and I think there is not the Least force in this argument than there would Be to argue that an imperfect Contexture of *parts,* or Base *Birth,* Should Deprive any from Gospel previleges; or Bring up any of those antiquated Ceremonies from oblivion, and reduse them into practise.

But you will say that Slave-keeping was practised Even under the Gospel, for we find *paul,* and the other apostles Exhorting *Servants to be obedient to their masters.* to which I reply, that it mite be they were Speaking to Servants in *minority* in General; But Doubtless it was practised in the Days of the Apostles from what *St. paul* Says, *1. Corin. 7 21. art thou called, being a servant? care not for it; but if thou mayest Be made free, use it rather.* So that the Apostle seems to recommend freedom if attainable, q.d. "if it is thy unhappy Lot to be a slave, yet if thou art Spiritually free Let the former appear so minute a thing when compared with the Latter that it is comparitively unworthy of notice; yet Since freedom is so Exelent a Jewel, which none have a right to Extirpate, and if there is any hope of attaining it, use all Lawfull measures for that purpose." So that however Extant or preval[e]nt it mite Be in that or this age; yet it does not in the Least reverse the unchangeable Laws of God, or of nature; or make that Become Lawfull which is in itself unlawfull; neither is it Strange, if we consider the moral Depravity of mans nature, thro'out all ages of the world, that mankind should Deviate from the unering rules of Heaven. But again, another argument which some use to maintain their intollerable opression upon others is this, viz., *that those Negros that are Brought into these plantations are Generally prisoners, taken in their wars, and would otherwise fall a sacrifice to the resentment of their own people.* But this argument, I think, is plainly confuted By the forecited account which Mr. *Boasman* gives, as well as many others. Again, some say they *Came honestly By their Slaves, Becaus they Bought them of their parents,* (that is, those that Brought them from Africa) *and rewarded them well for them.* But without Doubt this is, for the most part fals; But allowing they Did actually Buy them of their parents, yet I query, whether parents have any right to sel their Children for Slaves: if parents have a right to Be free, then it follows that their Children have Equally as good a right to their freedom, Even *Hereditary.* So, (to use the words of a Learned writer) "one has no Body to Blame But himself, in case he shall find himself Deprived of a man whome he tho't By Buying for a price he had made his own; for he Dealt in a trade which was illicit, and was prohibited by the most obvious Dictates of Humanity. for these resons Every one of those unfortunate men who are pretended to be Slaves, has a right to Be Declared free, for he never Lost his Liberty; he could not Lose it; his prince had no power to Dispose of him. of cours the Sale was *ipso Jure* void."

But I shall take notice of one argument more which these Slave-traders use, and it is this, viz. *that those Negros that are Emigrated into these colonies are brought out of a Land of Darkness under the meridian Light of the Gospel; and so it is a great Blessing instead of a Curs.* But I would ask, who is this that Darkneth counsel By words with out knoledg? Let us attend to the great appostle Speaking to us in *Rom. 3.8.* where he reproves some slanderers who told it as a maxim preached By the apostles that they said *Let us Do Evil that Good may come, whose Damnation* the inspired penman pronounces with an Emphasis *to Be Just.* And again *Chap.* 6 vers 1. where By way of interagation he asks, *Shall we continue in Sin that grace may abound?* The answer is obvious, *God forbid.* But that those Slavemerchants that trade upon the coasts of Africa do not aim at the Spiritual good of their Slaves, is Evident By their Behaviour towards them; if they had their Spiritual good at heart, we should Expect that those Slave-merchants that trade upon their coasts, would, insted of Causing quarrelings, and Blood-Shed among them, which is repugnant to Christianity, and below the Character of humanity, Be Sollicitous to Demean Exampleary among them, that By their wholesom conduct, those heathen mite be Enduced to Entertain hygh, and admiring tho'ts of our holy religion. Those Slaves in these Colonies are generally kept under the greatest ignorance, and Blindness, and they are scersly Ever told by their white masters whether there is a Supreme Being that governs the univers; or wheather there is any reward, or punishments Beyond the grave. Nay such are those restrictions that they are kept under that they Scersly know that they have a right to Be free, or if they Do they are not allowed to Speak in their defence; Such is their abject condission, that that *genius* that is peculiar to the human race, cannot have that Cultivation that the polite world is favour'd with, and therefore they are stiled the ignorant part of the world; whereas were they under the Same advantages to git knoledge with them, perhaps their progress in arts would not be inferior.

But should we give ourselves the trouble to Enquire into the grand motive that indulges men to concearn themselves in a trade So vile and abandon, we Shall find it to Be this, Namely, to Stimulate their Carnal avarice, and to maintain men in pride, Luxury, and idleness, and how much it hath Subserv'd to this vile purpose I Leave the Candid publick to Judge: I speak it with reverence yet I think all must give in that it hath such a tendency.

But altho god is of Long patience, yet it does not Last always, nay, he has *whet* his *glittering Sword, and his hand hath already taken hold on Judgement;* for who knows how far that the unjust Oppression which hath abounded in this Land, may be the procuring cause of this very Judgement that now impends, which so much portends *Slavery*?

for this is God's way of working, Often he brings the Same Judgements, or Evils upon men, as they unriteously Bring upon others. As is plain from *Judges* 1 and on.

But Adoni-bezek fled, and they persued after him, and caut him, and cut off his thumbs, and his great toes.

And Adoni-besek said, threescore and ten kings haveing their thumbs and their great toes cut off gathered their meat under my table: as I have Done, So god hath requited me.

And as wicked *Ahab,* and *Jezebel* to gratify their covetousness caused *Naboth* to be put to Death, and as *Dogs* licked the Blood of *Naboth,* the word of the Lord was By the prophet *Elijah, thus Saith the Lord, in the place where Dogs Licked the Blood of Naboth, Shall Dogs Lick thy Blood Even thine. See 1 Kings 21. 19. And of Jezebel also Spake the Lord, Saying, The Dogs Shall Eat Jezebel By the walls of Jezreel. vers 23.*

And we find the Judgement actually accomplished upon *Ahab* in the 22. Chap. & 38. vers.

And upon *Jezebel* in the 9 chap. 2 of *Kings.*

Again *Rev. 16.6. for they have Shed the Blood of Saints and prophets, and thou hast given them Blood to Drink; for they are worthy.* And *chap.* 18.6. *Reward her Even as She rewarded you.* I say this is often God's way of Dealing, by retaliating Back upon men the Same Evils that they unjustly Bring upon others. I Don't Say that we have reason to think that *Oppression* is the alone caus of this Judgement that God is pleas'd to Bring upon this Land, Nay, But we have the greatest reason to think that this is not one of the Least. And whatever some may think that I am instigated By a fals zeal; and all that I have Said upon the Subject is mere Novelty: yet I am not afraid to appeal to the consience of any rational and honnest man, as to the truth of what I have just hinted at; and if any will not confide in what I have humbly offer'd, I am persuaded it must be such Short-Sited persons whose Contracted Eyes never penitrate thro' the narrow confines of Self, and are mere Vassals to filthy Lucre.

But I Cannot persuade myself to make a period to this Small *Treatise,* without humbly addressing myself, more perticularly, unto all such as are Concearn'd in the practise of *Slave-keeping.*

Sirs, Should I persue the Dictates of nature, resulting from a sense of my own inability, I should be far from attempting to form this address: Nevertheless, I think that a mere Superficial reflection upon the merits of the Cause, may Serve as an ample apology, for this humble attempt. Therefore hopeing you will take it well at my hands, I persume, (tho' with the greatest Submission) to Crave your attention, while I offer you a few words.

Perhaps you will think the preceeding pages unworthy of Speculation: well, Let that be as it will; I would Sollicit you Seriously to reflect on your conduct, wheather you are not gilty of unjust Oppression. Can you wash your hands, and say, I am Clean from this Sin? Perhaps you will Dare to Say it Before men; But Dare you Say it Before the tremendous tribunal of that God Before Whome we must all, in a few precarious moments appear? then whatever fair glosses we may have put upon our Conduct, that god whose Eyes pervade the utmost Extent of human tho't, and Surveys with one intuitive view, the affairs of men; he will Examin into the matter himself, and will set Every thing upon its own Basis; and impartiallity Shall Be Seen flourishing throughout that Sollemn assembly. Alas! Shall men hazard their precious Souls for a little of the transetory things of time. O *Sirs!* Let that pity, and compassion, which is peculiar to mankind, Especially to Englishmen, no Longer Lie Dormant in your Breast: Let it run free thro' Disinterested Benevolence. then how would these iron yoaks Spontaneously fall from the gauled Necks of the oppress'd! And that Disparity, in point of Natural previlege, which is the Bane of Society, would Be Cast upon the utmost coasts of Oblivion. If this was the impulsive Exercise that animated all your actions, your Conscience's wold Be the onely Standard unto which I need appeal. think it nor uncharitable, nor Censorious to say, that whenever we Erect our Battery, so as it is Like to prove a Detriment to the intrest of any, we Loos their attention. or, if we Don't Entirely Loos that, yet if true Christian candour is wanting we cannot Be in a Sutiable frame for Speculation: So that the good Effect that these Otherwise mite have, will prove abortive. If I could once persuade you to reflect upon the matter with a Single, and an impartial Eye, I am almost assured that no more need to be Said upon the Subject: But whether I shall Be so happy as to persuade you to Cherish such an Exercise I know not: yet I think it is very obvious from what I have humbly offer'd, that so far forth as you have Been Concerned in the *Slave-trade,* so far it is that you have assumed an oppressive, and tyrannic power. Therefore is it not hygh time to undo these heavy Burdens, and Let the Oppressed go free? And while you manifest such a noble and magnanimous Spirit, to maintain inviobly your own Natural rights, and militate so much against Despotism, as it hath respect unto yourselves, you do not assume the Same usurpations, and are no Less tyrannic. Pray let there be a congruity amidst you Conduct, Least you fall amongst that Class the inspir'd pen-man Speaks of. *Rom.* 2.21 and on. *thou therefore which teacheth another, teachest thou not thy Self? thou that preachest a man Should not Steal, Dost thou Steal? thou that sayest, a man Should not Commit adultery, Dost thou Commit adultery? thou that abhoreth idols, Dost thou Commit Sacrilege? thou that makest thy Bost of the Law, through Breaking the Law Dishonnerest thou God?* While you thus Sway your tyrant Scepter over others, you have nothing to Expect But to Share in the Bitter pill. 'Twas an Exelent note that I Lately read in a modern peice, and it was this. "O when shall America be consistantly Engaged in the Cause of Liberty!" If you have any Love to yourselves, or any Love to this Land, if you have any Love to your fellow-men, Break these intollerable yoaks, and Let their names Be remembered no more, Least they Be retorted on your own necks, and you Sink under them; for god will not hold you guiltless.

Sirs, the important Caus in which you are Engag'd in is of a[n] Exelent nature, 'tis ornamental to your Characters, and will, undoubtedly, immortalize your names thro' the Latest posterity. And it is pleasing to Behold that patriottick Zeal which fire's your Breast; But it is Strange that you Should want the Least Stimulation to further Expressions of so noble a Spirit. Some gentlemen have Determined to Contend in a Consistant manner: they have *Let the oppressed go free;* and I cannot think it is for the want of such a generous princaple in you, But thro' some inadvertancy that [end of extant manuscript].

1990

Universal Salvation[1]

Preface

There is no greater folly than for men to express anger and resentment because their religious sentiments are attacked. If their characters are impeached by their own creed, they only are to blame.

All that the antagonists can say, cannot make falsehood truth, nor truth, falsehood. The following discourse was delivered at Rutland, Vt., June, 1805, immediately after hearing Mr. Ballou, an Universal Preacher, zealously exhibit his sentiments. The author had been repeatedly solicited to hear and dispute with the above Preacher: and had been charged with dishonesty and cowardice for refusing. He felt that some kind of testimony, in opposition to what he calls error, ought to be made; and has been urged to let the same appear in print. But whether, on the whole, it is for the interest of truth, is left to the judgment of the candid.

[1]The original title of Hayne's most famous sermon is: "Universal Salvation: A Very Ancient Doctrine; With Some Account of the Life and Character of Its Author. A Sermon. Delivered at Rutland, West Parish, in the Year 1805." It is reprinted from *Black Preacher in White America,* ed. Richard Newman; the copy was taken directly from the manuscript held by the Schomberg Center for Research in Black Culture.

A Sermon

Genesis 3, 4, And the serpent said unto the woman, ye shall not surely die.

The holy scriptures are a peculiar fund of instruction. They inform us of the origin of creation; of the primitive state of man; of his fall, or apostacy from God. It appears that he was placed in the garden of Eden, with full liberty to regale himself with all the delicious fruits that were to be found, except what grew on one tree—if he eat of that, that he should surely die, was the declaration of the Most High.

Happy were the human pair amidst this delightful Paradise, until a certain preacher, in his journey, came that way, and disturbed their peace and tranquility, by endeavoring to reverse the prohibition of the Almighty; as in our text, ye shall not surely dic.

> She pluck'd, she ate,
> Earth felt the wound; nature from her seat,
> Sighing through all her works, gave signs of woe,
> That all was lost.
>
> MILTON

We may attend,—To the character of the preacher; to the doctrines inculcated; to the hearer addressed; to the medium or instrument of the preaching.

I. As to the preacher, I shall observe, he has many names given him in the sacred writings; the most common is the devil. That it was he that disturbed the felicity of our first parents, is evident from 2 Cor. 11:3, and many other passages of Scripture. He was once an angel of light and knew better than to preach such doctrine; he did violence to his own reason.—But to be a little more particular, let it be observed:

1. He is an old preacher. He lived above one thousand seven hundred years before Abraham; above two thousand four hundred and thirty years before Moses; four thousand and four years before Christ. It is now five thousand eight hundred and nine years since he commenced preaching. By this time he must have acquired great skill in the art.

2. He is a very cunning, artful preacher. When Elymas the sorcerer, came to turn away people from the faith, he is said to be full of all subtlety, and a child of the devil, not only because he was an enemy to all righteousness, but on account of his carnal cunning and craftiness.

3. He is a very laborious, unweried preacher. He has been in the ministry almost six thousand years; and yet his zeal has not in the least abated. The apostle Peter compares him to a roaring lion, walking about seeking whom he may devour. When God inquired of this persevering preacher, Job 2:2, From whence camest thou? He answered the Lord, and said, From going to and fro in the earth, and from walking up and down in it. He is far from being circumscribed within the narrow limits of parish, state, or continental lines; but his haunt and travel is very large and extensive.

4. He is a heterogeneous preacher, if I may so express myself. He makes use of a Bible when he holds forth, as in his sermon to our Saviour; Matt. 4:6. He mixes truth with error, in order to make it go well, or to carry his point.

5. He is a very presumptuous preacher. Notwithstanding God had declared, in the most plain and positive terms, Thou shalt surely die, or In dying, thou shalt die,

yet this audacious wretch had the impudence to confront omnipotence, and says ye shall not surely die!

6. He is a very successful preacher. He draws a great number after him. No preacher can command hearers like him. He was successful with our first parents, with the old world. Noah once preached to those spirits who are now in the prison of hell; and told them from God, that they should surely die; but this preacher came along and declared the contrary, ye shall not surely die. The greater part it seems believed him and went to destruction. So it was with Sodom and Gomorrah. Lot preached to them; the substance of which was, up, get ye out of this place, for the Lord will destroy this city. Gen. 19:14. But this old declaimer told them, no danger, no danger, ye shall not surely die. To which they generally gave heed, and Lot seemed to them as one who mocked; they believed the universal preacher, and were consumed. Agreeably to the declaration of the apostle Jude, Sodom and Gomorrah and the cities about them, suffering the vengeance of eternal fire.

II. Let us attend to the doctrine inculcated by this preacher; ye shall not surely die. Bold assertion! without a single argument to support it. The death contained in the threatening was doubtless eternal death,—as nothing but this would express God's feelings towards sin, or render an infinite atonement necessary. To suppose it to be spiritual death, is to blend crime and punishment together; to suppose temporal death to be the curse of the law, then believers are not delivered from it, according to Gal. 3:13. What Satan meant to preach, was that there is no hell, and that the wages of sin is not death, but eternal life.

III. We shall now take notice of the hearer addressed by the preacher. This we have in the text, And the serpent said unto the woman, etc. That Eve had not so much experience as Adam, is evident; and so was not equally able to withstand temptation. This doubtless was the reason why the devil chose her, with whom he might hope to be successful. Doubtless he took a time when she was separated from her husband.

That this preacher has had the greatest success in the dark and ignorant parts of the earth, is evident: his kingdom is a kingdom of darkness. He is a great enemy to light. St. Paul gives us some account of him in his day, 2 Tim. 3:6. For of this sort are they which creep into houses, and lead captive silly women, laden with sin led away with divers lusts. The same apostle observes, Rom. 16:17, 18. Now I beseech you, brethren, mark them which cause divisions and offences, contrary to the doctrine which ye have learned, and avoid them. For they that are such serve not the Lord Jesus Christ, but their own belly; and by good words and fair speeches deceive the simple.

IV. The instrument or medium made use of by the preacher will now be considered. This we have in the text: And the serpent said etc. But how came the devil to preach through the serpent?

1. To save his own character, and the better to carry his point. Had the devil come to our first parents personally and unmasked, they would have more easily seen the deception. The reality of a future punishment is at times so clearly impressed on the human mind, that even Satan is constrained to own that there is a hell; altho' at other times he denies it. He does not wish to have it known that he is a liar; therefore he conceals himself, that he may the better accomplish his designs, and save his own character.

2. The devil is an enemy to all good, to all happiness and excellence. He is opposed to the felicity of the brutes. He took delight in tormenting the swine. The serpent, before he set up preaching Universal Salvation, was a cunning, beautiful, and happy creature; but now his glory is departed; for the Lord said unto the serpent, because thou hast done this, thou art cursed above all cattle, and above every beast of the field, upon thy belly shalt thou go, and dust shalt thou eat all the days of thy life. There is therefore, a kind of duplicate cunning in the matter, Satan gets the preacher and hearers also.

And is not this triumphant flattery,
And more than simple conquest in the foe?
YOUNG

3. Another reason why Satan employs instruments in his service is, because his empire is large and he cannot be every where himself.

4. He has a large number at his command, that love and approve of his work, delight in building up his kingdom, and stand ready to go at his call.

Inferences

1. The devil is not dead, but still lives; and is able to preach as well as ever, ye shall not surely die.

2. Universal Salvation is no new fangled scheme, but can boast of great antiquity.

3. See a reason why it ought to be rejected, because it is an ancient devilish doctrine.

4. See one reason why it is that Satan is such an enemy to the Bible, and to all who preach the gospel, because of that injunction, And he said unto them, go ye into all the world, and preach the gospel to every creature. He that believeth and is baptized shall be saved; but he that believeth not shall be damned.

5. See whence it was that Satan exerted himself so much to convince our first parents that there was no hell; because the denunciation of the Almighty was true, and he was afraid they would continue in the belief of it. Was there no truth in future punishment, or was it only a temporary evil, Satan would not be so busy, in trying to convince men that there is none. It is his nature and his element to lie. When he speaketh a lie, he speaketh of his own; for he is a liar, and the father of it.

6. We infer that ministers should not be proud of their preaching. If they preach the true gospel, they only, in substance, repeat Christ's sermons; if they preach ye shall not surely die, they only make use of the devil's old notes, that he delivered almost six thousand years ago.

7. It is probable that the doctrine of Universal Salvation will still prevail, since this preacher is yet alive, and not in the least superannuated; and every effort against him only enrages him more and more, and excites him to new inventions and exertions to build up his cause.

To close the subject: As the author of the foregoing discourse has confined himself wholly to the character of Satan, he trusts no one will feel himself personally injured by this short sermon: But should any imbibe a degree of friendship for this aged divine, and think that I have not treated this Universal Preacher with that respect and veneration which he justly deserves, let them be so kind as to point it out, and I will most cheerfully retract; for it has ever been a maxim with me, render unto all their dues.

1805

Joel Barlow 1754–1812

Echoing Leon Howard's assessment of Barlow in his 1943 study *The Connecticut Wits,* a commentator on Joel Barlow has more recently asserted that "it is as the poet of cornmeal mush that Barlow's popularity rests." The mention of "cornmeal mush" is an allusion to Barlow's immense popularity achieved with his 1793 poem, *The Hasty-Pudding,* traditionally considered the poet's nostalgic rendering of his memorable Connecticut boyhood. The mention of cornmeal mush, too, represents the attempt by historians of American literature to place Barlow within a peculiarly American context, one that provides for what has now become a "New Age" celebration of indigenous American products and peoples (cornmeal and Indians). In his own day, Barlow was indeed engaged in a celebration of America. But the celebration was in the context of his knowledge of countries other than America—France, England, Germany, and Algiers, for instance—countries for which he sought an equally free representative government, during the seventeen years he spent away from America as an international statesman.

Barlow was born the second-to-last child in the large family of a fairly well-to-do farmer, Samuel Barlow, and his second wife, Esther Hull. Given the size of both the family and their farm, Barlow could receive formal education only from the local minister, an education probably interspersed with farm and family chores. When Barlow was eighteen, his father arranged for his education at Moor's Indian School (later Dartmouth) in Hanover, New Hampshire; Barlow began his studies there in 1772. But his father's death shortly thereafter made it necessary (and financially possible) for Barlow to return home briefly and then to matriculate at Yale College with the class of 1778. It was here that Barlow began to evidence his interest in poetry, in moral and political philosophy, and in science as the key to the improvement of the human condition.

Barlow's college years were interrupted by the Revolutionary War, in which he took part during 1780–1781 as a chaplain to the Third Massachusetts Brigade. The chaplain's post enabled Barlow to continue writing poetry at the encouragement of family and friends. His secret engagement (secret engagements were punishable by Connecticut law) to Ruth Baldwin in 1779 led to their eventual (and enduring) marriage in 1781. Newly married, and with the war over in the early 1780s, Barlow sought patrons for his writing and opened a printing and stationer's store in Hartford. Upon the publication of *The Vision of Columbus* (1787), an "epic" poem about South and North American progress and promise, Barlow was selected by the Scioto Associates, a group of businessmen interested in land sales, to be their European representative. Barlow sailed for Europe in 1788.

Barlow's seventeen years abroad gave him the intellectual freedom and impetus to pursue projects that would not have been condoned in conservative, Federalist America. With the onset of the French Revolution in 1789, Barlow more openly continued his long career in social and political propaganda, moving from England to France and back again as the currents of revolution ebbed and flowed. When the Reign of Terror brought a bloodbath to some of his closest friends in 1793, Barlow made plans to leave France with Ruth Barlow (who had joined him in Europe in 1790). He took part in a shipping business in Hamburg, 1794–1795, and he became Minister to Algiers in 1796. Barlow's Algerian mission—to create treaties that would free the Mediterranean of piracy and to ensure the release of prisoners taken captive by pirates—lasted until late 1797, when he returned to Ruth in France. The Barlows bought a house in Paris and became patrons of the arts and sciences—and of Robert Fulton, who lived with them many months.

By 1805, when the intellectual climate in America had shifted so that it might accommodate the Republican tendencies of Joel Barlow, the Barlows returned to the United States and established themselves in the Washington community made inviting by the presidency of their friend, Thomas Jefferson. The Barlows remained in Washington in social and intellectual prominence. Barlow proposed, too much before its time, a national institution for the arts and sciences; Barlow's friends Jefferson, Monroe, and Madison encouraged him to write a history of America. But Barlow never completed his projects signaled by the republication of *The Vision of Columbus* (1787) as a much-altered poem, *The Columbiad* (1807). He was called upon for diplomacy once again, this time by President Madison in 1811, to negotiate a treaty with Napoleon. Barlow died, chasing the defeated and retreating Napoleon across the Russian steppes, in 1812.

The three selections below represent Barlow's career as a whole, for they include his patriotic promotion of America, his celebration of the indigenous America then entering the realm of myth, and a denunciation of the monarchist tendencies he sought to eradicate for future generations. It has been said that Barlow's life in Europe marked his transformation from a conservative Connecticut farmboy to a radical propagandist. Such an assessment occurs largely because—for about two years in his life, and evidently to promote his poem, *The Vision of Columbus*—Barlow engaged in collaborative writings with a group of Yale students and graduates who variably called themselves the Connecticut or Hartford Wits. But Barlow's earliest writings reveal the republicanism and anti-monarchist stance of his last writings. Barlow's early (pre-1788) writings are facilitated by the machinery of traditional Christianity, yet that machinery is less a sign of his belief in millennial prophecy (espoused by his nonelite contemporaries) than of his willingness to use rhetorical appeals (aimed at the nonelite) in order to promote his interest in freedom from injustice and tyranny—political, social, and moral. Barlow's pamphlet poem, *The Prospect of Peace* (1778), was his 1778 Yale commencement address as class poet. Barlow wrote *The Hasty-Pudding* (1793) while he was in Savoy, France, campaigning to become a deputy for Savoy to the French Republic. His manuscript poem, "Advice to a Raven in Russia," survives from his deputation to Napoleon, for the signing of a minor treaty. It was first published in 1938.

Carla Mulford
Pennsylvania State University

PRIMARY WORKS

Poems: *The Prospect of Peace,* 1778; *Poem, Spoken at the Public Commencement at Yale College,* 1781; *The Conspiracy of Kings,* 1792; *The Hasty-Pudding,* 1793; *Advice to a Raven in Russia,* written 1812, published 1938; Multi-book "epic" poems: *The Vision of Columbus,* 1787; *The Columbiad,* 1807; prose tracts: *Advice to the Privileged Orders in the Several States of Europe, Resulting from the Necessity and Propriety of a General Revolution in the Principle of Government,* 1792.

SECONDARY WORKS

Victor C. Miller, *Joel Barlow: Revolutionist London, 1791–92,* 1932; Leon Howard, *The Connecticut Wits,* 1943; James Woodress, *A Yankee's Odyssey: The Life of Joel Barlow,* 1958; Carla Mulford, "Joel Barlow's Radicalism in *The Conspiracy of Kings,*" *Deism, Masonry, and the Enlightenment: Essays Honoring Alfred Owen Aldridge,* ed. J. A. Leo Lemay, 1987.

The Prospect of Peace[1]

The closing scenes of Tyrants' fruitless rage,
The opening prospects of a golden age,
The dread events that crown th' important year,
Wake the glad song, and claim th' attentive ear.
Long has Columbia rung with dire alarms,
While Freedom call'd her injur'd sons to arms;
While various fortune fir'd th' embattled field,
Conquest delay'd, and victory stood conceal'd;
While closing legions mark'd their dreadful way,
And Millions trembled for the dubious day.
In this grand conflict heaven's Eternal Sire,
At whose dread frown the sons of guilt expire,
Bade vengeance rise, with sacred fury driven,
On those who war with Innocence and Heaven.
Behold, where late the trembling squadrons fled,
Hosts bow'd in chains, and hapless numbers bled,
In different fields our numerous heroes rouse,
To crop the wreath from Britain's impious brows.
Age following age shall these events relate
'Till Time's old empire yield to destin'd Fate;
Historic truth our guardian chiefs proclaim,
Their worth, their actions, and their deathless fame;
Admiring crouds their life-touch'd forms behold
In breathing canvass, or in sculptur'd gold,
And hail the Leader of the favorite throng,
The rapt'rous theme of some heroic song.
And soon, emerging from the orient skies,
The blisful morn in glorious pomp shall rise,
Wafting fair Peace from Europe's fated coast;
Where wand'ring long, in mazy factions lost,
From realm to realm, by rage and discord driven,

[1]Barlow's Yale commencement poem, *The Prospect of Peace,* was first published in 1778; this text, slightly modernized, is taken from the first edition.

She seem'd resolv'd to reascend her heaven.
This LEWIS view'd, and reach'd a friendly hand,[2]
Pointing her flight to this far-distant land;
Bade her extend her empire o'er the West,
And Europe's balance tremble on her crest!
Now, see the Goddess mounting on the day,
To these fair climes direct her circling way,
Willing to seek, once more, an earthly throne,
To cheer the globe, and emulate the sun.
With placid look she eyes the blissful shore,
Bids the loud-thundering cannon cease to roar;
Bids British navies from these ports be tost,
And hostile keels no more insult the coast;
Bids private feuds her sacred vengeance feel,
And bow submissive to the public weal;
Bids long, calm years adorn the happy clime,
And roll down blessings to remotest time.
Hail! heaven-born Peace, fair Nurse of Virtue hail!
Here, fix thy sceptre and exalt thy scale;
Hence, thro' the earth extend thy late domain,
'Till Heaven's own splendor shall absorb thy reign!
What scenes arise! what glories we behold!
See a broad realm its various charms unfold;
See crouds of patriots bless the happy land,
A godlike senate and a warlike band;
One friendly Genius fires the numerous whole,
From glowing Georgia to the frozen pole.
Along these shores, amid these flowery vales,
The woodland shout the joyous ear assails;
Industrious crouds in different labors toil,
Those ply the arts, and these improve the soil.
Here the fond merchant counts his rising gain,
There strides the rustic o'er the furrow'd plain,
Here walks the statesman, pensive and serene,
And there the school boys gambol round the green.
See ripening harvests gild the smiling plains,
Kind Nature's bounty and the pride of swains;
Luxuriant vines their curling tendrils shoot,
And bow their heads to drop the clustering fruit;
In the gay fields, with rich profusion strow'd,
The orchard bends beneath its yellow load,
The lofty boughs their annual burden pour,

[2]The French king Louis XVI (1754–1793) aided the colonies in the Revolutionary War. Barlow dedicated his epic poem *The Vision of Columbus* (1787) to Louis XVI, who in 1792 was driven by French revolutionaries from the throne and was beheaded in 1793.

And juicy harvests swell th' autumnal store.
These are the blessings of impartial Heaven,
To each fond heart in just proportion given.
No grasping lord shall grind the neighbouring poor,
Starve numerous vassals to increase his store;
No cringing slave shall at his presence bend,
Shrink at his frown, and at his nod attend;
Afric's unhappy children, now no more
Shall feel the cruel chains they felt before,
But every State in this just mean agree,
To bless mankind, and set th' oppressed free.
Then, rapt in transport, each exulting slave
Shall taste that Boon which God and nature gave,
And, fir'd with virtue, join the common cause,
Protect our freedom and enjoy our laws.
At this calm period, see, in pleasing view,
Art vies with Art, and Nature smiles anew:
On the long, winding strand that meets the tide,
Unnumber'd cities lift their spiry pride;
Gay, flowery walks salute th' inraptur'd eyes,
Tall, beauteous domes in dazzling prospect rise;
There thronging navies stretch their wanton sails,
Tempt the broad main and catch the driving gales;
There commerce swells from each remotest shore,
And wafts in plenty to the smiling store.
To these throng'd seats the country wide resorts,
And rolls her treasures to the op'ning ports;
While, far remote, gay health and pleasure flow,
And calm retirement cheers the laboring brow.
No din of arms the peaceful patriot hears,
No parting sigh the tender matron fears,
No field of fame invites the youth to rove,
Nor virgins know a harsher sound than love.
Fair Science then her laurel'd beauty rears,
And soars with Genius to the radiant stars.
Her glimmering dawn from Gothic darkness rose,
And nations saw her shadowy veil disclose;
She cheer'd fair Europe with her rising smiles,
Beam'd a bright morning o'er the British isles,
Now soaring reaches her meridian height,
And blest Columbia hails the dazzling light!
Here, rapt in tho't, the philosophic soul
Shall look thro' Nature's parts and grasp the whole.
See Genius kindling at a FRANKLIN's fame,
See unborn sages catch th' electric flame,
Bid hovering clouds the threatening blast expire,
Curb the fierce stream and hold th' imprison'd fire!
See the pleas'd youth, with anxious study, rove,

In orbs excentric thro' the realms above,
No more perplex'd, while RITTENHOUSE appears
To grace the museum with the rolling spheres.[3]
See that young Genius, that inventive soul,
Whose laws the jarring elements control;
Who guides the vengeance of mechanic power,
To blast the watery world & guard the peaceful shore.
And where's the rising Sage, the unknown name,
That new advent'rer in the lists of fame,
To find the cause, in secret nature bound,
The unknown cause, and various charms of sound?
What subtil medium leads the devious way;
Why different tensions different sounds convey;
Why harsh, rough tones in grating discord roll,
Or mingling concert charms th' enraptur'd soul.
And tell the cause why sluggish vapors rise,
And wave, exalted, thro' the genial skies;
What strange contrivance nature forms to bear
The ponderous burden thro' the lighter air.
These last Displays the curious mind engage,
And fire the genius of the rising age;
While moral tho'ts the pleas'd attention claim,
Swell the warm soul, and wake the virtuous flame;
While Metaphysics soar a boundless height,
And launch with EDWARDS[4] to the realms of light.
See the blest Muses hail their roseate bowers,
Their mansions blooming with poetic flowers;
See listening Seraphs join the epic throng,
And unborn JOSHUAS rise in future song.
Satire attends at Virtue's wakening call,
And Pride and Coquetry and Dulness fall.
Unnumber'd bards shall string the heavenly lyre,
To those blest strains which heavenly themes inspire;
Sing the rich Grace on mortal Man bestow'd,
The Virgin's Offspring and the *filial God*;
What love descends from heaven when JESUS dies!
What shouts attend him rising thro' the skies!
See Science now in lovelier charms appear,
Grac'd with new garlands from the blooming Fair.
See laurel'd nymphs in polish'd pages shine,
And Sapphic sweetness glow in every line.
No more the rougher Muse shall dare disgrace
The radiant charms that deck the blushing face;
But rising Beauties scorn the tinsel show,

[3]Benjamin Franklin and David Rittenhouse were the foremost scientists of their era in atmospheric studies.

[4]Jonathan Edwards.

The powder'd coxcomb and the flaunting beau;
While humble Merit, void of flattering wiles,
Claims the soft glance, and wakes th' enlivening smiles.
The opening lustre of an angel-mind,
Beauty's bright charms with sense superior join'd,
Bid Virtue shine, bid Truth and Goodness rise,
Melt from the voice, and sparkle from the eyes;
While the pleas'd Muse the gentle bosom warms,
The first in genius, as the first in charms.
Thus age and youth a smiling aspect wear,
Aw'd into virtue by the leading Fair;
While the bright offspring, rising to the stage,
Conveys the blessings to the future age.
  THESE are the views that Freedom's cause attend;
THESE shall endure 'till Time and Nature end.
With Science crown'd, shall Peace and Virtue shine,
And blest Religion beam a light divine.
Here the pure Church, descending from her God,
Shall fix on earth her long and last abode;
Zion arise, in radiant splendors dress'd,
By Saints admir'd, by Infidels confess'd;
Her opening courts, in dazzling glory, blaze,
Her walls salvation, and her portals praise.
  From each far corner of th' extended earth,
Her gathering sons shall claim their promis'd birth.
Thro' the drear wastes, beneath the setting day,
Where prowling natives haunt the wood for prey,
The swarthy Millions lift their wondring eyes,
And smile to see the Gospel morning rise:
Those who, thro' time, in savage darkness lay,
Wake to new light, and hail the glorious day!
In those dark regions, those uncultur'd wilds,
Fresh blooms the rose, the peaceful lilly smiles.
On the tall cliffs unnumber'd *Carmels* rise,
And in each vale some beauteous *Sharon* lies.
  From this fair Mount th' excinded stone shall roll,
Reach the far East and spread from pole to pole;
From one small Stock shall countless nations rise,
The world replenish and adorn the skies.
Earth's blood-stain'd empires, with their Guide the Sun,
From orient climes their gradual progress run;
And circling far, reach every western shore,
'Till earth-born empires rise and fall no more.
But see th' imperial GUIDE from heaven descend,
Whose beams are Peace, whose kingdom knows no end;
From calm Vesperia, thro' th' etherial way,
Back sweep the shades before th' effulgent day;

Thro' the broad East, the brightening splendor driven,
Reverses Nature and illumins heaven;
Astonish'd regions bless the gladdening sight,
And Suns and Systems own superior light.
As when th' asterial blaze o'er Bethl'em stood,
Which mark'd the birth-place of th' incarnate God;
When eastern priests the heavenly splendor view'd,
And numerous crouds the wonderous sign pursu'd:
So eastern kings shall view th' unclouded day
Rise in the West and streak its golden way:
That signal spoke a Savior's humble birth,
This speaks his long and glorious reign on earth!
THEN Love shall rule, and Innocence adore,
Discord shall cease, and Tyrants be no more;
'Till yon bright orb, and those celestial spheres,
In radiant circles, mark a thousand years;
'Till the grand *fiat* burst th' etherial frames,
Worlds crush on worlds, and Nature sink in flames!
The Church elect, from smouldering ruins, rise,
And sail triumphant thro' the yielding skies,
Hail'd by the Bridegroom! to the Father given,
The Joy of Angels, and the Queen of Heaven!

1778

The Hasty Pudding

A Poem, in Three Cantos

Omne tulit punctum qui miscuit utile dulci.[1]
He makes a good breakfast who mixes pudding with molasses.

Canto I

Ye Alps audacious, thro' the Heavens that rise,
To cramp the day and hide me from the skies;
Ye Gallic flags, that o'er their heights unfurl'd,[2]

[1]Barlow's motto is from Horace, *The Art of Poetry.* This text of the poem has been taken from the first American edition, 1796; the poem was originally published in France in 1793.

[2]Barlow refers to events of the French Revolution: Savoy, part of Sardinia, was overtaken by French troops and annexed to France in 1792.

Bear death to kings, and freedom to the world,
I sing not you. A softer theme I chuse,
A virgin theme, unconscious of the Muse,
But fruitful, rich, well suited to inspire
The purest frenzy of poetic fire.
  Despise it not, ye Bards to terror steel'd,
Who hurl'd your thunders round the epic field;
Nor ye who strain your midnight throats to sing
Joys that the vineyard and the still-house bring;
Or on some distant fair your notes employ,
And speak of raptures that you ne'er enjoy.
I sing the sweets I know, the charms I feel,
My morning incense, and my evening meal,
The sweets of Hasty-Pudding. Come, dear bowl,
Glide o'er my palate, and inspire my soul.
The milk beside thee, smoking from the kine,
Its substance mingled, married in with thine,
Shall cool and temper thy superior heat,
And save the pains of blowing while I eat.
  Oh! could the smooth, the emblematic song
Flow like thy genial juices o'er my tongue,
Could those mild morsels in my numbers chime,
And, as they roll in substance, roll in rhyme,
No more thy aukward unpoetic name
Should shun the Muse, or prejudice thy fame;
But rising grateful to the accustom'd ear,
All Bards should catch it, and all realms revere!
  Assist me first with pious toil to trace
Thro' wrecks of time thy lineage and thy race;
Declare what lovely squaw, in days of yore,
(Ere great Columbus sought thy native shore)
First gave thee to the world; her works of fame
Have liv'd indeed, but liv'd without a name.
Some tawny Ceres, goddess of her days,[3]
First learn'd with stones to crack the well-dry'd maize,
Thro' the rough sieve to shake the golden show'r,
In boiling water stir the yellow flour.
The yellow flour, bestrew'd and stir'd with haste,
Swells in the flood and thickens to a paste,
Then puffs and wallops, rises to the brim,
Drinks the dry knobs that on the surface swim:
The knobs at last the busy ladle breaks,
And the whole mass its true consistence takes.
  Could but her sacred name, unknown so long,
Rise like her labors, to the sons of song,

[3]Ceres is the Roman goddess of agriculture.

To her, to them, I'd consecrate my lays,
And blow her pudding with the breath of praise.
If 'twas Oella,[4] whom I sang before,
I here ascribe her one great virtue more.
Not thro' the rich Peruvian realms alone
The fame of Sol's sweet daughter should be known,
But o'er the world's wide climes should live secure,
Far as his rays extend, as long as they endure.

Dear Hasty-Pudding, what unpromis'd joy
Expands my heart, to meet thee in Savoy!
Doom'd o'er the world thro' devious paths to roam,
Each clime my country, and each house my home,
My soul is sooth'd, my cares have found an end,
I greet my long-lost, unforgotten friend.

For thee thro' Paris, that corrupted town,
How long in vain I wandered up and down,
Where shameless Bacchus,[5] with his drenching hoard
Cold from his cave usurps the morning board.
London is lost in smoke and steep'd in tea;
No Yankey there can lisp the name of thee:
The uncouth word, a libel on the town,
Would call a proclamation from the crown.[6]
For climes oblique, that fear the sun's full rays,
Chill'd in their fogs, exclude the generous maize;
A grain whose rich luxuriant growth requires
Short gentle showers, and bright etherial fires.

But here tho' distant from our native shore,
With mutual glee we meet and laugh once more,
The same! I know thee by that yellow face,
That strong complexion of true Indian race,
Which time can never change, nor soil impair,
Nor Alpine snows, nor Turkey's morbid air;
For endless years, thro' every mild domain,
Where grows the maize, there thou art sure to reign.

But man; more fickle, the bold licence claims,
In different realms to give thee different names.
Thee the soft nations round the warm Levant[7]
Palanta call, the French of course *Polante;*[8]

[4]Oella, a legendary Inca Indian, was considered to be the sun's daughter and the originator of spinning. Barlow had written of Oella in his *Vision of Columbus* (1787).

[5]Roman wine god.

[6]A certain king, at the time when this was written, was publishing proclamations to prevent American principles from being propagated in his country. [Barlow's note.] George III of England sought suppression of the democratic movement in his country. His ministers attacked many of England's chief propagandists; they attacked Barlow and Thomas Paine as well.

[7]Mediterranean.

[8]"Cooked cereal mush" in Italian and French, respectively.

E'en in thy native regions, how I blush
To hear the Pennsylvanians call thee *Mush!*
On Hudson's banks, while men of Belgic spawn
Insult and eat thee by the name *suppawn*.[9]
All spurious appellations, void of truth:
I've better known thee from my earliest youth,
Thy name is *Hasty-Pudding!* thus our sires
Were wont to greet thee fuming from their fires;
And while they argu'd in thy just defence
With logic clear, they thus explained the sense:—
"In *haste* the boiling cauldron o'er the blaze,
"Receives and cooks the ready-powder'd maize;
"In *haste* 'tis serv'd, and then in equal *haste,*
"With cooling milk, we make the sweet repast.
"No carving to be done, no knife to grate
"The tender ear, and wound the stony plate;
"But the smooth spoon, just fitted to the lip,
"And taught with art the yielding mass to dip,
"By frequent journies to the bowl well stor'd,
"Performs the hasty honors of the board."
Such is thy name, significant and clear,
A name, a sound to every Yankey dear,
But most to me, whose heart and palate chaste
Preserve my pure hereditary taste.
    There are who strive to stamp with disrepute
The luscious food, because it feeds the brute;
In tropes of high-strain'd wit, while gaudy prigs
Compare thy nursling man to pamper'd pigs;
With sovereign scorn I treat the vulgar jest,
Nor fear to share thy bounties with the beast.
What though the generous cow gives me to quaff
The milk nutritious; am I then a calf?
Or can the genius of the noisy swine,
Tho' nurs'd on pudding, thence lay claim to mine?
Sure the sweet song, I fashion to thy praise,
Runs more melodious than the notes they raise.
    My song resounding in its grateful glee,
No merit claims; I praise myself in thee.
My father lov'd thee through his length of days:
For thee his fields were shaded o'er with maize;
From thee what health, what vigour he possest,
Ten sturdy freemen sprung from him attest;
Thy constellation rul'd my natal morn,
And all my bones were made of Indian corn.

[9]The Dutch evidently adopted the Algonkian Indian word for mush.

Delicious grain! whatever form it take,
To roast or boil, to smother or to bake,
In every dish 'tis welcome still to me,
But most, my Hasty-Pudding, most in thee.
Let the green Succatash with thee contend,
Let beans and corn their sweetest juices blend,
Let butter drench them in its yellow tide,
And a long slice of bacon grace their side;
Not all the plate, how fam'd soe'er it be,
Can please my palate like a bowl of thee.
Some talk of Hoe-cake,[10] fair Virginia's pride,
Rich Johnny-cake[11] this mouth has often tri'd;
Both please me well, their virtues much the same;
Alike their fabric, as allied their fame,
Except in dear New-England, were the last
Receives a dash of pumpkin in the paste,
To give it sweetness and improve the taste.
But place them all before me, smoaking hot,
The big round dumplin rolling from the pot;
The pudding of the bag, whose quivering breast,
With suet lin'd leads on the Yankey feast;
The Charlotte[12] brown, within whose crusty sides
A belly soft the pulpy apple hides;
The yellow bread, whose face like amber glows,
And all of Indian that the bake-pan knows—
You tempt me not—my fav'rite greets my eyes,
To that lov'd bowl my spoon by instinct flies.

Canto II

To mix the food by vicious rules of art,
To kill the stomach and to sink the heart,
To make mankind, to social virtue sour,
Cram o'er each dish, and be what they devour;
For this the kitchen Muse first framed her book,
Commanding sweats to stream from every cook;
Children no more their antic gambols tried,
And friends to physic wonder'd why they died.
Not so the Yankey—his abundant feast,
With simples[13] furnished, and with plainness drest,

[10] A cake of cornmeal, water, and salt, which was originally baked upon a hoe blade over an open fire.

[11] A cake of cornmeal, wheat flour, eggs, and milk.

[12] A fruit-filled dessert cake or custard.

[13] Herbs and vegetables.

A numerous offspring gathers round the board,
And cheers alike the servant and the lord;
Whose well-bought hunger prompts the joyous taste,
And health attends them from the short repast.
  While the full pail rewards the milk-maid's toil,
The mother sees the morning cauldron boil;
To stir the pudding next demands their care,
To spread the table and the bowls prepare;
To feed the children, as their portions cool,
And comb their heads, and send them off to school.
  Yet may the simplest dish, some rules impart,
For nature scorns not all the aids of art.
E'en Hasty-Pudding, purest of all food,
May still be bad, indifferent, or good,
As sage experience the short process guides,
Or want of skill, or want of care presides.
Whoe'er would form it on the surest plan,
To rear the child and long sustain the man;
To shield the morals while it mends the size,
And all the powers of every food supplies,
Attend the lessons that the Muse shall bring,
Suspend your spoons, and listen while I sing.
  But since, O man! thy life and health demand
Not food alone, but labour from thy hand,
First in the field, beneath the sun's strong rays,
Ask of thy mother earth the needful maize;
She loves the race that courts her yielding soil,
And gives her bounties to the sons of toil.
  When now the ox, obedient to thy call,
Repays the loan that fill'd the winter stall,
Pursue his traces o'er the furrow'd plain,
And plant in measur'd hills the golden grain.
But when the tender germe begins to shoot,
And the green spire declares the sprouting root,
Then guard your nursling from each greedy foe,
Th' insidious worm, the all-devouring crow.
A little ashes, sprinkled round the spire,
Soon steep'd in rain, will bid the worm retire;
The feather'd robber with his hungry maw
Swift flies the field before your man of straw,
A frightful image, such as school boys bring
When met to burn the Pope, or hang the King.[14]

[14]During Guy Fawkes Day in England, effigies of the Pope, Fawkes, and others are burned, in celebration of the discovery of a Roman Catholic plot to blow up the King and Parliament. The allusion to the situation of the French King would not have been lost on Barlow's contemporary audience.

Thrice in the season, through each verdant row
Wield the strong plough-share and the faithful hoe;
The faithful hoe, a double task that takes,
To till the summer corn, and roast the winter cakes.[15]
Slow springs the blade, while check'd by chilling rains,
Ere yet the sun the seat of Cancer[16] gains;
But when his fiercest fires emblaze the land,
Then start the juices, then the roots expand;
Then, like a column of Corinthian mould,
The stalk struts upward, and the leaves unfold;
The bushy branches all the ridges fill,
Entwine their arms, and kiss from hill to hill.
Here cease to vex them, all your cares are done;
Leave the last labours to the parent sun;
Beneath his genial smiles the well-drest field,
When autumn calls, a plenteous crop shall yield.
Now the strong foliage bears the standards high,
And shoots the tall top-gallants to the sky;
The suckling ears their silky fringes bend,
And pregnant grown, their swelling coats distend;
The loaded stalk, while still the burthen grows,
O'erhangs the space that runs between the rows;
High as a hop field waves the silent grove,
A safe retreat for little thefts of love,
When the pledg'd roasting-ears invite the maid,
To meet her swain beneath the new-form'd shade;
His generous hand unloads the cumbrous hill,
And the green spoils her ready basket fill;
Small compensation for the two-fold bliss,
The promis'd wedding and the present kiss.
Slight depredations these; but now the moon
Calls from his hollow tree the sly raccoon;
And while by night he bears the prize away,
The bolder squirrel labours through the day.
Both thieves alike, but provident of time,
A virtue, rare, that almost hides their crime.
Then let them steal the little stores they can,
And fill their gran'ries from the toils of man;
We've one advantage where they take no part,—
With all their wiles they ne'er have found the art
To boil the Hasty-Pudding; here we shine
Superior far to tenants of the pine;
This envied boon to man shall still belong,

[15]Hoecakes.
[16]Zodiacal sign, the first point of which signals the summer solstice, June 21.

Unshar'd by them in substance or in song.
At last the closing season browns the plain,
And ripe October gathers in the grain;
Deep loaded carts the spacious corn-house fill,
The sack distended marches to the mill;
The lab'ring mill beneath the burthen groans,
And show'rs the future pudding from the stones;[17]
Till the glad house-wife greets the powder'd gold,
And the new crop exterminates the old.

Canto III

The days grow short; but tho' the falling sun
To the glad swain proclaims his day's work done,
Night's pleasing shades his various task prolong,
And yield new subjects to my various song.
For now, the corn-house fill'd, the harvest home,
Th' invited neighbours to the *Husking*[18] come;
A frolic scene, where work, and mirth, and play,
Unite their charms, to chace the hours away.
Where the huge heap lies center'd in the hall,
The lamp suspended from the cheerful wall,
Brown corn-fed nymphs, and strong hard-handed beaux,
Alternate rang'd, extend in circling rows,
Assume their seats, the solid mass attack;
The dry husks rustle, and the corn-cobs crack;
The song, the laugh, alternate notes resound,
And the sweet cider trips in silence round.
The laws of Husking ev'ry wight can tell;
And sure no laws he ever keeps so well:
For each red ear a general kiss he gains,
With each smut[19] ear she smuts the luckless swains;
But when to some sweet maid a prize is cast,
Red as her lips, and taper as her waist,
She walks the round, and culls one favor'd beau,
Who leaps, the luscious tribute to bestow.
Various the sport, as are the wits and brains
Of well pleas'd lasses and contending swains:
Till the vast mound of corn is swept away,
And he that gets the last ear, wins the day.
Meanwhile the house-wife urges all her care,
The well-earn'd feast to hasten and prepare.

[17]Grindstones.
[18]A husking party.
[19]An ear of corn that has the "smut," a fungus.

The sifted meal already waits her hand,
The milk is strain'd the bowls in order stand,
The fire flames high; and, as a pool (that takes
The headlong stream that o'er the mill-dam breaks)
Foams, roars and rages with incessant toils,
So the vext cauldron rages, roars and boils.
First with clean salt she seasons well the food,
Then strews the flour and thickens all the flood.
Long o'er the simmering fire she lets it stand:
To stir it well demands a stronger hand;
The husband takes his turn; and round and round
The ladle flies; at last the toil is crown'd;
When to the board the thronging huskers pour,
And take their seats as at the corn before.
I leave them to their feast. There still belong
More copious matters to my faithful song.
For rules there are, tho' ne'er unfolded yet,
Nice rules and wise, how pudding should be ate.
Some with molasses line the luscious treat,
And mix, like Bards, the useful with the sweet.
A wholesome dish, and well-deserving praise,
A great resource in those bleak wintry days,
When the chill'd earth lies buried deep in snow,
And raging Boreas[20] drives the shivering cow.
Blest cow! thy praise shall still my notes employ,
Great source of health, the only source of joy;
How oft thy teats these pious hands have prest!
How oft thy bounties prove my only feast!
How oft I've fed thee with my fav'rite grain!
And roar'd, like thee, to find thy children slain!
Ye swains who know her various worth to prize,
Ah! house her well from Winter's angry skies.
Potatoes, Pumpkins, should her sadness cheer,
Corn from your crib, and mashes[21] from your beer;
When Spring returns she'll well acquit the loan,
And nurse at once your infants and her own.
Milk then with pudding I should always chuse;
To this in future I confine my Muse,
Till she in haste some farther hints unfold,
Well for the young, nor useless to the old.
First in your bowl the milk abundant take,
Then drop with care along the silver lake
Your flakes of pudding; these at first will hide
Their little bulk beneath the swelling tide;

[20]In Greek mythology, the north (coldest) wind.

[21]Grain mixture resulting from the brewing process of beer.

But when their growing mass no more can sink,
When the soft island looms above the brink,
Then check your hand: you've got the portion's due,
So taught our sires, and what they taught is true.
There is a choice in spoons. Tho' small appear
The nice distinction, yet to me 'tis clear,
The deep bowl'd Gallic spoon, contriv'd to scoop
In ample draughts the thin diluted soup,
Performs not well in those substantial things,
Whose mass adhesive to the metal clings;
Where the strong labial muscles must embrace,
The gentle curve, and sweep the hollow space.
With ease to enter and discharge the freight,
A bowl less concave but still more dilate,
Becomes the pudding best. The shape, the size,
A secret rests unknown to vulgar eyes.
Experienc'd feeders can alone impart
A rule so much above the lore of art.
These tuneful lips, that thousand spoons have tried,
With just precision could the point decide,
Tho' not in song; the muse but poorly shines
In cones, and cubes, and geometric lines.
Yet the true form, as near as she can tell,
Is that small section of a goose-egg-shell,
Which in two equal portions shall divide
The distance from the centre to the side.
Fear not to slaver; 'tis no deadly sin,
Like the free Frenchman, from your joyous chin
Suspend the ready napkin; or, like me,
Poise with one hand your bowl upon your knee;
Just in the zenith your wise head project,
Your full spoon, rising in a line direct,
Bold as a bucket, heeds no drops that fall,
The wide mouth'd bowl will surely catch them all.

1793

Advice to a Raven in Russia[1]

December, 1812

Black fool, why winter here? These frozen skies,
Worn by your wings and deafened by your cries,
Should warn you hence, where milder suns invite,
And day alternates with his mother night.
You fear perhaps your food will fail you there,
Your human carnage, that delicious fare
That lured you hither, following still your friend
The great Napoleon to the world's bleak end.
You fear, because the southern climes poured forth
Their clustering nations to infest the north,
Bavarians, Austrians, those who drink the Po[2]
And those who skirt the Tuscan seas below,
With all Germania, Neustria, Belgia, Gaul,[3]
Doomed here to wade through slaughter to their fall,
You fear he left behind no wars, to feed
His feathered cannibals and nurse the breed.
Fear not, my screamer, call your greedy train,
Sweep over Europe, hurry back to Spain,
You'll find his legions there; the valiant crew
Please best their master when they toil for you.
Abundant there they spread the country o'er.
And taint the breeze with every nation's gore,
Iberian, Lusian,[4] British widely strown,
But still more wide and copious flows their own.
Go where you will; Calabria,[5] Malta, Greece,
Egypt and Syria still his fame increase,
Domingo's[6] fattened isle and India's plains
Glow deep with purple drawn from Gallic veins.
No raven's wing can stretch the flight so far
As the torn bandrols of Napoleon's war.
Choose then your climate, fix your best abode,

[1]Having gained almost all of Europe, Napoleon invaded Russia in June, 1812. He realized the futility of his Russian campaign in the winter of that year, and he was retreating across Russia when Barlow attempted to find him, in order to secure his signature on a minor treaty. Barlow died of pneumonia shortly after he wrote this poem, first published by Leon Howard in the *Huntingdon Library Quarterly,* 1938.

[2]An Italian river that flows from the Alps to the Adriatic.

[3]Germany, northern France, the Netherlands, France.

[4]Spanish, Portuguese.

[5]In southern Italy.

[6]West Indies.

He'll make you deserts and he'll bring you blood.
How could you fear a dearth? have not mankind,
Though slain by millions, millions left behind?
Has not conscription still the power to wield
Her annual falchion o'er the human field?
A faithful harvester! or if a man
Escape that gleaner, shall he scape the ban?
The triple ban, that like the hound of hell
Gripes with three joles, to hold his victim well.[7]
Fear nothing then, hatch fast your ravenous brood,
Teach them to cry to Bonaparte for food;
They'll be like you, of all his suppliant train,
The only class that never cries in vain.
For see what mutual benefits you lend!
(The surest way to fix the mutual friend)
While on his slaughtered troops your tribes are fed,
You cleanse his camp and carry off his dead.
Imperial scavenger! but now you know
Your work is vain amid these hills of snow.
His tentless troops are marbled through with frost
And change to crystal when the breath is lost.
Mere trunks of ice, though limbed like human frames
And lately warmed with life's endearing flames,
They cannot taint the air, the world impest,
Nor can you tear one fiber from their breast.
No! from their visual sockets, as they lie,
With beak and claws you cannot pluck an eye.
The frozen orb, preserving still its form,
Defies your talons as it braves the storm,
But stands and stares to God, as if to know
In what cursed hands He leaves His world below.
Fly then, or starve; though all the dreadful road
From Minsk[8] to Moscow with their bodies strowed
May count some myriads, yet they can't suffice
To feed you more beneath these dreary skies.
Go back, and winter in the wilds of Spain;
Feast there awhile, and in the next campaign
Rejoin your master; for you'll find him then,
With his new million of the race of men,
Clothed in his thunders, all his flags unfurled,

[7]The third ban or list was for the youngest draftees into the French army. Cerberus is the three-headed dog that guards the gates of Hades in roman mythology.

[8]City 400 miles southwest of Moscow. The Russian people burned Moscow when Napoleon took over the city in September, 1812. He began a retreat in October that left his troops open to guerilla attack, starvation, and the elements. Although 600,000 troops were engaged in retreat, only 24,000 managed to return in military order.

Raging and storming o'er the prostrate world.
War after war his hungry soul requires,
State after state shall sink beneath his fires,
Yet other Spains in victim smoke shall rise
And other Moscows suffocate the skies,
Each land lie reeking with its people's slain
And not a stream run bloodless to the main.
Till men resume their souls, and dare to shed
Earth's total vengeance on the monster's head,
Hurl from his blood-built throne this king of woes,
Dash him to dust, and let the world repose.

1938

Royall Tyler 1757–1826

Of Royall Tyler—who was courting her daughter—Abigail Adams wrote December 23, 1782, to John Adams (then on a diplomatic mission in Europe): "I am not acquainted with any young Gentleman whose attainments in literature are equal to his, who judges with greater accuracy or discovers a more delicate and refined taste. . . . I know not a young fellow upon the stage whose language is so pure or whose natural disposition is more agreeable." But John Adams was not charmed with the prospect of a writer for a son-in-law. To the approbation his wife seemed to give the courtship, he retorted January 22, 1783, "I confess I dont like the Subject at all." His daughter's husband "must be a Lawyer who spends his Midnights as well as Evenings at his Age over his Books not at any Lady's Fire Side." On March 28 he added, "My dear Daughters happiness employs my Thought night and Day. Dont let her form any Connections with any one, who is not devoted entirely to Study and to Business,—to honour & Virtue." Later that year, he ordered the women to come to him in Europe. Young Abigail married Adams's secretary to the legation, William Stephens Smith. Royall Tyler turned his attention to his burgeoning legal practice; became a celebrated author of works encouraging study, business, honor, and virtue; and rose to prominence as Chief Justice of the Supreme Court of Vermont (1807–1813).

Royall Tyler was born in Boston into a prosperous situation (his father was a merchant). He attended the Boston Latin School, then Harvard, achieving there—and in sporadic fighting in the Revolutionary War, which periodically broke up classes at Harvard—such renown that when he graduated, degrees were granted him from both Harvard and Yale. Admitted to the bar in 1780, Tyler set up a practice that by the mid-1780s won him the regard of the Massachusetts state government. Early in 1787, he helped quell, in the government's behalf, Shays's Rebellion, a farmers' disturbance over legal tender in western Massachusetts. After this success, he went on business matters to New York City. There Royall Tyler saw his first professional theatre production, Richard Brinsley Sheridan's *The School for Scandal.* And there he likely wrote and then saw his own play, *The Contrast,* produced on April 16, 1787.

For the rest of his life, Tyler would be a lawyer *and* a man of letters. His life would prove to doubters like John Adams that family men (he married Mary Palmer in 1794, and they had four children) could also be influential lawyers *and* writers. After settling as a lawyer in Vermont in 1791, Tyler went on to become state's attorney for Windham County, Chief Justice of the state Supreme Court, and a trustee and professor of law at the University of Vermont. He wrote several works: seven plays, three of which were produced; essays, alone and with Joseph Dennie; poems; a novel, *The Algerine Captive* (1797, and published in England in 1802); and a travel book, *The Yankey in London* (1809). Always one to satirize sham and hypocrisy and to celebrate "American" potential, Tyler is best remembered as the author of *The Contrast,* the first of his works produced and published.

The Contrast was lauded in the colonies, its author "proof," as a Baltimore reviewer wrote, "that these new climes are particularly favorable to the cultivation of arts and sciences." Several authors, including Judith Sargent Murray, praised Tyler in their own plays and play pieces. Tyler's themes—that sturdy, honest "Yankee" traits were more honorable, even in a country bumpkin (like Jonathan in *The Contrast*), than the foppish hypocrisy of aristocratic privilege in Europe—became the familiar pattern for many American writers of the nineteenth century. Although a pro-American message had been set forth in the writings of the earliest settlers, this message became more urgent as the United States sought its establishment as a world power. Tyler's play, reporting and instructing in a number of areas of concern in American society—from etiquette, courtship, and dress to politics and business—was a model for the proferring of Federal high-mindedness in an entertaining medium.

Carla Mulford
Pennsylvania State University

PRIMARY WORKS

The Contrast, 1790; "The Island of Barrataria," "The Origin of the Feast of Purim," "Joseph and His Brethren," and "The Judgement of Solomon" in *Four Plays,* eds. A.W. Peach and G.F. Newbrough, 1941; Marius B. Peladeau, *The Verse of Royall Tyler,* 1968, and *The Prose of Royall Tyler,* 1972.

SECONDARY WORKS

G. Thomas Tanselle, *Royall Tyler,* 1967; Ada L. and Herbert L. Carson, *Royall Tyler,* 1979. Jeffrey H. Richards, *Theatre Enough: American Culture and the Metaphor of the World Stage, 1607–1789,* 1991.

The Contrast, A Comedy in Five Acts

CHARACTERS

Col. Manly
Dimple
Van Rough
Jessamy
Jonathan

Charlotte
Maria
Letitia
Jenny

Servants

Scene. New York

Prologue

Written by a Young Gentleman of New York, and Spoken by Mr. Wignell[1]

EXULT, each patriot heart!—this night is shown
A piece, which we may fairly call our own;
Where the proud titles of "My Lord! Your Grace!"
To humble *Mr.* and plain *Sir* give place.
Our Author pictures not from foreign climes
The fashions or the follies of the times;
But has confin'd the subject of his work
To the gay scenes—the circles of New-York.
On native themes his Muse displays her pow'rs;
If ours the faults, the virtues too are ours.
Why should our thoughts to distant countries roam,
When each refinement may be found at home?
Who travels now to ape the rich or great
To deck an equipage and roll in state;
To court the graces, or to dance with ease,
Or by hypocrisy to strive to please?
Our free-born ancestors such arts despis'd;
Genuine sincerity alone they priz'd;
Their minds, with honest emulation fir'd;
To solid good—not ornament—aspir'd;
Or, if ambition rous'd a bolder flame,
Stern virtue throve, where indolence was shame.

But modern youths, with imitative sense,
Deem taste in dress the proof of excellence;
And spurn the meanness of your homespun arts,
Since homespun habits would obscure their parts;
Whilst all, which aims at splendour and parade,
Must come from Europe, *and be ready made.*
Strange! we should thus our native worth disclaim,
And check the progress of our rising fame.
Yet *one,* whilst imitation bears the sway,
Aspires to nobler heights, and points the way.
Be rous'd, my friends! his bold example view;
Let your own Bards be proud to copy *you!*
Should rigid critics reprobate our play,
At least the patriotic heart will say,
"Glorious our fall, since in a noble cause,
The bold *attempt alone* demands applause."
Still may the wisdom of the Comic Muse
Exalt your merits, or your faults accuse.
But think not, 't is her aim be severe;—

[1]Thomas Wignell (c. 1753–1803) played the role of Jonathan.

We all are mortals, and as mortals err.
If candour pleases, we are truly blest;
Vice trembles, when compell'd to stand confess'd.
Let not light Censure on your faults offend,
Which aims not to expose them, but amend.
Thus does our Author to your candour trust;
Conscious, the *free* are generous, as just.

ACT I

SCENE. *an Apartment at* CHARLOTTE'S. CHARLOTTE *and* LETITIA *discovered*

LETITIA. And so, Charlotte, you really think the pocket-hoop[2] unbecoming.

CHARLOTTE. No, I don't say so. It may be very becoming to saunter round the house of a rainy day; to visit my grand-mamma, or to go to Quakers' meeting: but to swim in a minuet, with the eyes of fifty well-dressed beaux upon me, to trip it in the Mall, or walk on the battery,[3] give me the luxurious, jaunty, flowing, bellhoop. It would have delighted you to have seen me the last evening, my charming girl! I was dangling o'er the battery with Billy Dimple; a knot of young fellows were upon the platform; as I passed them I faltered with one of the most bewitching false steps you ever saw, and then recovered myself with such a pretty confusion, flirting my hoop to discover a jet black shoe and brilliant buckle. Gad! how my little heart thrilled to hear the confused raptures of—*"Demme,[4] Jack, what a delicate foot!" "Ha! General, what a well-turned——"*

LETITIA. Fie! fie! Charlotte [*stopping her mouth*], I protest you are quite a libertine.

CHARLOTTE. Why, my dear little prude, are we not all such libertines? Do you think, when I sat tortured two hours under the hands of my friseur,[5] and an hour more at my toilet, that I had any thoughts of my aunt Susan, or my cousin Betsey? though they are both allowed to be critical judges of dress.

LETITIA. Why, who should we dress to please, but those who are judges of its merit?

CHARLOTTE. Why, a creature who does not know *Buffon* from *Soufflé*[6]—Man!—my Letitia—Man! for whom we dress, walk, dance, talk, lisp, languish, and smile. Does not the grave Spectator[7] assure us that even our much bepraised diffidence, modesty, and blushes are all directed to make ourselves good wives and mothers as fast as we can? Why, I'll undertake with one flirt of this hoop to bring more beaux to my feet in one week than the grave Maria, and her sentimental circle, can do, by sighing sentiment till their hairs are grey.

LETITIA. Well, I won't argue with you; you always out-talk me; let us change the subject. I hear that Mr. Dimple and Maria are soon to be married.

[2]Hoop skirt.
[3]A park at the southern end of Manhattan Island.
[4]"Damn me."
[5]Hairdresser.
[6]Georges de Buffon (1707–1788) was a French naturalist. Tyler creates a pun by substituting this name for "bouffant" (something puffy and light, usually a hairdo) and contrasting with "soufflé" (a puffy, light dish made with eggs).
[7]"Mr. Spectator" wrote on manners and morals in *The Spectator,* an eighteenth-century periodical.

CHARLOTTE. You hear true. I was consulted in the choice of the wedding clothes. She is to be married in a delicate white satin, and has a monstrous pretty brocaded lutestring[8] for the second day. It would have done you good to have seen with what an affected indifference the dear sentimentalist turned over a thousand pretty things, just as if her heart did not palpitate with her approaching happiness, and at last made her choice and arranged her dress with such apathy as if she did not know that plain white satin and a simple blond lace would show her clear skin and dark hair to the greatest advantage.

LETITIA. But they say her indifference to dress, and even to the gentleman himself, is not entirely affected.

CHARLOTTE. How?

LETITIA. It is whispered that if Maria gives her hand to Mr. Dimple, it will be without her heart.

CHARLOTTE. Though the giving the heart is one of the last of all laughable considerations in the marriage of a girl of spirit, yet I should like to hear what antiquated notions the dear little piece of old-fashioned prudery has got in her head.

LETITIA. Why, you know that old Mr. John-Richard-Robert-Jacob-Isaac-Abraham-Cornelius Van Dumpling, Billy Dimple's father (for he has thought fit to soften his name, as well as manners, during his English tour), was the most intimate friend of Maria's father. The old folks, about a year before Mr. Van Dumpling's death, proposed this match; the young folks were accordingly introduced, and told they must love one another. Billy was then a good-natured, decent-dressing young fellow, with a little dash of the coxcomb, such as our young fellows of fortune usually have. At this time, I really believe she thought she loved him; and had they then been married, I doubt not they might have jogged on, to the end of the chapter, a good kind of a sing-song lack-a-daysaical life, as other honest married folks do.

CHARLOTTE. Why did they not then marry?

LETITIA. Upon the death of his father, Billy went to England to see the world and rub off a little of the patroon rust. During his absence, Maria, like a good girl, to keep herself constant to her *nown true-love,* avoided company, and betook herself, for her amusement, to her books, and her dear Billy's letters. But, alas! how many ways has the mischievous demon of inconstancy of stealing into a woman's heart! Her love was destroyed by the very means she took to support it.

CHARLOTTE. How?—Oh! I have it—some likely young beau found the way to her study.

LETITIA. Be patient, Charlotte; your head so runs upon beaux. Why, she read *Sir Charles Grandison, Clarissa Harlowe,* Shenstone, and the *Sentimental Journey;*[9] and between whiles, as I said, Billy's letters. But, as her taste improved, her love declined. The contrast was so striking betwixt the good sense of her books and the flimsiness of her love-letters, that she discovered she had unthinkingly engaged her hand without her heart; and then the whole transaction, managed by the old folks, now appeared so unsentimental, and looked so like bargaining for a bale of

[8]Silk dress.

[9]*Sir Charles Grandison* (1753) and *Clarissa Harlowe* (1747) were sentimental novels by Samuel Richardson (1689–1761); William Shenstone (1714–1763) was a poet who wrote "Pastoral Ballad" (1755); *A Sentimental Journey* was the work of Laurence Sterne (1713–1768).

goods, that she found she ought to have rejected, according to every rule of romance, even the man of her choice, if imposed upon her in that manner. Clary Harlowe would have scorned such a match.

CHARLOTTE. Well, how was it on Mr. Dimple's return? Did he meet a more favourable reception than his letters?

LETITIA. Much the same. She spoke of him with respect abroad, and with contempt in her closet. She watched his conduct and conversation, and found that he had by travelling acquired the wickedness of Lovelace[10] without his wit, and the politeness of Sir Charles Grandison without his generosity. The ruddy youth, who washed his face at the cistern every morning, and swore and looked eternal love and constancy, was now metamorphosed into a flippant, palid, polite beau, who devotes the morning to his toilet, reads a few pages of Chesterfield's letters,[11] and then minces out, to put the infamous principles in practice upon every woman he meets.

CHARLOTTE. But, if she is so apt at conjuring up these sentimental bugbears, why does she not discard him at once?

LETITIA. Why, she thinks her word too sacred to be trifled with. Besides, her father, who has a great respect for the memory of his deceased friend, is ever telling her how he shall renew his years in their union, and repeating the dying injunctions of old Van Dumpling.

CHARLOTTE. A mighty pretty story! And so you would make me believe that the sensible Maria would give up Dumpling manor, and the all-accomplished Dimple as a husband, for the absurd, ridiculous reason, forsooth, because she despises and abhors him. Just as if a lady could not be privileged to spend a man's fortune, ride in his carriage, be called after his name, and call him her *nown dear lovee* when she wants money, without loving and respecting the great he-creature. Oh! my dear girl, you are a monstrous prude.

LETITIA. I don't say what I would do; I only intimate how I suppose she wishes to act.

CHARLOTTE. No, no, no! A fig of sentiment. If she breaks, or wishes to break, with Mr. Dimple, depend upon it, she has some other man in her eye. A woman rarely discards one lover until she is sure of another. Letitia little thinks what a clue I have to Dimple's conduct. The generous man submits to render himself disgusting to Maria, in order that she may leave him at liberty to address me. I must change the subject. [*Aside, and rings a bell.*

Enter SERVANT.

Frank, order the horses to.——Talking of marriage, did you hear that Sally Bloomsbury is going to be married next week to Mr. Indigo, the rich Carolinian?

LETITIA. Sally Bloomsbury married!—why, she is not yet in her teens.

CHARLOTTE. I do not know how this is, but you may depend upon it, 'tis a done affair. I have it from the best authority. There is my aunt Wyerly's Hannah. You know Hannah; though a black, she is a wench that was never caught in a lie in her life. Now, Hannah has a brother who courts Sarah, Mrs. Catgut the milliner's girl,

[10]The villain of *Clarissa Harlowe.*

[11]The letters of Philip Stanhope, Earl of Chesterfield (1694–1773), were written as instruction in good manners for his son. Once published in 1774, they were revealed to be hypocritical and shallow.

and she told Hannah's brother, and Hannah, who, as I said before, is a girl of undoubted veracity, told it directly to me, that Mrs. Catgut was making a new cap for Miss Bloomsbury, which, as it was very dressy, it is very probable is designed for a wedding cap. Now, as she is to be married, who can it be but to Mr. Indigo? Why, there is no other gentleman that visits at her papa's.

LETITIA. Say not a word more, Charlotte. Your intelligence is so direct and well grounded, it is almost a pity that it is not a piece of scandal.

CHARLOTTE. Oh! I am the pink of prudence. Though I cannot charge myself with ever having discredited a tea-party by my silence, yet I take care never to report anything of my acquaintance, especially if it is to their credit—*discredit,* I mean—until I have searched to the bottom of it. It is true, there is infinite pleasure in this charitable pursuit. Oh! how delicious to go and condole with the friends of some backsliding sister, or to retire with some old dowager or maiden aunt of the family, who love scandal so well that they cannot forbear gratifying their appetite at the expense of the reputation of their nearest relations! And then to return full fraught with a rich collection of circumstances, to retail to the next circle of our acquaintance under the strongest injunctions of secrecy—ha, ha, ha!—interlarding the melancholy tale with so many doleful shakes of the head, and more doleful "Ah! who would have thought it! so amiable, so prudent a young lady, as we all thought her, what a monstrous pity! well, I have nothing to charge myself with; I acted the part of a friend, I warned her of the principles of that rake, I told her what would be the consequence; I told her so, I told her so."—Ha, ha, ha!

LETITIA. Ha, ha, ha! Well, but, Charlotte, you don't tell me what you think of Miss Bloomsbury's match.

CHARLOTTE. Think! why I think it is probable she cried for a plaything, and they have given her a husband. Well, well, well, the puling chit[12] shall not be deprived of her plaything: 'tis only exchanging London dolls for American babies.—Apropos, of babies, have you heard what Mrs. Affable's high-flying notions of delicacy have come to?

LETITIA. Who, she that was Miss Lovely?

CHARLOTTE. The same; she married Bob Affable of Schenectady. Don't you remember?

Enter SERVANT.

SERVANT. Madam, the carriage is ready.

LETITIA. Shall we go to the stores first, or visiting?

CHARLOTTE. I should think it rather too early to visit, especially Mrs. Prim; you know she is so particular.

LETITIA. Well, but what of Mrs. Affable?

CHARLOTTE. Oh, I'll tell you as we go; come, come, let us hasten. I hear Mrs. Catgut has some of the prettiest caps arrived you ever saw. I shall die if I have not the first sight of them. [*Exeunt.*

[12]A childish woman.

SCENE II

A Room in VAN ROUGH'S *House*

MARIA sitting disconsolate at a Table, with Books, & c.

SONG

I

The sun sets in night, and the stars shun the day;
But glory remains when their lights fade away!
Begin, ye tormentors! your threats are in vain,
For the son of Alknomook shall never complain.

II

Remember the arrows he shot from his bow;
Remember your chiefs by his hatchet laid low:
Why so slow?—do you wait till I shrink from the pain?
No—the son of Alknomook will never complain.

III

Remember the wood where in ambush we lay,
And the scalps which we bore from your nation away:
Now the flame rises fast, you exult in my pain;
But the son of Alknomook can never complain.

IV

I go to the land where my father is gone;
His ghost shall rejoice in the fame of his son:
Death comes like a friend, he relieves me from pain;
And thy son, Oh Alknomook! has scorn'd to complain.

There is something in this song which ever calls forth my affections. The manly virtue of courage, that fortitude which steels the heart against the keenest misfortunes, which interweaves the laurel of glory amidst the instruments of torture and death, displays something so noble, so exalted, that in despite of the prejudices of education I cannot but admire it, even in a savage. The prepossession which our sex is supposed to entertain for the character of a soldier is, I know, a standing piece of raillery among the wits. A cockade, a lapell'd coat, and a feather, they will tell you, are irresistible by a female heart. Let it be so. Who is it that considers the helpless situation of our sex, that does not see that we each moment stand in need of a protector, and that a brave one too? Formed of the more delicate materials of nature, endowed only with the softer passions, incapable, from our ignorance of the world, to guard against the wiles of mankind, our security for happiness often depends upon their generosity and courage. Alas! how little of the former do we find! How inconsistent! that man should be leagued to destroy that honour upon which solely rests his respect and esteem. Ten thousand temptations allure us, ten thousand passions betray us; yet the smallest deviation from the path of rectitude is followed by the contempt and insult of man, and the more remorseless pity of woman; years of penitence and tears cannot wash away the stain, nor a life of virtue obliterate its remembrance. Reputation is the life of woman; yet courage to protect it is masculine and disgusting; and the only safe asylum a woman of delicacy can find is in the arms of a man of honour. How naturally, then, should we love the brave and the generous; how gratefully should we bless the arm raised for our protection, when nerv'd by virtue and directed by honour! Heaven grant that the man with whom I may be connected—may be connected! Whither has my imagination transported me—whither does it now lead me? Am I not indissolubly engaged, by every obligation of honour which my own consent and my father's approbation can give, to a man who can never share my affections, and whom a few days hence it will be criminal for me to disapprove—to disapprove! would to heaven that were all—to despise. For, can the most frivolous manners, actuated by the most depraved heart, meet, or merit, anything but contempt from every woman of delicacy and sentiment?

[VAN ROUGH *without.* Mary!

Ha! my father's voice—Sir!—

Enter VAN ROUGH

VAN ROUGH. What, Mary, always singing doleful ditties, and moping over these plaguy books.

MARIA. I hope, Sir, that it is not criminal to improve my mind with books, or to divert my melancholy with singing, at my leisure hours.

VAN ROUGH. Why, I don't know that, child; I don't know that. They us'd to say, when I was a young man, that if a woman knew how to make a pudding, and to keep herself out of fire and water, she knew enough for a wife. Now, what good have these books done you? have they not made you melancholy? as you call it. Pray, what right has a girl of your age to be in the dumps? haven't you everything your heart can wish; an't you going to be married to a young man of great fortune; an't you going to have the quit-rent of twenty miles square?

MARIA. One-hundredth part of the land, and a lease for life of the heart of a man I could love, would satisfy me.

VAN ROUGH. Pho, pho, pho! child; nonsense, downright nonsense, child. This comes of your reading your story-books; your Charles Grandisons, your Sentimental Journals, and your Robinson Crusoes,[13] and such other trumpery. No, no, no! child, it is money makes the mare go; keep your eye upon the main chance, Mary.

MARIA. Marriage, Sir, is, indeed, a very serious affair.

VAN ROUGH. You are right, child; you are right. I am sure I found it so, to my cost.

MARIA. I mean, Sir, that as marriage is a portion for life, and so intimately involves our happiness, we cannot be too considerate in the choice of our companion.

VAN ROUGH. Right, child; very right. A young woman should be very sober when she is making her choice, but when she has once made it, as you have done, I don't see why she should not be as merry as a grig; I am sure she has reason enough to be

[13]*Robinson Crusoe* (1719) was an adventure novel by Daniel Defoe (1660–1731).

so. Solomon says that "there is a time to laugh, and a time to weep."[14] Now, a time for a young woman to laugh is when she has made sure of a good rich husband. Now, a time to cry, according to you, Mary, is when she is making choice of him; but I should think that a young woman's time to cry was when she despaired of *getting* one. Why, there was your mother, now: to be sure, when I popp'd the question to her she did look a little silly; but when she had once looked down on her apron-strings, as all modest young women us'd to do, and drawled out ye-s, she was as brisk and as merry as a bee.

MARIA. My honoured mother, Sir, had no motive to melancholy; she married the man of her choice.

VAN ROUGH. The man of her choice! And pray, Mary, an't you going to marry the man of your choice—what trumpery notion is this? It is these vile books [*throwing them away*]. I'd have you to know, Mary, if you won't make young Van Dumpling the man of *your* choice, you shall marry him as the man of *my* choice.

MARIA. You terrify me, Sir. Indeed, Sir, I am all submission. My will is yours.

VAN ROUGH. Why, that is the way your mother us'd to talk. "My will is yours, my dear Mr. Van Rough, my will is yours"; but she took special care to have her own way, though, for all that.

MARIA. Do not reflect upon my mother's memory, Sir——

VAN ROUGH. Why not, Mary, why not? She kept me from speaking my mind all her *life,* and do you think she shall henpeck me now she is *dead* too? Come, come; don't go to sniveling; be a good girl, and mind the main chance. I'll see you well settled in the world.

MARIA. I do not doubt your love, Sir, and it is my duty to obey you. I will endeavour to make my duty and inclination go hand in hand.

VAN ROUGH. Well, well, Mary; do you be a good girl, mind the main chance, and never mind inclination. Why, do you know that I have been down in the cellar this very morning to examine a pipe of Madeira which I purchased the week you were born, and mean to tap on your wedding day?—That pipe cost me fifty pounds sterling. It was well worth sixty pounds; but I overreach'd Ben Bulkhead, the super-cargo. I'll tell you the whole story. You must know that——

Enter SERVANT

SERVANT. Sir, Mr. Transfer, the broker, is below. [*Exit.*

VAN ROUGH. Well, Mary, I must go. Remember, and be a good girl, and mind the main chance. [*Exit.*

MARIA [*alone*]. How deplorable is my situation! How distressing for a daughter to find her heart militating with her filial duty! I know my father loves me tenderly; why then do I reluctantly obey him? Heaven knows! with what reluctance I should oppose the will of a parent, or set an example of filial disobedience; at a parent's command, I could wed awkwardness and deformity. Were the heart of my husband good, I would so magnify his good qualities with the eye of conjugal affection, that the defects of his person and manners should be lost in the emanation of his virtues. At a father's command, I could embrace poverty. Were the poor man

[14]Ecclesiastes 3:4, "A time to weep, and a time to laugh."

my husband, I would learn resignation to my lot; I would enliven our frugal meal with good humour, and chase away misfortune from our cottage with a smile. At a father's command, I could almost submit to what every female heart knows to be the most mortifying, to marry a weak man, and blush at my husband's folly in every company I visited. But to marry a depraved wretch, whose only virtue is a polished exterior; who is actuated by the unmanly ambition of conquering the defenceless; whose heart, insensible to the emotions of patriotism, dilates at the plaudits of every unthinking girl; whose laurels are the sighs and tears of the miserable victims of his specious behaviour—can he, who has no regard for the peace and happiness of other families, ever have a due regard for the peace and happiness of his own? Would to heaven that my father were not so hasty in his temper? Surely, if I were to state my reasons for declining this match, he would not compel me to marry a man, whom, though my lips may solemnly promise to honour, I find my heart must ever despise. [*Exit.*

End of the First Act

ACT II. SCENE I

Enter CHARLOTTE *and* LETITIA

CHARLOTTE [*at entering*]. Betty, take those things out of the carriage and carry them to my chamber; see that you don't tumble them. My dear, I protest, I think it was the homeliest of the whole. I declare I was almost tempted to return and change it.

LETITIA. Why would you take it?

CHARLOTTE. Didn't Mrs. Catgut say it was the most fashionable?

LETITIA. But, my dear, it will never fit becomingly on you.

CHARLOTTE. I know that; but did not you hear Mrs. Catgut say it was fashionable?

LETITIA. Did you see that sweet airy cap with the white sprig?

CHARLOTTE. Yes, and I longed to take it; but, my dear, what could I do? Did not Mrs. Catgut say it was the most fashionable; and if I had not taken it, was not that awkward gawky, Sally Slender, ready to purchase it immediately?

LETITIA. Did you observe how she tumbled over the things at the next shop, and then went off without purchasing anything, nor even thanking the poor man for his trouble? But, of all the awkward creatures, did you see Miss Blouze endeavouring to thrust her unmerciful arm into those small kid gloves?

CHARLOTTE. Ha, ha, ha, ha!

LETITIA. Then did you take notice with what an affected warmth of friendship she and Miss Wasp met? when all their acquaintance know how much pleasure they take in abusing each other in every company.

CHARLOTTE. Lud![15] Letitia, is that so extraordinary? Why, my dear, I hope you are not going to turn sentimentalist. Scandal, you know, is but amusing ourselves with the faults, foibles, follies, and reputations of our friends; indeed, I don't know why we should have friends, if we are not at liberty to make use of them. But no person is so ignorant of the world as to suppose, because I amuse myself with a lady's

[15]Lord!

faults, that I am obliged to quarrel with her person every time we meet; believe me, my dear, we should have very few acquaintance at that rate.

SERVANT *enters and delivers a letter to* CHARLOTTE, *and——* [*Exit.*

CHARLOTTE. You'll excuse me, my dear.

[*Opens and reads to herself.*

LETITIA. Oh, quite excusable.

CHARLOTTE. As I hope to be married, my brother Henry is in the city.

LETITIA. What, your brother, Colonel Manly?

CHARLOTTE. Yes, my dear; the only brother I have in the world.

LETITIA. Was he never in this city?

CHARLOTTE. Never nearer than Harlem Heights, where he lay with his regiment.

LETITIA. What sort of a being is this brother of yours? If he is as chatty, as pretty, as sprightly as you, half the belles in the city will be pulling caps for him.

CHARLOTTE. My brother is the very counterpart and reverse of me: I am gay, he is grave; I am airy, he is solid; I am ever selecting the most pleasing objects for my laughter, he has a tear for every pitiful one. And thus, whilst he is plucking the briars and thorns from the path of the unfortunate, I am strewing my own path with roses.

LETITIA. My sweet friend, not quite so poetical, and a little more particular.

CHARLOTTE. Hands off, Letitia. I feel the rage of simile upon me; I can't talk to you in any other way. My brother has a heart replete with the noblest sentiments, but then, it is like—it is like—Oh! you provoking girl, you have deranged all my ideas—it is like—Oh! I have it—his heart is like an old maiden lady's bandbox; it contains many costly things, arranged with the most scrupulous nicety, yet the misfortune is that they are too delicate, costly, and antiquated for common use.

LETITIA. By what I can pick out of your flowery description, your brother is no beau.

CHARLOTTE. No, indeed, he makes no pretension to the character. He'd ride, or rather fly, an hundred miles to relieve a distressed object, or to do a gallant act in the service of his country; but should you drop your fan or bouquet in his presence, it is ten to one that some beau at the farther end of the room would have the honour of presenting it to you before he had observed that it fell. I'll tell you one of his antiquated, anti-gallant notions. He said once in my presence, in a room full of company—would you believe it?—in a large circle of ladies, that the best evidence a gentleman could give a young lady of his respect and affection was to endeavour in a friendly manner to rectify her foibles. I protest I was crimson to the eyes, upon reflecting that I was known as his sister.

LETITIA. Insupportable creature! tell a lady of her faults! if he is so grave, I fear I have no chance of captivating him.

CHARLOTTE. His conversation is like a rich, old-fashioned brocade—it will stand alone; every sentence is a sentiment. Now you may judge what a time I had with him, in my twelve months' visit to my father. He read me such lectures, out of pure brotherly affection, against the extremes of fashion, dress, flirting, and coquetry, and all the other dear things which he knows I dote upon, that I protest his conversation made me as melancholy as if I had been at church; and heaven knows, though I never prayed to go there but on one occasion, yet I would have exchanged his conversation for a psalm and a sermon. Church is rather melancholy, to be sure; but then I can ogle the beaux, and be regaled with "here endeth the first lesson," but his brotherly *here,* you would think had no end. You captivate him! Why, my dear, he would as soon fall in love with a box of Italian flowers. There is Maria, now, if she were not engaged, she might do something. Oh! how I should like to see that pair of pensorosos[16] together, looking as grave as two sailors' wives of a stormy night, with a flow of sentiment meandering through their conversation like purling streams in modern poetry.

LETITIA. Oh! my dear fanciful——

CHARLOTTE. Hush! I hear some person coming through the entry.

Enter SERVANT

SERVANT. Madam, there's a gentleman below who calls himself Colonel Manly; do you choose to be at home?

CHARLOTTE. Show him in. [*Exit* SERVANT.] Now for a sober face.

Enter COLONEL MANLY

MANLY. My dear Charlotte, I am happy that I once more enfold you within the arms of fraternal affection. I know you are going to ask (amiable impatience!) how our parents do—the venerable pair transmit you their blessing by me. They totter on the verge of a well-spent life, and wish only to see their children settled in the world, to depart in peace.

CHARLOTTE. I am very happy to hear that they are well. [*Coolly.*] Brother, will you give me leave to introduce you to our uncle's ward, one of my most intimate friends?

MANLY. [*saluting* LETITIA]. I ought to regard your friends as my own.

CHARLOTTE. Come, Letitia, do give us a little dash of your vivacity; my brother is so sentimental and so grave, that I protest he'll give us the vapours.[17]

MANLY. Though sentiment and gravity, I know, are banished the polite world, yet I hoped they might find some countenance in the meeting of such near connections as brother and sister.

CHARLOTTE. Positively, brother, if you go one step further in this strain, you will set me crying, and that, you know, would spoil my eyes; and then I should never get the husband which our good papa and mamma have so kindly wished me—never be established in the world.

MANLY. Forgive me, my sister—I am no enemy to mirth; I love your sprightliness; and I hope it will one day enliven the hours of some worthy man; but when I mention the respectable authors of my existence—the cherishers and protectors of my helpless infancy, whose hearts glow with such fondness and attachment that they would willingly lay down their lives for my welfare—you will excuse me if I am so unfashionable as to speak of them with some degree of respect and reverence.

[16]Persons deeply engaged in thought.
[17]The "blues."

CHARLOTTE. Well, well, brother; if you won't be gay, we'll not differ; I will be as grave as you wish. [*Affects gravity.*] And so, brother, you have come to the city to exchange some of your commutation notes[18] for a little pleasure?

MANLY. Indeed you are mistaken; my errand is not of amusement, but business; and as I neither drink nor game, my expenses will be so trivial, I shall have no occasion to sell my notes.

CHARLOTTE. Then you won't have occasion to do a very good thing. Why, here was the Vermont General—he came down some time since, sold all his musty notes at one stroke, and then laid the cash out in trinkets for his dear Fanny. I want a dozen pretty things myself; have you got the notes with you?

MANLY. I shall be ever willing to contribute, as far as it is in my power, to adorn or in any way to please my sister; yet I hope I shall never be obliged for this to sell my notes. I may be romantic, but I preserve them as a sacred deposit. Their full amount is justly due to me, but as embarrassments, the natural consequences of a long war, disable my country from supporting its credit, I shall wait with patience until it is rich enough to discharge them. If that is not in my day, they shall be transmitted as an honourable certificate to posterity, that I have humbly imitated our illustrious WASHINGTON, in having exposed my health and life in the service of my country, without reaping any other reward than the glory of conquering in so arduous a contest.

CHARLOTTE. Well said heroics. Why, my dear Henry, you have such a lofty way of saying things, that I protest I almost tremble at the thought of introducing you to the polite circles in the city. The belles would think you were a player run mad, with your head filled with old scraps of tragedy; and as to the beaux, they might admire, because they would not understand you. But, however, I must, I believe, introduce you to two or three ladies of my acquaintance.

LETITIA. And that will make him acquainted with thirty or forty beaux.

CHARLOTTE. Oh! brother, you don't know what a fund of happiness you have in store.

MANLY. I fear, sister, I have not refinement sufficient to enjoy it.

CHARLOTTE. Oh! you cannot fail being pleased.

LETITIA. Our ladies are so delicate and dressy.

CHARLOTTE. And our beaux so dressy and delicate.

LETITIA. Our ladies chat and flirt so agreeably.

CHARLOTTE. And our beaux simper and bow so gracefully.

LETITIA. With their hair so trim and neat.

CHARLOTTE. And their faces so soft and sleek.

LETITIA. Their buckles so tonish and bright.

CHARLOTTE. And their hands so slender and white.

LETITIA. I vow, Charlotte, we are quite poetical.

CHARLOTTE. And then, brother, the faces of the beaux are of such a lily-white hue! None of that horrid robustness of constitution, that vulgar cornfed glow of health, which can only serve to alarm an unmarried lady with apprehension, and prove a

[18]After the American Revolution, officers were given certificates promising payment of a sum equal to five years' full pay. Needy officers frequently cashed in such commutation notes before they were due—and at a sizable discount.

melancholy memento to a married one, that she can never hope for the happiness of being a widow. I will say this to the credit of our city beaux, that such is the delicacy of their complexion, dress, and address, that, even had I no reliance upon the honour of the dear Adonises,[19] I would trust myself in any possible situation with them, without the least apprehensions of rudeness.

MANLY. Sister Charlotte!

CHARLOTTE. Now, now, now, brother [*interrupting him*], now don't go to spoil my mirth with a dash of your gravity; I am so glad to see you, I am in tip-top spirits. Oh! that you could be with us at a little snug party. There is Billy Simper, Jack Chaffé, and Colonel Van Titter, Miss Promonade, and the two Miss Tambours, sometimes make a party, with some other ladies, in a side-box at the play. Everything is conducted with such decorum. First we bow round to the company in general, then to each one in particular, then we have so many inquiries after each other's health, and we are so happy to meet each other, and it is so many ages since we last had that pleasure, and if a married lady is in company, we have such a sweet dissertation upon her son Bobby's chin-cough; then the curtain rises, then our sensibility is all awake, and then, by the mere force of apprehension, we torture some harmless expression into a double meaning, which the poor author never dreamt of, and then we have recourse to our fans, and then we blush, and then the gentlemen jog one another, peep under the fan, and make the prettiest remarks; and then we giggle and they simper, and they giggle and we simper, and then the curtain drops, and then for nuts and oranges, and then we bow, and it's pray, Ma'am, take it, and pray, Sir, keep it, and oh! not for the world, Sir; and then the curtain rises again, and then we blush and giggle and simper and bow all over again. Oh! the sentimental charms of a side-box conversation! [*All laugh.*

MANLY. Well, sister, I join heartily with you in the laugh; for, in my opinion, it is as justifiable to laugh at folly as it is reprehensible to ridicule misfortune.

CHARLOTTE. Well, but, brother, positively I can't introduce you in these clothes: why, your coat looks as if it were calculated for the vulgar purpose of keeping yourself comfortable.

MANLY. This coat was my regimental coat in the late war. The public tumults of our state[20] have induced me to buckle on the sword in support of that government which I once fought to establish. I can only say, sister, that there was a time when this coat was respectable, and some people even thought that those men who had endured so many winter campaigns in the service of their country, without bread, clothing, or pay, at least deserved that the poverty of their appearance should not be ridiculed.

CHARLOTTE. We agree in opinion entirely, brother, though it would not have done for me to have said it: it is the coat makes the man respectable. In the time of the war, when we were almost frightened to death, why, your coat was respectable, that is, fashionable; now another kind of coat is fashionable, that is, respectable. And pray direct the tailor to make yours the height of the fashion.

MANLY. Though it is of little consequence to me of what shape my coat is, yet, as to the height of the fashion, there you will please to excuse me, sister. You know my

[19]Adonis was a beautiful young boy in Greek myth.

[20]Shays's Rebellion took place in Massachusetts in 1786.

sentiments on that subject. I have often lamented the advantage which the French have over us in that particular. In Paris, the fashions have their dawnings, their routine, and declensions, and depend as much upon the caprice of the day as in other countries; but there every lady assumes a right to deviate from the general *ton* as far as will be of advantage to her own appearance. In America, the cry is, what is the fashion? and we follow it indiscriminately, because it is so.

CHARLOTTE. Therefore it is, that when large hoops are in fashion, we often see many a plump girl lost in the immensity of a hoop-petticoat, whose want of height and *en-bon-point*[21] would never have been remarked in any other dress. When the high head-dress is the mode, how then do we see a lofty cushion, with a profusion of gauze, feathers, and ribbon, supported by a face no bigger than an apple! whilst a broad full-faced lady, who really would have appeared tolerably handsome in a large head-dress, looks with her smart chapeau[22] as masculine as a soldier.

MANLY. But remember, my dear sister, and I wish all my fair country-women would recollect, that the only excuse a young lady can have for going extravagantly into a fashion is because it makes her look extravagantly handsome.—Ladies, I must wish you a good morning.

CHARLOTTE. But, brother, you are going to make home with us.

MANLY. Indeed I cannot. I have seen my uncle and explained that matter.

CHARLOTTE. Come and dine with us, then. We have a family dinner about half-past four o'clock.

MANLY. I am engaged to dine with the Spanish ambassador. I was introduced to him by an old brother officer; and instead of freezing me with a cold card of compliment to dine with him ten days hence, he, with the true old Castilian frankness, in a friendly manner, asked me to dine with him to-day—an honour I could not refuse. Sister, adieu—Madam, you most obedient—— [*Exit.*

CHARLOTTE. I will wait upon you to the door, brother; I have something particular to say to you.

[*Exit.*

LETITIA [*alone*]. What a pair!—She the pink of flirtation, he the essence of everything that is *outré*[23] and gloomy.—I think I have completely deceived Charlotte by my manner of speaking of Mr. Dimple; she's too much the friend of Maria to be confided in. He is certainly rendering himself disagreeable to Maria, in order to break with her and proffer his hand to me. This is what the delicate fellow hinted in our last conversation. [*Exit.*

SCENE II. The Mall

Enter JESSAMY

JESSAMY. Positively this Mall is a very pretty place. I hope the cits[24] won't ruin it by repairs. To be sure, it won't do to speak of in the same day with Ranelagh or Vauxhall;[25] however, it's a fine place for a young fellow to display his person to

[21]Plumpness.
[22]Hat.
[23]Bizarre.
[24]A derogatory word for "citizens."
[25]Ranelagh Gardens and Vauxhall Gardens, public amusement parks in and near London.

advantage. Indeed, nothing is lost here; the girls have taste, and I am very happy to find they have adopted the elegant London fashion of looking back, after a genteel fellow like me has passed them.—Ah! who comes here? This, by his awkwardness, must be the Yankee colonel's servant. I'll accost him.

Enter JONATHAN

Votre très-humble serviteur, Monsieur.[26] I understand Colonel Manly, the Yankee officer, has the honour of your services.

JONATHAN. Sir!——

JESSAMY. I say, Sir, I understand that Colonel Manly has the honour of having you for a servant.

JONATHAN. Servant! Sir, do you take me for a neger—I am Colonel Manly's waiter.

JESSAMY. A true Yankee distinction, egad, without a difference. Why, Sir, do you not perform all the offices of a servant? do you not even blacken his boots?

JONATHAN. Yes; I do grease them a bit sometimes; but I am a true blue son of liberty, for all that. Father said I should come as Colonel Manly's waiter, to see the world, and all that; but no man shall master me. My father has as good a farm as the colonel.

JESSAMY. Well, Sir, we will not quarrel about terms upon the eye of an acquaintance from which I promise myself so much satisfaction—therefore, sans ceremonie[27]——

JONATHAN. What?——

JESSAMY. I say I am extremely happy to see Colonel Manly's waiter.

JONATHAN. Well, and I vow, too, I am pretty considerably glad to see you; but what the dogs need of all this outlandish lingo? Who may you be, Sir, if I may be so bold?

JESSAMY. I have the honour to be Mr. Dimple's servant, or, if you please, waiter. We lodge under the same roof, and should be glad of the honour of your acquaintance.

JONATHAN. You a waiter! by the living jingo, you look so topping, I took you for one of the agents to Congress.

JESSAMY. The brute has discernment, notwithstanding his appearance.—Give me leave to say I wonder then at your familiarity.

JONATHAN. Why, as to the matter of that, Mr.——; pray, what's your name?

JESSAMY. Jessamy, at your service.

JONATHAN. Why, I swear we don't make any great matter of distinction in our state between quality and other folks.

JESSAMY. This is, indeed, a levelling principle.—I hope, Mr. Jonathan, you have not taken part with the insurgents.

JONATHAN. Why, since General Shays has sneaked off and given us the bag to hold, I don't care to give my opinion; but you'll promise not to tell—put your ear this way—you won't tell?—I vow I did think the sturgeons were right.

JESSAMY. I thought, Mr. Jonathan, you Massachusetts men always argued with a gun in your hand. Why didn't you join them?

[26]French: Your most humble servant, Sir.
[27]French: without ceremony.

JONATHAN. Why, the colonel is one of those folks called the Shin—Shin[28]—dang it all, I can't speak them lignum vitæ[29] words—you know who I mean—there is a company of them—they wear a china goose at their button-hole—a kind of gilt thing.—Now the colonel told father and brother—you must know there are, let me see—there is Elnathan, Silas, and Barnabas, Tabitha—no, no, she's a she—tarnation, now I have it—there's Elnathan, Silas, Barnabas, Jonathan, that's I—seven of us, six went into the wars, and I stayed at home to take care of mother. Colonel said that it was a burning shame for the true blue Bunker Hill sons of liberty, who had fought Governor Hutchinson, Lord North,[30] and the Devil, to have any hand in kicking up a cursed dust against a government which we had, every mother's son of us, a hand in making.

JESSAMY. Bravo!—Well, have you been abroad in the city since your arrival? What have you seen that is curious and entertaining?

JONATHAN. Oh! I have seen a power of fine sights. I went to see two marblestone men and a leaden horse that stands out in doors in all weathers; and when I came where they was, one had got no head, and t'other weren't there. They said as how the leaden man was a damn'd tory,[31] and that he took wit in his anger and rode off in the time of the troubles.

JESSAMY. But this was not the end of your excursion?

JONATHAN. Oh, no; I went to a place they call Holy Ground. Now I counted this was a place where folks go to meeting; so I put my hymn-book in my pocket, and walked softly and grave as a minister; and when I came there, the dogs a bit of a meeting-house could I see. At last I spied a young gentlewoman standing by one of the seats which they have here at the doors. I took her to be the deacon's daughter, and she looked so kind, and so obliging, that I thought I would go and ask her the way to lecture, and—would you think it?—she called me dear, and sweeting, and honey, just as if we were married: by the living jingo, I had a month's mind to buss[32] her.

JESSAMY. Well, but how did it end?

JONATHAN. Why, as I was standing talking with her, a parcel of sailor men and boys got round me, the snarl-headed curs fell a-kicking and cursing of me at such a tarnal rate, that I vow I was glad to take to my heels and split home, right off, tail on end, like a stream of chalk.

JESSAMY. Why, my dear friend, you are not acquainted with the city; that girl you saw was a—— [*Whispers.*

JONATHAN. Mercy on my soul! was that young woman a harlot!—Well! if this is New-York Holy Ground, what must the Holy-day Ground be!

JESSAMY. Well, you should not judge of the city too rashly. We have a number of elegant, fine girls that make a man's leisure hours pass very agreeably. I would esteem it an honour to announce you to some of them.—Gad! that announce is a select word; I wonder where I picked it up.

JONATHAN. I don't want to know them.

[28]The Society of Cincinnati, an organization of officers of the American Revolution.

[29]Latin: wood of life.

[30]Thomas Hutchinson (1711–1780), governor of Massachusetts (1771–1774); Frederick North (1732–1792), prime minister of Britain (1770–1782).

[31]Person in support of continued allegiance with Britain during the American Revolution.

[32]Kiss.

JESSAMY. Come, come, my dear friend, I see that I must assume the honour of being the director of your amusements. Nature has given us passions, and youth and opportunity stimulate to gratify them. It is no shame, my dear Blueskin,[33] for a man to amuse himself with a little gallantry.

JONATHAN. Girl huntry! I don't altogether understand. I never played at that game. I know how to play hunt the squirrel, but I can't play anything with the girls; I am as good as married.

JESSAMY. Vulgar, horrid brute! Married, and above a hundred miles from his wife, and thinks that an objection to his making love to every woman he meets! He never can have read, no, he never can have been in a room with a volume of the divine Chesterfield.—So you are married?

JONATHAN. No, I don't say so, I said I was as good as married, a kind of promise.

JESSAMY. As good as married!——

JONATHAN. Why, yes; there's Tabitha Wymen, the deacon's daughter, at home; she and I have been courting a great while, and folks say as how we are to be married; and so I broke a piece of money with her when we parted, and she promised not to spark it with Solomon Dyer while I am gone. You wouldn't have me false to my true-love, would you?

JESSAMY. May be you have another reason for constancy; possibly the young lady has a fortune? Ha! Mr. Jonathan, the solid charms; the chains of love are never so binding as when the links are made of gold.

JONATHAN. Why, as to fortune, I must needs say her father is pretty dumb rich; he went representative for our town last year. He will give her—let me see—four times seven is—seven times four—nought and carry one—he will give her twenty acres of land—somewhat rocky though—a Bible, and a cow.

JESSAMY. Twenty acres of rock, a Bible, and a cow! Why, my dear Mr. Jonathan, we have servant-maids, or, as you would more elegantly express it, waitresses, in this city, who collect more in one year from their mistresses' cast clothes.

JONATHAN. You don't say so!——

JESSAMY. Yes, and I'll introduce you to one of them. There is a little lump of flesh and delicacy that lives at next door, waitress to Miss Maria; we often see her on the stoop.

JONATHAN. But are you sure she would be courted by me?

JESSAMY. Never doubt it; remember a faint heart never—blisters on my tongue—I was going to be guilty of a vile proverb; flat against the authority of Chesterfield. I say there can be no doubt that the brilliancy of your merit will secure you a favourable reception.

JONATHAN. Well, but what must I say to her?

JESSAMY. Say to her! why, my dear friend, though I admire your profound knowledge on every other subject, yet, you will pardon my saying that your want of opportunity has made the female heart escape the poignancy of your penetration. Say to her! Why, when a man goes a-courting, and hopes for success, he must begin with doing, and not saying.

JONATHAN. Well, what must I do?

[33]A slang term for an ardent supporter of the American Revolution.

JESSAMY. Why, when you are introduced you must make five or six elegant bows.

JONATHAN. Six elegant bows! I understand that; six, you say? Well——

JESSAMY. Then you must press and kiss her hand; then press a kiss, and so on to her lips and cheeks; then talk as much as you can about hearts, darts, flames, nectar and ambrosia—the more incoherent the better.

JONATHAN. Well, but suppose she should be angry with I?

JESSAMY. Why, if she should pretend—please to observe, Mr. Jonathan—if she should pretend to be offended, you must——But I'll tell you how my master acted in such a case: He was seated by a young lady of eighteen upon a sofa, plucking with a wanton hand the blooming sweets of youth and beauty. When the lady thought it necessary to check his ardour, she called up a frown upon her lovely face, so irresistibly alluring, that it would have warmed the frozen bosom of age; remember, said she, putting her delicate arm upon his, remember your character and my honour. My master instantly dropped upon his knees, with eyes swimming with love, cheeks glowing with desire, and in the gentlest modulation of voice he said: My dear Caroline, in a few months our hands will be indissolubly united at the altar; our hearts I feel are already so; the favours you now grant as evidence of your affection are favours indeed; yet, when the ceremony is once past, what will now be received with rapture will then be attributed to duty.

JONATHAN. Well, and what was the consequence?

JESSAMY. The consequence!—Ah! forgive me, my dear friend, but you New England gentlemen have such a laudable curiosity of seeing the bottom of everything—why, to be honest, I confess I saw the blooming cherub of a consequence smiling in its angelic mother's arms, about ten months afterwards.

JONATHAN. Well, if I follow all your plans, make them six bows, and all that, shall I have such little cherubim consequences?

JESSAMY. Undoubtedly.—What are you musing upon?

JONATHAN. You say you'll certainly make me acquainted?—Why, I was thinking then how I should contrive to pass this broken piece of silver—won't it buy a sugar-dram?

JESSAMY. What is that, the love-token from the deacon's daughter?—You come on bravely. But I must hasten to my master. Adieu, my dear friend.

JONATHAN. Stay, Mr. Jessamy—must I buss her when I am introduced to her?

JESSAMY. I told you, you must kiss her.

JONATHAN. Well, but must I buss her?

JESSAMY. Why kiss and buss, and buss and kiss, is all one.

JONATHAN. Oh! my dear friend, though you have a profound knowledge of all, a pugnency[34] of tribulation, you don't know everything. [*Exit.*

JESSAMY [*alone*]. Well, certainly I improve; my master could not have insinuated himself with more address into the heart of a man he despised. Now will this blundering dog sicken Jenny with his nauseous pawings, until she flies into my arms for very ease. How sweet will the contrast be between the blundering Jonathan and the courtly and accomplished Jessamy!

End of the Second Act

[34]Probably "poignancy."

ACT III. SCENE I

DIMPLE'S *Room*

DIMPLE *discovered at a Toilet*

DIMPLE [*reading*]: "Women have in general but one object, which is their beauty." Very true, my lord; positively very true. "Nature has hardly formed a woman ugly enough to be insensible to flattery upon her person." Extremely just, my lord; every day's delightful experience confirms this. "If her face is so shocking that she must, in some degree, be conscious of it, her figure and air, she thinks, make ample amends for it." The sallow Miss Wan is a proof of this. Upon my telling the distasteful wretch, the other day, that her countenance spoke the pensive language of sentiment, and that Lady Wortley Montagu[35] declared that if the ladies were arrayed in the garb of innocence, the face would be the last part which would be admired, as Monsieur Milton expresses it, she grinn'd horribly a ghastly smile.[36] "If her figure is deformed, she thinks her face counterbalances it."[37]

Enter JESSAMY *with letters*

Where got you these, Jessamy?

JESSAMY. Sir, the English packet is arrived.

DIMPLE [*opens and reads a letter enclosing notes*]:

"Sir,

"I have drawn bills on you in favour of Messers. Van Cash and Co. as per margin. I have taken up your note to Col. Piquet, and discharged your debts to my Lord Lurcher and Sir Harry Rook. I herewith enclose you copies of the bills, which I have no doubt will be immediately honoured. On failure, I shall empower some lawyer in your country to recover the amounts.

"I am, Sir,

"Your most humble servant,

"JOHN HAZARD."

Now, did not my lord expressly say that it was unbecoming a well-bred man to be in a passion, I confess I should be ruffled. [*Reads.*] "There is no accident so unfortunate, which a wise man may not turn to his advantage; nor any accident so fortunate, which a fool will not turn to his disadvantage." True, my lord; but how advantage can be derived from this I can't see. Chesterfield himself, who made, however, the worst practice of the most excellent precepts, was never in so embarrassing a situation. I love the person of Charlotte, and it is necessary I should command the fortune of Letitia. As to Maria!—I doubt not by my *sangfroid*[38] behaviour I shall compel her to decline the match; but the blame must not fall upon me. A prudent man, as my lord says, should take all the credit of a good action to

[35]English poet (1689–1762).

[36]*Paradise Lost, II* by John Milton (1608–1704).

[37]A quotation from Chesterfield's letters.

[38]Cool, composed.

himself, and throw the discredit of a bad one upon others. I must break with Maria, marry Letitia, and as for Charlotte—why, Charlotte must be a companion to my wife.—Here, Jessamy!

Enter JESSAMY

DIMPLE *folds and seals two letters*

DIMPLE. Here, Jessamy, take this letter to my love. [*Gives one.*

JESSAMY. To which of your honour's loves?—Oh! [*reading*] to Miss Letitia, your honour's rich love.

DIMPLE. And this [*delivers another*] to Miss Charlotte Manly. See that you deliver them privately.

JESSAMY. Yes, your honour. [*Going.*

DIMPLE. Jessamy, who are these strange lodgers that came to the house last night?

JESSAMY. Why, the master is a Yankee colonel; I have not seen much of him; but the man is the most unpolished animal your honour ever disgraced your eyes by looking upon. I have had one of the most *outré* conversations with him!—He really has a most prodigious effect upon my risibility.

DIMPLE. I ought, according to every rule of Chesterfield, to wait on him and insinuate myself into his good graces.——Jessamy, wait on the colonel with my compliments, and if he is disengaged I will do myself the honour of paying him my respects.—Some ignorant, unpolished boor——

JESSAMY *goes off and returns*

JESSAMY. Sir, the colonel is gone out, and Jonathan his servant says that he is gone to stretch his legs upon the Mall.—Stretch his legs! what an indelicacy of diction!

DIMPLE. Very well. Reach me my hat and sword. I'll accost him there, in my way to Letitia's, as by accident; pretend to be struck by his person and address, and endeavour to steal into his confidence. Jessamy, I have no business for you at present. [*Exit.*

JESSAMY. [*taking up the book*]. My master and I obtain our knowledge from the same source—though, gad! I think myself much the prettier fellow of the two. [*Surveying himself in the glass.*] That was a brilliant thought, to insinuate that I folded my master's letters for him; the folding is so neat, that it does honour to the operator. I once intended to have insinuated that I wrote his letters too; but that was before I saw them; it won't do now; no honour there, positively.—"Nothing looks more vulgar, [*reading affectedly*] ordinary, and illiberal than ugly, uneven, and ragged nails; the ends of which should be kept even and clean, not tipped with black, and cut in small segments of circles."—Segments of circles! surely my lord did not consider that he wrote for the beaux. Segments of circles; what a crabbed term! Now I dare answer that my master, with all his learning, does not know that this means, according to the present mode, let the nails grow long, and then cut them off even at top. [*Laughing without.*] Ha! that's Jenny's titter. I protest I despair of ever teaching that girl to laugh; she has something so execrably natural in her laugh, that I declare it absolutely discomposes my nerves. How came she into our house! [*Calls.*] Jenny!

Enter JENNY

Prythee, Jenny, don't spoil your fine face with laughing.

JENNY. Why, mustn't I laugh, Mr. Jessamy?

JESSAMY. You may smile, but, as my lord says, nothing can authorise a laugh.

JENNY. Well, but I can't help laughing.—Have you see him, Mr. Jessamy? ha, ha, ha!

JESSAMY. Seen whom?

JENNY. Why, Jonathan, the New England colonel's servant. Do you know he was at the play last night, and the stupid creature don't know where he has been. He would not go to a play for the world; he thinks it was a show, as he calls it.

JESSAMY. As ignorant and unpolished as he is, do you know, Miss Jenny, that I propose to introduce him to the honour of your acquaintance?

JENNY. Introduce him to me! for what?

JESSAMY. Why, my lovely girl, that you may take him under your protection, as Madame Rambouillet did young Stanhope;[39] that you may, by your plastic hand, mould this uncouth cub into a gentleman. He is to make love to you.

JENNY. Make love to me!——

JESSAMY. Yes, Mistress Jenny, make love to you; and, I doubt not, when he shall become *domesticated* in your kitchen, that this boor, under your auspices, will soon become *un amiable petit Jonathan*.[40]

JENNY. I must say, Mr. Jessamy, if he copies after me, he will be vastly, monstrously polite.

JESSAMY. Stay here one moment, and I will call him.—Jonathan!—Mr. Jonathan!— [*Calls.*

JONATHAN (*within*). Holla! there.—[*Enters.*] You promise to stand by me—six bows you say. [*Bows.*

JESSAMY. Mrs. Jenny, I have the honour of presenting Mr. Jonathan, Colonel Manly's waiter, to you. I am extremely happy that I have it in my power to make two worthy people acquainted with each other's merits.

JENNY. So, Mr. Jonathan, I hear you were at the play last night.

JONATHAN. At the play! why, did you think I went to the devil's drawing-room?

JENNY. The devil's drawing-room!

JONATHAN. Yes; why an't cards and dice the devil's device, and the play-house the shop where the devil hangs out the vanities of the world upon the tenterhooks of temptation? I believe you have not heard how they were acting the old boy one night, and the wicked one came among them sure enough, and went right off in a storm, and carried one quarter of the play-house with him. Oh! no, no, no! you won't catch me at a play-house, I warrant you.

JENNY. Well, Mr. Jonathan, though I don't scruple your veracity, I have some reasons for believing you were there: pray, where were you about six o'clock?

JONATHAN. Why, I went to see one Mr. Morrison, the *hocus pocus* man; they said as how he could eat a case knife.

JENNY. Well, and how did you find the place?

JONATHAN. As I was going about here and there, to and again, to find it, I saw a great crowd of folks going into a long entry that had lanterns over the door; so I asked

[39]Catherine de Vivonne Rambouillet (1588–1665) is said to have taught her age the art of gentility and conversation. But she died long before the birth of Philip Stanhope (1732–1768), the son of Lord Chesterfield (1694–1773).

[40]French: a courteous little Jonathan.

a man whether that was not the place where they played *hocus pocus?* He was a civil, kind man, though he did speak like the Hessians;[41] he lifted up his eyes and said, "They play *hocus pocus* tricks enough there, Got knows, mine friend."

JENNY. Well—

JONATHAN. So I went right in, and they showed me away, clean up to the garret, just like meeting-house gallery. And so I saw a power of topping folks, all sitting round in little cabins, "just like father's corn-cribs"; and then there was such a squeaking with the fiddles, and such a tarnal blaze with the lights, my head was near turned. At last the people that sat near me set up such a hissing—hiss—like so many mad cats; and then they went thump, thump, thump, just like our Peleg threshing wheat, and stamped away, just like the nation; and called out for one Mr. Langolee—I suppose he helps act the tricks.

JENNY. Well, and what did you do all this time?

JONATHAN. Gor, I—I liked the fun, and so I thumped away, and hiss'd as lustily as the best of 'em. One sailor-looking man that sat by me, seeing me stamp, and knowing I was a cute fellow, because I could make a roaring noise, clapped me on the shoulder and said, "You are a d——d hearty cock, smite my timbers!" I told him so I was, but I thought he need not swear so, and make use of such naughty words.

JESSAMY. The savage!—Well, and did you see the man with his tricks?

JONATHAN. Why, I vow, as I was looking out for him, they lifted up a great green cloth and let us look right into the next neighbour's house. Have you a good many houses in New-York made so in that 'ere way?

JENNY. Not many; but did you see the family?

JONATHAN. Yes, swamp it; I see'd the family.

JENNY. Well, and how did you like them?

JONATHAN. Why, I vow they were pretty much like other families—there was a poor, good-natured, curse of a husband, and a sad rantipole[42] of a wife.

JENNY. But did you see no other folks.

JONATHAN. Yes. There was one youngster; they called him Mr. Joseph; he talked as sober and as pious as a minister; but, like some ministers that I know, he was a sly tike in his heart for all that. He was going to ask a young woman to spark it with him, and—the Lord have mercy on my soul!—she was another man's wife.

JESSAMY. The Wabash!

JENNY. And did you see any more folks?

JONATHAN. Why, they came on as thick as mustard. For my part, I thought the house was haunted. There was a soldier fellow, who talked about his row de dow, dow, and courted a young woman; but, of all the cute folk I saw, I liked one little fellow——

JENNY. Aye! who was he?

JONATHAN. Why, he had red hair, and a little round plump face like mine, only not altogether so handsome. His name was—Darby—that was his baptizing name; his

[41]Germans.
[42]Wild, unruly.

other name I forgot. Oh! it was Wig—Wag—Wag-all Darby Wagall[43]—pray, do you know him?—I should like to take a sling with him, or a drap of cyder with a pepper-pod in it, to make it warm and confortable.

JENNY. I can't say I have that pleasure.

JONATHAN. I wish you did; he is a cute fellow. But there was one thing I didn't like in that Mr. Darby; and that was, he was afraid of some of them 'ere shooting irons, such as your troopers wear on training days. Now, I'm a true born Yankee American son of liberty, and I never was afraid of a gun yet in all my life.

JENNY. Well, Mr. Jonathan, you were certainly at the play-house.

JONATHAN. I at the play-house!—Why didn't I see the play then?

JENNY. Why, the people you saw were players.

JONATHAN. Mercy on my soul! did I see the wicked players?—Mayhap that 'ere Darby that I liked so was the old serpent himself, and had his cloven foot in his pocket. Why, I vow, now I come to think on't, the candles seemed to burn blue, and I am sure where I sat it smelt tarnally of brimstone.

JESSAMY. Well, Mr. Jonathan, from your account, which I confess is very accurate, you must have been at the play-house.

JONATHAN. Why, I vow, I began to smell a rat. When I came away, I went to the man for my money again; you want your money? says he; yes, says I; for what? says he; why, says I, no man shall jockey me out of my money; I paid my money to see sights, and the dogs a bit of a sight have I seen, unless you call listening to people's private business a sight. Why, says he, it is the School for Scandalization.[44]—The School for Scandalization!—Oh! ho! no wonder you New-York folks are so cute at it, when you go to school to learn it; and so I jogged off.

JESSAMY. My dear Jenny, my master's business drags me from you; would to heaven I knew no other servitude than to your charms.

JONATHAN. Well, but don't go; you won't leave me so——

JESSAMY. Excuse me.—Remember the cash.

[*Aside to him, and—Exit.*

JENNY. Mr. Jonathan, won't you please to sit down? Mr. Jessamy tells me you wanted to have some conversation with me.

[*Having brought forward two chairs, they sit.*

JONATHAN. Ma'am!—

JENNY. Sir!——

JONATHAN. Ma'am!——

JENNY. Pray, how do you like the city, Sir?

JONATHAN. Ma'am!——

JENNY. I say, Sir, how do you like New-York?

JONATHAN. Ma'am!——

[43]Darby Wagall is a combination of the names of Thomas Wignell and Darby, a character the actor played in *The Poor Soldier* (1783).

[44]*The School for Scandal* (1777) was written by Richard Sheridan (1751–1816) and opened in New York shortly before *The Contrast*.

JENNY. The stupid creature! but I must pass some little time with him, if it is only to endeavour to learn whether it was his master that made such an abrupt entrance into our house and my young mistress's heart, this morning. [*Aside.*] As you don't seem to like to talk, Mr. Jonathan—do you sing?

JONATHAN. Gor, I—I am glad she asked that, for I forgot what Mr. Jessamy bid me say, and I dare as well be hanged as act what he bid me do, I'm so ashamed. [*Aside.*] Yes, Ma'am, I can sing—I can sing "Mear," "Old Hundred," and "Bangor."

JENNY. Oh! I don't mean psalm tunes. Have you no little song to please the ladies, such as "Roslin Castle," or the "Maid of the Mill?"

JONATHAN. Why, all my tunes are go to meeting tunes, save one, and I count you won't altogether like that 'ere.

JENNY. What is it called?

JONATHAN. I am sure you have heard folks talk about it; it is called "Yankee Doodle."

JENNY. Oh! it is the tune I am fond of; and if I know anything of my mistress, she would be glad to dance to it. Pray, sing!

JONATHAN [*sings*].

Father and I went up to camp,
Along with Captain Goodwin;
And there we saw the men and boys,
As thick as hasty-pudding.
Yankee doodle do, etc.

And there we saw a swamping gun,
Big as log of maple,
On a little deuced cart,
A load for father's cattle.
Yankee doodle do, etc.

And every time they fired it off
It took a horn of powder
It made a noise—like father's gun,
Only a nation louder.
Yankee doodle do, etc.

There was a man in our town,
His name was——

No, no, that won't do. Now, if I was with Tabitha Wymen and Jemima Cawley down at father Chase's, I shouldn't mind singing this all out before them—you would be affronted if I was to sing that, though that's a lucky thought; if you should be affronted, I have something dang'd cute, which Jessamy told me to say to you.

JENNY. Is that all! I assure you I like it of all things.

JONATHAN. No, no; I can sing more; some other time, when you and I are better acquainted, I'll sing the whole of it—no, no—that's a fib—I can't sing but a hundred and ninety verses; our Tabitha at home can sing it all.—— [*Sings.*

Marblehead's rocky place,
And Cape-Cod is sandy;
Charlestown is burnt down,
Boston is the dandy.
Yankee doddle, doodle do, etc.

I vow, my own town song has put me into such topping spirits that I believe I'll begin to do a little, as Jessamy says we must when we go a-courting—[*Runs and kisses her.*] Burning rivers! cooling flames! red-hot roses! pig-nuts! hasty-pudding and ambrosia!

JENNY. What means this freedom? you insulting wretch. [*Strikes him.*

JONATHAN. Are you affronted?

JENNY. Affronted! with what looks shall I express my anger?

JONATHAN. Looks! why as to the matter of looks, you look as cross as a witch.

JENNY. Have you no feeling for the delicacy of my sex?

JONATHAN. Feeling! Gor, I—I feel the delicacy of your sex pretty smartly [*rubbing his cheek*], though, I vow, I thought when you city ladies courted and married, and all that, you put feeling out of the question. But I want to know whether you are really affronted, or only pretend to be so? 'Cause, if you are certainly right down affronted, I am at the end of my tether; Jessamy didn't tell me what to say to you.

JENNY. Pretend to be affronted!

JONATHAN. Aye aye, if you only pretend, you shall hear how I'll go to work to make cherubim consequences. [*Runs up to her.*

JENNY. Begone, you brute!

JONATHAN. That looks like mad; but I won't lose my speech. My dearest Jenny—your name is Jenny, I think?—My dearest Jenny, though I have the highest esteem for the sweet favours you have just now granted me—Gor, that's a fib, though; but Jessamy says it is not wicked to tell lies to the women. [*Aside.*] I say, though I have the highest esteem for the favours you have just now granted me, yet you will consider that, as soon as the dissolvable knot is tied, they will no longer be favours, but only matters of duty and matters of course.

JENNY. Marry you! you audacious monster! get out of my sight, or, rather, let me fly from you. [*Exit hastily.*

JONATHAN. Gor! she's gone off in a swinging passion, before I had time to think of consequences. If this is the way with your city ladies, give me the twenty acres of rock, the Bible, the cow, and Tabitha, and a little peaceable bundling.

SCENE II. The Mall

Enter MANLY

MANLY. It must be so, Montague! and it is not all the tribe of Mandevilles[45] that shall convince me that a nation, to become great, must first become dissipated. Luxury

[45]Edward Montagu (1713–1776), author of *Reflections on the Rise and Fall of Ancient Republics* (1759). Bernard de Mandeville (1670–1733), author of *The Fable of the Bees* (1705).

is surely the bane of a nation: Luxury! which enervates both soul and body, by opening a thousand new sources of enjoyment, opens, also, a thousand new sources of contention and want: Luxury! which renders a people weak at home, and accessible to bribery, corruption, and force from abroad. When the Grecian states knew no other tools than the axe and the saw, the Grecians were a great, a free and a happy people. The kings of Greece devoted their lives to the service of their country, and her senators knew no other superiority over their fellow-citizens than a glorious pre-eminence in danger and virtue. They exhibited to the world a noble spectacle—a number of independent states united by a similarity of language, sentiment, manners, common interest, and common consent in one grand mutual league of protection. And, thus united, long might they have continued the cherishers of arts and sciences, the protectors of the oppressed, the scourge of tyrants, and the safe asylum of liberty. But when foreign gold, and still more pernicious foreign luxury, had crept among them, they sapped the vitals of their virtue. The virtues of their ancestors were only found in their writings. Envy and suspicion, the vices of little minds, possessed them. The various states engendered jealousies of each other; and, more unfortunately, growing jealous of their great federal council, the Amphicytons, they forgot that their common safety had existed, and would exist, in giving them an honourable extensive prerogative. The common good was lost in the pursuit of private interest; and that people who, by uniting, might have stood against the world in arms, by dividing, crumbled into ruin—their name is now only known in the page of the historian, and what they once were is all we have left to admire. Oh! that America! Oh! that my country, would, in this her day, learn the things which belong to her peace!

Enter DIMPLE

DIMPLE. You are Colonel Manly, I presume?

MANLY. At your service, Sir.

DIMPLE. My name is Dimple, Sir. I have the honour to be a lodger in the same house with you, and, hearing you were in the Mall, came hither to take the liberty of joining you.

MANLY. You are very obliging, Sir.

DIMPLE. As I understand you are a stranger here, Sir, I have taken the liberty to introduce myself to your acquaintance, as possibly I may have it in my power to point out some things in this city worthy your notice.

MANLY. An attention to strangers is worthy a liberal mind, and must ever be gratefully received. But to a soldier, who has no fixed abode, such attentions are particularly pleasing.

DIMPLE. Sir, there is no character so respectable as that of a soldier. And, indeed, when we reflect how much we owe to those brave men who have suffered so much in the service of their country, and secured to us those inestimable blessings that we now enjoy, our liberty and independence, they demand every attention which gratitude can pay. For my own part, I never meet an officer, but I embrace him as my friend, nor a private in distress, but I insensibly extend my charity to him.——I have hit the Bumkin off very tolerably. [*Aside.*

MANLY. Give me your hand, Sir! I do not proffer this hand to everybody; but you steal into my heart. I hope I am as insensible to flattery as most men; but I declare (it may be my weak side) that I never hear the name of soldier mentioned with respect, but I experience a thrill of pleasure which I never feel on any other occasion.

DIMPLE. Will you give me leave, my dear Colonel, to confer an obligation on myself, by showing you some civilities during your stay here, and giving a similar opportunity to some of my friends?

MANLY. Sir, I thank you; but I believe my stay in this city will be very short.

DIMPLE. I can introduce you to some men of excellent sense, in whose company you will esteem yourself happy; and, by way of amusement, to some fine girls, who will listen to your soft things with pleasure.

MANLY. Sir, I should be proud of the honour of being acquainted with those gentlemen—but, as for the ladies, I don't understand you.

DIMPLE. Why, Sir, I need not tell you, that when a young gentleman is alone with a young lady he must say some soft things to her fair cheek—indeed, the lady will expect it. To be sure, there is not much pleasure when a man of the world and a finished coquette meet, who perfectly know each other; but how delicious is it to excite the emotions of joy, hope, expectation, and delight in the bosom of a lovely girl who believes every tittle of what you say to be serious!

MANLY. Serious, Sir! In my opinion, the man who, under pretensions of marriage, can plant thorns in the bosom of an innocent, unsuspecting girl is more detestable than a common robber, in the same proportion as private violence is more despicable than open force, and money of less value than happiness.

DIMPLE. How he awes me by the superiority of his sentiments. [*Aside.*] As you say, Sir, a gentleman should be cautious how he mentions marriage.

MANLY. Cautious, Sir! No person more approves of an intercourse between the sexes than I do. Female conversation softens our manners, whilst our discourse, from the superiority of our literary advantages, improves their minds. But, in our young country, where there is no such thing as gallantry, when a gentleman speaks of love to a lady, whether he mentions marriage or not, she ought to conclude either that he meant to insult her or that his intentions are the most serious and honourable. How mean, how cruel, is it, by a thousand tender assiduities, to win the affections of an amiable girl, and, though you leave her virtue unspotted, to betray her into the appearance of so many tender partialities, that every man of delicacy would suppress his inclination towards her, by supposing her heart engaged! Can any man, for the trivial gratification of his leisure hours, affect the happiness of a whole life! His not having spoken of marriage may add to his perfidy, but can be no excuse for his conduct.

DIMPLE. Sir, I admire your sentiments—they are mine. The light observations that fell from me were only a principle of the tongue; they came not from the heart; my practice has ever disapproved these principles.

MANLY. I believe you, sir. I should with reluctance suppose that those pernicious sentiments could find admittance into the heart of a gentleman.

DIMPLE. I am now, Sir, going to visit a family, where, if you please, I will have the honour of introducing you. Mr. Manly's ward, Miss Letitia, is a young lady of immense fortune; and his niece, Miss Charlotte Manly, is a young lady of great sprightliness and beauty.

MANLY. That gentleman, Sir, is my uncle, and Miss Manly my sister.

DIMPLE. The devil she is! [*Aside.*] Miss Manly your sister, Sir? I rejoice to hear it, and feel a double pleasure in being known to you.——Plague on him! I wish he was at Boston again, with all my soul. [*Aside.*

MANLY. Come, Sir, will you go?

DIMPLE. I will follow you in a moment, Sir. [*Exit* MANLY.] Plague on it! this is unlucky. A fighting brother is a cursed appendage to a fine girl. Egad! I just stopped in time; had he not discovered himself, in two minutes more I should have told him how well I was with his sister. Indeed, I cannot see the satisfaction of an intrigue, if one can't have the pleasure of communicating it to our friends. [*Exit.*

End of the Third Act

ACT IV. SCENE I

CHARLOTTE'S *Apartment*

CHARLOTTE *leading in* MARIA

CHARLOTTE. This is so kind, my sweet friend, to come to see me at this moment. I declare, if I were going to be married in a few days, as you are, I should scarce have found time to visit my friends.

MARIA. Do you think, then, that there is an impropriety in it?—How should you dispose of your time?

CHARLOTTE. Why, I should be shut up in my chamber; and my head would so run upon—upon—upon the solemn ceremony that I was to pass through!—I declare, it would take me above two hours merely to learn that little monosyllable—*Yes.* Ah! my dear, your sentimental imagination does not conceive what that little tiny word implies.

MARIA. Spare me your raillery, my sweet friend; I should love your agreeable vivacity at any other time.

CHARLOTTE. Why, this is the very time to amuse you. You grieve me to see you look so unhappy.

MARIA. Have I not reason to look so?

CHARLOTTE. What new grief distresses you?

MARIA. Oh! how sweet it is, when the heart is borne down with misfortune, to recline and repose on the bosom of friendship! Heaven knows that, although it is improper for a young lady to praise a gentleman, yet I have ever concealed Mr. Dimple's foibles, and spoke of him as of one whose reputation I expected would be linked with mine; but his late conduct towards me has turned my coolness into contempt. He behaves as if he meant to insult and disgust me; whilst my father, in the last conversation on the subject of our marriage, spoke of it as a matter which lay near his heart, and in which he would not bear contradiction.

CHARLOTTE. This works well; oh! the generous Dimple. I'll endeavour to excite her to discharge him. [*Aside.*] But, my dear friend, your happiness depends on yourself. Why don't you discard him? Though the match has been of long standing, I would not be forced to make myself miserable: no parent in the world should oblige me to marry the man I did not like.

MARIA. Oh! my dear, you never lived with your parents, and do not know what influence a father's frowns have upon a daughter's heart. Besides, what have I to alledge against Mr. Dimple, to justify myself to the world? He carries himself so smoothly, that every one would impute the blame to me, and call me capricious.

CHARLOTTE. And call her capricious! Did ever such an objection start into the heart of woman? For my part, I wish I had fifty lovers to discard, for no other reason than because I did not fancy them. My dear Maria, you will forgive me; I know your candour and confidence in me; but I have at times, I confess, been led to suppose that some other gentleman was the cause of your aversion to Mr. Dimple.

MARIA. No, my sweet friend, you may be assured, that though I have seen many gentlemen I could prefer to Mr. Dimple, yet I never saw one that I thought I could give my hand to, until this morning.

CHARLOTTE. This morning!

MARIA. Yes; one of the strangest accidents in the world. The odious Dimple, after disgusting me with his conversation, had just left me, when a gentleman, who, it seems, boards in the same house with him, saw him coming out of our door, and, the houses looking very much alike, he came into our house instead of his lodgings; nor did he discover his mistake until he got into the parlour, where I was; he then bowed so gracefully, made such a genteel apology, and looked so manly and noble!——

CHARLOTTE. I see some folks, though it is so great an impropriety, can praise a gentleman, when he happens to be the man of their fancy. [*Aside.*

MARIA. I don't know how it was—I hope he did not think me indelicate—but I asked him, I believe, to sit down, or pointed to a chair. He sat down, and, instead of having recourse to observations upon the weather, or hackneyed criticisms upon the theatre, he entered readily into a conversation worthy a man of sense to speak, and a lady of delicacy and sentiment to hear. He was not strictly handsome, but he spoke the language of sentiment, and his eyes looked tenderness and honour.

CHARLOTTE. Oh! [eagerly] you sentimental, grave girls, when your hearts are once touched, beat us rattles a bar's length. And so you are quite in love with this he-angel?

MARIA. In love with him! How can you rattle so, Charlotte? am I not going to be miserable? [*Sighs.*] In love with a gentleman I never saw but one hour in my life, and don't know his name! No; I only wished that the man I shall marry may look, and talk, and act, just like him. Besides, my dear, he is a married man.

CHARLOTTE. Why, that was good-natured—he told you so, I suppose, in mere charity, to prevent you falling in love with him?

MARIA. He didn't tell me so; [*peevishly*] he looked as if he was married.

CHARLOTTE. How, my dear; did he look sheepish?

MARIA. I am sure he has a susceptible heart, and the ladies of his acquaintance must be very stupid not to——

CHARLOTTE. Hush! I hear some person coming.

Enter LETITIA

LETITIA. My dear Maria, I am happy to see you. Lud! what a pity it is that you have purchased your wedding clothes.

MARIA. I think so. [*Sighing.*

LETITIA. Why, my dear, there is the sweetest parcel of silks come over you ever saw! Nancy Brilliant has a full suit come; she sent over her measure, and it fits her to a hair; it is immensely dressy, and made for a court-hoop. I thought they said the large hoops were going out of fashion.

CHARLOTTE. Did you see the hat? Is it a fact that the deep laces round the border is still the fashion?

DIMPLE. [*within*]. Upon my honour, Sir.

MARIA. Ha! Dimple's voice! My dear, I must take leave of you. There are some things necessary to be done at our house. Can't I go through the other room?

Enter DIMPLE *and* MANLY

DIMPLE. Ladies, your most obedient.

CHARLOTTE. Miss Van Rough, shall I present my brother Henry to you? Colonel Manly, Maria—Miss Van Rough, brother.

MARIA. Her brother! [*Turns and sees* MANLY.] Oh! my heart! the very gentleman I have been praising.

MANLY. The same amiable girl I saw this morning!

CHARLOTTE. Why, you look as if you were acquainted.

MANLY. I unintentionally intruded into this lady's presence this morning, for which she was so good as to promise me her forgiveness.

CHARLOTTE. Oh! ho! is that the case! Have these two penserosos been together? Were they Henry's eyes that looked so tenderly? [*Aside.*] And so you promised to pardon him? and could you be so good-natured? have you really forgiven him? I beg you would do it for my sake [*whispering loud to* MARIA]. But, my dear, as you are in such haste, it would be cruel to detain you; I can show you the way through the other room.

MARIA. Spare me, my sprightly friend.

MANLY. The lady does not, I hope, intend to deprive us of the pleasure of her company so soon.

CHARLOTTE. She has only a mantua-maker[46] who waits for her at home. But, as I am to give my opinion of the dress, I think she cannot go yet. We were talking of the fashions when you came in, but I suppose the subject must be changed to something of more importance now. Mr. Dimple, will you favour us with an account of the public entertainments?

DIMPLE. Why, really, Miss Manly, you could not have asked me a question more *mal-apropos.*[47] For my part, I must confess that, to a man who has travelled, there is nothing that is worthy the name of amusement to be found in this city.

CHARLOTTE. Except visiting the ladies.

DIMPLE. Pardon me, Madam; that is the avocation of a man of taste. But for amusement, I positively know of nothing that can be called so, unless you dignify with that title the hopping once a fortnight to the sound of two or three squeaking fiddles, and the clattering of the old tavern windows, or sitting to see the miserable mummers, whom you call actors, murder comedy and make a farce of tragedy.

MANLY. Do you never attend the theatre, Sir?

DIMPLE. I was tortured there once.

CHARLOTTE. Pray, Mr. Dimple, was it a tragedy or a comedy?

[46]Dressmaker.

[47]Inappropriate.

DIMPLE. Faith, Madam, I cannot tell; for I sat with my back to the stage all the time, admiring a much better actress than any there—a lady who played the fine woman to perfection; though, by the laugh of the horrid creatures round me, I suppose it was comedy. Yet, on second thoughts, it might be some hero in a tragedy, dying so comically as to set the whole house in an uproar. Colonel, I presume you have been in Europe?

MANLY. Indeed, Sir, I was never ten leagues from the continent.

DIMPLE. Believe me, Colonel, you have an immense pleasure to come; and when you shall have seen the brilliant exhibitions of Europe, you will learn to despise the amusements of this country as much as I do.

MANLY. Therefore I do not wish to see them; for I can never esteem that knowledge valuable which tends to give me a distaste for my native country.

DIMPLE. Well, Colonel, though you have not travelled, you have read.

MANLY. I have, a little; and by it have discovered that there is a laudable partiality which ignorant, untravelled men entertain for everything that belongs to their native country. I call it laudable; it injures no one; adds to their own happiness; and, when extended, becomes the noble principle of patriotism. Travelled gentlemen rise superior, in their own opinion, to this; but if the contempt which they contract for their country is the most valuable acquisition of their travels, I am far from thinking that their time and money are well spent.

MARIA. What noble sentiments!

CHARLOTTE. Let my brother set out where he will in the fields of conversation, he is sure to end his tour in the temple of gravity.

MANLY. Forgive me, my sister. I love my country; it has its foibles undoubtedly—some foreigners will with pleasure remark them—but such remarks fall very ungracefully from the lips of her citizens.

DIMPLE. You are perfectly in the right, Colonel—America has her faults.

MANLY. Yes, Sir; and we, her children, should blush for them in private, and endeavour, as individuals, to reform them. But, if our country has its errors in common with other countries, I am proud to say America—I mean the United States—has displayed virtues and achievements which modern nations may admire, but of which they have seldom set us the example.

CHARLOTTE. But, brother, we must introduce you to some of our gay folks, and let you see the city, such as it is. Mr. Dimple is known to almost every family in town; he will doubtless take a pleasure in introducing you?

DIMPLE. I shall esteem every service I can render your brother an honour.

MANLY. I fear the business I am upon will take up all my time, and my family will be anxious to hear from me.

MARIA. His family! but what is it to me that he is married! [*Aside.*]. Pray, how did you leave your lady, Sir?

CHARLOTTE. My brother is not married [*observing her anxiety*]; it is only an odd way he has of expressing himself. Pray, brother, is this business, which you make your continual excuse, a secret?

MANLY. No, sister; I came hither to solicit the honourable Congress, that a number of my brave old soldiers may be put upon the pension-list, who were, at first, not judged to be so materially wounded as to need the public assistance. My sister says true [*to* MARIA]; I call my late soldiers my family. Those who were not in the field in the late glorious contest, and those who were, have their respective merits; but, I confess, my older brother-soldiers are dearer to me than the former description. Friendships made in adversity are lasting; our countrymen may forget us, but that is no reason why we should forget one another. But I must leave you; my time of engagement approaches.

CHARLOTTE. Well, but, brother, if you will go, will you please to conduct my fair friend home? You live in the same street——I was to have gone with her myself—[*Aside.*] A lucky thought.

MARIA. I am obliged to your sister, Sir, and was just intending to go. [*Going.*

MANLY. I shall attend her with pleasure.

Exit with MARIA, *followed by* DIMPLE *and* CHARLOTTE.

MARIA. Now, pray, don't betray me to your brother.

CHARLOTTE. [*Just as she sees him make a motion to take his leave.*] One word with you, brother, if you please. [*Follows them out.*

Manent[48] DIMPLE *and* LETITIA.

DIMPLE. You received the billet I sent you, I presume?

LETITIA. Hush!—Yes.

DIMPLE. When shall I pay my respects to you?

LETITIA. At eight I shall be unengaged.

Reenter CHARLOTTE

DIMPLE. Did my lovely angel receive my billet? [*To* CHARLOTTE.]

CHARLOTTE. Yes.

DIMPLE. What hour shall I expect with impatience?

CHARLOTTE. At eight I shall be at home unengaged.

DIMPLE. Unfortunate! I have a horrid engagement of business at that hour. Can't you finish your visit earlier and let six be the happy hour?

CHARLOTTE. You know your influence over me. [*Exeunt severally.*

SCENE II

VAN ROUGH's House

VAN ROUGH [*alone*]. It cannot possibly be true! The son of my old friend can't have acted so unadvisedly. Seventeen thousand pounds! in bills! Mr. Transfer must have been mistaken. He always appeared so prudent, and talked so well upon money matters, and even assured me that he intended to change his dress for a suit of clothes which would not cost so much, and look more substantial, as soon as he married. No, no, no! it can't be; it cannot be. But, however, I must look out sharp. I did not care what his principles or his actions were, so long as he minded the main chance. Seventeen thousand pounds! If he had lost it in trade, why the best men may have ill-luck; but to game it away, as Transfer says—why, at this rate, his whole estate may go in one night, and, what is ten times worse, mine into the bar-

[48]"There remain."

gain. No, no; Mary is right. Leave women to look out in these matters; for all they look as if they didn't know a journal from a ledger, when their interest is concerned they know what's what; they mind the main chance as well as the best of us. I wonder Mary did not tell me she knew of his spending his money so foolishly. Seventeen thousand pounds! Why, if my daughter was standing up to be married, I would forbid the banns, if I found it was to a man who did not mind the main chance.—Hush! I hear somebody coming. 'Tis Mary's voice; a man with her too! I shouldn't be surprised if this should be the other string to her bow. Aye, aye, let them alone; women understand the main chance.—Though, i' faith, I'll listen a little. [*Retires into a closet.*

MANLY *leading in* MARIA

MANLY. I hope you will excuse my speaking upon so important a subject so abruptly; but, the moment I entered your room, you struck me as the lady whom I had long loved in imagination, and never hoped to see.

MARIA. Indeed, Sir, I have been led to hear more upon this subject than I ought.

MANLY. Do you, then, disapprove my suit, Madam, or the abruptness of my introducing it? If the latter, my peculiar situation, being obliged to leave the city in a few days, will, I hope, be my excuse; if the former, I will retire, for I am sure I would not give a moment's inquietude to her whom I could devote my life to please. I am not so indelicate as to seek your immediate approbation; permit me only to be near you, and by a thousand tender assiduities to endeavour to excite a grateful return.

MARIA. I have a father, whom I would die to make happy; he will disapprove——

MANLY. Do you think me so ungenerous as to seek a place in your esteem without his consent? You must—you ever ought to consider that man as unworthy of you seeks an interest in your heart contrary to a father's approbation. A young lady should reflect that the loss of a lover may be supplied, but nothing can compensate for the loss of a parent's affection. Yet, why do you suppose your father would disapprove? In our country, the affections are not sacrificed to riches or family aggrandizement; should you approve, my family is decent, and my rank honourable.

MARIA. You distress me, Sir.

MANLY. Then I will sincerely beg your excuse for obtruding so disagreeable a subject, and retire. [*Going.*

MARIA. Stay, Sir! your generosity and good opinion of me deserve a return; but why must I declare what, for these few hours, I have scarce suffered myself to think?—I am——

MANLY. What?

MARIA. Engaged, Sir; and, in a few days to be married to the gentleman you saw at your sister's.

MANLY. Engaged to be married! And I have been basely invading the rights of another? Why have you permitted this? Is this the return for the partiality I declared for you?

MARIA. You distress me, Sir. What would you have me say? you are too generous to wish the truth. Ought I to say that I dared not suffer myself to think of my engagement, and that I am going to give my hand without my heart? Would you have me confess a partiality for you? If so, your triumph is complete, and can be only more so when days of misery with the man I cannot love will make me think of him whom I could prefer.

MANLY [*after a pause*]. We are both unhappy; but it is your duty to obey your parent—mine to obey my honour. Let us, therefore, both follow the path of rectitude; and of this we may be assured, that if we are not happy, we shall, at least, deserve to be so. Adieu! I dare not trust myself longer with you. [*Exeunt severally.*

End of the Fourth Act

ACT V. SCENE I

DIMPLE'S *Lodgings*

JESSAMY *meeting* JONATHAN

JESSAMY. Well, Mr. Jonathan, what success with the fair?

JONATHAN. Why, such a tarnal cross tike you never saw! You would have counted she had lived upon crab-apples and vinegar for a fortnight. But what the rattle makes you look so tarnation glum?

JESSAMY. I was thinking, Mr. Jonathan, what could be the reason of her carrying herself so coolly to you.

JONATHAN. Coolly, do you call it? Why, I vow, she was fire-hot angry: may be it was because I buss'd her.

JESSAMY. No, no, Mr. Jonathan; there must be some other cause; I never yet knew a lady angry at being kissed.

JONATHAN. Well, if it is not the young woman's bashfulness, I vow I can't conceive why she shouldn't like me.

JESSAMY. May be it is because you have not the graces, Mr. Jonathan.

JONATHAN. Grace! Why, does the young woman expect I must be converted before I court her?

JESSAMY. I mean graces of person; for instance, my lord tells us that we must cut off our nails even at top, in small segments of circles—though you won't understand that; in the next place, you must regulate your laugh.

JONATHAN. Maple-log seize it! don't I laugh natural?

JESSAMY. That's the very fault, Mr. Jonathan. Besides, you absolutely misplace it. I was told by a friend of mine that you laughed outright at the play the other night, when you ought only to have tittered.

JONATHAN. Gor! I—what does one go to see fun for if they can't laugh.

JESSAMY. You may laugh; but you must laugh by rule.

JONATHAN. Swamp it—laugh by rule! Well, I should like that tarnally.

JESSAMY. Why, you know, Mr. Jonathan, that to dance, a lady to play with her fan, or a gentleman with his cane, and all other natural motions, are regulated by art. My master has composed an immensely pretty gamut, by which any lady or gentleman, with a few years' close application, may learn to laugh as gracefully as if they were born and bred to it.

JONATHAN. Mercy on my soul! A gamut for laughing—just like fa, la, sol?

JESSAMY. Yes. It comprises every possible display of jocularity, from an *affettuoso*[49]

[49]Italian: affectionate, smooth, loud.

smile to a *piano* titter, or full chorus *fortissimo* ha, ha, ha! My master employs his leisure hours in marking out the plays, like a cathedral chanting-book, that the ignorant may know where to laugh; and that pit, box, and gallery may keep time together, and not have a snigger in one part of the house, a broad grin in the other, and a d——d grum[50] look in the third. How delightful to see the audience all smile together, then look on their books, then twist their mouths into an agreeable simper, than altogether shake the house with a general ha, ha, ha! loud as a full chorus of Handel's[51] at an Abbey commemoration.

JONATHAN. Ha, ha, ha! that's dang'd cute, I swear.

JESSAMY. The gentlemen, you see, will laugh the tenor; the ladies will play the counter-tenor; the beaux will squeak the treble; and our jolly friends in the gallery a thorough base, ho, ho, ho!

JONATHAN. Well, can't you let me see that gamut?

JESSAMY. Oh! yes, Mr. Jonathan; here it is [*Takes out a book.*] Oh! no, this is only a titter with its variations. Ah, here it is. [*Takes out another.*] Now, you must know, Mr. Jonathan, this is a piece written by Ben Jonson,[52] which I have set to my master's gamut. The places where you must smile, look grave, or laugh outright, are marked below the line. Now look over me. "There was a certain man"—now you must smile.

JONATHAN. Well, read it again; I warrant I'll mind my eye.

JESSAMY. "There was a certain man, who had a sad scolding wife"—now you must laugh.

JONATHAN. Tarnation! That's no laughing matter though.

JESSAMY. "And she lay sick a-dying"—now you must titter.

JONATHAN. What, snigger when the good woman's a-dying! Gor, I——

JESSAMY. Yes, the notes say you must—"and she asked her husband leave to make a will"—now you must begin to look grave; "and her husband said"——

JONATHAN. Ay, what did her husband say? Something dang'd cute, I reckon.

JESSAMY. "And her husband said, you have had your will all your life-time, and would you have it after you are dead, too?"

JONATHAN. Ho, ho, ho! There the old man was even with her; he was up to the notch—ha, ha, ha!

JESSAMY. But, Mr. Jonathan, you must not laugh so. Why you ought to have tittered *piano,* and you have laughed *fortissimo.* Look here; you see these marks, A, B, C, and so on; these are the references to the other part of the book. Let us turn to it, and you will see the directions how to manage the muscles. This [*turns over*] was note D you blundered at.—You must purse the mouth into a smile, then titter, discovering the lower part of the three front upper teeth.

JONATHAN. How? read it again.

JESSAMY. "There was a certain man"—very well!—"who had a sad scolding wife"—why don't you laugh?

JONATHAN. Now, that scolding wife sticks in my gizzard so pluckily that I can't laugh for the blood and nowns of me. Let me look grave here, and I'll laugh your belly full, where the old creature's a-dying.

[50]Grim.

[51]George Frederick Handel (1685–1759), eminent composer.

[52]Ben Jonson (1572–1637), English dramatist.

JESSAMY. "And she asked her husband"—[*Bell rings.*] My master's bell! he's returned, I fear.—Here, Mr. Jonathan, take this gamut; and I make no doubt but with a few years' close application, you may be able to smile gracefully.

[*Exeunt severally.*

SCENE II

CHARLOTTE'S *Apartment*

Enter MANLY

MANLY. What, no one at home? How unfortunate to meet the only lady my heart was ever moved by, to find her engaged to another, and confessing her partiality for me! Yet engaged to a man who, by her intimation, and his libertine conversation with me, I fear, does not merit her. Aye! there's the sting; for, were I assured that Maria was happy, my heart is not so selfish but that it would dilate in knowing it, even though it were with another. But to know she is unhappy!—I must drive these thoughts from me. Charlotte has some books; and this is what I believe she calls her little library. [*Enters a closet.*

Enter DIMPLE *leading* LETITIA

LETITIA. And will you pretend to say now, Mr. Dimple, that you propose to break with Maria? Are not the banns published? Are not the clothes purchased? Are not the friends invited? In short, is it not a done affair?

DIMPLE. Believe me, my dear Letitia, I would not marry her.

LETITIA. Why have you not broke with her before this, as you all along deluded me by saying you would?

DIMPLE. Because I was in hopes she would, ere this, have broke with me.

LETITIA. You could not expect it.

DIMPLE. Nay, but be calm a moment; 'twas from my regard to you that I did not discard her.

LETITIA. Regard to me!

DIMPLE. Yes; I have done everything in my power to break with her, but the foolish girl is so fond of me that nothing can accomplish it. Besides, how can I offer her my hand when my heart is indissolubly engaged to you?

LETITIA. There may be reason in this; but why so attentive to Miss Manly?

DIMPLE. Attentive to Miss Manly! For heaven's sake, if you have no better opinion of my constancy, pay not so ill a compliment to my taste.

LETITIA. Did I not see you whisper her to-day?

DIMPLE. Possibly I might—but something of so very trifling a nature that I have already forgot what it was.

LETITIA. I believe she has not forgot it.

DIMPLE. My dear creature, how can you for a moment suppose I should have any serious thoughts of that trifling, gay, flighty coquette, that disagreeable——

Enter CHARLOTTE

My dear Miss Manly, I rejoice to see you; there is a charm in your conversation that always marks your entrance into company as fortunate.

LETITIA. Where have you been, my dear?

CHARLOTTE. Why, I have been about to twenty shops, turning over pretty things, and so have left twenty visits unpaid. I wish you would step into the carriage and whisk round, make my apology, and leave my cards where our friends are not at home; that, you know, will serve as a visit. Come, do go.

LETITIA. So anxious to get me out! but I'll watch you. [*Aside.*] Oh! yes, I'll go; I want a little exercise. Positively [DIMPLE *offering to accompany her*], Mr. Dimple, you shall not go; why, half my visits are cake and caudle visits; it won't do, you know, for you to go. [*Exit, but returns to the door in the back scene and listens.*]

DIMPLE. This attachment of your brother to Maria is fortunate.

CHARLOTTE. How did you come to the knowledge of it?

DIMPLE. I read it in their eyes.

CHARLOTTE. And I had it from her mouth. It would have amused you to have seen her! She, that thought it so great an impropriety to praise a gentleman that she could not bring out one word in your favour, found a redundancy to praise him.

DIMPLE. I have done everything in my power to assist his passion there: your delicacy, my dearest girl, would be shocked at half the instances of neglect and misbehaviour.

CHARLOTTE. I don't know how I should bear neglect; but Mr. Dimple must misbehave himself indeed, to forfeit my good opinion.

DIMPLE. Your good opinion, my angel, is the pride and pleasure of my heart; and if the most respectful tenderness for you, and an utter indifference for all your sex besides, can make me worthy of your esteem, I shall richly merit it.

CHARLOTTE. All my sex besides, Mr. Dimple!—you forgot your tête-à-tête[53] with Letitia.

DIMPLE. How can you, my lovely angel, cast a thought on that insipid, wry-mouthed, ugly creature!

CHARLOTTE. But her fortune may have charms.

DIMPLE. Not to a heart like mine. The man, who has been blessed with the good opinion of my Charlotte, must despise the allurements of fortune.

CHARLOTTE. I am satisfied.

DIMPLE. Let us think no more on the odious subject, but devote the present hour to happiness.

CHARLOTTE. Can I be happy, when I see the man I prefer going to be married to another?

DIMPLE. Have I not already satisfied my charming angel, that I can never think of marrying the puling Maria? But, even if it were so, could that be any bar to our happiness? for, as the poet sings,

> "Love, free as air, at sight of human ties,
> Spreads his light wings, and in a moment flies."[54]

Come, then, my charming angel! why delay our bliss? The present moment is ours; the next is in the hand of fate. [*Kissing her.*

[53] Private conversation.

[54] "Eloisa to Abelard" (1717) by Alexander Pope (1688–1744).

CHARLOTTE. Begone, Sir! By your delusions you had almost lulled my honour asleep.

DIMPLE. Let me lull the demon to sleep again with kisses.

[*He struggles with her; she screams.*

Enter MANLY

MANLY. Turn, villain! and defend yourself.—— [*Draws.*

VAN ROUGH *enters and beats down their swords*

VAN ROUGH. Is the devil in you? are you going to murder one another?

[*Holding* DIMPLE.

DIMPLE. Hold him, hold him—I can command my passion.

Enter JONATHAN

JONATHAN. What the rattle ails you? Is the old one in you? Let the colonel alone, can't you? I feel chock-full of fight—do you want to kill the colonel?——

MANLY. Be still, Jonathan; the gentleman does not want to hurt me.

JONATHAN. Gor! I—I wish he did; I'd show him Yankee boys play, pretty quick.— Don't you see you have frightened the young woman into the *hystrikes?*

VAN ROUGH. Pray, some of you explain this; what has been the occasion of all this racket?

MANLY. That gentleman can explain it to you; it will be a very diverting story for an intended father-in-law to hear.

VAN ROUGH. How was this matter, Mr. Van Dumpling?

DIMPLE. Sir—upon my honour—all I know is, that I was talking to this young lady, and this gentleman broke in on us in a very extraordinary manner.

VAN ROUGH. Why, all this is nothing to the purpose; can you explain it, Miss?

[*To* CHARLOTTE.

Enter LETITIA *through the back scene*

LETITIA. I can explain it to that gentleman's confusion. Though long betrothed to your daughter [*to* VAN ROUGH], yet, allured by my fortune, it seems (with shame do I speak it) he has privately paid his addresses to me, I was drawn in to listen to him by his assuring me that the match was made by his father without his consent, and that he proposed to break with Maria, whether he married me or not. But, whatever were his intentions respecting your daughter, Sir, even to me he was false; for he has repeated the same story, with some cruel reflections upon my person, to Miss Manly.

JONATHAN. What a tarnal curse!

LETITIA. Nor is this all, Miss Manly. When he was with me this very morning, he made the same ungenerous reflections upon the weakness of your mind as he has so recently done upon the defects of my person.

JONATHAN. What a tarnal curse and damn, too.

DIMPLE. Ha! since I have lost Letitia, I believe I had as good make it up with Maria. Mr. Van Rough, at present I cannot enter into particulars; but, I believe, I can explain everything to your satisfaction in private.

VAN ROUGH. There is another matter, Mr. Van Dumpling, which I would have you explain. Pray, Sir, have Messrs. Van Cash & Co. presented you those bills for acceptance?

DIMPLE. The deuce! Has he heard of those bills! Nay, then, all's up with Maria, too; but an affair of this sort can never prejudice me among the ladies; they will rather long to know what the dear creature possesses to make him so agreeable. [*Aside.*] Sir, you'll hear from me. [*To* MANLY.

MANLY. And you from me, Sir——

DIMPLE. Sir, you wear a sword——

MANLY. Yes, Sir. This sword was presented to me by that brave Gallic hero, the Marquis De la Fayette.[55] I have drawn it in the service of my country, and in private life, on the only occasion where a man is justified in drawing his sword, in defence of a lady's honour. I have fought too many battles in the service of my country to dread the imputation of cowardice. Death from a man of honour would be a glory you do not merit; you shall live to bear the insult of man and the contempt of that sex whose general smiles afforded you all your happiness.

DIMPLE. You won't meet me, Sir? Then I'll post you for a coward.

MANLY. I'll venture that, Sir. The reputation of my life does not depend upon the breath of a Mr. Dimple. I would have you to know, however, Sir, that I have a cane to chastise the insolence of a scoundrel, and a sword and the good laws of my country to protect me from the attempts of an assassin——

DIMPLE. Mighty well! Very fine, indeed! Ladies and gentlemen, I take my leave; and you will please to observe in the case of my deportment the contrast between a gentleman who has read Chesterfield and received the polish of Europe and an unpolished, untravelled American. [*Exit*

Enter MARIA

MARIA. Is he indeed gone?——

LETITIA. I hope, never to return.

VAN ROUGH. I am glad I heard of those bills; though it's plaguy unlucky; I hoped to see Mary married before I did.

MANLY. Will you permit a gentleman, Sir, to offer himself as a suitor to your daughter? Though a stranger to you, he is not altogether so to her, or unknown in this city. You may find a son-in-law of more fortune, but you can never meet with one who is richer in love for her, or respect for you.

VAN ROUGH. Why, Mary, you have not let this gentleman make love to you without my leave?

MANLY. I did not say, Sir——

MARIA. Say, Sir!——I—the gentleman, to be sure, met me accidentally.

VAN ROUGH. Ha, ha, ha! Mark me, Mary; young folks think old folks to be fools; but old folks know young folks to be fools. Why, I knew all about this affair. This was only a cunning way I had to bring it about. Hark ye! I was in the closet when you and he were at our house. [*Turns to the company.*] I heard that little baggage say she loved her old father, and would die to make him happy! Oh! how I loved the little baggage! And you talked very prudently, young man. I have inquired into

[55]French general and statesman (1757–1834) who served in the Continental Army during the American Revolution.

your character, and find you to be a man of punctuality and mind the main chance. And so, as you love Mary and Mary loves you, you shall have my consent immediately to be married. I'll settle my fortune on you, and go and live with you the remainder of my life.

MANLY. Sir, I hope——

VAN ROUGH. Come, come, no fine speeches; mind the main chance, young man, and you and I shall always agree.

LETITIA. I sincerely wish you joy [*advancing to* MARIA]; and hope your pardon for my conduct.

MARIA. I thank you for your congratulations, and hope we shall at once forget the wretch who has given us so much disquiet, and the trouble that he has occasioned.

CHARLOTTE. And I, my dear Maria—how shall I look up to you for forgiveness? I, who, in the practice of the meanest arts, have violated the most sacred rights of friendship? I never can forgive myself, or hope charity from the world; but, I confess, I have much to hope from such a brother; and I am happy that I may soon say, such a sister.

MARIA. My dear, you distress me; you have all my love.

MANLY. And mine.

CHARLOTTE. If repentance can entitle me to forgiveness, I have already much merit; for I despise the littleness of my past conduct. I now find that the heart of any worthy man cannot be gained by invidious attacks upon the rights and characters of others—by countenancing the addresses of a thousand—or that the finest assemblage of features, the greatest taste in dress, the genteelest address, or the most brilliant wit, cannot eventually secure a coquette from contempt and ridicule.

MANLY. And I have learned that probity, virtue, honour, though they should not have received the polish of Europe, will secure to an honest American the good graces of his fair countrywomen, and I hope, the applause of THE PUBLIC.

The End

1790

Hendrick Aupaumut (Mahican) 1757–1830

A native diplomat and grand sachem of the Mahicans, Hendrick Aupaumut was an important leader of the Stockbridge Indians during the last forty years of his life. He was described by Timothy Pickering, a special peace agent to the western tribes, as an intelligent man, fluent in English (which he wrote legibly). His elevation to leadership came at a critical time in Stockbridge history.

That history had been remarkable as an example of racial and cultural survival. The Stockbridges, of which the Mahicans formed the largest part, included remnants of tribal groups that had once inhabited the entire Hudson River Valley. At first contact, the Mahicans had controlled the territory on both sides of the river from the Catskills north to Lake Champlain. To the south were the Esopus, Wappingers, and other Munsee groups with whom the Mahicans had close relations and with whom they controlled the valley down to Manhattan. By 1700, however, they had been reduced from an estimated 4,000 to about 500 as a result of epidemic diseases, warfare, displacement, and amalgamation with other groups. Their decline continued in the eighteenth century. In 1735, missionaries were sent to the Mahicans and others on the Housatonic River in western Massachusetts, where they established a mission town at Stockbridge, to which were gathered the remnant tribes of the region. In 1740 Moravians established a mission for the Mahicans in New York; when New York officials ordered the Moravians to cease their efforts a few years later, the Mahicans dispersed to Pennsylvania, Canada, and elsewhere, including Stockbridge.

Aupaumut, born at Stockbridge, had been educated by the Moravians. At the outbreak of the Revolutionary War, he and many other Stockbridges enlisted in the Continental Army.

Following the battle of White Plains in 1778, he was commissioned captain and saw extensive service during the remainder of the war. After the war, the Stockbridges decided to move because of terrible losses during the war, the takeover of Stockbridge by whites, and the Stockbridges' susceptibility to the vices of their white neighbors. At the invitation of the Oneidas, they moved to Oneida Creek, New York, in the mid-1780s and established New Stockbridge.

Aupaumut became influential after the removal. By virtue of his loyalty to the United States, he served as an important go-between for the government and the Indians during the early 1790s. When the native groups of the Northwest Territory, encouraged by British intrigue, made war against the frontier settlements, Aupaumut was sent by General Arthur St. Clair in 1791 with a proclamation and offer of peace. At the request of Secretary of War Henry Knox in 1792, he traveled for eleven months among the Delawares, Miamis, Shawnees, and others. After this journey Aupaumut wrote "A Short Narration of My Last Journey to the Western Contry," a detailed account of his journey and negotiations with the various peoples. In 1794, he was at the Battle of Fallen Timbers with General Wayne and attended a session of the treaty negotiation with the Six Nations and others at Canadaigua; he signed the treaty that was drafted and continued to work as a negotiator for a number of years. In 1808 or 1809 he was seen in Washington with Nicholas Cusick, a Tuscarora, on their way to North Carolina to try to obtain reparations from the North Carolinians for lands that the Tuscaroras had been forced to abandon in the eighteenth century.

By the time of his travels to the Western country, Aupaumut was convinced that the Stockbridges must move farther west. He was afraid of the influence of not only the local whites but the Oneidas, who discouraged farming by the Stockbridge men. When the Oneidas attempted to introduce the religion of Handsome Lake to the Stockbridges, Aupaumut stopped them. In his search for a new home, Aupaumut sought out the Munsees and Delawares who had settled on the White River in Indiana, to whom he was appointed agent in 1808. Attempts of the Stockbridges to find a new home in the West were disrupted by the War of 1812, during which he adamantly opposed the efforts of Tecumseh to organize tribes on the frontier. In 1818 a group migrated to the White River to join the Munsees and Delawares, only to find that the lands had been sold. In 1821, Aupaumut's son Soloman took a small group to Wisconsin, where they settled on Menominee lands and were joined by others from Indiana and New York. In 1828, land was purchased for them on the Fox River, and in 1829, the year before Aupaumut's death, the last Stockbridges, including Aupaumut himself, removed to the West.

Aupaumut's "Narration," sprinkled with flaws in English idioms, attests to the struggle of a Native American, working in a second language, to record an Indian history full of speeches and dramatic episodes. The "Narration" provides the reader with rare insights into Indian manners, diplomacy, and protocol. Aupaumut himself takes on complex dimensions through his narrative. Despite what the colonists had done to his own people, Aupaumut was fiercely loyal to the United States. He had faith that the new nation would treat the Indians fairly. Always the diplomat, he carefully avoided discussing topics that might alienate the Indians, and he presented his hearers with logical arguments, stressing a preference of negotiation over warfare. Written about 1794, the manuscript went unpublished until 1827, after it was found among the papers of Isaac Zane of Philadelphia. Besides this piece, Aupaumut also recorded Mahican tribal traditions in 1791 and was author of a number of speeches and letters published during his lifetime.

Daniel F. Littlefield, Jr.
University of Arkansas at Little Rock

PRIMARY WORK

"History of the Muhheakunnuk Indians," in Jedediah Morse, ed., *First Annual Report of the American Society for Promoting the Civilization and General Improvement of the Indian Tribes of the United States,* 1824; *A Short Narration of My Last Journey to the Western Contry,* 1827.

SECONDARY WORK

T. J. Brasser, "Mahican," in Bruce G. Trigger, ed., *Handbook of North American Indians,* Vol. 15: Northeast, 1978; Jeanne Ronda and James P. Ronda, "'As They Were Faithful': Chief Hendrick Aupaumut and the Struggle for Stockbridge Survival, 1757–1830," *American Indian Culture and Research Journal* 3, 1979: 43–55.

from A Short Narration of My Last Journey to the Western Contry[1]

As I have propose to mention—The complaints or arguments of these Indians, and my arguments to convince them in several times, I will now put down.

First principal thing they argue is this—that the white people are deceitful in their dealings with us the Indians; (says they) The white people have taken all our lands from us, from time to time, until this time, and that they will continue the same way, &c. Then I reply and say it has been too much so, because these white people was governed by one Law, the Law of the great King of England; and by that Law they could hold our lands, in spite of our disatisfaction; and we were too fond of their liquors.[2] But now they have new Laws their own, and by these Laws Indians cannot

[1]Written about 1794, the *Narration* was not published until 1827 when it appeared in the second volume of the *Memoirs of the Pennsylvania Historical Society.* Accompanied by his brother and other Indians, Aupaumut met in council with a number of tribes including the Delaware, Shawnee, Miami, Wyandot, Ottawa, Chippewa, Potawatomi, and Kickapoo. His narrative is a record not only of speeches and negotiations but also of the complex tribal relations and the intrigues of some well-known historical figures such as Joseph Brant and Simon Girty. What follows is the conclusion of Aupaumut's narrative.

[2]A common complaint throughout Indian history has been that whites subverted Indian society through use of liquors.

be deceived as usual, &c. And they say, but these Big knifes have take away our lands since they have their own way.[3] And then I tell them, for this very reason the United Sachems[4] invite you to treat with them that you may settle these dificulties—for how can these dificulties settled without you treat with them?

Another thing they mention—says they, the Big knifes have used learning to Civilize Indians: and after they Christianize number of them so as to gain their attention, then they would killed them, and have killed of such 96 in one day at Cosuhkeck,[5] few years ago.

Another instance they mention—that one of the Chiefs of Shawany[6] was friendly to the Big knifes, and Big knifes gave him a flag, that where ever the chief should come a cross the Big knifes, he is to hoist up this flag, then they will meet together in peace. But soon after this agreement was made, the Big knifes came in the town of this Chief; some of the Indians could not trust the Big knifes and run off; but the Chief have such confidence in the words of the Big knifes he hoisted up his flag; but the Big knifes did not regarded, but killed the Chief and number of his friends.

Another instance they mention—that some of the Delawares was with the Big knifes on the service of Americans; but afterward the Big knifes have fall upon them and have killed number of them &c. And since that, every time the Big knifes get ready to come against us, they would sent message to us for peace—then they come to fight us—and they know how to speak good, but would not do good towards Indians &c.

Then I tell them I very sorry to hear these things. If the great men of the United States have the like principal or disposition as the Big knifes had, My nation and other Indians in the East would been along ago anihilated. But they are not so, Especially since they have their Liberty—they begin with new things, and now they endeavour to lift us up the Indians from the ground, that we may stand up and walk ourselves; because we the Indians, hitherto have lay flat as it were on the ground, by which we could not see great way; but if we could stand then we could see some distance. The United States in seeing our situation they put their hands on us, and lead us in the means of Life until we could stand and walk as they are. But on the other hand, the British seeing the Indians in their situation, they would just cover them with blanket and shirt every fall, and the Indians feel themselves warm, and esteem that usage very high—therefore they remain as it were on the ground and could not see great way these many years, &c.

And further I told them, the United Sachems will not speak wrong. Whatever they promise to Indians they will perform. Because out of 30,000 men, they chuse one men to attend in their great Council Fire—and such men must be very honest and wise, and they will do Justice to all people &c. In this way of converseing with them repeatly, make them willing to hear further.

[3]These Indians did not use the term "Big knifes" to apply to Americans in general but apparently restricted its use to frontiersmen.

[4]*I.e.,* the leaders of the United States.

[5]An apparent reference to Coshocton, the main town of the Turtle tribe of Delawares destroyed by whites in 1781 at the present site of Coshocton, Ohio.

[6]*I.e.,* Shawnee.

Another thing they urge that the United States could not govern the hostile Big knifes—and that they the Big knifes, will always have war with the Indians. If the United States could govern them, then the peace could stand sure. But the Big knifes are independent, and if we have peace with them, they would make slaves of us.

Then I told them, the reason the Big knifes are so bad, is this because they have run away from their own country of different States, because they were very mischivous, such as theives and robbers and murderes—and their laws are so strict these people could not live there without being often punished; therefore they run off in this contry and become lawless. They have lived such a distance from the United States, that in these several years the Law could not reached them because they would run in the woods, and no body could find them. But at length the people of the United States settle among them, and the Law now binds them; and if they would endeavour to run in the woods as usual, you would then have chance to knock their heads and they know this, therefore they oblige to set still, &c.

And further (says I,) we the Indians have such people also; for instance, here is Kuttoohwoh, or Cherekes;[7] they could not live among their own people in their own Contry, because they have strict Laws, so that if any steals, he must be whipt immediately; and if any commit adultery his ears will be cut off; and if any murders he will be instandly killed, &c. In all my arguments with these Indians, I have as if were oblige to say nothing with regard of the conduct of Yorkers, how they cheat my fathers, how they taken our lands Unjustly, and how my fathers were groaning as it were to their graves, in loseing their lands for nothing, although they were faithful friends to the Whites; and how the white people artfully got their Deeds confirm in their Laws, &c. I say had I mention these things to the Indians, it would agravate their prejudices against all white people, &c.

And here I will also mention the substance of my speech to these Nations, deliverd immediately after Brant's Prohibitory and Cautionary Message delivered.[8] And after the Indians been informed by some Emmissaries, that I and my Companions were sent by the Big knifes to number the Indians, and was to return again with the information, that the White people may judge how many men will be sufficient to fall upon the Indians, &c.

I begin with these words:—

Grandfathers—and Brothers—and friends—attend—[9]

As we have acquaint to each other many things, and as we have agreed that we would set together in council to manifest our sentiments to each other, I will now

[7]The Cherokees, an Iroquoian-speaking tribe, believed that they migrated from the north, from which they were expelled, and settled in the southeastern part of the continent where the Europeans found them. The Delawares and related tribes called them Kittuwa, after Kituhwa, one of their ancient towns.

[8]Joseph Brant (1747–1807) was a noted Mohawk chief, whose loyalties during and after the American Revolution rested with the British; hence he desired that the western tribes not make peace with the Americans. He did not attend Aupaumut's councils but on September 17, his nephew delivered a message in his behalf, urging the Indians not to be deceived by Aupaumut and declaring that George Washington had laid claim to all their lands.

[9]Common forms of address, indicating respect as well as the political and social relationship among tribal groups.

speak. We have heard various reports of many kinds, for which occasion I will now speak. The Prohibitory Voice of the Mohawks has reachd your ears, that you should not believe the Message I deliver to you, nor to what I say, that I was to deceive you, &c.

My Grandfathers Brothers and friends—

Let us consider the meaning of this Brant's Message—by the sound of it, he point at me as a deceiver or roag, that every nation must be warned. But let us now look back in the path of our forefathers, and see whether you can find one single instance wherein, or how my ancestors or myself have deceived you, or led you one step astray. I say Let us look narrowly, to see whether you can find one bone of yours lay on the ground, by means of my deceitfulness, and I now declare that you cannot found such instance. And further, you may reflect, and see wherein I have speak deceitfully since I come here, that Mohawks should have occasion to stop your ears. But you look back and see heaps of your bones, wherein the Mauquas[10] have deceived you repeatly. I think I could have good reason to tell you not to believe the Message or words of the Mohawks, for they will deceive you greatly as Usual—but I forbear.

Another information reached your ears, that I and my men were sent on purpose to number your nations &c. This also is a Dark Lye, for if you only consider whether I ever ask any of you how many warriors have you, you could easyly know whether I was sent on this Business.

My friends—

I now tell you that the white people well knew your numbers not only your warriors, but your women and children too. (How come they know you would say) because in every fall you gave your numbers to the whites therefore they knew it. Now consider, and think whether there is any need on the part of the Whites to sent me to number your nations, &c.

Six strings of wampom delivered.[11]

After this—then they talk among themselves, and then rehearse my speech and heartily thank me for the same.

And the Sachem of Delaware speak and said—

Grandchild—

It is true all what have said, we could not found any instance wherein your ancestors have deceived our fathers, and we cannot find any fault with your words since you meet us in this country &c. But on the other hand, our Uncles have injured us much these many years; and now after they divided, now they wanted to divide us also. And further, it is true we have gave our numbers to the English every year &c.

I have not mention several speeches with wampom delivered by these Indians to me while I was with them, and my last speech to Shawany &c. and many other affairs.

I now have occasion to say that I have been endeavouring to do my best in the business of peace and according to my best knowledge with regard of the desires of the United States, I have press in the minds of friends in the westward repeatly.

[10]*I.e.,* Mohawks.

[11]Wampum belts were commonly used during this time to confirm the authority of the message being delivered.

But since I arrived at home I understand that my Character is darkened by envious Indians who stayed but few days in Miamie. But for my conduct I will appeal to the nations whom I had Business with last summer, that is if any of my Brothers should doubt of my faithfulness. But this one thing, every wise men well knew, that to employ an enemy or half friend, will never speak well, &c.

With regard to myself, I think it is easy matter to find out whether I was not faithful with the United States in the late war, and whether I have not been faithfull in the work of peace according to abilities in these near two years. I have as it were sacrifice all my own affairs, and my family, for the sake of peace and this last time have gone from home better than Eleven months, and have gone thro a hazardous journeys, and have sufferd with sickness and hunger, and have left my Counsellors with the nations who are for peace, to promote peace and forward every means of peace while I am absent—not only so but I have been pleading and Justifying the Conduct of these people, for which they were well received at their arrival at Miamie. Notwithstand of all this, they brought my Name at Nought. The occasion of my speaking this sort, because of many evil and false reports sounded in the ears of my friends—and I am ready to answer any thing that may be asked respecting to the different Tribes of Indians, &c.—

Hendrick Aupaumut

1827

Hannah Webster Foster 1758–1840

Along with Susanna Rowson's *Charlotte Temple* (1794) and William H. Brown's *The Power of Sympathy* (1789), Foster's *The Coquette; or, The History of Eliza Wharton* (1797) topped the American best-seller lists of the 1790s. Frequently reprinted in the nineteenth century, the novel has had several twentieth-century printings as well. The success of her work did not bring Foster wide recognition, however; the book appeared anonymously, as written by "A Lady of Massachusetts." Not until 1866—twenty-six years after her death—did Hannah Foster's name appear on the title page.

Born in Salisbury, Massachusetts, the eldest daughter of Hannah Wainwright and Grant Webster, a prosperous merchant, Hannah Webster began life in comfortable surroundings. Her mother died in 1762, and it is likely that Hannah Webster was then enrolled in an academy for young women, somewhat like the one she later described in *The Boarding School; or, Lessons of a Preceptress to Her Pupils* (1798). The wide range of historical and literary allusions included in her works reflects an excellent education. By 1771 the young woman was living in Boston, where she began writing political articles for local newspapers. Her publications attracted the attention of John Foster, a graduate of Dartmouth, whom she married on April 7, 1785. The couple lived in Brighton, Massachusetts, where John Foster served as a pastor until his retirement in 1827.

Before she reached her tenth year of marriage, Foster bore six children. A year after the birth of her last child, she completed *The Coquette,* and the following year, *The Boarding School.* Thereafter, she returned to newspaper writing and devoted herself to encouraging young writers. When John Foster died in 1829, Foster moved to Montreal to be with her daughters Harriet Vaughan Cheney and Eliza Lanesford Cushing, both of whom were also writers.

The Coquette follows the epistolary tradition first used by Samuel Richardson in his novel *Pamela* (1740). The story of Eliza Wharton's temptation, seduction, distress, and doom is revealed in letters between friends and confidants. Eliza Wharton falls victim to the rake, Peter Sanford, referred to as "a second Lovelace"—an allusion to the seducer in Richardson's second novel, *Clarissa Harlowe* (1747–1748). Like the heroines of countless novels, Eliza dies in childbirth. Yet unlike those countless novels, *The Coquette* offers characters torn between love and their own worldly ambitions, between virtue and vice.

On another level, *The Coquette* serves as a prototype for the American quest-for-freedom novel, raising the question about the extent to which individuals can remain free in a society. Eliza is a coquette, but she is also an intelligent, spirited young woman unwilling to bury herself in a conventional marriage with a man (the Rev. Boyer) whom she finds interesting but immensely dull. She would gladly enter an egalitarian marriage like that enjoyed by her friends the Richmans, but she finds herself without such an opportunity. For Eliza, "Marriage is the tomb of friendship. It appears to me a very selfish state" (Letter 12).

The letters in *The Coquette* treat subjects ranging from friendship and marriage to economic security and social status. They expose, according to Cathy N. Davidson, the fundamental injustices of a patriarchal culture that places the opportunities for women within a limited domestic sphere. Given contemporary marriage laws and restrictive mores, the novel illustrates the extent to which women and men were constrained by social expectation. In this, the novel contrasts women's and men's views of marriage.

Foster's novel is deeply embedded in the American experience. Her claim that *The Coquette* was "founded on fact" was not merely a nod to the convention employed by early novelists to justify lurid or sensational works. She based her story on the experience, nearly a decade earlier, of her husband's distant cousin Elizabeth Whitman of Hartford, Connecticut, the daughter of parents highly respected in clerical, political, and social circles. After rejecting two ministerial suitors, Whitman engaged in a clandestine affair that left her pregnant and abandoned. Her story became public knowledge when the *Salem Mercury* (July 29, 1788) reported that "a female stranger," secluded at the Bell Tavern in Danvers to await her husband's arrival, had given birth to a stillborn child and had subsequently died. Reporters and preachers cited Whitman's story as "a good moral lecture to young ladies." Foster's contemporaries had no difficulty identifying the real-life counterparts of the "coquette" and her ministerial associates, though the identity of her seducer remains subject to dispute.

Foster's second work, *The Boarding School,* does not fit easily into any literary category. The subtitle, however, suggests a didactic commentary on female education. The first portion of the work fulfills that expectation: a description of the finishing school run by Mrs. Maria Williams, it includes exhortations on social conduct, reading, and general preparations for survival. The second part, containing letters from the students to the preceptress and to each other, demonstrates the beneficial effects of Mrs. William's instruction. A didactic textbook, *The Boarding School* might in Foster's own day have seemed a fitting result of the pen of a minister's wife. With *The Coquette,* however, Foster has stood the test of time.

Lucy M. Freibert
University of Louisville

PRIMARY WORKS

The Coquette; or, The History of Eliza Wharton. A Novel Founded on Fact, 1797, rpt. 1986; *The Boarding School; or, Lessons of a Preceptress to Her Pupils,* 1798.

SECONDARY WORKS

Walter P. Wenska, Jr., "*The Coquette* and the American Dream of Freedom," *Early American Literature* 12, 1977–1978; Cathy N. Davidson, *Revolution and the Word: The Rise of the Novel in America,* 1986; Frank Shuffelton, "Mrs. Foster's *Coquette,* and the Decline of the Brotherly Watch," *Studies in Eighteenth-Century Culture* 16, 1986; Kristie Hamilton, "An Assault on the Will: Republican Virtue and the City in Hannah Webster Foster's *The Coquette,*" *Early American Literature* 14, 1989; John Paul Tassoni, "'I can step out of myself a little': Feminine Virtue and Female Friendship in Hannah Foster's *The Coquette,*" in *Communication and Women's Friendships,* ed. Janet Doubler Ward and JoAnna Stephens Mink, 1993; Sharon M. Harris, "Hannah Webster Foster's *The Coquette:* Critiquing Franklin's America," in *Redefining the Political Novel,* ed. Sharon M. Harris, 1995.

from The Coquette; or, the History of Eliza Wharton

[As the novel opens, Eliza has just escaped an unwanted marriage with an elderly clergyman, Mr. Haly, who died before her parents could get him to the altar. Delighted to be launched into "society" again, Eliza visits General and Mrs. Richman. Eliza soon receives the attentions of a minister named Boyer, but she cannot bring herself to marry him immediately. She flirts with Sanford against the advice of her friends.]

Letter I
To Miss Lucy Freeman

New-Haven.

An unusual sensation possesses my breast; a sensation, which I once thought could never pervade it on any occasion whatever. It is *pleasure;* pleasure, my dear Lucy, on leaving my paternal roof! Could you have believed that the darling child of an indulgent and dearly beloved mother would feel a gleam of joy at leaving her? but so it is. The melancholy, the gloom, the condolence, which surrounded me for a month after the death of Mr. Haly, had depressed my spirits, and palled every enjoyment of life. Mr. Haly was a man of worth; a man of real and substantial merit. He is therefore deeply, and justly regreted by *his* friends; he was chosen to be a future guardian, and companion for me, and was, therefore, beloved by *mine.* As their choice; as a good man, and a faithful friend, I esteemed him. But no one acquainted with the disparity of our tempers and dispositions, our views and designs, can suppose my heart much engaged in the alliance. Both nature and education had instilled into my mind an implicit obedience to the will and desires of my parents. To them, of course, I sacrificed my fancy in this affair; determined that my reason should concur with theirs; and on that to risk my future happiness. I was the more encouraged, as I saw, from our first acquaintance, his declining health; and expected, that the event would prove as it has. Think not, however, that I rejoice in his death. No; far be it from me; for though I believe that I never felt the passion of love for Mr. Haly; yet a habit of conversing with him, of hearing daily the most virtuous, tender, and affectionate sentiments from his lips, inspired emotions of the sincerest friendship, and esteem.

He is gone. His fate is unalterably, and I trust, happily fixed. He lived the life, and died the death of the righteous. O that my last end may be like his! This event will, I hope, make a suitable and abiding impression upon my mind; teach me the fading nature of all sublunary enjoyments, and the little dependence which is to be placed on earthly felicity. Whose situation was more agreeable; whose prospects more flattering, then Mr. Haly's? Social, domestic, and connubial joys were fondly anticipated, and friends, and fortune seemed ready to crown every wish! Yet animated by still brighter hopes, he cheerfully bid them all adieu. In conversation with me, but a few days before his exit; "There is" said he, "but one link in the chain of life, undissevered; that, my dear Eliza, is my attachment to you. But God is wise and good in all his ways; and in this, as in all other respects, I would cheerfully say, His will be done."

You, my friend, were witness to the concluding scene; and therefore, I need not describe it.

I shall only add, on the subject, that if I have wisdom and prudence to follow his advice and example; if his prayers for my temporal and eternal welfare be heard and answered, I shall be happy indeed.

The disposition of mind, which I now feel, I wish to cultivate. Calm, placid, and serene; thoughtful of my duty, and benevolent to all around me, I wish for no other connection than that of friendship,

This Letter is all egotism, I have even neglected to mention the respectable, and happy friends, with whom I reside; but will do it in my next. Write soon, and often; and believe me sincerely yours,

Eliza Wharton.

Letter II

To the Same

New-Haven.

Time, which effaces every occasional impression, I find gradually dispelling the pleasing pensiveness, which the melancholy event, the subject of my last, had diffused over my mind. Naturally cheerful, volatile, and unreflecting, the opposite disposition, I have found to contain sources of enjoyment, which I was before unconscious of possessing.

My friends, here, are the picture of conjugal felicity. The situation is delightful. The visiting parties perfectly agreeable. Every thing tends to facilitate the return of my accustomed vivacity. I have written to my mother, and received an answer. She praises my fortitude, and admires the philosophy which I have exerted, under, what she calls, my heavy bereavement. Poor woman! She little thinks that my heart was untouched; and when that is unaffected, other sentiments and passions make but a transient impression. I have been, for a month or two, excluded from the gay world; and, indeed, fancied myself soaring above it. It is now that I begin to descend, and find my natural propensity for mixing in the busy scenes and active pleasures of life returning. I have received your letter; your moral lecture rather; and be assured, my dear, your monitorial lessons and advice shall be attended to. I believe I shall never again resume those airs, which you term *coquettish,* but which I think deserve a softer appellation; as they proceed from an innocent heart, and are the effusions of a youthful, and cheerful mind. We are all envited to spend the day, to morrow, at Col. Farington's, who has an elegant seat in this neighbourhood. Both he and his Lady are strangers to me; but the friends, by whom I am introduced, will procure me a welcome reception. Adieu.

Eliza Wharton.

Letter III
To the Same

New-Haven.

Is it time for me to talk again of conquests? or must I only enjoy them in silence? I must write to you the impulses of my mind; or I must not write at all. You are not so morose, as to wish me to become a nun, would our country, and religion allow it. I ventured yesterday to throw aside the habiliments of mourning, and to array myself in those more adapted to my taste. We arrived at Col. Farington's about one o'clock. The Col. handed me out of the carriage, and introduced me to a large company assembled in the Hall. My name was pronounced with an *emphasis;* and I was received with the most flattering tokens of respect. When we were summoned to dinner, a young gentleman in a clerical dress offered me his hand, and led me to a table furnished with an elegant, and sumptuous repast, with more gallantry, and address than commonly fall to the share of students. He sat opposite me at table; and whenever I raised my eye, it caught his. The ease, and politeness of his manners, with his particular attention to me, raised my curiosity, and induced me to ask Mrs. Laiton who he was? She told me that his name was Boyer; that he was descended from a worthy family; had passed with honor and applause through the university where he was educated; had since studied divinity with success; and now had a call to settle as a minister in one of the first parishes in a neighbouring state.

The gates of a spacious garden were thrown open, at this instant; and I accepted with avidity an invitation to walk in it. Mirth, and hilarity prevailed, and the moments fled on downy wings; while we traced the beauties of art and nature, so liberally displayed, and so happily blended in this delightful retreat. An enthusiastic admirer of scenes like these, I had rambled some way from the company, when I was followed by Mrs. Laiton to offer her condolence on the supposed loss, which I had sustained, in the death of Mr. Haly. My heart rose against the woman, so ignorant of human nature, as to think such conversation acceptable at such a time. I made her little reply, and waved the subject, though I could not immediately dispel the gloom which it excited.

The absurdity of a custom, authorising people at a first interview to revive the idea of griefs, which time has lulled, perhaps obliterated, is intolerable. To have our enjoyments arrested by the empty compliments of unthinking persons, for no other reason, than a compliance with fashion is to be treated in a manner, which the laws of humanity forbid.

We were soon joined by the gentlemen, who each selected his partner, and the walk was prolonged.

Mr. Boyer offered me his arm, which I gladly accepted; happy to be relieved from the impertinence of my female companion. We returned to tea, after which the ladies sung, and played by turns on the Piano Forte; while some of the gentlemen accompanied with the flute, the clarinet, and the violin, forming in the whole a very decent concert. An elegant supper, and half an hour's conversation after it, closed the evening; when we returned home, delighted with our entertainment and pleased with ourselves and each other. My imagination is so impressed with the festive scenes of the day, that Morpheus waves his ebon-wand in vain. The evening is fine beyond the power of description! all nature is serene and harmonious; in perfect unison with my present disposition of mind. I have been taking a retrospect of my past life; and a few juvenile follies excepted, which I trust the recording angel has blotted out with the tear of charity, find an approving conscience, and a heart at ease. Fortune, indeed, has not been very liberal of her gifts to me; but I presume on a large stock in the bank of friendship, which, united with health and innocence, give me some pleasing anticipations of future felicity.

Whatever my fate may be, I shall always continue your

Eliza Wharton.

Letter IV

To Mr. Selby

New-Haven.

You ask me, my friend, whether I am in pursuit of truth, or a lady? I answer, both. I hope and trust they are united; and really expect to find truth and the virtues and graces besides in a fair form. If you mean by the first part of your question, whether I am searching into the sublimer doctrines of religion? To these I would by no means be inattentive; but to be honest, my studies of that kind have been very much interrupted of late. The respectable circle of acquaintances with which I am honored here, has rendered my visits very frequent and numerous. In one of these I was introduced to Miss Eliza Wharton; a young lady whose elegant person, accomplished mind, and polished manners have been much celebrated. Her fame has often reached me; but, as the queen of Sheba said to Solomon, the half was not told me. You will think, that I talk in the style of a lover. I confess it, nor am I ashamed to rank myself among the professed admirers of this lovely fair one. I am in no danger, however, of becoming an enthusiastic devotee. No, I mean to act upon just and rational principles. Expecting soon to settle in an eligible situation, if such a companion as I am persuaded she will make me, may fall to my lot, I shall deem myself as happy as this state of imperfection will admit. She is now resident at Gen. Richman's. The general and his lady are her particular friends. They are warm in her praises. They tell me, however, that she is naturally of a gay disposition. No matter for that; it is an agreeable quality, where there is discretion sufficient for its regulation. A cheerful friend, much more a cheerful wife is peculiarly necessary to a person of a studious and sedentary life. They dispel the gloom of retirement, and exhilerate the spirits depressed by intense application. She was formerly addressed by the late Mr. Haly of Boston. He was not, it seems, the man of her choice; but her parents were extremely partial to him, and wished the connection to take place. She, like a dutiful child, sacrificed her own inclination to their pleasure, so far as to acquiesce in his visits. This she more easily accomplished, as his health, which declined from their first acquaintance, led her to suppose, as the event has proved, that he would not live to enter into any lasting engagements. Her father, who died some months before him, invited him to reside at his house, for the benefit of a change of air, agreeably to the advice of his physicians. She attended him during his last illness, with all the care and assiduity of a nurse; and with all the sympathising tenderness of a sister.

I have had several opportunities of conversing with her. She discovers an elevated mind, a ready apprehension, and an accurate knowledge of the various subjects which have been brought into view. I have not yet introduced the favorite subject of my heart. Indeed she seems studiously to avoid noticing any expression which leads towards it. But she must hear it soon. I am sure of the favor and interest of the friends with whom she resides. They have promised to speak previously in my behalf. I am to call as if accidentally this afternoon, just as they are to ride abroad. They are to refer me to Miss Wharton for entertainment, till their return. What a delightful opportunity for my purpose! I am counting the hours, nay, the very moments. Adieu. You shall soon hear again from your most obedient,

J. Boyer.

Letter V
To Miss Lucy Freeman

New-Haven.

These bewitching charms of mine have a tendency to keep my mind in a state of perturbation. I am so pestered with these admirers; not that I am so very handsome neither; but I don't know how it is, I am certainly very much the taste of the other sex. Followed, flattered, and caressed; I have cards and compliments in profusion. But I must try to be serious; for I have, alas! one serious lover. As I promised you to be particular in my writing, I suppose I must proceed methodically. Yesterday we had a party to dine. Mr. Boyer was of the number. His attention was immediately engrossed; and I soon perceived that every word, every action, and every look was studied to gain my approbation. As he sat next me at dinner, his assiduity and politeness were pleasing; and as we walked together afterwards, his conversation was improving. Mine was sentimental and sedate; perfectly adapted to the taste of my gallant. Nothing, however, was said particularly expressive of his apparent wishes. I studiously avoided every kind of discourse which might lead to this topic. I wish not for a declaration from any one, especially from one whom I could not repulse and do not intend to encourage at present. His conversation, so similar to what I had often heard from a similar character, brought a deceased friend to mind, and rendered me somewhat pensive. I retired directly after supper. Mr. Boyer had just taken leave.

Mrs. Richman came into my chamber as she was passing to her own. Excuse my intrusion, Eliza, said she; I thought I would just step in and ask you if you have passed a pleasant day?

Perfectly so, madam; and I have now retired to protract the enjoyment by recollection. What, my dear, is your opinion of our favorite Mr. Boyer? Declaring him your favorite, madam, is sufficient to render me partial to him. But to be frank, independent of that, I think him an agreeable man. Your heart, I presume, is now free? Yes, and I hope it will long remain so. Your friends, my dear, solicitous for your welfare, wish to see you suitably and agreeably connected. I hope my friends will never again interpose in my concerns of that nature. You, madam, who have ever known my heart, are sensible, that had the Almighty spared life, in a certain instance, I must have sacrificed my own happiness, or incurred their censure. I am young, gay, volatile. A melancholy event has lately extricated me from those shackles, which parental authority had imposed on my mind. Let me then enjoy that freedom which I so highly prize. Let me have opportunity, unbiassed by opinion, to gratify my natural disposition in a participation of those pleasures which youth and innocence afford. Of such pleasures, no one, my dear, would wish to deprive you. But beware, Eliza!—Though strowed[1] with flowers, when contemplated by your lively imagination, it is, after all, a slippery, thorny path. The round of fashionable dissipation is dangerous. A phantom is often pursued, which leaves its deluded votary the real form of wretchedness. She spoke with an emphasis, and taking up her candle, wished me a good night. I had not power to return the compliment. Something seemingly prophetic in her looks and expressions, cast a momentary gloom upon my mind! But I despise those contracted ideas which confine virtue to a cell. I have no notion of becoming a recluse. Mrs. Richman has ever been a beloved friend of mine; yet I always thought her rather prudish. Adieu,

Eliza Wharton.

Letter VI
To the Same

New-Haven.

I had scarcely seated myself at the breakfast table this morning, when a servant entered with a card of invitation from Major Sanford, requesting the happiness of my

[1]Strewn.

hand this evening, at a ball, given by Mr. Atkins, about three miles from this. I shewed the billet to Mrs. Richman, saying, I have not much acquaintance with this gentleman, madam; but I suppose his character sufficiently respectable to warrant an affirmative answer. He is a gay man, my dear, to say no more, and such are the companions we wish, when we join a party avowedly formed for pleasure. I then stepped into my apartment, wrote an answer, and dispatched the servant. When I returned to the parlour, something disapprobating appeared in the countenances of both my friends. I endeavored without seeming to observe, to dissipate it by chit chat; but they were better pleased with each other than with me; and soon rising, walked into the garden, and left me to amuse myself alone. My eyes followed them through the window. Happy pair, said I. Should it ever be my fate to wear the hymenial chain, may I be thus united! The purest and most ardent affection, the greatest consonance of taste and disposition, and the most congenial virtue and wishes distinguish this lovely couple. Health and wealth, with every attendant blessing preside over their favored dwelling, and shed their benign influence without alloy. The consciousness of exciting their displeasure gave me pain; but I consoled myself with the idea that it was ill founded.

They should consider, said I, that they have no satisfaction to look for beyond each other.

There every enjoyment is centered; but I am a poor solitary being, who need some amusement beyond what I can supply myself. The mind, after being confined at home for a while, sends the imagination abroad in quest of new treasures, and the body may as well accompany it, for ought I can see.

General Richman and lady have ever appeared solicitous to promote my happiness since I have resided with them. They have urged my acceptance of invitations to join parties, though they have not been much themselves, of late; as Mrs. Richman's present circumstances render her fond of retirement. What reason can be assigned for their apparent reluctance to this evening's entertainment is to me incomprehensible; but I shall apply the chymical powers of friendship and extract the secret from Mrs. Richman to morrow, if not before. Adieu. I am now summoned to dinner, and after that shall be engaged in preparation till the wished for hour of hilarity and mirth engrosses every faculty of your

Eliza Wharton.

Letter VIII

To Mr. Charles Deighton

New-Haven.

We had an elegant ball, last night, Charles; and what is still more to the taste of your old friend, I had an elegant partner; one exactly calculated to please my fancy; gay, volatile, apparently thoughtless of every thing but present enjoyment. It was Miss Eliza Wharton, a young lady, whose agreeable person, polished manners, and refined talents, have rendered her the toast of the country around for these two years; though for half that time she has had a clerical lover imposed on her by her friends;

for I am told it was not agreeable to her inclination. By this same clerical lover of hers, she was for several months confined as a nurse. But his death has happily relieved her, and she now returns to the world with redoubled lustre. At present she is a visitor to Mrs. Richman, who is a relation. I first saw her on a party of pleasure at Mr. Frazier's where we walked, talked, sung, and danced together. I thought her cousin watched her with a jealous eye; for she is, you must know, a prude; and immaculate, more so than you or I must be the man who claims admission to her society. But I fancy this young lady is a coquette; and if so, I shall avenge my sex, by retaliating the mischiefs, she meditates against us. Not that I have any ill designs; but only to play off her own artillery, by using a little unmeaning gallantry. And let her beware of the consequences. A young clergyman came in at Gen. Richman's yesterday, while I was waiting for Eliza, who was much more cordially received by the general and his lady, than was your humble servant: but I lay that up.

When she entered the room, an air of mutual embarrassment was evident. Thc lady recovered her assurance much more easily than the gentleman. I am just going to ride, and shall make it in my way to call and inquire after the health of my dulcinea. Therefore, adieu for the present.

Peter Sanford.

Letter XI
To Mr. Charles Deighton

New-Haven.

Well, Charles, I have been manoeuvring to day, a little revengefully. That, you will say, is out of character. So baleful a passion does not easily find admission among those softer ones, which you well know I cherish. However, I am a mere Proteus, and can assume any shape that will best answer my purpose.

I called this forenoon, as I told you I intended, at Gen. Richman's. I waited some time in the parlor alone, before Eliza appeared; and when she did appear, the distant reserve of her manners and the pensiveness of her countenance convinced me that she had been vexed, and I doubted not but Peter Sanford was the occasion. Her wise cousin, I could have sworn, had been giving her a detail of the vices of her gallant; and warning her against the danger of associating with him in future. Notwithstanding, I took no notice of any alteration in her behavior; but entered with the utmost facetiousness into a conversation which I thought most to her taste. By degrees, she assumed her usual vivacity; cheerfulness and good humor again animated her countenance. I tarried as long as decency would admit. She having intimated that they were to dine at my friend Lawrence's, I caught at this information; and determined to follow them, and teaze the jealous Mrs. Richman, by playing off all the gallantry I was master of in her presence.

I went, and succeeded to the utmost of my wishes, as I read in the vexation, visible in the one; and the ease and attention displayed by the other. I believe too, that I have charmed the eye at least, of the amiable Eliza. Indeed, Charles, she is a fine girl. I think it would hurt my conscience to wound her mind or reputation.

Were I disposed to marry, I am persuaded she would make an excellent wife; but that you know is no part of my plan, so long as I can keep out of the noose. Whenever I do submit to be shackled, it must be from a necessity of mending my fortune. This girl would be far from doing that. However, I am pleased with her acquaintance, and mean not to abuse her credulity and good nature, if I can help it.

Peter Sanford.

Letter XII
To Miss Lucy Freeman

New-Haven.

The heart of your friend is again besieged. Whether it will surrender to the assailants or not, I am unable at present to determine. Sometimes I think of becoming a predestinarian, and submitting implicitly to fate, without any exercise of free will; but, as mine seems to be a wayward one, I would counteract the operations of it, if possible.

Mrs. Richman told me this morning, that she hoped I should be as agreeably entertained this afternoon, as I had been the preceding; that she expected Mr. Boyer to dine, and take tea; and doubted not but he would be as attentive and sincere to me, if not as gay and polite as the gentleman who obtruded his civilities yesterday. I replied that I had no reason to doubt the sincerity of the one, or the other, having never put them to the test, nor did I imagine I ever should. Your friends, Eliza, said she, would be very happy to see you united to a man of Mr. Boyer's worth; and so agreeably settled, as he has a prospect of being. I hope, said I, that my friends are not so weary of my company, as to wish to dispose of me. I am too happy in my present connections to quit them for new ones. Marriage is the tomb of friendship. It appears to me a very selfish state. Why do people, in general, as soon as they are married, centre all their cares, their concerns, and pleasures in their own families? former acquaintances are neglected or forgotten. The tenderest ties between friends are weakened, or dissolved; and benevolence itself moves in a very limited sphere. It is the glory of the marriage state, she rejoined, to refine, by circumscribing our enjoyments. Here we can repose in safety.

"The friendships of the world are oft
Confed'racies in vice, or leagues in pleasure:
Our's has the purest virtue for its basis;
And such a friendship ends not but with life."

True, we cannot always pay that attention to former associates, which we may wish; but the little community which we superintend is quite as important an object; and certainly renders us more beneficial to the public. True benevolence, though it may change its objects, is not limited by time or place. Its effects are the same, and aided by a second self, are rendered more diffusive and salutary.

Some pleasantry passed, and we retired to dress. When summoned to dinner, I found Mr. Boyer below. If what is sometimes said be true, that love is diffident, reserved, and unassuming, this man must be tinctured with it. These symptoms were visible in his deportment when I entered the room. However, he soon recovered himself, and the conversation took a general turn. The festive board was crowned with sociability, and we found in reality, "The feast of reason, and the flow of soul." After we rose from table, a walk in the garden was proposed, an amusement we are all peculiarly fond of. Mr. Boyer offered me his arm. When at a sufficient distance from our company, he begged leave to congratulate himself on having an opportunity which he had ardently desired for some time, of declaring to me his attachment; and of soliciting an interest in my favor; or, if he might be allowed the term, affection. I replied, that, Sir, is indeed laying claim to an important interest. I believe you must substitute some more indifferent epithet for the present. Well then, said he, if it must be so, let it be esteem, or friendship. Indeed, Sir, said I, you are intitled to them both. Merit has always a share in that bank; and I know of none, who has a larger claim on that score, than Mr. Boyer. I suppose my manner was hardly serious enough for what he considered a weighty cause. He was a little disconcerted; but soon regaining his presence of mind, entreated me, with an air of earnestness, to encourage his suit, to admit his addresses, and, if possible, to reward his love. I told him, that this was rather a sudden affair to me; and that I could not answer him without consideration. Well then, said he, take what time you think proper, only relieve my suspense as soon as may be. Shall I visit you again to morrow? O, not so soon, said I. Next Monday, I believe will be early enough. I will endeavor to be at home. He thanked me even for that favor, recommended himself once more to my kindness; and we walked towards the company, returned with them to the house, and he soon took leave. I immediately retired to write this letter, which I shall close, without a single observation on the subject, until I know your opinion.

Eliza Wharton.

Letter XIII

To Miss Eliza Wharton

Hartford.

And so you wish to have my opinion before you know the result of your own. This is playing a little too much with my patience. But, however, I will gratify you this once, in hopes that my epistle may have a good effect. You will ask, perhaps, whether I would influence your judgment? I answer, no; provided you will exercise it yourself: but I am a little apprehensive that your fancy will mislead you. Methinks I can gather from your letters, a predilection for this Major Sanford. But he is a rake, my dear friend; and can a lady of your delicacy and refinement, think of forming a connection with a man of that character? I hope not. Nay, I am confident you do not. You mean only to exhibit a few more girlish airs, before you turn matron. But I am persuaded, if you wish to lead down the dance of life with regularity, you will not find a more excellent partner than Mr. Boyer. Whatever you can reasonably expect in a lover, husband, or friend, you may perceive to be united in this worthy man. His taste is undebauched, his manners not vitiated, his morals uncorrupted. His situation in life is, perhaps, as elevated as you have a right to claim. Forgive my plainness, Eliza. It is the task of friendship, sometimes to tell disagreeable truths. I know your ambition is to make a distinguished figure in the first class of polished society; to shine in the gay circle of fashionable amusements, and to bear off the palm amidst the votaries of pleasure. But these are fading honors, unsatisfactory enjoyments; incapable of gratifying those immortal principles of reason and religion, which have been implanted in your mind by nature; assiduously cultivated by the best of parents, and exerted, I trust, by yourself. Let me advise you then, in conducting this affair; an affair, big, perhaps, with your future fate, to lay aside those coquettish airs which you sometimes put on; and remember that you are not dealing with a fop, who will take advantage of every concession; but with a man of sense and honor, who will properly estimate your condescension, and frankness. Act then with that modest freedom, that dignified unreserve which bespeaks conscious rectitude and sincerity of heart.

I shall be extremely anxious to hear the process and progress of this business. Relieve my impatience, as soon as possible, and believe me yours, with undissembled affection.

Lucy Freeman.

Letter XVIII

To Mr. Charles Deighton

New-Haven.

Do you know, Charles, that I have commenced lover? I was always a general one; but now I am somewhat particular. I shall be the more interested, as I am likely to meet with difficulties; and it is the glory of a rake, as well as a Christian to combat obstacles. This same Eliza, of whom I have told you, has really made more impression on my heart, than I was aware of; or than the sex, take them as they rise, are wont to do. But she is besieged by a priest (a likely lad though.) I know not how it is, but they are commonly successful with the girls, even the gayest of them. This one, too, has the interest of all her friends, as I am told. I called yesterday, at General Richman's, and found this pair together, apparently too happy in each other's society for my wishes. I must own, that I felt a glow of jealousy, which I never experienced before; and vowed revenge for the pain it gave me, though but momentary. Yet Eliza's reception of me was visibly cordial; nay, I fancied my company as pleasing to her as that which she had before. I tarried not long, but left him to the enjoyment of that pleasure which I flatter myself will be short-lived. O, I have another plan in my head; a plan of necessity, which, you know, is the mother of invention. It is this: I am very much courted and caressed by the family of Mr. Lawrence, a man of large property in this neighborhood. He has only one child; a daughter, with whom I imagine the old folks intend to shackle me in the bonds of matrimony. The girl looks very well. She has no soul though, that I can discover. She is heiress, nevertheless, to a great fortune; and that is all the soul I wish for in a wife. In truth, Charles, I know of no other way to mend my circumstances. But lisp not a word of my embarrassments for your life. Show and equipage are my hobby-horse; and if any female wish to share them with me, and will furnish me with the means of supporting them, I have no objection. Could I conform to the sober rules of wedded life, and renounce those dear enjoyments of dissipation, in which I have so long indulged, I know not the lady in the world with whom I would sooner form a connection of this sort than with Eliza Wharton. But it will never do. If my fortune, or hers were better, I would risk a union; but as they are, no idea of the kind can be admitted. I shall endeavor, notwithstanding, to enjoy her company as long as possible. Though I cannot possess her wholly myself, I will not tamely see her the property of another.

I am now going to call at General Richman's, in hopes of an opportunity to profess my devotion to her. I know I am not a welcome visitor to the family; but I am independent of their censure or esteem, and mean to act accordingly.

Peter Sanford.

[After returning home, Eliza becomes engaged to Boyer yet continues to see Sanford. Boyer warns Eliza of the risk she is taking with her reputation. Finally, Boyer, discovering Eliza in intimate conversation with Sanford in her family's garden, breaks off the engagement. Eliza's efforts to retrieve Boyer's good will fail completely. Meanwhile, Sanford marries a wealthy woman but resumes his pursuit of Eliza. Eventually he seduces her. When she becomes pregnant, Eliza leaves home secretly with Sanford.]

Letter LXV

To Mr. Charles Deighton

Hartford.

Good news, Charles, good news! I have arrived to the utmost bounds of my wishes; the full possession of my adorable Eliza! I have heard a quotation from a certain book; but what book it was I have forgotten, if I ever knew. No matter for that; the quotation is, that "stolen waters are sweet, and bread eaten in secret is pleasant." If it has reference to the pleasures, which I have enjoyed with Eliza, I like it hugely, as Tristram Shandy's father said of Yorick's sermon; and I think it fully verified.

I had a long and tedious siege. Every method which love could suggest, or art invent, was adopted. I was sometimes ready to despair, under an idea that her resolution was unconquerable, her virtue impregnable. Indeed, I should have given over the pursuit long ago, but for the hopes of success I entertained from her parleying with me, and in reliance upon her own strength, endeavoring to combat, and counteract my designs. Whenever this has been the case, Charles, I have never yet been defeated in my plan. If a lady will consent to enter the lists against the antagonist of her honor, she may be sure of losing the prize. Besides, were her delicacy genuine, she would banish the man at once, who presumed to doubt, which he certainly does, who attempts to vanquish it!

But, far be it from me to criticise the pretensions of the sex. If I gain the rich reward of my dissimulation and gallantry, that you know is all I want.

To return then to the point. An unlucky, but not a miraculous accident, has taken place, which must soon expose our amour. What can be done? At the first discovery, absolute distraction seized the soul of Eliza, which has since terminated in a fixed melancholy. Her health too is much impaired. She thinks herself rapidly declining; and I tremble when I see her emaciated form!

My wife has been reduced very low, of late. She brought me a boy a few weeks past, a dead one though.

These circumstances give me neither pain nor pleasure. I am too much ingrossed by my divinity, to take an interest in any thing else. True, I have lately suffered myself to be somewhat engaged here and there by a few jovial lads, who assist me in dispelling the anxious thoughts, which my perplexed situation excites. I must, however, seek some means to relieve Eliza's distress. My finances are low; but the last fraction shall be expended in her service, if she need it.

Julia Granby is expected at Mrs. Wharton's every hour. I fear that her inquisitorial eye will soon detect our intrigue, and obstruct its continuation. Now there's a girl, Charles, I should never attempt to seduce; yet she is a most alluring object, I assure you. But the dignity of her manners forbid all assaults upon her virtue. Why, the very expression of her eye, blasts in the bud, every thought, derogatory to her honor; and tells you plainly, that the first insinuation of the kind, would be punished with eternal banishment and displeasure! Of her there is no danger! But I can write no more, except that I am, &c.

Peter Sanford.

Letter LXVIII

To Mrs. M. Wharton

Tuesday.

My Honored And Dear Mamma,

In what words, in what language shall I address you? What shall I say on a subject which deprives me of the power of expression? Would to God I had been totally deprived of that power before so fatal a subject required its exertion! Repentance comes too late, when it cannot prevent the evil lamented. For your kindness, your more than maternal affection towards me, from my infancy to the present moment, a long life of filial duty and unerring rectitude could hardly compensate. How greatly deficient in gratitude must I appear then, while I confess, that precept and example, counsel and advice, instruction and admonition, have been all lost upon me!

Your kind endeavors to promote my happiness have been repaid by the inexcusable folly of sacrificing it. The various emotions of shame, and remorse, penitence and regret, which torture and distract my guilty breast, exceed description. Yes, madam, your Eliza has fallen; fallen, indeed! She has become the victim of her own indiscretion, and of the intrigue and artifice of a designing libertine, who is the husband of another! She is polluted, and no more worthy of her parentage! She flies from you, not to conceal her guilt, that she humbly and penitently owns; but to avoid what she has never experienced, and feels herself unable to support, a mother's frown; to escape the heart-rending sight of a parent's grief, occasioned by the crimes of her guilty child!

I have become a reproach and disgrace to my friends. The consciousness of having forfeited their favor, and incurred their disapprobation and resentment, induces me to conceal from them the place of my retirement; but, lest your benevolence should render you anxious for my comfort in my present situation, I take the liberty to assure you that I am amply provided for.

I have no claim even upon your pity; but from my long experience of your tenderness, I presume to hope it will be extended to me. Oh, my mother, if you knew what the state of my mind is, and has been, for months past, you would surely compassionate my case! Could tears efface the stain, which I have brought upon my family, it would, long since have been washed away! But, alas, tears are vain; and vain is my bitter repentance! It cannot obliterate my crime, nor restore me to innocence and peace! In this life I have no ideas of happiness. These I have wholly resigned! The only hope which affords me any solace, is that of your forgiveness. If the deepest contrition can make an atonement; if the severest pains, both of body and mind, can restore me to your charity, you will not be inexorable! Oh, let my sufferings be deemed a sufficient punishment; and add not the insupportable weight of a parent's wrath! At present, I cannot see you. The effect of my crime is too obvious to be longer concealed, to elude the invidious eye of curiosity. This night, therefore, I leave your hospitable mansion! This night I become a wretched wanderer from thy paternal roof! Oh, that the grave were this night to be my lodging! Then should I lie down and be at rest! Trusting in the mercy of God, through the mediation of his son; I think I could meet my heavenly father with more composure and confidence, than my earthly parent!

Let not the faults and misfortunes of your daughter oppress your mind. Rather let the conviction of having faithfully discharged your duty to your lost child, support and console you in this trying scene.

Since I wrote the above, you have kindly granted me your forgiveness, though you knew not how great, how aggravated was my offence! You forgive me, you say: Oh, the harmonious, the transporting sound! It has revived my drooping spirits; and will enable me to encounter, with resolution, the trials before me!

Farewell, my dear mamma! pity and pray for your ruined child; and be assured, that affection and gratitude will be the last sentiments, which expire in the breast of your repenting daughter,

Eliza Wharton.

[Julia Granby, the friend who has been staying at the Wharton's, reports Eliza's demise to Lucy Freeman, now Mrs. Sumner.]

Letter LXXI

To Mrs. Lucy Sumner

Hartford.

The drama is now closed! A tragical one indeed it has proved!

How sincerely, my dear Mrs. Sumner, must the friends of our departed Eliza, sympathize with each other; and with her afflicted, bereaved parent!

You have doubtless seen the account, in the public papers, which gave us the melancholy intelligence. But I will give you a detail of circumstances.

A few days after my last was written, we heard that Major Sanford's property was attached, and he a prisoner in his own house. He was the last man, to whom we wished to apply for information respecting the forlorn wanderer; yet we had no other resource. And after waiting a fortnight in the most cruel suspense, we wrote a billet, entreating him, if possible, to give some intelligence concerning her. He replied, that he was unhappily deprived of all means of knowing himself; but hoped soon to relieve his own, and our anxiety about her.

In this situation we continued, till a neighbor (purposely, we since concluded) sent us a Boston paper. Mrs. Wharton took it, and inconscious of its contents, observed that the perusal might divert her, a few moments. She read for some time; when it suddenly dropped upon the floor. She clasped her hands together, and raising her streaming eyes to heaven, exclaimed, It is the Lord; let him do what he will! Be still, O my soul, and know that he is God!

What madam, said I, can be the matter? She answered not; but with inexpressible anguish depicted in her countenance, pointed to the paper. I took it up, and soon found the fatal paragraph. I shall not attempt to paint our heart felt grief and lamentation upon this occasion; for we had no doubt of Eliza's being the person described, as a stranger, who died at Danvers, last July. Her delivery of a child; her dejected state of mind; the marks upon her linen; indeed, every circumstance in the advertisement convinced us beyond dispute that it could be no other. Mrs. Wharton retired immediately to her chamber, where she continued overwhelmed with sorrow that night and the following day. Such, in fact, has been her habitual frame ever since; though the endeavors of her friends, who have sought to console her, have rendered her somewhat more conversable. My testimony of Eliza's penitence, before her departure, is a source of comfort to this disconsolate parent. She fondly cherished the idea, that having expiated her offence by sincere repentance and amendment, her deluded child finally made a happy exchange of worlds. But the desperate resolution, which she formed, and executed of becoming a fugitive; of deserting her mother's house and protection, and of wandering and dying among strangers, is a most distressing reflection to her friends; especially to her mother, in whose breast so many painful ideas arise, that she finds it extremely difficult to compose herself to that resignation, which she evidently strives to exemplify.

Eliza's brother has been to visit her last retreat; and to learn the particulars of her melancholy exit. He relates, that she was well accommodated, and had every attention and assistance, which her situation required. The people where she resided appear to have a lively sense of her merit and misfortunes. They testify her modest deportment, her fortitude under the sufferings to which she was called, and the serenity and composure, with which she bid a last adieu to the world. Mr. Wharton has brought back several scraps of her writing, containing miscellaneous reflections on her situation, the death of her babe, and the absence of her friends. Some of these were written before, some after her confinement. These valuable testimonies of the affecting sense, and calm expectation she entertained of her approaching dissolution, are calculated to sooth and comfort the minds of mourning connections. They greatly alleviate the regret occasioned by her absence, at this awful period.

Her elopement can be equalled only by the infatuation which caused her ruin.

> "But let no one reproach her memory.
> Her life has paid the forfeit of her folly.
> Let that suffice."

I am told that Major Sanford is quite frantic. Sure I am that he has reason to be. If the mischiefs he has brought upon others return upon his own head, dreadful indeed must be his portion! His wife has left him, and returned to her parents. His estate, which has been long mortgaged, is taken from him; and poverty and disgrace await him! Heaven seldom leaves injured innocence unavenged! Wretch, that he is, he ought for ever to be banished from human society! I shall continue with Mrs. Wharton, till the lenient hand of time has assuaged her sorrows; and then make my promised visit to you. I will bring Eliza's posthumous papers with me, when I come to Boston, as I have not time to copy them now.

I foresee, my dear Mrs. Sumner, that this disastrous affair will suspend your enjoyments, as it has mine. But what are our feelings, compared with the pangs which rend a parent's heart? This parent, I here behold, inhumanly stripped of the best solace of her declining years, by the ensnaring machinations of a profligate debauchee! Not only the life, but what was still dearer, the reputation and virtue of the unfortunate Eliza, have fallen victims at the shrine of *libertinism!* Detested be the epithet! Let it henceforth bear its true signature, and candor itself shall call it *lust* and *brutality!*

Execrable is the man, however arrayed in magnificence, crowned with wealth, or decorated with the external graces and accomplishments of fashionable life, who shall presume to display them, at the expense of virtue and innocence! Sacred names! attended with real blessings; blessings too useful and important to be trifled away! My resentment at the base arts, which must have been employed to complete the seduction of Eliza, I cannot suppress. I wish them to be exposed, and stamped with universal ignominy! Nor do I doubt but you will join with me in execrating the measures by which *we* have been robbed of so valuable a friend; and *society,* of so ornamental a member. I am, &c.

Julia Granby.

Letter LXXII
To Mr. Charles Deighton

Hartford.

Confusion, horror and despair are the portion of your wretched, unhappy friend! Oh, Deighton, I am undone! Misery irremediable is my future lot! She is gone; yes, she is gone for ever! The darling of my soul, the centre of all my wishes and enjoyments is no more! Cruel fate has snatched her from me; and she is irretrievably lost! I rave, and then reflect: I reflect, and then rave! I have not patience to bear this calamity, nor power to remedy it! Where shall I fly from the upbraidings of my mind, which accuses me as the murderer of my Eliza? I would fly to death, and seek a refuge in the grave; but the forebodings of a retribution to come, I cannot away with! Oh, that I had seen her; that I had once more asked her forgiveness! But even that privilege, that consolation was denied me! The day on which I meant to visit her, most of my property was attached, and to secure the rest, I was obliged to shut my doors, and become a prisoner in my own house! High living, and old debts, incurred by extravagance, had reduced the fortune of my wife to very little, and I could not satisfy the clamorous demands of my creditors.

I would have given millions, had I possessed them, to have been at liberty to see, and to have had power to preserve Eliza from death! But in vain was my anxiety; it could not relieve; it could not liberate me! When I first heard the dreadful tidings of her exit, I believe I acted like a madman! Indeed, I am little else now!

I have compounded with my creditors, and resigned the whole of my property.

Thus, that splendor and equipage, to secure which, I have sacrificed a virtuous woman, is taken from me; that poverty, the dread of which prevented my forming an honorable connection with an amiable and accomplished girl, the only one I ever loved, has fallen, with redoubled vengeance, upon my guilty head; and I must become a vagabond in the earth!

I shall fly my country as soon as possible; I shall go from every object which reminds me of my departed Eliza! But never, never shall I eradicate from my bosom the idea of her excellence; or the painful remembrance of the injuries I have done her! Her shade will perpetually haunt me! The image of her, as she appeared when mounting the carriage which conveyed her for ever from my sight, she waved her hand in token of a last adieu, will always be present to my imagination! The solemn counsel she gave me before we parted, never more to meet, will not cease to resound in my ears!

While my being is prolonged, I must feel the disgraceful, and torturing effects of my guilt in seducing her! How madly have I deprived her of happiness, of reputation, of life! Her friends, could they know the pangs of contrition, and the horror of conscience which attend me, would be amply revenged!

It is said, she quitted the world with composure and peace. Well she might! She had not that insupportable weight of iniquity, which sinks me to despair! She found consolation in that religion, which I have ridiculed as priestcraft and hypocrisy! But whether it be true, or false, would to heaven I could now enjoy the comforts, which its votaries evidently feel!

My wife has left me. As we lived together without love, we parted without regret.

Now, Charles, I am to bid you a long, perhaps, a last farewell. Where I shall roam in future, I neither know nor care; I shall go where the name of Sanford is unknown; and his person and sorrows unnoticed.

In this happy clime I have nothing to induce my stay. I have not money to support me with my profligate companions; nor have I any relish, at present, for their society. By the virtuous part of the community, I am shunned as the pest and bane of social enjoyment. In short I am debarred from every kind of happiness. If I look back, I recoil with horror from the black catalogue of vices, which have stained my past life, and reduced me to indigence and contempt. If I look forward, I shudder at the prospects which my foreboding mind presents to view, both in this and a coming world! This is a deplorable, yet just picture of myself! How totally the reverse of what I once appeared!

Let it warn you, my friend, to shun the dangerous paths which I have trodden, that you may never be involved in the hopeless ignominy and wretchedness of

Peter Sanford.

Letter LXXIII

To Miss Julia Granby

Boston.

A melancholy tale have you unfolded, my dear Julia; and tragic indeed is the concluding scene!

Is she then gone! gone in this most distressing manner! Have I lost my once loved friend; lost her in a way which I could never have conceived to be possible.

Our days of childhood were spent together in the same pursuits, in the same amusements. Our riper years encreased our mutual affection, and maturer judgment most firmly cemented our friendship. Can I then calmly resign her to so severe a fate! Can I bear the idea of her being lost to honor, to fame, and to life! No; she shall still live in the heart of her faithful Lucy; whose experience of her numerous virtues and engaging qualities, has imprinted her image too deeply on the memory to be obliterated. However she may have erred, her sincere repentance is sufficient to restore her to charity.

Your letter gave me the first information of this awful event. I had taken a short excursion into the country, where I had not seen the papers; or if I had, paid little or no attention to them. By your directions I found the distressing narrative of her exit. The poignancy of my grief, and the unavailing lamentations which the intelligence excited, need no delineation. To scenes of this nature, you have been habituated in the mansion of sorrow, where you reside.

How sincerely I sympathize with the bereaved parent of the dear, deceased Eliza, I can feel, but have not power to express. Let it be her consolation, that her child is at rest. The resolution which carried this deluded wanderer thus far from her friends, and supported her through her various trials, is astonishing! Happy would it have been, had she exerted an equal degree of fortitude in repelling the first attacks upon her virtue! But she is no more; and heaven forbid that I should accuse or reproach her!

Yet, in what language shall I express my abhorrence of the monster, whose detestable arts have blasted one of the fairest flowers in creation? I leave him to God, and his own conscience! Already is he exposed in his true colors! Vengeance already begins to overtake him! His sordid mind must now suffer the deprivation of those sensual gratifications, beyond which he is incapable of enjoyment!

Upon your reflecting and steady mind, my dear Julia, I need not inculcate the lessons which may be drawn from this woe-fraught tale; but for the sake of my sex in general, I wish it engraved upon every heart, that virtue alone, independent of the trappings of wealth, the parade of equipage, and the adulation of gallantry, can secure lasting felicity. From the melancholy story of Eliza Wharton, let the American fair learn to reject with disdain every insinuation derogatory to their true dignity and honor. Let them despise, and for ever banish the man, who can glory in the seduction of innocence and the ruin of reputation. To associate, is to approve; to approve, is to be betrayed!

I am, &c.

Lucy Sumner.

Letter LXXIV
To Mrs. M. Wharton

Boston.

Dear Madam,

We have paid the last tribute of respect to your beloved daughter. The day after my arrival, Mrs. Sumner proposed that we should visit the sad spot which contains the remains of our once amiable friend. The grave of Eliza Wharton, said she, shall not be unbedewed by the tears of friendship.

Yesterday we went accordingly, and were much pleased with the apparent sincerity of the people, in their assurances that every thing in their power had been done to render her situation comfortable. The minutest circumstances were faithfully related; and from the state of her mind, in her last hours, I think much comfort may be derived to her afflicted friends.

We spent a mournful hour, in the place where she is interred, and then returned to the inn, while Mrs. Sumner gave orders for a decent stone to be erected over her grave, with the following inscription:

> "THIS HUMBLE STONE,
> IN MEMORY OF
> ELIZA WHARTON,
> IS INSCRIBED BY HER WEEPING FRIENDS,
> TO WHOM SHE ENDEARED HERSELF BY UNCOMMON
> TENDERNESS AND AFFECTION.
> ENDOWED WITH SUPERIOR ACQUIREMENTS,
> SHE WAS STILL MORE DISTINGUISHED BY
> HUMILITY AND BENEVOLENCE.
> LET CANDOR THROW A VEIL OVER HER FRAILTIES,
> FOR GREAT WAS HER CHARITY TO OTHERS.
> SHE SUSTAINED THE LAST
> PAINFUL SCENE, FAR FROM EVERY FRIEND;
> AND EXHIBITED AN EXAMPLE
> OF CALM RESIGNATION.
> HER DEPARTURE WAS ON THE 25TH DAY OF
> JULY, A.D.——,
> IN THE 37TH YEAR OF HER AGE,
> AND THE TEARS OF STRANGERS WATERED HER
> GRAVE."

I hope, madam, that you will derive satisfaction from these exertions of friendship, and that, united to the many other sources of consolation with which you are furnished, they may alleviate your grief; and while they leave the pleasing remembrance of her virtues, add the supporting persuasion, that your Eliza is happy.

I am, &c.

Julia Granby.

1797

Susanna Haswell Rowson 1762–1824

Susanna Haswell Rowson's best-known work, *Charlotte Temple* (first published in London, 1791, as *Charlotte, A Tale of Truth*), became the first American best-selling novel when it was republished in 1794 by Matthew Carey of Philadelphia. Susanna Haswell was born in Portsmouth, England, in 1762. Her mother, Susanna Musgrave Haswell, died from complications of childbirth, an event that surely influenced Rowson's fiction. Her father, Lieutenant William Haswell, left Susanna to the care of relatives and went to Massachusetts. Late in 1766, he brought his daughter, then almost five years old, through a perilous sea voyage to the colonies. Haswell had remarried, and soon the young Susanna had two half-brothers.

The Haswells' loyalty to England made life in Massachusetts difficult for them during the Revolutionary War. They were first detained by an American guard and later conveyed by prisoner exchange to London. In England, Susanna Haswell worked as a governess, wrote novels and poetry, and married William Rowson, a hardware merchant. When the hardware business failed, the Rowsons decided to go on the stage. They toured in Britain, and then signed with Thomas Wignell's theater company. In 1793 the company went to the United States, where Susanna Rowson not only acted but was also a playwright and lyricist. Her song "America, Commerce and Freedom," in celebration of her adopted country, was especially popular.

When the American edition of *Charlotte Temple* appeared in 1794, it quickly sold out, and Carey had it reprinted at least once and possibly twice in the same year. It has been estimated that the book went through over 200 editions and was read by nearly a quarter to a half million people. Its subtitle may in part account for its immense popularity in a growing nation with a puritanical past; though novel-reading might have been regarded as a questionable activity, reading "a tale of truth," however melodramatic, could be excused, especially if that tale had been written by an author who took every possible occasion to drive home a moral point. In *Charlotte Temple,* moral points are frequently underscored for the "Dear reader," and Charlotte, a "fallen" woman, dies forsaken by the man she has loved.

After the successful publication of *Charlotte Temple* and other works, including *Rebecca, or, The Fille de Chambre,* Rowson gave up the stage and, in 1797, established "Mrs. Rowson's Young Ladies' Academy" in Boston, where she earned renown as an educator, textbook author, and columnist for the *Boston Weekly Magazine.* When Rowson died, she was one of the most celebrated women in America.

Though *Charlotte Temple* continued to be read throughout the nineteenth century, its literary merit was questioned. Some critics characterized Rowson's work as sentimental and melodramatic. Other critics, however, defended the novel, citing its psychological power and insight and its importance in portraying standards of morality prevalent in eighteenth-century America. Rowson's depiction of the Revolutionary War as the background of her romance was also seen as having significance in American literary history.

Literary scholars have also differed on the extent to which Rowson was a feminist. Certainly in her novels and even more strikingly in some of her poetry, Rowson confirms the established view of women as weak and in need of protection—either from parents or a husband—although experiences from her own life belied this traditional assessment. And yet there is in her depiction of the subjected and precarious situation of women an incipient protest against it. Interestingly, there is a connection between the controversial issues of Rowson's feminism and her literary power. Critics who have not taken Rowson seriously as a literary figure emphasize her appeal to an audience of "housemaids and shopgirls"—in other words to uneducated women employed in low-paying jobs—just the people who might be receptive to a protest, however mild and disguised, against the situation of women. For Rowson's feminism did not consist of an open rejection of any established order or sentiment; instead she vividly described a world of endless woes faced by women: deceitful friends, false advisers, heartless landlords, faithless lovers, disastrous pregnancies, and fatal childbirths. One can find in these melodramatic situations an incipient protest against the female condition and at the same time the source of her lasting power and appeal.

Laraine Fergenson
Bronx Community College
City University of New York

PRIMARY WORKS

Victoria, A Novel, 1786; *Mentoria, or the Young Ladies' Friend,* 1791; *Charlotte, a Tale of Truth,* published in London 1791, first American edition, 1794, later published as *Charlotte Temple,* rpt. 1986; *Rebecca, or, The Fille de Chambre,* 1792 in London, first American edition, 1794, rpt. 1987; *Trials of the Human Heart,* 1795; *Reuben and Rachel, or Tales of Old Times,* 1798.

SECONDARY WORKS

R. W. G. Vail, *Susanna Haswell Rowson, the Author of Charlotte Temple, A Bibliographical Study, American Antiquarian Society, Proceedings,* n.s. Vol. 42, 1933:47–160; Ellen B. Brandt, *Susanna Haswell Rowson: America's First Best-Selling Novelist,* 1975; Dorothy Weil, *In Defense of Women: Susanna Rowson,* 1976; Cathy N. Davidson, *Revolution and the Word: The Rise of the Novel in America,* 1986; Patricia L. Parker, *Susanna Rowson,* 1986.

from Charlotte Temple[1]

from Preface

For the perusal of the young and thoughtless of the fair sex, this Tale of Truth is designed; and I could wish my fair readers to consider it as not merely the effusion of Fancy, but as a reality. The circumstances on which I have founded this novel were related to me some little time since by an old lady who had personally known Charlotte, though she concealed the real names of the characters, and likewise the place where the unfortunate scenes were acted. . . . I have thrown over the whole a slight veil of fiction, and substituted names and places according to my own fancy. The principal characters in this little tale are now consigned to the silent tomb: it can therefore hurt the feelings of no one; and may, I flatter myself, be of service to some who are so unfortunate as to have neither friends to advise, or understanding to direct them, through the various and unexpected evils that attend a young and unprotected woman in her first entrance into life. . . .

Sensible as I am that a novel writer, at a time when such a variety of works are ushered into the world under that name, stands but a poor chance for fame in the annals of literature, but conscious that I wrote with a mind anxious for the happiness of that sex whose morals and conduct have so powerful an influence on mankind in

[1]The following excerpts are taken from the first American edition (1794), but the title *Charlotte Temple,* by which the novel is better known, has been used here.

general; and convinced that I have not wrote a line that conveys a wrong idea to the head or a corrupt wish to the heart, I shall rest satisfied in the purity of my own intentions, and if I merit not applause, I feel that I dread not censure.

If the following tale should save one hapless fair one from the errors which ruined poor Charlotte, or rescue from impending misery the heart of one anxious parent, I shall feel a much higher gratification in reflecting on this trifling performance, than could possibly result from the applause which might attend the most elegant finished piece of literature whose tendency might deprave the heart or mislead the understanding.

from Chapter I
A Boarding School

"Are you for a walk," said Montraville to his companion, as they arose from table; "are you for a walk? or shall we order the chaise and proceed to Portsmouth?" Belcour preferred the former; and they sauntered out to view the town, and to make remarks on the inhabitants, as they returned from church.

Montraville was a Lieutenant in the army: Belcour was his brother officer: they had been to take leave of their friends previous to their departure for America, and were now returning to Portsmouth, where the troops waited orders for embarkation. They had stopped at Chichester to dine; and knowing they had sufficient time to reach the place of destination before dark, and yet allow them a walk, had resolved, it being Sunday afternoon, to take a survey of the Chichester ladies as they returned from their devotions.

They had gratified their curiosity, and were preparing to return to the inn without honouring any of the belles with particular notice, when Madame Du Pont, at the head of her school, descended from the church. Such an assemblage of youth and innocence naturally attracted the young soldiers: they stopped; and, as the little cavalcade passed, almost involuntarily pulled off their hats. A tall, elegant girl looked at Montraville and blushed: he instantly recollected the features of Charlotte Temple, whom he had once seen and danced with at a ball at Portsmouth. At that time he thought on her only as a very lovely child, she being then only thirteen; but the improvement two years had made in her person, and the blush of recollection which suffused her cheeks as she passed, awakened in his bosom new and pleasing ideas. Vanity led him to think that pleasure at again beholding him might have occasioned the emotion he had witnessed, and the same vanity led him to wish to see her again.

"She is the sweetest girl in the world," said he, as he entered the inn. Belcour stared. "Did you not notice her?" continued Montraville: "she had on a blue bonnet, and with a pair of lovely eyes of the same colour, has contrived to make me feel devilish odd about the heart."

"Pho," said Belcour, "a musket ball from our friends, the Americans, may in less than two months make you feel worse."

"I never think of the future," replied Montraville; "but am determined to make the most of the present, and would willingly compound with any kind Familiar who would inform me who the girl is, and how I might be likely to obtain an interview."

But no kind Familiar at that time appearing, and the chaise which they had ordered, driving up to the door, Montraville and his companion were obliged to take leave of Chichester and its fair inhabitant, and proceed on their journey.

But Charlotte had made too great an impression on his mind to be easily eradicated: having therefore spent three whole days in thinking on her and in endeavouring to form some plan for seeing her, he determined to set off for Chichester, and trust to chance either to favour or frustrate his designs. Arriving at the verge of the town, he dismounted, and sending the servant forward with the horses, proceeded toward the place, where, in the midst of an extensive pleasure ground, stood the mansion which contained the lovely Charlotte Temple. Montraville leaned on a broken gate, and looked earnestly at the house. The wall which surrounded it was high, and perhaps the Argus's who guarded the Hesperian fruit within, were more watchful than those famed of old.

" 'Tis a romantic attempt," said he; "and should I even succeed in seeing and conversing with her, it can be productive of no good: I must of necessity leave England in a few days, and probably may never return; why then should I endeavour to engage the affections of this lovely girl, only to leave her a prey to a thousand inquietudes, of which at present she has no idea? I will return to Portsmouth and think no more about her."

The evening now was closed; a serene stillness reigned; and the chaste Queen of Night with her silver crescent faintly illuminated the hemisphere. The mind of Montraville was hushed into composure by the serenity of the surrounding objects. "I will think on her no more," said he, and turned with an intention to leave the place; but as he turned, he saw the gate which led to the pleasure grounds open, and two women come out, who walked arm-in-arm across the field.

"I will at least see who these are," said he. He overtook them, and giving them the compliments of the evening, begged leave to see them into the more frequented parts of the town: but how was he delighted, when, waiting for an answer, he discovered, under the concealment of a large bonnet, the face of Charlotte Temple.

He soon found means to ingratiate himself with her companion, who was a French teacher at the school, and, at parting, slipped a letter he had purposely written, into Charlotte's hand, and five guineas into that of Mademoiselle, who promised she would endeavour to bring her young charge into the field again the next evening. . . .

Chapter VI
An Intriguing Teacher

Madame Du Pont was a woman every way calculated to take the care of young ladies, had that care entirely devolved on herself; but it was impossible to attend the education of a numerous school without proper assistants; and those assistants were not always the kind of people whose conversation and morals were exactly such as parents of delicacy and refinement would wish a daughter to copy. Among the teachers at Madame Du Pont's school, was Mademoiselle La Rue, who added to a pleasing person and insinuating address, a liberal education and the manners of a gentlewoman. She was recommended to the school by a lady whose humanity overstepped the bounds of discretion: for though she knew Miss La Rue had eloped from a convent with a young officer, and, on coming to England, had lived with several different men in open defiance of all moral and religious duties; yet, finding her reduced to the most abject want, and believing the penitence which she professed to be sincere, she took her into her own family, and from thence recommended her to Madame Du Pont, as thinking the situation more suitable for a woman of her abilities. But Mademoiselle possessed too much of the spirit of intrigue to remain long without adventures. At church, where she constantly appeared, her person attracted the attention of a young man who was upon a visit at a gentleman's seat in the neighbourhood: she had met him several times clandestinely; and being invited to come out that evening, and eat some fruit and pastry in a summer-house belonging to the gentleman he was visiting, and requested to bring some of the ladies with her, Charlotte being her favourite, was fixed on to accompany her.

The mind of youth eagerly catches at promised pleasure: pure and innocent by nature, it thinks not of the dangers lurking beneath those pleasures, till too late to avoid them: when Mademoiselle asked Charlotte to go with her, she mentioned the gentleman as a relation, and spoke in such high terms of the elegance of his gardens, the sprightliness of his conversation, and the liberality with which he ever entertained his guests, that Charlotte thought only of the pleasure she should enjoy in the visit,—not on the imprudence of going without her governess's knowledge, or of the danger to which she exposed herself in visiting the house of a gay young man of fashion.

Madame Du Pont was gone out for the evening, and the rest of the ladies retired to rest, when Charlotte and the teacher stole out at the back gate, and in crossing the field, were accosted by Montraville, as mentioned in the first chapter.

Charlotte was disappointed in the pleasure she had promised herself from this visit. The levity of the gentlemen and the freedom of their conversation disgusted her. She was astonished at the liberties Mademoiselle permitted them to take; grew thoughtful and uneasy, and heartily wished herself at home again in her own chamber.

Perhaps one cause of that wish might be, an earnest desire to see the contents of the letter which had been put into her hand by Montraville.

Any reader who has the least knowledge of the world, will easily imagine the letter was made up of encomiums on her beauty, and vows of everlasting love and constancy; nor will he be surprised that a heart open to every gentle, generous sentiment, should feel itself warmed by gratitude for a man who professed to feel so much for her; nor is it improbable but her mind might revert to the agreeable person and martial appearance of Montraville.

In affairs of love, a young heart is never in more danger than when attempted by a handsome young soldier. A man of an indifferent appearance, will, when arrayed in a military habit, shew to advantage; but when beauty of person, elegance of manner, and an easy method of paying compliments, are united to the scarlet coat, smart cockade, and military sash, ah! well-a-day for the poor girl who gazes on him: she is in imminent danger; but if she listens to him with pleasure, 'tis all over with her, and from that moment she has neither eyes nor ears for any other object.

Now, my dear sober matron, (if a sober matron should deign to turn over these pages, before she trusts them to the eye of a darling daughter,) let me intreat you not to put on a grave face, and throw down the book in a passion and declare 'tis enough to turn the heads of half the girls in England; I do solemnly protest, my dear madam,

I mean no more by what I have here advanced, than to ridicule those romantic girls, who foolishly imagine a red coat and silver epaulet constitute the fine gentleman; and should that fine gentleman make half a dozen fine speeches to them, they will imagine themselves so much in love as to fancy it a meritorious action to jump out of a two pair of stairs window, abandon their friends, and trust entirely to the honour of a man, who perhaps hardly knows the meaning of the word, and if he does, will be too much the modern man of refinement, to practice it in their favour.

Gracious heaven! when I think on the miseries that must rend the heart of a doating parent, when he sees the darling of his age at first seduced from his protection, and afterwards abandoned, by the very wretch whose promises of love decoyed her from the paternal roof—when he sees her poor and wretched, her bosom torn between remorse for her crime and love for her vile betrayer—when fancy paints to me the good old man stooping to raise the weeping penitent, while every tear from her eye is numbered by drops from his bleeding heart, my bosom glows with honest indignation, and I wish for power to extirpate those monsters of seduction from the earth.

Oh my dear girls—for to such only am I writing—listen not to the voice of love, unless sanctioned by paternal approbation: be assured, it is now past the days of romance: no woman can be run away with contrary to her own inclination: then kneel down each morning, and request kind heaven to keep you free from temptation, or, should it please to suffer you to be tried, pray for fortitude to resist the impulse of inclination when it runs counter to the precepts of religion and virtue.

from Chapter VII
Natural Sense of Propriety Inherent in the Female Bosom

"I cannot think we have done exactly right in going out this evening, Mademoiselle," said Charlotte, seating herself when she entered her apartment: "nay, I am sure it was not right; for I expected to be very happy, but was sadly disappointed."

"It was your own fault, then," replied Mademoiselle: "for I am sure my cousin omitted nothing that could serve to render the evening agreeable."

"True," said Charlotte: "but I thought the gentlemen were very free in their manner: I wonder you would suffer them to behave as they did."

"Prithee, don't be such a foolish little prude," said the artful woman, affecting anger: "I invited you to go in hopes it would divert you, and be an agreeable change of scene; however, if your delicacy was hurt by the behaviour of the gentlemen, you need not go again; so there let it rest."

"I do not intend to go again," said Charlotte, gravely taking off her bonnet, and beginning to prepare for bed: "I am sure, if Madame Du Pont knew we had been out to-night, she would be very angry; and it is ten to one but she hears of it by some means or other."

"Nay, Miss," said La Rue, "perhaps your mighty sense of propriety may lead you to tell her yourself: and in order to avoid the censure you would incur, should she hear of it by accident, throw the blame on me: but I confess I deserve it: it will be a very kind return for that partiality which led me to prefer you before any of the rest of the ladies; but perhaps it will give you pleasure," continued she, letting fall some hypocritical tears, "to see me deprived of bread, and for an action which by the most rigid could only be esteemed an inadvertency, lose my place and character, and be driven again into the world, where I have already suffered all the evils attendant on poverty."

This was touching Charlotte in the most vulnerable part: she rose from her seat, and taking Mademoiselle's hand—"You know, my dear La Rue," said she, "I love you too well, to do anything that would injure you in my governess's opinion: I am only sorry we went out this evening."

"I don't believe it, Charlotte," said she, assuming a little vivacity; "for if you had not gone out, you would not have seen the gentleman who met us crossing the field; and I rather think you were pleased with his conversation."

"I had seen him once before," replied Charlotte, "and thought him an agreeable man; and you know one is always pleased to see a person with whom one has passed several chearful hours. "But," said she pausing, and drawing the letter from her pocket, while a gentle suffusion of vermillion tinged her neck and face, "he gave me this letter; what shall I do with it?"

"Read it, to be sure," returned Mademoiselle.

"I am afraid I ought not," said Charlotte: "my mother has often told me, I should never read a letter given me by a young man, without first giving it to her."

"Lord bless you, my dear girl," cried the teacher smiling, "have you a mind to be in leading strings all your life time. Prithee open the letter, read it, and judge for yourself; if you show it your mother, the consequence will be, you will be taken from school, and a strict guard kept over you; so you will stand no chance of ever seeing the smart young officer again."

"I should not like to leave school yet," replied Charlotte, "till I have attained a greater proficiency in my Italian and music. But you can, if you please, Mademoiselle, take the letter back to Montraville, and tell him I wish him well, but cannot, with any propriety, enter into a clandestine correspondence with him." She laid the letter on the table, and began to undress herself.

"Well," said La Rue, "I vow you are an unaccountable girl: have you no curiosity to see the inside now? for my part I could no more let a letter addressed to me lie unopened so long, than I could work miracles: he writes a good hand," continued she, turning the letter, to look at the superscription.

" 'Tis well enough," said Charlotte, drawing it towards her.

"He is a genteel young fellow," said La Rue carelessly, folding up her apron at the same time; "but I think he is marked with the small pox."

"Oh you are greatly mistaken," said Charlotte eagerly; "he has a remarkable clear skin and fine complexion."

"His eyes, if I could judge by what I saw," said La Rue, "are grey and want expression."

"By no means," replied Charlotte; "they are the most expressive eyes I ever saw."

"Well, child, whether they are grey or black is of no consequence: you have determined not to read his letter; so it is likely you will never either see or hear from him again."

Charlotte took up the letter, and Mademoiselle continued—

"He is most probably going to America; and if ever you should hear any account of him, it may possibly be that he is killed; and though he loved you ever so fervently, though his last breath should be spent in a prayer for your happiness, it can be nothing to you: you can feel nothing for the fate of the man, whose letters you will not open, and whose sufferings you will not alleviate, by permitting him to think you would remember him when absent, and pray for his safety."

Charlotte still held the letter in her hand: her heart swelled at the conclusion of Mademoiselle's speech, and a tear dropped upon the wafer that closed it.

"The wafer is not dry yet," said she, "and sure there can be no great harm—" She hesitated. La Rue was silent. "I may read it, Mademoiselle, and return it afterwards."

"Certainly," replied Mademoiselle.

"At any rate I am determined not to answer it," continued Charlotte, as she opened the letter.

Here let me stop to make one remark, and trust me my very heart aches while I write it; but certain I am, that when once a woman has stifled the sense of shame in her own bosom, when once she has lost sight of the basis on which reputation, honour, every thing that should be dear to the female heart, rests, she grows hardened in guilt, and will spare no pains to bring down innocence and beauty to the shocking level with herself: and this proceeds from that diabolical spirit of envy, which repines at seeing another in the full possession of that respect and esteem which she can no longer hope to enjoy.

Mademoiselle eyed the unsuspecting Charlotte, as she perused the letter, with a malignant pleasure. She saw, that the contents had awakened new emotions in her youthful bosom: she encouraged her hopes, calmed her fears, and before they parted for the night, it was determined that she should meet Montraville the ensuing evening. . . .

from Chapter IX
We Know Not What a Day May Bring Forth

Various were the sensations which agitated the mind of Charlotte, during the day preceding the evening in which she was to meet Montraville. Several times did she almost resolve to go to her governess, show her the letter, and be guided by her advice: but Charlotte had taken one step in the ways of imprudence; and when that is once done, there are always innumerable obstacles to prevent the erring person returning to the path of rectitude: yet these obstacles, however forcible they may appear in general, exist chiefly in imagination.

Charlotte feared the anger of her governess: she loved her mother, and the very idea of incurring her displeasure, gave her the greatest uneasiness: but there was a more forcible reason still remaining: should she show the letter to Madame Du Pont, she must confess the means by which it came into her possession; and what would be the consequence? Mademoiselle would be turned out of doors.

"I must not be ungrateful," said she. "La Rue is very kind to me; besides I can, when I see Montraville, inform him of the impropriety of our continuing to see or correspond with each other, and request him to come no more to Chichester."

However prudent Charlotte might be in these resolutions, she certainly did not take a proper method to confirm herself in them. Several times in the course of the day, she indulged herself in reading over the letter, and each time she read it, the contents sunk deeper in her heart. As evening drew near, she caught herself frequently consulting her watch. "I wish this foolish meeting was over," said she, by way of apology to her own heart, "I wish it was over; for when I have seen him, and convinced him my resolution is not to be shaken, I shall feel my mind much easier."

The appointed hour arrived. Charlotte and Mademoiselle eluded the eye of vigilance; and Montraville, who had waited their coming with impatience, received them with rapturous and unbounded acknowledgments for their condescension: he had wisely brought Belcour with him to entertain Mademoiselle, while he enjoyed an uninterrupted conversation with Charlotte. . . .

. . . Montraville was . . . generous in his disposition, liberal in his opinions, and good-natured almost to a fault; yet eager and impetuous in the pursuit of a favorite object, he staid not to reflect on the consequence which might follow the attainment of his wishes; with a mind ever open to conviction, had he been so fortunate as to possess a friend who would have pointed out the cruelty of endeavouring to gain the heart of an innocent artless girl, when he knew it was utterly impossible for him to marry her, and when the gratification of his passion would be unavoidable infamy and misery to her, and a cause of never-ceasing remorse to himself: had these dreadful consequences been placed before him in a proper light, the humanity of his nature would have urged him to give up the pursuit: but Belcour was not this friend; he rather encouraged the growing passion of Montraville; and being pleased with the vivacity of Mademoiselle, resolved to leave no argument untried, which he thought might prevail on her to be the companion of their intended voyage; and he made no doubt but her example, added to the rhetoric of Montraville, would persuade Charlotte to go with them.

Charlotte had, when she went out to meet Montraville, flattered herself that her resolution was not to be shaken, and that, conscious of the impropriety of her conduct in having a clandestine intercourse with a stranger, she would never repeat the indiscretion.

But alas! poor Charlotte, she knew not the deceitfulness of her own heart, or she would have avoided the trial of her stability.

Montraville was tender, eloquent, ardent, and yet respectful. . . .

from **Chapter XII**
[How thou art fall'n!]

[On the day that she plans to elope with Montraville, Charlotte receives a letter from her parents informing her that her grandfather will go to the school on the following day to take Charlotte home for a visit with her parents, who are planning a birthday celebration for her. This timely letter makes her reconsider her plan.]

. . . "Oh!" cried Charlotte . . . "let me reflect:—the irrevocable step is not yet taken: it is not too late to recede from the brink of a precipice, from which I can only behold the dark abyss of ruin, shame, and remorse!"

She arose from her seat, and flew to the apartment of La Rue. "Oh Mademoiselle!" said she, "I am snatched by a miracle from destruction! This letter has saved me: it has opened my eyes to the folly I was so near committing. I will not go, Mademoiselle; I will not wound the hearts of those dear parents who make my happiness the whole study of their lives."

"Well," said Mademoiselle, "do as you please, Miss; but pray understand that my resolution is taken, and it is not in your power to alter it. I shall meet the gentlemen at the appointed hour, and shall not be surprized at any outrage which Montraville may commit, when he finds himself disappointed. Indeed I should not be astonished, was he to come immediately here, and reproach you for your instability in the hearing of the whole school: and what will be the consequence? you will bear the odium of having formed the resolution of eloping, and every girl of spirit will laugh at your want of fortitude to put it in execution, while prudes and fools will load you with reproach and contempt. You will have lost the confidence of your parents, incurred their anger, and the scoffs of the world; and what fruit do you expect to reap from this piece of heroism, (for such no doubt you think it is?) you will have the pleasure to reflect, that you have deceived the man who adores you, and whom in your heart you prefer to all other men, and that you are separated from him for ever."

This eloquent harangue was given with such volubility, that Charlotte could not find an opportunity to interrupt her, or to offer a single word till the whole was finished, and then found her ideas so confused, that she knew not what to say.

At length she determined that she would go with Mademoiselle to the place of assignation, convince Montraville of the necessity of adhering to the resolution of remaining behind; assure him of her affection, and bid him adieu.

Charlotte formed this plan in her mind, and exulted in the certainty of its success. "How shall I rejoice," said she, "in this triumph of reason over inclination, and, when in the arms of my affectionate parents, lift up my soul in gratitude to heaven as I look back on the dangers I have escaped!"

The hour of assignation arrived: Mademoiselle put what money and valuables she possessed in her pocket, and advised Charlotte to do the same; but she refused; "my resolution is fixed," said she; "I will sacrifice love to duty."

Mademoiselle smiled internally; and they proceeded softly down the back stairs and out of the garden gate. Montraville and Belcour were ready to receive them.

"Now," said Montraville, taking Charlotte in his arms, "you are mine for ever."

"No," said she, withdrawing from his embrace, "I am come to take an everlasting farewell."

It would be useless to repeat the conversation that here ensued; suffice it to say, that Montraville used every argument that had formerly been successful, Charlotte's resolution began to waver, and he drew her almost imperceptibly towards the chaise.[2]

"I cannot go," said she: "cease, dear Montraville, to persuade. I must not: religion, duty, forbid."

"Cruel Charlotte," said he, "if you disappoint my ardent hopes, by all that is sacred, this hand shall put a period to my existence. I cannot—will not live without you."

[2]A light horse-drawn carriage.

"Alas! my torn heart!" said Charlotte, "how shall I act?"

"Let me direct you," said Montraville, lifting her into the chaise.

"Oh! my dear forsaken parents!" cried Charlotte.

The chaise drove off. She shrieked, and fainted into the arms of her betrayer.

[In the following scene the news of Charlotte's elopement is conveyed by Mr. Temple to his wife.]

from Chapter XIV
Maternal Sorrow

. . . "Temple," said she, assuming a look of firmness and composure, "tell me the truth I beseech you. I cannot bear this dreadful suspense. What misfortune has befallen my child? Let me know the worst, and I will endeavour to bear it as I ought."

"Lucy," replied Mr. Temple, "imagine your daughter alive, and in no danger of death: what misfortune would you then dread?"

"There is one misfortune which is worse than death. But I know my child too well to suspect—"

"Be not too confident, Lucy."

"Oh heavens!" said she, "what horrid images do you start: is it possible she should forget—"

"She has forgot us all, my love; she has preferred the love of a stranger to the affectionate protection of her friends."

"Not eloped?" cried she eagerly.[3]

Mr. Temple was silent.

"You cannot contradict it," said she. "I see my fate in those tearful eyes. Oh Charlotte! Charlotte! how ill have you requited our tenderness! But, Father of Mercies," continued she, sinking on her knees, and raising her streaming eyes and clasped hands to heaven, "this once vouchsafe to hear a fond, a distracted mother's prayer. Oh let thy bounteous Providence watch over and protect the dear thoughtless girl, save her from the miseries which I fear will be her portion, and oh! of thine infinite mercy, make her not a mother, lest she should one day feel what I now suffer." . . .

1794

Charles Brockden Brown 1771–1810

Like Royall Tyler before him, Charles Brockden Brown found himself, as he approached adulthood, facing the difficult reality that a new nation required men of the law rather than men of polite letters. Tyler seems to have accommodated himself to the situation, but Charles Brockden Brown seems to have tortured himself with it. His family pressured him to study law; he preferred not to do so. The family conflict brought Brown guilt, recrimination, and unhappiness, such that, at one crisis, he

[3]Anxiously.

wrote in a letter January 22, 1793, "I utterly despise myself. . . . Nothing but a wide vacuity presents itself," and he queried, "Was I born for nothing?" Such self-doubt hardly seems possible for the writer who would go on to write (and that, simultaneously) several novels within a brief amount of time; found and edit three literary journals; and become, in the minds of many later readers, America's first novelist of significance.

Born into a prosperous Quaker family engaged in the mercantile business in Philadelphia, Charles Brockden Brown studied at the prestigious Friends' Latin School until, at age sixteen, he took up study of the law. He lasted as a student in the Philadelphia legal establishment of a family friend until he reached his majority, at which point he finally made clear to his family that he could not bring himself to appear before the bar or to practice as a lawyer. The years in Philadelphia had brought him personal trouble and personal triumph. Although he castigated himself about his decision to displease his family, he was pleased with the acceptance he had received in Philadelphia literary circles like the Belles Lettres Club.

He traveled to New York, where he came under the influence of leading federalist intellectuals, including Timothy Dwight and Elihu Hubbard Smith, who would help further his career. With Smith, a medical student, poet, and playwright, Brown took rooms in New York City. He there met his future biographer, William Dunlap, a dramatist, painter, and art historian. Brown thus gained a circle of friends in fine arts who could offer him the tutelage and encouragement he would need to prosper as a writer.

Prosper as a writer he did. He became familiar with the writings of leading intellectuals in Europe and on the Continent. Specifically, his reading in the works of William Godwin and Mary Wollstonecraft would trigger the development of his own ideas about social responsibility and feminism, and would provide him a sense of wider audience sorely lacking in the narrow circles he had known in Philadelphia. His eclectic readings from this period—in Shakespeare and Milton, Isaac Newton and Erasmus Darwin, among many others—are evidenced in his writings, which were published in short succession in the late 1790s. During the year between the summers of 1798 and 1799 Brown was immensely prolific. He published *Wieland,* a novel concerning religious delusion and mass murder; *Ormond,* which celebrates a woman of patience and fortitude who faces the title character, a villainous seducer; and *Edgar Huntly,* the tale of a sleepwalker; *Alcuin,* a dialogue arguing in behalf of women's sexual freedom; and the first part of a novel, *Arthur Mervyn,* about the outbreak of yellow fever—which fascinated him—in Philadelphia in 1793 (the second part of the novel was published in 1800). Two other novels appeared in 1801 in rapid succession, *Clara Howard* and *Jane Talbot,* Brown's last novel, written in what seems to have been an attempt to gain a readership from the growing market in sentimental fiction.

Brown seems to have written unceasingly, but gaining a livelihood by way of imaginative literature proved less and less possible as each book appeared, so he turned to journalism. In 1799, he founded *The Monthly Magazine and American Review,* but that journal folded within the year. He was ready to try again in 1803 with *The Literary Magazine and American Register,* which lasted until 1806, when he started up the semiannual *American Register, or General Repository of History, Politics, and Science.* The last periodical marks the shift toward politics and history that characterized Brown's final years. He died of tuberculosis early in 1810.

Constantly testing the limits of rationality and the validity of basing moral judgment upon sense impressions, Brown's works treat human psychology and human fallibility again and again in story lines (usually first-person narratives) centered on patterns of hidden guilt, unaccountable thought and action, villainy, and treachery. In most works, Brown uses what has been called the gothic mode, replete with mysterious events and episodes of terror, often set at night in wild, dark, and sometimes cavernous places. He uses as well the devices of sentimental fiction—tales of heightened emotion featuring virtuous women in precarious situations with treacherous men who threaten dishonor and abandonment—popularized by Richardson in England and by William Hill Brown (*The Power of Sympathy,* 1789), Susanna Haswell Rowson (*Charlotte Temple,* 1791), and Hannah Webster Foster (*The Coquette,* 1797). "Somnambulism," the "fragment" Brown published in his own *Literary Magazine and American Register* for May, 1805, is a brief tale similar in tone and subject to his other works (especially *Edgar Huntly,* subtitled "Memoirs of a Sleepwalker"); yet it is less complex and ambiguous than most. At his best—*Wieland, Arthur Mervyn,* and *Edgar Huntly*—Brown offers surreal and imaginative studies of egotism, villainy, and abstraction like those of America's most celebrated writers: Poe, Hawthorne, Melville, James, Faulkner, and Porter.

Carla Mulford
Pennsylvania State University

PRIMARY WORK

The Novels of Charles Brockden Brown, 7 vols., 1827; 6 vols., 1887.

SECONDARY WORKS

H. R. Warfel, *Charles Brockden Brown: American Gothic Novelist,* 1949; D. A. Ringe, *Charles Brockden Brown,* 1966; N. S. Grabo, *The Coincidental Art of Charles Brockden Brown,* 1981; A. Axelrad, *Charles Brockden Brown: An American Tale,* 1983; S. Watts, *The Romance of Real Life: Charles Brockden Brown and the Origins of American Culture,* 1994.

Somnambulism[1]

A fragment

[The following fragment will require no other preface or commentary than an extract from the Vienna Gazette of June 14, 1784. "At Great Clogau, in Silesia, the attention of physicians, and of the people, has been excited by the case of a young man, whose behaviour indicates perfect health in all respects but one. He has a habit of rising in his sleep, and performing a great many actions with as much order and exactness as when awake. This habit for a long time shewed itself in freaks and achievements merely innocent, or, at least, only troublesome and inconvenient, till about six weeks ago. At that period a shocking event took place about three leagues from the town, and in the neighbourhood where the youth's family resides. A young lady, travelling with her father by night, was

[1]Published in the *Literary Magazine and American Register* 3 (May, 1805).

shot dead upon the road, by some person unknown. The officers of justice took a good deal of pains to trace the author of the crime, and at length, by carefully comparing circumstances, a suspicion was fixed upon this youth. After an accurate scrutiny, by the tribunal of the circle, he has been declared author of the murder: but what renders the case truly extraordinary is, that there are good reasons for believing that the deed was perpetrated by the youth while asleep, and was entirely unknown to himself. The young woman was the object of his affection, and the journey in which she had engaged had given him the utmost anxiety for her safety."]

——Our guests were preparing to retire for the night, when somebody knocked loudly at the gate. The person was immediately admitted, and presented a letter to Mr. Davis. This letter was from a friend, in which he informed our guest of certain concerns of great importance, on which the letter-writer was extremely anxious to have a personal conference with his friend; but knowing that he intended to set out from——four days previous to his writing, he was hindered from setting out by the apprehension of missing him upon the way. Meanwhile, he had deemed it best to send a special messenger to quicken his motions, should he be able to find him.

The importance of this interview was such, that Mr. Davis declared his intention of setting out immediately. No solicitations could induce him to delay a moment. His daughter, convinced of the urgency of his motives, readily consented to brave the perils and discomforts of a nocturnal journey.

This event had not been anticipated by me. The shock that it produced in me was, to my own apprehension, a subject of surprise. I could not help perceiving that it was greater than the occasion would justify. The pleasures of this intercourse were, in a moment, to be ravished from me. I was to part from my new friend, and when we should again meet it was impossible to foresee. It was then that I recollected her expressions, that assured me that her choice was fixed upon another. If I saw her again, it would probably be as a wife. The claims of friendship, as well as those of love, would then be swallowed up by a superior and hateful obligation.

But, though betrothed, she was not wedded. That was yet to come; but why should it be considered as inevitable? Our dispositions and views must change with circumstances. Who was he that Constantia Davis had chosen? Was he born to outstrip all competitors in ardour and fidelity? We cannot fail of chusing that which appears to us most worthy of choice. He had hitherto been unrivalled; but was not this day destined to introduce to her one, to whose merits every competitor must yield? He that would resign this prize, without an arduous struggle, would, indeed, be of all wretches the most pusillanimous and feeble.

Why, said I, do I cavil at her present choice? I will maintain that it does honour to her discernment. She would not be that accomplished being which she seems, if she had acted otherwise. It would be sacrilege to question the rectitude of her conduct. The object of her choice was worthy. The engagement of her heart in his favour was unavoidable, because her experience had not hitherto produced one deserving to be placed in competition with him. As soon as his superior is found, his claims will be annihilated. Has not this propitious accident supplied the defects of her former observation? But soft! is she not betrothed? If she be, what have I to dread? The engagement is accompanied with certain conditions. Whether they be openly expressed or not, they necessarily limit it. Her vows are binding on condition that the present situation continues, and that another does not arise, previously to marriage, by whose claims those of the present lover will be justly superseded.

But how shall I contend with this unknown admirer? She is going whither it will not be possible for me to follow her. An interview of a few hours is not sufficient to accomplish the important purpose that I meditate; but even this is now at an end. I shall speedily be forgotten by her. I have done nothing that entitles me to a place in her remembrance. While my rival will be left at liberty to prosecute his suit, I shall be abandoned to solitude, and have no other employment than to ruminate on the bliss that has eluded my grasp. If scope were allowed to my exertions, I might hope that they would ultimately be crowned with success; but, as it is, I am manacled and powerless. The good would easily be reached, if my hands were at freedom: now that they are fettered, the attainment is impossible.

But is it true that such is my forlorn condition? What is it that irrecoverably binds me to this spot? There are seasons of respite from my present occupations, in which I commonly indulge myself in journeys. This lady's habitation is not at an immeasurable distance from mine. It may be easily comprised within the sphere of my excursions. Shall I want a motive or excuse for paying her a visit? Her father has claimed to be better acquainted with my uncle. The lady has intimated, that the sight of me, at any future period, will give her pleasure. This will furnish ample apology for visiting their house. But why should I delay my visit? Why not immediately attend them on their way? If not on their whole journey, at least for a part of it? A journey in darkness is not unaccompanied with peril. Whatever be the caution or knowledge of their guide, they cannot be supposed to surpass mine, who have trodden this part of the way so often, that my chamber floor is scarcely more familiar to me. Besides, there is danger, from which, I am persuaded, my attendance would be a sufficient, an indispensable safeguard.

I am unable to explain why I conceived this journey to be attended with uncommon danger. My mind was, at first, occupied with the remoter consequences of this untimely departure, but my thoughts gradually returned to the contemplation of its immediate effects. There were twenty miles to a ferry, by which the travellers designed to cross the river, and at which they expected to arrive at sun-rise the next morning. I have said that the intermediate way was plain and direct. Their guide professed to be thoroughly acquainted with it.—From what quarter, then, could danger be expected to arise? It was easy to enumerate and magnify possibilities; that a tree, or ridge, or stone unobserved might overturn the carriage; that their horse might fail, or be urged, by some accident, to flight, were far from being impossible. Still they were such as justified caution. My vigilance would, at least, contribute to their security. But I could not for a moment divest myself of the belief, that my aid was indispensable. As I pondered on this image my emotions arose to terror.

All men are, at times, influenced by inexplicable sentiments. Ideas haunt them in spite of all their efforts to discard them. Prepossessions are entertained, for which their reason is unable to discover any adequate cause. The strength of a belief, when it is destitute of any rational foundation, seems, of itself, to furnish a new ground for credulity. We first admit a powerful persuasion, and then, from reflecting on the insufficiency of the ground on which it is built, instead of being prompted to dismiss it, we become more forcibly attached to it.

I had received little of the education of design. I owed the formation of my character chiefly to accident. I shall not pretend to determine in what degree I was credulous or superstitious. A belief, for which I could not rationally account, I was sufficiently prone to consider as the work of some invisible agent; as an intimation from the great source of existence and knowledge. My imagination was vivid. My passions, when I allowed them sway, were incontroulable. My conduct, as my feelings, was characterised by precipitation and headlong energy.

On this occasion I was eloquent in my remonstrances. I could not suppress my opinion, that unseen danger lurked in their way. When called upon to state the reasons of my apprehensions, I could only enumerate possibilities of which they were already apprised, but which they regarded in their true light. I made bold enquiries into the importance of the motives that should induce them to expose themselves to the least hazard. They could not urge their horse beyond his real strength. They would be compelled to suspend their journey for some time the next day. A few hours were all that they could hope to save by their utmost expedition. Were a few hours of such infinite moment?

In these representations I was sensible that I had over-leaped the bounds of rigid decorum. It was not my place to weigh his motives and inducements. My age and situation, in this family, rendered silence and submission my peculiar province. I had hitherto confined myself within bounds of scrupulous propriety, but now I had suddenly lost sight of all regards but those which related to the safety of the travellers.

Mr. Davis regarded my vehemence with suspicion. He eyed me with more attention than I had hitherto received from him. The impression which this unexpected interference made upon him, I was, at the time, too much absorbed in other considerations to notice. It was afterwards plain that he suspected my zeal to originate in a passion for his daughter, which it was by no means proper for him to encourage. If this idea occurred to him, his humanity would not suffer it to generate indignation or resentment in his bosom. On the contrary, he treated my arguments with mildness, and assured me that I had over-rated the inconveniences and perils of the journey. Some regard was to be paid to his daughter's ease and health. He did not believe them to be materially endangered. They should make suitable provision of cloaks and caps against the inclemency of the air. Had not the occasion been extremely urgent, and of that urgency he alone could be the proper judge, he should certainly not consent to endure even these trivial inconveniences. "But you seem," continued he, "chiefly anxious for my daughter's sake. There is, without doubt, a large portion of gallantry in your fears. It is natural and venial in a young man to take infinite pains for the service of the ladies; but, my dear, what say you? I will refer this important question to your decision. Shall we go, or wait till the morning?"

"Go, by all means," replied she. "I confess the fears that have been expressed appear to be groundless. I am bound to our young friend for the concern he takes in our welfare, but certainly his imagination misleads him. I am not so much a girl as to be scared merely because it is dark."

I might have foreseen this decision; but what could I say? My fears and my repugnance were strong as ever.

The evil that was menaced was terrible. By remaining where they were till the next day they would escape it. Was no other method sufficient for their preservation? My attendance would effectually obviate the danger.

This scheme possessed irresistible attractions. I was thankful to the danger for suggesting it. In the fervour of my conceptions, I was willing to run to the world's end to show my devotion to the lady. I could sustain, with alacrity, the fatigue of many nights of travelling and watchfulness. I should unspeakably prefer them to warmth and ease, if I could thereby extort from this lady a single phrase of gratitude or approbation.

I proposed to them to bear them company, at least till the morning light. They would not listen to it. Half my purpose was indeed answered by the glistening eyes and affectionate looks of Miss Davis, but the remainder I was pertinaciously bent on likewise accomplishing. If Mr. Davis had not suspected my motives, he would probably have been less indisposed to compliance. As it was, however, his objections were insuperable. They earnestly insisted on my relinquishing my design. My uncle, also, not seeing any thing that justified extraordinary precautions, added his injunctions. I was conscious of my inability to show any sufficient grounds for my fears. As long as their representations rung in my ears, I allowed myself to be ashamed of my weakness, and conjured up a temporary persuasion that my attendance was, indeed, superfluous, and that I should show most wisdom in suffering them to depart alone.

But this persuasion was transient. They had no sooner placed themselves in their carriage, and exchanged the parting adieus, but my apprehensions returned upon me as forcibly as ever. No doubt part of my despondency flowed from the idea of separation, which, however auspicious it might prove to the lady, portended unspeakable discomforts to me. But this was not all. I was breathless with fear of some unknown and terrible disaster that awaited them. A hundred times I resolved to disregard their remonstrances, and hover near them till the morning. This might be done without exciting their displeasure. It was easy to keep aloof and be unseen by them. I should doubtless have pursued this method if my fears had assumed any definite and consistent form; if, in reality, I had been able distinctly to tell what it was that I feared. My guardianship would be of no use against the obvious sources of danger in the ruggedness and obscurity of the way. For that end I must have tendered them my services, which I knew would be refused, and, if pertinaciously obtruded on them, might justly excite displeasure. I was not insensible, too, of the obedience that was due to my uncle. My absence would be remarked. Some anger and much disquietude would have been the consequences with respect to him. And after all, what was this groundless and ridiculous persuasion that governed me? Had I profited nothing by experience of the effects of similar follies? Was I never to attend to the lessons of sobriety and truth? How ignominious to be thus the slave of a fortuitous and inexplicable impulse! To be the victim of terrors more chimerical than those which haunt the dreams of idiots and children! *They* can describe clearly, and attribute a real existence to the object of their terrors. Not so can I.

Influenced by these considerations, I shut the gate at which I had been standing, and turned towards the house. After a few steps I paused, turned, and listened to the distant sounds of the carriage. My courage was again on the point of yielding, and new efforts were requisite before I could resume my first resolutions.

I spent a drooping and melancholy evening. My imagination continually hovered over our departed guests. I recalled every circumstance of the road. I reflected by what means they were to pass that bridge, or extricate themselves from this slough. I imagined the possibility of their guide's forgetting the position of a certain oak that grew in the road. It was an ancient tree, whose boughs extended, on all sides, to an extraordinary distance. They seemed disposed by nature in that way in which they would produce the most ample circumference of shade. I could not recollect any other obstruction from which much was to be feared. This indeed was several miles distant, and its appearance was too remarkable not to have excited attention.

The family retired to sleep. My mind had been too powerfully excited to permit me to imitate their example. The incidents of the last two days passed over my fancy like a vision. The revolution was almost incredible which my mind had undergone, in consequence of these incidents. It was so abrupt and entire that my soul seemed to have passed into a new form. I pondered on every incident till the surrounding scenes disappeared, and I forgot my real situation. I mused upon the image of Miss Davis till my whole soul was dissolved in tenderness, and my eyes overflowed with tears. There insensibly arose a sort of persuasion that destiny had irreversably decreed that I should never see her more.

While engaged in this melancholy occupation, of which I cannot say how long it lasted, sleep overtook me as I sat. Scarcely a minute had elapsed during this period without conceiving the design, more or less strenuously, of sallying forth, with a view to overtake and guard the travellers; but this design was embarrassed with invincible objections, and was alternately formed and laid aside. At length, as I have said, I sunk into profound slumber, if that slumber can be termed profound, in which my fancy was incessantly employed in calling up the forms, into new combinations, which had constituted my waking reveries.—The images were fleeting and transient, but the events of the morrow recalled them to my remembrance with sufficient distinctness. The terrors which I had so deeply and unaccountably imbibed could not fail of retaining some portion of their influence, in spite of sleep.

In my dreams, the design which I could not bring myself to execute while awake I embraced without hesitation. I was summoned, me-thought, to defend this lady from the attacks of an assassin. My ideas were full of confusion and inaccuracy. All that I can recollect is, that my efforts had been unsuccessful to avert the stroke of the murderer. This, however, was not accomplished without drawing on his head a bloody retribution. I imagined myself engaged, for a long time, in pursuit of the guilty, and, at last, to have detected him in an artful disguise. I did not employ the usual preliminaries which honour prescribes, but, stimulated by rage, attacked him with a pistol and terminated his career by a mortal wound.

I should not have described these phantoms had there not been a remarkable coincidence between them and the real events of that night. In the morning, my uncle, whose custom it was to rise first in the family, found me quietly reposing in the chair in which I had fallen asleep. His summons roused and startled me. This posture was so unusual that I did not readily recover my recollection, and perceive in what circumstances I was placed.

I shook off the dreams of the night. Sleep had refreshed and invigorated my frame, as well as tranquillized my thoughts. I still mused on yesterday's adventures, but my reveries were more cheerful and benign. My fears and bodements were dispersed with the dark, and I went into the fields, not merely to perform the duties of the day, but to ruminate on plans for the future.

My golden visions, however, were soon converted into visions of despair. A messenger arrived before noon, intreating my presence, and that of my uncle, at the house of Dr. Inglefield, a gentleman who resided at the distance of three miles from our house. The messenger explained the intention of this request. It appeared that the terrors of the preceding evening had some mysterious connection with truth. By some deplorable accident, Miss Davis had been shot on the road, and was still lingering in dreadful agonies at the house of this physician. I was in a field near the road when the messenger approached the house. On observing me, he called me. His tale was meagre and imperfect, but the substance of it was easy to gather. I stood for a moment motionless and aghast. As soon as I recovered my thoughts I set off full speed, and made not a moment's pause till I reached the house of Inglefield.

The circumstances of this mournful event, as I was able to collect them at different times, from the witnesses, were these. After they had parted from us, they proceeded on their way for some time without molestation. The clouds disappearing, the star-light enabled them with less difficulty to discern their path. They met not a human being till they came within less than three miles of the oak which I have before described. Here Miss Davis looked forward with some curiosity and said to her father, "Do you not see some one in the road before us? I saw him this moment move across from the fence on the right hand and stand still in the middle of the road."

"I see nothing, I must confess," said the father: "but that is no subject of wonder; your young eyes will of course see farther than my old ones."

"I see him clearly at this moment," rejoined the lady. "If he remain a short time where he is, or seems to be, we shall be able to ascertain his properties. Our horse's head will determine whether his substance be impassive or not."

The carriage slowly advancing, and the form remaining in the same spot, Mr. Davis at length perceived it, but was not allowed a clearer examination, for the person, having, as it seemed, ascertained the nature of the cavalcade, shot across the road, and disappeared. The behaviour of this unknown person furnished the travellers with a topic of abundant speculation.

Few possessed a firmer mind than Miss Davis; but whether she was assailed, on this occasion, with a mysterious foreboding of her destiny; whether the eloquence of my fears had not, in spite of resolution, infected her; or, whether she imagined evils that my incautious temper might draw upon me, and which might originate in our late interview, certain it was that her spirits were visibly depressed. This accident made no sensible alteration in her. She was still disconsolate and incommunicative. All the efforts of her father were insufficient to inspire her with cheerfulness. He repeatedly questioned her as to the cause of this unwonted despondency. Her answer was, that her spirits were indeed depressed, but she believed that the circumstance was casual. She knew of nothing that could justify despondency. But such is humanity. Cheerfulness and dejection will take their turns in the best regulated bosoms, and come and go when they will, and not at the command of reason. This observation was succeeded by a pause. At length Mr. Davis said, "A thought has just occurred to me. The person whom we just now saw is young Althorpe."

Miss Davis was startled: "Why, my dear father, should you think so? It is too dark to judge, at this distance, by resemblance of figure. Ardent and rash as he appears to be, I should scarcely suspect him on this occasion. With all the fiery qualities of youth, unchastised by experience, untamed by adversity, he is capable no doubt of extravagant adventures, but what could induce him to act in this manner?"

"You know the fears that he expressed concerning the issue of this night's journey. We know not what foundation he might have had for these fears. He told us of no danger that ought to deter us, but it is hard to conceive that he should have been thus vehement without cause. We know not what motives might have induced him to conceal from us the sources of his terror. And since he could not obtain our consent to his attending us, he has taken these means, perhaps, of effecting his purpose. The darkness might easily conceal him, from our observation. He might have passed us without our noticing him, or he might have made a circuit in the woods we have just passed, and come out before us."

"That I own," replied the daughter, "is not improbable. If it be true, I shall be sorry for his own sake, but if there be any danger from which his attendance can secure us, I shall be well pleased for all our sakes. He will reflect with some satisfaction, perhaps, that he has done or intended us a service. It would be cruel to deny him a satisfaction so innocent."

"Pray, my dear, what think you of this young man? Does his ardour to serve us flow from a right source?"

"It flows, I have no doubt, from a double source. He has a kind heart, and delights to oblige others: but this is not all. He is likewise in love, and imagines that he cannot do too much for the object of his passion."

"Indeed!" exclaimed Mr. Davis, in some surprise. "You speak very positively. That is more than I suspected; but how came you to know it with so much certainty?"

"The information came to me in the directest manner. He told me so himself."

"So ho! why, the impertinent young rogue!"

"Nay, my dear father, his behaviour did not merit that epithet. He is rash and inconsiderate. That is the utmost amount of his guilt. A short absence will show him the true state of his feelings. It was unavoidable, in one of his character, to fall in love with the first woman whose appearance was in any degree specious. But attachments like these will be extinguished as easily as they are formed. I do not fear for him on this account."

"Have you reason to fear for him on any account?"

"Yes. The period of youth will soon pass away. Overweening and fickle, he will go on committing one mistake after another, incapable of repairing his errors, or of profiting by the daily lessons of experience. His genius will be merely an implement of mischief. His greater capacity will be evinced merely by the greater portion of unhappiness that, by means of it, will accrue to others or rebound upon himself."

"I see, my dear, that your spirits are low. Nothing else, surely, could suggest such melancholy presages. For my part, I question not, but he will one day be a fine fellow and a happy one. I like him exceedingly. I shall take pains to be acquainted with his future adventures, and do him all the good that I can."

"That intention," said his daughter, "is worthy of the goodness of your heart. He is no less an object of regard to me than to you. I trust I shall want neither the power nor inclination to contribute to his welfare. At present, however, his welfare will be best promoted by forgetting me. Hereafter, I shall solicit a renewal of intercourse."

"Speak lower," said the father. "If I mistake not, there is the same person again." He pointed to the field that skirted the road on the left hand. The young lady's better eyes enabled her to detect his mistake. It was the trunk of a cherry-tree that he had observed.

They proceeded in silence. Contrary to custom, the lady was buried in musing. Her father, whose temper and inclinations were moulded by those of his child, insensibly subsided into the same state.

The re-appearance of the same figure that had already excited their attention diverted them anew from their contemplations. "As I live," exclaimed Mr. Davis, "that thing, whatever it be, haunts us. I do not like it. This is strange conduct for young Althorpe to adopt. Instead of being our protector, the danger, against which he so pathetically warned us, may be, in some inscrutable way, connected with this personage. It is best to be upon your guard."

"Nay, my father," said the lady, "be not disturbed. What danger can be dreaded by two persons from one? This thing, I dare say, means us no harm. What is at present inexplicable might be obvious enough if we were better acquainted with this neighbourhood. It is not worth a thought. You see it is now gone." Mr. Davis looked again, but it was no longer discernible.

They were now approaching a wood. Mr. Davis called to the guide to stop. His daughter enquired the reason of this command. She found it arose from his uncertainty as to the propriety of proceeding.

"I know not how it is," said he, "but I begin to be affected with the fears of young Althorpe. I am half resolved not to enter this wood.—That light yonder informs that a house is near. It may not be unadvisable to stop. I cannot think of delaying our journey till morning; but, by stopping a few minutes, we may possibly collect some useful information. Perhaps it will be expedient and practicable to procure the attendance of another person. I am not well pleased with myself for declining our young friend's offer."

To this proposal Miss Davis objected the inconveniences that calling at a farmer's house, at this time of night, when all were retired to rest, would probably occasion. "Besides," continued she, "the light which you saw is gone: a sufficient proof that it was nothing but a meteor."

At this moment they heard a noise, at a small distance behind them, as of shutting a gate. They called. Speedily an answer was returned in a tone of mildness. The person approached the chaise, and enquired who they were, whence they came, whither they were going, and, lastly, what they wanted.

Mr. Davis explained to this inquisitive person, in a few words, the nature of their situation, mentioned the appearance on the road, and questioned him, in his turn, as to what inconveniences were to be feared from prosecuting his journey. Satisfactory answers were returned to these enquiries.

"As to what you seed in the road," continued he, "I reckon it was nothing but a sheep or a cow. I am not more scary than some folks, but I never goes out a' nights without I sees some *sich* thing as that, that I takes for a man or woman, and am scared a little oftentimes, but not much. I'm sure after to find that it's not nothing but a cow, or hog, or tree, or something. If it wasn't some sich thing you seed, I reckon it was *Nick Handyside.*"

"Nick Handyside! who was he?"

"It was a fellow that went about the country a' nights. A shocking fool to be sure, that loved to plague and frighten people. Yes. Yes. It couldn't be nobody, he reckoned, but Nick. Nick was a droll thing. He wondered they'd never heard of Nick. He reckoned they were strangers in these here parts."

"Very true, my friend. But who is Nick? Is he a reptile to be shunned, or trampled on?"

"Why I don't know how as that. Nick is an odd soul to be sure; but he don't do nobody no harm, as ever I heard, except by scaring them. He is easily skeart though, for that matter, himself. He loves to frighten folks, but he's shocking apt to be frightened himself. I reckon you took Nick for a ghost. That's a shocking good story, I declare. Yet it's happened hundreds and hundreds of times, I guess, and more."

When this circumstance was mentioned, my uncle, as well as myself, was astonished at our own negligence. While enumerating, on the preceding evening, the obstacles and inconveniences which the travellers were likely to encounter, we entirely and unaccountably overlooked one circumstance, from which inquietude might reasonably have been expected. Near the spot where they now were, lived a Mr. Handyside, whose only son was an idiot. He also merited the name of monster, if a projecting breast, a mis-shapen head, features horrid and distorted, and a voice that resembled nothing that was ever before heard, could entitle him to that appellation. This being, besides the natural deformity of his frame, wore looks and practised gesticulations that were, in an inconceivable degree, uncouth and hideous. He was mischievous, but his freaks were subjects of little apprehension to those who were accustomed to them, though they were frequently occasions of alarm to strangers. He particularly delighted in imposing on the ignorance of strangers and the timidity of women. He was a perpetual rover. Entirely bereft of reason, his sole employment consisted in sleeping, and eating, and roaming. He would frequently escape at night, and a thousand anecdotes could have been detailed respecting the tricks which Nick Handyside had played upon way-farers.

Other considerations, however, had, in this instance, so much engrossed our minds, that Nick Handyside had never been once thought of or mentioned. This was the more remarkable, as there had very lately happened an adventure, in which this person had acted a principal part. He had wandered from home, and got bewildered in a desolate tract, known by the name of Norwood. It was a region, rude, sterile, and lonely, bestrewn with rocks, and embarrassed with bushes.

He had remained for some days in this wilderness. Unable to extricate himself, and, at length, tormented with hunger, he manifested his distress by the most doleful shrieks. These were uttered with most vehemence, and heard at greatest distance, by night. At first, those who heard them were panic-struck; but, at length, they furnished a clue by which those who were in search of him were guided to the spot. Notwithstanding the recentness and singularity of this adventure, and the probability that our guests would suffer molestation from this cause, so strangely forgetful had we been, that no caution on this head had been given. This caution, indeed, as the event testified, would have been superfluous, and yet I cannot enough wonder, that in hunting for some reason, by which I might justify my fears to them or to myself, I had totally overlooked this mischief-loving idiot. After listening to an ample description of Nick, being warned to proceed with particular caution in a part of the road that was near at hand, and being assured that they had nothing to dread from human-interference, they resumed their journey with new confidence.

Their attention was frequently excited by rustling leaves or stumbling footsteps; and the figure which they doubted not to belong to Nick Handyside, occasionally hovered in their sight. This appearance no longer inspired them with apprehension.

They had been assured that a stern voice was sufficient to reprise him, when most importunate. This antic being treated all others as children. He took pleasure in the effects which the sight of his own deformity produced, and betokened his satisfaction by a laugh, which might have served as a model to the poet who has depicted the ghastly risibilities of Death. On this occasion, however, the monster behaved with unusual moderation. He never came near enough for his peculiarities to be distinguished by star-light. There was nothing fantastic in his motions, nor any thing surprising, but the celebrity of his transitions. They were unaccompanied by those howls, which reminded you at one time of a troop of hungry wolves, and had, at another, something in them inexpressibly wild and melancholy. This monster possessed a certain species of dexterity. His talents, differently applied, would have excited rational admiration. He was fleet as a deer. He was patient, to an incredible degree, of watchfulness, and cold, and hunger. He had improved the flexibility of his voice, till his cries, always loud and rueful, were capable of being diversified without end. Instances had been known, in which the stoutest heart was appalled by them; and some, particularly in the case of women, in which they had been productive of consequences truly deplorable.

When the travellers had arrived at that part of the wood where, as they had been informed, it was needful to be particularly cautious, Mr. Davis for their greater security, proposed to his daughter to alight. The exercise of walking, he thought, after so much time spent in a close carriage, would be salutary and pleasant. The young lady readily embraced the proposal. They forthwith alighted, and walked at a small distance before the chaise, which was not conducted by the servant. From this moment the spectre, which, till now, had been occasionally visible, entirely disappeared. This incident naturally led the conversation to this topic. So singular a specimen of the forms which human nature is found to assume could not fail of suggesting a variety of remarks.

They pictured to themselves many combinations of circumstances in which Handyside might be the agent, and in which the most momentous effects might flow from his agency, without its being possible for others to conjecture the true nature of the agent. The propensities of this being might contribute to realize, on an American road, many of those imaginary tokens and perils which abound in the wildest romance. He would be an admirable machine, in a plan whose purpose was to generate or foster, in a given subject, the frenzy of quixotism.—No theatre was better adapted than Norwood to such an exhibition. This part of the country had long been deserted by beasts of prey. Bears might still, perhaps, be found during a very rigorous season, but wolves which, when the country was a desert, were extremely numerous, had now, in consequence of increasing population, withdrawn to more savage haunts. Yet the voice of Handyside, varied with the force and skill of which he was known to be capable, would fill these shades with outcries as ferocious as those which are to be heard in Siamese or Abyssinian forests. The tale of his recent elopement had been told by the man with whom they had just parted, in a rustic but picturesque style.

"But why," said the lady, "did not our kind host inform us of this circumstance? He must surely have been well acquainted with the existence and habits of this Handyside. He must have perceived to how many groundless alarms our ignorance, in this respect, was likely to expose us. It is strange that he did not afford us the slightest intimation of it."

Mr. Davis was no less surprised at this omission. He was at a loss to conceive how this should be forgotten in the midst of those minute directions, in which every cause had been laboriously recollected from which he might incur danger or suffer obstruction.

This person, being no longer an object of terror, began to be regarded with a very lively curiosity. They even wished for his appearance and near approach, that they might carry away with them more definite conceptions of his figure. The lady declared she should be highly pleased by hearing his outcries, and consoled herself with the belief, that he would not allow them to pass the limits which he had prescribed to his wanderings, without greeting them with a strain or two. This wish had scarcely been uttered, when it was completely gratified.

The lady involuntarily started, and caught hold of her father's arm. Mr. Davis himself was disconcerted. A scream, dismally loud, and piercingly shrill, was uttered by one at less than twenty paces from them.

The monster had shown some skill in the choice of a spot suitable to his design. Neighbouring precipices, and a thick umbrage of oaks, on either side, contributed to prolong and to heighten his terrible notes. They were rendered more awful by the profound stillness that preceded and followed them. They were able speedily to quiet the trepidations which this hideous outcry, in spite of preparation and foresight, had produced, but they had not foreseen one of its unhappy consequences.

In a moment Mr. Davis was alarmed by the rapid sound of footsteps behind him. His presence of mind, on this occasion, probably saved himself and his daughter from instant destruction. He leaped out of the path, and, by a sudden exertion, at the same moment, threw the lady to some distance from the tract. The horse that drew the chaise rushed by them with the celerity of lightning. Affrighted at the sounds which had been uttered at a still less distance from the horse than from Mr. Davis, possibly with a malicious design to produce this very effect, he jerked the bridle from the hands that held it, and rushed forward with headlong speed. The man, before he could provide for his own safety, was beaten to the earth. He was considerably bruised by the fall, but presently recovered his feet, and went in pursuit of the horse.

This accident happened at about a hundred yards from the *oak,* against which so many cautions had been given. It was not possible, at any time, without considerable caution, to avoid it. It was not to be wondered at, therefore, that, in a few seconds, the carriage was shocked against the trunk, overturned, and dashed into a thousand fragments. The noise of the crash sufficiently informed them of this event. Had the horse been inclined to stop, a repetition, for the space of some minutes, of the same savage and terrible shrieks would have added tenfold to his consternation and to the speed of his flight. After this dismal strain had ended, Mr. Davis raised his daughter from the ground. She had suffered no material injury. As soon as they recovered from the confusion into which this accident had thrown them, they began to consult upon the measures proper to be taken upon this emergency. They were left alone. The servant had gone in pursuit of the flying horse. Whether he would be able to retake him was extremely dubious. Meanwhile they were surrounded by darkness. What was the distance of the next house could not be known. At that hour of the night they could not hope to be directed, by the far-seen taper, to any hospitable roof. The only alternative, therefore, was to remain where they were, uncertain of the fate of their companion, or to go forward with the utmost expedition.

They could not hesitate to embrace the latter. In a few minutes they arrived at the oak. The chaise appeared to have been dashed against a knotty projecture of the trunk, which was large enough for a person to be conveniently seated on it. Here they again paused.—Miss Davis desired to remain here a few minutes to recruit her exhausted strength. She proposed to her father to leave her here, and go forward in quest of the horse and the servant. He might return as speedily as he thought proper. She did not fear to be alone. The voice was still. Having accomplished his malicious purposes, the spectre had probably taken his final leave of them. At all events, if the report of the rustic was true, she had no personal injury to fear from him.

Through some deplorable infatuation, as he afterwards deemed it, Mr. Davis complied with her intreaties, and went in search of the missing. He had engaged in a most unpromising undertaking. The man and horse were by this time at a considerable distance. The former would, no doubt, shortly return. Whether his pursuit succeeded or miscarried, he would surely see the propriety of hastening his return with what tidings he could obtain, and to ascertain his master's situation. Add to this, the impropriety of leaving a woman, single and unarmed, to the machinations of this demoniac. He had scarcely parted with her when these reflections occurred to him. His resolution was changed. He turned back with the intention of immediately seeking her. At the same moment, he saw the flash and heard the discharge of a pistol. The light proceeded from the foot of the oak. His imagination was filled with horrible forebodings. He ran with all his speed to the spot. He called aloud upon the name of his daughter, but, alas! she was unable to answer him. He found her stretched at the foot of the tree, senseless, and weltering in her blood. He lifted her in his arms, and seated her against the trunk. He found himself stained with blood, flowing from a wound, which either the darkness of the night, or the confusion of his thoughts, hindered him from tracing. Overwhelmed with a catastrophe so dreadful and unexpected, he was divested of all presence of mind. The author of his calamity had vanished. No human being was at hand to succour him in his uttermost distress. He beat his head against the ground, tore away his venerable locks, and rent the air with his cries.

Fortunately there was a dwelling at no great distance from this scene. The discharge of a pistol produces a sound too loud not to be heard far and wide, in this lonely region. This house belonged to a physician. He was a man noted for his humanity and sympathy. He was roused, as well as most of his family, by a sound so uncommon. He rose instantly, and calling up his people, proceeded with lights to the road. The lamentations of Mr. Davis directed them to the place. To the physician the scene was inexplicable. Who was the author of this distress; by whom the pistol was discharged; whether through some untoward chance or with design, he was as yet uninformed, nor could he gain any information from the incoherent despair of Mr. Davis.

Every measure that humanity and professional skill could suggest were employed on this occasion. The dying lady was removed to the house. The ball had lodged in her brain, and to extract it was impossible. Why should I dwell on the remaining incidents of this tale? She languished till the next morning, and then expired.——

1805

Federalist and Anti-Federalist Contentions

According to the Articles of Confederation, after the Revolutionary War, the states had entered "into a firm league of friendship with each other." The league was anything but "firm," however. Drafted in 1776 and finally ratified a full five years later, the Articles reflect the fear with which the thirteen states approached the idea of a strong, centralized government necessary to maintain a truly "United" States. With the memory of a powerful monarchy still lingering, the states entered into a confederation that left the national governing body—Congress—pitifully weak. Congressional sessions were often so poorly attended that there were not enough delegates to conduct legal business. And although Congress could declare war and peace and enter into alliances, it was not empowered to raise taxes, make laws, or create a national trade policy. On a theoretical level, the states justified this weak central government by arguing from the assumption that a truly republican government—a representative government without a hereditary executive—was only possible among people inhabiting a small land area populated by people with like interests. Therefore, the argument went, the individual states, rather than a centralized government combining all states, would best serve the interests of the people. The argument shows that a centralized power structure had proven, for the Revolutionary generation, untrustworthy.

The harsh economic and social realities of post-war life in the states seriously undermined visions of peaceful and prosperous confederation. The massive economic disruption in the wake of the war had left many in debt. Unable to repay their creditors, many debtors faced imprisonment, so they often turned to extreme measures to protect themselves. In Rhode Island, for instance, debtors gained control of the legislature and began printing large quantities of paper money, stipulating that creditors must accept the virtually worthless currency for the payment of debts. And in Massachusetts, in what has become known as Shays's Rebellion, armed farmers began surrounding courthouses, denying entrance to judges who would be ruling on their foreclosure and bankruptcy cases. In a standoff between roughly 1,500 farmers and 1,000 militiamen at a federal arsenal in Springfield, four farmers were killed. The rebellion, which occurred only a few months before the Federal Convention, played nicely into the hands of those calling for a more aggressive centralized government. John Adams (1735–1826), for instance, wrote about the "lawless tyrannical rabble" of Massachusetts in his *Defence of the Constitutions of Government of the United States of America* (1787, 1788).

When the Federal Convention finally convened in Philadelphia on May 25, 1787, only seven states—barely a majority—were represented. George Washington chaired the debates, which were conducted secretly so that the delegates could speak their minds freely. The secret deliberations were recorded by James Madison, whose Virginia Plan was influential in determining the ultimate ideology of the Constitution. The plan called for a bicameral (two-house) legislature with broad powers of legislative authority, a federal judiciary, and an executive. A system of checks and balances, by which none of the branches of government could gain supremacy over the others, allayed the fears of many who had worried that either the legislative or the executive branch would become tyrannical. On September 17 the Constitution was finally approved, and the state-by-state battle for ratification began.

Such a brief outline of the Convention debates perhaps incorrectly implies that the acceptance of the Constitution was a foregone conclusion, the inevitable end result of the Revolutionary War. However, the vigorous ratification debates suggest that the Constitution was considered a radical document, even though African-Americans, Native Americans, and women—the majority of the nation's inhabitants in 1787—were given no political voice in the Constitution. In the debates for ratification, supporters of the Constitution were called Federalists, while opposers came to be known as Anti-Federalists (a name given them by Federalists who realized the value of stigmatizing their opponents with the negative prefix). The Federalists found it difficult to allay common Anti-Federalist concerns—that individual states would lose their political autonomy under the new Constitution, that a national standing army was a threat to liberty, that officials in the new government would constitute an aristocracy, and that there was no bill of rights guaranteeing individual liberties.

The most famous defenses of the Constitution occur in a series of essays—now called the *Federalist Papers*—by Alexander Hamilton (1757–1804), James Madison (1731–1836), and John Jay (1745–1829). Written under the pseudonym *Publius* (for the Roman, Publius Valerianus, who was called *Publicola,* "people-lover"), the essays appeared first in New York newspapers between October 1787 and May 1788. New York was a crucial state in the ratification contest, for New York's influential governor, George Clinton, opposed the Constitution. If only because its citizens feared being the inhabitants of a lone, independent "nation," New York was eventually won over to the side of the Federalists, with the narrow vote of thirty in favor of the Constitution, twenty-seven opposed. The other states were slowly ratifying the Constitutional articles, perhaps under the influence of the *Publius* essays, which were being reprinted throughout the states. With full ratification (in 1790) by all thirteen states, the *Federalist Papers* entered literary history as important writings indeed.

In Federalist No. 6, Hamilton, echoing the beliefs of English philosopher Thomas Hobbes (1588–1679), argued that human beings are basically "ambitious, vindictive and rapacious." Hamilton used this theory of human nature to argue for a strong national government to check the "factions and convulsions" which would otherwise tear the states apart. And in Federalist No. 10, Madison argued that the only method to control faction without destroying individual liberty was to elect leaders whose "wisdom may best discern the true interest of their country." Although Madison acknowledged that the "unequal distribution of property" was the most prevalent source of faction, he nonetheless mocked "theoretic politicians" who had sought to end faction by "reducing mankind to a perfect equality in their political rights."

The Anti-Federalist argument is represented here in an essay by *Agrippa,* most likely written by one-time librarian of Harvard, James Winthrop. The objections to the Constitution raised by *Agrippa* were shared by many Anti-Federalists. Specifically, *Agrippa* argued that a bill of rights was absolutely necessary, because "we shall [not] always have good men to govern us." Thus, while Federalists like Hamilton used the theory of the innate corruptibility of humankind to argue for a strong central government, Anti-Federalists like *Agrippa* used this same theory to argue for a government whose powers would be restricted by a bill of rights.

On July 4, 1788, once it was learned that the crucial state of Virginia had ratified the Constitution, a large parade took place in Philadelphia. Virtually all classes and vocations were represented in the procession. Judges, lawyers, clergy, veterans, merchants, carpenters, sailors, apprentices, farmers, bricklayers (carrying a banner that read "Both Buildings and Rulers are the Works of our Hands"), coach painters, cabinet makers, food suppliers, bookbinders, printers, blacksmiths and others—all marched in the parade. Prominent Philadelphia doctor Benjamin Rush wrote of the procession that "rank for a while forgot all its claims." For that one moment, at least, it seemed as if the "We" of the Constitution truly represented the people themselves.

Nicholas D. Rombes, Jr.
University of Detroit Mercy

PRIMARY WORKS

The Federalist, ed. Jacob E. Cooke, 1961; *The Complete Anti-Federalist,* 7 vols., ed. Herbert J. Storing, 1981.

SECONDARY WORKS

Jackson Turner Main, *The Anti-Federalists: Critics of the Constitution, 1781–1788,* 1961; William Winslow Crosskey and William Jeffrey, Jr., *Politics and the Constitution in the History of the United States,* vol. 3, 1980; Alfred H. Kelly, et al., *The American Constitution: Its Origins and Development,* 1983; David F. Epstein, *The Political Theory of The Federalist,* 1984; Albert Furtwangler, *The Authority of Publius: A Reading of the Federalist Papers,* 1984; Terence Ball and J.G.A. Pocock, eds., *Conceptual Change and the Constitution,* 1988; George W. Carey, *The Federalist: Design for a Constitutional Republic,* 1989; Christopher M. Duncan, *The Anti-Federalists and Early American Political Thought,* 1995.

The Federalist No. 6 (Alexander Hamilton)

November 14, 1787

To the People of the State of New York.

The three last numbers of this Paper have been dedicated to an enumeration of the dangers to which we should be exposed, in a state of disunion, from the arms and arts of foreign nations. I shall now proceed to delineate dangers of a different, and, perhaps, still more alarming kind, those which will in all probability flow from dissentions between the States themselves, and from domestic factions and convulsions. These have been already in some instances slightly anticipated, but they deserve a more particular and more full investigation.

A man must be far gone in Utopian speculations who can seriously doubt, that if these States should either be wholly disunited, or only united in partial confederacies, the subdivisions into which they might be thrown would have frequent and violent contests with each other. To presume a want of motives for such contests, as an argument against their existence, would be to forget that men are ambitious, vindictive and rapacious. To look for a continuation of harmony between a number of independent unconnected sovereignties, situated in the same neighbourhood, would be to disregard the uniform course of human events, and to set at defiance the accumulated experience of ages.

The causes of hostility among nations are innumerable. There are some which have a general and almost constant operation upon the collective bodies of society: Of this description are the love of power or the desire of preeminence and dominion—the jealousy of power, or the desire of equality and safety. There are others which have a more circumscribed, though an equally operative influence, within their spheres: Such are the rivalships and competitions of commerce between commercial nations. And there are others, not less numerous than either of the former, which take their origin intirely in private passions; in the attachments, enmities, interests, hopes and fears of leading individuals in the communities of which they are members. Men of this class, whether the favourites of a king or of a people, have in too many instances abused the confidence they possessed; and assuming the pretext of some public motive, have not scrupled to sacrifice the national tranquility to personal advantage, or personal gratification.

The celebrated Pericles, in compliance with the resentments of a prostitute,[1] at the expense of much of the blood and treasure of his countrymen, attacked, vanquished and destroyed, the city of the *Samnians.* The same man, stimulated by private pique against the *Megarensians,*[2] another nation of Greece, or to avoid a prosecution with which he was threatened as an accomplice in a supposed theft of the statuary *Phidias,*[3] or to get rid of the accusations prepared to be brought against him for dissipating the funds of the State in the purchase of popularity,[4] or from a combination of all these causes, was the primitive author of that famous and fatal war, distinguished in the Grecian annals by the name of the *Pelopponesian* war; which, after various vicissitudes, intermissions and renewals, terminated in the ruin of the Athenian commonwealth.

The ambitious Cardinal,[5] who was Prime Minister to Henry VIIIth permitting his vanity to aspire to the Tripple-Crown[6] entertained hopes of succeeding in the acquisition of that splendid prize by the influence of the Emperor Charles Vth. To secure the favour and interest of this enterprising and powerful Monarch, he precipitated England into a war with France, contrary to the plainest dictates of Policy, and at the hazard of the safety and independence, as well of the Kingdom over which he presided by his councils, as of Europe in general. For if there ever was a Sovereign who bid fair to realise the project of universal monarchy it was the Emperor Charles Vth, of whose intrigues Wolsey was at once the instrument and the dupe.

The influence which the bigottry of one female,[7] the petulancies of another,[8] and the cabals of a third,[9] had in the co[n]temporary policy, ferments and pacifica-

[1]Aspasia, vide Plutarch's life of Pericles. (Publius)
[2]Idem. (Publius)
[3]Idem. Phidias was supposed to have stolen some public gold with the connivance of Pericles for the embellishment of the statue of Minerva. (Publius)
[4]Idem. (Publius)
[5]Thomas Wolsey (c. 1475–1530). (Cooke)
[6]Worn by the Popes. (Cooke)
[7]Madame De Maintenon. (Publius) She was secretly married to Louis XIV of France in 1684. The "bigotry" to which Hamilton referred was probably her successful attempt to persuade Louis to persecute the Huguenots. (Cooke)
[8]Dutchess of Marlborough. (Publius) As confidante and adviser to Queen Anne from 1702 to 1710, she was extremely influential in both court and state affairs until her political intrigues and personal arrogance led to a break with the Queen. (Cooke)
[9]Madame De Pompadoure. (Publius) As mistress to Louis XV in the years 1745–1765, she played a prominent part in the court intrigues by which France's ministers were chosen and the nation's policies determined. (Cooke)

tions of a considerable part of Europe are topics that have been too often descanted upon not to be generally known.

To multiply examples of the agency of personal considerations in the production of great national events, either foreign or domestic, according to their direction would be an unnecessary waste of time. Those who have but a superficial acquaintance with the sources from which they are to be drawn will themselves recollect a variety of instances; and those who have a tolerable knowledge of human nature will not stand in need of such lights, to form their opinion either of the reality or extent of that agency. Perhaps however a reference, tending to illustrate the general principle, may with propriety be made to a case which has lately happened among ourselves. If SHAYS had not been a *desperate debtor* it is much to be doubted whether Massachusetts would have been plunged into a civil war.[10]

But notwithstanding the concurring testimony of experience, in this particular, there are still to be found visionary, or designing men, who stand ready to advocate the paradox of perpetual peace between the States, though dismembered and alienated from each other. The genius of republics (say they) is pacific; the spirit of commerce has a tendency to soften the manners of men and to extinguish those inflammable humours which have so often kindled into wars. Commercial republics, like ours, will never be disposed to waste themselves in ruinous contentions with each other. They will be governed by mutual interest, and will cultivate a spirit of mutual amity and concord.

Is it not (we may ask these projectors in politics) the true interests of all nations to cultivate the same benevolent and philosophic spirit? If this be their true interest, have they in fact pursued it? Has it not, on the contrary, invariably been found, that momentary passions and immediate interests have a more active and imperious controul over human conduct than general or remote considerations of policy, utility or justice? Have republics in practice been less addicted to war than monarchies? Are not the former administered by men as well as the latter? Are there not aversions, predilections, rivalships and desires of unjust acquisition that affect nations as well as kings? Are not popular assemblies frequently subject to the impulses of rage, resentment, jealousy, avarice, and of other irregular and violent propensities? Is it not well known that their determinations are often governed by a few individuals, in whom they place confidence, and are of course liable to be tinctured by the passions and views of those individuals? Has commerce hitherto done anything more than change the objects of war? Is not the love of wealth as domineering and enterprising a passion as that of power or glory? Have there not been as many wars founded upon commercial motives, since that has become the prevailing system of nations, as were before occasioned b[y] the cupidity of territory or dominion? Has not the spirit of commerce in many instances administered

[10]Shays's Rebellion of 1786 and early 1787 in central and western Massachusetts expressed the discontent which was widespread throughout New England during the economic depression following the Revolution. Led by Daniel Shays, a Revolutionary War veteran and officeholder of Pelham, Massachusetts, the insurgents resorted to armed efforts to intimidate and close the courts to prevent action against debtors. By February of 1787 state troops, under the leadership of Major General Benjamin Lincoln, had suppressed the rebellion. (Cooke)

new incentives to the appetite both for the one and for the other? Let experience, the least fallible guide of human opinions, be appealed to for an answer to these inquiries.

Sparta, Athens, Rome and Carthage were all Republics; two of them, Athens and Carthage, of the commercial kind. Yet were they as often engaged in wars, offensive and defensive, as the neighbouring Monarchies of the same times. Sparta was little better than a well regulated camp; and Rome was never sated of carnage and conquest.

Carthage, though a commercial Republic, was the aggressor in the very war that ended in her destruction. Hannibal had carried her arms into the heart of Italy and to the gates of Rome, before Scipio, in turn, gave him an overthrow in the territories of Carthage and made a conquest of the Commonwealth.

Venice in latter times figured more than once in wars of ambition; 'till becoming an object of terror to the other Italian States, Pope Julius the Second found means to accomplish that formidable league,[11] which gave a deadly blow to the power and pride of this haughty Republic.

The Provinces of Holland, 'till they were overwhelmed in debts and taxes, took a leading and conspicuous part in the wars of Europe. They had furious contests with England for the dominion of the sea; and were among the most persevering and most implacable of the opponents of Louis XIV.

In the government of Britain the representatives of the people compose one branch of the national legislature. Commerce has been for ages the predominant pursuit of that country. Few nations, nevertheless, have been more frequently engaged in war; and the wars, in which that kingdom has been engaged, have in numerous instances proceeded from the people.

There have been, if I may so express it, almost as many popular as royal wars. The cries of the nation and the importunities of their representatives have, upon various occasions, dragged their monarchs into war, or continued them in it contrary to their inclinations, and, sometimes, contrary to the real interests of the State. In that memorable struggle for superiority, between the rival Houses of Austria and Bourbon which so long kept Europe in a flame, it is well known that the antipathies of the English against the avarice of a favourite leader,[12] protracted the war beyond the limits marked out by sound policy and for a considerable time in opposition to the views of the Court.[13]

The wars of these two last mentioned nations have in a great measure grown out of commercial considerations—The desire of supplanting and the fear of being supplanted either in particular branches of traffic or in the general advantages of trade and navigation; and sometimes even the more culpable desire of sharing in the commerce of other nations, without their consent.

[11]The League of Cambray, comprehending the Emperor, the King of France, the King of Arragon, and most of the Italian Princes and States. (Publius)

[12]The Duke of Marlborough. (Publius)

[13]The War of the Spanish Succession, 1701–1714. In 1709 Marlborough, commander-in-chief of the united British and Dutch armies, refused to consider a French plea for peace, although the Tory party in England was opposed to continuing the war. (Cooke)

The last war but two between Britain and Spain sprang from the attempts of the English merchants, to prosecute an illicit trade with the Spanish main.[14] These unjustifiable practices on their part produced severities on the part of the Spaniards, towards the subjects of Great Britain, which were not more justifiable; because they exceeded the bounds of a just retaliation, and were chargeable with inhumanity and cruelty. Many of the English who were taken on the Spanish coasts were sent to dig in the mines of Potosi; and by the usual progress of a spirit of resentment, the innocent were after a while confounded with the guilty in indiscriminate punishment. The complaints of the merchants kindled a violent flame throughout the nation, which soon after broke out in the house of commons, and was communicated from that body to the ministry. Letters of reprisal were granted and a war ensued, which in its consequences overthrew all the alliances[15] that but twenty years before had been formed, with sanguine expectations of the most beneficial fruits.

From this summary of what has taken place in other countries, whose situations have borne the nearest resemblance to our own, what reason can we have to confide in those reveries, which would seduce us into an expectation of peace and cordiality between the members of the present confederacy, in a state of separation? Have we not already seen enough of the fallacy and extravagance of those idle theories which have amused us with promises of an exemption from the imperfections, weaknesses and evils incident to society in every shape? Is it not time to awake from the deceitful dream of a golden age, and to adopt as a practical maxim for the direction of our political conduct, that we, as well as the other inhabitants of the globe, are yet remote from the happy empire of perfect wisdom and perfect virtue?

Let the point of extreme depression to which our national dignity and credit have sunk—let the inconveniences felt everywhere from a lax and ill administration of government—let the revolt of a part of the State of North Carolina[16]—the late menacing disturbances in Pennsylvania[17] and the actual insurrections and rebellions in Massachusetts declare![18]

So far is the general sense of mankind from corresponding with the tenets of those, who endeavor to lull asleep our apprehensions of discord and hostility be-

[14]The War of Jenkins's Ear, which began in 1739 and soon was absorbed into the War of the Austrian Succession (1740–1748). It arose from Spanish reprisals against repeated attempts by Englishmen to circumvent or defy the strict regulations under which Spain allowed a limited amount of trade with her American colonies. (Cooke)

[15]*I.e.,* the Continental balance-of-power system established by the Treaty of Utrecht in 1713. (Cooke)

[16]This refers to the establishment in 1784 of a separate state, Franklin, by the inhabitants of four western counties of North Carolina. The opposition of North Carolina and internal dissensions in the infant state led, at the end of 1787, to the submission of the inhabitants of Franklin to the authority of North Carolina. (Cooke)

[17]In 1787 many inhabitants of the Wyoming Valley sought to secede from Pennsylvania and establish a new state. The governor of Pennsylvania responded by ordering "a body of militia to hold themselves in readiness to march thither," an action approved by the state assembly less than a month before this essay was written. (Cooke)

[18]Shays's Rebellion, mentioned earlier in this paper. (Cooke)

tween the States, in the event of disunion, that it has from long observation of the progress of society become a sort of axiom in politics, that vicinity, or nearness of situation, constitutes nations natural enemies. An intelligent writer expresses himself on this subject to this effect—"NEIGHBOURING NATIONS (says he) are naturally ENEMIES of each other, unless their common weakness forces them to league in a CONFEDERATE REPUBLIC, and their constitution prevents the differences that neighbourhood occasions, extinguishing that secret jealousy, which disposes all States to aggrandise themselves at the expence of their neighbours."[19] This passage, at the same time points out the EVIL and suggests the REMEDY.

PUBLIUS.

1787

The Federalist No. 10 (James Madison)

November 22, 1787

To the People of the State of New York.

Among the numerous advantages promised by a well constructed Union, none deserves to be more accurately developed than its tendency to break and control the violence of faction. The friend of popular governments, never finds himself so much alarmed for their character and fate, as when he contemplates their propensity to this dangerous vice. He will not fail therefore to set a due value on any plan which, without violating the principles to which he is attached, provides a proper cure for it. The instability, injustice and confusion introduced in the public councils, have in truth been the mortal diseases under which popular governments have every where perished; as they continue to be the favorite and fruitful topics from which the adversaries to liberty derive their most specious declamations. The valuable improvements made by the American Constitutions on the popular models, both ancient and modern, cannot certainly be too much admired; but it would be an unwarrantable partiality, to contend that they have as effectually obviated the danger on this side as was wished and expected. Complaints are every where heard from our most considerate and virtuous citizens, equally the friends of public and private faith, and of public and personal liberty; that our governments are too unstable; that the public good is disregarded in the conflicts of rival parties; and that measures are too often decided, not according to the rules of justice, and the rights

[19]Vede Principes des Negotiations par L'Abbe de Mably. (Publius)

of the minor party; but by the superior force of an interested and over-bearing majority. However anxiously we may wish that these complaints had no foundation, the evidence of known facts will not permit us to deny that they are in some degree true. It will be found indeed, on a candid review of our situation, that some of the distresses under which we labor, have been erroneously charged on the operation of our governments; but it will be found, at the same time, that other causes will not alone account for many of our heaviest misfortunes; and particularly, for that prevailing and increasing distrust of public engagements, and alarm for private rights, which are echoed from one end of the continent to the other. These must be chiefly, if not wholly, effects of the unsteadiness and injustice, with which a factious spirit has tainted our public administrations.

By a faction I understand a number of citizens, whether amounting to a majority or minority of the whole, who are united and actuated by some common impulse of passion, or of interest, adverse to the rights of other citizens, or to the permanent and aggregate interests of the community.

There are two methods of curing the mischiefs of faction: the one, by removing its causes; the other, by controling its effects.

There are again two methods of removing the causes of faction: the one by destroying the liberty which is essential to its existence; the other, by giving to every citizen the same opinions, the same passions, and the same interests.

It could never be more truly said than of the first remedy, that it is worse than the disease. Liberty is to faction, what air is to fire, an aliment without which it instantly expires. But it could not be a less folly to abolish liberty, which is essential to political life, because it nourishes faction, than it would be to wish the annihilation of air, which is essential to animal life, because it imparts to fire its destructive agency.

The second expedient is as impracticable, as the first would be unwise. As long as the reason of man continues fallible, and he is at liberty to exercise it, different opinions will be formed. As long as the connection subsists between his reason and his self-love, his opinions and his passions will have a reciprocal influence on each other; and the former will be objects to which the latter will attach themselves. The diversity in the faculties of men from which the rights of property originate, is not less an insuperable obstacle to a uniformity of interests. The protection of these faculties is the first object of Government. From the protection of different and unequal faculties of acquiring property, the possession of degrees and kinds of property immediately results; and from the influence of these on the sentiments and views of the respective proprietors, ensues a division of the society into different interests and parties.

The latent causes of faction are thus sown in the nature of man; and we see them every where brought into different degrees of activity, according to the different circumstances of civil society. A zeal for different opinions concerning religion, concerning Government and many other points, as well of speculation as of practice; an attachment to different leaders ambitiously contending for pre-eminence and power; or to persons of other descriptions whose fortunes have been interesting to the human passions, have in turn divided mankind into parties, inflamed them with mutual animosity, and rendered them much more disposed to vex and oppress each other, than to cooperate for their common good. So strong is this propensity of mankind to fall into mutual animosities, that where no substantial occasion presents itself, the most frivolous and fanciful distinctions have been sufficient to kindle their unfriendly passions, and excite their most violent conflicts. But the most common and durable source of factions, has been the various and unequal distribution of property. Those who hold, and those who are without property, have ever formed distinct interests in society. Those who are creditors, and those who are debtors, fall under a like discrimination. A landed interest, a manufacturing interest, a mercantile interest, a monied interest, with many lesser interests, grow up of necessity in civilized nation, and divide them into different classes, actuated by different sentiments and views. The regulation of these various and interfering interests forms the principal task of modern Legislation, and involved the spirit of party and faction in the necessary and ordinary operations of Government.

No man is allowed to be a judge in his own cause; because his interest would certainly bias his judgment, and, not improbably, corrupt his integrity. With equal, nay with greater reason, a body of men, are unfit to be both judges and parties, at the same time; yet, what are many of the most important acts of legislation, but so many judicial determinations, not indeed concerning the rights of single persons, but concerning the rights of large bodies of citizens; and what are the different classes of legislators, but advocates and parties to the causes which they determine? Is a law proposed concerning private debts? It is a question to which the creditors are parties on one side, and the debtors on the other. Justice ought to hold the balance between them. Yet the parties are and must be themselves the judges; and the most numerous party, or in other words, the most powerful faction must be expected to prevail. Shall domestic manufactures be encouraged, and in what degree, by restrictions on foreign manufactures? are questions which would be differently decided by the landed and the manufacturing classes; and probably by neither, with a sole regard to justice and the public good. The apportionment of taxes on the various descriptions of poverty, is an act which seems to require the most exact impartiality; yet, there is perhaps no legislative act in which greater opportunity and temptation are given to a predominant party, to trample on the rules of justice. Every shilling with which they over-burden the inferior number, is a shilling saved to their own pockets.

It is in vain to say, that enlightened statesmen will be able to adjust these clashing interests, and render them all subservient to the public good. Enlightened statesmen will not always be at the helm: Nor, in many cases, can such an adjustment be made at all, without taking into view indirect and remote considerations, which will rarely prevail over the immediate interest which one party may find in disregarding the rights of another, or the good of the whole.

The inference to which we are brought, is, that the causes of faction cannot be removed; and that relief is only to be sought in the means of controling its effects.

If a faction consists of less than a majority, relief is supplied by the republican principle, which enables the majority to defeat its sinister views by regular vote: it may clog the administration, it may convulse the society; but it will be unable to execute and mask its violence under the forms of the Constitution. When a majority is included in a faction, the form of popular government on the other hand enables it to sacrifice to its ruling passion or interest, both the public good and the rights of other citizens. To secure the public good, and private rights, against the danger of such a faction, and at the same time to preserve the spirit and the form of popular government, is then the great object to which our enquiries are directed: Let me add that it is the great desideratum, by which alone this form of government can be rescued from the opprobrium under which it has so long labored, and be recommended to the esteem and adoption of mankind.

By what means is this object attainable? Evidently by one of two only. Either the existence of the same passion or interest in a majority at the same time, must be prevented; or the majority, having such co-existent passion or interest, must be rendered, by their number and local situation, unable to concert and carry into effect schemes of oppression. If the impulse and the opportunity be suffered to coincide, we well know that neither moral nor religious motives can be relied on as an adequate control. They are not found to be such on the injustice and violence of individuals, and lose their efficacy in proportion to the numbers combined together; that is, in proportion as their efficacy becomes needful.

From this view of the subject, it may be concluded, that a pure Democracy, by which I mean, a Society, consisting of a small number of citizens, who assemble and administer the Government in person, can admit of no cure for the mischiefs of faction. A common passion or interest will, in almost every case, be felt by a majority of the whole; a communication and concern results from the form of Government itself; and there is nothing to check the inducements to sacrifice the weaker party, or an obnoxious individual. Hence it is, that such Democracies have ever been spectacles of turbulence and contention; have ever been found incompatible with personal security, or the rights of property; and have in general been as short in their lives, as they have been violent in their deaths. Theoretic politicians, who have patronized this species of Government, have erroneously supposed, that by reducing mankind to a perfect equality in their political rights, they would at the same time, be perfectly equalized and assimilated in their possessions, their opinions, and their passions.

A Republic, by which I mean a Government in which the scheme of representation takes place, opens a different prospect, and promises the cure for which we are seeking. Let us examine the points in which it varies from pure Democracy, and we shall comprehend both the nature of the cure, and the efficacy which it must derive from the Union.

The two great points of difference between a Democracy and a Republic are, first, the delegation of the Government, in the latter, to a small number of citizens elected by the rest: secondly, the greater number of citizens, and greater sphere of country, over which the latter may be extended.

The effect of the first difference is, on the one hand to refine and enlarge the public views, by passing them through the medium of a chosen body of citizens, whose wisdom may best discern the true interest of their country, and whose patriotism and love of justice, will be least likely to sacrifice it to temporary or partial considerations. Under such a regulation, it may well happen that the public voice pronounced by the representatives of the people, will be more consonant to the public good, than if pronounced by the people themselves convened for the purpose. On the other hand, the effect may be inverted. Men of factious tempers, of local prejudices, or of sinister designs, may be intrigue, by corruption or by other means, first obtain the suffrages, and then betray the interests of the people. The question resulting is, whether small or extensive Republics are most favorable to the election of proper guardians of the public wealth and it is clearly decided in favor of the latter by two obvious considerations.

In the first place it is to be remarked that however small the Republic may be, the Representatives must be raised to a certain number, in order to guard against the cabals of a few; and that however large it may be, they must be limited to a certain number, in order to guard against the confusion of a multitude. Hence the number of Representatives in the two cases, not being in proportion to that of the Constituents, and being proportionally greatest in the small Republic, it follows, that if the proportion of fit characters, be not less, in the large than in the small Republic, the former will present a greater option, and consequently a greater probability of a fit choice.

In the next place, as each Representative will be chosen by a greater number of citizens in the large than in the small Republic, it will be more difficult for unworthy candidates to practise with success the vicious arts, by which elections are too often carried; and the suffrages of the people being more free, will be more likely to centre on men who possess the most attractive merit, and the most diffusive and established characters.

It must be confessed, that in this, as in most other cases, there is a mean, on both sides of which inconveniencies will be found to lie. By enlarging too much the number of electors, you render the representative too little acquainted with all their local circumstances and lesser interests; as by reducing it too much, you render him unduly attached to these, and too little fit to comprehend and pursue great and national objects. The Federal Constitution forms a happy combination in this respect; the great and aggregate interests being referred to the national, the local and particular, to the state legislatures.

The other point of difference is, the greater number of citizens and extent of territory which may be brought within the compass of Republican, than of Democratic Government; and it is this circumstance principally which renders factious combinations less to be dreaded in the former, than in the latter. The smaller the society, the fewer probably will be the distinct parties and interests composing it; the fewer the distinct parties and interests, the more frequently will a majority be found of the same party; and the smaller the numbers of individuals composing a majority, and the smaller the compass within which they are placed, the more easily will they concert and execute their plans of oppression. Extend the sphere, and you take in a greater variety of parties and interests; you make it less probable that a majority of the whole will have a common motive to invade the rights of other citizens; or if such a common motive exists, it will be more difficult for all who feel it to discover their own strength, and to act in unison with each other. Besides other impediments, it may be remarked, that where there is a consciousness of unjust or dishonorable purposes, communication is always checked by distrust, in proportion to the number whose concurrence is necessary.

Hence it clearly appears, that the same advantage, which a Republic has over a Democracy, in controling the effects of faction, is enjoyed by a large over a small Republic—is enjoyed by the Union over the States composing it. Does this advantage consist in the substitution of Representatives, whose enlightened views and virtuous sentiments render them superior to local prejudices, and to schemes of injustice? It will not be denied, that the Representation of the Union will be most likely to possess these requisite endowments. Does it consist in the greater security afforded by a greater variety of parties, against the event of any one party being able to outnumber and oppress the rest? In an equal degree does the encreased variety of parties, comprised within the Union, encrease this security? Does it, in fine, consist in the greater obstacles opposed to the concert and accomplishment of the secret wishes of an unjust and interested majority? Here, again, the extent of the Union gives it the most palpable advantage.

The influence of factious leaders may kindle a flame within their particular States but will be unable to spread a general conflagration through the other States: a religious sect, may degenerate into a political faction in a part of the confederacy; but the variety of sects dispersed over the entire face of it, must secure the national Councils against any danger from that source: a rage for paper money, for an abolition of debts, for an equal division of property, or for any other improper or wicked project, will be less apt to pervade the whole body of the Union, than a particular member of it; in the same proportion as such a malady is more likely to taint a particular county or district, than an entire State.

In the extent and proper structure of the Union, therefore, we behold a Republican remedy for the diseases most incident to Republican Government. And according to the degree of pleasure and pride, we feel in being Republicans, ought to be our zeal in cherishing the spirit, and supporting the character of Federalists.

PUBLIUS.

1787

An Anti-Federalist Paper

To the Massachusetts Convention.[1]

Gentlemen,

As it is essentially necessary to the happiness of a free people, that the constitution of government should be established in principles of truth, I have endeavoured, in a series of papers, to discuss the proposed form, with that degree of freedom which becomes a faithful citizen of the commonwealth. It must be obvious to the most careless observer, that the friends of the new plan appear to have nothing more in view than to establish it by a popular current, without any regard to the truth of its principles. Propositions, novel, erroneous and dangerous, are boldly advanced to support a system, which does not appear to be founded in, but in every instance to contradict, the experience of mankind. We are told, that a constitution is in itself a

[1]First published in the *Massachusetts Gazette,* January 29, 1788.

bill of rights; that all power not expressly given is reserved; that no powers are given to the new government which are not already vested in the state governments; and that it is for the security of liberty that the persons elected should have the absolute controul over the time, manner and place of election. These, and an hundred other things of the like kind, though they have gained the hasty assent of men, respectable for learning and ability, are false in themselves, and invented merely to serve a present purpose. This will, I trust, clearly appear from the following considerations.

It is common to consider man at first as in a state of nature, separate from all society. The only historical evidence, that the human species ever actually existed in this state, is derived from the book of Gen.[2] There, it is said, that Adam remained a while alone. While the whole species was comprehended in his person was the only instance in which this supposed state of nature really existed. Ever since the completion of the first pair, mankind appear as natural to associate with their own species, as animals of any other kind herd together. Wherever we meet with their settlements, they are found in clans. We are therefore justified in saying, that a state of society is the natural state of man. Wherever we find a settlement of men, we find also some appearance of government. The state of government is therefore as natural to mankind as a state of society. Government and society appear to be coeval. The most rude and artless form of government is probably the most ancient. This we find to be practised among the Indian tribes in America. With them the whole authority of government is vested in the whole tribe.[3] Individuals depend upon their reputation of valour and wisdom to give them influence. Their government is genuinely democratical. This was probably the first kind of government among mankind, as we meet with no mention of any other kind, till royalty was introduced in the person of Nimrod.[4] Immediately after that time, the Asiatick nations seem to have departed from the simple democracy, which is still retained by their American brethren, and universally adopted the kingly form. We do indeed meet with some vague rumors of an aristocracy in India so late as the time of Alexander the great.[5] But such stories are altogether uncertain and improbable. For in the time of Abraham,[6] who lived about sixteen hundred years before Alexander, all the little nations mentioned in the Mosaick history appear to be governed by kings. It does not appear from any accounts of the Asiatick kingdoms that they have practised at all upon the idea of a limitted monarchy. The whole power

[2]According to Genesis, Adam dwelled in Eden for a time before Eve was created. "And the Lord God said, It is not good that the man should be alone; I will make him a help meet for him" (Genesis 2:18).

[3]*Agrippa* is referring to the Iroquois nation, a confederacy made up of five tribes, each represented on the governing council. At the time of confederation and indeed even today, readers have commented on the similarity between the representative system of the Iroquois and that evident in the Constitution.

[4]Nimrod, famed as a great hunter, was a Babylonian leader who ruled several kingdoms. See Genesis 10:8–12.

[5]Alexander the Great (B.C. 356–323) was King of Macedonia, an ancient kingdom north of Greece, now part of Greece, Bulgaria, and Yugoslavia.

[6]According to the Bible, a covenant was established between Abraham's descendants and God, who told Abraham, "As for me, behold, my covenant is with thee, and thou shalt be a father of many nations" (Genesis 17:4).

of society has been delegated to the kings; and though they may be said to have constitutions of government, because the succession to the crown is limitted by certain rules, yet the people are not benefitted by their constitutions, and enjoy no share of civil liberty. The first attempt to reduce republicanism to a system, appears to be made by Moses when he led the Israelites out of Egypt.[7] This government stood a considerable time, about five centuries, till in a frenzy the people demanded a king, that they might resemble the nations about them. They were dissatisfied with their judges, and instead of changing the administration, they madly changed their constitution. However they might flatter themselves with the idea, that an high spirited people could get the power back again when they pleased; they never did get it back, and they fared like the nations about them. Their kings tyrannized over them for some centuries, till they fell under a foreign yoke. This is the history of that nation. With a change of names, it describes the progress of political changes in other countries. The people are dazzled with the splendour of distant monarchies, and a desire to share their glory induces them to sacrifice their domestick happiness.

From this general view of the state of mankind it appears, that all the power of government originally reside in the body of the people; and that when they appoint certain persons to administer the government, they delegate all the powers of government not expressly reserved. Hence it appears, that a constitution does not in itself imply any more than a declaration of the relation which the different parts of the government bear to each other, but does not in any degree imply security to the rights of individuals. This has been the uniform practice. In all doubtful cases the decision is in favour of the government. It is therefore impertinent to ask by what right government exercises powers not expressly delegated. Mr. Wilson,[8] the great oracle of federalism, acknowledges, in his speech to the Philadelphians, the truth of these remarks, as they respect the state governments, but attempts to set up a distinction between them and the continental government. To any body who will be at the trouble to read the new system, it is evidently in the same situation as the state constitutions now possess. It is a compact among the *people* for the purposes of government, and not a compact between states. It begins in the name of the people and not of the states.

It has been shown in the course of this paper, that when people institute government, they of course delegate all rights not expressly reserved. In our state constitution the bill of rights consists of thirty articles. It is evident therefore that the new constitution proposes to delegate greater powers than are granted to our own government, sanguine as the person was who denied it. The complaints against the separate governments, even by the friends of the new plan, are not that they have not power enough, but that they are disposed to make a bad use of what power they have. Surely then they reason badly, when they purpose to set up a govern-

[7]See Exodus, chapters 13 and 14, for an account of how Moses led the Israelites out of Egypt. See Judges for a description of the Hebrews' disaffection with their government.

[8]James Wilson (1742–1798) was a supporter of the Constitution. *Agrippa* refers to Wilson's "Address to the Citizens of Philadelphia," given on October 6, 1787.

ment possess'd of much more extensive powers than the present, and subject to much smaller checks.

Bills of rights, reserved by authority of the people, are, I believe, peculiar to America. A careful observance of the abuse practised in other countries has had its just effect by inducing our people to guard against them. We find the happiest consequences to flow from it. The separate governments know their powers, their objects, and operations. We are therefore not perpetually tormented with new experiments. For a single instance of abuse among us there are thousands in other countries. On the other hand, the people know their rights, and feel happy in the possession of their freedom, both civil and political. Active industry is the consequence of their security; and within one year the circumstances of the state and of individuals have improved to a degree never before known in this commonwealth. Though our bill of rights does not, perhaps, contain all the cases in which power might be safely reserved, yet it affords a protection to the persons and possessions of individuals not known in any foreign country. In some respects the power of government is a little too confined. In many other countries we find the people resisting their governours for exercising their power in an unaccustomed mode. But for want of a bill of rights the resistance is always by the principles of their government, a rebellion which nothing but success can justify. In our constitution we have aimed at delegating the necessary powers of government and confining their operation to beneficial purposes. At present we appear to have come very near the truth. Let us therefore have wisdom and virtue enough to preserve it inviolate. It is a stale contrivance to get the people into a passion, in order to make them sacrifice their liberty. Repentance always comes, but it comes too late. Let us not flatter ourselves that we shall always have good men to govern us. If we endeavour to be like other nations we shall have more bad men than good ones to exercise extensive powers. That circumstance alone will corrupt them. While they fancy themselves the vicegerents of God, they will resemble him only in power, but will always depart from his wisdom and goodness.

Agrippa.

1788

Missionary Voices of the Southwest

As evidenced by the selections elsewhere in the anthology, Spanish Catholic missionary efforts in the Southwest date to Fray Marcos de Niza's exploration of Zuni areas in 1539 and Francisco Vásquez de Coronado's expedition into the area in 1540. To be sure, these early missionary movements were haphazard and insecure: after Coronado withdrew from the Southwest in 1542, the three Franciscans who had volunteered to remain were killed by the Indians; in 1580, three others attempted to set up missions among the Pueblos, and they were eventually killed. The formal colonization of Pueblo Country was one involving both military and missionary designs. When Juan de Oñate arrived in 1598, he was able, within several months of his residence in the Pueblo area, to gain the formal submission of both Eastern and Western Pueblos. Dividing the region of New Mexico into seven districts, he declared, according to the commission given him, that it would be a missionary province of the Franciscan Order.

In the early seventeenth century, two missionary regions had been established in northwestern New Spain, one in the south (Sonora), where missionary work was under Jesuit auspices, and one in the north (New Mexico), where the Franciscans established their missions. According to estimates made by the fathers (who in 1630 claimed as many as 60,000 christianized Indians in ninety Pueblos served by fifty priests), the missionary efforts were flourishing among the Pueblos in the early seventeenth century. What became clear by the end of the century, however, is that Native Americans' nominal acceptance of the mission system (and of Catholicism generally) was not a result of actual conversion to Christianity. In proscribing native ceremonies and dances, in suppressing and destroying ceremonial objects (especially those associated with katchina practices), in publicly punishing native priests and medicine men, the reverend fathers and their military assistants merely pushed Native Americans underground in their efforts to retain native ways and ultimately initiated the backlash that resulted in the Pueblo Revolt of 1680. Resentment against Spanish rule and particularly against the friars continued, even after the Reconquest by Diego de Vargas from 1692 to 1694.

The eighteenth century brought less oppressive domination by the Spaniards and the missionaries who came to reside among the Indians in Pueblo Country. Fewer Franciscans were sent to live in New Mexico, and their resultant frustration was the greater when Indians seemed simply to accommodate Franciscan teachings to native ways. In what is called by some anthropologists "compartmentalization," natives tended to keep their own organization and viewpoints, quite apart from the teachings of the missionaries; they integrated into their activities some fragments—but not the system—of Catholicism. A residual distrust of the Franciscans, given the missionary effects of the previous century, is probably only a partial reason for the Indians' nonacceptance of Catholicism.

Another very real reason why native people were not integrally concerned with Catholicism resides in the efforts of local civil and military authorities to discredit the missionaries. Paraphrasing the biblical prophet Jeremiah in 1751, Fray Andrés Varo proclaimed his dismay to the crown:

"Oh land and kingdom of New Mexico! So long oppressed, humiliated, and persecuted, so often not governed, but tyrannized over by these unworthy chiefs." His complaints were not about the Native Americans over whom he served his missionary function but about the governmental officials, *alcaldes mayores* (who served, uncompensated, as local chief constables), who colluded with merchants for personal economic gain, leaving the missions and the converted Indians debt-ridden and thus poor. Varo's are among the most moving complaints, but they are not, with Fray Carlos José Delgado's, isolated comments about the missionary situation in mid-century. Varo's and Delgado's contentions are part of a wide literature—which includes events chronicled by Fray Juan Sanz de Lezaún in 1760, Fray Pedro Serrano in 1761, and Fray Agustín de Morfi in 1778—that voiced the continual troubles faced by missionaries in New Mexico who were attempting to bring their God to the native communities already there. The problems that these missionaries faced were not necessarily new to their endeavors, but they were problems that intensified in New Mexico, for a variety of reasons, from about the middle of the eighteenth century.

The Spanish crown was faced, mid-century, with increasing problems in the Americas. Revenues and exports were suffering, and territorial battles were adding to Spain's expenses of colonization. King Charles III, who ascended the throne in 1759 as the last Bourbon monarch of Spain, quickly established a series of reforms that would assist the political and economic situation of Spain. Known as the Bourbon Reforms, these efforts were intended by the crown to recolonize Spanish America by increasing taxation, by providing for industrialization of and better communications between existing colonized areas, by assisting the colonization especially of border areas, and by stripping the nobility, local farmers, and the Church of special status and privilege and of local autonomy.

The Spanish crown became acutely aware of the proximity of other European powers at its borders. Spain's silver-producing provinces—New Galicia, New Vizcaya, and New Léon—were at risk both from natives in the area and from the penetration inland by foreigners. Spanish fears of invasion were increased in 1763 when, at the end of the Great War for Empire, also called the French and Indian War (1754–1763), Spain received from France the trans-Mississippi West and the English took everything east of the Mississippi River. Spanish territory now clearly abutted English territory. Further, the French had already armed the Comanches and forced them southward from Illinois, into Apache hunting grounds. This heightened the military situation in New Mexico, as Apaches began a series of attacks on the Pueblos that would affect their strength and solidarity.

The Bourbon Reforms wrought havoc for the existing colonized areas of New Mexico, as local civil agents vied with the missionaries for increasingly diminishing power over the native populations. Reports on both sides pointed to ineptitude and moral infractions, laxity and selfishness. Local civil authorities claimed that the Franciscans rarely said Mass, were lax in administering the sacraments, and were seizing Indian lands and services for their own gain. On their side, the Franciscans charged the *alcaldes mayores* with profiteering and with exploitation of native peoples. The missionary voices of New Mexico represent a system in the midst of transformation from a religious community to a secularized civil body. The land and kingdom of New Mexico envisioned by Fray Andrés Varo as God's ideal Christian brotherhood was indeed disappearing while his lamentations over its loss were being voiced.

Even as Franciscan efforts in New Mexico were facing dwindling support, they were finding success in California. The Roman Catholic Church entered California in 1769, with the expedition of Gaspar de Portola and Junípero Serra as it crossed the border of Baja California and, while heading north, founded its first mission at San Diego. The immediate point of the expedition was twofold: military bases were sought so that Spain could resist aggression by other European powers and put off Russian trappers already hunting otter in Alta California; and missionary bases were sought for the conversion of the native peoples to Christianity. This group initiated a series of missions northward from San Diego. Two missions (San Diego de Alcalá in 1769 and San Carlos Borromeo de Carmelo in 1770) were founded upon the first entrance of the expedition, with others being established at intervals until the last, San Francisco Solano (Sonoma), was formed in 1823.

Initially, all contact with the native populations was in the hands of the friars. To establish a mission, the friars would immediately seek to convert and organize the Native Americans in the immediate vicinity. They then would extend their efforts so as to bring into their dominion Indian villages at a distance, but usually no more than a day's journey from the mission center. The process continued until the coastal strip was fully claimed, in about the year 1800. Eventually, the missionary efforts inland would require a military function, as natives increasingly refused to move from their homelands and take on ways not their own.

For the most part, it seems that the missionary efforts marking the work of the friars under Junípero Serra were pacific and fruitful for the Catholic Church. Following traditional Catholic theology, the friars spoke of the primacy of the spirit over the flesh. In the towns and villages where they fostered Christianity, they attempted to establish peace and order by developing a sense of community at the local mission, by celebrating Mass (their ultimate ritual of peace), by serving as ideal exemplars of virtuous living, and by mediating the community's relationship with its God. For those who adhered to the principles they taught, these priests could serve as moving testimony to the teachings of Christ. In writing his life of Junípero Serra, Francisco Palou was creating a model text of a model life which he himself was reputed to have enacted. Such was, for these priests, the vision of the mission upon which they had been sent.

Carla Mulford
Pennsylvania State University

Fray Carlos José Delgado 1677–post 1750

After the Pueblo Revolt of 1680, New Mexico was spared such violent clashes between Spanish colonizers and Native Americans in the pueblos. Yet the problems that contributed to the Revolt continued in the eighteenth century: civil and ecclesiastical leaders competed for the bodies and souls of Native Americans in the area, seeking to extend their control beyond the already captured areas where Christianized Indians worked for the Spanish. According to the civil officials, the missionaries undermined state authority; many officials wished, in fact, to see the religious affairs of the pueblos consolidated under fewer missionaries, whom they represented as being drains upon dwindling resources. The missionaries responded in kind, speaking of the civil officials' heinous, demoralizing, and un-Christian use of Native American peoples. One of the missionaries who spoke against the abusive civil leaders was Fray Carlos Delgado, who for many years was the resident missionary at the pueblo of San Agustin de Isleta.

According to his key editor, Charles W. Hackett, Fray Carlos Delgado was probably without peer as a true representative of the missionary order of St. Francis. He was reputed to be pious, penitent, and humble as he carried on his evangelical mission among the un-Christianized peoples surrounding the settled areas of northern and central New Mexico. His first successful missionizing seems to have been in 1742 among the Moqui Indians, who after the 1680 Pueblo Revolt had remained outside the circle of Spanish dominion. Two years later, in March 1744, he initiated another mission effort among the Navajos. In a letter to the Father Commissary General, Delgado reported that after six days, he and his assistant persuaded—with exhortations, good treatment, and gifts—5,000 Navajos to become Christians. That he was zealous in his efforts is clear; that he did not consider his own hardship also is evident. He wrote to the Father Commissary requesting more living space for those who had converted and more missionaries for assistance. For himself, he requested only that he be sent clothing and shoes, because the journey into Navajo territory had left him "without a habit, or sandals, or anything else, on account of the country's being so rough. . . . I ask, not a new habit or new sandals, but something old that may be spared there." The same letter reports his great surprise at his miraculous success—and his own unworthiness—in the missionary effort:

God and our holy father, Saint Francis, have permitted—for few of us would consider ourselves worthy—that I, the least individual shall have commenced these enterprises and won in them such good will among all the heathen, and even among the Christians, that in every pueblo they desired to have me as their minister, but I cannot because I am one only.

The missionary success among the Moquis and the Navajos convinced Delgado that he should attempt missionary work in El Gran Teguayo, in the far northeast of New Mexico. He wrote to the Father Commissary requesting permission to start on his journey in 1745, saying, "I am sixty-seven years of age, but, judging by the strength that I feel in myself I would say that I have seven and sixty spiritual arms to defend this *custodia* [realm] from so many enemies. They will be conquered, for envy and greed never prevail."

Delgado's report to Father Ximeno of March 27, 1750, telling of the injustices the Indians and the missionaries faced at the hands of civil authorities indicates that he indeed could not bear to see envy and greed prevail.

Carla Mulford
Pennsylvania State University

SECONDARY WORKS

Charles W. Hackett, ed., *Historical Documents Relating to New Mexico, Nueva Vizcaya, and Approaches Thereto, to 1773.* Vol. 3. Collected by Adolph F.A. Bandelier and Fanny Bandelier, 1937.

Report made by Rev. Father Fray Carlos Delgado to our Rev. Father Ximeno concerning the abominable hostilities and tyrannies of the governors and alcaldes mayores toward the Indians, to the consternation of the custodia. The year 1750.

Very Reverend Father and our Minister Provincial: I, Fray Carlos José Delgado, preacher general, commissary, notary, and censor of the Holy Office, apostolic notary, and missionary in the *custodia*[1] of the conversion of San Pablo of this province of El Santo Evangelio in the kingdom of New Mexico, appear before your reverence only for the purpose of lamenting before your paternal love the grave extortions that we, the ministers of these missions, are suffering, at the hands of the governors and alcaldes of that kingdom. I declare, that of the eleven governors and many *alcaldes mayores* whom I have known in the long period of forty years that I have served at the mission called San Agustín de la Isleta, most of them have hated, and do hate to the death, and insult and persecute the missionary religious, causing them all the troubles and annoyances that their passion dictates, without any other reason or fault than the opposition of the religious to the very serious injustices which the said governors and alcaldes inflict upon the helpless Indians recently received into the faith, so that the said converts shall not forsake our holy law and flee to the heathen, to take up anew their former idolatries. This is experienced every day, not without grave sorrow and heartfelt tears on the part of those evangelical sowers, who, on seeing that their work is wasted and that the fecund seed of their preaching to those souls is lost and bears no fruit, cry out to heaven and sorrowfully ask a remedy for this great evil. In order that your reverence's exalted understanding may regard as just the reasons which support the said missionaries in their opposition to the aforesaid extortions, even though it should be at the cost of their lives, and also in order that you may come to their aid with the measures best fitted for the total abolition of the said injuries and injustices, I shall specify them in the following manner:

The first annoyance with which the persons mentioned molest the Indians is to send agents every year (contrary to the royal ordinances, and especially to a decree of the most excellent señor, Don Francisco Fernández de la Cueva Henríquez, Duke of Albuquerque, and viceroy of New Spain, issued in this City of Mexico on May 18, 1709, whose content I present, the original being kept in the archive of the *custodia* mentioned) at the time of the harvest, to all the pueblos of the kingdom, under the pretext of buying maize for the support of their households, though most of it is really to be sold in the nearest villages. The said agents take from all the pueblos and missions eight hundred or a thousand *fanegas* [bushels], and compel the Indians to transport them to the place where the governor lives. Besides not paying them

[1]Guardianship.

anything for the said transportation, they do not pay them for the maize at once, and when the date arrives which they have designated for the payment, if the maize is worth two pesos a *fanega* they give them only one. Even this amount is not in coin or in any article that can be useful to the Indians, but in baubles, such as *chuchumates,* which are glass beads, ill-made knives, relics, awls, and a few handfuls of common tobacco, the value of which does not amount even to a tenth part of what the maize is worth which they extract from them by force, and this even though as has been said, they pay them only half the proper price that is charged throughout the kingdom. From this manifest injustice two very serious evils result: first, the unhappy Indians are left without anything to eat for the greater part of the year; and second, in order not to perish of hunger they are forced to go to the mountains and hunt for game or to serve on the ranches or farms for their food alone, leaving the missions abandoned.

The second oppression that the Indians frequently suffer at the hands of the governors is being compelled arbitrarily and by force, for the small price of an awl or other similar trifle, to work on the buildings that they need, whatever they may be and whether they require little or much time. The Indians also are required to drive cattle as far as the villa of Chihuahua,[2] which is more than two hundred leagues distant from the place where the governors live. They receive in payment for this service only a little ground corn, which they call *pinole,* and the Indian cattle drivers are compelled to pay for those [animals] that are lost or die for want of care or by any other accident. A pernicious evil arises from this cattle driving, for the Indians must abandon their families and leave their lands uncultivated, and, as a consequence, be dying of hunger during the greater part of the year.

The third oppression, and the most grievous and pernicious, from which originate innumerable evils and sins against God, and manifest injuries against the missionaries and Indians, is the wicked dissimulation of the governors in regard to the acts of the *alcaldes mayores,* for it is publicly known throughout the realm that when they give them their *varas,* or wands of office, they tell and advise them to make the Indians work without pity.

With such express license, your reverence can imagine how many disturbances will be caused by men who usually take the employment of *alcaldes mayores* solely for the purpose of advancing their own interests and acquiring property with which to make presents to the governors, so that the latter will countenance their unjust proceedings, even though they be denounced before them, and perhaps will even promote them in office. Every year they make the Indians weave four hundred blankets, or as many woolen sheets; they take from all the pueblos squads of thirty or forty Indians and work them the greater part of the year in planting maize and wheat, which they care for until it is placed in the granaries; they send them among the heathen Indians to trade indigo, knives, tobacco, and *chuchumates,* for cattle and for deer hides. Not even the women are exempt from this tyranny, for if the officials cannot make use of their work in any other way they compel them to spin almost all the wool needed for the said sheets and blankets. And the most lamentable thing about all this is that they recompense them for these tasks with only a handful of tobacco, which is divided among eighteen or twenty.

[2]City in northern Mexico.

The most grievous thing for the heathen Indians is that the alcaldes and even some of the governors, mix with their wives and daughters, often violating them, and this so openly that with a very little effort the violation of their consorts comes to the knowledge of the husbands, and as a result it often happens that they repudiate their wives and will not receive them until the missionary fathers labor to persuade them. The shameless way in which the officials conduct themselves in this particular is proved by an occasion when a certain governor was in conversation with some missionaries, and an Indian woman came into their presence to charge him with the rape of her daughter, and he, without changing countenance, ordered that she should be paid by merely giving her a buffalo skin that he had at hand.

Yet all that I have hitherto related does not drive the Indians to the limits of desperation or cause them to fall away from our holy faith so much as when the said alcaldes compel them to deliver to them a quantity of deer skins, lard, sheaves [of grain], chickens, and other things that their desires dictate, saying that they are for the governors, who ask for them. The Indian has to submit to this injustice, for they either take it from him without asking, or, if he does not have what the alcaldes ask for or does not give it promptly enough when he has it, he suffers either spoliation or punishment.

These punishments are so cruel and inhuman that sometimes for a slight offence, sometimes because the Indian resists the outrages that they inflict upon him, or sometimes because they are slow in doing what the alcaldes order, they are put in jail for many days, are confined in the stocks, or—and I cannot say it without tears—the officials flog them so pitilessly that, their wrath not being appeased by seeing them shed their blood, they inflict such deep scars upon them that they remain for many years. It is a proof of this second point that when I went among the heathen to reduce the apostates there were among them some who, with an aggrieved air, showed me their scars, thus giving me to understand that the reason why they fled and did not return to the pale of the church was their fear of these cruel punishments.

A further distressing proof of this practice is what was done in the past year at El Paso by a captain to a Catholic Indian of the Zuma nation, sacristan of the mission of El Real. A servant of the captain of El Paso had hidden three ears of corn which he had stolen from his master. The sacristan took them from him, and, without any more proof or reason than having found him with them in his hands, and because the said servant, to escape punishment, said that the innocent Indian often stole corn from the granaries, the said captain became so angered that, in violation of all natural and divine laws, he ordered six soldiers to take the Indian out and kill him in the fields.

They carried out the order, and when the unfortunate Zuma cried aloud for confession they did not yield to his entreaties, but gave him a violent death, perhaps being fearful that the missionary religious, whose duty it was to administer the holy sacrament to him, would prevent the execution of that unjust order, even though it might be at the cost of his life.

The outrage did not stop here, for when the Zuma Indians of the mission of El Real learned of the death of their countryman, they began to rise up, all crying out: "Why, since we are Christians, do they not permit us to confess at the hour of death? Let us flee to the mountains!" They did not flee, our father, either because the soldiers restrained them or because the fathers appealed to them. A still greater injury, however, arose from the remedy, for the governor having ordered a large troop of Zumas of both sexes to come to this city, simply because an Indian woman and two men were not able to travel as fast as the others, having crippled feet, the corporal who was leading them ordered them to be beheaded at a place called El Gallego, where he left the bodies unburied, to the intense grief of their companions and relatives, whose sorrow was not lessened on seeing that the said corporal and the rest of the escort robbed them of their little children in order to sell them as slaves in various places along the road.

Nor is it only the said alcaldes and governors that ill-treat the Indians in the manner described, but even the judges who enter to conduct the *residencias* of the alcaldes and governors who have completed their terms of office, inflict upon the Indians as much injury and hardship as may conduce to the advancement of their own interests and the success of their ambitious desires. It is public knowledge throughout the kingdom that such persons seek to conduct these *residencias* more for what they gain by unjust and violent spoliation of the Indians than for what they receive from the office that they exercise.

Finally, to such an extreme do the iniquities reach that are practiced against the Indians by governors and *alcaldes mayores,* as well as by the judges of *residencia,*[3] that, losing patience and possessed by fear, they turn their backs to our holy mother, the Church, abandon their pueblos and missions, and flee to the heathen, there to worship the devil, and, most lamentable of all, to confirm in idolatries those who have never been illumined by the light of our holy faith, so that they will never give ear or credit to the preaching of the gospel. Because of all this, every day new conversions become more difficult, and the zealous missionaries who in the service of both Majesties are anxiously seeking the propagation of the gospel, most often see their work wasted and do [not] accomplish the purpose of their extended wanderings.

Although it cannot be denied that those barbarous nations are stiffnecked, yet there have been many instances where thousands of them have entered joyfully through the requisite door of the holy sacrament of baptism, and most of the apostates would return to the bosom of the Church if they did not fear, with such good reason, the punishments and extortions that I have already spoken of. They have told me this on most of the occasions when I have entered in fulfillment of my obligation to reduce apostates and convert the heathen. In the year 1742, when, at the cost of indescribable labor and hardships, I reduced four hundred and forty odd among apostates and heathen in the province of Moqui, innumerable souls would have come to the bosom of our holy Church had they not been deterred by the reason that I have stated.

Although the missionary religious ought to oppose themselves to these grave injuries and their pernicious consequences, they often do not do it; first, because they never succeed in attaining their purpose, but on the contrary are insulted, disrespected, and held to be disturbers of the peace; second, because the governors and alcaldes impute and charge them with crimes that they have never committed, which they proceed to prove with false witnesses whom they have suborned before the fa-

[3]Official hearing on the conduct of officials.

ther custodian, and compel the latter to proceed against the religious whom they calumniate. And although the said custodians know very well that the denunciations are born of hatred, they proceed against the missionaries, changing them from one mission to another, in order to prevent the said governors from committing the excess of using their power to expel the missionaries from the kingdom, as has often happened; and also because, when the custodians do not agree to what the governors ask, the latter refuse to certify the allowance for the administration of the religious, which certification is necessary in order that the most excellent señor viceroy may issue the honorariums that his Majesty (whom may God preserve) assigns for the maintenance of the missionary religious. It has seemed to me that all that I have said ought to be presented before the charitable zeal of your reverence, so that, having it before you as father of those faithful sons, your apostolic missionaries, you may put into execution the means that your discretion may decide upon, with the purpose of ending this great abuse, of redeeming all those helpless people, and consoling your sorrowing sons. It is indisputable that whatever I have said is public, notorious, certain and true, as I swear *in verbo sacerdotis tacto pectore,* at this hospice of Santa Bárbara of the pueblo of Tlatelolco,[4] on March 27, 1750. Our very reverend father, your humblest subject, Fray CARLOS JOSE DELGADO, who venerates you, places himself at your feet.

1750

Francisco Palou 1723–1789

Had he been granted an honorary degree as colleges today grant such degrees, Palou, according to his editor Herbert E. Bolton, would have received this tribute: "Fray Francisco Palou, diligent student, devout Christian, loyal disciple, tireless traveler, zealous missionary, firm defender of the faith, resourceful pioneer, successful mission builder, able administrator, and fair-minded historian of California." Such a tribute seems apt for the man who so successfully memorialized his only rival in the California missionary effort, Fray Junípero Serra.

Born, like Serra (ten years earlier), at Majorca, Spain, Palou entered the Franciscan order in 1739 and was ordained in 1743. He eagerly joined Serra in the missionary program planned for the Americas; they and other future missionaries reached Vera Cruz, Mexico, in 1749. After several years in missions in Mexico, these Franciscans sought to extend their efforts northward, to replace the Jesuit missionaries who had been expelled from Spanish dominion in 1767 by King Charles III of Spain. Palou and Serra went first to the Baja California missions (1767). They reached Loreto, in Lower (Baja) California, in the spring of 1768. Serra was assigned the next year to Upper (Alta) California missions, which left those in Lower California to Palou's control until 1773.

Palou, wishing to serve with Serra again, chose to serve in the chain of missions in Upper California. He went first to San Diego, then on to Monterey-Carmel, Serra's headquarters. He assisted in the

[4]Town just north of Mexico City in the eighteenth century.

placement of friars, and he collected historical data that survives as some of the only record of these early California years. He was assigned in 1776 to the mission at San Francisco, where he stayed until 1784. Serra died in Carmel that year, which left open the presidency of the Upper California missions, a post Palou ably filled until, with failing health, he left in 1785. He died in Mexico, where he completed his life of Serra, most of which had been written in California.

Palou's two works, the *Noticias de la Nueva California* (published in the middle of the nineteenth century) and the biography of Serra, *Relacion historica* (1787), provide key information about early California and the missionary efforts there. He had nearly completed his life of Serra before returning to Mexico. He there added, after much research in the library at San Fernando, the long chapter on Serra's virtues. The book, published in Mexico City, was sent to the royal palace in Madrid, Spain, as well as to Majorca and to the missions of Sonora and California. It received high praise. Fray Junípero Serra's life can serve as a model of discipline and hard work, but more significant is Palou's project of transforming Serra's life into biography, a lengthy, detailed piece of writing, blending epistolary documentation, recreated dialogue, narrative, impassioned exposition, and moralizing. Palou's text stands well as a west-coast balance to Cotton Mather's earlier hagiographies of the early Puritan founders in *Magnalia Christi Americana.* Both texts are records of religious heroism in eras that seemed to be fast diminishing before the writers' eyes.

Carla Mulford
Pennsylvania State University

Juan Bruce-Novoa
University of California at Irvine

SECONDARY WORKS

Herbert E. Bolton, tr. and ed., *Historical Memoirs of New California,* 4 vols., 1926; Maynard J. Geiger, tr. and ed., *Palou's Life of Junípero Serra,* 1955; Geiger, *Franciscan Missionaries in Hispanic California,* 1969.

from Life of Junípero Serra

from Chapter XXII The Expeditions Arrive at the Port of Monterey— The Mission and Presidio of San Carlos Are Founded

What this chapter proposes will be taken care of by the following letter which the Venerable Father wrote to me, in which he announces his arrival at Monterey and what occurred at that port.

Live Jesus, Mary and Joseph!

Reverend Father Lector and President Fray Francisco Palóu

Most dear friend and esteemed Sir:

On May 31, by God's help, after a somewhat distressful sea voyage of a month and a half, this packet-boat, the *San Antonio,* with Don Juan Pérez as captain, arrived and anchored in this beautiful Port of Monterey. It is exactly the same in substance and features as the expedition of Don Sebastián Vizcaíno left it in the year 1603.[1] I was exceedingly comforted when that very night we learned that the over-land expedition had arrived fully eight days before. Father Fray Juan traveled with it. All are enjoying good health. I was further comforted when on the holyday of Pentecost, June 3, in the presence of all the officers of land and sea, together with all their subordinates, near the very same ravine and oak where the [Carmelite] Fathers of the said expedition had celebrated Mass, the altar was prepared, the bells were hung up and rung, the hymn *Veni, Creator* was sung, water was blessed, the large cross and the royal standards were set up and blessed, and I sang the first Mass known to have been celebrated here since that time. Afterwards we sang the *Salve Regina* to Our Lady before a statue given by His Excellency, which stood on the altar. During the Mass I preached to the men. We concluded the ceremonies by singing the *Te Deum.* Thereupon the civil officials performed the formal act of taking possession of the land in the name of the King, our Sovereign (may God save him!). After this we all ate together in the shade by the beach. The entire celebration was accompanied by frequent salvos from the guns aboard ship and ashore. . . .

I beg Your Reverence and earnestly request that two of the group be assigned to these missions, so as to make six with the four who are here, and to establish the Mission of San Buenaventura along the Santa Barbara Channel. It is a section of greater value than that of San Diego or Monterey or of the entire territory thus far discovered. Provisions for that mission have already been sent on two occasions. Up till now, no one has been able to blame the friars for not having established it; nor would I wish such blame to be attached once the guard is at hand for founding it. The truth is that as long as Father Fray Juan and I are on our feet, it shall not be delayed, because we shall then separate, each one going to his mission. For me it will be the greatest trial to remain alone, with the nearest priest at a distance of eighty leagues. Wherefore I beg Your Reverence to see to it that this utter loneliness of mine does not last too long a time. Father Lasuén ardently desires to come to these missions, and hence Your Reverence may keep him in mind when you have the opportunity to decide on the matter of assigning missionaries.

We are very short of wax for Mass-candles, both here and at San Diego. Nevertheless, tomorrow we are going to celebrate the feast and hold the procession of Corpus Christi, even though it be done in a poor fashion, in order to drive away whatever little devils there may be in this land. If it is possible to send some wax, it will be very helpful to us. Also the incense which I asked for on another occasion. Let Your Reverence not fail to write to His Illustrious Lordship, congratulating him on the discovery of this port and writing whatever may seem proper to you. Cease not to commend us to God. May He preserve Your Reverence for many years in His holy love and grace.

[1]Although Spaniards had sailed along the Pacific coast as far as Oregon as early as the 1540s, Monterey Bay was not discovered until the Vizcaíno expedition in 1602. Plans were made to settle the area, but nothing was done until Father Serra established his mission.

Mission San Carlos de Monterey
June [13], the feast of St. Anthony of Padua, 1770

Your most affectionate friend, companion and servant kisses the hand of Your Reverence.

Fray Junípero Serra

On the very day they took possession of the port, they began the Royal Presidio of San Carlos and founded the mission of the same name. Adjoining the presidio they built a chapel of palings to serve as a temporary church; likewise living quarters with their respective rooms or compartments for the use of the fathers, and the necessary workshops. Both establishments were surrounded by a stockade for their protection. The natives did not show themselves during those days, since the many volleys of artillery and muskets fired by the soldiers had frightened them. But they began to approach after a little while, and the Venerable Father began to offer them gifts to bring about their entrance into the fold of Holy Church and gain their souls, which was the principle purpose of his presence. . .

The lieutenant of the Catalonian volunteers, Don Pedro Fages, remained in charge of the New Presidio of San Carlos in Monterey. In consideration of the few soldiers he had at his disposal, in accord with the Venerable President he determined to suspend the founding of Mission San Buenaventura until a captain and nineteen soldiers should arrive. These had gone to Old California in February to return with some cattle. However, the captain with the soldiers and cattle returned only as far as San Diego, without sending to Monterey any notice of the fact. The news came only the following year by a ship, as will be seen a little further on. Since for this reason the third mission could not be established, our Venerable Father with his former pupil Fray Juan Crespí applied himself to the conversion of the Indians of Monterey, trying to attract with small gifts those who came to visit him. But since there was no one who knew their language, the missionaries experienced great difficulties in the beginning and up until the time when God desired to open the door to them by means of an Indian boy, a neophyte who had been brought along from Old California. Because of the association which the Venerable Father Junípero ordered him to maintain with the pagans for this precise purpose, he began to understand them and to pronounce some words in their tongue. So by means of this interpreter, Father Junípero was able to explain to the Indians the reason for his coming into their country, which was to guide their souls on the way to heaven.

On December 26 of that year he performed his first baptism in that pagan nation. For the fervent and ardent soul of our Venerable Father, this was the source of inexpressible joy. In time he succeeded in gaining others, and the number of Christians increased, so that three years afterwards, when I arrived at that mission, he had already baptized 165. By the time the Venerable Founder Fray Junípero closed his glorious career, he had baptized 1,014, of whom many had already died, to enjoy God in eternal life through the incessant efforts of that apostolic man.

What greatly aided these conversions, or better, what constituted the principal basis of this important conquest, were the singular marvels and prodigies which God our Lord wrought on behalf of the pagans to make them fear and love the Catholics: fear, so as to restrain them in order that so great a multitude might not treat with impudence so small a number of Christians; and love, that they might listen willingly to the evangelical doctrines which the missionaries had come to teach them, that they might embrace the sweet yoke of our holy law.

In his diary of the second over-land expedition to the Port of Monterey, Father Crespí states on May 24 (as the reader may see for himself) the following:

> *After marching about three leagues, at one o'clock in the afternoon we arrived at the lagoons of salt water by the Point of Pines, toward the northeast, where on the first expedition a second cross had been erected. Before we dismounted, the governor, a soldier and I went to inspect the cross, in order to determine whether we could find any sign of the arrival of the ship there; but we found none. We beheld the cross entirely surrounded by arrows and sticks with many feathers which had been stuck in the ground by the pagans. Also there was a string of sardines, still quite fresh, hanging from a pole at one side of the cross, and another stick with a piece of meat at the foot of the cross; also a little mound of mussels.*

That was a source of great wonder to all, but since they did not know the explanation, they suspended judgment.

Once the newly baptized began to converse in Spanish and the Lower California neophyte understood the Indians' language, the natives on several occasions declared the following: the very first time they saw our people the Indians noticed that all the Spaniards bore on their breasts a very resplendent cross; and when the Spaniards went away from there, leaving that large cross by the beach, the Indians were filled with such fear that they did not dare to approach so sacred an emblem. For they saw the cross shining with bright rays at a time when the rays of the sun which illumined the day were gone and were replaced by the shadows of night. They noticed, however, that the light of the cross grew so bright that it seemed to them to reach the very heavens. On beholding it during the day without these phenomena, and in its natural size, they approached it and tried to win its favor lest they suffer any harm, and in deference to it they made their offerings of meat, fish and mussels. When to their surprise it did not consume what they offered, they placed before it feathers and arrows, showing thereby they desired peace with the Holy Cross and with the people who had erected it there.

Various Indians made this statement at different times (as I have said), and again in the year 1774 when the Venerable Father President returned from Mexico City, before whom they repeated, without the slightest variation, what they had told me the preceding year. This the servant of God, for purposes of edification, wrote to His Excellency the Viceroy, in order to increase his fervor and to encourage him at the same time in the happy realization of this spiritual enterprise. Because of this prodigy and many others which the Lord showed, the conversion of these pagans has continued with all peacefulness and without the conflict of arms. Blessed be God, to Whom be all glory and praise.

from Chapter LVIII
The Exemplary Death of the Venerable Father Junípero

. . . I arrived on August 18 at his Mission San Carlos. There I found His Paternity in a very weakened condition, although he was up and around, and with great congestion of the chest. This condition, however, did not prevent him from going to church in the afternoon to recite the catechism and prayers with the neophytes. He concluded the devotions with the tender and pious hymns and versicles composed by the Venerable Father Margil in honor of the Assumption of the Blessed Virgin, whose octave we were celebrating. When I heard him sing with his voice as strong as usual, I remarked to a soldier who was talking to me: "It does not seem that the Father President is very sick." The soldier, who had known him since 1769, answered me: "Father, there is no basis for hope: he is ill. This saintly priest is always well when it comes to praying and singing, but he is nearly finished." . . .

We spoke leisurely on the matters for which he had called me, until the ship arrived. However, I was always in fear he would shortly die, for whenever I would enter into his little room or cell of adobes, I always found him quite interiorly recollected, although his companion told me he had acted this way ever since his faculty to confirm had expired. This, as I have stated before, was on the very day the ship anchored at these missions [of San Francisco]. Five days after I arrived at Monterey, the packet-boat anchored at that port. Immediately the royal surgeon went over to the mission to visit the Reverend Father President. Finding his chest in so bad a condition, he suggested hot poultices to expel the phlegm that had accumulated in the chest. The Father President told him to apply whatever remedy he chose. He did, but with no effect other than to cause further pain to that already worn-out body. But he did not show the least sign of pain, either at this strong application or at the agonies he was suffering. He acted as if he were not sick at all, always up and about as if he were well. When some of the cloth from the supplies of the ship was brought over, with his own hands he began to cut it up and distribute it to the neophytes to cover their nakedness.

On August 25 he told me he was disappointed that the fathers from Missions San Antonio and San Luis Obispo had not arrived, and that possibly the letters he had written them were delayed. I immediately sent word to the presidio, and the letters were brought over with the information that they had been overlooked. As soon as I saw their contents, an invitation to the fathers for a final farewell, I sent a courier with these letters, adding a message that the fathers should come posthaste, for I feared that our beloved superior would not be long with us because of his very weakened condition. And although the priests set out as soon as they received those letters, they did not arrive in time. The one from Mission San Antonio, which was twenty-five leagues away, arrived after his death and could assist only at his burial. The one from San Luis Obispo, fifty leagues away, arrived three days later and was able to be present at the commemorative services only on the seventh day after his death, as I shall point out later.

On August 26 he arose, weaker still. He told me he had passed a bad night. As a result, he desired to prepare himself for whatever God might decree with regard to him. He remained secluded the entire day, admitting not a single distraction. That night he made his general confession to me amid many tears, and with a clear mind just as if he were well. When this was over, after a brief period of reflection he took a cup of broth and then went to rest, his wish being that no one remain with him in his little room.

As soon as morning dawned on the 27th, I went to visit him and found him saying his breviary, since it was his custom always to commence Matins before daybreak.

On the road he always began it as soon as morning dawned. When I asked him how he had spent the night, he answered: "As usual." Nevertheless, he asked me to consecrate a Host and reserve It, and he would let me know when he wanted to receive. I did, and after finishing Mass I returned to tell him, and then he said he would like to receive the Most Holy Viaticum, and that for this he would go to the church. When I told him that was not necessary, that his cell could be fixed up in the best way possible and that the divine Majesty would come to visit him, he said, "No," that he wanted to receive Him in church, since if he could walk there, there was no need for the Lord to come to him. I had to give in and grant his holy desires. He went by himself to the church (more than a hundred yards distant), accompanied by the commandant of the presidio, who came to the ceremony with part of the soldiers (who were joined by the soldiers of the mission); and all the Indians of the town or mission accompanied the sick and devout priest to the church, all of them with great tenderness and piety.

When His Paternity reached the step of the sanctuary, he knelt down before a little table prepared for the ceremony. I came out of the sacristy vested, and on arriving at the altar, as soon as I prepared the incense to begin the devotional ceremony, the fervent servant of God intoned in his natural voice, as sonorous as when he was well, the verse *Tantum ergo Sacramentum,* singing it with tears in his eyes. I gave him the Holy Viaticum, according to the ceremonies of the ritual. When this very devotional function was over, which I had never seen in such circumstances, His Paternity remained in the same posture, kneeling, giving thanks to the Lord. When he was finished, he returned to his little cell accompanied by all the people. Some shed tears from devotion and tenderness, others out of sadness and sorrow because they feared they would be left without their beloved father. He remained alone in his cell in meditation, seated on the chair at the table. When I beheld him thus absorbed, I saw no reason to enter to talk to him. . . .

During the night he felt worse, and he asked to be anointed. This holy sacrament he received seated on an *equipal,* a little stool made of rushes. He recited with us the Litany of All Saints and the Penitential Psalms. He spent the entire night without sleep, the greater part of it on his knees, while he pressed his chest against the boards of his bed. When I suggested that he lie down awhile, he answered that in that position he felt more relieved. Other short periods of the night he spent seated on the floor, leaning against the lap of some of the neophytes. All night long his little cell was filled with these neophytes, drawn there by the great love they had for him as for the father who had begotten them anew in the Lord. When I saw him in this state of exhaustion and leaning against the arms of the Indians, I asked the surgeon how he thought he was. He answered (since the father appeared to be in a very critical state): "It seems to me that this blessed father wants to die on the floor."

I went in soon after and asked him if he wished absolution and the application of the plenary indulgence. He answered "Yes," and prepared himself. On his knees he received the plenary absolution, and I gave him also the plenary indulgence of the Order, with which he was most happy. He passed the entire night in the manner described. The feast of the Doctor of the Church St. Augustine dawned, August 28, and he appeared relieved. He did not experience so much congestion in his chest. During the whole night he had not slept or taken anything. He spent the morning seated on the rush stool, leaning against the bed. This bed consisted of some roughhewn boards, covered by a blanket serving more as a covering than as an aid to rest, for he never used even a sheepskin covering, such as was customary at our college. Along the road he used to do the same thing. He would stretch the blanket and a pillow on the ground, and he would lie down on these to get his necessary rest. He always slept with a crucifix upon his breast, in the embrace of his hands. It was about a foot in length. He had carried it with him from the time he was in the novitiate at the college, nor did he ever fail to have it with him. On all his journeys he carried it with him, together with the blanket and pillow. At his mission and whenever he stopped, as soon as he got up from bed he placed the crucifix upon the pillow. Thus he had it on this occasion when he did not wish to go to bed during the entire night or next morning, on the day when he was to deliver his soul to his Creator.

About ten o'clock in the morning on that feast of St. Augustine, the officers of the frigate came to visit him. . . .

After listening to them, he said: "Well, gentlemen, I thank you that after such a long time, during which we have not seen each other, and after making such a long voyage, you have come from so far off to this port to throw a little earth upon me." On hearing this, the gentlemen and all the rest of us present were surprised, seeing him seated on the little rush stool and hearing him answer everything with full mental faculties. But, scarcely concealing their tears which they could not restrain, they said: "No, Father, we trust that God will still make you well and enable you to continue this conquest." The servant of God (who, if he did not have a foreknowledge of the hour of his death, could not but know that it was near at hand) answered them: "Yes, yes, do me this favor and work of mercy; throw a little bit of earth upon my body, and I shall be greatly indebted to you." And casting his eyes upon me, he said: "I desire you to bury me in the church, quite close to Father Fray Juan Crespí for the present; and when the stone church is built, they may put me wherever they want."

When my tears allowed me to speak, I said to him: "Father President, if God is pleased to call you to Himself, it will be done as Your Paternity wishes. In that case, I ask Your Paternity out of love and the great affection you have always had for me, that when you arrive in the presence of the Most Blessed Trinity, you adore the Same in my name, and that you be not unmindful of me; and do not forget to pray for all the dwellers in these missions, particularly for those here present." He answered: "I promise, if the Lord in His infinite mercy grants me that eternal happiness, which I do not deserve because of my faults, that I shall pray for all and for the conversion of so many pagans whom I leave unconverted."

Within a short time he asked me to sprinkle his little room with holy water, and I did. When I asked him if he felt some pain, he said "No"; but he asked me to do it so he would have none. He remained in profound silence. All of a sudden, very frightened, he said to me: "Great fear has come upon me; I have a great fear. Read me the Commendation for a Departing Soul, and say it aloud so I can hear it." I did as he asked, while all the gentlemen from the ship assisted. Also present were his priest companion, Fray Matías Noriega, and the surgeon, and many others both from the ship and from the mission. I read for him the Commendation for a Departing Soul, to which the Venerable Father, though dying, responded as if he were well, just sitting there on his little rush stool, moving the hearts of us all to tenderness.

As soon as I finished, he broke out in words full of joy, saying: "Thanks be to

God, thanks be to God, all fear has now left me. Thanks be to God, I have no more fear, and so let us go outside." All of us retired to a little outside room with His Paternity. When we noticed this change, we were at one and the same time surprised and happy. . . .

He sat on the chair by the table, picked up his diurnal and began to pray. As soon as he was finished, I told him it was already after one o'clock in the afternoon, and asked him if he would like a cup of broth. He said "Yes." He took it and, after giving thanks, said: "Now, let us go to rest." He walked to his little room where he had his bed. He took off only his mantle and lay down over the boards covered with a blanket, with his holy crucifix mentioned above, in order to rest. We all thought he was going to sleep, as during the whole night he had not slept any. The gentlemen went out to eat. Since I was a little uneasy, after a short time I returned and approached his bed to see if he was sleeping. I found him just as we had left him a little before, but now asleep in the Lord, without having given any sign or trace of agony, his body showing no other sign of death than the cessation of breathing; on the contrary, he seemed to be sleeping. We piously believe that he went to sleep in the Lord a little before two in the afternoon, on the feast of St. Augustine in the year 1784, and that he went to receive in heaven the reward of his apostolic labors.

He ended his laborious life when he was seventy years, nine months and four days old. He lived in the world sixteen years, nine months and twenty-one days; as a religious fifty-three years, eleven months and thirteen days, of which he spent thirty-five years, four months and thirteen days as apostolic missionary. During this time he performed the glorious deeds of which we have read, in which his merits were more numerous than his steps. He lived in continuous activity, occupied in virtuous and holy exercises and in outstanding deeds, all directed to the greater glory of God and the salvation of souls. And would not one who labored so much for them, not labor much more for his own? Much there is that I could say, but this demands more time and more leisure. If God grants me this, and it is His most holy will, I shall not refuse the task of writing something about his heroic virtues for the sake of edification and good example.

As soon as I satisfied myself that we were now orphans, bereft of the amiable company of our venerable superior, that he was not sleeping but actually dead, I ordered the neophytes who were standing there to ring the bells in order to make the news known. As soon as the double peal rang out the sad news, the whole town assembled, weeping over the death of their beloved father who had begotten them anew in the Lord and who was more esteemed by them than if he had been their natural father. All wanted to see him in order to give vent to the sorrow that filled their hearts, and to express it in tears. So great was the crowd of people, including Indians and soldiers and sailors, that it was necessary to close the door in order to place him in the coffin that His Paternity had ordered to be made the day before. And in order to prepare his shroud, we had to do nothing else than to take off his sandals (which the captain of the packet-boat and the Father Chaplain, who were present, received as keepsakes). He remained in the shroud in which he died, that is, the habit, the cowl and the cord, but no inner tunic, for the two which he had for use on his journeys he had sent out to be washed six days before, together with a change of underclothing, which he did not care to use, for he wanted to die wearing only the habit, cowl and cord.

When the venerable corpse was placed in the coffin, and six burning candles were placed about it, the door of his cell was opened, which his saddened sons, the neophytes, immediately entered with their wreaths of wild flowers of varied hues, in order to grace the remains of the deceased Venerable Father. The remains were kept in the cell until nightfall, a continuous concourse of people entering and coming out. They were praying to him and touching rosaries and medals to his venerable hands and face, openly calling him "Holy Father," "Blessed Father," and other names dictated by the love they bore him, and by the heroic virtues which they had witnessed in him during life.

At nightfall we carried the remains to the church in procession. This was composed of the town of neophytes and the soldiers and sailors who remained. The remains were placed on a table surrounded by six lighted candles, and the ceremony was concluded with a response. They asked me to leave the church open in order to keep guard over the remains, and alternately to recite the Rosary for the soul of the deceased. They renewed the watch at set intervals, thus passing the whole night in continual prayer. I consented to this and left two soldiers as a guard to prevent any kind of indiscreet piety or theft, for all desired to obtain some little thing which the deceased had used. Chiefly the seamen and the soldiers, who had known him better and who had a great opinion of the virtue and sanctity of the deceased Venerable Father and who had dealt with him at sea and on land, asked me for some little article from among the things he had used. Although I promised all I would satisfy them after his burial, this was not enough to prevent them from cutting away small pieces of his habit from below, so it would not be noticed, and part of the hair of his tonsure, the guard being unable to restrain them, if it was not that he abetted them and participated in the pious theft. All wanted to obtain some memorial of the deceased, although such was the opinion they had of him that they called such items relics. I tried to correct them and explain it to them.

1787

Early Nineteenth Century

1800–1865

On the morning of August 31, 1837, Waldo and Lidian Emerson stepped into their buggy outside their home in Concord, Massachusetts, and drove the twenty or so miles into Cambridge. The day was bright and warm, the summer's dust having been settled by an earlier rainstorm. It was a festive time at Harvard: the class of 1837, which included future writers Henry David Thoreau and Richard Henry Dana, Jr., had graduated the previous day. And this afternoon, Emerson was to deliver the annual Phi Beta Kappa oration on what was already a somewhat hackneyed subject, "The American Scholar." Writers and commentators had often called for a distinctively American culture in the decades since political independence had been won. Indeed, William Ellery Channing, one of Harvard's better-known Overseers and perhaps a member of Emerson's audience, had written about the subject at length seven years before. For Emerson the occasion did not call for yet another appeal to literary nationalism; indeed, only the beginning and end of his lecture explicitly deal with American letters.

Still, almost fifty years later, Oliver Wendell Holmes would celebrate Emerson's speech as "our intellectual Declaration of Independence." And James Russell Lowell, a Harvard junior when he attended the talk, would speak of it as "an event without any former parallel in our literary annals." In *My Study Windows* (1871), Lowell dramatized the event: "What crowded and breathless aisles, what windows clustering with eager heads, what enthusiasm of approval, what grim silence of foregone dissent!" But these were recollections highly colored by the subsequent influence of "The American Scholar" and the fame of Emerson's many other essays and lectures. At the time, many in the audience found Emerson's ideas "misty, dreamy, unintelligible," as an older listener put it; "not very good and very transcendental," as a younger doubter wrote in his diary. The speech did not instantly liberate American letters from "the courtly muses of Europe," nor free the young scholars hearing it from the "disgust which the principles on which business is managed inspire."

And yet, "The American Scholar" serves usefully to signify a turning point in our culture. It can mark the beginning of what critics have named the "American Renaissance," a flourishing of literary art unprecedented in the brief history of the nation. Or more precisely, seen in retrospect, Emerson's talk came just as a remarkable cultural wave was gathering strength; it gave rhetorical form to that conjunction of publishing events, the establishment of institutions, and the development of personal networks that underlie such advances. Late in 1836, Henry Wadsworth Longfellow had returned from Europe to take up his literary professorship at Harvard; in that position, and as an anthologist and translator, he would introduce European literature to generations of American readers. As reviewer and arbiter of literary taste, he would also significantly shape the reputations and careers of American writers, including most notably those of his fellow Bowdoin graduate, Nathaniel Hawthorne, whose first volume, *Twice-Told Tales,* came out in 1837. Oliver Wendell Holmes, too, had returned to Harvard in 1836 to complete his medical degree and to publish his first volume, *Poems.* In 1836, just as Texas declared itself independent of Mexico and adopted a pro-slavery constitution, Angelina Grimké had issued her *Appeal to the Christian Women of the South,* a tract which helped introduce the idea of civil disobedience into the intensifying debate over slavery and, with Grimké's precedent-setting lectures to sexually mixed audiences, extended women's participation in the political and literary life of the republic. The following year, John Greenleaf Whittier had published his first volume, its politics explicit in its title, *Poems Written During the Progress of the Abolition Question.* Later in 1837, when Elijah P. Lovejoy was murdered and his anti-slavery newspaper, *The Observer,* destroyed by a mob in Alton, Illinois, the causes of abolition and a free press were even more closely linked and the political power of words tragically reaffirmed. Another year later, and young Frederick Douglass would escape from slavery and within a few years add his to the voices demanding its abolition.

Some months before Emerson delivered "The American Scholar," Horace Mann became the chief officer of the Massachusetts board of education; from that position he would initiate a series of studies and reforms that widened the scope of literacy, regularized curricula, extended the reading public, and otherwise influenced the shape of education across the country for at least the remainder of the century. By the Civil War, the principle of free, publicly funded primary education had been established almost everywhere but in the South, and the rate of school attendance was increasing more rapidly even than the population. In 1836, Mary Lyon had founded the Mt. Holyoke Female Seminary (later Mt. Holyoke College), the first such institution for women in the country; in 1837, Oberlin became the first co-educational college—and the first to admit black students—and Emma Willard formed the Willard Association for the Mutual Improvement of Female Teachers. Two of the Association's Honorary Vice Presidents were the poet and novelist, Lydia Sigourney, and Sarah Josepha Hale, who in 1836 had become editor of the merged *Ladies Magazine* and *Godey's Lady's Book.* The merger produced the most influential women's magazine of its time; it shaped a range of ideas from women's rights to women's fashions, and offered further opportunities for writers like Emerson, Longfellow, Poe, and Stowe, as well as many lesser-known women authors, to write for their living. The year 1836 also marks Margaret Fuller's introduction to Emerson and the birth of the Transcendentalists' informal "club," through which the members discussed and supported each other's ideas, and from which their journal, *The Dial* (1840–1844), emerged. In fact, Fuller met with the Emersons after Waldo's Phi Beta Kappa speech and returned with them to Concord. The next day she joined for the first time in the club's meeting—and feasting—at the Emersons' home, perhaps adding hers to others' praise for how his "noble discourse" emphasized the value of individual inspiration and an original relation to nature over the mass of unexamined tradition.

These historical details and many others one could list were not necessarily in the minds of Emerson or his listeners. It is only in looking back from a distance that one can be struck by the conjunction of events, to which "The American Scholar" seems to give point. In fact, many of Emerson's listeners were very likely more concerned with mundane problems. For 1837 had not been a happy year from an economic or social point of view. It had begun with a collapse in southern real estate and commodity prices, which had rapidly deepened into a widespread financial panic. By the time outgoing President Andrew Jackson had given his farewell address at the beginning of March, there had been riots in New York, and on May 10, banks in

New York and Boston had stopped redeeming their notes for silver or gold. Manufacturing was in decline, unemployment spreading, the investments and savings of thousands upon thousands of persons disappearing into the mysterious operations of a market economy few even claimed to understand. Though Emerson's listeners were probably not yet fully aware of it, seven lean years were coming upon the United States, an economic depression as deep as that of the 1930s.

Emerson had himself noted the multiplying problems in his journal:

Cold April; hard times; men breaking who ought not to break; banks bullied into the bolstering of desperate speculators; all the newspapers a chorus of owls. . . . Loud cracks in the social edifice.—Sixty thousand laborers, says rumor, to be presently thrown out of work, and these make a formidable mob to break open banks & rob the rich & brave the domestic government.

Yet it was not in Emerson's nature to turn gloomy at such prospects; besides, his comfortable situation in Concord sheltered him and his new family from the spreading distress. By the end of May he could write in his journal:

Still hard times. Yet how can I lament, when I see the resources of this continent in which three months will anywhere yield a crop of wheat or potatoes. On the bosom of this vast plenty, the blight of trade & manufactures seems to me a momentary mischance.

Perhaps nothing in Emerson so endeared him to his fellow Americans as this supreme optimism. In the face of vast changes in how and where people lived, worked, and played, practiced their religion, exchanged their ideas, obtained their clothing, Emerson retained an almost unqualified serenity about the future. He was not naive: America in 1837 was not "the best of all possible worlds." But like many of his countrymen, he seldom doubted that it could be made better, ever more perfect, through the efforts of individuals—individual "men," he would have said—acting on their deepest convictions in the belief that "what is true for you in your private heart is true for all men" ("Self-Reliance").

Edgar Allan Poe, even more recently married, had just moved to New York in 1837 after losing his job with the *Southern Literary Messenger.* In difficult financial circumstances, he was completing his novella *The Narrative of Arthur Gordon Pym,* a book whose central voyage ends, like Herman Melville's later *Moby-Dick,* in disaster and ambiguity:

And now we rushed into the embraces of the cataract, where a chasm threw itself open to receive us. But there arose in our pathway a shrouded human figure, very far larger in its proportions than any dweller among men. And the hue of the skin of the figure was of the perfect whiteness of the snow.

Perhaps the mutability of Poe's world, the wild cycles of commerce, the uncertainty of employment, the very rush of urban life evoked fear as well as confidence. Human ingenuity, unaided, might not always penetrate the deepest natural barriers, nor even the closer mysteries of our own passion and will. What was "true for you in your private heart" might not, as Emerson hoped, be "true for all men," but might instead express the imps of an altogether singular perversity. At any rate, for Poe, peril and loss remained dominant features of experience; the pit yawned fathomless, obscure at the feet of his heroes; the women of his poems and tales, like "Ligeia" (a story of that time), died mysteriously out of reach. In one of the few poems he wrote in 1837, he anticipates the better-known refrain of "The Raven," "nevermore":

How many scenes of what departed
    bliss!
  How many thoughts of what
    entombéd hopes!

How many visions of a maiden that is
No more—no more upon thy verdant slopes!
No more! alas, that magical sad sound
Transforming all! Thy charms shall please *no more,*—
Thy memory *no more!*

"Sonnet—To Zante"

However disparate, the views of Emerson and Poe by no means exhaust the range of responses to the vicissitudes of American society in the early nineteenth century. For a slave like Harriet Jacobs, change was neither a venture into possibility nor the threat of ruin; it would have been a blessing. But in 1837, her reality was confinement: hiding from her slave-master, she was suffering through a second year in the tiny attic of her grandmother's shed:

The garret was only nine feet long and seven wide. The highest part was three feet high, and sloped down abruptly to the loose board floor. There was no admission for either light or air. . . . The air was stifling; the darkness total. A bed had been spread on the floor. I could sleep quite comfortably on one side; but the slope was so sudden that I could not turn on the other without hitting the roof. The rats and mice ran over my bed; but I was weary, and I slept such sleep as the wretched may, when a tempest has passed over them. Morning came. I knew it only by the noises I heard; for in my small den day and night were all the same. I suffered for air even more than for light. But I was not comfortless. I heard the voices of my children.

Harriet Jacobs (Linda Brent),
Incidents in the Life of a Slave Girl

To say that the face of America was transformed in the first half of the nineteenth century is to tell much, and yet little. For how you experienced change—indeed, whether you did—and how you expressed those experiences depended critically on who you were—man or woman, slave or free, the owner of a mill or one of its "hands," a settler on the "virgin lands" of the West or an Indian defending on those lands the graves of your ancestors and the grounds of your hunt. Differing experiences, differing lives and cultures produced varieties of American literature. Thus, while it is important to perceive the world Emerson saw and articulated, it is equally important to perceive how dissimilar was Harriet Jacobs's world, how very different the aims, the opportunities, the audience, or even the *language* available for her writing. In short, as we think of the Emersons riding into Cambridge for Waldo's speech, we need simultaneously to think of Harriet Jacobs lying in that obscure crawl-space. And as we note the relationships between Emerson and those who knew and were influenced by him, we need to perceive the very different relationships and influences shaping the writing of many other Americans physically and intellectually distant from Concord. We shall return to these distinctions below. But first, it is useful to chart the dimensions of the changes that were reshaping the country in which Emerson, Poe, Jacobs, and their contemporaries lived.

Publishing—Growth and Goals

When the century began, the nation consisted of 16 states, mostly strung along the Atlantic coast; with the Gadsden Purchase in 1853, the United States had more than tripled its size, achieving the continental dimensions it would retain for over a century, until the admission of Alaska and Hawaii as states. In those fifty years the country's population grew from 5.3 million to over 23.1 million. Not only was that rate of increase extraordinary, but so was the rapidity with which those people moved on to ever-new frontiers. As the nineteenth century began, most knowledgeable Americans believed it would take a hundred years or more for white people to settle in the western territories even then claimed by the United States, much less in the vast areas further west claimed by Spain and populated primarily by Indians; nevertheless, by 1850,

California on the far Pacific had been sufficiently organized to be admitted as a state. At the same time, the urban population, especially in eastern cities, was climbing rapidly—mainly because of massive immigration from Ireland, Scandinavia, and elsewhere in western Europe.

This huge growth and spread of population offered new opportunities as well as presenting a variety of social problems. Urban expansion in particular generated a wide new audience for newspapers and magazines. The number of newspapers in the country increased during the first third of the century from about 200 to over 1200; in 1830, New York City alone had 47 newspapers (compared with perhaps a dozen today). These journals and a growing number of monthly and annual magazines served one of the most literate populations in the world. Similarly, debating societies and the lyceum movement, which combined the features of an entertainment and educational network, rapidly followed the spread of the white—and especially northern—population across the country. Founded by Josiah Holbrook in 1826, there were by 1835 lyceums in 15 states; by 1860, there were over 3,000 lyceums. People came to lyceum halls much as, a hundred years later, they would congregate at the movies. They heard lectures on the Oregon Trail and the South Seas, Napoleon and Black Elk, the new science of daguerreotyping and the pseudoscience of phrenology. They listened to debates on the burning issues of the time: who should be able to vote, chattel slavery versus wage slavery, the demon rum, whether married women could hold property, America's "manifest destiny" to extend its boundaries.

Such publishing and speaking outlets helped educate the majority of Americans who had had, up to that time, little formal schooling, and they probably fostered the national penchant for arguing issues large and small. They also at one time or another provided employment to almost every writer of this period. Bryant and Whitman ran newspapers, Fuller and Poe, Hawthorne and Higginson, Child, Whittier, Douglass and Ridge, among others, served as editors, often composing what they published. Emerson made much of his living as a star of the lyceum circuit; Phillips, Douglass, Angelina Grimké, Frances Harper, and others traveled as abolitionist "agents," lecturing across the cities and towns of the North. Nor was such editing and lecturing literary hackwork or simply political lobbying. Most of the best stories of Hawthorne and Stoddard first appeared in literary annuals, gift books, or similar magazines, the criticism of Poe and Fuller in newspapers and popular journals, and Emerson's essays were, for the most part, first developed as lectures.

Thinking perhaps of Hawthorne's complaints about how his career opportunities were blocked by the effusions of a "mob of scribbling women," commentators have argued that pre-Civil War America offered, at most, very limited opportunities for writers to live by their pens. There was no international copyright, the public generally preferred to buy cheaper pirated editions of popular British writers like Sir Walter Scott and Charles Dickens to home-grown products, and publishers paid American writers a pittance or were themselves paid by better-known authors like Washington Irving and James Fenimore Cooper to distribute their books. The conclusion drawn from these facts and from the further contention that the popular audience wished to read work different from what "serious" writers—the Hawthornes and Melvilles—had to offer is that pre-Civil War America provided an inhospitable climate for authors. But there were many overlapping audiences in the United States, and while an international copyright was not adopted until 1891, those audiences had long since found sustenance in and furnished support for many different groups of American writers.

In fact it was in the early nineteenth century that writing first became an available profession not only for white gentlemen but for others. *The Cherokee Phoenix,* established in Georgia in 1828, was the first newspaper published by an Indian tribe, and the first published in a native language as well as in English. It was succeeded in the West, after the Cherokees were forced out of their homes, by *The Cherokee Advocate,* founded in 1844. And George Copway, the well-known Ojibwa writer, published his newspaper, *Copway's American Indian,* in New York in 1851. In 1827, *Freedom's Journal* was established, the first of some seventeen black-owned and -edited newspapers in the pre-Civil War period. Begun by John B. Russwurm, the nation's first black college graduate, and Samuel E. Cornish, who edited a number of other weeklies, the *Journal,* like its successor, *The Rights of All,* and the other black newspapers, was abolitionist in sentiment and in much of its content, including many of the sketches and poems it published. The spread of abolitionist societies—by 1850 there were almost 2,000 with over 200,000 members—helped to provide further outlets for white and black writers like Child, Whittier, Douglass, Garnet, Harper, and Harriet Beecher Stowe; indeed, *Uncle Tom's Cabin* was initially serialized in the Washington-based *National Era.*

For white women in particular, writing opened new professional doors. A substantial portion of the novels published in the United States after 1820 were written by women—primarily for a female audience; indeed, most of the best-sellers before the Civil War were the works of writers like Susan Warner (*The Wide, Wide World,* 1850, the first American work to sell over a million copies), Maria Cummins (*The Lamplighter,* 1854), and E.D.E.N. Southworth (*The Hidden Hand,* 1859), not to speak of Stowe. In her autobiographical novel, *Ruth Hall* (1855), Fanny Fern (Sara Willis Parton) describes in often touching and satiric detail how, to keep her family together after her husband's death, she carved out a career as a writer against the advice, and often opposition, of her litterateur brother, Nathaniel P. Willis. Indeed, many of these women, and others included in this anthology, turned to writing in similar circumstances in order to earn their living.

Writing books that sold required entertaining as well as edifying their readers. But a living or not, writing was also for most authors an opportunity to shape the outlook, to mold the consciousness of their audience. In the twentieth century, most of us have been taught that "art" is a form of discourse that lays no claims on our actions, that a poem should not "mean but be," and that "literature" and "propaganda" are as different as elephants and ivy. But in the early nineteenth century there were few advocates of such "art for art's sake" theories in the United States. Thus Emerson writes that "it is not metres, but a metre-making argument that makes a poem—a thought so passionate and alive that like the spirit of a plant or animal it has an architecture of its own, and adorns nature with a new thing" ("The Poet"). And Thoreau says toward the beginning of *Walden:* "I do not propose to write an ode to dejection, but to brag as lustily as chanticleer in the morning, standing on his roost, if only to wake my neighbors up." Harriet Beecher Stowe is even more explicit in her "Concluding Remarks" to *Uncle Tom's Cabin:*

Nothing of tragedy can be written, can be spoken, can be conceived, that equals the frightful reality of scenes daily and hourly acting on our shores, beneath the shadow of American law, and the shadow of the cross of Christ.

And now, men and women of America, is this a thing to be trifled with, apologized for, and passed over in silence? . . . But, what can any individual do? Of that, every individual can judge. There is one thing that every individual can do,—they can see to it that they feel right. An atmosphere of sympathetic influence encircles every human be-

ing; and the man or woman who feels strongly, healthily and justly, on the great interests of humanity, is a constant benefactor to the human race. See, then, to your sympathies in this matter!

Even Hawthorne, whose *Twice-Told Tales* could hardly have seemed more distant from the daily pulse of American life, effectively drew certain morals about social change, the value of scientific progress, the sanctity of the human heart.

While the writing of the early nineteenth century is often shaped by these desires to influence how readers understand the world, it is also formed by the conditions of that world, as well as by the character of the literary traditions available to American authors. We shall turn shortly to the swiftly changing, increasingly complex material and intellectual circumstances affecting the writers of the time. But it is also important to recognize that how writers write, and about what, is in some measure a product of how their predecessors have written. Hawthorne, for example, adopted the ideas of the prose "Romance," which he develops in the "Custom-House" introduction to *The Scarlet Letter* and in his prefaces to *The House of the Seven Gables* and *The Blithedale Romance,* from earlier essays in English and American periodicals. These maintained that the Romance was an ideal form for depicting the past, providing the Romancer maintained a degree of verisimilitude even while creating the atmospheric and often dreamlike effects characteristic of the genre. Like other writers of their generation, Hawthorne and Poe were also influenced by the "Gothic" fictions of English and Continental authors like Matthew Lewis and Mrs. Ann Radcliffe, and domesticated in writings like those of Charles Brockden Brown. Such Gothic works as *The Monk* and *The Mysteries of Udolpho* featured remote castles, ghostly apparitions, mysterious villains, and imperiled maidens. Poe and Hawthorne, among others, adapted elements of such books, as well as material from the popular scientific and pseudoscientific literature concerned with phrenology, mesmerism, alchemy, and exploration of remote parts of the earth. By contrast, many women writers, for example, Caroline Kirkland and Alice Cary, were influenced by the realistic English village sketches of a writer like Mary Russell Mitford, and the focus on "love and money" of Jane Austen. Such literary traditions and the variety of popular forms in prose and verse existed side by side, but how writers chose to use them depended very much upon their responses to the worlds of change they faced and, as they often hoped, were molding.

Religion and Common Culture

In few areas was change more profound than in the religious and ethical life of the nation. By the end of the Revolution, most of the dominant churches, whether New England Presbyterian and Congregationalist or Virginia Anglican, were in decline. The rationalistic spirit of the Revolution undercut their credibility. Leaders like Ethan Allen and Thomas Paine wrote deistic attacks on the authority of the Bible and of the clergy, and Jefferson and Madison moved to disestablish state religions and to separate state from church. Besides, the war itself had scattered congregations, and the rapid westward expansion drew people even further from eastern church authority. Historians estimate that by the 1790s only one in twenty Americans was a church member.

Beginning late in the eighteenth century and continuing well into the nineteenth, the nation was swept by a series of religious revivals, called the Second Great Awakening. Such periodic revivals have continued with more or less intensity well into our own century, but this early nineteenth-century Awakening in many respects established the pattern of religious organization that has characterized the United States until recently. For it brought a large majority of Americans—perhaps as many as three in four by the 1830s—into some relationship with one or another of the evangelical Protestant churches. It confirmed that no one church would be dominant, much less established, in the United States, that, indeed, religion like business in America would thrive on a competition of denominations. Among these, newer groups that sought to recruit ordinary people who farmed and labored, principally the Baptists and the Methodists, would emerge by the 1820s as the largest.

But however fragmented, Protestantism came to provide a degree of common culture to much of the country. Most people were in some measure familiar with the Bible, with the language and meters of hymns, and many with Christian literary works like Bunyan's *Pilgrim's Progress.* Thus speakers and writers as diverse as Henry Highland Garnet and Emily Dickinson, Melville and Stowe could depend on their audience to recognize and respond to Biblical and other religious allusions and quotations. Traditions of Biblical citation and religious debate provided a basis for tracts like those of William Apes and David Walker. Religion, especially among southern black slaves, also provided a context for the creation of great works of art, the "spirituals" or sorrow songs. For many of today's readers, unfamiliarity with these traditions of religious discourse may in part block access to works of the nineteenth century.

Nineteenth-century evangelical Protestantism also displayed a strong millennial component, closely connecting the coming in of God's kingdom with the working out of the political future of the United States. The progress of democracy at home and abroad could be taken to demonstrate movement toward the millenium. And expansion of Protestant America into the territory of pagan Indians or Catholic French or Spaniards could be rationalized as fulfilling God's plan. Such pious justifications for, as well as criticisms of, American expansionism constituted a persistent note in many writings of the time.

To some extent, the Second Awakening, as well as subsequent revival campaigns, reflected a conscious organizing effort by clergymen and their supporters to win back ground lost in the Revolution. Large numbers of lay as well as institutionally trained preachers were ordained and sent to ride far-flung circuits. In the early nineteenth century, churches founded more than 70 denominational colleges, primarily to support their efforts. And all the denominations promoted great camp meetings at which thousands were urged to come forward, be "reborn," and find the "inner strength" needed to combat sin. In the years immediately following, as Elizabeth Cady Stanton reports, techniques for organizing revivals and for moving converts to respond—often with displays of uncontrolled emotion—repent, and be reborn were perfected by preachers like Charles Grandison Finney and Lyman Beecher, patriarch of the famous Beecher family. In other respects, however, the Awakenings reflected the search of Americans, especially on the frontier, for community and a source of order in a dangerous and often lawless society. The early nineteenth century saw the founding of many new denominations and sects, some of which, like the Mormons, tried to organize their converts into communities at once secular and religious. The periodic revivals also may have represented a desire to reinvest spiritual life with an emotional vitality missing from the well-humored, practical enlightenment prose of a Franklin.

That desire was also a significant component in the movement of Emerson and his Transcendentalist friends away from the bloodless Unitarianism of 1830s New

> Dr. Finney's . . . appearance in the pulpit on these memorable occasions is indelibly impressed on my mind. I can see him now, his great eyes rolling around the congregation and his arms flying about in the air like those of a windmill. One evening he described hell and the devil and the long procession of sinners being swept down the rapids, about to make the awful plunge into the burning depths of liquid fire below, and the rejoicing hosts in the inferno coming up to meet them with the shouts of the devils echoing through the vaulted arches. He suddenly halted, and, pointing his index finger at the supposed procession, he exclaimed:
>
> "There, do you not see them!"
>
> I was wrought up to such a pitch that I actually jumped up and gazed in the direction to which he pointed, while the picture glowed before my eyes and remained with me for months afterward. I cannot forbear saying that, although high respect is due to the intellectual, moral, and spiritual gifts of the venerable ex-president of Oberlin College, such preaching worked incalculable harm to the very souls he sought to save. Fear of the judgment seized my soul. Visions of the lost haunted my dreams. Mental anguish prostrated my health. Dethronement of my reason was apprehended by friends. But he was sincere, so peace to his ashes! Returning home, I often at night roused my father from his slumbers to pray for me, lest I should be cast into the bottomless pit before morning.
>
> Elizabeth Cady Stanton
> *Eighty Years and More, 1897*

England. In certain respects, Transcendentalism may be thought of as a secularized religion, an enthusiastic encounter with the "Over-Soul" entailing no outward display, an endless Sabbath kept, in Emily Dickinson's words,

> . . . staying at Home—
> With a Bobolink for a Chorister—
> And an Orchard, for a Dome—
>
> #324

Deeply influenced by English romantic writers like Coleridge and Wordsworth, and Continental thinkers like Kant and Swedenborg, the Transcendentalists, and those affected by them, opposed the reigning materialism and widespread conformity of American culture, trying instead to develop an "original relation to the universe." They believed that the commonplace, "the shop, the plough, and the ledger," could reveal the "form and order" of the mighty universe, for as Whitman put it:

> I believe a leaf of grass is no less
> perfect than the journey-work of
> the stars,
> And the pismire is equally perfect, and
> a grain of sand, and the egg of the
> wren,
>
> "Song of Myself," #31

For their sources of value and inspiration, they looked not to the past, as embodied in scriptures or creeds, but to the present encounter with nature and their own inner light. Again to quote Whitman:

> There was never any more inception
> than there is now,
> Nor any more youth or age than there
> is now,

And will never be any more perfection
than there is now,
Nor any more heaven or hell than there
is now.

"Song of Myself," #3

Not everyone shared this Transcendentalist vision of being at home in a universe open to one's intuitions. Emily Dickinson wrote that

. . . nature is a stranger yet;
The ones that cite her most
Have never passed her haunted house,
Nor simplified her ghost.

#1400

And Melville, like Hawthorne and Poe, presented a far more ambiguous picture of the power of the natural world in his white whale. Indeed, in later essays like "Circles," Emerson himself qualified his generally optimistic outlook, and as they increasingly engaged the political realities of slavery at home and revolution in Europe, writers like Thoreau and Fuller found a world less plastic and amenable to change.

In any case, whatever their longer-range impact, especially in literary circles, the Transcendentalists' immediate effect on their time was not extensive. The circulation of their journal, *The Dial,* never exceeded about 300, and most of the copies of Thoreau's first book were returned to him by the publisher. Emerson's Divinity School "Address" marked him among traditional clergymen as a heretic, Thoreau's neighbors viewed him as something of a crank, and Bronson Alcott's experiments with education were regarded as visionary failures. To the mainstream of evangelical Protestantism, they were intellectual bohemians, marginal if not altogether irrelevant.

This is not to say, however, that there was fundamental agreement among religious denominations. On the contrary, the divisions in American Protestantism reflected and helped widen growing sectional and political schisms. Take, for example, the question of what sorts of behavior being "born again" implied. For many churches, generally fundamentalist, and especially those in the South, salvation entailed struggling against sin, especially in oneself, in order that one might insure redemption in a life to come. For others, however, being reborn in the spirit of Christ entailed working to eradicate sin from *this world;* indeed, to evangelical Christians bringing in the kingdom of God depended upon perfecting the character of human society. Such believers developed a social gospel, which engaged them in efforts to eradicate the sources of human misery: poverty, alcoholism, war, discrimination against women, and above all slavery. These deep commitments to bring about fundamental change *in* the world invested the writing of activists like William Lloyd Garrison, John Greenleaf Whittier, Henry Highland Garnet, and Lydia Maria Child with a moral fervor and a sense of righteousness; these also helped carry them through poverty, obloquy, and even violent attacks on their persons. Garrison, for example, was at one point led down the streets of Boston with a rope around his neck by a mob of well-dressed "gentlemen." Such commitments also set these religious activists deeply at odds with their ostensibly Christian brethren, both North and South, especially over the issue of slavery.

To say this another way, Protestant Christianity provided certain common assumptions, a vocabulary and a set of images and allusions to the majority of Americans in the early nineteenth century. But the uses to which these commonalities were put were extremely diverse. Religion was in the hands of some a powerful censor: it was used to condemn the Grimké sisters for speaking in public, Melville for criticizing missionary activities in the Pacific, Whitman for extolling sexuality. It was used to defend (as well as to condemn) slavery, as Whittier's satire in "The Hunters of Men" and Douglass's attack in his *Narrative* show. Indeed, it was used to

More than fifty-seven years have elapsed since a band of patriots convened in this place to devise measures for the deliverance of this country from a foreign yoke. The cornerstone upon which they founded the temple of freedom was broadly this: "That all men are created equal; and they are endowed by their Creator with certain inalienable rights; that among these are life, LIBERTY, and the pursuit of happiness." At the sound of their trumpet call 3 million people rose up as from the sleep of death and rushed to the strife of blood, deeming it more glorious to die instantly as freemen than desirable to live one hour as slaves. They were few in number, poor in resources; but the honest conviction that TRUTH, JUSTICE, and RIGHT were on their side made them invincible.

We have met together for the achievement of an enterprise, without which that of our fathers is incomplete; and which, for its magnitude, solemnity, and probable results upon the destiny of the world as far transcends theirs as moral truth does physical force.

In purity of motive, in earnestness of zeal, in decision of purpose, in intrepidity of action, in steadfastness of faith, in sincerity of spirit, we would not be inferior to them.

Their principles led them to wage war against their oppressors and to spill human blood like water in order to be free. *Ours* forbid the doing of evil that good may come and lead us to reject, and to entreat the oppressed to reject the use of all carnal weapons for deliverance from bondage, relying solely upon those which are spiritual and mighty through God to the pulling down of strongholds.

"Declaration of the American Anti-Slavery Convention," 1834

rationalize violent attacks on Irish Catholic immigrants.

For many blacks, however, the Biblical stories of the Exodus, of Daniel, of Revelations provided images of consolation and hope. For a writer like Stowe, the primary problems of the nineteenth century were religious: how to sustain the moral seriousness of Puritanism without its terrorizing theology, a dilemma she dramatizes in *The Minister's Wooing.* Hawthorne selectively used the language and some of the imagery of Puritanism, but worked out questions of "sin and sorrow" so central to earlier New England religious life in newer psychological rather than theological terms. For an activist like Elizabeth Cady Stanton, religion was often an inhibitor, if not a downright enemy, to change. Yet to many nineteenth-century reformers, religion provided both the motivation and the moral energy to sustain a struggle for temperance, peace, and most of all the abolition of slavery.

The Debates Over Racism and Slavery

No issues during the middle decades of the nineteenth century so engaged the passions of Americans as those of slavery and race. Indeed, the period is marked by a series of political accords—the Missouri Compromise (1820), the Gag Rule (1836), the Compromise of 1850—designed to balance the interests of pro- and anti-slavery forces, and to postpone as long as possible the question of whether, in Lincoln's famous phrase, "A house divided against itself" could stand, whether the nation could "endure, permanently half *slave* and half *free*." The Founders had mainly assumed that slavery would in the course of time atrophy and that slaveholders, Constitutionally prevented from importing additional slaves, would ultimately turn to other, free sources of labor. But the invention of the cotton gin, which made practical the use of the kind of cotton grown in much of the South, the development of a device for pressing cotton into easily transported bales, and the vastly increased market for cotton resulting from the expansion of textile manufacturing in Great Britain and then in New England—these various factors actually began to increase the demand for slave labor early in the century. During the 1820s, while the living standards and hopes for the future of white American men were largely rising, those of black slaves were rapidly declining. Opportunities for slaves to become artisans or to hire out their time and, perhaps, earn freedom began to disappear. Laws against teaching slaves to read or write began to be harshly enforced, especially after the uprising led by Nat Turner in 1831 and the advent of militant abolitionism, as represented by David Walker and William Lloyd Garrison, among northern blacks and whites. In many areas of the upper South, slave-breeding became a major source of income. In the lower South, on the cotton, sugar, and indigo plantations, working conditions became increasingly harsh, as more and more labor was demanded from the larger corps of field hands.

Just as the character of slavery changed significantly over the half century preceding the Civil War, so the arguments for and against it altered. Initially, defenders of slavery—who were by no means confined to the South—argued that it was an institution as old as human history, dating back at least to Biblical and classical Greek civilizations, and sanctioned by Biblical texts. Then and now, they said, it had helped civilize and Christianize a childlike if not barbaric people. It was a more humane system than the "wage slavery" of the North and of Britain, which demanded that workers compete with one another to sell their one "possession," their labor, for a "wage," and which in hard times left them to fend for themselves in conditions of unrelenting poverty. In any case, southerners insisted, the several States had the right to define for themselves their forms of social organization without interference from a federal government. As the debate intensified, more racist theories came into play; in their extreme form, such arguments held that blacks (and other colored races) were less than human, incapable of full development even in freedom, and thus by nature cut out only to be drawers of water and hewers of wood.

Not all defenders of slavery were racists; nor were many abolitionists free of racist ideas. In the earlier part of the century, many of those opposing slavery believed that black people should be helped or more forcibly sent back to African colonies. With the circulation of powerful tracts like David Walker's *Appeal* (1829), and with Garrison's founding of *The Liberator* (1831), the vogue of colonization began to fade. If blacks were men, argued the abolitionists, and they were, as the lives of Toussaint and of Douglass testified, then the ideas of the Declaration of Independence—that "all men are created equal"—applied to them as well as to whites. "Life, liberty and the pursuit of happiness" were therefore "inalienable rights" which could not be infringed by law or custom. The issue at the center of stories like Douglass's "The Heroic Slave" and Melville's "Benito Cereno" was that of the full humanity of black people.

Because blacks were human—if supposedly "inferior"—in the eyes of most Americans, they stood before God as souls

> The brain of the Negro, as I have stated, is according to positive measurements, smaller than the Caucasian by a fultenth; and this deficiency exists particularly in the anterior portion of the brain, which is known to be the seat of the higher faculties. History and oservation, both teach that in accordance with this defective organization, he Mongol, the Malay, the Indian and Negro, are now and have been irall ages and all places, inferior to the Caucasian.
>
> Look at the world as it now stands and say where is civilization to be found except amongst the various branchs of the Caucasian race?
>
> Take Europe and start in the freezing limate of Russia, and come down to the straights of Gibralter, and yo find not a solitary exception, not one that excites a doubt.
>
> Take Asia in the same way, and the oly approximation to civilization, is found in the mixt, or in some of the Mogol tribes. Take China which is the nearest approximation—she has for cnturies had stability in her government, and many of the arts have been arried to a high state of perfection, but take her religion, her laws, her government, her literature, and how does the comparison stand? The mct you can say is, that the Chinese are an intermediate link between the Nego and Caucasian.
>
> Take Africa next and the picture preented is truly deplorable—with the exception of Egypt, and the Barbary States, which were in their palmy days occupied by Caucasian colonies, an now by their mixed descendants; and where I repeat, except here, will youfind from the Mediterranean to the Cape of Good Hope, a single record or a single monument to show that civilization has ever existed?
>
> Josiah C. Nott
>
> *Two Lectures on The Natural Historyof the Caucasian and Negro Races, 1844*

equally to be redeemed. To religious abolitionists, chattel slavery—claiming property in another human being—was the most fundamental violation of God's laws. For writers like Child, Jacobs, and Stowe, that was most vividly illustrated by the way in which slavery undermined and finally destroyed black families. In Stowe's *Uncle Tom's Cabin* the poles of the conflict are symbolized by Haley, the slavetrader, "a man alive to nothing but trade and profit," Halliday, the Quaker matri-

ing families apart, Halliday's religious home for reuniting them.

For some earlier writers, like Irving and Cooper, and others in the next generation like Hawthorne and, for a time, Emerson, the slavery issue was not central. But after the passage of the Fugitive Slave Act in 1850, which imposed on northerners the legal obligation of helping slaveholders regain their "property," and with the Dred Scott decision (1857), which held that Negroes were not citizens of the

slavery forces, and to postpone as long as possible the question of whether, in Lincoln's famous phrase, "A house divided against itself" could stand, whether the nation could "endure, permanently half *slave* and half *free.*" The Founders had mainly assumed that slavery would in the course of time atrophy and that slaveholders, Constitutionally prevented from importing additional slaves, would ultimately turn to other, free sources of labor. But the invention of the cotton gin, which made practical the use of the kind of cotton grown in much of the South, the development of a device for pressing cotton into easily transported bales, and the vastly increased market for cotton resulting from the expansion of textile manufacturing in Great Britain and then in New England—these various factors actually began to increase the demand for slave labor early in the century. During the 1820s, while the living standards and hopes for the future of white American men were largely rising, those of black slaves were rapidly declining. Opportunities for slaves to become artisans or to hire out their time and, perhaps, earn freedom began to disappear. Laws against teaching slaves to read or write began to be harshly enforced, especially after the uprising led by Nat Turner in 1831 and the advent of militant abolitionism, as represented by David Walker and William Lloyd Garrison, among northern blacks and whites. In many areas of the upper South, slave-breeding became a major source of income. In the lower South, on the cotton, sugar, and indigo plantations, working conditions became increasingly harsh, as more and more labor was demanded from the larger corps of field hands.

Just as the character of slavery changed significantly over the half century preceding the Civil War, so the arguments for and against it altered. Initially, defenders of slavery—who were by no means confined to the South—argued that it was an institution as old as human history, dating back at least to Biblical and classical Greek civilizations, and sanctioned by Biblical texts. Then and now, they said, it had helped civilize and Christianize a childlike if not barbaric people. It was a more humane system than the "wage slavery" of the North and of Britain, which demanded that workers compete with one another to sell their one "possession," their labor, for a "wage," and which in hard times left them to fend for themselves in conditions of unrelenting poverty. In any case, southerners insisted, the several States had the right to define for themselves their forms of social organization without interference from a federal government. As the debate intensified, more racist theories came into play; in their extreme form, such arguments held that blacks (and other colored races) were less than human, incapable of full development even in freedom, and thus by nature cut out only to be drawers of water and hewers of wood.

Not all defenders of slavery were racists; nor were many abolitionists free of racist ideas. In the earlier part of the century, many of those opposing slavery believed that black people should be helped or more forcibly sent back to African colonies. With the circulation of powerful tracts like David Walker's *Appeal* (1829), and with Garrison's founding of *The Liberator* (1831), the vogue of colonization began to fade. If blacks were men, argued the abolitionists, and they were, as the lives of Toussaint and of Douglass testified, then the ideas of the Declaration of Independence—that "all men are created equal"—applied to them as well as to whites. "Life, liberty and the pursuit of happiness" were therefore "inalienable rights" which could not be infringed by law or custom. The issue at the center of stories like Douglass's "The Heroic Slave" and Melville's "Benito Cereno" was that of the full humanity of black people.

Because blacks were human—if supposedly "inferior"—in the eyes of most Americans, they stood before God as souls

> The brain of the Negro, as I have stated, is, according to positive measurements, smaller than the Caucasian by a full tenth; and this deficiency exists particularly in the anterior portion of the brain, which is known to be the seat of the higher faculties. History and observation, both teach that in accordance with this defective organization, the Mongol, the Malay, the Indian and Negro, are now and have been in all ages and all places, inferior to the Caucasian.
>
> Look at the world as it now stands and say where is civilization to be found except amongst the various branches of the Caucasian race?
>
> Take Europe and start in the freezing climate of Russia, and come down to the straights of Gibralter, and you find not a solitary exception, not one that excites a doubt.
>
> Take Asia in the same way, and the only approximation to civilization, is found in the mixt, or in some of the Mongol tribes. Take China which is the nearest approximation—she has for centuries had stability in her government, and many of the arts have been carried to a high state of perfection, but take her religion, her laws, her government, her literature, and how does the comparison stand? The most you can say is, that the Chinese are an intermediate link between the Negro and Caucasian.
>
> Take Africa next and the picture presented is truly deplorable—with the exception of Egypt, and the Barbary States, which were in their palmy days occupied by Caucasian colonies, and now by their mixed descendants; and where I repeat, except here, will you find from the Mediterranean to the Cape of Good Hope, a single record or a single monument to show that civilization has ever existed?
>
> Josiah C. Nott
>
> *Two Lectures on The Natural History of the Caucasian and Negro Races, 1844*

equally to be redeemed. To religious abolitionists, chattel slavery—claiming property in another human being—was the most fundamental violation of God's laws. For writers like Child, Jacobs, and Stowe, that was most vividly illustrated by the way in which slavery undermined and finally destroyed black families. In Stowe's *Uncle Tom's Cabin* the poles of the conflict are symbolized by Haley, the slavetrader, "a man alive to nothing but trade and profit," and Rachel Halliday, the Quaker matriarch, whose face and dress and domestic [illegible]tions "showed at once the commu[illegible] [illegible] she belonged" Haley's com[illegible] [illegible]re responsible for tearing families apart, Halliday's religious home for reuniting them.

For some earlier writers, like Irving and Cooper, and others in the next generation like Hawthorne and, for a time, Emerson, the slavery issue was not central. But after the passage of the Fugitive Slave Act in 1850, which imposed on northerners the legal obligation of helping slaveholders regain their "property," and with the Dred Scott decision (1857), which held that Negroes were not citizens of the United States and that slaveholding could [illegible]ot be excluded from any of the states or [illegible]rritories, it became increasingly difficult [illegible] any public figure to avoid the issue.

other reform movements of the time, saw itself in conflict with organized religion. Thus the major appeal in the Seneca Falls "Declaration of Sentiments" is not to Christian virtue but to the Enlightenment ideas and rationalistic prose of the Declaration of Independence. Some traditionalists believed, and continued to argue well into the twentieth century, that the "excessive" thinking entailed in higher education would interfere with a woman's reproductive capacities; that, at best, women should learn domestic and cultural refinements like needlework and French. Others like Mary Lyon and Lucy Stone sought to break down the barriers that made female education separate from and unequal to that of males, even in the same institution. At Oberlin, which she attended, Stone insisted on taking the "full course," usually reserved for men, instead of the women's "literary" curriculum. Even women's clothing became an issue: Amelia Bloomer invented a costume, based on loose-fitting, Turkish-style pantaloons, designed to free women from the tight corsets and stays that restricted circulation and movement; but the "Bloomer" dress was too radical for its time.

The writing of women, and of many men, reflected these cross-currents. The end of *The Scarlet Letter* raises, at least in symbolic terms, the question of woman's role in the building of community in America; Hawthorne's later novel *The Blithedale Romance* brings into sharp contrast the dangerously "liberated" dark woman, Zenobia, with the fair and saving Priscilla. Many of the widely selling women's novels of the 1850s in effect promoted what were presumed to be female virtues of patience, submission to duty, obedience, and chastity; their plots rewarded young women displaying such values, though not so much by marriage as by the formation of a domestic community centered on them. Such patterns were not restricted to novels like Susan Warner's *The Wide, Wide World;* they provide structure to a book like Hawthorne's *The House of the Seven Gables,* as well. Still, many women writers felt it necessary—since the very act of a woman writing was regarded with suspicion by many—to deprecate their literary productions as, in Caroline Kirkland's phrases, work "too slight to need a preface," "straggling and cloudy crayon-sketches," a "rude attempt." Some hid their identities behind pen names, often male.

In asking "How Should Women Write?" (1860) Mary E. Bryan lamented that

> *Men, after much demur and hesitation have given women liberty to write; but they cannot yet consent to allow them full freedom. They may flutter out of the cage, but it must be with clipped wings; they may hop about the smooth-shaven lawn, but must, on no account, fly. With metaphysics they have nothing to do; it is too deep a sea for their lead to sound; nor must they grapple with those great social and moral problems with which every strong soul is now wrestling. They must not go beyond the surface of life, lest they should stir the impure sediment that lurks beneath.*
>
> . . . *Having prescribed these bounds to the female pen, men are the first to condemn her efforts as tame and commonplace, because they lack earnestness and strength.*

Bryan's complaint reflects the sense of restriction under which women writers of the period labored.

In fact, however, they often annulled such limitations. In *The Hidden Hand* (1859), E.D.E.N. Southworth created a female character, Capitola, who dons a boy's clothing in order to survive, fights a duel, rescues the passive heroine, and, like other adventurous female characters of the time, altogether defies the prescribed stereotypes for a proper woman. As early as the 1820s, women writers like Catharine Maria Sedgwick and Lydia Sigourney directed their attention to the public concerns of the new nation; later, Stowe and Child consciously engaged the great human ques-

tions of the time, like slavery and the growing disparities in wealth. Indeed, women writers of the period probably involved themselves more with daily concerns than their male counterparts, who, like Emerson, often existed in a world of abstractions and fancy. Fern and Child, among others, tried to bring to their audience the problems of urban homelessness, the exploitation of women workers, the experiences of prostitutes and female inmates, and Fuller placed before her readers not only those issues but her immediate experiences of revolution and its causes in Europe. Moreover, women fiction writers consciously worked in a more realistic mode, largely eschewing the "romances" and allegories preferred by Hawthorne. They focused on everyday lives in Ohio or Maine, rather than on the remote settings and mad heroes of Poe or on Melville's larger than life confrontation of Captain Ahab and the White Whale. In part, this realistic practice may have been imposed by the kinds of restrictions Bryan sketches; in part, it may have been a conscious choice, as Alice Cary suggests in concluding her second volume of stories, *Clovernook* (1853):

> *In our country, though all men are not "created equal," such is the influence of the sentiment of liberty and political equality, that:*
>
> *"All thoughts, all passions, all delights,*
> *Whatever stirs this mortal frame,"*
>
> *may with as much probability be supposed to affect conduct and expectation in the log cabin as in the marble mansion; and to illustrate this truth, to dispel that erroneous belief of the necessary baseness of the "common people" which the great masters in literature have in all ages labored to create, is a purpose and an object in our nationality to which the finest and highest genius may wisely be devoted; but which may be effected in a degree by writings as unpretending as these reminiscences of what occurred in the little village where I from childhood watched the pulsations of surrounding hearts.*

Just as many women writers of the period focused on subjects and adopted strategies somewhat different from those of men, so the forms in which women expressed themselves often differed. For example, writers like the Grimkés, Child, and Kirkland, adapted the letter—a form between private and public expression—for important published work. One thinks also of Emily Dickinson's conception of her poems, which almost entirely remained "unpublished," at least to the general public, throughout her life:

> This is my letter to the World
> That never wrote to Me—

Cary's stories seem, like life or dreams, to shift focus as they proceed. Many of Stowe's later works employ a narrator whose relationship to the reader is posed as that of a domestic friend speaking the language of kitchen conversation. Jacobs, unlike male slave narrators, employs many of the conventions and the language of the domestic novel.

The point is *not* that such differences absolutely divided female from male writing. It was not the case that men wrote the "serious" books and women the "popular"; men composed as many potboilers as women, and probably more best-sellers as the century went on. Nor was it true that women's fiction was inevitably "sentimental" or men's adventurous. Cooper, Child, and Sedgwick wrote adventure tales focused on the drama of Indian-white relations; what is striking, however, are the differences between their versions of those interactions. Cooper's is finally a vision of irreconcilably separate societies, the development of the white necessitating the destruction of the Indian. Sedgwick and Child, while not ignoring the reality of that destruction, explore social and sexual interactions—including those of white women with Indian men—as paths to a harmonious future. Similarly, a slave narra-

other reform movements of the time, saw itself in conflict with organized religion. Thus the major appeal in the Seneca Falls "Declaration of Sentiments" is not to Christian virtue but to the Enlightenment ideas and rationalistic prose of the Declaration of Independence. Some traditionalists believed, and continued to argue well into the twentieth century, that the "excessive" thinking entailed in higher education would interfere with a woman's reproductive capacities; that, at best, women should learn domestic and cultural refinements like needlework and French. Others like Mary Lyon and Lucy Stone sought to break down the barriers that made female education separate from and unequal to that of males, even in the same institution. At Oberlin, which she attended, Stone insisted on taking the "full course," usually reserved for men, instead of the women's "literary" curriculum. Even women's clothing became an issue: Amelia Bloomer invented a costume, based on loose-fitting, Turkish-style pantaloons, designed to free women from the tight corsets and stays that restricted circulation and movement; but the "Bloomer" dress was too radical for its time.

The writing of women, and of many men, reflected these cross-currents. The end of *The Scarlet Letter* raises, at least in symbolic terms, the question of woman's role in the building of community in America; Hawthorne's later novel *The Blithedale Romance* brings into sharp contrast the dangerously "liberated" dark woman, Zenobia, with the fair and saving Priscilla. Many of the widely selling women's novels of the 1850s in effect promoted what were presumed to be female virtues of patience, submission to duty, obedience, and chastity; their plots rewarded young women displaying such values, though not so much by marriage as by the formation of a domestic community centered on them. Such patterns were not restricted to novels like Susan Warner's *The Wide, Wide World;* they provide structure to a book like Hawthorne's *The House of the Seven Gables,* as well. Still, many women writers felt it necessary—since the very act of a woman writing was regarded with suspicion by many—to deprecate their literary productions as, in Caroline Kirkland's phrases, work "too slight to need a preface," "straggling and cloudy crayon-sketches," a "rude attempt." Some hid their identities behind pen names, often male.

In asking "How Should Women Write?" (1860) Mary E. Bryan lamented that

Men, after much demur and hesitation have given women liberty to write; but they cannot yet consent to allow them full freedom. They may flutter out of the cage, but it must be with clipped wings; they may hop about the smooth-shaven lawn, but must, on no account, fly. With metaphysics they have nothing to do; it is too deep a sea for their lead to sound; nor must they grapple with those great social and moral problems with which every strong soul is now wrestling. They must not go beyond the surface of life, lest they should stir the impure sediment that lurks beneath.

. . . Having prescribed these bounds to the female pen, men are the first to condemn her efforts as tame and commonplace, because they lack earnestness and strength.

Bryan's complaint reflects the sense of restriction under which women writers of the period labored.

In fact, however, they often annulled such limitations. In *The Hidden Hand* (1859), E.D.E.N. Southworth created a female character, Capitola, who dons a boy's clothing in order to survive, fights a duel, rescues the passive heroine, and, like other adventurous female characters of the time, altogether defies the prescribed stereotypes for a proper woman. As early as the 1820s, women writers like Catharine Maria Sedgwick and Lydia Sigourney directed their attention to the public concerns of the new nation; later, Stowe and Child consciously engaged the great human ques-

tions of the time, like slavery and the growing disparities in wealth. Indeed, women writers of the period probably involved themselves more with daily concerns than their male counterparts, who, like Emerson, often existed in a world of abstractions and fancy. Fern and Child, among others, tried to bring to their audience the problems of urban homelessness, the exploitation of women workers, the experiences of prostitutes and female inmates, and Fuller placed before her readers not only those issues but her immediate experiences of revolution and its causes in Europe. Moreover, women fiction writers consciously worked in a more realistic mode, largely eschewing the "romances" and allegories preferred by Hawthorne. They focused on everyday lives in Ohio or Maine, rather than on the remote settings and mad heroes of Poe or on Melville's larger than life confrontation of Captain Ahab and the White Whale. In part, this realistic practice may have been imposed by the kinds of restrictions Bryan sketches; in part, it may have been a conscious choice, as Alice Cary suggests in concluding her second volume of stories, *Clovernook* (1853):

> *In our country, though all men are not "created equal," such is the influence of the sentiment of liberty and political equality, that:*
>
> *"All thoughts, all passions, all delights,*
> *Whatever stirs this mortal frame,"*
>
> *may with as much probability be supposed to affect conduct and expectation in the log cabin as in the marble mansion; and to illustrate this truth, to dispel that erroneous belief of the necessary baseness of the "common people" which the great masters in literature have in all ages labored to create, is a purpose and an object in our nationality to ... finest and highest genius may ... which may be ef- ... unattend- ... childhood watched the pulsations of surrounding hearts.*

Just as many women writers of the period focused on subjects and adopted strategies somewhat different from those of men, so the forms in which women expressed themselves often differed. For example, writers like the Grimkés, Child, and Kirkland, adapted the letter—a form between private and public expression—for important published work. One thinks also of Emily Dickinson's conception of her poems, which almost entirely remained "unpublished," at least to the general public, throughout her life:

> This is my letter to the World
> That never wrote to Me—

Cary's stories seem, like life or dreams, to shift focus as they proceed. Many of Stowe's later works employ a narrator whose relationship to the reader is posed as that of a domestic friend speaking the language of kitchen conversation. Jacobs, unlike male slave narrators, employs many of the conventions and the language of the domestic novel.

The point is *not* that such differences absolutely divided female from male writing. It was not the case that men wrote the "serious" books and women the "popular"; men composed as many potboilers as women, and probably more best-sellers as the century went on. Nor was it true that women's fiction was inevitably "sentimental" or men's adventurous. Cooper, Child, and Sedgwick wrote adventure tales focused on the drama of Indian-white relations; what is striking, however, are the differences between their versions of those interactions. Cooper's is finally a vision of irreconcilably separate societies, the development of the white necessitating the destruction of the Indian. Sedgwick and Child, while not ignoring the reality of that destruction, explore social and sexual interactions—including those of white ... Indian men—as paths to a

other reform movements of the time, saw itself in conflict with organized religion. Thus the major appeal in the Seneca Falls "Declaration of Sentiments" is not to Christian virtue but to the Enlightenment ideas and rationalistic prose of the Declaration of Independence. Some traditionalists believed, and continued to argue well into the twentieth century, that the "excessive" thinking entailed in higher education would interfere with a woman's reproductive capacities; that, at best, women should learn domestic and cultural refinements like needlework and French. Others like Mary Lyon and Lucy Stone sought to break down the barriers that made female education separate from and unequal to that of males, even in the same institution. At Oberlin, which she attended, Stone insisted on taking the "full course," usually reserved for men, instead of the women's "literary" curriculum. Even women's clothing became an issue: Amelia Bloomer invented a costume, based on loose-fitting, Turkish-style pantaloons, designed to free women from the tight corsets and stays that restricted circulation and movement; but the "Bloomer" dress was too radical for its time.

The writing of women, and of many men, reflected these cross-currents. The end of *The Scarlet Letter* raises, at least in symbolic terms, the question of woman's role in the building of community in America; Hawthorne's later novel *The Blithedale Romance* brings into sharp contrast the dangerously "liberated" dark woman, Zenobia, with the fair and saving Priscilla. Many of the widely selling women's novels of the 1850s in effect promoted what were presumed to be female virtues of patience, submission to duty, obedience, and chastity; their plots rewarded young women displaying such values, though not so much by marriage as by the formation of a domestic community centered on them. Such patterns were not restricted to novels like Susan Warner's *The Wide, Wide World;* they provide structure to a book like Hawthorne's *The House of the Seven Gables,* as well. Still, many women writers felt it necessary—since the very act of a woman writing was regarded with suspicion by many—to deprecate their literary productions as, in Caroline Kirkland's phrases, work "too slight to need a preface," "straggling and cloudy crayon-sketches," a "rude attempt." Some hid their identities behind pen names, often male.

In asking "How Should Women Write?" (1860) Mary E. Bryan lamented that

> *Men, after much demur and hesitation have given women liberty to write; but they cannot yet consent to allow them full freedom. They may flutter out of the cage, but it must be with clipped wings; they may hop about the smooth-shaven lawn, but must, on no account, fly. With metaphysics they have nothing to do; it is too deep a sea for their lead to sound; nor must they grapple with those great social and moral problems with which every strong soul is now wrestling. They must not go beyond the surface of life, lest they should stir the impure sediment that lurks beneath.*
>
> *. . . Having prescribed these bounds to the female pen, men are the first to condemn her efforts as tame and commonplace, because they lack earnestness and strength.*

Bryan's complaint reflects the sense of restriction under which women writers of the period labored.

In fact, however, they often annulled such limitations. In *The Hidden Hand* (1859), E.D.E.N. Southworth created a female character, Capitola, who dons a boy's clothing in order to survive, fights a duel, rescues the passive heroine, and, like other adventurous female characters of the time, altogether defies the prescribed stereotypes for a proper woman. As early as the 1820s, women writers like Catharine Maria Sedgwick and Lydia Sigourney directed their attention to the public concerns of the new nation; later, Stowe and Child consciously engaged the great human ques-

tions of the time, like slavery and the growing disparities in wealth. Indeed, women writers of the period probably involved themselves more with daily concerns than their male counterparts, who, like Emerson, often existed in a world of abstractions and fancy. Fern and Child, among others, tried to bring to their audience the problems of urban homelessness, the exploitation of women workers, the experiences of prostitutes and female inmates, and Fuller placed before her readers not only those issues but her immediate experiences of revolution and its causes in Europe. Moreover, women fiction writers consciously worked in a more realistic mode, largely eschewing the "romances" and allegories preferred by Hawthorne. They focused on everyday lives in Ohio or Maine, rather than on the remote settings and mad heroes of Poe or on Melville's larger than life confrontation of Captain Ahab and the White Whale. In part, this realistic practice may have been imposed by the kinds of restrictions Bryan sketches; in part, it may have been a conscious choice, as Alice Cary suggests in concluding her second volume of stories, *Clovernook* (1853):

> *In our country, though all men are not "created equal," such is the influence of the sentiment of liberty and political equality, that:*
>
> *"All thoughts, all passions, all delights,*
> *Whatever stirs this mortal frame,"*
>
> *may with as much probability be supposed to affect conduct and expectation in the log cabin as in the marble mansion; and to illustrate this truth, to dispel that erroneous belief of the necessary baseness of the "common people" which the great masters in literature have in all ages labored to create, is a purpose and an object in our nationality to which the finest and highest genius may wisely be devoted; but which may be effected in a degree by writings as unpretending as these reminiscences of what occurred in and about the little village where I from childhood watched the pulsations of surrounding hearts.*

Just as many women writers of the period focused on subjects and adopted strategies somewhat different from those of men, so the forms in which women expressed themselves often differed. For example, writers like the Grimkés, Child, and Kirkland, adapted the letter—a form between private and public expression—for important published work. One thinks also of Emily Dickinson's conception of her poems, which almost entirely remained "unpublished," at least to the general public, throughout her life:

> This is my letter to the World
> That never wrote to Me—

Cary's stories seem, like life or dreams, to shift focus as they proceed. Many of Stowe's later works employ a narrator whose relationship to the reader is posed as that of a domestic friend speaking the language of kitchen conversation. Jacobs, unlike male slave narrators, employs many of the conventions and the language of the domestic novel.

The point is *not* that such differences absolutely divided female from male writing. It was not the case that men wrote the "serious" books and women the "popular"; men composed as many potboilers as women, and probably more best-sellers as the century went on. Nor was it true that women's fiction was inevitably "sentimental" or men's adventurous. Cooper, Child, and Sedgwick wrote adventure tales focused on the drama of Indian-white relations; what is striking, however, are the differences between their versions of those interactions. Cooper's is finally a vision of irreconcilably separate societies, the development of the white necessitating the destruction of the Indian. Sedgwick and Child, while not ignoring the reality of that destruction, explore social and sexual interactions—including those of white women with Indian men—as paths to a harmonious future. Similarly, a slave narrative like Harriet Jacobs's *Incidents* focuses directly on problems of family, sexuality, and relations between white and black women, matters seldom touched on in slave narratives by men. Nor is it that the work of women writers in this period is notably "better" than that of men, or vice versa. What we need to look at are the similarities and the differences in their work, where their subjects, their styles, and their audiences are alike and where they diverge. And we need to understand how those differences arose from the differing conditions of male and female life in the first half of the nineteenth century.

The Many Cultures of America

Needless to say, sexual differences constituted only one of the factors helping to create in the United States one of the world's most heterogeneous societies. Long before the advent of white settlers on the North American continent, of course, the "Indian" populations were themselves extremely diverse in language, culture, and social organization. With the coming of a variety of Europeans, the importation of African blacks as slaves, and, in the nineteenth century, the incorporation of large French- and Spanish-speaking areas into the United States and the arrival of Chinese workers and merchants, the pattern of racial and cultural diversity which has come to characterize twentieth-century America was established, though the full mosaic of ethnicity would not be seen until much later.

Differences in historical experience and cultural patterns are perhaps nowhere more clearly illustrated than in respect to American Indians during the first part of the nineteenth century. With the expansion of the white population westward between the Revolution and the Civil War, Indians—especially those east of the Mississippi River—faced intense pressure, first in the Northwest Territory, then in the Southeast. The result was a period of extreme social discontinuity, accompanied by dispossession, tragedy, bitterness, and sometimes violence. With the acquisition and rapid Anglo settlement of California, and the annexation of Texas, even those tribes remaining in the interior of America faced a white frontier on three sides.

The dominant policy adopted by the U.S. government during the first part of this period was removal. President James Monroe expressed the common view in an 1817 letter to Andrew Jackson: "The hunter or savage state requires a greater extent of territory to sustain it, than is compatible with the progress and just claims of civilized life, and must yield to it." In fact, however, when tribes like the Cherokees in Georgia adapted white agricultural models and organized themselves as a peaceful sovereign state, they were put under even more brutal pressure to leave. Under provisions of the Removal Act of 1830, tribes gave up their lands east of the Mississippi, willingly or otherwise, in exchange for lands in the West. And while the Supreme Court ruled in 1832 that the Indian nations were "distinct political communities" not subject to State jurisdiction, President Jackson refused to enforce that decision. Tricked and intimidated out of their lands, the southern Indians were forced to follow what became known as the "Trail of Tears" to the distant, and often barren, Oklahoma territory. By 1844, most tribes had been removed to the West. President Jackson had applauded his policy of removal by claiming that it had "at length placed [Indians] beyond the reach of injury and oppression," in areas where the "paternal care of the General Government [would] watch over them and protect them." In fact, however, the tide of white settlement rolled rapidly over the Mississippi, and within ten years the General Government had begun to embark on campaigns to concentrate Indians in ever-decreasing "reservations." The result was further decimation. Dispossessed of the lands that provided bases for their cultures, deprived of the means they had long used to sustain life and society, many tribes found it impossible to reestablish the old tribal ways.

Literary production in English indicates directly the degree of acculturation of the tribes and reflects the impact of removal and other assimilationist policies, such as Christian education, upon them. Most Indians who wrote in English belonged to tribes which had been displaced in the East or had been forced to remove to western lands. Cut off from traditional homelands and lifestyles, they were forced to acculturate in order to survive. Thus in the first half of the nineteenth century, the most significant Indian literary activity occurred among the rapidly acculturating Cherokees in the South and the Six Nations and Ojibwas in New York and the Great Lakes regions. Publishing outlets for Indians were limited. Writers often published their own work by subscription, but, because they were oddities, their works were sometimes printed by commercial presses, by national and religious newspapers and journals, as well as by the few Indian publishing outlets mentioned above.

Though most English works by Indians reflect the trends in popular writings by non-Indians, they have their own distinguishing characteristics. Much of the early poetry, by writers like Jane Schoolcraft and John Rollin Ridge, derives largely from romantic and early Victorian models. But not all work attempted to conform to the literary standards of the dominant society. Writers like David Cusick, Jane Schoolcraft, Nicholson Parker, and Nathaniel T. Strong attempted to record the oral traditions and lore of their people. Others served as informants to the growing number of non-Indian writers who took an anthropological interest in tribal cultures and sought to preserve the rehearsed traditions, legends, and chants, which remain popular among readers of American Indian literature today. Jane Schoolcraft, her mother, and brother, for instance, served as early informants for Jane's husband, Henry Rowe Schoolcraft, and Ely Parker was a major contributor to Lewis H. Morgan's work on the League of the Iroquois.

This new interest in Indian oral literatures reflected the convergence of several important themes in the development of a popular American national character. For one thing, a major current of American literary nationalism sought its source in aboriginal culture, which was appropriated by writers from Charles Brockden Brown to Henry Wadsworth Longfellow. In 1815, Walter Channing, writing in the first volume of the *North American Review,* which would quickly become a prestigious journal, argued that the only truly American literature was the "oral literature of the aborigines," whose common speech, he claimed, was "the very language of poetry." Second, expansion beyond the Trans-Appalachian and Trans-Mississippi frontiers coupled with Jackson's removal policy had precipitated armed conflict between the U.S. government and many Indian nations. Though the popular imagination later fixed on Custer and the Little Bighorn in thinking of Indian wars, the warfare of the 1840s and 1850s was far more widespread and destructive, in terms of the number of Indian casualties, than the post-Civil War battles. As would be the case after the Civil War, questions about the effectiveness and direction of Indian policy caused champions of the Indians to develop and publish evidence of the Indians' humanity and cultivation in the hope of affecting the public debate. Unfortunately, the sympathetic portrayals of Indian culture which aimed to accomplish this were linked with the popular but false notion that the Indians were a vanishing race. Neither the people themselves nor their culture were vanishing, however. While some formally educated Indians became prominent as culture brokers through their English language publications, within tribal settings tradition-bearers maintained the cultural legacy, represented by the oral poetry included in this volume. The advent of missions, English language education, vocational training, and acculturative measures altered but could not extinguish the native muse.

Despite the degree of acculturation that their works display, most Indian writers composing in English made some use of their native backgrounds, and they did not attempt to mask their sympathy for Indian causes. William Apess, for instance, wrote in behalf of Indian rights. Elias Boudinot proseletyzed for conscious acculturation as a means of resisting removal. George Harkins chided the Americans for paying lip service to freedom while calling for Indian removal. And George Copway, while supporting Christianization of Indians, condemned the whiskey trade and urged establishment of an Indian territory controlled by Indians in the upper Midwest. Such writers tried to focus on the realities of Indian life, attempting to cut through the stereotypical images of savages, noble or devilish, projected by popular white writers like Cooper and Longfellow. They were joined in such efforts by people like Child and Fuller, who rejected the common American views of Indian character and destiny. Fuller had, indeed, written that "at some distant day, [the Indians] will no doubt be considered as having acted the Roman or Carthaginian part of heroic and patriotic self-defence."

Other Indian writers, however, fed a part of the popular reading taste of the day. Biographical, autobiographical, and 'told-to" works by Indians enjoyed a good deal of popularity. Such works often helped to encourage the popular notion of the Indian as a vanishing race, the "Last of the Mohicans," an idea that was fully developed by mid-century, and that has persisted into recent times.

Most blacks in the United States remained slaves throughout the period. While slavery had deprived black people of their original African languages, it did not by any means succeed in extirpating all aspects of African culture—in music and dance, in folktales, in forms of extended family organization, for example. But southern law forbade and northern discrimination inhibited the teaching of reading and writing to blacks, and thus the production and consumption of traditional literary work was severely limited. It is all the more remarkable, therefore, that in this period two uniquely American art forms flourished among blacks. The spirituals were a singular blend of African and European music, of Hebrew and Christian religious images converted through slave experience into symbols of present torment and future hope. And the slave narratives were, with white women's narratives of Indian captivity, the first distinctively American forms of prose composition.

Almost all the writing of the period was produced by free blacks and by former slaves. George Moses Horton, who was a slave for much of his life, wrote verse—including love poetry for sale to undergraduates at Chapel Hill—in the thwarted hope that he might buy his freedom and emigrate. In important ways, literary production by free blacks before Emancipation was shaped by the conditions of its production and use. A number of writers like Frances Harper, James M. Whitfield, and James Madison Bell wrote poetry that was designed to be delivered from the platform more, perhaps, than silently read from a book. Their poems were in a sense "scripts," which they declaimed in churches, at public meetings, or at other events usually connected with the anti-slavery cause. Thus Whitfield's long poem "America" begins almost as a parody of patriotic verse:

America, it is to thee,
Thou boasted land of liberty,—
It is to thee I raise my song,
Thou land of blood, and crime, and
 wrong.

Many other poems and stories published in black newspapers or in abolitionist journals were designed to demonstrate by their very existence the abilities of their authors, often quite young, and the virtues of supporting their further education. Thus when Ann Plato's volume of prose and poetry (1841) was published she may have been as young as fifteen, and Frances Harper's *Forest Leaves* (no copy of which seems to have survived) came out when she was barely twenty. Furthermore, the poets set out to demonstrate that they could utilize the forms and cadences of British verse, and so their work is often quite as derivative as their white models.

In subject, in audience, and in intent, much of the writing by blacks in this period was thus closely tied to the movement for emancipation and to the efforts to develop and support black educational and religious institutions. Not surprisingly, therefore, the most widely used form was the slave narrative. The abolitionist and black presses published hundreds of these autobiographies, ranging in size from a few pages to whole volumes, like those of Gustavus Vassa, Frederick Douglass, James W.C. Pennington, Ellen and William Craft, and Harriet Jacobs. They describe firsthand the evils of slavery, and often of northern racism as well, narrate what are often thrilling escapes, and sometimes discuss the problems a former slave has in learning to read, getting a job, and adapting to northern ways. After the resounding success of *Uncle Tom's Cabin* in helping stir up anti-slavery sentiment, however, some black writers in the 1850s turned to fiction as an equally useful form. The decade saw the publication of the first four novels by black authors—William Wells Brown's *Clotel* (1853), Frank Webb's *The Garies and Their Friends* (1857), Martin Delany's *Blake* (1859), and Harriet Wilson's *Our Nig* (1859)—as well as Frederick Douglass's novella, "The Heroic Slave" (1853) and Frances Harper's short story "The Two Offers" (1859).

Apart from such work, almost all of it published in the Northeast, there existed a well-developed tradition of French Creole writing, primarily in New Orleans. And, of course, there was an extremely vital oral tradition of songs and tales throughout the South and wherever in northern communities black people gathered. Little of this oral material, which was after all the major expressive form among slaves, was collected until after the Civil War. Furthermore, slaves learned, as Douglass says, that "a still tongue makes a wise head," especially around whites. Thus, it is almost impossible to know precisely which stories were actually in circulation during slavery. What is clear, however, is that such oral traditions influenced post-Civil War black writers rather more than their earlier peers, for whose audience dialect and folk stories were too closely tied to the oppression and ignorance of slavery.

When the nineteenth century began, the United States stretched only one-third of the distance across the American continent, its dreams of further westward expansion thwarted by the colonial empires of France and Spain. France quickly retreated from the competition for American dominance with the sale of its vast Louisiana territory in 1803; the United States now found itself abutting, along its southwestern flank, the tantalizing provinces of New Spain, a colony soon to undergo its own revolutionary upheaval and emerge as the sovereign nation of Mexico.

No bordering countries could have been more dissimilar: one English-speaking and predominantly Protestant, the other Spanish-speaking and overwhelmingly Catholic. There were other seemingly irreconcilable differences as well, ranging from forms of social and political organization to relationships between the European colonizers and the native populations. And, of course, long-standing prejudices played a role in United States-Mexico relations. Mexicans took enormous pride in their folk and formal traditions which dated, on one side, to the Spain of Cervantes and Lope de Vega and, on the other, even farther back to the culture of the Aztecs. For Anglo-Americans, however, Mexicans and their customs were the despised products of decadent Europeans and barbarous American aborigines. But while Anglo-Americans scorned the Mexicans, they nevertheless coveted their land and over a thirty-year period, through settlement, purchase, deception, annexation, and the ultimate device of the Mexican War, systematically relieved the Mexicans of nearly half their territory: Texas, New Mexico, Arizona, California, Nevada, Utah, and half of Colorado.

As Anglo-Americans entered what is now the southwestern United States, the impact of their culture varied from one region to another. In Texas, for example, Anglo-American influences transformed the standing culture at a relatively moderate pace after 1821 when the Stephen Austin settlement was established. In California, the discovery of gold in 1848 precipitated a swarm of Anglo-American fortune hunters and settlers who virtually swamped much of *californio* culture. New Mexico, the third region of the Southwest which was well developed, held the least obvious appeal to Anglo-Americans and so maintained its predominantly Mexican character into the twentieth century.

Even after Anglo-American intervention and appropriation, however, the Spanish- and Mexican-based culture of the Southwest retained its distinctiveness and continued along its particular course of evolution. The Treaty of Guadalupe Hidalgo, which ended the Mexican War in 1848, granted American citizenship to the 80,000 Mexicans in the annexed territories, but with little immediate effect. The newly created Mexican-Americans long after maintained Spanish as their primary language, participated at minimal levels in the federal electoral process, and continued to look southward, toward Mexico City, for cultural reinvigoration.

Although Mexican-American settlements and towns of the Southwest from San Antonio to Monterey were never as isolated as generally depicted by American historians, they did exhibit many of the qualities of frontier or emerging cultures. In literary terms, this means that the prose produced was largely historical, personal, political, or religious in nature, with relatively little in the way of sustained fiction. Mexican-American writers mostly concerned themselves with tracing the establishment of Mexican culture from Texas to California, their roles in this grand historical spectacle, and God's blessing on the enterprise. As the presence of Anglo-Americans in their homelands increased, Mexican-Americans took up pens more anxiously, simultaneously eager to defend their culture against *yanqui* scorn and aware that the intruders would irreversibly transform precisely the customs and values they held dear. In California, where Anglo-American intervention was sudden and overwhelming, writers such as José María Amador, José Francisco Palomares and, especially, Mariano Vallejo mourned the passing of Mexican traditions. Occasionally, a Mexican-American would compose a narrative to defend his participation in Anglo-American causes; Juan Seguín of San Antonio prepared his "Personal Memoirs" to justify his role in the Texas war for independence.

Of the belletristic forms, poetry was by far the most popular mode of expression among Mexican-Americans. They wrote lyric poetry after the fashion of Spanish romanticism and political poetry treating every conceivable issue from bilingualism to statehood for New Mexico. The major outlets for Mexican-American poetry were the hundreds of Spanish-language newspapers in the Southwest that began to proliferate in the 1850s. These journals not only published information on contemporary political events but cultural news from the United States and Europe (especially Spain) and literary items by local writers. The submission of poetry to Spanish-language newspapers was so volu-

California will, probably, next fall away from the loose adhesion which, in such a country as Mexico, holds a remote province in a slight equivocal kind of dependence on the metropolis. Imbecile and distracted, Mexico never can exert any real government authority over such a country. The impotence of the one and the distance of the other, must make the relation one of virtual independence; unless, by stunting the province of all natural growth, and forbidding that immigration which can alone develope its capabilities and fulfill the purposes of its creation, tyranny may retain a military dominion, which is no government in the legitimate sense of the term.

In the case of California this is now impossible. The Anglo-Saxon foot is already on its borders. Already the advance guard of the irresistible army of Anglo-Saxon emigration has begun to pour down upon it, armed with the plough and the rifle, and marking its trail with schools and colleges, courts and representative halls, mills and meetinghouses. A population will soon be in actual occupation of California, over which it will be idle for Mexico to dream of dominion. They will necessarily become independent. All this without agency of our government, without responsibility of our people—in the natural flow of events, the spontaneous working of principles, and the adaptation of the tendencies and wants of the human race to the elemental circumstances in the midst of which they find themselves placed. . . .

Whether they will then attach themselves to our Union or not, is not to be predicted with any certainty. Unless the projected railroad across the continent to the Pacific be carried into effect, perhaps they may not; though even in that case, the day is not distant when the empires of the Atlantic and Pacific would again flow together into one, as soon as their inland border should approach each other. But that great work, colossal as appears the plan on its first suggestion, cannot remain long unbuilt.

"Annexation"
U.S. Magazine and Democratic Review, July, 1845

minous that one overworked Santa Fe editor published an item entitled "Remedies for Verse Mania." Mexican-American newspapers also regularly printed stories, many with a strong folkloric quality. As for the production of novels, the demanding, volatile nature of southwestern life did not easily allow for the sustained concentration necessary for their composition.

But the circumstances of southwestern culture so inimical to the production of long fiction were extremely conducive to the evolution of a rich folkloric tradition. Folk narratives, folk drama, and folk music all flourished in Mexican-American communities. Probably the most important expressive form used among Mexican-Americans in the nineteenth century was the *corrido.* This ballad type, in effect a legend set to music, was often used by Mexican-Americans to preserve their accounts of cultural conflict with Anglo-Americans. The *corrido* began to appear in the Southwest in the late 1850s, treating such issues as Mexican-American retribution for *yanqui* injustice and competition on the cattle trail between Anglo cowboys and Mexican-American *vaqueros.* The *cor-*

rido tradition thrives to the present day and constitutes a vast repertory of Mexican-American experience and consciousness.

While the original inhabitants of North America very likely came from Asia, and while Chinese were probably among the earliest modern explorers of the continent, Asians were among the latest and least welcomed immigrants to the United States. Trade between America and China, limited to the port of Guanzhou (Canton), had begun late in the eighteenth century; in the nineteenth, China was forced by European military powers to open additional ports. Initially, Chinese goods like tea, silk, and porcelain flowed outward, with little from the West being imported. But by 1807 western missionaries had begun work in China, and after its military defeat by Great Britain in the two Opium Wars (1839–42 and 1855–60), China was compelled to import goods from England (and other western nations, including the United States), particularly British opium. Additionally, China was forced to pay huge indemnities, to cede Hong Kong to England, and to make other humiliating concessions, like granting extraterritoriality to western citizens in China. The weakness of the Qing Dynasty, the burden of taxes levied to pay off indemnities, consequent civil rebellions (like the Taiping Revolution, 1851–1864), and massive floods and famine produced conditions encouraging emigration.

Like China, Japan in 1854 had been forced by military might to open its ports to western commerce. But unlike China, Japan readily began to import western technology and experts, strengthening itself militarily and economically until it emerged by the end of the century as a world power. With international standing and internal stability, there was little drive for emigration, and it was thus not until early in the twentieth century that significant numbers of Japanese immigrated to the continental United States.

Despite internal conditions, few Chinese had come to the United States before gold was discovered in California. Chum Ming, a merchant who had arrived in San Francisco in 1847, was one of the first to join the gold rush and to strike it rich. He wrote the news about "Gold Mountain" home to Sam Yup (Three Districts) near Guanzhou. In 1848, three Chinese had arrived in San Francisco; in 1849 there were 323. Their numbers increased gradually, peaking in 1854 at 13,100 and thereafter averaging 5,000 for the next twelve years. In all, about 35,000 Chinese, immigrants and sojourners, were in the United States during the 1850s, while about 2.5 million people immigrated from Europe. Yet for economic and racial reasons resentment mounted against the Chinese, and one discriminatory law after another was passed against them, mostly in California. In 1849, a law forbade any people of color from testifying against whites, thus effectively denying blacks and Indians, as well as Chinese, legal recourse. In 1854, a foreign miner's tax law was passed; it was levied almost exclusively against Chinese miners for the next twenty years. As the Chinese moved into other work, such as agriculture, cigar and shoe manufacturing, other laws were passed prohibiting their employment in these industries and preventing them from buying land. Finally, the only labor which Chinese could undertake without objection was largely "women's work": laundry, cooking, and domestic service.

It was precisely shortages of labor in Hawaii and the western states which led to the importation of Chinese workers, the so-called "coolies." The first group of 180 Chinese men was brought to work on Hawaii's sugar plantations in 1852; their wages were $3.00 a month. In 1868, pursuing a policy of divide and control, growers brought the first group of Japanese laborers to Hawaii, and in the early twentieth century Koreans and Filipinos. But it was in the construction of the transcontinental railroad that Chinese workers gained their greatest fame. They had helped build the California Central Railroad in 1858, but the Central Pacific, which had undertaken the challenging task of pushing the transcontinental line east from Sacramento through the Sierra Nevada and Rocky Mountains, would initially hire only whites. Failing to recruit a sufficient crew, Leland Stanford, president of the line, finally agreed to try out a group of 50 Chinese workers in 1865. They proved so industrious and efficient that fifty more were hired and within two years, 12,000 of the 13,500 workers on the railroad's payroll were Chinese. It was they who swung down from cliffs in straw baskets to set, and too often be blown up by, dynamite charges—thus coining the phrase "he didn't have a Chinaman's chance." It was they who lived and worked underground for months at a time during the bitter mountain winters, tunnelling the roadbed east. Ironically, their very efficiency in bringing the transcontinental railroad to completion on May 10, 1869, may have helped stifle other Chinese immigration, for the agitation which culminated in passage of the Chinese Exclusion Act of 1882 began soon after the last rail spike was driven.

The vast majority of the Chinese who came to the United States during this period were men, often hoping to make enough money to provide themselves with a stake at home. Many of the laborers were from peasant origins, not literate in Chinese, much less in English, a language they did not speak among themselves. Largely excluded from the society of westerners, and reviled by them, and proud of their own civilization, the Chinese immigrants retained a culture essentially Chinese in language as well as focus. Much of what they wrote, when they were able, was in the form of private letters back to families or brief Chinese poems about life in Gold Mountain.

A few Chinese were also able to study in eastern schools, mainly through the assistance of American missionaries. On April 12, 1847, Yung Wing arrived in New York City en route to Monson, Massachusetts, where he would enroll in the Monson Academy. He later graduated with Yale's class of 1854, the first Chinese to gain a degree from an American college. Yung Wing married an American woman and became a naturalized American citizen, though he frequently traveled between China and the United States, acting as a kind of bridge between his two countries. He purchased machinery in Fitchburg, Massachusetts, to establish an arms factory, which later became the famous Kiangnan Arsenal, near Shanghai. He also devised and directed the Chinese Educational Mission, a project which in the 1870s brought groups of Chinese boys to Hartford, Connecticut, to study at the expense of the Chinese government. The title of Yung Wing's graceful autobiography, *My Life in China and America* (1909), expresses something of the duality in his life.

The Rise of Industry

The immigration of Irish Catholics in the East and Chinese laborers in the West was met with mob violence, anti-foreign political organization, and new legal constraints. Yet in the long run, what was more deeply troubling to the young country were the related shifts of its economic base from agriculture to industry, and its population from rural to urban. Jeffersonian democrats had envisioned a country made up primarily of small landholders ("franklins") and artisans, educated, independent farmers, careful of their land, jealous of their political freedoms, dependent only on their own hard work for success. In fact, however, early in the nineteenth century the smaller, self-sufficient eastern-style family farm began a long decline, as growers increasingly turned to producing cash crops, like cotton, sugar, and wheat, for national and international markets. In the South, as we have pointed out, that meant an even harsher slave system. In the West, it meant the creation of huge, widely separated farms, which offered an efficient way of organizing growing but sacrificed most of the virtues of community. And since the young nation's single greatest exploitable resource was land, those living on the largest "unclaimed" tracts, American Indians, were by imposed treaties, callous chiseling, and continued violence pushed off into ever more remote and barren stretches of the West.

The new mills of the Northeast brought in their own social changes. At first they seemed to offer at least some opportunity to women from the declining Yankee farms; and they could certainly produce standardized products—clothing, boots, pots and pans—more cheaply than they could be produced even at home, much less by neighborhood artisans. But as competition increased, as the looms and spindles were speeded up, and as wages declined especially after the panic of 1837, the limited attractiveness of factory work disappeared. Independent artisans, who sold their product for a price, who could take pride in the work their hands created, who worked at times and at rates of their own choosing, whose family income was supplemented by a garden plot and by fishing and hunting, disappeared. They were replaced by the factory "hand," who had little or nothing to sell but his or her labor for a wage, and who worked the factory loom or wielded a pickaxe on the Erie Canal. The skills formerly learned and honed by craftspeople through apprentice systems began to be built into remarkably accurate machines, like those portrayed by Melville in "The Tartarus of Maids." They could be operated by relatively unskilled laborers, easily replaced in times of crisis by newcomers or even by cheaper child workers. Such laborers were mostly immigrants from Ireland or Germany crowding into eastern and developing midwestern cities. They had none of the skills, the small landholdings, the community connections, or the bases for family self-sufficiency which had seen independent artisans and farmers through hard times and helped set them on the road to success. Thus, there came into being—despite the misgivings even of some factory owners—a "permanent factory population." Differing in origins and religion, they were often at the edge of poverty, sometimes unemployed, subject to the new industrial discipline of the time-clock marking out fourteen-hour days, six days a week—"wage slaves," as southern planters liked to call them.

Many of the writers of the time tried to bring their concern for those afflicted by the changes in American society to a public largely ignorant of or indifferent to them. As journalists, Margaret Fuller, Fanny Fern, and Lydia Maria Child wrote about the conditions of life and work of this new urban working class, and the increasing disparities of income in the cities of the Northeast. Child's "Letters from New York" dealing with homeless families and the sharp contrasts of affluence and poverty can almost be read as accounts of urban America in the 1990s. In addition to Melville, Rebecca Harding Davis and Elizabeth Stuart Phelps (whose work appears in Volume 2) focus stories on the lives of people who labor in the mills, and *The Quaker City; or, the Monks of Monk Hall* by George Lippard, a working-class reformer, became a best-seller in 1845. Indeed, Melville's most famous book, *Moby-Dick,* can be read on one level as an industrial novel, deeply concerned with the processes by which raw materials are turned into commodities and with the complex interactions among those who work and those who increasingly determine their jobs. It deals with a variety of other themes, to be sure—men and nature, the existence of ultimate truths, the contest of fanaticism and liberalism—but Melville's intense concern with the processes of work suggests how deeply the changes wrought by the industrial revolution were affecting the consciousness of his contemporaries.

At the same time, the new accumulations of wealth, which permitted some Americans the leisure to read and learn, brought their own problems. While the belief persisted that every (white) American could make *his* fortune, the fact was that in the half century before the Civil War economic inequality increased rapidly—and noticeably. Preachers inveighed against Mammon, politicians denounced privilege, writers like Emerson deplored the "public and private avarice [which] make the air we breathe thick and fat," and Thoreau urged his readers to "simplify, simplify"; but the rich got richer, and the poor . . . well, they could at least "go west." Americans, whose grandparents had fought to overthrow the tyranny of king and nobles and "gentlemen," found themselves confronted with new forms of title based upon wealth—as well as with new forms of poverty, which persisted from generation to generation of factory hands and farm laborers.

But the underlying issue was whether the technological and social changes that were producing these effects were themselves finally beneficial, whatever their short-term impacts. No one could deny the enormity of these changes. Take, for example, the revolution in transportation. At the turn of the 19th century you traveled—if at all—along waterways cut over millions of years by natural forces, propelled—as human beings had always been propelled—by the current, by sail, or by oar and paddle. Or you followed narrow, rutted trails on foot or horseback, or perhaps in a lumbering Conestoga wagon that would, all too often, have to be pried out of deep mud sloughs. Writers like Cooper and Sedgwick, looking backward to earlier years, offer a sense of what such travel was like. A family moving from around Philadelphia to try its luck at farming in the northwest territories (Ohio or Indiana) could take many months—indeed, over a year, if it had to stop to construct its own fortified raft to float down the Ohio River—to reach its destination. Caroline Kirkland's *A New Home, Who'll Follow?* vividly pictures the hardships of travel to the West even in the 1830s. In 1843, the caravan of wagons traversing the Oregon trail from Independence, Missouri, to the Willamette Valley had taken over five months, and along the way at least seven of the migrants had been buried by the trailside. By 1857 our imaginary family could have made the trip from Philadelphia to St. Louis in a matter of *days* using the new "through line" organized by the Baltimore and Ohio Railroad; by then, of course, they would have had to move many hundreds of miles further to find land on which they could homestead. Just a dozen years later, passengers were making the railroad trip from Omaha to San Francisco in *four days.*

This revolution in transportation represents simply one aspect of the application of advanced industrial technologies. When in 1807 Robert Fulton first drove his steamboat Clermont up the Hudson River from New York to Albany in 30 hours, he was applying to transport a new motive power already being put to industrial uses. The adaptation and development of such technology was, even from the perspective of our own day, amazingly rapid; together with the exploitation of bountiful natural resources, it constituted a major reason for the country's mighty growth. For example, in 1830 Peter Cooper set an old pumping engine on a flatcar to create the first locomotive made in the United States; though it could manage the phenomenal speed of 12 miles per hour, his engine lost its first race against a horse. By 1840 there were about as many miles of railroad track, some 3328, as there were miles of canals—all built within the previous 25 years; by 1860, there were about 30,000 miles of rail. In certain respects, the locomotive became, as Walt Whitman called it, the "type of the modern." Not only had railroads—with steam-driven boats—utterly changed travel and trade, but they stimulated ancillary industries like coal-mining, lumbering, iron and machine tool production, as well as cash-crop farming. The building of the railroads also provided the basis for giant fortunes for their owners, entailed the importation of thousands of poor laborers, helped insure the settlement by white people of the vast territories between the Mississippi and the Rockies, and led to the final destruction of the Plains Indian ways of life.

Did all of this represent "progress" or "decline"? Whitman took the locomotive as an "emblem of motion and power—pulse of the continent," but his enthusiasm for the progress it represented was by no means universally shared. Emily Dickinson liked "to see it lap the Miles," a punctual though alarming steed. "But," asked Thoreau from Walden,

if we stay at home and mind our business, who will want railroads? We do not ride on the railroad; it rides upon us. Did you ever think what those sleepers are that underlie the railroad? Each one is a man, an Irishman, or a Yankee man. The rails are laid on them, and they are covered with sand, and the cars run smoothly over them. They are sound sleepers, I assure you. And every few years a new lot is laid down and run over; so that, if some have the pleasure of riding on a rail, others have the misfortune to be ridden upon.

In his sketch "The Celestial Railroad," Hawthorne portrays a modern railroad trip in terms of Bunyan's *Pilgrim's Progress*—headed not in a celestial, but in an opposite direction.

As the railroad provided an appropriately powerful and ambiguous symbol for modernizing America, so the scientist, the Frankenstein responsible for releasing this enormous power, became an equivocal figure. In another mood, Whitman wrote

When I heard the learn'd astronomer,
When the proofs, the figures, were
 ranged in columns before me,
When I was shown the charts and
 diagrams, to add, divide, and
 measure them,
When I sitting heard the astronomer
 where he lectured with much
 applause in the lecture-room,
How soon unaccountable I became tired
 and sick,
Till rising and gliding out I wander'd
 off by myself,
In the mystical moist night-air, and from
 time to time,
Look'd up in perfect silence at the stars.

Hawthorne created a series of "scientists" in works like "The Birthmark," "Rappaccini's Daughter," and *The House of the Seven Gables* who risk violating the most secret recesses of nature or of the human heart. Indeed, Chillingworth in *The Scarlet Letter* is a character cut in their image. So, in many respects, is Melville's Captain Ahab. Such figures are far distant from the happy image of Benjamin Franklin flying his innocent kite into the gathering thunderclouds above Philadelphia. But by the middle of the nineteenth century, the United States was no longer a nation of Franklins, and the society's power to understand and transform the world around it an increasingly enigmatic heritage.

Individualism and/vs. Community

What finally is that national heritage? That was perhaps the most conflicted of all the questions that emerged in the early nineteenth century. Walt Whitman best focuses the issue in the lines which came to open his book, *Leaves of Grass:*

One's-self I sing, a simple separate
 person,
Yet utter the word Democratic, the
 word En-masse.

"Inscriptions"

Does the word *yet* imply "still"—that is, that the poet must at once sing both the separate individual *and* the democratic mass? Or does it imply "but"—that is, a conflict between the writer as a separate "self" and the democratic "en masse"? In other words, is the relationship between individuals and society in a democracy harmonious and productive, or combative and draining? Do we say to our neighbors, "You are as good as I, so let us work together for our mutual betterment"? Or do we say, "I am as good as you, so get out of my way"?

Historians like David Brion Davis have rooted this tension in a change in the vision of the role of the United States from preserving the "virtuous republic" established by the Founders to ensuring above all "individual opportunity." In many ways the key to the intellectual and social life of the United States during the first half of the nineteenth century is defined precisely by this tension between the mission of a democratic community and the growing ideology of individual advancement. Obviously, many Americans saw no contradiction between these conceptions; indeed, for Benjamin Franklin, each entailed the other. Still, a certain discord emerges in writers concerned with the frontier, like Cooper and Kirkland, in the conflicts between the need for community and the imperatives of individual self-assertion. One hears it as a ground tone in the struggle over slavery: will the United States become what its founding documents promise—a blessed nation "dedicated to the proposition that all men are created equal"; or will it continue to recognize the "right" of one person to hold another as property?

Individual and community—with what scale do we balance their claims? We are transfixed by the unique expressive forms devised by individual artists like Dickinson, Whitman, and Melville. We are swayed, as indeed Americans in the nineteenth century were swayed, by the expression of individualist ideas in Emerson's electric language:

Society everywhere is in conspiracy against the manhood of every one of its members. Society is a joint-stock company, in which the members agree, for the better securing of his bread to each shareholder, to surrender the liberty and culture of the eater. The virtue in most request is conformity. Self- reliance is its

> In order more effectually to promote the great purposes of human culture; to establish the external relations of life on a basis of wisdom and purity; to apply the principles of justice and love to our social organization in accordance with the laws of Divine Providence; to substitute a system of brotherly cooperation for one of selfish competition; to secure to our children and those who may be entrusted to our care the benefits of the highest physical, intellectual, and moral education, which, in the progress of knowledge, the resources at our command will permit; to institute an attractive, efficient, and productive system of industry; to prevent the exercise of worldly anxiety by the competent supply of our necessary wants; to diminish the desire of excessive accumulation by making the acquisition of individual property subservient to upright and disinterested uses; to guarantee to each other forever the means of physical support and of spiritual progress; and thus to impart a greater freedom, simplicity, truthfulness, refinement, and moral dignity to our mode of life; we, the undersigned, do unite in a voluntary association, and adopt and ordain the following articles of agreement. . . .
>
> "Constitution of the Brook-Farm Association," 1841

aversion. . . . Whoso would be a man, must be a nonconformist. . . . Nothing is at last sacred but the integrity of your own mind. Absolve you to yourself, and you shall have the suffrage of the world. ("Self-Reliance")

Yet even as Emerson wrote, some of his closest friends were trying to establish at Brook Farm one among dozens of experiments in communitarian living, which entailed holding the land as a joint-stock company and working it together. It is not that such communities were popular with most Americans. The Mormons, like other religious collectives, were violently driven from upstate New York, then from Illinois, and finally to the then-wilds of Utah. Other secular communards were attacked, scorned, or satirized, as Hawthorne did for Brook Farm in his novel *The Blithedale Romance.* It is also possible that white hostility to the Cherokees of Georgia had to do not only with racism and greed for their land but with the fact that, organized as a separate nation, they conducted their business communally, and with great success.

Still, the efforts to establish communities based on shared values continued even in the face of hostility and the fundamental triumph of individualism. While Hawthorne mocked the Utopianism of Brook Farm, the themes of sustaining human community and the torment of individual isolation persist in much of his fiction. Melville suggests, in his final novel, *The Confidence-Man,* that a form of Emersonian individualism can easily become the "me-first" ethic of the entrepreneur. In Alice Cary's Uncle Christopher, individualism has become gnarled and destructive to those subject to it. And Alexis de Tocqueville, one of the keenest observers of nineteenth-century America, suggests that individualism too easily emerges as a "selfishness" that finally will confine a person "entirely within the solitude of his own heart." Tocqueville's view echoes precisely the criticism Margaret Fuller made of the insularity and self-absorption of her friend Emerson. She apparently shared the suspicion of him the Italian leader Giuseppe Mazzini expressed in a letter: "I feel fearful that he leads or will lead men to too much contemplation. . . . We stand in need of one who will . . . appeal to the collective influence and inspiring sources, more than to individual self-improvement."

Thus if individualism triumphed, it was not without a struggle, nor without its critics. Not, indeed, without alternatives being posed. Frederick Douglass writes of his fellow slaves on the plantation of Mr. Freeland:

We were linked and interlinked with each other. I loved them with a love stronger than any thing I have experienced since. It is sometimes said that we slaves do not love and confide in each other. In answer to this assertion, I can say, I never loved any or confided in any people more than my fellow slaves. . . . We never undertook to do any thing, of any importance, without a mutual consultation. We never moved separately. We were one; and as much so by our tempers and dispositions, as by the mutual hardships to which we were necessarily subjected by our condition as slaves.

Harriet Jacobs survives the rigors of nearly seven years hiding in an attic through the support of her family, which, much of the time, she can only hear. In *Uncle Tom's Cabin,* Stowe poses the Quaker community, led by its matriarch Rachel Halliday, as the center of values for her book. This idea of community was not simply her fiction; in *A New Home* Caroline Kirkland writes of her frontier experience:

In this newly-formed world, the earlier settler has a feeling of hostess-ship toward the new comer. I speak only of women—men look upon each one, newly arrived, merely as an additional business-automaton—a somebody more with whom to try the race of enterprize, i.e., money-making.

Even art might be created in and by a community; explaining the birth of a spiritual, an old former slave described a pre-Civil War religious meeting in these words:

I'd jump up dar and den and hollar and shout and sing and pat, and dey would all cotch de words and I'd sing it to some old shout song I'd heard 'em sing from Africa, and dey'd all take it up and keep at it, and keep a-addin' to it, and den it would be a spiritual.

In a way Emerson might have appreciated, this all-but-anonymous woman and her congregation were creating an art that as surely as Dickinson and Whitman turned from the "courtly muses of Europe" toward a distinctively American form and substance.

Individualism is a novel expression, to which a novel idea has given birth. Our fathers were only acquainted with *égoïsme* (selfishness). Selfishness is a passionate and exaggerated love of self, which leads a man to connect everything with himself and to prefer himself to everything in the world. Individualism is a mature and calm feeling, which disposes each member of the community to sever himself from the mass of his fellows and to draw apart with his family and his friends, so that after he has thus formed a little circle of his own, he willingly leaves society at large to itself. Selfishness originates in blind instinct; individualism proceeds from erroneous judgment more than from depraved feelings; it originates as much in deficiencies of mind as in perversity of heart.

Selfishness blights the germ of all virtue; individualism, at first, only saps the virtues of public life; but in the long run it attacks and destroys all others and is at length absorbed in downright selfishness. Selfishness is a vice as old as the world, which does not belong to one form of society more than to another; individualism is of democratic origin, and it threatens to spread in the same ratio as the equality of condition. . . .

As social conditions become more equal, the number of persons increases who, although they are neither rich nor powerful enough to exercise any great influence over their fellows, have nevertheless acquired or retained sufficient education and fortune to satisfy their own wants. They owe nothing to any man, they expect nothing from any man; they acquire the habit of always considering themselves as standing alone, and they are apt to imagine that their whole destiny is in their own hands.

Thus not only does democracy make every man forget his ancestors, but it hides his descendants and separates his contemporaries from him; it throws him back forever upon himself alone and threatens in the end to confine him entirely within the solitude of his own heart.

Alexis de Tocqueville, *Democracy in America,* Part II, 1840

Myths, Tales, and Legends

As it develops every society produces a series of images and narratives that in some sense become the common property of its members. These "myths" and "legends" serve a variety of functions in the society: they can offer an explanation of its physical and cultural origins; justify its hierarchies and other public arrangements; explain its beliefs, its rituals, its standards of morality and value; express its hopes as well as its fears. They present images of what the society regards as valued and deplored behavior, as in the stories of Miriam or of Cain and Abel in the Bible. They express what are often deep psychological and social conflicts, as in the story of Oedipus. They offer characters whom generations of readers can comfortably laugh at—as in "The Legend of Sleepy Hollow"—or can admire—as in "The Purloined Letter."

The origins of early tales, legends and images are a matter of considerable speculation, but they probably emerge from an interaction of historical events, individual creations, and what the society comes to feel is of value. No doubt, too, whatever the initial form of a story, as it gets told and retold it will gradually be developed, embellished, altered over time, take on the qualities of a legend, before it assumes a more or less definitive shape. Particularly in pre-literate cultures (i.e., cultures in which writing has not been developed), even well-developed myths seem to change over time as the conditions of life change. Divergent, indeed conflicting, myths can coexist within a culture, at least for a while. Different groups within a society construct and pass on stories they prefer. Ultimately the stories of the dominant group in a society themselves may come to dominate, though alternate myths often continue to live a kind of "underground" existence, offering a form of resistance to cultural extinction, especially among oppressed minorities.

The creation of myths is not a phenomenon of the dim past. They continue to be produced by accident and by design in any living society. "Rambo" is a contemporary example of a consciously created legendary character designed to express the unfulfilled desires of some American men. The strong, silent cowboy, familiar to us from the movies, was a similar invention of late-nineteenth-century male writers. The creators of such characters were, in effect, posing them as embodiments of what they saw as significant social values, and they are generally set against other figures who embody alternative values. Such was the case, for example, with Cooper's Leatherstocking, whose outlook on nature and human society contrasted sharply with that of the settlers. Whether over time such tales assume the proportions of true myths depends, in part, on how useful and significant they continue to be in the long-range cultural life of a society.

Myths, tales, and legends are not expected to be "realistic." That is, they do not depend for their impact on being "true to life" in any literal way. The Rambo version of combat is, of course, as removed from reality as are the tall tales of Paul Bunyan, or as Mike Fink's "Brags" printed below. The legendary exploits of the lone cowboy belied the harsh, boring conditions of his actual existence. Certain features of Leatherstocking's character and experiences are rooted in historic figures like David Crockett and Daniel Boone, but legends take on a life of their own, increasingly distant from whatever historic roots they had. The appeal of such tales is not that they did or could happen but that they express desires or fears or values held by some number of people in a culture; others, who do not share such emotions, may find them remote or even silly, as indeed, many have found Leatherstocking and Rambo and the lone cowhand.

Still, it is important to remember that the variety of myths, tales, and legends gathered here represent some of the differing cultures that were coming in the early nineteenth century to constitute American literature. Their differences tell us not only about the ideas and styles of individual authors but about the values and outlooks of these heterogeneous groups. The Ojibwa myths presented by Jane Johnston Schoolcraft and the tale about Mike Fink trying to scare Mrs. Davy Crockett relate combats between larger-than-life figures; but the conflicts embodied diverse world-views and societies, and the stories served distinct functions in their cultures. Even when members of the same society, like Cooper and Sedgwick, write about the same subject—the relationships of Indians and whites—their views and images can be significantly distinct and, of course, quite at variance with those of the Indians themselves. It is important to be aware of such differences, their sources, and their significance.

Africans and African-Americans, both slave and free, maintained a highly developed oral culture throughout the nineteenth century. We know, for example, that animal tales were told during slavery. But the tales of the contest of wits between black men and white men first appear in collections only in the twentieth century. Whether such stories were told *among* slaves, we do not know; if they were, it is not clear in what forms they appeared. And whether former slaves withheld these stories for fifty years after Emancipation, or early collectors intent on animal stories failed to seek them out, or they were fully developed later is not clear. In any case, the tales as they were later collected were not reproductions of older models; rather, they were part of an ongoing, living culture, shaped in response to the exigencies of African-American life in the periods after Emancipation.

We have therefore chosen to include African-American tales in the second volume of this anthology. As Susan Blake points out in her headnote, many of these tales, and certainly the oral tradition they represent, have roots in the slave period. But it would falsify them, and the oral tradition as it existed in the early nineteenth century, to suppose that the tales as we have them are precisely those that were being told among African-Americans in this period. Still, readers may wish to compare the tales printed in Volume 2 with those of other oral traditions available here.

In addition, a part of the African-American oral tradition is represented by the Spirituals, or "sorrow songs," printed later in this volume.

No hard-and-fast line divides the fictions gathered in this section and those presented under The Flowering of Narrative. These are, on the whole, earlier and—when they are not themselves myths or legends—more closely related to those forms. Most of the characters here are "unrealistic" and in a sense one-dimensional; they are not presented as growing and changing nor, on the whole, interacting with other richly developed characters. On the other hand, they often express deep and disturbing psychological states—as in Poe's tales—and powerful social conflicts—sometimes screened by humor, as in Washington Irving. Similarly, we do not turn to these narratives for "realistic" pictures of early nineteenth-century America. Yet read with imagination, they not only reflect the tensions of that world but in certain ways the fantasies of our own.

Paul Lauter
Trinity College

Jane Johnston Schoolcraft (Ojibwa) 1800–1841

Jane Johnston Schoolcraft (Bame-wa-was-ge-zhik-a-quay) was born in 1800 at Sault Ste. Marie, the daughter of John Johnston, an Irish fur trader, and Ozha-guscoday-way-quay (Susan) Johnston, daughter of the Chippewa chief Waub Ojeeg. Johnston met Ozha-guscoday-way-quay when he ran a trading post on Lake Superior near La Pointe, Wisconsin; after their marriage, the pair moved to the Sault. Jane, like her seven brothers and sisters, received her early education at home. She learned literature, history, and the classics from her father and read extensively in the large family library. In addition, Jane and the other children were educated in Ojibwa lore by their mother. They learned traditions, customs, and legends of their people and were well versed in the exploits of their grandfather, Waub Ojeeg, and great-grandfather, Ma Mongazida. Jane and the others were also taught the Ojibwa language. The young woman's well-rounded education was supplemented by travel with her father to Detroit, Quebec, and Montreal. Because there were no schools at Sault Ste. Marie at the time, Johnston took his daughter to Ireland in 1809 to complete her formal education.

In 1823 Jane Johnston married Henry Rowe Schoolcraft, the famous explorer, writer, and scholar. Schoolcraft's major interest was the American Indian, about whom he wrote over twenty volumes and hundreds of articles. The young Schoolcraft had come to the Sault in 1822 as Indian agent for the tribes living in the northern sections of Michigan, Wisconsin, and Minnesota. It was here, with the help of Jane and her family, that he began his lifelong study of Indian languages, customs, and traditions. Jane was Schoolcraft's research assistant until her death in 1841; she interpreted descriptions and accounts from native sources and helped him in his studies of the Ojibwa language.

In December, 1826, the Schoolcrafts began a reading society at the frontier outpost to foster the literary interests of the local inhabitants during the long winter. As an adjunct to this activity, Henry Schoolcraft with his wife's assistance began a manuscript magazine called "The Literary Voyager or Muzzenyegun." The magazine, which circulated in Detroit and New York as well as in Sault Ste. Marie, contained Ojibwa history, legends, and lore, as well as biographies of and speeches by contemporary Chippewas. Linguistic studies also appeared, as did essays on Ojibwa traits and customs. The magazine contained information on other Indian groups and on issues affecting all Indians, such as temperance. Finally, the "Literary Voyager" carried original poems and essays, many of which were written by Jane Schoolcraft, using the pen names Rosa and Leelinau.

For the most part, her style and diction are that of contemporary writers in the East. She does at times, however, experiment with rhyme and meter. One of Schoolcraft's main values as a writer is her ability to use her considerable literary skills in English to depict with accuracy and empathy the traditional lore of the Ojibwa.

James W. Parins
University of Arkansas at Little Rock

PRIMARY WORKS

"Character of Aboriginal Historical Tradition"; "To Sisters on a Walk in the Garden, After a Shower"; "Resignation"; "The Origin of the Robin—An Oral Allegory"; "Moowis, the Indian Coquette: A Chippewa Legend"; "Mishosha, or the Magician and His Daughters: A Chippewa Tale or Legend"; "Lines Written Under Severe Pain and Sickness"; "Origin of the Miscodeed or the Maid of Taquimenon"; "Otagamiad"; "Invocation to My Maternal Grandfather on Hearing His Descent from Chippewa Ancestors Misrepresented"; "To My Ever Beloved and Lamented Son William Henry"; "Say Dearest Friend, When Light Your Bark"; "Sonnet," 1827.

Mishosha, or the Magician and His Daughters

A Chippewa Tale or Legend[1]

In an early age of the world, when there were fewer inhabitants in the earth than there now are, there lived an Indian, who had a wife and two children, in a remote situation. Buried in the solitude of the forest, it was not often that he saw any one, out of the circle of his own family. Such a situation seemed favorable for his pursuits; and his life passed on in uninterrupted happiness, till he discovered a wanton disposition in his wife.

This woman secretly cherished a passion for a young man whom she accidentally met in the woods, and she lost no opportunity of courting his approaches. She even planned the death of her husband, who, she justly concluded, would put her to death, should he discover her infidelity. But this design was frustrated by the alertness of the husband, who having cause to suspect her, determined to watch narrowly, to ascertain the truth, before he should come to a determination how to act. He followed her silently one day, at a distance, and hid himself behind a tree. He soon beheld a tall, handsome man approach his wife, and lead her away.

He was now convinced of her crime, and thought of killing her, the moment she returned. In the meantime he went home, and pondered on his situation. At last he came to the determination of leaving her forever, thinking that her own conscience would in the end, punish her sufficiently; and relying on her maternal feelings, to take care of the two boys, whom he determined to leave behind.

When the wife returned, she was disappointed in not finding her husband, having concerted a plan to dispatch him. When she saw that day after day passed, and he did not return she at last guessed the true cause of his absence. She then returned to her paramour, leaving the two helpless boys behind, telling them that she was going a short distance, and would return; but determined never to see them more.

The children thus abandoned, soon made way with the food that was left in the lodge, and were compelled to quit it, in search of more. The eldest boy possessed much intrepidity, as well as great tenderness for his little brother, frequently carrying him when he became weary, and gathering all the wild fruit he saw. Thus they went deeper into the forest, soon losing all traces of their former habitation, till they were completely lost in the labyrinths of the wilderness.

The elder boy fortunately had a knife, with which he made a bow and arrows, and was thus enabled to kill a few birds for himself and brother. In this way they lived some time, still pressing on, they knew not whither. At last they saw an opening through the woods, and were shortly after delighted to find themselves on the borders of a broad lake. Here the elder boy busied himself in picking the seed pods of

[1]The first part of this story (through the episode of the great fish) appeared in the January, 1827, issue of *The Literary Voyager,* a manuscript magazine circulated by Henry Rowe Schoolcraft at Sault Ste. Marie, Michigan, in 1826 and 1827. According to Philip P. Mason, who edited the *Voyager* in 1962, Schoolcraft apparently planned to publish the tale in two installments. The entire tale appeared in Schoolcraft's *Algic Researches* (1839). Mason included the last half of the story in his edition, from which this version is reprinted. See his *The Literary Voyager or Muzzenyegun* (Lansing: Michigan State UP, 1962), 64–71.

the wild rose. In the meanwhile the younger, amused himself by shooting some arrows into the sand, one of which happened to fall into the lake. The elder brother, not willing to lose his time in making another, waded into the water to reach it. Just as he was about to grasp the arrow, a canoe passed by him with the rapidity of lightning. An old man, sitting in the centre, seized the affrighted youth, and placed him in the canoe. In vain the boy addressed him. "My grandfather" (a term of respect for old people) "pray take my little brother also. Alone, I cannot go with you; he will starve if I leave him." The old magician (for such was his real character) laughed at him. Then giving his canoe a slap, and commanding it to go, it glided through the water with inconceivable swiftness. In a few minutes they reached the habitation of Mishosha, standing on an island in the centre of the lake. Here he lived, with his two daughters, the terror of all the surrounding country.

Leading the young man up to the lodge "Here my eldest daughter," said he, "I have brought a young man who shall become your husband." The youth saw surprize depicted in the countenance of the daughter, but she made no reply, seeming thereby to acquiesce in the commands of her father. In the evening he overheard the daughters in conversation. "There again!" said the elder daughter, "our father has brought another victim, under the pretence of giving me a husband. When will his enmity to the human race cease; or when shall we be spared witnessing such scenes of vice and wickedness, as we are daily compelled to behold."

When the old magician was asleep, the youth told the elder daughter, how he had been carried off, and compelled to leave his helpless brother on the shore. She told him to get up and take her father's canoe, and using the charm he had observed, it would carry him quickly to his brother. That he could carry him food, prepare a lodge for him, and return by morning. He did in every thing as he had been directed, and after providing for the subsistence of his brother, told him that in a short time he should come for him. Then returning to the enchanted island, resumed his place in the lodge before the magician awoke. Once during the night Mishosha awoke, and not seeing his son in law, asked his eldest daughter what had become of him. She replied that he had merely stepped out, and would be back soon. This satisfied him. In the morning, finding the young man in the lodge, his suspicions were completely lulled. "I see, my daughter, you have told me the truth."

As soon as the sun rose, Mishosha thus addressed the young man. "Come, my son, I have a mind to gather gulls eggs. I am acquainted with an island where there are great quantities; and I wish your aid in gathering them." The young man, saw no reasonable excuse, and getting into the canoe, the magician gave it a slap, and bidding it go, in an instant they were at the island. They found the shore covered with gulls eggs, and the island surrounded with birds of this kind. "Go, my son," said the old man, "and gather them while I remain in the canoe." But the young man was no sooner ashore than Mishosha pushed his canoe a little from land and exclaimed: "Listen ye gulls! you have long expected something from me. I now give you an offering. Fly down, and devour him." Then striking his canoe, left the young man to his fate.

The birds immediately came in clouds around their victim, darkening all the air with their numbers. But the youth, seizing the first that came near him, and drawing his knife, cut off its head, and immediately skinning the bird, hung the feathers as a trophy on his breast. "Thus," he exclaimed, "will I treat every one of you who approaches me. Forbear, therefore, and listen to my words. It is not for you to eat human food. You have been given by the Great Spirit as food for man. Neither is it in the power of that old magician to do you any good. Take me on your beaks and carry me to his lodge, and you shall see that I am not ungrateful."

The gulls obeyed, collecting in a cloud for him to rest upon, and quickly flew to the lodge, where they arrived before the magician. The daughters were surprized at his return, but Mishosha conducted as if nothing extraordinary had taken place.

On the following day he again addressed the youth. "Come, my son," said he, "I will take you to an island covered with the most beautiful pebbles, looking like silver. I wish you to assist me in gathering some of them. They will make handsome ornaments, and are possessed of great virtues." Entering the canoe, the magician made use of his charm, and they were carried, in a few moments, to a solitary bay in an island, where there was a smooth sandy beach. The young man went ashore as usual. "A little further, a little further," cried the old man, "upon that rock you will get some finer ones." Then pushing his canoe from land, "Come thou great king of fishes," cried he, "you have long expected an offering from me. Come, and eat the stranger I have put ashore on your island." So saying, he commanded his canoe to return, and was soon out of sight. Immediately a monstrous fish shoved his long snout from the water, moving partially on the beach, and opening wide his jaws to receive his victim.

"When" exclaimed the young man, drawing his knife, and placing himself in a threatening attitude, "when did you ever taste human food. Have a care of yourself. You were given by the Great Spirit to man, and if you, or any of your tribes, taste human flesh, you will fall sick and die. Listen not to the words of that wicked old man, but carry me back to his island, in return for which, I shall present you a piece of red cloth."

The fish complied, raising his back out of water to allow the young man to get on. Then taking his way through the lake, landed his charge safely at the island, before the return of the magician.

The daughters were still more surprized to see him thus escaped a second time, from the arts of their father. But the old man maintained his taciturnity. He could not, however, help saying to himself, "What manner of boy is this, who ever escapes from my power. His spirit shall not however save him. I will entrap him tomorrow. Ha! ha! ha!"

Next day the magician addressed the young man as follows: "Come, my son," said he, "you must go with me to procure some young eagles. I wish to tame them. I have discovered an island where they are in great abundance." When they had reached the island, Mishosha led him inland until they came to the foot of a tall pine, upon which the nests were. "Now, my son," said he, "climb up this tree and bring down the birds." The young man obeyed. When he had with great difficulty got near the nest, "Now," exclaimed the magician, addressing the tree, "stretch yourself up and be very tall." The tree rose up at the command. "Listen, ye eagles," continued the old man, "you have long expected a gift from me. I now present you this boy, who has had the presumption to molest your young. Stretch forth your claws and seize him." So saying he left the young man to his fate, and returned.

But the intrepid youth drawing his knife, and cutting off the head of the first eagle that menaced him, raised his voice and exclaimed, "Thus will I deal with all who come near me. What right have you, ye ravenous birds, who were made to feed on beasts, to eat human flesh? Is it because that cowardly old canoe-man has bid you do so? He is an old woman. He can neither do you good nor harm. See, I have already slain one of your number. Respect my bravery, and carry me back that I may show you how I shall treat you."

The eagles, pleased with his spirit, assented, and clustering thick around him formed a seat with their backs, and flew toward the enchanted island. As they crossed the water they passed over the magician, lying half asleep in his canoe.

The return of the young man was hailed with joy by the daughters, who now plainly saw that he was under the guidance of a strong spirit. But the ire of the old man was excited, although he kept his temper under subjection. He taxed his wits for some new mode of ridding himself of the youth, who had so successfully baffled his skill. He next invited him to go a hunting.

Taking his canoe, they proceeded to an island and built a lodge to shelter themselves during the night. In the mean while the magician caused a deep fall of snow, with a storm of wind and severe cold. According to custom, the young man pulled off his moccasins and leggings and hung them before the fire to dry. After he had gone to sleep the magician, watching his opportunity, got up, and taking one moccasin and one legging, threw them into the fire. He then went to sleep. In the morning, stretching himself as he arose and uttering an exclamation of surprize, "My son," said he, "what has become of your moccasin and legging? I believe this is the moon in which fire attracts, and I fear they have been drawn in." The young man suspected the true cause of his loss, and rightly attributed it to a design of the magician to freeze him to death on the march. But he maintained the strictest silence, and drawing his conaus[2] over his head thus communed with himself: "I have full faith in the Manito[3] who has preserved me thus far, I do not fear that he will forsake me in this cruel emergency. Great is his power, and I invoke it now that he may enable me to prevail over this wicked enemy of mankind."

He then drew on the remaining moccasin and legging, and taking a dead coal from the fireplace, invoked his spirit to give it efficacy, and blackened his foot and leg as far as the lost garment usually reached. He then got up and announced himself ready for the march. In vain Mishosha led him through snows and over morasses, hoping to see the lad sink at every moment. But in this he was disappointed, and for the first time they returned home together.

Taking courage from this success, the young man now determined to try his own power, having previously consulted with the daughters. They all agreed that the life the old man led was detestable, and that whoever would rid the world of him, would entitle himself to the thanks of the human race.

On the following day the young man thus addressed his hoary captor. "My grandfather, I have often gone with you on perilous excursions and never murmured. I must now request that you will accompany me. I wish to visit my little brother, and to bring him home with me." They accordingly went on a visit to the main land, and found the little lad in the spot where he had been left. After taking him into the canoe, the young man again addressed the magician: "My grandfather, will you go and

[2]The meaning of this word is unknown. It may result from a misreading of Schoolcraft's manuscript.

[3]Spirit, or Great Spirit.

cut me a few of those red willows on the bank, I wish to prepare some smoking mixture." "Certainly, my son," replied the old man, "what you wish is not very hard. Ha, ha, ha! do you think me too old to get up there?" No sooner was Mishosha ashore, than the young man, placing himself in the proper position struck the canoe with his hand, and pronouncing the charm, N'CHIMAUN POLL, the canoe immediately flew through the water on its return to the island. It was evening when the two brothers arrived, and carried the canoe ashore. But the elder daughter informed the young man that unless he sat up and watched the canoe, and kept his hand upon it, such was the power of their father, it would slip off and return to him. Panigwun watched faithfully till near the dawn of day, when he could no longer resist the drowsiness which oppressed him, and fell into a short doze. In the meantime the canoe slipped off and sought its master, who soon returned in high glee. "Ha, ha, ha! my son," said he; "you thought to play me a trick. It was very clever. But you see I am too old for you."

A short time after, the young [man] again addressed the magician. "My grandfather, I wish to try my skill in hunting. It is said there is plenty of game on an island not far off, and I have to request that you will take me there in your canoe." They accordingly went to the island and spent the day in hunting. Night coming on they put up a temporary lodge. When the magician had sunk into a profound sleep, the young man got up, and taking one of Mishosha's leggings and moccasins from the place where they hung, threw them into the fire, thus retaliating the artifice before played upon himself. He had discovered that the foot and leg were the only vulnerable parts on the magician's body. Having committed these articles to the fire, he besought his Manito that he would raise a great storm of snow, wind, and hail, and then laid himself down beside the old man. Consternation was depicted on the countenance of the latter, when he awoke in the morning and found his moccasin and legging missing. "I believe, my grandfather," said the young man, "that this is the moon in which fire attracts, and I fear your foot and leg garments have been drawn in." Then rising and bidding the old man follow him, he began the morning's hunt, frequently turning to see how Mishosha kept up. He saw him faltering at every step, and almost benumbed with cold, but encouraged him to follow, saying, we shall soon get through and reach the shore; although he took pains, at the same time, to lead him in round-about ways, so as to let the frost take complete effect. At length the old man reached the brink of the island where the woods are succeeded by a border of smooth sand. But he could go no farther; his legs became stiff and refused motion, and he found himself fixed to the spot. But he still kept stretching out his arms and swinging his body to and fro. Every moment he found the numbness creeping higher. He felt his legs growing downward like roots, the feathers of his head turned to leaves, and in a few seconds he stood a tall and stiff sycamore, leaning toward the water.

Panigwun leaped into the canoe, and pronounced the charm, was soon transported to the island, where he related his victory to the daughters. They applauded the deed, agreed to put on mortal shapes, become wives to the two young men, and for ever quit the enchanted island. And passing immediately over to the main land, they lived lives of happiness and peace.

1827/1839

The Forsaken Brother

A Chippewa Tale[1]

It was a fine summer evening; the sun was scarcely an hour high,—its departing rays beamed through the foliage of the tall, stately elms, that skirted the little green knoll, on which a solitary Indian lodge stood. The deep silence that reigned in this sequest[er]ed and romantic spot, seemed to most of the inmates of that lonely hut, like the long sleep of death, that was now evidently fast sealing the eyes of the head of his poor family. His low breathing was answered by the sighs of his disconsolate wife and their children. Two of the latter were almost grown up, one was yet a mere child. These were the only human beings near the dying man. The door of the lodge was thrown open to admit the refreshing breeze of the lake, on the banks of which it stood; and as the cool air fanned the head of the poor man, he felt a momentary return of strength, and raising himself a little, he thus addressed his weeping family. "I leave you—thou, who hast been my partner in life, but you will not stay long to suffer in this world. But oh! my children, my poor children! you have just commenced life, and mark me, unkindness, and ingratitude, and every wickedness is in the scene before you. I left my kindred and my tribe, because I found what I have just warned you of. I have contented myself with the company of your mother and yourselves, for many years, and you will find my motives for separating from the haunts of men, were solicitude and anxiety to preserve you from the bad examples you would inevitably have followed. But I shall die content, if you, my children promise me, to cherish each other, and on no account to forsake your youngest brother, of him I give you both particular charge." The man became exhausted, and taking a hand of each of his eldest children, he continued—"My daughter! never forsake your little brother. My son, never forsake your little brother." "Never, never!" they both exclaimed. "Never—never!" repeated the father and expired.

The poor man died happy, because he thought his commands would be obeyed. The sun sank below the trees, and left a golden sky behind, which the family were wont to admire, but no one heeded it now. The lodge that was so still an hour before, was now filled with low and unavailing lamentations. Time wore heavily away—five long moons had passed and the sixth was nearly full, when the mother also died. In her last moments she pressed the fulfilment of their promise to their departed father. They readily renewed their promise, because they were yet free from any selfish motive. The winter passed away, and the beauties of spring cheered the drooping spirits of the bereft little family. The girl, being the eldest, dictated to her brothers, and seemed to feel a tender and sisterly affection for the youngest, who was rather sickly and delicate. The other boy soon showed symptoms of restlessness, and addressed the sister as follows. "My sister, are we always to live as if there were no other human

[1]Reprinted from Mason's edition of *The Literary Voyager or Muzzenyegun.* The tale first appeared in the February 13, 1827, issue of the *Voyager,* and Schoolcraft reprinted it in *Algic Researches* (1839) and *Historical and Statistical Information Respecting the History, Conditions and Prospects of the Indian Tribes of the United States* (1853) as well as in *Myth of Hiawatha* (1856) and *The Indian Fairy Book* (1856).

beings in the world. Must I deprive myself the pleasure of associating with my own kind? I shall seek the villages of men; I have determined, and you cannot prevent me." The girl replied, "My brother, I do not say no, to what you desire. We were not prohibited, the society of our fellow mortals, but we were told to cherish each other, and that we should not [do] nothing independent of each other—that neither pleasure nor pain ought ever to separate us, particularly from our helpless brother. If we follow our separate gratifications, it will surely make us forget *him* whom we are alike bound to support." The young man made no answer, but taking his bow and arrows left the lodge, and never returned.

Many moons had come and gone, after the young man's departure, and still the girl administered to the wants of her younger brother. At length, however, she began to be weary of her solitude, and of her charge. Years, which added to her strength and capability of directing the affairs of the household, also brought with them the desire of society, and made her solitude irksome. But in meditating a change of life, she thought only for herself, and cruelly sought to abandon her little brother, as her elder brother had done before.

One day after she had collected all the provisions she had set apart for emergencies, and brought a quantity of wood to the door, she said to her brother. "My brother, you must not stray far from the lodge. I am going to seek our brother: I shall soon be back." Then taking her bundle, she set off, in search of habitations. She soon found them, and was so much taken up with the pleasures and amusements of society, that all affection for her brother was obliterated. She accepted a proposal of marriage, and after that, never more thought of the helpless relative she had abandoned.

In the meantime the elder brother had also married, and settled on the shores of the same lake, which contained the bones of his parents, and the abode of his forsaken brother.

As soon as the little boy had eaten all the food left by his sister, he was obliged to pick berries and dig up roots. Winter came on, and the poor child was exposed to all its rigors. He was obliged to quit the lodge in search of food, without a shelter. Sometimes he passed the night in the clefts of old trees, and ate the refuse meats of the wolves. The latter soon became his only resource, and he became so fearless of these animals, that he would sit close to them whilst they devoured their prey, and the animals themselves seemed to pity his condition, and would always leave something. Thus he lived, as it were, on the bounty of fierce wolves until spring. As soon as the lake was free from ice, he followed his new found friends and companions to the shore. It happened his brother was fishing in his canoe in the lake, a considerable distance out, when he thought he heard the cry of a child, and wondered how any could exist on so bleak a part of the shore. He listened again more attentively, and distinctly heard the cry repeated. He made for shore as quick as possible, and as he approached land, discovered and recognized his little brother, and heard him singing in a plaintive voice—

Neesya, neesya, shyegwuh gushuh!
Ween ne myeengunish!
ne myeengunish!
My brother, my brother,
I am now turning into a Wolf!—
I am turning into a Wolf.

At the termination of his song he howled like a Wolf, and the young man was still more astonished when, on getting nearer shore, he perceived his poor brother half turned into that animal. He however, leapt on shore and strove to catch him in his arms, and soothingly said—"My brother, my brother, come to me." But the boy eluded his grasp, and fled, still singing as he fled—"I am turning into a Wolf—I am turning into a wolf," and howling in the intervals.

The elder brother, conscience struck, and feeling his brotherly affection returning with redoubled force, exclaimed in great anguish, "My brother, my brother, come to me." But the nearer he approached the child, the more rapidly his transformation went on, until he changed into a perfect wolf,—still singing and howling, and naming his brother and sister alternately in his song, as he fled into the woods, until his change was complete. At last he said. "I am a wolf," and bounded out of sight.

The young man felt the bitterness of remorse all his days, and the sister, when she heard of the fate of the little boy whom she had so cruelly left, and whom both she and her brother had solemnly promised to foster and protect, wept bitterly; and never ceased to mourn until she died.

1827/1839

Tales from the Hispanic Southwest

In his pioneering *Cuentos Españoles de Colorado y de Nuevo México (Spanish Tales from Colorado and New Mexico),* 1977, Professor Juan B. Rael points out that the majority of the 500 tales he collected between 1930–40 "represent a part of the cultural heritage that the first settlers of this former Spanish frontier brought with them, a heritage which their descendants have faithfully preserved through more than three centuries." The *cuentos,* or folktales, that Rael and his predecessor and teacher Aurelio M. Espinosa collected represent a huge repository of oral narratives that are old world in type-origin, but often adapted to the southwestern geographic and social ecology in which they were performed. The stories Hispanics related included morality tales alongside tales of picaresque rogues, tales of enchantment filled with witches, ghosts, enchanted princesses and tales in which animals with the gift of speech and wisdom reminded humans of their filial and social responsibilities.

"La comadre Sebastiana" (Doña Sebastiana) and "Los tres hermanos" (The Three Brothers) included here represent *cuentos morales* (morality tales) the function of which is to instill a complex religio-social sensibility in young listeners. There are scores of tales like "Los tres hermanos" in which characters who fail to consider the needs of the thirsty and hungry, the unsheltered, the old are justly served with moral ruin, death, and perhaps worst of all, eternal damnation. In "La comadre Sebastiana" death is personified, actually given full status as a character who functions to integrate the reality and certainty of death into everyday experience. Death is not imaged as the terrorizing grim reaper, but as a familial figure, *una comadre* or godparent, who maintains filial ties with an individual over a lifetime. Notice also that the *cuento* contains within its orthodox Christian configuration a space in which the social injustices Christianity has instituted over the centuries are exposed. For a poor man to openly chastise both Jesus and the Virgin Mary for failing to be equitable comprises a stunning class-conscious critique of Christian hypocrisy and the

Church's complicity with the rich. In this particular story, the woodcutter is rewarded for his charity with the gift of healing. As a *curandero* or folkhealer he assumes a revered position in traditional Chicano society, a position he must not abuse for material gain. When he does, the results are grave.

If these stories appear somewhat stiff in this textual edition it is because the intimate environment in which they were performed is lost in print. *Cuento* telling was a special event in which families, relatives, friends gathered after a long day's work, ate together, drank a few beers perhaps while the children roasted piñon nuts, and then listened with rapt attention as an uncle, ranch hand, or grandmother told story after story in nuanced tone, rich hand gestures, suspense-building pauses and meaningful glances at the children. The storytelling session often ended late, with the children clamoring for one more *cuento* ("uno más, tio, no más uno"/"one more, uncle, just one more") while the adults pulled them away and made for home. There would be other days and more tales another time.

However much the oral storytelling tradition has declined in recent decades, it remains a crucial narrative superstructure for numerous contemporary Chicano writers. In fact, New Mexico's preeminent Chicano novelist Rudolfo A. Anaya's *Bless Me, Ultima, Heart of Aztlan,* and numerous short stories resonate with the narrative apparatus that functions in the *cuento* tradition. One might say that the orally performed *cuento* has rather naturally imbricated itself upon the textual narratives writers like Anaya are creating. "Naturally," because Anaya was one of those children clamoring for one more *cuento.* The informality, verbal intimacy, even the melodramatic delight one discovers in Anaya and other Chicano writers seem a continuation of the tale telling strategies of the *cuento* performance.

Genaro M. Padilla
University of California at Berkeley

PRIMARY WORK

José Griego y Maestas, *Cuentos: Tales from the Hispanic Southwest,* retold in English by Rudolfo A. Anaya, 1980.

La comadre Sebastiana / Doña Sebastiana

Once there was a poor man who earned his living cutting wood in the common land of the land grant and selling it in the village. When he sold his wood his family ate well, when he couldn't sell it his family went hungry. He lived that way for a long time, but one day he was tempted by hunger and he decided to swipe one of his wife's setting hens.

He waited until everyone was asleep and then stole into the chicken coop, took a chicken and killed it. Then he stealthily made his way into the mountains where he planned to indulge himself. He made a big fire and put the chicken on a spit to roast. He was flavoring the chicken with a few spices and enjoying the drippings when he heard someone approach his camp.

God help me! he thought. Even here I can't be left alone to enjoy myself! Well, whoever it is, I'm not going to invite them to eat!

"How do you do, my friend," said the stranger as he approached the camp. The stranger's noble stature made the woodcutter cautious.

"Buenas noches," the woodcutter responded. "Who are you?"

"I am the Lord," the stranger answered. "Will you invite me to eat with you?"

The woodcutter looked at the small chicken and thought awhile. "No," he finally said, "I don't think I'll invite you to share my meal, and I'll tell you why. I think you neglect the poor. You give everything to the rich and so little to the poor. You don't treat us equally."

And so the woodcutter kept the chicken for himself, and the Lord went away saddened. The woodcutter was satisfied, but shortly he heard another person approaching.

"Good evening, my friend," said the woman as she drew near.

"Buenas noches, señora," the woodcutter replied. "And who might you be?"

"I am the Virgin Mary," the woman answered. "Will you share your food with me?"

The woodcutter scratched his beard, looked again at the small chicken and finally said, "No, I am not going to share my food with you, and I'll tell you why. I think your Son neglects the poor. Since you are the mother of God, you should intercede for us so He would make us all equal. Either we should all be rich, or we should all be poor. The way it is now, He makes some very rich and some very poor, and unfortunately I am one of the poor ones. For that reason I am not going to share my chicken with you."

So the Virgin Mary left, but it wasn't long before the woodcutter heard someone else approach. This time it was Doña Sebastiana, Death herself, who approached the woodcutter's fire.

"How goes it, friend?" Doña Sebastiana asked.

"Buenas noches," the woodcutter answered, trembling at the sight of the old hag in front of him. "Who are you?" he asked.

"I am Death," Doña Sebastiana answered as she slowly got down from her cart. "Will you share your meal with me?"

"I never realized Death was so thin!" the woodcutter said as he looked at the skeleton in front of him. "Of course you are welcome to share my food, and I'll tell you why. You do things very well. You don't play favorites with the wealthy because of their money, not the beautiful because of their beauty, nor do you play favorites with the ugly or the old or the young. No, you treat us all equally. Sit down and share my meal."

After they had finished eating the roasted chicken Doña Sebastiana was very pleased, so she told the woodcutter to ask for any favor he wished and it would be granted.

"Señora," the woodcutter said in his most humble voice, "I can't ask for a favor. If you wish to grant me one, then grant me what you will."

"Very well," Death answered, "I am going to grant you the power to be a healer, a *curandero.* You shall be able to cure all kinds of sickness. However, I leave you with one commandment: When you are asked to cure a sick person and you go to that patient's bed and see me standing at the head of the bed, don't cure that person regardless of what his relatives will pay or promise you. I warn you, if I am there, don't cure that person! That person has no remedy but to die. He has been called by God.

"But if you see me at the patient's feet, then go ahead and cure him. Use water or earth or curing powders, and the patient will get well. But remember, if you see me at the head of the bed, don't dare to attempt a cure, no matter what you are promised!"

So the curandero practiced his craft for many years and he cured many people and became famous for his powers. But one day the richest man in the region became ill and offered the curandero a fortune for a cure, and so the healer broke the commandment of Doña Sebastiana.

When the curandero arrived at the rich man's home he saw Doña Sebastiana seated at the head of the bed where the sick man lay. The curandero immediately grabbed her and wrestled her back and forth until she was so dizzy that he was able to move her to the foot of the bed. In that way Death was overpowered, and the curandero then cured the rich man.

But when the curandero was returning home Death met him on the road and reminded him that he had broken the one commandment he had promised not to break when she had given him the power to cure sickness.

"I warned you *never* to cure a sick person if I was at the head of his bed," Doña Sebastiana said angrily. "Now you must come with me."

She took the curandero to a dark room and showed him two candles. One candle had burned low and was flickering as if ready to go out, the other was a tall candle burning brightly.

"You have made a grave mistake," Death told the curandero. "Once you were like the tall candle and the sick man was like the short candle. But now you are the small candle and the man you cured is the tall one."

At that moment the flame of the short candle went out, and the curandero's soul was added to Doña Sebastiana's cart as it slowly made its way into eternity.

1980

Los tres hermanos / The Three Brothers

Once upon a time there lived an old couple who had three sons. When the eldest came of age, he asked his parents for permission to go where he could make his livelihood. His parents agreed and gave him their benediction and supplied him with provisions for his trip.

"May God bless you and keep you away from all evil," they said. "Be kind to old people and remember your parents."

So the young man set out on his journey. On the road he met a woman who asked him where he was going. He told her he was looking for work.

"You are a good son," she said. Then, as the day was very hot, she asked him for water, but he lied to her and told her he had no water.

"Very well," she said, "follow this road to the next city. There you will find a man who can help you. He is my son."

So he followed the road until he came to a simple but pleasing city. He knocked at the door where the woman had directed him and was received by the woman's son. The youth explained that he was looking for work.

"Very well," said the man, "in order to begin your work, go and catch that donkey and saddle him. I want you to deliver a letter to my mother. Take my dog with you. Wherever he stops you will know it is safe and you can rest there. But if he doesn't want to stop you should not stop there either."

So the boy mounted the donkey and started out. On the road he came upon a magnificent and dazzling city where there was every kind of entertainment. Everyone was singing and dancing or playing musical instruments. The youth wanted to stop awhile and join the wild entertainment of that tempting city, but the dog wouldn't stop there. They continued until they came to a river of blood. This strange sight filled the youth with dread and he would not cross the river. He returned and gave the letter back to the man.

"I didn't finish the errand," he explained. "I came upon a river of blood and I was afraid to cross it."

"Very well, I will pay you for your trouble anyway," the man answered. "What do you want as a reward for trying? A simple thanks which says, 'God repay your kindness,' or a bagful of money?"

"I'll take the money," replied the youth.

And as soon as he was paid he went straight to the beguiling city to indulge in its delights. He forgot all about his parents and never once thought of sharing his money with them.

* * *

In time the second son was eager to be on his own so he asked his parents for their blessing so that he might go out and make his way in life.

The old couple replied, "But what if what happened to your brother happens to you? He evidently had good luck, but he has forgotten us and never sent us a nickel."

He assured them he wouldn't forget them, so they blessed him and he went forth. He met the same gracious woman his brother had met on the road and, like his brother, he didn't share his water or food with her. Nevertheless she told him where he could find work. And so, like his brother before him, he arrived at the city and called at the door. The man came out, greeted him and offered him the same errand.

"Take the donkey and go deliver this letter," he said. "Take my small dog with you and wherever he stops you can rest, but if he doesn't stop you should not stop."

The second young man continued his journey, and like his brother before him he saw the city of many pleasures, and he too arrived at the river of blood, but wouldn't cross it. He returned to the house of the man and told him he had not delivered the letter because he had come to a river of blood which frightened him.

"Very well," the man replied, "now what do you want as your reward? A 'God repay your kindness' or a bagful of money?"

"The bagful of money," the second brother quickly replied, and from there he went immediately to the beautiful city where everyone sang, danced and played, and he forgot all about his parents.

* * *

Soon after, the youngest son asked for his parents' benediction so he could go out and look for work. But they cried and refused to allow him to go because they were afraid he might end up like his brothers. He pleaded with them until at last they gave him their blessing and their meager supply of bread and water for his journey.

The next day as he walked down the road he met the same woman, and she asked him where he was going. He told her he was looking for work in order to help his parents.

"In the city up the road you can work for my son," she said. Then she added, "I am hungry. Do you have bread or water?"

"Yes," he answered and he shared with her his loaf of bread and water. After eating he said to her, "Take what is left, *señora.*"

"No," she replied, "I cannot. You have a long way to walk yet."

"But I am a man and my parents taught me to share what I have with those who are in need. You are a woman and need the food."

The woman thanked him, took the food and the water and disappeared. The boy had walked only a short distance when he felt his pack grow heavy. He checked it and to his surprise it was replenished with food and water. He was mystified at what had happened, and he wondered if the woman was a witch or a saint.

He continued until he came to the city where he found the house the woman had described. He knocked at the door and a man came out and asked him what he wanted.

"I am looking for work," the boy replied.

"Very well," the man said, "I have an errand for you to do: Deliver a letter to my mother. Go catch that donkey so you can begin your journey, and take my little dog with you. He is a good companion. Wherever he stops you can stop to rest, but if he doesn't stop then you must continue."

The boy followed the road until he arrived at the beautiful and gay city where everyone sang, played, danced and laughed. He was tempted to stop and look for his two lost brothers, but the little dog wouldn't stop so he went on. Soon he arrived at the river of blood and he stopped; for a few minutes he didn't know what to do, then he remembered his parents' blessing.

"With the blessing of my father and mother I can overcome every obstacle in my way," he said, and with the little dog at his side he waded into the river and crossed safely to the other side.

"If God grants me life and health I will ask my master the meaning of this," he said to himself.

He continued his journey and came next to a river of swords.

"Ay, this is truly a dangerous place!" he whispered as he saw the sharp swords which filled the river. "But I have the blessing of my parents and that will keep me safe from all danger."

He jumped into the river, and with the little dog and the donkey at his side, he crossed safely. Once on the other side he marveled at the strange meaning of the river of swords.

"If God grants me life and health," he said, "I am going to ask my master the meaning of this obstacle."

Next he came to a place in the road blocked by two huge mountains which appeared to be fighting each other. The earth shook with their groans and huge boulders fell everywhere. As he had safely passed the treacherous rivers, so now he followed the little dog with his donkey, and they worked their way through the narrow canyon and the falling rocks until they were safely on the other side.

Up ahead he came upon a flock of very fat sheep grazing on a plain so desolate there wasn't a blade of grass on it. Yet in the distance there was a very green meadow, so the boy got down from his donkey and tried to drive the flock towards the grass. But the fat sheep wouldn't move towards the meadow and stayed in the dry desert. While trying to drive the sheep he lost the dog and he became very worried. It was strange, he thought, but the dog had not helped him while he had tried to drive the sheep to better pasture. Without his trusty dog he wouldn't know where to go, so he sat beneath a tree and said to himself, "I won't leave until my dog comes back."

Suddenly the little dog appeared and the boy was overjoyed to see him again. Together they continued their journey and it wasn't long before they came upon a flock of thin sheep grazing on grass so high it almost covered them.

"How can it be that the fat sheep are in a place so dry and desolate and these thin sheep are in such a beautiful meadow?" the boy wondered. "If God grants me life and health to return from this strange journey I will ask my master the meaning of this."

In the distance he caught sight of a marvelous city. He hoped it was the place where he was to deliver the letter so he hurried forward. He followed his little dog through the city until they came to the door of a certain house. The boy knocked at the door and a woman appeared. The boy thought she was the same woman he had met on the road and with whom he had shared his food, but he didn't say anything. He handed her the letter and she received it with a smile. Then she invited him in and fed him and gave him a place where he could rest. He felt happy and content that he had completed his errand, and he quickly fell asleep. He did not awaken until the woman called him softly.

"Wake up, my son, you have been asleep a long time."

"No, *señora,*" he said when he opened his eyes, "I just now fell asleep."

"No, you have been asleep for a hundred years," she said.

The way she said it made him jump up and run to the mirror. He saw that he was older and bearded. He grew very sad.

"Let me go quickly, my parents may already be dead!"

"Don't worry about your parents," she consoled him. "They are just as you left them."

But he did not yet believe her, so she sent him back to his master's home. On the return journey he didn't encounter any of the previous obstacles; instead, the road was straight to his master's house. The master received him warmly and asked him if he had done his work. The boy replied that he had.

"Now," the master said, "what do you want as your reward, a 'God bless you for your kindness,' or a bagful of money?"

"God's blessing is more valuable than money," the boy answered.

"Then you may ask for a favor," the man nodded.

* * *

"Before I ask my favor I would like to ask you some questions," the boy said. "What was the first city I came to when I left here? It was very beautiful and everyone was singing, dancing and laughing wildly."

"That is hell," his master answered.

"Farther on I came to a river of blood. What river was that?"

"That is the river of blood which Jesus shed for all sinners."

"Later I came to a river of swords. What river was that?"

"Those are the swords which wounded our Lord."

"Later I came upon two mountains which seemed to do battle with each other. What did that mean?"

"Those are two angry *compadres* who fight with each other instead of living in peace."

"Then I met a flock of fat sheep on a desolate plain. What did that strange sight mean?"

"Those are the poor people of the world who know there is a God and believe in Him."

"Up ahead I met a flock of thin sheep, and they were grazing in a beautiful meadow. What does this mean?"

"Those are the rich of the world who don't think there is a God nor believe in Him."

"And the city where I delivered the letter, what city is that?"

"That is heaven."

"And the woman who was in the house, who is she?"

"That is my mother."

"And you, master, you must be—"

"I am Jesus, the one who suffered for all sinners. Have you heard that the soldiers opened my side with a sword when I was on the cross?"

"Yes, my parents have told me the story."

Then the Lord lifted His arm and showed the boy the wound, and the boy understood all of the strange events which had occurred during his journey. He then made this request:

"The only favor I have to ask is that you take my parents and me, together with my two brothers, to the city where I delivered the letter."

"You and your parents will go to heaven, but not your brothers."

"But why, Lord?" the boy asked.

"Because they were bad sons, and did not take care of their parents, they deserve to spend eternity in the fires of hell."

1980

El obispo / The New Bishop

It had been many years since Archbishop Zubiría of Durango had crossed the Jornada del Muerto to visit his flock in the farthest part of his diocese in New Mexico. Thus people in a small and isolated village were very happy that his Excellency, the new bishop of Santa Fe, was coming to administer the sacrament of Confirmation to their children. A big feast was planned, and the local parish priest went about telling everyone to prepare for the visit of this very important church dignitary.

The people had never seen the bishop, so they were overjoyed to have the opportunity to meet him. The day the bishop arrived the priest took him to the sacristy where he could meet the people before he administered Confirmation to the children. But the people, in their excitement, forgot how to greet him.

The men came in first, but none remembered how to address the bishop, and in their awe of him they made many mistakes.

One bowed and said, "How do you do, your holiness San Joaquín."

Others greeted him by saying, "How do you do, most holy Saint Anthony."

And one woman was so flabbergasted she said, "How do you do, oh blessed Virgin Mary."

Finally one man entered and said, "How do you do, your Excellency."

When this man greeted him correctly the shocked bishop was pleased he had finally met someone who could speak good Castillian Spanish. He took the man aside and whispered confidently, "Isn't it a shame that these people are so backward and ignorant that they don't even know how to greet me?"

The man replied sarcastically, "Yes, my *paisanos* are a humble people. Who else would address Your Excellency as a saint or as the Virgin Mary, when it's plain to see you're neither a saint nor a virgin!"

1980

El indito de las cien vacas / The Indian and the Hundred Cows

In a small pueblo there once lived an Indian who was so devoted to the church he never missed mass on Sunday. One Sunday, during his homily, the priest said:

"Have charity, my children. Give alms to the poor. If you expect God's help it is necessary that you also help the church. You know that when you make a donation to God, He returns it a hundredfold."

The Indian, who was listening carefully, decided to give a cow that he had to the priest. That afternoon he brought his cow to the church and told the priest, "Padre, I have brought you my cow so that God will give me a hundred cows."

"Yes, yes, my son," the priest answered. "Have faith in God and he will repay your gift." Then the priest took the cow and added it to his own herd.

The Indian returned home very satisfied and he began to build a large corral where he could keep his hundred cows when they arrived. When he finished his corral he sat down to wait for the cows. He waited some time and then thought, "Perhaps the cows don't come on their own, maybe I should go for them." So he set out to look for his promised hundred cows. Near the church he came upon a large herd which he drove home and locked securely in his corral.

Later that afternoon the two *vaqueros* who took care of the priest's herd rode to the Indian's home.

"Why do you have these cattle locked up?" they asked gruffly. "Have they done some damage?"

"No, they haven't done any damage," the Indian answered. "I have them locked up because they're mine. I gave the priest a cow and he promised me God would give me a hundred, and here they are!"

"These are the priest's cattle, not yours," the cowboys answered.

"No, these are mine because he promised me a hundred for one!" the Indian insisted.

The cowboys returned to tell the priest what had happened. When he heard the news the priest became very angry. He got on his mule and the three rode to the Indian's home. When they arrived at the corral the Indian was sitting by the gate, his bow and quiver of arrows ready.

"Why have you locked up my cattle in your corral!" the priest shouted. "Is this the way you show your gratitude?"

"But these are my cows," the Indian answered.

"And who gave them to you?"

"You did. You said at mass whoever gave one cow would get a hundred in return!"

"That's not what I meant, you thief!" the priest cried angrily. "You are a thief and you must turn my cattle loose." He got down from his mule to open the gate but stopped when he saw the Indian put an arrow to his bow.

"Padre, if you dare touch the lock I will stick this arrow into your heart. Then the devils in hell will give you a hundred more."

The priest backed away. He realized the Indian meant to make him keep the promise he had made in church, and there was nothing he could do. So he got on his mule and quietly rode home, reminding himself to be more careful with what he said in his sermons.

1980

La Llorona, Malinche, and Guadalupe

Few, if any, tales from the Mexican oral tradition are as widespread as those of La Llorona (the "Weeping Woman"). In essence, the tale focuses on a poor woman whose well-to-do lover abandons her for a woman of his own class. Striken with grief—and in some versions longing for revenge—she murders their children and commits suicide. Thereafter, she roams the streets, wailing for their loss and frightening those who see or hear her. She is often said, in particular, to try getting close to crying babies.

This story, and related ones, have been localized and adapted in Latino communities. Folklorists have found versions of the tale in Mexican-American communities across the United States, from Oregon to Rhode Island. In *Spiders and Spinsters* (1982), Marta Weigle relates versions from New Mexico, Arizona, and California. In one La Llorona is portrayed as the "soul of a woman who went from house to house weeping at night to atone for her sins." In another, she is a mother driven mad by the loss of her son in a village drainage ditch; thereafter, she seeks to kidnap any small child she encounters. In another version related by Rosan Jordan, she was a woman who was married but who killed every baby she had, perhaps by feeding them to pigs or throwing them in a flooded river. In many of these versions, the weeping woman seems to hover between the image of woman as violator and woman as violated.

La Llorona is sometimes seen in relationship to another traditional female figure of the Mexican oral tradition, La Malinche. Historically, this image appears to derive from the Indian name for the person called by the Spaniards Doña Marina, the woman who was used by Cortés as interpreter and mistress during the first stages of the conquest of Mexico. In *The Labyrinth of Solitude* Octavio Paz links her to the Virgin of Guadalupe (see elsewhere in this volume); Paz writes:

> *If the Chingada is a representation of the violated Mother, it is appropriate to associate her with the Conquest, which was also a violation, not only in the historical sense but also in the very flesh of Indian women. The symbol of this violation is Doña Malinche, the mistress of Cortés. It is true that she gave herself voluntarily to the conquistador, but he forgot her as soon as her usefulness was over. Doña Marina becomes a figure representing the Indian women who were fascinated, violated or seduced by the Spaniards. And as a small boy will not forgive his mother if she abandons him to search for his father, the Mexican people have not forgiven La Malinche for her betrayal.*

Folklorists and others have questioned Paz's interpretation. Nevertheless, the figures of the La Llorona, Malinche, and Guadalupe have come to be increasingly significant, especially to Latina writers of the late twentieth century, who have recast these legends in their own terms in works like Sandra Cisneros's story "Woman Hollering Creek."

The contemporary writer Gloria Anzaldúa, for example, brings the three women figures together in her book *Borderlands/La Frontera* (see Volume 2):

> . . . La Virgen de Guadalupe *is the symbol of ethnic identity and of the tolerance for ambiguity that Chicanos-mexicanos, people of mixed race, people who have Indian blood, people who cross cultures, by necessity possess.*
>
> La gente Chicana tiene tres madres. *All three are mediators:* Guadalupe, *the virgin mother who has not abandoned us,* la Chingada (Malinche), *the raped mother whom we have abandoned, and la Llorona, the mother who seeks her lost children and is a combination of the other two.*
>
> *Ambiguity surrounds the symbols of these three "Our Mothers."* Guadalupe *has been used by the Church to mete out institutionalized oppression: to placate the Indians and mexicanos and Chicanos. In part, the true identity of all three has been subverted—*Guadalupe *to make us docile and enduring,* la Chingada *to make us ashamed of our Indian side, and* la Llorona *to make us long-suffering people. This obscuring has encouraged the virgen/puta (whore) dichotomy.*
>
> *Yet we have not all embraced this dichotomy. In the U.S. Southwest, Mexico, Central and South America the indio and the mestizo continue to worship the old spirit entities (including* Guadalupe*) and their supernatural power, under the guise of Christian saints.*

The versions of these tales which follow are contemporary renderings. But similar tales have been told at least since the period of Spanish colonization.

Paul Lauter
Trinity College

SECONDARY WORKS

Bert Almon, "Woman as Interpreter: Haniel Long's Malinche," *Southwest Review,* 1974; Sylvia A. Gonzales, "La Chicano: Guadalupe or Malinche" in *Comparative Perspectives of Third World Women,* 1980; Rachel Phillips, "Marina/ Malinche: Masks and Shadows" in *Women in Hispanic Literature,* 1983; Rosan A. Jordan and Susan J. Kalcik, *Women's Folklore, Women's Culture,* 1985; Gloria Anzaldúa, *Borderlands/La Frontera,* 1987; Pamela Jones, "'There Was a Woman': La Llorona in Oregon," 1988; Mariá Herrera-Sobek, *The Mexican Corrido: A Feminist Analysis,* 1990; Sandra Messinger Cypess, *La Malinche in Mexican Literature,* 1991; Tey Diana Rebolledo, *A Woman Singing in the Snow,* 1995.

La Llorona, Malinche, and the Unfaithful Maria[1]

In 1800 there was, in Spain, a Spaniard, who would visit a woman often without marrying her. His family did not approve. He saw her frequently but never married her. He fathered a child born of this woman.

When the child turned four years old, the father was to marry another, Dona Ana. When the father named the woman he was going to marry, the mother announced he could not, because she was his first love and he had fathered a child who was four years old. The marriage was cancelled. The mother took her son and went home.

The father then wanted to take the child from the mother. He befriended a man who was a close friend of the mother. He killed him, the friend of the mother. The mother later became known as the Llorona. When the mother found out the father had killed her friend, she too wanted to kill, because she had not been asked to marry the Spaniard, the father. She then took her son, and struck him, and slit his throat, killing him. She struck his little heart. She then took him by the feet and showed it to her lover, the father, and said, "Here is your son. Do you want to take him now?"

The father tore the door down, meaning to enter and kill her, but when he entered she had already killed herself. (The story of the Llorona, that involves a ring. That ring, whoever wears it, shall kill.) Then the dead woman's soul broke out of the body and it left through the bedroom window, dressed in a white gown. The soul started to scream, as if paying for what the woman had done.

Then, the maid took the ring from the dead woman's finger. The body was empty, for her soul was paying for her actions. (To this day she is paying in the name of the Llorona.) The maid put on this ring, then gave it to her daughter, whose name I cannot remember.

Her daughter was a girl the maid had cared for. She gave the ring to her, because she loved her. This girl later became known as the Malinche.[2] She had three children whom she loved. She drowned the first child in the river and threw the body away. She had another child and threw him in the river. She had still another one and did

[1]Spanish colonization brought about a mixture of European antecedents of this tale with the Aztec story of the Earth Mother, Tonantzin, who would visit Aztec communities and leave behind her cradle, empty except for a flint knife used in sacrifice. Later she would return, shrieking and wailing over the loss of her children, and then disappear into a river or lake. The story told here was translated by Patricia Ruiz.

[2]See headnote.

the same. She heard a voice telling her that her first child had become a doctor, that her second child had become a priest, and that the third child had become a lawyer. This woman, when the rains would fall and the river would overflow, would cry out, even after she had died, she would cry out, "Ohhhhh, my children. Where are they?"

When this woman was on her deathbed and death was near, her soul left her body, crying out. Then, another woman took the ring from the dead woman's finger. She was later known as Unfaithful Maria. She crept close to the body and whispered, "Now you are dead. I'm taking this ring, and we'll see what things I do."

This woman did not think good thoughts, but evil thoughts. A man appeared to her and said, "If you do this, I will make you beautiful." The woman took the ring and put it on her finger. She had three children and she killed them all, as the evil spirit had instructed.

Her head turned into that of a horse. When she would cry, she would cry as loud and as shrill as an ambulance. When she would cry far away, she would sound very near. When people would turn around to stare at her, whichever way they had turned, their twisted necks would stay that way until a healer could cure him. One of her feet was that of a horse, and one was that of a chicken. Those were the feet of Unfaithful Maria. This started back in 1800 and is still going on today in Mexico.

My grandparents told me this story. Then my stepfather. Then my grandmother, my father's mother, told me this story of the Llorona who was the first. My mother told me the second story of the Malinche. My stepfather told me about the third. My stepfather turned and looked at her and twisted his neck. His neck remained twisted for three years until a healer could cure him. His name was Rosendo Gonzales, my stepfather.

They applied a paste made of egg on his neck because he had twisted it looking at the Llorona. Then they bandaged his neck which was covered with a beaten egg. He wore that bandage for six or twelve days so he could once again move his neck, because he had twisted it looking at the Llorona.

1973

The Devil Woman[1]

My mother's cousin, Manuel Natividad, once saw the Devil. This was in the old days when people lived far from town and rode horseback. Manuel went to town every Saturday night and went to a dance. He was to be married one Sunday, but that Saturday night he got ready to go to the dance as usual. His parents and his sweetheart told him it was bad luck to go to a dance on the night before his wedding, but he laughed at them and rode off to town.

[1]This is a simpler and more common story of marital curse and revenge, yet its striking outcome shows the extent to which "The Llorona" and "The Devil Woman" likely have a common source. At heart, these stories of curse and revenge dramatize a deep belief in the sanctity of the family and the importance of the power of women. This story is a version told by Flo Sais.

As he was riding along in the dim moonlight, he saw a girl walking toward town. He stopped his horse and asked her where she was going.

"I'm going to the dance in town," she told him. "Why don't you let me ride behind you? It's a long way to walk."

"Well, I don't know," Manuel said. "I'm going to get married tomorrow and if my sweetheart hears about it, she might call off the wedding."

"Oh, it'll be all right," the girl told him. "I'll get off before we get there and nobody will know that I rode with you."

So Manuel pulled her up behind him. She looked like a very pretty girl. Under the shawl she wore over her head he could see that her hair was long and wavy. She had long polished fingernails.

When they were almost to town, the girl asked him for a cigarette and he gave her one.

"Well, light it for me, stupid," she said.

When he held the match to light her cigarette, he saw her face clearly for the first time. It was the hideous face of the Devil! He screamed and tried to jump off his horse, but she clawed at him with her long nails and tore the shirt from his back.

His friends found him the next day. He almost died from the terrible clawing. Everyone knew that the Devil had come for him because he hadn't listened to his old parents and his sweetheart. In fact, his sweetheart did call off the wedding and Manuel never married.

When he was an old man he would tell this story to his friends. "I know there is a Devil," he would say. "If anyone does not believe in these things, then let him look at the scars on my back."

The scars were clear and deep. My father saw them several times before Manuel died.

1959

Washington Irving 1783–1859

A merchant's son, born and raised in New York City, Washington Irving was writing satirical pieces for a local newspaper before he was twenty. It was not until he was thirty-seven, however, that he established himself as a professional author. The cheap importation and reproduction of English books made literature a precarious occupation in the United States at the beginning of the nineteenth century. Moreover American commercial society tended to equate art with idleness. For years Irving halfheartedly pursued a career in law and business, while stealing as much time from work as possible for his writing. Only in 1818, with the bankruptcy of his brothers' importing firm, on which he depended financially, did he risk authorship for a living. Two years later, however, the remarkable popularity of *The Sketch Book* made him a marketable commodity in both England and America, and his future as the nation's first successful professional writer was guaranteed.

In his youth, while essentially an amateur in literature, he wrote an abundance of broad, often irreverent burlesque humor, parody, and satire primarily to amuse a local New York audience. The comic periodical *Salmagundi,* on which he collaborated with his brother William and James Kirke Paulding, and the facetious *History of New York,* ostensibly written by the eccentric and highly unreliable antiquarian, Diedrich Knickerbocker, mocked literary conventions and simultaneously made fun of bourgeois manners, provincial high culture, American chauvinism, and republican politics—particularly Jefferson's.

From 1815 to 1832 Irving lived and traveled widely in England and on the European continent. Now much of his work shaped itself as a consciously American response to Old World culture. Seeking a large international audience, he became primarily a writer of short fiction and personalized sketches and essays. Burlesque satire gave way to a gentler, more subtle humor, and he developed the more ingratiating prose style for which he became famous. His persona Geoffrey Crayon, a shy, ironic, at times melancholy American bachelor writer traveling in Europe—a fictionalized version of Irving himself—gave a degree of thematic and tonal unity to his miscellanies, *The Sketch Book, Bracebridge Hall, Tales of a Traveller* and *The Alhambra.* In addition Crayon helped dramatize the author's ambivalent feelings towards both European aristocracy and American democracy.

Irving had grown up in a transitional America, a nation culturally unsure of itself and deeply divided as to how democratic it should become. He is often dismissed as a political reactionary, a would-be aristocrat in a democratic society. Such a view, however, overlooks complexities, if not contradictions, in his work. For him issues were seldom clear-cut, and he was prone to exploit his uncertainties. A mild (if not rampant) self-mockery is inherent in much of his satire and fiction.

By 1820 he had become a partial convert to romanticism, catering to the vogue for tearful sentimentality (though he made fun of it too) and exhibiting romantic interests in landscape, folklore, and the past. Subsequently as a historian and biographer, he was to focus on colorful drama, costumes, and pageantry. But though by temperament a dreamer, he lacked the high romantic's faith in imagination. The undermining of common sense by illusion and the shattering of visions against an unyielding reality are persistent themes in his work, as in "Rip Van Winkle" and "The Legend of Sleepy Hollow." With these narratives (both from *The Sketch Book*) Irving is usually seen as having created the short story as a new genre, distinct from the moral or sentimental tale and tales of headlong action and gothic mystery. Ironically both stories, with their evocative American settings, were partly inspired by German folk motifs and composed in England.

His going to Spain in 1826 and being given access to a mass of largely unused materials relating to Christopher Columbus led to his biography of the explorer. The book was well received, and thereafter Irving wrote more history and biography than fiction. A national celebrity upon his return to America in 1832, he traveled west, gathering material for "A Tour on the Prairies" (in *The Crayon Miscellany*), which he followed shortly with *Astoria* and *Bonneville,* histories of far-western furtrading and exploring ventures. From 1842 to 1846 he served as American minister to Spain. In his final years he continued to produce books and revised and published his complete works. He finished the five-volume *Life of Washington* shortly before his death.

William Hedges
Goucher College

PRIMARY WORKS

Salmagundi, 1807–08; *A History of New York . . . by Diedrich Knickerbocker,* 1809; *The Sketch Book of Geoffrey Crayon, Gent.,* 1819–20; *Bracebridge Hall,* 1822; *Tales of a Traveller,* 1824; *The Life and Voyages of Christopher Columbus,* 1828; *The Alhambra,* 1832; *The Crayon*

Miscellany, 1835; *Astoria,* 1836; *Adventures of Captain Bonneville,* 1837; *The Life of George Washington,* 1855–59.

SECONDARY WORKS

Stanley T. Williams, *The Life of Washington Irving,* 2 vols., 1935; William Hedges, *Washington Irving: An American Study, 1802–1832,* 1965; Andrew B. Meyers, *A Century of Commentary on the Works of Washington Irving,* 1976; Mary W. Bowden, *Washington Irving,* 1981; Stanley Brodwin, ed., *The Old and New World Romanticism of Washington Irving,* 1986; Jeffrey Rubin-Dorsky, *Adrift in the Old World: The Psychological Pilgrimage of Washington Irving,* 1988; Peter Antelyes, *Tales of Adventurous Enterprise: Washington Irving and the Poetics of Western Expansion,* 1990.

from A History of New York

From the Beginning of the World to the End of the Dutch Dynasty by Diedrich Knickerbocker

Book I

Chapter 5

In which the author puts a mighty question to the rout, by the assistance of the man in the moon—which not only delivers thousands of people from great embarrassment, but likewise concludes this introductory book

The writer of a history may, in some respects, be likened unto an adventurous knight, who having undertaken a perilous enterprise by way of establishing his fame, feels bound in honour and chivalry, to turn back for no difficulty nor hardship, and never to shrink or quail whatever enemy he may encounter. Under this impression, I resolutely draw my pen and fall to, with might and main, at those doughty questions and subtle paradoxes, which, like fiery dragons and bloody giants, beset the entrance to my history, and would fain repulse me from the very threshold. And at this moment a gigantic question has started up, which I must take by the beard and utterly subdue, before I can advance another step in my historic undertaking—but I trust this will be the last adversary I shall have to contend with, and that in the next book, I shall be enabled to conduct my readers in triumph into the body of my work.

The question which has thus suddenly arisen, is, what right had the first discoverers of America to land, and take possession of a country, without asking the consent of its inhabitants, or yielding them an adequate compensation for their territory?

My readers shall now see with astonishment, how easily I will vanquish this gigantic doubt, which has so long been the terror of adventurous writers; which has withstood so many fierce assaults, and has given such great distress of mind to multitudes of kind-hearted folks. For, until this mighty question is totally put to rest, the worthy people of America can by no means enjoy the soil they inhabit, with clear right and title, and quiet, unsullied consciences.

The first source of right, by which property is acquired in a country, is DISCOVERY. For as all mankind have an equal right to any thing, which has never before been appropriated, so any nation, that discovers an uninhabited country, and takes possession thereof, is considered as enjoying full property, and absolute, unquestionable empire therein.[1]

This proposition being admitted, it follows clearly, that the Europeans who first visited America, were the real discoverers of the same; nothing being necessary to the establishment of this fact, but simply to prove that it was totally uninhabited by man. This would at first appear to be a point of some difficulty, for it is well known, that this quarter of the world abounded with certain animals, that walked erect on two feet, had something of the human countenance, uttered certain unintelligible sounds, very much like language, in short, had a marvellous resemblance to human beings. But the host of zealous and enlightened fathers, who accompanied the discoverers, for the purpose of promoting the kingdom of heaven, by establishing fat monasteries and bishopricks on earth, soon cleared up this point, greatly to the satisfaction of his holiness the pope, and of all Christian voyagers and discoverers.

They plainly proved, and as there were no Indian writers arose on the other side, the fact was considered as fully admitted and established, that the two legged race of animals before mentioned, were mere cannibals, detestable monsters, and many of them giants—a description of vagrants, that since the times of Gog, Magog and Goliath,[2] have been considered as outlaws, and have received no quarter in either history, chivalry or song; indeed, even the philosopher Bacon, declared the Americans to be people proscribed by the laws of nature, inasmuch as they had a barbarous custom of sacrificing men, and feeding upon man's flesh.

Nor are these all the proofs of their utter barbarism: among many other writers of discernment, the celebrated Ulloa tells us "their imbecility is so visible, that one can hardly form an idea of them different from what one has of the brutes. Nothing disturbs the tranquillity of their souls, equally insensible to disasters, and to prosperity. Though half naked, they are as contented as a monarch in his most splendid array. Fear makes no impression on them, and respect as little."—All this is furthermore supported by the authority of M. Bouguer. "It is not easy," says he, "to describe the degree of their indifference for wealth and all its advantages. One does not well know what motives to propose to them when one would persuade them to any service. It is vain to offer them money, they answer that they are not hungry." And Vanegas confirms the whole, assuring us that "ambition, they have none, and are more desirous of being thought strong than valiant. The objects of ambition with us, honour, fame, reputation, riches, posts and distinctions, are unknown among them. So that this powerful spring of action, the cause of so much *seeming* good and *real* evil in the

[1]"Grotius. Pufendorf, b. 4. c. 4. Vattel, b. I. c. 18, et alii" [Irving's note]. Irving intended his notes and allusions to learned authorities in part as mock-pedantry. While generally more or less genuine, they are often difficult to decipher. Some are still unidentified. Here he refers to works by the legal authorities Hugo Grotius (1583–1645), Samuel von Pufendorf (1632–1694), Emmerich von Vattel (1714–1767), and vaguely to "others."

[2]See Ezekiel, 37–39; 1 Samuel, 17:4.

world has no power over them. In a word, these unhappy mortals may be compared to children, in whom the development of reason is not completed."[3]

Now all these peculiarities, though in the unenlightened states of Greece, they would have entitled their possessors to immortal honour, as having reduced to practice those rigid and abstemious maxims, the mere talking about which, acquired certain old Greeks the reputation of sages and philosophers;—yet were they clearly proved in the present instance, to betoken a most abject and brutified nature, totally beneath the human character. But the benevolent fathers, who had undertaken to turn these unhappy savages into dumb beasts, by dint of argument, advanced still stronger proofs; for as certain divines of the sixteenth century, and among the rest Lullus affirm—the Americans go naked, and have no beards!—"They have nothing," says Lullus, "of the reasonable animal, except the mask."—And even that mask was allowed to avail them but little, for it was soon found that they were of a hideous copper complexion—and being of a copper complexion, it was all the same as if they were negroes—and negroes are black, "and black" said the pious fathers, devoutly crossing themselves, "is the colour of the Devil!" Therefore so far from being able to own property, they had no right even to personal freedom, for liberty is too radiant a deity, to inhabit such gloomy temples. All which circumstances plainly convinced the righteous followers of Cortes and Pizarro, that these miscreants had no title to the soil that they infested—that they were a perverse, illiterate, dumb, beardless, bare-bottomed *black-seed*—mere wild beasts of the forests, and like them should either be subdued or exterminated.

From the foregoing arguments therefore, and a host of others equally conclusive, which I forbear to enumerate, it was clearly evident, that this fair quarter of the globe when first visited by Europeans, was a howling wilderness, inhabited by nothing but wild beasts; and that the transatlantic visitors acquired an incontrovertible property therein, by the *right of Discovery.*

This right being fully established, we now come to the next, which is the right acquired by *cultivation.* "The cultivation of the soil" we are told "is an obligation imposed by nature on mankind. The whole world is appointed for the nourishment of its inhabitants; but it would be incapable of doing it, was it uncultivated. Every nation is then obliged by the law of nature to cultivate the ground that has fallen to its share. Those people like the ancient Germans and modern Tartars, who having fertile countries, disdain to cultivate the earth, and choose to live by rapine, are wanting to themselves, and *deserve to be exterminated as savage and pernicious beasts.*"[4]

Now it is notorious, that the savages knew nothing of agriculture, when first discovered by the Europeans, but lived a most vagabond, disorderly, unrighteous life,—rambling from place to place, and prodigally rioting upon the spontaneous luxuries of nature, without tasking her generosity to yield them any thing more; whereas it has been most unquestionably shewn, that heaven intended the earth should be

[3]The quotations in this paragraph are taken by Irving from *History of America* (1777) by the Scottish historian William Robertson, who has made use of material from Ulloa, Bouguer, and Venegas (not Vanegas), authors of books on Spanish America.

[4]"Vattel—B. i, ch. 17. See likewise Grotius, Pufendorf, et alii" [Irving's note]. The reference, slightly incorrect, is to Vattel's *Le Droit des Gens.*

ploughed and sown, and manured, and laid out into cities and towns and farms, and country seats, and pleasure grounds, and public gardens, all which the Indians knew nothing about—therefore they did not improve the talents providence had bestowed on them—therefore they were careless stewards—therefore they had no right to the soil—therefore they deserved to be exterminated.

It is true the savages might plead that they drew all the benefits from the land which their simple wants required—they found plenty of game to hunt, which together with the roots and uncultivated fruits of the earth, furnished a sufficient variety for their frugal table;—and that as heaven merely designed the earth to form the abode, and satisfy the wants of man; so long as those purposes were answered, the will of heaven was accomplished.—But this only proves how undeserving they were of the blessings around them—they were so much the more savages, for not having more wants; for knowledge is in some degree an increase of desires, and it is this superiority both in the number and magnitude of his desires, that distinguishes the man from the beast. Therefore the Indians, in not having more wants, were very unreasonable animals; and it was but just that they should make way for the Europeans, who had a thousand wants to their one, and therefore would turn the earth to more account, and by cultivating it, more truly fulfil the will of heaven. Besides—Grotius and Lauterbach, and Pufendorf and Titius and a host of wise men besides, who have considered the matter properly, have determined, that the property of a country cannot be acquired by hunting, cutting wood, or drawing water in it—nothing but precise demarcation of limits, and the intention of cultivation, can establish the possession. Now as the savages (probably from never having read the authors above quoted) had never complied with any of these necessary forms, it plainly follows that they had no right to the soil, but that it was completely at the disposal of the first comers, who had more knowledge and more wants than themselves—who would portion out the soil, with churlish boundaries; who would torture nature to pamper a thousand fantastic humours and capricious appetites; and who of course were far more rational animals than themselves. In entering upon a newly discovered, uncultivated country therefore, the new comers were but taking possession of what, according to the aforesaid doctrine, was their own property—therefore in opposing them, the savages were invading their just rights, infringing the immutable laws of nature and counteracting the will of heaven—therefore they were guilty of impiety, burglary and trespass on the case,—therefore they were hardened offenders against God and man—therefore they ought to be exterminated.

But a more irresistible right than either that I have mentioned, and one which will be the most readily admitted by my reader, provided he is blessed with bowels of charity and philanthropy, is the right acquired by civilization. All the world knows the lamentable state in which these poor savages were found. Not only deficient in the comforts of life, but what is still worse, most piteously and unfortunately blind to the miseries of their situation. But no sooner did the benevolent inhabitants of Europe behold their sad condition than they immediately went to work to ameliorate and improve it. They introduced among them the comforts of life, consisting of rum, gin and brandy—and it is astonishing to read how soon the poor savages learnt to estimate these blessings—they likewise made known to them a thousand remedies by which the most inveterate diseases are alleviated and healed, and that they might comprehend the benefits and enjoy the comforts of these medicines they previously introduced among them the diseases which they were calculated to cure. By these and a variety of other methods was the condition of these poor savages, wonderfully improved; they acquired a thousand wants, of which they had before been ignorant, and as he has most sources of happiness, who has most wants to be gratified, they were doubtlessly rendered a much happier race of beings.

But the most important branch of civilization, and which has most strenuously been extolled, by the zealous and pious fathers of the Roman Church, is the introduction of the Christian faith. It was truly a sight that might well inspire horror, to behold these savages, stumbling among the dark mountains of paganism, and guilty of the most horrible ignorance of religion. It is true, they neither stole nor defrauded, they were sober, frugal, continent, and faithful to their word; but though they acted right habitually, it was all in vain, unless they acted so from precept. The new comers therefore used every method, to induce them to embrace and practice the true religion—except that of setting them the example.

But notwithstanding all these complicated labours for their good, such was the unparalleled obstinacy of these stubborn wretches, that they ungratefully refused, to acknowledge the strangers as their benefactors, and persisted in disbelieving the doctrines they endeavoured to inculcate; most insolently alledging, that from their conduct, the advocates of Christianity did not seem to believe in it themselves. Was not this too much for human patience?—would not one suppose, that the foreign emigrants from Europe, provoked at their incredulity and discouraged by their stiff-necked obstinacy, would forever have abandoned their shores, and consigned them to their original ignorance and misery?—But no——so zealous were they to effect the temporal comfort and eternal salvation of these pagan infidels, that they even proceeded from the milder means of persuasion, to the more painful and troublesome one of persecution——Let loose among them, whole troops of fiery monks and furious bloodhounds—purified them by fire and sword, by stake and faggot; in consequence of which indefatigable measures, the cause of Christian love and charity was so rapidly advanced, that in a very few years, not one fifth of the number of unbelievers existed in South America, that were found there at the time of its discovery.

Nor did the other methods of civilization remain unenforced. The Indians improved daily and wonderfully by their intercourse with the whites. They took to drinking rum, and making bargains. They learned to cheat, to lie, to swear, to gamble, to quarrel, to cut each other's throats, in short, to excel in all the accomplishments that had originally marked the superiority of their Christian visitors. And such a surprising aptitude have they shewn for these acquirements, that there is very little doubt that in a century more, provided they survive so long the irresistible effects of civilization; they will equal in knowledge, refinement, knavery, and debauchery, the most enlightened, civilized and orthodox nations of Europe.

What stronger right need the European settlers advance to the country than this. Have not whole nations of uninformed savages been made acquainted with a thousand imperious wants and indispensible comforts of which they were before wholly ignorant—Have they not been literally hunted and smoked out of the dens and lurking places of ignorance and infidelity, and absolutely scourged into the right path. Have not the temporal things, the vain baubles and filthy lucre of this world, which were too apt to engage their worldly and selfish thoughts, been benevolently taken from them; and have they not, in lieu thereof, been taught to set their affections on things above—And finally, to use the words of a reverend Spanish father, in a letter to his superior in Spain—"Can any one have the presumption to say, that these savage Pagans, have yielded any thing more than an inconsiderable recompense to their benefactors; in surrendering to them a little pitiful tract of this dirty sublunary planet, in exchange for a glorious inheritance in the kingdom of Heaven!"

Here then are three complete and undeniable sources of right established, any one of which was more than ample to establish a property in the newly discovered regions of America. Now, so it has happened in certain parts of this delightful quarter of the globe, that the right of discovery has been so strenuously asserted—the influence of cultivation so industriously extended, and the progress of salvation and civilization so zealously prosecuted, that, what with their attendant wars, persecutions, oppressions, diseases, and other partial evils that often hang on the skirts of great benefits—the savage aborigines have, some how or another, been utterly annihilated—and this all at once brings me to a fourth right, which is worth all the others put together—For the original claimants to the soil being all dead and buried, and no one remaining to inherit or dispute the soil, the Spaniards as the next immediate occupants entered upon the possession, as clearly as the hang-man succeeds to the clothes of the malefactor—and as they have Blackstone,[5] and all the learned expounders of the law on their side, they may set all actions of ejectment at defiance—and this last right may be entitled, the RIGHT BY EXTERMINATION, or in other words, the RIGHT BY GUNPOWDER.

But lest any scruples of conscience should remain on this head, and to settle the question of right forever, his holiness Pope Alexander VI, issued one of those mighty bulls, which bear down reason, argument and every thing before them; by which he generously granted the newly discovered quarter of the globe, to the Spaniards and Portuguese; who, thus having law and gospel on their side, and being inflamed with great spiritual zeal, shewed the Pagan savages neither favour nor affection, but prosecuted the work of discovery, colonization, civilization, and extermination, with ten times more fury than ever.

Thus were the European worthies who first discovered America, clearly entitled to the soil; and not only entitled to the soil, but likewise to the eternal thanks of these infidel savages, for having come so far, endured so many perils by sea and land, and taken such unwearied pains, for no other purpose under heaven but to improve their forlorn, uncivilized and heathenish condition—for having made them acquainted with the comforts of life, such as gin, rum, brandy, and the smallpox; for having introduced among them the light of religion, and finally——for having hurried them out of the world, to enjoy its reward!

But as argument is never so well understood by us selfish mortals, as when it comes home to ourselves, and as I am particularly anxious that this question should be put to rest forever, I will suppose a parallel case, by way of arousing the candid attention of my readers.

Let us suppose then, that the inhabitants of the moon, by astonishing advancement in science, and by a profound insight into that ineffable lunar philosophy, the

[5]"Black. *Com.* B II, c. i" [Irving's note]. That is *Commentaries on the Laws of England* (1765–1769) by William Blackstone, English jurist.

mere flickerings of which, have of late years, dazzled the feeble optics, and addled the shallow brains of the good people of our globe—let us suppose, I say, that the inhabitants of the moon, by these means, had arrived at such a command of their *energies,* such an enviable state of *perfectability,* as to controul the elements, and navigate the boundless regions of space. Let us suppose a roving crew of these soaring philosophers, in the course of an aerial voyage of discovery among the stars, should chance to alight upon this outlandish planet.

And here I beg my readers will not have the impertinence to smile, as is too frequently the fault of volatile readers, when perusing the grave speculations of philosophers. I am far from indulging in any sportive vein at present, nor is the supposition I have been making so wild as many may deem it. It has long been a very serious and anxious question with me, and many a time, and oft, in the course of my overwhelming cares and contrivances for the welfare and protection of this my native planet, have I lain awake whole nights, debating in my mind whether it was most probable we should first discover and civilize the moon, or the moon discover and civilize our globe. Neither would the prodigy of sailing in the air and cruising among the stars be a whit more astonishing and incomprehensible to us, than was the European mystery of navigating floating castles, through the world of waters, to the simple savages. We have already discovered the art of coasting along the aerial shores of our planet, by means of balloons, as the savages had, of venturing along their sea coasts in canoes; and the disparity between the former, and the aerial vehicles of the philosophers from the moon, might not be greater, than that, between the bark canoes of the savages, and the mighty ships of their discoverers. I might here pursue an endless chain of very curious, profound and unprofitable speculations; but as they would be unimportant to my subject, I abandon them to my reader, particularly if he is a philosopher, as matters well worthy his attentive consideration.

To return then to my supposition—let us suppose that the aerial visitants I have mentioned, possessed of vastly superior knowledge to ourselves; that is to say, possessed of superior knowledge in the art of extermination—riding on Hypogriffs,[6] defended with impenetrable armour—armed with concentrated sun beams, and provided with vast engines, to hurl enormous moon stones: in short, let us suppose them, if our vanity will permit the supposition, as superior to us in knowledge, and consequently in power, as the Europeans were to the Indians, when they first discovered them. All this is very possible, it is only our self-sufficiency that makes us think otherwise; and I warrant the poor savages, before they had any knowledge of the white men, armed in all the terrors of glittering steel and tremendous gunpowder, were as perfectly convinced that they themselves were the wisest, the most virtuous, powerful and perfect of created beings, as are, at this present moment, the lordly inhabitants of old England, the volatile populace of France, or even the self-satisfied citizens of this most enlightened republick.

Let us suppose, moreover, that the aerial voyagers, finding this planet to be nothing but a howling wilderness, inhabited by us, poor savages and wild beasts, shall take formal possession of it, in the name of his most gracious and philosophic excel-

[6]Usually "hippogriffs," fabulous beasts with the head and wings of an eagle and the body of a horse.

lency, the man in the moon. Finding however, that their numbers are incompetent to hold it in complete subjection, on account of the ferocious barbarity of its inhabitants; they shall take our worthy President, the King of England, the Emperor of Hayti, the mighty little Bonaparte, and the great King of Bantam, and returning to their native planet; shall carry them to court, as were the Indian chiefs led about as spectacles in the courts of Europe.

Then making such obeisance as the etiquette of the court requires, they shall address the puissant man in the moon, in, as near as I can conjecture, the following terms:

"Most serene and mighty Potentate, whose dominions extend as far as eye can reach, who rideth on the Great Bear, useth the sun as a looking glass and maintaineth unrivalled controul over tides, madmen and sea-crabs. We thy liege subjects have just returned from a voyage of discovery, in the course of which we have landed and taken possession of that obscure little scurvy planet, which thou beholdest rolling at a distance. The five uncouth monsters, which we have brought into this august presence, were once very important chiefs among their fellow savages; for the inhabitants of the newly discovered globe are totally destitute of the common attributes of humanity, inasmuch as they carry their heads upon their shoulders, instead of under their arms—have two eyes instead of one—are utterly destitute of tails, and of a variety of unseemly complexions, particularly of a horrible whiteness—whereas all the inhabitants of the moon are pea green!

"We have moreover found these miserable savages sunk into a state of the utmost ignorance and depravity, every man shamelessly living with his own wife, and rearing his own children, instead of indulging in that community of wives, enjoined by the law of nature, as expounded by the philosophers of the moon. In a word they have scarcely a gleam of true philosophy among them, but are in fact, utter heretics, ignoramuses and barbarians. Taking compassion therefore on the sad condition of these sublunary wretches, we have endeavoured, while we remained on their planet, to introduce among them the light of reason—and the comforts of the moon.—We have treated them to mouthfuls of moonshine and draughts of nitrous oxyde,[7] which they swallowed with incredible voracity, particularly the females; and we have likewise endeavoured to instil into them the precepts of lunar Philosophy. We have insisted upon their renouncing the contemptable shackles of religion and common sense, and adoring the profound, omnipotent, and all perfect energy, and the extatic, immutable, immoveable perfection. But such was the unparalleled obstinacy of these wretched savages, that they persisted in cleaving to their wives and adhering to their religion, and absolutely set at naught the sublime doctrines of the moon—nay, among other abominable heresies, they even went so far as blasphemously to declare, that this ineffable planet was made of nothing more nor less than green cheese!"

At these words, the great man in the moon (being a very profound philosopher) shall fall into a terrible passion, and possessing equal authority over things that do not belong to him, as did whilome his holiness the Pope, shall forthwith issue a formidable bull,——specifying, "That—whereas a certain crew of Lunatics have lately discovered and taken possession of that little dirty planet, called *the earth*—and that whereas it is inhabited by none but a race of two legged animals, that carry their

[7]Vernacularly called "laughing gas."

heads on their shoulders instead of under their arms; cannot talk the lunatic language; have two eyes instead of one; are destitute of tails, and of a horrible whiteness, instead of pea green——therefore and for a variety of other excellent reasons—they are considered incapable of possessing any property in the planet they infest, and the right and title to it are confirmed to its original discoverers.—And furthermore, the colonists who are now about to depart to the aforesaid planet, are authorized and commanded to use every means to convert these infidel savages from the darkness of Christianity, and make them thorough and absolute lunatics."

In consequence of this benevolent bull, our philosophic benefactors go to work with hearty zeal. They seize upon our fertile territories, scourge us from our rightful possession, relieve us from our wives, and when we are unreasonable enough to complain, they will turn upon us and say—miserable barbarians! ungrateful wretches!—have we not come thousands of miles to improve your worthless planet—have we not fed you with moonshine—have we not intoxicated you with nitrous oxyde——does not our moon give you light every night and have you the baseness to murmur, when we claim a pitiful return for all these benefits? But finding that we not only persist in absolute contempt to their reasoning and disbelief in their philosophy, but even go so far as daringly to defend our property, their patience shall be exhausted, and they shall resort to their superior powers of argument—hunt us with hypogriffs, transfix us with concentrated sun-beams, demolish our cities with moonstones; until having by main force, converted us to the true faith, they shall graciously permit us to exist in the torrid deserts of Arabia, or the frozen regions of Lapland, there to enjoy the blessings of civilization and the charms of lunar philosophy—in much the same manner as the reformed and enlightened savages of this country, are kindly suffered to inhabit the inhospitable forests of the north, or the impenetrable wilderness of South America.

Thus have I clearly proved, and I hope strikingly illustrated, the right of the early colonists to the possession of this country——and thus is this gigantic question, completely knocked in the head. . . .

1809

Rip Van Winkle

A Posthumous Writing of Diedrich Knickerbocker

By Woden, God of Saxons,
From whence comes Wensday, that is Wodensday.
Truth is a thing that ever I will keep
Unto thylke day in which I creep into
My sepulchre—

—CARTWRIGHT[1]

[1]Lines from *The Ordinary,* by William Cartwright, English dramatist (1611–1643).

The following Tale was found among the papers of the late Diedrich Knickerbocker, an old gentleman of New York, who was very curious in the Dutch history of the province, and the manners of the descendants from its primitive settlers. His historical researches, however, did not lie so much among books as among men; for the former are lamentably scanty on his favorite topics; whereas he found the old burghers, and still more their wives, rich in that legendary lore so invaluable to true history. Whenever, therefore, he happened upon a genuine Dutch family, snugly shut up in its low-roofed farmhouse, under a spreading sycamore, he looked upon it as a little clasped volume of black-letter, and studied it with the zeal of a bookworm.

The result of all these researches was a history of the province during the reign of the Dutch governors, which he published some years since. There have been various opinions as to the literary character of his work, and, to tell the truth, it is not a whit better than it should be. Its chief merit is its scrupulous accuracy, which indeed was a little questioned on its first appearance, but has since been completely established; and it is now admitted into all historical collections as a book of unquestionable authority.

The old gentleman died shortly after the publication of his work; and now that he is dead and gone, it cannot do much harm to his memory to say that his time might have been much better employed in weightier labor. He, however, was apt to ride his hobby his own way; and though it did now and then kick up the dust a little in the eyes of his neighbors, and grieve the spirit of some friends, for whom he felt the truest deference and affection, yet his errors and follies are remembered "more in sorrow than in anger,"[2] and it begins to be suspected that he never intended to injure or offend. But however his memory may be appreciated by critics, it is still held dear by many folk whose good opinion is well worth having; particularly by certain biscuit-bakers, who have gone so far as to imprint his likeness on their New-Year cakes; and have thus given him a chance for immortality, almost equal to the being stamped on a Waterloo Medal, or a Queen Anne's Farthing.[3]

Whoever has made a voyage up the Hudson must remember the Kaatskill mountains. They are a dismembered branch of the great Appalachian family, and are seen away to the west of the river, swelling up to a noble height, and lording it over the surrounding country. Every change of season, every change of weather, indeed, every hour of the day, produces some change in the magical hues and shapes of these mountains, and they are regarded by all the good wives, far and near, as perfect barometers. When the weather is fair and settled, they are clothed in blue and purple, and print their bold outlines on the clear evening sky; but sometimes, when the rest of the landscape is cloudless, they will gather a hood of gray vapors about their summits, which, in the last rays of the setting sun, will glow and light up like a crown of glory.

At the foot of these fairy mountains, the voyager may have descried the light smoke curling up from a village, whose shingle-roofs gleam among the trees, just where the blue tints of the upland melt away into the fresh green of the nearer landscape. It is a little village, of great antiquity, having been founded by some of the Dutch colonists in the early times of the province, just about the beginning of the government of the good Peter Stuyvesant, (may he rest in peace!) and there were some of the houses of the original settlers standing within a few years, built of small

[2]*Hamlet,* I, ii.

[3]Waterloo Medals and Queen Anne's Farthings were not scarce.

yellow bricks brought from Holland, having latticed windows and gable fronts, surmounted with weathercocks.

In that same village, and in one of these very houses (which, to tell the precise truth, was sadly time-worn and weather-beaten), there lived, many years since, while the country was yet a province of Great Britain, a simple, good-natured fellow, of the name of Rip Van Winkle. He was a descendant of the Van Winkles who figured so gallantly in the chivalrous days of Peter Stuyvesant, and accompanied him to the siege of Fort Christina. He inherited, however, but little of the martial character of his ancestors. I have observed that he was a simple, good-natured man; he was, moreover, a kind neighbor, and an obedient, hen-pecked husband. Indeed, to the latter circumstance might be owing that meekness of spirit which gained him such universal popularity; for those men are most apt to be obsequious and conciliating abroad, who are under the discipline of shrews at home. Their tempers, doubtless, are rendered pliant and malleable in the fiery furnace of domestic tribulation; and a curtain-lecture[4] is worth all the sermons in the world for teaching the virtues of patience and long-suffering. A termagant wife may, therefore, in some respects be considered a tolerable blessing; and if so, Rip Van Winkle was thrice blessed.

Certain it is, that he was a great favorite among all the good wives of the village, who, as usual with the amiable sex, took his part in all family squabbles; and never failed, whenever they talked those matters over in their evening gossipings, to lay all the blame on Dame Van Winkle. The children of the village, too, would shout with joy whenever he approached. He assisted at their sports, made their playthings, taught them to fly kites and shoot marbles, and told them long stories of ghosts, witches, and Indians. Whenever he went dodging about the village, he was surrounded by a troop of them, hanging on his skirts, clambering on his back, and playing a thousand tricks on him with impunity; and not a dog would bark at him throughout the neighborhood.

The great error in Rip's composition was an insuperable aversion to all kinds of profitable labor. It could not be from the want of assiduity or perseverance; for he would sit on a wet rock, with a rod as long and heavy as a Tartar's lance, and fish all day without a murmur, even though he should not be encouraged by a single nibble. He would carry a fowling-piece on his shoulder for hours together, trudging through woods and swamps, and up hill and down dale, to shoot a few squirrels or wild pigeons. He would never refuse to assist a neighbor even in the roughest toil, and was a foremost man at all country frolics for husking Indian corn, or building stone fences; the women of the village, too, used to employ him to run their errands, and to do such little odd jobs as their less obliging husbands would not do for them. In a word, Rip was ready to attend to anybody's business but his own; but as to doing family duty, and keeping his farm in order, he found it impossible.

In fact, he declared it was of no use to work on his farm; it was the most pestilent little piece of ground in the whole country; everything about it went wrong, and would go wrong, in spite of him. His fences were continually falling to pieces; his cow would either go astray, or get among the cabbages; weeds were sure to grow quicker in his fields than anywhere else; the rain always made a point of setting in just as he had some out-door work to do; so that though his patrimonial estate had dwindled

[4]A wife scolding her husband in bed.

away under his management, acre by acre, until there was little more left than a mere patch of Indian corn and potatoes, yet it was the worst conditioned farm in the neighborhood.

His children, too, were as ragged and wild as if they belonged to nobody. His son Rip, an urchin begotten in his own likeness, promised to inherit the habits, with the old clothes, of his father. He was generally seen trooping like a colt at his mother's heels, equipped in a pair of his father's cast-off galligaskins, which he had much ado to hold up with one hand, as a fine lady does her train in bad weather.

Rip Van Winkle, however, was one of those happy mortals, of foolish, well-oiled dispositions, who take the world easy, eat white bread or brown, whichever can be got with least thought or trouble, and would rather starve on a penny than work for a pound. If left to himself, he would have whistled life away in perfect contentment; but his wife kept continually dinning in his ears about his idleness, his carelessness, and the ruin he was bringing on his family. Morning, noon, and night, her tongue was incessantly going, and everything he said or did was sure to produce a torrent of household eloquence. Rip had but one way of replying to all lectures of the kind, and that, by frequent use, had grown into a habit. He shrugged his shoulders, shook his head, cast up his eyes, but said nothing. This, however, always provoked a fresh volley from his wife; so that he was fain to draw off his forces, and take to the outside of the house—the only side which, in truth, belongs to a hen-pecked husband.

Rip's sole domestic adherent was his dog Wolf, who was as much hen-pecked as his master; for Dame Van Winkle regarded them as companions in idleness, and even looked upon Wolf with an evil eye, as the cause of his master's going so often astray. True it is, in all points of spirit befitting an honorable dog, he was as courageous an animal as ever scoured the woods; but what courage can withstand the ever-during and all-besetting terrors of a woman's tongue? The moment Wolf entered the house his crest fell, his tail drooped to the ground, or curled between his legs, he sneaked about with a gallows air, casting many a sidelong glance at Dame Van Winkle, and at the least flourish of a broomstick or ladle he would fly to the door with yelping precipitation.

Times grew worse and worse with Rip Van Winkle as years of matrimony rolled on; a tart temper never mellows with age, and a sharp tongue is the only edged tool that grows keener with constant use. For a long while he used to console himself, when driven from home, by frequenting a kind of perpetual club of the sages, philosophers, and other idle personages of the village, which held its sessions on a bench before a small inn, designated by a rubicund portrait of His Majesty George the Third. Here they used to sit in the shade through a long, lazy summer's day, talking listlessly over village gossip, or telling endless sleepy stories about nothing. But it would have been worth any statesman's money to have heard the profound discussions that sometimes took place, when by chance an old newspaper fell into their hands from some passing traveller. How solemnly they would listen to the contents, as drawled out by Derrick Van Bummel, the schoolmaster, a dapper learned little man, who was not to be daunted by the most gigantic word in the dictionary; and how sagely they would deliberate upon public events some months after they had taken place.

The opinions of this junto were completely controlled by Nicholas Vedder, a patriarch of the village, and landlord of the inn, at the door of which he took his seat from morning till night, just moving sufficiently to avoid the sun and keep in the shade of a large tree; so that the neighbors could tell the hour by his movements as accurately as by a sun-dial. It is true he was rarely heard to speak, but smoked his pipe incessantly. His adherents, however (for every great man has his adherents), perfectly understood him, and knew how to gather his opinions. When anything that was read or related displeased him, he was observed to smoke his pipe vehemently, and to send forth short, frequent, and angry puffs; but when pleased, he would inhale the smoke slowly and tranquilly, and emit it in light and placid clouds; and sometimes, taking the pipe from his mouth, and letting the fragrant vapor curl about his nose, would gravely nod his head in token of perfect approbation.

From even this stronghold the unlucky Rip was at length routed by his termagant wife, who would suddenly break in upon the tranquillity of the assemblage and call the members all to naught; nor was that august personage, Nicholas Vedder himself, sacred from the daring tongue of this terrible virago, who charged him outright with encouraging her husband in habits of idleness.

Poor Rip was at last reduced almost to despair; and his only alternative, to escape from the labor of the farm and clamor of his wife, was to take gun in hand and stroll away into the woods. Here he would sometimes seat himself at the foot of a tree, and share the contents of his wallet with Wolf, with whom he sympathized as a fellow-sufferer in persecution. "Poor Wolf," he would say, "thy mistress leads thee a dog's life of it; but never mind, my lad, whilst I live thou shalt never want a friend to stand by thee!" Wolf would wag his tail, look wistfully in his master's face; and if dogs can feel pity, I verily believe he reciprocated the sentiment with all his heart.

In a long ramble of the kind on a fine autumnal day, Rip had unconsciously scrambled to one of the highest parts of the Kaatskill mountains. He was after his favorite sport of squirrel-shooting, and the still solitudes had echoed and re-echoed with the reports of his gun. Panting and fatigued, he threw himself, late in the afternoon, on a green knoll, covered with mountain herbage, that crowned the brow of a precipice. From an opening between the trees he could overlook all the lower country for many a mile of rich woodland. He saw at a distance the lordly Hudson, far, far below him, moving on its silent but majestic course, with the reflection of a purple cloud, or the sail of a lagging bark, here and there sleeping on its glassy bosom, and at last losing itself in the blue highlands.

On the other side he looked down into a deep mountain glen, wild, lonely, and shagged, the bottom filled with fragments from the impending cliffs, and scarcely lighted by the reflected rays of the setting sun. For some time Rip lay musing on this scene; evening was gradually advancing; the mountains began to throw their long blue shadows over the valleys; he saw that it would be dark long before he could reach the village, and he heaved a heavy sigh when he thought of encountering the terrors of Dame Van Winkle.

As he was about to descend, he heard a voice from a distance, hallooing, "Rip Van Winkle, Rip Van Winkle!" He looked round, but could see nothing but a crow winging its solitary flight across the mountain. He thought his fancy must have deceived him, and turned again to descend, when he heard the same cry ring through the still evening air: "Rip Van Winkle! Rip Van Winkle!"—at the same time Wolf bristled up his back, and giving a low growl, skulked to his master's side, looking fearfully down into the glen. Rip now felt a vague apprehension stealing over him; he looked anxiously in the same direction, and perceived a strange figure slowly toiling up the rocks, and bending under the weight of something he carried on his back. He was surprised to see any human being in this lonely and unfrequented place; but supposing it to be some one of the neighborhood in need of his assistance, he hastened down to yield it.

On nearer approach he was still more surprised at the singularity of the stranger's appearance. He was a short, square-built old fellow, with thick bushy hair, and a grizzled beard. His dress was of the antique Dutch fashion,—a cloth jerkin strapped round the waist—several pair of breeches, the outer one of ample volume, decorated with rows of buttons down the sides, and bunches at the knees. He bore on his shoulder a stout keg, that seemed full of liquor, and made signs for Rip to approach and assist him with the load. Though rather shy and distrustful of this new acquaintance, Rip complied with his usual alacrity; and mutually relieving one another, they clambered up a narrow gully, apparently the dry bed of a mountain torrent. As they ascended, Rip every now and then heard long, rolling peals, like distant thunder, that seemed to issue out of a deep ravine, or rather cleft, between lofty rocks, toward which their rugged path conducted. He paused for an instant, but supposing it to be the muttering of one of those transient thunder-showers which often take place in mountain heights, he proceeded. Passing through the ravine, they came to a hollow, like a small amphitheatre, surrounded by perpendicular precipices, over the brinks of which impending trees shot their branches, so that you only caught glimpses of the azure sky and the bright evening cloud. During the whole time Rip and his companion had labored on in silence; for though the former marvelled greatly what could be the object of carrying a keg of liquor up this wild mountain, yet there was something strange and incomprehensible about the unknown, that inspired awe and checked familiarity.

On entering the amphitheatre, new objects of wonder presented themselves. On a level spot in the centre was a company of odd-looking personages playing at ninepins. They were dressed in a quaint, outlandish fashion; some wore short doublets, others jerkins, with long knives in their belts, and most of them had enormous breeches, of similar style with that of the guide's. Their visages, too, were peculiar: one had a large beard, broad face, and small piggish eyes; the face of another seemed to consist entirely of nose, and was surmounted by a white sugar-loaf hat, set off with a little red cock's tail. They all had beards, of various shapes and colors. There was one who seemed to be the commander. He was a stout old gentleman, with a weather-beaten countenance; he wore a laced doublet, broad belt and hanger, high crowned hat and feather, red stockings, and high-heeled shoes, with roses in them. The whole group reminded Rip of the figures in an old Flemish painting, in the parlor of Dominie Van Shaick, the village parson, and which had been brought over from Holland at the time of the settlement.

What seemed particularly odd to Rip was, that, though these folks were evidently amusing themselves, yet they maintained the gravest faces, the most mysterious silence, and were, withal, the most melancholy party of pleasure he had ever witnessed. Nothing interrupted the stillness of the scene but the noise of the balls, which, whenever they were rolled, echoed along the mountains like rumbling peals of thunder.

As Rip and his companion approached them, they suddenly desisted from their play, and stared at him with such fixed, statue-like gaze, and such strange, uncouth, lack-lustre countenances, that his heart turned within him, and his knees smote together. His companion now emptied the contents of the keg into large flagons, and made signs to him to wait upon the company. He obeyed with fear and trembling; they quaffed the liquor in profound silence, and then returned to their game.

By degrees Rip's awe and apprehension subsided. He even ventured, when no eye was fixed upon him, to taste the beverage, which he found had much of the flavor of excellent Hollands. He was naturally a thirsty soul, and was soon tempted to repeat the draught. One taste provoked another; and he reiterated his visits to the flagon so often that at length his senses were overpowered, his eyes swam in his head, his head gradually declined, and he fell into a deep sleep.

On waking, he found himself on the green knoll whence he had first seen the old man of the glen. He rubbed his eyes—it was a bright sunny morning. The birds were hopping and twittering among the bushes, and the eagle was wheeling aloft, and breasting the pure mountain breeze. "Surely," thought Rip, "I have not slept here all night." He recalled the occurrences before he fell asleep. The strange man with a keg of liquor—the mountain ravine—the wild retreat among the rocks—the woe-begone party at ninepins—the flagon—"Oh! that flagon! that wicked flagon!" thought Rip,—"what excuse shall I make to Dame Van Winkle?"

He looked round for his gun, but in place of the clean, well-oiled fowling-piece, he found an old firelock lying by him, the barrel incrusted with rust, the lock falling off, and the stock worm-eaten. He now suspected that the grave roisters of the mountain had put a trick upon him, and, having dosed him with liquor, had robbed him of his gun. Wolf, too, had disappeared, but he might have strayed away after a squirrel or partridge. He whistled after him, and shouted his name, but all in vain; the echoes repeated his whistle and shout, but no dog was to be seen.

He determined to revisit the scene of the last evening's gambol, and if he met with any of the party, to demand his dog and gun. As he rose to walk, he found himself stiff in the joints, and wanting in his usual activity. "These mountain beds do not agree with me," thought Rip, "and if this frolic should lay me up with a fit of rheumatism, I shall have a blessed time with Dame Van Winkle." With some difficulty he got down into the glen: he found the gully up which he and his companion had ascended the preceding evening; but to his astonishment a mountain stream was now foaming down it, leaping from rock to rock, and filling the glen with babbling murmurs. He, however, made shift to scramble up its sides, working his toilsome way through thickets of birch, sassafras, and witch-hazel, and sometimes tripped up or entangled by the wild grape-vines that twisted their coils or tendrils from tree to tree, and spread a kind of network in his path.

At length he reached to where the ravine had opened through the cliffs to the amphitheatre; but no traces of such opening remained. The rocks presented a high, impenetrable wall, over which the torrent came tumbling in a sheet of feathery foam, and fell into a broad deep basin, black from the shadows of the surrounding forest. Here, then, poor Rip was brought to a stand. He again called and whistled after his dog; he was only answered by the cawing of a flock of idle crows, sporting high in air about a dry tree that overhung a sunny precipice; and who, secure in their elevation, seemed to look down and scoff at the poor man's perplexities. What was to be done?

the morning was passing away, and Rip felt famished for want of his breakfast. He grieved to give up his dog and gun he dreaded to meet his wife; but it would not do to starve among the mountains. He shook his head, shouldered the rusty firelock, and, with a heart full of trouble and anxiety, turned his steps homeward.

As he approached the village he met a number of people, but none whom he knew, which some what surprised him, for he had thought himself acquainted with every one in the country round. Their dress, too, was of a different fashion from that to which he was accustomed. They all stared at him with equal marks of surprise, and whenever they cast their eyes upon him, invariably stroked their chins. The constant recurrence of this gesture induced Rip, involuntarily, to do the same, when, to his astonishment, he found his beard had grown a foot long!

He had now entered the skirts of the village. A troop of strange children ran at his heels, hooting after him, and pointing at his gray beard. The dogs, too, not one of which he recognized for an old acquaintance, barked at him as he passed. The very village was altered; it was larger and more populous. There were rows of houses which he had never seen before, and those which had been his familiar haunts had disappeared. Strange names were over the doors—strange faces at the windows—everything was strange. His mind now misgave him; he began to doubt whether both he and the world around him were not bewitched. Surely this was his native village, which he had left but the day before. There stood the Kaatskill mountains—there ran the silver Hudson at a distance—there was every hill and dale precisely as it had always been. Rip was sorely perplexed. "That flagon last night," thought he, "has addled my poor head sadly!"

It was with some difficulty that he found the way to his own house, which he approached with silent awe, expecting every moment to hear the shrill voice of Dame Van Winkle. He found the house gone to decay—the roof fallen in, the windows shattered, and the doors off the hinges. A half-starved dog that looked like Wolf was skulking about it. Rip called him by name, but the cur snarled, showed his teeth, and passed on. This was an unkind cut indeed. "My very dog," sighed poor Rip, "has forgotten me!"

He entered the house, which, to tell the truth, Dame Van Winkle had always kept in neat order. It was empty, forlorn, and apparently abandoned. This desolateness overcame all his connubial fears—he called loudly for his wife and children—the lonely chambers rang for a moment with his voice, and then all again was silence.

He now hurried forth, and hastened to his old resort, the village inn—but it too was gone. A large rickety wooden building stood in its place, with great gaping windows, some of them broken and mended with old hats and petticoats, and over the door was painted, "The Union Hotel, by Jonathan Doolittle." Instead of the great tree that used to shelter the quiet little Dutch inn of yore, there now was reared a tall naked pole, with something on the top that looked like a red nightcap,[5] and from it was fluttering a flag, on which was a singular assemblage of stars and stripes;—all this was strange and incomprehensible. He recognized on the sign, however, the ruby face of King George, under which he had smoked so many a peaceful pipe; but even this was singularly metamorphosed. The red coat was changed for one of blue and

[5]Liberty poles and liberty caps were symbols used in the American and French Revolutions.

buff, a sword was held in the hand instead of a sceptre, the head was decorated with a cocked hat, and underneath was painted in large characters, GENERAL WASHINGTON.

There was, as usual, a crowd of folk about the door, but none that Rip recollected. The very character of the people seemed changed. There was a busy, bustling, disputatious tone about it, instead of the accustomed phlegm and drowsy tranquility. He looked in vain for the sage Nicholas Vedder, with his broad face, double chin, and fair long pipe, uttering clouds of tobacco-smoke instead of idle speeches; or Van Bummel, the schoolmaster, doling forth the contents of an ancient newspaper. In place of these, a lean, bilious-looking fellow, with his pockets full of hand-bills, was haranguing vehemently about rights of citizens—elections—members of congress—liberty—Bunker's Hill—heroes of seventy-six—and other words, which were a perfect Babylonish[6] jargon to the bewildered Van Winkle.

The appearance of Rip, with his long, grizzled beard, his rusty fowling-piece, his uncouth dress, and an army of women and children at his heels, soon attracted the attention of the tavern-politicians. They crowded round him, eyeing him from head to foot with great curiosity. The orator bustled up to him, and drawing him partly aside, inquired "On which side he voted?" Rip stared in vacant stupidity. Another short but busy little fellow pulled him by the arm, and, rising on tiptoe, inquired in his ear, "Whether he was Federal or Democrat?" Rip was equally at a loss to comprehend the question; when a knowing, self-important old gentleman, in a sharp cocked hat, made his way through the crowd, putting them to the right and left with his elbows as he passed, and planting himself before Van Winkle, with one arm akimbo, the other resting on his cane, his keen eyes and sharp hat penetrating, as it were, into his very soul, demanded, in an austere tone, "What brought him to the election with a gun on his shoulder, and a mob at his heels; and whether he meant to breed a riot in the village?"—"Alas! gentlemen," cried Rip, somewhat dismayed, "I am a poor quiet man, a native of the place, and a loyal subject of the King, God bless him!"

Here a general shout burst from the by-standers—"A tory! a tory! a spy! a refugee! hustle him! away with him!" It was with great difficulty that the self-important man in the cocked hat restored order; and, having assumed a tenfold austerity of brow, demanded again of the unknown culprit, what he came there for, and whom he was seeking? The poor man humbly assured him that he meant no harm, but merely came there in search of some of his neighbors, who used to keep about the tavern.

"Well—who are they?—name them."

Rip bethought himself a moment, and inquired, "Where's Nicholas Vedder?"

There was a silence for a little while, when an old man replied, in a thin piping voice, "Nicholas Vedder! why, he is dead and gone these eighteen years! There was a wooden tombstone in the churchyard that used to tell all about him, but that's rotten and gone too."

"Where's Brom Dutcher?"

"Oh, he went off to the army in the beginning of the war; some say he was killed at the storming of Stony Point—others say he was drowned in a squall at the foot of Antony's Nose. I don't know—he never came back again."

[6]Babel-like.

"Where's Van Bummel, the schoolmaster?"

"He went off to the wars too, was a great militia general, and is now in congress."

Rip's heart died away at hearing of these sad changes in his home and friends, and finding himself thus alone in the world. Every answer puzzled him too, by treating of such enormous lapses of time, and of matters which he could not understand: war—congress—Stony Point;—he had no courage to ask after any more friends, but cried out in despair, "Does nobody here know Rip Van Winkle?"

"Oh, Rip Van Winkle!" exclaimed two or three, "oh, to be sure! that's Rip Van Winkle yonder, leaning against the tree."

Rip looked, and beheld a precise counterpart of himself, as he went up the mountain; apparently as lazy, and certainly as ragged. The poor fellow was now completely confounded. He doubted his own identity, and whether he was himself or another man. In the midst of his bewilderment, the man in the cocked hat demanded who he was, and what was his name.

"God knows," exclaimed he, at his wit's end; "I'm not myself—I'm somebody else—that's me yonder—no—that's somebody else got into my shoes—I was myself last night, but I fell asleep on the mountain, and they've changed my gun, and everything's changed, and I'm changed, and I can't tell what's my name, or who I am!"

The by-standers began now to look at each other, nod, wink significantly, and tap their fingers against their foreheads. There was a whisper, also, about securing the gun, and keeping the old fellow from doing mischief, at the very suggestion of which the self-important man in the cocked hat retired with some precipitation. At this critical moment a fresh, comely woman pressed through the throng to get a peep at the gray-bearded man. She had a chubby child in her arms, which, frightened at his looks, began to cry. "Hush, Rip," cried she, "hush, you little fool; the old man won't hurt you." The name of the child, the air of the mother, the tone of her voice, all awakened a train of recollections in his mind. "What is your name, my good woman?" asked he.

"Judith Gardenier."

"And your father's name?"

"Ah, poor man, Rip Van Winkle was his name, but it's twenty years since he went away from home with his gun, and never has been heard of since,—his dog came home without him; but whether he shot himself, or was carried away by the Indians, nobody can tell. I was then but a little girl."

Rip had but one question more to ask; but he put it with a faltering voice:

"Where's your mother?"

Oh, she too had died but a short time since; she broke a bloodvessel in a fit of passion at a New-England pedler.

There was a drop of comfort, at least, in this intelligence. The honest man could contain himself no longer. He caught his daughter and her child in his arms. "I am your father!" cried he—"Young Rip Van Winkle once—old Rip Van Winkle now!—Does nobody know poor Rip Van Winkle?"

All stood amazed, until an old woman, tottering out from among the crowd, put her hand to her brow, and peering under it in his face for a moment, exclaimed, "Sure enough! it is Rip Van Winkle—it is himself! Welcome home again, old neighbor. Why, where have you been these twenty long years?"

Rip's story was soon told, for the whole twenty years had been to him but as one night. The neighbors stared when they heard it; some were seen to wink at each other, and put their tongues in their cheeks: and the self-important man in the cocked hat, who, when the alarm was over, had returned to the field, screwed down the corners of his mouth, and shook his head—upon which there was a general shaking of the head throughout the assemblage.

It was determined, however, to take the opinion of old Peter Vanderdonk, who was seen slowly advancing up the road. He was a descendant of the historian of that name, who wrote one of the earliest accounts of the province. Peter was the most ancient inhabitant of the village, and well versed in all the wonderful events and traditions of the neighborhood. He recollected Rip at once, and corroborated his story in the most satisfactory manner. He assured the company that it was a fact, handed down from his ancestor the historian, that the Kaatskill mountains had always been haunted by strange beings. That it was affirmed that the great Hendrick Hudson, the first discoverer of the river and country, kept a kind of vigil there every twenty years, with his crew of the Half-moon; being permitted in this way to revisit the scenes of his enterprise, and keep a guardian eye upon the river and the great city called by his name. That his father had once seen them in their old Dutch dresses playing at ninepins in a hollow of the mountain; and that he himself had heard, one summer afternoon, the sound of their balls, like distant peals of thunder.

To make a long story short, the company broke up and returned to the more important concerns of the election. Rip's daughter took him home to live with her; she had a snug, well-furnished house, and a stout, cheery farmer for a husband, whom Rip recollected for one of the urchins that used to climb upon his back. As to Rip's son and heir, who was the ditto of himself, seen leaning against the tree, he was employed to work on the farm; but evinced an hereditary disposition to attend to anything else but his business.

Rip now resumed his old walks and habits; he soon found many of his former cronies, though all rather the worse for the wear and tear of time; and preferred making friends among the rising generation, with whom he soon grew into great favor.

Having nothing to do at home, and being arrived at that happy age when a man can be idle with impunity, he took his place once more on the bench at the inn-door, and was reverenced as one of the patriarchs of the village, and a chronicle of the old times "before the war." It was some time before he could get into the regular track of gossip, or could be made to comprehend the strange events that had taken place during his torpor. How that there had been a revolutionary war,—that the country had thrown off the yoke of old England,—and that, instead of being a subject of his Majesty George the Third, he was now a free citizen of the United States. Rip, in fact, was no politician; the changes of states and empires made but little impression on him; but there was one species of despotism under which he had long groaned, and that was—petticoat government. Happily that was at an end; he had got his neck out of the yoke of matrimony, and could go in and out whenever he pleased, without dreading the tyranny of Dame Van Winkle. Whenever her name was mentioned, however, he shook his head, shrugged his shoulders, and cast up his eyes; which might pass either for an expression of resignation to his fate, or joy at his deliverance.

He used to tell his story to every stranger that arrived at Mr. Doolittle's hotel. He was observed, at first, to vary on some points every time he told it, which was, doubtless, owing to his having so recently awaked. It at last settled down precisely to the tale I have related, and not a man, woman, or child in the neighborhood but knew it by heart. Some always pretended to doubt the reality of it, and insisted that Rip had been out of his head, and that this was one point on which he always remained flighty. The old Dutch inhabitants, however, almost universally gave it full credit. Even to this day they never hear a thunder-storm of a summer afternoon about the Kaatskill, but they say Hendrick Hudson and his crew are at their game of ninepins; and it is a common wish of all hen-pecked husbands in the neighborhood, when life hangs heavy on their hands, that they might have a quieting draught out of Rip Van Winkle's flagon.

NOTE

The foregoing Tale, one would suspect, had been suggested to Mr. Knickerbocker by a little German superstition about the Emperor Frederick der Rothbart, and the Kypphäuser mountain:[7] *the subjoined note, however, which he had appended to the tale, shows that it is an absolute fact, narrated with his usual fidelity.*

"The story of Rip Van Winkle may seem incredible to many, but nevertheless I give it my full belief, for I know the vicinity of our old Dutch settlements to have been very subject to marvellous events and appearances. Indeed, I have heard many stranger stories than this, in the villages along the Hudson; all of which were too well authenticated to admit of a doubt. I have even talked with Rip Van Winkle myself, who, when last I saw him, was a very venerable old man, and so perfectly rational and consistent on every other point, that I think no conscientious person could refuse to take this into the bargain; nay, I have seen a certificate on the subject taken before a country justice and signed with a cross, in the justice's own handwriting. The story, therefore, is beyond the possibility of doubt.

D.K."

POSTSCRIPT

The following are travelling notes from a memorandum-book of Mr. Knickerbocker.

The Kaatsberg, or Catskill Mountains, have always been a region full of fable. The Indians considered them the abode of spirits, who influenced the weather, spreading sunshine or clouds over the landscape, and sending good or bad hunting-seasons. They were ruled by an old squaw spirit, said to be their mother. She dwelt on the highest peak of the Catskills, and had charge of the doors of day and night to open and shut them at the proper hour. She hung up the new moons in the skies, and cut up the old ones into stars. In times of drought, if properly propitiated, she would spin light summer clouds out of cobwebs and morning dew, and send them off from the crest of the mountain, flake after flake, like flakes of carded cotton, to float in the air; until, dissolved by the heat of the sun, they would fall in gentle showers, causing the grass to spring, the fruits to ripen, and the corn to grow an inch an hour. If displeased, however, she would brew up clouds black as ink, sitting in the midst of them like a bottle-bellied spider in the midst of its web; and when these clouds broke, woe betide the valleys!

In old times, say the Indian traditions, there was a kind of Manitou or Spirit, who kept about the wildest recesses of the Catskill Mountains, and took a mischievous pleasure in wreaking all kinds of evils and vexations upon the red men. Sometimes he

[7]The legend was that Frederick I (1152–1190) lay asleep in a mountain cave awaiting Germany's rise to world eminence, at which time he would re-emerge.

would assume the form of a bear, a panther, or a deer, lead the bewildered hunter a weary chase through tangled forests and among ragged rocks; and then spring off with a loud ho! ho! leaving him aghast on the brink of a beetling precipice or raging torrent.

The favorite abode of this Manitou is still shown. It is a great rock or cliff on the loneliest part of the mountains, and, from the flowering vines which clamber about it, and the wild flowers which abound in its neighborhood, is known by the name of the Garden Rock. Near the foot of it is a small lake, the haunt of the solitary bittern, with water-snakes basking in the sun on the leaves of the pond-lilies which lie on the surface. This place was held in great awe by the Indians, insomuch that the boldest hunter would not pursue his game within its precincts. Once upon a time, however, a hunter who had lost his way, penetrated to the Garden Rock, where he beheld a number of gourds placed in the crotches of trees. One of these he seized and made off with it, but in the hurry of his retreat he let it fall among the rocks, when a great stream gushed forth, which washed him away and swept him down precipices, where he was dashed to pieces, and the stream made its way to the Hudson, and continues to flow to the present day; being the identical stream known by the name of the Kaaters-kill.

1819/20

The Legend of Sleepy Hollow

Found among the Papers of the Late Diedrich Knickerbocker

A pleasing land of drowsy head it was,
Of dreams that wave before the half-shut eye;
And of gay castles in the clouds that pass,
For ever flushing round a summer sky.
—CASTLE OF INDOLENCE[1]

In the bosom of one of those spacious coves which indent the eastern shore of the Hudson, at that broad expansion of the river denominated by the ancient Dutch navigators the Tappan Zee, and where they always prudently shortened sail, and implored the protection of St. Nicholas when they crossed, there lies a small market-town or rural port, which by some is called Greensburgh, but which is more generally and properly known by the name of Tarry Town. This name was given, we are told, in former days, by the good housewives of the adjacent country, from the inveterate propensity of their husbands to linger about the village tavern on market-days. Be that as it may, I do not vouch for the fact, but merely advert to it for the sake of being precise and authentic. Not far from this village, perhaps about two miles, there is a little valley, or rather lap of land, among high hills, which is one of the quietest places in the whole world. A small brook glides through it, with just murmur

[1]Poem (1748) by James Thomson, British poet.

enough to lull one to repose; and the occasional whistle of a quail, or tapping of a woodpecker, is almost the only sound that ever breaks in upon the uniform tranquillity.

I recollect that, when a stripling, my first exploit in squirrel-shooting was in a grove of tall walnut-trees that shades one side of the valley. I had wandered into it at noon-time, when all nature is peculiarly quiet, and was startled by the roar of my own gun, as it broke the Sabbath stillness around, and was prolonged and reverberated by the angry echoes. If ever I should wish for a retreat, whither I might steal from the world and its distractions, and dream quietly away the remnant of a troubled life, I know of none more promising than this little valley.

From the listless repose of the place, and the peculiar character of its inhabitants, who are descendants from the original Dutch settlers, this sequestered glen has long been known by the name of SLEEPY HOLLOW, and its rustic lads are called the Sleepy Hollow Boys throughout all the neighboring country. A drowsy, dreamy influence seems to hang over the land, and to pervade the very atmosphere. Some say that the place was bewitched by a high German doctor, during the early days of the settlement; others, that an old Indian chief, the prophet or wizard of his tribe, held his pow-wows there before the country was discovered by Master Hendrick Hudson. Certain it is, the place still continues under the sway of some witching power, that holds a spell over the minds of the good people, causing them to walk in a continual reverie. They are given to all kinds of marvellous beliefs; are subject to trances and visions; and frequently see strange sights, and hear music and voices in the air. The whole neighborhood abounds with local tales, haunted spots, and twilight superstitions; stars shoot and meteors glare oftener across the valley than in any other part of the country, and the nightmare, with her whole ninefold,[2] seems to make it the favorite scene of her gambols.

The dominant spirit, however, that haunts this enchanted region, and seems to be commander-in-chief of all the powers of the air, is the apparition of a figure on horseback without a head. It is said by some to be the ghost of a Hessian trooper, whose head had been carried away by a cannonball, in some nameless battle during the Revolutionary War, and who is ever and anon seen by the country folk, hurrying along in the gloom of night, as if on the wings of the wind. His haunts are not confined to the valley, but extend at times to the adjacent roads, and especially to the vicinity of a church at no great distance. Indeed certain of the most authentic historians of those parts, who have been careful in collecting and collating the floating facts concerning this spectre, allege that the body of the trooper, having been buried in the churchyard, the ghost rides forth to the scene of battle in nightly quest of his head; and that the rushing speed with which he sometimes passes along the Hollow, like a midnight blast, is owing to his being belated, and in a hurry to get back to the church yard before daybreak.

Such is the general purport of this legendary superstition, which has furnished materials for many a wild story in that region of shadows; and the spectre is known, at all the country firesides, by the name of the Headless Horseman of Sleepy Hollow.

It is remarkable that the visionary propensity I have mentioned is not confined to the native inhabitants of the valley, but is unconsciously imbibed by every one who

[2]See *King Lear,* III, iv.

resides there for a time. However wide awake they may have been before they entered that sleepy region, they are sure, in a little time, to inhale the witching influence of the air, and begin to grow imaginative, to dream dreams, and see apparitions.

I mention this peaceful spot with all possible laud; for it is in such little retired Dutch valleys, found here and there embosomed in the great State of New York, that population, manners, and customs remain fixed; while the great torrent of migration and improvement, which is making such incessant changes in other parts of this restless country, sweeps by them unobserved. They are like those little nooks of still water which border a rapid stream; where we may see the straw and bubble riding quietly at anchor, or slowly revolving in their mimic harbor, undisturbed by the rush of the passing current. Though many years have elapsed since I trod the drowsy shades of Sleepy Hollow, yet I question whether I should not still find the same trees and the same families vegetating in its sheltered bosom.

In this by-place of nature, there abode, in a remote period of American history, that is to say, some thirty years since, a worthy wight of the name of Ichabod Crane; who sojourned, or, as he expressed it, "tarried," in Sleepy Hollow, for the purpose of instructing the children of the vicinity. He was a native of Connecticut, a State which supplies the Union with pioneers for the mind as well as for the forest, and sends forth yearly its legions of frontier woodsmen and country schoolmasters. The cognomen of Crane was not inapplicable to his person. He was tall, but exceedingly lank, with narrow shoulders, long arms and legs, hands that dangled a mile out of his sleeves, feet that might have served for shovels, and his whole frame most loosely hung together. His head was small, and flat at top, with huge ears, large green glassy eyes, and a long snipe nose, so that it looked like a weathercock perched upon his spindle neck, to tell which way the wind blew. To see him striding along the profile of a hill on a windy day, with his clothes bagging and fluttering about him, one might have mistaken him for the genius of famine descending upon the earth, or some scarecrow eloped from a cornfield.

His schoolhouse was a low building of one large room, rudely constructed of logs; the windows partly glazed, and partly patched with leaves of old copy-books. It was most ingeniously secured at vacant hours by a withe twisted in the handle of the door, and stakes set against the window-shutters; so that, though a thief might get in with perfect ease, he would find some embarrassment in getting out: an idea most probably borrowed by the architect, Yost Van Houten, from the mystery of an eel-pot. The schoolhouse stood in a rather lonely but pleasant situation, just at the foot of a woody hill, with a brook running close by, and a formidable birch-tree growing at one end of it. From hence the low murmur of his pupils' voices, conning over their lessons, might be heard in a drowsy summer's day, like the hum of a bee-hive; interrupted now and then by the authoritative voice of the master, in the tone of menace or command; or, peradventure, by the appalling sound of the birch, as he urged some tardy loiterer along the flowery path of knowledge. Truth to say, he was a conscientious man, and ever bore in mind the golden maxim, "Spare the rod and spoil the child."[3]—Ichabod Crane's scholars certainly were not spoiled.

[3]See *Hudibras* by Samuel Butler, English poet (1612–1680), bk. 2, canto 1; also Proverbs, 13:24.

I would not have it imagined, however, that he was one of those cruel potentates of the school, who joy in the smart of their subjects; on the contrary, he administered justice with discrimination rather than severity, taking the burden off the backs of the weak, and laying it on those of the strong. Your mere puny stripling, that winced at the least flourish of the rod, was passed by with indulgence; but the claims of justice were satisfied by inflicting a double portion on some little, tough, wrong-headed, broad-skirted Dutch urchin, who sulked and swelled and grew dogged and sullen beneath the birch. All this he called "doing his duty" by their parents; and he never inflicted a chastisement without following it by the assurance, so consolatory to the smarting urchin, that "he would remember it, and thank him for it the longest day he had to live."

When school-hours were over, he was even the companion and playmate of the larger boys; and on holiday afternoons would convoy some of the smaller ones home, who happened to have pretty sisters, or good housewives for mothers, noted for the comforts of the cupboard. Indeed it behooved him to keep on good terms with his pupils. The revenue arising from his school was small, and would have been scarcely sufficient to furnish him with daily bread, for he was a huge feeder, and, though lank, had the dilating powers of an anaconda; but to help out his maintenance, he was, according to country custom in those parts, boarded and lodged at the houses of the farmers, whose children he instructed. With these he lived successively a week at a time; thus going the rounds of the neighborhood, with all his worldly effects tied up in a cotten handkerchief.

That all this might not be too onerous on the purses of his rustic patrons, who are apt to consider the costs of schooling a grievous burden, and schoolmasters as mere drones, he had various ways of rendering himself both useful and agreeable. He assisted the farmers occasionally in the lighter labors of their farms; helped to make hay; mended the fences; took the horses to water; drove the cows from pasture; and cut wood for the winter fire. He laid aside, too, all the dominant dignity and absolute sway with which he lorded it in his little empire, the school, and became wonderfully gentle and ingratiating. He found favor in the eyes of the mothers, by petting the children, particularly the youngest; and like the lion bold, which whilom so magnanimously the lamb did hold,[4] he would sit with a child on one knee, and rock a cradle with his foot for whole hours together.

In addition to his other vocations, he was the singing-master of the neighborhood, and picked up many bright shillings by instructing the young folks in psalmody. It was a matter of no little vanity to him, on Sundays, to take his station in front of the church-gallery, with a band of chosen singers; where, in his own mind, he completely carried away the palm from the parson. Certain it is, his voice resounded far above all the rest of the congregation; and there are peculiar quavers still to be heard in that church, and which may even be heard half a mile off, quite to the opposite side of the mill-pond, on a still Sunday morning, which are said to be legitimately descended from the nose of Ichabod Crane. Thus, by divers little make-shifts in that ingenious way which is commonly denominated "by hook and by crook," the

[4]Alludes to the seventeenth-century *New England Primer,* under the letter *L.*

worthy pedagogue got on tolerably enough, and was thought, by all who understood nothing of the labor of headwork, to have a wonderfully easy life of it.

The schoolmaster is generally a man of some importance in the female circle of a rural neighborhood; being considered a kind of idle, gentleman-like personage, of vastly superior taste and accomplishments to the rough country swains, and, indeed, inferior in learning only to the parson. His appearance, therefore, is apt to occasion some little stir at the tea-table of a farm-house, and the addition of a supernumerary dish of cakes or sweetmeats, or, peradventure, the parade of a silver teapot. Our man of letters, therefore, was peculiarly happy in the smiles of all the country damsels. How he would figure among them in the churchyard, between services on Sundays! gathering grapes for them from the wild vines that overrun the surrounding trees; reciting for their amusement all the epitaphs on the tombstones; or sauntering, with a whole bevy of them, along the banks of the adjacent mill-pond; while the more bashful country bumpkins hung sheepishly back, envying his superior elegance and address.

From his half itinerant life, also, he was a kind of travelling gazette, carrying the whole budget of local gossip from house to house: so that his appearance was always greeted with satisfaction. He was, moreover, esteemed by the women as a man of great erudition, for he had read several books quite through, and was a perfect master of Cotton Mather's "History of New England Witchcraft,"[5] in which, by the way, he most firmly and potently believed.

He was, in fact, an odd mixture of small shrewdness and simple credulity. His appetite for the marvellous, and his powers of digesting it, were equally extraordinary; and both had been increased by his residence in this spellbound region. No tale was too gross or monstrous for his capacious swallow. It was often his delight, after his school was dismissed in the afternoon, to stretch himself on the rich bed of clover bordering the little brook that whimpered by his school-house, and there con over old Mather's direful tales, until the gathering dusk of the evening made the printed page a mere mist before his eyes. Then, as he wended his way, by swamp and stream, and awful woodland, to the farmhouse where he happened to be quartered, every sound of nature, at that witching hour, fluttered his excited imagination; the moan of the whippoorwill from the hill-side; the boding cry of the tree-toad, that harbinger of storm; the dreary hooting of the screech-owl, or the sudden rustling in the thicket of birds frightened from their roost. The fire-flies, too, which sparkled most vividly in the darkest places, now and then startled him, as one of uncommon brightness would stream across his path; and if, by chance, a huge blockhead of a beetle came winging his blundering flight against him, the poor varlet was ready to give up the ghost, with the idea that he was struck with a witch's token. His only resource on such occasions, either to drown thought or drive away evil spirits, was to sing psalm-tunes; and the good people of Sleepy Hollow, as they sat by their doors of an evening, were often filled with awe, at hearing his nasal melody, "in linked sweetness long drawn out,"[6] floating from the distant hill, or along the dusky road.

[5]An erroneous title, although Mather (1663–1728) did write extensively on witchcraft.

[6]Milton, *L'Allegro,* 1. 140.

Another of his sources of fearful pleasure was, to pass long winter evenings with the old Dutch wives, as they sat spinning by the fire, with a row of apples roasting and spluttering along the hearth, and listen to their marvellous tales of ghosts and goblins, and haunted fields, and haunted brooks, and haunted bridges, and haunted houses, and particularly of the headless horseman, or Galloping Hessian of the Hollow, as they sometimes called him. He would delight them equally by his anecdotes of witchcraft, and of the direful omens and portentous sights and sounds in the air, which prevailed in the earlier times of Connecticut; and would frighten them wofully with speculations upon comets and shooting stars, and with the alarming fact that the world did absolutely turn round, and that they were half the time topsy-turvy!

But if there was a pleasure in all this, while snugly cuddling in the chimney-corner of a chamber that was all of a ruddy glow from the crackling wood-fire, and where, of course, no spectre dared to show his face, it was dearly purchased by the terrors of his subsequent walk homewards. What fearful shapes and shadows beset his path amidst the dim and ghastly glare of a snowy night!—With what wistful look did he eye every trembling ray of light streaming across the waste fields from some distant window!—How often was he appalled by some shrub covered with snow, which, like a sheeted spectre, beset his very path!—How often did he shrink with curdling awe at the sound of his own steps on the frosty crust beneath his feet; and dread to look over his shoulder, lest he should behold some uncouth being tramping close behind him!—and how often was he thrown into complete dismay by some rushing blast, howling among the trees, in the idea that it was the Galloping Hessian on one of his nightly scourings!

All these, however, were mere terrors of the night, phantoms of the mind that walk in darkness; and though he had seen many spectres in his time, and been more than once beset by Satan in divers shapes, in his lonely perambulations, yet daylight put an end to all these evils; and he would have passed a pleasant life of it, in despite of the devil and all his works, if his path had not been crossed by a being that causes more perplexity to mortal man than ghosts, goblins, and the whole race of witches put together, and that was—a woman.

Among the musical disciples who assembled, one evening in each week, to receive his instructions in psalmody, was Katrina Van Tassel, the daughter and only child of a substantial Dutch farmer. She was a blooming lass of fresh eighteen; plump as a partridge; ripe and melting and rosy-cheeked as one of her father's peaches, and universally famed, not merely for her beauty, but her vast expectations. She was withal a little of a coquette, as might be perceived even in her dress, which was a mixture of ancient and modern fashions, as most suited to set off her charms. She wore the ornaments of pure yellow gold, which her great-great-grandmother had brought over from Saardam; the tempting stomacher of the olden time; and withal a provokingly short petticoat, to display the prettiest foot and ankle in the country round.

Ichabod Crane had a soft and foolish heart towards the sex; and it is not to be wondered at that so tempting a morsel soon found favor in his eyes; more especially after he had visited her in her paternal mansion. Old Baltus Van Tassel was a perfect picture of a thriving, contented, liberal-hearted farmer. He seldom, it is true, sent either his eyes or his thoughts beyond the boundaries of his own farm; but within those everything was snug, happy, and well-conditioned. He was satisfied with his wealth, but not proud of it; and piqued himself upon the hearty abundance rather than the style in which he lived. His stronghold was situated on the banks of the Hudson, in one of those green, sheltered, fertile nooks in which the Dutch farmers are so fond of nestling. A great elm-tree spread its broad branches over it; at the foot of which bubbled up a spring of the softest and sweetest water, in a little well, formed of a barrel; and then stole sparkling away through the grass, to a neighboring brook that bubbled along among alders and dwarf willows. Hard by the farm-house was a vast barn, that might have served for a church; every window and crevice of which seemed bursting forth with the treasures of the farm; the flail was busily resounding within it from morning till night; swallows and martins skimmed twittering about the eaves; and rows of pigeons, some with one eye turned up, as if watching the weather, some with their heads under their wings, or buried in their bosoms, and others swelling, and cooing, and bowing about their dames, were enjoying the sunshine on the roof. Sleek unwieldly porkers were grunting in the repose and abundance of their pens; whence sallied forth, now and then, troops of sucking pigs, as if to snuff the air. A stately squadron of snowy geese were riding in an adjoining pond, convoying whole fleets of ducks; regiments of turkeys were gobbling through the farm-yard, and guinea fowls fretting about it, like ill-tempered housewives, with their peevish discontented cry. Before the barn-door strutted the gallant cock, that pattern of a husband, a warrior, and a fine gentleman, clapping his burnished wings, and crowing in the pride and gladness of his heart—sometimes tearing up the earth with his feet, and then generously calling his ever-hungry family of wives and children to enjoy the rich morsel which he had discovered.

The pedagogue's mouth watered, as he looked upon this sumptuous promise of luxurious winter fare. In his devouring mind's eye he pictured to himself every roasting-pig running about with a pudding in his belly, and an apple in his mouth; the pigeons were snugly put to bed in a comfortable pie, and tucked in with a coverlet of crust; the geese were swimming in their own gravy; and the ducks pairing cosily in dishes, like snug married couples, with a decent competency of onion-sauce. In the porkers he saw carved out the future sleek side of bacon, and juicy relishing ham; not a turkey but he beheld daintily trussed up, with its gizzard under its wing, and, peradventure, a necklace of savory sausages; and even bright chanticleer himself lay sprawling on his back, in a side-dish, with uplifted claws, as if craving that quarter which his chivalrous spirit disdained to ask while living.

As the enraptured Ichabod fancied all this, and as he rolled his great green eyes over the fat meadow-lands, the rich fields of wheat, of rye, of buckwheat, and Indian corn, and the orchard burdened with ruddy fruit, which surrounded the warm tenement of Van Tassel, his heart yearned after the damsel who was to inherit these domains, and his imagination expanded with the idea how they might be readily turned into cash, and the money invested in immense tracts of wild land, and shingle palaces in the wilderness. Nay, his busy fancy already realized his hopes, and presented to him the blooming Katrina, with a whole family of children, mounted on the top of a wagon loaded with household trumpery, with pots and kettles dangling beneath; and he beheld himself bestriding a pacing mare, with a colt at her heels, setting out for Kentucky, Tennessee, or the Lord knows where.

When he entered the house, the conquest of his heart was complete. It was one of those spacious farm-houses, with high-ridged, but lowly-sloping roofs, built in the style handed down from the first Dutch settlers; the low projecting eaves forming a piazza along the front, capable of being closed up in bad weather. Under this were hung flails, harness, various utensils of husbandry, and nets for fishing in the neighboring river. Benches were built along the sides for summer use; and a great spinning-wheel at one end, and a churn at the other, showed the various uses to which this important porch might be devoted. From this piazza the wondering Ichabod entered the hall, which formed the centre of the mansion and the place of usual residence. Here, rows of resplendent pewter, ranged on a long dresser, dazzled his eyes. In one corner stood a huge bag of wool ready to be spun; in another a quantity of linsey-woolsey just from the loom; ears of Indian corn, and strings of dried apples and peaches, hung in gay festoons along the walls, mingled with the gaud of red peppers; and a door left ajar gave him a peep into the best parlor, where the claw-footed chairs and dark mahogany tables shone like mirrors; and irons, with their accompanying shovel and tongs, glistened from their covert of asparagus tops; mock-oranges and conch-shells decorated the mantel-piece; strings of various colored birds' eggs were suspended above it; a great ostrich egg was hung from the centre of the room, and a corner-cupboard, knowingly left open, displayed immense treasures of old silver and well-mended china.

From the moment Ichabod laid his eyes upon these regions of delight, the peace of his mind was at an end, and his only study was how to gain the affections of the peerless daughter of Van Tassel. In this enterprise, however, he had more real difficulties than generally fell to the lot of a knight-errant of yore, who seldom had anything but giants, enchanters, fiery dragons, and such like easily conquered adversaries, to contend with; and had to make his way merely through gates of iron and brass, and walls of adamant, to the castle-keep, where the lady of his heart was confined; all which he achieved as easily as a man would carve his way to the centre of a Christmas pie; and then the lady gave him her hand as a matter of course. Ichabod, on the contrary, had to win his way to the heart of a country coquette, beset with a labyrinth of whims and caprices, which were forever presenting new difficulties and impediments; and he had to encounter a host of fearful adversaries of real flesh and blood, the numerous rustic admirers, who beset every portal to her heart; keeping a watchful and angry eye upon each other, but ready to fly out in the common cause against any new competitor.

Among these the most formidable was a burly, roaring, roistering blade, of the name of Abraham, or, according to the Dutch abbreviation, Brom Van Brunt, the hero of the country round, which rang with his feats of strength and hardihood. He was broad-shouldered, and double-jointed, with short curly black hair, and a bluff but not unpleasant countenance, having a mingled air of fun and arrogance. From his Herculean frame and great powers of limb, he had received the nickname of BROM BONES, by which he was universally known. He was famed for great knowledge and skill in horsemanship, being as dexterous on horseback as a Tartar. He was foremost at all races and cockfights; and, with the ascendency which bodily strength acquires in rustic life, was the umpire in all disputes, setting his hat on one side, and giving his decisions with an air and tone admitting of no gainsay or appeal. He was always ready for either a fight or a frolic; but had more mischief than ill-will in his composition; and, with all his overbearing roughness, there was a strong dash of waggish good-humor at bottom. He had three or four boon companions, who regarded him as their model, and at the head of whom he scoured the country, attending every scene of feud or merriment for miles round. In cold weather he was distinguished by a fur cap, surmounted with a flaunting fox's tail; and when the folks at a country gathering descried this well-known crest at a distance, whisking about among a squad of hard riders, they always stood by for a squall. Sometimes his crew would be heard dashing along past the farmhouses at midnight, with whoop and halloo, like a troop of Don Cossacks; and the old dames, startled out of their sleep, would listen for a moment till the hurry-scurry had clattered by, and then exclaim, "Ay, there goes Brom Bones and his gang!" The neighbors looked upon him with a mixture of awe, admiration, and good-will; and when any madcap prank, or rustic brawl, occurred in the vicinity, always shook their heads, and warranted Brom Bones was at the bottom of it.

This rantipole[7] hero had for some time singled out the blooming Katrina for the object of his uncouth gallantries; and though his amorous toyings were something like the gentle caresses and endearments of a bear, yet it was whispered that she did not altogether discourage his hopes. Certain it is, his advances were signals for rival candidates to retire, who felt no inclination to cross a lion in his amours; insomuch, that, when his horse was seen tied to Van Tassel's paling, on a Sunday night, a sure sign that his master was courting, or, as it is termed, "sparking," within, all other suitors passed by in despair, and carried the war into other quarters.

Such was the formidable rival with whom Ichabod Crane had to contend, and, considering all things, a stouter man than he would have shrunk from the competition, and a wiser man would have despaired. He had, however, a happy mixture of pliability and perseverance in his nature; he was in form and spirit like a supple-jack—yielding, but tough; though he bent, he never broke; and though he bowed beneath the slightest pressure, yet, the moment it was away—jerk! he was as erect, and carried his head as high as ever.

To have taken the field openly against his rival would have been madness; for he was not a man to be thwarted in his amours, any more than that stormy lover, Achilles. Ichabod, therefore, made his advances in a quiet and gently insinuating manner. Under cover of his character of singing-master, he had made frequent visits at the farm-house; not that he had anything to apprehend from the meddlesome interference of parents, which is so often a stumbling-block in the path of lovers. Balt Van Tassel was an easy, indulgent soul; he loved his daughter better even than his pipe, and, like a reasonable man and an excellent father, let her have her way in everything. His notable little wife, too, had enough to do to attend to her housekeeping and manage her poultry; for, as she sagely observed, ducks and geese are foolish things, and must be looked after, but girls can take care of themselves. Thus while the busy dame bustled about the house, or plied her spinning-wheel at one end of the piazza, honest Balt would sit smoking his evening pipe at the other, watching the achievements of a little wooden warrior, who, armed with a sword in each hand, was most valiantly fighting the wind on the pinnacle of the barn. In the mean time, Ichabod would carry on his suit with the daughter by the side of the spring under the great elm, or sauntering along in the twilight,—that hour so favorable to the lover's eloquence.

[7]Wild, reckless.

I profess not to know how women's hearts are wooed and won. To me they have always been matters of riddle and admiration. Some seem to have but one vulnerable point, or door of access; while others have a thousand avenues, and may be captured in a thousand different ways It is a great triumph of skill to gain the former, but a still greater proof of generalship to maintain possession of the latter, for the man must battle for his fortress at every door and window. He who wins a thousand common hearts is therefore entitled to some renown; but he who keeps undisputed sway over the heart of a coquette, is indeed a hero. Certain it is, this was not the case with the redoubtable Brom Bones; and from the moment Ichabod Crane made his advances, the interests of the former evidently declined; his horse was no longer seen tied at the palings on Sunday nights, and a deadly feud gradually arose between him and the preceptor of Sleepy Hollow.

Brom, who had a degree of rough chivalry in his nature, would fain have carried matters to open warfare, and have settled their pretensions to the lady according to the mode of those most concise and simple reasoners, the knights-errant of yore—by single combat; but Ichabod was too conscious of the superior might of his adversary to enter the lists against him: he had overheard a boast of Bones, that he would "double the schoolmaster up, and lay him on a shelf of his own school-house"; and he was too wary to give him an opportunity. There was something extremely provoking in this obstinately pacific system; it left Brom no alternative but to draw upon the funds of rustic waggery in his disposition, and to play off boorish practical jokes upon his rival. Ichabod became the object of whimsical persecution to Bones and his gang of rough riders. They harried his hitherto peaceful domains; smoked out his singing-school, by stopping up the chimney; broke into the school-house at night, in spite of its formidable fastenings of withe and window-stakes, and turned everything topsy-turvy: so that the poor schoolmaster began to think all the witches in the country held their meetings there. But what was still more annoying, Brom took opportunities of turning him into ridicule in presence of his mistress, and had a scoundrel dog whom he taught to whine in the most ludicrous manner, and introduced as a rival of Ichabod's to instruct her in psalmody.

In this way matters went on for some time, without producing any material effect on the relative situation of the contending powers. On a fine autumnal afternoon, Ichabod, in pensive mood, sat enthroned on the lofty stool whence he usually watched all the concerns of his little literary realm. In his hand he swayed a ferule, that sceptre of despotic power; the birch of justice reposed on three nails, behind the throne, a constant terror to evil-doers; while on the desk before him might be seen sundry contraband articles and prohibited weapons, detected upon the persons of idle urchins; such as half-munched apples, popguns, whirligigs, fly-cages, and whole legions of rampant little paper game-cocks. Apparently there had been some appalling act of justice recently inflicted, for his scholars were all busily intent upon their books, or slyly whispering behind them with one eye kept upon the master; and a kind of buzzing stillness reigned throughout the school-room. It was suddenly interrupted by the appearance of a negro, in tow-cloth jacket and trousers, a round-crowned fragment of a hat, like the cap of Mercury, and mounted on the back of a ragged, wild, half-broken colt, which he managed with a rope by way of halter. He came clattering up to the school-door with an invitation to Ichabod to attend a merry-making or "quilting frolic," to be held that evening at Mynheer Van Tassel's;

and having delivered his message with that air of importance, and effort at fine language, which a negro is apt to display on petty embassies of the kind, he dashed over the brook, and was seen scampering away up the Hollow, full of the importance and hurry of his mission.

All was now bustle and hubbub in the late quiet school-room. The scholars were hurried through their lessons, without stopping at trifles; those who were nimble skipped over half with impunity, and those who were tardy had a smart application now and then in the rear, to quicken their speed, or help them over a tall word. Books were flung aside without being put away on the shelves, inkstands were overturned, benches thrown down, and the whole school was turned loose an hour before the usual time, bursting forth like a legion of young imps, yelping and racketing about the green, in joy at their early emancipation.

The gallant Ichabod now spent at least an extra half-hour at his toilet, brushing and furbishing up his best and indeed only suit of rusty black, and arranging his looks by a bit of broken looking-glass, that hung up in the school-house. That he might make his appearance before his mistress in the true style of a cavalier, he borrowed a horse from the farmer with whom he was domiciliated, a choleric old Dutchman, of the name of Hans Van Ripper, and, thus gallantly mounted, issued forth, like a knight-errant in quest of adventures. But it is meet I should, in the true spirit of romantic story, give some account of the looks and equipments of my hero and his steed. The animal he bestrode was a broken-down plough-horse, that had outlived almost everything but his viciousness. He was gaunt and shagged, with a ewe neck and a head like a hammer; his rusty mane and tail were tangled and knotted with burrs; one eye had lost its pupil, and was glaring and spectral; but the other had the gleam of a genuine devil in it. Still he must have had fire and mettle in his day, if we may judge from the name he bore of Gunpowder. He had, in fact, been a favorite steed of his master's, the choleric Van Ripper, who was a furious rider, and had infused, very probably, some of his own spirit into the animal; for, old and broken-down as he looked, there was more of the lurking devil in him than in any young filly in the country.

Ichabod was a suitable figure for such a steed. He rode with short stirrups, which brought his knees nearly up to the pommel of the saddle; his sharp elbows stuck out like grasshoppers'; he carried his whip perpendicularly in his hand, like a sceptre, and, as his horse jogged on, the motion of his arms was not unlike the flapping of a pair of wings. A small wool hat rested on the top of his nose, for so his scanty strip of forehead might be called; and the skirts of his black coat fluttered out almost to the horse's tail. Such was the appearance of Ichabod and his steed, as they shambled out of the gate of Hans Van Ripper, and it was altogether such an apparition as is seldom to be met with in broad daylight.

It was, as I have said, a fine autumnal day, the sky was clear and serene, and nature wore that rich and golden livery which we always associate with the idea of abundance. The forests had put on their sober brown and yellow, while some trees of the tenderer kind had been nipped by the frosts into brilliant dyes of orange, purple, and scarlet. Streaming files of wild ducks began to make their appearance high in the air; the bark of the squirrel might be heard from the groves of beech and hickory nuts, and the pensive whistle of the quail at intervals from the neighboring stubble-field.

The small birds were taking their farewell banquets. In the fulness of their revelry, they fluttered, chirping and frolicking, from bush to bush, and tree to tree, capricious from the very profusion and variety around them. There was the honest cockrobin, the favorite game of stripling sportsmen, with its loud querulous notes; and the twittering blackbirds flying in sable clouds; and the golden-winged woodpecker, with his crimson crest, his broad black gorget, and splendid plumage; and the cedar-bird, with its red-tipt wings and yellow-tipt tail, and its little monteiro cap of feathers; and the blue jay, that noisy coxcomb, in his gay light-blue coat and white under-clothes, screaming and chattering, nodding and bobbing and bowing, and pretending to be on good terms with every songster of the grove.

As Ichabod jogged slowly on his way, his eye, ever open to every symptom of culinary abundance, ranged with delight over the treasures of jolly autumn. On all sides he beheld vast store of apples; some hanging in oppressive opulence on the trees; some gathered into baskets and barrels for the market; others heaped up in rich piles for the cider-press. Farther on he beheld great fields of Indian corn, with its golden ears peeping from their leafy coverts, and holding out the promise of cakes and hasty-pudding; and the yellow pumpkins lying beneath them, turning up their fair round bellies to the sun, and giving ample prospects of the most luxurious of pies; and anon he passed the fragrant buckwheat fields, breathing the odor of the bee-hive, and as he beheld them, soft anticipations stole over his mind of dainty slapjacks, well buttered, and garnished with honey or treacle, by the delicate little dimpled hand of Katrina Van Tassel.

Thus feeding his mind with many sweet thoughts and "sugared suppositions," he journeyed along the sides of a range of hills which look out upon some of the goodliest scenes of the mighty Hudson. The sun gradually wheeled his broad disk down into the west. The wide bosom of the Tappan Zee lay motionless and glossy, excepting that here and there a gentle undulation waved and prolonged the blue shadow of the distant mountain. A few amber clouds floated in the sky, without a breath of air to move them. The horizon was of a fine golden tint, changing gradually into a pure apple-green, and from that into the deep blue of the mid-heaven. A slanting ray lingered on the woody crests of the precipices that overhung some parts of the river, giving greater depth to the dark-gray and purple of their rocky sides. A sloop was loitering in the distance, dropping slowly down with the tide, her sail hanging uselessly against the mast; and as the reflection of the sky gleamed along the still water, it seemed as if the vessel was suspended in the air.

It was toward evening that Ichabod arrived at the castle of the Heer Van Tassel, which he found thronged with the pride and flower of the adjacent country. Old farmers, a spare leathern-faced race, in homespun coats and breeches, blue stockings, huge shoes, and magnificent pewter buckles. Their brisk withered little dames, in close crimped caps, long-waisted shortgowns, homespun petticoats, with scissors and pincushions, and gay calico pockets hanging on the outside. Buxom lasses, almost as antiquated as their mothers, excepting where a straw hat, a fine ribbon, or perhaps a white frock, gave symptoms of city innovation. The sons, in short square-skirted coats with rows of stupendous brass buttons, and their hair generally queued in the fashion of the times, especially if they could procure an eel-skin for the purpose, it being esteemed, throughout the country, as a potent nourisher and strengthener of the hair.

Brom Bones, however, was the hero of the scene, having come to the gathering on his favorite steed, Daredevil, a creature, like himself, full of mettle and mischief, and which no one but himself could manage. He was, in fact, noted for preferring vicious animals, given to all kinds of tricks, which kept the rider in constant risk of his neck, for he held a tractable well-broken horse as unworthy of a lad of spirit.

Fain would I pause to dwell upon the world of charms that burst upon the enraptured gaze of my hero, as he entered the state parlor of Van Tassel's mansion. Not those of the bevy of buxom lasses, with their luxurious display of red and white; but the ample charms of a genuine Dutch country tea-table, in the sumptuous time of autumn. Such heaped-up platters of cakes of various and almost indescribable kinds, known only to experienced Dutch housewives! There was the doughty doughnut, the tenderer oly koek, and the crisp and crumbling cruller; sweet cakes and short cakes, ginger-cakes and honey-cakes, and the whole family of cakes. And then there were apple-pies and peach-pies and pumpkin-pies; besides slices of ham and smoked beef; and moreover delectable dishes of preserved plums, and peaches, and pears, and quinces; not to mention broiled shad and roasted chickens; together with bowls of milk and cream, all mingled higgledy-piggledy, pretty much as I have enumerated them, with the motherly tea-pot sending up its clouds of vapor from the midst—Heaven bless the mark! I want breath and time to discuss this banquet as it deserves, and am too eager to get on with my story. Happily, Ichabod Crane was not in so great a hurry as his historian, but did ample justice to every dainty.

He was a kind and thankful creature, whose heart dilated in proportion as his skin was filled with good cheer; and whose spirits rose with eating as some men's do with drink. He could not help, too, rolling his large eyes round him as he ate, and chuckling with the possibility that he might one day be lord of all this scene of almost unimaginable luxury and splendor. Then, he thought, how soon he'd turn his back upon the old school-house; snap his fingers in the face of Hans Van Ripper, and every other niggardly patron, and kick any itinerant pedagogue out-of-doors that should dare to call him comrade!

Old Baltus Van Tassel moved about among his guests with a face dilated with content and good-humor, round and jolly as the harvest-moon. His hospitable attentions were brief, but expressive, being confined to a shake of the hand, a slap on the shoulder, a loud laugh, and a pressing invitation to "fall to, and help themselves."

And now the sound of the music from the common room, or hall, summoned to the dance. The musician was an old gray-headed negro, who had been the itinerant orchestra of the neighborhood for more than half a century. His instrument was as old and battered as himself. The greater part of the time he scraped on two or three strings accompanying every movement of the bow with a motion of the head; bowing almost to the ground and stamping with his foot whenever a fresh couple were to start.

Ichabod prided himself upon his dancing as much as upon his vocal powers. Not a limb, not a fibre about him was idle; and to have seen his loosely hung frame in full motion, and clattering about the room, you would have thought Saint Vitus himself, that blessed patron of the dance, was figuring before you in person. He was the admiration of all the negroes; who, having gathered, of all ages and sizes, from the farm and the neighborhood, stood forming a pyramid of shining black faces at every door and window, gazing with delight at the scene, rolling their white eyeballs, and showing grinning rows of ivory from ear to ear. How could the flogger of urchins be otherwise than animated and joyous? the lady of his heart was his partner in the dance, and smiling graciously in reply to all his amorous oglings; while Brom Bones, sorely smitten with love and jealousy, sat brooding by himself in one corner.

When the dance was at an end, Ichabod was attracted to a knot of the sager folks, who, with old Van Tassel, sat smoking at one end of the piazza, gossiping over former times, and drawing out long stories about the war.

This neighborhood, at the time of which I am speaking, was one of those highly favored places which abound with chronicle and great men. The British and American line had run near it during the war; it had, therefore, been the scene of marauding, and infested with refugees, cow-boys,[8] and all kinds of border chivalry. Just sufficient time had elapsed to enable each story-teller to dress up his tale with a little becoming fiction, and, in the indistinctness of his recollection, to make himself the hero of every exploit.

There was the story of Doffue Martling, a large blue-bearded Dutchman, who had nearly taken a British frigate with an old iron nine-pounder from a mud breastwork, only that his gun burst at the sixth discharge. And there was an old gentleman who shall be nameless, being too rich a mynheer to be lightly mentioned, who, in the battle of Whiteplains, being an excellent master of defence, parried a musketball with a small sword, insomuch that he absolutely felt it whiz round the blade, and glance off at the hilt; in proof of which he was ready at any time to show the sword, with the hilt a little bent. There were several more that had been equally great in the field, not one of whom but was persuaded that he had a considerable hand in bringing the war to a happy termination.

But all these were nothing to the tales of ghosts and apparitions that succeeded. The neighborhood is rich in legendary treasures of the kind. Local tales and superstitions thrive best in these sheltered long-settled retreats; but are trampled underfoot by the shifting throng that forms the population of most of our country places. Besides, there is no encouragement for ghosts in most of our villages, for they have scarcely had time to finish their first nap, and turn themselves in their graves, before their surviving friends have travelled away from the neighborhood; so that when they turn out at night to walk their rounds, they have no acquaintance left to call upon. This is perhaps the reason why we so seldom hear of ghosts, except in our long-established Dutch communities.

The immediate cause, however, of the prevalence of supernatural stories in these parts was doubtless owing to the vicinity of Sleepy Hollow. There was a contagion in the very air that blew from that haunted region; it breathed forth an atmosphere of dreams and fancies infecting all the land. Several of the Sleepy Hollow people were present at Van Tassel's, and, as usual, were doling out their wild and wonderful legends. Many dismal tales were told about funeral trains, and mourning cries and wailings heard and seen about the great tree where the unfortunate Major André was taken,[9] and which stood in the neighborhood. Some mention was made also of the woman in white, that haunted the dark glen at Raven Rock, and was often heard to

[8]Guerrilla troops, active in the region during the Revolution.

[9]British officer involved in Benedict Arnold's desertion, executed as a spy by the Americans.

shriek on winter nights before a storm, having perished there in the snow. The chief part of the stories, however, turned upon the favorite spectre of Sleepy Hollow, the headless horseman, who had been heard several times of late, patrolling the country; and, it was said, tethered his horse nightly among the graves in the churchyard.

The sequestered situation of this church seems always to have made it a favorite haunt of troubled spirits. It stands on a knoll, surrounded by locust-trees and lofty elms, from among which its decent whitewashed walls shine modestly forth, like Christian purity beaming through the shades of retirement. A gentle slope descends from it to a silver sheet of water, bordered by high trees, between which, peeps may be caught at the blue hills of the Hudson. To look upon its grass-grown yard, where the sunbeams seem to sleep so quietly, one would think that there at least the dead might rest in peace. On one side of the church extends a wide woody dell, along which raves a large brook among broken rocks and trunks of fallen trees. Over a deep black part of the stream, not far from the church, was formerly thrown a wooden bridge; the road that led to it, and the bridge itself, were thickly shaded by overhanging trees, which cast a gloom about it, even in the daytime, but occasioned a fearful darkness at night. This was one of the favorite haunts of the headless horseman; and the place where he was most frequently encountered. The tale was told of old Brouwer, a most heretical disbeliever in ghosts, how he met the horseman returning from his foray into Sleepy Hollow, and was obliged to get up behind him; how they galloped over bush and brake, over hill and swamp, until they reached the bridge; when the horseman suddenly turned into a skeleton, threw old Brouwer into the brook, and sprang away over the tree-tops with a clap of thunder.

This story was immediately matched by a thrice marvellous adventure of Brom Bones, who made light of the galloping Hessian as an arrant jockey. He affirmed that, on returning one night from the neighboring village of Sing Sing, he had been overtaken by this midnight trooper; that he had offered to race with him for a bowl of punch, and should have won it too, for Daredevil beat the goblin horse all hollow, but, just as they came to the church-bridge, the Hessian bolted, and vanished in a flash of fire.

All these tales, told in that drowsy undertone with which men talk in the dark, the countenances of the listeners only now and then receiving a casual gleam from the glare of a pipe, sank deep in the mind of Ichabod. He repaid them in kind with large extracts from his invaluable author, Cotton Mather, and added many marvellous events that had taken place in his native State of Connecticut, and fearful sights which he had seen in his nightly walks about the Sleepy Hollow.

The revel now gradually broke up. The old farmers gathered together their families in their wagons, and were heard for some time rattling along the hollow roads, and over the distant hills. Some of the damsels mounted on pillions behind their favorite swains, and their light-hearted laughter, mingling with the clatter of hoofs, echoed along the silent woodlands, sounding fainter and fainter until they gradually died away—and the late scene of noise and frolic was all silent and deserted. Ichabod only lingered behind, according to the custom of country lovers, to have a *tête-à-tête* with the heiress, fully convinced that he was now on the high road to success. What passed at this interview I will not pretend to say, for in fact I do not know. Something, however, I fear me, must have gone wrong, for he certainly sallied forth, after no very great interval, with an air quite desolate and chop-fallen.—Oh, these women! these women! Could that girl have been playing off any of her coquettish tricks?—Was her encouragement of the poor pedagogue all a mere sham to secure her conquest of his rival?—Heaven only knows, not I!—Let it suffice to say, Ichabod stole forth with the air of one who had been sacking a hen-roost, rather than a fair lady's heart. Without looking to the right or left to notice the scene of rural wealth on which he had so often gloated, he went straight to the stable, and with several hearty cuffs and kicks, roused his steed most uncourteously from the comfortable quarters in which he was soundly sleeping, dreaming of mountains of corn and oats, and whole valleys of timothy and clover.

It was the very witching time of night[10] that Ichabod, heavy hearted and crest-fallen, pursued his travel homewards, along the sides of the lofty hills which rise above Tarry Town, and which he had traversed so cheerily in the afternoon. The hour was as dismal as himself. Far below him, the Tappan Zee spread its dusky and indistinct waste of waters, with here and there the tall mast of a sloop riding quietly at anchor under the land. In the dead hush of midnight he could even hear the barking of the watch-dog from the opposite shore of the Hudson; but it was so vague and faint as only to give an idea of his distance from this faithful companion of man. Now and then, too, the long-drawn crowing of a cock, accidentally awakened, would sound far, far off, from some farm-house away among the hills—but it was like a dreaming sound in his ear. No signs of life occurred near him, but occasionally the melancholy chirp of a cricket, or perhaps the guttural twang of a bull-frog, from a neighboring marsh, as if sleeping uncomfortably, and turning suddenly in his bed.

All the stories of ghosts and goblins that he had heard in the afternoon, now came crowding upon his recollection. The night grew darker and darker; the stars seemed to sink deeper in the sky, and driving clouds occasionally hid them from his sight. He had never felt so lonely and dismal. He was, moreover, approaching the very place where many of the scenes of the ghost-stories had been laid. In the centre of the road stood an enormous tulip-tree, which towered like a giant above all the other trees of the neighborhood, and formed a kind of landmark. Its limbs were gnarled, and fantastic, large enough to form trunks for ordinary trees, twisting down almost to the earth, and rising again into the air. It was connected with the tragical story of the unfortunate André, who had been taken prisoner hard by; and was universally known by the name of Major André's tree. The common people regarded it with a mixture of respect and superstition, partly out of sympathy for the fate of its ill-starred namesake, and partly from the tales of strange sights and doleful lamentations told concerning it.

As Ichabod approached this fearful tree, he began to whistle: he thought his whistle was answered,—it was but a blast sweeping sharply through the dry branches. As he approached a little nearer, he thought he saw something white, hanging in the midst of the tree,—he paused and ceased whistling; but on looking more narrowly, perceived that it was a place where the tree had been scathed by lightning, and the white wood laid bare. Suddenly he heard a groan,—his teeth chattered and his knees smote against the saddle: it was but the rubbing of one huge bough upon another, as they were swayed about by the breeze. He passed the tree in safety; but new perils lay before him.

[10]*Hamlet,* III, ii.

About two hundred yards from the tree a small brook crossed the road, and ran into a marshy and thickly wooded glen, known by the name of Wiley's swamp. A few rough logs, laid side by side, served for a bridge over this stream. On that side of the road where the brook entered the wood, a group of oaks and chestnuts, matted thick with wild grape-vines, threw a cavernous gloom over it. To pass this bridge was the severest trial. It was at this identical spot that the unfortunate André was captured, and under the covert of those chestnuts and vines were the sturdy yeomen concealed who surprised him. This has ever since been considered a haunted stream, and fearful are the feelings of the school boy who has to pass it alone after dark.

As he approached the stream, his heart began to thump; he summoned up, however, all his resolution, gave his horse half a score of kicks in the ribs, and attempted to dash briskly across the bridge; but instead of starting forward, the perverse old animal made a lateral movement, and ran broadside against the fence. Ichabod, whose fears increased with the delay, jerked the reins on the other side, and kicked lustily with the contrary foot: it was all in vain; his steed started, it is true, but it was only to plunge to the opposite side of the road into a thicket of brambles and alder bushes. The schoolmaster now bestowed both whip and heel upon the starveling ribs of old Gunpowder, who dashed forward, snuffling and snorting, but came to a stand just by the bridge, with a suddenness that had nearly sent his rider sprawling over his head. Just at this moment a plashy tramp by the side of the bridge caught the sensitive ear of Ichabod. In the dark shadow of the grove, on the margin of the brook, he beheld something huge, misshapen, black, and towering. It stirred not, but seemed gathered up in the gloom, like some gigantic monster ready to spring upon the traveller.

The hair of the affrighted pedagogue rose upon his head with terror. What was to be done? To turn and fly was not too late; and besides, what chance was there of escaping ghost or goblin, if such it was, which could ride upon the wings of the wind? Summoning up, therefore, a show of courage, he demanded in stammering accents—"Who are you?" He received no reply. He repeated his demand in a still more agitated voice. Still there was no answer. Once more he cudgelled the sides of the inflexible Gunpowder, and, shutting his eyes, broke forth with involuntary fervor into a psalm-tune. Just then the shadowy object of alarm put itself in motion, and, with a scramble and a bound, stood at once in the middle of the road. Though the night was dark and dismal, yet the form of the unknown might now in some degree be ascertained. He appeared to be a horseman of large dimensions, and mounted on a black horse of powerful frame. He made no offer of molestation or sociability, but kept aloof on one side of the road, jogging along on the blind side of old Gunpowder, who had now got over his fright and waywardness.

Ichabod, who had no relish for this strange midnight companion, and bethought himself of the adventure of Brom Bones with the Galloping Hessian, now quickened his steed, in hopes of leaving him behind. The stranger, however, quickened his horse to an equal pace. Ichabod pulled up, and fell into a walk, thinking to lag behind,—the other did the same. His heart began to sink within him; he endeavored to resume his psalm-tune, but his parched tongue clove to the roof of his mouth, and he could not utter a stave. There was something in the moody and dogged silence of this pertinacious companion, that was mysterious and appalling. It was soon fearfully accounted for. On mounting a rising ground, which brought the figure of his fellow-traveller in relief against the sky, gigantic in height, and muffled in a cloak, Ichabod was horror-struck, on perceiving that he was headless!—but his horror was still more increased, on observing that the head, which should have rested on his shoulders, was carried before him on the pommel of the saddle: his terror rose to desperation; he rained a shower of kicks and blows upon Gunpowder, hoping, by a sudden movement, to give his companion the slip,—but the spectre started full jump with him. Away then they dashed, through thick and thin; stones flying, and sparks flashing at every bound. Ichabod's flimsy garments fluttered in the air, as he stretched his long lank body away over his horse's head, in the eagerness of his flight.

They had now reached the road which turns off to Sleepy Hollow; but Gunpowder, who seemed possessed with a demon, instead of keeping up it, made an opposite turn, and plunged headlong downhill to the left. This road leads through a sandy hollow, shaded by trees for about a quarter of a mile, where it crosses the bridge famous in goblin story, and just beyond swells the green knoll on which stands the whitewashed church.

As yet the panic of the steed had given his unskilful rider an apparent advantage in the chase; but just as he had got half-way through the hollow, the girths of the saddle gave way, and he felt it slipping from under him. He seized it by the pommel, and endeavored to hold it firm, but in vain; and had just time to save himself by clasping old Gunpowder round the neck, when the saddle fell to the earth, and he heard it trampled underfoot by his pursuer. For a moment the terror of Hans Van Ripper's wrath passed across his mind—for it was his Sunday saddle; but this was no time for petty fears; the goblin was hard on his haunches; and (unskilful rider that he was!) he had much ado to maintain his seat; sometimes slipping on one side, sometimes on another, and sometimes jolted on the high ridge of his horse's backbone, with a violence that he verily feared would cleave him asunder.

An opening in the trees now cheered him with the hopes that the church-bridge was at hand. The wavering reflection of a silver star in the bosom of the brook told him that he was not mistaken. He saw the walls of the church dimly glaring under the trees beyond. He recollected the place where Brom Bones's ghostly competitor had disappeared. "If I can but reach that bridge," thought Ichabod, "I am safe." Just then he heard the black steed panting and blowing close behind him; he even fancied that he felt his hot breath. Another convulsive kick in the ribs, and old Gunpowder sprang upon the bridge; he thundered over the resounding planks; he gained the opposite side; and now Ichabod cast a look behind to see if his pursuer should vanish, according to rule, in a flash of fire and brimstone. Just then he saw the goblin rising in his stirrups, and in the very act of hurling his head at him. Ichabod endeavored to dodge the horrible missle, but too late. It encountered his cranium with a tremendous crash,—he was tumbled headlong into the dust, and Gunpowder, the black steed, and the goblin rider, passed by like a whirlwind.

The next morning the old horse was found without his saddle, and with the bridle under his feet, soberly cropping the grass at his master's gate. Ichabod did not make his appearance at breakfast;—dinner-hour came, but no Ichabod. The boys assembled at the school-house, and strolled idly about the banks of the brook; but no schoolmaster. Hans Van Ripper now began to feel some uneasiness about the fate of poor Ichabod, and his saddle. An inquiry was set on foot, and after diligent investigation they came upon his traces. In one part of the road leading to the church was found the saddle trampled in the dirt; the tracks of horses' hoofs deeply dented in the road, and evidently at furious speed, were traced to the bridge, beyond which, on the bank of a broad part of the brook, where the water ran deep and black, was found the hat of the unfortunate Ichabod, and close beside it a shattered pumpkin.

The brook was searched, but the body of the schoolmaster was not to be discovered. Hans Van Ripper, as executor of his estate, examined the bundle which contained all his worldly effects. They consisted of two shirts and a half; two stocks for the neck; a pair or two of worsted stockings; an old pair of corduroy small-clothes; a rusty razor; a book of psalm-tunes, full of dogs' ears, and a broken pitchpipe. As to the books and furniture of the school-house, they belonged to the community, excepting Cotton Mather's "History of Witchcraft," a "New England Almanac," and a book of dreams and fortune-telling; in which last was a sheet of foolscap much scribbled and blotted in several fruitless attempts to make a copy of verses in honor of the heiress of Van Tassel. These magic books and the poetic scrawl were forthwith consigned to the flames by Hans Van Ripper; who from that time forward determined to send his children no more to school; observing, that he never knew any good come of this same reading and writing. Whatever money the schoolmaster possessed, and he had received his quarter's pay but a day or two before, he must have had about his person at the time of his disappearance.

The mysterious event caused much speculation at the church on the following Sunday. Knots of gazers and gossips were collected in the churchyard, at the bridge, and at the spot where the hat and pumpkin had been found. The stories of Brouwer, of Bones, and a whole budget of others, were called to mind; and when they had diligently considered them all, and compared them with the symptoms of the present case, they shook their heads, and came to the conclusion that Ichabod had been carried off by the Galloping Hessian. As he was a bachelor, and in nobody's debt, nobody troubled his head any more about him. The school was removed to a different quarter of the Hollow, and another pedagogue reigned in his stead.

It is true, an old farmer, who had been down to New York on a visit several years after, and from whom this account of the ghostly adventure was received, brought home the intelligence that Ichabod Crane was still alive; that he had left the neighborhood, partly through fear of the goblin and Hans Van Ripper, and partly in mortification at having been suddenly dismissed by the heiress; that he had changed his quarters to a distant part of the country; had kept school and studied law at the same time, had been admitted to the bar, turned politician, electioneered, written for the newspapers, and finally had been made a justice of the Ten Pound Court. Brom Bones too, who shortly after his rival's disappearance conducted the blooming Katrina in triumph to the altar, was observed to look exceeding knowing whenever the story of Ichabod was related, and always burst into a hearty laugh at the mention of the pumpkin; which led some to suspect that he knew more about the matter than he chose to tell.

The old country wives, however, who are the best judges of these matters, maintain to this day that Ichabod was spirited away by supernatural means; and it is a favorite story often told about the neighborhood round the winter evening fire. The bridge became more than ever an object of superstitious awe, and that may be the reason why the road has been altered of late years, so as to approach the church by the border of the mill-pond. The school-house, being deserted, soon fell to decay, and was reported to be haunted by the ghost of the unfortunate pedagogue; and the ploughboy, loitering homeward of a still summer evening, has often fancied his voice at a distance, chanting a melancholy psalm-tune among the tranquil solitudes of Sleepy Hollow.

POSTSCRIPT,

Found in the Handwriting of Mr. Knickerbocker

The preceding Tale is given, almost in the precise words in which I heard it related at a Corporation meeting of the ancient city of Manhattoes, at which were present many of its sagest and most illustrious burghers. The narrator was a pleasant, shabby, gentlemanly old fellow, in pepper-and-salt clothes, with a sadly humorous face; and one whom I strongly suspected of being poor,—he made such efforts to be entertaining. When his story was concluded, there was much laughter and approbation, particularly from two or three deputy aldermen, who had been asleep the greater part of the time. There was, however, one tall, dry-looking old gentleman, with beetling eyebrows, who maintained a grave and rather severe face throughout: now and then folding his arms, inclining his head, and looking down upon the floor, as if turning a doubt over in his mind. He was one of your wary men, who never laugh, but upon good grounds—when they have reason and the law on their side. When the mirth of the rest of the company had subsided and silence was restored, he leaned one arm on the elbow of his chair, and sticking the other akimbo, demanded, with a slight but exceedingly sage motion of the head, and contraction of the brow, what was the moral of the story, and what it went to prove?

The story-teller, who was just putting a glass of wine to his lips, as a refreshment after his toils, paused for a moment, looked at his inquirer with an air of infinite deference, and, lowering the glass slowly to the table, observed, that the story was intended most logically to prove:—

"That there is no situation in life but has its advantages and pleasures—provided we will but take a joke as we find it:

"That, therefore, he that runs races with goblin troopers is likely to have rough riding of it.

"Ergo, for a country schoolmaster to be refused the hand of a Dutch heiress, is a certain step to high preferment in the state."

The cautious old gentleman knit his brows tenfold closer after this explanation, being sorely puzzled by the ratiocination of the syllogism; while, methought, the one in pepper-and-salt eyed him with something of a triumphant leer. At length he observed, that all this was very well, but still he thought the story a little on the extravagant—there were one or two points on which he had his doubts.

"Faith, sir," replied the story-teller, "as to that matter, I don't believe one half of it myself."

D.K.

1819/20

Mordecai Manuel Noah 1785–1851

In July of 1819, Mordecai Manuel Noah used his preface to *She Would Be a Soldier* to declare the importance of drawing upon exclusively American materials: "National plays should be encouraged. They have done everything for the British nation, and can do much for us. . . . We have a fine scope, and abundant materials to work with, and a noble country to justify the attempt." Noah's incredibly varied, somewhat controversial careers in politics, journalism, and theater were greatly shaped by his and America's ambivalence toward democracy and national identity—especially because he was Jewish. Born in Philadelphia to Revolutionary War veteran Manuel Noah and Zipporah Phillips but orphaned at age seven, Noah was raised by his maternal grandparents, Rebecca and Jonas Phillips, the latter a successful merchant who had already made a name for himself as a defender of Jewish rights. Much of Noah's childhood was spent at the theater in Philadelphia, and later, as a carver's apprentice, he traveled around upstate New York and Lower Canada selling wood products. These regions would later mark his adult life.

By the age of twenty-three, Noah had become self-educated in law and had written speeches for Simon Snyder, Pennsylvania's first non-aristocratic governor; through Snyder's influence, Noah was elected to the post of major in the Pennsylvania militia and from then on was commonly called "Major Noah." In 1809 he published his first play, *The Fortress of Sorrento,* which Noah himself declared awful, as well as *Shakspeare* [*sic*] *Illustrated,* a book that belittled Shakespeare's accomplishments supposedly in order to create a larger audience for original American plays. The never-completed second volume of that work was to include Noah's version of the non-Jewish roots of *The Merchant of Venice*'s "pound of flesh" motif. Noah's political voice gained momentum through work as a reporter in Harrisburg, Pennsylvania. Later, in Charleston, South Carolina, during the War of 1812, under the pseudonym Muly Malak, his war hawking led to being attacked as "a Jew" and as an "un-Christian Turk," which in turn led to several duels. Ironically, these skirmishes secured Noah's reputation as both an honorable southern gentleman and as a democratic activist. (Noah's "Southern honor" may have had something to do with his inconsistent stance toward slavery.) It was the War of 1812 that Noah, the first of several antebellum writers to do so, chose as *She Would Be a Soldier*'s backdrop, a stage device that helped sustain the play's national popularity and financial success, especially on July Fourth and Washington's Birthday, from 1819 to 1868.

Another popular literary setting of the early national era was the land of Algeria, where for years American and English soldiers had been captured and put into slavery. Having established a "double" reputation in Charleston as both scrappy nationalist and orientalized Jew, Noah, after an earlier referral by Joel Barlow, was appointed United States Consul to Tunis by then Secretary of State James Monroe, a position he held from 1813 to 1815. As consul, Noah's primary task was to use spies to negotiate secretly for the release of twelve U.S. war captives held in Algiers. After one of Noah's spies, Maryland native Richard Keene, mismanaged the allotted "three thousand dollars per man," Monroe and President James Madison released Noah of his consular duties. Their seemingly anti-Semitic justification was partly grounded on Noah's Jewishness interfering with his Americanness and his ability to represent America: "At the time of your appointment as consul at Tunis it was not known that the religion which you profess would form any obstacle to the exercise of your consular functions. Recent information, however, on which entire reliance may be placed, proves that it would produce a very unfavourable effect. IN CONSEQUENCE OF WHICH, the President has deemed it expedient to revoke your commission. On the receipt of this letter, therefore, you will consider yourself no longer in the public service." Shortly after, in 1815, a somewhat shaken and displaced Noah returned to New York, where he devoted more than a year to clearing his name. In the process, his creative and confrontational energies intensified, and led to his 1817 revitalizing Tammany Hall's *National Advocate* as its new editor. Although long-cleared of anti-Americanness and with his dreams of a prestigious diplomatic post clearly in the past, in 1819 Noah still needed to publish *Travels in England, France, Spain, and the Barbary States in the Years 1813–14 and 15,* as much a detailed account and defense of his (Jewish) American patriotism as it is a study of the contradictoriness of his firing. In it Noah seems baffled: "My religion was known to the government at the time of my appointment, and it constituted one of the prominent causes why I was sent to Barbary." Interestingly enough, *Travels* was published (in Noah's words, "to add to the stock of American literature") at around the same time that *She Would Be a Soldier* first took the stage.

Noah's life became even more crowded and his Jewish presence even more conspicuous in New York. Over the next few years, he would not only continue to produce plays for the New York stage, but in 1822 he was also appointed the city's sheriff (even though James Fenimore Cooper had written of Noah, "The sheriff of the city of New-York . . . , an officer elected by the people, was, a few years ago, a Jew!"). When the office was made elective in 1824, however, Noah was defeated; apparently anti-Semitic charges were a factor in that loss. Nevertheless, Noah would eventually become a New York City judge, and he remained, until his death in 1851, devoted to the theater. Chiefly, though, he was always a driven newspaper editor and at various times was associated with *The Enquirer, The Evening Star, The Commercial Advertiser, The Union, The Trangram or Fashionable Trifler, The Sunday Times,* and Noah's *Weekly Messenger* (partly edited by a then unknown Walt Whitman).

In 1837, Noah published his *Discourse on the Evidences of the American Indians Being the Descendants of the Lost Tribes of Israel,* a theory of Jewish-American roots at play since the colonization of America and still used by Noah's contemporaries, including William Apess. But perhaps Noah's most notable activity was the controversial Ararat Project, which overlapped with the peak viewing/reading times (1819–25) of *She Would Be a Soldier* and *Travels.* Ararat was Noah's celebrated, somewhat self-serving attempt to establish Grand Island, near Buffalo, New York, as a "City of Refuge for the Jews." Noah often used his editor's status to assert the need for a Jewish homeland. (He had previously tried to purchase Newport, Rhode Island.) In Ararat, Jews could be decolonized from regions such as post–Napoleonic Europe and be protected, empowered, and provided with help in adapting to the cultural—and agricultural—machinery of the modern world. The opening of Ararat truly signified Noah as dramatist and politician in search of a space for his Jewish and American selves. Garbed in crimson robes during the foundation-stone ceremonies on September 25, 1825, Noah asked his spectators, "Why should the parent of nations, the oldest of people, the founders of religion, wander among the governments of the earth, intreating succor and protection when we are capable of protecting ourselves?" But Ararat never made it past the spectacular performances surrounding the laying of the city's cornerstone.

Interestingly enough, despite Noah's assertions of Jewish identity, he does not include a single Jew in any of his plays. At the time, when most viewers saw a Jew on stage, they expected a stereotype (e.g., a greedy moneylender or a peddler). Since American audiences had been familiar with Shakespeare's *The Merchant of Venice* since 1750 and Cumberland's *The Jew* since 1794, one could argue that Noah, like his contemporary, Jewish-American playwright Isaac Harby of Charleston, resisted using Jewish characters as a way to forge a new American Jewish self. The absent presence of Jews and the desire for national identity should always be kept in mind when examining *She Would Be a Soldier,* but readers should also be aware that Noah was writing for the "popular" national stage as well as trying to provide a living for himself and his actors. In fact, he claimed to have written the play (in three days) for actress Catherine Leesugg, who starred as Christine (reads like "Christian"), the cross-dressed lead female character escaping from an arranged marriage. Like Royall Tyler's *The Contrast,* Noah's pro-American comedy mocks aristocratic privilege, etiquette, and fashion; it also brings attention to the use of food as a marker of national identity. Unlike Tyler's Jonathan, Noah's country bumpkin is Jerry Mayflower, a cowardly, drunk pig farmer—far from a sturdy "authentic" American. In other words, Noah points out that "American" virtue is not the sole property of a "Mayflower." Whereas Mayflower, the least desirable character in the play, is the one aligned with the pig, a role historically imposed upon Jews, the strongest character in the play is the Indian Chief, who is quite openly critical of whiteness in America. The Chief also manages to convince a snobbish British captain and his French aid to masquerade as Native American warriors. Along with the play's use of very American settings, potentially subversive Jewishness, and Shakespearean motifs and actors (notably Edwin Forrest as the Indian Chief), *She Would Be a Soldier* was also known to feature live horses on stage, another blending of "popular" and "high" culture on the early nineteenth-century stage. All in all, Noah's comedy blurs and then resolves a variety of national boundaries, identities, and responsibilities to display multiple cultural concerns and to produce new spaces in which to understand, critique, and enjoy the emerging American subject.

Craig Kleinman
City College of San Francisco

PRIMARY WORKS

The Fortress of Sorrento, 1809; *Shakspeare [sic] Illustrated,* 1809; *Paul and Alexis,* 1812; *She Would Be a Soldier, or The Plains of Chippewa,* 1819; *Travels in England, France, Spain, and the Barbary States in the Years 1813–14 and 15,* 1819; *The Siege of Tripoli,* 1820; *Essays of Howard on Domestic Economy,* 1820; *Marion, or The Hero of Lake George,* 1821; *The Grecian Captive,* 1822; *The Siege of Yorktown,* 1824; "Address by Mordecai M. Noah," 1825; *Discourse on the Evidences of the American Indians Being the Descendants of the Lost Tribes of Israel,* 1837; *Gleanings from a Gathered Harvest,* 1845; *She Would Be a Soldier, or The Plains of Chippewa,* in *Dramas from the American Theater, 1762–1909,* ed. Richard Moody, 1966.

SECONDARY WORKS

Isaac Goldberg, *Major Noah: American Jewish Pioneer,* 1936; Lee M. Friedman, "Mordecai M. Noah as Playwright," *Historia Judaica* 4.2 (October 1942); Anita Libman Lebeson, *Pilgrim People,* 1950; Louis Harap, *The Image of the Jew in American Literature: From Early Republic to Mass Migration,* 1974; Ronald Sanders, *Lost Tribes and Promised Lands,* 1978; Jonathon D. Sarna, *Jacksonian Jew: The Two Worlds of Mordecai Manuel Noah,* 1981; Lawrence W. Levine, *Highbrow/Lowbrow: The Emergence of Cultural Hierarchy in America,* 1988; Jacob Marcus, *United States Jewry, 1776–1985,* 1989; Craig Kleinman, "Pigging the Nation, Staging the Jew in M. M. Noah's *She Would Be a Soldier,*" *American Transcendental Quarterly* 10.3 (1996): 201–17.

She Would Be a Soldier

Characters

GENERAL	1ST OFFICER
JASPER	SOLDIER
LENOX	WAITER
HON. CAPTAIN PENDRAGON	JAILOR
JERRY	CHRISTINE
LAROLE	ADELA
JENKINS	MAID
INDIAN CHIEF	SOLDIERS, PEASANTS, INDIANS, ETC.

A Valley with a neat Cottage on the right, an Arbour on the left, and picturesque Mountains at a distance. Enter from the cottage, JASPER *and* JENKINS.

JENKINS: And so, neighbour, you are not then a native of this village?

JASPER: I am not, my friend; my story is short, and you shall hear it. It was my luck, call it bad or good, to be born in France, in the town of Castlenaudary, where my parents, good honest peasants, cultivated a small farm on the borders of the canal of Midi. I was useful, though young; we were well enough to live, and I received from the parish school a good education, was taught to love my country, my parents, and my friends; a happy temper, a common advantage in my country, made all things easy to me; I never looked for to-morrow to bring me more joy than I experienced to-day.

JENKINS: Pardon my curiosity, friend Jasper: how came you to leave your country, when neither want nor misfortune visited your humble dwelling?

JASPER: Novelty, a desire for change, an ardent disposition to visit foreign countries. Passing through the streets of Toulouse one bright morning in spring, the lively drum and fife broke on my ear, as I was counting my gains from a day's marketing. A company of soldiers neatly dressed, with white cockades, passed me with a brisk step; I followed them through instinct—the sergeant informed me that they were on their way to Bordeaux, from thence to embark for America, to aid the cause of liberty in the new world, and were commanded by the Marquis de la Fayette. That name was familiar to me; La Fayette was a patriot—I felt like a patriot, and joined the ranks immediately.

JENKINS: Well, you enlisted and left your country?

JASPER: I did. We had a boisterous passage to America, and endured many hardships during the revolution. I was wounded at Yorktown, which long disabled me, but what then? I served under great men, and for a great cause; I saw the independence of the thirteen states acknowledged, I was promoted to a sergeancy by the great Washington, and I sheathed my sword, with the honest pride of knowing, that I had aided in establishing a powerful and happy republic.

JENKINS: You did well, honest Jasper, you did well; and now you have the satisfaction of seeing your country still free and happy.

JASPER: I have, indeed. When the army was disbanded, I travelled on foot to explore the uncultivated territory which I had assisted in liberating, I purchased a piece of land near the great lakes, and with my axe levelled the mighty oaks, cleared my meadows, burnt out the wolves and bears, and then built that cottage there.

JENKINS: And thus became a settler and my neighbour; thanks to the drum and fife and the white cockade, that lured you from your home.

JASPER: In a short time, Jenkins, everything flourished; my cottage was neat, my cattle thriving, still I wanted something—it was a wife. I was tired of a solitary life, and married Kate, the miller's daughter; you knew her.

JENKINS: Ay, that I did; she was a pretty lass.

JASPER: She was a good wife—ever cheerful and industrious, and made me happy: poor Kate! I was without children for several years; at length my Christine was born, and I have endeavoured, in cultivating her mind, and advancing her happiness, to console myself for the loss of her mother.

JENKINS: Where is Christine? Where is your daughter, neighbour Jasper?

JASPER: She left the cottage early this morning with Lenox, to climb the mountains and see the sun rise; it is time for them to return to breakfast.

JENKINS: Who is this Mr. Lenox?

JASPER: An honest lieutenant of infantry, with a gallant spirit and a warm heart. He was wounded at Niagara, and one stormy night, he presented himself at our cottage door, pale and haggard. His arm had been shattered by a ball, and he had received a flesh wound from a bayonet: we took him in—for an old soldier never closes his door on a wounded comrade—Christine nursed him, and he soon recovered. But I wish they were here—it is growing late: besides, this is a busy day, friend Jenkins.

JENKINS: Ah, how so?

JASPER: You know Jerry Mayflower, the wealthy farmer; he has offered to marry my Christine. Girls must not remain single if they can get husbands, and I have consented to the match, and he will be here to-day to claim her hand.

JENKINS: But will Christine marry Jerry? She has been too well educated for the honest farmer.

JASPER: Oh, she may make a few wry faces, as she does when swallowing magnesia, but the dose will go down. There is some credit due to a wife who improves the intellect of her husband; aye, and there is some pride in it also. Girls should marry. Matrimony is like an old oak; age gives durability to the trunk, skill trims the branches, and affection keeps the foliage ever green. But come, let us in. [JASPER *and* JENKINS *enter the cottage*]

Pastoral Music.—LENOX *and* CHRISTINE *are seen winding down the mountains—his left arm is in a sling.*

CHRISTINE: At last we are at home.—O my breath is nearly gone. You soldiers are so accustomed to marching and counter-marching, that you drag me over hedge and briar, like an empty baggage-wagon. Look at my arm, young Mars, you've made it as red as pink, and as rough as—then my hand—don't attempt to kiss it, you—wild man of the woods.

LENOX: Nay, dear Christine, be not offended; if I have passed rapidly over rocks and mountains, it is because you were with me. My heart ever feels light and happy when I am permitted to walk with you; even the air seems newly perfumed, and the birds chaunt more melodiously; and see, I can take my arm out of confinement—your care has done this; your voice administered comfort, and your eyes affection. What do I not owe you?

CHRISTINE: Owe me? Nothing, only one of your best bows, and your prettiest compliments. But I do suspect, my serious cavalier, that your wounds were never as bad as you would have me think. Of late you have taken your recipes with so much grace, have swallowed so many bitter tinctures with a playful smile, that I believe you've been playing the invalid, and would make me your nurse for life—O sinner as you are, what have you to say for yourself?

LENOX: Why, I confess, dear Christine, that my time has passed with so much delight, that even the call of duty will find me reluctant to quit these scenes, so dear to memory, hospitality, and, let me add, to love. Be serious, then, dear Christine, and tell me what I have to hope; even now I expect orders from my commanding officer, requiring my immediate presence at the camp; we are on the eve of a battle—Speak!

CHRISTINE: Why, you soldiers are such fickle game, that if we once entangle you in the net, 'tis ten to one but the sight of a new face will be sufficiently tempting to break the mesh—you're just as true as the smoke of your cannon, and you fly off at the sight of novelty in petticoats, like one of your Congreve rockets—No, I won't love a soldier—that's certain.

LENOX: Nay, where is our reward then for deserving well of our country? Gratitude may wreath a chaplet of laurel, but trust me, Christine, it withers unless consecrated by beauty.

CHRISTINE: Well, that's a very pretty speech, and deserves one of my best courtesies. Now suppose I should marry you, my "dear ally Croaker," I shall expect to see myself placed on the summit of a baggage-wagon, with soldiers' wives and a few dear squalling brats, whose musical tones drown e'en the "squeaking of the wry-neck'd fife;" and if I should escape from the enemy at the close of a battle, I should be compelled to be ever ready, and "pack up my tatters and follow the drum."—No, no, I can't think of it.

LENOX: Prithee, be serious, dear Christine, your gaiety alarms me. Can you permit me to leave you without a sigh? Can I depart from that dear cottage and rush to battle without having the assurance that there is a heart within which beats in unison with mine? a heart which can participate in my glory, and sympathize in my misfortunes?

CHRISTINE: No—not so, Lenox; your glory is dear to me, your happiness my anxious wish. I have seen you bear pain like a soldier, and misfortune like a man. I am myself a soldier's daughter, and believe me, when I tell you that under the appearance of gaiety, my spirits are deeply depressed at your approaching departure. I have been taught, by a brave father, to love glory when combined with virtue. There is my hand;—be constant, and I am ever your friend; be true, and you shall find me ever faithful.

LENOX: Thanks—a thousand thanks, beloved Christine; you have removed a mountain of doubts and anxious wishes from my heart: I did hope for this reward, though it was a daring one. Love and honour must now inspire me, and should we again be triumphant in battle, I shall return to claim the reward of constancy—a reward dearer than thrones—the heart of a lovely and virtuous woman.

CHRISTINE: Enough, dear Lenox; I shall never doubt your faith. But come, let us in to breakfast—stay—my knight of the rueful countenance, where is the portrait which you have been sketching of me? Let me look at your progress.

LENOX: 'Tis here. [*Gives a small drawing book*]

CHRISTINE: [*Opening it*] Heavens, how unlike! Why Lenox, you were dreaming of the *Venus de Medici* when you drew this—Oh, you flatterer!

LENOX: Nay, 'tis not finished; now stand there, while I sketch the drapery.—[*Places her at a distance, takes out a pencil, and works at the drawing*]

CHRISTINE: Why, what a statue you are making of me. Pray, why not make a picture of it at once? Place me in that bower, with a lute and a lap dog, sighing for your return; then draw a soldier disguised as a pilgrim, leaning on his staff, and his cowl thrown back; let that pilgrim resemble thee, and then let the little dog bark, and I fainting, and there's a subject for the pencil and pallet.

LENOX: Sing, dear Christine, while I finish the drawing—it may be the last time I shall ever hear you.

CHRISTINE: Oh, do not say so, my gloomy cavalier; a soldier, and despair?

THE KNIGHT ERRANT

Written by the late Queen of Holland

It was Dunois, the young and brave, was bound to Palestine,
But first he made his orisons before St. Mary's shrine:
And grant, immortal Queen of Heav'n, was still the soldier's prayer,
That I may prove the bravest knight, and love the fairest fair.

His oath of honour on the shrine he grav'd it with his sword,
And follow'd to the Holy Land the banner of his Lord;
Where, faithful to his noble vow, his war-cry fill'd the air—
Be honour'd, aye, the bravest knight, beloved the fairest fair.

They ow'd the conquest to his arm, and then his liege lord said,
The heart that has for honour beat must be by bliss repaid:
My daughter Isabel and thou shall be a wedded pair,
For thou art bravest of the brave, she fairest of the fair.

And then they bound the holy knot before St. Mary's shrine,
Which makes a paradise on earth when hearts and hands combine;
And every lord and lady bright that was in chapel there,
Cry'd, Honour'd be the bravest knight, belov'd the fairest fair.

LENOX: There, 'tis finished—how do you like it?

CHRISTINE: Why, so, so—if you wish something to remind you of me, it will do.

LENOX: No, not so; your image is too forcibly impressed here to need so dull a monitor. But I ask it to reciprocate—wear this for my sake, [*Gives a miniature*] and think of him who, even in the battle's rage, will not forget thee. [*Bugle sounds at a distance*] Hark! 'tis a bugle of our army. [*Enter a* SOLDIER, *who delivers a letter to* LENOX *and retires*—LENOX *opens and reads it*] "The enemy, in force, has thrown up entrenchments near Chippewa; if your wounds will permit, join your corps without delay—a battle is unavoidable, and I wish you to share the glory of a victory. You have been promoted as an aid to the general for your gallantry in the last affair. It gives me pleasure to be the first who announces this grateful reward—lose not a moment.

Your friend, MANDEVILLE."

I must be gone immediately.

Enter JASPER *and* JENKINS *from the cottage*

JASPER: Ah! Lenox, my boy, good morning to you. Why Christine, you have had a long ramble with the invalid.

CHRISTINE: Lenox leaves us immediately, dear father; the army is on the march.

JASPER: Well, he goes in good time, and may success attend him. Ods my life, when I was young, the sound of the drum and fife was like the music of the spheres, and the noise and bustle of a battle was more cheering to me, than "the hunter's horn in the morning." You will not forget us, Lenox, will you?

LENOX: Forget ye? Never—I should be the most ungrateful of men, could I forget that endearing attention which poured oil into my wounds, and comforted the heart of a desponding and mutilated soldier. No, Jasper, no; while life remains, yourself and daughter shall never cease to live in my grateful remembrance. [CHRISTINE *and* LENOX *enter the cottage*]

*Pastoral Music.—*PEASANTS *are seen winding down the mountains, headed by* JERRY, *dressed for a festive occasion, with white favours, nosegays, etc.*

JERRY: Here I am, farmer Jasper—come to claim Miss Crissy as my wife, according to your promise, and have brought all my neighbours. How do you do?

JASPER: Well—quite well—and these are all your neighbours?

JERRY: Yes—there's Bob Short, the tanner; Nick Anvil, the blacksmith; Patty, the weaver's daughter—and the rest of 'em; come here, Patty, make a curtchey to the old soger—[PATTY *comes forward*]—a pretty girl! I could have had her, but she wanted edication—she wanted the airs and graces, as our schoolmaster says.

JASPER: Well, farmer, you are an honest man, but I fear my Christine will not approve this match, commenced without her advice, and concluded without her consent. Then her education has been so different from—

JERRY: O, fiddle-de-dee, I don't mind how larned she is, so much the better—she can teach me to parlyvoo, and dance solos and duets, and such elegant things, when I've done ploughing.

JASPER: But I'm not sure that she will like you.

JERRY: Not like me? Come, that's a good one; only look at my movements—why she can't resist me. I'm the boy for a race, for an apple-paring or quilting frolic—fight a cock, hunt an opossum, or snare a partridge with any one.—Then I'm a squire, and a county judge, and a *brevet* ossifer in the militia besides; and a devil of a fellow at an election to boot. Not have me? damme, that's an insult. Besides, sergeant Jasper, I've been to the wars since I've seen ye—got experience, laurels and lilies, and all them there things.

JASPER: Indeed!

JERRY: Yes—served a campaign, and was at the battle of Queenstown. What do you think of that?

JASPER: And did you share in the glory of that spirited battle?

JERRY: O yes, I shared in all the glory—that is—I didn't fight. I'll tell you how it was: I marched at the head of my village sogers, straight as the peacock in my farm yard, and I had some of the finest lads in our county, with rifles—well, we march'd and camp'd, and camp'd and march'd, and were as merry as grigs until we arrived at the river: half the troops had cross'd and were fighting away like young devils: ods life, what a smoke! what a popping of small arms, and roaring of big ones! and what a power of red coats!

JASPER: Well, and you panted to be at them? clubb'd your rifles, and dashed over?

JERRY: Oh no, I didn't—I was afear'd that in such a crowd, nobody would see how I fought, so I didn't cross at all. Besides, some one said, it were contrary to law and the constitution, to go into the enemy's country, but if they com'd into our country, it were perfectly lawful to flog 'em.

JASPER: And you did not cross?

JERRY: Oh no, I stood still and look'd on; it were contrary to the constitution of my country, and my own constitution to boot—so I took my post out of good gun shot, and felt no more fear nor you do now.

JASPER: No doubt. Admirable sophistry, that can shield cowards and traitors, under a mistaken principle of civil government! I've heard of those scruples, which your division felt when in sight of the enemy. Was that a time to talk of constitutions—when part of our gallant army was engaged with unequal numbers? Could you calmly behold your fellow citizens falling on all sides, and not avenge their death? Could you, with arms in your hands, the enemy in view, with the roar of cannon thundering on your ear, and the flag of your country waving amidst fire and smoke—could you find a moment to think of constitutions? Was that a time to pause and suffer coward scruples to unnerve the arm of freemen?

JERRY: Bravo! bravo! sergeant Jasper; that's a very fine speech—I'll vote for you for our assemblyman; now just go that over again, that I may get it by heart for our next town meeting—blazing flags—fiery cannon—smoking constitutions—

JASPER: I pray you pardon me. I am an old soldier, and fought for the liberty which you enjoy, and, therefore, claim some privilege in expressing my opinion. But come, your friends are idle, let us have breakfast before our cottage door.—Ah, Jerry, my Crissy would make a fine soldier's wife: do you know that I have given her a military education?

JERRY: No, surely—

JASPER: Aye, she can crack a bottle at twelve paces with a pistol.

JERRY: Crack a bottle! Come, that's a good one: I can crack a bottle too, but not so far off.

JASPER: And then she can bring down a buck, at any distance.

JERRY: Bring down a buck? I don't like that—can't say as how I like my wife to meddle with bucks. Can she milk—knit garters—make apple butter and maple sugar—dance a reel after midnight, and ride behind her husband on a pony, to see the trainings of our sogers—that's the wife for my money. Oh, here she comes.

Enter CHRISTINE *and* LENOX *from the cottage.*

JASPER: Christine, here is farmer Mayflower and his friends, who have come to visit our cottage, and you in particular.

CHRISTINE: They are all welcome. Good morning, Jerry—how is it with you?

JERRY: Purely, Miss Crissy, I'm stout and hearty, and you look as pretty and as rosy as a field of pinks on a sunshiny morning.

JASPER: Come here, farmer—give me your hand—Christine, yours—[*Joins them*]—there; may you live long and happy, and my blessings ever go with you.

CHRISTINE: [*Aside in amazement*] Heavens! what can this mean?

LENOX *is agitated—pause—*JASPER *and group retire—*LENOX *remains at a distance.*

JERRY: Why, Miss Crissy, your father has consented that I shall marry you, and I've come with my neighbours to have a little frolic, and carry you home with me.

CHRISTINE: And am I of so little moment as not to be consulted? Am I thus to be given away by my father without one anxious question? [*With decision*] Farmer, pardon my frankness; on this ocassion, sincerity alone is required—I do not like you, I will not marry you—nay, do not look surprised. I am a stranger to falsehood and dissimulation, and thus end at once all hopes of ever becoming my husband.

JERRY: Why, now, Miss Crissy, that's very cruel of you—I always had a sneaking kindness for you, and when your father gave his consent, I didn't dream as how you could refuse me.

CHRISTINE: My father has ever found me dutiful and obedient, but when he bestows my hand, without knowing whether my heart or inclinations accompany it, I feel myself bound to consult my own happiness. I cannot marry you, farmer.

LENOX: [*Advancing*] All things are prepared, and I am now about to depart. Christine, farewell! Friends, good fortune await you! [*Aside*] Dear Christine, remember me. [*Exit hastily*]

JERRY: Lack-a-daisy! What a disappointment to me, when I had put my house in such nice order—painted my walls—got a new chest upon chest—two new bed quilts, and a pair of pumps, and had the pig-sty and dairy whitewashed.—Hang me, after all, I believe, she is only a little shy. Oh, I see it now, she only wants a little coaxing—a little sparking or so—I've a great mind to kiss her. I will, too. [*Approaches* CHRISTINE, *who stands at a distance, buried in deep thought*]

CHRISTINE: Begone—dare not touch me! Heavens, am I reserved for this humiliation? Could my father be so cruel?

JERRY: Now, Crissy, don't be so shy—you know you like me—you know you said t'other day, when I were out training, that I held up my head more like a soger than anybody in the ranks; come now, let's make up; you'll always find me a dutiful husband, and if I ever flog you, then my name's not Jerry.

Enter JASPER *from the cottage, with a basket;* PEASANTS *following with fruit*

JASPER: Come, let us have breakfast in the open air—help me to arrange the table.

JERRY: Breakfast! Oh, true, I've a powerful appetite. [*Assists*]

CHRISTINE: [*Aside*] What is to be done? I have not a moment to lose; my father is stern and unyielding—I know his temper too well, to hope that my entreaties will prevail with him—the farmer is rich, and gold is a powerful tempter. I must be gone—follow Lenox, and in disguise, to avoid this hateful match. I'll in, whilst unobserved. [*Enters the cottage*]

JASPER: Come, sit down, farmer and neighbours; and you, my pretty lads and lasses, let's have a dance. Ah, here is a foraging party. [*Enter* SOLDIERS]

Party dance—several pastoral and fancy dances—and as the whole company retires, CHRISTINE *comes from the cottage with cautious steps—she is dressed in a frock coat, pantaloons and hat*

CHRISTINE: They are gone—now to escape. Scenes of my infancy—of many a happy hour, farewell! Oh, farewell, forever! [*Exit*]

JASPER *and* JERRY *return*

JERRY: She refused me plumply.

JASPER: Impossible!

JERRY: No, it's quite possible. Farmer, said she, I will *not* marry you—and hang me if there's any joke in that.

JASPER: Refuse an honest man? A wealthy one, too? And one whom her father gives to her? Trifling girl! Insensible to her happiness and interest. What objections had she to you, farmer?

JERRY: Objections! Oh, none in the world, only she wouldn't marry me; she didn't seem struck at all with my person.

JASPER: Mere coyness—maiden bashfulness.

JERRY: So I thought, sergeant Jasper, and was going to give her a little kiss, when she gave me such a look, and such a push, as quite astounded me.

JASPER: I will seek and expostulate with the stubborn girl. Ah, Jerry, times have strangely altered, when young women choose husbands for themselves, with as much ease and indifference, as a ribbon for their bonnet. [*Enters the cottage*]

JERRY: So they do—the little independent creatures as they are—but what Miss Crissy could see in me to refuse, hang me if I can tell. I'm call'd as sprightly a fellow as any in our county, and up to everything—always ready for fun, and perfectly goodnatured. [*Enter* JASPER *from the cottage, agitated*]

JASPER: She is nowhere to be found—she has gone off and left her poor old father. In her room, I found these lines scrawled with a pencil: "You have driven your daughter from you, by urging a match that was hateful to her. Was her happiness not worth consulting?" What's to be done? Where has she gone? Ah, a light breaks in upon me—to the camp—to the camp!

JERRY: Oho! I smell a rat too—she's gone after Mr. Lenox, the infantry ossifer. Oh, the young jade! But come along, old soger—get your hat and cane, and we'll go arter her—I'm a magistrate, and will bring her back by a habes corpus. [*They enter the cottage*]

Scene 2

A wood. Enter CHRISTINE *in haste, looking back with fear.*

CHRISTINE: On, on, or I shall be pursued and o'ertaken—I have lost my way. Ah, yonder is the camp—I see the flags and tents, a short time and I shall be with you, dear Lenox. [*Exit*]

Enter JASPER, JERRY, *and* PEASANTS

JERRY: We're on the right track, farmer; I know all tracks—used to 'em when I hunt 'possums.

JASPER: Cruel girl! to desert her old father, who has ever been kind and affectionate.

JERRY: Cruel girl! to desert me, who intended to be so very affectionate, if she had given me a chance.

JASPER: We cannot be far from the outposts, let us continue our search. [*Exeunt*]

Scene 3

A Camp. A row of tents in the rear with camp flags at equal distances; on the right wing is a neat marquee, and directly opposite to it another. Sentinels on duty at each marquee. Enter from the marquee, LENOX *and* ADELA.

LENOX: I never was more surprised! Just when I had brush'd up my arms, and prepared to meet the enemy, who should I find in camp but you, my old hoyden scholar. Why Adela, you have grown nearly as tall as a grenadier, and as pretty—zounds, I would kiss you, if I dare.

ADELA: I am delighted to see you dear Lenox; you are still as gay and amiable as when you taught your little Adela to conjugate verbs, and murder French; I heard of your gallantry and wounds, and imagined I should see you limping on crutches, with a green patch over one eye, and a wreath of laurel around your head, a kind of limping, one-eyed cupid; but I find you recovered from your wounds, and ready for new ones, my soldier.

LENOX: Bravo! the little skipping girl, who was once so full of mischief, has grown a tall and beautiful woman. But what brings you to camp, Adela? What have you to do with "guns and drums? heaven save the mark!"

ADELA: Why, my father wrote for me, expecting that the campaign was drawing to a close; but scarcely had I arrived here, when intelligence reached us that the enemy, in force, had occupied a position near Chippewa; it was too late to return, so I remained to see a little skirmishing.

LENOX: And are you prepared to endure the privations of a camp?

ADELA: Oh, it is delightful! it is something out of the common order of things, something new—such echoing of bugles—glistening of firearms, and nodding of plumes—such marchings and countermarchings—and such pretty officers too, Lenox; but then a terrible accident happened to me the other day.

LENOX: Aye, what was it?

ADELA: Why you must know, that I accompanied my father, who with his suite, and a small detachment, went out on a reconnoitering project.—Just as we *debouched* from the wood, according to the military phrase, we came suddenly and unexpectedly on a foraging party of the enemy, who began to fight and retreat at the same time.

LENOX: Well?

ADELA: My horse happening to be an old trooper, the moment the bugles sounded, and he heard the prattle of the small arms, he dashed in amongst them, and there was I screaming in a most delightful style, which, by some, must have been mistaken for a war-whoop, and to mend the matter, a very polite and accomplished Indian took aim at me with his rifle, and actually shot away the plume from my hat, which, I dare say, was as valuable a prize to him as I should have been.

LENOX: And how did you escape from your perilous situation?

ADELA: Oh, I soon recovered my fright, and reined in my old horse; my father and a few soldiers cut in before me, and covered my retreat, so that in the conclusion of this little affair, I gained a feather in my cap, though the enemy carried off the plume; and I found myself at last on the field of battle, as cool as any hero in the army.

LENOX: And so, my lively Adela, you have been fairly introduced to Mars and Bellona: how do you like them?

ADELA: Prodigiously. I find, after all, that courage is something like a cold bath; take the first plunge, and all is over. Lord, Lenox, how delightful it would have been, had I been armed and fought gallantly in that affair; my name would have been immortalized like Joan of Arc's. Congress would have voted me a medal, I should have had a public dinner at Tammany-Hall, and his honour the mayor would have made me one of his prettiest speeches, in presenting me with the freedom of the great city in a gold box.

LENOX: And so, then, you admire a military life?

ADELA: Oh, I'm in raptures with it! I am a perfect female Quixote, and would relinquish a thousand dandy beaux for one brave fellow; and, therefore, Lenox, don't be surprised, if you should see me going about from tent to tent, chaunting the old songs of

"Soldier, soldier, marry me,
With your fife and drum."

CHRISTINE *suddenly appears in the background and surveys the party with astonishment*

CHRISTINE: Heavens! what do I see? Lenox, and with a female so affectionately?

LENOX: Your spirits charm me, dear Adela, and revive those feelings for you, that time has impaired, but not destroyed. But come, let us in and see your worthy father. [*Leads her into the tent to the left*]

CHRISTINE: Cruel, unkind, false Lenox! Are these your vows of constancy? are these your protestations of love? Scarcely are you free from our cottage, when your vows and pledges are but air. Wretched Christine! what will become of you? I have deserted my father's house to avoid a hateful match, and seek the protection of the man I love; he is false, and I am lost. What's to be done? Return home a penitent, and meet the frowns of my father, and be wedded to the man I hate? Never. Seek out Lenox, and upbraid him with his falsehood? No, pride and wounded honour will not permit me. Let him go—he is a wretch who trifles with the affections of a woman. I care not what becomes of me, despair is all that I have left. Ha! a thought strikes me with the lightning's force—the army—I will enlist—this disguise is favourable, and in the battle's rage, seek that death which quickly awaits me—'tis resolved. [CORPORAL *passes over the stage*] Hist, corporal.

CORPORAL: Well, my lad, what would ye?

CHRISTINE: I would enlist, good corporal, and serve my country.

CORPORAL: Enlist! As a drummer or fifer, I suppose.

CHRISTINE: No; in the ranks—and though small, you will find me capable. Give me your musket. [CHRISTINE *takes the musket, shoulders, presents, and goes through a few motions*]

CORPORAL: Well done, my little fellow; you'll do, if it's only for a fugelman; come along to our sergeant, and receive the bounty. [*Exit*]

CHRISTINE: Now, Lenox, now am I fully revenged for your cruel desertion. [*Follows*]

End of the First Act

ACT II. Scene I

York, in Upper Canada; a Tavern meanly furnished. Enter LAROLE, *in pursuit of the chambermaid.*

LAROLE: Come here, you littel demoiselle—you bootiful sauvage, vy you run vay from me—hay?

MAID: I wish you would let me alone, mounsure, you officers' gentlemen are very disagreeable things.

LAROLE: Disagreeable? ma foi! I am one joli garçon, one pretti batchelor; disagreeable? I vill tell you, ma belle grizette, I am maître de mode, I give de lecons for dance, to speake de English, and de Francaise aussi; I can fence, aha! or fight de duel, or de enemi, je suis un soldat.

MAID: Well, if you're a soldier, you have no business to be following me up and down the house like a pet lamb. Why don't you go to camp?

LAROLE: Camp? vat is de camp? Oho, le champ de bataille; I shall tell you, mademoiselle, I did fight at the bataille de Vittoria, com un diable, like littel devil. I did kill beaucoup d'Anglais. Mai my maître, le capitain, he did give me a dam tump on my head wis his rapier, and did knock me down from on top of my horse, and make a me von prisonier.

MAID: Poor fellow! And so, mounsure, you were made prisoner?

LAROLE: Oui, ven I could not run avay, begar I surrender like von brave homme, and now I am jentiman to capitain Pendragoon; I do brus his coat, poudre his hair, and pull his corset tight, and ven he was order to come to Amérique, and fight wis de Yankee Doodel, begar me come too. I arrive ici, I am here, to make a littel de love to you.

MAID: Well now, once for all, I tell you not to be following me; I don't like Frenchmen—I can't parlyvoo.

LAROLE: You no like de Frenchiman? O quell barbare! vy you ave von abominable goût, mademoiselle, von shockin taste. I shall tell you, mademoiselle, en my contree, en France, de ladies are ver fond of me. O beaucoup, I am so charmant—so aimable, and so jentee, I have three five sweetheart, ami de coeur, mai for all dat I do love you ver mush, par example.

MAID: Let me go! [*Bell rings*] There, your master calls you. [*Exit*]

LAROLE: Dam de littel bell, I vill not come; mon maître he always interrupt me ven I make de love to the pretti ladi, he be jealous, begar I vill not come. [*Exit opposite side*]

Enter CAPTAIN PENDRAGON, *dressed in the British uniform, but in the extreme of fashion—throws himself into a chair*

PENDRAGON: Oh, curse such roads! My bones are making their way out of their sockets—such vile, abominable, detestable—Waiter!—If my friends at Castle Joram only knew the excruciating fatigues which I am undergoing in this barbarous land—Why, waiter!—or if his highness the commander-in-chief was only sensible of my great sacrifices to—Why, waiter! where the devil are you?

Enter WAITER

WAITER: Here I be, sir.

PENDRAGON: Why didn't you come when I first called? Do you think I've got lungs like a hunter? I'm fatigued and hungry. Get me an anchovy, a toast, and a bottle of old port.

WAITER: A what, sir? an ancho——

PENDRAGON: Yes, sir, an anchovy—small ones—delicate.

WAITER: Why, sir, we don't know what these are in this country.

PENDRAGON: The devil you don't! Then pray, sir, what have you to eat in this damn'd house fit for a gentleman?

WAITER: Why, sir, not much—the army eats us out of house and home. We have some very excellent fresh bear meat, sir.

PENDRAGON: Bear meat! Why, what the devil, fellow, do you take me for a Chickasaw, or an Esquimau? Bear meat! the honourable captain Pendragon, who never ate anything more gross than a cutlet at Molly's chop-house, and who lived on pigeons' livers at Very's, in Paris, offered bear meat in North America! I'll put that down in my travels.

WAITER: Why, sir, it is considered here a great delicacy.

PENDRAGON: The devil it is! Then pray, sir, what are your ordinary fares, if bear's meat is considered a delicacy?

WAITER: Why, truly, sir, this is but a young country, and we have to live upon what we can catch. Pray, would you fancy some 'possum fat and hominy?

PENDRAGON: Oh, shocking! begone, fellow—you'll throw me into a fever with your vile bill of fare. Get me a cup of tea—mix it, hyson and souchong, with cream and muffins.

WAITER: We can't give you any of those things, sir.—However, you can have an excellent cup of sage tea, sweetened with honey.

PENDRAGON: Sage tea! Why, you rascal, do you intend to throw me into a perspiration by way of curing my hunger? or do you take me for a goose or a duck, that you intend stuffing me with sage? Begone, get out, you little deformed fellow! [*Exit* WAITER] I shall perish in this barbarous land—bear meat, 'possum fat, and sage tea! O dear St. James! I wish I was snug in my old quarters. LaRole! [*Enter* LAROLE] Where the devil do you hide yourself in this damn'd house? Why, I shall starve—there's nothing to eat, fit for a gentleman.

LAROLE: Oui, monsieur, dis is von damn contree, I can find nosing to eat. I did look into all de pantri, mai parbleu, I find only a ver pretti demoiselle, mai, I could not eat her.

PENDRAGON: We must be off to the camp, LaRole, my quarters there will be infinitely more agreeable. I shall get the blue devils in this cursed place.

LAROLE: Vell, sair, I have all de devils ventre bleu, das you can imagine; dere is no politesse, no respect, nosing paid to me.

PENDRAGON: My fit of the blues is coming on me; sing me a song, LaRole.

LAROLE: A chanson? Vell, sair, I shall sing to frighten avay de littel blue devil; vill you I shall sing de English or de Française?

PENDRAGON: Oh, English, by all means—curse your foreign lingo.

LAROLE: Ahem! Ahem! you shall understand.

Vat is dis dull town to me,
Robin Hadair?

Vere is all de joys on earth, dat
Make dis town—

[*A bugle sounds without*] Ha! what is dat? who de devil intrup me in my chanson?

INDIAN CHIEF: [*Speaks without*] Have them all ready, with their rifles and tomahawks in order; [*Enters with another* INDIAN] and you, Coosewatchie, tell our priests to take their stand on yonder hill, and as my warriors pass them, examine whether they have fire in their eyes. [*Exit* INDIAN] How now, who have we here?

PENDRAGON: [*Examining him with his glass*] Where the devil did this character come from? he's one of the fancy, I suppose.

INDIAN: Who and what are you?

PENDRAGON: Who am I? Why, sir, I am the honourable captain Pendragon, of his majesty's guards, formerly of the buffs.

INDIAN: [*Aside*] The officer who is to be under my command. Well sir, you have lately arrived from across the great waters: How did you leave my father, the King of England?

PENDRAGON: How! call my most gracious sovereign your father? Why, sir, you are the most familiar—impertinent—s'death! I shall choke—What the devil do you mean?

INDIAN: [*Coolly*] What should I mean, young man, but to inquire after the health of my father, who commands my respect, who has honoured me with his favours, and in whose cause I am now fighting.

PENDRAGON: Well, sir, if you have the honour to hold a commission from his majesty, I desire that you will speak of him with proper awe, and not call him your father, but your gracious master.

INDIAN: Young man, the Indian warrior knows no master but the Great Spirit, whose voice is heard in thunder, and whose eye is seen in the lightning's flash; free as air, we bow the knee to no man; our forests are our home, our defence is our arms, our sustenance the deer and the elk, which we run down. White men encroach upon our borders, and drive us into war; we raise the tomahawk against your enemies, because your king has promised us protection and supplies. We fight for freedom, and in that cause, the great king and the poor Indian start upon equal terms.

PENDRAGON: A very clever spoken fellow, pon honour; I'll patronise him.

LAROLE: Parbleu, he is von very sensible sauvage; vill you take von pinch snuff?

INDIAN: Pshaw!

LAROLE: He say pshaw, I see he is born in de voods.

PENDRAGON: And are you prepared to fan these Yankees? We shall flog them without much fatigue, I understand.

INDIAN: Not so fast, young soldier; these pale-faced enemies of ours fight with obstinacy; accustomed to a hardy life, to liberty and laws, they are not willing to relinquish those blessings on easy terms; if we conquer them, it must be by no moderate exertions: it will demand force and cunning.

PENDRAGON: Oh, dry dogs, I suppose, not to be caught napping; well, I'm up to them, we'll fan them in high style; the ragged nabobs, I understand, are not far off, and our troops are in fine preservation.

INDIAN: True, preparation must be made to meet them. You are under my orders.

PENDRAGON: The devil I am!

INDIAN: Aye, sir; your general, at my request, has ordered you here to take command of a company of my warriors; but you must not appear in that dress: change it quickly, or they will not be commanded by you; they are men, and fight under the orders of men.

PENDRAGON: Change my dress! why what the devil do you mean, sir?

INDIAN: Mean? that you should appear in the ranks like a warrior, and not like a rabbit trussed for dressing—off with these garments, which give neither pleasure to the eye nor ease to the limbs—put on moccasins, wrap a blanket around you, put rings through your nose and ears, feathers in your head, and paint yourself like a soldier, with vermilion.

PENDRAGON: Why, this is the most impertinent and presuming savage in the wilds of North America. Harkee, sir, I'd have you to know, that I am a man of fashion, and one of the fancy—formerly of the buffs, nephew of a peer of the realm, and will be a member of parliament, in time; an officer of great merit and great services, Mr.—Red Jacket. Paint my face, and fight without clothes? I desire, sir, that you will please to take notice, that I fought at Badahoz with the immortal Wellington, and had the honour to be wounded, and promoted, and had a medal for my services in that affair, Mr.—Split-log. Put rings in my nose? a man of taste, and the *ne plus ultra* of Bond-street, the very mirror of fashion and elegance? Sir, I beg you to observe, that I am not to be treated in this manner—I shall resent this insult. Damme, I shall report you to the commander-in-chief at the Horse Guards, and have you courtmartialled for unfashionable deportment—Mr.—Walk-in-the-Water.

INDIAN: Come, come, sir, enough of this trifling; I do not understand it; you have heard my orders—obey them, or, after the battle, I'll roast you before a slow fire! [*Exit*]

LAROLE: O le barbare! O de dam sauvage! dis is de most impertinent dog in de vorld. Roast before de fire! Parbleu, mon maître, ve are not de littel pig.

PENDRAGON: I'm horrified! lost in amazement! but I'll resent it. Damme, I'll caricature him.

LAROLE: Oh, I vish I vas fight encore at Saragossa, vis mi lor Villainton; par example, I did get some hard tumps, mai I did get plenti to eat; but ici I ave nosing but de littel bear to mange.

PENDRAGON: Come along—courage, LaRole. We'll fan the Yankee Doodles in our best style, and then get a furlough, and be off to White-Hall, and the rings in our noses will afford anecdotes for the bon-ton for a whole year. Allons. [*Exeunt*]

Scene 2

The American Camp at daybreak. The drum and fife plays the reveille. Sentinels on duty before the tents. LENOX *enters from the tent on the right.* GENERAL *and* ADELA *from the left.*

LENOX: Good morning, general; you are "stirring with the lark"—and you also, Adela.

GENERAL: The times require the utmost vigilance, Lenox; the enemy cannot escape a battle now, and we must be prepared at all points to meet him. Decision and energy cannot fail to promote success.

ADELA: And what is to become of me, father, in the battle? Am I to ride the old trooper again, and run the risk of having the tip of my nose carried away by a musket ball, and left on the field of battle in all my glory?

GENERAL: You shall be taken care of, dear Adela; we will place you in the rear, among the baggage-wagons.

ADELA: And if they should be captured, I become also a prisoner, and probably a prize to some gallant Indian chief, who will make me his squaw, and teach me to kill deer. O delightful thought! [*Bugles sound*]

GENERAL: The troops are under arms, and approaching.

Quick march—the GENERAL, LENOX *and* ADELA *pass to the left, and stand near the tent; the troops advance;* CHRISTINE *is among them, dressed in uniform; they pass round the stage in regular order, then form the line two deep;* CHRISTINE *is in front on the right, and keeps her eye fixed anxiously on* Lenox; *drum beats the roll; the troops come to an order, and then proceed through the manual by the tap of drum, and finally to a present; the* GENERAL, LENOX, *and other officers advance, and pass through the line in review; the flags wave, and the band strikes up "Hail Columbia"*

GENERAL: Well—everything is right. And now, soldiers, to your posts; remember, discipline, subordination, courage, and country, and victory will be ours.

GENERAL, LENOX, *and* ADELA, *enter the tent to the left. The troops march off.* CHRISTINE *and a* SOLDIER, *headed by a* CORPORAL, *return to relieve guard at each tent. Port arms and whisper the countersign.* CHRISTINE *is placed before the tent on the right, her comrade on the left.* CORPORAL *retires with the two relieved sentries. After a pause, she beckons to her comrade*

CHRISTINE: Hist—comrade!

SOLDIER: Well, what is it?

CHRISTINE: Will you exchange places? There is no difference—and the sun will be too powerful for me presently. Look, here is a dollar.

SOLDIER: With all my heart. [*They cross quickly, the* SOLDIER *receives the money—* CHRISTINE *now paces before the tent into which* LENOX, ADELA *and the* GENERAL *have retired*]

CHRISTINE: Could I but see the false, perfidious Lenox, and upbraid him with his cruelty! [*She is in great uneasiness, pauses occasionally, and looks into the tent—her comrade is watching her.* LENOX *sings within*]

Shall the pleasures of life unknown fade away,
In viewing those charms so lovely and gay?
Shall the heart which has breath'd forth rapturous flame,
Be hid from the world and unsought for by fame?

Thus spoke the fond Roscoe to Scylla the fair,
As he gaz'd on her charms, with a love-soothing care:
Hear now the last wish, that fondly I sigh,
I'll conquer in love, or in battle I'll die.

He girded his armour and flew to the field,
Determin'd while life flow'd never to yield;
The foe was subdued, but death's cruel dart
Was aim'd at the valiant and fond Roscoe's heart:
But the blow was defeated—he lived to enjoy
The sight of his Scylla, no longer so coy,

And his laurels fresh bloom'd, as she smil'd on the youth,
And gave her fair hand in reward for his truth.

CHRISTINE: Ha, that false voice! I can no longer bear it!

Throws down her gun, and is about entering the tent, when her comrade, who has been attentively regarding her movements, rushes over and seizes her

SOLDIER: Where are you going?
CHRISTINE: Unhand me this instant! [*Struggles*]
SOLDIER: Guards, there!

Enter an OFFICER *with* SOLDIERS, *who attempts to seize* CHRISTINE—*she draws her sword and stands on the defensive, and after some resistance, escapes*

OFFICER: Pursue him quickly! [SOLDIERS *pursue*]
SOLDIER: He crosses the bridge.
OFFICER: The sentinels will reach him with their guns. [*Muskets discharged*]
SOLDIER: They have him—he is not hurt.

GENERAL, ADELA *and* LENOX *rush from the tent*

GENERAL: What means this confusion?
2ND OFFICER: The sentinel who was placed here on duty, attempted, for some desperate purpose, to enter your tent; but being discovered, he refused to surrender, drew his sword on me and the guard, and, after some resistance, has been disarmed and secured.
LENOX: Good heavens! What object could he have had?
2ND OFFICER: I know not—but he is a new recruit, probably a spy from the enemy.
GENERAL: It must be so—see that a court martial be called to try him, and bring the result to me without delay. If he is guilty, a dreadful example shall be made of him. Begone. [*Exeunt* GENERAL, SOLDIERS, *&C*]

Scene 3

Another Part of the Camp. Enter JASPER, JERRY *and* PEASANTS.

JASPER: Nowhere to be found. I have asked everybody in the camp in vain—she is lost to me. Unhappy, cruel girl! to quit her old and fond father thus.
JERRY: Unhappy girl! to leave me in such an ungenteel manner too, run away from me on my wedding day! but I'll find her out.
JASPER: Impossible! we must return, dejected and disappointed.
JERRY: I'll peep into every tent, bribe the sogers—I've got a little money left. [JASPER *and* PEASANTS *retire.* CORPORAL *crosses the stage*] Hist, corporal!
CORPORAL: Well, what would you?
JERRY: Why no, sure—it isn't—yes, it is—why Corporal Flash, how do you do? Don't you know me?
CORPORAL: Can't say I do, sir.
JERRY: Why, not know Jerry Mayflower? Don't you remember me at the battle of Queenstown, when you were in the boat and I on land, and you were crossing to fight Johnny Bull, and I didn't cross at all?

CORPORAL: Oh, I remember you now—I remember calling you a cowardly rascal at the time.

JERRY: So you did—how have you been? I am very glad to see you—you're not killed, I take it?

CORPORAL: No, not exactly killed—but I was wounded—an honour which you didn't seem to care much about.

JERRY: No, not much; I'm not very ambitious that way.

CORPORAL: What brings you to the camp, just when we are about having another brush with the enemy—do you want to run away again? Zounds! you deserve a round hundred at the halberts.

JERRY: Yes, I deserve many things that I don't get—but pray, corporal, mout you have seen a young woman in this here camp lately?

CORPORAL: Oh, plenty, among the suttlers.

JERRY: No, a kind of a pretty girl, a little ladylike, parlyvoos, and carries her head up straight.

CORPORAL: No—I've seen no such person.

JERRY: Well, Corporal Flash, I've a little cash, and what say you to a jug of whiskey punch? Brave men, you know, like you and I, should drink with one another.

CORPORAL: With all my heart; you're good for nothing else but to drink with.

JERRY: Then come along, my boy; we'll drown care, raise our spirits, and swallow the enemy in a bumper. [*Exeunt*]

Scene 4

A Prison. Enter two OFFICERS, GUARDS, *and* CHRISTINE. OFFICERS *seat themselves at a table, with pens and ink.*

1ST OFFICER: Young man, come forward. You have been charged with an act of mutiny, and with an attempt, for some unknown cause, to force your way, with arms in your hand, into the tent of the commanding general. We are convened for your trial—we have examined the testimony; and as you are a stranger in our ranks, no feelings of prejudice could have given a false colouring to that testimony. What have you to say?

CHRISTINE: Nothing.

OFFICER: Nothing?

CHRISTINE: Nothing! [*With firmness*] I am guilty!

OFFICER: Have a care, pause before you make this avowal of your guilt.

CHRISTINE: [*With settled firmness*] I have considered it well, and am ready to meet the consequences. I am guilty. [*With a burst of anguish*] Oh, most guilty!

OFFICER: Unhappy young man, what could have tempted you to this act? Who set you on?

CHRISTINE: Seek not to know the cause, 'tis buried here. Do your duty—I am prepared for the result.

OFFICER: [*To the Board*] The charge is fully admitted, and the rules of war prescribe the punishment. The object he had in view must yet be discovered; 'tis plain, however, that he is a spy, and has no hope of pardon. Record the verdict and sentence, for the inspection and concurrence of the general. [OFFICER *writes. The company rise from the table, and one approaches* CHRISTINE, *who appears buried in thought*]

OFFICER: Young man, I deeply commiserate your unhappy situation, but the rules of war are rigid, and must be enforced. You must prepare to die!

CHRISTINE: [*Starts, but recovers herself quickly*] I am ready.

OFFICER: I would offer you hope, but acts of mutiny, and when covering such suspicious motives as yours, cannot be pardoned. You have but a day to live. I deeply regret it, for you appear to have qualities which, in time, would have made you a valuable citizen. You are cut off in youth, probably from the hopes of a fond parent.

CHRISTINE: [*In agony*] Oh, no more—no more!

OFFICER: All the sympathy and indulgence which can be offered you shall be yours! Farewell. [*Exit* OFFICERS, GUARDS, *&C*]

CHRISTINE: At length 'tis concluded, and an ignominious death terminates my unmerited sufferings. Cruel father! and still more cruel Lenox! thus to have wounded the heart that loved you. Oh, what a situation is mine! separated from all I hold dear, sentenced to die, and in this disguise; to leave my poor father, and to know that death, alone, can tell my sad story. What's to be done? Discover all? No, no. Expose my weakness and folly—to see the false Lenox wedded to another, and I forced to accept the hand I loathe—to be pointed at for one who, lost to the delicacy of her sex, followed a perfidious lover in disguise, and, tortured by jealousy, enlisted, was mutinous, and sentenced to die; but who, to save a miserable life, avowed her situation, and recorded her disgrace at once? Never, never! let me die, and forever be forgotten—'tis but a blow, and it will end the pangs which torment me here. [*Enter a* SOLDIER, *who beckons*] I am ready, lead the way. [*Exit*]

Scene 5

Another part of the Prison. Enter the JAILOR, *driving* JERRY *before him.*

JAILOR: In, in, you mutinous dog! do you come here to breed a riot in our camp?

JERRY: Now, my dear good-natured jailor, only have pity on me, and I'll tell you all about it.

JAILOR: I won't hear you—didn't you breed a riot?

JERRY: Why no, it was not me. I am as innocent as a young lamb. I'll tell you how it was—come, sit down on this bench with me. [*They sit*] You must know that I'm a farmer, pretty well off, as a body mout say, and I wanted a wife; hard by our village, there lived an old soger with a pretty daughter, so I courted the old man for his daughter, and he consented to the match.

JAILOR: Well?

JERRY: And so I got together all my neighbours, and, with music, went to the old soger's to get my sweetheart, when, lo and behold! after all my trouble, she refused me plump.

JAILOR: No, did she?

JERRY: Aye, indeed; she didn't seem stricken with the proposal—and for fear her father would force her to marry me, egad, she run away.

JAILOR: And where did she go?

JERRY: I can't say, but her father and a whole *posse comitatus,* as we justices call 'em, went in search of her to the camp, and when I came here, I found some of my old comrades who fought with me at Queenstown; and so having a little money, we went to take a comfortable pitcher of whiskey punch together, and so, while over our cups, they doubted my valour, and hinted that I run away before the battle.

JAILOR: Well, and what did you do?

JERRY: Why, I offered to fight 'em single-handed all round, and we got into a dispute, and so when my money was all gone, they tweaked my nose, boxed my ears, and kick'd me out of the tent. So I then kick'd up a row, and—that's all.

JAILOR: A very pretty story, indeed! You look like a mutinous dog—so come, get into the black hole.

JERRY: Now, my dear jailor, do let me escape, and I'll give you the prettiest little pig in my farmyard.

JAILOR: What! bribe an honest and humane jailor, and with a pig? In with you.

JERRY: Well, but I've nothing to eat—I shall be half starved.

JAILOR: Oh no, you shall have something to employ your grinders on. [*Goes out, and returns with a black loaf, and a pitcher of water*] There!

JERRY: O dear, nothing else but black bread and cold water? Can't you get me a pickle?

JAILOR: I think you're in a devil of a pickle already—come, get in! [*Removes a board from the scene, which discovers a small dark hole.* JERRY *supplicates*]

JERRY: How long am I to be here, Mr. Jailor, in company with myself?

JAILOR: That depends on your good behaviour. [*Cannon are heard*] There! the battle has commenced.

JERRY: [*Putting his head out of the hole*] O dear, what's that? The great guns are going off. Are you sure, my dear jailor, that this prison is bomb proof?

JAILOR: Take your head in, you great land turtle.

JERRY: Oh, what will become of me?

End of the Second Act

ACT III. Scene I

Scene in front of a pavilion tent; trumpets and drums sounding. Enter GENERAL, LENOX, SOLDIERS, OFFICERS, *&C.*

GENERAL: At length victory has crown'd our arms, and the result of this action will keep alive the spirits of our troops, and the hopes of our country. Hark! the bugles are sounding a retreat, and the enemy has abandoned the field and taken to his entrenchments. Lenox, your hand—your conduct this day has confirmed our hopes—allow me in the name of our country to thank you.

LENOX: Not a word, dear general, not a word; I have merely done my duty, and done no more than every soldier in our ranks.

GENERAL: What is the result of this day's action?

LENOX: The enemy has lost upwards of 500 in killed and wounded, and several principal officers have been taken prisoners.

GENERAL: In what position were they when the attack became general?

LENOX: The British commander, pressed by our artillery under Towson, issued in all his force from his entrenchments. It was a gallant sight, to see his solid columns and burnished arms advance on the margin of the river, and his cavalry, with lightning's force, dart on our flanks to turn and throw them into confusion; but they were met by the volunteers under the brave Porter, and gallantly repulsed.

GENERAL: Go on.

LENOX: The enemy then condensed his forces and crossed the bridge, and was encountered on the plains of Chippewa by Scott, with his brigade, when the action became severe and general. No ambuscade or masked batteries were held in reserve—the enemy was not a moment concealed from our view—no tangled thicket or umbrageous groves gave effect or facility to our rifles: the battle was fought on a plain—where man grappled man, force was opposed to force, skill to skill, and eye to eye, in regular, disciplined, and admirable order.

GENERAL: How near were you to the British general?

LENOX: In sight and hearing. Charge the Yankees! said a hoarse voice which I knew to be his. Charge away! said our ardent troops, as they advanced with fixed bayonets; the fire became dreadful, and our stars and stripes were seen waving in the blaze. Scott rode through the lines cheering the men, and gallantly leading them on; Jessup and his third battalion turned the right flank of the enemy after a dreadful conflict; Ketchum had kept up a cross and ruinous fire; and Towson, from his dread artillery, scattered grape like hail amongst them. On, on! cried Leavenworth, the day's our own, my boys! Just then a shot struck down my comrade, Harrison, and shattered his leg.

GENERAL: Well?

LENOX: He grasped his sword and fought on his stump, clinging to the spot like fire-eyed Mars; the enemy, pressed on all sides, gave way; our troops pursued, and the flight became general. At length we drove them to their entrenchments, and remained masters of the field. Our trumpets sounded their retreat; victory perched on our eagles, and our bands struck up the soul-inspiring air of "Hail, Columbia, happy land!"

GENERAL: Well done, my brave fellows! This action will teach the enemy to respect that valour which they cannot subdue. See that the wounded prisoners are taken care of: give them all succor: victory loses half its value, when it is not tempered with mercy. [*Exit* GENERAL]

LENOX: Now to my dear Christine, to receive from her the reward which I hope I have fairly earned, and seek with her the joys of tranquillity and love.

Enter a SOLDIER

SOLDIER: Towards the conclusion of the battle we made two Indian warriors prisoners, who were fighting desperately; we have them with us.

LENOX: Bring them in; I will examine them, touching the number and force of their tribe. [*Exit* SOLDIER, *who returns with* PENDRAGON *and* LAROLE, *with a file of men; both are painted and dressed as Indians;* PENDRAGON *preserves his opera-glass, and* LAROLE *his snuff-box*]

PENDRAGON: What are we brought here for, fellow?

LENOX: Warriors, the fate of battle has placed you in our power; yet fear nothing, we shall treat you like men and soldiers. Deeply do we regret to see you take up arms against us, instigated by foreign influence, and bribed by foreign gold. How numerous is your tribe?

PENDRAGON: Why what the devil, sir, do you take us for Choctaws? Can't you tell a man of fashion in masquerade?

LENOX: Who and what are you?

PENDRAGON: I am the honourable Captain Pendragon, of his Majesty's Coldstream guards.

LENOX: The *honourable* Captain Pendragon, and taken prisoner fighting in the ranks with Indians, and in disguise? A man of rank and fashion, and a soldier, changing his complexion, his nature and his character—herding with savages—infuriating their horrid passions, and whetting their knives and tomahawks against their defenseless prisoners? Impossible! And who are you, sir? [*To* LAROLE]

LAROLE: [*Taking snuff*] Begar, sair, I am von man of fashion aussi, I am valet de sham to capitain Pendragoon; ve are in de masquerade, sair.

PENDRAGON: It's very true, sir, 'pon honour—we are in masquerade, though you look as if you doubt it. War, sir, is a kind of a—a singular science, and if you are to be knock'd on the head, 'tis of very little consequence whether your nose is tipped with blue or red, damme. I am in your power, sir, and a man of fashion, 'pon honour.

LENOX: Well, sir, if your example is to govern men of honour or men of fashion, I hope I am ignorant of the attributes of the one, or the eccentricities of the other. However, mercy to prisoners, even when they have forfeited mercy, may teach your nation lessons of toleration and humanity. Your life is safe, sir.

PENDRAGON: Sir, you speak very like a gentleman, and I shall be happy to taste Burgundy with you at the Horse Guards.

LENOX: I thank you, sir.

LAROLE: Par example, dis Yankee Doodel is von very pretti spoken jeune gentiman, I will give him de encouragement Sair, I vill be ver happy to serve you en my contree, to take un tasse de caffee at de Palais Royale en Paris wid you, to dress your hair, or pull your corset tight.

Enter GENERAL, ADELA *and* OFFICER

GENERAL: Who have we here?

LENOX: Prisoners, sir, and in disguise.

ADELA: As I live, an Indian dandy!

PENDRAGON: A lady? [*With an air of fashion*] Ma'am, your most devoted slave—inexpressibly happy to find a beautiful creature in this damn'd wilderness. You see, ma'am, I am a kind of a prisoner, but always at home, always at my ease, *à-la-mode* St. James—extremely rejoiced to have the honour of your acquaintance. A fine girl, LaRole, split me!

LAROLE: Oh, oui, she is very fine, I like her ver mush.

ADELA: Pray, sir, may I ask how came you to fancy that disguise?

PENDRAGON: Oh, it's not my fancy, 'pon honour, though I am one of the fancy; a mere *russe de guerre.* We on the other side of the water, have a kind of floating idea that you North Americans are half savages, and we must fight you after your own fashion.

ADELA: And have you discovered that any difference exists in the last affair in which you have been engaged?

PENDRAGON: Why, 'pon my soul, ma'am, this Yankee kind of warfare is inexpressibly inelegant, without flattery—no order—no military arrangement—no *deploying* in solid columns—but a kind of helter-skelter warfare, like a reel or a country-dance at a village inn, while the house is on fire.

ADELA: Indeed?

PENDRAGON: All true, I assure you. Why, do you know, ma'am, that one of your common soldiers was amusing himself with shooting at me for several minutes, although he saw from my air, and my dodging, that I was a man of fashion? Monstrous assurance! wasn't it?

ADELA: Why ay, it was rather impertinent for a common soldier to attempt to bring down a man of fashion.

LAROLE: Oui—it is dam impertinent, mai par example, de littel bullet of von common soldat, he sometime kill von great general.

PENDRAGON: Pray, ma'am, will you permit me to ask, when you arrived from England, and what family has the honour to boast of so beautiful a representative?

ADELA: Sir, I am not of England, I stand on my native soil.

PENDRAGON: Oh.

ADELA: And much as I esteem English women for their many amiable qualities, I hope that worth and virtue are not wholly centered in that country.

PENDRAGON: Why, 'pon my soul, ma'am, though it is not fashionable this year to be prejudiced, yet were I to admit that I saw any beauty or elegance in America, my Bond-Street friends would cut me—split me!

ADELA: I cannot admire their candour. Merit is the exclusive property of no country, and to form a just estimate of our own advantages, we should be ever prepared to admit the advantages possessed by others.

Enter a SOLDIER

SOLDIER: We have surprised and made captive the celebrated Indian chief, who fought so desperately against us.

GENERAL: Bring him before us. [*Exit* SOLDIER] He has long been the terror of the neighbourhood, and the crafty foe of our country.

Enter SOLDIERS *with the* INDIAN CHIEF

INDIAN: Who among you is the chief of these pale-faced enemies of our race?

GENERAL: I am he.

INDIAN: 'Tis well, sir; behold in me your captive, who has fallen into your power after a resistance becoming a warrior. I am ready to meet that death which I know awaits me.

GENERAL: Chief, your fears are groundless; we intend you no harm, but by our example, teach you the blessings of valour and mercy united.

INDIAN: Wherefore show me mercy? I ask it not of you.—Think you that I cannot bear the flames? that a warrior shrinks from the uplifted tomahawk? Try me—try how a great soul can smile on death. Or do you hope that I will meanly beg a life, which fate and evil fortune has thrown into your hands?

GENERAL: We ask no concessions of you, warrior; we wish to see you sensible of the delusions into which foreign nations have plunged you. We wish to see you our friend.

INDIAN: Your friend? Call back the times which we passed in liberty and happiness, when in the tranquil enjoyment of unrestrained freedom we roved through our forests, and only knew the bears as our enemy; call back our council fires, our fathers and pious priests; call back our brothers, wives and children, which cruel white men have destroyed.—Your friend? You came with the silver smile of peace, and we received you into our cabins; we hunted for you, toiled for you; our wives and daughters cherished and protected you; but when your numbers increased, you rose like wolves upon us, fired our dwellings, drove off our cattle, sent us in tribes to the wilderness, to seek for shelter; and now you ask me, while naked and a prisoner, to be your friend!

GENERAL: We have not done this, deluded man; your pretended advocates, over the great waters, have told you this tale.

INDIAN: Alas! it is a true one; I feel it here; 'tis no fiction: I was the chief of a great and daring tribe, which smiled on death with indifference and contempt; my cabin was the seat of hospitality and of love; I was first in council, and first in the field; my prosperity increased, my prospects brightened; but the white man came, and all was blasted.

GENERAL: What has been done, was the result of war.

INDIAN: Wherefore wage war against us? Was not your territory sufficiently ample, but did you sigh for our possessions? Were you not satisfied with taking our land from us, but would you hunt the lords of the soil into the den of the otter? Why drive to desperation a free and liberal people? Think you I would be your enemy unless urged by powerful wrongs? No, white man, no! the Great Spirit whom we worship, is also the God whom you adore; for friends we cheerfully lay down our lives; but against foes, our lives are staked with desperation. Had I taken you prisoner, death should have been your portion; death in cruel torments. Then why spare me? why spare the man whose knife was whetted against your life?

GENERAL: To show, by contrast, the difference of our principles. You would strike down the captive who implores your protection: we tender life and liberty to the prisoner, who asks himself for death.

INDIAN: Is this your vengeance?

GENERAL: It is. The Great Spirit delights in mercy. Be thou our friend, warrior; bury thy tomahawk deep in earth; let not jealous foreigners excite thy vengeance against us; but living as we do in one territory, let us smoke the calumet of peace, you and all your tribe, and let concord hereafter reign amongst us.—Be this the token. [*Gives a belt of wampum*]

INDIAN: Brother, I accept the token; forgive my rage, and pardon my unjust anger. Protect our warriors and wives; guard their wigwams from destruction; soften their prejudices and remove their jealousies. Do this, and the red man is your friend. I have urged you far to end my life: you have tempered your passions with mercy, and we are no longer foes. Farewell! [*Exit*]

LAROLE: Parbleu, dis general is like von great Roman. I vill speak von vord pour myself, I vill make de speech like de sauvage.

GENERAL: [*To* LAROLE] And you, sir, it appears, are in disguise, unlike a civilized soldier; you have been taken in the ranks with Indians.

LAROLE: Sair, mon general, you sall here vat I am goin to say. I am von Frenchiman; in my contree every Frenchiman he is von soldat.

GENERAL: Well?

LAROLE: Begar, sair, I must fight vid somebody, because it is my bisness. In de Egypt I did fight 'gainst de Turc; in Europe I did fight de whole vorld vis de Grand Napoleon, and in Amérique I did fight against you vid myself. Mais, you take a me de prisonier, I can fight no more; I vill trow myself on de protection of dis contree; I vill no more fight contree de Yankee Doodel; I vill stay here and eat de ros beef vid you, and mon capitain là, he may go to de devil.

GENERAL: Admirably concluded. And you, sir, what can we do to lighten your captivity?

PENDRAGON: Why sir, if war was not my profession, I'd sell out; but it's always my maxim to obey orders, whatever they may be: therefore, shall be happy to have a brush with you in war, and equally happy to crack a bottle of Burgundy with you in peace; a flash in the pan in one way, or a puff from a segar in another; a bullet under the ribs in battle, or a country dance in a ballroom; all's one to me, if it's only fashionably conducted.

GENERAL: Well, let's into my tent and partake of some refreshment. We may not always meet as enemies.

PENDRAGON: [*To* ADELA] Allow me the felicity of your little finger. [*Aside*] She's struck with my figure, split me! LaRole, take notice.

LAROLE: Oh, you are de littel devil among de ladies. [*Exeunt*]

Scene 2

A Prison. CHRISTINE *seated on a bench; her appearance betrays grief and despair.*

CHRISTINE: At length the weary night has passed away, and day dawns, but brings no joy or comfort to my aching heart. Alas! alas! Christine, where are all the bright visions thy fond fancy painted? where is that content and love which gleamed through the casement of our cottage, when my dear father smiled on his child, and entwined around her his protecting arms: when the false Lenox, too, with honeyed lips, and tones soft as zephyrs, vow'd eternal love? Let me not think of them, or I shall go mad. Oh, what a contrast! pent up in a vile prison, and in disguise! condemned to die, and perishing unknown and unprotected. On the one side, my grave yawns for me; and on the other, a false lover, and a cruel father, drive me to despair. My brain is on fire! [*Hurries about with rapid strides. Music loud and violent*] Ha! what is this? [*Tears the miniature from around her neck*] Lenox, these are thy features! thy mild looks beam hope and joy upon me. [*Kisses it*] Could such a face be false? Away with it! even now he weds another. [*Throws the miniature indignantly from her*] So, 'tis gone, and I am left alone in darkness and despair. [*She stands transfixed with grief—muffled drum rolls—she starts*] Ha! they come for me! Be firm, my heart!

Enter an OFFICER *and a file of* SOLDIERS

OFFICER: Young man, your hour has arrived: the detachment waits without to receive you.

CHRISTINE: [*Faintly*] I am ready.

OFFICER: Can I serve you in any manner? Is there no letter—no remembrance that you would wish sent to father or friend?

CHRISTINE: Oh, forbear!

SOLDIER: [*Picking up the miniature*] See, sir, here is a miniature.

OFFICER: [*Examining it*] By Heavens, they are the features of Captain Lenox! How came you by this? What! a thief too? 'Tis well your career is cut short.
CHRISTINE: Oh no, no! Give it me, I implore you; 'tis mine.
OFFICER: I shall restore it to the rightful owner. Come, we wait.
CHRISTINE: Lead on. A few fleeting moments, and all my troubles will be at an end. [*Exeunt*]

Scene 3

Before the Tent. Enter GENERAL, SOLDIERS, *&C., with papers.*

GENERAL: He has not confessed who set him on?
OFFICER: He has not, but admits the crime.
GENERAL: [*Returning papers*] 'Tis well—see him executed according to the sentence. Hard and imperious duty, which, at once, shuts out hope and mercy! [*Exit* GENERAL]
OFFICER: Now to seek for Lenox, and restore to him his miniature. [*Exit*]

Scene 4

The Camp, as in Act I, Scene 3; the stage is thrown open, drums roll, and the procession enters for the execution of CHRISTINE; *she is in the centre, between the two detachments; her coat is off, and the stock unloosened from her neck—her step is firm, until she reaches the tent of* LENOX, *when she clasps her hands and hangs down her head in despair. Procession makes the circuit of the stage with slow steps, and when opposite the tent she kneels; an* OFFICER *places the bandage over her eyes, and gives a sign to a detachment of four to advance; they step forward, and level their muskets at her; at the moment,* LENOX *rushes from the tent with the miniature in his hand and strikes up their guns.*

LENOX: Hold! for your lives! [*Rushes down to* CHRISTINE, *and tears the bandage from her eyes*] 'Tis she! 'tis she! 'tis my own, my beloved Christine! [*Holds her in his arms; she faints*]
2ND OFFICER: What means this?
LENOX: Stand off, ye cruel executioners, would you destroy a woman?
OFFICER: A woman? Heavens! how did this happen?

Enter GENERAL, ADELA, LAROLE, SOLDIERS, *&C*

LENOX: Support her, Adela, support my dear Christine! [ADELA *assists*]
CHRISTINE: [*Recovering*] Where am I? [*Sees* LENOX *and* ADELA] Hide me, save me from that horrid sight!
LENOX: Do you not know me, dear Christine?
CHRISTINE: Traitor, begone! let me die at once! Is she not your bride?
LENOX: No, by Heavens, no! 'tis my early friend, my dear companion. Could you doubt my love?
CHRISTINE: Not married? not your betrothed? O Lenox, are you then faithful?
LENOX: Could Christine doubt my vows?
CHRISTINE: I see it all—I have been deceived. Pardon me, dear Lenox; but driven to

despair by your supposed perfidy, I enlisted, and rushed on my fate—which in a moment (horrid thought!) would have terminated. But you are true, and I am happy. [*Embrace*]

LAROLE: Parbleu! it is a littel voman vidout de petticoat. Suppose she take a me von prisonier, O quell disgrâce!

Enter JASPER, JERRY *and* PEASANTS

JASPER: Where is she? where is my daughter?

CHRISTINE: My father? I dare not look upon him.

JASPER: Come to my arms, dear wanderer. Could you leave your poor old father thus? You've nearly broke my heart, Christine.

CHRISTINE: My sufferings have been equally severe; but do you pardon your child?

JASPER: I do—I do! and further prove my love, by making you happy. Take her, Lenox, she is yours; and never let father attempt to force his child into a marriage which her heart abhors.

JERRY: Well, I vow, Miss Crissy, you look very pretty in pantaloons, and make a fine soger; but after all, I'm glad to have escaped a wife who wears the breeches before marriage—so I consent that you shall have the infantry ossifer, because I can't help it; and so I'll marry Patty, the weaver's daughter, though she can't crack a bottle nor bring down a buck.

GENERAL: All things have terminated happily. Our arms have been triumphant, and our gallant soldiers rewarded with the approbation of their country. Love has intwined a wreath for your brows, Lenox, and domestic peace and happiness await you; and when old age draws on apace, may you remember the PLAINS OF CHIPPEWA, and feel toward Britain as freemen should feel towards all the world: *"Enemies in war—in peace, friends."*

Finis

1819

James Fenimore Cooper 1789–1851

James Fenimore Cooper was the first American novelist to gain international stature and the first to earn his living from royalties. A prodigious innovator, he has been credited with inventing sea fiction (Melville and Conrad expressed their indebtedness), the international novel, and distinctively American forms of the novel of manners and allegorical fiction. Cooper's thirty-two novels, spanning the period from 1820 to 1850, include works in all these genres. But, as Cooper himself knew, the novels for which he would be best remembered are his five Leather-stocking tales. In these tales, Cooper explored the meanings of American frontier experience, creating the prototypical Western hero, Natty Bumppo (the Leather-stocking), whose wilderness adventures dramatize some of the central cultural tensions of antebellum America.

The writer was the son of one of the early republic's most ambitious land speculators and developers, William Cooper, founder of Cooperstown in central New York State and later a U.S. congressman from that region. William Cooper, having struggled to surmount his lowly beginnings as a Philadelphia wheelwright, expected his sons to assume a place among America's Federalist gentry as lawyers, politicians, or gentleman farmers. Thus, James Fenimore Cooper seems an unlikely figure to have become a novelist. Indeed, he did not become one until he was thirty years old, after serving briefly in the merchant marine and the U.S. Navy and then living as a gentleman farmer in New York's Westchester County and in Cooperstown.

But during this period the vast real estate empire of William Cooper, who died in 1809, collapsed under the claims of creditors. By 1820, James Cooper (he added the Fenimore later) was the family's only surviving son and thus the primary bearer of its rapidly accumulating indebtedness. So desperate did his financial circumstances become by 1823 that in that year the sheriff of New York City, on behalf of creditors, inventoried the household possessions of Cooper's rented home in the city. Although Cooper may not have become a writer in order to gain solvency (family legend has it that he wrote his first novel in response to a dare from his wife), his literary career, once undertaken, was driven by both creative passion and financial necessity.

That career began in 1820 with *Precaution,* an unsuccessful and imitative novel of manners set in England and published anonymously. But in the following year, Cooper found his form and his audience with *The Spy.* In this best-seller, set in the Hudson River highlands above New York City during the American Revolution, the novelist exploited the immense appeal of American history, characters, and settings during a time when the Revolutionary era and its leaders (George Washington figures in the novel's action) had become a subject for reverence and nostalgia. If Cooper's paradigms of adventure action had derived from the works of Walter Scott, as contemporaries observed, his investment of those paradigms with American materials was welcomed by a grateful and appreciative reading public.

While *The Spy* established Cooper's reputation as a novelist, his next work, *The Pioneers,* published in 1823, more directly reveals his family legacy and his concerns for American life. In this first of the Leatherstocking tales, Cooper depicted the frontier settlement of Cooperstown, situated at the foot of Lake Otsego and called Templeton in the novel, as he remembered it from his childhood. (Born in New Jersey in 1789, Cooper was brought to Cooperstown in the first year of his life.) At the center of the novel, which probes the issue of rightful land ownership and use, stands Judge Marmaduke Temple—clearly a representation of William Cooper, the patriarchal founder and developer of Cooperstown.

The novel is organized around the perspectives of the land's historical claimants: old Indian John (Chingachgook), the last survivor of Native American life in the region; the seventy-year-old woodsman Natty Bumppo, whose spiritual claims to a free wilderness life long predate the property claims of Judge Temple; Oliver Effingham (known as Edwards for much of the novel), a descendant of an aristocratic Tory family dispossessed by the Revolution, who believes that Temple usurped his family's rights; and the multi-ethnic group of settlers attempting to secure their own more limited forms of land tenure. Although Temple ultimately is exonerated from the charge of usurpation, Cooper's ambivalence toward the authority of the patriarch—the novel both shores up such authority and undercuts it—is an interesting and energizing aspect of this novel and of the Leather-stocking tales as a whole.

After his publication of *The Pioneers,* widely admired by American readers for its close descriptions of frontier life, Cooper went on in the following year to repeat the success of *The Spy,* turning again to the materials of the American Revolution but this time in a nautical setting. *The Pilot,* one of whose central characters is John Paul Jones, is regarded by many literary historians as the first authentic novel of the sea.

Shortly thereafter, in 1826, Cooper published the second of the Leatherstocking tales, *The Last of the Mohicans,* set during the French and Indian War when Natty Bumppo was in vigorous middle age. Reviving Chingachgook (who had died in *The Pioneers*) and introducing his heroic son Uncas, this novel is centrally concerned with the issue of Indian dispossession and with the conflict of cultures. The novel's fast-paced action and its elegiac portrayal of Native Americans made it an enormous success with the reading public. Cooper's sympathetic and epic treatment of Native Americans in *The Last of the Mohicans* has been viewed in our time in two distinct ways: as a romantic strategy for dismissing Native Americans from national experience and as Cooper's authentic identification with and sympathy for Native American dispossession. These views, while opposing, are in fact not mutually exclusive and suggest the complexity of Cooper's literary legacy.

Soon after publication of *The Last of the Mohicans* in 1826, Cooper, now a national hero, left America for a European sojourn of seven years. In 1827 he published from Paris what he must have thought was the concluding volume in the Leather-stocking series, *The Prairie.* This novel, in which Natty Bumppo has become a fully mythic figure leading the nation's westward movement, is, like *The Pioneers,* concerned with issues of frontier justice and the future of the American experiment and, like *The Last of the Mohicans,* treats the displacement and reactive violence of Native Americans. A very old man now, Natty dies at the novel's conclusion in America's far west.

When Cooper returned to America from Europe in 1833, resuming residence in Cooperstown, he was shocked by what he regarded as the excesses of Jacksonian democracy, and from this point forward until the end of his life he waged an insistent argument—in his writings and in lawsuits (mostly against newspaper editors he believed had libeled him)—with his country. During the 1830s, in fact, Cooper published little fiction. Then, surprisingly, in the early 1840s, he brought the Leather-stocking hero back to life in two novels, *The Pathfinder* (1840) and *The Deerslayer* (1841) and thereby revived his own languishing career. These works, which show Natty Bumppo for the first time involved in romantic love, do not lack the violent frontier action that earlier had characterized *The Last of the Mohicans* and *The Prairie.* But their more classical depiction of the American wilderness reflects an altered sense of landscape that Cooper had derived from his European travels. *The Deerslayer,* set like *The Pioneers* at Lake Otsego but in a much earlier time (Natty here is a youth of twenty), renders a particularly serene and classical picture of the American forest prior to settlement. As much, however, as *The Deerslayer* communicates a sense of romantic retreat into a distant past, it also serves symbolically to attack Cooper's enemies—especially in its pointedly damaging portraits of the novel's unprincipled characters.

Later in the 1840s Cooper resumed his overt polemical attack on his enemies in a series of novels called the Littlepage Trilogy. In these works, he became the defender of landowners in the Hudson River Valley, taking their side against rebellious tenant farmers in the so-called anti-rent wars of this period. Cooper's late novel *The Crater* (1848), an allegory of the rise and fall of the United States, confirms the novelist's ever-deepening sense of historical doom. He ended his career with a bitter satire about American social life and legal practices called *The Ways of the Hour* (1850).

Through the course of his long career, Cooper explored in his fiction some of nineteenth-century America's most important issues, especially the role of elites in a democracy and the conflicting meanings of frontier experience. That experience was embodied and made mythic in Cooper's Leather-stocking hero, one of the most enduring and influential figures in American literature. Though many of Cooper's works are unread today, he was regarded throughout much of the nineteenth century as America's preeminent novelist, and in our own time his works are being vigorously reexamined as expressions of a troubled and ambivalent response to democratic culture.

H. Daniel Peck
Vassar College

PRIMARY WORKS

The Spy, 1821; *The Pioneers,* 1823; *The Pilot,* 1824; *The Last of the Mohicans,* 1826; *The Prairie,* 1827; *The Pathfinder,* 1840; *The Deerslayer,* 1841; in the State University of New York Press editions, edited by James F. Beard et al.; the Leather-stocking tales are reprinted in the following series: the Library of America, Oxford World's Classics, and Penguin Classics. *Letters and Journals,* ed. James F. Beard, 1960–68.

SECONDARY WORKS

James Grossman, *James Fenimore Cooper,* 1949; Kay Seymour House, *Cooper's Americans,* 1965; George Dekker, *James Fenimore Cooper the Novelist,* 1967; John P. McWilliams, *Political Justice in a Republic,* 1972; H. Daniel Peck, *A World by Itself: The Pastoral Moment in Cooper's Fiction,* 1977; Stephen Railton, *Fenimore Cooper: A Study of His Life and Imagination,* 1978; Wayne Franklin, *The New World of James Fenimore Cooper,* 1982; William Kelly, *Plotting America's Past: Fenimore Cooper and the Leather-stocking Tales,* 1983; Warren Motley, *The American Abraham: James Fenimore Cooper and the Frontier Patriarch,* 1987; Donald A. Ringe, *James Fenimore Cooper,* 1988; Charles Hanford Adams, *"The Guardian of the Law": Authority and Identity in James Fenimore Cooper,* 1990; Geoffrey Rans, *Cooper's Leather-stocking Novels: A Secular Reading,* 1991; H. Daniel Peck, ed., *New Essays on the Last of the Mohicans,* 1992; Alan Taylor, *William Cooper's Town: Power and Persuasion on the Frontier of the Early American Republic,* 1995.

[This selection from *The Pioneers*—three full continuous chapters showing the advance of spring in the frontier community of Templeton—renders the deep background of the novel's action. In chapter XXI, we find Judge Marmaduke Temple's daughter Elizabeth asking him to describe the moment, on Mount Vision, when he first looked down upon the future site of Templeton. After describing a period of deprivation (the "starving-time") in the early days of settlement (a story emphasizing Temple's role as village patriarch), the Judge complies. He renders his moment on the mountain as a visionary possession of a wilderness landscape. Implicitly pointing to Temple's erasure of earlier claimants, Oliver Effingham (Edwards) raises the issue of the Indians' rights (long ago "extinguished," Temple responds), and of Natty Bumppo's increasingly threatened rights to a life of wilderness freedom.

The ways in which that freedom, and the very environment that supports it, are being eroded by settlement are made vivid in the following two chapters. In chapter XXII the settlers bring down huge numbers of passenger pigeons by firing cannon shots into the flock, and in chapter XXIII they seine thousands of fish onto the shore where most are left to rot. Natty, scornful of the settlers' wastefulness, holds the Judge, and the process of settlement initiated by him, responsible for these actions. But Temple is himself a conservationist, sponsoring game laws and lamenting, as he does at the conclusion of chapter XXIII, "the wasteful extravagance of man." At issue here is the kind of law that best serves the future: the evolving and necessarily imperfect frontier law enforced by Judge Temple or the natural law represented by Natty.

These powerful chapters dramatizing environmental destruction reveal Cooper's prescience about such matters (the passenger pigeon, whose spectacular sky-covering migration was one of early America's most wondrous sights, would become extinct by the end of the nineteenth century) and suggest that, at times, his deeply engrained social conservatism could open out toward an enlightened spirit of conservation. His daughter Susan

Fenimore Cooper would carry that spirit into her own book, *Rural Hours* (1850), a pioneering work of bioregional literature also set in the Lake Otsego watershed.]

from The Pioneers, or the Sources of the Susquehanna; A Descriptive Tale

Chapter XXI

"Speed! Malise, speed! such cause of haste
Thine active sinews never brac'd."
–SCOTT, *THE LADY OF THE LAKE,* III.xiii.3–4.

The roads of Otsego, if we except the principal highways, were, at the early day of our tale, but little better than woodpaths. The high trees that were growing on the very verge of the wheel-tracks, excluded the sun's rays, unless at meridian, and the slowness of the evaporation, united with the rich mould of vegetable decomposition, that covered the whole country, to the depth of several inches, occasioned but an indifferent foundation for the footing of travellers. Added to these were the inequalities of a natural surface, and the constant recurrence of enormous and slippery roots, that were laid bare by the removal of the light soil, together with stumps of trees, to make a passage not only difficult, but dangerous. Yet the riders, among these numerous obstructions, which were such as would terrify an unpractised eye, gave no demonstrations of uneasiness, as their horses toiled through the sloughs, or trotted with uncertain paces along the dark route. In many places, the marks on the trees were the only indications of a road, with, perhaps, an occasional remnant of a pine, that, by being cut close to the earth, so as to leave nothing visible but its base of roots, spreading for twenty feet in every direction, was apparently placed there as a beacon, to warn the traveller that it was the centre of a highway.

Into one of these roads the active Sheriff led the way, first striking out of the footpath, by which they had descended from the sugar-bush, across a little bridge, formed of round logs laid loosely on sleepers of pine, in which large openings, of a formidable width, were frequent. The nag of Richard, when it reached one of these gaps, laid its nose along the logs, and stepped across the difficult passage with the sagacity of a man; but the blooded filly which Miss Temple rode disdained so humble a movement. She made a step or two with an unusual caution, and then, on reaching the broadest opening, obedient to the curb and whip of her fearless mistress, she bounded across the dangerous pass, with the activity of a squirrel.

"Gently, gently, my child," said Marmaduke, who was following in the manner of Richard—"this is not a country for equestrian feats. Much prudence is requisite, to journey through our rough paths with safety. Thou mayst practise thy skill in horsemanship on the plains of New-Jersey, with safety, but in the hills of Otsego, they must be suspended for a time."

"I may as well, then, relinquish my saddle at once, dear sir," returned his daughter; "for if it is to be laid aside until this wild country be improved, old age will overtake me, and put an end to what you term my equestrian feats."

"Say not so, my child," returned her father; "but if thou venturest again, as in crossing this bridge, old age will never overtake thee, but I shall be left to mourn thee, cut off in thy pride, my Elizabeth. If thou hadst seen this district of country, as I did, when it lay in the sleep of nature, and had witnessed its rapid changes, as it awoke to supply the wants of man, thou wouldst curb thy impatience for a little time, though thou shouldst not check thy steed."

"I recollect hearing you speak of your first visit to these woods, but the impression is faint, and blended with the confused images of childhood. Wild and unsettled as it may yet seem, it must have been a thousand times more dreary then. Will you repeat, dear sir, what you then thought of your enterprise, and what you felt?"

During this speech of Elizabeth, which was uttered with the fervour of affection, young Edwards rode more closely to the side of the Judge, and bent his dark eyes on his countenance, with an expression that seemed to read his thoughts.

"Thou wast then young, my child, but must remember when I left thee and thy mother, to take my first survey of these uninhabited mountains," said Marmaduke. "But thou dost not feel all the secret motives that can urge a man to endure privations in order to accumulate wealth. In my case they have not been trifling, and God has been pleased to smile on my efforts. If I have encountered pain, famine, and disease, in accomplishing the settlement of this rough territory, I have not the misery of failure to add to the grievances."

"Famine!" echoed Elizabeth; "I thought this was the land of abundance! had you famine to contend with?"

"Even so, my child," said her father. "Those who look around them now, and see the loads of produce that issue out of every wild path in these mountains, during the season of travelling, will hardly credit that no more than five years have elapsed, since the tenants of these woods were compelled to eat the scanty fruits of the forest to sustain life, and, with their unpractised skill, to hunt the beasts as food for their starving families."

"Ay!" cried Richard, who happened to overhear the last of this speech, between the notes of the wood-chopper's song, which he was endeavouring to breathe aloud; "that was the starving-time,[1] cousin Bess. I grew as lank as a weasel that fall, and my face was as pale as one of your fever-and-ague visages. Monsieur Le Quoi, there, fell away like a pumpkin in drying; nor do I think you have got fairly over it yet, Mon-

[1]The author has no better apology for interrupting the interest of a work of fiction by these desultory dialogues, than that they have reference to facts. In reviewing his work, after so many years, he is compelled to confess it is injured by too many allusions to incidents that are not at all suited to satisfy the just expectations of the general reader. One of these events is slightly touched on, in the commencement of this chapter.

More than thirty years since, a very near and dear relative of the writer, an elder sister and a second mother, was killed by a fall from a horse, in a ride among the very mountains mentioned in this tale. Few of her sex and years were more extensively known, or more universally beloved, than the admirable woman who thus fell a victim to the chances of the wilderness. [1832]

sieur. Benjamin, I thought, bore it with a worse grace than any of the family, for he swore it was harder to endure than a short allowance in the calm latitudes. Benjamin is a sad fellow to swear, if you starve him ever so little. I had half a mind to quit you then, 'duke, and to go into Pennsylvania to fatten; but, damn it, thinks I, we are sisters' children, and I will live or die with him, after all."

"I do not forget thy kindness," said Marmaduke, "nor that we are of one blood."

"But, my dear father," cried the wondering Elizabeth, "was there actual suffering? where were the beautiful and fertile vales of the Mohawk? could they not furnish food for your wants?"

"It was a season of scarcity; the necessities of life commanded a high price in Europe, and were greedily sought after by the speculators. The emigrants, from the east to the west, invariably passed along the valley of the Mohawk, and swept away the means of subsistence, like a swarm of locusts. Nor were the people on the Flats in a much better condition. They were in want themselves, but they spared the little excess of provisions, that nature did not absolutely require, with the justice of the German character. There was no grinding of the poor. The word speculator was then unknown to them. I have seen many a stout man, bending under the load of the bag of meal, which he was carrying from the mills of the Mohawk, through the rugged passes of these mountains, to feed his half-famished children, with a heart so light, as he approached his hut, that the thirty miles he had passed seemed nothing. Remember, my child, it was in our very infancy: we had neither mills, nor grain, nor roads, nor often clearings;——we had nothing of increase but the mouths that were to be fed; for, even at that inauspicious moment, the restless spirit of emigration was not idle; nay, the general scarcity, which extended to the east, tended to increase the number of adventurers."

"And how, dearest father, didst thou encounter this dreadful evil?" said Elizabeth, unconsciously adopting the dialect of her parent, in the warmth of her sympathy. "Upon thee must have fallen the responsibility, if not the suffering."

"It did, Elizabeth," returned the Judge, pausing for a single moment, as if musing on his former feelings. "I had hundreds at that dreadful time, daily looking up to me for bread. The sufferings of their families, and the gloomy prospect before them, had paralysed the enterprise and efforts of my settlers; hunger drove them to the woods for food, but despair sent them, at night, enfeebled and wan, to a sleepless pillow. It was not a moment for inaction. I purchased cargoes of wheat from the granaries of Pennsylvania; they were landed at Albany, and brought up the Mohawk in boats; from thence it was transported on pack-horses into the wilderness, and distributed amongst my people. Seines were made, and the lakes and rivers were dragged for fish. Something like a miracle was wrought in our favour, for enormous shoals of herrings were discovered to have wandered five hundred miles, through the windings of the impetuous Susquehanna, and the lake was alive with their numbers. These were at length caught, and dealt out to the people, with proper portions of salt; and from that moment, we again began to prosper."[2]

"Yes," cried Richard, "and I was the man who served out the fish and the salt. When the poor devils came to receive their rations, Benjamin, who was my deputy,

[2]All this was literally true. [1832]

was obliged to keep them off by stretching ropes around me, for they smelt so of garlic, from eating nothing but the wild onion, that the fumes put me out, often, in my measurement. You were a child then, Bess, and knew nothing of the matter, for great care was observed to keep both you and your mother from suffering. That year put me back, dreadfully, both in the breed of my hogs, and of my turkeys."

"No, Bess," cried the Judge, in a more cheerful tone, disregarding the interruption of his cousin, "he who hears of the settlement of a country, knows but little of the toil and suffering by which it is accomplished. Unimproved and wild as this district now seems to your eyes, what was it when I first entered the hills! I left my party, the morning of my arrival, near the farms of the Cherry Valley, and, following a deer-path, rode to the summit of the mountain, that I have since called Mount Vision; for the sight that there met my eyes seemed to me as the deceptions of a dream. The fire had run over the pinnacle, and, in a great measure, laid open the view. The leaves were fallen, and I mounted a tree, and sat for an hour looking on the silent wilderness. Not an opening was to be seen in the boundless forest, except where the lake lay, like a mirror of glass. The water was covered by myriads of the wild-fowl that migrate with the changes in the season; and, while in my situation on the branch of the beech, I saw a bear, with her cubs, descend to the shore to drink. I had met many deer, gliding through the woods, in my journey; but not the vestige of a man could I trace, during my progress, nor from my elevated observatory. No clearing, no hut, none of the winding roads that are now to be seen, were there; nothing but mountains rising behind mountains, and the valley, with its surface of branches, enlivened here and there with the faded foliage of some tree, that parted from its leaves with more than ordinary reluctance. Even the Susquehanna was then hid, by the height and density of the forest."

"And were you alone?" asked Elizabeth;——"passed you the night in that solitary state?"

"Not so, my child," returned her father. "After musing on the scene for an hour, with a mingled feeling of pleasure and desolation, I left my perch, and descended the mountain. My horse was left to browse on the twigs that grew within his reach, while I explored the shores of the lake, and the spot where Templeton stands. A pine of more than ordinary growth stood where my dwelling is now placed; a wind-row had been opened through the trees from thence to the lake, and my view was but little impeded. Under the branches of that tree I made my solitary dinner; I had just finished my repast as I saw a smoke curling from under the mountain, near the eastern bank of the lake. It was the only indication of the vicinity of man that I had then seen. After much toil, I made my way to the spot, and found a rough cabin of logs, built against the foot of a rock, and bearing the marks of a tenant, though I found no one within it.—"

"It was the hut of Leather-stocking," said Edwards, quickly.

"It was; though I, at first, supposed it to be a habitation of the Indians. But while I was lingering around the spot, Natty made his appearance, staggering under the carcass of a buck that he had slain. Our acquaintance commenced at that time; before, I had never heard that such a being tenanted the woods. He launched his bark canoe, and set me across the foot of the lake, to the place where I had fastened my horse, and pointed out a spot where he might get a scanty browsing until the morning; when I returned and passed the night in the cabin of the hunter."

Miss Temple was so much struck by the deep attention of young Edwards, during this speech, that she forgot to resume her interrogatories; but the youth himself continued the discourse, by asking—

"And how did the Leather-stocking discharge the duties of a host, sir?"

"Why, simply but kindly, until late in the evening, when he discovered my name and object, and the cordiality of his manner very sensibly diminished, or, I might better say, disappeared. He considered the introduction of the settlers as an innovation on his rights, I believe; for he expressed much dissatisfaction at the measure, though it was in his confused and ambiguous manner. I hardly understood his objections myself, but supposed they referred chiefly to an interruption of the hunting."

"Had you then purchased the estate, or were you examining it with an intent to buy?" asked Edwards, a little abruptly.

"It had been mine for several years. It was with a view to people the land that I visited the lake. Natty treated me hospitably, but coldly, I thought, after he learnt the nature of my journey. I slept on his own bear-skin, however, and in the morning joined my surveyors again."

"Said he nothing of the Indian rights, sir? The Leather-stocking is much given to impeach the justice of the tenure by which the whites hold the country."

"I remember that he spoke of them, but I did not clearly comprehend him, and may have forgotten what he said; for the Indian title was extinguished so far back as the close of the old war; and if it had not been at all, I hold under the patents of the Royal Governors, confirmed by an act of our own State Legislature, and no court in the country can affect my title."

"Doubtless, sir, your title is both legal and equitable," returned the youth, coldly, reining his horse back, and remaining silent till the subject was changed.

It was seldom Mr. Jones suffered any conversation to continue, for a great length of time, without his participation. It seems that he was of the party that Judge Temple had designated as his surveyors; and he embraced the opportunity of the pause that succeeded the retreat of young Edwards, to take up the discourse, and with it a narration of their further proceedings, after his own manner. As it wanted, however, the interest that had accompanied the description of the Judge, we must decline the task of committing his sentences to paper.

They soon reached the point where the promised view was to be seen. It was one of those picturesque and peculiar scenes, that belong to the Otsego, but which required the absence of the ice, and the softness of a summer's landscape, to be enjoyed in all its beauty. Marmaduke had early forewarned his daughter of the season, and of its effect on the prospect, and after casting a cursory glance at its capabilities, the party returned homeward, perfectly satisfied that its beauties would repay them for the toil of a second ride, at a more propitious season.

"The spring is the gloomy time of the American year," said the Judge; "and it is more peculiarly the case in these mountains. The winter seems to retreat to the fastnesses of the hills, as to the citadel of its dominion, and is only expelled, after a tedious siege, in which either party, at times, would seem to be gaining the victory."

"A very just and apposite figure, Judge Temple," observed the Sheriff; "and the garrison under the command of Jack Frost make formidable sorties—you understand what I mean by sorties, Monsieur; sallies, in English—and sometimes drive General Spring and his troops back again into the low countries."

"Yes, sair," returned the Frenchman, whose prominent eyes were watching the precarious footsteps of the beast he rode, as it picked its dangerous way among the roots of trees, holes, log-bridges, and sloughs, that formed the aggregate of the highway. "Je vous entend; de low countrie is freeze up for half de year."

The error of Mr. Le Quoi was not observed by the Sheriff; and the rest of the party were yielding to the influence of the changeful season, which was already teaching the equestrians that a continuance of its mildness was not to be expected for any length of time. Silence and thoughtfulness succeeded the gayety and conversation that had prevailed during the commencement of the ride, as clouds began to gather about the heavens, apparently collecting from every quarter, in quick motion, without the agency of a breath of air.

While riding over one of the cleared eminences that occurred in their route, the watchful eye of Judge Temple pointed out to his daughter the approach of a tempest. Flurries of snow already obscured the mountain that formed the northern boundary of the lake, and the genial sensation which had quickened the blood through their veins, was already succeeded by the deadening influence of an approaching *northwester.*

All of the party were now busily engaged in making the best of their way to the village, though the badness of the roads frequently compelled them to check the impatience of their horses, which often carried them over places that would not admit of any gait faster than a walk.

Richard continued in advance, followed by Mr. Le Quoi; next to whom rode Elizabeth, who seemed to have imbibed the distance which pervaded the manner of young Edwards, since the termination of the discourse between the latter and her father. Marmaduke followed his daughter, giving her frequent and tender warnings as to the management of her horse. It was, possibly, the evident dependence that Louisa Grant placed on his assistance, which induced the youth to continue by her side, as they pursued their way through a dreary and dark wood, where the rays of the sun could but rarely penetrate, and where even the daylight was obscured and rendered gloomy by the deep forests that surrounded them. No wind had yet reached the spot where the equestrians were in motion, but that dead stillness that often precedes a storm, contributed to render their situation more irksome than if they were already subjected to the fury of the tempest. Suddenly the voice of young Edwards was heard shouting, in those appalling tones that carry alarm to the very soul, and which curdle the blood of those that hear them—

"A tree! a tree! whip—spur for your lives! a tree! a tree!"

"A tree! a tree!" echoed Richard, giving his horse a blow, that caused the alarmed beast to jump nearly a rod, throwing the mud and water into the air, like a hurricane.

"Von tree! von tree!" shouted the Frenchman, bending his body on the neck of his charger, shutting his eyes, and playing on the ribs of his beast with his heels, at a rate that caused him to be conveyed, on the crupper of the Sheriff, with a marvellous speed.

Elizabeth checked her filly, and looked up, with an unconscious but alarmed air, at the very cause of their danger, while she listened to the crackling sounds that awoke the stillness of the forest; but, at the next instant, her bridle was seized by her father, who cried—

"God protect my child!" and she felt herself hurried onward, impelled by the vigour of his nervous arm.

Each one of the party bowed to his saddle-bows, as the tearing of branches was succeeded by a sound like the rushing of the winds, which was followed by a thundering report, and a shock that caused the very earth to tremble, as one of the noblest ruins of the forest fell directly across their path.

One glance was enough to assure Judge Temple that his daughter, and those in front of him, were safe, and he turned his eyes, in dreadful anxiety, to learn the fate of the others. Young Edwards was on the opposite side of the tree, his form thrown back in his saddle to its utmost distance, his left hand drawing up his bridle with its greatest force, while the right grasped that of Miss Grant, so as to draw the head of her horse under its body. Both the animals stood shaking in every joint with terror, and snorting fearfully. Louisa herself had relinquished her reins, and with her hands pressed on her face, sat bending forward in her saddle, in an attitude of despair mingled strangely with resignation.

"Are you safe?" cried the Judge, first breaking the awful silence of the moment.

"By God's blessing," returned the youth; "but if there had been branches to the tree we must have been lost—"

He was interrupted by the figure of Louisa, slowly yielding in her saddle; and but for his arm, she would have sunken to the earth. Terror, however, was the only injury that the clergyman's daughter had sustained, and, with the aid of Elizabeth, she was soon restored to her senses. After some little time was lost in recovering her strength, the young lady was replaced in her saddle, and, supported on either side, by Judge Temple and Mr. Edwards, she was enabled to follow the party in their slow progress.

"The sudden falling of the trees," said Marmaduke, "are the most dangerous accidents in the forest, for they are not to be foreseen, being impelled by no winds, nor any extraneous or visible cause, against which we can guard."

"The reason of their falling, Judge Temple, is very obvious," said the Sheriff. "The tree is old and decayed, and it is gradually weakened by the frosts, until a line drawn from the centre of gravity falls without its base, and then the tree comes of a certainty; and I should like to know, what greater compulsion there can be for any thing, than a mathematical certainty. I studied mathe——"

"Very true, Richard," interrupted Marmaduke; "thy reasoning is true, and, if my memory be not over treacherous, was furnished by myself, on a former occasion. But how is one to guard against the danger? canst thou go through the forests, measuring the bases, and calculating the centres of the oaks? answer me that, friend Jones, and I will say thou wilt do the country a service."

"Answer thee that, friend Temple!" returned Richard; "a well-educated man can answer thee any thing, sir. Do any trees fall in this manner, but such as are decayed? Take care not to approach the roots of a rotten tree, and you will be safe enough."

"That would be excluding us entirely from the forests," said Marmaduke. "But, happily, the winds usually force down most of these dangerous ruins, as their currents are admitted into the woods by the surrounding clearings, and such a fall as this has been is very rare."

Louisa, by this time, had recovered so much strength, as to allow the party to proceed at a quicker pace; but long before they were safely housed, they were overtaken by the storm; and when they dismounted at the door of the Mansion-house, the black plumes of Miss Temple's hat were drooping with the weight of a load of damp snow, and the coats of the gentlemen were powdered with the same material.

While Edwards was assisting Louisa from her horse, the warmhearted girl caught his hand with fervour, and whispered—

"Now, Mr. Edwards, both father and daughter owe their lives to you."

A driving, north-westerly storm succeeded; and before the sun was set, every vestige of spring had vanished; the lake, the mountains, the village, and the fields, being again hid under one dazzling coat of snow.

Chapter XXII

"Men, boys, and girls,
Desert th' unpeopled village; and wild crowds
Spread o'er the plain, by the sweet frenzy driven."
—SOMERVILLE, *THE CHACE,* II.197–99.

From this time to the close of April, the weather continued to be a succession of great and rapid changes. One day, the soft airs of spring seemed to be stealing along the valley, and, in unison with an invigorating sun, attempting, covertly, to rouse the dormant powers of the vegetable world; while on the next, the surly blasts from the north would sweep across the lake, and erase every impression left by their gentle adversaries. The snow, however, finally disappeared, and the green wheat fields were seen in every direction, spotted with the dark and charred stumps that had, the preceding season, supported some of the proudest trees of the forest. Ploughs were in motion, wherever those useful implements could be used, and the smokes of the sugar-camps were no longer seen issuing from the woods of maple. The lake had lost the beauty of a field of ice, but still a dark and gloomy covering concealed its waters, for the absence of currents left them yet hid under a porous crust, which, saturated with the fluid, barely retained enough strength to preserve the contiguity of its parts. Large flocks of wild geese were seen passing over the country, which hovered, for a time, around the hidden sheet of water, apparently searching for a resting-place; and then, on finding themselves excluded by the chill covering, would soar away to the north, filling the air with discordant screams, as if venting their complaints at the tardy operations of nature.

For a week, the dark covering of the Otsego was left to the undisturbed possession of two eagles, who alighted on the centre of its field, and sat eyeing their undisputed territory. During the presence of these monarchs of the air, the flocks of migrating birds avoided crossing the plain of ice, by turning into the hills, apparently seeking the protection of the forests, while the white and bald heads of the tenants of the lake were turned upward, with a look of contempt. But the time had come, when even these kings of birds were to be dispossessed. An opening had been gradually increasing, at the lower extremity of the lake, and around the dark spot where the current of the river prevented the formation of ice, during even the coldest weather; and the fresh southerly winds, that now breathed freely upon the valley, made an impression on the waters. Mimic waves begun to curl over the margin of the frozen field, which exhibited an outline of crystallizations, that slowly receded towards the north. At each step the power of the winds and the waves increased, until, after a struggle of a few hours, the turbulent little billows succeeded in setting the whole field in motion, when it was driven beyond the reach of the eye, with a rapidity, that was as magical as the change produced in the scene by this expulsion of the lingering remnant of winter. Just as the last sheet of agitated ice was disappearing in the distance, the eagles rose, and soared with a wide sweep above the clouds, while the waves tossed their little caps of snow into the air, as if rioting in their release from a thraldom of five months' duration.

The following morning Elizabeth was awakened by the exhilarating sounds of the martins, who were quarreling and chattering around the little boxes suspended above her windows, and the cries of Richard, who was calling, in tones animating as the signs of the season itself—

"Awake! awake! my fair lady! the gulls are hovering over the lake already, and the heavens are alive with pigeons. You may look an hour before you can find a hole, through which, to get a peep at the sun. Awake! awake! lazy ones! Benjamin is overhauling the ammunition, and we only wait for our breakfasts, and away for the mountains and pigeon-shooting."

There was no resisting this animated appeal, and in a few minutes Miss Temple and her friend descended to the parlour. The doors of the hall were thrown open, and the mild, balmy air of a clear spring morning was ventilating the apartment, where the vigilance of the ex-steward had been so long maintaining an artificial heat, with such unremitted diligence. The gentlemen were impatiently waiting for their morning's repast, each equipt in the garb of a sportsman. Mr. Jones made many visits to the southern door, and would cry—

"See, cousin Bess! see, 'duke! the pigeon-roosts of the south have broken up! They are growing more thick every instant. Here is a flock that the eye cannot see the end of. There is food enough in it to keep the army of Xerxes for a month, and feathers enough to make beds for the whole country. Xerxes, Mr. Edwards, was a Grecian king, who—no, he was a Turk, or a Persian, who wanted to conquer Greece, just the same as these rascals will overrun our wheat-fields, when they come back in the fall.—Away! away! Bess; I long to pepper them."

In this wish both Marmaduke and young Edwards seemed equally to participate, for the sight was exhilarating to a sportsman; and the ladies soon dismissed the party, after a hasty breakfast.

If the heavens were alive with pigeons, the whole village seemed equally in motion, with men, women, and children. Every species of fire-arms, from the French ducking-gun, with a barrel near six feet in length, to the common horseman's pistol, was to be seen in the hands of the men and boys; while bows and arrows, some made of the simple stick of a walnut sapling, and others in a rude imitation of the ancient cross-bows, were carried by many of the latter.

The houses, and the signs of life apparent in the village, drove the alarmed birds from the direct line of their flight, towards the mountains, along the sides and near the bases of which they were glancing in dense masses, equally wonderful by the rapidity of their motion, and their incredible numbers.

We have already said, that across the inclined plane which fell from the steep ascent of the mountain to the banks of the Susquehanna, ran the highway, on either side of which a clearing of many acres had been made, at a very early day. Over those clearings, and up the eastern mountain, and along the dangerous path that was cut into its side, the different individuals posted themselves, and in a few moments the attack commenced.

Amongst the sportsmen was the tall, gaunt form of Leather-stocking, walking over the field, with his rifle hanging on his arm, his dogs at his heels; the latter now scenting the dead or wounded birds, that were beginning to tumble from the flocks, and then crouching under the legs of their master, as if they participated in his feelings, at this wasteful and unsportsmanlike execution.

The reports of the fire-arms became rapid, whole volleys rising from the plain, as flocks of more than ordinary numbers darted over the opening, shadowing the field, like a cloud; and then the light smoke of a single piece would issue from among the leafless bushes on the mountain, as death was hurled on the retreat of the affrighted birds, who were rising from a volley, in a vain effort to escape. Arrows, and missiles of every kind, were in the midst of the flocks; and so numerous were the birds, and so low did they take their flight, that even long poles, in the hands of those on the sides of the mountain, were used to strike them to the earth.

During all this time, Mr. Jones, who disdained the humble and ordinary means of destruction used by his companions, was busily occupied, aided by Benjamin, in making arrangements for an assault of a more than ordinarily fatal character. Among the relics of the old military excursions, that occasionally are discovered throughout the different districts of the western part of New-York, there had been found in Templeton, at its settlement, a small swivel, which would carry a ball of a pound weight. It was thought to have been deserted by a war-party of the whites, in one of their inroads into the Indian settlements, when, perhaps, convenience or their necessity induced them to leave such an encumbrance behind them in the woods. This miniature cannon had been released from the rust, and being mounted on little wheels, was now in a state for actual service. For several years, it was the sole organ for extraordinary rejoicings used in those mountains. On the mornings of the Fourths of July, it would be heard ringing among the hills, and even Captain Hollister, who was the highest authority in that part of the country on all such occasions, affirmed that, considering its dimensions, it was no despicable gun for a salute. It was somewhat the worse for the service it had performed, it is true, there being but a trifling difference in size between the touch-hole and the muzzle. Still, the grand conceptions of Richard had suggested the importance of such an instrument, in hurling death at his nimble enemies. The swivel was dragged by a horse into a part of the open space, that the Sheriff thought most eligible for planting a battery of the kind, and Mr. Pump proceeded to load it. Several handfuls of duck-shot were placed on top of the powder, and the Major-domo announced that his piece was ready for service.

The sight of such an implement collected all the idle spectators to the spot, who, being mostly boys, filled the air with cries of exultation and delight. The gun was pointed high, and Richard, holding a coal of fire in a pair of tongs, patiently took his seat on a stump, awaiting the appearance of a flock worthy of his notice.

So prodigious was the number of the birds, that the scattering fire of the guns, with the hurling of missiles, and the cries of the boys, had no other effect than to break off small flocks from the immense masses that continued to dart along the valley, as if the whole of the feathered tribe were pouring through that one pass. None pretended to collect the game, which lay scattered over the fields in such profusion, as to cover the very ground with the fluttering victims.

Leather-stocking was a silent, but uneasy spectator of all these proceedings, but was able to keep his sentiments to himself until he saw the introduction of the swivel into the sports.

"This comes of settling a country!" he said—"here have I known the pigeons to fly for forty long years, and, till you made your clearings, there was nobody to skear or to hurt them. I loved to see them come into the woods, for they were company to a body; hurting nothing; being, as it was, as harmless as a garter-snake. But now it gives me sore thoughts when I hear the frighty things whizzing through the air, for I know it's only a motion to bring out all the brats in the village. Well! the Lord won't see the waste of his creaters for nothing, and right will be done to the pigeons, as well as others, by-and-by.——There's Mr. Oliver, as bad as the rest of them, firing into the flocks as if he was shooting down nothing but Mingo warriors."

Among the sportsmen was Billy Kirby, who, armed with an old musket, was loading, and, without even looking into the air, was firing, and shouting as his victims fell even on his own person. He heard the speech of Natty, and took upon himself to reply—

"What! old Leather-stocking," he cried, "grumbling at the loss of a few pigeons! If you had to sow your wheat twice, and three times, as I have done, you wouldn't be so massyfully feeling'd to'ards the divils.—Hurrah, boys! scatter the feathers. This is better than shooting at a turkey's head and neck, old fellow."

"It's better for you, maybe, Billy Kirby," replied the indignant old hunter, "and all them that don't know how to put a ball down a rifle-barrel, or how to bring it up ag'in with a true aim; but it's wicked to be shooting into flocks in this wastey manner; and none do it, who know how to knock over a single bird. If a body has a craving for pigeon's flesh, why! it's made the same as all other creater's, for man's eating, but not to kill twenty and eat one. When I want such a thing, I go into the woods till I find one to my liking, and then I shoot him off the branches without touching a feather of another, though there might be a hundred on the same tree. You couldn't do such a thing, Billy Kirby—you couldn't do it if you tried."

"What's that, old corn-stalk! you sapless stub!" cried the wood-chopper. "You've grown wordy, since the affair of the turkey; but if you're for a single shot, here goes at that bird which comes on by himself."

The fire from the distant part of the field had driven a single pigeon below the flock to which it belonged, and, frightened with the constant reports of the muskets, it was approaching the spot where the disputants stood, darting first from one side, and then to the other, cutting the air with the swiftness of lightning, and making a noise with its wings, not unlike the rushing of a bullet. Unfortunately for the wood-chopper, notwithstanding his vaunt, he did not see this bird until it was too late to fire as it approached, and he pulled his trigger at the unlucky moment when it was darting immediately over his head. The bird continued its course with the usual velocity.

Natty lowered the rifle from his arm, when the challenge was made, and, waiting a moment, until the terrified victim had got in a line with his eye, and had dropped near the bank of the lake, he raised it again with uncommon rapidity, and fired. It might have been chance, or it might have been skill, that produced the result; it was probably a union of both; but the pigeon whirled over in the air, and fell into the lake, with a broken wing. At the sound of his rifle, both his dogs started from his feet, and in a few minutes the "slut" brought out the bird, still alive.

The wonderful exploit of Leather-stocking was noised through the field with great rapidity, and the sportsmen gathered in to learn the truth of the report.

"What," said young Edwards, "have you really killed a pigeon on the wing, Natty, with a single ball?"

"Haven't I killed loons before now, lad, that dive at the flash?" returned the hunter. "It's much better to kill only such as you want, without wasting your powder and lead, than to be firing into God's creaters in this wicked manner. But I come out for a bird, and you know the reason why I like small game, Mr. Oliver, and now I have got one I will go home, for I don't relish to see these wasty ways that you are all practysing, as if the least thing was not made for use, and not to destroy."

"Thou sayest well, Leather-stocking," cried Marmaduke, "and I begin to think it time to put an end to this work of destruction."

"Put an ind, Judge, to your clearings. An't the woods his work as well as the pigeons? Use, but don't waste. Wasn't the woods made for the beasts and birds to harbour in? and when man wanted their flesh, their skins, or their feathers, there's the place to seek them. But I'll go to the hut with my own game, for I wouldn't touch one of the harmless things that kiver the ground here, looking up with their eyes on me, as if they only wanted tongues to say their thoughts."

With this sentiment in his mouth, Leather-stocking threw his rifle over his arm, and, followed by his dogs, stepped across the clearing with great caution, taking care not to tread on one of the wounded birds in his path. He soon entered the bushes on the margin of the lake, and was hid from view.

Whatever impression the morality of Natty made on the Judge, it was utterly lost on Richard. He availed himself of the gathering of the sportsmen, to lay a plan for one "fell swoop" of destruction. The musketmen were drawn up in battle array, in a line extending on each side of his artillery, with orders to await the signal of firing from himself.

"Stand by, my lads," said Benjamin, who acted as an aide-de-camp, on this occasion, "stand by, my hearties, and when Squire Dickens heaves out the signal to begin the firing, d'ye see, you may open upon them in a broadside. Take care and fire low, boys, and you'll be sure to hull the flock."

"Fire low!" shouted Kirby—"hear the old fool! If we fire low, we may hit the stumps, but not ruffle a pigeon."

"How should you know, you lubber?" cried Benjamin, with a very unbecoming heat, for an officer on the eve of battle—"how should you know, you grampus? Havn't I sailed aboard of the Boadishy for five years? and wasn't it a standing order to fire low, and to hull your enemy? Keep silence at your guns, boys, and mind the order that is passed."

The loud laughs of the musketmen were silenced by the more authoritative voice of Richard, who called for attention and obedience to his signals.

Some millions of pigeons were supposed to have already passed, that morning, over the valley of Templeton; but nothing like the flock that was now approaching had been seen before. It extended from mountain to mountain in one solid blue mass, and the eye looked in vain over the southern hills to find its termination. The front of this living column was distinctly marked by a line, but very slightly indented, so regular and even was the flight. Even Marmaduke forgot the morality of Leather-stocking as it approached, and, in common with the rest, brought his musket to a poise.

"Fire!" cried the Sheriff, clapping a coal to the priming of the cannon. As half of Benjamin's charge escaped through the touch-hole, the whole volley of the musketry preceded the report of the swivel. On receiving this united discharge of small-arms, the front of the flock darted upward, while, at the same instant, myriads of those in the rear rushed with amazing rapidity into their places, so that when the column of white smoke gushed from the mouth of the little cannon, an accumulated mass of objects was gliding over its point of direction. The roar of the gun echoed along the mountains, and died away to the north, like distant thunder, while the whole flock of alarmed birds seemed, for a moment, thrown into one disorderly and agitated mass. The air was filled with their irregular flight, layer rising above layer, far above the tops of the highest pines, none daring to advance beyond the dangerous pass; when, suddenly, some of the leaders of the feathered tribe shot across the valley, taking their flight directly over the village, and hundreds of thousands in their rear followed the example, deserting the eastern side of the plain to their persecutors and the slain.

"Victory!" shouted Richard, "victory! we have driven the enemy from the field."

"Not so, Dickon," said Marmaduke; "the field is covered with them; and, like the Leather-stocking, I see nothing but eyes, in every direction, as the innocent sufferers turn their heads in terror. Full one half of those that have fallen are yet alive: and I think it is time to end the sport; if sport it be."

"Sport!" cried the Sheriff; "it is princely sport. There are some thousands of the blue-coated boys on the ground, so that every old woman in the village may have a pot-pie for the asking."

"Well, we have happily frightened the birds from this side of the valley," said Marmaduke, "and the carnage must of necessity end, for the present.—Boys, I will give thee sixpence a hundred for the pigeons' heads only; so go to work, and bring them into the village."

This expedient produced the desired effect, for every urchin on the ground went industriously to work to wring the necks of the wounded birds. Judge Temple retired towards his dwelling with that kind of feeling, that many a man has experienced before him, who discovers, after the excitement of the moment has passed, that he has purchased pleasure at the price of misery to others. Horses were loaded with the dead; and, after this first burst of sporting, the shooting of pigeons became a business, with a few idlers, for the remainder of the season. Richard, however, boasted for many a year, of his shot with the "cricket;" and Benjamin gravely asserted, that he thought they killed nearly as many pigeons on that day, as there were Frenchmen destroyed on the memorable occasion of Rodney's victory.

Chapter XXIII

"Help, masters, help; here's a fish hangs in the net like a poor man's right in the law."

–*PERICLES,* II.i.116–17.

The advance of the season now became as rapid, as its first approach had been tedious and lingering. The days were uniformly mild, while the nights, though cool, were no longer chilled by frosts. The whip-poor-will was heard whistling his melancholy notes along the margin of the lake, and the ponds and meadows were sending forth the music of their thousand tenants. The leaf of the native poplar was seen quivering in the woods; the sides of the mountains began to lose their hue of brown, as the lively green of the different members of the forest blended their shades with the permanent colours of the pine and hemlock; and even the buds of the tardy oak were swelling with the promise of the coming summer. The gay and fluttering blue-bird, the social robin, and the industrious little wren, were all to be seen, enlivening the fields with their presence and their songs; while the soaring fish-hawk was already hovering over the waters of the Otsego, watching, with native voracity, for the appearance of his prey.

The tenants of the lake were far-famed for both their quantities and their quality, and the ice had hardly disappeared, before numberless little boats were launched from the shores, and the lines of the fishermen were dropped into the inmost recesses of its deepest caverns, tempting the unwary animals with every variety of bait, that the ingenuity or the art of man had invented. But the slow, though certain adventures with hook and line were ill-suited to the profusion and impatience of the settlers. More destructive means were resorted to; and, as the season had now arrived when the bass-fisheries were allowed by the provisions of the law, that Judge Temple had procured, the Sheriff declared his intention by availing himself of the first dark night, to enjoy the sport in person—

"And you shall be present, cousin Bess," he added, when he announced this design, "and Miss Grant, and Mr. Edwards; and I will show you what I call fishing—not nibble, nibble, nibble, as 'duke does, when he goes after the salmon-trout. There he will sit, for hours, in a broiling sun, or, perhaps, over a hole in the ice, in the coldest days in winter, under the lee of a few bushes, and not a fish will he catch, after all this mortification of the flesh. No, no—give me a good seine, that's fifty or sixty fathoms in length, with a jolly parcel of boatmen to crack their jokes, the while, with Benjamin to steer, and let us haul them in by thousands; I call that fishing."

"Ah! Dickon," cried Marmaduke, "thou knowest but little of the pleasure there is in playing with the hook and line, or thou wouldst be more saving of the game. I have known thee to leave fragments enough behind thee, when thou hast headed a night-party on the lake, to feed a dozen famishing families."

"I shall not dispute the matter, Judge Temple: this night will I go; and I invite the company to attend, and then let them decide between us."

Richard was busy, during most of the afternoon, making his preparations for the important occasion. Just as the light of the setting sun had disappeared, and a new moon had begun to throw its shadows on the earth, the fishermen took their departure in a boat, for a point that was situated on the western shore of the lake, at the distance of rather more than half a mile from the village. The ground had become settled, and the walking was good and dry. Marmaduke, with his daughter, her friend, and young Edwards, continued on the high, grassy banks, at the outlet of the placid sheet of water, watching the dark object that was moving across the lake, until it entered the shade of the western hills, and was lost to the eye. The distance round by land, to the point of destination, was a mile, and he observed—

"It is time for us to be moving; the moon will be down ere we reach the point, and then the miraculous hauls of Dickon will commence."

The evening was warm, and, after the long and dreary winter from which they had just escaped, delightfully invigorating. Inspirited by the scene, and their anticipated amusement, the youthful companions of the Judge followed his steps, as he led them along the shores of the Otsego, and through the skirts of the village.

"See!" said young Edwards; "they are building their fire already; it glimmers for a moment, and dies again, like the light of a fire-fly."

"Now it blazes," cried Elizabeth; "you can perceive figures moving around the light. Oh! I would bet my jewels against the gold beads of Remarkable, that my impatient cousin Dickon had an agency in raising that bright flame;—and see; it fades again, like most of his brilliant schemes."

"Thou hast guessed the truth, Bess," said her father; "he has thrown an armful of brush on the pile, which has burnt out as soon as lighted. But it has enabled them to find a better fuel, for their fire begins to blaze with a more steady flame. It is the true fisherman's beacon now; observe how beautifully it throws its little circle of light on the water."

The appearance of the fire urged the pedestrians on, for even the ladies had become eager to witness the miraculous draught. By the time they reached the bank which rose above the low point, where the fishermen had landed, the moon had sunk behind the tops of the western pines, and, as most of the stars were obscured by clouds, there was but little other light than that which proceeded from the fire. At the suggestion of Marmaduke, his companions paused to listen to the conversation of those below them, and examine the party, for a moment, before they descended to the shore.

The whole group were seated around the fire, with the exception of Richard and Benjamin; the former of whom occupied the root of a decayed stump, that had been drawn to the spot as part of their fuel, and the latter was standing, with his arms a-kimbo, so near to the flame, that the smoke occasionally obscured his solemn visage, as it waved around the pile, in obedience to the night-airs, that swept gently over the water.

"Why, look you, Squire," said the Major-domo, "you may call a lake-fish that will weigh twenty or thirty pounds a serious matter; but to a man who has hauled in a shovel-nosed shirk, d'ye see, it's but a poor kind of fishing, after all."

"I don't know, Benjamin," returned the Sheriff; "a haul of one thousand Otsego bass, without counting pike, pickerel, perch, bull-pouts, salmon-trouts, and suckers, is no bad fishing, let me tell you. There may be sport in sticking a shark, but what is he good for after you have got him? Now any one of the fish that I have named is fit to set before a king."

"Well, Squire," returned Benjamin, "just listen to the philosophy of the thing. Would it stand to reason, that such fish should live and be catched in this here little pond of water, where it's hardly deep enough to drown a man, as you'll find in the wide ocean, where, as every body knows, that is, every body that has followed the seas, whales and grampuses are to be seen, that are as long as one of them pine trees on yonder mountain?"

"Softly, softly, Benjamin," said the Sheriff, as if he wished to save the credit of his favourite; "why some of the pines will measure two hundred feet, and even more."

"Two hundred or two thousand, it's all the same thing," cried Benjamin, with an air which manifested that he was not easily to be bullied out of his opinion, on a subject like the present—"Haven't I been there, and haven't I seen? I have said that you fall in with whales as long as one of them there pines; and what I have once said I'll stand to!"

During this dialogue, which was evidently but the close of a much longer discussion, the huge frame of Billy Kirby was seen extended on one side of the fire, where he was picking his teeth with splinters of the chips near him, and occasionally shaking his head, with distrust of Benjamin's assertions.

"I've a notion," said the wood-chopper, "that there's water in this lake to swim the biggest whale that ever was invented; and, as to the pines, I think I ought to know so'thing consarning them; I have chopped many a one that was sixty times the length of my helve, without counting the eye; and I b'lieve, Benny, that if the old pine that stands in the hollow of the Vision Mountain, just over the village,—you may see the tree itself by looking up, for the moon is on its top yet;—well, now I b'lieve, if that same tree was planted out in the deepest part of the lake, there would be water enough for the biggest ship that ever was built to float over it, without touching its upper branches, I do."

"Did'ee ever see a ship, Master Kirby?" roared the steward—"did'ee ever see a ship, man? or any craft bigger than a limescow, or a wood-boat, on this here small bit of fresh water?"

"Yes, I have," said the wood-chopper, stoutly; "I can say that I have, and tell no lie."

"Did'ee ever see a British ship, Master Kirby? an English line-of-battle ship, boy? Where away did'ee ever fall in with a regular-built vessel, with starn-post and cutwater, garboard streak and plank-shear, gangways and hatchways, and waterways, quarter-deck and forecastle, ay, and flush-deck?—tell me that, man, if you can; where away did'ee ever fall in with a full-rigged, regular-built, decked vessel?"

The whole company were a good deal astounded with this overwhelming question, and even Richard afterwards remarked, that it "was a thousand pities that Benjamin could not read, or he must have made a valuable officer to the British marine. It is no wonder that they overcome the French so easily on the water, when even the lowest sailor so well understood the different parts of a vessel." But Billy Kirby was a fearless wight, and had great jealousy of foreign dictation; he had arisen on his feet, and turned his back to the fire, during the voluble delivery of this interrogatory, and when the steward ended, contrary to all expectation, he gave the following spirited reply:—

"Where! why on the North River, and maybe on Champlain. There's sloops on the river, boy, that would give a hard time on't to the stoutest vessel King George owns. They carry masts of ninety feet in the clear, of good, solid pine, for I've been at the chopping of many a one in Varmount state. I wish I was captain in one of them, and you was in that Board-dish that you talk so much about, and we'd soon see what good Yankee stuff is made on, and whether a Varmounter's hide an't as thick as an Englishman's."

The echoes from the opposite hills, which were more than half a mile from the fishing point, sent back the discordant laugh that Benjamin gave forth at this challenge; and the woods that covered their sides, seemed, by the noise that issued from their shades, to be full of mocking demons.

"Let us descend to the shore," whispered Marmaduke, "or there will soon be ill blood between them. Benjamin is a fearless boaster, and Kirby, though good-natured, is a careless son of the forest, who thinks one American more than a match for six Englishmen. I marvel that Dickon is silent, where there is such a trial of skill in the superlative!"

The appearance of Judge Temple and the ladies produced, if not a pacification, at least a cessation of hostilities. Obedient to the directions of Mr. Jones, the fishermen prepared to launch their boat, which had been seen in the back-ground of the view, with the net carefully disposed on a little platform in its stern, ready for service. Richard gave vent to his reproaches at the tardiness of the pedestrians, when all the turbulent passions of the party were succeeded by a calm, as mild and as placid as that which prevailed over the beautiful sheet of water, that they were about to rifle of its best treasures.

The night had now become so dark as to render objects, without the reach of the light of the fire, not only indistinct, but, in most cases, invisible. For a little distance the water was discernible, glistening, as the glare from the fire danced over its surface, touching it, here and there, with red, quivering streaks; but at a hundred feet from the shore, there lay a boundary of impenetrable gloom. One or two stars were shining through the openings of the clouds, and the lights were seen in the village, glimmering faintly, as if at an immeasurable distance. At times, as the fire lowered, or as the horizon cleared, the outline of the mountain, on the other side of the lake, might be traced, by its undulations; but its shadow was cast, wide and dense, on the bosom of the water, rendering the darkness, in that direction, trebly deep.

Benjamin Pump was invariably the cockswain and net-caster of Richard's boat, unless the Sheriff saw fit to preside in person; and, on the present occasion, Billy Kirby, and a youth of about half his strength, were assigned to the oars. The remainder of the assistants were stationed at the drag ropes. The arrangements were speedily made, and Richard gave the signal to "shove off."

Elizabeth watched the motion of the batteau, as it pulled from the shore, letting loose its rope as it went, but it very soon disappeared in the darkness, when the ear was her only guide to its evolutions. There was great affectation of stillness, during all these manœuvres, in order, as Richard assured them, "not to frighten the bass, who were running into the shoal waters, and who would approach the light, if not disturbed by the sounds from the fishermen."

The hoarse voice of Benjamin was alone heard, issuing out of the gloom, as he uttered, in authoritative tones, "pull larboard oar," "pull starboard," "give way together, boys," and such other dictative mandates as were necessary for the right disposition of his seine. A long time was passed in this necessary part of the process, for Benjamin prided himself greatly on his skill in throwing the net, and, in fact, most of the success of the sport depended on its being done with judgment. At length a loud splash in the water, as he threw away the "staff," or "stretcher," with a hoarse call from the steward, of "clear," announced that the boat was returning; when Richard seized a brand from the fire, and ran to a point, as far above the centre of the fishing ground, as the one from which the batteau had started was below it.

"Stick her in dead for the Squire, boys," said the steward, "and we'll have a look at what grows in this here pond."

In place of the falling net, were now to be heard the quick strokes of the oars, and the noise of the rope, running out of the boat. Presently the batteau shot into the circle of light, and in an instant she was pulled to shore. Several eager hands were extended, to receive the line, and, both ropes being equally well manned, the fishermen commenced hauling in, with slow and steady drags, Richard standing in the centre, giving orders, first to one party and then to the other, to increase or slacken their efforts, as occasion required. The visiters were posted near him, and enjoyed a fair view of the whole operation, which was slowly advancing to an end.

Opinions, as to the result of their adventure, were now freely hazarded by all the men, some declaring that the net came in as light as a feather, and others affirming that it seemed to be full of logs. As the ropes were many hundred feet in length, these opposing sentiments were thought to be of little moment by the Sheriff, who would go first to one line and then to the other, giving each a small pull, in order to enable him to form an opinion for himself.

"Why, Benjamin," he cried, as he made his first effort in this way, "you did not throw the net clear. I can move it with my little finger. The rope slackens in my hand."

"Did you ever see a whale, Squire?" responded the steward: "I say that if that there net is foul, the devil is in the lake in the shape of a fish, for I cast it as fair as ever rigging was rove over the quarter-deck of a flag-ship."

But Richard discovered his mistake, when he saw Billy Kirby before him, standing with his feet in the water, at an angle of forty-five degrees, inclining shorewards, and expending his gigantic strength in sustaining himself in that posture. He ceased his remonstrances, and proceeded to the party at the other line.

"I see the 'staffs,'" shouted Mr. Jones;—"gather in, boys, and away with it; to shore with her—to shore with her."

At this cheerful sound, Elizabeth strained her eyes, and saw the ends of the two sticks on the seine, emerging from the darkness, while the men closed near to each other, and formed a deep bag of their net. The exertions of the fishermen sensibly increased, and the voice of Richard was heard, encouraging them to make their greatest efforts, at the present moment.

"Now's the time, my lads," he cried, "let us get the ends to land, and all we have will be our own—away with her!"

"Away with her it is," echoed Benjamin—"hurrah! ho-a-hoy, ho-a-hoy, ho-a!"

"In with her," shouted Kirby, exerting himself in a manner that left nothing for those in his rear to do, but to gather up the slack of the rope which passed through his hands.

"Staff, ho!" shouted the steward.

"Staff, ho!" echoed Kirby, from the other rope.

The men rushed to the water's edge, some seizing the upper rope, and some the lower, or lead-rope, and began to haul with great activity and zeal. A deep semicircular sweep, of the little balls that supported the seine in its perpendicular position, was plainly visible to the spectators, and, as it rapidly lessened in size, the bag of the net appeared, while an occasional flutter on the water, announced the uneasiness of the prisoners it contained.

"Haul in, my lads," shouted Richard—"I can see the dogs kicking to get free. Haul in, and here's a cast that will pay for the labour."

Fishes of various sorts were now to be seen, entangled in the meshes of the net, as it was passed through the hands of the labourers, and the water, at a little distance from the shore, was alive with the movements of the alarmed victims. Hundreds of white sides were glancing up to the surface of the water, and glistening in the fire-light, when, frightened at the uproar and the change, the fish would again dart to the bottom, in fruitless efforts for freedom.

"Hurrah!" shouted Richard; "one or two more heavy drags, boys, and we are safe."

"Cheerily, boys, cheerily!" cried Benjamin; "I see a salmon-trout that is big enough for a chowder."

"Away with you, you varmint!" said Billy Kirby, plucking a bull-pout from the meshes, and casting the animal back into the lake with contempt. "Pull, boys, pull; here's all kinds, and the Lord condemn me for a liar, if there an't a thousand bass!"

Inflamed beyond the bounds of discretion at the sight, and forgetful of the season, the wood-chopper rushed to his middle into the water, and begun to drive the reluctant animals before him from their native element.

"Pull heartily, boys," cried Marmaduke, yielding to the excitement of the moment, and laying his hands to the net, with no trifling addition to the force. Edwards had preceded him, for the sight of the immense piles of fish, that were slowly rolling over on the gravelly beach, had impelled him also to leave the ladies, and join the fishermen.

Great care was observed in bringing the net to land, and, after much toil, the whole shoal of victims was safely deposited in a hollow of the bank, where they were left to flutter away their brief existence, in the new and fatal element.

Even Elizabeth and Louisa were greatly excited and highly gratified, by seeing two thousand captives thus drawn from the bosom of the lake, and laid as prisoners at their feet. But when the feelings of the moment were passing away, Marmaduke took in his hands a bass, that might have weighed two pounds, and, after viewing it a moment, in melancholy musing, he turned to his daughter, and observed—

"This is a fearful expenditure of the choicest gifts of Providence. These fish, Bess, which thou seest lying in such piles before thee, and which, by to-morrow evening, will be rejected food on the meanest table in Templeton, are of a quality and flavour that, in other countries, would make them esteemed a luxury on the tables of princes or epicures. The world has no better fish than the bass of Otsego: it unites the richness of the shad[3] to the firmness of the salmon."

"But surely, dear sir," cried Elizabeth, "they must prove a great blessing to the country, and a powerful friend to the poor."

"The poor are always prodigal, my child, where there is plenty, and seldom think of a provision against the morrow. But if there can be any excuse for destroying animals in this manner, it is in taking the bass. During the winter, you know, they are entirely protected from our assaults by the ice, for they refuse the hook; and during the hot months, they are not seen. It is supposed they retreat to the deep and cool waters of the lake, at that season; and it is only in the spring and autumn, that, for a few days, they are to be found, around the points where they are within the reach of a seine. But, like all the other treasures of the wilderness, they already begin to disappear, before the wasteful extravagance of man."

"Disappear, 'duke! disappear!" exclaimed the Sheriff; "if you don't call this appearing, I know not what you will. Here are a good thousand of the shiners, some hundreds of suckers, and a powerful quantity of other fry. But this is always the way with you, Marmaduke; first it's the trees, then it's the deer, after that it's the maple sugar, and so on to the end of the chapter. One day, you talk of canals, through a

[3]Of all the fish the writer has ever tasted, he thinks the one in question the best. [1832]

country where there's a river or a lake every half-mile, just because the water won't run the way you wish it to go; and the next, you say something about mines of coal, though any man who has good eyes, like myself—I say with good eyes—can see more wood than would keep the city of London in fuel for fifty years;—wouldn't it, Benjamin?"

"Why, for that, Squire," said the steward, "Lon'on is no small place. If it was stretched an end, all the same as a town on one side of a river, it would cover some such matter as this here lake. Thof I dar'st to say, that the wood in sight might sarve them a good turn, seeing that the Lon'oners mainly burn coal."

"Now we are on the subject of coal, Judge Temple," interrupted the Sheriff, "I have a thing of much importance to communicate to you; but I will defer it until to-morrow. I know that you intend riding into the eastern part of the Patent, and I will accompany you, and conduct you to a spot, where some of your projects may be realized. We will say no more now, for there are listeners; but a secret has this evening been revealed to me, 'duke, that is of more consequence to your welfare, than all your estate united."

Marmaduke laughed at the important intelligence, to which in a variety of shapes he was accustomed, and the Sheriff, with an air of great dignity, as if pitying his want of faith, proceeded in the business more immediately before them. As the labour of drawing the net had been very great, he directed one party of his men to commence throwing the fish into piles, preparatory to the usual division, while another, under the superintendence of Benjamin, prepared the seine for a second haul.

1823

Catharine Maria Sedgwick 1789–1867

Catharine Maria Sedgwick came from an important Federalist family in western Massachusetts. While Catharine always spoke with love and respect of her mother, Pamela Dwight Sedgwick suffered repeated periods of mental illness and does not seem to have been close to her daughter. Instead, Catharine admired her father, though he was often away for his political career, which culminated in his becoming Speaker of the House. In his absence Catharine was surrounded by her many siblings. She was particularly attached to her four brothers. Even when they had all married and become lawyers like their father, they remained the central figures in her emotional life. Single herself, she passed part of every year in the family of one or the other of her brothers, and was a favorite aunt to many children. It was her brothers who encouraged her to write. Together they worked to sustain her often failing self-confidence, and assisted her practically with contracts and reviews.

Sedgwick, who left the Calvinist church of her childhood to become a Unitarian, showed a consistent tolerance for members of minority groups. The hero of her first work, *A New-England Tale,* was a Quaker. A long section of *Redwood* concerns a Shaker community, and although Sedgwick analyzes the psychological pressures keeping members within the group, the religion is never condemned. Similarly, *Hope Leslie* shows a sympathetic understanding of Indians and Indian religious beliefs, based partly on her research into Mohawk customs. Unlike Cooper, whose

Last of the Mohicans appeared the year before *Hope Leslie,* Sedgwick countenances marriage between Indian and white woman: the heroine's sister, Faith Leslie, is carried into captivity as a child, marries an Indian and refuses the opportunity to rejoin the Puritan community. Sedgwick may have been influenced here by the similar legend of Eunice Williams, a remote ancestor of hers.

Sedgwick was immediately recognized as one of the writers creating an indigenous American literature. *A New-England Tale* was subtitled "Sketches of New-England Character and Manners," and two of her later novels, *Hope Leslie,* set among the Puritans, and *The Linwoods, Or "Sixty Years Since in America,"* set during the Revolution, mingled historical event with romantic invention. Praised as a woman writer, she was nevertheless associated equally with Bryant, Irving, and Cooper. On his European tour Cooper found he was assumed to be the author of *Redwood.*

Throughout her life Sedgwick was ambivalent about her position as a single woman. She told a favorite niece that "so many I have loved have made shipwreck of happiness in marriage or have found it a dreary joyless condition." Nevertheless, her fiction always depicts marriage as a young girl's goal and reward. Even in her final novel, *Married or Single?,* which she wrote to assuage depression after the death of her last remaining brother, she reveals her conflict. Though she wrote the novel to "drive away the smile . . . at the name of 'old maid'," she concluded the book by marrying off the heroine.

The central figures in Sedgwick's novels are women, often noted for their independence. In *Redwood* Aunt Debby, "a natural protector of the weak and oppressed" rescues a young girl held among the Shakers. Aunt Debby had decided to remain single after the Revolutionary War because she was "so imbued with the independent spirit of the times, that she would not then consent to the surrender of any of her rights." On two occasions Hope Leslie follows her own conscience and frees Indian women from unjust imprisonment. Both Hope and her Indian double Magawisca question political authority which does not include them: Hope, unable as a woman to work through the political system, defies it, and Magawisca denies a Puritan jury's jurisdiction over her people.

Though sympathetic to women's rights and abolition, Sedgwick never took an active part in those reforms. Towards the end of her life, however, she became the first director of the Women's Prison Association. Her novels show a horror of prisons and a hatred of slavery. In *The Linwoods* the heroine assists in releasing her brother from jail. She is aided by a free black family servant who tells the jailer she ties up, "remember, that you were strung up there by a 'd—n *nigger*'—a nigger *woman*!" In *Married or Single?* one heroine undertakes to free her brother from the New York Tombs, and another assists a runaway slave. Sedgwick's fiction repeatedly emphasized the political and personal need for liberty and independence.

Barbara A. Bardes
Suzanne Gossett
Loyola University Chicago

PRIMARY WORKS

A New-England Tale, 1822; *Redwood,* 1824; *Hope Leslie,* 1827 (reprint, Feminist Press, 1987); *Clarence,* 1830; *The Linwoods,* 1835; *Married or Single?,* 1857; *The Power of Her Sympathy: The Autobiography and Journal,* 1993.

SECONDARY WORKS

Michael Bell, "History and Romance Convention in Catharine Sedgwick's *Hope Leslie,*" *American Quarterly* 22, 1970; Mary Kelley, *Private Woman, Public Stage: Literary Domesticity in Nineteenth-Century America,* 1984; Sandra A. Zagarell, "Expanding 'America': Lydia Sigourney's *Sketch of Connecticut,* Catharine Sedgwick's *Hope Leslie,*" *Tulsa Studies in Women's Literature* 6, 1987; Barbara Bardes and Suzanne Gossett, *Declarations of Independence: Women and Political Power in Nineteenth-Century America,* 1990; *Redefining the Political Novel,* ed. Sharon Harris, 1995; Philip Gould, *Covenant and Republic: Historical Romance and the Politics of Puritanism,* 1996.

from Hope Leslie

[The first passage included here from *Hope Leslie* traces the consequences of an Indian attack on the Fletcher homestead outside Boston. Mr. Fletcher had emigrated to America in 1630 to join the Puritan settlements, but finding their community oppressive, he chose to build his home on the edge of the forest. During the attack, which occurs when Mr. Fletcher and his ward Hope Leslie are absent, the Pequod chief Mononotto reclaims his children, Magawisca and Oneco, and carries off Fletcher's eldest son, Everell, to avenge his own eldest son Samoset's murder by the English during a massacre of the Indians. Oneco takes with him his favorite, the child Faith Leslie. The scene, which recalls the story of Pocohontas, describes Magawisca's rescue of Everell Fletcher.]

from **Volume 1, Chapter 7**

It is not our purpose to describe, step by step, the progress of the Indian fugitives. Their sagacity in traversing their native forests, their skill in following and eluding an enemy, and all their politic devices, have been so well described in a recent popular work, that their usages have become familiar as household words, and nothing remains but to shelter defects of skill and knowledge under the veil of silence, since we hold it to be an immutable maxim, that a thing had better not be done than be ill done.

Suffice it to say, then, that the savages, after crossing the track of their pursuers, threaded the forest with as little apparent uncertainty as to their path as is now felt by travellers who pass through the same still romantic country in a stagecoach and on a broad turnpike. As they receded from the Connecticut the pine levels disappeared, the country was broken into hills, and rose into high mountains.

They traversed the precipitous sides of a river that, swollen by the vernal rains, wound its way among the hills, foaming and raging like an angry monarch. The river, as they traced its course, dwindled to a mountain rill, but still retaining its impetuous character, leaping and tumbling for miles through a descending defile, between high mountains, whose stillness, grandeur, and immobility contrasted with the noisy, reckless little stream as stern manhood with infancy. In one place, which the Indians called the throat of the mountain, they were obliged to betake themselves to the channel of the brook, there not being room on its margin for a footpath. The branches of the trees that grew from the rocky and precipitous declivities on each side met and interfaced, forming a sylvan canopy over the imprisoned stream. To Magawisca, whose imagination breathed a living spirit into all the objects of Nature, it seemed as if the spirits of the wood had stooped to listen to its sweet music.

After tracing this little sociable rill to its source, they again plunged into the silent forest, waded through marshy ravines, and mounted to the summits of steril hills, till at length, at the close of the third day, after having gradually descended for several miles, the hills on one side receded, and left a little interval of meadow, through which they wound into the lower valley of the Housatonic.

This continued and difficult march had been sustained by Everell with a spirit and fortitude that evidently won the favour of the savages, who always render homage to superiority over physical evil. There was something more than this common feeling in the joy with which Mononotto noted the boy's silent endurance, and even contempt of pain. One noble victim seemed to him better than a "human hecatomb." In proportion to his exultation in possessing an object worthy to avenge his son, was his fear that his victim would escape from him. During the march, Everell had twice, aided by Magawisca, nearly achieved his liberty. These detected conspiracies, though defeated, rendered the chief impatient to execute his vengeance, and he secretly resolved that it should not be delayed longer than the morrow. . . .

They had entered the expanded vale by following the windings of the Housatonic around a hill, conical and easy of ascent, excepting on that side which overlooked the river, where, half way from the base to the summit, rose a perpendicular rock, bearing on its beetling front the age of centuries. On every other side the hill was garlanded with laurels, now in full and profuse bloom, here and there surmounted by an intervening pine, spruce, or hemlock, whose seared winter foliage was fringed with the bright, tender sprouts of spring. We believe there is a chord even in the heart of savage man that responds to the voice of Nature. Certain it is, the party paused, as it appeared, from a common instinct, at a little grassy nook, formed by the curve of the hill, to gaze on this singularly beautiful spot. Everell looked on the smoke that curled from the huts of the village, imbosomed in pine-trees on the adjacent plain. The scene to him breathed peace and happiness, and gushing thoughts of home filled his eyes with tears. Oneco plucked clusters of laurels, and decked his little favourite, and the old chief fixed his melancholy eye on a solitary pine, scathed and blasted by tempests, that, rooted in the ground where he stood, lifted its topmost branches to the bare rock, where they seemed, in their wild desolation, to brave the elemental fury that had stripped them of beauty and life.

The leafless tree was truly, as it appeared to the eye of Mononotto, a fit emblem of the chieftain of a ruined tribe. "See you, child," he said, addressing Magawisca, "those unearthed roots? the tree must fall: hear you the death-song that wails through those blasted branches?"

"Nay, father, listen not to the sad strain; it is but the spirit of the tree mourning over its decay; rather turn thine ear to the glad song of this bright stream, image of the good. She nourishes the aged trees, and cherishes the tender flowerets, and her song is ever of happiness till she reaches the great sea, image of our eternity."

"Speak not to me of happiness, Magawisca; it has vanished with the smoke of our homes. I tell ye, the spirits of our race are gathered about this blasted tree. Samoset points to that rock—that sacrifice-rock." His keen glance turned from the rock to Everell.

Magawisca understood its portentous meaning, and she clasped her hands in mute and agonizing supplication. He answered to the silent entreaty. "It is in vain; my purpose is fixed, and here it shall be accomplished. Why hast thou linked thy heart, foolish girl, to this English boy? I have sworn, kneeling on the ashes of our hut, that I would never spare a son of our enemy's race. The lights of heaven witnessed my vow, and think you that, now this boy is given into my hands to avenge thy brother, I will spare him? no, not to *thy* prayer, Magawisca. No; though thou lookest on me with thy mother's eye, and speakest with her voice, I will not break my vow."

Mononotto had indeed taken a final and fatal resolution; and prompted, as he fancied, by supernatural intimations, and perhaps dreading the relentings of his own heart, he determined on its immediate execution. He announced his decision to the Mohawks. A brief and animated consultation followed, during which they brandished their tomahawks, and cast wild and threatening glances at Everell, who at once comprehended the meaning of these menacing looks and gestures. He turned an appealing glance to Magawisca. She did not speak. "Am I to die now?" he asked; she turned, shuddering, from him. . .

Magawisca and her companions were conducted to a wigwam standing on that part of the plain on which they had first entered. It was completely enclosed on three sides by dwarf oaks. In front there was a little plantation of the edible luxuries of the savages. On entering the hut they perceived it had but one occupant, a sick, emaciated old woman, who was stretched on her mat, covered with skins. She raised her head as the strangers entered, and at the sight of Faith Leslie uttered a faint exclamation, deeming the fair creature a messenger from the spirit-land; but, being informed who they were and whence they came, she made every sign and expression of courtesy to them that her feeble strength permitted.

Her hut contained all that was essential to savage hospitality. A few brands were burning on a hearthstone in the middle of the apartment. The smoke that found egress passed out by a hole in the centre of the roof, over which a mat was skilfully adjusted, and turned to the windward side by a cord that hung within. The old woman, in her long pilgrimage, had accumulated stores of Indian riches: piles of sleeping-mats lay in one corner; nicely-dressed skins garnished the walls; baskets of all shapes and sizes, gayly decorated with rude images of birds and flowers, contained dried fruits, medicinal herbs, Indian corn, nuts, and game. A covered pail, made of folds of birch bark, was filled with a kind of beer—a decoction of various roots and aromatic shrubs. Neatly-turned wooden spoons and bowls, and culinary utensils of clay, supplied all the demands of the inartificial housewifery of savage life.

The travellers, directed by their old hostess, prepared their evening repast—a short and simple process to an Indian; and, having satisfied the cravings of hunger, they were all, with the exception of Magawisca and one of the Mohawks, in a very short time stretched on their mats and fast asleep.

Magawisca seated herself at the feet of the old woman, and had neither spoken nor moved since she entered the hut. She watched anxiously and impatiently the movements of the Indian, whose appointed duty it appeared to be to guard her. He placed a wooden bench against the mat which served for a door, and stuffing his pipe with tobacco from a pouch slung over his shoulder, and then filling a gourd with the liquor in the pail, and placing it beside him he quietly sat himself down to his night-watch.

The old woman became restless, and her loud and repeated groans at last withdrew Magawisca from her own miserable thoughts. She inquired if she could do aught to allay her pain; the sufferer pointed to a jar that stood on the embers, in which a medicinal preparation was simmering. She motioned to Magawisca to give her a spoonful of the liquor; she did so; and as she took it, "It is made," she said, "of all the plants on which the spirit of sleep has breathed"; and so it seemed to be, for she had scarcely swallowed it when she fell asleep.

Once or twice she waked and murmured something, and once Magawisca heard her say, "Hark to the wekolis![1] he is perched on the old oak by the sacrifice-rock, and his cry is neither musical nor merry: a bad sign in a bird."

But all signs and portents were alike to Magawisca; every sound rung a death-peal to her ear, and the hissing silence had in it the mystery and fearfulness of death. The night wore slowly and painfully away, as if, as in the fairy tale, the moments were counted by drops of heart's blood. But the most wearisome nights will end; the morning approached; the familiar notes of the birds of earliest dawn were heard, and the twilight peeped through the crevices of the hut, when a new sound fell on Magawisca's startled ear. It was the slow, measured tread of many feet. The poor girl now broke silence, and vehemently entreated the Mohawk to let her pass the door, or at least to raise the mat.

He shook his head with a look of unconcern, as if it were the petulant demand of a child, when the old woman, awakened by the noise, cried out that she was dying; that she must have light and air; and the Mohawk started up, impulsively, to raise the mat. It was held between two poles that formed the doorposts; and, while he was disengaging it, Magawisca, as if inspired, and quick as thought, poured the liquor from the jar on the fire into the hollow of her hand, and dashed it into the gourd which the Mohawk had just replenished. The narcotic was boiling hot, but she did not cringe; she did not even feel it; and she could scarcely repress a cry of joy when the savage turned round and swallowed, at one draught, the contents of the cup.

Magawisca looked eagerly through the aperture, but, though the sound of the footsteps had approached nearer, she saw no one. She saw nothing but a gentle declivity that sloped to the plain, a few yards from the hut, and was covered with a grove of trees; beyond and peering above them were the hill and the sacrifice-rock; the morning star, its rays not yet dimmed in the light of day, shed a soft trembling beam on its summit. This beautiful star, alone in the heavens when all other lights were quenched, spoke to the superstitious, or, rather, the imaginative spirit of Magawisca. "Star of promise," she thought, "thou dost still linger with us when day is vanished, and now thou art there alone to proclaim the coming sun; thou dost send in upon my soul a ray of hope; and though it be but as the spider's slender pathway, it shall sustain my courage." She had scarcely formed this resolution when she needed all its efficacy, for the train whose footsteps she had heard appeared in full view.

First came her father, with the Housatonic chief; next, alone, and walking with a firm, undaunted step, was Everell, his arms folded over his breast, and his head a little inclined upward, so that Magawisca fancied she saw his full eye turned heavenward; after him walked all the men of the tribe, ranged according to their age, and the rank assigned to each by his own exploits.

[1]Whippoorwill.

They were neither painted nor ornamented according to the common usage at festivals and sacrifices, but everything had the air of hasty preparation. Magawisca gazed in speechless despair. The procession entered the wood, and for a few moments disappeared from her sight; again they were visible, mounting the acclivity of the hill by a winding, narrow footpath, shaded on either side by laurels. They now walked singly and slowly, but to Magawisca their progress seemed rapid as a falling avalanche. She felt that, if she were to remain pent in that prison-house, her heart would burst, and she sprang towards the doorway in the hope of clearing her passage; but the Mohawk caught her arm in his iron grasp, and putting her back, calmly retained his station. She threw herself on her knees to him; she entreated, she wept, but in vain: he looked on her with unmoved apathy. Already she saw the foremost of the party had reached the rock, and were forming a semicircle around it: again she appealed to her determined keeper, and again he denied her petition, but with a faltering tongue and a drooping eye.

Magawisca, in the urgency of a necessity that could brook no delay, had forgotten, or regarded as useless, the sleeping potion she had infused into the Mohawk's draught; she now saw the powerful agent was at work for her, and with that quickness of apprehension that made the operations of her mind as rapid as the impulses of instinct, she perceived that every emotion she excited but hindered the effect of the potion. Suddenly seeming to relinquish all purpose and hope of escape, she threw herself on a mat, and hid her face, burning with agonizing impatience, in her mantle. There we must leave her, and join that fearful company who were gathered together to witness what they believed to be the execution of exact and necessary justice.

Seated around their sacrifice-rock—their holy of holies—they listened to the sad story of the Pequod chief with dejected countenances and downcast eyes, save when an involuntary glance turned on Everell, who stood awaiting his fate, cruelly aggravated by every moment's delay, with a quiet dignity and calm resignation that would have become a hero or a saint. Surrounded by this dark cloud of savages, his fair countenance kindled by holy inspiration, he looked scarcely like a creature of earth.

There might have been among the spectators some who felt the silent appeal of the helpless, courageous boy; some whose hearts moved them to interpose to save the selected victim; but they were restrained by their interpretation of natural justice, as controlling to them as our artificial codes of laws to us.

Others, of a more cruel or more irritable disposition, when the Pequod described his wrongs and depicted his sufferings, brandished their tomahawks, and would have hurled them at the boy; but the chief said, "Nay, brothers, the work is mine; he dies by my hand—for my first-born—life for life; he dies by a single stroke, for thus was my boy cut off. The blood of sachems is in his veins. He has the skin, but not the soul of that mixed race, whose gratitude is like that vanishing mist," and he pointed to the vapour that was melting from the mountain tops into the transparent ether; "and their promises like this," and he snapped a dead branch from the pine beside which he stood, and broke it in fragments. "Boy as he is, he fought for his mother as the eagle fights for its young. I watched him in the mountain-path, when the blood gushed from his torn feet; not a word from his smooth lip betrayed his pain."

Mononotto embellished his victim with praises, as the ancients wreathed theirs with flowers. He brandished his hatchet over Everell's head, and cried exultingly, "See, he flinches not. Thus stood my boy when they flashed their sabres before his eyes and bade him betray his father. Brothers: My people have told me I bore a woman's heart towards the enemy. Ye shall see. I will pour out this English boy's blood to the last drop, and give his flesh and bones to the dogs and wolves."

He then motioned to Everell to prostrate himself on the rock, his face downward. In this position the boy would not see the descending stroke. Even at this moment of dire vengeance the instincts of a merciful nature asserted their rights.

Everell sunk calmly on his knees, not to supplicate life, but to commend his soul to God. He clasped his hands together. He did not—he could not speak; his soul was

"Rapt in still communion, that transcends
The imperfect offices of prayer."

At this moment a sunbeam penetrated the trees that enclosed the area, and fell athwart his brow and hair, kindling it with an almost supernatural brightness. To the savages, this was a token that the victim was accepted, and they sent forth a shout that rent the air. Everell bent forward and pressed his forehead to the rock. The chief raised the deadly weapon, when Magawisca, springing from the precipitous side of the rock, screamed "Forbear!" and interposed her arm. It was too late. The blow was levelled—force and direction given; the stroke, aimed at Everell's neck, severed his defender's arm, and left him unharmed. The lopped, quivering member dropped over the precipice. Mononotto staggered and fell senseless, and all the savages, uttering horrible yells, rushed towards the fatal spot.

"Stand back!" cried Magawisca. "I have bought his life with my own. Fly, Everell—nay, speak not, but fly—thither—to the east!" she cried, more vehemently.

Everell's faculties were paralyzed by a rapid succession of violent emotions. He was conscious only of a feeling of mingled gratitude and admiration for his preserver. He stood motionless, gazing on her. "I die in vain, then," she cried, in an accent of such despair that he was roused. He threw his arms around her, and pressed her to his heart as he would a sister that had redeemed his life with her own, and then, tearing himself from her, he disappeared. No one offered to follow him. The voice of nature rose from every heart, and, responding to the justice of Magawisca's claim, bade him "God speed!" To all it seemed that his deliverance had been achieved by miraculous aid. All—the dullest and coldest—paid involuntary homage to the heroic girl, as if she were a superior being, guided and upheld by supernatural power. . . .

from Volume 2, Chapter 1

[A number of years later, Hope, resisting both "the prejudices of the age" and conventional feminine behavior, secretly frees from prison the Indian woman Nelema, who has been condemned as a witch because she cured a case of snakebite with herbal medicine. Nelema promises to repay Hope by finding her long-lost sister, and months later Magawisca contacts Hope with news of the girl, who has been raised among the Pequods and married to Magawisca's brother Oneco. Meeting secretly at the cemetery where both their mothers are buried, Hope and Magawisca courageously plan a way for Hope to see her sister, although this action will violate colonial law. Sedgwick uses this meeting as well as Nelema's medical success to underscore her respect for Indian culture and to emphasize the strength and solidarity of women.]

The stranger seemed equally interested in Miss Leslie's appearance; and, fixing her eye intently on her, "Pray try my moccasins, lady," she said, earnestly.

"Oh, certainly; I should of all things like to buy a pair of you," said Hope; and, advancing, she was taking them from her shoulder, over which they were slung, when she, ascertaining by a quick glance that the servant had disappeared, gently repressed Miss Leslie's hand, saying at the same time, "Tell me thy name, lady."

"My name! Hope Leslie. But who art thou?" Hope asked in return, in a voice rendered almost inarticulate by the thought that flashed into her mind.

The stranger cast down her eyes, and for half an instant hesitated; then looking apprehensively around, she said, in low, distinct accents, "Hope Leslie, I am Magawisca."

"Magawisca!" echoed Hope. "Oh, Everell!" and she sprang towards the parlour door to summon Everell.

"Silence! stay," cried Magawisca, with a vehement gesture, and at the same time turning to escape should Hope prosecute her intention.

Hope perceived this, and again approached her. "It cannot, then, be Magawisca," she said; and she trembled as she spoke with doubts, hopes, and fears.

Magawisca might have at once identified herself by opening her blanket and disclosing her person; but that she did not, no one will wonder who knows that a savage feels more even than ordinary sensibility at personal deformity. She took from her bosom a necklace of hair and gold entwined together. "Dost thou know this?" she asked. "Is it not like that thou wearest?"

Hope grasped it, pressed it to her lips, and answered by exclaiming passionately, "My sister! my sister!"

"Yes, it is a token from thy sister. Listen to me, Hope Leslie: my time is brief; I may not stay here another moment; but come to me this evening at nine o'clock, at the burial-place, a little beyond the clump of pines, and I will give thee tidings of thy sister: keep what I say in thine own bosom; tell no one thou hast seen me; come *alone,* and fear not." . . .

She arrived at the appointed rendezvous, and there saw Magawisca, and Magawisca alone, kneeling before an upright stake planted at one end of a grave. She appeared occupied in delineating a figure on the stake with a small implement she held in her hand, which she dipped in a shell placed on the ground beside her.

Hope paused with a mingled feeling of disappointment and awe; disappointment that her sister was not there, and awe inspired by the solemnity of the scene before her: the spirit-stirring figure of Magawisca, the duty she was performing, the flickering light, the monumental stones, and the dark shadows that swept over them as the breeze bowed the tall pines. She drew her mantle, that fluttered in the breeze, close around her, and almost suppressed her breath, that she might not disturb what she believed to be an act of filial devotion.

Magawisca was not unconscious of Miss Leslie's approach, but she deemed the office in which she was engaged too sacred to be interrupted. She accompanied the movement of her hand with a low chant in her native tongue; and so sweet and varied were the tones of her voice, that it seemed to Hope they might have been breathed by an invisible spirit.

When she had finished her work, she leaned her head for a moment against the stake, and then rose and turned to Miss Leslie; a moonbeam shot across her face; it was wet with tears, but she spoke in a tranquil voice. "You have come—and alone?" she said, casting a searching glance around her.

"I promised to come alone," replied Hope.

"Yes, and I trusted you; and I will trust you farther, for the good deed you did Nelema."

"Nelema, then, lived to reach you."

"She did; wasted, faint, and dying, she crawled into my father's wigwam. She had but scant time and short breath; with that she cursed your race, and blessed you, Hope Leslie; her day was ended; the hand of death pressed her throat, and even then she made me swear to perform her promise to you."

"And you will, Magawisca," cried Hope, impetuously, "you will give me back my sister?"

"Nay, that she never promised—that I cannot do. I cannot send back the bird that has mated, to its parent nest—the stream that has mingled with other waters, to its fountain."

"Oh, do not speak to me in these dark sayings," replied Hope, her smooth brow contracting with impatience and apprehension, and her hurried manner and convulsed countenance contrasting strongly with the calmness of Magawisca; "what is it you mean? Where is my sister?"

"She is safe—she is near to you—and you shall see her, Hope Leslie."

"But when—and where, Magawisca? Oh, if I could once clasp her in my arms, she never should leave me—she never should be torn from me again."

"Those arms," said Magawisca, with a faint smile, "could no more retain thy sister than a spider's web. The lily of the Maqua's valley will never again make the English garden sweet."

"Speak plainer to me," cried Hope, in a voice of entreaty that could not be resisted. "Is my sister—" she paused, for her quivering lips could not pronounce the words that rose to them.

Magawisca understood her, and replied. "Yes, Hope Leslie, thy sister is married to Oneco."

"God forbid!" exclaimed Hope, shuddering as if a knife had been plunged in her bosom. "My sister married to an Indian!"

"An Indian!" exclaimed Magawisca, recoiling with a look of proud contempt, that showed she reciprocated with full measure the scorn expressed for her race. "Yes, an Indian, in whose veins runs the blood of the strongest, the fleetest of the children of the forest, who never turned their backs on friends or enemies, and whose souls have returned to the Great Spirit stainless as they came from him. Think ye that your blood will be corrupted by mingling with this stream?"

Long before Magawisca ceased to pour out her indignation, Hope's first emotion had given place to a burst of tears; she wept aloud, and her broken utterance of "O, my sister! my sister! My dear mother!" emitted but imperfect glimpses of the ruined hopes, the bitter feelings that oppressed her.

There was a chord in Magawisca's heart that needed but the touch of tenderness to respond in harmony; her pride vanished, and her indignation gave place to sympathy. She said in a low, soothing voice, "Now do not weep thus; your sister is well with us. She is cherished as the bird cherishes her young. The cold winds may not blow on her, nor the fierce sun scorch her, nor a harsh sound ever be spoken to her; she is dear to Mononotto as if his own blood ran in her veins; and Oneco—Oneco worships and serves her as if all good spirits dwelt in her. Oh, she is indeed well with us."

"There lies my mother," cried Hope, without seeming to have heard Magawisca's consolations; "she lost her life in bringing her children to this wild world, to secure them in the fold of Christ. O, God! restore my sister to the Christian family."

"And here," said Magawisca, in a voice of deep pathos, "here is my mother's grave; think ye not that the Great Spirit looks down on these sacred spots, where the good and the peaceful rest, with an equal eye? think ye not their children are His children, whether they are gathered in yonder temple where your people worship, or bow to him beneath the green boughs of the forest?"

There was certainly something thrilling in Magawisca's faith, and she now succeeded in riveting Hope's attention. "Listen to me," she said; "your sister is of what you call the Christian family. I believe ye have many names in that family. She hath been signed with the cross by a holy father from France; she bows to the crucifix."

"Thank God!" exclaimed Hope, fervently, for she thought that any Christian faith was better than none.

"Perhaps ye are right," said Magawisca, as if she read Hope's heart; "there may be those that need other lights; but to me, the Great Spirit is visible in the life-creating sun. I perceive him in the gentle light of the moon that steals in through the forest boughs. I feel him here," she continued, pressing her hand on her breast, while her face glowed with the enthusiasm of devotion. "I feel him in these ever-living, ever-wakeful thoughts—but we waste time. You must see your sister."

"When—and where?" again demanded Hope.

"Before I answer you, you must promise me by this sign," and she pointed to the emblem of her tribe, an eagle, which she had rudely delineated on the post that served as a headstone to her mother's grave; "you must promise me by the bright host of Heaven, that the door of your lips shall be fast; that none shall know that you have seen me, or are to see me again."

"I promise," said Hope, with her characteristic precipitancy.

"Then, when five suns have risen and set, I will return with your sister. But hush!" she said; suddenly stopping, and turning a suspicious eye towards the thicket of evergreens.

"It was but the wind," said Hope, rightly interpreting Magawisca's quick glance, and the slight inclination of her head.

"You would not betray me!" said Magawisca, in a voice of mingled assurance and inquiry. "Oh, more than ever entered into thy young thoughts hangs upon my safety."

"But why any fear for your safety? why not come openly among us? I will get the word of our good governor that you shall come and go in peace. No one ever feared to trust his word."

"You know not what you ask."

"Indeed I do; but you, Magawisca, know not what you refuse; and why refuse? are you afraid of being treated like a recovered prisoner? Oh, no! every one will delight to honour you, for your very name is dear to all Mr. Fletcher's friends—most dear to Everell."

"Dear to Everell Fletcher! Does he remember me? Is there a place in his heart for an Indian?" she demanded, with a blended expression of pride and melancholy.

"Yes, yes, Magawisca, indeed is there," replied Hope, for now she thought she had touched the right key. "It was but this morning that he said he had a mind to take an Indian guide, and seek you out among the Maquas." Magawisca hid her face in the folds of her mantle, and Hope proceeded with increasing earnestness. "There is nothing in the wide world—there is nothing that Everell thinks so good and so noble as you. Of, if you could but have seen his joy, when, after your parting on that horrid rock, he first heard you was living! He has described you so often and so truly, that the moment I saw you and heard your voice, I said to myself, 'this is surely Everell's Magawisca.'"

"Say no more, Hope Leslie, say no more," exclaimed Magawisca, throwing back the envelope from her face, as if she were ashamed to shelter emotions she ought not to indulge. "I have promised my father, I have repeated the vow here on my mother's grave, and if I were to go back from it, those bright witnesses," she pointed to the heavens, "would break their silence. Do not speak to me again of Everell Fletcher."

"Oh yes, once again, Magawisca: if you will not listen to me; if you will but give me this brief, mysterious meeting with my poor sister, at least let Everell be with me; for his sake, for my sake, for your own sake, do not refuse me."

Magawisca looked on Hope's glowing face for a moment, and then shook her head with a melancholy smile. "They tell me," she said, "that no one can look on you and deny you aught; that you can make old men's hearts soft, and mould them at your will; but I have learned to deny even the cravings of my own heart; to pursue my purpose like the bird that keeps her wing stretched to the toilsome flight, though the sweetest note of her mate recalls her to the nest. But ah! I do but boast," she continued, casting her eyes to the ground. "I may not trust myself; that was a childish scream that escaped me when I saw Everell; had my father heard it, his cheek would have been pale with shame. No, Hope Leslie, I may not listen to thee. You must come alone to the meeting, or never meet your sister: will you come?"

Hope saw in the determined manner of Magawisca that there was no alternative but to accept the boon on her own terms, and she no longer withheld her compliance. . . .

Before they separated, Hope said, "You will allow me, Magawisca, to persuade my sister, if I can, to remain with me?"

"Oh yes, if you can; but do not hope to persuade her. She and my brother are as if one life-chord bound them together; and, besides, your sister cannot speak to you and understand you as I do. She was very young when she was taken where she has only heard the Indian tongue: some, you know, are like water, that retains no mark; and others like the flinty rock, that never loses a mark." Magawisca observed Hope's look of disappointment, and, in a voice of pity, added, "Your sister hath a face that speaketh plainly what the tongue should never speak—her own goodness."

When these two romantic females had concerted every measure they deemed essential to the certainty and privacy of their meeting, Magawisca bowed her head and kissed the border of Hope's shawl with the reverent delicacy of an Oriental salutation; she then took from beneath her mantle some fragrant herbs, and strewed them over her mother's grave, then prostrated herself in deep and silent devotion, feeling (as others have felt on earth thus consecrated) as if the clods she pressed were instinct with life. When this last act of filial love was done, she rose, muffled herself closely in her dark mantle, and departed.

Hope lingered for a moment. "Mysteriously," she said, as her eye followed the noble figure of Magawisca till it was lost in the surrounding darkness, "mysteriously have our destinies been interwoven. Our mothers brought from a far distance to rest together here—their children connected in indissoluble bonds!"

from Volume 2, Chapter 8

[Hope's meeting with her sister leads to the capture of Magawisca as well as that of Faith Leslie. At her trial for "brewing conspiracy amongst us among the Indian tribes," Magawisca is assisted by John Eliot, "the apostle of New England," whom Sedgwick identifies as the "first Protestant missionary to the Indians." As the passage begins Magawisca is being slandered by Sir Philip Gardiner, a secret Catholic who has courted Hope unsuccessfully and attempts to take his revenge by harming her friend. In the dramatic climax of the scene, Magawisca denies the right of the Puritan magistrates to judge her or her people.]

He said "that, after conducting Miss Leslie to the governor's door, he had immediately returned to his own lodgings, and that, induced by the still raging storm to make his walk as short as possible, he took a cross-cut through the burial ground; that, on coming near the upper extremity of the enclosure, he fancied he heard a human voice mingling with the din of the storm; that he paused, and directly a flash of lightning discovered Magawisca kneeling on the bare wet earth, making those monstrous and violent contortions, which all who heard him well knew characterized the devil-worship of the powwows; he would not, he ought not repeat to Christian ears her invocations to the Evil One to aid her in the execution of her revenge on the English; nor would he more particularly describe her diabolical writhings and beatings of her person. His brethren might easily imagine his emotions at witnessing them by the sulphureous gleams of lightning, on which, doubtless, her prayers were sped."

Sir Philip had gained confidence as he proceeded in his testimony, for he perceived by the fearful and angry glances that were cast on the prisoner, that his tale was credited by many of his audience, and he hoped by all.

The notion that the Indians were the children of the devil was not confined to the vulgar; and the belief in a familiar intercourse with evil spirits, now rejected by all but the most ignorant and credulous, was then universally received.

All had, therefore, listened in respectful silence to Sir Philip's extraordinary testimony, and it was too evident that it had the effect to set the current of feeling and opinion against the prisoner. Her few friends looked despondent; but for herself, true to the spirit of her race, she manifested no surprise nor emotion of any kind.

The audience listened eagerly to the magistrate, who read from his note-book the particulars which had been received from the Indian informer, and which served to corroborate and illustrate Sir Philip's testimony. All the evidence being now before the court, the governor asked Magawisca "if she had aught to allege in her own defence."

"Speak humbly, maiden," whispered Mr. Eliot; "it will grace thy cause with thy judges."

"Say," said Everell, "that you are a stranger to our laws and usages, and demand some one to speak for you."

Magawisca bowed her head to both advisers, in token of acknowledgment of their interest, and then, raising her eyes to her judges, she said, "I am your prisoner, and ye may slay me, but I deny your right to judge me. My people have never passed under your yoke; not one of my race has ever acknowledged your authority."

"This excuse will not suffice thee," answered one of her judges; "thy pride is like the image of Nebuchadnezzar's dream—it standeth on feet of clay: thy race have been swift witnesses to that sure word of prophecy, 'Fear thou not, O Jacob, my servant, for I am with thee, and I will make a full end of the people whither I have driven thee'; thy people! truly, where are they?"

"My people! where are they?" she replied, raising her eyes to Heaven, and speaking in a voice that sounded like deep-toned music after the harsh tones addressed to her; "my people are gone to the isles of the sweet southwest—to those shores that the bark of an enemy can never touch: think ye I fear to follow them?"

There was a momentary silence throughout the assembly; all seemed, for an instant, to feel that no human power could touch the spirit of the captive. Sir Philip whispered to the magistrate who last spoke, "Is it not awful presumption for this woman thus publicly to glory in her heathen notions?"

The knight's prompting had the intended effect. "Has this Pequod woman," demanded the magistrate, "never been instructed in the principles of truth, that she dares thus to hold forth her heathenisms before us? Dost thou not know, woman," he continued, holding up a Bible, "that this book contains the only revelation of a future world—the only rule for the present life?"

"I know," she replied, "that it contains thy rule, and it may be needful for thy mixed race; but the Great Spirit hath written his laws on the hearts of his original children, and we need it not."

"She is of Satan's heritage, and our enemy—a proved conspirator against the peace of God's people, and I see not why she should not be cut off," said the same gentleman, addressing his brethren in office.

"The testimony," said another of the magistrates, in a low voice, in which reason and mildness mingled, and truly indicated the disposition of the speaker, "the testimony appeareth to me insufficient to give peace to our consciences in bringing her to extremity. She seems, after her own manner, to be guided by the truth. Let the governor put it to her whether she will confess the charges laid against her."

The governor accordingly appealed to the prisoner. "I neither confess nor deny aught," she said. "I stand here like a deer caught in a thicket, awaiting the arrow of the hunter." . . .

The governor replied, with a severe gravity, ominous to the knight, "That the circumstances he had alluded to certainly required explanation; if that should not prove satisfactory, they would demand a public investigation. In the mean time, he should suspend the trial of the prisoner, who, though the decision of her case might not wholly depend on the establishment of Sir Philip's testimony, was yet, at present, materially affected by it.

"He expressed a deep regret at the interruption that had occurred, as it must lead," he said, "to the suspension of the justice to be manifested, either in the acquittal or condemnation of the prisoner. Some of the magistrates being called away from town on the next morning, he found himself compelled to adjourn the sitting of the court till one month from the present date."

"Then," said Magawisca, for the first time speaking with a tone of impatience, "then, I pray you, send me to death now. Anything is better than wearing through another moon in my prison-house, thinking," she added, and cast down her eyelids, heavy with tears, "thinking of that old man—my father. I pray thee," she continued, bending low her head, "I pray thee now to set me free. Wait not for his testimony"—she pointed to Sir Philip: "as well may ye expect the green herb to spring up in your trodden streets, as the breath of truth to come from his false lips. Do you wait for him to prove that I am your enemy? Take my own word—I am your enemy; the sunbeam and the shadow cannot mingle. The white man cometh—the Indian vanisheth. Can we grasp in friendship the hand raised to strike us? Nay: and it matters not whether we fall by the tempest that lays the forest low, or are cut down alone by the stroke of the axe. I would have thanked you for life and liberty; for Mononotto's sake I would have thanked you; but if ye send me back to that dungeon—the grave of the living, feeling, thinking soul, where the sun never shineth, where the stars never rise nor set, where the free breath of Heaven never enters, where all is darkness without and within"—she pressed her hand on her breast—"ye will even now condemn me to death, but death more slow and terrible than your most suffering captive ever endured from Indian fires and knives." She paused; passed unresisted without the little railing that encompassed her, mounted the steps of the platform, and, advancing to the feet of the governor, threw back her mantle, and knelt before him. Her mutilated person, unveiled by this action, appealed to the senses of the spectators. Everell involuntarily closed his eyes, and uttered a cry of agony, lost, indeed, in the murmurs of the crowd. She spoke, and all again were as hushed as death. "Thou didst promise," she said, addressing herself to Governor Winthrop, "to my dying mother thou didst promise kindness to her children. In her name, I demand of thee death or liberty."

Everell sprang forward, and, clasping his hands, exclaimed, "In the name of God, liberty!"

The feeling was contagious, and every voice, save her judges, shouted "Liberty! liberty! Grant the prisoner liberty!" . . .

The governor bowed his assent. "Rise, Magawisca," he said, in a voice of gentle authority; "I may not grant thy prayer; but what I can do in remembrance of my solemn promise to thy dying mother, without leaving undone higher duty, I will do."

Edgar Allan Poe 1809–1849

Poe is one of the most popular American authors, but there is some confusion about an appropriate approach to reading his tales and poems. Because he so often wrote in the first person about vivid events, many people continue to make the mistake of assuming that the "I" in Poe narratives is Poe himself. Hence it is a temptation to think of him as a lunatic, a drug addict, an alcoholic, and if not an actual murderer, a morose and morbid individual who spent much time contemplating violent deeds against the unsuspecting. Actually Poe was a relatively sane, peace-loving, and hardworking author. To be sure, he probably used drugs on occasion and he certainly overindulged in alcohol; he also doubted his mental stability from time to time, especially during certain stressful periods of his career. Undoubtedly he made use of these feelings and experiences in his fiction.

But Poe's tales and poems are far more than the accidental products of a disordered fancy. On the contrary, what recent scholarship has shown is that Poe worked consciously and with great concentration to achieve certain effects. This impulse toward polishing and perfecting meant many sleepless hours of painstaking revision. Moreover, while Poe, more than most authors, drew upon the ideas and images in his imagination, he also borrowed themes and concepts from the popular culture of his time. He was influenced by Charles Brockden Brown, Washington Irving, and Nathaniel Hawthorne, to mention only a few of his inspirers, and a host of minor poets; but by overseas authors too: Sir Walter Scott, Lord Byron, E.T.A. Hoffmann, and the fictional style of the popular British journal, *Blackwood's.* He also incorporated into his works many of the fads popular during his lifetime, such as mesmerism and Egyptology. Often Poe took ideas circulating in popular books and magazines and used them in macabre, but artistic and strikingly original ways. In his literary practice Poe exemplifies the process whereby personal experience illuminated by imagination and nourished by the work of other authors is transmuted into art. There remains an element of mystery in this process; it cannot be reduced to mechanical steps. Yet we should bear it in mind when studying Poe, lest we fall into the error of earlier critics, who believed he was isolated, solitary, and self-inspired under the influence of narcotics.

Edgar Poe was born in Boston in 1809. His parents were actors in the stage dramas of the day, his mother performing her parts more professionally than his father, who disappeared from view before young Edgar was two. Orphaned at two and a half, Edgar was taken in and brought up (but never formally adopted) by the John Allan family of Richmond, Virginia. Poe was given a good primary education in Richmond and England, where the Allans spent five years (1815–1820) developing overseas business interests.

At the age of seventeen Poe entered the University of Virginia, where he spent only one year, his guardian Mr. Allan refusing to fund a second year of study. The subject of Poe's feud with John Allan deserves more detailed treatment than is possible here, but briefly it may be said that the hardheaded Allan disapproved of Poe's literary aspirations and had no patience with Poe's character, which—with some basis in fact—he took to be dreamy, impractical, and dissolute. On his side, Poe—again with some justification—thought Allan stingy and abusive. Though he continued for some years to write Allan letters that alternated between being assertive and truckling, eventually Poe accepted the fact that he was on his own and would receive no assistance from his guardian. Poe was in his early twenties when Allan died without mentioning his ward in his will.

Thereafter Poe would be associated professionally with five Eastern cities: Boston, Baltimore, Richmond, Philadelphia, and New York. In his late teens Poe traveled to Boston and enlisted in the army under the pseudonym Edgar A. Perry. Just around the time of his enlistment a Boston printer brought out Poe's first published work, a slim volume of poetry entitled *Tamerlane and Other Poems,* today one of the most highly prized collector's items in American belles lettres. After a stint in the armed forces, including a period at West Point, Poe went to live with family in Baltimore. The household consisted of Poe; his brother, William Henry Poe; his aunt, Maria Clemm; and her daughter, Poe's cousin, Virginia. Here Poe began writing experimentally, creating Gothic tales which were part serious fiction and part satire on German and British examples of the genre. These early efforts proved fruitful in the extreme: the stories were all published and one was awarded a prestigious prize.

On the strength of this early success, aided and abetted by a strong recommendation from an influential friend, Poe was offered an editorial post on a Richmond magazine. He accepted the offer, moved to Richmond and sent for Mrs. Clemm and Virginia, his brother having died in the meantime of tuberculosis. In order to establish some permanence for this improvised family, Poe married his cousin Virginia, who was then a girl of thirteen.

Poe's work for the *Southern Literary Messenger* increased circulation tenfold, and his career seemed to be settling down and stabilizing, except for two things: Poe's belief that his talents demanded a grander setting than Richmond afforded, and his drinking on the job, which his editorial boss told him would not be tolerated.

In 1837 Poe's restlessness, along with his boss's dissatisfaction, forced the young author to think about finding another position. Looking northward, Poe half quit and half had-to-leave the *Messenger.* The next eighteen months he spent in New York, freelancing and looking for editorial jobs that never materialized. It was during this period that he published his only full-length prose romance, *The Narrative of Arthur Gordon Pym.*

By 1839 Poe was in Philadelphia serving as assistant editor of the popular *Burton's Gentleman's Magazine* and writing some of his most famous tales, including "Ligeia" and "The Fall of the House of Usher." Once again Poe's drinking got him in trouble, and he was forced to leave *Burton's* and look for another position.

He soon found a place on *Graham's Magazine,* which was the old *Burton's* under new management. During his Philadelphia period (1839–1844) Poe's talents were at their peak. He wrote, among other tales, "The Tell-Tale Heart," "The Pit and the Pendulum," "The Masque of the Red Death," and "The Gold Bug," which won a $100 award from the Philadelphia *Dollar Newspaper.* Poe also wrote several important reviews which attracted much attention, not all of it friendly, from his literary colleagues.

In 1844 Poe moved to New York where he eventually settled in a country cottage in the Bronx, today a well-preserved historical landmark. Here he wrote more tales and several critical essays, which were to become influential after his death. He also wrote his philosophical treatise, *Eureka.* But his crowning achievement from these years was the composition of "The Raven," which made him famous, if not rich. Almost overnight this haunting hymn to bereavement with its striking rhythms became part of our literary heritage.

Around this time Poe realized one of his long-cherished ambitions: to be sole editor of a literary magazine. Under Poe, however, *The Broadway Journal* did not prosper. Not long after he had assumed the editorship, insurmountable financial problems shut down its presses. Bringing this period of Poe's life to a melancholy close was the death of his wife Virginia at the age of twenty-five. For years she had suffered from tuberculosis, with lapses and recoveries that Poe claimed were partly responsible for his heavy drinking.

Two years remained for Poe before he was found dying in the streets of Baltimore. During this time he indulged in flirtations with a number of literary ladies, on one occasion actually approaching the altar. But when the lady called off the engagement, Poe went south to Richmond, where he was greeted as something of a returning hero. In this Indian Summer of his life Poe was feted, admired, invited, and quoted. Not that he was put on a pedestal, but a photograph taken in 1849, the last year of his life, shows a handsome, relaxed, and healthy Poe, in contrast to earlier portraits where he appears stressed and ill. In Richmond Poe signed the pledge, became engaged to his childhood sweetheart, and formulated plans to open a new literary magazine.

But when he was returning to New York to gather up Mrs. Clemm and take her to Richmond, something went wrong. He never reached New York, but was found in a coma lying in the street in Baltimore during a local election, this last fact assuming some significance because Baltimore elections were notorious for rough times—for drinking and brawling and political skulduggery of all kinds. Poe died in a Baltimore hospital a few days later. In all probability he was not the victim of election touts, as is often reported. Most likely he stopped at Baltimore to see friends, drank more than he should have, and wandered about until he collapsed on the sidewalk. By the following morning he would have had pneumonia, which accords with the contemporary description of his symptoms.

Over the years Poe has been criticized relentlessly and admired extravagantly. The effort to see him plainly and realistically is ongoing, a challenge to each new generation of readers. His position in our literature is uncertain for two reasons: his subject matter seems bizarre and eccentric, even at times grotesque, and thus "outside the main currents of American thought." Second, his philosophy of a supernal realm of perfect beauty and understanding, which underlies several of the stories and poems, seems, to some, soft-minded and adolescent. On the other hand, more and more research is revealing the artistry of the tales, along with their solid links to American culture. Meanwhile, Poe's philosophy of Icarian idealism has proved itself in its appeal to thinkers worldwide. Poe opened up entire esthetic areas for subsequent authors, critics, poets, painters, and composers. He authorized fuller access to dreams, fantasies, and unconscious impulses than had been thought viable by previous artists. On these grounds his influence upon the French Symbolist poets and the later Surrealist painters is readily understandable. Poe's theory of superior insight impressed George Bernard Shaw and Frederick Nietzsche, while his interest in criminal psychology inspired some of the work of Dostoyevsky. His logician-detective influenced Conan Doyle's portrayal of Sherlock Holmes, while "The Gold Bug" was seed time for Robert Louis Stevenson's *Treasure Island.* Only recently have we begun to realize that major authors in many nations are in debt to Poe. It is time to set aside our patronizing attitude toward this great American author.

William Goldhurst
University of Florida at Gainesville

PRIMARY WORKS

James A. Harrison, ed., *The Complete Works of Edgar Allan Poe* ("The Virginia Edition") 1902; T.O. Mabbott et al., *Collected Works,* 3 volumes, 1969–78; Stuart and Susan Levine, eds., *The Short Fiction of Edgar Allan Poe: An Annotated Edition,* 1976; Burton R. Pollin, ed., *Collected Writings,* 2 volumes, 1981.

SECONDARY WORKS

Arthur Hobson Quinn, *Edgar Allan Poe: A Critical Biography,* 1940; T.O. Mabbott, "Annals" in *Collected Works,* Volume 1, 1969; Vincent Buranelli, *Edgar Allan Poe,* 2/e, 1977; *Critical Essays on Edgar Allan Poe,* ed. Eric W. Carlson, 1987; Joan Dayan, *Fables of Mind: An Inquiry into Poe's Fiction,* 1987; J. Gerald Kennedy, *Poe, Death, and the Life of Writing,* 1987; Michael J. S. Williams, *A World of Words: Language and Displacement in the Fiction of Edgar Allan Poe,* 1988; *The American Face of Edgar Allan Poe,* ed. Shawn Rosenheim and Stephen Rachman, 1995; *The Poe Encyclopedia,* 1997.

MS. Found in a Bottle

Qui n'a plus qu'un moment à vivre
N'a plus rien à dissimuler.
—QUINAULT—ATYS[1]

Of my country and of my family I have little to say. Ill usage and length of years have driven me from the one, and estranged me from the other. Hereditary wealth afforded me an education of no common order, and a contemplative turn of mind enabled me to methodize the stores which early study very diligently garnered up.—Beyond all things, the study of the German moralists gave me great delight; not from any ill-advised admiration of their eloquent madness, but from the ease with which my habits of rigid thought enabled me to detect their falsities. I have often been reproached with the aridity of my genius; a deficiency of imagination has been imputed to me as a crime; and the Pyrrhonism[2] of my opinions has at all times rendered me notorious. Indeed, a strong relish for physical philosophy has, I fear, tinctured my mind with a very common error of this age—I mean the habit of referring occurrences, even the least susceptible of such reference, to the principles of that science. Upon the whole, no person could be less liable than myself to be led away from the severe precincts of truth by the *ignes fatui*[3] of superstition. I have thought proper to premise thus much, lest the incredible tale I have to tell should be considered rather the raving of a crude imagination, than the positive experience of a mind to which the reveries of fancy have been a dead letter and a nullity.

After many years spent in foreign travel, I sailed in the year 18—, from the port of Batavia, in the rich and populous island of Java, on a voyage to the Archipelago of the Sunda islands. I went as passenger—having no other inducement than a kind of nervous restlessness which haunted me as a fiend.

Our vessel was a beautiful ship of about four hundred tons, copper-fastened, and built at Bombay of Malabar teak. She was freighted with cotton-wool and oil, from the Lachadive islands. We had also on board coir, jaggeree, ghee, cocoa-nuts,

[1]He who has but a moment to live
No longer wishes to deceive anyone.
The quotation is from an opera libretto by the French dramatist Philippe Quinault.

[2]Extreme skepticism.

[3]Literally "fatuous fire," but the phrase has come to signify a foolish distraction.

and a few cases of opium. The stowage was clumsily done, and the vessel consequently crank.[4]

We got under way with a mere breath of wind, and for many days stood along the eastern coast of Java, without any other incident to beguile the monotony of our course than the occasional meeting with some of the small grabs[5] of the Archipelago to which we were bound.

One evening, leaning over the taffrail, I observed a very singular, isolated cloud, to the N.W. It was remarkable, as well for its color, as from its being the first we had seen since our departure from Batavia. I watched it attentively until sunset, when it spread all at once to the eastward and westward, girting in the horizon with a narrow strip of vapor, and looking like a long line of low beach. My notice was soon afterwards attracted by the dusky-red appearance of the moon, and the peculiar character of the sea. The latter was undergoing a rapid change, and the water seemed more than usually transparent. Although I could distinctly see the bottom, yet, having the lead, I found the ship in fifteen fathoms. The air now became intolerably hot, and was loaded with spiral exhalations similar to those arising from heated iron. As night came on, every breath of wind died away, and a more entire calm it is impossible to conceive. The flame of a candle burned upon the poop without the least perceptible motion, and a long hair, held between the finger and thumb, hung without the possibility of detecting a vibration. However, as the captain said he could perceive no indication of danger, and as we were drifting in bodily to shore, he ordered the sails to be furled, and the anchor let go. No watch was set, and the crew, consisting principally of Malays, stretched themselves deliberately upon deck. I went below—not without a full presentiment of evil. Indeed, every appearance warranted me in apprehending a Simoom.[6] I told the captain my fears; but he paid no attention to what I said, and left me without deigning to give a reply. My uneasiness, however, prevented me from sleeping, and about midnight I went upon deck.—As I placed my foot upon the upper step of the companion-ladder, I was startled by a loud, humming noise, like that occasioned by the rapid revolution of a mill-wheel, and before I could ascertain its meaning, I found the ship quivering to its centre. In the next instant, a wilderness of foam hurled us upon our beam-ends, and, rushing over us fore and aft, swept the entire decks from stem to stern.

The extreme fury of the blast proved, in a great measure, the salvation of the ship. Although completely water-logged, yet, as her masts had gone by the board, she rose, after a minute, heavily from the sea, and, staggering awhile beneath the immense pressure of the tempest, finally righted.

By what miracle I escaped destruction, it is impossible to say. Stunned by the shock of the water, I found myself, upon recovery, jammed in between the sternpost and rudder. With great difficulty I gained my feet, and looking dizzily around, was, at first, struck with the idea of our being among breakers; so terrific, beyond the wildest imagination, was the whirlpool of mountainous and foaming ocean within which we were engulfed. After a while, I heard the voice of an old Swede, who had

[4]Coir is fiber made from the husk of coconuts; jaggeree is unrefined sugar made from the sap of a palm tree; ghee is a kind of butter made from buffalo milk. "Crank" is a nautical term meaning liable to heel or capsize.

[5]East Indian sailboats.

[6]A hot dry desert wind, used here to designate swiftness and violence.

shipped with us at the moment of our leaving port. I hallooed to him with all my strength, and presently he came reeling aft. We soon discovered that we were the sole survivors of the accident. All on deck, with the exception of ourselves, had been swept overboard;—the captain and mates must have perished as they slept, for the cabins were deluged with water. Without assistance, we could expect to do little for the security of the ship, and our exertions were at first paralyzed by the momentary expectation of going down. Our cable had, of course, parted like pack-thread, at the first breath of the hurricane, or we should have been instantaneously overwhelmed. We scudded with frightful velocity before the sea, and the water made clear breaches over us. The frame-work of our stern was shattered excessively, and, in almost every respect, we had received considerable injury; but to our extreme joy we found the pumps unchoked, and that we had made no great shifting of our ballast. The main fury of the blast had already blown over, and we apprehended little danger from the violence of the wind; but we looked forward to its total cessation with dismay; well believing, that, in our shattered condition, we should inevitably perish in the tremendous swell which would ensue. But this very just apprehension seemed by no means likely to be soon verified. For five entire days and nights—during which our only subsistence was a small quantity of jaggeree, procured with great difficulty from the forecastle—the hulk flew at a rate defying computation, before rapidly succeeding flaws of wind, which, without equalling the first violence of the Simoom, were still more terrific than any tempest I had before encountered. Our course for the first four days was, with trifling variations, S.E. and by S.; and we must have run down the coast of New Holland.[7]—On the fifth day the cold became extreme, although the wind had hauled round a point more to the northward.—The sun arose with a sickly yellow lustre, and clambered a very few degrees above the horizon—emitting no decisive light.—There were no clouds apparent, yet the wind was upon the increase, and blew with a fitful and unsteady fury. About noon, as nearly as we could guess, our attention was again arrested by the appearance of the sun. It gave out no light, properly so called, but a dull and sullen glow without reflection, as if all its rays were polarized. Just before sinking within the turgid sea, its central fires suddenly went out, as if hurriedly extinguished by some unaccountable power. It was a dim, silver-like rim, alone, as it rushed down the unfathomable ocean.

We waited in vain for the arrival of the sixth day—that day to me has not arrived—to the Swede, never did arrive. Thenceforward we were enshrouded in pitchy darkness, so that we could not have seen an object at twenty paces from the ship. Eternal night continued to envelop us, all unrelieved by the phosphoric sea-brilliancy to which we had been accustomed in the tropics. We observed too, that, although the tempest continued to rage with unabated violence, there was no longer to be discovered the usual appearance of surf, or foam, which had hitherto attended us. All around were horror, and thick gloom, and a black sweltering desert of ebony.—Superstitious terror crept by degrees into the spirit of the old Swede, and my own soul was wrapped up in silent wonder. We neglected all care of the ship, as worse than useless, and securing ourselves, as well as possible, to the stump of the mizen-mast, looked out bitterly into the world of ocean. We had no means of calculating time, nor could we form any guess of our situation. We were, however, well

[7]An old term for Australia.

aware of having made farther to the southward than any previous navigators, and felt great amazement at not meeting with the usual impediments of ice. In the meantime every moment threatened to be our last—every mountainous billow hurried to overwhelm us. The swell surpassed anything I had imagined possible, and that we were not instantly buried is a miracle. My companion spoke of the lightness of our cargo, and reminded me of the excellent qualities of our ship; but I could not help feeling the utter hopelessness of hope itself, and prepared myself gloomily for that death which I thought nothing could defer beyond an hour, as, with every knot of way the ship made, the swelling of the black stupendous seas became more dismally appalling. At times we gasped for breath at an elevation beyond the albatross—at times became dizzy with the velocity of our descent into some watery hell, where the air grew stagnant, and no sound disturbed the slumbers of the kraken.[8]

We were at the bottom of one of these abysses, when a quick scream from my companion broke fearfully upon the night. "See! see!" cried he, shrieking in my ears, "Almighty God! see! see!" As he spoke, I became aware of a dull, sullen glare of red light which streamed down the sides of the vast chasm where we lay, and threw a fitful brilliancy upon our deck. Casting my eyes upwards, I beheld a spectacle which froze the current of my blood. At a terrific height directly above us, and upon the very verge of the precipitous descent, hovered a gigantic ship of, perhaps, four thousand tons. Although upreared upon the summit of a wave more than a hundred times her own altitude, her apparent size still exceeded that of any ship of the line or East Indiaman in existence.[9] Her huge hull was of a deep dingy black, unrelieved by any of the customary carvings of a ship. A single row of brass cannon protruded from her open ports, and dashed from their polished surfaces the fires of innumerable battle-lanterns, which swung to and fro about her rigging. But what mainly inspired us with horror and astonishment, was that she bore up under a press of sail in the very teeth of that supernatural sea, and of that ungovernable hurricane. When we first discovered her, her bows were alone to be seen, as she rose slowly from the dim and horrible gulf beyond her. For a moment of intense terror she paused upon the giddy pinnacle, as if in contemplation of her own sublimity, then trembled and tottered, and—came down.

At this instant, I know not what sudden self-possession came over my spirit. Staggering as far aft as I could, I awaited fearlessly the ruin that was to overwhelm. Our own vessel was at length ceasing from her struggles, and sinking with her head to the sea. The shock of the descending mass struck her, consequently, in that portion of her frame which was already under water, and the inevitable result was to hurl me, with irresistible violence, upon the rigging of the stranger.

As I fell, the ship hove in stays, and went about;[10] and to the confusion ensuing I attributed my escape from the notice of the crew. With little difficulty I made my way unperceived to the main hatchway, which was partially open, and soon found an opportunity of secreting myself in the hold. Why I did so I can hardly tell. An indefinite sense of awe, which at first sight of the navigators of the ship had taken hold of

[8]A legendary sea monster noted for immense size and hostility to sailing ships.

[9]A ship of the line is a war ship; an East Indiaman is a ship in the employ of the Dutch East India Company. East Indiaman ships were bigger than other commercial vessels.

[10]"Hove in stays and went about" is nautical for tacked and headed into the wind.

my mind, was perhaps the principle of my concealment. I was unwilling to trust myself with a race of people who had offered, to the cursory glance I had taken, so many points of vague novelty, doubt, and apprehension. I therefore thought proper to contrive a hiding-place in the hold. This I did by removing a small portion of the shifting-boards, in such a manner as to afford me a convenient retreat between the huge timbers of the ship.

I had scarcely completed my work, when a footstep in the hold forced me to make use of it. A man passed by my place of concealment with a feeble and unsteady gait. I could not see his face, but had an opportunity of observing his general appearance. There was about it an evidence of great age and infirmity. His knees tottered beneath a load of years, and his entire frame quivered under the burthen. He muttered to himself, in a low broken tone, some words of a language which I could not understand, and groped in a corner among a pile of singular-looking instruments, and decayed charts of navigation. His manner was a wild mixture of the peevishness of second childhood, and the solemn dignity of a God. He at length went on deck, and I saw him no more.

* * *

A feeling, for which I have no name, has taken possession of my soul—a sensation which will admit of no analysis, to which the lessons of by-gone times are inadequate, and for which I fear futurity itself will offer me no key. To a mind constituted like my own, the latter consideration is an evil. I shall never—I know that I shall never—be satisfied with regard to the nature of my conceptions. Yet it is not wonderful that these conceptions are indefinite, since they have their origin in sources so utterly novel. A new sense—a new entity is added to my soul.

* * *

It is long since I first trod the deck of this terrible ship, and the rays of my destiny are, I think, gathering to a focus. Incomprehensible men! Wrapped up in meditations of a kind which I cannot divine, they pass me by unnoticed. Concealment is utter folly on my part, for the people *will not see.* It was but just now that I passed directly before the eyes of the mate—it was no long while ago that I ventured into the captain's own private cabin, and took thence the materials with which I write, and have written. I shall from time to time continue this journal. It is true that I may not find an opportunity of transmitting it to the world, but I will not fail to make the endeavour. At the last moment I will enclose the MS. in a bottle, and cast it within the sea.[11]

* * *

[11]Poe's narrator has been thrown by accident onto the *Flying Dutchman,* a legendary ghost ship that appears to seamen whose own vessel is sinking. It is likely that the *Flying Dutchman* was known as a slave-trading ship.

An incident has occurred which has given me new room for meditation. Are such things the operation of ungoverned Chance? I had ventured upon deck and thrown myself down, without attracting any notice, among a pile of ratlin-stuff and old sails, in the bottom of the yawl. While musing upon the singularity of my fate, I unwittingly daubed with a tar-brush the edges of a neatly-folded studding-sail which lay near me on a barrel. The studding-sail is now bent upon the ship, and the thoughtless touches of the brush are spread out into the word DISCOVERY. * * * I have made many observations lately upon the structure of the vessel. Although well armed, she is not, I think, a ship of war. Her rigging, build, and general equipment, all negative a supposition of this kind. What she *is not,* I can easily perceive—what she *is* I fear it is impossible to say. I know not how it is, but in scrutinizing her strange model and singular cast of spars, her huge size and overgrown suits of canvass, her severely simple bow and antiquated stern, there will occasionally flash across my mind a sensation of familiar things, and there is always mixed up with such indistinct shadows of recollection, an unaccountable memory of old foreign chronicles and ages long ago. * * * I have been looking at the timbers of the ship. She is built of a material to which I am a stranger. There is a peculiar character about the wood which strikes me as rendering it unfit for the purpose to which it has been applied. I mean its extreme *porousness,* considered independently of the worm-eaten condition which is a consequence of navigation in these seas, and apart from the rottenness attendant upon age. It will appear perhaps an observation somewhat over-curious, but this wood would have every characteristic of Spanish oak, if Spanish oak were distended by any unnatural means.

In reading the above sentence a curious apothegm of an old weather-beaten Dutch navigator comes full upon my recollection. "It is as sure," he was wont to say, when any doubt was entertained of his veracity, "as sure as there is a sea where the ship itself will grow in bulk like the living body of the seaman." * * * About an hour ago, I made bold to thrust myself among a group of the crew. They paid me no manner of attention, and, although I stood in the very midst of them all, seemed utterly unconscious of my presence. Like the one I had at first seen in the hold, they all bore about them the marks of a hoary old age. Their knees trembled with infirmity; their shoulders were bent double with decrepitude; their shrivelled skins rattled in the wind; their voices were low, tremulous and broken; their eyes glistened with the rheum of years; and their gray hairs streamed terribly in the tempest. Around them, on every part of the deck, lay scattered mathematical instruments of the most quaint and obsolete construction. * * * I mentioned some time ago the bending of a studding-sail. From that period the ship, being thrown dead off the wind, has continued her terrific course due south, with every rag of canvass packed upon her, from her trucks to her lower studding-sail booms, and rolling every moment her top-gallant yard-arms into the most appalling hell of water which it can enter into the mind of man to imagine. I have just left the deck, where I find it impossible to maintain a footing, although the crew seem to experience little inconvenience. It appears to me a miracle of miracles that our enormous bulk is not swallowed up at once and forever. We are surely doomed to hover continually upon the brink of Eternity, without taking a final plunge into the abyss. From billows a thousand times more stupendous than any I have ever seen, we glide away with the facility of the arrowy sea-gull; and the colossal waters rear their heads above us like demons of the deep, but like demons confined to simple threats and forbidden to destroy. I am led to attribute these frequent escapes to the only natural cause which can account for such effect.—I must suppose the ship to be within the influence of some strong current, or impetuous under-tow. * * * I have seen the captain face to face, and in his own cabin—but, as I expected, he paid no attention. Although in his appearance there is, to a casual observer, nothing which might bespeak him more or less than man—still a feeling of irrepressible reverence and awe mingled with the sensation of wonder with which I regarded him. In stature he is nearly my own height; that is, about five feet eight inches. He is of a well-knit and compact frame of body, neither robust nor remarkably otherwise. But it is the singularity of the expression which reigns upon the face—it is the intense, the wonderful, the thrilling evidence of old age, so utter, so extreme, which excites within my spirit a sense—a sentiment ineffable. His forehead, although little wrinkled, seems to bear upon it the stamp of a myriad of years.—His gray hairs are records of the past, and his grayer eyes are Sybils of the future. The cabin floor was thickly strewn with strange, iron-clasped folios, and mouldering instruments of science, and obsolete long-forgotten charts. His head was bowed down upon his hands, and he pored, with a fiery unquiet eye, over a paper which I took to be a commission, and which, at all events, bore the signature of a monarch. He muttered to himself, as did the first seaman whom I saw in the hold, some low peevish syllables of a foreign tongue, and although the speaker was close at my elbow, his voice seemed to reach my ears from the distance of a mile. * * * The ship and all in it are imbued with the spirit of Eld. The crew glide to and fro like the ghosts of buried centuries; their eyes have an eager and uneasy meaning; and when their fingers fall athwart my path in the wild glare of the battle-lanterns, I feel as I have never felt before, although I have been all my life a dealer in antiquities, and have imbibed the shadows of fallen columns at Balbec, and Tadmor, and Persepolis, until my very soul has become a ruin. * * * When I look around me I feel ashamed of my former apprehensions. If I trembled at the blast which has hitherto attended us, shall I not stand aghast at a warring of wind and ocean, to convey any idea of which the words tornado and simoom are trivial and ineffective? All in the immediate vicinity of the ship is the blackness of eternal night, and a chaos of foamless water; but, about a league on either side of us, may be seen, indistinctly and at intervals, stupendous ramparts of ice, towering away into the desolate sky, and looking like the walls of the universe. * * * As I imagined, the ship proves to be in a current; if that appellation can properly be given to a tide which, howling and shrieking by the white ice, thunders on to the southward with a velocity like the headlong dashing of a cataract. * * * To conceive the horror of my sensations is, I presume, utterly impossible; yet a curiosity to penetrate the mysteries of these awful regions, predominates even over my despair, and will reconcile me to the most hideous aspect of death. It is evident that we are hurrying onwards to some exciting knowledge—some never-to-be-imparted secret, whose attainment is destruction. Perhaps this current leads us to the southern pole itself. It must be confessed that a supposition apparently so wild has every probability in its favor. * * * The crew pace the deck with unquiet and tremulous step; but there is upon their countenances an expression more of the eagerness of hope than of the apathy of despair.

In the meantime the wind is still in our poop, and, as we carry a crowd of canvass, the ship is at times lifted bodily from out the sea—Oh, horror upon horror! the ice opens suddenly to the right, and to the left, and we are whirling dizzily, in immense concentric circles, round and round the borders of a gigantic amphitheatre,[12] the summit of whose walls is lost in the darkness and the distance. But little time will be left me to ponder upon my destiny—the circles rapidly grow small—we are plunging madly within the grasp of the whirlpool—and amid a roaring, and bellowing, and thundering of ocean and of tempest, the ship is quivering, oh God! and—going down.

NOTE.—The "MS. Found in a Bottle," was originally published in 1831 [1833], and it was not until many years afterwards that I became acquainted with the maps of Mercator, in which the ocean is represented as rushing, by four mouths, into the (northern) Polar Gulf, to be absorbed into the bowels of the earth; the Pole itself being represented by a black rock, towering to a prodigious height. [Poe's note]

1831

Ligeia

And the will therein lieth, which dieth not. Who knoweth the mysteries of the will, with its vigor? For God is but a great will pervading all things by nature of its intentness. Man doth not yield himself to the angels, nor unto death utterly, save only through the weakness of his feeble will.

—JOSEPH GLANVILL[1]

I cannot, for my soul, remember how, when, or even precisely where, I first became acquainted with the lady Ligeia. Long years have since elapsed, and my memory is feeble through much suffering. Or, perhaps, I cannot *now* bring these points to mind, because, in truth, the character of my beloved, her rare learning, her singular yet placid cast of beauty, and the thrilling and enthralling eloquence of her low musical language, made their way into my heart by paces so steadily and stealthily progressive that they have been unnoticed and unknown. Yet I believe that I met her first and most frequently in some large, old, decaying city near the Rhine. Of her family—I have surely heard her speak. That it is of a remotely ancient date cannot be doubted. Ligeia! Ligeia! Buried in studies of a nature more than all else adapted to deaden impressions of the outward world, it is by that sweet word alone—by Ligeia—that I bring before mine eyes in fancy the image of her who is no more. And now, while I write, a recollection flashes upon me that I have *never known* the paternal name of her who was my friend and my betrothed, and who became the partner of my studies, and finally the wife of my bosom. Was it a playful charge on the

[12]Poe is alluding to the image of a funnel-shaped opening at both North and South Poles—a fiction described as fact in the "scientific" books of Poe's day—especially Captain John C. Symmes's book *Symzonia* (1826).

[1]The Glanvill quote has never been located. Possibly Poe made it up to serve a very important function in the story.

part of my Ligeia? or was it a test of my strength of affection, that I should institute no inquiries upon this point? or was it rather a caprice of my own—a wildly romantic offering on the shrine of the most passionate devotion? I but indistinctly recall the fact itself—what wonder that I have utterly forgotten the circumstances which originated or attended it? And, indeed, if ever that spirit which is entitled *Romance*—if ever she, the wan and the misty-winged *Ashtophet*[2] of idolatrous Egypt, presided, as they tell, over marriages ill-omened, then most surely she presided over mine.

There is one dear topic, however, on which my memory fails me not. It is the *person* of Ligeia. In stature she was tall, somewhat slender, and, in her later days, even emaciated. I would in vain attempt to portray the majesty, the quiet ease, of her demeanor, or the incomprehensible lightness and elasticity of her footfall. She came and departed as a shadow. I was never made aware of her entrance into my closed study save by the dear music of her low sweet voice, as she placed her marble hand upon my shoulder. In beauty of face no maiden ever equalled her. It was the radiance of an opium-dream—an airy and spirit-lifting vision more wildly divine than the phantasies which hovered about the slumbering souls of the daughters of Delos.[3] Yet her features were not of that regular mould which we have been falsely taught to worship in the classical labors of the heathen. "There is no exquisite beauty," says Bacon, Lord Verulam, speaking truly of all the forms and *genera* of beauty, "without some *strangeness* in the proportion."[4] Yet, although I saw that the features of Ligeia were not of a classic regularity—although I perceived that her loveliness was indeed "exquisite," and felt that there was much of "strangeness" pervading it, yet I have tried in vain to detect the irregularity and to trace home my own perception of "the strange." I examined the contour of the lofty and pale forehead—it was faultless—how cold indeed that word when applied to a majesty so divine!—the skin rivalling the purest ivory, the commanding extent and repose, the gentle prominence of the regions above the temples; and then the raven-black, the glossy, the luxuriant and naturally-curling tresses, setting forth the full force of the Homeric epithet, "hyacinthine!" I looked at the delicate outlines of the nose—and nowhere but in the graceful medallions of the Hebrews had I beheld a similar perfection. There were the same luxurious smoothness of surface, the same scarcely perceptible tendency to the aquiline, the same harmoniously curved nostrils speaking the free spirit. I regarded the sweet mouth. Here was indeed the triumph of all things heavenly—the magnificent turn of the short upper lip—the soft, voluptuous slumber of the under—the dimples which sported, and the color which spoke—the teeth glancing back, with a brilliancy almost startling, every ray of the holy light which fell upon them in her serene and placid, yet most exultingly radiant of all smiles. I scrutinized the formation of the chin—and here, too, I found the gentleness of breadth, the softness and the majesty, the fullness and the spirituality, of the Greek—the contour which the god Apollo revealed but in a dream, to Cleomenes, the son of the Athenian.[5] And then I peered into the large eyes of Ligeia.

[2]A deity associated with Ashtoreth, love-goddess of the early Phoenecians.

[3]A poetic term for Greece.

[4]Poe was fond of the Francis Bacon quotation and used it several times in his works. He has changed one word. Bacon wrote: "There is no excellent beauty . . . ," which Poe transforms to "There is no exquisite beauty. . . ."

[5]Cleomenes was the sculptor of the Venus de Medici. The idea that Apollo appeared to the artist is Poe's invention.

For eyes we have no models in the remotely antique. It might have been, too, that in these eyes of my beloved lay the secret to which Lord Verulam alludes. They were, I must believe, far larger than the ordinary eyes of our own race. They were even fuller than the fullest of the gazelle eyes of the tribe of the valley of Nourjahad.[6] Yet it was only at intervals—in moments of intense excitement—that this peculiarity became more than slightly noticeable in Ligeia. And at such moments was her beauty—in my heated fancy thus it appeared perhaps—the beauty of beings either above or apart from the earth—the beauty of the fabulous Houri of the Turk.[7] The hue of the orbs was the most brilliant of black, and, far over them, hung jetty lashes of great length. The brows, slightly irregular in outline, had the same tint. The "strangeness," however, which I found in the eyes, was of a nature distinct from the formation, or the color, or the brilliancy of the features, and must, after all, be referred to the *expression*. Ah, word of no meaning! behind whose vast latitude of mere sound we intrench our ignorance of so much of the spiritual. The expression of the eyes of Ligeia! How for long hours have I pondered upon it! How have I, through the whole of a midsummer night, struggled to fathom it! What was it—that something more profound than the well of Democritus[8]—which lay far within the pupils of my beloved? What *was* it? I was possessed with a passion to discover. Those eyes! those large, those shining, those divine orbs! they became to me twin stars of Leda,[9] and I to them devoutest of astrologers.

There is no point, among the many incomprehensible anomalies of the science of mind, more thrillingly exciting than the fact—never, I believe, noticed in the schools—that, in our endeavors to recall to memory something long forgotten, we often find ourselves *upon the very verge* of remembrance, without being able, in the end, to remember. And thus how frequently, in my intense scrutiny of Ligeia's eyes, have I felt approaching the full knowledge of their expression—felt it approaching—yet not quite be mine—and so at length entirely depart! And (strange, oh strangest mystery of all!) I found, in the commonest objects of the universe, a circle of analogies to that expression. I mean to say that, subsequently to the period when Ligeia's beauty passed into my spirit, there dwelling as in a shrine, I derived, from many existences in the material world, a sentiment such as I felt always aroused within me by her large and luminous orbs. Yet not the more could I define that sentiment, or analyze, or even steadily view it. I recognized it, let me repeat, sometimes in the commonest objects of the universe. It has flashed upon me in the survey of a rapidly-growing vine—in the contemplation of a moth, a butterfly, a chrysalis, a stream of running water. I have felt it in the ocean; in the falling of a meteor. I have felt it in the glances of unusually aged people. And there are one or two stars in heaven—(one especially, a star of the sixth magnitude, double and changeable, to be found near the

[6]Poe's reference is to Frances Sheridan's *History of the Nourjahad,* an oriental novel.

[7]The houri are maidens in the Mohammedan Paradise.

[8]Actually what Democritus said was "Of truth we know nothing, for truth is in the depths." Democritus was a philosopher of ancient Greece noted for the theory that the world was composed of atoms.

[9]Leda was a beautiful mortal whom Zeus found irresistible. After Zeus, in the form of a swan, raped her, she gave birth to Helen of Troy (in one egg) and Castor and Pollux (in another egg).

large star in Lyra)[10] in a telescopic scrutiny of which I have been made aware of the feeling. I have been filled with it by certain sounds from stringed instruments, and not unfrequently by passages from books. Among innumerable other instances, I well remember something in a volume of Joseph Glanvill, which (perhaps merely from its quaintness—who shall say?) never failed to inspire me with the sentiment;—"And the will therein lieth, which dieth not. Who knoweth the mysteries of the will, with its vigor? For God is but a great will pervading all things by nature of its intentness. Man doth not yield him to the angels, nor unto death utterly, save only through the weakness of his feeble will."

Length of years, and subsequent reflection, have enabled me to trace, indeed, some remote connection between this passage in the English moralist and a portion of the character of Ligeia. An *intensity* in thought, action, or speech, was possibly, in her, a result, or at least an index, of that gigantic volition which, during our long intercourse, failed to give other and more immediate evidence of its existence. Of all the women whom I have ever known, she, the outwardly calm, the ever-placid Ligeia, was the most violently a prey to the tumultuous vultures of stern passion. And of such passion I could form no estimate, save by the miraculous expansion of those eyes which at once so delighted and appalled me—by the almost magical melody, modulation, distinctness and placidity of her very low voice—and by the fierce energy (rendered doubly effective by contrast with her manner of utterance) of the wild words which she habitually uttered.

I have spoken of the learning of Ligeia: it was immense—such as I have never known in woman. In the classical tongues was she deeply proficient, and as far as my own acquaintance extended in regard to the modern dialects of Europe, I have never known her at fault. Indeed upon any theme of the most admired, because simply the most abstruse of the boasted erudition of the academy, have I *ever* found Ligeia at fault? How singularly—how thrillingly, this one point in the nature of my wife has forced itself, at this late period only, upon my attention! I said her knowledge was such as I have never known in woman—but where breathes the man who has traversed, and successfully, *all* the wide areas of moral, physical, and mathematical science? I saw not then what I now clearly perceive, that the acquisitions of Ligeia were gigantic, were astounding; yet I was sufficiently aware of her infinite supremacy to resign myself, with a childlike confidence, to her guidance through the chaotic world of metaphysical investigation at which I was most busily occupied during the earlier years of our marriage. With how vast a triumph—with how vivid a delight—with how much of all that is ethereal in hope—did I *feel,* as she bent over me in studies but little sought—but less known—that delicious vista by slow degrees expanding before me, down whose long, gorgeous, and all untrodden path, I might at length pass onward to the goal of a wisdom too divinely precious not to be forbidden!

How poignant, then, must have been the grief with which, after some years, I beheld my well-grounded expectations take wings to themselves and fly away! Without Ligeia I was but as a child groping benighted. Her presence, her readings alone, ren-

[10]Lyra is a constellation of stars which form a heavenly harp.

dered vividly luminous the many mysteries of the transcendentalism[11] in which we were immersed. Wanting the radiant lustre of her eyes, letters, lambent and golden, grew duller than Saturnian lead.[12] And now those eyes shone less and less frequently upon the pages over which I pored. Ligeia grew ill. The wild eyes blazed with a too—too glorious effulgence; the pale fingers became of the transparent waxen hue of the grave, and the blue veins upon the lofty forehead swelled and sank impetuously with the tides of the most gentle emotion. I saw that she must die—and I struggled desperately in spirit with the grim Azrael.[13] And the struggles of the passionate wife were, to my astonishment, even more energetic than my own. There had been much in her stern nature to impress me with the belief that, to her, death would have come without its terrors;—but not so. Words are impotent to convey any just idea of the fierceness of resistance with which she wrestled with the Shadow. I groaned in anguish at the pitiable spectacle. I would have soothed—I would have reasoned; but, in the intensity of her wild desire for life,—for life—*but* for life—solace and reason were alike the uttermost of folly. Yet not until the last instance, amid the most convulsive writhings of her fierce spirit, was shaken the external placidity of her demeanor. Her voice grew more gentle—grew more low—yet I would not wish to dwell upon the wild meaning of the quietly uttered words. My brain reeled as I hearkened entranced, to a melody more than mortal—to assumptions and aspirations which mortality had never before known.

That she loved me I should not have doubted; and I might have been easily aware that, in a bosom such as hers, love would have reigned no ordinary passion. But in death only, was I fully impressed with the strength of her affection. For long hours, detaining my hand, would she pour out before me the overflowing of a heart whose more than passionate devotion amounted to idolatry. How had I deserved to be so blessed by such confession?—how had I deserved to be so cursed with the removal of my beloved in the hour of her making them? But upon this subject I cannot bear to dilate. Let me say only, that in Ligeia's more than womanly abandonment to a love, alas! all unmerited, all unworthily bestowed, I at length recognized the principle of her longing with so wildly earnest a desire for the life which was now fleeing so rapidly away. It is this wild longing—it is this eager vehemence of desire for life—*but* for life—that I have no power to portray—no utterance capable of expressing.

At high noon of the night in which she departed, beckoning me, peremptorily, to her side, she bade me repeat certain verses composed by herself not many days before. I obeyed her.—They were these:

> Lo! 't is a gala night
>   Within the lonesome latter years!
> An angel throng, bewinged, bedight
>   In veils, and drowned in tears,

[11]Poe refers here not to the New England school of thought headed by Emerson, but to spiritual realities above and beyond the physical world.

[12]A reference to alchemy, a medieval pseudoscience which contended that lead could be transformed into gold. Saturnine in alchemical terminology means lead-like.

[13]The Mohammedan angel of death.

Sit in a theatre, to see
A play of hopes and fears,
While the orchestra breathes fitfully
The music of the spheres.

Mimes, in the form of God on high,
Mutter and mumble low,
And hither and thither fly—
Mere puppets they, who come and go
At bidding of vast formless things
That shift the scenery to and fro,
Flapping from out their Condor wings
Invisible Wo!

That motley drama!—oh, be sure
It shall not be forgot!
With its Phantom chased forever more,
By a crowd that seize it not,
Through a circle that ever returneth in
To the self-same spot,
And much of Madness and more of Sin
And Horror the soul of the plot.

But see, amid the mimic rout,
A crawling shape intrude!
A blood-red thing that writhes from out
The scenic solitude!
It writhes!—it writhes!—with mortal pangs
The mimes become its food,
And the seraphs sob at vermin fangs
In human gore imbued.

Out—out are the lights—out all!
And over each quivering form,
The curtain, a funeral pall,
Comes down with the rush of a storm,
And the angels, all pallid and wan,
Uprising, unveiling, affirm
That the play is the tragedy, "Man,"
And its hero the Conqueror Worm.[14]

"O God!" half shrieked Ligeia, leaping to her feet and extending her arms aloft with a spasmodic movement, as I made an end of these lines—"O God! O Divine

[14]This poem, under the title "The Conqueror Worm," was written and published years earlier and then incorporated into "Ligeia."

Father!—shall these things be undeviatingly so?—shall this Conqueror be not once conquered? Are we not part and parcel in Thee? Who—who knoweth the mysteries of the will with its vigor? Man doth not yield him to the angels, *nor unto death utterly,* save only through the weakness of his feeble will."

And now, as if exhausted with emotion, she suffered her white arms to fall, and returned solemnly to her bed of death. And as she breathed her last sighs, there came mingled with them a low murmur from her lips. I bent to them my ear and distinguished, again, the concluding words of the passage in Glanvill—*"Man doth not yield him to the angels, nor unto death utterly, save only through the weakness of his feeble will."*

She died;—and I, crushed into the very dust with sorrow, could no longer endure the lonely desolation of my dwelling in the dim and decaying city by the Rhine. I had no lack of what the world calls wealth. Ligeia had brought me far more, very far more than ordinarily falls to the lot of mortals. After a few months, therefore, of weary and aimless wandering, I purchased, and put in some repair, an abbey, which I shall not name, in one of the wildest and least frequented portions of fair England. The gloomy and dreary grandeur of the building, the almost savage aspect of the domain, the many melancholy and time-honored memories connected with both, had much in unison with the feelings of utter abandonment which had driven me into that remote and unsocial region of the country. Yet although the external abbey, with its verdant decay hanging about it, suffered but little alteration, I gave way, with a child-like perversity, and perchance with a faint hope of alleviating my sorrows, to a display of more than regal magnificence within.—For such follies, even in childhood, I had imbibed a taste and now they came back to me as if in the dotage of grief. Alas, I feel how much even of incipient madness might have been discovered in the gorgeous and fantastic draperies, in the solemn carvings of Egypt, in the wild cornices and furniture, in the Bedlam patterns of the carpets of tufted gold! I had become a bounden slave in the trammels of opium, and my labors and my orders had taken a coloring from my dreams. But these absurdities I must not pause to detail. Let me speak only of that one chamber, ever accursed, whither in a moment of mental alienation, I led from the altar as my bride—as the successor of the unforgotten Ligeia—the fair-haired and blue-eyed Lady Rowena Trevanion, of Tremaine.

There is no individual portion of the architecture and decoration of that bridal chamber which is not now visibly before me. Where were the souls of the haughty family of the bride, when, through thirst of gold, they permitted to pass the threshold of an apartment *so* bedecked, a maiden and a daughter so beloved? I have said that I minutely remember the details of the chamber—yet I am sadly forgetful on topics of deep moment—and here there was no system, no keeping, in the fantastic display, to take hold upon the memory. The room lay in a high turret of the castellated abbey, was pentagonal in shape, and of capacious size. Occupying the whole southern face of the pentagon was the sole window—an immense sheet of unbroken glass from Venice—a single pane, and tinted of a leaden hue, so that the rays of either the sun or moon, passing through it, fell with a ghastly lustre on the objects within. Over the upper portion of this huge window, extended the trellice-work of an aged vine, which clambered up the massy walls of the turret. The ceiling, of gloomy-looking oak, was excessively lofty, vaulted, and elaborately fretted with the wildest and most grotesque specimens of a semi-Gothic, semi-Druidical device. From out the most central recess of this melancholy vaulting, depended, by a single chain of gold with long links, a huge censer of the same metal, Saracenic in pattern, and with many perforations so contrived that there writhed in and out of them, as if endued with a serpent vitality, a continual succession of parti-colored fires.[15]

Some few ottomans and golden candelabra, of Eastern figure, were in various stations about—and there was the couch, too—the bridal couch—of an Indian model, and low, and sculptured of solid ebony, with a pall-like canopy above. In each of the angles of the chamber stood on end a gigantic sarcophagus of black granite, from the tombs of the kings over against Luxor, with their aged lids full of immemorial sculpture. But in the draping of the apartment lay, alas! the chief phantasy of all. The lofty walls, gigantic in height—even unproportionably so—were hung from summit to foot, in vast folds, with a heavy and massive-looking tapestry—tapestry of a material which was found alike as a carpet on the floor, as a covering for the ottomans and the ebony bed, as a canopy for the bed, and as the gorgeous volutes of the curtains which partially shaded the window. The material was the richest cloth of gold. It was spotted all over, at irregular intervals, with arabesque figures, about a foot in diameter, and wrought upon the cloth in patterns of the most jetty black. But these figures partook of the true character of the arabesque only when regarded from a single point of view. By a contrivance now common, and indeed traceable to a very remote period of antiquity, they were made changeable in aspect. To one entering the room, they bore the appearance of simple monstrosities; but upon a farther advance, this appearance gradually departed; and step by step, as the visiter moved his station in the chamber, he saw himself surrounded by an endless succession of the ghastly forms which belong to the superstition of the Norman, or arise in the guilty slumbers of the monk. The phantasmagoric effect was vastly heightened by the artificial introduction of a strong continual current of wind behind the draperies—giving a hideous and uneasy animation to the whole.

In halls such as these—in a bridal chamber such as this—I passed, with the Lady of Tremaine, the unhallowed hours of the first month of our marriage—passed them with but little disquietude. That my wife dreaded the fierce moodiness of my temper—that she shunned me and loved me but little—I could not help perceiving; but it gave me rather pleasure than otherwise. I loathed her with a hatred belonging more to demon than to man. My memory flew back, (oh, with what intensity of regret!) to Ligeia, the beloved, the august, the beautiful, the entombed. I revelled in recollections of her purity, of her wisdom, of her lofty, her ethereal nature, of her passionate, her idolatrous love. Now, then, did my spirit fully and freely burn with more than all the fires of her own. In the excitement of my opium dreams (for I was habitually fettered in the shackles of the drug) I would call aloud upon her name, during the silence of the night, or among the sheltered recesses of the glens by day, as if, through the wild eagerness, the solemn passion, the consuming ardor of my longing for the

[15]Poe's mixture of Gothic, Druidic, and Saracenic decor is deliberate and perhaps calculated to suggest to readers familiar with the arcane a triumph over time and thus immortality.

departed, I could restore her to the pathway she had abandoned—ah, *could* it be forever?—upon the earth.

About the commencement of the second month of the marriage, the Lady Rowena was attacked with sudden illness, from which her recovery was slow. The fever which consumed her rendered her nights uneasy; and in her perturbed state of half-slumber, she spoke of sounds, and of motions, in and about the chamber of the turret, which I concluded had no origin save in the distemper of her fancy, or perhaps in the phantasmagoric influences of the chamber itself. She became at length convalescent—finally well. Yet but a brief period elapsed, ere a second more violent disorder again threw her upon a bed of suffering; and from this attack her frame, at all times feeble, never altogether recovered. Her illnesses were, after this epoch, of alarming character, and of more alarming recurrence, defying alike the knowledge and the great exertions of her physicians. With the increase of the chronic disease which had thus, apparently, taken too sure hold upon her constitution to be eradicated by human means, I could not fail to observe a similar increase in the nervous irritation of her temperament, and in her excitability by trivial causes of fear. She spoke again, and now more frequently and pertinaciously, of the sounds—of the slight sounds—and of the unusual motions among the tapestries, to which she had formerly alluded.

One night, near the closing in of September, she pressed this distressing subject with more than usual emphasis upon my attention. She had just awakened from an unquiet slumber, and I had been watching, with feelings half of anxiety, half of vague terror, the workings of her emaciated countenance. I sat by the side of her ebony bed, upon one of the ottomans of India. She partly arose, and spoke, in an earnest low whisper, of sounds which she *then* heard, but which I could not hear—of motions which she *then* saw, but which I could not perceive. The wind was rushing hurriedly behind the tapestries, and I wished to show her (what, let me confess it, I could not *all* believe) that those almost inarticulate breathings, and those very gentle variations of the figures upon the wall, were but the natural effects of that customary rushing of the wind. But a deadly pallor, overspreading her face, had proved to me that my exertions to reassure her would be fruitless. She appeared to be fainting, and no attendants were within call. I remembered where was deposited a decanter of light wine which had been ordered by her physicians, and hastened across the chamber to procure it. But, as I stepped beneath the light of the censer, two circumstances of a startling nature attracted my attention. I had felt that some palpable although invisible object had passed lightly by my person; and I saw that there lay upon the golden carpet, in the very middle of the rich lustre thrown from the censer, a shadow—a faint, indefinite shadow of angelic aspect—such as might be fancied for the shadow of a shade. But I was wild with the excitement of an immoderate dose of opium, and heeded these things but little, nor spoke of them to Rowena. Having found the wine, I recrossed the chamber, and poured out a goblet-ful, which I held to the lips of the fainting lady. She had now partially recovered, however, and took the vessel herself, while I sank upon an ottoman near me, with my eyes fastened upon her person. It was then that I became distinctly aware of a gentle foot-fall upon the carpet, and near the couch; and in a second thereafter, as Rowena was in the act of raising the wine to her lips, I saw, or may have dreamed that I saw, fall within the goblet, as if from some invisible spring in the atmosphere of the room, three or four large drops of a brilliant and ruby colored fluid.[16] If this I saw—not so Rowena. She swallowed the wine unhesitatingly, and I forbore to speak to her of a circumstance which must, after all, I considered, have been but the suggestion of a vivid imagination, rendered morbidly active by the terror of the lady, by the opium, and by the hour.

Yet I cannot conceal it from my own perception that, immediately subsequent to the fall of the ruby-drops, a rapid change for the worse took place in the disorder of my wife; so that, on the third subsequent night, the hands of her menials prepared her for the tomb, and on the fourth, I sat alone, with her shrouded body, in that fantastic chamber which had received her as my bride.—Wild visions, opium-engendered, flitted, shadow-like, before me. I gazed with unquiet eye upon the sarcophagi in the angles of the room, upon the varying figures of the drapery, and upon the writhing of the parti-colored fires in the censer overhead. My eyes then fell, as I called to mind the circumstances of a former night, to the spot beneath the glare of the censer where I had seen the faint traces of the shadow. It was there, however, no longer; and breathing with greater freedom, I turned my glances to the pallid and rigid figure upon the bed. Then rushed upon me a thousand memories of Ligeia—and then came back upon my heart, with the turbulent violence of a flood, the whole of that unutterable wo with which I had regarded *her* thus enshrouded. The night waned; and still, with a bosom full of bitter thoughts of the one only and supremely beloved, I remained gazing upon the body of Rowena.

It might have been midnight, or perhaps earlier, or later, for I had taken no note of time, when a sob, low, gentle, but very distinct, startled me from my revery.—I *felt* that it came from the bed of ebony—the bed of death. I listened in an agony of superstitious terror—but there was no repetition of the sound. I strained my vision to detect any motion in the corpse—but there was not the slightest perceptible. Yet I could not have been deceived. I *had* heard the noise, however faint, and my soul was awakened within me. I resolutely and perseveringly kept my attention riveted upon the body. Many minutes elapsed before any circumstance occurred tending to throw light upon the mystery. At length it became evident that a slight, a very feeble, and barely noticeable tinge of color had flushed up within the cheeks, and along the sunken small veins of the eyelids. Through a species of unutterable horror and awe, for which the language of mortality has no sufficiently energetic expression, I felt my heart cease to beat, my limbs grow rigid where I sat. Yet a sense of duty finally operated to restore my self-possession. I could no longer doubt that we had been precipitate in our preparations—that Rowena still lived. It was necessary that some immediate exertion be made; yet the turret was altogether apart from the portion of the abbey tenanted by the servants—there were none within call—I had no means of summoning them to my aid without leaving the room for many minutes—and this I could not venture to do. I therefore struggled alone in my endeavors to call back the spirit still hovering. In a short period it was certain, however, that a relapse had taken place; the color disappeared from both eyelid and cheek, leaving a wanness even more than that of marble; the lips became doubly shrivelled and pinched up in the ghastly expression of death; a repulsive clamminess and coldness overspread rapidly

[16]T.O. Mabbott suggests that the fluid is Ligeia's spirit made physical and not poison as many believe. Others associate it with blood.

the surface of the body; and all the usual rigorous stiffness immediately supervened. I fell back with a shudder upon the couch from which I had been so startlingly aroused, and again gave myself up to passionate waking visions of Ligeia.

An hour thus elapsed when (could it be possible?) I was a second time aware of some vague sound issuing from the region of the bed. I listened—in extremity of horror. The sound came again—it was a sigh. Rushing to the corpse, I saw—distinctly saw—a tremor upon the lips. In a minute afterward they relaxed, disclosing a bright line of the pearly teeth. Amazement now struggled in my bosom with the profound awe which had hitherto reigned there alone. I felt that my vision grew dim, that my reason wandered; and it was only by a violent effort that I at length succeeded in nerving myself to the task which duty thus once more had pointed out. There was now a partial glow upon the forehead and upon the cheek and throat; a perceptible warmth pervaded the whole frame; there was even a slight pulsation at the heart. The lady *lived;* and with redoubled ardor I betook myself to the task of restoration. I chafed and bathed the temples and the hands, and used every exertion which experience, and no little medical reading, could suggest. But in vain. Suddenly, the color fled, the pulsation ceased, the lips resumed the expression of the dead, and, in an instant afterward, the whole body took upon itself the icy chilliness, the livid hue, the intense rigidity, the sunken outline, and all the loathsome peculiarities of that which has been, for many days, a tenant of the tomb.

And again I sunk into visions of Ligeia—and again, (what marvel that I shudder while I write?) *again* there reached my ears a low sob from the region of the ebony bed. But why shall I minutely detail the unspeakable horrors of that night? Why shall I pause to relate how, time after time, until near the period of the gray dawn, this hideous drama of revification was repeated; how each terrific relapse was only into a sterner and apparently more irredeemable death; how each agony wore the aspect of a struggle with some invisible foe; and how each struggle was succeeded by I know not what of wild change in the personal appearance of the corpse? Let me hurry to a conclusion.

The greater part of the fearful night had worn away, and she who had been dead, once again stirred—and now more vigorously than hitherto, although arousing from a dissolution more appalling in its utter hopelessness than any. I had long ceased to struggle or to move, and remained sitting rigidly upon the ottoman, a helpless prey to a whirl of violent emotions, of which extreme awe was perhaps the least terrible, the least consuming. The corpse, I repeat, stirred, and now more vigorously than before. The hues of life flushed up with unwonted energy into the countenance—the limbs relaxed—and, save that the eyelids were yet pressed heavily together, and that the bandages and draperies of the grave still imparted their charnel character to the figure, I might have dreamed that Rowena had indeed shaken off, utterly, the fetters of Death. But if this idea was not, even then, altogether adopted, I could at least doubt no longer, when, arising from the bed, tottering, with feeble steps, with closed eyes, and with the manner of one bewildered in a dream, the thing that was enshrouded advanced boldly and palpably into the middle of the apartment.

I trembled not—I stirred not—for a crowd of unutterable fancies connected with the air, the stature, the demeanor of the figure, rushing hurriedly through my brain, had paralyzed—had chilled me into stone. I stirred not—but gazed upon the apparition. There was a mad disorder in my thoughts—a tumult unappeasable.

Could it, indeed, be the *living* Rowena who confronted me? Could it indeed be Rowena *at all*—the fair-haired, the blue-eyed Lady Rowena Trevanion of Tremaine? Why, *why* should I doubt it? The bandage lay heavily about the mouth—but then might it not be the mouth of the breathing Lady of Tremaine? And the cheeks—there were the roses as in her noon of life—yes, these might indeed be the fair cheeks of the living Lady of Tremaine. And the chin, with its dimples, as in health, might it not be hers?—but *had she then grown taller since her malady?* What inexpressible madness seized me with that thought? One bound, and I had reached her feet! Shrinking from my touch, she let fall from her head, unloosened, the ghastly cerements which had confined it, and there streamed forth, into the rushing atmosphere of the chamber, huge masses of long and dishevelled hair; *it was blacker than the raven wings of the midnight!* And now slowly opened *the eyes* of the figure which stood before me. "Here then, at least," I shrieked aloud, "can I never—can I never be mistaken—these are the full, and the black, and the wild eyes—of my lost love—of the lady—of the LADY LIGEIA."

1838

The Fall of the House of Usher

Son coeur est un luth suspendu;
Sitôt qu'on le touche il résonne.[1]
—DE BÉRANGER

During the whole of a dull, dark, and soundless day in the autumn of the year, when the clouds hung oppressively low in the heavens, I had been passing alone, on horseback, through a singularly dreary tract of country, and at length found myself, as the shades of the evening drew on, within view of the melancholy House of Usher. I know not how it was—but, with the first glimpse of the building, a sense of insufferable gloom pervaded my spirit. I say insufferable; for the feeling was unrelieved by any of that half-pleasurable, because poetic, sentiment, with which the mind usually receives even the sternest natural images of the desolate or terrible. I looked upon the scene before me—upon the mere house, and the simple landscape features of the domain—upon the bleak walls—upon the vacant eye-like windows—upon a few rank sedges—and upon a few white trunks of decayed trees—with an utter depression of soul which I can compare to no earthly sensation more properly than to the after-dream of the reveller upon opium—the bitter lapse into every-day life—the hideous dropping off of the veil. There was an iciness, a sinking, a sickening of the heart—an unredeemed dreariness of thought which no goading of the imagination could torture into aught of the sublime. What was it—I paused to think—what was

[1]Originally published in *Burton's Gentleman's Magazine* for Sept., 1839. The headnote, from the French poet Pierre-Jean de Béranger, translates, "His heart is a lute suspended; when touched, it resounds."

it that so unnerved me in the contemplation of the House of Usher? It was a mystery all insoluble; nor could I grapple with the shadowy fancies that crowded upon me as I pondered. I was forced to fall back upon the unsatisfactory conclusion, that while, beyond doubt, there *are* combinations of very simple natural objects which have the power of thus affecting us, still the analysis of this power lies among considerations beyond our depth. It was possible, I reflected, that a mere different arrangement of the particulars of the scene, of the details of the picture, would be sufficient to modify, or perhaps to annihilate its capacity for sorrowful impression; and, acting upon this idea, I reined my horse to the precipitous brink of a black and lurid tarn that lay in unruffled lustre by the dwelling, and gazed down—but with a shudder even more thrilling than before—upon the remodelled and inverted images of the gray sedge, and the ghastly tree-stems, and the vacant and eye-like windows.[2]

Nevertheless, in this mansion of gloom I now proposed to myself a sojourn of some weeks. Its proprietor, Roderick Usher, had been one of my boon companions in boyhood; but many years had elapsed since our last meeting. A letter, however, had lately reached me in a distant part of the country—a letter from him—which, in its wildly importunate nature, had admitted of no other than a personal reply. The MS. gave evidence of nervous agitation. The writer spoke of acute bodily illness—of a mental disorder which oppressed him—and of an earnest desire to see me, as his best, and indeed his only personal friend, with a view of attempting, by the cheerfulness of my society, some alleviation of his malady. It was the manner in which all this, and much more, was said—it was the apparent *heart* that went with his request—which allowed me no room for hesitation; and I accordingly obeyed forthwith what I still considered a very singular summons.

Although, as boys, we had been even intimate associates, yet I really knew little of my friend. His reserve had been always excessive and habitual. I was aware, however, that his very ancient family had been noted, time out of mind, for a peculiar sensibility of temperament, displaying itself, through long ages, in many works of exalted art, and manifested, of late, in repeated deeds of munificent yet unobtrusive charity, as well as in a passionate devotion to the intricacies, perhaps even more than to the orthodox and easily recognizable beauties, of musical science. I had learned, too, the very remarkable fact, that the stem of the Usher race, all time-honoured as it was, had put forth, at no period, any enduring branch; in other words, that the entire family lay in the direct line of descent, and had always, with very trifling and very temporary variation, so lain. It was this deficiency, I considered, while running over in thought the perfect keeping of the character of the premises with the accredited character of the people, and while speculating upon the possible influence which the one, in the long lapse of centuries, might have exercised upon the other—it was this deficiency, perhaps of collateral issue, and the consequent undeviating transmission, from sire to son, of the patrimony with the name, which had, at length, so identified the two as to merge the original title of the estate in the quaint and equivocal appel-

[2]The image of the house reflected in the water begins the pattern of occult correspondences which pervades the story throughout. The eye-like windows suggest the concept of the house as a human head which culminates in the allegorical poem "The Haunted Palace," located near the center of the story.

lation of the "House of Usher"—an appellation which seemed to include, in the minds of the peasantry who used it, both the family and the family mansion.

I have said that the sole effect of my somewhat childish experiment—that of looking down within the tarn—had been to deepen the first singular impression. There can be no doubt that the consciousness of the rapid increase of my superstition—for why should I not so term it?—served mainly to accelerate the increase itself. Such, I have long known, is the paradoxical law of all sentiments having terror as a basis. And it might have been for this reason only, that, when I again uplifted my eyes to the house itself, from its image in the pool, there grew in my mind a strange fancy—a fancy so ridiculous, indeed, that I but mention it to show the vivid force of the sensations which oppressed me. I had so worked upon my imagination as really to believe that about the whole mansion and domain there hung an atmosphere peculiar to themselves and their immediate vicinity—an atmosphere which had no affinity with the air of heaven, but which had reeked up from the decayed trees, and the gray wall, and the silent tarn—a pestilent and mystic vapour, dull, sluggish, faintly discernible, and leaden-hued.

Shaking off from my spirit what *must* have been a dream, I scanned more narrowly the real aspect of the building. Its principal feature seemed to be that of an excessive antiquity. The discoloration of ages had been great. Minute fungi overspread the whole exterior, hanging in a fine tangled web-work from the eaves. Yet all this was apart from an extraordinary dilapidation. No portion of the masonry had fallen; and there appeared to be a wild inconsistency between its still perfect adaptation of parts, and the crumbling condition of the individual stones. In this there was much that reminded me of the specious totality of old woodwork which has rotted for long years in some neglected vault, with no disturbance from the breath of the external air. Beyond this indication of extensive decay, however, the fabric gave little token of instability. Perhaps the eye of a scrutinizing observer might have discovered a barely perceptible fissure, which, extending from the roof of the building in front, made its way down the wall in a zigzag direction, until it became lost in the sullen waters of the tarn.

Noticing these things, I rode over a short causeway to the house. A servant in waiting took my horse, and I entered the Gothic archway of the hall. A valet, of stealthy step, thence conducted me, in silence, through many dark and intricate passages in my progress to the *studio* of his master. Much that I encountered on the way contributed, I know not how, to heighten the vague sentiments of which I have already spoken. While the objects around me—while the carvings of the ceilings, the sombre tapestries of the walls, the ebon blackness of the floors, and the phantasmagoric armorial trophies which rattled as I strode, were but matters to which, or to such as which, I had been accustomed from my infancy—while I hesitated not to acknowledge how familiar was all this—I still wondered to find how unfamiliar were the fancies which ordinary images were stirring up. On one of the staircases, I met the physician of the family. His countenance, I thought, wore a mingled expression of low cunning and perplexity. He accosted me with trepidation and passed on. The valet now threw open a door and ushered me into the presence of his master.

The room in which I found myself was very large and lofty. The windows were long, narrow, and pointed, and at so vast a distance from the black oaken floor as to be altogether inaccessible from within. Feeble gleams of encrimsoned light made their way through the trellissed panes, and served to render sufficiently distinct the more prominent objects around; the eye, however, struggled in vain to reach the remoter angles of the chamber, or the recesses of the vaulted and fretted ceiling. Dark draperies hung upon the walls. The general furniture was profuse, comfortless, antique, and tattered. Many books and musical instruments lay scattered about, but failed to give any vitality to the scene. I felt that I breathed an atmosphere of sorrow. An air of stern, deep, and irredeemable gloom hung over and pervaded all.

Upon my entrance, Usher arose from a sofa on which he had been lying at full length, and greeted me with a vivacious warmth which had much in it, I at first thought of an overdone cordiality—of the constrained effort of the *ennuyé*[3] man of the world. A glance, however, at his countenance convinced me of his perfect sincerity. We sat down; and for some moments, while he spoke not, I gazed upon him with a feeling half of pity, half of awe. Surely, man had never before so terribly altered, in so brief a period, as had Roderick Usher! It was with difficulty that I could bring myself to admit the identity of the wan being before me with the companion of my early boyhood. Yet the character of his face had been at all times remarkable. A cadaverousness of complexion; an eye large, liquid, and luminous beyond comparison; lips somewhat thin and very pallid, but of a surpassingly beautiful curve; a nose of a delicate Hebrew model, but with a breadth of nostril unusual in similar formations; a finely moulded chin, speaking, in its want of prominence, of a want of moral energy; hair of a more than web-like softness and tenuity; these features, with an inordinate expansion above the regions of the temple, made up altogether a countenance not easily to be forgotten. And now in the mere exaggeration of the prevailing character of these features, and of the expression they were wont to convey, lay so much of change that I doubted to whom I spoke. The now ghastly pallor of the skin, and the now miraculous lustre of the eye, above all things startled and even awed me. The silken hair, too, had been suffered to grow all unheeded, and as, in its wild gossamer texture, it floated rather than fell about the face, I could not, even with effort, connect its Arabesque[4] expression with any idea of simple humanity.

In the manner of my friend I was at once struck with an incoherence—an inconsistency; and I soon found this to arise from a series of feeble and futile struggles to overcome an habitual trepidancy—an excessive nervous agitation. For something of this nature I had indeed been prepared, no less by his letter, than by reminiscences of certain boyish traits, and by conclusions deducted from his peculiar physical conformation and temperament. His action was alternately vivacious and sullen. His voice varied rapidly from a tremulous indecision (when the animal spirits seemed utterly in abeyance) to that species of energetic concision—that abrupt, weighty, unhurried, and hollow-sounding enunciation—that leaden, self-balanced, and perfectly modulated guttural utterance, which may be observed in the lost drunkard, or the irreclaimable eater of opium, during the periods of his most intense excitement.

It was thus that he spoke of the object of my visit, of his earnest desire to see me, and of the solace he expected me to afford him. He entered, at some length, into what he conceived to be the nature of his malady. It was, he said, a constitutional and a family evil, and one for which he despaired to find a remedy—a mere nervous af-

[3]French for bored.
[4]Poe uses the word Arabesque to describe some of his fictional tales. Here it means unfamiliar, exotic.

fection, he immediately added, which would undoubtedly soon pass off. It displayed itself in a host of unnatural sensations. Some of these, as he detailed them, interested and bewildered me; although, perhaps, the terms and the general manner of their narration had their weight. He suffered much from a morbid acuteness of the senses; the most insipid food was alone endurable; he could wear only garments of certain texture; the odours of all flowers were oppressive; his eyes were tortured by even a faint light; and there were but peculiar sounds, and these from stringed instruments, which did not inspire him with horror.

To an anomalous species of terror I found him a bounden slave. "I shall perish," said he, "I *must* perish in this deplorable folly. Thus, thus, and not otherwise, shall I be lost. I dread the events of the future, not in themselves, but in their results. I shudder at the thought of any, even the most trivial, incident, which may operate upon this intolerable agitation of soul. I have, indeed, no abhorrence of danger, except in its absolute effect—in terror. In this unnerved—in this pitiable condition—I feel that the period will sooner or later arrive when I must abandon life and reason together, in some struggle with the grim phantasm, FEAR."[5]

I learned, moreover, at intervals, and through broken and equivocal hints, another singular feature of his mental condition. He was enchained by certain superstitious impressions in regard to the dwelling which he tenanted, and whence, for many years, he had never ventured forth—in regard to an influence whose suppositious force was conveyed in terms too shadowy here to be re-stated—an influence which some peculiarities in the mere form and substance of his family mansion had, by dint of long sufferance, he said, obtained over his spirit—an effect which the *physique* of the gray wall and turrets, and of the dim tarn into which they all looked down, had, at length, brought about upon the *morale* of his existence.

He admitted, however, although with hesitation, that much of the peculiar gloom which thus afflicted him could be traced to a more natural and far more palpable origin—to the severe and long-continued illness—indeed to the evidently approaching dissolution—of a tenderly beloved sister, his sole companion for long years, his last and only relative on earth. "Her decease," he said, with a bitterness which I can never forget, "would leave him (him the hopeless and the frail) the last of the ancient race of the Ushers." While he spoke, the lady Madeline (for so was she called) passed slowly through a remote portion of the apartment, and, without having noticed my presence, disappeared. I regarded her with an utter astonishment not unmingled with dread—and yet I found it impossible to account for such feelings. A sensation of stupor oppressed me, as my eyes followed her retreating steps. When a door, at length, closed upon her, my glance sought instinctively and eagerly the countenance of the brother—but he had buried his face in his hands, and I could only perceive that a far more than ordinary wanness had overspread the emaciated fingers through which trickled many passionate tears.

The disease of the lady Madeline had long baffled the skill of her physicians. A settled apathy, a gradual wasting away of the person, and frequent although transient affections of a partially cataleptical character were the unusual diagnosis. Hitherto she had steadily borne up against the pressure of her malady, and had not betaken

[5]Usher suffers from hyperesthesia, hypochondria, and acute anxiety—all disorders of the nervous system that can result in serious physical symptoms.

herself finally to bed; but on the closing in of the evening of my arrival at the house, she succumbed (as her brother told me at night with inexpressible agitation) to the prostrating power of the destroyer; and I learned that the glimpse I had obtained of her person would thus probably be the last I should obtain—that the lady, at least while living, would be seen by me no more.

For several days ensuing, her name was unmentioned by either Usher or myself: and during this period I was busied in earnest endeavours to alleviate the melancholy of my friend. We painted and read together, or I listened, as if in a dream, to the wild improvisations of his speaking guitar. And thus, as a closer and still closer intimacy admitted me more unreservedly into the recesses of his spirit, the more bitterly did I perceive the futility of all attempt at cheering a mind from which darkness, as if an inherent positive quality, poured forth upon all objects of the moral and physical universe in one unceasing radiation of gloom.

I shall ever bear about me a memory of the many solemn hours I thus spent alone with the master of the House of Usher. Yet I should fail in any attempt to convey an idea of the exact character of the studies, or of the occupations, in which he involved me, or led me the way. An excited and highly distempered ideality threw a sulphureous lustre over all. His long improvised dirges will ring forever in my ears. Among other things, I hold painfully in mind a certain singular perversion and amplification of the wild air of the last waltz of Von Weber.[6] From the paintings over which his elaborate fancy brooded, and which grew, touch by touch, into vagueness at which I shuddered the more thrillingly, because I shuddered knowing not why;—from these paintings (vivid as their images now are before me) I would in vain endeavour to educe more than a small portion which should lie within the compass of merely written words. By the utter simplicity, by the nakedness of his designs, he arrested and overawed attention. If ever mortal painted an idea, that mortal was Roderick Usher. For me at least—in the circumstances then surrounding me—there arose out of the pure abstractions which the hypochondriac contrived to throw upon his canvas, an intensity of intolerable awe, no shadow of which I felt ever yet in the contemplation of the certainly glowing yet too concrete reveries of Fuseli.[7]

One of the phantasmagoric conceptions of my friend, partaking not so rigidly of the spirit of abstraction, may be shadowed forth, although feebly, in words. A small picture presented the interior of an immensely long and rectangular vault or tunnel, with low walls, smooth, white, and without interruption or device. Certain accessory points of the design served well to convey the idea that this excavation lay at an exceeding depth below the surface of the earth. No outlet was observed in any portion of its vast extent, and no torch or other artificial source of light was discernible; yet a flood of intense rays rolled throughout, and bathed the whole in a ghastly and inappropriate splendour.

I have just spoken of that morbid condition of the auditory nerve which rendered all music intolerable to the sufferer, with the exception of certain effects of stringed instruments. It was, perhaps, the narrow limits to which he thus confined himself upon the guitar, which gave birth, in great measure, to the fantastic character of his performances. But the fervid *facility* of his *impromptus* could not be so ac-

[6]A German composer.

[7]A Swiss-English painter who specialized in fantastic scenes with grotesque figures.

counted for. They must have been, and were, in the notes, as well as in the words of his wild fantasias (for he not unfrequently accompanied himself with rhymed verbal improvisations), the result of that intense mental collectedness and concentration to which I have previously alluded as observable only in particular moments of the highest artificial excitement. The words of one of these rhapsodies I have easily remembered. I was, perhaps, the more forcibly impressed with it, as he gave it, because, in the under or mystic current of its meaning, I fancied that I perceived, and for the first time, a full consciousness on the part of Usher, of the tottering of his lofty reason upon her throne. The verses, which were entitled "The Haunted Palace," ran very nearly, if not accurately, thus:

I

In the greenest of our valleys,
  By good angels tenanted,
Once a fair and stately palace—
  Radiant palace—reared its head.
In the monarch Thought's dominion—
  It stood there!
Never seraph spread a pinion
  Over fabric half so fair.

II

Banners yellow, glorious, golden,
  On its roof did float and flow;
(This—all this—was in the olden
  Time long ago)
And every gentle air that dallied,
  In that sweet day,
Along the ramparts plumed and pallid,
  A winged odour went away.

III

Wanderers in that happy valley
  Through two luminous windows saw
Spirits moving musically
  To a lute's well-tunèd law,
Round about a throne where sitting
  (Porphyrogene!)[8]

[8]A word Poe coined from Greek roots meaning "born to the purple"—in other words, royal.

In state his glory well befitting,
The ruler of the realm was seen.

IV

And all with pearl and ruby glowing
Was the fair palace door,
Through which came flowing, flowing, flowing
And sparkling evermore,
A troop of Echoes whose sweet duty
Was but to sing,
In voices of surpassing beauty,
The wit and wisdom of their king.

V

But evil things, in robes of sorrow,
Assailed the monarch's high estate;
(Ah, let us mourn, for never morrow
Shall dawn upon him, desolate!)
And, round about his home, the glory
That blushed and bloomed
Is but a dim-remembered story
Of the old time entombed.

VI

And travellers now within that valley,
Through the red-litten windows see
Vast forms that move fantastically
To a discordant melody;
While, like a rapid ghastly river,
Through the pale door,
A hideous throng rush out forever,
And laugh—but smile no more.

I well remember that suggestions arising from this ballad, led us into a train of thought, wherein there became manifest an opinion of Usher's which I mention not so much on account of its novelty, (for other men have thought thus,) as on account of the pertinacity with which he maintained it. This opinion, in its general form, was that of the sentience of all vegetable things. But, in his disordered fancy, the idea had assumed a more daring character, and trespassed, under certain conditions, upon the kingdom of inorganization. I lack words to express the full extent, or the earnest *abandon* of his persuasion. The belief, however, was connected (as I have previously hinted) with the gray stones of the home of his forefathers. The conditions of the sentience had been here, he imagined, fulfilled in the method of collocation of these stones—in the order of their arrangement, as well as in that of the many *fungi* which overspread them, and of the decayed trees which stood around—above all, in the long undisturbed endurance of this arrangement, and in its reduplication in the still waters of the tarn. Its evidence—the evidence of the sentience—was to be seen, he said (and I here started as he spoke), in the gradual yet certain condensation of an atmosphere of their own about the waters and the walls. The result was discoverable, he added, in that silent yet importunate and terrible influence which for centuries had moulded the destinies of his family, and which made *him* what I now saw him—what he was. Such opinions need no comment, and I will make none.

Our books—the books which, for years, had formed no small portion of the mental existence of the invalid—were, as might be supposed, in strict keeping with his character of phantasm. We pored together over such works as the Ververt et Chartreuse of Gresset; the Belphegor of Machiavelli; the Heaven and Hell of Swedenborg; the Subterranean Voyage of Nicholas Klimm of Holberg; the Chiromancy of Robert Flud, of Jean D'Indaginé, and of De la Chambre; the Journey into the Blue Distance of Tieck; and the City of the Sun of Campanella. One favourite volume was a small octavo edition of the *Directorium Inquisitorum,* by the Dominican Eymeric de Gironne; and there were passages in Pomponius Mela, about the old African Satyrs and Œgipans, over which Usher would sit dreaming for hours. His chief delight, however, was found in the perusal of an exceedingly rare and curious book in quarto Gothic—the manual of a forgotten church—the *Vigiliæ Mortuorum secundum Chorum Ecclesiæ Maguntinæ.*[9]

I could not help thinking of the wild ritual of this work, and of its probable influence upon the hypochondriac, when, one evening, having informed me abruptly that the lady Madeline was no more, he stated his intention of preserving her corpse for a fortnight, (previously to its final interment,) in one of the numerous vaults within the main walls of the building. The worldly reason, however, assigned for this singular proceeding, was one which I did not feel at liberty to dispute. The brother had been led to his resolution (so he told me) by consideration of the unusual character of the malady of the deceased, of certain obtrusive and eager inquiries on the part of her medical men, and of the remote and exposed situation of the burial-ground of the family. I will not deny that when I called to mind the sinister countenance of the person whom I met upon the staircase, on the day of my arrival at the house, I had no desire to oppose what I regarded as at best but a harmless, and by no means an unnatural, precaution.[10]

At the request of Usher, I personally aided him in the arrangements for the temporary entombment. The body having been encoffined, we two alone bore it to its rest. The vault in which we placed it (and which had been so long unopened that our torches, half smothered in its oppressive atmosphere, gave us little opportunity for investigation) was small, damp, and entirely without means of admission for light; lying,

[9]All the books listed deal with pseudo-science, demonism, or persecution. Poe selects the titles carefully to suggest that Usher is devoted to obscure, frightening, and other-worldly works of history and fiction.

[10]Usher is afraid Lady Madeline's body will be dug up for instructional use in some medical college—a practice all too common in Poe's day. There were groups of men called resurrectionists who exhumed bodies for a living.

at great depth, immediately beneath that portion of the building in which was my own sleeping apartment. It had been used, apparently, in remote feudal times, for the worst purposes of a donjon-keep, and, in later days, as a place of deposit for powder, or some other highly combustible substance, as a portion of its floor, and the whole interior of a long archway through which we reached it, were carefully sheathed with copper. The door, of massive iron, had been, also, similarly protected. Its immense weight caused an unusually sharp grating sound, as it moved upon its hinges.

Having deposited our mournful burden upon tressels within this region of horror, we partially turned aside the yet unscrewed lid of the coffin, and looked upon the face of the tenant. A striking similitude between the brother and sister now first arrested my attention; and Usher, divining, perhaps, my thoughts, murmured out some few words from which I learned that the deceased and himself had been twins, and that sympathies of a scarcely intelligible nature had always existed between them. Our glances, however, rested not long upon the dead—for we could not regard her unawed. The disease which had thus entombed the lady in the maturity of youth, had left, as usual in all maladies of a strictly cataleptical character, the mockery of a faint blush upon the bosom and the face, and that suspiciously lingering smile upon the lip which is so terrible in death. We replaced and screwed down the lid, and, having secured the door of iron, made our way, with toil, into the scarcely less gloomy apartments of the upper portion of the house.

And now, some days of bitter grief having elapsed, an observable change came over the features of the mental disorder of my friend. His ordinary manner had vanished. His ordinary occupations were neglected or forgotten. He roamed from chamber to chamber with hurried, unequal, and objectless step. The pallor of his countenance had assumed, if possible, a more ghastly hue—but the luminousness of his eye had utterly gone out. The once occasional huskiness of his tone was heard no more; and a tremulous quaver, as if of extreme terror, habitually characterized his utterance. There were times, indeed, when I thought his unceasingly agitated mind was labouring with some oppressive secret, to divulge which he struggled for the necessary courage. At times, again, I was obliged to resolve all into the mere inexplicable vagaries of madness, for I beheld him gazing upon vacancy for long hours, in an attitude of the profoundest attention, as if listening to some imaginary sound. It was no wonder that his condition terrified—that it infected me. I felt creeping upon me, by slow yet certain degrees, the wild influences of his own fantastic yet impressive superstitions.

It was, especially, upon retiring to bed late in the night of the seventh or eighth day after the placing of the lady Madeline within the donjon, that I experienced the full power of such feelings. Sleep came not near my couch—while the hours waned and waned away. I struggled to reason off the nervousness which had dominion over me. I endeavoured to believe that much, if not all of what I felt, was due to the bewildering influence of the gloomy furniture of the room—of the dark and tattered draperies, which, tortured into motion by the breath of a rising tempest, swayed fitfully to and fro upon the walls, and rustled uneasily about the decorations of the bed. But my efforts were fruitless. An irrepressible tremour gradually pervaded my frame; and, at length, there sat upon my very heart an incubus of utterly causeless alarm. Shaking this off with a gasp and a struggle, I uplifted myself upon the pillows, and, peering earnestly within the intense darkness of the chamber, hearkened—I know not why, except that an instinctive spirit prompted me—to certain low and indefinite sounds which came, through the pauses of the storm, at long intervals, I knew not whence. Overpowered by an intense sentiment of horror, unaccountable yet unendurable, I threw on my clothes with haste, (for I felt that I should sleep no more during the night,) and endeavoured to arouse myself from the pitiable condition into which I had fallen, by pacing rapidly to and fro through the apartment.

I had taken but few turns in this manner, when a light step on an adjoining staircase arrested my attention. I presently recognised it as that of Usher. In an instant afterward he rapped, with a gentle touch, at my door, and entered, bearing a lamp. His countenance was, as usual, cadaverously wan—but, moreover, there was a species of mad hilarity in his eyes—an evidently restrained *hysteria* in his whole demeanour. His air appalled me—but anything was preferable to the solitude which I had so long endured, and I even welcomed his presence as a relief.

"And you have not seen it?" he said abruptly, after having stared about him for some moments in silence—"you have not then seen it?—but, stay! you shall." Thus speaking, and having carefully shaded his lamp, he hurried to one of the casements, and threw it freely open to the storm.

The impetuous fury of the entering gust nearly lifted us from our feet. It was, indeed, a tempestuous yet sternly beautiful night, and one wildly singular in its terror and its beauty. A whirlwind had apparently collected its force in our vicinity; for there were frequent and violent alterations in the direction of the wind; and the exceeding density of the clouds (which hung so low as to press upon the turrets of the house) did not prevent our perceiving the life-like velocity with which they flew careering from all points against each other, without passing away into the distance. I say that even their exceeding density did not prevent our perceiving this—yet we had no glimpse of the moon or stars—nor was there any flashing forth of the lightning. But the under surfaces of the huge masses of agitated vapour, as well as all terrestrial objects immediately around us, were glowing in the unnatural light of a faintly luminous and distinctly visible gaseous exhalation which hung about and enshrouded the mansion.

"You must not—you shall not behold this!" said I, shudderingly, to Usher, as I led him, with a gentle violence, from the window to a seat. "These appearances, which bewilder you, are merely electrical phenomena not uncommon—or it may be that they have their ghastly origin in the rank miasma of the tarn. Let us close this casement;—the air is chilling and dangerous to your frame. Here is one of your favourite romances. I will read, and you shall listen;—and so we will pass away this terrible night together."

The antique volume which I had taken up was the "Mad Trist" of Sir Launcelot Canning;[11] but I had called it a favourite of Usher's more in sad jest than in earnest; for, in truth, there is little in its uncouth and unimaginative prolixity which could have had interest for the lofty and spiritual ideality of my friend. It was, however, the only book immediately at hand; and I indulged a vague hope that the excitement which now agitated the hypochondriac, might find relief (for the history of mental

[11]Scholars have failed to find Canning's name among lists of real authors, although Poe used the reference on more than one occasion.

disorder is full of similar anomalies) even in the extremeness of the folly which I could read. Could I have judged, indeed, by the wild overstrained air of vivacity with which he hearkened, or apparently hearkened, to the words of the tale, I might well have congratulated myself upon the success of my design.

I had arrived at that well-known portion of the story where Ethelred, the hero of the Trist, having sought in vain for peaceable admission into the dwelling of the hermit, proceeds to make good an entrance by force. Here, it will be remembered, the words of the narrative run thus:[12]

"And Ethelred, who was by nature of a doughty heart, and who was now mighty withal, on account of the powerfulness of the wine which he had drunken, waited no longer to hold parley with the hermit, who, in sooth, was of an obstinate and maliceful turn, but, feeling the rain upon his shoulders, and fearing the rising of the tempest, uplifted his mace outright, and, with blows, made quickly room in the plankings of the door for his gauntleted hand; and now pulling therewith sturdily, he so cracked, and ripped, and tore all asunder, that the noise of the dry and hollow-sounding wood alarmed and reverberated throughout the forest."

At the termination of this sentence I started and, for a moment, paused; for it appeared to me (although I at once concluded that my excited fancy had deceived me)—it appeared to me that, from some very remote portion of the mansion, there came, indistinctly, to my ears, what might have been, in its exact similarity of character, the echo (but a stifled and dull one certainly) of the very cracking and ripping sound which Sir Launcelot had so particularly described. It was, beyond doubt, the coincidence alone which had arrested my attention; for, amid the rattling of the sashes of the casements, and the ordinary commingled noises of the still increasing storm, the sound, in itself, had nothing, surely, which should have interested or disturbed me. I continued the story:

"But the good champion Ethelred, now entering within the door, was sore enraged and amazed to perceive no signal of the maliceful hermit; but, in the stead thereof, a dragon of a scaly and prodigious demeanour, and of a fiery tongue, which sate in guard before a palace of gold, with a floor of silver; and upon the wall there hung a shield of shining brass with this legend enwritten—

> Who entereth herein, a conqueror hath bin;
> Who slayeth the dragon, the shield he shall win.

And Ethelred uplifted his mace, and struck upon the head of the dragon, which fell before him, and gave up his pesty breath, with a shriek so horrid and harsh, and withal so piercing, that Ethelred had fain to close his ears with his hands against the dreadful noise of it, the like whereof was never before heard."

Here again I paused abruptly, and now with a feeling of wild amazement—for there could be no doubt whatever that, in this instance, I did actually hear (although from what direction it proceeded I found it impossible to say) a low and apparently distant, but harsh, protracted, and most unusual screaming or grating sound—the

[12]Poe probably invented the story about Ethelred and the hermit-turned-dragon, details of which correspond to what is going on belowdecks with Lady Madeline.

exact counterpart of what my fancy had already conjured up for the dragon's unnatural shriek as described by the romancer.

Oppressed, as I certainly was, upon the occurrence of the second and most extraordinary coincidence, by a thousand conflicting sensations, in which wonder and extreme terror were predominant, I still retained sufficient presence of mind to avoid exciting, by any observation, the sensitive nervousness of my companion. I was by no means certain that he had noticed the sounds in question; although, assuredly, a strange alteration had, during the last few minutes, taken place in his demeanour. From a position fronting my own, he had gradually brought round his chair, so as to sit with his face to the door of the chamber; and thus I could but partially perceive his features, although I saw that his lips trembled as if he were murmuring inaudibly. His head had dropped upon his breast—yet I knew that he was not asleep, from the wide and rigid opening of the eye as I caught a glance of it in profile. The motion of his body, too, was at variance with this idea—for he rocked from side to side with a gentle yet constant and uniform sway. Having rapidly taken notice of all this, I resumed the narrative of Sir Launcelot, which thus proceeded:

"And now, the champion, having escaped from the terrible fury of the dragon, bethinking himself of the brazen shield, and of the breaking up of the enchantment which was upon it, removed the carcass from out of the way before him, and approached valorously over the silver pavement of the castle to where the shield was upon the wall; which in sooth tarried not for his full coming, but fell down at his feet upon the silver floor, with a mighty great and terrible ringing sound."

No sooner had these syllables passed my lips, than—as if a shield of brass had indeed, at the moment, fallen heavily upon a floor of silver—I became aware of a distinct, hollow, metallic, and clangorous, yet apparently muffled reverberation. Completely unnerved, I leaped to my feet; but the measured rocking movement of Usher was undisturbed. I rushed to the chair in which he sat. His eyes were bent fixedly before him, and throughout his whole countenance there reigned a stony rigidity. But, as I placed my hand upon his shoulder, there came a strong shudder over his whole person; a sickly smile quivered about his lips; and I saw that he spoke in a low, hurried, and gibbering murmur, as if unconscious of my presence. Bending closely over him, I at length drank in the hideous import of his words.

"Not hear it?—yes, I hear it, and *have* heard it. Long—long—long—many minutes, many hours, many days, have I heard it—yet I dared not—oh, pity me, miserable wretch that I am!—I dared not—I *dared* not speak! *We have put her living in the tomb!* Said I not that my senses were acute? I *now* tell you that I heard her first feeble movements in the hollow coffin. I heard them—many, many days ago—yet I dared not—I *dared not speak!* And now—to-night—Ethelred—ha! ha!—the breaking of the hermit's door, and the death-cry of the dragon, and the clangour of the shield!—say, rather, the rending of her coffin, and the grating of the iron hinges of her prison, and her struggles within the coppered archway of the vault! Oh whither shall I fly? Will she not be here anon? Is she not hurrying to upbraid me for my haste? Have I not heard her footsteps on the stair? Do I not distinguish that heavy and horrible beating of her heart? MADMAN!"—here he sprang furiously to his feet, and shrieked out his syllables, as if in the effort he were giving up his soul—"MADMAN! I TELL YOU THAT SHE NOW STANDS WITHOUT THE DOOR!"

As if in the superhuman energy of his utterance there had been found the potency of a spell—the huge antique panels to which the speaker pointed threw slowly back, upon the instant, their ponderous and ebony jaws. It was the work of the rushing gust—but then without those doors there DID stand the lofty and enshrouded figure of the lady Madeline of Usher. There was blood upon her white robes, and the evidence of some bitter struggle upon every portion of her emaciated frame. For a moment she remained trembling and reeling to and fro upon the threshold, then, with a low moaning cry, fell heavily inward upon the person of her brother, and in her violent and now final death-agonies, bore him to the floor a corpse, and a victim to the terrors he had anticipated.

From that chamber, and from that mansion, I fled aghast. The storm was still abroad in all its wrath as I found myself crossing the old causeway. Suddenly there shot along the path a wild light, and I turned to see whence a gleam so unusual could have issued; for the vast house and its shadows were alone behind me. The radiance was that of the full, setting, and blood-red moon, which now shone vividly through that once barely discernible fissure, of which I have before spoken as extending from the roof of the building, in a zigzag direction, to the base. While I gazed, this fissure rapidly widened—there came a fierce breath of the whirlwind—the entire orb of the satellite burst at once upon my sight—my brain reeled as I saw the mighty walls rushing asunder—there was a long tumultuous shouting sound like the voice of a thousand waters—and the deep and dank tarn at my feet closed sullenly and silently over the fragments of the "HOUSE OF USHER."

1839

Eleonora

Sub conservatione formæ specificæ salva anima.

—RAYMOND LULLY[1]

I am come of a race noted for vigor of fancy and ardor of passion. Men have called me mad; but the question is not yet settled, whether madness is or is not the loftiest intelligence—whether much that is glorious—whether all that is profound—does not spring from disease of thought—from *moods* of mind exalted at the expense of the general intellect. They who dream by day are cognizant of many things which escape those who dream only by night. In their grey visions they obtain glimpses of eternity, and thrill, in awaking, to find that they have been upon the verge of the great secret. In snatches, they learn something of the wisdom which is of good, and more of the mere knowledge which is of evil. They penetrate, however rudderless or compassless, into the vast ocean of the "light ineffable" and again, like the adven-

[1]Poe's headnote is taken from Victor Hugo, who quoted it in one of his novels. The original author was Ramon Llull, a thirteenth-century philosopher. The quotation translates: "As long as the specific form of a thing prevails, the spirit is safe." "Eleonora" first appeared in a number of periodicals and annuals for Fall, 1841.

turers of the Nubian geographer, "*agressi sunt mare tenebrarum, quid in eo esset exploraturi.*"[2]

We will say, then, that I am mad. I grant, at least, that there are two distinct conditions of my mental existence—the condition of a lucid reason, not to be disputed, and belonging to the memory of events forming the first epoch of my life—and a condition of shadow and doubt, appertaining to the present, and to the recollection of what constitutes the second great era of my being. Therefore, what I shall tell of the earlier period, believe; and to what I may relate of the later time, give only such credit as may seem due; or doubt it altogether; or, if doubt it ye cannot, then play unto its riddle the Oedipus.[3]

She whom I loved in youth, and of whom I now pen calmly and distinctly these remembrances, was the sole daughter of the only sister of my mother long departed. Eleonora was the name of my cousin. We had always dwelled together, beneath a tropical sun, in the Valley of the Many-Colored Grass. No unguided footstep ever came upon that vale; for it lay far away up among a range of giant hills that hung beetling around about it, shutting out the sunlight from its sweetest recesses. No path was trodden in its vicinity; and, to reach our happy home, there was need of putting back, with force, the foliage of many thousands of forest trees, and of crushing to death the glories of many millions of fragrant flowers. Thus it was that we lived all alone, knowing nothing of the world without the valley,—I, and my cousin, and her mother.

From the dim regions beyond the mountains at the upper end of our encircled domain, there crept out a narrow and deep river, brighter than all save the eyes of Eleonora; and, winding stealthily about in mazy courses, it passed away, at length, through a shadowy gorge, among hills still dimmer than those whence it had issued. We called it the "River of Silence"; for there seemed to be a hushing influence in its flow. No murmur arose from its bed, and so gently it wandered along, that the pearly pebbles upon which we loved to gaze, far down within its bosom, stirred not at all, but lay in a motionless content, each in its own old station, shining on gloriously forever.

The margin of the river, and of the many dazzling rivulets that glided, through devious ways, into its channel, as well as the spaces that extended from the margins away down into the depths of the streams until they reached the bed of pebbles at the bottom,—these spots, not less than the whole surface of the valley, from the river to the mountains that girdled it in, were carpeted all by a soft green grass, thick, short, perfectly even, and vanilla-perfumed, but so besprinkled throughout with the yellow buttercup, the white daisy, the purple violet, and the ruby-red asphodel, that

[2]Poe's reference to the Nubian geographer is taken from Jacob Bryant's *Mythology,* a popular commentary of the time, which says that the Arab chronicler calls the Atlantic Ocean the "Mare Tenebrarum" (the sea of darkness). The quotation as a whole translates "They ventured into the sea of Darkness in order to explore what it might contain" (Stuart and Susan Levine). The entire first paragraph of "Eleonora" is a capsule statement of Poe's mystical epistemology, essential for an understanding of his influence on French poets and Surrealist painters.

[3]Poe is asking readers to solve the riddle of the Sphinx. In Greek mythology, Oedipus answered the question posed by the Sphinx: what walks on four legs, then two legs, and finally three legs? The answer is man.

its exceeding beauty spoke to our hearts, in loud tones, of the love and of the glory of God.

And, here and there, in groves about this grass, like wildernesses of dreams, sprang up fantastic trees, whose tall slender stems stood not upright, but slanted gracefully towards the light that peered at noon-day into the centre of the valley. Their bark was speckled with the vivid alternate splendor of ebony and silver, and was smoother than all save the cheeks of Eleonora; so that but for the brilliant green of the huge leaves that spread from their summits in long tremulous lines, dallying with the Zephyrs, one might have fancied them giant serpents of Syria doing homage to their Sovereign the Sun.

Hand in hand about this valley, for fifteen years, roamed I with Eleonora before Love entered within our hearts. It was one evening at the close of the third lustrum[4] of her life, and of the fourth of my own, that we sat, locked in each other's embrace, beneath the serpent-like trees, and looked down within the waters of the River of Silence at our images therein. We spoke no words during the rest of that sweet day; and our words even upon the morrow were tremulous and few. We had drawn the god Eros from that wave, and now we felt that he had enkindled within us the fiery souls of our forefathers. The passions which had for centuries distinguished our race, came thronging with the fancies for which they had been equally noted, and together breathed a delirious bliss over the Valley of the Many-Colored Grass. A change fell upon all things. Strange brilliant flowers, star-shaped, burst out upon the trees where no flowers had been known before. The tints of the green carpet deepened; and when, one by one, the white daisies shrank away, there sprang up, in place of them, ten by ten of the ruby-red asphodel. And life arose in our paths; for the tall flamingo, hitherto unseen, with all gay glowing birds, flaunted his scarlet plumage before us. The golden and silver fish haunted the river, out of the bosom of which issued, little by little, a murmur that swelled, at length, into a lulling melody more divine than that of the harp of Æolus[5]—sweeter than all save the voice of Eleonora. And now, too, a voluminous cloud, which we had long watched in the regions of Hesper,[6] floated out thence, all gorgeous in crimson and gold, and settling in peace above us, sank, day by day, lower and lower, until its edges rested upon the tops of the mountains, turning all their dimness into magnificence, and shutting us up, as if forever, within a magic prison-house of grandeur and of glory.

The loveliness of Eleonora was that of the Seraphim; but she was a maiden artless and innocent as the brief life she had led among the flowers. No guile disguised the fervor of love which animated her heart, and she examined with me its inmost recesses as we walked together in the Valley of the Many-Colored Grass, and discoursed of the mighty changes which had lately taken place therein.

At length, having spoken one day, in tears, of the last sad change which must befall Humanity, she thenceforward dwelt only upon this one sorrowful theme, interweaving it into all our converse, as, in the songs of the bard of Schiraz,[7] the same images are found occurring, again and again, in every impressive variation of phrase.

[4]Five years. The term, one of Poe's favorites, exemplifies his "literary" style.
[5]Greek God of the winds.
[6]The evening star, usually the planet Venus.
[7]Poe's reference to Schiraz is probably an indirect allusion to Saadi, a twelfth century Persian poet born in Shiraz.

She had seen that the finger of Death was upon her bosom—that, like the ephemeron,[8] she had been made perfect in loveliness only to die; but the terrors of the grave, to her, lay solely in a consideration which she revealed to me, one evening at twilight, by the banks of the River of Silence. She grieved to think that, having entombed her in the Valley of the Many-Colored Grass, I would quit forever its happy recesses, transferring the love which now was so passionately her own to some maiden of the outer and every-day world. And, then and there, I threw myself hurriedly at the feet of Eleonora, and offered up a vow, to herself and to Heaven, that I would never bind myself in marriage to any daughter of Earth—that I would in no manner prove recreant to her dear memory, or to the memory of the devout affection with which she had blessed me. And I called the Mighty Ruler of the Universe to witness the pious solemnity of my vow. And the curse which I invoked of *Him* and of her, a saint in Helusion,[9] should I prove traitorous to that promise, involved a penalty the exceeding great horror of which will not permit me to make record of it here. And the bright eyes of Eleonora grew brighter at my words; and she sighed as if a deadly burthen had been taken from her breast; and she trembled and very bitterly wept; but she made acceptance of the vow, (for what was she but a child?) and it made easy to her the bed of her death. And she said to me, not many days afterwards, tranquilly dying, that, because of what I had done for the comfort of her spirit, she would watch over me in that spirit when departed, and, if so it were permitted her, return to me visibly in the watches of the night; but, if this thing were, indeed, beyond the power of the souls in Paradise, that she would, at least, give me frequent indications of her presence; sighing upon me in the evening winds, or filling the air which I breathed with perfume from the censers of the angels. And, with these words upon her lips, she yielded up her innocent life, putting an end to the first epoch of my own.

Thus far I have faithfully said. But as I pass the barrier in Time's path formed by the death of my beloved, and proceed with the second era of my existence, I feel that a shadow gathers over my brain, and I mistrust the perfect sanity of the record. But let me on.—Years dragged themselves along heavily, and still I dwelled within the Valley of the Many-Colored Grass;—but a second change had come upon all things. The star-shaped flowers shrank into the stems of the trees, and appeared no more. The tints of the green carpet faded; and, one by one, the ruby-red asphodels withered away; and there sprang up, in place of them, ten by ten, dark eye-like violets that writhed uneasily and were ever encumbered with dew. And Life departed from our paths; for the tall flamingo flaunted no longer his scarlet plumage before us, but flew sadly from the vale into the hills, with all the gay glowing birds that had arrived in his company. And the golden and silver fish swam down through the gorge at the lower end of our domain and bedecked the sweet river never again. And the lulling melody that had been softer than the wind-harp of Æolus and more divine than all save the voice of Eleonora, it died little by little away, in murmurs growing lower and lower, until the stream returned, at length, utterly, into the solemnity of its original silence. And then, lastly the voluminous cloud uprose, and, abandoning the tops of the mountains to the dimness of old, fell back into the regions of Hesper, and took away

[8]An insect that lives only one day in the mature state (Mabbott's note).

[9]Poe's variant spelling of Elysium, the Greek heaven.

all its manifold golden and gorgeous glories from the Valley of the Many-Colored Grass.

Yet the promises of Eleonora were not forgotten; for I heard the sounds of the swinging of the censers of the angels; and streams of a holy perfume floated ever and ever about the valley; and at lone hours, when my heart beat heavily, the winds that bathed my brow came unto me laden with soft sighs; and indistinct murmurs filled often the night air; and once—oh, but once only! I was awakened from a slumber like the slumber of death by the pressing of spiritual lips upon my own.

But the void within my heart refused, even thus, to be filled. I longed for the love which had before filled it to overflowing. At length the valley *pained* me through its memories of Eleonora, and I left it forever for the vanities and the turbulent triumphs of the world.

* * *

I found myself within a strange city, where all things might have served to blot from recollection the sweet dreams I had dreamed so long in the Valley of the Many-Colored Grass. The pomps and pageantries of a stately court, and the mad clangor of arms, and the radiant loveliness of woman, bewildered and intoxicated my brain. But as yet my soul had proved true to its vows, and the indications of the presence of Eleonora were still given me in the silent hours of the night. Suddenly, these manifestations they ceased; and the world grew dark before mine eyes; and I stood aghast at the burning thoughts which possessed—at the terrible temptations which beset me; for there came from some far, far distant and unknown land, into the gay court of the king I served, a maiden to whose beauty my whole recreant heart yielded at once—at whose footstool I bowed down without a struggle, in the most ardent, in the most abject worship of love. What indeed was my passion for the young girl of the valley in comparison with the fervor, and the delirium, and the spirit-lifting ecstasy of adoration with which I poured out my whole soul in tears at the feet of the ethereal Ermengarde?—Oh bright was the seraph Ermengarde! and in that knowledge I had room for none other.—Oh divine was the angel Ermengarde! and as I looked down into the depths of her memorial eyes I thought only of them—and *of her.*

I wedded;—nor dreaded the curse I had invoked; and its bitterness was not visited upon me. And once—but once again in the silence of the night, there came through my lattice the soft sighs which had forsaken me; and they modelled themselves into familiar and sweet voice, saying:

"Sleep in peace!—for the Spirit of Love reigneth and ruleth, and, in taking to thy passionate heart her who is Ermengarde, thou art absolved, for reasons which shall be made known to thee in Heaven, of thy vows unto Eleonora."

1841

The Oval Portrait[1]

The chateau into which my valet had ventured to make forcible entrance, rather than permit me, in my desperately wounded condition, to pass a night in the open air, was one of those piles of commingled gloom and grandeur which have so long frowned among the Apennines, not less in fact than in the fancy of Mrs. Radcliffe.[2] To all appearance it had been temporarily and very lately abandoned. We established ourselves in one of the smallest and least sumptuously furnished apartments. It lay in a remote turret of the building. Its decorations were rich, yet tattered and antique. Its walls were hung with tapestry and bedecked with manifold and multiform armorial trophies, together with an unusually great number of very spirited modern paintings in frames of rich golden arabesque.[3] In these paintings, which depended from the walls not only in their main surfaces, but in very many nooks which the bizarre architecture of the chateau rendered necessary—in these paintings my incipient delirium, perhaps, had caused me to take deep interest; so that I bade Pedro to close the heavy shutters of the room—since it was already night—to light the tongues of a tall candelabrum which stood by the head of my bed—and to throw open far and wide the fringed curtains of black velvet which enveloped the bed itself. I wished all this done that I might resign myself, if not to sleep, at least alternately to the contemplation of these pictures, and the perusal of a small volume which had been found upon the pillow, and which purported to criticise and describe them.

Long—long I read—and devoutly, devotedly I gazed. Rapidly and gloriously the hours flew by, and the deep midnight came. The position of the candelabrum displeased me, and outreaching my hand with difficulty, rather than disturb my slumbering valet, I placed it so as to throw its rays more fully upon the book.

But the action produced an effect altogether unanticipated. The rays of the numerous candles (for there were many) now fell within a niche of the room which had hitherto been thrown into deep shade by one of the bed-posts. I thus saw in vivid light a picture all unnoticed before. It was the portrait of a young girl just ripening into womanhood. I glanced at the painting hurriedly, and then closed my eyes. Why I did this was not at first apparent even to my own perception. But while my lids remained thus shut, I ran over in mind my reason for so shutting them. It was an impulsive movement to gain time for thought—to make sure that my vision had not deceived me—to calm and subdue my fancy for a more sober and more certain gaze. In a very few moments I again looked fixedly at the painting.

[1]The story first appeared in *Graham's* for April, 1842. This early version carried a headnote which read (in Italian) "He is alive and would speak were it not for his vow of silence" (attributed to a painting of St. Bruno). The first publication also included a lengthy introduction in which the narrator announces that he is (1) ill with fever (2) exhausted from lack of sleep (3) wounded and (4) under the influence of opium. These conditions were supposed to prepare the reader for the possibility of heightened imagination—or even delusion—in regard to what follows. In the later publication of the tale (1845) the author wisely omitted these overdone elements, retaining only the wound.

[2]Ann Radcliffe was a Gothic novelist of the previous century.

[3]That is, decorated with Moorish embellishments (Arabian art that flourished in medieval Spain).

That I now saw aright I could not and would not doubt; for the first flashing of the candles upon that canvas had seemed to dissipate the dreamy stupor which was stealing over my senses, and to startle me at once into waking life.

The portrait, I have already said, was that of a young girl. It was a mere head and shoulders, done in what is technically termed a *vignette* manner; much in the style of the favorite heads of Sully.[4] The arms, the bosom and even the ends of the radiant hair, melted imperceptibly into the vague yet deep shadow which formed the background of the whole. The frame was oval, richly gilded and filagreed in *Moresque*.[5] As a thing of art nothing could be more admirable than the painting itself. But it could have been neither the execution of the work, nor the immortal beauty of the countenance, which had so suddenly and so vehemently moved me. Least of all, could it have been that my fancy, shaken from its half slumber, had mistaken the head for that of a living person. I saw at once that the peculiarities of the design, of the *vignetting*,[6] and of the frame, must have instantly dispelled such idea—must have prevented even its momentary entertainment. Thinking earnestly upon these points, I remained, for an hour perhaps, half sitting, half reclining, with my vision riveted upon the portrait. At length, satisfied with the true secret of its effect, I fell back within the bed. I had found the spell of the picture in an absolute *life-likeliness* of expression, which at first startling, finally confounded, subdued and appalled me. With deep and reverent awe I replaced the candelabrum in its former position. The cause of my deep agitation being thus shut from view, I sought eagerly the volume which discussed the paintings and their histories. Turning to the number which designated the oval portrait, I there read the vague and quaint words which follow:

"She was a maiden of rarest beauty, and not more lovely than full of glee. And evil was the hour when she saw, and loved, and wedded the painter. He, passionate, studious, austere, and having already a bride in his Art; she a maiden of rarest beauty, and not more lovely than full of glee: all light and smiles, and frolicksome as the young fawn: loving and cherishing all things: hating only the Art which was her rival: dreading only the pallet and brushes and other untoward instruments which deprived her of the countenance of her lover. It was thus a terrible thing for this lady to hear the painter speak of his desire to pourtray even his young bride. But she was humble and obedient, and sat meekly for many weeks in the dark high turret-chamber where the light dripped upon the pale canvas only from overhead. But he, the painter, took glory in his work, which went on from hour to hour and from day to day. And he was a passionate, and wild and moody man, who became lost in reveries; so that he *would* not see that the light which fell so ghastlily in that lone turret withered the health and the spirits of his bride, who pined visibly to all but him. Yet she smiled on and still on, uncomplainingly, because she saw that the painter, (who had high renown,) took a fervid and burning pleasure in his task, and wrought day and night to depict her who so loved him, yet who grew daily more dispirited and weak. And in sooth some who beheld the portrait spoke of its resemblance in low words, as of a mighty marvel, and a proof not less of the power of the painter than of his deep love for her whom he depicted so surpassingly well. But at length, as the

[4]Thomas Sully was a leading portrait artist of Philadelphia, who (probably) was personally acquainted with Poe.

[5]Intricate embellishment in the Moorish style.

[6]Poe refers either to a painting style in which the figure shades off gradually into the background, or a portrait that implies a story—for example, early death, happy marriage, or other situation.

labor drew nearer to its conclusion there were admitted none into the turret; for the painter had grown wild with the ardor of his work, and turned his eyes from the canvas rarely, even to regard the countenance of his wife. And he *would* not see that the tints which he spread upon the canvas were drawn from the cheeks of her who sate beside him. And when many weeks had passed, and but little remained to do, save one brush upon the mouth and one tint upon the eye, the spirit of the lady again flickered up as the flame within the socket of the lamp. And then the brush was given, and then the tint was placed; and, for one moment, the painter stood entranced before the work which he had wrought; but in the next, while he yet gazed, he grew tremulous and very pallid, and aghast and crying with a loud voice, 'This is indeed *Life* itself!' turned suddenly to regard his beloved:—*She was dead!*"

1842

The Masque of the Red Death[1]

The "Red Death" had long devastated the country. No pestilence had ever been so fatal, or so hideous. Blood was its Avatar[2] and its seal—the redness and the horror of blood. There were sharp pains, and sudden dizziness, and then profuse bleeding at the pores, with dissolution. The scarlet stains upon the body and especially upon the face of the victim, were the pest ban which shut him out from the aid and from the sympathy of his fellow-men. And the whole seizure, progress and termination of the disease, were the incidents of half an hour.

But the Prince Prospero was happy and dauntless and sagacious. When his dominions were half depopulated, he summoned to his presence a thousand hale and light-hearted friends from among the knights and dames of his court, and with these retired to the deep seclusion of one of his castellated abbeys. This was an extensive and magnificent structure, the creation of the prince's own eccentric yet august taste. A strong and lofty wall girdled it in. This wall had gates of iron. The courtiers, having entered, brought furnaces and massy hammers and welded the bolts. They resolved to leave means neither of ingress or egress to the sudden impulses of despair or of frenzy from within. The abbey was amply provisioned. With such precautions the courtiers might bid defiance to contagion. The external world could take care of itself. In the meantime it was folly to grieve, or to think. The prince had provided all the appliances of pleasure. There were buffoons, there were improvisatori,[3] there were ballet-dancers, there were musicians, there was Beauty, there was wine. All these and security were within. Without was the "Red Death."

It was toward the close of the fifth or sixth month of his seclusion, and while the pestilence raged most furiously abroad, that the Prince Prospero entertained his thousand friends at a masked ball of the most unusual magnificence.

[1]The story first appeared in *Graham's* for May, 1842, then in *The Literary Souvenir* the following month.

[2]Embodiment, sign. The word originally was applied to the appearance of a Hindu god in human form.

[3]Clowns and unrehearsed entertainers.

It was a voluptuous scene, that masquerade. But first let me tell of the rooms in which it was held. There were seven—an imperial suite. In many palaces, however, such suites form a long and straight vista, while the folding doors slide back nearly to the walls on either hand, so that the view of the whole extent is scarcely impeded. Here the case was very different; as might have been expected from the duke's love of the *bizarre.* The apartments were so irregularly disposed that the vision embraced but little more than one at a time. There was a sharp turn at every twenty or thirty yards, and at each turn a novel effect. To the right and left, in the middle of each wall, a tall and narrow Gothic window looked out upon a closed corridor which pursued the windings of the suite. These windows were of stained glass whose color varied in accordance with the prevailing hue of the decorations of the chamber into which it opened. That at the eastern extremity was hung, for example, in blue—and vividly blue were its windows. The second chamber was purple in its ornaments and tapestries and here the panes were purple. The third was green throughout, and so were the casements. The fourth was furnished and lighted with orange—the fifth with white—the sixth with violet. The seventh apartment was closely shrouded in black velvet tapestries that hung all over the ceiling and down the walls, falling in heavy folds upon a carpet of the same material and hue. But in this chamber only, the color of the windows failed to correspond with the decorations. The panes here were scarlet—a deep blood color. Now in no one of the seven apartments was there any lamp or candelabrum, amid the profusion of golden ornaments that lay scattered to and fro or depended from the roof. There was no light of any kind emanating from lamp or candle within the suite of chambers. But in the corridors that followed the suite, there stood, opposite to each window, a heavy tripod, bearing a brazier of fire that projected its rays through the tinted glass and so glaringly illumined the room. And thus were produced a multitude of gaudy and fantastic appearances. But in the western or black chamber the effect of the fire-light that streamed upon the dark hangings through the blood-tinted panes, was ghastly in the extreme, and produced so wild a look upon the countenances of those who entered, that there were few of the company bold enough to set foot within its precincts at all.[4]

It was in this apartment, also, that there stood against the western wall, a gigantic clock of ebony. Its pendulum swung to and fro with a dull, heavy, monotonous clang; and when the minute-hand made the circuit of the face, and the hour was to be stricken, there came from the brazen lungs of the clock a sound which was clear and loud and deep and exceedingly musical, but of so peculiar a note and emphasis that, at each lapse of an hour, the musicians of the orchestra were constrained to pause, momentarily, in their performance, to hearken to the sound; and thus the waltzers perforce ceased their evolutions; and there was a brief disconcert of the whole gay company; and, while the chimes of the clock yet rang, it was observed that the giddiest grew pale, and the more aged and sedate passed their hands over their brows as if in confused reverie or meditation. But when the echoes had fully ceased, a light laughter at once pervaded the assembly; the musicians looked at each other and smiled as if at their own nervousness and folly, and made whispering vows, each

[4]Several critics have attempted to interpret Poe's fascinating color scheme: the ages of man is one such theory; a variation on the rainbow is another; the plague's inexorable progress through all social classes is a third.

to the other, that the next chiming of the clock should produce in them no similar emotion; and then, after the lapse of sixty minutes, (which embrace three thousand and six hundred seconds of the Time that flies,) there came yet another chiming of the clock, and then were the same disconcert and tremulousness and meditation as before.

But, in spite of these things, it was a gay and magnificent revel. The tastes of the duke were peculiar. He had a fine eye for colors and effects. He disregarded the *decora*[5] of mere fashion. His plans were bold and fiery, and his conceptions glowed with barbaric lustre. There are some who would have thought him mad. His followers felt that he was not. It was necessary to hear and see and touch him to be *sure* that he was not.

He had directed, in great part, the moveable embellishments of the seven chambers, upon occasion of this great *fête;*[6] and it was his own guiding taste which had given character to the masqueraders. Be sure they were grotesque. There were much glare and glitter and piquancy and phantasm—much of what has been since seen in "Hernani."[7] There were arabesque figures with unsuited limbs and appointments. There were delirious fancies such as the madman fashions. There was much of the beautiful, much of the wanton, much of the *bizarre,* something of the terrible, and not a little of that which might have excited disgust. To and fro in the seven chambers there stalked, in fact, a multitude of dreams. And these—the dreams—writhed in and about, taking hue from the rooms, and causing the wild music of the orchestra to seem as the echo of their steps. And, anon, there strikes the ebony clock which stands in the hall of the velvet. And then, for a moment, all is still, and all is silent save the voice of the clock. The dreams are stiff-frozen as they stand. But the echoes of the chime die away—they have endured but an instant—and a light, half-subdued laughter floats after them as they depart. And now again the music swells, and the dreams live, and writhe to and fro more merrily than ever, taking hue from the many-tinted windows through which stream the rays from the tripods. But to the chamber which lies most westwardly of the seven, there are now none of the maskers who venture; for the night is waning away; and there flows a ruddier light through the blood-colored panes; and the blackness of the sable drapery appals; and to him whose foot falls upon the sable carpet, there comes from the near clock of ebony a muffled peal more solemnly emphatic than any which reaches *their* ears who indulge in the more remote gaieties of the other apartments.

But these other apartments were densely crowded, and in them beat feverishly the heart of life. And the revel went whirlingly on, until at length there commenced the sounding of midnight upon the clock. And then the music ceased, as I have told; and the evolutions of the waltzers were quieted; and there was an uneasy cessation of all things as before. But now there were twelve strokes to be sounded by the bell of the clock; and thus it happened, perhaps, that more of thought crept, with more of time, into the meditations of the thoughtful among those who revelled. And thus, too, it happened, perhaps, that before the last echoes of the last chime had utterly sunk into silence, there were many individuals in the crowd who had found leisure

[5]Latin for fine items.
[6]French for banquet or formal dinner.
[7]A play by Victor Hugo.

to become aware of the presence of a masked figure which had arrested the attention of no single individual before. And the rumor of this new presence having spread itself whisperingly around, there arose at length from the whole company a buzz, or murmur, expressive of disapprobation and surprise—then, finally, of terror, of horror, and of disgust.

In an assembly of phantasms such as I have painted, it may well be supposed that no ordinary appearance could have excited such sensation. In truth the masquerade license of the night was nearly unlimited; but the figure in question had out-Heroded Herod, and gone beyond the bounds of even the prince's indefinite decorum. There are chords in the hearts of the most reckless which cannot be touched without emotion. Even with the utterly lost, to whom life and death are equally jests, there are matters of which no jest can be made. The whole company, indeed, seemed now deeply to feel that in the costume and bearing of the stranger neither wit nor propriety existed. The figure was tall and gaunt, and shrouded from head to foot in the habiliments of the grave. The mask which concealed the visage was made so nearly to resemble the countenance of a stiffened corpse that the closest scrutiny must have had difficulty in detecting the cheat. And yet all this might have been endured, if not approved, by the mad revellers around. But the mummer[8] had gone so far as to assume the type of the Red Death. His vesture was dabbled in *blood*—and his broad brow, with all the features of the face, was besprinkled with the scarlet horror.

When the eyes of Prince Prospero fell upon this spectral image (which with a slow and solemn movement, as if more fully to sustain its *rôle,* stalked to and fro among the waltzers) he was seen to be convulsed, in the first moment with a strong shudder either of terror or distaste; but, in the next, his brow reddened with rage.

"Who dares?" he demanded hoarsely of the courtiers who stood near him—"who dares insult us with this blasphemous mockery? Seize him and unmask him—that we may know whom we have to hang at sunrise, from the battlements!"

It was in the eastern or blue chamber in which stood the Prince Prospero as he uttered these words. They rang throughout the seven rooms loudly and clearly—for the prince was a bold and robust man, and the music had become hushed at the waving of his hand.

It was in the blue room where stood the prince, with a group of pale courtiers by his side. At first, as he spoke, there was a slight rushing movement of this group in the direction of the intruder, who at the moment was also near at hand, and now, with deliberate and stately step, made closer approach to the speaker. But from a certain nameless awe with which the mad assumptions of the mummer had inspired the whole party, there were found none who put forth hand to seize him; so that, unimpeded, he passed within a yard of the prince's person; and, while the vast assembly, as if with one impulse, shrank from the centres of the rooms to the walls, he made his way uninterruptedly, but with the same solemn and measured step which had distinguished him from the first, through the blue chamber to the purple—through the purple to the green—through the green to the orange—through this again to the white—and even thence to the violet, ere a decided movement had been made to

[8]Masked players who gave amateur performances, sometimes in the streets; the term is sometimes applied to actors in general.

arrest him. It was then, however, that the Prince Prospero, maddening with rage and the shame of his own momentary cowardice, rushed hurriedly through the six chambers, while none followed him on account of a deadly terror that had seized upon all. He bore aloft a drawn dagger, and had approached, in rapid impetuosity, to within three or four feet of the retreating figure, when the latter, having attained the extremity of the velvet apartment, turned suddenly and confronted his pursuer. There was a sharp cry—and the dagger dropped gleaming upon the sable carpet, upon which, instantly afterwards, fell prostrate in death the Prince Prospero. Then, summoning the wild courage of despair, a throng of the revellers at once threw themselves into the black apartment, and, seizing the mummer, whose tall figure stood erect and motionless within the shadow of the ebony clock, gasped in unutterable horror at finding the grave-cerements and corpse-like mask which they handled with so violent a rudeness, untenanted by any tangible form.[9]

And now was acknowledged the presence of the Red Death. He had come like a thief in the night. And one by one dropped the revellers in the blood-bedewed halls of their revel, and died each in the despairing posture of his fall. And the life of the ebony clock went out with that of the last of the gay. And the flames of the tripods expired. And Darkness and Decay and the Red Death held illimitable dominion over all.

1842

The Tell-Tale Heart[1]

True!—nervous—very, very dreadfully nervous I had been and am; but why *will* you say that I am mad? The disease had sharpened my senses—not destroyed—not dulled them. Above all was the sense of hearing acute. I heard all things in the heaven and in the earth. I heard many things in hell. How, then, am I mad? Hearken! and observe how healthily—how calmly I can tell you the whole story.

It is impossible to say how first the idea entered my brain; but once conceived, it haunted me day and night. Object there was none. Passion there was none. I loved the old man. He had never wronged me. He had never given me insult. For his gold I had no desire. I think it was his eye! yes, it was this! He had the eye of a vulture—a pale blue eye, with a film over it. Whenever it fell upon me, my blood ran cold; and so by degrees—very gradually—I made up my mind to take the life of the old man, and thus rid myself of the eye forever.[2]

[9]Poe's language in this climactic sentence is a bit indistinct. He means that inside the costume of the masked intruder there is nothing physical or material—only contagious plague germs.

[1]The story was first published in *The Pioneer* for January, 1843.

[2]Eyes possess a special mystique in European folklore, signifying, among other things, evil or irresistible influence. In Poe's story the filmed-over eye is a contrast to the luminous orbs of Ligeia and Roderick Usher. Possibly the vulture eye represents dull vision, blindness to reality.

Now this is the point. You fancy me mad. Madmen know nothing. But you should have seen *me.* You should have seen how wisely I proceeded—with what caution—with what foresight—with what dissimulation I went to work! I was never kinder to the old man than during the whole week before I killed him. And every night, about midnight, I turned the latch of his door and opened it—oh so gently! And then, when I had made an opening sufficient for my head, I put in a dark lantern, all closed, closed, so that no light shone out, and then I thrust in my head. Oh, you would have laughed to see how cunningly I thrust it in! I moved it slowly—very, very slowly, so that I might not disturb the old man's sleep. It took me an hour to place my whole head within the opening so far that I could see him as he lay upon his bed. Ha!—would a madman have been so wise as this? And then, when my head was well in the room, I undid the lantern cautiously—oh, so cautiously—cautiously (for the hinges creaked)—I undid it just so much that a single thin ray fell upon the vulture eye. And this I did for seven long nights—every night just at midnight—but I found the eye always closed; and so it was impossible to do the work; for it was not the old man who vexed me, but his Evil Eye. And every morning, when the day broke, I went boldly into the chamber, and spoke courageously to him, calling him by name in a hearty tone, and inquiring how he had passed the night. So you see he would have been a very profound old man, indeed, to suspect that every night, just at twelve, I looked in upon him while he slept.

Upon the eighth night I was more than usually cautious in opening the door. A watch's minute hand moves more quickly than did mine. Never before that night, had I *felt* the extent of my own powers—of my sagacity. I could scarcely contain my feelings of triumph. To think that there I was, opening the door, little by little, and he not even to dream of my secret deeds or thoughts. I fairly chuckled at the idea; and perhaps he heard me; for he moved on the bed suddenly, as if startled. Now you may think that I drew back—but no. His room was as black as pitch with the thick darkness, (for the shutters were close fastened, through fear of robbers,) and so I knew that he could not see the opening of the door, and I kept pushing it on steadily, steadily.

I had my head in, and was about to open the lantern, when my thumb slipped upon the tin fastening, and the old man sprang up in bed, crying out—"Who's there?"

I kept quite still and said nothing. For a whole hour I did not move a muscle, and in the meantime I did not hear him lie down. He was still sitting up in the bed listening;—just as I have done, night after night, hearkening to the death watches in the wall.[3]

Presently I heard a slight groan, and I knew it was the groan of mortal terror. It was not a groan of pain or of grief—oh, no!—it was the low stifled sound that arises from the bottom of the soul when overcharged with awe. I knew the sound well. Many a night, just at midnight, when all the world slept, it has welled up from my own bosom, deepening, with its dreadful echo, the terrors that distracted me.[4] I say

[3]The death watch was a beetle that was thought to make sounds predicting someone's death. But notice the application to the narrator's present action.

[4]More than once in this story Poe subtly implies that killer and victim are one, or that killer identifies with victim. Similar suggestions are planted in "The Cask of Amontillado" and "The Purloined Letter."

I knew it well. I knew what the old man felt, and pitied him, although I chuckled at heart. I knew that he had been lying awake ever since the first slight noise, when he had turned in the bed. His fears had been ever since growing upon him. He had been trying to fancy them causeless, but could not. He had been saying to himself—"It is nothing but the wind in the chimney—it is only a mouse crossing the floor," or "it is merely a cricket which has made a single chirp." Yes, he had been trying to comfort himself with these suppositions: but he had found all in vain. *All in vain;* because Death, in approaching him had stalked with his black shadow before him, and enveloped the victim. And it was the mournful influence of the unperceived shadow that caused him to feel—although he neither saw nor heard—to *feel* the presence of my head within the room.

When I had waited a long time, very patiently, without hearing him lie down, I resolved to open a little—a very, very little crevice in the lantern. So I opened it—you cannot imagine how stealthily, stealthily—until, at length a simple dim ray, like the thread of the spider, shot from out the crevice and fell full upon the vulture eye.

It was open—wide, wide open—and I grew furious as I gazed upon it. I saw it with perfect distinctness—all a dull blue, with a hideous veil over it that chilled the very marrow in my bones; but I could see nothing else of the old man's face or person: for I had directed the ray as if by instinct, precisely upon the damned spot.

And have I not told you that what you mistake for madness is but over acuteness of the senses?—now, I say, there came to my ears a low, dull, quick sound, such as a watch makes when enveloped in cotton. I knew *that* sound well, too. It was the beating of the old man's heart. It increased my fury, as the beating of a drum stimulates the soldier into courage.

But even yet I refrained and kept still. I scarcely breathed. I held the lantern motionless. I tried how steadily I could maintain the ray upon the eye. Meantime the hellish tattoo of the heart increased. It grew quicker and quicker, and louder and louder every instant. The old man's terror *must* have been extreme! It grew louder, I say, louder every moment!—do you mark me well? I have told you that I am nervous: so I am. And now at the dead hour of the night, amid the dreadful silence of that old house, so strange a noise as this excited me to uncontrollable terror. Yet, for some minutes longer I refrained and stood still. But the beating grew louder, louder! I thought the heart must burst. And now a new anxiety seized me—the sound would be heard by a neighbour! The old man's hour had come! With a loud yell, I threw open the lantern and leaped into the room. He shrieked once—once only. In an instant I dragged him to the floor, and pulled the heavy bed[5] over him. I then smiled gaily, to find the deed so far done. But, for many minutes, the heart beat on with a muffled sound. This, however, did not vex me; it would not be heard through the wall. At length it ceased. The old man was dead. I removed the bed and examined the corpse. Yes, he was stone, stone dead. I placed my hand upon the heart and held it there many minutes. There was no pulsation. He was stone dead. His eye would trouble me no more.

If still you think me mad, you will think so no longer when I describe the wise precautions I took for the concealment of the body. The night waned, and I worked

[5]Featherbed or heavy comforter, which in Poe's day sometimes served as a mattress.

hastily, but in silence. First of all I dismembered the corpse. I cut off the head and the arms and the legs.

I then took up three planks from the flooring of the chamber, and deposited all between the scantlings.[6] I then replaced the boards so cleverly, so cunningly, that no human eye—not even *his*—could have detected any thing wrong. There was nothing to wash out—no stain of any kind—no blood-spot whatever. I had been too wary for that. A tub had caught all—ha! ha!

When I had made an end of these labors, it was four o'clock—still dark as midnight. As the bell sounded the hour, there came a knocking at the street door. I went down to open it with a light heart,—for what had I *now* to fear? There entered three men, who introduced themselves, with perfect suavity, as officers of the police. A shriek had been heard by a neighbour during the night; suspicion of foul play had been aroused; information had been lodged at the police office, and they (the officers) had been deputed to search the premises.

I smiled,—for *what* had I to fear? I bade the gentlemen welcome. The shriek, I said, was my own in a dream. The old man, I mentioned, was absent in the country. I took my visitors all over the house. I bade them search—search *well.* I led them, at length, to *his* chamber. I showed them his treasures, secure, undisturbed. In the enthusiasm of my confidence, I brought chairs into the room, and desired them *here* to rest from their fatigues, while I myself, in the wild audacity of my perfect triumph, placed my own seat upon the very spot beneath which reposed the corpse of the victim.

The officers were satisfied. My *manner* had convinced them. I was singularly at ease. They sat, and while I answered cheerily, they chatted of familiar things. But, ere long, I felt myself getting pale and wished them gone. My head ached, and I fancied a ringing in my ears: but still they sat and still chatted. The ringing became more distinct:—it continued and became more distinct: I talked more freely to get rid of the feeling: but it continued and gained definiteness—until, at length, I found that the noise was *not* within my ears.

No doubt I now grew *very* pale;—but I talked more fluently, and with a heightened voice. Yet the sound increased—and what could I do? It was *a low, dull, quick sound—much such a sound as a watch makes when enveloped in cotton.* I gasped for breath—and yet the officers heard it not. I talked more quickly—more vehemently; but the noise steadily increased. I arose and argued about trifles, in a high key and with violent gesticulations; but the noise steadily increased. Why *would* they not be gone? I paced the floor to and fro with heavy strides, as if excited to fury by the observations of the men—but the noise steadily increased. Oh God! what *could* I do? I foamed—I raved—I swore! I swung the chair upon which I had been sitting, and grated it upon the boards, but the noise arose over all and continually increased. It grew louder—louder—*louder!* And still the men chatted pleasantly, and smiled. Was it possible they heard not? Almighty God!—no, no! They heard!—they suspected!—they *knew!*—they were making a mockery of my horror!—this I thought, and this I think. But anything was better than this agony! Anything was more tolerable than this derision! I could bear those hypocritical smiles no longer! I felt that I must scream or die! and now—again!—hark! louder! louder! louder! *louder!*

[6]Floor beams.

"Villains!" I shrieked, "dissemble no more! I admit the deed!—tear up the planks! here, here!—it is the beating of his hideous heart!"

1843

The Purloined Letter

Nil sapientiae odiosius acumine nimio.
—SENECA[1]

At Paris, just after dark one gusty evening in the autumn of 18—, I was enjoying the twofold luxury of meditation and a meerschaum, in company with my friend C. Auguste Dupin, in his little back library, or book-closet, *au troisième,*[2] *No. 33, Rue Dunôt, Faubourg St. Germain.* For one hour at least we had maintained a profound silence; while each, to any casual observer, might have seemed intently and exclusively occupied with the curling eddies of smoke that oppressed the atmosphere of the chamber. For myself, however, I was mentally discussing certain topics which had formed matter for conversation between us at an earlier period of the evening; I mean the affair of the Rue Morgue, and the mystery attending the murder of Marie Rogêt. I looked upon it, therefore, as something of a coincidence, when the door of our apartment was thrown open and admitted our old acquaintance, Monsieur G——, the Prefect of the Parisian police.

We gave him a hearty welcome; for there was nearly half as much of the entertaining as of the contemptible about the man, and we had not seen him for several years. We had been sitting in the dark, and Dupin now arose for the purpose of lighting a lamp, but sat down again, without doing so, upon G.'s saying that he had called to consult us, or rather to ask the opinion of my friend, about some official business which had occasioned a great deal of trouble.

"If it is any point requiring reflection," observed Dupin, as he forbore to enkindle the wick, "we shall examine it to better purpose in the dark."

"That is another of your odd notions," said the Prefect, who had a fashion of calling every thing "odd" that was beyond his comprehension, and thus lived amid an absolute legion of "oddities."

"Very true," said Dupin, as he supplied his visiter with a pipe, and rolled towards him a comfortable chair.

[1]The story was first printed in *The Gift* for December, 1844. A great favorite among storytellers and critics, it inspired fictional imitations by Wilkie Collins and Arthur Conan Doyle, as well as entire volumes of critical commentary, especially in recent years. The headnote reads "Nothing is more distasteful to good sense than too much cunning." The source of the saying is not Seneca, but Francis Bacon.

[2]French for "on the third." Americans would say "on the fourth floor."

"And what is the difficulty now?" I asked. "Nothing more in the assassination way, I hope?"

"Oh no; nothing of that nature. The fact is, the business is *very* simple indeed, and I make no doubt that we can manage it sufficiently well ourselves; but then I thought Dupin would like to hear the details of it, because it is so excessively *odd.*"

"Simple and odd," said Dupin.

"Why, yes; and not exactly that, either. The fact is, we have all been a good deal puzzled because the affair *is* so simple, and yet baffles us altogether."

"Perhaps it is the very simplicity of the thing which puts you at fault," said my friend.

"What nonsense you *do* talk!" replied the Prefect, laughing heartily.

"Perhaps the mystery is a little *too* plain," said Dupin.[3]

"Oh, good heavens! who ever heard of such an idea?"

"A little *too* self-evident."

"Ha! ha! ha!—ha! ha! ha!—ho! ho! ho!"—roared our visiter, profoundly amused, "oh, Dupin, you will be the death of me yet!"

"And what, after all, *is* the matter on hand?" I asked.

"Why, I will tell you," replied the Prefect, as he gave a long, steady, and contemplative puff, and settled himself in his chair. "I will tell you in a few words; but, before I begin, let me caution you that this is an affair demanding the greatest secrecy, and that I should most probably lose the position I now hold, were it known that I confided it to any one."

"Proceed," said I.

"Or not," said Dupin.

"Well, then; I have received personal information, from a very high quarter, that a certain document of the last importance, has been purloined from the royal apartments. The individual who purloined it is known; this beyond a doubt; he was seen to take it. It is known, also, that it still remains in his possession."

"How is this known?" asked Dupin.

"It is clearly inferred," replied the Prefect, "from the nature of the document, and from the nonappearance of certain results which would at once arise from its passing *out* of the robber's possession;—that is to say, from his employing it as he must design in the end to employ it."

"Be a little more explicit," I said.

"Well, I may venture so far as to say that the paper gives its holder a certain power in a certain quarter where such power is immensely valuable." The Prefect was fond of the cant of diplomacy.

"Still I do not quite understand," said Dupin.

"No? Well; the disclosure of the document to a third person, who shall be nameless, would bring in question the honor of a personage of most exalted station; and this fact gives the holder of the document an ascendancy over the illustrious personage whose honor and peace are so jeopardized."

"But this ascendancy," I interposed, "would depend upon the robber's knowledge of the loser's knowledge of the robber. Who would dare—"

[3]Dupin solves the problem before it is stated (Stuart and Susan Levine).

"The thief," said G., "is the Minister D——,[4] who dares all things, those unbecoming as well as those becoming a man. The method of the theft was not less ingenious than bold. The document in question—a letter, to be frank—has been received by the personage robbed while alone in the royal *boudoir.* During its perusal she was suddenly interrupted by the entrance of the other exalted personage from whom especially it was her wish to conceal it. After a hurried and vain endeavor to thrust it in a drawer, she was forced to place it, open as it was, upon a table. The address, however, was uppermost, and, the contents thus unexposed, the letter escaped notice. At this juncture enters the Minister D——. His lynx eye immediately perceives the paper, recognises the handwriting of the address, observes the confusion of the personage addressed, and fathoms her secret. After some business transactions, hurried through in his ordinary manner, he produces a letter somewhat similar to the one in question, opens it, pretends to read it, and then places it in close juxtaposition to the other. Again he converses, for some fifteen minutes, upon the public affairs. At length, in taking leave, he takes also from the table the letter to which he had no claim. Its rightful owner saw, but, of course, dared not call attention to the act, in the presence of the third personage who stood at her elbow. The minister decamped; leaving his own letter—one of no importance—upon the table."

"Here, then," said Dupin to me, "you have precisely what you demand to make the ascendancy complete—the robber's knowledge of the loser's knowledge of the robber."

"Yes," replied the Prefect; "and the power thus attained has, for some months past, been wielded, for political purposes, to a very dangerous extent. The personage robbed is more thoroughly convinced, every day, of the necessity of reclaiming her letter. But this, of course, cannot be done openly. In fine, driven to despair, she has committed the matter to me."

"Than whom," said Dupin, amid a perfect whirlwind of smoke, "no more sagacious agent could, I suppose, be desired, or even imagined."

"You flatter me," replied the Prefect; "but it is possible that some such opinion may have been entertained."

"It is clear," said I, "as you observe, that the letter is still in possession of the minister; since it is this possession, and not any employment of the letter, which bestows the power. With the employment the power departs."

"True," said G.; "and upon this conviction I proceeded. My first care was to make thorough search of the minister's hotel; and here my chief embarrassment lay in the necessity of searching without his knowledge. Beyond all things, I have been warned of the danger which would result from giving him reason to suspect our design."

"But," said I, "you are quite *au fait*[5] in these investigations. The Parisian police have done this thing often before."

[4]A convention of 19th-century fiction writers was to give the initial letters, rather than whole names, of story characters. The implication was that the characters had real-life identities, which the author concealed to protect the innocent. In the present case, the duplication of D—— with Dupin has inspired critical theories based on the idea that the detective and the thief are doubles or two aspects of the same mind.

[5]Well informed.

"O yes; and for this reason I did not despair. The habits of the minister gave me, too, a great advantage. He is frequently absent from home all night. His servants are by no means numerous. They sleep at a distance from their master's apartment, and, being chiefly Neapolitans, are readily made drunk. I have keys, as you know, with which I can open any chamber or cabinet in Paris. For three months a night has not passed, during the greater part of which I have not been engaged, personally, in ransacking the D—— Hôtel. My honor is interested, and, to mention a great secret, the reward is enormous. So I did not abandon the search until I had become fully satisfied that the thief is a more astute man than myself. I fancy that I have investigated every nook and corner of the premises in which it is possible that the paper can be concealed."

"But is it not possible," I suggested, "that although the letter may be in possession of the minister, as it unquestionably is, he may have concealed it elsewhere than upon his own premises?"

"This is barely possible," said Dupin. "The present peculiar condition of affairs at court, and especially of those intrigues in which D—— is known to be involved, would render the instant availability of the document—its susceptibility of being produced at a moment's notice—a point of nearly equal importance with its possession."

"Its susceptibility of being produced?" said I.

"That is to say, of being *destroyed,*" said Dupin.

"True," I observed; "the paper is clearly then upon the premises. As for its being upon the person of the minister, we may consider that as out of the question."

"Entirely," said the Prefect. "He has been twice waylaid, as if by footpads,[6] and his person rigorously searched under my own inspection."

"You might have spared yourself this trouble," said Dupin. "D——, I presume, is not altogether a fool, and, if not, must have anticipated these waylayings, as a matter of course."

"Not *altogether* a fool," said G., "but then he's a poet, which I take to be only one remove from a fool."

"True," said Dupin, after a long and thoughtful whiff from his meerschaum, "although I have been guilty of certain doggerel myself."

"Suppose you detail," said I, "the particulars of your search."

"Why the fact is, we took our time, and we searched *every where.* I have had long experience in these affairs. I took the entire building, room by room; devoting the nights of a whole week to each. We examined, first, the furniture of each apartment. We opened every possible drawer; and I presume you know that, to a properly trained police agent, such a thing as a *secret* drawer is impossible. Any man is a dolt who permits a 'secret' drawer to escape him in a search of this kind. The thing is *so* plain. There is a certain amount of bulk—of space—to be accounted for in every cabinet. Then we have accurate rules. The fiftieth part of a line could not escape us. After the cabinets we took the chairs. The cushions we probed with the fine long needles you have seen me employ. From the tables we removed the tops."

"Why so?"

"Sometimes the top of a table, or other similarly arranged piece of furniture, is removed by the person wishing to conceal an article; then the leg is excavated, the

[6]Pedestrian highwaymen.

article deposited within the cavity, and the top replaced. The bottoms and tops of bed-posts are employed in the same way."

"But could not the cavity be detected by sounding?" I asked.

"By no means, if, when the article is deposited, a sufficient wadding of cotton be placed around it. Besides, in our case, we were obliged to proceed without noise."

"But you could not have removed—you could not have taken to pieces *all* articles of furniture in which it would have been possible to make a deposit in the manner you mention. A letter may be compressed into a thin spiral roll, not differing much in shape or bulk from a large knitting-needle, and in this form it might be inserted into the rung of a chair, for example. You did not take to pieces all the chairs?"

"Certainly not; but we did better—we examined the rungs of every chair in the hotel, and, indeed, the jointings of every description of furniture, by the aid of a most powerful microscope.[7] Had there been any traces of recent disturbance we should not have failed to detect it instantly. A single grain of gimlet-dust, for example, would have been as obvious as an apple. Any disorder in the glueing—any unusual gaping in the joints—would have sufficed to insure detection."

"I presume you looked to the mirrors, between the boards and the plates, and you probed the beds and the bed-clothes, as well as the curtains and carpets."

"That of course; and when we had absolutely completed every particle of the furniture in this way, then we examined the house itself. We divided its entire surface into compartments, which we numbered, so that none might be missed; then we scrutinized each individual square inch throughout the premises, including the two houses immediately adjoining, with the microscope, as before."

"The two houses adjoining!" I exclaimed; "you must have had a great deal of trouble."

"We had; but the reward offered is prodigious."

"You include the *grounds* about the houses?"

"All the grounds are paved with brick. They gave us comparatively little trouble. We examined the moss between the bricks, and found it undisturbed."

"You looked among D——'s papers, of course, and into the books of the library?"

"Certainly; we opened every package and parcel; we not only opened every book, but we turned over every leaf in each volume, not contenting ourselves with a mere shake, according to the fashion of some of our police officers. We also measured the thickness of every book-*cover*, with the most accurate admeasurement, and applied to each the most jealous scrutiny of the microscope. Had any of the bindings been recently meddled with, it would have been utterly impossible that the fact should have escaped observation. Some five or six volumes, just from the hands of the binder, we carefully probed, longitudinally, with the needles."

"You explored the floors beneath the carpets?"

"Beyond doubt. We removed every carpet, and examined the boards with the microscope."

"And the paper on the walls?"

"Yes."

[7]Old fashioned term for magnifying glass.

"You looked into the cellars?"

"We did."

"Then," I said, "you have been making a miscalculation, and the letter is *not* upon the premises, as you suppose."

"I fear you are right there," said the Prefect. "And now, Dupin, what would you advise me to do?"

"To make a thorough re-search of the premises."

"That is absolutely needless," replied G——. "I am not more sure that I breathe than I am that the letter is not at the Hôtel."

"I have no better advice to give you," said Dupin. "You have, of course, an accurate description of the letter?"

"Oh, yes!"—And here the Prefect, producing a memorandum-book, proceeded to read aloud a minute account of the internal, and especially of the external appearance of the missing document. Soon after finishing the perusal of this description, he took his departure, more entirely depressed in spirits than I had ever known the good gentleman before.

In about a month afterwards he paid us another visit, and found us occupied very nearly as before. He took a pipe and a chair and entered into some ordinary conversation. At length I said,—

"Well, but G——, what of the purloined letter? I presume you have at last made up your mind that there is no such thing as overreaching the Minister?"

"Confound him, say I—yes; I made the reexamination, however, as Dupin suggested—but it was all labor lost, as I knew it would be."

"How much was the reward offered, did you say?" asked Dupin.

"Why, a very great deal—a *very* liberal reward—I don't like to say how much, precisely; but one thing I *will* say, that I would n't mind giving my individual check for fifty thousand francs to any one who could obtain me that letter. The fact is, it is becoming of more and more importance every day; and the reward has been lately doubled. If it were trebled, however, I could do no more than I have done."

"Why, yes," said Dupin, drawlingly, between the whiffs of his meerschaum, "I really—think, G——, you have not exerted yourself—to the utmost in this matter. You might—do a little more, I think, eh?"

"How?—in what way?"

"Why—puff, puff—you might—puff, puff—employ counsel in the matter, eh?—puff, puff, puff. Do you remember the story they tell of Abernethy?"

"No; hang Abernethy!"

"To be sure! hang him and welcome. But, once upon a time, a certain rich miser conceived the design of spunging upon this Abernethy for a medical opinion. Getting up, for this purpose, an ordinary conversation in a private company, he insinuated his case to the physician, as that of an imaginary individual.

"'We will suppose,' said the miser, 'that his symptoms are such and such; now, doctor, what would *you* have directed him to take?'

"'Take!' said Abernethy, 'why, take *advice,* to be sure.'"

"But," said the Prefect, a little discomposed, "I am *perfectly* willing to take advice, and to pay for it. I would *really* give fifty thousand francs to any one who would aid me in the matter."

"In that case," replied Dupin, opening a drawer, and producing a check-book, "you may as well fill me up a check for the amount mentioned. When you have signed it, I will hand you the letter."

I was astounded. The Prefect appeared absolutely thunder-stricken. For some minutes he remained speechless and motionless, looking incredulously at my friend with open mouth, and eyes that seemed starting from their sockets; then, apparently recovering himself in some measure, he seized a pen, and after several pauses and vacant stares, finally filled up and signed a check for fifty thousand francs, and handed it across the table to Dupin. The latter examined it carefully and deposited it in his pocket-book; then, unlocking an *escritoire,*[8] took thence a letter and gave it to the Prefect. This functionary grasped it in a perfect agony of joy, opened it with a trembling hand, cast a rapid glance at its contents, and then, scrambling and struggling to the door, rushed at length unceremoniously from the room and from the house, without having uttered a syllable since Dupin had requested him to fill up the check.

When he had gone, my friend entered into some explanations.

"The Parisian police," he said, "are exceedingly able in their way. They are persevering, ingenious, cunning, and thoroughly versed in the knowledge which their duties seem chiefly to demand. Thus, when G——detailed to us his mode of searching the premises at the Hôtel D——, I felt entire confidence in his having made a satisfactory investigation—so far as his labors extended."

"So far as his labors extended?" said I.

"Yes," said Dupin. "The measures adopted were not only the best of their kind, but carried out to absolute perfection. Had the letter been deposited within the range of their search, these fellows would, beyond a question, have found it."

I merely laughed—but he seemed quite serious in all that he said.

"The measures, then," he continued, "were good in their kind, and well executed; their defect lay in their being inapplicable to the case, and to the man. A certain set of highly ingenious resources are, with the Prefect, a sort of Procrustean bed,[9] to which he forcibly adapts his designs. But he perpetually errs by being too deep or too shallow, for the matter in hand; and many a schoolboy is a better reasoner than he. I knew one about eight years of age, whose success at guessing in the game of 'even and odd' attracted universal admiration. This game is simple, and is played with marbles. One player holds in his hand a number of these toys, and demands of another whether that number is even or odd. If the guess is right, the guesser wins one; if wrong, he loses one. The boy to whom I allude won all the marbles of the school. Of course he had some principle of guessing; and this lay in mere observation and admeasurement of the astuteness of his opponents. For example, an arrant simpleton is his opponent, and, holding up his closed hand, asks, 'are they even or odd?' Our schoolboy replies, 'odd,' and loses; but upon the second trial he wins, for he then says to himself, 'the simpleton had them even upon the first trial, and his amount of cunning is just sufficient to make him have them odd upon the second; I will therefore guess odd;'—he guesses odd, and wins. Now, with a simpleton a degree above the first, he would have reasoned thus: 'This fellow finds that in the first instance I guessed odd, and, in the second, he will propose to himself upon

[8]Writing desk.

[9]Procrustes (Greek mythology) took extreme measures to make his guests' body length fit his couch. He either stretched them to size or lopped off overhanging limbs. The reference to Procrustes no longer evokes a gruesome image, but is in common use among logicians.

the first impulse, a simple variation from even to odd, as did the first simpleton; but then a second thought will suggest that this is too simple a variation, and finally he will decide upon putting it even as before. I will therefore guess even;'—he guesses even, and wins. Now this mode of reasoning in the schoolboy, whom his fellows termed 'lucky,'—what, in its last analysis, is it?"

"It is merely," I said, "an identification of the reasoner's intellect with that of his opponent."

"It is," said Dupin; "and, upon inquiring of the boy by what means he effected the *thorough* identification in which his success consisted, I received answer as follows: 'When I wish to find out how wise, or how stupid, or how good, or how wicked is any one, or what are his thoughts at the moment, I fashion the expression of my face, as accurately as possible, in accordance with the expression of his, and then wait to see what thoughts or sentiments arise in my mind or heart, as if to match or correspond with the expression.' This response of the schoolboy lies at the bottom of all the spurious profundity which has been attributed to Rochefoucauld, to La Bougive, to Machiavelli, and to Campanella."[10]

"And the identification," I said, "of the reasoner's intellect with that of his opponent, depends, if I understand you aright, upon the accuracy with which the opponent's intellect is admeasured."

"For its practical value it depends upon this," replied Dupin; "and the Prefect and his cohort fail so frequently, first, by default of this identification, and, secondly, by ill-admeasurement, or rather through non-admeasurement, of the intellect with which they are engaged. They consider only their *own* ideas of ingenuity; and, in searching for anything hidden, advert only to the modes in which *they* would have hidden it. They are right in this much—that their own ingenuity is a faithful representative of that of *the mass;* but when the cunning of the individual felon is diverse in character from their own, the felon foils them, of course. This always happens when it is above their own, and very usually when it is below. They have no variation of principle in their investigations; at best, when urged by some unusual emergency—by some extraordinary reward—they extend or exaggerate their old modes of *practice,* without touching their principles. What, for example, in this case of D——, has been done to vary the principle of action? What is all this boring, and probing, and sounding, and scrutinizing with the microscope, and dividing the surface of the building into registered square inches—what is it all but an exaggeration *of the application* of the one principle or set of principles of search, which are based upon the one set of notions regarding human ingenuity, to which the Prefect, in the long routine of his duty, has been accustomed? Do you not see he has taken it for granted that *all* men proceed to conceal a letter,—not exactly in a gimlet-hole bored in a chair-leg—but, at least, in *some* out-of-the-way hole or corner suggested by the same tenor of thought which would urge a man to secrete a letter in a gimlet-hole bored in a chair-leg? And do you not see also, that such *recherchés*[11] nooks for concealment are adapted only for ordinary occasions, and would be adopted only by

[10]Rochefoucauld wrote *Reflexions,* a compendium of moral axioms; La Bougive remains unidentified; Machiavelli was an Italian courtier and author of a famous political handbook, *The Prince;* Campanella was a monk who wrote a controversial volume of philosophy. All these authors asked their readers to consider what "the other person" was thinking.

[11]Rare, obscure.

ordinary intellects; for, in all cases of concealment, a disposal of the article concealed—a disposal of it in this *recherché* manner,—is, in the very first instance, presumable and presumed; and thus its discovery depends, not at all upon the acumen, but altogether upon the mere care, patience, and determination of the seekers; and where the case is of importance—or, what amounts to the same thing in the policial eyes, when the reward is of magnitude,—the qualities in question have *never* been known to fail. You will now understand what I meant in suggesting that, had the purloined letter been hidden any where within the limits of the Prefect's examination—in other words, had the principle of its concealment been comprehended within the principles of the Prefect—its discovery would have been a matter altogether beyond question. This functionary, however, has been thoroughly mystified; and the remote source of his defeat lies in the supposition that the Minister is a fool, because he has acquired renown as a poet. All fools are poets; this the Prefect *feels;* and he is merely guilty of a *non distributio medii*[12] in thence inferring that all poets are fools."

"But is this really the poet?" I asked. "There are two brothers, I know; and both have attained reputation in letters. The Minister I believe has written learnedly on the Differential Calculus. He is a mathematician, and no poet."

"You are mistaken; I know him well; he is both. As poet *and* mathematician, he would reason well; as mere mathematician, he could not have reasoned at all, and thus would have been at the mercy of the Prefect."

"You surprise me," I said, "by these opinions, which have been contradicted by the voice of the world. You do not mean to set at naught the well-digested idea of centuries. The mathematical reason has long been regarded as *the* reason *par excellence.*"

"'*Il y a à parier,*'" replied Dupin, quoting from Chamfort, "'*que toute idée publique, toute convention reçue, est une sottise, car elle a convenu au plus grand nombre.*'[13] The mathematicians, I grant you, have done their best to promulgate the popular error to which you allude, and which is none the less an error for its promulgation as truth. With an art worthy a better cause, for example, they have insinuated the term 'analysis' into application to algebra. The French are the originators of this particular deception; but if a term is of any importance—if words derive any value from applicability—then 'analysis' conveys 'algebra' about as much as, in Latin, '*ambitus*' implies 'ambition,' '*religio*' 'religion,' or '*homines honesti,*' a set of *honorable* men."[14]

"You have a quarrel on hand, I see," said I, "with some of the algebraists of Paris; but proceed."

"I dispute the availability, and thus the value, of that reason which is cultivated in any especial form other than the abstractly logical. I dispute, in particular, the reason educed by mathematical study. The mathematics are the science of form and quantity; mathematical reasoning is merely logic applied to observation upon form

[12]Poe's Latin phrase translates "the undistributed middle"—an error in deductive logic in which the conclusion is not justified by the premises.

[13]"The odds are that every accepted idea is nonsense, since each one has been accepted by the multitude."

[14]Dupin says modern terms do not have the same denotation as their Latin roots. *Ambitus* meant "going around"; *religio* meant "to bind or relegate"; and *homines honesti* meant "distinguished" (Stuart and Susan Levine).

and quantity. The great error lies in supposing that even the truths of what is called *pure* algebra, are abstract or general truths. And this error is so egregious that I am confounded at the universality with which it has been received. Mathematical axioms are *not* axioms of general truth. What is true of *relation*—of form and quantity—is often grossly false in regard to morals, for example. In this latter science it is very usually *un*true that the aggregated parts are equal to the whole. In chemistry also the axiom fails. In the consideration of motive it fails; for two motives, each of a given value, have not, necessarily, a value when united, equal to the sum of their values apart. There are numerous other mathematical truths which are only truths within the limits of *relation.* But the mathematician argues, from his *finite truths,* through habit, as if they were of an absolutely general applicability—as the world indeed imagines them to be. Bryant, in his very learned 'Mythology,'[15] mentions an analogous source of error, when he says that 'although the Pagan fables are not believed, yet we forget ourselves continually, and make inferences from them as existing realities.' With the algebraists, however, who are Pagans themselves, the 'Pagan fables' *are* believed, and the inferences are made, not so much through lapse of memory, as through an unaccountable addling of the brains. In short, I never yet encountered the mere mathematician who could be trusted out of equal roots, or one who did not clandestinely hold it as a point of his faith that $x^2 + px$ was absolutely and unconditionally equal to q. Say to one of these gentlemen, by way of experiment, if you please, that you believe occasions may occur where $x^2 + px$ is *not* altogether equal to q, and, having made him understand what you mean, get out of his reach as speedily as convenient, for, beyond doubt, he will endeavor to knock you down.

"I mean to say," continued Dupin, while I merely laughed at his last observations, "that if the Minister had been no more than a mathematician, the Prefect would have been under no necessity of giving me this check. I knew him, however, as both mathematician and poet, and my measures were adapted to his capacity, with reference to the circumstances by which he was surrounded. I knew him as a courtier, too, and as a bold *intriguant.*[16] Such a man, I considered, could not fail to be aware of the ordinary policial modes of action. He could not have failed to anticipate—and events have proved that he did not fail to anticipate—the waylayings to which he was subjected. He must have foreseen, I reflected, the secret investigations of his premises. His frequent absences from home at night, which were hailed by the Prefect as certain aids to his success, I regarded only as *ruses,* to afford opportunity for thorough search to the police, and thus the sooner to impress them with the conviction to which G——, in fact, did finally arrive—the conviction that the letter was not upon the premises. I felt, also, that the whole train of thought, which I was at some pains in detailing to you just now, concerning the invariable principle of policial action in searches for articles concealed—I felt that this whole train of thought would necessarily pass through the mind of the Minister. It would imperatively lead him to despise all the ordinary *nooks* of concealment. *He* could not, I reflected, be so weak as not to see that the most intricate and remote recess of his hotel would be as open as his commonest closets to the eyes, to the probes, to the gimlets, and to the

[15]Jacob Bryant compiled and interpreted ancient myths in his *New System,* a book Poe knew well.

[16]Intriguer, opportunist.

microscopes of the Prefect. I saw, in fine, that he would be driven, as a matter of course, to *simplicity,* if not deliberately induced to it as a matter of choice. You will remember, perhaps, how desperately the Prefect laughed when I suggested, upon our first interview, that it was just possible this mystery troubled him so much on account of its being so *very* self-evident."

"Yes," said I, "I remember his merriment well. I really thought he would have fallen into convulsions."

"The material world," continued Dupin, "abounds with very strict analogies to the immaterial; and thus some color of truth has been given to the rhetorical dogma, that metaphor, or simile, may be made to strengthen an argument, as well as to embellish a description. The principle of the *vis inertiae,*[17] for example, seems to be identical in physics and metaphysics. It is not more true in the former, that a large body is with more difficulty set in motion than a smaller one, and that its subsequent *momentum* is commensurate with this difficulty, than it is, in the latter, that intellects of the vaster capacity, while more forcible, more constant, and more eventful in their movements than those of inferior grade, are yet the less readily moved, and more embarrassed and full of hesitation in the first few steps of their progress. Again: have you ever noticed which of the street signs, over the shop doors, are the most attractive of attention?"

"I have never given the matter a thought," I said.

"There is a game of puzzles," he resumed, "which is played upon a map. One party playing requires another to find a given word—the name of town, river, state or empire—any word, in short, upon the motley and perplexed surface of the chart. A novice in the game generally seeks to embarrass his opponents by giving them the most minutely lettered names; but the adept selects such words as stretch, in large characters, from one end of the chart to the other. These, like the over-largely lettered signs and placards of the street, escape observation by dint of being excessively obvious; and here the physical oversight is precisely analogous with the moral inapprehension by which the intellect suffers to pass unnoticed those considerations which are too obtrusively and too palpably self-evident. But this is a point, it appears, somewhat above or beneath the understanding of the Prefect. He never once thought it probable, or possible, that the Minister had deposited the letter immediately beneath the nose of the whole world, by way of best preventing any portion of that world from perceiving it.

"But the more I reflected upon the daring, dashing, and discriminating ingenuity of D——; upon the fact that the document must always have been *at hand,* if he intended to use it to good purpose; and upon the decisive evidence, obtained by the Prefect, that it was not hidden within the limits of that dignitary's ordinary search—the more satisfied I became that, to conceal this letter, the Minister had resorted to the comprehensive and sagacious expedient of not attempting to conceal it at all.

"Full of these ideas, I prepared myself with a pair of green spectacles, and called one fine morning, quite by accident, at the Ministerial hotel. I found D—— at home, yawning, lounging, and dawdling, as usual, and pretending to be in the last extremity of *ennui.*[18] He is, perhaps, the most really energetic human being now alive—but that is only when nobody sees him.

[17]Power of inertia. [18]Boredom.

"To be even with him, I complained of my weak eyes, and lamented the necessity of the spectacles, under cover of which I cautiously and thoroughly surveyed the apartment, while seemingly intent only upon the conversation of my host.

"I paid special attention to a large writing-table near which he sat, and upon which lay confusedly, some miscellaneous letters and other papers, with one or two musical instruments and a few books. Here, however, after a long and very deliberate scrutiny, I saw nothing to excite particular suspicion.

"At length my eyes, in going the circuit of the room, fell upon a trumpery fillagree card-rack of pasteboard, that hung dangling by a dirty blue ribbon, from a little brass knob just beneath the middle of the mantelpiece. In this rack, which had three or four compartments, were five or six visiting cards and a solitary letter. This last was much soiled and crumpled. It was torn nearly in two, across the middle—as if a design, in the first instance, to tear it entirely up as worthless, had been altered, or stayed, in the second. It had a large black seal, bearing the D—— cipher *very* conspicuously, and was addressed, in a diminutive female hand, to D——, the minister, himself. It was thrust carelessly, and even, as it seemed, contemptuously, into one of the upper divisions of the rack.

"No sooner had I glanced at this letter, than I concluded it to be that of which I was in search. To be sure, it was, to all appearance, radically different from the one of which the Prefect had read us so minute a description. Here the seal was large and black, with the D—— cipher; there it was small and red, with the ducal arms of the S—— family. Here, the address, to the Minister, was diminutive and feminine; there the superscription, to a certain royal personage, was markedly bold and decided; the size alone formed a point of correspondence. But, then, the *radicalness* of these differences, which was excessive; the dirt; the soiled and torn condition of the paper, so inconsistent with the *true* methodical habits of D——, and so suggestive of a design to delude the beholder into an idea of the worthlessness of the document; these things, together with the hyperobtrusive situation of this document, full in the view of every visitor, and thus exactly in accordance with the conclusions to which I had previously arrived; these things, I say, were strongly corroborative of suspicion, in one who came with the intention to suspect.

"I protracted my visit as long as possible, and, while I maintained a most animated discussion with the Minister, on a topic which I knew well had never failed to interest and excite him, I kept my attention really riveted upon the letter. In this examination, I committed to memory its external appearance and arrangement in the rack; and also fell, at length, upon a discovery which set at rest whatever trivial doubt I might have entertained. In scrutinizing the edges of the paper, I observed them to be more *chafed* than seemed necessary. They presented the *broken* appearance which is manifested when a stiff paper, having been once folded and pressed with a folder, is refolded in a reversed direction, in the same creases or edges which had formed the original fold. This discovery was sufficient. It was clear to me that the letter had been turned, as a glove, inside out, re-directed, and re-sealed. I bade the Minister good morning, and took my departure at once, leaving a gold snuff-box upon the table.

"The next morning I called for the snuff-box, when we resumed, quite eagerly, the conversation of the preceding day. While thus engaged, however, a loud report, as if of a pistol, was heard immediately beneath the windows of the hotel, and was succeeded by a series of fearful screams, and the shoutings of a mob. D—— rushed to a casement, threw it open, and looked out. In the meantime, I stepped to the card-rack, took the letter, put it in my pocket, and replaced it by a *fac-simile,* (so far as regards externals,) which I had carefully prepared at my lodgings; imitating the D—— cipher, very readily, by means of a seal formed of bread.

"The disturbance in the street had been occasioned by the frantic behavior of a man with a musket. He had fired it among a crowd of women and children. It proved, however, to have been without ball, and the fellow was suffered to go his way as a lunatic or a drunkard. When he had gone, D—— came from the window, whither I had followed him immediately upon securing the object in view. Soon afterwards I bade him farewell. The pretended lunatic was a man in my own pay."

"But what purpose had you," I asked, "in replacing the letter by a *fac-simile?* Would it not have been better, at the first visit, to have seized it openly, and departed?"

"D——," replied Dupin, "is a desperate man, and a man of nerve. His hotel, too, is not without attendants devoted to his interests. Had I made the wild attempt you suggest, I might never have left the Ministerial presence alive. The good people of Paris might have heard of me no more. But I had an object apart from these considerations. You know my political prepossessions. In this matter, I act as a partisan of the lady concerned. For eighteen months the Minister has had her in his power. She has now him in hers; since, being unaware that the letter is not in his possession, he will proceed with his exactions as if it was. Thus will he inevitably commit himself, at once, to his political destruction. His downfall, too, will not be more precipitate than awkward. It is all very well to talk about the *facilis descensus Averni;*[19] but in all kinds of climbing, as Catalani[20] said of singing, it is far more easy to get up than to come down. In the present instance I have no sympathy—at least no pity—for him who descends. He is that *monstrum horrendum,*[21] an unprincipled man of genius. I confess, however, that I should like very well to know the precise character of his thoughts, when, being defied by her whom the Prefect terms 'a certain personage,' he is reduced to opening the letter which I left for him in the card-rack."

"How? did you put any thing particular in it?"

"Why—it did not seem altogether right to leave the interior blank—that would have been insulting. D——, at Vienna once, did me an evil turn, which I told him, quite good-humoredly, that I should remember. So, as I knew he would feel some curiosity in regard to the identity of the person who had outwitted him, I thought it a pity not to give him a clue. He is well acquainted with my MS., and I just copied into the middle of the blank sheet the words—

—— Un dessein si funeste,
S'il n'est digne d'Atrée, est digne de Thyeste.[22]

They are to be found in Crébillon's 'Atrée.'"

1844

[19]"The easy descent to hell," from Vergil's *Aeneid.*
[20]A famous Italian opera singer.
[21]Horrible monster, another quote from Vergil.
[22]"A design so deadly, if not worthy of Atreus is worthy of Thyestes." The quote is from *Atrée et Thyeste* by the French playwright Crébillon. In this drama Thyestes seduces his brother's wife and in revenge Atreus kills the three sons of Thyestes and serves them up in a pie at a banquet honoring their father. The reference is over-gruesome for Poe's purpose, which is to suggest to D—— that "my revenge is better than your crime" (trans. Stuart and Susan Levine).

Sonnet—To Science[1]

Science! true daughter of Old Time thou art!
Who alterest all things with thy peering eyes.
Why preyest thou thus upon the poet's heart,
Vulture, whose wings are dull realities?
How should he love thee? or how deem thee wise,
Who wouldst not leave him in his wandering
To seek for treasure in the jewelled skies,
Albeit he soared with an undaunted wing?
Hast thou not dragged Diana from her car?
And driven the Hamadryad[2] from the wood
To seek a shelter in some happier star?
Hast thou not torn the Naiad[3] from her flood,
The Elfin from the green grass, and from me
The summer dream beneath the tamarind tree?[4]

1829

Romance[1]

Romance, who loves to nod and sing,
With drowsy head and folded wing,
Among the green leaves as they shake
Far down within some shadowy lake,
To me a painted paroquet[2]
Hath been—a most familiar bird—
Taught me my alphabet to say—
To lisp my very earliest word
While in the wild wood I did lie,
A child—with a most knowing eye.

Of late, eternal Condor[3] years
So shake the very Heaven on high

[1]First appeared in print in the collection *Al Aaraaf, Tamerlane, and Minor Poems,* 1829.
[2]Diana was an ancient Roman goddess associated with nature and fertility; Hamadryads are tree nymphs.
[3]Naiads are Greek female spirits who dwell in fresh water streams, lakes, etc.
[4]Tree noted for fragrance, found in the East and West Indies.

[1]First appeared in print in the collection *Al Aaraaf, Tamerlane, and Minor Poems,* 1829.
[2]Wooden bird hung from a pole outside a church tower to be shot at by archers (Mabbott).
[3]The condor is a scavenger with voracious appetite and vigorous flight. Poe's image is intentionally aggressive and distasteful.

With tumult as they thunder by,
I have no time for idle cares
Through gazing on the unquiet sky.
And when an hour with calmer wings
Its down upon my spirit flings—
That little time with lyre and rhyme
To while away—forbidden things!
My heart would feel to be a crime
Unless it trembled with the strings.

1829

Introduction[1]

Romance, who loves to nod and sing,
With drowsy head and folded wing,
Among the green leaves as they shake
Far down within some shadowy lake,
  To me a painted paroquet
Hath been—a most familiar bird—
  Taught me my alphabet to say,—
To lisp my very earliest word
While in the wild-wood I did lie
A child—with a most knowing eye
Succeeding years, too wild for song,
Then roll'd like tropic storms along,
Where, tho' the garish lights that fly,
Dying along the troubled sky
Lay bare, thro' vistas thunder-riven,
The blackness of the general Heaven,
That very blackness yet doth fling
Light on the lightning's silver wing.
For, being an idle boy lang syne,[2]
Who read Anacreon,[3] and drank wine,
I early found Anacreon rhymes
Were almost passionate sometimes—
And by strange alchemy of brain
His pleasures always turn'd to pain—
His naivete to wild desire—
His wit to love—his wine to fire—

[1]Poe incorporated the poem "Romance" into this longer effort in his *Poems* of 1831.
[2]Scottish for times past.
[3]Greek poet whose verses celebrate drinking and other pleasures.

And so, being young and dipt in folly
I fell in love with melancholy,
And used to throw my earthly rest
And quiet all away in jest—
I could not love except where Death
Was mingling his with Beauty's breath—
Or Hymen, Time, and Destiny
Were stalking between her and me.[4]

O, then the eternal Condor years,
So shook the very Heavens on high,
With tumult as they thunder'd by;
I had no time for idle cares,
Thro' gazing on the unquiet sky!
Or if an hour with calmer wing
Its down did on my spirit fling,
That little hour with lyre and rhyme
To while away—forbidden thing!
My heart half fear'd to be a crime
Unless it trembled with the string.

But *now* my soul hath too much room—
Gone are the glory and the gloom—
The black hath mellow'd into grey,
And all the fires are fading away.

My draught of passion hath been deep—
I revell'd, and I now would sleep—
And after-drunkenness of soul
Succeeds the glories of the bowl—
An idle longing night and day
To dream my very life away.[5]

But dreams—of those who dream as I,
Aspiringly, are damned, and die:
Yet should I swear I mean alone,
By notes so very shrilly blown,
To break upon Time's monotone,
While yet my vapid joy and grief
Are tintless of the yellow leaf—
Why not an imp the graybeard hath

[4]Poe does not mean he prefers lovers who are near death, but rather that early death seemed to single out the women he loved. The reference is probably to his mother, Elizabeth Arnold Poe; and an affectionate matron, Jane Stith Stanard, Poe knew in Richmond. The reference to Hymen, god of marriage, is a definite allusion to Sarah Elmira Royster, a childhood sweetheart Poe thought his fiancée, who without explanation married Alexander Shelton of Richmond.

[5]Poe strikes a fashionable pose of world-weariness popularized by Lord Byron.

Will shake his shadow in my path—
And even the graybeard will o'erlook
Connivingly my dreaming-book.

1831

To Helen[1]

Helen, thy beauty is to me
   Like those Nicéan[2] barks of yore,
That gently, o'er a perfumed sea,
   The weary, way-worn wanderer[3] bore
   To his own native shore.

On desperate seas long wont to roam,
   Thy hyacinth hair,[4] thy classic face,
Thy Naiad[5] airs have brought me home
   To the glory that was Greece,
   And the grandeur that was Rome.
Lo! in yon brilliant window-niche
   How statue-like I see thee stand,
The agate[6] lamp within thy hand!
   Ah, Psyche,[7] from the regions which
   Are Holy-Land![8]

1831

[1]First published in *Poems* (1831), but revised and polished to its present form over a period of twelve years. The title figure is certainly a reference to Helen of Troy, considered the most beautiful woman of antiquity; but the reader should bear in mind Poe's personal liking for the name Helen and variations on it, which he used in such works as "Lenore" and "Eleonora."

[2]Nicéan might refer to Nicea, an ancient city associated with Dionysus, Greek god of wine and frenzy; or to Nike, the Greek word for victory. These are the most likely explanations among many others that have been advanced by Poe scholars.

[3]The wanderer has been identified as Bacchus, Catullus, Menelaus, and Odysseus. The last two were travelers on missions of love.

[4]Hyacinth had special significance to Poe, and he used the term in other works. Hyacinthus was a beautiful Greek youth beloved of Apollo. At his death Apollo created the flower that bears his name. The term is also applied to the hair style of certain Greek statues and coins (Mabbott).

[5]Naiads are nymphs associated with fresh water lakes and rivers.

[6]The term "agate" is derived from "fidus Achates," a faithful friend of Aeneas in Vergil (Mabbott).

[7]Psyche was the Greek immortal who represented spirit.

[8]Since everyday usage would associate the term with Jerusalem, Holy Land in this line might refer to that city or to ancient Rome or Athens, the holy land of art and culture. Since the reference in line 12 is probably to Mrs. Stanard, Holy Land could also connote Richmond.

Israfel[1]

In Heaven a spirit doth dwell
"Whose heart-strings are a lute;"
None sing so wildly well
As the angel Israfel,[2]
And the giddy stars (so legends tell)
Ceasing their hymns, attend the spell
Of his voice, all mute.

Tottering above
In her highest noon,
The enamoured moon
Blushes with love,
While, to listen, the red levin[3]
(With the rapid Pleiads, even,
Which were seven,)[4]
Pauses in Heaven.

And they say (the starry choir
And the other listening things)
That Israfeli's fire
Is owing to that lyre[5]
By which he sits and sings—
The trembling living wire
Of those unusual strings.

But the skies that angel trod,
Where deep thoughts are a duty—
Where Love's a grown-up God—
Where the Houri[6] glances are
Imbued with all the beauty
Which we worship in a star.

[1]And the angel Israfel, whose heart-strings are a lute, and who has the sweetest voice of all God's creatures.—KORAN. [Poe's note]. This work was first published in *Poems* (1831), then revised and reprinted several times in the 1830s and 40s.

[2]Poe derived the name and the concept from Thomas Moore's *Lalla Rookh,* a popular Oriental tale.

[3]Lightning.

[4]The constellation Pleiades, which is supposed to represent seven sisters who were pursued by Orion.

[5]Probably to accommodate his rhyme scheme, Poe changes the basic image from a lute to a lyre, both stringed instruments with different frames. A lute looks like a mandolin with a bent neck, while a lyre is a small harp, the frame of which might be considered heart-shaped.

[6]Islamic maidens who dwell in Paradise.

Therefore, thou art not wrong,
 Israfeli, who despisest
An unimpassioned song;
To thee the laurels belong,
 Best bard, because the wisest!
Merrily live, and long

The ecstasies above
 With thy burning measures suit—
Thy grief, thy joy, thy hate, thy love,
 With the fervour of thy lute—
 Well may the stars be mute!

Yes, Heaven is thine; but this
 Is a world of sweets and sours;
 Our flowers are merely—flowers,
And the shadow of thy perfect bliss
 Is the sunshine of ours.

If I could dwell
Where Israfel
 Hath dwelt, and he where I,
He might not sing so wildly well
 A mortal melody,
While a bolder note than this might swell
 From my lyre within the sky.

1831

The City in the Sea[1]

Lo! Death has reared himself a throne
In a strange city lying alone
Far down within the dim West,
Where the good and the bad and the worst and the best
Have gone to their eternal rest.
There shrines and palaces and towers
(Time-eaten towers that tremble not!)
Resemble nothing that is ours.
Around, by lifting winds forgot,[2]

[1]First published in the 1831 collection, *Poems,* then revised and reprinted several times in the 1840s. The city Poe had in mind was Sodom or Gomorrah, sinful metropolises in the Bible destroyed for their wickedness and submerged in the Dead Sea.

[2]Contemporary descriptions of the Dead Sea claim that the waters are "so heavy that the winds cannot ruffle their surface."

Resignedly beneath the sky
The melancholy waters lie.

No rays from the holy heaven come down
On the long night-time of that town;
But light from out the lurid sea
Streams up the turrets silently—
Gleams up the pinnacles far and free—
Up domes—up spires—up kingly halls—
Up fanes—up Babylon-like walls—[3]
Up shadowy long-forgotten bowers
Of sculptured ivy and stone flowers—
Up many and many a marvellous shrine
Whose wreathéd friezes intertwine
The viol, the violet, and the vine.
Resignedly beneath the sky
The melancholy waters lie.
So blend the turrets and shadows there
That all seem pendulous in air,
While from a proud tower in the town
Death looks gigantically down.

There open fanes[4] and gaping graves
Yawn level with the luminous waves
But not the riches there that lie
In each idol's diamond eye—
Not the gaily-jewelled dead
Tempt the waters from their bed;
For no ripples curl, alas!
Along that wilderness of glass—
No swellings tell that winds may be
Upon some far-off happier sea—
No heavings hint that winds have been
On seas less hideously serene.

But lo, a stir is in the air!
The wave—there is a movement there![5]
As if the towers had thrust aside,
In slightly sinking, the dull tide—
As if their tops had feebly given
A void within the filmy Heaven.
The waves have now a redder glow—
The hours are breathing faint and low—

[3]They are Babylon-like because they are doomed to fall (Mabbott).

[4]Archaic for temple or church.

[5]Earthquakes are not unknown in the vicinity of the Dead Sea.

And when, amid no earthly moans,
Down, down that town shall settle hence,
Hell, rising from a thousand thrones,
Shall do it reverence.[6]

1831

The Sleeper[1]

At midnight, in the month of June,
I stand beneath the mystic moon.
An opiate vapour, dewy, dim,
Exhales from out her golden rim,
And, softly dripping, drop by drop,
Upon the quiet mountain top,
Steals drowsily and musically
Into the universal valley.
The rosemary nods upon the grave;
The lily lolls upon the wave;
Wrapping the fog about its breast,
The ruin moulders into rest;
Looking like Lethe,[2] see! the lake
A conscious slumber seems to take,
And would not, for the world, awake.
All Beauty sleeps!—and lo! where lies
Irene, with her Destinies!
Oh, lady bright! can it be right—
This window open to the night?
The wanton airs, from the tree-top,
Laughingly through the lattice drop—
The bodiless airs, a wizard rout,
Flit through thy chamber in and out,
And wave the curtain canopy
So fitfully—so fearfully—
Above the closed and fringéd lid
'Neath which thy slumb'ring soul lies hid,
That, o'er the floor and down the wall,

[6]The poem blends reality and fantasy in unique combination along with evoking emotions that are not quite familiar. This frontier-of-the-mind technique influenced later Surrealist painters.

[1]Originally entitled "Irene," published in 1831 and later revised and retitled in the late 1830s and early '40s.

[2]The river of forgetfulness in Greek mythology.

Like ghosts the shadows rise and fall!
Oh, lady dear, hast thou no fear?
Why and what art thou dreaming here?
Sure thou art come o'er far-off seas,
A wonder to these garden trees!
Strange is thy pallor! strange thy dress!
Strange, above all, thy length of tress,
And this all solemn silentness!

The lady sleeps! Oh, may her sleep,
Which is enduring, so be deep!
Heaven have her in its sacred keep!
This chamber changed for one more holy,
This bed for one more melancholy,
I pray to God that she may lie
Forever with unopened eye,
While the pale sheeted ghosts go by!

My love, she sleeps! Oh, may her sleep,
As it is lasting, so be deep!
Soft may the worms about her creep![3]
Far in the forest, dim and old,
For her may some tall vault unfold—
Some vault that oft hath flung its black
And wingéd panels fluttering back,
Triumphant, o'er the crested palls,
Of her grand family funerals—
Some sepulchre, remote, alone,
Against whose portal she hath thrown,
In childhood, many an idle stone—
Some tomb from out whose sounding door
She ne'er shall force an echo more,
Thrilling to think, poor child of sin!
It was the dead who groaned within.

1831

[3]To modern ears the line sounds disgusting and/or ludicrous, but it should be remembered that in Poe's day references to graveyard worms were common in popular literature and even in conversation. Ralph Waldo Emerson used to greet his aged aunt by "wishing her well of the worm."

The Valley of Unrest[1]

Once it smiled a silent dell
Where the people did not dwell;
They had gone unto the wars,
Trusting to the mild-eyed stars,
Nightly, from their azure towers,
To keep watch above the flowers,
In the midst of which all day
The red sun-light lazily lay.
Now each visiter shall confess
The sad valley's restlessness.
Nothing there is motionless—
Nothing save the airs that brood
Over the magic solitude.
Ah, by no wind are stirred those trees
That palpitate like the chill seas
Around the misty Hebrides!
Ah, by no wind those clouds are driven
That rustle through the unquiet Heaven
Uneasily, from morn till even,
Over the violets there that lie
In myriad types of the human eye—
Over the lilies three that wave
And weep above a nameless grave![2]
They wave:—from out their fragrant tops
Eternal dews come down in drops.
They weep:—from off their delicate stems
Perennial tears descend in gems.

1831

[1]Originally published in the 1831 collection, *Poems,* as "The Valley Nis," later revised and retitled in 1836 and 1845.

[2]Mabbott says the poem is a recollection of images impressed upon Poe during his visit to Scotland in 1815. The nameless grave was that of a dying soldier who asked a local farmer for assistance and died before mentioning his name. The poem is interesting not so much for its realistic content as for its imaginative and moody treatment of landscape.

Sonnet—Silence[1]

There are some qualities—some incorporate things,
That have a double life, which thus is made
A type of that twin entity which springs
From matter and light, evinced in solid and shade.
There is a two-fold *Silence*—sea and shore—
Body and soul. One dwells in lonely places,
Newly with grass o'ergrown; some solemn graces,
Some human memories and tearful lore,
Render him terrorless: his name's "No More."
He is the corporate Silence: dread him not!
No power hath he of evil in himself;
But should some urgent fate (untimely lot!)
Bring thee to meet his shadow (nameless elf,
That haunteth the lone regions where hath trod
No foot of man,) commend thyself to God![2]

1840

Dream-Land[1]

By a route obscure and lonely,
Haunted by ill angels only,
Where an Eidolon,[2] named NIGHT,
On a black throne reigns upright,
I have reached these lands but newly
From an ultimate dim Thule—[3]
From a wild weird clime that lieth, sublime,
Out of SPACE—out of TIME.

[1]First published in the *Philadelphia Saturday Courier* for January 4, 1840. Reprinted several times in the 1840s.

[2]The poet suggests that silence in the literal sense (corporate—that is, physical) is not to be feared; but silence of the spirit (depression or profound loneliness) can be devastating.

[1]Originally published in *Graham's Magazine* for June, 1844 and reprinted several times in the 1840s.

[2]A phantom.

[3]Thule was the Greek name for an island north of Britain and thus remote from the center of things. Vergil used the phrase "ultima Thule" in his *Georgics;* it has come to mean remote beyond literal geography, so far off as to be unrecorded on maps.

Bottomless vales and boundless floods,
And chasms, and caves and Titan[4] woods,
With forms that no man can discover
For the tears that drip all over;
Mountains toppling evermore
Into seas without a shore;
Seas that restlessly aspire,
Surging, unto skies of fire;
Lakes that endlessly outspread
Their lone waters—lone and dead,—
Their still waters—still and chilly
With the snows of the lolling lily.

By the lakes that thus outspread
Their lone waters, lone and dead,—
Their sad waters, sad and chilly
With the snows of the lolling lily,—
By the mountains—near the river
Murmuring lowly, murmuring ever,—
By the grey woods,—by the swamp
Where the toad and the newt encamp,—
By the dismal tarns and pools
    Where dwell the Ghouls,—
By each spot the most unholy—
In each nook most melancholy,—
There the traveller meets, aghast,
Sheeted Memories of the Past—
Shrouded forms that start and sigh
As they pass the wanderer by—
White-robed forms of friends long given,
In agony, to the Earth—and Heaven.

For the heart whose woes are legion
'T is a peaceful, soothing region—
For the spirit that walks in shadow
'T is—oh 't is an Eldorado![5]
But the traveller, travelling through it,
May not—dare not openly view it;
Never its mysteries are exposed
To the weak human eye unclosed;
So wills its King, who hath forbid
The uplifting of the fringéd lid;
And thus the sad Soul that here passes
Beholds it but through darkened glasses.

[4]Titans were Greek gods before the Olympians. They were enormous and forbidding deities.

[5]A mythical city of gold.

By a route obscure and lonely,
Haunted by ill angels only,
Where an Eidolon, named NIGHT,
On a black throne reigns upright,
I have wandered home but newly
From this ultimate dim Thule.

1844

The Raven[1]

Once upon a midnight dreary, while I pondered, weak and weary,
Over many a quaint and curious volume of forgotten lore—
While I nodded, nearly napping, suddenly there came a tapping,
As of some one gently rapping, rapping at my chamber door.
"'T is some visiter," I muttered, "tapping at my chamber door—
Only this and nothing more."

Ah, distinctly I remember it was in the bleak December;
And each separate dying ember wrought its ghost upon the floor.
Eagerly I wished the morrow;—vainly I had sought to borrow
From my books surcease of sorrow—sorrow for the lost Lenore—
For the rare and radiant maiden whom the angels name Lenore—
Nameless *here* for evermore.

And the silken, sad, uncertain rustling of each purple curtain
Thrilled me—filled me with fantastic terrors never felt before;
So that now, to still the beating of my heart, I stood repeating
"'T is some visiter entreating entrance at my chamber door—
Some late visiter entreating entrance at my chamber door;—
This it is and nothing more."

Presently my soul grew stronger; hesitating then no longer,
"Sir," said I, "or Madam, truly your forgiveness I implore;
But the fact is I was napping, and so gently you came rapping,
And so faintly you came tapping, tapping at my chamber door,
That I scarce was sure I heard you"—here I opened wide the door;—
Darkness there and nothing more.

[1]First published in 1845 in the *American Review;* thereafter published numerous times in the year of initial publication. Poe's best known poem in the U.S. and famous the world over. It has been reprinted, imitated, and satirized more than any other poem by an American, with the possible exception of Eliot's *Waste Land.*

Deep into that darkness peering, long I stood there wondering, fearing,
Doubting, dreaming dreams no mortal ever dared to dream before;
But the silence was unbroken, and the stillness gave no token,
And the only word there spoken was the whispered word, "Lenore!"
This I whispered, and an echo murmured back the word "Lenore!"
Merely this and nothing more.

Back into the chamber turning, all my soul within me burning,[2]
Soon again I heard a tapping somewhat louder than before.
"Surely," said I, "surely that is something at my window lattice;
Let me see, then, what thereat is, and this mystery explore—
Let my heart be still a moment and this mystery explore;—
'T is the wind and nothing more!"

Open here I flung the shutter, when, with many a flirt and flutter
In there stepped a stately Raven of the saintly days of yore.
Not the least obeisance made he; not a minute stopped or stayed he;
But, with mien of lord or lady, perched above my chamber door—
Perched upon a bust of Pallas[3] just above my chamber door—
Perched, and sat, and nothing more.

Then this ebony bird beguiling my sad fancy into smiling,
By the grave and stern decorum of the countenance it wore,
"Though thy crest be shorn and shaven, thou," I said, "art sure no craven,[4]
Ghastly grim and ancient Raven wandering from the Nightly shore—
Tell me what thy lordly name is on the Night's Plutonian shore!"[5]
Quoth the Raven, "Nevermore."

Much I marvelled this ungainly fowl to hear discourse so plainly,
Though its answer little meaning—little relevancy bore;
For we cannot help agreeing that no living human being
Ever yet was blessed with seeing bird above his chamber door—
Bird or beast upon the sculptured bust above his chamber door,
With such name as "Nevermore."

[2]The line might mean: I was thoroughly embarrassed by my complacent assumptions about the causes of the "rapping."

[3]Pallas Athene was the Greek goddess of wisdom. One of Poe's colleagues said that the raven on a bust of Pallas signifies the ascendancy of despair over reason.

[4]A cowardly knight sometimes had his head shaved as a sign of his disgrace (Mabbott).

[5]Relating to Pluto; thus the lower world, hellish.

But the Raven, sitting lonely on the placid bust, spoke only
That one word, as if his soul in that one word he did outpour.
Nothing farther then he uttered—not a feather then he fluttered—
Till I scarcely more than muttered "Other friends have flown before—
On the morrow *he* will leave me, as my hopes have flown before."
Then the bird said "Nevermore."

Startled at the stillness broken by reply so aptly spoken,
"Doubtless," said I, "what it utters is its only stock and store
Caught from some unhappy master whom unmerciful Disaster
Followed fast and followed faster till his songs one burden bore—
Till the dirges of his Hope that melancholy burden bore
Of 'Never—nevermore.'"

But the Raven still beguiling all my fancy into smiling,
Straight I wheeled a cushioned seat in front of bird, and bust and door;
Then, upon the velvet sinking, I betook myself to linking
Fancy unto fancy, thinking what this ominous bird of yore—
What this grim, ungainly, ghastly, gaunt, and ominous bird of yore
Meant in croaking "Nevermore."

This I sat engaged in guessing, but no syllable expressing
To the fowl whose fiery eyes now burned into my bosom's core;
This and more I sat divining, with my head at ease reclining
On the cushion's velvet lining that the lamp-light gloated o'er,
But whose velvet violet lining with the lamp-light gloating o'er,
She shall press, ah, nevermore!

Then, methought, the air grew denser, perfumed from an unseen censer
Swung by Seraphim[6] whose foot-falls tinkled on the tufted floor.
"Wretch," I cried, "thy God hath lent thee—by these angels he hath sent thee
Respite—respite and nepenthe[7] from thy memories of Lenore;
Quaff, oh quaff this kind nepenthe and forget this lost Lenore!"
Quoth the Raven "Nevermore."

"Prophet!" said I, "thing of evil! prophet still, if bird or devil!—
Whether Tempter sent, or whether tempest tossed thee here ashore,

[6]Angels.
[7]A legendary drink supposed to soothe the bereaved.

Desolate yet all undaunted, on this desert land enchanted—
On this home by Horror haunted—tell me truly, I implore—
Is there—*is* there balm in Gilead?[8]—tell me—tell me, I implore!"
Quoth the Raven "Nevermore."

"Prophet!" said I, "thing of evil!—prophet still, if bird or devil!
By that Heaven that bends above us—by that God we both adore—
Tell this soul with sorrow laden if, within the distant Aidenn,[9]
It shall clasp a sainted maiden whom the angels name Lenore—
Clasp a rare and radiant maiden whom the angels name Lenore."
Quoth the Raven "Nevermore."

"Be that word our sign of parting, bird or fiend!" I shrieked, upstarting—
"Get thee back into the tempest and the Night's Plutonian shore!
Leave no black plume as a token of that lie thy soul hath spoken!
Leave my loneliness unbroken!—quit the bust above my door!
Take thy beak from out my heart, and take thy form from off my door!"
Quoth the Raven "Nevermore."

And the Raven, never flitting, still is sitting, *still* is sitting
On the pallid bust of Pallas just above my chamber door;
And his eyes have all the seeming of a demon's that is dreaming,
And the lamp-light o'er him streaming throws his shadow on the floor;
And my soul from out that shadow that lies floating on the floor
Shall be lifted—nevermore![10]

1845

[8]A complex reference, meaning: is there solace in the future? or (Biblical) is there hope for me in heaven? Literally, the phrase denoted a fragrant tree grown in ancient Palestine; but there was a commercial salve in Poe's day called "Balm in Gilead," which was much like the modern Ben-Gay. Conceivably Poe is wondering whether a patent medicine might help if all else fails

[9]Poe's spelling of Eden; he meant heaven.

[10]Poe pointed out in one of his essays that the poem was a psychological study in self-torment, since the narrator knows in advance that the bird's answer will be negative and keeps on asking questions anyway.

Ulalume[1]

The skies they were ashen and sober;
The leaves they were crisped and sere—
The leaves they were withering and sere;
It was night in the lonesome October
Of my most immemorial year;
It was hard by the dim lake of Auber,
In the misty mid region of Weir—
It was down by the dank tarn of Auber,
In the ghoul-haunted woodland of Weir.[2]

Here once, through an alley Titanic,
Of cypress,[3] I roamed with my Soul—
Of cypress, with Psyche, my Soul.
These were days when my heart was volcanic
As the scoriac rivers that roll—[4]
As the lavas that restlessly roll
Their sulphurous currents down Yaanek
In the ultimate climes of the pole—
That groan as they roll down Mount Yaanek[5]
In the realms of the boreal[6] pole.

Our talk had been serious and sober,
But our thoughts they were palsied and sere—
Our memories were treacherous and sere—
For we knew not the month was October,
And we marked not the night of the year—
(Ah, night of all nights in the year!)
We noted not the dim lake of Auber—
(Though once we had journeyed down here)—
Remembered not the dank tarn of Auber,
Nor the ghoul-haunted woodland of Weir.

[1]First published in the *American Review* for December, 1847 and several times thereafter in 1848 and 1849. It is recorded that Poe wrote the poem on a friend's suggestion that he do something for public recitation expressing a variety of vocal effects. The content of the poem is more serious than this anecdote suggests. "Ulalume" derives from the Latin *ululare,* to wail; and *lumen,* light (Mabbott).

[2]Auber was a French composer whose ballet *Le lac du Fées* Poe might have seen. Weir was a landscape painter of the Hudson River School.

[3]In the flower and plant symbolism of the day, cypress meant mourning.

[4]Rivers full of scoriae, jagged boulders of loose lava (Mabbott).

[5]No mountain of this name has been discovered. Perhaps Poe invented the word to rhyme with volcanic.

[6]Northern.

And now, as the night was senescent
 And star-dials[7] pointed to morn—
 As the star-dials hinted of morn—
At the end of our path a liquescent
 And nebulous lustre was born,
Out of which a miraculous crescent
 Arose with a duplicate horn—
Astarte's bediamonded crescent[8]
 Distinct with its duplicate horn.

And I said—"She is warmer than Dian:[9]
 She rolls through an ether of sighs—
 She revels in a region of sighs:
She has seen that the tears are not dry on
 These cheeks, where the worm never dies
And has come past the stars of the Lion[10]
 To point us the path to the skies—
 To the Lethean[11] peace of the skies—
Come up, in despite of the Lion,
 To shine on us with her bright eyes—
Come up through the lair of the Lion,[12]
 With love in her luminous eyes."

But Psyche, uplifting her finger,
 Said—"Sadly this star I mistrust—
 Her pallor I strangely mistrust:—
Oh, hasten!—oh, let us not linger!
 Oh, fly!—let us fly!—for we must."
In terror she spoke, letting sink her
 Wings until they trailed in the dust—
In agony sobbed, letting sink her
 Plumes till they trailed in the dust—
 Till they sorrowfully trailed in the dust.

I replied—"This is nothing but dreaming:
 Let us on by this tremulous light!
 Let us bathe in this crystalline light!
Its Sibyllic[13] splendor is beaming

[7]The movement of the constellations (or apparent movement) can act as a clock to the knowledgeable.
[8]Astarte is here associated with the planet Venus, which sometimes presents a crescent shape like the moon.
[9]Poe intends Dian to represent the moon and asserts that Venus (love) is warmer than Diana (the hunt).
[10]The constellation Leo the Lion.
[11]Lethean means inducing forgetfulness.
[12]Venus in Leo in astrological terms, means trouble in love (Mabbott).
[13]The sibyls could foretell the future.

With Hope and in Beauty to-night:—
See!—it flickers up the sky through the night!
Ah, we safely may trust to its gleaming,
And be sure it will lead us aright—
We safely may trust to a gleaming
That cannot but guide us aright,
Since it flickers up to Heaven through the night."[14]

Thus I pacified Psyche and kissed her,
And tempted her out of her gloom—
And conquered her scruples and gloom;
And we passed to the end of the vista,
But were stopped by the door of a tomb—
By the door of a legended[15] tomb;
And I said—"What is written, sweet sister,
On the door of this legended tomb?"
She replied—"Ulalume—Ulalume—
'T is the vault of thy lost Ulalume!"

Then my heart it grew ashen and sober
As the leaves that were crisped and sere—
As the leaves that were withering and sere,
And I cried—"It was surely October
On *this* very night of last year
That I journeyed—I journeyed down here—
That I brought a dread burden down here—
On this night of all nights in the year,[16]
Ah, what demon has tempted me here?
Well I know, now, this dim lake of Auber—
This misty mid region of Weir—
Well I know, now, this dank tarn of Auber,
This ghoul-haunted woodland of Weir."

Said we, then—the two, then: "Ah, can it
Have been that the woodlandish ghouls—
The pitiful, the merciful ghouls—
To bar up our way and to ban it
From the secret that lies in these wolds—

[14]The narrator says in effect: let's keep going by the light of Venus; but Psyche warns him that love has been a dangerous guide in the past. The narrator replies that he trusts Venus since its light flickers "up to heaven" and thus cannot misguide.

[15]Legended means inscribed.

[16]The narrator has buried his sweetheart exactly one year earlier in the cemetery he is now visiting.

From the thing that lies hidden in these wolds—
Have drawn up the spectre of a planet
From the limbo of lunary souls—
This sinfully scintillant planet
From the Hell of the planetary souls?"

1847

Eldorado[1]

Gaily bedight,
A gallant knight,
In sunshine and in shadow,
Had journeyed long,
Singing a song,
In search of Eldorado.

But he grew old—
This knight so bold—
And o'er his heart a shadow
Fell as he found
No spot of ground
That looked like Eldorado.

And, as his strength
Failed him at length,
He met a pilgrim shadow—
"Shadow," said he,
"Where can it be—
This land of Eldorado?"

"Over the Mountains
Of the Moon,
Down the Valley of the Shadow,
Ride, boldly ride,"
The shade replied,—
"If you seek for Eldorado."

1849

[1]The poem, inspired by the California gold rush, was published in *The Flag of Our Union* in 1849, the last year of Poe's life. The title refers to a legend of a king who ruled a golden city; by Poe's day the term meant a place—a city of gold.

Annabel Lee[1]

It was many and many a year ago,
In a kingdom by the sea
That a maiden there lived whom you may know
By the name of ANNABEL LEE;
And this maiden she lived with no other thought
Than to love and be loved by me.

I was a child and *she* was a child,
In this kingdom by the sea,
But we loved with a love that was more than love—
I and my ANNABEL LEE—
With a love that the winged seraphs of heaven
Coveted her and me.

And this was the reason that, long ago,
In this kingdom by the sea,
A wind blew out of a cloud, chilling
My beautiful ANNABEL LEE;
So that her highborn kinsmen came[2]
And bore her away from me,
To shut her up in a sepulchre
In this kingdom by the sea.

The angels, not half so happy in heaven,
Went envying her and me—
Yes!—that was the reason (as all men know,
In this kingdom by the sea)
That the wind came out of the cloud by night,
Chilling and killing my ANNABEL LEE.

But our love it was stronger by far than the love
Of those who were older than we—
Of many far wiser than we—
And neither the angels in heaven above,

[1]Initial authorized publication was in *Sartain's Union Magazine* for January, 1850. But in his last summer Poe distributed copies to several friends, who assumed he intended them to publish the poem; or who rushed it into print when they heard of Poe's death in October. Thus some versions appeared late in 1849.

[2]Several women known to Poe have claimed to be the real-life Annabel Lee, each one encouraged (probably) by Poe's assurance that she was the one true inspiration. The likelihood is that the poet was dramatizing a universal situation common in earlier times when parents arranged marriages and took harsh measures against daughters who did not cooperate. *The Bride of Lammermoor* by Sir Walter Scott recounts a tragic tale somewhat similar to the plot of "Annabel Lee." It was Poe's favorite novel.

Nor the demons down under the sea,
Can ever dissever my soul from the soul
Of the beautiful ANNABEL LEE:

For the moon never beams, without bringing me dreams
Of the beautiful ANNABEL LEE;
And the stars never rise, but I feel the bright eyes
Of the beautiful ANNABEL LEE:
And so, all the night-tide, I lie down by the side
Of my darling—my darling—my life and my bride,
In the sepulchre there by the sea—
In her tomb by the sounding sea.

1849/50

Alone[1]

From childhood's hour I have not been
As others were—I have not seen
As others saw—I could not bring
My passions from a common spring—
From the same source I have not taken
My sorrow—I could not awaken
My heart to joy at the same tone—
And all I loved—*I* loved alone—
Then—in my childhood, in the dawn
Of a most stormy life—was drawn
From every depth of good and ill
The mystery which binds me still—
From the torrent, or the fountain—
From the red cliff of the mountain—
From the sun that round me rolled
In its autumn tint of gold—
From the lightning in the sky
As it pass'd me flying by—
From the thunder and the storm—
And the cloud that took the form
When the rest of Heaven was blue
Of a demon in my view.—

1875

[1]This poem has an interesting history. It was handwritten by Poe in 1829 in the album of a lady friend who later married a Baltimore judge. The original is now owned by the first owner's granddaughter. It was first published in 1875.

A Review: Twice-Told Tales. By Nathaniel Hawthorne.[1]

We said a few hurried words about Mr. Hawthorne in our last number, with the design of speaking more fully in the present. We are still, however, pressed for room, and must necessarily discuss his volumes more briefly and more at random than their high merits deserve.[2]

The book professes to be a collection of *tales,* yet is, in two respects, misnamed. These pieces are now in their third republication, and, of course, are thrice-told. Moreover, they are by no means *all* tales, either in the ordinary or in the legitimate understanding of the term. Many of them are pure essays; for example, "Sights from a Steeple," "Sunday at Home," "Little Annie's Ramble," "A Rill from the Town Pump," "The Toll-Gatherer's Day," "The Haunted Mind," "The Sister Years," "Snow-Flakes," "Night Sketches," and "Foot-Prints on the Sea-Shore." We mention these matters chiefly on account of their discrepancy with that marked precision and finish by which the body of the work is distinguished.

Of the essays just named, we must be content to speak in brief. They are each and all beautiful, without being characterised by the polish and adaptation so visible in the tales proper. A painter would at once note their leading or predominant feature, and style it *repose.* There is no attempt at effect. All is quiet, thoughtful, subdued. Yet this repose may exist simultaneously with high originality of thought; and Mr. Hawthorne has demonstrated the fact. At every turn we meet with novel combinations; yet these combinations never surpass the limits of the quiet. We are soothed as we read; and withal is a calm astonishment that ideas so apparently obvious have never occurred or been presented to us before. Herein our author differs materially from Lamb or Hunt or Hazlitt—who, with vivid originality of manner and expression, have less of the true novelty of thought than is generally supposed, and whose originality, at best, has an uneasy and meretricious quaintness, replete with startling effects unfounded in nature, and inducing trains of reflection which lead to no satisfactory result. The Essays of Hawthorne have much of the character of Irving, with more of originality, and less of finish; while, compared with the Spectator,[3] they have a vast superiority at all points. The Spectator, Mr. Irving, and Mr. Hawthorne have in common that tranquil and subdued manner which we have chosen to denominate *repose;* but, in the case of the two former, this repose is attained rather by the absence of novel combination, or of originality, than otherwise, and consists chiefly in the calm, quiet, unostentatious expression of commonplace thoughts, in an unambitious, unadulterated Saxon. In them, by strong effort, we are made to conceive the absence of all. In the essays before us the absence of effort is too obvious to be mistaken, and a strong under-current of *suggestion* runs continuously beneath the upper stream of the tranquil thesis. In short, these effusions of Mr. Hawthorne are the

[1]First published in *Graham's Magazine* for May, 1842.

[2]Poe had written a brief critique of Hawthorne in the April issue of *Graham's.*

[3]*The Spectator* was a famous English periodical which published the essays of Addison and Steele, masters of the essay form.

product of a truly imaginative intellect, restrained, and in some measure repressed, by fastidiousness of taste, by constitutional melancholy and by indolence.

But it is of his tales that we desire principally to speak. The tale proper, in our opinion, affords unquestionably the fairest field for the exercise of the loftiest talent, which can be afforded by the wide domains of mere prose. Were we bidden to say how the highest genius could be most advantageously employed for the best display of its own powers, we should answer, without hesitation—in the composition of a rhymed poem, not to exceed in length what might be perused in an hour. Within this limit alone can the highest order of true poetry exist. We need only here say, upon this topic, that, in almost all classes of composition, the unity of effect or impression is a point of the greatest importance. It is clear, moreover, that this unity cannot be thoroughly preserved in productions whose perusal cannot be completed at one sitting. We may continue the reading of a prose composition, from the very nature of prose itself, much longer than we can persevere, to any good purpose, in the perusal of a poem. This latter, if truly fulfilling the demands of the poetic sentiment, induces an exaltation of the soul which cannot be long sustained. All high excitements are necessarily transient. Thus a long poem is a paradox. And, without unity of impression, the deepest effects cannot be brought about. Epics were the offspring of an imperfect sense of Art, and their reign is no more. A poem *too* brief may produce a vivid, but never an intense or enduring impression. Without a certain continuity of effort—without a certain duration or repetition of purpose—the soul is never deeply moved. There must be the dropping of the water upon the rock. De Béranger has wrought brilliant things—pungent and spirit-stirring—but, like all immassive bodies, they lack *momentum,* and thus fail to satisfy the Poetic Sentiment. They sparkle and excite, but, from want of continuity, fail deeply to impress.[4] Extreme brevity will degenerate into epigrammatism; but the sin of extreme length is even more unpardonable. *In medio tutissimus ibis.*[5]

Were we called upon, however, to designate that class of composition which, next to such a poem as we have suggested, should best fulfil the demands of high genius—should offer it the most advantageous field of exertion—we should unhesitatingly speak of the prose tale, as Mr. Hawthorne has here exemplified it. We allude to the short prose narrative, requiring from a half-hour to one or two hours in its perusal. The ordinary novel is objectionable, from its length, for reasons already stated in substance. As it cannot be read at one sitting, it deprives itself, of course, of the immense force derivable from *totality.* Worldly interests intervening during the pauses of perusal, modify, annul, or counteract, in a greater or less degree, the impressions of the book. But simple cessation in reading, would, of itself, be sufficient to destroy the true unity. In the brief tale, however, the author is enabled to carry out the fulness of his intention, be it what it may. During the hour of perusal the soul of the reader is at the writer's control. There are no external or extrinsic influences—resulting from weariness or interruption.

[4]Jean-Pierre de Béranger was a French poet whose works Poe knew in translation. Poe refers to him several times elsewhere, and usually overrates his talent (Pollin).

[5]In a middle course you will go most safely.

A skilful literary artist has constructed a tale. If wise, he has not fashioned his thoughts to accommodate his incidents; but having conceived, with deliberate care, a certain unique or single *effect* to be wrought out, he then invents such incidents—he then combines such events as may best aid him in establishing this preconceived effect. If his very initial sentence tend not to the outbringing of this effect, then he has failed in his first step. In the whole composition there should be no word written, of which the tendency, direct or indirect, is not to the one pre-established design. And by such means, with such care and skill, a picture is at length painted which leaves in the mind of him who contemplates it with a kindred art, a sense of the fullest satisfaction. The idea of the tale has been presented unblemished, because undisturbed; and this is an end unattainable by the novel. Undue brevity is just as exceptionable here as in the poem; but undue length is yet more to be avoided.

We have said that the tale has a point of superiority even over the poem. In fact, while the *rhythm* of this latter is an essential aid in the development of the poet's highest idea—the idea of the Beautiful—the artificialities of this rhythm are an inseparable bar to the development of all points of thought or expression which have their basis in *Truth*. But Truth is often, and in very great degree, the aim of the tale. Some of the finest tales are tales of ratiocination. Thus the field of this species of composition, if not in so elevated a region on the mountain of Mind, is a tableland of far vaster extent than the domain of the mere poem. Its products are never so rich, but infinitely more numerous, and more appreciable by the mass of mankind. The writer of the prose tale, in short, may bring to his theme a vast variety of modes or inflections of thought and expression—(the ratiocinative, for example, the sarcastic, or the humorous) which are not only antagonistical to the nature of the poem, but absolutely forbidden by one of its most peculiar and indispensable adjuncts; we allude, of course, to rhythm. It may be added here, *par parenthèse,* that the author who aims at the purely beautiful in a prose tale is laboring at great disadvantage. For Beauty can be better treated in the poem. Not so with terror, or passion, or horror, or a multitude of such other points. And here it will be seen how full of prejudice are the usual animadversions against those *tales of effect,* many fine examples of which were found in the earlier numbers of Blackwood.[6] The impressions produced were wrought in a legitimate sphere of action, and constituted a legitimate although sometimes an exaggerated interest. They were relished by every man of genius: although there were found many men of genius who condemned them without just ground. The true critic will but demand that the design intended be accomplished, to the fullest extent, by the means most advantageously applicable.

We have very few American tales of real merit—we may say, indeed, none, with the exception of "The Tales of a Traveller" of Washington Irving, and these "Twice-Told Tales" of Mr. Hawthorne. Some of the pieces of Mr. John Neal abound in vigor and originality; but in general, his compositions of this class are excessively diffuse, extravagant, and indicative of an imperfect sentiment of Art. Articles at random are, now and then, met with in our periodicals which might be advantageously compared

[6]Poe read British magazines as a pastime in childhood and as a "professional duty" in his maturity. The periodical which had the strongest influence on his themes and style was *Blackwood's Edinburgh Magazine.*

with the best effusions of the British Magazines; but, upon the whole, we are far behind our progenitors in this department of literature.

Of Mr. Hawthorne's Tales we would say, emphatically, that they belong to the highest region of Art—an Art subservient to genius of a very lofty order. We had supposed, with good reason for so supposing, that he had been thrust into his present position by one of the impudent *cliques* which beset our literature, and whose pretensions it is our full purpose to expose at the earliest opportunity;[7] but we have been most agreeably mistaken. We know of few compositions which the critic can more honestly commend than these "Twice-Told Tales." As Americans, we feel proud of the book.

Mr. Hawthorne's distinctive trait is invention, creation, imagination, originality—a trait which, in the literature of fiction, is positively worth all the rest. But the nature of originality, so far as regards its manifestation in letters, is but imperfectly understood. The inventive or original mind as frequently displays itself in novelty of *tone* as in novelty of matter. Mr. Hawthorne is original at *all* points.

It would be a matter of some difficulty to designate the best of these tales; we repeat that, without exception, they are beautiful. "Wakefield" is remarkable for the skill with which an old idea—a well-known incident—is worked up or discussed. A man of whims conceives the purpose of quitting his wife and residing *incognito,* for twenty years, in her immediate neighborhood. Something of this kind actually happened in London. The force of Mr. Hawthorne's tale lies in the analysis of the motives which must or might have impelled the husband to such folly, in the first instance, with the possible causes of his perseverance. Upon this thesis a sketch of singular power has been constructed.

"The Wedding Knell" is full of the boldest imagination—an imagination fully controlled by taste. The most captious critic could find no flaw in this production.

"The Minister's Black Veil" is a masterly composition of which the sole defect is that to the rabble its exquisite skill will be *caviare.* The *obvious* meaning of this article will be found to smother its insinuated one. The *moral* put into the mouth of the dying minister will be supposed to convey the *true* import of the narrative; and that a crime of dark dye, (having reference to the "young lady") has been committed, is a point which only minds congenial with that of the author will perceive.

"Mr. Higginbotham's Catastrophe" is vividly original and managed most dexterously.

"Dr. Heidegger's Experiment" is exceedingly well imagined, and executed with surpassing ability. The artist breathes in every line of it.

"The White Old Maid" is objectionable, even more than the "Minister's Black Veil," on the score of its mysticism. Even with the thoughtful and analytic, there will be much trouble in penetrating its entire import.

"The Hollow of the Three Hills" we would quote in full, had we space;—not as evincing higher talent than any of the other pieces, but as affording an excellent example of the author's peculiar ability. The subject is commonplace. A witch subjects

[7]Poe's relations with New York literary coteries were complex and intense; some groups defended him in print while others attacked his character, appearance, and personal habits. Poe sued one of his detractors in 1847 and won a cash settlement.

the Distant and the Past to the view of a mourner. It has been the fashion to describe, in such cases, a mirror in which the images of the absent appear; or a cloud of smoke is made to arise, and thence the figures are gradually unfolded. Mr. Hawthorne has wonderfully heightened his effect by making the ear, in place of the eye, the medium by which the fantasy is conveyed. The head of the mourner is enveloped in the cloak of the witch, and within its magic folds there arise sounds which have an all-sufficient intelligence. Throughout this article also, the artist is conspicuous—not more in positive than in negative merits. Not only is all done that should be done, but (what perhaps is an end with more difficulty attained) there is nothing done which should not be. Every word *tells,* and there is not a word which does *not* tell.

In "Howe's Masquerade" we observe something which resembles plagiarism—but which *may be* a very flattering coincidence of thought. We quote the passage in question.

[We omit Poe's long quotation from Hawthorne.]

The idea here is, that the figure in the cloak is the phantom or reduplication of Sir William Howe; but in an article called "William Wilson," one of the "Tales of the Grotesque and Arabesque," we have not only the same idea, but the same idea similarly presented in several respects. We quote two paragraphs, which our readers may compare with what has been already given. We have italicized, above, the immediate particulars of resemblance.

[We omit Poe's long quotation from Hawthorne.]

Here it will be observed that, not only are the two general conceptions identical, but there are various *points* of similarity. In each case the figure seen is the wraith or duplication of the beholder. In each case the scene is a masquerade. In each case the figure is cloaked. In each, there is a quarrel—that is to say, angry words pass between the parties. In each the beholder is enraged. In each the cloak and sword fall upon the floor. The "villain, unmuffle yourself," of Mr. H. is precisely paralleled by a passage at page 56 of "William Wilson."[8]

In the way of objection we have scarcely a word to say of these tales. There is, perhaps, a somewhat too general or prevalent *tone*—a tone of melancholy and mysticism. The subjects are insufficiently varied. There is not so much of *versatility* evinced as we might well be warranted in expecting from the high powers of Mr. Hawthorne. But beyond these trivial exceptions we have really none to make. The style is purity itself. Force abounds. High imagination gleams from every page. Mr. Hawthorne is a man of the truest genius. We only regret that the limits of our Magazine will not permit us to pay him that full tribute of commendation, which, under other circumstances, we should be so eager to pay.[9]

1842

[8]If there were anything more than mere coincidence involved in the similarities between the two passages, the fault would have to be attributed to Poe. Hawthorne's story appeared in print a year earlier than Poe's.

[9]This critical essay has been widely and profoundly influential, especially in its description of the effective short story.

The Philosophy of Composition[1]

Charles Dickens, in a note now lying before me, alluding to an examination I once made of the mechanism of "Barnaby Rudge," says—"By the way, are you aware that Godwin wrote his 'Caleb Williams' backwards? He first involved his hero in a web of difficulties, forming the second volume, and then, for the first, cast about him for some mode of accounting for what had been done."

I cannot think this the *precise* mode of procedure on the part of Godwin—and indeed what he himself acknowledges,[2] is not altogether in accordance with Mr. Dickens' idea—but the author of "Caleb Williams" was too good an artist not to perceive the advantage derivable from at least a somewhat similar process. Nothing is more clear than that every plot, worth the name, must be elaborated to its *dénouement*[3] before anything be attempted with the pen. It is only with the *dénouement* constantly in view that we can give a plot its indispensable air of consequence, or causation, by making the incidents, and especially the tone at all points, tend to the development of the intention.

There is a radical error, I think, in the usual mode of constructing a story. Either history affords a thesis—or one is suggested by an incident of the day—or, at best, the author sets himself to work in the combination of striking events to form merely the basis of his narrative—designing, generally, to fill in with description, dialogue, or autorial comment, whatever crevices of fact, or action, may, from page to page, render themselves apparent.

I prefer commencing with the consideration of an *effect.* Keeping originality *always* in view—for he is false to himself who ventures to dispense with so obvious and so easily attainable a source of interest—I say to myself, in the first place, "Of the innumerable effects, or impressions, of which the heart, the intellect, or (more generally) the soul is susceptible, what one shall I, on the present occasion, select?" Having chosen a novel, first, and secondly a vivid effect, I consider whether it can be best wrought by incident or tone—whether by ordinary incidents and peculiar tone, or the converse, or by peculiarity both of incident and tone—afterward looking about me (or rather within) for such combinations of event, or tone, as shall best aid me in the construction of the effect.

I have often thought how interesting a magazine paper[4] might be written by any author who would—that is to say who could—detail, step by step, the processes by which any one of his compositions attained its ultimate point of completion. Why such a paper has never been given to the world, I am much at a loss to say—but, perhaps, the autorial vanity has had more to do with the omission than any one other cause. Most writers—poets in especial—prefer having it understood that they compose by a species of fine frenzy—an ecstatic intuition—and would

[1]Originally published in *Graham's Magazine* for April, 1846.

[2]Poe wrote a critical commentary on Dickens's *Barnaby Rudge* in which he predicted the conclusion before the last installment appeared in print. Godwin prefaces his *Caleb Williams* with the observation that he "invented" the third volume of his tale first, then the second, etc.

[3]Unravelling or final solution.

[4]That is, a magazine article.

positively shudder at letting the public take a peep behind the scenes, at the elaborate and vacillating crudities of thought—at the true purposes seized only at the last moment—at the innumerable glimpses of idea that arrived not at the maturity of full view—at the fully matured fancies discarded in despair as unmanageable—at the cautious selections and rejections—at the painful erasures and interpolations—in a word, at the wheels and pinions—the tackle for scene-shifting—the step-ladders and demon-traps—the cock's feathers, the red paint and the black patches, which, in ninety-nine cases out of the hundred, constitute the properties of the literary *histrio.*

I am aware, on the other hand, that the case is by no means common, in which an author is at all in condition to retrace the steps by which his conclusions have been attained. In general, suggestions, having arisen pell-mell, are pursued and forgotten in a similar manner.

For my own part, I have neither sympathy with the repugnance alluded to, nor, at any time the least difficulty in recalling to mind the progressive steps of any of my compositions; and, since the interest of an analysis, or reconstruction, such as I have considered a *desideratum,*[5] is quite independent of any real or fancied interest in the thing analyzed, it will not be regarded as a breach of decorum on my part to show the *modus operandi* by which some one of my own works was put together. I select "The Raven," as most generally known. It is my design to render it manifest that no one point in its composition is referrible either to accident or intuition—that the work proceeded, step by step, to its completion with the precision and rigid consequence of a mathematical problem.

Let us dismiss, as irrelevant to the poem, *per se,* the circumstance—or say the necessity—which, in the first place, gave rise to the intention of composing *a* poem that should suit at once the popular and the critical taste.

We commence, then, with this intention.

The initial consideration was that of extent. If any literary work is too long to be read at one sitting, we must be content to dispense with the immensely important effect derivable from unity of impression—for, if two sittings be required, the affairs of the world interfere, and every thing like totality is at once destroyed. But since, *ceteris paribus,*[6] no poet can afford to dispense with *any thing* that may advance his design, it but remains to be seen whether there is, in extent, any advantage to counterbalance the loss of unity which attends it. Here I say no, at once. What we term a long poem is, in fact, merely a succession of brief ones—that is to say, of brief poetical effects. It is needless to demonstrate that a poem is such, only inasmuch as it intensely excites, by elevating, the soul; and all intense excitements are, through a psychal necessity, brief. For this reason, at least one half of the "Paradise Lost" is essentially prose—a succession of poetical excitements interspersed, *inevitably,* with corresponding depressions—the whole being deprived, through the extremeness of its length, of the vastly important artistic element, totality, or unity, of effect.

It appears evident, then, that there is a distinct limit, as regards length, to all works of literary art—the limit of a single sitting—and that, although in certain classes of prose composition, such as "Robinson Crusoe," (demanding no unity,) this limit may be advantageously overpassed, it can never properly be overpassed in a

[5]Something needed.

[6]Other things being equal.

poem. Within this limit, the extent of a poem may be made to bear mathematical relation to its merit—in other words, to the excitement or elevation—again in other words, to the degree of the true poetical effect which it is capable of inducing; for it is clear that the brevity must be in direct ratio of the intensity of the intended effect:—this, with one proviso—that a certain degree of duration is absolutely requisite for the production of any effect at all.

Holding in view these considerations, as well as that degree of excitement which I deemed not above the popular, while not below the critical, taste, I reached at once what I conceived the proper *length* for my intended poem—a length of about one hundred lines. It is, in fact, a hundred and eight.

My next thought concerned the choice of an impression, or effect, to be conveyed: and here I may as well observe that, throughout the construction, I kept steadily in view the design of rendering the work *universally* appreciable. I should be carried too far out of my immediate topic were I to demonstrate a point upon which I have repeatedly insisted, and which, with the poetical, stands not in the slightest need of demonstration—the point, I mean, that Beauty is the sole legitimate province of the poem. A few words, however, in elucidation of my real meaning, which some of my friends have evinced a disposition to misrepresent. That pleasure which is at once the most intense, the most elevating, and the most pure, is, I believe, found in the contemplation of the beautiful. When, indeed, men speak of Beauty, they mean, precisely, not a quality, as is supposed, but an effect—they refer, in short, just to that intense and pure elevation of *soul*—*not* of intellect, or of heart—upon which I have commented, and which is experienced in consequence of contemplating "the beautiful." Now I designate Beauty as the province of the poem, merely because it is an obvious rule of Art that effects should be made to spring from direct causes—that objects should be attained through means best adapted for their attainment—no one as yet having been weak enough to deny that the peculiar elevation alluded to is *most readily* attained in the poem. Now the object, Truth, or the satisfaction of the intellect, and the object Passion, or the excitement of the heart, are, although attainable, to a certain extent, in poetry, far more readily attainable in prose. Truth, in fact, demands a precision, and Passion a *homeliness* (the truly passionate will comprehend me) which are absolutely antagonistic to that Beauty which, I maintain, is the excitement, or pleasurable elevation, of the soul. It by no means follows from any thing here said, that passion, or even truth, may not be introduced, and even profitably introduced, into a poem—for they may serve in elucidation, or aid the general effect, as do discords in music, by contrast—but the true artist will always contrive, first, to tone them into proper subservience to the predominant aim, and, secondly, to enveil them, as far as possible, in that Beauty which is the atmosphere and the essence of the poem.

Regarding, then, Beauty as my province, my next question referred to the *tone* of its highest manifestation—and all experience has shown that this tone is one of *sadness.* Beauty of whatever kind, in its supreme development, invariably excites the sensitive soul to tears. Melancholy is thus the most legitimate of all the poetical tones.[7]

[7]Poe's very dogmatic exposition of poetry's function demonstrates the fact—evidenced in some of his poems and tales—that he was more in tune with the sentimental literature of his time than is usually acknowledged.

The length, the province, and the tone, being thus determined, I betook myself to ordinary induction, with the view of obtaining some artistic piquancy which might serve me as a key-note in the construction of the poem—some pivot upon which the whole structure might turn. In carefully thinking over all the usual artistic effects—or more properly *points,* in the theatrical sense—I did not fail to perceive immediately that no one had been so universally employed as that of the *refrain.* The universality of its employment sufficed to assure me of its intrinsic value, and spared me the necessity of submitting it to analysis. I considered it, however, with regard to its susceptibility of improvement, and soon saw it to be in a primitive condition. As commonly used, the *refrain,* or burden, not only is limited to lyric verse, but depends for its impression upon the force of monotone—both in sound and thought. The pleasure is deduced solely from the sense of identity—of repetition. I resolved to diversify, and so heighten, the effect, by adhering, in general, to the monotone of sound, while I continually varied that of thought: that is to say, I determined to produce continuously novel effects, by the variation *of the application* of the *refrain*—the *refrain* itself remaining, for the most part, unvaried.

These points being settled, I next bethought me of the *nature* of my *refrain.* Since its application was to be repeatedly varied, it was clear that the *refrain* itself must be brief, for there would have been an insurmountable difficulty in frequent variations of application in any sentence of length. In proportion to the brevity of the sentence, would, of course, be the facility of the variation. This led me at once to a single word as the best *refrain.*

The question now arose as to the *character* of the word. Having made up my mind to a *refrain,* the division of the poem into stanzas was, of course, a corollary: the *refrain* forming the close of each stanza. That such a close, to have force, must be sonorous and susceptible of protracted emphasis, admitted no doubt: and these considerations inevitably led me to the long *o* as the most sonorous vowel, in connection with *r* as the most producible consonant.

The sound of the *refrain* being thus determined, it became necessary to select a word embodying this sound, and at the same time in the fullest possible keeping with that melancholy which I had predetermined as the tone of the poem. In such a search it would have been absolutely impossible to overlook the word "Nevermore." In fact, it was the very first which presented itself.

The next *desideratum* was a pretext for the continuous use of the one word "nevermore." In observing the difficulty which I at once found in inventing a sufficiently plausible reason for its continuous repetition, I did not fail to perceive that this difficulty arose solely from the pre-assumption that the word was to be so continuously or monotonously spoken by *a human* being—I did not fail to perceive, in short, that the difficulty lay in the reconciliation of this monotony with the exercise of reason on the part of the creature repeating the word. Here, then, immediately arose the idea of a *non*-reasoning creature capable of speech; and, very naturally, a parrot, in the first instance, suggested itself, but was superseded forthwith by a Raven, as equally capable of speech, and infinitely more in keeping with the intended *tone.*

I had now gone so far as the conception of a Raven—the bird of ill omen—monotonously repeating the one word, "Nevermore," at the conclusion of each stanza, in a poem of melancholy tone, and in length about one hundred lines. Now, never losing sight of the object *supremeness,* or perfection, at all points, I asked myself—

"Of all melancholy topics, what according to the *universal* understanding of mankind, is the *most* melancholy?" Death—was the obvious reply. "And when," I said, "is this most melancholy of topics most poetical?" From what I have already explained at some length, the answer here also, is obvious—"When it most closely allies itself to *Beauty:* the death, then, of a beautiful woman is, unquestionably, the most poetical topic in the world—and equally is it beyond doubt that the lips best suited for such topic are those of a bereaved lover."[8]

I had now to combine the two ideas, of a lover lamenting his deceased mistress and a Raven continuously repeating the word "Nevermore."—I had to combine these, bearing in mind my design of varying, at every turn, the *application* of the word repeated; but the only intelligible mode of such combination is that of imagining the Raven employing the word in answer to the queries of the lover. And here it was that I saw at once the opportunity afforded for the effect on which I had been depending—that is to say, the effect of the *variation of application.* I saw that I could make the first query propounded by the lover—the first query to which the Raven should reply "Nevermore"—that I could make this first query a commonplace one—the second less so—the third still less, and so on—until at length the lover, startled from his original *nonchalance* by the melancholy character of the word itself—by its frequent repetition—and by a consideration of the ominous reputation of the fowl that uttered it—is at length excited to superstition, and wildly propounds queries of a far different character—queries whose solution he has passionately at heart—propounds them half in superstition and half in that species of despair which delights in self-torture—propounds them not altogether because he believes in the prophetic or demoniac character of the bird (which, reason assures him, is merely repeating a lesson learned by rote) but because he experiences a phrenzied pleasure in so modeling his questions as to receive from the *expected* "Nevermore" the most delicious because the most intolerable of sorrow. Perceiving the opportunity thus afforded me—or, more strictly, thus forced upon me in the progress of the construction—I first established in mind the climax, or concluding query—that query to which "Nevermore" should be in the last place an answer—that in reply to which this word "Nevermore" should involve the utmost conceivable amount of sorrow and despair.

Here then the poem may be said to have its beginning—at the end, where all works of art should begin—for it was here, at this point of my preconsiderations, that I first put pen to paper in the composition of the stanza:

"Prophet," said I, "thing of evil! prophet still if bird or devil!
By that heaven that bends above us—by that God we both adore,
Tell this soul with sorrow laden, if within the distant Aidenn,
It shall clasp a sainted maiden whom the angels name Lenore—
Clasp a rare and radiant maiden whom the angels name Lenore."
Quoth the raven "Nevermore."

[8]Poe's pretense at logically selecting sounds, words, and themes must not be taken too literally. In striving to create the impression of self-inspiration, Poe omits mention of literary influence, which played a large part in his composition of "The Raven" and other works.

I composed this stanza, at this point, first that, by establishing the climax, I might the better vary and graduate, as regards seriousness and importance, the preceding queries of the lover—and, secondly, that I might definitely settle the rhythm, the metre, and the length and general arrangement of the stanza—as well as graduate the stanzas which were to precede, so that none of them might surpass this in rhythmical effect. Had I been able, in the subsequent composition, to construct more vigorous stanzas, I should, without scruple, have purposely enfeebled them, so as not to interfere with the climacteric effect.[9]

And here I may as well say a few words of the versification. My first object (as usual) was originality. The extent to which this has been neglected, in versification, is one of the most unaccountable things in the world. Admitting that there is little possibility of variety in mere *rhythm,* it is still clear that the possible varieties of metre and stanza are absolutely infinite—and yet, *for centuries, no man, in verse, has ever done, or ever seemed to think of doing, an original thing.* The fact is, that originality (unless in minds of very unusual force) is by no means a matter, as some suppose, of impulse or intuition. In general, to be found, it must be elaborately sought, and although a positive merit of the highest class, demands in its attainment less of invention than negation.

Of course, I pretend to no originality in either the rhythm or metre of the "Raven." The former is trochaic—the latter is octameter acatalectic, alternating with heptameter catalectic repeated in the *refrain* of the fifth verse, and terminating with tetrameter catalectic. Less pedantically—the feet employed throughout (trochees) consist of a long syllable followed by a short: the first line of the stanza consists of eight of these feet—the second of seven and a half (in effect two-thirds)—the third of eight—the fourth of seven and a half—the fifth the same—the sixth three and a half. Now, each of these lines, taken individually, has been employed before, and what originality the "Raven" has, is in their *combination into stanza;* nothing even remotely approaching this combination has ever been attempted.[10] The effect of this originality of combination is aided by other unusual, and some altogether novel effects, arising from an extension of the application of the principles of rhyme and alliteration.

The next point to be considered was the mode of bringing together the lover and the Raven—and the first branch of this consideration was the *locale.* For this the most natural suggestion might seem to be a forest, or the fields—but it has always appeared to me that a close *circumscription of space* is absolutely necessary to the effect of insulated incident:—it has the force of a frame to a picture. It has an indisputable moral power in keeping concentrated the attention, and, of course, must not be confounded with mere unity of place.

I determined, then, to place the lover in his chamber—in a chamber rendered sacred to him by memories of her who had frequented it. The room is represented as richly furnished—this in mere pursuance of the ideas I have already explained on the subject of Beauty, as the sole true poetical thesis.

[9]He means climactic.

[10]A slight exaggeration, as Poe well knew. He had recently read Elizabeth Barrett Browning's "Lady Geraldine's Courtship," which is quite close to "The Raven" in rhyme and meter.

The *locale* being thus determined, I had now to introduce the bird—and the thought of introducing him through the window, was inevitable. The idea of making the lover suppose, in the first instance, that the flapping of the wings of the bird against the shutter, is a "tapping" at the door, originated in a wish to increase, by prolonging, the reader's curiosity, and in a desire to admit the incidental effect arising from the lover's throwing open the door, finding all dark, and thence adopting the half-fancy that it was the spirit of his mistress that knocked.

I made the night tempestuous, first, to account for the Raven's seeking admission, and secondly, for the effect of contrast with the (physical) serenity within the chamber.

I made the bird alight on the bust of Pallas, also for the effect of contrast between the marble and the plumage—it being understood that the bust was absolutely *suggested* by the bird—the bust of *Pallas* being chosen, first, as most in keeping with the scholarship of the lover, and, secondly, for the sonorousness of the word, Pallas, itself.

About the middle of the poem, also, I have availed myself of the force of contrast, with a view of deepening the ultimate impression. For example, an air of the fantastic—approaching as nearly to the ludicrous as was admissible—is given to the Raven's entrance. He comes in "with many a flirt and flutter."

> Not the *least obeisance made he*—not a moment stopped or stayed he,
> *But with mien of lord or lady,* perched above my chamber door.

In the two stanzas which follow, the design is more obviously carried out:—

> Then this ebony bird beguiling my sad fancy into smiling
> By the *grave and stern decorum of the countenance it wore,*
> "Though thy *crest be shorn and shaven* thou," I said, "art sure no craven,
> Ghastly grim and ancient Raven wandering from the nightly shore—
> Tell me what thy lordly name is on the Night's Plutonian shore?"
> Quoth the Raven "Nevermore."
>
> Much I marvelled *this ungainly fowl* to hear discourse so plainly
> Though its answer little meaning—little relevancy bore;
> For we cannot help agreeing that no living human being
> *Ever yet was blessed with seeing bird above his chamber door—*
> *Bird or beast upon the sculptured bust above his chamber door,*
> With such name as "Nevermore."

The effect of the *dénouement* being thus provided for, I immediately drop the fantastic for a tone of the most profound seriousness:—this tone commencing in the stanza directly following the one last quoted, with the line,

> But the Raven, sitting lonely on that placid bust, spoke only, etc.

From this epoch the lover no longer jests—no longer sees any thing even of the fantastic in the Raven's demeanor. He speaks of him as a "grim, ungainly, ghastly, gaunt, and ominous bird of yore," and feels the "fiery eyes" burning into his "bosom's core." This revolution of thought, or fancy, on the lover's part, is intended to induce a similar one on the part of the reader—to bring the mind into a proper frame for the *dénouement*—which is now brought about as rapidly and as *directly* as possible.

With the *dénouement* proper—with the Raven's reply, "Nevermore," to the lover's final demand if he shall meet his mistress in another world—the poem, in its obvious phase, that of a simple narrative, may be said to have its completion. So far, every thing is within the limits of the accountable—of the real. A raven, having learned by rote the single word "Nevermore," and having escaped from the custody of its owner, is driven at midnight, through the violence of a storm, to seek admission at a window from which a light still gleams—the chamber-window of a student, occupied half in poring over a volume, half in dreaming of a beloved mistress deceased. The casement being thrown open at the fluttering of the bird's wings, the bird itself perches on the most convenient seat out of the immediate reach of the student, who, amused by the incident and the oddity of the visitor's demeanor, demands of it, in jest and without looking for a reply, its name. The raven addressed, answers with its customary word, "Nevermore"—a word which finds immediate echo in the melancholy heart of the student, who, giving utterance aloud to certain thoughts suggested by the occasion, is again startled by the fowl's repetition of "Nevermore." The student now guesses the state of the base, but is impelled, as I have before explained, by the human thirst for self-torture, and in part by superstition, to propound such queries to the bird as will bring him, the lover, the most of the luxury of sorrow, through the anticipated answer "Nevermore." With the indulgence, to the extreme, of this self-torture, the narration, in what I have termed its first or obvious phase, has a natural termination, and so far there has been no overstepping of the limits of the real.

But in subjects so handled, however skilfully, or with however vivid an array of incident, there is always a certain hardness or nakedness, which repels the artistical eye. Two things are invariably required—first, some amount of complexity, or more properly, adaptation; and, secondly, some amount of suggestiveness—some undercurrent, however indefinite, of meaning. It is this latter, in especial, which imparts to a work of art so much of that *richness* (to borrow from colloquy a forcible term) which we are too fond of confounding with *the ideal.* It is the *excess* of the suggested meaning—it is the rendering this the upper instead of the under current of the theme—which turns into prose (and that of the very flattest kind) the so called poetry of the so called transcendentalists.

Holding these opinions, I added the two concluding stanzas of the poem—their suggestiveness being thus made to pervade all the narrative which has preceded them. The under-current of meaning is rendered first apparent in the lines—

> "Take thy beak from out *my heart,* and take thy form from off my
> door!"
> Quoth the Raven "Nevermore!"

It will be observed that the words, "from out my heart," involve the first metaphorical expression in the poem. They, with the answer, "Nevermore," dispose the mind to seek a moral in all that has been previously narrated. The reader begins now to regard the Raven as emblematical[11]—but it is not until the very last line of the very last stanza, that the intention of making him emblematical of *Mournful and Never-ending Remembrance* is permitted distinctly to be seen:

> And the Raven, never flitting, still is sitting, still is sitting,
> On the pallid bust of Pallas, just above my chamber door;
> And his eyes have all the seeming of a demon's that is dreaming,
> And the lamplight o'er him streaming throws his shadow on the
> floor;
> And my soul *from out that shadow* that lies floating on the floor
> Shall be lifted—nevermore.

1846

HUMOR OF THE OLD SOUTHWEST

Davy Crockett, 1786–1836
Mike Fink, 1770?–1823?
Augustus Baldwin Longstreet, 1790–1870
George Washington Harris, 1814–1869

Southwest humor thrives on borders. It grew on a border, the Old Southwest frontier that before the Civil War ran through what is now the Southeast and then was generally identified with southern (rather than western) attitudes. As writing, it crossed the border with orality, coming from storytelling and in turn shaping the telling of tales. (In fact, the selections included here are well worth reading aloud.) It straddles the line, too, between "popular" and "high" literature; it appeared in newspapers and almanacs, in popular theater, and then in Mark Twain and William Faulkner. It lives on the border of realism, presenting as sober reality material that may be wildly exaggerated or clearly fantastic. Although almost exclusively the domain of white men, Southwest humor crosses traditional boundaries of gender as well, if only in one direction: some of its later ringtailed roarers are women. And it crosses cultural boundaries; it represents both genteel and frontier values, and it can mock and subvert either or both. From its place on so many borders, this style of humor has maintained a vitality that continues to excite interest in contemporary readers.

[11]A modern critic would use the term symbolic.

SUT LOVINGOOD.

YARNS SPUN

by a

"NAT'RAL BORN DURN'D FOOL.

WARPED AND WOVE FOR PUBLIC WEAR.

by

GEORGE W. HARRIS.

DEDICATORY.

"Well, Sut, your stories are all ready for the printer; to whom do you wish to dedicate the work?"

"I don't keer much, George; haint hit a kine ove lickskillet bisness, enyhow—sorter like the waggin ove a dorg's tail, when he sees yu eatin ove sassengers? But yere goes: How wud Anner Dickinson du tu pack hit ontu?"

"Oh, Sut, that would never do. What! dedicate such nonsense as yours to a woman? How will this do?

DEDICATED TO

THE MEMORY OF

ELBRIDGE GERRY EASTMAN,

THE ABLE EDITOR, AND FINISHED GENTLEMAN, THE FRIEND, WHOSE KINDLY VOICE FIRST INSPIRED MY TIMID PEN WITH HOPE.

GRATEFUL MEMORY

DROPS A TEAR AMONG THE FLOWERS, AS AFFECTION STREWS THEM O'ER HIS GRAVE."

"Won't begin tu du, George. The idear ove enybody bein grateful, ur rememberin a dead friend now-a-days! Why, if that wer tu git out onto me, I'd never be able tu mix in decent s'ciety while I lived. Tare that up, George."

"Well, what do you say to this, Sut?

TO

WILLIAM CRUTCHFIELD, OF CHATTANOOGA,

MY FRIEND IN STORM AND SUNSHINE, BRAVE ENOUGH TO BE TRUE, AND TRUE ENOUGH TO BE SINGULAR; ONE WHO SAYS WHAT HE THINKS, AND VERY OFTEN THINKS WHAT HE SAYS."

"That won't du either, hoss. 'Tis mos' es bad tu be grateful tu the livin es the dead. I tell yu hit ain't smart. Ef ever yu is grateful *at all,* show hit tu them what yu *expeck will* du a favor, *never* tu the 'tarnil fool what *hes dun hit.* Never es yu expeck tu git tu heaven, *never pay fur a ded hoss.* An' more, every fice ur houn dorg what either him ur me has wallop'd fur thar nastiness, wud open ontu our trail—ontu him fur buyin me, an' ontu me fur bein bought. No, George, I'll do ontill Bill gets poor ur dus sum devilmint. I'll tell yu what I'll du, I'll jis' dedercate this yere perduction *tu the durndest fool* in the United States, an' Massachusets too, he or she. An then, by golly, I'll jis' watch hu claims hit."

"Very well, Sut; how shall I write it? how designate the proper one?"

"Jis' this way; hits the easiest dun thing in the world:

DEDERCATED

WIF THE SYMPERTHYS OVE THE ORTHUR,

TU THE MAN UR 'OMAN, HUEVER THEY BE,

WHAT *DON'T* READ THIS YERE BOOK.

Don't *that* kiver the case tu a dot? Hu knows but what I'se dedercatin hit tu mysef at las'. Well, I don't keer a durn, I kin stan hit, ef the rest ove em kin."

The two voices in George Washington Harris's "Dedicatory" to his 1867 *Sut Lovingood* speak across several divides. Sut's hope to womanize with his writing opposes his friend's ideas about what is appropriate for a lady; Sut's language is as defiantly non-standard as his friend's is aggressively conventional, and Sut's morality is as Machiavellian as his friend's is pious. Yet despite the attacks on "decent s'ciety," the piece seems clearly written for an audience of exactly such folk.

Sut Lovingood, who made his first book appearance in 1867, is the latecomer in the Heath anthology's group of Southwest humorists. By then, this type of humor had already enjoyed its heyday, roughly the thirty years prior to the Civil War. One of the earliest practitioners, David Crockett (with the help of a ghostwriter) wrote the *Narrative* of his life as a campaign strategy when he was running for office in 1835. Most, if not all, of the rest of the Crockett writings come not from his pen but from numerous folk who wrote out of and thus contributed to the creation of the legendary Davy. The actual person David was born in Tennessee (though not on a mountain top), and metamorphosed into Davy, the legendary woodsman whose revival in the 1950s brought coontail hats and the popular "Ballad of Davy Crockett" into thousands of American homes. As a young man, David Crockett fought Indians under Andrew Jackson (whose policies he was later to oppose). He ran for and won a seat in the Tennessee state legislature in 1821; in 1827 he won a seat in Congress. By 1831 the legend-making had begun: James Kirke Paulding's *The Lion of the West* had as its leading character one Nimrod Wildfire, based on Crockett, and in 1833 Mathew St. Clair Clarke's *Life and Adventures of Colonel David Crockett of West Tennessee,* more famously reprinted as *Sketches and Eccentricities of Colonel David Crockett of West Tennessee,* was in print. After his heroic death at the Alamo in 1836, Crockett's fame spread through songs, poems, almanacs (known as Crockett Almanacs), plays, and silent movies. 1955 saw the Disney-inspired Crockett craze, and in 1986 his bicentennial was celebrated.

"Sunrise in His Pocket," taken from the posthumous Crockett Almanacs and clearly not attributable to David, shows the exuberant exaggeration typical of the tall-tale teller and hero Davy was made into. "A Pretty Predicament" and "Crockett's Daughters" simultaneously subvert cultural norms for women and perpetuate racial stereotyping.

The Crockett Almanacs contain stories about another legendary hero of the Old Southwest, Mike Fink. Although there is no evidence that Fink wrote down any stories himself, he apparently told them often and well. The earliest to claim to have heard and recorded Fink was Morgan Neville, whose *The Last of the Boatmen* appeared in 1829. Fink was a keelboatman on the Mississippi River. Before taking to the river he had worked, like Crockett, as an Indian scout; when he left the river, it was to move west as a trapper, where he died in the wilderness. Fink's exploits led him to be called (or call himself) "half-horse, half-alligator." Born around 1770 near Fort Pitt, Pennsylvania, Mike Fink had already earned a reputation for bravery and marksmanship when he took work poling keelboats, a sort of barge, down and up the Mississippi. On the river his violence, his brutal jokes, his competitive spirit, and his love life earned him legendary status. In 1822 Fink left for the west as a trapper; he may have died in the manner described in our account from Joseph M. Field in the *St. Louis Reveille* (1844). "Mike Fink Trying to Scare Mrs. Crockett" provides an interesting counterpoint to "Fink's Brag," and comes from the Crockett Almanacs, as does the story about Mike's daughter Sal Fink, "The Mississippi Screamer."

The first examples of literary rather than folkloristic Southwest humor came from a Georgia lawyer, judge, politician, minister, and secessionist, Augustus Baldwin Longstreet. An energetic and restless man, Longstreet was born in Augusta, Georgia. A friend of John C. Calhoun, Longstreet followed him to Yale and then into the law, which he practiced back home in Georgia. There he began *Georgia Scenes;* he published his first story in a Milledgeville paper in 1832. By 1838 Longstreet had taken on another profession: Methodist minister. In 1839, he took the presidency of Emory College, and moved after ten years to preside at Centenary College, followed by the University of Mississippi and the University of South Carolina. Longstreet's convictions and predilections remained typical for his class and region; he advocated secession and refused to attend an International Statistical Congress in London because of the presence of a black delegate.

The stories in *Georgia Scenes* are set in northeast Georgia, and Longstreet claimed that they represent "*real* incidents and characters" and "supply a chasm in history . . . the [Southern] society of the first thirty years of the republic." Edgar Allan Poe reviewed it in the *Southern Literary Messenger* for March, 1836, and the stories have since then enjoyed considerable success. "The Horse Swap" represents a situation that Faulkner would draw upon in "Spotted Horses" and *The Hamlet.* For Longstreet, it offers an opportunity to represent and through the narration to comment upon the conflict between frontier and genteel values, particularly as they concern the meaning of lying. Longstreet's use of a genteel narrator to frame the story is far more typical of the genre than Harris's later and more radical choice of a vernacular voice—Sut's—almost entirely free of framing.

George Washington Harris, like Longstreet both a talented and a restless man, was born in Pennsylvania but moved as a child to Tennessee, where he developed a fierce loyalty to the South. Like

Longstreet, he argued for secession; he wrote opposing Lincoln, Yankees, and Republicans in various newspapers. Harris worked in metal, captained a steamboat, farmed, superintended a glass works, worked as postmaster and alderman of Knoxville, Tennessee and for the railroad—and wrote. Sut stories began to appear in *Spirit of the Times* as early as 1843, though the volume of *Yarns* did not appear until 1867. Harris died in 1869 on a journey home from Lynchburg, Virginia, to arrange publication of his second book. *High Times and Hard Times* finally appeared 100 years after *Sut Lovingood,* in 1967. "Mrs. Yardley's Quilting Party" shows the character of Sut that led Faulkner to praise him in a *Paris Review* interview: "He had no illusions about himself, did the best he could; at certain times he was a coward and knew it and wasn't ashamed; he never blamed his misfortunes on anyone and never cursed God for them." Faulkner does not mention Sut's raucous, sometimes malicious brutality, but surely made use of it as well. The quilting story is of particular interest to feminists for several reasons: for the treatment of women, and for what it suggests—by means of Sut's profound desire to disrupt it—about the power of the quilting party.

Anne G. Jones
University of Florida at Gainesville

PRIMARY WORKS

Mathew St. Claire Clarke [?], *Sketches and Eccentricities of Col David Crockett, of West Tennessee,* 1833; Thomas Chilton, *A Narrative of the Life of David Crockett,* 1834, ed. James A. Shackford and Stanley J. Folmsbee, 1973; *Georgia Scenes,* 1835, ed. Richard Harwell, 1975; Anon., *The Crockett Almanacs,* 1835–56; *Sut Lovingwood. Yarns Spun by a "Nat'ral Born Durn'd Fool.["] Warped and Wove for Public Wear,* 1967; ed. M. Thomas Inge, [1868] 1988; J. Donald Wade, *Augustus Baldwin Longstreet,* 1924, ed. M. Thomas Inge, 1969; Constance M. Rourke, *Davy Crockett,* 1934; Richard M. Dorson, ed., *Davy Crockett, American Comic Legend,* 1939; Walter Blair and Franklin J. Meine, *Half Horse, Half Alligator: The Growth of the Mike Fink Legend,* 1956; James M. Shackford, *David Crockett, the Man and the Legend,* 1956; Ben H. McClary, ed., *The Lovingood Papers,* 1962–65; Milton Rickels, *George Washington Harris,* 1965; M. Thomas Inge, ed., *High Times and Hard Times. Sketches and Tales by GWH,* 1967; Michael A. Lofaro, ed., *Davy Crockett: The Man, the Legend, the Legacy, 1786–1986,* 1985.

SECONDARY WORKS

Spirit of the Times: A Chronicle of the Turf, Field Sports, Literature and the Stage, 1831–61; Franklin J. Meine, *Tall Tales of the Southwest,* 1930; Constance Rourke, *American Humor: A Study of the National Character,* 1931; Walter Blair, *Native American Humor, 1800–1900,* 1937; Elton Miles, *Southwest Humorists,* 1969; Louis D. Rubin, ed., *The Comic Imagination in American Literature,* 1973; Hennig Cohen and William B. Dillingham, eds., *Humor of the Old Southwest,* 1975; M. Thomas Inge, ed., *The Frontier Humorists: Critical Views,* 1975; Neil Schmitz, *Of Huck and Alice: Humorous Writing in American Literature,* 1983; W. Bedford Clark and W. Craig Turner, eds., *Critical Essays on American Humor,* 1984; Carroll Smith-Rosenberg, "Davy Crockett as Trickster: Pornography, Liminality, and Symbolic Inversion in Victorian America," in *Disorderly Conduct,* 1985; Carolyn S. Brown, *The Tall Tale in American Folklore and Literature,* 1987.

from The Crockett Almanacs

Sunrise in His Pocket

One January morning it was so all screwen cold that the forest trees were stiff and they couldn't shake, and the very daybreak froze fast as it was trying to dawn. The tinder box in my cabin would no more ketch fire than a sunk raft at the bottom of the sea. Well, seein' daylight war so far behind time I thought creation war in a fair way for freezen fast: so, thinks I, I must strike a little fire from my fingers, light my pipe, an' travel out a few leagues, and see about it. Then I brought my knuckles together like two thunderclouds, but the sparks froze up afore I could begin to collect 'em, so out I walked, whistlin' "Fire in the mountains!" as I went along in three double quick time. Well, arter I had walked about twenty miles up the Peak O'Day and Daybreak Hill I soon discovered what war the matter. The airth had actually friz fast on her axes, and couldn't turn round; the sun had got jammed between two cakes o' ice under the wheels, an' thar he had been shinin' an' workin' to get loose till he friz fast in his cold sweat. C-r-e-a-t-i-o-n! thought I, this ar the toughest sort of suspension, an' it mustn't be endured. Somethin' must be done, or human creation is done for. It war then so anteluvian an' premature cold that my upper and lower teeth an' tongue war all collapsed together as tight as a friz oyster; but I took a fresh twenty-pound bear off my back that I'd picked up on my road, and beat the animal agin the ice till the hot ile began to walk out on him at all sides. I then took an' held him over the airth's axes an' squeezed him till I'd thawed 'em loose, poured about a ton on't over the sun's face, give the airth's cog-wheel one kick backward till I got the sun loose—whistled "Push along, keep movin'!" an' in about fifteen seconds the airth gave a grunt, an' began movin'. The sun walked up beautiful, salutin' me with sich a wind o' gratitude that it made me sneeze. I lit my pipe by the blaze o' his top-knot, shouldered my bear, an' walked home, introducin' people to the fresh daylight with a piece of sunrise in my pocket.

1835–56

A Pretty Predicament

When I was a big boy, that had jist begun to go a galling, I got astray in the woods one arternoon; and being wandering about a good deel, and got pretty considerable soaked by a grist of rain, I sot down on to a stump, and begun to wring out my leggin's, and shake the drops off of my raccoon cap.

Whilst I was on the stump, I got kind of sleepy, and so laid my head back in the crotch of a young tree that growed behind me, and shot up my eyes. I had laid out of doors for many a night before, with a sky blanket over me—so I got to sleep pretty soon, and fell to snoring most beautiful. So somehow, or somehow else, I did not wake till near sundown; and I don't know when I should have waked, had it not been for somebody tugging at my hair. As soon as I felt this, though I wan't more than half awake, I begun to feel to see if my thum' nail was on, as that was all the ammunition I had about me. I lay still, to see what the feller would be at. The first idee I had was that a cussed Ingun was fixing to take off my scalp, so I thought I'd wait till I begun to feel the pint of his knife scraping against the skin, and then I should have full proof agin him, and could jerk out his copper-coloured liver with the law all on my side. At last I felt such a hard twitch, that I roared right out, but when I found my head was squeezed so tight in the crotch that I could not get it out, I felt like a gone sucker. I felt raal ridiculous, I can assure you; so I began to talk to the varmint, and telled him to help me get my head out, like a man, and I would give him five dollars before I killed him.

At last my hair begun to come out by the roots, and then I was mad to be took advantage of in that way. I swore at the varmint, till the tree shed all its leaves, and the sky turned yaller. So, in a few minutes, I heerd a voice, and then a gall cum running up, and axed what was the matter. She soon saw what was to pay, and telled me that the eagles were tearing out my hair to build nests with. I telled her I had endured more than a dead possum could stand already, and that if she would drive off the eagles, I would make her a present of an iron comb.

"That I will," says she; "for I am a she steamboat, and have doubled up a crocodile in my day."

So she pulled up a small sapling by the roots, and went to work as if she hadn't another minnit to live. She knocked down two of the varmints, and screamed the rest out of sight. Then I telled her the predicament I was in; and she said she would loosen the hold that the crotch had on my head. So she took and reached out her arm into a rattlesnake's hole, and pulled out three or four of them. She tied 'em awl together, and made a strong rope out of 'em. She tied one eend of the snakes to the top of one branch, and pulled as if she was trying to haul the multiplication table apart. The tightness about my head began to be different altogether, and I hauled out my cocoanut, though I left a piece of one of my ears behind.

As soon as I was clear, I could not tell which way to look for the sun, and I was afeared I should fall into the sky, for I did not know which way was up, and which way was down. Then I looked at the gal that had got me loose—she was a strapper: she was as tall as a sapling, and had an arm like a keel boat's tiller. So I looked at her like all wrath, and as she cum down from the tree, I says to her:

"I wish I may be utterly onswoggled if I don't know how to hate an Ingun or love a gal as well as any he this side of roaring river. I fell in love with three gals at once at a log rolling, and as for tea squalls my heart never shut pan for a minnit at a time; so if you will marry me, I will forgive the tree and the eagles for your sake."

Then she turned as white as an egg-shell, and I seed that her heart was busting, and I run up to her, like a squirrel to his hole, and gave her a buss that sounded louder than a musket. So her spunk was all gone, and she took my arm as tame as a pigeon, and we cut out for her father's house. She complained that I hung too heavy on her arm, for I was enermost used up after laying so long between the branches. So she took up a stone that would weigh about fifty pound, and put it in her pocket on the other side to balance agin my weight, and so she moved along as upright as a steamboat. She told me that her Sunday bonnet was a hornet's nest garnished with wolves' tails and eagles' feathers, and that she wore a bran new goun, made of a whole bear's-hide, the tail serving for a train. She said she could drink of the branch without a cup, could shoot a wild goose flying, and wade the Mississippi without wetting herself. She said she could not play on the piane, nor sing like a nightingale, but she could outscream a catamount and jump over her own shadow; she had good strong horse sense and new a woodchuck from a skunk. So I was pleased with her, and offered her all my plunder if she would let me split the difference and call her Mrs. Crockett.

She kinder said she must insult her father before she went so fur as to marry. So she took me into another room to introduce me to another beau that she had. He was setting on the edge of a grindstone at the back part of the room with his heels on the mantel-piece! He had the skullbone of a catamount for a snuff-box, and he was dressed like he had been used to seeing hard times. I got a side squint into one of his pockets, and saw it was full of eyes that had been gouged from people of my acquaintance. I knew my jig was up, for such a feller could outcourt me, and I thort the gal brot me in on proppus to have a fight. So I turned off, and threatened to call agin; and I cut through the bushes like a pint of whiskey among forty men.

1835–56

Crockett's Daughters

I always had the praise o' raisin the tallest and fattest, and sassyest gals in all America. They can out-run, out-jump, out-fight, and out-scream any crittur in creation; and for scratchin', thar's not a hungry painter, or a patent horse-rake can hold a claw to 'em.

The oldest one growed so etarnally tall that her head had got nearly out o' sight, when she got into an all-thunderin' fight with a thunder storm that stunted her growth, and now I am afraid that she'll never reach her natural size. Still, it takes a hull winter's weavin' to make her walkin' and bed clothes; and when she goes to bed, she's so tarnal long, and sleeps so sound, that we can only waken her by degrees, and that's by chopping fire wood on her shins.

An' I guess I shall never forget how all horrificaciously flumexed a hull party of Indians war, the time they surprised and seized my middle darter, Thebeann, when she war out gatherin' birch bark, to make a canoe. The varmints knew as soon as they got hold of her that she war one of my breed, by her thunderbolt kickin', and they determined to cook half of her and eat the other half alive, out of revenge for the many lickin's I gin 'em. At last they concluded to tie her to a tree, and kindle a fire around her. But they couldn't come it, for while they war gone for wood, a lot of painters that war looking on at the cowardly work, war so gal-vanised an' pleased with the gal's true grit that they formed a guard around her, and wouldn't allow the red niggers to come within smellin' distance; they actually gnawed her loose, an' 'scorted her half way home.

But the youngest o' my darters takes arter me, and is of the regular earthquake natur. Her body's flint rock, her soul's lightnin, her fist is a thunderbolt, and her teeth can out-cut any steam-mill saw in creation. She is a parfect infant prodigy, being only six years old; she has the biggest foot and widest mouth in all the west, and when she grins, she is splendifferous; she shows most beautiful intarnals, and can scare a flock o' wolves to total terrifications.

Well, one day, my sweet little infant was walking in the woods, and amusing herself by picking up walnuts, and cracking them with her front grindstones, when suddenaciously she stumbled over an a mitey great hungry he-barr. The critter seein' her fine red shoulders bare, sprung at her as if determined to feast upon Crockett meat. He gin her a savaggerous hug, and was jist about biting a regular buss out on her cheek, when the child, resentin' her insulted vartue, gin him a kick with her south fist in his digestion that made him hug the arth instanterly. Jist as he war a-comin' to her a second time, the little gal grinned sich a double streak o' blue lightnin into his mouth that it cooked the critter to death as quick as think. She brought him home for dinner.

She'll be a thunderin' fine gal when she gets her nateral growth, if her stock o' Crockett lightnin don't burst her biler, and blow her up.

1835–56

Mike Fink's Brag

I'm a Salt River roarer! I'm a ring-tailed squealer! I'm a reg'lar screamer from the ol' Massassip'! WHOOP! I'm the very infant that refused his milk before its eyes were open, and called out for a bottle of old Rye! I love the women an' I'm chockful o' fight! I'm half wild horse and half cock-eyed alligator and the rest o' me is crooked snags an' red-hot snappin' turtle. I can hit like fourth-proof lightnin' an' every lick I make in the woods lets in an acre o' sunshine. I can out-run, out-jump, out-shoot, out-brag, out-drink, an' out-fight, rough-an'-tumble, no holts barred, ary man on both sides the river from Pittsburgh to New Orleans an' back ag'in to St. Louiee. Come on, you flatters, you bargers, you milk-white mechanics, an' see how tough I am to chaw! I ain't had a fight for two days an' I'm spilein' for exercise. Cock-a-doddle-do!

1835–56

Mike Fink Trying to Scare Mrs. Crockett

You've all on you, heered of Mike Fink, the celebrated, an self-created, an never to be mated, Mississippi roarer, snag-lifter, an flatboat skuller. Well, I knowed the critter all round, an upside down; he war purty fair amongst squaws, cat-fish, an big niggers, but when it come to walkin into wild cats, bars, or alligators, he couldn't hold a taller candle to my young son, Hardstone Crockett. I'll never forget the time he tried to scare my wife Mrs. Davy Crockett. You see, the critter had tried all sorts of ways to scare her, but he had no more effect on her than droppen feathers on a barn floor; so he at last bet me a dozen wild cats that he would appear to her, an scare her teeth loose, an her toe nails out of joint; so the varmint one night arter a big freshet took an crept into an old alligator's skin, an met Mrs. Crockett jist as she was taken an evening's walk.

He spread open the mouth of the critter, an made sich a holler howl that he nearly scared himself out of the skin, but Mrs. Crockett didn't care any more for that, nor the alligator skin than she would for a snuff of lightnin, but when Mike got a leetle too close, and put out his paws with the idea of an embrace, then I tell you what, her indignation rose a little bit higher than a Mississippi flood, an she throwed a flash of eye-lightnen upon him that made it clear daylight for half an hour, but Mike thinkin of the bet an his fame for courage, still wagged his tail an walked out, when Mrs. Crockett out with a little teeth pick, and with a single swing of it sent the hull head and neck flyin fifty feet off, the blade jist shavin the top of Mike's head, and then seeing what it war, she trowed down her teeth pick, rolled up her sleeves, an battered poor Fink so that he fainted away in his alligator skin, an he war so all scaren mad, when he come too, that he swore he had been chawed up, and swallered by an alligator.

1850

Sal Fink, the Mississippi Screamer How She Cooked Injuns

I dar say you've all on you, if not more, frequently heerd this great she human crittur boasted of, an' pointed out as *"one o' the gals"*—but I tell you what, stranger, you have never really set your eyes on *"one of the gals,"* till you have seen Sal Fink, the Mississippi screamer, whose miniature pictur I here give, about as nat'ral as life, but not half as handsome—an' if thar ever was a gal that desarved to be christened *"one o' the gals,"* then this gal was that gal—and no mistake.

She fought a duel once with a thunderbolt, an' came off without a single, while at the fust fire she split the thunderbolt all to flinders, an' gave the pieces to Uncle Sam's artillerymen, to touch off their canon with. When a gal about six years old, she used to play see-saw on the Mississippi snags, and arter she war done she would snap 'em off, an' so cleared a large district of the river. She used to ride down the river on an alligator's back, standen upright, an' dancing *Yankee Doodle,* and could leave all the steamers behind. But the greatest feat she ever did, positively outdid anything that ever was did.

One day when she war out in the forest, making a collection o' wild cat skins for her family's winter beddin, she war captered in the most all-sneaken manner by about fifty Injuns, an' carried by 'em to Roast flesh Hollow, whar the blood drinkin wild varmits detarmined to skin her alive, sprinkle a leetle salt over her, an' devour her before her own eyes; so they took an' tied her to a tree, to keep till mornin' should bring the rest o' thar ring-nosed sarpints to enjoy the fun. Arter that, they lit a large fire in the Holler, turned the bottom o' thar feet towards the blaze, Injun fashion, and went to sleep to dream o' thar mornin's feast; well, after the critturs got into a somniferous snore, Sal got into an all-lightnin' of a temper, and burst all the ropes about her like an apron-string! She then found a pile o' ropes, too, and tied all the Injun's heels together all round the fire,—then fixin a cord to the shins of every two couple, she, with a suddenachous jerk, that made the intire woods tremble, pulled the intire lot o' sleepin' red-skins into that ar great fire, fast together, an' then sloped like a panther out of her pen, in the midst o' the tallest yellin, howlin, scramblin and singin', that war ever seen or heerd on, since the great burnin' o' Buffalo prairie!

1853

The Death of Mike Fink
(Joseph M. Field)

"The Last of the Boatmen" has not become altogether a *mythic* personage. There be around us those who still remember him as one of flesh and blood, as well of proportions simply human, albeit he lacked not somewhat of the *heroic* in stature, as well as in being a "perfect terror" to people!

As regards Mike, it has not yet become that favourite question of doubt—"Did such a being really live?" Nor have we heard the skeptic inquiry—"Did such a being really die?" But his death in half a dozen different ways and places has been asserted, and this, we take it, is the first gathering of the *mythic* haze—that shadowy and indistinct enlargement of outline, which, deepening through long ages, invests distinguished mortality with the sublimer attributes of the hero and the demi-god. Had Mike lived in "early Greece," his flat-boat feats would, doubtless, in poetry, have rivalled those of Jason in his ship; while in Scandinavian legends he would have been a river-god, to a certainty! The Sea-Kings would have sacrificed to him every time they "crossed the bar" on their return; and as for Odin himself, he would be duly advised, as far as any interference went, to "lay low and keep dark, or *pre*-haps," &c.

The story of Mike Fink, including a death, has been beautifully told by the late Morgan Neville of Cincinnati, a gentleman of the highest literary taste as well as of the most amiable and polished manners. "The Last of the Boatmen," as his sketch is entitled, is unexceptionable in style and, we believe, in *fact,* with one exception, and that is the statement as to the manner and place of Fink's death. He did *not die* on the Arkansas, but at Fort Henry, near the mouth of the Yellow Stone. Our informant is Mr. Chas. Keemle of this paper *[St. Louis Reveille],* who held a command in the neighbourhood at the time, and to whom every circumstance connected with the affair is most familiar. We give the story as it is told by himself.

In the year 1822, steamboats having left the "keels" and "broad-horns" entirely "out of sight," and Mike having, in consequence, fallen from his high estate—that of being "a little bit the almightiest man on the river, *any* how"—after a term of idleness, frolic and desperate rowdyism along the different towns, he, at St. Louis, entered the service of the Mountain Fur Company raised by our late fellow-citizen Gen. W.H. Ashley as a trapper and hunter; and in that capacity was he employed by Major Henry, in command of the Fort at the mouth of Yellow Stone river when the occurrence took place of which we write.

Mike, with many generous qualities, was always a reckless daredevil; but at this time, advancing in years and decayed in influence, above all become a victim of whisky, he was morose and desperate in the extreme. There was a government regulation which forbade the free use of alcohol at the trading posts on the Missouri river, and this was a continual source of quarrel between the men and the commandant,

Major Henry,—on the part of Fink, particularly. One of his freaks was to march with his rifle into the fort and demand a supply of spirits. Argument was fruitless, force not to be thought of, and when, on being positively denied, Mike drew up his rifle and sent a ball through the cask, deliberately walked up and filled his can, while his particular "boys" followed his example, all that could be done was to look upon the matter as one of his "queer ways," and that was the end of it.

This state of things continued for some time; Mike's temper and exactions growing more unbearable every day, until, finally, a "split" took place, not only between himself and the commandant, but many others in the fort, and the unruly boatman swore he would not live among them. Followed only by a youth named Carpenter, whom he had brought up, and for whom he felt a rude but strong attachment, he prepared a sort of cave in the river's bank, furnished it with a supply of whisky, and with his companion *turned in* to pass the winter, which was then closing upon them. In this place he buried himself, sometimes unseen for weeks, his *protege* providing what else was *necessary* beyond the whisky. At length attempts were used, on the part of those in the fort, to withdraw Carpenter from Fink; foul insinuations were made as to the nature of their connection; the youth was twitted with being a mere slave, & c., all which (Fink heard of it in spite of his retirement) served to breed distrust between the two, and though they did not separate, much of their cordiality ceased.

The winter wore away in this sullen state of torpor; spring came with its reviving influences, and to celebrate the season, a supply of alcohol was procured, and a number of his acquaintances from the fort coming to "rouse out" Mike, a desperate "frolic," of course, ensued.

There were river yarns and boatmen songs and "nigger breakdowns" interspersed with wrestling-matches, jumping, laugh, and yell, the can circulating freely, until Mike became somewhat mollified.

"I tell you what it is, boys," he cried, "the fort's a skunk-hole, and I rather live with the *bars* than stay in it. Some on ye's bin trying to part me and my boy, that I love like my own cub—but no matter. Maybe he's *pis*oned against me; but, Carpenter (striking the youth heavily on the shoulder), I took you by the hand when it had forgotten the touch of a father's or a mother's—you know me to be a man, and you ain't a going to turn out a dog!"

Whether it was that the youth fancied something insulting in the manner of the appeal, or not, we can't say; but it was not responded to very warmly, and a reproach followed from Mike. However, they drank together, and the frolic went on until Mike, filling his can, walked off some forty yards, placed it upon his head, and called to Carpenter to take his rifle.

This wild feat of shooting cans off each other's head was a favourite one with Mike—himself and "boy" generally winding up a hard frolic with this savage but deeply-meaning proof of continued confidence;—as for risk, their eagle eyes and iron nerves defied the might of whisky. After their recent alienation, a doubly generous impulse, without doubt, had induced Fink to propose and subject himself to the test.

Carpenter had been drinking wildly, and with a boisterous laugh snatched up his rifle. All present had seen the parties "shoot," and this desperate aim, instead of alarming, was merely made a matter of wild jest.

"Your grog is spilt, for ever, Mike!"

"Kill the old varmint, young 'un!"

"What'll his skin bring in St. Louis?" &c., &c.

Amid a loud laugh, Carpenter raised his piece—even the jesters remarked that he was unsteady,—crack!—the can fell,—a loud shout,—but, instead of a smile of pleasure, a dark frown settled upon the face of Fink! He made no motion except to clutch his rifle as though he would have crushed it, and there he stood, gazing at the youth strangely! Various shades of passion crossed his features—surprise, rage, suspicion—but at length they composed themselves into a sad expression; the ball had grazed the top of his head, cutting the scalp, and the thought of treachery had set his heart on fire.

There was a loud call upon Mike to know what he was waiting for, in which Carpenter joined, pointing to the can upon his head and bidding him fire, if he knew how!

"Carpenter, my son," said the boatman, "I taught you to shoot differently from that *last* shot! You've *missed* once, but you won't again!"

He fired, and his ball, crashing through the forehead of the youth, laid him a corpse amid his as suddenly hushed companions!

Time wore on—many at the fort spoke darkly of the deed. Mike Fink had never been known to miss his aim—he had grown afraid of Carpenter—he had murdered him! While this feeling was gathering against him, the unhappy boatman lay in his cave, shunning both sympathy and sustenance. He spoke to none—when he did come forth, 'twas as a spectre, and only to haunt the grave of his "boy," or, if he did break silence, 'twas to burst into a paroxysm of rage against the enemies who had "turned his boy's heart from him!"

At the fort was a man by the name of Talbott, the gunsmith of the station: he was very loud and bitter in his denunciations of the "murderer," as he called Fink, which, finally, reaching the ears of the latter, filled him with the most violent passion, and he swore that he would take the life of his defamer. This threat was almost forgotten, when one day, Talbott, who was at work in his shop, saw Fink enter the fort, his first visit since the death of Carpenter. Fink approached; he was careworn, sick, and wasted; there was no anger in his bearing, but he carried his rifle, (had he ever gone without it?) and the gunsmith was not a coolly brave man; moreover, his life had been threatened.

"Fink," cried he, snatching up a pair of pistols from his bench, "don't approach me—if you do, you're a dead man!"

"Talbott," said the boatman, in a sad voice, "you needn't be afraid; you've done me wrong—I'm come to talk to you about—Carpenter—my boy!"

He continued to advance, and the gunsmith again called to him:

"Fink! I know you; if you come three steps nearer, I'll fire, by——!"

Mike carried his rifle across his arm, and made no hostile demonstration, except in gradually getting nearer—*if* hostile his aim was.

"Talbott, you've accused me of murdering—my boy—Carpenter—that I raised from a child—that I loved like a son—that I can't live without! I'm not mad with you *now,* but you must let me show you that I *couldn't* do it—that I'd rather died than done it—that you've wronged me—"

By this time he was within a few steps of the door, and Talbott's agitation became extreme. Both pistols were pointed at Fink's breast, in expectation of a spring from the latter.

"By the Almighty above us, Fink, I'll fire—I don't want to speak to you now—don't put your foot on that step—don't."

Fink did put his foot on the step, and the same moment fell heavily within it, receiving the contents of both barrels in his breast! His last and only words were, "I didn't mean to kill my boy!"

Poor Mike! we are satisfied with our senior's conviction that you did *not* mean to kill him. Suspicion of treachery, doubtless, entered his mind, but cowardice and murder never dwelt there.

A few weeks after this event, Talbott himself perished in an attempt to cross the Missouri river in a skiff.

1844

from Georgia Scenes

The Horse Swap
(Augustus Baldwin Longstreet)

During the session of the Superior Court, in the village of——, about three weeks ago, when a number of people were collected in the principal street of the village, I observed a young man riding up and down the street, as I supposed, in a violent passion. He galloped this way, then that, and then the other. Spurred his horse to one group of citizens, then to another. Then dashed off at half speed, as if fleeing from danger; and suddenly checking his horse, returned—first in a pace, then in a trot, and then in a canter. While he was performing these various evolutions, he cursed, swore, whooped, screamed, and tossed himself in every attitude which man could assume on horse back. In short, he *cavorted* most magnanimously, (a term which, in our tongue, expresses all that I have described, and a little more) and seemed to be setting all creation at defiance. As I like to see all that is passing, I determined to take a position a little nearer to him, and to ascertain if possible, what it was that affected him so sensibly. Accordingly I approached a crowd before which he had stopt for a moment, and examined it with the strictest scrutiny.—But I could see nothing in it, that seemed to have any thing to do with the cavorter. Every man appeared to be in a good humor, and all minding their own business. Not one so much as noticed the principal figure. Still he went on. After a semicolon pause, which my appearance seemed to produce, (for he eyed me closely as I approached) he fetched a whoop, and swore that "he could out-swap any live man, woman or child, that ever walked these hills, or that ever straddled horse flesh since the days of old daddy Adam." "Stranger," said he to me, "did you ever see the *Yallow Blossom* from Jasper?"

"No," said I, "but I have often heard of him."

"I'm the boy," continued he; "perhaps a *leetle*—jist a *leetle* of the best man, at a horse swap, that ever trod shoe-leather."

I began to feel my situation a little awkward, when I was relieved by a man somewhat advanced in years, who stept up and began to survey the *"Yallow Blossom's"* horse with much apparent interest. This drew the rider's attention, and he turned the conversation from me to the stranger.

"Well, my old coon," said he, "do you want to swap *hosses?*"

"Why, I don't know," replied the stranger; "I believe I've got a beast I'd trade with you for that one, if you like him."

"Well, fetch up your nag, my old cock; you're jist the lark I wanted to get hold of. I am perhaps a *leetle,* jist a *leetle,* of the best man at a horse swap, that ever stole *cracklins* out of his mammy's fat gourd. Where's your *hoss?*"

"I'll bring him presently; but I want to examine your horse a little."

"Oh! look at him," said the Blossom, alighting and hitting him a cut—"look at him. He's the best piece of *hoss* flesh in the thirteen united universal worlds. There's no sort o' mistake in little Bullet. He can pick up miles on his feet and fling 'em behind him as fast as the next man's *hoss,* I don't care where he comes from.—And he can keep at it as long as the Sun can shine without resting."

During this harangue, little Bullet looked as if he understood it all, believed it, and was ready at any moment to verify it. He was a horse of goodly countenance, rather expressive of vigilance than fire; though an unnatural appearance of fierceness was thrown into it, by the loss of his ears, which had been cropt pretty close to his head. Nature had done but little for Bullet's head and neck; but he managed, in a great measure, to hide their defects, by bowing perpetually. He had obviously suffered severely for corn; but if his ribs and hip bones had not disclosed the fact, *he* never would have done it; for he was in all respects, as cheerful and happy, as if he commanded all the corn-cribs and fodder stacks in Georgia. His height was about twelve hands; but as his shape partook somewhat of that of the Giraffe, his haunches stood much lower. They were short, straight, peaked and concave. Bullet's tail, however, made amends for all his defects. All that the artist could do to beautify it, had been done; and all that horse could do to compliment the artist, Bullet did. His tail was nicked in superior style, and exhibited the line of beauty in so many directions, that it could not fail to hit the most fastidious taste in some of them. From the root it dropt into a graceful festoon; then rose in a handsome curve; then resumed its first direction; and then mounted suddenly upwards like a cypress knee to a perpendicular of about two and a half inches. The whole had a careless and bewitching inclination to the right. Bullet obviously knew where his beauty lay, and took all occasions to display it to the best advantage. If a stick cracked, or if any one moved suddenly about him, or coughed, or hawked, or spoke a little louder than common, up went Bullet's tail like lightning; and if the *going up* did not please, the *coming down* must of necessity, for it was as different from the other movement, as was its direction. The first, was a bold and rapid flight upward; usually to an angle of forty-five degrees. In this position he kept his interesting appendage, until he satisfied himself that nothing in particular was to be done; when he commenced dropping it by half inches, in second beats—then in triple time—then faster and shorter, and faster and shorter still; until it finally died away imperceptibly into its natural position. If I might compare sights to sounds, I should say, its *settling,* was more like the note of a locust than any thing else in nature.

Either from native sprightliness of disposition, from uncontrollable activity, or from an unconquerable habit of removing flies by the stamping of the feet, Bullet never stood still; but always kept up a gentle fly-scaring movement of his limbs, which was peculiarly interesting.

"I tell you, man," proceeded the Yellow Blossom, "he's the best live hoss that ever trod the grit of Georgia. Bob Smart knows the hoss. Come here, Bob, and mount this hoss and show Bullet's motions." Here, Bullet bristled up, and looked as if he had been hunting for Bob all day long, and had just found him. Bob sprang on his back. "Boo-oo-oo!" said Bob, with a fluttering noise of the lips; and away went Bullet, as if in a quarter race, with all his beauties spread in handsome style.

"Now fetch him back," said Blossom. Bullet turned and came in pretty much as he went out.

"Now trot him by." Bullet reduced his tail to *"customary"*—sidled to the right and left airily, and exhibited at least three varieties of trot, in the short space of fifty yards.

"Make him pace!" Bob commenced twitching the bridle and kicking at the same time. These inconsistent movements obviously (and most naturally) disconcerted Bullet; for it was impossible for him to learn, from them, whether he was to proceed or stand still. He started to trot—and was told that wouldn't do. He attempted a canter—and was checked again. He stopt—and was urged to go on. Bullet now rushed into the wide field of experiment, and struck out a gait of his own, that completely turned the tables upon his rider, and certainly deserved a patent. It seemed to have derived its elements from the jig, the minuet and the cotillon. If it was not a pace, it certainly had *pace* in it; and no man would venture to call it any thing else; so it passed off to the satisfaction of the owner.

"Walk him!" Bullet was now at home again; and he walked as if money was staked on him.

The stranger, whose name I afterwards learned was Peter Ketch, having examined Bullet to his heart's content, ordered his son Neddy to go and bring up Kit. Neddy soon appeared upon Kit; a well formed sorrel of the middle size, and in good order. His *tout ensemble* threw Bullet entirely in the shade; though a glance was sufficient to satisfy any one, that Bullet had the decided advantage of him in point of intellect.

"Why man," said Blossom, "do you bring such a hoss as that to trade for Bullet? Oh, I see you've no notion of trading."

"Ride him off, Neddy!" said Peter. Kit put off at a handsome lope.

"Trot him back!" Kit came in at a long, sweeping trot, and stopt suddenly at the crowd.

"Well," said Blossom, "let me look at him; may be he'll do to plough."

"Examine him!" said Peter, taking hold of the bridle close to the mouth; "He's nothing but a tacky. He an't as *pretty* a horse as Bullet, I know; but he'll do. Start 'em together for a hundred and fifty *mile;* and if Kit an't twenty mile ahead of him at the coming out, any man may take Kit for nothing. But he's a monstrous mean horse, gentlemen; any man may see that. He's the scariest horse, too, you ever saw. He won't do to hunt on, no how. Stranger, will you let Neddy have your rifle to shoot off him? Lay the rifle between his ears, Neddy, and shoot at the blaze in that stump. Tell me when his head is high enough."

Ned fired, and hit the blaze; and Kit did not move a hair's breadth.

"Neddy, take a couple of sticks and beat on that hogshead at Kit's tail."

Ned made a tremendous rattling; at which *Bullet* took fright, broke his bridle and dashed off in grand style; and would have stopt all farther negotiations, by going home in disgust, had not a traveller arrested him and brought him back; but Kit did not move.

"I tell you, gentlemen," continued Peter, "he's the scariest horse you ever saw. He an't as gentle as Bullet; but he won't do any harm if you watch him. Shall I put him in a cart, gig, or wagon for you, stranger? He'll cut the same capers there he does here. He's a monstrous mean horse."

During all this time, Blossom was examining him with the nicest scrutiny. Having examined his frame and limbs, he now looked at his eyes.

"He's got a curious look out of his eyes," said Blossom.

"Oh yes, sir," said Peter, "just as blind as a bat. Blind horses always have clear eyes. Make a motion at his eyes, if you please, sir."

Blossom did so, and Kit threw up his head rather as if something pricked him under the chin, than as if fearing a blow. Blossom repeated the experiment, and Kit jirked back in considerable astonishment.

"Stone blind, you see, gentlemen," proceeded Peter; "but he's just as good to travel of a dark night as if he had eyes."

"Blame my buttons," said Blossom, "if I like them eyes."

"No," said Peter, "nor I neither. I'd rather have 'em made of diamonds; but they'll do, if they don't show as much white as Bullet's."

"Well," said Blossom, "make a pass at me."

"No," said Peter; "you made the banter; now make your pass."

"Well, I'm never afraid to price my hosses. You must give me twenty-five dollars boot."

"Oh certainly; say fifty, and my saddle and bridle in. Here, Neddy, my son, take away daddy's horse."

"Well," said Blossom, "I've made my pass; now you make yours."

"I'm for short talk in a horse swap; and therefore always tell a gentleman, at once, what I mean to do. You must give me ten dollars."

Blossom swore absolutely, roundly and profanely, that he never would give boot.

"Well," said Peter, "I didn't care about trading; but you cut such high shines, that I thought I'd like to back you out; and I've done it. Gentlemen, you see I've brought him to a hack."

"Come, old man," said Blossom, "I've been joking with you. I begin to think you do want to trade; therefore, give me five dollars and take Bullet. I'd rather lose ten dollars, any time, than not make a trade; though I hate to fling away a good hoss."

"Well," said Peter, "I'll be as clever as you are. Just put the five dollars on Bullet's back and hand him over, it's a trade."

Blossom swore again, as roundly as before, that he would not give boot; and, said he, "Bullet wouldn't hold five dollars on his back, no how. But as I bantered you, if you say an even swap, here's at you."

"I told you," said Peter, "I'd be as clever as you; therefore, here goes two dollars more, just for trade sake. Give three dollars, and it's a bargain."

Blossom repeated his former assertion; and here the parties stood for a long time, and the by-standers (for many were now collected,) began to taunt both parties. After some time, however, it was pretty unanimously decided that the old man had backed Blossom out.

At length Blossom swore he "never would be backed out, for three dollars, after bantering a man;" and accordingly they closed the trade.

"Now," said Blossom, as he handed Peter the three dollars, "I'm a man, that when he makes a bad trade, makes the most of it until he can make a better. I'm for no rues and after-claps."

"That's just my way," said Peter; "I never goes to law to mend my bargains."

"Ah, you're the kind of boy I love to trade with. Here's your hoss, old man. Take the saddle and bridle off him, and I'll strip yours; but lift up the blanket easy from Bullet's back, for he's a mighty tenderbacked hoss."

The old man removed the saddle, but the blanket stuck fast. He attempted to raise it, and Bullet bowed himself, switched his tail, danced a little, and gave signs of biting.

"Don't hurt him, old man," said Blossom archly; "take it off easy. I am, perhaps, a leetle of the best man at a horse-swap that ever catched a coon."

Peter continued to pull at the blanket more and more roughly; and Bullet became more and more *cavortish:* in so much, that when the blanket came off, he had reached the *kicking* point in good earnest.

The removal of the blanket, disclosed a sore on Bullet's back-bone, that seemed to have defied all medical skill. It measured six full inches in length, and four in breadth; and had as many features as Bullet had motions. My heart sickened at the sight; and I felt that the brute who had been riding him in that situation, deserved the halter.

The prevailing feeling, however, was that of mirth. The laugh became loud and general, at the old man's expense; and rustic witticisms were liberally bestowed upon him and his late purchase. These, Blossom continued to provoke by various remarks. He asked the old man, "if he thought Bullet would let five dollars lie on his back." He declared most seriously, that he had owned that horse three months, and had never discovered before, that he had a sore back, "or he never should have thought of trading him," &c. &c.

The old man bore it all with the most philosophic composure. He evinced no astonishment at his late discovery, and made no replies. But his son, Neddy, had not disciplined his feelings quite so well. His eyes opened, wider and wider, from the first to the last pull of the blanket; and when the whole sore burst upon his view, astonishment and fright seemed to contend for the mastery of his countenance. As the blanket disappeared, he stuck his hands in his breeches pockets, heaved a deep sigh, and lapsed into a profound reverie; from which he was only roused by the cuts at his father. He bore them as long as he could; and when he could contain himself no longer, he began, with a certain wildness of expression, which gave a peculiar interest to what he uttered: "His back's mighty bad off; but dod drot my soul, if he's put it to daddy as bad as he thinks he has, for old Kit's both blind and *deef,* I'll be dod drot if he eint."

"The devil he is," said Blossom. "Yes, dod drot my soul if he *eint.* You walk him and see if he *eint.* His eyes don't look like it; but he *jist as live go agin* the house with you, or in a ditch, as any how. Now you go try him." The laugh was now turned on Blossom; and many rushed to test the fidelity of the little boy's report. A few experiments established its truth, beyond controversy.

"Neddy," said the old man, "you oughn't to try and make people discontented with their things." "Stranger, don't mind what the little boy says. If you can only get

Kit rid of them little failings, you'll find him all sorts of a horse. You are a *leetle* the best man, at a horse swap, that ever I got hold of; but don't fool away Kit. Come, Neddy, my son, let's be moving; the stranger seems to be getting snappish."

1835

from Sut Lovingood. Yarns Spun by a "Nat'ral Born Durn'd Fool." Warped and Wove for Public Wear.

Mrs. Yardley's Quilting (George Washington Harris)

"Thar's one durn'd nasty muddy job, an' I is jis' glad enuf tu take a ho'n ur two, on the straingth ove hit."

"What have you been doing, Sut?"

"Helpin tu salt ole Missis Yardley down."

"What do you mean by that?"

"Fixin her fur rotten cumfurtably, kiverin her up wif sile, tu keep the buzzards from cheatin the wurms."

"Oh, you have been helping to bury a woman."

"That's hit, by golly! Now why the devil can't I 'splain mysef like yu? I ladles out my words at randum, like a calf kickin at yaller-jackids; yu jis' rolls em out tu the pint, like a feller a-layin bricks—every one fits. How is it that bricks fits so clost enyhow? Rocks won't ni du hit."

"Becaze they'se all ove a size," ventured a man with a wen over his eye.

"The devil yu say, hon'ey-head! haint reapin-mersheens ove a size? I'd like tu see two ove em fit clost. Yu wait ontil yu sprouts tuther ho'n, afore yu venters tu 'splain mix'd questions. George, did yu know ole Missis Yardley?"

"No."

"Well, she wer a curious 'oman in her way, an' she wore shiney specks. Now jis' listen: Whenever yu see a ole 'oman ahine a par ove *shiney* specks, yu keep yer eye skinn'd; they am dang'rus in the extreme. Thar is jis' no knowin what they ken du. I hed one a-stradil ove me onst, fur kissin her gal. She went fur my har, an' she went fur my skin, ontil I tho't she ment tu kill me, an' wud a-dun hit, ef my hollerin hadent fotch ole Dave Jordan, a *bacheler,* tu my aid. He, like a durn'd fool, cotch her by the laig, an' drug her back'ards ofen me. She jis' kivered him, an' I run, by golly! The nex time I seed him he wer bald headed, an' his face looked like he'd been a-fitin wildcats.

"Ole Missis Yardley wer a great noticer ove littil things, that nobody else ever seed. She'd say right in the middil ove sumbody's serious talk: 'Law sakes! thar goes that yaller slut ove a hen, a-flingin straws over her shoulder; she's arter settin now, an' haint laid but seven aigs. I'll disapint *her,* see ef I don't; I'll put a punkin in her ne's, an' a feather in her nose. An' bless my soul! jis' look at that cow wif the wilted ho'n, a-flingin up dirt an' a-smellin the place whar hit cum frum, wif the rale ginuine still-wurim twis' in her tail, too; what upon the face ove the yeath kin she be arter now, the ole fool? watch her, Sally. An' sakes alive, jis' look at that ole sow; she's a-gwine in a fas' trot, wif her empty bag a-floppin agin her sides. Thar, she hes stop't, an's a-listenin! massy on us! what a long yearnis grunt she gin; hit cum frum way back ove her kidneys. Thar she goes agin; she's arter no good, sich kerryin on means no good.'

"An' so she wud gabble, no odds who wer a-listenin. She looked like she mout been made at fust 'bout four foot long, an' the common thickness ove wimen when they's at tharsefs, an' then had her har tied tu a stump, a par ove steers hitched to her heels, an' then straiched out a-mos' two foot more—mos' ove the straichin cumin outen her laigs an' naik. Her stockins, a-hangin on the clothes-line tu dry, looked like a par ove sabre scabbards, an' her naik looked like a dry beef shank smoked, an' mout been ni ontu es tough. I never felt hit mysef, I didn't, I jis' jedges by looks. Her darter Sal wer bilt at fust 'bout the laingth ove her mam, but wer never straiched eny by a par ove steers an' she wer fat enuf tu kill; she wer taller lyin down than she wer a-standin up. Hit wer her who gin me the 'hump shoulder.' Jis' look at me; haint I'se got a tech ove the dromedary back thar bad? haint I humpy? Well, a-stoopin tu kiss that squatty lard-stan ove a gal is what dun hit tu me. She wer the fairest-lookin gal I ever seed. She allers wore thick woolin stockins 'bout six inches too long fur her laig; they rolled down over her garters, lookin like a par ove life-presarvers up thar. I tell yu she wer a tarin gal enyhow. Luved kissin, wrastlin, an' biled cabbige, an' hated tite clothes, hot weather, an' suckit-riders. B'leved strong in married folk's ways, cradles, an' the remishun ove sins, an' didn't b'leve in corsets, fleas, peaners, nur the fashun plates."

"What caused the death of Mrs. Yardley, Sut?"

"Nuffin, only her heart stop't beatin 'bout losin a nine dimunt quilt. True, she got a skeer'd hoss tu run over her, but she'd a-got over that ef a quilt hadn't been mix'd up in the catastrophy. Yu see quilts wer wun ove her speshul gifts; she run strong on the bed-kiver question. Irish chain, star ove Texas, sun-flower, nine dimunt, saw teeth, checker board, an' shell quilts; blue, an' white, an' yaller an' black coverlids, an' callickercumfurts reigned triumphan' 'bout her hous'. They wer packed in drawers, layin in shelfs full, wer hung four dubbil on lines in the lof, packed in chists, piled on cheers, an' wer everywhar, even ontu the beds, an' wer changed every bed-makin. She told everybody she cud git tu listen tu hit that she ment tu give every durn'd one ove them tu Sal when she got married. Oh, lordy! what es fat a gal es Sal Yardley cud ever du wif half ove em, an' sleepin wif a husbun at that, is more nor I ever cud see through. Jis' think ove her onder twenty layer ove quilts in July, an' yu in thar too. Gewhillikins! George, look how I is sweatin' now, an' this is December. I'd 'bout es lief be shet up in a steam biler wif a three hundred pound bag ove lard, es tu make a bisiness ove sleepin wif that gal—'twould kill a glass-blower.

"Well, tu cum tu the serious part ove this conversashun, that is how the old quilt-mersheen an' coverlid-loom cum tu stop operashuns on this yeath. She hed narrated hit thru the neighborhood that nex Saterday she'd gin a quiltin—three quilts an' one cumfurt tu tie. 'Goblers, fiddils, gals, an' whisky,' wer the words she sent tu the men-folk, an' more tetchin ur wakenin words never drap't ofen an 'oman's tongue. She sed tu the gals, 'Sweet toddy, huggin, dancin, an' huggers in 'bundunce.' Them words struck the gals rite in the pit ove the stumick, an' spread a ticklin sensashun bof ways, ontil they scratched thar heads wif one han, an' thar heels wif tuther.

"Everybody, he an' she, what wer baptized b'levers in the righteousnes ove quiltins wer thar, an' hit jis' so happen'd that everybody in them parts, frum fifteen summers tu fifty winters, wer unannamus b'levers. Strange, warn't hit? Hit wer the bigges' quiltin ever Missis Yardley hilt, an' she hed hilt hundreds; everybody wer thar, 'scept the constibil an' suckit-rider, two dam easily-spared pussons; the numbers ni ontu even too; jis' a few more boys nur gals; that made hit more exhitin, fur hit gin the gals a chance tu kick an' squeal a littil, wifout runnin eny risk ove not gittin kissed at all, an' hit gin reasonabil grouns fur a few scrimmages amung the he's. Now es kissin an' fitin am the pepper an' salt ove all soshul getherins, so hit wer more espishully wif this ove ours. Es I swung my eyes over the crowd, George, I thought quiltins, managed in a morril an' sensibil way, truly am good things—good fur free drinkin, good fur free eatin, good fur free huggin, good fur free dancin, good fur free fitin, an' goodest ove all fur poperlatin a country fas'.

"Thar am a fur-seein wisdum in quiltins, ef they hes proper trimmins: 'vittils, fiddils, an' sperrits in 'bundunce.' One holesum quiltin am wuf three old pray'r meetins on the poperlashun pint, purtickerly ef hits hilt in the dark ove the moon, an' runs intu the night a few hours, an' April ur May am the time chosen. The moon don't suit quiltins whar everybody is well acquainted an' already fur along in courtin. She dus help pow'ful tu begin a courtin match onder, but when hit draws ni ontu a head, nobody wants a moon but the ole mammys.

"The mornin cum, still, saft, sunshiney; cocks crowin, hens singin, birds chirpin, tuckeys gobblin—jis' the day tu sun quilts, kick, kiss, squeal, an' make love.

"All the plow-lines an' clothes-lines wer straiched tu every post an' tree. Quilts purvailed. Durn my gizzard ef two acres roun that ar house warn't jis' one solid quilt, all out a-sunnin, an' tu be seed. They dazzled the eyes, skeered the hosses, gin wimen the heart-burn, an' perdominated.

"To'ards sundown the he's begun tu drap in. Yearnis' needil-driven cummenced tu lose groun; threads broke ofen, thimbils got los', an' quilts needed anuther roll. Gigglin, winkin, whisperin, smoofin ove har, an' gals a-ticklin one anuther, wer a-gainin every inch ove groun what the needils los'. Did yu ever notis, George, at all soshul getherins, when the he's begun tu gather, that the young she's begin tu tickil one anuther an' the ole maids swell thar tails, roach up thar backs, an' sharpen thar nails ontu the bed-posts an' door jams, an' spit an' groan sorter like cats a-courtin? Dus hit mean *rale* rath, ur is hit a dare tu the he's, sorter kivered up wif the outside signs ove danger? I honestly b'leve that the young shes' ticklin means, 'Cum an' take this job ofen our hans.' But that swellin I jis' don't onderstan; dus yu? Hit looks skeery, an' I never tetch one ove em when they am in the swellin way. I may be mistaken'd 'bout the ticklin bisiness too; hit may be dun like a feller chaws poplar bark when he haint got eny terbacker, a-sorter better nur nun make-shif. I dus know one thing tu a certainty: that is, when the he's take hold the ticklin quits, an' ef yu gits one ove the ole maids out tu hersef, then she subsides an' is the smoofes, sleekes, saft thing yu ever seed, an' dam ef yu can't hear her purr, jis' es plain!

"But then, George, gals an' ole maids haint the things tu fool time away on. Hits widders, by golly, what am the rale sensibil, steady-goin, never-skeerin, never-kickin, willin, sperrited, smoof pacers. They cum clost up tu the hoss-block, standin still wif thar purty silky years playin, an' the naik-veins a-throbbin, an' waits fur the word, which ove course yu gives, arter yu finds yer feet well in the stirrup, an' away they moves like a cradil on cushioned rockers, ur a spring buggy runnin in damp san'. A tetch ove the bridil, an' they knows yu wants em tu turn, an' they dus hit es willin es ef the idear wer thar own. I be dod rabbited ef a man can't 'propriate happiness by the skinful ef he is in contack wif sumbody's widder, an' is smart. Gin me a willin widder, the yeath over: what they don't know, haint worth larnin. They hes all been tu Jamakey an' larnt how sugar's made, an' knows how tu sweeten wif hit; an' by golly, they is always ready tu use hit. All yu hes tu du is tu find the spoon, an' then drink cumfort till yer blind. Nex tu good sperrits an' my laigs, I likes a twenty-five year ole widder, wif roun ankils, an' bright eyes, honestly an' squarly lookin intu yurn, an' sayin es plainly es a partrige sez 'Bob White,' 'Don't be afraid ove me; I hes been thar; yu know hit ef yu hes eny sense, an' thar's no use in eny humbug, ole feller—cum ahead!'

"Ef yu onderstans widder nater, they ken save yu a power ove troubil, onsartinty, an' time, an' ef yu is interprisin yu gits mons'rous well paid fur hit. The very soun ove thar littil shoe-heels speak full trainin, an' hes a knowin click as they tap the floor; an' the rustil ove thar dress sez, 'I dar you tu ax me.'

"When yu hes made up yer mind tu court one, jis' go at hit like hit wer a job ove rail-maulin. Ware yer workin close, use yer common, every-day moshuns an' words, an' abuv all, fling away yer cinamint ile vial an' burn all yer love songs. No use in tryin tu fool em, fur they sees plum thru yu, a durn'd sight plainer than they dus thru thar veils. No use in a pasted shut; she's been thar. No use in borrowin a cavortin fat hoss; she's been thar. No use in har-dye; she's been thar. No use in cloves, tu kill whisky breff; she's been thar. No use in buyin clost curtains fur yer bed, fur she has been thar. Widders am a speshul means, George, fur ripenin green men, killin off weak ones, an makin 'ternally happy the soun ones.

"Well, es I sed afore, I flew the track an' got ontu the widders. The fellers begun tu ride up an' walk up, sorter slow, like they warn't in a hurry, the durn'd 'saitful raskils, hitchin thar critters tu enything they cud find. One red-comb'd, long-spurr'd, dominecker feller, frum town, in a red an' white grid-iron jackid an' patent leather gaiters, hitched his hoss, a wild, skeery, wall-eyed devil, inside the yard palins, tu a cherry tree lim'. Thinks I, that hoss hes a skeer intu him big enuf tu run intu town, an' perhaps beyant hif, ef I kin only tetch hit off; so I sot intu thinkin.

"One aind ove a long clothes-line, wif nine dimunt quilts ontu hit, wer tied tu the same cherry tree that the hoss wer. I tuck my knife and socked hit thru every quilt, 'bout the middil, an' jis' below the rope, an' tied them thar wif bark, so they cudent slip. Then I went tu the back aind, an' ontied hit frum the pos', knottin in a hoe-handil, by the middil, tu keep the quilts frum slippin off ef my bark strings failed, an' laid hit on the groun. Then I went tu the tuther aind: thar wer 'bout ten foot tu spar, a-lyin on the groun arter tyin tu the tree. I tuck hit atwix Wall-eye's hine laigs, an' tied hit fas' tu bof stirrups, an' then cut the cherry tree lim' betwix his bridil an' the tree, almos' off. Now, mine yu thar wer two ur three uther ropes full ove quilts atween me an' the hous', so I wer purty well hid frum thar. I jis' tore off a palin frum the fence, an' tuck hit in bof hans, an' arter raisin hit 'way up yander, I fotch hit down, es hard es I cud, flatsided to'ards the groun, an' hit acksidentally happen'd tu hit Wall-eye, 'bout nine inches ahead ove the root ove his tail. Hit landed so hard that hit made my hans tingle, an' then busted intu splinters. The first thing I did, wer tu feel ove mysef, on the same spot whar hit hed hit the hoss. I cudent help duin hit tu save my life, an' I swar I felt sum ove Wall-eye's sensashun, jis' es plain. The fust thing he did, wer tu tare down the lim' wif a twenty footjump, his head to'ards the hous'. Thinks I, now yu hev dun hit, yu durn'd wall-eyed fool! tarin down that lim' wer the beginin ove all the troubil, an' the hoss did hit hissef; my conshuns felt clar es a mountin spring, an' I wer in a frame ove mine tu obsarve things es they happen'd, an' they soon begun tu happen purty clost arter one anuther rite then, an' thar, an' tharabouts, clean ontu town, thru hit, an' still wer a-happenin, in the woods beyant thar ni ontu eleven mile from ole man Yardley's gate, an' four beyant town.

"The fust line ove quilts he tried tu jump, but broke hit down; the nex one he ran onder; the rope cotch ontu the ho'n ove the saddil, broke at bof ainds, an' went along wif the hoss, the cherry tree lim' an' the fust line ove quilts, what I hed proverdensally tied fas' tu the rope. That's what I calls foresight, George. Right furnint the frunt door he cum in contack wif ole Missis Yardley hersef, an' anuther ole 'oman; they wer a-holdin a nine dimunt quilt spread out, a-'zaminin hit, an' a-praisin hits purfeckshuns. The durn'd onmanerly, wall-eyed fool run plum over Missis Yardley, frum ahine, stompt one hine foot through the quilt, takin hit along, a-kickin ontil he made hits corners snap like a whip. The gals screamed, the men hollered wo! an' the ole 'oman wer toted intu the hous' limber es a wet string, an' every word she sed wer, 'Oh, my preshus nine dimunt quilt.'

"Wall-eye busted thru the palins, an' Dominicker sed 'im, made a mortal rush fur his bitts, wer too late fur them, but in good time fur the strings ove flyin quilts, got tangled amung em, an' the gridiron jackid patren wer los' tu my sight amung star an' Irish chain quilts; he went from that quiltin at the rate ove thuty miles tu the hour. Nuffin lef on the lot ove the hole consarn, but a nine biler hat, a par ove gloves, an' the jack ove hearts.

"What a onmanerly, suddin way ove leavin places sum folks hev got, enyhow.

"Thinks I, well, that fool hoss, tarin down that cherry tree lim', hes dun sum good, enyhow; hit hes put the ole 'oman outen the way fur the balance ove the quiltin, an' tuck Dominicker outen the way an' outen danger, fur that gridiron jackid wud a-bred a scab on his nose afore midnite; hit wer morrily boun tu du hit.

"Two months arterwards, I tracked the route that hoss tuck in his kalamatus skeer, by quilt rags, tufts ove cotton, bunches ove har, (human an' hoss,) an' scraps ove a gridiron jackid stickin ontu the bushes, an' plum at the aind ove hit, whar all signs gin out, I foun a piece ove watch chain an' a hosses head. The places what know'd Dominicker, know'd 'im no more.

"Well, arter they'd tuck the ole 'oman up stairs an' camfired her tu sleep, things begun tu work agin. The widders broke the ice, an' arter a littil gigilin, goblin, an' gabblin, the kissin begun. *Smack!*—'Thar, now,' a widder sed that. *Pop!*—'Oh, don't!' *Pfip!*—'Oh, yu quit!' *Plosh!*—'Go *way* yu awkerd critter, yu kissed me in the eye!' anuther widder sed that. *Bop:* 'Now yu ar satisfied, I recon, big mouf!' *Vip!*—'That haint fair!' *Spat!*—'Oh, lordy! May, cum pull Bill away; he's a-tanglin my har.' *Thut!*—'I jis' d-a-r-e you tu du that agin!' a widder sed that, too. Hit sounded all 'roun that room like poppin co'n in a hot skillet, an' wer pow'ful sujestif.

"Hit kep on ontil I be durn'd ef *my* bristils didn't begin tu rise, an' sumthin like a cold buckshot wud run down the marrow in my back-bone 'bout every ten secons, an' then run up agin, tolerabil hot. I kep a swallerin wif nuthin tu swaller, an' my face felt swell'd; an' yet I wer fear'd tu make a bulge. Thinks I, I'll ketch one out tu hersef torreckly, an' then I guess we'll rastil. Purty soon Sal Yardley started fur the smoke 'ous, so I jis' gin my head I few short shakes, let down one ove my wings a-trailin, an' sirkiled roun her wif a side twis' in my naik, steppin sidewise, an' a-fetchin up my hinmos' foot wif a sorter jerkin slide at every step. Sez I, 'Too coo-took a-too.' She onderstood hit, an stopt, sorter spreadin her shoulders. An' jis' es I hed pouch'd out my mouf, an' wer a-reachin forrid wif hit, fur the article hitsef, sunthin interfared wif me, hit did. George, wer yu ever ontu yer hans an' knees, an' let a hell-tarin big, mad ram, wif a ten-yard run, but yu yearnis'ly, jis' onst, right squar ontu the pint ove yer back-bone?"

"No, you fool; why do you ask?"

"Kaze I wanted tu know ef yu cud hev a realizin' noshun ove my shock. Hits scarcely worth while tu try tu make yu onderstan the case by words only, onless yu hev been tetched in that way. Gr-eat golly! the fust thing I felt, I tuck hit tu be a back-ackshun yeathquake; an' the fust thing I seed wer my chaw'r terbacker a-flyin over Sal's head like a skeer'd bat. My mouf wer pouch'd out, ready fur the article hitsef, yu know, an' hit went outen the roun hole like the wad outen a pop-gun—thug! an' the fust thing I know'd, I wer a flyin over Sal's head too, an' a-gainin on the chaw'r terbacker fast. I wer straitened out strait, toes hinemos', middil fingernails foremos', an' the fust thing I hearn wer, 'Yu dam Shanghi!' Great Jerus-a-lam! I lit ontu my all fours jis' in time tu but the yard gate ofen hits hinges, an' skeer loose sum more hosses—kep on in a four-footed gallop, clean acrost the lane afore I cud straiten up, an' yere I cotch up wif my chaw'r terbacker, stickin flat agin a fence-rail. I hed got so good a start that I thot hit a pity tu spile hit, so I jis' jump'd the fence an' tuck thru the orchurd. I tell yu I dusted these yere close, fur I tho't hit wer arter me.

"Arter runnin a spell, I ventered tu feel roun back thar, fur sum signs ove what hed happened tu me. George, arter two pow'ful hardtugs, I pull'd out the vamp an' sole ove one ove ole man Yardley's big brogans, what he hed los' amung my coat-tails. Dre'ful! dre'ful! Arter I got hit away frum thar, my flesh went fas' asleep, frum abuv my kidneys tu my knees; about now, fur the fust time, the idear struck me, what hit wer that hed interfar'd wif me, an' los' me the kiss. Hit wer ole Yardley hed kicked me. I walked fur a month like I wer straddlin a thorn hedge. Sich a shock, at sich a time, an' on sich a place—jis' think ove hit! hit am tremenjus, haint hit? The place feels num, right now."

"Well, Sut, how did the quilting come out?"

"How the hell du yu 'speck me tu know? I warn't thar eny more."

1867

Explorations of an "American" Self

"What is an American?" When that question was asked, as it frequently was in the early part of the nineteenth century, it usually meant "in what ways, if at all, do white American men differ from their British forebearers?" Occasionally, a particularly perceptive commentator like Alexis de Tocqueville would write about the independent qualities of white American women. But even his *Democracy in America* (1835–1840) devotes only a single, though lengthy, chapter to "The Present and Probable Future Condition of the Three Races That Inhabit the Territory of the United States." And Mexicans, like the Irish immigrants, were not of significance to his subject. Indeed, the United States Constitution essentially excluded Indians from its definition of American citizenship and counted black slaves only as three-fifths of a person.

Nevertheless, throughout the period, Indians, blacks, and ultimately Mexicans and the new immigrants, as well as white women, scrutinized the same issues being examined by white men. In part, these concerned the question of nationality: What did it mean to be resident in the American democracy? How did that separate one from the person living in the old world, in France, perhaps, or in England, or even elsewhere in the new world, like Canada? And in literary terms, what did it mean, writers like Emerson and Fuller asked, to write an "American" book, or to create an "American" literature? Was it merely a colonial branch of the British stock or did it have qualities distinctively its own? But also, because even then the United States was an unusually heterogeneous country, such questions were extended to how the meaning of "American" might be different for those, like Indians, who were at once part and *not* part of the democracy. And for a black man like Frederick Douglass, how the experience of July 4, Independence Day, was distinct from that of whites.

In a larger sense, the basic issues concerned what it meant to be a "person," especially a person in this experimental social and political arrangement called "democracy." Gone, at least in theory, were the definitions of self once established by the hierarchy of king, nobles, and gentlemen. But then how, in this new, unformed world, did people define their "place" and consequently who they were or might become? And in a country largely to be created, how could, how should men and women effect a relationship with their fellow human beings or with nature? "Self-Reliance" may strike today's reader as inevitable in free enterprise America. But the individualism which Emerson so eloquently promoted was of rather recent invention, and the image he paints of himself standing in a woodland clearing and becoming a "transparent eyeball" open to all the "currents of the Universal Being" *(Nature)* would have appalled his grandparents' generation in its Pantheism and wild self-assertiveness.

For American intellectuals in the early nineteenth century were deeply affected by the revolutionary impulses of Romanticism, with its emphasis on openness to nature and to feeling, its idea of grand individual selves set free—or at least capable of being set free—from the constraints of tradition and decorum, with its view of society as a set of illegitimate constraints on free development of the self. But while such Romantic currents ran deep in American culture, certain consuming realities also heavily shaped conceptions of an American self. These determined the forms of self-definition in fact available to individuals. The frontier, for example, was on one side a synonym for individual opportunity, but on the other an ever-narrowing barbed-wire fence. Slave-masters were notorious for the extremes—of combativeness and hospitality, among other traits—they affected, but they were able to do so largely by constricting the world their slaves inhabited. This is by no means to suggest that the individual personalities of Indians or slaves were, as some once seemed to think, ground down into an undifferentiated mass. Rather, as one discovers in Harriet Jacobs's *Incidents* or in Douglass's *Narrative,* what some of us can take for granted in defining ourselves, those in fundamentally differing circumstances cannot. For even possession of one's body, much less one's land or traditions of language and culture, could not always be assumed. That Douglass remains uncertain, as the opening paragraphs of his book show, not only of the date of his birth but of the identity of his father may serve here as a symbol of such differences.

Still, the force of American society in the early nineteenth century was to atomize all groups into "simple, separate" persons, in Whitman's phrase. However differently, the writers of the time took up the question of an American self in ways that continue to shape our own understanding of the terms of the discussion.

Paul Lauter
Trinity College

George Copway (Kah-ge-ga-gah-bowh; Ojibwa) 1818–1869

Born in 1818 near the mouth of the Trent River in Upper Canada, Copway was raised as a traditional Ojibwa until 1827, when his parents converted to Christianity. In 1830, Copway became a Christian convert and later occasionally attended the Methodist Mission School at Rice Lake, Ontario. During 1834–37, he helped Methodist missionaries spread the gospel among the Lake Superior Ojibwa. In 1838 he entered Ebenezer Manual Labor School at Jacksonville, Illinois, where for the next nineteen months he received his only formal education. After he left school, Copway traveled in the East before returning to Rice Lake, where he met and married Elizabeth Howell, a white woman. An educated and genteel woman, who wrote numerous articles in her own right and whose letters reveal a polished writing style, Elizabeth Copway may have assisted her husband in his writing.

Until 1842 the Copways served as missionaries to the Indian tribes of Wisconsin and Minnesota. The high point of Copway's career in Canadian Indian affairs was his election in 1845 as vice president of the Grand Council of Methodist Ojibwas of Upper Canada. Later that year he was accused of embezzlement. After being imprisoned briefly in the summer of 1846, Copway was expelled from the Canadian Conference of the Wesleyan Methodist Church and left Canada for the United States. Befriended by American Methodists, Copway launched a new career as a lecturer and writer on Indian affairs. His first book was his autobiography, *The Life, History and Travels* (1847), later republished as *The Life, Letters and Speeches*

(New York: 1850) and as *Recollections of a Forest Life* (London: 1850). Enthusiasm for this autobiography was so great that it was reprinted in seven editions in one year.

In 1847, when the *Life, History and Travels* was published, William Medill, Commissioner of Indian Affairs, began efforts to secure Ojibwa removal from ceded territory to central Minnesota. Despite the plea of a delegation of headmen to regain villages in Wisconsin and upper Michigan, President Zachary Taylor in 1850 authorized immediate and total removal of the Ojibwas from the land set aside for them in 1842. These removal efforts aroused Copway to lecture in the East, South, and Midwest on his plan for a separate Indian state advocated in his pamphlet *Organization of a New Indian Territory, East of the Missouri River* (1850). His lectures in the East enabled him to meet the well-known scholars Henry Rowe Schoolcraft and Francis Parkman as well as such famous writers as Longfellow, Irving, and Cooper, who provided moral and financial encouragement for his later publishing projects. Copway's second book was *The Traditional History and Characteristic Sketches of the Ojibway Nation* (London, 1850; Boston, 1851), later republished as *Indian Life and Indian History* (1858). In this first published, book-length history of the Ojibwa, Copway is far more critical of whites than he was in his autobiography. Copway reached the zenith of his career in the years 1850–51, when he was selected to represent the Christian Indians at the Peace Congress held in Germany. He lectured in Great Britain and on the Continent before the Congress, where he created a great stir by delivering a lengthy anti-war speech while garbed in his Ojibwa finery.

Returning from Europe in December 1850, Copway hurriedly stitched together *Running Sketches of Men and Places, in England, France, Germany, Belgium, and Scotland* (1851), one of the first travel books by an Indian. Between July and fall 1851, Copway established the short-lived journal *Copway's American Indian.* Gradually abandoned by his eastern intellectual friends because of his constant pleas for money and beset by financial difficulties, he also endured the deaths of three of his four children from August 1849 to January 1850.

Copway's attempt to support his family by lecturing was unsuccessful because his novelty had worn off. Dropped by the eastern intellectuals, Copway was taken up by a nativist group who called themselves "native Americans." Members of this anti-immigrant, anti-Roman Catholic group later established the political party known as the "Know-Nothings." Little is known of Copway's later life. In 1864, he recruited Canadian Indians to serve in the American Civil War, for which he received a bounty. He surfaced again in 1867, when he advertised himself in the *Detroit Free Press* as a healer. The following year, having abandoned his wife and daughter, Copway arrived alone at the Lac-des-deux Montagnes, a large Algonquian-Iroquois mission near Montreal. Describing himself as a pagan, Copway became a Catholic convert and was baptized "Joseph-Antoine" on 17 January 1869. Several days later he died.

Copway's autobiography incorporates traditions from earlier personal narratives and American Indian oral narratives. It is divided into four parts: an ethnographic account of Ojibwa culture; the conversions of his band, family, and himself; his role as mediator between Indians and whites; and a history of Ojibwa white relations in the recent past. Copway's blending of myth, history, and personal experience created a structure that later American Indian autobiographies would follow.

In its nostalgia for the lost tribal past, Copway's autobiography bears a stronger relationship to the narratives published by African slaves in the late eighteenth century than to those by African-American slaves in the nineteenth. In the ethnographic sections on Ojibwa life, Copway adopts an overwhelmingly romantic and nostalgic tone. Appealing to American affection for the Indian as a child of nature, he also portrays himself as an example of the Indian's adaptability to white civilization. The ethnographic sections are designed to persuade his audience of the value of tribal culture and the essential humanity of Indian people.

A. LaVonne Brown Ruoff
University of Illinois at Chicago

PRIMARY WORKS

The Life, History and Travels of Kah-ge-ga-gah-bowh (George Copway), a Young Indian Chief of the Ojebwa Nation, . . . with a Sketch of the Present State of the Ojebwa Nation, in Regard to Christianity and Their Future Prospects, 1847. Repub. as *The Life, Letters and Speeches of Kah-ge-ga-gah-bowh, or G. Copway . . . ,* 2nd ed. rev. 1850; and as *Recollections of a Forest Life; or, The Life and Travels of Kah-ge-ga-gah-bowh, or George Copway . . . ,* 1850; 2nd ed. 1851; *Organization of a New Indian Territory, East of the Missouri River. Arguments and Reasons Submitted to the Honorable the Members of the Senate and House of Representatives to the 31st Congress of the United States; by the Indian Chief Kah-ge-ga-gah-bouh (sic), or Geo. Copway,* 1850; *Running Sketches of Men and Places, in England, France, Germany, Belgium, and Scotland,* 1851; *The Traditional History and Characteristic Sketches of the Ojibway Nation. By G. Copway, or, Kah-ge-ga-gah-bowh, Chief of the Ojibway Nation,* 1850; 1851. Repub. as *Indian Life and Indian History, by an Indian Author, Embracing the Traditions of the North American Indian Tribes Regarding Themselves, Particularly of that Most Important of all Tribes, the Ojibways,* 1858. *Copway's American Indian* (July–October 1851); *Life, Letters, and Speeches,* 1997.

SECONDARY WORKS

Dale T. Kobell, "Know-Nothings and Indians: Strange Bedfellows?" *The Western Historical Quarterly* 15 (1984):175–98; A. LaVonne Brown Ruoff, "George Copway: Nineteenth-Century American Indian Autobiographer," *Multi-cultural American Autobiography Issue,* ed. Robert J. Payne, Spec. Issue of *Auto-Biography* 3.2 (1987):6–17; Donald B. Smith, "The Life of George Copway or Kahgegagahbowh (1818–1869)—and a Review of His Writings," *Journal of Canadian Studies* 23 (1988):5–37: A. LaVonne Brown Ruoff, "Three Nineteenth-Century American Indian Autobiographers," *Redefining American Literary History,* eds. A. LaVonne Brown Ruoff and Jerry W. Ward, Jr., 1990:250–69; *Handbook of Native American Literature,* 1996.

from The Life of Kah-ge-ga-gah-bowh

Chapter I

The Christian will no doubt feel for my poor people, when he hears the story of one brought from that unfortunate race called the Indians. The lover of humanity will be glad to see that once powerful race can be made to enjoy the blessings of life.

What was once impossible—or rather thought to be—is made possible through my experience. I have made many close observations of men, and things around me; but, I regret to say, that I do not think I have made as good use of my opportunities as I might have done. It will be seen that I know but little—yet O how precious *that little!*—I would rather lose my right hand than be deprived of it.

I loved the woods, and the chase. I had the nature for it, and gloried in nothing else. The mind for letters was in me, *but was asleep,* till the dawn of Christianity arose, and awoke the slumbers of the soul into energy and action.

You will see that I served the imaginary gods of my poor blind father. I was out early and late in quest of the favors of the *Mon-e-doos* (spirits,) who, it was said, were numerous—who filled the air! At early dawn I watched the rising of the *palace* of the Great Spirit—*the sun*—who, it was said, made the world!

Early as I can recollect, I was taught that it was the gift of the many spirits to be a good hunter and warrior; and much of my time I devoted in search of their favors. On the mountain top, or along the valley, or the water brook, I searched for some kind intimation from the spirits who made their residence in the noise of the waterfalls.

I dreaded to hear the voice of the angry spirit in the gathering clouds. I looked with anxiety to catch a glimpse of the wings of the Great Spirit, who shrouded himself in rolling white and dark clouds—who, with his wings, fanned the earth, and laid low the tall pines and hemlock in his course—who rode in whirlwinds and tornadoes, and plucked the trees from their woven roots—who chased other gods from his course—who drove the Bad Spirit from the surface of the earth, down to the dark caverns of the deep. Yet he was a kind spirit. My father taught me to call that spirit Ke-sha-mon-e-doo—*Benevolent spirit*[1]—for his ancestors taught him no other name to give to that spirit who made the earth, with all its variety and smiling beauty. His benevolence I saw in the running of the streams, for the animals to quench their thirst and the fishes to live; the fruit of the earth teemed wherever I looked. Every thing I saw smilingly said Ke-sha-mon-e-doo nin-ge-oo-she-ig—*the Benevolent spirit made me.*

Where is he? My father pointed to the sun. What is his will concerning me, and the rest of the Indian race? This was a question that I found no one could answer, until a beam from heaven shone on my pathway, which was very dark, when first I saw that there was a true heaven—not in the far-setting sun, where the Indian anticipated a rest, a home for his spirit—but in the bosom of the Highest.

I view my life like the mariner on the wide ocean, without a compass, in the dark night, as he watches the heavens for the north star, which his eye having discovered, he makes his way amidst surging seas, and tossed by angry billows into the very jaws of death, till he arrives safely anchored at port. I have been tossed with hope and fear in this life; no star-light shone on my way, until the men of God pointed me to a Star in the East, as it rose with all its splendor and glory. It was the Star of Bethlehem. I could now say in the language of the poet—

"Once on the raging seas I rode,
    The storm was loud, the night was dark;
The ocean yawned, and rudely blowed
    The wind that tossed my foundering bark."

[1] *"Mone-doos* (spirits) . . . *Benevolent spirit"*—In Ojibwa world view, all elements are animate and contain potential hostility to men. However, they may be appeased through governing spirits. There are numerous eternal spirits of manitos who appear as spirit protectors of plants, birds, beasts, elemental forces, and life circumstances. Evil manitos are the cannibalistic windigos and underwater creatures. (See Ruth Landes, *Ojibwa Religion and the Midewiwin,* 1968).

Yes, I hope to sing some day in the realms of bliss—

"It was my guide, my light my all!
It bade my dark foreboding cease;
And through the storm and danger's thrall,
It led me to the port of peace."

I have not the happiness of being able to refer to written records in narrating the history of my forefathers; but I can reveal to the world what has long been laid up in my memory; so that when "I go the way of all the earth," the crooked and singular paths which I have made in the world, may not only be a warning to others, but may inspire them with a trust in God. And not only a warning and a trust, but also that the world may learn that there once lived such a man as Kah-ge-ga-gah-bowh, when they read his griefs and his joys.

My parents were of the Ojebwa nation, who lived on the lake back of Cobourg, on the shores of Lake Ontario Canada West. The lake was called Rice Lake,[2] where there was a quantity of wild rice, and much game of different kinds, before the whites cleared away the woods, where the deer and the bear then resorted.

My father and mother were taught the religion of their nation. My father became a medicine man in the early part of his life, and always had by him the implements of war, which generally distinguish our head men. He was a good hunter as any in the tribe. Very few brought more furs than he did in the spring. Every spring they returned from their hunting grounds. The Ojebwas each claimed, and claim to this day, hunting grounds, rivers, lakes, and whole districts of country. No one hunted on each other's ground. My father had the northern fork of the river Trent, above Bellmont lake.

My great-grandfather was the first who ventured to settle at Rice Lake, after the Ojebwa nation defeated the Hurons, who once inhabited all the lakes in Western Canada, and who had a large village just on the top of the hill of the Anderson farm, (which was afterwards occupied by the Ojebwas,) and which furnished a magnificent view of the lakes and surrounding country. He was of the *Crane tribe,* i.e. had a crane for totem—*coat of arms*—which now forms the totem of the villagers, excepting those who have since come amongst us from other villages by intermarriage, for there was a law that no one was to marry one of the same totem, for all considered each other as being related.[3] He must have been a daring adventurer—*a warrior*—for no

[2]Located northeast of Toronto and south of Peterborough, Ontario.

[3]"He was of the *Crane tribe,* . . . as being related."

According to William Whipple Warren, each Ojibwa clan is identified with a symbol of totem taken from nature, usually an animal, bird, fish, or reptile. Among the Ojibwa, clan membership descends through the male line. An individual is considered a close blood relation to all other Indians of the same clan, regardless of the band to which they belong. Consequently, intermarriage among clan members was formerly strictly forbidden (*History of the Ojibway Nation,* 1885; 1974).

The original five clans were expanded Warren lists 21 and Johnson, 27 (*Ojibway Heritage,* 1979). One of the original five clans, the most important bird clan was the crane. Warren notes that members of the Crane clan were numerous and that they resided mostly on the south shores of Lake Superior and toward the east in Canada. Warren translates the name for this clan, Bus-in-an-see, as "Echomaker," which alludes to the loud, clear, far-reaching cry of the crane. Johnston describes the crane as a symbol of leadership. Warren indicates that members of this clan were noted for possessing naturally a loud, ringing voice, and are the acknowledged orators of the tribe; in former times, when different tribes met in councils, they acted as interpreter of the wishes of their tribe. They claim, with some apparent justice, the chieftainship over the other clans of the Ojibways."

one would have ventured to go and settle down on the land from which they had just driven the Hurons, whom the Ojebwas conquered and reduced, unless he was a great hero. It is said that he lived about the islands of Rice Lake, secreting himself from the enemy for several years, until some others came and joined him, when they formed a settlement on one of the islands. He must have been a great hunter, for this was one of the principal inducements that made him venture there, for there must have been abundance of game of every kind. The Ojebwas are called, here and all around, Massissuagays, because they came from Me-sey Sah-gieng, at the head of Lake Huron, as you go up to Sault St. Marie falls.

Here he lived in jeopardy—with his life in his hand—enduring the unpleasant idea that he lived in the land of bones—*amidst the gloom,* which shrouded the once happy and populous village of the Hurons; here their bones lay broad-cast around his wigwam; where, among these woods once rang the war cry of the Hurons, echoing along the valley of the river Trent, but whose sinewed arms now laid low, with their badges and arms of war, in one common grave, near the residence of Peter Anderson, Esq. Their graves, forming a hillock, are now all that remain of this once powerful nation. Their bones, gun barrels, tomahawks, war spears, large scalping knives, are yet to be found there. This must have taken place soon after the formation of the settlement in Quebec.

The *Crane tribe* became the sole proprietors of this part of the Ojebwa land; the descendants of this tribe will continue to wear the distinguishing sign; except in a few instances, the chiefs are of this tribe.

My grandfather lived here about this time, and held some friendly intercourse with the whites. My father here learned the manners, customs, and worship of the nation. He, and others, became acquainted with the early settlers, and have ever been friendly with the whites. And I know the day when he used to shake the hand of the white man, and, *very friendly,* the white man would say, *"take some whiskey."* When he saw any hungering for venison, he gave them to eat; and some, in return for his kindness, have repaid him after they became good and great farmers.

My mother was of the *Eagle tribe;*[4] she was a sensible woman; she was as good a hunter as any of the Indians; she could shoot the deer, and the ducks flying as well as they. Nature had done a great deal for her, for she was active; and she was much more cleanly than the majority of our women in those days. She lived to see the day when most of her children were given up to the Lord in Christian baptism; while she experienced a change of heart, and the fulness of God in man, for she lived daily in the enjoyment of God's favors. I will speak more of her at a proper time, respecting her life and happy death.

My father still lives; he is from sixty-five to seventy years old, and is one of the chiefs of Rice Lake Indian Village. He used to love fire-water before he was converted to God, but now lives in the enjoyment of religion, and he is happy without the devil's spittal—*whiskey.* If Christianity had not come, and the grace of God had not taken possession of his heart, his head would soon have been laid low beneath the fallen leaves of the forest, and I, left, in my youthful days, an orphan. But to God be all the praise for his timely deliverance.

[4]According to Johnson, the Eagle clan was identified with foresight and courage. Warren indicates that this group was a branch of the Crane clan.

The reader will see that I cannot boast of an exalted parentage, nor trace the past history to some renowned warrior in days of yore; but let the above suffice. My fathers were those who endured much; who first took possession of the conquered lands of the Hurons.

I was born in *nature's wide domain!* The trees were all that sheltered my infant limbs—the blue heavens all that covered me. I am one of Nature's children; I have always admired her; she shall be my glory; her features—her robes, and the wreath about her brow—the seasons—her stately oaks, and the evergreen—her hair—ringlets over the earth, all contribute to my enduring love of her; and wherever I see her, emotions of pleasure roll in my breast, and swell and burst like waves on the shores of the ocean, in prayer and praise to Him who has placed me in her hand. It is thought great to be born in palaces, surrounded with wealth—but to be born in nature's wide domain is greater still!

I was born sometime in the fall of 1818, near the mouth of the river Trent, called in our language, Sah-ge-dah-we-ge-wah-noong, while my father and mother were attending the annual distribution of the presents from the government to the Indians. I was the third of our family; a brother and sister being older, both of whom died. My brother died without the knowledge of the Saviour, but my sister experienced the power of the loving grace of God. One brother, and two stepbrothers, are still alive.

I remember the tall trees, and the dark woods—the swamp just by, where the little wren sang so melodiously after the going down of the sun in the west—the current of the broad river Trent—the skipping of the fish, and the noise of the rapids a little above. It was here I first saw the light; a little fallen down shelter, made of evergreens, and a few dead embers, the remains of the last fire that shed its genial warmth around, were all that marked the spot. When I last visited it, nothing but fur poles stuck in the ground, and they were leaning on account of decay. Is this dear spot, made green by the tears of memory, any less enticing and hallowed than the palaces where princes are born? I would much more glory in this birth-place, with the broad canopy of heaven above me, and the giant arms of the forest trees for my shelter, than to be born in palaces of marble, studded with pillars of gold! Nature will be nature stil' while palaces shall decay and fall in ruins. Yes, Niagara will be Niagara a thousand years hence! the rainbow, a wreath over her brow, shall continue as long as the sun, and the flowing of the river! While the work of art, however impregnable, shall in atoms fall.

Our wigwam we always carried with us wherever we went. It was made in the following manner: Poles were cut about fifteen feet long; three with crotches at the end, which were stuck in the ground some distance apart, the upper ends meeting, and fastened with bark; and then other poles were cut in circular form and bound round the first, and then covered with plaited reeds, or sewed birch bark, leaving an opening on top for the smoke to escape. The skins of animals formed a covering for a gap, which answered for a door. The family all seated tailor-fashion on mats. In the fall and winter they were generally made more secure, for the purpose of keeping out the rain and cold. The covering of our wigwam was always carried by my mother, whenever we went through the woods. In the summer it was easier and pleasanter to move about from place to place, than in the winter. In the summer we had birch bark canoes, and with these we travelled very rapidly and easily. In the winter every thing was carried upon the back. I have known some Indians to carry a whole deer—not a small one, but a buck. If an Indian could lift up his pack off the ground by means of his arms, it was a good load, not too light nor too heavy. I once carried one hundred and ninety-six weight of flour, twelve pounds of shot, five pounds of coffee, and some sugar, about a quarter of a mile, without resting—the flour was in two bags. It felt very heavy. This was since I travelled with the missionaries, in going over one of the portages in the west.

Our summer houses were made like those in gardens among the whites, except that the skeleton is covered with bark.

The hunting grounds of the Indians were secured by right, a law and custom among themselves. No one was allowed to hunt on another's land, without invitation or permission. If any person was found trespassing on the ground of another, all his things were taken from him, except a handful of shot, powder sufficient to serve him in going *straight* home, a gun, a tomahawk, and a knife; all the fur, and other things, were taken from him. If he were found a second time trespassing, all his things were taken away from him, except food sufficient to subsist on while going home. And should he still come a third time to trespass on the same, or another man's hunting grounds, his nation, or tribe, are then informed of it, who take up his case. If still he disobey, he is banished from his tribe.

My father's hunting ground was at the head of Crow River, a branch of the River Trent, north of the Prince Edward District, Canada West. There are two branches to this river—one belongs to George Poudash, one of the principal chiefs of our nation; the other to my father; and the Crow River belongs to another chief by the name of John Crow. During the last war the Indians did not hunt or fish much for nearly six years, and at the end of that time there were large quantities of beaver, otter, minks, lynx, fishes, &c.

These hunting grounds abound with rivers and lakes; the face of the country is swampy and rocky; the deer and the bear abound in these woods; part of the surrendered territory is included in it. In the year 1818, 1,800,000 acres of it were surrendered to the British government For how much, do you ask? For 62,960 per annum! What a *great sum* for British generosity!

Much of the back country still remains unsold, and I hope the scales will be removed from the eyes of my poor countrymen, that they may see the robberies perpetrated upon them, before they surrender another foot of territory.

From these lakes and rivers come the best furs that are caught in Western Canada. Buyers of fur get large quantities from here. They are then shipped to New York city, or to England. Whenever fruit is plenty, bears are also plenty, and there is much bear hunting. Before the whites came amongst us, the skins of these animals served for clothing; they are now sold from three to eight dollars apiece.

My father generally took one or two families with him when he went to hunt; all were to hunt, and place their gains into one common stock till spring, (for they were often out all winter,) when a division took place.

Chapter II

In the fall we gathered the wild rice and in the winter we were in the interior. Some winters we suffered most severely, on account of the depth of snow, and the cold; our wigwams were often buried in snow. We not only suffered from the snow and the cold, but from hunger. Our party would be unable to hunt, and being far from the white settlements, we were often in want of food. I will narrate a circumstance of our sufferings, when I come to speak of the actual condition of our people, before Christianity was introduced among us, which, when I think of it, I cannot but bless God for his preserving kindness to us, in sparing us to hear his blessed word.

Soon after being Christianized, my father and another Indian, by the name of Big John, and myself, went out hunting; my father left his family near the mission station, living in the wigwam. While we were out on the hunting grounds, we found out that some Indians had gone before us on the route up the river, and every day we gained upon them: their tracks were fresh. The river and the lakes were frozen, and we had to walk on the ice. For some days together we did not fire a gun, for fear they would hear it and go from us, where we could not find them. At length we found them by the banks of the river, they were Nah-doo-ways or Mohawks, from Bay Quinty; they were seven of them, tall fellows. We shook hands with them: they received us kindly. My father had determined to take all they had, if we should overtake them. After they gave us a good dinner of boiled beaver, my father stepped across the fire and ripped open two packs of beaver furs, that were just by him. He said to them "We have only one custom among us, and that is well known to all; this river, and all that is in it are mine: I have come up the river behind you, and you appear to have killed all before you. This is mine, and this is mine," he said, as he touched with the handle of his tomahawk each of the packs of beaver, otter, and muskrat skins. I expected every moment to see my father knocked down with a tomahawk, but none dared touch him; he counted the skins and then threw them across the fire-place to us. After this was done, the same thing took place with the guns; only one was left them to use on their way home. He talked to them by signs, and bade them, as the sailors say, "weigh anchor and soon be under way;" they left, and we took possession of the temporary wigwam they had built. We never saw them afterwards on our hunting grounds, though some of them have been there since.

My father was ever kind and affectionate to me, particularly after the death of my brother, which was occasioned by the going off of a gun, the load passing through the arm, and so fractured it that it soon mortified and caused his death. He believed in persuasion; I know not that he ever used harsh means, but would talk to me for hours together. As soon as it was dark he would call me to his side and begin to talk, and tell me that the Great Spirit would bless me with a long life if I should love my friends, and particularly the aged. He would always take me with him when going any where near, and I learned his movements, for I watched him going through the woods. Often would he tell me that when I should be a man that I must do so, and so, and do as he did, while fording the rivers, shooting the deer, trapping the beaver, etc., etc. I always imitated him while I was a hunter.

My mother was also kind and affectionate; she seemed to be happy when she saw us enjoying ourselves by her; often she would not eat much for days together; she would leave all for us! She was an industrious woman; in the spring she made more sugar than any one else; she was never idle while the season for gathering wild rice lasted.

I was taught early to hunt the deer. It was a part of our father's duty to teach us how to handle the gun as well as the bow and arrow. I was early reminded to hunt for myself; a thirst to excel in hunting began to increase; no pains were spared, no fatigue was too great, and at all seasons I found something to stimulate me to exertion, that I might become a good hunter. For years I followed my father, observed how he approached the deer, the manner of getting it upon his shoulders to carry it home. The appearance of the sky, the sound of the distant water-falls in the morning, the appearance of the clouds and the winds, were to be noticed. The step, and the gesture, in travelling in search of the deer, were to be observed.

Many a lecture I received when the deer lay bleeding at the feet of my father; he would give me an account of the nobleness of the hunter's deeds, and said that I should never be in want whenever there was any game, and that many a poor aged man could be assisted by me. *"If you reverence the aged, many will be glad to hear of your name,"* were the words of my father. "The poor man will say to his children, 'my children, let us go to him, for he is a great hunter, and is kind to the poor, he will not turn us away empty.' The Great Spirit, who has given the aged a long life, will bless you. You must never laugh at any suffering object, for you know not how soon you may be in the same condition: never kill any game needlessly." Such was his language when we were alone in the woods. Ah! they were lessons directed from heaven.

In the spring but a few deer were killed, because they were not in good order, the venison being poor, and the skin so thin, that it was no object to kill them. To hunt deer in the summer was my great delight, which I did in the following manner:—During the day I looked for their tracks, as they came on the shore of the lake or river during the night; they came there to feed. If they came on the bank of the river, I lighted pitch pine, and the current of the river took the canoe along the shore. My lantern was so constructed that the light could not fall on one spot, but sweep along the shore. The deer could see the light, but were not alarmed by it, and continued feeding on the weeds. In this way, I have approached so close that I could have reached them with my paddle. In this manner our forefathers shot them, not with a gun, as I did, but with the bow and arrow. Bows were made strong enough, so that the arrows might pierce through them.

Another mode of hunting on the lakes, preferred by some, is shooting without a light. Many were so expert, and possessed such an accuracy in hearing, that they could shoot successfully in the dark, with no other guide than the noise of the deer in the water; the position of the deer being well known, in this way, the darkest night. I will here relate an occurrence which took place in 1834. My father and I were hunting on the river Trent, in the night; after we had shot two deer, and while returning homewards, we heard the noise of a deer's footsteps. The night was dark as pitch. We approached the deer. I asked my father at what part of the animal I should aim. He replied, "at the head or neck." I poised my gun and fired; hearing no noise, I concluded that my game was sure. I lighted some pitch pine and walked towards the spot from which the noise had come. The deer lay dead and bleeding. On examination I found that I had shot it just below the ear. In the fall of the year, also, I was accustomed to hunt; the meat was very fine, and the skins, (from which our moccasons were made,) were much thicker at this season. Those that could track the deer on fallen leaves and shoot one each day, were considered first rate hunters. The fall is the best time to determine the skill of the huntsman.

Of all animals the bear is the most dangerous to hunt. I had heard so many stories about its cunning that I dreaded to meet one. One day a party of us were going out to hunt the bear, just below Crooke's rapids. After we had made a temporary place to stay for several days, we marched in file; after a while we halted, each took a different direction. My father said, "my son you had better loiter behind the rest. Do not go far, for you may lose yourself." We parted—I took my course, and the rest theirs. I trembled for fear I should see what I was hunting for! I went only where I least expected to see a bear, and every noise I heard in the woods, I thought must be one. As I stood on an old mossy log, there was such a crack on the side of the hill that my heart leaped within me. As I turned and looked, there was a large bear running towards me! I hid myself behind a tree; but on he came; I watched him; he came like a hogshead rolling down hill; there were no signs of stopping; when a few feet from me, I jumped aside, and cried *Yah!* (an exclamation of fear.) I fired my gun without taking sight; in turning suddenly to avoid me, he threw up the earth and leaves; for an instant I was led to believe that the bear was upon me. I dropped my gun and fell backwards, while the bear lay sprawling just by me. Having recovered, I took up my gun and went a few feet from where I fell, and loaded my gun in a hurry. I then sought for a long pole, and with it, I poked it on its side, to see if it was really dead. It did not move, it was dead; but even then I had not courage to go and touch it with my hands. When all was over, and I had told my father I had killed a bear, I felt as though my little leggings could hardly contain me. In examining it, I found the ball had gone through its heart.

Bear meat is like pork. It can be kept a long time when cured. For some weeks together this was the only kind of food we used to eat.

The oil of the bear is used for various purposes. One use is, to prevent the falling out of the hair. The apothecaries buy it from the Indians for about five dollars a gallon.

The skins of bears are what our forefathers wore, before the white people came amongst us, as blankets; but now *land-sharks,* called traders, buy them from the Indians for a mere trifle.

I loved to hunt the bear, the beaver, and the deer but now, the occupation has no charms for me. I will now take the goose quil, for my *bow,* and its point for my *arrow.* If perchance I may yet speak; when my poor aching head lies low in the grave; when the hand that wrote these recollections shall have crumbled into dust; then these pages will not have been written in vain.

"O! Land of rest for thee I sigh—
When will the season come,
When I shall lay my armor by,
And dwell in peace at home."

The beaver was hunted in the spring and fall. They were either trapped or shot. Among all the animals that live in the water, the beaver is of the kindest disposition, when tamed; it is a very cleanly animal; sits on its broad tail on the ground while feeding; feeds all night, and sleeps most of the day. The beaver skin was once worth from eight to ten dollars apiece, or four dollars per pound.

The otter, too, is much valued. The whites buy the skins, and make caps of them. They are mostly caught in traps. In the fall and spring they are always on the move.

The otter is a greedy animal; it can be tamed, but when hungry becomes cross, and often bites. If it be a half a mile off, it will scent any food preparing in the wigwam.

When about five years old, I commenced shooting birds, with a small bow and arrow. I have shot many a bird, but am no more a marksman. I used to feel proud when I used to carry home my own game. The first thing that any of the hunters shot, was cooked by the grand-father and grand-mother, and there was great rejoicing, to inspire the youthful hunter with fresh ardor. Day after day I searched for the grey squirrel, the woodpecker, the snipe, and the snow bird, for this was all my employment.

The gun was another instrument put into my hands, which I was taught to use both carefully and skilfully. Seldom do accidents occur from the use of fire arms among our people. I delighted in running after the deer, in order to head and shoot them. It was a well known fact that I ranked high among the hunters. I remember the first deer I ever shot, it was about one mile north of the village of Keene. The Indians, as has just been said, once had a custom, which is now done away, of making a great feast of the first deer that a young hunter caught: the young hunter, however, was not to partake of any of it, but wait upon the others. All the satisfaction he could realize, was to thump his heels on the ground, while he and others were singing the following hunter's song:

"Ah yah ba wah, ne gah me koo nah vah!
Ah yah wa seeh, ne gah me koo nah nah."[5]

The fattest of the bucks I'll take,
The choicest of all animals I'll take

In the days of our ignorance we used to dance around the fire. I shudder when I think of those days of our darkness. I thought the Spirit would be kind to me if I danced before the old men; and day after day, or night after night, I have been employed with others in this way. I thank God that those days will never return.

Chapter III

The Ojebwas, as well as many others, acknowledged that there was but one Great Spirit, who made the world; they gave him the name of good or benevolent; *kesha* is benevolent, *monedoo* is spirit; Ke-sha-mon-e-doo. They supposed he lived in the heavens; but the most of the time he was in the *Sun*. They said it was from him they received all that was good through life, and that he seldom needs the offering of his Red children, for he was seldom angry.

They also said he could hear all his children, and see them. He was the author of all things that they saw, and made the other spirits that were acknowledged by the Ojebwas. It was said that these other spirits took special care of the various departments of nature. The god of the *hunter* was one who presided over the animals; the god of *war* was one who controlled the destinies of men; the god of *medicine* was one who presided over the herbs of the earth. The fishes had theirs, and there was another over the moon and stars!

[5]These lines are sung over and over again, for about half an hour.

"Millions of spiritual creatures walk the earth
Unseen, both when we sleep and when we wake."

There was one unappeasable spirit, called Bad Spirit, Mah-je-mah-ne-doo. He, it was thought, lived under the earth; and to him was attributed all that was not good, bad luck, sickness, even death. To him they offered sacrifices more than to any other spirit, things most dear to them. There were three things that were generally offered to the Bad Spirit, viz a dog, whiskey and tobacco, a fit offering, with the exception of the poor dog. The poor dog was painted red on its paws, with a large stone and five plugs of tobacco tied about its neck; it was then sunk in the water; while the beating of the drum took place upon the shore, and words were chanted to the Bad Spirit.

The whiskey was thus offered to the Bad Spirit:—When the Indians were seated around the wigwam, or on the grass, and the person who deals out the whiskey had given all the Indians a dram, then the devil was to have his share; it was poured on the ground, and if it went down quickly, it was thought he accepted the offering.

Fire water was sometimes poured out near the head of the graves of the deceased, that their spirits might drink with their former friends. I have often seen them sit around the grave, and, as they drank, make mention of the name of their dead, and pour some whiskey on the ground.

Our religion consisted in observing certain ceremonies every spring. Most of the Ojebwas around us used to come and worship the Great Spirit with us at Rice Lake. At this festival a great many of the youth were initiated into the medical mysteries of the nation. We were taught the virtues of herbs, and the various kinds of minerals used in our medicine. I will here describe the Me-tae-we-gah-mig or Grand Medicine Lodge. It was a wigwam 150 feet long and 15 feet wide. The clan of medicine men and women alone were allowed to be inside, at each sitting, with their medicine badge, on each side of the wigwam. Then there were four old men who took the lead in singing, and beating the drum, as they stood near the centre. Before them were a company who were to take degrees. There were four grades in the institution; and, as I have thought, somewhat similar to the Masonic institution.

After the singing commenced, the whole company arose and danced, as they moved from one end of the wigwam to the other. As they go round, one-half of them cast their heads down upon their bosoms, as if affected by the medicine, which was kept in small skins, and which they pretended to thrust at each other; this was done to deceive the ignorant. These forms were continued several days. The party to be made medicine men and women, looked on in the mean time, to see what they would have to do themselves. Then they are taken to another place with our medicine men, and are taught the science of medicine. After receiving instructions, another day was allotted to give them instruction on morality. They were advised on various subjects. All were to keep silence, and endeavor to retain what they were taught. I will here give some of the sayings of our medicine men:

"If you are a good hunter, warrior, and a medicine man, when you die, you will have no difficulty in getting to the far west in the spirit land."

"Listen to the words of your parents, never be impatient, then the Great Spirit will give you a long life."

"Never pass by any indigent person without giving him something to eat. Owh wah-yah-bak-mek ke-gah-shah-wa-ne-mig—the spirit that sees you will bless you."

"If you see an orphan in want, help him; for you will be rewarded by his friends here, or thanked by his parents in the land of spirits."

"If you own a good hunting dog, give it to the first poor man who really needs it."

"When you kill a deer, or bear never appropriate it to yourself alone, if others are in want; never withhold from them what the Great Spirit has blessed you with."

"When you eat, share with the poor children who are near you, for when you are old they will administer to your wants."

"Never use improper medicine to the injury of another, lest you yourself receive the same treatment."

"When an opportunity offers, call the aged together, and provide for them venison properly cooked, and give them a hearty welcome; then the gods that have favored them will be your friends."

These are a few specimens of the advice given by our fathers, and by adhering to their counsels the lives, peace, and happiness of the Indian race were secured; for then there was no whiskey among them. O! that accursed thing. O! why did the white man give it to my poor fathers? None but fiends in human shape could have introduced it among us.

I recollect the day when my people in Canada were both numerous and happy; and since then, to my sorrow, they have faded away like frost before the heat of the sun! Where are now that once numerous and happy people? The voice of but few is heard.

When I think of them, I feel pained to know that many have fallen a prey to its soul and body-destroying influence I could adopt the language of the poet:

> I will go to my tent and lie down in despair,
> I will paint me with black, and sever my hair,
> I will sit on the shore where the hurricane blows,
> And relate to the God of the tempest my woes;
> For my kindred are gone to the mounds of the dead,
> But they died not of hunger nor wasting decay,
> For the drink of the white man hath swept them away.

The Ojebwa nation, that unconquered nation, has fallen a prey to the withering influence of intemperance. Their buoyant spirits could once mount the air as on the wings of a bird. Now they have no spirits. They are hedged in, bound, and maltreated, by both the American and British governments. They have no other hope, than that at some day they will be relieved from their privations and trials by death. The fire-water has rolled towards them like the waves of the sea. Alas! alas! my poor people! The tribe became dissipated, and consequently improvident, and often suffered intensely.

It was in visiting the interior that we always suffered most. I will here narrate a single circumstance which will convey a correct idea of the sufferings to which the Indians were often exposed. To collect furs of different kinds for the traders, we had to travel far into the woods and remain there the whole winter. Once we left Rice Lake in the fall, and ascended the river in canoes, above Bellmont Lake. There were five families about to hunt with my father, on his grounds. The winter began to set in, and the river having frozen over, we left the canoes, the dried venison, the beaver, and some flour and pork; and when we had gone farther north, say about sixty miles from the whites, for the purpose of hunting, the snow fell for five days in succession to such a depth that it was impossible to shoot or trap anything. Our provisions were exhausted, and we had no means to procure any more. Here we were. The snow about five feet deep; our wigwam buried; the branches of the trees falling around us, and cracking from the weight of the snow.

Our mother boiled birch bark for my sister and myself, that we might not starve. On the seventh day some of them were so weak that they could not raise themselves, and others could not stand alone. They could only crawl in and out of the wigwam. We parched beaver skins and old moccasons for food. On the ninth day none of the men were able to go abroad, except my father and uncle. On the tenth day, still being without food, those only who were able to walk about the wigwam were my father, my grand-mother, my sister, and myself. O how distressing to see the starving Indians lying about the wigwam with hungry and eager looks; the children would cry for something to eat. My poor mother would heave *bitter sighs of despair,* the tears falling from her cheeks profusely as she kissed us. Wood, though plenty, could not be obtained, on account of the feebleness of our limbs.

My father, at times, would draw near the fire, and rehearse some prayer to the gods. It appeared to him that there was no way of escape; the men, women and children dying; some of them were speechless. The wigwam was cold and dark, and covered with snow. On the eleventh day, just before daylight, my father fell into a sleep; he soon awoke and said to me, "My son, the Great Spirit is about to bless us; this night in my dream I saw a person coming from the east, walking on tops of the trees. He told me that we should obtain two beavers this morning about nine o'clock. Put on your moccasons and go along with me to the river, and we will hunt the beaver, perhaps for the last time." I saw that his countenance beamed with delight; he was full of confidence. I put on my moccasons and carried my snow shoes, staggering along behind him, about half a mile. Having made a fire near the river, where there was an air hole, through which the beaver had come up during the night, my father tied a gun to a stump, with the muzzle towards the air hole; he also tied a string to the trigger, and said "should you see the beaver rise, pull the string and you will kill it." I stood by the fire with the string in my hand. I soon heard a noise occasioned by the blow of his tomahawk; he had killed a beaver, and he brought it to me. As he laid it down, he said "then the Great Spirit will not let us die here;" adding, as before, "if you see the beaver rise, pull the string." He left me, I soon saw the nose of one; but I did not shoot. Presently another came up; I pulled the trigger, and off the gun went. I could not see for sometime for the smoke. My father ran towards me, took the two beavers and laid them side by side; then pointing to the sun, said, "Do you see the sun? The Great Spirit informed me that we should kill these two about this time this morning. We will yet see our relatives at Rice Lake; now let us go home and see if they are still alive." We hastened home, and arrived just in time to save them from death. Since which, we visited the same spot, the year after the missionaries came among us. My father, with feelings of gratitude, knelt down on the spot where we had nearly perished. Glory to God! But what have I done for him since? Comparatively nothing. We were just at death's door, when Christianity rescued us. I have heard of many, who have perished in this way, far in the woods. In my travels to the west, I have met many whose families had perished, and who had themselves merely escaped starvation. May God forgive me, for my ingratitude and indolence in his blessed cause!

I will here introduce a favorite war song of the Ojebwa nation. It was accompanied by dancing, and an occasional war-whoop. At the end of each stanza, a warrior rehearsed some former victories, which inspired them with ardor for war. Unchristianized Indians are often like greedy lions after their prey; yes, at times they are indeed cruel and blood thirsty. I have met with warriors, who, when they had killed their enemies, cut open their breasts, took our their hearts, and drank their blood; and all this was out of mere *revenge* But to the *War Song,* which was first translated for Col McKinney, *"the Indian's friend,"* on the shore of Lake Superior.

"On that day when our heroes lay low—lay low—
On that day when our heroes lay low,
I fought by their side, and thought ere I died,
Just vengeance to take on the foe—the foe—
Just vengeance to take on the foe.

"On that day when our chieftains lay dead—lay dead—
On that day when our chieftains lay dead,
I fought hand to hand, at the head of my band,
And *here, on my breast,* have I bled—have I bled—
And here, on my breast, have I bled.

"Our chiefs shall return no more—no more—
Our chiefs shall return no more—
And their brothers in war who can't show scar for scar,
Like women their fates shall deplore—shall deplore—
Like women, their fates shall deplore.

"Five winters in hunting we'll spend—we'll spend—
Five winters in hunting we'll spend—
Then our youths grown to men, to the war lead again,
And our days like our fathers', we'll end—we'll end—
And our days like our fathers', we'll end."[6]

1850

[6]"Col McKinney, *'the Indian's friend,'* . . . And our days like our fathers', we'll end."] See Colonel Thomas L. McKenney's *Sketches of a Tour of the Lakes, of the Character and customs of the Chippeway Indians . . . ,* 1827. Copway and McKenney quote the war song of Wa-ba-jick, a great war chief of La Point, Lake Superior. The song was translated by his daughter, O-Shau-Guscoday-way-gua, wife of John Johnson (1762–1828). Their daughter, Jane Johnston, married Henry Rowe Schoolcraft (See her translations of the Ojibwa stories "Mishosha, or the Magician and his Daughters," and "The Forsaken Brother").

Ralph Waldo Emerson 1803–1882

Ralph Waldo Emerson is often positioned as the "father" of American literature. As a poet, preacher, orator, and essayist, he articulated the new nation's prospects and needs and became a weighty exemplum of the American artist. Throughout the 19th century, Emerson's portrait gazed down from schoolhouse and library walls, where he was enshrined as one of America's great poets. His daughter Ellen, accompanying her father on one of his frequent lecture tours, reported the fun of "seeing all the world burn incense to Father." His calls for a scholar and a poet who would exploit the untapped materials of the nation served as literary credos for subsequent generations of writers, from Rebecca Harding Davis, Walt Whitman, and Frederick Douglass, to Hart Crane, Robert Frost, and A.R. Ammons. He was known for his critique of conventional values of property and ambition, yet his formulation of the self-reliant American was used to authorize the *laissez-faire* individualism of Horatio Alger and Andrew Carnegie. He was one of the first American writers to be recognized by the British and European literary establishments, read enthusiastically by Carlyle and Nietzche. To Matthew Arnold, he is the "voice oracular" who challenges the "bitter knowledge" of his "monstrous, dead, unprofitable world." To Irving Howe, Emerson is the dominant spirit of his age, the proponent of "the American newness." In F.O. Matthiessen's formulation of the "American Renaissance," Emerson is the initiating force "on which Thoreau built, to which Whitman gave extension, and to which Hawthorne and Melville were indebted by being forced to react against its philosophical assumptions." To Whitman and, subsequently, to Alfred Kazin, Emerson is the "founder" of the "procession of American literature."

The eminence of his public position made Emerson's approval a valued commodity, as Whitman showed when he printed a congratulatory letter from Emerson with the second edition of *Leaves of Grass.* It also made him a formidable predecessor with whom younger writers had to contend. Writers as diverse as Thoreau, Louisa May Alcott, and Elizabeth Stuart Phelps describe their emergence onto the literary scene in relationship to Emerson, to his influence as a teacher or writer, a speaker or austere presence. Yet even such acknowledgments as Whitman's famous remark—"I was simmering, simmering, simmering, and Emerson brought me to a boil"—position Emerson primarily as a precursor, important for his influence on others, rather than for his own work. As Joel Porte has argued, "Emerson's fate, somewhat like Shakespeare's, was that he came to be treated as an almost purely allegorical personage whose real character and work got submerged in his function as a touchstone of critical opinion." He becomes the founder of "Transcendentalism" or the spokesman for "Nature," the "optimist" who does not understand the world's evil or pain. He is thus removed from the march of time, idealized as a "primordial" figure whose vision isolates him from the political and social struggles of his age.

But Emerson was never simply a distant patriarchal figure sheltered from the material problems of his age. He constructed his "optative" exuberance despite the early deaths of his father, two of his brothers, his beloved young wife, and his first son, and despite his own serious bouts with lung disease and eye strain. He was a child both of privilege and penury, of family position and dependence. As he wrote early on in his journal: "It is my own humor to despise pedigree. I was educated to prize it." His father, the minister William Emerson, died when he was eight, and his mother, Ruth Haskins Emerson, supported the five children (three others died young) by taking in boarders and by periodically living with relatives in Concord. Emerson's education vacillated between Boston Latin school and private tutoring by his aunt Mary Moody Emerson. At Harvard, which he attended on scholarship, Emerson struggled with the academic curriculum and with his expected future as either a teacher or minister. But he also conducted a more satisfying private education of reading and journal-writing that would prepare him to be a writer, an American scholar, and poet. Those aims had to wait, however, while Emerson helped support his family by teaching school. In 1825, he entered Harvard Divinity School, following nine generations of his family into the ministry. Yet six years after his ordination, he resigned the ministry, concerned that the "dogmatic theology" of "formal Christianity" looked only to past traditions and the words of the dead. "My business is with the living," he wrote in his journal. "I have sometimes thought that in order to be a good minister it was necessary to leave the ministry."

These years were full of personal tumult as well. In 1829, Emerson married Ellen Tucker, only to lose her sixteen months later to the tuberculosis that also threatened him. The pain of her death and his own sense of vulnerability may have hastened Emerson's decision to leave the ministry. With the substantial inheritance she left him, he had the means to make such a change, to travel on the continent, to buy books, and to write them. The inheritance, with the earnings he received from his lecture tours and his publications and with a lifetime of frugality and fiscal planning, made him financially secure. He supported an extended family, caring for his retarded brother for twenty years. In 1835, he married Lidian Jackson, and moved to Concord, where they had four children—Waldo, Ellen, Edith, and Edward Waldo, who later edited his father's works and journals. The death from scarlet fever of five-year-old Waldo was a blow to Emerson's faith in compensation. In his 1844 essay "Experience," he wrote from this loss, and from his urgent desire to regain the "practical power" that could persist despite personal and public griefs. "Life is not intellectual or critical, but sturdy," he argued. His subsequent career and personal life reflect a determined affirmation to be "an active soul." "I am *Defeated* all the time," he acknowledged, "yet to Victory I am born." Emerson continued his work into his seventies, relying on his daughter Ellen to help organize his last lectures and essays. He died in 1882, from pneumonia, and was buried in Concord, near Thoreau and Hawthorne.

Emerson's long career, and his financial and social security, allowed him to intervene decisively in the formation of American culture and letters. Although he generally resisted the call to public advocacy, he was sought after to support various social causes: he was urged to join the experimental commune of Brook Farm, prodded to take a leading role in the abolitionist movement and in the lobbying for women's rights. He spoke in defense of John Brown, in opposition to the Fugitive Slave Law. But, as Thoreau claimed in 1845, it was Emerson's "personal influence upon young persons [that was] greater than any man's." A follower praised "his magnanimous recognition of the work of others," adding that "no one ever came into personal contact with him without a new or renewed confidence in his own possibilities." Emerson's efforts on behalf of his fellow writers were of material importance, addressing the social impediments to publication and reputation. Through financial support, personal connections, or editorial efforts, he made possible publication of work by Thoreau and Bronson Alcott, Margaret Fuller and Jones Very. He loaned Thoreau the house at Walden Pond for his celebrated retreat and raised money to support the impoverished Alcott family, despite his own belief that a philosopher should earn his keep. He oversaw American printings of Carlyle's books and wrote prefaces for translations of Persian poets and of Plutarch. With Margaret Fuller, he edited *The Dial,* a short-lived but influential periodical. Young friends mined his eclectic library for books on "oriental topics" or the latest translation of Goethe. Americans traveling abroad carried introductions from Emerson, and foreign travelers met their American counterparts at his Concord house. Unlike many authors of his day, Emerson insisted on some control over his books' physical production, on their proofreading and revision, their reprinting and marketing. He was active in contemporary struggles to attain an international copyright, to secure better publishing contracts and royalties, and to curtail unsupervised reprints and piracies of books.

Emerson's initial fame came from his critique of the literary, religious, and educational establishments of his day. He was known as an experimenter who urged Americans to reject their deference to old modes and values, to continental traditions. His chiding lectures about Harvard's religious and literary training, and his resignation from the clergy, made him a spokesman for reformist positions, although it also aroused harsh criticism of him as a religious infidel, "a sort of mad dog," and a "dangerous man." At the first meeting of the Transcendental Club, Emerson decried the "tame" genius of the times that did not match the grandeur of "this Titanic continent," and he transformed Harvard's traditional Phi Beta Kappa oration on "The American Scholar" into a critique of the "meek young men" and "sluggard intellect of this continent" and a call for a new age when "we will walk on our own feet; we will work with our own hands; we will speak our own minds."

Emerson's work is characterized by a combination of homely metaphors and grandiose goals, by his insistence on the present and his expectations for the future. His outpouring of "private" writings reflects a practical economy of writing, in which journals serve as a "Savings Bank" for "deposit" of "earnings" to be reworked into lectures and essays. They demonstrate his incredible energy and discipline (he kept 182 journals and notebooks over his career, which he carefully reread, indexed, and cross-referenced for use in preparing his more "public" work); and they reflect an astounding ambition, evident in the titles of his college journals, "The Wide World" and "The Universe," and in such notebooks as "XO" ("Inexorable; Reality and Illusion").

Emerson's literary practices have always been provocative. A critic of his first book, *Nature,* was offended by language that is sometimes "coarse and blunt." He also protested that "the effort of perusal is often painful, the thoughts excited are frequently bewildering, and the results to which they lead us, uncertain and obscure. The reader feels as in a disturbed dream." Although modern readers are unlikely to be upset by Emerson's diction or references to sex and madness, he remains disturbing, seen as a "difficult" writer requiring vast annotation and philosophic glossing. Emerson was indeed an allusive writer, but his use of cultural materials provokes with a purpose. The context he constructs is adamantly untraditional, mixing quotations from classics and British poetry with oriental literature and Welsh bards. One metaphor will emerge from his interest in scientific or engineering experiments, another from local politics, and yet another from what his son Waldo said that morning. The problem in reading Emerson—as well as the pleasure—is in seeing how such eclecticism undermines conventions of authority and reference and challenges established modes of reading. His first book was hailed as wondrous, as the thunderous "original writings of an angel," and as the "forerunner of a new class of books, the harbinger of a new Literature." His essays propose conventional wisdom only to turn it inside out, to question and challenge it. They develop as conversations or as self-reflexive inquiries, refining and testing assumptions. Although the essays are often mined for their aphorisms, these "laws" have a dubious position in Emerson's work, serving less as universal truths than as cultural positions to be examined. His claims about his age and place, about the American poet, scholar, or preacher, are challenges to his fellow citizens and to himself. They suggest a practice, as Emily Dickinson would write, of dwelling in possibility, not in prose.

For himself, and for the American public, he advocated "creative reading as well as creative writing," rejecting traditional oppositions between thinking and acting, between the scholar and the worker, between the speculative and the practical. "Words are also actions," he wrote, "and actions are a kind of words." For despite the hopeful tone of much of the writing, Emerson's brand of self-reliance and his exuberant nationalism were an aspiration, to be achieved only through constant work, constant critique. He rejects poets who "are contented with a civil and conformed manner of living" and who "write poems from the fancy, at a safe distance from their own experience." To Emerson, the poet has a public role to fulfill, a "necessity to be published" so he "apprises us not of his wealth, but of the commonwealth." Although Emerson has been lionized as a man of learning and privilege, his ambition was to "write something which all can read, like *Robinson Crusoe.* And when I have written a paper or a book, I see with regret that it is not solid, with a right materialistic treatment, which delights everybody." He argued that writers must constantly scrutinize their own work, that they must refashion themselves in response to changing circumstances and audiences: "he is no master who cannot vary his forms and carry his own end triumphantly through the most difficult." The poet explores "the science of the real"; he "turns the world to glass, and shows us all things in their right series and procession." Emerson's aim as a writer was less to originate a tradition than to produce active readers, who would then refashion themselves and their culture: "Let me remind the reader that I am only an experimenter. Do not set the least value on what I do, or the least discredit on what I do not, as if I pretended to settle anything as true or false. I unsettle all things. No facts are to me sacred; none are profane; I simply experiment, an endless seeker, with no Past at my back."

Jean Ferguson Carr
University of Pittsburgh

PRIMARY WORKS

Ralph L. Rusk, ed., *The Letters of Ralph Waldo Emerson,* 1939; Joseph Slater, ed., *The Correspondence of Emerson and Carlyle,* 1964; Arthur C. McGiffert, Jr. *Young Emerson Speaks* [sermons]; Ralph H. Orth et al, eds., *The Poetry Notebooks of Ralph Waldo Emerson,* 1986; *The Journals of Ralph Waldo Emerson,* ed. Edward W. Emerson and Waldo Emerson Forbes, 10 vols., 1909–1914; William Gilman, Alfred R. Ferguson, Ralph H. Orth, et al, *The Journals and Miscellaneous Notebooks of R.W. Emerson,* 16 vols., 1960–86; Joel Porte, *Emerson in his Journals,* 1982; Stephen Whicher, Robert Spiller, and Wallace Williams, *The Early Lectures of R.W. Emerson,* 3 vols., 1959–71; *Emerson's Complete Works,* ed. J.E. Cabot, 12 vols., 1883–1893; *The Complete Works of Ralph Waldo Emerson,* ed. Edward W. Emerson, 12 vols., 1903–1904; Alfred R. Ferguson, Jean Ferguson Carr, Douglas E. Wilson, textual editors, *The Collected Works of R.W. Emerson,* 1971–

SECONDARY WORKS

Ralph L. Rusk, *The Life of Ralph Waldo Emerson,* 1949; Sherman Paul, *Emerson's Angle of Vision: Man and Nature in American Experience,* 1952; Hyatt H. Waggoner, *Emerson as Poet,*

1974; David T. Porter, *Emerson and Literary Change,* 1978; Gay Wilson Allen, *Waldo Emerson: A Biography,* 1981; Joel Porte, *Emerson, Prospect and Retrospect,* 1982; Donald Yannella, *Ralph Waldo Emerson,* 1982; Robert E. Burkholder and Joel Myerson, eds., *Critical Essays on Ralph Waldo Emerson,* 1983; Julie Ellison, *Emerson's Romantic Style,* 1984; Harold Bloom, ed., *Ralph Waldo Emerson,* 1985; Robert D. Richardson, *Emerson, The Mind on Fire: A Biography,* 1995; Christopher Newfield, *The Emerson Effect: Individualism and Submission in America,* 1996; Charles E. Mitchell, *Individualism and Its Discontents: Appropriations of Emerson, 1880–1950,* 1997; John Carlos Rowe, *At Emerson's Tomb: The Politics of Classic American Literature,* 1997.

Nature

A subtle chain of countless rings
The next unto the farthest brings;
The eye reads omens where it goes,
And speaks all languages the rose;
And, striving to be man, the worm
Mounts through all the spires of form.[1]

Introduction

Our age is retrospective. It builds the sepulchres of the fathers. It writes biographies, histories, and criticism. The foregoing generations beheld God and nature face to face; we, through their eyes. Why should not we also enjoy an original relation to the universe? Why should not we have a poetry and philosophy of insight and not of tradition, and a religion by revelation to us, and not the history of theirs? Embosomed for a season in nature, whose floods of life stream around and through us, and invite us by the powers they supply, to action proportioned to nature, why should we grope among the dry bones of the past, or put the living generation into masquerade out of its faded wardrobe? The sun shines to-day also. There is more wool and flax in the fields. There are new lands, new men, new thoughts. Let us demand our own works and laws and worship.

Undoubtedly we have no questions to ask which are unanswerable. We must trust the perfection of the creation so far, as to believe that whatever curiosity the order of things has awakened in our minds, the order of things can satisfy. Every man's condition is a solution in hieroglyphic to those inquiries he would put. He acts it as life, before he apprehends it as truth. In like manner, nature is already, in its forms and tendencies, describing its own design. Let us interrogate the great apparition, that shines so peacefully around us. Let us inquire, to what end is nature?

[1]The 1836 edition had as epigraph a quotation attributed to Plotinus: "Nature is but an image or imitation of wisdom, the last thing of the soul; nature being a thing which doth only do, but not know."

All science has one aim, namely, to find a theory of nature. We have theories of races and of functions, but scarcely yet a remote approach to an idea of creation. We are now so far from the road to truth, that religious teachers dispute and hate each other, and speculative men are esteemed unsound and frivolous. But to a sound judgment, the most abstract truth is the most practical. Whenever a true theory appears, it will be its own evidence. Its test is, that it will explain all phenomena. Now many are thought not only unexplained but inexplicable; as language, sleep, madness, dreams, beasts, sex.

Philosophically considered, the universe is composed of Nature and the Soul. Strictly speaking, therefore, all that is separate from us, all which Philosophy distinguishes as the NOT ME, that is, both nature and art, all other men and my own body, must be ranked under this name, NATURE. In enumerating the values of nature and casting up their sum, I shall use the word in both senses;—in its common and in its philosophical import. In inquiries so general as our present one, the inaccuracy is not material; no confusion of thought will occur. *Nature,* in the common sense, refers to essences unchanged by man; space, the air, the river, the leaf. *Art* is applied to the mixture of his will with the same things, as in a house, a canal, a statue, a picture. But his operations taken together are so insignificant, a little chipping, baking, patching, and washing, that in an impression so grand as that of the world on the human mind, they do not vary the result.

Chapter I
Nature

To go into solitude, a man needs to retire as much from his chamber as from society. I am not solitary whilst I read and write, though nobody is with me. But if a man would be alone, let him look at the stars. The rays that come from those heavenly worlds, will separate between him and what he touches. One might think the atmosphere was made transparent with this design, to give man, in the heavenly bodies, the perpetual presence of the sublime. Seen in the streets of cities, how great they are! If the stars should appear one night in a thousand years, how would men believe and adore; and preserve for many generations the remembrance of the city of God which had been shown! But every night come out these envoys of beauty, and light the universe with their admonishing smile.

The stars awaken a certain reverence, because though always present, they are inaccessible; but all natural objects make a kindred impression, when the mind is open to their influence. Nature never wears a mean appearance. Neither does the wisest man extort her secret, and lose his curiosity by finding out all her perfection. Nature never became a toy to a wise spirit. The flowers, the animals, the mountains, reflected the wisdom of his best hour, as much as they had delighted the simplicity of his childhood.

When we speak of nature in this manner, we have a distinct but most poetical sense in the mind. We mean the integrity of impression made by manifold natural objects. It is this which distinguishes the stick of timber of the wood-cutter, from the tree of the poet. The charming landscape which I saw this morning, is indubitably made up of some twenty or thirty farms. Miller owns this field, Locke that, and Manning the woodland beyond. But none of them owns the landscape. There is a property in the horizon which no man has but he whose eye can integrate all the parts, that is, the poet. This is the best part of these men's farms, yet to this their warranty-deeds give no title.

To speak truly, few adult persons can see nature. Most persons do not see the sun. At least they have a very superficial seeing. The sun illuminates only the eye of the man, but shines into the eye and the heart of the child. The lover of nature is he whose inward and outward senses are still truly adjusted to each other; who has retained the spirit of infancy even into the era of manhood. His intercourse with heaven and earth becomes part of his daily food. In the presence of nature, a wild delight runs through the man, in spite of real sorrows. Nature says,—he is my creature, and maugre[1] all his impertinent griefs, he shall be glad with me. Not the sun or the summer alone, but every hour and season yields its tribute of delight; for every hour and change corresponds to and authorizes a different state of the mind, from breathless noon to grimmest midnight. Nature is a setting that fits equally well a comic or a mourning piece. In good health, the air is a cordial of incredible virtue. Crossing a bare common, in snow puddles, at twilight, under a clouded sky, without having in my thoughts any occurrence of special good fortune, I have enjoyed a perfect exhilaration. I am glad to the brink of fear. In the woods too, a man casts off his years, as the snake his slough, and at what period soever of life, is always a child. In the woods, is perpetual youth. Within these plantations of God, a decorum and sanctity reign, a perennial festival is dressed, and the guest sees not how he should tire of them in a thousand years. In the woods, we return to reason and faith. There I feel that nothing can befall me in life,—no disgrace, no calamity, (leaving me my eyes,) which nature cannot repair. Standing on the bare ground,—my head bathed by the blithe air, and uplifted into infinite space,—all mean egotism vanishes. I become a transparent eye-ball; I am nothing; I see all; the currents of the Universal Being circulate through me; I am part or particle of God. The name of the nearest friend sounds then foreign and accidental: to be brothers, to be acquaintances,—master or servant, is then a trifle and a disturbance. I am the lover of uncontained and immortal beauty. In the wilderness, I find something more dear and connate than in streets or villages. In the tranquil landscape, and especially in the distant line of the horizon, man beholds somewhat as beautiful as his own nature.

The greatest delight which the fields and woods minister, is the suggestion of an occult relation between man and the vegetable. I am not alone and unacknowledged. They nod to me, and I to them. The waving of the boughs in the storm, is new to me and old. It takes me by surprise, and yet is not unknown. Its effect is like that of a higher thought or a better emotion coming over me, when I deemed I was thinking justly or doing right.

Yet it is certain that the power to produce this delight, does not reside in nature, but in man, or in a harmony of both. It is necessary to use these pleasures with great temperance. For, nature is not always tricked[2] in holiday attire, but the same scene which yesterday breathed perfume and glittered as for the frolic of the nymphs, is

[1]In spite of.
[2]Dressed.

overspread with melancholy today. Nature always wears the colors of the spirit. To a man laboring under calamity, the heat of his own fire hath sadness in it. Then, there is a kind of contempt of the landscape felt by him who has just lost by death a dear friend. The sky is less grand as it shuts down over less worth in the population.

Chapter II

Commodity

Whoever considers the final cause of the world, will discern a multitude of uses that enter as parts into that result. They all admit of being thrown into one of the following classes; Commodity; Beauty; Language; and Discipline.

Under the general name of Commodity, I rank all those advantages which our senses owe to nature. This, of course, is a benefit which is temporary and mediate, not ultimate, like its service to the soul. Yet although low, it is perfect in its kind, and is the only use of nature which all men apprehend. The misery of man appears like childish petulance, when we explore the steady and prodigal provision that has been made for his support and delight on this green ball which floats him through the heavens. What angels invented these splendid ornaments, these rich conveniences, this ocean of air above, this ocean of water beneath, this firmament of earth between? this zodiac of lights, this tent of dropping clouds, this striped coat of climates, this fourfold year? Beasts, fire, water, stones, and corn serve him. The field is at once his floor, his work-yard, his play-ground, his garden, and his bed.

> "More servants wait on man
> Than he'll take notice of."—[1]

Nature, in its ministry to man, is not only the material, but is also the process and the result. All the parts incessantly work into each other's hands for the profit of man. The wind sows the seed; the sun evaporates the sea; the wind blows the vapor to the field; the ice, on the other side of the planet, condenses rain on this; the rain feeds the plant; the plant feeds the animal; and thus the endless circulations of the divine charity nourish man.

The useful arts are reproductions or new combinations by the wit of man, of the same natural benefactors. He no longer waits for favoring gales, but by means of steam, he realizes the fable of Æolus's[2] bag, and carries the two and thirty winds in the boiler of his boat. To diminish friction, he paves the road with iron bars, and, mounting a coach with a ship-load of men, animals, and merchandise behind him, he darts through the country, from town to town, like an eagle or a swallow through the air. By the aggregate of these aids, how is the face of the world changed, from the era of Noah to that of Napoleon! The private poor man hath cities, ships, canals, bridges, built for him. He goes to the post-office, and the human race run on his errands; to the book-shop, and the human race read and write of all that happens, for

[1]From "Man" (1633) by the English poet George Herbert. The poem is also quoted in "Prospects," Chapter VIII.

[2]The wind god.

him; to the court-house, and nations repair his wrongs. He sets his house upon the road, and the human race go forth every morning, and shovel out the snow, and cut a path for him.

But there is no need of specifying particulars in this class of uses. The catalogue is endless, and the examples so obvious, that I shall leave them to the reader's reflection, with the general remark, that this mercenary benefit is one which has respect to a farther good. A man is fed, not that he may be fed, but that he may work.

Chapter III
Beauty

A nobler want of man is served by nature, namely, the love of Beauty.

The ancient Greeks called the world *κόσμος,*[1] beauty. Such is the constitution of all things, or such the plastic power of the human eye, that the primary forms, as the sky, the mountain, the tree, the animal, give us a delight *in and for themselves;* a pleasure arising from outline, color, motion, and grouping. This seems partly owing to the eye itself. The eye is the best of artists. By the mutual action of its structure and of the laws of light, perspective is produced, which integrates every mass of objects, of what character soever, into a well colored and shaded globe, so that where the particular objects are mean and unaffecting, the landscape which they compose, is round and symmetrical. And as the eye is the best composer, so light is the first of painters. There is no object so foul that intense light will not make beautiful. And the stimulus it affords to the sense, and a sort of infinitude which it hath, like space and time, make all matter gay. Even the corpse hath its own beauty. But besides this general grace diffused over nature, almost all the individual forms are agreeable to the eye, as is proved by our endless imitations of some of them, as the acorn, the grape, the pine-cone, the wheat-ear, the egg, the wings and forms of most birds, the lion's claw, the serpent, the butterfly, sea-shells, flames, clouds, buds, leaves, and the forms of many trees, as the palm.

For better consideration, we may distribute the aspects of Beauty in a threefold manner.

1. First, the simple perception of natural forms is a delight. The influence of the forms and actions in nature, is so needful to man, that, in its lowest functions, it seems to lie on the confines of commodity and beauty. To the body and mind which have been cramped by noxious work or company, nature is medicinal and restores their tone. The tradesman, the attorney comes out of the din and craft of the street, and sees the sky and the woods, and is a man again. In their eternal calm, he finds himself. The health of the eye seems to demand a horizon. We are never tired, so long as we can see far enough.

But in other hours, Nature satisfies by its loveliness, and without any mixture of corporeal benefit. I see the spectacle of morning from the hill-top over against my house, from day-break to sun-rise, with emotions which an angel might share. The

[1]Greek term suggesting order and harmony.

long slender bars of cloud float like fishes in the sea of crimson light. From the earth, as a shore, I look out into that silent sea. I seem to partake its rapid transformations: the active enchantment reaches my dust, and I dilate and conspire with the morning wind. How does Nature deify us with a few and cheap elements! Give me health and a day, and I will make the pomp of emperors ridiculous. The dawn is my Assyria, the sun-set and moon-rise my Paphos,[2] and unimaginable realms of faerie; broad noon shall be my England of the senses and the understanding; the night shall be my Germany of mystic philosophy and dreams.

Not less excellent, except for our less susceptibility in the afternoon, was the charm, last evening, of a January sunset. The western clouds divided and subdivided themselves into pink flakes modulated with tints of unspeakable softness; and the air had so much life and sweetness, that it was a pain to come within doors. What was it that nature would say? Was there no meaning in the live repose of the valley behind the mill, and which Homer or Shakspeare could not re-form for me in words? The leafless trees become spires of flame in the sunset, with the blue east for their background, and the stars of the dead calices[3] of flowers, and every withered stem and stubble rimed with frost, contribute something to the mute music.

The inhabitants of cities suppose that the country landscape is pleasant only half the year. I please myself with the graces of the winter scenery, and believe that we are as much touched by it as by the genial influences of summer. To the attentive eye, each moment of the year has its own beauty, and in the same field, it beholds, every hour, a picture which was never seen before, and which shall never be seen again. The heavens change every moment, and reflect their glory or gloom on the plains beneath. The state of the crop in the surrounding farms alters the expression of the earth from week to week. The succession of native plants in the pastures and roadsides, which makes the silent clock by which time tells the summer hours, will make even the divisions of the day sensible to a keen observer. The tribes of birds and insects, like the plants punctual to their time, follow each other, and the year has room for all. By water-courses, the variety is greater. In July, the blue pontederia or pickerel-weed blooms in large beds in the shallow parts of our pleasant river, and swarms with yellow butterflies in continual motion. Art cannot rival this pomp of purple and gold. Indeed the river is a perpetual gala, and boasts each month a new ornament.

But this beauty of Nature which is seen and felt as beauty, is the least part. The shows of day, the dewy morning, the rainbow, mountains, orchards in blossom, stars, moonlight, shadows in still water, and the like, if too eagerly hunted, become shows merely, and mock us with their unreality. Go out of the house to see the moon, and 't is mere tinsel; it will not please as when its light shines upon your necessary journey. The beauty that shimmers in the yellow afternoons of October, who ever could clutch it? Go forth to find it, and it is gone: 't is only a mirage as you look from the windows of diligence.

2. The presence of a higher, namely, of the spiritual element is essential to its perfection. The high and divine beauty which can be loved without effeminacy, is that which is found in combination with the human will. Beauty is the mark God sets upon virtue. Every natural action is graceful. Every heroic act is also decent, and causes the

[2]"Assyria . . . Paphos." Ancient civilizations.
[3]Calyxes, the outer coverings of flowers.

place and the bystanders to shine. We are taught by great actions that the universe is the property of every individual in it. Every rational creature has all nature for his dowry and estate. It is his, if he will. He may divest himself of it; he may creep into a corner, and abdicate his kingdom, as most men do, but he is entitled to the world by his constitution. In proportion to the energy of his thought and will, he takes up the world into himself. "All those things for which men plough, build, or sail, obey virtue," said Sallust. "The winds and waves," said Gibbon,[4] "are always on the side of the ablest navigators." So are the sun and moon and all the stars of heaven. When a noble act is done,—perchance in a scene of great natural beauty; when Leonidas[5] and his three hundred martyrs consume one day in dying, and the sun and moon come each and look at them once in the steep defile of Thermopylae; when Arnold Winkelried, in the high Alps, under the shadow of the avalanche, gathers in his side a sheaf of Austrian spears to break the line for his comrades; are not these heroes entitled to add the beauty of the scene to the beauty of the deed? When the bark of Columbus nears the shore of America;—before it, the beach lined with savages, fleeing out of all their huts of cane; the sea behind; and the purple mountains of the Indian Archipelago around, can we separate the man from the living picture? Does not the New World clothe his form with her palm-groves and savannahs as fit drapery? Ever does natural beauty steal in like air, and envelope great actions. When Sir Harry Vane was dragged up the Tower-hill, sitting on a sled, to suffer death, as the champion of the English laws, one of the multitude cried out to him, "You never sate on so glorious a seat." Charles II., to intimidate the citizens of London, caused the patriot Lord Russel to be drawn in an open coach, through the principal streets of the city, on his way to the scaffold. "But," his biographer says, "the multitude imagined they saw liberty and virtue sitting by his side." In private places, among sordid objects, an act of truth or heroism seems at once to draw to itself the sky as its temple, the sun as its candle. Nature stretcheth out her arms to embrace man, only let his thoughts be of equal greatness. Willingly does she follow his steps with the rose and the violet, and bend her lines of grandeur and grace to the decoration of her darling child. Only let his thoughts be of equal scope, and the frame will suit the picture. A virtuous man is in unison with her works, and makes the central figure of the visible sphere. Homer, Pindar, Socrates, Phocion,[6] associate themselves fitly in our memory with the geography and climate of Greece. The visible heavens and earth sympathize with Jesus. And in common life, whosoever has seen a person of powerful character and happy genius, will have remarked how easily he took all things along with him,—the persons, the opinions, and the day, and nature became ancillary to a man.

3. There is still another aspect under which the beauty of the world may be viewed, namely, as it becomes an object of the intellect. Beside the relation of things to virtue, they have a relation to thought. The intellect searches out the absolute order of things as they stand in the mind of God, and without the colors of affection. The intellectual and the active powers seem to succeed each other, and the exclusive

[4]"Sallust . . . Gibbon" Roman historian (86–34 B.C.) and British author of *Decline and Fall of the Roman Empire* (1788).

[5]Emerson gives several historical examples of "noble acts": Spartan King Leonidas who fought the Persians in 480 B.C., Swiss hero Winkelried who sacrificed himself in battle in 1386; Columbus, and two English politicians executed under Charles II.

[6]Greek poets (Homer and Pindar), philosopher (Socrates), and statesman (Phocion).

activity of the one, generates the exclusive activity of the other. There is something unfriendly in each to the other, but they are like the alternate periods of feeding and working in animals; each prepares and will be followed by the other. Therefore does beauty, which, in relation to actions, as we have seen, comes unsought, and comes because it is unsought, remain for the apprehension and pursuit of the intellect; and then again, in its turn, of the active power. Nothing divine dies. All good is eternally reproductive. The beauty of nature reforms itself in the mind, and not for barren contemplation, but for new creation.

All men are in some degree impressed by the face of the world; some men even to delight. This love of beauty is Taste. Others have the same love in such excess, that, not content with admiring, they seek to embody it in new forms. The creation of beauty is Art.

The production of a work of art throws a light upon the mystery of humanity. A work of art is an abstract or epitome of the world. It is the result or expression of nature, in miniature. For, although the works of nature are innumerable and all different, the result or the expression of them all is similar and single. Nature is a sea of forms radically alike and even unique. A leaf, a sun-beam, a landscape, the ocean, make an analogous impression on the mind. What is common to them all,—that perfectness and harmony, is beauty. The standard of beauty is the entire circuit of natural forms,—the totality of nature; which the Italians expressed by defining beauty "il piu nell' uno."[7] Nothing is quite beautiful alone: nothing but is beautiful in the whole. A single object is only so far beautiful as it suggests this universal grace. The poet, the painter, the sculptor, the musician, the architect, seek each to concentrate this radiance of the world on one point, and each in his several work to satisfy the love of beauty which stimulates him to produce. Thus is Art, a nature passed through the alembic[8] of man. Thus in art, does nature work through the will of a man filled with the beauty of her first works.

The world thus exists to the soul to satisfy the desire of beauty. This element I call an ultimate end. No reason can be asked or given why the soul seeks beauty. Beauty, in its largest and profoundest sense, is one expression for the universe. God is the all-fair. Truth, and goodness, and beauty, are but different faces of the same All. But beauty in nature is not ultimate. It is the herald of inward and eternal beauty, and is not alone a solid and satisfactory good. It must stand as a part, and not as yet the last or highest expression of the final cause of Nature.

Chapter IV

Language

Language is a third use which Nature subserves to man. Nature is the vehicle of thought, and in a simple, double, and threefold degree.

1. Words are signs of natural facts.
2. Particular natural facts are symbols of particular spiritual facts.
3. Nature is the symbol of spirit.

[7]"The many in one."

[8]Apparatus used for distilling or refining.

1. Words are signs of natural facts. The use of natural history is to give us aid in supernatural history: the use of the outer creation, to give us language for the beings and changes of the inward creation. Every word which is used to express a moral or intellectual fact, if traced to its root, is found to be borrowed from some material appearance. *Right* means *straight; wrong* means *twisted. Spirit* primarily means *wind; transgression,* the crossing of a *line; supercilious,* the *raising of the eyebrow.* We say the *heart* to express emotion, the *head* to denote thought; and *thought* and *emotion* are words borrowed from sensible things, and now appropriated to spiritual nature. Most of the process by which this transformation is made, is hidden from us in the remote time when language was framed; but the same tendency may be daily observed in children. Children and savages use only nouns or names of things, which they convert into verbs, and apply to analogous mental acts.

2. But this origin of all words that convey a spiritual import,—so conspicuous a fact in the history of language,—is our least debt to nature. It is not words only that are emblematic; it is things which are emblematic. Every natural fact is a symbol of some spiritual fact. Every appearance in nature corresponds to some state of the mind, and that state of the mind can only be described by presenting that natural appearance as its picture. An enraged man is a lion, a cunning man is a fox, a firm man is a rock, a learned man is a torch. A lamb is innocence; a snake is subtle spite; flowers express to us the delicate affections. Light and darkness are our familiar expression for knowledge and ignorance; and heat for love. Visible distance behind and before us, is respectively our image of memory and hope.

Who looks upon a river in a meditative hour, and is not reminded of the flux of all things? Throw a stone into the stream, and the circles that propagate themselves are the beautiful type of all influence. Man is conscious of a universal soul within or behind his individual life, wherein, as in a firmament, the natures of Justice, Truth, Love, Freedom, arise and shine. This universal soul, he calls Reason: it is not mine, or thine, or his, but we are its; we are its property and men. And the blue sky in which the private earth is buried, the sky with its eternal calm, and full of everlasting orbs, is the type of Reason. That which, intellectually considered, we call Reason, considered in relation to nature, we call Spirit. Spirit is the Creator. Spirit hath life in itself. And man in all ages and countries, embodies it in his language, as the FATHER.

It is easily seen that there is nothing lucky or capricious in these analogies, but that they are constant, and pervade nature. These are not the dreams of a few poets, here and there, but man is an analogist, and studies relations in all objects. He is placed in the centre of beings, and a ray of relation passes from every other being to him. And neither can man be understood without these objects, nor these objects without man. All the facts in natural history taken by themselves, have no value, but are barren, like a single sex. But marry it to human history, and it is full of life. Whole Floras, all Linnaeus' and Buffon's[1] volumes, are dry catalogues of facts; but the most trivial of these facts, the habit of a plant, the organs, or work, or noise of an insect, applied to the illustration of a fact in intellectual philosophy, or, in any way associated to human nature, affects us in the most lively and agreeable manner. The seed

[1]Eighteenth-century Swedish botanist and French naturalist, who wrote famous plant classifications.

of a plant,—to what affecting analogies in the nature of man, is that little fruit made use of, in all discourse, up to the voice of Paul, who calls the human corpse a seed,—"It is sown a natural body; it is raised a spiritual body."[2] The motion of the earth round its axis, and round the sun, makes the day, and the year. These are certain amounts of brute light and heat. But is there no intent of an analogy between man's life and the seasons? And do the seasons gain no grandeur or pathos from that analogy? The instincts of the ant are very unimportant, considered as the ant's; but the moment a ray of relation is seen to extend from it to man, and the little drudge is seen to be a monitor, a little body with a mighty heart, then all its habits, even that said to be recently observed, that it never sleeps, become sublime.

Because of this radical correspondence between visible things and human thoughts, savages, who have only what is necessary, converse in figures. As we go back in history, language becomes more picturesque, until its infancy, when it is all poetry; or all spiritual facts are represented by natural symbols. The same symbols are found to make the original elements of all languages. It has moreover been observed, that the idioms of all languages approach each other in passages of the greatest eloquence and power. And as this is the first language, so is it the last. This immediate dependence of language upon nature, this conversion of an outward phenomenon into a type of somewhat in human life, never loses its power to affect us. It is this which gives that piquancy to the conversation of a strong-natured farmer or back-woodsman, which all men relish.

A man's power to connect his thought with its proper symbol, and so to utter it, depends on the simplicity of his character, that is, upon his love of truth, and his desire to communicate it without loss. The corruption of man is followed by the corruption of language. When simplicity of character and the sovereignty of ideas is broken up by the prevalence of secondary desires, the desire of riches, of pleasure, of power, and of praise,—and duplicity and falsehood take place of simplicity and truth, the power over nature as an interpreter of the will, is in a degree lost; new imagery ceases to be created, and old words are perverted to stand for things which are not; a paper currency is employed, when there is no bullion in the vaults. In due time, the fraud is manifest, and words lose all power to stimulate the understanding or the affections. Hundreds of writers may be found in every long-civilized nation, who for a short time believe, and make others believe, that they see and utter truths, who do not of themselves clothe one thought in its natural garment, but who feed unconsciously on the language created by the primary writers of the country, those, namely, who hold primarily on nature.

But wise men pierce this rotten diction and fasten words again to visible things; so that picturesque language is at once a commanding certificate that he who employs it, is a man in alliance with truth and God. The moment our discourse rises above the ground line of familiar facts, and is inflamed with passion or exalted by thought, it clothes itself in images. A man conversing in earnest, if he watch his intellectual processes, will find that a material image, more or less luminous, arises in his mind, cotemporaneous with every thought, which furnishes the vestment of the thought. Hence, good writing and brilliant discourse are perpetual allegories. This imagery is spontaneous. It is the blending of experience with the present action of

[2]I Cor. 15:44.

the mind. It is proper creation. It is the working of the Original Cause through the instruments he has already made.

These facts may suggest the advantage which the country-life possesses for a powerful mind, over the artificial and curtailed life of cities. We know more from nature than we can at will communicate. Its light flows into the mind evermore, and we forget its presence. The poet, the orator, bred in the woods, whose senses have been nourished by their fair and appeasing changes, year after year, without design and without heed,—shall not lose their lesson altogether, in the roar of cities or the broil of politics. Long hereafter, amidst agitation and terror in national councils,—in the hour of revolution,—these solemn images shall reappear in their morning lustre, as fit symbols and words of the thoughts which the passing events shall awaken. At the call of a noble sentiment, again the woods wave, the pines murmur, the river rolls and shines, and the cattle low upon the mountains, as he saw and heard them in his infancy. And with these forms, the spells of persuasion, the keys of power are put into his hands.

3. We are thus assisted by natural objects in the expression of particular meanings. But how great a language to convey such pepper-corn informations! Did it need such noble races of creatures, this profusion of forms, this host of orbs in heaven, to furnish man with the dictionary and grammar of his municipal speech? Whilst we use this grand cipher to expedite the affairs of our pot and kettle, we feel that we have not yet put it to its use, neither are able. We are like travellers using the cinders of a volcano to roast their eggs. Whilst we see that it always stands ready to clothe what we would say, we cannot avoid the question, whether the characters are not significant of themselves. Have mountains, and waves, and skies, no significance but what we consciously give them, when we employ them as emblems of our thoughts? The world is emblematic. Parts of speech are metaphors, because the whole of nature is a metaphor of the human mind. The laws of moral nature answer to those of matter as face to face in a glass. "The visible world and the relation of its parts, is the dial plate of the invisible."[3] The axioms of physics translate the laws of ethics. Thus, "the whole is greater than its part;" "reaction is equal to action;" "the smallest weight may be made to lift the greatest, the difference of weight being compensated by time;" and many the like propositions, which have an ethical as well as physical sense. These propositions have a much more extensive and universal sense when applied to human life, than when confined to technical use.

In like manner, the memorable words of history, and the proverbs of nations, consist usually of a natural fact, selected as a picture or parable of a moral truth. Thus; A rolling stone gathers no moss; A bird in the hand is worth two in the bush; A cripple in the right way, will beat a racer in the wrong; Make hay while the sun

[3]This essay uses many of the quotations Emerson copied into his journals. He rarely cites the source, although he does mark with double quotations when a passage is a "*bona fide* quotation from any person" rather than an imagined or rhetorical comment. In some cases he paraphrases or quotes from memory. Here he cites the 18th-century philosopher Swedenborg; other quotations are from Shakespeare's plays and sonnets, the English Quaker George Fox, Coleridge, Francis Bacon, the Bible, Goethe, Plato, and Milton. Emerson could expect most of his contemporary readers to recognize Biblical passages, mythological allusions, and Shakespeare.

shines; 'T is hard to carry a full cup even; Vinegar is the son of wine; The last ounce broke the camel's back; Long-lived trees make roots first;—and the like. In their primary sense these are trivial facts, but we repeat them for the value of their analogical import. What is true of proverbs, is true of all fables, parables, and allegories.

This relation between the mind and matter is not fancied by some poet, but stands in the will of God, and so is free to be known by all men. It appears to men, or it does not appear. When in fortunate hours we ponder this miracle, the wise man doubts, if, at all other times, he is not blind and deaf;

——"Can these things be,
And overcome us like a summer's cloud,
Without our special wonder?"[4]

for the universe becomes transparent, and the light of higher laws than its own, shines through it. It is the standing problem which has exercised the wonder and the study of every fine genius since the world began; from the era of the Egyptians and the Brahmins,[5] to that of Pythagoras, of Plato, of Bacon, of Leibnitz,[6] of Swedenborg. There sits the Sphinx at the road-side, and from age to age, as each prophet comes by, he tries his fortune at reading her riddle. There seems to be a necessity in spirit to manifest itself in material forms; and day and night, river and storm, beast and bird, acid and alkali, preëxist in necessary Ideas in the mind of God, and are what they are by virtue of preceding affections, in the world of spirit. A Fact is the end or last issue of spirit. The visible creation is the terminus or the circumference of the invisible world. "Material objects," said a French philosopher, "are necessarily kinds of *scoriae*[7] of the substantial thoughts of the Creator, which must always preserve an exact relation to their first origin; in other words, visible nature must have a spiritual and moral side."[8]

This doctrine is abstruse, and though the images of "garment," "scoriae," "mirror," &c., may stimulate the fancy, we must summon the aid of subtler and more vital expositors to make it plain. "Every scripture is to be interpreted by the same spirit which gave it forth,"—is the fundamental law of criticism. A life in harmony with nature, the love of truth and of virtue, will purge the eyes to understand her text. By degrees we may come to know the primitive sense of the permanent objects of nature, so that the world shall be to us an open book, and every form significant of its hidden life and final cause.

A new interest surprises us, whilst, under the view now suggested, we contemplate the fearful extent and multitude of objects; since "every object rightly seen, unlocks a new faculty of the soul." That which was unconscious truth, becomes, when interpreted and defined in an object, a part of the domain of knowledge,—a new weapon in the magazine of power.

[4]*Macbeth,* III, iv, 110–112.
[5]Priests of 7th-century B.C. Indian religion.
[6]Seventeenth-century German mathematician and philosopher.
[7]Refuse from melting metals or ores.
[8]Quoted from Guillaume Oegger, *The True Messiah* (1829).

Chapter V

Discipline

In view of the significance of nature, we arrive at once at a new fact, that nature is a discipline. This use of the world includes the preceding uses, as parts of itself.

Space, time, society, labor, climate, food, locomotion, the animals, the mechanical forces, give us sincerest lessons, day by day, whose meaning is unlimited. They educate both the Understanding and the Reason. Every property of matter is a school for the understanding,—its solidity or resistance, its inertia, its extension, its figure, its divisibility. The understanding adds, divides, combines, measures, and finds nutriment and room for its activity in this worthy scene. Meantime, Reason transfers all these lessons into its own world of thought, by perceiving the analogy that marries Matter and Mind.

1. Nature is a discipline of the understanding in intellectual truths. Our dealing with sensible objects is a constant exercise in the necessary lessons of difference, of likeness, of order, of being and seeming, of progressive arrangement; of ascent from particular to general; of combination to one end of manifold forces. Proportioned to the importance of the organ to be formed, is the extreme care with which its tuition is provided,—a care pretermitted in no single case. What tedious training, day after day, year after year, never ending, to form the common sense; what continual reproduction of annoyances, inconveniences, dilemmas; what rejoicing over us of little men; what disputing of prices, what reckonings of interest,—and all to form the Hand of the mind;—to instruct us that "good thoughts are no better than good dreams, unless they be executed!"

The same good office is performed by Property and its filial systems of debt and credit. Debt, grinding debt, whose iron face the widow, the orphan, and the sons of genius fear and hate;—debt, which consumes so much time, which so cripples and disheartens a great spirit with cares that seem so base, is a preceptor whose lessons cannot be forgone, and is needed most by those who suffer from it most. Moreover, property, which has been well compared to snow,—"if it fall level to-day, it will be blown into drifts to-morrow,"—is the surface action of internal machinery, like the index on the face of a clock. Whilst now it is the gymnastics of the understanding, it is hiving in the foresight of the spirit, experience in profounder laws.

The whole character and fortune of the individual are affected by the least inequalities in the culture of the understanding; for example, in the perception of differences. Therefore is Space, and therefore Time, that man may know that things are not huddled and lumped, but sundered and individual. A bell and a plough have each their use, and neither can do the office of the other. Water is good to drink, coal to burn, wool to wear; but wool cannot be drunk, nor water spun, nor coal eaten. The wise man shows his wisdom in separation, in gradation, and his scale of creatures and of merits is as wide as nature. The foolish have no range in their scale, but suppose every man is as every other man. What is not good they call the worst, and what is not hateful, they call the best.

In like manner, what good heed, nature forms in us! She pardons no mistakes. Her yea is yea, and her nay, nay.

The first steps in Agriculture, Astronomy, Zoölogy, (those first steps which the farmer, the hunter, and the sailor take,) teach that nature's dice are always loaded; that in her heaps and rubbish are concealed sure and useful results.

How calmly and genially the mind apprehends one after another the laws of physics! What noble emotions dilate the mortal as he enters into the counsels of the creation, and feels by knowledge the privilege to BE! His insight refines him. The beauty of nature shines in his own breast. Man is greater that he can see this, and the universe less, because Time and Space relations vanish as laws are known.

Here again we are impressed and even daunted by the immense Universe to be explored. "What we know, is a point to what we do not know."[1] Open any recent journal of science, and weigh the problems suggested concerning Light, Heat, Electricity, Magnetism, Physiology, Geology, and judge whether the interest of natural science is likely to be soon exhausted.

Passing by many particulars of the discipline of nature, we must not omit to specify two.

The exercise of the Will or the lesson of power is taught in every event. From the child's successive possession of his several senses up to the hour when he saith, "Thy will be done!"[2] he is learning the secret, that he can reduce under his will, not only particular events, but great classes, nay the whole series of events, and so conform all facts to his character. Nature is thoroughly mediate. It is made to serve. It receives the dominion of man as meekly as the ass on which the Saviour rode. It offers all its kingdoms to man as the raw material which he may mould into what is useful. Man is never weary of working it up. He forges the subtile and delicate air into wise and melodious words, and gives them wing as angels of persuasion and command. One after another, his victorious thought comes up with and reduces all things, until the world becomes, at last, only a realized will,—the double of the man.

2. Sensible objects conform to the premonitions of Reason and reflect the conscience. All things are moral; and in their boundless changes have an unceasing reference to spiritual nature. Therefore is nature glorious with form, color, and motion, that every globe in the remotest heaven; every chemical change from the rudest crystal up to the laws of life; every change of vegetation from the first principle of growth in the eye of a leaf, to the tropical forest and antediluvian coal-mine; every animal function from the sponge up to Hercules, shall hint or thunder to man the laws of right and wrong, and echo the Ten Commandments. Therefore is nature ever the ally of Religion: lends all her pomp and riches to the religious sentiment. Prophet and priest, David, Isaiah, Jesus, have drawn deeply from this source. This ethical character so penetrates the bone and marrow of nature, as to seem the end for which it was made. Whatever private purpose is answered by any member or part, this is its public and universal function, and is never omitted. Nothing in nature is exhausted in its first use. When a thing has served an end to the uttermost, it is wholly new for an ulterior service. In God, every end is converted into a new means. Thus the use of com-

[1]Emerson's learned quotations often came from less elevated sources: he found this quote from Bishop Joseph Butler in a British novel *Tremaine* (1825) by Robert P. Ward.

[2]The Lord's Prayer, Matthew 6:10, 26:42.

modity, regarded by itself, is mean and squalid. But it is to the mind an education in the doctrine of Use, namely, that a thing is good only so far as it serves; that a conspiring of parts and efforts to the production of an end, is essential to any being. The first and gross manifestation of this truth, is our inevitable and hatred training in values and wants, in corn and meat.

It has already been illustrated, that every natural process is a version of a moral sentence. The moral law lies at the centre of nature and radiates to the circumference. It is the pith and marrow of every substance, every relation, and every process. All things with which we deal, preach to us. What is a farm but a mute gospel? The chaff and the wheat, weeds and plants, blight, rain, insects, sun,—it is a sacred emblem from the first furrow of spring to the last stack which the snow of winter overtakes in the fields. But the sailor, the shepherd, the miner, the merchant, in their several resorts, have each an experience precisely parallel, and leading to the same conclusion: because all organizations are radically alike. Nor can it be doubted that this moral sentiment which thus scents the air, grows in the grain, and impregnates the waters of the world, is caught by man and sinks into his soul. The moral influence of nature upon every individual is that amount of truth which it illustrates to him. Who can estimate this? Who can guess how much firmness the sea-beaten rock has taught the fisherman? how much tranquillity has been reflected to man from the azure sky, over whose unspotted deeps the winds forevermore drive flocks of stormy clouds, and leave no wrinkle or stain? how much industry and providence and affection we have caught from the pantomime of brutes? What a searching preacher of self-command is the varying phenomenon of Health!

Herein is especially apprehended the unity of Nature,—the unity in variety,—which meets us everywhere. All the endless variety of things make an identical impression. Xenophanes[3] complained in his old age, that, look where he would, all things hastened back to Unity. He was weary of seeing the same entity in the tedious variety of forms. The fable of Proteus[4] has a cordial truth. A leaf, a drop, a crystal, a moment of time is related to the whole, and partakes of the perfection of the whole. Each particle is a microcosm, and faithfully renders the likeness of the world.

Not only resemblances exist in things whose analogy is obvious, as when we detect the type of the human hand in the flipper of the fossil saurus,[5] but also in objects wherein there is great superficial unlikeness. Thus architecture is called "frozen music," by De Stael and Goethe. Vitruvius[6] thought an architect should be a musician. "A Gothic church," said Coleridge, "is a petrified religion." Michael Angelo maintained, that, to an architect, a knowledge of anatomy is essential. In Haydn's oratorios, the notes present to the imagination not only motions, as, of the snake, the stag, and the elephant, but colors also; as the green grass. The law of harmonic sounds reappears in the harmonic colors. The granite is differenced in its laws only by the more or less of heat, from the river that wears it away. The river, as it flows, resem-

[3]Sixth century B.C. Greek philosopher.
[4]Greek god who could change his shape.
[5]Extinct reptile, lizard.
[6]French writer Madame de Stael (1766–1817), German philosopher-author Goethe (1749–1832), and Roman architect Vitruvius (1st cent. B.C.).

bles the air that flows over it; the air resembles the light which traverses it with more subtile currents; the light resembles the heat which rides with it through Space. Each creature is only a modification of the other; the likeness in them is more than the difference, and their radical law is one and the same. A rule of one art, or a law of one organization, holds true throughout nature. So intimate is this Unity, that, it is easily seen, it lies under the undermost garment of nature, and betrays its source in Universal Spirit. For, it pervades Thought also. Every universal truth which we express in words, implies or supposes every other truth. *Omne verum vero consonat.*[7] It is like a great circle on a sphere, comprising all possible circles; which, however, may be drawn, and comprise it, in like manner. Every such truth is the absolute Ens[8] seen from one side. But it has innumerable sides.

The central Unity is still more conspicuous in actions. Words are finite organs of the infinite mind. They cannot cover the dimensions of what is in truth. They break, chop, and impoverish it. An action is the perfection and publication of thought. A right action seems to fill the eye, and to be related to all nature. "The wise man, in doing one thing, does all; or, in the one thing he does rightly, he sees the likeness of all which is done rightly."

Words and actions are not the attributes of brute nature. They introduce us to the human form, of which all other organizations appear to be degradations. When this appears among so many that surround it, the spirit prefers it to all others. It says, 'From such as this, have I drawn joy and knowledge; in such as this have I found and beheld myself; I will speak to it; it can speak again; it can yield me thought already formed and alive.'[9] In fact, the eye,—the mind,—is always accompanied by these forms, male and female; and these are incomparably the richest informations of the power and order that lie at the heart of things. Unfortunately, every one of them bears the marks as of some injury; is marred and superficially defective. Nevertheless, far different from the deaf and dumb nature around them, these all rest like fountain-pipes on the unfathomed sea of thought and virtue whereto they alone, of all organizations, are the entrances.

It were a pleasant inquiry to follow into detail their ministry to our education, but where would it stop? We are associated in adolescent and adult life with some friends, who, like skies and waters, are coextensive with our idea; who, answering each to a certain affection of the soul, satisfy our desire on that side; whom we lack power to put at such focal distance from us, that we can mend or even analyze them. We cannot choose but love them. When much intercourse with a friend has supplied us with a standard of excellence, and has increased our respect for the resources of God who thus sends a real person to outgo our ideal; when he has, moreover, become an object of thought, and, whilst his character retains all its unconscious effect, is converted in the mind into solid and sweet wisdom,—it is a sign to us that his office is closing, and he is commonly withdrawn from our sight in a short time.

[7]Every truth is consonant with all other truth.

[8]Latin term for "abstract being."

[9]The single quotation marks indicate that this is an imagined or rhetorical quotation.

Chapter VI
Idealism

Thus is the unspeakable but intelligible and practicable meaning of the world conveyed to man, the immortal pupil, in every object of sense. To this one end of Discipline, all parts of nature conspire.

A noble doubt perpetually suggests itself, whether this end be not the Final Cause of the Universe; and whether nature outwardly exists. It is a sufficient account of that Appearance we call the World, that God will teach a human mind, and so makes it the receiver of a certain number of congruent sensations, which we call sun and moon, man and woman, house and trade. In my utter impotence to test the authenticity of the report of my senses, to know whether the impressions they make on me correspond with outlying objects, what difference does it make, whether Orion is up there in heaven, or some god paints the image in the firmament of the soul? The relations of parts and the end of the whole remaining the same, what is the difference, whether land and sea interact, and worlds revolve and intermingle without number or end,—deep yawning under deep, and galaxy balancing galaxy, throughout absolute space,—or, whether, without relations of time and space, the same appearances are inscribed in the constant faith of man? Whether nature enjoy a substantial existence without, or is only in the apocalypse of the mind, it is alike useful and alike venerable to me. Be it what it may, it is ideal to me, so long as I cannot try the accuracy of my senses.

The frivolous make themselves merry with the Ideal theory, as if its consequences were burlesque; as if it affected the stability of nature. It surely does not. God never jests with us, and will not compromise the end of nature, by permitting any inconsequence in its procession. Any distrust of the permanence of laws, would paralyze the faculties of man. Their permanence is sacredly respected, and his faith therein is perfect. The wheels and springs of man are all set to the hypothesis of the permanence of nature. We are not built like a ship to be tossed, but like a house to stand. It is a natural consequence of this structure, that, so long as the active powers predominate over the reflective, we resist with indignation any hint that nature is more short-lived or mutable than spirit. The broker, the wheelwright, the carpenter, the toll-man, are much displeased at the intimation.

But whilst we acquiesce entirely in the permanence of natural laws, the question of the absolute existence of nature still remains open. It is the uniform effect of culture on the human mind, not to shake our faith in the stability of particular phenomena, as of heat, water, azote;[1] but to lead us to regard nature as a phenomenon, not a substance; to attribute necessary existence to spirit; to esteem nature as an accident and an effect.

To the senses and the unrenewed understanding, belongs a sort of instinctive belief in the absolute existence of nature. In their view, man and nature are indissolubly joined. Things are ultimates, and they never look beyond their sphere. The presence of Reason mars this faith. The first effort of thought tends to relax this despotism of

[1]Nitrogen.

the senses, which binds us to nature as if we were a part of it, and shows us nature aloof, and, as it were, afloat. Until this higher agency intervened, the animal eye sees, with wonderful accuracy, sharp outlines and colored surfaces. When the eye of Reason opens, to outline and surface are at once added, grace and expression. These proceed from imagination and affection, and abate somewhat of the angular distinctness of objects. If the Reason be stimulated to more earnest vision, outlines and surfaces become transparent, and are no longer seen; causes and spirits are seen through them. The best moments of life are these delicious awakenings of the higher powers, and the reverential withdrawing of nature before its God.

Let us proceed to indicate the effects of culture. 1. Our first institution in the Ideal philosophy is a hint from nature herself.

Nature is made to conspire with spirit to emancipate us. Certain mechanical changes, a small alteration in our local position apprizes us of a dualism. We are strangely affected by seeing the shore from a moving ship, from a balloon, or through the tints of an unusual sky. The least change in our point of view, gives the whole world a pictorial air. A man who seldom rides, needs only to get into a coach and traverse his own town, to turn the street into a puppet-show. The men, the women,—talking, running, bartering, fighting,—the earnest mechanic, the lounger, the beggar, the boys, the dogs, are unrealized at once, or, at least, wholly detached from all relation to the observer, and seen as apparent, not substantial beings. What new thoughts are suggested by seeing a face of country quite familiar, in the rapid movement of the rail-road car! Nay, the most wonted objects, (make a very slight change in the point of vision,) please us most. In a camera obscura,[2] the butcher's cart, and the figure of one of our own family amuse us. So a portrait of a well-known face gratifies us. Turn the eyes upside down, by looking at the landscape through your legs, and how agreeable is the picture, though you have seen it any time these twenty years!

In these cases, by mechanical means, is suggested the difference between the observer and the spectacle,—between man and nature. Hence arises a pleasure mixed with awe; I may say, a low degree of the sublime is felt from the fact, probably, that man is hereby apprized, that, whilst the world is a spectacle, something in himself is stable.

2. In a higher manner, the poet communicates the same pleasure. By a few strokes he delineates, as on air, the sun, the mountain, the camp, the city, the hero, the maiden, not different from what we know them, but only lifted from the ground and afloat before the eye. He unfixes the land and the sea, makes them revolve around the axis of his primary thought, and disposes them anew. Possessed himself by a heroic passion, he uses matter as symbols of it. The sensual man conforms thoughts to things; the poet conforms things to his thoughts. The one esteems nature as rooted and fast; the other, as fluid, and impresses his being thereon. To him, the refractory world is ductile and flexible; he invests dust and stones with humanity, and makes them the words of the Reason. The Imagination may be defined to be, the use which the Reason makes of the material world. Shakspeare possesses the power of subordinating nature for the purposes of expression, beyond all poets. His imperial

[2]Nineteenth-century forerunner of the camera.

muse tosses the creation like a bauble from hand to hand, and uses it to embody any caprice of thought that is uppermost in his mind. The remotest spaces of nature are visited, and the farthest sundered things are brought together, by a subtle spiritual connection. We are made aware that magnitude of material things is relative, and all objects shrink and expand to serve the passion of the poet. Thus, in his sonnets, the lays of birds, the scents and dyes of flowers, he finds to be the *shadow* of his beloved; time, which keeps her from him, is his *chest;* the suspicion she has awakened, is her *ornament;*

> The ornament of beauty is Suspect,
> A crow which flies in heaven's sweetest air.

His passion is not the fruit of chance; it swells, as he speaks, to a city, or a state.

> No, it was builded far from accident;
> It suffers not in smiling pomp, nor falls
> Under the brow of thralling discontent;
> It fears not policy, that heretic,
> That works on leases of short numbered hours,
> But all alone stands hugely politic.

In the strength of his constancy, the Pyramids seem to him recent and transitory. The freshness of youth and love dazzles him with its resemblance to morning.

> Take those lips away
> Which so sweetly were forsworn;
> And those eyes,—the break of day,
> Lights that do mislead the morn.[3]

The wild beauty of this hyperbole, I may say, in passing, it would not be easy to match in literature.

This transfiguration which all material objects undergo through the passion of the poet,—this power which he exerts to dwarf the great, to magnify the small,—might be illustrated by a thousand examples from his Plays. I have before me the Tempest, and will cite only these few lines.

> ARIEL. The strong based promontory
> Have I made shake, and by the spurs plucked up
> The pine and cedar.

Prospero calls for music to soothe the frantic Alonzo, and his companions;

> A solemn air, and the best comforter
> To an unsettled fancy, cure thy brains
> Now useless, boiled within thy skull.

[3]Shakespeare, Sonnets 70, 124, and *Measure for Measure,* IV, i, 1–4.

Again;

The charm dissolves apace,
And, as the morning steals upon the night,
Melting the darkness, so their rising senses
Begin to chase the ignorant fumes that mantle
Their clearer reason.
Their understanding
Begins to swell: and the approaching tide
Will shortly fill the reasonable shores
That now lie foul and muddy.[4]

The perception of real affinities between events, (that is to say, of *ideal* affinities, for those only are real,) enables the poet thus to make free with the most imposing forms and phenomena of the world, and to assert the predominance of the soul.

3. Whilst thus the poet animates nature with his own thoughts, he differs from the philosopher only herein, that the one proposes Beauty as his main end; the other Truth. But the philosopher, not less than the poet, postpones the apparent order and relations of things to the empire of thought. "The problem of philosophy," according to Plato, "is, for all that exists conditionally, to find a ground unconditioned and absolute." It proceeds on the faith that a law determines all phenomena, which being known, the phenomena can be predicted. That law, when in the mind, is an idea. Its beauty is infinite. The true philosopher and the true poet are one, and a beauty, which is truth, and a truth, which is beauty, is the aim of both. Is not the charm of one of Plato's or Aristotle's definitions, strictly like that of the Antigone of Sophocles? It is, in both cases, that a spiritual life has been imparted to nature; that the solid seeming block of matter has been pervaded and dissolved by a thought; that this feeble human being has penetrated the vast masses of nature with an informing soul, and recognized itself in their harmony, that is, seized their law. In physics, when this is attained, the memory disburthens itself of its cumbrous catalogues of particulars, and carries centuries of observation in a single formula.

Thus even in physics, the material is degraded before the spiritual. The astronomer, the geometer, rely on their irrefragable analysis, and disdain the results of observation. The sublime remark of Euler[5] on his law of arches, "This will be found contrary to all experience, yet is true;" had already transferred nature into the mind, and left matter like an outcast corpse.

4. Intellectual science has been observed to beget invariably a doubt of the existence of matter. Turgot[6] said, "He that has never doubted the existence of matter, may be assured he has no aptitude for metaphysical inquiries." It fastens the attention upon immortal necessary uncreated natures, that is, upon Ideas; and in their presence, we feel that the outward circumstance is a dream and a shade. Whilst we wait in this Olympus of gods, we think of nature as an appendix to the soul. We ascend

[4]Shakespeare, *The Tempest,* V, i. The opening lines are spoken not by Ariel but by Prospero.

[5]Eighteenth-century Swiss mathematician.

[6]Eighteenth-century French economist and statesman.

into their region, and know that these are the thoughts of the Supreme Being. "These are they who were set up from everlasting, from the beginning, or ever the earth was. When he prepared the heavens, they were there; when he established the clouds above, when he strengthened the fountains of the deep. Then they were by him, as one brought up with him. Of them took he counsel."[7]

Their influence is proportionate. As objects of science, they are accessible to few men. Yet all men are capable of being raised by piety or by passion, into their region. And no man touches these divine natures, without becoming, in some degree, himself divine. Like a new soul, they renew the body. We become physically nimble and lightsome; we tread on air; life is no longer irksome, and we think it will never be so. No man fears age or misfortune or death, in their serene company, for he is transported out of the district of change. Whilst we behold unveiled the nature of Justice and Truth, we learn the difference between the absolute and the conditional or relative. We apprehend the absolute. As it were, for the first time, *we exist.* We become immortal, for we learn that time and space are relations of matter; that, with a perception of truth, or a virtuous will, they have no affinity.

5. Finally, religion and ethics, which may be fitly called,—the practice of ideas, or the introduction of ideas into life,—have an analogous effect with all lower culture, in degrading nature and suggesting its dependence on spirit. Ethics and religion differ herein; that the one is the system of human duties commencing from man; the other, from God. Religion includes the personality of God; Ethics does not. They are one to our present design. They both put nature under foot. The first and last lesson of religion is, "The things that are seen, are temporal; the things that are unseen, are eternal."[8] It puts an affront upon nature. It does that for the unschooled, which philosophy does for Berkeley and Viasa.[9] The uniform language that may be heard in the churches of the most ignorant sects, is,—'Contemn the unsubstantial shows of the world; they are vanities, dreams, shadows, unrealities; seek the realities of religion.' The devotee flouts nature. Some theosophists have arrived at a certain hostility and indignation towards matter, as the Manichean[10] and Plotinus.[11] They distrusted in themselves any looking back to these flesh-pots of Egypt. Plotinus was ashamed of his body. In short, they might all say of matter, what Michael Angelo said of external beauty, "it is the frail and weary weed, in which God dresses the soul, which he has called into time."

It appears that motion, poetry, physical and intellectual science, and religion, all tend to affect our convictions of the reality of the external world. But I own there is something ungrateful in expanding too curiously the particulars of the general proposition, that all culture tends to imbue us with idealism. I have no hostility to nature, but a child's love to it. I expand and live in the warm day like corn and melons. Let us speak her fair. I do not wish to fling stones at my beautiful mother, nor soil my gentle nest. I only wish to indicate the true position of nature in regard to man, wherein to establish man, all right education tends; as the ground which to at-

[7]Paraphrase of Proverbs 8:23–30.
[8]II Cor. 4:18.
[9]Eighteenth-century idealist philosopher and British bishop, and the legendary author of the Sanscrit scriptures, the Vedas.
[10]A follower of the Third-century Babylonian mystic, Manes, who believes the world is divided between good and evil.
[11]Third-century Roman philosopher.

tain is the object of human life, that is, of man's connection with nature. Culture inverts the vulgar views of nature, and brings the mind to call that apparent, which it uses to call real, and that real, which it uses to call visionary. Children, it is true, believe in the external world. The belief that it appears only, is an afterthought, but with culture, this faith will as surely arise on the mind as did the first.

The advantage of the ideal theory over the popular faith, is this, that it presents the world in precisely that view which is most desirable to the mind. It is, in fact, the view which Reason, both speculative and practical, that is, philosophy and virtue, take. For, seen in the light of thought, the world always is phenomenal; and virtue subordinates it to the mind. Idealism sees the world in God. It beholds the whole circle of persons and things, of actions and events, of country and religion, not as painfully accumulated, atom after atom, act after act, in an aged creeping Past, but as one vast picture, which God paints on the instant eternity, for the contemplation of the soul. Therefore the soul holds itself off from a too trivial and microscopic study of the universal tablet. It respects the end too much, to immerse itself in the means. It sees something more important in Christianity, than the scandals of ecclesiastical history, or the niceties of criticism; and, very incurious concerning persons or miracles, and not at all disturbed by chasms of historical evidence, it accepts from God the phenomenon, as it finds it, as the pure and awful form of religion in the world. It is not hot and passionate at the appearance of what it calls its own good or bad fortune, at the union or opposition of other persons. No man is its enemy. It accepts whatsoever befalls, as part of its lesson. It is a watcher more than a doer, and it is a doer, only that it may the better watch.

Chapter VII
Spirit

It is essential to a true theory of nature and of man, that it should contain somewhat progressive. Uses that are exhausted or that may be, and facts that end in the statement, cannot be all that is true of this brave lodging wherein man is harbored, and wherein all his faculties find appropriate and endless exercise. And all the uses of nature admit of being summed in one, which yields the activity of man an infinite scope. Through all its kingdoms, to the suburbs and outskirts of things, it is faithful to the cause whence it had its origin. It always speaks of Spirit. It suggests the absolute. It is a perpetual effect. It is a great shadow pointing always to the sun behind us.

The aspect of nature is devout. Like the figure of Jesus, she stands with bended head, and hands folded upon the breast. The happiest man is he who learns from nature the lesson of worship.

Of that ineffable essence which we call Spirit, he that thinks most, will say least. We can foresee God in the coarse, and, as it were, distant phenomena of matter; but when we try to define and describe himself, both language and thought desert us, and we are as helpless as fools and savages. That essence refuses to be recorded in propositions, but when man has worshipped him intellectually, the noblest ministry of nature is to stand as the apparition of God. It is the organ through which the universal spirit speaks to the individual, and strives to lead back the individual to it.

When we consider Spirit, we see that the views already presented do not include the whole circumference of man. We must add some related thoughts.

Three problems are put by nature to the mind; What is matter? Whence is it? and Whereto? The first of these questions only, the ideal theory answers. Idealism saith: matter is a phenomenon, not a substance. Idealism acquaints us with the total disparity between the evidence of our own being, and the evidence of the world's being. The one is perfect; the other, incapable of any assurance; the mind is a part of the nature of things; the world is a divine dream, from which we may presently awake to the glories and certainties of day. Idealism is a hypothesis to account for nature by other principles than those of carpentry and chemistry. Yet, if it only deny the existence of matter, it does not satisfy the demands of the spirit. It leaves God out of me. It leaves me in the splendid labyrinth of my perceptions, to wander without end. Then the heart resists it, because it balks the affections in denying substantive being to men and women. Nature is so pervaded with human life, that there is something of humanity in all, and in every particular. But this theory makes nature foreign to me, and does not account for that consanguinity which we acknowledge to it.

Let it stand, then, in the present state of our knowledge, merely as a useful introductory hypothesis, serving to apprize us of the eternal distinction between the soul and the world.

But when, following the invisible steps of thought, we come to inquire, Whence is matter? and Whereto? many truths arise to us out of the recesses of consciousness. We learn that the highest is present to the soul of man, that the dread universal essence, which is not wisdom, or love, or beauty, or power, but all in one, and each entirely, is that for which all things exist, and that by which they are; that spirit creates; that behind nature, throughout nature, spirit is present; one and not compound, it does not act upon us from without, that is, in space and time, but spiritually, or through ourselves: therefore, that spirit, that is, the Supreme Being, does not build up nature around us, but puts it forth through us, as the life of the tree puts forth new branches and leaves through the pores of the old. As a plant upon the earth, so a man rests upon the bosom of God; he is nourished by unfailing fountains, and draws, at his need, inexhaustible power. Who can set bounds to the possibilities of man? Once inhale the upper air, being admitted to behold the absolute natures of justice and truth, and we learn that man has access to the entire mind of the Creator, is himself the creator in the finite. This view, which admonishes me where the sources of wisdom and power lie, and points to virtue as to

"The golden key
Which opes the palace of eternity,"[1]

carries upon its face the highest certificate of truth, because it animates me to create my own world through the purification of my soul.

The world proceeds from the same spirit as the body of man. It is a remoter and inferior incarnation of God, a projection of God in the unconscious. But it differs from the body in one important respect. It is not, like that, now subjected to the human will. Its serene order is inviolable by us. It is, therefore, to us, the present expositor of the divine mind. It is a fixed point whereby we may measure our

[1]Milton, *Comus,* 13–14.

departure. As we degenerate, the contrast between us and our house is more evident We are as much strangers in nature, as we are aliens from God. We do not understand the notes of birds. The fox and the deer run away from us; the bear and tiger rend us. We do not know the uses of more than a few plants, as corn and the apple, the potato and the vine. Is not the landscape, every glimpse of which hath a grandeur, a face of him? Yet this may show us what discord is between man and nature, for you cannot freely admire a noble landscape, if laborers are digging in the field hard by. The poet finds something ridiculous in his delight, until he is out of the sight of men.

Chapter VIII

Prospects

In inquiries respecting the laws of the world and the frame of things, the highest reason is always the truest. That which seems faintly possible—it is so refined, is often faint and dim because it is deepest seated in the mind among the eternal verities. Empirical science is apt to cloud the sight, and, by the very knowledge of functions and processes, to bereave the student of the manly contemplation of the whole. The savant becomes unpoetic. But the best read naturalist who lends an entire and devout attention to truth, will see that there remains much to learn of his relation to the world, and that it is not to be learned by any addition or subtraction or other comparison of known quantities, but is arrived at by untaught sallies of the spirit, by a continual self-recovery, and by entire humility. He will perceive that there are far more excellent qualities in the student than preciseness and infallibility; that a guess is often more fruitful than an indisputable affirmation, and that a dream may let us deeper into the secret of nature than a hundred concerted experiments.

For, the problems to be solved are precisely those which the physiologist and the naturalist omit to state. It is not so pertinent to man to know all the individuals of the animal kingdom, as it is to know whence and whereto is this tyrannizing unity in his constitution, which evermore separates and classifies things, endeavoring to reduce the most diverse to one form. When I behold a rich landscape, it is less to my purpose to recite correctly the order and superposition of the strata, than to know why all thought of multitude is lost in a tranquil sense of unity. I cannot greatly honor minuteness in details, so long as there is no hint to explain the relation between things and thoughts; no ray upon the *metaphysics* of conchology, of botany, of the arts, to show the relation of the forms of flowers, shells, animals, architecture, to the mind, and build science upon ideas. In a cabinet of natural history, we become sensible of a certain occult recognition and sympathy in regard to the most unwieldy and eccentric forms of beast, fish, and insect. The American who has been confined, in his own country, to the sight of buildings designed after foreign models, is surprised on entering York Minster or St. Peter's at Rome, by the feeling that these structures are imitations also,—faint copies of an invisible archetype. Nor has science sufficient humanity, so long as the naturalist overlooks that wonderful congruity which subsists between man and the world; of which he is lord, not because he is the most subtile inhabitant, but because he is its head and heart, and finds something of himself in every great and small thing, in every mountain stratum, in every new law of color, fact of astronomy, or atmospheric influence which observation or analysis lay open. A perception of this mystery inspires the muse of George Herbert, the beautiful psalmist of the seventeenth century. The following lines are part of his little poem on Man.

"Man is all symmetry,
Full of proportions, one limb to another,
And to all the world besides.
Each part may call the farthest, brother;
For head with foot hath private amity,
And both with moons and tides.

"Nothing hath got so far
But man hath caught and kept it as his prey;
His eyes dismount the highest star;
He is in little all the sphere.
Herbs gladly cure our flesh, because that they
Find their acquaintance there.

"For us, the winds do blow,
The earth doth rest, heaven move, and fountains flow;
Nothing we see, but means our good,
As our delight, or as our treasure;
The whole is either our cupboard of food,
Or cabinet of pleasure.

"The stars have us to bed:
Night draws the curtain; which the sun withdraws.
Music and light attend our head.
All things unto our flesh are kind,
In their descent and being; to our mind,
In their ascent and cause.

"More servants wait on man
Than he'll take notice of. In every path,
He treads down that which doth befriend him
When sickness makes him pale and wan.
Oh mighty love! Man is one world, and hath
Another to attend him."

The perception of this class of truths makes the attraction which draws men to science, but the end is lost sight of in attention to the means. In view of this half-sight of science, we accept the sentence of Plato, that, "poetry comes nearer to vital truth than history." Every surmise and vaticination of the mind is entitled to a certain respect, and we learn to prefer imperfect theories, and sentences, which contain glimpses of truth, to digested systems which have no one valuable suggestion. A wise writer will feel that the ends of study and composition are best answered by announcing undiscovered regions of thought, and so communicating, through hope, new activity to the torpid spirit.

I shall therefore conclude this essay with some traditions of man and nature, which a certain poet[1] sang to me; and which, as they have always been in the world, and perhaps reappear to every bard, may be both history and prophecy.

'The foundations of man are not in matter, but in spirit. But the element of spirit is eternity. To it, therefore, the longest series of events, the oldest chronologies are young and recent. In the cycle of the universal man, from whom the known individuals proceed, centuries are points, and all history is but the epoch of one degradation.

'We distrust and deny inwardly our sympathy with nature. We own and disown our relation to it, by turns. We are, like Nebuchadnezzar,[2] dethroned, bereft of reason, and eating grass like an ox. But who can set limits to the remedial force of spirit?

'A man is a god in ruins. When men are innocent, life shall be longer, and shall pass into the immortal, as gently as we awake from dreams. Now, the world would be insane and rabid, if these disorganizations should last for hundreds of years. It is kept in check by death and infancy. Infancy is the perpetual Messiah, which comes into the arms of fallen men, and pleads with them to return to paradise.

'Man is the dwarf of himself. Once he was permeated and dissolved by spirit. He filled nature with his overflowing currents. Out from him sprang the sun and moon; from man, the sun; from woman, the moon. The laws of his mind, the periods of his actions externized themselves into day and night, into the year and the seasons. But, having made for himself this huge shell, his waters retired; he no longer fills the veins and veinlets; he is shrunk to a drop. He sees, that the structure still fits him, but fits him colossally. Say, rather, once it fitted him, now it corresponds to him from far and on high. He adores timidly his own work. Now is man the follower of the sun, and woman the follower of the moon. Yet sometimes he starts in his slumber, and wonders at himself and his house, and muses strangely at the resemblance betwixt him and it. He perceives that if his law is still paramount, if still he have elemental power, if his word is sterling yet in nature, it is not conscious power, it is not inferior but superior to his will. It is Instinct.' Thus my Orphic poet sang.

At present, man applies to nature but half his force. He works on the world with his understanding alone. He lives in it, and masters it by a penny-wisdom; and he that works most in it, is but a half-man, and whilst his arms are strong and his digestion good, his mind is imbruted, and he is a selfish savage. His relation to nature, his power over it, is through the understanding; as by manure; the economic use of fire, wind, water, and the mariner's needle; steam, coal, chemical agriculture; the repairs of the human body by the dentist and the surgeon. This is such a resumption of power, as if a banished king should buy his territories inch by inch, instead of vaulting at once into his throne. Meantime, in the thick darkness, there are not wanting gleams of a better light,—occasional examples of the action of man upon nature with his entire force,—with reason as well as understanding. Such examples are; the traditions of miracles in the earliest antiquity of all nations; the history of Jesus Christ; the achievements of a principle, as in religious and political revolutions, and in the abolition of the Slave-trade; the miracles of enthusiasm, as those reported of

[1]Emerson here "quotes" an imaginary poet. Most of these "orphic" passages are drawn from his own journals.

[2]Cf. Daniel 4:25–33.

Swedenborg, Hohenlohe,[3] and the Shakers; many obscure and yet contested facts, now arranged under the name of Animal Magnetism;[4] prayer; eloquence; self-healing; and the wisdom of children. These are examples of Reason's momentary grasp of the sceptre; the exertions of a power which exists not in time or space, but an instantaneous in-streaming causing power. The difference between the actual and the ideal force of man is happily figured by the schoolmen, in saying, that the knowledge of man is an evening knowledge, *vespertina cognitio,* but that of God is a morning knowledge, *matutina cognitio.*

The problem of restoring to the world original and eternal beauty, is solved by the redemption of the soul. The ruin or the blank, that we see when we look at nature, is in our own eye. The axis of vision is not coincident with the axis of things, and so they appear not transparent but opake. The reason why the world lacks unity, and lies broken and in heaps, is, because man is disunited with himself. He cannot be a naturalist, until he satisfies all the demands of the spirit. Love is as much its demand, as perception. Indeed, neither can be perfect without the other. In the uttermost meaning of the words, thought is devout, and devotion is thought. Deep calls unto deep.[5] But in actual life, the marriage is not celebrated. There are innocent men who worship God after the tradition of their fathers, but their sense of duty has not yet extended to the use of all their faculties. And there are patient naturalists, but they freeze their subject under the wintry light of the understanding. Is not prayer also a study of truth,—a sally of the soul into the unfound infinite? No man ever prayed heartily, without learning something. But when a faithful thinker, resolute to detach every object from personal relations, and see it in the light of thought, shall, at the same time, kindle science with the fire of the holiest affections, then will God go forth anew into the creation.

It will not need, when the mind is prepared for study, to search for objects. The invariable mark of wisdom is to see the miraculous in the common. What is a day? What is a year? What is summer? What is woman? What is a child? What is sleep? To our blindness, these things seem unaffecting. We make fables to hide the baldness of the fact and conform it, as we say, to the higher law of the mind. But when the fact is seen under the light of an idea, the gaudy fable fades and shrivels. We behold the real higher law. To the wise, therefore, a fact is true poetry, and the most beautiful of fables. These wonders are brought to our own door. You also are a man. Man and woman, and their social life, poverty, labor, sleep, fear, fortune, are known to you. Learn that none of these things is superficial, but that each phenomenon has its roots in the faculties and affections of the mind. Whilst the abstract question occupies your intellect, nature brings it in the concrete to be solved by your hands. It were a wise inquiry for the closet, to compare, point by point, especially at remarkable crises in life, our daily history, with the rise and progress of ideas in the mind.

So shall we come to look at the world with new eyes. It shall answer the endless inquiry of the intellect,—What is truth? and of the affections,—What is good? by

[3]Nineteenth-century German bishop credited with miracle cures.

[4]Form of hypnotism or mesmerism, developed in 1775 by Friedrich Mesmer.

[5]Cf. Psalms 42:7.

yielding itself passive to the educated Will. Then shall come to pass what my poet said; 'Nature is not fixed but fluid. Spirit alters, moulds, makes it. The immobility or bruteness of nature, is the absence of spirit; to pure spirit, it is fluid, it is volatile, it is obedient. Every spirit builds itself a house; and beyond its house a world; and beyond its world, a heaven. Know then, that the world exists for you. For you is the phenomenon perfect. What we are, that only can we see. All that Adam had, all that Caesar could, you have and can do. Adam called his house, heaven and earth; Caesar called his house, Rome; you perhaps call yours, a cobler's trade; a hundred acres of ploughed land; or a scholar's garret. Yet line for line and point for point, your dominion is as great as theirs, though without fine names. Build, therefore, your own world. As fast as you conform your life to the pure idea in your mind, that will unfold its great proportions. A correspondent revolution in things will attend the influx of the spirit. So fast will disagreeable appearances, swine, spiders, snakes, pests, madhouses, prisons, enemies, vanish; they are temporary and shall be no more seen. The sordor and filths of nature, the sun shall dry up, and the wind exhale. As when the summer comes from the south; the snow-banks melt, and the face of the earth becomes green before it, so shall the advancing spirit create its ornaments along its path, and carry with it the beauty it visits, and the song which enchants it; it shall draw beautiful faces, warm hearts, wise discourse, and heroic acts, around its way, until evil is no more seen. The kingdom of man over nature, which cometh not with observation,—a dominion such as now is beyond his dream of God,—he shall enter without more wonder than the blind man feels who is gradually restored to perfect sight.'

1836, 1849

The American Scholar[1]

An Oration delivered before the Phi Beta Kappa Society, at Cambridge, August 31 1837

Mr. President and Gentlemen,

I greet you on the re-commencement of our literary year. Our anniversary is one of hope, and, perhaps, not enough of labor. We do not meet for games of strength or skill, for the recitation of histories, tragedies, and odes, like the ancient Greeks; for parliaments of love and poesy, like the Troubadours; nor for the advancement of science, like our cotemporaries in the British and European capitals. Thus far, our holiday has been simply a friendly sign of the survival of the love of letters amongst a people too busy to give to letters any more. As such, it is precious as the sign of an

[1]The original title for the address and 1837 pamphlet was "An Oration Delivered before the Phi Beta Kappa Society, at Cambridge, August 31, 1937." The 1849 title is the assigned topic of the annual Phi Beta Kappa lectures.

indestructible instinct. Perhaps the time is already come, when it ought to be, and will be, something else; when the sluggard intellect of this continent will look from under its iron lids, and fill the postponed expectation of the world with something better than the exertions of mechanical skill. Our day of dependence, our long apprenticeship to the learning of other lands, draws to a close. The millions, that around us are rushing into life, cannot always be fed on the sere remains of foreign harvests. Events, actions arise, that must be sung, that will sing themselves. Who can doubt, that poetry will revive and lead in a new age, as the star in the constellation Harp, which now flames in our zenith, astronomers announce, shall one day be the pole-star for a thousand years?

In this hope, I accept the topic which not only usage, but the nature of our association, seem to prescribe to this day,—the AMERICAN SCHOLAR. Year by year, we come up hither to read one more chapter of his biography. Let us inquire what light new days and events have thrown on his character, and his hopes.

It is one of those fables,[2] which, out of an unknown antiquity, convey an unlooked-for wisdom, that the gods, in the beginning, divided Man into men, that he might be more helpful to himself; just as the hand was divided into fingers, the better to answer its end.

The old fable covers a doctrine ever new and sublime; that there is One Man,—present to all particular men only partially, or through one faculty; and that you must take the whole society to find the whole man. Man is not a farmer, or a professor, or an engineer, but he is all. Man is priest, and scholar, and statesman, and producer, and soldier. In the *divided* or social state, these functions are parcelled out to individuals, each of whom aims to do his stint of the joint work, whilst each other performs his. The fable implies, that the individual, to possess himself, must sometimes return from his own labor to embrace all the other laborers. But unfortunately, this original unit, this fountain of power, has been so distributed to multitudes, has been so minutely subdivided and peddled out, that it is spilled into drops, and cannot be gathered. The state of society is one in which the members have suffered amputation from the trunk, and strut about so many walking monsters,—a good finger, a neck, a stomach, an elbow, but never a man.

Man is thus metamorphosed into a thing, into many things. The planter, who is Man sent out into the field to gather food, is seldom cheered by any idea of the true dignity of his ministry. He sees his bushel and his cart, and nothing beyond, and sinks into the farmer, instead of Man on the farm. The tradesman scarcely ever gives an ideal worth to his work, but is ridden by the routine of his craft, and the soul is subject to dollars. The priest becomes a form; the attorney, a statute-book; the mechanic, a machine; the sailor, a rope of a ship.

In this distribution of functions, the scholar is the delegated intellect. In the right state, he is, *Man Thinking*. In the degenerate state, when the victim of society, he tends to become a mere thinker, or, still worse, the parrot of other men's thinking.

In this view of him, as Man Thinking, the theory of his office is contained. Him nature solicits with all her placid, all her monitory pictures; him the past instructs; him the future invites. Is not, indeed, every man a student, and do not all things ex-

[2] A version of this fable appears in Plato and in Plutarch.

ist for the student's behoof? And, finally, is not the true scholar the only true master? But the old oracle[3] said, "All things have two handles: beware of the wrong one." In life, too often, the scholar errs with mankind and forfeits his privilege. Let us see him in his school, and consider him in reference to the main influences he receives.

I. The first in time and the first in importance of the influences upon the mind is that of nature. Every day, the sun; and, after sunset, night and her stars. Ever the winds blow; ever the grass grows. Every day, men and women, conversing, beholding and beholden. The scholar is he of all men whom this spectacle most engages. He must settle its value in his mind. What is nature to him? There is never a beginning, there is never an end, to the inexplicable continuity of this web of God, but always circular power returning into itself. Therein it resembles his own spirit, whose beginning, whose ending, he never can find,—so entire, so boundless. Far, too, as her splendors shine, system on system shooting like rays, upward, downward, without centre, without circumference,—in the mass and in the particle, nature hastens to render account of herself to the mind. Classification begins. To the young mind, every thing is individual, stands by itself. By and by, it finds how to join two things, and see in them one nature; then three, then three thousand; and so, tyrannized over by its own unifying instinct, it goes on tying things together, diminishing anomalies, discovering roots running under ground, whereby contrary and remote things cohere, and flower out from one stem. It presently learns, that, since the dawn of history, there has been a constant accumulation and classifying of facts. But what is classification but the perceiving that these objects are not chaotic, and are not foreign, but have a law which is also a law of the human mind? The astronomer discovers that geometry, a pure abstraction of the human mind, is the measure of planetary motion. The chemist finds proportions and intelligible method throughout matter; and science is nothing but the finding of analogy, identity, in the most remote parts. The ambitious soul sits down before each refractory fact; one after another, reduces all strange constitutions, all new powers, to their class and their law, and goes on for ever to animate the last fibre of organization, the outskirts of nature, by insight.

Thus to him, to this school-boy under the bending dome of day, is suggested, that he and it proceed from one root; one is leaf and one is flower; relation, sympathy, stirring in every vein. And what is that Root? Is not that the soul of his soul?—A thought too bold,—a dream too wild. Yet when this spiritual light shall have revealed the law of more earthly natures,—when he has learned to worship the soul, and to see that the natural philosophy that now is, is only the first gropings of its gigantic hand, he shall look forward to an ever expanding knowledge as to a becoming creator. He shall see, that nature is the opposite of the soul, answering to it part for part. One is seal, and one is print. Its beauty is the beauty of his own mind. Its laws are the laws of his own mind. Nature then becomes to him the measure of his attainments. So much of nature as he is ignorant of, so much of his own mind does he not yet possess. And, in fine, the ancient precept, "Know thyself," and the modern precept, "Study nature," become at last one maxim.

[3]The passage is from the Stoic philosopher Epictetus (1st–2nd century A.D.).

II. The next great influence into the spirit of the scholar, is, the mind of the Past,—in whatever form, whether of literature, of art, of institutions, that mind is inscribed. Books are the best type of the influence of the past, and perhaps we shall get at the truth,—learn the amount of this influence more conveniently,—by considering their value alone.

The theory of books is noble. The scholar of the first age received into him the world around; brooded thereon; gave it the new arrangement of his own mind, and uttered it again. It came into him, life; it went out from him, truth. It came to him, short-lived actions; it went out from him, immortal thoughts. It came to him, business; it went from him, poetry. It was dead fact; now, it is quick thought. It can stand, and it can go. It now endures, it now flies, it now inspires. Precisely in proportion to the depth of mind from which it issued, so high does it soar, so long does it sing.

Or, I might say, it depends on how far the process had gone, of transmuting life into truth. In proportion to the completeness of the distillation, so will the purity and imperishableness of the product be. But none is quite perfect. As no air-pump can by any means make a perfect vacuum, so neither can any artist entirely exclude the conventional, the local, the perishable from his book, or write a book of pure thought, that shall be as efficient, in all respects, to a remote posterity, as to cotemporaries, or rather to the second age. Each age, it is found, must write its own books; or rather, each generation for the next succeeding. The books of an older period will not fit this.

Yet hence arises a grave mischief. The sacredness which attaches to the act of creation,—the act of thought,—is transferred to the record. The poet chanting, was felt to be a divine man: henceforth the chant is divine also. The writer was a just and wise spirit: henceforward it is settled, the book is perfect; as love of the hero corrupts into worship of his statue. Instantly, the book becomes noxious: the guide is a tyrant. The sluggish and perverted mind of the multitude, slow to open to the incursions of Reason, having once so opened, having once received this book, stands upon it, and makes an outcry, if it is disparaged. Colleges are built on it. Books are written on it by thinkers, not by Man Thinking; by men of talent, that is, who start wrong, who set out from accepted dogmas, not from their own sight of principles. Meek young men grow up in libraries, believing it their duty to accept the views, which Cicero, which Locke, which Bacon, have given, forgetful that Cicero, Locke, and Bacon[4] were only young men in libraries, when they wrote these books.

Hence, instead of Man Thinking, we have the bookworm. Hence, the book-learned class, who value books, as such; not as related to nature and the human constitution, but as making a sort of Third Estate[5] with the world and the soul. Hence, the restorers of readings, the emendators, the bibliomaniacs of all degrees.

Books are the best of things, well used; abused, among the worst. What is the right use? What is the one end, which all means go to effect? They are for nothing but to inspire. I had better never see a book, than to be warped by its attraction clean

[4]Emerson lists "young men" who, as adults, altered Western intellectual practice: the Roman orator Cicero (106–43 B.C.), 17th-century British philosopher John Locke, and 17th-century essayist Francis Bacon.

[5]Term used in pre-revolutionary France and in England to define the political class of commoners.

out of my own orbit, and made a satellite instead of a system. The one thing in the world, of value, is the active soul. This every man is entitled to; this every man contains within him, although, in almost all men, obstructed, and as yet unborn. The soul active sees absolute truth; and utters truth, or creates. In this action, it is genius; not the privilege of here and there a favorite, but the sound estate of every man. In its essence, it is progressive. The book, the college, the school of art, the institution of any kind, stop with some past utterance of genius. This is good, say they,—let us hold by this. They pin me down. They look backward and not forward. But genius looks forward: the eyes of man are set in his forehead, not in his hindhead: man hopes: genius creates. Whatever talents may be, if the man create not, the pure efflux of the Diety is not his;—cinders and smoke there may be, but not yet flame. There are creative manners, there are creative actions, and creative words; manners, actions, words, that is, indicative of no custom or authority, but springing spontaneous from the mind's own sense of good and fair.

On the other part, instead of being its own seer, let it receive from another mind its truth, though it were in torrents of light, without periods of solitude, inquest, and self-recovery, and a fatal disservice is done. Genius is always sufficiently the enemy of genius by over influence. The literature of every nation bear me witness. The English dramatic poets have Shakspearized now for two hundred years.

Undoubtedly there is a right way of reading, so it be sternly subordinated. Man Thinking must not be subdued by his instruments. Books are for the scholar's idle times. When he can read God directly, the hour is too precious to be wasted in other men's transcripts of their readings. But when the intervals of darkness come, as come they must,—when the sun is hid, and the stars withdraw their shining,—we repair to the lamps which were kindled by their ray, to guide our steps to the East again, where the dawn is. We hear, that we may speak. The Arabian proverb says, "A fig tree, looking on a fig tree, becometh fruitful."

It is remarkable, the character of the pleasure we derive from the best books. They impress us with the conviction, that one nature wrote and the same reads. We read the verses of one of the great English poets, of Chaucer, of Marvell, of Dryden, with the most modern joy,—with a pleasure, I mean, which is in great part caused by the abstraction of all *time* from their verses. There is some awe mixed with the joy of our surprise, when this poet, who lived in some past world, two or three hundred years ago, says that which lies close to my own soul, that which I also had wellnigh thought and said. But for the evidence thence afforded to the philosophical doctrine of the identity of all minds, we should suppose some preëstablished harmony, some foresight of souls that were to be, and some preparation of stores for their future wants, like the fact observed in insects, who lay up food before death for the young grub they shall never see.

I would not be hurried by any love of system, by any exaggeration of instincts, to underrate the Book. We all know, that, as the human body can be nourished on any food, though it were boiled grass and the broth of shoes, so the human mind can be fed by any knowledge. And great and heroic men have existed, who had almost no other information than by the printed page. I only would say, that it needs a strong head to bear that diet. One must be an inventor to read well. As the proverb says, "He that would bring home the wealth of the Indies, must carry out the wealth of the Indies." There is then creative reading as well as creative writing. When the mind is braced by labor and invention, the page of whatever book we read becomes luminous with manifold allusion. Every sentence is doubly significant, and the sense of our author is as broad as the world. We then see, what is always true, that, as the seer's hour of vision is short and rare among heavy days and months, so is its record, perchance, the least part of his volume. The discerning will read, in his Plato or Shakspeare, only that least part,—only the authentic utterances of the oracle;—all the rest he rejects, were it never so many times Plato's and Shakspeare's.

Of course, there is a portion of reading quite indispensable to a wise man. History and exact science he must learn by laborious reading. Colleges, in like manner, have their indispensable office,—to teach elements. But they can only highly serve us, when they aim not to drill, but to create; when they gather from far every ray of various genius to their hospitable halls, and, by the concentrated fires, set the hearts of their youth on flame. Thought and knowledge are natures in which apparatus and pretension avail nothing. Gowns, and pecuniary foundations, though of towns of gold, can never countervail the least sentence or syllable of wit. Forget this, and our American colleges will recede in their public importance, whilst they grow richer every year.

III. There goes in the world a notion, that the scholar should be a recluse, a valetudinarian,—as unfit for any handiwork or public labor, as a penknife for an axe. The so-called 'practical men' sneer at speculative men, as if, because they speculate or *see,* they could do nothing. I have heard it said that the clergy,—who are always, more universally than any other class, the scholars of their day,—are addressed as women; that the rough, spontaneous conversation of men they do not hear, but only a mincing and diluted speech. They are often virtually disfranchised; and, indeed, there are advocates for their celibacy. As far as this is true of the studious classes, it is not just and wise. Action is with the scholar subordinate, but it is essential. Without it, he is not yet man. Without it, thought can never ripen into truth. Whilst the world hangs before the eye as a cloud of beauty, we cannot even see its beauty. Inaction is cowardice, but there can be no scholar without the heroic mind. The preamble of thought, the transition through which it passes from the unconscious to the conscious, is action. Only so much do I know, as I have lived. Instantly we know whose words are loaded with life, and whose not.

The world,—this shadow of the soul, or *other me,* lies wide around. Its attractions are the keys which unlock my thoughts and make me acquainted with myself. I run eagerly into this resounding tumult. I grasp the hands of those next me, and take my place in the ring to suffer and to work, taught by an instinct, that so shall the dumb abyss be vocal with speech. I pierce its order; I dissipate its fear; I dispose of it within the circuit of my expanding life. So much only of life as I know by experience, so much of the wilderness have I vanquished and planted, or so far have I extended my being, my dominion. I do not see how any man can afford, for the sake of his nerves and his nap, to spare any action in which he can partake. It is pearls and rubies to his discourse. Drudgery, calamity, exasperation, want, are instructors in eloquence and wisdom. The true scholar grudges every opportunity of action past by, as a loss of power.

It is the raw material out of which the intellect moulds her splendid products. A strange process too, this, by which experience is converted into thought, as a mulberry leaf is converted into satin. The manufacture goes forward at all hours.

The actions and events of our childhood and youth, are now matters of calmest observation. They lie like fair pictures in the air. Not so with our recent actions,—with the business which we now have in hand. On this we are quite unable to speculate. Our affections as yet circulate through it. We no more feel or know it, than we feel the feet, or the hand, or the brain of our body. The new deed is yet a part of life,—remains for a time immersed in our unconscious life. In some contemplative hour, it detaches itself from the life like a ripe fruit, to become a thought of the mind. Instantly, it is raised, transfigured; the corruptible has put on incorruption. Henceforth it is an object of beauty, however base its origin and neighborhood. Observe, too, the impossibility of antedating this act. In its grub state, it cannot fly, it cannot shine, it is a dull grub. But suddenly, without observation, the selfsame thing unfurls beautiful wings, and is an angel of wisdom. So is there no fact, no event, in our private history, which shall not, sooner or later, lose its adhesive, inert form, and astonish us by soaring from our body into the empyrean. Cradle and infancy, school and playground, the fear of boys, and dogs, and ferules, the love of little maids and berries, and many another fact that once filled the whole sky, are gone already; friend and relative, profession and party, town and country, nation and world, must also soar and sing.

Of course, he who has put forth his total strength in fit actions, has the richest return of wisdom. I will not shut myself out of this globe of action, and transplant an oak into a flower-pot, there to hunger and pine; nor trust the revenue of some single faculty, and exhaust one vein of thought, much like those Savoyards,[6] who, getting their livelihood by carving shepherds, shepherdesses, and smoking Dutchmen, for all Europe, went out one day to the mountain to find stock, and discovered that they had whittled up the last of their pine-trees. Authors we have, in numbers, who have written out their vein, and who, moved by a commendable prudence, sail for Greece or Palestine, follow the trapper into the prairie, or ramble round Algiers, to replenish their merchantable stock.

If it were only for a vocabulary, the scholar would be covetous of action. Life is our dictionary. Years are well spent in country labors; in town,—in the insight into trades and manufactures; in frank intercourse with many men and women; in science; in art; to the one end of mastering in all their facts a language by which to illustrate and embody our perceptions. I learn immediately from any speaker how much he has already lived, through the poverty or the splendor of his speech. Life lies behind us as the quarry from whence we get tiles and copestones for the masonry of to-day. This is the way to learn grammar. Colleges and books only copy the language which the field and the work-yard made.

But the final value of action, like that of books, and better than books, is, that it is a resource. That great principle of Undulation in nature, that shows itself in the inspiring and expiring of the breath; in desire and satiety; in the ebb and flow of the sea; in day and night; in heat and cold; and as yet more deeply ingrained in every atom and every fluid, is known to us under the name of Polarity,—these "fits of easy transmission and reflection," as Newton called them, are the law of nature because they are the law of spirit.

[6]Natives of Savoy, region in the French Alps.

The mind now thinks; now acts; and each fit reproduces the other. When the artist has exhausted his materials, when the fancy no longer paints, when thoughts are no longer apprehended, and books are a weariness,—he has always the resource *to live.* Character is higher than intellect. Thinking is the function. Living is the functionary. The stream retreats to its source. A great soul will be strong to live, as well as strong to think. Does he lack organ or medium to impart his truths? He can still fall back on this elemental force of living them. This is a total act. Thinking is a partial act. Let the grandeur of justice shine in his affairs. Let the beauty of affection cheer his lowly roof. Those 'far from fame,' who dwell and act with him, will feel the force of his constitution in the doings and passages of the day better than it can be measured by any public and designed display. Time shall teach him, that the scholar loses no hour which the man lives. Herein he unfolds the sacred germ of his instinct, screened from influence. What is lost in seemliness is gained in strength. Not out of those, on whom systems of education have exhausted their culture, comes the helpful giant to destroy the old or to build the new, but out of unhandselled[7] savage nature, out of terrible Druids and Berserkirs, come at last Alfred and Shakspeare.[8]

I hear therefore with joy whatever is beginning to be said of the dignity and necessity of labor to every citizen. There is virtue yet in the hoe and the spade, for learned as well as for unlearned hands. And labor is everywhere welcome; always we are invited to work; only be this limitation observed, that a man shall not for the sake of wider activity sacrifice any opinion to the popular judgments and modes of action.

I have now spoken of the education of the scholar by nature, by books, and by action. It remains to say somewhat of his duties.

They are such as become Man Thinking. They may all be comprised in self-trust. The office of the scholar is to cheer, to raise, and to guide men by showing them facts amidst appearances. He plies the slow, unhonored, and unpaid task of observation. Flamsteed and Herschel,[9] in their glazed observatories, may catalogue the stars with the praise of all men, and, the results being splendid and useful, honor is sure. But he, in his private observatory, cataloguing obscure and nebulous stars of the human mind, which as yet no man has thought of as such,—watching days and months, sometimes, for a few facts; correcting still his old records;—must relinquish display and immediate fame. In the long period of his preparation, he must betray often an ignorance and shiftlessness in popular arts, incurring the disdain of the able who shoulder him aside. Long he must stammer in his speech; often forego the living for the dead. Worse yet, he must accept,—how often! poverty and solitude. For the ease and pleasure of treading the old road, accepting the fashions, the education, the religion of society, he takes the cross of making his own, and, of course, the self-accusation, the faint heart, the frequent uncertainty and loss of time, which are the nettles and tangling vines in the way of the self-relying and self-directed; and the state of virtual hostility in which he seems to stand to society, and especially to educated

[7]Untamed, untouched by hand, inauspicious.

[8]Ancient Celtic priests and Norse warriors contrast with examples of British civilization, Shakespeare and Alfred, the 9th-century king who founded schools and instituted laws.

[9]Seventeenth and eighteenth-century English astronomers.

society. For all this loss and scorn, what offset? He is to find consolation in exercising the highest functions of human nature. He is one, who raises himself from private considerations, and breathes and lives on public and illustrious thoughts. He is the world's eye. He is the world's heart. He is to resist the vulgar prosperity that retrogrades ever to barbarism, by preserving and communicating heroic sentiments, noble biographies, melodious verse, and the conclusions of history. Whatsoever oracles the human heart, in all emergencies, in all solemn hours, has uttered as its commentary on the world of actions,—these he shall receive and impart. And whatsoever new verdict Reason from her inviolable seat pronounces on the passing men and events of to-day,—this he shall hear and promulgate.

These being his functions, it becomes him to feel all confidence in himself, and to defer never to the popular cry. He and he only knows the world. The world of any moment is the merest appearance Some great decorum, some fetish of a government, some ephemeral trade, or war, or man, is cried up by half mankind and cried down by the other half, as if all depended on this particular up or down. The odds are that the whole question is not worth the poorest thought which the scholar has lost in listening to the controversy. Let him not quit his belief that a popgun is a popgun, though the ancient and honorable of the earth affirm it to be the crack of doom. In silence, in steadiness, in severe abstraction, let him hold by himself; add observation to observation, patient of neglect, patient of reproach; and bide his own time,—happy enough, if he can satisfy himself alone, that this day he has seen something truly. Success treads on every right step. For the instinct is sure, that prompts him to tell his brother what he thinks. He then learns, that in going down into the secrets of his own mind, he has descended into the secrets of all minds. He learns that he who has mastered any law in his private thoughts, is master to that extent of all men whose language he speaks, and of all into whose language his own can be translated. The poet, in utter solitude remembering his spontaneous thoughts and recording them, is found to have recorded that, which men in crowded cities find true for them also. The orator distrusts at first the fitness of his frank confessions,—his want of knowledge of the persons he addresses,—until he finds that he is the complement of his hearers;—that they drink his words because he fulfills for them their own nature; the deeper he dives into his privatest, secretest presentiment, to his wonder he finds, this is the most acceptable, most public, and universally true. The people delight in it; the better part of every man feels, This is my music; this is myself.

In self-trust, all the virtues are comprehended. Free should the scholar be,—free and brave. Free even to the definition of freedom, "without any hindrance that does not arise out of his own constitution." Brave; for fear is a thing, which a scholar by his very function puts behind him. Fear always springs from ignorance. It is a shame to him if his tranquility, amid dangerous times, arise from the presumption, that, like children and women, his is a protected class; or if he seek a temporary peace by the diversion of his thoughts from politics or vexed questions, hiding his head like an ostrich in the flowering bushes, peeping into microscopes, and turning rhymes, as a boy whistles to keep his courage up. So is the danger a danger still; so is the fear worse. Manlike let him turn and face it. Let him look into its eye and search its nature, inspect its origin,—see the whelping of this lion,—which lies no great way back; he will then find in himself a perfect comprehension of its nature and extent; he will have made his hands meet on the other side, and can henceforth defy it, and pass on superior. The world is his, who can see through its pretension. What deafness, what stone-blind custom, what overgrown error you behold, is there only by sufferance,—by your sufferance. See it to be a lie, and you have already dealt it its mortal blow.

Yes, we are the cowed,—we the trustless. It is a mischievous notion that we are come late into nature; that the world was finished a long time ago. As the world was plastic and fluid in the hands of God, so it is ever to so much of his attributes as we bring to it. To ignorance and sin, it is flint. They adapt themselves to it as they may; but in proportion as a man has any thing in him divine, the firmament flows before him and takes his signet and form. Not he is great who can alter matter, but he who can alter my state of mind. They are the kings of the world who give the color of their present thought to all nature and all art, and persuade men by the cheerful serenity of their carrying the matter, that this thing which they do, is the apple which the ages have desired to pluck, now at last ripe, and inviting nations to the harvest. The great man makes the great thing. Wherever Macdonald sits, there is the head of the table. Linnæus makes botany the most alluring of studies, and wins it from the farmer and the herb-woman; Davy, chemistry; and Cuvier, fossils.[10] The day is always his, who works in it with serenity and great aims. The unstable estimates of men crowd to him whose mind is filled with a truth, as the heaped waves of the Atlantic follow the moon.

For this self-trust, the reason is deeper than can be fathomed,—darker than can be enlightened. I might not carry with me the feeling of my audience in stating my own belief. But I have already shown the ground of my hope, in adverting to the doctrine that man is one. I believe man has been wronged; he has wronged himself. He has almost lost the light, that can lead him back to his prerogatives. Men are become of no account. Men in history, men in the world of to-day are bugs, are spawn, and are called 'the mass' and 'the herd.' In a century, in a millennium, one or two men; that is to say,—one or two approximations to the right state of every man. All the rest behold in the hero or the poet their own green and crude being,—ripened; yes, and are content to be less, so *that* may attain to its full stature. What a testimony,—full of grandeur, full of pity, is borne to the demands of his own nature, by the poor clansman, the poor partisan, who rejoices in the glory of his chief. The poor and the low find some amends to their immense moral capacity, for their acquiescence in a political and social inferiority. They are content to be brushed like flies from the path of a great person, so that justice shall be done by him to that common nature which it is the dearest desire of all to see enlarged and glorified. They sun themselves in the great man's light, and feel it to be their own element. They cast the dignity of man from their downtrod selves upon the shoulders of a hero, and will perish to add one drop of blood to make that great heart beat, those giant sinews combat and conquer. He lives for us, and we live in him.

Men such as they are, very naturally seek money or power; and power because it is as good as money,—the "spoils," so called, "of office." And why not? for they aspire to the highest, and this, in their sleep-walking, they dream is highest. Wake them, and they shall quit the false good, and leap to the true, and leave governments

[10]Emerson extends the contemporary saying about a Scottish clan leader's authority to three influential scientists.

to clerks and desks. This revolution is to be wrought by the gradual domestication of the idea of Culture. The main enterprise of the world for splendor, for extent, is the upbuilding of a man. Here are the materials strown along the ground. The private life of one man shall be a more illustrious monarchy,—more formidable to its enemy, more sweet and serene in its influence to its friend, than any kingdom in history. For a man, rightly viewed, comprehendeth the particular natures of all men. Each philosopher, each bard, each actor, has only done for me, as by a delegate, what one day I can do for myself. The books which once we valued more than the apple of the eye, we have quite exhausted. What is that but saying, that we have come up with the point of view which the universal mind took through the eyes of one scribe; we have been that man, and have passed on. First, one; then, another; we drain all cisterns, and, waxing greater by all these supplies, we crave a better and more abundant food. The man has never lived that can feed us ever. The human mind cannot be enshrined in a person, who shall set a barrier on any one side to this unbounded, unboundable empire. It is one central fire, which, flaming now out of the lips of Etna, lightens the capes of Sicily; and, now out of the throat of Vesuvius, illuminates the towers and vineyards of Naples. It is one light which beams out of a thousand stars. It is one soul which animates all men.

But I have dwelt perhaps tediously upon this abstraction of the Scholar. I ought not to delay longer to add what I have to say, of nearer reference to the time and to this country.

Historically, there is thought to be a difference in the ideas which predominate over successive epochs, and there are data for marking the genius of the Classic, of the Romantic, and now of the Reflective or Philosophical age. With the views I have intimated of the oneness or the identity of the mind through all individuals, I do not much dwell on these differences. In fact, I believe each individual passes through all three. The boy is a Greek; the youth, romantic; the adult, reflective. I deny not, however, that a revolution in the leading idea may be distinctly enough traced.

Our age is bewailed as the age of Introversion. Must that needs be evil? We, it seems, are critical; we are embarrassed with second thoughts; we cannot enjoy any thing for hankering to know whereof the pleasure consists; we are lined with eyes; we see with our feet; the time is infected with Hamlet's unhappiness,—

> "Sicklied o'er with the pale cast of thought."[11]

Is it so bad then? Sight is the last thing to be pitied. Would we be blind? Do we fear lest we should outsee nature and God, and drink truth dry? I look upon the discontent of the literary class, as a mere announcement of the fact, that they find themselves not in the state of mind of their fathers, and regret the coming state as untried; as a boy dreads the water before he has learned that he can swim. If there is any period one would desire to be born in,—is it not the age of Revolution; when the old and the new stand side by side, and admit of being compared; when the energies of all men are searched by fear and by hope; when the historic glories of the old, can be compensated by the rich possibilities of the new era? This time, like all times, is a very good one, if we but know what to do with it.

[11]*Hamlet,* III, i. 85.

I read with joy some of the auspicious signs of the coming days, as they glimmer already through poetry and art, through philosophy and science, through church and state.

One of these signs is the fact, that the same movement which effected the elevation of what was called the lowest class in the state, assumed in literature a very marked and as benign an aspect. Instead of the sublime and beautiful; the near, the low, the common, was explored and poetized. That, which had been negligently trodden under foot by those who were harnessing and provisioning themselves for long journeys into far countries, is suddenly found to be richer than all foreign parts. The literature of the poor, the feelings of the child, the philosophy of the street, the meaning of household life, are the topics of the time. It is a great stride. It is a sign,—is it not? of new vigor, when the extremities are made active, when currents of warm life run into the hands and the feet. I ask not for the great, the remote, the romantic; what is doing in Italy or Arabia; what is Greek art, or Provençal minstrelsy; I embrace the common, I explore and sit at the feet of the familiar, the low. Give me insight into to-day, and you may have the antique and future worlds. What would we really know the meaning of? The meal in the firkin;[12] the milk in the pan; the ballad in the street; the news of the boat; the glance of the eye; the form and the gait of the body;—show me the ultimate reason of these matters; show me the sublime presence of the highest spiritual cause lurking, as always it does lurk, in these suburbs and extremities of nature; let me see every trifle bristling with the polarity that ranges it instantly on an eternal law; and the shop, the plough, and the leger, referred to the like cause by which light undulates and poets sing;—and the world lies no longer a dull miscellany and lumber-room, but has form and order; there is no trifle; there is no puzzle; but one design unites and animates the farthest pinnacle and the lowest trench.

This idea has inspired the genius of Goldsmith, Burns, Cowper, and, in a newer time, of Goethe, Wordsworth, and Carlyle. This idea they have differently followed and with various success. In contrast with their writing, the style of Pope, of Johnson, of Gibbon, looks cold and pedantic. This writing is blood-warm. Man is surprised to find that things near are not less beautiful and wondrous than things remote. The near explains the far. The drop is a small ocean. A man is related to all nature. This perception of the worth of the vulgar is fruitful in discoveries. Goethe, in this very thing the most modern of the moderns, has shown us, as none ever did, the genius of the ancients.

There is one man of genius, who has done much for this philosophy of life, whose literary value has never yet been rightly estimated;—I mean Emanuel Swedenborg. The most imaginative of men, yet writing with the precision of a mathematician, he endeavored to engraft a purely philosophical Ethics on the popular Christianity of his time. Such an attempt, of course, must have difficulty, which no genius could surmount. But he saw and showed the connection between nature and the affections of the soul. He pierced the emblematic or spiritual character of the visible, audible, tangible world. Especially did his shade-loving muse hover over and interpret the lower parts of nature; he showed the mysterious bond that allies moral

[12]Small wooden bowl.

evil to the foul material forms, and has given in epical parables a theory of insanity, of beasts, of unclean and fearful things.

Another sign of our times, also marked by an analogous political movement, is, the new importance given to the single person. Every thing that tends to insulate the individual,—to surround him with barriers of natural respect, so that each man shall feel the world is his, and man shall treat with man as a sovereign state with a sovereign state;—tends to true union as well as greatness. "I learned," said the melancholy Pestalozzi,[13] "that no man in God's wide earth is either willing or able to help any other man." Help must come from the bosom alone. The scholar is that man who must take up into himself all the ability of the time, all the contributions of the past, all the hopes of the future. He must be an university of knowledges. If there be one lesson more than another, which should pierce his ear, it is, The world is nothing, the man is all; in yourself is the law of all nature, and you know not yet how a globule of sap ascends; in yourself slumbers the whole of Reason; it is for you to know all, it is for you to dare all. Mr. President and Gentlemen, this confidence in the unsearched might of man belongs, by all motives, by all prophecy, by all preparation, to the American Scholar. We have listened too long to the courtly muses of Europe. The spirit of the American freeman is already suspected to be timid, imitative, tame. Public and private avarice make the air we breathe thick and fat. The scholar is decent, indolent, complaisant. See already the tragic consequence. The mind of this country, taught to aim at low objects, eats upon itself. There is no work for any but the decorous and the complaisant. Young men of the fairest promise, who begin life upon our shores, inflated by the mountain winds, shined upon by all the stars of God, find the earth below not in unison with these,—but are hindered from action by the disgust which the principles on which business is managed inspire, and turn drudges, or die of disgust,—some of them suicides. What is the remedy? They did not yet see, and thousands of young men as hopeful now crowding to the barriers for the career, do not yet see, that, if the single man plant himself indomitably on his instincts, and there abide, the huge world will come round to him. Patience,—patience;—with the shades of all the good and great for company; and for solace, the perspective of your own infinite life; and for work, the study and the communication of principles, the making those instincts prevalent, the conversion of the world. Is it not the chief disgrace in the world, not to be an unit;—not to be reckoned one character;—not to yield that peculiar fruit which each man was created to bear, but to be reckoned in the gross, in the hundred, or the thousand, of the party, the section, to which we belong; and our opinion predicted geographically, as the north, or the south? Not so, brothers and friends,—please God, ours shall not be so. We will walk on our own feet; we will work with our own hands; we will speak our own minds. The study of letters shall be no longer a name for pity, for doubt, and for sensual indulgence. The dread of man and the love of man shall be a wall of defence and a wreath of joy around all. A nation of men will for the first time exist, because each believes himself inspired by the Divine Soul which also inspires all men.

1837, 1849

[13]Swiss educator and theorist (1746–1827) who influenced Bronson Alcott.

Self-Reliance

"Ne te quæsiveris extra."[1]

"Man is his own star; and the soul that can
Render an honest and a perfect man,
Commands all light, all influence, all fate;
Nothing to him falls early or too late.
Our acts our angels are, or good or ill,
Our fatal shadows that walk by us still."
—EPILOGUE TO BEAUMONT AND FLETCHER'S *Honest Man's Fortune.*

Cast the bantling[2] *on the rocks,*
Suckle him with the she-wolf's teat;
Wintered with the hawk and fox,
Power and speed be hands and feet.[3]

I read the other day some verses written by an eminent painter[4] which were original and not conventional. The soul always hears an admonition in such lines, let the subject be what it may. The sentiment they instil is of more value than any thought they may contain. To believe your own thought, to believe that what is true for you in your private heart, is true for all men,—that is genius. Speak your latent conviction and it shall be the universal sense; for the inmost in due time[5] becomes the outmost,—and our first thought is rendered back to us by the trumpets of the Last Judgment. Familiar as the voice of the mind is to each, the highest merit we ascribe to Moses, Plato, and Milton, is that they set at naught books and traditions, and spoke not what men but what they thought. A man should learn to detect and watch that gleam of light which flashes across his mind from within, more than the lustre of the firmament of bards and sages. Yet he dismisses without notice his thought, because it is his. In every work of genius we recognize our own rejected thoughts: they come back to us with a certain alienated majesty. Great works of art have no more affecting lesson for us than this. They teach us to abide by our spontaneous impression with good-humored inflexibility then most when the whole cry of voices is on the other side. Else, tomorrow a stranger will say with masterly good sense precisely what we have thought and felt all the time, and we shall be forced to take with shame our own opinion from another.

There is a time in every man's education when he arrives at the conviction that envy is ignorance; that imitation is suicide; that he must take himself for better, for worse, as his portion; that though the wide universe is full of good, no kernel of nourishing corn can come to him but through his toil bestowed on that plot of ground

[1]"Look to no one outside yourself," from Persius, *Satires* (1st cent. A.D.).

[2]Young child.

[3]This verse is by Emerson.

[4]Probably refers to American painter Washington Allston (1779–1843).

[5]Emerson's replacement of the 1841 edition's more extreme "always" with "in due time" is an example of how he moderated descriptors in his 1847 revision. He also altered such words as "ever," "all," "great," "most," and "whole."

which is given to him to till. The power which resides in him is new in nature, and none but he knows what that is which he can do, nor does he know until he has tried. Not for nothing one face, one character, one fact makes much impression on him, and another none. This sculpture in the memory is not without preëstablished harmony. The eye was placed where one ray should fall, that it might testify of that particular ray. We but half express ourselves, and are ashamed of that divine idea which each of us represents. It may be safely trusted as proportionate and of good issues, so it be faithfully imparted, but God will not have his work made manifest by cowards. A man is relieved and gay when he has put his heart into his work and done his best; but what he has said or done otherwise, shall give him no peace. It is a deliverance which does not deliver. In the attempt his genius deserts him; no muse befriends; no invention, no hope.

Trust thyself: every heart vibrates to that iron string. Accept the place the divine Providence has found for you; the society of your contemporaries, the connexion of events. Great men have always done so and confided themselves childlike to the genius of their age, betraying their perception that the absolutely trustworthy was seated at their heart, working through their hands, predominating in all their being. And we are now men, and must accept in the highest mind the same transcendent destiny; and not minors and invalids in a protected corner, not cowards fleeing before a revolution, but guides, redeemers, and benefactors, obeying the Almighty effort, and advancing on Chaos and the Dark.

What pretty oracles nature yields us on this text in the face and behavior of children, babes and even brutes. That divided and rebel mind, that distrust of a sentiment because our arithmetic has computed the strength and means opposed to our purpose, these have not. Their mind being whole, their eye is as yet unconquered, and when we look in their faces, we are disconcerted. Infancy conforms to nobody: all conform to it, so that one babe commonly makes four or five out of the adults who prattle and play to it. So God has armed youth and puberty and manhood no less with its own piquancy and charm, and made it enviable and gracious and its claims not to be put by, if it will stand by itself. Do not think the youth has no force because he cannot speak to you and me. Hark! in the next room his voice is sufficiently clear and emphatic.[6] It seems he knows how to speak to his contemporaries. Bashful or bold, then, he will know how to make us seniors very unnecessary.

The nonchalance of boys who are sure of a dinner, and would disdain as much as a lord to do or say aught to conciliate one, is the healthy attitude of human nature. A boy is in the parlour what the pit[7] is in the playhouse; independent, irresponsible, looking out from his corner on such people and facts as pass by, he tries and sentences them on their merits, in the swift summary way of boys, as good, bad, interesting, silly, eloquent, troublesome. He cumbers himself never about consequences,

[6]Throughout the 1847 revision, Emerson altered the more colloquial and oral style of the 1841 first edition. Here he omits: "who spoke so clear and emphatic? Good Heaven! it is he! it is that very lump of bashfulness and phlegm which for weeks has done nothing but eat when you were by, that now rolls out these words like bellstrokes." Elsewhere, he revises: sewing up your "guarded lips" with "packthread," "words as hard as cannon balls," what the "aged ladies" say, a "right fool's word," "rambling round creation as a moth round a lamp," "gadding abroad," and "as the eyes of a maid follow her mistress."

[7]Cheap seats in Elizabethan theater.

about interests: he gives an independent, genuine verdict. You must court him: he does not court you. But the man is, as it were, clapped into jail by his consciousness. As soon as he has once acted or spoken with eclat, he is a committed person, watched by the sympathy or the hatred of hundreds whose affections must now enter into his account. There is no Lethe[8] for this. Ah, that he could pass again into his neutrality! Who can thus avoid all pledges, and having observed, observe again from the same unaffected, unbiassed, unbribable, unaffrighted innocence, must always be formidable. He would utter opinions on all passing affairs, which being seen to be not private but necessary, would sink like darts into the ear of men, and put them in fear.

These are the voices which we hear in solitude, but they grow faint and inaudible as we enter into the world. Society everywhere is in conspiracy against the manhood of every one of its members. Society is a joint-stock company in which the members agree for the better securing of his bread to each shareholder, to surrender the liberty and culture of the eater. The virtue in most request is conformity. Self-reliance is its aversion. It loves not realities and creators, but names and customs.

Whoso would be a man must be a nonconformist. He who would gather immortal palms must not be hindered by the name of goodness, but must explore if it be goodness. Nothing is at last sacred but the integrity of your own mind. Absolve you to yourself, and you shall have the suffrage of the world. I remember an answer which when quite young I was prompted to make to a valued adviser who was wont to importune me with the dear old doctrines of the church. On my saying, What have I to do with the sacredness of traditions, if I live wholly from within? my friend suggested—"But these impulses may be from below, not from above." I replied, "They do not seem to me to be such; but if I am the Devil's child, I will live then from the Devil." No law can be sacred to me but that of my nature. Good and bad are but names very readily transferable to that or this; the only right is what is after my constitution, the only wrong what is against it. A man is to carry himself in the presence of all opposition as if every thing were titular and ephemeral but he. I am ashamed to think how easily we capitulate to badges and names, to large societies and dead institutions. Every decent and well-spoken individual affects and sways me more than is right. I ought to go upright and vital, and speak the rude truth in all ways. If malice and vanity wear the coat of philanthropy, shall that pass? If an angry bigot assumes this bountiful cause of Abolition, and comes to me with his last news from Barbadoes,[9] why should I not say to him, 'Go love thy infant; love thy wood-chopper: be good-natured and modest: have that grace; and never varnish your hard, uncharitable ambition with this incredible tenderness for black folk a thousand miles off. Thy love afar is spite at home.' Rough and graceless would be such greeting, but truth is handsomer than the affectation of love. Your goodness must have some edge to it—else it is none. The doctrine of hatred must be preached as the counteraction of the doctrine of love when that pules and whines. I shun father and mother[10] and wife and brother, when my genius calls me. I would write on the lintels of the door-post,[11] *Whim.* I hope it is somewhat better than whim at last, but we cannot spend

[8]Mythological river that induces forgetfulness.

[9]Slavery was officially abolished in 1834 in the British West Indies.

[10]Cf. Matthew 10:37.

[11]Emerson refers to marking with blood the houses of believers so God would not "smite" them; cf. Deuteronomy 6:9 and Exodus 12:23.

the day in explanation. Expect me not to show cause why I seek or why I exclude company. Then, again, do not tell me, as a good man did to-day, of my obligation to put all poor men in good situations. Are they *my* poor? I tell thee, thou foolish philanthropist, that I grudge the dollar, the dime, the cent I give to such men as do not belong to me and to whom I do not belong. There is a class of persons to whom by all spiritual affinity I am bought and sold; for them I will go to prison, if need be; but your miscellaneous popular charities; the education at college of fools; the building of meeting-houses to the vain end to which many now stand; alms to sots; and the thousandfold Relief Societies;—though I confess with shame I sometimes succumb and give the dollar, it is a wicked dollar which by and by I shall have the manhood to withhold.

Virtues are in the popular estimate rather the exception than the rule. There is the man *and* his virtues. Men do what is called a good action, as some piece of courage or charity, much as they would pay a fine in expiation of daily non-appearance on parade. Their works are done as an apology or extenuation of their living in the world,—as invalids and the insane pay a high board. Their virtues are penances. I do not wish to expiate, but to live. My life is for itself and not for a spectacle. I much prefer that it should be of a lower strain, so it be genuine and equal, than that it should be glittering and unsteady. I wish it to be sound and sweet, and not to need diet and bleeding.[12] I ask primary evidence that you are a man, and refuse this appeal from the man to his actions. I know that for myself it makes no difference whether I do or forbear those actions which are reckoned excellent. I cannot consent to pay for a privilege where I have intrinsic right. Few and mean as my gifts may be, I actually am, and do not need for my own assurance or the assurance of my fellows any secondary testimony.

What I must do, is all that concerns me, not what the people think. This rule, equally arduous in actual and in intellectual life, may serve for the whole distinction between greatness and meanness. It is the harder, because you will always find those who think they know what is your duty better than you know it. It is easy in the world to live after the world's opinion; it is easy in solitude to live after our own; but the great man is he who in the midst of the crowd keeps with perfect sweetness the independence of solitude.

The objection to conforming to usages that have become dead to you, is, that it scatters your force. It loses your time and blurs the impression of your character. If you maintain a dead church, contribute to a dead Bible-Society, vote with a great party either for the Government or against it, spread your table like base housekeepers,—under all these screens, I have difficulty to detect the precise man you are. And, of course, so much force is withdrawn from your proper life. But do your work,[13] and I shall know you. Do your work, and you shall reinforce yourself. A man must consider what a blindman's-buff is this game of conformity. If I know your sect, I anticipate your argument. I hear a preacher announce for his text and topic the expediency of one of the institutions of his church. Do I not know beforehand that not possibly can he say a new and spontaneous word? Do I not know that with all this ostentation of examining the grounds of the institution, he will do no such thing? Do

[12]Bloodletting.
[13]In various versions of this passage, Emerson recommended doing your "work," "office," and "thing."

I not know that he is pledged to himself not to look but at one side,—the permitted side, not as a man, but as a parish minister? He is a retained attorney, and these airs of the bench are the emptiest affectation. Well, most men have bound their eyes with one or another handkerchief, and attached themselves to some one of these communities of opinion. This conformity makes them not false in a few particulars, authors of a few lies, but false in all particulars. Their every truth is not quite true. Their two is not the real two, their four not the real four: so that every word they say chagrins us, and we know not where to begin to set them right. Meantime nature is not slow to equip us in the prison-uniform of the party to which we adhere. We come to wear one cut of face and figure, and acquire by degrees the gentlest asinine expression. There is a mortifying experience in particular which does not fail to wreak itself also in the general history; I mean "the foolish face of praise,"[14] the forced smile which we put on in company where we do not feel at ease in answer to conversation which does not interest us. The muscles, not spontaneously moved, but moved by a low usurping wilfulness, grow tight about the outline of the face with the most disagreeable sensation.

For nonconformity the world whips you with its displeasure. And therefore a man must know how to estimate a sour face. The bystanders look askance on him in the public street or in the friend's parlor. If this aversation had its origin in contempt and resistance like his own, he might well go home with a sad countenance; but the sour faces of the multitude, like their sweet faces, have no deep cause, but are put on and off as the wind blows, and a newspaper directs. Yet is the discontent of the multitude more formidable than that of the senate and the college. It is easy enough for a firm man who knows the world to brook the rage of the cultivated classes. Their rage is decorous and prudent, for they are timid as being very vulnerable themselves. But when to their feminine rage the indignation of the people is added, when the ignorant and the poor are aroused, when the unintelligent brute force that lies at the bottom of society is made to growl and mow,[15] it needs the habit of magnanimity and religion to treat it godlike as a trifle of no concernment.

The other terror that scares us from self-trust is our consistency; a reverence for our past act or word, because the eyes of others have no other data for computing our orbit than our past acts, and we are loath to disappoint them.

But why should you keep your head over your shoulder? Why drag about this corpse of your memory, lest you contradict somewhat you have stated in this or that public place? Suppose you should contradict yourself; what then? It seems to be a rule of wisdom never to rely on your memory alone, scarcely even in acts of pure memory, but to bring the past for judgment into the thousand-eyed present, and live ever in a new day. In your metaphysics you have denied personality to the Deity; yet when the devout motions of the soul come, yield to them heart and life, though they should clothe God with shape and color. Leave your theory as Joseph his coat in the hand of the harlot,[16] and flee.

A foolish consistency is the hobgoblin of little minds, adored by little statesmen and philosophers and divines. With consistency a great soul has simply nothing to do. He may as well concern himself with his shadow on the wall. Speak what you

[14]Pope, "Epistle to Dr. Arbuthnot" (1735).
[15]Grimace.
[16]Joseph fled from the temptings of Potiphar's wife; cf. Genesis 39:12.

think now in hard words, and to-morrow speak what to-morrow thinks in hard words again, though it contradict every thing you said to-day.—'Ah, so you shall be sure to be misunderstood.'—Is it so bad then to be misunderstood? Pythagoras[17] was misunderstood, and Socrates, and Jesus, and Luther, and Copernicus, and Galileo, and Newton, and every pure and wise spirit that ever took flesh. To be great is to be misunderstood.

I suppose no man can violate his nature. All the sallies of his will are rounded in by the law of his being as the inequalities of Andes and Himmaleh are insignificant in the curve of the sphere. Nor does it matter how you gauge and try him. A character is like an acrostic or Alexandrian stanza;—read it forward, backward, or across, it still spells the same thing. In this pleasing contrite wood-life which God allows me, let me record day by day my honest thought without prospect or retrospect, and, I cannot doubt, it will be found symmetrical, though I mean it not, and see it not. My book should smell of pines and resound with the hum of insects. The swallow over my window should interweave that thread or straw he carries in his bill into my web also. We pass for what we are. Character teaches above our wills. Men imagine that they communicate their virtue or vice only by overt actions and do not see that virtue or vice emit a breath every moment.

There will be an agreement in whatever variety of actions, so they be each honest and natural in their hour. For of one will, the actions will be harmonious, however unlike they seem. These varieties are lost sight of at a little distance, at a little height of thought. One tendency unites them all. The voyage of the best ship is a zigzag line of a hundred tacks. See the line from a sufficient distance, and it straightens itself to the average tendency. Your genuine action will explain itself and will explain your other genuine actions. Your conformity explains nothing. Act singly, and what you have already done singly, will justify you now. Greatness appeals to the future. If I can be firm enough to-day to do right and scorn eyes, I must have done so much right before, as to defend me now. Be it how it will, do right now. Always scorn appearances, and you always may. The force of character is cumulative. All the foregone days of virtue work their health into this. What makes the majesty of the heroes of the senate and the field, which so fills the imagination? The consciousness of a train of great days and victories behind. They shed an united light on the advancing actor. He is attended as by a visible escort of angels. That is it which throws thunder into Chatham's voice, and dignity into Washington's port,[18] and America into Adams's eye.[19] Honor is venerable to us because it is no ephemeris. It is always ancient virtue. We worship it to-day, because it is not of to-day. We love it and pay it homage, because it is not a trap for our love and homage, but is self-dependent, self-derived, and therefore of an old immaculate pedigree, even if shown in a young person.

I hope in these days we have heard the last of conformity and consistency. Let the words be gazetted[20] and ridiculous henceforward. Instead of the gong for din-

[17]Like the rest of the list, the 6th-century Greek philosopher and mathematician met resistance for his radical positions.

[18]Demeanor, bearing.

[19]The list of politicians includes William Pitt (Earl of Chatham), George Washington, and one of the patriotic Adamses (Samuel, John, or John Quincy). In Emerson's journal, the thundering voice belonged to the American orator, William Ellery Channing.

[20]Published in a newspaper.

ner, let us hear a whistle from the Spartan fife. Let us never bow and apologize more. A great man is coming to eat at my house. I do not wish to please him: I wish that he should wish to please me. I will stand here for humanity, and though I would make it kind, I would make it true. Let us affront and reprimand the smooth mediocrity and squalid contentment of the times, and hurl in the face of custom, and trade, and office, the fact which is the upshot of all history, that there is a great responsible Thinker and Actor working wherever a man works; that a true man belongs to no other time or place, but is the centre of things. Where he is, there is nature. He measures you, and all men, and all events. Ordinarily every body in society reminds us of somewhat else or of some other person. Character, reality, reminds you of nothing else; it takes place of the whole creation. The man must be so much that he must make all circumstances indifferent. Every true man is a cause, a country, and an age; requires infinite spaces and numbers and time fully to accomplish his design;—and posterity seem to follow his steps as a train of clients. A man Cæsar is born, and for ages after, we have a Roman Empire. Christ is born, and millions of minds so grow and cleave to his genius, that he is confounded with virtue and the possible of man. An institution is the lengthened shadow of one man; as, Monachism, of the Hermit Antony; the Reformation, of Luther; Quakerism, of Fox; Methodism, of Wesley; Abolition, of Clarkson. Scipio,[21] Milton called "the height of Rome;" and all history resolves itself very easily into the biography of a few stout and earnest persons.

Let a man then know his worth, and keep things under his feet. Let him not peep or steal, or skulk up and down with the air of a charity-boy, a bastard, or an interloper, in the world which exists for him. But the man in the street finding no worth in himself which corresponds to the force which built a tower or sculptured a marble god, feels poor when he looks on these. To him a palace, a statue, or a costly book have an alien and forbidding air, much like a gay equipage, and seem to say like that, 'Who are you, sir?' Yet they all are his, suitors for his notice, petitioners to his faculties that they will come out and take possession. The picture waits for my verdict: it is not to command me, but I am to settle its claims to praise. That popular fable of the sot who was picked up dead drunk in the street, carried to the duke's house, washed and dressed and laid in the duke's bed, and, on his waking, treated with all obsequious ceremony like the duke, and assured that he had been insane, owes its popularity to the fact, that it symbolizes so well the state of man, who is in the world a sort of sot, but now and then wakes up, exercises his reason, and finds himself a true prince.

Our reading is mendicant and sycophantic. In history, our imagination plays us false. Kingdom and lordship, power and estate are a gaudier vocabulary than private John and Edward in a small house and common day's work: but the things of life are the same to both: the sum total of both is the same. Why all this deference to Alfred, and Scanderbeg, and Gustavus?[22] Suppose they were virtuous: did they wear out virtue? As great a stake depends on your private act to-day, as followed their public and renowned steps. When private men shall act with original views, the lustre will be transferred from the actions of kings to those of gentlemen.

[21]Roman general who conquered Carthage (201 B.C.).

[22]The list of national heroes includes Alfred the Great of England, Scanderbeg or Iskander Bey (the leader of a 15th-century Albanian rebellion against the Turks) and King Gustavus Adolphus of Sweden.

The world has been instructed by its kings, who have so magnetized the eyes of nations. It has been taught by this colossal symbol the mutual reverence that is due from man to man. The joyful loyalty with which men have everywhere suffered the king, the noble, or the great proprietor to walk among them by a law of his own, make his own scale of men and things, and reverse theirs, pay for benefits not with money but with honor, and represent the Law in his person, was the hieroglyphic by which they obscurely signified their consciousness of their own right and comeliness, the right of every man.

The magnetism which all original action exerts is explained when we inquire the reason of self-trust. Who is the Trustee? What is the aboriginal Self on which a universal reliance may be grounded? What is the nature and power of that science-baffling star, without parallax,[23] without calculable elements, which shoots a ray of beauty even into trivial and impure actions, if the least mark of independence appear? The inquiry leads us to that source, at once the essence of genius, of virtue, and of life, which we call Spontaneity or Instinct. We denote this primary wisdom as Intuition, whilst all later teachings are tuitions. In that deep force, the last fact behind which analysis cannot go, all things find their common origin. For the sense of being which in calm hours rises, we know not how, in the soul, is not diverse from things, from space, from light, from time, from man, but one with them, and proceeds obviously from the same source whence their life and being also proceed. We first share the life by which things exist, and afterwards see them as appearances in nature, and forget that we have shared their cause. Here is the fountain of action and of thought. Here are the lungs of that inspiration which giveth man wisdom, and which cannot be denied without impiety and atheism. We lie in the lap of immense intelligence, which makes us receivers of its truth and organs of its activity. When we discern justice, when we discern truth, we do nothing of ourselves, but allow a passage to its beams. If we ask whence this comes, if we seek to pry into the soul that causes, all philosophy is at fault. Its presence or its absence is all we can affirm. Every man discriminates between the voluntary acts of his mind, and his involuntary perceptions, and knows that to his involuntary perceptions a perfect faith is due. He may err in the expression of them, but he knows that these things are so, like day and night, not to be disputed. My wilful actions and acquisitions are but roving;—the idlest reverie, the faintest native emotion, command my curiosity and respect. Thoughtless people contradict as readily the statement of perceptions as of opinions, or rather much more readily; for, they do not distinguish between perception and notion. They fancy that I choose to see this or that thing. But perception is not whimsical, but fatal. If I see a trait, my children will see it after me, and in course of time, all mankind,—although it may chance that no one has seen it before me. For my perception of it is as much a fact as the sun.

The relations of the soul to the divine spirit are so pure that it is profane to seek to interpose helps. It must be that when God speaketh, he should communicate not one thing, but all things; should fill the world with his voice; should scatter forth light, nature, time, souls, from the centre of the present thought; and new date and new create the whole. Whenever a mind is simple, and receives a divine wisdom, old

[23]Star whose distance from the Earth cannot be measured.

things pass away,—means, teachers, texts, temples fall; it lives now and absorbs past and future into the present hour. All things are made sacred by relation to it,—one as much as another. All things are dissolved to their centre by their cause, and in the universal miracle petty and particular miracles disappear. If, therefore, a man claims to know and speak of God, and carries you backward to the phraseology of some old mouldered nation in another country, in another world, believe him not. Is the acorn better than the oak which is its fulness and completion? Is the parent better than the child into whom he has cast his ripened being? Whence then this worship of the past? The centuries are conspirators against the sanity and authority of the soul. Time and space are but physiological colors which the eye makes, but the soul is light; where it is, is day; where it was, is night; and history is an impertinence and an injury, if it be anything more than a cheerful apologue or parable of my being and becoming.

Man is timid and apologetic; he is no longer upright; he dares not say 'I think,' 'I am,' but quotes some saint or sage. He is ashamed before the blade of grass or the blowing rose. These roses under my window make no reference to former roses or to better ones; they are for what they are; they exist with God to-day. There is no time to them. There is simply the rose; it is perfect in every moment of its existence. Before a leaf-bud has burst, its whole life acts; in the full-blown flower, there is no more; in the leafless root, there is no less. Its nature is satisfied, and it satisfies nature, in all moments alike. But man postpones or remembers; he does not live in the present, but with reverted eye laments the past, or, heedless of the riches that surround him, stands on tiptoe to foresee the future. He cannot be happy and strong until he too lives with nature in the present, above time.

This should be plain enough. Yet see what strong intellects dare not yet hear God himself, unless he speak the phraseology of I know not what David, or Jeremiah, or Paul. We shall not always set so great a price on a few texts, on a few lives. We are like children who repeat by rote the sentences of grandames and tutors, and, as they grow older, of the men of talents and character they chance to see,—painfully recollecting the exact words they spoke; afterwards, when they come into the point of view which those had who uttered these sayings, they understand them, and are willing to let the words go; for, at any time, they can use words as good, when occasion comes. If we live truly, we shall see truly. It is as easy for the strong man to be strong, as it is for the weak to be weak. When we have new perception, we shall gladly disburden the memory of its hoarded treasures as old rubbish. When a man lives with God, his voice shall be as sweet as the murmur of the brook and the rustle of the corn.

And now at last the highest truth on this subject remains unsaid; probably, cannot be said; for all that we say is the far off remembering of the intuition. That thought, by what I can now nearest approach to say it, is this. When good is near you, when you have life in yourself, it is not by any known or accustomed way; you shall not discern the foot-prints of any other; you shall not see the face of man; you shall not hear any name;—the way, the thought, the good shall be wholly strange and new. It shall exclude example and experience. You take the way from man, not to man. All persons that ever existed are its forgotten ministers. Fear and hope are alike beneath it. There is somewhat low even in hope. In the hour of vision, there is nothing that can be called gratitude, nor properly joy. The soul raised over passion beholds identity and eternal causation, perceives the self-existence of Truth and Right, and calms itself with knowing that all things go well. Vast spaces of nature, the Atlantic Ocean, the South Sea,—long intervals of time, years, centuries,—are of no account. This which I think and feel underlay every former state of life and circumstances, as it does underlie my present, and what is called life, and what is called death.

Life only avails, not the having lived. Power ceases in the instant of repose; it resides in the moment of transition from a past to a new state, in the shooting of the gulf, in the darting to an aim. This one fact the world hates, that the soul *becomes;* for, that forever degrades the past, turns all riches to poverty, all reputation to a shame, confounds the saint with the rogue, shoves Jesus and Judas equally aside. Why then do we prate of self-reliance? Inasmuch as the soul is present, there will be power not confident but agent. To talk of reliance, is a poor external way of speaking. Speak rather of that which relies, because it works and is. Who has more obedience than I, masters me, though he should not raise his finger. Round him I must revolve by the gravitation of spirits. We fancy it rhetoric when we speak of eminent virtue. We do not yet see that virtue is Height, and that a man or a company of men plastic and permeable to principles, by the law of nature must overpower and ride all cities, nations, kings, rich men, poets, who are not.

This is the ultimate fact which we so quickly reach on this as on every topic, the resolution of all into the ever blessed ONE. Self-existence is the attribute of the Supreme Cause, and it constitutes the measure of good by the degree in which it enters into all lower forms. All things real are so by so much virtue as they contain. Commerce, husbandry, hunting, whaling, war, eloquence, personal weight, are somewhat, and engage my respect as examples of its presence and impure action. I see the same law working in nature for conservation and growth. Power is in nature the essential measure of right. Nature suffers nothing to remain in her kingdoms which cannot help itself. The genesis and maturation of a planet, its poise and orbit, the bended tree recovering itself from the strong wind, the vital resources of every animal and vegetable, are demonstrations of the self-sufficing, and therefore self-relying soul.

Thus all concentrates; let us not rove; let us sit at home with the cause. Let us stun and astonish the intruding rabble of men and books and institutions by a simple declaration of the divine fact. Bid the invaders take the shoes from off their feet, for God is here within.[24] Let our simplicity judge them, and our docility to our own law demonstrate the poverty of nature and fortune beside our native riches.

But now we are a mob. Man does not stand in awe of man, nor is his genius admonished to stay at home, to put itself in communication with the internal ocean, but it goes abroad to beg a cup of water of the urns of other men. We must go alone. I like the silent church before the service begins, better than any preaching. How far off, how cool, how chaste the persons look, begirt each one with a precinct or sanctuary. So let us always sit. Why should we assume the faults of our friend, or wife, or father, or child, because they sit around our hearth, or are said to have the same blood? All men have my blood, and I have all men's. Not for that will I adopt their

[24]In Exodus 3:5, God warns Moses not to profane the holy ground of the burning bush.

petulance or folly, even to the extent of being ashamed of it. But your isolation must not be mechanical, but spiritual, that is, must be elevation. At times the whole world seems to be in conspiracy to importune you with emphatic trifles. Friend, client, child, sickness, fear, want, charity, all knock at once at thy closet door and say,—'Come out unto us.' But keep thy state; come not into their confusion. The power men possess to annoy me, I give them by a weak curiosity. No man can come near me but through my act. "What we love that we have, but by desire we bereave ourselves of the love."[25]

If we cannot at once rise to the sanctities of obedience and faith, let us at least resist our temptations; let us enter into the state of war, and wake Thor and Woden,[26] courage and constancy, in our Saxon breasts. This is to be done in our smooth times by speaking the truth. Check this lying hospitality and lying affection. Live no longer to the expectation of these deceived and deceiving people with whom we converse. Say to them, O father, O mother, O wife, O brother, O friend, I have lived with you after appearances hitherto. Henceforward I am the truth's. Be it known unto you that henceforward I obey no law less than the eternal law. I will have no covenants but proximities. I shall endeavor to nourish my parents, to support my family, to be the chaste husband of one wife,—but these relations I must fill after a new and unprecedented way. I appeal from your customs. I must be myself. I cannot break myself any longer for you, or you. If you can love me for what I am, we shall be the happier. If you cannot, I will still seek to deserve that you should. I will not hide my tastes or aversions. I will so trust that what is deep is holy, that I will do strongly before the sun and moon whatever inly rejoices me, and the heart appoints. If you are noble, I will love you; if you are not, I will not hurt you and myself by hypocritical attentions. If you are true, but not in the same truth with me, cleave to your companions; I will seek my own. I do this not selfishly, but humbly and truly. It is alike your interest and mine and all men's, however long we have dwelt in lies, to live in truth. Does this sound harsh to-day? You will soon love what is dictated by your nature as well as mine, and if we follow the truth, it will bring us out safe at last.—But so you may give these friends pain. Yes, but I cannot sell my liberty and my power, to save their sensibility. Besides, all persons have their moments of reason when they look out into the region of absolute truth; then will they justify me and do the same thing.

The populace think that your rejection of popular standards is a rejection of all standard, and mere antinomianism;[27] and the bold sensualist will use the name of philosophy to gild his crimes. But the law of consciousness abides. There are two confessionals, in one or the other of which we must be shriven. You may fulfil your round of duties by clearing yourself in the *direct,* or, in the *reflex* way. Consider whether you have satisfied your relations to father, mother, cousin, neighbor, town, cat, and dog; whether any of these can upbraid you. But I may also neglect this reflex standard, and absolve me to myself. I have my own stern claims and perfect circle. It denies the name of duty to many offices that are called duties. But if I can discharge its debts, it enables me to dispense with the popular code. If any one imagines that this law is lax, let him keep its commandment one day.

[25]A paraphrase from the 18th-century German poet Schiller.

[26]Norse gods of thunder and war.

[27]Belief that faith rather than moral law achieves salvation; by extension, an opposition to moral laws.

And truly it demands something godlike in him who has cast off the common motives of humanity, and has ventured to trust himself for a taskmaster. High be his heart, faithful his will, clear his sight, that he may in good earnest be doctrine, society, law to himself, that a simple purpose may be to him as strong as iron necessity is to others.

If any man consider the present aspects of what is called by distinction *society,* he will see the need of these ethics. The sinew and heart of man seem to be drawn out, and we are become timorous desponding whimperers. We are afraid of truth, afraid of fortune, afraid of death, and afraid of each other. Our age yields no great and perfect persons. We want men and women who shall renovate life and our social state, but we see that most natures are insolvent, cannot satisfy their own wants, have an ambition out of all proportion to their practical force, and do lean and beg day and night continually. Our housekeeping is mendicant, our arts, our occupations, our marriages, our religion we have not chosen, but society has chosen for us. We are parlor soldiers. We shun the rugged battle of fate, where strength is born.

If our young men miscarry in their first enterprizes, they lose all heart. If the young merchant fails, men say he is *ruined.* If the finest genius studies at one of our colleges, and is not installed in an office within one year afterwards in the cities or suburbs of Boston or New York, it seems to his friends and to himself that he is right in being disheartened and in complaining the rest of his life. A sturdy lad from New Hampshire or Vermont, who in turn tries all the professions, who *teams it, farms it, peddles,* keeps a school, preaches, edits a newspaper, goes to Congress, buys a township, and so forth, in successive years, and always, like a cat, falls on his feet, is worth a hundred of these city dolls. He walks abreast with his days, and feels no shame in not 'studying a profession,' for he does not postpone his life, but lives already. He has not one chance, but a hundred chances. Let a Stoic[28] open the resources of man, and tell men they are not leaning willows, but can and must detach themselves; that with the exercise of self-trust, new powers shall appear; that a man is the word made flesh, born to shed healing to the nations,[29] that he should be ashamed of our compassion, and that the moment he acts from himself, tossing the laws, the books, idolatries, and customs out of the window, we pity him no more but thank and revere him,—and that teacher shall restore the life of man to splendor, and make his name dear to all History.

It is easy to see that a greater self-reliance must work a revolution in all the offices and relations of men; in their religion; in their education; in their pursuits; their modes of living; their association; in their property; in their speculative views.

1. In what prayers do men allow themselves! That which they call a holy office, is not so much as brave and manly. Prayer looks abroad and asks for some foreign addition to come through some foreign virtue, and loses itself in endless mazes of natural and supernatural, and mediatorial and miraculous. Prayer that craves a particular commodity,—any thing less than all good,—is vicious. Prayer is the contemplation of the facts of life from the highest point of view. It is the soliloquy of a beholding and jubilant soul. It is the spirit of God pronouncing his works good.[30] But

[28]Ancient Greek philosophers who advocated impassivity, independence, and adherence to natural law.

[29]Cf. John 1:14, and Revelation 22:2.

[30]God's pronouncement after creating the world; cf. Genesis 1:31.

prayer as a means to effect a private end, is meanness and theft. It supposes dualism and not unity in nature and consciousness. As soon as the man is at one with God, he will not beg. He will then see prayer in all action. The prayer of the farmer kneeling in his field to weed it, the prayer of the rower kneeling with the stroke of his oar, are true prayers heard throughout nature, though for cheap ends. Caratach, in Fletcher's Bonduca,[31] when admonished to inquire the mind of the god Audate, replies,—

> "His hidden meaning lies in our endeavors,
> Our valors are our best gods."

Another sort of false prayers are our regrets. Discontent is the want of self-reliance: it is infirmity of will. Regret calamities, if you can thereby help the sufferer; if not, attend your own work, and already the evil begins to be repaired. Our sympathy is just as base. We come to them who weep foolishly, and sit down and cry for company, instead of imparting to them truth and health in rough electric shocks; putting them once more in communication with their own reason. The secret of fortune is joy in our hands. Welcome evermore to gods and men is the self-helping man. For him all doors are flung wide: him all tongues greet, all honors crown, all eyes follow with desire. Our love goes out to him and embraces him, because he did not need it. We solicitously and apologetically caress and celebrate him, because he held on his way and scorned our disapprobation. The gods love him because men hated him. "To the persevering mortal," said Zoroaster,[32] "the blessed Immortals are swift."

As men's prayers are a disease of the will, so are their creeds a disease of the intellect. They say with those foolish Israelites, 'Let not God speak to us, lest we die. Speak thou, speak any man with us, and we will obey.'[33] Everywhere I am hindered of meeting God in my brother, because he has shut his own temple doors, and recites fables merely of his brother's, or his brother's brother's God. Every new mind is a new classification. If it prove a mind of uncommon activity and power, a Locke, a Lavoisier, a Hutton, a Bentham, a Fourier,[34] it imposes its classification on other men, and lo! a new system. In proportion to the depth of the thought, and so to the number of the objects it touches and brings within reach of the pupil, is his complacency. But chiefly is this apparent in creeds and churches, which are also classifications of some powerful mind acting on the elemental thought of Duty, and man's relation to the Highest. Such is Calvinism, Quakerism, Swedenborgianism. The pupil takes the same delight in subordinating every thing to the new terminology, as a girl who has just learned botany in seeing a new earth and new seasons thereby. It will happen for a time, that the pupil will find his intellectual power has grown by the study of his master's mind. But in all unbalanced minds, the classification is idolized, passes for the end, and not for a speedily exhaustible means, so that the walls of the system blend to their eye in the remote horizon with the walls of the universe; the luminaries of heaven seem to them hung on the arch their master built. They cannot

[31]Jacobean drama by John Fletcher.

[32]Persian religious leader (6th cent. B.C.).

[33]Cf. Exodus 20:9.

[34]List of pioneers in natural and social sciences. Instead of Fourier, the advocate of communitarianism, the 1841 edition included the phrenologist Spurzheim.

imagine how you aliens have any right to see,—how you can see; 'It must be somehow that you stole the light from us.' They do not yet perceive, that light, unsystematic, indomitable, will break into any cabin, even into theirs. Let them chirp awhile and call it their own. If they are honest and do well, presently their neat new pinfold[35] will be too strait and low, will crack, will lean, will rot and vanish, and the immortal light, all young and joyful, million-orbed, million-colored, will beam over the universe as on the first morning.

2. It is for want of self-culture that the superstition of Travelling, whose idols are Italy, England, Egypt, retains its fascination for all educated Americans. They who made England, Italy, or Greece venerable in the imagination, did so by sticking fast where they were, like an axis of the earth. In manly hours, we feel that duty is our place. The soul is no traveller: the wise man stays at home, and when his necessities, his duties, on any occasion call him from his house, or into foreign lands, he is at home still, and shall make men sensible by the expression of his countenance, that he goes the missionary of wisdom and virtue, and visits cities and men like a sovereign, and not like an interloper or a valet.

I have no churlish objection to the circumnavigation of the globe, for the purposes of art, of study, and benevolence, so that the man is first domesticated, or does not go abroad with the hope of finding somewhat greater than he knows. He who travels to be amused, or to get somewhat which he does not carry, travels away from himself, and grows old even in youth among old things. In Thebes, in Palmyra, his will and mind have become old and dilapidated as they. He carries ruins to ruins.

Travelling is a fool's paradise. Our first journeys discover to us the indifference of places. At home I dream that at Naples, at Rome, I can be intoxicated with beauty, and lose my sadness. I pack my trunk, embrace my friends, embark on the sea, and at last wake up in Naples, and there beside me is the stern Fact, the sad self, unrelenting, identical, that I fled from. I seek the Vatican, and the palaces. I affect to be intoxicated with sights and suggestions, but I am not intoxicated. My giant goes with me wherever I go.

3. But the rage of travelling is a symptom of a deeper unsoundness affecting the whole intellectual action. The intellect is vagabond, and our system of education fosters restlessness. Our minds travel when our bodies are forced to stay at home. We imitate; and what is imitation but the travelling of the mind? Our houses are built with foreign taste; our shelves are garnished with foreign ornaments; our opinions, our tastes, our faculties, lean, and follow the Past and the Distant. The soul created the arts wherever they have flourished. It was in his own mind that the artist sought his model. It was an application of his own thought to the thing to be done and the conditions to be observed. And why need we copy the Doric or the Gothic model? Beauty, convenience, grandeur of thought, and quaint expression are as near to us as to any, and if the American artist will study with hope and love the precise thing to be done by him, considering the climate, the soil, the length of the day, the wants of the people, the habit and form of the government, he will create a house in which all these will find themselves fitted, and taste and sentiment will be satisfied also.

Insist on yourself; never imitate. Your own gift you can present every moment with the cumulative force of a whole life's cultivation; but of the adopted talent of

[35]Animal enclosure.

another, you have only an extemporaneous, half possession. That which each can do best, none but his Maker can teach him. No man yet knows what it is, nor can, till that person has exhibited it. Where is the master who could have taught Shakspeare? Where is the master who could have instructed Franklin, or Washington, or Bacon, or Newton? Every great man is a unique. The Scipionism of Scipio is precisely that part he could not borrow. Shakspeare will never be made by the study of Shakspeare. Do that which is assigned you, and you cannot hope too much or dare too much. There is at this moment for you an utterance brave and grand as that of the colossal chisel of Phidias,[36] or trowel of the Egyptians, or the pen of Moses, or Dante, but different from all these. Not possibly will the soul all rich, all eloquent, with thousand-cloven tongue, deign to repeat itself; but if you can hear what these patriarchs say, surely you can reply to them in the same pitch of voice: for the ear and the tongue are two organs of one nature. Abide in the simple and noble regions of thy life, obey thy heart, and thou shalt reproduce the Foreworld again.

4. As our Religion, our Education, our Art look abroad, so does our spirit of society. All men plume themselves on the improvement of society, and no man improves.

Society never advances. It recedes as fast on one side as it gains on the other. It undergoes continual changes: it is barbarous, it is civilized, it is christianized, it is rich, it is scientific; but this change is not amelioration. For every thing that is given, something is taken. Society acquires new arts and loses old instincts. What a contrast between the well-clad, reading, writing, thinking American, with a watch, a pencil, and a bill of exchange in his pocket, and the naked New Zealander, whose property is a club, a spear, a mat, and an undivided twentieth of a shed to sleep under. But compare the health of the two men, and you shall see that the white man has lost his aboriginal strength. If the traveller tell us truly, strike the savage with a broad axe, and in a day or two the flesh shall unite and heal as if you struck the blow into soft pitch, and the same blow shall send the white to his grave.

The civilized man has built a coach, but has lost the use of his feet. He is supported on crutches, but lacks so much support of muscle. He has a fine Geneva watch, but he fails of the skill to tell the hour by the sun. A Greenwich nautical almanac he has, and so being sure of the information when he wants it, the man in the street does not know a star in the sky. The solstice he does not observe; the equinox he knows as little; and the whole bright calendar of the year is without a dial in his mind. His note-books impair his memory; his libraries overload his wit; the insurance office increases the number of accidents; and it may be a question whether machinery does not encumber; whether we have not lost by refinement some energy, by a christianity entrenched in establishments and forms, some vigor of wild virtue. For every stoic was a stoic; but in Christendom where is the Christian?

There is no more deviation in the moral standard than in the standard of height or bulk. No greater men are now than ever were. A singular equality may be observed between the great men of the first and of the last ages; nor can all the science, art, religion and philosophy of the nineteenth century avail to educate greater men than Plutarch's heroes, three or four and twenty centuries ago. Not in time is the race

[36]Greek sculptor (5th cent. B.C.).

progressive. Phocion, Socrates, Anaxagoras, Diogenes,[37] are great men, but they leave no class. He who is really of their class will not be called by their name, but will be his own man, and, in his turn the founder of a sect. The arts and inventions of each period are only its costume, and do not invigorate men. The harm of the improved machinery may compensate its good. Hudson and Behring accomplished so much in their fishing-boats, as to astonish Parry and Franklin,[38] whose equipment exhausted the resources of science and art. Galileo, with an opera-glass, discovered a more splendid series of celestial phenomena than any one since. Columbus found the New World in an undecked boat. It is curious to see the periodical disuse and perishing of means and machinery which were introduced with loud laudation, a few years or centuries before. The great genius returns to essential man. We reckoned the improvements of the art of war among the triumphs of science, and yet Napoleon conquered Europe by the Bivouac,[39] which consisted of falling back on naked valor, and disencumbering it of all aids. The Emperor held it impossible to make a perfect army, says Las Cases,[40] "without abolishing our arms, magazines, commissaries, and carriages, until in imitation of the Roman custom, the soldier should receive his supply of corn, grind it in his hand-mill, and bake his bread himself."

Society is a wave. The wave moves onward, but the water of which it is composed, does not. The same particle does not rise from the valley to the ridge. Its unity is only phenomenal. The persons who make up a nation to-day, next year die, and their experience with them.

And so the reliance on Property, including the reliance on governments which protect it, is the want of self-reliance. Men have looked away from themselves and at things so long, that they have come to esteem the religious, learned, and civil institutions, as guards of property, and they deprecate assaults on these, because they feel them to be assaults on property. They measure their esteem of each other, by what each has, and not by what each is. But a cultivated man becomes ashamed of his property, out of new respect for his nature. Especially he hates what he has, if he see that it is accidental,—came to him by inheritance, or gift, or crime; then he feels that it is not having; it does not belong to him, has no root in him, and merely lies there, because no revolution or no robber takes it away. But that which a man is, does always by necessity acquire, and what the man acquires is living property, which does not wait the beck of rulers, or mobs, or revolutions, or fire, or storm, or bankruptcies, but perpetually renews itself wherever the man breathes. "Thy lot or portion of life," said the Caliph Ali,[41] "is seeking after thee; therefore be at rest from seeking after it." Our dependence on these foreign goods leads us to our slavish respect for numbers. The political parties meet in numerous conventions; the greater the concourse, and with each new uproar of announcement, The delegation from Essex!

[37]Statesmen and philosophers of classical Greece.

[38]Emerson contrasts 16th- and 17th-century navigators with 19th-century Arctic explorers.

[39]Emerson capitalizes what would then have been a technical term introduced during the Napoleonic wars, and indicating a temporary encampment, without tents.

[40]French historian and biographer of Napoleon (1766–1842).

[41]Emerson found this sentence by the 7th-century successor of Mohammed in Ockley's *History of the Saracens* (1718).

The Democrats from New Hampshire! The Whigs of Maine! the young patriot feels himself stronger than before by a new thousand of eyes and arms. In like manner the reformers summon conventions, and vote and resolve in multitude. Not so, O friends! will the God deign to enter and inhabit you, but by a method precisely the reverse. It is only as a man puts off all foreign support, and stands alone, that I see him to be strong and to prevail. He is weaker by every recruit to his banner. Is not a man better than a town? Ask nothing of men, and in the endless mutation, thou only firm column must presently appear the upholder of all that surrounds thee. He who knows that power is inborn, that he is weak because he has looked for good out of him and elsewhere, and so perceiving, throws himself unhesitatingly on his thought, instantly rights himself, stands in the erect position, commands his limbs, works miracles; just as a man who stands on his feet is stronger than a man who stands on his head.

So use all that is called Fortune. Most men gamble with her, and gain all, and lose all, as her wheel rolls. But do thou leave as unlawful these winnings, and deal with Cause and Effect, the chancellors of God. In the Will work and acquire, and thou hast chained the wheel of Chance, and shalt sit hereafter out of fear from her rotations. A political victory, a rise of rents, the recovery of your sick, or the return of your absent friend, or some other favorable event, raises your spirits, and you think good days are preparing for you. Do not believe it. Nothing can bring you peace but yourself. Nothing can bring you peace but the triumph of principles.

1841, 1847

Circles

Nature centres into balls,
And her proud ephemerals,
Fast to surface and outside,
Scan the profile of the sphere;
Knew they what that signified,
A new genesis were here.[1]

The eye is the first circle; the horizon which it forms is the second; and throughout nature this primary figure is repeated without end. It is the highest emblem in the cipher of the world. St. Augustine[2] described the nature of God as a circle whose centre was everywhere, and its circumference nowhere. We are all our lifetime reading the copious sense of this first of forms. One moral we have already deduced in

[1]Emerson added the motto to this essay in 1847.

[2]Emerson copied this specific passage from John Norris's *Intelligible World* (1704), mistaking Augustine as the author. The metaphoric association of God with circles was widespread in early religious writings.

considering the circular or compensatory character of every human action. Another analogy we shall now trace; that every action admits of being outdone. Our life is an apprenticeship to the truth, that around every circle another can be drawn; that there is no end in nature, but every end is a beginning; that there is always another dawn risen on mid-noon,[3] and under every deep a lower deep opens.

This fact, as far as it symbolizes the moral fact of the Unattainable, the flying Perfect, around which the hands of man can never meet, at once the inspirer and the condemner of every success, may conveniently serve us to connect many illustrations of human power in every department.

There are no fixtures in nature. The universe is fluid and volatile. Permanence is but a word of degrees. Our globe seen by God, is a transparent law, not a mass of facts. The law dissolves the fact and holds it fluid. Our culture is the predominance of an idea which draws after it this train of cities and institutions. Let us rise into another idea: they will disappear. The Greek sculpture is all melted away, as if it had been statues of ice: here and there a solitary figure or fragment remaining, as we see flecks and scraps of snow left in cold dells and mountain clefts, in June and July. For, the genius that created it, creates now somewhat else. The Greek letters last a little longer, but are already passing under the same sentence, and tumbling into the inevitable pit which the creation of new thought opens for all that is old. The new continents are built out of the ruins of an old planet: the new races fed out of the decomposition of the foregoing. New arts destroy the old. See the investment of capital in aqueducts, made useless by hydraulics; fortifications, by gunpowder; roads and canals, by railways; sails, by steam; steam by electricity.

You admire this tower of granite, weathering the hurts of so many ages. Yet a little waving hand built this huge wall, and that which builds, is better than that which is built. The hand that built, can topple it down much faster. Better than the hand, and nimbler, was the invisible thought which wrought through it, and thus ever behind the coarse effect, is a fine cause, which, being narrowly seen, is itself the effect of a finer cause. Every thing looks permanent until its secret is known. A rich estate appears to women a firm and lasting fact; to a merchant, one easily created out of any materials, and easily lost. An orchard, good tillage, good grounds, seem a fixture, like a gold mine, or a river, to a citizen; but to a large farmer, not much more fixed than the state of the crop. Nature looks provokingly stable and secular, but it has a cause like all the rest; and when once I comprehend that, will these fields stretch so immovably wide, these leaves hang so individually considerable? Permanence is a word of degrees. Every thing is medial. Moons are no more bounds to spiritual power than bat-balls.

The key to every man is his thought. Sturdy and defying though he look, he has a helm which he obeys, which is, the idea after which all his facts are classified. He can only be reformed by showing him a new idea which commands his own. The life of man is a self-evolving circle, which, from a ring imperceptibly small, rushes on all sides outwards to new and larger circles, and that without end. The extent to which this generation of circles, wheel without wheel will go, depends on the force or truth of the individual soul. For, it is the inert effort of each thought having formed itself into a circular wave of circumstance,—as, for instance, an empire, rules of an art, a local usage, a religious rite,—to heap itself on that ridge, and to solidify, and hem in

[3]Cf. *Paradise Lost,* V, 310–11.

the life. But if the soul is quick and strong, it bursts over that boundary on all sides, and expands another orbit on the great deep, which also runs up into a high wave, with attempt again to stop and to bind. But the heart refuses to be imprisoned; in its first and narrowest pulses, it already tends outward with a vast force, and to immense and innumerable expansions.

Every ultimate fact is only the first of a new series. Every general law only a particular fact of some more general law presently to disclose itself. There is no outside, no enclosing wall, no circumference to us. The man finishes his story,—how good! how final! how it puts a new face on all things! He fills the sky. Lo! on the other side rises also a man, and draws a circle around the circle we had just pronounced the outline of the sphere. Then already is our first speaker, not man, but only a first speaker. His only redress is forthwith to draw a circle outside of his antagonist. And so men do by themselves. The result of to-day which haunts the mind and cannot be escaped, will presently be abridged into a word, and the principle that seemed to explain nature, will itself be included as one example of a bolder generalization. In the thought of to-morrow there is a power to upheave all thy creed, all the creeds, all the literatures of the nations, and marshal thee to a heaven which no epic dream has yet depicted. Every man is not so much a workman in the world, as he is a suggestion of that he should be. Men walk as prophecies of the next age.

Step by step we scale this mysterious ladder: the steps are actions; the new prospect is power. Every several result is threatened and judged by that which follows. Every one seems to be contradicted by the new; it is only limited by the new. The new statement is always hated by the old, and, to those dwelling in the old, comes like an abyss of skepticism. But the eye soon gets wonted to it, for the eye and it are effects of one cause; then its innocency and benefit appear, and, presently, all its energy spent, it pales and dwindles before the revelation of the new hour.

Fear not the new generalization. Does the fact look crass and material, threatening to degrade thy theory of spirit? Resist it not; it goes to refine and raise thy theory of matter just as much.

There are no fixtures to men, if we appeal to consciousness. Every man supposes himself not to be fully understood; and if there is any truth in him, if he rests at last on the divine soul, I see not how it can be otherwise. The last chamber, the last closet, he must feel, was never opened; there is always a residuum unknown, unanalyzable. That is, every man believes that he has a greater possibility.

Our moods do not believe in each other. To-day, I am full of thoughts, and can write what I please. I see no reason why I should not have the same thought, the same power of expression to-morrow. What I write, whilst I write it, seems the most natural thing in the world: but, yesterday, I saw a dreary vacuity in this direction in which now I see so much; and a month hence, I doubt not, I shall wonder who he was that wrote so many continuous pages. Alas for this infirm faith, this will not strenuous, this vast ebb of a vast flow! I am God in nature; I am a weed by the wall.

The continual effort to raise himself above himself, to work a pitch above his last height, betrays itself in a man's relations. We thirst for approbation, yet cannot forgive the approver. The sweet of nature is love; yet if I have a friend, I am tormented by my imperfections. The love of me accuses the other party. If he were high enough to slight me, then could I love him, and rise by my affection to new heights. A man's growth is seen in the successive choirs of his friends. For every friend whom he loses for truth, he gains a better. I thought, as I walked in the woods and mused on my friends, why should I play with them this game of idolatry? I know and see too well, when not voluntarily blind, the speedy limits of persons called high and worthy. Rich, noble, and great they are by the liberality of our speech, but truth is sad. O blessed Spirit, whom I forsake for these, they are not thou! Every personal consideration that we allow, costs us heavenly state. We sell the thrones of angels for a short and turbulent pleasure.

How often must we learn this lesson? Men cease to interest us when we find their limitations. The only sin is limitation. As soon as you once come up with a man's limitations, it is all over with him. Has he talents? has he enterprises? has he knowledge? it boots not. Infinitely alluring and attractive was he to you yesterday, a great hope, a sea to swim in; now, you have found his shores, found it a pond, and you care not if you never see it again.

Each new step we take in thought reconciles twenty seemingly discordant facts, as expressions of one law. Aristotle and Plato are reckoned the respective heads of two schools. A wise man will see that Aristotle Platonizes. By going one step farther back in thought, discordant opinions are reconciled, by being seen to be two extremes of one principle, and we can never go so far back as to preclude a still higher vision.

Beware when the great God lets loose a thinker on this planet. Then all things are at risk. It is as when a conflagration has broken out in a great city, and no man knows what is safe, or where it will end. There is not a piece of science, but its flank may be turned to-morrow; there is not any literary reputation, not the so-called eternal names of fame, that may not be revised and condemned. The very hopes of man, the thoughts of his heart, the religion of nations, the manners and morals of mankind, are all at the mercy of a new generalization. Generalization is always a new influx of the divinity into the mind. Hence the thrill that attends it.

Valor consists in the power of self-recovery, so that a man cannot have his flank turned, cannot be outgeneralled, but put him where you will, he stands. This can only be by his preferring truth to his past apprehension of truth; and his alert acceptance of it from whatever quarter; the intrepid conviction that his laws, his relations to society, his christianity, his world may at any time be superseded and decease.

There are degrees in idealism. We learn first to play with it academically, as the magnet was once a toy. Then we see in the heyday of youth and poetry that it may be true, that it is true in gleams and fragments. Then, its countenance waxes stern and grand, and we see that it must be true. It now shows itself ethical and practical. We learn that God IS; that he is in me; and that all things are shadows of him. The idealism of Berkeley[4] is only a crude statement of the idealism of Jesus, and that, again, is a crude statement of the fact that all nature is the rapid efflux of goodness executing and organizing itself. Much more obviously is history and the state of the world at any one time, directly dependent on the intellectual classification then existing in the minds of men. The things which are dear to men at this hour, are so on account

[4]Eighteenth-century English bishop and philosopher.

of the ideas which have emerged on their mental horizon, and which cause the present order of things as a tree bears its apples. A new degree of culture would instantly revolutionize the entire system of human pursuits.

Conversation is a game of circles. In conversation we pluck up the termini which bound the common of silence on every side. The parties are not to be judged by the spirit[5] they partake and even express under this Pentecost.[6] To-morrow they will have receded from this high-water mark. To-morrow you shall find them stooping under the old packsaddles. Yet let us enjoy the cloven flame whilst it glows on our walls. When each new speaker strikes a new light, emancipates us from the oppression of the last speaker, to oppress us with the greatness and exclusiveness of his own thought, then yields us to another redeemer, we seem to recover our rights, to become men. O what truths profound and executable only in ages and orbs, are supposed in the announcement of every truth! In common hours, society sits cold and statuesque. We all stand waiting, empty,—knowing, possibly, that we can be full, surrounded by mighty symbols which are not symbols to us, but prose and trivial toys. Then cometh the god, and converts the statues into fiery men, and by a flash of his eye burns up the veil which shrouded all things, and the meaning of the very furniture, of cup and saucer, of chair and clock and tester, is manifest. The facts which loomed so large in the fogs of yesterday,—property, climate, breeding, personal beauty, and the like, have strangely changed their proportions. All that we reckoned settled, shakes and rattles; and literatures, cities, climates, religions, leave their foundations, and dance before our eyes. And yet here again see the swift circumscription.[7] Good as is discourse, silence is better, and shames it. The length of the discourse indicates the distance of thought betwixt the speaker and the hearer. If they were at a perfect understanding in any part, no words would be necessary thereon. If at one in all parts, no words would be suffered.

Literature is a point outside of our hodiernal[8] circle, through which a new one may be described. The use of literature is to afford us a platform whence we may command a view of our present life, a purchase by which we may move it. We fill ourselves with ancient learning; install ourselves the best we can in Greek, in Punic,[9] in Roman houses, only that we may wiselier see French, English, and American houses and modes of living. In like manner, we see literature best from the midst of wild nature, or from the din of affairs, or from a high religion. The field cannot be well seen from within the field. The astronomer must have his diameter of the earth's orbit as a base to find the parallax of any star.

Therefore, we value the poet. All the argument, and all the wisdom, is not in the encyclopedia, or the treatise on metaphysics, or the Body of Divinity, but in the sonnet or the play. In my daily work I incline to repeat my old steps, and do not believe in remedial force, in the power of change and reform. But some Petrarch or Ariosto,[10] filled with the new wine of his imagination, writes me an ode, or a brisk

[5]the spirit . . . flame. Cf. Acts 2:1–4.
[6]Christian celebration of the coming of the Holy Ghost to the apostles.
[7]The 1847 edition's "circumspection," meaning to look around or to be cautious, was probably a printer's variant for the 1841 version, indicating the drawing of limits or boundaries, of *termini.*
[8]Of the present day.
[9]Ancient civilization of Carthage.
[10]Poets of the Italian Renaissance.

romance, full of daring thought and action. He smites and arouses me with his shrill tones, breaks up my whole chain of habits, and I open my eye on my own possibilities. He claps wings to the sides of all the solid old lumber of the world, and I am capable once more of choosing a straight path in theory and practice.

We have the same need to command a view of the religion of the world. We can never see christianity from the catechism:—from the pastures, from a boat in the pond, from amidst the songs of wood-birds, we possibly may. Cleansed by the elemental light and wind, steeped in the sea of beautiful forms which the field offers us, we may chance to cast a right glance back upon biography. Christianity is rightly dear to the best of mankind; yet was there never a young philosopher whose breeding had fallen into the christian church, by whom that brave text of Paul's, was not specially prized:—"Then shall also the Son be subject unto Him who put all things under him, that God may be all in all."[11] Let the claims and virtues of persons be never so great and welcome, the instinct of man presses eagerly onward to the impersonal and illimitable, and gladly arms itself against the dogmatism of bigots with this generous word, out of the book itself.

The natural world may be conceived of as a system of concentric circles, and we now and then detect in nature slight dislocations, which apprize us that this surface on which we now stand, is not fixed, but sliding. These manifold tenacious qualities, this chemistry and vegetation, these metals and animals, which seem to stand there for their own sake, are means and methods only,—are words of God, and as fugitive as other words. Has the naturalist or chemist learned his craft, who has explored the gravity of atoms and the elective affinities, who has not yet discerned the deeper law whereof this is only a partial or approximate statement, namely, that like draws to like; and that the goods which belong to you, gravitate to you, and need not be pursued with pains and cost? Yet is that statement approximate also, and not final. Omnipresence is a higher fact. Not through subtle, subterranean channels, need friend and fact be drawn to their counterpart, but, rightly considered, these things proceed from the eternal generation of the soul. Cause and effect are two sides of one fact.

The same law of eternal procession ranges all that we call the virtues, and extinguishes each in the light of a better. The great man will not be prudent in the popular sense; all his prudence will be so much deduction from his grandeur. But it behoves each to see when he sacrifices prudence, to what god he devotes it; if to ease and pleasure, he had better be prudent still: if to a great trust, he can well spare his mule and panniers, who has a winged chariot instead. Geoffrey draws on his boots to go through the woods, that his feet may be safer from the bite of snakes; Aaron never thinks of such a peril. In many years, neither is harmed by such an accident. Yet it seems to me that with every precaution you take against such an evil, you put yourself into the power of the evil. I suppose that the highest prudence is the lowest prudence. Is this too sudden a rushing from the centre to the verge of our orbit? Think how many times we shall fall back into pitiful calculations, before we take up our rest in the great sentiment, or make the verge of to-day the new centre. Besides, your bravest sentiment is familiar to the humblest men. The poor and the low have their way of expressing the last facts of philosophy as well as you. "Blessed be

[11] I Cor. 15:28.

nothing," and "the worse things are, the better they are," are proverbs which express the transcendentalism of common life.

One man's justice is another's injustice; one man's beauty, another's ugliness; one man's wisdom, another's folly; as one beholds the same objects from a higher point. One man thinks justice consists in paying debts, and has no measure in his abhorrence of another who is very remiss in this duty, and makes the creditor wait tediously. But that second man has his own way of looking at things; asks himself, which debt must I pay first, the debt to the rich, or the debt to the poor? the debt of money, or the debt of thought to mankind, of genius to nature? For you, O broker, there is no other principle but arithmetic. For me, commerce is of trivial import; love, faith, truth of character, the aspiration of man, these are sacred: nor can I detach one duty, like you, from all other duties, and concentrate my forces mechanically on the payment of moneys. Let me live onward: you shall find that, though slower, the progress of my character will liquidate all these debts without injustice to higher claims. If a man should dedicate himself to the payment of notes, would not this be injustice? Does he owe no debt but money? And are all claims on him to be postponed to a landlord's or a banker's?

There is no virtue which is final; all are initial. The virtues of society are vices of the saint. The terror of reform is the discovery that we must cast away our virtues, or what we have always esteemed such, into the same pit that has consumed our grosser vices.

> "Forgive his crimes, forgive his virtues too,
> Those smaller faults, half converts to the right."[12]

It is the highest power of divine moments that they abolish our contritions also. I accuse myself of sloth and unprofitableness, day by day; but when these waves of God flow into me, I no longer reckon lost time. I no longer poorly compute my possible achievement by what remains to me of the month or the year; for these moments confer a sort of omnipresence and omnipotence, which asks nothing of duration, but sees that the energy of the mind is commensurate with the work to be done, without time.

And thus, O circular philosopher, I hear some reader exclaim, you have arrived at a fine pyrrhonism,[13] at an equivalence and indifferency of all actions, and would fain teach us, that, *if we are true,* forsooth, our crimes may be lively stones out of which we shall construct the temple of the true God.[14]

I am not careful to justify myself. I own I am gladdened by seeing the predominance of the saccharine principle throughout vegetable nature, and not less by beholding in morals that unrestrained inundation of the principle of good into every chink and hole that selfishness has left open, yea, into selfishness and sin itself; so that no evil is pure, nor hell itself without its extreme satisfactions. But lest I should mislead any when I have my own head, and obey my whims, let me remind the reader that I am only an experimenter. Do not set the least value on what I do, or the least discredit on what I do not, as if I pretended to settle anything as true or false. I

[12]Edward Young, *The Complaint; or Night Thoughts* (1742–1745).

[13]Radical skepticism, suspension of judgment.

[14]Cf. I Peter 2:5.

unsettle all things. No facts are to me sacred; none are profane; I simply experiment, an endless seeker, with no Past at my back.

Yet this incessant movement and progression, which all things partake, could never become sensible to us, but by contrast to some principle of fixture or stability in the soul. Whilst the eternal generation of circles proceeds, the eternal generator abides. That central life is somewhat superior to creation, superior to knowledge and thought, and contains all its circles. Forever it labors to create a life and thought as large and excellent as itself, suggesting to our thought a certain development, as if that which is made, instructs how to make a better.

Thus there is no sleep, no pause, no preservation, but all things renew, germinate, and spring. Why should we import rags and relics into the new hour? Nature abhors the old, and old age seems the only disease: all others run into this one. We call it by many names,—fever, intemperance, insanity, stupidity, and crime: they are all forms of old age: they are rest, conservatism, appropriation, inertia, not newness, not the way onward. We grizzle[15] every day. I see no need of it. Whilst we converse with what is above us, we do not grow old, but grow young. Infancy, youth, receptive, aspiring, with religious eye looking upward, counts itself nothing, and abandons itself to the instruction flowing from all sides. But the man and woman of seventy assume to know all, they have outlived their hope, they renounce aspiration, accept the actual for the necessary, and talk down to the young. Let them then become organs of the Holy Ghost; let them be lovers; let them behold truth; and their eyes are uplifted, their wrinkles smoothed, they are perfumed again with hope and power. This old age ought not to creep on a human mind. In nature, every moment is new; the past is always swallowed and forgotten; the coming only is sacred. Nothing is secure but life, transition, the energizing spirit. No love can be bound by oath or covenant to secure it against a higher love. No truth so sublime but it may be trivial tomorrow in the light of new thoughts. People wish to be settled: only as far as they are unsettled, is there any hope for them.

Life is a series of surprises. We do not guess to-day the mood, the pleasure, the power of to-morrow, when we are building up our being. Of lower states,—of acts of routine and sense,—we can tell somewhat; but the masterpieces of God, the total growths and universal movements of the soul, he hideth; they are incalculable. I can know that truth is divine and helpful, but how it shall help me, I can have no guess, for, *so to be* is the sole inlet of *so to know.* The new position of the advancing man has all the powers of the old, yet has them all new. It carries in its bosom all the energies of the past, yet is itself an exhalation of the morning. I cast away in this new moment all my once hoarded knowledge, as vacant and vain. Now, for the first time, seem I to know any thing rightly. The simplest words,—we do not know what they mean, except when we love and aspire.

The difference between talents and character is adroitness to keep the old and trodden round, and power and courage to make a new road to new and better goals. Character makes an overpowering present, a cheerful, determined hour, which fortifies all the company, by making them see that much is possible and excellent, that was not thought of. Character dulls the impression of particular events. When we see

[15]To grow gray-haired, to age.

the conqueror, we do not think much of any one battle or success. We see that we had exaggerated the difficulty. It was easy to him. The great man is not convulsible or tormentable; events pass over him without much impression. People say sometimes, 'See what I have overcome; see how cheerful I am; see how completely I have triumphed over these black events.' Not if they still remind me of the black event. True conquest is the causing the calamity to fade and disappear as an early cloud of insignificant result in a history so large and advancing.

The one thing which we seek with insatiable desire, is to forget ourselves, to be surprised out of our propriety, to lose our sempiternal memory, and to do something without knowing how or why; in short, to draw a new circle. Nothing great was ever achieved without enthusiasm.[16] The way of life is wonderful: it is by abandonment. The great moments of history are the facilities of performance through the strength of ideas, as the works of genius and religion. "A man," said Oliver Cromwell,[17] "never rises so high as when he knows not whither he is going." Dreams and drunkenness, the use of opium and alcohol are the semblance and counterfeit of this oracular genius, and hence their dangerous attraction for men. For the like reason, they ask the aid of wild passions, as in gaming and war, to ape in some manner these flames and generosities of the heart.

1841, 1847

The Poet

A moody child and wildly wise
Pursued the game with joyful eyes,
Which chose, like meteors, their way,
And rived the dark with private ray:
They overleapt the horizon's edge,
Searched with Apollo's privilege;
Through man, and woman, and sea, and star,
Saw the dance of nature forward far;
Through worlds, and races, and terms, and times,
Saw musical order, and pairing rhymes.

Olympian bards who sung
Divine ideas below,
Which always find us young,
And always keep us so.[1]

[16]Quoted from Coleridge, *The Statesman's Manual* (1816).

[17]English general and Lord Protector (1599–1658).

[1]These two poetic mottoes are by Emerson. The first verse is taken from his unfinished masque, "A Discontented Poet," and the quatrain is from "Ode to Beauty."

Those who are esteemed umpires of taste, are often persons who have acquired some knowledge of admired pictures or sculptures, and have an inclination for whatever is elegant; but if you inquire whether they are beautiful souls, and whether their own acts are like fair pictures, you learn that they are selfish and sensual. Their cultivation is local, as if you should rub a log of dry wood in one spot to produce fire, all the rest remaining cold. Their knowledge of the fine arts is some study of rules and particulars, or some limited judgment of color or form, which is exercised for amusement or for show. It is a proof of the shallowness of the doctrine of beauty, as it lies in the minds of our amateurs, that men seem to have lost the perception of the instant dependence of form upon soul. There is no doctrine of forms in our philosophy. We were put into our bodies, as fire is put into a pan, to be carried about; but there is no accurate adjustment between the spirit and the organ, much less is the latter the germination of the former. So in regard to other forms, the intellectual men do not believe in any essential dependence of the material world on thought and volition. Theologians think it a pretty air-castle to talk of the spiritual meaning of a ship or a cloud, of a city or a contract, but they prefer to come again to the solid ground of historical evidence; and even the poets are contented with a civil and conformed manner of living, and to write poems from the fancy, at a safe distance from their own experience. But the highest minds of the world have never ceased to explore the double meaning, or, shall I say, the quadruple, or the centuple, or much more manifold meaning, of every sensuous fact: Orpheus,[2] Empedocles, Heraclitus,[3] Plato, Plutarch, Dante, Swedenborg, and the masters of sculpture, picture, and poetry. For we are not pans and barrows, nor even porters of the fire and torch-bearers, but children of the fire, made of it, and only the same divinity transmuted, and at two or three removes, when we know least about it. And this hidden truth, that the fountains whence all this river of Time, and its creatures, floweth, are intrinsically ideal and beautiful, draws us to the consideration of the nature and functions of the Poet, or the man of Beauty, to the means and materials he uses, and to the general aspect of the art in the present time.

The breadth of the problem is great, for the poet is representative. He stands among partial men for the complete man, and apprises us not of his wealth, but of the commonwealth. The young man reveres men of genius, because, to speak truly, they are more himself than he is. They receive of the soul as he also receives, but they more. Nature enhances her beauty to the eye of loving men, from their belief that the poet is beholding her shows at the same time. He is isolated among his contemporaries, by truth and by his art, but with this consolation in his pursuits, that they will draw all men sooner or later. For all men live by truth, and stand in need of expression. In love, in art, in avarice, in politics, in labor, in games, we study to utter our painful secret. The man is only half himself, the other half is his expression.

Notwithstanding this necessity to be published, adequate expression is rare. I know not how it is that we need an interpreter; but the great majority of men seem to be minors, who have not yet come into possession of their own, or mutes, who cannot report the conversation they have had with nature. There is no man who does not

[2]The list includes the mythological poet Orpheus, whom Emerson and contemporaries treated as a historic figure.

[3]Empedocles and Heraclitus were 5th-century Greek philosophers.

anticipate a supersensual utility in the sun, and stars, earth, and water. These stand and wait to render him a peculiar service.[4] But there is some obstruction, or some excess of phlegm in our constitution, which does not suffer them to yield the due effect. Too feeble fall the impressions of nature on us to make us artists. Every touch should thrill. Every man should be so much an artist, that he could report in conversation what had befallen him. Yet, in our experience, the rays or appulses have sufficient force to arrive at the senses, but not enough to reach the quick, and compel the reproduction of themselves in speech. The poet is the person in whom these powers are in balance, the man without impediment, who sees and handles that which others dream of, traverses the whole scale of experience, and is representative of man, in virtue of being the largest power to receive and to impart.

For the Universe has three children, born at one time, which reappear, under different names, in every system of thought, whether they be called cause, operation, and effect; or, more poetically, Jove, Pluto, Neptune; or, theologically, the Father, the Spirit, and the Son; but which we will call here, the Knower, the Doer, and the Sayer. These stand respectively for the love of truth, for the love of good, and for the love of beauty. These three are equal. Each is that which he is essentially, so that he cannot be surmounted or analyzed, and each of these three has the power of the others latent in him, and his own patent.

The poet is the sayer, the namer, and represents beauty. He is a sovereign, and stands on the centre. For the world is not painted, or adorned, but is from the beginning beautiful; and God has not made some beautiful things, but Beauty is the creator of the universe. Therefore the poet is not any permissive potentate, but is emperor in his own right. Criticism is infested with a cant of materialism, which assumes that manual skill and activity is the first merit of all men, and disparages such as say and do not, overlooking the fact, that some men, namely, poets, are natural sayers, sent into the world to the end of expression, and confounds them with those whose province is action, but who quit it to imitate the sayers. But Homer's words are as costly and admirable to Homer, as Agamemnon's victories are to Agamemnon. The poet does not wait for the hero or the sage, but, as they act and think primarily, so he writes primarily what will and must be spoken, reckoning the others, though primaries also, yet, in respect to him, secondaries and servants; as sitters or models in the studio of a painter, or as assistants who bring building materials to an architect.

For poetry was all written before time was, and whenever we are so finely organized that we can penetrate into that region where the air is music, we hear those primal warblings, and attempt to write them down, but we lose ever and anon a word, or a verse, and substitute something of our own, and thus miswrite the poem. The men of more delicate ear write down these cadences more faithfully, and these transcripts, though imperfect, become the songs of the nations. For nature is as truly beautiful as it is good, or as it is reasonable, and must as much appear, as it must be done, or be known. Words and deeds are quite indifferent modes of the divine energy. Words are also actions, and actions are a kind of words.

The sign and credentials of the poet are, that he announces that which no man foretold. He is the true and only doctor;[5] he knows and tells; he is the only teller of

[4]Cf. Milton, Sonnet XIX, line 14.
[5]Used in the earlier sense of "teacher."

news, for he was present and privy to the appearance which he describes. He is a beholder of ideas, and an utterer of the necessary and causal. For we do not speak now of men of poetical talents, or of industry and skill in metre, but of the true poet. I took part in a conversation the other day, concerning a recent writer of lyrics, a man of subtle mind, whose head appeared to be a music-box of delicate tunes and rhythms, and whose skill, and command of language, we could not sufficiently praise. But when the question arose, whether he was not only a lyrist, but a poet, we were obliged to confess that he is plainly a contemporary, not an eternal man. He does not stand out of our low limitations, like a Chimborazo under the line,[6] running up from the torrid base through all the climates of the globe, with belts of the herbage of every latitude on its high and mottled sides; but this genius is the landscape-garden of a modern house, adorned with fountains and statues, with well-bred men and women standing and sitting in the walks and terraces. We hear, through all the varied music, the ground-tone of conventional life. Our poets are men of talents who sing, and not the children of music. The argument is secondary, the finish of the verses is primary.

For it is not metres, but a metre-making argument, that makes a poem,—a thought so passionate and alive, that, like the spirit of a plant or an animal, it has an architecture of its own, and adorns nature with a new thing. The thought and the form are equal in the order of time, but in the order of genesis the thought is prior to the form. The poet has a new thought: he has a whole new experience to unfold; he will tell us how it was with him, and all men will be the richer in his fortune. For, the experience of each new age requires a new confession, and the world seems always waiting for its poet. I remember, when I was young, how much I was moved one morning by tidings that genius had appeared in a youth who sat near me at table. He had left his work, and gone rambling none knew whither, and had written hundreds of lines, but could not tell whether that which was in him was therein told: he could tell nothing but that all was changed,—man, beast, heaven, earth, and sea. How gladly we listened! how credulous! Society seemed to be compromised. We sat in the aurora of a sunrise which was to put out all the stars. Boston seemed to be at twice the distance it had the night before, or was much farther than that. Rome,—what was Rome? Plutarch and Shakspeare were in the yellow leaf,[7] and Homer no more should be heard of. It is much to know that poetry has been written this very day, under this very roof, by your side. What! that wonderful spirit has not expired! these stony moments are still sparkling and animated! I had fancied that the oracles were all silent,[8] and nature had spent her fires, and behold! all night, from every pore, these fine auroras have been streaming. Every one has some interest in the advent of the poet, and no one knows how much it may concern him. We know that the secret of the world is profound, but who or what shall be our interpreter, we know not. A mountain ramble, a new style of face, a new person, may put the key into our hands. Of course, the value of genius to us is in the veracity of its report. Talent may frolic

[6]Ecuadorian mountain located below the equator.

[7]Cf. *Macbeth,* Act V, iii, 22–23: "I have lived long enough. My way of life is fallen into the sere, the yellow leaf."

[8]Cf. Milton, "On the Morning of Christ's Nativity," line 173 "The oracles are dumb."

and juggle; genius realizes and adds. Mankind, in good earnest, have arrived so far in understanding themselves and their work, that the foremost watchman on the peak announces his news. It is the truest word ever spoken, and the phrase will be the fittest, most musical, and the unerring voice of the world for that time.

All that we call sacred history attests that the birth of a poet is the principal event in chronology. Man, never so often deceived, still watches for the arrival of a brother who can hold him steady to a truth, until he has made it his own. With what joy I begin to read a poem, which I confide in as an inspiration! And now my chains are to be broken; I shall mount above these clouds and opaque airs in which I live,—opaque, though they seem transparent,—and from the heaven of truth I shall see and comprehend my relations. That will reconcile me to life, and renovate nature, to see trifles animated by a tendency, and to know what I am doing. Life will no more be a noise; now I shall see men and women, and know the signs by which they may be discerned from fools and satans. This day shall be better than my birthday: then I became an animal: now I am invited into the science of the real. Such is the hope, but the fruition is postponed. Oftener it falls, that this winged man, who will carry me into the heaven, whirls me into mists, then leaps and frisks about with me as it were from cloud to cloud, still affirming that he is bound heavenward; and I, being myself a novice, am slow in perceiving that he does not know the way into the heavens, and is merely bent that I should admire his skill to rise, like a fowl or a flying fish, a little way from the ground or the water; but the all-piercing, all-feeding, and ocular air of heaven, that man shall never inhabit. I tumble down again soon into my old nooks, and lead the life of exaggerations as before, and have lost some faith[9] in the possibility of any guide who can lead me thither where I would be.

But leaving these victims of vanity, let us, with new hope, observe how nature, by worthier impulses, has ensured the poet's fidelity to his office of announcement and affirming, namely, by the beauty of things, which becomes a new, and higher beauty, when expressed. Nature offers all her creatures to him as a picture-language. Being used as a type, a second wonderful value appears in the object, far better than its old value, as the carpenter's stretched cord, if you hold your ear close enough, is musical in the breeze. "Things more excellent than every image," says Jamblichus,[10] "are expressed through images." Things admit of being used as symbols, because nature is a symbol, in the whole, and in every part. Every line we can draw in the sand, has expression; and there is no body without its spirit or genius. All form is an effect of character; all condition, of the quality of the life; all harmony, of health; (and, for this reason, a perception of beauty should be sympathetic, or proper only to the good). The beautiful rests on the foundations of the necessary. The soul makes the body, as the wise Spenser teaches:—

"So every spirit, as it is most pure,
And hath in it the more of heavenly light,
So it the fairer body doth procure
To habit in, and it more fairly dight,

[9]In a correction copy of the 1844 edition, Emerson marked the change from "lost my faith."

[10]Fourth-century Neo-Platonic philosopher.

With cheerful grace and amiable sight.
For, of the soul, the body form doth take,
For soul is form, and doth the body make."[11]

Here we find ourselves, suddenly, not in a critical speculation, but in a holy place, and should go very warily and reverently. We stand before the secret of the world, there where Being passes into Appearance, and Unity into Variety.

The Universe is the externization of the soul. Wherever the life is, that bursts into appearance around it. Our science is sensual, and therefore superficial. The earth, and the heavenly bodies, physics, and chemistry, we sensually treat, as if they were self-existent; but these are the retinue of that Being we have. "The mighty heaven," said Proclus,[12] "exhibits, in its transfigurations, clear images of the splendor of intellectual perceptions; being moved in conjunction with the unapparent periods of intellectual natures." Therefore, science always goes abreast with the just elevation of the man, keeping step with religion and metaphysics; or, the state of science is an index of our self-knowledge. Since everything in nature answers to a moral power, if any phenomenon remains brute and dark, it is because the corresponding faculty in the observer is not yet active.

No wonder, then, if these waters be so deep, that we hover over them with a religious regard. The beauty of the fable proves the importance of the sense; to the poet, and to all others; or, if you please, every man is so far a poet as to be susceptible of these enchantments of nature: for all men have the thoughts whereof the universe is the celebration. I find that the fascination resides in the symbol. Who loves nature? Who does not? Is it only poets, and men of leisure and cultivation, who live with her? No; but also hunters, farmers, grooms, and butchers, though they express their affection in their choice of life, and not in their choice of words. The writer wonders what the coachman or the hunter values in riding, in horses, and dogs. It is not superficial qualities. When you talk with him, he holds these at as slight a rate as you. His worship is sympathetic; he has no definitions, but he is commanded in nature, by the living power which he feels to be there present. No imitation, or playing of these things, would content him; he loves the earnest of the north wind, of rain, of stone, and wood, and iron. A beauty not explicable, is dearer than a beauty which we can see to the end of. It is nature the symbol, nature certifying the supernatural, body overflowed by life, which he worships, with coarse, but sincere rites.

The inwardness, and mystery, of this attachment, drive men of every class to the use of emblems. The schools of poets, and philosophers, are not more intoxicated with their symbols, than the populace with theirs. In our political parties, compute the power of badges and emblems. See the huge wooden ball[13] rolled by successive ardent crowds from Baltimore to Bunker hill! In the political processions, Lowell goes in a loom, and Lynn in a shoe, and Salem in a ship. Witness the cider-barrel, the log-cabin, the hickory-stick, the palmetto, and all the cognizances of party. See the power of national emblems. Some stars, lilies, leopards, a crescent, a lion, an eagle, or other figure, which came into credit God knows how, on an old rag of bunting,

[11]From Edmund Spenser's "An Hymn in Honour of Beauty" (1596).

[12]Fifth-century Greek Neo-Platonic philosopher.

[13]The political slogan "Keep the ball rolling" was used by the Whigs in the 1840 presidential campaign. The passage goes on to list other political and manufacturing emblems.

blowing in the wind, on a fort, at the ends of the earth, shall make the blood tingle under the rudest, or the most conventional exterior. The people fancy they hate poetry, and they are all poets and mystics!

Beyond this universality of the symbolic language, we are apprised of the divineness of this superior use of things, whereby the world is a temple, whose walls are covered with emblems, pictures, and commandments of the Diety, in this, that there is no fact in nature which does not carry the whole sense of nature; and the distinctions which we make in events, and in affairs, of low and high, honest and base, disappear when nature is used as a symbol. Thought makes everything fit for use. The vocabulary of an omniscient man would embrace words and images excluded from polite conversation. What would be base, or even obscene, to the obscene, becomes illustrious, spoken in a new connexion of thought. The piety of the Hebrew prophets purges their grossness. The circumcision is an example of the power of poetry to raise the low and offensive. Small and mean things serve as well as great symbols. The meaner the type by which a law is expressed, the more pungent it is, and the more lasting in the memories of men: just as we choose the smallest box, or case, in which any needful utensil can be carried. Bare lists of words are found suggestive, to an imaginative and excited mind; as it is related of Lord Chatham, that he was accustomed to read in Bailey's Dictionary,[14] when he was preparing to speak in Parliament. The poorest experience is rich enough for all the purposes of expressing thought. Why covet a knowledge of new facts? Day and night, house and garden, a few books, a few actions, serve us as well as would all trades and all spectacles. We are far from having exhausted the significance of the few symbols we use. We can come to use them yet with a terrible simplicity. It does not need that a poem should be long. Every word was once a poem. Every new relation is a new word. Also, we use defects and deformities to a sacred purpose, so expressing our sense that the evils of the world are such only to the evil eye. In the old mythology, mythologists observe, defects are ascribed to divine natures, as lameness to Vulcan, blindness to Cupid, and the like, to signify exuberances.

For, as it is dislocation and detachment from the life of God, that makes things ugly, the poet, who re-attaches things to nature and the Whole,—re-attaching even artificial things, and violations of nature, to nature, by a deeper insight,—disposes very easily of the most disagreeable facts. Readers of poetry see the factory-village, and the railway, and fancy that the poetry of the landscape is broken up by these; for these works of art are not yet consecrated in their reading; but the poet sees them fall within the great Order not less than the bee-hive, or the spider's geometrical web. Nature adopts them very fast into her vital circles, and the gliding train of cars she loves like her own. Besides, in a centred mind, it signifies nothing how many mechanical inventions you exhibit. Though you add millions, and never so surprising, the fact of mechanics has not gained a grain's weight. The spiritual fact remains unalterable, by many or by few particulars; as no mountain is of any appreciable height to break the curve of the sphere. A shrewd country-boy goes to the city for the first time, and the complacent citizen is not satisfied with his little wonder. It is not that

[14]Renowned orator William Pitt, Earl of Chatham (1708–1778); widely used etymological dictionary (1721) by Nathan Bailey.

he does not see all the fine houses, and know that he never saw such before, but he disposes of them as easily as the poet finds place for the railway. The chief value of the new fact, is to enhance the great and constant fact of Life, which can dwarf any and every circumstance, and to which the belt of wampum, and the commerce of America, are alike.

The world being thus put under the mind for verb and noun, the poet is he who can articulate it. For, though life is great, and fascinates, and absorbs,—and though all men are intelligent of the symbols through which it is named,—yet they cannot originally use them. We are symbols, and inhabit symbols; workmen, work, and tools, words and things, birth and death, all are emblems; but we sympathize with the symbols, and, being infatuated with the economical uses of things, we do not know that they are thoughts. The poet, by an ulterior intellectual perception, gives them a power which makes their old use forgotten, and puts eyes, and a tongue, into every dumb and inanimate object. He perceives the thought's independence of the symbol, the stability of the thought, the accidency and fugacity[15] of the symbol. As the eyes of Lyncæus[16] were said to see through the earth, so the poet turns the world to glass, and shows us all things in their right series and procession. For, through that better perception, he stands one step nearer to things, and sees the flowing or metamorphosis; perceives that thought is multiform; that within the form of every creature is a force impelling it to ascend into a higher form; and, following with his eyes the life, uses the forms which express that life, and so his speech flows with the flowing of nature. All the facts of the animal economy,—sex, nutriment, gestation, birth, growth—are symbols of the passage of the world into the soul of man, to suffer there a change, and reappear a new and higher fact. He uses forms according to the life, and not according to the form. This is true science. The poet alone knows astronomy, chemistry, vegetation, and animation, for he does not stop at these facts, but employs them as signs. He knows why the plain, or meadow of space, was strown with these flowers we call suns, and moons, and stars; why the great deep is adorned with animals, with men, and gods; for, in every word he speaks he rides on them as the horses of thought.

By virtue of this science the poet is the Namer, or Language-maker, naming things sometimes after their appearance, sometimes after their essence, and giving to every one its own name and not another's, thereby rejoicing the intellect, which delights in detachment or boundary. The poets made all the words, and therefore language is the archives of history, and, if we must say it, a sort of tomb of the muses. For, though the origin of most of our words is forgotten, each word was at first a stroke of genius, and obtained currency, because for the moment it symbolized the world to the first speaker and to the hearer. The etymologist finds the deadest word to have been once a brilliant picture. Language is fossil poetry. As the limestone of the continent consists of infinite masses of the shells of animalcules, so language is made up of images, or tropes, which now, in their secondary use, have long ceased to remind us of their poetic origin. But the poet names the thing because he sees it, or comes one step nearer to it than any other. This expression, or naming, is not art, but a second nature, grown out of the first, as a leaf out of a tree. What we call

[15]Transitoriness, volatility.

[16]One of the Argonauts, noted for his eyesight; from Apollonius Rhodius, *The Argonautica* (3rd–2nd cent B.C.).

nature, is a certain self-regulated motion, or change; and nature does all things by her own hands, and does not leave another to baptize her, but baptizes herself; and this through the metamorphosis again. I remember that a certain poet[17] described it to me thus:

Genius is the activity which repairs the decays of things, whether wholly or partly of a material and finite kind. Nature, through all her kingdoms, insures herself. Nobody cares for planting the poor fungus: so she shakes down from the gills of one agaric countless spores, any one of which, being preserved, transmits new billions of spores to-morrow or next day. The new agaric of this hour has a chance which the old one had not. This atom of seed is thrown into a new place, not subject to the accidents which destroyed its parent two rods off. She makes a man; and having brought him to ripe age, she will no longer run the risk of losing this wonder at a blow, but she detaches from him a new self, that the kind may be safe from accidents to which the individual is exposed. So when the soul of the poet has come to ripeness of thought, she detaches and sends away from it its poems or songs,—a fearless, sleepless, deathless progeny, which is not exposed to the accidents of the weary kingdom of time: a fearless, vivacious offspring, clad with wings (such was the virtue of the soul out of which they came), which carry them fast and far, and infix them irrecoverably into the hearts of men. These wings are the beauty of the poet's soul. The songs, thus flying immortal from their mortal parent, are pursued by clamorous flights of censures, which swarm in far greater numbers, and threaten to devour them; but these last are not winged. At the end of a very short leap they fall plump down, and rot, having received from the souls out of which they came no beautiful wings. But the melodies of the poet ascend, and leap, and pierce into the deeps of infinite time.

So far the bard taught me, using his freer speech. But nature has a higher end, in the production of new individuals, than security, namely, *ascension,* or, the passage of the soul into higher forms. I knew, in my younger days, the sculptor who made the statue of the youth which stands in the public garden. He was, as I remember, unable to tell, directly, what made him happy, or unhappy, but by wonderful indirections he could tell. He rose one day, according to his habit, before the dawn, and saw the morning break, grand as the eternity out of which it came, and, for many days after, he strove to express this tranquillity, and, lo! his chisel had fashioned out of marble the form of a beautiful youth, Phosphor,[18] whose aspect is such, that, it is said, all persons who look on it become silent. The poet also resigns himself to his mood, and that thought which agitated him is expressed, but *alter idem,*[19] in a manner totally new. The expression is organic, or, the new type which things themselves take when liberated. As, in the sun, objects paint their images on the retina of the eye, so they, sharing the aspiration of the whole universe, tend to paint a far more delicate copy of their essence in his mind. Like the metamorphosis of things into higher organic forms, is their change into melodies. Over everything stands its dæmon, or

[17]The framed passage is from Emerson's own journal.

[18]Greek god Lucifer, the morning star. In his journal, Emerson himself is the sculptor, cutting a statue of Hesperus, the evening star.

[19]Latin for "the same yet different."

soul, and, as the form of the thing is reflected by the eye, so the soul of the thing is reflected by a melody. The sea, the mountain-ridge, Niagara, and every flower-bed, pre-exist, or super-exist, in pre-cantations, which sail like odors in the air, and when any man goes by with an ear sufficiently fine, he overhears them, and endeavors to write down the notes, without diluting or depraving them. And herein is the legitimation of criticism, in the mind's faith, that the poems are a corrupt version of some text in nature, with which they ought to be made to tally. A rhyme in one of our sonnets should not be less pleasing than the iterated nodes of a sea-shell, or the resembling difference of a group of flowers. The pairing[20] of the birds is an idyl, not tedious as our idyls are; a tempest is a rough ode without falsehood or rant; a summer, with its harvest sown, reaped, and stored, is an epic song, subordinating how many admirably executed parts. Why should not the symmetry and truth that modulate these, glide into our spirits, and we participate the invention of nature?

This insight, which expresses itself by what is called Imagination, is a very high sort of seeing, which does not come by study, but by the intellect being where and what it sees, by sharing the path, or circuit of things through forms, and so making them translucid to others. The path of things is silent. Will they suffer a speaker to go with them? A spy they will not suffer; a lover, a poet, is the transcendency of their own nature,—him they will suffer. The condition of true naming, on the poet's part, is his resigning himself to the divine *aura* which breathes through forms, and accompanying that.

It is a secret which every intellectual man quickly learns, that, beyond the energy of his possessed and conscious intellect, he is capable of a new energy (as of an intellect doubled on itself), by abandonment to the nature of things; that, beside his privacy of power as an individual man, there is a great public power, on which he can draw, by unlocking, at all risks, his human doors, and suffering the ethereal tides to roll and circulate through him: then he is caught up into the life of the Universe, his speech is thunder, his thought is law, and his words are universally intelligible as the plants and animals. The poet knows that he speaks adequately, then only when he speaks somewhat wildly, or, "with the flower of the mind;"[21] not with the intellect, used as an organ, but with the intellect released from all service, and suffered to take its direction from its celestial life; or, as the ancients[22] were wont to express themselves, not with intellect alone, but with the intellect inebriated by nectar. As the traveller who has lost his way, throws his reins on his horse's neck, and trusts to the instinct of the animal to find his road, so must we do with the divine animal who carries us through this world. For if in any manner we can stimulate this instinct, new passages are opened for us into nature, the mind flows into and through things hardest and highest, and the metamorphosis is possible.

This is the reason why bards love wine, mead, narcotics, coffee, tea, opium, the fumes of sandal-wood and tobacco, or whatever other procurers of animal exhilaration. All men avail themselves of such means as they can, to add this extraordinary power to their normal powers; and to this end they prize conversation, music,

[20]Mating.

[21]Translation of a Greek phrase from the "Chaldean Oracles," selections of which appeared in translation in *The Dial* in 1844.

[22]Emerson is paraphrasing Plotinus and Proclus.

pictures, sculpture, dancing, theatres, travelling, war, mobs, fires, gaming, politics, or love, or science, or animal intoxication, which are several coarser or finer *quasi*-mechanical substitutes for the true nectar, which is the ravishment of the intellect by coming nearer to the fact. These are auxiliaries to the centrifugal tendency of a man, to his passage out into free space, and they help him to escape the custody of that body in which he is pent up, and of that jail-yard of individual relations in which he is enclosed. Hence a great number of such as were professionally expressors of Beauty, as painters, poets, musicians, and actors, have been more than others wont to lead a life of pleasure and indulgence; all but the few who received the true nectar; and, as it was a spurious mode of attaining freedom, as it was an emancipation not into the heavens, but into the freedom of baser places, they were punished for that advantage they won, by a dissipation and deterioration. But never can any advantage be taken of nature by a trick. The spirit of the world, the great calm presence of the creator, comes not forth to the sorceries of opium or of wine. The sublime vision comes to the pure and simple soul in a clean and chaste body. That is not an inspiration which we owe to narcotics, but some counterfeit excitement and fury. Milton says, that the lyric poet may drink wine and live generously, but the epic poet, he who shall sing of the gods, and their descent unto men, must drink water out of a wooden bowl.[23] For poetry is not 'Devil's wine,'[24] but God's wine. It is with this as it is with toys. We fill the hands and nurseries of our children with all manner of dolls, drums, and horses, withdrawing their eyes from the plain face and sufficing objects of nature, the sun, and moon, the animals, the water, and stones, which should be their toys. So the poet's habit of living should be set on a key so low, that the common influences should delight him. His cheerfulness should be the gift of the sunlight; the air should suffice for his inspiration, and he should be tipsy with water. That spirit which suffices quiet hearts, which seems to come forth to such from every dry knoll of sere grass, from every pine-stump, and half-imbedded stone, on which the dull March sun shines, comes forth to the poor and hungry, and such as are of simple taste. If thou fill thy brain with Boston and New York, with fashion and covetousness, and wilt stimulate thy jaded senses with wine and French coffee, thou shalt find no radiance of wisdom in the lonely waste of the pinewoods.

If the imagination intoxicates the poet, it is not inactive in other men. The metamorphosis excites in the beholder an emotion of joy. The use of symbols has a certain power of emancipation and exhilaration for all men. We seem to be touched by a wand, which makes us dance and run about happily, like children. We are like persons who come out of a cave or cellar into the open air. This is the effect on us of tropes, fables, oracles, and all poetic forms. Poets are thus liberating gods. Men have really got a new sense, and found within their world, another world, or nest of worlds; for, the metamorphosis once seen, we divine that it does not stop. I will not now consider how much this makes the charm of algebra and the mathematics, which also have their tropes, but it is felt in every definition; as, when Aristotle defines *space* to be an immovable vessel, in which things are contained;—or, when Plato defines a *line* to be a flowing point; or, *figure* to be a bound of solid; and many the

[23]Paraphrase of Milton's "Elegia Sexta" (1629).
[24]Emerson attributed this definition to the Church Fathers.

like. What a joyful sense of freedom we have, when Vitruvius announces the old opinion of artists, that no architect can build any house well, who does not know something of anatomy. When Socrates, in Charmides, tells us that the soul is cured of its maladies by certain incantations, and that these incantations are beautiful reasons, from which temperance is generated in souls; when Plato calls the world an animal; and Timæus affirms that the plants also are animals; or affirms a man to be a heavenly tree, growing with his root, which is his head, upward; and, as George Chapman, following him, writes,—

> "So in our tree of man, whose nervie root
> Springs in his top;"

when Orpheus speaks of hoariness as "that white flower which marks extreme old age;" when Proclus calls the universe the statue of the intellect; when Chaucer, in his praise of 'Gentilesse,' compares good blood in mean condition to fire, which, though carried to the darkest house betwixt this and the mount of Caucasus, will yet hold its natural office, and burn as bright as if twenty thousand men did it behold; when John saw, in the apocalypse, the ruin of the world through evil, and the stars fall from heaven, as the figtree casteth her untimely fruit; when Æsop reports the whole catalogue of common daily relations through the masquerade of birds and beasts;—we take the cheerful hint of the immortality of our essence, and its versatile habit and escapes, as when the gypsies say of themselves, "it is in vain to hang them, they cannot die."[25]

The poets are thus liberating gods. The ancient British bards had for the title of their order, "Those who are free throughout the world."[26] They are free, and they make free. An imaginative book renders us much more service at first, by stimulating us through its tropes, than afterward, when we arrive at the precise sense of the author. I think nothing is of any value in books, excepting the transcendental and extraordinary. If a man is inflamed and carried away by his thought, to that degree that he forgets the authors and the public, and heeds only this one dream, which holds him like an insanity, let me read his paper, and you may have all the arguments and histories and criticism. All the value which attaches to Pythagoras, Paracelsus, Cornelius Agrippa, Cardan, Kepler, Swedenborg, Schelling, Oken,[27] or any other who introduces questionable facts into his cosmogony, as angels, devils, magic, astrology, palmistry, mesmerism, and so on, is the certificate we have of departure from routine, and that here is a new witness. That also is the best success in conversation, the magic of liberty, which puts the world, like a ball, in our hands. How cheap even the liberty then seems; how mean to study, when an emotion communicates to the intellect the power to sap and upheave nature: how great the perspective! nations, times,

[25]Emerson's catalogue of "poets" is hardly the usual literary tradition; it includes Greek philosophers, a Roman architect, a translator of Homer, a mythological poet, as well as the authors of the Apocalypse, *The Canterbury Tales,* and Aesop's *Fables,* and ends with a saying of the "gypsies" taken from George Borrow's *The Zincali* (1842).

[26]Emerson found this "motto" in a biography of the popular English poet Felicia Hemans, in which she discussed her interest in "Welsh Melodies."

[27]Catalogue of scientific and religious theoreticians from ancient Greece to Emerson's own day.

systems, enter and disappear, like threads in tapestry of large figure and many colors; dream delivers us to dream, and, while the drunkenness lasts, we will sell our bed, our philosophy, our religion, in our opulence.

There is good reason why we should prize this liberation. The fate of the poor shepherd, who, blinded and lost in the snowstorm, perishes in a drift within a few feet of his cottage door, is an emblem of the state of man. On the brink of the waters of life and truth, we are miserably dying. The inaccessibleness of every thought but that we are in, is wonderful. What if you come near to it,—you are as remote, when you are nearest, as when you are farthest. Every thought is also a prison; every heaven is also a prison. Therefore we love the poet, the inventor, who in any form, whether in an ode, or in an action, or in looks and behavior, has yielded us a new thought. He unlocks our chains, and admits us to a new scene.

This emancipation is dear to all men, and the power to impart it, as it must come from greater depth and scope of thought, is a measure of intellect. Therefore all books of the imagination endure, all which ascend to that truth, that the writer sees nature beneath him, and uses it as his exponent. Every verse or sentence, possessing this virtue, will take care of its own immortality. The religions of the world are the ejaculations of a few imaginative men.

But the quality of the imagination is to flow, and not to freeze. The poet did not stop at the color, or the form, but read their meaning; neither may he rest in this meaning, but he makes the same objects exponents of his new thought. Here is the difference betwixt the poet and the mystic, that the last nails a symbol to one sense, which was a true sense for a moment, but soon becomes old and false. For all symbols are fluxional; all language is vehicular and transitive, and is good, as ferries and horses are, for conveyance, not as farms and houses are, for homestead. Mysticism consists in the mistake of an accidental and individual symbol for an universal one. The morning-redness happens to be the favorite meteor to the eyes of Jacob Behmen,[28] and comes to stand to him for truth and faith; and he believes should stand for the same realities to every reader. But the first reader prefers as naturally the symbol of a mother and child, or a gardener and his bulb, or a jeweller polishing a gem. Either of these, or of a myriad more, are equally good to the person to whom they are significant. Only they must be held lightly, and be very willingly translated into the equivalent terms which others use. And the mystic must be steadily told,—All that you say is just as true without the tedious use of that symbol as with it. Let us have a little algebra, instead of this trite rhetoric,—universal signs, instead of these village symbols,—and we shall both be gainers. The history of hierarchies seems to show, that all religious error consisted in making the symbol too stark and solid, and, at last, nothing but an excess of the organ of language.

Swedenborg, of all men in the recent ages, stands eminently for the translator of nature into thought. I do not know the man in history to whom things stood so uniformly for words. Before him the metamorphosis continually plays. Everything on which his eye rests, obeys the impulses of moral nature. The figs become grapes whilst he eats them. When some of his angels affirmed a truth, the laurel twig which they held blossomed in their hands. The noise which, at a distance, appeared like gnashing and thumping, on coming nearer was found to be the voice of disputants.

[28](Jakob Böhme), German mystic (1575–1624).

The men, in one of his visions, seen in heavenly light, appeared like dragons, and seemed in darkness; but, to each other, they appeared as men, and, when the light from heaven shone into their cabin, they complained of the darkness, and were compelled to shut the window that they might see.

There was this perception in him, which makes the poet or seer an object of awe and terror, namely, that the same man, or society of men, may wear one aspect to themselves and their companions, and a different aspect to higher intelligences. Certain priests, whom he describes as conversing very learnedly together, appeared to the children, who were at some distance, like dead horses; and many the like misappearances. And instantly the mind inquires, whether these fishes under the bridge, yonder oxen in the pasture, those dogs in the yard, are immutably fishes, oxen, and dogs, or only so appear to me, and perchance to themselves appear upright men; and whether I appear as a man to all eyes. The Bramins and Pythagoras propounded the same question, and if any poet has witnessed the transformation, he doubtless found it in harmony with various experiences. We have all seen changes as considerable in wheat and caterpillars. He is the poet, and shall draw us with love and terror, who sees, through the flowing vest, the firm nature, and can declare it.

I look in vain for the poet whom I describe. We do not, with sufficient plainness, or sufficient profoundness, address ourselves to life, nor dare we chaunt[29] our own times and social circumstance. If we filled the day with bravery, we should not shrink from celebrating it. Time and nature yield us many gifts, but not yet the timely man, the new religion, the reconciler, whom all things await. Dante's praise is, that he dared to write his autobiography in colossal cipher, or into universality. We have yet had no genius in America, with tyrannous eye, which knew the value of our incomparable materials, and saw, in the barbarism and materialism of the times, another carnival of the same gods whose picture he so much admires in Homer; then in the middle age; then in Calvinism. Banks and tariffs, the newspaper and caucus, methodism and unitarianism, are flat and dull to dull people, but rest on the same foundations of wonder as the town of Troy and the temple of Delphi, and are as swiftly passing away. Our logrolling, our stumps and their politics, our fisheries, our Negroes, and Indians, our boasts, and our repudiations,[30] the wrath of rogues, and the pusillanimity of honest men, the northern trade, the southern planting, the western clearing, Oregon, and Texas,[31] are yet unsung. Yet America is a poem in our eyes; its ample geography dazzles the imagination, and it will not wait long for metres. If I have not found that excellent combination of gifts in my countrymen which I seek, neither could I aid myself to fix the idea of the poet by reading now and then in Chalmers's[32] collection of five centuries of English poets. These are wits, more than poets, though there have been poets among them. But when we adhere to the ideal of the poet, we have our difficulties even with Milton and Homer. Milton is too literary, and Homer too literal and historical.

[29]Emerson's usual way of spelling "chant."

[30]William Gilman suggested this correction for the first-edition's "boats," to contrast with "repudiations," *i.e.,* refusals to acknowledge or pay debts.

[31]States involved in contemporary political disputes.

[32]Alexander Chalmers: *Works of the English Poets* (21 volumes; 1810).

But I am not wise enough for a national criticism, and must use the old largeness a little longer, to discharge my errand from the muse to the poet concerning his art.

Art is the path of the creator to his work. The paths, or methods, are ideal and eternal, though few men ever see them, not the artist himself for years, or for a lifetime, unless he come into the conditions. The painter, the sculptor, the composer, the epic rhapsodist, the orator, all partake one desire, namely, to express themselves symmetrically and abundantly, not dwarfishly and fragmentarily. They found or put themselves in certain conditions, as, the painter and sculptor before some impressive human figures; the orator, into the assembly of the people; and the others, in such scenes as each has found exciting to his intellect; and each presently feels the new desire. He hears a voice, he sees a beckoning. Then he is apprised, with wonder, what herds of dæmons hem him in. He can no more rest; he says, with the old painter, "By God, it is in me, and must go forth of me." He pursues a beauty, half seen, which flies before him. The poet pours out verses in every solitude. Most of the things he says are conventional, no doubt; but by and by he says something which is original and beautiful. That charms him. He would say nothing else but such things. In our way of talking, we say, 'That is yours, this is mine;' but the poet knows well that it is not his; that it is as strange and beautiful to him as to you; he would fain hear the like eloquence at length. Once having tasted this immortal ichor,[33] he cannot have enough of it, and, as an admirable creative power exists in these intellections, it is of the last importance that these things get spoken. What a little of all we know is said! What drops of all the sea of our science are baled up! and by what accident it is that these are exposed, when so many secrets sleep in nature! Hence the necessity of speech and song; hence these throbs and heart-beatings in the orator, at the door of the assembly, to the end, namely, that thought may be ejaculated as Logos, or Word.

Doubt not, O poet, but persist. Say, 'It is in me, and shall out.' Stand there, baulked and dumb, stuttering and stammering, hissed and hooted, stand and strive, until, at last, rage draw out of thee that *dream*-power which every night shows thee is thine own; a power transcending all limit and privacy, and by virtue of which a man is the conductor of the whole river of electricity. Nothing walks, or creeps, or grows, or exists, which must not in turn arise and walk before him as exponent of his meaning. Comes he to that power, his genius is no longer exhaustible. All the creatures, by pairs and by tribes, pour into his mind as into a Noah's ark, to come forth again to people a new world. This is like the stock of air for our respiration, or for the combustion of our fireplace, not a measure of gallons, but the entire atmosphere if wanted. And therefore the rich poets, as Homer, Chaucer, Shakspeare, and Raphael, have obviously no limits to their works, except the limits of their lifetime, and resemble a mirror carried through the street, ready to render an image of every created thing.

O poet! a new nobility is conferred in groves and pastures, and not in castles, or by the sword-blade, any longer. The conditions are hard, but equal. Thou shalt leave the world, and know the muse only. Thou shalt not know any longer the times, customs, graces, politics, or opinions of men, but shalt take all from the muse. For the time of towns is tolled from the world by funereal chimes, but in nature the univer-

[33]In Greek mythology, ethereal fluid that replaces the gods' blood.

sal hours are counted by succeeding tribes of animals and plants, and by growth of joy on joy. God wills also that thou abdicate a duplex and manifold life, and that thou be content that others speak for thee. Others shall be thy gentlemen, and shall represent all courtesy and worldly life for thee; others shall do the great and resounding actions also. Thou shalt lie close hid with nature, and canst not be afforded to the Capitol or the Exchange.[34] The world is full of renunciations and apprenticeships, and this is thine; thou must pass for a fool and a churl for a long season. This is the screen and sheath in which Pan has protected his well-beloved flower, and thou shalt be known only to thine own, and they shall console thee with tenderest love. And thou shalt not be able to rehearse the names of thy friends in thy verse, for an old shame before the holy ideal. And this is the reward: that the ideal shall be real to thee, and the impressions of the actual world shall fall like summer rain, copious, but not troublesome, to thy invulnerable essence. Thou shalt have the whole land for thy park and manor, the sea for thy bath and navigation, without tax and without envy; the woods and the rivers thou shalt own; and thou shalt possess that wherein others are only tenants and boarders. Thou true land-lord! sea-lord! air-lord! Wherever snow falls, or water flows, or birds fly, wherever day and night meet in twilight, wherever the blue heaven is hung by clouds, or sown with stars, wherever are forms with transparent boundaries, wherever are outlets into celestial space, wherever is danger, and awe, and love, there is Beauty, plenteous as rain, shed for thee, and though thou shouldst walk the world over, thou shalt not be able to find a condition inopportune or ignoble.

1844, 1847

Experience

The lords of life, the lords of life,—
I saw them pass,
In their own guise,
Like and unlike,
Portly and grim,
Use and Surprise,
Surface and Dream,
Succession swift, and spectral Wrong,
Temperament without a tongue,
And the inventor of the game
Omnipresent without name;—
Some to see, some to be guessed,
They marched from east to west:
Little man, least of all,
Among the legs of his guardians tall,
Walked about with puzzled look:—

[34]*I.e.,* to politics or banking.

Him by the hand dear nature took;
Dearest nature, strong and kind,
Whispered, 'Darling, never mind!
Tomorrow they will wear another face,
The founder thou! these are thy race!'[1]

Where do we find ourselves? In a series, of which we do not know the extremes, and believe that it has none. We wake and find ourselves on a stair: there are stairs below us, which we seem to have ascended; there are stairs above us, many a one, which go upward and out of sight. But the Genius which, according to the old belief, stands at the door by which we enter, and gives us the lethe[2] to drink, that we may tell no tales, mixed the cup too strongly, and we cannot shake off the lethargy now at noonday. Sleep lingers all our lifetime about our eyes, as night hovers all day in the boughs of the fir-tree. All things swim and glimmer. Our life is not so much threatened as our perception. Ghostlike we glide through nature, and should not know our place again. Did our birth fall in some fit of indigence and frugality in nature, that she was so sparing of her fire and so liberal of her earth, that it appears to us that we lack the affirmative principle, and though we have health and reason, yet we have no superfluity of spirit for new creation? We have enough to live and bring the year about, but not an ounce to impart or to invest. Ah that our Genius were a little more of a genius! We are like millers on the lower levels of a stream, when the factories above them have exhausted the water. We too fancy that the upper people must have raised their dams.

If any of us knew what we were doing, or where we are going, then when we think we best know! We do not know today whether we are busy or idle. In times when we thought ourselves indolent, we have afterwards discovered, that much was accomplished, and much was begun in us. All our days are so unprofitable while they pass, that 'tis wonderful where or when we ever got anything of this which we call wisdom, poetry, virtue. We never got it on any dated calendar day. Some heavenly days must have been intercalated somewhere, like those that Hermes won with dice of the Moon, that Osiris might be born.[3] It is said, all martyrdoms looked mean when they were suffered.[4] Every ship is a romantic object, except that we sail in. Embark, and the romance quits our vessel, and hangs on every other sail in the horizon. Our life looks trivial, and we shun to record it. Men seem to have learned of the horizon the art of perpetual retreating and reference. 'Yonder uplands are rich pasturage, and my neighbor has fertile meadow, but my field,' says the querulous farmer,[5] 'only holds the world together.' I quote another man's saying; unluckily, that other withdraws himself in the same way, and quotes me. 'Tis the trick of nature thus to degrade today; a good deal of buzz, and somewhere a result slipped magically in. Every roof is agreeable to the eye, until it is lifted; then we find tragedy and moaning women,

[1]The motto is by Emerson.
[2]In Greek mythology, drinking from the river Lethe produces forgetfulness.
[3]After the sun god had forbidden his wife to bear a child on any existing day, her lover Hermes won five extra days ("intercalated" or inserted) on which the Egyptian gods could be born. Cf. Plutarch's *Morals*.
[4]From Harriet Martineau's *Deerbrook: A Novel* (1839).
[5]The farmer's passages are from Emerson's journal.

and hard-eyed husbands, and deluges of lethe, and the men ask, 'What's the news?' as if the old were so bad. How many individuals can we count in society? how many actions? how many opinions? So much of our time is preparation, so much is routine, and so much retrospect, that the pith of each man's genius contracts itself to a very few hours. The history of literature—take the net result of Tiraboschi, Warton, or Schlegel,[6]—is a sum of very few ideas, and of very few original tales,—all the rest being variation of these. So in this great society wide lying around us, a critical analysis would find very few spontaneous actions. It is almost all custom and gross sense. There are even few opinions, and these seem organic in the speakers, and do not disturb the universal necessity.

What opium is instilled into all disaster! It shows formidable as we approach it, but there is at last no rough rasping friction, but the most slippery sliding surfaces: we fall soft on a thought: *Ate Dea* is gentle—

"Over men's heads walking aloft,
With tender feet treading so soft."[7]

People grieve and bemoan themselves, but it is not half so bad with them as they say. There are moods in which we court suffering, in the hope that here, at least, we shall find reality, sharp peaks and edges of truth. But it turns out to be scene-painting and counterfeit. The only thing grief has taught me, is to know how shallow it is. That, like all the rest, plays about the surface, and never introduces me into the reality, for contact with which, we would even pay the costly price of sons and lovers. Was it Boscovich[8] who found out that bodies never come in contact? Well, souls never touch their objects. An innavigable sea washes with silent waves between us and the things we aim at and converse with. Grief too will make us idealists. In the death of my son,[9] now more than two years ago, I seem to have lost a beautiful estate,—no more. I cannot get it nearer to me. If tomorrow I should be informed of the bankruptcy of my principal debtors, the loss of my property would be a great inconvenience to me, perhaps, for many years; but it would leave me as it found me,—neither better nor worse. So is it with this calamity: it does not touch me: something which I fancied was a part of me, which could not be torn away without tearing me, nor enlarged without enriching me, falls off from me, and leaves no scar. It was caducous. I grieve that grief can teach me nothing, nor carry me one step into real nature. The Indian[10] who was laid under a curse, that the wind should not blow on him, nor water flow to him, nor fire burn him, is a type of us all. The dearest events are summer-rain, and we the Para coats[11] that shed every drop. Nothing is left us now but death. We look to that with a grim satisfaction, saying, there at least is reality that will not dodge us.

I take this evanescence and lubricity of all objects, which lets them slip through our fingers then when we clutch hardest, to be the most unhandsome part of our condition. Nature does not like to be observed, and likes that we should be her fools

[6]Authors of Italian, English, and German literary histories.

[7]Goddess of mischief and discord as described in Homer's *Iliad,* XIX, 92–93.

[8]Eighteenth-century Italian physicist.

[9]Emerson's first child Waldo died in 1842 at the age of 5. His first wife Ellen had died in 1831, and his brother Edward in 1834.

[10]From Robert Southey's "The Curse of Kehama" (1810).

[11]Rubber coats, introduced after the development of vulcanization in 1839.

and playmates. We may have the sphere for our cricket-ball, but not a berry for our philosophy. Direct strokes she never gave us power to make; all our blows glance, all our hits are accidents. Our relations to each other are oblique and casual.

Dream delivers us to dream, and there is no end to illusion. Life is a train of moods like a string of beads, and, as we pass through them, they prove to be many-colored lenses which paint the world their own hue, and each shows only what lies in its focus. From the mountain you see the mountain. We animate what we can, and we see only what we animate. Nature and books belong to the eyes that see them. It depends on the mood of the man, whether he shall see the sunset or the fine poem. There are always sunsets, and there is always genius; but only a few hours so serene that we can relish nature or criticism. The more or less depends on structure or temperament. Temperament is the iron wire on which the beads are strung. Of what use is fortune or talent to a cold and defective nature? Who cares what sensibility or discrimination a man has at some time shown, if he falls asleep in his chair? or if he laugh and giggle? or if he apologize? or is infected with egotism? or thinks of his dollar? or cannot pass by food? or has gotten a child in his boyhood? Of what use is genius, if the organ is too convex or too concave, and cannot find a focal distance within the actual horizon of human life? Of what use, if the brain is too cold or too hot, and the man does not care enough for results, to stimulate him to experiment, and hold him up in it? or if the web is too finely woven, too irritable by pleasure and pain, so that life stagnates from too much reception, without due outlet? Of what use to make heroic vows of amendment, if the same old law-breaker is to keep them? What cheer can the religious sentiment yield, when that is suspected to be secretly dependent on the seasons of the year, and the state of the blood? I knew a witty physician who found the creed in the biliary duct, and used to affirm that if there was disease in the liver, the man became a Calvinist, and if that organ was sound, he became a Unitarian. Very mortifying is the reluctant experience that some unfriendly excess or imbecility neutralizes the promise of genius. We see young men who owe us a new world, so readily and lavishly they promise, but they never acquit the debt; they die young and dodge the account: or if they live, they lose themselves in the crowd.

Temperament also enters fully into the system of illusions, and shuts us in a prison of glass which we cannot see. There is an optical illusion about every person we meet. In truth, they are all creatures of given temperament, which will appear in a given character, whose boundaries they will never pass: but we look at them, they seem alive, and we presume there is impulse in them. In the moment, it seems impulse; in the year, in the lifetime, it turns out to be a certain uniform tune which the revolving barrel of the music-box must play. Men resist the conclusion in the morning, but adopt it as the evening wears on, that temper prevails over everything of time, place, and condition, and is inconsumable in the flames of religion. Some modifications the moral sentiment avails to impose, but the individual texture holds its dominion, if not to bias the moral judgments, yet to fix the measure of activity and of enjoyment.

I thus express the law as it is read from the platform of ordinary life, but must not leave it without noticing the capital exception. For temperament is a power which no man willingly hears any one praise but himself. On the platform of physics, we cannot resist the contracting influences of so-called science. Temperament puts all divinity to rout. I know the mental proclivity of physicians. I hear the chuckle of the phrenologists. Theoretic kidnappers and slave-drivers, they esteem each man the victim of another, who winds him round his finger by knowing the law of his being, and by such cheap signboards as the color of his beard, or the slope of his occiput, reads the inventory of his fortunes and character. The grossest ignorance does not disgust like this impudent knowingness. The physicians say, they are not materialists; but they are:—Spirit is matter reduced to an extreme thinness: O *so* thin!—But the definition of *spiritual* should be, *that which is its own evidence.* What notions do they attach to love! what to religion! One would not willingly pronounce these words in their hearing, and give them the occasion to profane them. I saw a gracious gentleman who adapts his conversation to the form of the head of the man he talks with! I had fancied that the value of life lay in its inscrutable possibilities; in the fact that I never know, in addressing myself to a new individual, what may befall me. I carry the keys of my castle in my hand, ready to throw them at the feet of my lord, whenever and in what disguise soever he shall appear. I know he is in the neighborhood, hidden among vagabonds. Shall I preclude my future, by taking a high seat, and kindly adapting my conversation to the shape of heads? When I come to that, the doctors shall buy me for a cent.—'But, sir, medical history; the report to the Institute; the proven facts!'—I distrust the facts and the inferences. Temperament is the veto or limitation-power in the constitution, very justly applied to restrain an opposite excess in the constitution, but absurdly offered as a bar to original equity. When virtue is in presence, all subordinate powers sleep. On its own level, or in view of nature, temperament is final. I see not, if one be once caught in this trap of so-called sciences, any escape for the man from the links of the chain of physical necessity. Given such an embryo, such a history must follow. On this platform, one lives in a sty of sensualism, and would soon come to suicide. But it is impossible that the creative power should exclude itself. Into every intelligence there is a door which is never closed, through which the creator passes. The intellect, seeker of absolute truth, or the heart, lover of absolute good, intervenes for our succor, and at one whisper of these high powers, we awake from ineffectual struggles with this nightmare. We hurl it into its own hell, and cannot again contract ourselves to so base a state.

The secret of the illusoriness is in the necessity of a succession of moods or objects. Gladly we would anchor, but the anchorage is quicksand. This onward trick of nature is too strong for us: *Pero si muove.*[12] When, at night, I look at the moon and stars, I seem stationary, and they to hurry. Our love of the real draws us to permanence, but health of body consists in circulation, and sanity of mind in variety or facility of association. We need change of objects. Dedication to one thought is quickly odious. We house with the insane, and must humor them; then conversation dies out. Once I took such delight in Montaigne, that I thought I should not need any other book; before that, in Shakspeare; then in Plutarch; then in Plotinus; at one time in Bacon; afterwards in Goethe; even in Bettine;[13] but now I turn the pages of either of them languidly, whilst I still cherish their genius. So with pictures; each will bear an

[12]"Nevertheless it moves": a variant of Galileo's famous comment after the Church forced him to deny that the earth moves around the sun.

[13]German writer Elizabeth von Arnim (1785–1859), whose book on Goethe Emerson described in 1842 as "the most remarkable book ever written by a woman."

emphasis of attention once, which it cannot retain, though we fain would continue to be pleased in that manner. How strongly I have felt of pictures, that when you have seen one well, you must take your leave of it; you shall never see it again. I have had good lessons from pictures, which I have since seen without emotion or remark. A deduction must be made from the opinion, which even the wise express of a new book or occurrence. Their opinion gives me tidings of their mood, and some vague guess at the new fact, but is nowise to be trusted as the lasting relation between that intellect and that thing. The child asks, 'Mamma, why don't I like the story as well as when you told it me yesterday?' Alas, child, it is even so with the oldest cherubim of knowledge. But will it answer thy question to say, Because thou wert born to a whole, and this story is a particular? The reason of the pain this discovery causes us (and we make it late in respect to works of art and intellect), is the plaint of tragedy which murmurs from it in regard to persons, to friendship and love.

That immobility and absence of elasticity which we find in the arts, we find with more pain in the artist. There is no power of expansion in men. Our friends early appear to us as representatives of certain ideas, which they never pass or exceed. They stand on the brink of the ocean of thought and power, but they never take the single step that would bring them there. A man is like a bit of Labrador spar,[14] which has no lustre as you turn it in your hand, until you come to a particular angle; then it shows deep and beautiful colors. There is no adaptation or universal applicability in men, but each has his special talent, and the mastery of successful men consists in adroitly keeping themselves where and when that turn shall be oftenest to be practised. We do what we must, and call it by the best names we can, and would fain have the praise of having intended the result which ensues. I cannot recall any form of man who is not superfluous sometimes. But is not this pitiful? Life is not worth the taking, to do tricks in.

Of course, it needs the whole society, to give the symmetry we seek. The parti-colored wheel must revolve very fast to appear white. Something is learned too by conversing with so much folly and defect. In fine, whoever loses, we are always of the gaining party. Divinity is behind our failures and follies also. The plays of children are nonsense, but very educative nonsense. So is it with the largest and solemnest things, with commerce, government, church, marriage, and so with the history of every man's bread, and the ways by which he is to come by it. Like a bird which alights nowhere, but hops perpetually from bough to bough, is the Power which abides in no man and in no woman, but for a moment speaks from this one, and for another moment from that one.

But what help from these fineries or pedantries? What help from thought? Life is not dialectics. We, I think, in these times, have had lessons enough of the futility of criticism. Our young people have thought and written much on labor and reform, and for all that they have written, neither the world nor themselves have got on a step. Intellectual tasting of life will not supersede muscular activity. If a man should consider the nicety of the passage of a piece of bread down his throat, he would starve. At Education-Farm,[15] the noblest theory of life sat on the noblest figures of

[14]Crystalline rock.

[15]Probably referring to Brook Farm, a commune Emerson had been invited to join.

young men and maidens, quite powerless and melancholy. It would not rake or pitch a ton of hay; it would not rub down a horse; and the men and maidens it left pale and hungry. A political orator wittily compared our party promises to western roads, which opened stately enough, with planted trees on either side, to tempt the traveller, but soon became narrow and narrower, and ended in a squirrel-track, and ran up a tree. So does culture with us; it ends in headache. Unspeakably sad and barren does life look to those, who a few months ago were dazzled with the splendor of the promise of the times. "There is now no longer any right course of action, nor any self-devotion left among the Iranis."[16] Objections and criticism we have had our fill of. There are objections to every course of life and action, and the practical wisdom infers an indifferency, from the omnipresence of objection. The whole frame of things preaches indifferency. Do not craze yourself with thinking, but go about your business anywhere. Life is not intellectual or critical, but sturdy. Its chief good is for well-mixed people who can enjoy what they find, without question. Nature hates peeping, and our mothers speak her very sense when they say, "Children, eat your victuals, and say no more of it." To fill the hour,—that is happiness; to fill the hour, and leave no crevice for a repentance or an approval. We live amid surfaces, and the true art of life is to skate well on them. Under the oldest mouldiest conventions, a man of native force prospers just as well as in the newest world, and that by skill of handling and treatment. He can take hold anywhere. Life itself is a mixture of power and form, and will not bear the least excess of either. To finish the moment, to find the journey's end in every step of the road, to live the greatest number of good hours, is wisdom. It is not the part of men but of fanatics, or of mathematicians, if you will, to say, that, the shortness of life considered, it is not worth caring whether for so short a duration we were sprawling in want, or sitting high. Since our office is with moments, let us husband them. Five minutes of today are worth as much to me, as five minutes in the next millennium. Let us be poised, and wise, and our own, today. Let us treat the men and women well: treat them as if they were real: perhaps they are. Men live in their fancy, like drunkards whose hands are too soft and tremulous for successful labor. It is a tempest of fancies, and the only ballast I know, is a respect to the present hour. Without any shadow of doubt, amidst this vertigo of shows and politics, I settle myself ever the firmer in the creed, that we should not postpone and refer and wish, but do broad justice where we are, by whomsoever we deal with, accepting our actual companions and circumstances, however humble or odious, as the mystic officials to whom the universe has delegated its whole pleasure for us. If these are mean and malignant, their contentment, which is the last victory of justice, is a more satisfying echo to the heart, than the voice of poets and the casual sympathy of admirable persons. I think that however a thoughtful man may suffer from the defects and absurdities of his company, he cannot without affectation deny to any set of men and women, a sensibility to extraordinary merit. The coarse and frivolous have an instinct of superiority, if they have not a sympathy, and honor it in their blind capricious way with sincere homage.

[16]From *Desatir,* a collection of ancient Persian prophetic works translated into English in 1818.

The fine young people despise life, but in me, and in such as with me are free from dyspepsia, and to whom a day is a sound and solid good, it is a great excess of politeness to look scornful and to cry for company. I am grown by sympathy a little eager and sentimental, but leave me alone, and I should relish every hour and what it brought me, the potluck of the day, as heartily as the oldest gossip in the bar-room. I am thankful for small mercies. I compared notes with one of my friends who expects everything of the universe, and is disappointed when anything is less than the best, and I found that I begin at the other extreme, expecting nothing, and am always full of thanks for moderate goods. I accept the clangor and jangle of contrary tendencies. I find my account in sots and bores also. They give a reality to the circumjacent picture, which such a vanishing meteorous appearance can ill spare. In the morning I awake, and find the old world, wife, babes, and mother, Concord and Boston, the dear old spiritual world, and even the dear old devil not far off. If we will take the good we find, asking no questions, we shall have heaping measures. The great gifts are not got by analysis. Everything good is on the highway. The middle region of our being is the temperate zone. We may climb into the thin and cold realm of pure geometry and lifeless science, or sink into that of sensation. Between these extremes is the equator of life, of thought, of spirit, of poetry,—a narrow belt. Moreover, in popular experience, everything good is on the highway. A collector peeps into all the picture-shops of Europe, for a landscape of Poussin, a crayon-sketch of Salvator;[17] but the Transfiguration, the Last Judgment, the Communion of St. Jerome, and what are as transcendent as these, are on the walls of the Vatican, the Uffizi, or the Louvre,[18] where every footman may see them; to say nothing of nature's pictures in every street, of sunsets and sunrises every day, and the sculpture of the human body never absent. A collector recently bought at public auction, in London, for one hundred and fifty-seven guineas, an autograph of Shakspeare: but for nothing a schoolboy can read Hamlet, and can detect secrets of highest concernment yet unpublished therein. I think I will never read any but the commonest books,—the Bible, Homer, Dante, Shakspeare, and Milton. Then we are impatient of so public a life and planet, and run hither and thither for nooks and secrets. The imagination delights in the wood-craft of Indians, trappers, and bee-hunters. We fancy that we are strangers, and not so intimately domesticated in the planet as the wild man, and the wild beast and bird. But the exclusion reaches them also; reaches the climbing, flying, gliding, feathered and four-footed man. Fox and woodchuck, hawk and snipe, and bittern, when nearly seen, have no more root in the deep world than man, and are just such superficial tenants of the globe. Then the new molecular philosophy shows astronomical interspaces betwixt atom and atom, shows that the world is all outside: it has no inside.

The mid-world is best. Nature, as we know her, is no saint. The lights of the church, the ascetics, Gentoos and corn-eaters,[19] she does not distinguish by any favor. She comes eating and drinking and sinning. Her darlings, the great, the strong,

[17]Seventeenth-century French and Italian painters.

[18]Paintings by Raphael, Michelangelo, and Domenichino; museums of Rome, Florence, and Paris.

[19]Hindus and vegetarians; in the first edition Emerson paired Gentoos with Grahamites, the cultish followers of Sylvester Graham (1794–1851), a New England reformer and inventor of the graham cracker.

the beautiful, are not children of our law, do not come out of the Sunday School, nor weigh their food, nor punctually keep the commandments. If we will be strong with her strength, we must not harbor such disconsolate consciences, borrowed too from the consciences of other nations. We must set up the strong present tense against all the rumors of wrath, past or to come. So many things are unsettled which it is of the first importance to settle,—and, pending their settlement, we will do as we do. Whilst the debate goes forward on the equity of commerce, and will not be closed for a century or two, New and Old England may keep shop. Law of copyright and international copyright[20] is to be discussed, and, in the interim, we will sell our books for the most we can. Expediency of literature, reason of literature, lawfulness of writing down a thought, is questioned; much is to say on both sides, and, while the fight waxes hot, thou, dearest scholar, stick to thy foolish task, add a line every hour, and between whiles add a line. Right to hold land, right of property, is disputed, and the conventions convene, and before the vote is taken, dig away in your garden, and spend your earnings as a waif or godsend to all serene and beautiful purposes. Life itself is a bubble and a skepticism, and a sleep within a sleep.[21] Grant it, and as much more as they will,—but thou, God's darling! heed thy private dream: thou wilt not be missed in the scorning and skepticism: there are enough of them: stay there in thy closet, and toil, until the rest are agreed what to do about it. Thy sickness, they say, and thy puny habit, require that thou do this or avoid that, but know that thy life is a flitting state, a tent for a night, and do thou, sick or well, finish that stint. Thou art sick, but shalt not be worse, and the universe, which holds thee dear, shall be the better.

Human life is made up of the two elements, power and form, and the proportion must be invariably kept, if we would have it sweet and sound. Each of these elements in excess makes a mischief as hurtful as its defect. Everything runs to excess: every good quality is noxious, if unmixed, and, to carry the danger to the edge of ruin, nature causes each man's peculiarity to super-abound. Here, among the farms, we adduce the scholars as examples of this treachery. They are nature's victims of expression. You who see the artist, the orator, the poet, too near, and find their life no more excellent than that of mechanics or farmers, and themselves victims of partiality, very hollow and haggard, and pronounce them failures,—not heroes, but quacks,—conclude very reasonably that these arts are not for man, but are disease. Yet nature will not bear you out. Irresistible nature made men such, and makes legions more of such, every day. You love the boy reading in a book, gazing at a drawing, or a cast: yet what are these millions who read and behold, but incipient writers and sculptors? Add a little more of that quality which now reads and sees, and they will seize the pen and chisel. And if one remembers how innocently he began to be an artist, he perceives that nature joined with his enemy. A man is a golden impossibility. The line he must walk is a hair's breadth. The wise through excess of wisdom is made a fool.

[20]The United States did not pass an international copyright law until 1891, after years of heated debates over unauthorized publications.

[21]Cf. *The Tempest,* IV, i, 156–158.

How easily, if fate would suffer it, we might keep forever these beautiful limits, and adjust ourselves, once for all, to the perfect calculation of the kingdom of known cause and effect. In the street and in the newspapers, life appears so plain a business, that manly resolution and adherence to the multiplication-table through all weathers, will insure success. But ah! presently comes a day—or is it only a half-hour, with its angel-whispering—which discomfits the conclusions of nations and of years! Tomorrow again, everything looks real and angular, the habitual standards are reinstated, common sense is as rare as genius,—is the basis of genius, and experience is hands and feet to every enterprise;—and yet, he who should do his business on this understanding, would be quickly bankrupt. Power keeps quite another road than the turnpikes of choice and will, namely, the subterranean and invisible tunnels and channels of life. It is ridiculous that we are diplomatists, and doctors, and considerate people: there are no dupes like these. Life is a series of surprises, and would not be worth taking or keeping, if it were not. God delights to isolate us every day, and hide from us the past and the future. We would look about us, but with grand politeness he draws down before us an impenetrable screen of purest sky, and another behind us of purest sky. 'You will not remember,' he seems to say, 'and you will not expect.' All good conversation, manners, and action, come from a spontaneity which forgets usages, and makes the moment great. Nature hates calculators; her methods are saltatory and impulsive. Man lives by pulses; our organic movements are such; and the chemical and ethereal agents are undulatory and alternate; and the mind goes antagonizing on, and never prospers but by fits. We thrive by casualties. Our chief experiences have been casual. The most attractive class of people are those who are powerful obliquely, and not by the direct stroke: men of genius, but not yet accredited: one gets the cheer of their light, without paying too great a tax. Theirs is the beauty of the bird, or the morning light, and not of art. In the thought of genius there is always a surprise; and the moral sentiment is well called "the newness," for it is never other; as new to the oldest intelligence as to the young child,—"the kingdom that cometh without observation."[22] In like manner, for practical success, there must not be too much design. A man will not be observed in doing that which he can do best. There is a certain magic about his properest action, which stupefies your powers of observation, so that though it is done before you, you wist not of it. The art of life has a pudency, and will not be exposed. Every man is an impossibility, until he is born; every thing impossible, until we see a success. The ardors of piety agree at last with the coldest skepticism,—that nothing is of us or our works,—that all is of God. Nature will not spare us the smallest leaf of laurel. All writing comes by the grace of God, and all doing and having. I would gladly be moral, and keep due metes and bounds, which I dearly love, and allow the most to the will of man, but I have set my heart on honesty in this chapter, and I can see nothing at last, in success or failure, than more or less of vital force supplied from the Eternal. The results of life are uncalculated and uncalculable. The years teach much which the days never know. The persons who compose our company, converse, and come and go, and design and execute many things, and somewhat comes of it all, but an unlooked-for result. The individual is always mistaken. He designed many things, and drew in other persons as coadjutors, quarrelled with some or all, blundered much, and something is done; all

[22]Cf. Luke 17:20–21.

are a little advanced, but the individual is always mistaken. It turns out somewhat new, and very unlike what he promised himself.

The ancients, struck with this irreducibleness of the elements of human life to calculation, exalted Chance into a divinity, but that is to stay too long at the spark,—which glitters truly at one point,—but the universe is warm with the latency of the same fire. The miracle of life which will not be expounded, but will remain a miracle, introduces a new element. In the growth of the embryo, Sir Everard Home,[23] I think, noticed that the evolution was not from one central point, but coactive from three or more points. Life has no memory. That which proceeds in succession might be remembered, but that which is coexistent, or ejaculated from a deeper cause, as yet far from being conscious, knows not its own tendency. So is it with us, now skeptical, or without unity, because immersed in forms and effects all seeming to be of equal yet hostile value, and now religious, whilst in the reception of spiritual law. Bear with these distractions, with this coetaneous[24] growth of the parts: they will one day be *members,* and obey one will. On that one will, on that secret cause, they nail our attention and hope. Life is hereby melted into an expectation or a religion. Underneath the inharmonious and trivial particulars, is a musical perfection, the Ideal journeying always with us, the heaven without rent or seam. Do but observe the mode of our illumination. When I converse with a profound mind, or if at any time being alone I have good thoughts, I do not at once arrive at satisfactions, as when, being thirsty, I drink water, or go to the fire, being cold: no! but I am at first apprised of my vicinity to a new and excellent region of life. By persisting to read or to think, this region gives further sign of itself, as it were in flashes of light, in sudden discoveries of its profound beauty and repose, as if the clouds that covered it parted at intervals, and showed the approaching traveller the inland mountains, with the tranquil eternal meadows spread at their base, whereon flocks graze, and shepherds pipe and dance. But every insight from this realm of thought is felt as initial, and promises a sequel. I do not make it; I arrive there, and behold what was there already. I make! O no! I clap my hands in infantine joy and amazement, before the first opening to me of this august magnificence, old with the love and homage of innumerable ages, young with the life of life, the sunbright Mecca of the desert. And what a future it opens! I feel a new heart beating with the love of the new beauty. I am ready to die out of nature, and be born again into this new yet unapproachable America I have found in the West.

> "Since neither now nor yesterday began
> These thoughts, which have been ever, nor yet can
> A man be found who their first entrance knew."[25]

If I have described life as a flux of moods, I must now add, that there is that in us which changes not, and which ranks all sensations and states of mind. The consciousness in each man is a sliding scale, which identifies him now with the First Cause, and now with the flesh of his body; life above life, in infinite degrees. The sentiment from which it sprung determines the dignity of any deed, and the question

[23]Scottish surgeon and anatomist (1756–1832).
[24]Simultaneous.
[25]Translation from Sophocles' *Antigone,* ll.455–457.

ever is, not, what you have done or forborne, but, at whose command you have done or forborne it.

Fortune, Minerva,[26] Muse, Holy Ghost,—these are quaint names, too narrow to cover this unbounded substance. The baffled intellect must still kneel before this cause, which refuses to be named,—ineffable cause, which every fine genius has essayed to represent by some emphatic symbol, as, Thales by water, Anaximenes by air, Anaxagoras by (Noûs) thought,[27] Zoroaster by fire, Jesus and the moderns by love: and the metaphor of each has become a national religion. The Chinese Mencius[28] has not been the least successful in his generalization. "I fully understand language," he said, "and nourish well my vast-flowing vigor."—"I beg to ask what you call vast-flowing vigor?" said his companion. "The explanation," replied Mencius, "is difficult. This vigor is supremely great, and in the highest degree unbending. Nourish it correctly, and do it no injury, and it will fill up the vacancy between heaven and earth. This vigor accords with and assists justice and reason, and leaves no hunger." In our more correct writing, we give to this generalization the name of Being, and therby confess that we have arrived as far as we can go. Suffice it for the joy of the universe, that we have not arrived at a wall, but at interminable oceans. Our life seems not present, so much as prospective; not for the affairs on which it is wasted, but as a hint of this vast-flowing vigor. Most of life seems to be mere advertisement of faculty: information is given us not to sell ourselves cheap; that we are very great. So, in particulars, our greatness is always in a tendency or direction, not in an action. It is for us to believe in the rule, not in the exception. The noble are thus known from the ignoble. So in accepting the leading of the sentiments, it is not what we believe concerning the immortality of the soul, or the like, but *the universal impulse to believe,* that is the material circumstance, and is the principal fact in the history of the globe. Shall we describe this cause as that which works directly? The spirit is not helpless or needful of mediate organs. It has plentiful powers and direct effects. I am explained without explaining, I am felt without acting, and where I am not. Therefore all just persons are satisfied with their own praise. They refuse to explain themselves, and are content that new actions should do them that office. They believe that we communicate without speech, and above speech, and that no right action of ours is quite unaffecting to our friends, at whatever distance; for the influence of action is not to be measured by miles. Why should I fret myself, because a circumstance has occurred, which hinders my presence where I was expected? If I am not at the meeting, my presence where I am should be as useful to the commonwealth of friendship and wisdom, as would be my presence in that place. I exert the same quality of power in all places. Thus journeys the mighty Ideal before us; it never was known to fall into the rear. No man ever came to an experience which was satiating, but his good is tidings of a better. Onward and onward! In liberated moments, we know that a new picture of life and duty is already possible; the elements already exist in many minds around you, of a doctrine of life which shall transcend any written record we have. The new statement will comprise the skepticisms, as well as the faiths of society, and out of unbeliefs a creed shall be formed. For, skepticisms are not gratuitous or law-

[26]Roman goddess of wisdom.

[27]Thales . . . Anaximenes . . . Anaxagoras. Greek philosophers.

[28]Confucian philosopher Meng-Tse (3rd cent. B.C.).

less, but are limitations of the affirmative statement, and the new philosophy must take them in, and make affirmations outside of them, just as much as it must include the oldest beliefs.

It is very unhappy, but too late to be helped, the discovery we have made, that we exist. That discovery is called the Fall of Man. Ever afterwards, we suspect our instruments. We have learned that we do not see directly, but mediately, and that we have no means of correcting these colored and distorting lenses which we are, or of computing the amount of their errors. Perhaps these subject-lenses have a creative power; perhaps there are no objects. Once we lived in what we saw; now, the rapaciousness of this new power, which threatens to absorb all things, engages us. Nature, art, persons, letters, religions,—objects, successively tumble in, and God is but one of its ideas. Nature and literature are subjective phenomena; every evil and every good thing is a shadow which we cast. The street is full of humiliations to the proud. As the fop contrived to dress his bailiffs in his livery, and make them wait on his guests at table, so the chagrins which the bad heart gives off as bubbles, at once take form as ladies and gentlemen in the street, shopmen or bar-keepers in hotels, and threaten or insult whatever is threatenable and insultable in us. 'Tis the same with our idolatries. People forget that it is the eye which makes the horizon, and the rounding mind's eye which makes this or that man a type or representative of humanity with the name of hero or saint. Jesus the "providential man," is a good man on whom many people are agreed that these optical laws shall take effect. By love on one part, and by forbearance to press objection on the other part, it is for a time settled, that we will look at him in the centre of the horizion, and ascribe to him the properties that will attach to any man so seen. But the longest love or aversion has a speedy term. The great and crescive[29] self, rooted in absolute nature, supplants all relative existence, and ruins the kingdom of mortal friendship and love. Marriage (in what is called the spiritual world) is impossible, because of the inequality between every subject and every object. The subject is the receiver of Godhead, and at every comparison must feel his being enhanced by that cryptic might. Though not in energy, yet by presence, this magazine[30] of substance cannot be otherwise than felt: nor can any force of intellect attribute to the object the proper deity which sleeps or wakes forever in every subject. Never can love make consciousness and ascription equal in force. There will be the same gulf between every me and thee, as between the original and the picture. The universe is the bride of the soul. All private sympathy is partial. Two human beings are like globes, which can touch only in a point, and, whilst they remain in contact, all other points of each of the spheres are inert; their turn must also come, and the longer a particular union lasts, the more energy of appetency the parts not in union acquire.[31]

Life will be imaged, but cannot be divided nor doubled. Any invasion of its unity would be chaos. The soul is not twin-born, but the only begotten, and though revealing itself as child in time, child in appearance, is of a fatal and universal power, admitting no co-life. Every day, every act betrays the ill-concealed deity. We believe

[29]Growing.
[30]Stored supply.
[31]Referring to contemporary physics experiments about static electricity. "Appetancy" meant both physical propulsion toward unity and sexual desire.

in ourselves, as we do not believe in others. We permit all things to ourselves, and that which we call sin in others, is experiment for us. It is an instance of our faith in ourselves, that men never speak of crime as lightly as they think: or, every man thinks a latitude safe for himself, which is nowise to be indulged to another. The act looks very differently on the inside, and on the outside; in its quality, and in its consequences. Murder in the murderer is no such ruinous thought as poets and romancers will have it; it does not unsettle him, or fright him from his ordinary notice of trifles: it is an act quite easy to be contemplated, but in its sequel, it turns out to be a horrible jangle and confounding of all relations. Especially the crimes that spring from love, seem right and fair from the actor's point of view, but, when acted, are found destructive of society. No man at last believes that he can be lost, nor that the crime in him is as black as in the felon. Because the intellect qualifies in our own case the moral judgments. For there is no crime to the intellect. That is antinomian or hypernomian,[32] and judges law as well as fact. "It is worse than a crime, it is a blunder," said Napoleon, speaking the language of the intellect. To it, the world is a problem in mathematics or the science of quantity, and it leaves out praise and blame, and all weak emotions. All stealing is comparative. If you come to absolutes, pray who does not steal? Saints are sad, because they behold sin, (even when they speculate,) from the point of view of the conscience, and not of the intellect; a confusion of thought. Sin seen from the thought, is a diminution or *less:* seen from the conscience or will, it is pravity or *bad.* The intellect names it shade, absence of light, and no essence. The conscience must feel it as essence, essential evil. This it is not: it has an objective existence, but no subjective.

Thus inevitably does the universe wear our color, and every object fall successively into the subject itself. The subject exists, the subject enlarges; all things sooner or later fall into place. As I am, so I see; use what language we will, we can never say anything but what we are; Hermes,[33] Cadmus,[34] Columbus, Newton, Bonaparte, are the mind's ministers. Instead of feeling a poverty when we encounter a great man, let us treat the new comer like a travelling geologist, who passes through our estate, and shows us good slate, or limestone, or anthracite, in our brush pasture. The partial action of each strong mind in one direction, is a telescope for the objects on which it is pointed. But every other part of knowledge is to be pushed to the same extravagance, ere the soul attains her due sphericity. Do you see that kitten chasing so prettily her own tail? If you could look with her eyes, you might see her surrounded with hundreds of figures performing complex dramas, with tragic and comic issues, long conversations, many characters, many ups and downs of fate,—and meantime it is only puss and her tail. How long before our masquerade will end its noise of tambourines, laughter, and shouting, and we shall find it was a solitary performance?—A subject and an object,—it takes so much to make the galvanic circuit complete, but magnitude adds nothing. What imports it whether it is Kepler[35] and the sphere; Columbus and America; a reader and his book; or puss with her tail?

[32]Against or beyond the control of law.

[33]Greek god who invented the lyre.

[34]Legendary founder of Thebes, who taught the Greeks the alphabet.

[35]German astronomer (1571–1630), who discovered basic laws of planetary motion.

It is true that all the muses and love and religion hate these developments, and will find a way to punish the chemist, who publishes in the parlor the secrets of the laboratory. And we cannot say too little of our constitutional necessity of seeing things under private aspects, or saturated with our humors. And yet is the God the native of these bleak rocks. That need makes in morals the capital virtue of self-trust. We must hold hard to this poverty, however scandalous, and by more vigorous self-recoveries, after the sallies of action, possess our axis more firmly. The life of truth is cold, and so far mournful; but it is not the slave of tears, contributions, and perturbations. It does not attempt another's work, nor adopt another's facts. It is a main lesson of wisdom to know your own from another's. I have learned that I cannot dispose of other people's facts; but I possess such a key to my own, as persuades me against all their denials, that they also have a key to theirs. A sympathetic person is placed in the dilemma of a swimmer among drowning men, who all catch at him, and if he give so much as a leg or a finger, they will drown him. They wish to be saved from the mischiefs of their vices, but not from their vices. Charity would be wasted on this poor waiting on the symptoms. A wise and hardy physician will say, *Come out of that,* as the first condition of advice.

In this our talking America, we are ruined by our good nature and listening on all sides. This compliance takes away the power of being greatly useful. A man should not be able to look other than directly and forthright. A preoccupied attention is the only answer to the importunate frivolity of other people: an attention, and to an aim which makes their wants frivolous. This is a divine answer, and leaves no appeal, and no hard thoughts. In Flaxman's[36] drawing of the Eumenides of Æschylus, Orestes supplicates Apollo, whilst the Furies sleep on the threshold. The face of the god expresses a shade of regret and compassion, but calm with the conviction of the irreconcilableness of the two spheres. He is born into other politics, into the eternal and beautiful. The man at his feet asks for his interest in turmoils of the earth, into which his nature cannot enter. And the Eumenides there lying express pictorially this disparity. The god is surcharged with his divine destiny.

Illusion, Temperament, Succession, Surface, Surprise, Reality, Subjectiveness,—these are threads on the loom of time, these are the lords of life. I dare not assume to give their order, but I name them as I find them in my way. I know better than to claim any completeness for my picture. I am a fragment, and this is a fragment of me. I can very confidently announce one or another law, which throws itself into relief and form, but I am too young yet by some ages to compile a code. I gossip for my hour concerning the eternal politics. I have seen many fair pictures not in vain. A wonderful time I have lived in. I am not the novice I was fourteen, nor yet seven years ago. Let who will ask, where is the fruit? I find a private fruit sufficient. This is a fruit,—that I should not ask for a rash effect from meditations, counsels, and the hiving of truths. I should feel it pitiful to demand a result on this town and county, an overt effect on the instant month and year. The effect is deep and secular as the cause. It works on periods in which mortal lifetime is lost. All I know is reception; I am and I have: but I do not get, and when I have fancied I had gotten anything, I found I did not. I worship with wonder the great Fortune. My reception has been so large, that

[36]British artist (1755–1826).

I am not annoyed by receiving this or that superabundantly. I say to the Genius, if he will pardon the proverb, *In for a mill, in for a million.* When I receive a new gift, I do not macerate[37] my body to make the account square, for, if I should die, I could not make the account square. The benefit overran the merit the first day, and has overran the merit ever since. The merit itself, so-called, I reckon part of the receiving.

Also, that hankering after an overt or practical effect seems to me an apostasy. In good earnest, I am willing to spare this most unnecessary deal of doing. Life wears to me a visionary face. Hardest, roughest action is visionary also. It is but a choice between soft and turbulent dreams. People disparage knowing and the intellectual life, and urge doing. I am very content with knowing, if only I could know. That is an august entertainment, and would suffice me a great while. To know a little, would be worth the expense of this world. I hear always the law of Adrastia,[38] "that every soul which had acquired any truth, should be safe from harm until another period."

I know that the world I converse with in the city and in the farms, is not the world I *think.* I observe that difference, and shall observe it. One day, I shall know the value and law of this discrepance. But I have not found that much was gained by manipular attempts to realize the world of thought. Many eager persons successively make an experiment in this way, and make themselves ridiculous. They acquire democratic manners, they foam at the mouth, they hate and deny. Worse, I observe, that, in the history of mankind, there is never a solitary example of success,—taking their own tests of success. I say this polemically, or in reply to the inquiry, why not realize your world? But far be from me the despair which prejudges the law by a paltry empiricism,—since there never was a right endeavor, but it succeeded. Patience and patience, we shall win at the last. We must be very suspicious of the deceptions of the element of time. It takes a good deal of time to eat or to sleep, or to earn a hundred dollars, and a very little time to entertain a hope and an insight which becomes the light of our life. We dress our garden, eat our dinners, discuss the household with our wives, and these things make no impression, are forgotten next week; but in the solitude to which every man is always returning, he has a sanity and revelations, which in his passage into new worlds he will carry with him. Never mind the ridicule, never mind the defeat: up again, old heart!—it seems to say,—there is victory yet for all justice; and the true romance which the world exists to realize, will be the transformation of genius into practical power.

1844, 1847

[37]Waste away from excessive fasting.
[38]Nemesis, Greek goddess of justice or destiny; cf. Plato's *Phaedrus.*

Concord Hymn[1]

Sung at the Completion of the Battle Monument, July 4, 1837

By the rude bridge that arched the flood,
Their flag to April's breeze unfurled,
Here once the embattled farmers stood
And fired the shot heard round the world.

The foe long since in silence slept;
Alike the conqueror silent sleeps;
And Time the ruined bridge has swept
Down the dark stream which seaward creeps.

On this green bank, by this soft stream,
We set to-day a votive stone;
That memory may their deed redeem,
When, like our sires, our sons are gone.

Spirit, that made those heroes dare
To die, and leave their children free,
Bid Time and Nature gently spare
The shaft we raise to them and thee.

1837

The Rhodora[1]

On Being Asked, Whence Is the Flower?

In May, when sea-winds pierced our solitudes,
I found the fresh Rhodora in the woods,
Spreading its leafless blooms in a damp nook,
To please the desert and the sluggish brook.

[1]Emerson's popular hymn was sung to the tune of Old Hundred at the dedication of the monument commemorating the Revolutionary War battles of April 19, 1775. First printed as a broadside and distributed at the 1837 ceremony, it was popularized in newspapers, memorized by schoolchildren, and carved on a memorial stone in Concord.

[1]Written in 1834, the poem was first published in James Freeman Clarke's *The Western Messenger* (Kentucky) in 1839. A rhodora is a shrub that grows in New England.

The purple petals, fallen in the pool,
Made the black water with their beauty gay;
Here might the red-bird come his plumes to cool,
And court the flower that cheapens his array.
Rhodora! if the sages ask thee why
This charm is wasted on the earth and sky,
Tell them, dear, that if eyes were made for seeing,
Then Beauty is its own excuse for being:
Why thou wert there, O rival of the rose!
I never thought to ask, I never knew:
But, in my simple ignorance, suppose
The self-same Power that brought me there brought you.

1839

The Snow-Storm[1]

Announced by all the trumpets of the sky,
Arrives the snow, and, driving o'er the fields,
Seems nowhere to alight: the whited air
Hides hills and woods, the river, and the heaven,
And veils the farm-house at the garden's end.
The sled and traveller stopped, the courier's feet
Delayed, all friends shut out, the housemates sit
Around the radiant fireplace, enclosed
In a tumultuous privacy of storm.

Come see the north wind's masonry.
Out of an unseen quarry evermore
Furnished with tile, the fierce artificer
Curves his white bastions with projected roof
Round every windward stake, or tree, or door.
Speeding, the myriad-handed, his wild work
So fanciful, so savage, nought cares he
For number or proportion. Mockingly,
On coop or kennel he hangs Parian[2] wreaths;
A swan-like form invests the hidden thorn;
Fills up the farmer's lane from wall to wall,

[1]Written in 1833–1834, the poem first appeared in *The Dial* in 1841.
[2]White marble used by Greek sculptors.

Maugre[3] the farmer's sighs; and, at the gate
A tapering turret overtops the work.
And when his hours are numbered, and the world
Is all his own, retiring, as he were not,
Leaves, when the sun appears, astonished Art
To mimic in slow structures, stone by stone,
Built in an age, the mad wind's night-work,
The frolic architecture of the snow.

1841

Compensation[1]

I

The wings of Time are black and white,
Pied[2] with morning and with night.
Mountain tall and ocean deep
Trembling balance duly keep.
In changing moon and tidal wave
Glows the feud of Want and Have.
Gauge of more and less through space,
Electric star or pencil plays,
The lonely Earth amid the balls
That hurry through the eternal halls,
A makeweight flying to the void,
Supplemental asteroid,
Or compensatory spark,
Shoots across the neutral Dark.

II

Man's the elm, and Wealth the vine;
Stanch and strong the tendrils twine:
Though the frail ringlets thee deceive,
None from its stock that vine can reave.
Fear not, then, though child infirm,
There's no god dare wrong a worm;

[3]In spite of.

[1]Emerson added these verses in 1847 as mottoes to his essay "Compensation."
[2]Multi-colored.

Laurel crowns cleave to deserts,
And power to him who power exerts.
Hast not thy share? On winged feet,
Lo! it rushes thee to meet;
And all that Nature made thy own,
Floating in air or pent in stone,
Will rive the hills and swim the sea,
And, like thy shadow, follow thee.

1841

Ode, Inscribed to W.H. Channing[1]

Though loath to grieve
The evil time's sole patriot,
I cannot leave
My honied thought
For the priest's cant,
Or statesman's rant.

If I refuse
My study for their politique,
Which at the best is trick,
The angry Muse
Puts confusion in my brain.

But who is he that prates
Of the culture of mankind,
Of better arts and life?
Go, blindworm, go,
Behold the famous States
Harrying Mexico[2]
With rifle and with knife!

Or who, with accent bolder,
Dare praise the freedom-loving mountaineer?

[1]First published in *Poems* (1847), the poem is an imaginary dialogue between one who "prates" of "culture" and "arts" and the time's "sole patriot." Emerson constructed the poem from many journal passages in which he worried through his own response to the troubling political crises of the day (the Mexican War, slavery, Polish rebellion). Dedicated to the noted abolitionist and reformer, William Henry Channing (1810–1884).

[2]States . . . Mexico: Mexican War of 1846–1848, which Emerson opposed as an attempt to extend slave-holding territory.

I found by thee, O rushing Contoocook!
And in thy valleys, Agiochook![3]
The jackals[4] of the negro-holder.

The God who made New Hampshire
Taunted the lofty land
With little men;—
Small bat and wren
House in the oak:—
If earth-fire cleave
The upheaved land, and bury the folk,
The southern crocodile would grieve.
Virtue palters; Right is hence;
Freedom praised, but hid;
Funeral eloquence
Rattles the coffin-lid.

What boots thy zeal,
O glowing friend,
That would indignant rend
The northland from the south?
Wherefore? to what good end?
Boston Bay and Bunker Hill
Would serve things still;—
Things are of the snake.

The horseman serves the horse,
The neatherd serves the neat,[5]
The merchant serves the purse,
The eater serves his meat;
'T is the day of the chattel,
Web to weave, and corn to grind;
Things are in the saddle,
And ride mankind.

There are two laws discrete,
Not reconciled,—
Law for man, and law for thing;
The last builds town and fleet,
But it runs wild,
And doth the man unking.

[3]Contoocook . . . Agiochook: Indian names for a river and the White Mountains of New Hampshire.

[4]Alluding to New Hampshire's support of proslavery laws.

[5]Archaic terms for cowherd and cows.

'T is fit the forest fall,
The steep be graded,
The mountain tunnelled,
The sand shaded,
The orchard planted,
The glebe[6] tilled,
The prairie granted,
The steamer built.

Let man serve law for man;
Live for friendship, live for love,
For truth's and harmony's behoof;
The state may follow how it can,
As Olympus follows Jove.

Yet do not I implore
The wrinkled shopman to my sounding woods,
Nor bid the unwilling senator
Ask votes of thrushes in the solitudes.
Every one to his chosen work;—
Foolish hands may mix and mar;
Wise and sure the issues are.
Round they roll till dark is light,
Sex to sex, and even to odd;—
The over-god
Who marries Right to Might,
Who peoples, unpeoples,—
He who exterminates
Races by stronger races,
Black by white faces,—
Knows to bring honey
Out of the lion;[7]
Grafts gentlest scion
On pirate and Turk.

The Cossack eats Poland,[8]
Like stolen fruit;
Her last noble is ruined,
Her last poet mute:
Straight, into double band

[6]Field.

[7]Reference to Samson, whose discovery of "honey in the carcase of the lion" suggested the riddle: "Out of the eater came forth meat, and out of the strong came forth sweetness"; cf. Judges, 14:8–14.

[8]Reference to Russian efforts to subjugate Poland.

The victors divide;
Half for freedom strike and stand;—
The astonished Muse finds thousands at her side.

1847

Hamatreya[1]

Bulkeley, Hunt, Willard, Hosmer, Meriam, Flint[2]
Possessed the land which rendered to their toil
Hay, corn, roots, hemp, flax, apples, wool, and wood.
Each of these landlords walked amidst his farm,
Saying, ''T is mine, my children's, and my name's.
How sweet the west wind sounds in my own trees!
How graceful climb those shadows on my hill!
I fancy these pure waters and the flags[3]
Know me, as does my dog: we sympathize;
And, I affirm, my actions smack of the soil.'

Where are these men? Asleep beneath their grounds:
And strangers, fond as they, their furrows plough.
Earth laughs in flowers, to see her boastful boys
Earth-proud, proud of the earth which is not theirs;
Who steer the plough, but cannot steer their feet
Clear of the grave.
They added ridge to valley, brook to pond,
And sighed for all that bounded their domain;
'This suits me for a pasture; that's my park;
We must have clay, lime, gravel, granite-ledge,
And misty lowland, where to go for peat.
The land is well,—lies fairly to the south.
'T is good, when you have crossed the sea and back,
To find the sitfast acres where you left them.'
Ah! the hot owner sees not Death, who adds
Him to his land, a lump of mould the more.
Hear what the Earth says:—

[1]First published in *Poems* (1847), and based on his reading the Hindu *Vishnu Purana.* In the Hindu source, the Earth chants a song to the god Maitreya (Hamatreya), "by listening to which ambition fades away like the snow before the sun."

[2]The first settlers of Concord, including Emerson's ancestor, Bulkeley.

[3]Wild irises.

EARTH-SONG

'Mine and yours;
Mine, not yours.
Earth endures;
Stars abide—
Shine down in the old sea;
Old are the shores;
But where are old men?
I who have seen much,
Such have I never seen.

'The lawyer's deed
Ran sure,
In tail,[4]
To them, and to their heirs
Who shall succeed,
Without fail,
Forevermore.

'Here is the land,
Shaggy with wood,
With its old valley,
Mound and flood.
But the heritors?—
Fled like the flood's foam.
The lawyer, and the laws,
And the kingdom,
Clean swept herefrom.

'They called me theirs,
Who so controlled me;
Yet every one
Wished to stay, and is gone.
How am I theirs,
If they cannot hold me,
But I hold them?'

When I heard the Earth-song,
I was no longer brave;
My avarice cooled
Like lust in the chill of the grave.

1847

[4]Variant of "entail," the legal system of restricting inheritance.

Merlin[1]

I

Thy trivial harp will never please
Or fill my craving ear;
Its chords should ring as blows the breeze,
Free, peremptory, clear.
No jingling serenader's art,
Nor tinkle of piano strings,
Can make the wild blood start
In its mystic springs.
The kingly bard
Must smite the chords rudely and hard,
As with hammer or with mace;
That they may render back
Artful thunder, which conveys
Secrets of the solar track,
Sparks of the supersolar blaze.
Merlin's blows are strokes of fate,
Chiming with the forest tone,
When boughs buffet boughs in the wood;
Chiming with the gasp and moan
Of the ice-imprisoned flood;
With the pulse of manly hearts;
With the voice of orators;
With the din of city arts;
With the cannonade of wars;
With the marches of the brave;
And prayers of might from martyrs' cave.

Great is the art,
Great be the manners, of the bard.
He shall not his brain encumber
With the coil of rhythm and number;
But, leaving rule and pale forethought,
He shall aye[2] climb
For his rhyme.
'Pass in, pass in,' the angels say,
'In to the upper doors,
Nor count compartments of the floors,

[1]First published in *Poems* (1847). Merlin is here one of the ancient Welsh bards Emerson often cited for their "freer speech."
[2]Always.

But mount to paradise
By the stairway of surprise.'

Blameless master of the games,
King of sport that never shames,
He shall daily joy dispense
Hid in song's sweet influence.
Things more cheerly live and go,
What time the subtle mind
Sings aloud the tune whereto
Their pulses beat,
And march their feet,
And their members are combined.

By Sybarites[3] beguiled,
He shall no task decline;
Merlin's mighty line
Extremes of nature reconciled,—
Bereaved a tyrant of his will,
And made the lion mild.
Songs can the tempest still,
Scattered on the stormy air,
Mould the year to fair increase,
And bring in poetic peace.

He shall not seek to weave,
In weak, unhappy times,
Efficacious rhymes;
Wait his returning strength.
Bird that from the nadir's floor
To the zenith's top can soar,—
The soaring orbit of the muse exceeds that journey's length.
Nor profane affect to hit
Or compass that, by meddling wit,
Which only the propitious mind
Publishes when 't is inclined.
There are open hours
When the God's will sallies free,
And the dull idiot might see
The flowing fortunes of a thousand years;—
Sudden, at unawares,
Self-moved, fly-to the doors,
Nor sword of angels could reveal
What they conceal.

[3]Wealthy and hedonistic Greeks.

II

The rhyme of the poet
Modulates the king's affairs;
Balance-loving Nature
Made all things in pairs.
To every foot its antipode;
Each color with its counter glowed;
To every tone beat answering tones,
Higher or graver;
Flavor gladly blends with flavor;
Leaf answers leaf upon the bough;
And match the paired cotyledons.[4]
Hands to hands, and feet to feet,
In one body grooms and brides;
Eldest rite, two married sides
In every mortal meet.
Light's far furnace shines,
Smelting balls and bars,
Forging double stars,
Glittering twins and trines.
The animals are sick with love,
Lovesick with rhyme;
Each with all propitious Time
Into chorus wove.

Like the dancers' ordered band,
Thoughts come also hand in hand;
In equal couples mated,
Or else alternated;
Adding by their mutual gage,
One to other, health and age.
Solitary fancies go
Short-lived wandering to and fro,
Most like to bachelors
Or an ungiven maid,
Not ancestors,
With no posterity to make the lie afraid,
Or keep truth undecayed.
Perfect-paired as eagle's wings,
Justice is the rhyme of things;
Trade and counting use
The self-same tuneful muse;
And Nemesis,[5]

[4]First leaves of a plant.
[5]Greek goddess of Fate.

Who with even matches odd,
Who arthwart space redresses
The partial wrong,
Fills the just period,
And finishes the song.

Subtle rhymes, with ruin rife,
Murmur in the house of life,
Sung by the Sisters[6] as they spin;
In perfect time and measure they
Build and unbuild our echoing clay,
As the two twilights of the day
Fold us music-drunken in.

1847

Brahma[1]

If the red slayer think he slays,
    Or if the slain think he is slain,
They know not well the subtle ways
    I keep, and pass, and turn again.

Far or forgot to me is near;
    Shadow and sunlight are the same;
The vanished gods to me appear;
    And one to me are shame and fame.

They reckon ill who leave me out;
    When me they fly, I am the wings;
I am the doubter and the doubt,
    And I the hymn the Brahmin sings.

The strong gods pine for my abode,
    And pine in vain the sacred Seven;[2]
But thou, meek lover of the good!
    Find me, and turn thy back on heaven.

1857

[6]In Greek mythology, the three fates.

[1]Derived from Emerson's reading in Hindu texts (*The Vishnu Purana, The Bhagavad-Gita,* and *The Upanishads*) and first published in *The Atlantic Monthly* (1857).

[2]The high saints of Hinduism.

Days[1]

Daughters of Time, the hypocritic Days,
Muffled and dumb, like barefoot dervishes,
And marching single in an endless file,
Bring diadems and fagots in their hands.
To each they offer gifts, after his will,
Bread, kingdoms, stars, and sky that holds them all.
I, in my pleached garden, watched the pomp,
Forgot my morning wishes, hastily
Took a few herbs and apples, and the Day
Turned and departed silent. I, too late,
Under her solemn fillet saw the scorn.

1857

Terminus[1]

It is time to be old
To take in sail:—
The god of bounds,
Who sets to seas ashore,
Came to me in his fatal rounds,
And said: 'No more!
No farther shoot
Thy broad ambitious branches, and thy root.
Fancy departs: no more invent;
Contract thy firmament
To compass of a tent.
There's not enough for this and that,
Make thy option which of two;
Economize the failing river,
Not the less revere the Giver,
Leave the many and hold the few.
Timely wise accept the terms,
Soften the fall with wary foot;
A little while
Still plan and smile,
And,—fault of novel germs,—
Mature the unfallen fruit.
Curse, if thou wilt, thy sires,

[1]First published in *The Atlantic Monthly* (1857).
[1]First published in *The Atlantic Monthly* (1867). Terminus was the Roman god of boundaries.

Bad husbands of their fires,
Who, when they gave thee breath,
Failed to bequeath
The needful sinew stark as once,
The Baresark[2] marrow to thy bones,
But left a legacy of ebbing veins,
Inconstant heat and nerveless reins,
Amid the Muses, left thee deaf and dumb,
Amid the gladiators, halt and numb.'

As the bird trims her to the gale,
I trim myself to the storm of time,
I man the rudder, reef the sail,
Obey the voice at eve obeyed at prime:
'Lowly faithful, banish fear,
Right onward drive unharmed;
The port, well worth the cruise, is near,
And every wave is charmed.'

1867

Sarah Margaret Fuller 1810–1850

Margaret Fuller's father had been disappointed when his first child was a girl. Still, when he was not away as a member of Congress or as Speaker of the Massachusetts House, he gave her the same education as any young man of their class might have received. At age fifteen, her daily schedule began at five in the morning, ended at eleven at night, and included reading literary and philosophical works in four languages, especially German, walking, singing, and playing the piano. The passages about "Miranda" in *Woman in the Nineteenth Century* reflect an idealized view of this upbringing, omitting the lifelong nightmares and headaches which may have been rooted in this imposing routine. When her family moved back to Cambridge in the early 1830s, Fuller met most of the people central to the Transcendentalist movement: Emerson, Thoreau, Bronson Alcott, W.H. Channing, among others. She was already on her way to what Thomas Carlyle called a "predetermination to *eat* this big universe as her oyster or her egg," and she made an instant impression on those around her.

The death of her father in 1835 forced Fuller to take up school-teaching to support herself and her family. After a brief stint in Alcott's progressive Temple School in Boston, she accepted a post in Providence, Rhode Island, moving there in 1837. But Fuller saw teaching as a means, not an end, and she keenly felt her isolation from the intellectual circles in

[2]The berserkers were fierce and brave Norse warriors, who fought "bare of shirt," i.e., without armor.

Boston, to which she returned in December, 1838.

There she flourished. In May, 1839, she published her translation of Eckermann's *Conversations With Goethe in the Last Years of His Life,* and in January, 1840, she began a two-year period as editor of *The Dial,* the semi-official journal of the Transcendentalists. During this period she supported herself by holding "Conversations" for women on topics such as poetry, ethics, Greek mythology, or the other subjects outlined in her letter to Sophia Ripley. Fuller believed that women had been educated solely for display and not to think. She saw herself as a catalyst for the women in her groups, and at her "Conversations" she attempted to guide and draw out the participants, to force them to realize the potential within themselves. Her "Conversations" between 1839 and 1844 were so popular—even though among the most expensive in Boston—that she was finally constrained to admit men. The "Conversations" anticipate the later organization of women's literary clubs and other efforts aimed at the self-development of women, who remained largely excluded from advanced educational institutions.

Between May and September, 1843, Fuller and some friends toured the midwest. Upon returning to Boston, Fuller set about writing up her account of the trip, and in June, 1844, published it as *Summer on the Lakes, in 1843.* The value of her book does not lie in its factual matter—Fuller had aimed at giving her "poetic impression of the country at large." In her commentary, she sympathized with the plight of the Indians and their betrayal by the whites, worried about attempts to imitate eastern standards of culture at the expense of losing what was unique to the West, and inserted many long passages of scenic description to convey her own sense of wonder at all the natural beauty she had seen.

Summer on the Lakes not only helped Fuller gain recognition as an author, it also brought her to the attention of Horace Greeley, who hired her as literary critic and general essayist for his New York *Tribune* and who offered to publish her next book. Fuller revised and expanded her essay "The Great Lawsuit. Man *versus* Men. Woman *versus* Women" from the July, 1843, *Dial,* and moved to New York in December, 1844, while still working on the book.

Woman in the Nineteenth Century, published in February, 1845, is Fuller's best-known work—indeed, the only one of her works generally made available to students. In it she attacks the hypocrisy of man, a hypocrisy that allowed him to champion freedom for blacks while maintaining legislation to restrict the rights of woman; a hypocrisy that saw man complain about woman's physical and emotional unsuitability for positions of responsibility in public life, yet insist that she be a field hand, a nurse, the one to raise and socialize children. She applied to "the woman question" ideas about self-development she shared with Emerson, and adapted something of his hortatory style to her social purposes. "What woman needs," she wrote,

> *is not as a woman to act or rule, but as a nature to grow, as an intellect to discern, as a soul to live freely, and unimpeded to unfold such powers as were given her when we left our common home.*

Fuller's arguments for full equality of opportunity, for abolishing stereotyped gender roles—"there is no wholly masculine man," she wrote, "no purely feminine woman"—and for women themselves to represent their own best interests may sound strikingly apt to today's readers. In any case, the book remains the fullest statement of women's rights to come out of the Boston-centered literary renaissance of mid-nineteenth-century America.

Fuller wrote nearly 250 reviews and occasional essays for the *Tribune* in the intense year and a half she worked in New York. *Papers on Literature and Art* (1846) collected only a few of these, including her famous essay surveying American literature, much of which is reprinted in this volume. But as a reporter she was also able to visit and write about women's prisons, Hopper Home, a halfway house for female convicts, immigrant slums, city hospitals. She focused her attention, as she had not before, on specific social issues of the day, like capital punishment, the abolitionist movement, the war on Mexico, treatment of madness.

In August, 1846, Fuller sailed for England as one of the first American "foreign correspondents," male or female. She began with the expected literary tour of England, where the recently issued *Papers* won her a warm reception among British writers. She also met, and was deeply influenced by, social activists like the Italian patriot Giuseppe Mazzini, and literary figures concerned with sexual liberation like the poet Adam Mickiewicz and the then-notorious French woman novelist George Sand. By the summer of 1847 she had taken up residence in Rome and had soon become involved in the revolutionary movements that were to shake Italy and all of Europe. She was swept up in the republican uprising, in her dispatches to the *Tribune* urging American support for the republican cause, and in the final siege of Rome running a military hospital. She also entered a relationship with Giovanni Ossoli, by whom she had a son, Angelo, in September, 1848; they apparently married the following year. When the Roman Republic fell to French troops in July, 1849, the Ossolis escaped to Rieti, where Angelo had almost been starved by a wet-nurse, and then to Florence, where many of their friends, including the poets Elizabeth and Robert Browning, appear to have been scandalized by their marriage and the fact that Giovanni was eleven years younger than Margaret. After a winter working on her history of the Roman Republic, Fuller set sail with Ossoli for America the following May. Their ship was caught in a storm, wrecked on a sandbar some fifty yards off Fire Island—almost within sight of New York City—and went down; only Angelo's body was ever found. Thoreau spent five days unsuccessfully combing the beach for their remains or for Fuller's missing manuscripts.

Although Fuller is famous today for *Woman in the Nineteenth Century,* she was best known by her contemporaries for her criticism—which attempted to establish well-defined standards—for her own personality—which some friends experienced as "the presence of a rather mountainous ME"—and for her conversation itself—which some found much superior to her writing. Indeed, she seems both to have intrigued and threatened many of her contemporaries: Hawthorne called her a "great humbug" in his journal and may have mocked her in the character of Zenobia in his novel about Brook Farm, *The Blithedale Romance.* While her friend Emerson lamented that he had "lost in her my audience," he, W.H. Channing, and James Freeman Clarke attempted to smooth away the social and political radicalism of her last years, bowdlerizing her journals and rewriting her letters in their *Memoirs of Margaret Fuller Ossoli* (1852). In the hands of such ambivalent editors, Fuller came to be regarded as, at best, a serio-comic footnote in American literary history, her style that—in the words of a prominent twentieth-century critic—of a headstrong "galloping filly." The emergence of a renewed women's movement in the 1960s helped revive interest in Fuller's work. Recent scholarship has shown the continuing influence of her writing on nineteenth-century feminists. And contemporary criticism has begun to understand the tensions in her life and work, the successes and failures of her prose, as reflections of her original effort to imagine "the woman who shall vindicate their birthright for all women; who shall teach them what to claim, and how to use what they obtain."

Joel Myerson
University of South Carolina

PRIMARY WORKS

Summer on the Lakes, in 1843, 1844; *Woman in the Nineteenth Century,* 1845; *Papers on Literature and Art,* 1846; *At Home and Abroad,* ed. Arthur B. Fuller, 1856; *The Letters of Margaret Fuller,* ed. Robert N. Hudspeth, 6 vols. to date, 1983–1994; *"These Sad But Glorious Days": Dispatches from Europe, 1846–1850,* ed. Larry J. Reynolds and Susan Belasco Smith, 1991; *The Essential Margaret Fuller,* ed. Jeffrey Steele, 1992; *The Portable Margaret Fuller,* ed. Mary Kelley, 1994.

SECONDARY WORKS

Memoirs of Margaret Fuller Ossoli, ed. Ralph Waldo Emerson, William Henry Channing, James Freeman Clarke, 2 vols., 1852; Madeleine B. Stern, *The Life of Margaret Fuller,* 1942; Bell Gale Chevigny, *The Woman and the Myth: Margaret Fuller's Life and Writings,* 1976; rev. ed., 1994; Joel Myerson, *Margaret Fuller: An Annotated Secondary Bibliography,* 1977; supplement in *Studies in the American Renaissance 1984*, 331–385; Paula Blanchard, *Margaret Fuller: From Transcendentalism to Revolution,* 1978; Joel Myerson, *Margaret Fuller: A Descriptive Primary Bibliography,* 1978; Margaret Vanderhaar Allen, *The Achievement of Margaret Fuller,* 1979; Joel Myerson, ed., *Critical Essays on Margaret Fuller;* 1980; Charles Capper, *Margaret Fuller: An American Romantic Life,* vol. 1: *The Private Years,* 1992; Joan von Mehren, *Minerva and the Muse: A Life of Margaret Fuller,* 1994; Christina Zwarg, *Feminist Conversations: Fuller, Emerson, and the Play of Reading,* 1995.

To [Sophia Ripley?][1]

Jamaica Plain,
27th August, 1839–

My dear friend,

I find it more difficult to give on paper a complete outline of my plan for the proposed conversations than I expected.[2] There is so much to say that I cannot make any statement satisfactory to myself within such limits as would be convenient for your purpose. As no one will wish to take the trouble of reading a long manuscript, I shall rather suggest than tell what I wish to do, and defer a full explanation to the first meeting. I wish you to use this communication according to

[1]Sophia Dana Ripley, daughter of Francis and Sophia Dana of Cambridge, married George Ripley in 1827. She was a force behind the creation of Brook Farm and a participant at Fuller's conversations.

[2]Each fall and spring from 1839 to 1844, Fuller conducted a series of "conversations" in Boston. Sarah Clarke noted that "there had been some fear expressed about town that it was a kind of infidel association, as several noted transcendentalists were engaged in it." Clarke described how Fuller managed the meetings: "One lady was insisting upon her sex's privilege to judge of things by her feelings, and to care not for the intellectual view of the matter. 'I am made so,' says she, 'and I cannot help it.' 'Yes,' says Margaret, gazing full upon her, 'but who are *you?* Were you an accomplished human being, were you all that a human being is capable of becoming, you might perhaps have a right to say, "I *like* it therefore it is good"—but, if you are not all that, your judgement must be partial and unjust if it is guided by your feelings alone.' Thus she speaketh plainly, and what in her lies; and we feel that, when she so generously opens her mind to us, we ought to do no less to her" (Sarah Clarke, "Letters of a Sister," 17 November and 14 December 1839).

your own judgment; if it seems to you too meagre to give any notion of the plan, lay it aside and interpret for me to whomsoever it may concern.

The advantages of such a weekly meeting might be great enough to repay the trouble of attendance if they consisted only in supplying a point of union to well-educated and thinking women in a city which, with great pretensions to mental refinement, boasts at present nothing of the kind and where I have heard many of mature age wish for some such means of stimulus and cheer, and these people for a place where they could state their doubts and difficulties with hope of gaining aid from the experience or aspirations of others. And if my office were only to suggest topicks which would lead to conversation of a better order than is usual at social meetings and to turn back the current when digressing into personalities or commonplaces so that—what is invaluable in the experience of each might be brought to bear upon all. I should think the object not unworthy of an effort. But my own ambition goes much farther. Thus to pass in review the departments of thought and knowledge and endeavor to place them in due relation to one another in our minds. To systematize thought and give a precision in which our sex are so deficient, chiefly, I think because they have so few inducements to test and classify what they receive. To ascertain what pursuits are best suited to us in our time and state of society, and how we may make best use of our means for building up the life of thought upon the life of action.

Could a circle be assembled in earnest desirous to answer the great questions. What were we born to do? How shall we do it? which so few ever propose to themselves 'till their best years are gone by. I should think the undertaking a noble one, and if my resources should prove sufficient to make me its moving spring, I should be willing to give it a large portion of those coming years which will as I hope be my best. I look upon it with no blind enthusiasm, nor unlimited faith, but with a confidence that I have attained a distinct perception of means which if there are persons competent to direct them, can supply a great want and promote really[?] high objects. So far as I have tried them yet they have met with success so much beyond my hopes, that my faith will not be easily shaken, or my earnestness chilled.

Should I however be disappointed in Boston I could hardly hope that such a plan could be brought to bear upon general society in any other city of the U.S. But I do not fear if a good beginning can be had, I am confident that twenty persons cannot be brought together for better motives than those of vanity or pedantry to talk upon such subjects as we propose without finding in themselves great deficiencies which they will be very desirous to supply. Should the enterprize fail, it will be either from incompetence in me or that sort of vanity in others which wears the garb of modesty. On the first of these points I need not speak. I can scarcely have felt the wants of others so much without feeling my own still more deeply. And from the depth of my feeling and the earnestness it gave such power as I have thus far exerted has come. Of course those who propose to meet me feel a confidence in me. And should they be disappointed I shall regret it not solely or most on my own account, I have not given my gage without weighing my capacity to sustain defeat. For the other I know it is very hard to lay aside the shelter of vague generalities, the cant of coterei criticism and the delicate disdains of *good society* and fearless meet the light although it flow from the sun of truth. Yet, as without such generous courage nothing can be done, or learned I cannot but hope to see many capable of it. Willing that others should think their sayings crude, shallow or tasteless if by such unpleasant means they may secure real health and vigor which may enable them to see their friends undefended by rouge or candlelight.

Since I saw you I have been told that several persons are desirous to join, if only they need not talk. I am so sure that the success of the whole depends on conversation being general that I do not wish any one to join who does not intend, *if possible,* to take an active part. No one will be forced, but those who do not talk will not derive the same advantages with those who openly state their impressions and consent to learn by blundering as is the destiny of Man here below. And general silence or side talks would paralyze me. I should feel coarse and misplaced if I were to be haranguing too much. In former instances I have been able to make it easy and even pleasant to twenty five out of thirty to bear their part, to question, to define, to state and examine their opinions. If I could not do as much now I should consider myself unsuccessful and should withdraw. But I should expect communication to be effected by degrees and to do a great deal myself at the first meetings.

My method has been to open a subject as for instance *Poetry* as expressed in
External Nature,
The Life of man
Literature
The Fine Arts
or History of a nation to be studied in
Its religious and civil institutions
Its literature and arts,
The characters of its great men
and after as good a general statement as I know how to make select a branch of the subject and lead others to give their thoughts upon it.

When they have not been successful in verbal utterance of their thoughts I have asked for them in writing. At the next meeting I read these aloud and canvassed their adequacy without mentioning the names of the writers. I found this less and less necessary as I proceeded and my companions acquired greater command both of thoughts and language, but for a time it was useful. I hope it may not be necessary now, but if it should great advantages may be derived from even this limited use of the pen.

I do not wish at present to pledge myself to any course of subjects. Except generally that they will be such as literature and the arts present in endless profusion. Should a class be brought together, I should wish first to ascertain our common ground and in a few meetings should see whether it be practicable to follow up the design in my mind which would look as yet too grand on paper. Let us see whether there will be any organ and if so note down the music to which it may give breath.

I believe I have said as much as any one will wish to read. I am ready to answer any questions which may be proposed Meanwhile put and will add nothing more here except always yours truly
S.M. Fuller.

1839

A Short Essay on Critics[1]

An essay on Criticism were a serious matter; for, though this age be emphatically critical, the writer would still find it necessary to investigate the laws of criticism as a science, to settle its conditions as an art. Essays entitled critical are epistles addressed to the public through which the mind of the recluse relieves itself of its impressions. Of these the only law is, "Speak the best word that is in thee." Or they are regular articles, got up to order by the literary hack writer, for the literary mart, and the only law is to make them plausible. There is not yet deliberate recognition of a standard of criticism, though we hope the always strengthening league of the republic of letters must ere long settle laws on which its Amphictyonic[2] council may act. Meanwhile let us not venture to write on criticism, but by classifying the critics imply our hopes, and thereby our thoughts.

First, there are the subjective class, (to make use of a convenient term, introduced by our German benefactors). These are persons to whom writing is no sacred, no reverend employment. They are not driven to consider, not forced upon investigation by the fact, that they are deliberately giving their thoughts an independent existence, and that it may live to others when dead to them. They know no agonies of conscientious research, no timidities of self-respect. They see no Ideal beyond the present hour, which makes its mood an uncertain tenure. How things affect them now they know; let the future, let the whole take care of itself. They state their impressions as they rise, of other men's spoken, written, or acted thoughts. They never dream of going out of themselves to seek the motive, to trace the law of another nature. They never dream that there are statures which cannot be measured from their point of view. They love, they like, or they hate; the book is detestable, immoral, absurd, or admirable, noble, of a most approved scope;—these statements they make with authority, as those who bear the evangel of pure taste and accurate judgment, and need be tried before no human synod. To them it seems that their present position commands the universe.

Thus the essays on the works of others, which are called criticisms, are often, in fact, mere records of impressions. To judge of their value you must know where the man was brought up, under what influences,—his nation, his church, his family even. He himself has never attempted to estimate the value of these circumstances, and find a law or raise a standard above all circumstances, permanent against all influence. He is content to be the creature of his place, and to represent it by his spoken and written word. He takes the same ground with the savage, who does not hesitate to say of the product of a civilization on which he could not stand, "It is bad," or "It is good."

The value of such comments is merely reflex. They characterize the critic. They give an idea of certain influences on a certain act of men in a certain time or place. Their absolute, essential value is nothing. The long review, the eloquent article by the

[1]This essay followed "The Editors to the Reader" as the opening article in the first issue of the *Dial.*

[2]There were several Amphictyonic Leagues in ancient Greece, the most famous being the one at Delphi, which controlled the oracle there.

man of the nineteenth century are of no value by themselves considered, but only as samples of their kind. The writers were content to tell what they felt, to praise or to denounce without needing to convince us or themselves. They sought not the divine truths of philosophy, and she proffers them not, if unsought.

Then there are the apprehensive. These can go out of themselves and enter fully into a foreign existence. They breathe its life; they live in its law; they tell what it meant, and why it so expressed its meaning. They reproduce the work of which they speak, and make it better known to us in so far as two statements are better than one. There are beautiful specimens in this kind. They are pleasing to us as bearing witness of the genial sympathies of nature. They have the ready grace of love with somewhat of the dignity of disinterested friendship. They sometimes give more pleasure than the original production of which they treat, as melodies will sometimes ring sweetlier in the echo. Besides there is a peculiar pleasure in a true response; it is the assurance of equipoise in the universe. These, if not true critics, come nearer the standard than the subjective class, and the value of their work is ideal as well as historical.

Then there are the comprehensive, who must also be apprehensive. They enter into the nature of another being and judge his work by its own law. But having done so, having ascertained his design and the degree of his success in fulfilling it, thus measuring his judgment, his energy and skill, they do also know how to put that aim in its place, and how to estimate its relations. And this the critic can only do who perceives the analogies of the universe, and how they are regulated by an absolute, invariable principle. He can see how far that work expresses this principle as well as how far it is excellent in its details. Sustained by a principle, such as can be girt within no rule, no formula, he can walk around the work, he can stand above it, he can uplift it, and try its weight. Finally he is worthy to judge it.

Critics are poets cut down, says some one by way of jeer; but, in truth, they are men with the poetical temperament to apprehend, with the philosophical tendency to investigate. The maker is divine; the critic sees this divine, but brings it down to humanity by the analytic process. The critic is the historian who records the order of creation. In vain for the maker, who knows without learning it, but not in vain for the mind of his race.

The critic is beneath the maker, but is his needed friend. What tongue could speak but to an intelligent ear, and every noble work demands its critic. The richer the work, the more severe would be its critic; the larger its scope, the more comprehensive must be his power of scrutiny. The critic is not a base caviller, but the younger brother of genius. Next to invention is the power of interpreting invention; next to beauty the power of appreciating beauty.

And of making others appreciate it; for the universe is a scale of infinite gradation, and below the very highest, every step is explanation down to the lowest. Religion, in the two modulations of poetry and music, descends through an infinity of waves to the lowest abysses of human nature. Nature is the literature and art of the divine mind; human literature and art the criticism on that; and they, too, find their criticism within their own sphere.

The critic, then, should be not merely a poet, not merely a philosopher, not merely an observer, but tempered of all three. If he criticize the poem, he must want nothing of what constitutes the poet, except the power of creating forms and speaking in music. He must have as good an eye and as fine a sense; but if he had as fine an organ for expression also, he would make the poem instead of judging it. He must be inspired by the philosopher's spirit of inquiry and need of generalization, but he must not be constrained by the hard cemented masonry of method to which philosophers are prone. And he must have the organic acuteness of the observer, with a love of ideal perfection, which forbids him to be content with mere beauty of details in the work or the comment upon the work.

There are persons who maintain, that there is no legitimate criticism, except the reproductive; that we have only to say what the work is or is to us, never what it is not. But the moment we look for a principle, we feel the need of a criterion, of a standard; and then we say what the work is *not,* as well as what it *is;* and this is as healthy though not as grateful and gracious an operation of the mind as the other. We do not seek to degrade but to classify an object by stating what it is not. We detach the part from the whole, lest it stand between us and the whole. When we have ascertained in what degree it manifests the whole we may safely restore it to its place, and love or admire it there ever after.

The use of criticism in periodical writing is to sift, not to stamp a work. Yet should they not be "sieves and drainers for the use of luxurious readers," but for the use of earnest inquirers, giving voice and being to their objections, as well as stimulus to their sympathies. But the critic must not be an infallible adviser to his reader. He must not tell him what books are not worth reading, or what must be thought of them when read, but what he read in them. Wo to that coterie where some critic sits despotic, intrenched behind the infallible "We." Wo to that oracle who has infused such soft sleepiness, such a gentle dulness into his atmosphere, that when he opes his lips no dog will bark. It is this attempt at dictatorship in the reviewers, and the indolent acquiescence of their readers, that has brought them into disrepute. With such fairness did they make out their statements, with such dignity did they utter their verdicts, that the poor reader grew all too submissive. He learned his lesson with such docility, that the greater part of what will be said at any public or private meeting can be foretold by any one who has read the leading periodical works for twenty years back. Scholars sneer at and would fain dispense with them altogether; and the public, grown lazy and helpless by this constant use of props and stays, can now scarce brace itself even to get through a magazine article, but reads in the daily paper laid beside the breakfast plate a short notice of the last number of the long established and popular review, and thereupon passes its judgment and is content.

Then the partisan spirit of many of these journals has made it unsafe to rely upon them as guide-books and expurgatory indexes. They could not be content merely to stimulate and suggest thought, they have at last become powerless to supersede it.

From these causes and causes like these, the journals have lost much of their influence. There is a languid feeling about them, an inclination to suspect the justice of their verdicts, the value of their criticisms. But their golden age cannot be quite past. They afford too convenient a vehicle for the transmission of knowledge; they are too natural a feature of our time to have done all their work yet. Surely they may be redeemed from their abuses, they may be turned to their true uses. But how?

It were easy to say what they should *not* do. They should not have an object to carry or a cause to advocate, which obliges them either to reject all writings which wear the distinctive traits of individual life, or to file away what does not suit them, till the essay, made true to their design, is made false to the mind of the writer. An external consistency is thus produced at the expense of all salient thought, all genuine emotion of life, in short, and living influences. Their purpose may be of value, but by such means was no valuable purpose ever furthered long. There are those, who have with the best intention pursued this system of trimming and adaptation, and thought it well and best to

"Deceive their country for their country's good."

But their country cannot long be so governed. It misses the pure, the full tone of truth; it perceives that the voice is modulated to coax, to persuade, and it turns from the judicious man of the world, calculating the effect to be produced by each of his smooth sentences to some earnest voice which is uttering thoughts, crude, rash, ill-arranged it may be, but true to one human breast, and uttered in full faith, that the God of Truth will guide them aright.

And here, it seems to me, has been the greatest mistake in the conduct of these journals. A smooth monotony has been attained, an uniformity of tone, so that from the title of a journal you can infer the tenor of all its chapters. But nature is ever various, ever new, and so should be her daughters, art and literature. We do not want merely a polite response to what we thought before, but by the freshness of thought in other minds to have new thought awakened in our own. We do not want stores of information only, but to be roused to digest these into knowledge. Able and experienced men write for us, and we would know what they think, as they think it not for us but for themselves. We would live with them, rather than be taught by them how to live; we would catch the contagion of their mental activity, rather than have them direct us how to regulate our own. In books, in reviews, in the senate, in the pulpit, we wish to meet thinking men, not schoolmasters or pleaders. We wish that they should do full justice to their own view, but also that they should be frank with us, and, if now our superiors, treat us as if we might some time rise to be their equals. It is this true manliness, this firmness in his own position, and this power of appreciating the position of others, that alone can make the critic our companion and friend. We would converse with him, secure that he will tell us all his thought, and speak as man to man. But if he adapts his work to us, if he stifles what is distinctively his, if he shows himself either arrogant or mean, or, above all, if he wants faith in the healthy action of free thought, and the safety of pure motive, we will not talk with him, for we cannot confide in him. We will go to the critic who trusts Genius and trusts us, who knows that all good writing must be spontaneous, and who will write out the bill of fare for the public as he read it for himself,—

"Forgetting vulgar rules, with spirit free
To judge each author by his own intent,
Nor think one standard for all minds is meant."

Such an one will not disturb us with personalities, with sectarian prejudices, or an undue vehemence in favor of petty plans or temporary objects. Neither will he disgust us by smooth obsequious flatteries and an inexpressive, lifeless gentleness. He will be free and make free from the mechanical and distorting influences we hear complained of on every side. He will teach us to love wisely what we before loved well, for he knows the difference between censoriousness and discernment, infatuation and reverence; and, while delighting in the genial melodies of Pan, can perceive, should Apollo bring his lyre into audience, that there may be strains more divine than those of his native groves.[3]

1840

from Summer on the Lakes

Chapter III

In the afternoon of this day we reached the Rock river, in whose neighborhood we proposed to make some stay, and crossed at Dixon's ferry.

This beautiful stream flows full and wide over a bed of rocks, traversing a distance of near two hundred miles, to reach the Mississippi. Great part of the country along its banks is the finest region of Illinois, and the scene of some of the latest romance of Indian warfare. To these beautiful regions Black Hawk returned with his band "to pass the summer," when he drew upon himself the warfare in which he was finally vanquished.[1] No wonder he could not resist the longing, unwise though its indulgence might be, to return in summer to this home of beauty.

Of Illinois, in general, it has often been remarked that it bears the character of country which has been inhabited by a nation skilled like the English in all the ornamental arts of life, especially in landscape gardening. That the villas and castles seem to have been burnt, the enclosures taken down, but the velvet lawns, the flower gardens, the stately parks, scattered at graceful intervals by the decorous hand of art, the frequent deer, and the peaceful herd of cattle that make picture of the plain, all suggest more of the masterly mind of man, than the prodigal, but careless, motherly love of nature. Especially is this true of the Rock river country. The river flows sometimes through these parks and lawns, then betwixt high bluffs, whose grassy ridges are covered with fine trees, or broken with crumbling stone, that easily assumes the forms of buttress, arch and clustered columns. Along the face of such crumbling rocks, swallows' nests are clustered, thick as cities, and eagles and deer do not disdain their summits. One morning, out in the boat along the base of these rocks, it was amusing, and affecting too, to see these swallows put their heads out to look at us. There was something very hospitable about it, as if man had never shown himself a tyrant near them. What a morning that was! Every sight is worth twice as much by the early morning light. We borrow something of the spirit of the hour to look upon them.

The first place where we stopped was one of singular beauty, a beauty of soft, luxuriant wildness. It was on the bend of the river, a place chosen by an Irish gentleman, whose absenteeship seems of the wisest kind, since for a sum which would have been but a drop of water to the thirsty fever of his native land, he commands a residence which has all that is desirable, in its independence, its beautiful retirement, and means of benefit to others.

[3]Pan, the Greek god of pastures and flocks. Apollo, the Greek god of light and life.

[1]Black Hawk (1767–1838), chief of the Sauks, who led an effort to reclaim traditional Sauk lands from white appropriation.

His park, his deer-chase, he found already prepared; he had only to make an avenue through it. This brought us by a drive, which in the heat of noon seemed long, though afterwards, in the cool of morning and evening, delightful, to the house. This is, for that part of the world, a large and commodious dwelling. Near it stands the log-cabin where its master lived while it was building, a very ornamental accessory.

In front of the house was a lawn, adorned by the most graceful trees. A few of these had been taken out to give a full view of the river, gliding through banks such as I have described. On this bend the bank is high and bold, so from the house or the lawn the view was very rich and commanding. But if you descended a ravine at the side to the water's edge, you found there a long walk on the narrow shore, with a wall above of the richest hanging wood, in which they said the deer lay hid. I never saw one, but often fancied that I heard them rustling, at daybreak, by these bright clear waters, stretching out in such smiling promise, where no sound broke the deep and blissful seclusion, unless now and then this rustling, or the plash of some fish a little gayer than the others; it seemed not necessary to have any better heaven, or fuller expression of love and freedom than in the mood of nature here.

Then, leaving the bank, you would walk far and far through long grassy paths, full of the most brilliant, also the most delicate flowers. The brilliant are more common on the prairie, but both kinds loved this place.

Amid the grass of the lawn, with a profusion of wild strawberries, we greeted also a familiar love, the Scottish harebell, the gentlest, and most touching form of the flower-world.

The master of the house was absent, but with a kindness beyond thanks had offered us a resting place there. Here we were taken care of by a deputy, who would, for his youth, have been assigned the place of a page in former times, but in the young west, it seems he was old enough for a steward. Whatever be called his function, he did the honors of the place so much in harmony with it, as to leave the guests free to imagine themselves in Elysium. And the three days passed here were days of unalloyed, spotless happiness.

There was a peculiar charm in coming here, where the choice of location, and the unobtrusive good taste of all the arrangements, showed such intelligent appreciation of the spirit of the scene, after seeing so many dwellings of the new settlers, which showed plainly that they had no thought beyond satisfying the grossest material wants. Sometimes they looked attractive, the little brown houses, the natural architecture of the country, in the edge of the timber. But almost always when you came near, the slovenliness of the dwelling and the rude way in which objects around it were treated, when so little care would have presented a charming whole, were very repulsive. Seeing the traces of the Indians, who chose the most beautiful sites for their dwellings, and whose habits do not break in on that aspect of nature under which they were born, we feel as if they were the rightful lords of a beauty they forbore to deform. But most of these settlers do not see it at all; it breathes, it speaks in vain to those who are rushing into its sphere. Their progress is Gothic, not Roman,[2] and their mode of cultivation will, in the course of twenty, perhaps ten, years, obliterate the natural expression of the country.

[2]That is, just as the Goths conquered Rome and tried to obliterate its civilization, easterners coming west would do the same.

This is inevitable, fatal; we must not complain, but look forward to a good result. Still, in travelling through this country, I could not but be struck with the force of a symbol. Wherever the hog comes, the rattlesnake disappears; the omnivorous traveller, safe in its stupidity, willingly and easily makes a meal of the most dangerous of reptiles, and one whom the Indian looks on with a mystic awe. Even so the white settler pursues the Indian, and is victor in the chase. But I shall say more upon the subject by-and-by.

While we were here we had one grand thunder storm, which added new glory to the scene.

One beautiful feature was the return of the pigeons every afternoon to their home. Every afternoon they came sweeping across the lawn, positively in clouds, and with a swiftness and softness of winged motion, more beautiful than anything of the kind I ever knew. Had I been a musician, such as Mendelssohn,[3] I felt that I could have improvised a music quite peculiar, from the sound they made, which should have indicated all the beauty over which their wings bore them. I will here insert a few lines left at this house, on parting, which feebly indicate some of the features.

Familiar to the childish mind were tales
  Of rock-girt isles amid a desert sea,
Where unexpected stretch the flowery vales
  To soothe the shipwrecked sailor's misery.
Fainting, he lay upon a sandy shore,
And fancied that all hope of life was o'er;
But let him patient climb the frowning wall,
Within, the orange glows beneath the palm tree tall,
And all that Eden boasted waits his call.

Almost these tales seem realized to-day,
When the long dullness of the sultry way,
Where "independent" settlers' careless cheer
Made us indeed feel we were "strangers" here,
Is cheered by sudden sight of this fair spot,
On which "improvement" yet has made no blot,
But Nature all-astonished stands, to find
Her plan protected by the human mind.

Blest be the kindly genius of the scene;
  The river, bending in unbroken grace,
The stately thickets, with their pathways green,
  Fair lonely trees, each in its fittest place.
Those thickets haunted by the deer and fawn;
Those cloudlike flights of birds across the lawn;
The gentlest breezes here delight to blow,
And sun and shower and star are emulous to deck the show.

[3]Felix Mendelssohn (1809–1847), German composer and musician.

Wondering, as Crusoe, we survey the land;[4]
Happier than Crusoe we, a friendly band;
Blest be the hand that reared this friendly home,
The heart and mind of him to whom we owe
Hours of pure peace such as few mortals know;
May he find such, should he be led to roam;
Be tended by such ministering sprites—
Enjoy such gaily childish days, such hopeful nights!
And yet, amid the goods to mortals given,
To give those goods again is most like heaven.

Hazelwood, Rock River, June 30th, 1843.

The only really rustic feature was of the many coops of poultry near the house, which I understood it to be one of the chief pleasures of the master to feed.

Leaving this place, we proceeded a day's journey along the beautiful stream, to a little town named Oregon. We called at a cabin, from whose door looked out one of those faces which, once seen, are never forgotten; young, yet touched with many traces of feeling, not only possible, but endured; spirited, too, like the gleam of a finely tempered blade. It was a face that suggested a history, and many histories, but whose scene would have been in courts and camps. At this moment their circles are dull for want of that life which is waning unexcited in this solitary recess.

The master of the house proposed to show us a "short cut," by which we might, to especial advantage, pursue our journey. This proved to be almost perpendicular down a hill, studded with young trees and stumps. From these he proposed, with a hospitality of service worthy an Oriental, to free our wheels whenever they should get entangled, also, to be himself the drag, to prevent our too rapid descent. Such generosity deserved trust; however, we women could not be persuaded to render it. We got out and admired, from afar, the process. Left by our guide—and prop! we found ourselves in a wide field, where, by playful quips and turns, an endless "creek," seemed to divert itself with our attempts to cross it. Failing in this, the next best was to whirl down a steep bank, which feat our charioteer performed with an air not unlike that of Rhesus, had he but been as suitably furnished with chariot and steeds![5]

At last, after wasting some two or three hours on the "short cut," we got out by following an Indian trail,—Black Hawk's! How fair the scene through which it led! How could they let themselves be conquered, with such a country to fight for!

Afterwards, in the wide prairie, we saw a lively picture of nonchalance, (to speak in the fashion of dear Ireland). There, in the wide sunny field, with neither tree nor umbrella above his head, sat a pedler, with his pack, waiting apparently for customers. He was not disappointed. We bought, what hold in regard to the human world, as unmarked, as mysterious, and as important an existence, as the infusoria to the natural, to wit, pins. This incident would have delighted those modern sages, who, in imitation of the sitting philosophers of ancient Ind, prefer silence to speech, waiting to going and scornfully smile in answer to the motions of earnest life,

[4]The castaway Robinson Crusoe, hero of Daniel Defoe's *The Life and Strange Surprizing Adventures of Robinson Crusoe* (1719).

[5]Rhesus, an ally who was killed and had his white horses taken in order to help defeat Troy.

"Of itself will nothing come,
That ye must still be seeking?"

However, it seemed to me to-day, as formerly on these sublime occasions, obvious that nothing would come, unless something would go; now, if we had been as sublimely still as the pedler, his pins would have tarried in the pack, and his pockets sustained an aching void of pence!

Passing through one of the fine, park-like woods, almost clear from underbrush and carpeted with thick grasses and flowers, we met (for it was Sunday,) a little congregation just returning from their service, which had been performed in a rude house in its midst. It had a sweet and peaceful air as if such words and thoughts were very dear to them. The parents had with them all their little children; but we saw no old people; that charm was wanting, which exists in such scenes in older settlements, of seeing the silver bent in reverence beside the flaxen head.

At Oregon, the beauty of the scene was of even a more sumptuous character than at our former "stopping place." Here swelled the river in its boldest course, interspersed by halcyon isles on which nature had lavished all her prodigality in tree, vine, and flower, banked by noble bluffs, three hundred feet high, their sharp ridges as exquisitely definite as the edge of a shell; their summits adorned with those same beautiful trees, and with buttresses of rich rock, crested with old hemlocks, which wore a touching and antique grace amid the softer and more luxuriant vegetation. Lofty natural mounds rose amidst the rest, with the same lovely and sweeping outline, showing everywhere the plastic power of water,—water, mother of beauty, which, by its sweet and eager flow, had left such lineaments as human genius never dreamt of.

Not far from the river was a high crag, called the Pine Rock, which looks out, as our guide observed, like a helmet above the brow of the country. It seems as if the water left here and there a vestige of forms and materials that preceded its course, just to set off its new and richer designs.

The aspect of this country was to me enchanting, beyond any I have ever seen, from its fullness of expression, its bold and impassioned sweetness. Here the flood of emotion has passed over and marked everywhere its course by a smile. The fragments of rock touch it with a wildness and liberality which give just the needed relief. I should never be tired here, though I have elsewhere seen country of more secret and alluring charms, better calculated to stimulate and suggest. Here the eye and heart are filled.

How happy the Indians must have been here! It is not long since they were driven away, and the ground, above and below, is full of their traces.

"The earth is full of men."

You have only to turn up the sod to find arrowheads and Indian pottery. On an island, belonging to our host, and nearly opposite his house, they loved to stay, and, no doubt, enjoyed its lavish beauty as much as the myriad wild pigeons that now haunt its flower-filled shades. Here are still the marks of their tomahawks, the troughs in which they prepared their corn, their caches.

A little way down the river is the site of an ancient Indian village, with its regularly arranged mounds. As usual, they had chosen with the finest taste. It was one of those soft shadowy afternoons when we went there, when nature seems ready to weep, not from grief, but from an overfull heart. Two prattling, lovely little girls, and an African boy, with glittering eye and ready grin, made our party gay; but all were still as we entered their little inlet and trod those flowery paths. They may blacken Indian life as they will, talk of its dirt, its brutality, I will ever believe that the men who chose that dwelling-place were able to feel emotions of noble happiness as they returned to it, and so were the women that received them. Neither were the children sad or dull, who lived so familiarly with the deer and the birds, and swam that clear wave in the shadow of the Seven Sisters.[6] The whole scene suggested to me a Greek splendor, a Greek sweetness, and I can believe that an Indian brave, accustomed to ramble in such paths, and be bathed by such sunbeams, might be mistaken for Apollo, as Apollo was for him by West.[7] Two of the boldest bluffs are called the Deer's Walk, (not because deer do *not* walk there,) and the Eagle's Nest. The latter I visited one glorious morning; it was that of the fourth of July, and certainly I think I had never felt so happy that I was born in America. Wo to all country folks that never saw this spot, never swept an enraptured gaze over the prospect that stretched beneath. I do believe Rome and Florence are suburbs compared to this capital of nature's art.

The bluff was decked with great bunches of a scarlet variety of the milkweed, like cut coral, and all starred with a mysterious-looking dark flower, whose cup rose lonely on a tall stem. This had, for two or three days, disputed the ground with the lupine and phlox. My companions disliked, I liked it.

Here I thought of, or rather saw, what the Greek expresses under the form of Jove's darling, Ganymede,[8] and the following stanzas took form.

GANYMEDE TO HIS EAGLE,

SUGGESTED BY A WORK OF THORWALDSEN'S.

Composed on the height called the Eagle's Nest, Oregon, Rock River, July 4th, 1843.

Upon the rocky mountain stood the boy,
   A goblet of pure water in his hand,
His face and form spoke him one made for joy,
   A willing servant to sweet love's command,
But a strange pain was written on his brow,
And thrilled throughout his silver accents now—

"My bird," he cries, "my destined brother friend,
   O wither fleets to-day thy wayward flight?
Hast thou forgotten that I here attend,
   From the full noon until this sad twilight?
A hundred times, at least, from the clear spring,
   Since the full noon o'er hill and valley glowed,

[6]The Seven Hills of Rome.
[7]Apollo, the Greek god of light and life. Benjamin West (1738–1820), American historical and portrait painter whose subjects often included Indians.
[8]Jove, the major Roman god, who, in the form of an eagle, made his cupbearer Ganymede immortal.

I've filled the vase which our Olympian king
  Upon my care for thy sole use bestowed;
That at the moment when thou should'st descend,
A pure refreshment might thy thirst attend.

Hast thou forgotten earth, forgotten me,
  Thy fellow bondsman in a royal cause,
Who, from the sadness of infinity,
  Only with thee can know that peaceful pause
In which we catch the flowing strain of love,
Which binds our dim fates to the throne of Jove?

Before I saw thee, I was like the May,
  Longing for summer that must mar its bloom,
Or like the morning star that calls the day,
  Whose glories to its promise are the tomb;
And as the eager fountain rises higher
  To throw itself more strongly back to earth,
Still, as more sweet and full rose my desire,
  More fondly it reverted to its birth,
For, what the rosebud seeks tells not the rose,
The meaning foretold by the boy the man cannot disclose.

I was all Spring, for in my being dwelt
  Eternal youth, where flowers are the fruit,
Full feeling was the thought of what was felt,
  Its music was the meaning of the lute;
But heaven and earth such life will still deny,
For earth, divorced from heaven, still asks the question
  Why?

Upon the highest mountains my young feet
  Ached, that no pinions from their lightness grew,
My starlike eyes the stars would fondly greet,
  Yet win no greeting from the circling blue;
Fair, self-subsistent each in its own sphere,
  They had no care that there was none for me;
Alike to them that I was far or near,
  Alike to them, time and eternity.

But, from the violet of lower air,
  Sometimes an answer to my wishing came,
Those lightning births my nature seemed to share,
  They told the secrets of its fiery frame,
The sudden messengers of hate and love,
The thunderbolts that arm the hand of Jove,

And strike sometimes the sacred spire, and strike the sacred grove.
Come in a moment, in a moment gone,
They answered me, then left me still more lone,
They told me that the thought which ruled the world,
As yet no sail upon its course had furled,
That the creation was but just begun,
New leaves still leaving from the primal one,
But spoke not of the goal to which *my* rapid wheels would run.

Still, still my eyes, though tearfully, I strained
To the far future which my heart contained,
And no dull doubt my proper hope profaned.

At last, O bliss, thy living form I spied,
Then a mere speck upon a distant sky,
Yet my keen glance discerned its noble pride
And the full answer of that sun-filled eye;
I knew it was the wing that must upbear
My earthlier form into the realms of air.

Thou knowest how we gained that beauteous height,
Where dwells the monarch of the sons of light,
Thou knowest he declared us two to be
The chosen servants of his ministry,
Thou as his messenger, a sacred sign
Of conquest, or with omen more benign,
To give its due weight to the righteous cause,
To express the verdict of Olympian laws.

And I to wait upon the lonely spring,
Which slakes the thirst of bards to whom 'tis given
The destined dues of hopes divine to sing,
And weave the needed chain to bind to heaven.
Only from such could be obtained a draught
For him who in his early home from Jove's own cup has quaffed.

To wait, to wait, but not to wait too long,
Till heavy grows the burthen of a song;
O bird! too long hast thou been gone to-day,
My feet are weary of their frequent way,
The spell that opes the spring my tongue no more can say.

If soon thou com'st not, night will fall around,
My head with a sad slumber will be bound,
And the pure draught be spilt upon the ground.

Remember that I am not yet divine,
Long years of service to the fatal Nine
Are yet to make a Delphian vigor mine.[9]

O, make them not too hard, thou bird of Jove,
Answer the stripling's hope, confirm his love,
Receive the service in which he delights,
And bear him often to the serene heights,
Where hands that were so prompt in serving thee,
Shall be allowed the highest ministry,
And Rapture live with bright Fidelity.

The afternoon was spent in a very different manner. The family, whose guests we were, possessed a gay and graceful hospitality that gave zest to each moment. They possessed that rare politeness which, while fertile in pleasant expedients to vary the enjoyment of a friend, leaves him perfectly free the moment he wishes to be so. With such hosts, pleasure may be combined with repose. They lived on the bank opposite the town, and, as their house was full, we slept in the town, and passed three days with them, passing to and fro morning and evening in their boats. (To one of these, called the Fairy, in which a sweet little daughter of the house moved about lighter than any Scotch Elien ever sung, I should indite a poem, if I had not been guilty of rhyme on the very last page.) At morning this was very pleasant; at evening, I confess I was generally too tired with the excitements of the day to think it so.

Their house—a double log cabin—was, to my eye, the model of a Western villa. Nature had laid out before it grounds which could not be improved. Within, female taste had veiled every rudeness—availed itself of every sylvan grace.

In this charming abode what laughter, what sweet thoughts, what pleasing fancies, did we not enjoy! May such never desert those who reared it and made us so kindly welcome to all its pleasures!

Fragments of city life were dexterously crumbled into the dish prepared for general entertainment. Ice creams followed the dinner drawn by the gentlemen from the river, and music and fireworks wound up the evening of days spent on the Eagle's Nest. Now they had prepared a little fleet to pass over to the Fourth of July celebration, which some queer drumming and fifing, from the opposite bank, had announced to be "on hand."

We found the free and independent citizens there collected beneath the trees, among whom many a round Irish visage dimpled at the usual puffs of Ameriky.

The orator was a New Englander, and the speech smacked loudly of Boston, but was received with much applause, and followed by a plentiful dinner, provided by and for the Sovereign People, to which Hail Columbia served as grace.

Returning, the gay flotilla hailed the little flag which the children had raised from a log-cabin, prettier than any president ever saw, and drank the health of their country and all mankind, with a clear conscience.

Dance and song wound up the day. I know not when the mere local habitation has seemed to me to afford so fair a chance of happiness as this. To a person of

[9]The Nine Muses were the daughters of Zeus (or Jove) and Mnemosyne. Delphos was a city in Greece world-renowned for being the home of an oracle.

unspoiled tastes, the beauty alone would afford stimulus enough. But with it would be naturally associated all kinds of wild sports, experiments, and the studies of natural history. In these regards, the poet, the sportsman, the naturalist, would alike rejoice in this wide range of untouched loveliness.

Then, with a very little money, a ducal estate may be purchased, and by a very little more, and moderate labor, a family be maintained upon it with raiment, food and shelter. The luxurious and minute comforts of a city life are not yet to be had without effort disproportionate to their value. But, where there is so great a counterpoise, cannot these be given up once for all? If the houses are imperfectly built, they can afford immense fires and plenty of covering; if they are small, who cares?—with such fields to roam in. In winter, it may be borne; in summer, is of no consequence. With plenty of fish, and game, and wheat, can they not dispense with a baker to bring "muffins hot" every morning to the door for their breakfast?

Here a man need not take a small slice from the landscape, and fence it in from the obtrusions of an uncongenial neighbor, and there cut down his fancies to miniature improvements which a chicken could run over in ten minutes. He may have water and wood and land enough, to dread no incursions on his prospect from some chance Vandal[10] that may enter his neighborhood. He need not painfully economise and manage how he may use it all; he can afford to leave some of it wild, and to carry out his own plans without obliterating those of nature.

Here, whole families might live together, if they would. The sons might return from their pilgrimages to settle near the parent hearth; the daughters might find room near their mother. Those painful separations, which already desecrate and desolate the Atlantic coast, are not enforced here by the stern need of seeking bread; and where they are voluntary, it is no matter. To me, too, used to the feelings which haunt a society of struggling men, it was delightful to look upon a scene where nature still wore her motherly smile and seemed to promise room not only for those favored or cursed with the qualities best adapting for the strifes of competition, but for the delicate, the thoughtful, even the indolent or eccentric. She did not say, Fight or starve; nor even, Work or cease to exist; but, merely showing that the apple was a finer fruit than the wild crab, gave both room to grow in the garden.

A pleasant society is formed of the families who live along the banks of this stream upon farms. They are from various parts of the world, and have much to communicate to one another. Many have cultivated minds and refined manners, all a varied experience, while they have in common the interests of a new country and a new life. They must traverse some space to get at one another, but the journey is through scenes that make it a separate pleasure. They must bear inconveniences to stay in one another's houses; but these, to the well-disposed, are only a source of amusement and adventure.

The great drawback upon the lives of these settlers, at present, is the unfitness of the women for their new lot. It has generally been the choice of the men, and the women follow, as women will, doing their best for affection's sake, but too often in heartsickness and weariness. Beside it frequently not being a choice or conviction of their own minds that it is best to be here, their part is the hardest, and they are least

[10]The Germanic tribe that sacked Rome in 455.

fitted for it. The men can find assistance in field labor, and recreation with the gun and fishing-rod. Their bodily strength is greater, and enables them to bear and enjoy both these forms of life.

The women can rarely find any aid in domestic labor. All its various and careful tasks must often be performed, sick or well, by the mother and daughters, to whom a city education has imparted neither the strength nor skill now demanded.

The wives of the poorer settlers, having more hard work to do than before, very frequently become slatterns; but the ladies, accustomed to a refined neatness, feel that they cannot degrade themselves by its absence, and struggle under every disadvantage to keep up the necessary routine of small arrangements.

With all these disadvantages for work, their resources for pleasure are fewer. When they can leave the housework, they have not learnt to ride, to drive, to row, alone. Their culture has too generally been that given to women to make them "the ornaments of society." They can dance, but not draw; talk French, but know nothing of the language of flowers; neither in childhood were allowed to cultivate them, lest they should tan their complexions. Accustomed to the pavement of Broadway, they dare not tread the wildwood paths for fear of rattlesnakes!

Seeing much of this joylessness, and inaptitude, both of body and mind, for a lot which would be full of blessings for those prepared for it, we could not but look with deep interest on the little girls, and hope they would grow up with the strength of body, dexterity, simple tastes, and resources that would fit them to enjoy and refine the western farmer's life.

But they have a great deal to war with in the habits of thought acquired by their mothers from their own early life. Everywhere the fatal spirit of imitation, of reference to European standards, penetrates, and threatens to blight whatever of original growth might adorn the soil.

If the little girls grow up strong, resolute, able to exert their faculties, their mothers mourn over their want of fashionable delicacy. Are they gay, enterprising, ready to fly about in the various ways that teach them so much, these ladies lament that "they cannot go to school, where they might learn to be quiet." They lament the want of "education" for their daughters, as if the thousand needs which call out their young energies, and the language of nature around, yielded no education.

Their grand ambition for their children, is to send them to school in some eastern city, the measure most likely to make them useless and unhappy at home. I earnestly hope that, ere long, the existence of good schools near themselves, planned by persons of sufficient thought to meet the wants of the place and time, instead of copying New York or Boston, will correct this mania. Instruction the children want to enable them to profit by the great natural advantages of their position; but methods copied from the education of some English Lady Augusta, are as ill suited to the daughter of an Illinois farmer, as satin shoes to climb the Indian mounds. An elegance she would diffuse around her, if her mind were opened to appreciate elegance; it might be of a kind new, original, enchanting as different from that of the city belle as that of the prairie torchflower from the shopworn article that touches the cheek of that lady within her bonnet.

To a girl really skilled to make home beautiful and comfortable, with bodily strength to enjoy plenty of exercise, the woods, the streams, a few studies, music, and the sincere and familiar intercourse, far more easily to be met here than elsewhere, would afford happiness enough. Her eyes would not grow dim, nor her cheeks sunken, in the absence of parties, morning visits, and milliners' shops.

As to music, I wish I could see in such places the guitar rather than the piano, and good vocal more than instrumental music.

The piano many carry with them, because it is the fashionable instrument in the eastern cities. Even there, it is so merely from the habit of imitating Europe, for not one in a thousand is willing to give the labor requisite to ensure any valuable use of the instrument.

But, out here, where the ladies have so much less leisure, it is still less desirable. Add to this, they never know how to tune their own instruments, and as persons seldom visit them who can do so, these pianos are constantly out of tune, and would spoil the ear of one who began by having any.

The guitar, or some portable instrument which requires less practice, and could be kept in tune by themselves, would be far more desirable for most of these ladies. It would give all they want as a household companion to fill up the gaps of life with a pleasant stimulus or solace, and be sufficient accompaniment to the voice in social meetings.

Singing in parts is the most delightful family amusement, and those who are constantly together can learn to sing in perfect accord. All the practice it needs, after some good elementary instruction, is such as meetings by summer twilight, and evening firelight naturally suggest. And, as music is an universal language, we cannot but think a fine Italian duet would be as much at home in the log cabin as one of Mrs. Gore's novels.[11]

The sixth July we left this beautiful place. It was one of those rich days of bright sunlight, varied by the purple shadows of large sweeping clouds. Many a backward look we cast, and left the heart behind.

Our journey to-day was no less delightful than before, still all new, boundless, limitless. Kinmont[12] says, that limits are sacred; that the Greeks were in the right to worship a god of limits. I say, that what is limitless is alone divine, that there was neither wall nor road in Eden, that those who walked there lost and found their way just as we did, and that all the gain from the Fall was that we had a wagon to ride in. I do not think, either, that even the horses doubted whether this last was any advantage.

Everywhere the rattlesnake-weed grows in profusion. The antidote survives the bane. Soon the coarser plantain, the "white man's footstep," shall take its place.

We saw also the compass plant, and the western tea plant. Of some of the brightest flowers an Indian girl afterwards told me the medicinal virtues. I doubt not those students of the soil knew a use to every fair emblem, on which we could only look to admire its hues and shape.

After noon we were ferried by a girl, (unfortunately not of the most picturesque appearance) across the Kishwaukie, the most graceful stream, and on whose bosom rested many full-blown water-lilies, twice as large as any of ours. I was told that, *en revanche,* they were scentless, but I still regret that I could not get at one of them to try.

[11]Mrs. Catherine Gore (1799–1861), prolific English novelist and playwright.

[12]Alexander Kinmont (1799–1838), best known for his *Twelve Lectures on the Natural History of Man, and the Rise and Progress of Philosophy* (1839).

Query, did the lilied fragrance which, in the miraculous times, accompanied visions of saints and angels, proceed from water or garden lilies?

Kishwaukie is, according to tradition, the scene of a famous battle, and its many grassy mounds contain the bones of the valiant. On these waved thickly the mysterious purple flower, of which I have spoken before. I think it springs from the blood of the Indians, as the hyacinth did from that of Apollo's darling.

The ladies of our host's family at Oregon, when they first went there, after all the pains and plagues of building and settling, found their first pastime in opening one of these mounds, in which they found, I think, three of the departed, seated in the Indian fashion.

One of these same ladies, as she was making bread one winter morning, saw from the window a deer directly before the house. She ran out, with her hands covered with dough, calling the others, and they caught him bodily before he had time to escape.

Here (at Kishwaukie) we received a visit from a ragged and barefoot, but bright-eyed gentleman, who seemed to be the intellectual loafer, the walking Will's coffee-house of the place. He told us many charming snake stories; among others, of himself having seen seventeen young ones reënter the mother snake, on the intrusion of a visiter.

This night we reached Belvidere, a flourishing town in Boone county, where was the tomb, now despoiled, of Big Thunder.[13] In this later day we felt happy to find a really good hotel.

From this place, by two days of very leisurely and devious journeying, we reached Chicago, and thus ended a journey, which one at least of the party might have wished unending.

I have not been particularly anxious to give the geography of the scene, inasmuch as it seemed to me no route, nor series of stations, but a garden interspersed with cottages, groves and flowery lawns, through which a stately river ran. I had no guidebook, kept no diary, do not know how many miles we travelled each day, nor how many in all. What I got from the journey was the poetic impression of the country at large; it is all I have aimed to communicate.

The narrative might have been made much more interesting, as life was at the time, by many piquant anecdotes and tales drawn from private life. But here courtesy restrains the pen, for I know those who received the stranger with such frank kindness would feel ill requited by its becoming the means of fixing many spyglasses, even though the scrutiny might be one of admiring interest, upon their private homes.

For many of these, too, I was indebted to a friend, whose property they more lawfully are. This friend was one of those rare beings who are equally at home in nature and with man. He knew a tale of all that ran and swam, and flew, or only grew, possessing that extensive familiarity with things which shows equal sweetness of sympathy and playful penetration. Most refreshing to me was his unstudied lore, the

[13]The Indian chief Big Thunder had been buried by placing his body in a blanket on top of a log pyre. Fuller is referring to the habit of visitors of taking a souvenir from the burial site.

unwritten poetry which common life presents to a strong and gentle mind. It was a great contrast to the subtleties of analysis, the philosophic strainings of which I had seen too much. But I will not attempt to transplant it. May it profit others as it did me in the region where it was born, where it belongs. The evening of our return to Chicago the sunset was of a splendor and calmness beyond any we saw at the West. The twilight that succeeded was equally beautiful; soft, pathetic, but just so calm. When afterwards I learned this was the evening of Allston's death, it seemed to me as if this glorious pageant was not without connection with that event;[14] at least, it inspired similar emotions,—a heavenly gate closing a path adorned with shows well worthy Paradise.

Farewell, ye soft and sumptuous solitudes!
Ye fairy distances, ye lordly woods,
Haunted by paths like those that Poussin[15] knew,
When after his all gazers' eyes he drew;
I go,—and if I never more may steep
An eager heart in your enchantments deep,
Yet ever to itself that heart may say,
Be not exacting; thou hast lived one day;
Hast looked on that which matches with thy mood,
Impassioned sweetness of full being's flood,
Where nothing checked the bold yet gentle wave,
Where nought repelled the lavish love that gave.
A tender blessing lingers o'er the scene,
Like some young mother's thought, fond, yet serene,
And through its life new-born our lives have been.
Once more farewell,—a sad, a sweet farewell:
And, if I never must behold you more,
In other worlds I will not cease to tell
The rosary I here have numbered o'er:
And bright-haired Hope will lend a gladdened ear,
And Love will free him from the grasp of Fear,
And Gorgon critics, while the tale they hear,[16]
Shall dew their stony glances with a tear,
If I but catch one echo from your spell;—
And so farewell,—a grateful, sad farewell!

1844

[14]The noted American painter Washington Allston (1779–1843) had died on 9 July.

[15]Nicholas Poussin (1594–1665), French historical and landscape painter.

[16]In Greek mythology, the Gorgons were three sisters with snakelike hair whose gaze could turn onlookers to stone.

from Woman in the Nineteenth Century

"Frei durch Venunft, stark durch Gesetze,
Durch Sanftmuth gross, und reich durch Schätze,
Die lange Zeit dein Busen dir verschwieg."[1]

"I meant the day-star should not brighter rise,
Nor lend like influence from its lucent seat;
I meant she should be courteous, facile, sweet,
Free from that solemn vice of greatness, pride;
I meant each softest virtue there should meet,
Fit in that softer bosom to reside;
Only a (heavenward and instructed) soul
I purposed her, that should, with evea powers,
The rock, the spindle, and the shears control
Of destiny, and spin her own free hours."[2]

Preface

The following essay is a reproduction, modified and expanded, of an article published in "The Dial, Boston, July, 1843," under the title of "The Great Lawsuit. Man versus Men: Woman versus Women."

This article excited a good deal of sympathy, and still more interest. It is in compliance with wishes expressed from many quarters, that it is prepared for publication in its present form.

Objections having been made to the former title, as not sufficiently easy to be understood, the present has been substituted as expressive of the main purpose of the essay; though, by myself, the other is preferred, partly for the reason others do not like it,—that is, that it requires some thought to see what it means, and might thus prepare the reader to meet me on my own ground. Beside, it offers a larger scope, and is, in that way, more just to my desire. I meant, by that title, to intimate the fact that, while it is the destiny of Man, in the course of the Ages, to ascertain and fulfil the law of his being, so that his life shall be seen, as a whole, to be that of an angel or messenger, the action of prejudices and passions, which attend, in the day, the growth of the individual, is continually obstructing the holy work that is to make the earth a part of heaven. By Man I mean both man and woman: these are the two halves of one thought. I lay no especial stress on the welfare of either. I believe that the development of the one cannot be effected without that of the other. My highest wish is that this truth should be distinctly and rationally apprehended, and the conditions of life and freedom recognized as the same for the daughters and the sons of time; twin exponents of a divine thought.

I solicit a sincere and patient attention from those who open the following pages at all. I solicit of women that they will lay it to heart to ascertain what is for them the

[1] "Free through understanding, strong through principles,/Great through gentleness, and enriched by loved ones,/This long time your bosom has concealed you." (Source unidentified.)

[2] Ben Jonson (ca. 1573–1637), English essayist and dramatist, quoted from Epigram No. 76, "On Lucy, Countess of Bedford."

liberty of law. It is for this, and not for any, the largest, extension of partial privileges that I seek. I ask them, if interested by these suggestions, to search their own experience and intuitions for better, and fill up with fit materials and trenches that hedge them in. From men I ask a noble and earnest attention to any thing that can be offered on this great and still obscure subject, such as I have met from many with whom I stand in private relations.

And may truth, unpolluted by prejudice, vanity, or selfishness, be granted daily more and more, as the due inheritance, and only valuable conquest for us all!

November, 1844.

. . . It should be remarked that, as the principle of liberty is better understood, and more nobly interpreted, a broader protest is made in behalf of Woman. As men become aware that few men have had a fair chance, they are inclined to say that no women have had a fair chance. The French Revolution, that strangely disguised angel, bore witness in favor of Woman, but interpreted her claims no less ignorantly than those of Man. Its idea of happiness did not rise beyond outward enjoyment, unobstructed by the tyranny of others. The title it gave was "citoyen," "citoyenne," and it is not unimportant to Woman that even this species of equality was awarded her. Before, she could be condemned to perish on the scaffold for treason, not as a citizen, but as a subject. The right with which this title then invested a human being, was that of bloodshed and license. The Goddess of Liberty was impure. As we read the poem addressed to her not long since, by Beranger, we can scarcely refrain from tears as painful as the tears of blood that flowed when "such crimes were committed in her name."[3] Yes! Man, born to purify and animate the unintelligent and the cold, can, in his madness, degrade and pollute no less the fair and the chaste. Yet truth was prophesied in the ravings of that hideous fever, caused by long ignorance and abuse. Europe is conning a valued lesson from the blood-stained page. The same tendencies, farther unfolded, will bear good fruit in this country.

Yet, by men in this country, as by the Jews, when Moses was leading them to the promised land, every thing has been done that inherited depravity could do, to hinder the promise of Heaven from its fulfilment. The cross, here as elsewhere, has been planted only to be blasphemed by cruelty and fraud. The name of the Prince of Peace has been profaned by all kinds of injustice toward the Gentile whom he said he came to save. But I need not speak of what has been done towards the Red Man, the Black Man. Those deeds are the scoff of the world; and they have been accompanied by such pious words that the gentlest would not dare to intercede with "Father, forgive them, for they know not what they do."

Here, as elsewhere, the gain of creation consists always in the growth of individual minds, which live and aspire, as flowers bloom and birds sing, in the midst of morasses; and in the continual development of that thought, the thought of human destiny, which is given to eternity adequately to express, and which ages of failure only seemingly impede. Only seemingly, and whatever seems to the contrary, this country is as surely destined to elucidate a great moral law, as Europe was to promote the mental culture of Man.

[3]Pierre-Jean de Béranger (1780–1857), French lyric poet known for his "La Liberté." The quotation is attributed to Madame Roland (1754–1793), a French revolutionist.

Though the national independence be blurred by the servility of individuals, though freedom and equality have been proclaimed only to leave room for a monstrous display of slave-dealing and slave-keeping; though the free American so often feels himself free, like the Roman, only to pamper his appetites and his indolence through the misery of his fellow beings; still it is not in vain that the verbal statement has been made, "All men are born free and equal." There it stands, a golden certainty wherewith to encourage the good, to shame the bad. The New World may be called clearly to perceive that it incurs the utmost penalty if it reject or oppress the sorrowful brother. And, if men are deaf, the angels hear. But men cannot be deaf. It is inevitable that an external freedom, an independence of the encroachments of other men, such as has been achieved for the nation, should be so also for every member of it. That which has once been clearly conceived in the intelligence cannot fail, sooner or later, to be acted out. It has become a law as irrevocable as that of the Medes in their ancient dominion;[4] men will privately sin against it, but the law, as expressed by a leading mind of the age,

"Tutti fatti a sembianza d'un Solo,
Figli tutti d'un solo riscatto,
In qual'ora, in qual parte del suolo
Transcorriamo quest' aura vital,
Siam fratelli, siam stretti ad un patto:
Maladetto colui che lo infrange,
Che s'innalza sul fiacco che piange
Che contrista uno spirto immortal.[5]

"All made in the likeness of the One,
All children of one ransom,
In whatever hour, in whatever part of the soil,
We draw this vital air,
We are brothers; we must be bound by one compact,
Accursed he who infringes it,
Who raises himself upon the weak who weep,
Who saddens an immortal spirit."

This law cannot fail of universal recognition. Accursed be he who willingly saddens an immortal spirit—doomed to infamy in later, wiser ages, doomed in future stages of his own being to deadly penance, only short of death. Accursed be he who sins in ignorance, if that ignorance be caused by sloth.

We sicken no less at the pomp than the strife of words. We feel that never were lungs so puffed with the wind of declamation, on moral and religious subjects, as now. We are tempted to implore these "word-heroes," these word-Catos,

[4]The inhabitants of Medea (in what is now northwest Iran) who were conquered by the Persians under Cyrus the Great.

[5]Manzoni [Fuller's note.] Alessandro Manzoni (1785–1873), Italian romantic novelist, quoted from "Coro Dell' Atto Secondo," *Il Conte di Carmagnola,* canto 45.

word-Christs, to beware of cant[6] above all things; to remember that hypocrisy is the most hopeless as well as the meanest of crimes, and that those must surely be polluted by it, who do not reserve a part of their morality and religion for private use. Landor[7] says that he cannot have a great deal of mind who cannot afford to let the larger part of it lie fallow, and what is true of genius is not less so of virtue. The tongue is a valuable member, but should appropriate but a small part of the vital juices that are needful all over the body. We feel that the mind may "grow black and rancid in the smoke" even "of altars." We start up from the harangue to go into our closet and shut the door. There inquires the spirit, "Is this rhetoric the bloom of healthy blood or a false pigment artfully laid on?" And yet again we know where is so much smoke, must be some fire; with so much talk about virtue and freedom, must be mingled some desire for them; that it cannot be in vain that such have become the common topics of conversation among men, rather than schemes for tyranny and plunder, that the very newspapers see it best to proclaim themselves "Pilgrims," "Puritans," "Heralds of Holiness." The king that maintains so costly a retinue cannot be a mere boast, or Carabbas fiction.[8] We have waited here long in the dust; we are tired and hungry, but the triumphal procession must appear at last.

Of all its banners, none has been more steadily upheld, and under none have more valor and willingness for real sacrifices been shown, than that of the champions of the enslaved African. And this band it is, which, partly from a natural following out of principles, partly because many women have been prominent in that cause, makes, just now, the warmest appeal in behalf of Woman.

Though there has been a growing liberality on this subject, yet society at large is not so prepared for the demands of this party, but that they are and will be for some time, coldly regarded as the Jacobins[9] of their day.

"Is it not enough," cries the irritated trader, "that you have done all you could to break up the national union, and thus destroy the prosperity of our country, but now you must be trying to break up family union, to take my wife away from the cradle and the kitchen hearth to vote at polls, and preach from a pulpit? Of course, if she does such things, she cannot attend to those of her own sphere. She is happy enough as she is. She has more leisure than I have, every means of improvement, every indulgence."

"Have you asked her whether she was satisfied with these *indulgences*?"

"No, but I know she is. She is too amiable to wish what would make me unhappy, and too judicious to wish to step beyond the sphere of her sex. I will never consent to have our peace disturbed by any such discussions."

[6]Dr. Johnson's one piece of advice should be written on every door; "Clear your mind of cant." But Byron, to whom it was so acceptable, in clearing away the noxious vine, shook down the building. Sterling's emendation is worthy of honor: "Realize your cant, not cast it off." [Fuller's note.] Samuel Johnson (1709–1784), English lexicographer and essayist, quoted from James Boswell, *The Life of Samuel Johnson* (1791), dated 15 May 1873. John Sterling (1806–1844), English poet and dramatist.

[7]Walter Savage Landor (1775–1864), English essayist.

[8]Carabbas, a character in Perrault's *Le Chat Botté (Puss in Boots),* whose name is synonymous with aristocratic pretension.

[9]Jacobins, the name given to a radical organization in the French Revolution and usually associated with the Reign of Terror under Robespierre.

"'Consent—you?' it is not consent from you that is in question, it is assent from your wife."

"Am not I the head of my house?"

"You are not the head of your wife. God has given her a mind of her own."

"I am the head and she the heart."

"God grant you play true to one another then. I suppose I am to be grateful that you did not say she was only the hand. If the head represses no natural pulse of the heart, there can be no question as to your giving your consent. Both will be of one accord, and there needs but to present any question to get a full and true answer. There is no need of precaution, of indulgence, or consent. But our doubt is whether the heart *does* consent with the head, or only obeys its decrees with a passiveness that precludes the exercise of its natural powers, or a repugnance that turns sweet qualities to bitter, or a doubt that lays waste the fair occasions of life. It is to ascertain the truth, that we propose some liberating measures."

Thus vaguely are these questions proposed and discussed at present. But their being proposed at all implies much thought and suggests more. Many women are considering within themselves, what they need that they have not, and what they can have, if they find they need it. Many men are considering whether women are capable of being and having more than they are and have, *and,* whether, if so, it will be best to consent to improvement in their condition.

This morning, I open the Boston "Daily Mail," and find in its "poet's corner," a translation of Schiller's "Dignity of Woman." In the advertisement of a book on America, I see in the table of contents this sequence, "Republican Institutions. American Slavery. American Ladies."

I open the *"Deutsche Schnellpost,"* published in New-York, and find at the head of a column, *Judenund Frauen-emancipation in Ungarn.* "Emancipation of Jews and Women in Hungary."

The past year has seen action in the Rhode-Island legislature, to secure married women rights over their own property, where men showed that a very little examination of the subject could teach them much; an article in the Democratic Review on the same subject more largely considered, written by a woman, impelled, it is said, by glaring wrong to a distinguished friend having shown the defects in the existing laws, and the state of opinion from which they spring; and an answer from the revered old man, J.Q. Adams, in some respects the Phocion of his time, to an address made him by some ladies.[10] To this last I shall again advert in another place.

These symptoms of the times have come under my view quite accidentally: one who seeks, may, each month or week, collect more.

The numerous party, whose opinions are already labelled and adjusted too much to their mind to admit of any new light, strive, by lectures on some model-woman of bride-like beauty and gentleness, by writing and lending little treatises, intended to mark out with precision the limits of Woman's sphere, and Woman's mission, to prevent other than the rightful shepherd from climbing the wall, or the flock from using any chance to go astray.

[10]The article is "The Legal Wrongs of Women," *United States Magazine and Democratic Review,* 14 (May 1844): 477–483. John Quincy Adams (1767–1848), sixth president of the United States. Phocion (ca. 402–317 B.C.), leader of the aristocratic party in Athens.

Without enrolling ourselves at once on either side, let us look upon the subject from the best point of view which to-day offers. No better, it is to be feared, than a high house-top. A high hill-top, or at least a cathedral spire, would be desirable.

It may well be an Anti-Slavery party that pleads for Woman, if we consider merely that she does not hold property on equal terms with men; so that, if a husband dies without making a will, the wife, instead of taking at once his place as head of the family, inherits only a part of his fortune, often brought him by herself, as if she were a child, or ward only, not an equal partner.

We will not speak of the innumerable instances in which profligate and idle men live upon the earnings of industrious wives; or if the wives leave them, and take with them the children, to perform the double duty of mother and father, follow from place to place, and threaten to rob them of the children, if deprived of the rights of a husband, as they call them, planting themselves in their poor lodgings, frightening them into paying tribute by taking from them the children, running into debt at the expense of these otherwise so overtasked helots. Such instances count up by scores within my own memory. I have seen the husband who had stained himself by a long course of low vice, till his wife was wearied from her heroic forgiveness, by finding that his treachery made it useless, and that if she would provide bread for herself and her children, she must be separate from his ill fame—I have known this man come to install himself in the chamber of a woman who loathed him and say she should never take food without his company. I have known these men steal their children whom they knew they had no means to maintain, take them into dissolute company, expose them to bodily danger, to frighten the poor woman, to whom, it seems, the fact that she alone had borne the pangs of their birth, and nourished their infancy, does not give an equal right to them. I do believe that this mode of kidnapping—and it is frequent enough in all classes of society—will be by the next age viewed as it is by Heaven now, and that the man who avails himself of the shelter of men's laws to steal from a mother her own children, or arrogate any superior right in them, save that of superior virtue, will bear the stigma he deserves, in common with him who steals grown men from their mother land, their hopes, and their homes.

I said, we will not speak of this now, yet I *have* spoken, for the subject makes me feel too much. I could give instances that would startle the most vulgar and callous, but I will not, for the public opinion of their own sex is already against such men, and where cases of extreme tyranny are made known, there is private action in the wife's favor. But she ought not to need this, nor, I think, can she long. Men must soon see that, on their own ground, that Woman is the weaker party, she ought to have legal protection, which would make such oppression impossible. But I would not deal with "atrocious instances" except in the way of illustration, neither demand from men a partial redress in some one matter, but go to the root of the whole. If principles could be established, particulars would adjust themselves aright. Ascertain the true destiny of Woman, give her legitimate hopes, and a standard within herself; marriage and all other relations would by degrees be harmonized with these.

But to return to the historical progress of this matter. Knowing that there exists in the minds of men a tone of feeling towards women as towards slaves, such as is expressed in the common phrase, "Tell that to women and children," that the infinite soul can only work through them in already ascertained limits; that the gift of reason, Man's highest prerogative, is allotted to them in much lower degree; that they must be kept from mischief and melancholy by being constantly engaged in active labor, which is to be furnished and directed by those better able to think, &c. &c,—we need not multiply instances, for who can review the experience of last week without recalling words which imply, whether in jest or earnest, these views or views like these,—knowing this, can we wonder that many reformers think that measures are not likely to be taken in behalf of women, unless their wishes could be publicly represented by women?

"That can never be necessary," cry the other side. "All men are privately influenced by women; each has his wife, sister, or female friends, and is too much biased by these relations to fail of representing their interests, and, if this is not enough, let them propose and enforce their wishes with the pen. The beauty of home would be destroyed, the delicacy of the sex be violated, the dignity of halls of legislation degraded by an attempt to introduce them there. Such duties are inconsistent with those of a mother"; and then we have ludicrous pictures of ladies in hysterics at the polls, and senate chambers filled with cradles.

But if, in reply, we admit as truth that Woman seems destined by nature rather for the inner circle, we must add that the arrangements of civilized life have not been, as yet, such as to secure it to her. Her circle, if the duller, is not the quieter. If kept from "excitement," she is not from drudgery. Not only the Indian squaw carries the burdens of the camp, but the favorites of Louis XIV accompany him in his journeys, and the washerwoman stands at her tub and carries home her work at all seasons, and in all states of health. Those who think the physical circumstances of Woman would make a part in the affairs of national government unsuitable, are by no means those who think it impossible for the negresses to endure field work, even during pregnancy, or the sempstresses to go through their killing labors.

As to the use of the pen, there was quite as much opposition to Woman's possessing herself of that help to free agency, as there is now to her seizing on the rostrum or the desk;[11] and she is likely to draw, from a permission to plead her cause that way, opposite inferences to what might be wished by those who now grant it.

As to the possibility of her filling with grace and dignity, any such position, we should think those who had seen the great actresses, and heard the Quaker preachers of modern times, would not doubt, that Woman can express publicly the fulness of thought and creation, without losing any of the peculiar beauty of her sex. What can pollute and tarnish is to act thus from any motive except that something needs to be said or done. Woman could take part in the processions, the songs, the dances of old religion; no one fancied their delicacy was impaired by appearing in public for such a cause.

As to her home, she is not likely to leave it more than she now does for balls, theatres, meetings for promoting missions, revival meetings, and others to which she flies, in hope of an animation for her existence, commensurate with what she sees enjoyed by men. Governors of ladies' fairs are no less engrossed by such a change, than the Governor of the state by his; presidents of Washingtonian societies[12] no less away from home than presidents of conventions. If men look straitly to it, they will find that, unless their lives are domestic, those of the women will not be. A house is

[11] That is, women were actively discouraged from speaking in public, especially to mixed audiences.

[12] Temperance societies named after George Washington, first president of the United States.

no home unless it contain food and fire for the mind as well as for the body. The female Greek, of our day, is as much in the street as the male to cry, "What news?" We doubt not it was the same in Athens of old. The women, shut out from the market-place, made up for it at the religious festivals. For human beings are not so constituted that they can live without expansion. If they do not get it one way, they must another, or perish.

As to men's representing women fairly at present, while we hear from men who owe to their wives not only all that is comfortable or graceful, but all that is wise in the arrangement of their lives, the frequent remark, "You cannot reason with a woman,"—when from those of delicacy, nobleness, and poetic culture, falls the contemptuous phrase "women and children," and that in no light sally of the hour, but in works intended to give a permanent statement of the best experiences,—when not one man, in the million, shall I say? no, not in the hundred million, can rise above the belief that Woman was made *for man,*—when such traits as these are daily forced upon the attention, can we feel that Man will always do justice to the interests of Woman? Can we think that he takes a sufficiently discerning and religious view of her office and destiny, *ever* to do her justice, except when prompted by sentiment,—accidentally or transiently, that is, for the sentiment will vary according to the relations in which he is placed. The lover, the poet, the artist, are likely to view her nobly. The father and the philosopher have some chance of liberality; the man of the world, the legislator for expediency, none.

Under these circumstances, without attaching importance, in themselves, to the changes demanded by the champions of Woman, we hail them as signs of the times. We would have every arbitrary barrier thrown down. We would have every path laid open to Woman as freely as to Man. Were this done and a slight temporary fermentation allowed to subside, we should see crystallizations more pure and of more various beauty. We believe the divine energy would pervade nature to a degree unknown in the history of former ages, and that no discordant collision, but a ravishing harmony of the spheres would ensue.

Yet, then and only then, will mankind be ripe for this, when inward and outward freedom for Woman as much as for Man shall be acknowledged as *a right,* not yielded as a concession. As the friend of the negro assumes that one man cannot by right, hold another in bondage, so should the friend of Woman assume that Man cannot, by right, lay even well-meant restrictions on Woman. If the negro be a soul, if the woman be a soul, apparelled in flesh, to one Master only are they accountable. There is but one law for souls, and if there is to be an interpreter of it, he must come not as man, or son of man, but as son of God.

Were thought and feeling once so far elevated that Man should esteem himself the brother and friend, but nowise the lord and tutor of Woman,—were he really bound with her in equal worship,—arrangements as to function and employment would be of no consequence. What Woman needs is not as a woman to act or rule, but as a nature to grow, as an intellect to discern, as a soul to live freely and unimpeded, to unfold such powers as were given her when we left our common home. If fewer talents were given her, yet if allowed the free and full employment of these, so that she may render back to the giver his own with usury, she will not complain; nay, I dare to say she will bless and rejoice in her earthly birth-place, her earthly lot. Let us consider what obstructions impede this good era, and what signs give reason to hope that it draws near.

I was talking on this subject with Miranda, a woman, who, if any in the world could, might speak without heat and bitterness of the position of her sex. Her father was a man who cherished no sentimental reverence for Woman, but a firm belief in the equality of the sexes. She was his eldest child, and came to him at an age when he needed a companion. From the time she could speak and go alone, he addressed her not as a plaything, but as a living mind. Among the few verses he ever wrote was a copy addressed to this child, when the first locks were cut from her head, and the reverence expressed on this occasion for that cherished head, he never belied. It was to him the temple of immortal intellect. He respected his child, however, too much to be an indulgent parent. He called on her for clear judgement, for courage, for honor and fidelity; in short, for such virtues as he knew. In so far as he possessed the keys to the wonders of this universe, he allowed free use of them to her, and by the incentive of a high expectation, he forbade, as far as possible, that she should let the privilege lie idle.

Thus this child was early led to feel herself a child of the spirit. She took her place easily, not only in the world of organized being, but in the world of mind. A dignified sense of self-dependence was given as all her portion, and she found it a sure anchor. Herself securely anchored, her relations with others were established with equal security. She was fortunate in a total absence of those charms which might have drawn to her bewildering flatteries, and in a strong electric nature, which repelled those who did not belong to her, and attracted those who did. With men and women her relations were noble,—affectionate without passion, intellectual without coldness. The world was free to her, and she lived freely in it. Outward adversity came, and inward conflict, but that faith and self-respect had early been awakened which must always lead at last, to an outward serenity and an inward peace.

Of Miranda I had always thought as an example, that the restraints upon the sex were insuperable only to those who think them so, or who noisily strive to break them. She had taken a course of her own, and no man stood in her way. Many of her acts had been unusual, but excited no uproar. Few helped, but none checked her; and the many men, who knew her mind and her life, showed to her confidence, as to a brother, gentleness as to a sister. And not only refined, but very coarse men approved and aided one in whom they saw resolution and clearness of design. Her mind was often the leading one, always effective.

When I talked with her upon these matters, and had said very much what I have written, she smilingly replied: "And yet we must admit that I have been fortunate, and this should not be. My good father's early trust gave the first bias, and the rest followed of course. It is true that I have had less outward aid, in after years, than most women; but that is of little consequence. Religion was early awakened in my soul,—a sense that what the soul is capable to ask it must attain, and that, though I might be aided and instructed by others, I must depend on myself as the only constant friend. This self-dependence, which was honored in me, is deprecated as a fault in most women. They are taught to learn their rule from without, not to unfold it from within.

"This is the fault to Man, who is still vain, and wishes to be more important to Woman than, by right, he should be."

"Men have not shown this disposition toward you," I said.

"No! because the position I early was enabled to take was one of self-reliance. And were all women as sure of their wants as I was, the result would be the same. But they are so overloaded with precepts by guardians, who think that nothing is so much to be dreaded for a woman as originality of thought or character, that their minds are impeded by doubts till they lose their chance of fair, free proportions. The difficulty is to get them to the point from which they shall naturally develope self-respect, and learn self-help.

"Once I thought that men would help to forward this state of things more than I do now. I saw so many of them wretched in the connections they had formed in weakness and vanity. They seemed so glad to esteem women whenever they could.

"'The soft arms of affection' said one of the most discerning spirits, 'will not suffice for me, unless on them I see the steel bracelets of strength.'

"But early I perceived that men never, in any extreme of despair, wished to be women. On the contrary they were ever ready to taunt one another, at any sign of weakness, with,

"'Art thou not like the women, who'—

The passage ends various ways, according to the occasion and rhetoric of the speaker. When they admired any woman they were inclined to speak of her as 'above her sex.' Silently I observed this, and feared it argued a rooted scepticism, which for ages had been fastening on the heart, and which only an age of miracles could eradicate. Ever I have been treated with great sincerity; and I look upon it as a signal instance of this, that an intimate friend of the other sex said, in a fervent moment, that I 'deserved in some star to be a man.' He was much surprised when I disclosed my view of my position and hopes, when I declared my faith that the feminine side, the side of love, of beauty, of holiness, was now to have its full chance, and that, if either were better, it was better now to be a woman, for even the slightest achievement of good was furthering an especial work of our time. He smiled incredulously. 'She makes the best she can of it,' thought he. 'Let Jews believe the pride of Jewry, but I am of the better sort, and know better.'

"Another used as highest praise, in speaking of a character in literature, the words 'a manly woman.'

"So in the noble passage of Ben Jonson:

'I meant the day-star should not brighter ride,
  Nor shed like influence from its lucent seat;
I meant she should be courteous, facile, sweet,
  Free from that solemn vice of greatness, pride;
I meant each softest virtue there should meet,
  Fit in that softer bosom to abide,
Only a learned and a *manly* soul
  I purposed her, that should with even powers
The rock, the spindle, and the shears control
  Of destiny, and spin her own free hours.'"

"Methinks," said I, "you are too fastidious in objecting to this. Jonson, in using the word 'manly,' only meant to heighten the picture of this, the true, the intelligent fate, with one of the deeper colors."

"And yet," said she, "so invariable is the use of this word where a heroic quality is to be described, and I feel so sure that persistence and courage are the most womanly no less than the most manly qualities, that I would exchange these words for others of a larger sense at the risk of marring the fine tissue of the verse. Read, 'A heavenward and instructed soul,' and I should be satisfied. Let it not be said, wherever there is energy or creative genius, 'She has a masculine mind.'"

This by no means argues a willing want of generosity toward Woman. Man is as generous towards her as he knows how to be.

Wherever she has herself arisen in national or private history, and nobly shone forth in any form of excellence, men have received her, not only willingly, but with triumph. Their encomiums, indeed, are always, in some sense, mortifying; they show too much surprise. "Can this be you?" he cries to the transfigured Cinderella; "well, I should never have thought it, but I am very glad. We will tell every one that you have *'surpassed your sex.'"*

In every-day life, the feelings of the many are stained with vanity. Each wishes to be lord in a little world, to be superior at least over one; and he does not feel strong enough to retain a life-long ascendency over a strong nature. Only a Theseus could conquer before he wed the Amazonian queen.[13] Hercules wished rather to rest with Dejanira, and received the poisoned robe as a fit guerdon. The tale should be interpreted to all those who seek repose with the weak.[14]

But not only is Man vain and fond of power, but the same want of development, which thus affects him morally, prevents his intellectually discerning the destiny of Woman. The boy wants no woman, but only a girl to play ball with him, and mark his pocket handkerchief.

Thus, in Schiller's Dignity of Woman,[15] beautiful as the poem is, there is no "grave and perfect man," but only a great boy to be softened and restrained by the influence of girls. Poets—the elder brothers of their race—have usually seen further; but what can you expect of every-day men, if Schiller was not more prophetic as to what women must be? Even with Richter,[16] one foremost thought about a wife was that she would "cook him something good." But as this is a delicate subject, and we are in constant danger of being accused of slighting what are called "the functions," let me say, in behalf of Miranda and myself, that we have high respect for those who "cook something good," who create and preserve fair order in houses, and prepare therein the shining raiment for worthy inmates, worthy guests. Only these "functions" must not be a drudgery, or enforced necessity, but a part of life. Let Ulysses drive the beeves home, while Penelope there piles up the fragrant loaves; they are both well employed if these be done in thought and love, willingly. But Penelope is no more meant for a baker or weaver solely, than Ulysses for a cattle-herd.[17]

[13]Theseus was a Greek hero; the Amazonian queen Hippolyte or Orethyia. Fuller seems to mean that it takes a man as strong as Theseus to wed a woman as strong as the Amazonian queen.

[14]The weak Dejanira, trying to win back the love of the wandering Greek demi-god Hercules, gave him as a gift a shirt she had obtained from Nessus. She had been led to believe that the shirt was steeped in a love potion; instead, it contained a caustic poison which devoured Hercules' flesh.

[15]A poem by the German writer Friedrich von Schiller (1759–1805). It praises women for docility by way of contrast with "masculine" aspiration and passion.

[16]The German fiction writer Jean Paul Richter (1763–1825) generally drew sympathetic portraits of women, but in some of his work he puts forward many of the patriarchal assumptions about woman's "place."

[17]Ulysses is the hero of Homer's epic, *The Odyssey,* and Penelope is the faithful wife who awaits his return.

The sexes should not only correspond to and appreciate, but prophesy to one another. In individual instances this happens. Two persons love in one another the future good which they aid one another to unfold. This is imperfectly or rarely done in the general life. Man has gone but little way; now he is waiting to see whether Woman can keep step with him; but, instead of calling out, like a good brother, "You can do it, if you only think so," or impersonally, "Any one can do what he tries to do"; he often discourages with school-boy brag: "Girls can't do that; girls can't play ball." But let any one defy their taunts, break through and be brave and secure, they rend the air with shouts. . . .

A little while since, I was at one of the most fashionable places of public resort. I saw there many women, dressed without regard to the season or the demands of the place, in apery, or, as it looked, in mockery, of European fashions. I saw their eyes restlessly courting attention. I saw the way in which it was paid: the style of devotion, almost an open sneer, which it pleased those ladies to receive from men whose expression marked their own low position in the moral and intellectual world. Those women went to their pillows with their heads full of folly, their hearts of jealousy, or gratified vanity; those men, with the low opinion they already entertained of Woman confirmed. These were American *ladies;* that is, they were of that class who have wealth and leisure to make full use of the day, and confer benefits on others. They were of that class whom the possession of external advantages makes of pernicious example to many, if these advantages be misused.

Soon after, I met a circle of women, stamped by society as among the most degraded of their sex. "How," it was asked of them, "did you come here?" for, by the society that I saw in the former place, they were shut up in a prison. The causes were not difficult to trace: love of dress, love of flattery, love of excitement. They had not dresses like the other ladies, so they stole them; they could not pay for flattery by distinctions, and the dower of a worldly marriage, so they paid by the profanation of their persons. In excitement, more and more madly sought from day to day, they drowned the voice of conscience.

Now I ask you, my sisters, if the women at the fashionable house be not answerable for those women being in the prison?

As to position in the world of souls, we may suppose the women of the prison stood fairest, both because they had misused less light, and because loneliness and sorrow had brought some of them to feel the need of better life, nearer truth and good. This was no merit in them, being an effect of circumstance, but it was hopeful. But you, my friends, (and some of you I have already met), consecrate yourselves without waiting for reproof, in free love and unbroken energy, to win and to diffuse a better life. Offer beauty, talents, riches, on the altar; thus shall ye keep spotless your own hearts, and be visibly or invisibly the angels to others.

I would urge upon those women who have not yet considered this subject, to do so. Do not forget the unfortunates who dare not cross your guarded way. If it do not suit you to act with those who have organized measures of reform, then hold not yourself excused from acting in private. Seek out these degraded women, give them tender sympathy, counsel, employment. Take the place of mothers, such as might have saved them originally.

If you can do little for those already under the ban of the world,—and the best considered efforts have often failed, from a want of strength in those unhappy ones to bear up against the sting of shame and the prejudices of the world, which makes them seek oblivion again in their old excitements,—you will at least leave a sense of love and justice in their hearts, that will prevent their becoming utterly embittered and corrupt. And you may learn the means of prevention for those yet uninjured. There will be found in a diffusion of mental culture, simple tastes, best taught by your example, a genuine self-respect, and above all, what the influence of Man tends to hide from Woman, the love and fear of a divine, in preference to a human tribunal.

But suppose you save many who would have lost their bodily innocence (for as to mental, the loss of that is incalculably more general,) through mere vanity and folly; there still remain many, the prey and spoil of the brute passions of Man; for the stories frequent in our newspapers outshame antiquity, and vie with the horrors of war.

As to this, it must be considered that, as the vanity and proneness to seduction of the imprisoned women represented a general degradation in their sex; so do these acts a still more general and worse in the male. Where so many are weak it is natural there should be many lost, where legislators admit that ten thousand prostitutes are a fair proportion to one city, and husbands tell their wives that it is folly to expect chastity from men, it is inevitable that there should be many monsters of vice. . . .

There are two aspects of Woman's nature, represented by the ancients as Muse and Minerva.[18] It is the former to which the writer in the Pathfinder looks.[19] It is the latter which Wordsworth has in mind, when he says,

> "With a placid brow,
> Which woman ne'er should forfeit, keep thy vow."[20]

The especial genius of Woman I believe to be electrical in movement, intuitive in function, spiritual in tendency. She excels not so easily in classification, or recreation, as in an instinctive seizure of causes, and a simple breathing out of what she receives, that has the singleness of life, rather than the selecting and energizing of art.

More native is it to her to be the living model of the artist than to set apart from herself any one form in objective reality; more native to inspire and receive the poem, than to create it. In so far as soul is in her completely developed, all soul is the same; but in so far as it is modified in her as Woman, it flows, it breathes, it sings, rather than deposits soil, or finishes work; and that which is especially feminine flushes, in blossom, the face of earth, and pervades, like air and water, all this seeming solid globe, daily renewing and purifying its life. Such may be the especially feminine element spoken of as Femality. But it is no more the order of nature that it should be incarnated pure in any form, than that the masculine energy should exist unmingled with it in any form.

Male and female represent the two sides of the great radical dualism. But, in fact, they are perpetually passing into one another. Fluid hardens to solid, solid rushes to fluid. There is no wholly masculine man, no purely feminine woman.

[18]The Muses were goddesses of the arts, poetry, song, the sciences; Fuller uses them to represent woman's artistic nature. Minerva, Roman goddess of wisdom and handicrafts, was sometimes portrayed in armor, and here represents intellectual strength.

[19]A New York newspaper writer had published two articles under the title "Femality."

[20]Slightly altered from *Liberty: Sequel to the Preceding* (1835) by the English poet William Wordsworth.

History jeers at the attempts of physiologists to bind great original laws by the forms which flow from them. They make a rule; they say from observation what can and cannot be. In vain! Nature provides exceptions to every rule. She sends women to battle, and sets Hercules spinning; she enables women to bear immense burdens, cold, and frost; she enables the man, who feels maternal love, to nourish his infant like a mother. Of late she plays still gayer pranks. Not only she deprives organizations, but organs, of a necessary end. She enables people to read with the top of the head, and see with the pit of the stomach. Presently she will make a female Newton, and a male Syren.[21]

Man partakes of the feminine in the Apollo, Woman of the masculine as Minerva.

What I mean by the Muse is that unimpeded clearness of the intuitive powers, which a perfectly truthful adherence to every admonition of the higher instincts would bring to a finely organized human being. It may appear as prophecy or as poesy. It enabled Cassandra[22] to foresee the results of actions passing round her; the Seeress to behold the true character of the person through the mask of his customary life. (Sometimes she saw a feminine form behind the man, sometimes the reverse.) It enabled the daughter of Linnaeus to see the soul of the flower exhaling from the flower.[23] It gave a man, but a poet-man, the power of which he thus speaks: "Often in my contemplation of nature, radiant intimations, and as it were sheaves of light, appear before me as to the facts of cosmogony, in which my mind has, perhaps, taken especial part." He wisely adds, "but it is necessary with earnestness to verify the knowledge we gain by these flashes of light." And none should forget this. Sight must be verified by light before it can deserve the honors of piety and genius. Yet sight comes first, and of this sight of the world of causes, this approximation to the region of primitive motions, women I hold to be especially capable. Even without equal freedom with the other sex, they have already shown themselves so; and should these faculties have free play, I believe they will open new, deeper and purer sources of joyous inspiration than have as yet refreshed the earth.

Let us be wise, and not impede the soul. Let her work as she will. Let us have one creative energy, one incessant revelation. Let it take what form it will, and let us not bind it by the past to man or woman, black or white. Jove sprang from Rhea, Pallas from Jove.[24] So let it be.

If it has been the tendency of these remarks to call Woman rather to the Minerva side,—if I, unlike the more generous writer, have spoken from society no less than the soul,—let it be pardoned! It is love that has caused this,—love for many incarcerated souls, that might be freed, could the idea of religious self-dependence be established in them, could the weakening habit of dependence on others be broken up.

[21]Isaac Newton (1642–1727), the British mathematician. In Greek mythology, the Sirens were sea nymphs who lured mariners into shipwreck.

[22]Daughter of Priam, King of Troy, she was gifted with the power of prophecy, but also fated not to be believed by those around her.

[23]The daughter of Linnaeus states, that, while looking steadfastly at the red lily, she saw its spirit hovering above it, as a red flame. It is true, this, like many fair spirit-stories, may be explained away as an optical illusion, but its poetic beauty and meaning would, even then, make it valuable, as an illustration of the spiritual fact. [Fuller's note.] Karl Linnaeus, Swedish botanist (1707–1778) developed a system for classifying plants.

[24]The chief Roman god, Jove or Jupiter, was born of Rhea. Pallas Athene sprang, fully armored, from his head.

Proclus[25] teaches that every life has, in its sphere, a totality or wholeness of the animating powers of the other spheres; having only, as its own characteristic, a predominance of some one power. Thus Jupiter comprises, within himself, the other twelve powers, which stand thus: The first triad is *demiurgic or fabricative,* that is, Jupiter, Neptune, Vulcan; the second, *defensive,* Vesta, Minerva, Mars; the third, *vivific,* Ceres, Juno, Diana; and the fourth, Mercury, Venus, Apollo, *elevating and harmonic.* In the sphere of Jupiter, energy is predominant—with Venus, beauty; but each comprehends and apprehends all the others.[26]

When the same community of life and consciousness of mind begin among men, humanity will have, positively and finally, subjugated its brute elements and Titanic childhood; criticism will have perished; arbitrary limits and ignorant censure be impossible; all will have entered upon the liberty of law, and the harmony of common growth.

Then Apollo will sing to his lyre what Vulcan forges on the anvil, and the Muse weave anew the tapestries of Minerva.

It is, therefore, only in the present crisis that the preference is given to Minerva. The power of continence must establish the legitimacy of freedom, the power of self-poise the perfection of motion.

Every relation, every gradation of nature is incalculably precious, but only to the soul which is poised upon itself, and to whom no loss, no change, can bring dull discord, for it is in harmony with the central soul.

If any individual live too much in relations, so that he becomes a stranger to the resources of his own nature, he falls, after a while, into a distraction, or imbecility, from which he can only be cured by a time of isolation, which gives the renovating fountains time to rise up. With a society it is the same. Many minds, deprived of the traditionary or instinctive means of passing a cheerful existence, must find help in self-impulse, or perish. It is therefore that, while any elevation, in the view of union, is to be hailed with joy, we shall not decline celibacy as the great fact of the time. It is one from which no vow, no arrangement, can at present save a thinking mind. For now the rowers are pausing on their oars; they wait a change before they can pull together. All tends to illustrate the thought of a wise contemporary. Union is only possible to those who are units. To be fit for relations in time, souls, whether of Man or Woman, must be able to do without them in the spirit.

It is therefore that I would have Woman lay aside all thought, such as she habitually cherishes, of being taught and led by men. I would have her, like the Indian girl, dedicate herself to the Sun, the Sun of Truth, and go nowhere if his beams did not make clear the path. I would have her free from compromise, from complaisance, from helplessness, because I would have her good enough and strong enough to love one and all beings, from the fulness, not the poverty of being.

Men, as at present instructed, will not help this work, because they also are under the slavery of habit. I have seen with delight their poetic impulses. A sister is the fairest ideal, and how nobly Wordsworth, and even Byron, have written of a sister![27]

[25]Greek philosopher (c. 410–485 B.C.).

[26]Fuller interprets Jupiter, the chief among Roman gods, as incorporating the qualities of all the other major Roman gods.

[27]William Wordsworth paid poetic tribute to his sister Dorothy; Byron to Augusta Leigh, his half-sister.

There is no sweeter sight than to see a father with his little daughter. Very vulgar men become refined to the eye when leading a little girl by the hand. At that moment, the right relation between the sexes seems established, and you feel as if the man would aid in the noblest purpose, if you ask him in behalf of his little daughter. Once, two fine figures stood before me, thus. The father of very intellectual aspect, his falcon eye softened by affection as he looked down on his fair child; she the image of himself, only more graceful and brilliant in expression. I was reminded of Southey's Kehama;[28] when, lo, the dream was rudely broken! They were talking of education, and he said,

"I shall not have Maria brought too forward. If she knows too much, she will never find a husband; superior women hardly ever can."

"Surely," said his wife, with a blush, "you wish Maria to be as good and wise as she can, whether it will help her to marriage or not."

"No," he persisted, "I want her to have a sphere and a home, and some one to protect her when I am gone."

It was a trifling incident, but made a deep impression. I felt that the holiest relations fail to instruct the unprepared and perverted mind. If this man, indeed, could have looked at it on the other side, he was the last that would have been willing to have been taken himself for the home and protection he could give, but would have been much more likely to repeat the tale of Alcibiades with his phials.

But men do *not* look at both sides, and women must leave off asking them and being influenced by them, but retire within themselves, and explore the groundwork of life till they find their peculiar secret. Then, when they come forth again, renovated and baptized, they will know how to turn all dross to gold, and will be rich and free though they live in a hut, tranquil if in a crowd. Then their sweet singing shall not be from passionate impulse, but the lyrical overflow of a divine rapture, and a new music shall be evolved from this many-chorded world.

Grant her, then, for a while, the armor and the javelin.[29] Let her put from her the press of other minds, and meditate in virgin loneliness. The same idea shall reäppear in due time as Muse, or Ceres,[30] the all-kindly, patient Earth-Spirit. . . .

And now I have designated in outline, if not in fulness, the stream which is ever flowing from the heights of my thought.

In the earlier tract, I was told, I did not make my meaning sufficiently clear. In this I have consequently tried to illustrate it in various ways, and may have been guilty of much repetition. Yet, as I am anxious to leave no room for doubt, I shall venture to retrace, once more, the scope of my design in points, as was done in old-fashioned sermons.

Man is a being of two-fold relations, to nature beneath, and intelligences above him. The earth is his school, if not his birth-place; God his object; life and thought his means of interpreting nature, and aspiring to God.

Only a fraction of this purpose is accomplished in the life of any one man. Its entire accomplishment is to be hoped only from the sum of the lives of men, or Man considered as a whole.

[28]A narrative poem, *The Curse of Kehama* (1810) by British poet Robert Southey (1774–1843).

[29]The defense and weapon of Pallas Athene, the Greek goddess of wisdom.

[30]Roman goddess of agriculture, grain, and harvest.

As this whole has one soul and one body, any injury or obstruction to a part, or to the meanest member, affects the whole. Man can never be perfectly happy or virtuous, till all men are so.

To address Man wisely, you must not forget that his life is partly animal, subject to the same laws with Nature.

But you cannot address him wisely unless you consider him still more as soul and appreciate the conditions and destiny of soul.

The growth of Man is two-fold, masculine and feminine.

As far as these two methods can be distinguished they are so as

Energy and Harmony;
Power and Beauty;
Intellect and Love;

or by some such rude classification; for we have not language primitive and pure enough to express such ideas with precision.

These two sides are supposed to be expressed in Man and Woman, that is, as the more and less, for the faculties have not been given pure to either, but only in preponderance. There are also exceptions in great number, such as men of far more beauty than power, and the reverse. But as a general rule, it seems to have been the intention to give a preponderance on the one side, that is called masculine, and on the other, one that is called feminine.

There cannot be a doubt that, if these two developments were in perfect harmony, they would correspond to and fulfil one another, like hemispheres, or the tenor and bass in music.

But there is no perfect harmony in human nature; and the two parts answer one another only now and then; or, if there be a persistent consonance, it can only be traced, at long intervals, instead of discoursing an obvious melody.

What is the cause of this?

Man, in the order of time, was developed first; as energy comes before harmony; power before beauty.

Woman was therefore under his care as an elder. He might have been her guardian and teacher.

But as human nature goes not straight forward, but by excessive action and then reaction in an undulated course, he misunderstood and abused his advantages, and became her temporal master instead of her spiritual sire.

On himself came the punishment. He educated Woman more as a servant than a daughter, and found himself a king without a queen.

The children of this unequal union showed unequal natures, and, more and more, men seemed sons of the hand-maid, rather than princess.

At last there were so many Ishmaelites that the rest grew frightened and indignant. They laid the blame on Hagar, and drove her forth into the wilderness.[31]

But there were none the fewer Ishmaelites for that.

At last men became a little wiser, and saw that the infant Moses was, in every case, saved by the pure instincts of Woman's breast.[32] For, as too much adversity is

[31]In Genesis, Hagar was Abraham's concubine, who bore him a son, Ishmael, when his wife, Sarah, proved barren. But after the birth of Sarah's son Isaac, the now-haughty Hagar was banished from Abraham's tents.

[32]A reference to the Biblical story in which Pharaoh's daughter saves Moses.

better for the moral nature than too much prosperity, Woman, in this respect, dwindled less than Man, though in other respects, still a child in leading strings.

So Man did her more and more justice, and grew more and more kind.

But yet, his habits and his will corrupted by the past—he did not clearly see that Woman was half himself, that her interests were identical with his, and that, by the law of their common being, he could never reach his true proportions while she remained in any wise shorn of hers.

And so it has gone on to our day; both ideas developing, but more slowly than they would under a clearer recognition of truth and justice, which would have permitted the sexes their due influence on one another, and mutual improvement from more dignified relations.

Wherever there was pure love, the natural influences were, for the time, restored.

Wherever the poet or artist gave free course to his genius, he saw the truth, and expressed it in worthy forms, for these men especially share and need the feminine principle. The divine birds need to be brooded into life and song by mothers.

Wherever religion (I mean the thirst for truth and good, not the love of sect and dogma) had its course, the original design was apprehended in its simplicity, and the dove presaged sweetly from Dodona's oak.[33]

I have aimed to show that no age was left entirely without a witness of the equality of the sexes in function, duty and hope.

Also, that when there was unwillingness or ignorance, which prevented this being acted upon, women had not the less power for their want of light and noble freedom. But it was power which hurt alike them and those against whom they made use of the arms of the servile,—cunning blandishment, and unreasonable emotion.

That now the time has come when a clearer vision and better action are possible—when Man and Woman may regard one another as brother and sister, the pillars of one porch, the priests of one worship.

I have believed and intimated that this hope would receive an ampler frution, than ever before, in our own land.

And it will do so if this land carry out the principles from which sprang our national life.

I believe that, at present, women are the best helpers of one another.

Let them think; let them act; till they know what they need.

We only ask of men to remove arbitrary barriers. Some would like to do more. But I believe it needs for Woman to show herself in her native dignity, to teach them how to aid her; their minds are so encumbered by tradition.

When Lord Edward Fitzgerald[34] travelled with the Indians, his manly heart obliged him at once to take the packs from the squaws and carry them. But we do not read that the red men followed his example, though they are ready enough to carry the pack of the white woman, because she seems to them a superior being.

Let Woman appear in the mild majesty of Ceres, and rudest churls will be willing to learn from her.

[33]The oak grove in Dodona, in ancient Greece, housed an oracle dedicated to Zeus.

[34]Lord Edward Fitzgerald (1763–1798), Irish politician who traveled down the Mississippi River.

You ask, what use will she make of liberty, when she has so long been sustained and restrained?

I answer; in the first place, this will not be suddenly given. I read yesterday a debate of this year on the subject of enlarging women's rights over property. It was a leaf from the class-book that is preparing for the needed instruction. The men learned visibly as they spoke. The champions of Woman saw the fallacy of arguments on the opposite side, and were startled by their own convictions. With their wives at home, and the readers of the paper, it was the same. And so the stream flows on; thought urging action, and action leading to the evolution of still better thought.

But, were this freedom to come suddenly, I have no fear of the consequences. Individuals might commit excesses, but there is not only in the sex a reverence for decorums and limits inherited and enhanced from generation to generation, which many years of other life could not efface, but a native love, in Woman as Woman, of proportion, of "the simple art of not too much,"—a Greek moderation, which would create immediately a restraining party, the natural legislators and instructors of the rest, and would gradually establish such rules as are needed to guard, without impeding, life.

The Graces would lead the choral dance, and teach the rest to regulate their steps to the measure of beauty.

But if you ask me what offices they may fill, I reply—any. I do not care what case you put; let them be sea-captains, if you will. I do not doubt there are women well fitted for such an office, and, if so, I should be glad to see them in it, as to welcome the maid of Saragossa, or the maid of Missolonghi, or the Suliote heroine, or Emily Plater.[35]

I think women need, especially at this juncture, a much greater range of occupation than they have, to rouse their latent powers. A party of travellers lately visited a lonely hut on a mountain. There they found an old woman that told them she and her husband had lived there forty years. "Why," they said, "did you choose so barren a spot?" She "did not know; *it was the man's notion.*"

And, during forty years, she had been content to act, without knowing why, upon "the man's notion." I would not have it so.

In families that I know, some little girls like to saw wood, others to use carpenters' tools. Where these tastes are indulged, cheerfulness and good humor are promoted. Where they are forbidden, because "such things are not proper for girls," they grow sullen and mischievous.

Fourier[36] had observed these wants of women, as no one can fail to do who watches the desires of little girls, or knows the ennui that haunts grown women, except where they make to themselves a serene little world by art of some kind. He,

[35]Sargossa, a city in northern Spain and capital of the kingdom of Aragon. Missolonghi, a town in Greece at which the British poet Lord Byron died (1824) during the struggle for Greek independence from Turkey. Suliotes, people of Greece who were defeated by the Turks in 1822 but who nevertheless played an important role in the Greek war of liberation. Countess Emily Plater was involved in the Polish war for independence.

[36]Charles Fourier (1772–1837), a French socialist on whose model a number of utopian communities were set up in the United States and who influenced George Ripley, a major force in establishing the Brook Farm community at West Roxbury, Massachusetts.

therefore, in proposing a great variety of employments, in manufactures or the care of plants and animals, allows for one third of women as likely to have a taste for masculine pursuits, one third of men for feminine.

Who does not observe the immediate glow and serenity that is diffused over the life of women, before restless or fretful, by engaging in gardening, building, or the lowest department of art. Here is something that is not routine, something that draws forth life toward the infinite.

I have no doubt, however, that a large proportion of women would give themselves to the same employments as now, because there are circumstances that must lead them. Mothers will delight to make the nest soft and warm. Nature would take care of that; no need to clip the wings of any bird that wants to soar and sing, or finds in itself the strength of pinion for a migratory flight unusual to its kind. The difference would be that *all* need not be constrained to employments for which *some* are unfit.

I have urged upon the sex self-subsistence in its two forms of self-reliance and self-impulse, because I believe them to be the needed means of the present juncture.

I have urged on Woman independence of Man, not that I do not think the sexes mutually needed by one another, but because in Woman this fact has led to an excessive devotion, which has cooled love, degraded marriage, and prevented either sex from being what it should be to itself or the other.

I wish Woman to live, *first* for God's sake. Then she will not make an imperfect man her god, and thus sink to idolatry. Then she will not take what is not fit for her from a sense of weakness and poverty. Then, if she finds what she needs in Man embodied, she will know how to love, and be worthy of being loved.

By being more a soul, she will not be less Woman, for nature is perfected through spirit.

Now there is no woman, only an overgrown child.

That her hand may be given with dignity, she must be able to stand alone. I wish to see men and women capable of such relations as are depicted by Landor[37] in his Pericles and Aspasia, where grace is the natural garb of strength, and the affections are calm, because deep. The softness is that of a firm tissue, as when

> "The gods approve
> The depth, but not the tumult of the soul,
> A fervent, not ungovernable love."

A profound thinker has said, "no married woman can represent the female world, for she belongs to her husband. The idea of Woman must be represented by a virgin."

But that is the very fault of marriage, and of the present relation between the sexes; that the woman *does* belong to the man, instead of forming a whole with him. Were it otherwise, there would be no such limitation to the thought.

Woman, self-centered, would never be absorbed by any relation; it would be only an experience to her as to man. It is a vulgar error that love, *a* love, to Woman is her whole existence; she also is born for Truth and Love in their universal energy.

[37]Walter Savage Landor (1775–1864), British author.

Would she but assume her inheritance, Mary would not be the only virgin mother. Not Manzoni alone would celebrate in his wife the virgin mind with the maternal wisdom and conjugal affections.[38] The soul is ever young, ever virgin.

And will not she soon appear?—the woman who shall vindicate their birthright for all women; who shall teach them what to claim, and how to use what they obtain? Shall not her name be for her era Victoria, for her country and life Virginia? Yet predictions are rash; she herself must teach us to give her the fitting name.

An idea not unknown to ancient times has of late been revived, that, in the metamorphoses of life, the soul assumes the form, first of Man, then of Woman, and takes the chances, and reaps the benefits of either lot. Why then, say some, lay such emphasis on the rights or needs of Woman? What she wins not as Woman, will come to her as Man.

That makes no difference. It is not Woman, but the law of right, the law of growth, that speaks in us, and demands the perfection of each being in its kind,—apple as apple, Woman as Woman. Without adopting your theory I know that I, a daughter, live through the life of Man; but what concerns me now is, that my life be a beautiful, powerful, in a word, a complete life in its kind. Had I but one more moment to live, I must wish the same.

Suppose, at the end of your cycle, your great world-year, all will be completed, whether I exert myself or not (and the supposition is *false*.—but suppose it true), am I to be indifferent about it? Not so! I must beat my own pulse true in the heart of the world; for *that* is virtue, excellence, health.

Thou, Lord of Day! didst leave us to-night so calmly glorious, not dismayed that cold winter is coming, not postponing thy beneficence to the fruitful summer! Thou didst smile on thy day's work when it was done, and adorn thy down-going as thy uprising, for thou art loyal, and it is thy nature to give life, if thou canst, and shine at all events!

I stand in the sunny noon of life. Objects no longer glitter in the dews of morning, neither are yet softened by the shadows of evening. Every spot is seen, every chasm revealed. Climbing the dusty hill, some fair effigies that once stood for symbols of human destiny have been broken; those I still have with me, show defects in this broad light. Yet enough is left, even by experience, to point distinctly to the glories of that destiny; faint, but not to be mistaken streaks of the future day. I can say with the bard,

> "Though many have suffered shipwreck, still beat noble hearts."[39]

Always the soul says to us all, Cherish your best hopes as a faith, and abide by them in action. Such shall be the effectual fervent means to their fulfilment;

> For the Power to whom we bow
> Has given its pledge that, if not now,
> They of pure and stedfast mind,
> By faith exalted, truth refined,
> *Shall* hear all music loud and clear,
> Whose first notes they ventured here.

[38]In the "Preface" to *Adelchi* (1822) a tragedy by Italian writer Alessandro Manzoni (1785–1873).

[39]From "Laodamia" by the British poet William Wordsworth (1770–1850).

Then fear not thou to wind the horn,
Though elf and gnome thy courage scorn;
Ask for the Castle's King and Queen;
Though rabble rout may rush between,
Beat thee senseless to the ground,
In the dark beset thee round;
Persist to ask and it will come,
Seek not for rest in humbler home;
So shalt thou see what few have seen,
The palace home of King and Queen.

1844

from American Literature;

Its Position in the Present Time, and Prospects for the Future

Some thinkers may object to this essay, that we are about to write of that which has, as yet, no existence.

For it does not follow because many books are written by persons born in America that there exists an American literature. Books which imitate or represent the thoughts and life of Europe do not constitute an American literature. Before such can exist, an original idea must animate this nation and fresh currents of life must call into life fresh thoughts along its shores.

We have no sympathy with national vanity. We are not anxious to prove that there is as yet much American literature. Of those who think and write among us in the methods and of the thoughts of Europe, we are not impatient; if their minds are still best adapted to such food and such action. If their books express life of mind and character in graceful forms, they are good and we like them. We consider them as colonists and useful schoolmasters to our people in a transition state; which lasts rather longer than is occupied in passing, bodily, the ocean which separates the new from the old world.

We have been accused of an undue attachment to foreign continental literature, and, it is true, that in childhood, we had well nigh "forgotten our English," while constantly reading in other languages. Still, what we loved in the literature of continental Europe was the range and force of ideal manifestation in forms of national and individual greatness. A model was before us in the great Latins of simple masculine minds seizing upon life with unbroken power. The stamp both of nationality and individuality was very strong upon them; their lives and thoughts stood out in clear and bold relief. The English character has the iron force of the Latins, but not the frankness and expansion. Like their fruits, they need a summer sky to give them more sweetness and a richer flavour. This does not apply to Shakspeare, who has all the fine side of English genius, with the rich colouring, and more fluent life, of the

Catholic countries. Other poets, of England also, are expansive more or less, and soar freely to seek the blue sky, but take it as a whole, there is in English literature, as in English character, a reminiscence of walls and ceilings, a tendency to the arbitrary and conventional that repels a mind trained in admiration of the antique spirit. It is only in later days that we are learning to prize the peculiar greatness which a thousand times outweighs this fault, and which has enabled English genius to go forth from its insular position and conquer such vast dominion in the realms both of matter and of mind.

Yet there is, often, between child and parent, a reaction from excessive influence having been exerted, and such an one we have experienced, in behalf of our country, against England. We use her language, and receive, in torrents, the influence of her thought, yet it is, in many respects, uncongenial and injurious to our constitution. What suits Great Britain, with her insular position and consequent need to concentrate and intensify her life, her limited monarchy, and spirit of trade, does not suit a mixed race, continually enriched with new blood from other stocks the most unlike that of our first descent, with ample field and verge enough to range in and leave every impulse free, and abundant opportunity to develope a genius, wide and full as our rivers, flowery, luxuriant and impassioned as our vast prairies, rooted in strength as the rocks on which the Puritan fathers landed.

That such a genius is to rise and work in this hemisphere we are confident; equally so that scarce the first faint streaks of that day's dawn are yet visible. It is sad for those that foresee, to know they may not live to share its glories, yet it is sweet, too, to know that every act and word, uttered in the light of that foresight, may tend to hasten or ennoble its fulfilment.

That day will not rise till the fusion of races among us is more complete. It will not rise till this nation shall attain sufficient moral and intellectual dignity to prize moral and intellectual, no less highly than political, freedom, not till, the physical resources of the country being explored, all its regions studded with towns, broken by the plow, netted together by railways and telegraph lines, talent shall be left at leisure to turn its energies upon the higher department of man's existence. Nor then shall it be seen till from the leisurely and yearning soul of that riper time national ideas shall take birth, ideas craving to be clothed in a thousand fresh and original forms.

Without such ideas all attempts to construct a national literature must end in abortions like the monster of Frankenstein, things with forms, and the instincts of forms, but soulless, and therefore revolting. We cannot have expression till there is something to be expressed.

The symptoms of such a birth may be seen in a longing felt here and there for the sustenance of such ideas. At present, it shows itself, where felt, in sympathy with the prevalent tone of society, by attempts at external action, such as are classed under the head of social reform. But it needs to go deeper, before we can have poets, needs to penetrate beneath the springs of action, to stir and remake the soil as by the action of fire.

Another symptom is the need felt by individuals of being even sternly sincere. This is the one great means by which alone progress can be essentially furthered. Truth is the nursing mother of genius. No man can be absolutely true to himself, eschewing cant, compromise, servile imitation, and complaisance, without becoming original, for there is in every creature a fountain of life which, if not choked back by stones and other dead rubbish, will create a fresh atmosphere, and bring to life fresh beauty. And it is the same with the nation as with the individual man.

The best work we do for the future is by such truth. By use of that, in whatever way, we harrow the soil and lay it open to the sun and air. The winds from all quarters of the globe bring seed enough, and there is nothing wanting but preparation of the soil, and freedom in the atmosphere, for ripening of a new and golden harvest.

We are sad that we cannot be present at the gathering in of this harvest. And yet we are joyous, too, when we think that though our name may not be writ on the pillar of our country's fame, we can really do far more towards rearing it, than those who come at a later period and to a seemingly fairer task. *Now,* the humblest effort, made in a noble spirit, and with religious hope, cannot fail to be even infinitely useful. Whether we introduce some noble model from another time and clime, to encourage aspiration in our own, or cheer into blossom the simplest wood-flower that ever rose from the earth, moved by the genuine impulse to grow, independent of the lures of money or celebrity; whether we speak boldly when fear or doubt keep others silent, or refuse to swell the popular cry upon an unworthy occasion, the spirit of truth, purely worshipped, shall turn our acts and forbearances alike to profit, informing them with oracles which the latest time shall bless.

Under present circumstances the amount of talent and labour given to writing ought to surprise us. Literature is in this dim and struggling state, and its pecuniary results exceedingly pitiful. From many well known causes it is impossible for ninety-nine out of the hundred, who wish to use the pen, to ransom, by its use, the time they need. This state of things will have to be changed in some way. No man of genius writes for money; but it is essential to the free use of his powers, that he should be able to disembarrass his life from care and perplexity. This is very difficult here; and the state of things gets worse and worse, as less and less is offered in pecuniary meed for works demanding great devotion of time and labour (to say nothing of the ether engaged) and the publisher, obliged to regard the transaction as a matter of business, demands of the author to give him only what will find an immediate market, for he cannot afford to take any thing else. This will not do! When an immortal poet was secure only of a few copyists to circulate his works, there were princes and nobles to patronize literature and the arts. Here is only the public, and the public must learn how to cherish the nobler and rarer plants, and to plant the aloe, able to wait a hundred years for its bloom, or its garden will contain, presently, nothing but potatoes and pot-herbs. We shall have, in the course of the next two or three years, a convention of authors to inquire into the causes of this state of things and propose measures for its remedy. Some have already been thought of that look promising, but we shall not announce them till the time be ripe; that date is not distant, for the difficulties increase from day to day, in consequence of the system of cheap publication, on a great scale.

The ranks that led the way in the first half century of this republic were far better situated than we, in this respect. The country was not so deluged with the dingy page, reprinted from Europe, and patriotic vanity was on the alert to answer the question, "Who reads an American book?" And many were the books written, worthy to be read, as any out of the first class in England. They were, most of them, except in their subject matter, English books.

The list is large, and, in making some cursory comments, we do not wish to be understood as designating *all* who are worthy of notice, but only those who present themselves to our minds with some special claims. In history there has been nothing done to which the world at large has not been eager to award the full meed of its deserts. Mr. Prescott,[1] for instance, has been greeted with as much warmth abroad as here. We are not disposed to undervalue his industry and power of clear and elegant arrangement. The richness and freshness of his materials is such that a sense of enchantment must be felt in their contemplation. We must regret, however, that they should have been first presented to the public by one who possesses nothing of the higher powers of the historian, great leading views, or discernment as to the motives of action and the spirit of an era. Considering the splendour of the materials the books are wonderfully tame, and every one must feel that having once passed through them and got the sketch in the mind, there is nothing else to which it will recur. The absence of thought, as to that great picture of Mexican life, with its heroisms, its terrible but deeply significant superstitions, its admirable civic refinement, seems to be quite unbroken.

Mr. Bancroft[2] is a far more vivid writer; he has great resources and great command of them, and leading thoughts by whose aid he groups his facts. But we cannot speak fully of his historical works, which we have only read and referred to here and there.

In the department of ethics and philosophy, we may inscribe two names as likely to live and be blessed and honoured in the later time. These are the names of Channing and of Emerson.

Dr. Channing[3] had several leading thoughts which corresponded with the wants of his time, and have made him in it a father of thought. His leading idea of "the dignity of human nature" is one of vast results, and the peculiar form in which he advocated it had a great work to do in this new world. The spiritual beauty of his writings is very great; they are all distinguished for sweetness, elevation, candour, and a severe devotion to truth. On great questions, he took middle ground, and sought a panoramic view; he wished also to stand high, yet never forgot what was above more than what was around and beneath him. He was not well acquainted with man on the impulsive and passionate side of his nature, so that his view of character was sometimes narrow, but it was always noble. He exercised an expansive and purifying power on the atmosphere, and stands a godfather at the baptism of this country.

The Sage of Concord[4] has a very different mind, in every thing except that he has the same disinterestedness and dignity of purpose, the same purity of spirit. He is a profound thinker. He is a man of ideas, and deals with causes rather than effects. His ideas are illustrated from a wide range of literary culture and refined observation, and embodied in a style whose melody and subtle fragrance enchant those who stand stupified before the thoughts themselves, because their utmost depths do not enable them to sound his shallows. His influence does not yet extend over a wide

[1]William Hickling Prescott (1796–1859), American historian.

[2]George Bancroft (1800–1891), American historian and statesman.

[3]William Ellery Channing (1780–1842), Unitarian minister and religious writer.

[4]Fuller was the first to call Ralph Waldo Emerson (1803–1882), American essayist and poet, the "Sage of Concord," after the town in which he lived.

space; he is too far beyond his place and his time, to be felt at once or in full, but it searches deep, and yearly widens its circles. He is a harbinger of the better day. His beautiful elocution has been a great aid to him in opening the way for the reception of his written word.

In that large department of literature which includes descriptive sketches, whether of character or scenery, we are already rich. Irving, a genial and fair nature, just what he ought to be, and would have been, at any time of the world, has drawn the scenes amid which his youth was spent in their primitive lineaments, with all the charms of his graceful jocund humour. He has his niche and need never be deposed; it is not one that another could occupy.

The first enthusiasm about Cooper[5] having subsided, we remember more his faults than his merits. His ready resentment and way of showing it in cases which it is the wont of gentlemen to pass by in silence, or meet with a good humoured smile, have caused unpleasant associations with his name, and his fellow citizens, in danger of being tormented by suits for libel, if they spoke freely of him, have ceased to speak of him at all. But neither these causes, nor the baldness of his plots, shallowness of thought, and poverty in the presentation of character, should make us forget the grandeur and originality of his sea-sketches, nor the redemption from oblivion of our forest-scenery, and the noble romance of the hunter-pioneer's life. Already, but for him, this fine page of life's romance would be almost forgotten. He has done much to redeem these irrevocable beauties from the corrosive acid of a semi-civilized invasion. [Omitted here is a paragraph on Cooper quoted by Fuller from William Gilmore Simms's *Views and Reviews*[6] (1846).]

Miss Sedgwick[7] and others have portrayed, with skill and feeling, scenes and personages from the revolutionary time. Such have a permanent value in proportion as their subject is fleeting. The same charm attends the spirited delineations of Mrs. Kirkland,[8] and that amusing book, "A New Purchase." The features of Hoosier, Sucker, and Wolverine life are worth fixing; they are peculiar to the soil, and indicate its hidden treasures; they have, also, that charm which simple life, lived for its own sake, always has, even in rude and all but brutal forms.

What shall we say of the poets? The list is scanty; amazingly so, for there is nothing in the causes that paralyze other kinds of literature that could affect lyrical and narrative poetry. Men's hearts beat, hope, and suffer always, and they must crave such means to vent them; yet of the myriad leaves garnished with smooth stereotyped rhymes that issue yearly from our press, you will not find, one time in a million, a little piece written from any such impulse, or with the least sincerity or sweetness of tone. They are written for the press, in the spirit of imitation or vanity, the paltriest offspring of the human brain, for the heart disclaims, as the ear is shut against them. This is the kind of verse which is cherished by the magazines as a correspondent to the tawdry pictures of smiling milliners' dolls in the frontispiece. Like these they are only a fashion, a fashion based on no reality of love or beauty. The inducement to write them consists in a little money, or more frequently the charm of seeing an anonymous name printed at the top in capitals.

[5]James Fenimore Cooper: see selection in this volume.

[6]William Gilmore Simms, southern writer of fiction and essays.

[7]Catharine Maria Sedgwick: see selection in this volume.

[8]Caroline Kirkland: see selection in this volume.

We must here, in passing, advert also to the style of story current in the magazines, flimsy beyond any texture that was ever spun or even dreamed of by the mind of man, in any other age and country. They are said to be "written for the seamstresses," but we believe that every way injured class could relish and digest better fare even at the end of long days of exhausting labour. There are exceptions to this censure; stories by Mrs. Child[9] have been published in the magazines, and now and then good ones by Mrs. Stephens[10] and others; but, take them generally, they are calculated to do a positive injury to the public mind, acting as an opiate, and of an adulterated kind, too.

But to return to the poets. At their head Mr. Bryant stands alone.[11] His range is not great, nor his genius fertile. But his poetry is purely the language of his inmost nature, and the simple lovely garb in which his thoughts are arranged, a direct gift from the Muse. He has written nothing that is not excellent, and the atmosphere of his verse refreshes and composes the mind, like leaving the highway to enter some green, lovely, fragrant wood.

Halleck and Willis are poets of society.[12] Though the former has written so little, yet that little is full of fire,—elegant, witty, delicate in sentiment. It is an honour to the country that these occasional sparks, struck off from the flint of commercial life, should have kindled so much flame as they have. It is always a consolation to see one of them sparkle amid the rubbish of daily life. One of his poems has been published within the last year, written, in fact, long ago, but new to most of us, and it enlivened the literary thoroughfare, as a green wreath might some dusty, musty hall of legislation.

Willis has not the same terseness or condensed electricity. But he has grace, spirit, at times a winning pensiveness, and a lively, though almost wholly sensuous, delight in the beautiful.

Dana[13] has written so little that he would hardly be seen in a more thickly garnished galaxy. But the masculine strength of feeling, the solemn tenderness and refined thought displayed in such pieces as the "Dying Raven," and the "Husband and Wife's Grave," have left a deep impression on the popular mind.

Longfellow[14] is artificial and imitative. He borrows incessantly, and mixes what he borrows, so that it does not appear to the best advantage. He is very faulty in using broken or mixed metaphors. The ethical part of his writing has a hollow, secondhand sound. He has, however, elegance, a love of the beautiful, and a fancy for what is large and manly, if not a full sympathy with it. His verse breathes at times much sweetness; and, if not allowed to supersede what is better may promote a taste for good poetry. Though imitative, he is not mechanical.

We cannot say as much for Lowell,[15] who, we must declare it, though to the grief of some friends, and the disgust of more, is absolutely wanting in the true spirit and tone of poesy. His interest in the moral questions of the day has supplied the want of

[9]Lydia Maria Child: see selection in this volume.

[10]Mrs. Anne Stephens (1813–1886) wrote over two dozen novels of English and American history.

[11]William Cullen Bryant: see selection in this volume.

[12]Fitz-Greene Halleck (1790–1867), New York poet. Nathaniel Parker Willis (1806–1867), New York newspaperman and poet.

[13]Richard Henry Dana, Sr. (1787–1879), poet and founder of the *North American Review.*

[14]Henry Wadsworth Longfellow: see selection in this volume.

[15]James Russell Lowell (1819–1891).

vitality in himself; his great facility at versification has enabled him to fill the ear with a copious stream of pleasant sound. But his verse is stereotyped; his thought sounds no depth, and posterity will not remember him.

R.W. Emerson, in melody, in subtle beauty of thought and expression, takes the highest rank upon this list. But his poems are mostly philosophical, which is not the truest kind of poetry. They want the simple force of nature and passion, and, while they charm the ear and interest the mind, fail to wake far-off echoes in the heart. The imagery wears a symbolical air, and serves rather as illustration, than to delight us by fresh and glowing forms of life.

We must here mention one whom the country has not yet learned to honour, perhaps never may, for he wants artistic skill to give complete form to his inspiration. This is William Ellery Channing,[16] nephew and namesake of Dr. C., a volume of whose poems, published three or four years ago in Boston, remains unknown, except to a few friends, nor, if known, would they probably excite sympathy, as those which have been published in the periodicals have failed to do so. Yet some of the purest tones of the lyre are his, the finest inspirations as to the feelings and passions of men, deep spiritual insight, and an entire originality in the use of his means. The frequently unfinished and obscure state of his poems, a passion for forcing words out of their usual meaning into one which they may appropriately bear, but which comes upon the reader with an unpleasing and puzzling surprise, may repel, at first glance, from many of these poems, but do not mar the following sublime description of the beings we want, to rule, to redeem, to re-create this nation, and under whose reign alone can there be an American literature, for then only could we have life worth recording. The simple grandeur of this poem as a whole, must be felt by every one, while each line and thought will be found worthy of earnest contemplation and satisfaction after the most earnest life and thought.

> Hearts of Eternity! hearts of the deep!
> Proclaim from land to sea your mighty fate;
> How that for you no living comes too late;
> How ye cannot in Theban labyrinth creep;
> How ye great harvests from small surface reap;
> Shout, excellent band, in grand primeval strain,
> Like midnight winds that foam along the main,
> And do all things rather than pause to weep.
> A human heart knows naught of littleness,
> Suspects no man, compares with no man's ways,
> Hath in one hour most glorious length of days,
> A recompense, a joy, a loveliness;
> Like eaglet keen, shoots into azure far,
> And always dwelling nigh is the remotest star.

A series of poems, called "Man in the Republic," by Cornelius Mathews,[17] deserves a higher meed of sympathy than it has received. The thoughts and views are strong and noble, the exhibition of them imposing. In plastic power this writer is

[16]William Ellery Channing (1818–1901), American poet and Fuller's brother-in-law.

[17]Cornelius Mathews (1817–1889), New York editor, novelist, and poet.

deficient. His prose works sin in exuberance, and need consolidating and chastening. We find fine things, but not so arranged as to be seen in the right places and by the best light. In his poems Mr. Mathews is unpardonably rough and rugged; the poetic substance finds no musical medium in which to flow. Yet there *is* poetic substance which makes full chords, if not a harmony. He holds a worthy sense of the vocation of the poet, and worthily expresses it thus:—

> To strike or bear, to conquer or to yield
> Teach thou! O topmost crown of duty, teach,
> What fancy whispers to the listening ear,
> At hours when tongue nor taint of care impeach
> The fruitful calm of greatly silent hearts;
> When all the stars for happy thought are set,
> And, in the secret chambers of the soul,
> All blessed powers of joyful truth are met;
> Though calm and garlandless thou mayst appear,
> The world shall know thee for its crowned seer.

A considerable portion of the hope and energy of this country still turns towards the drama, that greatest achievement when wrought to perfection of human power. For ourselves, we believe the day of the regular drama to be past; and, though we recognize the need of some kind of spectacle and dramatic representation to be absolutely coincident with an animated state of the public mind, we have thought that the opera, ballet, pantomime and briefer, more elastic forms, like the *vaudeville* of the French theatre, or the *proverb* of the social party, would take the place of elaborate tragedy and comedy. . . .

1846

from Things and Thoughts in Europe

Foreign Correspondence of the Tribune

Dispatch 17

ROME, October 18, 1847[1]

In the Spring, when I came to Rome, the people were in the intoxication of joy at the first serious measures of reform taken by the Pope.[2] I saw with pleasure their childlike joy and trust: I saw with pleasure the Pope, who has not in his expression the

[1]First published as "Things and Thoughts in Europe. No. XVII" in *New-York Daily Tribune,* 27 November 1847, p. 1:1–3.

[2]Fuller's initial enthusiasm for the role of the liberal Pope Pius IX in supporting reforms and the efforts to unite Italy were later reversed in response to his irresolution, his flight when a Roman Republic was declared, and his backing of a French invasion to restore him to the Papal throne.

signs of intellectual greatness so much as of nobleness and tenderness of heart, of large and liberal sympathies. Heart had spoken to heart between the Prince and the People; it was beautiful to see the immediate good influence of human feeling, generous designs, on the part of a ruler: he had wished to be a father, and the Italians, with that readiness of genius that characterizes them, entered at once into the relation; they, the Roman people, stigmatized by prejudice as so crafty and ferocious, showed themselves children, eager to learn, quick to obey, happy to confide.

Still, doubts were always present whether all this joy was not premature. The task undertaken by the Pope seemed to present insuperable difficulties. It is never easy to put new wine into old bottles, and our age is one where all things tend to a great crisis, not merely to revolution but to radical reform. From the people themselves the help must come, and not from princes: in the new state of things there will be none but natural princes, great men. From the aspirations of the general heart, from the teachings of conscience in individuals, and not from an old ivy-covered church, long since undermined, corroded by Time and gnawed by vermin, the help must come. Rome, to resume her glory, must cease to be an ecclesiastical Capital; must renounce all this gorgeous mummery, whose poetry, whose picture charms no one more than myself, but whose meaning is all of the Past and finds no echo in the Future. Although I sympathized warmly with the warm love of the people, the adulation of leading writers, who were so willing to take all from the hand of the prince, of the Church, as a gift and a bounty instead of implying steadily that it was the right of the people, was very repulsive to me. The Moderate party, like all who, in a transition state, manage affairs with a constant eye to prudence, lacks dignity always in its expositions; it is disagreeable and depressing to read them.

Passing into Tuscany, I found the Liberty of the Press just established, and a superior preparation to make use of it. The *'Alba,'* the *'Patria,'* were begun, and have been continued with equal judgment and spirit. Their aim is to educate the youth, to educate the lower people; they see that this is to be done by promoting Thought fearlessly, yet urge temperance in action while the time is yet so difficult, and many of its signs dubious. They aim at breaking down those barriers between the different States of Italy, relics of a barbarous state of polity, artificially kept up by the craft of her foes.[3] While anxious not to break down what is really native to the Italian character, defences and differences that give individual genius a chance to grow and the fruits of each region to ripen in their natural way, they aim at a harmony of spirit as to measures of education and for the affairs of business, without which Italy can never, as

[3]Fuller arrived in Italy during a period called the *Risorgimento,* or national revival. It expressed a generally nationalist and republican spirit, perhaps best articulated in the writings and speeches of Giuseppe Mazzini, who had been struggling in exile for some 15 years to develop the movement for change. In political terms, the movement underway by 1847 sought to free Italy from foreign domination—especially that of the Austrian empire—to unify the many little separate and sometimes hostile Italian states, and to develop at least a constitutional, if not a republican, form of government. After a number of initial successes, which were linked to the revolutionary movements taking place all over Europe in 1848, the Italian cause was temporarily defeated, primarily through French intervention in 1849. It would take another decade for the goal of Italian unification to be accomplished under the leadership of Garibaldi and Cavour.

one nation, present a front strong enough to resist foreign robbery, and for want of which so much time and talent are wasted here, and internal development almost wholly checked.

There is in Tuscany a large corps of enlightened minds, well prepared to be the instructors, the elder brothers and guardians of the lower people, and whose hearts burn to fulfil that noble office. Hitherto it had been almost impossible to them, for the reasons I have named in speaking of Lombardy; but, during these last four months that the way has been opened by the Freedom of the Press and establishment of the National Guard—so valuable, first of all, as giving occasion for public meetings and free interchange of thought between the different classes, it is surprising how much light they have been able to diffuse already.

A Bolognese, to whom I observed, "How can you be so full of trust when all your hopes depend, not on the recognition of principles and wants throughout the people, but on the life of one mortal man?" replied, "Ah! but you don't consider that his life gives us a chance to effect that recognition. If Pius IX. be spared to us five years, it will be impossible for his successors ever to take a backward course. Our people is of a genius so vivacious; we are unhappy but not stupid, we Italians; we can learn as much in two months as other nations in twenty years." This seemed to me no brag when I returned to Tuscany and saw the great development and diffusion of thought that had taken place during my brief absence. The Grand Duke, a well-intentioned, though dull man, had dared to declare himself *"an* ITALIAN *Prince,"* and the heart of Tuscany had bounded with hope. It is now deeply as justly felt that *the* curse of Italy is foreign intrusion, that if she could dispense with foreign aid and be free from foreign aggression, she would find the elements of salvation within herself. All her efforts tend that way, to reestablish the natural position of things: may Heaven grant them success! For myself I believe they will attain it. I see more reason for hope, as I know more of the people. Their rash and baffled struggles have taught them prudence; they are wanted in the civilized world as a peculiar influence; their leaders are thinking men, their cause is righteous. I believe that Italy will revive to new life, and probably a greater, a more truly rich and glorious, than at either epoch of her former greatness.

During the period of my absence, the Austrians had entered Ferrara. It is well that they hazarded this step, for it showed them the difficulties in acting against a Prince of the Church who is at the same time a friend to the People. The position was new, and they were probably surprised at the result, surprised at the firmness of the Pope, surprised at the indignation, tempered by calm resolve, on the part of the Italians. Louis Philippe's mean apostacy has this time turned to the advantage of Freedom. He renounced the good understanding with England which it had been one of the leading features of his policy to maintain, in the hope of aggrandizing and enriching his family (not France; he did not care for France) he did not know that he was paving the way for Italian Freedom. England now is led to play a part a little nearer her pretensions as the Guardian of Progress than she often comes, and the ghost of Lafayette looks down, not unappeased, to see the "Constitutional King" decried by the subjects he has cheated and lulled so craftily. The King of Sardinia is a worthless man, in whom nobody puts any trust so far as regards his heart or honor, but the stress of things seems likely to keep him on the right side. The little sovereigns blustered at first, then ran away affrighted when they found there was really a spirit risen at last within the charmed circle, a spirit likely to defy, to transcend, the spells of haggard premiers and imbecile monarchs.

I arrived in Florence, unhappily, too late for the great fete of the 12th September, in honor of the grant of the National Guard.[4] But I wept at the mere recital of the events of that day, which, if it should lead to no important results, must still be hallowed for ever in the memory of Italy for the great and beautiful emotions that flooded the hearts of her children. The National Guard is hailed with no undue joy by Italians, as the earnest of Progress, the first step toward truly national institutions and a representation of the people. Gratitude had done its natural work in their hearts; it had made them better. Some days before were passed by reconciling all strifes, composing all differences between cities, districts, and individuals. They wished to drop all petty, all local differences, to wash away all stains, to bathe and prepare for a new great covenant of brotherly love, where each should act for the good of all. On that day they all embraced in sign of this—strangers, foes, all, exchanged the kiss of faith and love; they exchanged banners as a token that they would fight for, would animate, one another. All was done in that beautiful poetic manner peculiar to this artist people, but it was the spirit, so great and tender, that melts my heart to think of. It was the spirit of true religion—such, my Country; as welling freshly from some great hearts in thy early hours, won for thee all of value that thou canst call thy own, whose ground-work is the assertion, still sublime though thou hast not been true to it, that all men have equal rights, and that these are *birth*-rights, derived from God alone.

I rejoice to say that the Americans took their share in this occasion, and that Greenough[5]—one of the few Americans who, living in Italy, takes the pains to know whether it is alive or dead; who penetrates beyond the cheats of tradesmen and the cunning of a mob corrupted by centuries of slavery, to know the real mind, the vital blood, of Italy—took a leading part. I am sorry to say that a large portion of my countrymen here take the same slothful and prejudiced view as the English, and, after many years' sojourn, betray entire ignorance of Italian literature and Italian life beyond what is attainable in a month's passage through the thoroughfares. However, they did show, this time, a becoming spirit, and erected the American Eagle where its cry ought to be heard from afar, where a Nation is striving for independent existence and a Government to represent the People. Crawford[6] here in Rome has had the just feeling to join the Guard, and it is a real sacrifice for an artist to spend time on the exercises; but it well becomes the sculptor of Orpheus,[7] of him who had such faith, such music of divine thought, that he made the stones move, turned the beasts from their accustomed haunts and shamed Hell itself into sympathy with the grief of love. I do not deny that such a spirit is wanted here in Italy; it is everywhere if anything great, anything permanent, is to be done. In reference to what I have said of many Americans in Italy, I will only add that they talk about the corrupt and degen-

[4]The establishment of such local popular militias was viewed as a significant step forward in asserting Italian pride and self-determination.

[5]Horatio Greenough (1805–1852), a well-known American sculptor.

[6]Thomas Crawford (1813?–1857), American sculptor.

[7]In Greek mythology a poet and musician whose playing of the lyre could calm savage beasts and make rocks move. His playing persuaded Pluto, king of the underworld, to return his wife, Euridice, to Orpheus.

erate state of Italy as they do about that of our slaves at home. They come ready trained to that mode of reasoning which affirms that, because men are degraded by bad institutions, they are not fit for better.

For the English, some of them, are full of generous, intelligent sympathy, as indeed what is more solidly, more wisely good than the right sort of Englishmen, but others are like a gentleman I traveled with the other day, a man of intelligence and refinement too as to the details of life and outside culture, who observed, "he did not see what the Italians wanted of a National Guard unless to wear these little caps." He was a man who had passed five years in Italy, but always covered with that non-conductor called by a witty French writer "the Britannic fluid."

Very sweet to my ear was the continual hymn in the streets of Florence, in honor of Pius IX. It is the Roman hymn, and none of the new ones written in Tuscany have been able to take its place.—The people thank the Grand Duke when he does them good, but they know well from whose mind that good originates, and all their love is for the Pope. Time presses, or I would fain describe in detail the troupe of laborers of the lowest class, marching home at night; keeping step as if they were in the National Guard, filling the air and cheering the melancholy moon, by the patriotic hymns sung, with the mellow tone and in the perfect time which belong to Italians. I would describe the extempore concerts in the streets, the rejoicings at the theatres, where the addresses of liberal souls to the people, through that best vehicle, the drama, may now be heard. But I am tired; what I have to write would fill volumes, and my letter must go. I will only add some words upon the happy augury I draw from the wise docility of the people. With what readiness they listened to wise counsel and the hopes of the Pope that they would give no advantage to his enemies at a time when they were so fevered by the knowledge that conspiracy was at work in their midst. That was a time of trial. On all these occasions of popular excitement their conduct is like music, in such order and with such union of the melody of feeling with discretion where to stop; but what is wonderful is that they acted in the same manner on that difficult occasion. The influence of the Pope here is without bounds; he can always calm the crowd at once. But in Tuscany where they have no such one idol, they listened in the same way on a very trying occasion. The first announcement of the regulation for the Tuscan National Guard terribly disappointed the people; they felt that the Grand Duke, after suffering them to demonstrate such trust and joy on this feast of the 12th, did not really trust, on his side; that he meant to limit them all he could; they felt baffled, cheated; hence young men in anger tore down at once the symbols of satisfaction and respect; but the leading men went among the people, begged them to be calm, and wait till a deputation had seen the Grand Duke. The people listened at once to men who, they were sure, had at heart their best good—waited; the Grand Duke became convinced, and all ended without disturbance. If the people continue to act thus, their hopes cannot be baffled. Certainly I, for one, do not think that the present road will suffice to lead Italy to her goal. But it *is* an onward, upward road, and the people learn as it advances. Where they can now seek and think fearless of prisons and bayonets, a healthy circulation of blood begins, and the heart frees itself from disease.

I earnestly hope some expression of sympathy from my country toward Italy. Take a good chance and do something; you have shown much good feeling toward the Old World in its physical difficulties—you ought to do so still more in its spiritual endeavor. This cause is OURS, above all others; we ought to show that we feel it to be so. At present there is no likelihood of war, but in case of it I trust the United States would not fail in some noble token of sympathy toward this country. The Soul of our Nation need not wait for its Government; these things are better done by the effort of individuals. I believe some in the United States will pay attention to these words of mine, will feel that I am not a person to be kindled by a childish, sentimental enthusiasm, but that I must be sure that I have seen something of Italy to speak as I do. I have been here only seven months, but my means of observation have been uncommon. I have been ardently desirous to judge fairly, and I had no prejudices to prevent; beside, I was not ignorant of the history and literature of Italy and had some common ground on which to stand with its inhabitants, and hear what they have to say. In many ways she is of kin to us; she is the country of Columbus, of Amerigo,[8] of Cabot.[9] It would please me much to see a cannon here bought by the contributions of Americans, at whose head should stand the name of Cabot, to be used by the Guard for salutes on festive occasions, if they should be so happy as to have no more serious need. In Tuscany they are casting one to be called the "Gioberti," from a writer who has given a great impulse to the present movement. I should like the gift of America to be called the AMERICA, the COLUMBO, or the WASHINGTON. Please think of this, some of my friends, who still care for the Eagle, the 4th July, and the old cries of Hope and Honor. See, if there are any objections that I do not think of, and do something if it is well and brotherly.[10] Ah! America, with all thy rich boons, thou hast a heavy account to render for the talent given; see in every way that thou be not found wanting.

Dispatch 18

[Undated][1]

This letter will reach the United States about the 1st of January; and it may not be impertinent to offer a few New-Year's reflections. Every new year, indeed, confirms the old thoughts, but also presents them under some new aspects.

The American in Europe, if a thinking mind, can only become more American. In some respects it is a great pleasure to be here. Although we have an independent political existence, our position toward Europe, as to Literature and the Arts, is still that of a colony, and one feels the same joy here that is experienced by the colonist in returning to the parent home. What was but picture to us becomes reality; remote allusions and derivations trouble no more: we see the pattern of the stuff, and understand the whole tapestry. There is a gradual clearing up on many points, and many baseless notions and crude fancies are dropped. Even the post-haste passage of the

[8]Amerigo Vespucci (Americus Vespucius, 1451–1512), Italian navigator, whose name we still bear.

[9]John Cabot, originally Giovanni Caboto (1450–1498), Italian navigator in English service, who discovered for Europeans the North American continent in 1497.

[10]In fact, her letter appears to have helped stimulate the first mass meeting in the United States in support of the Italian revolution. Horace Greeley, editor of the *Tribune,* was among its sponsors.

[1]First published as "Things and Thoughts in Europe No. XVIII" in *New-York Daily Tribune,* 1 January 1848, p. 1:1–3.

business American through the great cities, escorted by cheating couriers, and ignorant *valets de place,* unable to hold intercourse with the natives of the country, and passing all his leisure hours with his countrymen, who know no more than himself, clears his mind of some mistakes—lifts some mists from his horizon.

There are three species: first, the servile American—a being utterly shallow, thoughtless, worthless. He comes abroad to spend his money and indulge his tastes. His object in Europe is to have fashionable clothes, good foreign cookery, to know some titled persons, and furnish himself with coffee-house gossip, which he wins importance at home by retailing among those less traveled, and as uninformed as himself.

I look with unspeakable contempt on this class—a class which has all the thoughtlessness and partiality of the exclusive classes in Europe, without any of their refinement, or the chivalric feeling which still sparkles among them here and there. However, though these willing serfs in a free age do some little hurt, and cause some annoyance at present, it cannot last: our country is fated to a grand, independent existence, and as its laws develop, these parasites of a bygone period must wither and drop away.

Then there is the conceited American, instinctively bristling and proud of—he knows not what—He does not see, not he, that the history of Humanity for many centuries is likely to have produced results it requires some training, some devotion, to appreciate and profit by. With his great clumsy hands only fitted to work on a steam-engine, he seizes the old Cremona violin, makes it shriek with anguish in his grasp, and then declares he thought it was all humbug before he came, and now he knows it; that there is not really any music in these old things; that the frogs in one of our swamps make much finer, for *they* are young and alive. To him the etiquettes of courts and camps, the ritual of the Church, seem simply silly—and no wonder, profoundly ignorant as he is of their origin and meaning. Just so the legends which are the subjects of pictures, the profound myths which are represented in the antique marbles, amaze and revolt him; as, indeed, such things need to be judged of by another standard from that of the Connecticut Blue-Laws. He criticises severely pictures, feeling quite sure that his natural senses are better means of judgment than the rules of connoisseurs—not feeling that to see such objects mental vision as well as fleshly eyes are needed, and that something is aimed at in Art beyond the imitation of the commonest forms of Nature.

This is Jonathan in the sprawling state, the booby truant, not yet aspiring enough to be a good school-boy. Yet in his folly there is meaning; add thought and culture to his independence, and he will be a man of might: he is not a creature without hope, like the thick-skinned dandy of the class first specified.

The Artistes form a class by themselves. Yet among them, though seeking special aims by special means may also be found the lineaments of these two classes, as well as of the third, of which I am to speak.

3d. The thinking American—a man who, recognizing the immense advantage of being born to a new world and on a virgin soil, yet does not wish one seed from the Past to be lost. He is anxious to gather and carry back with him all that will bear a new climate and new culture. Some will dwindle; others will attain a bloom and stature unknown before. He wishes to gather them clean, free from noxious insects. He wishes to give them a fair trial in his new world. And that he may know the conditions under which he may best place them in that new world, he does not neglect to study their history in this.

The history of our planet in some moments seems so painfully mean and little, such terrible bafflings and failures to compensate some brilliant successes—such a crashing of the mass of men beneath the feet of a few, and these, too, of the least worthy—such a small drop of honey to each cup of gall, and, in many cases, so mingled, that it is never one moment in life purely tasted,—above all, so little achieved for Humanity as a whole, such tides of war and pestilence intervening to blot out the traces of each triumph, that no wonder if the strongest soul sometimes pauses aghast! No wonder if the many indolently console themselves with gross joys and frivolous prizes. Yes! those men *are* worthy of admiration who can carry this cross faithfully through fifty years; it is a great while for all the agonies that beset a lover of good, a lover of men; it makes a soul worthy of a speedier ascent, a more productive ministry in the next sphere. Blessed are they who ever keep that portion of pure, generous love with which they began life! How blessed those who have deepened the fountains, and have enough to spare for the thirst of others! Some such there are; and, feeling that, with all the excuses for failure, still only the sight of those who triumph gives a meaning to life or makes its pangs endurable, we must arise and follow.

Eighteen hundred years of this Christian culture in these European Kingdoms, a great theme never lost sight of, a mighty idea, an adorable history to which the hearts of men invariably cling, yet are genuine results rare as grains of gold in the river's sandy bed! Where is the genuine Democracy to which the rights of all men are holy? where the child-like wisdom learning all through life more and more of the will of God? where the aversion to falsehood in all its myriad disguises of cant, vanity, covetousness, so clear to be read in all the history of Jesus of Nazareth? Modern Europe is the sequel to that history, and see this hollow England, with its monstrous wealth and cruel poverty, its conventional life and low, practical aims; see this poor France, so full of talent, so adroit, yet so shallow and glossy still, which could not escape from a false position with all its baptism of blood; see that lost Poland and this Italy bound down by treacherous hands in all the force of genius; see Russia with its brutal Czar and innumerable slaves; see Austria and its royalty that represents nothing, and its people who, as people, are and have nothing! If we consider the amount of truth that has really been spoken out in the world, and the love that has beat in private hearts—how Genius has decked each spring-time with such splendid flowers, conveying each one enough of instruction in its life of harmonious energy, and how continually, unquenchably the spark of faith has striven to burst into flame and light up the Universe—the public failure seems amazing, seems monstrous.

Still Europe toils and struggles with her idea, and, at this moment, all things bode and declare a new outbreak of the fire, to destroy old palaces of crime! May it fertilize also many vineyards!—Here at this moment a successor of St. Peter, after the lapse of near two thousand years, is called "Utopian" by a part of this Europe, because he strives to get some food to the mouths of the *leaner* of his flock. A wonderful state of things, and which leaves as the best argument against despair that men do not, *cannot* despair amid such dark experiences—and thou, my country! will thou not be more true? does no greater success await thee? All things have so conspired to teach, to aid! A new world, a new chance, with oceans to wall in the new thought against interference from the old!—Treasures of all kinds, gold, silver, corn, marble, to provide for every physical need! A noble, constant, starlike soul, an Italian, led the way to its shores, and, in the first days, the strong, the pure, those too brave, too sincere for the life of the Old World hastened to people them. A generous struggle then shook off what was foreign and gave the nation a glorious start for a worthy goal. Men rocked the cradle of its hopes, great, firm, disinterested men who saw, who wrote, as the basis of all that was to be done, a statement of the rights, the inborn rights of men, which, if fully interpreted and acted upon, leaves nothing to be desired.

Yet, oh Eagle, whose early flight showed this clear sight of the Sun, how often dost thou near the ground, how show the vulture in these later days! Thou wert to be the advance-guard of Humanity, the herald of all Progress; how often hast thou betrayed this high commission! Fain would the tongue in clear triumphant accents draw example from thy story, to encourage the hearts of those who almost faint and die beneath the old oppressions. But we must stammer and blush when we speak of many things. I take pride here that I may really say the Liberty of the Press works well, and that checks and balances naturally evolve from it which suffice to its government. I may say the minds of our people are alert, and that Talent has a free chance to rise. It is much. But dare I say that political ambition is not as darkly sullied as in other countries? Dare I say that men of most influence in political life are those who represent most virtue or even intellectual power? Is it easy to find names in that career of which I can speak with enthusiasm? Must I not confess in my country to a boundless lust of gain? Must I not confess to the weakest vanity, which bristles and blusters at each foolish taunt of the foreign press; and must I not admit that the men who make these undignified rejoinders seek and find popularity so? Must I not confess that there is as yet no antidote cordially adopted that will defend even that great, rich country against the evils that have grown out of the commercial system in the old world? Can I say our social laws are generally better, or show a nobler insight into the wants of man and woman? I do, indeed, say what I believe, that voluntary association for improvement in these particulars will be the grand means for my nation to grow and give a nobler harmony to the coming age. But it is only of a small minority that I can say they as yet seriously take to heart these things; that they earnestly meditate on what is wanted for their country,—for mankind,—for our cause is, indeed, the cause of all mankind at present. Could we succeed, really succeed, combine a deep religious love with practical development, the achievements of Genius with the happiness of the multitude, we might believe Man had now reached a commanding point in his ascent, and would stumble and faint no more. Then there is this horrible cancer of Slavery, and this wicked War, that has grown out of it.[2] How dare I speak of these things here? I listen to the same arguments against the emancipation of Italy, that are used against the emancipation of our blacks; the same arguments in favor of the spoliation of Poland as for the conquest of Mexico. I find the cause of tyranny and wrong everywhere the same—and lo! my Country the darkest offender, because with the least excuse, foresworn to the high calling with which she was called,—no champion of the rights of men, but a robber and a jailer; the scourge

[2]Fuller refers to the Mexican War (1846–48), which many Americans saw as a means to extend slavery territory.

hid behind her banner; her eyes fixed, not on the stars, but on the possessions of other men.

How it pleases me here to think of the Abolitionists! I could never endure to be with them at home, they were so tedious, often so narrow, always so rabid and exaggerated in their tone.

But, after all, they had a high motive, something eternal in their desire and life; and, if it was not the only thing worth thinking of it was really something worth living and dying for to free a great nation from such a terrible blot, such a threatening plague. God strengthen them and make them wise to achieve their purpose!

I please myself, too, with remembering some ardent souls among the American youth who, I trust, will yet expand and help to give soul to the huge, over fed, too hastily grown-up body. May they be constant. "Were Man but constant he were perfect!" it has been said; and it is true that he who could be constant to those moments in which he has been truly human—not brutal, not mechanical—is on the sure path to his perfection and to effectual service of the Universe.

It is to the youth that Hope addresses itself, to those who yet burn with aspiration, who are not hardened in their sins. But I dare not expect too much of them. I am not very old, yet of those who, in life's morning, I saw touched by the light of a high hope, many have seceded. Some have become voluptuaries; some mere family men, who think it is quite life enough to win bread for half a dozen people and treat them decently; others are lost through indolence and vacillation. Yet some remain constant. "I have witnessed many a shipwreck, yet still beat noble hearts."

I have found many among the youth of England, of France—of Italy also—full of high desire, but will they have courage and purity to fight the battle through in the sacred, the immortal band? Of some of them I believe it and await the proof. If a few succeed amid the trial, we have not lived and loved in vain.

To these, the heart of my country, a Happy New Year! I do not know what I have written. I have merely yielded to my feelings in thinking of America; but something of true love must be in these lines—receive them kindly, my friends; it is, by itself, some merit for printed words to be sincere.

Frederick Douglass 1818–1895

Abolitionist, women's rights advocate, journalist and newspaper editor, social reformer and race leader, Frederick Douglass was unquestionably one of the most prominent black leaders of the nineteenth century and one of the most eloquent orators in American public life.

Frederick Augustus Washington Bailey was born a slave in Talbot County, Maryland in February 1818. His mother, Harriet Bailey, was a slave; his father, Douglass suspected, was probably Aaron Anthony, the general plantation superintendent for the Lloyd plantation, where Douglass spent his early childhood. A sensitive and intelligent child, Douglass was quick to observe the horrors and routine injustices of slavery and his passion for black liberation and women's rights was undoubtedly fueled by his early observations and experiences on the Lloyd plantation. When Douglass was eight years old, he was sent to Baltimore to live with and work for the Auld family. There he learned an important lesson about the relationship of reading and writing to a liberated consciousness. In the face of the adamant opposition of the Aulds to his receiving even the most elementary instruction, Douglass, through a series of ruses, slowly and painstakingly taught himself the rudiments of reading and writing.

Another step towards his liberation occurred at the age of sixteen, when he was hired out to Edward Covey, a notorious "Negro breaker." For the first time Douglass, who had until this point lived as either a house- or urban slave, became a field hand and, for the first time in his life, he was regularly whipped and his spirit almost broken. Douglass's decision to physically defend himself against Covey's brutality—a central moment in his 1845 *Narrative*—was a turning point in his life as a slave and the final rehearsal for his escape from bondage. In 1838, Douglass escaped from slavery in Baltimore to pursue his vision of freedom in the North. In New York City he married Anna Murray, a free black woman from Baltimore who had been instrumental in his escape; Douglass and his bride then made their way to New Bedford, Massachusetts, in search of a new life. Typical of many former slaves who had decisively broken away from the shackles of slavery, Douglass renamed himself shortly after he arrived in the North, choosing as his own the name of the hero of Sir Walter Scott's novel *The Lady of the Lake.*

In early 1839, Douglass purchased his first copy of William Lloyd Garrison's radical abolitionist newspaper, the *Liberator*—the initial step towards his transformation into an abolitionist leader. He read the *Liberator* religiously, began to attend anti-slavery meetings in the local black community and, by 1841, had emerged as an eloquent leader of the black people in New Bedford. Later that year, Douglass was electrified when he heard Garrison speak for the first time and decided to attend an anti-slavery convention at Nantucket, where Garrison was scheduled to speak again. It was at that meeting on August 12, 1841, that Douglass was encouraged to address the audience. In spite of his embarrassment, Douglass stood up and offered a very moving account of his experiences as a slave. Douglass addressed the convention again that evening and, when the meeting was over, John A. Collins, general agent of the Massachusetts Anti-Slavery Society, asked Douglass to join them as an agent. After some soul-searching, Douglass agreed. From that point on, Douglass committed his life to, in his words, the "great work" of abolition and black liberation.

Douglass's public career unfolded in several distinct phases. Between 1841 and 1845, he lectured extensively on the anti-slavery circuit. When he published his *Narrative* in 1845, it was so explicit in its details that it exposed him to the risks of capture and re-enslavement. He fled to England and spent the years between 1845 and 1847 lecturing and promoting the anti-slavery cause throughout the British Isles. His English friends raised the money which allowed Douglass to purchase his freedom and to publish his own journal.

When Douglass returned to the United States, he broke with William Lloyd Garrison, who was then advocating that New England secede from the United States—a strategy which, in Douglass's view, would allow slavery to flourish in the South unchallenged. Ultimately, Douglass came to differ with Garrisonian abolitionists on a number of other issues as well, including the usefulness of electoral politics and the centrality of non-resistance—indeed, Douglass became a supporter of John Brown's direct attacks on the slave power. Douglass moved to Rochester, New York, in 1847, where he established his newspaper, *The North Star* (later renamed *Frederick Douglass' Paper*) and vigorously resumed his efforts on behalf of the abolitionist movement. He also became a participant in the first women's rights conventions in 1848, at Seneca Falls and at Rochester.

Although his despair over the bleak condition of blacks during the 1850s led him to briefly consider emigration to another country as a solution, Douglass welcomed the outbreak of the Civil War as the moment in which the long-awaited opportunity for black emancipation and elevation had arrived. During the war, he functioned as a public spokesman for the position that this conflict should be seen as a war of emancipation and, along with Sojourner Truth, urged Abraham Lincoln to enlist blacks in the Union army. When Lincoln yielded to these demands in 1862, Douglass was at the forefront in urging blacks to join the army to fight for their freedom. Between 1865 and his death in 1895, Douglass continued to function as one of the most prominent black spokesmen in the country and as a political leader in the Republican Party. He served as U.S. Marshal of the District of Columbia (1877–1881), Recorder of Deeds for the District of Columbia (1881–1886) and chargé d'affaires for Santo Domingo and minister to Haiti (1889–1891). He also completed the third and final of his autobiographical writings, *The Life and Times of Frederick Douglass* (1892).

Frederick Douglass's life, politics and writings are inextricably linked. His first speeches were moving and powerful evocations of his experiences as a slave and, in his early public appearances, he was often presented as a showpiece for major abolitionist lectures. "Give us the facts," he was told by John Collins, "we will take care of the philosophy." As Douglass grew more confident of his speaking abilities, however, he increasingly chafed under these guidelines, and he began to expand the scope of his speeches, incorporating larger issues and elaborating his own philosophy. His mentors became concerned that Douglass's eloquence would undermine his authenticity as a former slave, and Collins even urged him to sprinkle his speech with a little plantation language to maintain his credibility with his audiences. To dispel growing public doubts about his experiences as a slave, Douglass spent the winter of 1844 to 1845 writing an account of his experiences. *Narrative of the Life of Frederick Douglass, An American Slave, Written by Himself* appeared in May, 1845, with a preface by William Lloyd Garrison and an introductory letter by Wendell Phillips. Douglass's narrative was an instant popular success. In the first five months 4,500 copies were sold and, over the next several years, editions appeared in England, Ireland, France, and Germany.

One of the reasons for the popular appeal of Douglass's *Narrative* would certainly be the skill with which he appropriated the language and symbolism of American middle-class culture and religion to denounce the evils of slavery and racism. Unlike David Walker, for example, whose *Appeal* was addressed to the black community and issued dire warnings of America's impending doom, Douglass's *Narrative* excoriated American society for its lapses at the same time that it affirmed its original promise. In this respect, as William L. Andrews has pointed out, Douglass's *Narrative* is a kind of American jeremiad. Throughout his autobiography, Douglass blends his personal experiences as a slave with sharp attacks on the inequities of slavery and racism. And he appropriates the rhetoric of the jeremiad to distinguish between true and false Americans and Christians, between those who would affirm the dream and those who would destroy it. In the process, particularly by appropriating the rhetoric and symbols of Christianity, Douglass establishes a convincing case for himself as a lonely outcast in his own land and, more importantly, as a prophet ordained to warn American society against perversity and error. Against the backdrop of his relationship with the abolitionist movement,

Douglass's *Narrative* can also be read as a step towards the declaration of his literary and political independence—the first step towards his ultimate break with the Garrisonians and his long and extraordinary public career.

James A. Miller
Trinity College

PRIMARY WORKS

Frederick Douglass, *Narrative of the Life of Frederick Douglass, Written by Himself,* 1845; Frederick Douglass, *My Bondage and My Freedom,* 1855; Frederick Douglass, *Life and Times of Frederick Douglass: Written by Himself,* 1892; Philip S. Foner, ed., *The Life and Writing of Frederick Douglass,* 5 vols., 1950, 1971; John W. Blassingame, ed., *The Frederick Douglass Papers,* Ser. 1, vols. 1 and 2, 1979, 1982.

SECONDARY WORKS

Henry Louis Gates, Jr., "Binary Oppositions in Chapter One of *Narrative of the Life of Frederick Douglass, An American Slave, Written by Himself,*" in Dexter Fisher and Robert Stepto, eds., *Afro-American Literature: The Reconstruction of Instruction,* 1979; Robert G. O'Meally, "Frederick Douglass's 1845 *Narrative:* The Text Was Meant to Be Preached," in Fisher and Stepto; Robert B. Stepto, "Narration, Authentication and Authorial Control in Frederick Douglass's *Narrative of 1845,*" in Fisher and Stepto; Waldo E. Martin, Jr., *The Mind of Frederick Douglass,* 1984; William L. Andrews, *To Tell a Free Story: The First Century of Afro-American Autobiography, 1760–1865,* 1986; *Frederick Douglass's Narrative of the Life of Frederick Douglass,* ed. Harold Bloom, 1988; *Frederick Douglass: New Literary and Historical Essays,* Eric Sundquist, ed., 1990; *Critical Essays on Frederick Douglass,* William L. Andrews, ed., 1991; William S. McFeely, *Frederick Douglass,* 1991; Eric Sundquist, *To Wake the Nations: Race in the Making of American Literature,* 1993.

Narrative of the Life of Frederick Douglass, an American Slave[1]

Preface[2]

In the month of August, 1841, I attended an anti-slavery convention in Nantucket, at which it was my happiness to become acquainted with FREDERICK DOUGLASS, the writer of the following Narrative. He was a stranger to nearly every member of that body; but, having recently made his escape from the southern prisonhouse of bondage, and feeling his curiosity excited to ascertain the principles and measures of the abolitionists,—of whom he had heard a somewhat vague description while he was a slave,—he was induced to give his attendance, on the occasion alluded to, though at that time a resident in New Bedford.

Fortunate, most fortunate occurrence!—fortunate for the millions of his mana-

[1]First printed in May 1845 by the Anti-Slavery Office in Boston; their 1847 edition is the source of the present text. The words "Written by Himself" were included in the title.

[2]The author of the "Preface" was William Lloyd Garrison; see the selection from Garrison's work elsewhere in this volume.

cled brethren, yet panting for deliverance from their awful thraldom!—fortunate for the cause of negro emancipation, and of universal liberty!—fortunate for the land of his birth, which he has already done so much to save and bless!—fortunate for a large circle of friends and acquaintances, whose sympathy and affection he has strongly secured by the many sufferings he has endured, by his virtuous traits of character, by his ever-abiding remembrance of those who are in bonds, as being bound with them!—fortunate for the multitudes, in various parts of our republic, whose minds he has enlightened on the subject of slavery, and who have been melted to tears by his pathos, or roused to virtuous indignation by his stirring eloquence against the enslavers of men!—fortunate for himself, as it at once brought him into the field of public usefulness, "gave the world assurance of a man," quickened the slumbering energies of his soul, and consecrated him to the great work of breaking the rod of the oppressor, and letting the oppressed go free!

I shall never forget his first speech at the convention—the extraordinary emotion it excited in my own mind—the powerful impression it created upon a crowded auditory, completely taken by surprise—the applause which followed from the beginning to the end of his felicitous remarks. I think I never hated slavery so intensely as at that moment; certainly, my perception of the enormous outrage which is inflicted by it, on the godlike nature of its victims, was rendered far more clear than ever. There stood one, in physical proportion and stature commanding and exact—in intellect richly endowed—in natural eloquence a prodigy—in soul manifestly "created but a little lower than the angels"[3]—yet a slave, ay, a fugitive slave,—trembling for his safety, hardly daring to believe that on the American soil, a single white person could be found who would befriend him at all hazards, for the love of God and humanity! Capable of high attainments as an intellectual and moral being—needing nothing but a comparatively small amount of cultivation to make him an ornament to society and a blessing to his race—by the law of the land, by the voice of the people, by the terms of the slave code, he was only a piece of property, a beast of burden, a chattel personal, nevertheless!

A beloved friend from New Bedford[4] prevailed on Mr. DOUGLASS to address the convention: He came forward to the platform with a hesitancy and embarrassment, necessarily the attendants of a sensitive mind in such a novel position. After apologizing for his ignorance, and reminding the audience that slavery was a poor school for the human intellect and heart, he proceeded to narrate some of the facts in his own history as a slave, and in the course of his speech gave utterance to many noble thoughts and thrilling reflections. As soon as he had taken his seat, filled with hope and admiration, I rose, and declared that PATRICK HENRY,[5] of revolutionary fame, never made a speech more eloquent in the cause of liberty, than the one we had just listened to from the lips of that hunted fugitive. So I believed at that time—such is my belief now. I reminded the audience of the peril which surrounded this self-

[3]Psalm 8:5.

[4]William C. Coffin, one of the town's leading abolitionists.

[5]Henry (1736–1799), the well-known statesman and orator, was perhaps best remembered for his March 23, 1775, speech to the Virginia House of Delegates, which included the following: "Is life so dear or peace so sweet as to be purchased at the price of chains and slavery? Forbid it, Almighty God! I know not what course others may take; but as for me, give me liberty, or give me death!"

emancipated young man at the North,—even in Massachusetts, on the soil of the Pilgrim Fathers, among the descendants of revolutionary sires; and I appealed to them, whether they would ever allow him to be carried back into slavery,—law or no law, constitution or no constitution. The response was unanimous and in thunder-tones—"NO!" "Will you succor and protect him as a brother-man—a resident of the old Bay State."[6] "YES!" shouted the whole mass, with an energy so startling, that the ruthless tyrants south of Mason and Dixon's line might almost have heard the mighty burst of feeling, and recognized it as the pledge of an invincible determination, on the part of those who gave it, never to betray him that wanders, but to hide the out-cast, and firmly to abide the consequences.

It was at once deeply impressed upon my mind, that, if Mr. DOUGLASS could be persuaded to consecrate his time and talents to the promotion of the anti-slavery enterprise, a powerful impetus would be given to it, and a stunning blow at the same time inflicted on northern prejudice against a colored complexion. I therefore endeavored to instill hope and courage into his mind, in order that he might dare to engage in a vocation so anomalous and responsible for a person in his situation; and I was seconded in this effort by warm-hearted friends, especially by the late General Agent of the Massachusetts Anti-Slavery Society, Mr. JOHN A. COLLINS, whose judgment in this instance entirely coincided with my own. At first, he could give no encouragement; with unfeigned diffidence, he expressed his conviction that he was not adequate to the performance of so great a task; the path marked out was wholly an untrodden one; he was sincerely apprehensive that he should do more harm than good. After much deliberation, however, he consented to make a trial; and ever since that period, he has acted as a lecturing agent, under the auspices either of the American or the Massachusetts Anti-Slavery Society. In labors he has been most abundant; and his success in combating prejudice, in gaining proselytes, in agitating the public mind, has far surpassed the most sanguine expectations that were raised at the commencement of his brilliant career. He has borne himself with gentleness and meekness, yet with true manliness of character. As a public speaker, he excels in pathos, wit, comparison, imitation, strength of reasoning, and fluency of language. There is in him that union of head and heart, which is indispensable to an enlightenment of the heads and a winning of the hearts of others. May his strength continue to be equal to his day! May he continue to "grow in grace, and in the knowledge of God," that he may be increasingly serviceable in the cause of bleeding humanity, whether at home or abroad!

It is certainly a very remarkable fact, that one of the most efficient advocates of the slave population, now before the public, is a fugitive slave, in the person of FREDERICK DOUGLASS; and that the free colored population of the United States are as ably represented by one of their own number, in the person of CHARLES LENOX REMOND,[7] whose eloquent appeals have extorted the highest applause of multitudes on both sides of the Atlantic. Let the calumniators of the colored race despise themselves for their baseness and illiberality of spirit, and henceforth cease to talk of the

[6]Massachusetts.

[7]Remond (1810–1873), one of the first black abolitionist lecturers, had returned from Britain and Ireland in 1842 and spoken on a number of occasions with Douglass.

natural inferiority of those who require nothing but time and opportunity to attain to the highest point of human excellence.

It may, perhaps, be fairly questioned, whether any other portion of the population of the earth could have endured the privations, sufferings and horrors of slavery, without having become more degraded in the scale of humanity than the slaves of African descent. Nothing has been left undone to cripple their intellects, darken their minds, debase their moral nature, obliterate all traces of their relationship to mankind; and yet how wonderfully they have sustained the mighty load of a most frightful bondage, under which they have been groaning for centuries! To illustrate the effect of slavery on the white man,—to show that he has no powers of endurance, in such a condition, superior to those of his black brother,—DANIEL O'CONNELL,[8] the distinguished advocate of universal emancipation, and the mightiest champion of prostrate but not conquered Ireland, relates the following anecdote in a speech delivered by him in the Conciliation Hall, Dublin, before the Loyal National Repeal Association, March 31, 1845. "No matter," said Mr. O'CONNELL, "under what specious term it may disguise itself, slavery is still hideous. *It has a natural, an inevitable tendency to brutalize every noble faculty of man.* An American sailor, who was cast away on the shore of Africa, where he was kept in slavery for three years, was at the expiration of that period, found to be imbruted and stultified—he had lost all reasoning power; and having forgotten his native language, could only utter some savage gibberish between Arabic and English, which nobody could understand, and which even he himself found difficulty in pronouncing. So much for the humanizing influence of THE DOMESTIC INSTITUTION!" Admitting this to have been an extraordinary case of mental deterioration, it proves at least that the white slave can sink as low in the scale of humanity as the black one.

Mr. DOUGLASS has very properly chosen to write his own Narrative, in his own style, and according to the best of his ability, rather than to employ some one else. It is, therefore, entirely his own production; and, considering how long and dark was the career he had to run as a slave,—how few have been his opportunities to improve his mind since he broke his iron fetters,—it is, in my judgment, highly creditable to his head and heart. He who can peruse it without a tearful eye, a heaving breast, an afflicted spirit,—without being filled with an unutterable abhorrence of slavery and all its abettors, and animated with a determination to seek the the immediate overthrow of that execrable system,—without trembling for the fate of this country in the hands of a righteous God, who is ever on the side of the oppressed, and whose arm is not shortened that it cannot save,—must have a flinty heart, and be qualified to act the part of a trafficker "in slaves and the souls of men." I am confident that it is essentially true in all its statements; that nothing has been set down in malice, nothing exaggerated, nothing drawn from the imagination; that it comes short of the reality, rather than overstates a single fact in regard to SLAVERY AS IT IS.[9] The experience of FREDERICK DOUGLASS, as a slave, was not a peculiar one; his lot was not especially a hard one; his case may be regarded as a very fair specimen of the treatment

[8]Daniel O'Connell (1775–1847), Irish leader often called the "Liberator," was elected a member of Parliament, but took his seat only after Catholic Emancipation in 1829.

[9]The title of a very important source-book and anti-slavery tract (1839) by Theodore Dwight Weld.

of slaves in Maryland, in which State it is conceded that they are better fed and less cruelly treated than in Georgia, Alabama, or Louisiana. Many have suffered incomparably more, while very few on the plantations have suffered less, than himself. Yet how deplorable was his situation! what terrible chastisements were inflicted upon his person! what still more shocking outrages were perpetrated upon his mind! with all his noble powers and sublime aspirations, how like a brute was he treated, even by those professing to have the same mind in them that was in Christ Jesus! to what dreadful liabilities was he continually subjected! how destitute of friendly counsel and aid, even in his greatest extremities! how heavy was the midnight of woe which shrouded in blackness the last ray of hope, and filled the future with terror and gloom! what longings after freedom took possession of his breast, and how his misery augmented, in proportion as he grew reflective and intelligent,—thus demonstrating that a happy slave is an extinct man! how he thought, reasoned, felt, under the lash of the driver, with the chains upon his limbs! what perils he encountered in his endeavors to escape from his horrible doom! and how signal have been his deliverance and preservation in the midst of a nation of pitiless enemies!

This Narrative contains many affecting incidents, many passages of great eloquence and power; but I think the most thrilling one of them all is the description DOUGLASS gives of his feelings, as he stood soliloquizing respecting his fate, and the chances of his one day being a freeman, on the banks of the Chesapeake Bay—viewing the receding vessels as they flew with their white wings before the breeze, and apostrophizing them as animated by the living spirit of freedom. Who can read that passage, and be insensible to its pathos and sublimity? Compressed into it is a whole Alexandrian library[10] of thought, feeling, and sentiment—all that can, all that need be urged, in the form of expostulation, entreaty, rebuke, against that crime of crimes,—making man the property of his fellow-man! O, how accursed is that system, which entombs the godlike mind of man, defaces the divine image, reduces those who by creation were crowned with glory and honor to a level with four-footed beasts, and exalts the dealer in human flesh above all that is called God! Why should its existence be prolonged one hour? Is it not evil, only evil, and that continually? What does its presence imply but the absence of all fear of God, all regard for man, on the part of the people of the United States? Heaven speed its eternal overthrow!

So profoundly ignorant of the nature of slavery are many persons, that they are stubbornly incredulous whenever they read or listen to any recital of the cruelties which are daily inflicted on its victims. They do not deny that the slaves are held as property; but that terrible fact seems to convey to their minds no idea of injustice, exposure to outrage, or savage barbarity. Tell them of cruel scourgings, of mutilations and brandings, of scenes of pollution and blood, of the banishment of all light and knowledge, and they affect to be greatly indignant at such enormous exaggerations, such wholesale misstatements, such abominable libels on the character of the southern planters! As if all these direful outrages were not the natural results of slavery! As if it were less cruel to reduce a human being to the condition of a thing, than to give him a severe flagellation, or to deprive him of necessary food and clothing!

[10]The library at Alexandria, in Egypt, contained what may well have been the greatest collection in the ancient world.

As if whips, chains, thumb-screws, paddles, bloodhounds, overseers, drivers, patrols, were not all indispensable to keep the slaves down, and to give protection to their ruthless oppressors! As if, when the marriage institution is abolished, concubinage, adultery, and incest, must not necessarily abound; when all the rights of humanity are annihilated, any barrier remains to protect the victim from the fury of the spoiler; when absolute power is assumed over life and liberty, it will not be wielded with destructive sway! Skeptics of this character abound in society. In some few instances, their incredulity arises from a want of reflection; but, generally, it indicates a hatred of the light, a desire to shield slavery from the assaults of its foes, a contempt of the colored race, whether bond or free. Such will try to discredit the shocking tales of slaveholding cruelty which are recorded in this truthful Narrative; but they will labor in vain. Mr. DOUGLASS has frankly disclosed the place of his birth, the names of those who claimed ownership in his body and soul, and the names also of those who committed the crimes which he has alleged against them. His statements, therefore, may easily be disproved, if they are untrue.

In the course of his Narrative, he relates two instances of murderous cruelty,—in one of which a planter deliberately shot a slave belonging to a neighboring plantation, who had unintentionally gotten within his lordly domain in quest of fish; and in the other, an overseer blew out the brains of a slave who had fled to a stream of water to escape a bloody scourging. Mr. DOUGLASS states that in neither of these instances was any thing done by way of legal arrest or judicial investigation. The Baltimore American, of March 17, 1845, relates a similar case of atrocity, perpetrated with similar impunity—as follows:—"*Shooting a Slave.*—We learn, upon the authority of a letter from Charles county, Maryland, received by a gentleman of this city, that a young man, named Matthews, a nephew of General Matthews, and whose father, it is believed, holds an office at Washington, killed one of the slaves upon his father's farm by shooting him. The letter states that young Matthews had been left in charge of the farm; that he gave an order to the servant, which was disobeyed, when he proceeded to the house, *obtained a gun, and, returning, shot the servant.* He immediately, the letter continues, fled to his father's residence, where he still remains unmolested."—Let it never be forgotten, that no slaveholder or overseer can be convicted of any outrage perpetrated on the person of a slave, however diabolical it may be, on the testimony of colored witnesses, whether bond or free. By the slave code, they are adjudged to be as incompetent to testify against a white man, as though they were indeed a part of the brute creation. Hence, there is no legal protection in fact, whatever there may be in form, for the slave population; and any amount of cruelty may be inflicted on them with impunity. Is it possible for the human mind to conceive of a more horrible state of society?

The effect of a religious profession on the conduct of southern masters is vividly described in the following Narrative, and shown to be any thing but salutary. In the nature of the case, it must be in the highest degree pernicious. The testimony of Mr. DOUGLASS, on this point, is sustained by a cloud of witnesses, whose veracity is unimpeachable. "A slaveholder's profession of Christianity is a palpable imposture. He is a felon of the highest grade. He is a man-stealer. It is of no importance what you put in the other scale."

Reader! are you with the man-stealers in sympathy and purpose, or on the side of their down-trodden victims? If with the former, then are you the foe of God and man. If with the latter, what are you prepared to do and dare in their behalf? Be faithful, be vigilant, be untiring in your efforts to break every yoke, and let the oppressed go free. Come what may—cost what it may—inscribe on the banner which you unfurl to the breeze, as your religious and political motto—"NO COMPROMISE WITH SLAVERY! NO UNION WITH SLAVEHOLDERS!"

WM. LLOYD GARRISON

Boston, *May* 1, 1845.

Letter from Wendell Phillips, Esq.[11]

BOSTON, *April* 22, 1845.

My Dear Friend:

You remember the old fable of "The Man and the Lion," where the lion complained that he should not be so misrepresented "when the lions wrote history."

I am glad the time has come when the "lions write history." We have been left long enough to gather the character of slavery from the involuntary evidence of the masters. One might, indeed, rest sufficiently satisfied with what, it is evident, must be, in general, the results of such a relation, without seeking farther to find whether they have followed in every instance. Indeed, those who stare at the half-peck of corn a week, and love to count the lashes on the slave's back, are seldom the "stuff" out of which reformers and abolitionists are to be made. I remember that, in 1838, many were waiting for the results of the West India experiment,[12] before they could come into our ranks. Those "results" have come long ago; but, alas! few of that number have come with them, as converts. A man must be disposed to judge of emancipation by other tests than whether it has increased the produce of sugar,—and to hate slavery for other reasons than because it starves men and whips women,—before he is ready to lay the first stone of his anti-slavery life.

I was glad to learn, in your story, how early the most neglected of God's children waken to a sense of their rights, and of the injustice done them. Experience is a keen teacher; and long before you had mastered your A B C, or knew where the "white sails" of the Chesapeake were bound, you began, I see, to gauge the wretchedness of the slave, not by his hunger and want, not by his lashes and toil, but by the cruel and blighting death which gathers over his soul.

In connection with this, there is one circumstance which makes your recollections peculiarly valuable, and renders your early insight the more remarkable. You come from that part of the country where we are told slavery appears with its fairest features. Let us hear, then, what it is at its best estate—gaze on its bright side, if it has one; and then imagination may task her powers to add

[11]For information about Phillips, see the headnote to his work elsewhere in this volume.

[12]Great Britain had abolished the African slave trade and then, as of August 1, 1834, had decreed an end to slavery in the British West Indies, thus inaugurating a period of significant change for the newly-freed black population of the islands.

dark lines to the picture, as she travels southward to that (for the colored man) Valley of the Shadow of Death, where the Mississippi sweeps along.

Again, we have known you long, and can put the most entire confidence in your truth, candor, and sincerity. Every one who has heard you speak has felt, and, I am confident, every one who reads your book will feel, persuaded that you give them a fair specimen of the whole truth. No one-sided portrait,—no wholesale complaints,—but strict justice done, whenever individual kindliness has neutralized, for a moment, the deadly system with which it was strangely allied. You have been with us, too, some years, and can fairly compare the twilight of rights, which your race enjoy at the North, with that "noon of night" under which they labor south of Mason and Dixon's line. Tell us whether, after all, the half-free colored man of Massachusetts is worse off than the pampered slave of the rice swamps!

In reading your life, no one can say that we have unfairly picked out some rare specimens of cruelty. We know that the bitter drops, which even you have drained from the cup, are no incidental aggravations, no individual ills, but such as must mingle always and necessarily in the lot of every slave. They are the essential ingredients, not the occasional results, of the system.

After all, I shall read your book with trembling for you. Some years ago, when you were beginning to tell me your real name and birthplace, you may remember I stopped you, and preferred to remain ignorant of all. With the exception of a vague description, so I continued, till the other day, when you read me your memoirs. I hardly knew, at the time, whether to thank you or not for the sight of them, when I reflected that it was still dangerous, in Massachusetts, for honest men to tell their names! They say the fathers, in 1776, signed the Declaration of Independence with the halter about their necks. You, too, publish your declaration of freedom with danger compassing you around. In all the broad lands which the Constitution of the United States overshadows, there is no single spot,—however narrow or desolate,—where a fugitive slave can plant himself and say, "I am safe." The whole armory of Northern Law has no shield for you. I am free to say that, in your place, I should throw the MS. into the fire.

You, perhaps, may tell your story in safety, endeared as you are to so many warm hearts by rare gifts, and a still rare devotion of them to the service of others. But it will be owing only to your labors, and the fearless efforts of those who, trampling the laws and Constitution of the country under their feet, are determined that they will "hide the outcast," and that their hearths shall be, spite of the law, an asylum for the oppressed, if, some time or other, the humblest may stand in our streets, and bear witness in safety against the cruelties of which he has been the victim.

Yet it is sad to think, that these very throbbing hearts which welcome your story, and form your best safeguard in telling it, are all beating contrary to the "statute in such case made and provided." Go on, my dear friend, till you, and those who, like you, have been saved, so as by fire, from the dark prisonhouse, shall stereotype these free, illegal pulses into statutes; and New England, cutting loose from a blood-stained Union, shall glory in being the house of refuge for the oppressed;—till we no longer merely "*hide* the outcast," or make a merit of standing idly by while he is hunted in our midst; but, consecrating anew the soil of the Pilgrims as an asylum for the oppressed, proclaim our *welcome* to the slave so loudly, that the tones shall reach every hut in the Carolinas, and make the broken-hearted bondman leap up at the thought of old Massachusetts.

God speed the day!

Till then, and ever,
Yours truly,
WENDELL PHILLIPS

Chapter I

I was born in Tuckahoe, near Hillsborough, and about twelve miles from Easton, in Talbot county, Maryland. I have no accurate knowledge of my age, never having seen any authentic record containing it. By far the larger part of the slaves know as little of their ages as horses know of theirs, and it is the wish of most masters within my knowledge to keep their slaves thus ignorant. I do not remember to have ever met a slave who could tell of his birthday. They seldom come nearer to it than planting-time, harvest-time, cherry-time, spring-time, or fall-time. A want of information concerning my own was a source of unhappiness to me even during childhood. The white children could tell their ages. I could not tell why I ought to be deprived of the same privilege. I was not allowed to make any inquiries of my master concerning it. He deemed all such inquiries on the part of a slave improper and impertinent, and evidence of a restless spirit. The nearest estimate I can give makes me now between twenty-seven and twenty-eight years of age. I come to this, from hearing my master say, some time during 1835, I was about seventeen years old.

My mother was named Harriet Bailey. She was the daughter of Isaac and Betsey Bailey, both colored, and quite dark. My mother was of a darker complexion than either my grandmother or grandfather.

My father was a white man. He was admitted to be such by all I ever heard speak of my parentage. The opinion was also whispered that my master was my father; but of the correctness of this opinion, I know nothing; the means of knowing was withheld from me. My mother and I were separated when I was but an infant—before I knew her as my mother. It is a common custom, in the part of Maryland from which I ran away, to part children from their mothers at a very early age. Frequently, before the child has reached its twelfth month, its mother is taken from it, and hired out on some farm a considerable distance off, and the child is placed under the care of an old woman, too old for field labor. For what this separation is done, I do not know, unless it be to hinder the development of the child's affection toward its mother, and to blunt and destroy the natural affection of the mother for the child. This is the inevitable result.

I never saw my mother, to know her as such, more than four or five times in my life; and each of these times was very short in duration, and at night. She was hired by a Mr. Stewart, who lived about twelve miles from my home. She made her journeys to see me in the night, travelling the whole distance on foot, after the performance of her day's work. She was a field hand, and a whipping is the penalty of not being in the field at sunrise, unless a slave has special permission from his or her master to the contrary—a permission which they seldom get, and one that gives to him that gives it the proud name of being a kind master. I do not recollect of ever seeing my mother by the light of day. She was with me in the night. She would lie down with me, and get me to sleep, but long before I waked she was gone. Very little communication ever took place between us. Death soon ended what little we could have while she lived, and with it her hardships and suffering. She died when I was about seven years old, on one of my master's farms, near Lee's Mill. I was not allowed to be present during her illness, at her death, or burial. She was gone long before I knew anything about it. Never having enjoyed, to any considerable extent, her soothing presence, her tender and watchful care, I received the tidings of her death with much the same emotions I should have probably felt at the death of a stranger.

Called thus suddenly away, she left me without the slightest intimation of who my father was. The whisper that my master was my father, may or may not be true; and, true or false, it is of but little consequence to my purpose whilst the fact remains, in all its glaring odiousness, that slaveholders have ordained, and by law established, that the children of slave women shall in all cases follow the condition of their mothers; and this is done too obviously to administer to their own lusts, and make a gratification of their wicked desires profitable as well as pleasurable; for by this cunning arrangement, the slaveholder, in cases not a few, sustains to his slaves the double relation of master and father.

I know of such cases; and it is worthy of remark that such slaves invariably suffer greater hardships, and have more to contend with, than others. They are, in the first place, a constant offence to their mistress. She is ever disposed to find fault with them; they can seldom do any thing to please her; she is never better pleased than when she sees them under the lash, especially when she suspects her husband of showing to his mulatto children favors which he withholds from his black slaves. The master is frequently compelled to sell this class of his slaves, out of deference to the feelings of his white wife; and, cruel as the deed may strike any one to be, for a man to sell his own children to human flesh-mongers, it is often the dictate of humanity for him to do so; for, unless he does this, he must not only whip them himself, but must stand by and see one white son tie up his brother, of but few shades darker complexion than himself, and ply the gory lash to his naked back; and if he lisp one word of disapproval, it is set down to his parental partiality, and only makes a bad matter worse, both for himself and the slave whom he would protect and defend.

Every year brings with it multitudes of this class of slaves. It was doubtless in consequence of a knowledge of this fact, that one great statesman of the south predicted the downfall of slavery by the inevitable laws of population. Whether this prophecy is ever fulfilled or not, it is nevertheless plain that a very different-looking class of people are springing up at the south, and are now held in slavery, from those originally brought to this country from Africa; and if their increase will do no other good, it will do away the force of the argument, that God cursed Ham, and therefore American slavery is right.[13] If the lineal descendants of Ham are alone to be scripturally enslaved, it is certain that slavery at the south must soon become unscriptural;

[13]In Genesis 9:20–27 Noah curses his son, Ham, consigning him to bondage to his brothers; the passage was cited as scriptural authority for slavery.

for thousands are ushered into the world, annually, who, like myself, owe their existence to white fathers, and those fathers most frequently their own masters.

I have had two masters. My first master's name was Anthony. I do not remember his first name. He was generally called Captain Anthony—a title which, I presume, he acquired by sailing a craft on the Chesapeake Bay. He was not considered a rich slaveholder. He owned two or three farms, and about thirty slaves. His farms and slaves were under the care of an overseer. The overseer's name was Plummer. Mr. Plummer was a miserable drunkard, a profane swearer, and a savage monster. He always went armed with a cowskin[14] and a heavy cudgel. I have known him to cut and slash the women's heads so horribly, that even master would be enraged at his cruelty, and would threaten to whip him if he did not mind himself. Master, however, was not a humane slaveholder. It required extraordinary barbarity on the part of an overseer to affect him. He was a cruel man, hardened by a long life of slaveholding. He would at times seem to take great pleasure in whipping a slave. I have often been awakened at the dawn of day by the most heartrending shrieks of an old aunt of mine, whom he used to tie up to a joist, and whip upon her naked back till she was literally covered with blood. No words, no tears, no prayers, from his gory victim, seemed to move his iron heart from its bloody purpose. The louder she screamed, the harder he whipped; and where the blood ran fastest, there he whipped longest. He would whip her to make her scream, and whip her to make her hush; and not until overcome by fatigue, would he cease to swing the blood-clotted cowskin. I remember the first time I ever witnessed this horrible exhibition. I was quite a child, but I well remember it. I never shall forget it whilst I remember any thing. It was the first of a long series of such outrages, of which I was doomed to be a witness and a participant. It struck me with awful force. It was the bloodstained gate, the entrance to the hell of slavery, through which I was about to pass. It was a most terrible spectacle. I wish I could commit to paper the feelings with which I beheld it.

This occurrence took place very soon after I went to live with my old master, and under the following circumstances. Aunt Hester went out one night,—where or for what I do not know,—and happened to be absent when my master desired her presence. He had ordered her not to go out evenings, and warned her that she must never let him catch her in company with a young man, who was paying attention to her belonging to Colonel Lloyd. The young man's named was Ned Roberts, generally called Lloyd's Ned. Why master was so careful of her, may be safely left to conjecture. She was a woman of noble form, and of graceful proportions, having very few equals, and fewer superiors, in personal appearance, among the colored or white women of our neighborhood.

Aunt Hester had not only disobeyed his orders in going out, but had been found in company with Lloyd's Ned; which circumstance, I found, from what he said while whipping her, was the chief offence. Had he been a man of pure morals himself, he might have been thought interested in protecting the innocence of my aunt; but those who knew him will not suspect him of any such virtue. Before he commenced whipping Aunt Hester, he took her into the kitchen, and stripped her from neck to waist, leaving her neck, shoulders, and back, entirely naked. He then told her to

[14]A cowhide whip.

cross her hands, calling her at the same time a d—d b—h. After crossing her hands, he tied them with a strong rope, and led her to a stool under a large hook in the joist, put in for the purpose. He made her get upon the stool, and tied her hands to the hook. She now stood fair for his infernal purpose. Her arms were stretched up at their full length, so that she stood upon the ends of her toes. He then said to her, "Now, you d—d b—h, I'll learn you how to disobey my orders!" and after rolling up his sleeves, he commenced to lay on the heavy cowskin, and soon the warm, red blood (amid heart-rending shrieks from her, and horrid oaths from him) came dripping to the floor. I was so terrified and horror-stricken at the sight, that I hid myself in a closet, and dared not venture out till long after the bloody transaction was over. I expected it would be my turn next. It was all new to me. I had never seen any thing like it before. I had always lived with my grandmother on the outskirts of the plantation, where she was put to raise the children of the younger women. I had therefore been, until now, out of the way of the bloody scenes that often occurred on the plantation.

Chapter II

My master's family consisted of two sons, Andrew and Richard; one daughter, Lucretia, and her husband, Captain Thomas Auld. They lived in one house, upon the home plantation of Colonel Edward Lloyd. My master was Colonel Lloyd's clerk and superintendent. He was what might be called the overseer of the overseers. I spent two years of childhood on this plantation in my old master's family. It was here that I witnessed the bloody transaction recorded in the first chapter; and as I received my first impressions of slavery on this plantation, I will give some description of it, and of slavery as it there existed. The plantation is about twelve miles north of Easton, in Talbot county, and is situated on the border of Miles River. The principal products raised upon it were tobacco, corn, and wheat. These were raised in great abundance; so that, with the products of this and the other farms belonging to him, he was able to keep in almost constant employment a large sloop, in carrying them to market at Baltimore. This sloop was named Sally Lloyd, in honor of one of the colonel's daughters. My master's son-in-law, Captain Auld, was master of the vessel; she was otherwise manned by the colonel's own slaves. Their names were Peter, Isaac, Rich, and Jake. These were esteemed very highly by the other slaves, and looked upon as the privileged ones of the plantation; for it was no small affair, in the eyes of the slaves, to be allowed to see Baltimore.

Colonel Lloyd kept from three to four hundred slaves on his home plantation, and owned a large number more on the neighboring farms belonging to him. The names of the farms nearest to the home plantation were Wye Town and New Design. "Wye Town" was under the overseership of a man named Noah Willis. New Design was under the overseership of a Mr. Townsend. The overseers of these, and all the rest of the farms, numbering over twenty, received advice and direction from the managers of the home plantation. This was the great business place. It was the seat of government for the whole twenty farms. All disputes among the overseers were settled here. If a slave was convicted of any high misdemeanor, became unmanageable, or evinced a determination to run away, he was brought immediately here, severely whipped, put on board the sloop, carried to Baltimore, and sold to Austin Woolfolk, or some other slave-trader, as a warning to the slaves remaining.

Here, too, the slaves of all the other farms received their monthly allowance of food, and their yearly clothing. The men and women slaves received, as their monthly allowance of food, eight pounds of pork, or its equivalent in fish, and one bushel of corn meal. Their yearly clothing consisted of two coarse linen shirts, one pair of linen trousers, like the shirts, one jacket, one pair of trousers for winter, made of coarse negro cloth, one pair of stockings, and one pair of shoes; the whole of which could not have cost more than seven dollars. The allowance of the slave children was given to their mothers, or the old women having the care of them. The children unable to work in the field had neither shoes, stockings, jackets, nor trousers, given to them; their clothing consisted of two coarse linen shirts per year. When these failed them, they went naked until the next allowance-day. Children from seven to ten years old, of both sexes, almost naked, might be seen at all seasons of the year.

There were no beds given the slaves, unless one coarse blanket be considered such, and none but the men and women had these. This, however, is not considered a very great privation. They find less difficulty from the want of beds, than from the want of time to sleep; for when their day's work in the field is done, the most of them having their washing, mending, and cooking to do, and having few or none of the ordinary facilities for doing either of these, very many of their sleeping hours are consumed in preparing for the field the coming day; and when this is done, old and young, male and female, married and single, drop down side by side, on one common bed,—the cold, damp floor,—each covering himself or herself with their miserable blankets; and here they sleep till they are summoned to the field by the driver's horn. At the sound of this, all must rise, and be off to the field. There must be no halting; every one must be at his or her post; and woe betides them who hear not this morning summons to the field; for if they are not awakened by the sense of hearing, they are by the sense of feeling: no age nor sex finds any favor. Mr. Severe, the overseer, used to stand by the door of the quarter, armed with a large hickory stick and heavy cowskin, ready to whip any one who was so unfortunate as not to hear, or, from any other cause, was prevented from being ready to start for the field at the sound of the horn.

Mr. Severe was rightly named: he was a cruel man. I have seen him whip a woman, causing the blood to run half an hour at the time; and this, too, in the midst of her crying children, pleading for their mother's release. He seemed to take pleasure in manifesting his fiendish barbarity. Added to his cruelty, he was a profane swearer. It was enough to chill the blood and stiffen the hair of an ordinary man to hear him talk. Scarce a sentence escaped him but that was commenced or concluded by some horrid oath. The field was the place to witness his cruelty and profanity. His presence made it both the field of blood and of blasphemy. From the rising till the going down of the sun, he was cursing, raving, cutting, and slashing among the slaves of the field, in the most frightful manner. His career was short. He died very soon after I went to Colonel Lloyd's; and he died as he lived, uttering, with his dying groans, bitter curses and horrid oaths. His death was regarded by the slaves as the result of a merciful providence.

Mr. Severe's place was filled by a Mr. Hopkins. He was a very different man. He was less cruel, less profane, and made less noise, than Mr. Severe. His course was characterized by no extraordinary demonstrations of cruelty. He whipped, but seemed to take no pleasure in it. He was called by the slaves a good overseer.

The home plantation of Colonel Lloyd wore the appearance of a country village. All the mechanical operations for all the farms were performed here. The shoemaking and mending, the black-smithing, cartwrighting, coopering, weaving, and grain-grinding, were all performed by the slaves on the home plantation. The whole place wore a business-like aspect very unlike the neighboring farms. The number of houses, too, conspired to give it advantage over the neighboring farms. It was called by the slaves the *Great House Farm.* Few privileges were esteemed higher, by the slaves of the out-farms, than that of being selected to do errands at the Great House Farm. It was associated in their minds with greatness. A representative could not be prouder of his election to a seat in the American Congress, than a slave on one of the out-farms would be of his election to do errands at the Great House Farm. They regarded it as evidence of great confidence reposed in them by their overseers; and it was on this account, as well as a constant desire to be out of the field from under the driver's lash, that they esteemed it a high privilege, one worth careful living for. He was called the smartest and most trusty fellow, who had this honor conferred upon him the most frequently. The competitors for this office sought as diligently to please their overseers, as the office-seekers in the political parties seek to please and deceive the people. The same traits of character might be seen in Colonel Lloyd's slaves, as are seen in the slaves of the political parties.

The slaves selected to go to the Great House Farm, for the monthly allowance for themselves and their fellow-slaves, were peculiarly enthusiastic. While on their way, they would make the dense old woods, for miles around, reverberate with their wild songs, revealing at once the highest joy and the deepest sadness. They would compose and sing as they went along, consulting neither time nor tune. The thought that came up, came out—if not in the word, in the sound;—and as frequently in the one as in the other. They would sometimes sing the most pathetic sentiment in the most rapturous tone, and the most rapturous sentiment in the most pathetic tone. Into all of their songs they would manage to weave something of the Great House Farm. Especially would they do this, when leaving home. They would then sing most exultingly the following words:—

"I am going away to the Great House Farm!
O, yea! O, yea! O!"

This they would sing, as a chorus, to words which to many would seem unmeaning jargon, but which, nevertheless, were full of meaning to themselves. I have sometimes thought that the mere hearing of those songs would do more to impress some minds with the horrible character of slavery, than the reading of whole volumes of philosophy on the subject could do.

I did not, when a slave, understand the deep meaning of those rude and apparently incoherent songs. I was myself within the circle; so that I neither saw nor heard as those without might see and hear. They told a tale of woe which was then altogether beyond my feeble comprehension; they were tones loud, long, and deep; they breathed the prayer and complaint of souls boiling over with the bitterest anguish.

Every tone was a testimony against slavery, and a prayer to God for deliverance from chains. The hearing of those wild notes always depressed my spirit, and filled me with ineffable sadness. I have frequently found myself in tears while hearing them. The mere recurrence to those songs, even now, afflicts me; and while I am writing these lines, an expression of feeling has already found its way down my cheek. To those songs I trace my first glimmering conception of the dehumanizing character of slavery. I can never get rid of that conception. Those songs still follow me, to deepen my hatred of slavery, and quicken my sympathies for my brethren in bonds. If any one wishes to be impressed with the soul-killing effects of slavery, let him go to Colonel Lloyd's plantation, and, on allowance-day, place himself in the deep pine woods, and there let him, in silence analyze the sounds that shall pass through the chambers of his soul,—and if he is not thus impressed, it will only be because "there is no flesh in his obdurate heart."

I have often been utterly astonished, since I came to the north, to find persons who could speak of the singing, among slaves, as evidence of their contentment and happiness. It is impossible to conceive of a greater mistake. Slaves sing most when they are most unhappy. The songs of the slave represent the sorrows of his heart; and he is relieved by them, only as an aching heart is relieved by its tears. At least, such is my experience. I have often sung to drown my sorrow, but seldom to express my happiness. Crying for joy, and singing for joy, were alike uncommon to me while in the jaws of slavery. The singing of a man cast away upon a desolate island might be as appropriately considered as evidence of contentment and happiness, as the singing of a slave; the songs of the one and of the other are prompted by the same emotion.

Chapter III

Colonel Lloyd kept a large and finely cultivated garden, which afforded almost constant employment for four men, besides the chief gardener, (Mr. M'Durmond.) This garden was probably the greatest attraction of the place. During the summer months, people came from far and near—from Baltimore, Easton, and Annapolis—to see it. It abounded in fruits of almost every description, from the hardy apple of the north to the delicate orange of the south. This garden was not the least source of trouble on the plantation. Its excellent fruit was quite a temptation to the hungry swarms of boys, as well as the older slaves, belonging to the colonel, few of whom had the virtue or the vice to resist it. Scarcely a day passed, during the summer, but that some slave had to take the lash for stealing fruit. The colonel had to resort to all kinds of stratagems to keep his slaves out of the garden. The last and most successful one was that of tarring his fence all around, after which, if a slave was caught with any tar upon his person, it was deemed sufficient proof that he had either been into the garden, or had tried to get in. In either case, he was severely whipped by the chief gardener. This plan worked well; the slaves became as fearful of tar as of the lash. They seemed to realize the impossibility of touching *tar* without being defiled.

The colonel also kept a splendid riding equipage. His stable and carriage-house presented the appearance of some of our large city livery establishments. His horses were of the finest form and noblest blood. His carriage-house contained three splendid coaches, three or four gigs, besides dearborns and barouches of the most fashionable style.[15]

This establishment was under the care of two slaves—old Barney and young Barney—father and son. To attend to this establishment was their sole work. But it was by no means an easy employment; for in nothing was Colonel Lloyd more particular than in the management of his horses. The slightest inattention to these was unpardonable, and was visited upon those, under whose care they were placed, with the severest punishment; no excuse could shield them, if the colonel only suspected any want of attention to his horses—a supposition which he frequently indulged, and one which, of course, made the office of old and young Barney a very trying one. They never knew when they were safe from punishment. They were frequently whipped when least deserving, and escaped whipping when most deserving it. Every thing depended upon the looks of the horses, and the state of Colonel Lloyd's own mind when his horses were brought to him for use. If a horse did not move fast enough, or hold his head high enough, it was owing to some fault of his keepers. It was painful to stand near the stabledoor, and hear the various complaints against the keepers when a horse was taken out for use. "This horse has not had proper attention. He has not been sufficiently rubbed and curried, or he has not been properly fed; his food was too wet or too dry; he got it too soon or too late; he was too hot or too cold; he had too much hay, and not enough of grain; or he had too much grain, and not enough of hay; instead of old Barney's attending to the horse, he had very improperly left it to his son." To all these complaints, no matter how unjust, the slave must answer never a word. Colonel Lloyd could not brook any contradiction from a slave. When he spoke, a slave must stand, listen, and tremble; and such was literally the case. I have seen Colonel Lloyd make old Barney, a man between fifty and sixty years of age, uncover his bald head, kneel down upon the cold, damp ground, and receive upon his naked and toil-worn shoulders more than thirty lashes at the time. Colonel Lloyd had three sons—Edward, Murray, and Daniel,—and three sons-in-law, Mr. Winder, Mr. Nicholson, and Mr. Lowndes. All of these lived at the Great House Farm, and enjoyed the luxury of whipping the servants when they pleased, from old Barney down to William Wilkes, the coach-driver. I have seen Winder make one of the house-servants stand off from him a suitable distance to be touched with the end of his whip, and at every stroke raise great ridges upon his back.

To describe the wealth of Colonel Lloyd would be almost equal to describing the riches of Job.[16] He kept from ten to fifteen house-servants. He was said to own a thousand slaves, and I think this estimate quite within the truth. Colonel Lloyd owned so many that he did not know them when he saw them; nor did all the slaves of the out-farms know him. It is reported of him, that, while riding along the road one day, he met a colored man, and addressed him in the usual manner of speaking to colored people on the public highways of the south: "Well, boy, whom do you belong to?" "To Colonel Lloyd," replied the slave. "Well, does the colonel treat you well?" "No, sir," was the ready reply. "What, does he work you too hard?" "Yes, sir." "Well, don't he give you enough to eat?" "Yes, sir, he gives me enough, such as it is."

[15]Various kinds of horse-drawn carriages.

[16]Before being visited with misfortunes, the Biblical Job was enormously wealthy.

The colonel, after ascertaining where the slave belonged, rode on; the man also went on about his business, not dreaming that he had been conversing with his master. He thought, said, and heard nothing more of the matter, until two or three weeks afterwards. The poor man was then informed by his overseer that, for having found fault with his master, he was now to be sold to a Georgia trader. He was immediately chained and handcuffed; and thus, without a moment's warning, he was snatched away, and forever sundered, from his family and friends, by a hand more unrelenting than death. This is the penalty of telling the truth, of telling the simple truth, in answer to a series of plain questions.

It is partly in consequence of such facts, that slaves, when inquired of as to their condition and the character of their masters, almost universally say they are contented, and that their masters are kind. The slaveholders have been known to send in spies among their slaves, to ascertain their views and feelings in regard to their condition. The frequency of this has had the effect to establish among the slaves the maxim, that a still tongue makes a wise head. They suppress the truth rather than take the consequences of telling it, and in so doing prove themselves a part of the human family. If they have any thing to say of their masters, it is generally in their masters' favor, especially when speaking to an untried man. I have been frequently asked, when a slave, if I had a kind master, and do not remember ever to have given a negative answer; nor did I, in pursuing this course, consider myself as uttering what was absolutely false; for I always measured the kindness of my master by the standard of kindness set up among slaveholders around us. Moreover, slaves are like other people, and imbibe prejudices quite common to others. They think their own better than that of others. Many, under the influence of this prejudice, think their own masters are better than the masters of other slaves; and this, too, in some cases, when the very reverse is true. Indeed, it is not uncommon for slaves even to fall out and quarrel among themselves about the relative goodness of their masters, each contending for the superior goodness of his own over that of the others. At the very same time, they mutually execrate their masters when viewed separately. It was so on our plantation. When Colonel Lloyd's slaves met the slaves of Jacob Jepson, they seldom parted without a quarrel about their masters; Colonel Lloyd's slaves contending that he was the richest, and Mr. Jepson's slaves that he was the smartest, and most of a man. Colonel Lloyd's slaves would boast his ability to buy and sell Jacob Jepson. Mr. Jepson's slaves would boast his ability to whip Colonel Lloyd. These quarrels would almost always end in a fight between the parties, and those that whipped were supposed to have gained the point at issue. They seemed to think that the greatness of their masters was transferable to themselves. It was considered as being bad enough to be a slave; but to be a poor man's slave was deemed a disgrace indeed!

Chapter IV

Mr. Hopkins remained but a short time in the office of overseer. Why his career was so short, I do not know, but suppose he lacked the necessary severity to suit Colonel Lloyd. Mr. Hopkins was succeeded by Mr. Austin Gore, a man possessing, in an eminent degree, all those traits of character indispensable to what is called a first-rate overseer. Mr. Gore had served Colonel Lloyd, in the capacity of overseer, upon one of the out-farms, and had shown himself worthy of the high station of overseer upon the home or Great House Farm.

Mr. Gore was proud, ambitious, and persevering. He was artful, cruel, and obdurate. He was just the man for such a place, and it was just the place for such a man. It afforded scope for the full exercise of all his powers, and he seemed to be perfectly at home in it. He was one of those who could torture the slightest look, word, or gesture, on the part of the slave, into impudence, and would treat it accordingly. There must be no answering back to him; no explanation was allowed a slave, showing himself to have been wrongfully accused. Mr. Gore acted fully up to the maxim laid down by slaveholders,—"It is better that a dozen slaves suffer under the lash, than that the overseer should be convicted, in the presence of the slaves, of having been at fault." No matter how innocent a slave might be—it availed him nothing, when accused by Mr. Gore of any misdemeanor. To be accused was to be convicted, and to be convicted was to be punished; the one always following the other with immutable certainty. To escape punishment was to escape accusation; and few slaves had the fortune to do either, under the overseership of Mr. Gore. He was just proud enough to demand the most debasing homage of the slave, and quite servile enough to crouch, himself, at the feet of the master. He was ambitious enough to be contented with nothing short of the highest rank of overseers, and persevering enough to reach the height of his ambition. He was cruel enough to inflict the severest punishment, artful enough to descend to the lowest trickery, and obdurate enough to be insensible to the voice of a reproving conscience. He was, of all the overseers, the most dreaded by the slaves. His presence was painful; his eye flashed confusion; and seldom was his sharp, shrill voice heard, without producing horror and trembling in their ranks.

Mr. Gore was a grave man, and, though a young man, he indulged in no jokes, said no funny words, seldom smiled. His words were in perfect keeping with his looks, and his looks were in perfect keeping with his words. Overseers will sometimes indulge in a witty word, even with the slaves; not so with Mr. Gore. He spoke but to command, and commanded but to be obeyed; he dealt sparingly with his words, and bountifully with his whip, never using the former where the latter would answer as well. When he whipped, he seemed to do so from a sense of duty, and feared no consequences. He did nothing reluctantly, no matter how disagreeable; always at his post, never inconsistent. He never promised but to fulfil. He was, in a word, a man of the most inflexible firmness and stone-like coolness.

His savage barbarity was equalled only by the consummate coolness with which he committed the grossest and most savage deeds upon the slaves under his charge. Mr. Gore once undertook to whip one of Colonel Lloyd's slaves, by the name of Demby. He had given Demby but few stripes, when, to get rid of the scourging, he ran and plunged himself into a creek, and stood there at the depth of his shoulders, refusing to come out. Mr. Gore told him that he would give him three calls, and that, if he did not come out at the third call, he would shoot him. The first call was given. Demby made no response, but stood his ground. The second and third calls were given with the same result. Mr. Gore then, without consultation or deliberation with any one, not even giving Demby an additional call, raised his musket to his face, taking deadly aim at his standing victim, and in an instant poor Demby was no more.

His mangled body sank out of sight, and blood and brains marked the water where he had stood.

A thrill of horror flashed through every soul upon the plantation, excepting Mr. Gore. He alone seemed cool and collected. He was asked by Colonel Lloyd and my old master, why he resorted to this extraordinary expedient. His reply was, (as well as I can remember,) that Demby had become unmanageable. He was setting a dangerous example to the other slaves,—one which, if suffered to pass without some such demonstration on his part, would finally lead to the total subversion of all rule and order upon the plantation. He argued that if one slave refused to be corrected, and escaped with his life, the other slaves would soon copy the example; the result of which would be, the freedom of the slaves, and the enslavement of the whites. Mr. Gore's defence was satisfactory. He was continued in his station as overseer upon the home plantation. His fame as an overseer went abroad. His horrid crime was not even submitted to judicial investigation. It was committed in the presence of slaves, and they of course could neither institute a suit, nor testify against him; and thus the guilty perpetrator of one of the bloodiest and most foul murders goes unwhipped of justice, and uncensured by the community in which he lives. Mr. Gore lived in St. Michael's, Talbot county, Maryland, when I left there; and if he is still alive, he very probably lives there now; and if so, he is now, as he was then, as highly esteemed and as much respected as though his guilty soul had not been stained with his brother's blood.

I speak advisedly when I say this,—that killing a slave, or any colored person, in Talbot county, Maryland, is not treated as a crime, either by the courts or the community. Mr. Thomas Lanman, of St Michael's, killed two slaves, one of whom he killed with a hatchet, by knocking his brains out. He used to boast of the commission of the awful and bloody deed. I have heard him do so laughingly, saying, among other things, that he was the only benefactor of his country in the company, and that when others would do as much as he had done, we should be relieved of "the d——d niggers."

The wife of Mr. Giles Hicks, living but a short distance from where I used to live, murdered my wife's cousin, a young girl between fifteen and sixteen years of age, mangling her person in the most horrible manner, breaking her nose and breastbone with a stick, so that the poor girl expired in a few hours afterward. She was immediately buried, but had not been in her untimely grave but a few hours before she was taken up and examined by the coroner, who decided that she had come to her death by severe beating. The offence for which this girl was thus murdered was this:—She had been set that night to mind Mrs. Hicks's baby, and during the night she fell asleep, and the baby cried. She, having lost her rest for several night previous, did not hear the crying. They were both in the room with Mrs. Hicks. Mrs. Hicks, finding the girl slow to move, jumped from her bed, seized an oak stick of wood by the fireplace, and with it broke the girl's nose and breastbone, and thus ended her life. I will not say that this most horrid murder produced no sensation in the community. It did produce sensation, but not enough to bring the murderess to punishment. There was a warrant issued for her arrest, but it was never served. Thus she escaped not only punishment, but even the pain of being arraigned before a court for her horrid crime.

Whilst I am detailing bloody deeds which took place during my stay on Colonel

Lloyd's plantation, I will briefly narrate another, which occurred about the same time as the murder of Demby by Mr. Gore.

Colonel Lloyd's slaves were in the habit of spending a part of their nights and Sundays in fishing for oysters, and in this way made up the deficiency of their scanty allowance. An old man belonging to Colonel Lloyd, while thus engaged, happened to get beyond the limits of Colonel Lloyd's, and on the premises of Mr. Beal Bondly. At this trespass, Mr. Bondly took offence, and with his musket came down to the shore, and blew its deadly contents into the poor old man.

Mr. Bondly came over to see Colonel Lloyd the next day, whether to pay him for his property, or to justify himself in what he had done, I know not. At any rate, this whole fiendish transaction was soon hushed up. There was very little said about it at all, and nothing done. It was a common saying, even among little white boys, that it was worth a half-cent to kill a "nigger," and a half-cent to bury one.

Chapter V

As to my own treatment while I lived on Colonel Lloyd's plantation, it was very similar to that of the other slave children. I was not old enough to work in the field, and there being little else than field work to do, I had a great deal of leisure time. The most I had to do was to drive up the cows at evening, keep the fowls out of the garden, keep the front yard clean, and run of errands for my old master's daughter, Mrs. Lucretia Auld. The most of my leisure time I spent in helping Master Daniel Lloyd in finding his birds, after he had shot them. My connection with Master Daniel was of some advantage to me. He became quite attached to me, and was a sort of protector of me. He would not allow the older boys to impose upon me, and would divide his cakes with me.

I was seldom whipped by my old master, and suffered little from any thing else than hunger and cold. I suffered much from hunger, but much more from cold. In hottest summer and coldest winter, I was kept almost naked—no shoes, no stockings, no jacket, no trousers, nothing on but a coarse tow linen shirt, reaching only to my knees. I had no bed. I must have perished with cold, but that, the coldest nights, I used to steal a bag which was used for carrying corn to the mill. I would crawl into this bag, and there sleep on the cold, damp, clay floor, with my head in and feet out. My feet have been so cracked with the frost, that the pen with which I am writing might be laid in the gashes.

We were not regularly allowanced. Our food was coarse corn meal boiled. This was called *mush.* It was put into a large wooden tray or trough, and set down upon the ground. The children were then called, like so many pigs, and like so many pigs they would come and devour the mush; some with oyster-shells, others with pieces of shingle, some with naked hands, and none with spoons. He that ate fastest got most; he that was strongest secured the best place; and few left the trough satisfied.

I was probably between seven and eight years old when I left Colonel Lloyd's plantation. I left it with joy. I shall never forget the ecstasy with which I received the intelligence that my old master (Anthony) had determined to let me go to Baltimore, to live with Mr. Hugh Auld, brother to my old master's son-in-law, Captain Thomas

Auld. I received this information about three days before my departure. They were three of the happiest days I ever enjoyed. I spent the most part of all these three days in the creek, washing off the plantation scurf, and preparing myself for my departure.

The pride of appearance which this would indicate was not my own. I spent the time in washing, not so much because I wished to, but because Mrs. Lucretia had told me I must get all the dead skin off my feet and knees before I could go to Baltimore; for the people in Baltimore were very cleanly, and would laugh at me if I looked dirty. Besides, she was going to give me a pair of trousers, which I should not put on unless I got all the dirt off me. The thought of owning a pair of trousers was great indeed! It was almost a sufficient motive, not only to make me take off what would be called by pigdrovers the mange, but the skin itself. I went at it in good earnest, working for the first time with the hope of reward.

The ties that ordinarily bind children to their homes were all suspended in my case. I found no severe trial in my departure. My home was charmless; it was not home to me; on parting from it, I could not feel that I was leaving any thing which I could have enjoyed by staying. My mother was dead, my grandmother lived far off, so that I seldom saw her. I had two sisters and one brother, that lived in the same house with me; but the early separation of us from our mother had well nigh blotted the fact of our relationship from our memories. I looked for home elsewhere, and was confident of finding none which I should relish less than the one which I was leaving. If, however, I found in my new home hardship, hunger, whipping, and nakedness, I had the consolation that I should not have escaped any one of them by staying. Having already had more than a taste of them in the house of my old master, and having endured them there, I very naturally inferred my ability to endure them elsewhere, and especially at Baltimore; for I had something of the feeling about Baltimore that is expressed in the proverb, that "being hanged in England is preferable to dying a natural death in Ireland." I had the strongest desire to see Baltimore. Cousin Tom, though not fluent in speech, had inspired me with that desire by his eloquent description of the place. I could never point out any thing at the Great House, no matter how beautiful or powerful, but that he had seen something at Baltimore far exceeding, both in beauty and strength, the object which I pointed out to him. Even the Great House itself, with all its pictures, was far inferior to many buildings in Baltimore. So strong was my desire, that I thought a gratification of it would fully compensate for whatever loss of comforts I should sustain by the exchange. I left without a regret, and with the highest hopes of future happiness.

We sailed out of Miles River for Baltimore on a Saturday morning. I remember only the day of the week, for at that time I had no knowledge of the days of the month, nor the months of the year. On setting sail, I walked aft, and gave to Colonel Lloyd's plantation what I hoped would be the last look. I then placed myself in the bows of the sloop, and there spent the remainder of the day in looking ahead, interesting myself in what was in the distance rather than in things near by or behind.

In the afternoon of that day, we reached Annapolis, the capital of the State. We stopped but a few moments, so that I had no time to go on shore. It was the first large town that I had ever seen, and though it would look small compared with some of our New England factory villages, I thought it a wonderful place for its size—more imposing even than the Great House Farm!

We arrived at Baltimore early on Sunday morning, landing at Smith's Wharf, not far from Bowley's Wharf. We had on board the sloop a large flock of sheep; and after aiding in driving them to the slaughterhouse of Mr. Curtis on Louden Slater's Hill, I was conducted by Rich, one of the hands belonging on board of the sloop to my new home in Alliciana Street, near Mr. Gardner's ship-yard, on Fells Point.

Mr. and Mrs. Auld were both at home, and met me at the door with their little son Thomas, to take care of whom I had been given. And here I saw what I had never seen before; it was a white face beaming with the most kindly emotions; it was the face of my new mistress, Sophia Auld. I wish I could describe the rapture that flashed through my soul as I beheld it. It was a new and strange sight to me, brightening up my pathway with the light of happiness. Little Thomas was told, there was his Freddy,—and I was told to take care of little Thomas; and thus I entered upon the duties of my new home with the most cheering prospect ahead.

I looked upon my departure from Colonel Lloyd's plantation as one of the most interesting events of my life. It is possible, and even quite probable, that but for the mere circumstance of being removed from that plantation to Baltimore, I should have to-day, instead of being here seated by my own table, in the enjoyment of freedom and the happiness of home, writing this Narrative, been confined in the galling chains of slavery. Going to live at Baltimore laid the foundation, and opened the gateway, to all my subsequent prosperity. I have ever regarded it as the first plain manifestation of that kind providence which has ever since attended me, and marked my life with so many favors. I regarded the selection of myself as being somewhat remarkable. There were a number of slave children that might have been sent from the plantation to Baltimore. There were those younger, those older, and those of the same age. I was chosen from among them all, and was the first, last, and only choice.

I may be deemed superstitious, and even egotistical, in regarding this event as a special interposition of divine Providence in my favor. But I should be false to the earliest sentiments of my soul, if I suppressed the opinion. I prefer to be true to myself, even at the hazard of incurring the ridicule of others, rather than to be false, and incur my own abhorrence. From my earliest recollection, I date the entertainment of a deep conviction that slavery would not always be able to hold me within its foul embrace; and in the darkest hours of my career in slavery, this living word of faith and spirit of hope departed [not] from me, but remained like ministering angels to cheer me through the gloom. This good spirit was from God, and to him I offer thanksgiving and praise.

Chapter VI

My new mistress proved to be all she appeared when I first met her at the door,—a woman of the kindest heart and finest feelings. She had never had a slave under her control previously to myself, and prior to her marriage she had been dependent upon her own industry for a living. She was by trade a weaver; and by constant application to her business, she had been in a good degree preserved from the blighting and dehumanizing effects of slavery. I was utterly astonished at her goodness. I scarcely knew how to behave towards her. She was entirely unlike any other white woman I had ever seen. I could not approach her as I was accustomed to approach other white ladies. My early instruction was all out of place. The crouching servility, usually so acceptable a quality in a slave, did not answer when manifested toward her. Her favor was not gained by it; she seemed to be disturbed by it. She did not deem it impudent or unmannerly for a slave to look her in the face. The meanest slave was put fully at ease in her presence, and none left without feeling better for having seen her. Her face was made of heavenly smiles, and her voice of tranquil music.

But, alas! this kind heart had but a short time to remain such. The fatal poison of irresponsible power was already in her hands, and soon commenced its infernal work. That cheerful eye, under the influence of slavery, soon became red with rage; that voice, made all of sweet accord, changed to one of harsh and horrid discord; and that angelic face gave place to that of a demon.

Very soon after I went to live with Mr. and Mrs. Auld, she kindly commenced to teach me the A, B, C. After I had learned this, she assisted me in learning to spell words of three or four letters. Just at this point of my progress, Mr. Auld found out what was going on, and at once forbade Mrs. Auld to instruct me further, telling her, among other things, that it was unlawful,[17] as well as unsafe, to teach a slave to read. To use his own words further, he said, "If you give a nigger an inch, he will take an ell. A nigger should know nothing but to obey his master—to do as he is told to do. Learning would *spoil* the best nigger in the world. Now," said he, "if you teach that nigger (speaking of myself) how to read, there would be no keeping him. It would forever unfit him to be a slave. He would at once become unmanageable, and of no value to his master. As to himself, it could do him no good, but a great deal of harm. It would make him discontented and unhappy." These words sank deep into my heart, stirred up sentiments within that lay slumbering, and called into existence an entirely new train of thought. It was a new and special revelation, explaining dark and mysterious things, with which my youthful understanding had struggled, but struggled in vain. I now understood what had been to me a most perplexing difficulty—to wit, the white man's power to enslave the black man. It was a grand achievement, and I prized it highly. From that moment, I understood the pathway from slavery to freedom. It was just what I wanted, and I got it at a time when I the least expected it. Whilst I was saddened by the thought of losing the aid of my kind mistress, I was gladdened by the invaluable instruction which, by the merest accident, I had gained from my master. Though conscious of the difficulty of learning without a teacher, I set out with high hope, and a fixed purpose, at whatever cost of trouble, to learn how to read. The very decided manner with which he spoke, and strove to impress his wife with the evil consequences of giving me instruction, served to convince me that he was deeply sensible of the truths he was uttering. It gave me the best assurance that I might rely with the utmost confidence on the results which, he said, would flow from teaching me to read. What he most dreaded, that I most desired. What he most loved, that I most hated. That which to him was a great evil, to be carefully shunned, was to me a great good, to be diligently sought; and the argument which he so warmly urged, against my learning to read, only served to inspire me with a desire and determination to learn. In learning to read, I owe almost as much to the bitter opposition of my master, as to the kindly aid of my mistress. I acknowledge the benefit of both.

[17]Most southern states had statutes making the teaching of slaves to read or write illegal.

I had resided but a short time in Baltimore before I observed a marked difference, in the treatment of slaves, from that which I had witnessed in the country. A city slave is almost a freeman, compared with a slave on the plantation. He is much better fed and clothed, and enjoys privileges altogether unknown to the slave on the plantation. There is a vestige of decency, a sense of shame, that does much to curb and check those outbreaks of atrocious cruelty so commonly enacted upon the plantation. He is a desperate slaveholder, who will shock the humanity of his non-slaveholding neighbors with the cries of his lacerated slave. Few are willing to incur the odium attaching to the reputation of being a cruel master; and above all things, they would not be known as not giving a slave enough to eat. Every city slaveholder is anxious to have it known of him, that he feeds his slaves well; and it is due to them to say, that most of them do give their slaves enough to eat. There are, however, some painful exceptions to this rule. Directly opposite to us, on Philpot Street, lived Mr. Thomas Hamilton. He owned two slaves. Their names were Henrietta and Mary. Henrietta was about twenty-two years of age, Mary was about fourteen; and of all the mangled and emaciated creatures I ever looked upon, these two were the most so. His heart must be harder than stone, that could look upon these unmoved. The head, neck, and shoulders of Mary were literally cut to pieces. I have frequently felt her head, and found it nearly covered with festering sores, caused by the lash of her cruel mistress. I do not know that her master ever whipped her, but I have been an eyewitness to the cruelty of Mrs. Hamilton. I used to be in Mr. Hamilton's house nearly every day. Mrs. Hamilton used to sit in a large chair in the middle of the room, with a heavy cowskin always by her side, and scarce an hour passed during the day but was marked by the blood of one of these slaves. The girls seldom passed her without her saying, "Move faster, you *black gip*!" at the same time giving them a blow with the cowskin over the head or shoulders, often drawing the blood. She would then say, "Take that, you *black gip*!"—continuing, "If you don't move faster, I'll move you!" Added to the cruel lashings to which these slaves were subjected, they were kept nearly half-starved. They seldom knew what it was to eat a full meal. I have seen Mary contending with the pigs for the offal thrown into the street. So much was Mary kicked and cut to pieces, that she was oftener called *"pecked"* than by her name.

Chapter VII

I lived in Master Hugh's family about seven years. During this time, I succeeded in learning to read and write. In accomplishing this, I was compelled to resort to various stratagems. I had no regular teacher. My mistress, who had kindly commenced to instruct me, had, in compliance with the advice and direction of her husband, not only ceased to instruct, but had set her face against my being instructed by any one else. It is due, however, to my mistress to say of her, that she did not adopt this course of treatment immediately. She at first lacked the depravity indispensable to shutting me up in mental darkness. It was at least necessary for her to have some training in the exercise of irresponsible power, to make her equal to the task of treating me as though I were a brute.

My mistress was, as I have said, a kind and tender-hearted woman; and in the simplicity of her soul she commenced, when I first went to live with her, to treat me as she supposed one human being ought to treat another. In entering upon the duties of a slaveholder, she did not seem to perceive that I sustained to her the relation of a mere chattel, and that for her to treat me as a human being was not only wrong, but dangerously so. Slavery proved as injurious to her as it did to me. When I went there, she was a pious, warm, and tender-hearted woman. There was no sorrow or suffering for which she had not a tear. She had bread for the hungry, clothes for the naked, and comfort for every mourner that came within her reach. Slavery soon proved its ability to divest her of these heavenly qualities. Under its influence, the tender heart became stone, and the lamblike disposition gave way to one of tigerlike fierceness. The first step in her downward course was in her ceasing to instruct me. She now commenced to practise her husband's precepts. She finally became even more violent in her opposition than her husband himself. She was not satisfied with simply doing as well as he had commanded; she seemed anxious to do better. Nothing seemed to make her more angry than to see me with a newspaper. She seemed to think that here lay the danger. I have had her rush at me with a face made all up of fury, and snatch from me a newspaper, in a manner that fully revealed her apprehension. She was an apt woman; and a little experience soon demonstrated, to her satisfaction, that education and slavery were incompatible with each other.

From this time I was most narrowly watched. If I was in a separate room any considerable length of time, I was sure to be suspected of having a book, and was at once called to give an account of myself. All this, however, was too late. The first step had been taken. Mistress, in teaching me the alphabet, had given me the *inch,* and no precaution could prevent me from taking the *ell.*

The plan which I adopted, and the one by which I was most successful, was that of making friends of all the little white boys whom I met in the street. As many of these as I could, I converted into teachers. With their kindly aid, obtained at different times and in different places, I finally succeeded in learning to read. When I was sent of errands, I always took my book with me, and by going one part of my errand quickly, I found time to get a lesson before my return. I used also to carry bread with me, enough of which was always in the house, and to which I was always welcome; for I was much better off in this regard than many of the poor white children in our neighborhood. This bread I used to bestow upon the hungry little urchins, who, in return, would give me that more valuable bread of knowledge. I am strongly tempted to give the names of two or three of those little boys, as a testimonial of the gratitude and affection I bear them; but prudence forbids;—not that it would injure me, but it might embarrass them; for it is almost an unpardonable offence to teach slaves to read in this Christian country. It is enough to say of the dear little fellows, that they lived on Philpot Street, very near Durgin and Bailey's ship-yard. I used to talk this matter of slavery over with them. I would sometimes say to them, I wished I could be as free as they would be when they got to be men. "You will be free as soon as you are twenty-one, *but I am a slave for life!* Have not I as good a right to be free as you have?" These words used to trouble them; they would express for me the liveliest sympathy, and console me with the hope that something would occur by which I might be free.

I was now about twelve years old, and the thought of being *a slave for life* began to bear heavily upon my heart. Just about this time, I got hold of a book entitled "The

Columbian Orator."[18] Every opportunity I got, I used to read this book. Among much of other interesting matter, I found in it a dialogue between a master and his slave. The slave was represented as having run away from his master three times. The dialogue represented the conversation which took place between them, when the slave was retaken the third time. In this dialogue, the whole argument in behalf of slavery was brought forward by the master, all of which was disposed of by the slave. The slave was made to say some very smart as well as impressive things in reply to his master—things which had the desired though unexpected effect; for the conversation resulted in the voluntary emanicipation of the slave on the part of the master.

In the same book, I met with one of Sheridan's[19] mighty speeches on and in behalf of Catholic emancipation. These were choice documents to me. I read them over and over again with unabated interest. They gave tongue to interesting thoughts of my own soul, which had frequently flashed through my mind, and died away for want of utterance. The moral which I gained from the dialogue was the power of truth over the conscience of even a slaveholder. What I got from Sheridan was a bold denunciation of slavery, and a powerful vindication of human rights. The reading of these documents enabled me to utter my thoughts, and to meet the arguments brought forward to sustain slavery; but while they relieved me of one difficulty, they brought on another even more painful than the one of which I was relieved. The more I read, the more I was led to abhor and detest my enslavers. I could regard them in no other light than a band of successful robbers, who had left their homes, and gone to Africa, and stolen us from our homes, and in a strange land reduced us to slavery. I loathed them as being the meanest as well as the most wicked of men. As I read and contemplated the subject, behold! that very discontentment which Master Hugh had predicted would follow my learning to read had already come, to torment and sting my soul to unutterable anguish. As I writhed under it, I would at times feel that learning to read had been a curse rather than a blessing. It had given me a view of my wretched condition, without the remedy. It opened my eyes to the horrible pit, but to no ladder upon which to get out. In moments of agony, I envied my fellow-slaves for their stupidity. I have often wished myself a beast. I preferred the condition of the meanest reptile to my own. Any thing, no matter what, to get rid of thinking! It was this everlasting thinking of my condition that tormented me. There was no getting rid of it. It was pressed upon me by every object within sight or hearing, animate or inanimate. The silver trump of freedom had roused my soul to eternal wakefulness. Freedom now appeared, to disappear no more forever. It was heard in every sound, and seen in every thing. It was ever present to torment me with a sense of my wretched condition. I saw nothing without seeing it, I heard nothing without hearing it, and felt nothing without feeling it. It looked from every star, it smiled in every calm, breathed in every wind and moved in every storm.

I often found myself regretting my own existence, and wishing myself dead; and but for the hope of being free, I have no doubt but that I should have killed myself, or done something for which I should have been killed. While in this state of mind,

[18] An anthology of speeches, poems, dialogues and plays which Douglass had obtained as a child.

[19] Richard Brinsley Sheridan (1751–1816). Irish-born playwright and satirist, became a Member of the British Parliament and spoke out on behalf of Catholic Emancipation.

I was eager to hear any one speak of slavery. I was a ready listener. Every little while, I could hear something about the abolitionists. It was some time before I found what the word meant. It was always used in such connections as to make it an interesting word to me. If a slave ran away and succeeded in getting clear, or if a slave killed his master, set fire to a barn, or did any thing very wrong in the mind of a slaveholder, it was spoken of as the fruit of *abolition.* Hearing the word in this connection very often, I set about learning what it meant. The dictionary afforded me little or no help. I found it was "the act of abolishing;" but then I did not know what was to be abolished. Here I was perplexed. I did not dare to ask any one about its meaning, for I was satisfied that it was something they wanted me to know very little about. After a patient waiting, I got one of our city papers, containing an account of the number of petitions from the north, praying for the abolition of slavery in the District of Columbia, and of the slave trade between the States. From this time I understood the words *abolition* and *abolitionist,* and always drew near when that word was spoken, expecting to hear something of importance to myself and fellow-slaves. The light broke in upon me by degrees. I went one day down on the wharf of Mr. Waters; and seeing two Irishmen unloading a scow of stone, I went, unasked, and helped them. When we had finished, one of them came to me and asked me if I were a slave. I told him I was. He asked, "Are ye a slave for life?" I told him that I was. The good Irishman seemed to be deeply affected by the statement. He said to the other that it was a pity so fine a little fellow as myself should be a slave for life. He said it was a shame to hold me. They both advised me to run away to the north; that I should find friends there, and that I should be free. I pretended not to be interested in what they said, and treated them as if I did not understand them; for I feared they might be treacherous. White men have been known to encourage slaves to escape, and then, to get the reward, catch them and return them to their masters. I was afraid that these seemingly good men might use me so; but I nevertheless remembered their advice, and from that time I resolved to run away. I looked forward to a time at which it would be safe for me to escape. I was too young to think of doing so immediately; besides, I wished to learn how to write, as I might have occasion to write my own pass. I consoled myself with the hope that I should one day find a good chance. Meanwhile, I would learn to write.

The idea as to how I might learn to write was suggested to me by being in Durgin and Bailey's ship-yard, and frequently seeing the ship carpenters, after hewing, and getting a piece of timber ready for use, write on the timber the name of that part of the ship for which it was intended. When a piece of timber was intended for the larboard side, it would be marked—"L." When a piece was for the starboard side, it would be marked thus—"S." A piece for the larboard side forward, would be marked thus—"L.F." When a piece was for starboard side forward, it would be marked thus—"S. F." For larboard aft, it would be marked thus—"L. A." For starboard aft, it would be marked thus—"S. A." I soon learned the names of these letters, and for what they were intended when placed upon a piece of timber in the ship-yard. I immediately commenced copying them, and in a short time was able to make the four letters named. After that, when I met with any boy who I knew could write, I would tell him I could write as well as he. The next word would be, "I don't believe you. Let me see you try it." I would then make the letters which I had been so fortunate as to learn, and ask him to beat that. In this way I got a good many lessons in writing, which it is quite possible I should never have gotten in any other way. During this time, my copy-book was the board fence, brick way, and pavement; my pen and ink was a lump of chalk. With these, I learned mainly how to write. I then commenced and continued copying the Italics in Webster's Spelling Book,[20] until I could make them all without looking on the book. By this time, my little Master Thomas had gone to school, and learned how to write, and had written over a number of copy-books. These had been brought home, and shown to some of our near neighbors, and then laid aside. My mistress used to go to class meeting at the Wilk Street meetinghouse every Monday afternoon, and leave me to take care of the house. When left thus, I used to spend the time in writing in the spaces left in Master Thomas's copy-book, copying what he had written. I continued to do this until I could write a hand very similar to that of Master Thomas. Thus, after a long, tedious effort for years, I finally succeeded in learning how to write.

Chapter VIII

In a very short time after I went to live at Baltimore, my old master's youngest son Richard died; and in about three years and six months after his death, my old master, Captain Anthony, died, leaving only his son, Andrew, and daughter, Lucretia, to share his estate. He died while on a visit to see his daughter at Hillsborough. Cut off thus unexpectedly, he left no will as to the disposal of his property. It was therefore necessary to have a valuation of the property, that it might be equally divided between Mrs. Lucretia and Master Andrew. I was immediately sent for, to be valued with the other property. Here again my feelings rose up in detestation of slavery. I had now a new conception of my degraded condition. Prior to this, I had become, if not insensible to my lot, at least partly so. I left Baltimore with a young heart overborne with sadness, and a soul full of apprehension. I took passage with Captain Rowe, in the schooner Wild Cat, and, after a sail of about twenty-four hours, I found myself near the place of my birth. I had now been absent from it almost, if not quite, five years. I, however, remembered the place very well. I was only about five years old when I left it, to go and live with my old master on Colonel Lloyd's plantation; so that I was now between ten and eleven years old.

We were all ranked together at the valuation. Men and women, old and young, married and single, were ranked with horses, sheep and swine. There were horses and men, cattle and women, pigs and children, all holding the same rank in the scale of being, and were all subjected to the same narrow examination. Silvery-headed age and sprightly youth, maids and matrons, had to undergo the same indelicate inspection. At this moment, I saw more clearly than ever the brutalizing effects of slavery upon both slave and slaveholder.

After the valuation, then came the division. I have no language to express the high excitement and deep anxiety which were felt among us poor slaves during this time. Our fate for life was now to be decided. We had no more voice in that decision than the brutes among whom we were ranked. A single word from the white men was

[20]A word-book (1782–1783) developed by lexicographer Noah Webster (1758–1843); it was used in virtually all American schools and sold perhaps as many as sixty million copies.

enough—against all our wishes, prayers, and entreaties—to sunder forever the dearest friends, dearest kindred, and strongest ties known to human beings. In addition to the pain of separation, there was the horrid dread of falling into the hands of Master Andrew. He was known to us all as being a most cruel wretch,—a common drunkard, who had, by his reckless mismanagement and profligate dissipation, already wasted a large portion of his father's property. We all felt that we might as well be sold at once to the Georgia traders, as to pass into his hands; for we knew that that would be our inevitable condition,—a condition held by us all in the utmost horror and dread.

I suffered more anxiety than most of my fellowslaves. I had known what it was to be kindly treated; they had known nothing of the kind. They had seen little or nothing of the world. They were in very deed men and women of sorrow, and acquainted with grief. Their backs had been made familiar with the bloody lash, so that they had become callous; mine was yet tender; for while at Baltimore I got few whippings, and few slaves could boast of a kinder master and mistress than myself; and the thought of passing out of their hands into those of Master Andrew—a man who, but a few days before, to give me a sample of his bloody disposition, took my little brother by the throat, threw him on the ground, and with the heel of his boot stamped upon his head till the blood gushed from his nose and ears—was well calculated to make me anxious as to my fate. After he had committed this savage outrage upon my brother, he turned to me, and said that was the way he meant to serve me one of these days,—meaning, I suppose, when I came into his possession.

Thanks to a kind Providence, I fell to the portion of Mrs. Lucretia, and was sent immediately back to Baltimore, to live again in the family of Master Hugh. Their joy at my return equalled their sorrow at my departure. It was a glad day to me. I had escaped a [fate] worse than lion's jaws. I was absent from Baltimore, for the purpose of valuation and division, just about one month, and it seemed to have been six.

Very soon after my return to Baltimore, my mistress, Lucretia, died, leaving her husband and one child, Amanda; and in a very short time after her death, Master Andrew died. Now all the property of my old master, slaves included, was in the hands of strangers,—strangers who had had nothing to do with accumulating it. Not a slave was left free. All remained slaves, from the youngest to the oldest. If any one thing in my experience, more than another, served to deepen my conviction of the infernal character of slavery, and to fill me with unutterable loathing of slaveholders, it was their base ingratitude to my poor old grandmother. She had served my old master faithfully from youth to old age. She had been the source of all his wealth; she had peopled his plantation with slaves; she had become a great grandmother in his service. She had rocked him in infancy, attended him in childhood, served him through life, and at his death wiped from his icy brow the cold death-sweat, and closed his eyes forever. She was nevertheless left a slave—a slave for life—a slave in the hands of strangers; and in their hands she saw her children, her grandchildren, and her great-grandchildren, divided, like so many sheep, without being gratified with the small privilege of a single word, as to their or her own destiny. And, to cap the climax of their base ingratitude and fiendish barbarity, my grandmother, who was now very old, having outlived my old master and all his children, having seen the beginning and end of all of them, and her present owners finding she was of but little value, her frame already racked with the pains of old age, and complete helplessness fast stealing over her once active limbs, they took her to the woods, built her a little hut, put up a little mud-chimney, and then made her welcome to the privilege of supporting herself there in perfect loneliness; thus virtually turning her out to die! If my poor old grandmother now lives, she lives to suffer in utter loneliness; she lives to remember and mourn over the loss of children, the loss of grandchildren, and the loss of great-grandchildren. They are, in the language of the slave's poet, Whittier,—

"Gone, gone, sold and gone
To the rice swamp dank and lone,
Where the slave-whip ceaseless swings,
Where the noisome insect stings,
Where the fever-demon strews
Poison with the falling dews,
Where the sickly sunbeams glare
Through the hot and misty air:—
  Gone, gone, sold and gone
To the rice swamp dank and lone,
From Virginia hills and waters—
Woe is me, my stolen daughters!"[21]

The hearth is desolate. The children, the unconscious children, who once sang and danced in her presence, are gone. She gropes her way, in the darkness of age, for a drink of water. Instead of the voices of her children, she hears by day the moans of the dove, and by night the screams of the hideous owl. All is gloom. The grave is at the door. And now, when weighed down by the pains and aches of old age, when the head inclines to the feet, when the beginning and ending of human existence meet, and helpless infancy and painful old age combine together—at this time, this most needful time, the time for the exercise of that tenderness and affection which children only can exercise toward a declining parent—my poor old grandmother, the devoted mother of twelve children, is left all alone, in yonder little hut, before a few dim embers. She stands—she sits—she staggers—she falls—she groans—she dies—and there are none of her children or grandchildren present, to wipe from her wrinkled brow the cold sweat of death, or to place beneath the sod her fallen remains. Will not a righteous God visit for these things?

In about two years after the death of Mrs. Lucretia, Master Thomas married his second wife. Her name was Rowena Hamilton. She was the eldest daughter of Mr. William Hamilton. Master now lived in St. Michael's. Not long after his marriage, a misunderstanding took place between himself and Master Hugh; and as a means of punishing his brother, he took me from him to live with himself at St. Michael's. Here I underwent another most painful separation. It, however, was not so severe as the one I dreaded at the division of property; for, during this interval, a great change had taken place in Master Hugh and his once kind and affectionate wife. The influence of brandy upon him, and of slavery upon her, had effected a disastrous change in the characters of both; so that, as far as they were concerned, I thought I had little to lose by the change. But it was not to them that I was attached. It was to those little

[21]From John Greenleaf Whittier's "The Farewell: Of a Virginia Slave Mother to Her Daughter Sold into Southern Bondage," the full text of which is printed elsewhere in this volume.

Baltimore boys that I felt the strongest attachment. I had received many good lessons from them, and was still receiving them, and the thought of leaving them was painful indeed. I was leaving, too, without the hope of ever being allowed to return. Master Thomas had said he would never let me return again. The barrier betwixt himself and brother he considered impassable.

I then had to regret that I did not at least make the attempt to carry out my resolution to run away; for the chances of success are tenfold greater from the city than from the country.

I sailed from Baltimore for St. Michael's in the sloop Amanda, Captain Edward Dodson. On my passage, I paid particular attention to the direction which the steamboats took to go to Philadelphia. I found, instead of going down, on reaching North Point they went up the bay, in a north-easterly direction. I deemed this knowledge of the utmost importance. My determination to run away was again revived. I resolved to wait only so long as the offering of a favorable opportunity. When that came, I was determined to be off.

Chapter IX

I have now reached a period of my life when I can give dates. I left Baltimore, and went to live with Master Thomas Auld, at St. Michael's, in March, 1832. It was now more than seven years since I lived with him in the family of my old master, on Colonel Lloyd's plantation. We of course were now almost entire strangers to each other. He was to me a new master, and I to him a new slave. I was ignorant of his temper and disposition; he was equally so of mine. A very short time, however, brought us into full acquaintance with each other. I was made acquainted with his wife not less than with himself. They were well matched, being equally mean and cruel. I was now, for the first time during a space of more than seven years, made to feel the painful gnawings of hunger—a something which I had not experienced before since I left Colonel Lloyd's plantation. It went hard enough with me then, when I could look back at no period at which I had enjoyed a sufficiency. It was tenfold harder after living in Master Hugh's family, where I had always had enough to eat, and of that which was good. I have said Master Thomas was a mean man. He was so. Not to give a slave enough to eat, is regarded as the most aggravated development of meanness even among slaveholders. The rule is, no matter how coarse the food, only let there be enough of it. This is the theory; and in the part of Maryland from which I came, it is the general practice,—though there are many exceptions. Master Thomas gave us enough of neither coarse nor fine food. There were four slaves of us in the kitchen—my sister Eliza, my aunt Priscilla, Henny, and myself; and we were allowed less than half of a bushel of cornmeal per week, and very little else, either in the shape of meat or vegetables. It was not enough for us to subsist upon. We were therefore reduced to the wretched necessity of living at the expense of our neighbors. This we did by begging and stealing, whichever came handy in the time of need, the one being considered as legitimate as the other. A great many times have we poor creatures been nearly perishing with hunger, when food in abundance lay mouldering in the safe and smoke-house,[22] and our pious mistress was aware of the fact; and yet that mistress and her husband would kneel every morning, and pray that God would bless them in basket and store!

Bad as all slaveholders are, we seldom meet one destitute of every element of character commanding respect. My master was one of this rare sort. I do not know of one single noble act ever performed by him. The leading trait in his character was meanness; and if there were any other element in his nature, it was made subject to this. He was mean; and, like most other mean men, he lacked the ability to conceal his meanness. Captain Auld was not born a slaveholder. He had been a poor man, master only of a Bay craft. He came into possession of all his slaves by marriage; and of all men, adopted slaveholders are the worst. He was cruel, but cowardly. He commanded without firmness. In the enforcement of his rules, he was at times rigid, and at times lax. At times, he spoke to his slaves with the firmness of Napoleon and the fury of a demon; at other times, he might well be mistaken for an inquirer who had lost his way. He did nothing of himself. He might have passed for a lion, but for his ears.[23] In all things noble which he attempted, his own meanness shone most conspicuous. His airs, words, and actions, were the airs, words, and actions of born slaveholders, and, being assumed, were awkward enough. He was not even a good imitator. He possessed all the disposition to deceive, but wanted the power. Having no resources within himself, he was compelled to be the copyist of many, and being such, he was forever the victim of inconsistency; and of consequence he was an object of contempt, and was held as such even by his slaves. The luxury of having slaves of his own to wait upon him was something new and unprepared for. He was a slaveholder without the ability to hold slaves. He found himself incapable of managing his slaves either by force, fear, or fraud. We seldom called him "master," we generally called him "Captain Auld," and were hardly disposed to title him at all. I doubt not that our conduct had much to do with making him appear awkward, and of consequence fretful. Our want of reverence for him must have perplexed him greatly. He wished to have us call him master, but lacked the firmness necessary to command us to do so. His wife used to insist upon our calling him so, but to no purpose. In August, 1832, my master attended a Methodist camp-meeting held in the Bay-side, Talbot county, and there experienced religion. I indulged a faint hope that his conversion would lead him to emancipate his slaves, and that, if he did not do this, it would at any rate, make him more kind and humane. I was disappointed in both these respects. It neither made him to be humane to his slaves, nor to emancipate them. If it had any effect on his character, it made him more cruel and hateful in all his ways; for I believe him to have been a much worse man after his conversion than before. Prior to his conversion, he relied upon his own depravity to shield and sustain him in his savage barbarity; but after his conversion, he found religious sanction and support for his slaveholding cruelty. He made the greatest pretensions to piety. His house was the house of prayer. He prayed morning, noon, and night. He very soon distinguished himself among his brethren, and was soon made a class-leader and exhorter. His activity in revivals was great, and he proved himself an instrument in the

[22]Meat and fish were cured by smoking in the smoke-house and then stored there or in a meat safe.

[23]Which, like those of a jackass, showed him to be something other than what he claimed.

hands of the church in converting many souls. His house was the preachers' home. They used to take great pleasure in coming there to put up; for while he starved us, he stuffed them. We have had three or four preachers there at a time. The names of those who used to come most frequently while I lived there, were Mr. Storks, Mr. Ewery, Mr. Humphry, and Mr. Hickey. I have also seen Mr. George Cookman at our house. We slaves loved Mr. Cookman. We believed him to be a good man. We thought him instrumental in getting Mr. Samuel Harrison, a very rich slaveholder, to emancipate his slaves; and by some means got the impression that he was laboring to effect the emancipation of all the slaves. When he was at our house, we were sure to be called in to prayers. When the others were there, we were sometimes called in and sometimes not. Mr. Cookman took more notice of us than either of the other ministers. He could not come among us without betraying his sympathy for us, and, stupid as we were, we had the sagacity to see it.

While I lived with my master in St. Michael's, there was a white young man, a Mr. Wilson, who proposed to keep a Sabbath school for the instruction of such slaves as might be disposed to learn to read the New Testament. We met but three times, when Mr. West and Mr. Fairbanks, both class-leaders, with many others, came upon with us with sticks and other missiles, drove us off, and forbade us to meet again. Thus ended our little Sabbath school in the pious town of St. Michael's.

I have said my master found religious sanction for his cruelty. As an example, I will state one of many facts going to prove the charge. I have seen him tie up a lame young woman, and whip her with a heavy cowskin upon her naked shoulders, causing the warm red blood to drip; and, in justification of the bloody deed, he would quote this passage of Scripture—"He that knoweth his master's will, and doeth it not, shall be beaten with many stripes."

Master would keep this lacerated young woman tied up in this horrid situation four or five hours at a time. I have known him to tie her up early in the morning, and whip her before breakfast; leave her, go to his store, return at dinner, and whip her again, cutting her in the places already made raw with his cruel lash. The secret of master's cruelty toward "Henny" is found in the fact of her being almost helpless. When quite a child, she fell into the fire, and burned herself horribly. Her hands were so burnt that she never got the use of them. She could do very little but bear heavy burdens. She was to master a bill of expense; and as he was a mean man, she was a constant offence to him. He seemed desirous of getting the poor girl out of existence. He gave her away once to his sister; but, being a poor gift, she was not disposed to keep her. Finally, my benevolent master, to use his own words, "set her adrift to take care of herself." Here was a recently-converted man, holding on upon the mother, and at the same time turning out her helpless child, to starve and die! Master Thomas was one of the many pious slaveholders who hold slaves for the very charitable purpose of taking care of them.

My master and myself had quite a number of differences. He found me unsuitable to his purpose. My city life, he said, had had a very pernicious effect upon me. It had almost ruined me for every good purpose, and fitted me for every thing which was bad. One of my greatest faults was that of letting his horse run away, and go down to his father-in-law's farm, which was about five miles from St. Michael's. I would then have to go after it. My reason for this kind of carelessness, or carefulness, was, that I could always get something to eat when I went there. Master William

Hamilton, my master's father-in-law, always gave his slaves enough to eat. I never left there hungry, no matter how great the need of my speedy return. Master Thomas at length said he would stand it no longer. I had lived with him nine months, during which time he had given me a number of severe whippings, all to no good purpose. He resolved to put me out, as he said, to be broken; and, for this purpose, he let me for one year to a man named Edward Covey. Mr. Covey was a poor man, a farm-renter. He rented the place upon which he lived, as also the hands with which he tilled it. Mr. Covey had acquired a very high reputation for breaking young slaves, and this reputation was of immense value to him. It enabled him to get his farm tilled with much less expense to himself than he could have had it done without such a reputation. Some slaveholders thought it not much loss to allow Mr. Covey to have their slaves one year, for the sake of the training to which they were subjected, without any other compensation. He could hire young help with great ease, in consequence of this reputation. Added to the natural good qualities of Mr. Covey, he was a professor of religion—a pious soul—a member and a class-leader in the Methodist church. All of this added weight to his reputation as a "nigger-breaker." I was aware of all the facts, having been made acquainted with them by a young man who had lived there. I nevertheless made the change gladly; for I was sure of getting enough to eat, which is not the smallest consideration to a hungry man.

Chapter X

I left Master Thomas's house, and went to live with Mr. Covey, on the 1st of January, 1833. I was now, for the first time in my life, a field hand. In my new employment, I found myself even more awkward than a country boy appeared to be in a large city. I had been at my new home but one week before Mr. Covey gave me a very severe whipping, cutting my back, causing the blood to run, and raising ridges on my flesh as large as my little finger. The details of this affair are as follows: Mr. Covey sent me, very early in the morning of one of our coldest days in the month of January, to the woods, to get a load of wood. He gave me a team of unbroken oxen. He told me which was the in-hand ox, and which the off-hand one. He then tied the end of a large rope around the horns of the in-hand ox, and gave me the other end of it, and told me, if the oxen started to run, that I must hold on upon the rope. I had never driven oxen before, and of course I was very awkward. I, however, succeeded in getting to the edge of the woods with little difficulty; but I had got a very few rods into the woods, when the oxen took fright, and started full tilt, carrying the cart against trees, and over stumps, in the most frightful manner. I expected every moment that my brains would be dashed out against the trees. After running thus for a considerable distance, they finally upset the cart, dashing it with great force against a tree, and threw themselves into a dense thicket. How I escaped death, I do not know. There I was, entirely alone, in a thick wood, in a place new to me. My cart was upset and shattered, my oxen were entangled among the young trees, and there was none to help me. After a long spell of effort, I succeeded in getting my cart righted, my oxen disentangled and again yoked to the cart. I now proceeded with my team to the place where I had, the day before, been chopping wood, and loaded my cart pretty heavily, thinking in this way to tame my oxen. I then proceeded on my way home. I had now consumed one half of the day. I got out of the woods safely, and now felt out of danger. I stopped my oxen to open the woods gate; and just as I did so, before I could get hold of my ox-rope, the oxen again started, rushed through the gate, catching it between the wheel and the body of the cart, tearing it to pieces, and coming within a few inches of crushing me against the gate-post. Thus twice, in one short day, I escaped death by the merest chance. On my return, I told Mr. Covey what had happened, and how it happened. He ordered me to return to the woods again immediately. I did so, and he followed on after me. Just as I got into the woods, he came up and told me to stop my cart, and that he would teach me how to trifle away my time, and break gates. He then went to a large gum-tree, and with his axe cut three large switches, and, after trimming them up neatly with his pocketknife, he ordered me to take off my clothes. I made him no answer, but stood with my clothes on. He repeated his order. I still made him no answer, nor did I move to strip myself. Upon this he rushed at me with the fierceness of a tiger, tore off my clothes, and lashed me till he had worn out his switches, cutting me so savagely as to leave the marks visible for a long time after. This whipping was the first of a number just like it, and for similar offences.

I lived with Mr. Covey one year. During the first six months, of that year, scarce a week passed without his whipping me. I was seldom free from a sore back. My awkwardness was almost always his excuse for whipping me. We were worked fully up to the point of endurance. Long before day we were up, our horses fed, and by the first approach of day we were off to the field with our hoes and ploughing teams. Mr. Covey gave us enough to eat, but scarce time to eat it. We were often less than five minutes taking our meals. We were often in the field from the first approach of day till its last lingering ray had left us; and at saving-fodder time, midnight often caught us in the field binding blades.[24]

Covey would be out with us. The way he used to stand it, was this. He would spend the most of his afternoons in bed. He would then come out fresh in the evening, ready to urge us on with his words, example, and frequently with the whip. Mr. Covey was one of the few slaveholders who could and did work with his hands. He was a hard-working man. He knew by himself just what a man or a boy could do. There was no deceiving him. His work went on in his absence almost as well as in his presence; and he had the faculty of making us feel that he was ever present with us. This he did by surprising us. He seldom approached the spot where we were at work openly, if he could do it secretly. He always aimed at taking us by surprise. Such was his cunning, that we used to call him, among ourselves, "the snake." When we were at work in the cornfield, he would sometimes crawl on his hands and knees to avoid detection, and all at once he would rise nearly in our midst, and scream out, "Ha, ha! Come, come! Dash on, dash on!" This being his mode of attack, it was never safe to stop a single minute. His comings were like a thief in the night. He appeared to us as being ever at hand. He was under every tree, behind every stump, in every bush, and at every window, on the plantation. He would sometimes mount his horse, as if bound to St. Michael's, a distance of seven miles, and in half an hour afterwards you would see him coiled up in the corner of the wood-fence, watching every motion of

[24]At harvest time, slaves might be in the fields until after mid-night binding sheaves or "blades."

the slaves. He would, for this purpose, leave his horse tied up in the woods. Again, he would sometimes walk up to us, and give us orders as though he was upon the point of starting on a long journey, turn his back upon us, and make as though he was going to the house to get ready; and, before he would get half way thither, he would turn short and crawl into a fence-corner, or behind some tree, and there watch us till the going down of the sun.

Mr. Covey's *forte* consisted in his power to deceive. His life was devoted to planning and perpetrating the grossest deceptions. Every thing he possessed in the shape of learning or religion, he made conform to his disposition to deceive. He seemed to think himself equal to deceiving the Almighty. He would make a short prayer in the morning, and a long prayer at night and, strange as it may seem, few men would at times appear more devotional than he. The exercises of his family devotions were always commenced with singing; and, as he was a very poor singer himself, the duty of raising the hymn generally came upon me. He would read his hymn, and nod at me to commence. I would at times do so; at others, I would not. My non-compliance would almost always produce much confusion. To show himself independent of me, he would start and stagger through with his hymn in the most discordant manner. In this state of mind, he prayed with more than ordinary spirit. Poor man! such was his disposition, and success at deceiving, I do verily believe that he sometimes deceived himself into the solemn belief, that he was a sincere worshipper of the most high God; and this, too, at a time when he may be said to have been guilty of compelling his woman slave to commit the sin of adultery. The facts in the case are these: Mr. Covey was a poor man; he was just commencing in life; he was only able to buy one slave; and, shocking as is the fact, he bought her, as he said, for a *breeder.* This woman was named Caroline. Mr. Covey bought her from Mr. Thomas Lowe, about six miles from St. Michael's. She was a large, able-bodied woman, about twenty years old. She had already given birth to one child, which proved her to be just what he wanted. After buying her, he hired a married man of Mr. Samuel Harrison, to live with him one year; and him he used to fasten up with her every night! The result was, that, at the end of the year, the miserable woman gave birth to twins. At this result Mr. Covey seemed to be highly pleased, both with the man and the wretched woman. Such was his joy, and that of his wife, that nothing they could do for Caroline during her confinement was too good, or too hard to be done. The children were regarded as being quite an addition to his wealth.

If at any one time of my life more than another, I was made to drink the bitterest dregs of slavery, that time was during the first six months of my stay with Mr. Covey. We were worked in all weathers. It was never too hot or too cold; it could never rain, blow, hail, or snow, too hard for us to work in the field. Work, work, work, was scarcely more the order of the day than of the night. The longest days were too short for him, and the shortest nights too long for him. I was somewhat unmanageable when I first went there, but a few months of this discipline tamed me. Mr. Covey succeeded in breaking me. I was broken in body, soul, and spirit. My natural elasticity was crushed, my intellect languished, the disposition to read departed, the cheerful spark that lingered about my eye died; the dark night of slavery closed in upon me, and behold a man transformed into a brute!

Sunday was my only leisure time. I spent this in a sort of beastlike stupor, between sleep and wake, under some large tree. At times I would rise up, a flash of energetic freedom would dart through my soul, accompanied with a faint beam of hope, that flickered for a moment, and then vanished. I sank down again, mourning over my wretched condition. I was sometimes prompted to take my life, and that of Covey, but was prevented by a combination of hope and fear. My sufferings on this plantation seem now like a dream rather than a stern reality.

Our house stood within a few rods of the Chesapeake Bay, whose broad bosom was ever white with sails from every quarter of the habitable globe. Those beautiful vessels, robed in purest white, so delightful to the eye of freemen, were to me so many shrouded ghosts, to terrify and torment me with thoughts of my wretched condition. I have often, in the deep stillness of a summer's Sabbath, stood all alone upon the lofty banks of that noble bay, and traced, with saddened heart and tearful eye, the countless number of sails moving off to the mighty ocean. The sight of these always affected me powerfully. My thoughts would compel utterance; and there, with no audience but the Almighty, I would pour out my soul's complaint, in my rude way, with an apostrophe to the moving multitude of ships:—

"You are loosed from your moorings, and are free; I am fast in my chains, and am a slave! You move merrily before the gentle gale, and I sadly before the bloody whip! You are freedom's swiftwinged angels, that fly round the world; I am confined in bands of iron! O that I were free! Oh, that I were on one of your gallant decks, and under your protecting wing! Alas! betwixt me and you, the turbid waters roll. Go on, go on. O that I could also go! Could I but swim! If I could fly! O, why was I born a man, of whom to make a brute! The glad ship is gone; she hides in the dim distance. I am left in the hottest hell of unending slavery. O God, save me! God, deliver me! Let me be free! Is there any God? Why am I a slave? I will run away. I will not stand it. Get caught, or get clear, I'll try it. I had as well die with ague as the fever. I have only one life to lose. I had as well be killed running as die standing. Only think of it; one hundred miles straight north, and I am free! Try it? Yes! God helping me, I will. It cannot be that I shall live and die a slave. I will take to the water. This very bay shall yet bear me into freedom. The steamboats steered in a north-east course from North Point. I will do the same; and when I get to the head of the bay, I will turn my canoe adrift, and walk straight through Delaware into Pennsylvania. When I get there, I shall not be required to have a pass; I can travel without being disturbed. Let but the first opportunity offer, and, come what will, I am off. Meanwhile, I will try to bear up under the yoke. I am not the only slave in the world. Why should I fret? I can bear as much as any of them. Besides, I am but a boy, and all boys are bound to some one. It may be that my misery in slavery will only increase my happiness when I get free. There is a better day coming."

Thus I used to think, and thus I used to speak to myself; goaded almost to madness at one moment, and at the next reconciling myself to my wretched lot.

I have already intimated that my condition was much worse, during the first six months of my stay at Mr. Covey's, than in the last six. The circumstances leading to the change in Mr. Covey's course toward me form an epoch in my humble history. You have seen how a man was made a slave; you shall see how a slave was made a man. On one of the hottest days of the month of August, 1833, Bill Smith, William Hughes, a slave named Eli, and myself, were engaged in fanning wheat.[25] Hughes was clearing the fanned wheat from before the fan. Eli was turning, Smith was

[25]Separating the wheat from the chaff.

feeding, and I was carrying wheat to the fan. The work was simple, requiring strength rather than intellect; yet, to one entirely unused to such work, it came very hard. About three o'clock of that day, I broke down; my strength failed me; I was seized with a violent aching of the head, attended with extreme dizziness; I trembled in every limb. Finding what was coming, I nerved myself up, feeling it would never do to stop work. I stood as long as I could stagger to the hopper with grain. When I could stand no longer, I fell, and felt as if held down by an immense weight. The fan of course stopped; every one had his own work to do; and no one could do the work of the other, and have his own go on at the same time.

Mr. Covey was at the house, about one hundred yards from the treading-yard where we were fanning. On hearing the fan stop, he left immediately, and came to the spot where we were. He hastily inquired what the matter was. Bill answered that I was sick, and there was no one to bring wheat to the fan. I had by this time crawled away under the side of the post and rail-fence by which the yard was enclosed, hoping to find relief by getting out of the sun. He then asked where I was. He was told by one of the hands. He came to the spot, and, after looking at me awhile, asked me what was the matter. I told him as well as I could, for I scarce had strength to speak. He then gave me a savage kick in the side, and told me to get up. I tried to do so, but fell back in the attempt. He gave me another kick, and again told me to rise. I again tried, and succeeded in gaining my feet; but, stooping to get the tub with which I was feeding the fan, I again staggered and fell. While down in this situation, Mr. Covey took up the hickory slat with which Hughes had been striking off the half-bushel measure, and with it gave me a heavy blow upon the head, making a large wound, and the blood ran freely; and with this again told me to get up. I made no effort to comply, having now made up my mind to let him do his worst. In a short time after receiving this blow, my head grew better. Mr. Covey had now left me to my fate. At this moment I resolved, for the first time, to go to my master, enter a complaint, and ask his protection. In order to do this, I must that afternoon walk seven miles; and this, under the circumstances, was truly a severe undertaking. I was exceedingly feeble; made so as much by the kicks and blows which I received, as by the severe fit of sickness to which I had been subjected. I, however, watched my chance, while Covey was looking in an opposite direction, and started for St. Michael's. I succeeded in getting a considerable distance on my way to the woods, when Covey discovered me, and called after me to come back, threatening what he would do if I did not come. I disregarded both his calls and his threats, and made my way to the woods as fast as my feeble state would allow; and thinking I might be overhauled by him if I kept the road, I walked through the woods, keeping far enough from the road to avoid detection, and near enough to prevent losing my way. I had not gone far before my little strength again failed me. I could go no farther. I fell down, and lay for a considerable time. The blood was yet oozing from the wound on my head. For a time I thought I should bleed to death; and think now that I should have done so, but that the blood so matted my hair as to stop the wound. After lying there about three quarters of an hour, I nerved myself up again, and started on my way, through bogs and briers, barefooted and bareheaded, tearing my feet sometimes at nearly every step; and after a journey of about seven miles, occupying some five hours to perform it, I arrived at master's store. I then presented an appearance enough to affect any but a heart of iron. From the crown of my head to my feet, I was covered with blood. My hair was all clotted with dust and blood; my shirt was stiff with blood. My legs and feet were torn in sundry places with briers and thorns, and were also covered with blood. I suppose I looked like a man who had escaped a den of wild beasts, and barely escaped them. In this state I appeared before my master, humbly entreating him to interpose his authority for my protection. I told him all the circumstances as well as I could, and it seemed, as I spoke, at times to affect him. He would then walk the floor, and seek to justify Covey by saying he expected I deserved it. He asked me what I wanted. I told him, to let me get a new home; that as sure as I lived with Mr. Covey again, I should live with but to die with him; that Covey would surely kill me; he was in a fair way for it. Master Thomas ridiculed the idea that there was any danger of Mr. Covey's killing me, and said that he knew Mr. Covey; that he was a good man, and that he could not think of taking me from him; that, should he do so, he would lose the whole year's wages; that I belonged to Mr. Covey for one year, and that I must go back to him, come what might; and that I must not trouble him with any more stories, or that he would himself *get hold of me.* After threatening me thus, he gave me a very large dose of salts, telling me that I might remain in St. Michael's that night, (it being quite late,) but that I must be off back to Mr. Covey's early in the morning; and that if I did not, he would *get hold of me,* which meant that he would whip me. I remained all night, and, according to his orders, I started off to Covey's in the morning, (Saturday morning), wearied in body and broken in spirit. I got no supper that night, or breakfast that morning. I reached Covey's about nine o'-cock; and just as I was getting over the fence that divided Mrs. Kemp's fields from ours, out ran Covey with his cowskin, to give me another whipping. Before he could reach me, I succeeded in getting to the cornfield; and as the corn was very high, it afforded me the means of hiding. He seemed very angry, and searched for me a long time. My behavior was altogether unaccountable. He finally gave up the chase, thinking, I suppose, that I must come home for something to eat; he would give himself no further trouble in looking for me. I spent that day mostly in the woods, having the alternative before me,—to go home and be whipped to death, or stay in the woods and be starved to death. That night, I fell in with Sandy Jenkins, a slave with whom I was somewhat acquainted. Sandy had a free wife who lived about four miles from Mr. Covey's; and it being Saturday, he was on his way to see her. I told him my circumstances, and he very kindly invited me to go home with him. I went home with him, and talked this whole matter over, and got his advice as to what course it was best for me to pursue. I found Sandy an old adviser.[26] He told me, with great solemnity, I must go back to Covey; but that before I went, I must go with him into another part of the woods, where there was a certain *root,*[27] which, if I would take some of it with me, carrying it *always on my right side,* would render it impossible for Mr. Covey, or any other white man, to whip me. He said he had carried it for years; and since he had done so, he had never received a blow, and never expected to while he carried it. I at first rejected the idea, that the simple carrying of a root in my pocket would have any such effect as he had said, and was not disposed to take it; but Sandy impressed the necessity with much earnestness, telling me it could do no harm, if it did no good. To please him, I at length took the root, and, according to his direction,

[26]A wise man—perhaps a conjure man.
[27]Perhaps a "High John the Conquer" root—see the African-American tales in Volume 2, and note no. 28, below.

carried it upon my right side. This was Sunday morning. I immediately started for home; and upon entering the yard gate, out came Mr. Covey on his way to meeting. He spoke to me very kindly, bade me drive the pigs from a lot near by, and passed on towards the church. Now, this singular conduct of Mr. Covey really made me begin to think that there was something in the *root* which Sandy had given me; and had it been on any other day than Sunday, I could have attributed the conduct to no other cause than the influence of that root; and as it was, I was half inclined to think the *root* to be something more than I at first had taken it to be. All went well till Monday morning. On this morning, the virtue of the *root* was fully tested. Long before daylight, I was called to go and rub, curry, and feed, the horses. I obeyed, and was glad to obey. But whilst thus engaged, whilst in the act of throwing down some blades from the loft, Mr. Covey entered the stable with a long rope; and just as I was half out of the loft, he caught hold of my legs, and was about tying me. As soon as I found what he was up to, I gave a sudden spring, and as I did so, he holding to my legs, I was brought sprawling on the stable floor. Mr. Covey seemed now to think he had me, and could do what he pleased; but at this moment—from whence came the spirit I don't know—I resolved to fight; and, suiting my action to the resolution, I seized Covey hard by the throat; and as I did so, I rose. He held on to me, and I to him. My resistance was so entirely unexpected, that Covey seemed taken all aback. He trembled like a leaf. This gave me assurance, and I held him uneasy, causing the blood to run where I touched him with the ends of my fingers. Mr. Covey soon called out to Hughes for help. Hughes came, and, while Covey held me, attempted to tie my right hand. While he was in the act of doing so, I watched my chance, and gave him a heavy kick close under the ribs. This kick fairly sickened Hughes, so that he left me in the hands of Mr. Covey. This kick had the effect of not only weakening Hughes, but Covey also. When he saw Hughes bending over with pain, his courage quailed. He asked me if I meant to persist in my resistance. I told him I did, come what might; that he had used me like a brute for six months, and that I was determined to be used so no longer. With that, he strove to drag me to a stick that was lying just out of the stable door. He meant to knock me down. But just as he was leaning over to get the stick, I seized him with both hands by his collar, and brought him by a sudden snatch to the ground. By this time, Bill came. Covey called upon him for assistance. Bill wanted to know what he could do. Covey said, "Take hold of him, take hold of him!" Bill said his master hired him out to work, and not to help to whip me; so he left Covey and myself to fight our own battle out. We were at it for nearly two hours. Covey at length let me go, puffing and blowing at a great rate, saying that if I had not resisted, he would not have whipped me half so much. The truth was, that he had not whipped me at all. I considered him as getting entirely the worst end of the bargain; for he had drawn no blood from me, but I had from him. The whole six months afterwards, that I spent with Mr. Covey, he never laid the weight of his finger upon me in anger. He would occasionally say, he didn't want to get hold of me again. "No," thought I, "you need not; for you will come off worse than you did before."

This battle with Mr. Covey was the turning-point in my career as a slave. It rekindled the few expiring embers of freedom, and revived within me a sense of my own manhood. It recalled the departed self-confidence, and inspired me again with a determination to be free. The gratification afforded by the triumph was a full compensation for whatever else might follow, even death itself. He only can understand the deep satisfaction which I experienced, who has himself repelled by force the bloody arm of slavery. I felt as I never felt before. It was a glorious resurrection, from the tomb of slavery, to the heaven of freedom. My long-crushed spirit rose, cowardice departed, bold defiance took its place; and I now resolved that, however long I might remain a slave in form, the day had passed forever when I could be a slave in fact. I did not hesitate to let it be known of me, that the white man who expected to succeed in whipping, must also succeed in killing me.

From this time I was never again what might be called fairly whipped, though I remained a slave four years afterwards. I had several fights, but was never whipped.

It was for a long time a matter of surprise to me why Mr. Covey did not immediately have me taken by the constable to the whipping-post, and there regularly whipped for the crime of raising my hand against a white man in defence of myself. And the only explanation I can now think of does not entirely satisfy me; but such as it is, I will give it. Mr. Covey enjoyed the most unbounded reputation for being a first-rate overseer and negro-breaker. It was of considerable importance to him. That reputation was at stake; and had he sent me—a boy about sixteen years old—to the public whipping-post, his reputation would have been lost; so, to save his reputation, he suffered me to go unpunished.

My term of actual service to Mr. Edward Covey ended on Christmas day, 1833. The days between Christmas and New Year's day are allowed as holidays; and, accordingly, we were not required to perform any labor, more than to feed and take care of the stock. This time we regarded as our own, by the grace of our masters; and we therefore used or abused it nearly as we pleased. Those of us who had families at a distance, were generally allowed to spend the whole six days in their society. This time, however, was spent in various ways. The staid, sober, thinking and industrious ones of our number would employ themselves in making corn-brooms, mats, horse-collars, and baskets; and another class of us would spend the time hunting opossums, hares, and coons. But by far the larger part engaged in such sports and merriments as playing ball, wrestling, running foot-races, fiddling, dancing, and drinking whisky; and this latter mode of spending the time was by far the most agreeable to the feelings of our master. A slave who would work during the holidays was considered by our masters as scarcely deserving them. He was regarded as one who rejected the favor of his master. It was deemed a disgrace not to get drunk at Christmas; and he was regarded as lazy indeed, who had not provided himself with the necessary means, during the year, to get whisky enough to last him through Christmas.

From what I know of the effect of these holidays upon the slave, I believe them to be among the most effective means in the hands of the slaveholder in keeping down the spirit of insurrection. Were the slaveholders at once to abandon this practice, I have not the slightest doubt it would lead to an immediate insurrection among the slaves. These holidays serve as conductors, or safety-valves, to carry off the rebellious spirit of enslaved humanity. But for these, the slave would be forced up to the wildest desperation; and woe betide the slaveholder, the day he ventures to remove or hinder the operation of those conductors! I warn him that, in such an event, a spirit will go forth in their midst, more to be dreaded than the most appalling earthquake.

The holidays are part and parcel of the gross fraud, wrong, and inhumanity of slavery. They are professedly a custom established by the benevolence of the slaveholders; but I undertake to say, it is the result of selfishness, and one of the grossest frauds committed upon the down-trodden slave. They do not give the slaves this time because they would not like to have their work during its continuance, but because they know it would be unsafe to deprive them of it. This will be seen by the fact, that the slaveholders like to have their slaves spend those days just in such a manner as to make them as glad of their ending as of their beginning. Their object seems to be, to disgust their slaves with freedom, by plunging them into the lowest depths of dissipation. For instance, the slaveholders not only like to see the slave drink of his own accord, but will adopt various plans to make him drunk. One plan is, to make bets on their slaves, as to who can drink the most whisky without getting drunk; and in this way they succeed in getting whole multitudes to drink to excess. Thus, when the slave asks for virtuous freedom, the cunning slaveholder, knowing his ignorance, cheats him with a dose of vicious dissipation, artfully labelled with the name of liberty. The most of us used to drink it down, and the result was just what might be supposed: many of us were led to think that there was little to choose between liberty and slavery. We felt, and very properly too, that we had almost as well be slaves to man as to rum. So, when the holidays ended, we staggered up from the filth of our wallowing, took a long breath, and marched to the field,—feeling, upon the whole, rather glad to go, from what our master had deceived us into a belief was freedom, back to the arms of slavery.

I have said that this mode of treatment is a part of the whole system of fraud and inhumanity of slavery. It is so. The mode here adopted to disgust the slave with freedom, by allowing him to see only the abuse of it, is carried out in other things. For instance, a slave loves molasses; he steals some. His master, in many cases, goes off to town, and buys a large quantity; he returns, takes his whip, and commands the slave to eat the molasses, until the poor fellow is made sick at the very mention of it. The same mode is sometimes adopted to make the slaves refrain from asking for more food than their regular allowance. A slave runs through his allowance, and applies for more. His master is enraged at him; but, not willing to send him off without food, gives him more than is necessary, and compels him to eat it within a given time. Then, if he complains that he cannot eat it, he is said to be satisfied neither full nor fasting, and is whipped for being hard to please! I have an abundance of such illustrations of the same principle, drawn from my own observation, but think the cases I have cited sufficient. The practice is a very common one.

On the first of January, 1834, I left Mr. Covey, and went to live with Mr. William Freeland, who lived about three miles from St. Michael's. I soon found Mr. Freeland a very different man from Mr. Covey. Though not rich, he was what would be called an educated southern gentleman. Mr. Covey, as I have shown, was a well-trained negro-breaker and slave-driver. The former (slaveholder though he was) seemed to possess some regard for honor, some reverence for justice, and some respect for humanity. The latter seemed totally insensible to all such sentiments. Mr. Freeland had many of the faults peculiar to slaveholders, such as being very passionate and fretful; but I must do him the justice to say, that he was exceedingly free from those degrading vices to which Mr. Covey was constantly addicted. The one was open and frank, and we always knew where to find him. The other was a most artful deceiver, and could be understood only by such as were skilful enough to detect his cunningly-devised frauds. Another advantage I gained in my new master was, he made no pretensions to, or profession of, religion; and this, in my opinion, was truly a great advantage. I assert most unhesitatingly, that the religion of the south is a mere covering for the most horrid crimes,—a justifier of the most appalling barbarity,—a sanctifier of the most hateful frauds,—and a dark shelter under, which the darkest, foulest, grossest, and most infernal deeds of slaveholders find the strongest protection. Were I to be again reduced to the chains of slavery, next to that enslavement, I should regard being the slave of a religious master the greatest calamity that could befall me. For of all slaveholders with whom I have ever met, religious slaveholders are the worst. I have ever found them the meanest and basest, the most cruel and cowardly, of all others. It was my unhappy lot not only to belong to a religious slaveholder, but to live in a community of such religionists. Very near Mr. Freeland lived the Rev. Daniel Weeden, and in the same neighborhood lived the Rev. Rigby Hopkins. These were members and ministers in the Reformed Methodist Church. Mr. Weeden owned, among others, a woman slave, whose name I have forgotten. This woman's back, for weeks, was kept literally raw, made so by the lash of this merciless, *religious* wretch. He used to hire hands. His maxim was, Behave well or behave ill, it is the duty of a master occasionally to whip a slave, to remind him of his master's authority. Such was his theory, and such his practice.

Mr. Hopkins was even worse than Mr. Weeden. His chief boast was his ability to manage slaves. The peculiar feature of his government was that of whipping slaves in advance of deserving it. He always managed to have one or more of his slaves to whip every Monday morning. He did this to alarm their fears, and strike terror into those who escaped. His plan was to whip for the smallest offences, to prevent the commission of large ones. Mr. Hopkins could always find some excuse for whipping a slave. It would astonish one, unaccustomed to a slave-holding life, to see with what wonderful ease a slave-holder can find things, of which to make occasion to whip a slave. A mere look, word, or motion,—a mistake, accident, or want of power,—are all matters for which a slave may be whipped at any time. Does a slave look dissatisfied? It is said, he has the devil in him, and it must be whipped out. Does he speak loudly when spoken to by his master? Then he is wanting in reverence, and should be whipped for it. Does he ever venture to vindicate his conduct, when censured for it? Then he is guilty of impudence,—one of the greatest crimes of which a slave can be guilty. Does he ever venture to suggest a different mode of doing things from that pointed out by his master? He is indeed presumptuous, and getting above himself; and nothing less than a flogging will do for him. Does he, while ploughing, break a plough,—or, while hoeing, break a hoe? It is owing to his carelessness, and for it a slave must always be whipped. Mr. Hopkins could always find something of this sort to justify the use of the lash, and he seldom failed to embrace such opportunities. There was not a man in the whole county, with whom the slaves who had the getting their own home, would not prefer to live, rather than with this Rev. Mr. Hopkins. And yet there was not a man any where round, who made higher professions of religion, or was more active in revivals,—more attentive to the class, love-feast, prayer and preaching meetings, or more devotional in his family,—that prayed earlier, later, louder, and longer,—than this same reverend slave-driver, Rigby Hopkins.

But to return to Mr. Freeland, and to my experience while in his employment. He, like Mr. Covey, gave us enough to eat; but, unlike Mr. Covey, he also gave us sufficient time to take our meals. He worked us hard, but always between sunrise and sunset. He required a good deal of work to be done, but gave us good tools with which to work. His farm was large, but he employed hands enough to work it, and with ease, compared with many of his neighbors. My treatment, while in his employment, was heavenly, compared with what I experienced at the hands of Mr. Edward Covey.

Mr. Freeland was himself the owner of but two slaves. Their names were Henry Harris and John Harris. The rest of his hands he hired. These consisted of myself, Sandy Jenkins,[28] and Handy Caldwell. Henry and John were quite intelligent, and in a very little while after I went there, I succeeded in creating in them a strong desire to learn how to read. This desire soon sprang up in the others also. They very soon mustered up some old spelling-books, and nothing would do but that I must keep a Sabbath school. I agreed to do so, and accordingly devoted my Sundays to teaching these my loved fellow-slaves how to read. Neither of them knew his letters when I went there. Some of the slaves of the neighboring farms found what was going on, and also availed themselves of this little opportunity to learn to read. It was understood, among all who came, that there must be as little display about it as possible. It was necessary to keep our religious masters at St. Michael's unacquainted with the fact, that, instead of spending the Sabbath in wrestling, boxing, and drinking whisky, we were trying to learn how to read the will of God; for they had much rather see us engaged in those degrading sports, than to see us behaving like intellectual, moral, and accountable beings. My blood boils as I think of the bloody manner in which Messrs. Wright Fairbanks and Garrison West, both class-leaders, in connection with many others, rushed in upon us with sticks and stones, and broke up our virtuous little Sabbath school, at St. Michael's—all calling themselves Christians! humble followers of the Lord Jesus Christ! But I am again digressing.

I held my Sabbath school at the house of a free colored man, whose name I deem it imprudent to mention; for should it be known, it might embarrass him greatly, though the crime of holding the school was committed ten years ago. I had at one time over forty scholars, and those of the right sort, ardently desiring to learn. They were of all ages, though mostly men and women. I look back to those Sundays with an amount of pleasure not to be expressed. They were great days to my soul. The work of instructing my dear fellow-slaves was the sweetest engagement with which I was ever blessed. We loved each other, and to leave them at the close of the Sabbath was a severe cross indeed. When I think that these precious souls are to-day shut up in the prison-house of slavery, my feelings overcome me, and I am almost ready to ask, "Does a righteous God govern the universe? and for what does he hold the thunders in his right hand, if not to smite the oppressor, and deliver the spoiled out of the hand of the spoiler?" These dear souls came not to Sabbath school because it was popular to do so, nor did I teach them because it was reputable to be thus engaged. Every moment they spent in that school, they were liable to be taken up, and given thirty-nine lashes. They came because they wished to learn. Their minds had been starved by their cruel masters. They had been shut up in mental darkness. I taught them, because it was the delight of my soul to be doing something that looked like bettering the condition of my race. I kept up my school nearly the whole year I lived

[28]This is the same man who gave the roots to prevent my being whipped by Mr. Covey. He was a "clever soul." We used frequently to talk about the fight with Covey, and as often as we did so, he would claim my success as the result of the roots which he gave me. This superstition is very common among the more ignorant slaves. A slave seldom dies but that his death is attributed to trickery. [Douglass's note.]

with Mr. Freeland; and, beside my Sabbath school, I devoted three evenings in the week, during the winter, to teaching the slaves at home. And I have the happiness to know, that several of those who came to Sabbath school learned how to read; and that one, at least, is now free through my agency.

The year passed off smoothly. It seemed only about half as long as the year which preceded it. I went through it without receiving a single blow. I will give Mr. Freeland the credit of being the best master I ever had, *till I became my own master.* For the ease with which I passed the year, I was, however, somewhat indebted to the society of my fellow-slaves. They were noble souls; they not only possessed loving hearts, but brave ones. We were linked and interlinked with each other. I loved them with a love stronger than any thing I have experienced since. It is sometimes said that we slaves do not love and confide in each other. In answer to this assertion, I can say, I never loved any or confided in any people more than my fellow-slaves, and especially those with whom I lived at Mr. Freeland's. I believe we would have died for each other. We never undertook to do any thing, of any importance, without a mutual consultation. We never moved separately. We were one; and as much so by our tempers and dispositions, as by the mutual hardships to which we were necessarily subjected by our condition as slaves.

At the close of the year 1834, Mr. Freeland again hired me of my master, for the year 1835. But, by this time, I began to want to live *upon free land* as well as *with Freeland;* and I was no longer content, therefore, to live with him or any other slaveholder. I began, with the commencement of the year, to prepare myself for a final struggle, which should decide my fate one way or the other. My tendency was upward. I was fast approaching manhood, and year after year had passed, and I was still a slave. These thoughts roused me—I must do something. I therefore resolved that 1835 should not pass without witnessing an attempt, on my part, to secure my liberty. But I was not willing to cherish this determination alone. My fellow-slaves were dear to me. I was anxious to have them participate with me in this, my life-giving determination. I therefore, though with great prudence, commenced early to ascertain their views and feelings in regard to their condition, and to imbue their minds with thoughts of freedom. I bent myself to devising ways and means for our escape, and meanwhile strove, on all fitting occasions, to impress them with the gross fraud and inhumanity of slavery. I went first to Henry, next to John, then to the others. I found, in them all, warm hearts and noble spirits. They were ready to hear, and ready to act when a feasible plan should be proposed. This was what I wanted. I talked to them of our want of manhood, if we submitted to our enslavement without at least one noble effort to be free. We met often, and consulted frequently, and told our hopes and fears, recounted the difficulties, real and imagined, which we should be called on to meet. At times we were almost disposed to give up and try to content ourselves with our wretched lot; at others, we were firm and unbending in our determination to go. Whenever we suggested any plan, there was shrinking—the odds were fearful. Our path was beset with the greatest obstacles; and if we succeeded in gaining the end of it, our right to be free was yet questionable—we were yet liable to be returned to bondage. We could see no spot, this side of the ocean, where we could be free. We knew nothing about Canada. Our knowledge of the north did not extend farther than New York; and to go there, and be forever harassed with the frightful liability of being returned to slavery—with the certainty of being treated tenfold worse than before—the thought was truly a horrible one, and one which it was not easy to overcome. The case sometimes stood thus: At every gate through which we were to pass, we saw a watchman—at every ferry a guard—on every bridge a sentinel—and in every wood a patrol. We were hemmed in upon every side. Here were the difficulties, real or imagined—the good to be sought, and the evil to be shunned. On the one hand, there stood slavery, a stern reality, glaring frightfully upon us,—its robes already crimsoned with the blood of millions, and even now feasting itself greedily upon our own flesh. On the other hand, away back in the dim distance, under the flickering light of the north star, behind some craggy hill or snow-covered mountain, stood a doubtful freedom—half frozen—beckoning us to come and share its hospitality. This in itself was sometimes enough to stagger us; but when we permitted ourselves to survey the road, we were frequently appalled. Upon either side we saw grim death, assuming the most horrid shapes. Now it was starvation, causing us to eat our own flesh;—now we were contending with the waves, and were drowned;—now we were overtaken, and torn to pieces by the fangs of the terrible bloodhound. We were stung by scorpions, chased by wild beasts, bitten by snakes, and finally, after having nearly reached the desired spot,—after swimming rivers, encountering wild beasts, sleeping in the woods, suffering hunger and nakedness,—we were overtaken by our pursuers, and in our resistance, we were shot dead upon the spot! I say, this picture sometimes appalled us, and made us

> "rather bear those ills we had,
> Than fly to others, that we knew not of."[29]

In coming to a fixed determination to run away, we did more than Patrick Henry, when he resolved upon liberty or death. With us it was a doubtful liberty at most, and almost certain death if we failed. For my part, I should prefer death to hopeless bondage.

Sandy, one of our number, gave up the notion, but still encouraged us. Our company then consisted of Henry Harris, John Harris, Henry Bailey, Charles Roberts, and myself. Henry Bailey was my uncle, and belonged to my master. Charles married my aunt: he belonged to my master's father-in-law, Mr. William Hamilton.

The plan we finally concluded upon was, to get a large canoe belonging to Mr. Hamilton, and upon the Saturday night previous to Easter holidays, paddle directly up the Chesapeake Bay. On our arrival at the head of the bay, a distance of seventy or eighty miles from where we lived, it was our purpose to turn our canoe adrift, and follow the guidance of the north star till we got beyond the limits of Maryland. Our reason for taking the water route was, that we were less liable to be suspected as runaways; we hoped to be regarded as fishermen; whereas, if we should take the land route, we should be subjected to interruptions of almost every kind. Any one having a white face, and being so disposed, could stop us, and subject us to examination.

The week before our intended start, I wrote several protections, one for each of us. As well as I can remember they were in the following words, to wit:—

> *"This is to certify that I, the undersigned, have given the bearer, my servant, full liberty to go to Baltimore, and spend the Easter holidays. Written with mine own hand &c., 1835.*
>
> "William Hamilton,
>
> "Near St. Michael's, in Talbot county, Maryland."

[29]Shakespeare, *Hamlet,* III, i, 81–82.

We were not going to Baltimore; but, in going up the bay, we went toward Baltimore, and these protections were only intended to protect us while on the bay.

As the time drew near for our departure, our anxiety became more and more intense. It was truly a matter of life and death with us. The strength of our determination was about to be fully tested. At this time, I was very active in explaining every difficulty, removing every doubt, dispelling every fear, and inspiring all with the firmness indispensable to success in our undertaking; assuring them that half was gained the instant we made the move; we had talked long enough; we were now ready to move; if not now, we never should be; and if we did not intend to move now, we had as well fold our arms, sit down, and acknowledge ourselves fit only to be slaves. This, none of us were prepared to acknowledge. Every man stood firm; and at our last meeting, we pledged ourselves afresh, in the most solemn manner, that at the time appointed, we would certainly start in pursuit of freedom. This was in the middle of the week, at the end of which we were to be off. We went, as usual, to our several fields of labor, but with bosoms highly agitated with thoughts of our truly hazardous undertaking. We tried to conceal our feelings as much as possible; and I think we succeeded very well.

After a painful waiting, the Saturday morning, whose night was to witness our departure, came. I hailed it with joy, bring what of sadness it might. Friday night was a sleepless one for me. I probably felt more anxious than the rest, because I was, by common consent, at the head of the whole affair. The responsibility of success or failure lay heavily upon me. The glory of the one, and the confusion of the other, were alike mine. The first two hours of that morning were such as I never experienced before, and hope never to again. Early in the morning, we went, as usual, to the field. We were spreading manure; and all at once, while thus engaged, I was overwhelmed with an indescribable feeling, in the fulness of which I turned to Sandy, who was near by, and said, "We are betrayed!" "Well," said he, "that thought has this moment struck me." We said no more. I was never more certain of any thing.

The horn was blown as usual, and we went up from the field to the house for breakfast. I went for the form, more than for want of any thing to eat that morning. Just as I got to the house, in looking out at the lane gate, I saw four white men, with two colored men. The white men were on horseback, and the colored ones were walking behind, as if tied. I watched them a few moments till they got up to our lane gate. Here they halted, and tied the colored men to the gate-post. I was not yet certain as to what the matter was. In a few moments, in rode Mr. Hamilton, with a speed betokening great excitement. He came to the door, and inquired if Master William was in. He was told he was at the barn. Mr. Hamilton, without dismounting, rode up to the barn with extraordinary speed. In a few moments, he and Mr. Freeland returned to the house. By this time, the three constables rode up, and in great haste dismounted, tied their horses, and met Master William and Mr. Hamilton returning from the barn; and after talking awhile, they all walked up to the kitchen door. There was no one in the kitchen but myself and John. Henry and Sandy were up at the barn. Mr. Freeland put his head in at the door, and called me by name, saying, there were some gentlemen at the door who wished to see me. I stepped to the door, and inquired what they wanted. They at once seized me, and, without giving me any satisfaction, tied me—lashing my hands closely together. I insisted upon knowing what the matter was. They at length said, that they had learned I had been in a "scrape," and that I was to be examined before my master; and if their information proved false, I should not be hurt.

In a few moments, they succeeded in tying John. They then turned to Henry, who had by this time returned, and commanded him to cross his hands. "I won't!" said Henry, in a firm tone, indicating his readiness to meet the consequences of his refusal. "Won't you?" said Tom Graham, the constable. "No, I won't!" said Henry, in a still stronger tone. With this, two of the constables pulled out their shining pistols, and swore, by their Creator, that they would make him cross his hands or kill him. Each cocked his pistol, and, with fingers on the trigger, walked up to Henry, saying, at the same time, if he did not cross his hands, they would blow his damned heart out. "Shoot me, shoot me!" said Henry; "you can't kill me but once. Shoot, shoot,—and be damned! *I won't be tied!"* This he said in a tone of loud defiance; and at the same time, with a motion as quick as lightning, he with one single stroke dashed the pistols from the hand of each constable. As he did this, all hands fell upon him, and, after beating him some time, they finally overpowered him, and got him tied.

During the scuffle, I managed, I know not how, to get my pass out, and, without being discovered, put it into the fire. We were all now tied; and just as we were to leave for Easton jail, Betsy Freeland, mother of William Freeland, came to the door with her hands full of biscuits, and divided them between Henry and John. She then delivered herself of a speech, to the following effect:—addressing herself to me, she said, *"You devil! You yellow devil!* it was you that put it into the heads of Henry and John to run away. But for you, you long-legged mulatto devil! Henry nor John would never have thought of such a thing." I made no reply, and was immediately hurried off towards St. Michael's. Just a moment previous to the scuffle with Henry, Mr. Hamilton suggested the propriety of making a search for the protections which he had understood Frederick had written for himself and the rest. But, just at the moment he was about carrying his proposal into effect, his aid was needed in helping to tie Henry; and the excitement attending the scuffle caused them either to forget, or to deem it unsafe, under the circumstances, to search. So we were not yet convicted of the intention to run away.

When we got about half way to St. Michael's, while the constables having us in charge were looking ahead, Henry inquired of me what he should do with his pass. I told him to eat it with his biscuit, and own nothing; and we passed the word around, *"Own nothing;"* and *"Own nothing!"* said we all. Our confidence in each other was unshaken. We were resolved to succeed or fail together, after the calamity had befallen us as much as before. We were now prepared for any thing. We were to be dragged that morning fifteen miles behind horses, and then to be placed in the Easton jail. When we reached St. Michael's, we underwent a sort of examination. We all denied that we ever intended to run away. We did this more to bring out the evidence against us, than from any hope of getting clear of being sold; for, as I have said, we were ready for that. The fact was, we cared but little where we went, so we went together. Our greatest concern was about separation. We dreaded that more than any thing this side of death. We found the evidence against us to be the testimony of one person; our master would not tell who it was; but we came to a unanimous decision among ourselves as to who their informant was.[30] We were sent off to the jail at Easton. When we got there, we were delivered up to the sheriff, Mr. Joseph

[30]In the 1892 version of his autobiography, *The Life and Times of Frederick Douglass,* Douglass explicitly names Sandy Jenkins as the suspect: ". . . We suspected *one* person only. Several circumstances seemed to point Sandy out as our betrayer."

Graham, and by him placed in jail. Henry, John, and myself, were placed in one room together—Charles, and Henry Bailey, in another. Their object in separating us was to hinder concert.

We had been in jail scarcely twenty minutes, when a swarm of slave traders, and agents for slave traders, flocked into jail to look at us, and to ascertain if we were for sale. Such a set of beings I never saw before! I felt myself surrounded by so many fiends from perdition. A band of pirates never looked more like their father, the devil. They laughed and grinned over us, saying, "Ah, my boys! we have got you, haven't we?" And after taunting us in various ways, they one by one went into an examination of us, with intent to ascertain our value. They would impudently ask us if we would not like to have them for our masters. We would make them no answer, and leave them to find out as best they could. Then they would curse and swear at us, telling us that they could take the devil out of us in a very little while, if we were only in their hands.

While in jail, we found ourselves in much more comfortable quarters than we expected when we went there. We did not get much to eat, nor that which was very good; but we had a good clean room, from the windows of which we could see what was going on in the street, which was very much better than though we had been placed in one of the dark, damp cells. Upon the whole, we got along very well, so far as the jail and its keeper were concerned. Immediately after the holidays were over, contrary to all our expectations, Mr. Hamilton and Mr. Freeland came up to Easton, and took Charles, the two Henrys, and John, out of jail, and carried them home, leaving me alone. I regarded this separation as a final one. It caused me more pain than any thing else in the whole transaction. I was ready for any thing rather than separation. I supposed that they had consulted together, and had decided that, as I was the whole cause of the intention of the others to run away, it was hard to make the innocent suffer with the guilty; and that they had, therefore, concluded to take the others home, and sell me, as a warning to the others that remained. It is due to the noble Henry to say, he seemed almost as reluctant at leaving the prison as at leaving home to come to the prison. But we knew we should, in all probability, be separated, if we were sold; and since he was in their hands, he concluded to go peaceably home.

I was now left to my fate. I was all alone, and within the walls of a stone prison. But a few days before, and I was full of hope. I expected to have been safe in a land of freedom; but now I was covered with gloom, sunk down to the utmost despair. I thought the possibility of freedom was gone. I was kept in this way about one week, at the end of which, Captain Auld, my master, to my surprise and utter astonishment, came up, and took me out, with the intention of sending me, with a gentleman of his acquaintance, into Alabama. But, from some cause or other, he did not send me to Alabama, but concluded to send me back to Baltimore, to live again with his brother Hugh, and to learn a trade.

Thus, after an absence of three years and one month, I was once more permitted to return to my old home at Baltimore. My master sent me away, because there existed against me a very great prejudice in the community, and he feared I might be killed.

In a few weeks after I went to Baltimore, Master Hugh hired me to Mr. William Gardner, an extensive ship-builder, on Fell's Point. I was put there to learn how to calk. It, however, proved a very unfavorable place for the accomplishment of this object. Mr. Gardner was engaged that spring in building two large man-of-war brigs, professedly for the Mexican government. The vessels were to be launched in the July of that year, and in failure thereof, Mr. Gardner was to lose a considerable sum; so that when I entered, all was hurry. There was no time to learn any thing. Every man had to do that which he knew how to do. In entering the shipyard, my orders from Mr. Gardner were, to do whatever the carpenters commanded me to do. This was placing me at the beck and call of about seventy-five men. I was to regard all these as masters. Their word was to be my law. My situation was a most trying one. At times I needed a dozen pair of hands. I was called a dozen ways in the space of a single minute. Three or four voices would strike my ear at the same moment. It was—"Fred., come help me to cant this timber here."—"Fred., come carry this timber yonder."—"Fred., bring that roller here."—"Fred., go get a fresh can of water."—"Fred., come help saw off the end of this timber."—"Fred., go quick, and get the crowbar."—"Fred., hold on the end of this fall."[31]—"Fred., go to the blacksmith's shop, and get a new punch."—"Hurra, Fred.! run and bring me a cold chisel."—"I say, Fred., bear a hand, and get up a fire as quick as lightning under that steam-box."—"Halloo, nigger! come, turn this grindstone."—"Come, come! move, move! and *bowse*[32] this timber forward."—"I say, darky, blast your eyes, why don't you heat up some pitch?"—"Halloo! halloo! halloo!" (Three voices at the same time.) "Come here!—Go there!—Hold on where you are! Damn you, if you move, I'll knock your brains out!"

This was my school for eight months; and I might have remained there longer, but for a most horrid fight I had with four of the white apprentices, in which my left eye was nearly knocked out and I was horribly mangled in other respects. The facts in the case were these: Until a very little while after I went there, white and black ship-carpenters worked side by side, and no one seemed to see any impropriety in it. All hands seemed to be very well satisfied. Many of the black carpenters were freemen. Things seemed to be going on very well. All at once, the white carpenters knocked off, and said they would not work with free colored workmen. Their reason for this, as alleged, was, that if free colored carpenters were encouraged, they would soon take the trade into their own hands, and poor white men would be thrown out of employment. They therefore felt called upon at once to put a stop to it. And, taking advantage of Mr. Gardner's necessities, they broke off, swearing they would work no longer, unless he would discharge his black carpenters. Now, though this did not extend to me in form, it did reach me in fact. My fellow-apprentices very soon began to feel it degrading to them to work with me. They began to put on airs, and talk about the "niggers" taking the country, saying we all ought to be killed; and, being encouraged by the journeymen, they commenced making my condition as hard as they could, by hectoring me around, and sometimes striking me. I, of course, kept the vow I made after the fight with Mr. Covey, and struck back again, regardless of consequences; and while I kept them from combining, I succeeded very well; for I could whip the whole of them, taking them separately. They, however, at length combined, and came upon me, armed with sticks, stones, and heavy handspikes. One came in front with a half brick. There was one at each side of me, and one behind

[31]The end of a tackle.
[32]Haul.

me. While I was attending to those in front, and on either side, the one behind ran up with the handspike, and struck me a heavy blow upon the head. It stunned me. I fell, and with this they all ran upon me, and fell to beating me with their fists. I let them lay on for a while, gathering strength. In an instant, I gave a sudden surge, and rose to my hands and knees. Just as I did that, one of their number gave me, with his heavy boot, a powerful kick in the left eye. My eyeball seemed to have burst. When they saw my eye closed, and badly swollen, they left me. With this I seized the handspike, and for a time pursued them. But here the carpenters interfered, and I thought I might as well give it up. It was impossible to stand my hand against so many. All this took place in sight of not less than fifty white ship-carpenters, and not one interposed a friendly word; but some cried, "Kill the damned nigger! Kill him! kill him! He struck a white person." I found my only chance for life was in flight. I succeeded in getting away without an additional blow, and barely so, for to strike a white man is death by Lynch law,—and that was the law in Mr. Gardner's ship-yard; nor is there much of any other out of Mr. Gardner's ship-yard.

I went directly home, and told the story of my wrongs to Master Hugh; and I am happy to say of him, irreligious as he was, his conduct was heavenly, compared with that of his brother Thomas under similar circumstances. He listened attentively to my narration of the circumstances leading to the savage outrage, and gave many proofs of his strong indignation at it. The heart of my once overkind mistress was again melted into pity. My puffed-out eye and blood-covered face moved her to tears. She took a chair by me, washed the blood from my face, and, with a mother's tenderness, bound up my head, covering the wounded eye with a lean piece of fresh beef. It was almost compensation for my suffering to witness, once more, a manifestation of kindness from this, my once affectionate old mistress. Master Hugh was very much enraged. He gave expression to his feelings by pouring out curses upon the heads of those who did the deed. As soon as I got a little the better of my bruises, he took me with him to Esquire Watson's, on Bond Street, to see what could be done about the matter. Mr. Watson inquired who saw the assault committed. Master Hugh told him it was done in Mr. Gardner's ship-yard, at midday, where there were a large company of men at work. "As to that," he said, "the deed was done, and there was no question as to who did it." His answer was, he could do nothing in the case, unless some white man would come forward and testify. He could issue no warrant on my word. If I had been killed in the presence of a thousand colored people, their testimony combined would have been insufficient to have arrested one of the murderers. Master Hugh, for once, was compelled to say this state of things was too bad. Of course, it was impossible to get any white man to volunteer his testimony in my behalf, and against the white young men. Even those who may have sympathized with me were not prepared to do this. It required a degree of courage unknown to them to do so; for just at that time, the slightest manifestation of humanity toward a colored person was denounced as abolitionism, and that name subjected its bearer to frightful liabilities. The watchwords of the bloody-minded in that region, and in those days, were, "Damn the abolitionists!" and "Damn the niggers!" There was nothing done, and probably nothing would have been done if I had been killed. Such was, and such remains, the state of things in the Christian city of Baltimore.

Master Hugh, finding he could get no redress, refused to let me go back again to Mr. Gardner. He kept me himself, and his wife dressed my wound till I was again restored to health. He then took me into the ship-yard of which he was foreman, in the employment of Mr. Walter Price. There I was immediately set to calking, and very soon learned the art of using my mallet and irons. In the course of one year from the time I left Mr. Gardner's, I was able to command the highest wages given to the most experienced calkers. I was now of some importance to my master. I was bringing him from six to seven dollars per week. I sometimes brought him nine dollars per week: my wages were a dollar and a half a day. After learning how to calk, I sought my own employment, made my own contracts, and collected the money which I earned. My pathway became much more smooth than before; my condition was now much more comfortable. When I could get no calking to do, I did nothing. During these leisure times, those old notions about freedom would steal over me again. When in Mr. Gardner's employment, I was kept in such a perpetual whirl of excitement, I could think of nothing, scarcely, but my life; and in thinking of my life, I almost forgot my liberty. I have observed this in my experience of slavery,—that whenever my condition was improved, instead of its increasing my contentment, it only increased my desire to be free, and set me to thinking of plans to gain my freedom. I have found that, to make a contented slave, it is necessary to make a thoughtless one. It is necessary to darken his moral and mental vision, and, as far as possible, to annihilate the power of reason. He must be able to detect no inconsistencies in slavery; he must be made to feel that slavery is right; and he can be brought to that only when he ceases to be a man.

I was now getting, as I have said, one dollar and fifty cents per day. I contracted for it; I earned it; it was paid to me it was rightfully my own; yet, upon each returning Saturday night, I was compelled to deliver every cent of that money to Master Hugh. And why? Not because he earned it,—not because he had any hand in earning it,—not because I owed it to him,—nor because he possessed the slightest shadow of a right to it; but solely because he had the power to compel me to give it up. The right of the grim-visaged pirate upon the high seas is exactly the same.

Chapter XI

I now come to that part of my life during which I planned, and finally succeeded in making, my escape from slavery. But before narrating any of the peculiar circumstances, I deem it proper to make known my intention not to state all the facts connected with the transaction. My reasons for pursuing this course may be understood from the following: First, were I to give a minute statement of all the facts, it is not only possible but quite probable, that others would thereby be involved in the most embarrassing difficulties. Secondly, such a statement would most undoubtedly induce greater vigilance on the part of slaveholders than has existed heretofore among them; which would, of course, be the means of guarding a door whereby some dear brother bondman might escape his galling chains. I deeply regret the necessity that impels me to suppress any thing of importance connected with my experience in slavery. It would afford me great pleasure indeed, as well as materially add to the interest of my narrative, were I at liberty to gratify a curiosity, which I know exists in the minds of many, by an accurate statement of all the facts pertaining to my most fortunate escape. But I must deprive myself of this pleasure, and the curious of the gratification which such a statement would afford. I would allow myself to suffer under the greatest imputations which evil-minded men might suggest, rather than exculpate myself, and thereby run the hazard of closing the slightest avenue by which a brother slave might clear himself of the chains and fetters of slavery.[33]

I have never approved of the very public manner in which some of our western friends have conducted what they call the *underground railroad,*[34] but which I think, by their open declarations, has been made most emphatically the *upperground railroad.* I honor those good men and women for their noble daring, and applaud them for willingly subjecting themselves to bloody persecution, by openly avowing their participation in the escape of slaves. I, however, can see very little good resulting from such a course, either to themselves or the slaves escaping; while, upon the other hand, I see and feel assured that those open declarations are a positive evil to the slaves remaining, who are seeking to escape. They do nothing towards enlightening the slave, whilst they do much towards enlightening the master. They stimulate him to greater watchfulness, and enhance his power to capture his slave. We owe something to the slave south of the line as well as to those north of it; and in aiding the latter on their way to freedom, we should be careful to do nothing which would be likely to hinder the former from escaping from slavery. I would keep the merciless slaveholder profoundly ignorant of the means of flight adopted by the slave. I would leave him to imagine himself surrounded by myriads of invisible tormentors, ever ready to snatch from his infernal grasp his trembling prey. Let him be left to feel his way in the dark; let darkness commensurate with his crime hover over him; and let him feel that at every step he takes, in pursuit of the flying bondman, he is running the frightful risk of having his hot brains dashed out by an invisible agency. Let us render the tyrant no aid; let us not hold the light by which he can trace the footprints of our flying brother. But enough of this. I will now proceed to the statement of those facts, connected with my escape, for which I am alone responsible, and for which no one can be made to suffer but myself.

In the early part of the year 1838, I became quite restless. I could see no reason why I should, at the end of each week, pour the reward of my toil into the purse of my master. When I carried to him my weekly wages, he would, after counting the money, look me in the face with a robber-like fierceness, and say, "Is this all?" He was satisfied with nothing less than the last cent. He would, however, when I made him six dollars, sometimes give me six cents, to encourage me. It had the opposite effect. I regarded it as a sort of admission of my right to the whole. The fact that he gave me any part of my wages was proof, to my mind, that he believed me entitled to the whole of them. I always felt worse for having received any thing; for I feared that the giving me a few cents would ease his conscience, and make him feel himself to be a pretty honorable sort of robber. My discontent grew upon me. I was ever on the look-out for means of escape; and, finding no direct means, I determined to try to hire my time, with a view of getting money with which to make my escape. In the spring of 1838, when Master Thomas came to Baltimore to purchase his spring

[33]In *The Life and Times of Frederick Douglass,* Douglass describes how he escaped: he borrowed the papers of a free black, an American sailor, boarded the Baltimore train dressed as a sailor, and proceeded to Philadelphia, then to New York.

[34]A system of safe-houses, conveyors, and supporters that worked to help slaves escape.

goods, I got an opportunity, and applied to him to allow me to hire my time. He unhesitatingly refused my request, and told me this was another stratagem by which to escape. He told me I could go nowhere but that he could get me; and that, in the event of my running away, he should spare no pains in his efforts to catch me. He exhorted me to content myself, and be obedient. He told me, if I would be happy, I must lay out no plans for the future. He said, if I behaved myself properly, he would take care of me. Indeed, he advised me to complete thoughtlessness of the future, and taught me to depend solely upon him for happiness. He seemed to see fully the pressing necessity of setting aside my intellectual nature, in order to [insure] contentment in slavery. But in spite of him, and even in spite of myself, I continued to think, and to think about the injustice of my enslavement, and the means of escape.

About two months after this, I applied to Master Hugh for the privilege of hiring my time. He was not acquainted with the fact that I had applied to Master Thomas, and had been refused. He too, at first, seemed disposed to refuse; but, after some reflection, he granted me the privilege, and proposed the following terms: I was to be allowed all my time, make all contracts with those for whom I worked, and find my own employment; and, in return for this liberty, I was to pay him three dollars at the end of each week; find myself in calking tools, and in board and clothing. My board was two dollars and a half per week. This, with the wear and tear of clothing and calking tools, made my regular expenses about six dollars per week. This amount I was compelled to make up, or relinquish the privilege of hiring my time. Rain or shine, work or no work, at the end of each week the money must be forthcoming, or I must give up my privilege. This arrangement, it will be perceived, was decidedly in my master's favor. It relieved him of all need of looking after me. His money was sure. He received all the benefits of slaveholding without its evils; while I endured all the evils of a slave, and suffered all the care and anxiety of a freeman. I found it a hard bargain. But, hard as it was I thought it better than the old mode of getting along. It was a step towards freedom to be allowed to bear the responsibilities of a freeman, and I was determined to hold on upon it. I bent myself to the work of making money. I was ready to work at night as well as day, and by the most untiring perservance and industry, I made enough to meet my expenses, and lay up a little money every week. I went on thus from May till August. Master Hugh then refused to allow me to hire my time longer. The ground for his refusal was a failure on my part, one Saturday night, to pay him for my week's time. This failure was occasioned by my attending a camp meeting about ten miles from Baltimore. During the week, I had entered into an engagement with a number of young friends to start from Baltimore to the camp ground early Saturday evening; and being detained by my employer, I was unable to get down to Master Hugh's without disappointing the company. I knew that Master Hugh was in no special need of the money that night. I therefore decided to go to the camp meeting, and upon my return pay him the three dollars. I staid at the camp meeting one day longer than I intended when I left. But as soon as I returned, I called upon him to pay him what he considered his due. I found him very angry; he could scarce restrain his wrath. He said he had a great mind to give me a severe whipping. He wished to know how I dared go out of the city without asking his permission. I told him I hired my time, and while I paid him the price which he asked for it, I did not know that I was bound to ask him when and where I should go. This reply troubled him; and, after reflecting a few moments, he turned to me, and said I should hire my time no longer; that the next thing he should know of, I would be running away. Upon the same plea, he told me to bring my tools and clothing home forthwith. I did so; but instead of seeking work, as I had been accustomed to do previously to hiring my time, I spent the whole week without the performance of a single stroke of work. I did this in retaliation. Saturday night, he called upon me as usual for my week's wages. I told him I had no wages; I had done no work that week. Here we were upon the point of coming to blows. He raved, and swore his determination to get hold of me. I did not allow myself a single word; but was resolved, if he laid the weight of his hand upon me, it should be blow for blow. He did not strike me, but told me that he would find me in constant employment in future. I thought the matter over during the next day, Sunday, and finally resolved upon the third day of September, as the day upon which I would make a second attempt to secure my freedom. I now had three weeks during which to prepare for my journey. Early on Monday morning, before Master Hugh had time to make any engagement for me, I went out and got employment of Mr. Butler, at his ship-yard near the drawbridge, upon what is called the City Block, thus making it unnecessary for him to seek employment for me. At the end of the week, I brought him between eight and nine dollars. He seemed very well pleased, and asked why I did not do the same the week before. He little knew what my plans were. My object in working steadily was to remove any suspicion he might entertain of my intent to run away; and in this I succeeded admirably. I suppose he thought I was never better satisfied with my condition than at the very time during which I was planning my escape. The second week passed, and again I carried him my full wages; and so well pleased was he, that he gave me twenty-five cents, (quite a large sum for a slaveholder to give a slave), and bade me to make a good use of it. I told him I would.

Things went on without very smoothly indeed, but within there was trouble. It is impossible for me to describe my feelings as the time of my contemplated start drew near. I had a number of warm-hearted friends in Baltimore,—friends that I loved almost as I did my life,—and the thought of being separated from them forever was painful beyond expression. It is my opinion that thousands would escape from slavery, who now remain, but for the strong cords of affection that bind them to their friends. The thought of leaving my friends was decidedly the most painful thought with which I had to contend. The love of them was my tender point, and shook my decision more than all things else. Besides the pain of separation, the dread and apprehension of a failure exceeded what I had experienced at my first attempt. The appalling defeat I then sustained returned to torment me. I felt assured that, if I failed in this attempt, my case would be a hopeless one—it would seal my fate as a slave forever. I could not hope to get off with any thing less than the severest punishment, and being placed beyond the means of escape. It required no very vivid imagination to depict the most frightful scenes through which I should have to pass, in case I failed. The wretchedness of slavery, and the blessedness of freedom, were perpetually before me. It was life and death with me. But I remained firm, and, according to my resolution, on the third day of September, 1838, I left my chains, and succeeded in reaching New York without the slightest interruption of any kind. How I did so,—what means I adopted,—what direction I travelled, and by what mode of conveyance,—I must leave unexplained, for the reasons before mentioned.

I have been frequently asked how I felt when I found myself in a free State. I have never been able to answer the question with any satisfaction to myself. It was a moment of the highest excitement I ever experienced. I suppose I felt as one may imagine the unarmed mariner to feel when he is rescued by a friendly man-of-war from the pursuit of a pirate. In writing to a dear friend, immediately after my arrival at New York, I said I felt like one who had escaped a den of hungry lions. This state of mind, however, very soon subsided; and I was again seized by a feeling of great insecurity and loneliness. I was yet liable to be taken back, and subjected to all the tortures of slavery. This in itself was enough to damp the ardor of my enthusiasm. But the loneliness overcame me. There I was in the midst of thousands, and yet a perfect stranger; without home and without friends, in the midst of thousands of my own brethren—children of a common Father, and yet I dared not to unfold to any one of them my sad condition. I was afraid to speak to any one for fear of speaking to the wrong one, and thereby falling into the hands of money-loving kidnappers, whose business it was to lie in wait for the panting fugitive, as the ferocious beasts of the forest lie in wait for their prey. The motto which I adopted when I started from slavery was this—"Trust no man!" I saw in every white man an enemy, and in almost every colored man cause for distrust. It was a most painful situation; and, to understand it, one must needs experience it, or imagine himself in similar circumstances. Let him be a fugitive slave in a strange land—a land given up to be the hunting-ground for slaveholders—whose inhabitants are legalized kidnappers—where he is every moment subjected to the terrible liability of being seized upon by his fellowmen, as the hideous crocodile seizes upon his prey!—I say, let him place himself in my situation—without home or friends—without money or credit—wanting shelter, and no one to give it—wanting bread, and no money to buy it,—and at the same time let him feel that he is pursued by merciless men-hunters, and in total darkness as to what to do, where to go, or where to stay,—perfectly helpless both as to the means of defence and means of escape,—in the midst of plenty, yet suffering the terrible gnawings of hunger,—in the midst of houses, yet having no home,—among fellowmen, yet feeling as if in the midst of wild beasts, whose greediness to swallow up the trembling and half-famished fugitive is only equalled by that with which the monsters of the deep swallow up the helpless fish upon which they subsist,—I say, let him be placed in this most trying situation,—the situation in which I was placed,—then, and not till then, will he fully appreciate the hardships of, and know how to sympathize with, the toil-worn and whip-scarred fugitive slave.

Thank Heaven, I remained but a short time in this distress situation. I was relieved from it by the humane hand of Mr. David Ruggles,[35] whose vigilance, kindness, and perseverance, I shall never forget. I am glad of an opportunity to express, as far as words can, the love and gratitude I bear him. Mr. Ruggles is now afflicted with blindness, and is himself in need of the same kind offices which he was once so forward in the performance of toward others. I had been in New York but a few days, when Mr. Ruggles sought me out, and very kindly took me to his boarding-house at the corner of Church and Lespenard Streets. Mr. Ruggles was then very deeply engaged in the memorable *Darg* case, as well as attending to a number of other fugitive

[35]David Ruggles (1810–1849) a black journalist, businessman, fund-raiser, and activist, became general secretary of the New York Committee of Vigilance in 1835. In that position he helped hundreds of runaways, including Douglass: he sheltered Douglass for two weeks, arranged for his marriage, and sent the newlywed couple on to New Bedford with a donation of five dollars and a letter of introduction.

slaves; devising ways and means for their successful escape; and, though watched and hemmed in on almost every side, he seemed to be more than a match for his enemies.

Very soon after I went to Mr. Ruggles, he wished to know of me where I wanted to go; as he deemed it unsafe for me to remain in New York. I told him I was a calker, and should like to go where I could get work. I thought of going to Canada; but he decided against it, and in favor of my going to New Bedford, thinking I should be able to get work there at my trade. At this time, Anna,[36] my intended wife, came on; for I wrote to her immediately after my arrival at New York, (notwithstanding my homeless, houseless, and helpless condition,) informing her of my successful flight, and wishing her to come on forthwith. In a few days after her arrival, Mr. Ruggles called in the Rev. J.W.C. Pennington, who, in the presence of Mr. Ruggles, Mrs. Michaels, and two or three others, performed the marriage ceremony, and gave us a certificate, of which the following is an exact copy:—

> *"This may certify, that I joined together in holy matrimony Frederick Johnson*[37] *and Anna Murray, as man and wife, in the presence of Mr. David Ruggles and Mrs. Michaels.*
>
> "James W.C. Pennington
> "New York, Sept. 15, 1838."

Upon receiving this certificate, and a five-dollar bill from Mr. Ruggles, I shouldered one part of our baggage, and Anna took up the other, and we set out forthwith to take passage on board of the steamboat John W. Richmond for Newport, on our way to New Bedford. Mr. Ruggles gave me a letter to a Mr. Shaw in Newport, and told me, in case my money did not serve me to New Bedford, to stop in Newport and obtain further assistance; but upon our arrival at Newport, we were so anxious to get to a place of safety, that, notwithstanding we lacked the necessary money to pay our fare, we decided to take seats in the stage, and promise to pay when we got to New Bedford. We were encouraged to do this by two excellent gentlemen, residents of New Bedford, whose names I afterward ascertained to be Joseph Ricketson and William C. Taber. They seemed at once to understand our circumstances, and gave us such assurance of their friendliness as put us fully at ease in their presence. It was good indeed to meet with such friends, at such a time. Upon reaching New Bedford, we were directed to the house of Mr. Nathan Johnson, by whom we were kindly received, and hospitably provided for. Both Mr. and Mrs. Johnson took a deep and lively interest in our welfare. They proved themselves quite worthy of the name of abolitionists. When the stage-driver found us unable to pay our fare, he held on upon our baggage as security for the debt. I had but to mention the fact to Mr. Johnson, and he forthwith advanced the money.

We now began to feel a degree of safety, and to prepare ourselves for the duties and responsibilities of a life of freedom. On the morning after our arrival at New Bedford, while at the breakfast-table, the question arose as to what name I should be called by. The name given me by my mother was, "Frederick Augustus Washington Bailey." I, however, had dispensed with the two middle names long before I left Maryland so that I was generally known by the name of "Frederick Bailey." I started

[36]She was free. [Douglass's note.]

[37]I had changed my name from Frederick *Bailey* to that of *Johnson.* [Douglass's note.]

from Baltimore bearing the name of "Stanley." When I got to New York I again changed my name to "Frederick Johnson," and thought that would be the last change. But when I got to New Bedford, I found it necessary again to change my name. The reason of this necessity was, that there were so many Johnsons in New Bedford, it was already quite difficult to distinguish between them. I gave Mr. Johnson the privilege of choosing me a name, but told him he must not take from me the name of "Frederick." I must hold on to that, to preserve a sense of my identity. Mr. Johnson had just been reading the "Lady of the Lake," and at once suggested that my name be "Douglass."[38] From that time until now I have been called "Frederick Douglass"; and as I am more widely known by that name than by either of the others, I shall continue to use it as my own.

I was quite disappointed at the general appearance of things in New Bedford. The impression which I had received respecting the character and condition of the people of the north, I found to be singularly erroneous. I had very strangely supposed, while in slavery, that few of the comforts, and scarcely any of the luxuries, of life were enjoyed at the north, compared with what were enjoyed by the slaveholders of the south. I probably came to this conclusion from the fact that northern people owned no slaves. I supposed that they were about upon a level with the non-slaveholding population of the south. I knew *they* were exceedingly poor, and I had been accustomed to regard their poverty as the necessary consequence of their being non-slaveholders. I had somehow imbibed the opinion that, in the absence of slaves, there could be no wealth, and very little refinement. And upon coming to the north, I expected to meet with a rough, hard-handed, and uncultivated population, living in the most Spartanlike simplicity, knowing nothing of the ease, luxury, pomp, and grandeur of southern slaveholders. Such being my conjectures, any one acquainted with the appearance of New Bedford may very readily infer how palpably I must have seen my mistake.

In the afternoon of the day when I reached New Bedford, I visited the wharves, to take a view of the shipping. Here I found myself surrounded with the strongest proofs of wealth. Lying at the wharves, and riding in the stream, I saw many ships of the finest model, in the best order, and of the largest size. Upon the right and left, I was walled in by granite warehouses of the widest dimensions, stowed to their utmost capacity with the necessaries and comforts of life. Added to this, almost every body seemed to be at work, but noiselessly so, compared with what I had been accustomed to in Baltimore. There were no loud songs heard from those engaged in loading and unloading ships. I heard no deep oaths or horrid curses on the laborer. I saw no whipping of men; but all seemed to go smoothly on. Every man appeared to understand his work, and went at it with a sober, yet cheerful earnestness, which betokened the deep interest which he felt in what he was doing, as well as a sense of his own dignity as man. To me this looked exceedingly strange. From the wharves I strolled around and over the town, gazing with wonder and admiration at the splendid churches, beautiful dwellings, and finely-cultivated gardens; evincing an amount of wealth, comfort, taste, and refinement, such as I had never seen in any part of slaveholding Maryland.

[38]A central character in Sir Walter Scott's poem *Lady of the Lake.*

Every thing looked clean, new, and beautiful. I saw few or no dilapidated houses, with poverty-stricken inmates; no half-naked children and barefooted women, such as I had been accustomed to see in Hillsborough, Easton, St. Michael's, and Baltimore. The people looked more able, stronger, healthier, and happier, than those of Maryland. I was for once made glad by a view of extreme wealth, without being saddened by seeing extreme poverty. But the most astonishing as well as the most interesting thing to me was the condition of the colored people, a great many of whom, like myself, had escaped thither as a refuge from the hunters of men. I found many, who had not been seven years out of their chains, living in finer houses, and evidently enjoying more of the comforts of life, than the average of slaveholders in Maryland. I will venture to assert, that my friend Mr. Nathan Johnson (of whom I can say with a grateful heart, "I was hungry, and he gave me meat; I was thirsty, and he gave me drink; I was a stranger, and he took me in"[39] lived in a neater house; dined at a better table; took, paid for, and read, more newspapers; better understood the moral, religious, and political character of the nation,—than nine tenths of the slaveholders in Talbot county Maryland. Yet Mr. Johnson was a working man. His hands were hardened by toil, and not his alone, but those also of Mrs. Johnson. I found the colored people much more spirited than I had supposed they would be. I found among them a determination to protect each other from the blood-thirsty kidnapper, at all hazards. Soon after my arrival, I was told a circumstance which illustrated their spirit. A colored man and a fugitive slave were on unfriendly terms. The former was heard to threaten the latter with informing his master of his whereabouts. Straightway a meeting was called among the colored people, under the stereotyped notice, "Business of importance!" The betrayer was invited to attend. The people came at the appointed hour, and organized the meeting by appointing a very religious old gentleman as president, who, I believe, made a prayer, after which he addressed the meeting as follows: *"Friends, we have got him here, and I would recommend that you young men just take him outside the door, and kill him!"* With this, a number of them bolted at him; but they were intercepted by some more timid than themselves, and the betrayer escaped their vengeance, and has not been seen in New Bedford since. I believe there have been no more such threats, and should there be hereafter, I doubt not that death would be the consequence.

I found employment, the third day after my arrival, in stowing a sloop with a load of oil. It was new, dirty, and hard work for me; but I went at it with a glad heart and a willing hand. I was now my own master. It was a happy moment, the rapture of which can be understood only by those who have been slaves. It was the first work, the reward of which was to be entirely my own. There was no Master Hugh standing ready, the moment I earned the money, to rob me of it. I worked that day with a pleasure I had never before experienced. I was at work for myself and newly-married wife. It was to me the starting-point of a new existence. When I got through with that job, I went in pursuit of a job of calking; but such was the strength of prejudice against color, among the white calkers, that they refused to work with me, and of course I could get no employment.[40] Finding my trade of no immediate benefit, I threw off my calking habiliments, and prepared myself to do any kind of work I

[39]Matthew 25:35.

[40]I am told that colored persons can now get employment at calking in New Bedford—a result of anti-slavery effort. [Douglass's note.]

could get to do. Mr. Johnson kindly let me have his wood-horse and saw, and I very soon found myself, a plenty of work. There was no work too hard—none too dirty. I was ready to saw wood, shovel coal, carry wood, sweep the chimney, or roll oil casks,—all of which I did for nearly three years in New Bedford, before I became known to the anti-slavery world.

In about four months after I went to New Bedford, there came a young man to me, and inquired if I did not wish to take the "Liberator."[41] I told him I did; but, just having made my escape from slavery, I remarked that I was unable to pay for it then. I, however, finally became a subscriber to it. The paper came, and I read it from week to week with such feelings as it would be quite idle for me to attempt to describe. The paper became my meat and my drink. My soul was set all on fire. Its sympathy for my brethren in bonds—its scathing denunciations of slaveholders—its faithful exposures of slavery—and its powerful attacks upon the upholders of the institution—sent a thrill of joy through my soul, such as I had never felt before!

I had not long been a reader of the "Liberator," before I got a pretty correct idea of the principles, measures and spirit of the anti-slavery reform. I took right hold of the cause. I could do but little; but what I could, I did with a joyful heart, and never felt happier than when in an anti-slavery meeting. I seldom had much to say at the meetings, because what I wanted to say was said so much better by others. But, while attending an anti-slavery convention at Nantucket, on the 11th of August, 1841, I felt strongly moved to speak, and was at the same time much urged to do so by Mr. William C. Coffin, a gentleman who had heard me speak in the colored people's meeting at New Bedford. It was a severe cross, and I took it up reluctantly. The truth was, I felt myself a slave, and the idea of speaking to white people weighed me down. I spoke but a few moments, when I felt a degree of freedom, and said what I desired with considerable ease. From that time until now, I have been engaged in pleading the cause of my brethren—with what success, and with what devotion, I leave those acquainted with my labors to decide.

Appendix

I find, since reading over the foregoing Narrative, that I have, in several instances, spoken in such a tone and manner, respecting religion, as may possibly lead those unacquainted with my religious views to suppose me an opponent of all religion. To remove the liability of such misapprehension, I deem it proper to append the following brief explanation. What I have said respecting and against religion, I mean strictly to apply to the *slaveholding religion* of this land, and with no possible reference to Christianity proper; for, between the Christianity of this land, and the Christianity of Christ, I recognize the widest possible difference—so wide, that to receive the one as good, pure, and holy, is of necessity to reject the other as bad, corrupt, and wicked. To be the friend of the one, is of necessity to be the enemy of the other. I love the pure, peaceable, and impartial Christianity of Christ: I therefore hate the corrupt,

[41]See headnote to William Lloyd Garrison, elsewhere in this volume. As this episode indicates, many of the newspaper's readers were black.

slaveholding, women-whipping, cradle-plundering, partial and hypocritical Christianity of this land. Indeed, I can see no reason, but the most deceitful one, for calling the religion of this land Christianity. I look upon it as the climax of all misnomers, the boldest of all frauds, and the grossest of all libels. Never was there a clearer case of "stealing the livery of the court of heaven to serve the devil in." I am filled with unutterable loathing when I contemplate the religious pomp and show, together with the horrible inconsistencies, which every where surrounded me. We have men-stealers for ministers, women-whippers for missionaries, and cradle-plunderers for church members. The man who wields the blood-clotted cowskin during the week fills the pulpit on Sunday, and claims to be a minister of the meek and lowly Jesus. The man who robs me of my earnings at the end of each week meets me as a class-leader on Sunday morning, to show me the way of life, and the path of salvation. He who sells my sister, for purposes of prostitution, stands forth as the pious advocate of purity. He who proclaims it a religious duty to read the Bible denies me the right of learning to read the name of the God who made me. He who is the religious advocate of marriage robs whole millions of its sacred influence, and leaves them to the ravages of wholesale pollution. The warm defender of the sacredness of the family relation is the same that scatters whole families,—sundering husbands and wives, parents and children, sisters and brothers,—leaving the hut vacant, and the hearth desolate. We see the thief preaching against theft, and the adulterer against adultery. We have men sold to build churches, women sold to support the gospel, and babes sold to purchase Bibles for the *poor heathen! all for the glory of God and the good of souls!* The slave auctioneer's bell and the church-going bell chime in with each other, and the bitter cries of the heart-broken slave are drowned in the religious shouts of his pious master. Revivals of religion and revivals in the slave-trade go hand in hand together. The slave prison and the church stand near each other. The clanking of fetters and the rattling of chains in the prison, and the pious psalm and solemn prayer in the church, may be heard at the same time. The dealers in the bodies and souls of men erect their stand in the presence of the pulpit, and they mutually help each other. The dealer gives his blood-stained gold to support the pulpit, and the pulpit, in return, covers his infernal business with the garb of Christianity. Here we have religion and robbery the allies of each other—devils dressed in angels' robes, and hell presenting the semblance of paradise.

"Just God! and these are they,
Who minister at thine altar, God of right!
Men who their hands, with prayer and blessing, lay
On Israel's ark of light.[42]

"What! preach, and kidnap men?
Give thanks, and rob thy own afflicted poor?
Talk of thy glorious liberty, and then
Bolt hard the captive's door?

[42]The ark of the covenant, which, in a synagogue, contains the Torah or holy scripture.

"What! servants of thy own
Merciful Son, who came to seek and save
The homeless and the outcast, fettering down
The tasked and plundered slave!

"Pilate and Herod friends[43]
Chief priests and rulers, as of old, combine!
Just God and holy! is that church which lends
Strength to the spoiler thine?"[44]

The Christianity of America is a Christianity, of whose votaries it may be as truly said, as it was of the ancient scribes and Pharisees,[45] "They bind heavy burdens, and grievous to be borne, and lay them on men's shoulders, but they themselves will not move them with one of their fingers. All their works they do for to be seen of men.—They love the uppermost rooms at feasts, and the chief seats in the synagogues, ... and to be called of men, Rabbi, Rabbi.—But woe unto you, scribes and Pharisees, hypocrites! for ye shut up the kingdom of heaven against men; for ye neither go in yourselves, neither suffer ye them that are entering to go in. Ye devour widows' houses, and for a pretence make long prayers; therefore ye shall receive the greater damnation. Ye compass sea and land to make one proselyte, and when he is made, ye make him twofold more the child of hell than yourselves.—Woe unto you, scribes and Pharisees, hypocrites! for ye pay tithe of mint, and anise, and cumin, and have omitted the weightier matters of the law, judgment, mercy, and faith; these ought ye to have done, and not to leave the other undone. Ye blind guides! which strain at a gnat, and swallow a camel. Woe unto you, scribes and Pharisees, hypocrites! for ye make clean the outside of the cup and of the platter; but within, they are full of extortion and excess.—Woe unto you, scribes and Pharisees, hypocrites! for ye are like unto whited sepulchres, which indeed appear beautiful outward, but are within full of dead men's bones, and of all uncleanness. Even so ye also outwardly appear righteous unto men, but within ye are full of hypocrisy and iniquity."[46]

Dark and terrible as is this picture, I hold it to be strictly true of the overwhelming mass of professed Christians in America. They strain at a gnat, and swallow a camel. Could any thing be more true of our churches? They would be shocked at the proposition of fellowshipping a *sheep*-stealer; and at the same time they hug to their communion a *man*-stealer, and brand me with being an infidel, if I find fault with them for it. They attend with Pharisaical strictness to the outward forms of religion, and at the same time neglect the weightier matters of the law, judgment, mercy, and faith. They are always ready to sacrifice, but seldom to show mercy. They are they who are represented as professing to love God whom they have not seen, whilst they hate their brother whom they have seen. They love the heathen on the other side of the globe. They can pray for him, pay money to have the Bible put into

[43]Pontius Pilate, Roman official who condemned Jesus Christ; Herod Antipater, tetrarch of Galilee, presented the head of John the Baptist on a platter to his stepdaughter, Salome.

[44]From J.G. Whitter's poem "Clerical Oppressors."

[45]The scribes were Jewish scholars and biblical interpreters often historically at odds with those, like Jesus, asserting prophetic authority; the Pharisees were a school of ascetics who came to look at themselves as better than other men.

[46]See Matthew 23.

his hand, and missionaries to instruct him; while they despise and totally neglect the heathen at their own doors.

Such is, very briefly, my view of the religion of this land; and to avoid any misunderstanding, growing out of the use of general terms, I mean, by the religion of this land, that which is revealed in the words, deeds, and actions, of those bodies, north and south, calling themselves Christian churches, and yet in union with slaveholders. It is against religion, as presented by these bodies, that I have felt it my duty to testify.

I conclude these remarks by copying the following portrait of the religion of the south, (which is, by communion and fellowship, the religion of the north,) which I soberly affirm is "true to the life," and without caricature or the slightest exaggeration. It is said to have been drawn, several years before the present anti-slavery agitation began, by a northern Methodist preacher, who, while residing at the south, had an opportunity to see slaveholding morals, manners, and piety, with his own eyes. "Shall I not visit for these things? saith the Lord. Shall not my soul be avenged on such a nation as this?"[47]

A PARODY[48]

"Come, saints and sinners, hear me tell
How pious priests whip Jack and Nell,
And women buy and children sell,
And preach all sinners down to hell,
And sing of heavenly union.

"They'll bleat and baa, dona like goats,
Gorge down black sheep, and strain at motes,
Array their backs in fine black coats,
Then seize their negroes by their throats,
And choke, for heavenly union.

"They'll church you if you sip a dram,
And damn you if you steal a lamb;
Yet rob old Tony, Doll, and Sam,
Of human rights, and bread and ham;
Kidnapper's heavenly union.

"They'll loudly talk of Christ's reward,
And bind his image with a cord
And scold, and swing the lash abhorred,
And sell their brother in the Lord
To handcuffed heavenly union.

"They'll read and sing a sacred song,
And make a prayer both loud and long,

[47]Jeremiah 5:9.

[48]In the poem, Douglass is parodying "Heavenly Union," a hymn popular in Southern churches at the time.

And teach the right and do the wrong,
Hailing the brother, sister throng,
  With words of heavenly union.

"We wonder how such saints can sing,
Or praise the Lord upon the wing,
Who roar, and scold, and whip, and sting,
And to their slaves and mammon cling,
  In guilty conscience union.

"They'll raise tobacco, corn, and rye,
And drive, and thieve, and cheat, and lie,
And lay up treasures in the sky,
By making switch and cowskin fly,
  In hope of heavenly union.

"They'll crack old Tony on the skull,
And preach and roar like Bashan bull,[49]
Or braying ass, of mischief full,
Then seize old Jacob by the wool,
  And pull for heavenly union.

"A roaring, ranting, sleek man-thief,
Who lived on mutton, veal, and beef,
Yet never would afford relief
To needy, sable sons of grief,
  Was big with heavenly union.

" 'Love not the world,' the preacher said,
And winked his eye, and shook his head;
He seized on Tom, and Dick, and Ned,
Cut short their meat, and clothes, and bread,
  Yet still loved heavenly union.

"Another preacher whining spoke
Of One whose heart for sinners broke:
He tied old Nanny to an oak,
And drew the blood at every stroke,
  And prayed for heavenly union.

"Two others oped their iron jaws,
And waved their children-stealing paws;
There sat their children in gewgaws;
By stinting negroes' backs and maws,
  They kept up heavenly union.

[49]In the Old Testament, proverbially powerful.

"All good from Jack another takes,
And entertains their flirts and rakes,
Who dress as sleek as glossy snakes,
And cram their mouths with sweetened cakes;
And this goes down for union."

Sincerely and earnestly hoping that this little book may do something toward throwing light on the American slave system, and hastening the glad day of deliverance to the millions of my brethren in bonds—faithfully relying upon the power of truth, love, and justice, for success in my humble efforts—and solemnly pledging my self anew to the sacred cause,—I subscribe myself,

FREDERICK DOUGLASS
Lynn, Mass., April 28, 1845.

What to the Slave Is the Fourth of July?

An Address Delivered in Rochester, New York, on 5 July 1852[1]

Mr. President, Friends and Fellow Citizens: He who could address this audience without a quailing sensation, has stronger nerves than I have. I do not remember ever to have appeared as a speaker before any assembly more shrinkingly, nor with greater distrust of my ability, than I do this day. A feeling has crept over me, quite unfavorable to the exercise of my limited powers of speech. The task before me is one which requires much previous thought and study for its proper performance. I know that apologies of this sort are generally considered flat and unmeaning. I trust, however, that mine will not be so considered. Should I seem at ease, my appearance would much misrepresent me. The little experience I have had in addressing public meetings, in country school houses, avails me nothing on the present occasion.

The papers and placards say, that I am to deliver a 4th of July oration. This certainly sounds large, and out of the common way, for me. It is true that I have often had the privilege to speak in this beautiful Hall, and to address many who now honor me with their presence. But neither their familiar faces, nor the perfect gage I think I have of Corinthian Hall, seems to free me from embarrassment.

The fact is, ladies and gentlemen, the distance between this platform and the slave plantation, from which I escaped, is considerable—and the difficulties to be overcome in getting from the latter to the former, are by no means slight. That I am here to-day is, to me, a matter of astonishment as well as of gratitude. You will not,

[1]The speech was delivered on July 5, 1852, at Corinthian Hall in Rochester, New York. The text is based on that of the pamphlet, published by Lee, Mann and Company, during the same year.

therefore, be surprised, if in what I have to say, I evince no elaborate preparation, nor grace my speech with any high sounding exordium. With little experience and with less learning, I have been able to throw my thoughts hastily and imperfectly together; and trusting to your patient and generous indulgence, I will proceed to lay them before you.

This, for the purpose of this celebration, is the 4th of July. It is the birthday of your National Independence, and of your political freedom. This, to you, is what the Passover was to the emancipated people of God. It carries your minds back to the day, and to the act of your great deliverance; and to the signs, and to the wonders, associated with that act, and that day. This celebration also marks the beginning of another year of your national life; and reminds you that the Republic of America is now 76 years old. I am glad, fellow-citizens, that your nation is so young. Seventy-six years, though a good old age for a man, is but a mere speck in the life of a nation. Three score years and ten is the allotted time for individual men; but nations number their years by thousands. According to this fact, you are, even now, only in the beginning of your national career, still lingering in the period of childhood. I repeat, I am glad this is so. There is hope in the thought, and hope is much needed, under the dark clouds which lower above the horizon. The eye of the reformer is met with angry flashes, portending disastrous times; but his heart may well beat lighter at the thought that America is young, and that she is still in the impressible stage of her existence. May he not hope that high lessons of wisdom, of justice and of truth, will yet give direction to her destiny? Were the nation older, the patriot's heart might be sadder, and the reformer's brow heavier. Its future might be shrouded in gloom, and the hope of its prophets go out in sorrow. There is consolation in the thought that America is young. Great streams are not easily turned from channels, worn deep in the course of ages. They may sometimes rise in quiet and stately majesty, and inundate the land, refreshing and fertilizing the earth with their mysterious properties. They may also rise in wrath and fury, and bear away, on their angry waves, the accumulated wealth of years of toil and hardship. They, however, gradually flow back to the same old channel, and flow on as serenely as ever. But, while the river may not be turned aside, it may dry up, and leave nothing behind but the withered branch, and the unsightly rock, to howl in the abyss-sweeping wind, the sad tale of departed glory. As with rivers so with nations.

Fellow-citizens, I shall not presume to dwell at length on the associations that cluster about this day. The simple story of it is that, 76 years ago, the people of this country were British subjects. The style and title of your "sovereign people" in which you now glory was not then born. You were under the British Crown. Your fathers esteemed the English Government as the home government; and England as the fatherland. This home government, you know, although a considerable distance from your home, did, in the exercise of its parental prerogatives, impose upon its colonial children, such restraints, burdens and limitations, as, in its mature judgement, it deemed wise, right and proper.

But, your fathers, who had not adopted the fashionable idea of this day, of the infallibility of government, and the absolute character of its acts, presumed to differ from the home government in respect to the wisdom and the justice of some of those burdens and restraints. They went so far in their excitement as to pronounce the measures of government unjust, unreasonable, and oppressive, and altogether such as ought not to be quietly submitted to. I scarcely need say, fellow-citizens, that my opinion of those measures fully accords with that of your fathers. Such a declaration of agreement on my part would not be worth much to anybody. It would, certainly, prove nothing, as to what part I might have taken, had I lived during the great controversy of 1776. To say *now* that America was right, and England wrong, is exceedingly easy. Everybody can say it; the dastard, not less than the noble brave, can flippantly discant on the tyranny of England towards the American Colonies. It is fashionable to do so; but there was a time when to pronounce against England, and in favor of the cause of the colonies, tried men's souls.[2] They who did so were accounted in their day, plotters of mischief, agitators and rebels, dangerous men. To side with the right, against the wrong, with the weak against the strong, and with the oppressed against the oppressor! *here* lies the merit, and the one which, of all others, seems unfashionable in our day. The cause of liberty may be stabbed by the men who glory in the deeds of your fathers. But, to proceed.

Feeling themselves harshly and unjustly treated by the home government, your fathers, like men of honesty, and men of spirit, earnestly sought redress. They petitioned and remonstrated; they did so in a decorous, respectful, and loyal manner. Their conduct was wholly unexceptionable. This, however, did not answer the purpose. They saw themselves treated with sovereign indifference, coldness and scorn. Yet they persevered. They were not the men to look back.

As the sheet anchor takes a firmer hold, when the ship is tossed by the storm, so did the cause of your fathers grow stronger, as it breasted the chilling blasts of kingly displeasure. The greatest and best of British statesmen admitted its justice, and the loftiest eloquence of the British Senate came to its support. But, with that blindness which seems to be the unvarying characteristic of tyrants, since Pharoah and his hosts were drowned in the Red Sea, the British Government persisted in the exactions complained of.

The madness of this course, we believe, is admitted now, even by England; but we fear the lesson is wholly lost on our present rulers.

Oppression makes a wise man mad. Your fathers were wise men, and if they did not go mad, they became restive under this treatment. They felt themselves the victims of grievous wrongs, wholly incurable in their colonial capacity. With brave men there is always a remedy for oppression. Just here, the idea of a total separation of the colonies from the crown was born! It was a startling idea, much more so, than we, at this distance of time, regard it. The timid and the prudent (as has been intimated) of that day, were, of course, shocked and alarmed by it.

Such people lived then, had lived before, and will, probably, ever have a place on this planet; and their course, in respect to any great change, (no matter how great the good to be attained, or the wrong to be redressed by it), may be calculated with as much precision as can be the course of the stars. They hate all changes, but silver, gold and copper change! Of this sort of change they are always strongly in favor.

These people were called tories in the days of your fathers; and the appellation, probably, conveyed the same idea that is meant by a more modern, though a

[2]Douglass is paraphrasing the First *Crisis* paper of Thomas Paine; see the earlier section of this volume.

somewhat less euphonious term, which we often find in our papers, applied to some of our old politicians.[3]

Their opposition to the then dangerous thought was earnest and powerful; but, amid all their terror and affrighted vociferations against it, the alarming and revolutionary idea moved on, and the country with it.

On the 2d of July, 1776, the old Continental Congress, to the dismay of the lovers of ease, and the worshippers of property, clothed that dreadful idea with all the authority of national sanction. They did so in the form of a resolution; and as we seldom hit upon resolutions, drawn up in our day, whose transparency is at all equal to this, it may refresh your minds and help my story if I read it.

> *"Resolved, That these united colonies are, and of right, ought to be free and Independent States; that they are absolved from all allegiance to the British Crown; and that all political connection between them and the State of Great Britain is, and ought to be, dissolved."*[4]

Citizens, your fathers made good that resolution. They succeeded; and to-day you reap the fruits of their success. The freedom gained is yours; and you, therefore, may properly celebrate this anniversary. The 4th of July is the first great fact in your nation's history—the very ring-bolt in the chain of your yet undeveloped destiny.

Pride and patriotism, not less than gratitude, prompt you to celebrate and to hold it in perpetual remembrance. I have said that the Declaration of Independence is the RING-BOLT to the chain of your nation's destiny; so, indeed, I regard it. The principles contained in that instrument are saving principles. Stand by those principles, be true to them on all occasions, in all places, against all foes, and at whatever cost.

From the round top of your ship of state, dark and threatening clouds may be seen. Heavy billows, like mountains in the distance, disclose to the leeward huge forms of flinty rocks! That *bolt* drawn, that *chain* broken, and all is lost. *Cling to this day—cling to it,* and to its principles, with the grasp of a storm-tossed mariner to a spar at midnight.

The coming into being of a nation, in any circumstances, is an interesting event. But, besides general considerations, there were peculiar circumstances which make the advent of this republic an event of special attractiveness.

The whole scene, as I look back to it, was simple, dignified and sublime.

The population of the country, at the time, stood at the insignificant number of three millions. The country was poor in the munitions of war. The population was weak and scattered, and the country a wilderness unsubdued. There were then no means of concert and combination, such as exist now. Neither steam nor lightning had then been reduced to order and discipline. From the Potomac to the Delaware was a journey of many days. Under these, and innumerable other disadvantages, your fathers declared for liberty and independence and triumphed.

Fellow Citizens, I am not wanting in respect for the fathers of this republic. The signers of the Declaration of Independence were brave men. They were great men

[3]The term may be "hunker," used to refer to conservative Democrats of the time.

[4]Here, and elsewhere, Douglass quotes from or paraphrases the "Declaration of Independence."

too—great enough to give fame to a great age. It does not often happen to a nation to raise, at one time, such a number of truly great men. The point from which I am compelled to view them is not, certainly, the most favorable; and yet I cannot contemplate their great deeds with less than admiration. They were statesmen, patriots and heroes, and for the good they did, and the principles they contended for, I will unite with you to honor their memory.

They loved their country better than their own private interests; and, though this is not the highest form of human excellence, all will concede that it is a rare virtue, and that when it is exhibited, it ought to command respect. He who will, intelligently, lay down his life for his country, is a man whom it is not in human nature to despise. Your fathers staked their lives, their fortunes, and their sacred honor, on the cause of their country. In their admiration of liberty, they lost sight of all other interests.

They were peace men; but they preferred revolution to peaceful submission to bondage. They were quiet men; but they did not shrink from agitating against oppression. They showed forbearance; but that they knew its limits. They believed in order; but not in the order of tyranny. With them, nothing was "*settled*" that was not right. With them, justice, liberty and humanity were "*final*"; not slavery and oppression. You may well cherish the memory of such men. They were great in their day and generation. Their solid manhood stands out the more as we contrast it with these degenerate times.

How circumspect, exact and proportionate were all their movements! How unlike the politicians of an hour! Their statesmanship looked beyond the passing moment, and stretched away in strength into the distant future. They seized upon eternal principles, and set a glorious example in their defence. Mark them!

Fully appreciating the hardship to be encountered, firmly believing in the right of their cause, honorably inviting the scrutiny of an on-looking world, reverently appealing to heaven to attest their sincerity, soundly comprehending the solemn responsibility they were about to assume, wisely measuring the terrible odds against them, your fathers, the fathers of this republic, did, most deliberately, under the inspiration of a glorious patriotism, and with a sublime faith in the great principles of justice and freedom, lay deep the corner-stone of the national superstructure, which has risen and still rises in grandeur around you.

Of this fundamental work, this day is the anniversary. Our eyes are met with demonstrations of joyous enthusiasm. Banners and pennants wave exultingly on the breeze. The din of business, too, is hushed. Even Mammon seems to have quitted his grasp on this day. The ear-piercing fife and the stirring drum unite their accents with the ascending peal of a thousand church bells. Prayers are made, hymns are sung, and sermons are preached in honor of this day; while the quick martial tramp of a great and multitudinous nation, echoed back by all the hills, valleys and mountains of a vast continent, bespeak the occasion one of thrilling and universal interest—a nation's jubilee.

Friends and citizens, I need not enter further into the causes which led to this anniversary. Many of you understand them better than I do. You could instruct me in regard to them. That is a branch of knowledge in which you feel, perhaps, a much deeper interest than your speaker. The causes which led to the separation of the colonies from the British crown have never lacked for a tongue. They have all been taught in your common schools, narrated at your firesides, unfolded from your pulpits, and thundered from your legislative halls, and are as familiar to you as household words. They form the staple of your national poetry and eloquence.

I remember, also, that, as a people, Americans are remarkably familiar with all facts which make in their own favor. This is esteemed by some as a national trait—perhaps a national weakness. It is a fact, that whatever makes for the wealth or for the reputation of Americans, and can be had *cheap!* will be found by Americans. I shall not be charged with slandering Americans, if I say I think the American side of any question may be safely left in American hands.

I leave, therefore, the great deeds of your fathers to other gentlemen whose claim to have been regularly descended will be less likely to be disputed than mine!

The Present

My business, if I have any here to-day, is with the present. The accepted time with God and his cause is the ever-living now.

"Trust no future, however pleasant,
Let the dead past bury its dead;
Act, act in the living present,
Heart within, and God overhead."[5]

We have to do with the past only as we can make it useful to the present and to the future. To all inspiring motives, to noble deeds which can be gained from the past, we are welcome. But now is the time, the important time. Your fathers have lived, died, and have done their work, and have done much of it well. You live and must die, and you must do your work. You have no right to enjoy a child's share in the labor of your fathers, unless your children are to be blest by your labors. You have no right to wear out and waste the hard-earned fame of your fathers to cover your indolence. Sydney Smith[6] tells us that men seldom eulogize the wisdom and virtues of their fathers, but to excuse some folly or wickedness of their own. This truth is not a doubtful one. There are illustrations of it near and remote, ancient and modern. It was fashionable, hundreds of years ago, for the children of Jacob to boast, we have "Abraham to our father," when they had long lost Abraham's faith and spirit.[7] That people contented themselves under the shadow of Abraham's great name, while they repudiated the deeds which made his name great. Need I remind you that a similar thing is being done all over this country to-day? Need I tell you that the Jews are not the only people who built the tombs of the prophets, and garnished the sepulchers of the righteous? Washington could not die till he had broken the chains of his slaves.[8] Yet his monument is built up by the price of human blood, and the traders in the bodies and souls of men, shout—"We have Washington to *our father.*" Alas! that it should be so; yet so it is.

[5]From Henry Wadsworth Longfellow, "A Psalm of Life."

[6]Anglican essayist and minister (1771–1845), best known in the United States for questioning who, anywhere, "reads an American book."

[7]Luke 3:8.

[8]George Washington's will provided that, at his wife's death, the 300 and more slaves he owned should be freed.

"The evil that men do, lives after them,
The good is oft' interred with their bones."[9]

Fellow-citizens, pardon me, allow me to ask, why am I called upon to speak here to-day? What have I, or those I represent, to do with your national independence? Are the great principles of political freedom and of natural justice, embodied in that Declaration of Independence, extended to us? and am I, therefore, called upon to bring our humble offering to the national altar, and to confess the benefits and express devout gratitude for the blessings resulting from your independence to us?

Would to God, both for your sakes and ours, that an affirmative answer could be truthfully returned to these questions! Then would my task be light, and my burden easy and delightful. For *who* is there so cold, that a nation's sympathy could not warm him? Who so obdurate and dead to the claims of gratitude, that would not thankfully acknowledge such priceless benefits? Who so stolid and selfish, that would not give his voice to swell the hallelujahs of a nation's jubilee, when the chains of servitude had been torn from his limbs? I am not that man. In a case like that, the dumb might eloquently speak, and the "lame man leap as an hart."

But, such is not the state of the case. I say it with a sad sense of the disparity between us. I am not included within the pale of this glorious anniversary! Your high independence only reveals the immeasurable distance between us. The blessings in which you, this day, rejoice, are not enjoyed in common. The rich inheritance of justice, liberty, prosperity and independence, bequeathed by your fathers, is shared by you, not by me. The sunlight that brought life and healing to you, has brought stripes and death to me. This Fourth [of] July is *yours,* not *mine. You* may rejoice, *I* must mourn. To drag a man in fetters into the grand illuminated temple of liberty, and call upon him to join you in joyous anthems, were inhuman mockery and sacrilegious irony. Do you mean, citizens, to mock me, by asking me to speak to-day? If so, there is a parallel to your conduct. And let me warn you that it is dangerous to copy the example of a nation whose crimes, towering up to heaven, were thrown down by the breath of the Almighty, burying that nation in irrecoverable ruin! I can to-day take up the plaintive lament of a peeled and woe-smitten people!

"By the rivers of Babylon, there we sat down. Yea! we wept when we remembered Zion. We hanged our harps upon the willows in the midst thereof. For there, they that carried us away captive, required of us a song; and they who wasted us required of us mirth, saying, Sing us one of the songs of Zion. How can we sing the Lord's song in a strange land? If I forget thee, O Jerusalem, let my right hand forget her cunning. If I do not remember thee, let my tongue cleave to the roof of my mouth."[10]

Fellow-citizens; above your national, tumultous joy, I hear the mournful wail of millions! whose chains, heavy and grievous yesterday, are, to-day, rendered more intolerable by the jubilee shouts that reach them. If I do forget, if I do not faithfully remember those bleeding children of sorrow this day, "may my right hand forget her cunning, and may my tongue cleave to the roof of my mouth!" To forget them, to pass lightly over their wrongs, and to chime in with the popular theme, would be

[9] *Julius Caesar,* III, ii, 76.
[10] Psalm 137:1–6.

treason most scandalous and shocking, and would make me a reproach before God and the world. My subject, then fellow-citizens, is AMERICAN SLAVERY. I shall see, this day, and its popular characteristics, from the slave's point of view. Standing, there, identified with the American bondman, making his wrongs mine, I do not hesitate to declare, with all my soul, that the character and conduct of this nation never looked blacker to me than on this 4th of July! Whether we turn to the declarations of the past, or to the professions of the present, the conduct of the nation seems equally hideous and revolting. America is false to the past, false to the present, and solemnly binds herself to be false to the future. Standing with God and the crushed and bleeding slave on this occasion, I will, in the name of humanity which is outraged, in the name of liberty which is fettered, in the name of the constitution and the Bible, which are disregarded and trampled upon, dare to call in question and to denounce, with all the emphasis I can command, everything that serves to perpetuate slavery—the great sin and shame of America! "I will not equivocate; I will not excuse"[11]; I will use the severest language I can command; and yet not one word shall escape me that any man, whose judgement is not blinded by prejudice, or who is not at heart a slaveholder, shall not confess to be right and just.

But I fancy I hear some one of my audience say, it is just in this circumstance that you and your brother abolitionists fail to make a favorable impression on the public mind. Would you argue more, and denounce less, would you persuade more, and rebuke less, your cause would be much more likely to succeed. But, I submit, where all is plain there is nothing to be argued. What point in the anti-slavery creed would you have me argue? On what branch of the subject do the people of this country need light? Must I undertake to prove that the slave is a man? That point is conceded already. Nobody doubts it. The slaveholders themselves acknowledge it in the enactment of law, for their government. They acknowledge it when they punish disobedience on the part of the slave. There are seventy-two crimes in the State of Virginia, which, if committed by a black man, (no matter how ignorant he be), subject him to the punishment of death; while only two of the same crimes will subject a white man to the like punishment. What is this but the acknowledgement that the slave is a moral, intellectual and responsible being? The manhood of the slave is conceded. It is admitted in the fact that Southern statute books are covered with enactments forbidding, under severe fines and penalties, the teaching of the slave to read or to write. When you can point to any such laws, in reference to the beasts of the field, then I may consent to argue the manhood of the slave. When the dogs in your streets, when the fowls of the air, when the cattle on your hills, when the fish of the sea, and the reptiles that crawl, shall be unable to distinguish the slave from a brute, *then* will I argue with you that the slave is a man!

For the present, it is enough to affirm the equal manhood of the negro race. Is it not astonishing that, while we are ploughing, planting and reaping, using all kinds of mechanical tools, erecting houses, constructing bridges, building ships, working in metals of brass, iron, copper, silver and gold; that, while we are reading, writing and cyphering, acting as clerks, merchants and secretaries, having among us lawyers, doctors, ministers, poets, authors, editors, orators and teachers; that, while we are

[11]Douglass is quoting William Lloyd Garrison's editorial from the first issue of the *Liberator;* see the Garrison selection in this volume for the full text.

engaged in all manner of enterprises common to other man, digging gold in California, capturing the whale in the Pacific, feeding sheep and cattle on the hill-side, living, moving, acting, thinking, planning, living in families as husbands, wives and children, and, above all, confessing and worshipping the Christian's God, and looking hopefully for life and immortality beyond the grave, we are called upon to prove that we are men!

Would you have me argue that man is entitled to liberty? that he is the rightful owner of his own body? You have already declared it. Must I argue the wrongfulness of slavery? Is that a question for Republicans? Is it to be settled by the rules of logic and argumentation, as a matter beset with great difficulty, involving a doubtful application of the principle of justice, hard to be understood? How should I look to-day, in the presence of Americans, dividing, and subdividing a discourse, to show that men have a natural right to freedom? speaking of it relatively, and positively, negatively, and affirmatively. To do so, would be to make myself ridiculous, and to offer an insult to your understanding. There is not a man beneath the canopy of heaven, that does not know that slavery is wrong *for him.*

What, am I to argue that it is wrong to make men brutes, to rob them of their liberty, to work them without wages, to keep them ignorant of their relations to their fellow men, to beat them with sticks, to flay their flesh with the lash, to load their limbs with irons, to hunt them with dogs, to sell them at auction, to sunder their families, to knock out their teeth, to burn their flesh, to starve them into obedience and submission to their masters? Must I argue that a system thus marked with blood, and stained with pollution, is *wrong?* No! I will not. I have better employments for my time and strength, than such arguments would imply.

What, then, remains to be argued? Is it that slavery is not divine; that God did not establish it; that our doctors of divinity are mistaken? There is blasphemy in the thought. That which is inhuman, cannot be divine! *Who* can reason on such a proposition? They that can, may; I cannot. The time for such argument is past.

At a time like this, scorching irony, not convincing argument, is needed. O! had I the ability, and could I reach the nation's ear, I would, to-day, pour out a fiery stream of biting ridicule, blasting reproach, withering sarcasm, and stern rebuke. For it is not light that is needed, but fire; it is not the gentle shower, but thunder. We need the storm, the whirlwind, and the earthquake. The feeling of the nation must be quickened; the conscience of the nation must be roused; the propriety of the nation must be startled; the hypocrisy of the nation must be exposed; and its crimes against God and man must be proclaimed and denounced.

What, to the American slave, is your 4th of July? I answer: a day that reveals to him, more than all other days in the year, the gross injustice and cruelty to which he is the constant victim. To him, your celebration is a sham; your boasted liberty, an unholy license; your national greatness, swelling vanity; your sounds of rejoicing are empty and heartless; your denunciations of tyrants, brass fronted impudence; your shouts of liberty and equality, hollow mockery; your prayers and hymns, your sermons and thanksgivings, with all your religious parade, and solemnity, are, to him, mere bombast, fraud, deception, impiety, and hypocrisy—a thin veil to cover up crimes which would disgrace a nation of savages. There is not a nation on the earth guilty of practices, more shocking and bloody, than are the people of these United States, at this very hour.

Go where you may, search where you will, roam through all the monarchies and despotisms of the old world, travel through South America, search out every abuse, and when you have found the last, lay your facts by the side of the everyday practices of this nation, and you will say with me, that, for revolting barbarity and shameless hypocrisy, America reigns without a rival.

The Internal Slave Trade

Take the American slave-trade, which, we are told by the papers, is especially prosperous just now. Ex-Senator Benton[12] tells us that the price of men was never higher than now. He mentions the fact to show that slavery is in no danger. This trade is one of the peculiarities of American institutions. It is carried on in all the large towns and cities in one-half of this confederacy; and millions are pocketed every year, by dealers in this horrid traffic. In several states, this trade is a chief source of wealth. It is called (in contradistinction to the foreign slave-trade) "*the internal slave-trade.*" It is, probably, called so, too, in order to divert from it the horror with which the foreign slave-trade is contemplated. That trade has long since been denounced by this government, as piracy. It has been denounced with burning words, from the high places of the nation, as an execrable traffic. To arrest it, to put an end to it, this nation keeps a squadron, at immense cost, on the coast of Africa. Everywhere, in this country, it is safe to speak of this foreign slave-trade, as a most inhuman traffic, opposed alike to the laws of God and of man. The duty to extirpate and destroy it, is admitted even by our DOCTORS OF DIVINITY. In order to put an end to it, some of these last have consented that their colored brethren (nominally free) should leave this country, and establish themselves on the western coast of Africa! It is, however, a notable fact that, while so much execration is poured out by Americans upon those engaged in the foreign slave-trade, the men engaged in the slave-trade between the states pass without condemnation, and their business is deemed honorable.

Behold the practical operation of this internal slave-trade, the American slave-trade, sustained by American politics and American religion. Here you will see men and women reared like swine for the market. You know what is a swine-drover? I will show you a man-drover. They inhabit all our Southern States. They perambulate the country, and crowd the highways of the nation, with droves of human stock. You will see one of these human flesh-jobbers, armed with pistol, whip and bowie-knife, driving a company of a hundred men, women, and children, from the Potomac to the slave market at New Orleans. These wretched people are to be sold singly, or in lots, to suit purchasers. They are food for the cotton-field, and the deadly sugar-mill. Mark the sad procession, as it moves wearily along, and the inhuman wretch who drives them. Hear his savage yells and his blood-chilling oaths, as he hurries on his affrighted captives! There, see the old man, with locks thinned and gray. Cast one glance, if you please, upon that young mother, whose shoulders are bare to the scorching sun, her briny tears falling on the brow of the babe in her arms. See, too, that girl of thirteen, weeping, *yes!* weeping, as she thinks of the mother from whom she has been torn! The drove moves tardily. Heat and sorrow have nearly consumed

[12]Thomas Hart Benton (1782–1858), United States Senator from Missouri, 1821–1851.

their strength; suddenly you hear a quick snap, like the discharge of a rifle; the fetters clank, and the chain rattles simultaneously; your ears are saluted with a scream, that seems to have torn its way to the centre of your soul! The crack you heard, was the sound of the slave-whip; the scream you heard, was from the woman you saw with the babe. Her speed had faltered under the weight of her child and her chains! that gash on her shoulder tells her to move on. Follow this drove to New Orleans. Attend the auction; see men examined like horses; see the forms of women rudely and brutally exposed to the shocking gaze of American slave-buyers. See this drove sold and separated forever; and never forget the deep, sad sobs that arose from that scattered multitude. Tell me citizens, WHERE, under the sun, you can witness a spectacle more fiendish and shocking. Yet this is but a glance at the American slave-trade, as it exists, at this moment, in the ruling part of the United States.

I was born amid such sights and scenes. To me the American slave-trade is a terrible reality. When a child, my soul was often pierced with a sense of its horrors. I lived on Philpot Street, Fell's Point, Baltimore, and have watched from the wharves, the slave ships in the Basin, anchored from the shore, with their cargoes of human flesh, waiting for favorable winds to waft them down the Chesapeake. There was, at that time, a grand slave mart kept at the head of Pratt Street, by Austin Woldfolk.[13] His agents were sent into every town and county in Maryland, announcing their arrival, through the papers, and on flaming "*hand-bills,*" headed CASH FOR NEGROES. These men were generally well dressed men, and very captivating in their manners. Ever ready to drink, to treat, and to gamble. The fate of many a slave has depended upon the turn of a single card; and many a child has been snatched from the arms of its mother by bargains arranged in a state of brutal drunkenness.

The flesh-mongers gather up their victims by dozens, and drive them, chained, to the general depot at Baltimore. When a sufficient number have been collected here, a ship is chartered, for the purpose of conveying the forlorn crew to Mobile, or to New Orleans. From the slave prison to the ship, they are usually driven in the darkness of night; for since the anti-slavery agitation, a certain caution is observed.

In the deep still darkness of midnight, I have been often aroused by the dead heavy footsteps, and the piteous cries of the chained gangs that passed our door. The anguish of my boyish heart was intense; and I was often consoled, when speaking to my mistress in the morning, to hear her say that the custom was very wicked; that she hated to hear the rattle of the chains, and the heart-rending cries. I was glad to find one who sympathised with me in my horror.

Fellow-citizens, this murderous traffic is, to-day, in active operation in this boasted republic. In the solitude of my spirit, I see clouds of dust raised on the highways of the South; I see the bleeding footsteps; I hear the doleful wail of fettered humanity, on the way to the slave-markets, where the victims are to be sold like *horses, sheep,* and *swine,* knocked off to the highest bidder. There I see the tenderest ties ruthlessly broken, to gratify the lust, caprice and rapacity of the buyers and sellers of men. My soul sickens at the sight.

[13]Actually Austin Woolfolk, a well-known slave trader in Baltimore, to whom Douglass refers in his 1845 *Narrative.*

"Is this the land your Fathers loved,
The freedom which they toiled to win?
Is this the earth whereon they moved?
Are these the graves they slumber in?[14]

But a still more inhuman, disgraceful, and scandalous state of things remains to be presented.

By an act of the American Congress, not yet two years old, slavery has been nationalized in its most horrible and revolting form. By that act, Mason & Dixon's line has been obliterated; New York has become as Virginia; and the power to hold, hunt, and sell men, women, and children as slaves remains no longer a mere state institution, but is now an institution of the whole United States. The power is co-extensive with the star-spangled banner and American Christianity. Where these go, may also go the merciless slave-hunter. Where these are, man is not sacred. He is a bird for the sportsman's gun. By that most foul and fiendish of all human decrees, the liberty and person of every man are put in peril. Your broad republican domain is hunting ground for *men. Not* for thieves and robbers, enemies of society, merely, but for men guilty of no crime. Your lawmakers have commanded all good citizens to engage in this hellish sport. Your President, your Secretary of State, your *lords, nobles,* and ecclesiastics, enforce, as a duty you owe to your free and glorious country, and to your God, that you do this accursed thing. Not fewer than forty Americans have, within the past two years, been hunted down and, without a moment's warning, hurried away in chains, and consigned to slavery and excruciating torture. Some of these have had wives and children, dependent on them for bread; but of this, no account was made. The right of the hunter to his prey stands superior to the right of marriage, and to *all* rights in this republic, the rights of God included! For black men there are neither law, justice, humanity, nor religion. The Fugitive Slave *Law* makes MERCY TO THEM, A CRIME; and bribes the judge who tries them. An American JUDGE GETS TEN DOLLARS FOR EVERY VICTIM HE CONSIGNS to slavery, and five, when he fails to do so. The oath of any two villains is sufficient, under this hell-black enactment, to send the most pious and exemplary black man into the remorseless jaws of slavery! His own testimony is nothing. He can bring no witnesses for himself. The minister of American justice is bound by the law to hear but *one* side; and *that* side, is the side of the oppressor. Let this damning fact be perpetually told. Let it be thundered around the world, that, in tyrant-killing, king-hating, people-loving, democratic, Christian America, the seats of justice are filled with judges, who hold their offices under an open and palpable *bribe,* and are bound, in deciding in the case of a man's liberty, *to hear only his accusers!*[15]

In glaring violation of justice, in shameless disregard of the forms of administering law, in cunning arrangement to entrap the defenceless, and in diabolical intent, this Fugitive Slave Law stands alone in the annals of tyrannical legislation. I doubt if there be another nation on the globe, having the brass and the baseness to put such a law on the statute-book. If any man in this assembly thinks differently from me in

[14]Douglass changes slightly the first four lines of John Greenleaf Whittier's "Stanzas for the Times."

[15]The Fugitive Slave Act of 1850 did, in fact, provide that the testimony of the alleged fugitive would not "be admitted in evidence"; nor could the person call witnesses.

this matter, and feels able to disprove my statements, I will gladly confront him at any suitable time and place he may select.

Religious Liberty

I take this law to be one of the grossest infringements of Christian Liberty, and, if the churches and ministers of our country were not stupidly blind, or most wickedly indifferent, they, too, would so regard it.

At the very moment that they are thanking God for the enjoyment of civil and religious liberty, and for the right to worship God according to the dictates of their own consciences, they are utterly silent in respect to a law which robs religion of its chief significance, and makes it utterly worthless to a world lying in wickedness. Did this law concern the "*mint, anise* and *cummin*"[16]—abridge the right to sing psalms, to partake of the sacrament, or to engage in any of the ceremonies of religion, it would be smitten by the thunder of a thousand pulpits. A general shout would go up from the church, demanding *repeal, repeal, instant repeal!* And it would go hard with that politician who presumed to solicit the votes of the people without inscribing this motto on his banner. Further, if this demand were not complied with, another Scotland would be added to the history of religious liberty, and the stern old Covenanters would be thrown into the shade. A John Knox[17] would be seen at every church door, and heard from every pulpit, and Fillmore[18] would have no more quarter than was shown by Knox, to the beautiful, but treacherous Queen Mary of Scotland. The fact that the church of our country, (with fractional exceptions), does not esteem "the Fugitive Slave Law" as a declaration of war against religious liberty, implies that that church regards religion simply as a form of worship, an empty ceremony, and *not* a vital principle, requiring active benevolence, justice, love and good will towards man. It esteems sacrifice above mercy; psalm-singing above right doing; solemn meetings above practical righteousness. A worship that can be conducted by persons who refuse to give shelter to the houseless, to give bread to the hungry, clothing to the naked, and who enjoin obedience to a law forbidding these acts of mercy, is a curse, not a blessing to mankind. The Bible addresses all such persons as "scribes, pharisees, hypocrites, who pay tithe of *mint, anise,* and *cummin,* and have omitted the weightier matters of the law, judgement, mercy and faith."

The Church Responsible

But the church of this country is not only indifferent to the wrongs of the slave, it actually takes sides with the oppressors. It has made itself the bulwark of American slavery, and the shield of American slave-hunters. Many of its most eloquent Divines, who stand as the very lights of the church, have shamelessly given the sanction of religion and the Bible to the whole slave system. They have taught that man may, properly, be a slave; that the relation of master and slave is ordained of God; that to send back an escaped bondman to his master is clearly the duty of all the followers of the

[16]See Matthew 23:23. Douglass quotes the full passage at the end of the paragraph.

[17]Scottish religious reformer (1505–1572), who frequently denounced Mary Queen of Scots as "Jezebel."

[18]President Millard Fillmore.

Lord Jesus Christ; and this horrible blasphemy is palmed off upon the world for Christianity.

For my part, I would say, welcome infidelity! welcome atheism! welcome anything! in preference to the gospel, *as preached by those Divines!* They convert the very name of religion into an engine of tyranny, and barbarous cruelty, and serve to confirm more infidels, in this age, than all the infidel writings of Thomas Paine, Voltaire, and Bolingbroke,[19] put together, have done! These ministers make religion a cold and flinty-hearted thing, having neither principles of right action, nor bowels of compassion. They strip the love of God of its beauty, and leave the throne of religion a huge, horrible, repulsive form. It is a religion for oppressors, tyrants, man-stealers, and *thugs.* It is not that "*pure and undefiled religion*" which is from above, and which is "*first pure, then peaceable, easy to be entreated,* full of mercy and good fruits, *without partiality, and without hypocrisy.*"[20] But a religion which favors the rich against the poor; which exalts the proud above the humble; which divides mankind into two classes, tyrants and slaves; which says to the man in chains, *stay there;* and to the oppressor, *oppress on;* it is a religion which may be professed and enjoyed by all the robbers and enslavers of mankind; it makes God a respecter of persons, denies his fatherhood of the race, and tramples in the dust the great truth of the brotherhood of man. All this we affirm to be true of the popular church, and the popular worship of our land and nation—a religion, a church, and a worship which, on the authority of inspired wisdom, we pronounce to be an abomination in the sight of God. In the language of Isaiah, the American church might be well addressed, "Bring no more vain oblations; incense is an abomination unto me: the new moons and Sabbaths, the calling of assemblies, I cannot away with; it is iniquity, even the solemn meeting. Your new moons and your appointed feasts my soul hateth. They are a trouble to me; I am weary to bear them; and when ye spread forth your hands I will hide mine eyes from you. Yea! when ye make many prayers, I will not hear. YOUR HANDS ARE FULL OF BLOOD; cease to do evil, learn to do well; seek judgement; relieve the oppressed; judge for the fatherless; plead for the widow."[21]

The American church is guilty, when viewed in connection with what it is doing to uphold slavery; but it is superlatively guilty when viewed in connection with its ability to abolish slavery.

The sin of which it is guilty is one of omission as well as of commission. Albert Barnes but uttered what the common sense of every man at all observant of the actual state of the case will receive as truth, when he declared that "There is no power out of the church that could sustain slavery an hour, if it were not sustained in it."[22]

Let the religious press, the pulpit, the Sunday school, the conference meeting, the great ecclesiastical, missionary, Bible and tract associations of the land array their immense powers against slavery and slave-holding; and the whole system of crime

[19]For Thomas Paine, see the selection elsewhere in this volume. Voltaire, the pseudonym of French satirist and playwright François Marie Arouet (1694–1778), and Henry St. John, Viscount Bolingbroke (1678–1751) were, like Paine, notorious in the 18th and 19th centuries for their unorthodox ideas especially with respect to religion.

[20]James 1:27.

[21]Isaiah 1:13–17.

[22]Douglass is quoting from *An Inquiry Into the Scriptural Views of Slavery* (1846) by Albert Barnes, a Philadelphia minister.

and blood would be scattered to the winds; and that they do not do this involves them in the most awful responsibility of which the mind can conceive.

In prosecuting the anti-slavery enterprise, we have been asked to spare the church, to spare the ministry; but *how,* we ask, could such a thing be done? We are met on the threshold of our efforts for the redemption of the slave, by the church and ministry of the country, in battle arrayed against us; and we are compelled to fight or flee. From what *quarter,* I beg to know, has proceeded a fire so deadly upon our ranks, during the last two years, as from the Northern pulpit? As the champions of oppressors, the chosen men of American theology have appeared—men, honored for their so-called piety, and their real learning. The LORDS of Buffalo, the SPRINGS of New York, the LATHROPS of Auburn, the COXES and SPENCERS of Brooklyn, the GANNETS and SHARPS of Boston, the DEWEYS of Washington,[23] and other great religious lights of the land, have, in utter denial of the authority of *Him,* by whom they professed to be called to the ministry, deliberately taught us, against the example of the Hebrews and against the remonstrance of the Apostles, they teach "*that we ought to obey man's law before the law of God.*"

My spirit wearies of such blasphemy; and how such men can be supported, as the "standing types and representatives of Jesus Christ," is a mystery which I leave others to penetrate. In speaking of the American church, however, let it be distinctly understood that I mean the *great mass* of the religious organizations of our land. There are exceptions, and I thank God that there are. Noble men may be found, scattered all over these Northern States, of whom Henry Ward Beecher[24] of Brooklyn, Samuel J. May of Syracuse, and my esteemed friend[25] on the platform, are shining examples; and let me say further, that upon these men lies the duty to inspire our ranks with high religious faith and zeal, and to cheer us on in the great mission of the slave's redemption from his chains.

Religion in England and Religion in America

One is struck with the difference between the attitude of the American church towards the anti-slavery movement, and that occupied by the churches in England towards a similar movement in that country. There, the church, true to its mission of ameliorating, elevating, and improving the condition of mankind, came forward promptly, bound up the wounds of the West Indian slave, and restored him to his liberty. There, the question of emancipation was a high[ly] religious question. It was demanded, in the name of humanity, and according to the law of the living God. The Sharps, the Clarksons, the Wilberforces, the Buxtons, and the Burchells and the Knibbs,[26] were alike famous for their piety, and for their philanthropy. The

[23]Respectively John Chase Lord, Gardiner Spring, Leonard Elijah Lathrop, Samuel Hanson Cox, Ichabod Smith Spencer, Ezra Stiles Gannett, Daniel Sharp, and Orville Dewey. These men did not necessarily approve of slavery but they did counsel obedience to the Fugitive Slave Act and generally opposed the call of abolitionists like Douglass and Garrison for "immediate emancipation."

[24]Henry Ward Beecher, brother of Harriet Beecher Stowe.

[25]The Rev. Robert R. Raymond, who had read the Declaration of Independence as part of the ceremony.

[26]Respectively, Granville Sharp, Thomas Clarkson, William Wilberforce, Thomas Fowell Buxton, Thomas Burchell, and William Knibb, leaders among Christians opposing slavery and the slave trade in Britain and its colonies.

anti-slavery movement *there* was not an anti-church movement, for the reason that the church took its full share in prosecuting that movement: and the anti-slavery movement in this country will cease to be an anti-church movement, when the church of this country shall assume a favorable, instead of a hostile position towards that movement.

Americans! your republican politics, not less than your republican religion, are flagrantly inconsistent. You boast of your love of liberty, your superior civilization, and your pure Christianity, while the whole political power of the nation (as embodied in the two great political parties), is solemnly pledged to support and perpetuate the enslavement of three millions of your countrymen. You hurl your anathemas at the crowned headed tyrants of Russia and Austria, and pride yourselves on your Democratic institutions, while you yourselves consent to be the mere *tools* and *body-guards* of the tyrants of Virginia and Carolina. You invite to your shores fugitives of oppression from abroad, honor them with banquets, greet them with ovations, cheer them, toast them, salute them, protect them, and pour out your money to them like water; but the fugitives from your own land you advertise, hunt, arrest, shoot and kill. You glory in your refinement and your universal education; yet you maintain a system as barbarous and dreadful as ever stained the character of a nation—a system begun in avarice, supported in pride, and perpetuated in cruelty. You shed tears over fallen Hungary, and make the sad story of her wrongs the theme of your poets, statesmen and orators, till your gallant sons are ready to fly to arms to vindicate her cause against her oppressors;[27] but, in regard to the ten thousand wrongs of the American slave, you would enforce the strictest silence, and would hail him as an enemy of the nation who dares to make those wrongs the subject of public discourse! You are all on fire at the mention of liberty for France or for Ireland; but are as cold as an iceberg at the thought of liberty for the enslaved of America. You discourse eloquently on the dignity of labor; yet, you sustain a system which, in its very essence, casts a stigma upon labor. You can bare your bosom to the storm of British artillery to throw off a threepenny tax on tea; and yet wring the last hard-earned farthing from the grasp of the black laborers of your country. You profess to believe "that, of one blood, God made all nations of men to dwell on the face of all the earth,"[28] and hath commanded all men, everywhere to love one another; yet you notoriously hate, (and glory in your hatred), all men whose skins are not colored like your own. You declare, before the world, and are understood by the world to declare, that you "*hold these truths to be self evident, that all men are created equal; and are endowed by their Creator with certain inalienable rights; and that, among these are, life, liberty, and the pursuit of happiness;*" and yet, you hold securely, in a bondage which, according to your own Thomas Jefferson, "*is worse than ages of that which your fathers rose in rebellion to oppose," a seventh part* of the inhabitants of your country.

Fellow-citizens! I will not enlarge further on your national inconsistencies. The existence of slavery in this country brands your republicanism as a sham, your humanity as a base pretence, and your Christianity as a lie. It destroys your moral power abroad; it corrupts your politicians at home. It saps the foundation of religion; it makes your name a hissing, and a byword to a mocking earth. It is the antagonistic

[27]Hungary had been invaded and its republican government crushed in 1849 by troops from Russia and Austria.

[28]See Acts 17:26.

force in your government, the only thing that seriously disturbs and endangers your *Union.* It fetters your progress; it is the enemy of improvement, the deadly foe of education; it fosters pride; it breeds insolence; it promotes vice; it shelters crime; it is a curse to the earth that supports it; and yet, you cling to it, as if it were the sheet anchor of all your hopes. Oh! be warned! be warned! a horrible reptile is coiled up in your nation's bosom; the venomous creature is nursing at the tender breast of your youthful republic; *for the love of God, tear away,* and fling from you the hideous monster, and *let the weight of twenty millions crush and destroy it forever!*

The Constitution

But it is answered in reply to all this, that precisely what I have now denounced is, in fact, guaranteed and sanctioned by the Constitution of the United States; that the right to hold and to hunt slaves is a part of that Constitution framed by the illustrious Fathers of this Republic.

Then, I dare to affirm, notwithstanding all I have said before, your fathers stooped, basely stooped

> "To palter with us in a double sense:
> And keep the word of promise to the ear,
> But break it to the heart."[29]

And instead of being the honest men I have before declared them to be, they were the veriest imposters that ever practised on mankind. *This* is the inevitable conclusion, and from it there is no escape. But I differ from those who charge this baseness on the framers of the Constitution of the United States. *It is a slander upon their memory,* at least, so I believe. There is not time now to argue the constitutional question at length; nor have I the ability to discuss it as it ought to be discussed. The subject has been handled with masterly power by Lysander Spooner, Esq., by William Goodell, by Samuel E. Sewall, Esq., and last, though not least, by Gerritt Smith, Esq.[30] These gentlemen have, as I think, fully and clearly vindicated the Constitution from any design to support slavery for an hour.

Fellow-citizens! there is no matter in respect to which, the people of the North have allowed themselves to be so ruinously imposed upon, as that of the pro-slavery character of the Constitution. In *that* instrument I hold there is neither warrant, license, nor sanction of the hateful thing; but, interpreted as it *ought* to be interpreted, the Constitution is a GLORIOUS LIBERTY DOCUMENT. Read its preamble, consider its purposes. Is slavery among them? Is it at the gateway? or is it in the temple? It is neither. While I do not intend to argue this question on the present occasion, let me ask, if it be not somewhat singular that, if the Constitution were intended to be, by its framers and adopters, a slave-holding instrument, why neither *slavery, slaveholding,* nor *slave* can anywhere be found in it. What would be thought of an instrument,

[29]*Macbeth* V, viii, 20–22.

[30]Lysander Spooner, had published *The Unconstitutionality of Slavery* in 1845; William Goodell, *Views of American Constitutional Law, Its Bearing Upon American Slavery* (1844); Samuel E. Sewell, *Remarks on Slavery in the United States* (1827), was also active as an anti-slavery lawyer and politician in Massachusetts; Gerrit Smith wrote frequently on the subject.

drawn up, *legally* drawn up, for the purpose of entitling the city of Rochester to a track of land, in which no mention of land was made? Now, there are certain rules of interpretation, for the proper understanding of all legal instruments. These rules are well established. They are plain, common-sense rules, such as you and I, and all of us, can understand and apply, without having passed years in the study of law. I scout the idea that the question of the constitutionality or unconstitutionality of slavery is not a question for the people. I hold that every American citizen has a right to form an opinion of the constitution, and to propagate that opinion, and to use all honorable means to make his opinion the prevailing one. Without this right, the liberty of an American citizen would be as insecure as that of a Frenchman. Ex-Vice-President Dallas[31] tells us that the constitution is an object to which no American mind can be too attentive, and no American heart too devoted. He further says, the constitution, in its words, is plain and intelligible, and is meant for the home-bred, unsophisticated understandings of our fellow-citizens. Senator Berrien[32] tells us that the Constitution is the fundamental law, that which controls all others. The charter of our liberties, which every citizen has a personal interest in understanding thoroughly. The testimony of Senator Breese, Lewis Cass,[33] and many others that might be named, who are everywhere esteemed as sound lawyers, so regard the constitution. I take it, therefore, that it is not presumption in a private citizen to form an opinion of that instrument.

Now, take the constitution according to its plain reading, and I defy the presentation of a single pro-slavery clause in it. On the other hand it will be found to contain principles and purposes, entirely hostile to the existence of slavery.

I have detained my audience entirely too long already. At some future period I will gladly avail myself of an opportunity to give this subject a full and fair discussion.

Allow me to say, in conclusion, notwithstanding the dark picture I have this day presented of the state of the nation, I do not despair of this country. There are forces in operation, which must inevitably work the downfall of slavery. "*The arm of the Lord is not shortened,*"[34] and the doom of slavery is certain. I, therefore, leave off where I began, with *hope.* While drawing encouragement from the Declaration of Independence, the great principles it contains, and the genius of American Institutions, my spirit is also cheered by the obvious tendencies of the age. Nations do not now stand in the same relation to each other that they did ages ago. No nation can now shut itself up from the surrounding world, and trot round in the same old path of its fathers without interference. The time *was* when such could be done. Long established customs of hurtful character could formerly fence themselves in, and do their evil work with social impunity. Knowledge was then confined and enjoyed by the privileged few, and the multitude walked on in mental darkness. But a change has now come over the affairs of mankind. Walled cities and empires have become

[31]George Mifflin Dallas (1792–1864) had served as vice-president (1845–1849) and was, at the time of this speech an active candidate for the Democratic nomination for President and committed to enforcement of the Fugitive Slave Law.

[32]Georgia Senator John MacPherson Berrien (1781–1856), known as a constitutional lawyer and compromiser on the slavery issue.

[33]Sidney Breese and Lewis Cass were United States senators from Illinois and Michigan respectively.

[34]Paraphrased from Isaiah 59:1.

unfashionable. The arm of commerce has borne away the gates of the strong city. Intelligence is penetrating the darkest corners of the globe. It makes its pathway over and under the sea, as well as on the earth. Wind, steam, and lightning are its chartered agents. Oceans no longer divide, but link nations together. From Boston to London is now a holiday excursion. Space is comparatively annihilated. Thoughts expressed on one side of the Atlantic are distinctly heard on the other.

The far off and almost fabulous Pacific rolls in grandeur at our feet. The Celestial Empire, the mystery of ages, is being solved. The fiat of the Almighty, "*Let there be Light,*" has not yet spent its force. No abuse, no outrage whether in taste, sport or avarice, can now hide itself from the all-pervading light. The iron shoe, and crippled foot of China must be seen, in contrast with nature. *Africa must rise and put on her yet unwoven garment. "Ethiopia shall stretch out her hand unto God."*[35] In the fervent aspirations of William Lloyd Garrison, I say, and let every heart join in saying it:

God speed the year of jubilee
  The wide world o'er!
When from their galling chains set free,
Th' oppress'd shall vilely bend the knee,
And wear the yoke of tyranny
  Like brutes no more.
That year will come, and freedom's reign,
To man his plundered rights again
  Restore.

God speed the day when human blood
  Shall cease to flow!
In every clime be understood,
The claims of human brotherhood,
And each return for evil, good,
  Not blow for blow;
That day will come all feuds to end,
And change into a faithful friend
  Each foe.

God speed the hour, the glorious hour,
  When none on earth
Shall exercise a lordly power,
Nor in a tyrant's presence cower;
But all to manhood's stature tower,
  By equal birth!
THAT HOUR WILL COME, to each, to all,
And from his prison-house, the thrall
  Go forth.

[35]See Psalm 68:31: "Princes shall come out of Egypt; Ethiopia shall soon stretch out her hands unto God."

Until that year, day, hour, arrive,
With head, and heart, and hand I'll strive,
To break the rod, and rend the gyve,
The spoiler of his prey deprive—
So witness Heaven!
And never from my chosen post,
Whate'er the peril or the cost,
Be driven.[36]

1852

Harriet Ann Jacobs 1813–1897

Harriet Ann Jacobs was born a slave in Edenton, North Carolina, in 1813. At six, after the death of her mother, Jacobs was taken into her mistress's home and taught to read and to sew. When she was eleven, she was willed to her mistress's little niece and sent to the nearby Norcom home to live. Her father died the following year. Aside from her younger brother, Jacobs's closest relative was her remarkable grandmother, Molly Horniblow, a freed woman who ran a bakery in her home. As Jacobs grew into adolescence, her master Dr. James Norcom subjected her to unrelenting sexual harrassment. To prevent him from forcing her into concubinage, at sixteen Jacobs became involved in a sexual liaison with a white neighbor, Samuel Tredwell Sawyer. Their son Joseph was born c. 1829–1830, and their daughter Louisa Matilda in 1833.

Jacobs was determined to free her children. When she was twenty-one, she again refused to become Dr. Norcom's concubine and was punished by being sent out to a plantation. Then, learning that Dr. Norcom planned to take the children from her grandmother's care, she decided to run away to save them from becoming plantation slaves. Reasoning that Norcom would sell the children if she were gone, she hid with sympathetic black and white neighbors. As she had hoped, Norcom sold the children to their father, who permitted them to continue to stay with her grandmother. But Norcom's zealous efforts to find her, and her grandmother's fear that she would be caught and returned in chains—as an uncle had been—combined to keep her in Edenton. For almost seven years, Jacobs hid in a tiny attic crawlspace in her grandmother's house. She spent her days reading the Bible, sewing clothes for her children, and planning ways to free them all.

In 1842, Jacobs escaped north, was reunited with her daughter (who had been sent to Brooklyn), and found work in New York in the home of the litterateur Nathaniel Parker Willis. She arranged for her son to be sent to her brother, John S. Jacobs, who had escaped from slavery and become an abolitionist lecturer. In 1849, Jacobs joined him in Rochester, New York to run the local Anti-Slavery Reading Room. In Rochester, she became part of a circle of anti-slavery feminists. Amy Post, who had attended the 1848 Women's Rights Convention at Seneca Falls and played a major role in the follow-up

[36]William Lloyd Garrison, "The Triumph of Freedom."

Rochester meeting, became Jacobs's friend. Post urged Jacobs to write her life story as a weapon in the struggle against chattel slavery.

After passage of the 1850 Fugitive Slave Law, Jacobs returned to her job with the Willis family. In New York, the Norcoms repeatedly attempted to catch her, and in 1852, Mrs. Willis bought Jacobs's freedom. Although glad to be free, Jacobs wrote to Post, "I was robbed of my victory." Early the next year, she was struggling with the idea of writing her story: "since I have no fear of my name coming before those whom I have lived in dread of I cannot be happy without trying to be useful in some way." After an abortive effort to involve as an amanuensis Harriet Beecher Stowe, whose *Uncle Tom's Cabin* had become a best-seller, Jacobs began writing her own life story. She finished her book in 1858, but could not find a publisher. Then in 1861, a firm agreed to get it out if the well-known writer and editor Lydia Maria Child would supply a preface. Child agreed, but the publisher went bankrupt, and *Incidents* was finally privately printed early in 1861. The book was well reviewed in the African-American press and in reform newspapers; an English edition appeared the following year.

Like other abolitionists, Jacobs eagerly involved herself in the effort to transform the developing Civil War into a war of emancipation. In 1862, she left New York to do relief work among the "contraband" (slaves who escaped to the Union army). Jacobs raised money for southern blacks, using the celebrity she had won among reformers as the author of *Incidents.* For the next six years she served in Washington, D.C., Alexandria, Virginia, and Savannah, Georgia, as an "agent" of Philadelphia and New York Quakers. She wrote her 1867 letter to Ednah Dow Cheney, Secretary of the New England Freedman's Aid Society, while visiting Reconstruction Edenton. After 1868, Jacobs returned north. She spent her last years with her daughter in Boston and Washington, D.C.

In letters to Amy Post, Jacobs expressed the conflict she felt about revealing her life story. To write a book politicizing the sexual exploitation of female slaves, she would have to expose her own sexual history and reveal herself an unwed mother. Ultimately, she solved this problem by creating an alter-ego, Linda Brent, who narrates her history in the first person. In and through Brent's narrative of her experiences in slavery as a sexual object and as a mother, Harriet Jacobs moved her book beyond the limits of genteel nineteenth-century discourse.

Incidents is unique among slave narratives in its double thrust: It is at once the first-person tale of a heroic mother who rescues her children from slavery, and the first-person confession of a "fallen woman." Distinctive discourses express these double themes. When writing as a triumphant slave mother, Jacobs's narrator recounts precise details and uses language directly; when confessing her sexual history, however, she presents herself as a repentant supplicant, omitting specifics and using the elevated vocabulary, elaborate sentence structures, and prose associated with the popular fiction of the period. But this narrator does not present herself as the passive victim of the seduction novel. On the contrary. Linda Brent takes responsibility for her mistakes, as well as for her triumphs.

Telling the story of her struggle for freedom, Jacobs's narrator locates herself within a densely patterned social context. In contrast to slave narratives by men like Frederick Douglass, which characteristically focus on a lone protagonist struggling against an unjust society, *Incidents* presents a protagonist enmeshed in family relationships who recounts her efforts to achieve freedom for herself and her children within the context of the struggle for freedom of an entire black community. In Linda Brent, Jacobs created a narrator with a voice that is new in African-American literature, in women's literature, and in American literature.

Both the Preface that Jacobs signed as Linda Brent and the Introduction her editor Lydia Maria Child supplied, make clear that *Incidents* was written for an audience of free white women, and that its purpose was to involve these women in political action against the institution of chattel slavery and the ideology of white racism. On one level, *Incidents* is a literary expression of the struggle of black and white abolitionists against slavery and white racism, and the attempt of nineteenth-century black and white feminists to move women to act collectively in the public sphere. On another, it is one woman's effort "to give a true and just account of my own life in Slavery."

Jean Fagan Yellin
Pace University

PRIMARY WORKS

Incidents in the Life of a Slave Girl. Written By Herself, ed. L. Maria Child, 1861. Republished as *The Deeper Wrong. Incidents in the Life of a Slave Girl,* 1862. The standard text was edited by Jean Fagan Yellin, 1987; Harriet A. Jacobs to Ednah Dow Cheney, Edenton [North Carolina] April 25th [1867]. ALS; Sophia Smith Collection. This, and several other of Jacobs's letters, are included in the Yellin edition, above, and in Dorothy Sterling, ed., *We Are Your Sisters: Black Women in the Nineteenth Century,* 1984.

SECONDARY WORKS

William L. Andrews, *To Tell a Free Story: The First Century of Afro-American Autobiography, 1760–1865,* 1986; Hazel Carby, *Reconstructing Womanhood,* 1987; Jean Fagan Yellin, "Introduction," *Incidents in the Life of a Slave Girl: Written by Herself,* 1987; Mary Helen Washington, "Meditations on History: The Slave Narrative of Linda Brent," *Invented Lives: Narratives of Black Women, 1860–1960,* 1987; Valerie Smith, *Self-Discovery and Authority in Afro-American Narrative,* 1988; Dana D. Nelson, *The Word in Black and White: Reading "Race" in American Literature, 1638–1867,* 1992; Frances Smith Foster, *Written by Herself: Literary Production of African-American Women, 1746–1892,* 1993; Carla Petersen, *"Doers of the Word": African-American Women Speakers and Writers in the North (1830–1880),* 1995; Deborah M. Garfield and Rafia Zafar, eds., *Harriet Jacobs and "Incidents in the Life of a Slave Girl": New Critical Essays,* 1996.

from Incidents in the Life of a Slave Girl

Seven Years Concealed

I Childhood

I was born a slave; but I never knew it till six years of happy childhood had passed away. My father[1] was a carpenter, and considered so intelligent and skilful in his trade, that, when buildings out of the common line were to be erected, he was sent for from long distances, to be head workman. On condition of paying his mistress two hundred dollars a year, and supporting himself, he was allowed to work at his

[1]The family members referred to in this chapter include Jacobs's father, Daniel Jacobs (?–c. 1826), her brother John S. Jacobs (1815?–1875), and her grandmother, Molly Horniblow (c. 1771–1853).

trade, and manage his own affairs. His strongest wish was to purchase his children; but, though he several times offered his hard earnings for that purpose, he never succeeded. In complexion my parents were a light shade of brownish yellow, and were termed mulattoes. They lived together in a comfortable home; and, though we were all slaves, I was so fondly shielded that I never dreamed I was a piece of merchandise, trusted to them for safe keeping, and liable to be demanded of them at any moment. I had one brother, William, who was two years younger than myself—a bright, affectionate child. I had also a great treasure in my maternal grandmother, who was a remarkable woman in many respects. She was the daughter of a planter in South Carolina, who, at his death, left her mother and his three children free, with money to go to St. Augustine, where they had relatives. It was during the Revolutionary War; and they were captured on their passage, carried back, and sold to different purchasers. Such was the story my grandmother used to tell me; but I do not remember all the particulars. She was a little girl when she was captured and sold to the keeper of a large hotel. I have often heard her tell how hard she fared during childhood. But as she grew older she evinced so much intelligence, and was so faithful, that her master and mistress could not help seeing it was for their interest to take care of such a valuable piece of property. She became an indispensable personage in the household, officiating in all capacities, from cook and wet nurse to seamstress. She was much praised for her cooking; and her nice crackers became so famous in the neighborhood that many people were desirous of obtaining them. In consequence of numerous requests of this kind, she asked permission of her mistress to bake crackers at night, after all the household work was done; and she obtained leave to do it, provided she would clothe herself and her children from the profits. Upon these terms, after working hard all day for her mistress, she began her midnight bakings, assisted by her two oldest children. The business proved profitable; and each year she laid by a little, which was saved for a fund to purchase her children. Her master died, and the property was divided among his heirs. The widow had her dower in the hotel, which she continued to keep open. My grandmother remained in her service as a slave; but her children were divided among her master's children. As she had five, Benjamin, the youngest one, was sold, in order that each heir might have an equal portion of dollars and cents. There was so little difference in our ages that he seemed more like my brother than my uncle. He was a bright, handsome lad, nearly white; for he inherited the complexion my grandmother had derived from Anglo-Saxon ancestors. Though only ten years old, seven hundred and twenty dollars were paid for him. His sale was a terrible blow to my grandmother; but she was naturally hopeful, and she went to work with renewed energy, trusting in time to be able to purchase some of her children. She had laid up three hundred dollars, which her mistress one day begged as a loan, promising to pay her soon. The reader probably knows that no promise or writing given to a slave is legally binding; for, according to Southern laws, a slave, *being* property, can *hold* no property. When my grandmother lent her hard earnings to her mistress, she trusted solely to her honor. The honor of a slaveholder to a slave!

To this good grandmother I was indebted for many comforts. My brother Willie and I often received portions of the crackers, cakes, and preserves, she made to sell; and after we ceased to be children we were indebted to her for many more important services.

Such were the unusually fortunate circumstances of my early childhood. When I was six years old, my mother died; and then, for the first time, I learned, by the talk around me, that I was a slave. My mother's mistress was the daughter of my grandmother's mistress. She was the foster sister of my mother; they were both nourished at my grandmother's breast. In fact, my mother had been weaned at three months old, that the babe of the mistress might obtain sufficient food. They played together as children; and, when they became women, my mother was a most faithful servant to her whiter foster sister. On her death-bed her mistress promised that her children should never suffer for any thing; and during her lifetime she kept her word. They all spoke kindly of my dead mother, who had been a slave merely in name, but in nature was noble and womanly. I grieved for her, and my young mind was troubled with the thought who would now take care of me and my little brother. I was told that my home was now to be with her mistress; and I found it a happy one. No toilsome or disagreeable duties were imposed upon me. My mistress was so kind to me that I was always glad to do her bidding, and proud to labor for her as much as my young years would permit. I would sit by her side for hours, sewing diligently, with a heart as free from care as that of any free-born white child. When she thought I was tired, she would send me out to run and jump; and away I bounded, to gather berries or flowers to decorate her room. Those were happy days—too happy to last. The slave child had no thought for the morrow; but there came that blight, which too surely waits on every human being born to be a chattel.

When I was nearly twelve years old, my kind mistress sickened and died. As I saw the cheek grow paler, and the eye more glassy, how earnestly I prayed in my heart that she might live! I loved her; for she had been almost like a mother to me. My prayers were not answered. She died, and they buried her in the little churchyard, where, day after day, my tears fell upon her grave.

I was sent to spend a week with my grandmother. I was now old enough to begin to think of the future; and again and again I asked myself what they would do with me. I felt sure I should never find another mistress so kind as the one who was gone. She had promised my dying mother that her children should never suffer for any thing; and when I remembered that, and recalled her many proofs of attachment to me, I could not help having some hopes that she had left me free. My friends were almost certain it would be so. They thought she would be sure to do it, on account of my mother's love and faithful service. But, alas! we all know that the memory of a faithful slave does not avail much to save her children from the auction block.

After a brief period of suspense, the will of my mistress was read, and we learned that she had bequeathed me to her sister's daughter, a child of five years old. So vanished our hopes. My mistress had taught me the precepts of God's Word: "Thou shalt love they neighbor as thyself." "Whatsoever ye would that men should do unto you, do ye even so unto them." But I was her slave, and I suppose she did not recognize me as her neighbor. I would give much to blot out from my memory that one great wrong. As a child, I loved my mistress; and, looking back on the happy days I spent with her, I try to think with less bitterness of this act of injustice. While I was with her, she taught me to read and spell; and for this privilege, which so rarely falls to the lot of a slave, I bless her memory.

She possessed but few slaves; and at her death those were all distributed among her relatives. Five of them were my grandmother's children, and had shared the same milk that nourished her mother's children. Notwithstanding my grandmother's long and faithful service to her owners, not one of her children escaped the auction block. These God-breathing machines are no more, in the sight of their masters, than the cotton they plant, or the horses they tend.

[Linda Brent was willed to her late mistress's little niece Emily Flint and sent to the Flint house to live.]

VI The Jealous Mistress

I would ten thousand times rather that my children should be the half-starved paupers of Ireland than to be the most pampered among the slaves of America.[1] I would rather drudge out my life on a cotton plantation, till the grave opened to give me rest, than to live with an unprincipled master and a jealous mistress. The felon's home in a penitentiary is preferable. He may repent, and turn from the error of his ways, and so find peace; but it is not so with a favorite slave. She is not allowed to have any pride of character. It is deemed a crime in her to wish to be virtuous.

Mrs. Flint possessed the key to her husband's character before I was born. She might have used this knowledge to counsel and to screen the young and the innocent among her slaves; but for them she had no sympathy. They were the objects of her constant suspicion and malevolence. She watched her husband with unceasing vigilance; but he was well practised in means to evade it. What he could not find opportunity to say in words he manifested in signs. He invented more than were ever thought of in a deaf and dumb asylum. I let them pass, as if I did not understand what he meant; and many were the curses and threats bestowed on me for my stupidity. One day he caught me teaching myself to write. He frowned, as if he was not well pleased; but I suppose he came to the conclusion that such an accomplishment might help to advance his favorite scheme. Before long, notes were often slipped into my hand. I would return them, saying, "I can't read them, sir." "Can't you?" he replied; "then I must read them to you." He always finished the reading by asking, "Do you understand?" Sometimes he would complain of the heat of the tea room, and order his supper to be placed on a small table in the piazza. He would seat himself there with a well-satisfied smile, and tell me to stand by and brush away the flies. He would eat very slowly, pausing between the mouthfuls. These intervals were employed in describing the happiness I was so foolishly throwing away, and in threatening me with the penalty that finally awaited my stubborn disobedience. He boasted much of the forbearance he had exercised towards me, and reminded me that there was a limit to his patience. When I succeeded in avoiding opportunities for him to talk to me at home, I was ordered to come to his office, to do some errand. When there, I was obliged to stand and listen to such language as he saw fit to address to me.

[1]Abolitionists regularly compared the plight of the Irish starving in the potato famine with the plight of African-Americans held in slavery.

Sometimes I so openly expressed my contempt for him that he would become violently enraged, and I wondered why he did not strike me. Circumstanced as he was, he probably thought it was better policy to be forbearing. But the state of things grew worse and worse daily. In desperation I told him that I must and would apply to my grandmother for protection. He threatened me with death, and worse than death, if I made any complaint to her. Strange to say, I did not despair. I was naturally of a buoyant disposition, and always I had a hope of somehow getting out of his clutches. Like many a poor, simple slave before me, I trusted that some threads of joy would yet be woven into my dark destiny.

I had entered my sixteenth year, and every day it became more apparent that my presence was intolerable to Mrs. Flint. Angry words frequently passed between her and her husband. He had never punished me himself, and he would not allow any body else to punish me. In that respect, she was never satisfied; but, in her angry moods, no terms were too vile for her to bestow upon me. Yet I, whom she detested so bitterly, had far more pity for her than he had, whose duty it was to make her life happy. I never wronged her, or wished to wrong her; and one word of kindness from her would have brought me to her feet.

After repeated quarrels between the doctor and his wife, he announced his intention to take his youngest daughter, then four years old, to sleep in his apartment. It was necessary that a servant should sleep in the same room, to be on hand if the child stirred. I was selected for that office, and informed for what purpose that arrangement had been made. By managing to keep within sight of people, as much as possible, during the day time, I had hitherto succeeded in eluding my master, though a razor was often held to my throat to force me to change this line of policy. At night I slept by the side of my great aunt, where I felt safe. He was too prudent to come into her room. She was an old woman, and had been in the family many years. Moreover, as a married man, and a professional man, he deemed it necessary to save appearances in some degree. But he resolved to remove the obstacle in the way of his scheme; and he thought he had planned it so that he should evade suspicion. He was well aware how much I prized my refuge by the side of my old aunt, and he determined to dispossess me of it. The first night the doctor had the little child in his room alone. The next morning, I was ordered to take my station as nurse the following night. A kind Providence interposed in my favor. During the day Mrs. Flint heard of this new arrangement, and a storm followed. I rejoiced to hear it rage.

After a while my mistress sent for me to come to her room. Her first question was, "Did you know you were to sleep in the doctor's room?"

"Yes, ma'am."

"Who told you?"

"My master."

"Will you answer truly all the questions I ask?"

"Yes, ma'am."

"Tell me, then, as you hope to be forgiven, are you innocent of what I have accused you?"

"I am."

She handed me a Bible, and said, "Lay your hand on your heart, kiss this holy book, and swear before God that you tell me the truth."

I took the oath she required, and I did it with a clear conscience.

"You have taken God's holy word to testify your innocence," said she. "If you have deceived me, beware! Now take this stool, sit down, look me directly in the face, and tell me all that has passed between your master and you."

I did as she ordered. As I went on with my account her color changed frequently, she wept, and sometimes groaned. She spoke in tones so sad, that I was touched by her grief. The tears came to my eyes; but I was soon convinced that her emotions arose from anger and wounded pride. She felt that her marriage vows were desecrated, her dignity insulted; but she had no compassion for the poor victim of her husband's perfidy. She pitied herself as a martyr; but she was incapable of feeling for the condition of shame and misery in which her unfortunate, helpless slave was placed.

Yet perhaps she had some touch of feeling for me; for when the conference was ended, she spoke kindly, and promised to protect me. I should have been much comforted by this assurance if I could have had confidence in it; but my experiences in slavery had filled me with distrust. She was not a very refined woman, and had not much control over her passions. I was an object of her jealousy, and, consequently, of her hatred; and I knew I could not expect kindness or confidence from her under the circumstances in which I was placed. I could not blame her. Slaveholders' wives feel as other women would under similar circumstances. The fire of her temper kindled from small sparks, and now the flame became so intense that the doctor was obliged to give up his intended arrangement.

I knew I had ignited the torch, and I expected to suffer for it afterwards; but I felt too thankful to my mistress for the timely aid she rendered me to care much about that. She now took me to sleep in a room adjoining her own. There I was an object of her especial care, though not of her especial comfort, for she spent many a sleepless night to watch over me. Sometimes I woke up, and found her bending over me. At other times she whispered in my ear, as though it was her husband who was speaking to me, and listened to hear what I would answer. If she startled me, on such occasions, she would glide stealthily away; and the next morning she would tell me I had been talking in my sleep, and ask who I was talking to. At last, I began to be fearful for my life. It had been often threatened; and you can imagine, better than I can describe, what an unpleasant sensation it must produce to wake up in the dead of night and find a jealous woman bending over you. Terrible as this experience was, I had fears that it would give place to one more terrible.

My mistress grew weary of her vigils; they did not prove satisfactory. She changed her tactics. She now tried the trick of accusing my master of crime, in my presence, and gave my name as the author of the accusation. To my utter astonishment, he replied, "I don't believe it: but if she did acknowledge it, you tortured her into exposing me." Tortured into exposing him! Truly, Satan had no difficulty in distinguishing the color of his soul! I understood his object in making this false representation. It was to show me that I gained nothing by seeking the protection of my mistress; that the power was still all in his own hands. I pitied Mrs. Flint. She was a second wife, many years the junior of her husband; and the hoary-headed miscreant was enough to try the patience of a wiser and better woman. She was completely foiled, and knew not how to proceed. She would gladly have had me flogged for my supposed false oath; but, as I have already stated, the doctor never allowed any one to whip me. The old sinner was politic. The application of the lash might have led to remarks that would have exposed him in the eyes of his children and grandchildren. How often did I rejoice that I lived in a town where all the inhabitants knew each other! If I had been on a remote plantation, or lost among the multitude of a crowded city, I should not be a living woman at this day.

The secrets of slavery are concealed like those of the Inquisition. My master was, to my knowledge, the father of eleven slaves. But did the mothers dare to tell who was the father of their children? Did the other slaves dare to allude to it, except in whispers among themselves? No, indeed! They knew too well the terrible consequences.

My grandmother could not avoid seeing things which excited her suspicions. She was uneasy about me, and tried various ways to buy me; but the neverchanging answer was always repeated: "Linda does not belong to *me.* She is my daughter's property, and I have no legal right to sell her." The conscientious man! He was too scrupulous to *sell* me; but he had no scruples whatever about committing a much greater wrong against the helpless young girl placed under his guardianship, as his daughter's property. Sometimes my persecutor would ask me whether I would like to be sold. I told him I would rather be sold to any body than to lead such a life as I did. On such occasions he would assume the air of a very injured individual, and reproach me for my ingratitude. "Did I not take you into the house, and make you the companion of my own children?" he would say. "Have I ever treated you like a negro? I have never allowed you to be punished, not even to please your mistress. And this is the recompense I get, you ungrateful girl!" I answered that he had reasons of his own for screening me from punishment, and that the course he pursued made my mistress hate me and persecute me. If I wept, he would say, "Poor child! Don't cry! don't cry! I will make peace for you with your mistress. Only let me arrange matters in my own way. Poor, foolish girl! you don't know what is for your own good. I would cherish you. I would make a lady of you. Now go, and think of all I have promised you."

I did think of it.

Reader, I draw no imaginary pictures of southern homes. I am telling you the plain truth. Yet when victims make their escape from this wild beast of Slavery, northerners consent to act the part of bloodhounds, and hunt the poor fugitive back into his den, "full of dead men's bones, and all uncleanness."[2] Nay, more, they are not only willing, but proud, to give their daughters in marriage to slaveholders. The poor girls have romantic notions of a sunny clime, and of the flowering vines that all the year round shade a happy home To what disappointments are they destined! The young wife soon learns that the husband in whose hands she has placed her happiness pays no regard to his marriage vows. Children of every shade of complexion play with her own fair babies, and too well she knows that they are born unto him of his own household. Jealousy and hatred enter the flowery home, and it is ravaged of its loveliness.

Southern women often marry a man knowing that he is the father of many little slaves. They do not trouble themselves about it. They regard such children as property, as marketable as the pigs on the plantation; and it is seldom that they do not

[2]"Woe unto you, scribes and Pharisees, hypocrites! for ye are like unto whited sepulchres, which indeed appear beautiful outward, but are within full of dead men's bones, and of all uncleanness." Matthew 23:27.

make them aware of this by passing them into the slavetrader's hands as soon as possible, and thus getting them out of their sight. I am glad to say there are some honorable exceptions.

I have myself known two southern wives who exhorted their husbands to free those slaves towards whom they stood in a "parental relation"; and their request was granted. These husbands blushed before the superior nobleness of their wives' natures. Though they had only counselled them to do that which it was their duty to do, it commanded their respect, and rendered their conduct more exemplary. Concealment was at an end, and confidence took the place of distrust.

Though this bad institution deadens the moral sense, even in white women, to a fearful extent, it is not altogether extinct. I have heard southern ladies say of Mr. Such a one, "He not only thinks it no disgrace to be the father of those little niggers, but he is not ashamed to call himself their master. I declare, such things ought not to be tolerated in any decent society!"

[Linda Brent was subjected to unrelenting sexual harassment by Dr. Flint. When she was in her early teens, she fell in love with a free Black man, but Flint, who wanted her for himself, forbade her to marry.]

X A Perilous Passage in the Slave Girl's Life

After my lover went away, Dr. Flint contrived a new plan. He seemed to have an idea that my fear of my mistress was his greatest obstacle. In the blandest tones, he told me that he was going to build a small house for me, in a secluded place, four miles away from the town. I shuddered; but I was constrained to listen, while he talked of his intention to give me a home of my own, and to make a lady of me. Hitherto, I had escaped my dreaded fate, by being in the midst of people. My grandmother had already had high words with my master about me. She had told him pretty plainly what she thought of his character, and there was considerable gossip in the neighborhood about our affairs, to which the open-mouthed jealousy of Mrs. Flint contributed not a little. When my master said he was going to build a house for me, and that he could do it with little trouble and expense, I was in hopes something would happen to frustrate his scheme; but I soon heard that the house was actually begun. I vowed before my Maker that I would never enter it. I had rather toil on the plantation from dawn til dark; I had rather live and die in jail, than drag on, from day to day, through such a living death. I was determined that the master, whom I so hated and loathed, who had blighted the prospects of my youth, and made my life a desert, should not, after my long struggle with him, succeed at last in trampling his victim under his feet. I would do any thing, every thing, for the sake of defeating him. What *could* I do? I thought and thought, til I became desperate, and made a plunge into the abyss.

And now, reader, I come to a period in my unhappy life, which I would gladly forget if I could. The remembrance fills me with sorrow and shame. It pains me to tell you of it; but I have promised to tell you the truth, and I will do it honestly, let it cost me what it may. I will not try to screen myself behind the plea of compulsion from a master; for it was not so. Neither can I plead ignorance or thoughtlessness. For years, my master had done his utmost to pollute my mind with foul images, and to destroy the pure principles inculcated by my grandmother, and the good mistress of my childhood. The influences of slavery had had the same effect on me that they had on other young girls; they had made me prematurely knowing, concerning the evil ways of the world. I knew what I did, and I did it with deliberate calculation.

But, O, ye happy women, whose purity has been sheltered from childhood, who have been free to choose the objects of your affection, whose homes are protected by law, do not judge the poor desolate slave girl too severely! If slavery had been abolished, I, also, could have married the man of my choice; I could have had a home shielded by the laws; and I should have been spared the painful task of confessing what I am now about to relate; but all my prospects had been blighted by slavery. I wanted to keep myself pure; and, under the most adverse circumstances, I tried hard to preserve my self-respect; but I was struggling alone in the powerful grasp of the demon Slavery; and the monster proved too strong for me. I felt as if I was forsaken by God and man; as if all my efforts must be frustrated; and I became reckless in my despair.

I have told you that Dr. Flint's persecutions and his wife's jealousy had given rise to some gossip in the neighborhood. Among others, it chanced that a white unmarried gentleman had obtained some knowledge of the circumstances in which I was placed. He knew my grandmother, and often spoke to me in the street. He became interested for me, and asked questions about my master, which I answered in part. He expressed a great deal of sympathy, and a wish to aid me. He constantly sought opportunities to see me, and wrote to me frequently. I was a poor slave girl, only fifteen years old.

So much attention from a superior person was, of course, flattering; for human nature is the same in all. I also felt grateful for his sympathy, and encouraged by his kind words. It seemed to me a great thing to have such a friend. By degrees, a more tender feeling crept into my heart. He was an educated and eloquent gentleman; too eloquent, alas, for the poor slave girl who trusted in him. Of course I saw whither all this was tending. I knew the impassable gulf between us; but to be an object of interest to a man who is not married, and who is not her master, is agreeable to the pride and feelings of a slave, if her miserable situation has left her any pride or sentiment. It seems less degrading to give one's self, than to submit to compulsion. There is something akin to freedom in having a lover who has no control over you, except that which he gains by kindness and attachment. A master may treat you as rudely as he pleases, and you dare not speak; moreover, the wrong does not seem so great with an unmarried man, as with one who has a wife to be made unhappy. There may be sophistry in all this; but the condition of a slave confuses all principles of morality, and, in fact, renders the practice of them impossible.

When I found that my master had actually begun to build the lonely cottage, other feelings mixed with those I have described. Revenge, and calculations of interest, were added to flattered vanity and sincere gratitude for kindness. I knew nothing would enrage Dr. Flint so much as to know that I favored another; and it was something to triumph over my tyrant even in that small way. I thought he would revenge himself by selling me, and I was sure my friend, Mr. Sands, would buy me. He was a man of more generosity and feeling than my master, and I thought my freedom could be easily obtained from him. The crisis of my fate now came so near that I was desperate. I shuddered to think of being the mother of children that should be owned by my old tyrant. I knew that as soon as a new fancy took him, his victims were sold far off to get rid of them; especially if they had children. I had seen several women sold, with his babies at the breast. He never allowed his offspring by slaves to remain long in sight of himself and his wife. Of a man who was not my master I could ask to have my children well supported; and in this case, I felt confident I should obtain the boon. I also felt quite sure they they would be made free. With all these thoughts revolving in my mind, and seeing no other way of escaping the doom I so much dreaded, I made a headlong plunge. Pity me, and pardon me, O virtuous reader! You never knew what it is to be a slave; to be entirely unprotected by law or custom; to have the laws reduce you to the condition of a chattel, entirely subject to the will of another. You never exhausted your ingenuity in avoiding the snares, and eluding the power of a hated tyrant; you never shuddered at the sound of his footsteps, and trembled within hearing of his voice. I know I did wrong. No one can feel it more sensibly than I do. The painful and humiliating memory will haunt me to my dying day. Still, in looking back, calmly, on the events of my life, I feel that the slave woman ought not to be judged by the same standard as others.

The months passed on. I had many unhappy hours. I secretly mourned over the sorrow I was bringing on my grandmother, who had so tried to shield me from harm. I knew that I was the greatest comfort of her old age, and that it was a source of pride to her that I had not degraded myself, like most of the slaves. I wanted to confess to her that I was no longer worthy of her love; but I could not utter the dreaded words.

As for Dr. Flint, I had a feeling of satisfaction and triumph in the thought of telling *him.* From time to time he told me of his intended arrangements, and I was silent. At last, he came and told me the cottage was completed, and ordered me to go to it. I told him I would never enter it. He said, "I have heard enough of such talk as that. You shall go, if you are carried by force; and you shall remain there."

I replied, "I will never go there. In a few months I shall be a mother."

He stood and looked at me in dumb amazement, and left the house without a word. I thought I should be happy in my triumph over him. But now that the truth was out, and my relatives would hear of it, I felt wretched. Humble as were their circumstances, they had pride in my good character. Now, how could I look them in the face? My self-respect was gone! I had resolved that I would be virtuous, though I was a slave. I had said, "Let the storm beat! I will brave it till I die." And now, how humiliated I felt!

I went to my grandmother. My lips moved to make confession, but the words stuck in my throat. I sat down in the shade of a tree at her door and began to sew. I think she saw something unusual was the matter with me. The mother of slaves is very watchful. She knows there is no security for her children. After they have entered their teens she lives in daily expectation of trouble. This leads to many questions. If the girl is of a sensitive nature, timidity keeps her from answering truthfully, and this well-meant course has a tendency to drive her from maternal counsels. Presently, in came my mistress, like a mad woman, and accused me concerning her husband. My grandmother, whose suspicions had been previously awakened, believed what she said. She exclaimed, "O Linda! has it come to this? I had rather see you dead than to see you as you are now. You are a disgrace to your dead mother." She tore from my fingers my mother's wedding ring and her silver thimble. "Go away!" she exclaimed, "and never come to my house, again." Her reproaches fell so hot and heavy, that they left me no chance to answer. Bitter tears, such as the eyes never shed but once, were my only answer. I rose from my seat, but fell back again, sobbing. She did not speak to me; but the tears were running down her furrowed cheeks, and they scorched me like fire. She had always been so kind to me! *So* kind! How I longed to throw myself at her feet, and tell her all the truth! But she had ordered me to go, and never to come there again. After a few minutes, I mustered strength, and started to obey her. With what feelings did I now close that little gate, which I used to open with such an eager hand in my childhood! It closed upon me with a sound I never heard before.

Where could I go? I was afraid to return to my master's. I walked on recklessly, not caring where I went, or what would become of me. When I had gone four or five miles, fatigue compelled me to stop. I sat down on the stump of an old tree. The stars were shining through the boughs above me. How they mocked me, with their bright, calm light! The hours passed by, and as I sat there alone a chilliness and deadly sickness came over me. I sank on the ground. My mind was full of horrid thoughts. I prayed to die; but the prayer was not answered. At last, with great-effort I roused myself, and walked some distance further, to the house of a woman who had been a friend of my mother. When I told her why I was there, she spoke soothingly to me; but I could not be comforted. I thought I could bear my shame if I could only be reconciled to my grandmother. I longed to open my heart to her. I thought if she could know the real state of the case, and all I had been bearing for years, she would perhaps judge me less harshly. My friend advised me to send for her. I did so; but days of agonizing suspense passed before she came. Had she utterly forsaken me? No. She came at last. I knelt before her, and told her the things that had poisoned my life; how long I had been persecuted; that I saw no way of escape; and in an hour of extremity I had become desperate. She listened in silence. I told her I would bear any thing and do any thing, if in time I had hopes of obtaining her forgiveness. I begged of her to pity me, for my dead mother's sake. And she did pity me. She did not say, "I forgive you"; but she looked at me lovingly, with her eyes full of tears. She laid her old hand gently on my head, and murmured, "Poor child! Poor child!"

[Mrs. Flint threw Linda Brent out of the house and her grandmother took her in. Brent's son Benjamin was born in her grandmother's house, as was her daughter Ellen. When Linda Brent was 21, Flint again tried to force her into concubinage. She objected and was sent out to the plantation.]

XVI Scenes at the Plantation

Early the next morning I left my grandmother's with my youngest child. My boy was ill, and I left him behind. I had many sad thoughts as the old wagon jolted on. Hitherto, I had suffered alone; now, my little one was to be treated as a slave. As we drew near the great house, I thought of the time when I was formerly sent there out of revenge. I wondered for what purpose I was now sent. I could not tell. I resolved to obey orders so far as duty required; but within myself, I determined to make my stay as short as possible. Mr. Flint was waiting to receive us, and told me to follow him up stairs to receive orders for the day. My little Ellen was left below in the kitchen. It was a change for her, who had always been so carefully tended. My young master said she might amuse herself in the yard. This was kind of him, since the child was hateful to his sight. My task was to fit up the house for the reception of the bride. In the midst of sheets, tablecloths, towels, drapery, and carpeting, my head was as busy planning, as were my fingers with the needle. At noon I was allowed to go to Ellen. She had sobbed herself to sleep. I heard Mr. Flint say to a neighbor, "I've got her down here, and I'll soon take the town notions out of her head. My father is partly to blame for her nonsense. He ought to have broke her in long ago." The remark was made within my hearing, and it would have been quite as manly to have made it to my face. He *had* said things to my face which might, or might not, have surprised his neighbor if he had known of them. He was "a chip of the old block."

I resolved to give him no cause to accuse me of being too much of a lady, so far as work was concerned. I worked day and night, with wretchedness before me. When I lay down beside my child, I felt how much easier it would be to see her die than to see her master beat her about, as I daily saw him beat other little ones. The spirit of the mothers was so crushed by the lash, that they stood by, without courage to remonstrate. How much more must I suffer, before I should be "broke in" to that degree?

I wished to appear as contented as possible. Sometimes I had an opportunity to send a few lines home; and this brought up recollections that made it difficult, for a time, to seem calm and indifferent to my lot. Notwithstanding my efforts, I saw that Mr. Flint regarded me with a suspicious eye. Ellen broke down under the trials of her new life. Separated from me, with no one to look after her, she wandered about, and in a few days cried herself sick. One day, she sat under the window where I was at work, crying that weary cry which makes a mother's heart bleed. I was obliged to steel myself to bear it. After a while it ceased. I looked out, and she was gone. As it was near noon, I ventured to go down in search of her. The great house was raised two feet above the ground. I looked under it, and saw her about midway, fast asleep. I crept under and drew her out. As I held her in my arms, I thought how well it would be for her if she never waked up; and I uttered my thought aloud. I was startled to hear some one say, "Did you speak to me?" I looked up, and saw Mr. Flint standing beside me. He said nothing further, but turned, frowning, away. That night he sent Ellen a biscuit and a cup of sweetened milk. This generosity surprised me. I learned afterwards, that in the afternoon he had killed a large snake, which crept from under the house; and I supposed that incident had prompted his unusual kindness.

The next morning the old cart was loaded with shingles for town. I put Ellen into it, and sent her to her grandmother. Mr. Flint said I ought to have asked his permission. I told him the child was sick, and required attention which I had no time to give. He let it pass; for he was aware that I had accomplished much work in a little time.

I had been three weeks on the plantation, when I planned a visit home. It must be at night, after every body was in bed. I was six miles from town, and the road was very dreary. I was to go with a young man, who, I knew, often stole to town to see his mother. One night, when all was quiet, we started. Fear gave speed to our steps, and we were not long in performing the journey. I arrived at my grandmother's. Her bed room was on the first floor, and the window was open, the weather being warm. I spoke to her and she awoke. She let me in and closed the window, lest some late passer-by should see me. A light was brought, and the whole household gathered round me, some smiling and some crying. I went to look at my children, and thanked God for their happy sleep. The tears fell as I leaned over them. As I moved to leave, Benny stirred. I turned back, and whispered, "Mother is here." After digging at his eyes with his little fist, they opened, and he sat up in bed, looking at me curiously. Having satisfied himself that it was I, he exclaimed, "O mother! you ain't dead, are you? They didn't cut off your head at the plantation, did they?"

My time was up too soon, and my guide was waiting for me. I laid Benny back in his bed, and dried his tears by a promise to come again soon. Rapidly we retraced our steps back to the plantation. About half way we were met by a company of four patrols.[1] Luckily we heard their horse's hoofs before they came in sight, and we had time to hide behind a large tree. They passed, hallooing and shouting in a manner that indicated a recent carousal. How thankful we were that they had not their dogs with them! We hastened our footsteps, and when we arrived on the plantation we heard the sound of the hand-mill. The slaves were grinding their corn. We were safely in the house before the horn summoned them to their labor. I divided my little parcel of food with my guide, knowing that he had lost the chance of grinding his corn, and must toil all day in the field.

Mr. Flint often took an inspection of the house, to see that no one was idle. The entire management of the work was trusted to me, because he knew nothing about it; and rather than hire a superintendent he contented himself with my arrangements. He had often urged upon his father the necessity of having me at the plantation to take charge of his affairs, and make clothes for the slaves; but the old man knew him too well to consent to that arrangement.

When I had been working a month at the plantation, the great aunt of Mr. Flint came to make him a visit. This was the good old lady who paid fifty dollars for my grandmother, for the purpose of making her free, when she stood on the auction block. My grandmother loved this old lady, whom we all called Miss Fanny. She often came to take tea with us. On such occasions the table was spread with a snow-white cloth, and the china cups and silver spoons were taken from the old-fashioned buffet. There were hot muffins, tea rusks, and delicious sweetmeats. My grandmother kept two cows, and the fresh cream was Miss Fanny's delight. She invariably declared that it was the best in town. The old ladies had cosey times together. They would work and chat, and sometimes, while talking over old times, their spectacles would get dim with tears, and would have to be taken off and wiped. When Miss Fanny bade us good by, her bag was filled with grandmother's best cakes, and she was urged to come again soon.

There had been a time when Dr. Flint's wife came to take tea with us, and when her children were also sent to have a feast of "Aunt Marthy's" nice cooking. But after I became an object of her jealousy and spite, she was angry with grandmother for giving a shelter to me and my children. She would not even speak to her in the street. This wounded my grandmother's feelings, for she could not retain ill will against the

[1] A system of patrols monitored the roads and periodically checked the slave quarters. Slaves leaving the plantation were required to have a pass signed by a master or overseer; if caught without such passes, they were summarily punished by the patrol.

woman whom she had nourished with her milk when a babe. The doctor's wife would gladly have prevented our intercourse with Miss Fanny if she could have done it, but fortunately she was not dependent on the bounty of the Flints. She had enough to be independent; and that is more than can ever be gained from charity, however lavish it may be.

Miss Fanny was endeared to me by many recollections, and I was rejoiced to see her at the plantation. The warmth of her large, loyal heart made the house seem pleasanter while she was in it. She staid a week, and I had many talks with her. She said her principal object in coming was to see how I was treated, and whether any thing could be done for me. She inquired whether she could help me in any way. I told her I believed not. She condoled with me in her own peculiar way; saying she wished that I and all my grandmother's family were at rest in our graves, for not until then should she feel any peace about us. The good old soul did not dream that I was planning to bestow peace upon her, with regard to myself and my children; not by death, but by securing our freedom.

Again and again I had traversed those dreary twelve miles, to and from the town; and all the way, I was meditating upon some means of escape for myself and my children. My friends had made every effort that ingenuity could devise to effect our purchase, but all their plans had proved abortive. Dr. Flint was suspicious, and determined not to loosen his grasp upon us. I could have made my escape alone; but it was more for my helpless children than for myself that I longed for freedom. Though the boon would have been precious to me, above all price, I would not have taken it at the expense of leaving them in slavery. Every trial I endured, every sacrifice I made for their sakes, drew them closer to my heart, and gave me fresh courage to beat back the dark waves that rolled and rolled over me in a seemingly endless night of storms.

The six weeks were nearly completed, when Mr. Flint's bride was expected to take possession of her new home. The arrangements were all completed, and Mr. Flint said I had done well. He expected to leave home on Saturday, and return with his bride the following Wednesday. After receiving various orders from him, I ventured to ask permission to spend Sunday in town. It was granted; for which favor I was thankful. It was the first I had ever asked of him, and I intended it should be the last. It needed more than one night to accomplish the project I had in view; but the whole of Sunday would give me an opportunity. I spent the Sabbath with my grandmother. A calmer, more beautiful day never came down out of heaven. To me it was a day of conflicting emotions. Perhaps it was the last day I should ever spend under that dear, old sheltering roof! Perhaps these were the last talks I should ever have with the faithful old friend of my whole life! Perhaps it was the last time I and my children should be together! Well, better so, I thought, than that they should be slaves. I knew the doom that awaited my fair baby in slavery, and I determined to save her from it, or perish in the attempt. I went to make this vow at the graves of my poor parents, in the burying-ground of the slaves. "There the wicked cease from troubling, and there the weary be at rest. There the prisoners rest together; they hear not the voice of the oppressor; the servant is free from his master."[2] I knelt by the graves of my parents, and thanked God, as I had often done before, that they had not lived to witness my trials, or to mourn over my sins. I had received my mother's blessing when she died; and in many an hour of tribulation I had seemed to hear her voice,

[2]Job 3:17–19.

sometimes chiding me, sometimes whispering loving words into my wounded heart. I have shed many and bitter tears, to think that when I am gone from my children they cannot remember me with such entire satisfaction as I remembered my mother.

The graveyard was in the woods, and twilight was coming on. Nothing broke the death-like stillness except the occasional twitter of a bird. My spirit was over-awed by the solemnity of the scene. For more than ten years I had frequented this spot, but never had it seemed to me so sacred as now. A black stump, at the head of my mother's grave, was all that remained of a tree my father had planted. His grave was marked by a small wooden board, bearing his name, the letters of which were nearly obliterated. I knelt down and kissed them, and poured forth a prayer to God for guidance and support in the perilous step I was about to take. As I passed the wreck of the old meeting house, where, before Nat Turner's time, the slaves had been allowed to meet for worship, I seemed to hear my father's voice come from it, bidding me not to tarry till I reached freedom or the grave.[3] I rushed on with renovated hopes. My trust in God had been strengthened by that prayer among the graves.

My plan was to conceal myself at the house of a friend, and remain there a few weeks till the search was over. My hope was that the doctor would get discouraged, and, for fear of losing my value, and also of subsequently finding my children among the missing, he would consent to sell us; and I knew somebody would buy us. I had done all in my power to make my children comfortable during the time I expected to be separated from them. I was packing my things, when grandmother came into the room, and asked what I was doing. "I am putting my things in order," I replied. I tried to look and speak cheerfully; but her watchful eye detected something beneath the surface. She drew me towards her, and asked me to sit down. She looked earnestly at me, and said, "Linda, do you want to kill your old grandmother? Do you mean to leave your little, helpless children? I am old now, and cannot do for your babies as I once did for you."

I replied, that if I went away, perhaps their father would be able to secure their freedom.

"Ah, my child," said she, "don't trust too much to him. Stand by your own children, and suffer with them till death. Nobody respects a mother who forsakes her children; and if you leave them, you will never have a happy moment. If you go, you will make me miserable the short time I have to live. You would be taken and brought back, and your sufferings would be dreadful. Remember poor Benjamin. Do give it up, Linda. Try to bear a little longer. Things may turn out better than we expect."

My courage failed me, in view of the sorrow I should bring on that faithful, loving old heart. I promised that I would try longer, and that I would take nothing out of her house without her knowledge.

Whenever the children climbed on my knee, or laid their heads on my lap, she would say, "Poor little souls! what would you do without a mother? She don't love you as I do." And she would hug them to her own bosom, as if to reproach me for my want of affection; but she knew all the while that I loved them better than my life. I slept with her that night, and it was the last time. The memory of it haunted me for many a year.

[3]In 1831 in Southampton County, Virginia (about 40 miles upstream from Edenton) Nat Turner had led the bloodiest slave insurrection in American history. Subsequently, the white South retaliated by passing and enforcing repressive laws against slaves and free Blacks.

On Monday I returned to the plantation, and busied myself with preparations for the important day. Wednesday came. It was a beautiful day, and the faces of the slaves were as bright as sunshine. The poor creatures were merry. They were expecting little presents from the bride, and hoping for better times under her administration. I had no such hopes for them. I knew that the young wives of slaveholders often thought their authority and importance would be best established and maintained by cruelty; and what I had heard of young Mrs. Flint gave me no reason to expect that her rule over them would be less severe than that of the master and overseer. Truly, the colored race are the most cheerful and forgiving people on the face of the earth. That their masters sleep in safety is owing to their superabundance of heart; and yet they look upon their sufferings with less pity than they would bestow on those of a horse or a dog.

I stood at the door with others to receive the bridegroom and bride. She was a handsome, delicate-looking girl, and her face flushed with emotion at sight of her new home. I thought it likely that visions of a happy future were rising before her. It made me sad; for I knew how soon clouds would come over her sunshine. She examined every part of the house, and told me she was delighted with the arrangements I had made. I was afraid old Mrs. Flint had tried to prejudice her against me, and I did my best to please her.

All passed off smoothly for me until dinner time arrived. I did not mind the embarrassment of waiting on a dinner party, for the first time in my life, half so much as I did the meeting with Dr. Flint and his wife, who would be among the guests. It was a mystery to me why Mrs. Flint had not made her appearance at the plantation during all the time I was putting the house in order. I had not met her, face to face, for five years, and I had no wish to see her now. She was a praying woman, and, doubtless, considered my present position a special answer to her prayers. Nothing could please her better than to see me humbled and trampled upon. I was just where she would have me—in the power of a hard, unprincipled master. She did not speak to me when she took her seat at table; but her satisfied, triumphant smile, when I handed her plate, was more eloquent than words. The old doctor was not so quiet in his demonstrations. He ordered me here and there, and spoke with peculiar emphasis when he said "your *mistress.*" I was drilled like a disgraced soldier. When all was over, and the last key turned, I sought my pillow, thankful that God had appointed a season of rest for the weary.

The next day my new mistress began her housekeeping. I was not exactly appointed maid of all work; but I was to do whatever I was told. Monday evening came. It was always a busy time. On that night the slaves received their weekly allowance of food. Three pounds of meat, a peck of corn, and perhaps a dozen herring were allowed to each man. Women received a pound and a half of meat, a peck of corn, and the same number of herring. Children over twelve years old had half the allowance of the women. The meat was cut and weighed by the foreman of the field hands, and piled on planks before the meat house. Then the second foreman went behind the building, and when the first foreman called out, "Who takes this piece of meat?" he answered by calling somebody's name. This method was resorted to as means of preventing partiality in distributing the meat. The young mistress came out to see how things were done on her plantation, and she soon gave a specimen of her character. Among those in waiting for their allowance was a very old slave, who had faithfully served the Flint family through three generations. When he hobbled up to get his bit of meat, the mistress said he was too old to have any allowance; that when niggers were too old to work, they ought to be fed on grass. Poor old man! He suffered much before he found rest in the grave.

My mistress and I got along very well together. At the end of a week, old Mrs. Flint made us another visit, and was closeted a long time with her daughter-in-law. I had my suspicions what was the subject of the conference. The old doctor's wife had been informed that I could leave the plantation on one condition, and she was very desirous to keep me there. If she had trusted me, as I deserved to be trusted by her, she would have had no fears of my accepting that condition. When she entered her carriage to return home, she said to young Mrs. Flint, "Don't neglect to send for them as quick as possible." My heart was on the watch all the time, and I at once concluded that she spoke of my children. The doctor came the next day, and as I entered the room to spread the tea table, I heard him say, "Don't wait any longer. Send for them to-morrow." I saw through the plan. They thought my children's being there would fetter me to the spot, and that it was a good place to break us all in to abject submission to our lot as slaves. After the doctor left, a gentleman called, who had always manifested friendly feelings towards my grandmother and her family. Mr. Flint carried him over the plantation to show him the results of labor performed by men and women who were unpaid, miserably clothed, and half famished. The cotton crop was all they thought of. It was duly admired, and the gentleman returned with specimens to show his friends. I was ordered to carry water to wash his hands. As I did so, he said, "Linda, how do you like your new home?" I told him I liked it as well as I expected. He replied, "They don't think you are contented, and to-morrow they are going to bring your children to be with you. I am sorry for you, Linda. I hope they will treat you kindly." I hurried from the room, unable to thank him. My suspicions were correct. My children were to be brought to the plantation to be "broke in."

To this day I feel grateful to the gentleman who gave me this timely information. It nerved me to immediate action.

> [Linda Brent ran away. All avenues of escape from the town were put under surveillance, and for several weeks she was sheltered by black and white neighbors. When Dr. Flint persisted in his hunt for her, Linda Brent's friends secreted her in a nearby swamp while her uncle prepared a hiding place in her grandmother's house.]

XXI The Loophole of Retreat[1]

A small shed had been added to my grandmother's house years ago. Some boards were laid across the joists at the top, and between these boards and the roof was a very small garret, never occupied by any thing but rats and mice. It was a pent roof,

[1]A reference to William Cowper's "The Task," IV, 88–90:

> 'Tis pleasant, through the loopholes of retreat,/ To peep at such a world,—to see the stir/ Of the great Babel, and not feel the crowd.

covered with nothing but shingles, according to the southern custom for such buildings. The garret was only nine feet long and seven wide. The highest part was three feet high, and sloped down abruptly to the loose board floor. There was no admission for either light or air. My uncle Philip, who was a carpenter, had very skilfully made a concealed trap-door, which communicated with the storeroom. He had been doing this while I was waiting in the swamp. The storeroom opened upon a piazza. To this hole I was conveyed as soon as I entered the house. The air was stifling; the darkness total. A bed had been spread on the floor. I could sleep quite comfortably on one side; but the slope was so sudden that I could not turn on the other without hitting the roof. The rats and mice ran over my bed; but I was weary, and I slept such sleep as the wretched may, when a tempest has passed over them. Morning came. I knew it only by the noises I heard; for in my small den day and night were all the same. I suffered for air even more than for light. But I was not comfortless. I heard the voices of my children. There was joy and there was sadness in the sound. It made my tears flow. How I longed to speak to them! I was eager to look on their faces; but there was no hole, no crack, through which I could peep. This continued darkness was oppressive. It seemed horrible to sit or lie in a cramped position day after day, without one gleam of light. Yet I would have chosen this, rather than my lot as a slave, though white people considered it an easy one; and it was so compared with the fate of others. I was never cruelly overworked; I was never lacerated with the whip from head to foot; I was never so beaten and bruised that I could not turn from one side to the other; I never had my heel-strings cut to prevent my running away; I was never chained to a log and forced to drag it about, while I toiled in the fields from morning till night; I was never branded with hot iron, or torn by bloodhounds. On the contrary, I had always been kindly treated, and tenderly cared for, until I came into the hands of Dr. Flint. I had never wished for freedom till then. But though my life in slavery was comparatively devoid of hardships, God pity the woman who is compelled to lead such a life!

My food was passed up to me through the trap-door my uncle had contrived; and my grandmother, my uncle Phillip, and aunt Nancy would seize such opportunities as they could, to mount up there and chat with me at the opening. But of course this was not safe in the daytime. It must all be done in darkness. It was impossible for me to move in an erect position, but I crawled about my den for exercise. One day I hit my head against something, and found it was a gimlet. My uncle had left it sticking there when he made the trap-door. I was as rejoiced as Robinson Crusoe could have been at finding such a treasure. It put a lucky thought into my head. I said to myself, "Now I will have some light. Now I will see my children." I did not dare to begin my work during the daytime, for fear of attracting attention. But I groped round; and having found the side next the street, where I could frequently see my children, I stuck the gimlet in and waited for evening. I bored three rows of holes, one above another; then I bored out the interstices between. I thus succeeded in making one hole about an inch long and an inch broad. I sat by it till late into the night, to enjoy the little whiff of air that floated in. In the morning I watched for my children. The first person I saw in the street was Dr. Flint. I had a shuddering, superstitious feeling that it was a bad omen. Several familiar faces passed by. At last I heard the merry laugh of children, and presently two sweet little faces were looking up at me, as though they knew I was there, and were conscious of the joy they imparted. How I longed to *tell* them I was there!

My condition was now a little improved. But for weeks I was tormented by hundreds of little red insects, fine as a needle's point, that pierced through my skin, and produced an intolerable burning. The good grandmother gave me herb teas and cooling medicines, and finally I got rid of them. The heat of my den was intense, for nothing but thin shingles protected me from the scorching summer's sun. But I had my consolations. Through my peeping-hole I could watch the children, and when they were near enough, I could hear their talk. Aunt Nancy brought me all the news she could hear at Dr. Flint's. From her I learned that the doctor had written to New York to a colored woman, who had been born and raised in our neighborhood, and had breathed his contaminating atmosphere. He offered her a reward if she could find out any thing about me. I know not what was the nature of her reply; but he soon after started for New York in haste, saying to his family that he had business of importance to transact. I peeped at him as he passed on his way to the steamboat. It was a satisfaction to have miles of land and water between us, even for a little while; and it was a still greater satisfaction to know that he believed me to be in the Free States. My little den seemed less dreary than it had done. He returned, as he did from his former journey to New York, without obtaining any satisfactory information. When he passed our house next morning, Benny was standing at the gate. He had heard them say that he had gone to find me, and he called out, "Dr. Flint, did you bring my mother home? I want to see her." The doctor stamped his foot at him in a rage, and exclaimed, "Get out of the way, you little damned rascal! If you don't, I'll cut off your head."

Benny ran terrified into the house, saying, "You can't put me in jail again. I don't belong to you now." It was well that the wind carried the words away from the doctor's ear. I told my grandmother of it, when we had our next conference at the trap-door; and begged of her not to allow the children to be impertinent to the irascible old man.

Autumn came, with a pleasant abatement of heat. My eyes had become accustomed to the dim light, and by holding my book or work in a certain position near the aperture I contrived to read and sew. That was a great relief to the tedious monotony of my life. But when winter came, the cold penetrated through the thin shingle roof, and I was dreadfully chilled. The winters there are not so long, or so severe, as in northern latitudes; but the houses are not built to shelter from cold, and my little den was peculiarly comfortless. The kind grandmother brought me bed-clothes and warm drinks. Often I was obliged to lie in bed all day to keep comfortable; but with all my precautions, my shoulders and feet were frostbitten. O, those long, gloomy days, with no object for my eye to rest upon, and no thoughts to occupy my mind, except the dreary past and the uncertain future! I was thankful when there came a day sufficiently mild for me to wrap myself up and sit at the loophole to watch the passers by. Southerners have the habit of stopping and talking in the streets, and I heard many conversations not intended to meet my ears. I heard slave-hunters planning how to catch some poor fugitive Several times I heard allusions to Dr. Flint, myself, and the history of my children, who, perhaps, were playing near the gate. One would say, "I wouldn't move my little finger to catch her, as old Flint's property." Another would say, "I'll catch *any* nigger for the reward. A man ought to have what belongs to him, if he *is* a damned brute." The opinion was often expressed that I was in the Free States. Very rarely did any one suggest that I might be in the vicinity. Had the least suspicion rested on my grandmother's house, it would have been burned to the ground. But it was the last place they thought of. Yet there was no place, where slavery existed, that could have afforded me so good a place of concealment.

Dr. Flint and his family repeatedly tried to coax and bribe my children to tell something they had heard said about me. One day the doctor took them into a shop, and offered them some bright little silver pieces and gay handkerchiefs if they would tell where their mother was. Ellen shrank away from him, and would not speak; but Benny spoke up, and said, "Dr. Flint, I don't know where my mother is. I guess she's in New York; and when you go there again, I wish you'd ask her to come home, for I want to see her; but if you put her in jail, or tell her you'll cut her head off, I'll tell her to go right back."

[After years in hiding, Linda Brent escaped to the North. She was reunited with her children, who had been bought by their white father, and found work in the Bruce household. The passage of the 1850 Fugitive Slave Law, however, made her and her children extremely vulnerable.]

XLI Free at Last[1]

Mrs. Bruce, and every member of her family, were exceedingly kind to me. I was thankful for the blessings of my lot, yet I could not always wear a cheerful countenance. I was doing harm to no one; on the contrary, I was doing all the good I could in my small way; yet I could never go out to breathe God's free air without trepidation at my heart. This seemed hard; and I could not think it was a right state of things in any civilized country.

From time to time I received news from my good old grandmother. She could not write; but she employed others to write for her. The following is an extract from one of her last letters:—

"Dear Daughter: I cannot hope to see you again on earth; but I pray to God to unite us above, where pain will no more rack this feeble body of mine; where sorrow and parting from my children will be no more.[2] *God has promised these things if we are faithful unto the end. My age and feeble health deprive me of going to church now; but God is with me here at home. Thank your brother for his kindness. Give much love to him, and tell him to remember the Creator in the days of his youth, and strive to meet me in the Father's kingdom.*[3] *Love to Ellen and Benjamin. Don't neglect him. Tell him for me, to be a good boy. Strive, my child, to train them for God's children. May he protect and provide for you, is the prayer of your loving old mother."*

[1] "Free at last, free at last,/ Thank God, almighty, I'm free at last." One version of a traditional spiritual.

[2] "And God shall wipe away all tears from their eyes; and there shall be no more death, neither sorrow, nor crying, neither shall there be any more pain; for the former things are passed away." Revelations 21:4.

[3] "Remember now thy Creator in the days of thy youth, while the evil days come not, nor the years draw nigh, when thou shalt say, I have no pleasure in them." Ecclesiastes 12:1.

These letters both cheered and saddened me. I was always glad to have tidings from the kind, faithful old friend of my unhappy youth; but her messages of love made my heart yearn to see her before she died, and I mourned over the fact that it was impossible. Some months after I returned from my flight to New England, I received a letter from her, in which she wrote, "Dr. Flint is dead. He has left a distressed family. Poor old man! I hope he made his peace with God."

I remembered how he had defrauded my grandmother of the hard earnings she had loaned; how he had tried to cheat her out of the freedom her mistress had promised her, and how he had persecuted her children; and I thought to myself that she was a better Christian than I was, if she could entirely forgive him. I cannot say, with truth, that the news of my old master's death softened my feelings towards him. There are wrongs which even the grave does not bury. The man was odious to me while he lived, and his memory is odious now.

His departure from this world did not diminish my danger. He had threatened my grandmother that his heirs should hold me in slavery after he was gone; that I never should be free so long as a child of his survived. As for Mrs. Flint, I had seen her in deeper afflictions than I supposed the loss of her husband would be, for she had buried several children; yet I never saw any signs of softening in her heart. The doctor had died in embarrassed circumstances, and had little to will to his heirs, except such property as he was unable to grasp. I was well aware what I had to expect from the family of Flints; and my fears were confirmed by a letter from the south, warning me to be on my guard, because Mrs. Flint openly declared that her daughter could not afford to lose so valuable a slave as I was.

I kept close watch of the newspapers for arrivals; but one Saturday night, being much occupied, I forgot to examine the Evening Express as usual. I went down into the parlor for it, early in the morning, and found the boy about to kindle a fire with it. I took it from him and examined the list of arrivals. Reader, if you have never been a slave, you cannot imagine the acute sensation of suffering at my heart, when I read the names of Mr. and Mrs. Dodge, at a hotel in Courtland Street. It was a third-rate hotel, and that circumstance convinced me of the truth of what I had heard, that they were short of funds and had need of my value, as *they* valued me; and that was by dollars and cents. I hastened with the paper to Mrs. Bruce. Her heart and hand were always open to every one in distress, and she always warmly sympathized with mine. It was impossible to tell how near the enemy was. He might have passed and repassed the house while we were sleeping. He might at that moment be waiting to pounce upon me if I ventured out of doors. I had never seen the husband of my young mistress, and therefore I could not distinguish him from any other stranger. A carriage was hastily ordered; and, closely veiled, I followed Mrs. Bruce, taking the baby again with me into exile. After various turnings and crossings, and returnings, the carriage stopped at the house of one of Mrs. Bruce's friends, where I was kindly received. Mrs. Bruce returned immediately, to instruct the domestics what to say if any one came to inquire for me.

It was lucky for me that the evening paper was not burned up before I had a chance to examine the list of arrivals. It was not long after Mrs. Bruce's return to her house, before several people came to inquire for me. One inquired for me, another asked for my daughter Ellen, and another said he had a letter from my grandmother, which he was requested to deliver in person.

They were told, "She *has* lived here, but she has left."

"How long ago?"

"I don't know, sir."

"Do you know where she went?"

"I do not, sir." And the door was closed.

This Mr. Dodge, who claimed me as his property, was originally a Yankee pedler in the south; then he became a merchant, and finally a slaveholder. He managed to get introduced into what was called the first society, and married Miss Emily Flint. A quarrel arose between him and her brother, and the brother cowhided him. This led to a family feud, and he proposed to remove to Virginia. Dr. Flint left him no property, and his own means had become circumscribed, while a wife and children depended upon him for support. Under these circumstances, it was very natural that he should make an effort to put me into his pocket.

I had a colored friend, a man from my native place, in whom I had the most implicit confidence. I sent for him, and told him that Mr. and Mrs. Dodge had arrived in New York. I proposed that he should call upon them to make inquiries about his friends at the south, with whom Dr. Flint's family were well acquainted. He thought there was no impropriety in his doing so, and he consented. He went to the hotel, and knocked at the door of Mr. Dodge's room, which was opened by the gentleman himself, who gruffly inquired, "What brought you here? How came you to know I was in the city?"

"Your arrival was published in the evening papers, sir; and I called to ask Mrs. Dodge about my friends at home. I didn't suppose it would give any offence."

"Where's that negro girl, that belongs to my wife?"

"What girl, sir?"

"You know well enough. I mean Linda, that ran away from Dr. Flint's plantation, some years ago. I dare say you've seen her, and know where she is."

"Yes, sir, I've seen her, and know where she is. She is out of your reach, sir."

"Tell me where she is, or bring her to me, and I will give her a chance to buy her freedom."

"I don't think it would be of any use, sir. I have heard her say she would go to the ends of the earth, rather than pay any man or woman for her freedom, because she thinks she has a right to it. Besides, she couldn't do it, if she would, for she has spent her earnings to educate her children."

This made Mr. Dodge very angry, and some high words passed between them. My friend was afraid to come where I was; but in the course of the day I received a note from him. I supposed they had not come from the south, in the winter, for a pleasure excursion; and now the nature of their business was very plain.

Mrs. Bruce came to me and entreated me to leave the city the next morning. She said her house was watched, and it was possible that some clew to me might be obtained. I refused to take her advice. She pleaded with an earnest tenderness, that ought to have moved me; but I was in a bitter, disheartened mood. I was weary of flying from pillar to post. I had been chased during half my life, and it seemed as if the chase was never to end. There I sat, in that great city, guiltless of crime, yet not daring to worship God in any of the churches. I heard the bells ringing for afternoon service, and, with contemptuous sarcasm, I said, "Will the preachers take for their text, 'Proclaim liberty to the captive, and the opening of prison doors to them that are bound'? or will they preach from the text. 'Do unto others as ye would they should do unto you'?"[4] Oppressed Poles and Hungarians could find a safe refuge in that city; John Mitchell was free to proclaim in the City Hall his desire for "a plantation well stocked with slaves;" but there I sat, an oppressed American, not daring to show my face.[5] God forgive the black and bitter thoughts I indulged on that Sabbath day! The Scripture says, "Oppression makes even a wise man mad"; and I was not wise.[6]

I had been told that Mr. Dodge said his wife had never signed away her right to my children, and if he could not get me, he would take them. This it was, more than any thing else, that roused such a tempest in my soul. Benjamin was with his uncle William in California, but my innocent young daughter had come to spend a vacation with me. I thought of what I had suffered in slavery at her age, and my heart was like a tiger's when a hunter tries to seize her young.

Dear Mrs. Bruce! I seem to see the expression of her face, as she turned away discouraged by my obstinate mood. Finding her expostulation unavailing, she sent Ellen to entreat me. When ten o'clock in the evening arrived and Ellen had not returned, this watchful and unwearied friend became anxious. She came to us in a carriage, bringing a well-filled trunk for my journey—trusting that by this time I would listen to reason. I yielded to her, as I ought to have done before.

The next day, baby and I set out in a heavy snow storm, bound for New England again. I received letters from the City of Iniquity, addressed to me under an assumed name. In a few days one came from Mrs. Bruce, informing me that my new master was still searching for me, and that she intended to put an end to this persecution by buying my freedom. I felt grateful for the kindness that prompted this offer, but the idea was not so pleasant to me as might have been expected. The more my mind had become enlightened, the more difficult it was for me to consider myself an article of property; and to pay money to those who had so grievously oppressed me seemed like taking from my sufferings the glory of triumph.[7] I wrote to Mrs. Bruce, thanking her, but saying that being sold from one owner to another seemed too much like slavery; that such a great obligation could not be easily cancelled; and that I preferred to go to my brother in California.

Without my knowledge, Mrs. Bruce employed a gentleman in New York to enter into negotiations with Mr. Dodge. He proposed to pay three hundred dollars down, if Mr. Dodge would sell me, and enter into obligations to relinquish all claim to me or my children forever after. He who called himself my master said he scorned so small an offer for such a valuable servant. The gentleman replied, "You can do as you choose, sir. If you reject this offer you will never get any thing; for the woman has friends who will convey her and her children out of the country."

[4]"The spirit of the Lord God is upon me because the Lord hath anointed one to preach good tidings unto the meek; he hath sent me to bind up the brokenhearted, to proclaim liberty to the captives, and the opening of the prison to them that are bound." Isaiah 61:1. "Therefore all things whatsoever ye would that men should do to you, do ye even so to them: for this is the law and the prophets." Matthew 7:12.

[5]In 1854 John Mitchell (1815–1875), Irish nationalist founder of the proslavery newspaper *The Citizen* of New York wrote: "We, for our part, wish we had a good plantation, well-stocked with healthy negroes, in Alabama."

[6]"Surely oppression maketh a wise man mad; and a gift destroyeth the heart." Ecclesiastes 7:17.

[7]"He hath stripped me of my glory, and taken the crown from my head." Job 19:9.

Mr. Dodge concluded that "half a loaf was better than no bread," and he agreed to the proffered terms. By the next mail I received this brief letter from Mrs. Bruce: "I am rejoiced to tell you that the money for your freedom has been paid to Mr. Dodge. Come home to-morrow. I long to see you and my sweet babe."

My brain reeled as I read these lines. A gentleman near me said, "It's true; I have seen the bill of sale." "The bill of sale!" Those words struck me like a blow. So I was *sold* at last! A human being *sold* in the free city of New York! The bill of sale is on record, and future generations will learn from it that women were articles of traffic in New York, late in the nineteenth century of the Christian religion. It may hereafter prove a useful document to antiquaries, who are seeking to measure the progress of civilization in the United States. I well know the value of that bit of paper; but much as I love freedom, I do not like to look upon it. I am deeply grateful to the generous friend who procured it, but I despise the miscreant who demanded payment for what never rightfully belonged to him or his.

I had objected to having my freedom bought, yet I must confess that when it was done I felt as if a heavy load had been lifted from my weary shoulders. When I rode home in the cars I was no longer afraid to unveil my face and look at people as they passed. I should have been glad to have met Daniel Dodge himself; to have had him seen me and known me, that he might have mourned over the untoward circumstances which compelled him to sell me for three hundred dollars.

When I reached home, the arms of my benefactress were thrown round me, and our tears mingled. As soon as she could speak, she said, "O Linda, I'm *so* glad it's all over! You wrote to me as if you thought you were going to be transferred from one owner to another. But I did not buy you for your services. I should have done just the same, if you had been going to sail for California tomorrow. I should, at least, have the satisfaction of knowing that you left me a free woman."

My heart was exceedingly full. I remembered how my poor father had tried to buy me, when I was a small child, and how he had been disappointed. I hoped his spirit was rejoicing over me now. I remembered how my good old grandmother had laid up her earnings to purchase me in later years, and how often her plans had been frustrated. How that faithful, loving old heart would leap for joy, if she could look on me and my children now that we were free! My relatives had been foiled in all their efforts, but God had raised me up a friend among strangers, who had bestowed on me the precious, long-desired boon. Friend! It is a common word, often lightly used. Like other good and beautiful things, It may be tarnished by careless handling; but when I speak of Mrs. Bruce as my friend, the word is sacred.

My grandmother lived to rejoice in my freedom; but not long after, a letter came with a black seal. She had gone "where the wicked cease from troubling, and the weary are at rest."[8]

Time passed on, and a paper came to me from the south, containing an obituary notice of my uncle Phillip. It was the only case I ever knew of such an honor conferred upon a colored person. It was written by one of his friends, and contained these words: "Now that death has laid him low, they call him a good man and a useful citizen; but what are eulogies to the black man, when the world has faded from

[8]Job 3:17.

his vision? It does not require man's praise to obtain rest in God's kingdom." So they called a colored man a *citizen!* Strange words to be uttered in that region![9]

Reader, my story ends with freedom; not in the usual way, with marriage. I and my children are now free! We are as free from the power of slaveholders as are the white people of the north; and though that, according to my ideas, is not saying a great deal, it is a vast improvement in *my* condition. The dream of my life is not yet realized. I do not sit with my children in a home of my own. I still long for a hearthstone of my own, however humble. I wish it for my children's sake far more than for my own. But God so orders circumstances as to keep me with my friend Mrs. Bruce. Love, duty, gratitude, also bind me to her side. It is a privilege to serve her who pities my oppressed people, and who has bestowed the inestimable boon of freedom on me and my children.

It has been painful to me, in many ways, to recall the dreary years I passed in bondage. I would gladly forget them if I could. Yet the retrospection is not altogether without solace; for with those gloomy recollections come tender memories of my good old grandmother, like light, fleecy clouds floating over a dark and troubled sea.

1861

Harriet Jacobs to Ednah Dow Cheney

Edenton [North Carolina] April 25th [1867]

Dear Mrs Cheney[1]

I felt I would like to write you a line from my old home. I am sitting under the old roof twelve feet from the spot where I suffered all the crushing weight of slavery. thank God the bitter cup is drained of its last dreg.[2] there is no more need of hiding places to conceal slave Mothers. yet it was little to purchase the blessings of freedom. I could have worn this poor life out there to save my Children from the misery and degradation of Slavery.

I had long thought I had no attachment to my old home. as I often sit here and think of those I loved of their hard struggle in life—their unfaltering love and devotion toward myself and Children. I love to sit here and think of them. they have made the few sunny spots in that dark life sacred to me.

[9]In 1844 the North Carolina Supreme Court had declared that "free persons of color in this State are not to be considered as citizens. . . ." An older law, referred to by David Walker, required that free black people wear a patch on their clothing.

[1]Ednah Dow Little Hale Cheney (1824–1904), Boston philanthropist, writer and abolitionist, served as Secretary of the New England Freedmen's Aid Society from 1867 until 1875. She evidently became acquainted with Jacobs in connection with Jacobs's relief work in Alexandria and Savannah. (*Notable American Women.*) The non-standard usage in this letter exists in the original.

[2]"Awake, awake, stand up, O Jerusalem, which hast drunk at the hand of the Lord, the cup of his fury; thou has drunken the dregs of the cup of trembling, and wrung them out." Isaiah 51:17.

I cannot tell you how I feel in this place. the change is so great I can hardly take it all in I was born here, and amid all these new born blessings, the old dark cloud comes over me, and I find it hard to have faith in rebels.

the past winter was very severe for this region of Country it caused much suffering, and the freedmen with but few exceptions were cheated out of their crop of cotton. their contract masters shipped it for them, and when they ask for a settlement, they are answered I am daily expecting the returns. these men have gone to work cheerfully, planted another crop without the returns to live on until their present crop is made. many of the large plantations of the once wealthy Planter, is worked under the control of Colored Men. the Owners let their Plantations to the freedmen in prefference to the poor Whites. they believe the Negro determined to make money, and they will get the largest portion of it. last years experience I think will be a proffitable lesson many will learn to act for themselves. Negro suffrage is making a stir in this place. the rebels are striving to make these people feel they are their true friends, and they must not be led astray by the Yankees. the freedmen ask if Abraham Lincoln[3] led them astray, that his friends is their friends his enemies their enemies.

I have spent much of my time on the Plantations distributing seed and trying to teach the women to make Yankee gardens.[4] they plant everything to mature in the summer, like their corn and cotton fields. I have hunted up all the old people, done what I could for them. I love to work for these old people. many of them I have known from Childhood

there is one School in Edenton well attended.[5] on some of the Plantations there is from 15 to 25 Children that cannot attend School, the distance is so far. some of the freedmen are very anxious to establish Plantation schools, as soon as the more advanced Schools, can send out teachers. many of the freedmen are willing and will sustain their teachers. at present there is a great revival in the colored Churches. the Whites say the Niggers sung and prayed until they got their freedom, and they are not satisfied. now they are singing and praying for judgment. the white members of the Baptist Church invited the colored members to their Church, to help them sing and pray. I assure you they have done it with a will. I never saw such a state of excitement the Churches have been open night and day. these people have time to think of their souls, now they are not compelled to think for the Negro.

my love to Miss Daisy.[6] I send her some Jassmine blossoms tell her they bear the fragrance of freedom.

Yours Truly
H Jacobs

1867

[3]Abraham Lincoln (1809–1865), sixteenth President of the United States and signer of the Emancipation Proclamation.

[4]Jacobs made a practice of this. Child noted, "I found eleven letters awaiting me . . . . One of them was from Mrs. Jacobs, asking for garden seeds for some freedmen in Georgia, where she is at present." (Child to [Lucy Osgood], April 1, 1866, Wayland [Massachusetts], L. M. Child Papers Microform 64/1715.)

[5]On October 23, 1866, it was ordered that the freedmen of the Town of Edenton be allowed to build a Schoolhouse in the Town Commons east of Oakum Street . . . ." In 1868, "The Sewing Society of colored persons" was granted use of the Town Hall for a fair to raise money to pay for the schoolhouse lot. (Edenton, N.C., Town Minutes, 1865–1887, October 13, 1866, p. 19; July 2, 1868, p. 32. North Carolina State Archives)

[6]Cheney's daughter Margaret Swan Cheney (b. 1855).

Issues and Visions in Pre–Civil War America

We suggested in the Introduction that much literature of the early nineteenth century was directed to influencing the audience's ideas about the issues of the time and thus their actions in the world. Today's readers have often been taught that such hortatory writing is inherently less valuable than what is called "belles lettres," which appear to make no claims on our actions. That is not a view of "literature" with which most nineteenth-century intellectuals would have agreed. Regardless of how one evaluates persuasive literature, however, a great deal of nineteenth-century writing aimed to move its readers to feel and to act. This section presents a sample of such work.

While much of this writing takes essay or speech form, some emerges as poetry or fiction, as in the case of John Greenleaf Whittier and Frances Ellen Watkins Harper. The Whittier poems included here were primarily efforts to mobilize sentiment against slavery. And a poem like Harper's "Free Labor" is, among other things, implicitly an argument against purchasing slave-produced fabrics. But "essay" is itself a broadly inclusive term, covering as it does work as varied as Fanny Fern's informal *Fern Leaves* and Thoreau's *Walden,* ceremonious addresses, and the religious controversy and public letters of the Grimké sisters. These works are also diverse in that they come from every corner of the United States and from very distinct cultures. They also illustrate the continuities with and changes from important forms of discourse developed in the seventeenth and eighteenth centuries. In fact, the forms of personal narrative and religious and political controversy did not disappear with the Revolution; rather, they evolved in the ways illustrated by the works in this section.

While this literature presents a mix of forms, it also offers a power of language too often obscured because those forms—essay, letter, and speech—have generally been placed at a discount relative to poetry or fiction. Nevertheless, we find here phrases that have entered the common culture, like Sojourner Truth's question, "Ain't I a woman?" And we find passages of prose as evocative as those in any fiction, like the conclusion of Thomas Wentworth Higginson's essay on Nat Turner's slave insurrection:

> *While these things were going on, the enthusiasm for the Polish Revolution was rising to its height. The nation was ringing with a peal of joy, on hearing that at Frankfort the Poles had killed fourteen thousand Russians. The* Southern Religious Telegraph *was publishing an impassioned address to Kosciuszko; standards were being consecrated for Poland in the larger cities; heroes like Skrzynecki, Czartoryski, Rozyski, Raminski were choking the trump of Fame with their complicated patronymics. These are all forgotten now; and this poor negro, who did not even possess a name, beyond one abrupt monosyllable,—for even the name of Turner was the master's property,—still lives, a memory of terror, and a symbol of wild retribution.*

The issues these works address remain alive today: racism, inequality between the sexes, nonviolence as a means for effecting change, the place of languages and cultures other than English in the United States, voting, individualism, how we treat nature. For the most part, we have organized the writing in this section on the basis of such issues. In that way, readers can, we think, see how the issues are differently addressed by the writers, and how over a period of time they develop. For example, Thoreau's essay called "Civil Disobedience" ("Resistance to Civil Government," 1849) is often thought of as the origin of the concept of non-violent resistance to tyranny. But we see the idea posed more than a decade before in Angelina Grimké's "Appeal to the Christian Women of the South" (1836). In fact, the concept was deeply embedded in the evangelical Christianity of the time, especially in the work of reformers like William Lloyd Garrison and his followers. In a different way, one can follow in these works the conflicts about women's roles and possibilities from the 1830s through the 1860s. These debates, apart from their inherent interest, also affected the conceptions of character and conflict in many of the period's fictions, like *The Scarlet Letter* and *Uncle Tom's Cabin*.

But while the issues provide our organizing principle, we have not included works simply because they are of historical interest. Rather, we feel that the essays, poems, sketches, and letters printed here continue to speak effectively to readers today.

Paul Lauter
Trinity College

INDIAN VOICES

William Apess[1] *(Pequot) 1798–?*

The earliest major Indian writer of the nineteenth century, William Apess was born in 1798 near Colrain, Massachusetts. Apess's mother may, however, have been Candace Apes, who was owned as a slave and listed as a "Negro" woman by Captain Joseph Taylor of Colchester until he freed her in 1805 at age twenty-eight. The author's father, whose name was probably William A. Apes, was half white. His paternal grandmother was a full-blooded Pequot, who Apess claimed was descended from Metacomet (Wampanoag; c. 1639–1676, given the name King Philip by the English). After his parents separated when Apess was around three, he was reared by his maternal grandparents. Badly beaten by his alcoholic grandmother, Apess was subsequently bound out to whites at age four or five—a common practice for dealing with homeless children. Apess's pranks and strong will resulted in his being transferred to a series of masters. During his service to his last master, Apess was converted to Methodism in March, 1813, at age fifteen. Forbidden by his master to attend any more Methodist revivals, Apess ran away. He subsequently enlisted in the army during the War of 1812 and served during the 1814 invasions of Canada and defense of Plattsburgh, New York. In 1817, Apess returned to Connecticut, where he was reunited with Pequot relatives. Between 1821 and 1822, after he rejoined his parents near Colrain, Apess began serving as a lay preacher to mixed audiences. Apess's preaching was opposed by both his father and the local Methodist circuit rider, who forbade him to preach. In 1821, Apess married Mary Wood, a woman "nearly the same color as himself" (*A Son of the Forest,*

[1]Although Apess spelled his name as *Apes* in his early publications, he changed it to *Apess* in the second editon of *The Eulogy on King Philip* (1836) published in 1837 and in the second edition of *The Experience of Five Christian Indians* (1835). In legal documents of 1836 and 1837, his name also appears as *Apess.* His parents and other family members are alluded to as *Apes.* See Barry O'Connell, *On Our Own Ground,* xiv.

98), and supported his wife and growing family with a variety of jobs. After Apess moved to Providence, Rhode Island, he became in 1825 a "class leader" in a Methodist church. He was regularly ordained in 1829 as a minister by the Methodist Society.

Apess's *A Son of the Forest* (1829) is the first published autobiography written by an Indian. It appeared during the controversy over the Indian Removal Bill (1830), which authorized the federal government to remove Indians from lands east of the Mississippi to Indian Territory and other areas deemed suitable. The autobiography is a testament both to the essential humanity of Indian people and to their potential for adapting to white concepts of civilization. *A Son of the Forest* follows the basic structure of the spiritual confession, popular at that time. Apess's account of his experiences is especially interesting because he was primarily raised by whites. He describes how he was terrified of his own people because whites filled him with stereotypical stories about Indian cruelty but never told him how cruelly they treated Indians.

Apess published a briefer life history in *The Experiences of Five Christian Indians of the Pequod Tribe* (1833). Probably written before *A Son of the Forest,* this account is more critical of whites than the autobiography; the first edition of this book contained the essay "An Indian's Looking-Glass for the White Man," which was omitted in the 1837 edition, published as *The Experiences of Five Christian Indians of the Pequod Tribe.* This essay illustrates the themes present in Apess's work and the forceful style which made him a persuasive speaker. Apess contrasts whites' savage treatment of non-whites with their professed Christianity—a frequent theme in nineteenth-century slave narratives and life histories of Indian converts. Here, as in *A Son of the Forest* and *The Experiences of Five Christian Indians,* Apess blames whites for the alcoholism that has decimated Indian families. His criticism of Indian agents is another theme common in Indian life histories. Apess effectively focuses the essay on the equality of people of color with whites. This concept of equality of all people under God made Christianity very appealing to Indian converts and to slaves.

Apess's last two books grew out of his commitment to the fight for Indian rights. He describes the Mashpee struggle to retain self government in *Indian Nullification of the Unconstitutional Laws of Massachusetts, Relative to the Marshpee [sic] Tribe* (1835), one of the most powerful pieces of Indian protest literature of the first half of the nineteenth century. A mixture of Indian, white, and black, the Mashpees were subjected to considerable white prejudice. Apess's contact with them and their fight for civil and political rights turned Apess into a dedicated social reformer. Apess organized a council to draw up grievances, moved his family to Mashpee, became a spokesman for the tribe, and publicized their case in the Boston press. By 1834, his efforts gained success, as evidenced by the large audience that heard his Boston speech on the subject. The same year William Lloyd Garrison, the abolitionist editor, took up the cause of the Mashpee in *The Liberator.* Apess's efforts helped the Mashpees regain their rights, one of the few such Indian victories in the 1830s. However, the nation's attention was increasingly drawn away from the plight of the American Indian to the debate over the abolition of slavery. To remind whites of what New England Indians had endured, Apess wrote his final work, the eloquent *Eulogy on King Philip* (1836). Originally delivered as a series of lectures at the Odeon in Boston, the *Eulogy on King Philip* is a study of White-Indian relations in seventeenth- and eighteenth-century New England. After this work was published, Apess disappeared from public view and the details of his later life are unknown.

A. LaVonne Brown Ruoff
University of Illinois at Chicago

PRIMARY WORK

On Our Own Ground: The Complete Writings of William Apess, a Pequot, ed. Barry O'Connell, 1992.

SECONDARY WORKS

Kim McQuaid, "William Apess, Pequot, An Indian Reformer in the Jackson Era," *New England Quarterly* 50 (1977):605–25; Arnold Krupat, *The Voice in the Margin: Native American Literature and the Canon,* 1989; A. LaVonne Brown Ruoff, "Three Nineteenth Century American Indian Autobiographers," *Redefining American Literary History,* eds. A. LaVonne Brown Ruoff and Jerry W. Ward, Jr., 1990; David Murray, *Forked Tongues: Speech, Writing and Representation in North American Indian Texts,* 1991; Barry O'Connell, Introduction, *On Our Own Ground,* 1992; *Handbook of Native American Literature,* 1996.

An Indian's Looking-Glass for the White Man

Having a desire to place a few things before my fellow creatures who are travelling with me to the grave, and to that God who is the maker and preserver both of the white man and the Indian, whose abilities are the same, and who are to be judged by one God, who will show no favor to outward appearances, but will judge righteousness. Now I ask if degradation has not been heaped long enough upon the Indians? And if so, can there not be a compromise; is it right to hold and promote prejudices? If not, why not put them all away? I mean here amongst those who are civilized. It may be that many are ignorant of the situation of many of my brethren within the limits of New England. Let me for a few moments turn your attention to the reservations in the different states of New England, and, with but few exceptions, we shall find them as follows: The most mean, abject, miserable race of beings in the world—a complete place of prodigality and prostitution.

Let a gentleman and lady, of integrity and respectability visit these places, and they would be surprised; as they wandered from one hut to the other they would view with the females who are left alone, children half starved, and some almost as naked as they came into the world. And it is a fact that I have seen them as much so—while the females are left without protection, and are seduced by white men, and are finally left to be common prostitutes for them, and to be destroyed by that burning, fiery curse, that has swept millions, both of red and white men, into the grave with sorrow and disgrace—Rum. One reason why they are left so is, because their most sensible and active men are absent at sea. Another reason is, because they are made to believe they are minors and have not the abilities given them from God, to take care of themselves, without it is to see to a few little articles, such as baskets and brooms. Their land is in common stock, and they have nothing to make them enterprising.

Another reason is because those men who are Agents, many of them are unfaithful, and care not whether the Indians live or die; they are much imposed upon by their neighbors who have no principle. They would think it no crime to go upon Indian lands and cut and carry off their most valuable timber, or any thing else they chose; and I doubt not but they think it clear gain. Another reason is because they have no education to take care of themselves; if they had, I would risk them to take care of their property.

Now I will ask, if the Indians are not called the most ingenious people amongst us? And are they not said to be men of talents? And I would ask, could there be a more efficient way to distress and murder them by inches than the way they have taken? And there is no people in the world but who may be destroyed in the same way. Now if these people are what they are held up in our view to be, I would take the liberty to ask why they are not brought forward and pains taken to educate them? to give them all a common education, and those of the brightest and first-rate talents put forward and held up to office. Perhaps some unholy, unprincipled men would cry out, the skin was not good enough; but stop friends—I am not talking about the skin, but about principles. I would ask if there cannot be as good feelings and principles under a red skin as there can be under a white? And let me ask, is it not on the account of a bad principle, that we who are red children have had to suffer so much as we have? And let me ask, did not this bad principle proceed from the whites or their forefathers? And I would ask, is it worth while to nourish it any longer? If not, then let us have a change; although some men no doubt will spout their corrupt principles against it, that are in the halls of legislation and elsewhere. But I presume this kind of talk will seem surprising and horrible. I do not see why it should so long as they (the whites) say that they think as much of us as they do of themselves.

This I have heard repeatedly, from the most respectable gentlemen and ladies—and having heard so much precept, I should now wish to see the example. And I would ask who has a better right to look for these things than the naturalist himself—the candid man would say none.

I know that many say that they are willing, perhaps the majority of the people, that we should enjoy our rights and privileges as they do. If so, I would ask why are not we protected in our persons and property throughout the Union? Is it not because there reigns in the breast of many who are leaders, a most unrighteous, unbecoming and impure black principle, and as corrupt and unholy as it can be—while these very same unfeeling, self-esteemed characters pretend to take the skin as a pretext to keep us from our unalienable and lawful rights? I would ask you if you would like to be disfranchised from all your rights, merely because your skin is white, and for no other crime? I'll venture to say, these very characters who hold the skin to be such a barrier in the way, would be the first to cry out, injustice! awful injustice!

But, reader, I acknowledge that this is a confused world, and I am not seeking for office; but merely placing before you the black inconsistency that you place before me—which is ten times blacker than any skin that you will find in the Universe. And now let me exhort you to do away that principle, as it appears ten times worse in the sight of God and candid men, than skins of color—more disgraceful than all the skins that Jehovah ever made. If black or red skins, or any other skin of color is disgraceful to God, it appears that he has disgraced himself a great deal—for he has made fifteen colored people to one white, and placed them here upon this earth.

Now let me ask you, white man, if it is a disgrace for to eat, drink and sleep with the image of God, or sit, or walk and talk with them? Or have you the folly to think that the white man, being one in fifteen or sixteen, are the only beloved images of God? Assemble all nations together in your imagination, and then let the whites be seated amongst them, and then let us look for the whites, and I doubt not it would be hard finding them; for to the rest of the nations, they are still but a handful. Now suppose these skins were put together, and each skin had its national crimes written upon it—which skin do you think would have the greatest? I will ask one question more. Can you charge the Indians with robbing a nation almost of their whole Continent, and murdering their women and children, and then depriving the remainder of their lawful rights, that nature and God require them to have? And to cap the climax, rob another nation to till their grounds, and welter out their days under the lash with hunger and fatigue under the scorching rays of a burning sun? I should look at all the skins, and I know that when I cast my eye upon that white skin, and if I saw those crimes written upon it, I should enter my protest against it immediately, and cleave to that which is more honorable. And I can tell you that I am satisfied with the manner of my creation, fully—whether others are or not.

But we will strive to penetrate more fully into the conduct of those who profess to have pure principles, and who tell us to follow Jesus Christ and imitate him and have his Spirit. Let us see if they come any where near him and his ancient disciples. The first thing we are to look at, are his precepts, of which we will mention a few. "Thou shalt love the Lord thy God with all thy heart, with all thy soul, with all thy mind, and with all thy strength." The second is like unto it. "Thou shalt love thy neighbor as thyself." On these two precepts hang all the law and the prophets.—Matt. xxii. 37, 38, 39, 40. "By this shall all men know that they are my disciples, if ye have love one to another"—John xiii. 35. Our Lord left this special command with his followers, that they should love one another.

Again, John in his Epistles says, "He who loveth God, loveth his brother also"—iv. 21. "Let us not love in word but in deed"—iii. 18. "Let your love be without dissimulation. See that ye love one another with a pure heart fervently"—1. Peter, viii. 22. "If any man say, I love God, and hateth his brother, he is a liar"—John iv. 20. "Whosoever hateth his brother is a murderer, and no murderer hath eternal life abiding in him." The first thing that takes our attention, is the saying of Jesus, "Thou shalt love," &c. The first question I would ask my brethren in the ministry, as well as that of the membership, What is love, or its effects? Now if they who teach are not essentially affected with pure love, the love of God, how can they teach as they ought? Again, the holy teachers of old said, "Now if any man have not the spirit of Christ, he is none of his"—Rom. viii. 9. Now my brethren in the ministry, let me ask you a few sincere questions. Did you ever hear or read of Christ teaching his disciples that they ought to despise one because his skin was different from theirs? Jesus Christ being a Jew, and those of his Apostles certainly were not whites,—and did not he who completed the plan of salvation complete it for the whites as well as for the Jews, and others? And were not the whites the most degraded people on the earth at that time, and none were more so; for they sacrificed their children to dumb idols! And did not St. Paul labor more abundantly for building up a christian nation amongst you than any of the Apostles. And you know as well as I that you are not indebted to a principle beneath a white skin for your religious services, but to a colored one.

What then is the matter now; is not religion the same now under a colored skin as it ever was? If so I would ask why is not a man of color respected; you may say as many say, we have white men enough. But was this the spirit of Christ and his Apostles? If it had been, there would not have been one white preacher in the world—for Jesus Christ never would have imparted his grace or word to them, for he could forever have withheld it from them. But we find that Jesus Christ and his Apostles never looked at the outward appearances. Jesus in particular looked at the hearts, and his Apostles through him being discerners of the spirit, looked at their fruit without any regard to the skin, color or nation; as St. Paul himself speaks, "Where there is neither Greek nor Jew, circumcision nor uncircumcision, Barbarian nor Scythian, bond nor free—but Christ is all and in all."[1] If you can find a spirit like Jesus Christ and his Apostles prevailing now in any of the white congregations, I should like to know it. I ask, is it not the case that every body that is not white is treated with contempt and counted as barbarians? And I ask if the word of God justifies the white man in so doing? When the prophets prophesied, of whom did they speak? When they spoke of heathens, was it not the whites and others who were counted Gentiles? And I ask if all nations with the exception of the Jews were not counted heathens? and according to the writings of some, it could not mean the Indians, for they are counted Jews. And now I would ask, why is all this distinction made among these christian societies? I would ask what is all this ado about Missionary Societies, if it be not to christianize those who are not christians? And what is it for? To degrade them worse, to bring them into society where they must welter out their days in disgrace merely because their skin is of a different complexion. What folly it is to try to make the state of human society worse than it is. How astonished some may be at this—but let me ask, is it not so? Let me refer you to the churches only. And my brethren, is there any agreement? Do brethren and sisters love one another?—Do they not rather hate one another? Outward forms and ceremonies, the lusts of the flesh, the lusts of the eye and pride of life is of more value to many professors, than the love of God shed abroad in their hearts, or an attachment to his altar, to his ordinances or to his children. But you may ask who are the children of God? perhaps you may say none but white. If so, the word of the Lord is not true.

I will refer you to St. Peter's precepts—Acts 10. "God is no respecter of persons"—&c. Now if this is the case, my white brother, what better are you than God? And if no better, why do you profess his gospel and to have his spirit, act so contrary to it? Let me ask why the men of a different skin are so dispised, why are not they educated and placed in your pulpits? I ask if his services well performed are not as good as if a white man performed them? I ask if a marriage or a funeral ceremony, or the ordinance of the Lord's house would not be as acceptable in the sight of God as though he was white? And if so, why is it not to you? I ask again, why is it not as acceptable to have men to exercise their office in one place as well as in another? Perhaps you will say that if we admit you to all of these privileges you will want more. I expect that I can guess what that is—Why, say you, there would be intermarriages. How that would be I am not able to say—and if it should be, it would be nothing strange or new to me; for I can assure you that I know a great many that have intermarried, both of the whites and the Indians—and many are their sons and daughters—and people too of the first respectability. And I could point to some in the famous city of Boston and elsewhere. You may now look at the disgraceful act in the statute law passed by the Legislature of Massachusetts, and behold the fifty pound fine levied upon any Clergyman or Justice of the Peace that dare to encourage the laws of God and nature by a legitimate union in holy wedlock between the Indians and whites. I would ask how this looks to your law makers. I would ask if this corresponds with your sayings—that you think as much of the Indians as you do of the whites. I do not wonder that you blush many of you while you read; for many

[1]Colossians 3:11.

have broken the ill-fated laws made by man to hedge up the laws of God and nature. I would ask if they who have made the law have not broken it—but there is no other state in New England that has this law but Massachusetts; and I think as many of you do not, that you have done yourselves no credit.

But as I am not looking for a wife, having one of the finest cast, as you no doubt would understand while you read her experience and travail of soul in the way to heaven, you will see that it is not my object. And if I had none, I should not want any one to take my right from me and choose a wife for me; for I think that I or any of my brethren have a right to choose a wife for themselves as well as the whites—and as the whites have taken the liberty to choose my brethren, the Indians, hundreds and thousands of them as partners in life, I believe the Indians have as much right to choose their partners amongst the whites if they wish. I would ask you if you can see any thing inconsistent in your conduct and talk about the Indians? And if you do, I hope you will try to become more consistent. Now if the Lord Jesus Christ, who is counted by all to be a Jew, and it is well known that the Jews are a colored people, especially those living in the East, where Christ was born—and if he should appear amongst us, would he not be shut out of doors by many, very quickly? and by those too, who profess religion?

By what you read, you may learn how deep your principles are. I should say they were skin deep. I should not wonder if some of the most selfish and ignorant would spout a charge of their principles now and then at me. But I would ask, how are you to love your neighbors as yourself? Is it to cheat them? is it to wrong them in any thing? Now to cheat them out of any of their rights is robbery. And I ask, can you deny that you are not robbing the Indians daily, and many others? But at last you may think I am what is called a hard and uncharitable man. But not so. I believe there are many who would not hesitate to advocate our cause; and those too who are men of fame and respectability—as well as ladies of honor and virtue. There is a Webster,[2] an Everett,[3] and a Wirt,[4] and many others who are distinguished characters—besides an host of my fellow citizens, who advocate our cause daily. And how I congratulate such noble spirits—how they are to be prized and valued; for they are well calculated to promote the happiness of mankind. They well know that man was made for society, and not for hissing stocks and outcasts. And when such a principle as this lies within the hearts of men, how much it is like its God—and how it honors its Maker—and how it imitates the feelings of the good Samaritan, that had his wounds bound up, who had been among thieves and robbers.

Do not get tired, ye noble-hearted—only think how many poor Indians want their wounds done up daily; the Lord will reward you, and pray you stop not till this tree of distinction shall be levelled to the earth, and the mantle of prejudice torn from every American heart—then shall peace pervade the Union.

1833

[2]Daniel Webster (1782–1852) was a senator, statesman, and orator. In 1827, serving as President John Quincy Adams's spokesperson in the House of Representatives, Webster strongly attacked the State of Georgia for asserting claim to Cherokee land.

[3]Edward Everett (1794–1865), Unitarian clergyman, famed orator, and teacher of Ralph Waldo Emerson. In 1831 Everett spoke for two days in the House of Representatives in a losing battle to secure the Cherokees their annuity.

[4]William Wirt (1772–1834), lawyer, U.S. Attorney General, and author of "Letters of a British Spy" (1803). Outraged by the passage of the Indian Removal Bill in 1830, Wirt became counsel to the Cherokees. A year later, he argued eloquently but unsuccessfully for the Cherokees when they brought to the Supreme Court a case against the State of Georgia based on the tribe's status as a foreign nation.

John Wannuaucon Quinney (Mahican) 1797–1855

In a speech at Reidsville, New York, on July 4, 1854, John W. Quinney (The Dish) sought to prick the consciences of his listeners by reminding them of the epidemic diseases, warfare, broken treaties, and land appropriations that had characterized Indian history throughout the eras of European colonialism and American domination on the continent. He recognized the irony of a grand sachem of the Stockbridge Indians as the featured speaker on Independence Day. Instead of the American promise of freedom, equality, progress, and self-determination, Stockbridge history was marked by genocide, injustice, displacement, and removals, and Quinney appealed for justice for the American Indians, no matter how long it might be delayed.

When Quinney was born at New Stockbridge, New York, in 1797, the Stockbridges, of which the Mahicans were a part, were in the second major phase of their development as a social group forged by more than a century and a half of contact with non-Indians. At first contact, the Mahicans occupied territory on both sides of the Hudson from Lake Champlain south to the Catskills and had close ties to the Esopus, Wappinger, and other Munsee groups, their southern neighbors. By 1700 they had been reduced to about 500, and amalgamation with other tribes had begun, mainly as a result of epidemic diseases, warfare, and the encroachments of Europeans. They continued to decline and disperse to other regions, and in the early 1730s missionaries went among the Mahicans and Housatonics on the Housatonic River in western Massachusetts and established a mission town called Stockbridge. By 1738 remnants of various tribes in the region had moved to Stockbridge, but the Mahicans dominated. It was during this period that the Quinney name became associated with Stockbridge affairs. By the close of the Revolutionary War, the Stockbridges were inclined to move because of continued attrition of numbers, the effects of the war, takeover of the Stockbridge community by whites, and the Stockbridges' propensity for the vices of nearby white neighbors. Thus, at the invitation of the Oneidas, in the mid-1780s they removed to Oneida Creek, New York, where they established New Stockbridge. There they formed the stable farming community into which John W. Quinney was born.

By that time, however, Stockbridge leader Hendrick Aupaumut was convinced that they must abandon New Stockbridge. He feared the disruptive influence of both the neighboring whites and the Oneidas, the former because of their vices and the latter because of their encouragment of Stockbridge men to abandon farming and their attempts to introduce Handsome Lake's religion into the community. From the 1790s onward, Aupaumut encouraged removal to the West, an idea that had become a plan by the time Quinney reached his mid-twenties; Quinney's role in carrying out that plan was his first step toward Stockbridge leadership.

When Quinney delivered his Independence Day address in 1854, he was near the end of a long career as a well-known Stockbridge diplomat, lobbyist, and political leader. In 1822 he was one of three agents who went to Green Bay to purchase land on which New York Indians who wished to remove could resettle. They bought land from the Menominees, and the Stockbridges began removing in groups, one each year, until removal was completed in 1829. By then, however, their future in Wisconsin was doubtful. In 1827, U.S. commissioners had met with the Indians ostensibly to settle their boundaries but instead had bought a tract from the Menominees, including the land on the Fox River they had previously sold to the Stockbridges. Quinney represented the Stockbridges in Washington in 1828 and

1830, attempting to secure a valid title to their lands, but in 1831, the Menominees repudiated their sale to the New York Indians. The Stockbridges and Munsees then separated from the rest of the New York Indians and negotiated on their own; thus Quinney returned to Washington in 1831 and was instrumental in securing a treaty in 1832 that granted them two townships on the east side of Lake Winnebago, where they settled and reestablished their community.

Their affairs did not remain settled very long. In 1837 Quinney drafted a constitution, which a majority of the Stockbridges adopted, giving up their system of governance by hereditary leadership. With each removal, beginning with the first one from their small villages to Stockbridge, Massachusetts, amalgamation had continued and the process of acculturation had accelerated. Among a part of the population, however, some of the old ideas were slow to die and retained considerable force. Thus contention resulted between the constitutional faction and those who were reluctant to give up traditional governance practices. The result was an agreement to sell half of their land so that those who wished to remove farther west could do so. During the next five years, Quinney represented the Stockbridges before Congress, where he sought settlement of their various claims for losses during their removals. In 1843 the Stockbridges were divided once more when Congress made them U.S. citizens and individual landowners. Quinney once again represented them in Washington, seeking a return to tribal status for those who wanted it. Restoration came in 1846, though not before much Stockbridge land had been lost through sales. In order to prevent further difficulties for his people, Quinney helped negotiate a treaty in 1848 by which they agreed to remove farther west if suitable land could be found. By 1852, however, no selection had been made. By then, Quinney concluded that he was too old and poor to face another removal, and he pleaded with Congress to grant him title to his home at Stockbridge. His plea, which Congress granted in 1854, meant that he was willing to accept U.S. citizenship. Quinney died at Stockbridge, Wisconsin, on July 21, 1855. The following year, a new treaty with the Menominees granted lands to the Stockbridges and Munsees in Shawano County, to which those who had not become citizens removed for the last time between 1856 and 1859.

In his memorial to Congress in 1852, Quinney called himself "a true Native American," the first use of that term, some scholars believe, in reference to the indigenous peoples of America. The term refers to more than racial or cultural identity. Quinney's memorial, like his speech, reflects his intense awareness of the Mahican presence in American history from King Phillip's War to Manifest Destiny. His personal history—his education, life style, acceptance of citizenship, even the popular oratorical style in which he delivered his public statement—attested to the acculturation that had been necessary for survival in the face of Euro-American expansion. It attested as well to the extinction or near extinction of many of the peoples who once inhabited the northeastern region of the new American nation. When he died, the Mahican nation had all but disappeared, and he was aptly referred as one of the "Last of the Mohicans."

Daniel F. Littlefield, Jr.
University of Arkansas at Little Rock

PRIMARY WORK

"Quinney's Speech," (1854).

SECONDARY WORKS

Levi Konkapot, Jr., "The Last of the Mohicans," *Wisconsin Historical Society Report and Collections 1857–58* 4 (1859):303–307; "Death of John W. Quinney," *Wisconsin Historical Society Report and Collections 1857–58* 4 (1859):309–311; Frederick J. Dockstader, *Great North American Indians,* 1977:227–228; T.J. Brasser, "Mahican," *Handbook of North American Indians,* vol. 15 Northeast, ed. Bruce G. Trigger. 1978:198–212.

Quinney's Speech

It may appear to those whom I have the honor to address, a singular taste, for me, an Indian, to take an interest in the triumphal days of a people, who occupy by conquest, or have usurped the possession of the territories of my fathers, and have laid and carefully preserved, a train of terrible miseries, to end when my race shall have ceased to exist. But thanks to the fortunate circumstances of my life, I have been taught in the schools, and been able to read your histories and accounts of Europeans, yourselves and the Red Man; which instruct me, that while your rejoicings today are commemorative of the free birth of this giant nation, they simply convey to my mind, the recollection of a transfer of the miserable weakness and dependance of my race from one great power to another.

My friends, I am getting old, and have witnessed, for many years, your increase in wealth and power, while the steady consuming decline of my tribe, admonishes me, that their extinction is inevitable—they know it themselves, and the reflection teaches them humility and resignation, directing their attention to the existence of those happy hunting-grounds which the Great Father has prepared for all his red children.

In this spirit, my friends (being invited to come here), as a Muh-he-con-new, and now standing upon the soil which once was, and now ought to be, the property of this tribe, I have thought for once, and certainly the last time, I would shake you by the hand, and ask you to listen, for a little while, to what I have to say.

In the documentary papers of this state, and in the various histories of early events in the settlement of this part of the country by the whites, the many traditions of my tribe, which are as firmly believed as written annals by you, inform me that there are many errors. Without, however, intending to refer to, and correct those histories, I will give you what those traditions are.

About the year 1645, and when King Ben (the last of the hereditary chiefs of the Muh-he-con-new Nation) was in his prime, a Grand Council was convened of the Muh-he-con-new tribe, for the purpose of conveying from the old to the young men, a knowledge of the past. Councils, for this object especially, had ever, at stated periods, been held. Here, for the space of two moons, the stores of memory were dispensed; corrections and comparisons made, and the results committed to faithful breasts, to be transmitted again to succeeding posterity.

Many years after, another, and the last, Council of this kind was held; and the traditions reduced to writing, by two of our young men, who had been taught to read and write, in the school of the Rev. John Sargeant, of Stockbridge, Massachusetts.[1] They were obtained, in some way, by a white man, for publication, who soon after dying, all trace of them became lost. The traditions of the tribe, however, have mainly been preserved; of which I give you substantially, the following:

"A great people came from the North-West: crossed over the salt-waters, and after long and weary pilgrimages (planting many colonies on their track), took possession, and built their fires upon the Atlantic coast, extending from the Delaware on the south, to the Penobscot in the north. They became, in process of time, divided into different tribes and interests; all, however, speaking one common dialect. This great confederacy, comprising Delawares, Munsees, Mohegans, Narragansetts, Pequots, Penobscots, and many others (of whom a few are now scattered among the distant wilds of the West—others supporting a weak, tottering existence; while, by far, a larger remainder have passed that bourne, to which their brethren are tending), held its Council once a year, to deliberate on the general welfare. Patriarchal delegates from each tribe attended, assisted by priests and wise men, who communicated the will, and invoked the blessing, of the Great and Good Spirit. The policy and decisions of this Council were every where respected, and inviolably observed. Thus contentment smiled upon their existence, and they were happy. Their religion, communicated by priests and prophets, was simple and true. The manner of worship is imperfectly transmitted; but their reverence for a Great and Good Spirit—(whom they referred to by looking or pointing upwards), the observance of feasts and fasts, in each year; the offering of beasts in thanksgiving and for atonement, is clearly expressed. They believed the soul to be immortal;—in the existence of a happy land beyond the view, inhabited by those whose lives had been blameless: while for the wicked had been a region of misery reserved, covered with thorns and thistles, where comfort and pleasure were unknown. Time was divided into years and seasons; twelve moons for a year, and a number of years by so many winters."

The tribe, to which your speaker belongs, and of which there were many bands, occupied and possessed the country from the sea-shore, at Manhattan, to Lake Champlain. Having found an ebb and flow of the tide, they said: "This is Muh-he-con-new,"—"like our waters, which are never still." From this expression, and by this name, they were afterwards known, until their removal to Stockbridge, in the year 1730. Housatonic River Indians, Mohegan, Manhattas, were all names of bands in different localities, but bound together, as one family, by blood, marriage and descent.

At a remote period, before the advent of the Europeans, their wise men foretold the coming of a strange race, from the sunrise, as numerous as the leaves upon the trees, who would eventually crowd them from their fair possessions. But apprehension was mitigated by the knowledge and belief, at that time entertained, that their original home was not there, and after a period of years, they would return to the West, from whence they had come; and, moreover, said they, "all the red men are

[1]John Sargeant (1710–1749) graduated from Yale in 1729 and from 1731 to 1735 served as a tutor there. In 1735, at the behest of the Boston commissioners of the Society for the Propagation of the Gospel in New England, Sargeant went to the Housatonic river Indian settlements and established the mission town of Stockbridge.

sprung from a common ancestor, made by the Great Spirit from red clay, who will unite their strength to avert a common calamity." This tradition is confirmed by the common belief, which prevails in our day with all the Indian tribes; for they recognize one another by their color, as brothers, and acknowledge one Great Creator.

Two hundred and fifty winters ago, this prophecy was verified, and the Muh-he-con-new, for the first time, beheld the "pale-face." Their number was small, but their canoes were big. In the select and exclusive circles of your rich men, of the present day, I should encounter the gaze of curiosity, but not such as overwhelmed the senses of the Aborigines, my ancestors. "Our visitors were white, and must be sick. They asked for rest and kindness, we gave them both. They were strangers, and we took them in—naked, and we clothed them."[2] The first impression of astonishment and pity, was succeeded by awe and admiration of superior art, intelligence and address. A passion for information and improvement possessed the Indian—a residence was freely offered—territory given—and covenants of friendship exchanged.

Your written accounts of events at this period are familiar to you, my friends. Your children read them every day in their school books; but they do not read—no mind at this time can conceive, and no pen record, the terrible story of recompense for kindness, which for two hundred years has been paid the simple, trusting, guileless Muh-he-con-new. I have seen much myself—have been connected with more, and, I tell you, I know all. The tradition of the wise men is figuratively true, "that our home, at last, will be found in the West;" for, another tradition informs us, that "far beyond the setting sun, upon the smiling, happy lands, we shall be gathered with our Fathers, and be at rest."

Promises and professions were freely given, and as ruthlessly—intentionally broken. To kindle your fires—to be of and with us, was sought as a privilege; and yet at that moment you were transmitting to your kings, beyond the water, intelligence of your possession, "by right of discovery," and demanding assistance to assert and maintain your hold.

Where are the twenty-five thousand in number, and the four thousand warriors, who constituted the power and population of the great Muh-he-con-new Nation in 1604? They have been victims to vice and disease, which the white man imported. The small-pox, measles, and "strong waters" have done the work of annihilation.

Divisions and feuds were insidiously promoted between the several bands. They were induced to thin each other's ranks without just cause; and subsequently were defeated and disorganized in detail.

It is curious, the history of my tribe, in its decline, during the last two centuries and a half. Nothing that deserved the name of purchase, was ever made. From various causes, they were induced to abandon their territory at intervals, and retire further to the inland. Deeds were given indifferently to the Government, or to individuals, for which little or no consideration was paid. The Indian was informed, in many instances, that he was selling one parcel, while the conveyance described other, and much larger limits. Should a particular band, for purposes of hunting or fishing, desert, for a time, its usual place of residence, the land was said to be abandoned, and

[2]"For I was an hungered, and ye gave me meat: I was thirsty, and ye gave me drink: I was a stranger, and ye took me in: Naked, and ye clothed me: I was sick, and ye visited me: I was in prison, and ye came unto me." Matthew 25:35–36. See also verses 37–40.

the Indian claim extinguished. To legalize and confirm titles thus acquired, laws and edicts were subsequently passed, and these laws were said then, and are now called, justice!! Oh! what a mockery!! to confound justice with law. Will you look steadily at the intrigues, bargains, corruption and log-rolling of your present Legislatures, and see any trace of the divinity of justice? And by what test shall be tried the acts of the old Colonial Courts and Councils?

Let it not surprise you, my friends, when I say, that the spot on which we stand, has never been purchased or rightly obtained; and that by justice, human and divine, it is the property now of the remnant of that great people from whom I am descended. They left it in the tortures of starvation, and to improve their miserable existence; but a cession was never made, and their title has never been extinguished.

The Indian is said to be the ward of the white man, and the negro his slave. Has it ever occurred to you, my friends, that while the slave is increasing, and increased by every appliance, the Indian is left to rot and die, before the humanities of this model *Republic!* You have your tears, and groans, and mobs, and riots, for individuals of the former, while your indifference of purpose, and vacillation of policy, is hurrying to extinction, whole communities of the latter.

What are the treaties of the general Government? How often, and when, has its plighted faith been kept? Indian occupation forever, is, next year, or by the next Commissioner, more wise than his predecessor, re-purchased. One removal follows another, and thus your sympathies and justice are evinced in speedily *fulfilling the terrible destinies of our race.*

My friends, your holy book, the Bible, teaches us, that individual offences are punished in an existence, when time shall be no more. And the annals of the earth are equally instructive, that national wrongs are avenged, and national crimes atoned for in this world, to which alone the conformations of existence adapt them.

These events are above our comprehension, and for wise purposes. For myself and for my tribe, I ask for justice—I believe it will sooner or later occur—and may the Great and Good Spirit enable me to die in hope.

WANNUAUCON, *the Muh-he-con-new*

1854

Elias Boudinot (Cherokee) c. 1802–1839

Buck Watie, who was later to adopt the name Elias Boudinot, was born about 1802 in the Cherokee Nation in Georgia, the oldest son of Oo-watie and his wife Susanna Reese. Buck, or Gallegina, grew up during a time of rapid and sometimes violent change in the Cherokee Nation. Instead of the traditional Cherokee upbringing, Gallegina was sent to a Moravian mission school at Spring Place, Georgia, in 1811, where he received an education in the practices and values of the white society. There, the young Cherokee was taught reading, writing, arithmetic, religion, geography, and history in addition to vocational skills such as farming in the manner of white settlers.

In 1817, Buck was one of a group of Indian students chosen to attend the American Board of Commissioners for

Foreign Missions school at Cornwall, Connecticut. On the way to the school, the party stopped at the home of Elias Boudinot, president of the American Bible Society and a supporter of the Cornwall School. Buck Watie enrolled as Elias Boudinot, after the Cherokee custom of adopting the name of a benefactor. Boudinot remained at the school until 1826. In that year, he married Harriet Ruggles Gold, a white woman, of Cornwall.

In spring, 1826, Boudinot was sent on a tour of the eastern United States by the General Council of the Cherokee Nation to solicit donations for a national academy and for printing equipment. It was during this tour that he delivered his famous *Address to the Whites.* The trip was successful, and after a brief stint as teacher at the Hightower mission in the Cherokee Nation, Boudinot was asked to become the editor of the *Cherokee Phoenix,* the first newspaper published by American Indians. Publication of the newspaper was made possible by the acquisition of a press and types in both the Roman alphabet and the Cherokee syllabary paid for with funds raised on Boudinot's tour. It was also supported by the American Board, which was convinced by Samuel Austin Worcester to do so. Worcester was a missionary with whom Boudinot collaborated in translations of the New Testament and a Cherokee hymnal. After its first appearance in February, 1828, the newspaper was distributed not only in the Cherokee Nation but in the eastern United States and in Europe as well. While some parts of it were printed in Cherokee, much of the content was in English and dealt with news of Cherokee progress in farming, education, and industry.

While the *Phoenix* was a news medium to inform its local readers, it was also a propaganda tool used to persuade the larger society of the strides toward civilization being taken by the Indian nation. The Cherokees needed such persuasion in 1828, too, because of the encroachments of whites from Georgia on Indian lands, especially after the discovery of gold there. A special militia group, the Georgia Guard, had been started to patrol the Cherokee land claimed by the state. The Guard engaged in a policy of harassment of the Indians designed to encourage their emigration to the West. Georgia had a strong ally in their cause, the federal government, which passed the Indian Removal Act of 1830. Provisions of the Act called for the removal of eastern Indians to lands west of the Mississippi. Like most of the Cherokees, at first Boudinot resisted such a move, arguing that the Cherokees had adapted to white civilization and should be allowed to remain on their lands and preserve their political integrity.

But as pressures from Georgia and the federal government continued, Boudinot concluded that the only way the nation could be saved was to remove to the West. Accordingly, he and other Cherokees with similar views signed the Treaty of New Echota in 1835, providing for the trade of Cherokee lands in the East for land in Indian Territory. The treaty was opposed by the majority of Cherokees, many of whom continued to refuse to move. When the government sent soldiers to enforce the treaty, the result was the Trail of Tears, the mass migration of the Cherokees in the winter of 1838–39, which resulted in death for many and suffering for all. On June 22, 1839, a group of Cherokees killed Boudinot at Park Hill, Indian Territory, in revenge for his having signed the treaty. On the same day his relatives Major Ridge and John Ridge, both of whom had signed the New Echota Treaty, were killed as well.

Boudinot was an eloquent speaker for his people. The rhetoric and persuasive language of his *Address* are a forecast of the propagandistic style of his editorials in the *Cherokee Phoenix.* His greatest significance in Cherokee letters rests in his editorship and in his work as a translator of English works into Cherokee.

James W. Parins
University of Arkansas at Little Rock

PRIMARY WORK

An Address to the Whites, 1826.

SECONDARY WORKS

Letters and Other Papers Relating to Cherokee Affairs; Being in Reply to Sundry Publications Authorized by John Ross, 1837; Ralph Henry Gabriel, *Elias Boudinot, Cherokee, and His America,* 1941; Theda Perdue, ed., *Cherokee Editor: The Writings of Elias Boudinot,* 1983; Frankie Hutton and Barbara Straus Reed, eds., *Outsiders in 19th-Century Press History: Multicultural Perspectives,* 1995; *Handbook of Native American Literature,* 1996.

An Address to the Whites[1]

To those who are unacquainted with the manners, habits, and improvements of the Aborigines of this country, the term *Indian* is pregnant with ideas the most repelling and degrading. But such impressions, originating as they frequently do, from infant prejudices, although they hold too true when applied to some, do great injustices to many of this race of beings.

Some there are, perhaps even in this enlightened assembly, who at the bare sight of an Indian, or at the mention of the name, would throw back their imaginations to ancient times, to the ravages of savage warfare, to the yells pronounced over the mangled bodies of women and children, thus creating an opinion, inapplicable and highly injurious to those for whose temporal interest and eternal welfare, I come to plead.

What is an Indian? Is he not formed of the same materials with yourself? For "of one blood God created all the nations that dwell on the face of the earth." Though it be true that he is ignorant, that he is a heathen, that he is a savage; yet he is no more than all others have been under similar circumstances. Eighteen centuries ago what were the inhabitants of Great Britain?

You here behold an *Indian,* my kindred are *Indians,* and my fathers sleeping in the wilderness grave—they too were *Indians*. But I am not as my fathers were—broader means and nobler influences have fallen upon me. Yet I was not born as thousands are, in a stately dome and amid the congratulations of the great, for on a little hill, in a lonely cabin, overspread by the forest oak, I first drew my breath; and in a language unknown to learned and polished nations, I learnt to lisp my fond mother's name. In after days, I have had greater advantages than most of my race; and I now stand before you delegated by my native country to seek her interest, to labour for her respectability, and by my public efforts to assist in raising her to an equal standing with other nations of the earth.

The time has arrived when speculations and conjectures as to the practicability of civilizing the Indians must forever cease. A period is fast approaching when the stale remark—"Do what you will, an Indian will still be an Indian," must be placed no more in speech. With whatever plausibility this popular objection may have

[1]The speech was delivered in Philadelphia, where it was published by William F. Geddes in 1826 with the subtitle *Delivered in the First Presbyterian Church on the 26th of May, 1826.*

heretofore been made, every candid mind must now be sensible that it can no longer be uttered, except by those who are uninformed with respect to us, who are strongly prejudiced against us, or who are filled with vindictive feelings towards us; for the present history of the Indians, particularly of that nation to which I belong, most incontrovertibly establishes the fallacy of this remark. I am aware of the difficulties which have ever existed to Indian civilization. I do not deny the almost insurmountable obstacles which we ourselves have thrown in the way of this improvement, nor do I say that difficulties no longer remain; but facts will permit me to declare that there are none which may not easily be overcome, by strong and continued exertions. It needs not abstract reasoning to prove this position. It needs not the display of language to prove to the minds of good men, that Indians are susceptible of attainments necessary to the formation of polished society. It needs not the power of argument on the nature of man, to silence forever the remark that "it is the purpose of the Almighty that the Indians should be exterminated." It needs only that the world should know what we have done in the few last years, to foresee what yet we may do with the assistance of our white brethren, and that of the common Parent of us all.

It is not necessary to present to you a detailed account of the various aboriginal tribes, who have been known to you only on the pages of history, and there but obscurely known. They have gone; and to revert back to their days, would be only to disturb their oblivious sleep; to darken these walls with deeds at which humanity must shudder; to place before your eyes the scenes of Muskingum Sahta-goo[2] and the plains of Mexico, to call up the crimes of the bloody Cortes and his infernal host;[3] and to describe the animosity and vengeance which have overthrown, and hurried into the shades of death those numerous tribes. But here let me say, that however guilty these unhappy nations may have been, yet many and unreasonable were the wrongs they suffered, many the hardships they endured, and many their wanderings through the trackless wilderness. Yes, "notwithstanding the obloquy with which the early historians of the colonies have overshadowed the character of the ignorant and unfortunate natives, some bright gleams will occasionally break through, that throw a melancholy lustre on their memories. Facts are occasionally to be met with in their rude annals, which, though recorded with all the colouring of prejudice and bigotry, yet speak for themselves, and will be dwelt upon with applause and sympathy when prejudice shall have passed away."

Nor is it my purpose to enter largely into the consideration of the remnants, of those who have fled with time and are no more—They stand as monuments of the Indian's fate. And should they ever become extinct, they must move off the earth, as did their fathers. My design is to offer a few disconnected facts relative to the present improved state, and to the ultimate prospects of that particular tribe called Cherokees to which I belong.

The Cherokee nation lies within the chartered limits of the states of Georgia, Tennessee, and Alabama. Its extent as defined by treaties is about 200 miles in length from East to West, and about 120 in breadth. This country which is supposed to contain about 10,000,000 of acres exhibits great varieties of surface, the most part being

[2]Boudinot probably refers to the execution of ninety unarmed Indians on the Muskingum River in 1782.

[3]The Spanish conquest of Mexico under Hernando Cortés was ruthless and bloody.

hilly and mountainous, affording soil of no value. The vallies, however, are well watered and afford excellent land, in many parts particularly on the large streams, that of the first quality. The climate is temperate and healthy, indeed I would not be guilty of exaggeration were I to say, that the advantages which this country possesses to render it salubrious, are many and superior. Those lofty and barren mountains, defying the labour and ingenuity of man, and supposed by some as placed there only to exhibit omnipotence, contribute to the healthiness and beauty of the surrounding plains, and give to us that free air and pure water which distinguish our country. Those advantages, calculated to make the inhabitants healthy, vigorous, and intelligent, cannot fail to cause this country to become interesting. And there can be no doubt that the Cherokee Nation, however obscure and trifling it may now appear, will finally become, if not under its present occupants, one of the Garden spots of America. And here, let me be indulged in the fond wish, that she may thus become under those who now possess her; and ever be fostered, regulated and protected by the generous government of the United States.

The population of the Cherokee Nation increased from the year 1810 to that of 1824, 2000 exclusive of those who emigrated in 1818 and 19 to the west of the Mississippi—of those who reside on the Arkansas the number is supposed to be about 5000.[4]

The rise of these people in their movement towards civilization may be traced as far back as the relinquishment of their towns; when game became incompetent to their support, by reason of the surrounding white population. They then betook themselves to the woods, commenced the opening of small clearings, and the raising of stock; still however following the chase. Game has since become so scarce that little dependence for subsistence can be placed upon it. They have gradually and I could almost say universally forsaken their ancient employment. In fact, there is not a single family in the nation, that can be said to subsist on the slender support which the wilderness would afford. The love and the practice of hunting are not now carried to a higher degree, than among all frontier people whether white or red. It cannot be doubted, however, that there are many who have commenced a life of agricultural labour from mere necessity, and if they could, would gladly resume their former course of living. But these are individual feelings and ought to be passed over.

On the other hand it cannot be doubted that the nation is improving, rapidly improving in all those particulars which must finally constitute the inhabitants an industrious and intelligent people.

It is a matter of surprise to me, and must be to all those who are properly acquainted with the condition of the Aborigines of this country, that the Cherokees have advanced so far and so rapidly in civilization. But there are yet powerful obstacles, both within and without, to be surmounted in the march of improvement. The prejudices in regard to them in the general community are strong and lasting. The evil effects of their intercourse with their immediate white neighbours, who differ from them chiefly in name, are easily to be seen, and it is evident that from this intercourse proceed those demoralizing practices which in order to surmount, peculiar and unremitting efforts are necessary. In defiance, however, of these obstacles the Cherokees have improved and are still rapidly improving. To give you

[4]In 1808–1809 the Eastern Cherokee numbered 12,395. In 1819 the total was 15,000, one third of whom were west of the Mississippi. And in 1825 there were 13,542 in the East.

a further view of their condition, I will here repeat some of the articles of the two statistical tables taken at different periods.

In 1810 There were 19,500 cattle; 6,100 horses; 19,600 swine; 1,037 sheep; 467 looms; 1,600 spinning wheels; 30 waggons; 500 ploughs; 3 saw-mills; 13 grist-mills etc. At this time there are 22,000 cattle; 7,600 Horses; 46,000 swine; 2,500 sheep; 762 looms; 2,488 spinning wheels; 172 waggons; 2,943 ploughs; 10 saw-mills; 31 grist-mills; 62 Blacksmith-shops; 8 cotton machines; 18 schools; 18 ferries; and a number of public roads. In one district there were, last winter, upwards of 0000[5] volumes of good books; and 11 different periodical papers both religious and political, which were taken and read. On the public roads there are many decent Inns, and few houses for convenience, etc., would disgrace any country. Most of the schools are under the care and tuition of christian missionaries, of different denominations, who have been of great service to the nation, by inculcating moral and religious principles into the minds of the rising generation. In many places the word of God is regularly preached and explained, both by missionaries and natives; and there are numbers who have publicly professed their belief and interest in the merits of the great Saviour of the world. It is worthy of remark, that in no ignorant country have the missionaries undergone less trouble and difficulty, in spreading a knowledge of the Bible, than in this. Here, they have been welcomed and encouraged by the proper authorities of the nation, their persons have been protected, and in very few instances have some individual vagabonds threatened violence to them. Indeed it may be said with truth, that among no heathen people has the faithful minister of God experienced greater success, greater reward for his labour, than in this. He is surrounded by attentive hearers, the words which flow from his lips are not spent in vain. The Cherokees have had no established religion of their own, and perhaps to this circumstance we may attribute, in part, the facilities with which missionaries have pursued their ends. They cannot be called idolators; for they never worshipped Images. They believed in a Supreme Being, the Creator of all, the God of the white, the red, and the black man. They also believed in the existence of an evil spirit who resided, as they thought, in the setting sun, the future place of all who in their life time had done iniquitously. Their prayers were addressed alone to the Supreme Being, and which if written would fill a large volume, and display much sincerity, beauty and sublimity. When the ancient customs of the Cherokees were in their full force, no warrior thought himself secure, unless he had addressed his guardian angel; no hunter could hope for success, unless before the rising sun he had asked the assistance of his God, and on his return at eve had offered his sacrifice to him.

There are three things of late occurance, which must certainly place the Cherokee Nation in a fair light, and act as a powerful argument in favor of Indian improvement.

First. The invention of letters.

Second. The translation of the New Testament into Cherokee.

And Third. The organization of a Government.

The Cherokee mode of writing lately invented by George Guest,[6] who could not read any language nor speak any other than his own, consists of eighty-six characters, principally syllabic, the combinations of which form all the words of the language.

[5]The number intended is unknown.

[6]Also Gist or Guess, better known as Sequoyah (c. 1760–c. 1840), who gave his syllabary to the Cherokees in 1821.

Their terms may be greatly simplified, yet they answer all the purposes of writing, and already many natives use them.

The translation of the New Testament, together with Guest's mode of writing, has swept away that barrier which has long existed, and opened a spacious channel for the instruction of adult Cherokees. Persons of all ages and classes may now read the precepts of the Almighty in their own language. Before it is long, there will scarcely be an individual in the nation who can say, "I know not God neither understand I what thou sayest," for all shall know him from the greatest to the least. The aged warrior over whom has rolled three score and ten years of savage life, will grace the temple of God with his hoary head; and the little child yet on the breast of its pious mother shall learn to lisp its Maker's name.

The shrill sound of the Savage yell shall die away as the roaring of far distant thunder; and Heaven wrought music will gladden the affrighted wilderness. "The solitary places will be glad for them, and the desert shall rejoice and blossom as a rose." Already do we see the morning star, forerunner of approaching dawn, rising over the tops of those deep forests in which for ages have echoed the warrior's whoop. But has not God said it, and will he not do it? The Almighty decrees his purposes, and man cannot with all his ingenuity and device countervail them. They are more fixed in their course than the rolling sun—more durable than the everlasting mountains.

The Government, though defective in many respects, is well suited to the condition of the inhabitants. As they rise in information and refinement, changes in it must follow, until they arrive at that state of advancement, when I trust they will be admitted into all the privileges of the American family.

The Cherokee Nation is divided into eight districts, in each of which are established courts of justice, where all disputed cases are decided by a Jury, under the direction of a circuit Judge, who has jurisdiction over two districts. Sheriffs and other public officers are appointed to execute the decisions of the courts, collect debts, and arrest thieves and other criminals. Appeals may be taken to the Superior Court, held annually at the seat of Government. The Legislative authority is vested in a General Court, which consists of the National Committee and Council. The National Committee consists of thirteen members, who are generally men of sound sense and fine talents. The National Council consists of thirty-two members, beside the speaker, who act as the representatives of the people. Every bill passing these two bodies, becomes the law of the land. Clerks are appointed to do the writings, and record the proceedings of the Council. The executive power is vested in two principal chiefs, who hold their office during good behaviour, and sanction all the decisions of the legislative council. Many of the laws display some degree of civilization, and establish the respectability of the nation.

Polygamy is abolished. Female chastity and honor are protected by law. The Sabbath is respected by the Council during session. Mechanics are encouraged by law. The practice of putting aged persons to death for witchcraft is abolished and murder has now become a governmental crime.

From what I have said, you will form but a faint opinion of the true state and prospects of the Cherokees. You will, however, be convinced of three important truths.

First, that the means which have been employed for the christianization and civilization of this tribe, have been greatly blessed. Second, that the increase of these means will meet with final success. Third, that it has now become necessary, that efficient and more than ordinary means should be employed.

Sensible of this last point, and wishing to do something for themselves, the Cherokees have thought it advisable that there should be established, a Printing Press and a Seminary of respectable character; and for these purposes your aid and patronage are now solicited. They wish the types, as expressed in their resolution, to be composed of English letters and Cherokee characters. These characters have now become extensively used in the nation; their religious songs are written in them; there is an astonishing eagerness in people of all classes and ages to acquire a knowledge of them; and the New Testament has been translated into their language. All this impresses on them the immediate necessity of procuring types. The most informed and judicious of our nation, believe that such a press would go further to remove ignorance, and her offspring superstition and prejudice, than all other means. The adult part of the nation will probably grovel on in ignorance and die in ignorance, without any fair trial upon them, unless the proposed means are carried into effect. The simplicity of this method of writing, and the eagerness to obtain a knowledge of it, are evinced by the astonishing rapidity with which it is acquired, and by the numbers who do so. It is about two years since its introduction, and already there are a great many who can read it. In the neighbourhood in which I live, I do not recollect a male Cherokee, between the ages of fifteen and twenty five, who is ignorant of this mode of writing. But in connexion with those for Cherokee characters, it is necessary to have types for English letters. There are many who already speak and read the English language, and can appreciate the advantages which would result from the publication of their laws and transactions in a well conducted newspaper. Such a paper, comprising a summary of religious and political events, etc. on the one hand; and on the other, exhibiting the feelings, disposition, improvements, and prospects of the Indians; their traditions, their true character, as it once was and as it now is; the ways and means most likely to throw the mantle of civilization over all tribes; and such other matter as will tend to diffuse proper and correct impressions in regard to their condition—such a paper could not fail to create much interest in the American community, favourable to the aborigines, and to have a powerful influence on the advancement of the Indians themselves. How can the patriot or the philanthropist devise efficient means, without full and correct information as to the subjects of his labour. And I am inclined to think, after all that has been written in narratives, professedly to elucidate the leading traits of their character, that the public knows little of that character. To obtain a correct and complete knowledge of these people, there must exist a vehicle of Indian Intelligence, altogether different from those which have heretofore been employed. Will not a paper published in an Indian country, under proper and judicious regulations, have the desired effect? I do not say that Indians will produce learned and elaborate dissertations in explanation and vindication of their own character; but they may exhibit specimens of their intellectual efforts, of their eloquence, of their moral, civil and physical advancement, which will do quite as much to remove prejudice and to give profitable information.[7]

The Cherokees wish to establish their Seminary, upon a footing which will insure to it all the advantages, that belong to such institutions in the states. Need I

[7]The *Cherokee Phoenix,* a weekly, was established in 1828. Printed in both English and Sequoyan script, the paper was edited by Boudinot.

spend one moment in arguments, in favour of such an institution; need I speak one word of the utility, of the necessity, of an institution of learning; need I do more than simply to ask the patronage of benevolent hearts, to obtain that patronage.[8]

When before did a nation of Indians step forward and ask for the means of civilization? The Cherokee authorities have adopted the measures already stated, with a sincere desire to make their nation an intelligent and a virtuous people, and with a full hope that those who have already pointed out to them the road of happiness, will now assist them to pursue it. With that assistance, what are the prospects of the Cherokees? Are they not indeed glorious, compared to that deep darkness in which the nobler qualities of their souls have slept. Yes, methinks I can view my native country, rising from the ashes of her degredation, wearing her purified and beautiful garments, and taking her seat with the nations of the earth. I can behold her sons bursting the fetters of ignorance and unshackling her from the vices of heathenism. She is at this instant, risen like the first morning sun, which grows brighter and brighter, until it reaches its fulness of glory.

She will become not a great, but a faithful ally of the United States. In times of peace she will plead the common liberties of America. In times of war her intrepid sons will sacrifice their lives in your defence. And because she will be useful to you in coming time, she asks you to assist her in her present struggles. She asks not for greatness; she seeks not wealth, she pleads only for assistance to become respectable as a nation, to enlighten and ennoble her sons, and to ornament her daughters with modesty and virtue. She pleads for this assistance, too, because on her destiny hangs that of many nations. If she completes her civilization—then may we hope that all our nations will—then, indeed, may true patriots be encouraged in their efforts to make this world of the West, one continuous abode of enlightened, free, and happy people.

But if the Cherokee Nation fail in her struggle, if she die away, then all hopes are blasted, and falls the fabric of Indian civilization. Their fathers were born in darkness, and have died in darkness; without your assistance so will their sons. You, see, however, where the probability rests. Is there a soul whose narrowness will not permit the exercise of charity on such an occasion? Where is he that can withhold his mite from an object so noble? Who can prefer a little of his silver and gold, to the welfare of nations of his fellow beings? Human wealth perishes with our clay, but that wealth gained in charity still remains on earth, to enrich our names, when we are gone, and will be remembered in Heaven, when the miser and his coffers have mouldered together in their kindred earth. The works of a generous mind sweeten the cup of affliction; they enlighten the dreary way to the cold tomb; they blunt the sting of death, and smooth his passage to the unknown world. When all the kingdoms of this earth shall die away and their beauty and power shall perish, his name shall live and shine as a twinkling star; those for whose benefit be done his deeds of charity shall call him blessed, and they shall add honor to his immortal head.

There are, with regard to the Cherokee and other tribes, two alternatives; they must either become civilized and happy, or sharing the fate of many kindred nations, become extinct. If the General Government continue its protection, and the

[8]Although the Cherokee Council appropriated money for seminaries (or high schools) for both boys and girls in 1846, they were not built until 1851.

American people assist them in their humble efforts, they will, they must rise. Yes, under such protection, and with such assistance, the Indian must rise like the Phoenix, after having wallowed for ages in ignorance and barbarity. But should this Government withdraw its care, and the American people their aid, then, to use the words of a writer, "they will go the way that so many tribes have gone before them; for the hordes that still linger about the shores of Huron, and the tributary streams of the Mississippi, will share the fate of those tribes that once lorded it along the proud banks of the Hudson; of that gigantic race that are said to have existed on the borders of the Susquehanna; of those various nations that flourished about the Potomac and the Rhappahannoc, and that peopled the forests of the vast valley of Shenandoah. They will vanish like a vapour from the face of the earth, their very history will be lost in forgetfulness, and places that now know them will know them no more."

There is, in Indian history, something very melancholy, and which seems to establish a mournful precedent for the future events of the few sons of the forest, now scattered over this vast continent. We have seen every where the poor aborigines melt away before the white population. I merely speak of the fact, without at all referring to the cause. We have seen, I say, one family after another, one tribe after another, nation after nation, pass away; until only a few solitary creatures are left to tell the sad story of extinction.

Shall this precedent be followed? I ask you, shall red men live, or shall they be swept from the earth? With you and this public at large, the decision chiefly rests. Must they perish? Must they all, like the unfortunate Creeks, (victims of the unchristian policy of certain persons,) go down in sorrow to their grave?[9]

They hang upon your mercy as to a garment. Will you push them from you, or will you save them? Let humanity answer.

1826

Seattle (Duwamish) 1786–1866

Seattle (or Seathl) was chief of the Duwamish and Suquamish tribes. Converted by Catholic missionaries in the 1830s, he was a powerful leader of Indian peoples in the Puget Sound area and supported peaceful coexistence with Anglo-American settlers. Shortly after the Washington territory was organized in 1853, the new governor, Isaac Stevens, visited the tribes to discuss treaty arrangements. Seattle's speech was a formal response to that of Stevens. In 1887, Dr. Henry A. Smith, who attended the meeting, published the speech from what he claimed were his notes taken at the time. Smith professed to understand the Suquamish language, though later commentators have questioned his linguistic capabilities; in any case, Smith himself suggested that his rendition of whatever Seattle said was a pale shade of the original. Thus the authenticity of "Chief Seattle's speech" has been in question since it was first printed more than thirty years after the event.

[9]The "unfortunate Creeks" were victims of the Creek War of 1813–14, also known as the Red Stick War. In this clash with American forces (and some Cherokees), Creek towns were burned, many Creek citizens were killed, and others took refuge in Florida.

The problem was even further compounded in recent years when other versions of a supposed speech by Seattle were fabricated, first by the poet William Arrowsmith, during the 1960s, and later by a script writer, Ted Perry, in the 1970s. Perry's version was widely circulated, primarily because it placed into Seattle's mouth sentiments popular in environmentalist circles. The speech has thus become a particularly vivid example of the problem of authenticity in dealing with many supposedly Indian texts, including famous ones like those of Black Hawk and Black Elk. Are these the words of Indian orators, or are they constituted by what white auditors wish to have heard, or thought they did hear, coming, often many years before, from an Indian speaker . . . or, in fact, from a translator? There are no easy answers to such questions, and they have been extensively debated (on the Internet as well as in scholarly publications).

In the present instance, it is reasonably clear that Seattle delivered a speech on the stated occasion, that he was a powerful orator and an imposing presence. And it is likely that some or much of what he said is contained in Smith's version. It is also true, perhaps ironically, that authentic or not, this speech has become a part of "Indian" culture, referred to, quoted, and used by Native American as well as white writers. This is not without reason, for the speech may profitably be compared with Lincoln's Gettysburg Address or his Second Inaugural, other, perhaps more familiar, reflections on the costs of history. Though the "vanishing Indian" was a common theme in the popular arts of the nineteenth century, as well as an expression of a politically expedient ideology, the speech penetrates to the genocidal guilt behind that image, a motivation well articulated in the twentieth century by D. H. Lawrence and William Faulkner.

In 1855 Seattle signed the Port Elliot Treaty, which confined his and other Washington tribes to a reservation. The city of Seattle is, of course, named after him, though he strongly objected to that appropriation of a part of himself and appears, thereafter, to have preferred not to use the name—though that story, too, may be a part of the complex legend that has been constructed about this man.

Andrew O. Wiget
New Mexico University

Paul Lauter
Trinity College

PRIMARY WORKS

Dr. Henry A. Smith, "Early Reminiscences," Seattle *Sunday Star,* October 29, 1887; W. C. Vanderwerth, *Indian Oratory,* 1971.

SECONDARY WORKS

Clarence B. Bagley, "Chief Seattle and Angeline," 1931; Rudolph Kaiser, "Chief Seattle's Speech(es): American Origin and European Reception," in Brian Swann and Arnold Krupat, eds., *Recovering the Words: Essays in Native American Literature,* 1987; Vi Hilbert, "When Chief Seattle Spoke," in Robin K. Wright, ed., *A Time of Gathering: Native Heritage in Washington State,* 1990.

Speech of Chief Seattle

Yonder sky that has wept tears of compassion upon my people for centuries untold, and which to us appears changeless and eternal, may change. Today is fair. Tomorrow it may be overcast with clouds. My words are like the stars that never change.

Whatever Seattle says the great chief at Washington can rely upon with as much certainty as he can upon the return of the sun or the seasons. The White Chief says that Big Chief at Washington sends us greetings of friendship and goodwill. This is kind of him for we know he has little need of our friendship in return. His people are many. They are like the grass that covers vast prairies. My people are few. They resemble the scattering trees of a storm-swept plain. The great—and I presume—good White Chief sends us word that he wishes to buy our lands but is willing to allow us enough to live comfortably. This indeed appears just, even generous, for the Red Man no longer has rights that he need respect, and the offer may be wise also, as we are no longer in need of an extensive country.

There was a time when our people covered the land as the waves of a wind-ruffled sea cover its shell paved floor, but that time long since passed away with the greatness of tribes that are now but a mournful memory. I will not dwell on, nor mourn over, our untimely decay, nor reproach my paleface brothers with hastening it as we too may have been somewhat to blame.

Youth is impulsive. When our young men grow angry at some real or imaginary wrong, and disfigure their faces with black paint, it denotes that their hearts are black, and that they are often cruel and relentless, and our old men and old women are unable to restrain them. Thus it has ever been. Thus it was when the white man first began to push our forefathers westward. But let us hope that the hostilities between us may never return. We would have everything to lose and nothing to gain. Revenge by young men is considered gain, even at the cost of their own lives, but old men who stay at home in times of war, and mothers who have sons to lose, know better.

Our good father at Washington—for I presume he is now our father as well as yours, since King George has moved his boundaries further north—our great and good father, I say, sends us word that if we do as he desires he will protect us. His brave warriors will be to us a bristling wall of strength, and his wonderful ships of war will fill our harbors so that our ancient enemies far to the northward—the Hydas and Tsimpsians—will cease to frighten our women, children, and old men. Then in reality will he be our father and we his children. But can that ever be? Your God is not our God! Your God loves your people and hates mine. He folds his strong protecting arms lovingly about the pale face and leads him by the hand as a father leads his infant son—but He has forsaken His red children—if they really are His. Our God, the Great Spirit, seems also to have forsaken us. Your God makes your people wax strong every day. Soon they will fill all the land. Our people are ebbing away like a rapidly receding tide that will never return. The white man's God cannot love our people or He would protect them. They seem to be orphans who can look nowhere for help. How then can we be brothers? How can your God become our God and renew our prosperity and awaken in us dreams of returning greatness. If we have a common heavenly father He must be partial—for He came to His paleface children. We never saw Him. He gave you laws but had no word for his red children whose teeming multitudes once filled this vast continent as stars fill the firmament. No; we are two distinct races with separate origins and separate destinies. There is little in common between us.

To us the ashes of our ancestors are sacred and their resting place is hallowed ground. You wander far from the graves of your ancestors and seemingly without regret. Your religion was written upon tables of stone by the iron finger of your God so that you could not forget. The Red Man could never comprehend nor remember it. Our religion is the traditions of our ancestors—the dreams of our old men, given them in the solemn hours of night by the Great Spirit; and the visions of our sachems, and is written in the hearts of our people.

Your dead cease to love you and the land of their nativity as soon as they pass the portals of the tomb and wander way beyond the stars. They are soon forgotten and never return. Our dead never forget the beautiful world that gave them being. They still love its verdant valleys, its murmuring rivers, its magnificent mountains, sequestered vales and verdant lined lakes and bays, and ever yearn in tender, fond affection over the lonely hearted living, and often return from the Happy Hunting Ground to visit, guide, console and comfort others.

Day and night cannot dwell together. The Red Man has ever fled the approach of the White Man, as the morning mist flees before the morning sun.

However, your proposition seems fair and I think that my people will accept it and will retire to the reservation you offer them. Then we will dwell in peace, for the words of the Great White Chief seem to be the words of nature speaking to my people out of dense darkness.

It matters little where we pass the remnant of our days. They will not be many. The Indians' night promises to be dark. Not a single star of hope hovers above his horizon. Sad-voiced winds moan in the distance. Grim fate seems to be on the Red Man's trail, and wherever he goes he will hear the approaching footsteps of his fell destroyer and prepare stolidly to meet his doom, as does the wounded doe that hears the approaching footsteps of the hunter.

A few more moons. A few more winters—and not one of the descendants of the mighty hosts that once moved over his broad land or lived in happy homes, protected by the Great Spirit, will remain to mourn over the graves of a people—once more powerful and hopeful than yours. But why should I mourn at the untimely fate of my people? Tribe follows tribe, and nation follows nation, like the waves of the sea. It is the order of nature, and regret is useless. Your time of decay may be distant, but it will surely come, for even the White Man whose God walked and talked with him as friend with friend, cannot be exempt from the common destiny. We may be brothers after all. We will see.

We will ponder your proposition and when we decide will let you know. But should we accept it, I here and now make this condition that we will not be denied the privilege without molestation of visiting at any time the tombs of our ancestors, friends and children. Every part of this soil is sacred in the estimation of my people. Every hillside, every valley, every plain and grove, has been hallowed by some sad or happy event in days long vanished. Even the rocks, which seem to be dumb and dead as they swelter in the sun along the silent shore, thrill with memories of stirring events connected with the lives of my people, and the very dust upon which you now stand responds more lovingly to their footsteps than to yours, because it is rich with the blood of our ancestors and our bare feet are conscious of the sympathetic touch. Our departed braves, fond mothers, glad, happy-hearted maidens, and even our little children who lived here and rejoiced here for a brief season, will love these somber solitudes and at eventide they greet shadowy returning spirits. And when the last Red Man shall have perished, and the memory of my tribe shall have become a myth among the White Men, these shores will swarm with the invisible dead of my tribe, and when your children's children think themselves alone in the field, the store, the shop, upon the highway, or in the silence of the pathless woods, they will not be alone. In all the earth there is no place dedicated to solitude. At night when the streets of your cities and villages are silent and you think them deserted, they will throng with the returning hosts that once filled them and still love this beautiful land. The White Man will never be alone.

Let him be just and deal kindly with my people, for the dead are not powerless. Dead, did I say? There is no death, only a change of worlds.

1855

John Rollin Ridge (Cherokee) 1827–1867

John Rollin Ridge was a member of the Treaty Party of Cherokees. His father and grandfather were among the founders of the Party, so designated because of its support for the Treaty of New Echota (1835), which provided for removal of the Cherokees from the South to Indian Territory. Much of Ridge's writing on American Indians argues for the need of all Indians to become "civilized," that is, to be assimilated into white society, in order to survive.

Born in Georgia in 1827, Ridge was no stranger to turmoil. During his childhood, the Cherokee Nation was under pressure from whites to vacate their traditional lands and move westward. The Cherokees protested, but despite their eloquent arguments, it eventually became clear to many tribesmen that the cause was lost. As a result, John Ridge, Major Ridge, his nephew Elias Boudinot, and others signed the removal treaty, which resulted in the displacement of most of the Cherokees to Indian Territory.

Shortly after removal was completed in 1839, the two elder Ridges and Boudinot were assassinated on the same day in separate incidents by Ross Party Cherokees, who had opposed removal. The assassins dragged John Ridge from his bed and, in full view of his wife and children, stabbed him repeatedly. The scene remained in John Rollin Ridge's mind all of his life. Fearing for their lives, the family fled to Arkansas where Ridge remained for ten years, except for a brief stint at Great Barrington Academy in Massachusetts. He received a classical education under Cephas Washburn in Arkansas, and, for a time, studied law. In 1846, Ridge married and settled down to farm in the Indian Territory. As the result of an argument that grew out of factional divisions in the tribe, Ridge killed a member of the Ross Party and was forced to flee once more. He lived for a while in Southern Missouri, where he agitated against the Ross faction and even announced plans for an armed invasion of the Cherokee Nation. In 1850, however, he joined a number of other Cherokees on their way to the California gold fields. He always planned to return to the Cherokee Nation and, on at least two different occasions, introduced schemes to establish an Indian newspaper in the area. Although he never returned to Indian Territory, he remained in contact with his family and members of the Treaty Party. He was obviously considered a member of the group since he was asked to lead the Cherokee Southern delegation in its treaty deliberations after the Civil War.

In California, Ridge edited several newspapers and was an outspoken opponent of the Republicans. A Douglas Democrat, he was heavily involved in California politics. He also continued his literary career in California. He had begun writing and publishing poetry in Indian Territory and Arkansas, and his writing earned him some degree of fame as a poet in California. In 1854 he published a volume of romance fiction, *Life and Adventures of Joaquin Murieta, the Celebrated California Bandit,* ostensibly a true story. While the book was very popular, and Ridge achieved some fame from it, it was not a financial success.

Ridge wrote and published poetry in Arkansas and California. Much of this poetry uses poetic conventions common in the works of English and American romantic poets. The themes and structures in his work are often similar to those of earlier writers, especially in Ridge's pieces that deal with nature. The nature poems attempt to recreate the poet's personal experiences with the natural environment, which often have mystical or transcendental qualities. Imagination is nearly always the force that makes these experiences possible. His other poems are autobiographical and intensely personal, again following romantic models. While in California, Ridge wrote occasional poems, many of which are testimonials to the nineteenth-century idea of progress and the doctrine of Manifest Destiny.

In both his poetry and his prose, John Rollin Ridge argued that the only chance for survival for the American Indian lay in assimilating into white society. Like many others in the nineteenth century, Ridge was convinced of the reality of Manifest Destiny. He believed that the march of European civilization and technological progress was inexorable and could not be ignored by Indian nations. Yet, like most assimilated Indians of his time, he argued that justice demanded that his less acculturated brothers be safeguarded from oppression while the gradual process of acculturation took place. That way they might be saved from extinction. No doubt in some measure the alienation projected by Ridge was part of the legacy of colonization and removal which had been the tragic fate of his people, the Cherokees.

James W. Parins
University of Arkansas at Little Rock

PRIMARY WORKS

Life and Adventures of Joaquin Murieta, the Celebrated California Bandit, 1854; *Poems,* 1868.

SECONDARY WORKS

Edward Everett Dale, "John Rollin Ridge," *Chronicles of Oklahoma* 4 (December, 1928): 312–321; M.A. Ranck, "John Rollin Ridge in California," *Chronicles of Oklahoma* 19 (December, 1932): 560–569; Carolyn Thomas Foreman, "Edward W. Bushyhead and John Rollin Ridge," *Chronicles of Oklahoma* 15 (September, 1936): 295–311; James W. Parins, *John Rollin Ridge: His Life and Works,* 1991; *Handbook of Native American Literature,* 1996.

Oppression of Digger Indians[1]

The Daily Bee
Tuesday Evening, July 12, 1857

A gentleman residing in this city, who has but recently returned from a hunting trip in Humboldt county, informs us of certain outrages committed upon the Digger Indians of that region, which ought to be made public. He went up to a valley about

[1]This essay appeared in the Sacramento *Daily Bee* on July 12, 1857. It was reprinted in Farmer and Strickland's *A Trumpet of Our Own,* from which it is reprinted.

thirty miles south of the mouth of Eel river, which empties into the Pacific, where, finding a plenty of elk, deer, and bear, he temporarily located. The region is filled at this season with American hunters. There is but one permanent white resident in the valley—a man who went there from Nevada county with a Digger squaw for his wife, and accompanied by the Indians of the rancheria from which he took her. He is living on a ranch, the limits of which have not yet been surveyed, and which is covered by a large number of cattle brought there and placed upon it, from time to time, by himself. The increase of his stock promises to be rapid; in fact, the man is already a wealthy individual, though occupying so isolated and semi-savage a condition. Losing some of his cattle recently, which our informant says he is certain were in some instances killed, and in others driven off, by the hunters, he attributed the depredations to the Indians belonging to that region, and requested the hunters to shoot down every Indian, (except those he brought with him from Nevada county,) that they should come across. Many of the hunters were more than ready to act upon the suggestion, for it gave them a still better chance for carrying on a traffic in which they had previously been engaged, to wit: kidnapping Digger children and selling them in different parts of the country. A great many Indians have thus been shot down in cold blood by these white savages, and the inhuman practice of kidnapping is now going on with the steadiness of a regular system.

It is a pity that these poor and imbecile people cannot better be protected than they are by the General Government. We do not think it is the fault of the Indian Superintendent or his agents, in every instance, that such outrages occur. Many of the tribes of Diggers straggle off from the main body of their people and hide themselves in the mountains in order to escape being put on the reservations, and by so doing place themselves completely in the power of the hundreds of lawless white men who pitch their camps from place to place through the mountains, and make their money partly by hunting, partly by stealing cattle and laying it to the Indians, and partly by the system of kidnapping above alluded to. This latter practice is common in various parts of the country.

There is no remedy for these impositions upon the unfortunate Diggers, but the one now at work, and that is the placing them, as fast as it can be done, upon the reservations for their reception. The fact that such flagrant impositions are committed should cause renewed energy and exertion in this regard by those whose business it is especially to attend to it. There is no plea for the poor Digger but that of humanity. He has none of the romance which gathers around the nobler savage of the western prairies—he cannot defend himself or his rights, and a prayer for mercy is his only argument against cruelty and oppression.

1857

The Atlantic Cable

Let Earth be glad! for that great work is done,
Which makes, at last the Old and New World one!
Let all mankind rejoice! for time nor space
Shall check the progress of the human race!

Though Nature heaved the Continents apart,
She cast in one great mould the human heart;
She framed on one great plan the human mind,
And gave man speech to link him to his kind;
So that, though plains and mountains intervene,
Or oceans, broad and stormy, roll between
If there but be a courier for the thought—
Soft-winged or slow—the land and seas are nought,
And man is nearer to his brother brought.

First, ere the dawn of letters was, or burst
The light of science on the world, men, nurs't
In distant solitudes apart, did send
Their skin-clad heralds forth to thread the woods,
Scale mountain-peaks, or swim the sudden floods,
And bear their messages of peace or war.

Next, beasts were tamed to drag the rolling car,
Or speed the mounted rider on his track;
And then came, too, the vessels, oar-propelled,
Which fled the ocean, as the clouds grew black,
And safe near shore their prudent courses held.
Next came the winged ships, which, brave and free,
Did skim the bosom of the bounding sea,
And dared the storms and darkness in their flight,
Yet drifted far before the winds and night,
Or lay within the dead calm's grasp of might.
Then, sea-divided nations nearer came,
Stood face to face, spake each the other's name,
In friendship grew, and learned the truth sublime,
That Man is Man in every age and clime!
They nearer were by months and years—but space
Must still be shortened in Improvement's race,
And steam came next to wake the world from sleep,
And launch her black-plumed warriors of the deep;
The which, in calm or storm, rode onward still,
And braved the raging elements at will.
Then distance, which from calms' and storms' delays
Grew into months, was shortened into days,
And Science' self declared her wildest dream
Reached not beyond this miracle of steam!
But steam hath not the lightning's wondrous power,
Though, Titan-like, mid Science' sons it tower
And wrestle with the ocean in his wrath,
And sweep the wild waves foaming from its path.
A mightier monarch is that subtler thing,
Which speaks in thunder like a God,

Or humbly stoops to kiss the lifted rod;
Ascends to Night's dim, solitary throne,
And clothes it with a splendor not its own
A ghastly grandeur and ghostly sheen,
Through which the pale stars tremble as they're seen;
Descends to fire the far horizon's rim,
And paints Mount Etnas[1] in the cloudland grim;
Or, proud to own fair Science' rightful sway,
Low bends along th' electric wire to play,
And, helping out the ever-wondrous plan,
Becomes, in sooth, an errand-boy for man!

This power it was, which, not content with aught
As yet achieved by human will or thought
Disdained the slow account of months or days,
In navigation of the ocean ways,
And days would shorten into hours, and these
To minutes, in the face of sounding seas.
If Thought might not be borne upon the foam
Of furrowing keel, with speed that Thought should roam,
It then should walk, like light, the ocean's bed,
And laugh to scorn the winds and waves o'er head!
Beneath the reach of storm or wreck, down where
The skeletons of men and navies are,
Its silent steps should be; while o'er its path
The monsters of the deep, in sport or wrath,
The waters lashed, till like a pot should boil
The sea, and fierce Arion[2] seize the upcast spoil.

America! to thee belongs the praise
Of this great crowning deed of modern days.
'Twas Franklin called the wonder from on high;[3]
'Twas Morse[4] who bade it on man's errand fly—
'Twas he foretold its pathway 'neath the sea:
A daring Field[5] fulfilled the prophecy!
'Twas fitting that a great, free land like this,
Should give the lightning's voice to Liberty;
Should wing the heralds of Earth's happiness,
And sing, beneath the ever-sounding sea,
The fair, the bright millenial days to be.

[1]A volcano in Sicily.
[2]In Greek myth a miraculous horse, offspring of the sea-god Poseidon.
[3]The reference is to Franklin's experiments with lightning.
[4]Samuel F.B. Morse (1791–1872), American artist and inventor of the telegraph.
[5]Cyrus West Field (1819–1892), American merchant and entrepreneur, who organized the first transatlantic cable.

Now may, ere long, the sword be sheathed to rust,
The helmet laid in undistinguished dust;
The thund'rous chariot pause in mid career.
Its crimsoned wheels no more through blood to steer;
The red-hoofed steed from fields of death be led,
Or turned to pasture where the armies bled;
For Nation unto Nation soon shall be
Together brought in knitted unity,
And man be bound to man by that strong chain,
Which, linking land to land, and main to main,
Shall vibrate to the voice of Peace, and be
A throbbing heartstring of Humanity!

1868

The Stolen White Girl

The prairies are broad, and the woodlands are wide
And proud on his steed the wild half-breed may ride,
With the belt round his waist and the knife at his side.
And no white man may claim his beautiful bride.

Though he stole her away from the land of the whites,
Pursuit is in vain, for her bosom delights
In the love that she bears the dark-eyed, the proud,
Whose glance is like starlight beneath a night-cloud.

Far down in the depths of the forest they'll stray,
Where the shadows like night are lingering all day;
Where the flowers are springing up wild at their feet,
And the voices of birds in the branches are sweet.

Together they'll roam by the streamlets that run,
O'ershadowed at times then meeting the sun—
The streamlets that soften their varying tune,
As up the blue heavens calm wanders the moon!

The contrast between them is pleasing and rare;
Her sweet eye of blue, and her soft silken hair,
Her beautiful waist, and her bosom of white
That heaves to the touch with a sense of delight;

His form more majestic and darker his brow,
Where the sun has imparted its liveliest glow—
An eye that grows brighter with passion's true fire,
As he looks on his loved one with earnest desire.

Oh, never let Sorrow's cloud darken their fate,
The girl of the "pale face," her Indian mate!
But deep in the forest of shadows and flowers,
Let Happiness smile, as she wings their sweet hours.

1868

A Scene Along the Rio de las Plumas

With solemn step I trace
A dark and dismal place,
Where moss with trailing ends,
From heavy boughs depends;
Where day resembles night,
And birds of sullen flight
Pierce darkness with their screams;
Where slow and sluggish streams
Crawl through the sleeping woods
And weirdful solitudes
In dreamy languor bound,
Upon their slimy breast
The lolling lilies rest,
And from their depths profound
Strange things, with staring eyes
And uncouth limbs, arise—
A moment gaze with mute surprise
Then sink adown like lead,
And seek their oozy bed.
What looks a spirit there,
Snow-white upon the air,
And hov'ring over these
Deep pools and drooping trees,
As if some heavenly sprite
Had come from Day to Night,
Is but the crane that feeds
When hungered 'mong the reeds
Or sloughs, flag-margined, wades,
Meandering 'neath the shades
And makes his vulgar dish
Of creeping things and fish.

Yon ermined owl that flits
Through dusky leaves, or sits
In somber silence now

On yonder ivyed bough
And looks a druid priest—
No higher thoughts inspire
Than lowest wants require,
As how to make his feast,
When lurking mouse or bird
Hath from its convert stirred.
Those flaming eyes awake
In yonder thorny brake,
Which dilate as I pass,
Illumining the grass
And lighting darksome ground,
Are not from that profound,
Where cries of woe resound
And Dante's damned abound,[1]
Nor yet the wandering ghouls,—
The dread of dead men's souls,—
(Because their flesh he craves,
And digs it from their graves),
But orbs of sinuous snake
Who from the neighboring lake,
Or vapor-breeding bog,
His victim soon shall take—
Some luckless dozing frog.
Nor will thy lither shape,
Thou rodent sly escape,
If once thine eye hath caught
The fire within that head,
From venomed sources fed,
With fascination fraught.

I reach a dimmer nook,
And warily I look,
For where you night-shades grow
And baneful blossoms blow,
Beneath the toadstools, well
I know ill-creatures dwell—
Tarantula, whose bite
Would strongest heart affright;
The stinging centipede,
Whose hundred-footed speed,
And hundred arm-ed feet
Bring death and danger fleet,
That, with Briarean clasp[2]

[1]The reference is to Dante's *Inferno,* the first part of his long poem *The Divine Comedy.*

[2]In Greek mythology Briareus was a monster of a hundred hands.

The fated victim grasp,
And scorpion, single-stinged,
Fabled erst as winged
And still reported wise,
If pressed, a suicide.
And here I see—but lo!
I can no further go,
For what's this hum I hear
Which fills the atmosphere,
And drums the tingling ear
Till, half distraught, I reel?
I heard, but no I feel!
Good sakes, what winged forms!
What singing, dizzying swarms!
Ten thousand needles flamed
Could not with them be named.

1868

THE LITERATURE OF SLAVERY AND ABOLITION

David Walker 1785–1830

Of David Walker it must be said that the sketchy details of his brief life blend inexorably into the historical process whereby, around 1830, a somewhat diffuse anti-slavery sentiment largely taken up with the notion of "colonizing" blacks back to Africa was annealed into an increasingly militant and organized abolitionist movement. No single factor accounted for this change; Garrison's starting of *The Liberator* in 1831 was involved, as was the slave revolt led by Nat Turner later that year. But David Walker's *Appeal,* coming from within and addressed primarily to the black community, and unprecedented both in its militance and for its extended argument against Colonization, was surely a critical ingredient in that process.

David Walker was born September 28, 1785, in Wilmington, North Carolina—a town which, over a century later, would be the scene of the bloody race riot which forms the basis for Charles Chesnutt's novel *The Marrow of Tradition.* His mother was a free black woman, his father—who died some months before he was born—a slave, and thus, in accord with the laws of the South's "peculiar institution," David followed the "condition of his mother." Of his youth we know virtually nothing: he traveled widely in the United States, somewhere acquired an education rare for a black person in that day, and developed an inveterate hatred of slavery and racism in all their manifestations. And yet we know much: in Wilmington, he and his mother would have been required by a law passed the year of his birth to wear a patch of cloth with the legend "FREE" upon their left shoulders. They were forbidden to testify against whites in court, could not gather in meetings without suspicion that they were planning insurrection, and constantly lived in fear that, marked by their "FREE" patches, they would be kidnapped and sold off as slaves. No surprise, then, that in the 1820s, Walker moved north, settling in Boston, where he became a dealer in new and used clothing.

In the few remaining years of his life there, Walker was one of the most active members of Boston's small community of free black people. He was assiduous in the Methodist church, sheltered fugitives, shared the little he earned with the poor, married a young woman named Eliza, and frequently spoke out in public against slavery. In 1827, he became an agent for the newly formed *Freedom's Journal,* which he distributed and wrote for. He issued his *Appeal* in 1829; by the next year, he was dead.

The cause of his death was unclear, though in his day such an early death was not unusual. Still, the suspicion lingered that he had been poisoned. Such speculation was fired by the intense responses to his *Appeal.* A price of $1,000 dead and $10,000 alive was put on his head in Georgia. The Governor of Georgia wrote to the Mayor of Boston demanding that he suppress circulation of the *Appeal;* the Mayor of Savannah requested Walker's arrest. Laws were passed across the South banning its distribution and reasserting the policy against teaching slaves to read or write. Even whites opposed to slavery, like Benjamin Lundy and William Lloyd Garrison, condemned the pamphlet as "injudicious" and inflammatory. Nevertheless, the tract continued to circulate, occasionally, it would seem, in the pockets of clothing that Walker sold to sailors shipping to southern ports. Before Walker's death, it had gone into three editions, each more militant, and it continued to be reprinted and circulated for many years after.

Why was—is—the *Appeal* so thoroughly provocative? In the first place, it utterly breaks in language, tone, and strategy with the moderation that had largely characterized the anti-slavery movement. It rejects an approach emphasizing moral suasion, or an appeal to the religious sentiments of whites. Indeed, it attacks the supposed Christianity and liberalism of white America, including that of founding fathers like Jefferson. It affirms the citizenship of black people in the Republic, scorning the central notion of the colonization Societies that black Americans should remove themselves to Africa. And it calls upon blacks to unite—not a popular concept among assimilationists of his day—to take action, in the extreme case, to kill or be killed if that proves necessary to achieve liberation. A century before these ideas were widely diffused, it invokes pride in being black, hope in militancy, not servility; in a certain sense, it is the first expression of black nationalism placed into print in the United States.

Walker's work should not, however, be taken as a diatribe against all whites. In the course of the four "Articles" which constitute the full text of the *Appeal,* he expresses gratitude toward the white Americans "who have volunteered their services for our redemption. . . ." "Though we are unable to compensate them for their labours," he writes, "we nevertheless thank them from the bottom of our hearts, and have our eyes steadfastly fixed upon them, and their labors of love for God and man." And while he denounces colonization as a "plot," he appeals to "our friends who have been imperceptibly drawn into this plot." He views them "with tenderness, and would not for the world injure their feelings"; he has "only to hope for the future, that they will withdraw themselves from it. . . ."

Still, it is one of the ironies of our history that Patrick Henry's cry—"Give me liberty or give me death"—evokes intense sentiments of patriotism; whereas, David Walker's assertion—"Yea, would I meet death with avidity far! far!! in preference to such *servile submission*"—has evoked primarily fear.

Paul Lauter
Trinity College

PRIMARY WORK

Herbert Aptheker, ed. *One Continual Cry: David Walker's Appeal to the Colored Citizens of the World,* 1965. Also reprinted by Arno, 1969; and ed. Charles M. Wiltse, 1965.

SECONDARY WORKS

Henry Highland Garnet, "A Brief Sketch of the Life and Character of David Walker," in both Aptheker and Arno texts; Donald M. Jacobs, "David Walker: Boston Race Leader, 1825–1830," *Essex Institute Historical Collections,* 107 (January, 1971), 94–107; Sterling Stuckey, "David Walker: In Defense of African Rights and Liberty," *Slave Culture: Nationalist Theory and the Foundations of Black America,* 1987.

from Appeal &c.

Preamble

My dearly beloved Brethren and Fellow Citizens:

Having travelled over a considerable portion of these United States, and having, in the course of my travels taken the most accurate observations of things as they exist—the result of my observations has warranted the full and unshakened conviction, that we, (colored people of these United States) are the most degraded, wretched, and abject set of beings that ever lived since the world began, and I pray God, that none like us ever may live again until time shall be no more. They tell us of the Israelites in Egypt, the Helots[1] in Sparta, and of the Roman Slaves, which last, were made up from almost every nation under heaven, whose sufferings under those ancient and heathen nations were, in comparison with ours, under this enlightened and christian nation, no more than a cypher—or in other words, those heathen nations of antiquity, had but little more among them than the name and form of slavery, while wretchedness and endless miseries were reserved, apparently in a phial, to be poured out upon our fathers, ourselves and our children by *christian* Americans!

These positions, I shall endeavour, by the help of the Lord, to demonstrate in the course of this *appeal,* to the satisfaction of the most incredulous mind—and may God Almighty who is the father of our Lord Jesus Christ, open your hearts to understand and believe the truth.

The *causes,* my brethren, which produce our wretchedness and miseries, are so very numerous and aggravating, that I believe the pen only of a Josephus[2] or a Plutarch,[3] can well enumerate and explain them. Upon subjects, then, of such incomprehensible magnitude, so impenetrable, and so notorious, I shall be obliged to omit a large class of, and content myself with giving you an exposition of a few of those, which do indeed rage to such an alarming pitch, that they cannot but be a perpetual source of terror and dismay to every reflecting mind.

[1]The lowest class among the Spartans. They were essentially serfs, tied to land held by upper-class Spartans, who rendered a portion of their production to their lords. They could not be sold and could be freed only by the State. They may have been the original inhabitants of the area.

[2]Jewish historian, 37–c. 100 A.D.

[3]Greek biographer and moralist, first century A.D.

I am fully aware, in making this appeal to my much afflicted and suffering brethren, that I shall not only be assailed by those whose greatest earthly desires are, to keep us in abject ignorance and wretchedness, and who are of the firm conviction that heaven has designed us and our children to be slaves and *beasts of burden* to them and their children.—I say, I do not only expect to be held up to the public as an ignorant, impudent and restless disturber of the public peace, by such avaricious creatures, as well as a mover of insubordination—and perhaps put in prison or to death, for giving a superficial exposition of our miseries, and exposing tyrants. But I am persuaded, that many of my brethren, particularly those who are ignorantly in league with slave-holders or tyrants, who acquire their daily bread by the blood and sweat of their more ignorant brethren—and not a few of those too, who are too ignorant to see an inch beyond their noses, will rise up and call me cursed—Yea, the jealous ones among us will perhaps use more abject subtlety by affirming that this work is not worth perusing; that we are well situated and there is no use in trying to better our condition, for we cannot. I will ask one question here.—Can our condition be any worse?—Can it be more mean and abject? If there are any changes, will they not be for the better, though they may appear for the worse at first? Can they get us any lower? Where can they get us? They are afraid to treat us worse, for they know well, the day they do it they are gone. But against all accusations which may or can be preferred against me, I appeal to heaven for my motive in writing—who knows that my object is, if possible, to awaken in the breasts of my afflicted, degraded and slumbering brethren, a spirit of enquiry and investigation respecting our miseries and wretchedness in this *Republican Land of Liberty!!!!!*

The sources from which our miseries are derived and on which I shall comment, I shall not combine in one, but shall put them under distinct heads and expose them in their turn; in doing which, keeping truth on my side, and not departing from the strictest rules of morality, I shall endeavor to penetrate, search out, and lay them open for your inspection. If you cannot or will not profit by them, I shall have done *my* duty to you, my country and my God.

And as the inhuman system of *slavery,* is the *source* from which most of our miseries proceed, I shall begin with that *curse to nations,* which has spread terror and devastation through so many nations of antiquity, and which is raging to such a pitch at the present day in Spain and in Portugal. It had one tug in England, in France, and in the United States of America; yet the inhabitants thereof, do not learn wisdom, and erase it entirely from their dwellings and from all with whom they have to do. The fact is, the labour of slaves comes so cheap to the avaricious usurpers, and is (as they think) of such great utility to the country where it exists, that those who are actuated by sordid avarice only, overlook the evils, which will as sure as the Lord lives, follow after the good. In fact, they are so happy to keep in ignorance and degradation, and to receive the homage and the labour of the slaves, they forget that God rules in the armies of heaven and among the inhabitants of the earth, having his ears continually open to the cries, tears and groans of his oppressed people; and being a just and holy Being will at one day appear fully in behalf of the oppressed, and arrest the progress of the avaricious oppressors; for although the destruction of the oppressors God may not effect by the oppressed, yet the Lord our God will bring other destructions upon them—for not unfrequently will he cause them to rise up one against another, to be split and divided, and to oppress each other, and sometimes to open hostilities with sword in hand. . . .

All persons who are acquainted with history, and particularly the Bible, who are not blinded by the God of this world, and are not actuated solely by avarice—who are able to lay aside prejudice long enough to view candidly and impartially, things as they were, are, and probably will be, who are willing to admit that God made man to serve him *alone,* and that man should have no other Lord or Lords but himself—that God Almighty is the *sole proprietor* or *master* of the WHOLE human family, and will not on any consideration admit of a colleague, being unwilling to divide his glory with another.—And who can dispense with prejudice long enough to admit that we are men, notwithstanding our *improminent noses* and *woolly heads,* and believe that we feel for our fathers, mothers, wives and children as well as they do for theirs.—I say, all who are permitted to see and believe these things, can easily recognize the judgments of God among the Spaniards. Though others may lay the cause of the fierceness with which they cut each other's throats, to some other circumstances, yet they who believe that God is a God of justice, will believe that SLAVERY *is the principal cause.*

While the Spaniards are running about upon the field of battle cutting each other's throats, has not the Lord an afflicted and suffering people in the midst of them whose cries and groans in consequence of oppression are continually pouring into the ears of the God of justice? Would they not cease to cut each others throats if they could? But how can they? The very support which they draw from government to aid them in perpetrating such enormities, does it not arise in a great degree from the wretched victims of oppression among them? And yet they are calling for *Peace!—Peace!!* Will any peace be given unto them? Their destruction may indeed be procrastinated awhile, but can it continue long while they are oppressing the Lord's people? Has He not the hearts of all men in His hand? Will he suffer one part of his creatures to go on oppressing another like brutes always, with impunity? And yet those avaricious wretches are calling for *Peace!!!!* I declare it does appear to me, as though some nations think God is asleep, or that he made the Africans for nothing else but to dig their mines and work their farms, or they cannot believe history, sacred or profane. I ask every man who has a heart and is blessed with the privilege of believing—Is not God a God of justice to all his creatures? Do you say he is? Then if he gives peace and tranquility to tyrants, and permits them to keep our fathers, our mothers, ourselves and our children in eternal ignorance and wretchedness to support them and their families, would he be to us a God of *justice?* I ask O ye *christians!!!* who hold us and our children, in the most abject ignorance and degradation, that ever a people were afflicted with since the world began—I say, if God gives you peace and tranquility, and suffers you thus to go on afflicting us and our children, who have never given you the least provocation,—Would he be to us *a God of justice?* If you will allow that we are MEN, who feel for each other, does not the blood of our fathers and of us their children, cry aloud to the Lord of Sabaoth against you, for the cruelties and murders with which you have, and do continue to afflict us. But it is time for me to close my remarks on the suburbs, just to enter more fully into the interior of this system of cruelty and oppression.

Article I

Our Wretchedness in Consequence of Slavery

My beloved brethren: The Indians of North and of South America—the Greeks—the Irish subjected under the king of Great Britain—the Jews that ancient people of the Lord—the inhabitants of the islands of the sea—in fine, all the inhabitants of the earth, (except however, the sons of Africa) are called *men,* and of course are, and ought to be free. But we, (coloured people) and our children are *brutes!!* and of course are and ought to be SLAVES to the American people and their children forever! to dig their mines and work their farms; and thus go on enriching them, from one generation to another with our blood and our tears!!

I promised in a preceding page to demonstrate to the satisfaction of the most incredulous, that we, (colored people of these United States of America) are the *most wretched, degraded* and abject set of beings that ever *lived* since the world began, and that the white Americans having reduced us to the wretched state of *slavery,* treat us in that condition *more cruel* (they being an enlightened and christian people) than any heathen nation did any people whom it had reduced to our condition. These affirmations are so well confirmed in the minds of all unprejudiced men who have taken the trouble to read histories, that they need no elucidation from me. But to put them beyond all doubt, I refer you in the first place to the children of Jacob, or of Israel in Egypt, under Pharaoh and his people. Some of my brethren do not know who Pharaoh and the Egyptians were—I know it to be a fact that some of them take the Egyptians to have been a gang of *devils,* not knowing any better, and that they (Egyptians) having got possession of the Lord's people, treated them *nearly* as cruel as *christians Americans* do us, at the present day. For the information of such, I would only mention that the Egyptians, were Africans or colored people, such as we are—some of them yellow and others dark—a mixture of Ethiopians and the natives of Egypt—about the same as you see the colored people of the United States at the present day,—I say, I call your attention then, to the children of Jacob, while I point out particularly to you his son Joseph among the rest, in Egypt.

"And Pharaoh, said unto Joseph, thou shalt be over my house, and according unto thy word shall all my people be ruled; only in the throne will I be greater than thou."[4]

"And Pharaoh said unto Joseph, see, I have set thee over all the land of Egypt."[5]

"And Pharaoh said unto Joseph, I am Pharaoh, and without thee shall no man lift up his hand or foot in all the land of Egypt."[6]

Now I appeal to heaven and to earth, and particularly to the American people themselves who cease not to declare that our condition is not *hard,* and that we are comparatively satisfied to rest in wretchedness and misery, under them and their children. Not, indeed, to show me a colored President, a Governor, a Legislator, a Senator, a Mayor, or an Attorney at the Bar.—But to show me a man of color, who holds the low office of a Constable, or one who sits in a Juror Box, even on a case of one of his wretched brethren, throughout this great Republic!!—But let us pass Joseph the son of Israel a little further in review, as he existed with that heathen nation.

[4]See Genesis, chap. xli, v. 40. [Walker's note]

[5]v. 41. [Walker's note]

[6]v. 44. [Walker's note]

"And Pharaoh called Joseph's name Zaphnathpaaneah; and he gave him to wife Asenath the daughter of Potipherah priest of On. And Joseph went out over all the land of Egypt."[7]

Compare the above, with the American institutions. Do they not institute laws to prohibit us from marrying among the whites? I would wish, candidly, however, before the Lord, to be understood, that I would not give a *pinch of snuff* to be married to any white person I ever saw in all the days of my life. And I do say it, that the black man, or man of color, who will leave his own color (provided he can get one who is good for any thing) and marry a white woman, to be a double slave to her just because she is *white,* ought to be treated by her as he surely will be, viz; as a NIGER!!! It is not indeed what I care about intermarriages with the whites, which induced me to pass this subject in review; for the Lord knows, that there is a day coming when they will be glad enough to get into the company of the blacks, notwithstanding, we are, in this generation, levelled by them almost on a level with the brute creation; and some of us they treat even worse than they do the brutes that perish. I only made this extract to show how much lower we are held, and how much more cruel we are treated by the Americans, than were the children of Jacob, by the Egyptians. We will notice the sufferings of Israel some further, under *heathen Pharaoh,* compared with ours under the *enlightened christians of America.*

"And Pharaoh spake unto Joseph, saying, thy father and thy brethren are come unto thee:

The land of Egypt is before thee: in the best of the land make thy father and brethren to dwell; in the land of Goshen let them dwell; and if thou knowest any men of activity among them, then make them rulers over my cattle."[8]

I ask those people who treat us so *well,* Oh! I ask them, where is the most barren spot of land which they have given unto us? Israel had the most fertile land in all Egypt. Need I mention the very notorious fact, that I have known a poor man of color, who labored night and day, to acquire a little money, and having acquired it, he vested it in a small piece of land, and got him a house erected thereon, and having paid for the whole, he moved his family into it, where he was suffered to remain but nine months, when he was cheated out of his property by a white man, and driven out of door!—And is not this the case generally? Can a man of color buy a piece of land and keep it peaceably? Will not some white man try to get it from him even if it is in a *mud hole?* I need not comment any farther on a subject, which all, both black and white, will readily admit. But I must, really, observe that in this very city, when a man of color dies, if he owned any real estate it must generally fall into the hands of some white person. The wife and children of the deceased may weep and lament if they please, but the estate will be kept snug enough by its white posessors.

But to prove farther that the conditions of the Israelites was better under the Egyptians than ours is under the whites. I call upon the professing christians, I call upon the philanthropist, I call upon the very tyrant himself, to show me a page of history, either sacred or profane, on which a verse can be found, which maintains, that the Egyptians heaped the *insupportable insult* upon the children of Israel by telling them that they were not of the *human family.* Can the whites deny this charge? Have they not, after having reduced us to the deplorable condition of slaves under

[7]v. 45. [Walker's note]

[8]Genesis, chap. xlvii. v. 5, 6. [Walker's note]

their feet, held us up as descending originally from the tribes of *Monkeys* or *Orang-Outangs?* O! my God! I appeal to every man of feeling—is not this insupportable? Is it not heaping the most gross insult upon our miseries, because they have got us under their feet and we cannot help ourselves? Oh! pity us we pray thee, Lord Jesus, Master.—Has Mr. Jefferson declared to the world, that we are inferior to the whites, both in the endowments of our bodies and of minds?[9] It is indeed surprising, that a man of such great learning, combined with such excellent natural parts, should speak so of a set of men in chains. I do not know what to compare it to, unless, like putting one wild deer in an iron cage, where it will be secured, and hold another by the side of the same, then let it go, and expect the one in the cage to run as fast as the one at liberty. So far, my brethren, were the Egyptians from heaping these insults upon their slaves, that Pharaoh's daughter took Moses, a son of Israel, for her own, as will appear by the following.

"And Pharaoh's daughter said unto her, [Moses' mother] take this child away, and nurse it for me and I will pay thee thy wages. And the woman took the child [Moses] and nursed it.

And the child grew, and she brought him unto Pharaoh's daughter and he became her son. And she called his name Moses: and she said because I drew him out of the water."[10]

In all probability, Moses would have become Prince Regent to the throne, and no doubt, in process of time but he would have been seated on the throne of Egypt. But he had rather suffer shame, with the people of God, than to enjoy pleasures with that wicked people for a season. O! that the colored people were long since of Moses' excellent disposition, instead of courting favor with, and telling news and lies to our *natural enemies,* against each other—aiding them to keep their hellish chains of slavery upon us. Would we not long before this time, have been respectable men, instead of such wretched victims of oppression as we are? Would they be able to drag our mothers, our fathers, our wives, our children and ourselves, around the world in chains and hand-cuffs as they do, to dig up gold and silver for them and theirs? This question, my brethren, I leave for you to digest; and may God Almighty force it home to your hearts. Remember that unless you are united, keeping your tongues within your teeth, you will be afraid to trust your secrets to each other, and thus perpetuate our miseries under the *christians!!!!!* [☞ ADDITION,—Remember, also to lay humble at the feet of our Lord and Master Jesus Christ, with prayers and fastings. Let our enemies go on with their butcheries, and at once fill up their cup. Never make an attempt to gain our freedom or *natural right,* from under our cruel oppressors and murderers, until you see your way clear;[11] when that hour arrives and you move, be

[9]The reference is to Jefferson's *Notes on the State of Virginia,* Query XIV, printed elsewhere in this volume.

[10]See Exodus, chap. ii. v. 9, 10. [Walker's note]

[11]Walker's note: "It is not to be understood here, that I mean for us to wait until God shall take us by the hair of our heads and drag us out of abject wretchedness and slavery, nor do I mean to convey the idea for us to wait until our enemies shall make preparations, and call us to seize those preparations, take it away from them, and put every thing before us to death, in order to gain our freedom which God has given us. For you must remember that we are men as well as they. God has been pleased to give us two eyes, two hands, two feet, and some sense in our heads as well as they. They have no more right to hold us in slavery than we have to hold them, we have just as much right, in the sight of God, to hold them and their children in slavery and wretchedness, as they have to hold us, and no more."

not afraid or dismayed; for be you assured that Jesus Christ the king of heaven and of earth who is the God of justice and of armies, will surely go before you. And those enemies who have for hundreds of years stolen our *rights,* and kept us ignorant of Him and His divine worship, he will remove. Millions of whom, are this day, so ignorant and avaricious, that they cannot conceive how God can have an attribute of justice, and show mercy to us because it pleased Him to make us black—which color, Mr. Jefferson calls unfortunate!!!!!! As though we are not as thankful to our God for having made us as it pleased himself, as they (the whites) are for having made them white. They think because they hold us in their infernal chains of slavery that we wish to be white, or of their color—but they are dreadfully deceived—we wish to be just as it pleased our Creator to have made us, and no avaricious and unmerciful wretches, have any business to make slaves of or hold us in slavery. How would they like for us to make slaves of, or hold them in cruel slavery, and murder them as they do us? But is Mr. Jefferson's assertion true? viz. "that it is unfortunate for us that our Creator has been pleased to make us black." We will not take his say so, for the fact. The world will have an opportunity to see whether it is unfortunate for us, that our Creator *has made us* darker than the *whites.*

Fear not the number and education of our *enemies,* against whom we shall have to contend for our lawful right; guaranteed to us by our Maker; for why should we be afraid, when God is, and will continue (if we continue humble) to be on our side?

The man who would not fight under our Lord and Master Jesus Christ, in the glorious and heavenly cause of freedom and of God—to be delivered from the most wretched, abject and servile slavery, that ever a people was afflicted with since the foundation of the world, to the present day—ought to be kept with all of his children or family, in slavery, or in chains, to be butchered by his *cruel enemies.*☜]

I saw a paragraph, a few years since, in a South Carolina paper, which, speaking of the barbarity of the Turks it said: "The Turks are the most "barbarous" people in the world—they treat the Greeks "more like *brutes* than human beings." And in the same paper was an advertisement, which said: "Eight well built Virginia and Maryland *Negro "fellows* and four *wenches* will positively be *sold* "for this day *to the highest bidder!*" And what astonished me still more was, to see in this same *humane* paper!! the cuts of three men, with clubs and budgets[12] on their backs, and an advertisement offering a considerable sum of money for their apprehension and delivery. I declare it is really so *funny* to hear the Southerners and Westerners of this country talk about *barbarity,* that it is positively, enough to make a man *smile.*

The sufferings of the Helots among the Spartans, were somewhat severe, it is true, but to say that theirs were as severe as ours among the Americans I do most strenuously deny—for instance, can any man show me an article on a page of ancient history which specifies, that, the Spartans chained, and hand-cuffed the Helots, and dragged them from their wives and children, children from their parents, mothers from their sucking babes, wives from their husbands, driving them from one end of the country to the other? Notice the Spartans were heathens, who lived long before our Divine Master made his appearance in the flesh. Can Christian Americans deny these barbarous cruelties? Have you not Americans, having subjected us under you, added to these miseries, by insulting us in telling us to our face, because we are helpless that we are not of the human family? I ask you, O! Americans, I ask you, in the

[12]A bag or sack.

name of the Lord, can you deny these charges? Some perhaps may deny, by saying, that they never thought or said that we were not men. But do not actions speak louder than words?—have they not made provisions for the Greeks and Irish? Nations who have never done the least thing for them, while *we* who have enriched their country with our blood and tears—have dug up gold and silver for them and their children, from generation to generation, and are in more miseries than any other people under heaven, are not seen, but by comparatively a handful of the American people? There are indeed, more ways to kill a dog besides choaking it to death with butter. Further. The Spartans or Lacedemonians, had some frivolous pretext for enslaving the Helots, for they (Helots) while being free inhabitants of Sparta, stirred up an intestine commotion, and were by the Spartans subdued, and made prisoners of war. Consequently they and their children were condemned to perpetual slavery.[13]

I have been for years troubling the pages of historians to find out what our fathers have done to the *white Christians of America,* to merit such condign punishment as they have inflicted on them, and do continue to inflict on us their children. But I must aver, that my researches have hitherto been to no effect. I have therefore come to the immovable conclusion, that they (Americans) have, and do continue to punish us for nothing else, but for enriching them and their country. For I cannot conceive of any thing else. Nor will I ever believe otherwise until the Lord shall convince me.

The world knows, that slavery as it existed among the Romans, (which was the primary cause of their destruction) was, comparatively speaking, no more than a *cypher,* when compared with ours under the Americans. Indeed, I should not have noticed the Roman slaves, had not the very learned and penetrating Mr. Jefferson said, "When a master was murdered, all his slaves in the same house or within hearing, were condemned to death."[14]—Here let me ask Mr. Jefferson, (but he is gone to answer at the bar of God, for the deeds done in his body while living,) I therefore ask the whole American people, had I not rather die, or be put to death than to be a slave to any tyrant, who takes not only my own, but my wife and children's lives by the inches? Yea, would I meet death with avidity far! far!! in preference to such *servile submission* to the murderous hands of tyrants. Mr. Jefferson's very severe remarks on us have been so extensively argued upon by men whose attainments in literature, I shall never be able to reach, that I would not have meddled with it, were it not to solicit each of my brethren, who has the spirit of a man, to buy a copy of Mr. Jefferson's "Notes on Virginia," and put it in the hand of his son. For let no one of us suppose that the refutations which have been written by our white friends are enough—they are *whites*—we are *blacks.* We, and the world wish to see the charges of Mr. Jefferson refuted by the blacks *themselves,* according to their chance: for we must remember that what the whites have written respecting this subject, is other men's labors and did not emanate from the blacks. I know well, that there are some talents and learning among the coloured people of this country, which we have not a chance to develope, in consequence of oppression; but our oppression ought not to hinder us from acquiring all we can.—For we will have a chance to develope them by and

[13]See Dr. Goldsmith's History of Greece—page 9. See also Plutarch's lives. The Helots subdued by Agis, king of Sparta. [Walker's note]

[14]See his Notes on Virginia, page 210. [Walker's note]

by. God will not suffer us, always to be oppressed. Our sufferings will come to an *end,* in spite of all the Americans this side of *eternity.* Then we will want all the learning and talents among ourselves, and perhaps more, to govern ourselves.—"Every dog must have its day," the American's is coming to an end.

But let us review Mr. Jefferson's remarks respecting us some further. Comparing our miserable fathers, with the learned philosophers of Greece, he says: "Yet notwithstanding these and other discouraging circumstances among the Romans, their slaves were often their rarest artists. They excelled too in science, insomuch as to be usually employed as tutors to their master's children; Epictetus, Terence and Phaedrus,[15] were slaves,—but they were of the race of whites. It is not their *condition* then, but *nature,* which has produced the distinction."[16] See this, my brethren!! Do you believe that this assertion is swallowed by millions of the whites? Do you know that Mr. Jefferson was one of as great characters as ever lived among the whites? See his writings for the world, and public labors for the United States of America. Do you believe that the assertions of such a man, will pass away into oblivion unobserved by this people and the world? If you do you are much mistaken—See how the American people treat us—have we souls in our bodies? are we men who have any spirits at all? I know that there are many *swell-bellied* fellows among us whose greatest object is to fill their stomachs. Such I do not mean—I am after those who know and feel, that we are MEN as well as other people; to them, I say, that unless we try to refute Mr. Jefferson's arguments respecting us, we will only establish them.

But the slaves among the Romans. Every body who has read history, knows, that as soon as a slave among the Romans obtained his freedom, he could rise to the greatest eminence in the State, and there was no law instituted to hinder a slave from buying his freedom. Have not the Americans instituted laws to hinder us from obtaining our freedom. Do any deny this charge? Read the laws of Virginia, North Carolina, &c. Further: have not the Americans instituted laws to prohibit a man of colour from obtaining and holding any office whatever, under the government of the United States of America? Now, Mr. Jefferson tells us that our condition is not so hard, as the slaves were under the Romans!!!

It is time for me to bring this article to a close. But before I close it, I must observe to my brethren that at the close of the first Revolution in this country with Great Britain, there were but thirteen States in the Union, now there are twenty-four, most of which are slave-holding States, and the whites are dragging us around in chains and hand-cuffs to their new States and Territories to work their mines and farms, to enrich them and their children, and millions of them believing firmly that we being a little darker than they, were made by our creator to be an inheritance to them and their children forever—the same as a parcel of *brutes!!*

Are we MEN!!—I ask you, O my brethren! are we MEN? Did our creator make us to be slaves to dust and ashes like ourselves? Are they not dying worms as well as we? Have they not to make their appearance before the tribunal of heaven, to answer for the deeds done in the body, as well as we? Have we any other master but Jesus Christ alone? Is he not their master as well as ours?—What right then, have we to

[15]Respectively, a Greek Stoic philosopher held in Rome; Roman writer of comic drama; Roman writer of fables.

[16]See his Notes on Virginia, page 211. [Walker's note]

obey and call any other master, but Himself? How we could be so *submissive* to a gang of men, whom we cannot tell whether they are as *good* as ourselves or not, I never could conceive. However, this is shut up with the Lord and we cannot precisely tell—but I declare, we judge men by their works.

The whites have always been an unjust, jealous unmerciful, avaricious and blood thirsty set of beings, always seeking after power and authority.—We view them all over the confederacy of Greece, where they were first known to be any thing, (in consequence of education) we see them there, cutting each other's throats—trying to subject each other to wretchedness and misery, to effect which they used all kinds of deceitful, unfair and unmerciful means. We view them next in Rome, where the spirit of tyranny and deceit raged still higher.—We view them in Gaul, Spain and in Britain—in fine, we view them all over Europe, together with what were scattered about in Asia and Africa, as heathens, and we see them acting more like devils than accountable men. But some may ask, did not the blacks of Africa, and the mulattoes of Asia, go on in the same way as did the whites of Europe. I answer no—they never were half so avaricious, deceitful and unmerciful as the whites, according to their knowledge.

But we will leave the whites or Europeans as heathens and take a view of them as christians, in which capacity we see them as cruel, if not more so than ever. In fact, take them as a body, they are ten times more cruel avaricious and unmerciful than ever they were; for while they were heathens they were bad enough it is true, but it is positively a fact that they were not quite so audacious as to go and take vessel loads of men, women and children, and in cold blood and through devilishness, throw them into the sea, and murder them in all kinds of ways. While they were heathens, they were too ignorant for such barbarity. But being christians, enlightened and sensible, they are completely prepared for such hellish cruelties. Now suppose God were to give them more sense, what would they do. If it were possible would they not *dethrone* Jehovah and seat themselves upon his throne? I therefore, in the name and fear of the Lord God of heaven and of earth, divested of prejudice either on the side of my colour or that of the whites, advance my suspicion of them, whether they are *as good by nature* as we are or not. Their actions, since they were known as a people, have been the reverse, I do indeed suspect them, but this, as I before observed, is shut up with the Lord, we cannot exactly tell, it will be proved in succeeding generations.—The whites have had the essence of the gospel as it was preached by my master and his apostles—the Ethiopians have not, who are to have it in its meridian splendor—the Lord will give it to them to their satisfaction. I hope and pray my God, that they will make good use of it, that it may be well with them.[17]

1829

[17]Walker's note: "It is my solemn belief, that if ever the world becomes Christianized, (which must certainly take place before long) it will be through the means, under God of the *Blacks,* who are now held in wretchedness, and degradation, by the white *Christians* of the world, who before they learn to do justice to us before our Maker—and be reconciled to us, and reconcile us to them, and by that means have clear consciences before God and man.—Send out Missionaries to convert the Heathens, many of whom after they cease to worship gods, which neither see nor hear, become ten times more the children of Hell, then ever they were, why what is the reason? Why the reason is obvious, they must learn to do justice at home, before they go into distant lands, to display their charity, Christianity, and benevolence; when they learn to do justice, God will accept their offering, (no man may think that I am against Missionaries for I am not, my object is to see justice done at home, before we go to convert the Heathens.)"

William Lloyd Garrison 1805–1879

Like Benjamin Franklin, William Lloyd Garrison came from a poor New England family, was apprenticed to a printer, thus developed his skills in editing and writing, and applied them to a revolutionary cause. Both also believed that human beings were capable of infinite improvement and both devoted themselves to their divergent ideas of doing good in a wide variety of arenas. There the similarities cease. Indeed, it would be difficult to find two men more unlike in temperament, habits of mind, and prose. Franklin—worldly, conscious of image, ever ready to compromise, to seize the main chance, to accept the politic bird in the hand; given a bit to fat and a bit to smugness; a man who brought others together with humor, hard work, a touch of irony. Garrison—provincial, indifferent to opinion, as uncompromising with friend as with foe, ever demanding the "last full measure of devotion": spare, humorless in public, and self-righteous, it may be; a man who brought others together with the goad of his rhetoric and the heat of his passion. Franklin, whose final political act was to persuade the Constitutional delegates to accept the imperfect document they had created; Garrison, who came to denounce that document as a "covenant with Death and an agreement with Hell."

Garrison's father, an amiable sailing master somewhat given to drink, abandoned the family in 1808, three years after the birth of William Lloyd in Newburyport, Massachusetts. Reduced to poverty, Garrison's mother sought employment as a nurse in Lynn, then in Baltimore. At age 13, Garrison secured an apprenticeship in the office of the Newburyport *Herald,* where he learned printing and began to write anonymously for the paper. Concluding his apprenticeship in 1826, Garrison worked as a compositor and editor of newspapers committed to temperance and political causes. In 1828, however, he met Benjamin Lundy, editor of *The Genius of Universal Emancipation,* virtually the only national newspaper devoted solely to the somnolent anti-slavery cause. Garrison would, they agreed, become associate editor. But by the time he took up that task, he had abandoned the position Lundy held, that slavery would be ended by gradually emancipating blacks and colonizing them in Africa. Instead, Garrison began to argue for immediate emancipation without colonization or compensation. He also denounced a Newburyport merchant for transporting slaves from Baltimore to New Orleans. Convicted of libel, Garrison was, in lieu of payment of a fine and costs, sent to jail for forty-nine days. Characteristically, he turned confinement into a platform for a stream of anti-slavery poems and letters affirming his right to free speech.

In January of 1831, he had established himself in Boston where, with Isaac Knapp, he began issuing the *Liberator.* Set in the few hours they could spare from their jobs, printed with borrowed type, issued from a dingy office that also served as their lodging, the paper had within a few years effected a sea change in anti-slavery sentiment. Garrison succeeded in confronting Americans with stark moral choices. Slavery, he argued, was a crime against God and man—*the* most heinous of crimes. Gradualism and colonization merely perpetuated that crime; indeed, compounded it by maintaining that whites and blacks could not live together in one harmonious society. Only immediate emancipation could eradicate that crime, restore the moral integrity of American society, and bring to fruition the promise of the Declaration of Independence. To this position Garrison held unswervingly, insistently, clamorously for over thirty years. If friends held out political compromises for the sake of "ultimate" progress, he rejected them; if the Constitution was interpreted as sustaining slaveholding, he denounced it. And if others could not see the moral revolution entailed in immediate, unconditional emancipation, he would enlighten them.

He was effective. Quickened by his rhetoric and by his influence in organizing the American Anti-Slavery Society in 1833, Southern militants began defending slavery as a positive good and arguing for its extension into new territories. In turn, Northerners came to regard the South as aggressively pushing its peculiar institution throughout the democracy. In the North, the militance of Garrison and his supporters was often met with mob actions by proslavery forces, which helped mobilize moderates to defend at least the right of abolitionists to be heard. Garrison was, in short, a burr under the political saddle of ante-bellum America, which no amount of careful riding could dislodge; a "practical agitator," as John Jay Chapman later described him, keeping the issues to which he devoted himself at a boil.

These encompassed every significant reform posed in his time: temperance, women's rights, pacifism. The American Anti-Slavery Society split in 1840, largely because the Garrisonians insisted that women could not on principle be excluded from full participation in the work of reform. Indeed, Garrison joined Elizabeth Cady Stanton and Lucretia Mott in the gallery at the World Anti-Slavery Congress in London because they had not been allowed to take their seats as delegates. He broke with Frederick Douglass over the latter's espousal of political action apart from appeals to conscience, and Douglass's growing doubts about the practicality of Garrisonian non-resistance as a means for overcoming the slave power.

These were, for Garrison, not miscellaneous positions. Rather, they were rooted in the millenial beliefs of the Great Awakening that God's kingdom would be brought in by people actively committed to eradicating not just their own wrongdoings but sinfulness from the world. To be a Christian was, for Garrison, to carry out literally the injunctions of the Sermon on the Mount. In particular, he was committed to the principle of "non-resistance to evil by violence," for "he denied the right of any man whatsoever, or any body of men, forcibly to coerce another man in any way," to quote Leo Tolstoi, who was strongly influenced by him. Garrison, Tolstoi continues, "was the first to proclaim this principle as a rule for the organization of the life of men." For coercion, Garrison would substitute what he perceived as ultimately human: the rational and loving persuasion of one person by another. He saw in slavery, in male domination, in the practice of politics, instances of forcible coercion, and thus he opposed them, not so much because they were impractical or unlawful or cruel, but because they perpetuated inhuman relationships among people. The difficulties Garrison presents for today's readers may thus be less a matter of his alleged shrillness and fanaticism than our skepticism that non-violence, whether articulated by Thoreau or practiced by Martin Luther King, Jr., is a ground upon which we can construct peaceful and free societies.

Paul Lauter
Trinity College

PRIMARY WORKS

Selections from the Writings and Speeches of William Lloyd Garrison, 1852, reprinted 1968; Wendell Phillips Garrison and Francis Jackson Garrison, *William Lloyd Garrison: The Story of His Life,* 4 vols., 1885–1889; Truman Nelson, ed., *Document of Upheaval,* 1966; George M. Frederickson, ed., *William Lloyd Garrison,* 1968; Walter M. Merrill and Louis Ruchames, eds., *Letters of William Lloyd Garrison,* 6 vols. 1971–1981.

SECONDARY WORKS

John Jay Chapman, *William Lloyd Garrison,* 1921; Fanny Garrison Villard, *William Lloyd Garrison on Non-Resistance,* 1924; Walter M. Merrill, *Against Wind and Tide: A Biography of William Lloyd Garrison,* 1963; John L. Thomas, *The Liberator: William Lloyd Garrison, A Biography,* 1963; Archibald Henry Grimke, *William Lloyd Garrison: The Abolitionist,* 1969; Aileen S. Kraditor, *Means and Ends in American Abolitionism: Garrison and His Critics on Strategy and Tactics, 1834–1850,* 1969; James Brewer Stewart, *William Lloyd Garrison and the Challenge of Emancipation,* 1992; William B. Rogers, *"We Are All Together Now": Frederick Douglass, William Lloyd Garrison and the Prophetic Tradition,* 1995.

from William Lloyd Garrison: The Story of His Life

To the Public

In the month of August, I issued proposals for publishing "THE LIBERATOR" in Washington City; but the enterprise, though hailed in different sections of the country, was palsied by public indifference. Since that time, the removal of the *Genius of Universal Emancipation* to the Seat of Government has rendered less imperious the establishment of a similar periodical in that quarter.

During my recent tour for the purpose of exciting the minds of the people by a series of discourses on the subject of slavery, every place that I visited gave fresh evidence of the fact, that a greater revolution in public sentiment was to be effected in the free States—*and particularly in New-England*—than at the South. I found contempt more bitter, opposition more active, detraction more relentless, prejudice more stubborn, and apathy more frozen, than among slave-owners themselves. Of course, there were individual exceptions to the contrary. This state of things afflicted, but did not dishearten me. I determined, at every hazard, to lift up the standard of emancipation in the eyes of the nation, *within sight of Bunker Hill and in the birthplace of liberty.* That standard is now unfurled; and long may it float, unhurt by the spoliations of time or the missiles of a desperate foe—yea, till every chain be broken, and every bondman set free! Let Southern oppressors tremble—let their secret abettors tremble—let their Northern apologists tremble—let all the enemies of the persecuted blacks tremble.

I deem the publication of my original Prospectus unnecessary, as it has obtained a wide circulation. The principles therein inculcated will be steadily pursued in this paper, excepting that I shall not array myself as the political partisan of any man. In defending the great cause of human rights, I wish to derive the assistance of all religions and of all parties.

Assenting to the "self-evident truth" maintained in the American Declaration of Independence, "that all men are created equal, and endowed by their Creator with certain inalienable rights—among which are life, liberty and the pursuit of happiness," I shall strenuously contend for the immediate enfranchisement of our slave population. In Park-Street Church, on the Fourth of July, 1829, in an address on slavery, I unreflectingly assented to the popular but pernicious doctrine of *gradual* abolition. I seize this opportunity to make a full and unequivocal recantation, and thus publicly to ask pardon of my God, of my country, and of my brethren the poor slaves, for having uttered a sentiment so full of timidity, injustice, and absurdity. A similar recantation, from my pen, was published in the *Genius of Universal Emancipation* at Baltimore, in September, 1829. My conscience is now satisfied.

I am aware that many object to the severity of my language; but is there not cause for severity? I *will be* as harsh as truth, and as uncompromising as justice. On this subject, I do not wish to think, or speak, or write, with moderation. No! no! Tell a man whose house is on fire to give a moderate alarm; tell him to moderately rescue his wife from the hands of the ravisher; tell the mother to gradually extricate her babe from the fire into which it has fallen;—but urge me not to use moderation in a cause like the present. I am in earnest—I will not equivocate—I will not excuse—I will not retreat a single inch—AND I WILL BE HEARD. The apathy of the people is enough to make every statue leap from its pedestal, and to hasten the resurrection of the dead.

It is pretended, that I am retarding the cause of emancipation by the coarseness of my invective and the precipitancy of my measures. *The charge is not true.* On this question my influence,—humble as it is,—is felt at this moment to a considerable extent, and shall be felt in coming years—not perniciously, but beneficially—not as a curse, but as a blessing; and posterity will bear testimony that I was right. I desire to thank God, that he enables me to disregard "the fear of man which bringeth a snare," and to speak his truth in its simplicity and power. And here I close with this fresh dedication:

"Oppression! I have seen thee, face to face,
And met thy cruel eye and cloudy brow;
But thy soul-withering glance I fear not now—
For dread to prouder feelings doth give place
Of deep abhorrence! Scorning the disgrace
Of slavish knees that at thy footstool bow,
I also kneel—but with far other vow
Do hail thee and thy herd of hirelings base:—
I swear, while life-blood warms my throbbing veins,
Still to oppose and thwart, with heart and hand,
Thy brutalising sway—till Afric's chains
Are burst, and Freedom rules the rescued land,—
Trampling Oppression and his iron rod:
Such is the vow I take—SO HELP ME GOD"[1]

William Lloyd Garrison.
Boston, January 1, 1831.

1885

[1]The author of this sonnet was Thomas Pringle, the Scottish poet, 1789–1834, one of the founders of *Blackwood's Magazine,* and Secretary of the London Society for the Abolition of Slavery throughout the British Dominions.

Lydia Maria Child 1802–1880

Lydia Maria Child was one of America's first women of letters. For a half-century, she edited anthologies and annuals and wrote poetry, novels, short fiction, history, essays, and juvenile works. Among the Garrisonian abolitionists, Garrison himself was the most significant journalist, Wendell Phillips the most influential speaker, and Child the most important writer. The selections that follow focus on her anti-slavery writings.

Child was a popular author when young. In 1824, at age twenty-two, she had written a novel, *Hobomok, A Tale of Early Times,* based on the experiences of the Puritan settlers and their relationships to the Indians. The book presents the marriage of a young Puritan woman to an Indian man, Hobomok; while their happy union ends after Mary's youthful white lover returns from overseas and her Indian husband nobly disappears into the forest, the novel offers an altogether different mythic view of interracial relations from that of Cooper. The book was sufficiently well-received to allow Child to obtain library privileges at the all-male Boston Athenaeum and to write a second novel in 1825, *The Rebels, or Boston Before the Revolution.* In the same year, she opened a school for girls, and in the next produced the first periodical for children in the United States, the *Juvenile Miscellany,* most of which she wrote. In 1828, she married David Child, an idealistic but profoundly impractical young man, whose projects invariably ran the family into debt. In part to survive financially, Child began writing books of practical advice for women, like *The Frugal Housewife* (1829) and *The Mother's Book* (1831). She conceived a grand project, *The Ladies' Family Library,* designed to provide women with biographical models, information, and ideas about their history and lives. Of the four volumes completed by 1835, her *History of the Condition of Women, In Various Ages and Nations* was perhaps the most influential, both as a source for later writers and in its broad view of women's accomplishments.

By 1833, however, she had met William Lloyd Garrison and had committed herself to immediate and unconditional emancipation of the slaves. Her first effort toward that end was *An Appeal in Favor of that Class of Americans Called Africans.* In her "Preface" Child addressed the problem she faced as a woman writing about a public political issue in a society that restricted middle-class females to the "domestic sphere." Addressing an audience familiar with her fiction and her domestic how-to books (well within the accepted range of women's writing), she challenges them to read her inflammatory pamphlet. In doing so, Child does not adopt the "masculine" stance of a polemicist. Instead, she uses traditional patterns of female discourse and presents herself as a supplicant. Despite this conciliatory stance, the literary establishment rejected both the *Appeal* and its author. Its publication in 1833 marked Child as a "radical," and "decent" people began to shun her works: the Athenaeum revoked her library privileges, the *Juvenile Miscellany* failed for lack of subscribers, and the promise of her literary career disappeared. But the *Appeal* was a major force in persuading a generation of young New England intellectuals to support immediate emancipation, and for the rest of her long life, Child did much of her writing for that and other reform movements.

In 1841, Child left Northampton, Massachusetts, where she had been involved with David in his plan to grow sugar beets as a substitute for the cane sugar produced by slave labor in the South. She moved to New York City to edit the Garrisonian abolitionist newspaper *The National Anti-Slavery Standard.*

Child published in the *Standard* her informal weekly "Letters from New York," which appeared next to her own editorials, and later edited and republished these columns in an effort to make some money. "Letter 14," one of these, voices an affirmation of nature and of mankind that heralds Child's connections with Transcendentalism. Yet this sketch of poverty in New York City also suggests Dickens's London in its juxtaposition of urban wealth and poverty. Mixing mid-century appeals to sentiment with advanced social consciousness, Child condemns society for causing poverty—which, she asserts, is the source of urban crime—and she condemns the penal system for re-creating this crime. "Woman's Rights," another "New York Letter," addresses an issue that already in 1843 appeared urgent to her and to her reformer-readers. "Number Thirty-Three" is a third "New York Letter." Perhaps because of its radical content, she did not anthologize this account of her efforts to protect the British abolitionist speaker George Thompson from anti-abolitionist rioters. In this Letter, the tensions between traditional literary forms and untraditional political content—disjunctions that characterized Child's "Preface" to the *Appeal*—again appear. Beginning from a recollection occasioned by the note of a katydid, Child provides an extraordinary account of racist violence. These tensions are repeated several paragraphs later when, after a concrete and detailed account of a riot, Child republishes the conventional poem it occasioned.

Her short story "Slavery's Pleasant Homes," which appeared in 1843 in a literary annual published by the Boston Female Anti-Slavery Society, presents Slavery as a web of private relationships, not as a forced labor system in a capitalist economy. Here Child uses characters and plotlines that have become mythic in American literature and culture. Like other mythologists, she presents types, concentrating on patterns of actions in her dramas of blacks and whites, slaves and masters, men and women.

In 1843 Child resigned from her position as editor of the *Standard,* wearied of the internal struggles that had increasingly split the abolitionist movement. In an effort to reestablish her literary career, she published two series of her *Letters from New York* (1843, 1845), a collection of stories, *Fact and Fiction* (1846), and began a huge work, *The Progress of Religious Ideas Through Successive Ages* (1855). She also continued to write on behalf of Indians, as in her story "A Legend of the Falls of St. Anthony" (1846) and her *Appeal for the Indians* (1868). And she pursued her advocacy of blacks. Some 300,000 copies of her exchange of letters with Governor Wise and Mrs. Mason of Virginia, occasioned by John Brown's raid, were circulated in 1860, and were important in preparing northern consciousness for what would be a war against slavery. In 1865 with her own funds she had printed and circulated especially among blacks, *The Freedmen's Book,* a collection of essays, biographical sketches, and poems by and about black people. It was designed, in the tradition of Child's commitment to "art for truth's sake," as a literacy text and to promote the ideas of votes for blacks and of black pride. Many of her works, like her last novel, *A Romance of the Republic* (1867), focus on interracial marriages, which Child seemed to offer as a symbol for her vision of a nation to be made one out of many. Indeed, after Emancipation, Child's dramas of racial and sexual power relationships under slavery were adopted by later generations of American writers to figure power relationships in a racist, sexist society. Her mythic characters and plots appear and reappear in American letters from Mark Twain's *Pudd'nhead Wilson* to William Faulkner's *Absalom! Absalom!*

Jean Fagan Yellin
Pace University

PRIMARY WORKS

Fact and Fiction: A Collection of Stories, 1846; *A Romance of the Republic,* 1867; *An Appeal in Favor of that Class of Americans Called Africans,* 1833; *The History of the Condition of Women, in Various Ages and Nations,* vols. 4 and 5, *Ladies' Family Library,* 1835; *Letters from New York, First Series,* 1843; *Second Series,* 1845; *Correspondence Between Lydia Maria Child and Gov. Wise and Mrs. Mason of Virginia,* 1860; *The Freedmen's Book,* 1865; *An Appeal for the Indians,* 1868; *The Collected Correspondence of Lydia Maria Child,* 1817–1880, ed. Patricia G. Holland, Milton Meltzer, and Francine Krasno, 1980; *Lydia Maria Child: Selected Letters, 1817–1880,* ed. Milton Meltzer, Patricia G. Holland, and Francine Krasno, 1982; *A Lydia Child Reader,* 1997.

SECONDARY WORKS

Helene G. Baer, *The Heart Is Like Heaven: The Life of Lydia Maria Child,* 1964; Milton Meltzer, *Tongue of Flame: The Life of Lydia Maria Child,* 1965; Carolyn L. Karcher, "Introduction," Lydia Maria Child, *Hobomok and Other Writings on Indians,* 1986; Jean Fagan Yellin, *Women and Sisters: The Antislavery Feminists in American Culture,* 1989; Carolyn L. Karcher, "Rape, Murder and Revenge in 'Slavery's Pleasant Homes,'" in *The Aesthetics of Sentiment,* ed. Shirley Samuels, 1992; Deborah Pickman Clifford, *Crusader for Reform: A Life of Lydia Maria Child,* 1992; Carolyn L. Karcher, *The First Woman of the Republic: A Cultural Biography of Lydia Maria Child,* 1994; Bruce Mills, *Cultural Reformations: Lydia Maria Child and the Literature of Reform,* 1994.

from Appeal in Favor of that Class of Americans Called Africans

Preface

READER, I beseech you not to throw down this volume as soon as you have glanced at the title. Read it, if your prejudices will allow, for the very truth's sake. If I have the most trifling claims upon your good will, for an hour's amusement to yourself, or benefit to your children, read it for *my* sake:—Read it, if it be merely to find fresh occasion to sneer at the vulgarity of the cause;—Read it, from sheer curiosity to see what a woman who had much better attend to her household concerns will say upon such a subject;—Read it, on any terms, and my purpose will be gained.

The subject I have chosen admits of no encomiums on my country; but as I generally make it an object to supply what is most needed, this circumstance is unimportant; the market is so glutted with flattery, that a little truth may be acceptable, were it only for its rarity.

I am fully aware of the unpopularity of the task I have undertaken; but though I *expect* ridicule and censure, it is not in my nature to *fear* them.

A few years hence, the opinion of the world will be a matter in which I have not even the most transient interest; but this book will be abroad on its mission of humanity, long after the hand that wrote it is mingling with the dust.

Should it be the means of advancing, even one single hour, the inevitable progress of truth and justice, I would not exchange the consciousness for all Rothschild's wealth,[1] or Sir Walter's fame.[2]

Chapter VIII

Prejudices Against People Of Color, And Our Duties In Relation To This Subject.

While we bestow our earnest disapprobation on the system of slavery, let us not flatter ourselves that we are in reality any better than our brethren of the South. Thanks to our soil and climate, and the early exertions of the excellent Society of Friends, the *form* of slavery does not exist among us; but the very *spirit* of the hateful and mischievous thing is here in all its strength. . . . Our prejudice against colored people is even more inveterate than it is at the South. The planter is often attached to his negroes, and lavishes caresses and kind words upon them, as he would on a favorite hound: but our cold-hearted, ignoble prejudice admits of no exception—no intermission. . . . In order that my readers may not be ignorant of the extent of this tyrannical prejudice, I will as briefly as possible state the evidence, and leave them to judge of it, as their hearts and consciences may dictate.

In the first place, an unjust law exists in this Commonwealth, by which marriage between persons of different color is pronounced illegal. . . . The government ought not to be invested with power to control the affections, any more than the consciences of citizens. A man has at least as good a right to choose his wife, as he has to choose his religion. . . .

There is among the colored people an increasing desire for information, and laudable ambition to be respectable in manners and appearance. . . . But in the public schools, colored children are subject to many discouragements and difficulties; and into the private schools they cannot gain admission. . . .

In the theatre, it is not possible for respectable colored people to obtain a decent seat. They must either be excluded, or herd with the vicious.

A fierce excitement prevailed, not long since, because a colored man had bought a pew in one of our churches. . . . Even at the communion-table, the mockery of human pride is mingled with the worship of Jehovah. . . .

Will any candid person tell me why respectable colored people should not be allowed to make use of public conveyances, open to all who are able and willing to pay for the privilege? Those who enter a vessel, or a stage-coach, cannot expect to select their companions. If they can afford to take a carriage or boat for themselves, then, and then only, they have a right to be exclusive. . . .

The state of public feeling not only makes it difficult for the Africans to obtain information, but it prevents them from making profitable use of what knowledge they

[1]The wealth of the European financial house of Rothschild had, by Child's time, become legendary.

[2]Sir Walter Scott (1771–1832), prolific poet and novelist, was the most popular writer of the day.

have. A colored man, however intelligent, is not allowed to pursue any business more lucrative than that of a barber, a shoe-black, or a waiter. These, and all other employments, are truly respectable, whenever the duties connected with them are faithfully performed; but it is unjust that a man should, on account of his complexion, be prevented from performing more elevated uses in society. Every citizen ought to have a fair chance to try his fortune in any line of business, which he thinks he has ability to transact. . . .

If it be disagreeable to allow colored people the same right and privileges as other citizens, we can do with our prejudice, what most of us often do with better feeling—we can conceal it.

Our almanacs and newspapers can fairly show both sides of the question; and if they lean to either party, let it not be the strongest. Our preachers can speak of slavery, as they do of other evils. Our poets can find in this subject abundant room for sentiment and pathos. Our orators (provided they do not want office) may venture an allusion to our *in*-"glorious institutions."

The union of individual influence produces a vast amount of moral force, which is not the less powerful because it is often unperceived. A mere change in the *direction* of our efforts, without any increased exertion, would in the course of a few years, produce an entire revolution of public feeling. This slow but sure way of doing good is almost the only means by which benevolence can effect its purpose. . . .

By publishing this book I have put my mite into the treasury. The expectation of displeasing all classes has not been unaccompanied with pain. But it has been strongly impressed upon my mind that it was a duty to fulfil this task; and worldly considerations should never stifle the voice of conscience.

1833

Letters from New York

#14

Weeks have passed since I wrote you; not from want of inclination, but because the wrangling at Washington leaves no room for gentle thoughts and poetic fancies. I know not whether you long as earnestly as I do to have Congress stop its discord, and the birds begin their harmony.[1] I was always impatient for the spring-time, but never so much as now; compelled as I am to watch the vile game of venality and passion, which men dignify with the name of government. Patience yet a few months longer, and Congress will *disband;* I do not think it will ever *rise,* until slavery is abolished; unless, indeed, a portion of them "rise" in the *southern* sense of the phrase, to cut up facts with bowie-knives, and exterminate truth with rifle-balls.

[1]Child is referring to the Congressional debate over the "gag rule" to block consideration of anti-slavery petitions.

Patience yet a little longer! and I shall find delicate bells of trailing arbutus, fragrant as an infant's breath, hidden deep, under their coverlid of autumn leaves, like modest worth in this pretending world. My spirit is weary for rural rambles. It is sad walking in the city. The streets shut out the sky, even as commerce comes between the soul and heaven. The busy throng, passing and repassing, fetter freedom, while they offer no sympathy. The loneliness of the soul is deeper, and far more restless, than in the solitude of the mighty forest. Wherever are woods and fields I find a home; each tinted leaf and shining pebble is to me a friend; and wherever I spy a wild flower, I am ready to leap up, clap my hands, and exclaim, "Cockatoo! he know me very well!" as did the poor New Zealander, when he recognized a bird of his native clime, in the menageries of London.

But amid these magnificent masses of sparkling marble, hewn *in prison,* I am alone. For eight weary months, I have met in the crowded streets but two faces I had ever seen before. Of some, I would I could say that I should never see them again; but they haunt me in my sleep, and come between me and the morning. Beseeching looks, begging the comfort and the hope I have no power to give. Hungry eyes, that look as if they had pleaded long for sympathy, and at last gone mute in still despair. Through what woful, what frightful masks, does the human soul look forth, leering, peeping, and defying, in this thoroughfare of nations. Yet in each and all lie the capacities of an archangel; as the majestic oak lies enfolded in the acorn that we tread carelessly under foot, and which decays, perchance, for want of soil to root in.

The other day, I went forth for exercise merely, without other hope of enjoyment than a farewell to the setting sun, on the now deserted Battery, and a fresh kiss from the breezes of the sea, ere they passed through the polluted city, bearing healing on their wings. I had not gone far, when I met a little ragged urchin, about four years old, with a heap of newspapers, "more big as he could carry," under his little arm, and another clenched in his small, red fist. The sweet voice of childhood was prematurely cracked into shrillness, by screaming street cries, at the top of his lungs; and he looked blue, cold, and disconsolate. May the angels guard him! How I wanted to warm him in my heart. I stood, looking after him, as he went shivering along. Imagination followed him to the miserable cellar where he probably slept on dirty straw; I saw him flogged, after his day of cheerless toil, because he had failed to bring home pence enough for his parents' grog; I saw wicked ones come muttering and beckoning between his young soul and heaven; they tempted him to steal to avoid the dreaded beating. I saw him, years after, bewildered and frightened, in the police-office, surrounded by hard faces. Their law-jargon conveyed no meaning to his ear, awakened no slumbering moral sense, taught him no clear distinction between right and wrong; but from their cold, harsh tones, and heartless merriment, he drew the inference that they were enemies; and, as such, he hated them. At that moment, one tone like a mother's voice might have wholly changed his earthly destiny; one kind word of friendly counsel might have saved him—as if an angel standing in the genial sunlight, had thrown to him one end of a garland, and gently diminishing the distance between them, had drawn him safely out of the deep and tangled labyrinth, where all false echoes and winding paths conspired to make him lose his way.

But watchmen and constables were around him; and they have small fellowship with angels. The strong impulses that might have become overwhelming love for his race, are perverted to the bitterest hatred. He tries the universal resort of weakness against force; if they are too strong for *him,* he will be too cunning for *them. Their* cunning is roused to detect *his* cunning: and thus the gallows-game is played, with interludes of damnable merriment from police reports, whereat the heedless multitude laugh; while angels weep over the slow murder of a human soul.

When, O when, will men learn that society makes and cherishes the very crimes it so fiercely punishes, and *in* punishing reproduces?

> The key of knowledge first ye take away,
> And then, because ye've robbed him, ye enslave;
> Ye shut out from him the sweet light of day,
> And then, because he's in the dark, ye pave
> The road, that leads him to his wished-for grave,
> With stones of stumbling: then, if he but tread
> Darkling and slow, ye call him "fool" and "knave";—
> Doom him to toil, and yet deny him bread:
> Chains round his limbs ye throw, and curses on his head.

God grant the little shivering carrier-boy a brighter destiny than I have foreseen for him.

A little further on, I encountered two young boys fighting furiously for some coppers, that had been given them and had fallen on the pavement. They had matted black hair, large, lustrous eyes, and an olive complexion. They were evidently foreign children, from the sunny climes of Italy or Spain, and nature had made them subjects for an artist's dream. Near by on the cold stone steps, sat a ragged, emaciated woman, whom I conjectured, from the resemblance of her large, dark eyes, might be their mother; but she looked on their fight with languid indifference, as if seeing, she saw it not. I spoke to her, and she shook her head in a mournful way, that told me she did not understand my language. Poor, forlorn wanderer! would I could place thee and thy beautiful boys under shelter of sun-ripened vines, surrounded by the music of thy motherland! Pence I will give thee, though political economy reprove the deed. They can but appease the hunger of the body; they cannot soothe the hunger of thy heart; that I obey the kindly impulse may make the world none the better—perchance some iota the worse; yet I must needs follow it—I cannot otherwise.

I raised my eyes above the woman's weather-beaten head, and saw, behind the window of clear, plate glass, large vases of gold and silver, curiously wrought. They spoke significantly of the sad contrasts in this disordered world; and excited in my mind whole volumes, not of political, but of angelic economy. "Truly," said I, "if the Law of Love prevailed, vases of gold and silver might even more abound—but no homeless outcast would sit shivering beneath their glittering mockery. All would be richer, and no man the poorer. When will the world learn its best wisdom? When will the mighty discord come into heavenly harmony?" I looked at the huge stone structures of commercial wealth, and they gave an answer that chilled my heart. Weary of city walks, I would have turned homeward; but nature, ever true and harmonious, beckoned to me from the Battery,[2] and the glowing twilight gave

[2]The southern tip of Manhattan Island, so named for a fort located there.

me friendly welcome. It seemed as if the dancing Spring Hours had thrown their rosy mantles on old silvery winter in the lavishness of youthful love.

I opened my heart to the gladsome influence, and forgot that earth was not a mirror of the heavens. It was but for a moment; for there, under the leafless trees, lay two ragged little boys, asleep in each other's arms. I remembered having read in the police reports, the day before, that two little children, thus found, had been taken up as vagabonds. They told, with simple pathos, how both their mothers had been dead for months; how they had formed an intimate friendship, had begged together, ate together, hungered together, and together slept uncovered beneath the steel-cold stars.

The twilight seemed no longer warm; and brushing away a tear, I walked hastily homeward. As I turned into the street where God has provided me with a friendly shelter, something lay across my path. It was a woman, apparently dead; with garments all draggled in New-York gutters, blacker than waves of the infernal rivers. Those who gathered around, said she had fallen in intoxication, and was rendered senseless by the force of the blow. They carried her to the watch-house, and the doctor promised she should be well attended. But alas, for watch-house charities to a breaking heart! I could not bring myself to think otherwise than that hers *was* a breaking heart! Could she but give a full revelation of early emotions checked in their full and kindly flow, of affections repressed, of hopes blighted, and energies misemployed through ignorance, the heart would kindle and melt, as it does when genius stirs its deepest recesses.

It seemed as if the voice of human wo was destined to follow me through the whole of that unblest day. Late in the night I heard the sound of voices in the street, and raising the window, saw a poor, staggering woman in the hands of a watchman. My ear caught the words, "Thank you kindly, sir. I should *like* to go home." The sad and humble accents in which the simple phrase was uttered, the dreary image of the watch-house, which that poor wretch dreamed was her *home,* proved too much for my overloaded sympathies. I hid my face in the pillow, and wept; for "my heart was almost breaking with the misery of my kind."

I thought, then, that I would walk no more abroad, till the fields were green. But my mind and body grow alike impatient of being inclosed within four walls; both ask for the free breeze, and the wide, blue dome that overarches and embraces *all.* Again I rambled forth, under the February sun, as mild and genial as the breath of June. Heart, mind, and frame grew glad and strong, as we wandered on, past the old Stuyvesant church, which a few years agone was surrounded by fields and Dutch farmhouses, but now stands in the midst of peopled streets;—and past the trim, new houses, with their green verandahs, in the airy suburbs. Following the railroad, which lay far beneath our feet, as we wound our way over the hills, we came to the burying-ground of the poor. Weeds and brambles grew along the sides, and the stubble of last year's grass waved over it, like dreary memories of the past; but the sun smiled on it, like God's love on the desolate soul. It was inexpressibly touching to see the frail memorials of affection, placed there by hearts crushed under the weight of poverty. In one place was a small rude cross of wood, with the initials J.S. cut with a penknife, and apparently filled with ink. In another a small hoop had been bent into the form of a heart, painted green, and nailed on a stick at the head of the grave. On one upright shingle was painted only "MUTTER"; the

German word for MOTHER. On another was scrawled, as if with charcoal, *So ruhe wohl, du unser liebes kind.* (Rest well, our beloved child.) One recorded life's brief history thus: "H.G. born in Bavaria; died in New-York." Another short epitaph, in French, told that the sleeper came from the banks of the Seine.

The predominance of foreign epitaphs affected me deeply. Who could now tell with what high hopes those departed ones had left the heart-homes of Germany, the sunny hills of Spain, the laughing skies of Italy, or the wild beauty of Switzerland? Would not the friends they had left in their childhood's home, weep scalding tears to find them in a pauper's grave, with their initials rudely carved on a fragile shingle? Some had not even these frail memorials. It seemed there was none to care whether they lived or died. A wide, deep trench was open; and there I could see piles of unpainted coffins heaped one upon the other, left uncovered with earth, till the yawning cavity was filled with its hundred tenants.

Returning homeward, we passed a Catholic burying-ground. It belonged to the upper classes, and was filled with marble monuments, covered with long inscriptions. But none of them touched my heart like that rude shingle, with the simple word "Mutter" inscribed thereon. The gate was open, and hundreds of Irish, in their best Sunday clothes, were stepping reverently among the graves, and kissing the very sods. Tenderness for the dead is one of the loveliest features of their nation and their church.

The evening was closing in, as we returned, thoughtful but not gloomy. Bright lights shone through crimson, blue, and green, in the apothecaries' windows, and were reflected in prismatic beauty from the dirty pools in the street. It was like poetic thoughts in the minds of the poor and ignorant; like the memory of pure aspirations in the vicious; like a rainbow of promise, that God's spirit never leaves even the most degraded soul. I smiled, as my spirit gratefully accepted this love-token from the outward; and I thanked our heavenly Father for a world beyond this.

1842

#33

It is curious how a single note in the great hymn of Nature sometimes recalls the memories of years—opens whole galleries of soul-painting, stretching far off into the remote perspective of the past. Rambling on the Brooklyn side of the ferry the other evening, I heard the note of a Katy-did. Instantly it flashed upon my recollection, under what impressive circumstances I, for the first time in my life, heard the angular note of that handsome insect. Six years ago, George Thompson[1] accompanied us to New-York. It was August, a month which the persecuted abolitionists were wont to observe brought out a multitude of snakes and southerners. . . .

The steamboat, which brought us to New-York, was filled with our masters.[2] We saw one after another pointing out George Thompson; and never has it been my fortune to witness such fierce manifestations of hatred written on the human

[1]George Thompson (1804–1878), a British abolitionist, toured the U.S. at Garrison's invitation from 1834 to 1835; he again visited America in 1850 and in 1864.

[2]This is an ironic reference to slaveholders, whom Child suggests were ruling over all Americans.

countenance. Men, who a few moments before seemed like polished gentlemen, were suddenly transformed into demons.—They followed close behind us, as we walked the deck, with clenched fists, and uttering the most fearful imprecations. One man, from Georgia, drew a sword from his case, and swore he would kill whoever dares say a word against slavery. It was our intention to stop at Newport, to visit a relative; and I was glad that it so happened; for had we gone on, the boat whould have arrived in New-York just at dusk; and I, for one, had no inclination to land at that hour, with such a set of ferocious characters, to whom our persons were well known, and whom we had observed in whispered consultation, ominous of mischief. We pursued our route the next day, without attracting attention; and fearing that George Thompson would bring ruin to the dwelling of any acquaintance we might wish to visit in the city, we crossed over to Brooklyn, to the house of a friend who had known and loved him in Europe. The katydids were then in full concert; and their name was legion. It was the first time I had ever heard them; and my mind was in that excited state, which made all sounds discordant. . . .

Mr. Thompson seemed, as he did on all similar occasions, very little disturbed concerning his own danger; but our host was so obviously anxious, that it imparted a degree of uneasiness to us all. That night, I started at every sound, and when the harsh and unusual notes of that army of katydids met my ear, I was again and again deceived by the impression that they were the shouts of a mob in the distance. I shall never be able to get rid of the image this engraved; to my mind the katydids will forever speak of mobs. . . .

Our host was by no means quite reassured, even when Thompson and my husband[3] had both left. I was not of sufficient consequence to endanger anybody; but should I be recognized, it might naturally be reported that Thompson was in the same house. Resolving that no one should incur risk on my account, and being utterly without friends in New-York, I went to a hotel at Bath, and staid there alone. Never, before or since, have I experienced such utter desolation, as I did the few days I remained there. It seemed to me as if anti-slavery had cut me off from all the sympathies of my kind. As I sat there alone, I wrote the following lines, for George Thompson's magnificent album. They have been several times printed; but as my reminiscences are busy with him, I will repeat them:

I've heard thee when thy powerful words
Were like the cataract's roar—
Or like the ocean's mighty waves
Resounding on the shore

But even in reproof of sin,
Love brooded over all—
As the mild rainbow's heavenly arch
Rests on the waterfall.

I've heard thee in the hour of prayer
When dangers were around,

[3]David Lee Child (1794–1874) was, like Child, a staunch Garrisonian abolitionist.

Thy voice was like the royal harp,
That breathed a charmed sound.

The evil spirit felt its powers
And howling turned away;
And some, perchance, "who came to scoff
Remained with thee to pray."

I've seen thee, too, in playful mood,
When words of magic spell
Dropped from thy lips like fairy gems,
That sparkled as they fell.

Still great and good in every change!
Magnificent and mild!
As if a saraph's god-like power
Dwealt in a little child.

Among the various exciting recollections with which Thompson is associated, no one is as deeply on my mind as the 1st of August, 1835. It was the first anniversary of emancipation in the British West Indies; and the abolitionists of Boston proposed to hold a meeting in commemoration of that glorious event. The Tremont House[4] was swarming with southerners; and they swore that George Thompson should not be allowed to speak. The meeting was, however, held at Julian Hall. Few people were there, and I had a chance to observe them all. Near the stairs, was a line of men in fine broadcloth, whom I saw at once were slaveholders; the fact was plainly enough written in the clenched fist, the fiercely compressed lip, and the haughty carriage of the head. In front of them were a dozen or more stout truckmen, in shirtsleeves; there seemed to be an understanding between them; there were in fact "the glorious Union." . . .

[Thompson, aware that there "were well-managed preparations for a savage mob," poured out "torrents of eloquence." The Southerners raged out of the hall, with the truckmen after them.]

When the meeting closed, the heart of every abolitionist beat with a quickened pulse, for Thompson's safety. From time to time, the fierce, impatient faces of the truckmen were seen above the staircase; their courage evidently reinforced by fresh supplies of rum, paid for by southern generosity. Abolitionists, who left the meeting, came back to tell that the stairway and entry were lined with desperate-looking fellows, brandishing clubs and cart-whips; and that a carriage, with the steps down, stood close to the door. I did not then know that a train was laid by our friends for Thompson's escape. All I could do, was to join the women, who formed a dense circle around him; a species of troops in much requisition at that period, and well known by the name of "Quaker militia" . . . . Near the platform, where the speaker had stood, was a private door, leading, by a flight of back stairs, into a store-room,

[4]A Boston hotel.

that opened into another street than the front entrance. The mob were either ignorant of this entrance, or forgetful; but our friends were neither. One of our number held the key; a second had engaged a carriage, with swift horses, and a colored driver; a third made a signal from a window, for the carriage to approach the store communicating with the back passage. Holding Thompson in friendly chat, the women, as it were quite accidentally, approached the private door. The circle opened—the door opened—a volley of oaths from the truckmen, and a deafening rush down the front stairs—but where was *he?*

For a few moments, we who remained in the hall could not answer. But presently, S.J. May[5] came to us, with a face like Carara marble, and breathed, rather than uttered, the welcome words, "Thank God! he's safe!". . . .

I never saw George Thompson again, after that hurried farewell at morning twilight, when "Judge Lynch" was lying in wait for him. He left the country a few months after.

1842

Women's Rights

#50

. . . *Every* subject, bearing any relationship to the contesting influences of moral attraction and physical force, is a *branch* of anti-slavery, or more properly speaking, a branch *with* anti-slavery. All truths flow from one, and then to one; and whosoever has a mind sufficiently comprehensive to follow to one great principle, reaches another in the process. I do not perceive, however, that the doctrine of Women's Rights, as it is called, has a more immediate connection with anti-slavery, than several other subjects, which bring in question the law of physical force. . . .

I am not ultra enough to suit the reformer, and too reforming to please the conservative.

That the present position of women in society is the result of physical force, is obvious enough; whosoever doubts it, let her reflect why she is afraid to go in the evening without the protection of a man. What constitutes the danger of aggression? Superior physical strength, uncontrolled by the moral sentiments. If physical strength were in complete subjection to moral influence, there would be no need of outward protection. That animal instinct and brute force now govern the world, is painfully apparent in the condition of women everywhere; from the Morduan Tartars,[1] whose ceremony of marriage consists in placing the bride on a mat, and consigning her to the bridegroom, with the words, "Here, wolf, take thy lamb,"—to the German remark, that "stiff ale, stinging tobacco, and a girl in her smart dress, are the best things." The same thing, softened by the refinements of civilization,

[5]Unitarian minister Samuel J. May (1794–1871), the uncle of writer Louisa May Alcott, was a founder of the American Antislavery Society.

[1]Historically the Tartars, a nomadic people, were widely located in the steppes connecting Europe and Asia, in the north of China, and on the shores of the Caspian and Black seas.

peeps out in Stephen's remark, that "woman never looks so interesting, as when leaning on the arm of a soldier"; and in Hazlitt's complaint that "it is not easy to keep up a conversation with women in company. It is thought a piece of rudeness to differ from them; it is not quite fair to ask them a reason for what they say."[2]

This sort of politeness to women is what men call gallantry; an odious word to every sensible woman, because she sees that it is merely the flimsy veil which foppery throws over sensuality, to conceal its grossness. So far is it from indicating sincere esteem and affection for women, that the profligacy of a nation may, in general, be fairly measured by its gallantry. This taking away rights, and condescending to grant privileges, is an old trick of the physical-force principle; and with the immense majority, who only look on the surface of things, this mask effectually disguises an ugliness, which would otherwise be abhorred. The most inveterate slaveholders are probably those who take most pride in dressing their household servants handsomely, and who would be most ashamed to have the name of being unnecessarily cruel. And profligates, who form the lowest and most sensual estimate of women, are the very ones to treat them with an excess of outward deference.

There are few books which I can read through, without feeling insulted as a woman; but this insult is almost universally conveyed through that which was intended for praise. Just imagine, for a moment, what impression it would make on men, if women authors should write about their "rosy lips," and "melting eyes," and "voluptuous forms," as they write about us! That women in general do not feel this kind of flattery to be an insult, I readily admit; for, in the first place, they do not perceive the gross chattel-principle, of which it is the utterance; moreover, they have, from long habit, become accustomed to consider themselves as household conveniences, or gilded toys. Hence, they consider it feminine and pretty to abjure all such use of their faculties, as would make them co-workers with man in the advancement of those great principles, on which the progress of society depends. "There is perhaps no animal," says Hannah More, "so much indebted to subordination, for its good behaviour, as woman."[3] Alas, for the animal age, in which such utterance could be tolerated by public sentiment! . . .

I have said enough to show that I consider prevalent opinions and customs highly unfavourable to the moral and intellectual development of women; and I need not say, that, in proportion to their true culture, women will be more useful and happy, and domestic life more perfected. True culture, in them, as in men, consists in the full and free development of individual character, regulated by their own perceptions of what is true, and their own love of what is good.

This individual responsibility is rarely acknowledged, even by the most refined, as necessary to the spiritual progress of women. I once heard a very beautiful lecture from R.W. Emerson,[4] on Being and Seeming. In the course of many remarks, as true as they were graceful, he urged women to be, rather than seem. He told them that all their laboured education of forms, strict observance of genteel etiquette, tasteful arrangement of the toilette, etc., all this seeming would not gain

[2]William Hazlitt (1778–1830), English essayist and critic, was known for his epigrams and invective.

[3]Hannah More (1745–1831), an English writer, produced moral and religious works.

[4]Ralph Waldo Emerson: see selection in this volume.

hearts like being truly what God made them; that earnest simplicity, the sincerity of nature, would kindle the eye, light up the countenance, and give an inexpressible charm to the plainest features.

The advice was excellent, but the motive, by which it was urged, brought a flush of indignation over my face. Men were exhorted to be, rather than to seem, that they might fulfil the sacred mission for which their souls were embodied; that they might, in God's freedom, grow up into the full stature of spiritual manhood; but women were urged to simplicity and truthfulness, that they might become more pleasing.

Are we not all immortal beings? Is not each one responsible for himself and herself? There is no measuring the mischief done by the prevailing tendency to teach women to be virtuous as a duty to man rather than to God—for the sake of pleasing the creature, rather than the Creator. "God is thy law, thou mine," said Eve to Adam.[5] May Milton be forgiven for sending that thought "out into everlasting time" in such a jewelled setting. . . .

But while I see plainly that society is on a false foundation, and that prevailing views concerning women indicate the want of wisdom and purity, which they serve to perpetuate—still, I must acknowledge that much of the talk about Women's Rights offends both my reason and my taste. I am not of those who maintain there is no sex in souls; nor do I like the results deducible from that doctrine. I believe that the natures of man and woman are spiritually different, yet the same. Two flutes on the same key do not produce harmony; but on different keys they do. There is no inferiority or superiority. The same tune is played, and with the same skill; but it is played on different keys, and the unity of variety is harmony.

I do not think the paths of man and woman identical; but in a true order of society they must ever run side by side, start from the same point, run the same length, and reach the same end. Kinmont, in his admirable book, called the Nature of Man, expresses my views more completely than I can myself. Speaking of the warlike courage of the ancient German women, and of their being respectfully consulted on important public affairs, he says: "You ask me if I consider all this right, and deserving of approbation? or that women were here engaged in their appropriate tasks? I answer, yes; it is just as right that they should take this interest in the honour of their country, as the other sex. Of course, I do not think that women were made for war and battle; neither do I believe that men were. But since the fashion of the times had made it so, and settled it that war was a necessary element of greatness, and that no safety was to be procured without it, I argue that it shows a healthful state of feeling in other respects, that the feelings of both sexes were equally enlisted in the cause: that there was no division in the house, or the state; and that the serious pursuits and objects of the one were also the serious pursuits and objects of the other."

The nearer society approaches to divine order, the less separation will there be in the characters, duties, and pursuits of men and women. Women will not become less gentle and graceful, but men will become more so. Women will not neglect the care and education of their children, but men will find themselves ennobled and refined by sharing those duties with them; and will receive, in return, co-operation and sympathy in the discharge of various other duties, now deemed inappropriate

[5]In John Milton's *Paradise Lost.*

to women. The more women become rational companions, partners in business and in thought, as well as in affection and amusement, the more highly will men appreciate *home*—that blessed word, which opens to the human heart the most perfect glimpse of Heaven, and helps to carry it thither, as on an angel's wings. . . .

The conviction that woman's present position in society is a false one, and therefore re-acts disastrously on the happiness and improvement of man, is pressing by slow degrees on the common consciousness, through all the obstacles of bigotry, sensuality, and selfishness. As man approaches to the truest life, he will perceive more and more that there is no separation or discord in their mutual duties. They will be one; but it will be as affection and thought are one; the treble and bass of the same harmonious tune.

1843

Slavery's Pleasant Homes

A Faithful Sketch

"Thy treasures of gold
Are dim with the blood of the hearts thou hast sold;
Thy home may be lovely, but round it I hear
The crack of the whip, and the footsteps of fear."

When Frederic Dalcho brought his young bride from New-Orleans to her Georgian home, there were great demonstrations of joy among the slaves of the establishment,—dancing, shouting, clapping of hands, and eager invocations of blessing on the heads of "massa and missis"; for well they knew that he who manifested most zeal was likely to get the largest coin, or the brightest handkerchief.

The bride had been nurtured in seclusion, almost as deep as that of the oriental harem. She was a pretty little waxen plaything, as fragile and as delicate as the white Petunia blossom. She brought with her two slaves. Mars, a stalwart mulatto, of good figure, but a cunning and disagreeable expression of countenance. Rosa, a young girl, elegantly formed, and beautiful as a dark velvet carnation. The blush, so easily excited, shone through the transparent brown of her smooth cheek, like claret through a bottle in the sunshine. It was a beautiful contrast to see her beside her mistress, like a glittering star in attendance upon the pale and almost vanishing moonsickle. They had grown up from infancy together; for the mother of Rosa was foster-mother of Marion; and soon as the little white lady could speak, she learned to call Rosa *her* slave. As they grew older, the wealthy planter's daughter took pride in her servant's beauty, and loved to decorate her with jewels. "You shall wear my golden ornaments whenever you ask for them," said she; "they contrast so well with the soft, brown satin of your neck and arms. I will wear pearls and amethysts; but gold needs the dark complexion to show its richness. Besides, you are a handsome creature, Rosa, and gold is none too good for you."

Her coachman, Mars, was of the same opinion: but the little petted coquette tossed her graceful head at him, and paid small heed to his flattering words. Not so with George, the handsome quadroon brother of Frederic Dalcho, and his favorite slave; but the master and mistress were too much absorbed with their own honeymoon, to observe them. Low talks among the rose-bushes, and stolen meetings by moonlight, passed unnoticed, save by the evil eyes of Mars. Thus it passed on for months. The young slaves had uttered the marriage vow to each other, in the silent presence of the stars.

It chanced, one day, that Rosa was summoned to the parlor to attend her mistress, while George stood respectfully, hat in hand, waiting for a note, which his master was writing. She wore about her neck a small heart and cross of gold, which her lover had given her the night before. He smiled archly, as he glanced at it, and the answer from her large, dark eyes was full of joyful tenderness. Unfortunately, the master looked up at that moment, and at once comprehended the significance of that beaming expression. He saw that it spoke whole volumes of mutual, happy love; and it kindled in him an unholy fire. He had never before realized that the girl was so very handsome. He watched her, as she pursued her work, until she felt uneasy beneath his look. From time to time, he glanced at his young wife. She, too, was certainly very lovely; but the rich, mantling beauty of the slave had the charm of novelty. The next day, he gave her a gay dress; and when he met her among the garden shrubbery, he turned her glossy ringlets over his finger, and called her a pretty darling. Poor Rosa hastened away, filled with terror. She wanted to tell her mistress all this, and claim her protection; but she dared not. As for George, he was of a proud and fiery nature, and she dreaded the storm it would raise in his breast. Her sleeping apartment adjoined that of her mistress, and she was now called to bring water to her master at a much later hour than had been usual with him. One night, no answer was given to the summons. Rosa was not in her room. When questioned in the morning, she stammered out an incoherent excuse, and burst into tears. She was ordered, somewhat sternly, to be very careful not to be again absent when called for.

Marion took an early opportunity to plead her favorite's cause. "I have suspected, for some time," said she, "that George and Rosa are courting; and for my part, I should like very well to have them married." Her husband made no reply, but abruptly left the room. His conduct towards George became singularly capricious and severe. Rosa wept much in secret, and became shy as a startled fawn. Her mistress supposed it was because Mr. Dalcho objected to her marriage, and suspected nothing more. She tried to remonstrate with him, and learn the nature of his objections; but he answered sharply, and left her in tears.

One night, Marion was awakened by the closing of the door, and found that Frederic was absent. She heard voices in Rosa's apartment, and the painful truth flashed upon her. Poor young wife, what a bitter hour was that!

In the morning, Rosa came to dress her, as usual, but she avoided looking in her face, and kept her eyes fixed on the ground. As she *knelt* to tie the satin shoe, Marion spoke angrily of her awkwardness, and gave her a blow. It was the first time she had ever struck her; for they really loved each other. The beautiful slave looked up with an expression of surprise, which was answered by a strange, wild stare. Rosa fell at her feet, and sobbed out, "Oh, mistress, I am not to blame. Indeed, indeed, I am very wretched." Marion's fierce glance melted into tears. "Poor child," said she, "I ought not to have struck you; but, oh, Rosa, I am wretched, too." The foster-sisters embraced each other, and wept long and bitterly; but neither sought any further to learn the other's secrets.

At breakfast, George was in attendance, but he would not look at Rosa, though she watched for a glance with anxious love. When she found an opportunity to see him alone, he was sullen, and rejected her proffered kiss. "Rosa, where were you last night?" said he, hastily. The poor girl blushed deeply, and strove to take his hand; but he flung her from him, with so much force that she reeled against the wall. "Oh, George," said she, with bitter anguish, "what *can* I do? I am his *slave.*" The justice of her plea, and the pathos of her tones, softened his heart. He placed her head on his shoulder, and said more kindly, "Keep out of his way, dear Rosa; keep out of his way."

Rosa made strong efforts to follow this injunction; and dearly did she rue it. George was sent away from the house, to work on the plantation, and they were forbidden to see each other, under penalty of severe punishment. His rival, Mars, watched them, and gave information of every attempt to transgress this cruel edict. But love was more omnipotent than fear of punishment, and the lovers did sometimes catch a stolen interview. The recurrence of this disobedience exasperated their master beyond endurance. He swore he would overcome her obstinacy, or kill her; and one severe flogging succeeded another, till the tenderly-nurtured slave fainted under the cruel infliction, which was rendered doubly dangerous by the delicate state of her health. Maternal pains came on prematurely, and she died a few hours after.

George wandered into the woods, and avoided the sight of his reckless master, who, on his part, seemed willing to avoid an interview. Four days had passed since Rosa's death, and the bereaved one had scarcely tasted food enough to sustain his wretched life. He stood beside the new-made grave, which he himself had dug. "Oh, Father in Heaven!" he exclaimed, "what would I give, if I had not flung her from me! Poor girl, *she* was not to blame." He leaned his head against a tree, and looked mournfully up to the moon struggling through clouds. Cypresses reared their black forms against the sky, and the moss hung from bough to bough, in thick, funereal festoons. But a few months ago, how beautiful and bright was Nature—and now, how inexpressibly gloomy. The injustice of the past, and the hopelessness of the future, came before him with dreary distinctness. "He is my brother," thought he, "we grew up side by side, children of the same father; but I am his slave. Handsomer, stronger, and more intelligent than he; yet I am his *slave.* And now he will sell me, because the murdered one will forever come up between us."

He thought of Rosa as he first saw her, so happy, and so beautiful; of all her gushing tenderness; of her agonized farewell, when they last met; of her graceful form bleeding under the lash, and now lying cold and dead beneath his feet.

He looked toward his master's house. "Shall I escape now and forever?" said he; "or shall I first"—he paused, threw his arms widely upward, gnashed his teeth, and groaned aloud, "God, pity me! He murdered my poor Rosa."

On that night, Marion's sleep was disturbed and fitful. The memory of her foster-sister mingled darkly with all her dreams. Was that a shriek she heard? It was fearfully shrill in the night-silence! Half sleeping and half waking, she called wildly, "Rosa! Rosa!" But a moment after, she remembered that Rosa's light step would never again come at her call. At last a drowsy slave answered the loud summons of her bell. "I left your master reading in the room below," said she; "go and see if he is ill." The girl came back, pallid and frightened. "Oh, mistress, he is dead!" she exclaimed; "there is a dagger through his heart."

Neighbors were hastily summoned, and the slaves secured. Among them was George, who, with a fierce and haggard look, still lingered around Rosa's grave.

The dagger found in Frederic Dalcho's heart was the one he had himself been accustomed to wear. He lay upon the sofa, with an open book beside him, as if he had fallen asleep reading. A desk in the room was broken open, and a sum of money gone. Near it, was dropped a ragged handkerchief, known to belong to Mars. Suspicion hovered between him and George. Both denied the deed. Mars tried hard to fix the guilt on his hated rival, and swore to many falsehoods. But as some of these falsehoods were detected, and the stolen money was found hidden in his bed, the balance turned against him. After the brief, stern trial awarded to slaves, with slaveholders for judges and jurors, Mars was condemned to be hung. George thought of his relentless persecutions, and for a moment triumphed over the cunning enemy, who had so often dogged poor Rosa's steps; but his soul was too generous to retain this feeling.

The fatal hour came. Planters rode miles to witness the execution, and stood glaring at their trembling victim, with the fierceness of tigers. The slaves from miles around were assembled, to take warning by his awful punishment. The rope was adjusted on the strong bough of a tree. Mars shook like a leaf in the wind. The countenance of George was very pale and haggard, and his breast was heaving with tumultuous thoughts. "He is my enemy." said he to himself; "tis an awful thing to die thus. The *theft* I did not commit; but if I take all the blame, they can do no more than hang me."

They led the shivering wretch towards the tree, and were about to fasten the fatal noose. But George rushed forward with a countenance ghastly pale, and exclaimed, "Mars is innocent. I murdered him—for he killed my wife, and hell was in my bosom."

No voice praised him for the generous confession. They kicked and cursed him; and hung up, like a dog or a wolf, a man of nobler soul than any of them all.

The Georgian papers thus announced the deed: "*Fiend-like Murder.* Frederic Dalcho, one of our most wealthy and respected citizens, was robbed and murdered last week, by one of his slaves. The black demon was caught and hung; and hanging was too good for him."

The Northern papers copied this version; merely adding, "These are the black-hearted monsters, which abolition philanthropy would let loose upon our brethren of the South."

Not one was found to tell how the slave's young wife had been torn from him by his own brother, and murdered with slow tortures. Not one recorded the heroism that would not purchase life by another's death, though the victim was his enemy. His very *name* was left unmentioned; he was only Mr. Dalcho's *slave!*

1843

John Greenleaf Whittier 1807–1892

He is now remembered as an early local colorist, whose example and support blessed the careers of later regional artists (such as Sarah Orne Jewett, whom he championed and advised), and whose warm depictions of American rural life rise occasionally above the patterned sentimentality which makes so much nineteenth-century poetry inaccessible to twentieth-century readers. His present reputation rests largely on a single poem—the nostalgic *Snowbound* (1866), in which the poet re-creates a scene of his childhood on the weatherbeaten, isolated Massachusetts farmstead where he was born; describing the family "snowbound" indoors together, the poet dwells with poignant affection on the firelit faces of beloved family members, now long dead, but then gathered in the midst of life around a winter fireside. Although he produced many volumes of poetry and prose, and was widely published throughout his career, it was *Snowbound* which brought him national recognition as a poet and, after a lifetime of poverty, a comfortable income as a writer. But in his own time, and his own estimation, John Greenleaf Whittier was an abolitionist first, and a poet second.

Whittier was born in 1807 to a devout, debt-ridden Quaker farm family, which was struggling to retain the homestead near Haverhill, Massachusetts, where the Whittiers had been farmers since 1648. It was a costly battle: heavy physical labor in childhood broke Whittier's constitution, and in later life he would be subject to chronic headaches and, on several occasions, severe physical breakdowns. His formal education was necessarily limited, and though as a Quaker he was encouraged to study and express himself, few books were allowed him beyond the Bible and the journals of the early Friends; however, when at fourteen he was exposed to the poetry of Robert Burns, he was inspired—for he, too, was poor and ill-educated, and yet could use his rough dialect and rural environment as the medium and subject for poetic expression.

But the habits of mind and spirit which he developed in that Quaker homestead drew Whittier into a life dedicated to social reform. Though Quakers were no longer openly persecuted, their history and faith still set them on the margin of New England society, and gave them a critical perspective on that society as well as a tendency to look with compassion and understanding on the outcast and the oppressed. Their belief in the Inner Light, by which God's grace may move in any human being, regardless of outward condition, led them to honor all souls—including women, native Americans, and blacks—as equally precious in God's sight, and therefore in man's: to treat a human being as property was an outrageous violation of both man and God. When in 1826 the young Whittier published his first poem, he met William Lloyd Garrison, the journal's editor—and they became comrades in the movement to end slavery in the United States.

Encouraged by Garrison to pursue his writing, Whittier threw off the cobbling trade for which he had been training, and wrote—surviving by teaching school and editing an assortment of newspapers while his poetry and articles were being published in a number of publications. But with *Justice and Expediency* (1833), a significant abolitionist tract, he cast his lot—and his creative energies—with the then-outcast and abominated anti-slavery movement, a choice which exposed him to much abuse—and, during the 1830s, physical danger: he and the British abolitionist George Thompson were attacked and stoned on a New Hampshire lecture tour in 1835, and on another occasion in 1838 he joined in secret a raid on his own offices in order to salvage his papers from the flames. He was elected as a delegate to the National Anti-Slavery Convention in Philadelphia, which in turn led to his election in 1835 to a term in the Massachusetts legislature; and while he poured out anti-slavery poetry for political journals, he was a tireless and skillful manipulator of politicians in the Whig party and later the anti-slavery Liberty party (which he helped found in 1839).

In 1836 he moved with his mother and sisters to Amesbury, Massachusetts, where he soon settled permanently; and from this rural hamlet he sent forth his tracts, articles, broadsides—and poems and fiction. In the 1850s, when abolition became more fashionable and the Movement developed a larger following, Whittier's reputation improved considerably; with the publication of *Snowbound* in 1868 he achieved national reknown as a poet; and over the remaining two decades of his life his work enjoyed steadily increasing popularity.

Whittier is sometimes eulogized as an inadequately trained artist whose talents were martyred to mere topical journalism. His association with the abolition movement doomed for several decades any hopes he might have had for popular acceptance as a poet, but it also monopolized his creative energies throughout the 1830s and much of the '40s and '50s. Often-quoted lines from Whittier's meditative *Tent on the Beach* (1867) offer the self-portrait of "a dreamer born/ Who, with a mission to fulfil,/Had left the Muses' haunts to turn/The crank of an opinion-mill,/Making his rustic reed of song/A weapon in the war with wrong." But perhaps more representative of his own self-perception is his remark that he placed a "higher value on my name as appended to the Anti-Slavery Declaration . . . than on any title-page of any book." He threw himself into the emancipation movement with fierce commitment, for the fact of slavery simply enraged him; and as a devout Quaker, he believed that his verses should not be ends in themselves but *means* to the ends of spiritual understanding and practical piety—means by which good works in the world could be generated.

But it was also through his labors in the "opinion mill" that he found and developed his own simple, passionate poetic voice. In the poetry Whittier devoted to the struggle against slavery, the occasion demanded not just expression but *persuasion;* to achieve his goal, the poet learned in some degree to discipline his language for effect, and, by lacing his verse with small inversions of language and eerily ironic impersonations, he hoped to stimulate thought and encourage the reader to examine his conscience. The poems here should be read not as imperfect precursors of some later and purer art, but *as topical poems:* they draw their power as much from Whittier's political theme as they do from his artistic techniques. In the abolition poems, strategies for compression and self-control are employed to express feelings of profound moral outrage—a combination which yields some of Whittier's most affecting and expressive poetry.

Elaine Sargent Apthorp
San Jose State University

PRIMARY WORKS

Complete Writings, 7 vols., 1904; *Legends of New England,* 1831, reprinted with intro. by John B. Pickard, 1965; *Letters of John Greenleaf Whitter,* ed. John B. Pickard, 3 vols., 1975; *Whittier on Writers and Writing; The Uncollected Critical Writings of John Greenleaf Whitter,* ed. Edwin H. Cady and Harry Hayden Clark, 1950.

SECONDARY WORKS

Samuel T. Pickard, *Life and Letters of John Greenleaf Whittier,* 2 vols., 1894; Albert Mordell, *Quaker Militant, John Greenleaf Whittier,* 1933; John Pickard, *John Greenleaf Whittier: An Introduction and Interpretation,* 1961; Edward C. Wagenknecht, *John Greenleaf Whittier: A Portrait in Paradox,* 1967; Robert Penn Warren, *John Greenleaf Whittier's Poetry: An Appraisal and Selection,* 1971; Jayne K. Kribbs, ed., *Critical Essays on John Greenleaf Whittier,* 1980; Charlotte Lindgren, "Barnes and Whittier: Early Folklorists," *Tennessee Folklore Society Bulletin,* 1981; Miller E. Burdick, "The Immortalizing Power of Imagination: A Reading of Whittier's 'Snowbird,'" *ESQ: A Journal of the American Renaissance,* 1985; James H. Justus, "The Fireside Poets: Hearthside Values and the Language of Care," *Nineteenth Century American Poetry,* 1985; James Rocks, "Whittier's 'Snowbound': 'The Circle of the Hearth' and the Discourse on Domesticity," *Studies in the American Renaissance,* 1993.

The Hunters of Men[1]

Have ye heard of our hunting, o'er mountain and glen,
Through cane-brake[2] and forest,—the hunting of men?
The lords of our land to this hunting have gone,
As the fox-hunter follows the sound of the horn;
Hark! the cheer and the hallo! the crack of the whip,
And the yell of the hound as he fastens his grip!
All blithe are our hunters, and noble their match,
Though hundreds are caught, there are millions to catch.
So speed to their hunting, o'er mountain and glen,
Through cane-brake and forest,—the hunting of men!

Gay luck to our hunters! how nobly they ride
In the glow of their zeal, and the strength of their pride!
The priest with his cassock flung back on the wind,
Just screening the politic[3] statesman behind;
The saint and the sinner, with cursing and prayer,
The drunk and the sober, ride merrily there.
And woman, kind woman, wife, widow, and maid,
For the good of the hunted, is lending her aid:
Her foot's in the stirrup, her hand on the rein,
How blithely she rides to the hunting of men!

Oh, goodly and grand is our hunting to see,
In this "land of the brave and this home of the free."
Priest, warrior, and statesman, from Georgia to Maine,
All mounting the saddle, all grasping the rein;
Right merrily hunting the black man, whose sin
Is the curl of his hair and the hue of his skin!
Woe, now, to the hunted who turns him at bay!
Will our hunters be turned from their purpose and prey?
Will their hearts fail within them? their nerves tremble, when
All roughly they ride to the hunting of men?

Ho! alms for our hunters! all weary and faint,
Wax the curse of the sinner and prayer of the saint.
The horn is wound faintly, the echoes are still,
Over cane-brake and river, and forest and hill.
Haste, alms for our hunters! the hunted once more

[1]These lines were written when the orators of the American Colonization Society were demanding that the free blacks should be sent to Africa, and opposing Emancipation unless expatriation followed. See the report of the proceedings of the society at its annual meeting in 1834. [Whittier's note]

[2]A thicket of cane.

[3]Shrewd, artful, concerned with expediency.

Have turned from their flight with their backs to the shore:
What right have they here in the home of the white,
Shadowed o'er by our banner of Freedom and Right?
Ho! alms for the hunters! or never again
Will they ride in their pomp to the hunting of men!

Alms, alms for our hunters! why will ye delay,
When their pride and their glory are melting away?
The parson has turned; for, on charge of his own,
Who goeth a warfare, or hunting, alone?
The politic statesman looks back with a sigh,
There is doubt in his heart, there is fear in his eye.
Oh, haste, lest that doubting and fear shall prevail,
And the head of his steed take the place of the tail.
Oh, haste, ere he leave us! for who will ride then,
For pleasure or gain, to the hunting of men?

1835

The Farewell

of a Virginia Slave Mother to Her Daughters Sold into Southern Bondage

Gone, gone,—sold and gone,
To the rice-swamp dank and lone.
Where the slave-whip ceaseless swings,
Where the noisome insect stings,
Where the fever demon strews
Poison with the falling dews,
Where the sickly sunbeams glare
Through the hot and misty air;
Gone, gone,—sold and gone,
To the rice-swamp dank and lone,
From Virginia's hills and waters;
Woe is me, my stolen daughters!

Gone, gone,—sold and gone,
To the rice-swamp dank and lone.
There no mother's eye is near them,
There no mother's ear can hear them;
Never, when the torturing lash
Seams their back with many a gash,

Shall a mother's kindness bless them,
Or a mother's arms caress them.
   Gone, gone,—sold and gone,
   To the rice-swamp dank and lone,
   From Virginia's hills and waters;
   Woe is me, my stolen daughters!

   Gone, gone,—sold and gone,
   To the rice-swamp dank and lone.
Oh, when weary, sad and slow,
From the fields at night they go,
Faint with toil, and racked with pain,
To their cheerless homes again,
There no brother's voice shall greet them;
There no father's welcome meet them.
   Gone, gone,—sold and gone,
   To the rice-swamp dank and lone,
   From Virginia's hills and waters;
   Woe is me, my stolen daughters!

   Gone, gone,—sold and gone,
   To the rice-swamp dank and lone.
From the tree whose shadow lay
On their childhood's place of play;
From the cool spring where they drank;
Rock, and hill, and rivulet bank;
From the solemn house of prayer,
And the holy counsels there;
   Gone, gone,—sold and gone,
   To the rice-swamp dank and lone,
   From Virginia's hills and waters;
   Woe is me, my stolen daughters!

   Gone, gone,—sold and gone,
   To the rice-swamp dank and lone;
Toiling through the weary day,
And at night the spoiler's prey.[1]
Oh, that they had earlier died,
Sleeping calmly, side by side,
Where the tyrant's power is o'er,
And the fetter galls no more!
   Gone, gone,—sold and gone,
   To the rice-swamp dank and lone,
   From Virginia's hills and waters;
   Woe is me, my stolen daughters!

[1]Victim of plunderer; vulnerable to violation.

Gone, gone,—sold and gone,
To the rice-swamp dank and lone.
By the holy love He beareth;
By the bruised reed He spareth;
Oh, may He, to whom alone
All their cruel wrongs are known,
Still their hope and refuge prove,
With a more than mother's love.
Gone, gone,—sold and gone,
To the rice-swamp dank and lone,
From Virginia's hills and waters;
Woe is me, my stolen daughters!

1838

Massachusetts to Virginia[1]

The blast from Freedom's Northern hills, upon its Southern way,
Bears greeting to Virginia from Massachusetts Bay:
No word of haughty challenging, nor battle bugle's peal,
Nor steady tread of marching files, nor clang of horsemen's steel.

No trains of deep-mouthed cannon along our highways go;
Around our silent arsenals untrodden lies the snow;
And to the land-breeze of our ports, upon their errands far,
A thousand sails of commerce swell, but none are spread for war.

We hear thy threats, Virginia! thy stormy words and high,
Swell harshly on the Southern winds which melt along our sky;
Yet, not one brown, hard hand foregoes its honest labor here,
No hewer of our mountain oaks suspends his axe in fear.

Wild are the waves which lash the reefs along St. George's bank;
Cold on the shore of Labrador the fog lies white and dank;

[1]Written on reading an account of the proceedings of the citizens of Norfolk, Va., in reference to George Latimer, the alleged fugitive slave, who was seized in Boston without warrant at the request of James B. Grey, of Norfolk, claiming to be his master. The case caused great excitement North and South, and led to the presentation of a petition to Congress, signed by more than fifty thousand citizens of Massachusetts, calling for such laws and proposed amendments to the Constitution as should relieve the Commonwealth from all further participation in the crime of oppression. George Latimer himself was finally given free papers for the sum of four hundred dollars. [Whittier's note]

Through storm, and wave, and blinding mist, stout are the hearts
which man
The fishing-smacks of Marblehead, the sea-boats of Cape Ann.[2]

The cold north light and wintry sun glare on their icy forms,
Bent grimly o'er their straining lines or wrestling with the storms;
Free as the winds they drive before, rough as the waves they roam,
They laugh to scorn the slaver's threat against their rocky home.

What means the Old Dominion?[3] Hath she forgot the day
When o'er her conquered valleys swept the Briton's steel array?
How side by side, with sons of hers, the Massachusetts men
Encountered Tarleton's charge of fire, and stout Cornwallis, then?[4]

Forgets she how the Bay State,[5] in answer to the call
Of her old House of Burgesses, spoke out from Faneuil Hall?[6]
When, echoing back her Henry's cry, came pulsing on each breath
Of Northern winds, the thrilling sounds of "Liberty or Death!"[7]

What asks the Old Dominion? If now her sons have proved
False to their fathers' memory, false to the faith they loved;
If she can scoff at Freedom, and its great charter[8] spurn,
Must we of Massachusetts from truth and duty turn?

We hunt your bondmen, flying from Slavery's hateful hell;
Our voices, at your bidding, take up the blood-hound's yell;
We gather, at your summons, above our fathers' graves,
From Freedom's holy altar-horns[9] to tear your wretched slaves!

Thank God! not yet so vilely can Massachusetts bow;
The spirit of her early time is with her even now;
Dream not because her Pilgrim blood moves slow and calm and
cool,
She thus can stoop her chainless neck, a sister's slave and tool!

All that a sister State should do, all that a free State may,
Heart, hand, and purse we proffer, as in our early day;

[2]This and other place-names in this stanza refer to sections of the Massachusetts coastline, and to fishing grounds to the north.

[3]Virginia.

[4]British generals defeated in the War for Independence. Reference recalls Massachusetts' military aid to Virginia at critical moments in the War.

[5]Massachusetts.

[6]Refers to Virginia's colonial House of Burgesses and to the Boston meeting house where community leaders met during the Revolution.

[7]Virginia Revolutionary Patrick Henry, who in addressing the House of Burgesses exclaimed, "I know not what course others may take, but as for me, give me liberty or give me death!"

[8]Refers to the Declaration of Independence, drafted by Virginia's Thomas Jefferson, which asserted that "all men are created equal."

[9]Sanctuary.

But that one dark loathsome burden ye must stagger with alone,
And reap the bitter harvest which ye yourselves have sown!

Hold, while ye may, your struggling slaves, and burden God's free air
With woman's shriek beneath the lash, and manhood's wild despair;
Cling closer to the "cleaving curse" that writes upon your plains
The blasting of Almighty wrath against a land of chains.

Still shame your gallant ancestry, the cavaliers of old,
By watching round the shambles[10] where human flesh is sold;
Gloat o'er the new-born child, and count his market value, when
The maddened mother's cry of woe shall pierce the slaver's den!

Lower than plummet soundeth,[11] sink the Virginia name;
Plant, if ye will, your fathers' graves with rankest weeds of shame;
Be, if ye will, the scandal of God's fair universe;
We wash our hands forever of your sin and shame and curse.

A voice from lips whereon the coal from Freedom's shrine hath been,
Thrilled, as but yesterday, the hearts of Berkshire's mountain men:[12]
The echoes of that solemn voice are sadly lingering still
In all our sunny valleys, on every wind-swept hill.

And when the prowling man-thief came hunting for his prey
Beneath the very shadow of Bunker's shaft of gray,[13]
How, through the free lips of the son, the father's warning spoke;
How, from its bonds of trade and sect, the Pilgrim city broke![14]

A hundred thousand right arms were lifted up on high,
A hundred thousand voices sent back their loud reply;
Through the thronged towns of Essex[15] the startling summons rang,
And up from bench and loom and wheel her young mechanics[16] sprang!

[10]A slaughterhouse.
[11]Refers to a line in Shakespeare's *The Tempest* (Act III, sc. 3, 1.101).
[12]Refers to the farmers and trappers of the Berkshire mountains in western Massachusetts.
[13]Bunker Hill was the site of a famous battle of the Revolution, in which six hundred colonial soldiers held the hilltop successfully against the onslaught of a British force more than twice their number.
[14]Boston, which was founded by nonseparatist Puritan "pilgrims."
[15]Whittier's home county, where this poem was being read.
[16]Craft and trade workers; skilled laborers.

The voice of free, broad Middlesex,[17] of thousands as of one,
The shaft of Bunker calling to that of Lexington;
From Norfolk's ancient villages, from Plymouth's rocky bound
To where Nantucket feels the arms of ocean close her round;
From rich and rural Worcester, where through the calm repose
Of cultured vales and fringing woods the gentle Nashua flows,
To where Wachuset's wintry blasts the mountain larches stir,
Swelled up to Heaven the thrilling cry of "God save Latimer!"[18]

And sandy Barnstable rose up, wet with the salt sea spray;
And Bristol sent her answering shout down Narragansett Bay!
Along the broad Connecticut old Hampden felt the thrill,
And the cheer of Hampshire's woodmen swept down from
Holyoke Hill.

The voice of Massachusetts! Of her free sons and daughters,
Deep calling unto deep aloud, the sound of many waters!
Against the burden of that voice what tyrant power shall stand?
No fetters in the Bay State! No slave upon her land!

Look to it well, Virginians! In calmness we have borne,
In answer to our faith and trust, your insult and your scorn;
You've spurned our kindest counsels; you've hunted for our lives;
And shaken round our hearths and homes your manacles and
gyves![19]

We wage no war, we lift no arm, we fling no torch within[20]
The fire-damps of the quaking mine beneath your soil of sin;[21]
We leave ye with your bondmen, to wrestle, while ye can,
With the strong upward tendencies and godlike soul of man!

But for us and for our children, the vow which we have given
For freedom and humanity is registered in heaven;
No slave-hunt in our borders,—no pirate on our strand!
No fetters in the Bay State,—no slave upon our land!

1843

[17]Massachusetts county. In the verses which follow, a number of other Massachusetts counties, towns, and natural landmarks are named (Lexington, scene of the first battle of the Revolutionary War; Norfolk; Plymouth; Nantucket; Worcester; the river Naushua; Wachuset mountain; Barnstable; Bristol; Narragansett Bay; the Connecticut River, which flows past Hampden, Hampshire, and Holyoke Hill) to indicate the breadth of the Massachusetts protest against the seizure of Latimer.

[18]George Latimer. See Whittier's headnote.

[19]Shackles.

[20]Explosive mixture formed by the release of methane gas into the air of underground mines.

[21]Whittier probably intended a double meaning here: soil as earth (above a mine), as well as moral stain.

At Port Royal[1]

The tent-lights glimmer on the land,
The ship-lights on the sea;
The night-wind smooths with drifting sand
Our track on lone Tybee.

At last our grating keels outslide,
Our good boats forward swing;
And while we ride the land-locked tide,
Our negroes row and sing.

For dear the bondman holds his gifts
Of music and of song:
The gold that kindly Nature sifts
Among his sands of wrong;

The power to make his toiling days
And poor home-comforts please;
The quaint relief of mirth that plays
With sorrow's minor keys.

Another glow than sunset's fire
Has filled the west with light,
Where field and garner, barn and byre,[2]
Are blazing through the night.

The land is wild with fear and hate,
The rout runs mad and fast;
From hand to hand, from gate to gate
The flaming brand is passed.

The lurid glow falls strong across
Dark faces broad with smiles:
Not theirs the terror, hate, and loss
That fire yon blazing piles.

With oar-strokes timing to their song,
They weave in simple lays

[1]In November, 1861, a Union force under Commodore Dupont and General Sherman captured Port Royal, and from this point as a basis of operations, the neighboring islands between Charleston and Savannah were taken possession of. The early occupation of this district, where the negro population was greatly in excess of the white, gave an opportunity which was at once seized upon, of practically emancipating the slaves and of beginning that work of civilization which was accepted as the grave responsibility of those who had labored for freedom. [Whittier's note]

[2]Garner is a granary, byre a cow barn.

The pathos of remembered wrong,
  The hope of better days,—

The triumph-note that Miriam sung,[3]
  The joy of uncaged birds:
Softening with Afric's mellow tongue
  Their broken Saxon words.[4]

SONG OF THE NEGRO BOATMEN

Oh, praise an' tanks! De Lord he come
  To set de people free;
An' massa tink it day ob doom,[5]
  An' we ob jubilee.[6]
De Lord dat heap de Red Sea waves[7]
  He jus' as 'trong as den;
He say de word: we las' night slaves;
  To-day, de Lord's freemen.
    De yam will grow, de cotton blow,
      We'll hab de rice an' corn;
    Oh nebber you fear, if nebber you hear
      De driver[8] blow his horn!

Ole massa on he trabbels gone;
  He leaf de land behind:
De Lord's breff blow him furder on,
  Like corn-shuck[9] in de wind.
We own de hoe, we own de plough,
  We own de hands dat hold;

We sell de pig, we sell de cow,
  But nebber chile be sold.
    De yam will grow, de cotton blow,
      We'll hab de rice an' corn;
    Oh nebber you fear, if nebber you hear
      De driver blow his horn!

We pray de Lord: he gib us signs
  Dat some day we be free;

[3]See Exodus 15:20–21.

[4]Colloquial for English, which was the language of the Angles and Saxons of the British isles.

[5]Refers to the return of Christ on Judgment Day; for the unredeemed sinner, the moment of final damnation.

[6]Refers to the return of Christ on Judgment Day; for the saint and redeemed sinner, the moment of rejoicing and deliverance.

[7]To aid Moses and the Israelites as they fled from Egyptian persecution, Jehovah parted the waters of the Red Sea that they might pass across safely.

[8]Slave-driver.

[9]The outer husk of an ear of corn, usually stripped away and discarded.

De norf-wind tell it to de pines,
De wild-duck to de sea;
We tink it when de church-bell ring,
We dream it in de dream;
De rice-bird mean it when he sing,
De eagle when he scream.
De yam will grow, de cotton blow,
We'll hab de rice an' corn:
Oh nebber you fear, if nebber you hear
De driver blow his horn!

We know de promise nebber fail,
An' nebber lie de word;
So like de 'postles in de jail,[10]
We waited for de Lord:
An' now he open ebery door,
An' trow away de key;
He tink we lub him so before,
We lub him better free.
De yam will grow, de cotton blow,
He'll gib de rice an' corn;
Oh nebber you fear, if nebber you hear
De driver blow his horn!

So sing our dusky gondoliers;[11]
And with a secret pain,
And smiles that seem akin to tears,
We hear the wild refrain.

We dare not share the negro's trust,
Nor yet his hope deny;
We only know that God is just,
And every wrong shall die.

Rude seems the song; each swarthy[12] face,
Flame-lighted, ruder still:
We start to think that hapless[13] race
Must shape our good or ill;

That laws of changeless justice bind
Oppressor with oppressed;
And, close as sin and suffering joined,
We march to Fate abreast.

[10]Paul and Silas, early leaders of the Christian church, who when imprisoned for their faith prayed in their cell continuously for release.
[11]Dark-skinned (African) boatmen, guiding long, narrow, flat-bottomed barges.
[12]Black.
[13]Unlucky.

Sing on, poor hearts! your chant shall be
Our sign of blight or bloom,
The Vala-song[14] of Liberty,
Or death-rune of our doom!

1862

Angelina Grimké Weld 1805–1879
Sarah Moore Grimké 1792–1873

In the 1830s, the Grimké sisters became major publicists on behalf of women's rights and anti-slavery. They had earlier shocked their prominent South Carolina slaveholding family by publicly aligning themselves with Garrisonian abolitionism. Because they lectured in public to "promiscuous" audiences of men and women, they then placed themselves beyond the boundaries defining women's decent behavior in nineteenth-century America.

The slavery system had long distressed both women. After Sarah moved to Philadelphia and joined the Society of Friends, her younger sister followed. Then in 1835, reading that anti-slavery women had been mobbed in Boston, Angelina impulsively wrote to abolitionist William Lloyd Garrison and embraced the cause of the anti-slavery activists. When Garrison published her letter in his newspaper *The Liberator* (without her knowledge or her consent), even Sarah condemned her. Nonetheless, Angelina persisted in her untraditional behavior and politics. In *An Appeal to the Christian Women of the South* (1836), she argues the validity of her new-found public role and urges her southern "sisters" to act to end chattel slavery and to break the laws, if necessary, to do so.

Angelina became an "agent" of the American Anti-Slavery Society, speaking to small groups of women in the New York City area. Increasingly, curious men came to listen. Sarah soon joined her on the platform, and in the summer of 1837 both Grimké sisters lectured throughout New England for the anti-slavery movement. When the educator Catharine Beecher attacked them by arguing that women should restrict themselves to the domestic sphere, Angelina Grimké responded in ringing tones with *Letters to Catharine Beecher* asserting the correctness of the abolitionist cause and arguing that women can act appropriately wherever and however men can—both in private and in public.

While her younger sister composed a vigorous reply to Beecher, Sarah Grimké was framing *Letters on the Equality of the Sexes, and the Condition of Woman.*[1] Sarah Grimké's pioneering feminist arguments are rooted in her lifelong study of theology. Even the electric phrases that sometimes flash from her Latinate prose—such as the "root of bitterness" she identifies as "the mistaken notion of the inequality of the sexes"—are scriptural.

The public careers of the Grimké sisters functionally ended in 1838, when Angelina married abolitionist Theodore

[14]Perhaps health-song, as in "valedictory."

[1]Excerpts from these *Letters* are printed below in the section on Sarah Moore Grimké.

Weld. The sisters' anti-slavery arguments, however, came to define abolitionism to many Americans, and their writings on women's rights became the grounding of later works by Margaret Fuller and the women who established an American feminist movement at Seneca Falls in 1848. In addition, the presence of the Grimké sisters on the public platform inspired a new generation, like Abby Kelley Foster and Lucy Stone, to speak in public and to assert women's presence in public life.

Jean Fagan Yellin
Pace University

PRIMARY WORKS

"Letter to William Lloyd Garrison, 30 August, 1835," published in the *Liberator,* copied in other publications, and reprinted as a broadside; Angelina Grimké, *Appeal to the Christian Women of the South,* 1836; *Appeal to the Women of the Nominally Free States,* 1837; *Letters to Catharine Beecher, in reply to an Essay on Slavery and Abolition, Addressed to A. E. Grimké,* revised edition 1838; Sarah Grimké, *Letters on the Equality of the Sexes, and the Condition of Woman,* 1838, first published in a series in the *New England Spectator,* 1938; "Letter to the Women's Rights Convention, Syracuse, 1852," Women's Rights Tract No. 8, 1852.

SECONDARY WORKS

Gerda Lerner, *The Grimké Sisters from South Carolina: Rebels Against Slavery,* 1967; Katharine Du Pre Lumpkin, *The Emancipation of Angelina Grimké,* 1974; Jean Fagan Yellin, *Women and Sisters: The Antislavery Feminists in American Culture,* 1989.

from Appeal to the Christian Women of the South

> *Then Mordecai commanded to answer Esther, Think not within thyself that thou shalt escape in the king's house more than all the Jews. For if thou altogether holdest thy peace at this time, then shall there enlargement and deliverance arise to the Jews from another place: but thou and thy father's house shall be destroyed; and who knoweth whether thou art come to the kingdom for such a time as this. And Esther bade them return Mordecai this answer:—and so will I go in unto the king, which is not according to law, and if I perish, I perish."* Esther IV. 13–16.

Respected Friends,

It is because I feel a deep and tender interest in your present and eternal welfare that I am willing thus publicly to address you. Some of you have loved me as a relative, and some have felt bound to me in Christian sympathy, and Gospel fellowship; and even when compelled by a strong sense of duty, to break those outward bonds of union which bound us together as members of the same community, and members of the same religious denomination, you were generous enough to give me credit, for sincerity as a Christian, though you believed I had been most strangely deceived. . . .

But there are other Christian women scattered over the Southern States, a very large number of whom have never seen me, and never heard my name, and who feel *no* interest whatever in *me.* But I feel an interest in *you,* as branches of the same vine from whose root I daily draw the principle of spiritual vitality—Yes! Sisters in Christ I feel an interest in *you,* and often has the secret prayer arisen on your behalf, Lord "open thou their eyes that they may see wondrous things out of thy Law"—It is then, because I *do feel* and *do pray* for you, that I thus address you upon a subject about which of all others, perhaps you would rather not hear any thing; but, "would to God ye could bear with me a little in my folly, and indeed bear with me, for I am jealous over you with godly jealousy." Be not afraid then to read my appeal; it is *not* written in the heat of passion or prejudice, but in that solemn calmness which is the result of conviction and duty. It is true, I am going to tell you unwelcome truths, but I mean to speak those *truths in love,* and remember Solomon says, "faithful are the *wounds* of a friend." I do not believe the time has yet come when *Christian women* "will not endure sound doctrine," even on the subject of Slavery, if it is spoken to them in tenderness and love, therefore I now address *you. . . .*

I have thus, I think, clearly proved to you seven propositions, viz.: First, that slavery is contrary to the declaration of our independence. Second, that it is contrary to the first charter of human rights given to Adam, and renewed to Noah. Third, that the fact of slavery having been the subject of prophecy, furnishes *no* excuse whatever to slavedealers. Fourth, that no such system existed under the patriarchal dispensation. Fifth, that *slavery never* existed under the Jewish dispensation; but so far otherwise, that every servant was placed under the *protection of law,* and care taken not only to prevent all *involuntary* servitude, but all *voluntary perpetual* bondage. Sixth, that slavery in America reduces a *man* to a *thing,* a "chattel personal," *robs him* of *all* his rights as a *human being,* fetters both his mind and body, and protects the *master* in the most unnatural and unreasonable power, whilst it *throws him out* of the protection of law. Seventh, that slavery is contrary to the example and precepts of our holy and merciful Redeemer, and of his apostles.

But perhaps you will be ready to query, why appeal to *women* on this subject? *We* do not make the laws which perpetuate slavery. *No* legislative power is vested in *us; we* can do nothing to overthrow the system, even if we wished to do so. To this I reply, I know you do not make the laws, but I also know that *you are the wives and mothers, the sisters and daughters of those who do,* and if you really suppose *you* can do nothing to overthrow slavery, you are greatly mistaken. You can do much in every way: four things I will name. 1st. You can read on this subject. 2d. You can pray over this subject. 3d. You can speak on this subject. 4th. You can *act* on this subject. I have not placed reading before praying because I regard it more important, but because, in order to pray aright, we must understand what we are praying for; it is only then we can "pray with the understanding and the spirit also."

1. Read then on the subject of slavery. Search the Scriptures daily, whether the things I have told you are true. Other books and papers might be a great help to you in this investigation, but they are not necessary, and it is hardly probable that your Committees of Vigilance[1] will allow you to have any other. The *Bible* then is the book I want you to read in the spirit of inquiry, and the spirit of prayer. Even the enemies

[1]Citizens' groups which, in the white South, attempted to buttress the institution of chattel slavery by preventing the publication or distribution of abolitionist writings and speeches; the black North later organized committees of vigilance to protect fugitive slaves from slave-catchers.

of Abolitionists, acknowledge that their doctrines are drawn from it. In the great mob in Boston, last autumn, when the books and papers of the Anti-Slavery Society, were thrown out of the windows of their office, one individual laid hold of the Bible and was about tossing it out to the ground, when another reminded him that it was the Bible he had in his hand. "*O! 'tis all one,*" he replied, and out went the sacred volume, along with the rest. We thank him for the acknowledgment. Yes, "*it is all one,*" for our books and papers are mostly commentaries on the Bible, and the Declaration.[2] Read the *Bible* then, it contains the words of Jesus, and they are spirit and life. Judge for yourselves whether *he sanctioned* such a system of oppression and crime.

2. Pray over this subject. When you have entered into your closets, and shut to the doors, then pray to your father, who seeth in secret, that he would open your eyes to see whether slavery is *sinful,* and if it is, that he would enable you to bear a faithful, open and unshrinking testimony against it, and to do whatsoever your hands find to do, leaving the consequences entirely to him, who still says to us whenever we try to reason away duty from the fear of consequences, "*What is that to thee, follow thou me.*" Pray also for that poor slave, that he may be kept patient and submissive under his hard lot, until God is pleased to open the door of freedom to him without violence or bloodshed. Pray too for the master that his heart may be softened. and he made willing to acknowledge, as Joseph's brethren[3] did, "Verily we are guilty concerning our brother," before he will be compelled to add in consequence of Divine judgment, "therefore is all this evil come upon us." Pray also for all your brethren and sisters who are laboring in the righteous cause of Emancipation in the Northern States, England and the world. There is great encouragement for prayer in these words of our Lord. "Whatsoever ye shall ask the Father *in my name,* he *will give* it to you"—Pray then without ceasing, in the closet and the social circle.

3. Speak on this subject. It is through the tongue, the pen, and the press, that truth is principally propagated. Speak then to your relatives, your friends, your acquaintances on the subject of slavery; be not afraid if you are conscientiously convinced it is *sinful,* to say so openly, but calmly, and to let your sentiments be known. If you are served by the slaves of others, try to ameliorate their condition as much as possible; never aggravate their faults, and thus add fuel to the fire of anger already kindled, in a master and mistress's bosom; remember their extreme ignorance, and consider them as your Heavenly Father does the *less* culpable on this account, even when they do wrong things. Discountenance *all* cruelty to them, all starvation, all corporal chastisement; these may brutalize and *break* their spirits, but will never bend them to willing, cheerful obedience. If possible, see that they are comfortably and *seasonably* fed, whether in the house or the field; it is unreasonable and cruel to expect slaves to wait for their breakfast until eleven o'clock, when they rise at five or six. Do all you can, to induce their owners to clothe them well, and to allow them many little indulgences which would contribute to their comfort. Above all, try to persuade your husband, father, brothers and sons, that *slavery is a crime against God and man,* and that it is a great sin to keep *human beings* in such abject ignorance; to deny them the privilege of learning to read and write. The Catholics are universally condemned, for denying the Bible to the common people, but, *slaveholders must not* blame them, for *they* are doing the *very same thing,* and for the very same reason,

[2]Declaration of Independence.
[3]Genesis 42:21.

neither of these systems can bear the light which bursts from the pages of that Holy Book. And lastly, endeavour to inculcate submission on the part of the slaves, but whilst doing this be faithful in pleading the cause of the oppressed.

"Will *you* behold unheeding,
Life's holiest feelings crushed,
Where *woman's* heart is bleeding,
Shall *woman's* voice be hushed?"[4]

4. Act on this subject. Some of you *own* slaves yourselves. If you believe slavery is *sinful,* set them at liberty, "undo the heavy burdens and let the oppressed go free." If they wish to remain with you, pay them wages, if not let them leave you. Should they remain teach them, and have them taught the common branches of an English education; they have minds and those minds, *ought to be improved.* So precious a talent as intellect, never was given to be wrapt in a napkin and buried in the earth. It is the *duty* of all, as far as they can, to improve their own mental faculties, because we are commanded to love God with *all our minds,* as well as with all our hearts, and we commit a great sin, if we *forbid or prevent* that cultivation of the mind in others, which would enable them to perform this duty. Teach your servants then to read &c, and encourage them to believe it is their *duty* to learn, if it were only that they might read the Bible.

But some of you will say, we can neither free our slaves nor teach them to read, for the laws of our state forbid it. Be not surprised when I say such wicked laws *ought to be no barrier* in the way of your duty, and I appeal to the Bible to prove this position. What was the conduct of Shiphrah and Puah, when the king of Egypt issued his cruel mandate, with regard to the Hebrew children? "*They* feared *God,* and did *not* as the King of Egypt commanded them, but saved the men children alive." Did these *women* do right in disobeying that monarch? "*Therefore* (says the sacred text,) *God dealt well* with them, and made them houses" Ex. i. What was the conduct of Shadrach, Meshach, and Abednego, when Nebuchadnezzar set up a golden image in the plain of Dura, and commanded all people, nations, and languages, to fall down and worship it? "Be it known, unto thee, (said these faithful *Jews*) O king, that *we will not* serve thy gods, nor worship the image which thou hast set up." Did these men *do right in disobeying the law* of their sovereign? Let their miraculous deliverance from the burning fiery furnace answer; Dan. iii. . . .

But some of you may say, if we do free our slaves, they will be taken up and sold, therefore there will be no use in doing it. Peter and John might just as well have said, we will not preach the gospel, for if we do, we shall be taken up and put in prison, therefore there will be no use in our preaching. *Consequences,* my friends, belong no more to *you,* than they did to these apostles. Duty is ours and events are God's. If you think slavery is sinful, all *you* have to do is to set your slaves at liberty, do all you can to protect them, and in humble faith and fervent prayer, commend them to your common Father. He can take care of them; but if for wise purposes he sees fit to allow them to be sold, this will afford you an opportunity of testifying openly, wherever you go, against the crime of *manstealing.* Such an act will be *clear robbery,* and if exposed, might, under the Divine direction, do the cause of Emancipation more

[4]Elizabeth Margaret Chandler, "Think of our Country's Glory," *Poetical Works,* ed. Benjamin Lundy (Philadelphia: Howell, 1836), p. 64.

good, than any thing that could happen, for, "He makes even the wrath of man to praise him, and the remainder of wrath he will restrain."[5]

I know that this doctrine of obeying *God,* rather than man, will be considered as dangerous, and heretical by many, but I am not afraid openly to avow it, because it is the doctrine of the Bible; but I would not be understood to advocate resistance to any law however oppressive, if, in obeying it, I was not obliged to commit *sin.* If for instance, there was a law, which imposed imprisonment or a fine upon me if I manumitted a slave, I would on no account resist that law, I would set the slave free, and then go to prison or pay the fine. If a law commands me to *sin I will break it;* if it calls me to *suffer,* I will let it take its course *unresistingly.* The doctrine of blind obedience and unqualified submission to *any human* power, whether civil or ecclesiastical, is the doctrine of despotism, and ought to have no place among Republicans and Christians.

But you will perhaps say, such a course of conduct would inevitably expose us to great suffering. Yes! my christian friends, I believe it would, but this will *not* excuse you or any one else for the neglect of *duty.* If Prophets and Apostles, Martyrs, and Reformers had not been willing to suffer for the truth's sake, where would the world have been now? If they had said, we cannot speak the truth, we cannot do what we believe is right, because the *laws of our country or public opinion are against us,* where would our holy religion have been now? . . .

But you may say we are *women,* how can *our* hearts endure persecution? And why not? Have not *women* stood up in all the dignity and strength of moral courage to be the leaders of the people, and to bear a faithful testimony for the truth whenever the providence of God has called them to do so? Are there no *women* in that noble army of martyrs who are now singing the song of Moses and the Lamb? Who led out the women of Israel from the house of bondage, striking the timbrel, and singing the song of deliverance on the banks of that sea whose waters stood up like walls of crystal to open a passage for their escape? It was a *woman;* Miriam, the prophetess, the sister of Moses and Aaron. Who went up with Barak to Kadesh to fight against Jabin, King of Canaan, into whose hand Israel had been sold because of their iniquities? It was a *woman!* Deborah the wife of Lapidoth, the judge, as well as the prophetess of that backsliding people; Judges iv, 9. Into whose hands was Sisera, the captain of Jabin's host delivered? Into the hand of a *woman.* Jael the wife of Heber! Judges vi, 21. Who dared to *speak the truth* concerning those judgments which were coming upon Judea, when Josiah, alarmed at finding that his people "had not kept the word of the Lord to do after all that was written in the book of the Law," sent to enquire of the Lord concerning these things? It was a *woman.* Huldah the prophetess, the wife of Shallum; 2, Chron. xxxiv, 22. Who was chosen to deliver the whole Jewish nation from that murderous decree of Persia's King, which wicked Haman had obtained by calumny and fraud? It was a *woman;* Esther the Queen; yes, weak and trembling *woman* was the instrument appointed by God, to reverse the bloody mandate of the eastern monarch, and save the *whole visible church* from destruction. What human voice first proclaimed to Mary that she should be the mother of our Lord? It was a *woman!* Elizabeth, the wife of Zacharias; Luke i, 42, 43. Who united with the good old Simeon in giving thanks publicly in the temple, when the child, Jesus, was presented there by his parents, "and spake of him to all them that

[5] "Surely the wrath of man shall praise thee:
The remainder of wrath shalt thou restrain." Psalms 76:10.

looked for redemption in Jerusalem?" It was a *woman!* Anna the prophetess. Who first proclaimed Christ as the true Messiah in the streets of Samaria, once the capital of the ten tribes? It was a *woman!* Who ministered to the Son of God whilst on earth, a despised and persecuted Reformer, in the humble garb of a carpenter? They were *women!* Who followed the rejected King of Israel, as his fainting footsteps trod the road to Calvary? "A great company of people and of *women;*" and it is remarkable that to *them alone,* he turned and addressed the pathetic language, "Daughters of Jerusalem, weep not for me, but weep for yourselves and your children". . . .

To whom did he *first* appear after his resurrection? It was to a *woman!* Mary Magdalene; Mark xvi, 9. Who gathered with the apostles to wait at Jerusalem, in prayer and supplication, for "the promise of the Father;" the spiritual blessing of the Great High Priest of his Church, who had entered, *not* into the splendid temple of Solomon, there to offer the blood of bulls, and of goats, and the smoking censer upon the golden altar, but into Heaven itself, there to present his intercessions, after having "given himself for us, an offering and a sacrifice to God for a sweet smelling savor?" *Women* were among that holy company; Acts i, 14. And did *women* wait in vain? Did those who had ministered to his necessities, followed in his train, and wept at his crucifixion, wait in vain? No! No! Did the cloven tongues of fire descend upon the heads of *women* as well as men? Yes, my friends, "it sat upon *each one of them;*" Acts ii, 3. *Women* as well as men were to be living stones in the temple of grace, and therefore *their* heads were consecrated by the descent of the Holy Ghost as well as those of men. Were *women* recognized as fellow laborers in the gospel field? They were! Paul says in his epistle to the Philippians, "help those *women* who labored with me, in the gospel;" Phil. iv, 3. . . .

And what, I would ask in conclusion, have *women* done for the great and glorious cause of Emancipation? Who wrote that pamphlet which moved the heart of Wilberforce[6] to pray over the wrongs, and his tongue to plead the cause of the oppressed African? It was a *woman,* Elizabeth Heyrick.[7] Who labored assiduously to keep the sufferings of the slave continually before the British public? They were *women.* And how did they do it? By their needles, paint brushes and pens, by speaking the truth, and petitioning Parliament for the abolition of slavery. And what was the effect of their labors? Read it in the Emancipation bill of Great Britain. Read it, in the present state of her West India Colonies. Read it, in the impulse which has been given to the cause of freedom, in the United States of America. Have English women then done so much for the negro, and shall American women do nothing? Oh no! Already are there sixty female Anti-Slavery Societies in operation. These are doing just what the English women did, telling the story of the colored man's wrongs, praying for his deliverance, and presenting his kneeling image constantly before the public eye on bags and needle-books, card-racks, pen-wipers, pin-cushions, &c. Even the children of the north are inscribing on their handy work, "May the points of our needles prick the slaveholder's conscience." Some of the reports of these Societies exhibit not only considerable talent, but a deep sense of religious duty, and a determination to persevere through evil as well as good report, until every scourge, and every shackle, is buried under the feet of the manumitted slave.

[6]The British abolitionist William Wilberforce (1759–1833), a member of Parliament, led the Committee to Abolish the Slave Trade.

[7]The English Quaker Elizabeth Heyrick first urged the doctrine of Immediate Emancipation in an 1825 pamphlet; British abolitionists, who had previously argued for gradual emancipation, adopted her principles.

The Ladies' Anti-Slavery Society of Boston was called last fall, to a severe trial of their faith and constancy. They were mobbed by "the gentlemen of property and standing," in that city at their anniversary meeting, and their lives were jeoparded by an infuriated crowd; but their conduct on that occasion did credit to our sex, and affords a full assurance that they will *never* abandon the cause of the slave. . . . The Northern women may labor to produce a correct public opinion at the North, but if Southern women sit down in listless indifference and criminal idleness, public opinion cannot be rectified and purified at the South. It is manifest to every reflecting mind, that slavery must be abolished; the era in which we live, and the light which is overspreading the whole world on this subject, clearly show that the time cannot be distant when it will be done. Now there are only two ways in which it can be effected, by moral power or physical force, and it is for *you* to choose which of these you prefer. Slavery always has, and always will produce insurrections wherever it exists, because it is a violation of the natural order of things, and no human power can much longer perpetuate it. . . .

Well may the poet exclaim in bitter sarcasm,

> "The fustian flag that proudly waves
> In solemn mockery o'er *a land of slaves.*"[8]

Can you not, my friends, understand the signs of the times; do you not see the sword of retributive justice hanging over the South, or are you still slumbering at your posts?—Are there no Shiphrahs, no Puahs[9] among you, who will dare in Christian firmness and Christian meekness, to refuse to obey the *wicked laws* which require *woman to enslave, to degrade and to brutalize woman?* Are there no Miriams,[10] who would rejoice to lead out the captive daughters of the Southern States to liberty and light? Are there no Huldahs[11] there who will dare to *speak the truth* concerning the sins of the people and those judgments, which it requires no prophet's eye to see, must follow if repentance is not speedily sought? Is there no Esther[12] among you who will plead for the poor devoted slave? Read the history of this Persian queen, it is full of instruction; she at first refused to plead for the Jews; but, hear the words of Mordecai, "Think not within thyself, that *thou* shalt escape in the king's house more than all the Jews, for *if thou altogether holdest thy peace at this time,* then shall there enlargement and deliverance arise to the Jews from another place: but *thou and thy father's house shall be destroyed.*" Listen, too, to her magnanimous reply to this powerful appeal; "*I will* go unto the king, which is *not* according to law, and if I perish, I perish." Yes! if there were but *one* Esther at the South, she *might* save her country from ruin; but let the Christian women there arise, as the Christian women of Great

[8]Thomas Moore (1779–1852), "To the Lord Viscount Forbes, Written from the City of Washington": "Where bastard Freedom waves/The fustian flag in mockery over slaves."

[9]Hebrew midwives who disobeyed Pharaoh's command to slay sons born to Hebrew women. Exodus 1:15–20.

[10]Sister of Moses, who led a dance celebrating the Lord's victory over the Egyptians. She is cited as an example of truly enthusiastic worship of God. See Exodus 15:20–21.

[11]Speaks the Lord's prophecy of the destruction of the kingdom of Judah. 2 Chronicles 34:22–28.

[12]Intervened with her husband, the king of Persia, at considerable personal risk, to save Mordecai and all the Jews from the slaughter planned for them by Haman. See particularly Esther 4:16: "Then I will go to the King, though it is against the law; and if I perish, I perish."

Britain did, in the majesty of moral power, and that salvation is certain. Let them embody themselves in societies, and send petitions up to their different legislatures, entreating their husbands, fathers, brothers and sons, to abolish the institution of slavery; no longer to subject *woman* to the scourge and the chain, to mental darkness and moral degradation; no longer to tear husbands from their wives, and children from their parents; no longer to make men, women, and children, work *without wages;* no longer to make their lives bitter in hard bondage; no longer to reduce *American citizens* to the abject condition of *slaves,* of "chattels personal;" no longer to barter the *image of God* in human shambles for corruptible things such as silver and gold.

The *women of the South can overthrow* this horrible system of oppression and cruelty, licentiousness and wrong. Such appeals to your legislatures would be irresistible, for there is something in the heart of man which *will bend under moral suasion.* There is a swift witness for truth in his bosom, which *will respond to truth* when it is uttered with calmness and dignity. If you could obtain but six signatures to such a petition in only one state, I would say, send up that petition, and be not in the least discouraged by the scoffs and jeers of the heartless, or the resolution of the house to lay it on the table. It will be a great thing if the subject can be introduced into your legislatures in any way, even by *women,* and *they* will be the most likely to introduce it there in the best possible manner, as a matter of *morals* and *religion,* not of expediency or politics. You may petition, too, the different ecclesiastical bodies of the slave states. Slavery must be attacked with the whole power of truth and the sword of the spirit. You must take it up on *Christian* ground, and fight against it with Christian weapons, whilst your feet are shod with the preparation of the gospel of peace. And *you are now* loudly called upon by the cries of the widow and the orphan, to arise and gird yourselves for this great moral conflict, with the whole armour of righteousness upon the right hand and on the left. . . .

Sisters in Christ, I have done. As a Southerner, I have felt it was my duty to address you. I have endeavoured to set before you the exceeding sinfulness of slavery, and to point you to the example of those noble women who have been raised up in the church to effect great revolutions, and to suffer for the truth's sake. I have appealed to your sympathies as women, to your sense of duty as *Christian women.* I have attempted to vindicate the Abolitionists, to prove the entire safety of immediate Emancipation, and to plead the cause of the poor and oppressed. I have done—I have sowed the seeds of truth, but I well know, that even if an Apollos were to follow in my steps to water them, "*God only* can give the increase." To Him then who is able to prosper the work of his servant's hand, I commend this Appeal in fervent prayer, that as he "hath *chosen the weak things of the world,* to confound the things which are mighty," so He may cause His blessing, to descend and carry conviction to the hearts of many Lydias[13] through these speaking pages. Farewell—Count me not your "enemy because I have told you the truth," but believe me in unfeigned affection,

Your sympathizing Friend,
Angelina E. Grimké.

1836

[13]A successful businesswoman of Philippi who extended her hospitality and help to the ministry of Paul and Silas and received them when they were released from prison. Acts 16:14–15, 40.

from Letters to Catharine Beecher

Letter XI

Brookline, Mass. *8th mo. 28th,* 1837.

Dear Friend:

. . . I trust my sisters may always be permitted to *petition* for a redress of grievances. Why not? The right of petition is the only political right that women have: why not let them exercise it whenever they are aggrieved? Our fathers waged a bloody conflict with England, because *they* were taxed without being represented. This is just what unmarried women of property now are. *They* were not willing to be governed by laws which *they* had no voice in making; but this is the way in which women are governed in this Republic. If, then, *we* are taxed without being represented, and governed by laws *we* have no voice in framing, then, surely, we ought to be permitted at least to remonstrate against "every political measure that may tend to injure and oppress our sex in various parts of the nation, and under the various public measures that may hereafter be enforced."[1] Why not? Art thou afraid to trust the women of this country with discretionary power as to petitioning? Is there not sound principle and common sense enough among them, to regulate the exercise of this right? I believe they will always use it wisely. I am not afraid to trust my sisters—not I.

Thou sayest, "In this country, petitions to Congress, in reference to official duties of legislators, seem, IN ALL CASES, to fall entirely without the sphere of female duty. Men are the proper persons to make appeals to the rulers whom they appoint," &c. Here I entirely dissent from thee. The fact that women are denied the right of voting for members of Congress, is but a poor reason why they should also be deprived of the right of petition. If their numbers are counted to swell the number of Representatives in our State and National Legislatures, the *very least* that can be done is to give them the right of petition in all cases whatsoever; and without any abridgement. If not, they are mere slaves, known only through their masters. . . .

Thy Friend,
A.E. Grimké
1837

[1]Here, and throughout these *Letters,* Grimké is quoting from Beecher to refute her.

Letter XII
Human Rights Not Founded on Sex

East Boylston, Mass. 10*th mo.* 2*d,* 1837.

Dear Friend:

. . . The investigation of the rights of the slave has led me to a better understanding of my own. . . . Human beings have *rights,* because they are *moral* beings: the rights of *all* men grow out of their moral nature; and as all men have the same moral nature, they have essentially the same rights. . . . Now if rights are founded in the nature of our moral being, then the *mere circumstance of sex* does not give to man higher rights and responsibilities, than to woman. To suppose that it does, would be to deny the self-evident truth, that the "physical constitution is the mere instrument of the moral nature." To suppose that it does, would be to break up utterly the relations, of the two natures, and to reverse their functions, exalting the animal nature into a monarch, and humbling the moral into a slave; making the former a proprietor, and the latter its property. When human beings are regarded as *moral* beings, *sex,* instead of being enthroned upon the summit, administering upon rights and responsibilities, sinks into insignificance and nothingness. My doctrine then is, that whatever it is morally right for man to do, it is morally right for woman to do. Our duties originate, not from difference of sex, but from the diversity of our relations in life, the various gifts and talents committed to our care, and the different eras in which we live.

This regulation of duty by the mere circumstance of sex, rather than by the fundamental principle of moral being, has led to all that multifarious train of evils flowing out of the anti-christian doctrine of masculine and feminine virtues. By this doctrine, man has been converted into the warrior, and clothed with sternness, and those other kindred qualities, which in common estimation belong to his character as a *man;* whilst woman has been taught to lean upon an arm of flesh, to sit as a doll arrayed in "gold, and pearls, and costly array," to be admired for her personal charms, and caressed and humored like a spoiled child, or converted into a mere drudge to suit the convenience of her lord and master. Thus have all the diversified relations of life been filled with "confusion and every evil work." This principle has given to man a charter for the exercise of tyranny and selfishness, pride and arrogance, lust and brutal violence. It has robbed woman of essential rights, the right to think and speak and act on all great moral questions, just as men think and speak and act; the right to share their responsibilities, perils and toils, the right to fulfil the great end of her being, as a moral, intellectual and immortal creature, and of glorifying God in her body and her spirit which are His. Hitherto, instead of being a help meet to man, in the highest, noblest sense of the term, as a companion, a co-worker, an equal; she has been a mere appendage of his being, an instrument of his convenience and pleasure, the pretty toy with which he wiled away his leisure moments, or the pet animal whom he humored into playfulness and submission. Woman, instead of being regarded as the equal of man, has uniformly been looked down upon as his inferior, a mere gift to fill up the measure of his happiness. In "the poetry of romantic gallantry," it is true, she has been called "the last *best* gift of God to man";[1] but I believe I speak forth the words of truth and soberness when I affirm, that woman never was given to man. She was created, like him, in the image of God, and crowned with glory and honor; created only a little lower than the angels,[2]—not, as is almost universally assumed, a little lower than man; on her brow, as well as on his, was placed the "diadem of beauty," and in her hand the sceptre of universal dominion. Gen: i. 27, 28. "The last *best gift* of God to man!" Where is the scripture warrant for this "rhetorical flourish, this splendid absurdity"? Let us examine the account of her creation. "And the rib which the Lord God had taken from man, made he a woman, and brought her unto the man." Not as a gift—for Adam immediately recognized her *as a part of himself*—("this is now bone of my bone, and flesh of my flesh")—a companion and equal, not one hair's breadth beneath him in the majesty and glory of her moral being; not placed under his authority as a *subject,* but by his side, on the same platform of human rights, under the government of God only. This idea of woman's being "the last best gift of God to man," however pretty it may sound to the ears of those who love to discourse upon "the poetry of romantic gallantry, and the generous promptings of chivalry," has nevertheless been the means of sinking her from an *end* into a mere *means*—of turning her into an *appendage* to man, instead of recognizing her as *a part of man*—of destroying her individuality, and rights, and responsibilities, and merging her moral being in that of man. Instead of *Jehovah* being *her* king, *her* lawgiver, and *her* judge, she has been taken out of the exalted scale of existence in which He placed her, and subjected to the despotic control of man. . . .

I recognize no rights but *human* rights—I know nothing of men's rights and women's rights; for in Christ Jesus, there is neither male nor female. It is my solemn conviction, that, until this principle of equality is recognised and embodied in practice, the church can do nothing effectual for the permanent reformation of the world. Woman was the first transgressor, and the first victim of power. In all heathen nations, she has been the slave of man, and Christian nations have never acknowledged her rights. . . . Now, I believe it is woman's right to have a voice in all the laws and regulations by which she is to be *governed,* whether in Church or State; and that the present arrangements of society, on these points, are *a violation of human rights, a rank usurpation of power,* a violent seizure and confiscation of what is sacredly and inalienably hers—thus inflicting upon woman outrageous wrongs, working mischief incalculable in the social circle, and in its influence on the world producing only evil, and that continually. *If* Ecclesiastical and Civil governments are ordained of God, *then* I contend that woman has just as much right to sit in solemn counsel in Conventions, Conferences, Associations and General Assemblies, as man—just as much right to sit upon the throne of England, or in the Presidential chair of the United States. . . .

1837

[1]John Milton, "Paradise Lost," Book V, line 19: "Heaven's last, best gift; my ever new delight."

[2]Psalms viii, 5.

Henry Highland Garnet 1815–1882

Less well-known than Frederick Douglass or Charles Lenox Remond, who were his contemporaries, Henry Highland Garnet was early identified as a radical within the abolitionist movement because he argued for active resistance to slavery. Prior to Garnet, the prevailing strategy adopted by Black abolitionists had been to oppose slavery by appealing to Christian morality and to conduct that opposition largely within the bounds of law: thus, for example, Charles Lenox Remond focused his attention on social conditions in Massachusetts and Frederick Douglass made a point of purchasing his own freedom. Although Garnet's position, reflected here in *An Address to the Slaves of the United States of America* (1843), was initially rejected as extreme and dangerous, enactment of the Fugitive Slave Law, the Dred Scott Case the Mexican War, and the general political climate which led to the Civil War eventually made Garnet's advocacy of civil disobedience, indeed resistance, appear appropriate, if not also moderate or mainstream, as a response to slavery.

Garnet had known slavery. Born in 1815, on the Maryland estate of Colonel William Spencer, he escaped with his father, the son of a Mandingo chieftan, when he was nine years old. The family fled to Wilmington, traveling by night, and then, aided by Quakers in the underground railway, escaped to New Hope, Pennsylvania and finally settled in New York City. Garnet attended the New York African Free School on Mulberry Street, a school of some three hundred black students, between 1826 and 1828. But education did not bring Free School students better jobs in New York, so in 1828 Garnet went to sea as a cabin boy, making at least two voyages to Cuba. The following year, when he returned to New York, he found that the family home had been looted by slave-hunters and that his sister had been arrested as a "fugitive from labor." Although his sister was eventually released, the experience had a permanent and radical effect on Garnet. He bought a large knife, which he wore openly, and stalked up Broadway, looking for the men who had invaded his home. Fearing for his safety, friends persuaded him to go to Long Island, where he remained for a few years, working and studying. During that period, Garnet suffered a knee injury which left him permanently crippled and eventually required the amputation of his leg. Hobbled, dependent on a crutch, he turned his attention fully to study.

For the next several years, Garnet attended school in New York, went briefly to a school in Canaan, New Hampshire, where he and other black students were driven out of town by angry citizens, and finally to the Oneida Institute in upstate New York. Following his graduation in 1840, Garnet married, taught school and began to study theology. In 1843, the year of his ordination as a Presbyterian minister, Garnet attended the Negro national convention in Buffalo. Although Garnet was by this time well known in abolitionist circles, this was his first direct encounter with Frederick Douglass, and the meeting marked the beginning of a rivalry which persisted until the 1850s. Douglass, who embraced William Lloyd Garrison's approach to abolition and who endorsed women's rights as well, was opposed to supporting the Liberty Party, to which Garnet belonged, and believed that the use of violence was contrary to Christian teaching. In Garnet's view, abolition of slavery was vastly more important than any other cause, and in *An Address to the Slaves of the United States of America* he argued that it was sinful not to use violence if it were necessary to end submission to slave owners.

Garnet's speech took a set of ideas earlier and more radically expressed in David

Walker's *Appeal.* Walker had said that slaves should wait for an opportunity and then "kill or be killed" to restore their natural rights. Garnet, subtly adapting Walker's entreaty, claimed that the condition of servitude effectively made it impossible for slaves to obey the Ten Commandments. Thus, it was their Christian obligation to resist, and resist violently if necessary: "You had far better all die—*die immediately,* than live slaves and entail your wretchedness upon your posterity." Garnet's many detractors feared that he was encouraging actions which might lead to a blood bath, and in fact, John Brown, who in 1859 led the raid on Harper's Ferry, had the speech printed and widely circulated.

Garnet's disagreements with Douglass and the Garrisonians were not limited to the use of violence, for he later became a supporter of voluntary emigration to Africa, and Douglass found occasion to argue with him from the pages of his newspaper, *The North Star.* But in 1850, Garnet removed himself from the American scene, going to Germany and Britain to lecture, and finally to Jamaica as a Presbyterian missionary. Yet, after his return to America, political sentiments had shifted, and many of Garnet's ideas seemed less alien and threatening. By 1863, Garnet and Douglass were united in recruiting Negro troops for the Union Army, and they later joined in efforts to raise funds for Mary Todd Lincoln. In February, 1865, when Congress enacted the bill which became the Thirteenth Amendment, President Lincoln invited Garnet to deliver a sermon in the House of Representatives. He was the first of his race to speak before that body, the first black to enter the House except as a servant.

Garnet's address, widely and favorably reported, brought him national fame. For the next several years, he continued to lecture on economic subjects and on civil rights, and in 1881, having been appointed Minister Resident and Consul General, he travelled to Liberia, where he died. Throughout his life, Garnet was drawn to ideas which were received with suspicion by centrist abolitionists. Before Frederick Douglass founded the *North Star,* Garnet had recommended establishment of a national printing press. His support of voluntary emigration, which was vehemently opposed by the Garrisonians, arose from his interest in opposing slavery both in the United States and abroad. He argued that the Christian Church, through its silence, had supported the institution of slavery. Although he worked to end slavery in America, he looked to Cuba and Haiti and Jamaica and Africa to understand the international character of the "peculiar institution," for his perspective was always global in scope. His intellectual independence set him apart from others equally dedicated to his cause, and his passion sometimes frightened even those who agreed with him in principle, but he broadened and deepened the debate over slavery, and he deserves to be better remembered as a genuinely radical black voice for abolition.

Allison Heisch
San Jose State University

PRIMARY WORKS

Herbert Aptheker, *A Documentary History of the Negro People in the United States,* 1951; Ernest Bormann, *Forerunners of Black Power,* 1971; Earl Ofari, *"Let Your Motto Be Resistance": The Life and Thought of Henry Highland Garnet,* 1972.

SECONDARY WORKS

Benjamin Quarles, *Black Abolitionists,* 1969; Robert Haynes, *Blacks in White America Before 1865,* 1972; Joel Schor, *Henry Highland Garnet,* 1977; Sterling Stuckey, *Going Through the Storm: The Influence of African American Art in History,* 1994; Martin B. Pasternak, *Rise Now and Fly to Arms: The Life of Henry Highland Garnet,* 1995.

An Address to the Slaves of the United States of America, Buffalo, N.Y., 1843

Brethren and Fellow-Citizens:—Your brethren of the North, East, and West have been accustomed to meet together in National Conventions, to sympathize with each other, and to weep over your unhappy condition. In these meetings we have addressed all classes of the free, but we have never, until this time, sent a word of consolation and advice to you. We have been contented in sitting still and mourning over your sorrows, earnestly hoping that before this day your sacred liberties would have been restored. But, we have hoped in vain. Years have rolled on, and tens of thousands have been borne on streams of blood and tears, to the shores of eternity. While you have been oppressed, we have also been partakers with you; nor can we be free while you are enslaved. We, therefore, write to you as being bound with you.

Many of you are bound to us, not only by the ties of a common humanity, but we are connected by the more tender relations of parents, wives, husbands, children, brothers, and sisters, and friends. As such we most affectionately address you.

Slavery has fixed a deep gulf between you and us, and while it shuts out from you the relief and consolation which your friends would willingly render, it afflicts and persecutes you with a fierceness which we might not expect to see in the fiends of hell. But still the Almighty Father of mercies has left to us a glimmering ray of hope, which shines out like a lone star in a cloudy sky. Mankind are becoming wiser, and better—the oppressor's power is fading, and you, every day, are becoming better informed, and more numerous. Your grievances, brethren, are many. We shall not attempt, in this short address, to present to the world all the dark catalogue of this nation's sins, which have been committed upon an innocent people. Nor is it indeed necessary, for you feel them from day to day, and all the civilized world look upon them with amazement.

Two hundred and twenty-seven years ago, the first of our injured race were brought to the shores of America. They came not with glad spirits to select their homes in the New World. They came not with their own consent, to find an unmolested enjoyment of the blessings of this fruitful soil. The first dealings they had with men calling themselves Christians, exhibited to them the worst features of corrupt and sordid hearts: and convinced them that no cruelty is too great, no villainy and no robbery too abhorrent for even enlightened men to perform, when influenced by avarice and lust. Neither did they come flying upon the wings of Liberty, to a land of freedom. But they came with broken hearts, from their beloved native land, and were doomed to unrequited toil and deep degradation. Nor did the evil of their bondage end at their emancipation by death. Succeeding generations inherited their chains, and millions have come from eternity into time, and have returned again to the world of spirits, cursed and ruined by American slavery.

The propagators of the system, or their immediate ancestors, very soon discovered its growing evil, and its tremendous wickedness, and secret promises were made to destroy it. The gross inconsistency of a people holding slaves, who had themselves "ferried o'er the wave" for freedom's sake, was too apparent to be entirely overlooked. The voice of Freedom cried, "Emancipate your slaves." Humanity supplicated with tears for the deliverance of the children of Africa. Wisdom urged her solemn plea. The bleeding captive pleaded his innocence, and pointed to Christianity who stood weeping at the cross. Jehovah frowned upon the nefarious institution, and thunderbolts, red with vengeance, struggled to leap forth to blast the guilty wretches who maintained it. But all was vain. Slavery had stretched its dark wings of death over the land, the Church stood silently by—the priests prophesied falsely, and the people loved to have it so. Its throne is established, and now it reigns triumphant.

Nearly three millions of your fellow-citizens are prohibited by law and public opinion (which in this country is stronger than law) from reading the Book of Life. Your intellect has been destroyed as much as possible, and every ray of light they have attempted to shut out from your minds. The oppressors themselves have become involved in the ruin. They have become weak, sensual, and rapacious—they have cursed you—they have cursed themselves—they have cursed the earth which they have trod.

The colonists threw the blame upon England. They said that the mother country entailed the evil upon them, and that they would rid themselves of it if they could. The world thought they were sincere, and the philanthropic pitied them. But time soon tested their sincerity. In a few years the colonists grew strong, and severed themselves from the British Government. Their independence was declared, and they took their station among the sovereign powers of the earth. The declaration was a glorious document. Sages admired it, and the patriotic of every nation reverenced the God-like sentiments which it contained. When the power of Government returned to their hands, did they emancipate the slaves? No; they rather added new links to our chains. Were they ignorant of the principles of Liberty? Certainly they were not. The sentiments of their revolutionary orators fell in burning eloquence upon their hearts, and with one voice they cried, *Liberty or Death.*[1] Oh what a sentence was that! It ran from soul to soul like electric fire, and nerved the arm of thousands to fight in the holy cause of Freedom. Among the diversity of opinions that are entertained in regard to physical resistance, there are but a few found to gainsay that stern declaration. We are among those who do not.

Slavery! How much misery is comprehended in that single word. What mind is there that does not shrink from its direful effects? Unless the image of God be obliterated from the soul, all men cherish the love of Liberty. The nice discerning political economist does not regard the sacred right more than the untutored African who roams in the wilds of Congo. Nor has the one more right to the full enjoyment of his freedom than the other. In every man's mind the good seeds of liberty are planted, and he who brings his fellow down so low, as to make him contented with a condition of slavery, commits the highest crime against God and man. Brethren, your oppressors aim to do this. They endeavor to make you as much like brutes as possible. When they have blinded the eyes of your mind—when they have embittered the sweet waters of life—when they have shut out the light which shines from the word of God—then, and not till then, has American slavery done its perfect work.

To such Degradation it is sinful in the Extreme for you to make voluntary Submission. The divine commandments you are in duty bound to reverence and obey. If

[1]A reference to Patrick Henry's speech to the Virginia House of Burgesses: "I know not what course others may take, but as for me, give me liberty or give me death."

you do not obey them, you will surely meet with the displeasure of the Almighty. He requires you to love him supremely, and your neighbor as yourself—to keep the Sabbath day holy—to search the Scriptures—and bring up your children with respect for his laws, and to worship no other God but him. But slavery sets all these at nought, and hurls defiance in the face of Jehovah. The forlorn condition in which you are placed, does not destroy your moral obligation to God. You are not certain of heaven, because you suffer yourselves to remain in a state of slavery, where you cannot obey the commandments of the Sovereign of the universe. If the ignorance of slavery is a passport to heaven, then it is a blessing, and no curse, and you should rather desire its perpetuity than its abolition. God will not receive slavery, nor ignorance, nor any other state of mind, for love and obedience to him. Your condition does not absolve you from your moral obligation. The diabolical injustice by which your liberties are cloven down, *neither God, nor angels, or just men, command you to suffer for a single moment. Therefore it is your solemn and imperative duty to use every means, both moral, intellectual, and physical, that promises success.* If a band of heathen men should attempt to enslave a race of Christians, and to place their children under the influence of some false religion, surely, Heaven would frown upon the men who would not resist such aggression, even to death. If, on the other hand, a band of Christians should attempt to enslave a race of heathen men, and to entail slavery upon them, and to keep them in heathenism in the midst of Christianity, the God of heaven would smile upon every effort which the injured might make to disenthral themselves.

Brethren, it is as wrong for your lordly oppressors to keep you in slavery, as it was for the man thief to steal our ancestors from the coast of Africa. You should therefore now use the same manner of resistance, as would have been just in our ancestors, when the bloody footprints of the first remorseless soul-thief was placed upon the shores of our fatherland. The humblest peasant is as free in the sight of God as the proudest monarch that ever swayed a sceptre. Liberty is a spirit sent out from God, and like its great Author, is no respecter of persons.

Brethren, the time has come when you must act for yourselves. It is an old and true saying that, "if hereditary bondmen would be free, they must themselves strike the blow." You can plead your own cause, and do the work of emancipation better than any others. The nations of the old world are moving in the great cause of universal freedom, and some of them at least will, ere long, do you justice. The combined powers of Europe have placed their broad seal of disapprobation upon the African slave-trade. But in the slave-holding parts of the United States, the trade is as brisk as ever. They buy and sell you as though you were brute beasts. The North has done much—her opinion of slavery in the abstract is known. But in regard to the South, we adopt the opinion of the *New York Evangelist*—"We have advanced so far, that the cause apparently waits for a more effectual door to be thrown open than has been yet." We are about to point you to that more effectual door. Look around you, and behold the bosoms of your loving wives heaving with untold agonies! Hear the cries of your poor children! Remember the stripes your fathers bore. Think of the torture and disgrace of your noble mothers. Think of your wretched sisters, loving virtue and purity, as they are driven into concubinage and are exposed to the unbridled lusts of incarnate devils. Think of the undying glory that hangs around the ancient name of Africa:—and forget not that you are native-born

American citizens, and as such, you are justly entitled to all the rights that are granted to the freest. Think how many tears you have poured out upon the soil which you have cultivated with unrequited toil and enriched with your blood; and then go to your lordly enslavers and tell them plainly, that you *are determined to be free.* Appeal to their sense of justice, and tell them that they have no more right to oppress you, than you have to enslave them. Entreat them to remove the grievous burdens which they have imposed upon you, and to remunerate you for your labor. Promise them renewed diligence in the cultivation of the soil, if they will render to you an equivalent for your services. Point them to the increase of happiness and prosperity in the British West-Indies since the Act of Emancipation.[2] Tell them in language which they cannot misunderstand, of the exceeding sinfulness of slavery, and of a future judgment, and of the righteous retributions of an indignant God. Inform them that all you desire is *freedom,* and that nothing else will suffice. Do this, and for ever after cease to toil for the heartless tyrants, who give you no other reward but stripes and abuse. If they then commence the work of death, they, and not you, will be responsible for the consequences. You had far better all die—*die immediately,* than live slaves, and entail your wretchedness upon your posterity. If you would be free in this generation, here is your only hope. However much you and all of us may desire it, there is not much hope of redemption without the shedding of blood. If you must bleed, let it all come at once—rather *die freemen, than live to be the slaves.* It is impossible, like the children of Israel, to make a grand exodus from the land of bondage. The Pharaohs are on both sides of the blood-red waters! You cannot move *en masse,* to the dominions of the British Queen—nor can you pass through Florida and overrun Texas, and at last find peace in Mexico. The propagators of American slavery are spending their blood and treasure, that they may plant the black flag in the heart of Mexico and riot in the halls of the Montezumas. In the language of the Rev. Robert Hall, when addressing the volunteers of Bristol, who were rushing forth to repel the invasion of Napoleon, who threatened to lay waste the fair homes of England, "Religion is too much interested in your behalf, not to shed over you her most gracious influences."

You will not be compelled to spend much time in order to become inured to hardships. From the first moment that you breathed the air of heaven, you have been accustomed to nothing else but hardships. The heroes of the American Revolution were never put upon harder fare than a peck of corn and a few herrings per week. You have not become enervated by the luxuries of life. Your sternest energies have been beaten out upon the anvil of severe trial. Slavery has done this, to make you subservient to its own purposes; but it has done more than this, it has prepared you for any emergency. If you receive good treatment, it is what you could hardly expect; if you meet with pain, sorrow, and even death, these are the common lot of the slaves.

Fellow-men! patient sufferers! behold your dearest rights crushed to the earth! See your sons murdered, and your wives, mothers and sisters doomed to prostitution. In the name of the merciful God, and by all that life is worth, let it no longer be a debatable question, whether it is better to choose *Liberty* or *death.*

[2]The Act freeing the slaves in the British West Indies had been passed ten years before, in 1833.

In 1822, Denmark Veazie, of South Carolina, formed a plan for the liberation of his fellow-men.[3] In the whole history of human efforts to overthrow slavery, a more complicated and tremendous plan was never formed. He was betrayed by the treachery of his own people, and died a martyr to freedom. Many a brave hero fell, but history, faithful to her high trust, will transcribe his name on the same monument with Moses, Hampden, Tell, Bruce and Wallace, Toussaint L'Ouverture, Lafayette and Washington. That tremendous movement shook the whole empire of slavery. The guilty soul-thieves were overwhelmed with fear. It is a matter of fact, that at that time, and in consequence of the threatened revolution, the slave States talked strongly of emancipation. But they blew but one blast of the trumpet of freedom, and then laid it aside. As these men became quiet, the slaveholders ceased to talk about emancipation: and now behold your condition today! Angels sigh over it, and humanity has long since exhausted her tears in weeping on your account!

The patriotic Nathaniel Turner[4] followed Denmark Veazie. He was goaded to desperation by wrong and injustice. By despotism, his name has been recorded on the list of infamy, and future generations will remember him among the noble and brave.

Next arose the immortal Joseph Cinque, the hero of the *Amistad*.[5] He was a native African, and by the help of God he emancipated a whole ship-load of his fellow-men on the high seas. And he now sings of liberty on the sunny hills of Africa and beneath his native palm-trees, where he hears the lion roar and feels himself as free as that king of the forest.

Next arose Madison Washington,[6] that bright star of freedom, and took his station in the constellation of true heroism. He was a slave on board the brig *Creole,* of Richmond, bound to New Orleans, that great slave mart, with a hundred and four others. Nineteen struck for liberty or death. But one life was taken, and the whole were emancipated, and the vessel was carried into Nassau, New Providence.

Noble men! Those who have fallen in freedom's conflict, their memories will be cherished by the true-hearted and the God-fearing in all future generations; those who are living, their names are surrounded by a halo of glory.

Brethren, arise, arise! Strike for your lives and liberties. Now is the day and the hour. Let every slave throughout the land do this, and the days of slavery are numbered. You cannot be more oppressed than you have been—you cannot suffer greater cruelties than you have already. *Rather die freemen than live to be slaves.* Remember that you are *four millions!*

It is in your power so to torment the God-cursed slaveholders, that they will be glad to let you go free. If the scale was turned, and black men were the masters and white men the slaves, every destructive agent and element would be employed to lay

[3]Denmark Vesey led the organization of a planned slave insurrection in Charleston, South Carolina in 1822; it was betrayed before it was put into action.

[4]See the essay by Thomas Wentworth Higginson elsewhere in this volume.

[5]The *Amistad* was a Spanish schooner that was seized, in the summer of 1839, by its "cargo" of fifty-four slaves, led by Joseph Cinque. By a ruse, the whites who had been spared to navigate the ship back to Africa steered it instead to Long Island, where the Africans were seized and charged with piracy. After an eighteen-month legal battle, the Supreme Court freed the Africans and they were able to return to Mendi, their homeland.

[6]See Frederick Douglass's story "The Heroic Slave," printed elsewhere in this volume.

the oppressor low. Danger and death would hang over their heads day and night. Yes, the tyrants would meet with plagues more terrible than those of Pharaoh. But you are a patient people. You act as though you were made for the special use of these devils. You act as though your daughters were born to pamper the lusts of your

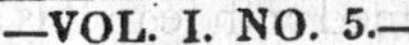
—VOL. I. NO. 5.—

THE

AMERICAN ANTI-SLAVERY ALMANAC,

FOR

1840,

BEING BISSEXTILE OR LEAP-YEAR, AND THE 64TH OF AMERICAN INDEPENDENCE. CALCULATED FOR NEW YORK; ADAPTED TO THE NORTHERN AND MIDDLE STATES.

NORTHERN HOSPITALITY—NEW YORK NINE MONTHS' LAW.
The slave steps out of the slave-state, and his chains fall. A free state, with another chain, stands ready to re-enslave him.

Thus saith the Lord, Deliver him that is spoiled out of the hands of the oppressor.

NEW YORK:
PUBLISHED BY THE AMERICAN ANTI-SLAVERY SOCIETY,
NO. 143 NASSAU STREET.

masters and overseers. And worse than all, you tamely submit while your lords tear your wives from your embraces and defile them before your eyes. In the name of God, we ask, are you men? Where is the blood of your fathers? Has it all run out of your veins? Awake, awake; millions of voices are calling you! Your dead fathers speak to you from their graves. Heaven, as with a voice of thunder, calls on you to arise from the dust.

Let your motto be resistance! *resistance! resistance!* No oppressed people have ever secured their liberty without resistance. What kind of resistance you had better make, you must decide by the circumstances that surround you, and according to the suggestion of expediency. Brethren, adieu! Trust in the living God. Labor for the peace of the human race, and remember that you are *four millions.*

1848

Wendell Phillips 1811–1884

The eighth of nine children, Wendell Phillips was born in a Beacon Hill mansion into one of Boston's distinguished old families. The Reverend George Phillips, his ancestor, had arrived with John Winthrop on the *Arbella* in 1630, and the family fortune had been established before the Revolutionary War. His father John Phillips, a lawyer, had both inherited and married wealth, and he saw to it that Wendell received the education and cultural exposure appropriate to the son of a Boston Brahmin. He attended the Boston Latin School and went on to Harvard College and Harvard Law School. Handsome and athletic, Phillips was elected to the Porcellan the Gentleman's Club, and the Hasty Pudding Club, certain signs of his aristocratic status. When he graduated from college in 1831 he had served as president of each of those elite organizations. Except for a report that he watched the English actress Fanny Kemble at the Tremont Theatre nineteen nights in a row, everything recorded of Phillips's early life was conservative and conventional; there were no hints of passion or political commitment. He took up the law with a classmate in Lowell, Massachusetts, in 1834, but returned to Boston the following year and rented an office from which he tried, and apparently failed, to establish a law practice.

Although his private income was such that he did not need to work, Wendell Phillips was at that juncture professionally adrift, in want of a vocation. Yet in November, 1837, with the brother and sister-in-law of William Lloyd Garrison serving as best man and matron of honor, he married a member of the Female Anti-Slavery Society, Ann Greene, who he later said had ". . . made an out and out abolitionist of me. . . ." The following month, at a meeting in Faneuil Hall organized by William Ellery Channing to protest the mob murder of the abolitionist Elijah Lovejoy in Alton, Illinois, Phillips spoke eloquently in opposition to the Massachusetts Attorney General, James T. Austin, who had defended the killing, and thus he began his career as a public orator against slavery.

In succeeding years, allied with Garrison, Phillips wrote and spoke locally, but in November, 1854, he undertook the first of his "abolitionizing trips," following a speech-making circuit which took him to Utica, Rochester, Syracuse, Detroit, Cleveland, and Cincinnati. The circuit later widened to include Chicago, Madison, and Milwaukee. For the next twenty-five years he made these journeys over and over, collecting fees of 250 dollars for his appearances. In the early years, his speaker's fees, like much of his extensive private wealth, found their way into the hands of persons whose causes he espoused. But in the waning years of his life, his personal fortune expended, Phillips was forced to continue his public speaking in order to support himself and his invalid wife.

It was the Lyceum lecture series that brought Phillips wide recognition as a speaker. Although he was principally known for his abolitionist speeches, his repertoire included such topics as "Water," "Geology," "Chartism," and a very famous historical piece called "The Lost Arts." Often, when Phillips was engaged to deliver one of these "improving" lectures to his audiences of middle-class northerners, on a succeeding evening he would speak without fee on abolition. While the substance of his orations was set down in his "commonplace book," Phillips spoke from memory, without notes, and in a manner which dazzled his audiences. Thoreau called him "an eloquent speaker and a righteous man." A southern newspaper, the Richmond *Enquirer,* called him an "infernal machine set to music." Frequently transcribed and reprinted, many of his speeches became set pieces re-enacted in school recitations. In 1887, the black poet James Weldon Johnson heard his classmate "Shiny" recite "Toussaint L'Ouverture" as the centerpiece of his grammar school graduation exercises.

The special characteristic of Phillips's orations on black heroes was their insistence on qualitative racial equality. Unlike him, many of the abolitionists opposed slavery simply on the grounds of Christian charity. Thus, for example, some part of the sympathy engendered by Stowe's depiction of Eliza and George, the young couple in *Uncle Tom's Cabin,* had to do with the fact that they were mulatto, and therefore partly white. Many of Phillips's contemporaries held views like those of Louis Agassiz, the Harvard biologist, who came to the conclusion that the negro race was separate from and inferior to the white race, but who was nevertheless opposed to the institution of slavery.

Two speeches in particular, "Crispus Attucks" and "Toussaint L'Ouverture," represent Wendell Phillips's uncompromising support of racial equality. These speeches were delivered literally hundreds of times. In Crispus Attucks, who fought and died in the Boston Massacre in 1770, Phillips finds his example of a black man who liberated colonials from British slavery. In Toussaint L'Ouverture, who led the revolution against the French in Haiti, Phillips does not come far short of making a case for black supremacy, for he sees in Toussaint a man whose vision rivals Edmund Burke's, a man greater than Cromwell, greater far than Napolean, both a genius and a saint. The real purpose of Phillips's speech is, however, revealed by its date: 1863. A debate was raging about whether or not to enlist black men as Union soldiers; there were those who argued either that they would not fight or that they would fight like savages. Phillips offers Toussaint's military genius and his humanitarian conduct to exemplify the capabilities of black soldiers.

Allison Heisch
San Jose State University

PRIMARY WORKS

Speeches, Lectures, and Letters, 1863, 1968; *Speeches, Lectures, and Letters:* Second series, 1891, 1969; *Wendell Phillips on Civil Rights and Freedom,* ed. Louis Filler, 1982.

SECONDARY WORKS

Ralph Korngold, *Two Friends of Man: The Story of William Lloyd Garrison and Wendell Phillips and Their Relationship With Abraham Lincoln,* 1950; Carl Bode, *The American*

Lyceum: Town Meetings of the Mind, 1956; Irving H. Bartlett, *Wendell Phillips, Brahmin Radical,* 1961; Lorenzo Sears, *Wendell Phillips, Orator and Agitator,* 1967; Irving H. Bartlett, *Wendell and Ann Phillips: The Community of Reform, 1840–1880,* 1979; James Brewer Stewart, *Wendell Phillips, Liberty's Hero,* 1986.

from Toussaint L'Ouverture

. . . He had been born a slave on a plantation in the north of the island, an unmixed Negro, his father stolen from Africa If anything, therefore, that I say of him tonight moves your admiration, remember, the black race claims it all—we have no part nor lot in it. He was fifty years old at this time. An old Negro had taught him to read. His favorite books were Epictetus, Raynal, military memoirs, Plutarch.[1] In the woods, he learned some of the qualities of herbs, and was village doctor. On the estate, the highest place he ever reached was that of coachman. At fifty, he joined the army as physician. Before he went, he placed his master and mistress on shipboard, freighted the vessel with a cargo of sugar and coffee, and sent them to Baltimore, and never afterward did he forget to send them, year by year, ample means of support. And I might add that, of all the leading Negro generals, each one saved the man under whose roof he was born, and protected the family. [Cheering.]

Let me add another thing. If I stood here tonight to tell the story of Napoleon, I should take it from the lips of Frenchmen, who find no language rich enough to paint the great captain of the nineteenth century. Were I here to tell you the story of Washington, I should take it from your hearts—you, who think no marble white enough on which to carve the name of the Father of His Country. [Applause.] I am about to tell you the story of a Negro who has left hardly one written line. I am to glean it from the reluctant testimony of Britons, Frenchmen, Spaniards—men who despised him as a Negro and a slave, and hated him because he had beaten them in many a battle. All the materials for his biography are from the lips of his enemies.

The second story told of him is this. About the time he reached the camp, the army had been subjected to two insults. First, their commissioners, summoned to meet the French Committee, were ignominiously and insultingly dismissed; and when, afterward, François, their general, was summoned to a second conference, and went to it on horseback, accompanied by two officers; a young lieutenant, who had known him as a slave, angered at seeing him in the uniform of an officer, raised his riding whip and struck him over the shoulders. If he had been the savage which the Negro is painted to us, he had only to breathe the insult to his twenty-five thousand soldiers, and they would have trodden out the Frenchmen in blood. But the indignant chief rode back in silence to his tent, and it was twenty-four hours before his troops heard of this insult to their general. Then the word went forth, "Death to every white man!" They had fifteen hundred prisoners. Ranged in front of the camp,

[1]Greek, French, and Latin philosophers and historians. Epictetus was a 1st-century Greek stoic philosopher; Guillaume Raynal, an 18th-century historian wrote on the Europeans in the West Indies; Plutarch, a 1st-century biographer and moral philosopher.

they were about to be shot. Toussaint, who had a vein of religious fanaticism, like most great leaders—like Mohammed, like Napoleon, like Cromwell, like John Brown [cheers], he could preach as well as fight—mounting a hillock, and getting the ear of the crowd, exclaimed: "Brothers, this blood will not wipe out the insult to our chief; only the blood in yonder French camp can wipe it out. To shed that is courage; to shed this is cowardice and cruelty besides"; and he saved fifteen hundred lives. [Applause.]

I cannot stop to give in detail every one of his efforts. This was in 1793. Leap with me over seven years; come to 1800; what has he achieved? He has driven the Spaniard back into his own cities, conquered him there, and put the French banner over every Spanish town; and for the first time, and almost the last, the island obeys one law. He has put the mulatto under his feet. He has attacked Maitland,[2] defeated him in pitched battles, and permitted him to retreat to Jamaica; and when the French army rose upon Laveaux, their general, and put him in chains, Toussaint defeated them, took Laveaux out of prison, and put him at the head of his own troops. The grateful French in return named him General in Chief. *"Cet homme fait l'ouverture partout,"* said one—"This man makes an opening everywhere,"—hence his soldiers named him L'Ouverture, *the opening.*

This was the work of seven years. Let us pause a moment, and find something to measure him by. You remember Macaulay[3] says, comparing Cromwell with Napoleon, that Cromwell showed the greater military genius, if we consider that he never saw an army till he was forty; while Napoleon was educated from a boy in the best military schools in Europe. Cromwell manufactured his own army; Napoleon at the age of twenty-seven was placed at the head of the best troops Europe ever saw. They were both successful; but, says Macaulay, with such disadvantages, the Englishman showed the greater genius. Whether you allow the inference or not, you will at least grant that it is a fair mode of measurement. Apply it to Toussaint. Cromwell never saw an army till he was forty; this man never saw a soldier till he was fifty. Cromwell manufactured his own army—out of what? Englishmen, the best blood in Europe. Out of the middle class of Englishmen, the best blood of the island. And with it he conquered what? Englishmen, their equals. This man manufactured his army out of what? Out of what you call the despicable race of Negroes, debased, demoralized by two hundred years of slavery, one hundred thousand of them imported into the island within four years, unable to speak a dialect intelligible even to each other. Yet out of this mixed, and, as you say, despicable mass, he forged a thunderbolt and hurled it at what? At the proudest blood in Europe, the Spaniard, and sent him home conquered [cheers]; at the most warlike blood in Europe, the French, and put them under his feet; at the pluckiest blood in Europe, the English, and they skulked home to Jamaica. [Applause.] Now if Cromwell was a general, at least this man was a soldier. I know it was a small territory; it was not as large as the continent; but it was as large as that Attica, which, with Athens for a capital, has filled the earth with its fame for two thousand years. We measure genius by quality, not by quantity.

Further—Cromwell was only a soldier; his fame stops there. Not one line in the statute book of Britain can be traced to Cromwell; not one step in the social life

[2]British general.

[3]Nineteenth-century British historian who wrote *History of England.*

of England finds its motive power in his brain. The state he founded went down with him to his grave. But this man no sooner put his hand on the helm of state than the ship steadied with an upright keel, and he began to evince a statesmanship as marvelous as his military genius. History says that the most statesmanlike act of Napoleon was his proclamation of 1802, at the Peace of Amiens, when, believing that the indelible loyalty of a native-born heart is always a sufficient basis on which to found an empire, he said: "Frenchmen, come home. I pardon the crimes of the last twelve years; I blot out its parties; I found my throne on the hearts of all Frenchmen,"—and twelve years of unclouded success showed how wisely he judged. That was in 1802. In 1800 this Negro made a proclamation; it runs thus: "Sons of St. Domingo, come home. We never meant to take your houses or your lands. The Negro only asked that liberty which God gave him. Your houses wait for you; your lands are ready; come and cultivate them"; and from Madrid and Paris, from Baltimore and New Orleans, the emigrant planters crowded home to enjoy their estates, under the pledged word that was never broken of a victorious slave. [Cheers.]

Again, Carlyle[4] has said, "The natural king is one who melts all wills into his own." At this moment he turned to his armies—poor, ill-clad, and half-starved—and said to them: Go back and work on these estates you have conquered; for an empire can be founded only on order and industry, and you can learn these virtues only there. And they went. The French admiral, who witnessed the scene, said that in a week his army melted back into peasants.

It was 1800. The world waited fifty years before, in 1846, Robert Peel[5] dared to venture, as a matter of practical statesmanship, the theory of free trade. Adam Smith[6] theorized, the French statesmen dreamed, but no man at the head of affairs had ever dared to risk it as a practical measure. Europe waited till 1846 before the most practical intellect in the world, the English, adopted the great economic formula of unfettered trade. But in 1800 this black, with the instinct of statesmanship, said to the committee who were drafting for him a Constitution: "Put at the head of the chapter of commerce that the ports of St. Domingo are open to the trade of the world." [Cheers.] With lofty indifference to race, superior to all envy or prejudice, Toussaint had formed this committee of eight white proprietors and one mulatto—not a soldier nor a Negro on the list, although Haitian history proves that, with the exception of Rigaud,[7] the rarest genius has always been shown by pure Negroes.

Again, it was 1800, at a time when England was poisoned on every page of her statute book with religious intolerance, when a man could not enter the House of Commons without taking an Episcopal communion, when every State in the Union, except Rhode Island, was full of the intensest religious bigotry. This man was a Negro. You say that is a superstitious blood. He was uneducated. You say that makes a man narrow-minded. He was a Catholic. Many say that is but another name for intolerance. And yet—Negro, Catholic, slave—he took his place by the side of Roger

[4]Author of the monumental history *The French Revolution.*

[5]Tory Prime Minister of Britain (1788–1850) who repealed taxes to encourage free trade.

[6]Eighteenth-century Scot who wrote *The Wealth of Nations;* father of *laissez faire* economics.

[7]Mulatto general who defeated the British in the Southern part of Haiti.

Williams, and said to his committee: "Make it the first line of my Constitution that I know no difference between religious beliefs." [Applause.]

Now, blue-eyed Saxon, proud of your race, go back with me to the commencement of the century, and select what statesman you please. Let him be either American or European; let him have a brain the result of six generations of culture; let him have the ripest training of university routine; let him add to it the better education of practical life; crown his temples with the silver of seventy years; and show me the man of Saxon lineage for whom his most sanguine admirer will wreathe a laurel rich as embittered foes have placed on the brow of this Negro—rare military skill, profound knowledge of human nature, content to blot out all party distinctions, and trust a state to the blood of its sons—anticipating Sir Robert Peel fifty years, and taking his station by the side of Roger Williams before any Englishman or American had won the right; and yet this is the record which the history of rival states makes up for this inspired black of St. Domingo. [Cheers.]

It was 1801. The Frenchmen who lingered on the island described its prosperity and order as almost incredible. You might trust a child with a bag of gold to go from Samana to Port-au-Prince without risk. Peace was in every household; the valleys laughed with fertility; culture climbed the mountains; the commerce of the world was represented in its harbors. At this time Europe concluded the Peace of Amiens, and Napoleon took his seat on the throne of France. He glanced his eyes across the Atlantic, and, with a single stroke of his pen, reduced Cayenne and Martinique back into chains. He then said to his Council, "What shall I do with St. Domingo?" The slaveholders said, "Give it to us." Napoleon turned to the Abbé Gregoire, "What is your opinion?" "I think those men would change their opinions, if they changed their skins." Colonel Vincent, who had been private secretary to Toussaint, wrote a letter to Napoleon, in which he said: "Sire, leave it alone; it is the happiest spot in your dominions; God raised this man to govern; races melt under his hand. He has saved you this island; for I know of my own knowledge that, when the Republic could not have lifted a finger to prevent it, George III offered him any title and any revenue if he would hold the island under the British crown. He refused, and saved it for France." Napoleon turned away from his Council, and is said to have remarked, "I have sixty thousand idle troops; I must find them something to do." He meant to say, "I am about to seize the crown; I dare not do it in the faces of sixty thousand republican soldiers: I must give them work at a distance to do." The gossip of Paris gives another reason for his expedition against St. Domingo. It is said that the satirists of Paris had christened Toussaint, the Black Napoleon; and Bonaparte hated his black shadow. Toussaint had unfortunately once addressed him a letter, "The first of the blacks to the first of the whites." He did not like the comparison. You would think it too slight a motive. But let me remind you of the present Napoleon, that when the epigrammatists of Paris christened his wasteful and tasteless expense at Versailles, *Soulouquerie,* from the name of Soulouque, the Black Emperor, he deigned to issue a specific order forbidding the use of the word. The Napoleon blood is very sensitive. So Napoleon resolved to crush Toussaint from one motive or another, from the prompting of ambition, or dislike of this resemblance, which was very close. If either imitated the other, it must have been the white, since the Negro preceded him several years. They were very much alike, and they were very French—French even in vanity, common to both. You remember Bonaparte's vainglorious words to his soldiers at the Pyramids: "Forty centuries look down upon us." In the same mood, Toussaint said to the French captain who urged him to go to France in his frigate, "Sir, your ship is not large enough to carry me." Napoleon, you know, could never bear the military uniform. He hated the restraint of his rank; he loved to put on the gray coat of the Little Corporal, and wander in the camp. Toussaint also never could bear a uniform. He wore a plain coat, and often the yellow Madras handkerchief of the slaves. A French lieutenant once called him a maggot in a yellow handkerchief. Toussaint took him prisoner next day, and sent him home to his mother. Like Napoleon, he could fast many days; could dictate to three secretaries at once; could wear out four or five horses. Like Napoleon, no man ever divined his purpose or penetrated his plan. He was only a Negro, and so, in him, they called it hypocrisy. In Bonaparte we style it diplomacy. For instance, three attempts made to assassinate him all failed, from not firing at the right spot. If they thought he was in the north in a carriage, he would be in the south on horseback; if they thought he was in the city in a house, he would be in the field in a tent. They once riddled his carriage with bullets; he was on horseback on the other side. The seven Frenchmen who did it were arrested. They expected to be shot. The next day was some saint's day; he ordered them to be placed before the high altar, and, when the priest reached the prayer for forgiveness, came down from his high seat, repeated it with him, and permitted them to go unpunished. [Cheers.] He had that wit common to all great commanders, which makes its way in a camp. His soldiers getting disheartened, he filled a large vase with powder, and, scattering six grains of rice in it, shook them up, and said: "See, there is the white, there is the black; what are you afraid of?" So when people came to him in great numbers for office, as it is reported they do sometimes even in Washington, he learned the first words of a Catholic prayer in Latin, and, repeating it, would say, "Do you understand that?" "No, sir." "What! want an office, and not know Latin? Go home and learn it!"

Then, again, like Napoleon—like genius always—he had confidence in his power to rule men. You remember when Bonaparte returned from Elba, and Louis XVIII sent an army against him, Bonaparte descended from his carriage, opened his coat, offering his breast to their muskets and saying, "Frenchmen, it is the Emperor!" and they ranged themselves behind him, *his* soldiers, shouting, *"Vive l'Empereur!"* That was in 1815. Twelve years before, Toussaint, finding that four of his regiments had deserted and gone to Leclerc,[8] drew his sword, flung it on the grass, went across the field to them, folded his arms, and said, "Children, can you point a bayonet at me?" The blacks fell on their knees, praying his pardon. His bitterest enemies watched him, and none of them charged him with love of money, sensuality, or cruel use of power. The only instance in which his sternest critic has charged him with severity is this. During a tumult, a few white proprietors who had returned, trusting his proclamation, were killed. His nephew, General Moise, was accused of indecision in quelling the riot. He assembled a court-martial, and, on its verdict, ordered his own nephew to be shot, sternly Roman in thus keeping his promise of protection to the whites. Above the lust of gold, pure in private life, generous in the use

[8]Brother-in-law of Napoleon Bonaparte and head of the French expeditionary forces in Haiti.

of his power, it was against such a man that Napoleon sent his army, giving to General Leclerc, the husband of his beautiful sister Pauline, thirty thousand of his best troops, with orders to reintroduce slavery. Among these soldiers came all of Toussaint's old mulatto rivals and foes.

Holland lent sixty ships. England promised by special message to be neutral; and you know neutrality means sneering at freedom and sending arms to tyrants. [Loud and long-continued applause.] England promised neutrality, and the black looked out on the whole civilized world marshaled against him. America, full of slaves, of course was hostile. Only the Yankee sold him poor muskets at a very high price. [Laughter.] Mounting his horse, and riding to the eastern end of the island, Samana, he looked out on a sight such as no native had ever seen before. Sixty ships of the line, crowded by the best soldiers of Europe, rounded the point. They were soldiers who had never yet met an equal, whose tread, like Caesar's, had shaken Europe—soldiers who had scaled the Pyramids, and planted the French banners on the walls of Rome. He looked a moment, counted the flotilla, let the reins fall on the neck of his horse, and, turning to Christophe, exclaimed: "All France is come to Haiti; they can only come to make us slaves; and we are lost!" He then recognized the only mistake of his life—his confidence in Bonaparte, which had led him to disband his army.

Returning to the hills, he issued the only proclamation which bears his name and breathes vengeance: "My children, France comes to make us slaves. God gave us liberty; France has no right to take it away. Burn the cities, destroy the harvests, tear up the roads with cannon, poison the wells, show the white man the hell he comes to make"; and he was obeyed. [Applause.] When the great William of Orange saw Louis XIV cover Holland with troops, he said, "Break down the dikes, give Holland back to ocean"; and Europe said, "Sublime!" When Alexander saw the armies of France descend upon Russia, he said, "Burn Moscow, starve back the invaders"; and Europe said, "Sublime!" This black saw all Europe marshaled to crush him, and gave to his people the same heroic example of defiance.

It is true, the scene grows bloodier as we proceed. But, remember, the white man fitly accompanied his infamous attempt to *reduce freemen to slavery* with every bloody and cruel device that bitter and shameless hate could invent. Aristocracy is always cruel. The black man met the attempt, as every such attempt should be met, with war to the hilt. In his first struggle to gain his freedom, he had been generous and merciful, saved lives and pardoned enemies, as the people in every age and clime have always done when rising against aristocrats. Now, to save his liberty, the Negro exhausted every means, seized every weapon, and turned back the hateful invaders with a vengeance as terrible as their own, though even now he refused to be cruel.

Leclerc sent word to Christophe that he was about to land at Cape City. Christophe said, "Toussaint is governor of the island. I will send to him for permission. If without it a French soldier sets foot on shore, I will burn the town, and fight over its ashes."

Leclerc landed. Christophe took two thousand *white* men, women, and children, and carried them to the mountains in safety, then with his own hands set fire to the splendid palace which French architects had just finished for him, and in forty hours the place was in ashes. The battle was fought in its streets, and the French driven back to their boats. [Cheers.] Wherever they went, they were met with fire and sword. Once, resisting an attack, the blacks, Frenchmen born, shouted the "Marseilles Hymn," and the French soldiers stood still; they could not fight the "Marseillaise." And it was not till their officers sabered them on that they advanced, and then they were beaten. Beaten in the field, the French then took to lies. They issued proclamations, saying, "We do not come to make you slaves; this man Toussaint tells you lies. Join us, and you shall have the rights you claim." They cheated every one of his officers, except Christophe and Dessalines, and his own brother Pierre, and finally these also deserted him, and he was left alone. He then sent word to Leclerc, "I will submit. I could continue the struggle for years—could prevent a single Frenchman from safely quitting your camp. But I hate bloodshed. I have fought only for the liberty of my race. Guarantee that, I will submit and come in." He took the oath to be a faithful citizen; and on the same crucifix Leclerc swore that he should be faithfully protected, and that the island should be free. As the French general glanced along the line of his splendidly equipped troops, and saw, opposite, Toussaint's ragged, ill-armed followers, he said to him, "L'Ouverture, had you continued the war, where could you have got arms?" "I would have taken yours" was the Spartan reply. [Cheers.] He went down to his house in peace; it was summer, Leclerc remembered that the fever months were coming, when his army would be in hospitals, and when one motion of that royal hand would sweep his troops into the sea. He was too dangerous to be left at large. So they summoned him to attend a council; and here is the only charge made against him—the only charge. They say he was fool enough to go. Grant it; what was the record? The white man lies shrewdly to cheat the Negro. Knight-errantry was truth. The foulest insult you can offer a man since the Crusades is, You lie. Of Toussaint, Hermona, the Spanish general, who knew him well, said, "He was the purest soul God ever put into a body." Of him history bears witness, "He never broke his word." Maitland was traveling in the depths of the woods to meet Toussaint, when he was met by a messenger, and told that he was betrayed. He went on, and met Toussaint, who showed him two letters—one from the French general, offering him any rank if he would put Maitland in his power, and the other his reply. It was, "Sir, I have promised the Englishman that he shall go back." [Cheers.] Let it stand, therefore, that the Negro, truthful as a knight of old, was cheated by his lying foe. Which race has reason to be proud of such a record?

But he was not cheated. He was under espionage. Suppose he had refused: the government would have doubted him, would have found some cause to arrest him. He probably reasoned thus: "If I go willingly, I shall be treated accordingly"; and he went. The moment he entered the room, the officers drew their swords, and told him he was prisoner; and one young lieutenant who was present says, "He was not at all surprised, but seemed very sad." They put him on shipboard, and weighed anchor for France. As the island faded from his sight, he turned to the captain, and said, "You think you have rooted up the tree of liberty, but I am only a branch; I have planted the tree so deep that all France can never root it up." [Cheers.] Arrived in Paris, he was flung into jail, and Napoleon sent his secretary, Caffarelli, to him, supposing he had buried large treasures. He listened a while, then replied, "Young man, it is true I have lost treasures, but they are not such as you come to seek." He was then sent to the Castle of St. Joux, to a dungeon twelve feet by twenty, built wholly of stone, with a narrow window, high up on the side, looking out on the snows of Switzerland. In winter, ice covers the floor; in summer, it is damp and wet. In this living tomb the child of the sunny tropic was left to die. From this dungeon he wrote two letters to Napoleon. One of them ran thus:

> *Sire, I am a French citizen. I never broke a law. By the grace of God, I have saved for you the best island of your realm. Sire, of your mercy grant me justice.*

Napoleon never answered the letters. The commandant allowed him five francs a day for food and fuel. Napoleon heard of it, and reduced the sum to three. The luxurious usurper, who complained that the English government was stingy because it allowed him only six thousand dollars a month, stooped from his throne to cut down a dollar to a half, and still Toussaint did not die quick enough.

This dungeon was a tomb. The story is told that, in Josephine's time, a young French marquis was placed there, and the girl to whom he was betrothed went to the Empress and prayed for his release. Said Josephine to her, "Have a model of it made, and bring it to me." Josephine placed it near Napoleon. He said, "Take it away—it is horrible!" She put it on his footstool, and he kicked it from him. She held it to him the third time, and said, "Sire, in this horrible dungeon you have put a man to die." "Take him out," said Napoleon, and the girl saved her lover. In this tomb Toussaint was buried, but he did not die fast enough. Finally, the commandant was told to go into Switzerland, to carry the keys of the dungeon with him, and to stay four days; when he returned, Toussaint was found starved to death. That imperial assassin was taken twelve years after to his prison at St. Helena, planned for a tomb, as he had planned that of Toussaint, and there he whined away his dying hours in pitiful complaints of curtains and titles, of dishes and rides. God grant that when some future Plutarch shall weigh the great men of our epoch, the whites against the blacks, he do not put that whining child at St. Helena into one scale, and into the other the Negro meeting death like a Roman, without a murmur, in the solitude of his icy dungeon!

From the moment he was betrayed, the Negroes began to doubt the French, and rushed to arms. Soon every Negro but Maurepas deserted the French. Leclerc summoned Maurepas to his side. He came, loyally bringing with him five hundred soldiers. Leclerc spiked his epaulettes to his shoulders, shot him, and flung him into the sea. He took his five hundred soldiers on shore, shot them on the edge of a pit, and tumbled them in. Desalines from the mountain saw it, and, selecting five hundred French officers from his prisons, hung them on separate trees in sight of Leclerc's camp; and born, as I was, not far from Bunker Hill, I have yet found no reason to think he did wrong. [Cheers.] They murdered Pierre Toussaint's wife at his own door, and after such treatment that it was mercy when they killed her. The maddened husband, who had but a year before saved the lives of twelve hundred white men, carried his next thousand prisoners and sacrificed them on her grave.

The French exhausted every form of torture. The Negroes were bound together and thrown into the sea; anyone who floated was shot, others sunk with cannon balls tied to their feet; some smothered with sulphur fumes, others strangled, scourged to death, gibbeted; sixteen of Toussaint's officers were chained to rocks in desert islands, others in marshes, and left to be devoured by poisonous reptiles and insects. Rochambeau sent to Cuba for bloodhounds. When they arrived, the young girls went down to the wharf, decked the hounds with ribbons and flowers, kissed their necks, and, seated in the amphitheater, the women clapped their hands to see a Negro thrown to these dogs, previously starved to rage. But the Negroes besieged this very city so closely that these same girls, in their misery, ate the very hounds they had welcomed.

Then flashed forth that defying courage and sublime endurance which show how alike all races are when tried in the same furnace. The Roman wife, whose husband faltered when Nero ordered him to kill himself, seized the dagger and, mortally wounding her own body, cried, "Poetus, it is not hard to die." The world records it with proud tears. Just in the same spirit, when a Negro colonel was ordered to execution and trembled, his wife seized his sword and, giving herself a death wound, said, "Husband, death is sweet when liberty is gone."

The war went on. Napoleon sent over thirty thousand more soldiers. But disaster still followed his efforts. What the sword did not devour, the fever ate up. Leclerc died. Pauline carried his body back to France. Napoleon met her at Bordeaux, saying, "Sister, I gave you an army—you bring me back ashes." Rochambeau—the Rochambeau of our history—left in command of eight thousand troops, sent word to Dessalines: "When I take you, I will not shoot you like a soldier, or hang you like a white man; I will whip you to death like a slave." Dessalines chased him from battlefield to battlefield, from fort to fort, and finally shut him up in Samana. Heating cannon balls to destroy his fleet, Dessalines learned that Rochambeau had begged of the British admiral to cover his troops with the English flag, and the generous Negro suffered the boaster to embark undisturbed.

Some doubt the courage of the Negro. Go to Haiti, and stand on those fifty thousand graves of the best soldiers France ever had, and ask them what they think of the Negro's sword. And if that does not satisfy you, go to France, to the splendid mausoleum of the Counts of Rochambeau, and to the eight thousand graves of Frenchmen who skulked home under the English flag, and ask them. And if that does not satisfy you, come home, and if it had been October 1859, you might have come by way of quaking Virginia, and asked her what she thought of Negro courage.

You may also remember this—that we Saxons were slaves about four hundred years, sold with the land, and our fathers never raised a finger to end that slavery. They waited till Christianity and civilization, till commerce and the discovery of America, melted away their chains. Spartacus in Italy led the slaves of Rome against the empress of the world. She murdered him, and crucified them. There never was a slave rebellion successful but once, and that was in St. Domingo. Every race has been, some time or other, in chains. But there never was a race that, weakened and degraded by such chattel slavery, unaided, tore off its own fetters, forged them into swords, and won its liberty on the battlefield, but one, and that was the black race of St. Domingo. God grant that the wise vigor of our government may avert that necessity from our land, may raise into peaceful liberty the four million committed to our care, and show under democratic institutions a statesmanship as farsighted as that of England, as brave as the Negro of Haiti!

So much for the courage of the Negro. Now look at his endurance. In 1805 he said to the white men, "This island is ours; not a white foot shall touch it." Side by side with him stood the South American republics, planted by the best blood of the countrymen of Lope de Vega and Cervantes. They topple over so often that you could no more daguerreotype their crumbling fragments than you could the waves of the ocean. And yet, at their side, the Negro has kept his island sacredly to himself. It is said that at first, with rare patriotism, the Haitian government ordered the destruction of all the sugar plantations remaining, and discouraged its culture, deeming that the temptation which lured the French back again to attempt their enslavement. Burn over New York tonight, fill up her canals, sink every ship, destroy her railroads, blot out every remnant of education from her sons, let her be ignorant and penniless, with nothing but her hands to begin the world again—how much could she do in sixty years? And Europe, too, would lend you money, but she will not lend Haiti a dollar. Haiti, from the ruins of her colonial dependence, is become a civilized state, the seventh nation in the catalogue of commerce with this country, inferior in morals and education to none of the West Indian isles. Foreign merchants trust her courts as willingly as they do our own. Thus far, she has foiled the ambition of Spain, the greed of England, and the malicious statesmanship of Calhoun. Toussaint made her what she is. In this work there was grouped around him a score of men, mostly of pure Negro blood, who ably seconded his efforts. They were able in war and skillful in civil affairs, but not, like him, remarkable for that rare mingling of high qualities which alone makes true greatness, and insures a man leadership among those otherwise almost his equals. Toussaint was indisputably their chief. Courage, purpose, endurance—these are the tests. He did plant a state so deep that all the world has not been able to root it up.

I would call him Napoleon, but Napoleon made his way to empire over broken oaths and through a sea of blood. This man never broke his word. "NO RETALIATION" was his great motto and the rule of his life; and the last words uttered to his son in France were these: "My boy, you will one day go back to St. Domingo; forget that France murdered your father." I would call him Cromwell, but Cromwell was only a soldier, and the state he founded went down with him into his grave. I would call him Washington, but the great Virginian held slaves. This man risked his empire rather than permit the slave trade in the humblest village of his dominions.

You think me a fanatic tonight, for you read history, not with your eyes, but with your prejudices. But fifty years hence, when Truth gets a hearing, the Muse of History will put Phocion for the Greek, and Brutus for the Roman, Hampden for England, Fayette for France, choose Washington as the bright, consummate flower of our earlier civilization, and John Brown the ripe fruit of our noonday [thunders of applause], then, dipping her pen in the sunlight, will write in the clear blue, above them all, the name of the soldier, the statesman, the martyr, TOUSSAINT L'OUVERTURE. [Long-continued applause.]

1863

Thomas Wentworth Higginson 1823–1911

He is remembered, when he is remembered at all, as Emily Dickinson's well-meaning but short-sighted "preceptor," who in co-editing the first collection of her poetry smoothed away the vivid irregularity of her genius. By profession he was a Protestant clergyman; yet he organized and commanded the first regiment of black troops in the Civil War. By heritage, he was a Boston Brahmin; yet in 1854 he led a vigilante assault to free a fugitive slave from a federal courthouse, in the course of which a marshal was shot to death. He was one of nineteenth-century America's best-known essayists and speakers; yet it was political activism on behalf of abolition, women's rights, and the demands of working people that gave joy to much of his life. His long career may seem to our later eyes filled with paradoxes if not outright contradictions, yet to Thomas Wentworth Higginson, it was a life which, in looking back, he could describe as *Cheerful Yesterdays*.

The Higginsons, Stephen and Louisa Storrow, were descended from old Massachusetts and New Hampshire families. Wentworth, as he came to be called was their tenth and last child, born December 22, 1823, in their home on "Professor's Row" in Cambridge, Massachusetts. The extensive Higginson library, the intellectual community of Cambridge, and later the broad education provided by Harvard College, which Higginson entered in 1837 when he was 13, helped prepare him for life as an intellectual in what was then America's intellectual capital. He credited to his mother the development of the "leading motives" of his life: "the love of personal liberty, of religious freedom, and of the equality of the sexes." But like many of his friends, Higginson was deeply influenced by the Transcendentalism of Emerson, Theodore Parker, and Margaret Fuller. Whatever its specific doctrines, the movement seemed to sweep away the constraints of tradition and to offer to a new generation the opportunity for carrying out "numberless projects of social reform."

After graduating with the class of 1841, Higginson vacillated between the life of a Poet and that of a Preacher. He found little to interest him in Christian doctrine and was rather put off by church ritual. Still, the ministry did seem to provide opportunities for pursuing his passion for liberal reform, and especially the abolitionism to which he had become increasingly committed. "Preaching alone I should love," he wrote, "but I feel inwardly that something more will be sought of me—An aesthetic life—how beautiful—but the life of a Reformer, a People's Guide 'battling for the right'—glorious, but, oh how hard!" This question of a vocation—or even an appropriate subject—would haunt Higginson throughout his life and perhaps explains why, despite his many talents and vigorous style, he never emerged as one of the outstanding writers of the century.

In 1847, Higginson was chosen by the First Religious Society of Newburyport as its pastor; the essentially conservative parishioners came to regard him and his new bride, Mary Channing, "as if we were handsome spotted panthers, good to look at and roaring finely—something to be proud of, perhaps—but not to be approached incautiously, or too near." His ministry would last only a year—he later served six years at the decidedly unorthodox Free Church of Worcester—but Higginson quickly became involved with the concerns that would shape his life. He preached effectively against drink, and played an active role in the state Temperance Convention, as he later would in national temperance organizations. He opened an evening school for working people, and urged labor reforms, like the ten-hour day. He became active on behalf of women, in 1850 signing the call for the first national women's rights convention; later, after breaking with Elizabeth Cady Stanton and Susan B. Anthony over the issue of the Fifteenth Amendment, Higginson became a founder of the American Women's Suffrage Association and was for fourteen years co-editor of its periodical, *Women's Journal.*

But his primary commitment before the Civil War was to the abolition of slavery. While minister at Newburyport, he accepted John Greenleaf Whittier's nomination to run for Congress as the candidate of the anti-slavery Free Soil party—an action which essentially ended that ministry. After the passage of the Fugitive Slave Act in 1850, he again ran for Congress, urging Newburyport voters to disobey the Act. In

May of 1854 he was one of the main planners, and as events transpired a primary actor, in an attack on the Boston Court House designed, unsuccessfully, to free the fugitive Anthony Burns from the slave power. Later, Higginson would travel and preach on behalf of the anti-slavery forces in "Bloody Kansas," and he would become one of the "Secret Six" who raised money and support for John Brown's raid. Late in the 1850s he wrote a series of essays on black rebellions, which would not be published in the *Atlantic* until after the war had broken out—part of one of these, on Nat Turner, is printed here. But his major contribution to the work of Emancipation was to undertake the training and command of the First South Carolina Volunteers. Higginson's account of his command—and his education—is contained in *Army Life in a Black Regiment,* one of the most fascinating books to come out of the Civil War.

In the 46 years he lived after the war, Higginson remained active in a variety of causes, though he devoted himself increasingly to the pen and the lectern. He wrote volumes of history for adults and children, biographies of Margaret Fuller, Longfellow, and Whittier, an unsuccessful novel, *Malbone* (1870), interesting regional sketches, *Oldport Days* (1869), one of the few sensible books on women by a man, *Common Sense About Women* (1881), and a flow of essays about writing and writers.

One of these, a "Letter to a Young Contributer" published in the *Atlantic* just as he was leaving to take up his army command, brought a flood of responses, among them an enigmatic note from a young woman named Emily Dickinson, who wrote asking "if my verse is alive." Thus began an irregular correspondence of twenty-five years, during which Dickinson played the role of pupil and Higginson that of "a preceptorship which," he wrote, "it is almost needless to say did not exist." His account of their only extended meeting is included below, as are a number of her letters to him. Higginson's advice to delay publication until she had "mastered" poetic orthodoxy has been accused of being the cause of Dickinson's failure to print her poems during her lifetime—rather an insubstantial notion, given Dickinson's own ideas about publication and how she chose to share her poems. Undoubtedly, Higginson did not fully appreciate her work and he certainly took objectionable liberties in "regularizing" and titling her poems when he co-edited the first volume of her verse after her death. That is, he shared many of the critical limits of his time—including a distaste for Whitman. But he did recognize in Dickinson a "wholly new and original poetic genius" and he played a significant role in bringing her into print.

But history is nothing, if not ironic. Perhaps Higginson would have smiled to know that his long life had narrowed in literary history to a footnote in the tale of Emily Dickinson. And, perhaps, he would smile again to find his own work restored to a little of its independent value.

Paul Lauter
Trinity College

PRIMARY WORKS

The Writings of Thomas Wentworth Higginson, 7 vols, 1900; *Letters and Journals of Thomas Wentworth Higginson,* ed. Mary Thacher Higginson, 1921, 1969; *Black Rebellion,* ed. James M. McPherson, 1969.

SECONDARY WORKS

Anna Mary Wells, *Dear Preceptor: The Life and Times of Thomas Wentworth Higginson,* 1963; Howard N. Meyer, *Colonel of the Black Regiment: The Life of Thomas Wentworth Higginson,* 1967; Tilden G. Edelstein, *Strange Enthusiasm: A Life of Thomas Wentworth Higginson,* 1968; James W. Tuttleton, *Thomas Wentworth Higginson,* 1978.

from Nat Turner's Insurrection

During the year 1831, up to the 23d of August, the Virginia newspapers seem to have been absorbed in the momentous problems which then occupied the minds of intelligent American citizens: What Gen. Jackson should do with the scolds, and what with the disreputables?[1] should South Carolina be allowed to nullify?[2] and would the wives of cabinet ministers call on Mrs. Eaton?[3] It is an unfailing opiate to turn over the drowsy files of the Richmond *Enquirer,* until the moment when those dry and dusty pages are suddenly kindled into flame by the torch of Nat Turner. Then the terror flared on increasing, until the remotest Southern States were found shuddering at nightly rumors of insurrection; until far-off European colonies—Antigua, Martinique, Caraccas, Tortola—recognized by some secret sympathy the same epidemic alarms; until the very boldest words of freedom were reported as uttered in the Virginia House of Delegates with unclosed doors; until an obscure young man named Garrison was indicted at common law in North Carolina, and had a price set upon his head by the Legislature of Georgia.[4]

Near the south-eastern border of Virginia, in Southampton County, there is a neighborhood known as "The Cross Keys." It lies fifteen miles from Jerusalem, the county-town, or "court-house," seventy miles from Norfolk, and about as far from Richmond. It is some ten or fifteen miles from Murfreesborough in North Carolina, and about twenty-five from the Great Dismal Swamp. Up to Sunday, the 21st of August, 1831, there was nothing to distinguish it from any other rural, lethargic, slipshod Virginia neighborhood, with the due allotment of mansion-houses and log huts, tobacco-fields and "old-fields," horses, dogs, negroes, "poor white folks," so called, and other white folks, poor without being called so. One of these last was Joseph Travis, who had recently married the widow of one Putnam Moore, and had unfortunately wedded to himself her negroes also.

In the woods on the plantation of Joseph Travis, upon the Sunday just named, six slaves met at noon for what is called in the Northern States a picnic, and in the Southern a barbecue. The bill of fare was to be simple: one brought a pig, and another some brandy, giving to the meeting an aspect so cheaply convivial that no one would have imagined it to be the final consummation of a conspiracy which had been for six months in preparation. In this plot four of the men had been already initiated,—Henry, Hark or Hercules, Nelson, and Sam. Two others were novices, Will and Jack by name. The party had remained together from twelve to three o'clock, when a seventh man joined them,—a short, stout, powerfully built person, of dark mulatto complexion, and strongly marked African features, but with a face full of expression and resolution. This was Nat Turner.

He was at this time nearly thirty-one years old, having been born on the 2d of

[1]Political factions during Andrew Jackson's presidency.

[2]The doctrine that states had the right, within their territory, to nullify a federal law.

[3]Peggy O'Neale, originally a bar-maid, had married President Andrew Jackson's Secretary of War, John H. Eaton. Other members of the cabinet, notably John C. Calhoun, and their wives tried to ostracize her socially, and the conflict carried over into political infighting within the administration.

[4]William Lloyd Garrison had, indeed, had a price set on his head after he began publishing *The Liberator.*

October, 1800. He had belonged originally to Benjamin Turner,—from whom he took his last name, slaves having usually no patronymic;—had then been transferred to Putnam Moore, and then to his present owner. He had, by his own account, felt himself singled out from childhood for some great work; and he had some peculiar marks on his person, which, joined to his mental precocity, were enough to occasion, among his youthful companions, a superstitious faith in his gifts and destiny. He had some mechanical ingenuity also; experimentalized very early in making paper, gunpowder, pottery, and in other arts, which, in later life, he was found thoroughly to understand. His moral faculties appeared strong, so that white witnesses admitted that he had never been known to swear an oath, to drink a drop of spirits, or to commit a theft. And, in general, so marked were his early peculiarities that people said "he had too much sense to be raised; and, if he was, he would never be of any use as a slave." This impression of personal destiny grew with his growth: he fasted, prayed, preached, read the Bible, heard voices when he walked behind his plough, and communicated his revelations to the awe-struck slaves. They told him, in return, that, "If they had his sense, they would not serve any master in the world."

The biographies of slaves can hardly be individualized; they belong to the class. We know bare facts; it is only the general experience of human beings in like condition which can clothe them with life. The outlines are certain, the details are inferential. Thus, for instance, we know that Nat Turner's young wife was a slave; we know that she belonged to a different master from himself; we know little more than this, but this is much. For this is equivalent to saying, that, by day or by night, her husband had no more power to protect her than the man who lies bound upon a plundered vessel's deck has power to protect his wife on board the pirate schooner disappearing in the horizon. She may be well treated, she may be outraged; it is in the powerlessness that the agony lies. There is, indeed, one thing more which we do know of this young woman: the Virginia newspapers state that she was tortured under the lash, after her husband's execution, to make her produce his papers: this is all.

What his private experiences and special privileges or wrongs may have been, it is therefore now impossible to say. Travis was declared to be "more humane and fatherly to his slaves than any man in the county;" but it is astonishing how often this phenomenon occurs in the contemporary annals of slave insurrections. The chairman of the county court also stated, in pronouncing sentence, that Nat Turner had spoken of his master as "only too indulgent;" but this, for some reason, does not appear in his printed Confession, which only says, "He was a kind master, and placed the greatest confidence in me." It is very possible that it may have been so, but the printed accounts of Nat Turner's person look suspicious: he is described in Gov. Floyd's proclamation as having a scar on one of his temples, also one on the back of his neck, and a large knot on one of the bones of his right arm, produced by a blow; and although these were explained away in Virginia newspapers as having been produced by fights with his companions, yet such affrays are entirely foreign to the admitted habits of the man. It must therefore remain an open question, whether the scars and the knot were produced by black hands or by white.

Whatever Nat Turner's experiences of slavery might have been, it is certain that his plans were not suddenly adopted, but that he had brooded over them for years. To this day there are traditions among the Virginia slaves of the keen devices of "Prophet Nat." If he was caught with lime and lampblack in hand, conning over a half-finished county-map on the barn-door, he was always "planning what to do if he were blind;" or, "studying how to get to Mr. Francis's house." When he had called a meeting of slaves, and some poor whites came eavesdropping, the poor whites at once became the subjects for discussion: he incidentally mentioned that the masters had been heard threatening to drive them away; one slave had been ordered to shoot Mr. Jones's pigs, another to tear down Mr. Johnson's fences. The poor whites, Johnson and Jones, ran home to see to their homesteads, and were better friends than ever to Prophet Nat.

He never was a Baptist preacher, though such vocation has often been attributed to him. The impression arose from his having immersed himself, during one of his periods of special enthusiasm, together with a poor white man named Brantley. "About this time," he says in his Confession, "I told these things to a white man, on whom it had a wonderful effect; and he ceased from his wickedness, and was attacked immediately with a cutaneous eruption, and the blood oozed from the pores of his skin, and after praying and fasting nine days he was healed. And the Spirit appeared to me again, and said, as the Saviour had been baptized, so should we be also; and when the white people would not let us be baptized by the church, we went down into the water together, in the sight of many who reviled us, and were baptized by the Spirit. After this I rejoiced greatly, and gave thanks to God."

The religious hallucinations narrated in his Confession seem to have been as genuine as the average of such things, and are very well expressed. The account reads quite like Jacob Behmen. He saw white spirits and black spirits contending in the skies; the sun was darkened, the thunder rolled. "And the Holy Ghost was with me, and said, 'Behold me as I stand in the heavens!' And I looked, and saw the forms of men in different attitudes. And there were lights in the sky, to which the children of darkness gave other names than what they really were; for they were the lights of the Saviour's hands, stretched forth from east to west, even as they were extended on the cross on Calvary, for the redemption of sinners." He saw drops of blood on the corn: this was Christ's blood, shed for man. He saw on the leaves in the woods letters and numbers and figures of men,—the same symbols which he had seen in the skies. On May 12, 1828, the Holy Spirit appeared to him, and proclaimed that the yoke of Jesus must fall on him, and he must fight against the serpent when the sign appeared. Then came an eclipse of the sun in February, 1831: this was the sign; then he must arise and prepare himself, and slay his enemies with their own weapons; then also the seal was removed from his lips, and then he confided his plans to four associates.

When he came, therefore, to the barbecue on the appointed Sunday, and found not these four only, but two others, his first question to the intruders was, how they came thither. To this Will answered manfully, that his life was worth no more than the others, and "his liberty was as dear to him." This admitted him to confidence; and as Jack was known to be entirely under Hark's influence, the strangers were no bar to their discussion. Eleven hours they remained there, in anxious consultation: one can imagine those dusky faces, beneath the funereal woods, and amid the flickering of pine-knot torches, preparing that stern revenge whose shuddering echoes should ring through the land so long. Two things were at last decided: to begin their work that night; and to begin it with a massacre so swift and irresistible as to create in a few days more terror than many battles, and so spare the need of future bloodshed. "It was agreed that we should commence at home on that night, and, until we had armed and equipped ourselves and gained sufficient force, neither age nor sex was to be spared: which was invariably adhered to."

John Brown invaded Virginia with nineteen men, and with the avowed resolution to take no life but in self-defence. Nat Turner attacked Virginia from within, with six men, and with the determination to spare no life until his power was established. John Brown intended to pass rapidly through Virginia, and then retreat to the mountains.[5] Nat Turner intended to "conquer Southampton County as the white men did in the Revolution, and then retreat, if necessary, to the Dismal Swamp." Each plan was deliberately matured; each was in its way practicable; but each was defeated by a single false step, as will soon appear.

We must pass over the details of horror, as they occurred during the next twenty-four hours. Swift and stealthy as Indians, the black men passed from house to house,—not pausing, not hesitating, as their terrible work went on. In one thing they were humaner than Indians, or than white men fighting against Indians: there was no gratuitous outrage beyond the death-blow itself, no insult, no mutilation; but in every house they entered, that blow fell on man, woman, and child,—nothing that had a white skin was spared. From every house they took arms and ammunition, and from a few money. On every plantation they found recruits: those dusky slaves, so obsequious to their master the day before, so prompt to sing and dance before his Northern visitors, were all swift to transform themselves into fiends of retribution now; show them sword or musket, and they grasped it, though it were an heirloom from Washington himself. The troop increased from house to house,—first to fifteen, then to forty, then to sixty. Some were armed with muskets, some with axes, some with scythes, some came on their master's horses. As the numbers increased, they could be divided, and the awful work was carried on more rapidly still. The plan then was for an advanced guard of horsemen to approach each house at a gallop, and surround it till the others came up. Meanwhile, what agonies of terror must have taken place within, shared alike by innocent and by guilty! what memories of wrongs inflicted on those dusky creatures, by some,—what innocent participation, by others, in the penance! The outbreak lasted for but forty-eight hours; but, during that period, fifty-five whites were slain, without the loss of a single slave.

One fear was needless, which to many a husband and father must have intensified the last struggle. These negroes had been systematically brutalized from childhood; they had been allowed no legalized or permanent marriage; they had beheld around them an habitual licentiousness, such as can scarcely exist except under slavery; some of them had seen their wives and sisters habitually polluted by the husbands and the brothers of these fair white women who were now absolutely in their power. Yet I have looked through the Virginia newspapers of that time in vain for one charge of an indecent outrage on a woman against these triumphant and terrible slaves. Wherever they went, there went death, and that was all. It is reported by some of the contemporary newspapers, that a portion of this abstinence was the result of deliberate consultation among the insurrectionists; that some of them were resolved on taking the white women for wives, but were overruled by Nat Turner. If so, he is the only American slave-leader of whom we know certainly that he rose above the ordinary level of slave vengeance; and Mrs. Stowe's picture of Dred's[6] purposes is then precisely typical of his: "Whom the Lord saith unto us, 'Smite,' them will we smite.

[5]Higginson knew whereof he spoke; he had been among Brown's most intimate confidants prior to the raid on Harpers Ferry.

[6]In *Dred,* a novel by Harriet Beecher Stowe.

We will not torment them with the scourge and fire, nor defile their women as they have done with ours. But we will slay them utterly, and consume them from off the face of the earth."[7]

When the number of adherents had increased to fifty or sixty, Nat Turner judged it time to strike at the county-seat, Jerusalem. Thither a few white fugitives had already fled, and couriers might thence be despatched for aid to Richmond and Petersburg, unless promptly intercepted. Besides, he could there find arms, ammunition, and money; though they had already obtained, it is dubiously reported, from eight hundred to one thousand dollars. On the way it was necessary to pass the plantation of Mr. Parker, three miles from Jerusalem. Some of the men wished to stop here and enlist some of their friends. Nat Turner objected, as the delay might prove dangerous; he yielded at last, and it proved fatal.

He remained at the gate with six or eight men; thirty or forty went to the house, half a mile distant. They remained too long, and he went alone to hasten them. During his absence a party of eighteen white men came up suddenly, dispersing the small guard left at the gate; and when the main body of slaves emerged from the house, they encountered, for the first time, their armed masters. The blacks halted; the whites advanced cautiously within a hundred yards, and fired a volley; on its being returned, they broke into disorder, and hurriedly retreated, leaving some wounded on the ground. The retreating whites were pursued, and were saved only by falling in with another band of fresh men from Jerusalem, with whose aid they turned upon the slaves, who in their turn fell into confusion. Turner, Hark, and about twenty men on horseback retreated in some order; the rest were scattered. The leader still planned to reach Jerusalem by a private way, thus evading pursuit; but at last decided to stop for the night, in the hope of enlisting additional recruits.

During the night the number increased again to forty, and they encamped on Major Ridley's plantation. An alarm took place during the darkness,—whether real or imaginary, does not appear,—and the men became scattered again. Proceeding to make fresh enlistments with the daylight, they were resisted at Dr. Blunt's house, where his slaves, under his orders, fired upon them; and this, with a later attack from a party of white men near Capt. Harris's, so broke up the whole force that they never re-united. The few who remained together agreed to separate for a few hours to see if any thing could be done to revive the insurrection, and meet again that evening at their original rendezvous. But they never reached it.

Gloomily came Nat Turner at nightfall into those gloomy woods where forty-eight hours before he had revealed the details of his terrible plot to his companions. At the outset all his plans had succeeded; every thing was as he predicted: the slaves had come readily at his call; the masters had proved perfectly defenceless. Had he not been persuaded to pause at Parker's plantation, he would have been master before now of the arms and ammunition at Jerusalem; and with these to aid, and the Dismal Swamp for a refuge, he might have sustained himself indefinitely against his pursuers.

Now the blood was shed, the risk was incurred, his friends were killed or captured, and all for what? Lasting memories of terror, to be sure, for his oppressors;

[7]The passage contains Old Testament phrases, but is not a precise quotation. It does illustrate Nat Turner's biblical style.

but, on the other hand, hopeless failure for the insurrection, and certain death for him. What a watch he must have kept that night! To that excited imagination, which had always seen spirits in the sky and blood-drops on the corn and hieroglyphic marks on the dry leaves, how full the lonely forest must have been of signs and solemn warnings! Alone with the fox's bark, the rabbit's rustle, and the screech-owl's scream, the self-appointed prophet brooded over his despair. Once creeping to the edge of the wood, he saw men stealthily approach on horseback. He fancied them some of his companions; but before he dared to whisper their ominous names, "Hark" or "Dred,"—for the latter was the name, since famous, of one of his more recent recruits,—he saw them to be white men, and shrank back stealthily beneath his covert.

There he waited two days and two nights,—long enough to satisfy himself that no one would rejoin him, and that the insurrection had hopelessly failed. The determined, desperate spirits who had shared his plans were scattered forever, and longer delay would be destruction for him also. He found a spot which he judged safe, dug a hole under a pile of fence-rails in a field, and lay there for six weeks, only leaving it for a few moments at midnight to obtain water from a neighboring spring. Food he had previously provided, without discovery, from a house near by. . . .

But the immediate danger was at an end, the short-lived insurrection was finished, and now the work of vengeance was to begin. In the frank phrase of a North-Carolina correspondent, "The massacre of the whites was over, and the white people had commenced the destruction of the negroes, which was continued after our men got there, from time to time, as they could fall in with them, all day yesterday." A postscript adds, that "passengers by the Fayetteville stage say, that, by the latest accounts, one hundred and twenty negroes had been killed,"—this being little more than one day's work. . . .

Men were tortured to death, burned, maimed, and subjected to nameless atrocities. The overseers were called on to point out any slaves whom they distrusted, and if any tried to escape they were shot down. Nay, worse than this. "A party of horsemen started from Richmond with the intention of killing every colored person they saw in Southampton County. They stopped opposite the cabin of a free colored man, who was hoeing in his little field. They called out, 'Is this Southampton County?' He replied, 'Yes, sir, you have just crossed the line, by yonder tree.' They shot him dead, and rode on." This is from the narrative of the editor of the Richmond *Whig,* who was then on duty in the militia, and protested manfully against these outrages. "Some of these scenes," he adds, "are hardly inferior in barbarity to the atrocities of the insurgents."

These were the masters' stories. If even these conceded so much, it would be interesting to hear what the slaves had to report. I am indebted to my honored friend, Lydia Maria Child, for some vivid recollections of this terrible period, as noted down from the lips of an old colored woman, once well known in New York, Charity Bowery. "At the time of the old Prophet Nat," she said, "the colored folks was afraid to pray loud; for the whites threatened to punish 'em dreadfully, if the least noise was heard. The patrols was low drunken whites; and in Nat's time, if they heard any of the colored folks praying, or singing a hymn, they would fall upon 'em and abuse 'em, and sometimes kill 'em, afore master or missis could get to 'em. The brightest and best was killed in Nat's time. The whites always suspect such ones. They killed a great many at a place called Duplon. They killed Antonio, a slave of Mr. J. Stanley, whom they shot; then they pointed their guns at him, and told him to confess about the insurrection. He told 'em he didn't know any thing about any insurrection. They shot several balls through him, quartered him, and put his head on a pole at the fork of the road leading to the court." (This is no exaggeration, if the Virginia newspapers may be taken as evidence.) "It was there but a short time. He had no trial. They never do. In Nat's time, the patrols would tie up the free colored people, flog 'em, and try to make 'em lie against one another, and often killed them before anybody could interfere. Mr. James Cole, high sheriff, said, if any of the patrols came on his plantation, he would lose his life in defence of his people. One day he heard a patroller boasting how many niggers he had killed. Mr. Cole said, 'If you don't pack up, as quick as God Almighty will let you, and get out of this town, and never be seen in it again, I'll put you where dogs won't bark at you.' He went off, and wasn't seen in them parts again"[8]. . . .

It is astonishing to discover, by laborious comparison of newspaper files, how vast was the immediate range of these insurrectionary alarms. Every Southern State seems to have borne its harvest of terror. . . .

Meanwhile the cause of all this terror was made the object of desperate search. On Sept. 17 the governor offered a reward of five hundred dollars for his capture; and there were other rewards, swelling the amount to eleven hundred dollars,—but in vain. No one could track or trap him. On Sept. 30 a minute account of his capture appeared in the newspapers, but it was wholly false. On Oct. 7 there was another, and on Oct. 18 another; yet all without foundation. Worn out by confinement in his little cave, Nat Turner grew more adventurous, and began to move about stealthily by night, afraid to speak to any human being, but hoping to obtain some information that might aid his escape. Returning regularly to his retreat before daybreak, he might possibly have continued this mode of life until pursuit had ceased, had not a dog succeeded where men had failed. The creature accidentally smelt out the provisions hid in the cave, and finally led thither his masters, two negroes, one of whom was named Nelson. On discovering the formidable fugitive, they fled precipitately, when he hastened to retreat in an opposite direction. This was on Oct. 15; and from this moment the neighborhood was all alive with excitement, and five or six hundred men undertook the pursuit.

It shows a more than Indian adroitness in Nat Turner to have escaped capture any longer. The cave, the arms, the provisions, were found; and, lying among them, the notched stick of this miserable Robinson Crusoe,[9] marked with five weary weeks and six days. But the man was gone. For ten days more he concealed himself among the wheat-stacks on Mr. Francis's plantation, and during this time was reduced almost to despair. Once he decided to surrender himself, and walked by night within two miles of Jerusalem before his purpose failed him. Three times he tried to get out of that neighborhood, but in vain: travelling by day was of course out of the question, and by night he found it impossible to elude the patrol. Again and again, therefore, he returned to his hiding-place; and, during his whole two months' liberty,

[8]Higginson had solicited information on Nat Turner from Lydia Maria Child and is here quoting from her letter.

[9]The reference here is to the hero of Daniel Defoe's novel of that name, who was cast away on a barren island.

never went fives miles from the Cross Keys. On the 25th of October, he was at last discovered by Mr. Francis as he was emerging from a stack. A load of buckshot was instantly discharged at him, twelve of which passed through his hat as he fell to the ground. He escaped even then; but his pursuers were rapidly concentrating upon him, and it is perfectly astonishing that he could have eluded them for five days more.

On Sunday, Oct. 30, a man named Benjamin Phipps, going out for the first time on patrol duty, was passing at noon a clearing in the woods where a number of pine-trees had long since been felled. There was a motion among their boughs; he stopped to watch it; and through a gap in the branches he saw, emerging from a hole in the earth beneath, the face of Nat Turner. Aiming his gun instantly, Phipps called on him to surrender. The fugitive, exhausted with watching and privation, entangled in the branches, armed only with a sword, had nothing to do but to yield,—sagaciously reflecting, also, as he afterwards explained, that the woods were full of armed men, and that he had better trust fortune for some later chance of escape, instead of desperately attempting it then. He was correct in the first impression, since there were fifty armed scouts within a circuit of two miles. His insurrection ended where it began; for this spot was only a mile and a half from the house of Joseph Travis.

Torn, emaciated, ragged, "a mere scarecrow," still wearing the hat perforated with buckshot, with his arms bound to his sides, he was driven before the levelled gun to the nearest house, that of a Mr. Edwards. He was confined there that night; but the news had spread so rapidly that within an hour after his arrival a hundred persons had collected, and the excitement became so intense "that it was with difficulty he could be conveyed alive to Jerusalem." The enthusiasm spread instantly through Virginia; M. Trezvant, the Jerusalem postmaster, sent notices of it far and near; and Gov. Floyd himself wrote a letter to the Richmond *Enquirer* to give official announcement of the momentous capture.

When Nat Turner was asked by Mr. T.R. Gray, the counsel assigned him, whether, although defeated, he still believed in his own Providential mission, he answered, as simply as one who came thirty years after him, "Was not Christ crucified?" In the same spirit, when arraigned before the court, "he answered, 'Not guilty,' saying to his counsel that he did not feel so." But apparently no argument was made in his favor by his counsel, nor were any witnesses called,—he being convicted on the testimony of Levi Waller, and upon his own confession, which was put in by Mr. Gray, and acknowledged by the prisoner before the six justices composing the court, as being "full, free, and voluntary." He was therefore placed in the paradoxical position of conviction by his own confession, under a plea of "Not guilty." The arrest took place on the 30th of October, 1831, the confession on the 1st of November, the trial and conviction on the 5th, and the execution on the following Friday, the 11th of November, precisely at noon. He met his death with perfect composure, declined addressing the multitude assembled, and told the sheriff in a firm voice that he was ready. Another account says that he "betrayed no emotion, and even hurried the executioner in the performance of his duty." "Not a limb nor a muscle was observed to move. His body, after his death, was given over to the surgeons for dissection."

The confession of the captive was published under authority of Mr. Gray, in a pamphlet, at Baltimore. Fifty thousand copies of it are said to have been printed; and it was "embellished with an accurate likeness of the brigand, taken by Mr. John

Crawley, portrait-painter, and lithographed by Endicott & Swett, at Baltimore." The newly established *Liberator* said of it, at the time, that it would "only serve to rouse up other leaders, and hasten other insurrections," and advised grand juries to indict Mr. Gray. I have never seen a copy of the original pamphlet; it is not easily to be found in any of our public libraries; and I have heard of but one as still existing, although the Confession itself has been repeatedly reprinted. Another small pamphlet, containing the main features of the outbreak, was published at New York during the same year, and this is in my possession. But the greater part of the facts which I have given were gleaned from the contemporary newspapers.

Who now shall go back thirty years, and read the heart of this extraordinary man, who, by the admission of his captors, "never was known to swear an oath, or drink a drop of spirits," who, on the same authority, "for natural intelligence and quickness of apprehension was surpassed by few men," "with a mind capable of attaining any thing;" who knew no book but his Bible, and that by heart; who devoted himself soul and body to the cause of his race, without a trace of personal hope or fear; who laid his plans so shrewdly that they came at last with less warning than any earthquake on the doomed community around; and who, when that time arrived, took the life of man, woman, and child, without a throb of compunction, a word of exultation, or an act of superfluous outrage? Mrs. Stowe's "Dred" seems dim and melodramatic beside the actual Nat Turner, and De Quincey's "Avenger"[10] is his only parallel in imaginative literature. Mr. Gray, his counsel, rises into a sort of bewildered enthusiasm with the prisoner before him. "I shall not attempt to describe the effect of his narrative, as told and commented on by himself, in the condemned-hole of the prison. The calm, deliberate composure with which he spoke of his late deeds and intentions, the expression of his fiend-like face when excited by enthusiasm, still bearing the stains of the blood of helpless innocence about him, clothed with rags and covered with chains, yet daring to raise his manacled hands to heaven, with a spirit soaring above the attributes of man,—I looked on him, and the blood curdled in my veins."

But, the more remarkable the personal character of Nat Turner, the greater the amazement felt that he should not have appreciated the extreme felicity of his position as a slave. In all insurrections, the standing wonder seems to be that the slaves most trusted and best used should be most deeply involved. So in this case, as usual, men resorted to the most astonishing theories of the origin of the affair. One attributed it to Free-Masonry, and another to free whiskey,—liberty appearing dangerous, even in these forms. The poor whites charged it upon the free colored people, and urged their expulsion; forgetting that in North Carolina the plot was betrayed by one of this class, and that in Virginia there were but two engaged, both of whom had slave wives. The slaveholding clergymen traced it to want of knowledge of the Bible, forgetting that Nat Turner knew scarcely any thing else. On the other hand, "a distinguished citizen of Virginia" combined in one sweeping denunciation "Northern incendiaries, tracts, Sunday schools, religion, reading, and writing."

But whether the theories of its origin were wise or foolish, the insurrection made its mark; and the famous band of Virginia emancipationists, who all that winter made

[10]Central character in a highly romantic work by English author Thomas De Quincey.

the House of Delegates ring with unavailing eloquence,—till the rise of slave-exportation to new cotton regions stopped their voices,—were but the unconscious mouthpieces of Nat Turner. In January, 1832, in reply to a member who had called the outbreak a "petty affair," the eloquent James McDowell thus described the impression it left behind:—

"Now, sir, I ask you, I ask gentlemen in conscience to say, was that a 'petty affair' which startled the feelings of your whole population; which threw a portion of it into alarm, a portion of it into panic; which wrung out from an affrighted people the thrilling cry, day after day, conveyed to your executive, *'We are in peril of our lives; send us an army for defence'?* Was that a 'petty affair' which drove families from their homes,—which assembled women and children in crowds, without shelter, at places of common refuge, in every condition of weakness and infirmity, under every suffering which want and terror could inflict, yet willing to endure all, willing to meet death from famine, death from climate, death from hardships, preferring any thing rather than the horrors of meeting it from a domestic assassin? Was that a 'petty affair' which erected a peaceful and confiding portion of the State into a military camp; which outlawed from pity the unfortunate beings whose brothers had offended; which barred every door, penetrated every bosom with fear or suspicion; which so banished every sense of security from every man's dwelling, that, let but a hoof or horn break upon the silence of the night, and an aching throb would be driven to the heart, the husband would look to his weapon, and the mother would shudder and weep upon her cradle? Was it the fear of Nat Turner, and his deluded, drunken handful of followers, which produced such effects? Was it this that induced distant counties, where the very name of Southampton was strange, to arm and equip for a struggle? No, sir: it was the suspicion eternally attached to the slave himself,—the suspicion that a Nat Turner might be in every family; that the same bloody deed might be acted over at any time and in any place; that the materials for it were spread through the land, and were always ready for a like explosion. Nothing but the force of this withering apprehension,—nothing but the paralyzing and deadening weight with which it falls upon and prostrates the heart of every man who has helpless dependants to protect,—nothing but this could have thrown a brave people into consternation, or could have made any portion of this powerful Commonwealth, for a single instant, to have quailed and trembled."

While these things were going on, the enthusiasm for the Polish Revolution was rising to its height. The nation was ringing with a peal of joy, on hearing that at Frankfort the Poles had killed fourteen thousand Russians. The *Southern Religious Telegraph* was publishing an impassioned address to Kosciuszko; standards were being consecrated for Poland in the larger cities; heroes like Skrzynecki, Czartoryski, Rozyski, Raminski, were choking the trump of Fame with their complicated patronymics. These are all forgotten now; and this poor negro, who did not even possess a name, beyond one abrupt monosyllable,—for even the name of Turner was the master's property,—still lives, a memory of terror, and a symbol of wild retribution.

1861

Letter to Mrs. Higginson on Emily Dickinson

I shan't sit up tonight to write you all about E.D. dearest but if you had read Mrs. Stoddard's[1] novels you could understand a house where each member runs his or her own selves. Yet I only saw her.

A large county lawyer's house, brown brick, with great trees & a garden—I sent up my card. A parlor dark & cool & stiffish, a few books & engravings & an open piano—Malbone & O D [Out Door] Papers[2] among other books.

A step like a pattering child's in entry & in glided a little plain woman with two smooth bands of reddish hair & a face a little like Belle Dove's; not plainer—with no good feature—in a very plain & exquisitely clean white pique & a blue net worsted shawl. She came to me with two day lilies which she put in a sort of childlike way into my hand & said "These are my introduction" in a soft frightened breathless childlike voice—& added under her breath Forgive me if I am frightened; I never see strangers & hardly know what I say—but she talked soon & thenceforward continuously—& deferentially—sometimes stopping to ask me to talk instead of her—but readily recommencing. Manner between Angie Tilton & Mr. Alcott[3]—but thoroughly ingenuous & simple which they are not & saying many things which you would have thought foolish & I wise—& some things you wd. hv. liked. I add a few over the page.

This is a lovely place, at least the view Hills everywhere, hardly mountains. I saw Dr. Stearns the Pres't of College—but the janitor cd. not be found to show me into the building I may try again tomorrow. I called on Mrs. Banfield & saw her five children—She looks much like H.H. *when ill* & was very cordial & friendly. Goodnight darling I am very sleepy & do good to write you this much. Thine am I

I got here at 2 & leave at 9. E.D. dreamed all night of *you* (not me) & next day got my letter proposing to come here!! She only knew of you through a mention in my notice of Charlotte Hawes.[4]

"Women talk: men are silent: that is why I dread women."

"My father only reads on Sunday—he reads lonely & rigorous books."

"If I read a book [and] it makes my whole body so cold no fire ever can warm me I know that is poetry. If I feel physically as if the top of my head were taken off, I know that is poetry. These are the only way I know it. Is there any other way."

"How do most people live without any thoughts. There are many people in the world (you must have noticed them in the street) How do they live. How do they get strength to put on their clothes in the morning"

"When I lost the use of my Eyes it was a comfort to think there were so few real books that I could easily find some one to read me all of them"

"Truth is such a rare thing it is delightful to tell it."

[1]The fiction of Elizabeth Drew Stoddard is represented elsewhere in this volume.

[2]The books are, respectively, a novel and a collection of essays by Higginson.

[3]Bronson Alcott, American Transcendentalist and educational reformer, known for his other-worldliness.

[4]Higginson had published a tribute to the memory of Charlotte Prince Hawes, a magazine writer, in the *Boston Radical* in 1867.

"I find ecstasy in living—the mere sense of living is joy enough"

I asked if she never felt want of employment, never going off the place & never seeing any visitor "I never thought of conceiving that I could ever have the slightest approach to such a want in all future time" (& added) "I feel that I have not expressed myself strongly enough."

She makes all the bread for her father only likes hers & says "& people must have puddings" this very dreamily, as if they were comets—so she makes them. . . .

She said to me at parting "Gratitude is the only secret that cannot reveal itself". . . .

I saw Mr. Dickinson this morning a little—thin dry & speechless—I saw what her life has been. Dr. S[tearns] says her sister is proud of her. . . .

This picture of Mrs Browning's tomb is from E.D. "Timothy Titcomb" [Dr. Holland] gave it to her.

I think I will mail this here as I hv. found time to write so much. I miss you little woman & wish you were here but you'd hate travelling.

Ever

E D again

"Could you tell me what home is"

"I never had a mother. I suppose a mother is one to whom you hurry when you are troubled."

"I never knew how to tell time by the clock till I was 15. My father thought he had taught me but I did not understand & I was afraid to say I did not & afraid to ask any one else lest he should know."

Her father was not severe I should think but remote. He did not wish them to read anything but the Bible. One day her brother brought home Kavanagh[5] hid it under the piano cover & made signs to her & they read it: her father at last found it & was displeased. Perhaps it was before this that a student of his was amazed that they had never heard of Mrs. [Lydia Maria] Child[6] & used to bring them books & hide in a bush by the door. They were then little things in short dresses with their feet on the rungs of the chair. After the first book she thought in ecstasy "This then is a book! And there are more of them!"

"Is it oblivion or absorption when things pass from our minds?"

Major Hunt[7] interested her more than any man she ever saw. She remembered two things he said—that her great dog "understood gravitation" & when he said he should come again "in a year. If I say a shorter time it will be longer."

When I said I would come again *some time* she said "Say in a long time, that will be nearer. Some time is nothing."

After long disuse of her eyes she read Shakespeare & thought why is any other book needed.

I never was with any one who drained my nerve power so much. Without touching her, she drew from me. I am glad not to live near her. She often thought me *tired* & seemed very thoughtful of others.

[5]A romance by Longfellow set in a small New England town.

[6]The work of Lydia Maria Child is represented elsewhere in this volume.

[7]Edward Bissell Hunt, an army engineer killed during the Civil War, and husband of Helen Hunt Jackson, author of *Ramona.*

[The postscript of a letter Higginson wrote his sisters (HCL) on Sunday, 21 August, adds:]

Of course I hv. enjoyed my trip very very much. In Amherst I had a nice aftn & evng with my singular poet.c correspondent & the remarkable cabinets of the College.

1921

Caroline Lee Hentz 1800–1856

As Rhoda Ellison has pointed out, the life of Caroline Hentz bears remarkable similarities to that of her fellow domestic novelist and primary antagonist in the writing of *The Planter's Northern Bride,* Harriet Beecher Stowe. Both came from Massachusetts, married "scholarly, unprosperous" men, and taught with their husbands; they even moved to the same town, Cincinnati, in the same year (1832), and probably belonged to the same literary society there. Both became major national figures in the flourishing of women's fiction; Hentz wrote her publisher in 1851, "I am compelled to turn my brains to gold and to sell them to the highest bidder" (Kelley, 164). But after Cincinnati, their geographical—and to some extent thematic—paths diverged: Stowe moved back to New England, and Hentz went south, to Chapel Hill, North Carolina, Covington, Kentucky, Florence, Alabama, and other points south. She died in Marianna, Florida, two years after publishing her most interesting fictional defense of slavery, *The Planter's Northern Bride.*

Hentz used her experience in the South as the basis for her claim that she, far better than Stowe, knew slavery intimately. "Slavery, as [Stowe] describes it, is an entirely new institution to us," she wrote (Kelley, 168). Yet the demands of rhetoric clearly (and of course inevitably) dictated the shape of her defense. Unlike many other novels of the plantation romance, Hentz's novel is more like Stowe's in its set of characters. There is a kindly planter, a northern bride, a black preacher, and loyal, lighter-skinned "servants" (the term southern slaveholders preferred to "slave"). The major implied opposition, as Ellison points out, is that between the bad guys: Stowe's slave-driver versus Hentz's abolitionist. But Hentz's effort to discredit abolitionism by exposing the personal motives of its spokespersons does not stop with one villain: she offers "two other types: the good man who rides a hobby and the busybody who is determined to free the slaves against their will" (Ellison, xiii). As Stowe had Southerners criticize slavery, so Hentz had Northerners defend it.

And unlike many other proslavery apologias, Hentz's—perhaps, ironically, more effectively for her purposes—eschews sectionalism and attacks on the North, using instead a moderate tone to mediate the fierce oppositions by then in force. Her two themes, typical of the proslavery arguments more generally, had to do with slavery's humaneness to all concerned and its economic benefits to the entire nation. The first chapter of *The Planter's Northern Bride* shows Moreland's (slavery's) humanity by contrasting, as so many apologists did, the "personal" and "intimate" bond constructed within plantation households with the cold cash nexus relation constructed by capitalism. While Albert and his master treat one another with courtesy and concern, notwithstanding their clearly defined and obviously very different roles, the white Northern woman worker has been abandoned by her community in the interests of industrial capitalism. The economic benefits are less dramatically rendered, in "long speeches by the planter and in occasional auctorial outbursts" (Ellison, xvi).

Hentz came to the explicit defense of slavery in *The Planter's Northern Bride* after establishing a solid reputation as a domestic novelist of the "scribbling mob" that so famously irritated Nathaniel Hawthorne. Her first big hit had come in 1850 with *Linda, or, The Young Pilot of the Belle Creole.* By 1854 her numerous publications included *Lovell's Folly* (1833), *De Lara, or, The Moorish Bride* (1843), *Aunt Patty's Scrap-bag* (1846), *Rena, or, The Snow Bird* (1851), *Eoline* (1852), *Ugly Effie, or, the Neglected One and the Pet Beauty* (1852), and *Marcus Warland* (1852). There is little mention of slavery, or even African-Americans, in the earlier works, consistent with the patterns of national domestic fiction. Another more ardent pro-South writer, August Evans (Wilson), whose *Macaria* (1863) defended the Confederacy in the midst of the war, barely mentions race or slavery in her best known *Beulah* (1859) or even her immediately post-war best seller *St. Elmo* (1866). After *The Planter's Northern Bride* and even before the Civil War, Hentz, too, returned to the list of concerns of the domestic novel, on which race and slavery took low priority, and before her death in 1856 wrote *The Banished Son* (1856), *Courtship and Marriage* (1856), *Ernest Linwood* (1856), and *The Lost Daughter* (1857).

The field is open for scholarship on Hentz; though she is included in various studies of domestic or women's fiction, there is more to be said about how she negotiated regional concerns with gender and racial identity. She said, interestingly, that she could not "conceive how a woman could write such a work" as Stowe's *Uncle Tom's Cabin,* aligning gender with southern apologetics. Yet her career suggests that she finally disconnected gender from other issues. Her works that do address race and slavery, then, might be looked at with an eye to the relation between gender and race/slavery as a white woman read it. Given the narrow and inferior place allotted to white women in most male apologias for the system, one might expect some interesting problematics as white women defended a system that confined both themselves and blacks and slaves to positions of little authority.

Anne G. Jones
University of Florida

PRIMARY SOURCE

Caroline Lee Hentz, *The Planter's Northern Bride,* [1854], 1970.

SECONDARY SOURCES

Rhoda Coleman Ellison, "Introduction," Caroline Lee Hentz, *The Planter's Northern Bride,* 1970; Miriam J. Shillingsburg, "The Ascent of Woman, Southern Style: Hentz, King, Chopin," in *Southern Literature in Transition,* ed. Philip Castille, et al., 1983; Mary Kelley, *Private Woman, Public Stage,* New York, 1984; Iman Lababidi, "The Life and Literary Works of C. L. Hentz," *Dissertation Abstracts International* 1991, Mar., vol. 51 (9), 3073A.

from The Planter's Northern Bride

Chapter I

Mr. Moreland, a Southern planter, was travelling through the New England States in the bright season of a Northern spring. Business with some of the merchant princes of Boston had brought him to the North; but a desire to become familiar with the beautiful surroundings of the metropolis induced him to linger long after it was transacted, to gratify the taste and curiosity of an intelligent and liberal mind. He was rich and independent, had leisure as well as wealth at his command, and there was something in the deep green fields and clear blue waters of New England that gave a freshness, and brightness, and elasticity to his spirits, wanting in his milder, sunnier latitude.

He found himself one Saturday night in a sweet country village, whose boundaries were marked by the most luxuriant shubbery and trees, in the midst of which a thousand silver rills were gushing. He was pleased with the prospect of passing the ensuing Sunday in a valley so serene and quiet, that it seemed as if Nature enjoyed in its shades the repose of an eternal Sabbath. The inn where he stopped was a neat, orderly place, and though the landlord impressed him, at first, as a hard, repulsive looking man, with a dark, Indian face, and large, iron-bound frame, he found him ready to perform all the duties of a host. Requesting to be shown to a private apartment, he ordered Albert, a young mulatto, who accompanied him on his journey, to follow him with his valise. Albert was a handsome, golden-skinned youth, with shining black hair and eyes, dressed very nearly as genteelly as his master, and who generally attracted more attention on their Northern tour. Accustomed to wait on his master and listen to the conversation of refined and educated gentlemen, he had very little of the dialect of the negro, and those familiar with the almost unintelligible jargon which delineators of the sable character put into their lips, could not but be astonished at the propriety of his language and pronunciation.

When Mr. Moreland started on his journey to the North, his friends endeavoured to dissuade him from taking a servant with him, as he would incur the danger of losing him among the granite hills to which he was bound:—they especially warned him of the risk of taking Albert, whose superior intelligence and cultivation would render him more accessible to the arguments which would probably be brought forward to lure him from his allegiance.

"I defy all the eloquence of the North to induce Albert to leave me," exclaimed Mr. Moreland. "Let them do it if they can. Albert," he said, calling the boy to him, who was busily employed in brushing and polishing his master's boots, with a friction quick enough to create sparkles of light. "Albert,—I am going to the North,—would you like to go with me?"

"To be sure I would, master, I would like to go anywhere in the world with you."

"You know the people are all free at the North, Albert."

"Yes, master."

"And when you are there, they will very likely try to persuade you that you are free too, and tell you it is your duty to run away from me, and set up for a gentleman yourself. What do you think of all this?"

Albert suspended his brush in the air, drew up his left shoulder with a significant shrug, darted an oblique glance at his master from his bright black eyes, and then renewed his friction with accelerated velocity.

"Well, my boy, you have not answered me," cried Mr. Moreland, in a careless, yet interested manner, peculiar to himself.

"Why, you see, Mars. Russell (when he addressed his master by his Christian name, he always abbreviated his title in this manner, though when the name was omitted he uttered the title in all its dignity),—"you see, Mars. Russell,"—here the mulatto slipped the boot from his arm, placed it on the floor, and still retaining the brush in his right hand, folded his arms across his breast, and spoke deliberately and earnestly,—"they couldn't come round this boy with that story; I've hearn it often enough already; I ain't afraid of anything they can say and do, to get me away from you as long as you want me to stay with you. But if you are afraid to trust me, master, that's another thing. You'd better leave me, if you think I'd be mean enough to run away."

"Well said, Albert!" exclaimed Mr. Moreland, laughing at the air of injured honour and conscious self-appreciation he assumed; "I do trust you, and shall surely take you with me; you can make yourself very amusing to the people, by telling them of your home frolics, such as being chained, handcuffed, scourged, flayed, and burned alive, and all those little trifles they are so much interested in."

"Oh! master, I wish I may find everybody as well off as I am. If there's no lies told on you but what I tell, you'll be mighty safe, I know. Ever since Miss Claudia"—

"Enough," cried Mr. Moreland, hastily interrupting him. He had breathed a name which evidently awakened painful recollections, for his sunshiny countenance became suddenly dark and cold. Albert, who seemed familiar with his master's varying moods, respectfully resumed his occupation, while Mr. Moreland took up his hat and plunged into the soft, balmy atmosphere of a Southern spring morning.

It is not our intention to go back and relate the past history of Mr. Moreland. It will be gathered in the midst of unfolding events, at least all that is necessary for the interest of our story. We will therefore return to the white-walled inn of the fair New England village, where our traveller was seated, enjoying the long, dewy twilight of the new region in which he was making a temporary rest. The sun had gone down, but the glow of his parting smile lingered on the landscape and reddened the stream that gleamed and flashed through the distant shrubbery. Not far from the inn, on a gradual eminence, rose the village church, whose tall spire, surmounted by a horizontal vane, reposed on the golden clouds of sunset, resembling the crucifix of some gorgeous cathedral. This edifice was situated far back from the road, surrounded by a common of the richest green, in the centre of which rose the swelling mound, consecrated by the house of God. Some very handsome buildings were seen at regular intervals, on either side of the road, among which the court-house stood conspicuous, with its freestone-coloured wall and lofty cupola. There was something in the aspect of that church, with its heaven-ascending spire, whose glory-crown of lingering day-beams glittered with a kind of celestial splendour, reminding him of the halo which encircles the brows of saints; something in the deep tranquillity of the hour, the soft, hazy, undulating outline of the distant horizon, the swaying motion of the tall poplars that margined the street far as his eye could reach, and through whose darkening vista a solitary figure gradually lessened on the eye, that solemnized and even saddened the spirits of our traveller. The remembrances of early youth and opening manhood pressed upon him with suddenly awakened force. Hopes, on which so sad and awful a blight had fallen, raised themselves like faded flowers sprinkled with dew, and mocked him with their visionary bloom. In the excitement of travelling, the realities of business, the frequent collision of interests, the championship of oft invaded rights, he had lost much of that morbidness of feeling and restlessness of character, which, being more accidental than inherent, would naturally yield to the force of circumstances counter to those in which they were born. But at the close of any arbitrary division of time, such as the last day of the week or the year, the mind is disposed to deeper meditation, and the mental burden, whose weight has been equipoised by worldly six-day cares, rolls back upon the mind with leaden oppression.

Moreland had too great a respect for the institutions of religion, too deep an inner sense of its power, to think of continuing his journey on the Sabbath, and he was glad that the chamber which he occupied looked out upon that serene landscape, and that the morning shadow of the lofty church-spire would be thrown across his window. It seemed to him he had seen this valley before, with its beautiful green, grassy slopes, its sunset-gilded church, and dark poplar avenue. And it seemed to him also, that he had seen a fair maiden form gliding through the central aisle of that temple, in robes of virgin white, and soft, down-bending eyes of dark brown lustre, and brow of moonlight calmness. It was one of those dim reminiscences, those vague, dream-like consciousnesses of a previous existence, which every being of poetic temperament is sometimes aware of, and though they come, faint shadows of a far-off world, quick and vanishing as lightning, they nevertheless leave certain traces of their presence, "trails of glory," as a great poet has called them, proceeding from the spirit's home.

While he sat leaning in silence against the window frame, the bell of the church began to toll slowly and solemnly, and as the sounds rolled heavily and gloomily along, then reverberated and vibrated with melancholy prolongation, sending out a sad, dying echo, followed by another majestic, startling peal, he wondered to hear such a funeral knell at that twilight hour, and looked up the shadowy line of poplars for the dark procession leading to the grave. Nothing was seen, however, and nothing heard but those monotonous, heavy, mournful peals, which seemed to sweep by him with the flaps of the raven's wings. Twenty times the bell tolled, and then all was still.

"What means the tolling of the bell?" asked he of the landlord, who was walking beneath the window. "Is there a funeral at this late hour?"

"A young woman has just died," replied the landlord. "They are tolling her age. It is a custom of our village."

Moreland drew back with a shudder. Just twenty. That was *her* age. *She* had not died, and yet the deathbell might well ring a deeper knell over her than the being who had just departed. In the grave the remembrance of the bitterest wrongs are buried, and the most vindictive cease to thirst for vengeance. Moreland was glad when a summons to supper turned his thoughts into a different channel.

There might have been a dozen men seated around the table, some whose dress and manners proclaimed that they were gentlemen, others evidently of a coarser grain. They all looked up at the entrance of Moreland, who, with a bow, such as the courteous stranger is always ready to make, took his seat, while Albert placed himself behind his master's chair.

"Take a seat," said Mr. Grimby, the landlord, looking at Albert. "There's one by the gentleman. Plenty of room for us all."*

"My boy will wait," cried Mr. Moreland, with unconscious haughtiness, while his pale cheek visibly reddened. "I would thank you to leave the arrangement of such things to myself."

"No offence, I hope, sir," rejoined Mr. Grimby. "We look upon everybody here as free and equal. This is a free country, and when folks come among us we don't see why they can't conform to our ways of thinking. There's a proverb that says—'when you're with the Romans, it's best to do as the Romans do.'"

"Am I to understand," said Mr. Moreland, fixing his eye deliberately on his Indian-visaged host, "that you wish my servant to sit down with yourself and these gentlemen?"

"To be sure I do," replied the landlord, winking his small black eye knowingly at his left-hand neighbour. "I don't see why he isn't as good as the rest of us. I'm an enemy to all distinctions myself, and I'd like to bring everybody round to my opinion."

"Albert!" cried his master, "obey the landlord's wishes. *I* want no supper; take my seat and see that you are well attended to."

"Mars. Russell," said the mulatto, in a confused and deprecating tone.

"Do as I tell you," exclaimed Mr. Moreland, in a tone of authority, which, though tempered by kindness, Albert understood too well to resist. As Moreland passed from the room, a gentleman, with a very prepossessing countenance and address, who was seated on the opposite side of the table, rose and followed him.

"I am sorry you have had so poor a specimen of Northern politeness," said the gentleman, accosting Moreland, with a slight embarrassment of manner. "I trust you do not think we all endorse such sentiments."

"I certainly must make you an exception, sir," replied Moreland, holding out his hand with involuntary frankness; "but I fear there are but very few. This is, however, the first direct attack I have received, and I hardly knew in what way to meet it. I have too much self-respect to place myself on a level with a man so infinitely my inferior. That he intended to insult me, I know by his manner. He knows our customs at home, and that nothing could be done in more positive violation of them than his unwarrantable proposition."

They had walked out in the open air while they were speaking, and continued their walk through the poplar avenue, through whose stiff and stately branches the first stars of evening were beginning to glisten.

"I should think you would fear the effect of these things on your servant," said the gentleman,—"that it would make him insolent and rebellious. Pardon me, sir, but I think you were rather imprudent in bringing him with you, and exposing him to the influences which must meet him on every side. You will not be surprised, after the instance which has just occurred, when I tell you, that, in this village, you are in the very hot-bed of fanaticism; and that a Southern planter, accompanied by his slave, can meet but little sympathy, consideration, or toleration; I fear there will be strong efforts made to induce your boy to leave you."

*A fact.

"I fear nothing of that kind," answered Moreland. "If they can bribe him from me, let him go. I brought him far less to minister to my wants than to test his fidelity and affection. I believe them proof against any temptation or assault; if I am deceived I wish to know it, though the pang would be as severe as if my own brother should lift his hand against me."

"Indeed!—I did not imagine that the feelings were ever so deeply interested. While I respect your rights, and resent any ungentlemanlike infringement of them, as in the case of our landlord, I cannot conceive how beings, who are ranked as goods and chattels, things of bargain and traffic, can ever fill the place of a friend or brother in the heart."

"Nevertheless, I assure you, that next to our own kindred, we look upon our slaves as our best friends."

As they came out of the avenue into the open street, they perceived the figure of a woman, walking with slow steps before them, bearing a large bundle under her arm; she paused several times, as if to recover breath, and once she stopped and leaned against the fence, while a dry, hollow cough rent her frame.

"Nancy," said the gentleman, "is that you?—you should not be out in the night air."

The woman turned round, and the starlight fell on a pale and wasted face.

"I can't help it," she answered,—"I can't hold out any longer,—I can't work any more;—I ain't strong enough to do a single chore now; and Mr. Grimby says he hain't got any room for me to lay by in. My wages stopped three weeks ago. He says there's no use in my hanging on any longer, for I'll never be good for anything any more."

"Where are you going now?" said the gentleman.

"Home!" was the reply, in a tone of deep and hopeless despondency,—"Home, to my poor old mother. I've supported her by my wages ever since I've been hired out; that's the reason I haven't laid up any. God knows——"

Here she stopped, for her words were evidently choked by an awful realization of the irremediable misery of her condition. Moreland listened with eager interest. His compassion was awakened, and so were other feelings. Here was a problem he earnestly desired to solve, and he determined to avail himself of the opportunity thrown in his path.

"How far is your home from here?" he asked.

"About three-quarters of a mile."

"Give me your bundle—I'll carry it for you, you are too feeble; nay, I insist upon it."

Taking the bundle from the reluctant hand of the poor woman, he swung it lightly upward and poised it on his left shoulder. His companion turned with a look of unfeigned surprise towards the elegant and evidently high-bred stranger, thus courteously relieving poverty and weakness of an oppressive burden.

"Suffer me to assist you," said he. "You must be very unaccustomed to services of this kind; I ought to have anticipated you."

"I am not accustomed to do such things for myself," answered Moreland, "because there is no occasion; but it only makes me more willing to do them for others. You look upon us as very self-indulging beings, do you not?"

"We think your institutions calculated to promote the growth of self-indulgence and selfishness. The virtues that resist their opposing influences must have more than common vitality."

"We, who know the full length and breadth of our responsibilities, have less time than any other men for self-indulgence. We feel that life is too short for the performance of our duties, made doubly arduous and irksome by the misapprehension and prejudice of those who ought to know us better and judge us more justly and kindly. My good woman, do we walk too fast?"

"Oh, no, sir. I so long to get home, but I am so ashamed to have you carry that bundle."

He had forgotten the encumbrance in studying the domestic problem, presented to him for solution. Here was a poor young woman, entirely dependent on her daily labour for the support of herself and aged mother, incapacitated by sickness from ministering to their necessities, thrown back upon her home, without the means of subsistence: in prospective, a death of lingering torture for herself, for her mother a life of destitution or a shelter in the almshouse. For every comfort, for the bare necessaries of life, they must depend upon the compassion of the public; the attendance of a physician must be the work of charity, their existence a burden on others.

She had probably been a faithful labourer in her employer's family, while health and strength lasted. He was an honest man in the common acceptation of the word, and had doled out her weekly wages as long as they were earned; but he was not rich, he had no superfluous gold, and could not afford to pay to her what was due to her stronger and more healthy successor; he could not afford to give her even the room which was required by another. What could she do but go to her desolate home and die? She could not murmur. She had no claim on the affection of the man in whose service she had been employed. She had lived with him in the capacity of a hireling, and he, satisfied that he paid her the utmost farthing which justice required, dismissed her, without incurring the censure of unkindness or injustice. We ought to add, without deserving it. There were others far more able than himself to take care of her, and a home provided by the parish for every unsheltered head.

Moreland, whose moral perceptions were rendered very acute by observation, drew a contrast in his own mind, between the Northern and Southern labourer, when reduced to a state of sickness and dependence. He brought his own experience in comparison with the lesson of the present hour, and thought that the sick and dying negro, retained under his master's roof, kindly nursed and ministered unto, with no sad, anxious lookings forward into the morrow for the supply of nature's wants, no fears of being cast into the pauper's home, or of being made a member of that unhappy family, consecrated by no head, hallowed by no domestic relationship, had in contrast a far happier lot. In the latter case there was sickness, without its most horrible concomitant, poverty, without the harrowing circumstances connected with public charity, or the capricious influence of private compassion. It is true, the nominal bondage of the slave was wanting, but there was the bondage of poverty, whose iron chains are heard clanking in every region of God's earth, whose dark links are wrought in the forge of human suffering, eating slowly into the quivering flesh, till they reach and dry up the life-blood of the heart. It has often been said that there need be no such thing as poverty in this free and happy land; that here it is only the offspring of vice and intemperance; that the avenues of wealth and distinction are open to all, and that all who choose may arrive at the golden portals of success and honour, and enter boldly in. Whether this be true or not, let the thousand toiling operatives of the Northern manufactories tell; let the poor, starving seamstresses, whose pallid faces mingle their chill, wintry gleams with the summer glow and splendour of the Northern cities, tell; let the free negroes, congregated in the suburbs of some of our modern Babylons, lured from their homes by hopes based on sand, without forethought, experience, or employment, without sympathy, influence, or caste, let them also tell.

When Moreland reached the low, dark-walled cottage which Nancy pointed out as her home, he gave her back her bundle, and at the same time slipped a bill into her hand, of whose amount she could not be aware. But she knew by the soft, yielding paper the nature of the gift, and something whispered her that it was no niggard boon.

"Oh, sir," she cried, "you are too good. God bless you, sir, over and over again!"

She stood in the doorway of the little cabin, and the dull light within played luridly on her sharpened and emaciated features. Her large black eyes were burning with consumption's wasting fires, and a deep red, central spot in each concave cheek, like the flame of the magic cauldron, was fed with blood alone. Large tears were now sparkling in those glowing flame-spots, but they did not extinguish their wasting brightness.

"Poor creature!" thought Moreland. "Her day of toil is indeed over. There is nothing left for her but to endure and to die. She has learned to *labour,* she must now learn to *wait.*"

As he turned from the door, resolving to call again before he left the village, he saw his companion step back and speak to her, extending his hand at the same time. Perceiving that he was actuated by the Christian spirit, which does not wish the left hand to know what the right hand doeth, he walked slowly on, through an atmosphere perfumed by the delicious but oppressive fragrance of the blossoming lilacs, that lent to this obscure habitation a certain poetic charm.

During their walk back to the inn, he became more and more pleased with his new acquaintance, whose name he ascertained was Brooks, by profession an architect of bridges. He was not a resident of the village, but was now engaged in erecting a central bridge over the river that divided the village from the main body of the town. As his interests were not identified with the place or the people, his opinions were received by Moreland with more faith and confidence than if they issued from the lips of a native inhabitant.

When they returned to the inn, they found Albert waiting at the door, with a countenance of mingled vexation and triumph. The landlord and several other men were standing near him, and had evidently been engaged in earnest conversation. The sudden cessation of this, on the approach of Mr. Moreland, proved that he had been the subject of it, and from the manner in which they drew back as he entered the passage, he imagined their remarks were not of the most flattering nature.

"Well, Albert, my boy," said he, when they were alone in his chamber, "I hope you relished your supper."

"Please, Mars. Russell, don't do that again. I made 'em wait on me this time, but it don't seem right. Besides, I don't feel on an equality with 'em, no way. They are no gentlemen."

Moreland laughed.

"What were they talking to you about so earnestly as I entered?" asked he.

"About how you treated me and the rest of us. Why, Mars. Russell, they don't know nothing about us. They want to know if we don't wear chains at home and manacles about our wrists. One asked if you didn't give us fodder to eat. Another wanted to strip off my coat, to see if my back wa'n't all covered with scars. I wish you'd heard what I told 'em. Master, I wish you'd heard the way I give it to 'em."

"I have no doubt you did me justice, Albert. My feelings are not in the least wounded, though my sense of justice is pained. Why, I should think the sight of your round, sleek cheeks, and sound, active limbs would be the best argument in my favour. They must believe you thrive wonderfully on fodder."

"What you think one of 'em said, Mars. Russell? They say you fatten me up, you dress me up, and carry me 'bout as a show-boy, to make folks think you treat us all well, but that the niggers at home are treated worse than dogs or cattle, a heap worse. I tell 'em it's all one big lie. I tell 'em you're the best—"

"Never mind, Albert. That will do. I want to think—"

Albert never ventured to intrude on his master's thinking moments, and, turning away in respectful silence, he soon stretched himself on the carpet and sunk in a profound sleep. In the mean time Moreland waded through a deep current of thought, that swelled as it rolled, and ofttimes it was turbid and foaming, and sometimes it seemed of icy chillness. He was a man of strong intellect and strong passions; but the latter, being under the control of principle, gave force and energy and warmth to a character which, if unrestrained, they would have defaced and laid waste. He was a searcher after truth, and felt ready and brave enough to plunge into the cold abyss, where it is said to be hidden, or to encounter the fires of persecution, the thorns of prejudice, to hazard everything, to suffer everything, rather than relinquish the hope of attaining it. He pondered much on the condition of mankind, its inequalities and wrongs. He thought of the poor and subservient in other lands, and compared them with our own. He thought of the groaning serfs of Russia; the starving sons of Ireland; the squalid operatives of England, its dark, subterranean workshops, sunless abodes of want, misery, and sin, its toiling millions, doomed to drain their hearts' best blood to add to the splendours and luxuries of royalty and rank; of the free hirelings of the North, who, as a *class,* travail in discontent and repining, anxious to throw off the yoke of servitude, sighing for an equality which exists only in name; and then he turned his thoughts homeward, to the enslaved children of Africa, and, taking them as a *class,* as a *distinct race* of beings, he came to the irresistible conclusion, that they were the happiest *subservient* race that were found on the face of the globe. He did not seek to disguise to himself the evils which were inseparably connected with their condition, or that man too oft abused the power he owned; but in view of all this, in view of the great, commanding truth, that wherever civilized man exists, there is the dividing line of the high and the low, the rich and the poor, the thinking and the labouring, in view of the God-proclaimed fact that "all Creation toileth and groaneth to gether," and that labour and suffering are the solemn sacraments of life, he believed that the slaves of the South were blest beyond the pallid slaves of Europe, or the anxious, care-worn labourers of the North.

With this conviction he fell asleep, and in his dreams he still tried to unravel the mystery of life, and to reconcile its inequalities with the justice and mercy of an omnipotent God.

1854

George Fitzhugh 1804–1881

George Fitzhugh lived out, before the Civil War, a decline of the sort that would more be more typical of his class and race in the South after the war's end: the family's plantation in Virginia had to be sold in the 1820s, and his education came almost entirely by his own hand. Yet Fitzhugh became a lawyer, and by the 1850s, began to publish what became a "steady stream" of defenses of the institution of slavery. Fitzhugh's thinking is notable in that it took the characteristic arguments for slavery to their logical extremes. If slavery was a positive good, if its effects were benevolent for the entire society, then—argued Fitzhugh—race should make no difference. Slavery was as good for whites as it was for blacks. "To justify her own social system," he wrote, "the South . . . will have to justify the slavery principle . . . as natural, normal, and necessitous. . . . In the absence of negro slavery there must be white slavery, else the white laboring class are remitted to slavery to capital, which is much more cruel and exacting than domestic slavery," he wrote (Faust, 277).

By 1856 Fitzhugh's work was well enough known to send him on a tour of the North to spread the word. Northerners were horrified at his "professed support for white as well as black slavery" (Faust, 273). Yet as the selection in this anthology shows, this argument does not deviate from so much as it extends the arguments for slavery that typified southern thought. For slavery as a system was logically separable from race as a system.

Southerners rejected the "social contractual theories of Locke and the 'absurd' and 'dangerous' principles of the Declaration of Independence" (Faust, 273), believing instead that the healthy community depended on a particular sort of interdependence among its members. That interdependence in turn depended on very clear boundaries between social and economic entities—slave and master, for example, male and female, and—in many other apologists' thinking—black and white. Southern thought ascribed to each group a set of roles and responsibilities that it saw as natural and normal for that group's identity. The identities—seen to be equally natural and normal—established biological differences between sexes and races as well.

Contemporary interest in Fitzhugh and other less radical proslavery apologists comes in part from an awareness that these notions did not die with the Confederacy. The Agrarians, whose *I'll Take My Stand* is excerpted in the introduction to the modern period, picked up on their notions of interdependency and hierarchy, and in particular used these ideas—as had the proslavery apologists—to mount a critique of industrial capitalism. Thus the interest in proslavery today derives in part also from what these arguments shared with other critiques of the atomization of modern society, primarily Marxism. However "interested" their position, proslavery apologists saw, or said they saw, slavery to be a humane, and economically feasible antidote to the dissociations of wage employment. In slavery, with its paternalistic "family black and white," even (they would say especially) a slave's needs were met by the system holistically, from birth to death, at work and away from it, in a community setting for which the factory could be no match. Of course the fact of human ownership of other humans played a light part in these arguments; however, such ownership was justified by the Bible, according to the apologists, who pointed out their precedents in detail.

Fitzhugh, the most radical of the apologists, managed to eke out a living in various minor government positions—before the war in Washington at the attorney general's office, during it in the Confederacy in

Richmond, and after it in the Freedmen's Bureau. In 1866 he left the Freedmen's Bureau to return to his war-devastated home in Port Royal, Virginia. His arguments against Reconstruction and emancipation began to take a virulently racist cast missing from his earlier separation of the issues. He sank into poverty and increasing silence, and died in 1881.

Anne G. Jones
University of Florida

PRIMARY WORKS

Slavery Justified, 1851; *Sociology for the South,* 1854; "Southern Thought," *DeBow's Review* 23 (1857):338–350; "Southern Thought Again," *DeBow's Review* 23 (1857):449–462; *Cannibals All!,* 1957; Harvey Wish, ed., *Ante-Bellum,* 1960; Eric McKitrick, ed., *Slavery Defended,* 1963; Drew Gilpin Faust, ed., *The Ideology of Slavery,* 1981.

SECONDARY WORKS

Harvey Wish, *George Fitzhugh,* 1943; Louis Hartz, *The Liberal Tradition in America,* 1955; C. Vann Woodward, "George Fitzhugh," in *Cannibals All!,* 1960; Eugene Genovese, *The World the Slaveholders Made,* 1969; Larry E. Tise, *Proslavery,* 1987.

from Southern Thought

Twenty years ago the South had no thought—no opinions of her own. Then she stood behind all christendom, admitted her social structure, her habits, her economy, and her industrial pursuits to be wrong, deplored them as a necessity, and begged pardon for their existence. Now she is about to lead the thought and direct the practices of christendom; for christendom sees and admits that she has acted a silly and suicidal part in abolishing African slavery—the South a wise and prudent one in retaining it. France and England, who fairly represent the whole of so-called free society, are actively engaged in the slave-trade under more odious and cruel forms than were ever known before. They must justify their practices; and, to do so, must adopt and follow Southern thought. This, of itself, would put the South at the lead of modern civilization.

In the sneering ridicule of the false and fallacious philanthropy of Lord Brougham by the London Times, the leading paper of Western Europe, we see that they are breaking ground to condemn and repudiate the "rose-water philanthropy" of Clarkson, Wilbeforce, Howard, and Hannah More, that nursed scoundrels and savages at the expense of the honest, industrious, laboring whites.

The next inevitable step will be to approve and vindicate the conduct of Hercules, and Moses, and Joshua, and the discoverers and settlers of America, who have conquered, enslaved, and exterminated savages, just as fast as might be necessary to make room for free civilized whites. This is the only philosophy that can justify the subjugation of Algiers or the hundred southern conquests and annexations of England; and this philosophy is consistent with Southern thought and practices, but wholly at war with the maudlin sentimentality of Hannah More, Wilbeforce, and Lord Brougham. Southern thought alone can justify European practices, and Southern practices alone save Western Europe from universal famine; for cotton, sugar, rice, molasses, and other slave products are intolerably dear and intolerably scarce, and France and England must have slaves to increase their production, or starve. They have begun to follow in our wake, instead of our humbly imitating them. It is true they are still impertinent and presumptious, and loud in their abuse of our form of slavery, whilst they are busily adopting worse forms. But the veil of hypocrisy with which they would conceal their conduct is too transparent to avail them long. Besides, they can use no arguments to justify their conduct that will not equally justify ours. In any view of the subject Southern thought and Southern example must rule the world.

The South has acted wisely and prudently, acted according to the almost universal usage of civilized mankind, and the injunctions of the Bible, and she is about to gather her reward for so doing. She flourishes like the bay tree, whilst Europe starves, and she is as remarkable for her exemption from crime as her freedom from poverty. She is by far, very far, the most prosperous and happy country in the world. Her jealous and dependent rivals have begun to imitate her. They must soon openly approve her course in order to vindicate themselves.

But there is no narrow philosophy to justify slavery. No human or divine authority to vindicate mere negro slavery as an exceptional institution. All the authority is the other way. White slavery, not black, has been the normal element of civilized society. It is true that the authorities and the philosophy which approve white slavery, are still stronger authorities in favor of negro slavery, for the principle and the practices of mankind in the general have been to make inferior races and individuals slaves to their superiors. How fortunate for the South that she has this inferior race, which enables her to make the whites a privileged class, and to exempt them from all servile, menial, and debasing employments.

But we must force the reluctant admission from Western Europe that the emancipation of the white serfs or villians was a far more cruel failure, so far as those serfs were concerned, than West India emancipations. In truth, the admission is made in fact, though not in form, in almost every review, newspaper, and work of fiction, that emanates from the press of Western Europe or our North. They concur in describing the emancipated whites as starving from year to year, and from generation to generation, whilst nobody pretends that the liberated negroes of the West Indies are starving. As for crime and ignorance, we suspect that the laboring liberated poor of Western Europe may well claim to rival, if not surpass, the negroes of Jamaica. But the liberated whites work harder and cheaper as freemen, or rather as slaves to capital, than they did as serfs; and, therefore, the rich who employ them think white emancipation a successful experiment, a glorious change for the better. Because, although it starves and brings to untimely graves some half million of the laboring poor annually, it nevertheless makes labor cheaper, and increases the profits of the rich.

We despise this flood of crocodile tears which England is shedding over the free negroes of the West Indies, whilst she has not one tear to shed on account of her laboring poor at home, who are ten times worse off than the free negroes.

In the absence of negro slavery there must be white slavery, else the white laboring class are remitted to slavery to capital, which is much more cruel and exacting than domestic slavery.

Southern thought must justify the slavery principle, justify slavery as natural, normal, and necessitous. He who justifies mere negro slavery, and condemns other forms of slavery, does not think at all—no, not in the least. To prove that such men do not think, we have only to recur to the fact that they always cite the usages of antiquity and the commands of the Bible to prove that negro slavery is right. Now if these usages and commands prove anything, they prove that all kinds of slavery are right.

By Southern thought, we mean a Southern philosophy, not excuses, apologies, and palliations.

The South has much work before her, for to justify her own social system, she will have to disprove and refute the whole social, ethical, political, and economical philosophy of the day. These philosophies have grown up in societies whose social relations are different from hers, and are intended to enforce and justify those relations. They all inculcate selfishness and competition as the great duties of man, and success in getting the better of our fellow beings in the war of the wits as the chiefest, if not the only merit. The opposite or protective philosophy, which takes care of the weak whilst it governs them, is the philosophy of the South.

The free trade or competitive philosophy is an admitted failure, and most of the literature of Europe is employed in exposing and condemning it. From the writings of the socialists, (and almost everybody is a socialist in Western Europe,) we can derive both facts and arguments quite sufficient to upset the whole moral philosophy of the day. From the Bible and Aristotle we can deduce (added to our own successful experiment) quite enough to build up a new philosophy on the ruins of the present false and vicious system.

The South is fulfilling her destiny and coming up to her work beautifully. She is multiplying her academies, her colleges, and her universities, and they are all well patronised and conducted by able professors. Several of these professors have written works defending slavery with great ability, on general and scientific principles. All of them are true to Southern institutions. From these schools thousands of educated and influential men annually proceed to every quarter of the South. They will mould and control thought and opinion, whether they settle down as private citizens or become editors, lawyers, divines, or politicians.

Female schools and colleges are also rapidly increasing in numbers, and this is an important gain, for it is the mother who first affects opinions, and it is difficult in after life to get rid even of erroneous principles which have been taught by the mother in the nursery. It is not safe, wise, or prudent, to commit the education of our daughters to Northern schools, nor to female teachers brought from the North.

Fashion is one of the most powerful engines in controlling opinion, and fashion will soon cease to be borrowed from the North. Southern watering places are full to overflowing, and few go to the North to be insulted by the helps in their hotels. These Southern watering places annually bring together intelligent and influential persons from the various States of the South, who form friendships, unite various sections in stronger bonds of amity, and confirm each other in the support of Southern institutions, by comparison and concurrence of opinion. People do not like to be out of the fashion in thought any more than in dress, and hence the prevalent anti-slavery doctrines at Northern watering places, must exercise a baleful and dangerous influence on Southerners who visit them.

The educational conventions held in various parts of the South exercise a similar influence to our watering places, but a far more important and potent one, for they are attended by the ablest men in the nation, whose every day business, duty, and occupation, is to form opinion, and to inaugurate a Southern thought. The importance of these conventions in cutting us off from imitative allegiance to the North and to Europe can hardly be overrated. Nay, they will do more; they will teach our revilers to respect, admire, and imitate us, by the unanswerable facts and arguments which they will adduce to justify our institutions.

Another fact for congratulation to the South is, that our people are beginning to write books—to build up a literature of our own. This is an essential prerequisite to the establishment of independence of thought amongst us. All Northern and European books teach abolition either directly or indirectly. The indirect method is more dangerous than the direct one. It consists in inculcating doctrines at war with slavery, without expressly assailing the institution. Now, all authors who write about law, religion, politics, ethics, social or political economy, if not pro-slavery men themselves, are continually inculcating doctrines accordant with their own social forms, and therefore at war with ours. Hence it follows, that all books in the whole range of moral science, if not written by Southern authors, within the last twenty or thirty years, inculcate abolition either directly or indirectly. If written before that time, even by Southern authors, they are likely to be as absurd and as dangerous as the Declaration of Independence, or the Virginia Bill of Rights.

It is all important that we should write our own books. It matters little who makes our shoes. Indeed, the South will commit a fatal blunder, if, in its haste to become nominally independent, it loses its present engines of power, and thereby ceases to be really independent. Cotton is king; and rice, sugar, Indian corn, wheat, and tobacco, are his chief ministers. It is our great agricultural surplus that gives us power, commands respect, and secures independence. The world is pinched now for agricultural products. The rebellion in India will increase the scarcity. Then, take away our surplus from the world's supply, and famine and nakedness would be the consequence. We should not jeopard this great lever of power in the haste to become, like Englishmen, shop-keepers, cobblers, and common carriers for the universe. Our present pursuits are more honorable, more lucrative, and more generative of power and independence than those we fondly aspire to. We cannot do double work. If we become a commercial and manufacturing people, we must cease to be an agricultural one, or at least we shall cease to have an agricultural surplus. We should become as feeble, as isolated and contemptible as Chinese or Japanese. Actual independence would be bartered off for formal independence, which no one would respect. An increase in our commerce and manufactures, so gradual as not to affect the amount of our agricultural surplus, would be desirable, provided that increase never extends so far as to make us a commercial and manufacturing people. That we can be all three is one of the most palpable absurdities ever conceived by the human brain. Foreigners cannot buy from us unless we buy an equivalent amount from them. If they should do so, our agricultural surplus would absorb the whole currency of the world in less than a century, and we should be oppressed with a plethora of money that would necessitate the carrying about a cart-load of silver to buy an ox.

We can afford to let foreigners be our cobblers, and carriers, and tradesmen for a while longer, but we cannot safely delay writing our own books for an hour.

In Congress, and in the courts of Europe, in the conflict of debate, and in the war of diplomacy, Southerners have always shown themselves the equals, generally the superiors, of the first intellects of the world. This is easily accounted for.

All true power, whether in speaking, writing, or fighting, proceeds quite as much from strength of will as from power of mind or body; and no men have half the strength of will that Southerners possess. We are accustomed to command from our cradle. To command becomes a want and a necessity of our nature, and this begets that noble strength of will that nerves the mind for intellectual conflict and intellectual exertion, just as it nerves the body for physical contest. We are sure to write well, because we shall write boldly, fearlessly, and energetically.

We have already made a start. A great many Southern books have been written within the last three or four years. They are almost all distinguished by that boldness of thought, and close and energetic logic, which characterizes the Southern mind. The North surpasses us in taste and imagination, equals us in learning, but is far behind us in logic. No doubt our greater intensity of will gives us this advantage, for in no intellectual effort is force of will so absolutely necessary as in moral reasoning. It is the most difficult intellectual exercise, and therefore the most perfect self-control and self-command are required to nerve to high effort in this direction.

Several of our distinguished professors are employed in preparing school books for academies and common schools, and text books for our colleges. It is all important to "teach the young idea how to shoot," and to give it, in early life, a Southern bent. We have been guilty of great remissness on this subject, but we shall speedily repair it, and soon no more school books from Europe or the North will be seen south of Mason's and Dixon's line.

Last, not least, of the causes, in busy operation to beget a Southern thought, are our annual commercial conventions. We have little practical acquaintance with trade or commerce, and do not know that conventions can direct industry, or control trade, any more than they can stop or divert the tide. We shrewdly suspect, however, that despite of conventions, private individuals will direct their industry and invest their capital in such manner as they think most profitable. Nay, more—we are so irreverent as to believe that each man is the best judge in such matters for himself. Besides, we think it far more dignified to let a starving and naked world come to our Egyptian granaries, as Joseph's brethren came to him, than for us to be hawking, peddling, and drumming like Englishmen through the universe. The character of drummer, hawker, and peddler, does not suit Southern taste or Southern talent. We have no turn whatever for swapping, drumming, and bargaining; and if we went from home with our products, might get cheated out of our eyes. Besides, we should neglect our crops, and in a short time would have nothing to employ our commerce.

But poorly as we think of these conventions as commercial stimulants or agencies, we know that they are invaluable as a means, and by far the most potent means, of uniting the South, begetting a common public opinion, and preparing us for any crisis or emergency that may arise. Let the South but be prepared and united, and her rights will always be respected, and the Union secure. But apathy and inertness beget aggression; and any further aggression by the North will precipitate disunion. The cup of our endurance is filled to the brim.

These conventions are composed of able, patriotic, and conservative men. Their proceeding, though firm, are calm, dignified, and moderate. They represent Southern feeling and opinion correctly, and excluding Russia, the South is the only conservative section of civilized christendom. The democracy of the North, it is true, are conservative, but there Black Republicanism is in the ascendant, and that is radical and revolutionary in the extreme. The Pope of Rome is a radical reformer. Louis Napoleon and Victoria are halfway socialists, and Henry the Fifth, the Bourbon heir to the French throne, is a thorough socialist. So desperate is the condition of the people throughout Western Europe, that no one in power dare tell them that there shall be no change, that all things shall remain as they are. The South is the only conservative section of christendom, because it is the only section satisfied with its own condition. Every where else, except in our North, the people are suffering intolerable ills, and ripe, at any moment, for revolution. There is no occasion for radicalism and revolutionary spirit at the North. Next to the South, it is the most prosperous, and should be the most contented country in the world. All of its discontent, and its political, moral, and religious heresies have grown out of abolition. Men who begin by assailing negro slavery find that all government begets slavery in some form, and hence all abolitionists are socialists, who propose to destroy all the institutions of society.

That slavery to capital, so intolerable in densely settled countries, where lands are monopolised by the few, can never be felt at the North, until our vast possessions in the West are peopled to the Pacific, and a refluent population begins to pour back upon the East. Then, like Western Europe, the North would have a laboring population slaves to capital, "slaves without masters." Famine would become perennial, and revolution the common order of the day, as in Western Europe. Nay, the condition of the laboring class of the North-east, would be far worse than in Europe, because there would be no checks to competition, no limitations to the despotism of capital over labor. The spirit of trade and commerce is universal, and it is as much the business of trade to devour the poor, as of the whales to swallow herrings. All its profits are derived from unjust exacting or "exploitation" of the common poor laboring class; for the professional and capitalist, and skilful laboring classes, manage to exact five times as much from the poor, as they pay to the tradesmen in way of profit. The poor produce everything and enjoy nothing. The people of the North are hugging to their breasts a silly delusion, in the belief that the poor can tax the rich, and thus prevent those evils that are starving and maddening the masses in Western Europe. You can't tax a rich man unless he be a slave-holder, because he produces nothing. You can't tax property, except in slave society, because it does not breed or produce anything itself. Labor pays all taxes, pays the rich man's income, educates his children, pays the professional man's fees, the merchant's profits, and pays all the taxes which support the Government; a property tax must take a part of the property proposed to be taxed, and such a tax never will be imposed; a property tax would soon divest all men of their property.

Gerrit Smith said most truly in Congress: "The poor pay all taxes, we (meaning the rich) are the mere conduits who pass them over to government." This was the noblest and the grandest truth that ever was uttered on the floor of legislative hall. It is this awful truth that is shaking free society to its base, and it will never recover from the shock. 'Tis now tottering to its fall. Property and not labor is taxed in slave society. 'Tis true the negro produces the wherewithal to pay the tax, but he loses nothing by it. Neither his food or his raiment are abridged. Both humanity and self-interest prevent the master from lowering his wages. The master pays the tax by abridging his own expenses. He has less of food and raiment, not the slave. The capitalist charges higher rents and profits to meet increased taxation, and lives as expensively as ever. The employer reduces the wages of his laborers for the same purpose, and dines and sups as luxuriously as ever.

Labor pays all taxes, but labor in slave society is property, and men will take care of their property. In free society, labor is not property, and there is nothing to shield the laborer from the grinding weight of taxation—all of which he pays, because he produces everything valuable.

We have made this digression to show that if the North ever becomes densely settled, there is no mode of escaping from the evils of free competition and from the taxing power or exploitation of skill and capital. In Europe, competition is not so fierce, the spirit of trade not so universal. They have still kings, nobles, and established churches, stripped, it is true of their fair proportions, reduced somewhat to the semblance of shadowy "phantasms;" yet, still, as the natural friends of the poor, interposing some check to the unfeeling exactions of the landholder, the tradesman, and the employer. In the palmy days of royalty, of feudal nobility, and of catholic rule, there were no poor in Europe. Every man had his house and his home, and both his brave and his pious protectors. The baron and the priest vied with each other in their care of the vassal. This was feudal slavery; and what is modern liberty? Why, quietly, slowly, almost insensibly, the poor have been turned over from the parental and protective rule of kings, barons, and churchmen, to the unfeeling despotism of capitalists, employers, usurers, and extortioners; and this was called emancipation!

Although, in the event of a dense population cooped up in the North, without means of escape, the evils which we have depicted, would occur more virulently there than in Europe; yet, it is not worth while to anticipate evils that may never happen. The North is now doing well. Her poor are not the slaves of capital, and never will be whilst there are vacant lands in the North. Population does not always increase. It has its ebbs and flows. Very large countries, such as America, are not likely to be overstocked with inhabitants. Secret causes at work will diminish population in some sections, whilst it is increasing in others. The situation of the North is natural, healthful, and progressive, but for the abolitionists and other agrarian isms. 'Tis treason in them to disturb society by the unnecessary agitation of questions as to contingent and future evils. But this is not their only treason. They propose, in their conventions, to dissolve the Union, not for any evils with which it afflicts them, but because the South hold slaves. Now, Black Republicans, who are under the rule of abolitionists, if not all abolitionists themselves, are radical and revolutionary in their doctrines, and dangerous to the Union; whilst Southern Commercial Conventions are composed entirely of men of the opposite character, of enlightened conservatives.

We differ from what are called the extremists of the South; but would not shoot down the sentinels of our camp. If not the wisest, most far-seeing, and most prudent, they are the most zealous friends of the South. They believe, that eventually, the aggressions of Northern abolition will force disunion upon us, and look to disunion as probably the only ultimate redress for the wrongs inflicted on us. We think a victory may yet, perhaps, be won by the South, not by arms, but by Southern thought and European necessities. Thought, by means of the press and the mail, has now become almost omnipotent. It rules the world. Thought, with hunger and nakedness to prompt, stimulate, and direct it, will prove irresistable. That thought has commenced and begotten a counter-current in Europe, that impels France to renew the slave-trade under a new form, and induced a debate in the British Parliament which evinces a universal change of opinion as to abolition and squints most obviously towards the renewal of the slave-trade. Revolutions of opinion do not go backwards, nor do they stand still in a half-way course. England sees, admits, and deplores the error of West India emancipation. This admission is but a step in a chain of argument, which must ultimately carry her further from abolition, and bring her nearer to slavery. For a while, she will try to maintain some middle ground between emancipation and slavery, and substitute coolies, and African apprentices, for negro slaves. But there are two reasons why she cannot long occupy this ground. First, its falsity and hypocrisy are too obvious; and secondly, coolies and apprentices do not answer the purpose of slaves. Her necessities will compel her to reinstate African slavery in its old and mildest form. Thus will Southern thought triumph, Southern morality be vindicated, and Southern wisdom, prudence, and foresight, be rendered apparent. The crusades lasted for a century. Those who conducted them had stronger convictions, and a clearer sense of duty, than modern abolitionists, for they laid down their lives by the million in the cause, whilst modern abolitionists, from Wilbeforce to Greely, have not evinced the slightest taste for martyrdom. All Europe then believed the crusades a righteous and holy undertaking. Abolition has never commanded such universal assent, nor such self-denying sacrifices. So far from marching a thousand or more miles to fight for their cause, they have not been willing to give up a cup of coffee, an ounce of sugar, or a pound of cotton, to speed it; no, they have been encouraging slavery, whilst abusing it, by consuming slave products. Europe and the North can any day abolish slavery by disusing slave products. They should try the experiment, for should they succeed in abolishing it, they will have none of those products thereafter—Jamaica and Hayti prove this.

The crusades lasted for a century, and their signal failure opened men's eyes to the folly and wickedness of such expeditions; and soon men began to wonder at the infatuation of their crusading ancestry. So it will be with abolition. It has lasted nearly a hundred years. It has failed as signally as the crusades, and brought hunger and nakedness on its votaries, or at least on the laboring poor at their doors. As in the case of the crusades, abolition will soon be considered a mad infatuation—for want, brought on by it, combines with failure, to open men's eyes.

Southern thought must be a distinct thought—not a half thought, but a whole thought. Domestic slavery must be vindicated in the abstract, and in the general, as a normal, natural, and, *in general,* necessitous element of civilized society, without regard to race or color.

This argument about races is an infidel procedure, and we had better give up the negroes than the Bible. It is a double assertion of the falsity of the Bible—first, as it maintains that mankind have not sprang from a common parentage; and, secondly, as it contends that it is morally wrong to enslave white men, who, the Bible informs us, were enslaved by the express command of God. But it is also utterly falsified by history. The little States of Greece, in their intestine wars, made slaves of their prisoners, and there was no complaint that they did not make good slaves; whilst the Macedonians, an inferior race, were proverbially unfit for slavery. The Georgians and Circassians, the most beautiful of the human family, make excellent slaves, whilst the Bedouin Arab and American Indian are as unfit for slavery as the Bengal tiger, or those tribes in Palestine whom God commanded Moses and Joshua to put to the sword without discrimination or mercy.

Again: to defend and justify mere negro slavery, and condemn other forms of slavery, is to give up expressly the whole cause of the South—for mulattoes, quadroons, and men with as white skins as any of us, may legally be, and in fact are, held in slavery in every State of the South. The abolitionists well know this, for almost the whole interest of Mrs. Stowe's Uncle Tom's Cabin, arises from the fact, that a man and woman, with fair complexion, are held as slaves.

We are all in the habit of maintaining that our slaves are far better off than the common laborers of Europe, and that those laborers were infinitely better situated as feudal serfs or slaves than as freemen, or rather as slaves to capital. Now, we stultify ourselves if we maintain it would be wrong to remit them back to domestic slavery, which we always argue is much milder and protective than that slavery to capital, to which emancipation has subjected them. They have been wronged and injured by emancipation, would we not restore them to slavery? Or are we, too, to become Socialists, and coop them up in Greely's Free-Love phalansteries? There are no other alternatives.

Again: every Southern man in defending slavery, habitually appeals to the almost universal usages of civilized man, and argues that slavery must be natural to man, and intended by Providence as the condition of the larger portion of the race, else it could not have been so universal. What a ridiculous and absurd figure does the defender of mere negro slavery cut, who uses this argument, when the abolitionist turns round on him and says—"why, you have just admitted that white slavery was wrong, and this universal usage which you speak of has been white, not black slavery. The latter is a very recent affair."

We must defend the principle of slavery as part of the constitution of man's nature. The defence of mere negro slavery, will, nay, has involved us in a thousand absurdities and contradictions. We must take high philosophical, biblical, and historical grounds, and soar beyond the little time and space around us to the earliest records of time, and the farthest verge of civilization. Let us quit the narrow boundaries of the rice, the sugar and the cotton field, and invite the abolitionists to accompany us in our flight to the tent of Abraham, to the fields of Judea, to the halls of David and of Solomon, to the palaces and the farms of Athens and of Rome, and to the castles of the grim Barons of medieval time. Let us point to their daily routine of domestic life. Then, not till then, may we triumphantly defend negro slavery. "You see slavery everywhere, and throughout all times: you see men subjected to it by express command or by permission of God, with skins as white and intellects as good as yours. Can it be wrong to enslave the poor negro, who needs a master more than any of these?" Less than this is inconsiderate assertion, not Southern thought; nay, not thought at all.

The temptation to confine the defence of slavery to mere negro slavery is very strong, for it is obvious that they require masters under all circumstances, whilst the whites need them only under peculiar circumstances, and those circumstances such as we can hardly realize the existence of in America. May the day never arrive when our lands shall be so closely monopolized, and our population become so dense, that the poor would find slavery a happy refuge from the oppression of capital.

In the South, there is another and a stronger reason for the feeling of indignation at the bare suggestion of white slavery—that is pride of caste. No man loves liberty and hates slavery so cordially as the Southerner. Liberty is with him a privilege, or distinction, belonging to all white men. Slavery a badge of disgrace attached to an inferior race. Accustomed from childhood to connect the idea of slavery with the negro, and of liberty with the white man, it shocks his sensibilities barely to mention white slavery. 'Tis vain to talk to him of the usages of mankind, for his prejudices and prepossessions were formed long before he heard of history, and they are too strong to be reasoned away.

This peculiarity of Southerners, and other slaveholders, is admirably described by Burke, who was the most philosophic and farseeing statesman of modern times. He says, "in Virginia and the Carolinas they have a vast multitude of slaves. Where this is the case in any part of the world, those who are free are by far the most proud and jealous of their freedom. Freedom is to them not only an enjoyment, but a kind of rank and privilege. Not seeing then that freedom, as in countries where it is a common blessing, and as broad and general as the air, may be united with much abject toil, with great misery, with all the exterior of servitude, liberty looks among them as something more noble and liberal. I do not mean to commend the superior morality of this sentiment, which has at least as much pride as virtue in it; but I cannot alter the nature of man. The fact is so; and those people of the Southern colonies are much more strongly, and with a more stubborn spirit attached to liberty, than those to the Northward. Such were all the ancient commonwealths; such were our Gothic ancestry; such, in our days, were the Poles; and such will be all masters of slaves who are not slaves themselves. In such a people, haughtiness of domination combines with the spirit of freedom, fortifies it, and renders it invisible."

1857

Mary Boykin Chesnut 1823–1886

Historians and literary critics alike have praised Mary Boykin Chesnut's "diary" for its vivid and sweeping narrative of Confederate life during the Civil War. As her editor C. Vann Woodward points out, the enduring value of Chesnut's autobiographical writing lies not so much in the information it contains, but "in the life and reality with which it endows people and events and with which it evokes the chaos and complexity of a society at war." A politically astute, well-educated, and gregarious woman whose father and husband were southern political figures, Mary Chesnut was in an ideal position to observe and record the intricacies of her society and her era. Born in Statesburg, South Carolina, she was the oldest daughter of Mary Boykin and Stephen Miller. Her father was, at various periods, a U.S. Congressman and Senator, governor and state senator.

According to her biographer Elisabeth Muhlenfeld, young Mary Miller received an unusually solid education for a nineteenth-century southern woman. She attended Madame Talvande's French School for Young Ladies in Charleston where she excelled in a course of study which stressed foreign language, history, rhetoric, literature, and science, as well as traditional female "accomplishments." While in attendance at Madame Talvande's, she met James Chesnut Jr., whom she married when she was barely seventeen. From a wealthy Camden family, her husband, a Princeton graduate and lawyer, served in various political positions before the war, including a U.S. Senate seat which he gave up in 1860 when differences between the North and South became insurmountable. His connections with such figures as Jefferson Davis during the war years opened windows of opportunity for his wife's observations of and relationships with key figures in the national drama, as did her own enjoyment of friendships with a broad spectrum of the Confederacy's most prominent men and women. After the war the Chesnuts' land and plantation near Camden were lost to debt; and after James's death in 1884, Mary was left with a struggling dairy farm and a strong desire to complete her memoirs. Always in danger from heart trouble, she died of an attack before seeing her work published.

Like many other southern autobiographers writing about the Civil War, many of them women who struggled through the vicissitudes of a war on home territory, Chesnut created her "diary" out of a complexly rendered combination of an actual diary written during the war and her memories of the past. The 1984 publication of *The Private Mary Chesnut,* edited by Woodward and Muhlenfeld, makes the original, and highly personal, diary available for the first time. This actual diary, which she kept under lock and key, was not meant for publication; and the autobiographical book known as her "diary" was actually written twenty years after the war, in 1881 – 1884. Woodward's 1981 edition, entitled *Mary Chesnut's Civil War,* incorporates part of the original diary with the retrospective memoirs. Mary Chesnut's writing was first published in 1905 and later in 1949 in an edition by Ben Ames Williams with the title (not one of Chesnut's choosing) *A Diary from Dixie.* Unlike Williams's *Diary,* Woodward's edition provides a synthesis of the two forms of autobiography, the diary and the memoir, in a responsibly edited combination of what Chesnut actually wrote during the war and twenty years later. One of her stated purposes in her revision of the eighties, Woodward discovers through her correspondence, was what she called "leaving myself out." To whatever extent she succeeded, Woodward attempts to right the balance by reinserting personal comments which the previous editions have left unpublished. In the selections reprinted below from Woodward's edition, deleted passages have been indicated by brackets. *Mary Chesnut's Civil War* thus captures the sweep and chaos of a society at war, as did Williams's *A Diary from Dixie,* but the more recent edition also allows an intimate picture of the woman as writer of her own story of that society.

Chesnut describes herself as writing "like a spider, spinning [her] own entrails." This web of self, like Chesnut's sense of history, is complexly attached to and woven out of a keen awareness of the white woman's position in a patriarchal slave society. At a personal level Chesnut, who was childless and married to the only son of a wealthy planter family, was painfully cognizant of white woman's role as the bearer of legitimate heirs. Her attitude toward slavery and patriarchal ideology has been seen as radically feminist for the times, and it has become commonplace to point out that Chesnut saw miscegenation as the embodiment of the evil of slavery and of the double standard that allowed the white southern male sexual freedom and marital infidelity while his wife and daughter were bound by the prohibitions of chastity. In her frequently quoted diatribes against this aspect of slavery, such as the one reproduced below, though, Chesnut seems so intent on pitying the white women whose husbands are involved in philanderings in the slave quarters that she has no sympathy left for the black women who became their victims. She views black women instead as symbols of sexuality, ironically with freedoms not allowed "respectable" white women. Moreover, she seems to blame black women for a sexual coercion only white men could instigate or force, thereby focusing her bitterness at the victims of slavery, not the victimizers.

Thus Chesnut, a member of the wealthy planter class, abhorred slavery and its sexual vices; but, like many white women of her time and position, seemed to remain blind, or at least myopic, concerning the intersections of gender and race with the power structures of the system in which she lived much of her life. Yet, despite her limited critique of the patriarchal underpinnings of slavery, Mary Boykin Chesnut's massive volume paints a valuable portrait, interior as well as exterior, of the Old South's physical and ideological struggle to survive, its ultimate failure to do so, and perhaps some of the reasons behind that failure.

Minrose C. Gwin
University of New Mexico

PRIMARY WORKS

Mary Chesnut's Civil War, ed. C. Vann Woodward, 1981; *The Private Mary Chesnut: The Unpublished Civil War Diaries,* ed. Woodward and Elisabeth Muhlenfeld, 1984.

SECONDARY WORKS

Elisabeth Muhlenfeld, *Mary Boykin Chesnut: A Biography,* 1981; C. Vann Woodward, "Mary Chesnut in Search of Her Genre," *Yale Review* 73 (Winter 1984): 199–209; Minrose C. Gwin, *Black and White Women of the Old South: The Peculiar Sisterhood in American Literature,* 1985, pp. 81–109; Clara Junker, "Writing Herstory: Mary Chesnut's Civil War," *Southern Studies* 26 (1987): 18–27; Elizabeth Fox-Genovese, *Within the Plantation Household: Black and White Women of the Old South,* 1988, pp. 334–371.

from Mary Chesnut's Civil War

March 18, 1861

. . . ⟨⟨I wonder if it be a sin to think slavery a curse to any land. Sumner said not one word of this hated institution which is not true. Men and women are punished when their masters and mistresses are brutes and not when they do wrong—and then we live surrounded by prostitutes. An abandoned woman is sent out of any decent house elsewhere. Who thinks any worse of a negro or mulatto woman for being a thing we can't name? God forgive us, but ours is a *monstrous* system and wrong and iniquity. Perhaps the rest of the world is as bad—this *only* I see. Like the patriarchs of old our men live all in one house with their wives and their concubines, and the mulattoes one sees in every family exactly resemble the white children—and every lady tells you who is the father of all the mulatto children in everybody's household, but those in her own she seems to think drop from the clouds, or pretends so to think. Good women we have, *but* they talk of all *nastiness*—tho' they never do wrong, they talk day and night of [*erasures illegible save for the words* "all unconsciousness"] my disgust sometimes is boiling over—but they are, I believe, in conduct the purest women God ever made. Thank God for my countrywomen—alas for the men! No worse than men everywhere, but the lower their mistresses, the more degraded they must be.

⟨⟨My mother-in-law told me when I was first married not to send my female servants in the street on errands. They were then tempted, led astray—and then she said placidly, so they told *me* when I came here, and I was very particular, *but you see with what result.*

⟨⟨Mr. Harris said it was so patriarchal. So it is—flocks and herds and slaves—and wife Leah does not suffice. Rachel must be *added,* if not *married.*[1] And all the time they seem to think themselves patterns—models of husbands and fathers.

⟨⟨Mrs. Davis told me everybody described my husband's father as an odd character—"a millionaire who did nothing for his son whatever, left him to struggle with poverty, &c." I replied—"Mr. Chesnut Senior thinks himself the best of fathers—and his son thinks likewise. I have nothing to say—but it is true. He has no money but what he makes as a lawyer." And again I say, my countrywomen are as pure as angels, tho' surrounded by another race who are the social evil!⟩⟩

August 26, 1861

. . . Now, this assemblage of army women or Confederate matrons talked pretty freely today. Let us record. . . .

"You people who have been everywhere, stationed all over the U.S.—states, frontiers—been to Europe and all that, tell us homebiding ones: are our men worse than the others? Does Mrs. Stowe know? You know?"

"No, Lady Mary Montagu did. After all, only men and women—everywhere.[2] But Mrs. Stowe's exceptional cases may be true. You can pick out horrors from any criminal court record or newspaper in any country."

"You see, irresponsible men, county magnates, city millionaires, princes, &c do pretty much as they please. They are above law and morals."

Russell once more, to whom London and Paris and India have been an everyday sight—and every night, too, streets and all—for him to go on in indignation because there are women on negro plantations who were not vestal virgins! Negro women are married and after marriage behave as well as other people. Marrying is the amusement of their life. They take life easily. So do their class everywhere. Bad men are hated here as elsewhere.

"I hate slavery. I hate a man who—You say there are no more fallen women on a plantation than in London, in proportion to numbers. What do you say to this? A magnate who runs a hideous black harem and its consequences under the same roof with his lovely white wife and his beautiful and accomplished daughters? He holds his head as high and poses as the model of all human virtues to these poor women whom God and the laws have given him. From the height of his awful majesty he scolds and thunders at them, as if he never did wrong in his life.

"Fancy such a man finding his daughter reading *Don Juan.*[3] 'You with that unmoral book!' And he orders her out of his sight.

[1]In Genesis 29–30, Jacob, unhappy with his wife Leah, also marries her sister Rachel. He has children by both women and by their handmaidens as well. M.B.C. apparently believed old Mr. Chesnut had children by a slave whom she calls "Rachel" (p. 72). She confesses no such suspicions of her husband.

[2]"This world consists of men, women, and Herveys." Lady Mary (Wortley) Montagu, *Letters* (1763), volume 1. Lady Montagu, the wife of an adviser to George I, chronicled the scandals of London society.

[3]Lord Byron, *Don Juan* (1824).

"You see, Mrs. Stowe did not hit the sorest spot. She makes Legree[4] a bachelor. Remember George II and his like."[5]

"Oh, I knew half a Legree, a man said to be as cruel as Legree—but the other half of him did not correspond. He was a man of polished manners. And the best husband and father and member of the church in the world."

"Can that be so?"

"Yes, I know it. Exceptional case, that sort of thing, always."

"And I knew the dissolute half of Legree well. He was high and mighty. But the kindest creature to his slaves—and the unfortunate results of his bad ways were not sold, had not to jump over ice blocks. They were kept in full view and provided for handsomely in his will.

"His wife and daughters in the might of their purity and innocence are supposed never to dream of what is as plain before their eyes as the sunlight, and they play their parts of unsuspecting angels to the letter. They prefer to adore their father as model of all earthly goodness."

"Well, yes. If he is rich, he is the fountain from whence all blessings flow."

"The one I have in my eye—my half of Legree, the dissolute half—was so furious in his temper and thundered his wrath so at the poor women they were glad to let him do as he pleased in peace, if they could only escape his everlasting faultfinding and noisy bluster. Making everybody so uncomfortable."

"*Now.* Now, do you know any woman of this generation who would stand that sort of thing?"

"No, never—not for one moment. The make-believe angels were of the last century. We know—and we won't have it."

"Condition of women is improving, it seems. These are old-world stories."

"Women were brought up not to judge their fathers or their husbands. They took them as the Lord provided—and were thankful."

"If they should not go to heaven, after all—think of what lives most women lead."

"No heaven, no purgatory, no——, the other thing—never. I believe in future rewards and punishments."

"How about the wives of drunkards? I heard a woman say once to a friend of her husband, tell it as a cruel matter of fact, without bitterness, without comment: 'Oh, you have not seen him. He is changed. He has not gone to bed sober in thirty years.' She has had her purgatory—if not what Mrs.——calls 'the other thing'—here in this world. We all know what a drunken man is. To think, *for no crime* a person may be condemned to live with one thirty years."

"You wander from the question I asked. Are Southern men worse because of the slave system and the—facile black women?"

"Not a bit. They see too much of them. The barroom people don't drink. The confectionary people loathe candy. They are sick of the black sight of them."

"You think a nice man from the South is the nicest thing in the world."

"I know it. Put him by any other man and see!"

"And you say no saints and martyrs now—those good women who stand by bad husbands? Eh?"

[4]Simon Legree of *Uncle Tom's Cabin.*

[5]The ten-year relationship of George II with Mrs. Henrietta Howard was an open secret, as were several more casual liaisons.

"No use to mince matters—no use to pick words—everybody knows the life of a woman whose husband drinks."

"Some men have a hard time, too. I know women who are—well, the very devil and all his imps."

"And have you not seen girls cower and shrink away from a fierce brute of a father? Men are dreadful animals."

"Seems to me those of you who are hardest on men here are soft enough with them when they are present. Now, everybody knows I am 'the friend of man,' and I defend them behind their backs, as I take pleasure in their society—well—before their faces." . . .

October 13, 1861

Went to hear Tom Davis[6] preach. It was a political sermon. He ended it by commenting on a remark made by a celebrated person from Washington who said he was bored with politics all the week. And if he could not hear a little pure religion, undefiled, on Sunday, he would not go to church.

Nudged me: "That's you. You are always grumbling at political sermons." "But I am not the least celebrated." However, the whispered dispute was soon settled. Henry Clay was the man who hoped to eschew politics one day in seven.

Our parson cited Lord Nelson as a case of good prayer from a bad man. At the battle of Trafalgar he prayed fervently, and his prayer was answered. And there he died, saying, "Thank God I die doing my duty." Again my whisper: "He prayed, too, for Lady Hamilton, and he left her a legacy to his country—ungrateful country would not accept the bequest."[7]

At Mulberry we went in the afternoon to the negro church on the plantation. Manning Brown,[8] Methodist minister, preached to a very large black congregation. Though glossy black, they were well dressed—some very stylishly gotten up. They were stout, comfortable-looking Christians. The house women in white aprons and white turbans were the nicest looking. How snow-white the turbans on their heads appeared. But the youthful sisters flaunted in pink and sky blue bonnets which tried their complexions. For *the family* they had a cushioned seat near the pulpit, neatly covered with calico.

Manning Brown preached hell fire—so hot I felt singed, if not parboiled, though I could not remember any of my many sins worthy of an eternity in torment. But if all the world's misery, sin, and suffering came from so small a sin as eating that apple, what mighty proportions mine take.

Jim Nelson, the driver—the stateliest darky I ever saw. He is tall and straight as a pine tree, with a fair face—not so very black, but full-blooded African. His forefathers must have been of royal blood over there.

[6]Thomas Frederick Davis, Jr., was associate pastor of the Grace Episcopal Church in Camden. His wife was M.B.C.'s first cousin.

[7]The night before his death at the battle of Trafalgar, Horatio Nelson added a codicil to his will, leaving his mistress Lady Emma Hamilton and their daughter Horatia "a legacy to my king and country" and asking that they be given a pension. The will was not made public, and no such grant was ever made.

[8]A nephew of Old Colonel Chesnut who lived in Sumter District.

This distinguished gentleman was asked to "lead in prayer." He became wildly excited. Though on his knees, facing us, with his eyes shut, he clapped his hands at the end of every sentence, and his voice rose to the pitch of a shrill shriek. Still, his voice was strangely clear and musical, occasionally in a plaintive minor key that went to your heart. Sometimes it rung out like a trumpet. I wept bitterly. It was all sound, however, and emotional pathos. There was literally nothing in what he said. The words had no meaning at all. It was the devotional passion of voice and manner which was so magnetic. The negroes sobbed and shouted and swayed backward and forward, some with aprons to their eyes, most clapping their hands and responding in shrill tones, "Yes, my God! Jesus!" "Aeih! Savior! Bless de Lord, amen—&c."

It was a little too exciting for me. I would very much have liked to shout, too. Jim Nelson, when he rose from his knees, trembled and shook as one in a palsy. And from his eye you could see the ecstasy had not left him yet. He could not stand at all—sunk back on his bench.

Now, all this leaves not a trace behind. Jim Nelson is a good man—honest and true. And so he continues. Those who stole before steal on, in spite of sobs and shouts on Sunday. Those who drink continue to drink when they can get it. Except that for any open, *detected* sin they are turned out of church. A Methodist parson is practical—no mealy-mouth creature. He requires them to keep the commandments. If they are not married and show they ought to be, out of the church they go. If married members are not true to their vows and it is made plain to him by their conduct, he has them up before the church. They are devoted to their church membership. And it is a keen police court.

Suddenly, as I sat wondering what next, they broke out into one of those soul-stirring negro camp-meeting hymns To me this is the saddest of all earthly music—weird and depressing beyond my powers to describe.

The wrestling of the world asketh a fall;
Here is no home: here is a wildernesse.
Forth Pilgrim! forth! Oh! beast out of thy stall!
Look up on high—And thank thy God for all.
—Chaucer

October 20, 1861

. . . Hume says, "Mighty governments are built up by a great deal of accident with a very little of human foresight and wisdom."[9]

We have seen the building of one lately with no end of Jefferson and a constant sprinkling of Calhoun, &c&c&c. Which is the wisdom—where the accident or foresight? Somebody said Jefferson and Calhoun were the stern lights and did not help us to see what is before us.

One thing Mrs. Browne and I discussed. There were in Richmond and in Montgomery the safe, sober, second thoughts of the cool, wise morning hours. There in that drawing room after dinner—how much more in the smoking congresses where women were not—came what we called ideas preserved in alcohol. The self-same

[9]David Hume, *History of England* (1754–62), volume 2, chapter 23.

wild schemes, mad talk, exaggerated statements, inflamed and irrational views—our might and the enemies' weakness, &c&c. If "in vino veritas," God help us. After all it was not, could not be, unadulterated truth—it was truth, alcoholized.

I care no more for alcoholized wisdom than I do for the chattering of blackbirds—[*remainder of page cut off*].

Hard on the poor innocent birds! They were made so. And the great statesmen and soldiers deliberately drink down their high inheritance of reason and with light hearts become mere gabbling geese. *Alcools*—

Hume, after his kind, talks of *accident*. Lamartine says, "Dieu est Dieu—ce que les hommes appellent *rencontre,* les anges l'appellent Providence."[10]

Thank God for pine knots. Gas and candles and oil are all disappearing in the Confederacy. Lamb thinks for social purposes candles so much better than the garish light of the sun.[11] The unsocial nights of our ancestors in their dark caves. They must have laid about and abused one another in the dark. No, they went to sleep. And women then were too much slaves to dream of curtain lectures—which is one form of lying about and abusing one another in the dark. "What repartees could have passed, when you had to feel around for a smile and had to handle your neighbor's cheek to see if he understood you?"

Fool enough to attempt to advise.
Ah, gentle dames! It gars me greet,
To think how many counsels sweet,
How many lengthened sage advices
The husband from the wife despises.[12]

⟨⟨poor me—⟩⟩

January 16, 1865

My husband is at home once more—for how long, I do not know. And his aides fill the house, and a group of hopelessly wounded haunt the place. And the drilling and the marching goes on—and as far as I can see, for. bats. happily forgotten.

It rains a flood—freshet after freshet. The forces of nature are befriending us, for our enemies have to make their way through swamps.

A month ago my husband wrote me a letter which I promptly suppressed after showing it to Mrs. McCord. He warned us to make ready—for the end had come. Our resources were exhausted—and the means of resistance could not be found.

It was what we could not bring ourselves to believe. And now—he thinks, with the RR all blown up, the swamps impassable by freshets which have no time to subside, so constant is the rain. The negroes are utterly apathetic (would they be so, if

[10]A paraphrase from *Geneviève,* part 116. "God is God—what people call meeting, the angels call Providence."

[11]Paraphrased from Charles Lamb, "Popular Fallacies, XV.—That We Should Lie Down with the Lamb," in *The Last Essays of Elia* (1833). The quotation at the end of this paragraph derives from the same essay, although M.B.C. does not reproduce Lamb's wording exactly.

[12]Slightly misquoted from Robert Burns, "Tam o' Shanter" (1791).

they saw us triumphant!), and if we had but an army to seize the opportunity. No troops—that is the real trouble. Dr. Gibbes took it on himself to send a telegram. Some people are cool enough—and fools enough for anything.

"Does Jeff Davis so hate South Carolina that he means to abandon her to her fate?" I wonder if they showed Mr. Davis this.

The answer has come.

"No. Jeff Davis loves South Carolina—only Yankees hate her. He will do all he can to save her."

Hardee—he of Hardee's *Tactics*[13]—he has a head for tactics, but it is not large enough to plan a campaign. He can only fight well when under orders.

We seem utterly without a head down here—utterly at sea. If some heavenborn genius would rush in and take command—

The pilot in calm weather lets any sea boy toy with his rudder—but when the winds howl and the waves rise, he seizes the helm himself.

And our pilot? Where is he?

"Napoleon had to go to St. Helena when he had exhausted his levies. No more soldiers until France could grow them."

"Suppose we try Stephen Elliott—everybody trusts him."

Today Mrs. McCord exchanged 16,000 dollars, Confederate bills, for gold—300 dollars. Sixteen thousand—for three hundred.

The bazaar will be a Belshazzar affair.[14] The handwriting is on the wall. Bad news everywhere.

Miss Garnett was in agony.

"I fear the very worst—before they find out, those stupid Yankees, that I am Irish."

The fears of old maids increase, apparently in proportion to their age and infirmities—and hideous ugliness.

Isabella fairly white and shining—resplendent in apparel—has gone down to Millwood.

She reproved the "weary heart" for dragging so in the road of life, or as she put it: "What do you mean to do if your father dies—or anybody that you really care for dies? You leave yourself no margin for proper affliction—when the time comes."

January 17, 1865

Bazaar opens today.

Sherman marches always—all RR's smashed.

And if I laugh at any mortal thing, it is that I may not weep.

Generals as plenty as blackberries, none in command. Beauregard with his Shiloh green sickness again. Bad time for a general seized by *melancholia*.

And this refrain is beating in my brain—

> March—March—Ettrick and Teviotdale—
> Why the de'il do ye not march all in order,

[13]William Joseph Hardee was the author of a standard textbook, *Rifle and Light Infantry Tactics* (1853–55).

[14]Daniel 5.

March—March—Teviot and Clydesdale—
All the blue bonnets are over the Border.[15]

1981

Abraham Lincoln 1809–1865

Tom Lincoln, born to poverty, almost illiterate, and raised to the mastery of a limited body of farming skills, struggled to squeeze, from a succession of small farms in Kentucky, Indiana, and Illinois, a livelihood for his family. But his son Abraham, burdened with the gift of an extraordinary intelligence, sensed nothing but weary futility in what seemed to him a treadmill of squatting and moving on; and though his formal schooling was as minimal as his father's, Abraham was inspired to educate himself by the few books that came his way and by the support of his sensitive and ambitious mother and stepmother. From these resources and from his own native sensitivity he gleaned that he ought to make his life, like the books he had cherished, a story with a meaningful end.

To say that he succeeded in this would be an understatement. At twenty-one he was on his own, working as laborer, storekeeper, and postmaster in the small town of New Salem, Illinois—and teaching himself the law; by his mid-twenties he was not only a successful practicing lawyer but a member of the state legislature (in which he served four terms); at thirty-eight he was elected to Congress; at fifty-two, he was elected president of the United States; and by the time of his death by assassination—only a few weeks after the inauguration of his second presidential term—he had made of himself so extraordinary a statesman that his end was all too painfully meaningful.

The ideals of the Republic which were celebrated in the histories he read as a child instilled in Lincoln the faith that, despite the poverty and squalor of his birth, he could determine his own destiny, and that the Constitution of his country guaranteed him the right to do so. Consequently he both revered the Constitution and labored, in his legal and political career, to assure that the Constitution's guarantees extended as far in practice as they did in ideal. That these two concerns were incompatible—that the compromise with slavery which was written into the Constitution made the United States (as he was to describe it) "a house divided against itself," a union which could not honor the rights of its southern states without making a mockery of its own Bill of Rights—occurred to him only gradually: for though he was vocal in his disapproval of slavery, throughout most of his political career he stood for free soil in the new territories but not for Abolition. When he campaigned for the presidency in 1860 his platform emphasized not the problem of slavery, but the preservation of the Union, as his primary concern.

It seemed clear enough that the new president was not the avenging angel of liberty the abolitionists had waited for, but rather an adroit politician whose appearance of flexible moderation made him tolerable to many though satisfactory to few: not the man anyone really wanted, but the only man who could command a tentative majority among the now bitterly divided

[15]The first lines, slightly misquoted, of a "ditty" sung to "the ancient air of 'Blue Bonnets over the Border,'" in Sir Walter Scott, *The Monastery. A Romance* (1820), volume 2, chapter 11.

population. He was quick and resourceful in appeasing the conflicting interests of his constituents—as ready to paint himself a defender of segregation as of universal liberty, where doing either would persuade his audience to accept his vision of the Constitution.

Yet the hysterical dread and outrage with which his opponents—both North and South—viewed his candidacy, which caused them to brand him the "blackest" of the "black Republicans," and which caused seven southern states to secede from the Union in response to his election in 1861, was not unfounded. Adherents of slavery had good reason to fear him, for in Lincoln the worldly pragmatism that made him a skillful manipulator of men was coupled with an extraordinary intellectual independence. He had demonstrated in Congress his willingness to jeopardize his own political future by taking an unpopular stand on principle, once the reins of power were in his hands; and the stand he had taken then indicated that as president he would be the enemy of slaveholders, despite his protestations of moderation. During his presidency he was besieged as much by the defenders of slavery as by its enemies, but in 1862, at a critically unstable moment in the war, he cast the weight of his administration with immediate emancipation of the slaves in the Confederate states, against the wishes of what seemed an overwhelming majority of the people. In his efforts to preserve the Union, he was willing to appease, and reluctant to offend, the powerful adherents of slavery—a posture which dictated a number of half-measures and dubious compromises. But the Union he envisioned was one in which slavery—and all artificial perpetuation of inequality among men—should have no lasting place.

Lincoln's rhetorical posture shifted with the needs of the moment much as his policies did; but like his policies, the language of Lincoln's presidential speeches has about it a ring of enlightened purposiveness which seems to reach beyond the merely strategic dimension of rhetoric. In early speeches he employed the precise language and humorous illustrative fables appropriate to an attorney arguing a case in law, but in the later speeches—of which the selections offered here are the most famous examples—he turned steadily toward the rhetoric of the Bible, both in style and reference. This shift from the legal to the religious parallels Lincoln's shift from the legislative to the executive branches of government and from a posture of legislative compromise to one of military force; his Biblical rhetoric, which had characterized the speeches of abolitionists for decades, appeals as they did to an authority that could not finally be found in the Constitution, but which might be counted on to unite a politically divided people under the banner of the Christianity they still shared.

The *Address at the Dedication of the Gettysburg National Cemetery* and the *Second Inaugural Address* are remarkable, however, not for their employment of Biblical cadence and reference but for the simplicity and clarity with which that rhetoric is fused with the self-educated lawyer's measured concern for justice in the affairs of men. Two addresses were given on November 19, 1863, at the dedication of the national cemetery at Gettysburg—site, only three months before, of the bloodiest battle of the War—and *both* appealed to the Christian sentiments of the fifteen thousand Americans who gathered for the ceremonies: but it was Edward Everett's two-hour paean to the forces of armed righteousness which met the public standard for eloquence and piety. Lincoln's two-minute speech, over almost before the crowd could gather that the president was speaking, seemed a failure—for it was concise and simple, barren of the florid language which would demonstrate the speaker's passionate response to the occasion. The piece, however, like Lincoln himself, gained after a time the regard of a people who (as Lincoln once jested) could be fooled some of the time but not forever; and his little speech has gradually come to seem more eloquent than any less restrained or more complex statement could have been. The author seems to speak from a place above narrow rational self-interest yet below blind adherence to an extrarational authority, so that these pleas for unity and support become reassertions of faith in the rational humanist principles on which his precious, precarious Republic had been founded.

Elaine Sargent Apthorp
San Jose State University

PRIMARY WORKS

Roy Basler, ed., *The Collected Works of Abraham Lincoln,* 9 volumes, 1953–1955; *Supplement 1832–1865,* 1974.

SECONDARY WORKS

Jacques Barzun, *Lincoln the Literary Genius,* 1960; Steven B. Oates, *With Malice Toward None,* 1978; Charles B. Strozier, *Lincoln's Quest for Union: Public and Private Meanings,* 1982, 1987.

Address at the Dedication of the Gettysburg National Cemetery

Four score and seven years ago our fathers brought forth on this continent, a new nation, conceived in Liberty, and dedicated to the proposition that all men are created equal.

Now we are engaged in a great civil war; testing whether that nation, or any nation so conceived and so dedicated, can long endure. We are met on a great battle-field of that war. We have come to dedicate a portion of that field as a final resting-place for those who here gave their lives that that nation might live. It is altogether fitting and proper that we should do this.

But, in a larger sense, we cannot dedicate—we cannot consecrate—we cannot hallow—this ground. The brave men, living and dead, who struggled here have consecrated it, far above our poor power to add or detract. The world will little note, nor long remember, what we say here, but it can never forget what they did here. It is for us the living, rather, to be dedicated here to the unfinished work which they who fought here have thus far so nobly advanced. It is rather for us to be here dedicated to the great task remaining before us—that from these honored dead we take increased devotion to that cause for which they gave the last full measure of devotion; that we here highly resolve that these dead shall not have died in vain; that this nation, under God, shall have a new birth of freedom; and that government of the people, by the people, for the people, shall not perish from the earth.

Second Inaugural Address

FELLOW-COUNTRYMEN:

At this second appearing to take the oath of the presidential office, there is less occasion for an extended address than there was at the first. Then a statement, somewhat in detail, of a course to be pursued, seemed fitting and proper. Now, at the expiration of four years, during which public declarations have been constantly called forth on every point and phase of the great contest which still absorbs the attention and engrosses the energies of the nation, little that is new could be presented. The progress of our arms,[1] upon which all else chiefly depends, is as well known to the public as to myself; and it is, I trust, reasonably satisfactory and encouraging to all. With high hope for the future, no prediction in regard to it is ventured.

On the occasion corresponding to this four years ago, all thoughts were anxiously directed to an impending civil war. All dreaded it—all sought to avert it. While the inaugural address was being delivered from this place, devoted altogether to saving the Union without war, insurgent agents were in the city seeking to destroy it without war—seeking to dissolve the Union, and divide effects, by negotiation. Both parties deprecated war; but one of them would make war rather than let the nation survive; and the other would accept war rather than let it perish. And the war came.

One-eighth of the whole population were colored slaves, not distributed generally over the Union, but localized in the Southern part of it. These slaves constituted a peculiar and powerful interest. All knew that this interest was, somehow, the cause of the war. To strengthen, perpetuate, and extend this interest was the object for which the insurgents would rend the Union, even by war; while the government claimed no right to do more than to restrict the territorial enlargement of it.

Neither party expected for the war the magnitude or the duration which it has already attained. Neither anticipated that the cause of the conflict might cease with, or even before, the conflict itself should cease.[2] Each looked for an easier triumph, and a result less fundamental and astounding. Both read the same Bible, and pray to the same God; and each invokes his aid against the other. It may seem strange that any men should dare to ask a just God's assistance in wringing their bread from the sweat of other men's faces; but let us judge not, that we be not judged.[3] The prayers of both could not be answered—that of neither has been answered fully.

The Almighty has his own purposes. "Woe unto the world because of offences! for it must needs be that offences come; but woe to that man by whom the offence cometh."[4] If we shall suppose that American slavery is one of those offences which, in the providence of God, must needs come, but which, having continued through His appointed time, He now wills to remove, and that He gives to both North and South this terrible war, as the woe due to those by whom the offence came, shall we discern therein any departure from those divine attributes which the believers in a

[1]The success of our armies. At the time of Lincoln's second inaugural, the Civil War was essentially over, the Union forces victorious.

[2]That the slaves would be freed before the war to decide their future was ended. Lincoln's Emancipation Proclamation went into effect on January 1, 1863.

[3]Reference to the Book of Matthew, 7:1.

[4]Reference to the Book of Matthew, 17:7.

Living God always ascribe to Him? Fondly do we hope—fervently do we pray—that this mighty scourge of war may speedily pass away. Yet, if God wills that it continue until all the wealth piled by the bondman's two hundred and fifty years of unrequited toil shall be sunk, and until every drop of blood drawn with the lash shall be paid by another drawn with the sword, as was said three thousand years ago, so still it must be said, "The judgments of the Lord are true and righteous altogether."[5]

With malice toward none; with charity for all; with firmness in the right, as God gives us to see the right, let us strive on to finish the work we are in; to bind up the nation's wounds; to care for him who shall have borne the battle, and for his widow, and his orphan—to do all which may achieve and cherish a just and lasting peace, among ourselves, and with all nations.

LITERATURE AND THE "WOMAN QUESTION"

Sarah Moore Grimké 1792–1873

See headnote to Angelina Grimké, pages 1945 through 1946.

from Letters on the Equality of the Sexes, and the Condition of Woman

Letter VIII
The Condition of Women in the United States

Brookline, 1837

. . . I shall now proceed to make a few remarks on the condition of women in my own country.

During the early part of my life, my lot was cast among the butterflies of the *fashionable* world; and of this class of women, I am constrained to say, both from experience and observation, that their education is miserably deficient; that they are taught to regard marriage as the one thing needful, the only avenue to distinction; hence to attract the notice and win the attention of men, by their external charms, is the chief business of fashionable girls. They seldom think that men will be allured by intellectual acquirements, because they find, that where any mental superiority exists, a woman is generally shunned and regarded as stepping out of her "appropriate sphere," which, in their view, is to dress, to dance, to set out to the best possible advantage her person, to read the novels which inundate the press, and which do more to destroy her character as a rational creature, than any thing else. Fashionable women regard themselves, and are regarded by men,

[5]Reference to the Book of Psalms 9:9.

as pretty toys or as mere instruments of pleasure; and the vacuity of mind, the heartlessness, the frivolity which is the necessary result of this false and debasing estimate of women, can only be fully understood by those who have mingled in the folly and wickedness of fashionable life. . . .

There is another and much more numerous class in this country, who are withdrawn by education or circumstances from the circle of fashionable amusements, but who are brought up with the dangerous and absurd idea, that *marriage* is a kind of preferment; and that to be able to keep their husband's house, and render his situation comfortable, is the end of her being. Much that she does and says and thinks is done in reference to this situation; and to be married is too often held up to the view of girls as the sine qua non of human happiness and human existence. For this purpose more than for any other, I verily believe the majority of girls are trained. This is demonstrated by the imperfect education which is bestowed upon them, and the little pains taken to cultivate their minds, after they leave school, by the little time allowed them for reading, and by the idea being constantly inculcated, that although all household concerns should be attended to with scrupulous punctuality at particular seasons, the improvement of their intellectual capacities is only a secondary consideration, and may serve as an occupation to fill up the odds and ends of time. In most families, it is considered a matter of far more consequence to call a girl off from making a pie, or a pudding, than to interrupt her whilst engaged in her studies. This mode of training necessarily exalts, in their view, the animal above the intellectual and spiritual nature, and teaches women to regard themselves as a kind of machinery, necessary to keep the domestic engine in order, but of little value as the *intelligent* companions of men.

Let no one think, from these remarks, that I regard a knowledge of housewifery as beneath the acquisition of women. Far from it: I believe that a complete knowledge of household affairs is an indispensable requisite in a woman's education,—that by the mistress of a family, whether married or single, doing her duty thoroughly and *understandingly,* the happiness of the family is increased to an incalculable degree, as well as a vast amount of time and money saved. All I complain of is, that our education consists so almost exclusively in culinary and other manual operations. I do long to see the time, when it will no longer be necessary for women to expend so many precious hours in furnishing "a well spread table," but that their husbands will forego some of their accustomed indulgences in this way, and encourage their wives to devote some portion of their time to mental cultivation, even at the expense of having to dine sometimes on baked potatoes, or bread and butter. . . .

The influence of women over the minds and character of *children* of both sexes, is allowed to be far greater than that of men. This being the case by the very ordering of nature, women should be prepared by education for the performance of their sacred duties as mothers and as sisters. . . .

There is another way in which the general opinion, that women are inferior to men, is manifested, that bears with tremendous effect on the laboring class, and indeed on almost all who are obliged to earn a subsistence, whether it be by mental or physical exertion—I allude to the disproportionate value set on the time and labor of men and of women. A man who is engaged in teaching, can always, I believe, command a higher price for tuition than a woman—even when he teaches the same branches, and is not in any respect superior to the woman. This I know is the case in boarding and other schools with which I have been acquainted, and it is so in every occupation in which the sexes engage indiscriminately. As for example, in tailoring, a man has twice, or three times as much for making a waistcoat or pantaloons as a woman, although the work done by each may be equally good. In those employments which are peculiar to women, their time is estimated at only half the value of that of men. A woman who goes out to wash, works as hard in proportion as a wood sawyer, or a coal heaver, but she is not generally able to make more than half as much by a day's work. The low remuneration which women receive for their work, has claimed the attention of a few philanthropists, and I hope it will continue to do so until some remedy is applied for this enormous evil. . . . There is yet another and more disastrous consequence arising from this unscriptural notion—women being educated, from earliest childhood, to regard themselves as inferior creatures, have not that self-respect which conscious equality would engender, and hence when their virtue is assailed, they yield to temptation with facility, under the idea that it rather exalts than debases them, to be connected with a superior being.

There is another class of women in this country, to whom I cannot refer, without feelings of the deepest shame and sorrow. I allude to our female slaves. Our southern cities are whelmed beneath a tide of pollution; the virtue of female slaves is wholly at the mercy of irresponsible tyrants, and women are bought and sold in our slave markets, to gratify the brutal lust of those who bear the name of Christians. In our slave States, if amid all her degradation and ignorance, a woman desires to preserve her virtue unsullied, she is either bribed or whipped into compliance, or if she dares resist her seducer, her life by the laws of some of the slave States may be, and has actually been sacrificed to the fury of disappointed passion. Where such laws do not exist, the power which is necessarily vested in the master over his property, leaves the defenceless slave entirely at his mercy, and the sufferings of some females on this account, both physical and mental, are intense. Mr. Gholson,[1] in the House of Delegates of Virginia, in 1832, said, "He really had been under the impression that he owned his slaves. He had lately purchased four women and ten children, in whom he thought he had obtained a great bargain; for he supposed they were his own property, *as were his brood mares.*" But even if any laws existed in the United States, as in Athens formerly, for the protection of female slaves, they would be null and void, because the evidence of a colored person is not admitted against a white, in any of our Courts of Justice in the slave States. "In Athens, if a female slave had cause to complain of any want of respect to the laws of modesty, she could seek the protection of the temple, and demand a change of owners; and such appeals were never discountenanced, or neglected by the magistrate." In Christian America, the slave has no refuge from unbridled cruelty and lust.

S.A. Forrall, speaking of the state of morals at the South, says, "Negresses when young and likely, are often employed by the planter, or his friends, to administer to their sensual desires. This frequently is a matter of speculation, for if the

[1]"It has always (perhaps erroneously) been considered by steady and old-fashioned people, that the owner of land had a reasonable right to its annual profits . . . the owner of *brood mares,* to their product; and the owner of *female slaves, to their increase.*" Mr. Gohlson's speech to the Virginia legislature, January 18, 1831, as reported in the Richmond *Whig* and quoted in *American Slavery As It Is* (1839; rpt. New York: Arno Press, 1969), p. 182.

offspring, a mulatto, be a handsome female, 800 or 1000 dollars may be obtained for her in the New Orleans market. It is an occurrence of no uncommon nature to see a Christian father sell his own daughter and the brother his own sister." . . . I will add but one more from the numerous testimonies respecting the degradation of female slaves, and the licentiousness of the South. It is from the Circular of the Kentucky Union, for the moral and religious improvement of the colored race. "To the female character among our black population, we cannot allude but with feelings of the bitterest shame. A similar condition of moral pollution and utter disregard of a pure and virtuous reputation, is to be found *only without the pale of Christendom.* That such a state of society should exist in a Christian nation, claiming to be the most enlightened upon earth, without calling forth any *particular attention* to its existence, though ever before our eyes and *in our* families, is a moral phenomenon at once unaccountable and disgraceful." Nor does the colored woman suffer alone: the moral purity of the white woman is deeply contaminated. In the daily habit of seeing the virtue of her enslaved sister sacrificed without hesitancy or remorse, she looks upon the crimes of seduction and illicit intercourse without horror, and although not personally involved in the guilt, she loses that value for innocence in her own, as well as the other sex, which is one of the strongest safeguards to virtue. She lives in habitual intercourse with men, whom she knows to be polluted by licentiousness, and often is she compelled to witness in her own domestic circle, those disgusting and heartsickening jealousies and strifes which disgraced and distracted the family of Abraham. In addition to all this, the female slaves suffer every species of degradation and cruelty, which the most wanton barbarity can inflict; they are indecently divested of their clothing, sometimes tied up and severely whipped, sometimes prostrated on the earth, while their naked bodies are torn by the scorpion lash.

"The whip on WOMAN's shrinking flesh!
Our soil yet reddening with the stains
Caught from her scourging warm and fresh."[2]

Can any American woman look at these scenes of shocking licentiousness and cruelty, and fold her hands in apathy, and say, "I have nothing to do with slavery"? *She cannot and be guiltless.*

I cannot close this letter, without saying a few words on the benefits to be derived by men, as well as women, from the opinions I advocate relative to the equality of the sexes. Many women are now supported, in idleness and extravagance, by the industry of their husbands, fathers, or brothers, who are compelled to toil out their existence, at the counting house, or in the printing office, or some other laborious occupation, while the wife and daughters and sisters take no part in the support of the family, and appear to think that their sole business is to spend the hard bought earnings of their male friends. I deeply regret such a state of things, because I believe that if women felt their responsibility, for the support of themselves, or their families it would add strength and dignity to their characters, and teach them more true sympathy for their husbands, than is now generally manifested,—a sympathy which would be exhibited by actions as well as words. Our brethren may

[2]John Greenleaf Whittier, "Stanzas."

reject my doctrine, because it runs counter to common opinions, and because it wounds their pride; but I believe they would be "partakers of the benefit" resulting from the Equality of the Sexes, and would find that woman, as their equal, was unspeakably more valuable than woman as their inferior, both as a moral and an intellectual being.

Thine in the bonds of womanhood,

Sarah M. Grimké

1838

Letter XV
Man Equally Guilty with Woman in the Fall

Uxbridge, 10th Mo. 20th, 1837.

. . . To perform our duties, we must comprehend our rights and responsibilities; and it is because we do not understand, that we now fall so far short in the discharge of our obligations. Unaccustomed to think for ourselves, and to search the sacred volume, to see how far we are living up to the design of Jehovah in our creation, we have rested satisfied with the sphere marked out for us by man, never detecting the fallacy of that reasoning which forbids woman to exercise some of her noblest faculties, and stamps with the reproach of indelicacy those actions by which women were formerly dignified and exalted in the church.

I should not mention this subject again, if it were not to point out to my sisters what seems to me an irresistible conclusion from the literal interpretation of St. Paul, without reference to the context, and the peculiar circumstances and abuses which drew forth the expressions, "I suffer not a woman to teach"[1]— "Let your women keep silence in the church,"[2] i.e. congregation. It is manifest, that if the apostle meant what his words imply, when taken in the strictest sense, then women have no right to *teach* Sabbath or day schools, or to open their lips to sing in the assemblies of the people; yet young and delicate women are engaged in all these offices; they are expressly trained to exhibit themselves, and raise their voices to a high pitch in the choirs of our places of worship. I do not intend to sit in judgment on my sisters for doing these things; I only want them to see, that they are as really infringing a *supposed* divine command, by instructing their pupils in the Sabbath or day schools, and by singing in the congregation, as if they were engaged in preaching the unsearchable riches of Christ to a lost and perishing world. Why, then, are we permitted to break this injunction in some points, and so seduously warned not to overstep the bounds set for us by our *brethren* in another? Simply, as I believe, because in the one case we subserve *their* views and *their* interests, and act *in subordination to them;* whilst in the other, we come in contact with their interests, and claim to be on an equality with them in the highest and most important trust ever committed to man, namely, the ministry of the word. It is manifest, that if women were permitted to be ministers of the gospel, as they unquestionably were in the primitive ages of the Christian church, it would interfere materially with the

[1] 1 Timothy 2:12.

[2] 1 Corinthians 14:34.

present organized system of spiritual power and ecclesiastical authority, which is now vested solely in the hands of men. It would either show that all the paraphernalia of theological seminaries, &c &c. to prepare men to become evangelists, is wholly unnecessary, or it would create a necessity for similar institutions in order to prepare women for the same office; and this would be an encroachment on that learning, which our kind brethren have so ungenerously monopolized. I do not ask any one to believe my statements, or adopt my conclusions, because they are mine; but I do earnestly entreat my sisters to lay aside their prejudices, and examine these subjects *for themselves,* regardless of the "traditions of men," because they are intimately connected with their duty and their usefulness in the present important crisis.

All who know any thing of the present system of benevolent and religious operations, know that women are performing an important part in them, in *subserviency to men,* who guide our labors, and are often the recipients of those benefits of education we toil to confer, and which we rejoice they can enjoy, although it is their mandate which deprives us of the same advantages. Now, whether our brethren have defrauded us intentionally, or unintentionally, the wrong we suffer is equally the same. For years, they have been spurring us up to the performance of our duties. The immense usefulness and the vast influence of woman have been eulogized and called into exercise, and many a blessing has been lavished upon us, and many a prayer put up for us, because we have labored by day and by night to clothe and feed and educate young men, whilst our own bodies sometimes suffer for want of comfortable garments, and our minds are left in almost utter destitution of that improvement which we are toiling to bestow upon the brethren. . . .

If the sewing societies, the avails of whose industry are now expended in supporting and educating young men for the ministry, were to withdraw their contributions to these objects, and give them where they are *more needed,* to the advancement of their *own sex* in useful learning, the next generation might furnish sufficient proof, that in intelligence and ability to master the whole circle of sciences, woman is not inferior to man; and instead of a sensible woman being regarded as she now is, as a *lusses naturae,*[3] they would be quite as common as sensible men. I confess, considering the high claim men in this country make to great politeness and deference to women, it does seem a little extraordinary that we should be urged to work for the brethren. I should suppose it would be more in character with "the generous promptings of chivalry, and the poetry of romantic gallantry," for which Catharine E. Beecher gives them credit, for them to form societies to educate their sisters, seeing our inferior capacities require more cultivation to bring them into use, and qualify us to be helps meet for them. However, though I think this would be but a just return for all our past kindnesses in this way, I should be willing to balance our accounts, and begin a new course. Henceforth, let the benefit be reciprocated, or else let each sex provide for the education of their own poor, whose talents ought to be rescued from the oblivion of ignorance. Sure I am, the young men who are now benefitted by the handy work of their sisters, will not be less honorable if they occupy half their time in earning enough to pay for their own education, instead of depending on the industry of women, who not

[3]Freak of nature.

unfrequently deprive themselves of the means of purchasing valuable books which might enlarge their stock of useful knowledge, and perhaps prove a blessing to the family by furnishing them with instructive reading. If the minds of women were enlightened and improved, the domestic circle would be more frequently refreshed by intelligent conversation, a means of edification now deplorably neglected, for want of that cultivation which these intellectual advantages would confer. . . .

I have now, my dear sister, completed my series of letters. I am aware, they contain some new views; but I believe they are based on the immutable truths of the Bible. All I ask for them is, the candid and prayerful consideration of Christians. If they strike at some of our bosom sins, our deep-rooted prejudices, our long cherished opinions, let us not condemn them on that account, but investigate them fearlessly and prayerfully, and not shrink from the examination; because, if they are true, they place heavy responsibilities upon women. In throwing them before the public, I have been actuated solely by the belief, that if they are acted upon, they will exalt the character and enlarge the usefulness of my own sex, and contribute greatly to the happiness and virtue of the other. That there is a root of bitterness continually springing up in families and troubling the repose of both men and women, (must be manifest to even a superficial observer; and I believe) it is the mistaken notion of the inequality of the sexes.[4] As there is an assumption of superiority on the one part, which is not sanctioned by Jehovah, there is an incessant struggle on the other to rise to that degree of dignity, which God designed women to possess in common with men, and to maintain those rights and exercise those privileges which every woman's common sense, apart from the prejudices of education, tells her are inalienable; they are a part of her moral nature, and can only cease when her immortal mind is extinguished.

One word more. I feel that I am calling upon my sex to sacrifice what has been, what is still dear to their hearts, the adulation, the flattery, the attentions of trifling men. I am asking them to repel these insidious enemies whenever they approach them; to manifest by their conduct, that, although they value highly the society of pious and intelligent men, they have no taste for idle conversation, and for that silly preference which is manifested for their personal accommodation, often at the expense of great inconvenience to their male companions. As an illustration of what I mean, I will state a fact.

I was traveling lately in a stage coach. A gentleman, who was also a passenger, was made sick by riding with his back to the horses. I offered to exchange seats, assuring him it did not affect me at all unpleasantly; but he was too polite to permit a lady to run the risk of being discommoded. I am sure he meant to be very civil, but I really thought it was a foolish piece of civility. This kind of attention encourages selfishness in woman, and is only accorded as a sort of quietus, in exchange for those *rights* of which we are deprived. Men and women are equally bound to cultivate a spirit of accommodation; but I exceedingly deprecate her being treated like a spoiled child, and sacrifices made to her selfishness and vanity. In lieu of these flattering but injurious attentions, yielded to her as an inferior, as a mark of benevolence and courtesy, I want my sex to claim nothing from their brethren but what

[4]"Looking diligently lest any man fail of the grace of God; lest any root of bitterness springing up trouble *you,* and thereby may be defiled. Hebrews 12:15.

their brethren may justly claim from them, in their intercourse as Christians. I am persuaded woman can do much in this way to elevate her own character. And that we may become duly sensible of the dignity of our nature, only a little lower than the angels, and bring forth fruit to the glory and honor of Emanuel's name, is the fervent prayer of

Thine in the bonds of womanhood,

Sarah M. Grimké

1838

Elizabeth Cady Stanton 1815–1902

Elizabeth Cady Stanton became one of the best known and most radical women's rights advocates of the nineteenth century. If Susan B. Anthony became the movement's most effective organizer, Stanton became its leading philosopher.

No one would have predicted Stanton's public role from the circumstances of her birth. She was born in Johnstown, New York, on November 12, 1815. Her father, Daniel Cady, was a judge, "a conservative of the conservatives," as Stanton later recalled. Her mother, Margaret, came from the landed Livingston family of eastern New York and remained, according to her daughter, "blue-blooded, socially as well as physically."

As a young girl, she was reminded often that sons would have been more welcome in her family than daughters. Of eleven children born to her parents, six died young, including all five of the Cady sons. When her eldest brother, Eleazer, died in 1826, Stanton tried desperately to comfort her father. All he would say was, "Oh, my daughter, I wish you were a boy!" Stanton learned early that such gender stereotyping was not personal but structural. In her father's law office, where she acted as assistant, she discovered that everywhere, men had legal, political, and economic dominance.

In the 1830s, Stanton saw a far different vision of the world when she visited her cousins, Gerrit and Ann Smith. The Smiths were committed anti-slavery activists, and there Stanton met her future husband, Henry Brewster Stanton, a tireless and enthusiastic abolitionist lecturer. Henry and Elizabeth were married, despite strong parental misgivings, in May, 1840.

The Stantons spent their honeymoon in England, where they attended the World Anti-Slavery Convention. Among the delegates to the meeting, Lucretia Mott most attracted Stanton's attention. Quaker minister from Philadelphia, founder of the Philadelphia Female Anti-Slavery Society, and mother of six, Mott epitomized for Stanton the freedom and independence for women that Stanton had dreamed about but had never before seen.

The World Anti-Slavery Convention decided on the first day of its meeting not to seat women delegates. Angered by such discrimination, Stanton and Mott resolved to organize a convention, as soon as they returned home, solely to discuss women's rights.

For eight years, however, they postponed action. The Stantons were immersed in starting a new career and a new family, first in Johnstown and then in Boston, where Henry began work as a lawyer and politician. Not until the Stantons moved to Seneca Falls would Elizabeth and Lucretia carry out their plan. There in Seneca Falls, the Stantons would raise four more children, to make seven in all. There, too, Elizabeth would begin her active career as a women's rights reformer.

Perhaps three hundred people attended the Seneca Falls convention. One hundred of them (sixty-eight women and thirty-two men) signed the Declaration of Sentiments, asserting that "all men and women are created equal." While Stanton discussed her own reasons for organizing this meeting, she said very little about why so many other people, on such short notice, would attend such a radical gathering.

Local people were in fact inspired to support women's rights by their participation in three other reform movements. The first was the effort to pass a Married Women's Property Act. For twelve years, the right of married women to own property had been seriously discussed throughout New York State. Wealthy men supported it so that they could give land to their daughters. Yet such an act had unsettling implications. Public debate over the Married Women's Property Act was also a debate over the equality of women and men and, in fact, over the meaning of the Declaration of Independence itself. As republicans, Americans linked citizenship rights (including the right to vote) with economic independence. If married women could be economically self-sufficient, what would prevent them from demanding political independence, as well? This debate over women's rights occurred simultaneously with efforts to give black males equal voting rights with white men in New York State. Both issues forced New Yorkers to consider the essential meaning of citizenship in their democratic republic.

Against this general background, two more reform efforts hit Seneca Falls and the neighboring village of Waterloo with particular intensity. In Waterloo, a large Quaker meeting split apart over issues relating to equality. One group formed the new Congregational Friends. Active in both abolitionism and women's rights, almost every family in this group would attend the Seneca Falls convention. In Seneca Falls at the same time, traditional political parties exploded under the impact of the new Free Soil party, whose goal was to eliminate slavery in the western territories. Free Soilers in Seneca Falls would also support the women's rights convention.

Because the Seneca Falls convention used the language of the Declaration of Independence, people reacted to its demands for women's equality more positively than Stanton remembered. Many Americans agreed with Horace Greeley, editor of the nation's most influential newspaper, the *New York Tribune,* when he admitted that "when a sincere republican is asked to say in sober earnest, what adequate reason he can give for refusing the demand of women to an equal participation with men in political rights, he must answer, None at all. . . . it is but the assertion of a natural right, and as such must be conceded."

The Seneca Falls convention raised issues that Americans would debate through the mid-twentieth century. It touched off a series of local and national conventions that led to the formation of national women's rights organizations, to women's active presence in public life, and finally, seventy-two years later, to the passage of the Nineteenth Amendment on August 26, 1920, giving women the right to vote. Americans remain ambivalent, however, about whether or not "all men and women are created equal."

Stanton herself never deviated from her uncompromising commitment to women's rights, which she called "the greatest revolution the world has ever known." In her last public act before her death in 1902, she wrote one letter to President Theodore Roosevelt and another, the day before she died, to his wife, Edith K. Roosevelt, asking them to support a constitutional amendment for women's right to vote.

Judith Wellman
State University of New York at Oswego

PRIMARY WORKS

Eighty Years & More: Reminiscences, 1815–1897, 1898, reprint 1971; Theodore Stanton and Harriot Stanton Blatch, *Elizabeth Cady Stanton as Revealed in Her Letters, Diary and Reminiscences,* 2 vols., 1922; Ellen Carol DuBois, ed., *Elizabeth Cady Stanton, Susan B. Anthony: Correspondence, Writings, Speeches,* 1981; *The Selected Papers of Elizabeth Cady Stanton and Susan B. Anthony,* 1977.

SECONDARY WORKS

Lois Banner, *Elizabeth Cady Stanton, a Radical for Women's Rights,* 1980; Elisabeth Griffith, *In Her Own Right: The Life of Elizabeth Cady Stanton,* 1984; Beth Marie Waggenspack, *The Search for Self-Sovereignty: the Oratory of Elizabeth Cady Stanton,* 1989.

from Eighty Years and More: Reminiscences

Up to this time life had glided by with comparative ease, but now the real struggle was upon me. My duties were too numerous and varied, and none sufficiently exhilarating or intellectual to bring into play my higher faculties. I suffered with mental hunger, which, like an empty stomach, is very depressing. I had books, but no stimulating companionship. To add to my general dissatisfaction at the change from Boston, I found that Seneca Falls was a malarial region, and in due time all the children were attacked with chills and fever which, under homeopathic treatment in those days, lasted three months. The servants were afflicted in the same way. Cleanliness, order, the love of the beautiful and artistic, all faded away in the struggle to accomplish what was absolutely necessary from hour to hour. Now I understood, as I never had before, how women could sit down and rest in the midst of general disorder. Housekeeping, under such conditions, was impossible, so I packed our clothes, locked up the house, and went to that harbor of safety, home, as I did ever after in stress of weather.

I now fully understood the practical difficulties most women had to contend with in the isolated household, and the impossibility of woman's best development if in contact, the chief part of her life, with servants and children. Fourier's phalansterie community life and co-operative households[1] had a new significance for me. Emerson says, "A healthy discontent is the first step to progress." The general discontent I felt with woman's portion as wife, mother, housekeeper, physician, and spiritual guide, the chaotic conditions into which everything fell without her constant supervision, and the wearied, anxious look of the majority of women impressed me with a strong feeling that some active measures should be taken to remedy the wrongs of society in general, and of women in particular. My experience at the World's Anti-slavery Convention, all I had read of the legal status of women, and the oppression I saw everywhere, together swept across my soul, intensified now by many personal experiences. It seemed as if all the elements had conspired to impel

[1]Frenchman Charles Fourier developed a scheme for organizing harmonious cooperative communities. Inspired by articles in the *New York Tribune,* Americans established several of these in the 1840s, including one in nearby Skaneateles, New York.

me to some onward step. I could not see what to do or where to begin—my only thought was a public meeting for protest and discussion.

In this tempest-tossed condition of mind I received an invitation to spend the day with Lucretia Mott, at Richard Hunt's, in Waterloo. There I met several members of different families of Friends, earnest, thoughtful women. I poured out, that day, the torrent of my long-accumulating discontent, with such vehemence and indignation that I stirred myself, as well as the rest of the party, to do and dare anything. My discontent, according to Emerson, must have been healthy, for it moved us all to prompt action, and we decided, then and there, to call a "Woman's Rights Convention." We wrote the call that evening and published it in the *Seneca County Courier* the next day, the 14th of July, 1848,[2] giving only five days' notice, as the convention was to be held on the 19th and 20th. The call was inserted without signatures,—in fact it was a mere announcement of a meeting,—but the chief movers and managers were Lucretia Mott, Mary Ann McClintock, Jane Hunt, Martha C. Wright, and myself. The convention, which was held two days in the Methodist Church,[3] was in every way a grand success. The house was crowded at every session, the speaking good, and a religious earnestness dignified all the proceedings.

These were the hasty initiative steps of "the most momentous reform that had yet been launched on the world—the first organized protest against the injustice which had brooded for ages over the character and destiny of one-half the race." No words could express our astonishment on finding, a few days afterward, that what seemed to us so timely, so rational, and so sacred, should be a subject for sarcasm and ridicule to the entire press of the nation. With our Declaration of Rights and Resolutions for a text, it seemed as if every man who could wield a pen prepared a homily on "woman's sphere." All the journals from Maine to Texas seemed to strive with each other to see which could make our movement appear the most ridiculous. The anti-slavery papers stood by us manfully and so did Frederick Douglass,[4] both in the convention and in his paper, *The North Star,* but so pronounced was the popular voice against us, in the parlor, press, and pulpit, that most of the ladies who had attended the convention and signed the declaration, one by one, withdrew their names and influence and joined our persecutors. Our friends gave us the cold shoulder and felt themselves disgraced by the whole proceeding.

If I had had the slightest premonition of all that was to follow that convention, I fear I should not have had the courage to risk it, and I must confess that it was with fear and trembling that I consented to attend another, one month afterward, in Rochester. Fortunately, the first one seemed to have drawn all the fire, and of the second but little was said. But we had set the ball in motion, and now, in quick succession, conventions were held in Ohio, Indiana, Massachusetts, Pennsylvania, and in the City of New York, and have been kept up nearly every year since.

. . . The most noteworthy of the early conventions were those held in Massachusetts, in which such men as Garrison, Phillips, Channing, Parker, and Emerson

[2]This actually appeared first on July 11, 1848.

[3]The women's rights conventions actually met in the Wesleyan Methodist Church.

[4]Escaped slave, abolitionist orator, and editor of *The North Star* in Rochester, New York, Douglass was the only known black person to attend the Seneca Falls meeting. He remained committed to women's rights throughout his life.

took part.[5] It was one of these that first attracted the attention of Mrs. John Stuart Mill, and drew from her pen that able article on "The Enfranchisement of Woman," in the *Westminster Review* of October, 1852.[6] . . .

Declaration of Sentiments

When, in the course of human events, it becomes necessary for one portion of the family of man to assume among the people of the earth a position different from that which they have hitherto occupied, but one to which the laws of nature and of nature's God entitle them, a decent respect to the opinions of mankind requires that they should declare the causes that impel them to such a course.

We hold these truths to be self-evident: that all men and women are created equal; that they are endowed by their Creator with certain inalienable rights; that among these are life, liberty, and the pursuit of happiness; that to secure these rights governments are instituted, deriving their just powers from the consent of the governed. Whenever any form of government becomes destructive of these ends, it is the right of those who suffer from it to refuse allegiance to it, and to insist upon the institution of a new government, laying its foundation on such principles, and organizing its powers in such form, as to them shall seem most likely to effect their safety and happiness. Prudence, indeed, will dictate that governments long established should not be changed for light and transient causes; and accordingly all experience hath shown that mankind are more disposed to suffer, while evils are sufferable, than to right themselves by abolishing the forms to which they were accustomed. But when a long train of abuses and usurpations, pursuing invariably the same object evinces a design to reduce them under absolute despotism, it is their duty to throw off such government, and to provide new guards for their future security. Such has been the patient sufferance of the women under this government, and such is now the necessity which constrains them to demand the equal station to which they are entitled.

The history of mankind is a history of repeated injuries and usurpations on the part of man toward woman, having in direct object the establishment of an absolute tyranny over her. To prove this, let facts be submitted to a candid world.

He has never permitted her to exercise her inalienable right to the elective franchise.

[5]William Lloyd Garrison, Wendell Phillips, William Henry Channing, and Theodore Parker were all nationally known radical abolitionists from the Boston area. Garrison edited *The Liberator;* Phillips was a brilliant anti-slavery orator; Channing and Parker were Unitarian ministers. Ralph Waldo Emerson of Concord, Massachusetts, was perhaps America's best-known essayist and philosopher.

[6]Mrs. John Stuart Mill: Harriet Taylor married John Stuart Mill in 1851, after a twenty-one year intimate friendship. Mill attributed much of his commitment to women's rights to Harriet's influence, including "all that is most striking and profound" in his influential *The Subjection of Women* (1869).

He has compelled her to submit to laws, in the formation of which she had no voice.

He has withheld from her rights which are given to the most ignorant and degraded men—both natives and foreigners.

Having deprived her of this first right of a citizen, the elective franchise, thereby leaving her without representation in the halls of legislation, he has oppressed her on all sides.

He has made her, if married, in the eye of the law, civilly dead.

He has taken from her all right in property, even to the wages she earns.

He has made her, morally, an irresponsible being, as she can commit many crimes with impunity, provided they be done in the presence of her husband. In the covenant of marriage, she is compelled to promise obedience to her husband, he becoming, to all intents and purposes, her master—the law giving him power to deprive her of her liberty, and to administer chastisement.

He has so framed the laws of divorce, as to what shall be the proper causes, and in case of separation, to whom the guardianship of the children shall be given, as to be wholly regardless of the happiness of women—the law, in all cases, going upon a false supposition of the supremacy of man, and giving all power into his hands.

After depriving her of all rights as a married woman, if single, and the owner of property, he has taxed her to support a government which recognizes her only when her property can be made profitable to it.

He has monopolized nearly all the profitable employments, and from those she is permitted to follow, she receives but a scanty remuneration. He closes against her all the avenues to wealth and distinction which he considers most honorable to himself. As a teacher of theology, medicine, or law, she is not known.

He has denied her the facilities for obtaining a thorough education, all colleges being closed against her.

He allows her in Church, as well as State, but a subordinate position, claiming Apostolic authority for her exclusion from the ministry, and, with some exceptions, from any public participation in the affairs of the Church.

He has created a false public sentiment by giving to the world a different code of morals for men and women, by which moral delinquencies which exclude women from society, are not only tolerated, but deemed of little account in man.

He has usurped the prerogative of Jehovah himself, claiming it as his right to assign for her a sphere of action, when that belongs to her conscience and to her God.

He has endeavored, in every way that he could, to destroy her confidence in her own powers, to lessen her self-respect, and to make her willing to lead a dependent and abject life.

Now, in view of this entire disfranchisement of one-half the people of this country, their social and religious degradation—in view of the unjust laws above mentioned, and because women do feel themselves aggrieved, oppressed, and fraudulently deprived of their most sacred rights, we insist that they have immediate admission to all the rights and privileges which belong to them as citizens of the United States.

In entering upon the great work before us, we anticipate no small amount of misconception, misrepresentation, and ridicule; but we shall use every instrumentality within our power to effect our object. We shall employ agents, circulate tracts, petition the State and National legislatures, and endeavor to enlist the pulpit and the press in our behalf. We hope this Convention will be followed by a series of Conventions embracing every part of the country.

1898

Fanny Fern (Sara Willis Parton)[1] *1811–1872*

Born in Portland, Maine, the daughter of Nathaniel and Hannah Parker Willis, Fern spent her early years in Boston, where her father established a religious newspaper and founded *Youth's Companion.* Fern learned journalism from him but preferred her more broadminded mother to whom she later attributed her literary talents. Fern was educated at the famous Beecher seminary; Catharine Beecher and her sister Harriet recalled her as a mischief-maker who neglected her studies but wrote witty essays.

Fern lived happily with her first husband, Charles Eldredge, a bank cashier whom she married in 1837. But when he died in 1846, soon after the deaths of her mother and the eldest of her three daughters, she was reduced to relative poverty with only grudging support from her father and in-laws. In 1849 she married Samuel Farrington, a Boston merchant; they quickly separated, and Fern later portrayed him as a "hypocrite" who tricks a reluctant widow into marriage and then deserts her.

Fern tried unsuccessfully to earn a living sewing and teaching and had to give up a daughter to her in-laws before she decided to make use of her background and write short sketches for Boston papers. She appealed to her brother, N.P. Willis, a successful poet and editor, for help in launching a literary career; apparently he pronounced her writing vulgar and advised making shirts instead. But Fern's sketches proved so popular that when she collected them in 1853, *Fern Leaves from Fanny's Portfolio* became an instant best-seller. She continued the next year with a second series and a juvenile.

Fern's early sketches are heavily autobiographical: they treat the deaths of husbands or children, as in "A Thanksgiving Story," or the failings of family members, as in "Apollo Hyacinth," where she satirizes her brother as a dandy and social climber. One prominent theme, which appears below in "Mrs. Adolphus Smith Sporting the 'Blue Stocking'" and "Critics" and would become a Fern staple, is the difficult situation of the female writer; Fern's aspiring authors have trouble finding decent writing conditions, proper remuneration from editors, or fair treatment by critics.

Fern used material from her early sketches in *Ruth Hall* (1855), a novel about the struggles of a widow to gain financial security. Fern had thought herself protected by her pseudonym, but *Ruth Hall* caused a sensation when her identity was discovered—and apparently hinted at by her publisher's ads—and Ruth's mean father, in-laws, and brother "Hyacinth" recognized as the author's own. While Nathaniel Hawthorne admired the novel, making Fern the one exception to his sweeping indictment of his female rivals as a "d—d mob of scribbling women," most critics attacked it for the same reason he praised it: the lack of "female delicacy" involved in satirizing one's relatives and allowing one's heroine to evolve from tearful victim to aggressive author and businesswoman. Fern was widely thought to have "demeaned herself" in creating "Ruthless Hall."

[1]Although "Fanny Fern" was a pen name, Parton preferred it to her real name and used it even in her personal life, becoming "Fanny" to her family and friends.

Neither disapproving critics nor the publication of *Life and Beauties of Fanny Fern* (1855), an anonymously authored book denouncing her, affected Fern's popularity with readers. She accepted the extravagant sum of $100 a week to write for the New York *Ledger,* reclaimed her daughter, and moved to New York. In 1856 she again broke with convention, marrying a man eleven years her junior (James Parton, the biographer) and publicly praising Walt Whitman's scandalous *Leaves of Grass.* She also published an inferior novel, *Rose Clark,* but thereafter restricted herself to the form she excelled at, the short, informal essay; from 1857 to her death in 1872 she published several collections of these from her *Ledger* columns.

Because her early work is best known (or because women writing in mid-nineteenth-century America have been lumped together), Fanny Fern has been mistakenly classified as a "sentimentalist." Fred Pattee in *The Feminine Fifties* calls her a "tearful moralizer," claiming she produced "goody-goody inanity." However, Fern's writing changed significantly after her initial success. The first three-quarters of *Fern Leaves* may be too lachrymose for modern taste but the last quarter contains humorous and satirical pieces, and in the second series the proportion is exactly reversed. Fern was known to her contemporaries for her non-goody-goody wit and humor expressed in the "noisy, rattling" style—full of italics and exclamation points—that her brother deplored.

By 1859 and the publication of *Folly As It Flies,* Fern had developed a surer voice, still direct and fresh but more relaxed and unified. She also broadened her range of subject matter. Although her trademark continued to be women's and children's rights and everyday domestic topics, like the annoying habits of husbands, Fern became more conscious of urban social and economic conditions. She began to express her empathy with working women, which had earlier revealed itself in pieces like "Soliloquy of a Housemaid," in greater detail, depicting poverty, prostitution, exploitation of workers, and prison life.

Barbara A. White
University of New Hampshire

PRIMARY WORKS

Joyce W. Warren, ed., *Ruth Hall and Other Writings,* 1986.

SECONDARY WORKS

Lucy M. Freibert and Barbara A. White, eds., *Hidden Hands: An Anthology of American Women Writers, 1790–1870,* 1985; Judith Fetterley, *Provisions: A Reader from 19th-Century American Women,* 1985; Joyce W. Warren, *Fanny Fern: An Independent Woman,* 1992; Sharon Harris, ed., *Redefining the Political Novel: American Women Writers, 1797–1901,* 1995.

Hints to Young Wives

Shouldn't I like to make a bon-fire of all the "Hints to Young Wives," "Married Woman's Friend," etc., and throw in the authors after them? I have a little neighbor who believes all they tell her is gospel truth, and lives up to it. The minute she sees her husband coming up the street, she makes for the door, as if she hadn't another minute to live, stands in the entry with her teeth chattering in her head till he gets all his coats and mufflers, and overshoes, and what-do-you-call'-ems off, then chases round (like a cat in a fit) after the boot-jack; warms his slippers and puts 'em on, and dislocates her wrist carving at the table for fear it will tire him.

Poor little innocent fool! she imagines that's the way to preserve his affection. Preserve a fiddlestick! The consequence is, he's sick of the sight of her; snubs her when she asks him a question, and after he has eaten her good dinners takes himself off as soon as possible, bearing in mind the old proverb "that too much of a good thing is good for nothing." Now the truth is just this, and I wish all the women on earth had but one ear in common, so that I could put this little bit of gospel into it:—Just so long as a man isn't quite as sure as if he knew for certain, whether nothing on earth could ever disturb your affection for him, he is your humble servant, but the very second he finds out (or thinks he does) that he has possession of every inch of your heart, and no neutral territory—he will turn on his heel and march off whistling "Yankee Doodle!"

Now it's no use to take your pocket handkerchief and go snivelling round the house with a pink nose and red eyes; not a bit of it! If you have made the interesting discovery that you were married for a sort of upper servant or housekeeper, just *fill that place and no other,* keep your temper, keep all his strings and buttons and straps on; and then keep him at a distance as a housekeeper should—"them's my sentiments!" I have seen one or two men in my life who could bear to be loved (as a woman with a soul knows how), without being spoiled by it, or converted into a tyrant—but they are rare birds, and should be caught, stuffed and handed over to Barnum! Now as the ministers say, "I'll close with an interesting little incident that came under my observation."

Mr. Fern came home one day when I had such a crucifying headache that I couldn't have told whether I was married or single, and threw an old coat into my lap to mend. Well, I tied a wet bandage over my forehead, "left all flying," and sat down to it—he might as well have asked me to make a *new* one; however I new lined the sleeves, mended the buttonholes, sewed on new buttons down the front, and all over the coat tails—when finally it occurred to me (I believe it was a suggestion of Satan), that the *pocket* might need mending so I turned it inside out, and *what do you think I found?* A *love-letter from him to my dress-maker!!* I dropped the coat, I dropped the work-basket, I dropped the buttons, I dropped the baby (it was a *female,* and I thought it just as well to put her out of future misery) and then I hopped up into a chair front of the looking-glass, and remarked to the young woman I saw there, *"F-a-n-n-y F-e-r-n! if you—are—ever—such—a—confounded fool again"—and I wasn't.*

Olive Branch
Feb. 14, 1852

from Fern Leaves, 1st Series

Thanksgiving Story

"Mary!" said the younger of two little girls, as they nestled under a coarse coverlid, one cold night in December, "tell me about Thanksgiving-day before papa went to heaven. I'm cold and hungry, and I can't go to sleep;—I want something nice to think about."

"Hush!" said the elder child, "don't let dear mamma hear you; come nearer to me;"—and they laid their cheeks together.

"I fancy papa was rich. We lived in a very nice house. I know there were pretty pictures on the wall; and there were nice velvet chairs, and the carpet was thick and soft, like the green moss-patches in the wood;—and we had pretty gold-fish on the side-table, and Tony, my black nurse, used to feed them. And papa!—you can't remember papa, Letty,—he was tall and grand, like a prince, and when he smiled he made me think of angels. He brought me toys and sweetmeats, and carried me out to the stable, and set me on Romeo's live back, and laughed because I was afraid! And I used to watch to see him come up the street, and then run to the door to jump in his arms;—he was a dear, kind papa," said the child, in a faltering voice.

"Don't cry," said the little one; "please tell me some more."

"Well, Thanksgiving-day we were so happy; we sat around such a large table, with so many people,—aunts and uncles and cousins,—I can't think why they never come to see us now, Letty,—and Betty made such sweet pies, and we had a big—big turkey; and papa would have me sit next to him, and gave me the wishbone, and all the plums out of his pudding; and after dinner he would take me in his lap, and tell me 'Red Riding Hood,' and call me 'pet,' and 'bird,' and 'fairy.' O, Letty, I can't tell any more; I believe I'm going to cry."

"I'm very cold," said Letty. "Does papa know, up in heaven, that we are poor and hungry now?"

"Yes—no—I can't tell," answered Mary, wiping away her tears; unable to reconcile her ideas of heaven with such a thought. "Hush!—mamma will hear!"

Mamma had "heard." The coarse garment, upon which she had toiled since sunrise, dropped from her hands, and tears were forcing themselves, thick and fast, through her closed eyelids. The simple recital found but too sad an echo in that widowed heart.

1853

from Fern Leaves, 2nd Series

Soliloquy of a Housemaid

Oh, dear, dear! Wonder if my mistress *ever* thinks I am made of flesh and blood? Five times, within half an hour, I have trotted up stairs, to hand her things, that were only four feet from her rocking-chair. Then, there's her son, Mr. George,—it does seem to me, that a great able-bodied man like him, need n't call a poor tired woman up four pair of stairs to ask "what's the time of day?" Heigho!—its "*Sally* do this," and "*Sally* do that," till I wish I never had been baptized at all; and I might as well go farther back, while I am about it, and wish I had never been born.

Now, instead of ordering me round so like a dray horse, if they would only look up smiling-like, now and then; or ask me how my "rheumatiz" did; or say good morning, Sally; or show some sort of interest in a fellow-cretur, I could pluck up a bit of heart to work for them. A kind word would ease the wheels of my treadmill amazingly, and wouldn't cost *them* anything, either.

Look at my clothes, all at sixes and sevens. I can't get a minute to sew on a string or button, except at night; and then I'm so sleepy it is as much as ever I can find the way to bed: and what a bed it is, to be sure! Why, even the pigs are now and then allowed clean straw to sleep on; and as to bed-clothes, the less said about them the better; my old cloak serves for a blanket, and the sheets are as thin as a charity school soup. Well, well; one wouldn't think it, to see all the fine glittering things down in the drawing-room. Master's span of horses, and Miss Clara's diamond ear-rings, and mistresses rich dresses. I *try* to think it is all right, but it is no use.

To-morrow is Sunday—"day of *rest,*" I believe they *call* it. H-u-m-p-h!—more cooking to be done—more company—more confusion than on any other day in the week. If I own a soul I have not heard how to take care of it for many a long day. Wonder if my master and mistress calculate to pay me for *that,* if I lose it? It is a *question* in my mind. Land of Goshen! I aint sure I've got a mind—there's the bell again!

1854

Apollo Hyacinth

"There is no better test of moral excellence, than the keenness of one's sense, and the depth of one's love, of all that is beautiful."

—DONOHUE.

I don't endorse that sentiment. I am acquainted with Apollo Hyacinth. I have read his prose, and I have read his poetry; and I have cried over both, till my heart was as soft as my head, and my eyes were as red as a rabbit's. I have listened to him in public, when he was, by turns, witty, sparkling, satirical, pathetic, till I could have added a codicil to my will, and left him all my worldly possessions; and possibly you have done the same. He has, perhaps, grasped you cordially by the hand, and, with a beaming smile, urged you, in his musical voice, to "call on him and Mrs. Hyacinth"; and you have called: but, did you ever find him "in"? You have invited him to visit you, and have received a "gratified acceptance," in his elegant chirography; but, *did he ever come?* He has borrowed money of you, in the most elegant manner possible; and, as he deposited it in his beautiful purse, he has assured you, in the choicest and most happily chosen language, that he "should never forget your kindness"; but, *did he ever pay?*

Should you die to-morrow, Apollo would write a poetical obituary notice of you, which would raise the price of pocket-handkerchiefs; but should your widow call on him in the course of a month, to solicit his patronage to open a school, she would be told "he was out of town," and that it was "quite uncertain when he would return."

Apollo has a large circle of relatives; but his "keenness of perception, and deep love, of the beautiful" are so great, that none of them *exactly* meet his views. His "moral excellence," however, does not prevent his making the most of them. He has a way of dodging them adroitly, when they call for a reciprocation, either in a business or a social way; or, if, at any time, there is a necessity for inviting them to his house, he does it when he is at his *country* residence, where their *greenness* will not be out of place.

Apollo never says an uncivil thing—never; he prides himself on that, as well as on his perfect knowledge of human nature; therefore, his sins are all sins of omission. His tastes are very exquisite, and his nature peculiarly sensitive; consequently, he cannot bear trouble. He will tell you, in his elegant way, that trouble "annoys" him, that it "bores" him; in short, that it unfits him for life—for business; so, should you hear that a friend or relative of his, even a brother or a sister, was in distress, or persecuted in any manner, you could not do Apollo a greater injury (in his estimation) than to inform him of the fact. It would so grate upon his sensitive spirit,—it would so "annoy" him; whereas, did he not hear of it until the friend, or brother, or sister, were relieved or buried, he could manage the matter with his usual urbanity and without the slightest draught upon his exquisitely sensitive nature, by simply writing a pathetic and elegant note, expressing the keenest regret at not having known "all about it" in time to have "flown to the assistance of his dear"—&c.

Apollo prefers friends who can stand grief and annoyance, as a rhinoceros can stand flies—friends who can bear their own troubles and all his—friends who will stand between him and everything disagreeable in life, and never ask anything in return. To such friends he clings with the most touching tenacity—as long as he can use them; but let their good name be assailed, let misfortune once overtake them, and his "moral excellence" compels him, at once, to ignore their existence, until they have been extricated from all their troubles, and it has become perfectly safe and *advantageous* for him to renew the acquaintance.

Apollo is keenly alive to the advantages of social position, (not having always enjoyed them;) and so, his Litany reads after this wise: From all questionable, unfashionable, unpresentable, and vulgar persons, Good Lord, deliver us!

1854

Critics

"Bilious wretches, who abuse you because you write better than they."

Slander and detraction! Even I, Fanny, know better than that. *I* never knew an editor to nib[1] his pen with a knife as sharp as his temper, and write a scathing criticism on a book, because the authoress had declined contributing to his paper. I never knew a man who had fitted himself to a promiscuous coat, cut out in merry mood by taper fingers, to seize his porcupine quill, under the agony of too tight a *self-inflicted* fit, to annihilate the offender. I never saw the bottled-up hatred of years, concentrated in a single venomous paragraph. I never heard of an unsuccessful masculine author, whose books were drugs in the literary market, speak with a sneer of successful literary feminity, and insinuate that it was by *accident,* not *genius,* that they hit the popular favor!

By the memory of "seventy-six," No! Do you suppose a *man's* opinions are in the market—to be bought and sold to the highest bidder? Do you suppose he would laud a vapid book, because the fashionable authoress once laved his toadying

[1]To mend the point of a pen.

temples with the baptism of upper-tendom? or, do you suppose he'd lash a poor, but self-reliant wretch, who had presumed to climb to the topmost round of Fame's ladder, without *his* royal permission or assistance, and in despite of his repeated attempts to discourage her? No—no—bless your simple soul; a man never stoops to a meanness. There never was a criticism yet, born of envy, or malice, or repulsed love, or disappointed ambition. No—no. Thank the gods, *I* have a more exalted opinion of masculinity.

1854

Mrs. Adolphus Smith Sporting the "Blue Stocking"

Well, I think I'll finish that story for the editor of the "Dutchman." Let me see; where did I leave off? The setting sun was just gilding with his last ray—"Ma, I want some bread and molassees"—(yes, dear,) gilding with his last ray the church spire—"Wife, where's my Sunday pants?" *(Under the bed, dear,)* the church spire of Inverness, when a—"There's nothing under the bed, dear, but your lace cap"—(Perhaps they are in the coal hod in the closet,) when a horseman was seen approaching—"Ma'am, the *pertators* is out; not one for dinner"—(Take some turnips,) approaching, covered with dust, and—"Wife! the baby has swallowed a button"—(*Reverse him,* dear—take him by the heels,) and waving in his hand a banner, on which was written—"Ma! I've torn my pantaloons"—liberty or death! The inhabitants rushed *en masse*—"Wife! WILL you leave off scribbling?" (Don't be disagreeable, Smith, I'm just getting inspired,) to the public square, where De Begnis, who had been secretly—"Butcher wants to see you, ma'am"—secretly informed of the traitors'—"Forgot *which* you said, ma'am, sausages or mutton chop"—movements, gave orders to fire; not less than twenty—My gracious! Smith, you have n't been *reversing* that child all this time; he's as black as your coat; and that boy of YOURS has torn up the first sheet of my manuscript. There! it's no use for a married woman to cultivate her intellect.—Smith, hand me those twins.

1854

Independence

"FOURTH OF JULY." Well—I don't feel patriotic. Perhaps I might if they would stop that deafening racket. Washington was very well, if he *couldn't* spell, and I'm glad we are all free; but as a woman—I shouldn't know it, didn't some orator tell me. Can I go out of an evening without a hat at my side? Can I go out with one on my head without danger of a station-house? Can I clap my hands at some public speaker when I am nearly bursting with delight? Can I signify the contrary when my hair stands on end with vexation? Can I stand up in the cars "like a gentleman" without being immediately invited "to sit down"? Can I get into an omnibus without having

my sixpence taken from my hand and given to the driver? Can I cross Broadway without having a policeman tackled to my helpless elbow? Can I go to see anything *pleasant,* like an execution or a dissection? Can I drive that splendid "Lantern,"[1] distancing—like his owner—all competitors? Can I have the nomination for "Governor of Vermont," like our other contributor, John G. Saxe?[2] Can I be a Senator, that I may hurry up that millennial International Copyright Law?[3] Can I *even* be President? Bah—you know I can't. *"Free!"* Humph!

New York Ledger
July 30, 1859

The Working-Girls of New York

Nowhere more than in New York does the contest between squalor and splendor so sharply present itself. This is the first reflection of the observing stranger who walks its streets. Particularly is this noticeable with regard to its women. Jostling on the same pavement with the dainty fashionist is the care-worn working-girl. Looking at both these women, the question arises, which lives the more miserable life—she whom the world styles "fortunate," whose husband belongs to three clubs, and whose only meal with his family is an occasional breakfast, from year's end to year's end; who is as much a stranger to his own children as to the reader; whose young son of seventeen has already a detective on his track employed by his father to ascertain where and how he spends his nights and his father's money; swift retribution for that father who finds food, raiment, shelter, equipages for his household; but love, sympathy, companionship—never? Or she—this other woman—with a heart quite as hungry and unappeased, who also faces day by day the same appalling question: *Is this all life has for me?*

A great book is yet unwritten about women. Michelet has aired his wax-doll theories regarding them.[1] The defender of "woman's rights" has given us her views. Authors and authoresses of little, and big repute, have expressed themselves on this subject, and none of them as yet have begun to grasp it: men—because they lack spirituality, rightly and justly to interpret women; women—because they dare not, or will not tell us that which most interests us to know. Who shall write this bold, frank, truthful book remains to be seen. Meanwhile woman's millennium is yet a great way off; and while it slowly progresses, conservatism and indifference gaze through their spectacles at the seething elements of to-day, and wonder "what ails all our women?"

Let me tell you what ails the working-girls. While yet your breakfast is progressing, and your toilet unmade, comes forth through Chatham Street and the

[1]A horse belonging to Robert Bonner, Fern's editor.

[2]John Godfrey Saxe (1816–1887), a poet and frequent contributor to magazines, ran for Governor of Vermont in 1859 and 1860.

[3]Fern supported an international copyright law to protect authors from having their works pirated in other countries.

[1]Refers to misogynist writings of Jules Michelet (1798–1894), a French historian who preferred women to be docile and obedient.

Bowery, a long procession of them by twos and threes to their daily labor. Their breakfast, so called, has been hastily swallowed in a tenement house, where two of them share, in a small room, the same miserable bed. Of its quality you may better judge, when you know that each of these girls pays but three dollars a week for board, to the working man and his wife where they lodge.

The room they occupy is close and unventilated, with no accommodations for personal cleanliness, and so near to the little Flinegans that their Celtic night-cries are distinctly heard. They have risen unrefreshed, as a matter of course, and their ill-cooked breakfast does not mend the matter. They emerge from the doorway where their passage is obstructed by "nanny goats" and ragged children rooting together in the dirt, and pass out into the street. They shiver as the sharp wind of early morning strikes their temples. There is no look of youth on their faces; hard lines appear there. Their brows are knit; their eyes are sunken; their dress is flimsy, and foolish, and tawdry; always a hat, and feather or soiled artificial flower upon it; the hair dressed with an abortive attempt at style; a soiled petticoat; a greasy dress, a well-worn sacque or shawl, and a gilt breast-pin and earrings.

Now follow them to the large, black-looking building, where several hundred of them are manufacturing hoop-skirts. If you are a woman you have worn plenty; but you little thought what passed in the heads of these girls as their busy fingers glazed the wire, or prepared the spools for covering them, or secured the tapes which held them in their places. *You* could not stay five minutes in that room, where the noise of the machinery used is so deafening, that only by the motion of the lips could you comprehend a person speaking.

Five minutes! Why, these young creatures bear it, from seven in the morning till six in the evening; week after week, month after month, with only half an hour at midday to eat their dinner of a slice of bread and butter or an apple, which they usually eat in the building, some of them having come a long distance. As I said, the roar of machinery in that room is like the roar of Niagara. Observe them as you enter. Not one lifts her head. They might as well be machines, for any interest or curiosity they show, save always to know *what o'clock it is.* Pitiful! pitiful, you almost sob to yourself, as you look at these young girls. *Young?* Alas! it is only in years that they are young.

Folly As It Flies

1868

Sojourner Truth c. 1797–1883

In the 1960s, the revival of the women's movement was greeted with ambivalence and hostility by some black women, for they regarded the demands of feminists to be concerns chiefly of middle-class white women and they feared that issues bearing upon gender would divert attention from the cause of black civil rights. The situation paralleled the conflict which had arisen over a century earlier, when the struggles for abolition and for women's rights had been intertwined. Suffragists had assumed, or at least hoped, that by working to gain the vote for blacks, they would guarantee the same rights for women, and thus they stayed in the vanguard of abolition. After the end of the Civil War, when women were excluded from the Fourteenth and Fifteenth Amendments, advocates of women's rights such as Frederick Douglass urged patience, saying that it was "the Negro's hour." Some abolitionists took the position that race was a more fundamental issue than sex and that in any case women could exert due influence simply by enforcing their views on enfranchised husbands. Nearly alone in her vocal opposition to this perspective was Sojourner Truth, a self-named ex-slave, a wandering evangelist, a woman nearly six feet tall with a great, resounding voice and a presence so extraordinary that one of her listeners wrote that in describing her one might "as well attempt to report the seven apocalyptic thunders."

Much of what is known of her is drawn from the autobiography she dictated and sold and from transcriptions of her speeches and accounts of her appearances. Given the name Isabella Baumfree, she was born in slavery in Hurley, Ulster County, New York, the property of a Dutch patroon, and sold three times before she was twelve. She was raped by one of her masters, John Dumont, and she later had five children from her union with Thomas, another slave. In 1827, the year before slavery was outlawed in New York, Dumont sold her five-year-old son Peter, and "Bell" fled with her infant, contracting to work for a year for another master and then successfully suing in Kingston, New York, for the custody of her son. She took the name of Van Wagener from her last employer, and in 1829 moved to New York City with her two youngest children. Over the next fifteen years, as Isabella Van Wagener, she worked as a domestic servant and became deeply involved with mystical cults and with evangelical religion. Periodically, she had visions and heard voices from beyond, and in 1843 she listened to a summons from God directing her to go forth and preach. After changing her name to reflect her mission, which was to be a traveler who shows people their sins and tells them what is true, Sojourner Truth took to the road.

Her travels took her first through Long Island and Connecticut and then to Northampton, Massachusetts, where she joined a communal farm called the Northampton Association of Education and Industry, a project started by William Lloyd Garrison's brother-in-law, George Benson. By 1850, Sojourner Truth was touring Indiana, Missouri, Ohio, and Kansas, supporting herself by selling copies of her autobiography, the *Narrative of Sojourner Truth* (1850), which she had dictated to a woman named Olive Gilbert. Although she became a folk heroine through her appearances and sometimes spoke in the company of well-known abolitionists such as Frederick Douglass, her fame was most firmly established by Harriet Beecher Stowe, who described her as a "Lybian Sibyl" in an article published in *The Atlantic Monthly* (1863). During the 1850s, she bought a house in Battle Creek, Michigan, and thereafter she used it as a headquarters from which she periodically emerged to go on tour. During the Civil War she raised supplies for Negro soldiers, and she was presented to President Lincoln at the White House in 1864. For a time after the war, she worked as an adviser to emancipated slaves through the National Freedman's Relief Association, and she thereafter campaigned for establishment of a "Negro State," a project which did lead to substantial Negro migration west. In 1875, when her grandson and traveling companion, Sammy Banks, became ill, she retired to Battle Creek, but through letters written for her by her friends and the hundreds of visitors she had, Sojourner Truth remained in contact with her admirers in the women's rights movement.

Her speeches were spontaneous, frequently humorous, full of biblical allusions and memorable biographical references, and she preached a combination of feminist Christianity, abolition, temperance and women's rights. Often, she depicted herself as a figure like the Old Testament prophets, as someone sent to warn: "I am sittin' among you to watch; and every once and awhile I will come out and tell you what time of night it is." She delighted in weaving her versions of biblical stories into her admonitions and in using the Bible as a way of making her points: she argued that women should have their rights, for example, because God and a woman produced Jesus Christ and there was not a single man involved. In general, her view of the social relation of the sexes differed radically from the prevailing philosophy that women should be a silent, "improving" influence on their husbands, for she did not accept either the notion of physical inferiority of women or the idea that women would or should be placed on pedestals. If institutions in the public sphere, such as the courts, were not fit places for women, she thought they were unfit for men as well. Unlike middle-class black women who might hope to gain social dignity and security through marriage, Sojourner Truth did not envision women and men as husbands and wives, but more as parallel entities. In fact, although she spoke of having borne thirteen children, if she considered the role of men important in their production, she never mentioned it. And while she said that she was glad that black men were getting their rights, she regarded the restriction of voting rights to men as pure meanness: "Now that there is a great stir about colored men's getting their rights is the time for women to step in and have theirs. I am sometimes told that 'Women aint fit to vote. What, don't you know that a woman had seven devils in her: and do you suppose a woman is fit to rule the nation?' . . . man is so selfish that he has got women's rights and his own, too, and yet he won't give women their rights. He keeps them all to himself. . . ."

In the stories she told of herself and those told about her, Sojourner Truth emerged as fearless, unfettered, exuberant, and utterly indifferent to convention. Accused of being a man, she bared her breast before an audience in Indiana, and in Washington, after the war, she fought Jim Crow laws by conducting a noisy and physical personal campaign to integrate public transport. An apocryphal figure who created her own apocrypha, she sometimes presented herself as quasi-immortal. In her 1867 speech, she claimed to be over eighty years old, and said that she would live another forty years to see women get their rights. In her last public letter, published in the Chicago *Inter-Ocean* (1880), Sojourner Truth said that she had seen over a hundred New Years, and in *The History of Woman Suffrage* (1886) it was solemnly reported that she died at the age of one hundred and ten. Although her race and appearance were sufficient grounds for her to be scorned by some, the very same qualities inspired unbounded admiration from scores of women who had worked first for abolition and then for female suffrage, only to discover that there was little support for their cause. In the years after the Civil War, Sojourner Truth remained among the black defenders of women's rights. She was called "the Miriam of the later Exodus . . . the most wonderful woman the colored race has ever produced," a remark which now strikes us as unintentionally patronizing. Yet, the sentiments were genuine, and Sojourner Truth would not have disagreed. If she was not, after all, immortal, she was certainly larger than life. The nation had never seen or heard anything quite like her.

Allison Heisch
San Jose State University

PRIMARY WORK

Olive Gilbert, *Narrative of Sojourner Truth (1850),* ed. Frances W. Titus, 1853, 1884, 1970, 1991.

SECONDARY WORKS

Hertha Pauli, *Her Name Was Sojourner Truth,* 1962; Elizabeth Cady Stanton, et al., *History of Woman Suffrage,* 3 vols., 1881–1886, 1970; Gerda Lerner, *Black Women in White America: A Documentary History,* 1973; Jean Fagan Yellin, *Women and Sisters: The Antislavery Feminists in American Culture,* 1989; Jacqueline Bernard, *Journey Toward Freedom: The Story of Sojourner Truth,* 1990.

Reminiscences by Frances D. Gage of Sojourner Truth, for May 28–29, 1851

The leaders of the movement trembled on seeing a tall, gaunt black woman in a gray dress and white turban, surmounted with an uncouth sun-bonnet, march deliberately into the church, walk with the air of a queen up the aisle, and take her seat upon the pulpit steps. A buzz of disapprobation was heard all over the house, and there fell on the listening ear, "An abolition affair!" "Woman's rights and niggers!" "I told you so!" "Go it, darkey!"

I chanced on that occasion to wear my first laurels in public life as president of the meeting. At my request order was restored, and the business of the Convention went on. Morning, afternoon, and evening exercises came and went. Through all these sessions old Sojourner, quiet and reticent as the "Lybian Statue," sat crouched against the wall on the corner of the pulpit stairs, her sun-bonnet shading her eyes, her elbows on her knees, her chin resting upon her broad, hard palms. At intermission she was busy selling the "Life of Sojourner Truth," a narrative of her own strange and adventurous life. Again and again, timorous and trembling ones came to me and said, with earnestness, "Don't let her speak, Mrs. Gage, it will ruin us. Every newspaper in the land will have our cause mixed up with abolition and niggers, and we shall be utterly denounced." My only answer was, "We shall see when the time comes."

The second day the work waxed warm. Methodist, Baptist, Episcopal, Presbyterian, and Universalist ministers came in to hear and discuss the resolutions presented. One claimed superior rights and privileges for man, on the ground of "superior intellect"; another, because of the "manhood of Christ; if God had desired the equality of woman, He would have given some token of His will through the birth, life, and death of the Saviour." Another gave us a theological view of the "sin of our first mother."

There were very few women in those days who dared to "speak in meeting"; and the august teachers of the people were seemingly getting the better of us, while the boys in the galleries, and the sneerers among the pews, were hugely enjoying the discomfiture, as they supposed, of the "strong-minded." Some of the tender-skinned friends were on the point of losing dignity, and the atmosphere betokened a storm. When, slowly from her seat in the corner rose Sojourner Truth, who, till now, had scarcely lifted her head. "Don't let her speak!" gasped half a dozen in my ear. She moved slowly and solemnly to the front, laid her old bonnet at her feet, and turned her great speaking eyes to me. There was a hissing sound of disapprobation above and below. I rose and announced "Sojourner Truth," and begged the audience to keep silence for a few moments.

The tumult subsided at once, and every eye was fixed on this almost Amazon form, which stood nearly six feet high, head erect, and eyes piercing the upper air like one in a dream. At her first word there was a profound hush. She spoke in deep tones, which, though not loud, reached every ear in the house, and away through the throng at the doors and windows.

"Wall, chilern, whar dar is so much racket dar must be somethin' out o' kilter. I tink dat 'twixt de niggers of de Souf and de womin at de Norf, all talkin' 'bout rights, de white men will be in a fix pretty soon. But what's all dis here talkin' 'bout?

"Dat man ober dar say dat womin needs to be helped into carriages, and lifted ober ditches, and to hab de best place everywhar. Nobody eber helps me into carriages, or ober mud-puddles, or gibs me any best place!" And raising herself to her full height, and her voice to a pitch like rolling thunder, she asked. "And a'n't I a woman? Look at me! Look at my arm! (and she bared her right arm to the shoulder, showing her tremendous muscular power). I have ploughed, and planted, and gathered into barns, and no man could head me! And a'n't I a woman? I could work as much and eat as much as a man—when I could get it—and bear de lash as well! And a'n't I a woman? I have borne thirteen chilern, and seen 'em mos' all sold off to slavery, and when I cried out with my mother's grief, none but Jesus heard me! And a'n't I a woman?

"Den dey talks 'bout dis ting in de head; what dis dey call it?" ("Intellect," whispered some one near.) "Dat's it, honey. What's dat got to do wid womin's rights or nigger's rights? If my cup won't hold but a pint, and yourn holds a quart, wouldn't ye be mean not to let me have my little half-measure full?" And she pointed her significant finger, and sent a keen glance at the minister who had made the argument. The cheering was long and loud.

"Den dat little man in black dar he say women can't have as much rights as men, 'cause Christ wan't a woman! Whar did your Christ come from?" Rolling thunder couldn't have stilled that crowd, as did those deep, wonderful tones, as she stood there with outstretched arms and eyes of fire. Raising her voice still louder, she repeated, "Whar did your Christ come from? From God and a woman! Man had nothin' to do wid Him." Oh, what a rebuke that was to that little man.

Turning again to another objector, she took up the defense of Mother Eve. I can not follow her through it all. It was pointed, and witty, and solemn; eliciting at almost every sentence deafening applause; and she ended by asserting: "If de fust woman God ever made was strong enough to turn de world upside down all alone, dese women togedder (and she glanced her eye over the platform) ought to be able to turn it back, and get it right side up again! And now dey is asking to do it, de men better let 'em." Long-continued cheering greeted this. "'Bleeged to ye for hearin' on me, and now ole Sojourner han't got nothin' more to say."

Amid roars of applause, she returned to her corner, leaving more than one of us with streaming eyes, and hearts beating with gratitude. She had taken us up in her strong arms and carried us safely over the slough of difficulty turning the whole tide in our favor. I have never in my life seen anything like the magical influence that subdued the mobbish spirit of the day, and turned the sneers and jeers of an excited crowd into notes of respect and admiration. Hundreds rushed up to shake hands with her, and congratulate the glorious old mother, and bid her God-speed on her mission of "testifyin' agin concerning the wickedness of this 'ere people."

1881

Speech at New York City Convention

. . . Sojourner Truth, a tall colored woman, well known in anti-slavery circles, and called the Lybian Sybil, made her appearance on the platform. This was the signal for a fresh outburst from the mob; for at every session every man of them was promptly in his place, at twenty-five cents a head. And this was the one redeeming feature of this mob—it paid all expenses, and left a surplus in the treasury. Sojourner combined in herself, as an individual, the two most hated elements of humanity. She was black, and she was a woman, and all the insults that could be cast upon color and sex were together hurled at her; but there she stood, calm and dignified, a grand, wise woman, who could neither read nor write, and yet with deep insight could penetrate the very soul of the universe about her. As soon as the terrible turmoil was in a measure quelled

She said: Is it not good for me to come and draw forth a spirit, to see what kind of spirit people are of? I see that some of you have got the spirit of a goose, and some have got the spirit of a snake. I feel at home here. I come to you, citizens of New York, as I suppose you ought to be. I am a citizen of the State of New York; I was born in it, and I was a slave in the State of New York; and now I am a good citizen of this State. I was born here, and I can tell you I feel at home here. I've been lookin' round and watchin' things, and I know a little mite 'bout Woman's Rights, too. I come forth to speak 'bout Woman's Rights, and want to throw in my little mite, to keep the scales a-movin'. I know that it feels a kind o' hissin' and ticklin' like to see a colored woman get up and tell you about things, and Woman's Rights. We have all been thrown down so low that nobody thought we'd ever get up again; but we have been long enough trodden now; we will come up again, and now I am here.

I was a-thinkin', when I see women contendin' for their rights, I was a-thinkin' what a difference there is now, and what there was in old times. I have only a few minutes to speak; but in the old times the kings of the earth would hear a woman. There was a king in the Scriptures; and then it was the kings of the earth would kill a woman if she come into their presence; but Queen Esther[1] come forth, for she was oppressed, and felt there was a great wrong, and she said I will die or I will bring my

[1]The Old Testament King Ahasuerus offered to fulfill any request made by his Jewish wife Esther, even if she asked for half of his kingdom. Esther asked for justice for her people. Prince Haman was slaughtering the Jews because he believed he had been insulted by the king's adviser, Mordecai. King Ahasuerus hanged Haman on the gallows Haman had built for Mordecai.

complaint before the king. Should the king of the United States be greater, or more crueler, or more harder? But the king, he raised up his sceptre and said: "Thy request shall be granted unto thee—to the half of my kingdom will I grant it to thee!" Then he said he would hang Haman on the gallows he had made up high. But that is not what women come forward to contend. The women want their rights as Esther. She only wanted to explain her rights. And he was so liberal that he said, "the half of my kingdom shall be granted to thee," and he did not wait for her to ask, he was so liberal with her.

Now, women do not ask half of a kingdom, but their rights, and they don't get 'em. When she comes to demand 'em, don't you hear how sons hiss their mothers like snakes, because they ask for their rights; and can they ask for anything less? The king ordered Haman to be hung on the gallows which he prepared to hang others; but I do not want any man to be killed, but I am sorry to see them so short-minded. But we'll have our rights; see if we don't; and you can't stop us from them; see if you can. You may hiss as much as you like, but it is comin'. Women don't get half as much rights as they ought to; we want more, and we will have it. Jesus says: "What I say to one, I say to all—watch!" I'm a-watchin'. God says: "Honor your father and your mother." Sons and daughters ought to behave themselves before their mothers, but they do not. I can see them a-laughin', and pointin' at their mothers up here on the stage. They hiss when an aged woman comes forth. If they'd been brought up proper they'd have known better than hissing like snakes and geese. I'm 'round watchin' these things, and I wanted to come up and say these few things to you, and I'm glad of the hearin' you give me. I wanted to tell you a mite about Woman's Rights, and so I came out and said so. I am sittin' among you to watch; and every once and awhile I will come out and tell you what time of night it is.

1881

Address to the First Annual Meeting of the American Equal Rights Association

New York City, May 9, 1867

My friends, I am rejoiced that you are glad, but I don't know how you will feel when I get through. I come from another field—the country of the slave. They have got their liberty—so much good luck to have slavery partly destroyed; not entirely. I want it root and branch destroyed. Then we will all be free indeed. I feel that if I have to answer for the deeds done in my body just as much as a man, I have a right to have just as much as a man. There is a great stir about colored men getting their rights, but not a word about the colored women; and if colored men get their rights, and not colored women theirs, you see the colored men will be masters over the women, and it will be just as bad as it was before. So I am for keeping the thing going while things are stirring; because if we wait till it is still, it will take a great while to get it going again. White women are a great deal smarter, and know more than colored women, while colored women do not know scarcely anything. They go out washing, which is about as high as a colored woman gets, and their men go about idle, strutting up and down; and when the women come home, they ask for their money and take it all, and then scold because there is no food. I want you to consider on that, chil'n. I call you chil'n; you are somebody's chil'n, and I am old enough to be mother of all that is here. I want women to have their rights. In the courts women have no right, no voice; nobody speaks for them. I wish woman to have her voice there among the pettifoggers. If it is not a fit place for women, it is unfit for men to be there.

I am above eighty years old; it is about time for me to be going. I have been forty years a slave and forty years free, and would be here forty years more to have equal rights for all. I suppose I am kept here because something remains for me to do; I suppose I am yet to help to break the chain. I have done a great deal of work; as much as a man, but did not get so much pay. I used to work in the field and bind grain, keeping up with the cradler; but men doing no more, got twice as much pay; so with the German women. They work in the field and do as much work, but do not get the pay. We do as much, we eat as much, we want as much. I suppose I am about the only colored woman that goes about to speak for the rights of the colored women. I want to keep the thing stirring, now that the ice is cracked. What we want is a little money. You men know that you get as much again as women when you write, or for what you do. When we get our rights we shall not have to come to you for money, for then we shall have money enough in our own pockets; and may be you will ask us for money. But help us now until we get it. It is a good consolation to know that when we have got this battle once fought we shall not be coming to you any more. You have been having our rights so long, that you think, like a slaveholder, that you own us. I know that it is hard for one who has held the reins for so long to give up; it cuts like a knife. It will feel all the better when it closes up again. I have been in Washington about three years, seeing about these colored people. Now colored men have the right to vote. There ought to be equal rights now more than ever, since colored people have got their freedom. I am going to talk several times while I am here; so now I will do a little singing. I have not heard any singing since I came here.

Accordingly, suiting the action to the word, Sojourner sang, "We are going home." "There, children," said she, "in heaven we shall rest from all our labors; first do all we have to do here. There I am determined to go, not to stop short of that beautiful place, and I do not mean to stop till I get there, and meet you there, too."

1881

Frances Ellen Watkins Harper 1825–1911

The long and remarkable career of Frances Ellen Watkins Harper ran from the middle of the nineteenth into the beginning of the twentieth century. Therefore, she appears in both volumes of this anthology, with different selections from her work in each. Over her lifetime she was directly involved in abolitionism, the Underground Railroad, the temperance movement, the labor for black education and economic self-determination, the anti-lynching movement, and the campaign for women's suffrage. Harper demonstrated in her life and work a fusion between her artistic and her political lives. She refused to separate the two. Political issues suffused her literary creations; literary selections (especially poems that she wrote) laced her political speeches. Ardent activist, groundbreaking writer, and brilliant artist in the oral tradition, she stands as a model of integrated aesthetic and political commitment.

The only child of free parents, Frances Ellen Watkins was born in Baltimore, Maryland, a slaveholding state, where she witnessed slavery firsthand as she was growing up. Orphaned at three, she was adopted by an aunt and uncle, who ran a school for free blacks which she attended until the age of fourteen. At that time she hired out as a domestic to a Baltimore family. Already a writer while still in her teens, she published a volume of poetry at sixteen, *Forest Leaves* (also cited as *Autumn Leaves*), no copies of which are known to exist.

She left the South in 1850, settling in a free state, Ohio, where she took a teaching job at Union Seminary near Columbus (relocated, this institution would become Wilberforce University). After a few years she moved to Little York, Pennsylvania, and when a law was passed in 1853 forbidding free blacks to enter Maryland without risking capture and sale, she became intensely involved in anti-slavery work. Vowing to fight slavery in whatever way she could, she immersed herself in the stories of runaway slaves arriving on the Underground Railroad and became a friend and colleague of William Still, later famous as the author of the monumental 1872 history *The Underground Railroad.*

Probably at this point political passion and her calling as an artist truly began to fuse for Harper. With the delivery of her first anti-slavery speech in August of 1854 in New Bedford, Massachusetts, "The Education and Elevation of the Colored Race," she inaugurated the long and brilliant public-speaking career that before the Civil War would carry her through Massachusetts, Pennsylvania, New York, New Jersey, Ohio, and Maine, where she was engaged by the state Anti-Slavery Society as a full-time lecturer. In 1860 in Cincinnati she married a widower, Fenton Harper, who had two children, and settled with him on a farm she helped purchase outside Columbus. When he died four years later, she and their baby, Mary, moved to Philadelphia where she resumed the teaching and anti-slavery work she had begun before her marriage.

Harper's brilliance as an artist in the oral tradition is testified to by contemporary descriptions. She spoke at length—up to two hours—without a written text (thereby leaving few verbatim records of her speeches). She is pictured by one audience member, Grace Greenwood (Sara J. Lippincott), quoted in William Still's book, as standing quietly beside her desk "with gestures few and fitting. Her manner is marked by dignity and composure. She is never assuming, never theatrical. . . . The woe of two hundred years sighed through her tones. Every glance of her sad eyes was a mournful remonstrance against injustice and wrong." Although she met with discrimination—she would later report some listeners refusing to believe she was a woman or that she was really black—Harper was hugely successful as an orator, at one point in 1854 giving at least thirty-three speeches in twenty-one different towns and cities in a six-week period.

Highly gifted as well in the written tradition, Harper was America's best-known and most popular black poet between Phillis Wheatley and Paul Laurence Dunbar. Publishing four volumes of poetry as an adult, she wrote about many topics, characteristically focusing on black characters and experiences, slavery, lynching, temperance, Christianity, or moral reform. As a poet she worked in both the popular and high-culture traditions, often aiming in her work to stimulate a vivid emotional response in the reader, such as anger, pity, horror, exaltation, or compassion. She incorporated into her poetry African-American oral subject matter and techniques and also used the conventions of sentimentalism—ultra regular rhyme and rhythm, elaborate and even artificial language, direct apostrophal exclamations—to bring black and poor people's experiences into the mainstream, which in terms of popular published poetry in the United States in the nineteenth century prized rather than avoided the indulgence of feeling. Her poems on slavery in this volume, for example, appeal directly and boldly to her readers' emotions of sympathy, outrage, shame, and patriotic pride.

As a fiction writer Harper's position in American literary history is preeminent. Her 1859 short story "The Two Offers" is thought to be the first short story published by a black person in the United States. It appeared in the *Anglo-African Magazine,* a publication founded in 1859 by Thomas Hamilton and committed to printing the work only of black writers. Perhaps because of the freedom created by that policy, the story does not deal with racial issues; it focuses instead on the problems of drunkenness, wife abuse, and child neglect, and the pressure on women to marry, even if the marriage in question is destructive. Grounded in the middle-class nineteenth-century feminine ideology which some historians have labeled the cult of "true womanhood," an ideology which praised the superior piety, domesticity, and moral rectitude of Christian womanhood, the story argues that dignity and happiness are available to the woman who remains single.

Following the Civil War, Harper did not diminish her commitment as a political activist, orator, poet, and fiction writer, continuing to be celebrated as the most popular and well-known black American poet of the nineteenth century and publishing her best-known long work, *Iola Leroy,* in 1892. She died of heart disease in Philadelphia at the age of eighty-six and is buried there in Eden Cemetery.

Elizabeth Ammons
Tufts University

PRIMARY WORKS

Poems on Miscellaneous Subjects, 1854; "The Two Offers," 1859 (short story); *Sketches of Southern Life,* 1872 (poems); *Iola Leroy; or Shadows Uplifted,* 1892 (novel); *The Martyr of Alabama and Other Poems,* 1894; *Complete Poems of Frances E.W. Harper,* Maryemma Graham, ed., 1988; *A Brighter Day Coming: A Frances Ellen Watkins Harper Reader,* Frances Smith Foster, ed., 1990.

SECONDARY WORKS

Patricia Liggins Hill, "'Let Me Make the Songs for the People': A Study of Frances Watkins Harper's Poetry," *Black American Literature Forum* 15:2 (1981): 60–65; Hazel Carby, *Reconstructing Womanhood: The Emergence of the African-American Woman Novelist,* 1987; Paul Lauter, "Is Frances Ellen Watkins Harper Good Enough to Teach?" *Legacy* 5 (1988): 27–32; Frances Smith Foster, *Written by Herself: Literary Production by African American Women,*

1746–1892, 1993; Carla L. Peterson, *"Doers of the Word": African-American Women Speakers and Writers in the North (1830–1880),* 1995.

The Slave Mother

Heard you that shriek? It rose
So wildly on the air,
It seemed as if a burden'd heart
Was breaking in despair.

Saw you those hands so sadly clasped—
The bowed and feeble head—
The shuddering of that fragile form—
That look of grief and dread?

Saw you the sad, imploring eye?
Its every glance was pain,
As if a storm of agony
Were sweeping through the brain.

She is a mother, pale with fear,
Her boy clings to her side,
And in her kirtle vainly tries
His trembling form to hide.

He is not hers, although she bore
For him a mother's pains;
He is not hers, although her blood
Is coursing through his veins!

He is not hers, for cruel hands
May rudely tear apart
The only wreath of household love
That binds her breaking heart.

His love has been a joyous light
That o'er her pathway smiled,
A fountain gushing ever new,
Amid life's desert wild.

His lightest word has been a tone
Of music round her heart,

Their lives a streamlet blent in one—
Oh, Father! must they part?

They tear him from her circling arms,
Her last and fond embrace.
Oh! never more may her sad eyes
Gaze on his mournful face.

No marvel, then, these bitter shrieks
Disturb the listening air:
She is a mother, and her heart
Is breaking in despair.

1857

The Tennessee Hero

"He had heard his comrades plotting to obtain their liberty, and rather than betray them he received 750 lashes and died."

He stood before the savage throng,
The base and coward crew;
A tameless light flashed from his eye,
His heart beat firm and true.

He was the hero of his band,
The noblest of them all;
Though fetters galled his weary limbs,
His spirit spurned their thrall.

And towered, in its manly might,
Above the murderous crew.
Oh! liberty had nerved his heart,
And every pulse beat true.

"Now tell us," said the savage troop,
"And life thy gain shall be!
Who are the men that plotting, say—
'They must and will be free!'"

Oh, could you have seen the hero then,
As his lofty soul arose,

And his dauntless eyes defiance flashed
On his mean and craven foes!

"I know the men who would be free;
They are the heroes of your land;
But death and torture I defy,
Ere I betray that band.

And what! oh, what is life to me,
Beneath your base control?
Nay! do your worst. Ye have no chains
To bind my free-born soul."

They brought the hateful lash and scourge,
With murder in each eye.
But a solemn vow was on his lips—
He had resolved to die.

Yes, rather than betray his trust,
He'd meet a death of pain;
'T was sweeter far to meet it thus
Than wear a treason stain!

Like storms of wrath, of hate and pain,
The blows rained thick and fast;
But the monarch soul kept true
Till the gates of life were past.

And the martyr spirit fled
To the throne of God on high,
And showed his gaping wounds
Before the unslumbering eye.

1857

Free Labor

I wear an easy garment,
O'er it no toiling slave
Wept tears of hopeless anguish,
In his passage to the grave.

And from its ample folds
Shall rise no cry to God,

Upon its warp and woof shall be
No stain of tears and blood.

Oh, lightly shall it press my form,
Unladened with a sigh,
I shall not 'mid its rustling hear,
Some sad despairing cry.

This fabric is too light to bear
The weight of bondsmen's tears,
I shall not in its texture trace
The agony of years.

Too light to bear a smother'd sigh,
From some lorn woman's heart,
Whose only wreath of household love
Is rudely torn apart.

Then lightly shall it press my form,
Unburden'd by a sigh;
And from its seams and folds shall rise,
No voice to pierce the sky,

And witness at the throne of God,
In language deep and strong,
That I have nerv'd Oppression's hand,
For deeds of guilt and wrong.

1857

An Appeal to the American People

When a dark and fearful strife
Raged around the nation's life,
And the traitor plunged his steel
Where your quivering hearts could feel,
When your cause did need a friend,
We were faithful to the end.

When we stood with bated breath,
Facing fiery storms of death,
And the war-cloud, red with wrath,
Fiercely swept around our path,
Did our hearts with terror quail?
Or our courage ever fail?

When the captive, wanting bread,
Sought our poor and lowly shed,
And the blood-hounds missed his way,
Did we e'er his path betray?
Filled we not his heart with trust
As we shared with him our crust?

With your soldiers, side by side,
Helped we turn the battle's tide,
Till o'er ocean, stream and shore,
Waved the rebel flag no more,
And above the rescued sod
Praises rose to freedom's God.

But to-day the traitor stands
With the crimson on his hands,
Scowling 'neath his brow of hate,
On our weak and desolate,
With the blood-rust on the knife
Aiméd at the nation's life.

Asking you to weakly yield
All we won upon the field,
To ignore, on land and flood,
All the offerings of our blood,
And to write above our slain
"They have fought and died in vain."

To your manhood we appeal,
Lest the traitor's iron heel
Grind and trample in the dust
All our new-born hope and trust,
And the name of freedom be
Linked with bitter mockery.

1858

The Colored People in America

Having been placed by a dominant race in circumstances over which we have had no control, we have been the butt of ridicule and the mark of oppression. Identified with a people over whom weary ages of degradation have passed, whatever concerns them, as a race, concerns me. I have noticed among our people a disposition to censure and upbraid each other, a disposition which has its foundation rather, perhaps, in a want of common sympathy and consideration, than mutual hatred, or other unholy passions. Born to an inheritance of misery, nurtured in degradation, and cradled in oppression, with the scorn of the white man upon their souls, his fetters upon their limbs, his scourge upon their flesh, what can be expected from their offspring, but a mournful reaction of that cursed system which spreads its baneful influence over body and soul; which dwarfs the intellect, stunts its development, debases the spirit, and degrades the soul? Place any nation in the same condition which has been our hapless lot, fetter their limbs and degrade their souls, debase their sons and corrupt their daughters, and when the restless yearnings for liberty shall burn through heart and brain—when, tortured by wrong and goaded by oppression, the hearts that would madden with misery, or break in despair, resolve to break their thrall, and escape from bondage, then let the bay of the bloodhound and the scent of the human tiger be upon their track;—let them feel that, from the ceaseless murmur of the Atlantic to the sullen roar of the Pacific, from the thunders of the rainbow-crowned Niagara to the swollen waters of the Mexican gulf, they have no shelter for their bleeding feet, or resting-place for their defenceless heads;—let them, when nominally free, feel that they have only exchanged the iron yoke of oppression for the galling fetters of a vitiated public opinion;—let prejudice assign them the lowest places and the humblest positions, and make them "hewers of wood and drawers of water;"—let their income be so small that they must from necessity bequeath to their children an inheritance of poverty and a limited education,—and tell me, reviler of our race! censurer of our people! if there is a nation in whose veins runs the purest Caucasian blood, upon whom the same causes would not produce the same effects; whose social condition, intellectual and moral character, would present a more favorable aspect than ours? But there is hope; yes, blessed be God! for our down-trodden and despised race. Public and private schools accommodate our children; and in my own southern home, I see women, whose lot is unremitted labor, saving a pittance from their scanty wages to defray the expense of learning to read. We have papers edited by colored editors, which we may consider it an honor to possess, and a credit to sustain. We have a church that is extending itself from east to west, from north to south, through poverty and reproach, persecution and pain. We have our faults, our want of union and concentration of purpose; but are there not extenuating circumstances around our darkest faults—palliating excuses for our most egregious errors? and shall we not hope, that the mental and moral aspect which we present is but the first step of a mighty advancement, the faintest corruscations of the day that will dawn with unclouded splendor upon our down-trodden and benighted race, and that ere long we may present to the admiring gaze of those who wish us well, a people to whom knowledge has given power, and righteousness exaltation?

1857

Speech: On the Twenty-Fourth Anniversary of the American Anti-Slavery Society

Could we trace the record of every human heart, the aspirations of every immortal soul, perhaps we would find no man so imbruted and degraded that we could not trace the word liberty either written in living characters upon the soul or hidden away in some nook or corner of the heart. The law of liberty is the law of God, and is antecedent to all human legislation. It existed in the mind of Deity when He hung the first world upon its orbit and gave it liberty to gather light from the central sun.

Some people say set the slaves free. Did you ever think, if the slaves were free, they would steal everything they could lay their hands on from now till the day of their death—that they would steal more than two thousand millions of dollars (applause)! Ask Maryland, with her tens of thousands of slaves, if she is not prepared for freedom, and hear her answer: "I help supply the coffle-gangs of the South." Ask Virginia, with her hundreds of thousands of slaves, if she is not weary with her merchandise of blood and anxious to shake the gory traffic from her hands, and hear her reply: "Though fertility has covered my soil, though a genial sky bends over my hills and vales, though I hold in my hand a wealth of waterpower, enough to turn the spindles to clothe the world, yet, with all these advantages, one of my chief staples has been the sons and daughters I send to the human market and human shambles" (applause). Ask the farther South, and all the cotton-growing States chime in, "We have need of fresh supplies to fill the ranks of those whose lives have gone out in unrequited toil on our distant plantations."

A hundred thousand new-born babes are annually added to the victims of slavery; twenty thousand lives are annually sacrificed on the plantations of the South. Such a sight should send a thrill of horror through the nerves of civilization and impel the heart of humanity to lofty alchemy by which this blood can be transformed into gold. Instead of listening to the cry of agony, they listen to the ring of dollars and stoop down to pick up the coin (applause).

But a few months since a man escaped from bondage and found a temporary shelter almost beneath the shadow of Bunker Hill. Had that man stood upon the deck of an Austrian ship, beneath the shadow of the house of the Hapsburgs, he would have found protection. Had he been wrecked upon an island or colony of Great Britain, the waves of the tempest-lashed ocean would have washed him deliverance. Had he landed upon the territory of vine-encircled France and a Frenchman had reduced him to a thing and brought him here beneath the protection of our institutions and our laws, for such a nefarious deed that Frenchman would have lost his citizenship in France. Beneath the feebler light which glimmers from the Koran, the Bey of Tunis would have granted him freedom in his own dominions. Beside the ancient pyramids of Egypt he would have found liberty, for the soil laved by the glorious Nile is now consecrated to freedom. But from Boston harbour, made memorable by the infusion of three-penny taxed tea, Boston in its proximity to the plains of Lexington and Concord, Boston almost beneath the shadow of Bunker Hill and almost in sight of Plymouth Rock, he is thrust back from liberty and manhood and reconverted into a chattel. You have heard that, down South, they keep bloodhounds to hunt slaves. Ye bloodhounds, go back to your kennels; when you fail to catch the flying fugitive, when his stealthy tread is heard in the place where the bones of the revolutionary sires repose, the ready North is base enough to do your shameful service (applause).

Slavery is mean, because it tramples on the feeble and weak. A man comes with his affidavits from the South and invites me before a commissioner; upon that evidence *ex parte* and alone he hitches me to the car of slavery and trails my womanhood in the dust. I stand at the threshold of the Supreme Court and ask for justice, simple justice. Upon my tortured heart is thrown the mocking words, "You are a negro; you have no rights which white men are bound to respect"[1] (loud and long-continued applause)! Had it been my lot to have lived beneath the Crescent instead of the Cross, had injustice and violence been heaped upon my head as a Mohammedan woman, as a member of a common faith, I might have demanded justice and been listened to by the Pasha, the Bey or the Vizier; but when I come here to ask for justice, men tell me, "We have no higher law than the Constitution" (applause).

But I will not dwell on the dark side of the picture. God is on the side of freedom; and any cause that has God on its side, I care not how much it may be trampled upon, how much it may be trailed in the dust, is sure to triumph. The message of Jesus Christ is on the side of freedom, "I come to preach deliverance to the captives, the opening of the prison doors to them that are bound." The truest and noblest hearts in the land are on the side of freedom. They may be hissed at by slavery's minions, their names cast out as evil, their characters branded with fanaticism, but O,

"To side with Truth is noble when we share her humble crust
Ere the cause bring fame and profit and it's prosperous to be just."

May I not, in conclusion, ask every honest, noble heart, every seeker after truth and justice, if they will not also be on the side of freedom. Will you not resolve that you will abate neither heart nor hope till you hear the death-knoll of human bondage sounded, and over the black ocean of slavery shall be heard a song, more exulting than the song of Miriam when it floated o'er Egypt's dark sea,[2] the requiem of Egypt's ruined hosts and the anthem of the deliverance of Israel's captive people? (great applause)

(We have attempted to give a full report of Miss Watkins's speech.)

1857

[1]It was still true in 1857 that not even free blacks could assume any constitutional rights. An 1819 Virginia law restricted the mobility of free blacks and forbade them to "speak provocatively" to whites. An 1820 South Carolina law decreed that free Negroes on ships coming into state harbors be imprisoned until the ships departed. And although the Massachusetts State Constitution said that "all men, without distinction of color or race, are equal before the law," a Massachusetts Supreme Court ruling of 1849 upheld racial segregation in schools. Not until a new law was passed in 1855 did the school segregation end.

[2]Miriam, the sister of Moses and Aaron and an important leader of the Jews, led her people in singing and dancing after they had safely crossed the Red Sea and escaped from bondage to the Egyptians (Exodus 15:20–21).

The Two Offers

"What is the matter with you, Laura, this morning? I have been watching you this hour, and in that time you have commenced a half dozen letters and torn them all up. What matter of such grave moment is puzzling your dear little head, that you do not know how to decide?"

"Well, it is an important matter: I have two offers for marriage, and I do not know which to choose."

"I should accept neither, or to say the least, not at present."

"Why not?"

"Because I think a woman who is undecided between two offers, has not love enough for either to make a choice; and in that very hesitation, indecision, she has a reason to pause and seriously reflect, lest her marriage, instead of being an affinity of souls or a union of hearts, should only be a mere matter of bargain and sale, or an affair of convenience and selfish interest."

"But I consider them both very good offers, just such as many a girl would gladly receive. But to tell you the truth, I do not think that I regard either as a woman should the man she chooses for her husband. But then if I refuse, there is the risk of being an old maid, and that is not to be thought of."

"Well, suppose there is, is that the most dreadful fate that can befall a woman? Is there not more intense wretchedness in an ill-assorted marriage—more utter loneliness in a loveless home, than in the lot of the old maid who accepts her earthly mission as a gift from God, and strives to walk the path of life with earnest and unfaltering steps?"

"Oh! what a little preacher you are. I really believe that you were cut out for an old maid; that when nature formed you, she put in a double portion of intellect to make up for a deficiency of love; and yet you are kind and affectionate. But I do not think that you know anything of the grand, over-mastering passion, or the deep necessity of woman's heart for loving."

"Do you think so?" resumed the first speaker; and bending over her work she quietly applied herself to the knitting that had lain neglected by her side, during this brief conversation; but as she did so, a shadow flitted over her pale and intellectual brow, a mist gathered in her eyes, and a slight quivering of the lips, revealed a depth of feeling to which her companion was a stranger.

But before I proceed with my story, let me give you a slight history of the speakers. They were cousins, who had met life under different auspices. Laura Lagrange, was the only daughter of rich and indulgent parents, who had spared no pains to make her an accomplished lady. Her cousin, Janette Alston, was the child of parents, rich only in goodness and affection. Her father had been unfortunate in business, and dying before he could retrieve his fortunes, left his business in an embarrassed state. His widow was unacquainted with his business affairs, and when the estate was settled, hungry creditors had brought their claims and the lawyers had received their fees, she found herself homeless and almost penniless, and she who had been sheltered in the warm clasp of loving arms, found them too powerless to shield her from the pitiless pelting storms of adversity. Year after year she struggled with poverty and wrestled with want, till her toil-worn hands became too feeble to hold the shattered chords of existence, and her tear-dimmed eyes grew heavy with the slumber of death. Her daughter had watched over her with untiring devotion, had closed her eyes in death, and gone out into the busy, restless world, missing a precious tone from the voices of earth, a beloved step from the paths of life. Too self reliant to depend on the charity of relations, she endeavored to support herself by her own exertions, and she had succeeded. Her path for a while was marked with struggle and trial, but instead of uselessly repining, she met them bravely, and her life became not a thing of ease and indulgence, but of conquest, victory, and accomplishments. At the time when this conversation took place, the deep trials of her life had passed away. The achievements of her genius had won her a position in the literary world, where she shone as one of its bright particular stars. And with her fame came a competence of worldly means, which gave her leisure for improvement, and the riper development of her rare talents. And she, that pale intellectual woman, whose genius gave life and vivacity to the social circle, and whose presence threw a halo of beauty and grace around the charmed atmosphere in which she moved, had at one period of her life, known the mystic and solemn strength of an all-absorbing love. Years faded into the misty past, had seen the kindling of her eye, the quick flushing of her cheek, and the wild throbbing of her heart, at tones of a voice long since hushed to the stillness of death. Deeply, wildly, passionately, she had loved. Her whole life seemed like the pouring out of rich, warm and gushing affections. This love quickened her talents, inspired her genius, and threw over her life a tender and spiritual earnestness. And then came a fearful shock, a mournful waking from that "dream of beauty and delight." A shadow fell around her path; it came between her and the object of her heart's worship; first a few cold words, estrangement, and then a painful separation; the old story of woman's pride—digging the sepulchre of her happiness, and then a new-made grave, and her path over it to the spirit world; and thus faded out from that young heart her bright, brief and saddened dream of life. Faint and spirit-broken, she turned from the scenes associated with the memory of the loved and lost. She tried to break the chain of sad associations that bound her to the mournful past; and so, pressing back the bitter sobs from her almost breaking heart, like the dying dolphin, whose beauty is born of its death anguish, her genius gathered strength from suffering and wonderous power and brilliancy from the agony she hid within the desolate chambers of her soul. Men hailed her as one of earth's strangely gifted children, and wreathed the garlands of fame for her brow, when it was throbbing with a wild and fearful unrest. They breathed her name with applause, when through the lonely halls of her stricken spirit, was an earnest cry for peace, a deep yearning for sympathy and heart-support.

But life, with its stern realities, met her; its solemn responsibilities confronted her, and turning, with an earnest and shattered spirit, to life's duties and trials, she found a calmness and strength that she had only imagined in her dreams of poetry and song. We will now pass over a period of ten years, and the cousins have met again. In that calm and lovely woman, in whose eyes is a depth of tenderness, tempering the flashes of her genius, whose looks and tones are full of sympathy and love, we recognize the once smitten and stricken Janette Alston. The bloom of her girlhood had given way to a higher type of spiritual beauty, as if some unseen hand had been polishing and refining the temple in which her lovely spirit found its habitation;

and this had been the fact. Her inner life had grown beautiful, and it was this that was constantly developing the outer. Never, in the early flush of womanhood, when an absorbing love had lit up her eyes and glowed in her life, had she appeared so interesting as when, with a countenance which seemed overshadowed with a spiritual light, she bent over the death-bed of a young woman, just lingering at the shadowy gates of the unseen land.

"Has he come?" faintly but eagerly exclaimed the dying woman. "Oh! how I have longed for his coming, and even in death he forgets me."

"Oh, do not say so, dear Laura, some accident may have detained him," said Janette to her cousin; for on that bed, from whence she will never rise, lies the once-beautiful and light-hearted Laura Lagrange, the brightness of whose eyes has long since been dimmed with tears, and whose voice had become like a harp whose every chord is tuned to sadness—whose faintest thrill and loudest vibrations are but the variations of agony. A heavy hand was laid upon her once warm and bounding heart, and a voice came whispering through her soul, that she must die. But, to her, the tidings was a message of deliverance—a voice, hushing her wild sorrows to the calmness of resignation and hope. Life had grown so weary upon her head—the future looked so hopeless—she had no wish to tread again the track where thorns had pierced her feet, and clouds overcast her sky; and she hailed the coming of death's angel as the footsteps of a welcome friend. And yet, earth had one object so very dear to her weary heart. It was her absent and recreant husband; for, since that conversation, she had accepted one of her offers, and become a wife. But, before she married, she learned that great lesson of human experience and woman's life, to love the man who bowed at her shrine, a willing worshipper. He had a pleasing address, raven hair, flashing eyes, a voice of thrilling sweetness, and lips of persuasive eloquence; and being well versed in the ways of the world, he won his way to her heart, and she became his bride, and he was proud of his prize. Vain and superficial in his character, he looked upon marriage not as a divine sacrament for the soul's development and human progression, but as the title-deed that gave him possession of the woman he thought he loved. But alas for her, the laxity of his principles had rendered him unworthy of the deep and undying devotion of a purehearted woman; but, for awhile, he hid from her his true character, and she blindly loved him, and for a short period was happy in the consciousness of being beloved; though sometimes a vague unrest would fill her soul, when, overflowing with a sense of the good, the beautiful, and the true, she would turn to him, but find no response to the deep yearnings of her soul—no appreciation of life's highest realities—its solemn grandeur and significant importance. Their souls never met, and soon she found a void in her bosom, that his earth-born love could not fill. He did not satisfy the wants of her mental and moral nature—between him and her there was no affinity of minds, no intercommunion of souls.

Talk as you will of woman's deep capacity for loving, of the strength of her affectional nature. I do not deny it; but will the mere possession of any human love, fully satisfy all the demands of her whole being? You may paint her in poetry or fiction, as a frail vine, clinging to her brother man for support, and dying when deprived of it; and all this may sound well enough to please the imaginations of school-girls, or love-lorn maidens. But woman—the true woman—if you would render her happy, it needs more than the mere development of her affectional nature. Her conscience should be enlightened, her faith in the true and right established, and scope given to her Heaven-endowed and God-given faculties. The true aim of female education should be, not a development of one or two, but all the faculties of the human soul, because no perfect womanhood is developed by imperfect culture. Intense love is often akin to intense suffering, and to trust the whole wealth of a woman's nature on the frail bark of human love, may often be like trusting a cargo of gold and precious gems, to a bark that has never battled with the storm, or buffetted the waves. Is it any wonder, then, that so many life-barks go down, paving the ocean of time with precious hearts and wasted hopes? that so many float around us, shattered and dismasted wrecks? that so many are stranded on the shoals of existence, mournful beacons and solemn warnings for the thoughtless, to whom marriage is a careless and hasty rushing together of the affections? Alas that an institution so fraught with good for humanity should be so perverted, and that state of life, which should be filled with happiness, become so replete with misery. And this was the fate of Laura Lagrange. For a brief period after her marriage her life seemed like a bright and beautiful dream, full of hope and radiant with joy. And then there came a change—he found other attractions that lay beyond the pale of home influences. The gambling saloon had power to win him from her side, he had lived in an element of unhealthy and unhallowed excitements, and the society of a loving wife, the pleasures of a well-regulated home, were enjoyments too tame for one who had vitiated his tastes by the pleasures of sin. There were charmed houses of vice, built upon dead men's loves, where, amid a flow of song, laughter, wine, and careless mirth, he would spend hour after hour, forgetting the cheek that was paling through his neglect, heedless of the tear-dimmed eyes, peering anxiously into the darkness, waiting, or watching his return.

The influence of old associations was upon him. In early life, home had been to him a place of ceilings and walls, not a true home, built upon goodness, love and truth. It was a place where velvet carpets hushed his tread, where images of loveliness and beauty invoked into being by painter's art and sculptor's skill, pleased the eye and gratified the taste, where magnificence surrounded his way and costly clothing adorned his person; but it was not the place for the true culture and right development of his soul. His father had been too much engrossed in making money, and his mother in spending it, in striving to maintain a fashionable position in society, and shining in the eyes of the world, to give the proper direction to the character of their wayward and impulsive son. His mother put beautiful robes upon his body, but left ugly scars upon his soul; she pampered his appetite, but starved his spirit. Every mother should be a true artist, who knows how to weave into her child's life images of grace and beauty, the true poet capable of writing on the soul of childhood the harmony of love and truth, and teaching it how to produce the grandest of all poems—the poetry of a true and noble life. But in his home, a love for the good, the true and right, had been sacrificed at the shrine of frivolity and fashion. That parental authority which should have been preserved as a string of precious pearls, unbroken and unscattered, was simply the administration of chance. At one time obedience was enforced by authority, at another time by flattery and promises, and just as often it was not enforced [at] all. His early associations were formed as chance directed, and from his want of home-training, his character received a bias, his life a shade, which ran through every avenue of his existence, and darkened all his future hours. Oh, if we would trace the history of all the crimes that have o'ershadowed this sin-shrouded and sorrow-darkened world of ours, how many might be seen arising from the wrong home influences, or the weakening of the home ties. Home should always be the best school for the affections, the birth-place of high resolves, and the altar upon which lofty aspirations are kindled, from whence the soul may go forth strengthened, to act its part aright in the great drama of life, with conscience enlightened, affections cultivated, and reason and judgment dominant. But alas for the young wife. Her husband had not been blessed with such a home. When he entered the arena of life, the voices from home did not linger around his path as angels of guidance about his steps; they were not like so many messages to invite him to deeds of high and holy worth. The memory of no sainted mother arose between him and deeds of darkness; the earnest prayers of no father arrested him in his downward course: and before a year of his married life had waned, his young wife had learned to wait and mourn his frequent and uncalled-for absence. More than once had she seen him come home from his midnight haunts, the bright intelligence of his eye displaced by the drunkard's stare, and his manly gait changed to the inebriate's stagger; and she was beginning to know the bitter agony that is compressed in the mournful words, a drunkard's wife. And then there came a bright but brief episode in her experience; the angel of life gave to her existence a deeper meaning and loftier significance: she sheltered in the warm clasp of her loving arms, a dear babe, a precious child, whose love filled every chamber of her heart, and felt the fount of maternal love gushing so new within her soul. That child was hers. How overshadowing was the love with which she bent over its helplessness, how much it helped to fill the void and chasms in her soul. How many lonely hours were beguiled by its winsome ways, its answering smiles and fond caresses. How exquisite and solemn was the feeling that thrilled her heart when she clasped the tiny hands together and taught her dear child to call God "Our Father."

What a blessing was that child. The father paused in his headlong career, awed by the strange beauty and precocious intellect of his child; and the mother's life had a better expression through her ministrations of love. And then there came hours of bitter anguish, shading the sunlight of her home and hushing the music of her heart. The angel of death bent over the couch of her child and beaconed it away. Closer and closer the mother strained her child to her wildly heaving breast, and struggled with the heavy hand that lay upon its heart. Love and agony contended with death, and the language of the mother's heart was,

> Oh, Death, away! that innocent is mine;
> I cannot spare him from my arms
> To lay him, Death, in thine.
> I am a mother, Death; I gave that darling birth
> I could not bear his lifeless limbs
> Should moulder in the earth.

But death was stronger than love and mightier than agony and won the child for the land of crystal founts and deathless flowers, and the poor, stricken mother sat down beneath the shadow of her mighty grief, feeling as if a great light had gone out from her soul, and that the sunshine had suddenly faded around her path. She turned in her deep anguish to the father of her child, the loved and cherished dead. For awhile his words were kind and tender, his heart seemed subdued, and his tenderness fell upon her worn and weary heart like rain on perishing flowers, or cooling waters to lips all parched with thirst and scorched with fever; but the change was evanescent, the influence of unhallowed associations and evil habits had vitiated and poisoned the springs of his existence. They had bound him in their meshes, and he lacked the moral strength to break his fetters, and stand erect in all the strength and dignity of a true manhood, making life's highest excellence his ideal, and striving to gain it.

And yet moments of deep contrition would sweep over him, when he would resolve to abandon the wine-cup forever, when he was ready to forswear the handling of another card, and he would try to break away from the associations that he felt were working his ruin; but when the hour of temptation came his strength was weakness, his earnest purposes were cobwebs, his well-meant resolutions ropes of sand, and thus passed year after year of the married life of Laura Lagrange. She tried to hide her agony from the public gaze, to smile when her heart was almost breaking. But year after year her voice grew fainter and sadder, her once light and bounding step grew slower and faltering. Year after year she wrestled with agony, and strove with despair, till the quick eyes of her brother read, in the paling of her cheek and the dimming eye, the secret anguish of her worn and weary spirit. On that wan, sad face, he saw the death-tokens, and he knew the dark wing of the mystic angel swept coldly around her path. "Laura," said her brother to her one day, "you are not well, and I think you need our mother's tender care and nursing. You are daily losing strength, and if you will go I will accompany you." At first, she hesitated, she shrank almost instinctively from presenting that pale sad face to the loved ones at home. That face was such a tell-tale; it told of heart-sickness, of hope deferred, and the mournful story of unrequited love. But then a deep yearning for home sympathy woke within her a passionate longing for love's kind words, for tenderness and heart-support, and she resolved to seek the home of her childhood, and lay her weary head upon her mother's bosom, to be folded again in her loving arms, to lay that poor, bruised and aching heart where it might beat and throb closely to the loved ones at home. A kind welcome awaited her. All that love and tenderness could devise was done to bring the bloom to her cheek and the light to her eye; but it was all in vain; hers was a disease that no medicine could cure, no earthly balm would heal. It was a slow wasting of the vital forces, the sickness of the soul. The unkindness and neglect of her husband, lay like a leaden weight upon her heart, and slowly oozed away its life-drops. And where was he that had won her love, and then cast it aside as a useless thing, who rifled her heart of its wealth and spread bitter ashes upon its broken altars? He was lingering away from her when the death-damps were gathering on her brow, when his name was trembling on her lips! lingering away! when she was watching his coming, though the death films were gathering before her eyes, and earthly things were fading from her vision. "I think I hear him now," said the dying woman, "surely that is his step;" but the sound died away in the distance. Again she started from an uneasy slumber, "that is his voice! I am so glad he has come." Tears gathered in the eyes of the sad watchers by that dying bed, for they knew that she was deceived. He had not returned. For her sake they wished his coming. Slowly the hours waned away, and then came the sad, soul-sickening thought that she was forgotten, forgotten in the last hour of human need, forgotten when the spirit, about to be dissolved, paused for the last time on the threshold of existence, a weary watcher at the gates of death. "He has forgotten me," again she faintly murmured, and the last tears she would ever shed on earth sprung to her mournful eyes, and clasping her hands together in silent anguish, a few broken sentences issued from her pale and quivering lips. They were prayers for strength and earnest pleading for him who had desolated her young life, by turning its sunshine to shadows, its smiles to tears. "He has forgotten me," she murmured again, "but I can bear it, the bitterness of death is passed, and soon I hope to exchange the shadows of death for the brightness of eternity, the rugged paths of life for the golden streets of glory, and the care and turmoils of earth for the peace and rest of heaven." Her voice grew fainter and fainter, they saw the shadows that never deceive flit over her pale and faded face, and knew that the death angel waited to soothe their weary one to rest, to calm the throbbing of her bosom and cool the fever of her brain. And amid the silent hush of their grief the freed spirit, refined through suffering, and brought into divine harmony through the spirit of the living Christ, passed over the dark waters of death as on a bridge of light, over whose radiant arches hovering angels bent. They parted the dark locks from her marble brow, closed the waxen lids over the once bright and laughing eye, and left her to the dreamless slumber of the grave. Her cousin turned from that death-bed a sadder and wiser woman. She resolved more earnestly than ever to make the world better by her example, gladden by her presence, and to kindle the fires of her genius on the altars of universal love and truth. She had a higher and better object in all her writings than the mere acquisition of gold, or acquirement of fame. She felt that she had a high and holy mission on the battle-field of existence, that life was not given her to be frittered away in nonsense, or wasted away in trifling pursuits. She would willingly espouse an unpopular cause but not an unrighteous one. In her the downtrodden slave found an earnest advocate; the flying fugitive remembered her kindness as he stepped cautiously through our Republic, to gain his freedom in a monarchial land, having broken the chains on which the rust of centuries had gathered. Little children learned to name her with affection, the poor called her blessed, as she broke her bread to the pale lips of hunger. Her life was like a beautiful story, only it was clothed with the dignity of reality and invested with the sublimity of truth. True, she was an old maid, no husband brightened her life with his love, or shaded it with his neglect. No children nestling lovingly in her arms called her mother. No one appended Mrs. to her name; she was indeed an old maid, not vainly striving to keep up an appearance of girlishness, when departed was written on her youth. Not vainly pining at her loneliness and isolation, the world was full of warm, loving hearts and her own beat in unison with them. Neither was she always sentimentally sighing for something to love, objects of affection were all around her, and the world was not so wealthy in love that it had no use for hers; in blessing others she made a life and benediction, and as old age descended peacefully and gently upon her, she had learned one of life's most precious lessons, that true happiness consists not so much in the fruition of our wishes as in the regulation of desires and the full development and right culture of our whole natures.

1859

VOICES FROM THE SOUTHWEST

Juan Nepomuceno Seguin 1806–1890

Juan Nepomuceno Seguin was born into the prominent Seguin family of San Fernando de Bexar (San Antonio) in 1806. He came into early contact with the Anglo-Americans immigrating into Texas in the 1820s and sided with his father and other Mexican elites to welcome the Americans. By the 1830s his friendship with Stephen Austin led to public opposition against Mexican President Santa Anna and complicity with the Americans in plans to secede from Mexico to form the Republic of Texas. In January, 1836, Seguin received a commission from Austin to serve as a captain in the Texas cavalry, with orders to report to the Alamo in San Antonio. He escaped the battle of the Alamo and certain death only because he had been sent through the Mexican lines for reinforcements.

After the successful Texas rebellion, Seguin was seated in the Texas Senate in 1838, where he argued that laws be published in both Spanish and English. In 1841, he was elected mayor of San Antonio. Although he was a generally popular mayor, a number of recently arrived Anglos circulated rumors that he was a Mexican spy conspiring with Santa Anna to regain Texas. Ultimately, daily troublesome encounters with certain Anglos, coupled with outright threats of violence against him and his family, forced him from San Antonio into Mexico in 1842.

Once in Mexico he was immediately captured by Santa Anna's forces. As Seguin explains in his *Personal Memoirs* (1858): "Thrown into prison, in a foreign country, I had no alternative left, but, to linger in a loathsome confinement, or to accept military service. On one hand, my wife and children, reduced to beggary, and separated from me; on the other hand, to turn my arms against my own country. The alternative was sad, the struggle of feelings violent; at last the father triumphed over the citizen; I seized a sword that galled my hand."

The *Personal Memoirs* is characterized by just such self-division. It is an autobiographical account of Seguin's divided loyalties to Texas and Mexico that may be said to represent the kind of ambivalence, often outright cultural schizophrenia, that appears in many early accounts by Mexican(American)s. Seguin writes that he remained in Mexico until 1848 when the Treaty of Guadalupe-Hidalgo was signed and then sought permission of Sam Houston to return to his native Texas. His narrative discloses an accommodating voice in addressing "the American people" from whom he seems to be begging acceptance, but the narrative also assumes an oppositional posture in its description of the injustices and hostilities perpetrated against him and other Texas Mexican families who were socially and economically displaced during the period. Seguin's *Memoirs,* therefore, has all the marks of a narrative that engages in multiple address. That is, the narrative may read like a self-serving political apologia for his Anglo audience, while for his Mexican "posterity" it serves as a warning that despite their proclamations of loyalty to the American state, their social position, if not their very lives, would remain tenuous and always imperiled.

That Seguin remained nationally and culturally self-divided is evidenced by the fact that he built a ranch home in Texas in 1855 but then just a few years after the publication of his *Personal Memoirs* moved to Monterey (1862) to accept a post in the army of Benito Juárez, serving as a colonel until 1871. In the 1870s he again lived in Texas, and then returned to Mexico in 1883, to be with his son, Santiago, who was the mayor of Nuevo Laredo. Whereas he had successfully applied for a pension in Texas in 1873, in 1887 he was denied a military pension in Mexico on the grounds that he had been a Texas rebel. Seguin remained in Mexico, however, until he died and was buried in Nuevo Laredo on August 27, 1890.

Even after death Juan Nepomuceno Seguin has not remained nationally settled. In recognition of his loyal service to Texas in rebelling against Mexico his remains were removed from Mexico on September 20, 1974, and reinterred in Seguin, Texas, a town that in 1838, when he was still highly popular, changed its name from Walnut Creek to Seguin in his honor.

Genaro Padilla
University of California at Berkeley

PRIMARY WORKS

Personal Memoirs, 1858; *A Revolution Remembered: The Memoirs and Selected Correspondence of Juan N. Seguin,* Jesus F. de la Teja, ed., 1991.

SECONDARY WORKS

Leonard Pitt, *The Decline of Californios*, 1969; Genaro M. Padilla, "The Recovery of Chicano Nineteenth Century Autobiography," *American Quarterly* 40, no. 3 (September 1988).

from Personal Memoirs

Preface

A native of the City of San Antonio de Bexar, I embraced the cause of Texas at the report of the first cannon which foretold her liberty; filled an honorable situation in the ranks of the conquerors of San Jacinto,[1] and was a member of the legislative body of the Republic. I now find myself, in the very land, which in other times bestowed on me such bright and repeated evidences of trust and esteem, exposed to the attacks of scribblers and personal enemies, who, to serve *political purposes,* and engender strife, falsify historical facts, with which they are but imperfectly acquainted. I owe it to myself, my children and friends, to answer them with a short, but true exposition of my acts, from the beginning of my public career, to the time of the return of General Woll from the Rio Grande,[2] with the Mexican forces, amongst which I was then serving.

I address myself to the American people; to that people impetuous, as the whirlwind, when aroused by the hypocritical clamors of designing men, but just, impartial and composed, whenever men and facts are submitted to their judgment.

[1]The site of the decisive military battle of the Texas insurgents against Mexico in 1836 in which General Santa Anna's troops were defeated by Sam Houston's forces. Seguin counts himself as one of the Texas independence fighters.

[2]General Woll, a French soldier of fortune in the employ of the Mexican army, recaptured San Antonio briefly in 1842.

I have been the object of the hatred and passionate attacks of some few disorganisers, who, for a time, ruled, as masters, over the poor and oppressed population of San Antonio. Harpy-like, ready to pounce on every thing that attracted the notice of their rapacious avarice, I was an obstacle to the execution of their vile designs. They, therefore, leagued together to exasperate and ruin me, spread against me malignant calumnies, and made use of odious machinations to sully my honor, and tarnish my well earned reputation.

A victim to the wickedness of a few men, whose imposture was favored by their origin, and recent domination over the country; a foreigner in my native land; could I be expected stoically to endure their outrages and insults? Crushed by sorrow, convinced that my death alone would satisfy my enemies, I sought for a shelter amongst those against whom I had fought; I separated from my country, parents, family, relatives and friends, and what was more, from the institutions, on behalf of which I had drawn my sword, with an earnest wish to see Texas free and happy.

In that involuntary exile, my only ambition was to devote my time, far from the tumult of war, to the support of my family, who shared in my sad condition.

Fate, however, had not exhausted its cup of bitterness. Thrown into a prison, in a foreign country, I had no alternative left, but, to linger in a loathsome confinement, or to accept military service. On one hand, my wife and children, reduced to beggary, and separated from me; on the other hand, to turn my arms against my own country. The alternative was sad, the struggle of feelings violent; at last the father triumphed over the citizen; I seized a sword that galled my hand. (Who amongst my readers will not understand my situation?) I served Mexico; I served her loyally and faithfully; I was compelled to fight my own countrymen, but I was never guilty of the barbarous and unworthy deeds of which I am accused by my enemies.

Ere the tomb closes over me and my contemporaries, I wish to lay open to publicity this stormy period of my life; I do it for friends as well as for my enemies, I challenge the latter to contest, with facts, the statements I am about to make, and I leave the decision unhesitatingly to the witnesses of the events.

Memoirs

In October 1834, I was Political Chief of the Department of Bejar.[3] Dissatisfied with the reactionary designs of General Santa Anna,[4] who was at that time President of the Republic of Mexico, and endeavored to overthrow the Federal system, I issued a circular, in which I urged every Municipality in Texas to appoint delegates to a convention that was to meet at San Antonio, for the purpose of taking into consideration the impending dangers, and for devising the means to avert them.

[3]Bejar, commonly called Bexar, is a county in south-central Texas in which San Antonio is located.

[4]Antonio López de Santa Anna (1794–1876), a career military man, was elected President of Mexico in 1833. He led the Mexican forces against the Texas upstarts in 1836 and was captured by Sam Houston's army after the battle of San Jacinto. After being sent to Washington, D.C., he returned to Mexico, regained power and popularity, but was overthrown and exiled to Cuba in 1845. During the 1840s–1850s Santa Anna was either in power or in exile, and was perpetually trying to secure control of the government until shortly before his death.

All the Municipalities appointed their delegates, but the convention never met, the General Government having ordered Col. José Maria Mendoza[5] to march with his forces from Matamoras to San Antonio, and prevent the meeting of the delegates. The proofs of the above facts exist in the archives of the County of Bejar.

In April 1835, the Governor of Coahuila[6] and Texas called for assistance from the various Departments, to resist the aggressions of Santa Anna against that State. I volunteered my services, and received from the Political Chief, Don Angel Navarro,[7] the command of a party of National Guards, sent from San Antonio to Monclova. In our encounters with the troops of Santa Anna, I was efficiently assisted by Col. B. R. Milam and Maj. John R. Allen. On our withdrawal from Monclova, disgusted with the weakness of the Executive, who had given up the struggle, we pledged ourselves to use all our influence to rouse Texas against the tyrannical government of Santa Anna.

We returned to San Antonio in the beginning of June. The Military Commander, Col. Domingo Ugartchea, considering me opposed to the existing government, ordered two officers to watch secretly my motions. This, however, did not prevent me from working diligently to prepare for the intended movement.

We had agreed that the movement should begin in the center of Texas, but, not hearing from that quarter, I determined to send an agent to Brazoria,[8] Juan A. Zambrano, with directions to sound the disposition of the people. On the return of the agent, we were apprized that there was a great deal of talk about a revolution, in public meetings, but that the moment for an armed movement was still remote. Our agent was sent to Victoria,[9] and he there called a meeting of the citizens, but the Military Commander of Goliad sent down a detachment of troops to prevent the assembly and arrest the promoters.

We were despairing of a successful issue, when the Military Commander of Texas, informed of the revolutionary feelings which were spreading over the colonies, determined upon removing from the town of Gonzales a piece of artillery, lent to that Corporation by the Political Chief Saucedo. This was at the time a delicate undertaking. A lieutenant was detailed to carry it into execution, with orders to use force if necessary. On the same day that the military detachment started for Gonzales, I went to the lower ranchos on the San Antonio River, at Salvador Flores I held a meeting of the neighbors, and induced several to take up arms, well satisfied that the beginning of the revolution was close at hand. The officer sent to Gonzales met some resistance at the "Perra," and thought it prudent to beat a hasty retreat. Col.

[5]A Mexican military officer sent to restore order in Texas in 1835.

[6]The Mexican provinces of Coahuila and Tejas were united as one state by the Mexican Constitution (1824), but different regional factions remained at odds through the 1830s creating an unstable situation for the central government. President Santa Anna intervened in 1833 with the result that some of the influential Mexican elite—the Seguin family amongst them—declared against Santa Anna's interference in local matters.

[7]The patriarch of the influential Navarro family of the San Antonio areas whose political sway in Texas lasted until the end of the 19th century. José Antonio Navarro, his son, was crucial in fomenting the Texas rebellion against Santa Anna and was influential in organizing the state's government.

[8]Brazoria County was the area at the mouth of the Brazos river where some of the first American pioneers, under the colonization scheme of Stephen F. Austin, settled Texas.

[9]A small settlement on the Guadalupe River in South Texas.

Ugartchea was making preparations to proceed in person towards Gonzales, with a respectable force, when he received orders from Gen. Cos to await his arrival.[10]

A few days after the entry of Gen. Cos into San Antonio, Major Collinsworth, surprising the garrison of Goliad, took possession of that place. So soon as I was informed of that circumstance, I marched with my company to reinforce the Major, but, at the "Conquista" crossing on the San Antonio River, I was overtaken by an express from General Stephen F. Austin,[11] who informed me that he was marching on San Antonio, and requested me to join him, in order to attack General Cos. I retraced my steps, after having requested Captain Manuel Flores to go and meet General Austin and inform him of my readiness to comply with his wishes, and that I would take with me all the men I could possibly enlist on my route.

On the 13th of October, I met Austin on the Salado, at the crossing of the Gonzales road, and joined my forces with his small army. Upon this occasion I had the honor to become acquainted with General Sam Houston,[12] who accompanied Austin. On the same day we had a slight encounter with the forces under Cos, who retired into San Antonio. Austin, as Commander-in-Chief of the army, gave me the appointment of Captain.

I was commanded to accompany Col. Bowie to the Mission of San José, with my company, with orders to approach the city as nearly as possible, following the banks of the river. We arrived, on the evening of the 21st of November, at the Mission of Concepcion, and noticing that we had been observed by the scouts of Gen. Cos, passed the night in making preparations to resist an attack which we considered imminent. We were not deceived; on the morning of the 22d a force was seen moving along the road from San Antonio to the Mission. A few men, sent by Bowie to reconnoitre, made such a rash charge, that they were cut off from their line of retreat, and had to shut themselves up in the steeple of the church, where they remained during the action. The day was soon ours; the enemy retreating, with the loss of one piece of artillery.

I was detailed to forage for the army, and was successful in doing so, returning to the camp with a liberal supply of provisions. Our camp was shortly moved to

[10]Martín Perfecto de Cós, military commander of the northern Mexican army, was sent by Santa Anna to quell the Texas rebellion in 1835.

[11]Stephen F. Austin (1793–1836) was perhaps the most important figure in the Anglo-American settlement of Texas. Stephen carried out his father Moses Austin's colonization plan to provide land parcels for some three hundred American families in the 1820s. The Austin enterprise was so successful that by 1830 Texas was inhabited largely by Americans, a situation that led to the military annexation of the territory in the mid-1830s.

[12]Sam Houston (1793–1863) was a towering figure in Texas political life from 1836, when as commander-in-chief of the Texas army he defeated Santa Anna's forces at San Jacinto, to his forced retirement from the governorship of Texas in 1861 because he resisted secession from the Union. After the battle of San Jacinto, Houston was elected first President of the Republic of Texas (1836), and immediately upon its annexation to the U.S. in 1846 he was elected to the U.S. Senate where he served for nearly fourteen years. Houston remained firmly opposed to southern secession during the 1850s and, hence, his last years in the Senate were troubled by the erosion of support in the Texas legislature. Notwithstanding his anti-South stand, he was elected Governor of Texas in 1859, but when the secession vote passed he was deposed and resigned from the governorship.

within one mile of the Alamo,[13] whence we proceeded to the "Molino Blanco," and established head-quarters. On the 11th of December we entered the city, and after having taken possession of the houses of the Curate Garza, Veramendi, Garza, Flores, and others, we obliged the enemy to capitulate and withdraw towards Laredo.

After the capture of San Antonio, Captain Travis' company and mine were detailed to go in pursuit of the Mexican forces, and capture from them a cavallado[14] which they had in the Parrita, Laredo road; we succeeded, taking nearly one hundred head of horses, which were sent to San Felipe de Austin, for the benefit of the public service. I was afterwards detailed to the ranchos on the San Antonio river, to see if I could find more horses belonging to the Mexican troops.

On the 2d of January, 1836, I received from the Provisional Government[15] the commission of Captain of Regular Cavalry, with orders to report to Lieutenant-Colonel Travis in San Antonio.

On the 22d of February, at 2 o'clock P. M., General Santa Anna took possession of the city, with over 4000 men, and in the mean time we fell back on the Alamo.

On the 28th, the enemy commenced the bombardment, meanwhile we met in a Council of War, and taking into consideration our perilous situation, it was resolved by a majority of the council, that I should leave the fort, and proceed with a communication to Colonel Fannin, requesting him to come to our assistance. I left the Alamo on the night of the council; on the following day I met, at the Ranch of San Bartolo, on the Cibolo, Captain Desac, who, by orders of Fannin, had foraged on my ranch, carrying off a great number of beeves, corn, &c. Desac informed me that Fannin could not delay more than two days his arrival at the Cibolo, on his way to render assistance to the defenders of the Alamo. I therefore determined to wait for him. I sent Fannin, by express, the communication from Travis, informing him at the same time of the critical position of the defenders of the Alamo. Fannin answered me, through Lieutenant Finley, that he had advanced as far as "Rancho Nuevo," but, being informed of the movements of General Urrea, he had countermarched to Goliad, to defend that place; adding, that he could not respond to Travis' call, their respective commands being separate, and depending upon General Houston, then at Gonzales, with whom he advised me to communicate. I lost no time in repairing to Gonzales, and reported myself to the General, informing him of the purport of my mission. He commanded me to wait at Gonzales for further orders. General Houston ordered Captain Salvador Flores with 25 men of my company to the lower ranchos on the San Antonio river, to protect the inhabitants from the depredations of the Indians.

Afterwards, I was ordered to take possession, with the balance of my company, of the "Perra," distant about four miles on the road to San Antonio, with instructions

[13]The Alamo, a mission church situated in San Antonio, was the site of the famous thirteen-day battle in 1836 between General Santa Anna's forces and a ragged group of Texas rebels.

[14]A herd of horses.

[15]Seguin is referring here to the provisional government established by the Mexican elite and the American settlers which opposed the central Mexican government and agitated for an independent republic.

to report every evening at head-quarters. Thus my company was forming the vanguard of the Texan army, on the road to San Antonio.

On the 6th of March, I received orders to go to San Antonio with my company and a party of American citizens, carrying, on the horses, provisions for the defenders of the Alamo.

Arrived at the Cibolo, and not hearing the signal gun which was to be discharged every fifteen minutes, as long as the place held out, we retraced our steps to convey to the General-in-Chief the sad tidings. A new party was sent out, which soon came back, having met with Anselmo Vergara and Andres Barcena, both soldiers of my company, whom I had left for purposes of observation in the vicinity of San Antonio; they brought the intelligence of the fall of the Alamo. Their report was so circumstantial as to preclude any doubts about that disastrous event.

The Texan army began its retreat towards the centre of the country. I was put in command of the rear-guard, with orders not to leave any families behind. I continued covering the rear-guard, until we had crossed the Arenoso creek, near the Brazos, where I was, by orders of the General, detached with Captain Mosley Baker, to the town of San Felipe de Austin, to cut off the enemy from the passage of the river. We remained in that position, and within sight of the Brigade of General Ramirez, who occupied San Felipe. I was subsequently ordered to occupy with my company Gross' house, farther up the river. Our main army was then encamped in the bottom of the Paloma or Molino Creek, on the Western bank of the Brazos River, where it remained until information was received that the enemy had crossed the river at Fort Bend, and was marching towards Harrisburg. Our army began at once to cross the river, on board the steamer Yellow Stone, and when the whole force had crossed, took up the march, with the intention of harassing the enemy's rear-guard.

The army was taking its noon rest, near Buffalo Bayou, when two soldiers of my company, who had gone out to water horses, reported that they had seen three Mexicans riding at full speed over the prairie. Without delay, I advised the General, who immediately sent Captains Karnes and —— in pursuit. These officers returned shortly, bringing as prisoners a captain, a citizen, and an express bearer of despatches from Mexico to the enemy.

We were apprised by the prisoners that Santa Anna was at Harrisburg with 800 men; and a perusal of their papers made us acquainted with the fact that Cos was to bring him reinforcements. To prevent the concentration of forces, General Sam Houston gave the order to resume the march. The army, artillery, and train, crossed over Buffalo Bayou on rafts, during which operation, General Rusk,[16] then Secretary of War, did not spare his personal labor. It was dark when the crossing was effected. In the course of the night we passed through Harrisburg, the ruins of which were still smoking, having been set on fire by the enemy. We continued our march all night. At daybreak a man was taken prisoner, who, on discovering us, had attempted to escape. He was a printer belonging to San Felipe, and informed us that the enemy were at a distance of about 8 miles, on the way back to Harrisburg. Our scouts came in

[16]Thomas Jefferson Rusk, along with Sam Houston, was one of the military commanders during the Texas rebellion. He was influential in organizing the Texas Republic and later the state government. Rusk was elected to the U.S. Senate in 1846 and served until his death by suicide in 1857.

soon with the information that the enemy were countermarching towards Buffalo Bayou.

Conscious of the starving condition of the troops, who had not eaten for twenty-four hours, General Houston resolved on camping, in a small mott, contiguous to the San Jacinto River.

We were beginning to cook our meal, when the enemy showed themselves close to us. We rushed to arms, and formed in line of battle. On their nearer approach we were ordered to lay down on the ground, thus concealing ourselves in the grass. A height, adjacent to our position, was soon occupied by the enemy, upon which, the General ordered the band to strike up "Will you come to the bower."[17] The enemy answered with its artillery, and we joined the chorus with a brisk musketry. We were soon charged by a skirmishing party on foot, detached from the right wing of the enemy; they were quickly driven back by a party of our cavalry, supported by the artillery. The enemy kept up their fire until they had selected a camping ground, distant about 400 steps from ours, and protected by two motts. Both armies ceased firing; we resumed the cooking of our meal, composed of meat only, but had the good fortune to capture a boat loaded with provisions, which afforded some seasoning to a repast that otherwise would have been rather scanty.

On the same evening General Lamar went out with a party of Cavalry, to draw the enemy into a fight; the result was a slight skirmish, ending in the wounding of two or three on each side.

On the morning of the 21st of April, General Houston, for the purpose of cutting off the communication of General Cos' forces with those of Santa Anna, ordered deaf Smith to burn the bridge over the river, but, on reaching it, he saw that he had come too late, the enemy's reinforcements had already crossed. However, the bridge was destroyed, and Smith returned to our camp at the very moment when Cos united with Santa Anna.

At noon, General Rusk came to partake of dinner in my tent. When he had done eating, he asked me if the Mexicans were not in the habit of taking a siesta at that hour. I answered in the affirmative, adding, moreover, that in such cases they kept under arms their main and advanced guards, with a line of sentinels. General Rusk observed that he thought so; however, the moment seemed to him favorable to attack the enemy, and he further said: "Do you feel like fighting?" I answered that I was always ready and willing to fight, upon which the General rose, saying: "Well, let us go!" I made at once my dispositions; the General proceeded along the line, speaking to the Captains, and our force was soon under arms. Generals Houston and Rusk delivered short addresses, and we formed into line of battle in front of the enemy. My company was in the left wing, under Colonel Sherman. We marched onward on the prairie, and were met by a column of infantry, which we drove back briskly. Before falling in with that column, we had dispersed an ambuscade that had opened their fire against us within pistol shot. The whole enemy's line, panic struck, took to flight. We were already on the bank of the river, in pursuit of the fugitives, when my attention was called to a Mexican officer, who, emerging from the river where he had kept himself concealed, gave himself up and requested me to spare his life. Being shel-

[17]A popular melody of the period.

tered by weeds and grass, he seemed afraid to leave his retreat, owing to the fire which was kept up against the fugitives. I ordered those who were close to me to cease firing, which order was extended along the line to a considerable distance. Then, the officer who had addressed me came out, followed by Colonels Bringas, Almonte, Dias, and quite a number of other officers.

On my way to the camp with the prisoners, an officer, named Sanchez, conducted me to a place where $25,000 had been concealed. I reached the camp at dark, presented my prisoners to the General, who congratulated me, and I reported to him the discovery of the money. Colonel Forbes was at once detailed to go and bring it in.

On this great and glorious day my company was conspicuous for efficiency and gallantry; however, we did not lose one single man, to the surprise of those who had witnessed our honorable and perilous situation.

1858

Mariano Guadalupe Vallejo 1808–1890

In the 1870s Hubert Howe Bancroft, bookdealer, document collector, and professional historian, solicited scores of personal narratives by "Californios," as the native California Mexicans called themselves, that would comprise the material for his massive *History of California,* published between 1884 and 1890. As Bancroft himself wrote of the project in *Literary Industries* (1888), he and his field assistants collected some "two hundred volumes of original narrative from memory by as many early Californians, native and pioneers, written by themselves or taken down from their lips . . . the vivid narratives of their experiences." Such were the people, such are the narrative titles—María Innocente Avila, "Cosas de California"; Juan Bernal, "Memoria de un Californio"; Rafael Gonzalez, "Experiencias de un soldado"; Apolinaria Lorenzana, "Memorias de la Beata"; Eulalia Pérez, "Una vieja y sus recuerdos"; Pio Pico, "Narración histórica"; Vincente Sanchez, "Cartas de un Angelino"; Felipe Osuna de Marron, "Recuerdos del pasado"; Victoriano Vega, "Vida Californiana"; Pablo Véjar, "Recuerdos de un viejo." In this collection are some 140 Hispano personal histories, or autobiographic utterances, of lengths varying from ten or so pages to a fair number that are hundreds of pages long, and a handful that comprise as many as five volumes.

As oral history, these personal narratives provide a broad field of information on Hispano-Mexicano life before the loss of California and much of northern Mexico to the United States in the war of 1846–48. Given the kind of information Bancroft wished to elicit, the narratives tend to describe the significant historical, political, and social events of the day. In the act of testimonial compliance, many of the narratives present a picture of an idyllic pre-American California. This nostalgic tendency is especially conspicuous in the recollections of the social elite; however, even those narratives recorded by members of the lower classes, men who were soldiers and women who worked in the mission system, produce an image of a generally stable, self-sufficient society—at least before the American invasion and subsequent social transformation. The nostalgic tendency of the narratives must be understood as a direct result of sociocultural rupture, since nearly all are characterized by a general sense of malaise, evident in those sections that describe political, economic, and cultural displacement.

It is the disjuncture between a valorized pre-American life and the profound sense of loss after the invasion which provided the autobiographic moment through which the past and the present could be reconsidered, conjoined, reconciled in some degree. The narratives bequeathed by these individuals may have been used by Bancroft as social history, but it is the ever present "I" that transforms them from oral history proper into that genre of life history—autobiography. Whereas for Bancroft the collection of these personal narratives was foundational research for his *History of California* project, for the narrators themselves it was the critical and perhaps only occasion for recreating the life of the self, together with the world inhabited by that self. Such was the case because an established way of life was disintegrating, being rubbed out, erased even at the moment the life was being narrated, transcribed, textualized.

One exemplary narrative, Mariano Guadalupe Vallejo's *Recuerdos históricos y personales tocante a la alta California* (1875), comprises five folio volumes, or nearly one-thousand pages of personal, familial, social, and cultural history. Vallejo is nostalgic at moments, acquiescent although not passive at others, embittered toward the Americanos and yet aware of his own self-betrayal. As a man in his sixties relating the history of California from 1769–1849 with a clear view of its social formation, its transition from Spanish to Mexican influence, and its radical transformation under the American regime, his is a narrative that fuses his own story with the larger social history of his times.

Vallejo is, perhaps, the prime example of the social, economic, and political Californio entrepreneur in the nineteenth century whose inverse fortunes measurably reflect the shifting socio-economic politics of his time. From his youth always quick to take the main chance, Vallejo parlayed his soldiering under the Mexican regime into ascending rank and ever expanding property titlement, building an estate in northern California that began with nothing (no familial titles) and eventually grew into 175,000 acres of land, thousands of cattle and horses, luxurious homes and furnishings, scores of servants, a vast library of the classics, even a carriage delivered from Paris. By the time he composed his *Recuerdos* in the mid-1870s his estate had been stripped to the acreage surrounding his home in Sonoma; he had lost his wealth to lawyers, venture capitalists, and other "ingrates," with the result that he was left roaming San Francisco and the Sonoma countryside asking old friends for small loans.

Like Seguin's *Personal Memoirs,* Vallejo's *Recuerdos* is an ambivalent autobiographical text, which for all of its class-related rationalizing struggles with itself to reconcile history and the individual life. The *Recuerdos,* unlike the Franklinian autobiographical text which charts the rise of the individual from obscurity and poverty to fame and wealth, is a history of the individual's fall from power and his gradual loss of wealth. Hence, by virtue of the author's social displacement, Vallejo's "Recuerdos" is pushed into an antithetical relation with other nineteenth-century American autobiographies which tend to celebrate the conjuncture between the progress of the American nation and that of the American individual. As text it is forced into opposition against the classic American autobiography, the mode of which is generally celebratory. In the case of some of the Californios like Vallejo, the reformation of the self into an American is opposed by external social and cultural forces which simultaneously preclude the individual's movement into American society and distance her or him from their own original culture by denying the value of language, history, and communal affiliation. The autobiographical act thus becomes a tense ritual of gathering and sorting the relics of the communal past, textually extending the cultural legacy while rearranging the national one, proclaiming a desire to become American but doing so in a language and discourse of opposition.

Genaro Padilla
University of California at Berkeley

PRIMARY WORK

Recuerdos históricos y personales tocante a la alta California, 1875.

SECONDARY WORKS

Leonard Pitt, *The Decline of the Californios,* 1969; Genaro M. Padilla, "The Recovery of Chicano Nineteenth-Century Autobiography," *American Quarterly* 40 (September 1988) No. 3; Alan Rosenus, *General M. G. Vallejo and the Advent of the Americans: A Biography,* 1995.

from Recuerdos históricos y personales tocante a la alta California

[Vallejo, who had earlier favored American annexation, records the dismay and sense of betrayal he felt when a group of ragged "thieves" led by Captain John C. Frémont imprisoned him and other men during the Bear Flag insurrection (June 1846) that hastened the U.S.-Mexican War in California.]

All during the first week of the month of June various interviews took place between Captain Frémont and his compatriots. What passed between them is not public knowledge, but if the antecedents may be drawn from what followed, it is easy to presume that they were perfecting the plans they thought most appropriate for seizing Alta California and devising the means to come off victorious in their undertaking. That such may have been the object of their frequent meeting is proved by the fact that on the afternoon of June 11th Frémont and his men, without a previous declaration of war and under no other pretext than their own caprice or necessity, seized the three hundred horses (two hundred of which belonged to the Indians emancipated from San Rafael ex-mission, the interests of whom were managed by Timothy Murphy) which on the account and by the order of Commanding General Castro were grazing to the north of the Cosumnes River in charge of Lieutenant Francisco Arce and several soldiers.

This was the first hostile act that Captain Frémont committed against the property of the inhabitants of California, and although the enormity of his conduct is somewhat mitigated by the fact of his having allowed the cowboys to return to San José mounted upon the horses, the impartial historian should not for that reason fail to censure in severe terms a soldier who belies his glorious mission and becomes a leader of thieves. In spite of my desire to palliate as much as I can the conduct of the individuals who participated in the theft of the Indians' horses, I cannot but stigmatize them with the anathema which society fulminates against those who without legal right to do so appropriate the property of others.

After distributing the horses as they thought most advantageous to their plans, the gentlemen under Captain Frémont's command took the road leading through the Napa Hills to Sonoma and at dawn on the fourteenth of June they surrounded my house located on the *plaza* at Sonoma. At daybreak they raised the shout of alarm and when I heard it, I looked out of my bedroom window. To my great surprise, I made out groups of armed men scattered to the right and left of my residence. The recent arrivals were not in uniform, but were all armed and presented a fierce aspect. Some of them wore on their heads a visorless cap of coyote skin, some a low-crowned plush hat, [and] some a red cotton handkerchief. As for the balance of the clothing of the assaulters of my residence, I shall not attempt to describe it, for I acknowledge that I am incapable of doing the task justice. I suspected that the intruders had intentions harmful not to my [property] interests alone, but to my life and that of the members of my family. I realized that my situation was desperate. My wife advised me to try and flee by the rear door, but I told her that such a step was unworthy and that under no circumstances could I decide to desert my young family at such a critical time. I had my uniform brought, dressed quickly and then ordered the large vestibule door thrown open. The house was immediately filled with armed men. I went with them into the parlor of my residence. I asked them what the trouble was and who was heading the party, but had to repeat that question a second time, because almost all of those who were in the parlor replied at once, "Here we are all heads." When I again asked with whom I should take the matter up, they pointed out William B. Ide who was the eldest of all. I then addressed that gentleman and informed him that I wanted to know to what happy circumstance *I owed the visit of so many individuals.*

In reply he stated that both Captain Merritt and the other gentlemen who were in his company had decided not to continue living any longer under the Mexican government, whose representatives Castro and Pío Pico, did not respect the rights of American citizens living in the *Departamento;* that Castro was every once in a while issuing proclamations treating them all as bandits and, in a desire to put a stop to all these insults, they had decided to declare California independent; that while he held none but sentiments of regard for me, he would be forced to take me prisoner along with all my family.

We were at this point when there appeared in the room *don* Salvador Vallejo, *don* Pepe de la Rosa, Jacob P. Leese, and *don* Victor Prudon, all friends of mine for whom an order of arrest was suggested until it was decided what should be my fate. I thought for a moment that through some sacrifice on my part I might get rid of so many and such little desired guests, but my hopes were frustrated by the unworthy action of the Canadian, Olivier Beaulieu, who, knowing from his own experiences that liquor is an incentive for all kinds of villainous acts, had gone to his house and procured there a barrel full of brandy, which he distributed among the companions of Merritt and Ide. Once under the influence of the liquor, they forgot the chief object of their mission and broke into shouts of "Get the loot, get the loot!"

Fortunately, these seditious cries emitted by Scott, Beaulieu, Sears and others attracted the attention of Doctor Semple who stepped very angrily to the door of the entrance vestibule and by means of a speech of much feeling, in which there were not a few threats, gave them to understand that he would kill the first man who by committing robbery would cast a blot upon the expedition he had helped organize to advance a political end and that, so long as he was alive, he would not allow it to be turned into a looting expedition. . . .

Shortly after Lieutenant Misroon's arrival at Sonoma, he endeavored to enter into extra-official relations with William B. Ide and the companions of that impoverished commander, but his advances met with no response, because Ide and the others sheltered under the fateful "Bear Flag" did not leave the barracks, the entrance to which was protected by nine cannon of different calibers that they had taken away from me at dawn on June 14th and which they kept loaded to the muzzle. These were all in charge of their respective gunners (the artillerymen did not know their business, for they had been improvised) who never for a single instant relaxed their vigilance over the war materials of which they had been left in charge.

When Lieutenant Misroon had arranged everything as best he could, he left instructions for his subordinate and returned on board the frigate "Portsmouth," where it is to be presumed that he submitted to Captain Montgomery an account of all he had heard and witnessed at Sonoma.

Shortly after Doctor Semple had set out for the Sacramento, the *plaza* at Sonoma was taken in charge by William B. Ide, whom the rest of the force that had invaded my residence had agreed to obey. The number of those who along with William B. Ide remained in charge of the Sonoma garrison was at least fifty. I am aware that various historians have fixed the number at eighteen, but I absolutely know that they are in error. It only remains to determine whether the mistake has been accidental or intentional. I am of the opinion that it has been intentional, for it seems that a hidden but powerful hand has taken great pains to garble all the facts relative to the capture of the Sonoma *plaza* by the group of adventurers to whom history has given the name of "The Bear Flag Party." I, who was made the chief victim those *patriotic gentlemen* sacrificed upon the altar of their well-laid plans, have no interest whatsoever in bespattering them with mud, nor do I aspire to ennoble myself at the expense of their reputation. All I desire is that the impartial public may know what took place at Sonoma on fateful June 14th, 1846, and that it may, after learning all there is to know in regard to this scandalous violation of law that deprived of liberty those who for years had been making countless sacrifices to redeem from the hands of the barbarous heathen the territory known as the Sonoma Frontier, decide in favor of one or the other of the participants in the events I have just related. All I demand is that the decision arrived at may be upon a basis of fact.

On the fourth day that Mr. Ide was in command at the Sonoma *plaza* and when he saw that a great number of Americans and foreigners had hurried in to place themselves under his protection, being fearful lest the Californians would attack them on their *ranchos* should they continue to live scattered over the country, he issued a document in which he set forth the reasons that had impelled him to refuse to recognize the authority of the Mexican government. The original proclamation, which was very brief, merely stated that, since the lives of foreigners were in imminent danger, he had felt it his duty to declare Alta California independent and that, counting as he did upon the definite support and cooperation of the "fighting men" who had rallied around him, he aimed to do all he could to prevent the Californians or the Mexicans from recovering the military post and arms which the valor of his men had seized from them. This is approximately what "Captain" Ide read aloud before the flagpole in the Sonoma *plaza.* I am fully aware that the original proclamation was destroyed and that a few weeks later another was drawn up which, it was said, contained a list of the wrongs which the Mexican authorities had perpetrated against United States citizens.

After the reading of the Commander-in-chief's proclamation, they proceeded with great ceremony to hoist the flag by virtue of which those who had assaulted my home and who had by that time appropriated to themselves two hundred fifty muskets and nine cannon proposed to carry on their campaign.

This flag was nothing more nor less than a strip of white cotton stuff with a red edge and upon the white part, almost in the center, were written the words "California Republic." Also on the white part, almost in the center, there was painted a bear with lowered head. The bear was so badly painted, however, that it looked more like a pig than a bear. The material for the flag was furnished, according to some, by Mrs. Elliot; according to others by Mrs. Sears. I also heard it said that Mrs. Grigsby furnished it.

Those who helped to prepare, sew and paint the flag were the following young men: Alexander Todd, Thomas Cowie and Benjamin Duell. The latter was the one who suggested that a star be painted near the mouth of the bear. Of course, both the bear and the star were very badly drawn, but that should not be wondered at, if one takes into consideration the fact that they lacked brushes and suitable colors.

The running up of this queer flag caused much fear to the families of the Californians established in the neighborhood of Sonoma, Petaluma and San Rafael, for they realized that the instigators of the uprising that had disturbed the tranquility of the frontier had made up their minds to rule, come what might, and, as the rumor had been spread far and wide that Ide and his associates had raised the bear flag in order to enjoy complete liberty and not be obliged to render any account of their activities to any civilized governments, the ranchers, who would have remained unperturbed should the American flag have been run up in Sonoma and who would have considered it as the harbinger of a period of progress and enlightenment, seized their *machetes* and guns and fled to the woods, determined to await a propitious moment for getting rid of the disturbers of the peace. Strange to relate, the first victim that the ranchers sacrificed was the painter of the "Bear Flag," young Thomas Cowie who, along with P. Fowler, was on his way to Fitch's ranch to get one-eyed Moses Carson (brother of the famous explorer Colonel Kit Carson), who was employed as an overseer by Captain Henry Fitch, to give them a half barrel of powder he had locked up in one of the storage closets of his farmhouse. Fowler and Cowie were taken by surprise at the Yulupa Rancho by the party operating under the command of Captains Padilla and Ramón Carrillo, who at the request of the people had assumed direction of the hostilities it had been decided to undertake against "the Bears." Neither of the two extemporaneous commanders thought it right to take the lives of their young captives, upon whom there had been found letters that proved beyond any doubt that Moses Carson and certain others of the Americans employed at the Fitch Ranch were in accord with Ide, Merritt and others of those who had made up their minds to put an end to Mexican domination in California; so they decided to tie them up to a couple of trees while they deliberated as to what should be done with the captives, whose fate was to be decided at the meeting that night to which had been summoned all the ranchers who by their votes had shared in entrusting command of the Californian forces to those wealthy citizens, Padilla and Carrillo. I am of the opinion that the lives of Cowie and Fowler would have been spared, had it not been that a certain Bernardo García, better known under the name of "Three-fingered Jack," taken advantage of the darkness of the night, approached the trees to which the captives were tied and put an end to their existence with his well-sharpened dagger.

After committing the two murders I have just told about, Bernardo García entered the lonely hut in which Padilla, Carrillo and others had met and were discussing as to what disposition should be made of the prisoners. Without waiting for them to ask him any questions, he said to his compatriots, "I thought you here were going to decide to free the prisoners and, as that is not for the good of my country, I got ahead of you and took the lives of the Americans who were tied to the trees."

Those few words, spoken with the greatest of sang-froid by the wickedest man that California had produced up to that time, caused all who heard him to shudder. No one dared to object to what had been done, however, for they knew that such a step would have exposed them to falling under the knife of the dreaded Bernardo García, who for years past had been the terror of the Sonoma frontier.

Equally with the relatives of the unfortunate youths, Cowie and Fowler, I regretted their premature death, for, in spite of the fact that they belonged to a group of audacious men who had torn me from the bosom of my family and done as they pleased with my horses, saddles and arms, I did not consider that the simple fact that they were the bearers of a few letters made them deserving of the supreme penalty. Until that fatal June 21st, neither they nor their companions had shed any Mexican blood and it was not right for the Mexicans to begin a war *à outrance,* that could not help but bring very grievous consequences upon them and their families. . . .

When we reached New Helvetia, the Canadian, Alexis, who was heading our escort, gave three knocks upon the main gate with his lance and it was immediately thrown open by Captain Sutter, who, feigning surprise at seeing us as prisoners, led us into his living quarters. He then promised to comply with the orders that Captain Frémont had delivered to him by the mouth of his lieutenant, Alexis, who had said in our presence, "Captain Frémont is turning these gentlemen over to you for you to keep as prisoners behind these walls and upon your own responsibility."

"All right," said Sutter, and without any further ceremony he turned to us and suggested that we accompany him to a large room situated on the second floor where the only furniture was a kind of rude benches. When we were all inside this room, Sutter locked the door and thought no more about us that night.

I leave my readers to imagine how we cursed at finding ourselves locked up in a narrow room and forced to sleep upon the floor, without a mattress and without a blanket, even without water with which to quench our burning thirst. There, seated upon a bench, I ran over in my mind all that I had witnessed since that fatal June 14th and I assure you I regretted very much not having accepted the offer of that brave captain of militia, *don* Cayetano Juárez, had ordered made to me through his brother, Vicente Juárez.

On June 14, 1846, Captain Juárez was at his Tulcay *hacienda,* when he learned that a group of adventurers had assaulted the Sonoma *plaza.* No sooner did he learn of it than, arming himself, he came to an understanding with Citizens Victorino Altamirano, Antonio Wilson, Vicente and Francisco Juárez, Andrés Vaca, Pancho Cibrián and others. He went and took up a position in Portezuelo Pass, where he awaited the reply that was to be brought to him by a brother of his whom he had sent, disguised as a woman, to take up a position where I was to pass and ask me if I desired that he (Cayetano Juárez) should make an effort to snatch me from the hands of my guards. I do not recall what it was that caused me to refuse the generous offer of that devoted soldier who had made up his mind to risk his life to procure my freedom. I think that I was influenced above all by the thought I held as to the misfortunes that would inevitably overtake my family, if Captain Juárez and his friends had killed the comrades of those who had remained behind in Sonoma in possession of the *plaza* and war materials. My repentance came too late, for I was in the hands of a foresworn man, a foreigner who had received many favors from me and mine, [but] who had deliberately forgotten them all and, to cap the climax of [his] infamy, had consented to become my jailor, in order to curry favor with a lot of men who had nothing to their names but an extraordinary dose of boldness, who were not fighting under any recognized flag, and who apparently had no other object than robbery and looting.

After a sleepless night, I greeted the dawn of the new day with enthusiasm, for we were by then beginning to experience the urge of a voracious appetite. Our jailor, however, who had doubtless made up his mind to make us drain the last drop of gall which a perverse fate had meted out to us, sent us no food until eleven o'clock in the morning, at which time he came and opened the door to permit the entrance of an Indian carrying a jar filled with broth and pieces of meat. He did not send us a spoon, knives and forks, for Captain Sutter no doubt thought that since we had lost our liberty we had also ceased to retain our dignity. Such behavior on the part of a companion in arms (at that time Captain Sutter was still an official of the Mexican Government) could not help but inspire our disgust, for we all recognized the insult that he was inflicting upon us by taking advantage of the circumstances. There are times in life, however, when man should resign himself to suffering every kind of adversity. Doubtless, God had decreed that the month of June, 1846, should be the blackest month of my life.

Four days after our arrival at New Helvetia, Citizen Julio Carrillo appeared at that place. Furnished with a passport issued to him by Lieutenant Misroon, he had undertaken the journey to bring me news of my family. Inasmuch as my jailors did not have any great respect for officials of the United States, they paid no attention to the passport and locked *señor* Carrillo up in the same room in which I was enjoying Captain Sutter's hospitality, along with Victor Prudon, Jacob Leese and Salvador Vallejo. I regretted very much the imprisonment of that friend who, moved by a desire to put an end to my wife's worry, had undertaken the dangerous mission of entering the enemy's camp. . . .

Some years ago (in 1868) when I was in Monterey, my friend, David Spence, showed me a book entitled "History of California," written by an author of recognized merit by the name of Franklin Tuthill, and called my attention to that part of the gentleman's narrative where he expresses the assurance that the guerrilla men whom Captain Frémont sent in pursuit of the Californian, Joaquín de la Torre, took nine field pieces from the latter. I could not help but be surprised when I read such a story, for I know for a fact that Captain de la Torre had only thirty cavalrymen under his command who as their only weapons carried a lance, carbine, saber and pistol. I think that Mr. Tuthill would have done better if, instead of inventing the capture of nine cannon, he had devoted a few lines to describing the vandal-like manner in which the "Bear" soldiers sacked the Olompalí Rancho and maltreated the eighty year old Dámaso Rodríguez, alférez retired, whom they beat so badly as to cause his death in the presence of his daughters and granddaughters. Filled with dismay, they gathered into their arms the body of the venerable old man who had fallen as a victim of the thirst for blood that was the prime mover of the guerrilla men headed by Mr. Ford.

I should indeed like to draw a veil over such a black deed, but the inexorable impartiality that is the guiding light of the historian prevents me from passing over a fact that so helps to reveal the true character of the men who on June 14, 1846, assaulted the *plaza* at Sonoma at a time when its garrison was in the central part of the *Departamento* busy curbing raids by the barbarous heathen. Let my readers not think that it is my desire to open up wounds that have healed over by now. I am very far from harboring any such thought, for ever since Alta California became a part of the great federation of the United States of North [America], I have spared no effort to establish upon a solid and enduring basis those sentiments of union and concord which are so indispensible for the progress and advancement of all those who dwell in my native land, and, so long as I live, I propose to use all the means at my command to see to it that both races cast a stigma upon the disagreeable events that took place on the Sonoma frontier in 1846. If before I pass on to render an account of my acts to the Supreme Creator, I succeed in being a witness to a reconciliation between victor and vanquished, conquerors and conquered, I shall die with the conviction of not having striven in vain.

In bringing this chapter to a close, I will remark that, if the men who hoisted the "Bear Flag" had raised the flag that Washington sanctified by his abnegation and patriotism, there would have been no war on the Sonoma frontier, for all our minds were prepared to give a brotherly embrace to the sons of the Great Republic, whose enterprising spirit had filled us with admiration. Ill-advisedly, however, as some say, or dominated by a desire to rule without let or hindrance, as others say, they placed themselves under the shelter of a flag that pictured a bear, an animal that we took as the emblem of rapine and force. This mistake was the cause of all the trouble, for when the Californians saw parties of men running over their plains and forests under the "Bear Flag," they thought that they were dealing with robbers and took the steps they thought most effective for the protection of their lives and property.

[An Account of the Gold Rush]

Gold in the mines! This cry, resounding throughout the length and breadth of California, created a veritable revolution, social and financial. The farmer left his plough in the furrow, the schoolmaster abandoned his books and blackboards, the sailor deserted his ship, the barber flung down his razor and the tailor his shears. Even the lover relinquished the hand of his sweetheart to clutch the pick and shovel and rush forth in search of the longed-for metal.

Some of the adventurers left Monterey mounted on fine horses. Speeding along the roads at twenty miles a day, they were not long in reaching their destination. Others, with an eye to the future, set out in oxcarts loaded with provisions; they spent more time on the road, but on reaching the goal of their desires found themselves in far better circumstances than those who had preceded them, since their carts served them as bedrooms, dining rooms, reception halls and kitchens. As rains fell frequently at the mines, it was not only a comfort but a necessity to have places in which to take refuge from the storms.

Shortly after the discovery of the gold diggings, San Diego, Los Angeles, Monterey, Branciforte [Santa Cruz] and San José lost the greater part of their population, for everyone who could dispose of his property left his home and took the road to the mines or "placers," as they called the spots where the coveted metal could be gathered by the handful.

The few wooden houses which existed in the country were torn apart and loaded into small coasting vessels and sent to Sacramento, whence the lumber went forward to the mines by oxcart. Picks, shovels, sheets of tinplate, nails, rubber boots and medicines . . . sold at fabulous prices. But it must be remembered that as many of the miners were producing more than two hundred pesos in a day of twelve hours, they were not minded to resent the inflated prices which they were forced to pay for tools, medicines and food.

At this time, when the populous cities of the southern part of the state were deserted by their inhabitants, the frontier town of Sonoma, an essentially agricultural community, which up to that time had figured only as an outpost against the raids of the heathen savages, rose to the first rank among the cities of Alta California.[1]

All the caravans from Monterey and other parts of the state, and even those which arrived from the state of Sonora,[2] broke their journey at Sonoma, where they rested the wearied animals, repaired harness and wagons, shod their saddle horses and bought fresh provisions before resuming their march. On the other hand, the miners who had met with good fortune in the diggings came, for the most part, to Sonoma to dispose of their gold, to buy new clothing and to make other necessary preparations for their return to the mines.

In December, 1848, and during all of the year 1849, gold in dust or flakes was so abundant in Sonoma that it was difficult to obtain six dollars an ounce in exchange for coined money. This low rate was attributed in part to the large amount of gold brought in by the Indians. . . .

At the diggings the food consisted of the flesh of wild animals, of ship biscuit or bread made by the miners, onions, potatoes, dried beans, salt pork, and from time to time, of salmon. This fish abounded in the Sacramento River, and at that time could be caught with astonishing ease. The fishermen loaded great carts with salmon and, traveling day and night, brought them still fresh to the mining camps, where they sold them for twenty *reales* [$2.50] a pound.

As a rule, a four-horse wagon carried to the mines a ton of salmon, which produced for its owner, when he had sold it to the miners, about $5,000.00. When it is

[1]Early in the Spanish colonial period, California was geographically sectioned, politically and imaginatively, into Baja or Lower, and Alta or Upper, provinces, with Monterey as the approximate dividing line. These designations remain in popular use today as Southern and Northern California.

[2]A state in northern Mexico that borders what is now California and Arizona.

taken into consideration that the round trip could be made in eight days, and sometimes in even shorter time, it can be seen that the earnings of the fishermen were on a level with those of the miners, without the exposure to the calamitous and unpleasant experiences peculiar to the life of the gold diggers.

When the rainy season drew near, the miners who had been fortunate came down from the diggings to spend the winter in Sacramento, which, by reason of its proximity to San Francisco, offered a thousand comforts which one would have sought in vain in the towns of the interior. There were undoubtedly many cases of miners, owners of rich placers, who feared to lose their claims if they abandoned them during the winter, and so remained in the diggings during the rainy season.

Some of these men lost their lives, buried under the snow, some were drowned in the rivers and some were devoured by wild beasts. Misfortunes of this sort were very frequent in the district behind Downieville, where in the winter the snow lies to a depth of eight, ten or twelve feet, and wild animals are abundant.

In the winter Sacramento was always crowded, since it was there that the gamblers assembled in droves to fleece the unwary. Gaming tables were set up everywhere; faro, monte, rouge et noire and lasquinet were the favorite games. The amounts waged on a single card were very great, and there were times when they reached five or six hundred ounces of gold.

To attract many persons to their gambling halls, the proprietors engaged musicians and singers to whom they paid high wages. I remember that one such family, composed of four persons, was paid a hundred dollars a day, in addition to lodging, meals, liquor and laundry. Anyone had the right to enter the houses of play and demand liquor and cigars without payment, since the astute proprietors knew that the fumes of tobacco and liquor were powerful auxiliaries in upsetting the judgment of those who came to risk their money. Of course, the bankers cheated continually and those who laid their money on the green cloth rarely won.

. . . Many Californians, drawn by the novelty of the spectacle (for gambling in public was not permitted under Mexican rule, although in private the common people played until they lost the clothes off their backs) and deluded into believing that they could easily enrich themselves by guessing the cards, lost in half an hour cattle and ranches that had been owned for half a century, perhaps, by their ancestors. Blinded by the passion for the game, they did not awaken to the truth of the situation until it was already too late to remedy.

Disputes frequently arose among those who played, and these disputes developed into blows, shootings or stabbings. The police never interfered until hostilities were concluded, and the judges, in fear of their lives, refrained from punishing the guilty if they belonged to the great society of Hounds.[3]

[3]The Hounds were a group of thugs—many of them were former Australian penal convicts—who, ironically, were commissioned by the mayor of San Francisco to patrol the streets of the city. As Vallejo indicates, these Hounds actually swaggered through the streets intimidating and beating "foreigners." On July 14, 1849, they attacked a Chilean and Peruvian encampment, destroying personal property, robbing and terrifying people, raping women, and killing a few "greasers." After this outrage, the Law and Order party was formed to arrest and try them.

This society, at the beginning of 1849, ruled San Francisco and, by means of its ramifications, dominated all California. The Society of Hounds had been founded under the name of "Society for Mutual Aid" but it was in reality nothing but an organization of soulless wretches whose only object was pillage, robbery and banditry; naturally, human life had no value in the eyes of these malefactors.

The Californians living in San Francisco and its environs, and the Europeans of Latin race furnished most of the victims of the Hounds; but when the supply of "foreigners" began to run low, the Hounds were not above robbing their countrymen, the North Americans. . . .

Malefactors who fell into the hands of the miners seldom escaped with their lives. As at that time there were no laws, everyone did justice for himself, either alone or with the aid of his friends and neighbors. It is well known that '48 and '49 were terrible times for bandits, as the industrious miners hanged them as fast as they caught them, without distinction of sex. A woman was hanged in Downieville, and in Placerville (alias Hangtown) also they hanged a young woman who had caused human blood to flow. . . .

When gold was discovered, the flag of stars already waved over Alta California. No longer were we ruled by the Mexican laws, under whose shadow some had advanced while others fell back, but under which no one had perished of hunger, and only two individuals had been by law deprived of their lives, a very common event during the early years of the North American domination in California.

The language now spoken in our country, the laws which govern us, the faces which we encounter daily, are those of the masters of the land, and, of course, antagonistic to our interests and rights,[4] but what does that matter to the conqueror? He wishes his own well-being and not ours!—a thing that I consider only natural in individuals, but which I condemn in a government which has promised to respect and make respected our rights, and to treat us as its own sons. But what does it avail us to complain. The thing has happened and there is no remedy.

. . . I ask, what has the state government done for the Californians since the victory over Mexico? Have they kept the promises with which they deluded us? I do not ask for miracles; I am not and never have been exacting; I do not demand gold, a pleasing gift only to abject peoples. But I ask and I have a right to ask for an answer.

1875

[4]Vallejo is referring to disputes over language use, land tenure and ownership, and to a wide feeling on the part of Mexican Californians that they had been politically disfranchised by the American newcomers after California had become a state in 1849.

A CONCORD INDIVIDUALIST

Henry David Thoreau 1817–1862

Henry Thoreau was the second son and third child of John Thoreau, whose father Jean had emigrated to America from the Isle of Jersey about the time of the American Revolution. The Thoreaus were of Huguenot stock, having been driven from France in the Protestant persecutions of the late seventeenth century, culminating in the revocation by Louis XIV of the Edict of Nantes in 1685. Thoreau's energetic mother, Cynthia Dunbar Thoreau, was of hardy Scotch lineage. Growing up in Concord, Massachusetts, home also to Nathaniel Hawthorne and Ralph Waldo Emerson, Thoreau attended Harvard College in nearby Cambridge from 1833 to 1837, graduating without conspicuous honors. The remainder of his life, except for visits to Canada, Maine, Minnesota, and nearby locales, he spent in his home community, whose flora and fauna he explored with a microscopic eye, recording his observations in a compendious journal which he faithfully kept from 1837 to 1860. Early interpreters of Thoreau understandably thought of him as a naturalist, since his observations of botanical phenomena were copious, and since he spent much of his time roaming the environs of Concord with spyglass, notebook, and pencil, recording the seasonal changes and life cycles of hundreds of plants.

But this interpretation of Thoreau is now universally adjudged to have been too narrow. The mistake lay in part in the failure to perceive in Thoreau his immersion in the world view of his "Transcendentalist" friend and neighbor, Ralph Waldo Emerson, who had propounded in his seminal book, *Nature,* the doctrine that every physical fact is but the facade of a spiritual truth. Emerson had counseled his generation to look *through* the transparency of nature in order to grasp the essential spirituality of the universe embosomed there; and Thoreau, of all Emerson's followers, acted upon Emerson's teachings most consistently. His most dramatic act was his retirement for two years, two months, and two days in 1845, 1846, and 1847 to Walden Pond, where he built a hut and studied nature to discover what she had to teach of moral and spiritual truth, the record of which he narrated in one of the most influential books of the nineteenth century—*Walden*—a triumph of refined, condensed, figurative prose that has provided the base for his distinguished twentieth-century literary reputation.

Thoreau's "Transcendental" premises led him to take a negative view of the dominant values of pre–Civil-War America. He wrote disparagingly of the destruction of the natural environment, of which human beings were an integral part; he deplored the implications of the rise of industrialism, with its emphasis upon materialistic values; he condemned the institution of black slavery, which debased people to the level of property, and as a corollary, the government which fostered and perpetuated the institution. Astute readers will also discern in Thoreau an awareness of the philosophical systems of his day, particularly of Kant and Coleridge; of the political and economic theories of the time; and even of many scientific assumptions that were to flower in the twentieth century. In short, Thoreau was not only a writer of great skill, but a man remarkably alert to the thinking of his age, who with remarkable prescience anticipated the crisis in values of the century to follow him. He is a man of his time, it is true, but he is a man of our time also; and it is his perceptiveness of the human problems of all times that makes him such an engaging literary figure to the student today.

Though Thoreau considered his profession to be that of writer, he published only two books in his short lifetime of 44 years. The first, *A Week on the Concord and Merrimack Rivers* (1849) is the record of a two-week river excursion by rowboat taken by Thoreau and his brother, John, in the fall of 1839, condensed in the book to one week, and embellished by Thoreau's reflections on a variety of subjects for the most part suggested to him by his wide reading in world literature. For many readers, the book is a collection of remarkable essays that lack cohesion and relatedness. It is, however, the second book, *Walden* (1854), that has elevated Thoreau into the first rank of American authors, and distinguished him throughout the world as an artist and philosopher of unique perceptiveness and vision. *Walden* breaks out of the structure of Emersonian Transcendentalism current at the time (though influenced by it), lifting the perceptive reader to a rare and exhilarating self-knowledge, as Thoreau's romantic contemporary John Keats observed that poetry should do, "surprising by a fine excess." That is to say, by employing many of the devices of poetry—allusion, figures of speech, imagery—and through a disciplined process of refinement and constriction of his text that took portions of the book through seven versions, Thoreau achieved a work of such subtlety and suggestiveness that repeated readings do not exhaust its meanings or dim the brilliance of its insights. Though only a few chapters can be excerpted for inclusion in an anthology such as this, students of American literature should secure a copy of the complete *Walden,* perennially available in multiple inexpensive editions, and enjoy the coherence and unity of the book as a whole.

Next to *Walden,* Thoreau is best known for his essay, "Resistance to Civil Government," often mistakenly called "Civil Disobedience," which delineates his view in 1849 of the legitimate role of the private individual in a society whose government sanctions the immorality of black slavery. Published in a soon to be defunct journal, *Aesthetic Papers,* edited by Elizabeth Peabody, Thoreau's contentions that private morality is a privileged sanctuary that governments have no right to intrude upon, and that such intrusion by government should be passively resisted by the individual, have elicited sympathetic responses in widely separated parts of the world, from Gandhi's India to Martin Luther King's American South. The immediate occasion that provoked the essay was Thoreau's incarceration in the Concord jail for one night for his refusal to pay his poll tax to a government which supported black slavery, a story that he narrates in his essay; but what chiefly interests the modern reader is Thoreau's perceptive definition of the line of demarcation between individual prerogative and the power of the state. In other words, Thoreau universalizes his experience, seeking not so much to justify his own actions and motives, as to illuminate the principles that provide the cutting edge that separates individual rights from state authority. Black slavery is to him a moral issue, and a government that condones it and even abets it has intruded into an area where governments, according to his principle, have no authority. Over against the American Constitution, which condones black slavery, Thoreau superimposes an eighteenth-century "higher law" resembling that of Jefferson in the Declaration of Independence, which accords supremacy to individual morality.

By 1859, Thoreau's passive resistance to governmental intrusion upon individual rights, so eloquently argued in 1849, had changed to a methodology of militancy. When John Brown made his abortive assault upon the armory at Harpers Ferry, Thoreau applauded Brown's resort to arms, tacitly admitting, it would seem, that so entrenched an evil as southern slavery was unresponsive to the passive resistance he had offered earlier as the appropriate weapon to use to confront state authority. Thoreau had met John Brown in Concord and had been impressed by his single-minded aversion to human slavery; and in "A Plea for Captain John Brown," delivered by Thoreau as a lecture on several occasions before Brown was executed by hanging on December 2, 1859, Thoreau elevates Brown to the level of mythical hero, a "man of principle" who defied personal danger in order to shock both North and South into a recognition of the moral obliquy that black slavery typified. Thoreau had written earlier of his horror of the institution of slavery, notably in "Slavery in Massachusetts" (1854), which excoriated the Fugitive Slave Law that permitted southern sheriffs to pursue fleeing blacks across the boundaries of northern states; but Thoreau's John Brown essays are perhaps the most polemic that he ever wrote, charged with outrage at the social institution that was soon to provoke the American Civil War. Ironically, Thoreau was not to live to see the day when the Emancipation Proclamation would extinguish the American government's approval of a practice he found so heinous.

He died in 1862 of tuberculosis, the scourge of his family, at the age of 44. Within four years, four books of his writings were in print, edited and published by his sister, Sophia, his friend, Ellery Channing, and by Emerson. His remarkable journal was issued in 1906, adding to his growing fame. As he declined into death in the spring months of 1862, just as nature was renewing herself around him, he expressed no regrets for the life he had lived. To the deathbed question, "Have you made your peace with God?" he allegedly replied, "We never quarrelled." "Are you ready for the next world?" another acquaintance asked. Thoreau's response was: "One world at a time."

Wendell P. Glick
University of Minnesota

PRIMARY WORKS

A Week on the Concord and Merrimack Rivers, 1849; *Walden,* 1854. Posthumously published: *The Maine Woods,* 1864; *Cape Cod,* 1865; *Letters to Various Persons* (edited by Emerson), 1865; *A Yankee in Canada, with Anti-Slavery and Reform Papers,* 1866. *The Writings of Henry David Thoreau,* 1906, 20 vols., which includes the *Journal,* is currently being superseded by the Princeton Edition of *The Writings of Henry David Thoreau,* 1971–, which will also include the *Journal* in augmented form.

SECONDARY WORKS

Walter Harding, *The Days of Henry Thoreau,* 1965, 1966; Stanley Cavell, *The Senses of Walden,* 1972, 1974, 1980, 1981 (soon to be reissued); Walter Harding and Michael Meyer, *The New Thoreau Handbook,* 1980; Raymond R. Borst, ed., *Henry David Thoreau/A Descriptive Bibliography,* 1982; William Howarth, *The Book of Concord/Thoreau's Life as a Writer,* 1982; Leonard N. Neufeldt, *The Economist: Henry Thoreau and Enterprise,* 1988; H. Daniel Peck, *Thoreau's Morning Work,* 1990; Frederick Garber, *Thoreau's Fable of Inscribing,* 1991.

Resistance to Civil Government[1]

I heartily accept the motto,—"That government is best which governs least;"[2] and I should like to see it acted up to more rapidly and systematically. Carried out, it finally amounts to this, which also I believe,—"That government is best which governs not at all;" and when men are prepared for it, that will be the kind of government which they will have. Government is at best but an expedient; but most governments are usually, and all governments are sometimes, inexpedient. The objections which have been brought against a standing army, and they are many and weighty, and deserve to prevail, may also at last be brought against a standing government. The standing army is only an arm of the standing government. The government itself, which is only the mode which the people have chosen to execute their will, is equally liable to be abused and perverted before the people can act through it. Witness the present Mexican war, the work of comparatively a few individuals using the standing government as their tool; for, in the outset, the people would not have consented to this measure.[3]

This American government,—what is it but a tradition, though a recent one, endeavoring to transmit itself unimpaired to posterity, but each instant losing some of its integrity? It has not the vitality and force of a single living man; for a single man can bend it to his will. It is a sort of wooden gun to the people themselves; and, if ever they should use it in earnest as a real one against each other, it will surely split. But it is not the less necessary for this; for the people must have some complicated machinery or other, and hear its din to satisfy that idea of government which they have. Governments show thus how successfully men can be imposed on, even impose on themselves, for their own advantage. It is excellent, we must all allow; yet this government never of itself furthered any enterprise, but by the alacrity with which it got out of its way. *It* does not keep the country free. *It* does not settle the West. *It* does not educate. The character inherent in the American people has done all that has been accomplished; and it would have done somewhat more, if the government had not sometimes got in its way. For government is an expedient by which men would fain succeed in letting one another alone; and, as has been said, when it is most expedient, the governed are most let alone by it. Trade and commerce, if they were not made of India rubber, would never manage to bounce over the obstacles which legislators are continually putting in their way; and, if one were to judge these men wholly by the effects of their actions, and not partly by their intentions, they would deserve to be classed and punished with those mischievous persons who put obstructions on the railroads.

But, to speak practically and as a citizen, unlike those who call themselves no-government men, I ask for, not at once no government, but *at once* a better government. Let every man make known what kind of government would command his respect, and that will be one step toward obtaining it.

[1]This is the title Thoreau gave his essay when he published it in 1849. Diligent search has unearthed no evidence that the often used title, "Civil Disobedience," was Thoreau's.

[2]The motto Thoreau quotes would have been recognized by many of his readers as a quotation from the masthead of the journal, *The Democratic Review.*

[3]There was much citizen protest over the United States' involvement in the Mexican War (1845–1848), in many respects similar to the protest over the war in Viet Nam.

After all, the practical reason why, when the power is once in the hands of the people, a majority are permitted, and for a long period continue, to rule, is not because they are most likely to be in the right, not because this seems fairest to the minority, but because they are physically the strongest. But a government in which the majority rule in all cases cannot be based on justice, even as far as men understand it. Can there not be a government in which majorities do not virtually decide right and wrong, but conscience?—in which majorities decide only those questions to which the rule of expediency is applicable? Must the citizen ever for a moment, or in the least degree, resign his conscience to the legislator? Why has every man a conscience, then? I think that we should be men first, and subjects afterward. It is not desirable to cultivate a respect for the law, so much as for the right. The only obligation which I have a right to assume, is to do at any time what I think right. It is truly enough said, that a corporation has no conscience; but a corporation of conscientious men is a corporation *with* a conscience. Law never made men a whit more just; and, by means of their respect for it, even the well-disposed are daily made the agents of injustice. A common and natural result of an undue respect for law is, that you may see a file of soldiers, colonel, captain, corporal, privates, powder-monkeys and all, marching in admirable order over hill and dale to the wars, against their wills, aye, against their common sense and consciences, which makes it very steep marching indeed, and produces a palpitation of the heart. They have no doubt that it is a damnable business in which they are concerned; they are all peaceably inclined. Now, what are they? Men at all? or small moveable forts and magazines, at the service of some unscrupulous man in power? Visit the Navy Yard, and behold a marine, such a man as an American government can make, or such as it can make a man with its black arts, a mere shadow and reminiscence of humanity, a man laid out alive and standing, and already, as one may say, buried under arms with funeral accompaniments, though it may be

"Not a drum was heard, not a funeral note,
    As his corse to the rampart we hurried;
Not a soldier discharged his farewell shot
    O'er the grave where our hero we buried."[4]

The mass of men serve the State thus, not as men mainly, but as machines, with their bodies. They are the standing army, and the militia, jailers, constables, *posse comitatus,* &c. In most cases there is no free exercise whatever of the judgment or of the moral sense; but they put themselves on a level with wood and earth and stones, and wooden men can perhaps be manufactured that will serve the purpose as well. Such command no more respect than men of straw, or a lump of dirt. They have the same sort of worth only as horses and dogs. Yet such as these even are commonly esteemed good citizens. Others, as most legislators, politicians, lawyers, ministers, and office-holders, serve the State chiefly with their heads; and, as they rarely make any moral distinctions, they are as likely to serve the devil, without intending it, as God. A very few, as heroes, patriots, martyrs, reformers in the great sense, and *men,* serve the State with their consciences also, and so necessarily resist it for the most part; and they are commonly treated by it as enemies. A wise man will only be useful as a man,

[4]The poem is by Charles Wolfe.

and will not submit to be "clay," and "stop a hole to keep the wind away,"[5] but leave that office to his dust at least:—

> "I am too high-born to be propertied,
> To be a secondary at control,
> Or useful serving-man and instrument
> To any sovereign state throughout the world."[6]

He who gives himself entirely to his fellow-men appears to them useless and selfish; but he who gives himself partially to them is pronounced a benefactor and philanthropist.

How does it become a man to behave toward this American government today? I answer that he cannot without disgrace be associated with it. I cannot for an instant recognize that political organization as *my* government which is the *slave's* government also.

All men recognize the right of revolution; that is, the right to refuse allegiance to and to resist the government, when its tyranny or its inefficiency are great and unendurable. But almost all say that such is not the case now. But such was the case, they think, in the Revolution of '75. If one were to tell me that this was a bad government because it taxed certain foreign commodities brought to its ports, it is most probable that I should not make an ado about it, for I can do without them: all machines have their friction; and possibly this does enough good to counterbalance the evil. At any rate, it is a great evil to make a stir about it. But when the friction comes to have its machine, and oppression and robbery are organized, I say, let us not have such a machine any longer. In other words, when a sixth of the population of a nation which has undertaken to be the refuge of liberty are slaves, and a whole country is unjustly overrun and conquered by a foreign army, and subjected to military law, I think that it is not too soon for honest men to rebel and revolutionize. What makes this duty the more urgent is the fact, that the country so overrun is not our own, but ours is the invading army.

Paley, a common authority with many on moral questions, in his chapter on the "Duty of Submission to Civil Government,"[7] resolves all civil obligation into expediency; and he proceeds to say, "that so long as the interest of the whole society requires it, that is, so long as the established government cannot be resisted or changed without public inconveniency, it is the will of God that the established government be obeyed, and no longer." . . . "This principle being admitted, the justice of every particular case of resistance is reduced to a computation of the quantity of the danger and grievance on the one side, and of the probability and expense of redressing it on the other." Of this, he says, every man shall judge for himself. But Paley appears never to have contemplated those cases to which the rule of expediency does not apply, in which a people, as well as an individual, must do justice, cost what it may. If I have unjustly wrested a plank from a drowning man, I must restore it to him though

[5]Shakespeare, *Hamlet.*

[6]Shakespeare, *King John.*

[7]Paley, an English philosopher, taught that resistance to government which caused "public inconveniency" was an affront to God. The effect of such teaching, obviously, was to make resistance to the government in power very difficult, however corrupt such a government might be.

I drown myself. This, according to Paley, would be inconvenient. But he that would save his life, in such a case, shall lose it. This people must cease to hold slaves, and to make war on Mexico, though it cost them their existence as a people.

In their practice, nations agree with Paley; but does any one think that Massachusetts does exactly what is right at the present crisis?

> "A drab of state, a cloth-o'-silver slut,
> To have her train borne up, and her soul trail in the dirt."[8]

Practically speaking, the opponents to a reform in Massachusetts are not a hundred thousand politicians at the South, but a hundred thousand merchants and farmers here, who are more interested in commerce and agriculture than they are in humanity, and are not prepared to do justice to the slave and to Mexico, *cost what it may.* I quarrel not with far-off foes, but with those who, near at home, co-operate with, and do the bidding of those far away, and without whom the latter would be harmless. We are accustomed to say, that the mass of men are unprepared; but improvement is slow, because the few are not materially wiser or better than the many. It is not so important that many should be as good as you, as that there be some absolute goodness somewhere; for that will leaven the whole lump. There are thousands who are *in opinion* opposed to slavery and to the war, who yet in effect do nothing to put an end to them; who, esteeming themselves children of Washington and Franklin, sit down with their hands in their pockets, and say that they know not what to do, and do nothing; who even postpone the question of freedom to the question of free-trade, and quietly read the prices-current along with the latest advices from Mexico, after dinner, and, it may be, fall asleep over them both. What is the price-current of an honest man and patriot to-day? They hesitate, and they regret, and sometimes they petition; but they do nothing in earnest and with effect. They will wait, well-disposed, for others to remedy the evil, that they may no longer have it to regret. At most, they give only a cheap vote, and a feeble countenance and God-speed, to the right, as it goes by them. There are nine hundred and ninety-nine patrons of virtue to one virtuous man; but it is easier to deal with the real possessor of a thing than with the temporary guardian of it.

All voting is a sort of gaming, like chequers or backgammon, with a slight moral tinge to it, a playing with right and wrong, with moral questions; and betting naturally accompanies it. The character of the voters is not staked. I cast my vote, perchance, as I think right; but I am not vitally concerned that that right should prevail. I am willing to leave it to the majority. Its obligation, therefore, never exceeds that of expediency. Even voting *for the right* is *doing* nothing for it. It is only expressing to men feebly your desire that it should prevail. A wise man will not leave the right to the mercy of chance, nor wish it to prevail through the power of the majority. There is but little virtue in the action of masses of men. When the majority shall at length vote for the abolition of slavery, it will be because they are indifferent to slavery, or because there is but little slavery left to be abolished by their vote. *They* will then be

[8]Cyril Tourneur, the playwright from whose *The Revenger's Tragedy* (IV, iv) Thoreau is quoting, was a contemporary of Shakespeare.

the only slaves. Only *his* vote can hasten the abolition of slavery who asserts his own freedom by his vote.

I hear of a convention to be held at Baltimore, or elsewhere, for the selection of a candidate for the Presidency, made up chiefly of editors, and men who are politicians by profession; but I think, what is it to any independent, intelligent, and respectable man what decision they may come to, shall we not have the advantage of his wisdom and honesty, nevertheless? Can we not count upon some independent votes? Are there not many individuals in the country who do not attend conventions? But no: I find that the respectable man, so called, has immediately drifted from his position, and despairs of his country, when his country has more reason to despair of him. He forthwith adopts one of the candidates thus selected as the only *available* one, thus proving that he is himself *available* for any purposes of the demagogue. His vote is of no more use than that of any unprincipled foreigner or hireling native, who may have been bought. Oh for a man who is a *man,* and, as my neighbor says, has a bone in his back which you cannot pass your hand through! Our statistics are at fault: the population has been returned too large. How many *men* are there to a square thousand miles in this country? Hardly one. Does not America offer any inducement for men to settle here? The American has dwindled into an Odd Fellow,—one who may be known by the development of his organ of gregariousness, and a manifest lack of intellect and cheerful self-reliance; whose first and chief concern, on coming into the world, is to see that the alms-houses are in good repair; and, before yet he has lawfully donned the virile garb, to collect a fund for the support of the widows and orphans that may be: who, in short, ventures to live only by the aid of the mutual insurance company, which has promised to bury him decently.

It is not a man's duty, as a matter of course, to devote himself to the eradication of any, even the most enormous wrong; he may still properly have other concerns to engage him; but it is his duty, at least, to wash his hands of it, and, if he gives it no thought longer, not to give it practically his support. If I devote myself to other pursuits and contemplations, I must first see, at least, that I do not pursue them sitting upon another man's shoulders. I must get off him first, that he may pursue his contemplations too. See what gross inconsistency is tolerated. I have heard some of my townsmen say, "I should like to have them order me out to help put down an insurrection of the slaves, or to march to Mexico,—see if I would go;" and yet these very men have each, directly by their allegiance, and so indirectly, at least, by their money, furnished a substitute. The soldier is applauded who refuses to serve in an unjust war by those who do not refuse to sustain the unjust government which makes the war; is applauded by those whose own act and authority he disregards and sets at nought; as if the State were penitent to that degree that it hired one to scourge it while it sinned, but not to that degree that it left off sinning for a moment. Thus, under the name of order and civil government, we are all made at last to pay homage to and support our own meanness. After the first blush of sin, comes its indifference and from immoral it becomes, as it were, *un*moral, and not quite unnecessary to that life which we have made.

The broadest and most prevalent error requires the most disinterested virtue to sustain it. The slight reproach to which the virtue of patriotism is commonly liable, the noble are most likely to incur. Those who, while they disapprove of the character and measures of a government, yield to it their allegiance and support, are undoubtedly its most conscientious supporters, and so frequently the most serious obstacles to reform. Some are petitioning the State to dissolve the Union, to disregard the requisitions of the President. Why do they not dissolve it themselves,—the union between themselves and the State,—and refuse to pay their quota into its treasury? Do not they stand in the same relation to the State, that the State does to the Union? And have not the same reasons prevented the State from resisting the Union, which have prevented them from resisting the State?

How can a man be satisfied to entertain an opinion merely, and enjoy *it?* Is there any enjoyment in it, if his opinion is that he is aggrieved? If you are cheated out of a single dollar by your neighbor, you do not rest satisfied with knowing that you are cheated, or with saying that you are cheated, or even with petitioning him to pay you your due; but you take effectual steps at once to obtain the full amount, and see that you are never cheated again. Action from principle,—the perception and the performance of right,—changes things and relations; it is essentially revolutionary, and does not consist wholly with any thing which was. It not only divides states and churches, it divides families; aye, it divides the *individual,* separating the diabolical in him from the divine.

Unjust laws exist: shall we be content to obey them, or shall we endeavor to amend them, and obey them until we have succeeded, or shall we transgress them at once? Men generally, under such a government as this, think that they ought to wait until they have persuaded the majority to alter them. They think that, if they should resist, the remedy would be worse than the evil. But it is the fault of the government itself that the remedy *is* worse than the evil. *It* makes it worse. Why is it not more apt to anticipate and provide for reform? Why does it not cherish its wise minority? Why does it cry and resist before it is hurt? Why does it not encourage its citizens to be on the alert to point out its faults, and *do* better than it would have them? Why does it always crucify Christ, and excommunicate Copernicus and Luther, and pronounce Washington and Franklin rebels?

One would think, that a deliberate and practical denial of its authority was the only offence never contemplated by government; else, why has it not assigned its definite, its suitable and proportionate penalty? If a man who has no property refuses but once to earn nine shillings for the State, he is put in prison for a period unlimited by any law that I know, and determined only by the discretion of those who placed him there; but if he should steal ninety times nine shillings from the State, he is soon permitted to go at large again.

If the injustice is part of the necessary friction of the machine of government, let it go, let it go: perchance it will wear smooth,—certainly the machine will wear out. If the injustice has a spring, or a pulley, or a rope, or a crank, exclusively for itself, then perhaps you may consider whether the remedy will not be worse than the evil; but if it is of such a nature that it requires you to be the agent of injustice to another, then, I say, break the law. Let your life be a counter friction to stop the machine. What I have to do is to see, at any rate, that I do not lend myself to the wrong which I condemn.

As for adopting the ways which the State has provided for remedying the evil, I know not of such ways. They take too much time, and a man's life will be gone. I have other affairs to attend to. I came into this world, not chiefly to make this a good place to live in, but to live in it, be it good or bad. A man has not every thing to do, but something; and because he cannot do *every thing,* it is not necessary that he should do *something* wrong. It is not my business to be petitioning the governor or the legislature any more than it is theirs to petition me; and, if they should not hear my petition, what should I do then? But in this case the State has provided no way: its very Constitution is the evil. This may seem to be harsh and stubborn and unconciliatory; but it is to treat with the utmost kindness and consideration the only spirit that can appreciate or deserves it. So is all change for the better, like birth and death which convulse the body.

I do not hesitate to say, that those who call themselves abolitionists should at once effectually withdraw their support, both in person and property, from the government of Massachusetts, and not wait till they constitute a majority of one, before they suffer the right to prevail through them. I think that it is enough if they have God on their side, without waiting for that other one. Moreover, any man more right than his neighbors, constitutes a majority of one already.

I meet this American government, or its representative the State government, directly, and face to face, once a year, no more, in the person of its tax-gatherer; this is the only mode in which a man situated as I am necessarily meets it; and it then says distinctly, Recognize me; and the simplest, the most effectual, and, in the present posture of affairs, the indispensablest mode of treating with it on this head, of expressing your little satisfaction with and love for it, is to deny it then. My civil neighbor, the tax-gatherer, is the very man I have to deal with,—for it is, after all, with men and not with parchment that I quarrel,—and he has voluntarily chosen to be an agent of the government. How shall he ever know well what he is and does as an officer of the government, or as a man, until he is obliged to consider whether he shall treat me, his neighbor, for whom he has respect, as a neighbor and well-disposed man, or as a maniac and disturber of the peace, and see if he can get over this obstruction to his neighborliness without a ruder and more impetuous thought or speech corresponding with his action? I know this well, that if one thousand, if one hundred, if ten men whom I could name,—if ten *honest* men only,—aye, if *one* HONEST man, in this State of Massachusetts, *ceasing to hold slaves,* were actually to withdraw from this copartnership, and be locked up in the county jail therefor, it would be the abolition of slavery in America. For it matters not how small the beginning may seem to be: what is once well done is done for ever. But we love better to talk about it: that we say is our mission. Reform keeps many scores of newspapers in its service, but not one man. If my esteemed neighbor, the State's ambassador, who will devote his days to the settlement of the question of human rights in the Council Chamber, instead of being threatened with the prisons of Carolina, were to sit down the prisoner of Massachusetts, that State which is so anxious to foist the sin of slavery upon her sister,[9]—though at present she can discover only an act of inhospitality to be the ground of a quarrel with her,—the Legislature would not wholly waive the subject the following winter.

Under a government which imprisons any unjustly, the true place for a just man is also a prison. The proper place to-day, the only place which Massachusetts has pro-

[9]Thoreau's "esteemed neighbor," Samuel Hoar, was expelled from South Carolina for defending black sailors from Massachusetts.

vided for her freer and less desponding spirits, is in her prisons, to be put out and locked out of the State by her own act, as they have already put themselves out by their principles. It is there that the fugitive slave, and the Mexican prisoner on parole, and the Indian come to plead the wrongs of his race, should find them; on that separate, but more free and honorable ground, where the State places those who are not *with* her but *against* her,—the only house in a slave-state in which a free man can abide with honor. If any think that their influence would be lost there, and their voices no longer afflict the ear of the State, that they would not be as an enemy within its walls, they do not know by how much truth is stronger than error, nor how much more eloquently and effectively he can combat injustice who has experienced a little in his own person. Cast your whole vote, not a strip of paper merely, but your whole influence. A minority is powerless while it conforms to the majority; it is not even a minority then; but it is irresistible when it clogs by its whole weight. If the alternative is to keep all just men in prison, or give up war and slavery, the State will not hesitate which to choose. If a thousand men were not to pay their tax-bills this year, that would not be a violent and bloody measure, as it would be to pay them, and enable the State to commit violence and shed innocent blood. This is, in fact, the definition of a peaceable revolution, if any such is possible. If the tax-gatherer, or any other public officer, asks me, as one has done, "But what shall I do?" my answer is, "If you really wish to do any thing, resign your office." When the subject has refused allegiance, and the officer has resigned his office, then the revolution is accomplished. But even suppose blood should flow. Is there not a sort of blood shed when the conscience is wounded? Through this wound a man's real manhood and immortality flow out, and he bleeds to an everlasting death. I see this blood flowing now.

I have contemplated the imprisonment of the offender, rather than the seizure of his goods,—though both will serve the same purpose,—because they who assert the purest right, and consequently are most dangerous to a corrupt State, commonly have not spent much time in accumulating property. To such the State renders comparatively small service, and a slight tax is wont to appear exorbitant, particularly if they are obliged to earn it by special labor with their hands. If there were one who lived wholly without the use of money, the State itself would hesitate to demand it of him. But the rich man—not to make any invidious comparison—is always sold to the institution which makes him rich. Absolutely speaking, the more money, the less virtue; for money comes between a man and his objects, and obtains them for him; and it was certainly no great virtue to obtain it. It puts to rest many questions which he would otherwise be taxed to answer; while the only new question which it puts is the hard but superfluous one, how to spend it. Thus his moral ground is taken from under his feet. The opportunities of living are diminished in proportion as what are called the "means" are increased. The best thing a man can do for his culture when he is rich is to endeavour to carry out those schemes which he entertained when he was poor. Christ answered the Herodians according to their condition. "Show me the tribute-money," said he;—and one took a penny out of his pocket;—If you use money which has the image of Caesar on it, and which he has made current and valuable, that is, *if you are men of the State,* and gladly enjoy the advantages of Caesar's government, then pay him back some of his own when he demands it; "Render therefore to Caesar that which is Caesar's, and to God those things which are God's,"—leaving them no wiser than before as to which was which; for they did not wish to know.

When I converse with the freest of my neighbors, I perceive that, whatever they may say about the magnitude and seriousness of the question, and their regard for the public tranquillity, the long and the short of the matter is, that they cannot spare the protection of the existing government, and they dread the consequences of disobedience to it to their property and families. For my own part, I should not like to think that I ever rely on the protection of the State. But, if I deny the authority of the State when it presents its tax-bill, it will soon take and waste all my property, and so harass me and my children without end. This is hard. This makes it impossible for a man to live honestly and at the same time comfortably in outward respects. It will not be worth the while to accumulate property; that would be sure to go again. You must hire or squat somewhere, and raise but a small crop, and eat that soon. You must live within yourself, and depend upon yourself, always tucked up and ready for a start, and not have many affairs. A man may grow rich in Turkey even, if he will be in all respects a good subject of the Turkish government. Confucius said,—"If a State is governed by the principles of reason, poverty and misery are subjects of shame; if a State is not governed by the principles of reason, riches and honors are the subjects of shame." No: until I want the protection of Massachusetts to be extended to me in some distant southern port, where my liberty is endangered, or until I am bent solely on building up an estate at home by peaceful enterprise, I can afford to refuse allegiance to Massachusetts, and her right to my property and life. It costs me less in every sense to incur the penalty of disobedience to the State, than it would to obey. I should feel as if I were worth less in that case.

Some years ago, the State met me in behalf of the church, and commanded me to pay a certain sum toward the support of a clergyman whose preaching my father attended, but never I myself. "Pay it," it said, "or be locked up in the jail." I declined to pay. But, unfortunately, another man saw fit to pay it. I did not see why the schoolmaster should be taxed to support the priest, and not the priest the schoolmaster; for I was not the State's schoolmaster, but I supported myself by voluntary subscription. I did not see why the lyceum[10] should not present its tax-bill, and have the State to back its demand, as well as the church. However, at the request of the selectmen, I condescended to make some such statement as this in writing:—"Know all men by these presents, that I, Henry Thoreau, do not wish to be regarded as a member of any incorporated society which I have not joined." This I gave to the town-clerk; and he has it. The State, having thus learned that I did not wish to be regarded as a member of that church, has never made a like demand on me since; though it said that it must adhere to its original presumption that time. If I had known how to name them, I should then have signed off in detail from all the societies which I never signed on to; but I did not know where to find a complete list.

I have paid no poll-tax for six years. I was put into a jail once on this account, for one night; and, as I stood considering the walls of solid stone, two or three feet thick, the door of wood and iron, a foot thick, and the iron grating which strained the light, I could not help being struck with the foolishness of that institution which treated me as if I were mere flesh and blood and bones, to be locked up. I wondered

[10]Thoreau was active in the Concord Lyceum, a forum in which invited lecturers spoke on topics of interest to people in the community.

that it should have concluded at length that this was the best use it could put me to, and had never thought to avail itself of my services in some way. I saw that, if there was a wall of stone between me and my townsmen, there was a still more difficult one to climb or break through, before they could get to be as free as I was. I did not for a moment feel confined, and the walls seemed a great waste of stone and mortar. I felt as if I alone of all my townsmen had paid my tax. They plainly did not know how to treat me, but behaved like persons who are underbred. In every threat and in every compliment there was a blunder; for they thought that my chief desire was to stand the other side of that stone wall. I could not but smile to see how industriously they locked the door on my meditations, which followed them out again without let or hinderance, and *they* were really all that was dangerous. As they could not reach me, they had resolved to punish my body; just as boys, if they cannot come at some person against whom they have a spite, will abuse his dog. I saw that the State was half-witted, that it was timid as a lone woman with her silver spoons, and that it did not know its friends from its foes, and I lost all my remaining respect for it, and pitied it.

Thus the State never intentionally confronts a man's sense, intellectual or moral, but only his body, his senses. It is not armed with superior wit or honesty, but with superior physical strength. I was not born to be forced. I will breathe after my own fashion. Let us see who is the strongest. What force has a multitude? They only can force me who obey a higher law than I. They force me to become like themselves. I do not hear of *men* being *forced* to live this way or that by masses of men. What sort of life were that to live? When I meet a government which says to me, "Your money or your life," why should I be in haste to give it my money? It may be in a great strait, and not know what to do: I cannot help that. It must help itself; do as I do. It is not worth the while to snivel about it. I am not responsible for the successful working of the machinery of society. I am not the son of the engineer. I perceive that, when an acorn and a chestnut fall side by side, the one does not remain inert to make way for the other, but both obey their own laws, and spring and grow and flourish as best they can, till one, perchance, overshadows and destroys the other. If a plant cannot live according to its nature, it dies; and so a man.

The night in prison was novel and interesting enough. The prisoners in their shirt-sleeves were enjoying a chat and the evening air in the door-way, when I entered. But the jailer said, "Come, boys, it is time to lock up;" and so they dispersed, and I heard the sound of their steps returning into the hollow apartments. My roommate was introduced to me by the jailer, as "a first-rate fellow and a clever man." When the door was locked, he showed me where to hang my hat, and how he managed matters there. The rooms were whitewashed once a month; and this one, at least, was the whitest, most simply furnished, and probably the neatest apartment in the town. He naturally wanted to know where I came from, and what brought me there; and, when I had told him, I asked him in turn how he came there, presuming him to be an honest man, of course; and, as the world goes, I believe he was. "Why," said he, "they accused me of burning a barn; but I never did it." As near as I could discover, he had probably gone to bed in a barn when drunk, and smoked his pipe there; and so a barn was burnt. He had the reputation of being a clever man, had been there some three months waiting for his trial to come on, and would have to wait as much longer; but he was quite domesticated and contented, since he got his board for nothing, and thought that he was well treated.

He occupied one window, and I the other; and I saw, that, if one stayed there long, his principal business would be to look out the window. I had soon read all the tracts that were left there, and examined where former prisoners had broken out, and where a grate had been sawed off, and heard the history of the various occupants of that room; for I found that even here there was a history and a gossip which never circulated beyond the walls of the jail. Probably this is the only house in the town where verses are composed, which are afterward printed in a circular form, but not published. I was shown quite a long list of verses which were composed by some young men who had been detected in an attempt to escape, who avenged themselves by singing them.

I pumped my fellow-prisoner as dry as I could, for fear I should never see him again; but at length he showed me which was my bed, and left me to blow out the lamp.

It was like travelling into a far country, such as I had never expected to behold, to lie there for one night. It seemed to me that I never had heard the town-clock strike before, nor the evening sounds of the village; for we slept with the windows open, which were inside the grating. It was to see my native village in the light of the middle ages, and our Concord was turned into a Rhine stream, and visions of knights and castles passed before me. They were the voices of old burghers that I heard in the streets. I was an involuntary spectator and auditor of whatever was done and said in the kitchen of the adjacent village-inn,—a wholly new and rare experience to me. It was a closer view of my native town. I was fairly inside of it. I never had seen its institutions before. This is one of its peculiar institutions; for it is a shire town. I began to comprehend what its inhabitants were about.

In the morning, our breakfasts were put through the hole in the door, in small oblong-square tin pans, made to fit, and holding a pint of chocolate, with brown bread, and an iron spoon. When they called for the vessels again, I was green enough to return what bread I had left; but my comrade seized it, and said that I should lay that up for lunch or dinner. Soon after, he was let out to work at haying in a neighboring field, whither he went every day, and would not be back till noon; so he bade me good-day, saying that he doubted if he should see me again.

When I came out of prison,—for some one interfered, and paid the tax,—I did not perceive that great changes had taken place on the common, such as he observed who went in a youth, and emerged a tottering and grayheaded man; and yet a change had to my eyes come over the scene,—the town, and State, and country,—greater than any that mere time could effect. I saw yet more distinctly the State in which I lived. I saw to what extent the people among whom I lived could be trusted as good neighbors and friends; that their friendship was for summer weather only; that they did not greatly purpose to do right; that they were a distinct race from me by their prejudices and superstitions, as the Chinamen and Malays are; that, in their sacrifices to humanity, they ran no risks, not even to their property; that, after all, they were not so noble but they treated the thief as he had treated them, and hoped, by a certain outward observance and a few prayers, and by walking in a particular straight though useless path from time to time, to save their souls. This may be to judge my neighbors harshly; for I believe that most of them are not aware that they have such an institution as the jail in their village.

It was formerly the custom in our village, when a poor debtor came out of jail, for his acquaintances to salute him, looking through their fingers, which were crossed to represent the grating of a jail window, "How do ye do?" My neighbors did not thus salute me, but first looked at me, and then at one another, as if I had returned from a long journey. I was put into jail as I was going to the shoemaker's to get a shoe which was mended. When I was let out the next morning, I proceeded to finish my errand, and, having put on my mended shoe, joined a huckleberry party, who were impatient to put themselves under my conduct; and in half an hour,—for the horse was soon tackled,[11] *was in the midst of a huckleberry field, on one of our highest hills, two miles off; and then the State was nowhere to be seen.*

This is the whole history of "My Prisons."[12]

I have never declined paying the highway tax, because I am as desirous of being a good neighbor as I am of being a bad subject; and, as for supporting schools, I am doing my part to educate my fellow-countrymen now. It is for no particular item in the tax-bill that I refuse to pay it. I simply wish to refuse allegiance to the State, to withdraw and stand aloof from it effectually. I do not care to trace the course of my dollar, if I could, till it buys a man, or a musket to shoot one with,—the dollar is innocent,—but I am concerned to trace the effects of my allegiance. In fact, I quietly declare war with the State, after my fashion, though I will still make what use and get what advantage of her I can, as is usual in such cases.

If others pay the tax which is demanded of me,[13] from a sympathy with the State, they do but what they have already done in their own case, or rather they abet injustice to a greater extent than the State requires. If they pay the tax from a mistaken interest in the individual taxed, to save his property or prevent his going to jail, it is because they have not considered wisely how far they let their private feelings interfere with the public good.

This, then, is my position at present. But one cannot be too much on his guard in such a case, lest his action be biassed by obstinacy, or an undue regard for the opinions of men. Let him see that he does only what belongs to himself and to the hour.

I think sometimes, Why, this people mean well; they are only ignorant; they would do better if they knew how: why give your neighbors this pain to treat you as they are not inclined to? But I think, again, this is no reason why I should do as they do, or permit others to suffer much greater pain of a different kind. Again, I sometimes say to myself, When many millions of men, without heat, without ill-will, without personal feeling of any kind, demand of you a few shillings only, without the possibility, such is their constitution, of retracting or altering their present demand, and without the possibility, on your side, of appeal to any other millions, why expose yourself to this overwhelming brute force? You do not resist cold and hunger, the winds and the waves, thus obstinately; you quietly submit to a thousand similar necessities. You do not put your head into the fire. But just in proportion as I regard this as not wholly a brute force, but partly a human force, and consider that I have relations to those millions as to so many millions of men, and not of mere brute or inanimate things, I see that appeal is possible, first and instantaneously, from them to the Maker of them, and, secondly, from them to themselves. But, if I put my head deliberately into the fire, there is no appeal to fire or to the Maker of fire, and I have only myself to blame. If I could convince myself that I have any right to be satisfied

[11] *I.e.,* harnessed.

[12] "My Prisons" was the title of a book written by the Italian poet Silvio Pellico after he had spent years in prison.

[13] It is not known for certain who paid Thoreau's tax and thus secured his release from jail.

with men as they are, and to treat them accordingly, and not according, in some respects, to my requisitions and expectations of what they and I ought to be, then, like a good Mussulman[14] and fatalist, I should endeavor to be satisfied with things as they are, and say it is the will of God. And, above all, there is this difference between resisting this and a purely brute or natural force, that I can resist this with some effect; but I cannot expect, like Orpheus, to change the nature of the rocks and trees and beasts.[15]

I do not wish to quarrel with any man or nation. I do not wish to split hairs, to make fine distinctions, or set myself up as better than my neighbors. I seek rather, I may say, even an excuse for conforming to the laws of the land. I am but too ready to conform to them. Indeed I have reason to suspect myself on this head; and each year, as the tax-gatherer comes round, I find myself disposed to review the acts and position of the general and state governments, and the spirit of the people, to discover a pretext for conformity. I believe that the State will soon be able to take all my work of this sort out of my hands, and then I shall be no better a patriot than my fellow-countrymen. Seen from a lower point of view, the Constitution, with all its faults, is very good; the law and the courts are very respectable; even this State and this American government are, in many respects, very admirable and rare things, to be thankful for, such as a great many have described them; but seen from a point of view a little higher, they are what I have described them; seen from a higher still, and the highest, who shall say what they are, or that they are worth looking at or thinking of at all?

However, the government does not concern me much, and I shall bestow the fewest possible thoughts on it. It is not many moments that I live under a government, even in this world. If a man is thought-free, fancy-free, imagination-free, that which *is not* never for a long time appearing *to be* to him, unwise rulers or reformers cannot fatally interrupt him.

I know that most men think differently from myself; but those whose lives are by profession devoted to the study of these or kindred subjects, content me as little as any. Statesmen and legislators, standing so completely within the institution, never distinctly and nakedly behold it. They speak of moving society, but have no resting-place without it. They may be men of a certain experience and discrimination, and have no doubt invented ingenious and even useful systems, for which we sincerely thank them; but all their wit and usefulness lie within certain not very wide limits. They are wont to forget that the world is not governed by policy and expediency. Webster[16] never goes behind government, and so cannot speak with authority about it. His words are wisdom to those legislators who contemplate no essential reform in the existing government; but for thinkers, and those who legislate for all time, he never once glances at the subject. I know of those whose serene and wise speculations on this theme would soon reveal the limits of his mind's range and hospitality.

[14]A Mussulman was a Mohammedan.

[15]Orpheus, according to Greek Mythology, could play his lyre so beautifully that trees and rocks moved.

[16]Thoreau's objection to Daniel Webster, one of the most powerful senators in the 1840s, was that Webster considered the American Constitution, which condoned black slavery, to be the ultimate authority on moral issues. In the final paragraphs of this essay, Thoreau argues for a moral order transcending the Constitution.

Yet, compared with the cheap professions of most reformers, and the still cheaper wisdom and eloquence of politicians in general, his are almost the only sensible and valuable words, and we thank Heaven for him. Comparatively, he is always strong, original, and, above all, practical. Still his quality is not wisdom, but prudence. The lawyer's truth is not Truth, but consistency, or a consistent expediency. Truth is always in harmony with herself, and is not concerned chiefly to reveal the justice that may consist with wrong-doing. He well deserves to be called, as he has been called, the Defender of the Constitution. There are really no blows to be given by him but defensive ones. He is not a leader, but a follower. His leaders are the men of '87. "I have never made an effort," he says, "and never propose to make an effort; I have never countenanced an effort, and never mean to countenance an effort, to disturb the arrangement as originally made, by which the various States came into the Union." Still thinking of the sanction which the Constitution gives to slavery, he says, "Because it was a part of the original compact,—let it stand." Notwithstanding his special acuteness and ability, he is unable to take a fact out of its merely political relations, and behold it as it lies absolutely to be disposed of by the intellect,—what, for instance, it behoves a man to do here in America to-day with regard to slavery,—but ventures, or is driven, to make some such desperate answer as the following, while professing to speak absolutely, and as a private man,—from which what new and singular code of social duties might be inferred?—"The manner," says he, "in which the governments of those States where slavery exists are to regulate it, is for their own consideration, under their responsibility to their constituents, to the general laws of propriety, humanity, and justice, and to God. Associations formed elsewhere, springing from a feeling of humanity, or any other cause, have nothing whatever to do with it. They have never received any encouragement from me, and they never will."[17]

They who know of no purer sources of truth, who have traced up its stream no higher, stand, and wisely stand, by the Bible and the Constitution, and drink at it there with reverence and humility; but they who behold where it comes trickling into this lake or that pool, gird up their loins once more, and continue their pilgrimage toward its fountain-head.

No man with a genius for legislation has appeared in America. They are rare in the history of the world. There are orators, politicians, and eloquent men, by the thousand; but the speaker has not yet opened his mouth to speak, who is capable of settling the much-vexed questions of the day. We love eloquence for its own sake, and not for any truth which it may utter, or any heroism it may inspire. Our legislators have not yet learned the comparative value of free-trade and of freedom, of union, and of rectitude, to a nation. They have no genius or talent for comparatively humble questions of taxation and finance, commerce and manufactures and agriculture. If we were left solely to the wordy wit of legislators in Congress for our guidance, uncorrected by the seasonable experience and the effectual complaints of the people, America would not long retain her rank among the nations. For eighteen hundred years, though perchance I have no right to say it, the New Testament has been writ-

[17]These extracts have been inserted since the Lecture was read. [Thoreau's note.]

ten; yet where is the legislator who has wisdom and practical talent enough to avail himself of the light which it sheds on the science of legislation?

The authority of government, even such as I am willing to submit to,—for I will cheerfully obey those who know and can do better than I, and in many things even those who neither know nor can do so well,—is still an impure one: to be strictly just, it must have the sanction and consent of the governed. It can have no pure right over my person and property but what I concede to it. The progress from an absolute to a limited monarchy, from a limited monarchy to a democracy, is a progress toward a true respect for the individual. Is a democracy, such as we know it, the last improvement possible in government? Is it not possible to take a step further towards recognizing and organizing the rights of man? There will never be a really free and enlightened State, until the State comes to recognize the individual as a higher and independent power, from which all its own power and authority are derived, and treats him accordingly. I please myself with imagining a State at last which can afford to be just to all men, and to treat the individual with respect as a neighbor; which even would not think it inconsistent with its own repose, if a few were to live aloof from it, not meddling with it, nor embraced by it, who fulfilled all the duties of neighbors and fellow-men. A State which bore this kind of fruit, and suffered it to drop off as fast as it ripened, would prepare the way for a still more perfect and glorious State, which also I have imagined, but not yet anywhere seen.

1849

from Walden

Where I Lived, and What I Lived For

At a certain season of our life we are accustomed to consider every spot as the possible site of a house. I have thus surveyed the country on every side within a dozen miles of where I live. In imagination I have bought all the farms in succession, for all were to be bought, and I knew their price. I walked over each farmer's premises, tasted his wild apples, discoursed on husbandry with him, took his farm at his price, at any price, mortgaging it to him in my mind; even put a higher price on it,—took every thing but a deed of it,—took his word for his deed, for I dearly love to talk,—cultivated it, and him too to some extent, I trust, and withdrew when I had enjoyed it long enough, leaving him to carry it on. This experience entitled me to be regarded as a sort of real-estate broker by my friends. Wherever I sat, there I might live, and the landscape radiated from me accordingly. What is a house but a *sedes,* a seat?—better if a country seat. I discovered many a site for a house not likely to be soon improved, which some might have thought too far from the village, but to my eyes the village was too far from it. Well, there I might live, I said; and there I did live, for an hour, a summer and a winter life; saw how I could let the years run off, buffet the winter through, and see the spring come in. The future inhabitants of this region, wherever they may place their houses, may be sure that they have been anticipated.

An afternoon sufficed to lay out the land into orchard woodlot and pasture, and to decide what fine oaks or pines should be left to stand before the door, and whence each blasted tree could be seen to the best advantage; and then I let it lie, fallow perchance, for a man is rich in proportion to the number of things which he can afford to let alone.

My imagination carried me so far that I even had the refusal of several farms,—the refusal was all I wanted,—but I never got my fingers burned by actual possession. The nearest that I came to actual possession was when I bought the Hollowell Place, and had begun to sort my seeds, and collected materials with which to make a wheelbarrow to carry it on or off with; but before the owner gave me a deed of it, his wife—every man has such a wife—changed her mind and wished to keep it, and he offered me ten dollars to release him. Now, to speak the truth, I had but ten cents in the world, and it surpassed my arithmetic to tell, if I was that man who had ten cents, or who had a farm, or ten dollars, or all together. However, I let him keep the ten dollars and the farm too, for I had carried it far enough; or rather, to be generous, I sold him the farm for just what I gave for it, and, as he was not a rich man, made him a present of ten dollars, and still had my ten cents, and seeds, and materials for a wheelbarrow left. I found thus that I had been a rich man without any damage to my poverty. But I retained the landscape, and I have since annually carried off what it yielded without a wheelbarrow. With respect to landscapes,—

> "I am monarch of all I *survey,*
> My right there is none to dispute."[1]

I have frequently seen a poet withdraw, having enjoyed the most valuable part of a farm, while the crusty farmer supposed that he had got a few wild apples only. Why, the owner does not know it for many years when a poet has put his farm in rhyme, the most admirable kind of invisible fence, has fairly impounded it, milked it, skimmed it, and got all the cream, and left the farmer only the skimmed milk.

The real attractions of the Hollowell farm, to me, were; its complete retirement, being about two miles from the village, half a mile from the nearest neighbor, and separated from the highway by a broad field; its bounding on the river, which the owner said protected it by its fogs from frosts in the spring, though that was nothing to me; the gray color and ruinous state of the house and barn, and the dilapidated fences, which put such an interval between me and the last occupant; the hollow and lichen-covered apple trees, gnawed by rabbits, showing what kind of neighbors I should have; but above all, the recollection I had of it from my earliest voyages up the river, when the house was concealed behind a dense grove of red maples, through which I heard the house-dog bark. I was in haste to buy it, before the proprietor finished getting out some rocks, cutting down the hollow apple trees, and grubbing up some young birches which had sprung up in the pasture, or, in short, had made any more of his improvements. To enjoy these advantages I was ready to carry it on; like

[1]Thoreau was himself a surveyor; in italicizing *"survey"* in the quotation from William Cowper's *Verses Supposed to be Written by Alexander Selkirk* he is punning on Cowper's meaning. Puns are frequent in his writings.

Atlas,[2] to take the world on my shoulders,—I never heard what compensation he received for that,—and do all those things which had no other motive or excuse but that I might pay for it and be unmolested in my possession of it; for I knew all the while that it would yield the most abundant crop of the kind I wanted if I could only afford to let it alone. But it turned out as I have said.

All that I could say, then, with respect to farming on a large scale, (I have always cultivated a garden,) was, that I had had my seeds ready. Many think that seeds improve with age. I have no doubt that time discriminates between the good and the bad; and when at last I shall plant, I shall be less likely to be disappointed. But I would say to my fellows, once for all, As long as possible live free and uncommitted. It makes but little difference whether you are committed to a farm or the county jail.

Old Cato, whose "De Re Rusticâ" is my "Cultivator,"[3] says, and the only translation I have seen makes sheer nonsense of the passage, "When you think of getting a farm, turn it thus in your mind, not to buy greedily; nor spare your pains to look at it, and do not think it enough to go round it once. The oftener you go there the more it will please you, if it is good." I think I shall not buy greedily, but go round and round it as long as I live, and be buried in it first, that it may please me the more at last.

The present was my next experiment of this kind, which I purpose to describe more at length; for convenience, putting the experience of two years into one. As I have said, I do not propose to write an ode to dejection, but to brag as lustily as chanticleer in the morning, standing on his roost, if only to wake my neighbors up.

When first I took up my abode in the woods, that is, began to spend my nights as well as days there, which, by accident, was on Independence Day, or the fourth of July, 1845, my house was not finished for winter, but was merely a defence against the rain, without plastering or chimney, the walls being of rough weather-stained boards, with wide chinks, which made it cool at night. The upright white hewn studs and freshly planed door and window casings gave it a clean and airy look, especially in the morning, when its timbers were saturated with dew, so that I fancied that by noon some sweet gum would exude from them. To my imagination it retained throughout the day more or less of this auroral character, reminding me of a certain house on a mountain which I had visited the year before. This was an airy and unplastered cabin, fit to entertain a traveling god, and where a goddess might trail her garments. The winds which passed over my dwelling were such as sweep over the ridges of mountains, bearing the broken strains, or celestial parts only, of terrestrial music. The morning wind forever blows, the poem of creation is uninterrupted; but few are the ears that hear it. Olympus is but the outside of the earth every where.

The only house I had been the owner of before, if I except a boat, was a tent, which I used occasionally when making excursions in the summer, and this is still rolled up in my garret; but the boat, after passing from hand to hand, has gone down

[2]Atlas, according to Greek mythology was compelled by Zeus to support the heavens on his shoulders as a punishment.

[3]A journal on farming being published at the time was called the *Cultivator.* Cato was a Roman writer on agriculture.

the stream of time. With this more substantial shelter about me, I had made some progress toward settling in the world. This frame, so slightly clad, was a sort of crystallization around me, and reacted on the builder. It was suggestive somewhat as a picture in outlines. I did not need to go out doors to take the air, for the atmosphere within had lost none of its freshness. It was not so much within doors as behind a door where I sat, even in the rainiest weather. The Harivansa[4] says, "An abode without birds is like a meat without seasoning." Such was not my abode, for I found myself suddenly neighbor to the birds; not by having imprisoned one, but having caged myself near them. I was not only nearer to some of those which commonly frequent the garden and the orchard, but to those wilder and more thrilling songsters of the forest which never, or rarely, serenade a villager,—the wood-thrush, the veery, the scarlet tanager, the field-sparrow, the whippoorwill, and many others.

I was seated by the shore of a small pond, about a mile and a half south of the village of Concord and somewhat higher than it, in the midst of an extensive wood between that town and Lincoln, and about two miles south of that our only field known to fame, Concord Battle Ground; but I was so low in the woods that the opposite shore, half a mile off, like the rest, covered with wood, was my most distant horizon. For the first week, whenever I looked out on the pond it impressed me like a tarn high up on the side of a mountain, its bottom far above the surface of other lakes, and, as the sun arose, I saw it throwing off its nightly clothing of mist, and here and there, by degrees, its soft ripples or its smooth reflecting surface was revealed, while the mists, like ghosts, were stealthily withdrawing in every direction into the woods, as at the breaking up of some nocturnal conventicle. The very dew seemed to hang upon the trees later into the day than usual, as on the sides of mountains.

This small lake was of most value as a neighbor in the intervals of a gentle rain storm in August, when, both air and water being perfectly still, but the sky overcast, mid-afternoon had all the serenity of evening, and the wood-thrush sang around, and was heard from shore to shore. A lake like this is never smoother than at such a time; and the clear portion of the air above it being shallow and darkened by clouds, the water, full of light and reflections, becomes a lower heaven itself so much the more important. From a hill top near by, where the wood had been recently cut off, there was a pleasing vista southward across the pond, through a wide indentation in the hills which form the shore there, where their opposite sides sloping toward each other suggested a stream flowing out in that direction through a wooded valley, but stream there was none. That way I looked between and over the near green hills to some distant and higher ones in the horizon, tinged with blue. Indeed, by standing on tiptoe I could catch a glimpse of some of the peaks of the still bluer and more distant mountain ranges in the north-west, those true-blue coins from heaven's own mint, and also of some portion of the village. But in other directions, even from this point, I could not see over or beyond the woods which surrounded me. It is well to have some water in your neighborhood, to give buoyancy to and float the earth. One value even of the smallest well is, that when you look into it you see that earth is not

[4]Thoreau read widely in Hindu literature. The Harivansa was a Hindu poem.

continent but insular. This is as important as that it keeps butter cool.[5] When I looked across the pond from this peak toward the Sudbury meadows, which in time of flood I distinguished elevated perhaps by a mirage in their seething valley, like a coin in a basin, all the earth beyond the pond appeared like a thin crust insulated and floated even by this small sheet of intervening water, and I was reminded that this on which I dwelt was but *dry land.*

Though the view from my door was still more contracted, I did not feel crowded or confined in the least. There was pasture enough for my imagination. The low shrub-oak plateau to which the opposite shore arose, stretched away toward the prairies of the West and the steppes of Tartary, affording ample room for all the roving families of men. "There are none happy in the world but beings who enjoy freely a vast horizon,"—said Damodara, when his herds required new and larger pastures.[6]

Both place and time were changed, and I dwelt nearer to those parts of the universe and to those eras in history which had most attracted me. Where I lived was as far off as many a region viewed nightly by astronomers. We are wont to imagine rare and delectable places in some remote and more celestial corner of the system, behind the constellation of Cassiopeia's Chair, far from noise and disturbance. I discovered that my house actually had its site in such a withdrawn, but forever new and unprofaned, part of the universe. If it were worth the while to settle in those parts near to the Pleiades or the Hyades, to Aldebaran or Altair,[7] then I was really there, or at an equal remoteness from the life which I had left behind, dwindled and twinkling with as fine a ray to my nearest neighbor, and to be seen only in moonless nights by him. Such was that part of creation where I had squatted—

"There was a shepherd that did live,
And held his thoughts as high
As were the mounts whereon his flocks
Did hourly feed him by."

What should we think of the shepherd's life if his flocks always wandered to higher pastures than his thoughts?

Every morning was a cheerful invitation to make my life of equal simplicity, and I may say innocence, with Nature herself. I have been as sincere a worshipper of Aurora as the Greeks.[8] I got up early and bathed in the pond; that was a religious exercise, and one of the best things which I did. They say that characters were engraven on the bathing tub of king Tching-thang to this effect: "Renew thyself completely each day; do it again, and again, and forever again." I can understand that. Morning brings back the heroic ages. I was as much affected by the faint hum of a mosquito making its invisible and unimaginable tour through my apartment at earliest dawn,

[5]Thoreau is saying that the perspective that comes from studying Nature is more important than the narrow uses we put Nature to. Butter was preserved in cool wells because there was no refrigeration.

[6]The steppes of Tartary are prairie-like areas of Russia. Damodara was Krishna, in Hindu mythology one of the deities of Hinduism

[7]Thoreau is referring in this passage to stars and constellations of stars.

[8]Aurora was the goddess of the dawn in Roman mythology (Eos in Greek). Memnon was her son.

when I was sitting with door and windows open, as I could be by any trumpet that ever sang of fame. It was Homer's requiem; itself an Iliad and Odyssey in the air, singing its own wrath and wanderings. There was something cosmical about it; a standing advertisement, till forbidden, of the everlasting vigor and fertility of the world. The morning, which is the most memorable season of the day, is the awakening hour. Then there is least somnolence in us; and for an hour, at least, some part of us awakes which slumbers all the rest of the day and night. Little is to be expected of that day, if it can be called a day, to which we are not awakened by our Genius, but by the mechanical nudgings of some servitor, are not awakened by our own newly-acquired force and aspirations from within, accompanied by the undulations of celestial music, instead of factory bells, and a fragrance filling the air—to a higher life than we fell asleep from; and thus the darkness bear its fruit, and prove itself to be good, no less than the light. That man who does not believe that each day contains an earlier, more sacred, and auroral hour than he has yet profaned, has despaired of life, and is pursuing a descending and darkening way. After a partial cessation of his sensuous life, the soul of man, or its organs rather, are reinvigorated each day, and his Genius tries again what noble life it can make. All memorable events, I should say, transpire in morning time and in a morning atmosphere. The Vedas say, "All intelligences awake with the morning." Poetry and art, and the fairest and most memorable of the actions of men, date from such an hour. All poets and heroes, like Memnon, are the children of Aurora, and emit their music at sunrise. To him whose elastic and vigorous thought keeps pace with the sun, the day is a perpetual morning. It matters not what the clocks say or the attitudes and labors of men. Morning is when I am awake and there is a dawn in me. Moral reform is the effort to throw off sleep. Why is it that men give so poor an account of their day if they have not been slumbering? They are not such poor calculators. If they had not been overcome with drowsiness they would have performed something. The millions are awake enough for physical labor; but only one in a million is awake enough for effective intellectual exertion, only one in a hundred millions to a poetic or divine life. To be awake is to be alive. I have never yet met a man who was quite awake. How could I have looked him in the face?

We must learn to reawaken and keep ourselves awake, not by mechanical aids, but by an infinite expectation of the dawn, which does not forsake us in our soundest sleep. I know of no more encouraging fact than the unquestionable ability of man to elevate his life by a conscious endeavor. It is something to be able to paint a particular picture, or to carve a statue, and so to make a few objects beautiful; but it is far more glorious to carve and paint the very atmosphere and medium through which we look, which morally we can do. To affect the quality of the day, that is the highest of arts. Every man is tasked to make his life, even in its details, worthy of the contemplation of his most elevated and critical hour. If we refused, or rather used up, such paltry information as we get, the oracles would distinctly inform us how this might be done.

I went to the woods because I wished to live deliberately, to front only the essential facts of life, and see if I could not learn what it had to teach, and not, when I came to die, discover that I had not lived. I did not wish to live what was not life, living is so dear; nor did I wish to practise resignation, unless it was quite necessary. I wanted to live deep and suck out all the marrow of life, to live so sturdily and

Spartan-like as to put to rout all that was not life, to cut a broad swath and shave close, to drive life into a corner, and reduce it to its lowest terms, and, if it proved to be mean, why then to get the whole and genuine meanness of it, and publish its meanness to the world; or if it were sublime, to know it by experience, and be able to give a true account of it in my next excursion. For most men, it appears to me, are in a strange uncertainty about it, whether it is of the devil or of God, and have *somewhat hastily* concluded that it is the chief end of man here to "glorify God and enjoy him forever."

Still we live meanly, like ants; though the fable tells us that we were long ago changed into men; like pygmies we fight with cranes; it is error upon error, and clout upon clout, and our best virtue has for its occasion a superfluous and evitable wretchedness. Our life is frittered away by detail. An honest man has hardly need to count more than his ten fingers, or in extreme cases he may add his ten toes, and lump the rest. Simplicity, simplicity, simplicity! I say, let your affairs be as two or three, and not a hundred or a thousand; instead of a million count half a dozen, and keep your accounts on your thumb nail. In the midst of this chopping sea of civilized life, such are the clouds and storms and quicksands and thousand-and-one items to be allowed for, that a man has to live, if he would not founder and go to the bottom and not make his port at all, by dead reckoning, and he must be a great calculator indeed who succeeds. Simplify, simplify. Instead of three meals a day, if it be necessary eat but one; instead of a hundred dishes, five; and reduce other things in proportion. Our life is like a German Confederacy,[9] made up of petty states, with its boundary forever fluctuating, so that even a German cannot tell you how it is bounded at any moment. The nation itself, with all its so called internal improvements, which, by the way, are all external and superficial, is just such an unwieldy and overgrown establishment, cluttered with furniture and tripped up by its own traps, ruined by luxury and heedless expense, by want of calculation and a worthy aim, as the million households in the land; and the only cure for it as for them is in a rigid economy, a stern and more than Spartan simplicity of life and elevation of purpose. It lives too fast. Men think that it is essential that the *Nation* have commerce, and export ice, and talk through a telegraph, and ride thirty miles an hour, without a doubt, whether *they* do or not; but whether we should live like baboons or like men, is a little uncertain. If we do not get out sleepers,[10] and forge rails, and devote days and nights to the work, but go to tinkering upon our *lives* to improve *them,* who will build railroads? And if railroads are not built, how shall we get to heaven in season? But if we stay at home and mind our business, who will want railroads? We do not ride on the railroad; it rides upon us. Did you ever think what those sleepers are that underlie the railroad? Each one is a man, an Irish-man, or a Yankee man. The rails are laid on them, and they are covered with sand, and the cars run smoothly over them. They are sound sleepers, I assure you. And every few years a new lot is laid down and run over; so that, if some have the pleasure of riding on a rail, others have the misfortune to be

[9]The German nation as we know it did not exist in Thoreau's time; what is now Germany consisted of many warring states that were not unified until 1871.

[10]Sleepers were railroad ties. Thoreau is punning.

ridden upon. And when they run over a man that is walking in his sleep, a supernumerary sleeper in the wrong position, and wake him up, they suddenly stop the cars, and make a hue and cry about it, as if this were an exception. I am glad to know that it takes a gang of men for every five miles to keep the sleepers down and level in their beds as it is, for this is a sign that they may sometime get up again.

Why should we live with such hurry and waste of life? We are determined to be starved before we are hungry. Men say that a stitch in time saves nine, and so they take a thousand stitches to-day to save nine to-morrow. As for *work,* we haven't any of any consequence. We have the Saint Vitus' dance, and cannot possibly keep our heads still. If I should only give a few pulls at the parish bell-rope, as for a fire, that is, without setting the bell, there is hardly a man on his farm in the outskirts of Concord, notwithstanding that press of engagements which was his excuse so many times this morning, nor a boy, nor a woman, I might almost say, but would forsake all and follow that sound, not mainly to save property from the flames, but, if we will confess the truth, much more to see it burn, since burn it must, and we, be it known, did not set it on fire,—or to see it put out, and have a hand in it, if that is done as handsomely; yes, even if it were the parish church itself. Hardly a man takes a half hour's nap after dinner, but when he wakes he holds up his head and asks, "What's the news?" as if the rest of mankind had stood his sentinels. Some give directions to be waked every half hour, doubtless for no other purpose; and then, to pay for it, they tell what they have dreamed. After a night's sleep the news is as indispensable as the breakfast. "Pray tell me any thing new that has happened to a man any where on this globe",—and he reads it over his coffee and rolls, that a man has had his eyes gouged out this morning on the Wachito River; never dreaming the while that he lives in the dark unfathomed mammoth cave of this world, and has but the rudiment of an eye himself.[11]

For my part, I could easily do without the postoffice. I think that there are very few important communications made through it. To speak critically, I never received more than one or two letters in my life—I wrote this some years ago—that were worth the postage. The penny-post is, commonly, an institution through which you seriously offer a man that penny for his thoughts which is so often safely offered in jest. And I am sure that I never read any memorable news in a newspaper. If we read of one man robbed, or murdered, or killed by accident, or one house burned, or one vessel wrecked, or one steamboat blown up, or one cow run over on the Western Railroad, or one mad dog killed, or one lot of grasshoppers in the winter,—we never need read of another. One is enough. If you are acquainted with the principle, what do you care for a myriad instances and applications? To a philosopher all *news,* as it is called, is gossip, and they who edit and read it are old women over their tea. Yet not a few are greedy after this gossip. There was such a rush, as I hear, the other day at one of the offices to learn the foreign news by the last arrival, that several large squares of plate glass belonging to the establishment were broken by the pressure,—news which I seriously think a ready wit might write a twelve-month or twelve years beforehand with sufficient accuracy. As for Spain, for instance, if you know how to throw in Don Carlos and the Infanta, and Don Pedro and Seville and Granada, from

[11]Thoreau's reference is to Mammoth Cave in Kentucky, where the fish were blind.

time to time in the right proportions,—they may have changed the names a little since I saw the papers,—and serve up a bull-fight when other entertainments fail, it will be true to the letter, and give us as good an idea of the exact state or ruin of things in Spain as the most succinct and lucid reports under this head in the newspapers: and as for England, almost the last significant scrap of news from that quarter was the revolution of 1649; and if you have learned the history of her crops for an average year, you never need attend to that thing again, unless your speculations are of a merely pecuniary character. If one may judge who rarely looks into the newspapers, nothing new does ever happen in foreign parts, a French revolution not excepted.

What news! how much more important to know what that is which was never old! "Kieou-pe-yu (great dignitary of the state of Wei) sent a man to Khoung-tseu to know his news. Khoung-tseu caused the messenger to be seated near him, and questioned him in these terms: What is your master doing? The messenger answered with respect: My master desires to diminish the number of his faults, but he cannot accomplish it. The messenger being gone, the philosopher remarked: What a worthy messenger! What a worthy messenger!" The preacher, instead of vexing the ears of drowsy farmers on their day of rest at the end of the week,—for Sunday is the fit conclusion of an ill-spent week, and not the fresh and brave beginning of a new one,—with this one other draggle-tail of a sermon, should shout with thundering voice,—"Pause! Avast! Why so seeming fast, but deadly slow?"

Shams and delusions are esteemed for soundest truths, while reality is fabulous. If men would steadily observe realities only, and not allow themselves to be deluded, life, to compare it with such things as we know, would be like a fairy tale and the Arabian Nights' Entertainments. If we respected only what is inevitable and has a right to be, music and poetry would resound along the streets. When we are unhurried and wise, we perceive that only great and worthy things have any permanent and absolute existence,—that petty fears and petty pleasures are but the shadow of the reality. This is always exhilarating and sublime. By closing the eyes and slumbering, and consenting to be deceived by shows, men establish and confirm their daily life of routine and habit every where, which still is built on purely illusory foundations. Children, who play life, discern its true law and relations more clearly than men, who fail to live it worthily, but who think that they are wiser by experience, that is, by failure. I have read in a Hindoo book, that "there was a king's son, who, being expelled in infancy from his native city, was brought up by a forester, and, growing up to maturity in that state, imagined himself to belong to the barbarous race with which he lived. One of his father's ministers having discovered him, revealed to him what he was, and the misconception of his character was removed, and he knew himself to be a prince. So soul," continues the Hindoo philosopher, "from the circumstances in which it is placed, mistakes its own character, until the truth is revealed to it by some holy teacher, and then it knows itself to be *Brahme*."[12] I perceive that we inhabitants of New England live this mean life that we do because our vision does not penetrate the surface of things. We think that that *is* which *appears* to be. If a man should walk through this town and see only the reality, where, think you, would the "Mill-dam"[13]

[12] *I.e.,* Brahma, in Hindu mythology the creator.

[13] The Mill-dam was the central business section of Concord.

go to? If he should give us an account of the realities he beheld there, we should not recognize the place in his description. Look at a meeting-house, or a court-house, or a jail, or a shop, or a dwelling-house, and say what that thing really is before a true gaze, and they would all go to pieces in your account of them. Men esteem truth remote, in the outskirts of the system, behind the farthest star, before Adam and after the last man. In eternity there is indeed something true and sublime. But all these times and places and occasions are now and here. God himself culminates in the present moment, and will never be more divine in the lapse of all the ages. And we are enabled to apprehend at all what is sublime and noble only by the perpetual instilling and drenching of the reality which surrounds us. The universe constantly and obediently answers to our conceptions; whether we travel fast or slow, the track is laid for us. Let us spend our lives in conceiving then. The poet or the artist never yet had so fair and noble a design but some of his posterity at least could accomplish it.

Let us spend one day as deliberately as Nature, and not be thrown off the track by every nutshell and mosquito's wing that falls on the rails. Let us rise early and fast, or break fast, gently and without perturbation; let company come and let company go, let the bells ring and the children cry,—determined to make a day of it. Why should we knock under and go with the stream? Let us not be upset and overwhelmed in that terrible rapid and whirlpool called a dinner, situated in the meridian shallows. Weather this danger and you are safe, for the rest of the way is down hill. With unrelaxed nerves, with morning vigor, sail by it, looking another way, tied to the mast like Ulysses.[14] If the engine whistles, let it whistle till it is hoarse for its pains. If the bell rings, why should we run? We will consider what kind of music they are like. Let us settle ourselves, and work and wedge our feet downward through the mud and slush of opinion, and prejudice, and tradition, and delusion, and appearance, that alluvion which covers the globe, through Paris and London, through New York and Boston and Concord, through church and state, through poetry and philosophy and religion, till we come to a hard bottom and rocks in place, which we can call *reality,* and say, This is, and no mistake; and then begin, having a *point d'appui,*[15] below freshet and frost and fire, a place where you might found a wall or a state, or set a lamp-post safely, or perhaps a gauge, not a Nilometer, but a Realometer,[16] that future ages might know how deep a freshet of shams and appearances had gathered from time to time. If you stand right fronting and face to face to a fact, you will see the sun glimmer on both its surfaces, as if it were a cimeter,[17] and feel its sweet edge dividing you through the heart and marrow, and so you will happily conclude your mortal career. Be it life or death, we crave only reality. If we are really dying, let us hear the rattle in our throats and feel cold in the extremities; if we are alive, let us go about our business.

Time is but the stream I go a-fishing in. I drink at it; but while I drink I see the sandy bottom and detect how shallow it is. Its thin current slides away, but eternity

[14]Ulysses, returning from Troy in Homer's *Odyssey,* had ordered his men to tie him to the mast of his ship, so that he would be able to resist the seductive songs of the Sirens.

[15]A firm point of support.

[16]By "Nilometer" Thoreau means a gauge used by Egyptians at the head of the Nile to measure the water depth. Thoreau is punning between "Nil" (nothing) and "real" as in "reality."

[17]"Cimeter" is the obsolete form of "scimitar," a sharp, curved, single-edged sword. Compare below, the reference to "cleaver."

remains. I would drink deeper; fish in the sky, whose bottom is pebbly with stars. I cannot count one. I know not the first letter of the alphabet. I have always been regretting that I was not as wise as the day I was born. The intellect is a cleaver; it discerns and rifts its way into the secret of things. I do not wish to be any more busy with my hands than is necessary. My head is hands and feet. I feel all my best faculties concentrated in it. My instinct tells me that my head is an organ for burrowing, as some creatures use their snout and fore-paws, and with it I would mine and burrow my way through these hills. I think that the richest vein is somewhere hereabouts; so by the divining rod and thin rising vapors I judge; and here I will begin to mine.

Higher Laws

As I came home through the woods with my string of fish, trailing my pole, it being now quite dark, I caught a glimpse of a woodchuck stealing across my path, and felt a strange thrill of savage delight, and was strongly tempted to seize and devour him raw; not that I was hungry then, except for that wildness which he represented. Once or twice, however, while I lived at the pond, I found myself ranging the woods, like a half-starved hound, with a strange abandonment, seeking some kind of venison which I might devour, and no morsel could have been too savage for me. The wildest scenes had become unaccountably familiar. I found in myself, and still find, an instinct toward a higher, or, as it is named, spiritual life, as do most men, and another toward a primitive rank and savage one, and I reverence them both.[18] I love the wild not less than the good. The wildness and adventure that are in fishing still recommended it to me. I like sometimes to take rank hold on life and spend my day more as the animals do. Perhaps I have owed to this employment and to hunting, when quite young, my closest acquaintance with Nature. They early introduce us to and detain us in scenery with which otherwise, at that age, we should have little acquaintance. Fishermen, hunters, woodchoppers, and others, spending their lives in the fields and woods, in a peculiar sense a part of Nature themselves, are often in a more favorable mood for observing her, in the intervals of their pursuits, than philosophers or poets even, who approach her with expectation. She is not afraid to exhibit herself to them. The traveller on the prairie is naturally a hunter, on the head waters of the Missouri and Columbia a trapper, and at the Falls of St. Mary[19] a fisherman. He who is only a traveller learns things at second-hand and by the halves, and is poor authority. We are most interested when science reports what those men already know practically or instinctively, for that alone is a true *humanity,* or account of human experience.

They mistake who assert that the Yankee has few amusements, because he has not so many public holidays, and men and boys do not play so many games as they

[18]In reverencing both the physical and spiritual in himself, Thoreau departs from the Christian tradition of disparaging the carnal desires of the body.

[19]The Falls of St. Mary are probably those in British Columbia associated with salmon fishing, though Thoreau may have had in mind the St. Mary's River in Nova Scotia, also known for its fisheries.

do in England, for here the more primitive but solitary amusements of hunting fishing and like have not yet given place to the former. Almost every New England boy among my contemporaries shouldered a fowling piece[20] between the ages of ten and fourteen; and his hunting and fishing grounds were not limited like the preserves of an English nobleman, but were more boundless even than those of a savage. No wonder, then, that he did not oftener stay to play on the common. But already a change is taking place, owing, not to an increased humanity, but to an increased scarcity of game, for perhaps the hunter is the greatest friend of the animals hunted, not excepting the Humane Society.

Moreover, when at the pond, I wished sometimes to add fish to my fare for variety. I have actually fished from the same kind of necessity that the first fishers did. Whatever humanity I might conjure up against it was all factitious, and concerned my philosophy more than my feelings. I speak of fishing only now, for I had long felt differently about fowling, and sold my gun before I went to the woods. Not that I am less humane than others, but I did not perceive that my feelings were much affected. I did not pity the fishes nor the worms. This was habit. As for fowling, during the last years that I carried a gun my excuse was that I was studying ornithology, and sought only new or rare birds. But I confess that I am now inclined to think that there is a finer way of studying ornithology than this. It requires so much closer attention to the habits of the birds, that, if for that reason only, I have been willing to omit the gun. Yet notwithstanding the objection on the score of humanity, I am compelled to doubt if equally valuable sports are ever substituted for these; and when some of my friends have asked me anxiously about their boys, whether they should let them hunt, I have answered, yes,—remembering that it was one of the best parts of my education,—*make* them hunters, though sportsmen only at first, if possible, mighty hunters at last, so that they shall not find game large enough for them in this or any vegetable wilderness,—hunters as well as fishers of men.[21] Thus far I am of the opinion of Chaucer's nun, who

"yave not of the text a pulled hen
That saith that hunters ben not holy men."

There is a period in the history of the individual, as of the race, when the hunters are the "best men," as the Algonquins called them. We cannot but pity the boy who has never fired a gun; he is no more humane, while his education has been sadly neglected. This was my answer with respect to those youths who were bent on this pursuit, trusting that they would soon outgrow it. No humane being, past the thoughtless age of boyhood, will wantonly murder any creature, which holds its life by the same tenure that he does. The hare in its extremity cries like a child. I warn you, mothers, that my sympathies do not always make the usual phil-*anthropic* distinctions.[22]

[20]An archaic name for "gun."

[21]Christ, in calling Simon and Andrew from their fishing to follow him, told them: "I will make you to become fishers of men." Mark 1:17.

[22]As he does so often, Thoreau is playing with the etymology of words. He is saying that his love of animals is not limited to "love of man" only.

Such is oftenest the young man's introduction to the forest, and the most original part of himself. He goes thither at first as a hunter and fisher, until at last, if he has the seeds of a better life in him, he distinguishes his proper objects, as a poet or naturalist it may be, and leaves the gun and fish-pole behind. The mass of men are still and always young in this respect. In some countries a hunting parson is no uncommon sight. Such a one might make a good shepherd's dog, but is far from being the Good Shepherd. I have been surprised to consider that the only obvious employment, except wood-chopping, ice-cutting, or the like business, which ever to my knowledge detained at Walden Pond for a whole half day any of my fellow-citizens, whether fathers or children of the town, with just one exception, was fishing. Commonly they did not think that they were lucky, or well paid for their time, unless they got a long string of fish, though they had the opportunity of seeing the pond all the while. They might go there a thousand times before the sediment of fishing would sink to the bottom and leave their purpose pure; but no doubt such a clarifying process would be going on all the while. The governor and his council faintly remember the pond, for they went a-fishing there when they were boys; but now they are too old and dignified to go a-fishing, and so they know it no more forever. Yet even they expect to go to heaven at last. If the legislature regards it, it is chiefly to regulate the number of hooks to be used there; but they know nothing about the hook of hooks with which to angle for the pond itself, impaling the legislature for a bait. Thus, even in civilized communities, the embryo man passes through the hunter stage of development.

I have found repeatedly, of late years, that I cannot fish without falling a little in self-respect. I have tried it again and again. I have skill at it, and, like many of my fellows, a certain instinct for it, which revives from time to time, but always when I have done I feel that it would have been better if I had not fished. I think that I do not mistake. It is a faint intimation, yet so are the first streaks of morning. There is unquestionably this instinct in me which belongs to the lower orders of creation; yet with every year I am less a fisherman, though without more humanity or even wisdom; at present I am no fisherman at all. But I see that if I were to live in a wilderness I should again be tempted to become a fisher and hunter in earnest. Beside, there is something essentially unclean about this diet and all flesh, and I began to see where housework commences, and whence the endeavor, which costs so much, to wear a tidy and respectable appearance each day, to keep the house sweet and free from all ill odors and sights. Having been my own butcher and scullion and cook, as well as the gentleman for whom the dishes were served up, I can speak from an unusually complete experience. The practical objection to animal food in my case was its uncleanness; and, besides, when I had caught and cleaned and cooked and eaten my fish, they seemed not to have fed me essentially. It was insignificant and unnecessary, and cost more than it came to. A little bread or a few potatoes would have done as well, with less trouble and filth. Like many of my contemporaries, I had rarely for many years used animal food, or tea, or coffee, &c.; not so much because of any ill effects which I had traced to them, as because they were not agreeable to my imagination. The repugnance to animal food is not the effect of experience, but is an instinct. It appeared more beautiful to live low and fare hard in many respects; and though I never did so, I went far enough to please my imagination. I believe that every man who has ever been earnest to preserve his higher or poetic faculties in the best condition has been particularly inclined to abstain from animal food, and from much food of any kind. It is a significant fact, stated by entomologists, I find it in Kirby and Spence, that "some insects in their perfect state, though furnished with organs of feeding, make no use of them;" and they lay it down as "a general rule, that almost all insects in this state eat much less than in that of larvae. The voracious caterpillar when transformed into a butterfly," . . . "and the gluttonous maggot when become a fly," content themselves with a drop or two of honey or some other sweet liquid. The abdomen under the wings of the butterfly still represents the larva. This is the tid-bit which tempts his insectivorous fate. The gross feeder is a man in the larva state; and there are whole nations in that condition, nations without fancy or imagination, whose vast abdomens betray them.

It is hard to provide and cook so simple and clean a diet as will not offend the imagination; but this, I think, is to be fed when we feed the body; they should both sit down at the same table. Yet perhaps this may be done. The fruits eaten temperately need not make us ashamed of our appetites, nor interrupt the worthiest pursuits. But put an extra condiment into your dish, and it will poison you. It is not worth the while to live by rich cookery. Most men would feel shame if caught preparing with their own hands precisely such a dinner, whether of animal or vegetable food, as is every day prepared for them by others. Yet till this is otherwise we are not civilized, and, if gentlemen and ladies, are not true men and women. This certainly suggests what change is to be made. It may be vain to ask why the imagination will not be reconciled to flesh and fat. I am satisfied that it is not. Is it not a reproach that man is a carnivorous animal? True, he can and does live, in a great measure, by preying on other animals; but this is a miserable way,—as any one who will go to snaring rabbits, or slaughtering lambs, may learn,—and he will be regarded as a benefactor of his race who shall teach man to confine himself to a more innocent and wholesome diet. Whatever my own practice may be, I have no doubt that it is a part of the destiny of the human race, in its gradual improvement, to leave off eating animals, as surely as the savage tribes have left off eating each other when they came in contact with the more civilized.

If one listens to the faintest but constant suggestions of his genius,[23] which are certainly true, he sees not to what extremes, or even insanity, it may lead him; and yet that way, as he grows more resolute and faithful, his road lies. The faintest assured objection which one healthy man feels will at length prevail over the arguments and customs of mankind. No man ever followed his genius till it misled him. Though the result were bodily weakness, yet perhaps no one can say that the consequences were to be regretted, for these were a life in conformity to higher principles. If the day and the night are such that you greet them with joy, and life emits a fragrance like flowers and sweet-scented herbs, is more elastic, more starry, more immortal,—that is your success. All nature is your congratulation, and you have cause momentarily to bless yourself. The greatest gains and values are farthest from being appreciated. We easily come to doubt if they exist. We soon forget them. They are the highest reality. Perhaps the facts most astounding and most real are never communicated by man to man. The true harvest of my daily life is somewhat as intangible and indescribable as

[23]By "genius" Thoreau means an innate faculty in all people which, he believes, identifies the good, the true, the right, the beautiful. These are the "highest reality."

the tints of morning or evening. It is a little star-dust caught, a segment of the rainbow which I have clutched.

Yet, for my part, I was never unusually squeamish; I could sometimes eat a fried rat with a good relish, if it were necessary. I am glad to have drunk water so long, for the same reason that I prefer the natural sky to an opium-eater's heaven. I would fain keep sober always; and there are infinite degrees of drunkenness. I believe that water is the only drink for a wise man; wine is not so noble a liquor; and think of dashing the hopes of a morning with a cup of warm coffee, or of an evening with a dish of tea! Ah, how low I fall when I am tempted by them! Even music may be intoxicating. Such apparently slight causes destroyed Greece and Rome, and will destroy England and America. Of all ebriosity, who does not prefer to be intoxicated by the air he breathes? I have found it to be the most serious objection to coarse labors long continued, that they compelled me to eat and drink coarsely also. But to tell the truth, I find myself at present somewhat less particular in these respects. I carry less religion to the table, ask no blessing; not because I am wiser than I was, but, I am obliged to confess, because, however much it is to be regretted, with years I have grown more coarse and indifferent. Perhaps these questions are entertained only in youth, as most believe of poetry. My practice is "nowhere," my opinion is here. Nevertheless I am far from regarding myself as one of those privileged ones to whom the Ved refers when it says, that "he who has true faith in the Omnipresent Supreme Being may eat all that exists," that is, is not bound to inquire what is his food, or who prepares it; and even in their case it is to be observed, as a Hindoo commentator has remarked, that the Vedant limits this privilege to "the time of distress."

Who has not sometimes derived an inexpressible satisfaction from his food in which appetite had no share? I have been thrilled to think that I owed a mental perception to the commonly gross sense of taste, that I have been inspired through the palate, that some berries which I had eaten on a hill-side had fed my genius. "The soul not being mistress of herself," says Thseng-tseu, "one looks, and one does not see; one listens, and one does not hear; one eats, and one does not know the savor of food." He who distinguishes the true savor of his food can never be a glutton; he who does not cannot be otherwise. A puritan may go to his brown-bread crust with as gross an appetite as ever an alderman to his turtle. Not that food which entereth into the mouth defileth a man, but the appetite with which it is eaten. It is neither the quality nor the quantity, but the devotion to sensual savors; when that which is eaten is not a viand to sustain our animal, or inspire our spiritual life, but food for the worms that possess us. If the hunter has a taste for mud-turtles, muskrats, and other such savage tid-bits, the fine lady indulges a taste for jelly made of a calf's foot, or for sardines from over the sea, and they are even. He goes to the mill-pond, she to her preserve-pot. The wonder is how they, how you and I, can live this slimy beastly life, eating and drinking.

Our whole life is startlingly moral. There is never an instant's truce between virtue and vice. Goodness is the only investment that never fails. In the music of the harp which trembles round the world it is the insisting on this which thrills us. The harp is the travelling patterer for the Universe's Insurance Company, recommending its laws, and our little goodness is all the assessment that we pay. Though the youth at last grows indifferent, the laws of the universe are not indifferent, but are forever on the side of the most sensitive. Listen to every zephyr for some reproof, for it is surely there, and he is unfortunate who does not hear it. We cannot touch a string or move a stop but the charming moral transfixes us. Many an irksome noise, go a long way off, is heard as music, a proud sweet satire on the meanness of our lives.

We are conscious of an animal in us, which awakens in proportion as our higher nature slumbers. It is reptile and sensual, and perhaps cannot be wholly expelled; like the worms which, even in life and health, occupy our bodies. Possibly we may withdraw from it, but never change its nature. I fear that it may enjoy a certain health of its own; that we may be well, yet not pure. The other day I picked up the lower jaw of a hog, with white and sound teeth and tusks, which suggested that there was an animal health and vigor distinct from the spiritual. This creature succeeded by other means than temperance and purity. "That in which men differ from brute beasts," says Mencius, "is a thing very inconsiderable; the common herd lose it very soon; superior men preserve it carefully." Who knows what sort of life would result if we had attained to purity? If I knew so wise a man as could teach me purity I would go to seek him forthwith. "A command over our passions, and over the external senses of the body, and good acts, are declared by the Ved to be indispensable in the mind's approximation to God." Yet the spirit can for the time pervade and control every member and function of the body, and transmute what in form is the grossest sensuality into purity and devotion. The generative energy, which, when we are loose, dissipates and makes us unclean, when we are continent invigorates and inspires us. Chastity is the flowering of man; and what are called Genius, Heroism, Holiness, and the like, are but various fruits which succeed it. Man flows at once to God when the channel of purity is open. By turns our purity inspires and our impurity casts us down. He is blessed who is assured that the animal is dying out in him day by day, and the divine being established. Perhaps there is none but has cause for shame on account of the inferior and brutish nature to which he is allied. I fear that we are such gods or demigods only as fauns and satyrs, the divine allied to beasts, the creatures of appetite, and that, to some extent, our very life is our disgrace.—

"How happy's he who hath due place assigned
To his beasts and disaforested his mind!

* * *

Can use his horse, goat, wolf, and ev'ry beast,
And is not ass himself to all the rest!
Else man not only is the herd of swine,
But he's those devils too which did incline
Them to a headlong rage, and made them worse."[24]

All sensuality is one, though it takes many forms; all purity is one. It is the same whether a man eat, or drink, or cohabit, or sleep sensually. They are but one appetite,

[24]The passage of poetry quoted from John Donne alludes to the Biblical story of Christ's casting out the devils from afflicted persons and transferring them into a herd of swine, which then plunged headlong into the sea. Thoreau is warning against the danger of giving ourselves up completely to sensuality and failing to strive for "wisdom and purity."

and we only need to see a person do any one of these things to know how great a sensualist he is. The impure can neither stand nor sit with purity. When the reptile is attacked at one mouth of his burrow, he shows himself at another. If you would be chaste, you must be temperate. What is chastity? How shall a man know if he is chaste? He shall not know it. We have heard of this virtue, but we know not what it is. We speak conformably to the rumor which we have heard. From exertion come wisdom and purity; from sloth ignorance and sensuality. In the student sensuality is a sluggish habit of mind. An unclean person is universally a slothful one, one who sits by a stove, whom the sun shines on prostrate, who reposes without being fatigued. If you would avoid uncleanness, and all the sins, work earnestly, though it be at cleaning a stable. Nature is hard to be overcome, but she must be overcome. What avails it that you are Christian, if you are not purer than the heathen, if you deny yourself no more, if you are not more religious? I know of many systems of religion esteemed heathenish whose precepts fill the reader with shame, and provoke him to new endeavors, though it be to the performance of rites merely.

I hesitate to say these things, but it is not because of the subject,—I care not how obscene my *words* are,—but because I cannot speak of them without betraying my impurity. We discourse freely without shame of one form of sensuality, and are silent about another. We are so degraded that we cannot speak simply of the necessary functions of human nature. In earlier ages, in some countries, every function was reverently spoken of and regulated by law. Nothing was too trivial for the Hindoo lawgiver, however offensive it may be to modern taste. He teaches how to eat, drink, cohabit, void excrement and urine, and the like, elevating what is mean, and does not falsely excuse himself by calling these things trifles.

Every man is the builder of a temple, called his body, to the god he worships, after a style purely his own, nor can he get off by hammering marble instead. We are all sculptors and painters, and our material is our own flesh and blood and bones. Any nobleness begins at once to refine a man's features, any meanness or sensuality to imbrute them.

John Farmer sat at his door one September evening, after a hard day's work, his mind still running on his labor more or less. Having bathed he sat down to recreate his intellectual man. It was a rather cool evening, and some of his neighbors were apprehending a frost. He had not attended to the train of his thoughts long when he heard some one playing on a flute, and that sound harmonized with his mood. Still he thought of his work; but the burden of his thought was, that though this kept running in his head, and he found himself planning and contriving it against his will, yet it concerned him very little. It was no more than the scurf of his skin, which was constantly shuffled off. But the notes of the flute came home to his ears out of a different sphere from that he worked in, and suggested work for certain faculties which slumbered in him. They gently did away with the street, and the village, and the state in which he lived. A voice said to him,—Why do you stay here and live this mean moiling life, when a glorious existence is possible for you? Those same stars twinkle over other fields than these.—But how to come out of this condition and actually migrate thither? All that he could think of was to practise some new austerity, to let his mind descend into his body and redeem it, and treat himself with ever increasing respect.

Spring

The opening of large tracts by the ice-cutters commonly causes a pond to break up earlier; for the water, agitated by the wind, even in cold weather, wears away the surrounding ice. But such was not the effect on Walden that year, for she had soon got a thick new garment to take the place of the old. This pond never breaks up so soon as the others in this neighborhood, on account both of its greater depth and its having no stream passing through it to melt or wear away the ice. I never knew it to open in the course of a winter, not excepting that of '52–3, which gave the ponds so severe a trial. It commonly opens about the first of April, a week or ten days later than Flint's Pond and Fair-Haven, beginning to melt on the north side and in the shallower parts where it began to freeze. It indicates better than any water hereabouts the absolute progress of the season, being least affected by transient changes of temperature. A severe cold of a few days' duration in March may very much retard the opening of the former ponds, while the temperature of Walden increases almost uninterruptedly. A thermometer thrust into the middle of Walden on the 6th of March, 1847, stood at 32°, or freezing point; near the shore at 33°; in the middle of Flint's Pond, the same day, at 32½°; at a dozen rods from the shore, in shallow water, under ice a foot thick, at 36°. This difference of three and a half degrees between the temperature of the deep water and the shallow in the latter pond, and the fact that a great proportion of it is comparatively shallow, show why it should break up so much sooner than Walden. The ice in the shallowest part was at this time several inches thinner than in the middle. In mid-winter the middle had been the warmest and the ice thinnest there. So, also, every one who has waded about the shores of a pond in summer must have perceived how much warmer the water is close to the shore, where only three or four inches deep, than a little distance out, and on the surface where it is deep, than near the bottom. In spring the sun not only exerts an influence through the increased temperature of the air and earth, but its heat passes through ice a foot or more thick, and is reflected from the bottom in shallow water, and so also warms the water and melts the under side of the ice, at the same time that it is melting it more directly above, making it uneven, and causing the air bubbles which it contains to extend themselves upward and downward until it is completely honey-combed, and at last disappears suddenly in a single spring rain. Ice has its grain as well as wood, and when a cake begins to rot or "comb," that is, assume the appearance of honey-comb, whatever may be its position, the air cells are at right angles with what was the water surface. Where there is a rock or a log rising near to the surface the ice over it is much thinner, and is frequently quite dissolved by this reflected heat; and I have been told that in the experiment at Cambridge to freeze water in a shallow wooden pond, though the cold air circulated underneath, and so had access to both sides, the reflection of the sun from the bottom more than counterbalanced this advantage. When a warm rain in the middle of the winter melts off the snow-ice from Walden, and leaves a hard dark or transparent ice on the middle, there will be a strip of rotten though thicker white ice, a rod or more wide, about the shores, created by this reflected heat. Also, as I have said, the bubbles themselves within the ice operate as burning glasses to melt the ice beneath.

The phenomena of the year take place every day in a pond on a small scale. Every morning, generally speaking, the shallow water is being warmed more rapidly than the deep, though it may not be made so warm after all, and every evening it is being cooled more rapidly until the morning. The day is an epitome of the year. The night is the winter, the morning and evening are the spring and fall, and the noon is the summer. The cracking and booming of the ice indicate a change of temperature. One pleasant morning after a cold night, February 24th, 1850, having gone to Flint's Pond to spend the day, I noticed with surprise, that when I struck the ice with the head of my axe, it resounded like a gong for many rods around, or as if I had struck on a tight drum-head. The pond began to boom about an hour after sunrise, when it felt the influence of the sun's rays slanted upon it from over the hills; it stretched itself and yawned like a waking man with a gradually increasing tumult, which was kept up three or four hours. It took a short siesta at noon, and boomed once more toward night, as the sun was withdrawing his influence. In the right stage of the weather a pond fires its evening gun with great regularity. But in the middle of the day, being full of cracks, and the air also being less elastic, it had completely lost its resonance, and probably fishes and muskrats could not then have been stunned by a blow on it. The fishermen say that the "thundering of the pond" scares the fishes and prevents their biting. The pond does not thunder every evening, and I cannot tell surely when to expect its thundering; but though I may perceive no difference in the weather, it does. Who would have suspected so large and cold and thick-skinned a thing to be so sensitive? Yet it has its law to which it thunders obedience when it should as surely as the buds expand in the spring. The earth is all alive and covered with papillae. The largest pond is as sensitive to atmospheric changes as the globule of mercury in its tube.

One attraction in coming to the woods to live was that I should have leisure and opportunity to see the spring come in. The ice in the pond at length begins to be honey-combed, and I can set my heel in it as I walk. Fogs and rains and warmer suns are gradually melting the snow; the days have grown sensibly longer; and I see how I shall get through the winter without adding to my wood-pile, for large fires are no longer necessary. I am on the alert for the first signs of spring, to hear the chance note of some arriving bird, or the striped squirrel's chirp, for his stores must be now nearly exhausted, or see the woodchuck venture out of his winter quarters. On the 13th of March, after I had heard the bluebird, song-sparrow, and red-wing, the ice was still nearly a foot thick. As the weather grew warmer, it was not sensibly worn away by the water, nor broken up and floated off as in rivers, but, though it was completely melted for half a rod in width about the shore, the middle was merely honey-combed and saturated with water, so that you could put your foot through it when six inches thick; but by the next day evening, perhaps, after a warm rain followed by fog, it would have wholly disappeared, all gone off with the fog, spirited away. One year I went across the middle only five days before it disappeared entirely. In 1845 Walden was first completely open on the 1st of April; in '46, the 25th of March; in '47, the 8th of April; in '51, the 28th of March; in '52, the 18th of April; in '53, the 23d of March; in '54, about the 7th of April

Every incident connected with the breaking up of the rivers and ponds and the settling of the weather is particularly interesting to us who live in a climate of so great extremes. When the warmer days come, they who dwell near the river hear the ice crack at night with a startling whoop as loud as artillery, as if its icy fetters were rent from end to end, and within a few days see it rapidly going out. So the alligator comes out of the mud with quakings of the earth. One old man, who has been a close observer of Nature, and seems as thoroughly wise in regard to all her operations as if she had been put upon the stocks when he was a boy, and he had helped to lay her keel,—who has come to his growth, and can hardly acquire more of a natural lore if he should live to the age of Methuselah,[25]—told me, and I was surprised to hear him express wonder at any of Nature's operations, for I thought that there were no secrets between them, that one spring day he took his gun and boat, and thought that he would have a little sport with the ducks. There was ice still on the meadows, but it was all gone out of the river, and he dropped down without obstruction from Sudbury, where he lived, to Fair-Haven Pond, which he found, unexpectedly, covered for the most part with a firm field of ice. It was a warm day, and he was surprised to see so great a body of ice remaining. Not seeing any ducks, he hid his boat on the north or back side of an island in the pond, and then concealed himself in the bushes on the south side, to await them. The ice was melted for three or four rods from the shore, and there was a smooth and warm sheet of water, with a muddy bottom, such as the ducks love, within, and he thought it likely that some would be along pretty soon. After he had lain still there about an hour he heard a low and seemingly very distant sound, but singularly grand and impressive, unlike any thing he had ever heard, gradually swelling and increasing as if it would have a universal and memorable ending, a sullen rush and roar, which seemed to him all at once like the sound of a vast body of fowl coming in to settle there, and, seizing his gun, he started up in haste and excited; but he found, to his surprise, that the whole body of the ice had started while he lay there, and drifted in to the shore, and the sound he had heard was made by its edge grating on the shore,—at first gently nibbled and crumbled off, but at length heaving up and scattering its wrecks along the island to a considerable height before it came to a stand still.

At length the sun's rays have attained the right angle, and warm winds blow up mist and rain and melt the snow banks, and the sun dispersing the mist smiles on a checkered landscape of russet and white smoking with incense, through which the traveller picks his way from islet to islet, cheered by the music of a thousand tinkling rills and rivulets whose veins are filled with the blood of winter which they are bearing off.

Few phenomena gave me more delight than to observe the forms which thawing sand and clay assume in flowing down the sides of a deep cut on the railroad through which I passed on my way to the village, a phenomenon not very common on so large a scale, though the number of freshly exposed banks of the right material must have been greatly multiplied since railroads were invented. The material was sand of every degree of fineness and of various rich colors, commonly mixed with a little clay. When the frost comes out in the spring, and even in a thawing day in the winter, the sand begins to flow down the slopes like lava, sometimes bursting out through the snow and overflowing it where no sand was to be seen before. Innumerable little streams overlap and interlace one with another, exhibiting a sort of hybrid product, which obeys half way the law of currents, and half way that of vegetation. As it flows

[25]According to Genesis 5:27, he lived 969 years.

it takes the forms of sappy leaves or vines, making heaps of pulpy sprays a foot or more in depth, and resembling, as you look down on them, the laciniated lobed and imbricated thalluses of some lichens; or you are reminded of coral, of leopards' paws or birds' feet, of brains or lungs or bowels, and excrements of all kinds. It is a truly *grotesque* vegetation, whose forms and color we see imitated in bronze, a sort of architectural foliage more ancient and typical than acanthus, chiccory, ivy, vine, or any vegetable leaves; destined perhaps, under some circumstances, to become a puzzle to future geologists. The whole cut impressed me as if it were a cave with its stalactites laid open to the light. The various shades of the sand are singularly rich and agreeable, embracing the different iron colors, brown, gray, yellowish, and reddish. When the flowing mass reaches the drain at the foot of the bank it spreads out flatter into *strands,* the separate streams losing their semi-cylindrical form and gradually becoming more flat and broad, running together as they are more moist, till they form an almost flat *sand,* still variously and beautifully shaded, but in which you can trace the original forms of vegetation; till at length, in the water itself, they are converted into *banks,* like those formed off the mouths of rivers, and the forms of vegetation are lost in the ripple marks on the bottom.

The whole bank, which is from twenty to forty feet high, is sometimes overlaid with a mass of this kind of foliage, or sandy rupture, for a quarter of a mile on one or both sides, the produce of one spring day. What makes this sand foliage remarkable is its springing into existence thus suddenly. When I see on the one side the inert bank,—for the sun acts on one side first,—and on the other this luxuriant foliage, the creation of an hour, I am affected as if in a peculiar sense I stood in the laboratory of the Artist who made the world and me,—had come to where he was still at work, sporting on this bank, and with excess of energy strewing his fresh designs about. I feel as if I were nearer to the vitals of the globe, for this sandy overflow is something such a foliaceous mass as the vitals of the animal body. You find thus in the very sands an anticipation of the vegetable leaf. No wonder that the earth expresses itself outwardly in leaves, it so labors with the idea inwardly. The atoms have already learned this law, and are pregnant by it. The overhanging leaf sees here its prototype. *Internally,* whether in the globe or animal body, it is a moist thick *lobe,* a word especially applicable to the liver and lungs and the *leaves* of fat, (λείβω, *labor, lapsus,* to flow or slip downward, a lapsing; λοβος, *globus,* lobe, globe; also lap, flap, and many other words,) *externally* a dry thin *leaf,* even as the *f* and *v* are a pressed and dried *b.* The radicals of lobe are *lb,* the soft mass of the *b* (single lobed, or B, double lobed,) with a liquid *l* behind it pressing it forward. In globe, *glb,* the guttural *g* adds to the meaning the capacity of the throat. The feathers and wings of birds are still drier and thinner leaves. Thus, also, you pass from the lumpish grub in the earth to the airy and fluttering butterfly. The very globe continually transcends and translates itself, and becomes winged in its orbit. Even ice begins with delicate crystal leaves, as if it had flowed into moulds which the fronds of water plants have impressed on the watery mirror. The whole tree itself is but one leaf, and rivers are still vaster leaves whose pulp is intervening earth, and towns and cities are the ova of insects in their axils.

When the sun withdraws the sand ceases to flow, but in the morning the streams will start once more and branch and branch again into a myriad of others. You here see perchance how blood vessels are formed. If you look closely you observe that first there pushes forward from the thawing mass a stream of softened sand with a drop-like point, like the ball of the finger, feeling its way slowly and blindly downward, until at last with more heat and moisture, as the sun gets higher, the most fluid portion, in its effort to obey the law to which the most inert also yields, separates from the latter and forms for itself a meandering channel or artery within that, in which is seen a little silvery stream glancing like lightning from one stage of pulpy leaves or branches to another, and ever and anon swallowed up in the sand. It is wonderful how rapidly yet perfectly the sand organizes itself as it flows, using the best material its mass affords to form the sharp edges of its channel. Such are the sources of rivers. In the silicious matter which the water deposits is perhaps the bony system, and in the still finer soil and organic matter the fleshy fibre or cellular tissue. What is man but a mass of thawing clay? The ball of the human finger is but a drop congealed. The fingers and toes flow to their extent from the thawing mass of the body. Who knows what the human body would expand and flow out to under a more genial heaven? Is not the hand a spreading *palm* leaf with its lobes and veins? The ear may be regarded, fancifully, as a lichen, *umbilicaria,* on the side of the head, with its lobe or drop. The lip (*labium* from *labor* (?)) laps or lapses from the sides of the cavernous mouth. The nose is a manifest congealed drop or stalactite. The chin is a still larger drop, the confluent dripping of the face. The cheeks are a slide from the brows into the valley of the face, opposed and diffused by the cheek bones. Each rounded lobe of the vegetable leaf, too, is a thick and now loitering drop, larger or smaller; the lobes are the fingers of the leaf; and as many lobes as it has, in so many directions it tends to flow, and more heat or other genial influences would have caused it to flow yet farther.

Thus it seemed that this one hillside illustrated the principle of all the operations of Nature. The Maker of this earth but patented a leaf. What Champollion will decipher this hieroglyphic for us,[26] that we may turn over a new leaf at last? This phenomenon is more exhilarating to me than the luxuriance and fertility of vineyards. True, it is somewhat excrementitious in its character, and there is no end to the heaps of liver lights and bowels, as if the globe were turned wrong side outward; but this suggests at least that Nature has some bowels, and there again is mother of humanity. This is the frost coming out of the ground; this is Spring. It precedes the green and flowery spring, as mythology precedes regular poetry. I know of nothing more purgative of winter fumes and indigestions. It convinces me that Earth is still in her swaddling clothes, and stretches forth baby fingers on every side. Fresh curls spring from the baldest brow. There is nothing inorganic. These foliaceous heaps lie along the bank like the slag of a furnace, showing that Nature is "in full blast" within. The earth is not a mere fragment of dead history, stratum upon stratum like the leaves of a book, to be studied by geologists and antiquaries chiefly, but living poetry like the leaves of a tree, which precede flowers and fruit,—not a fossil earth, but a living earth; compared with whose great central life all animal and vegetable life is merely parasitic. Its throes will heave our exuviae from their graves. You may melt your metals and cast them into the most beautiful moulds you can; they will never excite me like the forms which this molten earth flows out into. And not only it, but the institutions upon it, are plastic like clay in the hands of the potter.

[26]Jean François Champollion (1790–1832) deciphered the hieroglyphics on the Rosetta Stone, thus providing a key to ancient Egyptian culture.

Ere long, not only on these banks, but on every hill and plain and in every hollow, the frost comes out of the ground like a dormant quadruped from its burrow, and seeks the sea with music, or migrates to other climes in clouds. Thaw with his gentle persuasion is more powerful than Thor with his hammer.[27] The one melts, the other but breaks in pieces.

When the ground was partially bare of snow, and a few warm days had dried its surface somewhat, it was pleasant to compare the first tender signs of the infant year just peeping forth with stately beauty of the withered vegetation which had withstood the winter,—life-everlasting, golden-rods, pinweeds, and graceful wild grasses, more obvious and interesting frequently than in summer even, as if their beauty was not ripe till then; even cotton-grass, cat-tails, mulleins, johnswort, hardhack, meadow-sweet, and other strong stemmed plants, those unexhausted granaries which entertain the earliest birds,—decent weeds, at least, which widowed Nature wears. I am particularly attracted by the arching and sheaf-like top of the wool-grass; it brings back the summer to our winter memories, and is among the forms which art loves to copy, and which, in the vegetable kingdom, have the same relation to types already in the mind of man that astronomy has. It is an antique style older than Greek or Egyptian. Many of the phenomena of Winter are suggestive of an inexpressible tenderness and fragile delicacy. We are accustomed to hear this king described as a rude and boisterous tyrant; but with the gentleness of a lover he adorns the tresses of Summer.

At the approach of spring the red-squirrels got under my house, two at a time, directly under my feet as I sat reading or writing, and kept up the queerest chuckling and chirruping and vocal pirouetting and gurgling sounds that ever were heard; and when I stamped they only chirruped the louder, as if past all fear and respect in their mad pranks, defying humanity to stop them. No you don't—chickaree—chickaree. They were wholly deaf to my arguments, or failed to perceive their force, and fell into a strain of invective that was irresistible.

The first sparrow of spring! The year beginning with younger hope than ever! The faint silvery warblings heard over the partially bare and moist fields from the blue-bird, the song-sparrow, and the red-wing, as if the last flakes of winter tinkled as they fell! What at such a time are histories, chronologies, traditions, and all written revelations? The brooks sing carols and glees to the spring. The marsh-hawk sailing low over the meadow is already seeking the first slimy life that awakes. The sinking sound of melting snow is heard in all dells, and the ice dissolves apace in the ponds. The grass flames up on the hillsides like a spring fire,—"et primitus oritur herba imbribus primoribus evocata,"[28]—as if the earth sent forth an inward heat to greet the returning sun; not yellow but green is the color of its flame;—the symbol of perpetual youth, the grass-blade, like a long green ribbon, streams from the sod into the summer, checked indeed by the frost, but anon pushing on again, lifting its spear of last year's hay with the fresh life below. It grows as steadily as the rill oozes out of the ground. It is almost identical with that, for in the growing days of June, when the rills are dry, the grass blades are their channels, and from year to year the herds drink at this perennial green stream, and the mower draws from it betimes their winter

[27]Norse god of Thunder.

[28]From the Latin poem *De Re Rustica* by Varro, c. 25 B.C.: "The grass starts to grow, summoned by the early rains."

supply. So our human life but dies down to its root, and still puts forth its green blade to eternity.

Walden is melting apace. There is a canal two rods wide along the northerly and westerly sides, and wider still at the east end. A great field of ice has cracked off from the main body. I hear a song-sparrow singing from the bushes on the shore,—*olit, olit, olit,—chip, chip, chip, che char,—che wiss, wiss, wiss.* He too is helping to crack it. How handsome the great sweeping curves in the edge of the ice, answering somewhat to those of the shore, but more regular! It is unusually hard, owing to the recent severe but transient cold, and all watered or waved like a palace floor. But the wind slides eastward over its opaque surface in vain, till it reaches the living surface beyond. It is glorious to behold this ribbon of water sparkling in the sun, the bare face of the pond full of glee and youth, as if it spoke the joy of the fishes within it, and of the sands on its shore,—a silvery sheen as from the scales of a *leuciscus,* as it were all one active fish. Such is the contrast between winter and spring. Walden was dead and is alive again. But this spring it broke up more steadily, as I have said.

The change from storm and winter to serene and mild weather, from dark and sluggish hours to bright and elastic ones, is a memorable crisis which all things proclaim. It is seemingly instantaneous at last. Suddenly an influx of light filled my house, though the evening was at hand, and the clouds of winter still overhung it, and the eaves were dripping with sleety rain. I looked out the window, and lo! where yesterday was cold gray ice there lay the transparent pond already calm and full of hope as on a summer evening, reflecting a summer evening sky in its bosom, though none was visible overhead, as if it had intelligence with some remote horizon. I heard a robin in the distance, the first I had heard for many a thousand years, methought, whose note I shall not forget for many a thousand more,—the same sweet and powerful song of yore. O the evening robin, at the end of a New England summer day! If I could ever find the twig he sits upon! I mean *he;* I mean *the twig.* This at least is not the *Turdus migratorius.*[29] The pitch-pines and shrub-oaks about my house, which had so long drooped, suddenly resumed their several characters, looked brighter, greener, and more erect and alive, as if effectually cleansed and restored by the rain. I knew that it would not rain any more. You may tell by looking at any twig of the forest, ay, at your very wood-pile, whether its winter is past or not. As it grew darker, I was startled by the *honking* of geese flying low over the woods, like weary travellers getting in late from southern lakes, and indulging at last in unrestrained complaint and mutual consolation. Standing at my door, I could hear the rush of their wings; when, driving toward my house, they suddenly spied my light, and with hushed clamor wheeled and settled in the pond. So I came in, and shut the door, and passed my first spring night in the woods.

In the morning I watched the geese from the door through the mist, sailing in the middle of the pond, fifty rods off, so large and tumultuous that Walden appeared like an artificial pond for their amusement. But when I stood on the shore they at once rose up with a great flapping of wings at the signal of their commander, and when they had got into rank circled about over my head, twenty-nine of them, and then steered straight to Canada, with a regular *honk* from the leader at intervals,

[29]The American robin.

trusting to break their fast in muddier pools. A "plump"[30] of ducks rose at the same time and took the route to the north in the wake of their noisier cousins.

For a week I heard the circling groping clangor of some solitary goose in the foggy mornings, seeking its companion, and still peopling the woods with the sound of a larger life than they could sustain. In April the pigeons were seen again flying express in small flocks, and in due time I heard the martins twittering over my clearing, though it had not seemed that the township contained so many that it could afford me any, and I fancied that they were peculiarly of the ancient race that dwelt in hollow trees ere white men came. In almost all climes the tortoise and the frog are among the precursors and heralds of this season, and birds fly with song and glancing plumage, and plants spring and bloom, and winds blow, to correct this slight oscillation of the poles and preserve the equilibrium of Nature.

As every season seems best to us in its turn, so the coming in of spring is like the creation of Cosmos out of Chaos and the realization of the Golden Age.—

"Eurus ad Auroram, Nabathaeaque regna recessit,
Persidaque, et radiis juga subdita matutinis."[31]

"The East-Wind withdrew to Aurora and the Nabathaean kingdom,
And the Persian, and the ridges placed under the morning rays.

* * *

Man was born. Whether that Artificer of things,
The origin of a better world, made him from the divine seed;
Or the earth being recent and lately sundered from the high
Ether, retained some seeds of cognate heaven."

A single gentle rain makes the grass many shades greener. So our prospects brighten on the influx of better thoughts. We should be blessed if we lived in the present always, and took advantage of every accident that befell us, like the grass which confesses the influence of the slightest dew that falls on it; and did not spend our time in atoning for the neglect of past opportunities, which we call doing our duty. We loiter in winter while it is already spring. In a pleasant spring morning all men's sins are forgiven. Such a day is a truce to vice. While such a sun holds out to burn, the vilest sinner may return. Through our own recovered innocence we discern the innocence of our neighbors. You may have known your neighbor yesterday for a thief, a drunkard, or a sensualist, and merely pitied or despised him, and despaired of the world; but the sun shines bright and warm this first spring morning, re-creating the world, and you meet him at some serene work, and see how his exhausted and debauched veins expand with still joy and bless the new day, feel the spring influence with the innocence of infancy, and all his faults are forgotten. There is not only an atmosphere of good will about him, but even a savor of holiness groping for expression, blindly and ineffectually perhaps, like a new-born instinct, and for a short hour the south hill-side echoes to no vulgar jest. You see some innocent fair shoots preparing to

[30]Flock.
[31]From Ovid, *Metamorphoses,* Book 1.

burst from his gnarled rind and try another year's life, tender and fresh as the youngest plant. Even he has entered into the joy of his Lord. Why the jailer does not leave open his prison doors,—why the judge does not dismiss his case,—why the preacher does not dismiss his congregation! It is because they do not obey the hint which God gives them, nor accept the pardon which he freely offers to all.

"A return to goodness produced each day in the tranquil and beneficent breath of the morning, causes that in respect to the love of virtue and the hatred of vice, one approaches a little the primitive nature of man, as the sprouts of the forest which has been felled. In like manner the evil which one does in the interval of a day prevents the germs of virtues which began to spring up again from developing themselves and destroys them.

"After the germs of virtue have thus been prevented many times from developing themselves, then the beneficent breath of evening does not suffice to preserve them. As soon as the breath of evening does not suffice longer to preserve them, then the nature of man does not differ much from that of the brute. Men seeing the nature of this man like that of the brute, think that he has never possessed the innate faculty of reason. Are those the true and natural sentiments of man?"[32]

"The Golden Age was first created, which without any avenger
Spontaneously without law cherished fidelity and rectitude.
Punishment and fear were not; nor were threatening words read
On suspended brass; nor did the suppliant crowd fear
The words of their judge; but were safe without an avenger.
Not yet the pine felled on its mountains had descended
To the liquid waves that it might see a foreign world,
And mortals knew no shores but their own.

* * *

There was eternal spring, and placid zephyrs with warm
Blasts soothed the flowers born without seed."[33]

On the 29th of April, as I was fishing from the bank of the river near the Nine-Acre-Corner bridge, standing on the quaking grass and willow roots, where the muskrats lurk, I heard a singular rattling sound, somewhat like that of the sticks which boys play with their fingers, when, looking up, I observed a very slight and graceful hawk, like a night-hawk, alternately soaring like a ripple and tumbling a rod or two over and over, showing the underside of its wings, which gleamed like a satin ribbon in the sun, or like the pearly inside of a shell. This sight reminded me of falconry and what nobleness and poetry are associated with that sport. The Merlin it seemed to me it might be called: but I care not for its name. It was the most ethereal flight I had ever witnessed. It did not simply flutter like a butterfly, nor soar like the larger hawks, but it sported with proud reliance in the fields of air; mounting again and again with its strange chuckle, it repeated its free and beautiful fall, turning over and over like a kite, and then recovering from its lofty tumbling, as if it had never set

[32]From *The Book of Mencius.*
[33]From Ovid, *Metamorphoses,* Book 1.

its foot on *terra firma.* It appeared to have no companion in the universe,—sporting there alone,—and to need none but the morning and the ether with which it played. It was not lonely, but made all the earth lonely beneath it. Where was the parent which hatched it, its kindred, and its father in the heavens? The tenant of the air, it seemed related to the earth but by an egg hatched some time in the crevice of a crag;—or was its native nest made in the angle of a cloud, woven of the rainbow's trimmings and the sunset sky, and lined with some soft midsummer haze caught up from earth? Its eyry now some cliffy cloud.

Beside this I got a rare mess of golden and silver and bright cupreous fishes, which looked like a string of jewels. Ah! I have penetrated to those meadows on the morning of many a first spring day, jumping from hummock to hummock, from willow root to willow root, when the wild river valley and the woods were bathed in so pure and bright a light as would have waked the dead, if they had been slumbering in their graves, as some suppose. There needs no stronger proof of immortality. All things must live in such a light. O Death, where was thy sting? O Grave, where was thy victory, then?[34]

Our village life would stagnate if it were not for the unexplored forests and meadows which surround it. We need the tonic of wildness,—to wade sometimes in marshes where the bittern and the meadow-hen lurk, and hear the booming of the snipe; to smell the whispering sedge where only some wilder and more solitary fowl builds her nest, and the mink crawls with its belly close to the ground. At the same time that we are earnest to explore and learn all things, we require that all things be mysterious and unexplorable, that land and sea be infinitely wild, unsurveyed and unfathomed by us because unfathomable. We can never have enough of Nature. We must be refreshed by the sight of inexhaustible vigor, vast and Titanic features, the sea-coast with its wrecks, the wilderness with its living and its decaying trees, the thunder cloud, and the rain which lasts three weeks and produces freshets. We need to witness our own limits transgressed, and some life pasturing freely where we never wander. We are cheered when we observe the vulture feeding on the carrion which disgusts and disheartens us and deriving health and strength from the repast. There was a dead horse in the hollow by the path to my house, which compelled me sometimes to go out of my way, especially in the night when the air was heavy, but the assurance it gave me of the strong appetite and inviolable health of Nature was my compensation for this. I love to see that Nature is so rife with life that myriads can be afforded to be sacrificed and suffered to prey on one another; that tender organizations can be so serenely squashed out of existence like pulp,—tadpoles which herons gobble up, and tortoises and toads run over in the road; and that sometimes it has rained flesh and blood! With the liability to accident, we must see how little account is to be made of it. The impression made on a wise man is that of universal innocence. Poison is not poisonous after all, nor are any wounds fatal. Compassion is a very untenable ground. It must be expeditious. Its pleadings will not bear to be stereotyped.

Early in May, the oaks, hickories, maples, and other trees, just putting out amidst the pine woods around the pond, imparted a brightness like sunshine to the landscape, especially in cloudy days, as if the sun were breaking through mists and shining faintly on the hill-sides here and there. On the third or fourth of May I saw a loon

[34]I Corinthians 15:55.

in the pond, and during the first week of the month I heard the whippoorwill, the brown-thrasher, the veery, the wood-pewee, the chewink, and other birds. I had heard the wood-thrush long before. The phoebe had already come once more and looked in at my door and window, to see if my house was cavern-like enough for her, sustaining herself on humming wings with clinched talons, as if she held by the air, while she surveyed the premises. The sulphur-like pollen of the pitch-pine soon covered the pond and the stones and rotten wood along the shore, so that you could have collected a barrel-ful. This is the "sulphur showers" we hear of. Even in Calidas' drama of Sacontala, we read of "rills dyed yellow with the golden dust of the lotus."[35] And so the seasons went rolling on into summer, as one rambles into higher and higher grass.

Thus was my first year's life in the woods completed; and the second year was similar to it. I finally left Walden September 6th, 1847.

Conclusion

To the sick the doctors wisely recommend a change of air and scenery. Thank Heaven, here is not all the world. The buck-eye does not grow in New England, and the mocking-bird is rarely heard here. The wild-goose is more of a cosmopolite than we; he breaks his fast in Canada, takes a luncheon in the Ohio, and plumes himself for the night in a southern bayou. Even the bison, to some extent, keeps pace with the seasons, cropping the pastures of the Colorado only till a greener and sweeter grass awaits him by the Yellowstone. Yet we think that if rail-fences are pulled down, and stone-walls piled up on our farms, bounds are henceforth set to our lives and our fates decided. If you are chosen town-clerk, forsooth, you cannot go to Tierra del Fuego this summer: but you may go to the land of infernal fire nevertheless. The universe is wider than our views of it.

Yet we should oftener look over the tafferel of our craft, like curious passengers, and not make the voyage like stupid sailors picking oakum.[36] The other side of the globe is but the home of our correspondent. Our voyaging is only great-circle sailing, and the doctors prescribe for diseases of the skin merely. One hastens to Southern Africa to chase the giraffe; but surely that is not the game he would be after. How long, pray, would a man hunt giraffes if he could? Snipes and woodcocks also may afford rare sport; but I trust it would be nobler game to shoot one's self.—

> "Direct your eye sight inward, and you'll find
> A thousand regions in your mind
> Yet undiscovered. Travel them, and be
> Expert in home-cosmography."[37]

[35] A fifth-century Sanskrit drama by the Hindu poet Kalidasa.

[36] Picking oakum meant, literally, twisting caulking material used to stuff cracks to prevent leakage of the boat. Sailors were assigned to do it when there were no important tasks to be done. In effect, picking oakum meant killing time.

[37] The poem quoted from William Habington reinforces Thoreau's insistence upon people's acknowledgement of the spiritual reality within them.

What does Africa,—what does the West stand for? Is not our own interior white on the chart? black though it may prove, like the coast, when discovered. Is it the source of the Nile, or the Niger, or the Mississippi, or a North-West Passage around this continent, that we would find? Are these the problems which most concern mankind? Is Franklin the only man who is lost, that his wife should be so earnest to find him? Does Mr. Grinnell know where he himself is?[38] Be rather the Mungo Park, the Lewis and Clarke and Frobisher, of your own streams and oceans; explore your own higher latitudes,—with shiploads of preserved meats to support you, if they be necessary; and pile the empty cans sky-high for a sign. Were preserved meats invented to preserve meat merely? Nay, be a Columbus to whole new continents and worlds within you, opening new channels, not of trade, but of thought. Every man is the lord of a realm beside which the earthly empire of the Czar is but a petty state, a hummock left by the ice. Yet some can be patriotic who have no *self*-respect, and sacrifice the greater to the less. They love the soil which makes their graves, but have no sympathy with the spirit which may still animate their clay. Patriotism is a maggot in their heads. What was the meaning of that South-Sea Exploring Expedition, with all its parade and expense, but an indirect recognition of the fact, that there are continents and seas in the moral world, to which every man is an isthmus or an inlet, yet unexplored by him, but that it is easier to sail many thousand miles through cold and storm and cannibals, in a government ship, with five hundred men and boys to assist one, than it is to explore the private sea, the Atlantic and Pacific Ocean of one's being alone.—

> "Erret, et extremos alter scrutetur Iberos.
> Plus habet hic vitae, plus habet ille viae."
> Let them wander and scrutinize the outlandish Australians.
> I have more of God, they more of the road.[39]

It is not worth the while to go round the world to count the cats in Zanzibar. Yet do this even till you can do better, and you may perhaps find some "Symmes' Hole" by which to get at the inside at last.[40] England and France, Spain and Portugal, Gold Coast and Slave Coast, all front on this private sea; but no bark from them has ventured out of sight of land, though it is without doubt the direct way to India. If you would learn to speak all tongues and conform to the customs of all nations, if you would travel farther than all travellers, be naturalized in all climes, and cause the Sphinx to dash her head against a stone, even obey the precept of the old philosopher, and Explore thyself. Herein are demanded the eye and the nerve. Only the defeated and deserters go to the wars, cowards that run away and enlist. Start now on that farthest western way, which does not pause at the Mississippi or the Pacific, nor conduct toward a worn-out China or Japan, but leads on direct a tangent to this

[38]Grinnell was a New York citizen who supported the search for the lost explorer, Sir John Franklin. The other persons mentioned in this passage were all explorers.

[39]The quotation from the Roman poet Claudian (which alters "Spaniards" to "Australians") reiterates Thoreau's point in the "Conclusion" of *Walden* that it is more profitable to explore the treasures within ourselves than to explore the remote areas of the Earth.

[40]Symmes was an Englishman who argued that the Earth was hollow.

sphere, summer and winter, day and night, sun down, moon down, and at last earth down too.

It is said that Mirabeau took to highway robbery "to ascertain what degree of resolution was necessary in order to place one's self in formal opposition to the most sacred laws of society." He declared that "a soldier who fights in the ranks does not require half so much courage as a foot-pad,"—"that honor and religion have never stood in the way of a well-considered and a firm resolve." This was manly, as the world goes; and yet it was idle, if not desperate. A saner man would have found himself often enough "in formal opposition" to what are deemed "the most sacred laws of society," through obedience to yet more sacred laws, and so have tested his resolution without going out of his way. It is not for a man to put himself in such an attitude to society, but to maintain himself in whatever attitude he find himself through obedience to the laws of his being, which will never be one of opposition to a just government, if he should chance to meet with such.

I left the woods for as good a reason as I went there. Perhaps it seemed to me that I had several more lives to live, and could not spare any more time for that one. It is remarkable how easily and insensibly we fall into a particular route, and make a beaten track for ourselves. I had not lived there a week before my feet wore a path from my door to the pond-side; and though it is five or six years since I trod it, it is still quite distinct. It is true, I fear that others may have fallen into it, and so helped to keep it open. The surface of the earth is soft and impressible by the feet of men; and so with the paths which the mind travels. How worn and dusty, then, must be the highways of the world, how deep the ruts of tradition and conformity! I did not wish to take a cabin passage, but rather to go before the mast and on the deck of the world, for there I could best see the moonlight amid the mountains. I do not wish to go below now.

I learned this, at least, by my experiment;[41] that if one advances confidently in the direction of his dreams, and endeavors to live the life which he has imagined, he will meet with a success unexpected in common hours. He will put some things behind, will pass an invisible boundary; new, universal, and more liberal laws will begin to establish themselves around and within him; or the old laws be expanded, and interpreted in his favor in a more liberal sense, and he will live with the license of a higher order of beings. In proportion as he simplifies his life, the laws of the universe will appear less complex, and solitude will not be solitude, nor poverty poverty, nor weakness weakness. If you have built castles in the air, your work need not be lost; that is where they should be. Now put the foundations under them.

It is a ridiculous demand which England and America make, that you shall speak so that they can understand you. Neither men nor toad-stools grow so. As if that were important, and there were not enough to understand you without them. As if Nature could support but one order of understandings, could not sustain birds as well as quadrupeds, flying as well as creeping things, and *hush* and *who,* which Bright can understand, were the best English.[42] As if there were safety in stupidity

[41]His "experiment," *i.e.,* his attempt to discover what it meant to live well, in his two-year stay at Walden Pond.

[42]"Bright" was a common name for oxen, while *hush* and *who* were apparently terms used in driving them. Thoreau expresses his concern in this paragraph that language may be inadequate to express the magnitude of human potential.

alone. I fear chiefly lest my expression may not be *extra- vagant* enough, may not wander far enough beyond the narrow limits of my daily experience, so as to be adequate to the truth of which I have been convinced. *Extra vagance!* it depends on how you are yarded. The migrating buffalo, which seeks new pastures in another latitude, is not extravagant like the cow which kicks over the pail, leaps the cowyard fence, and runs after her calf, in milking time. I desire to speak somewhere *without* bounds; like a man in a waking moment, to men in their waking moments; for I am convinced that I cannot exaggerate enough even to lay the foundation of a true expression. Who that has heard a strain of music feared then lest he should speak extravagantly any more forever? In view of the future or possible, we should live quite laxly and undefined in front, our outlines dim and misty on that side; as our shadows reveal an insensible perspiration toward the sun. The volatile truth of our words should continually betray the inadequacy of the residual statement. Their truth is instantly *translated;* its literal monument alone remains. The words which express our faith and piety are not definite; yet they are significant and fragrant like frankincense to superior natures.

Why level downward to our dullest perception always, and praise that as common sense? The commonest sense is the sense of men asleep, which they express by snoring. Sometimes we are inclined to class those who are once-and-a-half witted with the half-witted, because we appreciate only a third part of their wit. Some would find fault with the morning-red, if they ever got up early enough. "They pretend," as I hear, "that the verses of Kabir have four different senses; illusion, spirit, intellect, and the exoteric doctrine of the Vedas;" but in this part of the world it is considered a ground for complaint if a man's writings admit of more than one interpretation. While England endeavors to cure the potato-rot, will not any endeavor to cure the brain-rot, which prevails so much more widely and fatally?

I do not suppose that I have attained to obscurity, but I should be proud if no more fatal fault were found with my pages on this score than was found with the Walden ice. Southern customers objected to its blue color, which is the evidence of its purity, as if it were muddy, and preferred the Cambridge ice, which is white, but tastes of weeds. The purity men love is like the mists which envelop the earth, and not like the azure ether beyond.

Some are dinning in our ears that we Americans, and moderns generally, are intellectual dwarfs compared with the ancients, or even the Elizabethan men. But what is that to the purpose? A living dog is better than a dead lion. Shall a man go and hang himself because he belongs to the race of pygmies, and not be the biggest pygmy that he can? Let every one mind his own business, and endeavor to be what he was made.

Why should we be in such desperate haste to succeed, and in such desperate enterprises? If a man does not keep pace with his companions, perhaps it is because he hears a different drummer. Let him step to the music which he hears, however measured or far away. It is not important that he should mature as soon as an apple-tree or an oak. Shall he turn his spring into summer? If the condition of things which we were made for is not yet, what were any reality which we can substitute? We will not be shipwrecked on a vain reality. Shall we with pains erect a heaven of blue glass over ourselves, though when it is done we shall be sure to gaze still at the true ethereal heaven far above, as if the former were not?

There was an artist in the city of Kouroo who was disposed to strive after perfection. One day it came into his mind to make a staff. Having considered that in an imperfect work time is an ingredient, but into a perfect work time does not enter, he said to himself, It shall be perfect in all respects, though I should do nothing else in my life. He proceeded instantly to the forest for wood, being resolved that it should not be made of unsuitable material; and as he searched for and rejected stick after stick, his friends gradually deserted him, for they grew old in their works and died, but he grew not older by a moment. His singleness of purpose and resolution, and his elevated piety, endowed him, without his knowledge, with perennial youth. As he made no compromise with Time, Time kept out of his way, and only sighed at a distance because he could not overcome him. Before he had found a stock in all respects suitable the city of Kouroo was a hoary ruin, and he sat on one of its mounds to peel the stick. Before he had given it the proper shape the dynasty of the Candahars was at an end, and with the point of the stick he wrote the name of the last of that race in the sand, and then resumed his work. By the time he had smoothed and polished the staff Kalpa was no longer the pole-star; and ere he had put on the ferule and the head adorned with precious stones, Brahma had awoke and slumbered many times.[43] But why do I stay to mention these things? When the finishing stroke was put to his work, it suddenly expanded before the eyes of the astonished artist into the fairest of all the creations of Brahma. He had made a new system in making a staff, a world with full and fair proportions; in which, though the old cities and dynasties had passed away, fairer and more glorious ones had taken their places. And now he saw by the heap of shavings still fresh at his feet, that, for him and his work, the former lapse of time had been an illusion, and that no more time had elapsed than is required for a single scintillation from the brain of Brahma to fall on and inflame the tinder of a mortal brain. The material was pure, and his art was pure; how could the result be other than wonderful?

No face which we can give to a matter will stead us so well at last as the truth. This alone wears well. For the most part, we are not where we are, but in a false position. Through an infirmity of our natures, we suppose a case, and put ourselves into it, and hence are in two cases at the same time, and it is doubly difficult to get out. In sane moments we regard only the facts, the case that is. Say what you have to say, not what you ought. Any truth is better than make-believe. Tom Hyde, the tinker, standing on the gallows, was asked if he had any thing to say. "Tell the tailors," said he, "to remember to make a knot in their thread before they take the first stitch." His companion's prayer is forgotten.

However mean your life is, meet it and live it; do not shun it and call it hard names. It is not so bad as you are. It looks poorest when you are richest. The fault-finder will find faults even in paradise. Love your life, poor as it is. You may perhaps have some pleasant, thrilling, glorious hours, even in a poorhouse. The setting sun is reflected from the windows of the alms-house as brightly as from the rich man's abode; the snow melts before its door as early in the spring. I do not see but a quiet mind may live as contentedly there, and have as cheering thoughts, as in a palace. The town's poor seem to me often to live the most independent lives of any. May be

[43]Kalpa . . . Brahma: Thoreau's emphasis is upon the passage of aeons of time.

they are simply great enough to receive without misgiving. Most think that they are above being supported by the town; but it oftener happens that they are not above supporting themselves by dishonest means, which should be more reputable. Cultivate poverty like a garden herb, like sage. Do not trouble yourself much to get new things, whether clothes or friends. Turn the old; return to them. Things do not change; we change. Sell your clothes and keep your thoughts. God will see that you do not want society. If I were confined to a corner of a garret all my days, like a spider, the world would be just as large to me while I had my thoughts about me. The philosopher said: "From an army of three divisions one can take away its general, and put it in disorder; from the man the most abject and vulgar one cannot take away his thought." Do not seek so anxiously to be developed, to subject yourself to many influences to be played on; it is all dissipation. Humility like darkness reveals the heavenly lights. The shadows of poverty and meanness gather around us, "and lo! creation widens to our view." We are often reminded that if there were bestowed on us the wealth of Croesus, our aims must still be the same, and our means essentially the same. Moreover, if you are restricted in your range by poverty, if you cannot buy books and newspapers, for instance, you are but confined to the most significant and vital experiences; you are compelled to deal with the material which yields the most sugar and the most starch. It is life near the bone where it is sweetest. You are defended from being a trifler. No man loses ever on a lower level by magnanimity on a higher. Superfluous wealth can buy superfluities only. Money is not required to buy one necessary of the soul.

I live in the angle of a leaden wall, into whose composition was poured a little alloy of bell metal. Often, in the repose of my mid-day, there reaches my ears a confused *tintinnabulum*[44] from without. It is the noise of my contemporaries. My neighbors tell me of their adventures with famous gentlemen and ladies, what notabilities they met at the dinner-table; but I am no more interested in such things than in the contents of the Daily Times. The interest and the conversation are about costume and manners chiefly; but a goose is a goose still, dress it as you will. They tell me of California and Texas, of England and the Indies, of the Hon. Mr.——of Georgia or of Massachusetts, all transient and fleeting phenomena, till I am ready to leap from their court-yard like the Mameluke bey.[45] I delight to come to my bearings,—not walk in procession with pomp and parade, in a conspicuous place, but to walk even with the Builder of the universe, if I may,—not to live in this restless, nervous, bustling, trivial Nineteenth Century, but stand or sit thoughtfully while it goes by. What are men celebrating? They are all on a committee of arrangements, and hourly expect a speech from somebody. God is only the president of the day, and Webster is his orator. I love to weigh, to settle, to gravitate toward that which most strongly and rightfully attracts me;—not hang by the beam of the scale and try to weigh less,—not suppose a case, but take the case that is; to travel the only path I can, and that on which no power can resist me. It affords me no satisfaction to commence to spring an arch before I have got a solid foundation. Let us not play at kittly-benders.[46] There is a solid bottom every where. We read that the traveller asked the boy

[44]Din, racket.

[45]An Egyptian bey, or officer, who escaped capture by leaping from a wall onto his horse.

[46]A game of children which involved running over thin ice.

if the swamp before him had a hard bottom. The boy replied that it had. But presently the traveller's horse sank in up to the girths, and he observed to the boy, "I thought you said that this bog had a hard bottom." "So it has," answered the latter, "but you have not got half way to it yet." So it is with the bogs and quicksands of society; but he is an old boy that knows it. Only what is thought said or done at a certain rare coincidence is good. I would not be one of those who will foolishly drive a nail into mere lath and plastering; such a deed would keep me awake nights. Give me a hammer, and let me feel for the furring.[47] Do not depend on the putty. Drive a nail home and clinch it so faithfully that you can wake up in the night and think of your work with satisfaction,—a work at which you would not be ashamed to invoke the Muse. So will help you God, and so only. Every nail driven should be as another rivet in the machine of the universe, you carrying on the work.

Rather than love, than money, than fame, give me truth. I sat at a table where were rich food and wine in abundance, and obsequious attendance, but sincerity and truth were not; and I went away hungry from the inhospitable board. The hospitality was as cold as the ices. I thought that there was no need of ice to freeze them. They talked to me of the age of the wine and the fame of the vintage; but I thought of an older, a newer, and purer wine, of a more glorious vintage, which they had not got, and could not buy. The style, the house and grounds and "entertainment" pass for nothing with me. I called on the king, but he made me wait in his hall, and conducted like a man incapacitated for hospitality. There was a man in my neighborhood who lived in a hollow tree. His manners were truly regal. I should have done better had I called on him.

How long shall we sit in our porticoes practising idle and musty virtues, which any work would make impertinent? As if one were to begin the day with long-suffering, and hire a man to hoe his potatoes; and in the afternoon go forth to practise Christian meekness and charity with goodness aforethought! Consider the China pride and stagnant self-complacency of mankind.[48] This generation reclines a little to congratulate itself on being the last of an illustrious line; and in Boston and London and Paris and Rome, thinking of its long descent, it speaks of its progress in art and science and literature with satisfaction. There are the Records of the Philosophical Societies, and the public Eulogies of *Great Men!* It is the good Adam contemplating his own virtue. "Yes, we have done great deeds, and sung divine songs, which shall never die,"—that is, as long as *we* can remember them. The learned societies and great men of Assyria,—where are they? What youthful philosophers and experimentalists we are! There is not one of my readers who has yet lived a whole human life. These may be but the spring months in the life of the race. If we have had the seven-years' itch, we have not seen the seventeen-year locust yet in Concord. We are acquainted with a mere pellicle of the globe on which we live. Most have not delved six feet beneath the surface, nor leaped as many above it. We know not where we are. Beside, we are sound asleep nearly half our time. Yet we esteem ourselves wise, and have an established order on the surface. Truly, we are deep thinkers, we are ambitious spirits! As I stand over the insect crawling amid the pine needles on the forest

[47]The solid structure of a wall in which a driven nail will hold firm, unlike a nail driven only into plaster.

[48]China and the East were in Thoreau's time largely cut off economically and culturally from the West.

floor, and endeavoring to conceal itself from my sight, and ask myself why it will cherish those humble thoughts, and hide its head from me who might perhaps be its benefactor, and impart to its race some cheering information, I am reminded of the greater Benefactor and Intelligence that stands over me the human insect.

There is an incessant influx of novelty into the world, and yet we tolerate incredible dulness. I need only suggest what kind of sermons are still listened to in the most enlightened countries. There are such words as joy and sorrow, but they are only the burden of a psalm, sung with a nasal twang, while we believe in the ordinary and mean. We think that we can change our clothes only. It is said that the British Empire is very large and respectable, and that the United States are a first-rate power. We do not believe that a tide rises and falls behind every man which can float the British Empire like a chip, if he should ever harbor it in his mind. Who knows what sort of seventeen-year locust will next come out of the ground? The government of the world I live in was not framed, like that of Britain, in after-dinner conversations over the wine.

The life in us is like the water in the river. It may rise this year higher than man has ever known it, and flood the parched uplands; even this may be the eventful year, which will drown out all our muskrats. It was not always dry land where we dwell. I see far inland the banks which the stream anciently washed, before science began to record its freshets. Every one has heard the story which has gone the rounds of New England, of a strong and beautiful bug which came out of the dry leaf of an old table of apple-tree wood, which had stood in a farmer's kitchen for sixty years, first in Connecticut, and afterward in Massachusetts,—from an egg deposited in the living tree many years earlier still, as appeared by counting the annual layers beyond it; which was heard gnawing out for several weeks, hatched perchance by the heat of an urn. Who does not feel his faith in a resurrection and immortality strengthened by hearing of this? Who knows what beautiful and winged life, whose egg has been buried for ages under many concentric layers of woodenness in the dead dry life of society, deposited at first in the alburnum of the green and living tree, which has been gradually converted into the semblance of its well-seasoned tomb,—heard perchance gnawing out now for years by the astonished family of man, as they sat round the festive board,—may unexpectedly come forth from amidst society's most trivial and handselled furniture, to enjoy its perfect summer life at last!

I do not say that John or Jonathan[49] will realize all this; but such is the character of that morrow which mere lapse of time can never make to dawn. The light which puts out our eyes is darkness to us. Only that day dawns to which we are awake. There is more day to dawn. The sun is but a morning star.

THE END

1854

[49]John (John Bull) was a common nickname for an Englishman, Jonathan for an American

A Plea for Captain John Brown[1]

I trust that you will pardon me for being here. I do not wish to force my thoughts upon you, but I feel forced myself. Little as I know of Captain Brown, I would fain do my part to correct the tone and the statements of the newspapers, and of my countrymen generally, respecting his character and actions. It costs us nothing to be just. We can at least express our sympathy with, and admiration of, him and his companions, and that is what I now propose to do.

First, as to his history.

I will endeavor to omit, as much as possible, what you have already read. I need not describe his person to you, for probably most of you have seen and will not soon forget him. I am told that his grandfather, John Brown, was an officer in the Revolution; that he himself was born in Connecticut about the beginning of this century, but early went with his father to Ohio. I heard him say that his father was a contractor who furnished beef to the army there, in the war of 1812; that he accompanied him to the camp, and assisted him in that employment, seeing a good deal of military life, more, perhaps, than if he had been a soldier, for he was often present at the councils of the officers. Especially, he learned by experience how armies are supplied and maintained in the field—a work which, he observed, requires at least as much experience and skill as to lead them in battle. He said that few persons had any conception of the cost, even the pecuniary cost, of firing a single bullet in war. He saw enough, at any rate, to disgust him with a military life, indeed to excite in him a great abhorrence of it; so much so, that though he was tempted by the offer of some petty office in the army, when he was about eighteen, he not only declined that, but he also refused to train when warned, and was fined for it. He then resolved that he would never have anything to do with war, unless it were a war for liberty.

When the troubles in Kansas began, he sent several of his sons thither to strengthen the party of the Free State men, fitting them out with such weapons as he had; telling them that if the troubles should increase, and there should be need of him, he would follow to assist them with his hand and counsel. This, as you all know, he soon after did; and it was through his agency, far more than any other's that Kansas was made free.

For a part of his life he was a surveyor,[2] and at one time he was engaged in wool-growing, and he went to Europe as an agent about that business. There, as every where, he had his eyes about him, and made many original observations. He said, for

[1]John Brown attacked the federal arsenal at Harpers Ferry on October 16, 1859 with 22 heavily armed men, hoping that the attack would incite the slaves in the South to revolt. He was wounded, was captured on October 18, was tried immediately, convicted, and hanged on December 2. Thoreau had met Brown earlier on two occasions when Brown was in Concord raising money to purchase arms to carry on attacks against pro-slavery settlers in Kansas. Delivered first as a lecture on October 30, 1859 in the Concord Town Hall, the "Plea" was published early in February, 1860, in *Echoes of Harper's Ferry,* a collection of essays and poems on Brown edited by James Redpath.
Read to the citizens of Concord, Mass., Sunday Evening, October 30, 1859. Also as the fifth lecture of the Fraternity Course in Boston, November 1; and at Worcester, November 3. [Thoreau's note]

[2]Both Brown and Thoreau were surveyors.

instance, that he saw why the soil of England was so rich, and that of Germany (I think it was) so poor, and he thought of writing to some of the crowned heads about it. It was because in England the peasantry live on the soil which they cultivate, but in Germany they are gathered into villages, at night. It is a pity that he did not make a book of his observations.

I should say that he was an old-fashioned man in his respect for the Constitution, and his faith in the permanence of this Union. Slavery he deemed to be wholly opposed to these, and he was its determined foe.

He was by descent and birth a New England farmer, a man of great common sense, deliberate and practical as that class is, and tenfold more so. He was like the best of those who stood at Concord Bridge once, on Lexington Common, and on Bunker Hill, only he was firmer and higher principled than any that I have chanced to hear of as there. It was no abolition lecturer that converted him. Ethan Allen and Stark, with whom he may in some respects be compared, were rangers in a lower and less important field.[3] They could bravely face their country's foes, but he had the courage to face his country herself, when she was in the wrong. A Western writer says, to account for his escape from so many perils, that he was concealed under a "rural exterior;" as if, in that prairie land, a hero should, by good rights, wear a citizen's dress only.

He did not go to the college called Harvard, good old Alma Mater as she is. He was not fed on the pap that is there furnished. As he phrased it, "I know no more of grammar than one of your calves." But he went to the great university of the West, where he sedulously pursued the study of Liberty, for which he had early betrayed a fondness, and having taken many degrees, he finally commenced the public practice of Humanity in Kansas, as you all know. Such were *his humanities,* and not any study of grammar. He would have left a Greek accent slanting the wrong way, and righted up a falling man.

He was one of that class of whom we hear a great deal, but, for the most part, see nothing at all—the Puritans. It would be in vain to kill him. He died lately in the time of Cromwell, but he reappeared here.[4] Why should he not? Some of the Puritan stock are said to have come over and settled in New England. They were a class that did something else than celebrate their forefathers' day, and eat parched corn in remembrance of that time. They were neither Democrats nor Republicans, but men of simple habits, straightforward, prayerful; not thinking much of rulers who did not fear God, not making many compromises, nor seeking after available candidates.

"In his camp," as one has recently written, and as I have myself heard him state, "he permitted no profanity; no man of loose morals was suffered to remain there, unless, indeed, as a prisoner of war. 'I would rather,' said he, 'have the small-pox, yellow fever, and cholera, all together in my camp, than a man without principle. . . . It is a mistake, sir, that our people make, when they think that bullies are the best fighters, or that they are the fit men to oppose these Southerners. Give me men of good

[3]The early battles of the American Revolution mentioned by Thoreau were fought by hardy citizen-soldiers of New England who opposed British domination. Ethan Allen and John Stark distinguished themselves at the battles of Ticonderoga and Bunker Hill, respectively.

[4]Thoreau compares Brown to Oliver Cromwell, the stern, religious military leader who overthrew the English monarchy, executed Charles I. and ruled England from 1653 to 1658.

principles,—God-fearing men,—men who respect themselves, and with a dozen of them I will oppose any hundred such men as these Buford ruffians.'"[5] He said that if one offered himself to be a soldier under him, who was forward to tell what he could or would do, if he could only get sight of the enemy, he had but little confidence in him.

He was never able to find more than a score or so of recruits whom he would accept, and only about a dozen, among them his sons, in whom he had perfect faith. When he was here, some years ago, he showed to a few a little manuscript book,—his "orderly book" I think he called it,—containing the names of his company in Kansas, and the rules by which they bound themselves; and he stated that several of them had already sealed the contract with their blood. When some one remarked that, with the addition of a chaplain, it would have been a perfect Cromwellian troop, he observed that he would have been glad to add a chaplain to the list, if he could have found one who could fill that office worthily. It is easy enough to find one for the United States army. I believe that he had prayers in his camp morning and evening, nevertheless.

He was a man of Spartan habits, and at sixty was scrupulous about his diet at your table, excusing himself by saying that he must eat sparingly and fare hard, as became a soldier or one who was fitting himself for difficult enterprises, a life of exposure.

A man of rare common sense and directness of speech, as of action; a transcendentalist above all, a man of ideas and principles,—that was what distinguished him. Not yielding to a whim or transient impulse, but carrying out the purpose of a life. I noticed that he did not overstate any thing, but spoke within bounds. I remember, particularly, how, in his speech here, he referred to what his family had suffered in Kansas, without ever giving the least vent to his pent-up fire. It was a volcano with an ordinary chimney-flue. Also referring to the deeds of certain Border Ruffians, he said, rapidly paring away his speech, like an experienced soldier, keeping a reserve of force and meaning, "They had a perfect right to be hung." He was not in the least a rhetorician, was not talking to Buncombe[6] or his constituents any where, had no need to invent any thing, but to tell the simple truth, and communicate his own resolution; therefore he appeared incomparably strong, and eloquence in Congress and elsewhere seemed to me at a discount. It was like the speeches of Cromwell compared with those of an ordinary king.

As for his tact and prudence, I will merely say, that at a time when scarcely a man from the Free States was able to reach Kansas by any direct route, at least without having his arms taken from him, he, carrying what imperfect guns and other weapons he could collect, openly and slowly drove an ox-cart through Missouri, apparently in the capacity of a surveyor, with his surveying compass exposed in it, and so passed unsuspected, and had ample opportunity to learn the designs of the enemy. For some time after his arrival he still followed the same profession. When, for instance, he saw a knot of the ruffians on the prairie, discussing, of course, the single topic which then

[5]Buford was a leader of pro-slavery men into what is now Kansas. Settlers from both North and South moved into this area in an attempt to form majorities that would bring Kansas into the union as a state supporting their viewpoint on slavery. Tensions were very high.

[6]A pompous speaker who says nothing.

occupied their minds, he would, perhaps, take his compass and one of his sons, and proceed to run an imaginary line right through the very spot on which that conclave had assembled, and when he came up to them, he would naturally pause and have some talk with them, learning their news, and, at last, all their plans perfectly; and having thus completed his real survey, he would resume his imaginary one, and run on his line till he was out of sight.

When I expressed surprise that he could live in Kansas at all, with a price set upon his head, and so large a number, including the authorities, exasperated against him, he accounted for it by saying, "It is perfectly well understood that I will not be taken." Much of the time for some years he has had to skulk in swamps, suffering from poverty and from sickness, which was the consequence of exposure, befriended only by Indians and a few whites. But though it might be known that he was lurking in a particular swamp, his foes commonly did not care to go in after him. He could even come out into a town where there were more Border Ruffians[7] than Free State men, and transact some business, without delaying long, and yet not be molested; for said he, "No little handful of men were willing to undertake it, and a large body could not be got together in season."

As for his recent failure, we do not know the facts about it. It was evidently far from being a wild and desperate attempt. His enemy, Mr. Vallandigham,[8] is compelled to say, that "it was among the best planned and executed conspiracies that ever failed."

Not to mention his other successes, was it a failure, or did it show a want of good management, to deliver from bondage a dozen human beings, and walk off with them by broad daylight, for weeks if not months, at a leisurely pace, through one State after another, for half the length of the North, conspicuous to all parties, with a price set upon his head, going into a court room on his way and telling what he had done, thus convincing Missouri that it was not profitable to try to hold slaves in his neighborhood?—and this, not because the government menials were lenient, but because they were afraid of him.

Yet he did not attribute his success, foolishly, to "his star," or to any magic. He said, truly, that the reason why such greatly superior numbers quailed before him, was, as one of his prisoners confessed, because they *lacked a cause*—a kind of armor which he and his party never lacked. When the time came, few men were found willing to lay down their lives in defence of what they knew to be wrong; they did not like that this should be their last act in this world.

But to make haste to *his* last act, and its effects.

The newspapers seem to ignore, or perhaps are really ignorant of the fact, that there are at least as many as two or three individuals to a town throughout the North, who think much as the present speaker does about him and his enterprise. I do not hesitate to say that they are an important and growing party. We aspire to be something more than stupid and timid chattels, pretending to read history and our bibles, but desecrating every house and every day we breathe in. Perhaps anxious politicians may prove that only seventeen white men and five negroes were concerned in the late enterprise, but their very anxiety to prove this might suggest to themselves that all is

[7]Pro-slavery partisans in Kansas.

[8]Vallandigham was an Ohio congressman who, along with Senator Mason of Virginia, interviewed Brown after his capture.

not told. Why do they still dodge the truth? They are so anxious because of a dim consciousness of the fact, which they do not distinctly face, that at least a million of the free inhabitants of the United States would have rejoiced if it had succeeded. They at most only criticise the tactics. Though we wear no crape, the thought of that man's position and probable fate is spoiling many a man's day here at the North for other thinking. If any one who has seen him here can pursue successfully any other train of thought, I do not know what he is made of. If there is any such who gets his usual allowance of sleep, I will warrant him to fatten easily under any circumstances which do not touch his body or purse. I put a piece of paper and a pencil under my pillow, and when I could not sleep, I wrote in the dark.

On the whole, my respect for my fellow-men, except as one may outweigh a million, is not being increased these days. I have noticed the cold-blooded way in which newspaper writers and men generally speak of this event, as if an ordinary malefactor, though one of unusual "pluck,"—as the Governor of Virginia is reported to have said, using the language of the cock-pit, "the gamest man he ever saw,"—had been caught, and were about to be hung. He was not dreaming of his foes when the governor thought he looked so brave. It turns what sweetness I have to gall, to hear, or hear of, the remarks of some of my neighbors. When we heard at first that he was dead, one of my townsmen observed that "he died as the fool dieth;" which, pardon me, for an instant suggested a likeness in him dying to my neighbor living. Others, craven-hearted, said disparagingly, that "he threw his life away," because he resisted the government. Which way have they thrown *their* lives, pray?—Such as would praise a man for attacking singly an ordinary band of thieves or murderers. I hear another ask, Yankee-like, "What will he gain by it?" as if he expected to fill his pockets by this enterprise. Such a one has no idea of gain but in this worldly sense. If it does not lead to a "surprise" party, if he does not get a new pair of boots, or a vote of thanks, it must be a failure. "But he won't gain any thing by it." Well, no, I don't suppose he could get four-and-sixpence a day for being hung, take the year round; but then he stands a chance to save a considerable part of his soul—and *such* a soul!—when *you* do not. No doubt you can get more in your market for a quart of milk than for a quart of blood, but that is not the market that heroes carry their blood to.

Such do not know that like the seed is the fruit, and that, in the moral world, when good seed is planted, good fruit is inevitable, and does not depend on our watering and cultivating; that when you plant, or bury, a hero in his field, a crop of heroes is sure to spring up. This is a seed of such force and vitality, that it does not ask our leave to germinate.

The momentary charge at Balaclava,[9] in obedience to a blundering command, proving what a perfect machine the soldier is, has, properly enough, been celebrated by a poet laureate; but the steady, and for the most part successful charge of this man, for some years, against the legions of Slavery, in obedience to an infinitely higher command, is as much more memorable than that, as an intelligent and conscientious man is superior to a machine. Do you think that that will go unsung?

[9]The charge by outnumbered British cavalry in the Crimean War of 1854, celebrated as "The Charge of the Light Brigade" in a well-known poem by Tennyson.

"Served him right"—"A dangerous man"—"He is undoubtedly insane." So they proceed to live their sane, and wise, and altogether admirable lives, reading their Plutarch a little, but chiefly pausing at that feat of Putnam,[10] who was let down into a wolf's den; and in this wise they nourish themselves for brave and patriotic deeds some time or other. The Tract Society could afford to print that story of Putnam. You might open the district schools with the reading of it, for there is nothing about Slavery or the Church in it; unless it occurs to the reader that some pastors are *wolves* in sheep's clothing. "The American Board of Commissioners for Foreign Missions" even, might dare to protest against *that* wolf. I have heard of boards, and of American boards, but it chances that I never heard of this particular lumber till lately. And yet I hear of Northern men, women, and children, by families, buying a "life membership" in such societies as these;—a life-membership in the grave! You can get buried cheaper than that.

Our foes are in our midst and all about us. There is hardly a house but is divided against itself, for our foe is the all but universal woodenness of both head and heart, the want of vitality in man, which is the effect of our vice; and hence are begotten fear, superstition, bigotry, persecution, and slavery of all kinds. We are mere figure-heads upon a hulk, with livers in the place of hearts. The curse is the worship of idols, which at length changes the worshipper into a stone image himself; and the New Englander is just as much an idolater as the Hindoo. This man was an exception, for he did not set up even a political graven image between him and his God.

A church that can never have done with excommunicating Christ while it exists! Away with your broad and flat churches, and your narrow and tall churches! Take a step forward, and invent a new style of out-houses. Invent a salt that will save you, and defend our nostrils.

The modern Christian is a man who has consented to say all the prayers in the liturgy, provided you will let him go straight to bed and sleep quietly afterward. All his prayers begin with "Now I lay me down to sleep," and he is forever looking forward to the time when he shall go to his "*long* rest." He has consented to perform certain old established charities, too, after a fashion, but he does not wish to hear of any new-fangled ones; he doesn't wish to have any supplementary articles added to the contract, to fit it to the present time. He shows the whites of his eyes on the Sabbath, and the blacks all the rest of the week. The evil is not merely a stagnation of blood, but a stagnation of spirit. Many, no doubt, are well disposed, but sluggish by constitution and by habit, and they cannot conceive of a man who is actuated by higher motives than they are. Accordingly they pronounce this man insane, for they know that *they* could never act as he does, as long as they are themselves.

We dream of foreign countries, of other times and races of men, placing them at a distance in history or space; but let some significant event like the present occur in our midst, and we discover, often, this distance and this strangeness between us and our nearest neighbors. *They* are our Austrias, and Chinas, and South Sea Islands. Our crowded society becomes well spaced all at once, clean and handsome to the eye, a city of magnificent distances. We discover why it was that we never got beyond

[10]Israel Putnam, a hero of the American Revolution, allegedly crawled into a cave at night and killed a savage wolf. Thoreau in this passage is ridiculing religious organizations and individuals who fail to take a stand—as Brown had done—against slavery.

compliments and surfaces with them before; we become aware of as many versts between us and them as there are between a wandering Tartar and a Chinese town. The thoughtful man becomes a hermit in the thorough-fares of the marketplace. Impassable seas suddenly find their level between us, or dumb steppes stretch themselves out there. It is the difference of constitution, of intelligence, and faith, and not streams and mountains, that make the true and impassable boundaries between individuals and between states. None but the like-minded can come plenipotentiary to our court.

I read all the newspapers I could get within a week after this event, and I do not remember in them a single expression of sympathy for these men. I have since seen one noble statement, in a Boston paper, not editorial. Some voluminous sheets decided not to print the full report of Brown's words to the exclusion of other matter. It was as if a publisher should reject the manuscript of the New Testament, and print Wilson's last speech.[11] The same journal which contained this pregnant news, was chiefly filled, in parallel columns, with the reports of the political conventions that were being held. But the descent to them was too steep. They should have been spared this contrast, been printed in an extra at least. To turn from the voices and deeds of earnest men to the *cackling* of political conventions! Office seekers and speech-makers, who do not so much as lay an honest egg, but wear their breasts bare upon an egg of chalk! Their great game is the game of straws, or rather that universal aboriginal game of the platter, at which the Indians cried *hub, bub!*[12] Exclude the reports of religious and political conventions, and publish the words of a living man.

But I object not so much to what they have omitted as to what they have inserted. Even the *Liberator*[13] called it "a misguided, wild, and apparently insane . . . effort." As for the herd of newspapers and magazines, I do not chance to know an editor in the country who will deliberately print anything which he knows will ultimately and permanently reduce the number of his subscribers. They do not believe that it would be expedient. How then can they print truth? If we do not say pleasant things, they argue, nobody will attend to us. And so they do like some travelling auctioneers, who sing an obscene song in order to draw a crowd around them. Republican editors, obliged to get their sentences ready for the morning edition, and accustomed to look at every thing by the twilight of politics, express no admiration, nor true sorrow even, but call these men "deluded fanatics"—"mistaken men"—"insane," or "crazed." It suggests what a *sane* set of editors we are blessed with, *not* "mistaken men"; who know very well on which side their bread is buttered, at least.

A man does a brave and humane deed, and at once, on all sides, we hear people and parties declaring, "I didn't do it, nor countenance *him* to do it, in any conceivable way. It can't be fairly inferred from my past career." I, for one, am not interested to hear you define your position. I don't know that I ever was, or ever shall be. I think it is mere egotism, or impertinent at this time. Ye needn't take so much pains to wash your skirts of him. No intelligent man will ever be convinced that he was any creature of yours. He went and came, as he himself informs us, "under the auspices of

[11]Wilson was a senator from Massachusetts.

[12]*Hub, bub* was a name applied by New Englanders to a native Indian game played with bones.

[13]The *Liberator* was the best known and most radical of the Abolitionist newspapers. William Lloyd Garrison was founder and editor.

John Brown and nobody else." The Republican party does not perceive how many his *failure* will make to vote more correctly than they would have them. They have counted the votes of Pennsylvania & Co., but they have not correctly counted Captain Brown's vote. He has taken the wind out of their sails, the little wind they had, and they may as well lie to and repair.

What though he did not belong to your clique! Though you may not approve of his method or his principles, recognize his magnanimity. Would you not like to claim kindredship with him in that, though in no other thing he is like, or likely, to you? Do you think that you would lose your reputation so? What you lost at the spile, you would gain at the bung.[14]

If they do not mean all this, then they do not speak the truth, and say what they mean. They are simply at their old tricks still.

"It was always conceded to him," *says one who calls him crazy,* "that he was a conscientious man, very modest in his demeanor, apparently inoffensive, until the subject of Slavery was introduced, when he would exhibit a feeling of indignation unparalleled."

The slave-ship is on her way, crowded with its dying victims; new cargoes are being added in mid ocean; a small crew of slaveholders, countenanced by a large body of passengers, is smothering four millions under the hatches, and yet the politician asserts that the only proper way by which deliverance is to be obtained, is by "the quiet diffusion of the sentiments of humanity," without any "outbreak." As if the sentiments of humanity were ever found unaccompanied by its deeds, and you could disperse them, all finished to order, the pure article, as easily as water with a watering-pot, and so lay the dust. What is that that I hear cast overboard? The bodies of the dead that have found deliverance. That is the way we are "diffusing" humanity, and its sentiments with it.

Prominent and influential editors, accustomed to deal with politicians, men of an infinitely lower grade, say, in their ignorance, that he acted "on the principle of revenge." They do not know the man. They must enlarge themselves to conceive of him. I have no doubt that the time will come when they will begin to see him as he was. They have got to conceive of a man of faith and of religious principle, and not a politician or an Indian; of a man who did not wait till he was personally interfered with, or thwarted in some harmless business, before he gave his life to the cause of the oppressed.

If Walker[15] may be considered the representative of the South, I wish I could say that Brown was the representative of the North. He was a superior man. He did not value his bodily life in comparison with ideal things. He did not recognize unjust human laws, but resisted them as he was bid. For once we are lifted out of the trivialness and dust of politics into the region of truth and manhood. No man in America has ever stood up so persistently and effectively for the dignity of human nature, knowing himself for a man, and the equal of any and all governments. In that sense he was the most American of us all. He needed no babbling lawyer, making false issues, to defend him. He was more than a match for all the judges that American

[14]In other words, what you lose of the liquid at the top (vent) hole of a barrel, you gain at the spout (below) where the liquid is drawn.

[15]Robert Walker was Governor of the Kansas Territory.

voters, or office-holders of whatever grade, can create. He could not have been tried by a jury of his peers, because his peers did not exist. When a man stands up serenely against the condemnation and vengeance of mankind, rising above them literally *by a whole body,*—even though he were of late the vilest murderer, who has settled that matter with himself,—the spectacle is a sublime one,—didn't ye know it, ye Liberators, ye Tribunes, ye Republicans?[16]—and we become criminal in comparison. Do yourselves the honor to recognize him. He needs none of your respect.

As for the Democratic journals, they are not human enough to affect me at all. I do not feel indignation at any thing they may say.

I am aware that I anticipate a little, that he was still, at the last accounts, alive in the hands of his foes; but that being the case, I have all along found myself thinking and speaking of him as physically dead.

I do not believe in erecting statues to those who still live in our hearts, whose bones have not yet crumbled in the earth around us, but I would rather see the statue of Captain Brown in the Massachusetts State-House yard, than that of any other man whom I know. I rejoice that I live in this age—that I am his contemporary.

What a contrast, when we turn to that political party which is so anxiously shuffling him and his plot out of its way,[17] and looking around for some available slaveholder, perhaps, to be its candidate, at least for one who will execute the Fugitive Slave Law, and all those other unjust laws which he took up arms to annul![18]

Insane! A father and six sons, and one son-in-law, and several more men besides,—as many at least as twelve disciples,—all struck with insanity at once; while the sane tyrant holds with a firmer gripe than ever his four millions of slaves, and a thousand sane editors, his abettors, are saving their country and their bacon! Just as insane were his efforts in Kansas. Ask the tyrant who is his most dangerous foe, the sane man or the insane. Do the thousands who know him best, who have rejoiced at his deeds in Kansas, and have afforded him material aid there, think him insane? Such a use of this word is a mere trope with most who persist in using it, and I have no doubt that many of the rest have already in silence retracted their words.

Read his admirable answers to Mason and others. How they are dwarfed and defeated by the contrast! On the one side, half brutish, half timid questioning; on the other, truth, clear as lightning, crashing into their obscene temples. They are made to stand with Pilate, and Gessler, and the Inquisition.[19] How ineffectual their speech and action! and what a void their silence! They are but helpless tools in this great work. It was no human power that gathered them about this preacher.

What have Massachusetts and the North sent a few *sane* representatives to Congress for, of late years?—to declare with effect what kind of sentiments? All their speeches put together and boiled down,—and probably they themselves will confess it,—do not match for manly directness and force, and for simple truth, the few

[16]Liberators, Tribunes, Republicans: names of three New England newspapers.

[17]"That political party," *i.e.,* the newly organized Republican Party.

[18]The Fugitive Slave Law of 1850 required northern states and their citizens to aid in capturing black slaves fleeing from their southern masters.

[19]Pontius Pilate, the Roman governor of Palestine, allowed Jesus to be crucified. Gessler, an Austrian tyrant, was killed by William Tell. The Inquisition of the Roman Catholic Church oppressed dissenters, executing many.

casual remarks of crazy John Brown, on the floor of the Harper's Ferry engine house;—that man whom you are about to hang, to send to the other world, though not to represent *you* there. No, he was not our representative in any sense. He was too fair a specimen of a man to represent the like of us. Who, then, *were* his constituents? If you read his words understandingly you will find out. In his case there is no idle eloquence, no made, nor maiden speech, no compliments to the oppressor. Truth is his inspirer, and earnestness the polisher of his sentences. He could afford to lose his Sharps' rifles, while he retained his faculty of speech, a Sharps' rifle of infinitely surer and longer range.

And the *New York Herald* reports the conversation *"verbatim"!* It does not know of what undying words it is made the vehicle.

I have no respect for the penetration of any man who can read the report of that conversation, and still call the principal in it insane. It has the ring of a saner sanity than an ordinary discipline and habits of life, than an ordinary organization, secure. Take any sentence of it—"Any questions that I can honorably answer, I will; not otherwise. So far as I am myself concerned, I have told every thing truthfully. I value my word, sir." The few who talk about his vindictive spirit, while they really admire his heroism, have no test by which to detect a noble man, no amalgam to combine with his pure gold. They mix their own dross with it.

It is a relief to turn from these slanders to the testimony of his more truthful, but frightened, jailers and hangmen. Governor Wise speaks far more justly and appreciatingly of him than any Northern editor, or politician, or public personage, that I chance to have heard from. I know that you can afford to hear him again on this subject. He says: "They are themselves mistaken who take him to be a madman. . . . He is cool, collected, and indomitable, and it is but just to him to say, that he was humane to his prisoners. . . . And he inspired me with great trust in his integrity as a man of truth. He is a fanatic, vain and garrulous," (I leave that part to Mr. Wise) "but firm, truthful, and intelligent. His men, too, who survive, are like him. . . . Colonel Washington[20] says that he was the coolest and firmest man he ever saw in defying danger and death. With one son dead by his side, and another shot through, he felt the pulse of his dying son with one hand, and held his rifle with the other, and commanded his men with the utmost composure, encouraging them to be firm, and to sell their lives as dear as they could. Of the three white prisoners, Brown, Stevens, and Coppoc,[21] it was hard to say which was most firm. . . ."

Almost the first Northern men whom the slaveholder has learned to respect!

The testimony of Mr. Vallandigham, though less valuable, is of the same purport, that "it is vain to underrate either the man or his conspiracy. . . . He is the farthest possible remove from the ordinary ruffian, fanatic, or madman."

"All is quiet at Harper's Ferry," say the journals. What is the character of that calm which follows when the law and the slaveholder prevail? I regard this event as a touchstone designed to bring out, with glaring distinctness, the character of this government. We needed to be thus assisted to see it by the light of history. It needed to see itself. When a government puts forth its strength on the side of injustice, as ours to maintain Slavery and kill the liberators of the slave, it reveals itself a merely

[20]Colonel Washington was a landowner near Harpers Ferry, kidnapped by Brown.

[21]Stevens and Coppoc were two of Brown's men. They were captured and later executed.

brute force, or worse, a demoniacal force. It is the head of the Plug Uglies.[22] It is more manifest than ever that tyranny rules. I see this government to be effectually allied with France and Austria in oppressing mankind. There sits a tyrant holding fettered four millions of slaves; here comes their heroic liberator. This most hypocritical and diabolical government looks up from its seat on the gasping four millions, and inquires with an assumption of innocence, "What do you assault me for? Am I not an honest man? Cease agitation on this subject, or I will make a slave of you, too, or else hang you."

We talk about a *representative* government; but what a monster of a government is that where the noblest faculties of the mind, and the *whole* heart, are not *represented.* A semi-human tiger or ox, stalking over the earth, with its heart taken out and the top of its brain shot away. Heroes have fought well on their stumps when their legs were shot off, but I never heard of any good done by such a government as that.

The only government that I recognize,—and it matters not how few are at the head of it, or how small its army,—is that power that establishes justice in the land, never that which establishes injustice. What shall we think of a government to which all the truly brave and just men in the land are enemies, standing between it and those whom it oppresses? A government that pretends to be Christian and crucifies a million Christs every day!

Treason! Where does such treason take its rise? I cannot help thinking of you as you deserve, ye governments. Can you dry up the fountains of thought? High treason, when it is resistance to tyranny here below, has its origin in, and is first committed by the power that makes and forever recreates man. When you have caught and hung all these human rebels, you have accomplished nothing but your own guilt, for you have not struck at the fountain head. You presume to contend with a foe against whom West Point cadets and rifled cannon *point* not. Can all the art of the cannon-founder tempt matter to turn against its maker? Is the form in which the founder thinks he casts it more essential than the constitution of it and of himself?

The United States have a coffle of four millions of slaves. They are determined to keep them in this condition; and Massachusetts is one of the confederated overseers to prevent their escape. Such are not all the inhabitants of Massachusetts, but such are they who rule and are obeyed here. It was Massachusetts, as well as Virginia, that put down this insurrection at Harper's Ferry. She sent the marines there, and she will have to pay the penalty of her sin.

Suppose that there is a society in this State that out of its own purse and magnanimity saves all the fugitive slaves that run to us, and protects our colored fellow-citizens, and leaves the other work to the Government, so-called. Is not that government fast losing its occupation, and becoming contemptible to mankind? If private men are obliged to perform the offices of government, to protect the weak and dispense justice, then the government becomes only a hired man, or clerk, to perform menial or indifferent services. Of course, that is but the shadow of a government whose existence necessitates a Vigilant Committee.[23] What should we think of the oriental Cadi even, behind whom worked in secret a Vigilant Committee? But such is the character of our Northern States generally; each has its Vigilant Committee.

[22]*I.e.,* gangs of ruffians.

[23]*I.e.,* a citizen group assuming law enforcement responsibilities. Thoreau is thinking of the abolitionists.

And, to a certain extent, these crazy governments recognize and accept this relation. They say, virtually, "We'll be glad to work for you on these terms, only don't make a noise about it." And thus the government, its salary being insured, withdraws into the back shop, taking the constitution with it, and bestows most of its labor on repairing that. When I hear it at work sometimes, as I go by, it reminds me, at best, of those farmers who in winter contrive to turn a penny by following the coopering business. And what kind of spirit is their barrel made to hold? They speculate in stocks, and bore holes in mountains, but they are not competent to lay out even a decent highway. The only *free* road, the Underground Railroad,[24] is owned and managed by the Vigilant Committee. *They* have tunnelled under the whole breadth of the land. Such a government is losing its power and respectability as surely as water runs out of a leaky vessel, and is held by one that can contain it.

I hear many condemn these men because they were so few. When were the good and the brave ever in a majority? Would you have had him wait till that time came?—till you and I came over to him? The very fact that he had no rabble or troop of hirelings about him would alone distinguish him from ordinary heroes. His company was small indeed, because few could be found worthy to pass muster. Each one who there laid down his life for the poor and oppressed, was a picked man, called out of many thousands, if not millions; apparently a man of principle, of rare courage and devoted humanity, ready to sacrifice his life at any moment for the benefit of his fellow man. It may be doubted if there were as many more their equals in these respects in all the country—I speak of his followers only—for their leader, no doubt, scoured the land far and wide, seeking to swell his troop. These alone were ready to step between the oppressor and the oppressed. Surely, they were the very best men you could select to be hung. That was the greatest compliment which this country could pay them. They were ripe for her gallows. She has tried a long time, she has hung a good many, but never found the right one before.

When I think of him, and his six sons, and his son in law,—not to enumerate the others,—enlisted for this fight; proceeding coolly, reverently, humanely to work, for months if not years, sleeping and waking upon it, summering and wintering the thought, without expecting any reward but a good conscience, while almost all America stood ranked on the other side, I say again that it affects me as a sublime spectacle. If he had had any journal advocating *"his cause,"* any organ as the phrase is, monotonously and wearisomely playing the same old tune, and then passing round the hat, it would have been fatal to his efficiency. If he had acted in any way so as to be let alone by the government, he might have been suspected. It was the fact that the tyrant must give place to him, or he to the tyrant, that distinguished him from all the reformers of the day that I know.

It was his peculiar doctrine that a man has a perfect right to interfere by force with the slaveholder, in order to rescue the slave. I agree with him. They who are continually shocked by slavery have some right to be shocked by the violent death of the slaveholder, but no others. Such will be more shocked by his life than by his death. I shall not be forward to think him mistaken in his method who quickest succeeds to

[24]The Underground Railroad consisted of a loose chain of people dedicated to aiding runaway slaves to escape to Canada.

liberate the slave. I speak for the slave when I say, that I prefer the philanthropy of Captain Brown to that philanthropy which neither shoots me nor liberates me. At any rate, I do not think it is quite sane for one to spend his whole life in talking or writing about this matter, unless he is continuously inspired, and I have not done so. A man may have other affairs to attend to. I do not wish to kill nor to be killed, but I can foresee circumstances in which both these things would be by me unavoidable. We preserve the so-called "peace" of our community by deeds of petty violence every day. Look at the policeman's billy and hand cuffs! Look at the jail! Look at the gallows! Look at the chaplain of the regiment! We are hoping only to live safely on the outskirts of *this* provisional army. So we defend ourselves and our hen roosts, and maintain slavery. I know that the mass of my countrymen think that the only righteous use that can be made of Sharps' rifles and revolvers is to fight duels with them, when we are insulted by other nations, or to hunt Indians, or shoot fugitive slaves with them, or the like. I think that for once the Sharps' rifles and the revolvers were employed in a righteous cause. The tools were in the hands of one who could use them.

The same indignation that is said to have cleared the temple once will clear it again.[25] The question is not about the weapon, but the spirit in which you use it. No man has appeared in America as yet who loved his fellow man so well, and treated him so tenderly. He lived for him. He took up his life and he laid it down for him. What sort of violence is that which is encouraged, not by soldiers but by peaceable citizens, not so much by lay-men as by ministers of the gospel, and not so much by the fighting sects as by the Quakers, and not so much by Quaker men as by Quaker women?

This event advertises me that there is such a fact as death—the possibility of a man's dying. It seems as if no man had ever died in America before, for in order to die you must first have lived. I don't believe in the hearses and palls and funerals that they have had. There was no death in the case, because there had been no life; they merely rotted or sloughed off, pretty much as they had rotted or sloughed along. No temple's vail was rent,[26] only a hole dug somewhere. Let the dead bury their dead. The best of them fairly ran down like a clock. Franklin—Washington—they were let off without dying; they were merely missing one day. I hear a good many pretend that they are going to die;—or that they have died for aught that I know. Nonsense! I'll defy them to do it. They haven't got life enough in them. They'll deliquesce like fungi, and keep a hundred eulogists mopping the spot where they left off. Only half a dozen or so have died since the world began. Do you think that you are going to die, sir? No! there's no hope of you. You haven't got your lesson yet. You've got to stay after school. We make a needless ado about capital punishment—taking lives, when there is no life to take. *Memento mori!*[27] We don't understand that sublime sentence which some worthy got sculptured on his gravestone once. We've interpreted it in a grovelling and snivelling sense; we've wholly forgotten how to die.

But be sure you do die, nevertheless. Do your work, and finish it. If you know how to begin, you will know when to end.

[25]Christ, in anger, drove the money-changers from the temple in Jerusalem.

[26]According to the New Testament, when Christ died on the cross the veil of the temple was torn.

[27]Remember that you must die.

These men, in teaching us how to die, have at the same time taught us how to live. If this man's acts and words do not create a revival, it will be the severest possible satire on the acts and words that do. It is the best news that America has ever heard. It has already quickened the feeble pulse of the North, and infused more and more generous blood into her veins and heart, than any number of years of what is called commercial and political prosperity could. How many a man who was lately contemplating suicide has now something to live for!

One writer says that Brown's peculiar monomania made him to be "dreaded by the Missourians as a supernatural being." Sure enough, a hero in the midst of us cowards is always so dreaded. He is just that thing. He shows himself superior to nature. He has a spark of divinity in him.

"Unless above himself he can
Erect himself, how poor a thing is man!"

Newspaper editors argue also that it is a proof of his *insanity* that he thought he was appointed to do this work which he did—that he did not suspect himself for a moment! They talk as if it were impossible that a man could be "divinely appointed" in these days to do any work whatever; as if vows and religion were out of date as connected with any man's daily work,—as if the agent to abolish Slavery could only be somebody appointed by the President, or by some political party. They talk as if a man's death were a failure, and his continued life, be it of whatever character, were a success.

When I reflect to what a cause this man devoted himself, and how religiously, and then reflect to what cause his judges and all who condemn him so angrily and fluently devote themselves, I see that they are as far apart as the heavens and earth are asunder.

The amount of it is, our *"leading men"* are a harmless kind of folk, and they know *well enough* that *they* were not divinely appointed, but elected by the votes of their party.

Who is it whose safety requires that Captain Brown be hung? Is it indispensable to any Northern man? Is there no resource but to cast these men also to the Minotaur?[28] If you do not wish it say so distinctly. While these things are being done, beauty stands veiled and music is a screeching lie. Think of him—of his rare qualities! such a man as it takes ages to make, and ages to understand; no mock hero, nor the representative of any party. A man such as the sun may not rise upon again in this benighted land. To whose making went the costliest material, the finest adamant; sent to be the redeemer of those in captivity. And the only use to which you can put him is to hang him at the end of a rope! You who pretend to care for Christ crucified, consider what you are about to do to him who offered himself to be the savior of four millions of men.

Any man knows when he is justified, and all the wits in the world cannot enlighten him on that point. The murderer always knows that he is justly punished; but when a government takes the life of a man without the consent of his conscience, it is an audacious government, and is taking a step towards its own dissolution. Is it not

[28]A monster in Greek mythology who devoured youths.

possible that an individual may be right and a government wrong? Are laws to be enforced simply because they were made? or declared by any number of men to be good, if they are *not* good? Is there any necessity for a man's being a tool to perform a deed of which his better nature disapproves? Is it the intention of law-makers that *good* men shall be hung ever? Are judges to interpret the law according to the letter, and not the spirit? What right have *you* to enter into a compact with yourself that you *will* do thus or so, against the light within you? Is it for *you* to *make up* your mind—to form any resolution whatever—and not accept the convictions that are forced upon you, and which ever pass your understanding? I do not believe in lawyers, in that mode of attacking or defending a man, because you descend to meet the judge on his own ground, and, in cases of the highest importance, it is of no consequence whether a man breaks a human law or not. Let lawyers decide trivial cases. Business men may arrange that among themselves. If they were the interpreters of the everlasting laws which rightfully bind man, that would be another thing. A counterfeiting law-factory, standing half in a slave land and half in a free! What kind of laws for free men can you expect from that?

I am here to plead his cause with you. I plead not for his life, but for his character—his immortal life; and so it becomes your cause wholly, and is not his in the least. Some eighteen hundred years ago Christ was crucified; this morning, perchance, Captain Brown was hung. These are the two ends of a chain which is not without its links. He is not Old Brown any longer; he is an Angel of Light.

I see now that it was necessary that the bravest and humanest man in all the country should be hung. Perhaps he saw it himself. I *almost fear* that I may yet hear of his deliverance, doubting if a prolonged life, if *any* life, can do as much good as his death.

"Misguided"! "Garrulous"! "Insane"! "Vindictive"! So ye write in your easy chairs, and thus the wounded responds from the floor of the Armory, clear as a cloudless sky, true as the voice of nature is: "No man sent me here; it was my own prompting and that of my Maker. I acknowledge no master in human form."

And in what a sweet and noble strain he proceeds, addressing his captors, who stand over him: "I think, my friends, you are guilty of a great wrong against God and humanity, and it would be perfectly right for any one to interfere with you so far as to free those you wilfully and wickedly hold in bondage."

And referring to his movement: "It is, in my opinion, the greatest service a man can render to God."

"I pity the poor in bondage that have none to help them; that is why I am here; not to gratify any personal animosity, revenge, or vindictive spirit. It is my sympathy with the oppressed and the wronged, that are as good as you, and as precious in the sight of God."

You don't know your testament when you see it.

"I want you to understand that I respect the rights of the poorest and weakest of colored people, oppressed by the slave power, just as much as I do those of the most wealthy and powerful."

"I wish to say, furthermore, that you had better, all you people at the South, prepare yourselves for a settlement of that question, that must come up for settlement sooner than you are prepared for it. The sooner you are prepared the better. You may dispose of me very easily. I am nearly disposed of now; but this question is still to be settled—this negro question, I mean; the end of that is not yet."

I foresee the time when the painter will paint that scene, no longer going to Rome for a subject;[29] the poet will sing it; the historian record it; and, with the Landing of the Pilgrims and the Declaration of Independence, it will be the ornament of some future national gallery, when at least the present form of Slavery shall be no more here. We shall then be at liberty to weep for Captain Brown. Then, and not till then, we will take our revenge.

1860

Walking

I wish to speak a word for Nature, for absolute freedom and wildness, as contrasted with a freedom and culture merely civil,—to regard man as an inhabitant, or a part and parcel of Nature, rather than a member of society. I wish to make an extreme statement, if so I may make an emphatic one, for there are enough champions of civilization: the minister, and the school-committee, and every one of you will take care of that.

I have met with but one or two persons in the course of my life who understood the art of Walking, that is, of taking walks,—who had a genius, so to speak, for *sauntering:* which word is beautifully derived "from idle people who roved about the country, in the Middle Ages, and asked charity, under pretence of going *à la Sainte Terre,*" to the Holy Land, till the children exclaimed, "There goes a *Sainte-Terrer,*" a Saunterer,—a Holy-Lander. They who never go to the Holy Land in their walks, as they pretend, are indeed mere idlers and vagabonds; but they who do go there are saunterers in the good sense, such as I mean. Some, however, would derive the word from *sans terre,* without land or a home, which, therefore, in the good sense, will mean, having no particular home, but equally at home everywhere. For this is the secret of successful sauntering. He who sits still in a house all the time may be the greatest vagrant of all; but the saunterer, in the good sense, is no more vagrant than the meandering river, which is all the while sedulously seeking the shortest course to the sea. But I prefer the first, which, indeed, is the most probable derivation. For every walk is a sort of crusade, preached by some Peter the Hermit in us, to go forth and reconquer this Holy Land from the hands of the Infidels.[1]

It is true, we are but faint-hearted crusaders, even the walkers, nowadays, who undertake no perservering, never-ending enterprises. Our expeditions are but tours, and come round again at evening to the old hearth-side from which we set out. Half the walk is but retracing our steps. We should go forth on the shortest walk, perchance, in the spirit of undying adventure, never to return,—prepared to send back our embalmed hearts only as relics to our desolate kingdoms. If you are ready to leave father and mother, and brother and sister, and wife and child and friends, and

[29]John Stewart Curry's famous mural of Brown with the flowing beard would seem to bear out Thoreau's prophecy.

[1]Peter the Hermit was a zealot who led an unsuccessful crusade to Jerusalem in 1096 to free the Holy Land from the "infidels."

never see them again,[2]—if you have paid your debts, and made your will, and settled all your affairs, and are a free man, then you are ready for a walk.

To come down to my own experience, my companion and I, for I sometimes have a companion, take pleasure in fancying ourselves knights of a new, or rather an old, order,—not Equestrians or Chevaliers, not Ritters or Riders,[3] but Walkers, a still more ancient and honorable class, I trust. The chivalric and heroic spirit which once belonged to the Rider seems now to reside in, or perchance to have subsided into, the Walker,—not the Knight, but Walker Errant.[4] He is a sort of fourth estate,[5] outside of Church and State and People.

We have felt that we almost alone hereabouts practised this noble art; though, to tell the truth, at least, if their own assertions are to be received, most of my townsmen would fain walk sometimes, as I do, but they cannot. No wealth can buy the requisite leisure, freedom, and independence, which are the capital in this profession. It comes only by the grace of God. It requires a direct dispensation from Heaven to become a walker. You must be born into the family of the Walkers. *Ambulator nascitur, non fit.*[6] Some of my townsmen, it is true, can remember and have described to me some walks which they took ten years ago, in which they were so blessed as to lose themselves for half an hour in the woods; but I know very well that they have confined themselves to the highway ever since, whatever pretensions they may make to belong to this select class. No doubt they were elevated for a moment as by the reminiscence of a previous state of existence, when even they were foresters and outlaws.

"When he came to grene wode,
  In a mery mornynge,
There he herde the notes small

  Of byrdes mery syngynge.
"It is ferre gone, sayd Robyn,[7]
  That I was last here;
Me lyste a lytell for to shote
  At the donne dere."

I think that I cannot preserve my health and spirits, unless I spend four hours a day at least—and it is commonly more than that—sauntering through the woods and over the hills and fields, absolutely free from all worldly engagements. You may safely say, A penny for your thoughts, or a thousand pounds. When sometimes I am reminded that the mechanics and shopkeepers stay in their shops not only all the forenoon, but all the afternoon too, sitting with crossed legs, so many of them,—as if the legs were made to sit upon, and not to stand or walk upon,—I think that they deserve some credit for not having all committed suicide long ago.

[2]Christ so charged his disciples as a prerequisite to following Him.

[3]Thoreau may have been thinking of Karl Ritter, father of modern human geography. A Chevalier was a member of one of the orders of knighthood.

[4]Thoreau is punning on "Knight Errant," a knight who traveled in search of heroic exploits.

[5]The press.

[6]A walker is born, not made.

[7]Robyn (Robin Hood) was a legendary twelfth-century hero who lived in the forest and robbed the rich to give to the poor. He illegally hunted deer on the preserves of the nobility.

I, who cannot stay in my chamber for a single day without acquiring some rust, and when sometimes I have stolen forth for a walk at the eleventh hour of four o'clock in the afternoon, too late to redeem the day, when the shades of night were already beginning to be mingled with the daylight, have felt as if I had committed some sin to be atoned for,—I confess that I am astonished at the power of endurance, to say nothing of the moral insensibility, of my neighbors who confine themselves to shops and offices the whole day for weeks and months, ay, and years almost together. I know now what manner of stuff they are of,—sitting there now at three o'clock in the afternoon, as if it were three o'clock in the morning. Bonaparte[8] may talk of the three-o'clock-in-the-morning courage, but it is nothing to the courage which can sit down cheerfully at this hour in the afternoon over against one's self whom you have known all the morning, to starve out a garrison to whom you are bound by such strong ties of sympathy. I wonder that about this time, or say between four and five o'clock in the afternoon, too late for the morning papers and too early for the evening ones, there is not a general explosion heard up and down the street, scattering a legion of antiquated and housebred notions and whims to the four winds for an airing,—and so the evil cure itself.

How womankind, who are confined to the house still more than men, stand it I do not know; but I have ground to suspect that most of them do not *stand* it at all. When, early in a summer afternoon, we have been shaking the dust of the village from the skirts of our garments, making haste past those houses with purely Doric or Gothic fronts,[9] which have such an air of repose about them, my companion whispers that probably about these times their occupants are all gone to bed. Then it is that I appreciate the beauty and the glory of architecture, which itself never turns in, but forever stands out and erect, keeping watch over the slumberers.

No doubt temperament, and, above all, age, have a good deal to do with it. As a man grows older, his ability to sit still and follow in-door occupations increases. He grows vespertinal in his habits as the evening of life approaches, till at last he comes forth only just before sundown, and gets all the walk that he requires in half an hour.

But the walking of which I speak has nothing in it akin to taking exercise, as it is called, as the sick take medicine at stated hours,—as the swinging of dumbbells or chairs; but is itself the enterprise and adventure of the day. If you would get exercise, go in search of the springs of life. Think of a man's swinging dumbbells for his health, when those springs are bubbling up in far-off pastures unsought by him!

Moreover, you must walk like a camel, which is said to be the only beast which ruminates when walking.[10] When a traveller asked Wordsworth's servant to show him her master's study, she answered, "Here is his library, but his study is out of doors."

Living much out of doors, in the sun and wind, will no doubt produce a certain roughness of character,—will cause a thicker cuticle to grow over some of the finer qualities of our nature, as on the face and hands, or as severe manual labor robs the hands of some of their delicacy of touch. So staying in the house, on the other hand,

[8]Napoleon.

[9]Doric: an early architectural form developed by the Greeks. Gothic: the dominant architectural mode of the Middle Ages.

[10]Thoreau is using "ruminates" as a pun; the principal meaning he has in mind is "contemplates."

may produce a softness and smoothness, not to say thinness of skin, accompanied by an increased sensibility to certain impressions. Perhaps we should be more susceptible to some influences important to our intellectual and moral growth, if the sun had shone and the wind blown on us a little less; and no doubt it is a nice matter to proportion rightly the thick and thin skin. But methinks that is a scurf that will fall off fast enough,—that the natural remedy is to be found in the proportion which the night bears to the day, the winter to the summer, thought to experience. There will be so much the more air and sunshine in our thoughts. The callous palms of the laborer are conversant with finer tissues of self-respect and heroism, whose touch thrills the heart, than the languid fingers of idleness. That is mere sentimentality that lies abed by day and thinks itself white, far from the tan and callus of experience.

When we walk, we naturally go to the fields and woods: what would become of us, if we walked only in a garden or a mall? Even some sects of philosophers have felt the necessity of importing the woods to themselves, since they did not go to the woods. "They planted groves and walks of Platanes," where they took *subdiales ambulationes*[11] in porticos open to the air. Of course it is of no use to direct our steps to the woods, if they do not carry us thither. I am alarmed when it happens that I have walked a mile into the woods bodily, without getting there in spirit. In my afternoon walk I would fain forget all my morning occupations and my obligations to society. But it sometimes happens that I cannot easily shake off the village. The thought of some work will run in my head, and I am not where my body is,—I am out of my senses. In my walks I would fain return to my senses. What business have I in the woods, if I am thinking of something out of the woods? I suspect myself, and cannot help a shudder, when I find myself so implicated even in what are called good works,—for this may sometimes happen.

My vicinity affords many good walks; and though for so many years I have walked almost every day, and sometimes for several days together, I have not yet exhausted them. An absolutely new prospect is a great happiness, and I can still get this any afternoon. Two or three hours' walking will carry me to as strange a country as I expect ever to see. A single farm-house which I had not seen before is sometimes as good as the dominions of the King of Dahomey.[12] There is in fact a sort of harmony discoverable between the capabilities of the landscape within a circle of ten miles' radius, or the limits of an afternoon walk, and the threescore years and ten of human life. It will never become quite familiar to you.

Nowadays almost all man's improvements, so called, as the building of houses, and the cutting down of the forest and of all large trees, simply deform the landscape, and make it more and more tame and cheap. A people who would begin by burning the fences and let the forest stand! I saw the fences half consumed, their ends lost in the middle of the prairie, and some worldly miser with a surveyor looking after his bounds, while heaven had taken place around him, and he did not see the angels going to and fro, but was looking for an old post-hole in the midst of paradise. I looked again, and saw him standing in the middle of a boggy, stygian fen, surrounded by devils, and he had found his bounds without a doubt, three little stones, where a

[11]Walks in the open air.

[12]Presumably King Gezo of the West African kingdom whose economy was based on the export of slaves.

stake had been driven, and looking nearer, I saw that the Prince of Darkness[13] was his surveyor.

I can easily walk ten, fifteen, twenty, any number of miles, commencing at my own door, without going by any house, without crossing a road except where the fox and the mink do: first along by the river, and then the brook, and then the meadow and the wood-side. There are square miles in my vicinity which have no inhabitant. From many a hill I can see civilization and the abodes of man afar. The farmers and their works are scarcely more obvious than woodchucks and their burrows. Man and his affairs, church and state and school, trade and commerce, and manufactures and agriculture, even politics, the most alarming of them all,—I am pleased to see how little space they occupy in the landscape. Politics is but a narrow field, and that still narrower highway yonder leads to it. I sometimes direct the traveller thither. If you would go to the political world, follow the great road,—follow that market-man, keep his dust in your eyes, and it will lead you straight to it; for it, too, has its place merely, and does not occupy all space. I pass from it as from a beanfield into the forest, and it is forgotten. In one half-hour I can walk off to some portion of the earth's surface where a man does not stand from one year's end to another, and there, consequently, politics are not, for they are but as the cigar-smoke of a man.

The village is the place to which the roads tend, a sort of expansion of the highway, as a lake of a river. It is the body of which roads are the arms and legs,—a trivial or quadrivial place, the thoroughfare and ordinary of travellers. The word is from the Latin *villa,* which, together with *via,* a way, or more anciently *ved* and *vella,* Varro derives from *veho,* to carry, because the villa is the place to and from which things are carried. They who got their living by teaming were said *vellaturam facere.*[14] Hence, too, apparently, the Latin word *vilis* and our vile; also *villain.* This suggests what kind of degeneracy villagers are liable to. They are wayworn by the travel that goes by and over them, without travelling themselves.

Some do not walk at all; others walk in the highways; a few walk across lots. Roads are made for horses and men of business. I do not travel in them much, comparatively, because I am not in a hurry to get to any tavern or grocery or livery-stable or depot to which they lead. I am a good horse to travel, but not from choice a roadster. The landscape-painter uses the figures of men to mark a road. He would not make that use of my figure. I walk out into a Nature such as the old prophets and poets, Menu, Moses, Homer, Chaucer, walked in. You may name it America, but it is not America: neither Americus Vespucius,[15] nor Columbus, nor the rest were the discoverers of it. There is a truer account of it in mythology than in any history of America, so called, that I have seen.

However, there are a few old roads that may be trodden with profit, as if they led somewhere now that they are nearly discontinued. There is the Old Marlborough Road,[16] which does not go to Marlborough now, methinks, unless that is Marlborough where it carries me. I am the bolder to speak of it here, because I presume that there are one or two such roads in every town.

[13]Satan.

[14]Literally, "to make a cart."

[15]The Italian navigator who gave America its name.

[16]A deserted road that once led from Concord to Marlborough.

THE OLD MARLBOROUGH ROAD

Where they once dug for money,
But never found any;
Where sometimes Martial Miles
Singly flies,
And Elijah Wood,
I fear for no good:
No other man,
Save Elisha Dugan,—
O man of wild habits,
Partridges and rabbits,
Who hast no cares
Only to set snares,
Who liv'st all alone,
Close to the bone,
And where life is sweetest
Constantly eatest.
When the spring stirs my blood
With the instinct to travel,
I can get enough gravel
On the Old Marlborough Road.
Nobody repairs it,
For nobody wears it;
It is a living way,
As the Christians say.
Not many there be
Who enter therein,
Only the guests of the
Irishman Quin.
What is it, what is it,
But a direction out there,
And the bare possibility
Of going somewhere?
Great guide-boards of stone,
But travellers none;
Cenotaphs of the towns
Named on their crowns.
It is worth going to see
Where you *might* be.
What king
Did the thing,
I am still wondering;
Set up how or when,
By what selectmen,
Gourgas or Lee,
Clark or Darby?
They're a great endeavor
To be something forever;
Blank tablets of stone,

Where a traveller might groan,
And in one sentence
Grave all that is known;
Which another might read,
In his extreme need.
I know one or two
Lines that would do,
Literature that might stand
All over the land,
Which a man could remember
Till next December,
And read again in the spring,
After the thawing.
If with fancy unfurled
You leave your abode,
You may go round the world
By the Old Marlborough Road.

At present, in this vicinity, the best part of the land is not private property; the landscape is not owned, and the walker enjoys comparative freedom. But possibly the day will come when it will be partitioned off into so-called pleasure-grounds, in which a few will take a narrow and exclusive pleasure only,—when fences shall be multiplied, and man-traps and other engines invented to confine men to the *public* road, and walking over the surface of God's earth shall be construed to mean trespassing on some gentleman's grounds. To enjoy a thing exclusively is commonly to exclude yourself from the true enjoyment of it. Let us improve our opportunities, then, before the evil days come.

What is it that makes it so hard sometimes to determine whither we will walk? I believe that there is a subtle magnetism in Nature, which, if we unconsciously yield to it, will direct us aright. It is not indifferent to us which way we walk. There is a right way; but we are very liable from heedlessness and stupidity to take the wrong one. We would fain take that walk, never yet taken by us through this actual world, which is perfectly symbolical of the path which we love to travel in the interior and ideal world; and sometimes, no doubt, we find it difficult to choose our direction, because it does not yet exist distinctly in our idea.

When I go out of the house for a walk, uncertain as yet whither I will bend my steps, and submit myself to my instinct to decide for me, I find, strange and whimsical as it may seem, that I finally and inevitably settle southwest, toward some particular wood or meadow or deserted pasture or hill in that direction. My needle[17] is slow to settle,—varies a few degrees, and does not always point due southwest, it is true, and it has good authority for this variation, but it always settles between west and south-southwest. The future lies that way to me, and the earth seems more unexhausted and richer on that side. The outline which would bound my walks would be, not a circle, but a parabola, or rather like one of those cometary orbits which have been thought to be non-returning curves, in this case opening westward, in which my

[17]Thoreau means his inner "compass."

house occupies the place of the sun. I turn round and round irresolute sometimes for a quarter of an hour, until I decide, for the thousandth time, that I will walk into the southwest or west. Eastward I go only by force; but westward I go free. Thither no business leads me. It is hard for me to believe that I shall find fair landscapes or sufficient wildness and freedom behind the eastern horizon. I am not excited by the prospect of a walk thither; but I believe that the forest which I see in the western horizon stretches uninterruptedly towards the setting sun, and that there are no towns nor cities in it of enough consequence to disturb me. Let me live where I will, on this side is the city, on that the wilderness, and ever I am leaving the city more and more, and withdrawing into the wilderness. I should not lay so much stress on this fact, if I did not believe that something like this is the prevailing tendency of my countrymen. I must walk toward Oregon, and not toward Europe. And that way the nation is moving, and I may say that mankind progress from east to west. Within a few years we have witnessed the phenomenon of a southeastward migration, in the settlement of Australia; but this affects us as a retrograde movement, and, judging from the moral and physical character of the first generation of Australians, has not yet proved a successful experiment. The eastern Tartars[18] think that there is nothing west beyond Thibet. "The world ends there," say they; "beyond there is nothing but a shoreless sea." It is unmitigated East where they live.

We go eastward to realize history and study the works of art and literature, retracing the steps of the race; we go westward as into the future, with a spirit of enterprise and adventure. The Atlantic is a Lethean stream,[19] in our passage over which we have had an opportunity to forget the Old World and its institutions. If we do not succeed this time, there is perhaps one more chance for the race left before it arrives on the banks of the Styx;[20] and that is in the Lethe of the Pacific, which is three times as wide.

I know not how significant it is, or how far it is an evidence of singularity, that an individual should thus consent in his pettiest walk with the general movement of the race; but I know that something akin to the migratory instinct in birds and quadrupeds,—which, in some instances, is known to have affected the squirrel tribe, impelling them to a general and mysterious movement, in which they were seen, say some, crossing the broadest rivers, each on its particular chip, with its tail raised for a sail, and bridging narrower streams with their dead,—that something like the *furor* which affects the domestic cattle in the spring,[21] and which is referred to a worm in their tails,—affects both nations and individuals, either perennially or from time to time. Not a flock of wild geese cackles over our town, but it to some extent unsettles the value of real estate here, and, if I were a broker, I should probably take that disturbance into account.

[18]Nomads that once roamed over what is now Mongolia.

[19]In Greek mythology the river Lethe flowed in Hades. Persons who drank the water forgot the past.

[20]The Styx, in Greek mythology, was a river in the world of the dead.

[21]The *"furor"* Thoreau is speaking of results from the itching in the hides of cattle when eggs laid there by cattle flies begin to hatch. The cattle are very restless during this period in the spring.

"Than longen folk to gon on pilgrimages,
And palmeres for to seken strange strondes."[22]

Every sunset which I witness inspires me with the desire to go to a West as distant and as fair as that into which the sun goes down. He appears to migrate westward daily, and tempt us to follow him. He is the Great Western Pioneer whom the nations follow. We dream all night of those mountain-ridges in the horizon, though they may be of vapor only, which were last gilded by his rays. The island of Atlantis,[23] and the islands and gardens of the Hesperides, a sort of terrestrial paradise, appear to have been the Great West of the ancients, enveloped in mystery and poetry. Who has not seen in imagination, when looking into the sunset sky, the gardens of the Hesperides, and the foundation of all those fables?

Columbus felt the westward tendency more strongly than any before. He obeyed it, and found a New World for Castile and Leon. The herd of men in those days scented fresh pastures, from afar.

"And now the sun had stretched out all the hills,
And now was dropped into the western bay;
At last *he* rose, and twitched his mantle blue;
To-morrow to fresh woods and pastures new."[24]

Where on the globe can there be found an area of equal extent with that occupied by the bulk of our States, so fertile and so rich and varied in its productions, and at the same time so habitable by the European, as this is? Michaux,[25] who knew but part of them, says that "the species of large trees are much more numerous in North America than in Europe; in the United States there are more than one hundred and forty species that exceed thirty feet in height; in France there are but thirty that attain this size." Later botanists more than confirm his observations. Humboldt came to America to realize his youthful dreams of a tropical vegetation, and he beheld it in its greatest perfection in the primitive forests of the Amazon, the most gigantic wilderness on the earth, which he has so eloquently described. The geographer Guyot, himself a European, goes farther,—farther than I am ready to follow him; yet not when he says,—"As the plant is made for the animal, as the vegetable world is made for the animal world, America is made for the man of the Old World. . . . The man of the Old World sets out upon his way. Leaving the highlands of Asia, he descends from station to station towards Europe. Each of his steps is marked by a new civilization superior to the preceding, by a greater power of development. Arrived at the Atlantic, he pauses on the shore of this unknown ocean, the bounds of which he knows not, and turns upon his footprints for an instant." When he has exhausted the rich soil of Europe, and reinvigorated himself, "then recommences his adventurous career westward as in the earliest ages." So far Guyot.

[22]The quotation is from Chaucer's *Canterbury Tales* in which the characters narrate tales while pilgrimaging from London to Canterbury.

[23]Atlantis was, according to the ancients, a lost sunken island, often sought for. The Hesperides was an imaginary garden that produced golden apples.

[24]Thoreau quotes the final four lines of Milton's pastoral elegy, "Lycidas."

[25]André Michaux was a French botanist who traveled extensively in America; Alexander Humboldt was a German naturalist and traveler.

From this western impulse coming in contact with the barrier of the Atlantic sprang the commerce and enterprise of modern times. The younger Michaux, in his "Travels West of the Alleghanies in 1802," says that the common inquiry in the newly settled West was, "'From what part of the world have you come?' As if these vast and fertile regions would naturally be the place of meeting and common country of all the inhabitants of the globe."

To use an obsolete Latin word, I might say, *Ex Oriente lux; ex Occidente* FRUX. From the East light; from the West fruit.

Sir Francis Head, an English traveller and a Governor-General of Canada, tells us that "in both the northern and southern hemispheres of the New World, Nature has not only outlined her works on a larger scale, but has painted the whole picture with brighter and more costly colors than she used in delineating and in beautifying the Old World. . . . The heavens of America appear infinitely higher, the sky is bluer, the air is fresher, the cold is intenser, the moon looks larger, the stars are brighter, the thunder is louder, the lightning is vivider, the wind is stronger, the rain is heavier, the mountains are higher, the rivers longer, the forests bigger, the plains broader." This statement will do at least to set against Buffon's account of this part of the world and its productions.[26]

Linnaeus said long ago, "Nescio quæ facies *lœta, glabra* plantis Americanis: I know not what there is of joyous and smooth in the aspect of American plants"; and I think that in this country there are no, or at most very few, *Africanœ bestiœ,* African beasts, as the Romans called them, and that in this respect also it is peculiarly fitted for the habitation of man. We are told that within three miles of the centre of the East-Indian city of Singapore, some of the inhabitants are annually carried off by tigers; but the traveller can lie down in the woods at night almost anywhere in North America without fear of wild beasts.

These are encouraging testimonies. If the moon looks larger here than in Europe, probably the sun looks larger also. If the heavens of America appear infinitely higher, and the stars brighter, I trust that these facts are symbolical of the height to which the philosophy and poetry and religion of her inhabitants may one day soar. At length, perchance, the immaterial heaven will appear as much higher to the American mind, and the intimations that star it as much brighter. For I believe that climate does thus react on man,—as there is something in the mountain-air that feeds the spirit and inspires. Will not man grow to greater perfection intellectually as well as physically under these influences? Or is it unimportant how many foggy days there are in his life? I trust that we shall be more imaginative, that our thoughts will be clearer, fresher, and more ethereal, as our sky,—our understanding more comprehensive and broader, like our plains,—our intellect generally on a grander scale, like our thunder and lightning, our rivers and mountains and forests,—and our hearts shall even correspond in breadth and depth and grandeur to our inland seas. Perchance there will appear to the traveller something, he knows not what, of *lœta* and *glabra,* of joyous and serene, in our very faces. Else to what end does the world go on, and why was America discovered?

[26]Buffon was an eighteenth-century French writer on natural history. Linnaeus was a well known Swedish botanist.

To Americans I hardly need to say,—

"Westward the star of empire takes its way."

As a true patriot, I should be ashamed to think that Adam in paradise was more favorably situated on the whole than the backwoodsman in this country.

Our sympathies in Massachusetts are not confined to New England; though we may be estranged from the South, we sympathize with the West. There is the home of the younger sons, as among the Scandinavians they took to the sea for their inheritance. It is too late to be studying Hebrew; it is more important to understand even the slang of to-day.

Some months ago I went to see a panorama of the Rhine. It was like a dream of the Middle Ages. I floated down its historic stream in something more than imagination, under bridges built by the Romans, and repaired by later heroes, past cities and castles whose very names were music to my ears, and each of which was the subject of a legend. There were Ehrenbreitstein and Rolandseck and Coblentz, which I knew only in history. They were ruins that interested me chiefly. There seemed to come up from its waters and its vine-clad hills and valleys a hushed music as of Crusaders departing for the Holy Land. I floated along under the spell of enchantment, as if I had been transported to an heroic age, and breathed an atmosphere of chivalry.

Soon after, I went to see a panorama of the Mississippi, and as I worked my way up the river in the light of today, and saw the steamboats wooding up, counted the rising cities, gazed on the fresh ruins of Nauvoo,[27] beheld the Indians moving west across the stream, and, as before I had looked up the Moselle, now looked up the Ohio and the Missouri, and heard the legends of Dubuque and of Wenona's Cliff,—still thinking more of the future than of the past or present,—I saw that this was a Rhine stream of a different kind; that the foundations of castles were yet to be laid, and the famous bridges were yet to be thrown over the river; and I felt that *this was the heroic age itself,* though we know it not, for the hero is commonly the simplest and obscurest of men.

The West of which I speak is but another name for the Wild; and what I have been preparing to say is, that in Wildness is the preservation of the world. Every tree sends its fibres forth in search of the Wild. The cities import it at any price. Men plough and sail for it. From the forest and wilderness come the tonics and barks which brace mankind. Our ancestors were savages. The story of Romulus and Remus being suckled by a wolf is not a meaningless fable.[28] The founders of every State which has risen to eminence have drawn their nourishment and vigor from a similar wild source. It was because the children of the Empire were not suckled by the wolf that they were conquered and displaced by the children of the Northern forests who were.

I believe in the forest, and in the meadow, and in the night in which the corn grows. We require an infusion of hemlock-spruce or arbor-vitæ in our tea. There is

[27]The Illinois city founded by the Mormons; it was attacked and destroyed by their opponents.

[28]Romulus and Remus, according to Roman legend, were twin sons of the God, Mars. Discarded as infants, they were suckled by a she-wolf until found and raised by a shepherd.

a difference between eating and drinking for strength and from mere gluttony. The Hottentots eagerly devour the marrow of the koodoo and other antelopes raw, as a matter of course. Some of our Northern Indians eat raw the marrow of the Arctic reindeer, as well as various other parts, including the summits of the antlers, as long as they are soft. And herein, perchance, they have stolen a march on the cooks of Paris. They get what usually goes to feed the fire. This is probably better than stall-fed beef and slaughter-house pork to make a man of. Give me a wildness whose glance no civilization can endure,—as if we lived on the marrow of koodoos devoured raw.

There are some intervals which border the strain of the wood-thrush, to which I would migrate,—wild lands where no settler has squatted; to which, methinks, I am already acclimated.

The African hunter Cummings tells us that the skin of the eland, as well as that of most other antelopes just killed, emits the most delicious perfume of trees and grass. I would have every man so much like a wild antelope, so much a part and parcel of Nature, that his very person should thus sweetly advertise our senses of his presence, and remind us of those parts of Nature which he most haunts. I feel no disposition to be satirical, when the trapper's coat emits the odor of musquash even; it is a sweeter scent to me than that which commonly exhales from the merchant's or the scholar's garments. When I go into their wardrobes and handle their vestments, I am reminded of no grassy plains and flowery meads which they have frequented, but of dusty merchants' exchanges and libraries rather.

A tanned skin is something more than respectable, and perhaps olive is a fitter color than white for a man,—a denizen of the woods. "The pale white man!" I do not wonder that the African pitied him. Darwin the naturalist says, "A white man bathing by the side of a Tahitian was like a plant bleached by the gardener's art, compared with a fine, dark green one, growing vigorously in the open fields."

Ben Jonson exclaims,—

> "How near to good is what is fair!"

So I would say,—

> "How near to good is what is *wild!*"

Life consists with wildness. The most alive is the wildest. Not yet subdued to man, its presence refreshes him. One who pressed forward incessantly and never rested from his labors, who grew fast and made infinite demands on life, would always find himself in a new country or wilderness, and surrounded by the raw material of life. He would be climbing over the prostrate stems of primitive forest-trees.

Hope and the future for me are not in lawns and cultivated fields, not in towns and cities, but in the impervious and quaking swamps. When, formerly, I have analyzed my partiality for some farm which I had contemplated purchasing, I have frequently found that I was attracted solely by a few square rods of impermeable and unfathomable bog,—a natural sink in one corner of it. That was the jewel which dazzled me. I derive more of my subsistence from the swamps which surround my native town than from the cultivated gardens in the village. There are no richer parterres to my eyes than the dense beds of dwarf andromeda *(Cassandra calyculata)* which cover these tender places on the earth's surface. Botany cannot go farther than tell me the names of the shrubs which grow there,—the high-blueberry, panicled andromeda, lamb-kill, azalea, and rhodora,—all standing in the quaking sphagnum. I often think that I should like to have my house front on this mass of dull red bushes, omitting other flower plots and borders, transplanted spruce and trim box, even gravelled walks,—to have this fertile spot under my windows, not a few imported barrow-fulls of soil only to cover the sand which was thrown out in digging the cellar. Why not put my house, my parlor, behind this plot, instead of behind that meagre assemblage of curiosities, that poor apology for a Nature and Art, which I call my front-yard? It is an effort to clear up and make a decent appearance when the carpenter and mason have departed, though done as much for the passer-by as the dweller within. The most tasteful front-yard fence was never an agreeable object of study to me; the most elaborate ornaments, acorn-tops, or what not, soon wearied and disgusted me. Bring your sills up to the very edge of the swamp, then, (though it may not be the best place for a dry cellar,) so that there be no access on that side to citizens. Front-yards are not made to walk in, but, at most, through, and you could go in the back way.

Yes, though you may think me perverse, if it were proposed to me to dwell in the neighborhood of the most beautiful garden that ever human art contrived, or else of a dismal swamp, I should certainly decide for the swamp. How vain, then, have been all your labors, citizens, for me!

My spirits infallibly rise in proportion to the outward dreariness. Give me the ocean, the desert, or the wilderness! In the desert, pure air and solitude compensate for want of moisture and fertility. The traveller Burton says of it,—"Your *morale* improves; you become frank and cordial, hospitable and single-minded. . . . In the desert, spirituous liquors excite only disgust. There is a keen enjoyment in a mere animal existence." They who have been travelling long on the steppes of Tartary say,—"On reëntering cultivated lands, the agitation, perplexity, and turmoil of civilization oppressed and suffocated us; the air seemed to fail us, and we felt every moment as if about to die of asphyxia." When I would recreate myself, I seek the darkest wood, the thickest and most interminable, and, to the citizen, most dismal swamp. I enter a swamp as a sacred place,—a *sanctum sanctorum.* There is the strength, the marrow of Nature. The wild-wood covers the virgin mould,—and the same soil is good for men and for trees. A man's health requires as many acres of meadow to his prospect as his farm does loads of muck. There are the strong meats on which he feeds. A town is saved, not more by the righteous men in it than by the woods and swamps that surround it. A township where one primitive forest waves above, while another primitive forest rots below,—such a town is fitted to raise not only corn and potatoes, but poets and philosophers for the coming ages. In such a soil grew Homer and Confucius and the rest, and out of such a wilderness comes the Reformer eating locusts and wild honey.[29]

To preserve wild animals implies generally the creation of a forest for them to dwell in or resort to. So is it with man. A hundred years ago they sold bark in our

[29]In the New Testament John the Baptist, who lived in the wilderness where he ate locusts and wild honey, announced the coming of Christ.

streets peeled from our own woods. In the very aspect of those primitive and rugged trees, there was, methinks, a tanning principle which hardened and consolidated the fibres of men's thoughts. Ah! already I shudder for these comparatively degenerate days of my native village, when you cannot collect a load of bark of good thickness,—and we no longer produce tar and turpentine.

The civilized nations—Greece, Rome, England—have been sustained by the primitive forests which anciently rotted where they stand. They survive as long as the soil is not exhausted. Alas for human culture! little is to be expected of a nation, when the vegetable mould is exhausted, and it is compelled to make manure of the bones of its fathers. There the poet sustains himself merely by his own superfluous fat, and the philosopher comes down on his marrow-bones.

It is said to be the task of the American "to work the virgin soil," and that "agriculture here already assumes proportions unknown everywhere else." I think that the farmer displaces the Indian even because he redeems the meadow, and so makes himself stronger and in some respects more natural. I was surveying for a man the other day a single straight line one hundred and thirty-two rods long, through a swamp, at whose entrance might have been written the words which Dante read over the entrance to the infernal regions,—"Leave all hope, ye that enter,"—that is, of ever getting out again; where at one time I saw my employer actually up to his neck and swimming for his life in his property, though it was still winter. He had another similar swamp which I could not survey at all, because it was completely under water, and nevertheless, with regard to a third swamp, which I did *survey* from a distance, he remarked to me, true to his instincts, that he would not part with it for any consideration, on account of the mud which it contained. And that man intends to put a girdling ditch round the whole in the course of forty months, and so redeem it by the magic of his spade. I refer to him only as the type of a class.

The weapons with which we have gained our most important victories, which should be handed down as heirlooms from father to son, are not the sword and the lance, but the bush-whack, the turf-cutter, the spade, and the bog-hoe, rusted with the blood of many a meadow, and begrimed with the dust of many a hard-fought field. The very winds blew the Indian's cornfield into the meadow, and pointed out the way which he had not the skill to follow. He had no better implement with which to intrench himself in the land than a clamshell. But the farmer is armed with plough and spade.

In Literature it is only the wild that attracts us. Dulness is but another name for tameness. It is the uncivilized free and wild thinking in "Hamlet" and the "Iliad," in all the Scriptures and Mythologies, not learned in the schools, that delights us. As the wild duck is more swift and beautiful than the tame, so is the wild—the mallard—thought, which 'mid falling dews wings it way above the fens.[30] A truly good book is something as natural, and as unexpectedly and unaccountably fair and perfect, as a wild flower discovered on the prairies of the West or in the jungles of the East. Genius is a light which makes the darkness visible, like the lightning's flash, which perchance shatters the temple of knowledge itself,—and not a taper lighted at the hearth-stone of the race, which pales before the light of common day.

[30]Thoreau is paraphrasing from Bryant's poem "To a Waterfowl."

English literature, from the days of the minstrels to the Lake Poets,—Chaucer and Spenser and Milton, and even Shakespeare, included,—breathes no quite fresh and in this sense wild strain. It is an essentially tame and civilized literature, reflecting Greece and Rome. Her wilderness is a green-wood,—her wild man a Robin Hood. There is plenty of genial love of Nature, but not so much of Nature herself. Her chronicles inform us when her wild animals, but not when the wild man in her, became extinct.

The science of Humboldt is one thing, poetry is another thing. The poet to-day, notwithstanding all the discoveries of science, and the accumulated learning of mankind, enjoys no advantage over Homer.

Where is the literature which gives expression to Nature? He would be a poet who could impress the winds and streams into his service, to speak for him; who nailed words to their primitive senses, as farmers drive down stakes in the spring, which the frost has heaved; who derived his words as often as he used them,—transplanted them to his page with earth adhering to their roots; whose words were so true and fresh and natural that they would appear to expand like the buds at the approach of spring, though they lay half-smothered between two musty leaves in a library,—ay, to bloom and bear fruit there, after their kind, annually, for the faithful reader, in sympathy with surrounding Nature.

I do not know of any poetry to quote which adequately expresses this yearning for the Wild. Approached from this side, the best poetry is tame. I do not know where to find in any literature, ancient or modern, any account which contents me of that Nature with which even I am acquainted. You will perceive that I demand something which no Augustan nor Elizabethan age, which no *culture,* in short, can give. Mythology comes nearer to it than anything. How much more fertile a Nature, at least, has Grecian mythology its root in than English literature! Mythology is the crop which the Old World bore before its soil was exhausted, before the fancy and imagination were affected with blight; and which it still bears, wherever its pristine vigor is unabated. All other literatures endure only as the elms which overshadow our houses; but this is like the great dragon-tree of the Western Isles, as old as mankind, and, whether that does or not, will endure as long; for the decay of other literatures makes the soil in which it thrives.

The West is preparing to add its fables to those of the East. The valleys of the Ganges, the Nile, and the Rhine, having yielded their crop, it remains to be seen what the valleys of the Amazon, the Plate, the Orinoco, the St. Lawrence, and the Mississippi will produce. Perchance, when, in the course of ages, American liberty has become a fiction of the past,—as it is to some extent a fiction of the present,—the poets of the world will be inspired by American mythology.

The wildest dreams of wild men, even, are not the less true, though they may not recommend themselves to the sense which is most common among Englishmen and Americans to-day. It is not every truth that recommends itself to the common sense. Nature has a place for the wild clematis as well as for the cabbage. Some expressions of truth are reminiscent,—others merely *sensible,* as the phrase is,—others prophetic. Some forms of disease, even, may prophesy forms of health. The geologist has discovered that the figures of serpents, griffins, flying dragons, and other fanciful embellishments of heraldry, have their prototypes in the forms of fossil species which were extinct before man was created, and hence "indicate a faint and shadowy knowledge of a previous state of organic existence." The Hindoos dreamed that the earth rested on an elephant, and the elephant on a tortoise, and the tortoise on a serpent; and though it may be an unimportant coincidence, it will not be out of place here to state, that a fossil tortoise has lately been discovered in Asia large enough to support an elephant. I confess that I am partial to these wild fancies, which transcend the order of time and development. They are the sublimest recreation of the intellect. The partridge loves peas, but not those that go with her into the pot.

In short, all good things are wild and free. There is something in a strain of music, whether produced by an instrument or by the human voice,—take the sound of a bugle in a summer night, for instance,—which by its wildness, to speak without satire, reminds me of the cries emitted by wild beasts in their native forests. It is so much of their wildness as I can understand. Give me for my friends and neighbors wild men, not tame ones. The wildness of the savage is but a faint symbol of the awful ferity with which good men and lovers meet.

I love even to see the domestic animals reassert their native rights,—any evidence that they have not wholly lost their original wild habits and vigor; as when my neighbor's cow breaks out of her pasture early in the spring and boldly swims the river, a cold, gray tide, twenty-five or thirty rods wide, swollen by the melted snow. It is the buffalo crossing the Mississippi. This exploit confers some dignity on the herd in my eyes,—already dignified. The seeds of instinct are preserved under the thick hides of cattle and horses, like seeds in the bowels of the earth, an indefinite period.

Any sportiveness in cattle is unexpected. I saw one day a herd of a dozen bullocks and cows running about and frisking in unwieldly sport, like huge rats, even like kittens. They shook their heads, raised their tails, and rushed up and down a hill, and I perceived by their horns, as well as by their activity, their relation to the deer tribe. But, alas! a sudden loud *Whoa!* would have damped their ardor at once, reduced them from venison to beef, and stiffened their sides and sinews like the locomotive. Who but the Evil One has cried, "Whoa!" to mankind? Indeed, the life of cattle, like that of many men, is but a sort of locomotiveness; they move a side at a time, and man, by his machinery, is meeting the horse and ox halfway. Whatever part the whip has touched is thenceforth palsied. Who would ever think of a *side* of any of the supple cat tribe, as we speak of a *side* of beef?

I rejoice that horses and steers have to be broken before they can be made the slaves of men, and that men themselves have some wild oats still left to sow before they become submissive members of society. Undoubtedly, all men are not equally fit subjects for civilization; and because the majority, like dogs and sheep, are tame by inherited disposition, this is no reason why the others should have their natures broken that they may be reduced to the same level. Men are in the main alike, but they were made several in order that they might be various. If a low use is to be served, one man will do nearly or quite as well as another; if a high one, individual excellence is to be regarded. Any man can stop a hole to keep the wind away,[31] but no other man could serve so rare a use as the author of this illustration did. Confucius says,—"The skins of the tiger and the leopard, when they are tanned, are as the skins of the

[31]Thoreau's phrase "stop a hole to keep the wind away" is from Hamlet (V, i, 236).

dog and the sheep tanned." But it is not the part of a true culture to tame tigers, any more than it is to make sheep ferocious; and tanning their skins for shoes is not the best use to which they can be put.

When looking over a list of men's names in a foreign language, as of military officers, or of authors who have written on a particular subject, I am reminded once more that there is nothing in a name. The name Menschikoff, for instance, has nothing in it to my ears more human than a whisker, and it may belong to a rat. As the names of the Poles and Russians are to us, so are ours to them. It is as if they had been named by the child's rigmarole,—*I cry wiery ichery van, tittle-tol-tan.* I see in my mind a herd of wild creatures swarming over the earth, and to each the herdsman has affixed some barbarous sound in his own dialect. The names of men are of course as cheap and meaningless as *Bose* and *Tray,* the names of dogs.

Methinks it would be some advantage to philosophy, if men were named merely in the gross, as they are known. It would be necessary only to know the genus, and perhaps the race or variety, to know the individual. We are not prepared to believe that every private soldier in a Roman army had a name of his own,—because we have not supposed that he had a character of his own. At present our only true names are nicknames. I knew a boy who, from his peculiar energy, was called "Buster" by his playmates, and this rightly supplanted his Christian name. Some travellers tell us that an Indian had no name given him at first, but earned it, and his name was his fame; and among some tribes he acquired a new name with every new exploit. It is pitiful when a man bears a name for convenience merely, who has earned neither name nor fame.

I will not allow mere names to make distinctions for me, but still see men in herds for all them. A familiar name cannot make a man less strange to me. It may be given to a savage who retains in secret his own wild title earned in the woods. We have a wild savage in us, and a savage name is perchance somewhere recorded as ours. I see that my neighbor, who bears the familiar epithet William, or Edwin, takes it off with his jacket. It does not adhere to him when asleep or in anger, or aroused by any passion or inspiration. I seem to hear pronounced by some of his kin at such a time his original wild name in some jaw-breaking or else melodious tongue.

Here is this vast, savage, howling mother of ours, Nature, lying all around, with such beauty, and such affection for her children, as the leopard; and yet we are so early weaned from her breast to society, to that culture which is exclusively an interaction of man on man,—a sort of breeding in and in, which produces at most a merely English nobility, a civilization destined to have a speedy limit.

In society, in the best institutions of men, it is easy to detect a certain precocity. When we should still be growing children, we are already little men. Give me a culture which imports much muck from the meadows, and deepens the soil,—not that which trusts to heating manures, and improved implements and modes of culture only!

Many a poor sore-eyed student that I have heard of would grow faster, both intellectually and physically, if, instead of sitting up so very late, he honestly slumbered a fool's allowance.

There may be an excess even of informing light. Niépce, a Frenchman, discovered "actinism," that power in the sun's rays which produces a chemical effect,—that granite rocks, and stone structures, and statues of metal, "are all alike destructively acted upon during the hours of sunshine, and, but for provisions of Nature no less wonderful, would soon perish under the delicate touch of the most subtile of the agencies of the universe." But he observed that "those bodies which underwent this change during the daylight possessed the power of restoring themselves to their original conditions during the hours of night, when this excitement was no longer influencing them." Hence it has been inferred that "the hours of darkness are as necessary to the inorganic creation as we know night and sleep are to the organic kingdom." Not even does the moon shine every night, but gives place to darkness.

I would not have every man nor every part of a man cultivated, any more than I would have every acre of earth cultivated: part will be tillage, but the greater part will be meadow and forest, not only serving an immediate use, but preparing a mould against a distant future, by the annual decay of the vegetation which it supports.

There are other letters for the child to learn than those which Cadmus invented.[32] The Spaniards have a good term to express this wild and dusky knowledge,—*Gramática parda,* tawny grammar,—a kind of mother-wit derived from that same leopard to which I have referred.

We have heard of a Society for the Diffusion of Useful Knowledge. It is said that knowledge is power; and the like. Methinks there is equal need of a Society for the Diffusion of Useful Ignorance, what we will call Beautiful Knowledge, a knowledge useful in a higher sense: for what is most of our boasted so-called knowledge but a conceit that we know something, which robs us of the advantage of our actual ignorance? What we call knowledge is often our positive ignorance; ignorance our negative knowledge. By long years of patient industry and reading of the newspapers—for what are the libraries of science but files of newspapers?—a man accumulates a myriad facts, lays them up in his memory, and then when in some spring of his life he saunters abroad into the Great Fields of thought, he, as it were, goes to grass like a horse, and leaves all his harness behind in the stable. I would say to the Society for the Diffusion of Useful Knowledge, sometimes,—Go to grass. You have eaten hay long enough. The spring has come with its green crop. The very cows are driven to their country pastures before the end of May; though I have heard of one unnatural farmer who kept his cow in the barn and fed her on hay all the year round. So, frequently, the Society for the Diffusion of Useful Knowledge treats its cattle.

A man's ignorance sometimes is not only useful, but beautiful,—while his knowledge, so called, is oftentimes worse than useless, besides being ugly. Which is the best man to deal with,—he who knows nothing about a subject, and, what is extremely rare, knows that he knows nothing, or he who really knows something about it, but thinks that he knows all?

My desire for knowledge is intermittent; but my desire to bathe my head in atmospheres unknown to my feet is perennial and constant. The highest that we can attain to is not Knowledge, but Sympathy with Intelligence. I do not know that this higher knowledge amounts to anything more definite than a novel and grand surprise on a sudden revelation of the insufficiency of all that we called Knowledge

[32]Cadmus was the character in Greek legend who sowed dragon's teeth from which sprang the ancestors of the nobility of Thebes.

before,—a discovery that there are more things in heaven and earth than are dreamed of in our philosophy. It is the lighting up of the mist by the sun. Man cannot *know* in any higher sense than this, any more than he can look serenely, and with impunity in the face of the sun: *'Ως τὶ νοῶν, οὐκεὶνον νοήσεις,*—"You will not perceive that, as perceiving a particular thing," say the Chaldean Oracles.[33]

There is something servile in the habit of seeking after a law which we may obey. We may study the laws of matter at and for our convenience, but a successful life knows no law. It is an unfortunate discovery certainly, that of a law which binds us where we did not know before that we were bound. Live free, child of the mist,—and with respect to knowledge we are all children of the mist. The man who takes the liberty to live is superior to all the laws, by virtue of his relation to the lawmaker. "That is active duty," says the Vishnu Purana, "which is not for our bondage; that is knowledge which is for our liberation: all other duty is good only unto weariness; all other knowledge is only the cleverness of an artist."[34]

It is remarkable how few events or crises there are in our histories; how little exercised we have been in our minds, how few experiences we have had. I would fain be assured that I am growing apace and rankly, though my very growth disturb this dull equanimity,—though it be with struggle through long, dark, muggy nights or seasons of gloom. It would be well, if all our lives were a divine tragedy even, instead of this trivial comedy or farce. Dante, Bunyan, and others, appear to have been exercised in their minds more than we: they were subjected to a kind of culture such as our district schools and colleges do not contemplate. Even Mahomet, though many may scream at his name, had a good deal more to live for, ay, and to die for, than they have commonly.[35]

When, at rare intervals, some thought visits one, as perchance he is walking on a railroad, then indeed the cars go by without his hearing them. But soon, by some inexorable law, our life goes by and the cars return.

"Gentle breeze, that wanderest unseen,
And bendest the thistles round Loira of storms,
Traveller of the windy glens,
Why hast thou left my ear so soon?"

While almost all men feel an attraction drawing them to society, few are attracted strongly to Nature. In their relation to Nature men appear to me for the most part, notwithstanding their arts, lower than the animals. It is not often a beautiful relation, as in the case of the animals. How little appreciation of the beauty of the landscape there is among us! We have to be told that the Greeks called the world *Κόσμος*, Beauty, or Order, but we do not see clearly why they did so, and we esteem it at best only a curious philological fact.

[33]The empire of the Chaldeans flourished in what is now Iran about 600 B.C. Oracles were sayings of persons, usually priestesses in touch with the Gods, that revealed hidden knowledge.

[34]The Vishnu Paranas elaborated the myths of Vishnu, one of the greatest gods of the Hindu religion.

[35]Dante was the Italian author of *The Divine Comedy;* John Bunyan was the English author of *Pilgrim's Progress.* Mahomet was founder of the religion of Islam.

For my part, I feel that with regard to Nature I live a sort of border life, on the confines of a world into which I make occasional and transient forays only, and my patriotism and allegiance to the State into whose territories I seem to retreat are those of a moss-trooper. Unto a life which I call natural I would gladly follow even a will-o'-the-wisp through bogs and sloughs unimaginable, but no moon nor fire-fly has shown me the causeway to it. Nature is a personality so vast and universal that we have never seen one of her features. The walker in the familiar fields which stretch around my native town sometimes finds himself in another land than is described in their owners' deeds, as it were in some faraway field on the confines of the actual Concord, where her jurisdiction ceases, and the idea which the word Concord suggests ceases to be suggested. These farms which I have myself surveyed, those bounds which I have set up appear dimly still as through a mist; but they have no chemistry to fix them; they fade from the surface of the glass; and the picture which the painter painted stands out dimly from beneath. The world with which we are commonly acquainted leaves no trace, and it will have no anniversary.

I took a walk on Spaulding's Farm the other afternoon. I saw the setting sun lighting up the opposite side of a stately pine wood. Its golden rays straggled into the aisles of the wood as into some noble hall. I was impressed as if some ancient and altogether admirable and shining family had settled there in that part of the land called Concord, unknown to me,—to whom the sun was servant,—who had not gone into society in the village,—who had not been called on. I saw their park, their pleasure-ground, beyond through the wood, in Spaulding's cranberry-meadow. The pines furnished them with gables as they grew. Their house was not obvious to vision; the trees grew through it. I do not know whether I heard the sounds of a suppressed hilarity or not. They seemed to recline on the sunbeams. They have sons and daughters. They are quite well. The farmer's cart-path, which leads directly through their hall, does not in the least put them out,—as the muddy bottom of a pool is sometimes seen through the reflected skies. They never heard of Spaulding, and do not know that he is their neighbor,—notwithstanding I heard him whistle as he drove his team through the house. Nothing can equal the serenity of their lives. Their coat of arms is simply a lichen. I saw it painted on the pines and oaks. Their attics were in the tops of the trees. They are of no politics. There was no noise of labor. I did not perceive that they were weaving or spinning. Yet I did detect, when the wind lulled and hearing was done away, the finest imaginable sweet musical hum,—as of a distant hive in May, which perchance was the sound of their thinking. They had no idle thoughts, and no one without could see their work, for their industry was not as in knots and excrescences embayed.

But I find it difficult to remember them. They fade irrevocably out of my mind even now while I speak and endeavor to recall them, and recollect myself. It is only after a long and serious effort to recollect my best thoughts that I become again aware of their cohabitancy. If it were not for such families as this, I think I should move out of Concord.

We are accustomed to say in New England that few and fewer pigeons visit us every year. Our forests furnish no mast for them. So, it would seem, few and fewer thoughts visit each growing man from year to year, for the grove in our minds is laid waste,—sold to feed unnecessary fires of ambition, or sent to mill, and there is scarcely a twig left for them to perch on. They no longer build nor breed with us. In some more genial season, perchance, a faint shadow flits across the landscape of the mind, cast by the *wings* of some thought in its vernal or autumnal migration, but, looking up, we are unable to detect the substance of the thought itself. Our winged thoughts are turned to poultry. They no longer soar, and they attain only to a Shanghai and Cochin-China grandeur.[36] Those *gra-a-ate thoughts,* those *gra-a-ate men* you hear of!

We hug the earth,—how rarely we mount! Methinks we might elevate ourselves a little more. We might climb a tree, at least. I found my account in climbing a tree once. It was a tall white pine, on the top of a hill; and though I got well pitched, I was well paid for it, for I discovered new mountains in the horizon which I had never seen before,—so much more of the earth and the heavens. I might have walked about the foot of the tree for threescore years and ten, and yet I certainly should never have seen them. But, above all, I discovered around me,—it was near the end of June,—on the ends of the topmost branches only, a few minute and delicate red cone-like blossoms, the fertile flower of the white pine looking heavenward. I carried straightway to the village the topmost spire, and showed it to stranger jurymen who walked the streets,—for it was court-week,—and to farmers and lumber-dealers and woodchoppers and hunters, and not one had ever seen the like before, but they wondered as at a star dropped down. Tell of ancient architects finishing their works on the tops of columns as perfectly as on the lower and more visible parts! Nature has from the first expanded the minute blossoms of the forest only toward the heavens, above men's heads and unobserved by them. We see only the flowers that are under our feet in the meadows. The pines have developed their delicate blossoms on the highest twigs of the wood every summer for ages, as well over the heads of Nature's red children as of her white ones; yet scarcely a farmer or hunter in the land has ever seen them.

Above all, we cannot afford not to live in the present. He is blessed over all mortals who loses no moment of the passing life in remembering the past. Unless our philosophy hears the cock crow in every barn-yard within our horizon, it is belated. That sound commonly reminds us that we are growing rusty and antique in our employments and habits of thought. His philosophy comes down to a more recent time than ours. There is something suggested by it that is a newer treatment,—the gospel according to this moment. He has not fallen astern; he has got up early, and kept up early, and to be where he is is to be in season, in the foremost rank of time. It is an expression of the health and soundness of Nature, a brag for all the world,—healthiness as of a spring burst forth, a new fountain of the Muses,[37] to celebrate this last instant of time. Where he lives no fugitive slave laws are passed. Who has not betrayed his master many times since last he heard that note?

The merit of this bird's strain is in its freedom from all plaintiveness. The singer can easily move us to tears or to laughter, but where is he who can excite in us a pure morning joy? When, in doleful dumps, breaking the awful stillness of our wooden sidewalk on a Sunday, or, perchance, a watcher in the house of mourning, I hear a

[36]Shanghai and Cochin-China are breeds of heavy, domestic poultry.

[37]In Greek mythology, certain fountains in Greece were sacred to the nine Muses, patron goddesses of the arts.

cockerel crow far or near, I think to myself, "There is one of us well, at any rate,"—and with a sudden gush return to my senses.

We had a remarkable sunset one day last November. I was walking in a meadow, the source of a small brook, when the sun at last, just before setting, after a cold gray day, reached a clear stratum in the horizon, and the softest, brightest morning sunlight fell on the dry grass and on the stems of the trees in the opposite horizon, and on the leaves of the shrub-oaks on the hill-side, while our shadows stretched long over the meadow castward, as if we were the only motes in its beams. It was such a light as we could not have imagined a moment before, and the air also was so warm and serene that nothing was wanting to make a paradise of that meadow. When we reflected that this was not a solitary phenomenon, never to happen again, but that it would happen forever and ever an infinite number of evenings, and cheer and reassure the latest child that walked there, it was more glorious still.

The sun sets on some retired meadow, where no house is visible, with all the glory and splendor that it lavishes on cities, and, perchance, as it has never set before,—where there is but a solitary marsh-hawk to have his wings gilded by it, or only a musquash[38] looks out from his cabin, and there is some little black-veined brook in the midst of the marsh, just beginning to meander, winding slowly round a decaying stump. We walked in so pure and bright a light, gilding the withered grass and leaves, so softly and serenely bright, I thought I had never bathed in such a golden flood, without a ripple or a murmur to it. The west side of every wood and rising ground gleamed like the boundary of Elysium,[39] and the sun on our backs seemed like a gentle herdsman driving us home at evening.

So we saunter toward the Holy Land, till one day the sun shall shine more brightly than ever he has done, shall perchance shine into our minds and hearts, and light up our whole lives with a great awakening light, as warm and serene and golden as on a bank-side in autumn.

1862

Letters to H. G. O. Blake

Concord, March 27, 1848.

I am glad to hear that any words of mine, though spoken so long ago that I can hardly claim identity with their author, have reached you. It gives me pleasure, because I have therefore reason to suppose that I have uttered what concerns men, and that it is not in vain that man speaks to man. This is the value of literature. Yet those days are so distant, in every sense, that I have had to look at that page again, to learn what was the tenor of my thoughts then. I should value that article, however, if only because it was the occasion of your letter.

[38]"Musquash" was Thoreau's name for the muskrat, which burrowed into the banks of streams.

[39]In Greek mythology, Paradise.

I do believe that the outward and the inward life correspond; that if any should succeed to live a higher life, others would not know of it; that difference and distance are one. To set about living a true life is to go a journey to a distant country, gradually to find ourselves surrounded by new scenes and men; and as long as the old are around me, I know that I am not in any true sense living a new or a better life. The outward is only the outside of that which is within. Men are not concealed under habits,[1] but are revealed by them; they are their true clothes. I care not how curious a reason they may give for their abiding by them. Circumstances are not rigid and unyielding, but our habits are rigid. We are apt to speak vaguely sometimes, as if a divine life were to be grafted on to or built over this present as a suitable foundation. This might do if we could so build over our old life as to exclude from it all the warmth of our affection, and addle it, as the thrush builds over the cuckoo's egg, and lays her own atop, and hatches that only; but the fact is, we—so thin is the partition—hatch them both, and the cuckoo's always by a day first, and that young bird crowds the young thrushes out of the nest. No. Destroy the cuckoo's egg, or build a new nest.

Change is change. No new life occupies the old bodies,—they decay. *It* is born, and grows, and flourishes. Men very pathetically inform the old, accept and wear it. Why put up with the almshouse when you may go to heaven? It is embalming,—no more. Let alone your ointments and your linen swathes, and go into an infant's body. You see in the catacombs of Egypt the result of that experiment,—that is the end of it.

I do believe in simplicity. It is astonishing as well as sad, how many trivial affairs even the wisest man thinks he must attend to in a day; how singular an affair he thinks he must omit. When the mathematician would solve a difficult problem, he first frees the equation of all incumbrances, and reduces it to its simplest terms. So simplify the problem of life, distinguish the necessary and the real. Probe the earth to see where your main roots run. I would stand upon facts. Why not see,—use our eyes? Do men know nothing? I know many men who, in common things, are not to be deceived; who trust no moonshine; who count their money correctly, and know how to invest it; who are said to be prudent and knowing, who yet will stand at a desk the greater part of their lives, as cashiers in banks, and glimmer and rust and finally go out there. If they *know* anything, what under the sun do they do that for? Do they know what *bread* is? or what it is for? Do they know what life is? If they *knew* something, the places which know them now would know them no more forever.

This, our respectable daily life, on which the man of common sense, the Englishman of the world, stands so squarely, and on which our institutions are founded, is in fact the veriest illusion, and will vanish like the baseless fabric of a vision; but that faint glimmer of reality which sometimes illuminates the darkness of daylight for all men, reveals something more solid and enduring than adamant, which is in fact the corner-stone of the world.

Men cannot conceive of a state of things so fair that it cannot be realized. Can any man honestly consult his experience and say that it is so? Have we any facts to

[1]Thoreau is using the word "habits" in the usual sense, but also to mean "clothing."

appeal to when we say that our dreams are premature? Did you ever hear of a man who had striven all his life faithfully and singly toward an object and in no measure obtained it? If a man constantly aspires, is he not elevated? Did ever a man try heroism, magnanimity, truth, sincerity, and find that there was no advantage in them? that it was a vain endeavor? Of course we do not expect that our paradise will be a garden. We know not what we ask. To look at literature,—how many fine thoughts has every man had! how few fine thoughts are expressed! Yet we never have a fantasy so subtle and ethereal, but that *talent merely,* with more resolution and faithful persistency, after a thousand failures, might fix and engrave it in distinct and enduring words, and we should see that our dreams are the solidest facts that we know. But I speak not of dreams.

What can be expressed in words can be expressed in life.

My actual life is a fact, in view of which I have no occasion to congratulate myself; but for my faith and aspiration I have respect. It is from these that I speak. Every man's position is in fact too simple to be described. I have sworn no oath. I have no designs on society, or nature, or God. I am simply what I am, or I begin to be that. I *live* in the *present.* I only remember the past, and anticipate the future. I love to live. I love reform better than its modes. There is no history of how bad became better. I believe something, and there is nothing else but that. I know that I am. I know that another is who knows more than I, who takes interest in me, whose creature, and yet whose kindred, in one sense, am I. I know that the enterprise is worthy. I know that things work well. I have heard no bad news.

As for positions, combinations, and details,—what are they? In clear weather, when we look into the heavens, what do we see but the sky and the sun?

If you would convince a man that he does wrong, do right. But do not care to convince him. Men will believe what they see. Let them see.

Pursue, keep up with, circle round and round your life, as a dog does his master's chaise. Do what you love. Know your own bone; gnaw at it, bury it, unearth it, and gnaw it still. Do not be too moral. You may cheat yourself out of much life so. Aim above morality. Be not simply good; be good for something. All fables, indeed, have their morals; but the innocent enjoy the story. Let nothing come between you and the light. Respect men and brothers only. When you travel to the Celestial City, carry no letter of introduction. When you knock, ask to see God,—none of the servants. In what concerns you much, do not think that you have companions: know that you are alone in the world.

Thus I write at random. I need to see you, and I trust I shall, to correct my mistakes. Perhaps you have some oracles for me.

Henry Thoreau
1848

Concord, November 16, 1857.

Mr. Blake,—You have got the start again. It was I that owed you a letter or two, if I mistake not.

They make a great ado nowadays about hard times; but I think that the community generally, ministers and all, take a wrong view of the matter, though some of the ministers preaching according to a formula may pretend to take a right one. This general failure, both private and public, is rather occasion for rejoicing, as reminding us whom we have at the helm,—that justice is always done. If our merchants did not most of them fail, and the banks too, my faith in the old laws of the world would be staggered. The statement that ninety-six in a hundred doing such business surely break down is perhaps the sweetest fact that statistics have revealed,—exhilarating as the fragrance of sallows in spring. Does it not say somewhere, "The Lord reigneth, let the earth rejoice"? If thousands are thrown out of employment, it suggests that they were not well employed. Why don't they take the hint? It is not enough to be industrious; so are the ants. What are you industrious about?

The merchants and company have long laughed at transcendentalism, higher laws, etc., crying, "None of your moonshine," as if they were anchored to something not only definite, but sure and permanent. If there was any institution which was presumed to rest on a solid and secure basis, and more than any other represented this boasted common sense, prudence, and practical talent, it was the bank; and now those very banks are found to be mere reeds shaken by the wind. Scarcely one in the land has kept its promise. It would seem as if you only need live forty years in any age of this world, to see its most promising government become the government of Kansas, and banks nowhere. Not merely the Brook Farm and Fourierite communities,[1] but now the community generally has failed. But there is the moonshine still, serene, beneficent, and unchanged. Hard times, I say, have this value, among others, that they show us what such promises are worth,—where the *sure* banks are. I heard some Mr. Eliot praised the other day because he had paid some of his debts, though it took nearly all he had (why, I've done as much as that myself many times, and a little more), and then gone to board. What if he has? I hope he's got a good boarding-place, and can pay for it. It's not everybody that can. However, in my opinion, it is cheaper to keep house,—*i.e.,* if you don't keep too big a one.

Men will tell you sometimes that "money's hard." That shows it was not made to eat, I say. Only think of a man in this new world, in his log cabin, in the midst of a corn and potato patch, with a sheepfold on one side, talking about money being hard! So are flints hard; there is no alloy in them. What has that to do with his raising his food, cutting his wood (or breaking it), keeping in-doors when it rains, and, if need be, spinning and weaving his clothes? Some of those who sank with the steamer the other day found out that money was *heavy* too. Think of a man's priding himself on this kind of wealth, as if it greatly enriched him. As if one struggling in mid-ocean with a bag of gold on his back should gasp out, "I am worth a hundred thousand dollars." I see them struggling just as ineffectually on dry land, nay, even more hopelessly, for, in the former case, rather than sink, they will finally let the bag go; but in the latter they are pretty sure to hold and go down with it. I see them swimming about in their great-coats, collecting their rents, really *getting their dues,* drinking bitter draughts which only increase their thirst, becoming more and

[1]The "Brook Farm and Fourierite Communities" resembled present-day communes in that they attracted people who, for various reasons, wished to remain aloof from the dominant society.

more water-logged, till finally they sink plumb down to the bottom. But enough of this.

Have you ever read Ruskin's books?[2] If not, I would recommend you to try the second and third volumes (not parts) of his "Modern Painters." I am now reading the fourth, and have read most of his other books lately. They are singularly good and encouraging, though not without crudeness and bigotry. The themes in the volumes referred to are Infinity, Beauty, Imagination, Love of Nature, etc.,—all treated in a very living manner. I am rather surprised by them. It is remarkable that these things should be said with reference to painting chiefly, rather than literature. The "Seven Lamps of Architecture," too, is made of good stuff; but, as I remember, there is too much about art in it for me and the Hottentots. We want to know about matters and things in general. Our house is as yet a hut.

You must have been enriched by your solitary walk over the mountains. I suppose that I feel the same awe when on their summits that many do on entering a church. To see what kind of earth that is on which you have a house and garden somewhere, perchance! It is equal to the lapse of many years. You must ascend a mountain to learn your relation to matter, and so to your own body, for *it* is at home there, though *you* are not. It might have been composed there, and will have no farther to go to return to dust there, than in your garden; but your spirit inevitably comes away, and brings your body with it, if it lives. Just as awful really, and as glorious, is your garden. See how I can play with my fingers! They are the funniest companions I have ever found. Where did they come from? What strange control I have over them! *Who* am I? What are they?—those little peaks—call them Madison, Jefferson, Lafayette. What is *the matter? My* fingers do I say? Why, erelong, they may form the top-most crystal of Mount Washington.[3] I go up there to see my body's cousins. There are some fingers, toes, bowels, etc., that I take an interest in, and therefore I am interested in all their relations.

Let me suggest a theme for you: to state to yourself precisely and completely what that walk over the mountains amounted to for you,—returning to this essay again and again, until you are satisfied that all that was important in your experience is in it. Give this good reason to yourself for having gone over the mountains, for mankind is ever going over a mountain. Don't suppose that you can tell it precisely the first dozen times you try, but at 'em again, especially when, after a sufficient pause, you suspect that you are touching the heart or summit of the matter, reiterate your blows there, and account for the mountain to yourself. Not that the story need be long, but it will take a long while to make it short. It did not take very long to get over the mountain, you thought; but have you got over it indeed? If you have been to the top of Mount Washington, let me ask, what did you find there? That is the way they prove witnesses, you know. Going up there and being blown on is nothing. We never do much climbing while we are there, but we eat our luncheon, etc., very much as at home. It is after we get home that we really

[2]John Ruskin was a popular contemporary British writer on the arts, principally on painting.

[3]Mt. Washington, in Northern New Hampshire, is the highest mountain in New England.

go over the mountain, if ever. What did the mountain say? What did the mountain do?

I keep a mountain anchored off eastward a little way, which I ascend in my dreams both awake and asleep. Its broad base spreads over a village or two, which do not know it; neither does it know them, nor do I when I ascend it. I can see its general outline as plainly now in my mind as that of Wachusett.[4] I do not invent in the least, but state exactly what I see. I find that I go up it when I am light-footed and earnest. It ever smokes like an altar with its sacrifice. I am not aware that a single villager frequents it or knows of it. I keep this mountain to ride instead of a horse.

Do you not mistake about seeing Moosehead Lake from Mount Washington? That must be about one hundred and twenty miles distant, or nearly twice as far as the Atlantic, which last some doubt if they can see thence. Was it not Umbagog?

Dr. Solger has been lecturing in the vestry in this town on Geography, to Sanborn's scholars,[5] for several months past, at five P.M. Emerson and Alcott have been to hear him. I was surprised when the former asked me, the other day, if I was not going to hear Dr. Solger. What, to be sitting in a meeting-house cellar at that time of day, when you might possibly be out-doors! I never thought of such a thing. What was the sun made for? If he does not prize daylight, I do. Let him lecture to owls and dormice. He must be a wonderful lecturer indeed who can keep me indoors at such an hour, when the night is coming in which no man can walk.

Are you in want of amusement nowadays? Then play a little at the game of getting a living. There never was anything equal to it. Do it temperately, though, and don't sweat. Don't let this secret out, for I have a design against the Opera.[6] OPERA!! Pass along the exclamations, devil.

Now is the time to become conversant with your woodpile (this comes under Work for the Month), and be sure you put some warmth into it by your mode of getting it. Do not consent to be passively warmed. An intense degree of that is the hotness that is threatened. But a positive warmth within can withstand the fiery furnace,[7] as the vital heat of a living man can withstand the heat that cooks meat.

1857

[4] A mountain about 30 miles west of Concord.

[5] Franklin Sanborn for many years conducted a private school for Concord, and New England, children.

[6] Thoreau is using the word in its Latin meaning, *i.e.,* "work."

[7] Thoreau is here alluding to the delivery of Daniel and his friends from the fiery furnace where they were thrown upon their refusal to worship the golden image set up by the Chaldean king, Nebuchadnezzar.

from The Journal

Catching a Pig

August 8, 1856

3:30 P.M.—When I came forth, thinking to empty my boat and go a-meditating along the river,—for the full ditches and drenched grass forbade other routes, except the highway,—and this is one advantage of a boat,—I learned to my chagrin that Father's pig was gone. He had leaped out of the pen some time since his breakfast, but his dinner was untouched. Here was an ugly duty not to be shirked,—a wild shoat that weighed but ninety to be tracked, caught, and penned,—an afternoon's work, at least (if I were lucky enough to accomplish it so soon), prepared for me, quite different from what I had anticipated. I felt chagrined, it is true, but I could not ignore the fact nor shirk the duty that lay so near to me. Do the duty that lies nearest to thee. I proposed to Father to sell the pig as he was running (somewhere) to a neighbor who had talked of buying him, making a considerable reduction. But my suggestion was not acted on, and the responsibilities of the case all devolved on me, for I could run faster than Father. Father looked to me, and I ceased to look to the river. Well, let us see if we can track him. Yes, this is the corner where he got out, making a step of his trough. Thanks to the rain, his tracks are quite distinct. Here he went along the edge of the garden over the water and muskmelons, then through the beans and potatoes, and even along the front-yard walk I detect the print of his divided hoof, his two sharp toes *(ungulæ).* It's a wonder we did not see him. And here he passed out under the gate, across the road,—how naked he must have felt!—into a grassy ditch, and whither next? Is it of any use to go hunting him up unless you have devised some mode of catching him when you have found? Of what avail to know where he has been, even where he is? He was so shy the little while we had him, of course he will never come back; he cannot be tempted by a swill-pail. Who knows how many miles off he is! Perhaps he has taken the back track and gone to Brighton, or Ohio! At most, probably we shall only have the satisfaction of glimpsing the nimble beast at a distance, from time to time, as he trots swiftly through the green meadows and cornfields. But, now I speak, what is that I see pacing deliberately up the middle of the street forty rods off? It is *he.* As if to tantalize, to tempt us to waste our afternoon without further hesitation, he thus offers himself. He roots a foot or two and then lies down on his belly in the middle of the street. But think not to catch him a-napping. He has his eyes about, and his ears too. He has already been chased. He gives that wagon a wide berth, and now, seeing me, he turns and trots back down the street. He turns into a front yard. Now if I can only close that gate upon him ninety-nine hundredths of the work is done, but ah! he hears me coming afar off, he foresees the danger, and, with swinish cunning and speed, he scampers out. My neighbor in the street tries to head him; he jumps to this side the road, then to that, before him; but the third time the pig was there first and went by. "Whose is it?" he shouts. "It's ours." He bolts into that neighbor's yard and so across his premises. He has been twice there before, it seems; he knows the road; see what work he has made in his flower-garden! He must be fond of bulbs. Our neighbor picks up one tall flower with its bulb attached, holds it out at arm's length. He is excited about the pig; it is a subject he is interested in. But where is [he] gone now? The last glimpse I had of him was as he went through the cow-yard; here are his tracks again in this cornfield, but they are lost in the grass. We lose him; we beat the bushes in vain; he may be far away. But hark! I heard a grunt. Nevertheless for half an hour I do not see him that grunted. At last I find fresh tracks along the river, and again lose them. Each neighbor whose garden I traverse tells me some anecdote of losing pigs, or the attempt to drive them, by which I am not encouraged. Once more he crosses our first neighbor's garden and is said to be in the road. But I am not there yet; it is a good way off. At length my eyes rest on him again, after three quarters of an hour's separation. There he trots with the whole road to himself, and now again drops on his belly in a puddle. Now he starts again, seeing me twenty rods [off], deliberates, considers which way I want him to go, and goes the other. There was some chance of driving him along the sidewalk, or letting him go rather, till he slipped under our gate again, but of what avail would that be? How corner and catch him who keeps twenty rods off? He never lets the open side of the triangle be less than half a dozen rods wide. There was one place where a narrower street turned off at right angles with the main one, just this side our yard, but I could not drive him past that. Twice he ran up the narrow street, for he knew I did not wish it, but though the main street was broad and open and no traveller in sight, when I tried to drive him past this opening he invariably turned his piggish head toward me, dodged from side to side, and finally ran up the narrow street or down the main one, as if there were a high barrier erected before him. But really he is no more obstinate than I. I cannot but respect his tactics and his independence. He will be he, and I may be I. He is not unreasonable because he thwarts me, but only the more reasonable. He has a strong will. He stands upon his idea. There is a wall across the path not where a man bars the way, but where he is resolved not to travel. Is he not superior to man therein? Once more he glides down the narrow street, deliberates at a corner, chooses wisely for him, and disappears through an openwork fence eastward. He has gone to fresh gardens and pastures new. Other neighbors stand in the doorways but half sympathizing, only observing, "Ugly thing to catch." "You have a job on your hands." I lose sight of him, but hear that he is far ahead in a large field. And there we try to let him alone a while, giving him a wide berth.

At this stage an Irishman was engaged to assist. "I can catch him," says he, with Buonapartean confidence.[1] He thinks him a family Irish pig. His wife is with him, bare-headed, and his little flibbertigibbet of a boy, seven years old. "Here, Johnny, do you run right off there" (at the broadest possible angle with his own course). "Oh, but he can't do anything." "Oh, but I only want him to tell me where he is,—to keep sight of him." Michael soon discovers that he is not an Irish pig, and his wife and Johnny's occupation are soon gone. Ten minutes afterward I am patiently tracking him step by step through a corn-field, a near-sighted man helping me, and then into garden after garden far eastward, and finally into the highway, at the grave-yard; but hear and see nothing. One suggests a dog to track him. Father is meanwhile selling him to the blacksmith, who also is trying to get sight of him. After fifteen minutes since he disappeared eastward, I hear that he has been to the river twice far on [?]

[1]*I.e.,* with the confidence of Napoleon.

the north, through the first neighbor's premises. I wend that way. He crosses the street far ahead, Michael behind; he dodges up an avenue. I stand in the gap there, Michael at the other end, and now he tries to corner him. But it is a vain hope to corner him in a yard. I see a carriage-manufactory door open. "Let him go in there, Flannery." For once the pig and I are of one mind; he bolts in, and the door is closed. Now for a rope. It is a large barn, crowded with carriages. The rope is at length obtained; the windows are barred with carriages lest he bolt through. He is resting quietly on his belly in the further corner, thinking unutterable things.

Now the course recommences within narrower limits. Bump, bump, bump he goes, against wheels and shafts. We get no hold yet. He is all ear and eye. Small boys are sent under the carriages to drive him out. He froths at the mouth and deters them. At length he is stuck for an instant between the spokes of a wheel, and I am securely attached to his hind leg. He squeals deafeningly, and is silent. The rope is attached to a hind leg. The door is opened, and the *driving* commences. Roll an egg as well. You may drag him, but you cannot drive him. But he is in the road, and now another thunder-shower greets us. I leave Michael with the rope in one hand and a switch in the other and go home. He seems to be gaining a little westward. But, after long delay, I look out and find that he makes but doubtful progress. A boy is made to face him with a stick, and it is only when the pig springs at him savagely that progress is made homeward. He will be killed before he is driven home. I get a wheelbarrow and go to the rescue. Michael is alarmed. The pig is rabid, snaps at him. We drag him across the barrow, hold him down, and so, at last, get him home.

If a wild shoat like this gets loose, first track him if you can, or otherwise discover where he is. Do not scare him more than you can help. Think of some yard or building or other inclosure that will hold him and, by showing your forces—yet as if uninterested parties—fifteen or twenty rods off, let him of his own accord enter it. Then slightly shut the gate. Now corner and tie him and put him into a cart or barrow.

All progress in driving at last was made by facing and endeavoring to switch him from home. He rushed upon you and made a few feet in the desired direction. When I approached with the barrow he advanced to meet it with determination.

So I get home at dark, wet through and supperless, covered with mud and wheel-grease, without any rare flowers.

Last Friday (the 22d) afternoon (when I was away), Father's pig got out again and took to the riverside. The next day he was heard from, but not found. That night he was seen on an island in the meadow, in the midst of the flood, but thereafter for some time no account of him. J. Farmer advised to go to Ai Hale, just over the Carlisle line. He has got a dog which, if you put him on the track of the pig not more than four hours' old, will pursue and catch him and hold him by the ear without hurting him till you come up. That's the best way. Ten men cannot stop him in the road, but he will go by them. It was generally conceded that the right kind of dog was all that was wanted, like Ai Hale's, one that would hold him by the ear, but not uselessly maim him. One or two said, "If I only had such a one's dog, I'd catch him for so much."

Neighbors sympathized as much as in them lay. It was the town talk; the meetings were held at Wolcott & Holden's. Every man told of his losses and disappointments in this line. One had heard of his pig last up in Westford, but never saw him again; another had only caught his pig by his running against a post so hard as to stun himself for a few moments. It was thought this one must have been born in the woods, for he would run and leap like a wolf. Some advised not to build so very high, but lay the upper board flat over the pen, for then, when he caught by his fore feet, his body would swing under to no purpose. One said you would not catch him to buy a pig out of a drove. Our pig ran as if he *still* had the devil in him. It was generally conceded that a good dog was the desideratum. But thereupon Lawrence, the harness-maker, came forward and told his experience. He once helped hunt a pig in the next town. He weighed two hundred; had been out some time (though not in '75), but they learned where he resorted; but they got a capital dog of the right kind. They had the dog tied lest he should scare the pig too soon. They crawled along very carefully near to the hollow where the pig was till they could hear him. They knew that if he should hear them and he was wide awake, he would dash off with a grunt, and that would be the last of him, but what more could they do? They consulted in a whisper and concluded to let the dog go. They did so, and directly heard an awful yelp; rushed up; the pig was gone, and there lay the dog torn all to pieces! At this there was a universal *haw! haw!* and the reputation of dogs fell, and the chance of catching the pig seemed less.

Two dollars reward was offered to him who would catch and return him without maiming him. At length, the 26th, he was heard from. He was caught and tied in north part of the town. Took to a swamp, as they say they are inclined. He was chased two hours with a spaniel dog, which never faced him, nor touched him, but, as the man said, "tuckered him out," kept him on the go and showed where he was. When at a distance the pig stopped and faced the dog until the pursuers came up. He was brought home the 27th, all his legs tied, and put into his new pen. It was a very deep one. It might have been made deeper, but Father did not wish to build a wall, and the man who caught him and got his two dollars for it thought it ought to hold any decent pig. Father said he didn't wish to keep him in a well.

1906

The Flowering of Narrative

For many years students of American literature generally assumed that the only serious narratives of the "American Renaissance" were composed by Hawthorne, Melville, and perhaps Poe—the "major" successors to Irving and Cooper—and that almost everything else written at the time could be placed in the category of "popular" fiction, whose leading practitioner was Harriet Beecher Stowe. The problem with this account was not only that it dismissed Stowe and many other white women and black writers, but that it was also inaccurate because it lost the richness of literary production in the period in the large shadows cast by the "major" figures. The strength of Hawthorne, Melville, and Poe as writers does not at all depend on obscuring their contemporaries. On the contrary, seeing them more fully in the context of the wide range of narratives produced in the decades before the Civil War offers a fresh view of their achievements and at the same time reestablishes the value of the other writers, many of them women, with whom they shared the artistic stage, especially in the 1850s.

In the twentieth century Hawthorne and Melville have been linked as writers and, in turn, contrasted with Harriet Beecher Stowe. The men were friends and read, appreciated, and wrote about each other's work. Unlike Stowe, neither man could really make a decent living by writing; each finally depended on political appointment to survive financially. And it is usually argued that Hawthorne's and Melville's concerns and fictional methods were similar: they composed romances about the darker side of human experience, about "sin and sorrow," creating striking symbols—like the scarlet letter, the minister's black veil, and the white whale, Moby-Dick—to express the powerful ambiguity of their visions. There is much that is true in this account. And yet, seen in the context of their times the significant differences between Hawthorne and Melville come into focus as sharply as their similarities.

The history of their reputations illustrates that point. From the early 1840s, Hawthorne was seen by critics as America's "classic" writer of fiction, and he has retained that esteem over a century and a half, even though, as Jane Tompkins has pointed out, the measures of a "classic" have substantially changed. Melville, on the other hand, was regarded by his contemporaries as something of a failed teller of South Seas island tales, was largely forgotten from the beginning of the Civil War until the 1920s, and then was rapidly revived as the country's preeminent novelist.

In fact, if we view Hawthorne's longer fiction together with that being written by the "mob of scribbling women" he often deplored, their similarities are striking—as is their distance from Melville and Poe. Like Hawthorne, women writers such as Stowe in *The Minister's Wooing* and Alice Cary or Elizabeth Drew Stoddard in stories like those in this section focused on social and sexual interactions of people not unlike ourselves, living in relatively familiar contemporary or recognizable historical settings. They were concerned with matters like love, jealousy, property, marriage, careers. They wrote fictions about society, that is, some more realistic, others touched with the imaginative moonlight of what Hawthorne termed the "romance."

To be sure, women like Cary and Caroline Kirkland, among others, were less drawn to elaborate symbols or allegory than Hawthorne. And they generally composed in a plainer, somewhat conversational style. They had learned a realistic approach to writing about everyday events from predecessors like the British writer of village sketches, Mary Russell Mitford, little known to American readers today. Kirkland and Cary helped extend the influence of this realistic strategy through the literary salons they convened at their New York homes in the 1850s. Indeed, realism became the dominant approach of many women writers, especially when their subject was domestic life.

Such "domestic" fictions reached a wide, predominantly female audience. The development of the power-driven rotary press in the 1840s had enabled the circulation of hundreds of thousands of copies of successful novels in the next decade. Many, though by no means all, of these were written by women, for whom novel writing offered a whole new line of work. They knew their audience: women much like themselves often seeking through the reading of fiction to extend their experience beyond the shut doors of their middle-class homes. Many of these books offered an ideology that supported the virtues of domesticity and, within that, images of female steadfastness and strength. Some appear to today's reader as heavily sentimental, focused on the tearfully difficult story of a girl alone in *The Wide, Wide World*—to use the title of Susan Warner's best seller. Others, however, were presented with the humor of a Fanny Fern and the moral intensity represented by Stowe in *The Minister's Wooing.* Despite their popularity and the critical respect they obtained in the 1850s, women like Stowe, E.D.E.N. Southworth, Susan Warner, and Alice Cary suffered an even longer eclipse than did Melville; they are only now being rediscovered and reprinted in response to the concerns of the women's movement.

By contrast with this more realistic tradition, the fictions of Melville and Poe were influenced by the extravagancies of "Gothic" novels, with their remote settings, unlikely events, larger-than-life characters, and ambience of hallucination, danger, and fear. Their often mysterious worlds are inhabited largely by men, few of whom we would ordinarily encounter in everyday life—elements which may help to explain the limits of their popularity with a largely female readership of fiction in the 1850s. Their language is often as fanciful as their settings and characters. Particularly in his long fictions, Melville spreads a wide and colorful canvas before us, laced with many dark and ambiguous shadows. His political concerns with slavery and racism, or with the oppression of women, are akin to Stowe's, though rather at variance with the conservative views of his friend Hawthorne. To be sure, Melville's later work approaches political issues obliquely, unlike Stowe, who generally takes them head-on.

Still other writers found models in the broad panorama of events and personages drawn in British eighteenth-century adventure novels like Henry Fielding's *Tom Jones,* in the contemporary works of Charles Dickens, or in American historical narratives of travel to exotic climes, like Richard Henry Dana's *Three Years Before the Mast.* In terms of scope, eventfulness of action, and variety of characters Stowe's *Uncle Tom's Cabin* or, less successfully, E.D.E.N. Southworth's *The Hidden Hand* reflect such influences. *Uncle Tom's Cabin,* shaped by both "domestic" and "adventure" traditions, was itself instrumental in stimulating black novelists, like William Wells Brown, as well as a host of attempted "answers" to Stowe's indictment of slavery. Black authors had long composed autobiographical slave narratives; only in the 1850s, however, did they begin to write *fictions,* like Brown's *Clotel* and autobiographically based narratives like Harriet Wilson's *Our Nig,* perhaps because a market had emerged, perhaps because they appreciated the value of *Uncle Tom's Cabin* in the struggle against slavery and racism.

As we can see, then, in the decades before the Civil War narratives developed along a number of lines and in a variety of forms. This section is designed to suggest something of that diversity, in its strengths and weaknesses, as well as to convey a somewhat fuller picture of the period's fiction than has usually been available.

Paul Lauter
Trinity College

Nathaniel Hawthorne 1804–1864

Since the publication of *The Scarlet Letter* in 1850, Nathaniel Hawthorne has been recognized as one of America's most important writers, both a "romancer" who probed inner mysteries and a "realist" who assessed the American character and experience.

Born in Massachusetts on the Fourth of July, 1804, he was the descendant of Puritan worthies and the son of a ship's captain who died at sea in 1808. His mother then brought her son and two daughters to live with her own family, the Mannings. Books freed Hawthorne's imagination, but the Eden of his youth was the lakeside wilderness of Raymond, Maine, where from 1816 to 1819 he lived with his mother and sisters, "free as a bird." Summoned back to Salem to prepare for college, and working part-time in the Mannings stagecoach office, he complained, "No Man can be a Poet & a Book-Keeper at the same time." The problem would recur.

From 1821 to 1825, Hawthorne was a student at Bowdoin College, graduating in the middle of his class of thirty-eight. From the Scottish Philosophers, he absorbed the concepts of faculty psychology which would recur in his fiction: belief in a unitary mind with separate but interacting powers (including perception, reason, memory, association of ideas, and imagination) regulated by the will during waking hours but not in dreams; and a conviction that fulfillment requires living throughout the entire range of our faculties and sensibilities. Three classmates would become lifelong friends—Bridge (who helped arrange publication of his first book), Longfellow (who reviewed it), and Pierce (who became President of the United States and appointed Hawthorne Consul to Liverpool).

Even before college, Hawthorne had rejected the major careers open to graduates—the ministry, medicine, and law. He mistrusted institutionalized authority, including organized religion, though he would always provisionally believe in a beneficent deity. "What do you think of my becoming an Author, and relying for support upon my pen," he had asked his mother, musing how proud she would be "to see my works praised." Although that ambition was unrealistic in mercantile America—since most books were imported from England or pirated, and most magazine fiction was low-paid and published anonymously—the new graduate was determined to pursue it. In the tales he produced in the Mannings's "chamber under the eaves," he exaggerated his plight as a lonely writer-dreamer, though his problems were real enough. In 1828, at his own expense, he published a slender novel drawn from his college experience entitled *Fanshawe,* but it is characteristic of his lifelong diffidence that he soon repudiated it and tried to destroy all copies. He linked some of his tales into collections, but for lack of a publisher, he burned some and submitted others to periodicals and gift-books. Editors were eager for his stories and one offered hackwork: in 1836, with the assistance of his sister Elizabeth, Hawthorne edited *The American Magazine of Useful and Entertaining Knowledge* and wrote a best-selling children's text, *Peter Parley's Universal History.*

In 1837, Hawthorne's "twelve lonely years" as "the obscurest man of letters in America" came to an end when *Twice-told Tales* was published with his name on the cover. Longfellow, already well established as a man of letters, enthusiastically praised the author's poetic imagination, his style, and his use of New England materials, and other critics followed suit, though neither this collection nor the expanded 1842 version attracted a large audience. The volume included "The Minister's Black Veil," a historically grounded parable about the guilt we hide from one another and about the dangers of self-absorption (which anticipates *The Scarlet Letter*). But Hawthorne had not chosen to include two even more complex early stories, "My Kinsman, Major Molineux" or "Young Goodman Brown": both probe the individual's complex inner life and interrelationships with society, warning against simplistic moral judgments and challenging pious assumptions about Puritanism and revolutionary America. Both present eruptions of what had been suppressed; and the narrator, who asks if the guilt-obsessed Brown had "only dreamed a wild dream of a witch-meeting" and answers "Be it so if you will," requires the reader to participate in moral judgment. For the castles of Gothic romance, Hawthorne substituted the American wilderness and the wilderness of the mind. As in a dream, his fiction pushes beyond surface reality, conveying knowledge that resists complete understanding.

Eighteen hundred thirty-seven brought another milestone: Hawthorne met Sophia Peabody, a frail amateur artist to whom he became secretly engaged the following year. He was still writing stories for the magazines; but in January, 1839, to supplement his income, Hawthorne sought political appointment, and became Measurer in the Boston Custom House. Predictably complaining that his imagination was dulled by routine, he produced only a few tales and two collections of children's stories (*Grandfather's Chair* and *Famous Old People*), as well as entries in the notebooks he used as literary storehouses and long letters telling Sophia (his "Dove" and his "Wife") how love had wakened him to life.

He left the Custom House in November, 1840. The following April, he began what he would call "the most romantic episode of his own life—essentially a daydream and yet a fact": he joined the Utopian commune of Brook Farm. Although skeptical about the community's socialist ideals, he hoped their way of life would enable him to combine authorship and marriage. But the drudgery of farm work made writing impossible, and he left after half a year. His third novel, *The Blithedale Romance,* would dramatize that venture.

Next came an idyl that would last over three years: in July, 1842, Hawthorne married Sophia and moved into the Old Manse in Concord. He contentedly gardened, ice-skated with Emerson, and rowed with Thoreau. He also wrote prolifically, producing twenty published works, among them two of his most challenging stories—"The Birth-mark" and "Rappaccini's Daughter." Both explore the dark side of nineteenth-century scientific and technological change by means of experiments that go awry, and both portray men's anxieties about women's sexuality. Perhaps working out his own apprehensions as a new groom, Hawthorne presented obsessed and cold-hearted men who destroy the innocent women who love and trust them. He had no trouble selling what he wrote; but his pen did not provide enough support, especially after the birth of his daughter Una in 1844. Political appointment was again the recourse.

In April, 1846, Hawthorne became Surveyor of the Salem Custom House and returned to his birthplace. That June, *Mosses from an Old Manse* was published and his son Julian was born; but predictably, Hawthorne's imagination was inhibited by routine duty. Nonetheless, he was earning a comfortable living; and when the victorious Whigs dismissed him in 1849, Hawthorne struggled for reinstatement on the grounds that as a Surveyor and a man of letters, he was apolitical. Then, anguished by his mother's death and frustrated by his dismissal, he wrote *The Scarlet Letter.*

His first novel, his masterpiece, is an indictment of Puritan America, but also of his own society. Its introductory essay, "The Custom-House," purportedly a straightforward account of his experience as Surveyor, attacks officials who connived in his dismissal while vindicating himself as an artist. Like his heroine Hester, Hawthorne emerges from confrontation with a self-righteous society as an individual of integrity, passion, and moral superiority. The introduction also defines his requisites for writing romance: "a neutral territory, somewhere between the real world and fairy-land, where the Actual and the Imaginary may meet, and each imbue itself with the nature of the other"; enlivened by the heart, fiction could then "flow out on the brightening page." The romance itself also expresses Hawthorne's "romantic" belief in subjective perception, showing how imagination participates in creating the world we inhabit. Thus in the central scaffold scene, Dimmesdale perceives a meteor as an immense scarlet letter which signifies his guilt.

Leaving Salem forever, Hawthorne moved his family to a small house in the Berkshires in the spring of 1850, and soon produced his second novel, *The House of the Seven Gables,* centering on a Salem family burdened by ancestral guilt. He also wrote most of his third novel, *The Blithedale Romance,* drawing on his Brook Farm experience; his third major collection of short fiction, *The Snow-Image;* and a collection of Greek myths retold for children entitled *A Wonder-Book.* This was also the period of his friendship with Herman Melville—an ideal reader, whose review of *Mosses from an Old Manse* praised Hawthorne's "power of blackness," and who would dedicate *Moby-Dick* to him with "admiration for his genius."

Hawthorne's third child, Rose, was born in Lenox in 1851, and a year later, he bought a house in Concord, the only one he ever owned. The following year, however, the family would sail for England: as a reward for writing Pierce's campaign biography, Hawthorne was appointed Consul to Liverpool, serving from 1853 to 1857. As in his other political positions, Hawthorne worked conscientiously, but his imagination became stultified; except for his notebooks, he wrote almost nothing. Then from 1857 to 1859, he lived in Rome and Florence, where his immersion in art and acquaintance with artists generated the last romance he would complete—*The Marble Faun.*

Returning to Concord in 1860, Hawthorne struggled to complete three other romances; but his health was broken and he was distraught by the prospect and then the actuality of civil war. Though he believed slavery was evil and hoped for Union victory, he remained skeptical about what abolitionists (or any other reformers) could accomplish. Except for the eyewitness report "Chiefly About War Matters," he published only a series of sketches drawn from his English notebooks (collected as *Our Old Home*). He died on May 19, 1864. Soon afterward, Sophia augmented her slim income by editing his American notebooks for publication; and memoirs by Julian and Rose Hawthorne expanded the biographical record.

For more than a century, despite changes in perspective and methodology, the verdict on Hawthorne's stature has remained virtually constant. For Henry

James, Hawthorne was a great imaginative writer who was limited by the thinness of American culture and sometimes trapped into allegory; early twentieth-century critics saw him as a dreamer of dreamlike fiction and the heir of Puritan gloom; mid-century "new critics" concentrated on the symbolism and the organic unity of his fiction and analyzed recurring character types and themes. More recently, Hawthorne has been studied by poststructuralists, feminists, and new literary historians. Reader-response theorists show how Hawthorne's texts "create" his readers; semioticians examine such signifiers as the scarlet letter; deconstructionists read his texts as hieroglyphs that resist final interpretation; and his conception of romance and his rhetorical performance are reassessed. Scholars ask how he used history, how family constellations shaped him and how marketplace values controlled him, and trace his status as a literary celebrity from his time to ours. He is understood as a self-aware writer who conceals even while revealing himself through his narrators and his characters, as in the fictionalized autobiography of "The Custom House" and the novel it introduces.

Feminists point out that through such sympathetic characters as Beatrice Rappaccini and Hester Prynne, Hawthorne indicted patriarchal society by showing how it victimizes women. They note that he expressed greater respect for women's individuality and autonomy than most male writers, and thought marriage should be an equal partnership. Yet they also note his uneasiness about women's sexuality and his conflicted attitudes toward independent women (such as Margaret Fuller). His much-criticized remark about the "mob of scribbling women" expressed resentment at the popularity of women's novels and contempt for what such popularity required, though he praised "genuine" writing by men and women alike.

For everyone, textual analysis has been abetted by the Centenary editions; and biographical study has become easier with the publication of Hawthorne's letters. The critical consensus continues to be that Hawthorne was a shrewd and large-minded writer who read widely and pondered deeply about the human condition and American identity from Puritan times to his own. Though afflicted by self-doubt and constrained by a materialistic society that did not adequately reward serious artists, he created texts whose power, profundity, and artistry command our attention.

Hawthorne's structured irresolutions require his readers to become collaborators who examine character and behavior, attentive to the narrator's voice and developments of plot, character, theme, and imagery. He makes us probe beneath surface appearances and permits no simplistic judgments: characters are not simply good or bad but mixed. We evaluate them in terms of their interfusion of mind, heart, and imagination, and what they nurture or destroy. The admired minister Dimmesdale proves to be a hypocritical self-absorbed adulterer, while the condemned adulteress Hester emerges as a woman of noble integrity.

Hawthorne's recurrent themes include the interpenetration of past and present; the antagonism between the individual and society; the dangers of isolation; the importance of self-knowledge; the "fortunate fall," or lost innocence as the price of mature awareness; and the impossibility of earthly perfection. Themes are usually veiled and layered, as in "Young Goodman Brown" (about a journey into evil undertaken by a "good man" whose imagination has been distorted by the stern morality of his Puritan society) and "My Kinsman, Major Molineux" (about a youth on the verge of adulthood, and about America on the verge of Revolution).

Readers quickly recognize many of Hawthorne's recurrent images: light and dark, masks and veils, shadows and mirrors, the labyrinthine path, the moonlight of imagination, the fire of passion, the cave of the heart. But interpretation rarely remains stable. Thus the scarlet letter is a badge of shame transformed into an emblem of triumph, the A itself suggesting not only *adulteress* but a range of other meanings, while its color suggests life-giving blood and sexual passion but also hellfire. Confronting Hawthorne's art of ironic multiplicity expands the reader's imagination. He wrote about his own society and its antecedents, but it turns out that he also wrote about ours.

Rita K. Gollin
State University of New York College at Geneseo

PRIMARY WORKS

The Complete Works of Nathaniel Hawthorne, 12 vols, 1883; *The English Notebooks of Nathaniel Hawthorne,* ed. R. Stewart, 1941; *The Centenary Edition of the Works of Nathaniel Hawthorne,* 18 vols, ed. W. Charvat et al., 1962–1987; *Hawthorne's Lost Notebooks 1835–41,* ed. B. Mouffe, 1978.

SECONDARY WORKS

Henry James, *Hawthorne,* 1879; Marian Kesselring, *Hawthorne's Reading, 1828–1850,* 1949; Hyatt Waggoner, *Hawthorne: A Critical Study,* 1955; Nina Baym, *The Shape of Hawthorne's Career,* 1976; Rita K. Gollin, *Nathaniel Hawthorne and the Truth of Dreams,* 1979; James R. Mellow, *Nathaniel Hawthorne in His Times,* 1980; Arlin Turner, *Nathaniel Hawthorne: A Biography,* 1980; Gloria Erlich, *Family Themes and Hawthorne's Fiction: The Tenacious Web,* 1984; Michael Colacurcio, *The Province of Piety,* 1984; Richard H. Brodhead, *The School of Hawthorne,* 1986; Albert J. von Frank, ed., *Critical Essays on Hawthorne's Short Stories,* 1990; Sacvan Bercovitch, *The Office of the Scarlet Letter,* 1991; Charles Swann, *Nathaniel Hawthorne, Tradition and Revolution,* 1991; Edwin Haviland Miller, *Salem Is My Dwelling Place,* 1991; T. Walter Herbert, *Dearest Beloved: The Hawthornes and the Making of the Middle Class Family,* 1993.

My Kinsman, Major Molineux[1]

After the kings of Great Britain had assumed the right of appointing the colonial governors, the measures of the latter seldom met with the ready and general approbation, which had been paid to those of their predecessors, under the original charters.[2] The people looked with most jealous scrutiny to the exercise of power, which did not emanate from themselves, and they usually rewarded the rulers with slender gratitude, for the compliances, by which, in softening their instructions from beyond the sea, they had incurred the reprehension of those who gave them. The annals of Massachusetts Bay will inform us, that of six governors, in the space of about forty years from the surrender of the old charter, under James II., two were imprisoned by a popular insurrection; a third, as Hutchinson[3] inclines to believe, was driven from

[1]First published in the *Token* (1832) but not collected until *The Snow-Image, and Other Tales* (1851).

[2]Charles II annulled the Massachusetts Charter in 1684; James II appointed the first royal governor in 1685.

[3]Thomas Hutchinson (1711–1780), the last royal governor, who wrote *The History of the Colony and Province of Massachusetts-Bay* (1764, 1767).

the province by the whizzing of a musket ball; a fourth, in the opinion of the same historian, was hastened to his grave by continual bickerings with the House of Representatives; and the remaining two, as well as their successors, till the Revolution, were favored with few and brief intervals of peaceful sway. The inferior members of the court party,[4] in times of high political excitement, led scarcely a more desirable life. These remarks may serve as preface to the following adventures, which chanced upon a summer night, not far from a hundred years ago. The reader, in order to avoid a long and dry detail of colonial affairs, is requested to dispense with an account of the train of circumstances, that had caused much temporary inflammation of the popular mind.

It was near nine o'clock of a moonlight evening, when a boat crossed the ferry with a single passenger, who had obtained his conveyance, at that unusual hour, by the promise of an extra fare. While he stood on the landing-place, searching in either pocket for the means of fulfilling his agreement, the ferryman lifted a lantern, by the aid of which, and the newly risen moon, he took a very accurate survey of the stranger's figure. He was a youth of barely eighteen years, evidently countrybred, and now, as it should seem, upon his first visit to town. He was clad in a coarse grey coat, well worn, but in excellent repair; his under garments were durably constructed of leather, and sat tight to a pair of serviceable and well-shaped limbs; his stockings of blue yarn, were the incontrovertible handiwork of a mother or a sister; and on his head was a three-cornered hat, which in its better days had perhaps sheltered the graver brow of the lad's father. Under his left arm was a heavy cudgel, formed of an oak sapling, and retaining a part of the hardened root; and his equipment was completed by a wallet,[5] not so abundantly stocked as to incommode the vigorous shoulders on which it hung. Brown, curly hair, well-shaped features, and bright, cheerful eyes, were nature's gifts, and worth all that art could have done for his adornment.

The youth, one of whose names was Robin, finally drew from his pocket the half of a little province-bill of five shillings, which, in the depreciation of that sort of currency, did but satisfy the ferryman's demand, with the surplus of a sexangular piece of parchment valued at three pence.[6] He then walked forward into the town, with as light a step, as if his day's journey had not already exceeded thirty miles, and with as eager an eye, as if he were entering London city, instead of the little metropolis of a New England colony. Before Robin had proceeded far, however, it occurred to him, that he knew not whither to direct his steps; so he paused, and looked up and down the narrow street, scrutinizing the small and mean wooden buildings, that were scattered on either side.

"This low hovel cannot be my kinsman's dwelling," thought he, "nor yonder old house, where the moonlight enters at the broken casement; and truly I see none hereabouts that might be worthy of him. It would have been wise to inquire my way of the ferryman, and doubtless he would have gone with me, and earned a shilling from the Major for his pains. But the next man I meet will do as well."

He resumed his walk, and was glad to perceive that the street now became wider, and the houses more respectable in their appearance. He soon discerned a figure

[4]Supporters of the royal government.
[5]Knapsack.
[6]Colonial paper money.

moving on moderately in advance, and hastened his steps to overtake it. As Robin drew nigh, he saw that the passenger was a man in years, with a full periwig of grey hair, a wide-skirted coat of dark cloth, and silk stockings rolled about his knees. He carried a long and polished cane, which he struck down perpendicularly before him, at every step; and at regular intervals he uttered two successive hems, of a peculiarly solemn and sepulchral intonation. Having made these observations, Robin laid hold of the skirt of the old man's coat, just when the light from the open door and windows of a barber's shop, fell upon both their figures.

"Good evening to you, honored Sir," said he, making a low bow, and still retaining his hold of the skirt. "I pray you to tell me whereabouts is the dwelling of my kinsman, Major Molineux?"

The youth's question was uttered very loudly; and one of the barbers, whose razor was descending on a well-soaped chin, and another who was dressing a Ramillies[7] wig, left their occupations, and came to the door. The citizen, in the meantime, turned a long favored countenance upon Robin, and answered him in a tone of excessive anger and annoyance. His two sepulchral hems, however, broke into the very centre of his rebuke, with most singular effect, like a thought of the cold grave obtruding among wrathful passions.

"Let go my garment, fellow! I tell you, I know not the man you speak of. What! I have authority, I have—hem, hem—authority; and if this be the respect you show your betters, your feet shall be brought acquainted with the stocks,[8] by daylight, to-morrow morning!"

Robin released the old man's skirt, and hastened away, pursued by an ill-mannered roar of laughter from the barber's shop. He was at first considerably surprised by the result of his question, but, being a shrewd youth, soon thought himself able to account for the mystery.

"This is some country representative," was his conclusion, "who has never seen the inside of my kinsman's door, and lacks the breeding to answer a stranger civilly. The man is old, or verily—I might be tempted to turn back and smite him on the nose. Ah, Robin, Robin! even the barber's boys laugh at you, for choosing such a guide! You will be wiser in time, friend Robin."

He now became entangled in a succession of crooked and narrow streets, which crossed each other, and meandered at no great distance from the water-side. The smell of tar was obvious to his nostrils, the masts of vessels pierced the moonlight above the tops of the buildings, and the numerous signs, which Robin paused to read, informed him that he was near the centré of business. But the streets were empty, the shops were closed, and lights were visible only in the second stories of a few dwelling-houses. At length, on the corner of a narrow lane, through which he was passing, he beheld the broad countenance of a British hero swinging before the door of an inn,[9] whence proceeded the voices of many guests. The casement of one of the lower windows was thrown back, and a very thin curtain permitted Robin to distinguish a party at supper, round a well-furnished table. The fragrance of the good cheer steamed forth into the outer air, and the youth could not fail to recollect, that

[7]Elaborate wig with a braided tail named for a British victory in Ramillies, Belgium.
[8]Wooden instrument of punishment with holes for confining ankles and sometimes wrists.
[9]On a signboard.

the last remnant of his travelling stock of provision had yielded to his morning appetite, and that noon had found, and left him, dinnerless.

"Oh, that a parchment three-penny might give me a right to sit down at yonder table," said Robin, with a sigh. "But the Major will make me welcome to the best of his victuals; so I will even step boldly in, and inquire my way to his dwelling."

He entered the tavern, and was guided by the murmur of voices, and fumes of tobacco, to the public room. It was a long and low apartment, with oaken walls, grown dark in the continual smoke, and a floor, which was thickly sanded, but of no immaculate purity. A number of persons, the larger part of whom appeared to be mariners, or in some way connected with the sea, occupied the wooden benches, or leather-bottomed chairs, conversing on various matters, and occasionally lending their attention to some topic of general interest. Three or four little groups were draining as many bowls of punch, which the great West India trade had long since made a familiar drink in the colony. Others, who had the aspect of men who lived by regular and laborious handicraft, preferred the insulated bliss of an unshared potation, and became more taciturn under its influence. Nearly all, in short, evinced a predilection for the Good Creature[10] in some of its various shapes, for this is a vice, to which, as the Fast-day sermons of a hundred years ago will testify, we have a long hereditary claim. The only guests to whom Robin's sympathies inclined him, were two or three sheepish countrymen, who were using the inn somewhat after the fashion of a Turkish Caravansary; they had gotten themselves into the darkest corner of the room, and, heedless of the Nicotian atmosphere,[11] were supping on the bread of their own ovens, and the bacon cured in their own chimney-smoke. But though Robin felt a sort of brotherhood with these strangers, his eyes were attracted from them, to a person who stood near the door, holding whispered conversation with a group of ill-dressed associates. His features were separately striking almost to grotesqueness, and the whole face left a deep impression in the memory. The forehead bulged out into a double prominence, with a vale between; the nose came boldly forth in an irregular curve, and its bridge was of more than a finger's breadth; the eyebrows were deep and shaggy, and the eyes glowed beneath them like fire in a cave.

While Robin deliberated of whom to inquire respecting his kinsman's dwelling, he was accosted by the innkeeper, a little man in a stained white apron, who had come to pay his professional welcome to the stranger. Being in the second generation from a French Protestant, he seemed to have inherited the courtesy of his parent nation; but no variety of circumstance was ever known to change his voice from the one shrill note in which he now addressed Robin.

"From the country, I presume, Sir?" said he, with a profound bow. "Beg to congratulate you on your arrival, and trust you intend a long stay with us. Fine town here, Sir, beautiful buildings, and much that may interest a stranger. May I hope for the honor of your commands in respect to supper?"

"The man sees a family likeness! the rogue has guessed that I am related to the Major!" thought Robin, who had hitherto experienced little superfluous civility.

[10]"For every creature of God is good, and nothing to be refused, if it be received with thanksgiving" (2 Timothy 4:4).

[11]Filled with tobacco smoke (from Jean Nicot, who introduced tobacco into France in 1560, when he was an ambassador at Lisbon).

All eyes were now turned on the country lad, standing at the door, in his worn three-cornered hat, grey coat, leather breeches, and blue yarn stockings, leaning on an oaken cudgel, and bearing a wallet on his back.

Robin replied to the courteous innkeeper, with such an assumption of consequence, as befitted the Major's relative.

"My honest friend," he said, "I shall make it a point to patronize your house on some occasion, when—"here he could not help lowering his voice—"I may have more than a parchment three-pence in my pocket. My present business," continued he, speaking with lofty confidence, "is merely to inquire the way to the dwelling of my kinsman, Major Molineux."

There was a sudden and general movement in the room, which Robin interpreted as expressing the eagerness of each individual to become his guide. But the innkeeper turned his eyes to a written paper on the wall, which he read, or seemed to read, with occasional recurrences to the young man's figure.

"What have we here?" said he, breaking his speech into little dry fragments. 'Left the house of the subscriber, bounden servant,[12] Hezekiah Mudge—had on, when he went away, grey coat, leather breeches, master's third best hat. One pound currency reward to whoever shall lodge him in any jail in the province.' Better trudge, boy, better trudge!"

Robin had begun to draw his hand towards the lighter end of the oak cudgel, but a strange hostility in every countenance, induced him to relinquish his purpose of breaking the courteous innkeeper's head. As he turned to leave the room, he encountered a sneering glance from the bold-featured personage whom he had before noticed; and no sooner was he beyond the door, than he heard a general laugh, in which the innkeeper's voice might be distinguished, like the dropping of small stones into a kettle.

"Now is it not strange," thought Robin, with his usual shrewdness, "is it not strange, that the confession of an empty pocket, should outweigh the name of my kinsman, Major Molineux? Oh, if I had one of these grinning rascals in the woods, where I and my oak sapling grew up together, I would teach him that my arm is heavy, though my purse be light!"

On turning the corner of the narrow lane, Robin found himself in a spacious street, with an unbroken line of lofty houses on each side, and a steepled building at the upper end, whence the ringing of a bell announced the hour of nine. The light of the moon, and the lamps from numerous shop windows, discovered people promenading on the pavement, and amongst them, Robin hoped to recognize his hitherto inscrutable relative. The result of his former inquiries made him unwilling to hazard another, in a scene of such publicity, and he determined to walk slowly and silently up the street, thrusting his face close to that of every elderly gentleman, in search of the Major's lineaments. In his progress, Robin encountered many gay and gallant figures. Embroidered garments, of showy colors, enormous periwigs, gold-laced hats, and silver hilted swords, glided past him and dazzled his optics. Travelled youths, imitators of the European fine gentlemen of the period, trod jauntily along, half-dancing to the fashionable tunes which they hummed, and making poor Robin ashamed

[12]A person who contracts to exchange a period of servitude for transportation to the colonies.

of his quiet and natural gait. At length, after many pauses to examine the gorgeous display of goods in the shop windows, and after suffering some rebukes for the impertinence of his scrutiny into people's faces, the Major's kinsman found himself near the steepled building, still unsuccessful in his search. As yet, however, he had seen only one side of the thronged street; so Robin crossed, and continued the same sort of inquisition down the opposite pavement, with stronger hopes than the philosopher seeking an honest man,[13] but with no better fortune. He had arrived about midway towards the lower end, from which his course began, when he overheard the approach of some one, who struck down a cane on the flag-stones at every step, uttering, at regular intervals, two sepulchral hems.

"Mercy on us!" quoth Robin, recognizing the sound.

Turning a corner, which chanced to be close at his right hand, he hastened to pursue his researches, in some other part of the town. His patience was now wearing low, and he seemed to feel more fatigue from his rambles since he crossed the ferry, than from his journey of several days on the other side. Hunger also pleaded loudly within him, and Robin began to balance the propriety of demanding, violently and with lifted cudgel, the necessary guidance from the first solitary passenger, whom he should meet. While a resolution to this effect was gaining strength, he entered a street of mean appearance, on either side of which, a row of ill-built houses was straggling towards the harbor. The moonlight fell upon no passenger along the whole extent, but in the third domicile which Robin passed, there was a half-opened door, and his keen glance detected a woman's garment within.

"My luck may be better here," said he to himself.

Accordingly, he approached the door, and beheld it shut closer as he did so; yet an open space remained, sufficing for the fair occupant to observe the stranger, without a corresponding display on her part. All that Robin could discern was a strip of scarlet petticoat, and the occasional sparkle of an eye, as if the moonbeams were trembling on some bright thing.

"Pretty mistress,"—for I may call her so with a good conscience, thought the shrewd youth, since I know nothing to the contrary—"my sweet pretty mistress, will you be kind enough to tell me whereabouts I must seek the dwelling of my kinsman, Major Molineux?"

Robin's voice was plaintive and winning, and the female, seeing nothing to be shunned in the handsome country youth, thrust open the door, and came forth into the moonlight. She was a dainty little figure, with a white neck, round arms, and a slender waist, at the extremity of which her scarlet petticoat jutted out over a hoop, as if she were standing in a balloon. Moreover, her face was oval and pretty, her hair dark beneath the little cap, and her bright eyes possessed a sly freedom, which triumphed over those of Robin.

"Major Molineux dwells here," said this fair woman.

Now her voice was the sweetest Robin had heard that night, the airy counterpart of a stream of melted silver; yet he could not help doubting whether that sweet voice spoke Gospel truth. He looked up and down the mean street, and then surveyed the house before which they stood. It was a small, dark edifice of two stories, the second

[13]The fifth-century Greek Cynic philosopher Diogenes supposedly roamed the world seeking an honest man.

of which projected over the lower floor; and the front apartment had the aspect of a shop for petty commodities.

"Now truly I am in luck," replied Robin, cunningly, "and so indeed is my kinsman, the Major, in having so pretty a housekeeper. But I prithee trouble him to step to the door; I will deliver him a message from his friends in the country, and then go back to my lodgings at the inn."

"Nay, the Major has been a-bed this hour or more," said the lady of the scarlet petticoat; "and it would be to little purpose to disturb him to-night, seeing his evening draught was of the strongest. But he is a kind-hearted man, and it would be as much as my life's worth, to let a kinsman of his turn away from the door. You are the good old gentleman's very picture, and I could swear that was his rainy-weather hat. Also, he has garments very much resembling those leather—But come in, I pray, for I bid you hearty welcome in his name."

So saying, the fair and hospitable dame took our hero by the hand; and though the touch was light, and the force was gentleness, and though Robin read in her eyes what he did not hear in her words, yet the slender waisted woman, in the scarlet petticoat, proved stronger than the athletic country youth. She had drawn his half-willing footsteps nearly to the threshold, when the opening of a door in the neighborhood, startled the Major's housekeeper, and, leaving the Major's kinsman, she vanished speedily into her own domicile. A heavy yawn preceded the appearance of a man, who, like the Moonshine of Pyramus and Thisbe, carried a lantern,[14] needlessly aiding his sister luminary in the heavens. As he walked sleepily up the street, he turned his broad, dull face on Robin, and displayed a long staff, spiked at the end.

"Home, vagabond, home!" said the watchman, in accents that seemed to fall asleep as soon as they were uttered. "Home, or we'll set you in the stocks by peep of day!"

"This is the second hint of the kind," thought Robin. "I wish they would end my difficulties, by setting me there to-night."

Nevertheless, the youth felt an instinctive antipathy towards the guardian of midnight order, which at first prevented him from asking his usual question. But just when the man was about to vanish behind the corner, Robin resolved not to lose the opportunity, and shouted lustily after him—

"I say, friend! will you guide me to the house of my kinsman, Major Molineux?"

The watchman made no reply, but turned the corner and was gone; yet Robin seemed to hear the sound of drowsy laughter stealing along the solitary street. At that moment, also, a pleasant titter saluted him from the open window above his head; he looked up, and caught the sparkle of a saucy eye; a round arm beckoned to him, and next he heard light footsteps descending the staircase within. But Robin, being of the household of a New England clergyman, was a good youth, as well as a shrewd one; so he resisted temptation, and fled away.

He now roamed desperately, and at random, through the town, almost ready to believe that a spell was on him, like that, by which a wizard of his country, had once kept three pursuers wandering, a whole winter night, within twenty paces of the cottage which they sought. The streets lay before him, strange and desolate, and the

[14]In the blundering enactment of the story of Pyramus and Thisbe in Shakespeare's *Midsummer Night's Dream,* one character plays the role of Moonshine.

lights were extinguished in almost every house. Twice, however, little parties of men, among whom Robin distinguished individuals in outlandish attire, came hurrying along, but though on both occasions they paused to address him, such intercourse did not at all enlighten his perplexity. They did but utter a few words in some language of which Robin knew nothing, and perceiving his inability to answer, bestowed a curse upon him in plain English, and hastened away. Finally, the lad determined to knock at the door of every mansion that might appear worthy to be occupied by his kinsman, trusting that perseverance would overcome the fatality which had hitherto thwarted him. Firm in this resolve, he was passing beneath the walls of a church, which formed the corner of two streets, when, as he turned into the shade of its steeple, he encountered a bulky stranger, muffled in a cloak. The man was proceeding with the speed of earnest business, but Robin planted himself full before him, holding the oak cudgel with both hands across his body, as a bar to further passage.

"Halt, honest man, and answer me a question," said he, very resolutely. "Tell me, this instant, whereabouts is the dwelling of my kinsman, Major Molineux?"

"Keep your tongue between your teeth, fool, and let me pass," said a deep, gruff voice, which Robin partly remembered. "Let me pass, I say, or I'll strike you to the earth!"

"No, no, neighbor!" cried Robin, flourishing his cudgel, and then thrusting its larger end close to the man's muffled face. "No, no, I'm not the fool you take me for, nor do you pass, till I have an answer to my question. Whereabouts is the dwelling of my kinsman, Major Molineux?"

The stranger, instead of attempting to force his passage, stept back into the moonlight, unmuffled his own face and stared full into that of Robin.

"Watch here an hour, and Major Molineux will pass by," said he.

Robin gazed with dismay and astonishment, on the unprecedented physiognomy of the speaker. The forehead with its double prominence, the broad-hooked nose, the shaggy eyebrows, and fiery eyes, were those which he had noticed at the inn, but the man's complexion had undergone a singular, or, more properly, a twofold change. One side of the face blazed of an intense red, while the other was black as midnight, the division line being in the broad bridge of the nose; and a mouth, which seemed to extend from ear to ear, was black or red, in contrast to the color of the cheek. The effect was as if two individual devils, a fiend of fire and a fiend of darkness, had united themselves to form this infernal visage. The stranger grinned in Robin's face, muffled his parti-colored features, and was out of sight in a moment.

"Strange things we travellers see!" ejaculated Robin.

He seated himself, however, upon the steps of the church-door, resolving to wait the appointed time for his kinsman's appearance. A few moments were consumed in philosophical speculations, upon the species of the *genus homo,* who had just left him, but having settled this point shrewdly, rationally, and satisfactorily, he was compelled to look elsewhere for amusement. And first he threw his eyes along the street; it was of more respectable appearance than most of those into which he had wandered, and the moon, "creating, like the imaginative power, a beautiful strangeness in familiar objects," gave something of romance to a scene, that might not have possessed it in the light of day. The irregular, and often quaint architecture of the houses, some of whose roofs were broken into numerous little peaks; while others ascended, steep and narrow, into a single point; and others again were square; the pure milk-white of some of their complexions, the aged darkness of others, and the thousand sparklings, reflected from bright substances in the plastered walls of many; these matters engaged Robin's attention for awhile, and then began to grow wearisome. Next he endeavored to define the forms of distant objects, starting away with almost ghostly indistinctness, just as his eye appeared to grasp them; and finally he took a minute survey of an edifice, which stood on the opposite side of the street, directly in front of the church-door, where he was stationed. It was a large square mansion, distinguished from its neighbors by a balcony, which rested on tall pillars, and by an elaborate Gothic window, communicating therewith.

"Perhaps this is the very house I have been seeking," thought Robin.

Then he strove to speed away the time, by listening to a murmur, which swept continually along the street, yet was scarcely audible, except to an unaccustomed ear like his; it was a low, dull, dreamy sound, compounded of many noises, each of which was at too great a distance to be separately heard. Robin marvelled at this snore of a sleeping town, and marvelled more, whenever its continuity was broken, by now and then a distant shout, apparently loud where it originated. But altogether it was a sleep-inspiring sound, and to shake off its drowsy influence, Robin arose, and climbed a window-frame, that he might view the interior of the church. There the moonbeams came trembling in, and fell down upon the deserted pews, and extended along the quiet aisles. A fainter, yet more awful radiance, was hovering round the pulpit, and one solitary ray had dared to rest upon the opened page of the great Bible. Had Nature, in that deep hour, become a worshipper in the house, which man had builded? Or was that heavenly light the visible sanctity of the place, visible because no earthly and impure feet were within the walls? The scene made Robin's heart shiver with a sensation of loneliness, stronger than he had ever felt in the remotest depths of his native woods; so he turned away, and sat down again before the door. There were graves around the church, and now an uneasy thought obtruded into Robin's breast. What if the object of his search, which had been so often and so strangely thwarted, were all the time mouldering in his shroud? What if his kinsman should glide through yonder gate, and nod and smile to him in passing dimly by?

"Oh, that any breathing thing were here with me!" said Robin.

Recalling his thoughts from this uncomfortable track, he sent them over forest, hill, and stream, and attempted to imagine how that evening of ambiguity and weariness, had been spent by his father's household. He pictured them assembled at the door, beneath the tree, the great old tree, which had been spared for its huge twisted trunk, and venerable shade, when a thousand leafy brethren fell. There, at the going down of the summer sun, it was his father's custom to perform domestic worship, that the neighbors might come and join with him like brothers of the family, and that the wayfaring man might pause to drink at that fountain, and keep his heart pure by freshening the memory of home. Robin distinguished the seat of every individual of the little audience; he saw the good man in the midst, holding the Scriptures in the golden light that shone from the western clouds; he beheld him close the book, and all rise up to pray. He heard the old thanksgivings for daily mercies, the old supplications for their continuance, to which he had so often listened in weariness, but which were now among his dear remembrances. He perceived the slight inequality of his father's voice when he came to speak of the Absent One; he noted how his mother turned her face to the broad and knotted trunk; how his elder brother scorned, because the beard was rough upon his upper lip, to permit his features to be moved; how his younger sister drew down a low hanging branch before her eyes; and how the little one of all, whose sports had hitherto broken the decorum of the scene, understood the prayer for her playmate, and burst into clamorous grief. Then he saw them go in at the door; and when Robin would have entered also, the latch tinkled into its place, and he was excluded from his home.

"Am I here, or there?" cried Robin, starting; for all at once, when his thoughts had become visible and audible in a dream, the long, wide, solitary street shone out before him.

He aroused himself, and endeavored to fix his attention steadily upon the large edifice which he had surveyed before. But still his mind kept vibrating between fancy and reality; by turns, the pillars of the balcony lengthened into the tall, bare stems of pines, dwindled down to human figures, settled again in their true shape and size, and then commenced a new succession of changes. For a single moment, when he deemed himself awake, he could have sworn that a visage, one which he seemed to remember, yet could not absolutely name as his kinsman's, was looking towards him from the Gothic window. A deeper sleep wrestled with, and nearly overcame him, but fled at the sound of footsteps along the opposite pavement. Robin rubbed his eyes, discerned a man passing at the foot of the balcony, and addressed him in a loud, peevish, and lamentable cry.

"Halloo, friend! must I wait here all night for my kinsman, Major Molineux?"

The sleeping echoes awoke, and answered the voice; and the passenger, barely able to discern a figure sitting in the oblique shade of the steeple, traversed the street to obtain a nearer view. He was himself a gentleman in his prime, of open, intelligent, cheerful, and altogether prepossessing countenance. Perceiving a country youth, apparently homeless and without friends, he accosted him in a tone of real kindness, which had become strange to Robin's ears.

"Well, my good lad, why are you sitting here?" inquired he. "Can I be of service to you in any way?"

"I am afraid not, Sir," replied Robin, despondingly; "yet I shall take it kindly, if you'll answer me a single question. I've been searching half the night for one Major Molineux; now, Sir, is there really such a person in these parts, or am I dreaming?"

"Major Molineux! The name is not altogether strange to me," said the gentleman, smiling. "Have you any objection to telling me the nature of your business with him?"

Then Robin briefly related that his father was a clergyman, settled on a small salary, at a long distance back in the country, and that he and Major Molineux were brothers' children. The Major, having inherited riches, and acquired civil and military rank, had visited his cousin in great pomp a year or two before; had manifested much interest in Robin and an elder brother, and, being childless himself, had thrown out hints respecting the future establishment of one of them in life. The elder brother was destined to succeed to the farm, which his father cultivated, in the interval of sacred duties; it was therefore determined that Robin should profit by his kinsman's generous intentions, especially as he had seemed to be rather the favorite, and was thought to possess other necessary endowments.

"For I have the name of being a shrewd youth," observed Robin, in this part of his story.

"I doubt not you deserve it," replied his new friend, good naturedly; "but pray proceed."

"Well, Sir, being nearly eighteen years old, and well-grown, as you see," continued Robin, raising himself to his full height, "I thought it high time to begin the world. So my mother and sister put me in handsome trim, and my father gave me half the remnant of his last year's salary, and five days ago I started for this place, to pay the Major a visit. But would you believe it, Sir? I crossed the ferry a little after dusk, and have yet found nobody that would show me the way to his dwelling; only an hour or two since, I was told to wait here, and Major Molineux would pass by."

"Can you describe the man who told you this?" inquired the gentleman.

"Oh, he was a very ill-favored fellow, Sir," replied Robin, "with two great bumps on his forehead, a hook nose, fiery eyes, and, what struck me as the strangest, his face was of two different colors. Do you happen to know such a man, Sir?"

"Not intimately," answered the stranger, "but I chanced to meet him a little time previous to your stopping me. I believe you may trust his word, and that the Major will very shortly pass through this street. In the mean time, as I have a singular curiosity to witness your meeting, I will sit down here upon the steps, and bear you company."

He seated himself accordingly, and soon engaged his companion in animated discourse. It was but of brief continuance, however, for a noise of shouting, which had long been remotely audible, drew so much nearer, that Robin inquired its cause.

"What may be the meaning of this uproar?" asked he. "Truly, if your town be always as noisy, I shall find little sleep, while I am an inhabitant."

"Why, indeed, friend Robin, there do appear to be three or four riotous fellows abroad to-night," replied the gentleman. "You must not expect all the stillness of your native woods, here in our streets. But the watch will shortly be at the heels of these lads, and—"

"Aye, and set them in the stocks by peep of day," interrupted Robin, recollecting his own encounter with the drowsy lantern-bearer. "But, dear Sir, if I may trust my ears, an army of watchmen would never make head against such a multitude of rioters. There were at least a thousand voices went to make up that one shout."

"May not one man have several voices, Robin, as well as two complexions?" said his friend.

"Perhaps a man may; but Heaven forbid that a woman should!" responded the shrewd youth, thinking of the seductive tones of the Major's housekeeper.

The sounds of a trumpet in some neighboring street now became so evident and continual, that Robin's curiosity was strongly excited. In addition to the shouts, he heard frequent bursts from many instruments of discord, and a wild and confused laughter filled up the intervals. Robin rose from the steps, and looked wistfully towards a point, whither several people seemed to be hastening.

"Surely some prodigious merrymaking is going on," exclaimed he. "I have laughed very little since I left home, Sir, and should be sorry to lose an opportunity. Shall we just step round the corner by that darkish house, and take our share of the fun?"

"Sit down again, sit down, good Robin," replied the gentleman, laying his hand on the skirt of the grey coat. "You forget that we must wait here for your kinsman; and there is reason to believe that he will pass by, in the course of a very few moments."

The near approach of the uproar had now disturbed the neighborhood; windows flew open on all sides; and many heads, in the attire of the pillow, and confused by sleep suddenly broken, were protruded to the gaze of whoever had leisure to observe them. Eager voices hailed each other from house to house, all demanding the explanation, which not a soul could give. Half-dressed men hurried towards the unknown commotion, stumbling as they went over the stone steps, that thrust themselves into the narrow foot-walk. The shouts, the laughter, and the tuneless bray, the antipodes of music, came onward with increasing din, till scattered individuals, and then denser bodies, began to appear round a corner, at the distance of a hundred yards.

"Will you recognize your kinsman, Robin, if he passes in this crowd?" inquired the gentleman.

"Indeed, I can't warrant it, Sir; but I'll take my stand here, and keep a bright look out," answered Robin, descending to the outer edge of the pavement.

A mighty stream of people now emptied into the street, and came rolling slowly towards the church. A single horseman wheeled the corner in the midst of them, and close behind him came a band of fearful wind-instruments, sending forth a fresher discord, now that no intervening buildings kept it from the ear. Then a redder light disturbed the moonbeams, and a dense multitude of torches shone along the street, concealing by their glare whatever object they illuminated. The single horseman, clad in a military dress, and bearing a drawn sword, rode onward as the leader, and, by his fierce and variegated countenance, appeared like war personified; the red of one cheek was an emblem of fire and sword; the blackness of the other betokened the mourning which attends them. In his train, were wild figures in the Indian dress, and many fantastic shapes without a model, giving the whole march a visionary air, as if a dream had broken forth from some feverish brain, and were sweeping visibly through the midnight streets. A mass of people, inactive, except as applauding spectators, hemmed the procession in, and several women ran along the sidewalks, piercing the confusion of heavier sounds, with their shrill voices of mirth or terror.

"The double-faced fellow has his eye upon me," muttered Robin, with an indefinite but uncomfortable idea, that he was himself to bear a part in the pageantry.

The leader turned himself in the saddle, and fixed his glance full upon the country youth, as the steed went slowly by. When Robin had freed his eyes from those fiery ones, the musicians were passing before him, and the torches were close at hand; but the unsteady brightness of the latter formed a veil which he could not penetrate. The rattling of wheels over the stones sometimes found its way to his ear, and confused traces of a human form appeared at intervals, and then melted into the vivid light. A moment more, and the leader thundered a command to halt; the trumpets vomited a horrid breath, and held their peace; the shouts and laughter of the people died away, and there remained only a universal hum, nearly allied to silence. Right before Robin's eyes was an uncovered cart. There the torches blazed the brightest, there the moon shone out like day, and there, in tar-and-feathery dignity, sate his kinsman, Major Molineux!

He was an elderly man, of large and majestic person, and strong, square features, betokening a steady soul; but steady as it was, his enemies had found the means to shake it. His face was pale as death, and far more ghastly; the broad forehead was contracted in his agony, so that his eyebrows formed one grizzled line; his eyes were red and wild, and the foam hung white upon his quivering lip. His whole frame was agitated by a quick, and continual tremor, which his pride strove to quell, even in those circumstances of overwhelming humiliation. But perhaps the bitterest pang of all was when his eyes met those of Robin; for he evidently knew him on the instant, as the youth stood witnessing the foul disgrace of a head that had grown grey in honor. They stared at each other in silence, and Robin's knees shook, and his hair bristled, with a mixture of pity and terror. Soon, however, a bewildering excitement began to seize upon his mind; the preceding adventures of the night, the unexpected appearance of the crowd, the torches, the confused din, and the hush that followed, the spectre of his kinsman reviled by that great multitude, all this, and more than all, a perception of tremendous ridicule in the whole scene, affected him with a sort of mental inebriety. At that moment a voice of sluggish merriment saluted Robin's ears; he turned instinctively, and just behind the corner of the church stood the lantern-bearer, rubbing his eyes, and drowsily enjoying the lad's amazement. Then he heard a peal of laughter like the ringing of silvery bells; a woman twitched his arm, a saucy eye met his, and he saw the lady of the scarlet petticoat. A sharp, dry cachinnation appealed to his memory, and, standing on tiptoe in the crowd, with his white apron over his head, he beheld the courteous little innkeeper. And lastly, there sailed over the heads of the multitude a great, broad laugh, broken in the midst by two sepulchral hems; thus—

"Haw, haw, haw—hem, hem—haw, haw, haw, haw."

The sound proceeded from the balcony of the opposite edifice, and thither Robin turned his eyes. In front of the Gothic window stood the old citizen, wrapped in a wide gown, his grey periwig exchanged for a nightcap, which was thrust back from his forehead, and his silk stockings hanging down about his legs. He supported himself on his polished cane in a fit of convulsive merriment, which manifested itself on his solemn old features, like a funny inscription on a tombstone. Then Robin seemed to hear the voices of the barbers; of the guests of the inn; and of all who had made sport of him that night. The contagion was spreading among the multitude, when, all at once, it seized upon Robin, and he sent forth a shout of laughter that echoed through the street; every man shook his sides, every man emptied his lungs, but Robin's shout was the loudest there. The cloud-spirits peeped from their silvery islands, as the congregated mirth went roaring up the sky! The Man in the Moon heard the far bellow; "Oho," quoth he, "the old Earth is frolicsome to-night!"

When there was a momentary calm in that tempestuous sea of sound, the leader gave the sign, the procession resumed its march. On they went, like fiends that throng in mockery round some dead potentate, mighty no more, but majestic still in his agony. On they went, in counterfeited pomp, in senseless uproar, in frenzied merriment, trampling all on an old man's heart. On swept the tumult, and left a silent street behind.

"Well, Robin, are you dreaming?" inquired the gentleman, laying his hand on the youth's shoulder.

Robin started, and withdrew his arm from the stone post, to which he had instinctively clung, while the living stream rolled by him. His cheek was somewhat pale, and his eye not quite so lively as in the earlier part of the evening.

"Will you be kind enough to show me the way to the ferry?" said he, after a moment's pause.

"You have then adopted a new subject of inquiry?" observed his companion, with a smile.

"Why, yes, Sir," replied Robin, rather dryly. "Thanks to you, and to my other friends, I have at last met my kinsman, and he will scarce desire to see my face again. I begin to grow weary of a town life, Sir. Will you show me the way to the ferry?"

"No, my good friend Robin, not to-night, at least," said the gentleman. "Some few days hence, if you continue to wish it, I will speed you on your journey. Or, if you prefer to remain with us, perhaps, as you are a shrewd youth, you may rise in the world, without the help of your kinsman, Major Molineux."

1832

Young Goodman Brown[1]

Young Goodman[2] Brown came forth, at sunset, into the street of Salem village, but put his head back, after crossing the threshold, to exchange a parting kiss with his young wife. And Faith, as the wife was aptly named, thrust her own pretty head into the street, letting the wind play with the pink ribbons of her cap, while she called to Goodman Brown.

"Dearest heart," whispered she, softly and rather sadly, when her lips were close to his ear, "pr'y thee, put off your journey until sunrise, and sleep in your own bed to-night. A lone woman is troubled with such dreams and such thoughts, that she's afeard of herself, sometimes. Pray, tarry with me this night, dear husband, of all nights in the year!"

"My love and my Faith," replied young Goodman Brown, "of all nights in the year, this one night must I tarry away from thee. My journey, as thou callest it, forth and back again, must needs be done 'twixt now and sunrise. What, my sweet, pretty wife, dost thou doubt me already, and we but three months married!"

"Then, God bless you!" said Faith, with the pink ribbons, "and may you find all well, when you come back."

"Amen!" cried Goodman Brown. "Say thy prayers, dear Faith, and go to bed at dusk, and no harm will come to thee."

So they parted; and the young man pursued his way, until, being about to turn the corner by the meeting-house, he looked back, and saw the head of Faith still peeping after him, with a melancholy air, in spite of her pink ribbons.

"Poor little Faith!" thought he, for his heart smote him. "What a wretch am I, to leave her on such an errand! She talks of dreams, too. Methought, as she spoke, there was trouble in her face, as if a dream had warned her what work is to be done to-night. But, no, no! 'twould kill her to think it. Well; she's a blessed angel on earth; and after this one night, I'll cling to her skirts and follow her to Heaven."

[1]First published in 1835 in *The New England Magazine* and included in *Mosses from an Old Manse* (1846).

[2]A polite term of address for a man of humble status who was head of a household.

With this excellent resolve for the future, Goodman Brown felt himself justified in making more haste on his present evil purpose. He had taken a dreary road, darkened by all the gloomiest trees of the forest, which barely stood aside to let the narrow path creep through, and closed immediately behind. It was all as lonely as could be; and there is this peculiarity in such a solitude, that the traveller knows not who may be concealed by the innumerable trunks and the thick boughs overhead; so that, with lonely footsteps, he may yet be passing through an unseen multitude.

"There may be a devilish Indian behind every tree," said Goodman Brown, to himself; and he glanced fearfully behind him, as he added, "What if the devil himself should be at my very elbow!"

His head being turned back, he passed a crook of the road, and looking forward again, beheld the figure of a man, in grave and decent attire, seated at the foot of an old tree. He arose, at Goodman Brown's approach, and walked onward, side by side with him.

"You are late, Goodman Brown," said he. "The clock of the Old South was striking as I came through Boston; and that is full fifteen minutes agone."[3]

"Faith kept me back awhile," replied the young man, with a tremor in his voice, caused by the sudden appearance of his companion, though not wholly unexpected.

It was now deep dusk in the forest, and deepest in that part of it where these two were journeying. As nearly as could be discerned, the second traveller was about fifty years old, apparently in the same rank of life as Goodman Brown, and bearing a considerable resemblance to him, though perhaps more in expression than features. Still, they might have been taken for father and son. And yet, though the elder person was as simply clad as the younger, and as simple in manner too, he had an indescribable air of one who knew the world, and would not have felt abashed at the governor's dinner-table, or in King William's court,[4] were it possible that his affairs should call him thither. But the only thing about him, that could be fixed upon as remarkable, was his staff, which bore the likeness of a great black snake, so curiously wrought, that it might almost be seen to twist and wriggle itself, like a living serpent. This, of course, must have been an ocular deception, assisted by the uncertain light.

"Come, Goodman Brown!" cried his fellow-traveller, "this is a dull pace for the beginning of a journey. Take my staff, if you are so soon weary."

"Friend," said the other, exchanging his slow pace for a full stop, "having kept covenant by meeting thee here, it is my purpose now to return whence I came. I have scruples, touching the matter thou wot'st of."

"Sayest thou so?" replied he of the serpent, smiling apart. "Let us walk on, nevertheless, reasoning as we go, and if I convince thee not, thou shalt turn back. We are but a little way in the forest, yet."

"Too far, too far!" exclaimed the goodman, unconsciously resuming his walk. "My father never went into the woods on such an errand, nor his father before him. We have been a race of honest men and good Christians, since the days of the martyrs.[5] And shall I be the first of the name of Brown, that ever took this path, and kept—"

[3]The Old South Church in Boston; such speed suggests supernatural power.

[4]King William III and his wife Queen Mary II jointly ruled England from 1689 to 1702.

[5]Allusion to the murder of English Protestants during the reign of the Catholic monarch Mary Tudor (1553–1558).

"Such company, thou wouldst say," observed the elder person, interpreting his pause. "Well said, Goodman Brown! I have been as well acquainted with your family as with ever a one among the Puritans; and that's no trifle to say. I helped your grandfather, the constable, when he lashed the Quaker woman so smartly through the streets of Salem. And it was I that brought your father a pitch-pine knot, kindled at my own hearth, to set fire to an Indian village, in King Philip's war.[6] They were my good friends, both; and many a pleasant walk have we had along this path, and returned merrily after midnight. I would fain be friends with you, for their sake."

"If it be as thou sayest," replied Goodman Brown, "I marvel they never spoke of these matters. Or, verily, I marvel not, seeing that the least rumor of the sort would have driven them from New-England. We are a people of prayer, and good works, to boot, and abide no such wickedness."

"Wickedness or not," said the traveller with the twisted staff, "I have a very general acquaintance here in New-England. The deacons of many a church have drunk the communion wine with me; the selectmen, of divers towns, make me their chairman; and a majority of the Great and General Court[7] are firm supporters of my interest. The governor and I, too—but these are state-secrets."

"Can this be so!" cried Goodman Brown, with a stare of amazement at his undisturbed companion. "Howbeit, I have nothing to do with the governor and council; they have their own ways, and are no rule for a simple husbandman,[8] like me. But, were I to go on with thee, how should I meet the eye of that good old man, our minister, at Salem village? Oh, his voice would make me tremble, both Sabbath-day and lecture-day!"[9]

Thus far, the elder traveller had listened with due gravity, but now burst into a fit of irrepressible mirth, shaking himself so violently, that his snake-like staff actually seemed to wriggle in sympathy.

"Ha! ha! ha!" shouted he, again and again; then composing himself, "Well, go on, Goodman Brown, go on; but pr'y thee, don't kill me with laughing!"

"Well, then, to end the matter at once," said Goodman Brown, considerably nettled, "there is my wife, Faith. It would break her dear little heart; and I'd rather break my own!"

"Nay, if that be the case," answered the other, "e'en go thy ways, Goodman Brown. I would not, for twenty old women like the one hobbling before us, that Faith should come to any harm."

As he spoke, he pointed his staff at a female figure on the path, in whom Goodman Brown recognized a very pious and exemplary dame, who had taught him his catechism, in youth, and was still his moral and spiritual adviser, jointly with the minister and Deacon Gookin.

"A marvel, truly, that Goody Cloyse[10] should be so far in the wilderness, at night-fall!" said he. "But, with your leave, friend, I shall take a cut through the woods, until we have left this Christian woman behind. Bring a stranger to you, she might ask whom I was consorting with, and whither I was going."

[6]Uprising of the Wampanoag Indians (1675–1676) led by the chief called by settlers "King Philip."

[7]Colonial legislature.

[8]Farmer or small landowner.

[9]Midweek sermon day.

[10]Abbreviation of goodwife, a polite term for a married woman of humble status. Goody Cloyse, like Goody Cory and Martha Carrier, was sentenced to death at the Salem witchcraft trials of 1692. Hawthorne's chief sources of information include Cotton Mather's *Wonders of the Invisible World* and *Magnalia Christi Americana,* written soon after the trials ended.

"Be it so," said his fellow-traveller. "Betake you to the woods, and let me keep the path."

Accordingly, the young man turned aside, but took care to watch his companion, who advanced softly along the road, until he had come within a staff's length of the old dame. She, meanwhile, was making the best of her way, with singular speed for so aged a woman, and mumbling some indistinct words, a prayer, doubtless, as she went. The traveller put forth his staff, and touched her withered neck with what seemed the serpent's tail.

"The devil!" screamed the pious old lady.

"Then Goody Cloyse knows her old friend?" observed the traveller, confronting her, and leaning on his writhing stick.

"Ah, forsooth, and is it your worship, indeed?" cried the good dame. "Yea, truly is it, and in the very image of my old gossip, Goodman Brown, the grandfather of the silly fellow that now is. But—would your worship believe it?—my broomstick hath strangely disappeared, stolen, as I suspect, by that unhanged witch, Goody Cory, and that, too, when I was all anointed with the juice of smallage and cinque-foil and wolf's-bane—"

"Mingled with fine wheat and the fat of a new-born babe," said the shape of old Goodman Brown.

"Ah, your worship knows the receipt," cried the old lady, cackling aloud. "So, as I was saying, being all ready for the meeting, and no horse to ride on, I made up my mind to foot it; for they tell me, there is a nice young man to be taken into communion to-night. But now your good worship will lend me your arm, and we shall be there in a twinkling."

"That can hardly be," answered her friend. "I may not spare you my arm, Goody Cloyse, but here is my staff, if you will."

So saying, he threw it down at her feet, where, perhaps, it assumed life, being one of the rods which its owner had formerly lent to the Egyptian Magi.[11] Of this fact, however, Goodman Brown could not take cognizance. He had cast up his eyes in astonishment, and looking down again, beheld neither Goody Cloyse nor the serpentine staff, but his fellow-traveller alone, who waited for him as calmly as if nothing had happened.

"That old woman taught me my catechism!" said the young man; and there was a world of meaning in this simple comment.

They continued to walk onward, while the elder traveller exhorted his companion to make good speed and persevere in the path, discoursing so aptly, that his arguments seemed rather to spring up in the bosom of his auditor, than to be suggested by himself. As they went, he plucked a branch of maple, to serve for a walking-stick, and began to strip it of the twigs and little boughs, which were wet with evening dew. The moment his fingers touched them, they became strangely withered and dried up, as with a week's sunshine. Thus the pair proceeded, at a good free pace, until suddenly, in a gloomy hollow of the road, Goodman Brown sat himself down on the stump of a tree, and refused to go any farther.

[11] Duplicating Aaron's feat, Egyptian magicians turned rods into serpents, but his rod swallowed theirs (Exodus 7:11–12).

"Friend," said he, stubbornly, "my mind is made up. Not another step will I budge on this errand. What if a wretched old woman do choose to go to the devil, when I thought she was going to Heaven! Is that any reason why I should quit my dear Faith, and go after her?"

"You will think better of this, by-and-by," said his acquaintance, composedly. "Sit here and rest yourself awhile; and when you feel like moving again, there is my staff to help you along."

Without more words, he threw his companion the maple stick, and was as speedily out of sight, as if he had vanished into the deepening gloom. The young man sat a few moments, by the road-side, applauding himself greatly, and thinking with how clear a conscience he should meet the minister, in his morning-walk, nor shrink from the eye of good old Deacon Gookin. And what calm sleep would be his, that very night, which was to have been spent so wickedly, but purely and sweetly now, in the arms of Faith! Amidst these pleasant and praiseworthy meditations, Goodman Brown heard the tramp of horses along the road, and deemed it advisable to conceal himself within the verge of the forest, conscious of the guilty purpose that had brought him thither, though now so happily turned from it.

On came the hoof-tramps and the voices of the riders, two grave old voices, conversing soberly as they drew near. These mingled sounds appeared to pass along the road, within a few yards of the young man's hiding-place; but owing, doubtless, to the depth of the gloom, at that particular spot, neither the travellers nor their steeds were visible. Though their figures brushed the small boughs by the way-side, it could not be seen that they intercepted, even for a moment, the faint gleam from the strip of bright sky, athwart which they must have passed. Goodman Brown alternately crouched and stood on tip-toe, pulling aside the branches, and thrusting forth his head as far as he durst, without discerning so much as a shadow. It vexed him the more, because he could have sworn, were such a thing possible, that he recognized the voices of the minister and Deacon Gookin, jogging along quietly, as they were wont to do, when bound to some ordination or ecclesiastical council. While yet within hearing, one of the riders stopped to pluck a switch.

"Of the two, reverend Sir," said the voice like the deacon's, "I had rather miss an ordination-dinner than to-night's meeting. They tell me that some of our community are to be here from Falmouth[12] and beyond, and others from Connecticut and Rhode-Island; besides several of the Indian powows, who, after their fashion, know almost as much deviltry as the best of us. Moreover, there is a goodly young woman to be taken into communion."

"Mighty well, Deacon Gookin!" replied the solemn old tones of the minister. "Spur up, or we shall be late. Nothing can be done, you know, until I get on the ground."

The hoofs clattered again, and the voices, talking so strangely in the empty air, passed on through the forest, where no church had ever been gathered, nor solitary Christian prayed. Whither, then, could these holy men be journeying, so deep into the heathen wilderness? Young Goodman Brown caught hold of a tree, for support, being ready to sink down on the ground, faint and overburthened with the heavy

[12]Cape Cod town about seventy miles from Salem.

sickness of his heart. He looked up to the sky, doubting whether there really was a Heaven above him. Yet, there was the blue arch, and the stars brightening in it.

"With Heaven above, and Faith below, I will yet stand firm against the devil!" cried Goodman Brown.

While he still gazed upward, into the deep arch of the firmament, and had lifted his hands to pray, a cloud, though no wind was stirring, hurried across the zenith, and hid the brightening stars. The blue sky was still visible, except directly overhead, where this black mass of cloud was sweeping swiftly northward. Aloft in the air, as if from the depths of the cloud, came a confused and doubtful sound of voices. Once, the listener fancied that he could distinguish the accents of town's-people of his own, men and women, both pious and ungodly, many of whom he had met at the communion-table, and had seen others rioting at the tavern. The next moment, so indistinct were the sounds, he doubted whether he had heard aught but the murmur of the old forest, whispering without a wind. Then came a stronger swell of those familiar tones, heard daily in the sunshine, at Salem village, but never, until now, from a cloud of night. There was one voice, of a young woman, uttering lamentations, yet with an uncertain sorrow, and entreating for some favor, which, perhaps, it would grieve her to obtain. And all the unseen multitude, both saints and sinners, seemed to encourage her onward.

"Faith!" shouted Goodman Brown, in a voice of agony and desperation; and the echoes of the forest mocked him, crying—"Faith! Faith!" as if bewildered wretches were seeking her, all through the wilderness.

The cry of grief, rage, and terror, was yet piercing the night, when the unhappy husband held his breath for a response. There was a scream, drowned immediately in a louder murmur of voices, fading into far-off laughter, as the dark cloud swept away, leaving the clear and silent sky above Goodman Brown. But something fluttered lightly down through the air, and caught on the branch of a tree. The young man seized it, and beheld a pink ribbon.

"My Faith is gone!" cried he, after one stupefied moment. "There is no good on earth; and sin is but a name. Come, devil! for to thee is this world given."

And maddened with despair, so that he laughed loud and long, did Goodman Brown grasp his staff and set forth again, at such a rate, that he seemed to fly along the forest-path, rather than to walk or run. The road grew wilder and drearier, and more faintly traced, and vanished at length, leaving him in the heart of the dark wilderness, still rushing onward, with the instinct that guides mortal man to evil. The whole forest was peopled with frightful sounds; the creaking of the trees, the howling of wild beasts, and the yell of Indians; while, sometimes, the wind tolled like a distant church-bell, and sometimes gave a broad roar around the traveller, as if all Nature were laughing him to scorn. But he was himself the chief horror of the scene, and shrank not from its other horrors.

"Ha! ha! ha!" roared Goodman Brown, when the wind laughed at him. "Let us hear which will laugh loudest! Think not to frighten me with your deviltry! Come witch, come wizard, come Indian powow,[13] come devil himself! and here comes Goodman Brown. You may as well fear him as he fear you!"

[13]Medicine man.

In truth, all through the haunted forest, there could be nothing more frightful than the figure of Goodman Brown. On he flew, among the black pines, brandishing his staff with frenzied gestures, now giving vent to an inspiration of horrid blasphemy, and now shouting forth such laughter, as set all the echoes of the forest laughing like demons around him. The fiend in his own shape is less hideous, than when he rages in the breast of man. Thus sped the demoniac on his course, until, quivering among the trees, he saw a red light before him, as when the felled trunks and branches of a clearing have been set on fire, and throw up their lurid blaze against the sky, at the hour of midnight. He paused, in a lull of the tempest that had driven him onward, and heard the swell of what seemed a hymn, rolling solemnly from a distance, with the weight of many voices. He knew the tune; it was a familiar one in the choir of the village meeting-house. The verse died heavily away, and was lengthened by a chorus, not of human voices, but of all the sounds of the benighted wilderness, pealing in awful harmony together. Goodman Brown cried out; and his cry was lost to his own ear, by its unison with the cry of the desert.

In the interval of silence, he stole forward, until the light glared full upon his eyes. At one extremity of an open space, hemmed in by the dark wall of the forest, arose a rock, bearing some rude, natural resemblance either to an altar or a pulpit, and surrounded by four blazing pines, their tops aflame, their stems untouched, like candles at an evening meeting. The mass of foliage, that had overgrown the summit of the rock, was all on fire, blazing high into the night, and fitfully illuminating the whole field. Each pendent twig and leafy festoon was in a blaze. As the red light arose and fell, a numerous congregation alternately shone forth, then disappeared in shadow, and again grew, as it were, out of the darkness, peopling the heart of the solitary woods at once.

"A grave and dark-clad company!" quoth Goodman Brown.

In truth, they were such. Among them, quivering to-and-fro, between gloom and splendor, appeared faces that would be seen, next day, at the council-board of the province, and others which, Sabbath after Sabbath, looked devoutly heavenward, and benignantly over the crowded pews, from the holiest pulpits in the land. Some affirm, that the lady of the governor was there. At least, there were high dames well known to her, and wives of honored husbands, and widows, a great multitude, and ancient maidens, all of excellent repute, and fair young girls, who trembled, lest their mothers should espy them. Either the sudden gleams of light, flashing over the obscure field, bedazzled Goodman Brown, or he recognized a score of the church-members of Salem village, famous for their especial sanctity. Good old Deacon Gookin had arrived, and waited at the skirts of that venerable saint, his revered pastor. But, irreverently consorting with these grave, reputable, and pious people, these elders of the church, these chaste dames and dewy virgins, there were men of dissolute lives and women of spotted fame, wretches given over to all mean and filthy vice, and suspected even of horrid crimes. It was strange to see, that the good shrank not from the wicked, nor were the sinners abashed by the saints. Scattered, also, among their pale-faced enemies, were the Indian priests, or powows, who had often scared their native forest with more hideous incantations than any known to English witchcraft.

"But, where is Faith?" thought Goodman Brown; and, as hope came into his heart, he trembled.

Another verse of the hymn arose, a slow and mournful strain, such as the pious love, but joined to words which expressed all that our nature can conceive of sin, and darkly hinted at far more. Unfathomable to mere mortals is the lore of fiends. Verse after verse was sung, and still the chorus of the desert swelled between, like the deepest tone of a mighty organ. And, with the final peal of that dreadful anthem, there came a sound, as if the roaring wind, the rushing streams, the howling beasts, and every other voice of the unconverted wilderness, were mingling and according with the voice of guilty man, in homage to the prince of all. The four blazing pines threw up a loftier flame, and obscurely discovered shapes and visages of horror on the smoke-wreaths, above the impious assembly. At the same moment, the fire on the rock shot redly forth, and formed a glowing arch above its base, where now appeared a figure. With reverence be it spoken, the figure bore no slight similitude, both in garb and manner, to some grave divine of the New-England churches.

"Bring forth the converts!" cried a voice, that echoed through the field and rolled into the forest.

At the word, Goodman Brown stept forth from the shadow of the trees, and approached the congregation, with whom he felt a loathful brotherhood, by the sympathy of all that was wicked in his heart. He could have well nigh sworn, that the shape of his own dead father beckoned him to advance, looking downward from a smoke-wreath, while a woman, with dim features of despair, threw out her hand to warn him back. Was it his mother? But he had no power to retreat one step, nor to resist, even in thought, when the minister and good old Deacon Gookin seized his arms, and led him to the blazing rock. Thither came also the slender form of a veiled female, led between Goody Cloyse, that pious teacher of the catechism, and Martha Carrier, who had received the devil's promise to be queen of hell. A rampant hag was she! And there stood the proselytes, beneath the canopy of fire.

"Welcome, my children," said the dark figure, "to the communion of your race! Ye have found, thus young, your nature and your destiny. My children, look behind you!"

They turned; and flashing forth, as it were, in a sheet of flame, the fiend-worshippers were seen; the smile of welcome gleamed darkly on every visage.

"There," resumed the sable form, "are all whom ye have reverenced from youth. Ye deemed them holier than yourselves, and shrank from your own sin, contrasting it with their lives of righteousness, and prayerful aspirations heavenward. Yet, here are they all, in my worshipping assembly! This night it shall be granted you to know their secret deeds; how hoary-bearded elders of the church have whispered wanton words to the young maids of their households; how many a woman, eager for widow's weeds, has given her husband a drink at bedtime, and let him sleep his last sleep in her bosom; how beardless youths have made haste to inherit their fathers' wealth; and how fair damsels—blush not, sweet ones!—have dug little graves in the garden, and bidden me, the sole guest, to an infant's funeral. By the sympathy of your human hearts for sin, ye shall scent out all the places—whether in church, bed-chamber, street, field, or forest—where crime has been committed, and shall exult to behold the whole earth one stain of guilt, one mighty blood-spot. Far more than this! It shall be yours to penetrate, in every bosom, the deep mystery of sin, the fountain of all wicked arts, and which inexhaustibly supplies more evil impulses than human power—than my power, at its utmost!—can make manifest in deeds. And now, my children, look upon each other."

They did so; and, by the blaze of the hell-kindled torches, the wretched man beheld his Faith, and the wife her husband, trembling before that unhallowed altar.

"Lo! there ye stand, my children," said the figure, in a deep and solemn tone, almost sad, with its despairing awfulness, as if his once angelic nature could yet mourn for our miserable race. "Depending upon one another's hearts, ye had still hoped, that virtue were not all a dream. Now are ye undeceived! Evil is the nature of mankind. Evil must be your only happiness. Welcome, again, my children, to the communion of your race!"

"Welcome!" repeated the fiend-worshippers, in one cry of despair and triumph.

And there they stood, the only pair, as it seemed, who were yet hesitating on the verge of wickedness, in this dark world. A basin was hollowed, naturally, in the rock. Did it contain water, reddened by the lurid light? or was it blood? or, perchance, a liquid flame? Herein did the Shape of Evil dip his hand, and prepare to lay the mark of baptism upon their foreheads, that they might be partakers of the mystery of sin, more conscious of the secret guilt of others, both in deed and thought, than they could now be of their own. The husband cast one look at his pale wife, and Faith at him. What polluted wretches would the next glance shew them to each other, shuddering alike at what they disclosed and what they saw!

"Faith! Faith!" cried the husband. "Look up to Heaven, and resist the Wicked One!"

Whether Faith obeyed, he knew not. Hardly had he spoken, when he found himself amid calm night and solitude, listening to a roar of the wind, which died heavily away through the forest. He staggered against the rock and felt it chill and damp, while a hanging twig, that had been all on fire, besprinkled his cheek with the coldest dew.

The next morning, young Goodman Brown came slowly into the street of Salem village, staring around him like a bewildered man. The good old minister was taking a walk along the grave-yard, to get an appetite for breakfast and meditate his sermon, and bestowed a blessing, as he passed, on Goodman Brown. He shrank from the venerable saint, as if to avoid an anathema. Old Deacon Gookin was at domestic worship, and the holy words of his prayer were heard through the open window. "What God doth the wizard pray to?" quoth Goodman Brown. Goody Cloyse, that excellent old Christian, stood in the early sunshine, at her own lattice, catechising a little girl, who had brought her a pint of morning's milk. Goodman Brown snatched away the child, as from the grasp of the fiend himself. Turning the corner by the meeting-house, he spied the head of Faith, with the pink ribbons, gazing anxiously forth, and bursting into such joy at sight of him, that she skipt along the street, and almost kissed her husband before the whole village. But, Goodman Brown looked sternly and sadly into her face, and passed on without a greeting.

Had Goodman Brown fallen asleep in the forest, and only dreamed a wild dream of a witch-meeting?

Be it so, if you will. But, alas! it was a dream of evil omen for young Goodman Brown. A stern, a sad, a darkly meditative, a distrustful, if not a desperate man, did he become, from the night of that fearful dream. On the Sabbath-day, when the congregation were singing a holy psalm, he could not listen, because an anthem of sin rushed loudly upon his ear, and drowned all the blessed strain. When the minister spoke from the pulpit, with power and fervid eloquence, and, with his hand on the open Bible, of the sacred truths of our religion, and of saint-like lives and triumphant deaths, and of future bliss or misery unutterable, then did Goodman Brown turn pale, dreading, lest the roof should thunder down upon the gray blasphemer and his hearers. Often, awakening suddenly at midnight, he shrank from the bosom of Faith, and at morning or eventide, when the family knelt down at prayer, he scowled, and muttered to himself, and gazed sternly at his wife, and turned away. And when he had lived long, and was borne to his grave, a hoary corpse, followed by Faith, an aged woman, and children and grand-children, a goodly procession, besides neighbors, not a few, they carved no hopeful verse upon his tomb-stone; for his dying hour was gloom.

1835

The Minister's Black Veil[1]

A Parable[2]

The sexton stood in the porch of Milford[3] meeting-house, pulling lustily at the bell-rope. The old people of the village came stooping along the street. Children, with bright faces, tript merrily beside their parents, or mimicked a graver gait, in the conscious dignity of their Sunday clothes. Spruce bachelors looked sidelong at the pretty maidens, and fancied that the Sabbath sunshine made them prettier than on week-days. When the throng had mostly streamed into the porch, the sexton began to toll the bell, keeping his eye on the Reverend Mr. Hooper's door. The first glimpse of the clergyman's figure was the signal for the bell to cease its summons.

"But what has good Parson Hooper got upon his face?" cried the sexton in astonishment.

All within hearing immediately turned about, and beheld the semblance of Mr. Hooper, pacing slowly his meditative way towards the meeting-house. With one accord they started, expressing more wonder than if some strange minister were coming to dust the cushions of Mr. Hooper's pulpit.

"Are you sure it is our parson?" inquired Goodman Gray of the sexton.

"Of a certainty it is good Mr. Hooper," replied the sexton. "He was to have exchanged pulpits with Parson Shute of Westbury; but Parson Shute sent to excuse himself yesterday, being to preach a funeral sermon."

The cause of so much amazement may appear sufficiently slight. Mr. Hooper, a gentlemanly person of about thirty, though still a bachelor, was dressed with due clerical neatness, as if a careful wife had starched his band, and brushed the weekly

[1]First published in the *Token* (1836) and included in *Twice-told Tales* (1837).

[2]Another clergyman in New England, Mr. Joseph Moody, of York, Maine, who died about eighty years since, made himself remarkable by the same eccentricity that is here related of the Reverend Mr. Hooper. In his case, however, the symbol had a different import. In early life he had accidentally killed a beloved friend; and from that day till the hour of his own death, he hid his face from men [Hawthorne's note].

[3]A town southwest of Boston.

dust from his Sunday's garb. There was but one thing remarkable in his appearance. Swathed about his forehead, and hanging down over his face, so low as to be shaken by his breath, Mr. Hooper had on a black veil. On a nearer view, it seemed to consist of two folds of crape, which entirely concealed his features, except the mouth and chin, but probably did not intercept his sight, farther than to give a darkened aspect to all living and inanimate things. With this gloomy shade before him, good Mr. Hooper walked onward, at a slow and quiet pace, stooping somewhat and looking on the ground, as is customary with abstracted men, yet nodding kindly to those of his parishioners who still waited on the meeting-house steps. But so wonder-struck were they, that his greeting hardly met with a return.

"I can't really feel as if good Mr. Hooper's face was behind that piece of crape," said the sexton.

"I don't like it," muttered an old woman, as she hobbled into the meeting-house. "He has changed himself into something awful, only by hiding his face."

"Our parson has gone mad!" cried Goodman Gray, following him across the threshold.

A rumor of some unaccountable phenomenon had preceded Mr. Hooper into the meeting-house, and set all the congregation astir. Few could refrain from twisting their heads towards the door; many stood upright, and turned directly about; while several little boys clambered upon the seats, and came down again with a terrible racket. There was a general bustle, a rustling of the women's gowns and shuffling of the men's feet, greatly at variance with that hushed repose which should attend the entrance of the minister. But Mr. Hooper appeared not to notice the perturbation of his people. He entered with an almost noiseless step, bent his head mildly to the pews on each side, and bowed as he passed his oldest parishioner, a white-haired great-grandsire, who occupied an arm-chair in the centre of the aisle. It was strange to observe, how slowly this venerable man became conscious of something singular in the appearance of his pastor. He seemed not fully to partake of the prevailing wonder, till Mr. Hooper had ascended the stairs, and showed himself in the pulpit, face to face with his congregation, except for the black veil. That mysterious emblem was never once withdrawn. It shook with his measured breath as he gave out the psalm; it threw its obscurity between him and the holy page, as he read the Scriptures; and while he prayed, the veil lay heavily on his uplifted countenance. Did he seek to hide it from the dread Being whom he was addressing?

Such was the effect of this simple piece of crape, that more than one woman of delicate nerves was forced to leave the meeting-house. Yet perhaps the pale-faced congregation was almost as fearful a sight to the minister, as his black veil to them.

Mr. Hooper had the reputation of a good preacher, but not an energetic one: he strove to win his people heavenward, by mild persuasive influences, rather than to drive them thither, by the thunders of the Word. The sermon which he now delivered, was marked by the same characteristics of style and manner, as the general series of his pulpit oratory. But there was something, either in the sentiment of the discourse itself, or in the imagination of the auditors, which made it greatly the most powerful effort that they had ever heard from their pastor's lips. It was tinged, rather more darkly than usual, with the gentle gloom of Mr. Hooper's temperament. The subject had reference to secret sin, and those sad mysteries which we hide from our nearest and dearest, and would fain conceal from our own consciousness, even forgetting that the Omniscient can detect them. A subtle power was breathed into his words. Each member of the congregation, the most innocent girl, and the man of hardened breast, felt as if the preacher had crept upon them, behind his awful veil, and discovered their hoarded iniquity of deed or thought. Many spread their clasped hands on their bosoms. There was nothing terrible in what Mr. Hooper said; at least, no violence; and yet, with every tremor of his melancholy voice, the hearers quaked. An unsought pathos came hand in hand with awe. So sensible were the audience of some unwonted attribute in their minister, that they longed for a breath of wind to blow aside the veil, almost believing that a stranger's visage would be discovered, though the form, gesture, and voice were those of Mr. Hooper.

At the close of the services, the people hurried out with indecorous confusion, eager to communicate their pent-up amazement, and conscious of lighter spirits, the moment they lost sight of the black veil. Some gathered in little circles, huddled closely together, with their mouths all whispering in the centre; some went homeward alone, wrapt in silent meditation; some talked loudly, and profaned the Sabbath-day with ostentatious laughter. A few shook their sagacious heads, intimating that they could penetrate the mystery; while one or two affirmed that there was no mystery at all, but only that Mr. Hooper's eyes were so weakened by the midnight lamp, as to require a shade. After a brief interval, forth came good Mr. Hooper also, in the rear of his flock. Turning his veiled face from one group to another, he paid due reverence to the hoary heads, saluted the middle-aged with kind dignity, as their friend and spiritual guide, greeted the young with mingled authority and love, and laid his hands on the little children's heads to bless them. Such was always his custom on the Sabbath-day. Strange and bewildered looks repaid him for his courtesy. None, as on former occasions, aspired to the honor of walking by their pastor's side. Old Squire Saunders, doubtless by an accidental lapse of memory, neglected to invite Mr. Hooper to his table, where the good clergyman had been wont to bless the food, almost every Sunday since his settlement. He returned, therefore, to the parsonage, and, at the moment of closing the door, was observed to look back upon the people, all of whom had their eyes fixed upon the minister. A sad smile gleamed faintly from beneath the black veil, and flickered about his mouth, glimmering as he disappeared.

"How strange," said a lady, "that a simple black veil, such as any woman might wear on her bonnet, should become such a terrible thing on Mr. Hooper's face!"

"Something must surely be amiss with Mr. Hooper's intellects," observed her husband, the physician of the village. "But the strangest part of the affair is the effect of this vagary, even on a sober-minded man like myself. The black veil, though it covers only our pastor's face, throws its influence over his whole person, and makes him ghost-like from head to foot. Do you not feel it so?"

"Truly do I," replied the lady; "and I would not be alone with him for the world. I wonder he is not afraid to be alone with himself!"

"Men sometimes are so," said her husband.

The afternoon service was attended with similar circumstances. At its conclusion, the bell tolled for the funeral of a young lady. The relatives and friends were assembled in the house, and the more distant acquaintances stood about the door, speaking of the good qualities of the deceased, when their talk was interrupted by the appearance of Mr. Hooper, still covered with his black veil. It was now an appropriate emblem. The clergyman stepped into the room where the corpse was laid, and bent over the coffin, to take a last farewell of his deceased parishioner. As he stooped, the veil hung straight down from his forehead, so that, if her eye-lids had not been closed for ever, the dead maiden might have seen his face. Could Mr. Hooper be fearful of her glance, that he so hastily caught back the black veil? A person, who watched the interview between the dead and living, scrupled not to affirm, that, at the instant when the clergyman's features were disclosed, the corpse had slightly shuddered, rustling the shroud and muslin cap, though the countenance retained the composure of death. A superstitious old woman was the only witness of this prodigy. From the coffin, Mr. Hooper passed into the chamber of the mourners, and thence to the head of the staircase, to make the funeral prayer. It was a tender and heart-dissolving prayer, full of sorrow, yet so imbued with celestial hopes, that the music of a heavenly harp, swept by the fingers of the dead, seemed faintly to be heard among the saddest accents of the minister. The people trembled, though they but darkly understood him, when he prayed that they, and himself, and all of mortal race, might be ready, as he trusted this young maiden had been, for the dreadful hour that should snatch the veil from their faces. The bearers went heavily forth, and the mourners followed, saddening all the street, with the dead before them, and Mr. Hooper in his black veil behind.

"Why do you look back?" said one in the procession to his partner.

"I had a fancy," replied she, "that the minister and the maiden's spirit were walking hand in hand."

"And so had I, at the same moment," said the other.

That night, the handsomest couple in Milford village were to be joined in wedlock. Though reckoned a melancholy man, Mr. Hooper had a placid cheerfulness for such occasions, which often excited a sympathetic smile, where livelier merriment would have been thrown away. There was no quality of his disposition which made him more beloved than this. The company at the wedding awaited his arrival with impatience, trusting that the strange awe, which had gathered over him throughout the day, would now be dispelled. But such was not the result. When Mr. Hooper came, the first thing that their eyes rested on was the same horrible black veil, which had added deeper gloom to the funeral, and could portend nothing but evil to the wedding. Such was its immediate effect on the guests, that a cloud seemed to have rolled duskily from beneath the black crape, and dimmed the light of the candles. The bridal pair stood up before the minister. But the bride's cold fingers quivered in the tremulous hand of the bridegroom, and her deathlike paleness caused a whisper, that the maiden who had been buried a few hours before, was come from her grave to be married. If ever another wedding were so dismal, it was that famous one, where they tolled the wedding-knell.[4] After performing the ceremony, Mr. Hooper raised a glass of wine to his lips, wishing happiness to the new-married couple, in a strain of mild pleasantry that ought to have brightened the features of the guests, like a cheerful gleam from the hearth. At that instant, catching a glimpse of his figure in the looking-glass, the black veil involved his own spirit in the horror with which it

[4]Hawthorne's story "The Wedding Knell," also published in the 1836 *Token* and included in *Twice-told Tales.*

overwhelmed all others. His frame shuddered—his lips grew white—he spilt the untasted wine upon the carpet—and rushed forth into the darkness. For the Earth, too, had on her Black Veil.

The next day, the whole village of Milford talked of little else than Parson Hooper's black veil. That, and the mystery concealed behind it, supplied a topic for discussion between acquaintances meeting in the street, and good women gossiping at their open windows. It was the first item of news that the tavern-keeper told to his guests. The children babbled of it on their way to school. One imitative little imp covered his face with an old black handkerchief, thereby so affrighting his playmates, that the panic seized himself, and he well nigh lost his wits by his own waggery.

It was remarkable, that, of all the busy-bodies and impertinent people in the parish, not one ventured to put the plain question to Mr. Hooper, wherefore he did this thing. Hitherto, whenever there appeared the slightest call for such interference, he had never lacked advisers, nor shown himself averse to be guided by their judgment. If he erred at all, it was by so painful a degree of self-distrust, that even the mildest censure would lead him to consider an indifferent action as a crime. Yet, though so well acquainted with this amiable weakness, no individual among his parishioners chose to make the black veil a subject of friendly remonstrance. There was a feeling of dread, neither plainly confessed nor carefully concealed, which caused each to shift the responsibility upon another, till at length it was found expedient to send a deputation of the church, in order to deal with Mr. Hooper about the mystery, before it should grow into a scandal. Never did an embassy so ill discharge its duties. The minister received them with friendly courtesy, but became silent, after they were seated, leaving to his visiters the whole burthen of introducing their important business. The topic, it might be supposed, was obvious enough. There was the black veil, swathed round Mr. Hooper's forehead, and concealing every feature above his placid mouth, on which, at times, they could perceive the glimmering of a melancholy smile. But that piece of crape, to their imagination, seemed to hang down before his heart, the symbol of a fearful secret between him and them. Were the veil but cast aside, they might speak freely of it, but not till then. Thus they sat a considerable time, speechless, confused, and shrinking uneasily from Mr. Hooper's eye, which they felt to be fixed upon them with an invisible glance. Finally, the deputies returned abashed to their constituents, pronouncing the matter too weighty to be handled, except by a council of the churches, if, indeed, it might not require a general synod.

But there was one person in the village, unappalled by the awe with which the black veil had impressed all beside herself. When the deputies returned without an explanation, or even venturing to demand one, she, with the calm energy of her character, determined to chase away the strange cloud that appeared to be settling round Mr. Hooper, every moment more darkly than before. As his plighted wife, it should be her privilege to know what the black veil concealed. At the minister's first visit, therefore, she entered upon the subject, with a direct simplicity, which made the task easier both for him and her. After he had seated himself, she fixed her eyes steadfastly upon the veil, but could discern nothing of the dreadful gloom that had so overawed the multitude: it was but a double fold of crape, hanging down from his forehead to his mouth, and slightly stirring with his breath.

"No," said she aloud, and smiling, "there is nothing terrible in this piece of crape, except that it hides a face which I am always glad to look upon. Come, good sir, let the sun shine from behind the cloud. First lay aside your black veil: then tell me why you put it on."

Mr. Hooper's smile glimmered faintly.

"There is an hour to come," said he, "when all of us shall cast aside our veils. Take it not amiss, beloved friend, if I wear this piece of crape till then."

"Your words are a mystery too," returned the young lady. "Take away the veil from them, at least."

"Elizabeth, I will," said he, "so far as my vow may suffer me. Know, then, this veil is a type and a symbol, and I am bound to wear it ever, both in light and darkness, in solitude and before the gaze of multitudes, and as with strangers, so with my familiar friends. No mortal eye will see it withdrawn. This dismal shade must separate me from the world: even you, Elizabeth, can never come behind it!"

"What grievous affliction hath befallen you," she earnestly inquired, "that you should thus darken your eyes for ever?"

"If it be a sign of mourning," replied Mr. Hooper, "I, perhaps, like most other mortals, have sorrows dark enough to be typified by a black veil."

"But what if the world will not believe that it is the type of an innocent sorrow?" urged Elizabeth. "Beloved and respected as you are, there may be whispers, that you hide your face under the consciousness of secret sin. For the sake of your holy office, do away this scandal!"

The color rose into her cheeks, as she intimated the nature of the rumors that were already abroad in the village. But Mr. Hooper's mildness did not forsake him. He even smiled again—that same sad smile, which always appeared like a faint glimmering of light, proceeding from the obscurity beneath the veil.

"If I hide my face for sorrow, there is cause enough," he merely replied; "and if I cover it for secret sin, what mortal might not do the same?"

And with this gentle, but unconquerable obstinacy, did he resist all her entreaties. At length Elizabeth sat silent. For a few moments she appeared lost in thought, considering, probably, what new methods might be tried, to withdraw her lover from so dark a fantasy, which, if it had no other meaning, was perhaps a symptom of mental disease. Though of a firmer character than his own, the tears rolled down her cheeks. But, in an instant, as it were, a new feeling took the place of sorrow: her eyes were fixed insensibly on the black veil, when, like a sudden twilight in the air, its terrors fell around her. She arose, and stood trembling before him.

"And do you feel it then at last?" said he mournfully.

She made no reply, but covered her eyes with her hand, and turned to leave the room. He rushed forward and caught her arm.

"Have patience with me, Elizabeth!" cried he passionately. "Do not desert me, though this veil must be between us here on earth. Be mine, and hereafter there shall be no veil over my face, no darkness between our souls! It is but a mortal veil—it is not for eternity! Oh! you know not how lonely I am, and how frightened to be alone behind my black veil. Do not leave me in this miserable obscurity for ever!"

"Lift the veil but once, and look me in the face," said she.

"Never! It cannot be!" replied Mr. Hooper.

"Then, farewell!" said Elizabeth.

She withdrew her arm from his grasp, and slowly departed, pausing at the door, to give one long, shuddering gaze, that seemed almost to penetrate the mystery of the black veil. But, even amid his grief, Mr. Hooper smiled to think that only a material emblem had separated him from happiness, though the horrors which it shadowed forth, must be drawn darkly between the fondest of lovers.

From that time no attempts were made to remove Mr. Hooper's black veil, or, by a direct appeal, to discover the secret which it was supposed to hide. By persons who claimed a superiority to popular prejudice, it was reckoned merely an eccentric whim, such as often mingles with the sober actions of men otherwise rational, and tinges them all with its own semblance of insanity. But with the multitude, good Mr. Hooper was irreparably a bugbear. He could not walk the streets with any peace of mind, so conscious was he that the gentle and timid would turn aside to avoid him, and that others would make it a point of hardihood to throw themselves in his way. The impertinence of the latter class compelled him to give up his customary walk, at sunset, to the burial ground; for when he leaned pensively over the gate, there would always be faces behind the grave-stones, peeping at his black veil. A fable went the rounds, that the stare of the dead people drove him thence. It grieved him, to the very depth of his kind heart, to observe how the children fled from his approach, breaking up their merriest sports, while his melancholy figure was yet afar off. Their instinctive dread caused him to feel, more strongly than aught else, that a preternatural horror was interwoven with the threads of the black crape. In truth, his own antipathy to the veil was known to be so great, that he never willingly passed before a mirror, nor stooped to drink at a still fountain, lest, in its peaceful bosom, he should be affrighted by himself. This was what gave plausibility to the whispers, that Mr. Hooper's conscience tortured him for some great crime, too horrible to be entirely concealed, or otherwise than so obscurely intimated. Thus, from beneath the black veil, there rolled a cloud into the sunshine, an ambiguity of sin or sorrow, which enveloped the poor minister, so that love or sympathy could never reach him. It was said, that ghost and fiend consorted with him there. With self-shudderings and outward terrors, he walked continually in its shadow, groping darkly within his own soul, or gazing through a medium that saddened the whole world. Even the lawless wind, it was believed, respected his dreadful secret, and never blew aside the veil. But still good Mr. Hooper sadly smiled, at the pale visages of the worldly throng as he passed by.

Among all its bad influences, the black veil had the one desirable effect, of making its wearer a very efficient clergyman. By the aid of his mysterious emblem—for there was no other apparent cause—he became a man of awful power, over souls that were in agony for sin. His converts always regarded him with a dread peculiar to themselves, affirming, though but figuratively, that, before he brought them to celestial light, they had been with him behind the black veil. Its gloom, indeed, enabled him to sympathize with all dark affections. Dying sinners cried aloud for Mr. Hooper, and would not yield their breath till he appeared; though ever, as he stooped to whisper consolation, they shuddered at the veiled face so near their own. Such were the terrors of the black veil, even when Death had bared his visage! Strangers came long distances to attend service at his church, with the mere idle purpose of gazing at his figure, because it was forbidden them to behold his face. But many were made to quake ere they departed! Once, during Governor Belcher's administration,

Mr. Hooper was appointed to preach the election sermon.[5] Covered with his black veil, he stood before the chief magistrate, the council, and the representatives, and wrought so deep an impression, that the legislative measures of that year, were characterized by all the gloom and piety of our earliest ancestral sway.

In this manner Mr. Hooper spent a long life, irreproachable in outward act, yet shrouded in dismal suspicions; kind and loving, though unloved, and dimly feared; a man apart from men, shunned in their health and joy, but ever summoned to their aid in mortal anguish. As years wore on, shedding their snows above his sable veil, he acquired a name throughout the New-England churches, and they called him Father Hooper. Nearly all his parishioners, who were of mature age when he was settled, had been borne away by many a funeral: he had one congregation in the church, and a more crowded one in the church-yard; and having wrought so late into the evening, and done his work so well, it was now good Father Hooper's turn to rest.

Several persons were visible by the shaded candlelight, in the death-chamber of the old clergyman. Natural connections he had none. But there was the decorously grave, though unmoved physician, seeking only to mitigate the last pangs of the patient whom he could not save. There were the deacons, and other eminently pious members of his church. There, also, was the Reverend Mr. Clark, of Westbury, a young and zealous divine, who had ridden in haste to pray by the bed-side of the expiring minister. There was the nurse, no hired handmaiden of death, but one whose calm affection had endured thus long, in secresy, in solitude, amid the chill of age, and would not perish, even at the dying hour. Who, but Elizabeth! And there lay the hoary head of good Father Hooper upon the death-pillow, with the black veil still swathed about his brow and reaching down over his face, so that each more difficult gasp of his faint breath caused it to stir. All through life that piece of crape had hung between him and the world: it had separated him from cheerful brotherhood and woman's love, and kept him in that saddest of all prisons, his own heart; and still it lay upon his face, as if to deepen the gloom of his darksome chamber, and shade him from the sunshine of eternity.

For some time previous, his mind had been confused, wavering doubtfully between the past and the present, and hovering forward, as it were, at intervals, into the indistinctness of the world to come. There had been feverish turns, which tossed him from side to side, and wore away what little strength he had. But in his most convulsive struggles, and in the wildest vagaries of his intellect, when no other thought retained its sober influence, he still showed an awful solicitude lest the black veil should slip aside. Even if his bewildered soul could have forgotten, there was a faithful woman at his pillow, who, with averted eyes, would have covered that aged face, which she had last beheld in the comeliness of manhood. At length the death-stricken old man lay quietly in the torpor of mental and bodily exhaustion, with an imperceptible pulse, and breath that grew fainter and fainter, except when a long, deep, and irregular inspiration seemed to prelude the flight of his spirit.

[5]Jonathan Belcher (1682–1757) was Governor of both Massachusetts and New Hampshire between 1730 and 1741, which sets Hawthorne's story during the period of religious fervor known as "The Great Awakening." The annual election sermon was delivered by an eminent minister to solemnize the inauguration of a newly elected governor.

The minister of Westbury approached the bedside.

"Venerable Father Hooper," said he, "the moment of your release is at hand. Are you ready for the lifting of the veil, that shuts in time from eternity?"

Father Hooper at first replied merely by a feeble motion of his head; then, apprehensive, perhaps, that his meaning might be doubtful, he exerted himself to speak.

"Yea," said he, in faint accents, "my soul hath a patient weariness until that veil be lifted."

"And is it fitting," resumed the Reverend Mr. Clark, "that a man so given to prayer, of such a blameless example, holy in deed and thought, so far as mortal judgment may pronounce; is it fitting that a father in the church should leave a shadow on his memory, that may seem to blacken a life so pure? I pray you, my venerable brother, let not this thing be! Suffer us to be gladdened by your triumphant aspect, as you go to your reward. Before the veil of eternity be lifted, let me cast aside this black veil from your face!"

And thus speaking, the Reverend Mr. Clark bent forward to reveal the mystery of so many years. But, exerting a sudden energy, that made all the beholders stand aghast, Father Hooper snatched both his hands from beneath the bed-clothes, and pressed them strongly on the black veil, resolute to struggle, if the minister of Westbury would contend with a dying man.

"Never!" cried the veiled clergyman. "On earth, never!"

"Dark old man!" exclaimed the affrighted minister, "with what horrible crime upon your soul are you now passing to the judgment?"

Father Hooper's breath heaved; it rattled in his throat; but, with a mighty effort, grasping forward with his hands, he caught hold of life, and held it back till he should speak. He even raised himself in bed; and there he sat, shivering with the arms of death around him, while the black veil hung down, awful, at that last moment, in the gathered terrors of a life-time. And yet the faint, sad smile, so often there, now seemed to glimmer from its obscurity, and linger on Father Hooper's lips.

"Why do you tremble at me alone?" cried he, turning his veiled face round the circle of pale spectators. "Tremble also at each other! Have men avoided me, and women shown no pity, and children screamed and fled, only for my black veil? What, but the mystery which it obscurely typifies, has made this piece of crape so awful? When the friend shows his inmost heart to his friend; the lover to his best-beloved; when man does not vainly shrink from the eye of his Creator, loathsomely treasuring up the secret of his sin; then deem me a monster, for the symbol beneath which I have lived, and die! I look around me, and, lo! on every visage a Black Veil!"

While his auditors shrank from one another, in mutual affright, Father Hooper fell back upon his pillow, a veiled corpse, with a faint smile lingering on the lips. Still veiled, they laid him in his coffin, and a veiled corpse they bore him to the grave. The grass of many years has sprung up and withered on that grave, the burial-stone is moss-grown, and good Mr. Hooper's face is dust; but awful is still the thought, that it mouldered beneath the Black Veil!

1836

The Birth-mark[1]

In the latter part of the last century there lived a man of science—an eminent proficient in every branch of natural philosophy—who, not long before our story opens, had made experience of a spiritual affinity, more attractive than any chemical one. He had left his laboratory to the care of an assistant, cleared his fine countenance from the furnace-smoke, washed the stain of acids from his fingers, and persuaded a beautiful woman to become his wife. In those days, when the comparatively recent discovery of electricity, and other kindred mysteries of nature, seemed to open paths into the region of miracle, it was not unusual for the love of science to rival the love of woman, in its depth and absorbing energy. The higher intellect, the imagination, the spirit, and even the heart, might all find their congenial aliment in pursuits which, as some of their ardent votaries believed, would ascend from one step of powerful intelligence to another, until the philosopher should lay his hand on the secret of creative force, and perhaps make new worlds for himself. We know not whether Aylmer possessed this degree of faith in man's ultimate control over nature. He had devoted himself, however, too unreservedly to scientific studies, ever to be weaned from them by any second passion. His love for his young wife might prove the stronger of the two; but it could only be by intertwining itself with his love of science, and uniting the strength of the latter to its own.

Such a union accordingly took place, and was attended with truly remarkable consequences, and a deeply impressive moral. One day, very soon after their marriage, Aylmer sat gazing at his wife, with a trouble in his countenance that grew stronger, until he spoke.

"Georgiana," said he, "has it never occurred to you that the mark upon your cheek might be removed?"

"No, indeed," said she, smiling; but perceiving the seriousness of his manner, she blushed deeply. "To tell you the truth, it has been so often called a charm, that I was simple enough to imagine it might be so."

"Ah, upon another face, perhaps it might," replied her husband. "But never on yours! No, dearest Georgiana, you came so nearly perfect from the hand of Nature, that this slightest possible defect—which we hesitate whether to term a defect or a beauty—shocks me, as being the visible mark of earthly imperfection."

"Shocks you, my husband!" cried Georgiana, deeply hurt; at first reddening with momentary anger, but then bursting into tears. "Then why did you take me from my mother's side? You cannot love what shocks you!"

To explain this conversation, it must be mentioned, that, in the centre of Georgiana's left cheek, there was a singular mark, deeply interwoven, as it were, with the texture and substance of her face. In the usual state of her complexion,—a healthy, though delicate bloom,—the mark wore a tint of deeper crimson, which imperfectly defined its shape amid the surrounding rosiness. When she blushed, it gradually became more indistinct, and finally vanished amid the triumphant rush of blood, that

[1]First published in 1843 in the *Pioneer Magazine* and included in *Mosses from an Old Manse* (1846).

bathed the whole cheek with its brilliant glow. But, if any shifting emotion caused her to turn pale, there was the mark again, a crimson stain upon the snow, in what Aylmer sometimes deemed an almost fearful distinctness. Its shape bore not a little similarity to the human hand, though of the smallest pigmy size. Georgiana's lovers were wont to say, that some fairy, at her birth-hour, had laid her tiny hand upon the infant's cheek, and left this impress there, in token of the magic endowments that were to give her such sway over all hearts. Many a desperate swain would have risked life for the privilege of pressing his lips to the mysterious hand. It must not be concealed, however, that the impression wrought by this fairy sign-manual varied exceedingly, according to the difference of temperament in the beholders. Some fastidious persons—but they were exclusively of her own sex—affirmed that the Bloody Hand, as they chose to call it, quite destroyed the effect of Georgiana's beauty, and rendered her countenance even hideous. But it would be as reasonable to say, that one of those small blue stains, which sometimes occur in the purest statuary marble, would convert the Eve of Powers[2] to a monster. Masculine observers, if the birth-mark did not heighten their admiration, contented themselves with wishing it away, that the world might possess one living specimen of ideal loveliness, without the semblance of a flaw. After his marriage—for he thought little or nothing of the matter before—Aylmer discovered that this was the case with himself.

Had she been less beautiful—if Envy's self could have found aught else to sneer at—he might have felt his affection heightened by the prettiness of this mimic hand, now vaguely portrayed, now lost, now stealing forth again, and glimmering to-and-fro with every pulse of emotion that throbbed within her heart. But, seeing her otherwise so perfect, he found this one defect grow more and more intolerable, with every moment of their united lives.[3] It was the fatal flaw of humanity, which Nature, in one shape or another, stamps ineffaceably on all her productions, either to imply that they are temporary and finite, or that their perfection must be wrought by toil and pain. The Crimson Hand expressed the ineludible gripe, in which mortality clutches the highest and purest of earthly mould, degrading them into kindred with the lowest, and even with the very brutes, like whom their visible frames return to dust. In this manner, selecting it as the symbol of his wife's liability to sin, sorrow, decay, and death, Aylmer's sombre imagination was not long in rendering the birth-mark a frightful object, causing him more trouble and horror than ever Georgiana's beauty, whether of soul or sense, had given him delight.

At all the seasons which should have been their happiest, he invariably, and without intending it—nay, in spite of a purpose to the contrary—reverted to this one disastrous topic. Trifling as it at first appeared, it so connected itself with innumerable trains of thought, and modes of feeling, that it became the central point of all. With the morning twilight, Aylmer opened his eyes upon his wife's face, and recognized the symbol of imperfection; and when they sat together at the evening hearth, his eyes wandered stealthily to her cheek, and beheld, flickering with the blaze of the

[2]America's most famous sculptor Hiram Powers (1805–1873), working in Florence, produced his nude marble statue of *Eve Tempted* in 1842 and the even more famous *Greek Slave* in 1843. During Hawthorne's stay in Italy, he and Powers were good friends.

[3]Hawthorne's story evolves from ideas in his notebooks, e.g., the 1837 entry, "A person to be in the possession of something as perfect as mortal man has a right to demand; he tries to make it better, and ruins it entirely."

wood fire, the spectral Hand that wrote mortality, where he would fain have worshipped. Georgiana soon learned to shudder at his gaze. It needed but a glance, with the peculiar expression that his face often wore, to change the roses of her cheek into a deathlike paleness, amid which the Crimson Hand was brought strongly out, like a bas-relief of ruby on the whitest marble.

Late, one night, when the lights were growing dim, so as hardly to betray the stain on the poor wife's cheek, she herself, for the first time, voluntarily took up the subject.

"Do you remember, my dear Aylmer," said she, with a feeble attempt at a smile—"have you any recollection of a dream, last night, about this odious Hand?"

"None!—none whatever!" replied Aylmer, starting; but then he added in a dry, cold tone, affected for the sake of concealing the real depth of his emotion:—"I might well dream of it; for before I fell asleep, it had taken a pretty firm hold of my fancy."

"And you did dream of it," continued Georgiana, hastily; for she dreaded lest a gush of tears should interrupt what she had to say—"A terrible dream! I wonder that you can forget it. Is it possible to forget this one expression?—'It is in her heart now—we must have it out!'—Reflect, my husband; for by all means I would have you recall that dream."

The mind is in a sad note, when Sleep, the all-involving, cannot confine her spectres within the dim region of her sway, but suffers them to break forth, affrighting this actual life with secrets that perchance belong to a deeper one. Aylmer now remembered his dream. He had fancied himself, with his servant Aminadab, attempting an operation for the removal of the birth-mark. But the deeper went the knife, the deeper sank the Hand, until at length its tiny grasp appeared to have caught hold of Georgiana's heart; whence, however, her husband was inexorably resolved to cut or wrench it away.

When the dream had shaped itself perfectly in his memory, Aylmer sat in his wife's presence with a guilty feeling. Truth often finds its way to the mind close-muffled in robes of sleep, and then speaks with uncompromising directness of matters in regard to which we practise an unconscious self-deception, during our waking moments. Until now, he had not been aware of the tyrannizing influence acquired by one idea over his mind, and of the lengths which he might find in his heart to go, for the sake of giving himself peace.

"Aylmer," resumed Georgiana, solemnly, "I know not what may be the cost to both of us, to rid me of this fatal birth-mark. Perhaps its removal may cause cureless deformity. Or, it may be, the stain goes as deep as life itself. Again, do we know that there is a possibility, on any terms, of unclasping the firm gripe of this little Hand, which was laid upon me before I came into the world?"

"Dearest Georgiana, I have spent much thought upon the subject," hastily interrupted Aylmer—"I am convinced of the perfect practicability of its removal."

"If there be the remotest possibility of it," continued Georgiana, "let the attempt be made, at whatever risk. Danger is nothing to me; for life—while this hateful mark makes me the object of your horror and disgust—life is a burthen which I would fling down with joy. Either remove this dreadful Hand, or take my wretched life! You have deep science! All the world bears witness of it. You have achieved great wonders! Cannot you remove this little, little mark, which I cover with the tips of two small fingers? Is this beyond your power, for the sake of your own peace, and to save your poor wife from madness?"

"Noblest—dearest—tenderest wife!" cried Aylmer, rapturously. "Doubt not my power. I have already given this matter the deepest thought—thought which might almost have enlightened me to create a being less perfect than yourself. Georgiana, you have led me deeper than ever into the heart of science. I feel myself fully competent to render this dear cheek as faultless as its fellow; and then, most beloved, what will be my triumph, when I shall have corrected what Nature left imperfect, in her fairest work! Even Pygmalion, when his sculptured woman assumed life, felt not greater ecstasy than mine will be."

"It is resolved, then," said Georgiana, faintly smiling,—"And, Aylmer, spare me not, though you should find the birth-mark take refuge in my heart at last."

Her husband tenderly kissed her cheek—her right cheek—not that which bore the impress of the Crimson Hand.

The next day, Aylmer apprized his wife of a plan that he had formed, whereby he might have opportunity for the intense thought and constant watchfulness, which the proposed operation would require; while Georgiana, likewise, would enjoy the perfect repose essential to its success. They were to seclude themselves in the extensive apartments occupied by Aylmer as a laboratory, and where, during his toilsome youth, he had made discoveries in the elemental powers of nature, that had roused the admiration of all the learned societies in Europe. Seated calmly in this laboratory, the pale philosopher had investigated the secrets of the highest cloud-region, and of the profoundest mines; he had satisfied himself of the causes that kindled and kept alive the fires of the volcano; and had explained the mystery of fountains, and how it is that they gush forth, some so bright and pure, and others with such rich medicinal virtues, from the dark bosom of the earth. Here, too, at an earlier period, he had studied the wonders of the human frame, and attempted to fathom the very process by which Nature assimilates all her precious influences from earth and air, and from the spiritual world, to create and foster Man, her masterpiece. The latter pursuit, however, Aylmer had long laid aside, in unwilling recognition of the truth, against which all seekers sooner or later stumble, that our great creative Mother, while she amuses us with apparently working in the broadest sunshine, is yet severely careful to keep her own secrets, and, in spite of her pretended openness, shows us nothing but results. She permits us indeed, to mar, but seldom to mend, and, like a jealous patentee, on no account to make. Now, however, Aylmer resumed these half-forgotten investigations; not, of course, with such hopes or wishes as first suggested them; but because they involved much physiological truth, and lay in the path of his proposed scheme for the treatment of Georgiana.

As he led her over the threshold of the laboratory, Georgiana was cold and tremulous. Aylmer looked cheerfully into her face, with intent to reassure her, but was so startled with the intense glow of the birth-mark upon the whiteness of her cheek, that he could not restrain a strong convulsive shudder. His wife fainted.

"Aminadab! Aminadab!" shouted Aylmer, stamping violently on the floor.

Forthwith, there issued from an inner apartment a man of low stature, but bulky frame, with shaggy hair hanging about his visage, which was grimed with the vapors of the furnace. This personage had been Aylmer's under-worker during his whole scientific career, and was admirably fitted for that office by his great mechanical readiness, and the skill with which, while incapable of comprehending a single principle, he executed all the practical details of his master's experiments. With his vast strength, his shaggy hair, his smoky aspect, and the indescribable earthiness that incrusted him, he seemed to represent man's physical nature; while Aylmer's slender figure, and pale, intellectual face, were no less apt a type of the spiritual element.

"Throw open the door of the boudoir, Aminadab," said Aylmer, "and burn a pastille."

"Yes, master," answered Aminadab, looking intently at the lifeless form of Georgiana; and then he muttered to himself:—"If she were my wife, I'd never part with that birth-mark."

When Georgiana recovered consciousness, she found herself breathing an atmosphere of penetrating fragrance, the gentle potency of which had recalled her from her deathlike faintness. The scene around her looked like enchantment. Aylmer had converted those smoky, dingy, sombre rooms, where he had spent his brightest years in recondite pursuits, into a series of beautiful apartments, not unfit to be the secluded abode of a lovely woman. The walls were hung with gorgeous curtains, which imparted the combination of grandeur and grace, that no other species of adornment can achieve; and as they fell from the ceiling to the floor, their rich and ponderous folds, concealing all angles and straight lines, appeared to shut in the scene from infinite space. For aught Georgiana knew, it might be a pavilion among the clouds. And Aylmer, excluding the sunshine, which would have interfered with his chemical processes, had supplied its place with perfumed lamps, emitting flames of various hue, but all uniting in a soft, empurpled radiance. He now knelt by his wife's side, watching her earnestly, but without alarm; for he was confident in his science, and felt that he could draw a magic circle round her, within which no evil might intrude.

"Where am I?—Ah, I remember!" said Georgiana, faintly; and she placed her hand over her cheek, to hide the terrible mark from her husband's eyes.

"Fear not, dearest!" exclaimed he. "Do not shrink from me! Believe me, Georgiana, I even rejoice in this single imperfection, since it will be such rapture to remove it."

"Oh, spare me!" sadly replied his wife—"Pray do not look at it again. I never can forget that convulsive shudder."

In order to soothe Georgiana, and, as it were, to release her mind from the burthen of actual things, Aylmer now put in practice some of the light and playful secrets, which science had taught him among its profounder lore. Airy figures, absolutely bodiless ideas, and forms of unsubstantial beauty, came and danced before her, imprinting their momentary footsteps on beams of light. Though she had some indistinct idea of the method of these optical phenomena, still the illusion was almost perfect enough to warrant the belief, that her husband possessed sway over the spiritual world. Then again, when she felt a wish to look forth from her seclusion, immediately, as if her thoughts were answered, the procession of external existence flitted across a screen. The scenery and the figures of actual life were perfectly represented, but with that bewitching, yet indescribable difference, which always makes a picture, an image, or a shadow, so much more attractive than the original. When wearied of this, Aylmer bade her cast her eyes upon a vessel, containing a quantity of earth. She did so, with little interest at first, but was soon startled, to perceive the germ of a plant, shooting upward from the soil. Then came the slender stalk—the leaves gradually unfolded themselves—and amid them was a perfect and lovely flower.

"It is magical!" cried Georgiana, "I dare not touch it."

"Nay, pluck it," answered Aylmer, "pluck it, and inhale its brief perfume while you may. The flower will wither in a few moments, and leave nothing save its brown seed-vessels—but thence may be perpetuated a race as ephemeral as itself."

But Georgiana had no sooner touched the flower than the whole plant suffered a blight, its leaves turning coal-black, as if by the agency of fire.

"There was too powerful a stimulus," said Aylmer thoughtfully.

To make up for this abortive experiment, he proposed to take her portrait by a scientific process of his own invention. It was to be effected by rays of light striking upon a polished plate of metal. Georgiana assented—but, on looking at the result, was affrighted to find the features of the portrait blurred and indefinable,[4] while the minute figure of a hand appeared where the cheek should have been. Aylmer snatched the metallic plate, and threw it into a jar of corrosive acid.

Soon, however, he forgot these mortifying failures. In the intervals of study and chemical experiment, he came to her, flushed and exhausted, but seemed invigorated by her presence, and spoke in glowing language of the resources of his art. He gave a history of the long dynasty of the Alchemists, who spent so many ages in quest of the universal solvent, by which the Golden Principle might be elicited from all things vile and base. Aylmer appeared to believe, that, by the plainest scientific logic, it was altogether within the limits of possibility to discover this long-sought medium; but, he added, a philosopher who should go deep enough to acquire the power, would attain too lofty a wisdom to stoop to the exercise of it. Not less singular were his opinions in regard to the Elixir Vitæ.[5] He more than intimated, that it was his option to concoct a liquid that should prolong life for years—perhaps interminably—but that it would produce a discord in nature, which all the world, and chiefly the quaffer of the immortal nostrum, would find cause to curse.

"Aylmer, are you in earnest?" asked Georgiana, looking at him with amazement and fear; "it is terrible to possess such power, or even to dream of possessing it!"

"Oh, do not tremble, my love!" said her husband, "I would not wrong either you or myself by working such inharmonious effects upon our lives. But I would have you consider how trifling, in comparison, is the skill requisite to remove this little Hand."

At the mention of the birth-mark, Georgiana, as usual, shrank, as if a red-hot iron had touched her cheek.

Again Aylmer applied himself to his labors. She could hear his voice in the distant furnace-room, giving directions to Aminadab, whose harsh, uncouth, misshapen tones were audible in response, more like the grunt or growl of a brute than human speech. After hours of absence, Aylmer reappeared, and proposed that she should

[4]In a daguerreotype—the first practical photographic process, introduced in 1839—a sitter's reflected image was fixed onto a silvered and sensitized metal plate after about thirty seconds. Any movement produced a blurred image.

[5]The main project of alchemy was to transmute base metals into gold, but also involved seeking a panacea (or cure for all illnesses) and an elixir (or liquid) that might prolong life indefinitely.

now examine his cabinet of chemical products, and natural treasures of the earth. Among the former he showed her a small vial, in which, he remarked, was contained a gentle yet most powerful fragrance, capable of impregnating all the breezes that blow across a kingdom. They were of inestimable value, the contents of that little vial; and, as he said so, he threw some of the perfume into the air, and filled the room with piercing and invigorating delight.

"And what is this?" asked Georgiana, pointing to a small crystal globe, containing a gold-colored liquid. "It is so beautiful to the eye, that I could imagine it the Elixir of Life."

"In one sense it is," replied Aylmer, "or rather the Elixir of Immortality. It is the most precious poison that ever was concocted in this world. By its aid, I could apportion the lifetime of any mortal at whom you might point your finger. The strength of the dose would determine whether he were to linger out years, or drop dead in the midst of a breath. No king, on his guarded throne, could keep his life, if I, in my private station, should deem that the welfare of millions justified me in depriving him of it."

"Why do you keep such a terrific drug?" inquired Georgiana in horror.

"Do not mistrust me, dearest!" said her husband, smiling; "its virtuous potency is yet greater than its harmful one. But, see! here is a powerful cosmetic. With a few drops of this, in a vase of water, freckles may be washed away as easily as the hands are cleansed. A stronger infusion would take the blood out of the cheek, and leave the rosiest beauty a pale ghost."

"Is it with this lotion that you intend to bathe my cheek?" asked Georgiana anxiously.

"Oh, no!" hastily replied her husband—"this is merely superficial. Your case demands a remedy that shall go deeper."

In his interviews with Georgiana, Aylmer generally made minute inquiries as to her sensations, and whether the confinement of the rooms, and the temperature of the atmosphere, agreed with her. These questions had such a particular drift, that Georgiana began to conjecture that she was already subjected to certain physical influences, either breathed in with the fragrant air, or taken with her food. She fancied, likewise—but it might be altogether fancy—that there was a stirring up of her system,—a strange indefinite sensation creeping through her veins, and tingling, half painfully, half pleasurably, at her heart. Still, whenever she dared to look into the mirror, there she beheld herself, pale as a white rose, and with the crimson birth-mark stamped upon her cheek. Not even Aylmer now hated it so much as she.

To dispel the tedium of the hours which her husband found it necessary to devote to the processes of combination and analysis, Georgiana turned over the volumes of his scientific library. In many dark old tomes, she met with chapters full of romance and poetry. They were the works of the philosophers of the middle ages, such as Albertus Magnus, Cornelius Agrippa, Paracelsus, and the famous friar who created the prophetic Brazen Head.[6] All these antique naturalists stood in advance of their centuries, yet were imbued with some of their credulity, and therefore were

[6]Medieval and Renaissance philosophers and scientists whose experiments were associated with magic. The friar was Roger Bacon.

believed, and perhaps imagined themselves, to have acquired from the investigation of nature a power above nature, and from physics a sway over the spiritual world. Hardly less curious and imaginative were the early volumes of the Transactions of the Royal Society,[7] in which the members, knowing little of the limits of natural possibility, were continually recording wonders, or proposing methods whereby wonders might be wrought.

But, to Georgiana, the most engrossing volume was a large folio from her husband's own hand, in which he had recorded every experiment of his scientific career, with its original aim, the methods adopted for its development, and its final success or failure, with the circumstances to which either event was attributable. The book, in truth, was both the history and emblem of his ardent, ambitious, imaginative, yet practical and laborious, life. He handled physical details, as if there were nothing beyond them; yet spiritualized them all, and redeemed himself from materialism, by his strong and eager aspiration towards the infinite. In his grasp, the veriest clod of earth assumed a soul. Georgiana, as she read, reverenced Aylmer, and loved him more profoundly than ever, but with a less entire dependence on his judgment than heretofore. Much as he had accomplished, she could not but observe that his most splendid successes were almost invariably failures, if compared with the ideal at which he aimed. His brightest diamonds were the merest pebbles, and felt to be so by himself, in comparison with the inestimable gems which lay hidden beyond his reach. The volume, rich with achievements that had won renown for its author, was yet as melancholy a record as ever mortal hand had penned. It was the sad confession, and continual exemplification, of the short-comings of the composite man—the spirit burthened with clay and working in matter—and of the despair that assails the higher nature, at finding itself so miserably thwarted by the earthly part. Perhaps every man of genius, in whatever sphere, might recognize the image of his own experience in Aylmer's journal.

So deeply did these reflections affect Georgiana, that she laid her face upon the open volume, and burst into tears. In this situation she was found by her husband.

"It is dangerous to read in a sorcerer's books," said he, with a smile, though his countenance was uneasy and displeased. "Georgiana, there are pages in that volume, which I can scarcely glance over and keep my senses. Take heed lest it prove as detrimental to you!"

"It has made me worship you more than ever," said she.

"Ah! wait for this one success," rejoined he, "then worship me if you will. I shall deem myself hardly unworthy of it. But, come! I have sought you for the luxury of your voice. Sing to me, dearest!"

So she poured out the liquid music of her voice to quench the thirst of his spirit. He then took his leave, with a boyish exuberance of gaiety, assuring her that her seclusion would endure but a little longer, and that the result was already certain. Scarcely had he departed, when Georgiana felt irresistibly impelled to follow him. She had forgotten to inform Aylmer of a symptom, which, for two or three hours past, had begun to excite her attention. It was a sensation in the fatal birth-mark, not painful, but which induced a restlessness throughout her system. Hastening after her husband, she intruded, for the first time, into the laboratory.

[7]The Royal Society, founded in London in 1662, was committed to scientific experiment.

The first thing that struck her eye was the furnace, that hot and feverish worker, with the intense glow of its fire, which, by the quantities of soot clustered above it, seemed to have been burning for ages. There was a distilling apparatus in full operation. Around the room were retorts, tubes, cylinders, crucibles, and other apparatus of chemical research. An electrical machine stood ready for immediate use. The atmosphere felt oppressively close, and was tainted with gaseous odors, which had been tormented forth by the processes of science. The severe and homely simplicity of the apartment, with its naked walls and brick pavement, looked strange, accustomed as Georgiana had become to the fantastic elegance of her boudoir. But what chiefly, indeed almost solely, drew her attention, was the aspect of Aylmer himself.

He was pale as death, anxious, and absorbed, and hung over the furnace as if it depended upon his utmost watchfulness whether the liquid, which it was distilling, should be the draught of immortal happiness or misery. How different from the sanguine and joyous mien that he had assumed for Georgiana's encouragement!

"Carefully now, Aminadab! Carefully, thou human machine! Carefully, thou man of clay!" muttered Aylmer, more to himself than his assistant. "Now, if there be a thought too much or too little, it is all over!"

"Hoh! hoh!" mumbled Aminadab—"look, master, look!"

Aylmer raised his eyes hastily, and at first reddened, then grew paler than ever, on beholding Georgiana. He rushed towards her, and seized her arm with a gripe that left the print of his fingers upon it.

"Why do you come hither? Have you no trust in your husband?" cried he impetuously. "Would you throw the blight of that fatal birth-mark over my labors? It is not well done. Go, prying woman, go!"

"Nay, Aylmer," said Georgiana, with the firmness of which she possessed no stinted endowment, "it is not you that have a right to complain. You mistrust your wife! You have concealed the anxiety with which you watch the development of this experiment. Think not so unworthily of me, my husband! Tell me all the risk we run; and fear not that I shall shrink, for my share in it is far less than your own!"

"No, no, Georgiana!" said Aylmer impatiently, "it must not be."

"I submit," replied she calmly. "And, Aylmer, I shall quaff whatever draught you bring me; but it will be on the same principle that would induce me to take a dose of poison, if offered by your hand."

"My noble wife," said Aylmer, deeply moved, "I knew not the height and depth of your nature, until now. Nothing shall be concealed. Know, then, that this Crimson Hand, superficial as it seems, has clutched its grasp into your being, with a strength of which I had no previous conception. I have already administered agents powerful enough to do aught except to change your entire physical system. Only one thing remains to be tried. If that fail us, we are ruined!"

"Why did you hesitate to tell me this?" asked she.

"Because, Georgiana," said Aylmer, in a low voice, "there is danger!"

"Danger? There is but one danger—that this horrible stigma shall be left upon my cheek!" cried Georgiana. "Remove it! remove it!—whatever be the cost—or we shall both go mad!"

"Heaven knows, your words are too true," said Aylmer, sadly. "And now, dearest, return to your boudoir. In a little while, all will be tested."

He conducted her back, and took leave of her with a solemn tenderness, which spoke far more than his words how much was now at stake. After his departure,

Georgiana became wrapt in musings. She considered the character of Aylmer, and did it completer justice than at any previous moment. Her heart exulted, while it trembled, at his honorable love, so pure and lofty that it would accept nothing less than perfection, nor miserably make itself contented with an earthlier nature than he had dreamed of. She felt how much more precious was such a sentiment, than that meaner kind which would have borne with the imperfection for her sake, and have been guilty of treason to holy love, by degrading its perfect idea to the level of the actual. And, with her whole spirit, she prayed, that, for a single moment, she might satisfy his highest and deepest conception. Longer than one moment, she well knew, it could not be; for his spirit was ever on the march—ever ascending—and each instant required something that was beyond the scope of the instant before.

The sound of her husband's footsteps aroused her. He bore a crystal goblet, containing a liquor colorless as water, but bright enough to be the draught of immortality. Aylmer was pale; but it seemed rather the consequence of a highly wrought state of mind, and tension of spirit, than of fear or doubt.

"The concoction of the draught has been perfect," said he, in answer to Georgiana's look. "Unless all my science have deceived me, it cannot fail."

"Save on your account, my dearest Aylmer," observed his wife, "I might wish to put off this birth-mark of mortality by relinquishing mortality itself, in preference to any other mode. Life is but a sad possession to those who have attained precisely the degree of moral advancement at which I stand. Were I weaker and blinder, it might be happiness. Were I stronger, it might be endured hopefully. But, being what I find myself, methinks I am of all mortals the most fit to die."

"You are fit for heaven without tasting death!" replied her husband. "But why do we speak of dying? The draught cannot fail. Behold its effect upon this plant!"

On the window-seat there stood a geranium, diseased with yellow blotches, which had overspread all its leaves. Aylmer poured a small quantity of the liquid upon the soil in which it grew. In a little time, when the roots of the plant had taken up the moisture, the unsightly blotches began to be extinguished in a living verdure.

"There needed no proof," said Georgiana, quietly. "Give me the goblet. I joyfully stake all upon your word."

"Drink, then, thou lofty creature!" exclaimed Aylmer, with fervid admiration. "There is no taint of imperfection on thy spirit. Thy sensible frame, too, shall soon be all perfect!"

She quaffed the liquid, and returned the goblet to his hand.

"It is grateful," said she, with a placid smile. "Methinks it is like water from a heavenly fountain; for it contains I know not what of unobtrusive fragrance and deliciousness. It allays a feverish thirst, that had parched me for many days. Now, dearest, let me sleep. My earthly senses are closing over my spirit, like the leaves round the heart of a rose, at sunset."

She spoke the last words with a gentle reluctance, as if it required almost more energy than she could command to pronounce the faint and lingering syllables. Scarcely had they loitered through her lips, ere she was lost in slumber. Aylmer sat by her side, watching her aspect with the emotions proper to a man, the whole value of whose existence was involved in the process now to be tested. Mingled with this mood, however, was the philosophic investigation, characteristic of the man of science. Not the minutest symptom escaped him. A heightened flush of the cheek—a slight irregularity of breath—a quiver of the eyelid—a hardly perceptible tremor through the frame—such were the details which, as the moments passed, he wrote down in his folio volume. Intense thought had set its stamp upon every previous page of that volume; but the thoughts of years were all concentrated upon the last.

While thus employed, he failed not to gaze often at the fatal Hand, and not without a shudder. Yet once, by a strange and unaccountable impulse, he pressed it with his lips. His spirit recoiled, however, in the very act, and Georgiana, out of the midst of her deep sleep, moved uneasily and murmured, as if in remonstrance. Again, Aylmer resumed his watch. Nor was it without avail. The Crimson Hand, which at first had been strongly visible upon the marble paleness of Georgiana's cheek now grew more faintly outlined. She remained not less pale than ever; but the birth-mark, with every breath that came and went, lost somewhat of its former distinctness. Its presence had been awful; its departure was more awful still. Watch the stain of the rainbow fading out of the sky; and you will know how that mysterious symbol passed away.

"By Heaven, it is well nigh gone!" said Aylmer to himself, in almost irrepressible ecstasy. "I can scarcely trace it now Success! Success! And now it is like the faintest rose-color. The slightest flush of blood across her cheek would overcome it. But she is so pale!"

He drew aside the window-curtain, and suffered the light of natural day to fall into the room, and rest upon her cheek. At the same time, he heard a gross, hoarse chuckle, which he had long known as his servant Aminadab's expression of delight.

"Ah, clod! Ah, earthly mass!" cried Aylmer, laughing in a sort of frenzy. "You have served me well! Matter and Spirit—Earth and Heaven—have both done their part in this! Laugh, thing of senses! You have earned the right to laugh."

These exclamations broke Georgiana's sleep. She slowly unclosed her eyes, and gazed into the mirror, which her husband had arranged for that purpose. A faint smile flitted over her lips, when she recognized how barely perceptible was now that Crimson Hand, which had once blazed forth with such disastrous brilliancy as to scare away all their happiness. But then her eyes sought Aylmer's face, with a trouble and anxiety that he could by no means account for.

"My poor Aylmer!" murmured she.

"Poor? Nay, richest! Happiest! Most favored!" exclaimed he. "My peerless bride, it is successful! You are perfect!"

"My poor Aylmer!" she repeated, with a more than human tenderness. "You have aimed loftily!—you have done nobly! Do not repent, that, with so high and pure a feeling, you have rejected the best that earth could offer. Aylmer—dearest Aylmer—I am dying!"

Alas, it was too true! The fatal Hand had grappled with the mystery of life, and was the bond by which an angelic spirit kept itself in union with a mortal frame. As the last crimson tint of the birth-mark—that sole token of human imperfection—faded from her cheek, the parting breath of the now perfect woman passed into the atmosphere, and her soul, lingering a moment near her husband, took its heavenward flight. Then a hoarse, chuckling laugh was heard again! Thus ever does the gross Fatality of Earth exult in its invariable triumph over the immortal essence, which, in this dim sphere of half-development, demands the completeness of a higher state. Yet, had Aylmer reached a profounder wisdom, he need not thus have flung away the happiness, which would have woven his mortal life of the self-same texture with the celestial. The momentary circumstance was too strong for him; he failed to look beyond the shadowy scope of Time, and living once for all in Eternity, to find the perfect Future in the present.

1843

Rappaccini's Daughter[1]

From the Writings of Aubépine[2]

We do not remember to have seen any translated specimens of the productions of M. de l'Aubépine; a fact the less to be wondered at, as his very name is unknown to many of his own countrymen, as well as to the student of foreign literature. As a writer, he seems to occupy an unfortunate position between the Transcendentalists (who, under one name or another, have their share in all the current literature of the world), and the great body of pen-and-ink men who address the intellect and sympathies of the multitude. If not too refined, at all events too remote, too shadowy and unsubstantial in his modes of development, to suit the taste of the latter class, and yet too popular to satisfy the spiritual or metaphysical requisitions of the former, he must necessarily find himself without an audience; except here and there an individual, or possibly an isolated clique. His writings, to do them justice, are not altogether destitute of fancy and originality; they might have won him greater reputation but for an inveterate love of allegory, which is apt to invest his plots and characters with the aspect of scenery and people in the clouds, and to steal away the human warmth out of his conceptions. His fictions are sometimes historical, sometimes of the present day, and sometimes, so far as can be discovered, have little or no reference either to time or space. In any case, he generally contents himself with a very slight embroidery of outward manners,—the faintest possible counterfeit of real life,—and endeavors to create an interest by some less obvious peculiarity of the subject. Occasionally, a breath of nature, a rain-drop of pathos and tenderness, or a gleam of humor, will find its way into the midst of his fantastic imagery, and make us feel as if, after all, we were yet within the limits of our native earth. We will only add to this very cursory notice, that M. de l'Aubépine's productions, if the reader chance to take them in precisely the proper point of view, may amuse a leisure hour as well as those of a brighter man; if otherwise, they can hardly fail to look excessively like nonsense.

Our author is voluminous; he continues to write and publish with as much praiseworthy and indefatigable prolixity, as if his efforts were crowned with the brilliant success that so justly attends those of Eugene Sue.[3] His first appearance was by a collection of stories, in a long series of volumes, entitled *"Contes deux fois*

[1]First published in 1844 in *The United States Magazine and Democratic Review* and included in *Mosses from an Old Manse* (1846).

[2]Hawthorne.

[3]A popular French novelist (1804–1857).

recontées." The titles of some of his more recent works (we quote from memory) are as follows:—*"Le Voyage Céleste à Chemin de Fer,"* 3 tom. 1838. *"Le nouveau Père Adam et la nouvelle Mère Eve,"* 2 tom. 1839. *"Roderic; ou le Serpent à l'estomac,"* 2 tom. 1840. *"Le Culte de Feu,"* a folio volume of ponderous research into the religion and ritual of the old Persian Ghebers, published in 1841. *"La Soirée du Château en Espagne,"* 1 tom. 8 vo. 1842; and *"L'Artiste du Beau; ou le Papillon Mécanique,"* 5 tom. 4to. 1843. Our somewhat wearisome perusal of this startling catalogue of volumes has left behind it a certain personal affection and sympathy, though by no means admiration, for M. de l'Aubépine; and we would fain do the little in our power towards introducing him favorably to the American public. The ensuing tale is a translation of his *"Beatrice; ou la Belle Empoisonneuse,"* recently published in *"La Revue Anti-Aristocratique."* This journal, edited by the Comte de Bearhaven, has, for some years past, led the defence of liberal principles and popular rights, with a faithfulness and ability worthy of all praise.[4]

A young man, named Giovanni Guasconti, came, very long ago, from the more southern region of Italy, to pursue his studies at the University of Padua. Giovanni, who had but a scanty supply of gold ducats in his pocket, took lodgings in a high and gloomy chamber of an old edifice, which looked not unworthy to have been the palace of a Paduan noble, and which, in fact, exhibited over its entrance the armorial bearings of a family long since extinct. The young stranger, who was not unstudied in the great poem of his country, recollected that one of the ancestors of this family, and perhaps an occupant of this very mansion, had been pictured by Dante as a partaker of the immortal agonies of his Inferno. These reminiscences and associations, together with the tendency to heart-break natural to a young man for the first time out of his native sphere, caused Giovanni to sigh heavily, as he looked around the desolate and ill-furnished apartment.

"Holy Virgin, Signor," cried old dame Lisabetta, who, won by the youth's remarkable beauty of person, was kindly endeavoring to give the chamber a habitable air, "what a sigh was that to come out of a young man's heart! Do you find this old mansion gloomy? For the love of heaven, then, put your head out of the window, and you will see as bright sunshine as you have left in Naples."

Guasconti mechanically did as the old woman advised, but could not quite agree with her that the Paduan sunshine was as cheerful as that of southern Italy. Such as it was, however, it fell upon a garden beneath the window, and expended its fostering influences on a variety of plants, which seemed to have been cultivated with exceeding care.

"Does this garden belong to the house?" asked Giovanni.

"Heaven forbid, Signor!—unless it were fruitful of better pot-herbs than any that grow there now," answered old Lisabetta. "No; that garden is cultivated by the own hands of Signor Giacomo Rappaccini, the famous Doctor, who, I warrant him, has been heard of as far as Naples. It is said that he distils these plants into medicines that are as potent as a charm. Oftentimes you may see the Signor Doctor at work, and perchance the Signora his daughter, too, gathering the strange flowers that grow in the garden."

[4]Hawthorne's mock review of himself gives French renderings of *Twice-told Tales*, the titles of individual stories, and *The Democratic Review* (edited by his friend John O'Sullivan).

The old woman had now done what she could for the aspect of the chamber, and, commending the young man to the protection of the saints, took her departure.

Giovanni still found no better occupation than to look down into the garden beneath his window. From its appearance, he judged it to be one of those botanic gardens, which were of earlier date in Padua than elsewhere in Italy, or in the world. Or, not improbably, it might once have been the pleasure-place of an opulent family; for there was the ruin of a marble fountain in the centre, sculptured with rare art, but so wofully shattered that it was impossible to trace the original design from the chaos of remaining fragments. The water, however, continued to gush and sparkle into the sunbeams as cheerfully as ever. A little gurgling sound ascended to the young man's window, and made him feel as if the fountain were an immortal spirit, that sung its song unceasingly, and without heeding the vicissitudes around it; while one century embodied it in marble, and another scattered the perishable garniture on the soil. All about the pool into which the water subsided, grew various plants, that seemed to require a plentiful supply of moisture for the nourishment of gigantic leaves, and, in some instances, flowers gorgeously magnificent. There was one shrub in particular, set in a marble vase in the midst of the pool, that bore a profusion of purple blossoms, each of which had the lustre and richness of a gem; and the whole together made a show so resplendent that it seemed enough to illuminate the garden, even had there been no sunshine. Every portion of the soil was peopled with plants and herbs, which, if less beautiful, still bore tokens of assiduous care; as if all had their individual virtues, known to the scientific mind that fostered them. Some were placed in urns, rich with old carving, and others in common garden-pots; some crept serpent-like along the ground, or climbed on high, using whatever means of ascent was offered them. One plant had wreathed itself round a statue of Vertumnus,[5] which was thus quite veiled and shrouded in a drapery of hanging foliage, so happily arranged that it might have served a sculptor for a study.

While Giovanni stood at the window, he heard a rustling behind a screen of leaves, and became aware that a person was at work in the garden. His figure soon emerged into view, and showed itself to be that of no common laborer, but a tall, emaciated, sallow, and sickly-looking man, dressed in a scholar's garb of black. He was beyond the middle term of life, with grey hair, a thin grey beard, and a face singularly marked with intellect and cultivation, but which could never, even in his more youthful days, have expressed much warmth of heart.

Nothing could exceed the intentness with which this scientific gardener examined every shrub which grew in his path; it seemed as if he was looking into their inmost nature, making observations in regard to their creative essence, and discovering why one leaf grew in this shape, and another in that, and wherefore such and such flowers differed among themselves in hue and perfume. Nevertheless, in spite of this deep intelligence on his part, there was no approach to intimacy between himself and these vegetable existences. On the contrary, he avoided their actual touch, or the direct inhaling of their odors, with a caution that impressed Giovanni most

[5]The Roman god of changing seasons and thus of flowers and fruits, married to Pomona. Hawthorne's garden imagery includes allusions not only to classical myth but to the Garden of Eden, the Song of Songs, the Romance of the Rose, Dante, Spenser, and the University of Padua's experimental botanical gardens (founded in 1545).

disagreeably; for the man's demeanor was that of one walking among malignant influences, such as savage beasts, or deadly snakes, or evil spirits, which, should he allow them one moment of license, would wreak upon him some terrible fatality. It was strangely frightful to the young man's imagination, to see this air of insecurity in a person cultivating a garden, that most simple and innocent of human toils, and which had been alike the joy and labor of the unfallen parents of the race. Was this garden, then, the Eden of the present world?—and this man, with such a perception of harm in what his own hands caused to grow, was he the Adam?

The distrustful gardener, while plucking away the dead leaves or pruning the too luxuriant growth of the shrubs, defended his hands with a pair of thick gloves. Nor were these his only armor. When, in his walk through the garden, he came to the magnificent plant that hung its purple gems beside the marble fountain, he placed a kind of mask over his mouth and nostrils, as if all this beauty did but conceal a deadlier malice. But finding his task still too dangerous, he drew back, removed the mask, and called loudly, but in the infirm voice of a person affected with inward disease:

"Beatrice!—Beatrice!"[6]

"Here am I, my father! What would you?" cried a rich and youthful voice from the window of the opposite house; a voice as rich as a tropical sunset, and which made Giovanni, though he knew not why, think of deep hues of purple or crimson, and of perfumes heavily delectable.—"Are you in the garden?"

"Yes, Beatrice," answered the gardener, "and I need your help."

Soon there emerged from under a sculptured portal the figure of a young girl, arrayed with as much richness of taste as the most splendid of the flowers, beautiful as the day, and with a bloom so deep and vivid that one shade more would have been too much. She looked redundant with life, health, and energy; all of which attributes were bound down and compressed, as it were, and girdled tensely, in their luxuriance, by her virgin zone.[7] Yet Giovanni's fancy must have grown morbid, while he looked down into the garden; for the impression which the fair stranger made upon him was as if here were another flower, the human sister of those vegetable ones, as beautiful as they—more beautiful than the richest of them—but still to be touched only with a glove, nor to be approached without a mask. As Beatrice came down the garden path, it was observable that she handled and inhaled the odor of several of the plants, which her father had most sedulously avoided.

"Here, Beatrice," said the latter,—"see how many needful offices require to be done to our chief treasure. Yet, shattered as I am, my life might pay the penalty of approaching it so closely as circumstances demand. Henceforth, I fear, this plant must be consigned to your sole charge."

"And gladly will I undertake it," cried again the rich tones of the young lady, as she bent towards the magnificent plant, and opened her arms as if to embrace it. "Yes, my sister, my splendor, it shall be Beatrice's task to nurse and serve thee; and thou shalt reward her with thy kisses and perfumed breath, which to her is as the breath of life!"

[6]The name, literally "she who makes happy," is also that of Dante's beloved Beatrice Portonari (1266–1290), immortalized in his *Divine Comedy.*

[7]Belt worn by a young unmarried woman.

Then, with all the tenderness in her manner that was so strikingly expressed in her words, she busied herself with such attentions as the plant seemed to require; and Giovanni, at his lofty window, rubbed his eyes, and almost doubted whether it were a girl tending her favorite flower, or one sister performing the duties of affection to another. The scene soon terminated. Whether Doctor Rappaccini had finished his labors in the garden, or that his watchful eye had caught the stranger's face, he now took his daughter's arm and retired. Night was already closing in; oppressive exhalations seemed to proceed from the plants, and steal upward past the open window; and Giovanni, closing the lattice, went to his couch, and dreamed of a rich flower and beautiful girl. Flower and maiden were different and yet the same, and fraught with some strange peril in either shape.

But there is an influence in the light of morning that tends to rectify whatever errors of fancy, or even of judgment, we may have incurred during the sun's decline, or among the shadows of the night, or in the less wholesome glow of moonshine. Giovanni's first movement on starting from sleep, was to throw open the window, and gaze down into the garden which his dreams had made so fertile of mysteries. He was surprised, and a little ashamed, to find how real and matter-of-fact an affair it proved to be, in the first rays of the sun, which gilded the dew-drops that hung upon leaf and blossom, and, while giving a brighter beauty to each rare flower, brought everything within the limits of ordinary experience. The young man rejoiced, that, in the heart of the barren city, he had the privilege of overlooking this spot of lovely and luxuriant vegetation. It would serve, he said to himself, as a symbolic language, to keep him in communion with Nature. Neither the sickly and thought-worn Doctor Giacomo Rappaccini, it is true, nor his brilliant daughter, were now visible; so that Giovanni could not determine how much of the singularity which he attributed to both, was due to their own qualities, and how much to his wonder-working fancy. But he was inclined to take a most rational view of the whole matter.

In the course of the day, he paid his respects to Signor Pietro Baglioni, professor of medicine in the University, a physician of eminent repute, to whom Giovanni had brought a letter of introduction. The Professor was an elderly personage, apparently of genial nature, and habits that might almost be called jovial; he kept the young man to dinner, and made himself very agreeable by the freedom and liveliness of his conversation, especially when warmed by a flask or two of Tuscan wine. Giovanni, conceiving that men of science, inhabitants of the same city, must needs be on familiar terms with one another, took an opportunity to mention the name of Doctor Rappaccini. But the Professor did not respond with so much cordiality as he had anticipated.

"Ill would it become a teacher of the divine art of medicine," said Professor Pietro Baglioni, in answer to a question of Giovanni, "to withhold due and well-considered praise of a physician so eminently skilled as Rappaccini. But, on the other hand, I should answer it but scantily to my conscience, were I to permit a worthy youth like yourself, Signor Giovanni, the son of an ancient friend, to imbibe erroneous ideas respecting a man who might hereafter chance to hold your life and death in his hands. The truth is, our worshipful Doctor Rappaccini has as much science as any member of the faculty—with perhaps one single exception—in Padua, or all Italy. But there are certain grave objections to his professional character."

"And what are they?" asked the young man.

"Has my friend Giovanni any disease of body or heart, that he is so inquisitive about physicians?" said the Professor, with a smile. "But as for Rappaccini, it is said of him—and I, who know the man well, can answer for its truth—that he cares infinitely more for science than for mankind. His patients are interesting to him only as subjects for some new experiment. He would sacrifice human life, his own among the rest, or whatever else was dearest to him, for the sake of adding so much as a grain of mustard-seed to the great heap of his accumulated knowledge."

"Methinks he is an awful man, indeed," remarked Guasconti, mentally recalling the cold and purely intellectual aspect of Rappaccini. "And yet, worshipful Professor, is it not a noble spirit? Are there many men capable of so spiritual a love of science?"

"God forbid," answered the Professor, somewhat testily—"at least, unless they take sounder views of the healing art than those adopted by Rappaccini. It is his theory, that all medicinal virtues are comprised within those substances which we term vegetable poisons. These he cultivates with his own hands, and is said even to have produced new varieties of poison, more horribly deleterious than Nature, without the assistance of this learned person, would ever have plagued the world withal. That the Signor Doctor does less mischief than might be expected, with such dangerous substances, is undeniable. Now and then, it must be owned, he has effected—or seemed to effect—a marvellous cure. But, to tell you my private mind, Signor Giovanni, he should receive little credit for such instances of success—they being probably the work of chance—but should be held strictly accountable for his failures, which may justly be considered his own work."

The youth might have taken Baglioni's opinions with many grains of allowance, had he known that there was a professional warfare of long continuance between him and Doctor Rappaccini, in which the latter was generally thought to have gained the advantage. If the reader be inclined to judge for himself, we refer him to certain black-letter tracts on both sides, preserved in the medical department of the University of Padua.

"I know not, most learned Professor," returned Giovanni, after musing on what had been said of Rappaccini's exclusive zeal for science—"I know not how dearly this physician may love his art; but surely there is one object more dear to him. He has a daughter."

"Aha!" cried the Professor with a laugh. "So now our friend Giovanni's secret is out. You have heard of this daughter, whom all the young men in Padua are wild about, though not half a dozen have ever had the good hap to see her face. I know little of the Signora Beatrice, save that Rappaccini is said to have instructed her deeply in his science, and that, young and beautiful as fame reports her, she is already qualified to fill a professor's chair. Perchance her father destines her for mine! Other absurd rumors there be, not worth talking about, or listening to. So now, Signor Giovanni, drink off your glass of Lacryma."[8]

Guasconti returned to his lodgings somewhat heated with the wine he had quaffed, and which caused his brain to swim with strange fantasies in reference to

[8]Lachryma Christi ("Tears of Christ"), a famous Italian white wine.

Doctor Rappaccini and the beautiful Beatrice. On his way, happening to pass by a florist's, he bought a fresh bouquet of flowers.

Ascending to his chamber, he seated himself near the window, but within the shadow thrown by the depth of the wall, so that he could look down into the garden with little risk of being discovered. All beneath his eye was a solitude. The strange plants were basking in the sunshine, and now and then nodding gently to one another, as if in acknowledgment of sympathy and kindred. In the midst, by the shattered fountain, grew the magnificent shrub, with its purple gems clustering all over it; they glowed in the air, and gleamed back again out of the depths of the pool, which thus seemed to overflow with colored radiance from the rich reflection that was steeped in it. At first, as we have said, the garden was a solitude. Soon, however,—as Giovanni had half-hoped, half-feared, would be the case,—a figure appeared beneath the antique sculptured portal, and came down between the rows of plants, inhaling their various perfumes, as if she were one of those beings of old classic fable, that lived upon sweet odors. On again beholding Beatrice, the young man was even startled to perceive how much her beauty exceeded his recollection of it; so brilliant, so vivid was its character, that she glowed amid the sunlight, and, as Giovanni whispered to himself, positively illuminated the more shadowy intervals of the garden path. Her face being now more revealed than on the former occasion, he was struck by its expression of simplicity and sweetness; qualities that had not entered into his idea of her character, and which made him ask anew, what manner of mortal she might be. Nor did he fail again to observe, or imagine, an analogy between the beautiful girl and the gorgeous shrub that hung its gem-like flowers over the fountain; a resemblance which Beatrice seemed to have indulged a fantastic humor in heightening, both by the arrangement of her dress and the selection of its hues.

Approaching the shrub, she threw open her arms, as with a passionate ardor, and drew its branches into an intimate embrace; so intimate, that her features were hidden in its leafy bosom, and her glistening ringlets all intermingled with the flowers.

"Give me thy breath, my sister," exclaimed Beatrice; "for I am faint with common air! And give me this flower of thine, which I separate with gentlest fingers from the stem, and place it close beside my heart."

With these words, the beautiful daughter of Rappaccini plucked one of the richest blossoms of the shrub, and was about to fasten it in her bosom. But now, unless Giovanni's draughts of wine had bewildered his senses, a singular incident occurred. A small orange-colored reptile, of the lizard or chameleon species, chanced to be creeping along the path, just at the feet of Beatrice. It appeared to Giovanni—but, at the distance from which he gazed, he could scarcely have seen anything so minute—it appeared to him, however, that a drop or two of moisture from the broken stem of the flower descended upon the lizard's head. For an instant, the reptile contorted itself violently, and then lay motionless in the sunshine. Beatrice observed this remarkable phenomenon, and crossed herself, sadly, but without surprise; nor did she therefore hesitate to arrange the fatal flower in her bosom. There it blushed, and almost glimmered with the dazzling effect of a precious stone, adding to her dress and aspect the one appropriate charm, which nothing else in the world could have supplied. But Giovanni, out of the shadow of his window, bent forward and shrank back, and murmured and trembled.

"Am I awake? Have I my senses?" said he to himself. "What is this being?—beautiful, shall I call her?—or inexpressibly terrible?"

Beatrice now strayed carelessly through the garden, approaching closer beneath Giovanni's window, so that he was compelled to thrust his head quite out of its concealment in order to gratify the intense and painful curiosity which she excited. At this moment, there came a beautiful insect over the garden wall; it had perhaps wandered through the city and found no flowers nor verdure among those antique haunts of men, until the heavy perfumes of Doctor Rappaccini's shrubs had lured it from afar. Without alighting on the flowers, this winged brightness seemed to be attracted by Beatrice, and lingered in the air and fluttered about her head. Now, here it could not be but that Giovanni Guasconti's eyes deceived him. Be that as it might, he fancied that while Beatrice was gazing at the insect with childish delight, it grew faint and fell at her feet;—its bright wings shivered; it was dead—from no cause that he could discern, unless it were the atmosphere of her breath. Again Beatrice crossed herself and sighed heavily, as she bent over the dead insect.

An impulsive movement of Giovanni drew her eyes to the window. There she beheld the beautiful head of the young man—rather a Grecian than an Italian head, with fair, regular features, and a glistening of gold among his ringlets—gazing down upon her like a being that hovered in midair. Scarcely knowing what he did, Giovanni threw down the bouquet which he had hitherto held in his hand.

"Signora," said he, "there are pure and healthful flowers. Wear them for the sake of Giovanni Guasconti!"

"Thanks, Signor," replied Beatrice, with her rich voice, that came forth as it were like a gush of music; and with a mirthful expression half childish and half womanlike. "I accept your gift, and would fain recompense it with this precious purple flower; but if I toss it into the air, it will not reach you. So Signor Guasconti must even content himself with my thanks."

She lifted the bouquet from the ground, and then as if inwardly ashamed at having stepped aside from her maidenly reserve to respond to a stranger's greeting, passed swiftly homeward through the garden. But, few as the moments were, it seemed to Giovanni when she was on the point of vanishing beneath the sculptured portal, that his beautiful bouquet was already beginning to wither in her grasp. It was an idle thought; there could be no possibility of distinguishing a faded flower from a fresh one at so great a distance.

For many days after this incident, the young man avoided the window that looked into Doctor Rappaccini's garden, as if something ugly and monstrous would have blasted his eyesight, had he been betrayed into a glance. He felt conscious of having put himself, to a certain extent, within the influence of an unintelligible power, by the communication which he had opened with Beatrice. The wisest course would have been, if his heart were in any real danger, to quit his lodgings and Padua itself, at once; the next wiser, to have accustomed himself, as far as possible, to the familiar and day-light view of Beatrice; thus bringing her rigidly and systematically within the limits of ordinary experience. Least of all, while avoiding her sight, ought Giovanni to have remained so near this extraordinary being, that the proximity and possibility even of intercourse, should give a kind of substance and reality to the wild vagaries which his imagination ran riot continually in producing. Guasconti had not a deep heart—or at all events, its depths were not sounded now—but he had a quick fancy, and an ardent southern temperament, which rose every instant to a higher fever-pitch. Whether or no Beatrice possessed those terrible attributes—that fatal breath—the affinity with those so beautiful and deadly flowers—which were indicated by what Giovanni had witnessed, she had at least instilled a fierce and subtle poison into his system. It was not love, although her rich beauty was a madness to him; nor horror, even while he fancied her spirit to be imbued with the same baneful essence that seemed to pervade her physical frame; but a wild offspring of both love and horror that had each parent in it, and burned like one and shivered like the other. Giovanni knew not what to dread; still less did he know what to hope; yet hope and dread kept a continual warfare in his breast, alternately vanquishing one another and starting up afresh to renew the contest. Blessed are all simple emotions, be they dark or bright! It is the lurid intermixture of the two that produces the illuminating blaze of the infernal regions.

Sometimes he endeavored to assuage the fever of his spirit by a rapid walk through the streets of Padua, or beyond its gates; his footsteps kept time with the throbbings of his brain, so that the walk was apt to accelerate itself to a race. One day, he found himself arrested; his arm was seized by a portly personage who had turned back on recognizing the young man, and expended much breath in overtaking him.

"Signor Giovanni!—stay, my young friend!" cried he. "Have you forgotten me? That might well be the case, if I were as much altered as yourself."

It was Baglioni, whom Giovanni had avoided, ever since their first meeting, from a doubt that the Professor's sagacity would look too deeply into his secrets. Endeavoring to recover himself, he stared forth wildly from his inner world into the outer one, and spoke like a man in a dream:

"Yes; I am Giovanni Guasconti. You are Professor Pietro Baglioni. Now let me pass!"

"Not yet—not yet, Signor Giovanni Guasconti," said the Professor, smiling, but at the same time scrutinizing the youth with an earnest glance.—"What; did I grow up side by side with your father, and shall his son pass me like a stranger, in these old streets of Padua? Stand still, Signor Giovanni; for we must have a word or two, before we part."

"Speedily, then, most worshipful Professor, speedily!" said Giovanni, with feverish impatience. "Does not your worship see that I am in haste?"

Now, while he was speaking, there came a man in black along the street, stooping and moving feebly, like a person in inferior health. His face was all overspread with a most sickly and sallow hue, but yet so pervaded with an expression of piercing and active intellect, that an observer might easily have overlooked the merely physical attributes, and have seen only this wonderful energy. As he passed, this person exchanged a cold and distant salutation with Baglioni, but fixed his eyes upon Giovanni with an intentness that seemed to bring out whatever was within him worthy of notice. Nevertheless, there was a peculiar quietness in the look, as if taking merely a speculative, not a human, interest in the young man.

"It is Doctor Rappaccini!" whispered the Professor, when the stranger had passed.—"Has he ever seen your face before?"

"Not that I know," answered Giovanni, starting at the name.

"He *has* seen you!—he must have seen you!" said Baglioni, hastily. "For some purpose or other, this man of science is making a study of you. I know that look of his! It is the same that coldly illuminates his face, as he bends over a bird, a mouse, or a butterfly, which, in pursuance of some experiment, he has killed by the perfume of a flower;—a look as deep as nature itself, but without Nature's warmth of love. Signor Giovanni, I will stake my life upon it, you are the subject of one of Rappaccini's experiments!"

"Will you make a fool of me?" cried Giovanni, passionately. "*That,* Signor Professor, were an untoward experiment."

"Patience, patience!" replied the imperturbable Professor.—"I tell thee, my poor Giovanni, that Rappaccini has a scientific interest in thee. Thou hast fallen into fearful hands! And the Signora Beatrice? What part does she act in this mystery?"

But Guasconti, finding Baglioni's pertinacity intolerable, here broke away, and was gone before the Professor could again seize his arm. He looked after the young man intently, and shook his head.

"This must not be," said Baglioni to himself. "The youth is the son of my old friend, and shall not come to any harm from which the arcana of medical science can preserve him. Besides, it is too insufferable an impertinence in Rappaccini, thus to snatch the lad out of my own hands, as I may say, and make use of him for his infernal experiments. This daughter of his! It shall be looked to. Perchance, most learned Rappaccini, I may foil you where you little dream of it!"

Meanwhile, Giovanni had pursued a circuitous route, and at length found himself at the door of his lodgings. As he crossed the threshold, he was met by old Lisabetta, who smirked and smiled, and was evidently desirous to attract his attention; vainly, however, as the ebullition of his feelings had momentarily subsided into a cold and dull vacuity. He turned his eyes full upon the withered face that was puckering itself into a smile, but seemed to behold it not. The old dame, therefore, laid her grasp upon his cloak.

"Signor!—Signor!" whispered she, still with a smile over the whole breadth of her visage, so that it looked not unlike a grotesque carving in wood, darkened by centuries—"Listen, Signor! There is a private entrance into the garden!"

"What do you say?" exclaimed Giovanni, turning quickly about, as if an inanimate thing should start into feverish life.—"A private entrance into Doctor Rappaccini's garden!"

"Hush! hush!—not so loud!" whispered Lisabetta, putting her hand over his mouth. "Yes; into the worshipful Doctor's garden, where you may see all his fine shrubbery. Many a young man in Padua would give gold to be admitted among those flowers."

Giovanni put a piece of gold into her hand.

"Show me the way," said he.

A surmise, probably excited by his conversation with Baglioni, crossed his mind, that this interposition of old Lisabetta might perchance be connected with the intrigue, whatever were its nature, in which the Professor seemed to suppose that Doctor Rappaccini was involving him. But such a suspicion, though it disturbed Giovanni, was inadequate to restrain him. The instant that he was aware of the possibility of approaching Beatrice, it seemed an absolute necessity of his existence to do so. It mattered not whether she were angel or demon; he was irrevocably within her sphere, and must obey the law that whirled him onward, in ever lessening circles, towards a result which he did not attempt to foreshadow. And yet, strange to say, there came across him a sudden doubt, whether this intense interest on his part were not delusory—whether it were really of so deep and positive a nature as to justify him in now thrusting himself into an incalculable position—whether it were not merely the fantasy of a young man's brain, only slightly, or not at all, connected with his heart!

He paused—hesitated—turned half about—but again went on. His withered guide led him along several obscure passages, and finally undid a door, through which, as it was opened, there came the sight and sound of rustling leaves, with the broken sunshine glimmering among them. Giovanni stepped forth, and forcing himself through the entanglement of a shrub that wreathed its tendrils over the hidden entrance, he stood beneath his own window, in the open area of Doctor Rappaccini's garden.

How often is it the case, that, when impossibilities have come to pass, and dreams have condensed their misty substance into tangible realities, we find ourselves calm, and even coldly self-possessed, amid circumstances which it would have been a delirium of joy or agony to anticipate! Fate delights to thwart us thus. Passion will choose his own time to rush upon the scene, and lingers sluggishly behind, when an appropriate adjustment of events would seem to summon his appearance. So was it now with Giovanni. Day after day, his pulses had throbbed with feverish blood, at the improbable idea of an interview with Beatrice, and of standing with her, face to face, in this very garden, basking in the Oriental sunshine of her beauty, and snatching from her full gaze the mystery which he deemed the riddle of his own existence. But now there was a singular and untimely equanimity within his breast. He threw a glance around the garden to discover if Beatrice or her father were present, and perceiving that he was alone, began a critical observation of the plants.

The aspect of one and all of them dissatisfied him; their gorgeousness seemed fierce, passionate, and even unnatural. There was hardly an individual shrub which a wanderer, straying by himself through a forest, would not have been startled to find growing wild, as if an unearthly face had glared at him out of the thicket. Several, also, would have shocked a delicate instinct by an appearance of artificialness, indicating that there had been such commixture, and, as it were, adultery of various vegetable species, that the production was no longer of God's making, but the monstrous offspring of man's depraved fancy, glowing with only an evil mockery of beauty. They were probably the result of experiment, which, in one or two cases, had succeeded in mingling plants individually lovely into a compound possessing the questionable and ominous character that distinguished the whole growth of the garden. In fine, Giovanni recognized but two or three plants in the collection, and those of a kind that he well knew to be poisonous. While busy with these contemplations, he heard the rustling of a silken garment, and turning, beheld Beatrice emerging from beneath the sculptured portal.

Giovanni had not considered with himself what should be his deportment; whether he should apologize for his intrusion into the garden, or assume that he was there with the privity, at least, if not by the desire, of Doctor Rappaccini or his daughter. But Beatrice's manner placed him at his ease, though leaving him still in doubt by what agency he had gained admittance. She came lightly along the path, and met him near the broken fountain. There was surprise in her face, but brightened by a simple and kind expression of pleasure.

"You are a connoisseur in flowers, Signor," said Beatrice with a smile, alluding to the bouquet which he had flung her from the window. "It is no marvel, therefore, if the sight of my father's rare collection has tempted you to take a nearer view. If he were here, he could tell you many strange and interesting facts as to the nature and habits of these shrubs, for he has spent a life-time in such studies, and this garden is his world."

"And yourself, lady"—observed Giovanni—"if fame says true—you, likewise, are deeply skilled in the virtues indicated by these rich blossoms, and these spicy perfumes. Would you deign to be my instructress, I should prove an apter scholar than if taught by Signor Rappaccini himself."

"Are there such idle rumors?" asked Beatrice, with the music of a pleasant laugh. "Do people say that I am skilled in my father's science of plants? What a jest is there! No; though I have grown up among these flowers, I know no more of them than their hues and perfume; and sometimes, methinks I would fain rid myself of even that small knowledge. There are many flowers here, and those not the least brilliant, that shock and offend me, when they meet my eye. But, pray, Signor, do not believe these stories about my science. Believe nothing of me save what you see with your own eyes."

"And must I believe all that I have seen with my own eyes?" asked Giovanni pointedly, while the recollection of former scenes made him shrink. "No, Signora, you demand too little of me. Bid me believe nothing, save what comes from your own lips."

It would appear that Beatrice understood him. There came a deep flush to her cheek; but she looked full into Giovanni's eyes, and responded to his gaze of uneasy suspicion with a queen-like haughtiness.

"I do so bid you, Signor!" she replied. "Forget whatever you may have fancied in regard to me. If true to the outward senses, still it may be false in its essence. But the words of Beatrice Rappaccini's lips are true from the depths of the heart outward. Those you may believe!"

A fervor glowed in her whole aspect, and beamed upon Giovanni's consciousness like the light of truth itself. But while she spoke, there was a fragrance in the atmosphere around her, rich and delightful, though evanescent, yet which the young man, from an indefinable reluctance, scarcely dared to draw into his lungs. It might be the odor of the flowers. Could it be Beatrice's breath, which thus embalmed her words with a strange richness, as if by steeping them in her heart? A faintness passed like a shadow over Giovanni, and flitted away; he seemed to gaze through the beautiful girl's eyes into her transparent soul, and felt no more doubt or fear.

The tinge of passion that had colored Beatrice's manner vanished; she became gay, and appeared to derive a pure delight from her communion with the youth, not unlike what the maiden of a lonely island might have felt, conversing with a voyager from the civilized world. Evidently her experience of life had been confined within the limits of that garden. She talked now about matters as simple as the day-light or summer-clouds, and now asked questions in reference to the city, or Giovanni's distant home, his friends, his mother, and his sisters; questions indicating such seclusion, and such lack of familiarity with modes and forms, that Giovanni responded as if to an infant. Her spirit gushed out before him like a fresh rill, that was just catching its first glimpse of the sunlight, and wondering at the reflections of earth and sky which were flung into its bosom. There came thoughts, too, from a deep source, and fantasies of a gem-like brilliancy, as if diamonds and rubies sparkled upward among the bubbles of the fountain. Ever and anon, there gleamed across the young man's mind a sense of wonder, that he should be walking side by side with the being who had so wrought upon his imagination—whom he had idealized in such hues of terror—in whom he had positively witnessed such manifestations of dreadful attributes—that he should be conversing with Beatrice like a brother, and should find her so human and so maiden-like. But such reflections were only momentary; the effect of her character was too real, not to make itself familiar at once.

In this free intercourse, they had strayed through the garden, and now, after many turns among its avenues, were come to the shattered fountain, beside which grew the magnificent shrub with its treasury of glowing blossoms. A fragrance was diffused from it, which Giovanni recognized as identical with that which he had attributed to Beatrice's breath, but incomparably more powerful. As her eyes fell upon it, Giovanni beheld her press her hand to her bosom, as if her heart were throbbing suddenly and painfully.

"For the first time in my life," murmured she, addressing the shrub, "I had forgotten thee!"

"I remember, Signora," said Giovanni, "that you once promised to reward me with one of these living gems for the bouquet, which I had the happy boldness to fling to your feet. Permit me now to pluck it as a memorial of this interview."

He made a step towards the shrub, with extended hand. But Beatrice darted forward, uttering a shriek that went through his heart like a dagger. She caught his hand, and drew it back with the whole force of her slender figure. Giovanni felt her touch thrilling through his fibres.

"Touch it not!" exclaimed she, in a voice of agony. "Not for thy life! It is fatal!"

Then, hiding her face, she fled from him, and vanished beneath the sculptured portal. As Giovanni followed her with his eyes, he beheld the emaciated figure and pale intelligence of Doctor Rappaccini, who had been watching the scene, he knew not how long, within the shadow of the entrance.

No sooner was Guasconti alone in his chamber, than the image of Beatrice came back to his passionate musings, invested with all the witchery that had been gathering around it ever since his first glimpse of her, and now likewise imbued with a tender warmth of girlish womanhood. She was human: her nature was endowed with all gentle and feminine qualities; she was worthiest to be worshipped; she was capable, surely, on her part, of the height and heroism of love. Those tokens, which he had hitherto considered as proofs of a frightful peculiarity in her physical and moral system, were now either forgotten, or, by the subtle sophistry of passion, transmuted into a golden crown of enchantment, rendering Beatrice the more admirable, by so much as she was the more unique. Whatever had looked ugly, was now beautiful; or, if incapable of such a change, it stole away and hid itself among those shapeless half-ideas, which throng the dim region beyond the daylight of our perfect consciousness. Thus did he spend the night, nor fell asleep, until the dawn had begun to awake the slumbering flowers in Doctor Rappaccini's garden, whither Giovanni's dreams doubtless led him. Up rose the sun in his due season, and flinging his beams upon the young man's eyelids, awoke him to a sense of pain. When thoroughly aroused, he became sensible of a burning and tingling agony in his hand—in his right hand—the very hand which Beatrice had grasped in her own, when he was on the point of plucking one of the gem-like flowers. On the back of that hand there was now a purple print, like that of four small fingers, and the likeness of a slender thumb upon his wrist.

Oh, how stubbornly does love—or even that cunning semblance of love which flourishes in the imagination, but strikes no depth of root into the heart—how stubbornly does it hold its faith, until the moment come, when it is doomed to vanish into thin mist! Giovanni wrapt a handkerchief about his hand, and wondered what evil thing had stung him, and soon forgot his pain in a reverie of Beatrice.

After the first interview, a second was in the inevitable course of what we call fate. A third; a fourth; and a meeting with Beatrice in the garden was no longer an incident in Giovanni's daily life, but the whole space in which he might be said to live; for the anticipation and memory of that ecstatic hour made up the remainder. Nor was it otherwise with the daughter of Rappaccini. She watched for the youth's appearance, and flew to his side with confidence as unreserved as if they had been playmates from early infancy—as if they were such playmates still. If, by any unwonted chance, he failed to come at the appointed moment, she stood beneath the window, and sent up the rich sweetness of her tones to float around him in his chamber, and echo and reverberate throughout his heart—"Giovanni! Giovanni! Why tarriest thou? Come down!"—And down he hastened into that Eden of poisonous flowers.

But, with all this intimate familiarity, there was still a reserve in Beatrice's demeanor, so rigidly and invariably sustained, that the idea of infringing it scarcely occurred to his imagination. By all appreciable signs, they loved; they had looked love, with eyes that conveyed the holy secret from the depths of one soul into the depths of the other, as if it were too sacred to be whispered by the way; they had even spoken love, in those gushes of passion when their spirits darted forth in articulated breath, like tongues of long-hidden flame; and yet there had been no seal of lips, no clasp of hands, nor any slightest caress, such as love claims and hallows. He had never touched one of the gleaming ringlets of her hair; her garment—so marked was the physical barrier between them—had never been waved against him by a breeze. On the few occasions when Giovanni had seemed tempted to overstep the limit, Beatrice grew so sad, so stern, and withal wore such a look of desolate separation, shuddering at itself, that not a spoken word was requisite to repel him. At such times, he was startled at the horrible suspicions that rose, monster-like, out of the caverns of his heart, and stared him in the face; his love grew thin and faint as the morning-mist; his doubts alone had substance. But when Beatrice's face brightened again, after the momentary shadow, she was transformed at once from the mysterious, questionable being, whom he had watched with so much awe and horror; she was now the beautiful and unsophisticated girl, whom he felt that his spirit knew with a certainty beyond all other knowledge.

A considerable time had now passed since Giovanni's last meeting with Baglioni. One morning, however, he was disagreeably surprised by a visit from the Professor, whom he had scarcely thought of for whole weeks, and would willingly have forgotten still longer. Given up, as he had long been, to a pervading excitement, he could tolerate no companions, except upon condition of their perfect sympathy with his present state of feeling. Such sympathy was not to be expected from Professor Baglioni.

The visitor chatted carelessly, for a few moments, about the gossip of the city and the University, and then took up another topic.

"I have been reading an old classic author lately," said he, "and met with a story that strangely interested me. Possibly you may remember it. It is of an Indian prince, who sent a beautiful woman as a present to Alexander the Great.[9] She was as lovely as the dawn, and gorgeous as the sunset; but what especially distinguished her was a certain rich perfume in her breath—richer than a garden of Persian roses. Alexander, as was natural to a youthful conqueror, fell in love at first sight with this magnificent stranger. But a certain sage physician, happening to be present, discovered a terrible secret in regard to her."

"And what was that?" asked Giovanni, turning his eyes downward to avoid those of the Professor.

"That this lovely woman," continued Baglioni, with emphasis, "had been nourished with poisons from her birth upward, until her whole nature was so imbued with them, that she herself had become the deadliest poison in existence. Poison was her element of life. With that rich perfume of her breath, she blasted the very air. Her love would have been poison!—her embrace death! Is not this a marvelous tale?"

"A childish fable," answered Giovanni, nervously starting from his chair. "I marvel how your worship finds time to read such nonsense, among your graver studies."

"By the bye," said the Professor, looking uneasily about him, "what singular fragrance is this in your apartment? Is it the perfume of your gloves? It is faint, but delicious, and yet, after all, by no means agreeable. Were I to breathe it long, methinks it would make me ill. It is like the breath of a flower—but I see no flowers in the chamber."

"Nor are there any," replied Giovanni, who had turned pale as the Professor spoke; "nor, I think, is there any fragrance, except in your worship's imagination. Odors, being a sort of element combined of the sensual and the spiritual, are apt to deceive us in this manner. The recollection of a perfume—the bare idea of it—may easily be mistaken for a present reality."

"Aye; but my sober imagination does not often play such tricks," said Baglioni; "and were I to fancy any kind of odor, it would be that of some vile apothecary drug, wherewith my fingers are likely enough to be imbued. Our worshipful friend Rappaccini, as I have heard, tinctures his medicaments with odors richer than those of Araby. Doubtless, likewise, the fair and learned Signora Beatrice would minister to her patients with draughts as sweet as a maiden's breath. But wo to him that sips them!"

Giovanni's face evinced many contending emotions. The tone in which the Professor alluded to the pure and lovely daughter of Rappaccini was a torture to his soul; and yet, the intimation of a view of her character, opposite to his own, gave instantaneous distinctness to a thousand dim suspicions, which now grinned at him like so many demons. But he strove hard to quell them, and to respond to Baglioni with a true lover's perfect faith.

"Signor Professor," said he, "you were my father's friend—perchance, too, it is your purpose to act a friendly part towards his son. I would fain feel nothing towards you, save respect and deference. But I pray you to observe, Signor, that there is one

[9]Reported by the English doctor and writer Sir Thomas Brown in *Vulgar Errors* (1646), whom Hawthorne quotes in an 1839 notebook entry.

subject on which we must not speak. You know not the Signora Beatrice. You cannot, therefore, estimate the wrong—the blasphemy, I may even say—that is offered to her character by a light or injurious word."

"Giovanni!—my poor Giovanni!" answered the Professor, with a calm expression of pity, "I know this wretched girl far better than yourself. You shall hear the truth in respect to the poisoner Rappaccini, and his poisonous daughter. Yes; poisonous as she is beautiful! Listen; for even should you do violence to my grey hairs, it shall not silence me. That old fable of the Indian woman has become a truth, by the deep and deadly science of Rappaccini, and in the person of the lovely Beatrice!"

Giovanni groaned and hid his face.

"Her father," continued Baglioni, "was not restrained by natural affection from offering up his child, in this horrible manner, as the victim of his insane zeal for science. For—let us do him justice—he is as true a man of science as ever distilled his own heart in an alembic. What, then, will be your fate? Beyond a doubt, you are selected as the material of some new experiment. Perhaps the result is to be death—perhaps a fate more awful still! Rappaccini, with what he calls the interest of science before his eyes, will hesitate at nothing."

"It is a dream!" muttered Giovanni to himself, "surely it is a dream!"

"But," resumed the Professor, "be of good cheer, son of my friend! It is not yet too late for the rescue. Possibly, we may even succeed in bringing back this miserable child within the limits of ordinary nature, from which her father's madness has estranged her. Behold this little silver vase! It was wrought by the hands of the renowned Benvenuto Cellini,[10] and is well worthy to be a love-gift to the fairest dame in Italy. But its contents are invaluable. One little sip of this antidote would have rendered the most virulent poisons of the Borgias innocuous.[11] Doubt not that it will be as efficacious against those of Rappaccini. Bestow the vase, and the precious liquid within it, on your Beatrice, and hopefully await the result."

Baglioni laid a small, exquisitely wrought silver phial on the table, and withdrew, leaving what he had said to produce its effect upon the young man's mind.

"We will thwart Rappaccini yet!" thought he, chuckling to himself, as he descended the stairs. "But, let us confess the truth of him, he is a wonderful man!—a wonderful man indeed! A vile empiric, however, in his practice, and therefore not to be tolerated by those who respect the good old rules of the medical profession!"

Throughout Giovanni's whole acquaintance with Beatrice, he had occasionally, as we have said, been haunted by dark surmises as to her character. Yet, so thoroughly had she made herself felt by him as a simple, natural, most affectionate and guileless creature, that the image now held up by Professor Baglioni, looked as strange and incredible, as if it were not in accordance with his own original conception. True, there were ugly recollections connected with his first glimpses of the beautiful girl; he could not quite forget the bouquet that withered in her grasp, and the insect that perished amid the sunny air, by no ostensible agency, save the fragrance of her breath. These incidents, however, dissolving in the pure light of her character, had no longer the efficacy of facts, but were acknowledged as mistaken

[10]Italian sculptor and goldsmith, and author of a famous autobiography (1500–1571).

[11]An influential Italian aristocratic family that was notorious for corruption and licentiousness during the Renaissance.

fantasies, by whatever testimony of the senses they might appear to be substantiated. There is something truer and more real, than what we can see with the eyes, and touch with the finger. On such better evidence, had Giovanni founded his confidence in Beatrice, though rather by the necessary force of her high attributes, than by any deep and generous faith, on his part. But, now, his spirit was incapable of sustaining itself at the height to which the early enthusiasm of passion had exalted it; he fell down, grovelling among earthly doubts, and defiled therewith the pure whiteness of Beatrice's image. Not that he gave her up; he did but distrust. He resolved to institute some decisive test that should satisfy him, once for all, whether there were those dreadful peculiarities in her physical nature, which could not be supposed to exist without some corresponding monstrosity of soul. His eyes, gazing down afar, might have deceived him as to the lizard, the insect, and the flowers. But if he could witness, at the distance of a few paces, the sudden blight of one fresh and healthful flower in Beatrice's hand, there would be room for no further question. With this idea, he hastened to the florist's, and purchased a bouquet that was still gemmed with the morning dew-drops.

It was now the customary hour of his daily interview with Beatrice. Before descending into the garden, Giovanni failed not to look at his figure in the mirror; a vanity to be expected in a beautiful young man, yet, as displaying itself at that troubled and feverish moment, the token of a certain shallowness of feeling and insincerity of character. He did gaze, however, and said to himself, that his features had never before possessed so rich a grace, nor his eyes such vivacity, nor his cheeks so warm a hue of superabundant life.

"At least," thought he, "her poison has not yet insinuated itself into my system. I am no flower to perish in her grasp!"

With that thought, he turned his eyes on the bouquet, which he had never once laid aside from his hand. A thrill of indefinable horror shot through his frame, on perceiving that those dewy flowers were already beginning to droop; they wore the aspect of things that had been fresh and lovely, yesterday. Giovanni grew white as marble, and stood motionless before the mirror, staring at his own reflection there, as at the likeness of something frightful. He remembered Baglioni's remark about the fragrance that seemed to pervade the chamber. It must have been the poison in his breath! Then he shuddered—shuddered at himself! Recovering from his stupor, he began to watch, with curious eye, a spider that was busily at work, hanging its web from the antique cornice of the apartment, crossing and re-crossing the artful system of interwoven lines, as vigorous and active a spider as ever dangled from an old ceiling. Giovanni bent towards the insect, and emitted a deep, long breath. The spider suddenly ceased its toil; the web vibrated with a tremor originating in the body of the small artisan. Again Giovanni sent forth a breath, deeper, longer, and imbued with a venomous feeling out of his heart; he knew not whether he were wicked or only desperate. The spider made a convulsive gripe with his limbs, and hung dead across the window.

"Accursed! Accursed!" muttered Giovanni, addressing himself. "Hast thou grown so poisonous, that this deadly insect perishes by thy breath?"

At that moment, a rich, sweet voice came floating up from the garden:—

"Giovanni! Giovanni! It is past the hour! Why tarriest thou! Come down!"

"Yes," muttered Giovanni again. "She is the only being whom my breath may not slay! Would that it might!"

He rushed down, and in an instant, was standing before the bright and loving eyes of Beatrice. A moment ago, his wrath and despair had been so fierce that he could have desired nothing so much as to wither her by a glance. But, with her actual presence, there came influences which had too real an existence to be at once shaken off; recollections of the delicate and benign power of her feminine nature, which had so often enveloped him in a religious calm; recollections of many a holy and passionate outgush of her heart, when the pure fountain had been unsealed from its depths, and made visible in its transparency to his mental eye; recollections which, had Giovanni known how to estimate them, would have assured him that all this ugly mystery was but an earthly illusion, and that, whatever mist of evil might seem to have gathered over her, the real Beatrice was a heavenly angel. Incapable as he was of such high faith, still her presence had not utterly lost its magic. Giovanni's rage was quelled into an aspect of sullen insensibility. Beatrice, with a quick spiritual sense, immediately felt that there was a gulf of blackness between them, which neither he nor she could pass. They walked on together, sad and silent, and came thus to the marble fountain, and to its pool of water on the ground, in the midst of which grew the shrub that bore gem-like blossoms. Giovanni was affrighted at the eager enjoyment—the appetite, as it were—with which he found himself inhaling the fragrance of the flowers.

"Beatrice," asked he abruptly, "whence came this shrub?"

"My father created it," answered she, with simplicity.

"Created it! created it!" repeated Giovanni. "What mean you, Beatrice?"

"He is a man fearfully acquainted with the secrets of nature," replied Beatrice; "and, at the hour when I first drew breath, this plant sprang from the soil, the offspring of his science, of his intellect, while I was but his earthly child. Approach it not!" continued she, observing with terror that Giovanni was drawing nearer to the shrub. "It has qualities that you little dream of. But I, dearest Giovanni,—I grew up and blossomed with the plant, and was nourished with its breath. It was my sister, and I loved it with a human affection: for—alas! hast thou not suspected it? there was an awful doom."

Here Giovanni frowned so darkly upon her that Beatrice paused and trembled. But her faith in his tenderness reassured her, and made her blush that she had doubted for an instant.

"There was an awful doom," she continued,—"the effect of my father's fatal love of science—which estranged me from all society of my kind. Until Heaven sent thee, dearest Giovanni, Oh! how lonely was thy poor Beatrice!"

"Was it a hard doom?" asked Giovanni, fixing his eyes upon her.

"Only of late have I known how hard it was," answered she tenderly. "Oh, yes; but my heart was torpid, and therefore quiet."

Giovanni's rage broke forth from his sullen gloom like a lightning-flash out of a dark cloud.

"Accursed one!" cried he, with venomous scorn and anger. "And finding thy solitude wearisome, thou hast severed me, likewise, from all the warmth of life, and enticed me into thy region of unspeakable horror!"

"Giovanni!" exclaimed Beatrice, turning her large bright eyes upon his face. The force of his words had not found its way into her mind; she was merely thunderstruck.

"Yes, poisonous thing!" repeated Giovanni, beside himself with passion. "Thou hast done it! Thou hast blasted me! Thou hast filled my veins with poison! Thou hast made me as hateful, as ugly, as loathsome and deadly a creature as thyself,—a world's wonder of hideous monstrosity! Now—if our breath be happily as fatal to ourselves as to all others—let us join our lips in one kiss of unutterable hatred, and so die!"

"What has befallen me?" murmured Beatrice, with a low moan out of her heart. "Holy Virgin pity me, a poor heart-broken child!"

"Thou! Dost thou pray?" cried Giovanni, still with the same fiendish scorn. "Thy very prayers, as they come from thy lips, taint the atmosphere with death. Yes, yes; let us pray! Let us to church, and dip our fingers in the holy water at the portal! They that come after us will perish as by a pestilence. Let us sign crosses in the air! It will be scattering curses abroad in the likeness of holy symbols!"

"Giovanni," said Beatrice calmly, for her grief was beyond passion, "why dost thou join thyself with me thus in those terrible words? I, it is true, am the horrible thing thou namest me. But thou!—what hast thou to do, save with one other shudder at my hideous misery, to go forth out of the garden and mingle with thy race, and forget that there ever crawled on earth such a monster as poor Beatrice?"

"Dost thou pretend ignorance?" asked Giovanni, scowling upon her. "Behold! This power have I gained from the pure daughter of Rappaccini!"

There was a swarm of summer-insects flitting through the air, in search of the food promised by the flower-odors of the fatal garden. They circled round Giovanni's head, and were evidently attracted towards him by the same influence which had drawn them, for an instant, within the sphere of several of the shrubs. He sent forth a breath among them, and smiled bitterly at Beatrice, as at least a score of the insects fell dead upon the ground.

"I see it! I see it!" shrieked Beatrice. "It is my father's fatal science! No, no, Giovanni; it was not I! Never, never! I dreamed only to love thee, and be with thee a little time, and so to let thee pass away, leaving but thine image in mine heart. For, Giovanni—believe it—though my body be nourished with poison, my spirit is God's creature, and craves love as its daily food. But my father!—he has united us in this fearful sympathy. Yes; spurn me!—tread upon me!—kill me! Oh, what is death, after such words as thine? But it was not I! Not for a world of bliss would I have done it!"

Giovanni's passion had exhausted itself in its outburst from his lips. There now came across him a sense, mournful, and not without tenderness, of the intimate and peculiar relationship between Beatrice and himself. They stood, as it were, in an utter solitude, which would be made none the less solitary by the densest throng of human life. Ought not, then, the desert of humanity around them to press this insulated pair closer together? If they should be cruel to one another, who was there to be kind to them? Besides, thought Giovanni, might there not still be a hope of his returning within the limits of ordinary nature, and leading Beatrice—the redeemed Beatrice—by the hand? Oh, weak, and selfish, and unworthy spirit, that could dream of an earthly union and earthly happiness as possible, after such deep love had been so bitterly wronged as was Beatrice's love by Giovanni's blighting words! No, no; there could be no such hope. She must pass heavily, with that broken heart, across the borders of Time—she must bathe her hurts in some fount of Paradise, and forget her grief in the light of immortality—and *there* be well!

But Giovanni did not know it.

"Dear Beatrice," said he, approaching her, while she shrank away, as always at his approach, but now with a different impulse—"dearest Beatrice, our fate is not yet so desperate. Behold! There is a medicine, potent, as a wise physician has assured me, and almost divine in its efficacy. It is composed of ingredients the most opposite to those by which thy awful father has brought this calamity upon thee and me. It is distilled of blessed herbs. Shall we not quaff it together, and thus be purified from evil?"

"Give it me!" said Beatrice, extending her hand to receive the little silver phial which Giovanni took from his bosom. She added, with a peculiar emphasis: "I will drink—but do thou await the result."

She put Baglioni's antidote to her lips; and, at the same moment, the figure of Rappaccini emerged from the portal, and came slowly towards the marble fountain. As he drew near, the pale man of science seemed to gaze with a triumphant expression at the beautiful youth and maiden, as might an artist who should spend his life in achieving a picture or a group of statuary, and finally be satisfied with his success. He paused—his bent form grew erect with conscious power, he spread out his hands over them, in the attitude of a father imploring a blessing upon his children. But those were the same hands that had thrown poison into the stream of their lives! Giovanni trembled. Beatrice shuddered nervously, and pressed her hand upon her heart.

"My daughter," said Rappaccini, "thou art no longer lonely in the world! Pluck one of those precious gems from thy sister shrub, and bid thy bridegroom wear it in his bosom. It will not harm him now! My science, and the sympathy between thee and him, have so wrought within his system, that he now stands apart from common men, as thou dost, daughter of my pride and triumph, from ordinary women. Pass on, then, through the world, most dear to one another, and dreadful to all besides!"

"My father," said Beatrice, feebly—and still, as she spoke, she kept her hand upon her heart—"wherefore didst thou inflict this miserable doom upon thy child?"

"Miserable!" exclaimed Rappaccini. "What mean you, foolish girl? Dost thou deem it misery to be endowed with marvellous gifts, against which no power nor strength could avail an enemy? Misery, to be able to quell the mightiest with a breath? Misery, to be as terrible as thou art beautiful? Wouldst thou, then, have preferred the condition of a weak woman, exposed to all evil, and capable of none?"

"I would fain have been loved, not feared," murmured Beatrice, sinking down upon the ground.—"But now it matters not; I am going, father, where the evil, which thou hast striven to mingle with my being, will pass away like a dream—like the fragrance of these poisonous flowers, which will no longer taint my breath among the flowers of Eden. Farewell, Giovanni! Thy words of hatred are like lead within my heart—but they, too, will fall away as I ascend. Oh, was there not, from the first, more poison in thy nature than in mine?"

To Beatrice—so radically had her earthly part been wrought upon by Rappaccini's skill—as poison had been life, so the powerful antidote was death. And thus the poor victim of man's ingenuity and of thwarted nature, and of the fatality that attends all such efforts of perverted wisdom, perished there, at the feet of her father and Giovanni. Just at that moment, Professor Pietro Baglioni looked forth from the window, and called loudly, in a tone of triumph mixed with horror, to the thunder-stricken man of science:

"Rappaccini! Rappaccini! And is *this* the upshot of your experiment?"

1844

The Artist of the Beautiful

An elderly man, with his pretty daughter on his arm, was passing along the street, and emerged from the gloom of the cloudy evening into the light that fell across the pavement from the window of a small shop. It was a projecting window; and on the inside were suspended a variety of watches,—pinchbeck, silver, and one or two of gold,—all with their faces turned from the street, as if churlishly disinclined to inform the wayfarers what o'clock it was. Seated within the shop, sidelong to the window, with his pale face bent earnestly over some delicate piece of mechanism, on which was thrown the concentrated lustre of a shade-lamp, appeared a young man.

"What can Owen Warland be about?" muttered old Peter Hovenden,—himself a retired watchmaker, and the former master of this same young man, whose occupation he was now wondering at. "What can the fellow be about? These six months past, I have never come by his shop without seeing him just as steadily at work as now. It would be a flight beyond his usual foolery to seek for the Perpetual Motion. And yet I know enough of my old business to be certain, that what he is now so busy with is no part of the machinery of a watch."

"Perhaps, father," said Annie, without showing much interest in the question, "Owen is inventing a new kind of timekeeper. I am sure he has ingenuity enough."

"Poh, child! he has not the sort of ingenuity to invent anything better than a Dutch toy," answered her father, who had formerly been put to much vexation by Owen Warland's irregular genius. "A plague on such ingenuity! All the effect that ever I knew of it, was to spoil the accuracy of some of the best watches in my shop. He would turn the sun out of its orbit, and derange the whole course of time, if, as I said before, his ingenuity could grasp anything bigger than a child's toy!"

"Hush, father! he hears you," whispered Annie, pressing the old man's arm. "His ears are as delicate as his feelings, and you know how easily disturbed they are. Do let us move on."

So Peter Hovenden and his daughter Annie plodded on without further conversation, until, in a by-street of the town, they found themselves passing the open door of a blacksmith's shop. Within was seen the forge, now blazing up, and illuminating the high and dusky roof, and now confining its lustre to a narrow precinct of the coal-strewn floor, according as the breath of the bellows was puffed forth, or again inhaled into its vast leathern lungs. In the intervals of brightness, it was easy to distinguish objects in remote corners of the shop, and the horse-shoes that hung upon the wall; in the momentary gloom, the fire seemed to be glimmering amidst the vagueness of unenclosed space. Moving about in this red glare and alternate dusk, was the figure of the blacksmith, well worthy to be viewed in so picturesque an aspect of light and shade, where the bright blaze struggled with the black night, as if each would have snatched his comely strength from the other. Anon, he drew a white-hot bar of iron from the coals, laid it on the anvil, uplifted his arm of might, and was soon enveloped in the myriads of sparks which the strokes of his hammer scattered into the surrounding gloom.

"Now, that is a pleasant sight," said the old watchmaker. "I know what it is to work in gold, but give me the worker in iron, after all is said and done. He spends his labor upon a reality. What say you, daughter Annie?"

"Pray don't speak so loud, father," whispered Annie. "Robert Danforth will hear you."

"And what if he should hear me?" said Peter Hovenden; "I say again, it is a good and a wholesome thing to depend upon main strength and reality, and to earn one's bread with the bare and brawny arm of a blacksmith. A watchmaker gets his brain puzzled by his wheels within a wheel, or loses his health or the nicety of his eyesight, as was my case; and finds himself, at middle age, or a little after, past labor at his own trade, and fit for nothing else, yet too poor to live at his ease. So, I say once again, give me main strength for my money. And then, how it takes the nonsense out of a man! Did you ever hear of a blacksmith being such a fool as Owen Warland, yonder?"

"Well said, uncle Hovenden!" shouted Robert Danforth, from the forge, in a full, deep, merry voice, that made the roof re-echo. "And what says Miss Annie to that doctrine? She, I suppose, will think it a genteeler business to tinker up a lady's watch, than to forge a horse-shoe or make a grid-iron!"

Annie drew her father onward, without giving him time for reply.

But we must return to Owen Warland's shop, and spend more meditation upon his history and character than either Peter Hovenden, or probably his daughter Annie, or Owen's old schoolfellow, Robert Danforth, would have thought due to so slight a subject. From the time that his little fingers could grasp a pen-knife, Owen had been remarkable for a delicate ingenuity, which sometimes produced pretty shapes in wood, principally figures of flowers and birds, and sometimes seemed to aim at the hidden mysteries of mechanism. But it was always for purposes of grace, and never with any mockery of the useful. He did not, like the crowd of school-boy artizans, construct little windmills on the angle of a barn, or watermills across the neighboring brook. Those who discovered such peculiarity in the boy, as to think it worth their while to observe him closely, sometimes saw reason to suppose that he was attempting to imitate the beautiful movements of Nature, as exemplified in the flight of birds or the activity of little animals. It seemed, in fact, a new development of the love of the Beautiful, such as might have made him a poet, a painter, or a sculptor, and which was as completely refined from all utilitarian coarseness, as it could have been in either of the fine arts. He looked with singular distaste at the stiff and regular processes of ordinary machinery. Being once carried to see a steam-engine, in the expectation that his intuitive comprehension of mechanical principles would be gratified, he turned pale, and grew sick, as if something monstrous and unnatural had been presented to him. This horror was partly owing to the size and terrible energy of the Iron Laborer; for the character of Owen's mind was microscopic, and tended naturally to the minute, in accordance with his diminutive frame, and the marvellous smallness and delicate power of his fingers. Not that his sense of beauty was thereby diminished into a sense of prettiness. The Beautiful Idea has no relation to size, and may be as perfectly developed in a space too minute for any but microscopic investigation, as within the ample verge that is measured by the arc of the rainbow. But, at all events, this characteristic minuteness in his objects and accomplishments made the world even more incapable, than it might otherwise have been, of appreciating Owen Warland's genius. The boy's relatives saw nothing better to be done—as perhaps there was not—than to bind him apprentice to a watchmaker, hoping that his strange ingenuity might thus be regulated, and put to utilitarian purposes.

Peter Hovenden's opinion of his apprentice has already been expressed. He could make nothing of the lad. Owen's apprehension of the professional mysteries, it is true, was inconceivably quick. But he altogether forgot or despised the grand object of a watchmaker's business, and cared no more for the measurement of time than if it had been merged into eternity. So long, however, as he remained under his old master's care, Owen's lack of sturdiness made it possible, by strict injunctions and sharp oversight, to restrain his creative eccentricities within bounds. But when his apprenticeship was served out, and he had taken the little shop which Peter Hovenden's failing eyesight compelled him to relinquish, then did people recognize how unfit a person was Owen Warland to lead old blind Father Time along his daily course. One of his most rational projects was, to connect a musical operation with the machinery of his watches, so that all the harsh dissonances of life might be rendered tuneful, and each flitting moment fall into the abyss of the Past in golden drops of harmony. If a family-clock was entrusted to him for repair—one of those tall, ancient clocks that have grown nearly allied to human nature, by measuring out the lifetime of many generations—he would take upon himself to arrange a dance or funeral procession of figures, across its venerable face, representing twelve mirthful or melancholy hours. Several freaks of this kind quite destroyed the young watchmaker's credit with that steady and matter-of-fact class of people who hold the opinion that time is not to be trifled with, whether considered as the medium of advancement and prosperity in this world, or preparation for the next. His custom rapidly diminished—a misfortune, however, that was probably reckoned among his better accidents by Owen Warland, who was becoming more and more absorbed in a secret occupation, which drew all his science and manual dexterity into itself, and likewise gave full employment to the characteristic tendencies of his genius. This pursuit had already consumed many months.

After the old watchmaker and his pretty daughter had gazed at him, out of the obscurity of the street, Owen Warland was seized with a fluttering of the nerves, which made his hand tremble too violently to proceed with such delicate labor as he was now engaged upon.

"It was Annie herself!" murmured he. "I should have known it, by this throbbing of my heart, before I heard her father's voice. Ah, how it throbs! I shall scarcely be able to work again on this exquisite mechanism to-night. Annie—dearest Annie—thou shouldst give firmness to my heart and hand, and not shake them thus; for if I strive to put the very spirit of Beauty into form, and give it motion, it is for thy sake alone. Oh, throbbing heart, be quiet! If my labor be thus thwarted, there will come vague and unsatisfied dreams, which will leave me spiritless to-morrow."

As he was endeavoring to settle himself again to his task, the shop-door opened, and gave admittance to no other than the stalwart figure which Peter Hovenden had paused to admire, as seen amid the light and shadow of the blacksmith's shop. Robert Danforth had brought a little anvil of his own manufacture, and peculiarly constructed, which the young artist had recently bespoken. Owen examined the article, and pronounced it fashioned according to his wish.

"Why, yes," said Robert Danforth, his strong voice filling the shop as with the sound of a bass-viol, "I consider myself equal to anything in the way of my own trade; though I should have made but a poor figure at yours, with such a fist as this,"—

added he, laughing, as he laid his vast hand beside the delicate one of Owen. "But what then? I put more main strength into one blow of my sledge-hammer, than all that you have expended since you were a 'prentice. Is not that the truth?"

"Very probably," answered the low and slender voice of Owen. "Strength is an earthly monster. I make no pretensions to it. My force, whatever there may be of it, is altogether spiritual."

"Well; but, Owen, what are you about!" asked his old schoolfellow, still in such a hearty volume of tone that it made the artist shrink; especially as the question related to a subject so sacred as the absorbing dream of his imagination. "Folks do say, that you are trying to discover the Perpetual Motion."

"The Perpetual Motion?—nonsense!" replied Owen Warland, with a movement of disgust; for he was full of little petulances. "It can never be discovered! It is a dream that may delude men whose brains are mystified with matter, but not me. Besides, if such a discovery were possible, it would not be worth my while to make it, only to have the secret turned to such purposes as are now effected by steam and water-power. I am not ambitious to be honored with the paternity of a new kind of cotton-machine."

"That would be droll enough!" cried the blacksmith, breaking out into such an uproar of laughter, that Owen himself, and the bell-glasses on his work-board, quivered in unison. "No, no, Owen! No child of yours will have iron joints and sinews. Well, I won't hinder you any more. Good night, Owen, and success; and if you need any assistance, so far as a downright blow of hammer upon anvil will answer the purpose, I'm your man!"

And with another laugh, the man of main strength left the shop.

"How strange it is," whispered Owen Warland to himself, leaning his head upon his hand, "that all my musings, my purposes, my passion for the Beautiful, my consciousness of power to create it—a finer, more ethereal power, of which this earthly giant can have no conception—all all, look so vain and idle, whenever my path is crossed by Robert Danforth! He would drive me mad, were I to meet him often. His hard, brute force darkens and confuses the spiritual element within me. But I, too, will be strong in my own way. I will not yield to him!"

He took from beneath a glass, a piece of minute machinery, which he set in the condensed light of his lamp, and, looking intently at it through a magnifying glass, proceeded to operate with a delicate instrument of steel. In an instant, however, he fell back in his chair, and clasped his hands, with a look of horror on his face, that made its small features as impressive as those of a giant would have been.

"Heaven! What have I done!" exclaimed he. "The vapor!—the influence of that brute force!—it has bewildered me, and obscured my perception. I have made the very stroke—the fatal stroke—that I have dreaded from the first! It is all over—the toil of months—the object of my life! I am ruined!"

And there he sat, in strange despair, until his lamp flickered in the socket, and left the Artist of the Beautiful in darkness.

Thus it is, that ideas which grow up within the imagination, and appear so lovely to it, and of a value beyond whatever men call valuable, are exposed to be shattered and annihilated by contact with the Practical. It is requisite for the ideal artist to possess a force of character that seems hardly compatible with its delicacy; he must keep his faith in himself, while the incredulous world assails him with its utter disbelief; he must stand up against mankind and be his own sole disciple, both as respects his genius, and the objects to which it is directed.

For a time, Owen Warland succumbed to this severe, but inevitable test. He spent a few sluggish weeks, with his head so continually resting in his hands, that the townspeople had scarcely an opportunity to see his countenance. When, at last, it was again uplifted to the light of day, a cold, dull, nameless change was perceptible upon it. In the opinion of Peter Hovenden, however, and that order of sagacious understandings who think that life should be regulated, like clock-work, with leaden weights, the alteration was entirely for the better. Owen now indeed, applied himself to business with dogged industry. It was marvellous to witness the obtuse gravity with which he would inspect the wheels of a great, old silver watch; thereby delighting the owner, in whose fob it had been worn till he deemed it a portion of his own life, and was accordingly jealous of its treatment. In consequence of the good report thus acquired, Owen Warland was invited by the proper authorities to regulate the clock in the church-steeple. He succeeded so admirably in this matter of public interest, that the merchants gruffly acknowledged his merits on 'Change; the nurse whispered his praises, as she gave the potion in the sick-chamber; the lover blessed him at the hour of appointed interview; and the town in general thanked Owen for the punctuality of dinner-time. In a word, the heavy weight upon his spirits kept everything in order, not merely within his own system, but wheresoever the iron accents of the church-clock were audible. It was a circumstance, though minute, yet characteristic of his present state, that, when employed to engrave names or initials on silver spoons, he now wrote the requisite letters in the plainest possible style; omitting a variety of fanciful flourishes, that had heretofore distinguished his work in this kind.

One day, during the era of this happy transformation, old Peter Hovenden came to visit his former apprentice.

"Well, Owen," said he, "I am glad to hear such good accounts of you from all quarters; and especially from the town-clock yonder, which speaks in your commendation every hour of the twenty-four. Only get rid altogether of your nonsensical trash about the Beautiful—which I, nor nobody else, nor yourself to boot, could never understand—only free yourself of that, and your success in life is as sure as daylight. Why, if you go on in this way, I should even venture to let you doctor this precious old watch of mine; though, except my daughter Annie, I have nothing else so valuable in the world."

"I should hardly dare touch it, sir," replied Owen in a depressed tone; for he was weighed down by his old master's presence.

"In time," said the latter, "in time, you will be capable of it."

The old watchmaker, with the freedom naturally consequent on his former authority, went on inspecting the work which Owen had in hand at the moment, together with other matters that were in progress. The artist, meanwhile, could scarcely lift his head. There was nothing so antipodal to his nature as this man's cold, unimaginative sagacity, by contact with which everything was converted into a dream, except the densest matter of the physical world. Owen groaned in spirit, and prayed fervently to be delivered from him.

"But what is this?" cried Peter Hovenden abruptly, taking up a dusty bell-glass, beneath which appeared a mechanical something, as delicate and minute as the system of a butterfly's anatomy. "What have we here! Owen, Owen! there is witchcraft in these little chains, and wheels, and paddles! See! with one pinch of my finger and thumb, I am going to deliver you from all future peril."

"For Heaven's sake," screamed Owen Warland, springing up with wonderful energy, "as you would not drive me mad—do not touch it! The slightest pressure of your finger would ruin me for ever."

"Aha, young man! And is it so?" said the old watchmaker, looking at him with just enough of penetration to torture Owen's soul with the bitterness of worldly criticism. "Well; take your own course. But I warn you again, that in this small piece of mechanism lives your evil spirit. Shall I exorcise him?"

"You are my Evil Spirit," answered Owen, much excited—"you, and the hard, coarse world! The leaden thoughts and the despondency that you fling upon me are my clogs. Else, I should long ago have achieved the task that I was created for."

Peter Hovenden shook his head, with the mixture of contempt and indignation which mankind, of whom he was partly a representative, deem themselves entitled to feel towards all simpletons who seek other prizes than the dusty ones along the highway. He then took his leave with an uplifted finger, and a sneer upon his face, that haunted the artist's dreams for many a night afterwards. At the time of his old master's visit, Owen was probably on the point of taking up the relinquished task; but, by this sinister event, he was thrown back into the state whence he had been slowly emerging.

But the innate tendency of his soul had only been accumulating fresh vigor, during its apparent sluggishness. As the summer advanced, he almost totally relinquished his business, and permitted Father Time, so far as the old gentleman was represented by the clocks and watches under his control, to stray at random through human life, making infinite confusion among the train of bewildered hours. He wasted the sunshine, as people said, in wandering through the woods and fields, and along the banks of streams. There, like a child, he found amusement in chasing butterflies, or watching the motions of water-insects. There was something truly mysterious in the intentness with which he contemplated these living playthings, as they sported on the breeze; or examined the structure of an imperial insect whom he had imprisoned. The chase of butterflies was an apt emblem of the ideal pursuit in which he had spent so many golden hours. But, would the Beautiful Idea ever be yielded to his hand, like the butterfly that symbolized it? Sweet, doubtless, were these days, and congenial to the artist's soul. They were full of bright conceptions, which gleamed through his intellectual world, as the butterflies gleamed through the outward atmosphere, and were real to him for the instant, without the toil, and perplexity, and many disappointments, of attempting to make them visible to the sensual eye. Alas, that the artist, whether in poetry or whatever other material, may not content himself with the inward enjoyment of the Beautiful, but must chase the flitting mystery beyond the verge of his ethereal domain, and crush its frail being in seizing it with a material grasp! Owen Warland felt the impulse to give external reality to his ideas, as irresistibly as any of the poets or painters, who have arrayed the world in a dimmer and fainter beauty, imperfectly copied from the richness of their visions.

The night was now his time for the slow process of recreating the one Idea, to which all his intellectual activity referred itself. Always at the approach of dusk, he stole into the town, locked himself within his shop, and wrought with patient delicacy of touch, for many hours. Sometimes he was startled by the rap of the watchman, who, when all the world should be asleep, had caught the gleam of lamp-light through the crevices of Owen Warland's shutters. Daylight, to the morbid sensibility of his mind, seemed to have an intrusiveness that interfered with his pursuits. On cloudy and inclement days, therefore, he sat with his head upon his hands, muffling, as it were, his sensitive brain in a mist of indefinite musings; for it was a relief to escape from the sharp distinctness with which he was compelled to shape out his thoughts, during his nightly toil.

From one of these fits of torpor, he was aroused by the entrance of Annie Hovenden, who came into the shop with the freedom of a customer, and also with something of the familiarity of a childish friend. She had worn a hole through her silver thimble, and wanted Owen to repair it.

"But I don't know whether you will condescend to such a task," said she, laughing, "now that you are so taken up with the notion of putting spirit into machinery."

"Where did you get that idea, Annie?" said Owen, starting in surprise.

"Oh, out of my own head," answered she, "and from something that I heard you say, long ago, when you were but a boy, and I a little child. But, come! will you mend this poor thimble of mine?"

"Anything for your sake, Annie," said Owen Warland—"anything; even were it to work at Robert Danforth's forge."

"And that would be a pretty sight!" retorted Annie, glancing with imperceptible slightness at the artist's small and slender frame. "Well; here is the thimble."

"But that is a strange idea of yours," said Owen, "about the spiritualization of matter!"

And then the thought stole into his mind, that this young girl possessed the gift to comprehend him, better than all the world beside. And what a help and strength would it be to him, in his lonely toil, if he could gain the sympathy of the only being whom he loved! To persons whose pursuits are insulated from the common business of life—who are either in advance of mankind, or apart from it—there often comes a sensation of moral cold, that makes the spirit shiver, as if it had reached the frozen solitudes around the pole. What the prophet, the poet, the reformer, the criminal, or any other man, with human yearnings, but separated from the multitude by a peculiar lot, might feel, poor Owen Warland felt.

"Annie," cried he, growing pale as death at the thought, "how gladly would I tell you the secret of my pursuit! You, methinks, would estimate it rightly. You, I know, would hear it with a reverence that I must not expect from the harsh, material world."

"Would I not? to be sure I would!" replied Annie Hovenden, lightly laughing. "Come; explain to me quickly what is the meaning of this little whirligig, so delicately wrought that it might be a plaything for Queen Mab. See; I will put it in motion."

"Hold," exclaimed Owen, "hold!"

Annie had but given the slightest possible touch, with the point of a needle, to the same minute portion of complicated machinery which has been more than once mentioned, when the artist seized her by the wrist with a force that made her scream aloud. She was affrighted at the convulsion of intense rage and anguish that writhed across his features. The next instant he let his head sink upon his hands.

"Go, Annie," murmured he, "I have deceived myself, and must suffer for it. I yearned for sympathy—and thought—and fancied—and dreamed—that you might give it me. But you lack the talisman, Annie, that should admit you into my secrets. That touch has undone the toil of months, and the thought of a lifetime! It was not your fault, Annie—but you have ruined me!"

Poor Owen Warland! He had indeed erred, yet pardonably; for if any human spirit could have sufficiently reverenced the processes so sacred in his eyes, it must have been a woman's. Even Annie Hovenden, possibly, might not have disappointed him, had she been enlightened by the deep intelligence of love.

The artist spent the ensuing winter in a way that satisfied any persons, who had hitherto retained a hopeful opinion of him, that he was, in truth, irrevocably doomed to inutility as regarded the world, and to an evil destiny on his own part. The decease of a relative had put him in possession of a small inheritance. Thus freed from the necessity of toil, and having lost the steadfast influence of a great purpose—great, at least to him—he abandoned himself to habits from which, it might have been supposed, the mere delicacy of his organization would have availed to secure him. But when the ethereal portion of a man of genius is obscured, the earthly part assumes an influence the more uncontrollable, because the character is now thrown off the balance to which Providence had so nicely adjusted it, and which, in coarser natures, is adjusted by some other method. Owen Warland made proof of whatever show of bliss may be found in riot. He looked at the world through the golden medium of wine, and contemplated the visions that bubble up so gaily around the brim of the glass, and that people the air with shapes of pleasant madness, which so soon grow ghostly and forlorn. Even when this dismal and inevitable change had taken place, the young man might still have continued to quaff the cup of enchantments, though its vapor did but shroud life in gloom, and fill the gloom with spectres that mocked at him. There was a certain irksomeness of spirit, which, being real, and the deepest sensation of which the artist was now conscious, was more intolerable than any fantastic miseries and horrors that the abuse of wine could summon up. In the latter case, he could remember, even out of the midst of his trouble, that all was but a delusion; in the former, the heavy anguish was his actual life.

From this perilous state, he was redeemed by an incident which more than one person witnessed, but of which the shrewdest could not explain nor conjecture the operation on Owen Warland's mind. It was very simple. On a warm afternoon of spring, as the artist sat among his riotous companions, with a glass of wine before him, a splendid butterfly flew in at the open window, and fluttered about his head.

"Ah!" exclaimed Owen, who had drank freely, "Are you alive again, child of the sun, and playmate of the summer breeze, after your dismal winter's nap! Then it is time for me to be at work!"

And leaving his unemptied glass upon the table, he departed, and was never known to sip another drop of wine.

And now, again, he resumed his wanderings in the woods and fields. It might be fancied that the bright butterfly, which had come so spiritlike into the window, as Owen sat with the rude revellers, was indeed a spirit, commissioned to recall him to the pure, ideal life that had so etherealized him among men. It might be fancied, that he went forth to seek this spirit, in its sunny haunts; for still, as in the summer-time gone by, he was seen to steal gently up, wherever a butterfly had alighted, and lose himself in contemplation of it. When it took flight, his eyes followed the winged vision, as if its airy track would show the path to heaven. But what could be the purpose of the unseasonable toil, which was again resumed, as the watchman knew by the lines of lamp-light through the crevices of Owen Warland's shutters? The townspeople had one comprehensive explanation of all these singularities. Owen Warland had gone mad! How universally efficacious—how satisfactory, too, and soothing to the injured sensibility of narrowness and dullness—is this easy method of accounting for whatever lies beyond the world's most ordinary scope! From Saint Paul's days, down to our poor little Artist of the Beautiful, the same talisman has been applied to the elucidation of all mysteries in the words or deeds of men, who spoke or acted too wisely or too well. In Owen Warland's case, the judgment of his townspeople may have been correct. Perhaps he was mad. The lack of sympathy—that contrast between himself and his neighbors, which took away the restraint of example—was enough to make him so. Or, possibly, he had caught just so much of ethereal radiance as served to bewilder him, in an earthly sense, by its intermixture with the common daylight.

One evening, when the artist had returned from a customary ramble, and had just thrown the lustre of his lamp on the delicate piece of work, so often interrupted, but still taken up again, as if his fate were embodied in its mechanism, he was surprised by the entrance of old Peter Hovenden. Owen never met this man without a shrinking of the heart. Of all the world, he was most terrible, by reason of a keen understanding, which saw so distinctly what it did see, and disbelieved so uncompromisingly in what it could not see. On this occasion, the old watchmaker had merely a gracious word or two to say.

"Owen, my lad," said he, "we must see you at my house to-morrow night."

The artist began to mutter some excuse.

"Oh, but it must be so," quoth Peter Hovenden, "for the sake of the days when you were one of the household. What, my boy, don't you know that my daughter Annie is engaged to Robert Danforth? We are making an entertainment, in our humble way, to celebrate the event."

"Ah!" said Owen.

That little monosyllable was all he uttered; its tone seemed cold and unconcerned, to an ear like Peter Hovenden's; and yet there was in it the stifled outcry of the poor artist's heart, which he compressed within him like a man holding down an evil spirit. One slight outbreak, however, imperceptible to the old watchmaker, he allowed himself. Raising the instrument with which he was about to begin his work, he let it fall upon the little system of machinery that had, anew, cost him months of thought and toil. It was shattered by the stroke!

Owen Warland's story would have been no tolerable representation of the troubled life of those who strive to create the Beautiful, if, amid all other thwarting influences, love had not interposed to steal the cunning from his hand. Outwardly, he had been no ardent or enterprising lover; the career of his passion had confined its tumults and vicissitudes so entirely within the artist's imagination, that Annie herself had scarcely more than a woman's intuitive perception of it. But, in Owen's view, it covered the whole field of his life. Forgetful of the time when she had shown herself incapable of any deep response, he had persisted in connecting all his dreams of artistical success with Annie's image; she was the visible shape in which the spiritual power that he worshipped, and on whose altar he hoped to lay a not unworthy offering, was made manifest to him. Of course he had deceived himself; there were no such attributes in Annie Hovenden as his imagination had endowed her with. She, in the aspect which she wore to his inward vision, was as much a creation of his own, as the mysterious piece of mechanism would be were it ever realized. Had he become convinced of his mistake through the medium of successful love; had he won Annie to his bosom, and there beheld her fade from angel into ordinary woman, the disappointment might have driven him back, with concentrated energy, upon his sole remaining object. On the other hand, had he found Annie what he fancied, his lot would have been so rich in beauty, that, out of its mere redundancy, he might have wrought the Beautiful into many a worthier type than he had toiled for. But the guise in which his sorrow came to him, the sense that the angel of his life had been snatched away and given to a rude man of earth and iron, who could neither need nor appreciate her ministrations; this was the very perversity of fate, that makes human existence appear too absurd and contradictory to be the scene of one other hope or one other fear. There was nothing left for Owen Warland but to sit down like a man that had been stunned.

He went through a fit of illness. After his recovery, his small and slender frame assumed an obtuser garniture of flesh than it had ever before worn. His thin cheeks became round; his delicate little hand, so spiritually fashioned to achieve fairy task-work, grew plumper than the hand of a thriving infant. His aspect had a childishness, such as might have induced a stranger to pat him on the head—pausing, however, in the act, to wonder what manner of child was here. It was as if the spirit had gone out of him, leaving the body to flourish in a sort of vegetable existence. Not that Owen Warland was idiotic. He could talk, and not irrationally. Somewhat of a babbler, indeed, did people begin to think him; for he was apt to discourse at wearisome length, of marvels of mechanism that he had read about in books, but which he had learned to consider as absolutely fabulous. Among them he enumerated the Man of Brass, constructed by Albertus Magnus, and the Brazen Head of Friar Bacon; and, coming down to later times, the automata of a little coach and horses, which, it was pretended, had been manufactured for the Dauphin of France; together with an insect that buzzed about the ear like a living fly, and yet was but a contrivance of minute steel springs. There was a story, too, of a duck that waddled, and quacked, and ate; though, had any honest citizen purchased it for dinner, he would have found himself cheated with the mere mechanical apparition of a duck.

"But all these accounts," said Owen Warland, "I am now satisfied, are mere impositions."

Then, in a mysterious way, he would confess that he once thought differently. In his idle and dreamy days, he had considered it possible, in a certain sense, to spiritualize machinery; and to combine with the new species of life and motion, thus produced, a beauty that should attain to the ideal which Nature has proposed to herself, in all her creatures, but has never taken pains to realize. He seemed, however, to retain no very distinct perception either of the process of achieving this object, or of the design itself.

"I have thrown it all aside now," he would say. "It was a dream, such as young men are always mystifying themselves with. Now that I have acquired a little common sense, it makes me laugh to think of it."

Poor, poor, and fallen Owen Warland! These were the symptoms that he had ceased to be an inhabitant of the better sphere that lies unseen around us. He had lost his faith in the invisible, and now prided himself, as such unfortunates invariably do, in the wisdom which rejected much that even his eye could see, and trusted confidently in nothing but what his hand could touch. This is the calamity of men whose spiritual part dies out of them, and leaves the grosser understanding to assimilate them more and more to the things of which alone it can take cognizance. But, in Owen Warland, the spirit was not dead, nor past away; it only slept.

How it awoke again, is not recorded. Perhaps, the torpid slumber was broken by a convulsive pain. Perhaps, as in a former instance, the butterfly came and hovered about his head, and reinspired him—as, indeed, this creature of the sunshine had always a mysterious mission for the artist—reinspired him with the former purpose of his life. Whether it were pain or happiness that thrilled through his veins, his first impulse was to thank Heaven for rendering him again the being of thought, imagination, and keenest sensibility, that he had long ceased to be.

"Now for my task," said he. "Never did I feel such strength for it as now."

Yet, strong as he felt himself, he was incited to toil the more diligently, by an anxiety lest death should surprise him in the midst of his labors. This anxiety, perhaps, is common to all men who set their hearts upon anything so high, in their own view of it, that life becomes of importance only as conditional to its accomplishment. So long as we love life for itself, we seldom dread the losing it. When we desire life for the attainment of an object, we recognize the frailty of its texture. But, side by side with this sense of insecurity, there is a vital faith in our invulnerability to the shaft of death, while engaged in any task that seems assigned by Providence as our proper thing to do, and which the world would have cause to mourn for, should we leave it unaccomplished. Can the philosopher, big with the inspiration of an idea that is to reform mankind, believe that he is to be beckoned from this sensible existence, at the very instant when he is mustering his breath to speak the word of light? Should he perish so, the weary ages may pass away—the world's whole life-sand may fall, drop by drop—before another intellect is prepared to develop the truth that might have been uttered then. But history affords many an example, where the most precious spirit, at any particular epoch manifested in human shape, has gone hence untimely, without space allowed him, so far as mortal judgment could discern, to perform his mission on the earth. The prophet dies; and the man of torpid heart and sluggish brain lives on. The poet leaves his song half sung, or finishes it, beyond the scope of mortal ears, in a celestial choir. The painter—as Allston did—leaves half his conception on the canvass, to sadden us with its imperfect beauty, and goes to picture forth the whole, if it be no irreverence to say so, in the hues of Heaven. But, rather, such incomplete designs of this life will be perfected nowhere. This so frequent abortion of man's dearest projects must be taken as a proof, that the deeds of earth, however etherealized by piety or genius, are without value, except as exercises and manifestations of the spirit. In Heaven, all ordinary thought is higher and more melodious than Milton's song. Then, would he add another verse to any strain that he had left unfinished here?

But to return to Owen Warland. It was his fortune, good or ill, to achieve the purpose of his life. Pass we over a long space of intense thought, yearning effort, minute toil, and wasting anxiety, succeeded by an instant of solitary triumph; let all this be imagined; and then behold the artist, on a winter evening, seeking admittance to Robert Danforth's fireside circle. There he found the Man of Iron, with his massive substance thoroughly warmed and attempered by domestic influences. And there was Annie, too, now transformed into a matron, with much of her husband's plain and sturdy nature, but imbued, as Owen Warland still believed, with a finer grace, that might enable her to be the interpreter between Strength and Beauty. It happened, likewise, that old Peter Hovenden was a guest, this evening, at his daughter's fireside; and it was his well-remembered expression of keen, cold criticism, that first encountered the artist's glance.

"My old friend Owen!" cried Robert Danforth, starting up, and compressing the artist's delicate fingers within a hand that was accustomed to grip bars of iron. "This is kind and neighborly, to come to us at last! I was afraid your Perpetual Motion had bewitched you out of the remembrance of old times."

"We are glad to see you!" said Annie, while a blush reddened her matronly cheek. "It was not like a friend, to stay from us so long."

"Well, Owen," inquired the old watchmaker, as his first greeting, "how comes on the Beautiful? Have you created it at last?"

The artist did not immediately reply, being startled by the apparition of a young child of strength, that was tumbling about on the carpet; a little personage who had come mysteriously out of the infinite, but with something so sturdy and real in his composition that he seemed moulded out of the densest substance which earth could supply. This hopeful infant crawled towards the new-comer, and setting himself on end—as Robert Danforth expressed the posture—stared at Owen with a look of such sagacious observation, that the mother could not help exchanging a proud glance with her husband. But the artist was disturbed by the child's look, as imagining a resemblance between it and Peter Hovenden's habitual expression. He could have fancied that the old watchmaker was compressed into this baby-shape, and was looking out of those baby-eyes, and repeating—as he now did—the malicious question:

"The Beautiful, Owen! How comes on the Beautiful? Have you succeeded in creating the Beautiful?"

"I have succeeded," replied the artist, with a momentary light of triumph in his eyes, and a smile of sunshine, yet steeped in such depth of thought that it was almost sadness. "Yes, my friends, it is the truth. I have succeeded!"

"Indeed!" cried Annie, a look of maiden mirthfulness peeping out of her face again. "And it is lawful, now, to inquire what the secret is?"

"Surely; it is to disclose it, that I have come," answered Owen Warland. "You shall know, and see, and touch, and possess, the secret! For Annie—if by that name I may still address the friend of my boyish years—Annie, it is for your bridal gift that I have wrought this spiritualized mechanism, this harmony of motion, this Mystery of Beauty! It comes late, indeed; but it is as we go onward in life, when objects begin to lose their freshness of hue, and our souls their delicacy of perception, that the spirit of Beauty is most needed. If—forgive me, Annie—if you know how to value this gift, it can never come too late!"

He produced, as he spoke, what seemed a jewel-box. It was carved richly out of ebony by his own hand, and inlaid with a fanciful tracery of pearl, representing a boy in pursuit of a butterfly, which, elsewhere, had become a winged spirit, and was flying heavenward; while the boy, or youth, had found such efficacy in his strong desire, that he ascended from earth to cloud, and from cloud to celestial atmosphere, to win the Beautiful. This case of ebony the artist opened, and bade Annie place her finger on its edge. She did so, but almost screamed, as a butterfly fluttered forth, and alighting on her finger's tip, sat waving the ample magnificence of its purple and gold-speckled wings, as if in prelude to a flight. It is impossible to express by words the glory, the splendor, the delicate gorgeousness, which were softened into the beauty of this object. Nature's ideal butterfly was here realized in all its perfection; not in the pattern of such faded insects as flit among earthly flowers, but of those which hover across the meads of Paradise, for child-angels and the spirits of departed infants to disport themselves with. The rich down was visible upon its wings; the lustre of its eyes seemed instinct with spirit. The firelight glimmered around this wonder—the candles gleamed upon it—but it glistened apparently by its own radiance, and illuminated the finger and outstretched hand on which it rested, with a white gleam like that of precious stones. In its perfect beauty, the consideration of size was entirely lost. Had its wings overarched the firmament, the mind could not have been more filled or satisfied.

"Beautiful! Beautiful!" exclaimed Annie. "Is it alive? Is it alive?"

"Alive? To be sure it is," answered her husband. "Do you suppose any mortal has skill enough to make a butterfly,—or would put himself to the trouble of making one, when any child may catch a score of them in a summer's afternoon? Alive? Certainly! But this pretty box is undoubtedly of our friend Owen's manufacture; and really it does him credit."

At this moment, the butterfly waved its wings anew, with a motion so absolutely lifelike that Annie was startled, and even awe-stricken; for, in spite of her husband's opinion, she could not satisfy herself whether it was indeed a living creature, or a piece of wondrous mechanism.

"Is it alive?" she repeated, more earnestly than before.

"Judge for yourself," said Owen Warland, who stood gazing in her face with fixed attention.

The butterfly now flung itself upon the air, fluttered round Annie's head, and soared into a distant region of the parlor, still making itself perceptible to sight by the starry gleam in which the motion of its wings enveloped it. The infant on the floor, followed its course with his sagacious little eyes. After flying about the room, it returned, in a spiral curve, and settled again on Annie's finger.

"But is it alive?" exclaimed she again; and the finger, on which the gorgeous mystery had alighted, was so tremulous that the butterfly was forced to balance himself with his wings. "Tell me if it be alive, or whether you created it?"

"Wherefore ask who created it, so it be beautiful?" replied Owen Warland. "Alive? Yes, Annie; it may well be said to possess life, for it absorbed my own being into itself; and in the secret of that butterfly, and in its beauty—which is not merely outward, but deep as its whole system—is represented the intellect, the imagination, the sensibility, the soul, of an Artist of the Beautiful! Yes, I created it. But"—and here his countenance somewhat changed—"this butterfly is not now to me what it was when I beheld it afar off, in the day-dreams of my youth."

"Be it what it may, it is a pretty plaything," said the blacksmith, grinning with childlike delight. "I wonder whether it would condescend to alight on such a great clumsy finger as mine? Hold it hither, Annie!"

By the artist's direction, Annie touched her finger's tip to that of her husband;

and, after a momentary delay, the butterfly fluttered from one to the other. It preluded a second flight by a similar, yet not precisely the same waving of wings, as in the first experiment; then, ascending from the blacksmith's stalwart finger, it rose in a gradually enlarging curve to the ceiling, made one wide sweep around the room, and returned with an undulating movement to the point whence it had started.

"Well, that does beat all nature!" cried Robert Danforth, bestowing the heartiest praise that he could find expression for; and, indeed, had he paused there, a man of finer words and nicer perception, could not easily have said more. "That goes beyond me, I confess! But what then? There is more real use in one downright blow of my sledge-hammer, than in the whole five years' labor that our friend Owen has wasted on this butterfly!"

Here the child clapped his hands, and made a great babble of indistinct utterance, apparently demanding that the butterfly should be given him for a plaything.

Owen Warland, meanwhile, glanced sidelong at Annie, to discover whether she sympathized in her husband's estimate of the comparative value of the Beautiful and the Practical. There was, amid all her kindness towards himself, amid all the wonder and admiration with which she contemplated the marvelous work of his hands, and incarnation of his idea, a secret scorn; too secret, perhaps, for her own consciousness, and perceptible only to such intuitive discernment as that of the artist. But Owen, in the latter stages of his pursuit, had risen out of the region in which such a discovery might have been torture. He knew that the world, and Annie as the representative of the world, whatever praise might be bestowed, could never say the fitting word, nor feel the fitting sentiment which should be the perfect recompense of an artist who, symbolizing a lofty moral by a material trifle—converting what was earthly, to spiritual gold—had won the Beautiful into his handiwork. Not at this latest moment, was he to learn that the reward of all high performance must be sought within itself, or sought in vain. There was, however, a view of the matter, which Annie, and her husband, and even Peter Hovenden, might fully have understood, and which would have satisfied them that the toil of years had here been worthily bestowed. Owen Warland might have told them, that this butterfly, this plaything, this bridal-gift of a poor watchmaker to a blacksmith's wife, was, in truth, a gem of art that a monarch would have purchased with honors and abundant wealth, and have treasured it among the jewels of his kingdom, as the most unique and wondrous of them all! But the artist smiled, and kept the secret to himself.

"Father," said Annie, thinking that a word of praise from the old watchmaker might gratify his former apprentice, "do come and admire this pretty butterfly!"

"Let us see," said Peter Hovenden, rising from his chair, with the sneer upon his face that always made people doubt, as he himself did, in everything but a material existence. "Here is my finger for it to alight upon. I shall understand it better when once I have touched it."

But, to the increased astonishment of Annie, when the tip of her father's finger was pressed against that of her husband, on which the butterfly still rested, the insect drooped its wings, and seemed on the point of falling to the floor. Even the bright spots of gold upon its wings and body, unless her eyes deceived her, grew dim, and the glowing purple took a dusky hue, and the starry lustre that gleamed around the blacksmith's hand, became faint, and vanished.

"It is dying! it is dying!" cried Annie, in alarm.

"It has been delicately wrought," said the artist calmly. "As I told you, it has imbibed a spiritual essence—call it magnetism, or what you will. In an atmosphere of doubt and mockery, its exquisite susceptibility suffers torture, as does the soul of him who instilled his own life into it. It has already lost its beauty; in a few moments more, its mechanism would be irreparably injured."

"Take away your hand, father!" entreated Annie, turning pale. "Here is my child; let it rest on his innocent hand. There, perhaps, its life will revive, and its colors grow brighter than ever."

Her father, with an acrid smile, withdrew his finger. The butterfly then appeared to recover the power of voluntary motion; while its hues assumed much of their original lustre, and the gleam of starlight, which was its most ethereal attribute, again formed a halo round about it. At first, when transferred from Robert Danforth's hand to the small finger of the child, this radiance grew so powerful that it positively threw the little fellow's shadow back against the wall. He, meanwhile, extended his plump hand as he had seen his father and mother do, and watched the waving of the insect's wings, with infantine delight. Nevertheless, there was a certain odd expression of sagacity, that made Owen Warland feel as if here were old Peter Hovenden, partially, and but partially, redeemed from his hard scepticism into childish faith.

"How wise the little monkey looks!" whispered Robert Danforth to his wife.

"I never saw such a look on a child's face," answered Annie, admiring her own infant, and with good reason, far more than the artistic butterfly. "The darling knows more of the mystery than we do."

As if the butterfly, like the artist, were conscious of something not entirely congenial in the child's nature, it alternately sparkled and grew dim. At length, it arose from the small hand of the infant with an airy motion, that seemed to bear it upward without an effort; as if the ethereal instincts, with which its master's spirit had endowed it, impelled this fair vision involuntarily to a higher sphere. Had there been no obstruction, it might have soared into the sky, and grown immortal. But its lustre gleamed upon the ceiling; the exquisite texture of its wings brushed against that earthly medium; and a sparkle or too, as of star-dust, floated downward and lay glimmering on the carpet. Then the butterfly came fluttering down, and instead of returning to the infant, was apparently attracted towards the artist's hand.

"Not so, not so!" murmured Owen Warland, as if his handiwork could have understood him. "Thou hast gone forth out of thy master's heart. There is no return for thee!"

With a wavering movement, and emitting a tremulous radiance, the butterfly struggled, as it were, towards the infant, and was about to alight upon his finger. But, while it still hovered in the air, the little Child of Strength, with his grandsire's sharp and shrewd expression in his face, made a snatch at the marvellous insect, and compressed it in his hand. Annie screamed! Old Peter Hovenden burst into a cold and scornful laugh. The blacksmith, by main force, unclosed the infant's hand, and found within the palm a small heap of glittering fragments, whence the Mystery of Beauty had fled for ever. And as for Owen Warland, he looked placidly at what seemed the ruin of his life's labor, and which was yet no ruin. He had caught a far other butterfly than this. When the artist rose high enough to achieve the Beautiful, the symbol by which he made it perceptible to mortal senses became of little value in his eyes, while his spirit possessed itself in the enjoyment of the Reality.

1844

Preface to *The House of the Seven Gables*

When a writer calls his work a Romance, it need hardly be observed that he wishes to claim a certain latitude, both as to its fashion and material, which he would not have felt himself entitled to assume had he professed to be writing a Novel. The latter form of composition is presumed to aim at a very minute fidelity, not merely to the possible, but to the probable and ordinary course of man's experience. The former—while, as a work of art, it must rigidly subject itself to laws, and while it sins unpardonably so far as it may swerve aside from the truth of the human heart—has fairly a right to present that truth under circumstances, to a great extent, of the writer's own choosing or creation. If he think fit, also, he may so manage his atmospherical medium as to bring out or mellow the lights and deepen and enrich the shadows of the picture. He will be wise, no doubt, to make a very moderate use of the privileges here stated, and, especially, to mingle the Marvellous rather as a slight, delicate, and evanescent flavor, that as any portion of the actual substance of the dish offered to the public. He can hardly be said, however, to commit a literary crime even if he disregard this caution.

In the present work, the author has proposed to himself—but with what success, fortunately, it is not for him to judge—to keep undeviatingly within his immunities. The point of view in which this tale comes under the Romantic definition lies in the attempt to connect a bygone time with the very present that is flitting away from us. It is a legend prolonging itself, from an epoch now gray in the distance, down into our own broad daylight, and bringing along with it some of its legendary mist, which the reader, according to his pleasure, may either disregard, or allow it to float almost imperceptibly about the characters and events for the sake of a picturesque effect. The narrative, it may be, is woven of so humble a texture as to require this advantage, and, at the same time, to render it the more difficult of attainment.

Many writers lay very great stress upon some definite moral purpose, at which they profess to aim their works. Not to be deficient in this particular, the author has provided himself with a moral,—the truth, namely, that the wrong-doing of one generation lives into the successive ones, and, divesting itself of every temporary advantage, becomes a pure and uncontrollable mischief; and he would feel it a singular gratification if this romance might effectually convince mankind—or, indeed, any one man—of the folly of tumbling down an avalanche of ill-gotten gold, or real estate, on the heads of an unfortunate posterity, thereby to maim and crush them, until the accumulated mass shall be scattered abroad in its original atoms. In good faith, however, he is not sufficiently imaginative to flatter himself with the slightest hope of this kind. When romances do really teach anything, or produce any effective operation, it is usually through a far more subtile process than the ostensible one. The author has considered it hardly worth his while, therefore, relentlessly to impale the story with its moral as with an iron rod,—or, rather, as by sticking a pin through a butterfly,—thus at once depriving it of life, and causing it to stiffen in an ungainly and unnatural attitude. A high truth, indeed, fairly, finely, and skilfully wrought out, brightening at every step, and crowning the final development of a work of fiction, may add an artistic glory, but is never any truer, and seldom any more evident, at the last page than at the first.

The reader may perhaps choose to assign an actual locality to the imaginary events of this narrative. If permitted by the historical connection,—which, though slight, was essential to his plan,—the author would very willingly have avoided anything of this nature. Not to speak of other objections, it exposes the romance to an inflexible and exceedingly dangerous species of criticism, by bringing his fancy-pictures almost into positive contact with the realities of the moment. It has been no part of his object, however, to describe local manners, nor in any way to meddle with the characteristics of a community for whom he cherishes a proper respect and a natural regard. He trusts not to be considered as unpardonably offending by laying out a street that infringes upon nobody's private rights, and appropriating a lot of land which had no visible owner, and building a house of materials long in use for constructing castles in the air. The personages of the tale—though they give themselves out to be of ancient stability and considerable prominence—are really of the author's own making, or, at all events, of his own mixing; their virtues can shed no lustre, nor their defects redound, in the remotest degree, to the discredit of the venerable town of which they profess to be inhabitants. He would be glad, therefore, if—especially in the quarter to which he alludes—the book may be read strictly as a Romance, having a great deal more to do with the clouds overhead than with any portion of the actual soil of the County of Essex.

Lenox, January 27, 1851

Mrs. Hutchinson[1]

The character of this female suggests a train of thought which will form as natural an introduction to her story as most of the prefaces to Gay's Fables[2] or the tales of Prior,[3] besides that the general soundness of the moral may excuse any want of present applicability. We will not look for a living resemblance of Mrs. Hutchinson, though the search might not be altogether fruitless.—But there are portentous indications, changes gradually taking place in the habits and feelings of the gentle sex, which seem to threaten our posterity with many of those public women, whereof one was a burthen too grievous for our fathers. The press, however, is now the medium through which feminine ambition chiefly manifests itself, and we will not anticipate the period, (trusting to be gone hence ere it arrive,) when fair orators shall be as numerous as the fair authors of our own day. The hastiest glance may show, how much of the texture and body of cisatlantic literature is the work of those slender fingers, from which only a light and fanciful embroidery has heretofore been required, that might sparkle upon the garment without enfeebling the web. Woman's intellect should never give the tone to that of man, and even her morality is not exactly the

[1]"Mrs. Hutchinson," first published in the *Salem Gazette* (7 December 1830).

[2]John Gay (1688–1732), English poet and playwright, author of *The Beggar's Opera.*

[3]Matthew Prior (1664–1721), English poet, essayist, and diplomat.

material for masculine virtue. A false liberality which mistakes the strong division lines of Nature for arbitrary distinctions, and a courtesy, which might polish criticism but should never soften it, have done their best to add a girlish feebleness to the tottering infancy of our literature. The evil is likely to be a growing one. As yet, the great body of American women are a domestic race; but when a continuance of ill-judged incitements shall have turned their hearts away from the fireside, there are obvious circumstances which will render female pens more numerous and more prolific than those of men, though but equally encouraged; and (limited of course by the scanty support of the public, but increasing indefinitely within those limits) the ink-stained Amazons will expel their rivals by actual pressure, and petticoats wave triumphant over all the field. But, allowing that such forebodings are slightly exaggerated, is it good for woman's self that the path of feverish hope, of tremulous success, of bitter and ignominious disappointment, should be left wide open to her? Is the prize worth her having if she win it? Fame does not increase the peculiar respect which men pay to female excellence, and there is a delicacy, (even in rude bosoms, where few would think to find it) that perceives, or fancies, a sort of impropriety in the display of woman's naked mind to the gaze of the world, with indications by which its inmost secrets may be searched out. In fine, criticism should examine with a stricter, instead of a more indulgent eye, the merits of females at its bar, because they are to justify themselves for an irregularity which men do not commit in appearing there; and woman, when she feels the impulse of genius like a command of Heaven within her, should be aware that she is relinquishing a part of the loveliness of her sex, and obey the inward voice with sorrowing reluctance, like the Arabian maid who bewailed the gift of Prophecy. Hinting thus imperfectly at sentiments which may be developed on a future occasion, we proceed to consider the celebrated subject of this sketch.

Mrs. Hutchinson was a woman of extraordinary talent and strong imagination, whom the latter quality, following the general direction taken by the enthusiasm of the times, prompted to stand forth as a reformer in religion. In her native country, she had shown symptoms of irregular and daring thought, but, chiefly by the influence of a favorite pastor, was restrained from open indiscretion. On the removal of this clergyman, becoming dissatisfied with the ministry under which she lived, she was drawn in by the great tide of Puritan emigration, and visited Massachusetts within a few years after its first settlement. But she bore trouble in her own bosom, and could find no peace in this chosen land.—She soon began to promulgate strange and dangerous opinions, tending, in the peculiar situation of the colony, and from the principles which were its basis and indispensable for its temporary support, to eat into its very existence. We shall endeavor to give a more practical idea of this part of her course.

It is a summer evening. The dusk has settled heavily upon the woods, the waves, and the Trimontane peninsula, increasing that dismal aspect of the embryo town which was said to have drawn tears of despondency from Mrs. Hutchinson, though she believed that her mission thither was divine. The houses, straw-thatched and lowly roofed, stand irregularly along streets that are yet roughened by the roots of the trees, as if the forest, departing at the approach of man, had left its reluctant foot prints behind. Most of the dwellings are lonely and silent; from a few we may hear the reading of some sacred text, or the quiet voice of prayer; but nearly all the sombre life of the scene is collected near the extremity of the village. A crowd of hooded women, and of men in steeple-hats and close cropt hair, are assembled at the door and open windows of a house newly built. An earnest expression glows in every face, and some press inward as if the bread of life were to be dealt forth, and they feared to lose their share, while others would fain hold them back, but enter with them since they may not be restrained. We also will go in, edging through the thronged doorway to an apartment which occupies the whole breadth of the house. At the upper end, behind a table on which are placed the Scriptures and two glimmering lamps, we see a woman, plainly attired as befits her ripened years; her hair, complexion, and eyes are dark, the latter somewhat dull and heavy, but kindling up with a gradual brightness. Let us look round upon the hearers. At her right hand, his countenance suiting well with the gloomy light which discovers it, stands Vane the youthful governor, preferred by a hasty judgment of the people over all the wise and hoary heads that had preceded him to New-England. In his mysterious eyes we may read a dark enthusiasm, akin to that of the woman whose cause he has espoused, combined with a shrewd worldly foresight, which tells him that her doctrines will be productive of change and tumult, the elements of his power and delight. On her left, yet slightly drawn back so as to evince a less decided support, is Cotton, no young and hot enthusiast, but a mild, grave man in the decline of life, deep in all the learning of the age, and sanctified in heart and made venerable in feature by the long exercise of his holy profession. He also is deceived by the strange fire now laid upon the altar, and he alone among his brethren is excepted in the denunciation of the new Apostle, as sealed and set apart by Heaven to the work of the ministry. Others of the priesthood stand full in front of the woman, striving to beat her down with brows of wrinkled iron, and whispering sternly and significantly among themselves, as she unfolds her seditious doctrines and grows warm in their support. Foremost is Hugh Peters, full of holy wrath, and scarce containing himself from rushing forward to convict her of damnable heresies; there also is Ward, meditating a reply of empty puns, and quaint antitheses, and tinkling jests that puzzle us with nothing but a sound. The audience are variously affected, but none indifferent. On the foreheads of the aged, the mature, and strong-minded, you may generally read steadfast disapprobation, though here and there is one, whose faith seems shaken in those whom he had trusted for years; the females, on the other hand, are shuddering and weeping, and at times they cast a desolate look of fear around them; while the young men lean forward, fiery and impatient, fit instruments for whatever rash deed may be suggested. And what is the eloquence that gives rise to all these passions? The woman tells them, (and cites texts from the Holy Book to prove her words,) that they have put their trust in unregenerated and uncommissioned men, and have followed them into the wilderness for naught. Therefore their hearts are turning from those whom they had chosen to lead them to Heaven, and they feel like children who have been enticed far from home, and see the features of their guides change all at once, assuming a fiendish shape in some frightful solitude.

These proceedings of Mrs. Hutchinson could not long be endured by the provincial government. The present was a most remarkable case, in which religious freedom was wholly inconsistent with public safety, and where the principles of an illiberal age indicated the very course which must have been pursued by worldly policy and enlightened wisdom. Unity of faith was the star that had guided these people over the deep, and a diversity of sects would either have scattered them from the land to which they had as yet so few attachments, or perhaps have excited a diminutive civil war among those who had come so far to worship together. The opposition to what may be termed the established church had now lost its chief support, by the removal of Vane from office and his departure for England, and Mr. Cotton began to have that light in regard to his errors, which will sometimes break in upon the wisest and most pious men, when their opinions are unhappily discordant with those of the Powers that be. A Synod, the first in New England, was speedily assembled, and pronounced its condemnation of the obnoxious doctrines. Mrs. Hutchinson was next summoned before the supreme civil tribunal, at which, however, the most eminent of the clergy were present, and appear to have taken a very active part as witnesses and advisers. We shall here resume the more picturesque style of narration.

It is a place of humble aspect where the Elders of the people are met, sitting in judgment upon the disturber of Israel. The floor of the low and narrow hall is laid with planks hewn by the axe,—the beams of the roof still wear the rugged bark with which they grew up in the forest, and the hearth is formed of one broad unhammered stone, heaped with logs that roll their blaze and smoke up a chimney of wood and clay. A sleety shower beats fitfully against the windows, driven by the November blast, which comes howling onward from the northern desert, the boisterous and unwelcome herald of a New England winter. Rude benches are arranged across the apartment and along its sides, occupied by men whose piety and learning might have entitled them to seats in those high Councils of the ancient Church, whence opinions were sent forth to confirm or supersede the Gospel in the belief of the whole world and of posterity.—Here are collected all those blessed Fathers of the land, who rank in our veneration next to the Evangelists of Holy Writ, and here also are many, unpurified from the fiercest errors of the age and ready to propagate the religion of peace by violence. In the highest place sits Winthrop, a man by whom the innocent and the guilty might alike desire to be judged, the first confiding in his integrity and wisdom, the latter hoping in his mildness. Next is Endicott, who would stand with his drawn sword at the gate of Heaven, and resist to the death all pilgrims thither, except they travelled his own path. The infant eyes of one in this assembly beheld the faggots blazing round the martyrs, in bloody Mary's time; in later life he dwelt long at Leyden, with the first who went from England for conscience sake; and now, in his weary age, it matters little where he lies down to die. There are others whose hearts were smitten in the high meridian of ambitious hope, and whose dreams still tempt them with the pomp of the old world and the din of its crowded cities, gleaming and echoing over the deep. In the midst, and in the centre of all eyes, we see the Woman. She stands loftily before her judges, with a determined brow, and, unknown to herself, there is a flash of carnal pride half hidden in her eye, as she surveys the many learned and famous men whom her doctrines have put in fear. They question her, and her answers are ready and acute; she reasons with them shrewdly, and brings scripture in support of every argument; the deepest controversialists of that scholastic day find here a woman, whom all their trained and sharpened intellects are inadequate to foil. But by the excitement of the contest, her heart is made to rise and swell within her, and she bursts forth into eloquence. She tells them of the long unquietness which she had endured in England perceiving the corruption of the church, and yearning for a purer and more perfect light, and how, in a day of solitary prayer, that light was given; she claims for herself the peculiar power of distinguishing between the chosen of man and the Sealed of Heaven, and affirms that her gifted eye can see the glory round the foreheads of the Saints, sojourning in their mortal state. She declares herself commissioned to separate the true shepherds from the false, and denounces present and future judgments on the land, if she be disturbed in her celestial errand. Thus the accusations are proved from her own mouth. Her judges hesitate, and some speak faintly in her defence; but, with a few dissenting voices, sentence is pronounced, bidding her go out from among them, and trouble the land no more.

Mrs. Hutchinson's adherents throughout the colony were now disarmed, and she proceeded to Rhode Island, an accustomed refuge for the exiles of Massachusetts, in all seasons of persecution. Her enemies believed that the anger of Heaven was following her, of which Governor Winthrop does not disdain to record a notable instance, very interesting in a scientific point of view, but fitter for his old and homely narrative than for modern repetition. In a little time, also, she lost her husband, who is mentioned in history only as attending her footsteps, and whom we may conclude to have been (like most husbands of celebrated women) a mere insignificant appendage of his mightier wife. She now grew uneasy among the Rhode-Island colonists, whose liberality towards her, at an era when liberality was not esteemed a christian virtue, probably arose from a comparative insolicitude on religious matters, more distasteful to Mrs. Hutchinson than even the uncompromising narrowness of the Puritans. Her final movement was to lead her family within the limits of the Dutch Jurisdiction, where, having felled the trees of a virgin soil, she became herself the virtual head, civil and ecclesiastical, of a little colony.

Perhaps here she found the repose, hitherto so vainly sought. Secluded from all whose faith she could not govern, surrounded by the dependents over whom she held an unlimited influence, agitated by none of the tumultuous billows which were left swelling behind her, we may suppose, that, in the stillness of Nature, her heart was stilled. But her impressive story was to have an awful close. Her last scene is as difficult to be portrayed as a shipwreck, where the shrieks of the victims die unheard along a desolate sea, and a shapeless mass of agony is all that can be brought home to the imagination. The savage foe was on the watch for blood. Sixteen persons assembled at the evening prayer; in the deep midnight, their cry rang through the forest; and daylight dawned upon the lifeless clay of all but one. It was a circumstance not to be unnoticed by our stern ancestors, in considering the fate of her who had so troubled their religion, that an infant daughter, the sole survivor amid the terrible destruction of her mother's household, was bred in a barbarous faith, and never learned the way to the Christian's Heaven. Yet we will hope, that there the mother and the child have met.

1830

from Abraham Lincoln[1]

(March–April 1862)

By and by there was a little stir on the staircase and in the passage-way, and in lounged a tall, loose-jointed figure, of an exaggerated Yankee port and demeanor, whom (as being about the homeliest man I ever saw, yet by no means repulsive or disagreeable) it was impossible not to recognize as Uncle Abe.

Unquestionably, Western man though he be, and Kentuckian by birth, President Lincoln is the essential representative of all Yankees, and the veritable specimen, physically, of what the world seems determined to regard as our characteristic qualities. It is the strangest and yet the fittest thing in the jumble of human vicissitudes, that he, out of so many millions, unlooked for, unselected by any intelligible process that could be based upon his genuine qualities, unknown to those who chose him, and unsuspected of what endowments may adapt him for his tremendous responsibility, should have found the way open for him to fling his lank personality into the chair of state,—where, I presume, it was his first impulse to throw his legs on the council-table, and tell the Cabinet Ministers a story. There is no describing his lengthy awkwardness, nor the uncouthness of his movement; and yet it seemed as if I had been in the habit of seeing him daily, and had shaken hands with him a thousand times in some village street; so true was he to the aspect of the pattern American, though with a certain extravagance which, possibly, I exaggerated still further by the delighted eagerness with which I took it in. If put to guess his calling and livelihood, I should have taken him for a country schoolmaster as soon as anything else. He was dressed in a rusty black frock-coat and pantaloons, unbrushed, and worn so faithfully that the suit had adapted itself to the curves and angularities of his figure, and had grown to be an outer skin of the man. He had shabby slippers on his feet. His hair was black, still unmixed with gray, stiff, somewhat bushy, and had apparently been acquainted with neither brush nor comb that morning, after the disarrangement of the pillow; and as to a nightcap, Uncle Abe probably knows nothing of such effeminacies. His complexion is dark and sallow, betokening, I fear, an insalubrious atmosphere around the White House; he has thick black eyebrows and an impending brow; his nose is large, and the lines about his mouth are very strongly defined.

The whole physiognomy is as coarse a one as you would meet anywhere in the length and breadth of the States; but, withal, it is redeemed, illuminated, softened, and brightened by a kindly though serious look out of his eyes, and an expression of homely sagacity, that seems weighted with rich results of village experience. A great deal of native sense; no bookish cultivation, no refinement; honest at heart, and thor-

[1]Three of the five paragraphs Hawthorne reluctantly agreed to omit from "Chiefly About War Matters" (published in the *Atlantic Monthly* in 1862) after his publisher James T. Fields thought the description of Lincoln's "uncouth aspect" would outrage readers. Nine years later in his memoir of Hawthorne (prepared for the *Atlantic* in 1871 and then included in *Yesterdays with Authors*), Fields printed the censored paragraphs, granting that he might have been too squeamish.

oughly so, and yet, in some sort, sly,—at least, endowed with a sort of tact and wisdom that are akin to craft, and would impel him, I think, to take an antagonist in flank, rather than to make a bull-run at him right in front. But, on the whole, I liked this sallow, queer, sagacious visage, with the homely human sympathies that warmed it; and, for my small share in the matter, would as lief have Uncle Abe for a ruler as any man whom it would have been practicable to put in his place. . . .

1872

Letters

Letter to Henry Wadsworth Longfellow

Salem, June 4th, 1837

Dear Sir,

Not to burthen you with my correspondence, I have delayed a rejoinder to your very kind and cordial letter, until now. It gratifies me to find that you have occasionally felt an interest in my situation; but your quotation from Jean Paul,[1] about the "lark's nest," makes me smile. You would have been nearer the truth if you had pictured me as dwelling in an owl's nest; for mine is about as dismal; and, like the owl I seldom venture abroad till after dark. By some witchcraft or other—for I really cannot assign any reasonable why and wherefore—I have been carried apart from the main current of life, and find it impossible to get back again. Since we last met—which, I remember, was in Sawtell's[2] room, where you read a farewell poem to the relics of the class—ever since that time, I have secluded myself from society; and yet I never meant any such thing, nor dreamed what sort of life I was going to lead. I have made a captive of myself and put me into a dungeon and now I cannot find the key to let myself out—and if the door were open, I should be almost afraid to come out. You tell me that you have met with troubles and changes. I know not what they may have been; but I can assure you that trouble is the next best thing to enjoyment, and that there is no fate in this work so horrible as to have no share in either its joys or sorrows. For the last ten years, I have not lived, but only dreamed about living. It may be true that there have been some unsubstantial pleasures here in the shade, which I should have missed in the sunshine, but you cannot conceive how utterly devoid of satisfaction all my retrospects are. I have laid up no treasure of pleasant remembrances, against old age; but there is some comfort in thinking that my future years can hardly fail to be more varied, and therefore more tolerable, than the past.

You give me more credit than I deserve, in supposing that I have led a studious life. I have, indeed, turned over a good many books, but in so desultory a

[1]Johann Paul Friedrich Richter (1763–1825), well-known German romantic novelist, called Jean Paul.

[2]Cullen Sawtelle (1805–1887); like Longfellow, one of Hawthorne's classmates at Bowdoin College.

way that it cannot be called study, nor has it left me the fruits of study. As to my literary efforts, I do not think much of them—neither is it worth while to be ashamed of them. They would have been better, I trust, if written under more favorable circumstances. I have had no external excitement—no consciousness that the public would like what I wrote, nor much hope nor a very passionate desire that they should do so. Nevertheless, having nothing else to be ambitious of, I have felt considerably interested in literature; and if my writings had made any decided impression, I should probably have been stimulated to greater exertions; but there has been no warmth of approbation, so that I have always written with benumbed fingers. I have another great difficulty, in the lack of materials; for I have seen so little of the world, that I have nothing but thin air to concoct my stories of, and it is not easy to give a lifelike semblance to such shadowy stuff. Sometimes, through a peephole, I have caught a glimpse of the real world; and the two or three articles in which I have portrayed such glimpses, please me better than the others. I have now, or shall soon have, one sharp spur to exertion, which I lacked at an earlier period; for I see little prospect but that I must scribble for a living. But this troubles me much less than you would suppose. I can turn my pen to all sorts of drudgery, such as children's books, etc., and by and by, I shall get some editorship that will answer my purpose. Frank Pierce, who was with us at college, offered me his influence to obtain an office in the Exploring Expedition; but I believe that he was mistaken in supposing that a vacancy existed. If such a post were attainable, I should certainly accept it; for, though fixed so long to one spot, I have always had a desire to run around the world.

The copy of my Tales[3] was sent to Mr. Owen's, the bookseller's in Cambridge. I am glad to find that you had read and liked some of the stories. To be sure, you could not well help flattering me a little; but I value your praise too highly not to have faith in its sincerity. When I last heard from the publisher—which was not very recently—the book was doing pretty well. Six or seven hundred copies had been sold. I suppose, however, these awful times have now stopped the sale.

I intend in a week or two to come out of my owl's nest, and not return to it till late in the summer—employing the interval in making a tour somewhere in New England. You, who have the dust of distant countries on your "sandal-shoon," cannot imagine how much enjoyment I shall have in this little excursion. Whenever I get abroad, I feel just as young as I did, ten years ago. What a letter I am inflicting on you! I trust you will answer it.

Yours sincerely,
Nath. Hawthorne.

1837

[3]*Twice-Told Tales,* whose publication provided the occasion for Hawthorne's letter and ultimately for a laudatory review by Longfellow.

Letter to Sophia Peabody

Oak Hill, April 13th, 1841

Ownest love,

Here is thy poor husband in a polar Paradise! I know not how to interpret this aspect of Nature—whether it be of good or evil omen to our enterprise. But I reflect that the Plymouth pilgrims arrived in the midst of storm and stept ashore upon mountain snow-drifts; and nevertheless they prospered, and became a great people—and doubtless it will be the same with us. I laud my stars, however, that thou wilt not have thy first impressions of our future home from such a day as this. Thou wouldst shiver all thy life afterwards, and never realise that there could be bright skies, and green hills and meadows, and trees heavy with foliage, when now the whole scene is a great snow-bank, and the sky full of snow likewise. Through faith, I persist in believing that spring and summer will come in their due season; but the unregenerated man shivers within me, and suggests a doubt whether I may not have wandered within the precincts of the Arctic circle, and chosen my heritage among everlasting snows. Dearest, provide thyself with a good stock of furs; and if thou canst obtain the skin of a polar bear, thou wilt find it a very suitable summer dress for this region. Thou must not hope ever to walk abroad, except upon snow-shoes, nor to find any warmth, save in thy husband's heart.

Belovedest, I have not yet taken my first lesson in agriculture, as thou mayst well suppose—except that I went to see our cows foddered, yesterday afternoon. We have eight of our own; and the number is now increased by a transcendental heifer, belonging to Miss Margaret Fuller. She is very fractious, I believe, and apt to kick over the milk pail. Thou knowest best, whether in these traits of character, she resembles her mistress.[1] Thy husband intends to convert himself into a milk-maid, this evening; but I pray heaven that Mr. Ripley[2] may be moved to assign him the kindliest cow in the herd—otherwise he will perform his duty with fear and trembling:

Ownest wife, I like my brethren in affliction very well; and couldst thou see us sitting round our table, at meal-times, before the great kitchen-fire, thou wouldst call it a cheerful sight. Mrs. Parker is a most comfortable woman to behold; she looks as if her ample person were stuffed full of tenderness—indeed, as if she were all one great, kind heart. Wert thou here, I should ask for nothing more—not even for sunshine and summer weather; for thou wouldst be both, to thy husband. And how is that cough of thine, my belovedest? Hast thou thought of me, in my perils and wanderings? I trust that thou dost muse upon me with hope and joy; not with repining. Think that I am gone before, to prepare a home for my Dove, and will return for her, all in good time.

Thy husband has the best chamber in the house, I believe; and though not quite so good as the apartment I have left, it will do very well. I have hung up thy two pictures; and they give me a glimpse of summer and of thee. The vase I intended to have brought in my arms, but could not very conveniently do it yester-

[1]Fuller's work is represented elsewhere in this volume. Hawthorne's attitude toward her was, at best, ambivalent.

[2]The Reverend George Ripley (1802–1880), American reformer and journalist instrumental in organizing Brook Farm.

day; so that it still remains at Mrs. Hillard's,[3] together with my carpet. I shall bring them [at] the next opportunity.

Now farewell, for the present, most beloved. I have been writing this in my chamber; but the fire is getting low, and the house is old and cold: so that the warmth of my whole person has retreated to my heart, which burns with love for thee. I must run down to the kitchen or parlor hearth, when thy image shall sit beside me—yea, be pressed to my breast. At bed-time, thou shalt have a few lines more. Now I think of it, dearest, wilt thou give Mrs. Ripley a copy of Grandfather's Chair and Liberty Tree;[4] she wants them for some boys here. I have several copies of Famous Old People.

April 14th, 10 A.M. Sweetest, I did not milk the cows last night, because Mr. Ripley was afraid to trust them to my hands, or me to their horns—I know not which. But this morning, I have done wonders. Before breakfast, I went out to the barn, and began to chop hay for the cattle; and with such "righteous vehemence" (as Mr. Ripley says) did I labor, that in the space of ten minutes, I broke the machine. Then I brought wood and replenished the fires; and finally sat down to breakfast and ate up a huge mound of buckwheat cakes. After breakfast, Mr. Ripley put a four-pronged instrument into my hands, which he gave me to understand was called a pitch-fork; and he and Mr. Farley[5] being armed with similar weapons, we all then commenced a gallant attack upon a heap of manure. This office being concluded, and thy husband having purified himself, he sits down to finish this letter to his most beloved wife. Dearest, I will never consent that thou come within half a mile of me, after such an encounter as that of this morning. Pray Heaven that his letter retain none of the fragrance with which the writer was imbued. As for thy husband himself, he is peculiarly partial to the odor; but that whimsical little nose of thine might chance to quarrel with it.

Belovedest, Miss Fuller's cow hooks the other cows, and has made herself ruler of the herd, and behaves in a very tyrannical manner. Sweetest, I know not when I shall see thee; but I trust it will not be longer than the end of next week. I love thee! I love thee! I wouldst thou wert with me; for then would my labor be joyful—and even now it is not sorrowful. Dearest, I shall make an excellent husbandman. I feel the original Adam reviving within me.

Miss Sophia A. Peabody,
13 West street,
Boston.

1841

Letter to H.W. Longfellow, Cambridge

[Salem] Custom House, June 5th. 1849

Dear Longfellow,

I meant to have written you before now about Kavanaugh,[1] but have had no quiet time, during my letter-writing hours; and now the freshness of my thoughts has ex-

[3]Susan Howe Hillard, a friend of the Peabodys and Hawthorne's Boston landlady.

[4]Books by Hawthorne.

[5]Another participant in the Brook Farm experiment.

[1]A romance by Longfellow.

haled away. It is a most precious and rare book—as fragrant as a bunch of flowers, and as simple as one flower. A true picture of life, moreover—as true as those reflections of the trees and banks that I used to see in the Concord, but refined to a higher degree than they; as if the reflection were itself reflected. Nobody but yourself would dare to write so quiet a book; nor could any other succeed in it. It is entirely original; a book by itself; a true work of genius, if ever there were one; and yet I should not wonder if many people (God confound them!) were to see no such matter in it. In fact, I doubt whether hardly anybody else has enjoyed it so much as I; although I have heard or seen none but favorable opinions.

I should like to have written a long notice of it, and would have done so for the Salem Advertiser; but, on the strength of my notice of Evangeline[2] and some half-dozen other books, I have been accused of a connection with the editorship of that paper, and of writing political articles—which I never did one single time in my whole life! I must confess, it stirs up a little of the devil within me, to find myself hunted by these political bloodhounds. If they succeed in getting me out of office, I will surely immolate one or two of them. Not that poor monster of a Conolly,[3] whom I desire only to bury in oblivion, far out of my own remembrance. Nor any of the common political brawlers, who work on their own level, and can conceive of no higher ground than what they occupy. But if there be among them (as there must be, if they succeed) some men who claim a higher position, and ought to know better, I may perhaps select a victim, and let fall one little drop of venom on his heart, that shall make him writhe before the grin of the multitude for a considerable time to come. This I will do, not as an act of individual vengeance, but in your behalf as well as mine, because he will have violated the sanctity of the priesthood to which we both, in our different degrees, belong. I do not claim to be a poet; and yet I cannot but feel that some of the sacredness of that character adheres to me, and ought to be respected in me, unless I step out of its immunities, or make it a plea for violating any of the rules of ordinary life. When other people concede me this privilege, I never think that I possess it; but when they disregard it, the consciousness makes itself felt. If they will pay no reverence to the imaginative power when it causes herbs of grace and sweet-scented flowers to spring up along their pathway, then they should be taught what it can do in the way of producing nettles, skunk-cabbage, deadly nightshade, wolf's bane, dog-wood.[4] If they will not be grateful for its works of beauty and beneficence, then let them dread it as a pervasive and penetrating mischief, that can reach them at their firesides and in their bedchambers, follow them to far countries, and make their very graves refuse to hide them. I have often thought that there must be a good deal of enjoyment in writing personal satire; but, never having felt the slightest ill-will towards any human being, I have hitherto been debarred from this peculiar source of pleasure. I almost hope I shall be turned out, so as to have an opportunity of trying it. I cannot help smiling in anticipation of the astonishment of some of these local magnates here, who suppose themselves quite out of the reach of any retribution on my part.

I have spent a good deal of time in Boston, within a few weeks; my two children having been ill of the scarlet-fever there; and the little boy was in quite an alarming way. I could not have submitted in the least, had it gone ill with him; but

[2]Another of Longfellow's well-known narrative poems.

[3]A local political figure.

[4]Various poisonous or evil-sounding plants.

God spared me that trial—and there was no real misfortunes, save such as that. Other troubles may irritate me superficially; nothing else can go near the heart.

I mean to come and dine with you, the next time you invite me; and Hillard said he would come too. Do not let it be within a week, however; for Bridge and his wife expect to be here in the course of that time.

Please to present my regards to Mrs. Longfellow, and believe me

ever your friend,
Nath Hawthorne.

1849

Letter to J.T. Fields, Boston

Salem, January 20th. 1850.

My dear Fields,[1]

I am truly glad that you like the introduction; for I was rather afraid that it might appear absurd and impertinent to be talking about myself, when nobody, that I know of, has requested any information on that subject.

As regards the size of the book, I have been thinking a good deal about it. Considered merely as a matter of taste and beauty, the form of publication which you recommend seems to me much preferable to that of the 'Mosses.'[2] In the present case, however, I have some doubts of the expediency; because, if the book is made up entirely of 'The Scarlet Letter,' it will be too sombre. I found it impossible to relieve the shadows of the story with so much light as I would gladly have thrown in. Keeping so close to its point as the tale does, and diversified no otherwise than by turning different sides of the same dark idea to the reader's eye, it will weary very many people, and disgust some. Is it safe, then, to stake the fate of the book entirely on this one chance? A hunter loads his gun with a bullet and several buck-shot; and, following his sagacious example, it was my purpose to conjoin the one long story with half a dozen shorter ones; so that, failing to kill the public outright with my biggest and heaviest lump of lead, I might have other chances with the smaller bits, individually and in the aggregate.

However, I am willing to leave these considerations to your judgment, and should not be sorry to have you decide for the separate publication.

In this latter event, it appears to me that the only proper title for the book would be 'The Scarlet Letter'; for 'The Custom House' is merely introductory—an entrance-hall to the magnificent edifice which I throw open to my guests. It would be funny, if, seeing the further passages so dark and dismal, they should all choose to stop there!

If 'The Scarlet Letter' is to be the title, would it not be well to print it on the title-page in red ink? I am not quite sure about the good taste of so doing; but it

[1]James Thomas Fields (1817–1881), the junior partner in Boston's major publishing firm, Ticknor and Fields, who published all Hawthorne's books from this point on. By encouraging Hawthorne to expand *The Scarlet Letter* for separate book publication instead of inclusion in a collection of tales, Fields helped launch Hawthorne's career as a romancer. He was a shrewd literary promoter but also Hawthorne's trusted friend.

[2]Hawthorne's collection of tales, *Mosses From An Old Manse.*

would certainly be piquant and appropriate—and, I think, attractive to the great gull whom we are endeavoring to circumvent.

Very truly Yours,
Nath[l]. Hawthorne

J.T. Fields, Esq.

1850

[*An undated draft of the letter:*]

As regards the book, I have been thinking and considering—I was rather afraid that it appears sagacious absurd and impertinent to have some doubts, of the introduction to the book, which you recommend. I have found it impossible to relieve the shadows of the story with so much light as I would gladly stake the fate of the book entirely on the public. However, I am willing to leave these considerations to your judgment, and should not be sorry to have you decide for the separate publication.

If the Judgment Letter is to be the title—print it on the title page in red ink. I think that the only proper title for the book would be the Scarlet Letter. I am quite sure about the taste of so doing. I think it is attractive and appropriate—

from Letter to H.W. Longfellow, Cambridge

Concord, Jan[y] 2[d] 1864.

Dear Longfellow . . .

. . . I have been much out of sorts of late, and do not well know what is the matter with me, but am inclined to draw the conclusion that I shall have little more to do with pen and ink. One more book I should like well enough to write, and have indeed begun it, but with no assurance of ever bringing it to an end. As is always the case, I have a notion that this last book would be my best; and full of wisdom about matters of life and death—and yet it will be no deadly disappointment if I am compelled to drop it. You can tell, far better than I, whether there is ever anything worth having a literary reputation, and whether the best achievements seem to have any substance after they grow cold.

Your friend,
Nath[l] Hawthorne.

1864

Caroline Kirkland 1801–1864

Caroline Stansbury Kirkland, eldest of eleven children of Eliza Alexander and Samuel Stansbury, was born on January 11, 1801, in New York City where she spent most of her childhood and adolescence in a family noted for its interest in literature and education. Kirkland's mother was herself a writer and Kirkland later revised and published some of her mother's work in her own gift books. An aunt headed a series of distinguished schools which Caroline attended and in which she later taught. In 1828 Caroline married William Kirkland, previously a teacher of classics at Hamilton College, and together they opened a girls' school in Geneva, New York. In 1835, however, they emigrated to Detroit, Michigan, for William, tired of teaching, had dreams of buying land and founding a "city" on the Michigan frontier. By 1837 they had acquired sufficient land and capital to move to the village of Pinckney where they began the experience in frontier living recorded in *A New Home—Who'll Follow?* (1839).

After five years on the frontier, the Kirklands returned to New York City where Caroline continued to pursue the writing career she had begun in Michigan. She had by this time published both *A New Home* and its sequel, *Forest Life* (1842), as well as essays and sketches in a variety of magazines. In 1846, William Kirkland died and at forty-five Kirkland became the sole support of herself and her four children. To make a living, she managed and taught in several girls' schools and wrote. She collected many of her essays in the various gift books she edited; in contrast to many similar offerings, Kirkland's collections were deservedly popular for their intellectual and aesthetic superiority. In 1847, Kirkland became editor of the *Union Magazine of Literature and Art.* As an editor, Kirkland demonstrated a strong commitment to realism in the materials she accepted for publication and considerable critical skill in her reviews, including an enthusiastic response to Melville's early books. Moreover, Kirkland was seriously interested in women as writers. In her long review essay of Susan Warner's *The Wide, Wide World* (1851) and *Queechy* (1852), and Anna Warner's *Dollars and Cents* (1852), published in the *North American Review* in 1853, she provided, in addition to detailed analyses of the strengths and weaknesses of these books, a survey of the state of the art of the novel in America with particular reference to women writers. Kirkland herself was part of a social and professional friendship network of women writers and her home frequently functioned as a literary salon. She died in New York City on April 6, 1864, and was buried in Greenwood Cemetery in Brooklyn.

A New Home—Who'll Follow?, published under the pseudonym Mary Clavers, describes the experience of a relatively well-educated middle-class white woman transported to the American frontier by virtue of her husband's ambition. As a follower, Kirkland takes advantage of the accident of her presence on the Michigan frontier to become a recorder of American social history. Defining herself against the romanticism of previous western chroniclers, Kirkland consciously asserts her commitment to realism. But what kind of a "story" can one tell if she has "never seen a cougar—nor been bitten by a rattlesnake?" In meeting the dual challenge posed by writing as a woman and a realist, Kirkland recognizes that she is doing something new in American literature. At the heart of her enterprise is the education of her readers to the significance of the American frontier. For Kirkland, the frontier is a true text, revealing a national character obsessed with issues of class and gender. The pressure exerted by the frontier toward "levelling downwards" derives its intensity from the fact that upward mobility is the prevailing motive for western emigration. Thus settlers who have come to Michigan to improve their class status wish no reminders of the class system they think they have left behind.

As a follower, Kirkland can view with some detachment those masculine impulses that have brought her to the frontier. While Mrs. Clavers as a woman struggles to establish a community with her neighbors, the desire to make money at the expense of one's neighbors dominates the male world that Mr. Clavers enters. The "factotum" who offers to build Montacute for Mr. Clavers clears out after having gotten rich on his money, and if Mrs. Jenkins does not effect the "thorough reformation" of Simeon, similar schemes will no doubt ensue from his presence in the "arena of public life." Kirkland's detachment from masculine "madness," however, does not blind her to the degree to which this madness shapes her life. Unable to save the fine oaks, she is granted only the symbolic power of naming the venture to be erected on their stumps. But her detachment does enable her to focus on the lives of women and to recognize that the experience of those who follow is not necessarily the experience of those who lead. Though the frontier may enlarge women's sphere to some degree, woman's world is still primarily the home. Kirkland devotes much of her text to describing the physical and material hardship of housekeeping in the wilderness. More seriously, she records the homelessness frequently experienced by women on the frontier. Since the westering impulse originates in the masculine agenda of upward mobility, men have little incentive to make homes; rather they view their land as counters in the status game, and they are prepared to sell out and move on at the first good offer, leaving women to pay the hidden costs. *A New Home—Who'll Follow?* signals a realism in American fiction designed to counter not simply previous romanticism but equally that masculine "realism" which believes the whole story is told when the man's story is told. In the portrait of Eloise Fidler, which precedes Mark Twain's Emmeline Grangerford by almost fifty years, Kirkland insists on telling her own story about women and writing. Satirizing through Eloise conventional masculine stereotypes of the woman writer, Kirkland in *A New Home* provides her readers with an alternative persona and style, distinctively female but clearly not feminine.

Judith Fetterley
State University of New York at Albany

PRIMARY WORKS

A New Home—Who'll Follow?, 1939, 1990; *Forest Life,* 1842; *Western Clearings,* 1845; *The Evening Book,* 1852; *A Book for the Home Circle,* 1853.

SECONDARY WORKS

William S. Osborne, *Caroline M. Kirkland,* 1972; Audrey Roberts, "The Letters of Caroline M. Kirkland" (Ph.D. dissertation, U of Wisconsin), 1976; Annette Kolodny, *The Land Before Her,* 1984; Judith Fetterley, ed., *Provisions: A Reader from Nineteenth-Century American Women,* 1985; Sandra Zagarell, "Introduction" to *A New Home—Who'll Follow?,* 1990.

from A New Home—Who'll Follow?

or, Glimpses of Western Life by Mrs. Mary Clavers, An Actual Settler.

Preface

I am glad to be told by those who live in the world, that it has lately become fashionable to read prefaces. I wish to say a few words, by way of introduction, to a work which may be deemed too slight to need a preface, but which will doubtless be acknowledged to require some recommendation.

I claim for these straggling and cloudy crayon sketches of life and manners in the remoter parts of Michigan the merit of general truth of outline. Beyond this I venture not to aspire. I felt somewhat tempted to set forth my little book as being entirely—what it is very nearly—a veritable history; an unimpeachable transcript of reality; a rough picture, in detached parts, but pentagraphed from the life; a sort of "Emigrant's Guide";—considering with myself that these my adventurous journeyings and tarryings beyond the confines of civilization might fairly be held to confer the traveller's privilege. But conscience prevailed, and I must honestly confess, that there be glosses, and colorings, and lights, if not shadows, for which the author is alone accountable. Journals, published entire and unaltered, should be Parthian darts, sent abroad only when one's back is turned. To throw them in the teeth of one's every-day associates might diminish one's popularity rather inconveniently. I would desire the courteous reader to bear in mind, however, that whatever is quite unnatural, or absolutely incredible, in the few incidents which diversify the following pages, is to be received as literally true. It is only in the most common-place parts (if there be comparisons) that I have any leasing-making to answer for.

It will of course be observed that Miss Mitford's[1] charming sketches of village life must have suggested the form of my rude attempt. I dare not flatter myself that any one will be led to accuse me of further imitation of a deservedly popular writer. And with such brief salvo, I make my humble curtsey.

M.C.

Preface to the Fourth Edition

The improvements which have taken place in the social aspect of the great West since these unvarnished records were written, may lead some who observe the present to doubt the truthfulness of such delineations of the past; but much observation subsequent to the publication of this book, and much after reflection upon it, suggest to me nothing to be retracted or altered in the sketches, as an honest portraiture of rural life in a new country.

No peculiarity of custom or expression is here introduced which was not drawn directly from fact, and if the picture lack verity in any particular, it is not through exaggeration, but the opposite. Indeed, the immediate appropriation of the book in a dozen different parts of the country, before the authorship was known, is a sufficient voucher for its truth.

I am, therefore, much pleased to be able to present a New Edition; the fourth public favor has called for, with illustrations by a pencil which never fails to add grace to any subject, however homely.

C.M.K.

New York, November, 1849.

[1]Mary Russell Mitford, an early nineteenth-century English writer of village stories and sketches.

Chapter I

Here are seen
No traces of man's pomp and pride; no silks
Rustle, nor jewels shine, nor envious eyes
Encounter.

Oh, there is not lost
One of earth's charms; upon her bosom yet
After the flight of untold centuries
The freshness of her far beginning lies.
—BRYANT[2]

Our friends in the "settlements" have expressed so much interest in such of our letters to them as happened to convey any account of the peculiar features of western life, and have asked so many questions, touching particulars which we had not thought worthy of mention that I have been for some time past contemplating the possibility of something like a detailed account of our experiences. And I have determined to give them to the world, in a form not very different from that in which they were originally recorded for our private delectation; nothing doubting, that a veracious history of actual occurrences, an unvarnished transcript of real characters, and an impartial record of every-day forms of speech (taken down in many cases from the lips of the speaker) will be pronounced "graphic" by at least a fair proportion of the journalists of the day.

It is true there are but meagre materials for anything that might be called a story. I have never seen a cougar—nor been bitten by a rattlesnake. The reader who has patience to go with me to the close of my desultory sketches, must expect nothing beyond a meandering recital of common-place occurrences—mere gossip about every-day people, little enhanced in value by any fancy or ingenuity of the writer; in short, a very ordinary pen-drawing; which, deriving no interest from coloring, can be valuable only for its truth.

A home on the outskirts of civilization—habits of society which allow the maid and her mistress to do the honors in complete equality, and to make the social tea visit in loving conjunction—such a distribution of the duties of life as compels all, without distinction, to rise with the sun or before him—to breakfast with the chickens—then,

"Count the slow clock, and dine exact at noon"—

to be ready for tea at four, and for bed at eight—may certainly be expected to furnish some curious particulars for the consideration of those whose daily course almost reverses this primitive arrangement—who "call night day and day night," and who are apt occasionally to forget, when speaking of a particular class, that "those creatures" are partakers with themselves of a common nature.

I can only wish, like other modest chroniclers, my respected prototypes, that so fertile a theme had fallen into worthier hands. If Miss Mitford, who has given us such

[2]William Cullen Bryant, "A Forest Hymn."

charming glimpses of Aberleigh, Hilton Cross, and the Loddon, had, by some happy chance, been translated to Michigan, what would she not have made of such materials as Tinkerville, Montacute, and the Turnip?

When my husband purchased two hundred acres of wild land on the banks of this to-be-celebrated stream, and drew with a piece of chalk on the bar-room table at Danforth's the plan of a village, I little thought I was destined to make myself famous by handing down to posterity a faithful record of the advancing fortunes of that favored spot.

"The madness of the people" in those days of golden dreams took more commonly the form of city-building; but there were a few who contented themselves with planning villages, on the banks of streams which certainly never could be expected to bear navies, but which might yet be turned to account in the more homely way of grinding or sawing—operations which must necessarily be performed somewhere, for the well-being of those very cities. It is of one of these humble attempts that it is my lot to speak, and I make my confession at the outset, warning any fashionable reader, who may have taken up my book, that I intend to be "decidedly low."

Whether the purchaser of *our* village would have been as moderate under all possible circumstances, I am not prepared to say, since, never having enjoyed a situation under government, his resources have not been unlimited; and for this reason any remark which may be hazarded in the course of these my lucubrations touching the more magnificent plans of wealthier aspirants, must be received with some grains of allowance. "Il est plus aisé d'être sage pour les autres, que de l'être pour soi-même."[3]

When I made my first visit to these remote and lonely regions, the scattered woods through which we rode for many miles were gay in their first gosling-green suit of half-opened leaves, and the forest odors which exhaled with the dews of morning and evening, were beyond measure delicious to one "long in populous cities pent." I desired much to be a little sentimental at the time, and feel tempted to indulge to some small extent even here—but I forbear; and shall adhere closely to matters more in keeping with my subject.

I think, to be precise, the time was the last, the very last of April, and I recollect well that even at that early season, by availing myself with sedulous application, of those times when I was fain to quit the vehicle through fear of the perilous mud-holes, or still more perilous half-bridged marshes, I picked upwards of twenty varieties of wild-flowers—some of them of rare and delicate beauty;—and sure I am, that if I had succeeded in inspiring my companion with one spark of my own floral enthusiasm, our hundred miles of travel would have occupied a week's time.

The wild-flowers of Michigan deserve a poet of their own. Shelley[4] who sang so quaintly of "the pied wind-flowers and the tulip tall," would have found many a fanciful comparison and deep-drawn meaning for the thousand gems of the roadside. Charles Lamb[5] could have written charming volumes about the humblest among them. Bulwer[6] would find means to associate the common three-leaved white lily so

[3]It is easier to be wise about others than about one's self.

[4]Percy Bysshe Shelley (1792–1822), English Romantic poet, wrote many poems about natural objects and phenomena.

[5]Charles Lamb (1775–1834), whose informal essays were widely read.

[6]Edward Bulwer-Lytton (1803–1873), an English writer, composed historical novels, among other works.

closely with the Past, the Present, and the Future—the Wind, the Stars, and the Tripod of Delphos,[7] that all future botanists, and eke[8] all future philosophers, might fail to unravel the "linked sweetness." We must have a poet of our own.

Since I have casually alluded to a Michigan mud-hole, I may as well enter into a detailed memoir on the subject, for the benefit of future travellers, who, flying over the soil on railroads, may look slightingly back upon the achievements of their predecessors. In the "settlements," a mud-hole is considered as apt to occasion an unpleasant jolt—a breaking of the thread of one's reverie—or in extreme cases, a temporary stand-still, or even an overturn of the rash and unwary. Here, on approaching one of these characteristic features of the "West"—(how much does that expression mean to include? I have never been able to discover its limits)—the driver stops—alights—walks up to the dark gulf—and around it, if he can get around it. He then seeks a long pole and sounds it, measures it across to ascertain how its width compares with the length of his wagon—tries whether its sides are perpendicular, as is usually the case if the road is much used. If he find it not more than three feet deep, he remounts cheerily, encourages his team, and in they go, with a plunge and a shock, rather apt to damp the courage of the inexperienced. If the hole be narrow, the hinder wheels will be quite lifted off the ground by the depression of their precedents, and so remain until by unwearied chiruping and some judicious touches of "the string" the horses are induced to struggle as for their lives; and if the Fates are propitious they generally emerge on the opposite side, dragging the vehicle, or, at least, the forewheels, after them. When I first "penetrated the interior," (to use an indigenous phrase,) all I knew of the wilds was from Hoffman's Tour, or Captain Hall's "graphic" delineations. I had some floating idea of "driving a barouche-and-four any where through the oak-openings"—and seeing "the murdered Banquos[9] of the forest" haunting the scenes of their departed strength and beauty. But I confess these pictures, touched by the glowing pencil of fancy, gave me but incorrect notions of a real journey through Michigan.

Our vehicle was not perhaps very judiciously chosen—at least we have since thought so. It was a light, high-hung carriage—of the description commonly known as a buggy or shandrydan—names, of which I would be glad to learn the etymology. I seriously advise any of my friends, who are about flitting to Wisconsin or Oregon, to prefer a heavy lumber wagon, even for the use of the ladies of the family; very little aid or consolation being derived from making a "genteel" appearance in such cases.

At the first encounter of such a mud-hole as I have attempted to describe, we stopped in utter despair. My companion indeed would fain have persuaded me that the many wheel tracks which passed through the formidable gulf were proof positive that it might be forded. I insisted with all a woman's obstinacy that I could not and would not make the attempt, and alighted accordingly, and tried to find a path on one side or the other. But in vain, even putting out of the question my paper-soled shoes—sensible things for the woods. The ditch on each side was filled with water and quite too wide to jump over; and we were actually contemplating a return, when

[7]Among the accouterments of the oracle at Delphi.

[8]Archaic for "also."

[9]Whose ghost appears in Shakespeare's *Macbeth.*

a man in an immense bear-skin cap and a suit of deer's hide, sprang from behind a stump just within the edge of the forest. He "poled" himself over the ditch in a moment, and stood beside us, rifle in hand, as wild and rough a specimen of humanity as one would wish to encounter in a strange and lonely road, just at the shadowy dusk of the evening. I did *not* scream, though I own I was prodigiously frightened. But our stranger said immediately, in a gentle tone and with a French accent, "Me watch deer—you want to cross?" On receiving an answer in the affirmative, he ran in search of a rail, which he threw over the terrific mud-hole—aided me to walk across by the help of his pole—showed my husband where to plunge—waited till he had gone safely through, and "slow circles dimpled o'er the quaking mud"—then took himself off by the way he came, declining any compensation with a most polite "rien! rien!" This instance of true and genuine and generous politeness I record for the benefit of all bearskin caps, leathern jerkins, and cowhide boots, which ladies from the eastward world may hereafter encounter in Michigan.

Our journey was marked by no incident more alarming than the one I have related, though one night passed in a wretched inn, deep in the "timbered land"—as all woods are called in Michigan—was not without its terrors, owing to the horrible drunkenness of the master of the house, whose wife and children were in constant fear of their lives from his insane fury. I can never forget the countenance of that desolate woman, sitting trembling, and with white compressed lips, in the midst of her children. The father raving all night, and coming through our sleeping apartment with the earliest ray of morning in search of more of the poison already boiling in his veins. The poor wife could not forbear telling me her story—her change of lot—from a well-stored and comfortable home in Connecticut to this wretched den in the wilderness—herself and children worn almost to shadows with the ague, and her husband such as I have described him. I may mention here, that not very long after, I heard of this man in prison in Detroit, for stabbing a neighbor in a drunken brawl, and ere the year was out, he died of delirium tremens, leaving his family destitute. So much for turning our fields of golden grain into "fire water"—a branch of business in which Michigan is fast improving.

Our ride being a deliberate one, I felt, after the third day, a little wearied, and began to complain of the sameness of the oak openings, and to wish we were fairly at our journey's end. We were crossing a broad expanse of what seemed, at a little distance, a smooth shaven lawn of the most brilliant green, but which proved on trial little better than a quaking bog—embracing within its ridgy circumference all possible varieties of

"Muirs and mosses, slaps and styles"—

I had just indulged in something like a yawn, and wished that I could see our hotel. At the word, my companion's face assumed rather a comical expression, and I was preparing to inquire somewhat testily what there was so laughable—I was getting tired and cross, reader—when down came our good horse to the very chin in a bog-hole, green as Erin on the top, but giving way on the touch, and seeming deep enough to have engulfed us entirely, if its width had been proportionate. Down came the horse—and this was not all—down came the driver; and I could not do less than follow, though at a little distance—our good steed kicking and floundering—covering us with hieroglyphics, which would be readily deciphered by any Wolverine we should meet, though perchance strange to the eyes of our friends at home. This mishap was soon amended. Tufts of long marsh grass served to assoilize our habiliments a little, and a clear stream which rippled through the marsh aided in removing the eclipse from our faces. We journeyed on cheerily, watching the splendid changes in the west, but keeping a bright look out for bog-holes.

Chapter XV

Honester men have stretch'd a rope, or the law has been sadly cheated. But this unhappy business of yours? Can nothing be done? Let me see the charge.

He took the papers, and as he read them, his countenance grew hopelessly dark and disconsolate.

—*ANTIQUARY*

A strange fish! Were I in England now, and had but this fish painted, not a holiday fool there but would give me a piece of silver.

—SHAKSPEARE—*TEMPEST*

Sorrow chang'd to solace, and solace mixed with sorrow.

—*THE PASSIONATE PILGRIM*

Several lots had already been purchased in Montacute and some improvement marked each succeeding day. The mill had grown to its full stature, the dam was nearly completed; the tavern began to exhibit promise of its present ugliness, and all seemed prosperous as our best dreams, when certain rumours were set afloat touching the solvency of our disinterested friend Mr. Mazard. After two or three days' whispering, a tall black-browed man who "happened in" from Gullsborough, the place which had for some time been honoured as the residence of the Dousterswivel of Montacute, stated boldly that Mr. Mazard had absconded; or, in Western language "cleared." It seemed passing strange that he should run away from the large house which was going on under his auspices; the materials all on the ground and the work in full progress. Still more unaccountable did it appear to us that his workmen should go on so quietly, without so much as expressing any anxiety about their pay.

Mr. Clavers had just been telling me of these things, when the long genius above mentioned, presented himself at the door of the loggery. His *abord* was a singular mixture of coarseness, and an attempt at being civil; and he sat for some minutes looking round and asking various questions before he touched the mainspring of his visit.

At length, after some fumbling in his pocket, he produced a dingy sheet of paper, which he handed to Mr. Clavers.

"There; I want you to read that, and tell me what you think of it."

I did not look at the paper, but at my husband's face, which was black enough. He walked away with the tall man, "and I saw no more of them at that time."

Mr. Clavers did not return until late in the evening, and it was then I learned that Mr. Mazard had been getting large quantities of lumber and other materials on his account, and as his agent; and that the money which had been placed in the agent's hands, for the purchase of certain lands to be flowed by the mill-pond, had gone into government coffers in payment for sundry eighty acre lots, which were intended for his, Mr. Mazard's, private behoof and benefit. These items present but a sample of our amiable friends trifling mistakes. I will not fatigue the reader by dwelling on the subject. The results of all this were most unpleasant to us. Mr. Clavers found himself involved to a large amount; and his only remedy seemed to prosecute Mr. Mazard. A consultation with his lawyer, however, convinced him, that even by this most disagreeable mode, redress was out of the question, since he had through inadvertence rendered himself liable for whatever that gentleman chose to buy or engage in his name. All that could be done, was to get out of the affair with as little loss as possible, and to take warning against land sharks in future.

An immediate journey to Detroit became necessary, and I was once more left alone, and in no overflowing spirits. I sat,

> "Revolving in *my* altered soul
> The various turns of fate below,"

when a tall damsel, of perhaps twenty-eight or thirty came in to make a visit. She was tastefully attired in a blue gingham dress, with broad cuffs of black morocco, and a black cambric apron edged with orange worsted lace. Her oily black locks were cut quite short round the ears, and confined close to her head by a black ribbon, from one side of which depended, almost in her eye, two very long tassels of black silk, intended to do duty as curls. Prunelle[10] slippers with high heels, and a cotton handkerchief tied under the chin, finished the costume, which I have been thus particular in describing, because I have observed so many that were nearly similar.

The lady greeted me in the usual style, with a familiar nod, and seated herself at once in a chair near the door.

"Well, how do like Michig*an?*"

This question received the most polite answer which my conscience afforded; and I asked the lady in my turn, if she was one of my neighbours?

"Why, massy, yes!" she replied; "do n't you know me? I tho't every body know'd me. Why, I'm the school ma'am, Simeon Jenkins' sister, Cleory Jenkins."

Thus introduced, I put all my civility in requisition to entertain my guest, but she seemed quite independent, finding amusement for herself, and asking questions on every possible theme.

"You're doing your own work now, a'n't ye?"

This might not be denied; and I asked if she did not know of a girl whom I might be likely to get.

"Well, I do n't know; I'm looking for a place where I can board and do chores myself. I have a good deal of time before school, and after I get back; and I did n't know but I might suite ye for a while."

I was pondering on this proffer, when the sallow damsel arose from her seat, took a short pipe from her bosom, (not "Pan's reedy pipe,"[11] reader) filled it with tobacco, which she carried in her 'work-pocket," and reseating herself, began to smoke with the greatest gusto, turning ever and anon to spit at the hearth.

[10] A smooth woolen or mixed fabric.

[11] A Greek god of forests, pastures, and wild life, famous for playing on the syrinx, or "Pan's Pipes."

Incredible again? alas, would it were not true! I have since known a girl of seventeen, who was attending a neighbour's sick infant, smoke the live-long day, and take snuff besides; and I can vouch for it, that a large proportion of the married women in the interior of Michigan use tobacco in some form, usually that of the odious pipe.

I took the earliest decent opportunity to decline the offered help, telling the school-ma'am plainly, that an inmate who smoked would make the house uncomfortable to me.

"Why, law!" said she, laughing; "that's nothing but pride now: folks is often too proud to take comfort. For my part, I could n't do without my pipe to please nobody."

Mr. Simeon Jenkins, the brother of this independent young lady now made his appearance on some trifling errand; and his sister repeated to him what I had said.

Mr. Jenkins took his inch of cigar from his mouth, and asked if I really disliked tobacco-smoke, seeming to think it scarcely possible.

"Do n't your old man smoke?" said he.

"No, indeed," said I, with more than my usual energy; "I should hope he never would."

"Well," said neighbour Jenkins, "I tell you what, I'm *boss* at home; and if my old woman was to stick up that fashion, I'd keep the house so blue she could n't see to snuff the candle."

His sister laughed long and loud at this sally, which was uttered rather angrily, and with an air of most manful bravery; and, Mr. Jenkins, picking up his end of cigar from the floor, walked off with an air evidently intended to be as expressive as the celebrated and oft-quoted nod of Lord Burleigh[12] in the Critic.

Chapter XVII

The house's form within was rude and strong,
Like an huge cave hewn out of rocky clift;
From whose rough vault the ragged breaches hung:—

* * *

And over them Arachne high did lift
Her cunning web, and spread her subtle net,
Enwrapped in foul smoke, and clouds more black than jet.

—SPENCER—*FAERY QUEENE*

It were good that men, in their innovations, would follow the example of time itself, which, indeed, innovateth greatly, but quietly, and by degrees scarce to be perceived.

—BACON

[12]A character in Richard Sheridan's *The Critic* (1799) who has no lines, only a celebrated nod.

It was on one of our superlatively doleful ague days, when a cold drizzling rain had sent mildew into our unfortunate bones; and I lay in bed, burning with fever, while my stronger half sat by the fire, taking his chill with his great-coat, hat, and boots on, that Mr. Rivers came to introduce his young daughter-in-law. I shall never forget the utterly disconsolate air, which, in spite of the fair lady's politeness, would make itself visible in the pauses of our conversation. She *did* try not to cast a curious glance round the room. She fixed her eyes on the fire-place—but there were the clay-filled sticks, instead of a chimney-piece—the half-consumed wooden *crane,* which had, more than once, let our dinner fall—the Rocky-Mountain hearth, and the reflector, baking biscuits for tea—so she thought it hardly polite to appear to dwell too long there. She turned towards the window: there were the shelves, with our remaining crockery, a grotesque assortment! and, just beneath, the unnameable iron and tin affairs, that are reckoned among the indispensables, even of the half-civilized state. She tried the other side, but there was the ladder, the flour-barrel, and a host of other things—rather odd parlour furniture—and she cast her eyes on the floor, with its gaping cracks, wide enough to admit a massasauga from below, and its inequalities, which might trip any but a sylph. The poor thing looked absolutely confounded, and I exerted all the energy my fever had left me, to try to say something a little encouraging.

"Come to-morrow morning, Mrs. Rivers," said I, "and you shall see the aspect of things quite changed; and I shall be able to tell you a great deal in favour of this wild life."

She smiled faintly, and tried not to look miserable, but I saw plainly that she was sadly depressed, and I could not feel surprised that she should be so. Mr. Rivers spoke very kindly to her, and filled up all the pauses in our forced talk with such cheering observations as he could muster.

He had found lodgings, he said, in a farm-house, not far from us, and his son's house would, ere long, be completed, when we should be quite near neighbours.

I saw tears swelling in the poor girl's eyes, as she took leave, and I longed to be well for her sake. In this newly-formed world, the earlier settler has a feeling of hostess-ship toward the new comer. I speak only of women—men look upon each one, newly arrived, merely as an additional business-automaton—a somebody more with whom to try the race of enterprize, i.e., money-making.

The next day Mrs. Rivers came again, and this time her husband was with her. Then I saw at a glance why it was that life in the wilderness looked so peculiarly gloomy to her. Her husband's face shewed but too plainly the marks of early excess; and there was at intervals, in spite of an evident effort to play the agreeable, an appearance of absence, of indifference, which spoke volumes of domestic history. He made innumerable inquiries, touching the hunting and fishing facilities of the country around us, expressed himself enthusiastically fond of those sports, and said the country was a living death without them, regretting much that Mr. Clavers was not of the same mind.

Meanwhile, I had begun to take quite an interest in his little wife. I found that she was as fond of novels and poetry, as her husband was of field-sports. Some of her flights of sentiment went quite beyond my sobered-down views. But I saw we should get on admirably, and so we have done ever since. I did not mistake that pleasant smile, and that soft sweet voice. They are even now as attractive as ever. And I had a neighbour.

Chapter XXVII

Smelling so sweetly (all musk,) and so rushling, I warrant you, in silk and gold; and in such alligant terms.

—SHAKSPEARE—*MERRY WIVES OF WINDSOR*

Art thou not Romeo, and a Montague?

—SHAKSPEARE

My brain's in a fever, my pulses beat quick
I shall die, or at least be exceedingly sick!
Oh what do you think! after all my romancing
My visions of glory, my sighing, my glancing—

—MISS BIDDY FUDGE

An addition to our Montacute first circle had lately appeared in the person of Miss Eloise Fidler, an elder sister of Mrs. Rivers, who was to spend some months "in this peaceful retreat,"—to borrow one of her favourite expressions.

This young lady was not as handsome as she would fain have been, if I may judge by the cataracts of ash-coloured ringlets which shaded her cheeks, and the exceeding straitness of the stays which restrained her somewhat exuberant proportions. Her age was at a stand; but I could never discover exactly where, for this point proved an exception to the general communicativeness of her disposition. I guessed it at eight-and-twenty; but perhaps she would have judged this uncharitable, so I will not insist. Certain it is that it must have taken a good while to read as many novels and commit to memory as much poetry, as lined the head and exalted the sensibilities of our fair visitant.

Her dress was in the height of fashion, and all her accoutrements *point de vice.*[13] A gold pencil-case of the most delicate proportions was suspended by a kindred chain round a neck which might be called whity-brown; and a note-book of corresponding lady-like-ness was peeping from the pocket of her highly-useful apron of blue silk—ever ready to secure a passing thought or an elegant quotation. Her album—she was just the person to have an album—was resplendent in gold and satin, and the verses which meandered over its emblazoned pages were of the most unexceptionable quality, overlaid with flowers and gems—love and despair. To find any degree of appropriateness in these various offerings, one must allow the fortunate possessor of the purple volume, at least all the various perfections of an Admirable Crichton,[14] allayed in some small measure by the trifling faults of coldness, fickleness, and deceit; and to judge of Miss Fidler's friends by their handwriting, they must have been able to offer an edifying variety of bumps to the fingers of the phrenologist. But here is the very book itself at my elbow, waiting these three months, I blush to say, for a contribution which has yet to be pumped up from my unwilling brains; and I have a mind to steal a few specimens from its already loaded pages, for the benefit of the distressed, who may, like myself, be at their wits' end for something to put in just such a book.

[13]Perfectly correct.

[14]A sixteenth-century Scottish prodigy, well-known for his beauty and accomplishments.

The first page, rich with embossed lilies, bears the invocation, written in a great black spattering hand, and wearing the air of a defiance. It runs thus:

If among the names of the stainless few
 Thine own hath maintain'd a place,
Come dip thy pen in the sable dew
 And with it this volume grace.

But oh! if thy soul e'er encouraged a thought
 Which purity's self might blame,
Close quickly the volume, and venture not
 To sully its snows with thy name.

Then we come to a wreath of flowers of gorgeous hues, within whose circle appears in a *miminee piminee*[15] hand, evidently a young lady's—

The Wreath of Sleep.

Oh let me twine this glowing wreath
 Amid those rings of golden hair,
'T will soothe thee with its odorous breath
 To sweet forgetfulness of care.

'T is form'd of every scented flower
 That flings its fragrance o'er the night;
And gifted with a fairy power
 To fill thy dreams with forms of light.

'T was braided by an angel boy
 When fresh from Paradise he came
To fill our earth-born hearts with joy—
 Ah! need I tell the cherub's name?

This contributor I have settled in my own mind to be a descendant of Anna Matilda, the high-priestess of the Della Cruscan order.[16] The next blazon[17] is an interesting view of a young lady, combing her hair. As she seems not to have been long out of bed, the lines which follow are rather appropriate, though I feel quite sure they come from the expert fingers of a merchant's clerk—from the finished elegance, and very sweeping tails of the chirography.[18]

Morning.

Awake! arise! art thou slumbering still?
When the sun is above the mapled hill,
And the shadows are flitting fast away,
And the dews are diamond beneath his ray,

[15]Absurdly nice.

[16]A school of affected English poets who had named themselves after the Accademia Della Crusa, established in the sixteenth century to purify the Italian language. Here, as elsewhere in this section, Kirkland is spoofing Miss Fidler's pretentions, partly by adopting her affected language.

[17]A description or ostentatious display.

[18]A fancy word for handwriting.

And every bird in our vine-roofed bower
Is waked into song by the joyous hour;
Come, banish sleep from thy gentle eyes,
Sister! sweet sister! awake! arise!

Yet I love to gaze on thy lids of pearl,
And to mark the wave of the single curl
That shades in its beauty thy brow of snow,
And the cheek that lies like a rose below;
And to list to the murmuring notes that fall
From thy lips, like music in fairy hall.
But it must not be—the sweet morning flies
Ere thou hast enjoyed it; awake! arise!

There is balm on the wings of this freshen'd air;
'T will make thine eye brighter, thy brow more fair,
And a deep, deep rose on thy cheek shall be
The meed of an early walk with me.
We will seek the shade by the green hill side,
Or follow the clear brook's whispering tide;
And brush the dew from the violet's eyes—
Sister! sweet sister! awake! arise!

This I transcribe for the good advice which it contains. And what have we here? It is tastefully headed by an engraving of Hero and Ursula in the "pleached bower,"[19] and Beatrice running "like a lap-wing"[20] in the background. It begins ominously.

To—.

Oh, look upon this pallid brow!
  Say, canst thou there discern one trace
Of that proud soul which oft ere now
  Thou'st sworn shed radiance o'er my face?
Chill'd is that soul—its darling themes,
  Thy manly honour, virtue, truth
Prove now to be but fleeting dreams,
  Like other lovely thoughts of youth.

Meet, if thy coward spirit dare,
  This sunken eye; say, dost thou see
The rays thou saidst were sparkling there
  When first its gaze was turn'd on thee?
That eye's young light is quench'd forever;
  No change its radiance can repair:
Will Joy's keen touch relume it? Never!
  It gleams the watch-light of Despair.

[19]A Shakespearean phrase; a bower formed by intertwining boughs.

[20]A plover notable for its irregular flight and jumping behavior.

I find myself growing hoarse by sympathy, and I shall venture only a single extract more, and this because Miss Fidler declares it, without exception, the sweetest thing she ever read. It is written with a crow-quill, and has other marks of femininity. Its vignette[21] is a little girl and boy playing at battle-door.[22]

Ballad.

The deadly strife was over, and across the field of fame,
With anguish in his haughty eye, the Moor Almanzor came;
He prick'd his fiery courser on among the scatter'd dead,
Till he came at last to what he sought, a sever'd human head.

It might have seem'd a maiden's, so pale it was, and fair;
But the lip and chin were shaded till they match'd the raven hair.
There lingered yet upon the brow a spirit bold and high,
And the stroke of death had scarcely closed the piercing eagle eye.

Almanzor grasp'd the flowing locks, and he staid not in his flight,
Till he reach'd a lonely castle's gate where stood a lady bright.
"Inez! behold thy paramour!" he loud and sternly cried,
And threw his ghastly burden down, close at the lady's side.

"I sought thy bower at even-tide, thou syren, false as fair!"
"And, would that I had rather died! I found yon stripling there.
"I turn'd me from the hated spot, but I swore by yon dread Heaven,
"To know no rest until my sword the traitor's life had riven."

The lady stood like stone until he turn'd to ride away,
And then she oped her marble lips, and wildly thus did say:
"Alas, alas! thou cruel Moor, what is it thou hast done!
"This was my brother Rodriguez, my father's only son."

And then before his frenzied eyes, like a crush'd lily bell,
Lifeless upon the bleeding head, the gentle Inez fell.
He drew his glittering ataghan—he sheath'd it in his side—
And for his Spanish ladye-love the Moor Almanzor died.

This is not a very novel incident, but young ladies like stories of love and murder, and Miss Fidler's tastes were peculiarly young-lady-like. She praised Ainsworth and James, but thought Bulwer's works "very immoral," though I never could discover that she had more than skimmed the story from any of them. Cooper she found "pretty;" Miss Sedgwick, "pretty well, only her characters are such common sort of people."[23]

Miss Fidler wrote her own poetry, so that she had ample employment for her

[21]A decorative design or picture.
[22]What we would today call badminton.
[23]William Harrison Ainsworth, English author of *Old Saint Paul's* and other novels. George P.R. James, English novelist and critic. Edward Bulwer-Lytton (see note 6). James Fenimore Cooper and Catharine Maria Sedgwick, the American novelists, are represented in this volume.

time while with us in the woods. It was unfortunate that she could not walk out much on account of her shoes. She was obliged to make out with diluted inspiration. The nearest approach she usually made to the study of Nature, was to sit on the wood-pile, under a girdled tree, and there, with her gold pencil in hand, and her "eyne,[24] grey as glas," rolled upwards, poefy by the hour. Several people, and especially one marriageable lady of a certain age, felt afraid Miss Fidler was "kind o' crazy."

And, standing marvel of Montacute, no guest at morning or night ever found the fair Eloise ungloved. Think of it! In the very wilds to be always like a cat in nutshells, alone useless where all are so busy! I do not wonder our good neighbours thought the damsel a little touched. And then her shoes! "Saint Crispin Crispianus"[25] never had so self-sacrificing a votary. No shoemaker this side of New-York could make a sole papery enough; no tannery out of France could produce materials for this piece of exquisite feminine foppery. Eternal imprisonment within doors, except in the warmest and driest weather, was indeed somewhat of a price to pay, but it was ungrudged. The sofa and its footstool, finery and novels, *would* have made a delicious world for Miss Eloise Fidler, *if*—

But alas! "all this availeth me nothing," has been ever the song of poor human nature. The mention of that unfortunate name includes the only real, personal, pungent distress which had as yet shaded the lot of my interesting heroine. Fidler! In the mortification adhering to so unpoetical, so unromantic, so inelegant a surname—a name irredeemable even by the highly classical elegance of the Eloise, or as the fair lady herself pronounced it, "Elovees;" in this lay all her wo; and the grand study of her life had been to sink this hated cognomen in one more congenial to her taste. Perhaps this very anxiety had defeated itself; at any rate, here she was at—I did not mean to touch on the ungrateful guess again, but at least at mateable years; neither married, nor particularly likely to be married.

Mrs. Rivers was the object of absolute envy to the pining Eloise. "Anna had been so fortunate," she said; "Rivers was the sweetest name! and Harley was such an elegant fellow!"

We thought poor Anna had been any thing but fortunate. She might better have been Fidler or Fiddlestring all her life than to have taken the name of an indifferent and dissipated husband. But not so thought Miss Fidler. It was not long after the arrival of the elegant Eloise, that the Montacute Lyceum[26] held its first meeting in Mr. Simeon Jenkins's shop, lighted by three candles, supported by candelabra of scooped potatoes; Mr. Jenkins himself sitting on the head of a barrel, as president. At first the debates of the institute were held with closed doors; but after the youthful or less practised speakers had tried their powers for a few evenings, the Lyceum was thrown open to the world every Tuesday evening, at six o'clock. The list of members was not very select as to age, character, or standing; and it soon included the entire gentility of the town, and some who scarce claimed rank elsewhere. The attendance of the ladies was particularly requested; and the whole fair sex of Montacute made a point of showing occasionally the interest they undoubtedly felt in the gallant knights who tilted in this field of honour.

[24]Archaic for eyes.

[25]The patron saint of shoemakers.

[26]Meetings for lectures, debates, and discussions, which provided important educational opportunities as well as entertainment to frontier communities. See Introduction.

But I must not be too diffuse—I was speaking of Miss Fidler. One evening—I hope that beginning prepares the reader for something highly interesting—one evening the question to be debated was the equally novel and striking one which regards the comparative mental capacity of the sexes; and as it was expected that some of the best speakers on both sides would be drawn out by the interesting nature of the subject, every body was anxious to attend.

Among the rest was Miss Fidler, much to the surprise of her sister and myself, who had hitherto been so unfashionable as to deny ourselves this gratification.

"What new whim possesses you, Eloise?" said Mrs. Rivers; "you who never go out in the day-time."

"Oh, just *per passy le tong,*"[27] said the young lady, who was a great French scholar; and go she would and did.

The debate was interesting to absolute breathlessness, both of speakers and hearers, and was gallantly decided in favour of the fair by a youthful member who occupied the barrel as president for the evening. He gave it as his decided opinion, that if the natural and social disadvantages under which woman laboured and must ever continue to labour, could be removed; if their education could be entirely different, and their position in society the reverse of what it is at present, they would be very nearly, if not quite, equal to the nobler sex, in all but strength of mind, in which very useful quality it was his opinion that man would still have the advantage, especially in those communities whose energies were developed by the aid of debating societies.

This decision was hailed with acclamations, and as soon as the question for the ensuing debate, "which is the more useful animal the ox or the ass?" was announced, Miss Eloise Fidler returned home to rave of the elegant young man who sat on the barrel, whom she had decided to be one of "Nature's aristocracy," and whom she had discovered to bear the splendid appellative of Dacre. "Edward Dacre," said she, "for I heard the rude creature Jenkins call him Ed."

The next morning witnessed another departure from Miss Fidler's usual habits. She proposed a walk; and observed that she had never yet bought an article at the store, and really felt as if she ought to purchase something. Mrs. Rivers chancing to be somewhat occupied, Miss Fidler did me the honour of a call, as she could not think of walking without a chaperon.

Behind the counter at Skinner's I saw for the first time a spruce clerk, a really well-looking young man, who made his very best bow to Miss Fidler, and served us with much assiduity. The young lady's purchases occupied some time, and I was obliged gently to hint home-affairs before she could decide between two pieces of muslin, which she declared to be so nearly alike, that it was almost impossible to say which was the best.

When we were at length on our return, I was closely questioned as to my knowledge of "that gentleman," and on my observing that he seemed to be a very decent young man, Miss Fidler warmly justified him from any such opinion, and after a glowing eulogium on his firm countenance, his elegant manners and his grace as a debater, concluded by informing me, as if to cap the climax, that his name was Edward Dacre.

[27]A very corrupt French for passing the time.

I had thought no more of the matter for some time, though I knew Mr. Dacre had become a frequent visitor at Mr. Rivers', when Mrs. Rivers came to me one morning with a perplexed brow, and confided to me her sisterly fears that Eloise was about to make a fool of herself, as she had done more than once before.

"My father," she said, "hoped in this remote corner of creation Eloise might forget her nonsense and act like other people; but I verily believe she is bent upon encouraging this low fellow, whose principal charm in her bewildered eyes is his name."

"His name?" said I, "pray explain;" for I had not then learned all the boundless absurdity of this new Cherubina's[28] fancies.

"Edward Dacre?" said my friend, "this is what enchants my sister, who is absolutely mad on the subject of her own homely appellation."

"Oh, is that all?" said I, "send her to me, then; and I engage to dismiss her cured."

And Miss Fidler came to spend the day. We talked of all novels without exception, and all poetry of all magazines, and Miss Fidler asked me if I had read the "Young Duke." Upon my confessing as much, she asked my opinion of the heroine, and then if I had ever heard so sweet a name. "May Dacre—May Dacre," she repeated, as if to solace her delighted ears.

"Only think how such names are murdered in this country," said I, tossing carelessly before her an account of Mr. Skinner's which bore, "Edkins Daker" below the receipt. I never saw a change equal to that which seemed to "come o'er the spirit of her dream." I went on with my citations of murdered names, telling how Rogers was turned into Rudgers, Conway into Coniway, and Montague into Montaig, but poor Miss Fidler was no longer in talking mood; and, long before the day was out, she complained of a head-ache and returned to her sister's. Mr. Daker found her "not at home" that evening; and when I called next morning, the young lady was in bed, steeping her long ringlets in tears, real tears.

To hasten to the catastrophe: it was discovered ere long that Mr. Edkins Daker's handsome face, and really pleasant manners, had fairly vanquished Miss Fidler's romance, and she had responded to his professions of attachment with a truth and sincerity, which while it vexed her family inexpressibly, seemed to me to atone for all her follies. Mr. Daker's prospects were by no means despicable, since a small capital employed in merchandize in Michigan, is very apt to confer upon the industrious and fortunate possessor that crowning charm, without which handsome faces, and even handsome names, are quite worthless in our Western eyes.

Some little disparity of age existed between Miss Fidler and her adorer; but this was conceded by all to be abundantly made up by the superabounding gentility of the lady; and when Mr. Daker returned from New-York with his new stock of goods and his stylish bride, I thought I had seldom seen a happier or better mated couple. And at this present writing, I do not believe Eloise, with all her whims, would exchange her very nice Edkins for the proudest Dacre of the British Peerage.

[28]A reference to *The Heroine, or Adventures of Cherubina* (1813), by Eaton Stannard Barrett, a British writer. A parody of romances, it was quite popular at the time.

Chapter XLIII

On ne doit pas juger du merite d'un homme par ses grandes qualités, mais par l'usage qu'il en sait faire.[29]

—ROCHEFOUCAULT

Des mots longs d'une toise,
De grands mots qui tiendroient d'ici jusqu' à Pontoise[30]

—RACINE—*LES PLAIDEURS*

But what he chiefly valued himself on, was his knowledge of metaphysics, in which, having once upon a time ventured too deeply, he came well nigh being smothered in a slough of unintelligible learning.

—W. IRVING—*KNICKERBOCKER*

Mr. Simeon Jenkins entered at an early stage of his career upon the arena of public life, having been employed by his honoured mother to dispose of a basket full of hard-boiled eggs, on election day, before he was eight years old. He often dwells with much unction upon this his debût; and declares that even at that dawning period, he had cut his eye-teeth.

"There was n't a feller there," Mr. Jenkins often says, "that could find out which side I was on, for all they tried hard enough. They thought I was soft, but I let 'em know I was as much baked as any on 'em. 'Be you a dimocrat?' says one. Buy some eggs and I'll tell ye, says I; and by the time he'd bought his eggs, I could tell well enough which side *he* belonged to, and I'd hand him out a ticket according, for I had blue ones in one end o' my basket, and white ones in the other, and when night come, and I got off the stump to go home, I had eighteen shillin' and four pence in my pocket."

From this auspicious commencement may be dated Mr. Jenkins' glowing desire to serve the public. Each successive election day saw him at his post. From eggs he advanced to pies, from pies to almanacs, whiskey, powder and shot, foot-balls, playing-cards, and at length, for ambition ever "did grow with what it fed on," he brought into the field a large turkey, which was tied to a post and stoned to death at twenty-five cents a throw. By this time the still youthful aspirant had become quite the man of the world; could smoke twenty four cigars per diem, if any body else would pay for them; play cards, in old Hurler's shop, from noon till daybreak, and rise winner; and all this with suitable trimmings of gin and hard words. But he never lost sight of the main chance. He had made up his mind to serve his country, and he was all this time convincing his fellow-citizens of the disinterested purity of his sentiments.

"Patriotism," he would say, "patriotism is the thing! any man that's too proud to serve his country aint fit to live. Some thinks so much o' themselves, that if they can't have just what they think they're fit for, they wont take nothing; but for my part, I

[29]One can't judge a man's merits by his major qualities, but by the way in which he knows how to use them.

[30]Words a fathom long, huge words that stretch from here to Pontoise.

call myself an American citizen; and any office that's in the gift o' the people will suit *me.* I'm up to any thing. And as there aint no other man about here,—no suitable man, I mean—that's got a horse, why I'd be willing to be constable, if the people's a mind to, though it would be a dead loss to me in my business, to be sure; but I could do any thing for my country. Hurra for patriotism! them's my sentiments."

It can scarcely be doubted that Mr. Jenkins became a very popular citizen, or that he usually played a conspicuous part at the polls. Offices began to fall to his share, and though they were generally such as brought more honour than profit, office is office, and Mr. Jenkins did not grumble. Things were going on admirably.

> The spoils of office glitter in his eyes,
> He climbs, he pants, he grasps them—

Or thought he was just going to grasp them, when, presto! he found himself in the minority; the wheel of fortune turned, and Mr. Jenkins and his party were left undermost. Here was a dilemma! His zeal in the public service was ardent as ever, but how could he get a chance to show it unless his party was in power? His resolution was soon taken. He called his friends together, mounted a stump, which had fortunately been left standing not far from the door of his shop, and then and there gave "reasons for my ratting" in terms sublime enough for any meridian.[31]

"My friends and feller-citizens," said this self-sacrificing patriot, "I find myself conglomerated in sich a way, that my feelin's suffers severely. I'm sitivated in a peculiar sitivation. O' one side, I see my dear friends, pussonal friends—friends, that's stuck to me like wax, through thick and thin, never shinnyin' off and on, but up to the scratch, and no mistake. O' t' other side I behold my country, my bleedin' country, the land that fetch'd me into this world o' trouble. Now, sence things be as they be, and can't be no otherways as I see, I feel kind o' screwed into an augerhold to know what to do. If I hunt over the history of the universal world from the creation of man to the present day, I see that men has always had difficulties; and that some has took one way to get shut of 'em, and some another. My candid and unrefragable opinion is, that rather than remain useless, buckled down to the shop, and indulging in selfishness, it is my solemn dooty to change my ticket. It is severe, my friends, but dooty is dooty. And now, if any man calls me a turn-coat," continued the orator, gently spitting in his hands, rubbing them together, and rolling his eyes round the assembly, "all I say is, let him say it so that I can hear him."

The last argument was irresistible, if even the others might have brooked discussion, for Mr. Jenkins stands six feet two in his stockings, when he wears any, and gesticulates with a pair of arms as long and muscular as Rob Roy's.[32] So, though the audience did not cheer him, they contented themselves with dropping off one by one, without calling in question the patriotism of the rising statesman.

The very next election saw Mr. Jenkins justice of the peace, and it was in this honourable capacity that I have made most of my acquaintance with him, though we began with threatenings of a storm. He called to take the acknowledgement of a deed, and I, anxious for my country's honour, for I too am something of a patriot in

[31]Highest point.
[32]The title character in a novel by Sir Walter Scott.

my own way, took the liberty of pointing out to his notice a trifling slip of the pen; videlicet,[33] "Justas of Piece," which manner of writing those words I informed him had gone out of fashion.

He reddened, looked at me very sharp for a moment, and then said he thanked me; but subjoined,

"Book-learning is a good thing enough where there aint too much of it. For my part, I've seen a good many that know'd books that did n't know much else. The proper cultivation and edication of the human intellect, has been the comprehen*sive* study of the human understanding from the original creation of the universal world to the present day, and there has been a good many ways tried besides book-learning. Not but what that's very well in its place."

And the justice took his leave with somewhat of a swelling air. But we are excellent friends, notwithstanding this hard rub; and Mr. Jenkins favours me now and then with half an hour's conversation, when he has had leisure to read up for the occasion in an odd volume of the Cyclopedia, which holds an honoured place in the corner of his shop. He ought, in fairness, to give me previous notice, that I might study the dictionary a little, for the hard words with which he arms himself for these "keen encounters," often push me to the very limits of my English.

I ought to add, that Mr. Jenkins has long since left off gambling, drinking, and all other vices of that class, except smoking; in this point he professes to be incorrigible. But as his wife, who is one of the nicest women in the world, and manages him admirably, pretends to like the smell of tobacco, and takes care never to look at him when he disfigures her well-scoured floor, I am not without hopes of his thorough reformation.

1839

Harriet Beecher Stowe 1811–1896

Harriet Beecher Stowe was the sister of seven ministers and the daughter of an eighth. Her father, Lyman Beecher, of enthusiastic temperament and Calvinist convictions, was one of the most influential churchmen of his day, and her brother, Henry Ward, became the best-known pulpit orator of his. Harriet's elder sister, Catharine, pioneered the movement for women's education in this country, and her half-sister, Isabella, became an outspoken advocate of women's suffrage. Harriet's husband, Calvin Stowe, was a respected theologian, sought after by institutions of higher learning. But by the time she was in her thirties, all Harriet had done was the normal thing—she had married and had children. One would have thought that, weighed down by the cares of child-rearing (she had six children) and housekeeping (without electricity or central heating or very much money), and subject to depression and ill-health, a person in Harriet's position could not possibly have surpassed the other members of her family in moral leadership and worldly renown. In fact, she wrote to her husband, at the age of thirty-one: "Life is half gone! What have we done? . . . It is time to prepare to die." But Harriet Beecher Stowe became the

[33]Namely.

most famous member of her illustrious family, and the greatest crusader of them all.

Her father had predicted it . . . sort of. He had said that if Harriet were a boy "she would do more than any of them." *How* she did it is hard to get hold of. For most of her life Harriet lived in an atmosphere dominated by ministers and educators, alive with theological and intellectual debate, so her cultural background had certainly prepared her for authorship. At the age of thirteen, she was sent from her home in Litchfield, Connecticut to the female seminary her sister had founded in Hartford and spent eight years there under Catharine's care, learning Latin and French and Italian, studying history and moral theology, and teaching in the seminary herself. In 1832, when the whole family moved to Cincinnati (a city then considered the "Athens of the West"), where her father had been appointed president of the Lane Theological Seminary, she and Catharine taught school together again and joined the Semi-Colon Club, where they met the city's literati. But it was not long before she met Calvin Stowe, a professor of theology at Lane, and began her long stint as a mother and household drudge.

The Stowes were poor by middle-class standards and couldn't always afford to have domestic help. Because of her husband's frequent trips, Harriet often had the whole menage on her hands, though she was currently in poor health herself and had very little money. The picture her letters give of her at this time is of a person half-humourously, half-desperately trying to keep things going. Torn between babies to nurse and diapers to change, overturned chamber pots to clean up after, untrained servant girls to instruct, half-written stories to finish, puddings to make, children to mind, clothe, comfort, and teach, letters to write, dishes to wash, bills to pay, Harriet seems to have led the most fragmented and harried existence imaginable, emotionally teetering back and forth between depression and hilarity. In order to put something between herself and this constant attrition, she began to write. Her sketches—published in magazines like the New York *Evangelist* and *Godey's Lady's Book*—paid for basic furniture (she bought mattresses with her first check) and minimal household help.

It was during this period in Cincinnati, while she was struggling to keep house, bring up babies, and earn money writing, that she first became acquainted with runaway slaves, the underground railroad, and the ferment surrounding abolition. In 1834 the major portion of Lane Theological Seminary's student body resigned because the school's Board of Trustees had forbidden them to live with and work on behalf of the city's black population. In 1836 violent anti-abolitionist riots broke out in Cincinnati. In 1838, on a visit to her brother, William, in Putnam, Ohio, Harriet became convinced of the urgency of the abolitionist cause (her father was what was then known as a gradualist). And in 1845 she wrote her first sketch on the subject, adopting a position that was both dangerous and unfashionable. She entitled it "Immediate Emancipation." Slavery and abolition were not only abstract moral issues for Stowe. Lane Theological Seminary, on which her entire family depended for a livelihood, never recovered from the student resignations and was hard put to pay its faculty salaries. So when Calvin was appointed to a chair at Bowdoin College, it must have been with some sense of relief that Harriet set off, pregnant, three children in tow, to make the long journey by rail and steamboat to Brunswick, Maine. (There is a story that she and her children were so shabbily dressed that a stationmaster along the way refused to let them inside the waiting room.) Harriet's letter describing the work involved in refurbishing the large, old, unlived-in house they had rented reproduces some of the chaotic scenes of her domestic life in Cincinnati.

She describes the birth of her son, Charles Edward, as a welcome relief from the frantic effort. But the move to Brunswick began a new era in her life.

By the time she left for Maine, Harriet had managed to publish a score or so of short pieces, some of which she collected in a volume called *The Mayflower* (1843). These sketches give no indication of the power she would achieve later, but their sense of local color and didactic flavor persist throughout her career. What they lacked was passion. And this was sparked by two incidents that occurred after the Stowes had settled in Brunswick. When the Compromise of 1850 put the Fugitive Slave Law into effect, requiring northerners to help slave-owners recover escaped slaves, Harriet's sister-in-law, a committed abolitionist, wrote to her saying that if she could write the way Harriet did she would "write something that [would] make this whole nation feel what an accursed thing slavery is." Harriet's response was to rise to her feet and declare, "I *will* write something. I will if I live." The second incident occurred one Sunday in church, when, during communion, Harriet had a vision of a black slave being beaten to death: she walked home, oblivious of everything, and, tears streaming down her face, wrote the scene that would become the capstone of her great masterpiece.

Stowe is best known for writing *Uncle Tom's Cabin,* an almost miraculously successful book whose fame has overshadowed the rest of her literary output. The writing of *Uncle Tom's Cabin* released in Stowe a deep well of passion and eloquence which animated her the rest of her working life. After *Uncle Tom's Cabin* she wrote a documentary source on American slavery, several more novels, biographical sketches of famous men, many journalistic sketches on a variety of topics, mostly domestic, a literary-biographical polemic, children's books, theological essays, travel pieces, a book about Florida, poems, hymns (one of which became famous), and a great deal of what might be called inspirational literature. In a sense, almost everything that Stowe wrote was inspirational. Whether she was writing humorous social commentary ("The Ravages of a Carpet"), or recording her meeting with a famous Negro orator ("Sojourner Truth—The Libyan Sybil"), or describing the habits of a New England housekeeper ("Miss Asphyxia"), her moral earnestness shone through. Like her New England housekeepers, Stowe was always improving the time, which meant that she never ceased to entreat, warn, reprove, encourage, and otherwise instruct her readers.

As her career progressed, her style became more literary and her subjects less directly concerned with religion and reform, but the drive towards edification remained the motive force behind her work. *A Key to Uncle Tom's Cabin* (1853) and *Dred: A Tale of the Dismal Swamp* (1856) continue her polemic against slavery. *The Minister's Wooing* (1859), one of the great portrayals of life in early New England, mounts a ferocious attack against Calvinist doctrine (see "Views of Divine Government" reprinted below), celebrates the potency of female culture, and puts forward a theory that unites divine and sexual love. *The Pearl of Orr's Island* (1862) and *Oldtown Folks* (1869), though more celebratory than critical, use characters and situations from New England life as moral examples to imitate or shun. In *Lady Byron Vindicated* (1870) Stowe exposes herself to ridicule by defending the honor of a woman she felt the world had unjustly scorned. And though her later novels, *Pink and White Tyranny* (1871), *My Wife and I* (1871), and *We and Our Neighbors* (1875), resemble novels of manners more than anything else, Stowe didn't think of them that way. The Preface to *Pink and White Tyranny* announces: "this story is not to be a novel as the world understands the word, . . . it is . . . a story with a moral; and for fear that you shouldn't find out exactly what the moral is . . . we shall tell you in the proper time succinctly . . . and send you off edified as if you had been hearing a sermon."

By openly declaring her writing desk a pulpit, Stowe may have been trying to reassure herself that in portraying personal relationships among the urban middle classes she was still doing the Lord's work. Yet such anxiety was natural, given her family background, the evangelical impulse that had always motivated her, and the moralizing temper of the society she wrote for. American literature for most of the nineteenth century bore the imprint of an evangelical Protestant culture, Calvinist in its belief in submission to the will of an all-powerful Providence, and reformist in its hope that all human beings would some day be "one with the sympathies of Christ" and would work to make the country's institutions more merciful and just. It was because *Uncle Tom's Cabin* sprang from such mainstream moral and religious beliefs that it was able to galvanize national opinion as dramatically as it did.

When Stowe began writing that book, she had no idea that its influence would reach so far. The novel started out as a series of sketches, scheduled to run for about fourteen weeks in an anti-slavery newspaper called the *National Era.* As Stowe said in a letter to the editor, Gamaliel Bailey, the series was intended "to hold up in the most lifelike and graphic manner possible Slavery. . . . There is no arguing with *pictures,* and everybody is impressed by them, whether they mean to be or not." Everybody *was* impressed. Letters started flooding in, and soon Stowe's original fourteen weeks stretched to ten months. The chapters that poured out were not composed under the same conditions that had produced the sketches. Catharine came to take care of the children so that Harriet would have time to work, and Calvin gave up his office at Bowdoin so that she would have a place to work in. Harriet wrote like a person possessed, or inspired. Later, she would say of the novel "God wrote it."

Despite the success of the serial version of *Uncle Tom's Cabin,* the Stowes had a hard time finding a publisher for the book because of its abolitionism. But when the book came out it sold like wildfire—ten thousand copies in the first few days, three hundred thousand in the first year. No book except the Bible had ever sold so well. The adulation Stowe received for her work was tremendous not only in this country but abroad as well, where it was immediately pirated and translated into dozens of languages. Letters came from famous people all over the world. Scores of stage versions appeared (it was these versions that made the "Eliza crossing the ice" episode famous; in the novel it occupies only half a sentence). Perhaps the most dramatic illustration of Stowe's popularity occurred on her first trip to Britain, when all through the night people thronged the stations of small towns on her route from London to Scotland just to see her train go by.

Although *Uncle Tom's Cabin* is still irresistible reading, its belief system no longer corresponds to the one that is dominant today. Its racial stereotypes are offensive—Stowe believed that Negroes as a race were emotional, spiritually gifted, loyal, and childlike—and her characterization of Uncle Tom has become a touchstone for modern critiques of racism. But the moral force of her attack on slavery remains, and it is important to understand why the particular form of her attack had such an unparalleled effect in her own day. In writing *Uncle Tom's Cabin* Stowe took the most sacred beliefs of her culture—the sanctity of the family and redemption through Christian love—and turned them into an attack on the evils of slavery. The original sub-title of the novel *(The Man Who Was a Thing)* presents her case succinctly. By treating slaves as things to be bought and sold, rather than as human beings, slavery implicitly denies that slaves have souls to save, and therefore it is a sin. As a sin, it destroys not only the soul of the slave-owner, but the social fabric as well, for in separating wife from husband and parent from child, it destroys the institution on which human society rests—the family. In showing how slavery subverts Christianity and attacks the family at the same time, Stowe appealed to the wealth of feeling her age had invested in the sacredness of the home and of family ties. It was a brilliant strategy. After *Uncle Tom's Cabin* appeared, Northern legislators used its arguments to convince their colleagues of slavery's evils.

But despite, or rather, because of its enormous popularity, *Uncle Tom's Cabin* has not come down to us as an American literary classic. Its power to move millions of people has been held against it by a critical tradition that, since the 1940s, has identified formal complexity and difficulty of apprehension with literary merit. The fact that it was written by a woman, in language that made overt appeals to the emotions, carried a political message, and asked its readers to change put it squarely in the category labelled "propaganda." That the most powerful book ever written by an American has been excluded from our literary canon precisely *because* of its power, should make us question the grounds on which some of our present "classics" have been chosen.

Jane Tompkins
Duke University

PRIMARY WORKS

Uncle Tom's Cabin, 1852; *The Key to Uncle Tom's Cabin,* 1853; *Dred,* 1856; *The Minister's Wooing,* 1859; *The Pearl of Orr's Island,* 1862; *Oldtown Folks,* 1869; *Lady Byron Vindicated,* 1870; *Pink and White Tyranny,* 1871; *Sam Lawson's Oldtown Fireside Stories,* 1872; *Poganuc People,* 1878; *The Writings of Harriet Beecher Stowe,* 1896; *Life and Letters of Harriet Beecher Stowe,* ed. Annie Fields, 1897.

SECONDARY WORKS

Robert Forrest Wilson, *Crusader in Crinoline,* 1941; Jean W. Ashton, *Harriet Beecher Stowe: A Reference Guide,* 1977; Elizabeth Ammons, ed., *Critical Essays on Harriet Beecher Stowe,* 1980; Jane Tompkins, "Sentimental Power: *Uncle Tom's Cabin* and the Politics of Literary History," *Sensational Designs: The Cultural Work of American Fiction,* 1985; Lawrence Buell, "Hawthorne and Stowe as Rival Interpreters of New England Puritanism," *New England Literary Culture,* 1986; Eric Sundquist, ed., *New Essays on Uncle Tom's Cabin,* 1986; Amy Schrager Lang, "Feel Right and Pray," *Prophetic Woman: Anne Hutchinson and the Problem of Dissent in the Literature of New England,* 1987; Joan Hedrick, "'Peaceable Fruits'" The Ministry of Harriet Beecher Stowe," *American Quarterly* 40:3 (September, 1988): 307–332; Jeanne Boydston, Mary Kelley and Anne Margolis, *The Limits of Sisterhood: The Beecher Sisters on Women's Rights and Woman's Sphere,* 1988; Gillian Brown, *Domestic Individualism,* 1990; Joan D. Hedrick, *Harriet Beecher Stowe: A Life,* 1994; Lora Romero, *Home Fronts: Nineteenth-Century Domesticity and Its Critics,* 1997.

from Uncle Tom's Cabin

or Life Among the Lowly

I In Which the Reader Is Introduced to a Man of Humanity

Late in the afternoon of a chilly day in February, two gentlemen were sitting alone over their wine, in a well-furnished dining parlor, in the town of P——, in Kentucky. There were no servants present, and the gentlemen, with chairs closely approaching, seemed to be discussing some subject with great earnestness.

For convenience sake, we have said, hitherto, two *gentlemen.* One of the parties, however, when critically examined, did not seem, strictly speaking, to come under the species. He was a short, thick-set man, with coarse, commonplace features, and that swaggering air of pretension which marks a low man who is trying to elbow his way upward in the world. He was much over-dressed, in a gaudy vest of many colors, a blue neckerchief, bedropped gayly with yellow spots, and arranged with a flaunting tie, quite in keeping with the general air of the man. His hands, large and coarse, were plentifully bedecked with rings; and he wore a heavy gold watch-chain, with a bundle of seals of portentous size, and a great variety of colors, attached to it,—which, in the ardor of conversation, he was in the habit of flourishing and jingling with evident satisfaction. His conversation was in free and easy defiance of Murray's Grammar, and was garnished at convenient intervals with various profane expressions, which not even the desire to be graphic in our account shall induce us to transcribe.

His companion, Mr. Shelby, had the appearance of a gentleman; and the arrangements of the house, and the general air of the housekeeping, indicated easy, and even opulent circumstances. As we before stated, the two were in the midst of an earnest conversation.

"That is the way I should arrange the matter," said Mr. Shelby.

"I can't make trade that way—I positively can't, Mr. Shelby," said the other, holding up a glass of wine between his eye and the light.

"Why, the fact is, Haley, Tom is an uncommon fellow; he is certainly worth that sum anywhere,—steady, honest, capable, manages my whole farm like a clock."

"You mean honest, as niggers go," said Haley, helping himself to a glass of brandy.

"No; I mean, really, Tom is a good, steady, sensible, pious fellow. He got religion at a camp-meeting, four years ago; and I believe he really *did* get it. I've trusted him, since then, with everything I have,—money, house, horses,—and let him come and go round the country; and I always found him true and square in everything."

"Some folks don't believe there is pious niggers, Shelby," said Haley, with a candid flourish of his hand, "but *I do.* I had a fellow, now, in this yer last lot I took to Orleans—'t was as good as a meetin, now, really; to hear that critter pray; and he was quite gentle and quiet like. He fetched me a good sum, too, for I bought him cheap of a man that was 'bliged to sell out; so I realized six hundred on him. Yes, I consider religion a valeyable thing in a nigger, when it's the genuine article, and no mistake."

"Well, Tom's got the real article, if ever a fellow had," rejoined the other. "Why, last fall, I let him go to Cincinnati alone, to do business for me, and bring home five hundred dollars. 'Tom,' says I to him, 'I trust you, because I think you're a Christian—I know you would n't cheat.' Tom comes back, sure enough; I knew he would. Some low fellows, they say, said to him—'Tom, why don't you make tracks for Canada?' 'Ah, master trusted me, and I could n't,'—they told me about it. I am sorry to part with Tom, I must say. You ought to let him cover the whole balance of the debt; and you would, Haley, if you had any conscience."

"Well, I've got just as much conscience as any man in business can afford to keep,—just a little, you know, to swear by, as 't were," said the trader, jocularly; "and, then, I'm ready to do anything in reason to 'blige friends; but this yer, you see, is a leetle too hard on a fellow—a leetle too hard." The trader sighed contemplatively, and poured out some more brandy.

"Well, then, Haley, how will you trade?" said Mr. Shelby, after an uneasy interval of silence.

"Well, have n't you a boy or gal that you could throw in with Tom?"

"Hum!—none that I could well spare; to tell the truth, it's only hard necessity makes me willing to sell at all. I don't like parting with any of my hands, that's a fact."

Here the door opened, and a small quadroon boy, between four and five years of age, entered the room. There was something in his appearance remarkably beautiful and engaging. His black hair, fine as floss silk, hung in glossy curls about his round, dimpled face, while a pair of large dark eyes, full of fire and softness, looked out from beneath the rich, long lashes, as he peered curiously into the apartment. A gay robe of scarlet and yellow plaid, carefully made and neatly fitted, set off to advantage the dark and rich style of his beauty; and a certain comic air of assurance, blended with bashfulness, showed that he had been not unused to being petted and noticed by his master.

"Hulloa, Jim Crow!" said Mr. Shelby, whistling, and snapping a bunch of raisins towards him, "pick that up, now!"

The child scampered, with all his little strength, after the prize, while his master laughed.

"Come here, Jim Crow," said he. The child came up, and the master patted the curly head, and chucked him under the chin.

"Now, Jim, show this gentleman how you can dance and sing." The boy commenced one of those wild, grotesque songs common among the negroes, in a rich, clear voice, accompanying his singing with many comic evolutions of the hands, feet, and whole body, all in perfect time to the music.

"Bravo!" said Haley, throwing him a quarter of an orange.

"Now, Jim, walk like old Uncle Cudjoe, when he has the rheumatism," said his master.

Instantly the flexible limbs of the child assumed the appearance of deformity and distortion, as, with his back humped up, and his master's stick in his hand, he hobbled about the room, his childish face drawn into a doleful pucker, and spitting from right to left, in imitation of an old man.

Both gentlemen laughed uproariously.

"Now, Jim," said his master, "show us how old Elder Robbins leads the psalm." The boy drew his chubby face down to a formidable length, and commenced toning a psalm tune through his nose, with imperturbable gravity.

"Hurrah! bravo! what a young 'un!" said Haley; "that chap's a case, I'll promise. Tell you what," said he, suddenly clapping his hand on Mr. Shelby's shoulder, "fling in that chap, and I'll settle the business—I will. Come, now, if that ain't doing the thing up about the rightest!"

At this moment, the door was pushed gently open, and a young quadroon woman, apparently about twenty-five, entered the room.

There needed only a glance from the child to her, to identify her as its mother. There was the same rich, full, dark eye, with its long lashes; the same ripples of silky black hair. The brown of her complexion gave way on the cheek to a perceptible flush, which deepened as she saw the gaze of the strange man fixed upon her in bold and undisguised admiration. Her dress was of the neatest possible fit, and set off to advantage her finely moulded shape;—a delicately formed hand and a trim foot and ankle were items of appearance that did not escape the quick eye of the trader, well used to run up at a glance the points of a fine female article.

"Well, Eliza?" said her master, as she stopped and looked hesitatingly at him.

"I was looking for Harry, please, sir;" and the boy bounded toward her, showing his spoils, which he had gathered in the skirt of his robe.

"Well, take him away, then," said Mr. Shelby; and hastily she withdrew, carrying the child on her arm.

"By Jupiter," said the trader, turning to him in admiration, "there's an article, now! You might make your fortune on that ar gal in Orleans, any day. I've seen over a thousand, in my day, paid down for gals not a bit handsomer."

"I don't want to make my fortune on her," said Mr. Shelby, dryly; and, seeking to turn the conversation, he uncorked a bottle of fresh wine, and asked his companion's opinion of it.

"Capital, sir,—first chop!" said the trader; then turning, and slapping his hand familiarly on Shelby's shoulder, he added—

"Come, how will you trade about the gal?—what shall I say for her—what'll you take?"

"Mr. Haley, she is not to be sold," said Shelby. "My wife would not part with her for her weight in gold."

"Ay, ay! women always say such things, cause they ha'nt no sort of calculation. Just show'em how many watches, feathers, and trinkets, one's weight in gold would buy, and that alters the case, *I* reckon."

"I tell you, Haley, this must not be spoken of; I say no, and I mean no," said Shelby, decidedly.

"Well, you'll let me have the boy, though," said the trader; "you must own I've come down pretty handsomely for him."

"What on earth can you want with the child?" said Shelby.

"Why, I've got a friend that's going into this yer branch of the business—wants to buy up handsome boys to raise for the market. Fancy articles entirely—sell for waiters, and so on, to rich 'uns, that can pay for handsome 'uns. It sets off one of yer great places—a real handsome boy to open door, wait, and tend. They fetch a good sum; and this little devil is such a comical, musical concern, he's just the article."

"I would rather not sell him," said Mr. Shelby, thoughtfully; "the fact is, sir, I'm a humane man, and I hate to take the boy from his mother, sir."

"O, you do?—La! yes—something of that ar natur. I understand, perfectly. It is mighty onpleasant getting on with women, sometimes. I al'ays hates these yer screachin', screamin' times. They are *mighty* onpleasant; but, as I manages business, I generally avoids 'em, sir. Now, what if you get the girl off for a day, or a week, or so; then the thing's done quietly,—all over before she comes home. Your wife might get her some ear-rings, or a new gown, or some such truck, to make up with her."

"I'm afraid not."

"Lor bless ye, yes! These critters an't like white folks, you know; they gets over things, only manage right. Now, they say," said Haley, assuming a candid and confidential air, "that this kind o' trade is hardening to the feelings; but I never found it so. Fact is, I never could do things up the way some fellers manage the business. I've seen 'em as would pull a woman's child out of her arms, and set him up to sell, and she screechin' like mad all the time;—very bad policy—damages the article—makes 'em quite unfit for service sometimes. I knew a real handsome gal once, in Orleans, as was entirely ruined by this sort o' handling. The fellow that was trading for her did n't want her baby; and she was one of your real high sort, when her blood was up. I tell you, she squeezed up her child in her arms, and talked, and went on real awful. It kinder makes my blood run cold to think on't; and when they carried off the child, and locked her up, she jest went ravin' mad, and died in a week. Clear waste, sir, of a thousand dollars, just for want of management,—there's where 't is. It's always best to do the humane thing, sir; that's been *my* experience." And the trader leaned back in his chair, and folded his arm, with an air of virtuous decision, apparently considering himself a second Wilberforce.[1]

The subject appeared to interest the gentleman deeply; for while Mr. Shelby was thoughtfully peeling an orange, Haley broke out afresh, with becoming diffidence, but as if actually driven by the force of truth to say a few words more.

"It don't look well, now, for a feller to be praisin' himself; but I say it jest because it's the truth. I believe I'm reckoned to bring in about the finest droves of niggers that is brought in,—at least, I've been told so; if I have once, I reckon I have a hundred times,—all in good case,—fat and likely, and I lose as few as any man in the business. And I lays it all to my management, sir; and humanity, sir, I may say, is the great pillar of *my* management."

Mr. Shelby did not know what to say, and so he said, "Indeed!"

"Now, I've been laughed at for my notions, sir, and I've been talked to. They an't pop'lar, and they an't common; but I stuck to 'em, sir; I've stuck to 'em, and realized well on 'em; yes, sir, they have paid their passage, I may say," and the trader laughed at his joke.

There was something so piquant and original in these elucidations of humanity, that Mr. Shelby could not help laughing in company. Perhaps you laugh too, dear reader; but you know humanity comes out in a variety of strange forms now-a-days, and there is no end to the odd things that humane people will say and do.

Mr. Shelby's laugh encouraged the trader to proceed.

"It's strange, now, but I never could beat this into people's heads. Now, there was Tom Loker, my old partner, down in Natchez; he was a clever fellow, Tom was,

[1]William Wilberforce (1759–1833)—English philanthropist and member of Parliament whose anti-slavery speeches and support of the "Divine Light" missionary movement influenced the New Light Evangelical Reform movement in the United States.

only the very devil with niggers,—on principle 't was, you see, for a better hearted feller never broke bread; 't was his *system,* sir. I used to talk to Tom. 'Why, Tom,' I used to say, 'when your gals takes on and cry, what's the use o' crackin on 'em over the head, and knockin' on 'em round? It's ridiculous,' says I, 'and don't do no sort o' good. Why, I don't see no harm in their cryin',' says I; 'it's natur,' says I, 'and if natur can't blow off one way, it will another. Besides, Tom,' says I, 'it jest spiles your gals; they get sickly, and down in the mouth; and sometimes they gets ugly,—particular yallow gals do,—and it's the devil and all gettin' on 'em broke in. Now,' says I, 'why can't you kinder coax 'em up, and speak 'em fair? Depend on it, Tom, a little humanity, thrown in along, goes a heap further than all your jawin' and crackin'; and it pays better,' says I, 'depend on 't.' But Tom could n't get the hang on 't; and he spiled so many for me, that I had to break off with him, though he was a good-hearted fellow, and as fair a business hand as is goin'."

"And do you find your ways of managing do the business better than Tom's?" said Mr. Shelby.

"Why, yes, sir, I may say so. You see, when I any ways can, I takes a leetle care about the onpleasant parts, like selling young uns and that,—get the gals out of the way—out of sight, out of mind, you know,—and when it's clean done, and can't be helped, they naturally gets used to it. 'Tan't, you know, as if it was white folks, that's brought up in the way of 'spectin' to keep their children and wives, and all that. Niggers, you know, that's fetched up properly, ha' n't no kind of 'spectations of no kind; so all these things comes easier."

"I'm afraid mine are not properly brought up, then," said Mr. Shelby.

"S'pose not; you Kentucky folks spile your niggers. You mean well by 'em, but 'tan't no real kindness, arter all. Now, a nigger, you see, what's got to be hacked and tumbled round the world, and sold to Tom, and Dick, and the Lord knows who, 'tan't no kindness to be givin' on him notions and expectations, and bringin' on him up too well, for the rough and tumble comes all the harder on him arter. Now, I venture to say, your niggers would be quite chop-fallen in a place where some of your plantation niggers would be singing and whooping like all possessed. Every man, you know, Mr. Shelby, naturally thinks well of his own ways, and I think I treat niggers just about as well as it's ever worth while to treat 'em."

"It's a happy thing to be satisfied," said Mr. Shelby, with a slight shrug, and some perceptible feelings of a disagreeable nature.

"Well," said Haley, after they had both silently picked their nuts for a season, "what do you say?"

"I'll think the matter over, and talk with my wife," said Mr. Shelby. "Meantime, Haley, if you want the matter carried on in the quiet way you speak of, you'd best not let your business in this neighborhood be known. It will get out among my boys, and it will not be a particularly quiet business getting away any of my fellows, if they know it, I'll promise you."

"O! certainly, by all means, mum! of course. But I'll tell you, I'm in a devil of a hurry, and shall want to know, as soon as possible, what I may depend on," said he, rising and putting on his overcoat.

"Well, call up this evening, between six and seven, and you shall have my answer," said Mr. Shelby, and the trader bowed himself out of the apartment.

"I'd like to have been able to kick the fellow down the steps," said he to himself, as he saw the door fairly closed, "with his impudent assurance; but he knows how much he has me at advantage. If anybody had ever said to me that I should sell Tom down south to one of those rascally traders, I should have said, 'Is thy servant a dog, that he should do this thing?' And now it must come, for aught I see. And Eliza's child, too! I know that I shall have some fuss with wife about that; and, for that matter, about Tom, too. So much for being in debt,—heigho! The fellow sees his advantage, and means to push it."

Perhaps the mildest form of the system of slavery is to be seen in the State of Kentucky. The general prevalence of agricultural pursuits of a quiet and gradual nature, not requiring those periodic seasons of hurry and pressure that are called for in the business of more southern districts, makes the task of the negro a more healthful and reasonable one; while the master, content with a more gradual style of acquisition, has not those temptations to hardheartedness which always overcome frail human nature when the prospect of sudden and rapid gain is weighed in the balance, with no heavier counterpoise than the interests of the helpless and unprotected.

Whoever visits some estates there, and witnesses the good-humored indulgence of some masters and mistresses, and the affectionate loyalty of some slaves, might be tempted to dream the oft-fabled poetic legend of a patriarchal institution, and all that; but over and above the scene there broods a portentous shadow—the shadow of *law.* So long as the law considers all these human beings, with beating hearts and living affections, only as so many *things* belonging to a master,—so long as the failure, or misfortune, or imprudence, or death of the kindest owner, may cause them any day to exchange a life of kind protection and indulgence for one of hopeless misery and toil,—so long it is impossible to make anything beautiful or desirable in the best regulated administration of slavery.

Mr. Shelby was a fair average kind of man, good-natured and kindly, and disposed to easy indulgence of those around him, and there had never been a lack of anything which might contribute to the physical comfort of the negroes on his estate. He had, however, speculated largely and quite loosely; had involved himself deeply, and his notes to a large amount had come into the hands of Haley; and this small piece of information is the key to the preceding conversation.

Now, it had so happened that, in approaching the door, Eliza had caught enough of the conversation to know that a trader was making offers to her master for somebody.

She would gladly have stopped at the door to listen, as she came out; but her mistress just then calling, she was obliged to hasten away.

Still she thought she heard the trader make an offer for her boy;—could she be mistaken? Her heart swelled and throbbed, and she involuntarily strained him so tight that the little fellow looked up into her face in astonishment.

"Eliza, girl, what ails you to-day?" said her mistress, when Eliza had upset the wash-pitcher, knocked down the workstand, and finally was abstractedly offering her mistress a long night-gown in place of the silk dress she had ordered her to bring from the wardrobe.

Eliza started. "O, missis!" she said, raising her eyes; then, bursting into tears, she sat down in a chair, and began sobbing.

"Why, Eliza, child! what ails you?" said her mistress.

"O! missis, missis," said Eliza, "there's been a trader talking with master in the parlor! I heard him."

"Well, silly child, suppose there has."

"O, missis, *do* you suppose mas'r would sell my Harry?" And the poor creature threw herself into a chair, and sobbed convulsively.

"Sell him! No, you foolish girl! You know your master never deals with those southern traders, and never means to sell any of his servants, as long as they behave well. Why, you silly child, who do you think would want to buy your Harry? Do you think all the world are set on him as you are, you goosie? Come, cheer up, and hook my dress. There now, put my back hair up in that pretty braid you learnt the other day, and don't go listening at doors any more."

"Well, but, missis, *you* never would give your consent—to—to—"

"Nonsense, child! to be sure, I should n't. What do you talk so for? I would as soon have one of my own children sold. But really, Eliza, you are getting altogether too proud of that little fellow. A man can't put his nose into the door, but you think he must be coming to buy him."

Reassured by her mistress' confident tone, Eliza proceeded nimbly and adroitly with her toilet, laughing at her own fears, as she proceeded.

Mrs. Shelby was a woman of a high class, both intellectually and morally. To that natural magnanimity and generosity of mind which one often marks as characteristic of the women of Kentucky, she added high moral and religious sensibility and principle, carried out with great energy and ability into practical results. Her husband, who made no professions to any particular religious character, nevertheless reverenced and respected the consistency of hers, and stood, perhaps, a little in awe of her opinion. Certain it was that he gave her unlimited scope in all her benevolent efforts for the comfort, instruction, and improvement of her servants, though he never took any decided part in them himself. In fact, if not exactly a believer in the doctrine of the efficiency of the extra good works of saints, he really seemed somehow or other to fancy that his wife had piety and benevolence enough for two—to indulge a shadowy expectation of getting into heaven through her superabundance of qualities to which he made no particular pretension.

The heaviest load on his mind, after his conversation with the trader, lay in the foreseen necessity of breaking to his wife the arrangement contemplated,—meeting the importunities and opposition which he knew he should have reason to encounter.

Mrs. Shelby, being entirely ignorant of her husband's embarrassments, and knowing only the general kindliness of his temper, had been quite sincere in the entire incredulity with which she had met Eliza's suspicions. In fact, she dismissed the matter from her mind, without a second thought; and being occupied in preparations for an evening visit, it passed out of her thoughts entirely.

VII The Mother's Struggle

[Eliza has been married to George Harris, a slave at a neighboring plantation, who has recently escaped from slavery. When Eliza overhears Mr. Shelby tell his wife that he has sold both Uncle Tom and Eliza's son Harry to a slave trader, Eliza decides to flee, but not before she stops by Uncle Tom's cabin to warn him that he has been sold. Tom declines Eliza's suggestion that he escape with her. The next day, Mrs. Shelby and two of the other slaves on the plantation covertly obstruct the slave trader's attempts to go after Eliza, thus buying her time to escape.]

It is impossible to conceive of a human creature more wholly desolate and forlorn than Eliza, when she turned her footsteps from Uncle Tom's cabin.

Her husband's suffering and dangers, and the danger of her child, all blended in her mind, with a confused and stunning sense of the risk she was running, in leaving the only home she had ever known, and cutting loose from the protection of a friend whom she loved and revered. Then there was the parting from every familiar object,—the place where she had grown up, the trees under which she had played, the groves where she had walked many an evening in happier days, by the side of her young husband,—everything, as it lay in the clear, frosty starlight, seemed to speak reproachfully to her, and ask her whither could she go from a home like that?

But stronger than all was maternal love, wrought into a paroxysm of frenzy by the near approach of a fearful danger. Her boy was old enough to have walked by her side, and, in an indifferent case, she would only have led him by the hand; but now the bare thought of putting him out of her arms made her shudder, and she strained him to her bosom with a convulsive grasp, as she went rapidly forward.

The frosty ground creaked beneath her feet, and she trembled at the sound; every quaking leaf and fluttering shadow sent the blood backward to her heart, and quickened her footsteps. She wondered within herself at the strength that seemed to be come upon her; for she felt the weight of her boy as if it had been a feather, and every flutter of fear seemed to increase the supernatural power that bore her on, while from her pale lips burst forth, in frequent ejaculations, the prayer to a Friend above—"Lord, help! Lord, save me!"

If it were *your* Harry, mother, or your Willie, that were going to be torn from you by a brutal trader, to-morrow morning,—if you had seen the man, and heard that the papers were signed and delivered, and you had only from twelve o'clock till morning to make good your escape,—how fast could *you* walk? How many miles could you make in those few brief hours, with the darling at your bosom,—the little sleepy head on your shoulder,—the small, soft arms trustingly holding on to your neck?

For the child slept. At first, the novelty and alarm kept him waking; but his mother so hurriedly repressed every breath or sound, and so assured him that if he were only still she would certainly save him, that he clung quietly round her neck, only asking, as he found himself sinking to sleep,

"Mother, I don't need to keep awake, do I?"

"No, my darling; sleep, if you want to."

"But, mother, if I do get asleep, you won't let him get me?"

"No! so may God help me!" said his mother, with a paler cheek, and a brighter light in her large dark eyes.

"You're *sure,* an't you, mother?"

"Yes, *sure!*" said the mother, in a voice that startled herself; for it seemed to her to come from a spirit within, that was no part of her; and the boy dropped his little weary head on her shoulder, and was soon asleep. How the touch of those warm arms, the gentle breathings that came in her neck, seemed to add fire and spirit to her movements! It seemed to her as if strength poured into her in electric streams, from every gentle touch and movement of the sleeping, confiding child. Sublime is the dominion of the mind over the body, that, for a time, can make flesh and nerve impregnable, and string the sinews like steel, so that the weak become so mighty.

The boundaries of the farm, the grove, the wood-lot, passed by her dizzily, as she walked on; and still she went, leaving one familiar object after another, slacking not, pausing not, till reddening daylight found her many a long mile from all traces of any familiar objects upon the open highway.

She had often been, with her mistress, to visit some connections, in the little village of T——, not far from the Ohio river, and knew the road well. To go thither, to escape across the Ohio river, were the first hurried outlines of her plan of escape; beyond that, she could only hope in God.

When horses and vehicles began to move along the highway, with that alert perception peculiar to a state of excitement, and which seems to be a sort of inspiration, she became aware that her headlong pace and distracted air might bring on her remark and suspicion. She therefore put the boy on the ground, and, adjusting her dress and bonnet, she walked on at as rapid a pace as she thought consistent with the preservation of appearances. In her little bundle she had provided a store of cakes and apples, which she used as expedients for quickening the speed of the child, rolling the apple some yards before them, when the boy would run with all his might after it; and this ruse, often repeated, carried them over many a half-mile.

After a while, they came to a thick patch of woodland, through which murmured a clear brook. As the child complained of hunger and thirst, she climbed over the fence with him; and, sitting down behind a large rock which concealed them from the road, she gave him a breakfast out of her little package. The boy wondered and grieved that she could not eat; and when, putting his arms round her neck, he tried to wedge some of his cake into her mouth, it seemed to her that the rising in her throat would choke her.

"No, no, Harry darling! mother can't eat till you are safe! We must go on—on—till we come to the river!" And she hurried again into the road, and again constrained herself to walk regularly and composedly forward.

She was many miles past any neighborhood where she was personally known. If she should chance to meet any who knew her, she reflected that the well-known kindness of the family would be of itself a blind to suspicion, as making it an unlikely supposition that she could be a fugitive. As she was also so white as not to be known as of colored lineage, without a critical survey, and her child was white also, it was much easier for her to pass on unsuspected.

On this presumption, she stopped at noon at a neat farmhouse, to rest herself, and buy some dinner for her child and self; for, as the danger decreased with the distance, the supernatural tension of the nervous system lessened, and she found herself both weary and hungry.

The good woman, kindly and gossipping, seemed rather pleased than otherwise with having somebody come in to talk with; and accepted, without examination, Eliza's statement, that she "was going on a little piece, to spend a week with her friends,"—all which she hoped in her heart might prove strictly true.

An hour before sunset, she entered the village of T——, by the Ohio river, weary and foot-sore, but still strong in heart. Her first glance was at the river, which lay, like Jordan, between her and the Canaan of liberty on the other side.

It was now early spring, and the river was swollen and turbulent; great cakes of floating ice were swinging heavily to and fro in the turbid waters. Owing to the peculiar form of the shore on the Kentucky side, the land bending far out into the water, the ice had been lodged and detained in great quantities, and the narrow channel which swept round the bend was full of ice, piled one cake over another, thus forming a temporary barrier to the descending ice, which lodged, and formed a great, undulating raft, filling up the whole river, and extending almost to the Kentucky shore.

Eliza stood, for a moment, contemplating this unfavorable aspect of things, which she saw at once must prevent the usual ferry-boat from running, and then turned into a small public house on the bank, to make a few inquiries.

The hostess, who was busy in various fizzing and stewing operations over the fire, preparatory to the evening meal, stopped, with a fork in her hand, as Eliza's sweet and plaintive voice arrested her.

"What is it?" she said.

"Is n't there any ferry or boat, that takes people over to B——, now?" she said.

"No, indeed!" said the woman; "the boats has stopped running."

Eliza's look of dismay and disappointment struck the woman, and she said, inquiringly,

"May be you're wanting to get over?—anybody sick? Ye seem mighty anxious?"

"I've got a child that's very dangerous," said Eliza. "I never heard of it till last night, and I've walked quite a piece to-day, in hopes to get to the ferry."

"Well, now, that's onlucky," said the woman, whose motherly sympathies were much aroused; "I'm re'lly consarned for ye. Solomon!" she called, from the window, towards a small back building. A man, in leather apron and very dirty hands, appeared at the door.

"I say, Sol," said the woman, "is that ar man going to tote them bar'ls over tonight?"

"He said he should try, if 't was any way prudent," said the man.

"There's a man a piece down here, that's going over with some truck this evening, if he durs' to; he'll be in here to supper to-night, so you'd better set down and wait. That's a sweet little fellow," added the woman, offering him a cake.

But the child, wholly exhausted, cried with weariness.

"Poor fellow! he is n't used to walking, and I've hurried him on so," said Eliza.

"Well, take him into this room," said the woman, opening into a small bedroom, where stood a comfortable bed. Eliza laid the weary boy upon it, and held his hands in hers till he was fast asleep. For her there was no rest. As a fire in her bones, the thought of the pursuer urged her on; and she gazed with longing eyes on the sullen, surging waters that lay between her and liberty. . . .

In consequence of all the various delays, it was about three-quarters of an hour after Eliza had laid her child to sleep in the village tavern that the party came riding into the same place. Eliza was standing by the window, looking out in another direction, when Sam's quick eye caught a glimpse of her. Haley and Andy were two yards behind. At this crisis, Sam contrived to have his hat blown off, and uttered a loud and characteristic ejaculation, which startled her at once; she drew suddenly back; the whole train swept by the window, round to the front door.

A thousand lives seemed to be concentrated in that one moment to Eliza. Her room opened by a side door to the river. She caught her child, and sprang down the steps towards it. The trader caught a full glimpse of her, just as she was disappearing down the bank; and throwing himself from his horse, and calling loudly on Sam and Andy, he was after her like a hound after a deer. In that dizzy moment her feet to her scarce seemed to touch the ground, and a moment brought her to the water's edge. Right on behind they came; and, nerved with strength such as God gives only to the desperate, with one wild cry and flying leap, she vaulted sheer over the turbid current by the shore, on to the raft of ice beyond. It was a desperate leap—impossible to anything but madness and despair; and Haley, Sam, and Andy, instinctively cried out, and lifted up their hands, as she did it.

The huge green fragment of ice on which she alighted pitched and creaked as her weight came on it, but she staid there not a moment. With wild cries and desperate energy she leaped to another and still another cake;—stumbling—leaping—slipping—springing upwards again! Her shoes are gone—her stockings cut from her feet—while blood marked every step; but she saw nothing, felt nothing, till dimly, as in a dream, she saw the Ohio side, and a man helping her up the bank.

"Yer a brave gal, now, whoever ye ar!" said the man, with an oath.

Eliza recognized the voice and face of a man who owned a farm not far from her old home.

"O, Mr. Symmes!—save me—do save me—do hide me!" said Eliza.

"Why, what's this?" said the man. "Why, if 'tan't Shelby's gal!"

"My child!—this boy!—he'd sold him! There is his Mas'r," said she, pointing to the Kentucky shore. "O, Mr. Symmes, you've got a little boy!"

"So I have," said the man, as he roughly, but kindly, drew her up the steep bank. "Besides, you're a right brave gal. I like grit, wherever I see it."

When they had gained the top of the bank, the man paused.

"I'd be glad to do something for ye," said he; "but then there's nowhar I could take ye. The best I can do is to tell ye to go *thar,*" said he, pointing to a large white house which stood by itself, off the main street of the village. "Go thar; they're kind folks. Thar's no kind o' danger but they'll help you,—they're up to all that sort o' thing."

"The Lord bless you!" said Eliza, earnestly.

"No 'casion, no 'casion in the world," said the man. "What I've done 's of no 'count."

"And, oh, surely, sir, you won't tell any one!"

"Go to thunder, gal! What do you take a feller for? In course not," said the man. "Come, now, go along like a likely, sensible gal, as you are. You've arnt your liberty, and you shall have it, for all me."

The woman folded her child to her bosom, and walked firmly and swiftly away. The man stood and looked after her.

"Shelby, now, mebbe won't think this yer the most neighborly thing in the world; but what's a feller to do? If he catches one of my gals in the same fix, he's welcome to pay back. Somehow I never could see no kind o' critter a strivin' and pantin', and trying to clar theirselves, with the dogs arter 'em, and go agin 'em. Besides, I don't see no kind of 'casion for me to be hunter and catcher for other folks, neither."

So spoke this poor, heathenish Kentuckian, who had not been instructed in his constitutional relations, and consequently was betrayed into acting in a sort of Christianized manner, which, if he had been better situated and more enlightened, he would not have been left to do.

Haley had stood a perfectly amazed spectator of the scene, till Eliza had disappeared up the bank, when he turned a blank, inquiring look on Sam and Andy.

"That ar was a tolable fair stroke of business," said Sam.

"The gal's got seven devils in her, I believe!" said Haley. "How like a wildcat she jumped!"

"Wal, now," said Sam, scratching his head, "I hope Mas'r 'll 'scuse us tryin' dat ar road. Don't think I feel spry enough for dat ar, no way!" and Sam gave a hoarse chuckle.

"*You* laugh!" said the trader, with a growl.

"Lord bless you, Mas'r, I could n't help it, now," said Sam, giving way to the long pent-up delight of his soul. "She looked so curi's, a leapin' and springin'—ice a crackin'—and only to hear her,—plump! ker chunk! ker splash! Spring! Lord! how she goes it!" said Sam and Andy laughed till the tears rolled down their cheeks.

"I'll make ye laugh t' other side yer mouths!" said the trader, laying about their heads with his riding-whip.

Both ducked, and ran shouting up the bank, and were on their horses before he was up.

"Good-evening, Mas'r!" said Sam, with much gravity. "I berry much spect Missis be anxious 'bout Jerry. Mas'r Haley won't want us no longer. Missis would n't hear of our ridin' the critters over Lizy's bridge to-night;" and, with a facetious poke into Andy's ribs, he started off, followed by the latter, at full speed,—their shouts of laughter coming faintly on the wind.

XI In Which Property Gets into an Improper State of Mind

It was late in a drizzly afternoon that a traveller alighted at the door of a small country hotel, in the village of N——, in Kentucky. In the bar-room he found assembled quite a miscellaneous company, whom stress of weather had driven to harbor, and the place presented the usual scenery of such reunions. Great, tall, raw-boned Kentuckians, attired in hunting-shirts, and trailing their loose joints over a vast extent of territory, with the easy lounge peculiar to the race,—rifles stacked away in the corner, shot-pouches, game-bags, hunting-dogs, and little negroes, all rolled together in the corners,—were the characteristic features in the picture. At each end of the fireplace sat a long-legged gentleman, with his chair tipped back, his hat on his head, and the heels of his muddy boots reposing sublimely on the mantel-piece,—a position, we will inform our readers, decidedly favorable to the turn of reflection incident to western taverns, where travellers exhibit a decided preference for this particular mode of elevating their understandings.

Mine host, who stood behind the bar, like most of his countrymen, was great of stature, good-natured, and loose-jointed, with an enormous shock of hair on his head, and a great tall hat on the top of that.

In fact, everybody in the room bore on his head this characteristic emblem of man's sovereignty; whether it were felt hat, palm-leaf, greasy beaver, or fine new chapeau, there it reposed with true republican independence. In truth, it appeared to be the characteristic mark of every individual. Some wore them tipped rakishly to one side—these were your men of humor, jolly, free-and-easy dogs; some had them jammed independently down over their noses—these were your hard characters, thorough men, who, when they wore their hats, *wanted* to wear them, and to wear them just as they had a mind to; there were those who had them set far over back—wide-awake men, who wanted a clear prospect; while careless men, who did not know, or care, how their hats sat, had them shaking about in all directions. The various hats, in fact, were quite a Shakspearean study.

Divers negroes, in very free-and-easy pantaloons, and with no redundancy in the shirt line, were scuttling about, hither and thither, without bringing to pass any very particular results, except expressing a generic willingness to turn over everything in creation generally for the benefit of Mas'r and his guests. Add to this picture a jolly, crackling, rollicking fire, going rejoicingly up a great wide chimney,—the outer door and every window being set wide open, and the calico window-curtain flopping and snapping in a good stiff breeze of damp raw air,—and you have an idea of the jollities of a Kentucky tavern.

Your Kentuckian of the present day is a good illustration of the doctrine of transmitted instincts and peculiarities. His fathers were mighty hunters,—men who lived in the woods, and slept under the free, open heavens, with the stars to hold their candles; and their descendant to this day always acts as if the house were his camp,—wears his hat at all hours, tumbles himself about, and puts his heels on the tops of chairs or mantel-pieces, just as his father rolled on the green sward, and put his upon trees and logs,—keeps all the windows and doors open, winter and summer, that he may get air enough for his great lungs,—calls everybody "stranger," with nonchalant bonhommie, and is altogether the frankest, easiest, most jovial creature living.

Into such an assembly of the free and easy our traveller entered. He was a short, thick-set man, carefully dressed, with a round, good-natured countenance, and something rather fussy and particular in his appearance. He was very careful of his valise and umbrella, bringing them in with his own hands, and resisting, pertinaciously, all offers from the various servants to relieve him of them. He looked round the bar-room with rather an anxious air, and, retreating with his valuables to the warmest corner, disposed them under his chair, sat down, and looked rather apprehensively up at the worthy whose heels illustrated the end of the mantel-piece, who was spitting from right to left, with a courage and energy rather alarming to gentlemen of weak nerves and particular habits.

"I say, stranger, how are ye?" said the aforesaid gentleman, firing an honorary salute of tobacco-juice in the direction of the new arrival.

"Well, I reckon," was the reply of the other, as he dodged, with some alarm, the threatening honor.

"Any news?" said the respondent, taking out a strip of tobacco and a large hunting-knife from his pocket.

"Not that I know of," said the man.

"Chaw?" said the first speaker, handing the old gentleman a bit of his tobacco, with a decidedly brotherly air.

"No, thank ye—it don't agree with me," said the little man, edging off.

"Don't, eh?" said the other, easily, and stowing away the morsel in his own mouth, in order to keep up the supply of tobacco-juice, for the general benefit of society.

The old gentleman uniformly gave a little start whenever his long-sided brother fired in his direction; and this being observed by his companion, he very good-naturedly turned his artillery to another quarter, and proceeded to storm one of the fire-irons with a degree of military talent fully sufficient to take a city.

"What's that?" said the old gentleman, observing some of the company formed in a group around a large handbill.

"Nigger advertised!" said one of the company, briefly.

Mr. Wilson, for that was the old gentleman's name, rose up, and, after carefully adjusting his valise and umbrella, proceeded deliberately to take out his spectacles and fix them on his nose; and, this operation being performed, read as follows:

> *"Ran away from the subscriber, my mulatto boy, George. Said George six feet in height, a very light mulatto, brown curly hair; is very intelligent, speaks handsomely, can read and write; will probably try to pass for a white man; is deeply scarred on his back and shoulders; has been branded in his right hand with the letter H.*
>
> *"I will give four hundred dollars for him alive, and the same sum for satisfactory proof that he has been killed."*

The old gentleman read this advertisement from end to end, in a low voice, as if he were studying it.

The long-legged veteran, who had been besieging the fire-iron, as before related, now took down his cumbrous length, and rearing aloft his tall form, walked up to the advertisement, and very deliberately spit a full discharge of tobacco-juice on it.

"There's my mind upon that!" said he, briefly, and sat down again.

"Why, now, stranger, what's that for?" said mine host.

"I'd do it all the same to the writer of that ar paper, if he was here," said the long man, coolly resuming his old employment of cutting tobacco. "Any man that owns a boy like that, and can't find any better way o' treating on him, *deserves* to lose him. Such papers as these is a shame to Kentucky; that's my mind right out, if anybody wants to know!"

"Well, now, that's a fact," said mine host, as he made an entry in his book.

"I've got a gang of boys, sir," said the long man, resuming his attack on the fire-irons, "and I jest tells 'em—'Boys,' says I,—'*run* now! dig! put! jest when ye want to! I never shall come to look after you!' That's the way I keep mine. Let 'em know they are free to run any time, and it jest breaks up their wanting to. More'n all, I've got free papers for 'em all recorded, in case I gets keeled up any o' these times, and they knows it; and I tell ye, stranger, there an't a fellow in our parts gets more out of his niggers than I do. Why, my boys have been to Cincinnati, with five hundred dollars' worth of colts, and brought me back the money, all straight, time and agin. It stands to reason they should. Treat 'em like dogs, and you'll have dogs' works and dogs' actions. Treat 'em like men, and you'll have men's works." And the honest drover, in his warmth, endorsed this moral sentiment by firing a perfect *feu de joie* at the fireplace.

"I think you're altogether right, friend," said Mr. Wilson; "and this boy described here *is* a fine fellow—no mistake about that. He worked for me some half-dozen years in my bagging factory, and he was my best hand, sir. He is an ingenious fellow, too: he invented a machine for the cleaning of hemp—a really valuable affair; it's gone into use in several factories. His master holds the patent of it."

"I'll warrant ye," said the drover, "holds it and makes money out of it, and then turns round and brands the boy in his right hand. If I had a fair chance, I'd mark him, I reckon, so that he'd carry it *one* while."

"These yer knowin' boys is allers aggravatin' and sarcy," said a coarse-looking fellow, from the other side of the room; "that's why they gets cut up and marked so. If they behaved themselves, they would n't."

"That is to say, the Lord made 'em men, and it's a hard squeeze getting 'em down into beasts," said the drover, dryly.

"Bright niggers is n't no kind of 'vantage to their masters," continued the other, well intrenched, in a coarse, unconscious obtuseness, from the contempt of his opponent; "what's the use o' talents and them things, if you can't get the use on 'em yourself? Why, all the use they make on 't is to get round you. I've had one or two of these fellers, and I jest sold 'em down river. I knew I'd got to lose 'em, first or last, if I did n't."

"Better send orders up to the Lord, to make you a set, and leave out their souls entirely," said the drover.

Here the conversation was interrupted by the approach of a small one-horse buggy to the inn. It had a genteel appearance, and a well-dressed, gentlemanly man sat on the seat, with a colored servant driving.

The whole party examined the new comer with the interest with which a set of loafers in a rainy day usually examine every new comer. He was very tall, with a dark, Spanish complexion, fine, expressive black eyes, and close-curling hair, also of a glossy blackness. His well-formed aquiline nose, straight thin lips, and the admirable contour of his finely-formed limbs, impressed the whole company instantly with the idea of something uncommon. He walked easily in among the company, and with a nod indicated to his waiter where to place his trunk, bowed to the company, and, with his hat in his hand, walked up leisurely to the bar, and gave in his name as Henry Butler, Oaklands, Shelby County. Turning, with an indifferent air, he sauntered up to the advertisement, and read it over.

"Jim," he said to his man, "seems to me we met a boy something like this, up at Bernan's, did n't we?"

"Yes, Mas'r," said Jim, "only I an't sure about the hand."

"Well, I did n't look, of course," said the stranger, with a careless yawn. Then, walking up to the landlord, he desired him to furnish him with a private apartment, as he had some writing to do immediately.

The landlord was all obsequious, and a relay of about seven negroes, old and young, male and female, little and big, were soon whizzing about, like a covey of partridges, bustling, hurrying, treading on each other's toes, and tumbling over each other, in their zeal to get Mas'r's room ready, while he seated himself easily on a chair in the middle of the room, and entered into conversation with the man who sat next to him.

The manufacturer, Mr. Wilson, from the time of the entrance of the stranger, had regarded him with an air of disturbed and uneasy curiosity. He seemed to himself to have met and been acquainted with him somewhere, but he could not recollect. Every few moments, when the man spoke, or moved, or smiled, he would start and fix his eyes on him, and then suddenly withdraw them, as the bright, dark eyes met his with such unconcerned coolness. At last, a sudden recollection seemed to flash upon him, for he stared at the stranger with such an air of blank amazement and alarm, that he walked up to him.

"Mr. Wilson, I think," said he, in a tone of recognition, and extending his hand. "I beg your pardon, I did n't recollect you before. I see you remember me,—Mr. Butler, of Oaklands, Shelby County."

"Ye—yes—yes, sir," said Mr. Wilson, like one speaking in a dream.

Just then a negro boy entered, and announced that Mas'r's room was ready.

"Jim, see to the trunks," said the gentleman, negligently; then addressing himself to Mr. Wilson, he added—"I should like to have a few moments' conversation with you on business, in my room, if you please."

Mr. Wilson followed him, as one who walks in his sleep; and they proceeded to a large upper chamber, where a new-made fire was crackling, and various servants flying about, putting finishing touches to the arrangements.

When all was done, and the servants departed, the young man deliberately locked the door, and putting the key in his pocket, faced about, and folding his arms on his bosom, looked Mr. Wilson full in the face.

"George!" said Mr. Wilson.

"Yes, George," said the young man.

"I could n't have thought it!"

"I am pretty well disguised, I fancy," said the young man, with a smile. "A little walnut bark has made my yellow skin a genteel brown, and I've dyed my hair black; so you see I don't answer to the advertisement at all."

"O, George! but this is a dangerous game you are playing. I could not have advised you to it."

"I can do it on my own responsibility," said George, with the same proud smile.

We remark, *en passant,* that George was, by his father's side, of white descent. His mother was one of those unfortunates of her race, marked out by personal beauty to be the slave of the passions of her possessor, and the mother of children who may never know a father. From one of the proudest families in Kentucky he had inherited a set of fine European features, and a high, indomitable spirit. From his mother he had received only a slight mulatto tinge, amply compensated by its accompanying rich, dark eye. A slight change in the tint of the skin and the color of his hair had metamorphosed him into the Spanish-looking fellow he then appeared; and as gracefulness of movement and gentlemanly manners had always been perfectly natural to him, he found no difficulty in playing the bold part he had adopted—that of a gentleman travelling with his domestic.

Mr. Wilson, a good-natured but extremely fidgety and cautious old gentleman, ambled up and down the room, appearing, as John Bunyan hath it, "much tumbled up and down in his mind," and divided between his wish to help George, and a certain confused notion of maintaining law and order: so, as he shambled about, he delivered himself as follows:

"Well, George, I s'pose you 're running away—leaving your lawful master, George—(I don't wonder at it)—at the same time, I'm sorry, George,—yes, decidedly—I think I must say that, George—it's my duty to tell you so."

"Why are you sorry, sir?" said George, calmly.

"Why, to see you, as it were, setting yourself in opposition to the laws of your country."

"*My* country!" said George, with a strong and bitter emphasis; "what country have I, but the grave,—and I wish to God that I was laid there!"

"Why, George, no—no—it won't do; this way of talking is wicked—unscriptural. George, you've got a hard master—in fact, he is—well he conducts himself reprehensibly—I can't pretend to defend him. But you know how the angel commanded Hagar to return to her mistress, and submit herself under her hand; and the apostle sent back Onesimus to his master."

"Don't quote Bible at me that way, Mr. Wilson," said George, with a flashing eye, "don't! for my wife is a Christian, and I mean to be, if ever I get to where I can; but to quote Bible to a fellow in my circumstances, is enough to make him give it up altogether. I appeal to God Almighty;—I'm willing to go with the case to Him, and ask Him if I do wrong to seek my freedom."

"These feelings are quite natural, George," said the good-natured man, blowing his nose. "Yes they're natural, but it is my duty not to encourage 'em in you. Yes, my boy, I'm sorry for you, now; it's a bad case—very bad; but the apostle says, 'Let every one abide in the condition in which he is called.' We must all submit to the indications of Providence, George,—don't you see?"

George stood with his head drawn back, his arms folded tightly over his broad breast, and a bitter smile curling his lips.

"I wonder, Mr. Wilson, if the Indians should come and take you a prisoner away from your wife and children, and want to keep you all your life hoeing corn for them, if you'd think it your duty to abide in the condition in which you were called. I rather think that you'd think the first stray horse you could find an indication of Providence—should n't you?"

The little old gentleman stared with both eyes at this illustration of the case; but, though not much of a reasoner, he had the sense in which some logicians on this particular subject do not excel,—that of saying nothing, where nothing could be said. So, as he stood carefully stroking his umbrella, and folding and patting down all the creases in it, he proceeded on with his exhortations in a general way.

"You see, George, you know, now, I always have stood your friend; and whatever I've said, I've said for your good. Now, here, it seems to me, you're running an awful risk. You can't hope to carry it out. If you're taken, it will be worse with you than ever; they'll only abuse you, and half kill you, and sell you down river."

"Mr. Wilson, I know all this," said George. "I *do* run a risk, but—" he threw open his overcoat, and showed two pistols and a bowie-knife. "There!" he said, "I'm ready for 'em! Down south I never *will* go. No! if it comes to that, I can earn myself at least six feet of free soil,—the first and last I shall ever own in Kentucky!"

"Why, George, this state of mind is awful; it's getting really desperate, George. I'm concerned. Going to break the laws of your country!"

"My country again! Mr. Wilson, *you* have a country; but what country have *I,* or any one like me, born of slave mothers? What laws are there for us? We don't make them,—we don't consent to them,—we have nothing to do with them; all they do for us is to crush us, and keep us down. Have n't I heard your Fourth-of-July speeches? Don't you tell us all, once a year, that governments derive their just power from the consent of the governed? Can't a fellow *think,* that hears such things? Can't he put this and that together, and see what it comes to?"

Mr. Wilson's mind was one of those that may not unaptly be represented by a bale of cotton,—downy, soft, benevolently fuzzy and confused. He really pitied George with all his heart, and had a sort of dim and cloudy perception of the style of feeling that agitated him; but he deemed it his duty to go on talking *good* to him, with infinite pertinacity.

"George, this is bad. I must tell you, you know, as a friend, you'd better not be meddling with such notions; they are bad, George, very bad, for boys in your condition,—very;" and Mr. Wilson sat down to a table, and began nervously chewing the handle of his umbrella.

"See here, now, Mr. Wilson," said George, coming up and sitting himself determinately down in front of him; "look at me, now. Don't I sit before you, every way, just as much a man as you are? Look at my face,—look at my hands,—look at my body," and the young man drew himself up proudly; "why am I *not* a man, as much as anybody? Well, Mr. Wilson, hear what I can tell you. I had a father—one of your Kentucky gentlemen—who did n't think enough of me to keep me from being sold with his dogs and horses, to satisfy the estate, when he died. I saw my mother put up at sheriff's sale, with her seven children. They were sold before her eyes, one by one, all to different masters; and I was the youngest. She came and kneeled down before old Mas'r, and begged him to buy her with me, that she might have at least one child with her; and he kicked her away with his heavy boot. I saw him do it; and the last that I heard was her moans and screams, when I was tied to his horse's neck, to be carried off to his place."

"Well, then?"

"My master traded with one of the men, and bought my oldest sister. She was a pious, good girl,—a member of the Baptist church,—and as handsome as my poor mother had been. She was well brought up, and had good manners. At first, I was glad she was bought, for I had one friend near me. I was soon sorry for it. Sir, I have stood at the door and heard her whipped, when it seemed as if every blow cut into my naked heart, and I could n't do anything to help her; and she was whipped, sir, for wanting to live a decent Christian life, such as your laws give no slave girl a right to live; and at last I saw her chained with a trader's gang, to be sent to market in Orleans,—sent there for nothing else but that,—and that's the last I know of her. Well, I grew up,—long years and years,—no father, no mother, no sister, not a living soul that cared for me more than a dog; nothing but whipping, scolding, starving. Why, sir, I've been so hungry that I have been glad to take the bones they threw to their dogs; and yet, when I was a little fellow, and laid awake whole nights and cried, it was n't the hunger, it was n't the whipping, I cried for. No, sir; it was for *my mother* and *my sisters,*—it was because I had n't a friend to love me on earth. I never knew what peace or comfort was. I never had a kind word spoken to me till I came to work in your factory. Mr. Wilson, you treated me well; you encouraged me to do well, and to learn to read and write, and to try to make something of myself; and God knows how grateful I am for it. Then, sir, I found my wife; you've seen her,—you know how beautiful she is. When I found she loved me, when I married her, I scarcely could believe I was alive, I was so happy; and, sir, she is as good as she is beautiful. But now what? Why, now comes my master, takes me right away from my work, and my friends, and all I like, and grinds me down into the very dirt! And why? Because, he says, I forgot who I was; he says, to teach me that I am only a nigger! After all, and last of all, he comes between me and my wife, and says I shall give her up, and live with another woman. And all this your laws give him power to do, in spite of God or man. Mr. Wilson, look at it! There is n't *one* of all these things, that have broken the hearts of my mother and my sister, and my wife and myself, but your laws allow, and give every man power to do, in Kentucky, and none can say to him nay! Do you call these the laws of *my* country? Sir, I have n't any country, any more than I have any father. But I'm going to have one. I don't want anything of *your* country, except to be let alone,—to go peaceably out of it; and when I get to Canada, where the laws will own me and protect me, *that* shall be my country, and its laws I will obey. But if any man tries to stop me, let him take care, for I am desperate. I'll fight for my liberty to the last breath I breathe. You say your fathers did it; if it was right for them, it is right for me!"

This speech, delivered partly while sitting at the table, and partly walking up and down the room,—delivered with tears, and flashing eyes, and despairing gestures,—was altogether too much for the good-natured old body to whom it was addressed, who had pulled out a great yellow silk pocket-handkerchief, and was mopping up his face with great energy.

"Blast 'em all!" he suddenly broke out. "Have n't I always said so—the infernal old cusses! I hope I an't swearing, now. Well! go ahead, George, go ahead; but be careful, my boy; don't shoot anybody, George, unless—well—you'd *better* not shoot, I reckon; at least, I would n't *hit* anybody, you know. Where is your wife, George?" he added, as he nervously rose, and began walking the room.

"Gone, sir, gone, with her child in her arms, the Lord only knows where;—gone after the north star; and when we ever meet, or whether we meet at all in this world, no creature can tell."

"Is it possible! astonishing! from such a kind family?"

"Kind families get in debt, and the laws of *our* country allow them to sell the child out of its mother's bosom to pay its master's debts," said George, bitterly.

"Well, well," said the honest old man, fumbling in his pocket. "I s'pose, perhaps, I an't following my judgment,—hang it, I *won't* follow my judgment!" he added, suddenly; "so here, George," and, taking out a roll of bills from his pocketbook, he offered them to George.

"No, my kind, good sir!" said George, "you've done a great deal for me, and this might get you into trouble. I have money enough, I hope, to take me as far as I need it."

"No; but you must, George. Money is a great help everywhere;—can't have too much, if you get it honestly. Take it,—*do* take it, *now,*—do, my boy!"

"On condition, sir, that I may repay it at some future time, I will," said George, taking up the money.

"And now, George, how long are you going to travel in this way?—not long or far, I hope. It's well carried on, but too bold. And this black fellow,—who is he?"

"A true fellow, who went to Canada more than a year ago. He heard, after he got there, that his master was so angry at him for going off that he had whipped his poor old mother; and he has come all the way back to comfort her, and get a chance to get her away."

"Has he got her?"

"Not yet; he has been hanging about the place, and found no chance yet. Meanwhile, he is going with me as far as Ohio, to put me among friends that helped him, and then he will come back after her."

"Dangerous, very dangerous!" said the old man.

George drew himself up, and smiled disdainfully.

The old gentleman eyed him from head to foot, with a sort of innocent wonder. "George, something has brought you out wonderfully. You hold up your head, and speak and move like another man," said Mr. Wilson.

"Because I'm a *freeman!*" said George, proudly. "Yes, sir; I've said Mas'r for the last time to any man. *I'm free!*"

"Take care! You are not sure,—you may be taken."

"All men are free and equal *in the grave,* if it comes to that, Mr. Wilson," said George.

"I'm perfectly dumb-foundered with your boldness!" said Mr. Wilson,—"to come right here to the nearest tavern!"

"Mr. Wilson, it is *so* bold, and this tavern is so near, that they will never think of it; they will look for me on ahead, and you yourself would n't know me. Jim's master don't live in this county; he is n't known in these parts. Besides, he is given up; nobody is looking after him, and nobody will take me up from the advertisement, I think."

"But the mark in your hand?"

George drew off his glove, and showed a newly-healed scar in his hand.

"That is a parting proof of Mr. Harris' regard," he said, scornfully. "A fortnight ago, he took it into his head to give it to me, because he said he believed I should try to get away one of these days. Looks interesting, does n't it?" he said, drawing his glove on again.

"I declare, my very blood runs cold when I think of it,—your condition and your risks!" said Mr. Wilson.

"Mine has run cold a good many years, Mr. Wilson; at present, it's about up to the boiling point," said George.

"Well, my good sir," continued George, after a few moments' silence, "I saw you knew me; I thought I'd just have this talk with you, lest your surprised looks should bring me out. I leave early to-morrow morning, before daylight; by tomorrow night I hope to sleep safe in Ohio. I shall travel by daylight, stop at the best hotels, go to the dinner-tables with the lords of the land. So, good-by, sir; if you hear that I'm taken, you may know that I'm dead!"

George stood up like a rock, and put out his hand with the air of a prince. The friendly little old man shook it heartily, and after a little shower of caution, he took his umbrella, and fumbled his way out of the room.

George stood thoughtfully looking at the door, as the old man closed it. A thought seemed to flash across his mind. He hastily stepped to it, and opening it, said,

"Mr. Wilson, one word more."

The old gentleman entered again, and George, as before, locked the door, and then stood for a few moments looking on the floor, irresolutely. At last, raising his head with a sudden effort—

"Mr. Wilson, you have shown yourself a Christian in your treatment of me,—I want to ask one last deed of Christian kindness of you."

"Well, George."

"Well, sir,—what you said was true. I *am* running a dreadful risk. There is n't, on earth, a living soul to care if I die," he added, drawing his breath hard, and speaking with a great effort,—"I shall be kicked out and buried like a dog, and nobody'll think of it a day after,—*only my poor wife!* Poor soul! she'll mourn and grieve; and if you'd only contrive, Mr. Wilson, to send this little pin to her. She gave it to me for a Christmas present, poor child! Give it to her, and tell her I loved her to the last. Will you? *Will* you?" he added, earnestly.

"Yes, certainly—poor fellow!" said the old gentleman, taking the pin, with watery eyes, and a melancholy quiver in his voice.

"Tell her one thing," said George; "it's my last wish, if she *can* get to Canada, to go there. No matter how kind her mistress is,—no matter how much she loves her home; beg her not to go back,—for slavery always ends in misery. Tell her to bring up our boy a free man, and then he won't suffer as I have. Tell her this, Mr. Wilson, will you?"

"Yes, George, I'll tell her; but I trust you won't die; take heart,—you're a brave fellow. Trust in the Lord, George. I wish in my heart you were safe through, though,—that's what I do."

"*Is* there a God to trust in?" said George, in such a tone of utter despair as arrested the old gentleman's words. "O, I've seen things all my life that have made me feel that there can't be a God. You Christians don't know how these things look to us. There's a God for you, but is there any for us?"

"O, now, don't—don't, my boy!" said the old man, almost sobbing as he spoke; "don't feel so! There is—there is; clouds and darkness are around about him, but righteousness and judgment are the habitation of his throne. There's a *God,* George,—believe it; trust in Him, and I'm sure He'll help you. Everything will be set right,—if not in this life, in another."

The real piety and benevolence of the simple old man invested him with a temporary dignity and authority, as he spoke. George stopped his distracted walk up and down the room, stood thoughtfully a moment, and then said, quietly,

"Thank you for saying that, my good friend; I'll *think of that.*"

XIII The Quaker Settlement

A quiet scene now rises before us. A large, roomy, neatly-painted kitchen, its yellow floor glossy and smooth, and without a particle of dust; a neat, well-blacked cooking-stove; rows of shining tin, suggestive of unmentionable good things to the appetite; glossy green wood chairs, old and firm; a small flag-bottomed rocking-chair, with a patch-work cushion in it, neatly contrived out of small pieces of different colored woollen goods, and a larger sized one, motherly and old, whose wide arms breathed hospitable invitation, seconded by the solicitation of its feather cushions,—a real comfortable, persuasive old chair, and worth, in the way of honest, homely enjoyment, a dozen of your plush or brochetelle drawing-room gentry; and in the chair, gently swaying back and forward, her eyes bent on some fine sewing, sat our old friend Eliza. Yes, there she is, paler and thinner than in her Kentucky home, with a world of quiet sorrow lying under the shadow of her long eyelashes, and marking the outline of her gentle mouth! It was plain to see how old and firm the girlish heart was grown under the discipline of heavy sorrow; and when, anon, her large dark eye was raised to follow the gambols of her little Harry, who was sporting, like some tropical butterfly, hither and thither over the floor, she showed a depth of firmness and steady resolve that was never there in her earlier and happier days.

By her side sat a woman with a bright tin pan in her lap, into which she was carefully sorting some dried peaches. She might be fifty-five or sixty; but hers was one of those faces that time seems to touch only to brighten and adorn. The snowy lisse crape cap, made after the strait Quaker pattern,—the plain white muslin handkerchief, lying in placid folds across her bosom,—the drab shawl and dress,—showed at once the community to which she belonged. Her face was round and rosy, with a healthful downy softness, suggestive of a ripe peach. Her hair, partially silvered by age, was parted smoothly back from a high placid forehead, on which time had written no inscription, except peace on earth, good will to men, and beneath shone a large pair of clear, honest, loving brown eyes; you only needed to look straight into them, to feel that you saw to the bottom of a heart as good and true as ever throbbed in woman's bosom. So much has been said and sung of beautiful young girls, why don't somebody wake up to the beauty of old women? If any want to get up an inspiration under this head, we refer them to our good friend Rachel Halliday, just as she sits there in her little rocking-chair. It had a turn for quacking and squeaking,—that chair had,—either from having taken cold in early life, or from some asthmatic affection, or perhaps from nervous derangement; but, as she gently swung backward and forward, the chair kept up a kind of subdued "creechy crawchy," that would have been intolerable in any other chair. But old Simeon Halliday often declared it was as good as any music to him, and the children all avowed that they would n't miss of hearing mother's chair for anything in the world. For why? for twenty years or more, nothing but loving words, and gentle moralities, and motherly loving kindness, had come from that chair;—head-aches and heart-aches innumerable had been cured there,—difficulties spiritual and temporal solved there,—all by one good, loving woman, God bless her!

"And so thee still thinks of going to Canada, Eliza?" she said, as she was quietly looking over her peaches.

"Yes, ma'am," said Eliza, firmly. "I must go onward. I dare not stop."

"And what'll thee do, when thee gets there? Thee must think about that, my daughter."

"My daughter" came naturally from the lips of Rachel Halliday; for hers was just the face and form that made "mother" seem the most natural word in the world.

Eliza's hands trembled, and some tears fell on her fine work; but she answered, firmly,

"I shall do—anything I can find. I hope I can find something."

"Thee knows thee can stay here, as long as thee pleases," said Rachel.

"O, thank you," said Eliza, "but"—she pointed to Harry—"I can't sleep nights; I can't rest. Last night I dreamed I saw that man coming into the yard," she said, shuddering.

"Poor child!" said Rachel, wiping her eyes; "but thee must n't feel so. The Lord hath ordered it so that never hath a fugitive been stolen from our village. I trust thine will not be the first."

The door here opened, and a little short, round, pincushiony woman stood at the door, with a cheery, blooming face, like a ripe apple. She was dressed, like Rachel, in sober gray, with the muslin folded neatly across her round, plump little chest.

"Ruth Stedman," said Rachel, coming joyfully forward; "how is thee, Ruth?" she said, heartily taking both her hands.

"Nicely," said Ruth, taking off her little drab bonnet, and dusting it with her handkerchief, displaying, as she did so, a round little head, on which the Quaker cap sat with a sort of jaunty air, despite all the stroking and patting of the small fat hands, which were busily applied to arranging it. Certain stray locks of decidedly curly hair, too, had escaped here and there, and had to be coaxed and cajoled into their place again; and then the new comer, who might have been five-and-twenty, turned from the small looking-glass, before which she had been making these arrangements, and looked well pleased,—as most people who looked at her might have been,—for she was decidedly a wholesome, whole-hearted, chirruping little woman, as ever gladdened man's heart withal.

"Ruth, this friend is Eliza Harris; and this is the little boy I told thee of."

"I am glad to see thee, Eliza,—very," said Ruth, shaking hands, as if Eliza were an old friend she had long been expecting; "and this is thy dear boy,—I brought a cake for him," she said, holding out a little heart to the boy, who came up, gazing through his curls, and accepted it shyly.

"Where's thy baby, Ruth?" said Rachel.

"O, he's coming; but thy Mary caught him as I came in, and ran off with him to the barn, to show him to the children."

At this moment, the door opened, and Mary, an honest, rosy-looking girl, with large brown eyes, like her mother's, came in with the baby.

"Ah! ha!" said Rachel, coming up, and taking the great, white, fat fellow in her arms; "how good he looks, and how he does grow!"

"To be sure, he does," said little bustling Ruth, as she took the child, and began taking off a little blue silk hood, and various layers and wrappers of outer garments; and having given a twitch here, and a pull there, and variously adjusted and arranged him, and kissed him heartily, she set him on the floor to collect his thoughts. Baby seemed quite used to this mode of proceeding, for he put his thumb in his mouth (as if it were quite a thing of course), and seemed soon absorbed in his own reflections, while the mother seated herself, and taking out a long stocking of mixed blue and white yarn, began to knit with briskness.

"Mary, thee 'd better fill the kettle, had n't thee?" gently suggested the mother.

Mary took the kettle to the well, and soon reäppearing, placed it over the stove, where it was soon purring and steaming, a sort of censer of hospitality and good cheer. The peaches, moreover, in obedience to a few gentle whispers from Rachel, were soon deposited, by the same hand, in a stew-pan over the fire.

Rachel now took down a snowy moulding-board, and, tying on an apron, proceeded quietly to making up some biscuits, first saying to Mary,—"Mary, had n't thee better tell John to get a chicken ready?" and Mary disappeared accordingly.

"And how is Abigail Peters?" said Rachel, as she went on with her biscuits.

"O, she's better," said Ruth; "I was in, this morning; made the bed, tidied up the house. Leah Hills went in, this afternoon, and baked bread and pies enough to last some days; and I engaged to go back to get her up, this evening."

"I will go in to-morrow, and do any cleaning there may be, and look over the mending," said Rachel.

"Ah! that is well," said Ruth. "I've heard," she added, "that Hannah Stanwood is sick. John was up there, last night,—I must go there to-morrow."

"John can come in here to his meals, if thee needs to stay all day," suggested Rachel.

"Thank thee, Rachel; will see, to-morrow; but, here comes Simeon."

Simeon Halliday, a tall, straight, muscular man, in drab coat and pantaloons, and broad-brimmed hat, now entered.

"How is thee, Ruth?" he said, warmly, as he spread his broad open hand for her little fat palm; "and how is John?"

"O! John is well, and all the rest of our folks," said Ruth, cheerily.

"Any news, father?" said Rachel, as she was putting her biscuits into the oven.

"Peter Stebbins told me that they should be along to-night, with *friends,*" said Simeon, significantly, as he was washing his hands at a neat sink, in a little back porch.

"Indeed!" said Rachel, looking thoughtfully, and glancing at Eliza.

"Did thee say thy name was Harris?" said Simeon to Eliza, as he reëntered.

Rachel glanced quickly at her husband, as Eliza tremulously answered "yes;" her fears, ever uppermost, suggesting that possibly there might be advertisements out for her.

"Mother!" said Simeon, standing in the porch, and calling Rachel out.

"What does thee want, father?" said Rachel, rubbing her floury hands, as she went into the porch.

"This child's husband is in the settlement, and will be here to-night," said Simeon.

"Now, thee does n't say that, father?" said Rachel, all her face radiant with joy.

"It's really true. Peter was down yesterday, with the wagon, to the other stand, and there he found an old woman and two men; and one said his name was George Harris; and, from what he told of his history, I am certain who he is. He is a bright, likely fellow, too."

"Shall we tell her now?" said Simeon.

"Let's tell Ruth," said Rachel. "Here, Ruth,—come here."

Ruth laid down her knitting-work, and was in the back porch in a moment.

"Ruth, what does thee think?" said Rachel. "Father says Eliza's husband is in the last company, and will be here to-night."

A burst of joy from the little Quakeress interrupted the speech. She gave such a bound from the floor, as she clapped her little hands, that two stray curls fell from under her Quaker cap, and lay brightly on her white neckerchief.

"Hush thee, dear!" said Rachel, gently; "hush, Ruth! Tell us, shall we tell her now?"

"Now! to be sure,—this very minute. Why, now, suppose 't was my John, how should I feel? Do tell her, right off."

"Thee uses thyself only to learn how to love thy neighbor, Ruth," said Simeon, looking, with a beaming face, on Ruth.

"To be sure. Is n't it what we are made for? If I did n't love John and the baby, I should not know how to feel for her. Come, now, do tell her,—do!" and she laid her hands persuasively on Rachel's arm. "Take her into thy bed-room, there, and let me fry the chicken while thee does it."

Rachel came out into the kitchen, where Eliza was sewing, and opening the door of a small bed-room, said, gently, "Come in here with me, my daughter; I have news to tell thee."

The blood flushed in Eliza's pale face; she rose, trembling with nervous anxiety, and looked towards her boy.

"No, no," said little Ruth, darting up, and seizing her hands. "Never thee fear; it's good news, Eliza,—go in, go in!" And she gently pushed her to the door, which closed after her; and then, turning round, she caught little Harry in her arms, and began kissing him.

"Thee'll see thy father, little one. Does thee know it? Thy father is coming," she said, over and over again, as the boy looked wonderingly at her.

Meanwhile, within the door, another scene was going on. Rachel Halliday drew Eliza toward her, and said, "The Lord hath had mercy on thee, daughter; thy husband hath escaped from the house of bondage."

The blood flushed to Eliza's cheek in a sudden glow, and went back to her heart with as sudden a rush. She sat down, pale and faint.

"Have courage, child," said Rachel, laying her hand on her head. "He is among friends, who will bring him here to-night."

"To-night!" Eliza repeated, "to-night!" The words lost all meaning to her; her head was dreamy and confused; all was mist for a moment.

When she awoke, she found herself snugly tucked up on the bed, with a blanket over her, and little Ruth rubbing her hands with camphor. She opened her eyes in a state of dreamy, delicious languor, such as one has who has long been bearing a heavy load, and now feels it gone, and would rest. The tension of the nerves, which had never ceased a moment since the first hour of her flight, had given way, and a strange feeling of security and rest came over her; and, as she lay, with her large, dark eyes open, she followed, as in a quiet dream, the motions of those about her. She saw the door open into the other room; saw the supper-table, with its snowy cloth; heard the dreamy murmur of the singing tea-kettle; saw Ruth tripping backward and forward, with plates of cake and saucers of preserves, and ever and anon stopping to put a cake into Harry's hand, or pat his head, or twine his long curls round her snowy fingers. She saw the ample, motherly form of Rachel, as she ever and anon came to the bed-side, and smoothed and arranged something about the bed-clothes, and gave a tuck here and there, by way of expressing her good-will; and was conscious of a kind of sunshine beaming down upon her from her large, clear, brown eyes. She saw Ruth's husband come in,—saw her fly up to him, and commence whispering very earnestly, ever and anon, with impressive gesture, pointing her little finger toward the room. She saw her, with the baby in her arms, sitting down to tea; she saw them all at table, and little Harry in a high chair, under the shadow of Rachel's ample wing; there were low murmurs of talk, gentle tinkling of tea-spoons, and musical clatter of cups and saucers, and all mingled in a delightful dream of rest; and Eliza slept, as she had not slept before, since the fearful midnight hour when she had taken her child and fled through the frosty star-light.

She dreamed of a beautiful country,—a land, it seemed to her, of rest,—green shores, pleasant islands, and beautifully glittering water; and there, in a house which kind voices told her was a home, she saw her boy playing, a free and happy child. She heard her husband's footsteps; she felt him coming nearer; his arms were around her, his tears falling on her face, and she awoke! It was no dream. The daylight had long faded; her child lay calmly sleeping by her side; a candle was burning dimly on the stand, and her husband was sobbing by her pillow.

The next morning was a cheerful one at the Quaker house. "Mother" was up betimes, and surrounded by busy girls and boys, whom we had scarce time to introduce to our readers yesterday, and who all moved obediently to Rachel's gentle "Thee had better," or more gentle "Had n't thee better?" in the work of getting breakfast; for a breakfast in the luxurious valleys of Indiana is a thing complicated and multiform, and, like picking up the rose-leaves and trimming the bushes in Paradise, asking other hands than those of the original mother. While, therefore, John ran to the spring for fresh water, and Simeon the second sifted meal for corn-cakes, and Mary ground coffee, Rachel moved gently and quietly about, making biscuits, cutting up chicken, and diffusing a sort of sunny radiance over the whole proceeding generally. If there was any danger of friction or collision from the ill-regulated zeal of so many young operators, her gentle "Come! come!" or "I would n't, now," was quite sufficient to allay the difficulty. Bards have written of the cestus of Venus, that turned the heads of all the world in successive generations. We had rather, for our part, have the cestus of Rachel Halliday, that kept heads from being turned, and made everything go on harmoniously. We think it is more suited to our modern days, decidedly.

While all other preparations were going on, Simeon the elder stood in his shirt-sleeves before a little looking-glass in the corner, engaged in the anti-patriarchal operation of shaving. Everything went on so sociably, so quietly, so harmoniously, in the great kitchen,—it seemed so pleasant to every one to do just what they were doing, there was such an atmosphere of mutual confidence and good fellowship everywhere,—even the knives and forks had a social clatter as they went on to the table; and the chicken and ham had a cheerful and joyous fizzle in the pan, as if they rather enjoyed being cooked than otherwise;—and when George and Eliza and little Harry came out, they met such a hearty, rejoicing welcome, no wonder it seemed to them like a dream.

At last, they were all seated at breakfast, while Mary stood at the stove, baking griddle-cakes, which, as they gained the true exact golden-brown tint of perfection, were transferred quite handily to the table.

Rachel never looked so truly and benignly happy as at the head of her table. There was so much motherliness and full-heartedness even in the way she passed a plate of cakes or poured a cup of coffee, that it seemed to put a spirit into the food and drink she offered.

It was the first time that ever George had sat down on equal terms at any white man's table; and he sat down, at first, with some constraint and awkwardness; but they all exhaled and went off like fog, in the genial morning rays of this simple, overflowing kindness.

This, indeed, was a home,—*home,*—a word that George had never yet known a meaning for; and a belief in God, and trust in his providence, began to encircle his heart, as, with a golden cloud of protection and confidence, dark, misanthropic, pining, atheistic doubts, and fierce despair, melted away before the light of a living Gospel, breathed in living faces, preached by a thousand unconscious acts of love and good will, which, like the cup of cold water given in the name of a disciple, shall never lose their reward.

"Father, what if thee should get found out again?" said Simeon second, as he buttered his cake.

"I should pay my fine," said Simeon, quietly.

"But what if they put thee in prison?"

"Could n't thee and mother manage the farm?" said Simeon, smiling.

"Mother can do almost everything," said the boy. "But is n't it a shame to make such laws?"

"Thee must n't speak evil of thy rulers, Simeon," said his father, gravely. "The Lord only gives us our worldly goods that we may do justice and mercy; if our rulers require a price of us for it, we must deliver it up."

"Well, I hate those old slaveholders!" said the boy, who felt as unchristian as became any modern reformer.

"I am surprised at thee, son," said Simeon; "thy mother never taught thee so. I would do even the same for the slaveholder as for the slave, if the Lord brought him to my door in affliction."

Simeon second blushed scarlet; but his mother only smiled, and said, "Simeon is my good boy; he will grow older, by and by, and then he will be like his father."

"I hope, my good sir, that you are not exposed to any difficulty on our account," said George, anxiously.

"Fear nothing, George, for therefore are we sent into the world. If we would not meet trouble for a good cause, we were not worthy of our name."

"But, for *me,*" said George, "I could not bear it."

"Fear not, then, friend George; it is not for thee, but for God and man, we do it," said Simeon. "And now thou must lie by quietly this day, and to-night, at ten o'clock, Phineas Fletcher will carry thee onward to the next stand,—thee and the rest of thy company. The pursuers are hard after thee; we must not delay."

"If that is the case, why wait till evening?" said George.

"Thou art safe here by daylight, for every one in the settlement is a Friend, and all are watching. It has been found safer to travel by night."

XIV Evangeline

[Uncle Tom is taken into custody by Haley, the slave trader. Young George Shelby, who has taught Uncle Tom to read and write, is devastated by the sale and vows to get Tom back some day. Haley and Tom board a boat for New Orleans, where Haley plans to sell Tom.]

"A young star! which shone
O'er life—too sweet an image for such glass!
A lovely being, scarcely formed or moulded;
A rose with all its sweetest leaves yet folded."

The Mississippi! How, as by an enchanted wand, have its scenes been changed, since Chateaubriand wrote his prose-poetic description of it, as a river of mighty, unbroken solitudes, rolling amid undreamed wonders of vegetable and animal existence.

But, as in an hour, this river of dreams and wild romance has emerged to a reality scarcely less visionary and splendid. What other river of the world bears on its bosom to the ocean the wealth and enterprise of such another country?—a country whose products embrace all between the tropics and the poles! Those turbid waters, hurrying, foaming, tearing along, an apt resemblance of that headlong tide of business which is poured along its wave by a race more vehement and energetic than any the old world ever saw. Ah! would that they did not also bear along a more fearful freight,—the tears of the oppressed, the sighs of the helpless, the bitter prayers of poor, ignorant hearts to an unknown God—unknown, unseen and silent, but who will yet "come out of his place to save all the poor of the earth!"

The slanting light of the setting sun quivers on the sea-like expanse of the river; the shivery canes, and the tall, dark cypress, hung with wreaths of dark, funereal moss, glow in the golden ray, as the heavily-laden steamboat marches onward.

Piled with cotton-bales, from many a plantation, up over deck and sides, till she seems in the distance a square, massive block of gray, she moves heavily onward to the nearing mart. We must look some time among its crowded decks before we shall find again our humble friend Tom. High on the upper deck, in a little nook among the everywhere predominant cotton-bales, at last we may find him.

Partly from confidence inspired by Mr. Shelby's representations, and partly from the remarkably inoffensive and quiet character of the man, Tom had insensibly won his way far into the confidence even of such as man as Haley.

At first he had watched him narrowly through the day, and never allowed him to sleep at night unfettered; but the uncomplaining patience and apparent contentment of Tom's manner led him gradually to discontinue these restraints, and for some time Tom had enjoyed a sort of parole of honor, being permitted to come and go freely where he pleased on the boat.

Ever quiet and obliging, and more than ready to lend a hand in every emergency which occurred among the workmen below, he had won the good opinion of all the hands, and spent many hours in helping them with as hearty a good will as ever he worked on a Kentucky farm.

When there seemed to be nothing for him to do, he would climb to a nook among the cotton-bales of the upper deck, and busy himself in studying over his Bible,—and it is there we see him now.

For a hundred or more miles above New Orleans, the river is higher than the surrounding country, and rolls its tremendous volume between massive levees twenty feet in height. The traveller from the deck of the steamer, as from some floating castle top, overlooks the whole country for miles and miles around. Tom, therefore, had spread out full before him, in plantation after plantation, a map of the life to which he was approaching.

He saw the distant slaves at their toil; he saw afar their villages of huts gleaming out in long rows on many a plantation, distant from the stately mansions and pleasure-grounds of the master;—and as the moving picture passed on, his poor, foolish heart would be turning backward to the Kentucky farm, with its old shadowy beeches,—to the master's house, with its wide, cool halls, and, near by, the little cabin, overgrown with the multiflora and bignonia. There he seemed to see familiar faces of comrades, who had grown up with him from infancy; he saw his busy wife, bustling in her preparations for his evening meals; he heard the merry laugh of his boys at their play, and the chirrup of the baby at his knee; and then, with a start, all faded, and he saw again the cane-brakes and cypresses and gliding plantations, and heard again the creaking and groaning of the machinery, all telling him too plainly that all that phase of life had gone by forever.

In such a case, you write to your wife, and send messages to your children; but

Tom could not write,—the mail for him had no existence, and the gulf of separation was unbridged by even a friendly word or signal.

Is it strange, then, that some tears fall on the pages of his Bible, as he lays it on the cotton-bale, and, with patient finger, threading his slow way from word to word, traces out its promises? Having learned late in life, Tom was but a slow reader, and passed on laboriously from verse to verse. Fortunate for him was it that the book he was intent on was one which slow reading cannot injure,—nay, one whose words, like ingots of gold, seem often to need to be weighed separately, that the mind may take in their priceless value. Let us follow him a moment, as, pointing to each word, and pronouncing each half aloud, he reads,

"Let—not—your—heart—be—troubled. In—my—Father's—house—are—many—mansions. I—go—to—prepare—a—place—for—you."

Cicero, when he buried his darling and only daughter, had a heart as full of honest grief as poor Tom's,—perhaps no fuller, for both were only men;—but Cicero could pause over no such sublime words of hope, and look to no such future reünion; and if he *had* seen them, ten to one he would not have believed,—he must fill his head first with a thousand questions of authenticity of manuscript, and correctness of translation. But, to poor Tom, there it lay, just what he needed, so evidently true and divine that the possibility of a question never entered his simple head. It must be true; for, if not true, how could he live?

As for Tom's Bible, though it had no annotations and helps in margin from learned commentators, still it had been embellished with certain way-marks and guide-boards of Tom's own invention, and which helped him more than the most learned expositions could have done. It had been his custom to get the Bible read to him by his master's children, in particular by young Master George; and, as they read, he would designate, by bold, strong marks and dashes, with pen and ink, the passages which more particularly gratified his ear or affected his heart. His Bible was thus marked through, from one end to the other, with a variety of styles and designations; so he could in a moment seize upon his favorite passages, without the labor of spelling out what lay between them;—and while it lay there before him, every passage breathing of some old home scene, and recalling some past enjoyment, his Bible seemed to him all of this life that remained, as well as the promise of a future one.

Among the passengers on the boat was a young gentleman of fortune and family, resident in New Orleans, who bore the name of St. Clare. He had with him a daughter between five and six years of age, together with a lady who seemed to claim relationship to both, and to have the little one especially under her charge.

Tom had often caught glimpses of this little girl,—for she was one of those busy, tripping creatures, that can be no more contained in one place than a sunbeam or a summer breeze,—nor was she one that, once seen, could be easily forgotten.

Her form was the perfection of childish beauty, without its usual chubbiness and squareness of outline. There was about it an undulating and aërial grace, such as one might dream of for some mythic and allegorical being. Her face was remarkable less for its perfect beauty of feature than for a singular and dreamy earnestness of expression, which made the ideal start when they looked at her, and by which the dullest and most literal were impressed, without exactly knowing why. The shape of her head and the turn of her neck and bust was peculiarly noble, and the long golden-brown hair that floated like a cloud around it, the deep spiritual gravity of her violet blue eyes, shaded by heavy fringes of golden brown,—all marked her out from other children, and made every one turn and look after her, as she glided hither and thither on the boat. Nevertheless, the little one was not what you would have called either a grave child or a sad one. On the contrary, an airy and innocent playfulness seemed to flicker like the shadow of summer leaves over her childish face, and around her buoyant figure. She was always in motion, always with a half smile on her rosy mouth, flying hither and thither, with an undulating and cloud-like tread, singing to herself as she moved as in a happy dream. Her father and female guardian were incessantly busy in pursuit of her,—but, when caught, she melted from them again like a summer cloud; and as no word of chiding or reproof ever fell on her ear for whatever she chose to do, she pursued her own way all over the boat. Always dressed in white, she seemed to move like a shadow through all sorts of places, without contracting spot or stain; and there was not a corner or nook, above or below, where those fairy footsteps had not glided, and that visionary golden head, with its deep blue eyes, fleeted along.

The fireman, as he looked up from his sweaty toil, sometimes found those eyes looking wonderingly into the raging depths of the furnace, and fearfully and pityingly at him, as if she thought him in some dreadful danger. Anon the steersman at the wheel paused and smiled, as the picture-like head gleamed through the window of the round house, and in a moment was gone again. A thousand times a day rough voices blessed her, and smiles of unwonted softness stole over hard faces, as she passed; and when she tripped fearlessly over dangerous places, rough, sooty hands were stretched involuntarily out to save her, and smooth her path.

Tom, who had the soft, impressible nature of his kindly race, ever yearning toward the simple and childlike, watched the little creature with daily increasing interest. To him she seemed something almost divine; and whenever her golden head and deep blue eyes peered out upon him from behind some dusky cotton-bale, or looked down upon him over some ridge of packages, he half believed that he saw one of the angels stepped out of his New Testament.

Often and often she walked mournfully round the place where Haley's gang of men and women sat in their chains. She would glide in among them, and look at them with an air of perplexed and sorrowful earnestness; and sometimes she would lift their chains with her slender hands, and then sigh wofully, as she glided away. Several times she appeared suddenly among them, with her hands full of candy, nuts, and oranges, which she would distribute joyfully to them, and then be gone again.

Tom watched the little lady a great deal, before he ventured on any overtures towards acquaintanceship. He knew an abundance of simple acts to propitiate and invite the approaches of the little people, and he resolved to play his part right skilfully. He could cut cunning little baskets out of cherry-stones, could make grotesque faces on hickory-nuts, or odd-jumping figures out of elder-pith, and he was a very Pan in the manufacture of whistles of all sizes and sorts. His pockets were full of miscellaneous articles of attraction, which he had hoarded in days of old for his master's children, and which he now produced, with commendable prudence and economy, one by one, as overtures for acquaintance and friendship.

The little one was shy, for all her busy interest in everything going on, and it was not easy to tame her. For a while, she would perch like a canary-bird on some box or package near Tom, while busy in the little arts afore-named, and take from him, with a kind of grave bashfulness, the little articles he offered. But at last they got on quite confidential terms.

"What's little missy's name?" said Tom, at last, when he thought matters were ripe to push such an inquiry.

"Evangeline St. Clare," said the little one, "though papa and everybody else call me Eva. Now, what's your name?"

"My name 's Tom; the little chil'en used to call me Uncle Tom, way back thar in Kentuck."

"Then I mean to call you Uncle Tom, because, you see, I like you," said Eva. "So, Uncle Tom, where are you going?"

"I don't know, Miss Eva."

"Don't know?" said Eva.

"No. I am going to be sold to somebody. I don't know who."

"My papa can buy you," said Eva, quickly; "and if he buys you, you will have good times. I mean to ask him to, this very day."

"Thank you, my little lady," said Tom.

The boat here stopped at a small landing to take in wood, and Eva, hearing her father's voice, bounded nimbly away. Tom rose up, and went forward to offer his service in wooding, and soon was busy among the hands.

Eva and her father were standing together by the railings to see the boat start from the landing-place, the wheel had made two or three revolutions in the water, when, by some sudden movement, the little one suddenly lost her balance, and fell sheer over the side of the boat into the water. Her father, scarce knowing what he did, was plunging in after her, but was held back by some behind him, who saw that more efficient aid had followed his child.

Tom was standing just under her on the lower deck, as she fell. He saw her strike the water, and sink, and was after her in a moment. A broad-chested, strong-armed fellow, it was nothing for him to keep afloat in the water, till, in a moment or two, the child rose to the surface, and he caught her in his arms, and, swimming with her to the boat-side, handed her up, all dripping, to the grasp of hundreds of hands, which, as if they had all belonged to one man, were stretched eagerly out to receive her. A few moments more, and her father bore her, dripping and senseless, to the ladies' cabin, where, as is usual in cases of the kind, there ensued a very well-meaning and kind-hearted strife among the female occupants generally, as to who should do the most things to make a disturbance, and to hinder her recovery in every way possible.

It was a sultry, close day, the next day, as the steamer drew near to New Orleans. A general bustle of expectation and preparation was spread through the boat; in the cabin, one and another were gathering their things together, and arranging them, preparatory to going ashore. The steward and chambermaid, and all, were busily engaged in cleaning, furbishing, and arranging the splendid boat, preparatory to a grand entree.

On the lower deck sat our friend Tom, with his arms folded, and anxiously, from time to time, turning his eyes towards a group on the other side of the boat.

There stood the fair Evangeline, a little paler than the day before, but otherwise exhibiting no traces of the accident which had befallen her. A graceful, elegantly-formed young man stood by her, carelessly leaning one elbow on a bale of cotton, while a large pocket-book lay open before him. It was quite evident, at a glance, that the gentleman was Eva's father. There was the same noble cast of head, the same large blue eyes, the same golden-brown hair; yet the expression was wholly different. In the large, clear blue eyes, though in form and color exactly similar, there was wanting that misty, dreamy depth of expression; all was clear, bold, and bright, but with a light wholly of this world: the beautifully cut mouth had a proud and somewhat sarcastic expression, while an air of free-and-easy superiority sat not ungracefully in every turn and movement of his fine form. He was listening, with a good-humored, negligent air, half comic, half contemptuous, to Haley, who was very volubly expatiating on the quality of the article for which they were bargaining.

"All the moral and Christian virtues bound in black morocco, complete!" he said, when Haley had finished. "Well, now, my good fellow, what's the damage, as they say in Kentucky; in short, what's to be paid out for this business? How much are you going to cheat me, now? Out with it!"

"Wal," said Haley, "if I should say thirteen hundred dollars for that ar fellow, I should n't but just save myself; I should n't, now, re'ly."

"Poor fellow!" said the young man, fixing his keen, mocking blue eye on him; "but I suppose you'd let me have him for that, out of a particular regard for me."

"Well, the young lady here seems to be sot on him, and nat'lly enough."

"O! certainly, there's a call on your benevolence, my friend. Now, as a matter of Christian charity, how cheap could you afford to let him go, to oblige a young lady that's particular sot on him?"

"Wal, now, just think on't," said the trader; "just look at them limbs,—broad-chested, strong as a horse. Look at his head; them high forrads allays shows calculatin niggers, that'll do any kind o' thing. I've marked that ar. Now, a nigger of that ar heft and build is worth considerable, just, as you may say, for his body, supposin he's stupid; but come to put in his calculatin faculties, and them which I can show he has oncommon, why, of course, it makes him come higher. Why, that ar fellow managed his master's whole farm. He has a strornary talent for business."

"Bad, bad, very bad; knows altogether too much!" said the young man, with the same mocking smile playing about his mouth. "Never will do, in the world. Your smart fellows are always running off, stealing horses, and raising the devil generally. I think you'll have to take off a couple of hundred for his smartness."

"Wal, there might be something in that ar, if it warnt for his character; but I can show recommends from his master and others, to prove he is one of your real pious,—the most humble, prayin, pious crittur ye ever did see. Why, he's been called a preacher in them parts he came from."

"And I might use him for a family chaplain, possibly," added the young man, dryly. "That 's quite an idea. Religion is a remarkably scarce article at our house."

"You're joking, now."

"How do you know I am? Did n't you just warrant him for a preacher? Has he been examined by any synod or council? Come, hand over your papers."

If the trader had not been sure, by a certain good-humored twinkle in the large blue eye, that all this banter was sure, in the long run, to turn out a cash concern, he might have been somewhat out of patience; as it was, he laid down a greasy pocket-book on the cotton-bales, and began anxiously studying over certain papers in it, the young man standing by, the while, looking down on him with an air of careless, easy drollery.

"Papa, do buy him! it's no matter what you pay," whispered Eva, softly, getting up on a package, and putting her arm around her father's neck. "You have money enough, I know. I want him."

"What for, pussy? Are you going to use him for a rattlebox, or a rocking-horse, or what?"

"I want to make him happy."

"An original reason, certainly."

Here the trader handed up a certificate, signed by Mr. Shelby, which the young man took with the tips of his long fingers, and glanced over carelessly.

"A gentlemanly hand," he said, "and well spelt, too. Well, now, but I'm not sure, after all, about this religion," said he, the old wicked expression returning to his eye; "the country is almost ruined with pious white people: such pious politicians as we have just before elections,—such pious goings on in all departments of church and state, that a fellow does not know who'll cheat him next. I don't know, either, about religion's being up in the market, just now. I have not looked in the papers lately, to see how it sells. How many hundred dollars, now, do you put on for this religion?"

"You like to be a jokin, now," said the trader; "but, then, there 's *sense* under all that ar. I know there's differences in religion. Some kinds is mis'rable: there's your meetin pious; there's your singin, roarin pious; them ar an't no account, in black or white;—but these rayly is; and I've seen it in niggers as often as any, your rail softly, quiet, stiddy, honest, pious, that the hull world could n't tempt 'em to do nothing that they thinks is wrong; and ye see in this letter what Tom's old master says about him."

"Now," said the young man, stooping gravely over his book of bills, "if you can assure me that I really can buy *this* kind of pious, and that it will be set down to my account in the book up above, as something belonging to me, I would n't care if I did go a little extra for it. How d'ye say?"

"Wal, raily, I can't do that," said the trader. "I'm a thinkin that every man 'll have to hang on his own hook, in them ar quarters."

"Rather hard on a fellow that pays extra on religion, and can't trade with it in the state where he wants it most, an't it, now?" said the young man, who had been making out a roll of bills while he was speaking. "There, count your money, old boy!" he added, as he handed the roll to the trader.

"All right," said Haley, his face beaming with delight; and pulling out an old inkhorn, he proceeded to fill out a bill of sale, which, in a few moments, he handed to the young man.

"I wonder, now, if I was divided up and inventoried," said the latter, as he ran over the paper, "how much I might bring. Say so much for the shape of my head, so much for a high forehead, so much for arms, and hands, and legs, and then so much for education, learning, talent, honesty, religion! Bless me! there would be small charge on that last, I'm thinking. But come, Eva," he said; and taking the hand of his daughter, he stepped across the boat, and carelessly putting the tip of his finger under Tom's chin, said, good-humoredly, "Look up, Tom, and see how you like your new master."

Tom looked up. It was not in nature to look into that gay, young, handsome face, without a feeling of pleasure; and Tom felt the tears start in his eyes as he said, heartily, "God bless you, Mas'r!"

"Well, I hope he will. What's your name? Tom? Quite as likely to do it for your asking as mine, from all accounts. Can you drive horses, Tom?"

"I've been allays used to horses," said Tom. "Mas'r Shelby raised heaps on 'em."

"Well, I think I shall put you in coachy, on condition that you won't be drunk more than once a week, unless in cases of emergency, Tom."

Tom looked surprised, and rather hurt, and said, "I never drink, Mas'r."

"I've heard that story before, Tom; but then we'll see. It will be a special accommodation to all concerned, if you don't. Never mind, my boy," he added, good-humoredly, seeing Tom still looked grave; "I don't doubt you mean to do well."

"I sartin do, Mas'r," said Tom.

"And you shall have good times," said Eva. "Papa is very good to everybody, only he always will laugh at them."

"Papa is much obliged to you for his recommendation," said St. Clare, laughing, as he turned on his heel and walked away.

XXX The Slave Warehouse

[Tom is happy with the St. Clares, though he misses his family and his home. When Eva grows sick and dies, her family and the servants are devastated, especially her father and Tom. St. Clare seriously considers Eva's deathbed request to free his slaves, but before he can do so, he is killed trying to stop two drunken men from fighting. St. Clare's widow decides that freeing the slaves would be wrong, so she sells several, among them Tom, to pay her late husband's debts.]

A slave warehouse! Perhaps some of my readers conjure up horrible visions of such a place. They fancy some foul, obscure den, some horrible *Tartarus "informis, ingens, cui lumen ademptum."*[1] But no, innocent friend; in these days men have learned the art of sinning expertly and genteelly, so as not to shock the eyes and senses of respectable society. Human property is high in the market; and is, therefore, well fed, well cleaned, tended, and looked after, that it may come to sale sleek, and strong, and shining. A slave-warehouse in New Orleans is a house externally not much unlike many others, kept with neatness; and where every day you may see arranged, under a sort of shed along the outside, rows of men and women, who stand there as a sign of the property sold within.

Then you shall be courteously entreated to call and examine, and shall find an abundance of husbands, wives, brothers, sisters, fathers, mothers, and young children, to be "sold separately, or in lots to suit the convenience of the purchaser;" and that soul immortal, once bought with blood and anguish by the Son of God, when the earth shook, and the rocks rent, and the graves were opened, can be sold, leased, mortgaged, exchanged for groceries or dry goods, to suit the phases of trade, or the fancy of the purchaser.

It was a day or two after the conversation between Marie and Miss Ophelia, that Tom, Adolph, and about half a dozen others of the St. Clare estate, were turned over to the loving kindness of Mr. Skeggs, the keeper of a depot on——street, to await the auction, next day.

[1]A hell "hideous, vast, deprived of light."

Tom had with him quite a sizable trunk full of clothing, as had most others of them. They were ushered, for the night, into a long room, where many other men, of all ages, sizes, and shades of complexion, were assembled, and from which roars of laughter and unthinking merriment were proceeding.

"Ah, ha! that's right. Go it, boys,—go it!" said Mr. Skeggs, the keeper. "My people are always so merry! Sambo, I see!" he said, speaking approvingly to a burly negro who was performing tricks of low buffoonery, which occasioned the shouts which Tom had heard.

As might be imagined, Tom was in no humor to join these proceedings; and, therefore, setting his trunk as far as possible from the noisy group, he sat down on it, and leaned his face against the wall.

The dealers in the human article make scrupulous and systematic efforts to promote noisy mirth among them, as a means of drowning reflection, and rendering them insensible to their condition. The whole object of the training to which the negro is put, from the time he is sold in the northern market till he arrives south, is systematically directed towards making him callous, unthinking, and brutal. The slave-dealer collects his gang in Virginia or Kentucky, and drives them to some convenient, healthy place,—often a watering place,—to be fattened. Here they are fed full daily; and, because some incline to pine, a fiddle is kept commonly going among them, and they are made to dance daily; and he who refuses to be merry—in whose soul thoughts of wife, or child, or home, are too strong for him to be gay—is marked as sullen and dangerous, and subjected to all the evils which the ill will of an utterly irresponsible and hardened man can inflict upon him. Briskness, alertness, and cheerfulness of appearance, especially before observers, are constantly enforced upon them, both by the hope of thereby getting a good master, and the fear of all that the driver may bring upon them, if they prove unsalable.

"What dat ar nigger doin here?" said Sambo, coming up to Tom, after Mr. Skeggs had left the room. Sambo was a full black, of great size, very lively, voluble, and full of trick and grimace.

"What you doin here?" said Sambo, coming up to Tom, and poking him facetiously in the side. "Meditatin', eh?"

"I am to be sold at the auction, to-morrow!" said Tom, quietly.

"Sold at auction,—haw! haw! boys, an't this yer fun? I wish't I was gwine that ar way!—tell ye, would n't I make em laugh? But how is it,—dis yer whole lot gwine to-morrow?" said Sambo, laying his hand freely on Adolph's shoulder.

"Please to let me alone!" said Adolph, fiercely, straightening himself up, with extreme disgust.

"Law, now, boys! dis yer's one o' yer white niggers,—kind o' cream color, ye know, scented!" said he, coming up to Adolph and snuffing. "O, Lor! he 'd do for a tobaccer-shop; they could keep him to scent snuff! Lor, he'd keep a whole shop agwine,—he would!"

"I say, keep off, can't you?" said Adolph, enraged.

"Lor, now, how touchy we is,—we white niggers! Look at us, now!" and Sambo gave a ludicrous imitation of Adolph's manner; "here's de airs and graces. We's been in a good family, I specs."

"Yes," said Adolph; "I had a master that could have bought you all for old truck!"

"Laws, now, only think," said Sambo, "the gentlemens that we is!"

"I belonged to the St. Clare family," said Adolph, proudly.

"Lor, you did! Be hanged if they ar' n't lucky to get shet of ye. Spects they's gwine to trade ye off with a lot o' cracked tea-pots and sich like!" said Sambo, with a provoking grin.

Adolph, enraged at this taunt, flew furiously at his adversary, swearing and striking on every side of him. The rest laughed and shouted, and the uproar brought the keeper to the door.

"What now, boys? Order,—order!" he said, coming in and flourishing a large whip.

All fled in different directions, except Sambo, who, presuming on the favor which the keeper had to him as a licensed wag, stood his ground, ducking his head with a facetious grin, whenever the master made a dive at him.

"Lor, Mas'r, 'tan't us,—we's reglar stiddy,—it's these yer new hands; they's real aggravatin',—kinder pickin' at us, all time!"

The keeper, at this, turned upon Tom and Adolph, and distributing a few kicks and cuffs without much inquiry, and leaving general orders for all to be good boys and go to sleep, left the apartment.

While this scene was going on in the men's sleeping-room, the reader may be curious to take a peep at the corresponding apartment allotted to the women. Stretched out in various attitudes over the floor, he may see numberless sleeping forms of every shade of complexion, from the purest ebony to white, and of all years, from childhood to old age, lying now asleep. Here is a fine bright girl, of ten years, whose mother was sold out yesterday, and who to-night cried herself to sleep when nobody was looking at her. Here, a worn old negress, whose thin arms and callous fingers tell of hard toil, waiting to be sold to-morrow, as a cast-off article, for what can be got for her; and some forty or fifty others, with heads variously enveloped in blankets or articles of clothing, lie stretched around them. But, in a corner, sitting apart from the rest, are two females of a more interesting appearance than common. One of these is a respectably-dressed mulatto woman between forty and fifty, with soft eyes and a gentle and pleasing physiognomy. She has on her head a high-raised turban, made of a gay red Madras handkerchief, of the first quality, and her dress is neatly fitted, and of good material, showing that she has been provided for with a careful hand. By her side, and nestling closely to her, is a young girl of fifteen,—her daughter. She is a quadroon, as may be seen from her fairer complexion, though her likeness to her mother is quite discernible. She has the same soft, dark eye, with longer lashes, and her curling hair is of a luxuriant brown. She also is dressed with great neatness, and her white, delicate hands betray very little acquaintance with servile toil. These two are to be sold to-morrow, in the same lot with the St. Clare servants; and the gentleman to whom they belong, and to whom the money for their sale is to be transmitted, is a member of a Christian church in New York, who will receive the money, and go thereafter to the sacrament of his Lord and theirs, and think no more of it.

These two, whom we shall call Susan and Emmeline, had been the personal attendants of an amiable and pious lady of New Orleans, by whom they had been carefully and piously instructed and trained. They had been taught to read and write, diligently instructed in the truths of religion, and their lot had been as happy an one as in their condition it was possible to be. But the only son of their protectress had the management of her property; and, by carelessness and extravagance involved it to a large amount, and at last failed. One of the largest creditors was the respectable firm of B. & Co., in New York. B. & Co. wrote to their lawyer in New Orleans, who attached the real estate (these two articles and a lot of plantation hands formed the most valuable part of it), and wrote word to that effect to New York. Brother B., being, as we have said, a Christian man, and a resident in a free State, felt some uneasiness on the subject. He did n't like trading in slaves and souls of men,—of course, he did n't; but, then, there were thirty thousand dollars in the case, and that was rather too much money to be lost for a principle; and so, after much considering, and asking advice from those that he knew would advise to suit him, Brother B. wrote to his lawyer to dispose of the business in the way that seemed to him the most suitable, and remit the proceeds.

The day after the letter arrived in New Orleans, Susan and Emmeline were attached, and sent to the depot to await a general auction on the following morning; and as they glimmer faintly upon us in the moonlight which steals through the grated window, we may listen to their conversation. Both are weeping, but each quietly, that the other may not hear.

"Mother, just lay your head on my lap, and see if you can't sleep a little," says the girl, trying to appear calm.

"I have n't any heart to sleep, Em; I can't; it's the last night we may be together!"

"O, mother, don't say so! perhaps we shall get sold together,—who knows?"

"If 't was anybody's else case, I should say so, too, Em," said the woman; "but I'm so feard of losin' you that I don't see anything but the danger."

"Why, mother, the man said we were both likely, and would sell well."

Susan remembered the man's looks and words. With a deadly sickness at her heart, she remembered how he had looked at Emmeline's hands, and lifted up her curly hair, and pronounced her a first-rate article. Susan had been trained as a Christian, brought up in the daily reading of the Bible, and had the same horror of her child's being sold to a life of shame that any other Christian mother might have; but she had no hope,—no protection.

"Mother, I think we might do first rate, if you could get a place as cook, and I as chamber-maid or seamstress, in some family. I dare say we shall. Let's both look as bright and lively as we can, and tell all we can do, and perhaps we shall," said Emmeline.

"I want you to brush your hair all back straight, to-morrow," said Susan.

"What for, mother? I don't look near so well, that way."

"Yes, but you'll sell better so."

"I don't see why!" said the child.

"Respectable families would be more apt to buy you, if they saw you looked plain and decent, as if you was n't trying to look handsome. I know their ways better 'n you do," said Susan.

"Well, mother, then I will."

"And, Emmeline, if we should n't ever see each other again, after to-morrow,—if I'm sold way up on a plantation somewhere, and you somewhere else,—always remember how you 've been brought up, and all Missis has told you; take your Bible with you, and your hymn-book; and if you're faithful to the Lord, he 'll be faithful to you."

So speaks the poor soul, in sore discouragement; for she knows that to-morrow any man, however vile and brutal, however godless and merciless, if he only has money to pay for her, may become owner of her daughter, body and soul; and then, how is the child to be faithful? She thinks of all this, as she holds her daughter in her arms, and wishes that she were not handsome and attractive. It seems almost an aggravation to her to remember how purely and piously, how much above the ordinary lot, she has been brought up. But she has no resort but to *pray;* and many such prayers to God have gone up from those same trim, neatly-arranged, respectable slave-prisons,—prayers which God has not forgotten, as a coming day shall show; for it is written, "Who causeth one of these little ones to offend, it were better for him that a mill-stone were hanged about his neck, and that he were drowned in the depths of the sea."

The soft, earnest, quiet moonbeam looks in fixedly, marking the bars of the grated windows on the prostrate, sleeping forms. The mother and daughter are singing together a wild and melancholy dirge, common as a funeral hymn among the slaves:

"O, where is weeping Mary?
O, where is weeping Mary?
'Rived in the goodly land.
She is dead and gone to Heaven;
She is dead and gone to Heaven;
'Rived in the goodly land."

These words, sung by voices of a peculiar and melancholy sweetness, in an air which seemed like the sighing of earthly despair after heavenly hope, floated through the dark prison rooms with a pathetic cadence, as verse after verse was breathed out:

"O, where are Paul and Silas?
O, where are Paul and Silas?
Gone to the goodly land.
They are dead and gone to Heaven;
They are dead and gone to Heaven;
'Rived in the goodly land."

Sing on, poor souls! The night is short, and the morning will part you forever!

But now it is morning, and everybody is astir; and the worthy Mr. Skeggs is busy and bright, for a lot of goods is to be fitted out for auction. There is a brisk look-out on the toilet; injunctions passed around to every one to put on their best face and be spry; and now all are arranged in a circle for a last review, before they are marched up to the Bourse.

Mr. Skeggs, with his palmetto on and his cigar in his mouth, walks around to put farewell touches on his wares.

"How's this?" he said, stepping in front of Susan and Emmeline. "Where's your curls, gal?"

The girl looked timidly at her mother, who, with the smooth adroitness common among her class, answers,

"I was telling her, last night, to put up her hair smooth and neat, and not havin' it flying about in curls; looks more respectable so."

"Bother!" said the man, peremptorily, turning to the girl; "you go right along, and curl yourself real smart!" He added, giving a crack to a rattan he held in his hand, "And be back in quick time, too!"

"You go and help her," he added, to the mother. "Them curls may make a hundred dollars difference in the sale of her."

Beneath a splendid dome were men of all nations, moving to and fro, over the marble pave. On every side of the circular area were little tribunes, or stations, for the use of speakers and auctioneers. Two of these, on opposite sides of the area, were now occupied by brilliant and talented gentlemen, enthusiastically forcing up, in English and French commingled, the bids of connoisseurs in their various wares. A third one, on the other side, still unoccupied, was surrounded by a group, waiting the moment of sale to begin. And here we may recognize the St. Clare servants,—Tom, Adolph, and others; and there, too, Susan and Emmeline, awaiting their turn with anxious and dejected faces. Various spectators, intending to purchase, or not intending, as the case might be, gathered around the group, handling, examining, and commenting on their various points and faces with the same freedom that a set of jockeys discuss the merits of a horse.

"Hulloa, Alf! what brings you here?" said a young exquisite, slapping the shoulder of a sprucely-dressed young man, who was examining Adolph through an eye-glass.

"Well, I was wanting a valet, and I heard that St. Clare's lot was going. I thought I'd just look at his—"

"Catch me ever buying any of St. Clare's people! Spoilt niggers, every one. Impudent as the devil!" said the other.

"Never fear that!" said the first. "If I get 'em, I'll soon have their airs out of them; they'll soon find that they've another kind of master to deal with than Monsieur St. Clare. 'Pon my word, I'll buy that fellow. I like the shape of him."

"You'll find it 'll take all you've got to keep him. He's deucedly extravagant!"

"Yes, but my lord will find that he *can't* be extravagant with *me.* Just let him be sent to the calaboose a few times, and thoroughly dressed down! I'll tell you if it don't bring him to a sense of his ways! O, I'll reform him, up hill and down,—you'll see. I buy him, that's flat!"

Tom had been standing wistfully examining the multitude of faces thronging around him, for one whom he would wish to call master. And if you should ever be under the necessity, sir, of selecting, out of two hundred men, one who was to become your absolute owner and disposer, you would, perhaps, realize, just as Tom did, how few there were that you would feel at all comfortable in being made over to. Tom saw abundance of men,—great, burly, gruff men; little, chirping, dried men; long-favored, lank, hard men; and every variety of stubbed-looking, common-place men, who pick up their fellow-men as one picks up chips, putting them into the fire or a basket with equal unconcern, according to their convenience; but he saw no St. Clare.

A little before the sale commenced, a short, broad, muscular man, in a checked shirt considerably open at the bosom, and pantaloons much the worse for dirt and wear, elbowed his way through the crowd, like one who is going actively into a business; and, coming up to the group, began to examine them systematically. From the moment that Tom saw him approaching, he felt an immediate and revolting horror at him, that increased as he came near. He was evidently, though short, of gigantic strength. His round, bullet head, large, light-gray eyes, with their shaggy, sandy eyebrows, and stiff, wiry, sun-burned hair, were rather unprepossessing items, it is to be confessed; his large, coarse mouth was distended with tobacco, the juice of which, from time to time, he ejected from him with great decision and explosive force; his hands were immensely large, hairy, sun-burned, freckled, and very dirty, and garnished with long nails, in a very foul condition. This man proceeded to a very free personal examination of the lot. He seized Tom by the jaw, and pulled open his mouth to inspect his teeth; made him strip up his sleeve, to show his muscle; turned him round, made him jump and spring, to show his paces.

"Where was you raised?" he added, briefly, to these investigations.

"In Kintuck, Mas'r," said Tom, looking about, as if for deliverance.

"What have you done?"

"Had care of Mas'r's farm," said Tom.

"Likely story!" said the other, shortly, as he passed on. He paused a moment before Dolph; then spitting a discharge of tobacco-juice on his well-blacked boots, and giving a contemptuous umph, he walked on. Again he stopped before Susan and Emmeline. He put out his heavy, dirty hand, and drew the girl towards him; passed it over her neck and bust, felt her arms, looked at her teeth, and then pushed her back against her mother, whose patient face showed the suffering she had been going through at every motion of the hideous stranger.

The girl was frightened, and began to cry.

"Stop that, you minx!" said the salesman; "no whimpering here,—the sale is going to begin." And accordingly the sale begun.

Adolph was knocked off, at a good sum, to the young gentleman who had previously stated his intention of buying him; and the other servants of the St. Clare lot went to various bidders.

"Now, up with you, boy! d'ye hear?" said the auctioneer to Tom.

Tom stepped upon the block, gave a few anxious looks round; all seemed mingled in a common, indistinct noise,—the clatter of the salesman crying off his qualifications in French and English, the quick fire of French and English bids; and almost in a moment came the final thump of the hammer, and the clear ring on the last syllable of the word *"dollars,"* as the auctioneer announced his price, and Tom was made over.—He had a master!

He was pushed from the block;—the short, bullet-headed man seizing him roughly by the shoulder, pushed him to one side, saying, in a harsh voice, "Stand there, *you*!"

Tom hardly realized anything; but still the bidding went on,—rattling, clattering, now French, now English. Down goes the hammer again,—Susan is sold! She goes down from the block, stops, looks wistfully back,—her daughter stretches her hands towards her. She looks with agony in the face of the man who has bought her,—a respectable middle-aged man, of benevolent countenance.

"O, Mas'r, please do buy my daughter!"

"I'd like to, but I'm afraid I can't afford it!" said the gentleman, looking, with painful interest, as the young girl mounted the block, and looked around her with a frightened and timid glance.

The blood flushes painfully in her otherwise colorless cheek, her eye has a feverish fire, and her mother groans to see that she looks more beautiful than she ever saw her before. The auctioneer sees his advantage, and expatiates volubly in mingled French and English, and bids rise in rapid succession.

"I'll do anything in reason," said the benevolent-looking gentleman, pressing in and joining with the bids. In a few moments they have run beyond his purse. He is silent; the auctioneer grows warmer; but bids gradually drop off. It lies now between an aristocratic old citizen and our bullet-headed acquaintance. The citizen bids for a few turns, contemptuously measuring his opponent; but the bullet-head has the advantage over him, both in obstinacy and concealed length of purse, and the controversy lasts but a moment; the hammer falls,—he has got the girl, body and soul, unless God help her!

Her master is Mr. Legree, who owns a cotton plantation on the Red river. She is pushed along into the same lot with Tom and two other men, and goes off, weeping as she goes.

The benevolent gentleman is sorry; but, then, the thing happens every day! One sees girls and mothers crying, at these sales, *always*! it can't be helped, &c.; and he walks off, with his acquisition, in another direction.

Two days after, the lawyer of the Christian firm of B. & Co., New York, sent on their money to them. On the reverse of that draft, so obtained, let them write these words of the great Paymaster, to whom they shall make up their account in a future day: *"When he maketh inquisition for blood, he forgetteth not the cry of the humble!"*

XL The Martyr

[Simon Legree is a cruel man who drinks heavily and treats his slaves brutally. One night, one of his slaves, Cassy, drugs him and escapes, taking with her another slave, Emmeline, and urging Tom to escape also. Tom refuses to go, and after Legree is unsuccessful in catching the two women, he decides to question Tom.]

. . . Tom heard the message with a forewarning heart; for he knew all the plan of the fugitives' escape, and the place of their present concealment;—he knew the deadly character of the man he had to deal with, and his despotic power. But he felt strong in God to meet death, rather than betray the helpless.

He sat his basket down by the row, and, looking up, said, "Into thy hands I commend my spirit! Thou hast redeemed me, oh Lord God of truth!" and then quietly yielded himself to the rough, brutal grasp with which Quimbo seized him.

"Ay, ay!" said the giant, as he dragged him along; "ye'll cotch it, now! I'll boun' Mas'r's back's up *high*! No sneaking out, now! Tell ye, ye'll get it, and no mistake! See how ye'll look, now, helpin' Mas'r's niggers to run away! See what ye'll get!"

The savage words none of them reached that ear!—a higher voice there was saying, "Fear not them that kill the body, and, after that, have no more that they can do." Nerve and bone of that poor man's body vibrated to those words, as if touched by the finger of God; and he felt the strength of a thousand souls in one. As he passed along, the trees and bushes, the huts of his servitude, the whole scene of his degradation, seemed to whirl by him as the landscape by the rushing car. His soul throbbed,—his home was in sight,—and the hour of release seemed at hand.

"Well, Tom!" said Legree, walking up, and seizing him grimly by the collar of his coat, and speaking through his teeth, in a paroxysm of determined rage, "do you know I've made up my mind to KILL you?"

"It's very likely, Mas'r," said Tom calmly.

"I *have,*" said Legree, with grim, terrible calmness, "*done—just—that—thing,* Tom, unless you'll tell me what you know about these yer gals!"

Tom stood silent.

"D'ye hear?" said Legree, stamping, with a roar like that of an incensed lion. "Speak!"

"I han't got nothing to tell, Mas'r," said Tom, with a slow, firm, deliberate utterance.

"Do you dare to tell me, ye old black Christian, ye don't *know?"* said Legree.

Tom was silent.

"Speak!" thundered Legree, striking him furiously. "Do you know anything?"

"I know, Mas'r; but I can't tell anything. *I can die!"*

Legree drew in a long breath; and, suppressing his rage, took Tom by the arm, and, approaching his face almost to his, said, in a terrible voice, "Hark 'e, Tom!—ye think, 'cause I've let you off before, I don't mean what I say; but, this time, I've *made up my mind,* and counted the cost. You've always stood it out agin' me: now, I'll *conquer ye; or kill ye!*—one or t'other. I'll count every drop of blood there is in you, and take 'em, one by one, till ye give up!"

Tom looked up to his master, and answered, "Mas'r, if you was sick, or in trouble, or dying, and I could save ye, I'd *give* ye my heart's blood; and, if taking every drop of blood in this poor old body would save your precious soul, I'd give 'em freely, as the Lord gave his for me. O, Mas'r! don't bring this great sin on your soul! It will hurt you more than 't will me! Do the worst you can, my troubles'll be over soon; but, if ye don't repent, yours won't *never* end!"

Like a strange snatch of heavenly music, heard in the lull of a tempest, this burst of feeling made a moment's blank pause. Legree stood aghast, and look at Tom; and there was such a silence, that the tick of the old clock could be heard, measuring, with silent touch, the last moments of mercy and probation to that hardened heart.

It was but a moment. There was one hesitating pause,—one irresolute, relenting thrill,—and the spirit of evil came back, with seven-fold vehemence; and Legree, foaming with rage, smote his victim to the ground.

Scenes of blood and cruelty are shocking to our ear and heart. What man has nerve to do, man has not nerve to hear. What brother-man and brother-Christian must suffer, cannot be told us, even in our secret chamber, it so harrows up the soul! And yet, oh my country! these things are done under the shadow of thy laws! O, Christ! thy church sees them, almost in silence!

But, of old, there was One whose suffering changed an instrument of torture, degradation and shame, into a symbol of glory, honor, and immortal life; and, where His spirit is, neither degrading stripes, nor blood, nor insults, can make the Christian's last struggle less than glorious.

Was he alone, that long night, whose brave, loving spirit was bearing up, in that old shed, against buffeting and brutal stripes?

Nay! There stood by him ONE,—seen by him alone,—"like unto the Son of God."

The tempter stood by him, too,—blinded by furious, despotic will,—every moment pressing him to shun that agony by the betrayal of the innocent. But the brave, true heart was firm on the Eternal Rock. Like his Master, he knew that, if he saved others, himself he could not save; nor could utmost extremity wring from him words, save of prayer and holy trust.

"He's most gone, Mas'r," said Sambo, touched, in spite of himself, by the patience of his victim.

"Pay away, till he gives up! Give it to him!—give it to him!" shouted Legree. "I'll take every drop of blood he has, unless he confesses!"

Tom opened his eyes, and looked upon his master. "Ye poor miserable critter!" he said, "there an't no more ye can do! I forgive ye, with all my soul!" and he fainted entirely away.

"I b'lieve, my soul, he's done for, finally," said Legree, stepping forward, to look at him. "Yes, he is! Well, his mouth's shut up, at last,—that's one comfort!"

Yes, Legree; but who shall shut up that voice in thy soul? that soul, past repentance, past prayer, past hope, in whom the fire that never shall be quenched is already burning!

Yet Tom was not quite gone. His wondrous words and pious prayers had struck upon the hearts of the imbruted blacks, who had been the instruments of cruelty upon him; and, the instant Legree withdrew, they took him down, and, in their ignorance, sought to call him back to life,—as if *that* were any favor to him.

"Sartin, we 's been doin' a drefful wicked thing!" said Sambo; "hopes Mas'r 'll have to 'count for it, and not we."

They washed his wounds,—they provided a rude bed, of some refuse cotton, for him to lie down on; and one of them, stealing up to the house, begged a drink of brandy of Legree, pretending that he was tired, and wanted it for himself. He brought it back, and poured it down Tom's throat.

"O, Tom!" said Quimbo, "we's been awful wicked to ye!"

"I forgive ye, with all my heart!" said Tom, faintly.

"O, Tom! do tell us who is *Jesus,* anyhow?" said Sambo;—"Jesus, that's been a standin' by you so, all this night!—Who is he?"

The word roused the failing, fainting spirit. He poured forth a few energetic sentences of that wondrous One,—his life, his death, his everlasting presence, and power to save.

They wept,—both the two savage men.

"Why did n't I never hear this before?" said Sambo; "but I do believe!—I can't help it! Lord Jesus, have mercy on us!"

"Poor critters!" said Tom, "I'd be willing to bar' all I have, if it 'll only bring ye to Christ! O, Lord! give me these two more souls, I pray!"

That prayer was answered!

XLI The Young Master

. . . Tom had been lying two days since the fatal night; not suffering, for every nerve of suffering was blunted and destroyed. He lay, for the most part, in a quiet stupor; for the laws of a powerful and well-knit frame would not at once release the imprisoned spirit. By stealth, there had been there, in the darkness of the night, poor desolated creatures, who stole from their scanty hours' rest, that they might repay to him some of those ministrations of love in which he had always been so abundant. Truly, those poor disciples had little to give,—only the cup of cold water; but it was given with full hearts.

Tears had fallen on that honest, insensible face,—tears of late repentance in the poor, ignorant heathen, whom his dying love and patience had awakened to repentance, and bitter prayers, breathed over him to a late-found Saviour, of whom they scarce knew more than the name, but whom the yearning ignorant heart of man never implores in vain.

Cassy, who had glided out of her place of concealment, and, by over-hearing, learned the sacrifice that had been made for her and Emmeline, had been there, the night before, defying the danger of detection; and, moved by the few last words which the affectionate soul had yet strength to breathe, the long winter of despair, the ice of years, had given way, and the dark, despairing woman had wept and prayed.

When George entered the shed, he felt his head giddy and his heart sick.

"Is it possible,—is it possible?" said he, kneeling down by him. "Uncle Tom, my poor, poor old friend!"

Something in the voice penetrated to the ear of the dying. He moved his head gently, smiled, and said,

> "Jesus can make a dying-bed
> Feel soft as downy pillows are."

Tears which did honor to his manly heart fell from the young man's eyes, as he bent over his poor friend.

"O, dear Uncle Tom! do wake,—do speak once more! Look up! Here's Mas'r George,—your own little Mas'r George. Don't you know me?"

"Mas'r George!" said Tom, opening his eyes, and speaking in a feeble voice; "Mas'r George!" He looked bewildered.

Slowly the idea seemed to fill his soul; and the vacant eye became fixed and brightened, the whole face lighted up, the hard hands clasped, and tears ran down the cheeks.

"Bless the Lord! it is,—it is,—it's all I wanted! They have n't forgot me. It warms my soul; it does my old heart good! Now I shall die content! Bless the Lord, oh my soul!"

"You shan't die! you *must n't* die, nor think of it! I've come to buy you, and take you home," said George, with impetuous vehemence.

"O, Mas'r George, ye're too late. The Lord's bought me, and is going to take me home,—and I long to go. Heaven is better than Kintuck."

"O, don't die! It'll kill me!—it'll break my heart to think what you've suffered,—and lying in this old shed, here! Poor, poor fellow!"

"Don't call me poor fellow!" said Tom, solemnly. "I *have* been poor fellow; but that's all past and gone, now. I'm right in the door, going into glory! O, Mas'r George! *Heaven has come!* I've got the victory!—the Lord Jesus has given it to me! Glory be to His name!"

George was awe-struck at the force, the vehemence, the power, with which these broken sentences were uttered. He sat gazing in silence.

Tom grasped his hand, and continued,—"Ye must n't, now, tell Chloe, poor soul! how ye found me;—'t would be so drefful to her. Only tell her ye found me going into glory; and that I could n't stay for no one. And tell her the Lord's stood by me everywhere and al'ays, and made everything light and easy. And oh, the poor chil'en, and the baby!—my old heart's been most broke for 'em, time and agin! Tell 'em all to follow me—follow me! Give my love to Mas'r, and dear good Missis, and everybody in the place! Ye don't know! 'Pears like I loves 'em all! I loves every creatur', everywhar!—it's nothing *but* love! O, Mas'r George! what a thing 't is to be a Christian!"

At this moment, Legree sauntered up to the door of the shed, looked in, with a dogged air of affected carelessness, and turned away.

"The old satan!" said George, in his indignation. "It 's a comfort to think the devil will pay *him* for this, some of these days!"

"O, don't!—oh, ye must n't!" said Tom, grasping his hand; "he's a poor mis'able critter! it's awful to think on 't! O, if he only could repent, the Lord would forgive him now; but I'm 'feared he never will!"

"I hope he won't!" said George; "I never want to see *him* in heaven!"

"Hush, Mas'r George!—it worries me! Don't feel so! He an't done me no real harm,—only opened the gate of the kingdom for me; that's all!"

At this moment, the sudden flush of strength which the joy of meeting his young master had infused into the dying man gave way. A sudden sinking fell upon him; he closed his eyes; and that mysterious and sublime change passed over his face, that told the approach of other worlds.

He began to draw his breath with long, deep inspirations; and his broad chest rose and fell, heavily. The expression of his face was that of a conqueror.

"Who,—who,—who shall separate us from the love of Christ?" he said, in a voice that contended with mortal weakness; and, with a smile, he fell asleep.

George sat fixed with solemn awe. It seemed to him that the place was holy; and, as he closed the lifeless eyes, and rose up from the dead, only one thought possessed him,—that expressed by his simple old friend,—"What a thing it is to be a Christian!"

He turned: Legree was standing, sullenly, behind him.

Something in that dying scene had checked the natural fierceness of youthful passion. The presence of the man was simply loathsome to George; and he felt only an impulse to get away from him, with as few words as possible.

Fixing his keen dark eyes on Legree, he simply said, pointing to the dead, "You have got all you ever can of him. What shall I pay you for the body? I will take it away, and bury it decently."

"I don't sell dead niggers," said Legree doggedly. "You are welcome to bury him where and when you like."

"Boys," said George, in an authoritative tone, to two or three negroes, who were looking at the body, "help me lift him up, and carry him to my wagon; and get me a spade."

One of them ran for a spade; the other two assisted George to carry the body to the wagon.

George neither spoke to nor looked at Legree, who did not countermand his orders, but stood, whistling, with an air of forced unconcern. He sulkily followed them to where the wagon stood at the door.

George spread his cloak in the wagon, and had the body carefully disposed of in it,—moving the seat, so as to give it room. Then he turned, fixed his eyes on Legree, and said, with forced composure,

"I have not, as yet, said to you what I think of this most atrocious affair;—this is not the time and place. But, sir, this innocent blood shall have justice. I will proclaim this murder. I will go to the very first magistrate, and expose you."

"Do!" said Legree, snapping his fingers, scornfully. "I'd like to see you doing it. Where you going to get witnesses?—how you going to prove it?—Come, now!"

George saw, at once, the force of this defiance. There was not a white person on the place; and, in all southern courts, the testimony of colored blood is nothing. He felt, at that moment, as if he could have rent the heavens with his heart's indignant cry for justice; but in vain.

"After all, what a fuss, for a dead nigger!" said Legree.

The word was as a spark to a powder magazine. Prudence was never a cardinal virtue of the Kentucky boy. George turned, and, with one indignant blow, knocked Legree flat upon his face; and, as he stood over him, blazing with wrath and defiance, he would have formed no bad personification of his great namesake triumphing over the dragon.

Some men, however, are decidedly bettered by being knocked down. If a man lays them fairly flat in the dust, they seem immediately to conceive a respect for him; and Legree was one of this sort. As he rose, therefore, and brushed the dust from his clothes, he eyed the slowly-retreating wagon with some evident consideration; nor did he open his mouth till it was out of sight.

Beyond the boundaries of the plantation, George had noticed a dry, sandy knoll, shaded by a few trees: there they made the grave.

"Shall we take off the cloak, Mas'r?" said the negroes, when the grave was ready.

"No, no,—bury it with him! It's all I can give you, now, poor Tom, and you shall have it."

They laid him in; and the men shovelled away, silently. They banked it up, and laid green turf over it.

"You may go, boys," said George, slipping a quarter into the hand of each. They lingered about, however.

"If young Mas'r would please buy us—" said one.

"We'd serve him so faithful!" said the other.

"Hard times here, Mas'r!" said the first. "Do, Mas'r, buy us, please!"

"I can't!—I can't!" said George, with difficulty, motioning them off; "it's impossible!"

The poor fellows looked dejected, and walked off in silence.

"Witness, eternal God!" said George, kneeling on the grave of his poor friend; "oh, witness, that, from this hour, I will do *what one man can* to drive out this curse of slavery from my land!"

There is no monument to mark the last resting-place of our friend. He needs none! His Lord knows where he lies, and will raise him up, immortal, to appear with him when he shall appear in his glory.

Pity him not! Such a life and death is not for pity! Not in the riches of omnipotence is the chief glory of God; but in self-denying, suffering love! And blessed are the men whom he calls to fellowship with him, bearing their cross after him with patience. Of such it is written, "Blessed are they that mourn, for they shall be comforted."

1852

from Preface to the First Illustrated Edition of *Uncle Tom's Cabin*

. . . "The author of 'Uncle Tom' had for many years lived in Ohio on the confines of a slave state, and had thus been made familiar with facts and occurrences in relation to the institution of American slavery. Some of the most harrowing incidents related in the story had from time to time come to her knowledge in conversation with former slaves now free in Ohio. The cruel sale and separation of a married woman from her husband, narrated in Chapter XII., 'Select Incidents of Lawful Trade,' had passed under her own eye while passenger on a steamboat on the Ohio River. Her husband and brother had once been obliged to flee with a fugitive slave woman by night, as described in Chapter IX., and she herself had been called to write the letters for a former slave woman, servant in her own family, to a slave husband in Kentucky, who, trusted with unlimited liberty, free to come and go on business between Kentucky and Ohio, still refused to break his pledge of honor to his master, though that master from year to year deferred the keeping of his promise of freedom to the slave. It was the simple honor and loyalty of this Christian black man, who remained in slavery rather than violate a trust, that first impressed her with the possibility of such a character as, years after, was delineated in Uncle Tom.

"From time to time incidents were brought to her knowledge which deepened her horror of slavery. In her own family she had a private school for her children, and as there was no provision for the education of colored children in her vicinity, she allowed them the privilege of attending. One day she was suddenly surprised by a visit from the mother of one of the brightest and most amusing of these children. It appeared that the child had never been emancipated, and was one of the assets of an estate in Kentucky, and had been seized and carried off by one of the executors, and was to be sold by the sheriff at auction to settle the estate. The sum for the little one's ransom was made up by subscription in the neighborhood, but the incident left a deep mark in Mrs. Stowe's mind as to the practical workings of the institution of slavery.

"But it was not for many years that she felt any call to make use of the materials thus accumulating. In fact, it was a sort of general impression upon her mind, as upon that of many humane people in those days, that the subject was so dark and painful a one, so involved in difficulty and obscurity, so utterly beyond human hope or help, that it was of no use to read, or think, or distress one's self about it. There was a class of professed Abolitionists in Cincinnati and the neighboring regions, but they were unfashionable persons and few in number. Like all asserters of pure abstract right as applied to human affairs, they were regarded as a species of moral monomaniacs, who, in the consideration of one class of interests and wrongs, had lost sight of all proportion and all good judgment. Both in church and in state they were looked upon as 'those that troubled Israel.'

"It was a general saying among conservative and sagacious people that this subject was a dangerous one to investigate, and that nobody could begin to read and think upon it without becoming practically insane; moreover, that it was a subject of such delicacy that no discussion of it could be held in the free States without impinging upon the sensibilities of the slave States, to whom alone the management of the matter belonged.

"So when Dr. Bailey—a wise, temperate, and just man, a model of courtesy in speech and writing—came to Cincinnati and set up an anti-slavery paper, proposing a fair discussion of the subject, there was an immediate excitement. On two occasions a mob led by slaveholders from Kentucky attacked his office, destroyed his printing-press, and threw his types into the Ohio River. The most of the Cincinnati respectability, in church and state, contented themselves on this occasion with reprobating the imprudence of Dr. Bailey in thus 'arousing the passions of our fellow-citizens of Kentucky.' In these mobs and riots the free colored people were threatened, maltreated, abused, and often had to flee for their lives. Even the servants of good families were often chased to the very houses of their employers, who rescued them with difficulty; and the story was current in those days of a brave little woman who defended her black waiter, standing, pistol in hand, on her own doorstep, and telling the mob face to face that they should not enter except over her dead body.

"Professor Stowe's house was more than once a refuge for frightened fugitives on whom the very terrors of death had fallen, and the inmates slept with arms in the house and a large bell ready to call the young men of the adjoining Institution, in case the mob should come up to search the house. Nor was this a vain or improbable suggestion, for the mob in their fury had more than once threatened to go up and set fire to Lane Seminary, where a large body of the students were known to be abolitionists. Only the fact that the Institution was two miles from the city, with a rough and muddy road up a long hill, proved its salvation. Cincinnati mud, far known for its depth and tenacity, had sometimes its advantages.

"The general policy of the leaders of society, in cases of such disturbances, was after the good old pattern in Judæa, where a higher One had appeared, who disturbed the traders in swine; 'they besought him that he would depart out of their coasts.' Dr. Bailey at last was induced to remove his paper to Washington, and to conduct his investigation under the protection of the national Capitol,—and there for years he demonstrated the fact that the truth may be spoken plainly yet courteously, and with all honorable and Christian fairness, on the most exciting of subjects. In justice to the South it must be said that his honesty, courage, and dignity of character won for him friends even among the most determined slaveholders. Manly men have a sort of friendship for an open, honest opponent, like that of Richard Coeur de Lion for Saladin.

"Far otherwise was the fate of Lovejoy, who essayed an anti-slavery paper at Alton, Illinois. A mob from Missouri besieged the office, set the house on fire, and shot him at the door. It was for some days reported that Dr. Beecher's son, Rev. Edward Beecher, known to have been associated with Lovejoy at this period, had been killed at the same time. Such remembrances show how well grounded were the fears which attended every effort to agitate this subject. People who took the side of justice and humanity in those days had to count the cost and pay the price of their devotion. In those times, when John G. Fee, a young Kentucky student in Lane Seminary, liberated his slaves, and undertook to preach the gospel of emancipation in Kentucky, he was chased from the State, and disinherited by his own father. Berea College, for the education of colored and white, stands to-day a triumphant monument of his persistence in well-doing. Mr. Van Zandt, a Kentucky farmer, set free his slaves and came over and bought a farm in Ohio. Subsequently, from an impulse of humanity, he received and protected fugitive slaves in the manner narrated in Chapter IX. of 'Uncle Tom's Cabin.' For this he was seized, imprisoned, his property attached, and he was threatened with utter ruin. Salmon P. Chase, then a rising young lawyer in Cincinnati, had the bravery to appear as his lawyer. As he was leaving the court-room, after making his plea, one of the judges remarked, 'There goes a young man who has *ruined* himself to-day,' and the sentiment was echoed by the general voice of society. The case went against Van Zandt, and Mr. Chase carried it up to the Supreme Court of the United States, which, utterly ignoring argument and justice, decided it against him. But a few years more, and Salmon P. Chase was himself Chief Justice of the United States. It was one of those rare dramatic instances in which courage and justice sometimes bring a reward even in this life.

"After many years' residence in Ohio, Mrs. Stowe returned to make her abode in New England, just in the height of the excitement produced by the Fugitive Slave Law.[1] Settled in Brunswick, Maine, she was in constant communication with friends in Boston, who wrote to her from day to day of the terror and despair which that law had occasioned to industrious, worthy colored people who had from time to time escaped to Boston, and were living in peace and security. She heard of families broken up and fleeing in the dead of winter to the frozen shores of Canada. But what seemed to her more inexplicable, more dreadful, was the apparent apathy of the Christian world of the free North to these proceedings. The pulpits that denounced them were exceptions; the voices raised to remonstrate few and far between.

"In New England, as at the West, professed abolitionists were a small, despised, unfashionable band, whose constant remonstrances from year to year had been disregarded as the voices of impracticable fanatics. It seemed now as if the system once confined to the Southern States was rousing itself to new efforts to extend itself all over the North, and to overgrow the institutions of free society.

"With astonishment and distress Mrs. Stowe heard on all sides, from humane and Christian people, that the slavery of the blacks was a guaranteed constitutional right, and that all opposition to it endangered the national Union. With this conviction she saw that even earnest and tender-hearted Christian people seemed to feel it a duty to close their eyes, ears, and hearts to the harrowing details of slavery, to put down all discussion of the subject, and even to assist slave owners to recover fugitives in Northern States. She said to herself, these people cannot know what slavery is; they do not see what they are defending; and hence arose a purpose to write some sketches which should show to the world slavery as she had herself seen it.

[1]The Fugitive Slave Act of 1850, part of the Missouri Compromise, allowed fugitive slaves in free states to be hunted, captured and returned to their owners.

Pondering this subject, she was one day turning over a little bound volume of an anti-slavery magazine, edited by Mrs. Dr. Bailey, of Washington, and there she read the account of the escape of a woman with her child on the ice of the Ohio River from Kentucky. The incident was given by an eye-witness, one who had helped the woman to the Ohio shore. This formed the first salient point of the story. She began to meditate. The faithful slave husband in Kentucky occurred to her as a pattern of Uncle Tom, and the scenes of the story began gradually to form themselves in her mind.

"The first part of the book ever committed to writing, was the death of Uncle Tom. This scene presented itself almost as a tangible vision to her mind while sitting at the communion table in the little church in Brunswick. She was perfectly overcome by it, and could scarcely restrain the convulsion of tears and sobbings that shook her frame. She hastened home and wrote it, and her husband being away she read it to her two sons of ten and twelve years of age. The little fellows broke out into convulsions of weeping, one of them saying, through his sobs, 'Oh! mamma, slavery is the most cursed thing in the world!' From that time the story can less be said to have been composed by her than imposed upon her. Scenes, incidents, conversations rushed upon her with a vividness and importunity that would not be denied. The book insisted upon getting itself into being, and would take no denial. After the two or three first chapters were written, she wrote to Dr. Bailey of the 'National Era' that she was planning a story that might probably run through several numbers of the 'Era.' In reply she received an instant application for it, and began immediately to send off weekly installments. She was then in the midst of heavy domestic cares, with a young infant, with a party of pupils in her family to whom she was imparting daily lessons with her own children, and with untrained servants requiring constant supervision, but the story was so much more intense a reality to her than any other earthly thing that the weekly installment never failed. It was there in her mind day and night waiting to be written, and requiring but a few moments to bring it into visible characters.

"The weekly number was always read to the family circle before it was sent away, and all the household kept up an intense interest in the progress of the story.

"As the narrative appeared in the 'Era,' sympathetic words began to come to her from old workers who had long been struggling in the anti-slavery cause. She visited Boston, went to the Anti-Slavery rooms, and reinforced her répertoire of facts by such documents as Theodore D. Weld's 'Slavery As It Is,' the Lives of Josiah Henson and Lewis Clarke, particulars from both whose lives were inwoven with the story in the characters of Uncle Tom and George Harris.

"In shaping her material the author had but one purpose, to show the institution of slavery truly, just as it existed. She had visited in Kentucky, had formed the acquaintance of people who were just, upright, and generous, and yet slaveholders. She had heard their views and appreciated their situation; she felt that justice required that their difficulties should be recognized and their virtues acknowledged. It was her object to show that the evils of slavery were the inherent evils of a bad *system,* and not always the fault of those who had become involved in it and were its actual administrators.

"Then she was convinced that the presentation of slavery alone, in its most dreadful forms, would be a picture of such unrelieved horror and darkness as nobody could be induced to look at. Of set purpose, she sought to light up the darkness by humorous and grotesque episodes, and the presentation of the milder and more amusing phases of slavery, for which her recollection of the never-failing wit and drollery of her former colored friends in Ohio gave her abundant material. As the story progressed, a young publisher, J.P. Jewett, of Boston, set his eye upon it, and made overtures for the publication of it in book form, to which she consented. After a while she had a letter from him expressing his fears that she was making the story too long for a one-volume publication. He reminded her that it was an unpopular subject, and that people would not willingly hear much about it; that one short volume might possibly sell, but if it grew to two it might prove a fatal obstacle to its success. Mrs. Stowe replied that she did not make the story, that the story made itself, and that she could not stop it till it was done. The feeling that pursued her increased in intensity to the last, till with the death of Uncle Tom it seemed as if the whole vital force had left her. A feeling of profound discouragement came over her. Would anybody read it? Would anybody listen? Would this appeal, into which she had put heart, soul, mind, and strength, which she had written with her heart's blood,—would it, too, go for nothing, as so many prayers and groans and entreaties of these poor suffering souls had already gone? There had just been a party of slaves who had been seized and thrown into prison in Washington for a vain effort to escape. They were, many of them, partially educated, cultivated young men and women, to whom slavery was intolerable. When they were retaken and marched through the streets of Washington, followed by a jeering crowd, one of them, named Emily Edmonson, answered one man who cried shame upon her, that she was not ashamed,—that she was proud that she and all the rest of them had made an effort for liberty! It was the sentiment of a heroine, but she and her sisters were condemned no less to the auction-block.

"'Uncle Tom's Cabin' was published March 20, 1852. The despondency of the author as to the question whether anybody would read or attend to her appeal was soon dispelled. Ten thousand copies were sold in a few days, and over three hundred thousand within a year, and eight power-presses, running day and night, were barely able to keep pace with the demand for it. It was read everywhere, apparently, and by everybody, and she soon began to hear echoes of sympathy all over the land. The indignation, the pity, the distress, that had long weighed upon her soul seemed to pass off from her, and into the readers of the book. . . ."

1897

from Life and Letters of Harriet Beecher Stowe

Poverty and Sickness

. . . In the spring of 1842 Mrs. Stowe visited Hartford, taking her six-year-old daughter Hatty with her. In writing from there to her husband she confides some of her literary plans and aspirations to him, and he answers:—

"My dear, you must be a literary woman. It is so written in the book of fate. Make all your calculations accordingly. Get a good stock of health and brush up your mind. Drop the E. out of your name. It only incumbers it and interferes with the flow and euphony. Write yourself fully and always Harriet Beecher Stowe, which is a name euphonious, flowing, and full of meaning. Then my word for it, your husband will lift up his head in the gate, and your children will rise up and call you blessed. . . .

"And now, my dear wife, I want you to come home as quick as you can. The fact is I cannot live without you, and if we were not so prodigious poor I would come for you at once. There is no woman like you in this wide world. Who else has so much talent with so little self-conceit; so much reputation with so little affectation; so much literature with so little nonsense; so much enterprise with so little extravagance; so much tongue with so little scold; so much sweetness with so little softness; so much of so many things and so little of so many other things?"

In answer to this letter Mrs. Stowe writes from Hartford:—

"I have seen Johnson of the 'Evangelist.' He is very liberally disposed, and I may safely reckon on being paid for all I do there. Who is that Hale, Jr., that sent me the 'Boston Miscellany,' and will he keep his word with me? His offers are very liberal,—twenty dollars for three pages, not very close print. Is he to be depended on? If so, it is the best offer I have received yet. I shall get something from the Harpers some time this winter or spring. Robertson, the publisher here, says the book ('The Mayflower') will sell, and though the terms they offer me are very low, that I shall make something on it. For a second volume I shall be able to make better terms. On the whole, my dear, if I choose to be a literary lady, I have, I think, as good a chance of making profit by it as any one I know of. But with all this, I have my doubts whether I shall be able to do so.

"Our children are just coming to the age when everything depends on my efforts. They are delicate in health, and nervous and excitable, and need a mother's whole attention. Can I lawfully divide my attention by literary efforts?

"There is one thing I must suggest. If I am to write, I must have a room to myself, which shall be *my* room. I have in my own mind pitched on Mrs. Whipple's room. I can put the stove in it. I have bought a cheap carpet for it, and I have furniture enough at home to furnish it comfortably, and I only beg in addition that you will let me change the glass door from the nursery into that room and keep my plants there, and then I shall be quite happy.

"All last winter I felt the need of some place where I could go and be quiet and satisfied. I could not there, for there was all the setting of tables, and clearing up of tables, and dressing and washing of children, and everything else going on, and the constant falling of soot and coal dust on everything in the room was a constant annoyance to me, and I never felt comfortable there though I tried hard. Then if I came into the parlor where you were I felt as if I were interrupting you, and you know you sometimes thought so too.

"Now this winter let the cooking-stove be put into that room, and let the pipe run up through the floor into the room above. We can eat by our cooking-stove, and the children can be washed and dressed and keep their playthings in the room above, and play there when we don't want them below. You can study by the parlor fire, and I and my plants, etc., will take the other room. I shall keep my work and all my things there and feel settled and quiet. I intend to have a regular part of each day devoted to the children, and then I shall take them in there."

In his reply to this letter Professor Stowe says:—

"The little magazine ('The Souvenir') goes ahead finely. Fisher sent down to Fulton the other day and got sixty subscribers. He will make the June number as handsome as possible, as a specimen number for the students, several of whom will take agencies for it during the coming vacation. You have it in your power by means of this little magazine to form the mind of the West for the coming generation. It is just as I told you in my last letter. God has written it in his book that you must be a literary woman, and who are we that we should contend against God? You must therefore make all your calculations to spend the rest of your life with your pen.

"If you only could come home to-day how happy should I be. I am daily finding out more and more (what I knew very well before) that you are the most intelligent and agreeable woman in the whole circle of my acquaintance." . . .

June 16, 1845.

My Dear Husband,—It is a dark, sloppy, rainy, muddy, disagreeable day, and I have been working hard (for me) all day in the kitchen, washing dishes, looking into closets, and seeing a great deal of that dark side of domestic life which a housekeeper may who will investigate too curiously into minutiæ in warm, damp weather, especially after a girl who keeps all clean on the *outside* of cup and platter, and is very apt to make good the rest of the text in the *inside* of things.

I am sick of the smell of sour milk, and sour meat, and sour everything, and then the clothes *will* not dry, and no wet thing does, and everything smells mouldy; and altogether I feel as if I never wanted to eat again.

Your letter, which was neither sour nor mouldy, formed a very agreeable contrast to all these things; the more so for being unexpected. I am much obliged to you for it. As to my health, it gives me very little solicitude, although I am bad enough and daily growing worse. I feel no life, no energy, no appetite, or rather a growing distaste for food; in fact, I am becoming quite ethereal. Upon reflection I perceive that it pleases my Father to keep me in the fire, for my whole situation is excessively harassing and painful. I suffer with sensible distress in the brain, as I have done more or less since my sickness last winter, a distress which some days takes from me all power of planning or executing anything; and you know that, except this poor head, my unfortunate household has no mainspring, for nobody feels any kind of responsibility to do a thing in time, place, or manner, except as I oversee it.

Georgiana[1] is so excessively weak, nervous, cross, and fretful, night and day, that she takes all Anna's strength and time with her; and then the children are, like other little sons and daughters of Adam, full of all kinds of absurdity and folly.

When the brain gives out, as mine often does, and one cannot think or remember anything, then what is to be done? All common fatigue, sickness, and exhaustion is nothing to this distress. Yet do I rejoice in my God and know in whom I believe, and only pray that the fire may consume the dross; as to the gold, that is imperishable. No real evil can happen to me, so I fear nothing for the future, and only suffer in the present tense.

[1]Georgiana May Stowe (b. 1843)—Harriet's fourth child.

God, the mighty God, is mine, of that I am sure, and I know He knows that though flesh and heart fail, I am all the while desiring and trying for his will alone. As to a journey, I need not ask a physician to see that it is needful to me as far as health is concerned, that is to say, all human appearances are that way, but I feel no particular choice about it. If God wills I go. He can easily find means. Money, I suppose, is as plenty with Him now as it always has been, and if He sees it is really best He will doubtless help me. . . .

My Dear Husband,—This week has been unusually fatal. The disease in the city has been malignant and virulent. Hearse drivers have scarce been allowed to unharness their horses, while furniture carts and common vehicles are often employed for the removal of the dead The sable trains which pass our windows, the frequent indications of crowding haste, and the absence of reverent decency have, in many cases, been most painful. Of course all these things, whether we will or no, bring very doleful images to the mind.

On Tuesday one hundred and sixteen deaths from cholera were reported, and that night the air was of that peculiarly oppressive, deathly kind that seems to lie like lead on the brain and soul.

As regards your coming home, I am decidedly opposed to it. First, because the chance of your being taken ill is just as great as the chance of your being able to render us any help. To exchange the salubrious air of Brattleboro' for the pestilent atmosphere of this place with your system rendered sensitive by water-cure treatment would be extremely dangerous. It is a source of constant gratitude to me that neither you nor father are exposed to the dangers here.

Second, none of us are sick, and it is very uncertain whether we shall be.

Third, if we were sick there are so many of us that it is not at all likely we shall all be taken at once.

July 1. Yesterday Mr. Stagg went to the city and found all gloomy and discouraged, while a universal panic seemed to be drawing nearer than ever before. Large piles of coal were burning on the cross walks and in the public squares, while those who had talked confidently of the cholera being confined to the lower classes and those who were imprudent began to feel as did the magicians of old, "This is the finger of God."

Yesterday, upon the recommendation of all the clergymen of the city, the mayor issued a proclamation for a day of general fasting, humiliation, and prayer, to be observed on Tuesday next.

July 3. We are all in good health and try to maintain a calm and cheerful frame of mind. The doctors are nearly used up. Dr. Bowen and Dr. Peck are sick in bed. Dr. Potter and Dr. Pulte ought, I suppose, to be there also. The younger physicians have no rest night or day. Mr. Fisher is laid up from his incessant visitations with the sick and dying. Our own Dr. Brown is likewise prostrated, but we are all resolute to stand by each other, and there are so many of us that it is not likely we can all be taken sick together.

July 4. All well. The meeting yesterday was very solemn and interesting. There is more or less sickness about us, but no very dangerous cases One hundred and twenty burials from cholera alone yesterday, yet to-day we see parties bent on pleasure or senseless carousing, while to-morrow and next day will witness a fresh harvest of death from them. How we can become accustomed to anything! Awhile ago ten a day dying of cholera struck terror to all hearts; but now the tide has surged up gradually until the deaths average over a hundred daily, and everybody is getting accustomed to it. Gentlemen make themselves agreeable to ladies by reciting the number of deaths in this house or that. This together with talk of funerals, cholera medicines, cholera dietetics, and chloride of lime form the ordinary staple of conversation. Serious persons of course throw in moral reflections to their taste.

July 10. Yesterday little Charley[2] was taken ill, not seriously, and at any other season I should not be alarmed. Now, however, a slight illness seems like a death sentence, and I will not dissemble that I feel from the outset very little hope. I still think it best that you should not return. By so doing you might lose all you have gained. You might expose yourself to a fatal incursion of disease. It is decidedly not your duty to do so.

July 12. Yesterday I carried Charley to Dr. Pulte, who spoke in such a manner as discouraged and frightened me. He mentioned dropsy on the brain as a possible result. I came home with a heavy heart, sorrowing, desolate, and wishing my husband and father were here.

About one o'clock this morning Miss Stewart suddenly opened my door crying, "Mrs. Stowe, Henry is vomiting." I was on my feet in an instant, and lifted up my heart for help. He was, however, in a few minutes relieved. Then I turned my attention to Charley, who was also suffering, put him into a wet sheet, and kept him there until he was in a profuse perspiration. He is evidently getting better, and is auspiciously cross. Never was crossness in a baby more admired. Anna[3] and I have said to each other exultingly a score of times, "How cross the little fellow is! How he does scold!"

July 15. Since I last wrote our house has been a perfect hospital. Charley apparently recovering, but still weak and feeble, unable to walk or play, and so miserably fretful and unhappy. Sunday Anna and I were fairly stricken down, as many others are, with no particular illness, but with such miserable prostration. I lay on the bed all day reading my hymn-book and thinking over passages of Scripture.

July 17. To-day we have been attending poor old Aunt Frankie's[4] funeral. She died yesterday morning, taken sick the day before while washing. Good, honest, trustful old soul! She was truly one who hungered and thirsted for righteousness.

Yesterday morning our poor little dog, Daisy, who had been ailing the day before, was suddenly seized with frightful spasms and died in half an hour. Poor little affectionate thing! If I were half as good for my nature as she for hers I should be much better than I am. While we were all mourning over her the news came that Aunt Frankie was breathing her last. Hatty, Eliza, Anna, and I made her shroud yesterday, and this morning I made her cap. We have just come from her grave.

July 23. At last, my dear, the hand of the Lord hath touched us. We have been watching all day by the dying bed of little Charley, who is gradually sinking. After a partial recovery from the attack I described in my last letter he continued for some days very feeble, but still we hoped for recovery. About four days ago he was taken with decided cholera, and now there is no hope of his surviving this night.

[2]Samuel Charles Stowe (b. 1849)—Harriet's fifth child.

[3]Anna Smith—an English girl who took care of Stowe's children in Cincinnati.

[4]Aunt Frankie—an elderly black woman who worked for Stowe.

Every kindness is shown us by the neighbors. Do not return. All will be over before you could possibly get here, and the epidemic is now said by the physicians to prove fatal to every new case. Bear up. Let us not faint when we are rebuked of Him. I dare not trust myself to say more but shall write again soon.

July 26.

My Dear Husband,—At last it is over and our dear little one is gone from us. He is now among the blessed. My Charley—my beautiful, loving, gladsome baby, so loving, so sweet, so full of life and hope and strength—now lies shrouded, pale and cold, in the room below. Never was he anything to me but a comfort. He has been my pride and joy. Many a heartache has he cured for me. Many an anxious night have I held him to my bosom and felt the sorrow and loneliness pass out of me with the touch of his little warm hands. Yet I have just seen him in his death agony, looked on his imploring face when I could not help nor soothe nor do one thing, not one, to mitigate his cruel suffering, do nothing but pray in my anguish that he might die soon. I write as though there were no sorrow like my sorrow, yet there has been in this city, as in the land of Egypt, scarce a house without its dead. This heartbreak, this anguish, has been everywhere, and when it will end God alone knows.

Removal to Brunswick

My Dear Sister,—Is it really true that snow is on the ground and Christmas coming, and I have not written unto thee, most dear sister? No, I don't believe it! I have n't been so naughty—it 's all a mistake—yes, written I must have—and written I have, too—in the night-watches as I lay on my bed—such beautiful letters—I wish you had only gotten them; but by day it has been hurry, hurry, hurry, and drive, drive, drive! or else the calm of a sick-room, ever since last spring.[1]

I put off writing when your letter first came because I meant to write you a long letter—a full and complete one, and so days slid by,—and became weeks,—and my little Charlie came . . . etc. and etc.!!! Sarah, when I look back, I wonder at myself, not that I forget any one thing that I should remember, but that I have remembered anything. From the time that I left Cincinnati with my children to come forth to a country that I knew not of almost to the present time, it has seemed as if I could scarcely breathe, I was so pressed with care. My head dizzy with the whirl of railroads and steamboats; then ten days' sojourn in Boston, and a constant toil and hurry in buying my furniture and equipments; and then landing in Brunswick in the midst of a drizzly, inexorable northeast storm, and beginning the work of getting in order a deserted, dreary, damp old house. All day long running from one thing to another, as for example, thus:—

Mrs. Stowe, how shall I make this lounge, and what shall I cover the back with first?

Mrs. Stowe. With the coarse cotton in the closet.

[1]In 1849, Calvin Stowe received a call to the Collins Professorship at Bowdoin College in Brunswick, Maine. The family moved there in 1850. This letter to her sister-in-law, Mrs. George Beecher, whose husband had died, describes the events of Stowe's first summer in Brunswick.

Woman. Mrs. Stowe, there is n't any more soap to clean the windows.

Mrs. Stowe. Where shall I get soap?

Here H., run up to the store and get two bars.

There is a man below wants to see Mrs. Stowe about the cistern. Before you go down, Mrs. Stowe, just show me how to cover this round end of the lounge.

There's a man up from the depot, and he says that a box has come for Mrs. Stowe, and it 's coming up to the house; will you come down and see about it?

Mrs. Stowe, don't go till you have shown the man how to nail that carpet in the corner. He 's nailed it all crooked; what shall he do? The black thread is all used up, and what shall I do about putting gimp on the back of that sofa? Mrs. Stowe, there is a man come with a lot of pails and tinware from Furbish; will you settle the bill now?

Mrs. Stowe, here is a letter just come from Boston inclosing that bill of lading; the man wants to know what he shall do with the goods. If you will tell me what to say I will answer the letter for you.

Mrs. Stowe, the meat-man is at the door. Had n't we better get a little beef-steak, or something, for dinner?

Shall Hatty go to Boardman's for some more black thread?

Mrs. Stowe, this cushion is an inch too wide for the frame. What shall we do now?

Mrs. Stowe, where are the screws of the black walnut bedstead?

Here's a man has brought in these bills for freight. Will you settle them now?

Mrs. Stowe, I don't understand using this great needle. I can't make it go through the cushion; it sticks in the cotton.

Then comes a letter from my husband saying he is sick abed, and all but dead; don't ever expect to see his family again; wants to know how I shall manage, in case I am left a widow; knows we shall get in debt and never get out; wonders at my courage; thinks I am very sanguine; warns me to be prudent, as there won't be much to live on in case of his death, etc., etc., etc. I read the letter and poke it into the stove, and proceed. . . .

Some of my adventures were quite funny; as for example: I had in my kitchen elect no sink, cistern, or any other water privileges, so I bought at the cotton factory two of the great hogsheads they bring oil in, which here in Brunswick are often used for cisterns, and had them brought up in triumph to my yard, and was congratulating myself on my energy, when lo and behold! it was discovered that there was no cellar door except one in the kitchen, which was truly a strait and narrow way, down a long pair of stairs. Hereupon, as saith John Bunyan, I fell into a muse,—how to get my cisterns into my cellar. In days of chivalry I might have got a knight to make me a breach through the foundation walls, but that was not to be thought of now, and my oil hogsheads standing disconsolately in the yard seemed to reflect no great credit on my foresight. In this strait I fell upon a real honest Yankee cooper, whom I besought, for the reputation of his craft and mine, to take my hogsheads to pieces, carry them down in staves, and set them up again, which the worthy man actually accomplished one fair summer forenoon, to the great astonishment of "us Yankees." When my man came to put up the pump, he stared very hard to see my hogsheads thus translated and standing as innocent and quiet as could be in the cellar, and then I told him, in a very mild, quiet way, that I got 'em taken to pieces and put together—just as if I had been always in the habit of doing such things. Professor Smith came down and looked very hard at them and then said, "Well, nothing can beat a willful woman." . . .

Then came on Mr. Stowe; and then came the eighth of July and my little Charley.[2] I was really glad for an excuse to lie in bed, for I was full tired, I can assure you. Well, I was what folks call very comfortable for two weeks, when my nurse had to leave me. . . .

During this time I have employed my leisure hours in making up my engagements with newspaper editors. I have written more than anybody, or I myself, would have thought. I have taught an hour a day in our school, and I have read two hours every evening to the children. The children study English history in school, and I am reading Scott's historic novels in their order. Tonight I finish the "Abbot;" shall begin "Kenilworth" next week; yet I am constantly pursued and haunted by the idea that I don't do anything. Since I began this note I have been called off at least a dozen times; once for the fishman, to buy a codfish; once to see a man who had brought me some barrels of apples; once to see a book-man; then to Mrs. Upham, to see about a drawing I promised to make for her; then to nurse the baby; then into the kitchen to make a chowder for dinner; and now I am at it again, for nothing but deadly determination enables me ever to write; it is rowing against wind and tide.

I suppose you think now I have begun, I am never going to stop, and in truth it looks like it; but the spirit moves now and I must obey.

Christmas is coming, and our little household is all alive with preparations; every one collecting their little gifts with wonderful mystery and secrecy. . . .

To tell the truth, dear, I am getting tired; my neck and back ache, and I must come to a close.

Your ready kindness to me in the spring I felt very much; and *why* I did not have the sense to have sent you one line just by way of acknowledgment, I 'm sure I don't know; I felt just as if I had, till I awoke, and behold! I had not. But, my dear, if my wits are somewhat wool-gathering and unsettled, my heart is as true as a star. I love you, and have thought of you often.

This fall I have felt often *sad,* lonesome, both very unusual feelings with me in these busy days; but the breaking away from my old home, and leaving father and mother, and coming to a strange place affected me naturally. In those sad hours my thoughts have often turned to George; I have thought with encouragement of his blessed state, and hoped that I should soon be there too. I have many warm and kind friends here, and have been treated with great attention and kindness. Brunswick is a delightful residence, and if you come East next summer you must come to my new home. George would delight to go a-fishing with the children, and see the ships, and sail in the sailboats, and all that.

Give Aunt Harriet's love to him, and tell him when he gets to be a painter to send me a picture.

Affectionately yours,
H. Stowe

[2]Charles Edward Stowe, Harriet's sixth child, who would become her biographer, is born.

BRUNSWICK, *July* 9, 1851.

Frederick Douglass, Esq.:

Sir,—You may perhaps have noticed in your editorial readings a series of articles that I am furnishing for the "Era" under the title of "Uncle Tom's Cabin, or Life among the Lowly."

In the course of my story the scene will fall upon a cotton plantation. I am very desirous, therefore, to gain information from one who has been an actual laborer on one, and it occurred to me that in the circle of your acquaintance there might be one who would be able to communicate to me some such information as I desire. I have before me an able paper written by a Southern planter, in which the details and *modus operandi* are given from his point of sight. I am anxious to have something more from another standpoint. I wish to be able to make a picture that shall be graphic and true to nature in its details. Such a person as Henry Bibb, if in the country, might give me just the kind of information I desire. You may possibly know of some other person. I will subjoin to this letter a list of questions, which in that case you will do me a favor by inclosing to the individual, with the request that he will at earliest convenience answer them.

For some few weeks past I have received your paper through the mail, and have read it with great interest, and desire to return my acknowledgments for it. It will be a pleasure to me at some time when less occupied to contribute something to its columns. I have noticed with regret your sentiments on two subjects—the church and African colonization, . . . with the more regret because I think you have a considerable share of reason for your feelings on both these subjects; but I would willingly, if I could, modify your views on both points.

In the first place you say the church is "pro-slavery." There is a sense in which this may be true. The American church of all denominations, taken as a body, comprises the best and most conscientious people in the country. I do not say it comprises none but these, or that none such are found out of it, but only if a census were taken of the purest and most high principled men and women of the country, the majority of them would be found to be professors of religion in some of the various Christian denominations. This fact has given to the church great weight in this country—the general and predominant spirit of intelligence and probity and piety of its majority has given it that degree of weight that it has the power to decide the great moral questions of the day. Whatever it unitedly and decidedly sets itself against as moral evil it can put down. In this sense the church is responsible for the sin of slavery. Dr. Barnes has beautifully and briefly expressed this on the last page of his work on slavery, when he says: "Not all the force out of the church could sustain slavery an hour if it were not sustained in it." It then appears that the church has the power to put an end to this evil and does not do it. In this sense she may be said to be pro-slavery. But the church has the same power over intemperance, and Sabbath-breaking, and sin of all kinds. There is not a doubt that if the moral power of the church were brought up to the New Testament standpoint it is sufficient to put an end to all these as well as to slavery. But I would ask you, Would you consider it a fair representation of the Christian church in this country to say that it is pro-intemperance, pro-Sabbath-breaking, and pro everything that it might put down if it were in a higher state of moral feeling? If you should make a list of all the abolitionists of the country, I think that you would find a majority of them in the church—certainly some of the most influential and efficient ones are ministers.

I am a minister's daughter, and a minister's wife, and I have had six brothers in the ministry (one is in heaven); I certainly ought to know something of the feelings of ministers on this subject. I was a child in 1820 when the Missouri question was agitated, and one of the strongest and deepest impressions on my mind was that made by my father's sermons and prayers, and the anguish of his soul for the poor slave at that time. I remember his preaching drawing tears down the hardest faces of the old farmers in his congregation.

I well remember his prayers morning and evening in the family for "poor, oppressed, bleeding Africa," that the time of her deliverance might come; prayers offered with strong crying and tears, and which indelibly impressed my heart and made me what I am from my very soul, the enemy of all slavery. Every brother I have has been in his sphere a leading anti-slavery man. One of them was to the last the bosom friend and counselor of Lovejoy.[3] As for myself and husband, we have for the last seventeen years lived on the border of a slave State, and we have never shrunk from the fugitives, and we have helped them with all we had to give. I have received the children of liberated slaves into a family school, and taught them with my own children, and it has been the influence that we found in the church and by the altar that has made us do all this. Gather up all the sermons that have been published on this offensive and unchristian Fugitive Slave Law, and you will find that those against it are numerically more than those in its favor, and yet some of the strongest opponents have not published their sermons. Out of thirteen ministers who meet with my husband weekly for discussion of moral subjects, only three are found who will acknowledge or obey this law in any shape.

After all, my brother, the strength and hope of your oppressed race does lie in the church—in hearts united to Him of whom it is said, "He shall spare the souls of the needy, and precious shall their blood be in his sight." Everything is against you, but Jesus Christ is for you, and He has not forgotten his church, misguided and erring though it be. I have looked all the field over with despairing eyes; I see no hope but in Him. This movement must and will become a purely religious one. The light will spread in churches, the tone of feeling will rise, Christians North and South will give up all connection with, and take up their testimony against, slavery, and thus the work will be done.

First Trip to Europe

. . . The preceding month Mrs. Stowe had received a letter from Mrs. Follen[1] in London, asking for information with regard to herself, her family, and the circumstances of her writing "Uncle Tom's Cabin."

In reply Mrs. Stowe sent the following very characteristic letter, which may be safely given at the risk of some repetition:—

ANDOVER, *February* 16, 1853.

[3]Elijah Lovejoy—published an anti-slavery paper in Alton, Illinois. He was shot and killed by a pro-slavery mob that burned his office and printing press.

[1]Mrs. Follen, Eliza Lee Cabot—a Boston aristocrat and ardent abolitionist, editor of *Child's Friend* and author of the juvenile classic, *The Well-Spent Hour.*

My Dear Madam,—I hasten to reply to your letter, to me the more interesting that I have long been acquainted with you, and during all the nursery part of my life made daily use of your poems for children.

I used to think sometimes in those days that I would write to you, and tell you how much I was obliged to you for the pleasure which they gave us all.

So you want to know something about what sort of a woman I am! Well, if this is any object, you shall have statistics free of charge. To begin, then, I am a little bit of a woman,—somewhat more than forty, about as thin and dry as a pinch of snuff; never very much to look at in my best days, and looking like a used-up article now.

I was married when I was twenty-five years old to a man rich in Greek and Hebrew, Latin and Arabic, and, alas! rich in nothing else. When I went to housekeeping, my entire stock of china for parlor and kitchen was bought for eleven dollars. That lasted very well for two years, till my brother was married and brought his bride to visit me. I then found, on review, that I had neither plates nor teacups to set a table for my father's family; wherefore I thought it best to reinforce the establishment by getting me a tea-set that cost ten dollars more, and this, I believe, formed my whole stock in trade for some years.

But then I was abundantly enriched with wealth of another sort.

I had two little, curly-headed twin daughters to begin with, and my stock in this line has gradually increased, till I have been the mother of seven children, the most beautiful and the most loved of whom lies buried near my Cincinnati residence. It was at his dying bed and at his grave that I learned what a poor slave mother may feel when her child is torn away from her. In those depths of sorrow which seemed to me immeasurable, it was my only prayer to God that such anguish might not be suffered in vain. There were circumstances about his death of such peculiar bitterness, of what seemed almost cruel suffering, that I felt that I could never be consoled for it, unless this crushing of my own heart might enable me to work out some great good to others. . . .

I allude to this here because I have often felt that much that is in that book ("Uncle Tom") had its root in the awful scenes and bitter sorrows of that summer. It has left now, I trust, no trace on my mind, except a deep compassion for the sorrowful, especially for mothers who are separated from their children.

During long years of struggling with poverty and sickness, and a hot, debilitating climate, my children grew up around me. The nursery and the kitchen were my principal fields of labor. Some of my friends, pitying my trials, copied and sent a number of little sketches from my pen to certain liberally paying "Annuals" with my name. With the first money that I earned in this way I bought a feather-bed! for as I had married into poverty and without a dowry, and as my husband had only a large library of books and a great deal of learning, the bed and pillows were thought the most profitable investment. After this I thought that I had discovered the philosopher's stone. So when a new carpet or mattress was going to be needed, or when, at the close of the year, it began to be evident that my family accounts, like poor Dora's, "would n't add up," then I used to say to my faithful friend and factotum Anna, who shared all my joys and sorrows, "Now, if you will keep the babies and attend to the things in the house for one day, I 'll write a piece, and then we shall be out of the scrape." So I became an author,—very modest at first, I do assure you, and remonstrating very seriously with the friends who had thought it best to put my name to the pieces by way of getting up a reputation; and if you ever see a woodcut of me, with an immoderately long nose, on the cover of all the U.S. Almanacs, I wish you to take notice, that I have been forced into it contrary to my natural modesty by the imperative solicitations of my dear five thousand friends and the public generally. One thing I must say with regard to my life at the West, which you will understand better than many English women could.

I lived two miles from the city of Cincinnati, in the country, and domestic service, not always you know to be found in the city, is next to an impossibility to obtain in the country, even by those who are willing to give the highest wages; so what was to be expected for poor me, who had very little of this world's goods to offer?

Had it not been for my inseparable friend Anna, a noble-hearted English girl, who landed on our shores in destitution and sorrow, and clave to me as Ruth to Naomi, I had never lived through all the trials which this uncertainty and want of domestic service imposed on both: you may imagine, therefore, how glad I was when, our seminary property being divided out into small lots which were rented at a low price, a number of poor families settled in our vicinity, from whom we could occasionally obtain domestic service. About a dozen families of liberated slaves were among the number, and they became my favorite resort in cases of emergency. If anybody wishes to have a black face look handsome, let them be left, as I have been, in feeble health in oppressive hot weather, with a sick baby in arms, and two or three other little ones in the nursery, and not a servant in the whole house to do a single turn. Then, if they could see my good old Aunt Frankie coming with her honest, bluff, black face, her long, strong arms, her chest as big and stout as a barrel, and her hilarious, hearty laugh, perfectly delighted to take one's washing and do it at a fair price, they would appreciate the beauty of black people.

My cook, poor Eliza Buck,—how she would stare to think of her name going to England!—was a regular epitome of slave life in herself; fat, gentle, easy, loving and lovable, always calling my very modest house and door-yard "The Place," as if it had been a plantation with seven hundred hands on it. She had lived through the whole sad story of a Virginia-raised slave's life. In her youth she must have been a very handsome mulatto girl. Her voice was sweet, and her manners refined and agreeable. She was raised in a good family as a nurse and seamstress. When the family became embarrassed, she was suddenly sold on to a plantation in Louisiana. She has often told me how, without any warning, she was suddenly forced into a carriage, and saw her little mistress screaming and stretching her arms from the window towards her as she was driven away. She has told me of scenes on the Louisiana plantation, and she has often been out at night by stealth ministering to poor slaves who had been mangled and lacerated by the lash. Hence she was sold into Kentucky, and her last master was the father of all her children. On this point she ever maintained a delicacy and reserve that always appeared to me remarkable. She always called him her husband; and it was not till after she had lived with me some years that I discovered the real nature of the connection. I shall never forget how sorry I felt for her, nor my feelings at her humble apology, "You know, Mrs. Stowe, slave women cannot help themselves." She had two very pretty quadroon daughters, with her beautiful hair and eyes, interesting children, whom I had instructed in the family school with my children. Time would fail to tell you all that I learned incidentally of the slave system in the history of various slaves who came into my family, and of the underground railroad which, I may say, ran through our house. But the letter is already too long.

You ask with regard to the remuneration which I have received for my work here in America. Having been poor all my life and expecting to be poor the rest of it, the idea of making money by a book which I wrote just because I could not help it, never occurred to me. It was therefore an agreeable surprise to receive ten thousand dollars as the first-fruits of three months' sale. I presume as much more is now due. Mr. Bosworth in England, the firm of Clarke & Co., and Mr. Bentley, have all offered me an interest in the sales of their editions in London. I am very glad of it, both on account of the value of what they offer, and the value of the example they set in this matter, wherein I think that justice has been too little regarded.

I have been invited to visit Scotland, and shall probably spend the summer there and in England.

I have very much at heart a design to erect in some of the Northern States a normal school, for the education of colored teachers in the United States and in Canada. I have very much wished that some permanent memorial of good to the colored race might be created out of the proceeds of a work which promises to have so unprecedented a sale. My own share of the profits will be less than that of the publishers', either English or American; but I am willing to give largely for this purpose, and I have no doubt that the publishers, both American and English, will unite with me; for nothing tends more immediately to the emancipation of the slave than the education and elevation of the free.

I am now writing a work which will contain, perhaps, an equal amount of matter with "Uncle Tom's Cabin." It will contain all the facts and documents on which that story was founded, and an immense body of facts, reports of trials, legal documents, and testimony of people now living South, which will more than confirm every statement in "Uncle Tom's Cabin."

I must confess that till I began the examination of facts in order to write this book, much as I thought I knew before, I had not begun to measure the depth of the abyss. The law records of courts and judicial proceedings are so incredible as to fill me with amazement whenever I think of them. It seems to me that the book cannot but be felt, and, coming upon the sensibility awaked by the other, do something.

I suffer exquisitely in writing these things. It may be truly said that I write with my heart's blood. Many times in writing "Uncle Tom's Cabin" I thought my health would fail utterly; but I prayed earnestly that God would help me till I got through, and still I am pressed beyond measure and above strength.

This horror, this nightmare abomination! can it be in my country! It lies like lead on my heart, it shadows my life with sorrow; the more so that I feel, as for my own brothers, for the South, and am pained by every horror I am obliged to write, as one who is forced by some awful oath to disclose in court some family disgrace. Many times I have thought that I must die, and yet I pray God that I may live to see something done. I shall in all probability be in London in May: shall I see you?

It seems to me so odd and dream-like that so many persons desire to see me, and now I cannot help thinking that they will think, when they do, that God hath chosen "the weak things of this world."

If I live till spring I shall hope to see Shakespeare's grave, and Milton's mulberry-tree, and the good land of my fathers,—old, old England! May that day come!

Yours affectionately,
H.B. STOWE

Closing Scenes

. . . In 1882 Mrs. Stowe writes to her son certain impressions derived from reading the "Life and Letters of John Quincy Adams," which are given as containing a retrospect of the stormy period of her own life-experience.

"Your father enjoys his proximity to the Boston library. He is now reading the twelve or fourteen volumes of the life and diary of John Q. Adams. It is a history of our country through all the period of slavery usurpation that led to the war. The industry of the man in writing is wonderful. Every day's doings in the house are faithfully daguerreotyped,—all the mean tricks, contrivances of the slave-power, and the pusillanimity of the Northern members from day to day recorded. Calhoun was then secretary of state. Under his connivance even the United States census was falsified, to prove that freedom was bad for negroes. Records of deaf, dumb, and blind, and insane colored people were distributed in Northern States, and in places where John Q. Adams had means of *proving* there were no negroes. When he found that these falsified figures had been used with the English embassador as reasons for admitting Texas as a slave State, the old man called on Calhoun, and showed him the industriously collected *proofs* of the falsity of this census. He says: 'He writhed like a trodden rattlesnake, but said the census was full of mistakes; but one part balanced another,—it was not worth while to correct them.' His whole life was an incessant warfare with the rapidly advancing spirit of slavery, that was coiling like a serpent around everything.

"At a time when the Southerners were like so many excited tigers and rattlesnakes,—when they bullied, and scoffed, and sneered, and threatened, this old man rose every day in his place, and, knowing every parliamentary rule and tactic of debate, found means to make himself heard. Then he presented a petition from *negroes,* which raised a storm of fury. The old man claimed that the right of petition was the right of every human being. They moved to expel him. By the rules of the house a man, before he can be expelled, may have the floor to make his defense. This was just what he wanted. He held the floor for *fourteen days,* and used his wonderful powers of memory and arrangement to give a systematic, scathing history of the usurpations of slavery; he would have spoken fourteen days more, but his enemies, finding the thing getting hotter and hotter, withdrew their motion, and the right of petition was gained.

"What is remarkable in this journal is the minute record of going to church every Sunday, and an analysis of the text and sermon. There is something about these so simple, so humble, so earnest. Often differing from the speaker—but with gravity and humility—he seems always to be so self-distrustful; to have such a sense of sinfulness and weakness, but such trust in God's fatherly mercy, as is most beautiful to see. Just the record of his Sunday sermons, and his remarks upon them, would be most instructive to a preacher. He was a regular communicant, and, beside, attended church on Christmas and Easter,—I cannot but love the old man. He died without seeing even the dawn of liberty which God has brought; but oh! I am sure he sees it from above. He died in the Capitol, in the midst of his labors, and the last words he said were, 'This is the last of earth; I am content.' And now, I trust, he is with God.

"All, all are gone. All that raged; all that threatened; all the cowards that yielded; truckled, sold their country for a mess of pottage; all the *men* that stood and bore infamy and scorn for the truth; all are silent in dust; the fight is over, but eternity will never efface from their souls whether they did well or ill—whether they fought bravely or failed like cowards. In a sense, our lives are irreparable. If we shrink, if we fail, if we choose the fleeting instead of the eternal, God may forgive us; but there must be an eternal regret! This man lived for humanity when hardest bestead; for truth when truth was unpopular; for Christ when Christ stood chained and scourged in the person of the slave."

1890

from The Minister's Wooing

XXIII Views of Divine Government

[*The Minister's Wooing* is a romance about young Mary Scudder, a devout New England girl who is wooed by three men: Calvinist preacher Samuel Hopkins, the profligate colonel Aaron Burr, and her true love James Marvyn. But the conventional romance plot provides a backdrop for Stowe's critique of traditional Calvinist doctrine.

The following selection describes the spiritual dilemma at the heart of the novel. News of James Marvyn's death at sea has reached the Marvyns and the Scudders. Mrs. Marvyn is distraught not only because her son is dead, but also because he has died unregenerate, without assurance that he has been saved. Mrs. Marvyn is not comforted by the Calvinist doctrine that has been preached to her by the abstract, highly intellectualized Reverend Hopkins. This doctrine states that the test of regeneration, or salvation, is the willingness to be damned and to undergo tremendous personal trials and self-sacrifice. Those who die unregenerate, and according to Hopkins there are only a few elect, will suffer greatly, sinners in the hands of an angry Edwardsian God.

This key chapter reveals the limitations of Calvinist doctrine as applied to the lives of women, particularly mothers. In its place, Stowe offers an alternative theological possibility, a gospel based on the faith that Jesus Christ died for the sins of all humans and that he is a God of love and mercy. This modern, evangelical model of conversion is preached by Candace, a black servant who shares the name of an African queen, and is grounded in the emotional realities of women's lives and their love for their families. It is this gospel which is finally able to comfort and heal Mrs. Marvyn.]

We have said before, what we now repeat, that it is impossible to write a story of New England life and manners for superficial thought or shallow feeling. They who would fully understand the springs which moved the characters with whom we now associate must go down with us to the very depths.

Never was there a community where the roots of common life shot down so deeply, and were so intensely grappled around things sublime and eternal. The founders of it were a body of confessors and martyrs, who turned their backs on the whole glory of the visible, to found in the wilderness a republic of which the God of Heaven and Earth should be the sovereign power. For the first hundred years grew this community, shut out by a fathomless ocean from the existing world, and divided by an antagonism not less deep from all the reigning ideas of nominal Christendom.

In a community thus unworldly must have arisen a mode of thought, energetic, original, and sublime. The leaders of thought and feeling were the ministry, and we boldly assert that the spectacle of the early ministry of New England was one to which the world gives no parallel. Living an intense, earnest, practical life, mostly tilling the earth with their own hands, they yet carried on the most startling and original religious investigations with a simplicity that might have been deemed audacious, were it not so reverential. All old issues relating to government, religion, ritual, and forms of church organization having for them passed away, they went straight to the heart of things, and boldly confronted the problem of universal being. They had come out from the world as witnesses to the most solemn and sacred of human rights. They had accustomed themselves boldly to challenge and dispute all sham pretensions and idolatries of past ages,—to question the right of kings in the State, and of prelates in the Church; and now they turned the same bold inquiries towards the Eternal Throne, and threw down their glove in the lists as authorized defenders of every mystery in the Eternal Government. The task they proposed to themselves was that of reconciling the most tremendous facts of sin and evil, present and eternal, with those conceptions of Infinite Power and Benevolence which their own strong and generous natures enabled them so vividly to realize. In the intervals of planting and harvesting, they were busy with the toils of adjusting the laws of a universe. Solemnly simple, they made long journeys in their old one-horse chaises, to settle with each other some nice point of celestial jurisprudence, and to compare their maps of the Infinite. Their letters to each other form a literature altogether unique. Hopkins sends to Edwards[1] the younger his scheme of the universe, in which he starts with the proposition, that God is infinitely above all obligations of any kind to his creatures. Edwards replies with the brusque comment,—"This is wrong; God has no more right to injure a creature than a creature has to injure God;" and each probably about that time preached a sermon on his own views, which was discussed by every farmer, in intervals of plough and hoe, by every woman and girl, at loom, spinning-wheel, or wash-tub. New England was one vast sea, surging from depths to heights with thought and discussion on the most insoluble of mysteries. And it is

[1]Jonathan Edwards (1703–1758) and Samuel Hopkins (1721–1803)—theologians who had a dramatic influence on New England religious life. Edwards was known for "fire and brimstone" sermons that combined Calvinism with Locke's empiricism. Hopkins's extended study on the New Divinity led him to the doctrine that only those who had experienced religious conversion were redeemed. He was also an outspoken critic of slavery.

to be added, that no man or woman accepted any theory or speculation simply *as* theory or speculation; all was profoundly real and vital,—a foundation on which actual life was based with intensest earnestness.

The views of human existence which resulted from this course of training were gloomy enough to oppress any heart which did not rise above them by triumphant faith or sink below them by brutish insensibility; for they included every moral problem of natural or revealed religion, divested of all those softening poetries and tender draperies which forms, ceremonies, and rituals had thrown around them in other parts and ages of Christendom. The human race, without exception, coming into existence "under God's wrath and curse," with a nature so fatally disordered, that, although perfect free agents, men were infallibly certain to do nothing to Divine acceptance until regenerated by the supernatural aid of God's Spirit,—this aid being given only to a certain decreed number of the human race, the rest, with enough free agency to make them responsible, but without this indispensable assistance exposed to the malignant assaults of evil spirits versed in every art of temptation, were sure to fall hopelessly into perdition. The standard of what constituted a true regeneration, as presented in such treatises as Edwards on the Affections, and others of the times, made this change to be something so high, disinterested, and superhuman, so removed from all natural and common habits and feelings, that the most earnest and devoted, whose whole life had been a constant travail of endeavor, a tissue of almost unearthly disinterestedness, often lived and died with only a glimmering hope of its attainment.

According to any views then entertained of the evidences of a true regeneration, the number of the whole human race who could be supposed as yet to have received this grace was so small, that, as to any numerical valuation, it must have been expressed as an infinitesimal. Dr. Hopkins in many places distinctly recognizes the fact, that the greater part of the human race, up to his time, had been eternally lost,—and boldly assumes the ground, that this amount of sin and suffering, being the best and most necessary means of the greatest final amount of happiness, was not merely permitted, but distinctly chosen, decreed, and provided for, as essential in the schemes of Infinite Benevolence. He held that this decree not only *permitted* each individual act of sin, but also took measures to make it certain, though, by an exercise of infinite skill, it accomplished this result without violating human free agency.

The preaching of those times was animated by an unflinching consistency which never shrank from carrying an idea to its remotest logical verge. The sufferings of the lost were not kept from view, but proclaimed with a terrible power. Dr. Hopkins boldly asserts, that "all the use which God will have for them is to suffer; this is all the end they can answer; therefore all their faculties, and their whole capacities, will be employed and used for this end. . . . . . The body can by omnipotence be made capable of suffering the greatest imaginable pain, without producing dissolution, or abating the least degree of life or sensibility. . . . . One way in which God will show his power in punishing the wicked will be in strengthening and upholding their bodies and souls in torments which otherwise would be intolerable."

The sermons preached by President Edwards on this subject are so terrific in their refined poetry of torture, that very few persons of quick sensibility could read them through without agony; and it is related, that, when, in those calm and tender tones which never rose to passionate enunciation, he read these discourses, the house was often filled with shrieks and wailings, and that a brother minister once laid hold of his skirts, exclaiming, in an involuntary agony, "Oh! Mr. Edwards! Mr. Edwards! is God not a God of mercy?"

Not that these men were indifferent or insensible to the dread words they spoke; their whole lives and deportment bore thrilling witness to their sincerity. Edwards set apart special days of fasting, in view of the dreadful doom of the lost, in which he was wont to walk the floor, weeping and wringing his hands. Hopkins fasted every Saturday. David Brainerd[2] gave up every refinement of civilized life to weep and pray at the feet of hardened savages, if by any means he might save *one.* All, by lives of eminent purity and earnestness, gave awful weight and sanction to their words.

If we add to this statement the fact, that it was always proposed to every inquiring soul, as an evidence of regeneration, that it should truly and heartily accept all the ways of God thus declared right and lovely, and from the heart submit to Him as the only just and good, it will be seen what materials of tremendous internal conflict and agitation were all the while working in every bosom. Almost all the histories of religious experience of those times relate paroxysms of opposition to God and fierce rebellion, expressed in language which appalls the very soul,—followed, at length, by mysterious elevations of faith and reactions of confiding love, the result of Divine interposition, which carried the soul far above the region of the intellect, into that of direct spiritual intuition.

President Edwards records that he was once in this state of enmity,—that the facts of the Divine administration seemed horrible to him,—and that this opposition was overcome by no course of reasoning, but by an *"inward and sweet sense,"* which came to him once when walking alone in the fields, and, looking up into the blue sky, he saw the blending of the Divine majesty with a calm, sweet, and almost infinite meekness.

The piety which grew up under such a system was, of necessity, energetic,—it was the uprousing of the whole energy of the human soul, pierced and wrenched and probed from her lowest depths to her topmost heights with every awful life-force possible to existence. He whose faith in God came clear through these terrible tests would be sure never to know greater ones. He might certainly challenge earth or heaven, things present or things to come, to swerve him from this grand allegiance.

But it is to be conceded, that these systems, so admirable in relation to the energy, earnestness, and acuteness of their authors, when received as absolute truth, and as a basis of actual life, had, on minds of a certain class, the effect of a slow poison, producing life-habits of morbid action very different from any which ever followed the simple reading of the Bible. They differ from the New Testament as the living embrace of a friend does from his lifeless body, mapped out under the knife of the anatomical demonstrator;—every nerve and muscle is there, but to a sensitive spirit there is the very chill of death in the analysis.

All systems that deal with the infinite are, besides, exposed to danger from small, unsuspected admixtures of human error, which become deadly when carried to such vast results. The smallest speck of earth's dust, in the focus of an infinite lens, appears magnified among the heavenly orbs as a frightful monster.

[2]David Brainerd (1718–1747)—a missionary to the Indians whose pietistic life, recorded in his journal, inspired others to enter the field.

Thus it happened, that, while strong spirits walked, palm-crowned, with victorious hymns, along these sublime paths, feebler and more sensitive ones lay along the track, bleeding away in life-long despair. Fearful to them were the shadows that lay over the cradle and the grave. The mother clasped her babe to her bosom, and looked with shuddering to the awful coming trial of free agency, with its terrible responsibilities and risks; and, as she thought of the infinite chances against her beloved, almost wished it might die in infancy. But when the stroke of death came, and some young, thoughtless head was laid suddenly low, who can say what silent anguish of loving hearts sounded the dread depths of eternity with the awful question, *Where?*

In no other time or place of Christendom have so fearful issues been presented to the mind. Some church interposed its protecting shield; the Christian born and baptized child was supposed in some wise rescued from the curse of the fall, and related to the great redemption,—to be a member of Christ's family, and, if ever so sinful, still infolded in some vague sphere of hope and protection. Augustine solaced the dread anxieties of trembling love by prayers offered for the dead, in times when the Church above and on earth presented itself to the eye of the mourner as a great assembly with one accord lifting interceding hands for the parted soul.

But the clear logic and intense individualism of New England deepened the problems of the Augustinian faith, while they swept away all those softening provisions so earnestly clasped to the throbbing heart of that great poet of theology. No rite, no form, no paternal relation, no faith or prayer of church, earthly or heavenly, interposed the slightest shield between the trembling spirit and Eternal Justice. The individual entered eternity alone, as if he had no interceding relation in the universe.

This, then, was the awful dread which was constantly underlying life. This it was which caused the tolling bell in green hollows and lonely dells to be a sound which shook the soul and searched the heart with fearful questions. And this it was that was lying with mountain weight on the soul of the mother, too keenly agonized to feel that doubt in such a case was any less a torture than the most dreadful certainty.

Hers was a nature more reasoning than creative and poetic; and whatever she believed bound her mind in strictest chains to its logical results. She delighted in the regions of mathematical knowledge, and walked them as a native home, but the commerce with abstract certainties fitted her mind still more to be stiffened and enchained by glacial reasonings, in regions where spiritual intuitions are as necessary as wings to birds.

Mary was by nature of the class who never reason abstractly, whose intellections all begin in the heart which sends them colored with its warm life-tint to the brain. Her perceptions of the same subjects were as different from Mrs. Marvyn's as his who revels only in color from his who is busy with the dry details of mere outline. The one mind was arranged like a map, and the other like a picture. In all the system which had been explained to her, her mind selected points on which it seized with intense sympathy, which it dwelt upon and expanded till all else fell away. The sublimity of disinterested benevolence,—the harmony and order of a system tending in its final results to infinite happiness,—the goodness of God,—the love of a self-sacrificing Redeemer,—were all so many glorious pictures, which she revolved in her mind with small care for their logical relations.

Mrs. Marvyn had never, in all the course of their intimacy, opened her mouth to Mary on the subject of religion. It was not an uncommon incident of those times for persons of great elevation and purity of character to be familiarly known and spoken of as living under a cloud of religious gloom; and it was simply regarded as one more mysterious instance of the workings of that infinite decree which denied to them the special illumination of the Spirit.

When Mrs. Marvyn had drawn Mary with her into her room, she seemed like a person almost in frenzy. She shut and bolted the door, drew her to the foot of the bed, and, throwing her arms round her, rested her hot and throbbing forehead on her shoulder. She pressed her thin hand over her eyes, and then, suddenly drawing back, looked her in the face as one resolved to speak something long suppressed. Her soft brown eyes had a flash of despairing wildness in them, like that of a hunted animal turning in its death-struggle on its pursuer.

"Mary," she said, "I can't help it,—don't mind what I say, but I must speak or die! Mary, I cannot, will not, be resigned!—it is all hard, unjust, cruel!—to all eternity I will say so! To me there is no goodness, no justice, no mercy in anything! Life seems to me the most tremendous doom that can be inflicted on a helpless being! *What had we done,* that it should be sent upon us? Why were we made to love so, to hope so,—our hearts so full of feeling, and all the laws of Nature marching over us,—never stopping for our agony? Why, we can suffer so in this life that we had better never have been born!

"But, Mary, think what a moment life is! think of those awful ages of eternity! and then think of all God's power and knowledge used on the lost to make them suffer! think that all but the merest fragment of mankind have gone into this,—are in it now! The number of the elect is so small we can scarce count them for anything! Think what noble minds, what warm, generous hearts, what splendid natures are wrecked and thrown away by thousands and tens of thousands! How we love each other! how our hearts weave into each other! how more than glad we should be to die for each other! And all this ends—O God, how must it end?—Mary! it isn't *my* sorrow only! What right have I to mourn? Is *my* son any better than any other mother's son? Thousands of thousands, whose mothers loved them as I love mine, are gone there!—Oh, my wedding-day! Why did they rejoice? Brides should wear mourning,—the bells should toll for every wedding; every new family is built over this awful pit of despair, and only one in a thousand escapes!"

Pale, aghast, horror-stricken, Mary stood dumb, as one who in the dark and storm sees by the sudden glare of lightning a chasm yawning under foot. It was amazement and dimness of anguish,—the dreadful words struck on the very centre where her soul rested. She felt as if the point of a wedge were being driven between her life and her life's life,—between her and her God. She clasped her hands instinctively on her bosom, as if to hold there some cherished image, and said, in a piercing voice of supplication, "*My* God! *my* God! oh, where art Thou?"

Mrs. Marvyn walked up and down the room with a vivid spot of red in each cheek, and a baleful fire in her eyes, talking in rapid soliloquy, scarcely regarding her listener, absorbed in her own enkindled thoughts.

"Dr. Hopkins says that this is all best,—better than it would have been in any other possible way,—that God *chose* it because it was for a greater final good,—that He not only chose it, but took means to make it certain,—that He ordains every sin, and does all that is necessary to make it certain,—that He creates the vessels of wrath and fits them for destruction, and that He has an infinite knowledge by which He can do it without violating their free agency.—So much the worse! What a use of infinite knowledge! What if men should do so? What if a father should take means to make it certain that his poor little child should be an abandoned wretch, without violating his free agency? So much the worse, I say!—They say He does this so that He may show to all eternity, by their example, the evil nature of sin and its consequences! This is all that the greater part of the human race have been used for yet; and it is all right, because an overplus of infinite happiness is yet to be wrought out by it!—It is *not* right! No possible amount of good to ever so many can make it right to deprave ever so few;—happiness and misery cannot be measured so! I never can think it right,—never!—Yet they say our salvation depends on our loving God,—loving Him better than ourselves,—loving Him better than our dearest friends.—It is impossible!—it is contrary to the laws of my nature! I can never love God! I can never praise Him!—I am lost! lost! lost! And what is worse, I cannot redeem my friends! Oh, I *could* suffer forever,—how willingly!—if I could save *him!*—But oh, eternity, eternity! Frightful, unspeakable woe! No end!—no bottom!—no shore!—no hope!—O God! O God!"

Mrs. Marvyn's eyes grew wilder,—she walked the floor, wringing her hands,—and her words, mingled with shrieks and moans, became whirling and confused, as when in autumn a storm drives the leaves in dizzy mazes.

Mary was alarmed,—the ecstacy of despair was just verging on insanity. She rushed out and called Mr. Marvyn.

"Oh! come in! do! quick!—I'm afraid her mind is going!" she said.

"It is what I feared," he said, rising from where he sat reading his great Bible, with an air of heartbroken dejection. "Since she heard this news, she has not slept nor shed a tear. The Lord hath covered us with a cloud in the day of his fierce anger."

He came into the room, and tried to take his wife into his arms. She pushed him violently back, her eyes glistening with a fierce light. "Leave me alone!" she said,—"I am a lost spirit!"

These words were uttered in a shriek that went through Mary's heart like an arrow.

At this moment, Candace, who had been anxiously listening at the door for an hour past, suddenly burst into the room.

"Lor' bress ye, Squire Marvyn, we won't hab her goin' on dis yer way," she said. "Do talk *gospel* to her, can't ye?—ef you can't, I will.

"Come, ye poor little lamb," she said, walking straight up to Mrs. Marvyn, "come to old Candace!"—and with that she gathered the pale form to her bosom, and sat down and began rocking her, as if she had been a babe. "Honey, darlin', ye a'n't right,—dar's a drefful mistake somewhar," she said. "Why, de Lord a'n't like what ye tink,—He *loves* ye, honey! Why, jes' feel how *I* loves ye,—poor ole black Candace,—an' I a'n't better'n Him as made me! Who was it wore de crown o' thorns, lamb?—who was it sweat great drops o' blood?—who was it said, 'Father, forgive dem'? Say, honey!—wasn't it de Lord dat made ye?—Dar, dar, now ye'r' cryin'!—cry away, and ease yer poor little heart! He died for Mass'r Jim,—loved him and *died* for him,—jes' give up his sweet, precious body and soul for him on de cross! Laws, jes' *leave* him in Jesus's hands! Why, honey, dar's de very print o' de nails in his hands now!"

The flood-gates were rent; and healing sobs and tears shook the frail form, as a faded lily shakes under the soft rains of summer. All in the room wept together.

"Now, honey," said Candace, after a pause of some minutes, "I knows our Doctor's a mighty good man, an' larned,—an' in fair weather I ha'n't no 'bjection to yer hearin' all about dese yer great an' mighty tings he's got to say. But, honey, dey won't do for you now; sick folks mus'n't hab strong meat; an' times like dese, dar jest a'n't but one ting to come to, an' dat ar's *Jesus*. Jes' come right down to whar poor ole black Candace has to stay allers,—it's a good place, darlin'! *Look right at Jesus.* Tell ye, honey, ye can't live no other way now. Don't ye 'member how He looked on His mother, when she stood faintin' an' tremblin' under de cross, jes' like you? He knows all about mothers' hearts; He won't break yours. It was jes' 'cause He know'd we'd come into straits like dis yer, dat he went through all dese tings,—Him, de Lord o' Glory! Is dis Him you was a-talkin' about?—Him you can't love? Look at Him, an' see ef you can't. Look an' see what He is!—don't ask no questions, and don't go to no reasonin's,—jes' look at *Him,* hangin' dar, so sweet and patient, on de cross! All dey could do couldn't stop his lovin' 'em; he prayed for 'em wid all de breath he had. Dar's a God you can love, a'n't dar? Candace loves Him,—poor, ole, foolish, black, wicked Candace,—and she knows He loves her,"—and here Candace broke down into torrents of weeping.

They laid the mother, faint and weary, on her bed, and beneath the shadow of that suffering cross came down a healing sleep on those weary eyelids.

"Honey," said Candace, mysteriously, after she had drawn Mary out of the room, "don't ye go for to troublin' yer mind wid dis yer. I'm clar Mass'r James is one o' de 'lect; and I'm clar dar's consid'able more o' de 'lect dan people tink. Why, Jesus didn't die for nothin',—all dat love a'n't gwine to be wasted. De 'lect is more'n you or I knows, honey! Dar's de *Spirit,*—He'll give it to 'em; and ef Mass'r James *is* called an' took, depend upon it de Lord has got him ready,—course He has,—so don't ye go to layin' on your poor heart what no mortal creetur can live under; 'cause, as we's got to live in dis yer world, it's quite clar de Lord must ha' fixed it so we *can;* and ef tings was as some folks suppose, why, we *couldn't* live, and dar wouldn't be no sense in anyting dat goes on."

The sudden shock of these scenes was followed, in Mrs. Marvyn's case, by a low, lingering fever. Her room was darkened, and she lay on her bed, a pale, suffering form, with scarcely the ability to raise her hand. The shimmering twilight of the sick-room fell on white napkins, spread over stands, where constantly appeared new vials, big and little, as the physician made his daily visit, and prescribed now this drug and now that, for a wound that had struck through the soul.

Mary remained many days at the white house, because, to the invalid, no step, no voice, no hand was like hers. We see her there now, as she sits in the glimmering by the bed-curtains,—her head a little drooped, as droops a snowdrop over a grave;—one ray of light from a round hole in the closed shutters falls on her smooth-parted hair, her small hands are clasped on her knees, her mouth has lines of sad compression, and in her eyes are infinite questionings.

1859

Sojourner Truth, the Libyan Sibyl[1]

Many years ago, the few readers of radical abolitionist papers must often have seen the singular name of Sojourner Truth announced as a frequent speaker at anti-slavery meetings, and as traveling on a sort of self-appointed agency through the country. I had myself often remarked the name, but never met the individual. On one occasion, when our house was filled with company, several eminent clergymen being our guests, notice was brought up to me that Sojourner Truth was below and requested an interview. Knowing nothing of her but her singular name, I went down, prepared to make this interview short, as the pressure of many other engagements demanded.

When I went into the room, a tall, spare form arose to meet me. She was evidently a full-blooded African, and, though now aged and worn with many hardships, still gave the impression of a physical development which in early youth must have been as fine a specimen of the torrid zone as Cumberworth's celebrated statuette of the Negro Woman at the Fountain. Indeed, she so strongly reminded me of that figure, that, when I recall the events of her life, as she narrated them to me, I imagine her as a living, breathing impersonation of that work of art.

I do not recollect ever to have been conversant with any one who had more of that silent and subtle power which we call personal presence than this woman. In the modern spiritualistic phraseology, she would be described as having a strong sphere. Her tall form, as she rose up before me, is still vivid to my mind. She was dressed in some stout, grayish stuff, neat and clean, though dusty from travel. On her head she wore a bright Madras handkerchief, arranged as a turban, after the manner of her race. She seemed perfectly self-possessed and at her ease,—in fact, there was almost an unconscious superiority, not unmixed with a solemn twinkle of humor, in the odd, composed manner in which she looked down on me. Her whole air had at times a gloomy sort of drollery which impressed one strangely.

"So this is *you?*" she said.

"Yes," I answered.

"Well, honey, de Lord bless ye! I jes' thought I'd like to come an' have a look at ye. You's heerd o' me, I reckon?" she added.

"Yes, I think I have. You go about lecturing, do you not?"

"Yes, honey, that's what I do. The Lord has made me a sign unto this nation, an' I go round a-testifyin', an' showin' on 'em their sins agin my people."

So saying, she took a seat, and, stooping over and crossing her arms on her knees, she looked down on the floor, and appeared to fall into a sort of reverie. Her great gloomy eyes and her dark face seemed to work with some undercurrent of feeling; she sighed deeply, and occasionally broke out,—

"O Lord ! O Lord! O the tears, an' the groans, an' the moans! O Lord!"

I should have said that she was accompanied by a little grandson of ten years,—the fattest, jolliest woolly-headed little specimen of Africa that one can imagine. He

[1]Sojourner Truth (1797?–1883)—evangelist, abolitionist, reformer, and women's rights activist, traveled and spoke out against social injustice from the time of her emancipation in 1826 until her death. See selection this volume.

was grinning and showing his glistening white teeth in a state of perpetual merriment, and at this moment broke out into an audible giggle, which disturbed the reverie into which his relative was falling.

She looked at him with an indulgent sadness, and then at me.

"Laws, ma'am, *he* don't know nothin' about it,—*he* don't. Why, I've seen them poor critturs, beat an' 'bused an' hunted, brought in all torn,—ears hangin' all in rags, where the dogs been a-bitin' of 'em!"

This set off our little African Puck into another giggle, in which he seemed perfectly convulsed.

She surveyed him soberly, without the slightest irritation.

"Well, you may bless the Lord you *can* laugh; but I tell you, 'twa'n't no laughin' matter."

By this time I thought her manner so original that it might be worth while to call down my friends; and she seemed perfectly well pleased with the idea. An audience was what she wanted,—it mattered not whether high or low, learned or ignorant. She had things to say, and was ready to say them at all times, and to any one.

I called down Dr. Beecher, Professor Allen, and two or three other clergymen, who, together with my husband and family, made a roomful. No princess could have received a drawing-room with more composed dignity than Sojourner her audience. She stood among them, calm and erect, as one of her own native palm-trees waving alone in the desert. I presented one after another to her, and at last said,—

"Sojourner, this is Dr. Beecher. He is a very celebrated preacher."

"*Is* he?" she said, offering her hand in a condescending manner, and looking down on his white head. "Ye dear lamb, I'm glad to see ye! De Lord bless ye! I loves preachers. I'm a kind o' preacher myself."

"You are?" said Dr. Beecher. "Do you preach from the Bible?"

"No, honey, can't preach from de Bible,—can't read a letter."

"Why, Sojourner, what do you preach from, then?"

Her answer was given with a solemn power of voice, peculiar to herself, that hushed every one in the room.

"When I preaches, I has just one text to preach from, an' I always preaches from this one. *My* text is, 'WHEN I FOUND JESUS.'"

"Well, you couldn't have a better one," said one of the ministers.

She paid no attention to him, but stood and seemed swelling with her own thoughts, and then began this narration:—

"Well, now, I'll jest have to go back, an' tell ye all about it. Ye see, we was all brought over from Africa, father an' mother an' I, an' a lot more of us; an' we was sold up an' down, an' hither an' yon; an' I can 'member when I was a little thing, not bigger than this 'ere," pointing to her grandson, "how my old mammy would sit out o' doors in the evenin', an' look up at the stars an' groan. She'd groan an' groan, an' says I to her,—

"'Mammy, what makes you groan so?'

"An' she'd say,—

"'Matter enough, chile! I'm groanin' to think o' my poor children: they don't know where I be, an' I don't know where they be; they looks up at the stars, an' I looks up at the stars, but I can't tell where they be.

"'Now,' she said, 'chile, when you're grown up, you may be sold away from your mother an' all your ole friends, an' have great troubles come on ye; an' when you has these troubles come on ye, ye jes' go to God, an' He'll help ye.'

"An' says I to her,—

"'Who is God anyhow, mammy?'

"An' says she,—

"'Why, chile, you jes' look up *dar!* It's Him that made all *dem!*'

"Well, I didn't mind much 'bout God in them days. I grew up pretty lively an' strong, an' could row a boat, or ride a horse, or work round, an' do 'most anything.

"At last I got sold away to a real hard massa an' missis. Oh, I tell you, they *was* hard! 'Peared like I couldn't please 'em, nohow. An' then I thought o' what my old mammy told me about God; an' I thought I'd got into trouble, sure enough, an' I wanted to find God, an' I heerd some one tell a story about a man that met God on a threshin'-floor, an' I thought, 'Well an' good, I'll have a threshin'-floor, too.' So I went down in the lot, an' I threshed down a place real hard, an' I used to go down there every day an' pray an' cry with all my might, a-prayin' to the Lord to make my massa an' missis better, but it didn't seem to do no good; an' so says I, one day,—

"'O God, I been a-askin' ye, an' askin' ye, for all this long time, to make my massa an' missis better, an' you don't do it, an' what *can* be the reason? Why, maybe you *can't.* Well, I shouldn't wonder ef you couldn't. Well, now, I tell you, I'll make a bargain with you. Ef you'll help me to git away from my massa an' missis, I'll agree to be good; but ef you don't help me, I really don't think I can be. Now,' says I, 'I want to git away; but the trouble's jest here: ef I try to git away in the night, I can't see; an' ef I try to git away in the daytime, they'll see me, an' be after me.'

"Then the Lord said to me, 'Git up two or three hours afore daylight, an' start off.'

"An' says I, 'Thank 'ee, Lord! that's a good thought.'

"So up I got, about three o'clock in the mornin,' an' I started an' traveled pretty fast, till, when the sun rose, I was clear away from our place an' our folks, an' out o'sight. An' then I begun to think I didn't know nothin' where to go. So I kneeled down, and says I,—

"'Well, Lord, you've started me out, an' now please to show me where to go.'

"Then the Lord made a house appear to me, an' He said to me that I was to walk on till I saw that house, an' then go in an' ask the people to take me. An' I traveled all day, an' didn't come to the house till late at night; but when I saw it, sure enough, I went in, an' I told the folks that the Lord sent me; an' they was Quakers, an' real kind they was to me. They jes' took me in, an' did for me as kind as ef I'd been one of 'em; an' after they'd give me supper, they took me into a room where there was a great, tall, white bed; an' they told me to sleep there. Well, honey, I was kind o' skeered when they left me alone with that great white bed; 'cause I never had been in a bed in my life. It never came into my mind they could mean me to sleep in it. An' so I jes' camped down under it on the floor, an' then I slep' pretty well. In the mornin', when they came in, they asked me ef I hadn't been asleep; an' I said, 'Yes, I never slep' better.' An' they said, 'Why, you haven't been in the bed!' An' says I, 'Laws, you didn't think o' sech a thing as my sleepin' in dat ar *bed,* did you? I never heerd o' sech a thing in my life.'

"Well, ye see, honey, I stayed an' lived with 'em. An' now jes' look here: instead o' keepin' my promise an' bein' good, as I told the Lord I would, jest as soon as everything got a-goin' easy, *I forgot all about God.*

"Pretty well don't need no help; an' I gin up prayin'. I lived there two or three years, an' then the slaves in New York were all set free, an' ole massa came to our house to make a visit, an' he asked me ef I didn't want to go back an' see the folks on the ole place. An' I told him I did. So he said, ef I'd jes' git into the wagon with him, he'd carry me over. Well, jest as I was goin' out to git into the wagon, *I met God!* an' says I, 'O God, I didn't know as you was so great!' An' I turned right round an' come into the house, an' set down in my room; for 't was God all around me. I could feel it burnin', burnin', burnin' all around me, an' goin' through me; an' I saw I was so wicked, it seemed as ef it would burn me up. An' I said, 'Oh, somebody, somebody, stand between God an' me, for it burns me!' Then, honey, when I said so, I felt as it were somethin' like an *amberill* [umbrella] that came between me an' the light, an' I felt it was *somebody,*—somebody that stood between me an' God; an' it felt cool, like a shade; an' says I, 'Who's this that stands between me an' God? Is it old Cato?' He was a pious old preacher; but then I seemed to see Cato in the light, an' he was all polluted an' vile, like me; an' I said, 'Is it old Sally?' an' then I saw her, an' she seemed jes' so. An' then says I, '*Who* is this?' An' then, honey, for a while it was like the sun shinin' in a pail o' water, when it moves up an' down; for I begun to feel 't was somebody that loved me; an' I tried to know him. An' I said, 'I know you! I know you! I know you!'—an' then I said, 'I don't know you! I don't know you! I don't know you!' An' when I said, 'I know you, I know you,' the light came; an' when I said, 'I don't know you, I don't know you,' it went, jes' like the sun in a pail o' water. An' finally somethin' spoke out in me an' said, *'This is Jesus!'* an' I spoke out with all my might, an' says I, '*This is Jesus!* Glory be to God!' An' then the whole world grew bright, an' the trees they waved an' waved in glory, an' every little bit o' stone on the ground shone like glass; an' I shouted an' said, 'Praise, praise, praise to the Lord!' An' I begun to feel sech a love in my soul as I never felt before,—love to all creatures. An' then, all of a sudden, it stopped, an' I said, 'Dar's de white folks, that have abused you an' beat you an' abused your people,—think o' them!' But then there came another rush of love through my soul, an' I cried out loud, 'Lord, Lord, I can love *even de white folks!*'

"Honey, I jes' walked round an' round in a dream. Jesus loved me! I knowed it,—I felt it. Jesus was my Jesus. Jesus would love me always. I didn't dare tell nobody; 't was a great secret. Everything had been got away from me that I ever had; an' I thought that ef I let white folks know about this, maybe they'd get *Him* away,—so I said, 'I'll keep this close. I won't let any one know.'"

"But, Sojourner, had you never been told about Jesus Christ?"

"No, honey. I hadn't heerd no preachin',—been to no meetin'. Nobody hadn't told me. I'd kind o' heerd of Jesus, but thought he was like Gineral Lafayette, or some o' them. But one night there was a Methodist meetin' somewhere in our parts, an' I went; an' they got up an' begun for to tell der 'speriences; an' de fust one begun to speak. I started, 'cause he told about Jesus. 'Why,' says I to myself, 'dat man's found him, too!' An' another got up an' spoke, an' I said, 'He's found him, too!' An' finally I said, 'Why, they all know him!' I was so happy! An' then they sung this hymn" (here Sojourner sang, in a strange, cracked voice, but evidently with all her soul and might, mispronouncing the English, but seeming to derive as much elevation and comfort from bad English as from good):—

"There is a holy city,
 A world of light above,

Above the stairs and regions,[2]
   Built by the God of love.

"An everlasting temple,
   And saints arrayed in white
There serve their great Redeemer
   And dwell with him in light.

"The meanest child of glory
   Outshines the radiant sun;
But who can speak the splendor
   Of Jesus on his throne?

"Is this the man of sorrows
   Who stood at Pilate's bar,
Condemned by haughty Herod
   And by his men of war?

"He seems a mighty conqueror,
   Who spoiled the powers below,
And ransomed many captives
   From everlasting woe.

"The hosts of saints around him
   Proclaim his work of grace,
The patriarchs and prophets,
   And all the godly race,

"Who speak of fiery trials
   And tortures on their way;
They came from tribulation
   To everlasting day.

"And what shall be my journey,
   How long I'll stay below,
Or what shall be my trials,
   Are not for me to know.

"In every day of trouble
   I'll raise my thoughts on high,
I'll think of that bright temple
   And crowns above the sky."

I put in this whole hymn, because Sojourner, carried away with her own feeling, sang it from beginning to end with a triumphant energy that held the whole circle around her intently listening. She sang with the strong barbaric accent of the native African, and with those indescribable upward turns and those deep gutterals which

[2]Starry regions.

give such a wild, peculiar power to the negro singing,—but, above all, with such an overwhelming energy of personal appropriation that the hymn seemed to be fused in the furnace of her feelings and come out recrystallized as a production of her own.

It is said that Rachel was wont to chant the Marseillaise in a manner that made her seem, for the time, the very spirit and impersonation of the gaunt, wild, hungry, avenging mob which rose against aristocratic oppression; and in like manner Sojourner, singing this hymn, seemed to impersonate the fervor of Ethiopia, savage, hunted of all nations, but burning after God in her tropic heart, and stretching her scarred hands towards the glory to be revealed.

"Well, den, ye see, after a while I thought I'd go back an' see de folks on de ole place. Well, you know, de law had passed dat de cullud folks was all free; an' my old missis, she had a daughter married about dis time who went to live in Alabama,—an' what did she do but give her my son, a boy about de age of dis yer, for her to take down to Alabama? When I got back to de ole place, they told me about it, an' I went right up to see ole missis, an' says I,—

"'Missis, have you been an' sent my son away down to Alabama?'

"'Yes, I have,' says she; 'he's gone to live with your young missis.'

"'Oh, missis,' says I, 'how could you do it?'

"'Poh!' says she 'what a fuss you make about a little nigger! Got more of 'em now than you know what to do with.'

"I tell you, I stretched up. I felt as tall as the world!

"'Missis,' says I, *'I'll have my son back agin!'*

"She laughed.

"'*You* will, you nigger? How you goin' to do it? You ha'n't got no money.'

"'No, missis, but *God* has, an' you'll see He'll help me!' An' I turned round, an' went out.

"Oh, but I *was* angry to have her speak to me so haughty an' so scornful, as ef my chile wasn't worth anything. I said to God, 'O Lord, render unto her double!' It was a dreadful prayer, an' I didn't know how true it would come.

"Well, I didn't rightly know which way to turn; but I went to the Lord, an' I said to Him, 'O Lord, ef I was as rich as you be, an' you was as poor as I be, I'd help you,—you *know* I would; and, oh, do help me!' An' I felt sure then that He would.

"Well, I talked with people, an' they said I must git the case before a grand jury. So I went into the town, when they was holdin' a court, to see ef I could find any grand jury. An' I stood round the court-house, an' when they was a-comin' out I walked right up to the grandest-lookin' one I could see, an' says I to him,—

"'Sir, be you a grand jury?'

"An' then he wanted to know why I asked, an' I told him all about it; an' he asked me all sorts of questions, an' finally he says to me,—

"'I think, ef you pay me ten dollars, that I'd agree to git your son for you.' An' says he, pointin' to a house over the way, 'You go long an' tell your story to the folks in that house, an' I guess they'll give you the money.'

"Well, I went, an' I told them, an' they gave me twenty dollars; an' then I thought to myself, 'Ef ten dollars will git him, twenty dollars will git him *sartin*.' So I carried it to the man all out, an' said,—

"'Take it all,—only be sure an' git him.'

"Well, finally they got the boy brought back; an' then they tried to frighten him, an' to make him say that I wasn't his mammy, an' that he didn't know me; but they couldn't make it out. They gave him to me, an' I took him an' carried him home; an' when I came to take off his clothes, there was his poor little back all covered with scars an' hard lumps, where they'd flogged him.

"Well, you see, honey, I told you how I prayed the Lord to render unto her double. Well, it came true; for I was up at ole missis' house not long after, an' I heerd 'em readin' a letter to her how her daughter's husband had murdered her,—how he'd thrown her down an' stamped the life out of her when he was in liquor; an' my ole missis, she giv' a screech an' fell flat on the floor. Then says I, 'O Lord, I didn't mean all that! You took me up too quick.'

"Well, I went in an' tended that poor critter all night. She was out of her mind,—a-cryin,' an' callin' for her daughter; an' I held her poor ole head on my arm, an' watched for her as ef she'd been my babby. An' I watched by her, an' took care on her all through her sickness after that, an' she died in my arms, poor thing!"

"Well, Sojourner, did you always go by this name?"

"No, 'deed! My name was Isabella; but when I left the house of bondage, I left everything behind. I wa'n't goin' to keep nothin' of Egypt on me, an' so I went to the Lord an' asked Him to give me a new name. And the Lord gave me Sojourner, because I was to travel up an' down the land, showin' the people their sins, an' bein' a sign unto them. Afterwards I told the Lord I wanted another name, 'cause everybody else had two names; and the Lord gave me Truth, because I was to declare the truth to the people.

"Ye see, some ladies have given me a white satin banner," she said, pulling out of her pocket and unfolding a white banner, printed with many texts, such as, "Proclaim liberty throughout all the land unto all the inhabitants thereof," and others of like nature. "Well," she said, "I journeys round to camp-meetin's, an' wherever folks is, an' I sets up my banner, an' then I sings, an' then folks always comes up round me, an' then I preaches to 'em. I tells 'em about Jesus, an' I tells 'em about the sins of this people. A great many always comes to hear me; an' they're right good to me, too, an' say they want to hear me agin."

We all thought it likely; and as the company left her, they shook hands with her, and thanked her for her very original sermon; and one of the ministers was overheard to say to another, "There's more of the gospel in that story than in most sermons."

Sojourner stayed several days with us, a welcome guest. Her conversation was so strong, simple, shrewd, and with such a droll flavoring of humor, that the Professor was wont to say of an evening, "Come, I am dull, can't you get Sojourner up here to talk a little?" She would come up into the parlor, and sit among pictures and ornaments, in her simple stuff gown, with her heavy traveling-shoes, the central object of attention both to parents and children, always ready to talk or to sing, and putting into the common flow of conversation the keen edge of some shrewd remark.

"Sojourner, what do you think of Women's Rights?"

"Well, honey, I's ben to der meetings, an' harked a good deal. Dey wanted me fur to speak. So I got up. Says I, 'Sisters, I ain't clear what you'd be after. Ef women want any rights more'n dey's got, why don't dey jes' *take 'em,* an' not be talkin' about it?' Some on 'em came round me, an' asked why I didn't wear bloomers. An' I told 'em I had bloomers enough when I was in bondage. You see," she said, "dey used to weave what dey called niggercloth, an' each one of us got jes' sech a strip, an' had to wear it width-wise. Them that was short got along pretty well, but as for me"—She gave an indescribably droll glance at her long limbs and then at us, and added, "Tell *you,* I had enough of bloomers in them days."

Sojourner then proceeded to give her views of the relative capacity of the sexes, in her own way.

"S'pose a man's mind holds a quart, an' a woman's don't hold but a pint; ef her pint is *full,* it's as good as his quart."

Sojourner was fond of singing an extraordinary lyric, commencing,—

"I'm on my way to Canada,
That cold but happy land;
The dire effects of slavery
I can no longer stand

O righteous Father,
Do look down on me,
And help me on to Canada,
Where colored folks are free!"

The lyric ran on to state that, when the fugitive crosses the Canada line,

"The Queen comes down unto the shore,
With arms extended wide,
To welcome the poor fugitive
Safe on to Freedom's side."

In the truth thus set forth she seemed to have the most simple faith.

But her chief delight was to talk of "glory," and to sing hymns whose burden was,—

"O glory, glory, glory,
Won't you come along with me?"

and when left to herself she would often hum these with great delight, nodding her head.

On one occasion I remember her sitting at a window singing, and fervently keeping time with her head, the little black Puck of a grandson meanwhile amusing himself with ornamenting her red-and-yellow turban with green dandelion curls, which shook and trembled with her emotions, causing him perfect convulsions of delight.

"Sojourner," said the Professor to her one day when he heard her singing, "you seem to be very sure about heaven."

"Well, I be," she answered triumphantly.

"What makes you so sure there is any heaven?"

"Well, 'cause I got such a hankerin' arter it in here," she said, giving a thump on her breast with her usual energy.

There was at the time an invalid in the house, and Sojourner, on learning it, felt a mission to go and comfort her. It was curious to see the tall, gaunt, dusky figure stalk up to the bed, with such an air of conscious authority, and take on herself the office of consoler with such a mixture of authority and tenderness. She talked as from above, and at the same time if a pillow needed changing, or any office to be rendered, she did it with a strength and handiness that inspired trust. One felt as if the dark, strange woman were quite able to take up the invalid in her bosom and bear her as a lamb, both physically and spiritually. There was both power and sweetness in that great warm soul and that vigorous frame.

At length Sojourner, true to her name, departed. She had her mission elsewhere. Where now she is, I know not; but she left deep memories behind her.

To these recollections of my own, I will add one more anecdote, related by Wendell Phillips. Speaking of the power of Rachel to move and bear down a whole audience by a few simple words, he said he never knew but one other human being that had that power, and that other was Sojourner Truth. He related a scene of which he was witness. It was at a crowded public meeting in Faneuil Hall, where Frederick Douglass was one of the chief speakers. Douglass had been describing the wrongs of the black race, and as he proceeded he grew more and more excited, and finally ended by saying that they had no hope of justice from the whites, no possible hope except in their own right arms. It must come to blood; they must fight for themselves, and redeem themselves, or it would never be done. Sojourner was sitting, tall and dark, on the very front seat, facing the platform; and in the hush of deep feeling, after Douglass sat down, she spoke out in her deep, peculiar voice, heard all over the house,—

"Frederick, *is God dead?*"

The effect was perfectly electrical, and thrilled through the whole house, changing as by a flash the whole feeling of the audience. Not another word she said or needed to say; it was enough. . . .

1863

from Oldtown Folks

[Another of Stowe's New England novels, *Oldtown Folks,* depicts life in a small village in Connecticut. Told from the perspective of Horace Holyoke (modelled after Stowe's husband), the novel recounts in convincing detail the lives of many of the village's inhabitants. Among these are the orphaned Tina and Harry, whose experiences with Miss Asphyxia are described in the following selection. In this chapter, Stowe retreats from her fond detailing of regional mores and critiques New England child-rearing with a vehemence and precision that may be read in the context of present day concern about domestic violence and child abuse.]

VIII Miss Asphyxia

"There won't be no great profit in this 'ere these ten year."

The object denominated "this 'ere" was the golden-haired child whom we have spoken of before,—the little girl whose mother lay dying. That mother is dead now; and the thing to be settled is, What is to be done with the children? The morning after the scene we have described looked in at the window and saw the woman, with a pale, placid face, sleeping as one who has found eternal rest, and the two weeping children striving in vain to make her hear.

Old Crab had been up early in his design of "carting the 'hull lot over to the poor-house," but made a solemn pause when his wife drew him into the little chamber. Death has a strange dignity, and whatsoever child of Adam he lays his hand on is for the time ennobled,—removed from the region of the earthly and commonplace to that of the spiritual and mysterious. And when Crab found, by searching the little bundle of the deceased, that there was actually money enough in it to buy a coffin and pay 'Zekiel Stebbins for digging the grave, he began to look on the woman as having made a respectable and edifying end, and the whole affair as coming to a better issue than he had feared.

And so the event was considered in the neighborhood, in a melancholy way, rather an interesting and auspicious one. It gave something to talk about in a region where exciting topics were remarkably scarce. The Reverend Jabez Periwinkle found in it a moving Providence which started him favorably on a sermon, and the funeral had been quite a windfall to all the gossips about; and now remained the question, What was to be done with the children?

"Now that we are diggin' the 'taters," said Old Crab, "that 'ere chap might be good for suthin', pickin' on 'em out o' the hills. Poor folks like us can't afford to keep nobody jest to look at, and so he'll have to step spry and work smart to airn his keep." And so at early dawn, the day after the funeral, the little boy was roused up and carried into the fields with the men.

But "this 'ere"—that is to say, a beautiful little girl of seven years—had greatly puzzled the heads of the worthy gossips of the neighborhood. Miss Asphyxia Smith, the elder sister of old Crab, was at this moment turning the child round, and examining her through a pair of large horn spectacles, with a view to "taking her to raise," as she phrased it.

Now all Miss Asphyxia's ideas of the purpose and aim of human existence were comprised in one word,—work. She was herself a working machine, always wound up and going,—up at early cock-crowing, and busy till bedtime, with a rampant and fatiguing industry that never paused for a moment. She conducted a large farm by the aid of a hired man, and drove a flourishing dairy, and was universally respected in the neighborhood as a smart woman.

Latterly, as her young cousin, who had shared the toils of the house with her, had married and left her, Miss Asphyxia had talked of "takin' a child from the poor-house, and so raisin' her own help"; and it was with the view of this "raisin' her help," that she was thus turning over and inspecting the little article which we have spoken of.

Apparently she was somewhat puzzled, and rather scandalized, that Nature should evidently have expended so much in a merely ornamental way on an article which ought to have been made simply for service. She brushed up a handful of the clustering curls in her large, bony hand, and said, with a sniff, "These'll have to come right off to begin with; gracious me, what a tangle!"

"Mother always brushed them out every day," said the child.

"And who do you suppose is going to spend an hour every day brushing your hair, Miss Pert?" said Miss Asphyxia. "That ain't what I take ye for, I tell you. You've got to learn to work for your living; and you ought to be thankful if I'm willing to show you how."

The little girl did not appear particularly thankful. She bent her soft, pencilled eyebrows in a dark frown, and her great hazel eyes had gathering in them a cloud of sullen gloom. Miss Asphyxia did not mind her frowning,—perhaps did not notice it. She had it settled in her mind, as a first principle, that children never liked anything that was good for them, and that, of course, if she took a child, it would have to be made to come to her by forcible proceedings promptly instituted. So she set her little subject before her by seizing her by her two shoulders and squaring her round and looking in her face, and opened direct conversation with her in the following succinct manner.

"What's your name?"

Then followed a resolved and gloomy silence, as the large bright eyes surveyed, with a sort of defiant glance, the inquisitor.

"Don't you hear?" said Miss Asphyxia, giving her a shake.

"Don't be so ha'sh with her," said the little old woman. "Say, my little dear, tell Miss Asphyxia your name," she added, taking the child's hand.

"Eglantine Percival," said the little girl, turning towards the old woman, as if she disdained to answer the other party in the conversation.

"Wh—a—t?" said Miss Asphyxia. "If there ain't the beatin'est name ever I heard. Well, I tell you *I* ain't got time to fix *my* mouth to say all that 'ere every time I want ye, now I tell ye."

"Mother and Harry called me Tina," said the child.

"Teny! Well, I should think so," said Miss Asphyxia. "That showed she'd got a grain o' sense left, anyhow. She's tol'able strong and well-limbed for her age," added that lady, feeling of the child's arms and limbs; "her flesh is solid. I think she'll make a strong woman, only put her to work early and keep her at it. I could rub out clothes at the wash-tub afore I was at her age."

"O, she can do considerable many little chores," said Old Crab's wife.

"Yes," said Miss Asphyxia; "there can a good deal be got out of a child if you keep at 'em, hold 'em in tight, and never let 'em have their head a minute; push right hard on behind 'em, and you get considerable. That's the way I was raised."

"But I want to play," said the little girl, bursting out in a sobbing storm of mingled fear and grief.

"Want to play, do you? Well, you must get over that. Don't you know that that's as bad as stealing? You haven't got any money, and if you eat folks's bread and butter, you've got to work to pay for it; and if folks buy your clothes, you've got to work to pay for them."

"But I've got some clothes of my own," persisted the child, determined not to give up her case entirely.

"Well, so you have; but there ain't no sort of wear in 'em," said Miss Asphyxia, turning to Mrs. Smith. "Them two dresses o' hern might answer for Sundays and sich, but I'll have to make her up a regular linsey working dress this fall, and check aprons; and she must set right about knitting every minute she is n't doing anything else. Did you ever learn how to knit?"

"No," said the child.

"Or to sew?" said Miss Asphyxia.

"Yes; mother taught me to sew," said the child.

"No! Yes! Hain't you learned manners? Do you say yes and no to people?"

The child stood a moment, swelling with suppressed feeling, and at last she opened her great eyes full on Miss Asphyxia, and said, "I don't like you. You ain't pretty, and I won't go with you."

"O now," said Mrs. Smith, "little girls mustn't talk so; that's naughty."

"Don't like me?—ain't I pretty?" said Miss Asphyxia, with a short, grim laugh.

"May be I ain't; but I know what I'm about, and you'd as goods know it first as last. I'm going to take ye right out with me in the waggin, and you'd best not have none of your cuttin's up. I keep a stick at home for naughty girls. Why, where do you suppose you're going to get your livin' if I don't take you?"

"I want to live with Harry," said the child, sobbing. "Where is Harry?"

"Harry's to work,—and there's where he's got to be," said Miss Asphyxia. "He's got to work with the men in the fields, and you've got to come home and work with me."

"I want to stay with Harry,—Harry takes care of me," said the child, in a piteous tone.

Old Mother Smith now toddled to her milk-room, and, with a melting heart, brought out a doughnut. "There now, eat that," she said; "and mebbe, if you're good, Miss Asphyxia will bring you down here some time."

"O laws, Polly, you allers was a fool!" said Miss Asphyxia. "It's all for the child's good, and what's the use of fussin' on her up? She'll come to it when she knows she's got to. 'Tain't no more than I was put to at her age, only the child's been fooled with and babied."

The little one refused the doughnut, and seemed to gather herself up in silent gloom.

"Come, now, don't stand sulking; let me put your bonnet on," said Miss Asphyxia, in a brisk, metallic voice. "I can't be losin' the best part of my day with this nonsense!" And forthwith she clawed up the child in her bony grasp, as easily as an eagle might truss a chick-sparrow.

"Be a good little girl, now," said the little gray woman, who felt a strange swelling and throbbing in her poor old breast. To be sure, she knew she was a fool; her husband had told her so at least three times every day for years; and Miss Asphyxia only confirmed what she accepted familiarly as the truth. But yet she could not help these unprofitable longings to coddle and comfort something,—to do some of those little motherly tendernesses for children which go to no particular result, only to make them happy; so she ran out after the wagon with a tempting seed-cake, and forced it into the child's hand.

"Take it, do take it," she said; "eat it, and be a good girl, and do just as she tells you to."

"I'll see to that," said Miss Asphyxia, as she gathered up the reins and gave a cut to her horse, which started that quadruped from a dream of green grass into a most animated pace. Every creature in her service—horse, cow, and pig—knew at once the touch of Miss Asphyxia, and the necessity of being up and doing when she was behind them; and the horse, who under other hands would have been the slowest and most reflective of beasts, now made the little wagon spin and bounce over the rough, stony road, so that the child's short legs flew up in the air every few moments.

"You must hold on tight," was Miss Asphyxia's only comment on this circumstance. "If you fall out, you'll break your neck!"

It was a glorious day of early autumn, the sun shining as only an autumn sun knows how to shine. The blue fields of heaven were full of fleecy flocks of clouds, drifting higher and thither at their lazy will. The golden-rod and the aster hung their plumage over the rough, rocky road; and now and then it wound through a sombre piece of woods, where scarlet sumachs and maples flashed out among the gloomy green hemlocks with a solemn and gorgeous light. So very fair was the day, and so full of life and beauty was the landscape, that the child, who came of a beauty-loving lineage, felt her little heart drawn out from under its burden of troubles, and springing and bounding with that elastic habit of happiness which seems hard to kill in children.

Once she laughed out as a squirrel, with his little chops swelled with a nut on each side, sat upon the fence and looked after them, and then whisked away behind the stone wall; and once she called out, "O, how pretty!" at a splendid clump of blue fringed gentian, which stood holding up its hundred azure vases by the wayside. "Oh, I do wish I could get some of that!" she cried out, impulsively.

"Some of what?" said Miss Asphyxia.

"O, those *beautiful* flowers!" said the child, leaning far out to look back.

"O, that's nothing but gentian," said Miss Asphyxia; "can't stop for that. Them blows is good to dry for weakness," she added. "By and by, if you're good, mebbe I'll let you get some of 'em."

Miss Asphyxia had one word for all flowers. She called them all "blows," and they were divided in her mind, in a manner far more simple than any botanical system, into two classes; namely, blows that were good to dry, and blows that were not. Elder-blow, catnip, hoarhound, hardhack, gentian, ginseng, and various other vegetable tribes, she knew well and had a great respect for; but all the other little weeds that put on obtrusive colors and flaunted in the summer breeze, without any pretensions to further usefulness, Miss Asphyxia completely ignored. It would not be describing her state to say she had a contempt for them: she simply never saw or thought of them at all. The idea of beauty as connected with any of them never entered her mind,—it did not exist there.

The young cousin who shared her housework had, to be sure, planted a few flowers in a corner of the garden; there were some peonies and pinks and a rosebush, which often occupied a spare hour of the girl's morning or evening; but Miss Asphyxia watched these operations with a sublime contempt, and only calculated the loss of potatoes and carrots caused by this unproductive beauty. Since the marriage of this girl, Miss Asphyxia had often spoken to her man about "clearing out them things"; but somehow he always managed to forget it, and the thriftless beauties still remained.

It wanted but about an hour of noon when Miss Asphyxia set down the little girl on the clean-scrubbed floor of a great kitchen, where everything was even desolately orderly and neat. She swung her at once into a chair. "Sit there," she said, "till I'm ready to see to ye." And then, marching up to her own room, she laid aside her bonnet, and, coming down, plunged into active preparations for the dinner.

An irrepressible feeling of desolation came over the child. The elation produced by the ride died away; and, as she sat dangling her heels from the chair, and watching the dry, grim form of Miss Asphyxia, a sort of terror of her began slowly to usurp the place of that courage which had at first inspired the child to rise up against the assertion of so uncongenial a power.

All the strange, dreadful events of the last few days mingled themselves, in her childish mind, in a weird mass of uncomprehended gloom and mystery. Her mother, so changed,—cold, stiff, lifeless, neither smiling nor speaking nor looking at her: the people coming to the house, and talking and singing and praying, and then putting her in a box in the ground, and saying that she was dead; and then, right upon that, to be torn from her brother, to whom she had always looked for protection and counsel,—all this seemed a weird, inexplicable cloud coming over her heart and darkening all her little life. Where was Harry? Why did he let them take her? Or perhaps equally dreadful people had taken him, and would never bring him back again.

There was a tall black clock in a corner of the kitchen, that kept its invariable monotone of tick-tack, tick-tack, with a persistence that made her head swim; and she watched the quick, decisive movements of Miss Asphyxia with somewhat of the same respectful awe with which one watches the course of a locomotive engine.

It was late for Miss Asphyxia's dinner preparations, but she instituted prompt measures to make up for lost time. She flew about the kitchen with such long-armed activity and fearful celerity, that the child began instinctively to duck and bob her little head when she went by, lest she should hit her and knock her off her chair.

Miss Asphyxia raked open the fire in the great kitchen chimney, and built it up with a liberal supply of wood; then she rattled into the back room, and a sound was heard of a bucket descending into a well with such frantic haste as only an oaken bucket under Miss Asphyxia's hands could be frightened into. Back she came with a stout black iron tea-kettle, which she hung over the fire; and then, flopping down a ham on the table, she cut off slices with a martial and determined air, as if she would like to see the ham try to help itself; and, before the child could fairly see what she was doing, the slices of ham were in the frying-pan over the coals, the ham hung up in its place, the knife wiped and put out of sight, and the table drawn out into the middle of the floor, and invested with a cloth for dinner.

During these operations the child followed every movement with awe-struck eyes, and studied with trembling attention every feature of this wonderful woman.

Miss Asphyxia was tall and spare. Nature had made her, as she often remarked of herself, entirely for use. She had allowed for her muscles no cushioned repose of fat, no redundant smoothness of outline. There was nothing to her but good, strong, solid bone, and tough, wiry, well-strung muscle. She was past fifty, and her hair was already well streaked with gray, and so thin that, when tightly combed and tied, it still showed bald cracks, not very sightly to the eye. The only thought that Miss Asphyxia ever had had in relation to the *coiffure* of her hair was that it was to be got out of her way. Hair she considered principally as something that might get into people's eyes, if not properly attended to; and accordingly, at a very early hour every morning, she tied all hers in a very tight knot, and then secured it by a horn comb on the top of her head. To tie this knot so tightly that, once done, it should last all day, was Miss Asphyxia's only art of the toilet, and she tried her work every morning by giving her head a shake, before she left her looking-glass, not unlike that of an unruly cow. If this process did not start the horn comb from its moorings, Miss Asphyxia was well pleased. For the rest, her face was dusky and wilted,—guarded by gaunt, high cheek-bones, and watched over by a pair of small gray eyes of unsleeping vigilance. The shaggy eyebrows that overhung them were grizzled, like her hair.

It would not be proper to say that Miss Asphyxia looked ill-tempered; but her features could never, by any stretch of imagination, be supposed to wear an expression of tenderness. They were set in an austere, grim gravity, whose lines had become more deeply channelled by every year of her life. As related to her fellow-creatures, she was neither passionate nor cruel. We have before described her as a working machine, forever wound up to high-pressure working-point; and this being her nature, she trod down and crushed whatever stood in the way of her work, with as little compunction as if she had been a steam-engine or a power-loom.

Miss Asphyxia had a full conviction of what a recent pleasant writer has denominated the total depravity of matter. She was not given to many words, but it might often be gathered from her brief discourses that she had always felt herself, so to speak, sword in hand against a universe where everything was running to disorder,—everything was tending to slackness, shiftlessness, unthrift, and she alone was left on the earth to keep things in their places. Her hired men were always too late up in the morning,—always shirking,—always taking too long a nap at noon; everybody was watching to cheat her in every bargain; her horse, cow, pigs,—all her possessions,—were ready at the slightest winking of her eye, or relaxing of her watch, to fall into all sorts of untoward ways and gyrations; and therefore she slept, as it were, in her armor, and spent her life as a sentinel on duty.

In taking a child, she had had her eyes open only to one patent fact,—that a child was an animal who would always be wanting to play, and that she must make all her plans and calculations to keep her from playing. To this end she had beforehand given out word to her brother, that, if she took the girl, the boy must be kept away. "Got enough on my hands now, without havin' a boy trainin' round my house, and upsettin' all creation," said the grim virgin.

"Wal, wal," said Old Crab, "'t ain't best; they'll be a consultin' together, and cuttin' up didos. I'll keep the boy tight enough, I tell you."

Little enough was the dinner that the child ate that day. There were two hulking, square-shouldered men at the table, who stared at her with great round eyes like oxen; and so, though Miss Asphyxia dumped down Indian pudding, ham, and fried potatoes before her, the child's eating was scarcely that of a blackbird.

Marvellous to the little girl was the celerity with which Miss Asphyxia washed and cleared up the dinner-dishes. How the dishes rattled, the knives and forks clinked, as she scraped and piled and washed and wiped and put everything in a trice back into such perfect place, that it looked as if nothing had ever been done on the premises!

After this Miss Asphyxia produced thimble, thread, needle, and scissors, and, drawing out of a closet a bale of coarse blue home-made cloth, proceeded to measure the little girl for a petticoat and short gown of the same. This being done to her mind, she dumped her into a chair beside her, and, putting a brown towel into her hands to be hemmed, she briefly said, "There, keep to work"; while she, with great despatch and resolution, set to work on the little garments aforesaid.

The child once or twice laid down her work to watch the chickens who came up around the door, or to note a bird which flew by with a little ripple of song. The first time, Miss Asphyxia only frowned, and said, "Tut, tut." The second time, there came three thumps of Miss Asphyxia's thimble down on the little head, with the admonition, "Mind your work." The child now began to cry, but Miss Asphyxia soon put an end to that by displaying a long birch rod, with a threatening movement, and saying succinctly, "Stop that, this minute, or I'll whip you." And the child was so certain of this that she swallowed her grief and stitched away as fast as her little fingers could go.

As soon as supper was over that night, Miss Asphyxia seized upon the child, and, taking her to a tub in the sink-room, proceeded to divest her of her garments and subject to her to a most thorough ablution.

"I'm goin' to give you one good scrubbin' to start with," said Miss Asphyxia; and, truth to say, no word could more thoroughly express the character of the ablution than the term "scrubbing." The poor child was deluged with soap and water, in mouth, nose, ears, and eyes, while the great bony hands rubbed and splashed, twisted her arms, turned her ears wrong side out, and dashed on the water with unsparing vigor. Nobody can tell the torture which can be inflicted on a child in one of these vigorous old New England washings, which used to make Saturday night a terror in good families. But whatever they were, the little martyr was by this time so thoroughly impressed with the awful reality of Miss Asphyxia's power over her, that she endured all with only a few long-drawn and convulsed sighs, and an inaudible "O dear!"

When well scrubbed and wiped, Miss Asphyxia put on a coarse homespun nightgown, and, pinning a cloth round the child's neck, began with her scissors the work of cutting off her hair. Snip, snip, went the fatal shears, and down into the towel fell bright curls, once the pride of a mother's heart, till finally the small head was despoiled completely. Then Miss Asphyxia, shaking up a bottle of camphor, proceeded to rub some vigorously upon the child's head. "There," she said, "that's to keep ye from catchin' cold."

She then proceeded to the kitchen, raked open the fire, and shook the golden curls into the bed of embers, and stood grimly over them while they seethed and twisted and writhed, as if they had been living things suffering a fiery torture, meanwhile picking diligently at the cloth that had contained them, that no stray hair might escape.

"I wonder now," she said to herself, "if any of this will rise and get into the next pudding?" She spoke with a spice of bitterness, poor woman, as if it would be just the way things usually went on, if it did.

She buried the fire carefully, and then, opening the door of a small bedroom adjoining, which displayed a single bed, she said, "Now get into bed."

The child immediately obeyed, thankful to hide herself under the protecting folds of a blue checked coverlet, and feeling that at last the dreadful Miss Asphyxia would leave her to herself.

Miss Asphyxia clapped to the door, and the child drew a long breath. In a moment, however, the door flew open. Miss Asphyxia had forgotten something. "Can you say your prayers?" she demanded.

"Yes, ma'am," said the child.

"Say 'em, then," said Miss Asphyxia; and bang went the door again.

"There, now, if I hain't done up my duty to that child, then I don't know," said Miss Asphyxia.

1869

Herman Melville 1819–1891

When Herman Melville was twelve years old, his merchant father died bankrupt. The tragedy plunged young Herman from the comfortable, patrician world of his Melvill and Gansevoort ancestors into the precarious, drudging world of the sailors, clerks, farm laborers, factory workers, paupers, and slaves who would subsequently people his fiction. Melville's unique perspective on his society derives from his experience of living at the intersection of these opposing worlds.

As the impoverished grandson of two well-connected Revolutionary War heroes—the Brahmin Thomas Melvill, veteran of the Boston Tea Party, and the slave-owning Dutch patroon Peter Gansevoort, defender of Fort Stanwix—Melville acquired a first-hand understanding of what it meant to be excluded from the Revolution's promised benefits. Forced to drop out of school, temporarily after his father's death in 1832, permanently after his elder brother Gansevoort likewise fell victim to bankruptcy in the Panic of 1837, Melville launched on a fruitless search for stable employment, sampling the range of low-paid jobs open to young men with few marketable skills. He worked as a clerk in a bank and in his brother's fur store, as a laborer on his uncle's farm, as a district schoolteacher in rural Massachusetts and New York, where he boarded with the families of his pupils and found himself defrauded of his salary on his second stint. He studied surveying and engineering, in the vain hope of procuring employment with the Erie Canal's engineering department. Finally, having exhausted all other options, he went to sea as a common sailor, first on a four-month voyage to Liverpool aboard the merchant ship *St. Lawrence* in 1839, then on a three-year voyage to the South Seas aboard a series of whaleships beginning with the *Acushnet* in 1841.

Ten years later Melville would write in *Moby-Dick,* "if, at my death, my executors, or more properly my creditors, find any precious MSS. in my desk, then here I prospectively ascribe all the honor and the glory to whaling; for a whale-ship was my Yale College and my Harvard." Indeed Melville's roving life as a sailor, which provided the material for his first six books, also schooled his imagination. Exposed to brutal working conditions alongside men of all races, Melville learned to identify with slaves and to draw analogies between different forms of oppression. Confronted in the Marquesas, Tahiti, and Hawaii with warships training their guns on naked islanders, and with "rapacious hordes of enlightened individuals" rushing to seize the "depopulated land" from natives reduced to starving "interloper[s]" in their own country, Melville came to view "the white civilized man as the most ferocious animal on the face of the earth." Above all, a sojourn among one of the peoples his society denigrated as "savages" taught Melville to question his deepest cultural assumptions.

In July, 1842, eighteen months of "tyrannical" usage at sea drove Melville and a shipmate named Toby Greene to jump ship at Nukahiva in the Marquesas. Falling into the hands of the Typee tribe, Melville discovered that these reputed cannibals "deal more kindly with each other, and are more humane" than many self-professed Christians. Although Melville chose to escape after four weeks of "indulgent captivity," he would never again take for granted either the superiority of white Christian civilization or the benefit of imposing it on others. Instead he began reexamining his own society through the eyes of "savages."

The Australian whaler *Lucy Ann,* on which Melville left Nukahiva, proved worse than the *Acushnet,* and he ended up embroiled in a mutiny that landed him in a Tahitian jail. Together with another shipmate, John Troy, Melville once more escaped and spent several weeks roaming around Tahiti and nearby Eimeo before shipping aboard the whaler *Charles and Henry.* Discharged in Hawaii, he clerked in a store for two and a half months. Finally, in August, 1843, he joined the crew of the homeward bound warship *United States* as an ordinary seaman, arriving in Boston the following October, 1844.

It was while narrating his adventures to his family that Melville found the métier he had sought for so long. His first book, *Typee: A Peep at Polynesian Life* (1846), was an instant success, but Melville's American publishers insisted on expurgating his attacks on the missionary and imperialist despoilers of Polynesia. "Try to get a living by the Truth," he would later complain in a famous letter to his friend Nathaniel Hawthorne "—and go to the Soup Societies." Melville struggled with this dilemma throughout his literary career. His next book, *Omoo* (1847), a fictionalized account of the mutiny aboard the *Lucy Ann* and his ensuing adventures in Tahiti, retracted the concessions he had made to the censors of *Typee* and exposed white depredations in the South Seas more unsparingly than ever. Thereafter, he started experimenting with increasingly elaborate strategies for subverting his readers' prejudices and conveying unwelcome truths.

In 1847 Melville married Elizabeth Shaw, daughter of the Massachusetts Supreme Court's influential Chief Justice, Lemuel Shaw. A family friend and surrogate father, Shaw also emerged in the controversial Roberts and Sims cases of 1849 and 1851 as a staunch defender of racial segregation and of the infamous Fugitive Slave Law. Family obligations thus added to the pressures impelling Melville toward indirection.

His experimental allegory *Mardi* (1849) combined metaphysical speculation, political satire, and anti-slavery protest. Melville's public rebelled against his formal innovations, however, forcing him to return to realistic narrative in *Redburn* (1849) and *White-Jacket: or The World in a Man-of-War* (1850). Based respectively on Melville's voyage to Liverpool and his stint on the frigate *United States,* these two books delineate scenes that underlie Melville's brilliant critiques of capitalism, slavery, war, and imperialism in his short fiction: "hollow-eyed and decrepit" children begging in the streets of Liverpool alongside "puny mothers, holding up puny babes in the glare of the sun" and "sturdy men, with the gallows in their eyes"; European emigrants "stowed away like bales of cotton, and packed like slaves in a slave-ship"; sailors degraded and flogged like slaves, ground into "implicit, unquestioning, dog-like devotion to whoever may be lord and master." Besides expressing Melville's passionate fellow-feeling for "classes of men . . . who bear the same relation to society at large, that the wheels do to a coach," *Redburn* and *White-Jacket* foreshadow such mature works as "Bartleby," "The Paradise of Bachelors and The Tartarus of Maids," "Benito Cereno," and *Billy Budd* in startling ways. For example, the harrowing sight *Redburn* describes of a family dying of starvation, hidden in a "vault" beneath a warehouse in a street where "the dingy wall was on every side," recurs in the wall imagery that pervades "Bartleby," most strikingly in the climactic tableau of Bartleby "huddled at the base of the wall" in the Tombs, having starved to death after being evicted from the narrator's Wall Street office. It also recurs in "The Tartarus of Maids," where the "figure of what had been a woman," her "blue arms" folding to her "livid bosom two shrunken things like children," metamorphoses into factory girls "pale with work, and blue with cold," their bodies controlled by machinery that has preempted their child-bearing faculties. Similarly, *Redburn*'s association of slave-trading with piracy—an association frequently made by abolitionists—reverberates through "Benito Cereno," where the Yankee Captain Delano ironically practices the piracy he fears, and views both European emigrants and slaves as "living freight." Finally, the central trope of *White-Jacket*—the world as a man-of-war—informs the posthumous *Billy Budd,* with its prescient evocation of a world dominated by the forces of militarism and imperialism masquerading as the guardians of peace.

The new technique Melville developed of fusing fact and symbol reached fruition in his most powerful and original work, *Moby-Dick* (1851). Conferring epic dignity on a class of men hitherto barred from the purview of literature, and elevating their despised occupation, the whale hunt, to mythic stature, *Moby-Dick*'s matchless achievement was to transform the implements, raw materials, and processes of a lucrative, gory industry, which subsisted on the plunder of nature, into rich symbols of the struggle to fulfill humanity's potential under conditions threatening apocalyptic destruction. The book's Shakespearean grandeur, philosophical depth, and daring mixture of genres and forms reflected Melville's omnivorous reading since entering literary circles. Its dedication to Hawthorne, whom he had met while writing *Moby-Dick,* also indicated a debt to the allegorist he had hailed in his review "Hawthorne and His Mosses" (1850) as an American Shakespeare.

Unlike Hawthorne, however, Melville violated his public's literary tastes and offended its religious and political sensibilities. Thus his ambitious epic did not win him the acclaim he hoped for, let alone the financial rewards he needed to support his growing family. In a desperate attempt to recapture the literary marketplace, Melville set out to produce a psychological romance of the type Hawthorne had popularized. Perversely, *Pierre; or, The Ambiguities* (1852) burlesqued the very form it sought to emulate. Featuring incest, satirizing Christianity, lampooning the literary establishment, and even caricaturing Melville's own family, it called down a storm of abuse and convinced many that Melville had gone mad.

In the year that intervened before Melville's next publication, he apparently wrote two works he was "prevented from printing," which have since been lost: a story or novel about a deserted sailor's wife named Agatha, with whose "great patience, & endurance, & resignedness"—like the Chola widow Hunilla's in "The Encantadas"—he seems to have strongly identified, and a book about tortoise-hunting, perhaps partly salvaged in "The Encantadas" (1854). The latter, comprising ten sketches of the Galápagos Islands, marked a transition in Melville's art—a valedictory by his sailor narrator, now bereft of his youthful resilience; a farewell to the seafaring world of his first six books, now reduced to ashes; and a final tribute to the human spirit he had apotheosized in *Moby-Dick,* now incarnated by a "vanquished," but unbowed woman.

With his re-emergence as a contributor to two of the period's leading monthly magazines, *Harper's* and *Putnam's,* Melville entered on a new phase of his literary career. Among his earliest ventures in serial publication was another transitional work, *Israel Potter* (1854–1855). Ironically, dedicated to the Bunker Hill Monument and offered to *Putnam's* as a Fourth of July narrative, it paid homage to the common soldiers who had fought in the American Revolution, but had never tasted its fruits.

Meanwhile Melville had turned to short fiction and begun perfecting a very different literary style, exemplified at its best by "Bartleby," "Benito Cereno," and "The Paradise of Bachelors and The Tartarus of Maids." In these stories, Melville depicted the victims of capitalism and slavery no longer through the eyes of a sympathetic sailor narrator, but through the eyes of an obtuse observer representing the class of "gentlemen" whose smug prosperity rested on the extorted labor of the workers they dehumanized—the class constituting Melville's public and closest associates in the social milieu he had rejoined. Mouthing their racist clichés, mimicking their social snobbery, echoing their pious platitudes, and exposing their sublime obliviousness to the suffering on which they fattened, Melville mercilessly anatomized the readers he had given up hope of converting. Yet he also jarred them out of their complacency through language that persistently provoked discomfort, and through the warning vision he held up again and again of the apocalyptic doom overtaking their society.

That vision culminated in *The Confidence-Man: His Masquerade* (1857). An allegorical apocalypse set on April Fools' Day, it imaged nineteenth-century America as a soot-streaked steamer heading down the Mississippi toward the financial capital of slavery, New Orleans, which the passengers have mistaken for the New Jerusalem. After a mysterious "advent" evoking Biblical prophecies of the Last Judgment, the book's title character assumes the guise, first of a crippled black beggar, then of various white gentlemen he describes as his friends, and proceeds to test the professed ideals of passengers and readers and to unmask the racism, class bias, and greed that belie them.

The Confidence-Man and the volume of his *Putnam's* stories that Melville collected in *The Piazza Tales* (1856) were his last published works of prose fiction. By 1856, he had reached a psychological nadir, which his family attributed to the strain of writing. Stepping into the breach, his father-in-law Judge Shaw financed a trip to Europe and the Middle East. On his return in 1857, Melville tried for three years to support his family by lecturing, and underwent a drawn-out repeat of the demoralizing search for remunerative employment that had driven him to sea. This time, however, the search led him in 1866 to a job as a Customs Inspector, which he held for nineteen years. The decade of trauma took a heavy toll, climaxing in 1867, when Melville's wife Elizabeth considered leaving him, fearing that he had gone insane, and their eldest son Malcolm committed suicide at age eighteen.

Melville's personal crisis converged with the national crisis of the Civil War, which elicited his volume of poetry *Battle-Pieces* (1866), an attempt to speak for all parties to the conflict. In the interstices of his custom-house work, Melville continued to write poetry. *Clarel: A Poem and Pilgrimage in the Holy Land,* articulating the era's religious and political disillusionment, appeared in 1876. Two privately published volumes followed: *John Marr and Other Sailors* (1888) and *Timoleon* (1891).

In 1886, a legacy finally made it possible for Melville to retire from the Custom House. The result was *Billy Budd,* found in manuscript on Melville's death in 1891. His most poignant protest against the sacrifice of humanity to the god of war, Melville dedicated it to his heroic mentor aboard the *United States,* the British sailor Jack Chase, "a stickler for the Rights of Man, and the liberties of the world."

Since Melville died forgotten by his American contemporaries, it is fitting that he should at last be set in company with other long forgotten writers, whose neglect derived from similar causes. Prophetically, Melville's rediscovery coincided with the discovery of black writers during the 1920s, and one of the first critics to rescue him from oblivion—Carl Van Vechten—played a prominent role in the Harlem Renaissance. The implications of this coincidence should become clearer in an anthology that allows us to compare Melville with writers who shared his vision of social justice. For among the authors with whom Melville has traditionally been anthologized, he was unique in exploring the connections linking slavery, patriarchy, capitalism, and imperialism, and in centering his art on the experience of a class invisible to his peers: the men and women of all races assigned the function of wheels bearing the coach in which comfortable white gentlemen and ladies were obliviously riding.

Carolyn L. Karcher
Temple University

PRIMARY WORKS

Merrell R. Davis and William H. Gilman, eds., *The Letters of Herman Melville,* 1960; Sidney Kaplan, ed., *Battle-Pieces,* 1960; Harrison Hayford and Merton M. Sealts, Jr., eds., *Billy Budd, Sailor,* 1962; Harrison Hayford, Hershel Parker, and G. Thomas Tanselle, eds., *Writings of Herman Melville,* 1968–(in progress); Jay Leyda, ed., *The Melville Log: A Documentary Life of Herman Melville,* 2 vols., 1951, 1969; Charles Haberstroth, ed., *John Marr and Other Stories,* 1975; Charles Haberstroth, ed., *Timoleon,* 1976; Harrison Hayford, Alma A. MacDougall, and G. Thomas Tanselle, eds., *The Piazza Tales and Other Prose Pieces, 1839–1860,* 1987; Harrison Hayford, Alma A. MacDougall, Hershel Parker, and G. Thomas Tanselle, eds., *Clarel,* 1991

SECONDARY WORKS

Charles Anderson, *Melville in the South Seas,* 1939, 1966; William H. Gilman, *Melville's Early Life and "Redburn,"* 1951; Leon Howard, *Herman Melville: A Biography,* 1951; Merton M. Sealts, *Melville as Lecturer,* 1957, 1970; Beatrice Ricks and Joseph D. Adams, *Herman Melville: A Reference Bibliography, 1900–1972,* 1973; Merton M. Sealts, *The Early Lives of Melville,* 1974; Lea Bertani Vozar Newman, *A Reader's Guide to the Short Stories of Herman Melville,* 1986; Elizabeth Renker, *Strike Through the Mask: Herman Melville and the Scene of Writing,* 1996; Hershel Parker, *Herman Melville: A Biography,* 1996.

Bartleby, the Scrivener

A Story of Wall-Street[1]

I am a rather elderly man. The nature of my avocations for the last thirty years has brought me into more than ordinary contact with what would seem an interesting and somewhat singular set of men, of whom as yet nothing that I know of has ever been written:—I mean the law-copyists or scriveners. I have known very many of them, professionally and privately, and if I pleased, could relate divers histories, at which good-natured gentlemen might smile, and sentimental souls might weep. But I waive the biographies of all other scriveners for a few passages in the life of Bartleby, who was a scrivener the strangest I ever saw or heard of. While of other law-copyists I might write the complete life, of Bartleby nothing of that sort can be done. I believe that no materials exist for a full and satisfactory biography of this man. It is an irreparable loss to literature. Bartleby was one of those beings of whom nothing is ascertainable, except from the original sources, and in his case those are very small. What my own astonished eyes saw of Bartleby, *that* is all I know of him, except, indeed, one vague report which will appear in the sequel.

Ere introducing the scrivener, as he first appeared to me, it is fit I make some mention of myself, my *employés,* my business, my chambers, and general surroundings;

[1]"Bartleby" was the first short story Melville published (though according to Merton Sealts's chronology of Melville's short fiction, it was the fourth story he wrote). It was serialized in the November and December, 1853, issues of *Putnam's Monthly Magazine* and later collected in *The Piazza Tales,* where the subtitle was omitted. The present text is from the standard Northwestern-Newberry edition of *The Piazza Tales and Other Prose Pieces, 1839–1860.*

because some such description is indispensable to an adequate understanding of the chief character about to be presented.

Imprimis:[2] I am a man who, from his youth upwards, has been filled with a profound conviction that the easiest way of life is the best. Hence, though I belong to a profession proverbially energetic and nervous, even to turbulence, at times, yet nothing of that sort have I ever suffered to invade my peace. I am one of those unambitious lawyers who never addresses a jury, or in any way draws down public applause; but in the cool tranquillity of a snug retreat, do a snug business among rich men's bonds and mortgages and title-deeds. All who know me, consider me an eminently *safe* man. The late John Jacob Astor,[3] a personage little given to poetic enthusiasm, had no hesitation in pronouncing my first grand point to be prudence; my next, method. I do not speak it in vanity, but simply record the fact, that I was not unemployed in my profession by the late John Jacob Astor; a name which, I admit, I love to repeat, for it hath a rounded and orbicular sound to it, and rings like unto bullion. I will freely add, that I was not insensible to the late John Jacob Astor's good opinion.

Some time prior to the period at which this little history begins, my avocations had been largely increased. The good old office, now extinct in the State of New-York, of a Master in Chancery,[4] had been conferred upon me. It was not a very arduous office, but very pleasantly remunerative. I seldom lose my temper; much more seldom indulge in dangerous indignation at wrongs and outrages; but I must be permitted to be rash here and declare, that I consider the sudden and violent abrogation of the office of Master in Chancery, by the new Constitution, as a——premature act; inasmuch as I had counted upon a life-lease of the profits, whereas I only received those of a few short years. But this is by the way.

My chambers were up stairs at No.—Wall-street. At one end they looked upon the white wall of the interior of a spacious sky-light shaft, penetrating the building from top to bottom. This view might have been considered rather tame than otherwise, deficient in what landscape painters call "life." But if so, the view from the other end of my chambers offered, at least, a contrast, if nothing more. In that direction my windows commanded an unobstructed view of a lofty brick wall, black by age and everlasting shade; which wall required no spy-glass to bring out its lurking beauties, but for the benefit of all near-sighted spectators, was pushed up to

[2]In the first place: used to introduce the first in a number of items, as in an inventory or will.

[3]German-born American multi-millionaire (1763–1848), who made his vast fortune in the fur trade and in real estate speculation. On his death he willed $350,000 (out of an estate totaling more than $20 million) to the founding of the New York Public Library. Astor's will had elicited much public comment only five years before the publication of "Bartleby." Stephen Zelnick has described Astor as a hated symbol of monopoly power, political corruption, antidemocratic values, and a new style of capitalist wage slavery. Also relevant, as Mario D'Avanzo has pointed out, is Astor's patronage of literary men, among them Washington Irving, whom he commissioned to write *Astoria,* a history of Astor's fur-trading colony in Oregon.

[4]A lucrative sinecure that guaranteed the Master his fees, regardless of which party won a case. Irving Adler has pointed out that the Court of Chancery, or Equity, was originally established in England "to provide remedies based on natural rights," rather than on "strict adherence to the written law." Its abolition expedited property settlements, but also subordinated natural rights to property rights, a central theme in the story.

within ten feet of my window panes. Owing to the great height of the surrounding buildings, and my chambers being on the second floor, the interval between this wall and mine not a little resembled a huge square cistern.

At the period just preceding the advent of Bartleby, I had two persons as copyists in my employment, and a promising lad as an office-boy. First, Turkey; second, Nippers; third, Ginger Nut. These may seem names, the like of which are not usually found in the Directory. In truth they were nicknames, mutually conferred upon each other by my three clerks, and were deemed expressive of their respective persons or characters. Turkey was a short, pursy[5] Englishman of about my own age, that is, somewhere not far from sixty. In the morning, one might say, his face was of a fine florid hue, but after twelve o'clock, meridian—his dinner hour—it blazed like a grate full of Christmas coals; and continued blazing—but, as it were, with a gradual wane—till 6 o'clock, P.M. or thereabouts, after which I saw no more of the proprietor of the face, which gaining its meridian with the sun, seemed to set with it, to rise, culminate, and decline the following day, with the like regularity and undiminished glory. There are many singular coincidences I have known in the course of my life, not the least among which was the fact, that exactly when Turkey displayed his fullest beams from his red and radiant countenance, just then, too, at that critical moment, began the daily period when I considered his business capacities as seriously disturbed for the remainder of the twenty-four hours. Not that he was absolutely idle, or averse to business then; far from it. The difficulty was, he was apt to be altogether too energetic. There was a strange, inflamed, flurried, flighty recklessness of activity about him. He would be incautious in dipping his pen into his inkstand. All his blots upon my documents, were dropped there after twelve o'clock, meridian. Indeed, not only would he be reckless and sadly given to making blots in the afternoon, but some days he went further, and was rather noisy. At such times, too, his face flamed with augmented blazonry, as if cannel[6] coal had been heaped on anthracite. He made an unpleasant racket with his chair; spilled his sand-box; in mending his pens, impatiently split them all to pieces, and threw them on the floor in a sudden passion; stood up and leaned over his table, boxing his papers about in a most indecorous manner, very sad to behold in an elderly man like him. Nevertheless, as he was in many ways a most valuable person to me, and all the time before twelve o'clock, meridian, was the quickest, steadiest creature too, accomplishing a great deal of work in a style not easy to be matched—for these reasons, I was willing to overlook his eccentricities, though indeed, occasionally, I remonstrated with him. I did this very gently, however, because, though the civilest, nay, the blandest and most reverential of men in the morning, yet in the afternoon he was disposed, upon provocation, to be slightly rash with his tongue, in fact, insolent. Now, valuing his morning services as I did, and resolved not to lose them; yet, at the same time made uncomfortable by his inflamed ways after twelve o'clock; and being a man of peace, unwilling by my admonitions to call forth unseemly retorts from him; I took upon me, one Saturday noon (he was always worse on Saturdays), to hint to him, very kindly, that perhaps now that he was growing old, it might be well to abridge his labors; in short, he need not come to my

[5]Short-winded due to obesity.

[6]A bituminous coal, rich in volatile matter, which burns with a very bright flame.

chambers after twelve o'clock, but, dinner over, had best go home to his lodgings and rest himself till tea-time. But no; he insisted upon his afternoon devotions. His countenance became intolerably fervid, as he oratorically assured me—gesticulating with a long ruler at the other end of the room—that if his services in the morning were useful, how indispensable, then, in the afternoon?

"With submission, sir," said Turkey on this occasion, "I consider myself your right-hand man. In the morning I but marshal and deploy my columns; but in the afternoon I put myself at their head, and gallantly charge the foe, thus!"—and he made a violent thrust with the ruler.

"But the blots, Turkey," intimated I.

"True,—but, with submission, sir, behold these hairs! I am getting old. Surely, sir, a blot or two of a warm afternoon is not to be severely urged against gray hairs. Old age—even if it blot the page—is honorable. With submission, sir, we *both* are getting old."

This appeal to my fellow-feeling was hardly to be resisted. At all events, I saw that go he would not. So I made up my mind to let him stay, resolving, nevertheless, to see to it, that during the afternoon he had to do with my less important papers.

Nippers, the second on my list, was a whiskered, sallow, and, upon the whole, rather piratical-looking young man of about five and twenty. I always deemed him the victim of two evil powers—ambition and indigestion. The ambition was evinced by a certain impatience of the duties of a mere copyist, an unwarrantable usurpation of strictly professional affairs, such as the original drawing up of legal documents. The indigestion seemed betokened in an occasional nervous testiness and grinning irritability, causing the teeth to audibly grind together over mistakes committed in copying; unnecessary maledictions, hissed, rather than spoken, in the heat of business; and especially by a continual discontent with the height of the table where he worked. Though of a very ingenious mechanical turn, Nippers could never get this table to suit him. He put chips under it, blocks of various sorts, bits of pasteboard, and at last went so far as to attempt an exquisite adjustment by final pieces of folding blotting-paper. But no invention would answer. If, for the sake of easing his back, he brought the table lid at a sharp angle well up towards his chin, and wrote there like a man using the steep roof of a Dutch house for his desk:—then he declared that it stopped the circulation in his arms. If now he lowered the table to his waistbands, and stooped over it in writing, then there was a sore aching in his back. In short, the truth of the matter was, Nippers knew not what he wanted. Or, if he wanted any thing, it was to be rid of a scrivener's table altogether. Among the manifestations of his diseased ambition was a fondness he had for receiving visits from certain ambiguous-looking fellows in seedy coats, whom he called his clients. Indeed I was aware that not only was he, at times, considerable of a ward-politician, but he occasionally did a little business at the Justices' courts, and was not unknown on the steps of the Tombs.[7] I have good reason to believe, however, that one individual who called upon him at my chambers, and who, with a grand air, he insisted was his client, was no other than a dun,[8] and the alleged title-deed, a bill. But with all his failings,

[7]In short Nippers is acting as a lawyer for the poor, the most numerous class held in the Tombs, the New York prison built in 1839. The Tombs received its name from the Egyptian tomb architecture it imitated, a style known as Egyptian Revival.

[8]An importunate creditor or agent employed to collect debts.

and the annoyances he caused me, Nippers, like his compatriot Turkey, was a very useful man to me; wrote a neat, swift hand; and, when he chose, was not deficient in a gentlemanly sort of deportment. Added to this, he always dressed in a gentlemanly sort of way; and so, incidentally, reflected credit upon my chambers. Whereas with respect to Turkey, I had much ado to keep him from being a reproach to me. His clothes were apt to look oily and smell of eating-houses. He wore his pantaloons very loose and baggy in summer. His coats were execrable; his hat not to be handled. But while the hat was a thing of indifference to me, inasmuch as his natural civility and deference, as a dependent Englishman, always led him to doff it the moment he entered the room, yet his coat was another matter. Concerning his coats, I reasoned with him; but with no effect. The truth was, I suppose, that a man with so small an income, could not afford to sport such a lustrous face and a lustrous coat at one and the same time. As Nippers once observed, Turkey's money went chiefly for red ink. One winter day I presented Turkey with a highly-respectable looking coat of my own, a padded gray coat, of a most comfortable warmth, and which buttoned straight up from the knee to the neck. I thought Turkey would appreciate the favor, and abate his rashness and obstreperousness of afternoons. But no. I verily believe that buttoning himself up in so downy and blanket-like a coat had a pernicious effect upon him; upon the same principle that too much oats are bad for horses. In fact, precisely as a rash, restive horse is said to feel his oats, so Turkey felt his coat. It made him insolent. He was a man whom prosperity harmed.

Though concerning the self-indulgent habits of Turkey I had my own private surmises, yet touching Nippers I was well persuaded that whatever might be his faults in other respects, he was, at least, a temperate young man. But indeed, nature herself seemed to have been his vintner, and at his birth charged him so thoroughly with an irritable, brandy-like disposition, that all subsequent potations were needless. When I consider how, amid the stillness of my chambers, Nippers would sometimes impatiently rise from his seat, and stooping over his table, spread his arms wide apart, seize the whole desk, and move it, and jerk it, with a grim, grinding motion on the floor, as if the table were a perverse voluntary agent, intent on thwarting and vexing him; I plainly perceive that for Nippers, brandy and water were altogether superfluous.

It was fortunate for me that, owing to its peculiar cause—indigestion—the irritability and consequent nervousness of Nippers, were mainly observable in the morning, while in the afternoon he was comparatively mild. So that Turkey's paroxysms only coming on about twelve o'clock, I never had to do with their eccentricities at one time. Their fits relieved each other like guards. When Nippers' was on, Turkey's was off; and *vice versa.* This was a good natural arrangement under the circumstances.

Ginger Nut, the third on my list, was a lad some twelve years old. His father was a carman,[9] ambitious of seeing his son on the bench instead of a cart, before he died. So he sent him to my office as student at law, errand boy, and cleaner and sweeper, at the rate of one dollar a week. He had a little desk to himself, but he did not use it much. Upon inspection, the drawer exhibited a great array of the shells of various sorts of nuts. Indeed, to this quick-witted youth the whole noble science of the law was contained in a nut-shell. Not the least among the employments of Ginger Nut,

[9]Carter, teamster.

as well as one which he discharged with the most alacrity, was his duty as cake and apple purveyor for Turkey and Nippers. Copying law papers being proverbially a dry, husky sort of business, my two scriveners were fain to moisten their mouths very often with Spitzenbergs[10] to be had at the numerous stalls nigh the Custom House and Post Office. Also, they sent Ginger Nut very frequently for that peculiar cake—small, flat, round, and very spicy—after which he had been named by them. Of a cold morning when business was but dull, Turkey would gobble up scores of these cakes, as if they were mere wafers—indeed they sell them at the rate of six or eight for a penny—the scrape of his pen blending with the crunching of the crisp particles in his mouth. Of all the fiery afternoon blunders and flurried rashnesses of Turkey, was his once moistening a ginger-cake between his lips, and clapping it on to a mortgage for a seal. I came within an ace of dismissing him then. But he mollified me by making an oriental bow, and saying—"With submission, sir, it was generous of me to find you in stationery on my own account."

Now my original business—that of a conveyancer[11] and title hunter, and drawer-up of recondite documents of all sorts—was considerably increased by receiving the master's office. There was now great work for scriveners. Not only must I push the clerks already with me, but I must have additional help. In answer to my advertisement, a motionless young man one morning, stood upon my office threshold, the door being open, for it was summer. I can see that figure now—pallidly neat, pitiably respectable, incurably forlorn! It was Bartleby.

After a few words touching his qualifications, I engaged him, glad to have among my corps of copyists a man of so singularly sedate an aspect, which I thought might operate beneficially upon the flighty temper of Turkey, and the fiery one of Nippers.

I should have stated before that ground glass folding-doors divided my premises into two parts, one of which was occupied by my scriveners, the other by myself. According to my humor I threw open these doors, or closed them. I resolved to assign Bartleby a corner by the folding-doors, but on my side of them, so as to have this quiet man within easy call, in case any trifling thing was to be done. I placed his desk close up to a small side-window in that part of the room, a window which originally had afforded a lateral view of certain grimy back-yards and bricks, but which, owing to subsequent erections, commanded at present no view at all, though it gave some light. Within three feet of the panes was a wall, and the light came down from far above, between two lofty buildings, as from a very small opening in a dome. Still further to a satisfactory arrangement, I procured a high green folding screen, which might entirely isolate Bartleby from my sight, though not remove him from my voice. And thus, in a manner, privacy and society were conjoined.

At first Bartleby did an extraordinary quantity of writing. As if long famishing for something to copy, he seemed to gorge himself on my documents. There was no pause for digestion. He ran a day and night line, copying by sun-light and by candle-light. I should have been quite delighted with his application, had he been cheerfully industrious. But he wrote on silently, palely, mechanically.

It is, of course, an indispensable part of a scrivener's business to verify the accuracy of his copy, word by word. Where there are two or more scriveners in an office,

[10]A variety of apple.

[11]A lawyer who prepares documents for the conveyance (transfer) of property and who investigates titles to property.

they assist each other in this examination, one reading from the copy, the other holding the original. It is a very dull, wearisome, and lethargic affair. I can readily imagine that to some sanguine temperaments it would be altogether intolerable. For example, I cannot credit that the mettlesome poet Byron would have contentedly sat down with Bartleby to examine a law document of, say five hundred pages, closely written in a crimpy hand.

Now and then, in the haste of business, it had been my habit to assist in comparing some brief document myself, calling Turkey or Nippers for this purpose. One object I had in placing Bartleby so handy to me behind the screen, was to avail myself of his services on such trivial occasions. It was on the third day, I think, of his being with me, and before any necessity had arisen for having his own writing examined, that, being much hurried to complete a small affair I had in hand, I abruptly called to Bartleby. In my haste and natural expectancy of instant compliance, I sat with my head bent over the original on my desk, and my right hand sideways, and somewhat nervously extended with the copy, so that immediately upon emerging from his retreat, Bartleby might snatch it and proceed to business without the least delay.

In this very attitude did I sit when I called to him, rapidly stating what it was I wanted him to do—namely, to examine a small paper with me. Imagine my surprise, nay, my consternation, when without moving from his privacy, Bartleby in a singularly mild, firm voice, replied, "I would prefer not to."

I sat awhile in perfect silence, rallying my stunned faculties. Immediately it occurred to me that my ears had deceived me, or Bartleby had entirely misunderstood my meaning. I repeated my request in the clearest tone I could assume. But in quite as clear a one came the previous reply, "I would prefer not to."

"Prefer not to," echoed I, rising in high excitement, and crossing the room with a stride. "What do you mean? Are you moon-struck? I want you to help me compare this sheet here—take it," and I thrust it towards him.

"I would prefer not to," said he.

I looked at him steadfastly. His face was leanly composed; his gray eye dimly calm. Not a wrinkle of agitation rippled him. Had there been the least uneasiness, anger, impatience or impertinence in his manner; in other words, had there been any thing ordinarily human about him, doubtless I should have violently dismissed him from the premises. But as it was, I should have as soon thought of turning my pale plaster-of-paris bust of Cicero out of doors. I stood gazing at him awhile, as he went on with his own writing, and then reseated myself at my desk. This is very strange, thought I. What had one best do? But my business hurried me. I concluded to forget the matter for the present, reserving it for my future leisure. So calling Nippers from the other room, the paper was speedily examined.

A few days after this, Bartleby concluded four lengthy documents, being quadruplicates of a week's testimony taken before me in my High Court of Chancery. It became necessary to examine them. It was an important suit, and great accuracy was imperative. Having all things arranged I called Turkey, Nippers and Ginger Nut from the next room, meaning to place the four copies in the hands of my four clerks, while I should read from the original. Accordingly, Turkey, Nippers and Ginger Nut had taken their seats in a row, each with his document in hand, when I called to Bartleby to join this interesting group.

"Bartleby! quick, I am waiting."

I heard a slow scrape of his chair legs on the uncarpeted floor, and soon he appeared standing at the entrance of his hermitage.

"What is wanted?" said he mildly.

"The copies, the copies," said I hurriedly. "We are going to examine them. There"—and I held towards him the fourth quadruplicate.

"I would prefer not to," he said, and gently disappeared behind the screen.

For a few moments I was turned into a pillar of salt,[12] standing at the head of my seated column of clerks. Recovering myself, I advanced towards the screen, and demanded the reason for such extraordinary conduct.

"*Why* do you refuse?"

"I would prefer not to."

With any other man I should have flown outright into a dreadful passion, scorned all further words, and thrust him ignominiously from my presence. But there was something about Bartleby that not only strangely disarmed me, but in a wonderful manner touched and disconcerted me. I began to reason with him.

"These are your own copies we are about to examine. It is labor saving to you, because one examination will answer for your four papers. It is common usage. Every copyist is bound to help examine his copy. Is it not so? Will you not speak? Answer!"

"I prefer not to," he replied in a flute-like tone. It seemed to me that while I had been addressing him, he carefully revolved every statement that I made; fully comprehended the meaning; could not gainsay the irresistible conclusion; but, at the same time, some paramount consideration prevailed with him to reply as he did.

"You are decided, then, not to comply with my request—a request made according to common usage and common sense?"

He briefly gave me to understand that on that point my judgment was sound. Yes: his decision was irreversible.

It is not seldom the case that when a man is browbeaten in some unprecedented and violently unreasonable way, he begins to stagger in his own plainest faith. He begins, as it were, vaguely to surmise that, wonderful as it may be, all the justice and all the reason is on the other side. Accordingly, if any disinterested persons are present, he turns to them for some reinforcement for his own faltering mind.

"Turkey," said I, "what do you think of this? Am I not right?"

"With submission, sir," said Turkey, with his blandest tone, "I think that you are."

"Nippers," said I, "what do *you* think of it?"

"I think I should kick him out of the office."

(The reader of nice perceptions will here perceive that, it being morning, Turkey's answer is couched in polite and tranquil terms, but Nippers replies in ill-tempered ones. Or, to repeat a previous sentence, Nippers's ugly mood was on duty, and Turkey's off.)

"Ginger Nut," said I, willing to enlist the smallest suffrage in my behalf, "what do *you* think of it?"

[12]In Genesis 19:26, God turns Lot's wife into a pillar of salt when she disobeys the command not to look back toward her home, the city of Sodom, destroyed for its wickedness. Ironically, here it is the narrator, and not the disobedient Bartleby, who has been turned into a pillar of salt.

"I think, sir, he's a little *luny,*" replied Ginger Nut, with a grin.

"You hear what they say," said I, turning towards the screen, "come forth and do your duty."

But he vouchsafed no reply. I pondered a moment in sore perplexity. But once more business hurried me. I determined again to postpone the consideration of this dilemma to my future leisure. With a little trouble we made out to examine the papers without Bartleby, though at every page or two, Turkey deferentially dropped his opinion that this proceeding was quite out of the common; while Nippers, twitching in his chair with a dyspeptic nervousness, ground out between his set teeth occasional hissing maledictions against the stubborn oaf behind the screen. And for his (Nippers's) part, this was the first and the last time he would do another man's business without pay.

Meanwhile Bartleby sat in his hermitage, oblivious to every thing but his own peculiar business there.

Some days passed, the scrivener being employed upon another lengthy work. His late remarkable conduct led me to regard his ways narrowly. I observed that he never went to dinner; indeed that he never went any where. As yet I had never of my personal knowledge known him to be outside of my office. He was a perpetual sentry in the corner. At about eleven o'clock though, in the morning, I noticed that Ginger Nut would advance toward the opening in Bartleby's screen, as if silently beckoned thither by a gesture invisible to me where I sat. The boy would then leave the office jingling a few pence, and reappear with a handful of ginger-nuts which he delivered in the hermitage, receiving two of the cakes for his trouble.

He lives, then, on ginger-nuts, thought I; never eats a dinner, properly speaking; he must be a vegetarian then; but no; he never eats even vegetables, he eats nothing but ginger-nuts. My mind then ran on in reveries concerning the probable effects upon the human constitution of living entirely on ginger-nuts. Ginger-nuts are so called because they contain ginger as one of their peculiar constituents, and the final flavoring one. Now what was ginger? A hot, spicy thing. Was Bartleby hot and spicy? Not at all. Ginger, then, had no effect upon Bartleby. Probably he preferred it should have none.

Nothing so aggravates an earnest person as a passive resistance. If the individual so resisted be of a not inhumane temper, and the resisting one perfectly harmless in his passivity; then, in the better moods of the former, he will endeavor charitably to construe to his imagination what proves impossible to be solved by his judgment. Even so, for the most part, I regarded Bartleby and his ways. Poor fellow! thought I, he means no mischief; it is plain he intends no insolence; his aspect sufficiently evinces that his eccentricities are involuntary. He is useful to me. I can get along with him. If I turn him away, the chances are he will fall in with some less indulgent employer, and then he will be rudely treated, and perhaps driven forth miserably to starve. Yes. Here I can cheaply purchase a delicious self-approval. To befriend Bartleby; to humor him in his strange wilfulness, will cost me little or nothing, while I lay up in my soul what will eventually prove a sweet morsel for my conscience. But this mood was not invariable with me. The passiveness of Bartleby sometimes irritated me. I felt strangely goaded on to encounter him in new opposition, to elicit some angry spark from him answerable to my own. But indeed I might as well have essayed to strike fire with my knuckles against a bit of Windsor soap. But one afternoon the evil impulse in me mastered me, and the following little scene ensued:

"Bartleby," said I, "when those papers are all copied, I will compare them with you."

"I would prefer not to."

"How? Surely you do not mean to persist in that mulish vagary?"

No answer.

I threw open the folding-doors near by, and turning upon Turkey and Nippers, exclaimed:

"Bartleby a second time says, he won't examine his papers. What do you think of it, Turkey?"

It was afternoon, be it remembered. Turkey sat glowing like a brass boiler, his bald head steaming, his hands reeling among his blotted papers.

"Think of it?" roared Turkey; "I think I'll just step behind his screen, and black his eyes for him!"

So saying, Turkey rose to his feet and threw his arms into a pugilistic position. He was hurrying away to make good his promise, when I detained him, alarmed at the effect of incautiously rousing Turkey's combativeness after dinner.

"Sit down, Turkey," said I, "and hear what Nippers has to say. What do you think of it, Nippers? Would I not be justified in immediately dismissing Bartleby?"

"Excuse me, that is for you to decide, sir. I think his conduct quite unusual, and indeed unjust, as regards Turkey and myself. But it may only be a passing whim."

"Ah," exclaimed I, "you have strangely changed your mind then—you speak very gently of him now."

"All beer," cried Turkey; "gentleness is effects of beer—Nippers and I dined together to-day. You see how gentle *I* am, sir. Shall I go and black his eyes?"

"You refer to Bartleby, I suppose. No, not to-day, Turkey," I replied; "pray, put up your fists."

I closed the doors, and again advanced towards Bartleby. I felt additional incentives tempting me to my fate. I burned to be rebelled against again. I remembered that Bartleby never left the office.

"Bartleby," said I, "Ginger Nut is away; just step round to the Post Office, won't you? (it was but a three minutes walk,) and see if there is any thing for me."

"I would prefer not to."

"You *will* not?"

"I *prefer* not."

I staggered to my desk, and sat there in a deep study. My blind inveteracy returned. Was there any other thing in which I could procure myself to be ignominiously repulsed by this lean, penniless wight?—my hired clerk? What added thing is there, perfectly reasonable, that he will be sure to refuse to do?

"Bartleby!"

No answer.

"Bartleby," in a louder tone.

No answer.

"Bartleby," I roared.

Like a very ghost, agreeably to the laws of magical invocation, at the third summons, he appeared at the entrance of his hermitage.

"Go to the next room, and tell Nippers to come to me."

"I prefer not to," he respectfully and slowly said, and mildly disappeared.

"Very good, Bartleby," said I, in a quiet sort of serenely severe self-possessed tone, intimating the unalterable purpose of some terrible retribution very close at hand. At the moment I half intended something of the kind. But upon the whole, as it was drawing towards my dinner-hour, I thought it best to put on my hat and walk home for the day, suffering much from perplexity and distress of mind.

Shall I acknowledge it? The conclusion of this whole business was, that it soon became a fixed fact of my chambers, that a pale young scrivener, by the name of Bartleby, had a desk there; that he copied for me at the usual rate of four cents a folio (one hundred words); but he was permanently exempt from examining the work done by him, that duty being transferred to Turkey and Nippers, out of compliment doubtless to their superior acuteness; moreover, said Bartleby was never on any account to be dispatched on the most trivial errand of any sort; and that even if entreated to take upon him such a matter, it was generally understood that he would prefer not to—in other words, that he would refuse point-blank.

As days passed on, I became considerably reconciled to Bartleby. His steadiness, his freedom from all dissipation, his incessant industry (except when he chose to throw himself into a standing revery behind his screen), his great stillness, his unalterableness of demeanor under all circumstances, made him a valuable acquisition. One prime thing was this,—*he was always there;*—first in the morning, continually through the day, and the last at night. I had a singular confidence in his honesty. I felt my most precious papers perfectly safe in his hands. Sometimes to be sure I could not, for the very soul of me, avoid falling into sudden spasmodic passions with him. For it was exceeding difficult to bear in mind all the time those strange peculiarities, privileges, and unheard of exemptions, forming the tacit stipulations on Bartleby's part under which he remained in my office. Now and then, in the eagerness of dispatching pressing business, I would inadvertently summon Bartleby, in a short, rapid tone, to put his finger, say, on the incipient tie of a bit of red tape with which I was about compressing some papers. Of course, from behind the screen the usual answer, "I prefer not to," was sure to come; and then, how could a human creature with the common infirmities of our nature, refrain from bitterly exclaiming upon such perverseness—such unreasonableness. However, every added repulse of this sort which I received only tended to lessen the probability of my repeating the inadvertence.

Here it must be said, that according to the custom of most legal gentlemen occupying chambers in densely-populated law buildings, there were several keys to my door. One was kept by a woman residing in the attic, which person weekly scrubbed and daily swept and dusted my apartments. Another was kept by Turkey for convenience sake. The third I sometimes carried in my own pocket. The fourth I knew not who had.

Now, one Sunday morning I happened to go to Trinity Church, to hear a celebrated preacher, and finding myself rather early on the ground, I thought I would walk round to my chambers for a while. Luckily I had my key with me; but upon applying it to the lock, I found it resisted by something inserted from the inside. Quite surprised, I called out; when to my consternation a key was turned from within; and thrusting his lean visage at me, and holding the door ajar, the apparition of Bartleby appeared, in his shirt sleeves, and otherwise in a strangely tattered dishabille, saying quietly that he was sorry, but he was deeply engaged just then, and—preferred not admitting me at present. In a brief word or two, he moreover added, that perhaps I had better walk round the block two or three times, and by that time he would probably have concluded his affairs.

Now, the utterly unsurmised appearance of Bartleby, tenanting my law-chambers of a Sunday morning, with his cadaverously gentlemanly *nonchalance,* yet withal firm and self-possessed, had such a strange effect upon me, that incontinently I slunk away from my own door, and did as desired. But not without sundry twinges of impotent rebellion against the mild effrontery of this unaccountable scrivener. Indeed, it was his wonderful mildness chiefly, which not only disarmed me, but unmanned me, as it were. For I consider that one, for the time, is a sort of unmanned when he tranquilly permits his hired clerk to dictate to him, and order him away from his own premises. Furthermore, I was full of uneasiness as to what Bartleby could possibly be doing in my office in his shirt sleeves, and in an otherwise dismantled condition of a Sunday morning. Was any thing amiss going on? Nay, that was out of the question. It was not to be thought of for a moment that Bartleby was an immoral person. But what could he be doing there?—copying? Nay again, whatever might be his eccentricities, Bartleby was an eminently decorous person. He would be the last man to sit down to his desk in any state approaching to nudity. Besides, it was Sunday; and there was something about Bartleby that forbade the supposition that he would by any secular occupation violate the proprieties of the day.

Nevertheless, my mind was not pacified; and full of a restless curiosity, at last I returned to the door. Without hindrance I inserted my key, opened it, and entered. Bartleby was not to be seen. I looked round anxiously, peeped behind his screen; but it was very plain that he was gone. Upon more closely examining the place, I surmised that for an indefinite period Bartleby must have ate, dressed, and slept in my office, and that too without plate, mirror, or bed. The cushioned seat of a ricketty old sofa in one corner bore the faint impress of a lean, reclining form. Rolled away under his desk, I found a blanket; under the empty grate, a blacking box and brush; on a chair, a tin basin, with soap and a ragged towel; in a newspaper a few crumbs of ginger-nuts and a morsel of cheese. Yes, thought I, it is evident enough that Bartleby has been making his home here, keeping bachelor's hall all by himself. Immediately then the thought came sweeping across me, What miserable friendlessness and loneliness are here revealed! His poverty is great; but his solitude, how horrible! Think of it. Of a Sunday, Wall-street is deserted as Petra;[13] and every night of every day it is an emptiness. This building too, which of week-days hums with industry and life, at nightfall echoes with sheer vacancy, and all through Sunday is forlorn. And here Bartleby makes his home; sole spectator of a solitude which he has seen all populous—a sort of innocent and transformed Marius brooding among the ruins of Carthage![14]

[13]Ancient fortress-city of the Edom desert, uninhabited for centuries. Its discovery in 1812 was a major archaeological event.

[14]Gaius Marius (157–86 B.C.), plebeian general and consul of Rome, after victorious campaigns in Africa and Gaul, lost a power struggle in Rome to patricians and fled back to Africa. When the Roman governor refused him the right to land in the territory he had conquered for Rome, Marius charged the messenger to "'Go tell him that you have seen Gaius Marius sitting in exile among the ruins of Carthage'; appositely applying the example of the fortune of that city to the change of his own condition" (Plutarch). A popular democratic symbol, he appeared frequently in nineteenth-century literature and art.

For the first time in my life a feeling of overpowering stinging melancholy seized me. Before, I had never experienced aught but a not-unpleasing sadness. The bond of a common humanity now drew me irresistibly to gloom. A fraternal melancholy! For both I and Bartleby were sons of Adam. I remembered the bright silks and sparkling faces I had seen that day, in gala trim, swan-like sailing down the Mississippi of Broadway; and I contrasted them with the pallid copyist, and thought to myself, Ah, happiness courts the light, so we deem the world is gay; but misery hides aloof, so we deem that misery there is none. These sad fancyings—chimeras, doubtless, of a sick and silly brain—led on to other and more special thoughts, concerning the eccentricities of Bartleby. Presentiments of strange discoveries hovered round me. The scrivener's pale form appeared to me laid out, among uncaring strangers, in its shivering winding sheet.

Suddenly I was attracted by Bartleby's closed desk, the key in open sight left in the lock.

I mean no mischief, seek the gratification of no heartless curiosity, thought I; besides, the desk is mine, and its contents too, so I will make bold to look within. Every thing was methodically arranged, the papers smoothly placed. The pigeon holes were deep, and removing the files of documents, I groped into their recesses. Presently I felt something there, and dragged it out. It was an old bandanna handkerchief, heavy and knotted. I opened it, and saw it was a savings' bank.

I now recalled all the quiet mysteries which I had noted in the man. I remembered that he never spoke but to answer; that though at intervals he had considerable time to himself, yet I had never seen him reading—no, not even a newspaper; that for long periods he would stand looking out, at his pale window behind the screen, upon the dead brick wall; I was quite sure he never visited any refectory or eating house; while his pale face clearly indicated that he never drank beer like Turkey, or tea and coffee even, like other men; that he never went any where in particular that I could learn; never went out for a walk, unless indeed that was the case at present; that he had declined telling who he was, or whence he came, or whether he had any relatives in the world; that though so thin and pale, he never complained of ill health. And more than all, I remembered a certain unconscious air of pallid—how shall I call it?—of pallid haughtiness, say, or rather an austere reserve about him, which had positively awed me into my tame compliance with his eccentricities, when I had feared to ask him to do the slightest incidental thing for me, even though I might know, from his long-continued motionlessness, that behind his screen he must be standing in one of those dead-wall reveries of his.

Revolving all these things, and coupling them with the recently discovered fact that he made my office his constant abiding place and home, and not forgetful of his morbid moodiness; revolving all these things, a prudential feeling began to steal over me. My first emotions had been those of pure melancholy and sincerest pity; but just in proportion as the forlornness of Bartleby grew and grew to my imagination, did that same melancholy merge into fear, that pity into repulsion. So true it is, and so terrible too, that up to a certain point the thought or sight of misery enlists our best affections; but, in certain special cases, beyond that point it does not. They err who would assert that invariably this is owing to the inherent selfishness of the human heart. It rather proceeds from a certain hopelessness of remedying excessive and organic ill. To a sensitive being, pity is not seldom pain. And when at last it is perceived that such pity cannot lead to effectual succor, common sense bids the soul be rid of it. What I saw that morning persuaded me that the scrivener was the victim of innate and incurable disorder. I might give alms to his body; but his body did not pain him; it was his soul that suffered, and his soul I could not reach.

I did not accomplish the purpose of going to Trinity Church that morning. Somehow, the things I had seen disqualified me for the time from church-going. I walked homeward, thinking what I would do with Bartleby. Finally, I resolved upon this;—I would put certain calm questions to him the next morning, touching his history, &c., and if he declined to answer them openly and unreservedly (and I supposed he would prefer not), then to give him a twenty dollar bill over and above whatever I might owe him, and tell him his services were no longer required; but that if in any other way I could assist him, I would be happy to do so, especially if he desired to return to his native place, wherever that might be, I would willingly help to defray the expenses. Moreover, if, after reaching home, he found himself at any time in want of aid, a letter from him would be sure of a reply.

The next morning came.

"Bartleby," said I, gently calling to him behind his screen.

No reply.

"Bartleby," said I, in a still gentler tone, "come here; I am not going to ask you to do any thing you would prefer not to do—I simply wish to speak to you."

Upon this he noiselessly slid into view.

"Will you tell me, Bartleby, where you were born?"

"I would prefer not to."

"Will you tell me *any thing* about yourself?"

"I would prefer not to."

"But what reasonable objection can you have to speak to me? I feel friendly towards you."

He did not look at me while I spoke, but kept his glance fixed upon my bust of Cicero, which as I then sat, was directly behind me, some six inches above my head.

"What is your answer, Bartleby?" said I, after waiting a considerable time for a reply, during which his countenance remained immovable, only there was the faintest conceivable tremor of the white attenuated mouth.

"At present I prefer to give no answer," he said, and retired into his hermitage.

It was rather weak in me I confess, but his manner on this occasion nettled me. Not only did there seem to lurk in it a certain calm disdain, but his perverseness seemed ungrateful, considering the undeniable good usage and indulgence he had received from me.

Again I sat ruminating what I should do. Mortified as I was at his behavior, and resolved as I had been to dismiss him when I entered my office, nevertheless I strangely felt something superstitious knocking at my heart, and forbidding me to carry out my purpose, and denouncing me for a villain if I dared to breathe one bitter word against this forlornest of mankind. At last, familiarly drawing my chair behind his screen, I sat down and said: "Bartleby, never mind then about revealing your history; but let me entreat you, as a friend, to comply as far as may be with the usages of this office. Say now you will help to examine papers to-morrow or next day: in short, say now that in a day or two you will begin to be a little reasonable:—say so, Bartleby."

"At present I would prefer not to be a little reasonable," was his mildly cadaverous reply.

Just then the folding-doors opened, and Nippers approached. He seemed suffering from an unusually bad night's rest, induced by severer indigestion than common. He overheard those final words of Bartleby.

"*Prefer not,* eh?" gritted Nippers—"I'd *prefer* him, if I were you, sir," addressing me—"I'd *prefer* him; I'd give him preferences, the stubborn mule! What is it, sir, pray, that he *prefers* not to do now?"

Bartleby moved not a limb.

"Mr. Nippers," said I, "I'd prefer that you would withdraw for the present."

Somehow, of late I had got into the way of involuntarily using this word "prefer" upon all sorts of not exactly suitable occasions. And I trembled to think that my contact with the scrivener had already and seriously affected me in a mental way. And what further and deeper aberration might it not yet produce? This apprehension had not been without efficacy in determining me to summary measures.

As Nippers, looking very sour and sulky, was departing, Turkey blandly and deferentially approached.

"With submission, sir," said he, "yesterday I was thinking about Bartleby here, and I think that if he would but prefer to take a quart of good ale every day, it would do much towards mending him, and enabling him to assist in examining his papers."

"So you have got the word too," said I, slightly excited.

"With submission, what word, sir," asked Turkey, respectfully crowding himself into the contracted space behind the screen, and by so doing, making me jostle the scrivener. "What word, sir?"

"I would prefer to be left alone here," said Bartleby, as if offended at being mobbed in his privacy.

"*That's* the word, Turkey," said I—"*that's* it."

"Oh, *prefer?* oh yes—queer word. I never use it myself. But, sir, as I was saying, if he would but prefer—"

"Turkey," interrupted I, "you will please withdraw."

"Oh certainly, sir, if you prefer that I should."

As he opened the folding-doors to retire, Nippers at his desk caught a glimpse of me, and asked whether I would prefer to have a certain paper copied on blue paper or white. He did not in the least roguishly accent the word prefer. It was plain that it involuntarily rolled from his tongue. I thought to myself, surely I must get rid of a demented man, who already has in some degree turned the tongues, if not the heads of myself and clerks. But I thought it prudent not to break the dismission at once.

The next day I noticed that Bartleby did nothing but stand at his window in his dead-wall revery. Upon asking him why he did not write, he said that he had decided upon doing no more writing.

"Why, how now? what next?" exclaimed I, "do no more writing?"

"No more."

"And what is the reason?"

"Do you not see the reason for yourself," he indifferently replied.

I looked steadfastly at him, and perceived that his eyes looked dull and glazed. Instantly it occurred to me, that his unexampled diligence in copying by his dim window for the first few weeks of his stay with me might have temporarily impaired his vision.

I was touched. I said something in condolence with him. I hinted that of course he did wisely in abstaining from writing for a while; and urged him to embrace that opportunity of taking wholesome exercise in the open air. This, however, he did not do. A few days after this, my other clerks being absent, and being in a great hurry to dispatch certain letters by the mail, I thought that, having nothing else earthly to do, Bartleby would surely be less inflexible than usual, and carry these letters to the post-office. But he blankly declined. So, much to my inconvenience, I went myself.

Still added days went by. Whether Bartleby's eyes improved or not, I could not say. To all appearance, I thought they did. But when I asked him if they did, he vouchsafed no answer. At all events, he would do no copying. At last, in reply to my urgings, he informed me that he had permanently given up copying.

"What!" exclaimed I; "suppose your eyes should get entirely well—better than ever before—would you not copy then?"

"I have given up copying," he answered, and slid aside.

He remained as ever, a fixture in my chamber. Nay—if that were possible—he became still more of a fixture than before. What was to be done? He would do nothing in the office: why should he stay there? In plain fact, he had now become a mill-stone to me, not only useless as a necklace, but afflictive to bear. Yet I was sorry for him. I speak less than truth when I say that, on his own account, he occasioned me uneasiness. If he would but have named a single relative or friend, I would instantly have written, and urged their taking the poor fellow away to some convenient retreat. But he seemed alone, absolutely alone in the universe. A bit of wreck in the mid Atlantic. At length, necessities connected with my business tyrannized over all other considerations. Decently as I could, I told Bartleby that in six days' time he must unconditionally leave the office. I warned him to take measures, in the interval, for procuring some other abode. I offered to assist him in this endeavor, if he himself would but take the first step towards a removal. "And when you finally quit me, Bartleby," added I, "I shall see that you go not away entirely unprovided. Six days from this hour, remember."

At the expiration of that period, I peeped behind the screen, and lo! Bartleby was there.

I buttoned up my coat, balanced myself; advanced slowly towards him, touched his shoulder, and said, "The time has come; you must quit this place; I am sorry for you; here is money; but you must go."

"I would prefer not," he replied, with his back still towards me.

"You *must.*"

He remained silent.

Now I had an unbounded confidence in this man's common honesty. He had frequently restored to me sixpences and shillings carelessly dropped upon the floor, for I am apt to be very reckless in such shirt-button affairs. The proceeding then which followed will not be deemed extraordinary.

"Bartleby," said I, "I owe you twelve dollars on account; here are thirty-two; the odd twenty are yours.—Will you take it?" and I handed the bills towards him.

But he made no motion.

"I will leave them here then," putting them under a weight on the table. Then taking my hat and cane and going to the door I tranquilly turned and added—"After you have removed your things from these offices, Bartleby, you will of course lock the door—since every one is now gone for the day but you—and if you please, slip your key underneath the mat, so that I may have it in the morning. I shall not see you again; so good-bye to you. If hereafter in your new place of abode I can be of any service to you, do not fail to advise me by letter. Good-bye, Bartleby, and fare you well."

But he answered not a word; like the last column of some ruined temple,[15] he remained standing mute and solitary in the middle of the otherwise deserted room.

As I walked home in a pensive mood, my vanity got the better of my pity. I could not but highly plume myself on my masterly management in getting rid of Bartleby. Masterly I call it, and such it must appear to any dispassionate thinker. The beauty of my procedure seemed to consist in its perfect quietness. There was no vulgar bullying, no bravado of any sort, no choleric hectoring, and striding to and fro across the apartment, jerking out vehement commands for Bartleby to bundle himself off with his beggarly traps. Nothing of the kind. Without loudly bidding Bartleby depart—as an inferior genius might have done—I *assumed* the ground that depart he must; and upon that assumption built all I had to say. The more I thought over my procedure, the more I was charmed with it. Nevertheless, next morning, upon awakening, I had my doubts,—I had somehow slept off the fumes of vanity. One of the coolest and wisest hours a man has, is just after he awakes in the morning. My procedure seemed as sagacious as ever,—but only in theory. How it would prove in practice—there was the rub. It was truly a beautiful thought to have assumed Bartleby's departure; but, after all, that assumption was simply my own, and none of Bartleby's. The great point was, not whether I had assumed that he would quit me, but whether he would prefer so to do. He was more a man of preferences than assumptions.

After breakfast, I walked down town, arguing the probabilities *pro* and *con.* One moment I thought it would prove a miserable failure, and Bartleby would be found all alive at my office as usual; the next moment it seemed certain that I should find his chair empty. And so I kept veering about. At the corner of Broadway and Canal-street, I saw quite an excited group of people standing in earnest conversation.

"I'll take odds he doesn't," said a voice as I passed.

"Doesn't go?—done!" said I, "put up your money."

I was instinctively putting my hand in my pocket to produce my own, when I remembered that this was an election day.[16] The words I had overheard bore no reference to Bartleby, but to the success or non-success of some candidate for the

[15]Donald M. Fiene has pointed out the relevance of Matthew 24:1–2: "And Jesus went out, and departed from the temple: and his disciples came to him for to shew him the buildings of the temple. And Jesus said unto them, See ye not all these things? verily I say unto you, There shall not be left here one stone upon another, that shall not be thrown down."

[16]A complicated pun suggesting that this may be Judgment Day for the narrator, whose "election," in the religious sense of being chosen for salvation, may depend on how he chooses to treat Bartleby. H. Bruce Franklin and Donald M. Fiene have interpreted the story in the light of Matthew 25:31–42, where Christ prophesies that he will return at the end of the world to consign his professed disciples to heaven or to hell, according to whether they have treated those in need as they would treat Christ himself: "For I was an hungred, and ye gave me meat: I was thirsty, and ye gave me drink: I was a stranger, and ye took me in: Naked, and ye clothed me: I was sick, and ye visited me: I was in prison, and ye came unto me. . . . Inasmuch as ye have done it unto one of the least of these my brethren, ye have done it unto me." I have drawn on their articles in identifying other relevant Biblical passages below.

mayoralty. In my intent frame of mind, I had, as it were, imagined that all Broadway shared in my excitement, and were debating the same question with me. I passed on, very thankful that the uproar of the street screened my momentary absent-mindedness.

As I had intended, I was earlier than usual at my office door. I stood listening for a moment. All was still. He must be gone. I tried the knob. The door was locked. Yes, my procedure had worked to a charm; he indeed must be vanished. Yet a certain melancholy mixed with this: I was almost sorry for my brilliant success. I was fumbling under the door mat for the key, which Bartleby was to have left there for me, when accidentally my knee knocked against a panel, producing a summoning sound, and in response a voice came to me from within—"Not yet; I am occupied."

It was Bartleby.

I was thunderstruck. For an instant I stood like the man who, pipe in mouth, was killed one cloudless afternoon long ago in Virginia, by summer lightning; at his own warm open window he was killed, and remained leaning out there upon the dreamy afternoon, till some one touched him, when he fell.

"Not gone!" I murmured at last. But again obeying that wondrous ascendancy which the inscrutable scrivener had over me, and from which ascendancy, for all my chafing, I could not completely escape, I slowly went down stairs and out into the street, and while walking round the block, considered what I should next do in this unheard-of perplexity. Turn the man out by an actual thrusting I could not; to drive him away by calling him hard names would not do; calling in the police was an unpleasant idea; and yet, permit him to enjoy his cadaverous triumph over me,—this too I could not think of. What was to be done? or, if nothing could be done, was there any thing further that I could *assume* in the matter? Yes, as before I had prospectively assumed that Bartleby would depart, so now I might retrospectively assume that departed he was. In the legitimate carrying out of this assumption, I might enter my office in a great hurry, and pretending not to see Bartleby at all, walk straight against him as if he were air. Such a proceeding would in a singular degree have the appearance of a home-thrust. It was hardly possible that Bartleby could withstand such an application of the doctrine of assumptions. But upon second thoughts the success of the plan seemed rather dubious. I resolved to argue the matter over with him again.

"Bartleby," said I, entering the office, with a quietly severe expression, "I am seriously displeased. I am pained, Bartleby. I had thought better of you. I had imagined you of such a gentlemanly organization, that in any delicate dilemma a slight hint would suffice—in short, an assumption. But it appears I am deceived. Why," I added, unaffectedly starting, "you have not even touched that money yet," pointing to it, just where I had left it the evening previous.

He answered nothing.

"Will you, or will you not, quit me?" I now demanded in a sudden passion, advancing close to him.

"I would prefer *not* to quit you," he replied, gently emphasizing the *not*.

"What earthly right have you to stay here? Do you pay any rent? Do you pay my taxes? Or is this property yours?"

He answered nothing.

"Are you ready to go on and write now? Are your eyes recovered? Could you copy a small paper for me this morning? or help examine a few lines? or step round to the post-office? In a word, will you do any thing at all, to give a coloring to your refusal to depart the premises?"

He silently retired into his hermitage.

I was now in such a state of nervous resentment that I thought it but prudent to check myself at present from further demonstrations. Bartleby and I were alone. I remembered the tragedy of the unfortunate Adams and the still more unfortunate Colt[17] in the solitary office of the latter; and how poor Colt, being dreadfully incensed by Adams, and imprudently permitting himself to get wildly excited, was at unawares hurried into his fatal act—an act which certainly no man could possibly deplore more than the actor himself. Often it had occurred to me in my ponderings upon the subject, that had that altercation taken place in the public street, or at a private residence, it would not have terminated as it did. It was the circumstance of being alone in a solitary office, up stairs, of a building entirely unhallowed by humanizing domestic associations—an uncarpeted office, doubtless, of a dusty, haggard sort of appearance;—this it must have been, which greatly helped to enhance the irritable desperation of the hapless Colt.

But when this old Adam of resentment rose in me and tempted me concerning Bartleby, I grappled him and threw him. How? Why, simply by recalling the divine injunction: "A new commandment give I unto you, that ye love one another."[18] Yes, this it was that saved me. Aside from higher considerations, charity often operates as a vastly wise and prudent principle—a great safeguard to its possessor. Men have committed murder for jealousy's sake, and anger's sake, and hatred's sake, and selfishness' sake, and spiritual pride's sake; but no man that ever I heard of, ever committed a diabolical murder for sweet charity's sake. Mere self-interest, then, if no better motive can be enlisted, should, especially with high-tempered men, prompt all beings to charity and philanthropy. At any rate, upon the occasion in question, I strove to drown my exasperated feelings towards the scrivener by benevolently construing his conduct. Poor fellow, poor fellow! thought I, he don't mean any thing; and besides, he has seen hard times, and ought to be indulged.

I endeavored also immediately to occupy myself, and at the same time to comfort my despondency. I tried to fancy that in the course of the morning, at such time as might prove agreeable to him, Bartleby, of his own free accord, would emerge from his hermitage, and take up some decided line of march in the direction of the door. But no. Half-past twelve o'clock came; Turkey began to glow in the face, overturn his inkstand, and become generally obstreperous; Nippers abated down into quietude and courtesy; Ginger Nut munched his noon apple; and Bartleby

[17]John C. Colt, brother of the Colt revolver's inventor, murdered the printer Samuel Adams with a hatchet when Adams called on him in his Broadway office to collect a debt. Adams's body was found salted and crated for shipment to New Orleans in September, 1841, and Colt was convicted of murder and sentenced to hanging in November, 1842. On the day of his execution, he married his mistress in his jail cell and was found dead of stab wounds shortly afterwards, in the wake of a mysterious fire that broke out following her departure. The death was called a suicide, but circumstances pointed to murder, and it was later revealed that the mistress had been secretly married to Colt's brother. The irony, however, is that the narrator views the murderer, Colt, as more unfortunate than the murdered man, Adams, whom he blames for provoking the murder. The same irony applies to his view of himself and Bartleby.

[18]John 13:34.

remained standing at his window in one of his profoundest dead-wall reveries. Will it be credited? Ought I to acknowledge it? That afternoon I left the office without saying one further word to him.

Some days now passed, during which, at leisure intervals I looked a little into "Edwards on the Will," and "Priestley on Necessity."[19] Under the circumstances, those books induced a salutary feeling. Gradually I slid into the persuasion that these troubles of mine touching the scrivener, had been all predestinated from eternity, and Bartleby was billeted upon me for some mysterious purpose of an all-wise Providence, which it was not for a mere mortal like me to fathom. Yes, Bartleby, stay there behind your screen, thought I; I shall persecute you no more; you are harmless and noiseless as any of these old chairs; in short, I never feel so private as when I know you are here. At last I see it, I feel it; I penetrate to the predestinated purpose of my life. I am content. Others may have loftier parts to enact; but my mission in this world, Bartleby, is to furnish you with office-room for such period as you may see fit to remain.

I believe that this wise and blessed frame of mind would have continued with me, had it not been for the unsolicited and uncharitable remarks obtruded upon me by my professional friends who visited the rooms. But thus it often is, that the constant friction of illiberal minds wears out at last the best resolves of the more generous. Though to be sure, when I reflected upon it, it was not strange that people entering my office should be struck by the peculiar aspect of the unaccountable Bartleby, and so be tempted to throw out some sinister observations concerning him. Sometimes an attorney having business with me, and calling at my office, and finding no one but the scrivener there, would undertake to obtain some sort of precise information from him touching my whereabouts; but without heeding his idle talk, Bartleby would remain standing immovable in the middle of the room. So after contemplating him in that position for a time, the attorney would depart, no wiser than he came.

Also, when a Reference[20] was going on, and the room full of lawyers and witnesses and business was driving fast, some deeply occupied legal gentlemen present, seeing Bartleby wholly unemployed, would request him to run round to his (the legal gentleman's) office and fetch some papers for him. Thereupon, Bartleby would tranquilly decline, and yet remain idle as before. Then the lawyer would give a great stare, and turn to me. And what could I say? At last I was made aware that all through the circle of my professional acquaintance, a whisper of wonder was running round, having reference to the strange creature I kept at my office. This worried me very much. And as the idea came upon me of his possibly turning out a long-lived man, and keep occupying my chambers, and denying my authority; and perplexing my visitors; and scandalizing my professional reputation; and casting a general gloom over the premises; keeping soul and body together to the last upon his savings (for doubtless he spent but half a dime a day), and in the end perhaps outlive me, and

[19]Arguing respectively from the premises of Calvinist theology and of philosophical determinism, the Massachusetts minister Jonathan Edwards, in his *Freedom of the Will* (1754), and the British clergyman-scientist Joseph Priestley, in his *Doctrine of Philosophical Necessity Illustrated* (1777), both maintained that the will was not free, and that all history had been preordained. Both also believed that the apocalyptic prophecies in the Bible were being fulfilled in their lifetime.

[20]The act of referring a disputed matter to a referee.

claim possession of my office by right of his perpetual occupancy: as all these dark anticipations crowded upon me more and more, and my friends continually intruded their relentless remarks upon the apparition in my room; a great change was wrought in me. I resolved to gather all my faculties together, and for ever rid me of this intolerable incubus.

Ere revolving any complicated project, however, adapted to this end, I first simply suggested to Bartleby the propriety of his permanent departure. In a calm and serious tone, I commended the idea to his careful and mature consideration. But having taken three days to meditate upon it, he apprised me that his original determination remained the same; in short, that he still preferred to abide with me.

What shall I do? I now said to myself, buttoning up my coat to the last button. What shall I do? what ought I to do? what does conscience say I *should* do with this man, or rather ghost? Rid myself of him, I must; go, he shall. But how? You will not thrust him, the poor, pale, passive mortal,—you will not thrust such a helpless creature out of your door? you will not dishonor yourself by such cruelty? No, I will not, I cannot do that. Rather would I let him live and die here, and then mason up his remains in the wall. What then will you do? For all your coaxing, he will not budge. Bribes he leaves under your own paper-weight on your table; in short, it is quite plain that he prefers to cling to you.

Then something severe, something unusual must be done. What! surely you will not have him collared by a constable, and commit his innocent pallor to the common jail? And upon what ground could you procure such a thing to be done?—a vagrant, is he? What! he a vagrant, a wanderer, who refuses to budge? It is because he will *not* be a vagrant, then, that you seek to count him *as* a vagrant. That is too absurd. No visible means of support: there I have him. Wrong again: for indubitably he *does* support himself, and that is the only unanswerable proof that any man can show of his possessing the means so to do. No more then. Since he will not quit me, I must quit him. I will change my offices; I will move elsewhere; and give him fair notice, that if I find him on my new premises I will then proceed against him as a common trespasser.

Acting accordingly, next day I thus addressed him: "I find these chambers too far from the City Hall; the air is unwholesome. In a word, I propose to remove my offices next week, and shall no longer require your services. I tell you this now, in order that you may seek another place."

He made no reply, and nothing more was said.

On the appointed day I engaged carts and men, proceeded to my chambers, and having but little furniture, every thing was removed in a few hours. Throughout, the scrivener remained standing behind the screen, which I directed to be removed the last thing. It was withdrawn; and being folded up like a huge folio, left him the motionless occupant of a naked room. I stood in the entry watching him a moment, while something from within me upbraided me.

I re-entered, with my hand in my pocket—and—and my heart in my mouth.

"Good-bye, Bartleby; I am going—good-bye, and God some way bless you; and take that," slipping something in his hand. But it dropped upon the floor, and then,—strange to say—I tore myself from him whom I had so longed to be rid of.

Established in my new quarters, for a day or two I kept the door locked, and started at every footfall in the passages. When I returned to my rooms after any little absence, I would pause at the threshold for an instant, and attentively listen, ere applying my key. But these fears were needless. Bartleby never came nigh me.

I thought all was going well, when a perturbed looking stranger visited me, inquiring whether I was the person who had recently occupied rooms at No.— Wall-street.

Full of forebodings, I replied that I was.

"Then sir," said the stranger, who proved a lawyer, "you are responsible for the man you left there. He refuses to do any copying; he refuses to do any thing; he says he prefers not to; and he refuses to quit the premises."

"I am very sorry, sir," said I, with assumed tranquillity, but an inward tremor, "but, really, the man you allude to is nothing to me[21]—he is no relation or apprentice of mine, that you should hold me responsible for him."

"In mercy's name, who is he?"

"I certainly cannot inform you. I know nothing about him. Formerly I employed him as a copyist; but he has done nothing for me now for some time past."

"I shall settle him then,—good morning, sir."

Several days passed, and I heard nothing more; and though I often felt a charitable prompting to call at the place and see poor Bartleby, yet a certain squeamishness of I know not what withheld me.

All is over with him, by this time, thought I at last, when through another week no further intelligence reached me But coming to my room the day after, I found several persons waiting at my door in a high state of nervous excitement.

"That's the man—here he comes," cried the foremost one, whom I recognized as the lawyer who had previously called upon me alone.

"You must take him away, sir, at once," cried a portly person among them, advancing upon me, and whom I knew to be the landlord of No.—Wall-street. "These gentlemen, my tenants, cannot stand it any longer; Mr. B——" pointing to the lawyer, "has turned him out of his room, and he now persists in haunting the building generally, sitting upon the banisters of the stairs by day, and sleeping in the entry by night. Every body is concerned; clients are leaving the offices; some fears are entertained of a mob; something you must do, and that without delay."

Aghast at this torrent, I fell back before it, and would fain have locked myself in my new quarters. In vain I persisted that Bartleby was nothing to me—no more than to any one else. In vain:—I was the last person known to have any thing to do with him, and they held me to the terrible account. Fearful then of being exposed in the papers (as one person present obscurely threatened) I considered the matter, and at length said, that if the lawyer would give me a confidential interview with the scrivener, in his (the lawyer's) own room, I would that afternoon strive my best to rid them of the nuisance they complained of.

Going up stairs to my old haunt, there was Bartleby silently sitting upon the banister at the landing.

"What are you doing here, Bartleby?" said I.

"Sitting upon the banister," he mildly replied.

[21]Cf. Peter's denial of Christ, Mark 14:68, 70–71: "But he denied, saying, I know not, neither understand I what thou sayest. . . . And he denied it again. . . . But he began to curse and to swear, saying, I know not this man of whom ye speak."

I motioned him into the lawyer's room, who then left us.

"Bartleby," said I, "are you aware that you are the cause of great tribulation to me, by persisting in occupying the entry after being dismissed from the office?"

No answer.

"Now one of two things must take place. Either you must do something, or something must be done to you. Now what sort of business would you like to engage in? Would you like to re-engage in copying for some one?"

"No; I would prefer not to make any change."

"Would you like a clerkship in a dry-goods store?"[22]

"There is too much confinement about that. No, I would not like a clerkship; but I am not particular."

"Too much confinement," I cried, "why you keep yourself confined all the time!"

"I would prefer not to take a clerkship," he rejoined, as if to settle that little item at once.

"How would a bar-tender's business suit you? There is no trying of the eyesight in that."

"I would not like it at all; though, as I said before, I am not particular."

His unwonted wordiness inspirited me. I returned to the charge.

"Well then, would you like to travel through the country collecting bills for the merchants? That would improve your health."

"No, I would prefer to be doing something else."

"How then would going as a companion to Europe, to entertain some young gentleman with your conversation,—how would that suit you?"

"Not at all. It does not strike me that there is any thing definite about that. I like to be stationary. But I am not particular."

"Stationary you shall be then," I cried, now losing all patience, and for the first time in all my exasperating connection with him fairly flying into a passion. "If you do not go away from these premises before night, I shall feel bound—indeed I *am* bound—to—to—to quit the premises myself!" I rather absurdly concluded, knowing not with what possible threat to try to frighten his immobility into compliance. Despairing of all further efforts, I was precipitately leaving him, when a final thought occurred to me—one which had not been wholly unindulged before.

"Bartleby," said I, in the kindest tone I could assume under such exciting circumstances, "will you go home with me now—not to my office, but my dwelling—and remain there till we can conclude upon some convenient arrangement for you at our leisure? Come, let us start now, right away."

"No: at present I would prefer not to make any change at all."

I answered nothing; but effectually dodging every one by the suddenness and rapidity of my flight, rushed from the building, ran up Wall-street towards Broadway, and jumping into the first omnibus was soon removed from pursuit. As soon as tranquillity returned I distinctly perceived that I had now done all that I possibly could, both in respect to the demands of the landlord and his tenants, and with regard to my own desire and sense of duty, to benefit Bartleby, and shield him from rude persecution. I now strove to be entirely care-free and quiescent; and my conscience justified me in the attempt; though indeed it was not so successful as I

[22]Melville had clerked in his brother's fur store, as well as in a dry-goods store in Honolulu.

could have wished. So fearful was I of being again hunted out by the incensed landlord and his exasperated tenants, that, surrendering my business to Nippers, for a few days I drove about the upper part of the town and through the suburbs, in my rockaway; crossed over to Jersey City and Hoboken, and paid fugitive visits to Manhattanville and Astoria. In fact I almost lived in my rockaway[23] for the time.

When again I entered my office, lo, a note from the landlord lay upon the desk. I opened it with trembling hands. It informed me that the writer had sent to the police, and had Bartleby removed to the Tombs as a vagrant. Moreover, since I knew more about him than any one else, he wished me to appear at that place, and make a suitable statement of the facts. These tidings had a conflicting effect upon me. At first I was indignant; but at last almost approved. The landlord's energetic, summary disposition, had led him to adopt a procedure which I do not think I would have decided upon myself; and yet as a last resort, under such peculiar circumstances, it seemed the only plan.

As I afterwards learned, the poor scrivener, when told that he must be conducted to the Tombs, offered not the slightest obstacle, but in his pale unmoving way, silently acquiesced.

Some of the compassionate and curious bystanders joined the party; and headed by one of the constables arm in arm with Bartleby, the silent procession filed its way through all the noise, and heat, and joy of the roaring thoroughfares at noon.

The same day I received the note I went to the Tombs, or to speak more properly, the Halls of Justice.[24] Seeking the right officer, I stated the purpose of my call, and was informed that the individual I described was indeed within. I then assured the functionary that Bartleby was a perfectly honest man, and greatly to be compassionated, however unaccountably eccentric. I narrated all I knew, and closed by suggesting the idea of letting him remain in as indulgent confinement as possible till something less harsh might be done—though indeed I hardly knew what. At all events, if nothing else could be decided upon, the alms-house must receive him. I then begged to have an interview.

Being under no disgraceful charge, and quite serene and harmless in all his ways, they had permitted him freely to wander about the prison, and especially in the inclosed grass-platted yards thereof. And so I found him there, standing all alone in the quietest of the yards, his face towards a high wall, while all around, from the narrow slits of the jail windows, I thought I saw peering out upon him the eyes of murderers and thieves.[25]

"Bartleby!"

"I know you," he said, without looking round,—"and I want nothing to say to you."

"It was not I that brought you here, Bartleby," said I, keenly pained at his implied suspicion. "And to you, this should not be so vile a place. Nothing reproachful attaches to you by being here. And see, it is not so sad a place as one might think. Look, there is the sky, and here is the grass."

"I know where I am," he replied, but would say nothing more, and so I left him.

[23]A light, low carriage with open sides and a fixed top.

[24]Melville is playing on the irony that the Tombs, officially designated the Halls of Justice and House of Detention, fulfilled two incompatible functions.

[25]Cf. Mark 15:27–28: "And with him they crucify two thieves. . . . And the scripture was fulfilled, which saith, And he was numbered with the transgressors."

As I entered the corridor again, a broad meat-like man, in an apron, accosted me, and jerking his thumb over his shoulder said—"Is that your friend?"

"Yes."

"Does he want to starve? If he does, let him live on the prison fare, that's all."

"Who are you?" asked I, not knowing what to make of such an unofficially speaking person in such a place.

"I am the grub-man. Such gentlemen as have friends here, hire me to provide them with something good to eat."

"Is this so?" said I, turning to the turnkey.

He said it was.

"Well then," said I, slipping some silver into the grub-man's hands (for so they called him). "I want you to give particular attention to my friend there; let him have the best dinner you can get. And you must be as polite to him as possible."

"Introduce me, will you?" said the grub-man, looking at me with an expression which seemed to say he was all impatience for an opportunity to give a specimen of his breeding.

Thinking it would prove of benefit to the scrivener, I acquiesced; and asking the grub-man his name, went up with him to Bartleby.

"Bartleby, this is Mr. Cutlets; you will find him very useful to you."

"Your sarvant, sir, your sarvant," said the grub-man, making a low salutation behind his apron. "Hope you find it pleasant here, sir; nice grounds—cool apartments, sir—hope you'll stay with us some time—try to make it agreeable. May Mrs. Cutlets and I have the pleasure of your company to dinner, sir, in Mrs. Cutlets' private room?"

"I prefer not to dine to-day," said Bartleby, turning away. "It would disagree with me; I am unused to dinners." So saying he slowly moved to the other side of the inclosure, and took up a position fronting the dead-wall.

"How's this?" said the grub-man, addressing me with a stare of astonishment. "He's odd, aint he?"

"I think he is a little deranged," said I, sadly.

"Deranged? deranged is it? Well now, upon my word, I thought that friend of yourn was a gentleman forger; they are always pale and genteel-like, them forgers. I can't help pity 'em—can't help it, sir. Did you know Monroe Edwards?"[26] he added touchingly, and paused. Then, laying his hand pityingly on my shoulder, sighed, "he died of consumption at Sing-Sing. So you weren't acquainted with Monroe?"

"No, I was never socially acquainted with any forgers. But I cannot stop longer. Look to my friend yonder. You will not lose by it. I will see you again."

Some few days after this, I again obtained admission to the Tombs, and went through the corridors in quest of Bartleby; but without finding him.

"I saw him coming from his cell not long ago," said a turnkey, "may be he's gone to loiter in the yards."

So I went in that direction.

"Are you looking for the silent man?" said another turnkey passing me. "Yonder he lies—sleeping in the yard there. 'Tis not twenty minutes since I saw him lie down."

The yard was entirely quiet. It was not accessible to the common prisoners. The

[26]A financier convicted of using forged letters of credit to defraud two firms of $25,000 each. His trial in June, 1842, caused as much of a sensation as that of Colt.

surrounding walls, of amazing thickness, kept off all sounds behind them. The Egyptian character of the masonry weighed upon me with its gloom. But a soft imprisoned turf grew under foot. The heart of the eternal pyramids, it seemed, wherein, by some strange magic, through the clefts, grass-seed, dropped by birds, had sprung.

Strangely huddled at the base of the wall, his knees drawn up, and lying on his side, his head touching the cold stones, I saw the wasted Bartleby. But nothing stirred. I paused; then went close up to him; stooped over, and saw that his dim eyes were open; otherwise he seemed profoundly sleeping. Something prompted me to touch him. I felt his hand, when a tingling shiver ran up my arm and down my spine to my feet.

The round face of the grub-man peered upon me now. "His dinner is ready. Won't he dine to-day, either? Or does he live without dining?"

"Lives without dining," said I, and closed the eyes.

"Eh!—He's asleep, aint he?"

"With kings and counsellors,"[27] murmured I.

* * * * *

There would seem little need for proceeding further in this history. Imagination will readily supply the meagre recital of poor Bartleby's interment. But ere parting with the reader, let me say, that if this little narrative has sufficiently interested him, to awaken curiosity as to who Bartleby was, and what manner of life he led prior to the present narrator's making his acquaintance, I can only reply, that in such curiosity I fully share, but am wholly unable to gratify it. Yet here I hardly know whether I should divulge one little item of rumor, which came to my ear a few months after the scrivener's decease. Upon what basis it rested, I could never ascertain; and hence, how true it is I cannot now tell. But inasmuch as this vague report has not been without a certain strange suggestive interest to me, however sad, it may prove the same with some others; and so I will briefly mention it. The report was this: that Bartleby had been a subordinate clerk in the Dead Letter Office at Washington, from which he had been suddenly removed by a change in the administration. When I think over this rumor, hardly can I express the emotions which seize me. Dead letters! does it not sound like dead men? Conceive a man by nature and misfortune prone to a pallid hopelessness, can any business seem more fitted to heighten it than that of continually handling these dead letters, and assorting them for the flames? For by the cart-load they are annually burned. Sometimes from out the folded paper the pale clerk takes a ring:—the finger it was meant for, perhaps, moulders in the grave; a bank-note sent in swiftest charity:—he whom it would relieve, nor eats nor hungers any more; pardon for those who died despairing; hope for those who died unhoping; good tidings for those who died stifled by unrelieved calamities. On errands of life, these letters speed to death.

Ah Bartleby! Ah humanity!

1853

[27]Job 3:14. After being smitten by God with boils, Job curses the day he was born and says that had he died in the womb or in infancy, he would have been "at rest, With kings and counsellors of the earth, which built desolate places for themselves."

from The Encantadas

Sketch Eighth
Norfolk Isle and the Chola Widow[1]

"At last they in an island did espy
A seemly woman sitting by the shore,
That with great sorrow and sad agony
Seemed some great misfortune to deplore,
And loud to them for succor called evermore."

"Black his eye as the midnight sky,
White his neck as the driven snow,
Red his cheek as the morning light;—
Cold he lies in the ground below.
My love is dead,
Gone to his death-bed,
All under the cactus tree."

"Each lonely scene shall thee restore,
For thee the tear be duly shed;
Belov'd till life can charm no more,
And mourned till Pity's self be dead."[2]

Far to the northeast of Charles' Isle, sequestered from the rest, lies Norfolk Isle; and, however insignificant to most voyagers, to me, through sympathy, that lone island has become a spot made sacred by the strongest trials of humanity.

It was my first visit to the Encantadas. Two days had been spent ashore in hunting tortoises. There was not time to capture many; so on the third afternoon we loosed our sails. We were just in the act of getting under way, the uprooted anchor yet suspended and invisibly swaying beneath the wave, as the good ship gradually turned on her heel to leave the isle behind, when the seaman who heaved with me at the windlass paused suddenly, and directed my attention to something moving on the land, not along the beach, but somewhat back, fluttering from a height.

In view of the sequel of this little story, be it here narrated how it came to pass,

[1]Begun in late 1853, Melville's ten sketches of the Galápagos Islands, which he had visited in 1841 and 1842, were serialized in the March, April, and May, 1854, issues of *Putnam's Monthly Magazine,* under the pseudonym "Salvator R. Tarnmoor," and later reprinted in *The Piazza Tales* (1856). The present text is from the standard Northwestern-Newberry edition of *The Piazza Tales and Other Prose Pieces, 1839–1860.*

According to Robert Sattelmeyer and James Barbour, Melville may have based the story of Hunilla partly on newspaper accounts in November, 1853, of an Indian woman, described as a "female Robinson Crusoe," recently rescued from an island off Santa Barbara after eighteen years of abandonment there.

[2]Spenser, *The Faerie Queene,* 2.12.27 (Melville changed the word "Maiden" in the original to "woman"). Thomas Chatterton, "The Mynstrelle's Songe," from *Aella: A Tragycal Enterlude,* also slightly altered. William Collins, "Dirge in Cymbeline," an epigraph Melville added to *The Piazza Tales* version of the story.

that an object which partly from its being so small was quite lost to every other man on board, still caught the eye of my handspike[3] companion. The rest of the crew, myself included, merely stood up to our spikes in heaving; whereas, unwontedly exhilarated at every turn of the ponderous windlass, my belted comrade leaped atop of it, with might and main giving a downward, thewey, perpendicular heave, his raised eye bent in cheery animation upon the slowly receding shore. Being high lifted above all others was the reason he perceived the object, otherwise unperceivable: and this elevation of his eye was owing to the elevation of his spirits; and this again—for truth must out—to a dram of Peruvian pisco,[4] in guerdon for some kindness done, secretly administered to him that morning by our mulatto steward. Now, certainly, pisco does a deal of mischief in the world; yet seeing that, in the present case, it was the means, though indirect, of rescuing a human being from the most dreadful fate, must we not also needs admit that sometimes pisco does a deal of good?

Glancing across the water in the direction pointed out, I saw some white thing hanging from an inland rock, perhaps half a mile from the sea.

"It is a bird; a white-winged bird; perhaps a——no; it is ——it is a handkerchief!"

"Aye, a handkerchief!" echoed my comrade, and with a louder shout apprised the captain.

Quickly now—like the running out and training of a great gun—the long cabin spy-glass was thrust through the mizzen rigging from the high platform of the poop; whereupon a human figure was plainly seen upon the inland rock, eagerly waving towards us what seemed to be the handkerchief.

Our captain was a prompt, good fellow. Dropping the glass, he lustily ran forward, ordering the anchor to be dropped again; hands to stand by a boat, and lower away.

In a half-hour's time the swift boat returned. It went with six and came with seven; and the seventh was a woman.

It is not artistic heartlessness, but I wish I could but draw in crayons; for this woman was a most touching sight; and crayons, tracing softly melancholy lines, would best depict the mournful image of the dark-damasked Chola widow.

Her story was soon told, and though given in her own strange language was as quickly understood, for our captain from long trading on the Chilian coast was well versed in the Spanish. A Chola, or half-breed Indian woman of Payta in Peru, three years gone by, with her young new-wedded husband Felipe, of pure Castilian blood, and her one only Indian brother, Truxill, Hunilla had taken passage on the main in a French whaler, commanded by a joyous man; which vessel, bound to the cruising grounds beyond the Enchanted Isles, proposed passing close by their vicinity. The object of the little party was to procure tortoise oil, a fluid which for its great purity and delicacy is held in high estimation wherever known; and it is well known all along this part of the Pacific coast. With a chest of clothes, tools, cooking utensils, a rude apparatus for trying out the oil,[5] some casks of biscuit, and other things, not omitting two favorite dogs, of which faithful animal all the Cholos are very fond,

[3]Bar or lever for turning the windlass, the mechanism used to hoist the anchor.

[4]Brandy made in Pisco, Peru, given in recompense (guerdon).

[5]Rendering fat into oil by boiling.

Hunilla and her companions were safely landed at their chosen place; the Frenchman, according to the contract made ere sailing, engaged to take them off upon returning from a four months' cruise in the westward seas; which interval the three adventurers deemed quite sufficient for their purposes.

On the isle's lone beach they paid him in silver for their passage out, the stranger having declined to carry them at all except upon that condition; though willing to take every means to insure the due fulfilment of his promise. Felipe had striven hard to have this payment put off to the period of the ship's return. But in vain. Still, they thought they had, in another way, ample pledge of the good faith of the Frenchman. It was arranged that the expenses of the passage home should not be payable in silver, but in tortoises; one hundred tortoises ready captured to the returning captain's hand. These the Cholos meant to secure after their own work was done, against the probable time of the Frenchman's coming back; and no doubt in prospect already felt, that in those hundred tortoises—now somewhere ranging the isle's interior—they possessed one hundred hostages. Enough: the vessel sailed; the gazing three on shore answered the loud glee of the singing crew; and ere evening, the French craft was hull down in the distant sea, its masts three faintest lines which quickly faded from Hunilla's eye.

The stranger had given a blithesome promise, and anchored it with oaths; but oaths and anchors equally will drag; nought else abides on fickle earth but unkept promises of joy. Contrary winds from out unstable skies, or contrary moods of his more varying mind, or shipwreck and sudden death in solitary waves; whatever was the cause, the blithe stranger never was seen again.

Yet, however dire a calamity was here in store, misgivings of it ere due time never disturbed the Cholos' busy mind, now all intent upon the toilsome matter which had brought them hither. Nay, by swift doom coming like the thief at night, ere seven weeks went by, two of the little party were removed from all anxieties of land or sea. No more they sought to gaze with feverish fear, or still more feverish hope, beyond the present's horizon line; but into the furthest future their own silent spirits sailed. By persevering labor beneath that burning sun, Felipe and Truxill had brought down to their hut many scores of tortoises, and tried out the oil, when, elated with their good success, and to reward themselves for such hard work, they, too hastily, made a catamaran, or Indian raft, much used on the Spanish main, and merrily started on a fishing trip, just without a long reef with many jagged gaps, running parallel with the shore, about half a mile from it. By some bad tide or hap, or natural negligence of joyfulness (for though they could not be heard, yet by their gestures they seemed singing at the time), forced in deep water against that iron bar, the ill-made catamaran was overset, and came all to pieces; when, dashed by broad-chested swells between their broken logs and the sharp teeth of the reef, both adventurers perished before Hunilla's eyes.

Before Hunilla's eyes they sank. The real woe of this event passed before her sight as some sham tragedy on the stage. She was seated on a rude bower among the withered thickets, crowning a lofty cliff, a little back from the beach. The thickets were so disposed, that in looking upon the sea at large she peered out from among the branches as from the lattice of a high balcony. But upon the day we speak of here, the better to watch the adventure of those two hearts she loved, Hunilla had withdrawn the branches to one side, and held them so. They formed an oval frame, through which the bluely boundless sea rolled like a painted one. And there, the invisible painter painted to her view the wave-tossed and disjointed raft, its once level logs slantingly upheaved, as raking masts, and the four struggling arms undistinguishable among them; and then all subsided into smooth-flowing creamy waters, slowly drifting the splintered wreck; while first and last, no sound of any sort was heard. Death in a silent picture; a dream of the eye; such vanishing shapes as the mirage shows.

So instant was the scene, so trance-like its mild pictorial effect, so distant from her blasted bower and her common sense of things, that Hunilla gazed and gazed, nor raised a finger or a wail. But as good to sit thus dumb, in stupor staring on that dumb show, for all that otherwise might be done. With half a mile of sea between, how could her two enchanted arms aid those four fated ones? The distance long, the time one sand. After the lightning is beheld, what fool shall stay the thunderbolt? Felipe's body was washed ashore, but Truxill's never came; only his gay, braided hat of golden straw—that same sunflower thing he waved to her, pushing from the strand—and now, to the last gallant, it still saluted her. But Felipe's body floated to the marge, with one arm encirclingly outstretched. Lock-jawed in grim death, the lover-husband, softly clasped his bride, true to her even in death's dream. Ah, Heaven, when man thus keeps his faith, wilt thou be faithless who created the faithful one? But they cannot break faith who never plighted it.

It needs not to be said what nameless misery now wrapped the lonely widow. In telling her own story she passed this almost entirely over, simply recounting the event. Construe the comment of her features, as you might; from her mere words little would you have weened that Hunilla was herself the heroine of her tale. But not thus did she defraud us of our tears. All hearts bled that grief could be so brave.

She but showed us her soul's lid, and the strange ciphers thereon engraved; all within, with pride's timidity, was withheld. Yet was there one exception. Holding out her small olive hand before our captain, she said in mild and slowest Spanish, "Señor, I buried him;" then paused, struggled as against the writhed coilings of a snake, and cringing suddenly, leaped up, repeating in impassioned pain, "I buried him, my life, my soul!"

Doubtless it was by half-unconscious, automatic motions of her hands, that this heavy-hearted one performed the final offices for Felipe, and planted a rude cross of withered sticks—no green ones might be had—at the head of that lonely grave, where rested now in lasting uncomplaint and quiet haven he whom untranquil seas had overthrown.

But some dull sense of another body that should be interred, of another cross that should hallow another grave—unmade as yet;—some dull anxiety and pain touching her undiscovered brother now haunted the oppressed Hunilla. Her hands fresh from the burial earth, she slowly went back to the beach, with unshaped purposes wandered there, her spell-bound eye bent upon the incessant waves. But they bore nothing to her but a dirge, which maddened her to think that murderers should mourn. As time went by, and these things came less dreamingly to her mind, the strong persuasions of her Romish faith, which sets peculiar store by consecrated urns, prompted her to resume in waking earnest that pious search which had but been begun as in somnambulism. Day after day, week after week, she trod the cindery beach, till at length a double motive edged every eager glance. With equal longing she now looked for the living and the dead; the brother and the captain; alike vanished, never to return. Little accurate note of time had Hunilla taken under such emotions as were hers, and little, outside herself, served for calendar or dial. As to poor Crusoe in the self-same sea,[6] no saint's bell pealed forth the lapse of week or month; each day went by unchallenged; no chanticleer announced those sultry dawns, no lowing herds those poisonous nights. All wonted and steadily recurring sounds, human, or humanized by sweet fellowship with man, but one stirred that torrid trance,—the cry of dogs; save which nought but the rolling sea invaded it, an all pervading monotone; and to the widow that was the least loved voice she could have heard.

No wonder that as her thoughts now wandered to the unreturning ship, and were beaten back again, the hope against hope so struggled in her soul, that at length she desperately said, "Not yet, not yet; my foolish heart runs on too fast." So she forced patience for some further weeks. But to those whom earth's sure indraft[7] draws, patience or impatience is still the same.

Hunilla now sought to settle precisely in her mind, to an hour, how long it was since the ship had sailed; and then, with the same precision, how long a space remained to pass. But this proved impossible. What present day or month it was she could not say. Time was her labyrinth, in which Hunilla was entirely lost.

And now follows——

Against my own purposes a pause descends upon me here. One knows not whether nature doth not impose some secrecy upon him who has been privy to certain things. At least, it is to be doubted whether it be good to blazon such. If some books are deemed most baneful and their sale forbid, how then with deadlier facts, not dreams of doting men? Those whom books will hurt will not be proof against events. Events, not books, should be forbid. But in all things man sows upon the wind, which bloweth just there whither it listeth; for ill or good man cannot know. Often ill comes from the good, as good from ill.

When Hunilla——

Dire sight it is to see some silken beast long dally with a golden lizard ere she devour. More terrible, to see how feline Fate will sometimes dally with a human soul, and by a nameless magic make it repulse a sane despair with a hope which is but mad. Unwittingly I imp this cat-like thing, sporting with the heart of him who reads; for if he feel not, he reads in vain.

—"The ship sails this day, to-day," at last said Hunilla to herself; "this gives me certain time to stand on; without certainty I go mad. In loose ignorance I have hoped and hoped; now in firm knowledge I will but wait. Now I live and no longer perish in bewilderings. Holy Virgin, aid me! Thou wilt waft back the ship. Oh, past length of weary weeks—all to be dragged over—to buy the certainty of to-day, I freely give ye, though I tear ye from me!"

As mariners tossed in tempest on some desolate ledge patch them a boat out of the remnants of their vessel's wreck, and launch it in the self-same waves, see here Hunilla, this lone shipwrecked soul, out of treachery invoking trust. Humanity, thou strong thing, I worship thee, not in the laurelled victor, but in this vanquished one.

[6]Defoe's Robinson Crusoe (1719) was marooned on a Caribbean island, but his historical prototype, Alexander Selkirk, had spent five years on Juan Fernandez, an island west of Chile.

[7]A current drawing or pulling in.

Truly Hunilla leaned upon a reed, a real one; no metaphor; a real Eastern reed. A piece of hollow cane, drifted from unknown isles, and found upon the beach, its once jagged ends rubbed smoothly even as by sand-paper; its golden glazing gone. Long ground between the sea and land, upper and nether stone, the unvarnished substance was filed bare, and wore another polish now, one with itself, the polish of its agony. Circular lines at intervals cut all round this surface, divided it into six panels of unequal length. In the first were scored the days, each tenth one marked by a longer and deeper notch; the second was scored for the number of sea-fowl eggs for sustenance, picked out from the rocky nests; the third, how many fish had been caught from the shore; the fourth, how many small tortoises found inland; the fifth, how many days of sun; the sixth, of clouds; which last, of the two, was the greater one. Long night of busy numbering, misery's mathematics, to weary her too-wakeful soul to sleep; yet sleep for that was none.

The panel of the days was deeply worn, the long tenth notches half effaced, as alphabets of the blind. Ten thousand times the longing widow had traced her finger over the bamboo; dull flute, which played on, gave no sound; as if counting birds flown by in air, would hasten tortoises creeping through the woods.

After the one hundred and eightieth day no further mark was seen; that last one was the faintest, as the first the deepest.

"There were more days," said our Captain; "many, many more; why did you not go on and notch them too, Hunilla?"

"Señor, ask me not."

"And meantime, did no other vessel pass the isle?"

"Nay, Señor;—but——"

"You do not speak; but *what,* Hunilla?"

"Ask me not, Señor."

"You saw ships pass, far away; you waved to them; they passed on;—was that it, Hunilla?"

"Señor, be it as you say."

Braced against her woe, Hunilla would not, durst not trust the weakness of her tongue. Then when our Captain asked whether any whale-boats had——

But no, I will not file this thing complete for scoffing souls to quote, and call it firm proof upon their side. The half shall here remain untold. Those two unnamed events which befell Hunilla on this isle, let them abide between her and her God. In nature, as in law, it may be libellous to speak some truths.

Still, how it was that although our vessel had lain three days anchored nigh the isle, its one human tenant should not have discovered us till just upon the point of sailing, never to revisit so lone and far a spot; this needs explaining ere the sequel come.

The place where the French captain had landed the little party was on the farther and opposite end of the isle. There too it was that they had afterwards built their hut. Nor did the widow in her solitude desert the spot where her loved ones had dwelt with her, and where the dearest of the twain now slept his last long sleep, and all her plaints awaked him not, and he of husbands the most faithful during life.

Now, high broken land rises between the opposite extremities of the isle. A ship anchored at one side is invisible from the other. Neither is the isle so small, but a considerable company might wander for days through the wilderness of one side, and never be seen, or their halloos heard, by any stranger holding aloof on the other. Hence Hunilla, who naturally associated the possible coming of ships with her own part of the isle, might to the end have remained quite ignorant of the presence of our vessel, were it not for a mysterious presentiment, borne to her, so our mariners averred, by this isle's enchanted air. Nor did the widow's answer undo the thought.

"How did you come to cross the isle this morning then, Hunilla?" said our Captain.

"Señor, something came flitting by me. It touched my cheek, my heart, Señor."

"What do you say, Hunilla?"

"I have said, Señor; something came through the air."

It was a narrow chance. For when in crossing the isle Hunilla gained the high land in the centre, she must then for the first have perceived our masts, and also marked that their sails were being loosed, perhaps even heard the echoing chorus of the windlass song. The strange ship was about to sail, and she behind. With all haste she now descends the height on the hither side, but soon loses sight of the ship among the sunken jungles at the mountain's base. She struggles on through the withered branches, which seek at every step to bar her path, till she comes to the isolated rock, still some way from the water. This she climbs, to reassure herself. The ship is still in plainest sight. But now worn out with over tension, Hunilla all but faints; she fears to step down from her giddy perch; she is feign to pause, there where she is, and as a last resort catches the turban from her head, unfurls and waves it over the jungles towards us.

During the telling of her story the mariners formed a voiceless circle round Hunilla and the Captain; and when at length the word was given to man the fastest boat, and pull round to the isle's thither side, to bring away Hunilla's chest and the tortoise-oil; such alacrity of both cheery and sad obedience seldom before was seen. Little ado was made. Already the anchor had been recommitted to the bottom, and the ship swung calmly to it.

But Hunilla insisted upon accompanying the boat as indispensable pilot to her hidden hut. So being refreshed with the best the steward could supply, she started with us. Nor did ever any wife of the most famous admiral in her husband's barge receive more silent reverence of respect, than poor Hunilla from this boat's crew.

Rounding many a vitreous cape and bluff, in two hours' time we shot inside the fatal reef; wound into a secret cove, looked up along a green many-gabled lava wall, and saw the island's solitary dwelling.

It hung upon an impending cliff, sheltered on two sides by tangled thickets, and half-screened from view in front by juttings of the rude stairway, which climbed the precipice from the sea. Built of canes, it was thatched with long, mildewed grass. It seemed an abandoned hay-rick whose haymakers were now no more. The roof inclined but one way; the eaves coming to within two feet of the ground. And here was a simple apparatus to collect the dews, or rather doubly-distilled and finest winnowed rains, which, in mercy or in mockery, the night-skies sometimes drop upon these blighted Encantadas. All along beneath the eaves, a spotted sheet, quite weather-stained, was spread, pinned to short, upright stakes, set in the shallow sand. A small clinker, thrown into the cloth, weighed its middle down, thereby straining all moisture into a calabash placed below. This vessel supplied each drop of water ever drunk upon the isle by the Cholos. Hunilla told us the calabash would sometimes, but not often, be half filled over-night. It held six quarts, perhaps. "But," said she, "we were used to thirst. At sandy Payta, where I live, no shower from heaven ever fell; all the water there is brought on mules from the inland vales."

Tied among the thickets were some twenty moaning tortoises, supplying Hunilla's lonely larder; while hundreds of vast tableted black bucklers, like displaced, shattered tomb-stones of dark slate, were also scattered round. These were the skeleton backs of those great tortoises from which Felipe and Truxill had made their precious oil. Several large calabashes and two goodly kegs were filled with it. In a pot near by were the caked crusts of a quantity which had been permitted to evaporate. "They meant to have strained it off next day," said Hunilla, as she turned aside.

I forgot to mention the most singular sight of all, though the first that greeted us after landing.

Some ten small, soft-haired, ringleted dogs, of a beautiful breed, peculiar to Peru, set up a concert of glad welcomings when we gained the beach, which was responded to by Hunilla. Some of these dogs had, since her widowhood, been born upon the isle, the progeny of the two brought from Payta. Owing to the jagged steeps and pitfalls, tortuous thickets, sunken clefts and perilous intricacies of all sorts in the interior; Hunilla, admonished by the loss of one favorite among them, never allowed these delicate creatures to follow her in her occasional birds'-nests climbs and other wanderings; so that, through long habituation, they offered not to follow, when that morning she crossed the land; and her own soul was then too full of other things to heed their lingering behind. Yet, all along she had so clung to them, that, besides what moisture they lapped up at early daybreak from the small scoop-holes among the adjacent rocks, she had shared the dew of her calabash among them; never laying by any considerable store against those prolonged and utter droughts, which in some disastrous seasons warp these isles.

Having pointed out, at our desire, what few things she would like transported to the ship—her chest, the oil, not omitting the live tortoises which she intended for a grateful present to our Captain—we immediately set to work, carrying them to the boat down the long, sloping stair of deeply-shadowed rock. While my comrades were thus employed, I looked, and Hunilla had disappeared.

It was not curiosity alone, but, it seems to me, something different mingled with it, which prompted me to drop my tortoise, and once more gaze slowly around. I remembered the husband buried by Hunilla's hands. A narrow pathway led into a dense part of the thickets. Following it through many mazes, I came out upon a small, round, open space, deeply chambered there.

The mound rose in the middle; a bare heap of finest sand, like that unverdured heap found at the bottom of an hour-glass run out. At its head stood the cross of withered sticks; the dry, peeled bark still fraying from it; its transverse limb tied up with rope, and forlornly adroop in the silent air.

Hunilla was partly prostrate upon the grave; her dark head bowed, and lost in her long, loosened Indian hair; her hands extended to the cross-foot, with a little brass crucifix clasped between; a crucifix worn featureless, like an ancient graven knocker long plied in vain. She did not see me, and I made no noise, but slid aside, and left the spot.

A few moments ere all was ready for our going, she reappeared among us. I looked into her eyes, but saw no tear. There was something which seemed strangely haughty in her air, and yet it was the air of woe. A Spanish and an Indian grief, which would not visibly lament. Pride's height in vain abased to proneness on the rack; nature's pride subduing nature's torture.

Like pages the small and silken dogs surrounded her, as she slowly descended towards the beach. She caught the two most eager creatures in her arms:—"Mia Teeta! Mia Tomoteeta!" and fondling them, inquired how many could we take on board.

The mate commanded the boat's crew; not a hard-hearted man, but his way of life had been such that in most things, even in the smallest, simple utility was his leading motive.

"We cannot take them all, Hunilla; our supplies are short; the winds are unreliable; we may be a good many days going to Tombez. So take those you have, Hunilla; but no more."

She was in the boat; the oarsmen too were seated; all save one, who stood ready to push off and then spring himself. With the sagacity of their race, the dogs now seemed aware that they were in the very instant of being deserted upon a barren strand. The gunwales of the boat were high; its prow—presented inland—was lifted; so owing to the water, which they seemed instinctively to shun, the dogs could not well leap into the little craft. But their busy paws hard scraped the prow, as it had been some farmer's door shutting them out from shelter in a winter storm. A clamorous agony of alarm. They did not howl, or whine; they all but spoke.

"Push off! Give way!" cried the mate. The boat gave one heavy drag and lurch, and next moment shot swiftly from the beach, turned on her heel, and sped. The dogs ran howling along the water's marge; now pausing to gaze at the flying boat, then motioning as if to leap in chase, but mysteriously withheld themselves; and again ran howling along the beach. Had they been human beings hardly would they have more vividly inspired the sense of desolation. The oars were plied as confederate feathers of two wings. No one spoke. I looked back upon the beach, and then upon Hunilla, but her face was set in a stern dusky calm. The dogs crouching in her lap vainly licked her rigid hands. She never looked behind her; but sat motionless, till we turned a promontory of the coast and lost all sights and sounds astern. She seemed as one, who having experienced the sharpest of mortal pangs, was henceforth content to have all lesser heart-strings riven, one by one. To Hunilla, pain seemed so necessary, that pain in other beings, though by love and sympathy made her own, was unrepiningly to be borne. A heart of yearning in a frame of steel. A heart of earthly yearning, frozen by the frost which falleth from the sky.

The sequel is soon told. After a long passage, vexed by calms and baffling winds, we made the little port of Tombez in Peru, there to recruit the ship. Payta was not very distant. Our captain sold the tortoise oil to a Tombez merchant; and adding to the silver a contribution from all hands, gave it to our silent passenger, who knew not what the mariners had done.

The last seen of lone Hunilla she was passing into Payta town, riding upon a small gray ass; and before her on the ass's shoulders, she eyed the jointed workings of the beast's armorial cross.[8]

1854

[8]Charles F. Briggs, editor of *Putnam's,* apologized to Melville in a letter of May 12, 1854, for having deleted "a few" words in this last sentence. Hershel Parker has called attention to a passage in *Clarel* that suggests what the deleted words might have been. In II.i, Melville refers to the legend that the ass acquired its cross by carrying Christ into Jerusalem, and describes it as "innocent," but "untrue."

The Paradise of Bachelors and the Tartarus of Maids[1]

I. *The Paradise of Bachelors*

It lies not far from Temple-Bar.[2]

Going to it, by the usual way, is like stealing from a heated plain into some cool, deep glen, shady among harboring hills.

Sick with the din and soiled with the mud of Fleet Street—where the Benedick[3] tradesmen are hurrying by, with ledger-lines ruled along their brows, thinking upon rise of bread and fall of babies—you adroitly turn a mystic corner—not a street—glide down a dim, monastic way, flanked by dark, sedate, and solemn piles, and still wending on, give the whole care-worn world the slip, and, disentangled, stand beneath the quiet cloisters of the Paradise of Bachelors.

[1]Published in the April, 1855, issue of *Harper's New Monthly Magazine,* this is one of three paired sketches that Melville wrote in spring, 1854. The others are "Poor Man's Pudding and Rich Man's Crumbs," which compares the rural poor of preindustrial America with the urban poor of industrial England and indicts the hollow charity of the rich in both countries; and "The Two Temples," which contrasts a wealthy New York church congregation with the working-class audience of a London theater gallery and finds true Christian charity only in the latter (the sketch was regretfully turned down by *Putnam's,* whose editors feared "offending the religious sensibilities of the public"). The present text is from the standard Northwestern-Newberry edition of *The Piazza Tales and Other Prose Pieces, 1839–1860.*

"The Paradise of Bachelors" is based on Melville's experiences of dining at Elm Court, Temple, and of visiting the Temple and being feted by Robert Francis Cooke at a dinner for nine guests on December 19, 20, and 21, 1849, while peddling the manuscript of *White-Jacket* in London. Melville's *Journal of a Visit to London and the Continent, 1849–1850* conveys a vivid sense of the contradictory position in which he found himself on revisiting England ten years after his first voyage to Liverpool: "*then* a sailor, *now* H.M. author of 'Peedee' 'Hullabaloo' & 'Pog-Dog.'" Punctuating it are frequent complaints of homesickness for Elizabeth and "the Little One"; accounts of "dodging about town to get a cheap dinner," cheap lodgings, and second-class travel accommodations; and comments on the "stiffness, formality & coldness" of the English upper classes. The *Journal* also indicates that although Melville "had a glorious time" and enjoyed the "fine dinner" and "exceedingly agreeable company" of his hosts at the "Paradise of Batchelors" (as he had already dubbed the Temple), he also regarded his contacts with England's social elites as grist for his literary mill. An invitation from the Duke of Rutland to visit him at his Castle elicited this response, for example: "here I have before me an open prospect to get some curious ideas of a style of life, which in all probability I shall never have again. I should much like to know what the highest English aristocracy really & practically is. . . . If I do not go, I am confident that hereafter I shall upbraid myself for neglecting such an opportunity of procuring 'material.'" Ultimately, however, ruefully admitting that his brother and friends would consider him a "ninny," Melville turned down the invitation, because it would have delayed his return home for an "intolerable" three weeks.

Likewise autobiographical in origin, the second half of the diptych, "The Tartarus of Maids," was inspired by Melville's trip to Carson's Mill in Dalton, Massachusetts, to get "a sleigh-load of paper" in late January, 1851. Critics have speculated that Elizabeth Melville's frequent pregnancies and their painful complications may have helped suggest the sketch's sexual symbolism.

[2]Stone gateway designed by Christopher Wren (1632–1723), separating Fleet Street, a publishers' and booksellers' district, from its prolongation, the Strand.

[3]A newly married man, once a confirmed bachelor, from Benedick in Shakespeare's *Much Ado about Nothing.*

Sweet are the oases in Sahara; charming the isle-groves of August prairies; delectable pure faith amidst a thousand perfidies: but sweeter, still more charming, most delectable, the dreamy Paradise of Bachelors, found in the stony heart of stunning London.

In mild meditation pace the cloisters;[4] take your pleasure, sip your leisure, in the garden waterward; go linger in the ancient library; go worship in the sculptured chapel: but little have you seen, just nothing do you know, not the sweet kernel have you tasted, till you dine among the banded Bachelors, and see their convivial eyes and glasses sparkle. Not dine in bustling commons, during term-time, in the hall; but tranquilly, by private hint, at a private table; some fine Templar's hospitably invited guest.

Templar? That's a romantic name. Let me see. Brian de Bois Guilbert was a Templar,[5] I believe. Do we understand you to insinuate that those famous Templars still survive in modern London? May the ring of their armed heels be heard, and the rattle of their shields, as in mailed prayer the monk-knights kneel before the consecrated Host? Surely a monk-knight were a curious sight picking his way along the Strand, his gleaming corselet and snowy surcoat spattered by an omnibus. Long-bearded, too, according to his order's rule; his face fuzzy as a pard's;[6] how would the grim ghost look among the crop-haired, close-shaven citizens? We know indeed—sad history recounts it—that a moral blight tainted at last this sacred Brotherhood. Though no sworded foe might outskill them in the fence, yet the worm of luxury crawled beneath their guard, gnawing the core of knightly troth, nibbling the monastic vow, till at last the monk's austerity relaxed to wassailing, and the sworn knights-bachelors grew to be but hypocrites and rakes.

But for all this, quite unprepared were we to learn that Knights-Templars (if at all in being) were so entirely secularized as to be reduced from carving out immortal fame in glorious battling for the Holy Land, to the carving of roast-mutton at a dinner-board. Like Anacreon,[7] do these degenerate Templars now think it sweeter far to fall in banquet than in war? Or, indeed, how can there be any survival of that famous order? Templars in modern London! Templars in their red-cross mantles smoking cigars at the Divan![8] Templars crowded in a railway train, till, stacked with steel helmet, spear, and shield, the whole train looks like one elongated locomotive!

[4]London's four Inns of Court (comprising Inner Temple, Middle Temple, Lincoln's Inn, and Gray's Inn), occupied by lawyers and law students.

[5]The Knights-Templars were monks of a military religious order established in twelfth-century Jerusalem to protect pilgrims and the Holy Sepulchre during the Crusades. Charges of sexual laxity, including sodomy, led to the order's disbanding in 1312. According to Beryl Rowland, several books published in the 1840s, one of which Melville owned, had revived the debate over the truth of those charges. The most popular source of information on the Templars, however, was Sir Walter Scott's novel *Ivanhoe* (1819), in which the evil Templar Brian de Bois-Guilbert abducts and tries to rape the Jewess Rebecca, and then has her tried for witchcraft when she resists. One of the central questions Melville raises is whether the modern Templars, the lawyers occupying the medieval order's London headquarters, share the sexual degeneracy of their predecessors.

[6]Leopard.

[7]Late sixth-century B.C. Greek poet whose lyrics celebrated wine and love. According to legend, he died by choking on a grape seed.

[8]Melville is punning on the two main definitions of Divan: Oriental council chamber and smoking room.

No. The genuine Templar is long since departed. Go view the wondrous tombs in the Temple Church;[9] see there the rigidly-haughty forms stretched out, with crossed arms upon their stilly hearts, in everlasting and undreaming rest. Like the years before the flood, the bold-Knights-Templars are no more. Nevertheless, the name remains, and the nominal society, and the ancient grounds, and some of the ancient edifices. But the iron heel is changed to a boot of patent-leather; the long two-handed sword to a one-handed quill; the monk-giver of gratuitous ghostly counsel now counsels for a fee; the defender of the sarcophagus (if in good practice with his weapon) now has more than one case to defend; the vowed opener and clearer of all highways leading to the Holy Sepulchre, now has it in particular charge to check, to clog, to hinder, and embarrass all the courts and avenues of Law; the knight-combatant of the Saracen, breasting spear-points at Acre, now fights law-points in Westminster Hall. The helmet is a wig. Struck by Time's enchanter's wand, the Templar is to-day a Lawyer.[10]

But, like many others tumbled from proud glory's height—like the apple, hard on the bough but mellow on the ground—the Templar's fall has but made him all the finer fellow.

I dare say those old warrior-priests were but gruff and grouty at the best; cased in Birmingham[11] hardware, how could their crimped arms give yours or mine a hearty shake? Their proud, ambitious, monkish souls clasped shut, like horn-book missals;[12] their very faces clapped in bomb-shells; what sort of genial men were these? But best of comrades, most affable of hosts, capital diner is the modern Templar. His wit and wine are both of sparkling brands.

The church and cloisters, courts and vaults, lanes and passages, banquet-halls, refectories, libraries, terraces, gardens, broad walks, domicils, and dessert-rooms, covering a very large space of ground, and all grouped in central neighborhood, and quite sequestered from the old city's surrounding din; and every thing about the place being kept in most bachelor-like particularity, no part of London offers to a quiet wight so agreeable a refuge.

The Temple is, indeed, a city by itself. A city with all the best appurtenances, as the above enumeration shows. A city with a park to it, and flower-beds, and a riverside—the Thames flowing by as openly, in one part, as by Eden's primal garden flowed the mild Euphrates. In what is now the Temple Garden the old Crusaders used to exercise their steeds and lances; the modern Templars now lounge on the benches beneath the trees, and, switching their patent-leather boots, in gay discourse exercise at repartee.

Long lines of stately portraits in the banquet-halls, show what great men of mark—famous nobles, judges, and Lord Chancellors—have in their time been Templars. But all Templars are not known to universal fame; though, if the having

[9]The Round Church of the Knights-Templars (1185), modeled on the Church of the Holy Sepulchre in Jerusalem, and dedicated to St. Mary.

[10]Jerusalem's Holy Sepulchre, believed to be the Tomb of Jesus, and the Palestinian seaport of Acre, the last Christian stronghold of the Crusades, were two of the most famous sites in the struggle between Christians and Saracens (Moslems) for control of the Holy Land. London's Westminster Hall was used as a law court in the nineteenth century.

[11]English industrial city.

[12]Missals: devotional books used during mass; horn-books: children's primers consisting of parchment sheets mounted on boards, with handles and a protective covering of transparent horn.

warm hearts and warmer welcomes, full minds and fuller cellars, and giving good advice and glorious dinners, spiced with rare divertisements of fun and fancy, merit immortal mention, set down, ye muses, the names of R.F.C.[13] and his imperial brother.

Though to be a Templar, in the one true sense, you must needs be a lawyer, or a student at the law, and be ceremoniously enrolled as member of the order, yet as many such, though Templars, do not reside within the Temple's precincts, though they may have their offices there, just so, on the other hand, there are many residents of the hoary old domicils who are not admitted Templars. If being, say, a lounging gentleman and bachelor, or a quiet, unmarried, literary man, charmed with the soft seclusion of the spot, you much desire to pitch your shady tent among the rest in this serene encampment, then you must make some special friend among the order, and procure him to rent, in his name but at your charge, whatever vacant chamber you may find to suit.

Thus, I suppose, did Dr. Johnson,[14] that nominal Benedick and widower but virtual bachelor, when for a space he resided here. So, too, did that undoubted bachelor and rare good soul, Charles Lamb.[15] And hundreds more, of sterling spirits, Brethren of the Order of Celibacy, from time to time have dined, and slept, and tabernacled here. Indeed, the place is all a honeycomb of offices and domicils. Like any cheese, it is quite perforated through and through in all directions with the snug cells of bachelors. Dear, delightful spot! Ah! when I bethink me of the sweet hours there passed, enjoying such genial hospitalities beneath those time-honored roofs, my heart only finds due utterance through poetry; and, with a sigh, I softly sing, "Carry me back to old Virginny!"[16]

Such then, at large, is the Paradise of Bachelors. And such I found it one pleasant afternoon in the smiling month of May, when, sallying from my hotel in Trafalgar Square, I went to keep my dinner-appointment with that fine Barrister, Bachelor, and Bencher,[17] R.F.C. (he *is* the first and second, and *should be* the third; I hereby nominate him), whose card I kept fast pinched between my gloved forefinger and thumb, and every now and then snatched still another look at the pleasant address inscribed beneath the name, "No.—, Elm Court, Temple."

At the core he was a right bluff, care-free, right comfortable, and most companionable Englishman. If on a first acquaintance he seemed reserved, quite icy in his air—patience; this Champagne will thaw. And if it never do, better frozen Champagne than liquid vinegar.

There were nine gentlemen, all bachelors, at the dinner. One was from "No.—, King's Bench Walk, Temple;" a second, third, and fourth, and fifth, from various courts or passages christened with some similarly rich resounding syllables. It was indeed a sort of Senate of the Bachelors, sent to this dinner from widely-scattered districts, to represent the general celibacy of the Temple. Nay it was, by representation, a Grand Parliament of the best Bachelors in universal London; several of those

[13]Robert Francis Cooke, Melville's dinner host at Elm Court, Temple.

[14]Samuel Johnson (1709–1784), English writer and lexicographer, whose haunts in Fleet Street Melville visited.

[15]English essayist (1775–1834), whose works Melville had begun reading on the sea passage to London.

[16]A pun on the virgin (bachelor) state, as well as one of several allusions linking the ruling classes of England and America and the systems of oppression over which they preside.

[17]One of the senior members presiding over the Inns of Court; a judge.

present being from distant quarters of the town, noted immemorial seats of lawyers and unmarried men—Lincoln's Inn, Furnival's Inn; and one gentleman, upon whom I looked with a sort of collateral awe, hailed from the spot where Lord Verulam[18] once abode a bachelor—Gray's Inn.

The apartment was well up toward heaven. I know not how many strange old stairs I climbed to get to it. But a good dinner, with famous company, should be well earned. No doubt our host had his dining-room so high with a view to secure the prior exercise necessary to the due relishing and digesting of it.

The furniture was wonderfully unpretending, old, and snug. No new shining mahogany, sticky with undried varnish; no uncomfortably luxurious ottomans, and sofas too fine to use, vexed you in this sedate apartment. It is a thing which every sensible American should learn from every sensible Englishman, that glare and glitter, gimcracks and gewgaws, are not indispensable to domestic solacement. The American Benedick snatches, down-town, a tough chop in a gilded show-box; the English bachelor leisurely dines at home on that incomparable South Down of his, off a plain deal board.[19]

The ceiling of the room was low. Who wants to dine under the dome of St. Peter's? High ceilings! If that is your demand, and the higher the better, and you be so very tall, then go dine out with the topping giraffe in the open air.

In good time the nine gentlemen sat down to nine covers, and soon were fairly under way.

If I remember right, ox-tail soup inaugurated the affair. Of a rich russet hue, its agreeable flavor dissipated my first confounding of its main ingredient with teamster's gads and the raw-hides of ushers.[20] (By way of interlude, we here drank a little claret.) Neptune's was the next tribute rendered—turbot[21] coming second; snow-white, flaky, and just gelatinous enough, not too turtleish in its unctuousness.

(At this point we refreshed ourselves with a glass of sherry.) After these light skirmishers had vanished, the heavy artillery of the feast marched in, led by that well-known English generalissimo, roast beef. For aids-de-camp we had a saddle of mutton, a fat turkey, a chicken-pie, and endless other savory things; while for avant-couriers[22] came nine silver flagons of humming ale. This heavy ordnance having departed on the track of the light skirmishers, a picked brigade of game-fowl encamped upon the board, their camp-fires lit by the ruddiest of decanters.

Tarts and puddings followed, with innumerable niceties; then cheese and crackers. (By way of ceremony, simply, only to keep up good old fashions, we here each drank a glass of good old port.)

The cloth was now removed; and like Blucher's[23] army coming in at the death on the field of Waterloo, in marched a fresh detachment of bottles, dusty with their hurried march.

[18]Francis Bacon (1561–1626), English philosopher and statesman.

[19]Mutton from the Southdown breed of sheep, served on wooden trencher.

[20]Both ushers (assistant schoolmasters) and teamsters use gads (goads) or rawhide whips, made from ox tails.

[21]Rich, gelatinous white fish.

[22]The advance guard of an army. Note the elaborate military imagery.

[23]Gebhard Leberecht von Blucher (1742–1819), leader of the Prussian troops allied with the English against Napoleon at the Battle of Waterloo, 1815. The victory over Napoleon inaugurated the era of British imperial rule.

All these manœuvrings of the forces were superintended by a surprising old field-marshal (I can not school myself to call him by the inglorious name of waiter), with snowy hair and napkin, and a head like Socrates. Amidst all the hilarity of the feast, intent on important business, he disdained to smile. Venerable man!

I have above endeavored to give some slight schedule of the general plan of operations. But any one knows that a good, genial dinner is a sort of pell-mell, indiscriminate affair, quite baffling to detail in all particulars. Thus, I spoke of taking a glass of claret, and a glass of sherry, and a glass of port, and a mug of ale—all at certain specific periods and times. But those were merely the state bumpers,[24] so to speak. Innumerable impromptu glasses were drained between the periods of those grand imposing ones.

The nine bachelors seemed to have the most tender concern for each other's health. All the time, in flowing wine, they most earnestly expressed their sincerest wishes for the entire well-being and lasting hygiene of the gentlemen on the right and on the left. I noticed that when one of these kind bachelors desired a little more wine (just for his stomach's sake, like Timothy),[25] he would not help himself to it unless some other bachelor would join him. It seemed held something indelicate, selfish, and unfraternal, to be seen taking a lonely, unparticipated glass. Meantime, as the wine ran apace, the spirits of the company grew more and more to perfect genialness and unconstraint. They related all sorts of pleasant stories. Choice experiences in their private lives were now brought out, like choice brands of Moselle or Rhenish, only kept for particular company. One told us how mellowly he lived when a student at Oxford; with various spicy anecdotes of most frank-hearted noble lords, his liberal companions. Another bachelor, a gray-headed man, with a sunny face, who, by his own account, embraced every opportunity of leisure to cross over into the Low Countries,[26] on sudden tours of inspection of the fine old Flemish architecture there—this learned, white-haired, sunny-faced old bachelor, excelled in his descriptions of the elaborate splendors of those old guild-halls, town-halls, and stadtholdhouses, to be seen in the land of the ancient Flemings. A third was a great frequenter of the British Museum, and knew all about scores of wonderful antiquities, of Oriental manuscripts, and costly books without a duplicate. A fourth had lately returned from a trip to Old Granada, and, of course, was full of Saracenic scenery. A fifth had a funny case in law to tell. A sixth was erudite in wines. A seventh had a strange characteristic anecdote of the private life of the Iron Duke,[27] never printed, and never before announced in any public or private company. An eighth had lately been amusing his evenings, now and then, with translating a comic poem of Pulci's.[28] He quoted for us the more amusing passages.

And so the evening slipped along, the hours told, not by a water-clock,[29] like King Alfred's, but a wine-chronometer. Meantime the table seemed a sort of Epsom Heath;[30] a regular ring, where the decanters galloped round. For fear one decanter

[24]Large drinking glasses, filled to the brim; here used in the sense of official toasts.

[25]I Timothy 5:23: "Drink no longer water, but use a little wine for thy stomach's sake and thine often infirmities."

[26]Hershel Parker suggests that Melville may intend a bawdy Shakespearean pun on the lower parts of the body. (Holland was similarly used by Shakespeare as a pun on Hole-land, anus).

[27]The Duke of Wellington (1769–1852), leader of the English army that defeated Napoleon at Waterloo.

[28]Luigi Pulci (1432–1484), Florentine comic poet.

[29]Instrument designed to measure time by the fall or flow of a quantity of water.

[30]English racetrack.

should not with sufficient speed reach his destination, another was sent express after him to hurry him; and then a third to hurry the second; and so on with a fourth and fifth. And throughout all this nothing loud, nothing unmannerly, nothing turbulent. I am quite sure, from the scrupulous gravity and austerity of his air, that had Socrates, the field-marshal, perceived aught of indecorum in the company he served, he would have forthwith departed without giving warning. I afterward learned that, during the repast, an invalid bachelor in an adjoining chamber enjoyed his first sound refreshing slumber in three long, weary weeks.

It was the very perfection of quiet absorption of good living, good drinking, good feeling, and good talk. We were a band of brothers. Comfort—fraternal, household comfort, was the grand trait of the affair. Also, you could plainly see that these easy-hearted men had no wives or children to give an anxious thought. Almost all of them were travelers, too; for bachelors alone can travel freely, and without any twinges of their consciences touching desertion of the fire-side.

The thing called pain, the bugbear styled trouble—those two legends seemed preposterous to their bachelor imaginations. How could men of liberal sense, ripe scholarship in the world, and capacious philosophical and convivial understandings—how could they suffer themselves to be imposed upon by such monkish fables? Pain! Trouble! As well talk of Catholic miracles. No such thing.—Pass the sherry, Sir.—Pooh, pooh! Can't be!—The port, Sir, if you please. Nonsense; don't tell me so.—The decanter stops with you, Sir, I believe.

And so it went.

Not long after the cloth was drawn our host glanced significantly upon Socrates, who, solemnly stepping to a stand, returned with an immense convolved horn, a regular Jericho horn,[31] mounted with polished silver, and otherwise chased and curiously enriched; not omitting two life-like goat's heads, with four more horns of solid silver, projecting from opposite sides of the mouth of the noble main horn.

Not having heard that our host was a performer on the bugle, I was surprised to see him lift this horn from the table as if he were about to blow an inspiring blast. But I was relieved from this, and set quite right as touching the purposes of the horn, by his now inserting his thumb and forefinger into its mouth; whereupon a slight aroma was stirred up, and my nostrils were greeted with the smell of some choice Rappee. It was a mull of snuff.[32] It went the rounds. Capital idea this, thought I, of taking snuff about this juncture. This goodly fashion must be introduced among my countrymen at home, further ruminated I.

[31]Joshua 6:1–21 tells the story of how God delivered the city of Jericho into the hands of the Israelites. Carrying the ark and blowing "seven trumpets of rams' horns," seven priests circled the city for seven days, and on the seventh day, when they made a "long blast with the ram's horn," the people lifted up a "great shout" and "the wall of the city [fell] down flat." In the aftermath, the Israelites "utterly destroyed all that was in the city, both man and woman, young and old, and ox, and sheep, and ass, with the edge of the sword." Hence the Jericho horn is an apocalyptic symbol warning this decadent ruling class of the judgment to come.

[32]Rappee: a moist, pungent snuff made from dark, rank tobacco leaves. Mull: a snuff-box (derived from mill; the verbs "to mull" and "to mill" both mean "to grind"). Beryl Rowland has pointed out the ancient sexual connotations of the mill, and the link between the mull in the first sketch and the paper mill in the second.

The remarkable decorum of the nine bachelors—a decorum not to be affected by any quantity of wine—a decorum unassailable by any degree of mirthfulness—this was again set in a forcible light to me, by now observing that, though they took snuff very freely, yet not a man so far violated the proprieties, or so far molested the invalid bachelor in the adjoining room as to indulge himself in a sneeze. The snuff was snuffed silently, as if it had been some fine innoxious powder brushed off the wings of butterflies.

But fine though they be, bachelors' dinners, like bachelors' lives, can not endure forever. The time came for breaking up. One by one the bachelors took their hats, and two by two, and arm-in-arm they descended, still conversing, to the flagging of the court; some going to their neighboring chambers to turn over the Decameron[33] ere retiring for the night; some to smoke a cigar, promenading in the garden on the cool river-side; some to make for the street, call a hack, and be driven snugly to their distant lodgings.

I was the last lingerer.

"Well," said my smiling host, "what do you think of the Temple here, and the sort of life we bachelors make out to live in it?"

"Sir," said I, with a burst of admiring candor—"Sir, this is the very Paradise of Bachelors!"

II. *The Tartarus of Maids*

It lies not far from Woedolor Mountain in New England. Turning to the east, right out from among bright farms and sunny meadows, nodding in early June with odorous grasses, you enter ascendingly among bleak hills. These gradually close in upon a dusky pass, which, from the violent Gulf Stream of air unceasingly driving between its cloven walls of haggard rock, as well as from the tradition of a crazy spinster's hut having long ago stood somewhere hereabouts, is called the Mad Maid's Bellows'-pipe.[1]

Winding along at the bottom of the gorge is a dangerously narrow wheel-road, occupying the bed of a former torrent. Following this road to its highest point, you stand as within a Dantean gateway.[2] From the steepness of the walls here, their strangely ebon hue, and the sudden contraction of the gorge, this particular point is called the Black Notch. The ravine now expandingly descends into a great, purple, hopper-shaped hollow, far sunk among many Plutonian, shaggy-wooded mountains.

[33] A collection of bawdy tales by the Italian writer Giovanni Boccaccio (1313–1375). The title refers to the ten days that the ten narrators have spent telling stories, in order to while away their seclusion in a country villa during the plague in Florence. Both the fictional content and the historical context of the *Decameron* are highly relevant to Melville's sketch.

[1] Note the elaborate parallels linking the second sketch to the first, and the equally elaborate sexual symbolism, both inaugurated here and developed throughout.

[2] The gateway to hell, described in *The Inferno* by the Italian poet Dante Alighieri (1265–1321) as bearing the inscription: "Through me you pass into the city of woe: / Through me you pass into eternal pain / . . . / All hope abandon, ye who enter here." This is the infernal counterpart of the Temple Bar gateway by Wren.

By the country people this hollow is called the Devil's Dungeon. Sounds of torrents fall on all sides upon the ear. These rapid waters unite at last in one turbid brick-colored stream, boiling through a flume among enormous boulders. They call this strange-colored torrent Blood River. Gaining a dark precipice it wheels suddenly to the west, and makes one maniac spring of sixty feet into the arms of a stunted wood of gray-haired pines, between which it thence eddies on its further way down to the invisible lowlands.

Conspicuously crowning a rocky bluff high to one side, at the cataract's verge, is the ruin of an old saw-mill, built in those primitive times when vast pines and hemlocks superabounded throughout the neighboring region. The black-mossed bulk of those immense, rough-hewn, and spike-knotted logs, here and there tumbled all together, in long abandonment and decay, or left in solitary, perilous projection over the cataract's gloomy brink, impart to this rude wooden ruin not only much of the aspect of one of rough-quarried stone, but also a sort of feudal, Rhineland, and Thurmberg[3] look, derived from the pinnacled wildness of the neighboring scenery.

Not far from the bottom of the Dungeon stands a large white-washed building, relieved, like some great whited sepulchre,[4] against the sullen background of mountain-side firs, and other hardy evergreens, inaccessibly rising in grim terraces for some two thousand feet.

The building is a paper-mill.

Having embarked on a large scale in the seedsman's business (so extensively and broadcast, indeed, that at length my seeds were distributed through all the Eastern and Northern States, and even fell into the far soil of Missouri and the Carolinas), the demand for paper at my place became so great, that the expenditure soon amounted to a most important item in the general account. It need hardly be hinted how paper comes into use with seedsmen, as envelopes. These are mostly made of yellowish paper, folded square; and when filled, are all but flat, and being stamped, and superscribed with the nature of the seeds contained, assume not a little the appearance of business-letters ready for the mail. Of these small envelopes I used an incredible quantity—several hundreds of thousands in a year. For a time I had pur-

[3]A fourteenth-century fortified castle whose ruins dominated the Rhine near Welmich, south of Koblenz. Melville probably cited it for its legend, which he would have found mentioned in the books he purchased on legends and panoramas of the Rhine. Thurmberg's wicked lord, annoyed by the ringing of the Sunday church bell, had it hung around the neck of the village priest, whom he ordered thrown into a deep well. The bell continued to toll, however, until the lord went mad and died. The parallel between the ruins left by medieval barons and by their capitalist successors has many implications, besides recalling the continuities between medieval and modern Templars in the first sketch.

[4]Cf. Matthew 23:27: "Woe unto you, scribes and Pharisees, hypocrites! for ye are like unto whited sepulchres, which indeed appear beautiful outward, but are within full of dead men's bones, and of all uncleanness." Preceding Jesus' denunciations of the Pharisees is the prophecy, "whosoever shall exalt himself shall be abased; and he that shall humble himself shall be exalted," and immediately following them are the apocalyptic prophecies foretelling the destruction of the Jerusalem temple and describing the signs of Jesus' Second Advent. Note the historical continuities linking the Jerusalem temple, the Holy Sepulchre for which the Templars fought, the Temple Church modeled on it, and the present "whited sepulchre."

chased my paper from the wholesale dealers in a neighboring town. For economy's sake, and partly for the adventure of the trip, I now resolved to cross the mountains, some sixty miles, and order my future paper at the Devil's Dungeon paper-mill.

The sleighing being uncommonly fine toward the end of January, and promising to hold so for no small period, in spite of the bitter cold I started one gray Friday noon in my pung,[5] well fitted with buffalo and wolf robes; and, spending one night on the road, next noon came in sight of Woedolor Mountain.

The far summit fairly smoked with frost; white vapors curled up from its white-wooded top, as from a chimney. The intense congelation made the whole country look like one petrifaction. The steel shoes of my pung craunched and gritted over the vitreous, chippy snow, as if it had been broken glass. The forests here and there skirting the route, feeling the same all-stiffening influence, their inmost fibres penetrated with the cold, strangely groaned—not in the swaying branches merely, but likewise in the vertical trunk—as the fitful gusts remorselessly swept through them. Brittle with excessive frost, many colossal tough-grained maples, snapped in twain like pipe-stems, cumbered the unfeeling earth.

Flaked all over with frozen sweat, white as a milky ram, his nostrils at each breath sending forth two horn-shaped shoots of heated respiration, Black, my good horse, but six years old, started at a sudden turn, where, right across the track—not ten minutes fallen—an old distorted hemlock lay, darkly undulatory as an anaconda.[6]

Gaining the Bellows'-pipe, the violent blast, dead from behind, all but shoved my high-backed pung up-hill. The gust shrieked through the shivered pass, as if laden with lost spirits bound to the unhappy world. Ere gaining the summit, Black, my horse, as if exasperated by the cutting wind, slung out with his strong hind legs, tore the light pung straight up-hill, and sweeping grazingly through the narrow notch, sped downward madly past the ruined saw-mill. Into the Devil's Dungeon horse and cataract rushed together.

With might and main, quitting my seat and robes, and standing backward, with one foot braced against the dash-board, I rasped and churned the bit, and stopped him just in time to avoid collision, at a turn, with the bleak nozzle of a rock, couchant like a lion in the way—a road-side rock.

At first I could not discover the paper-mill.

The whole hollow gleamed with the white, except, here and there, where a pinnacle of granite showed one wind-swept angle bare. The mountains stood pinned in shrouds—a pass of Alpine corpses. Where stands the mill? Suddenly a whirling, humming sound broke upon my ear. I looked, and there, like an arrested avalanche, lay the large whitewashed factory. It was subordinately surrounded by a cluster of other and smaller buildings, some of which, from their cheap, blank air, great length, gregarious windows, and comfortless expression, no doubt were boarding-houses of the operatives. A snow-white hamlet amidst the snows. Various rude, irregular squares and courts resulted from the somewhat picturesque clusterings of these buildings, owing to the broken, rocky nature of the ground, which forbade all method in their relative arrangement. Several narrow lanes and alleys, too, partly blocked with snow fallen from the roof, cut up the hamlet in all directions.

[5]One-horse sleigh used in New England.

[6]A large snake of the boa constrictor type. The runaway horse is a common symbol of uncontrolled sexuality. Note the verbal echoes of the passage describing the Jericho horn.

When, turning from the traveled highway, jingling with bells of numerous farmers—who, availing themselves of the fine sleighing, were dragging their wood to market—and frequently diversified with swift cutters dashing from inn to inn of the scattered villages—when, I say, turning from that bustling main-road, I by degrees wound into the Mad Maid's Bellows'-pipe, and saw the grim Black Notch beyond, then something latent, as well as something obvious in the time and scene, strangely brought back to my mind my first sight of dark and grimy Temple-Bar. And when Black, my horse, went darting through the Notch, perilously grazing its rocky wall, I remembered being in a runaway London omnibus, which in much the same sort of style, though by no means at an equal rate, dashed through the ancient arch of Wren. Though the two objects did by no means completely correspond, yet this partial inadequacy but served to tinge the similitude not less with the vividness than the disorder of a dream. So that, when upon reining up at the protruding rock I at last caught sight of the quaint groupings of the factory-buildings, and with the traveled highway and the Notch behind, found myself all alone, silently and privily stealing through deep-cloven passages into this sequestered spot, and saw the long, high-gabled main factory edifice, with a rude tower—for hoisting heavy boxes—at one end, standing among its crowded outbuildings and boarding-houses, as the Temple Church amidst the surrounding offices and dormitories, and when the marvelous retirement of this mysterious mountain nook fastened its whole spell upon me, then, what memory lacked, all tributary imagination furnished, and I said to myself, "This is the very counterpart of the Paradise of Bachelors, but snowed upon, and frost-painted to a sepulchre."

Dismounting, and warily picking my way down the dangerous declivity—horse and man both sliding now and then upon the icy ledges—at length I drove, or the blast drove me, into the largest square, before one side of the main edifice. Piercingly and shrilly the shotted blast blew by the corner; and redly and demoniacally boiled Blood River at one side. A long wood-pile, of many scores of cords, all glittering in mail of crusted ice, stood crosswise in the square. A row of horse-posts, their north sides plastered with adhesive snow, flanked the factory wall. The bleak frost packed and paved the square as with some ringing metal.

The inverted similitude recurred—"The sweet, tranquil Temple garden, with the Thames bordering its green beds," strangely meditated I.

But where are the gay bachelors?

Then, as I and my horse stood shivering in the wind-spray, a girl ran from a neighboring dormitory door, and throwing her thin apron over her bare head, made for the opposite building.

"One moment, my girl; is there no shed hereabouts which I may drive into?"

Pausing, she turned upon me a face pale with work, and blue with cold; an eye supernatural with unrelated misery.

"Nay," faltered I, "I mistook you. Go on; I want nothing."

Leading my horse close to the door from which she had come, I knocked. Another pale, blue girl appeared, shivering in the doorway as, to prevent the blast, she jealously held the door ajar.

"Nay, I mistake again. In God's name shut the door. But hold, is there no man about?"

That moment a dark-complexioned well-wrapped personage passed, making for the factory door, and spying him coming, the girl rapidly closed the other one.

"Is there no horse-shed here, Sir?"

"Yonder, to the wood-shed," he replied, and disappeared inside the factory.

With much ado I managed to wedge in horse and pung between the scattered piles of wood all sawn and split. Then, blanketing my horse, and piling my buffalo on the blanket's top, and tucking in its edges well around the breast-band and breeching, so that the wind might not strip him bare, I tied him fast, and ran lamely for the factory door, stiff with frost, and cumbered with my driver's dread-naught.[7]

Immediately I found myself standing in a spacious place, intolerably lighted by long rows of windows, focusing inward the snowy scene without.

At rows of blank-looking counters sat rows of blank-looking girls, with blank, white folders in their blank hands, all blankly folding blank paper.

In one corner stood some huge frame of ponderous iron, with a vertical thing like a piston periodically rising and falling upon a heavy wooden block. Before it—its tame minister—stood a tall girl, feeding the iron animal with half-quires[8] of rose-hued note paper, which, at every downward dab of the piston-like machine, received in the corner the impress of a wreath of roses. I looked from the rosy paper to the pallid cheek, but said nothing.

Seated before a long apparatus, strung with long, slender strings like any harp, another girl was feeding it with foolscap sheets, which, so soon as they curiously traveled from her on the cords, were withdrawn at the opposite end of the machine by a second girl. They came to the first girl blank; they went to the second girl ruled.

I looked upon the first girl's brow, and saw it was young and fair; I looked upon the second girl's brow, and saw it was ruled and wrinkled. Then, as I still looked, the two—for some small variety to the monotony—changed places; and where had stood the young, fair brow, now stood the ruled and wrinkled one.

Perched high upon a narrow platform, and still higher upon a high stool crowning it, sat another figure serving some other iron animal; while below the platform sat her mate in some sort of reciprocal attendance.

Not a syllable was breathed. Nothing was heard but the low, steady, overruling hum of the iron animals. The human voice was banished from the spot. Machinery—that vaunted slave of humanity—here stood menially served by human beings, who served mutely and cringingly as the slave serves the Sultan. The girls did not so much seem accessory wheels to the general machinery as mere cogs to the wheels.[9]

All this scene around me was instantaneously taken in at one sweeping glance—even before I had proceeded to unwind the heavy fur tippet from around my neck. But as soon as this fell from me the dark-complexioned man, standing close by, raised a sudden cry, and seizing my arm, dragged me out into the open air, and without pausing for a word instantly caught up some congealed snow and began rubbing both my cheeks.

"Two white spots like the whites of your eyes," he said; "man, your cheeks are frozen."

[7]Warm garment of thick cloth.

[8]Twelve sheets of folded paper.

[9]Cf. the famous passage in *The Communist Manifesto* explaining how laborers under capitalism become "a commodity" and "an appendage of the machine": "Not only are they slaves of the bourgeois class and the bourgeois state; they are daily and hourly enslaved by the machine, by the supervisor, and above all, by the individual bourgeois manufacturer himself."

"That may well be," muttered I; "'tis some wonder the frost of the Devil's Dungeon strikes in no deeper. Rub away."

Soon a horrible, tearing pain caught at my reviving cheeks. Two gaunt bloodhounds, one on each side, seemed mumbling them. I seemed Actæon.[10]

Presently, when all was over, I re-entered the factory, made known my business, concluded it satisfactorily, and then begged to be conducted throughout the place to view it.

"Cupid is the boy for that," said the dark-complexioned man. "Cupid!" and by this odd fancy-name calling a dimpled, red-cheeked, spirited-looking, forward little fellow, who was rather impudently, I thought, gliding about among the passive-looking girls—like a gold fish through hueless waves—yet doing nothing in particular that I could see, the man bade him lead the stranger through the edifice.

"Come first and see the water-wheel," said this lively lad, with the air of boyishly-brisk importance.

Quitting the folding-room, we crossed some damp, cold boards, and stood beneath a great wet shed, incessantly showering with foam, like the green barnacled bow of some East Indiaman[11] in a gale. Round and round here went the enormous revolutions of the dark colossal water-wheel, grim with its one immutable purpose.

"This sets our whole machinery a-going, Sir; in every part of all these buildings; where the girls work and all."

I looked, and saw that the turbid waters of Blood River had not changed their hue by coming under the use of man.

"You make only blank paper; no printing of any sort, I suppose? All blank paper, don't you?"

"Certainly; what else should a paper-factory make?"

The lad here looked at me as if suspicious of my common-sense.

"Oh, to be sure!" said I, confused and stammering; "it only struck me as so strange that red waters should turn out pale chee—paper, I mean."

He took me up a wet and rickety stair to a great light room, furnished with no visible thing but rude, manger-like receptacles running all round its sides; and up to these mangers, like so many mares haltered to the rack, stood rows of girls. Before each was vertically thrust up a long, glittering scythe, immovably fixed at bottom to the manger-edge. The curve of the scythe, and its having no snath[12] to it, made it look exactly like a sword. To and fro, across the sharp edge, the girls forever dragged long strips of rags, washed white, picked from baskets at one side; thus ripping asunder every seam, and converting the tatters almost into lint. The air swam with the fine, poisonous particles, which from all sides darted, subtilely, as motes in sun-beams, into the lungs.

[10]Hunter in classical mythology who watched the goddess Artemis (Diana) bathing and was punished by being turned into a stag and torn apart by his own dogs. The roles of Artemis as patroness of childbirth, chastity, and unmarried women are particularly relevant to Melville's story.

[11]Large sailing ship used in trade with India. That trade played a crucial role in the Industrial Revolution, first by contributing to capital accumulation, then by providing raw materials and a market for the British textile industry. During the very years when British military forces were busy defeating Napoleon, British manufacturing interests were gaining the upper hand over mercantile interests and developing the colonial policy that systematically destroyed the Indian hand-loom industry and transformed India from a major exporter into an importer of cotton textiles.

[12]Handle.

"This is the rag-room," coughed the boy.

"You find it rather stifling here," coughed I, in answer; "but the girls don't cough."

"Oh, they are used to it."

"Where do you get such hosts of rags?" picking up a handful from a basket.

"Some from the country round about; some from far over sea—Leghorn[13] and London."

"'Tis not unlikely, then," murmured I, "that among these heaps of rags there may be some old shirts, gathered from the dormitories of the Paradise of Bachelors. But the buttons are all dropped off. Pray, my lad, do you ever find any bachelor's buttons hereabouts?"

"None grow in this part of the country. The Devil's Dungeon is no place for flowers."

"Oh! you mean the *flowers* so called—the Bachelor's Buttons?"

"And was not that what you asked about? Or did you mean the gold bosom-buttons of our boss, Old Bach,[14] as our whispering girls all call him?"

"The man, then, I saw below is a bachelor, is he?"

"Oh, yes, he's a Bach."

"The edges of those swords, they are turned outward from the girls, if I see right; but their rags and fingers fly so, I can not distinctly see."

"Turned outward."

Yes, murmured I to myself; I see it now; turned outward; and each erected sword is so borne, edge-outward, before each girl. If my reading fails me not, just so, of old, condemned state-prisoners went from the hall of judgment to their doom: an officer before, bearing a sword, its edge turned outward, in significance of their fatal sentence. So, through consumptive pallors of this blank, raggy life, go these white girls to death.

"Those scythes look very sharp," again turning toward the boy.

"Yes; they have to keep them so. Look!"

That moment two of the girls, dropping their rags, plied each a whet-stone up and down the sword-blade. My unaccustomed blood curdled at the sharp shriek of the tormented steel.

Their own executioners; themselves whetting the very swords that slay them; meditated I.

"What makes those girls so sheet-white, my lad?"

"Why"—with a roguish twinkle, pure ignorant drollery, not knowing heartlessness—"I suppose the handling of such white bits of sheets all the time makes them so sheety."

"Let us leave the rag-room now, my lad."

More tragical and more inscrutably mysterious than any mystic sight, human or machine, throughout the factory, was the strange innocence of cruel-heartedness in this usage-hardened boy.

"And now," said he, cheerily, "I suppose you want to see our great machine, which cost us twelve thousand dollars only last autumn. That's the machine that makes the paper, too. This way, Sir."

[13]Livorno, third-ranking west coast port of Italy, after Genoa and Naples.

[14]As in bachelor.

Following him, I crossed a large, bespattered place, with two great round vats in it, full of a white, wet, woolly-looking stuff, not unlike the albuminous part of an egg, soft-boiled.

"There," said Cupid, tapping the vats carelessly, "these are the first beginnings of the paper; this white pulp you see. Look how it swims bubbling round and round, moved by the paddle here. From hence it pours from both vats into that one common channel yonder; and so goes, mixed up and leisurely, to the great machine. And now for that."

He led me into a room, stifling with a strange, blood-like, abdominal heat, as if here, true enough, were being finally developed the germinous particles lately seen.

Before me, rolled out like some long Eastern manuscript, lay stretched one continuous length of iron frame-work—multitudinous and mystical, with all sorts of rollers, wheels, and cylinders, in slowly-measured and unceasing motion.

"Here first comes the pulp now," said Cupid, pointing to the nighest end of the machine. "See; first it pours out and spreads itself upon this wide, sloping board; and then—look—slides, thin and quivering, beneath the first roller there. Follow on now, and see it as it slides from under that to the next cylinder. There; see how it has become just a very little less pulpy now. One step more, and it grows still more to some slight consistence. Still another cylinder, and it is so knitted—though as yet mere dragon-fly wing—that it forms an air-bridge here, like a suspended cobweb, between two more separated rollers; and flowing over the last one, and under again, and doubling about there out of sight for a minute among all those mixed cylinders you indistinctly see, it reappears here, looking now at last a little less like pulp and more like paper, but still quite delicate and defective yet awhile. But—a little further onward, Sir, if you please—here now, at this further point, it puts on something of a real look, as if it might turn out to be something you might possibly handle in the end. But it's not yet done, Sir. Good way to travel yet, and plenty more of cylinders must roll it."

"Bless my soul!" said I, amazed at the elongation, interminable convolutions, and deliberate slowness of the machine; "it must take a long time for the pulp to pass from end to end, and come out paper."

"Oh! not so long," smiled the precocious lad, with a superior and patronizing air; "only nine minutes. But look; you may try it for yourself. Have you a bit of paper? Ah! here's a bit on the floor. Now mark that with any word you please, and let me dab it on here, and we'll see how long before it comes out at the other end."

"Well, let me see," said I, taking out my pencil; "come, I'll mark it with your name."

Bidding me take out my watch Cupid adroitly dropped the inscribed slip on an exposed part of the incipient mass.

Instantly my eye marked the second-hand on my dial-plate.

Slowly I followed the slip, inch by inch; sometimes pausing for full half a minute as it disappeared beneath inscrutable groups of the lower cylinders, but only gradually to emerge again; and so, on, and on, and on—inch by inch; now in open sight, sliding along like a freckle on the quivering sheet; and then again wholly vanished; and so, on, and on, and on—inch by inch; all the time the main sheet growing more and more to final firmness—when, suddenly, I saw a sort of paper-fall, not wholly unlike a water-fall; a scissory sound smote my ear, as of some cord being snapped;

and down dropped an unfolded sheet of perfect foolscap,[15] with my "Cupid" half faded out of it, and still moist and warm.

My travels were at an end, for here was the end of the machine.

"Well, how long was it?" said Cupid.

"Nine minutes to a second," replied I, watch in hand.

"I told you so."

For a moment a curious emotion filled me, not wholly unlike that which one might experience at the fulfillment of some mysterious prophecy. But how absurd, thought I again; the thing is a mere machine, the essence of which is unvarying punctuality and precision.

Previously absorbed by the wheels and cylinders, my attention was now directed to a sad-looking woman standing by.

"That is rather an elderly person so silently tending the machine-end here. She would not seem wholly used to it either."

"Oh," knowingly whispered Cupid, through the din, "she only came last week. She was a nurse[16] formerly. But the business is poor in these parts, and she's left it. But look at the paper she is piling there."

"Ay, foolscap," handling the piles of moist, warm sheets, which continually were being delivered into the woman's waiting hands. "Don't you turn out any thing but foolscap at this machine?"

"Oh, sometimes, but not often, we turn out finer work—cream-laid and royal sheets, we call them. But foolscap being in chief demand, we turn out foolscap most."

It was very curious. Looking at that blank paper continually dropping, dropping, dropping, my mind ran on in wonderings of those strange uses to which those thousand sheets eventually would be put. All sorts of writings would be writ on those now vacant things—sermons, lawyers' briefs, physicians' prescriptions, love-letters, marriage certificates, bills of divorce, registers of births, death-warrants, and so on, without end. Then, recurring back to them as they here lay all blank, I could not but bethink me of that celebrated comparison of John Locke, who, in demonstration of his theory that man had no innate ideas, compared the human mind at birth to a sheet of blank paper; something destined to be scribbled on, but what sort of characters no soul might tell.[17]

Pacing slowing to and fro along the involved machine, still humming with its play, I was struck as well by the inevitability as the evolvement-power in all its motions.

"Does that thin cobweb there," said I, pointing to the sheet in its more imperfect stage, "does that never tear or break? It is marvelous fragile, and yet this machine it passes through is so mighty."

"It never is known to tear a hair's point."

[15]Cheap writing paper, typically 16 by 13 inches. Derived from the watermark of a dunce's cap formerly applied to such paper.

[16]In the original meaning of the word, a woman employed to suckle and otherwise care for an infant.

[17]John Locke, English philosopher (1632–1704). His *Essay Concerning Human Understanding* (1690) denied the existence of innate ideas and compared the mind of a newborn infant to a "tabula rasa," or blank page.

"Does it never stop—get clogged?"

"No. It *must* go. The machinery makes it go just *so;* just that very way, and at that very pace you there plainly *see* it go. The pulp can't help going."

Something of awe now stole over me, as I gazed upon this inflexible iron animal. Always, more or less, machinery of this ponderous, elaborate sort strikes, in some moods, strange dread into the human heart, as some living, panting Behemoth might. But what made the thing I saw so specially terrible to me was the metallic necessity, the unbudging fatality which governed it. Though, here and there, I could not follow the thin, gauzy vail of pulp in the course of its more mysterious or entirely invisible advance, yet it was indubitable that, at those points where it eluded me, it still marched on in unvarying docility to the autocratic cunning of the machine. A fascination fastened on me. I stood spell-bound and wandering in my soul. Before my eyes—there, passing in slow procession along the wheeling cylinders, I seemed to see, glued to the pallid incipience of the pulp, the yet more pallid faces of all the pallid girls I had eyed that heavy day. Slowly, mournfully, beseechingly, yet unresistingly, they gleamed along, their agony dimly outlined on the imperfect paper, like the print of the tormented face on the handkerchief of Saint Veronica.[18]

"Halloa! the heat of the room is too much for you," cried Cupid, staring at me.

"No—I am rather chill, if any thing."

"Come out, Sir—out—out," and, with the protecting air of a careful father, the precocious lad hurried me outside.

In a few moments, feeling revived a little, I went into the folding-room—the first room I had entered, and where the desk for transacting business stood, surrounded by the blank counters and blank girls engaged at them.

"Cupid here has led me a strange tour," said I to the dark-complexioned man before mentioned, whom I had ere this discovered not only to be an old bachelor, but also the principal proprietor. "Yours is a most wonderful factory. Your great machine is a miracle of inscrutable intricacy."

"Yes, all our visitors think it so. But we don't have many. We are in a very out-of-the-way corner here. Few inhabitants, too. Most of our girls come from far-off villages."

"The girls," echoed I, glancing round at their silent forms. "Why is it, Sir, that in most factories, female operatives, of whatever age, are indiscriminately called girls, never women?"

"Oh! as to that—why, I suppose, the fact of their being generally unmarried—that's the reason, I should think. But it never struck me before. For our factory here, we will not have married women; they are apt to be off-and-on too much. We want none but steady workers: twelve hours to the day, day after day, through the three hundred and sixty-five days, excepting Sundays, Thanksgiving, and Fast-days. That's our rule. And so, having no married women, what females we have are rightly enough called girls."

"Then these are all maids," said I, while some pained homage to their pale virginity made me involuntarily bow.

"All maids."

18. According to legend, when Christ was carrying his cross on the way to Calvary, she wiped his face with her veil or handkerchief, which miraculously retained its imprint.

Again the strange emotion filled me.

"Your cheeks look whitish yet, Sir," said the man, gazing at me narrowly. "You must be careful going home. Do they pain you at all now? It's a bad sign, if they do."

"No doubt, Sir," answered I, "when once I have got out of the Devil's Dungeon, I shall feel them mending."

"Ah, yes; the winter air in valleys, or gorges, or any sunken place, is far colder and more bitter than elsewhere. You would hardly believe it now, but it is colder here than at the top of Woedolor Mountain."

"I dare say it is, Sir. But time presses me; I must depart."

With that, remuffling myself in dread-naught and tippet, thrusting my hands into my huge seal-skin mittens, I sallied out into the nipping air, and found poor Black, my horse, all cringing and doubled up with the cold.

Soon, wrapped in furs and meditations, I ascended from the Devil's Dungeon.

At the Black Notch I paused, and once more bethought me of Temple-Bar. Then, shooting through the pass, all alone with inscrutable nature, I exclaimed—Oh! Paradise of Bachelors! and oh! Tartarus of Maids!

1855

Benito Cereno[1]

In the year 1799, Captain Amasa Delano,[2] of Duxbury, in Massachusetts, commanding a large sealer[3] and general trader, lay at anchor, with a valuable cargo, in the harbor of St. Maria—a small, desert, uninhabited island toward the southern extremity of the long coast of Chili. There he had touched for water.

On the second day, not long after dawn, while lying in his berth, his mate came below, informing him that a strange sail was coming into the bay. Ships were then not so plenty in those waters as now. He rose, dressed, and went on deck.

The morning was one peculiar to that coast. Everything was mute and calm; everything gray. The sea, though undulated into long roods of swells, seemed fixed, and was sleeked at the surface like waved lead that has cooled and set in the smelter's mould. The sky seemed a gray surtout. Flights of troubled gray fowl, kith and kin with flights of troubled gray vapors among which they were mixed, skimmed low and fitfully over the waters, as swallows over meadows before storms. Shadows present, foreshadowing deeper shadows to come.

[1]"Benito Cereno" was serialized in the October, November, and December, 1855, issues of *Putnam's Monthly* and collected the following year in *The Piazza Tales.* At one stage, Melville had intended to title his collection "Benito Cereno and Other Sketches." The present text is from the standard Northwestern-Newberry edition of *The Piazza Tales and Other Prose Pieces, 1839–1860.*

[2]As Horace Scudder first noted, Melville based his plot primarily on Chapter 18 of Captain Amasa Delano's *Narrative of Voyages and Travels, in the Northern and Southern Hemispheres* (1817), but altered and amplified his source in significant ways. Two of his many changes were to backdate the events from 1805 to 1799 and to rechristen the Spanish ship *Tryal* the *San Dominick*

[3]Seal-hunting ship.

To Captain Delano's surprise, the stranger, viewed through the glass, showed no colors; though to do so upon entering a haven, however uninhabited in its shores, where but a single other ship might be lying, was the custom among peaceful seamen of all nations. Considering the lawlessness and loneliness of the spot, and the sort of stories, at that day, associated with those seas, Captain Delano's surprise might have deepened into some uneasiness had he not been a person of a singularly undistrustful good nature, not liable, except on extraordinary and repeated incentives, and hardly then, to indulge in personal alarms, any way involving the imputation of malign evil in man. Whether, in view of what humanity is capable, such a trait implies, along with a benevolent heart, more than ordinary quickness and accuracy of intellectual perception, may be left to the wise to determine.

But whatever misgivings might have obtruded on first seeing the stranger, would almost, in any seaman's mind, have been dissipated by observing that, the ship, in navigating into the harbor, was drawing too near the land, for her own safety's sake, owing to a sunken reef making out off her bow. This seemed to prove her a stranger, indeed, not only to the sealer, but the island; consequently, she could be no wonted freebooter on that ocean. With no small interest, Captain Delano continued to watch her—a proceeding not much facilitated by the vapors partly mantling the hull, through which the far matin[4] light from her cabin streamed equivocally enough; much like the sun—by this time hemisphered on the rim of the horizon, and apparently, in company with the strange ship, entering the harbor—which, wimpled[5] by the same low, creeping clouds, showed not unlike a Lima intriguante's one sinister eye peering across the Plaza from the Indian loop-hole of her dusk *saya-y-manta.*[6]

It might have been but a deception of the vapors, but, the longer the stranger was watched, the more singular appeared her maneuvers. Ere long it seemed hard to decide whether she meant to come in or no—what she wanted, or what she was about. The wind, which had breezed up a little during the night, was now extremely light and baffling, which the more increased the apparent uncertainty of her movements.

Surmising, at last, that it might be a ship in distress, Captain Delano ordered his whale-boat to be dropped, and, much to the wary opposition of his mate, prepared to board her, and, at the least, pilot her in. On the night previous, a fishing-party of the seamen had gone a long distance to some detached rocks out of sight from the sealer, and, an hour or two before day-break, had returned, having met with no small success. Presuming that the stranger might have been long off soundings, the good captain put several baskets of the fish, for presents, into his boat, and so pulled away. From her continuing too near the sunken reef, deeming her in danger, calling to his men, he made all haste to apprise those on board of their situation. But, some time ere the boat came up, the wind, light though it was, having shifted, had headed the vessel off, as well as partly broken the vapors from about her.

[4]Early morning.

[5]Veiled; covered as with a wimple, the head-dress worn by nuns to cover the head, neck, and sides of the face.

[6]Skirt and shawl combination; the shawl could be used to veil the face of a woman involved in an intrigue, or illicit love affair.

Upon gaining a less remote view, the ship, when made signally visible on the verge of the leaden-hued swells, with the shreds of fog here and there raggedly furring her, appeared like a white-washed monastery after a thunder-storm, seen perched upon some dun cliff among the Pyrenees. But it was no purely fanciful resemblance which now, for a moment, almost led Captain Delano to think that nothing less than a ship-load of monks was before him. Peering over the bulwarks were what really seemed, in the hazy distance, throngs of dark cowls; while, fitfully revealed through the open port-holes, other dark moving figures were dimly descried, as of Black Friars[7] pacing the cloisters.

Upon a still nigher approach, this appearance was modified, and the true character of the vessel was plain—a Spanish merchantman of the first class; carrying negro slaves, amongst other valuable freight, from one colonial port to another. A very large, and, in its time, a very fine vessel, such as in those days were at intervals encountered along that main; sometimes superseded Acapulco treasure-ships, or retired frigates of the Spanish king's navy, which, like superannuated Italian palaces, still, under a decline of masters, preserved signs of former state.

As the whale-boat drew more and more nigh, the cause of the peculiar pipe-clayed[8] aspect of the stranger was seen in the slovenly neglect pervading her. The spars, ropes, and great part of the bulwarks, looked woolly, from long unacquaintance with the scraper, tar, and the brush. Her keel seemed laid, her ribs put together, and she launched, from Ezekiel's Valley of Dry Bones.[9]

In the present business in which she was engaged, the ship's general model and rig appeared to have undergone no material change from their original war-like and Froissart[10] pattern. However, no guns were seen.

The tops were large, and were railed about with what had once been octagonal net-work, all now in sad disrepair. These tops hung overhead like three ruinous

[7]Dominicans, an order of mendicant preaching monks, called Black Friars because of the black mantles they wore. The Spanish priest St. Dominic founded the order in 1215 to combat the Albigenisan heresy, but in Spain the Dominicans' main targets were the Moors, the North African Moslems who had conquered Spain in the eighth century A.D., and the Jews. When the Spanish Inquisition was launched under Ferdinand and Isabella, the Dominicans were entrusted with its execution, which involved the denunciation, torture, and burning at stake of heretics, the confiscation of their property, and the forced mass conversion or expulsion of Moors and Jews.

The Dominican missionary Bartolomé de las Casas also played a key role in the history of the Americas, by proposing that slaves be imported from Africa in order to save the Indians from slavery and extinction.

[8]Whitened, from the grayish white clay used for making tobacco pipes and for whitening leather.

[9]Ezekiel 37:1–14, tells of how God set the prophet down in the midst of a valley full of dry bones and instructed him to prophesy to them that God would restore them to life. Accordingly, the dry bones "lived, and stood up upon their feet, an exceeding great army." God then explains that "these bones are the whole house of Israel," whose "bones are dried" because their "hope is lost," but who are shortly to be resurrected and restored to the land of Israel. The Biblical allusion suggests an analogy between the Israelites and the African slaves on board the *San Dominick,* as captive nations seeking to be restored to their homeland.

[10]Jean Froissart (c. 1333–c. 1405), medieval historian of the wars between France and England; hence medieval, feudal, or pertaining to national conquest.

aviaries, in one of which was seen perched, on a ratlin,[11] a white noddy, a strange fowl, so called from its lethargic, somnambulistic character, being frequently caught by hand at sea. Battered and mouldy, the castellated forecastle seemed some ancient turret, long ago taken by assault, and then left to decay. Toward the stern, two high-raised quarter galleries—the balustrades here and there covered with dry, tindery sea-moss—opening out from the unoccupied state-cabin, whose dead lights,[12] for all the mild weather, were hermetically closed and calked—these tenantless balconies hung over the sea as if it were the grand Venetian canal. But the principal relic of faded grandeur was the ample oval of the shield-like stern-piece, intricately carved with the arms of Castile and Leon,[13] medallioned about by groups of mythological or symbolical devices; uppermost and central of which was a dark satyr in a mask, holding his foot on the prostrate neck of a writhing figure, likewise masked.

Whether the ship had a figure-head, or only a plain beak, was not quite certain, owing to canvas wrapped about that part, either to protect it while undergoing a re-furbishing, or else decently to hide its decay. Rudely painted or chalked, as in a sailor freak, along the forward side of a sort of pedestal below the canvas, was the sentence, *"Seguid vuestro jefe,"* (follow your leader); while upon the tarnished head-boards, near by, appeared, in stately capitals, once gilt, the ship's name, "SAN DOMINICK," each letter streakingly corroded with tricklings of copper-spike rust; while, like mourning weeds, dark festoons of sea-grass slimily swept to and fro over the name, with every hearse-like roll of the hull.

As at last the boat was hooked from the bow along toward the gangway amid-ship, its keel, while yet some inches separated from the hull, harshly grated as on a sunken coral reef. It proved a huge bunch of conglobated barnacles adhering below the water to the side like a wen; a token of baffling airs and long calms passed somewhere in those seas.

Climbing the side, the visitor was at once surrounded by a clamorous throng of whites and blacks, but the latter outnumbering the former more than could have been expected, negro transportation-ship as the stranger in port was. But, in one language, and as with one voice, all poured out a common tale of suffering; in which the negresses, of whom there were not a few, exceeded the others in their dolorous vehemence. The scurvy, together with a fever, had swept off a great part of their number, more especially the Spaniards. Off Cape Horn, they had narrowly escaped shipwreck; then, for days together, they had lain tranced without wind; their provisions were low; their water next to none; their lips that moment were baked.

While Captain Delano was thus made the mark of all eager tongues, his one eager glance took in all the faces, with every other object about him.

Always upon first boarding a large and populous ship at sea, especially a foreign one, with a nondescript crew such as Lascars[14] or Manilla men, the impression varies in a peculiar way from that produced by first entering a strange house with strange

[11]Small transverse rope attached to the shrouds of a ship and forming the steps of a rope ladder.

[12]Metal covers or shutters fitted to portholes to keep out light and water.

[13]Ancient kingdoms of Spain, united after 1230. Their arms included a closed castle symbolizing Castile and a rampant lion symbolizing Leon (see the description of the Spanish flag later in the story).

[14]East Indian sailors.

inmates in a strange land. Both house and ship, the one by its walls and blinds, the other by its high bulwarks like ramparts, hoard from view their interiors till the last moment; but in the case of the ship there is this addition; that the living spectacle it contains, upon its sudden and complete disclosure, has, in contrast with the blank ocean which zones it, something of the effect of enchantment. The ship seems unreal; these strange costumes, gestures, and faces, but a shadowy tableau just emerged from the deep, which directly must receive back what it gave.

Perhaps it was some such influence as above is attempted to be described, which, in Captain Delano's mind, heightened whatever, upon a staid scrutiny, might have seemed unusual; especially the conspicuous figures of four elderly grizzled negroes, their heads like black, doddered[15] willow tops, who, in venerable contrast to the tumult below them, were couched sphynx-like, one on the starboard cat-head,[16] another on the larboard, and the remaining pair face to face on the opposite bulwarks above the main-chains. They each had bits of unstranded old junk in their hands, and, with a sort of stoical self-content, were picking the junk into oakum,[17] a small heap of which lay by their sides. They accompanied the task with a continuous, low, monotonous chant; droning and druling away like so many gray-headed bagpipers playing a funeral march.

The quarter-deck rose into an ample elevated poop, upon the forward verge of which, lifted, like the oakum-pickers, some eight feet above the general throng, sat along in a row, separated by regular spaces, the cross-legged figures of six other blacks; each with a rusty hatchet in his hand, which, with a bit of brick and a rag, he was engaged like a scullion in scouring; while between each two was a small stack of hatchets, their rusted edges turned forward awaiting a like operation. Though occasionally the four oakum-pickers would briefly address some person or persons in the crowd below, yet the six hatchet-polishers neither spoke to others, nor breathed a whisper among themselves, but sat intent upon their task, except at intervals, when, with the peculiar love in negroes of uniting industry with pastime, two and two they sideways clashed their hatchets together, like cymbals, with a barbarous din. All six, unlike the generality, had the raw aspect of unsophisticated Africans.

But that first comprehensive glance which took in those ten figures, with scores less conspicuous, rested but an instant upon them, as, impatient of the hubbub of voices, the visitor turned in quest of whomsoever it might be that commanded the ship.

But as if not unwilling to let nature make known her own case among his suffering charge, or else in despair of restraining it for the time, the Spanish captain, a gentlemanly, reserved-looking, and rather young man to a stranger's eye, dressed with singular richness, but bearing plain traces of recent sleepless cares and disquietudes, stood passively by, leaning against the main-mast, at one moment casting a

[15]Deprived of branches through age or decay. The word "sphynx-like" hints at a riddle of life-and-death importance to be solved, as in the Greek legend of Oedipus, in which the sphinx of Thebes destroyed all passers-by who could not solve the riddle she posed. A mythological creature, the sphinx was of Egyptian origin—one of many allusions in the story to this ancient African civilization, which abolitionists pointed to as evidence that Africans were not mere savages.

[16]A projecting piece of timber or iron near the bow of a ship, to which the anchor is hoisted and secured. One is on the starboard (right) side, another on the larboard (left).

[17]Pieces of worn hemp rope impregnated with tar and used in caulking seams.

dreary, spiritless look upon his excited people, at the next an unhappy glance toward his visitor. By his side stood a black of small stature, in whose rude face, as occasionally, like a shepherd's dog, he mutely turned it up into the Spaniard's, sorrow and affection were equally blended.

Struggling through the throng, the American advanced to the Spaniard, assuring him of his sympathies, and offering to render whatever assistance might be in his power. To which the Spaniard returned, for the present, but grave and ceremonious acknowledgments, his national formality dusked by the saturnine mood of ill health.

But losing no time in mere compliments, Captain Delano returning to the gangway, had his baskets of fish brought up; and as the wind still continued light, so that some hours at least must elapse ere the ship could be brought to the anchorage, he bade his men return to the sealer, and fetch back as much water as the whale-boat could carry, with whatever soft bread the steward might have, all the remaining pumpkins on board, with a box of sugar, and a dozen of his private bottles of cider.

Not many minutes after the boat's pushing off, to the vexation of all, the wind entirely died away, and the tide turning, began drifting back the ship helplessly seaward. But trusting this would not long last, Captain Delano sought with good hopes to cheer up the strangers, feeling no small satisfaction that, with persons in their condition he could—thanks to his frequent voyages along the Spanish main—converse with some freedom in their native tongue.

While left alone with them, he was not long in observing some things tending to heighten his first impressions; but surprise was lost in pity, both for the Spaniards and blacks, alike evidently reduced from scarcity of water and provisions; while long-continued suffering seemed to have brought out the less good-natured qualities of the negroes, besides, at the same time, impairing the Spaniard's authority over them. But, under the circumstances, precisely this condition of things was to have been anticipated. In armies, navies, cities, or families, in nature herself, nothing more relaxes good order than misery. Still, Captain Delano was not without the idea, that had Benito Cereno been a man of greater energy, misrule would hardly have come to the present pass. But the debility, constitutional or induced by the hardships, bodily and mental, of the Spanish captain, was too obvious to be overlooked. A prey to settled dejection, as if long mocked with hope he would not now indulge it, even when it had ceased to be a mock, the prospect of that day or evening at furthest, lying at anchor, with plenty of water for his people, and a brother captain to counsel and befriend, seemed in no perceptible degree to encourage him. His mind appeared unstrung, if not still more seriously affected. Shut up in these oaken walls, chained to one dull round of command, whose unconditionality cloyed him, like some hypochondriac abbot he moved slowly about, at times suddenly pausing, starting, or staring, biting his lip, biting his finger-nail, flushing, paling, twitching his beard, with other symptoms of an absent or moody mind. This distempered spirit was lodged, as before hinted, in as distempered a frame. He was rather tall, but seemed never to have been robust, and now with nervous suffering was almost worn to a skeleton. A tendency to some pulmonary complaint appeared to have been lately confirmed. His voice was like that of one with lungs half gone, hoarsely suppressed, a husky whisper. No wonder that, as in this state he tottered about, his private servant apprehensively followed him. Sometimes the negro gave his master his arm, or took his handkerchief out of his pocket for him; performing these and similar offices with that affectionate zeal which transmutes into something filial or fraternal acts in themselves but menial; and which has gained for the negro the repute of making the most pleasing body servant in the world; one, too, whom a master need be on no stiffly superior terms with, but may treat with familiar trust; less a servant than a devoted companion.

Marking the noisy indocility of the blacks in general, as well as what seemed the sullen inefficiency of the whites, it was not without humane satisfaction that Captain Delano witnessed the steady good conduct of Babo.

But the good conduct of Babo, hardly more than the ill-behavior of others, seemed to withdraw the half-lunatic Don Benito from his cloudy languor. Not that such precisely was the impression made by the Spaniard on the mind of his visitor. The Spaniard's individual unrest was, for the present, but noted as a conspicuous feature in the ship's general affliction. Still, Captain Delano was not a little concerned at what he could not help taking for the time to be Don Benito's unfriendly indifference towards himself. The Spaniard's manner, too, conveyed a sort of sour and gloomy disdain, which he seemed at no pains to disguise. But this the American in charity ascribed to the harassing effects of sickness, since, in former instances, he had noted that there are peculiar natures on whom prolonged physical suffering seems to cancel every social instinct of kindness; as if forced to black bread themselves, they deemed it but equity that each person coming nigh them should, indirectly, by some slight or affront, be made to partake of their fare.

But ere long Captain Delano bethought him that, indulgent as he was at the first, in judging the Spaniard, he might not, after all, have exercised charity enough. At bottom it was Don Benito's reserve which displeased him; but the same reserve was shown towards all but his faithful personal attendant. Even the formal reports which, according to sea-usage, were, at stated times, made to him by some petty underling, either a white, mulatto or black, he hardly had patience enough to listen to, without betraying contemptuous aversion. His manner upon such occasions was, in its degree, not unlike that which might be supposed to have been his imperial countryman's, Charles V., just previous to the anchoritish retirement of that monarch from the throne.[18]

This splenetic disrelish of his place was evinced in almost every function pertaining to it. Proud as he was moody, he condescended to no personal mandate. Whatever special orders were necessary, their delivery was delegated to his body-servant, who in turn transferred them to their ultimate destination, through runners, alert Spanish boys or slave boys, like pages or pilot-fish[19] within easy call continually hovering round Don Benito. So that to have beheld this undemonstrative invalid gliding about, apathetic and mute, no landsman could have dreamed that in him was lodged a dictatorship beyond which, while at sea, there was no earthly appeal.

Thus, the Spaniard, regarded in his reserve, seemed as the involuntary victim of mental disorder. But, in fact, his reserve might, in some degree, have proceeded from design. If so, then here was evinced the unhealthy climax of that icy though consci-

[18]Charles V (1500–1558) succeeded Ferdinand and Isabella to the throne of Spain in 1517 and became Holy Roman Emperor two years later. He inaugurated the importation of African slaves to the American colonies in 1517. After involving Spain in a long series of territorial wars with France and religious wars against the Ottoman Turks and German Protestants, Charles V abdicated the throne and retired to a monastery in the last years of his life, disappointed in his hopes and broken in health.

[19]Smaller fish that often swim in the company of sharks, seeming to pilot them.

entious policy, more or less adopted by all commanders of large ships, which, except in signal emergencies, obliterates alike the manifestation of sway with every trace of sociality; transforming the man into a block, or rather into a loaded cannon, which, until there is call for thunder, has nothing to say.

Viewing him in this light, it seemed but a natural token of the perverse habit induced by a long course of such hard self-restraint, that, notwithstanding the present condition of his ship, the Spaniard should still persist in a demeanor, which, however harmless, or, it may be, appropriate, in a well appointed vessel, such as the San Dominick might have been at the outset of the voyage, was anything but judicious now. But the Spaniard perhaps thought that it was with captains as with gods: reserve, under all events, must still be their cue. But more probably this appearance of slumbering dominion might have been but an attempted disguise to conscious imbecility—not deep policy, but shallow device. But be all this as it might, whether Don Benito's manner was designed or not, the more Captain Delano noted its pervading reserve, the less he felt uneasiness at any particular manifestation of that reserve towards himself.

Neither were his thoughts taken up by the captain alone. Wonted to the quiet orderliness of the sealer's comfortable family of a crew, the noisy confusion of the San Dominick's suffering host repeatedly challenged his eye. Some prominent breaches not only of discipline but of decency were observed. These Captain Delano could not but ascribe, in the main, to the absence of those subordinate deck-officers to whom, along with higher duties, is entrusted what may be styled the police department of a populous ship. True, the old oakum-pickers appeared at times to act the part of monitorial constables to their countrymen, the blacks; but though occasionally succeeding in allaying trifling outbreaks now and then between man and man, they could do little or nothing toward establishing general quiet. The San Dominick was in the condition of a transatlantic emigrant ship, among whose multitude of living freight are some individuals, doubtless, as little troublesome as crates and bales; but the friendly remonstrances of such with their ruder companions are of not so much avail as the unfriendly arm of the mate. What the San Dominick wanted was, what the emigrant ship has, stern superior officers.[20] But on these decks not so much as a fourth mate was to be seen.

The visitor's curiosity was roused to learn the particulars of those mishaps which had brought about such absenteeism, with its consequences; because, though deriving some inkling of the voyage from the wails which at the first moment had greeted him, yet of the details no clear understanding had been had. The best account would, doubtless, be given by the captain. Yet at first the visitor was loth to ask it, unwilling to provoke some distant rebuff. But plucking up courage, he at last accosted Don Benito, renewing the expression of his benevolent interest, adding, that did he (Captain Delano) but know the particulars of the ship's misfortunes, he would, perhaps, be better able in the end to relieve them. Would Don Benito favor him with the whole story?

Don Benito faltered; then, like some somnambulist suddenly interfered with, vacantly stared at his visitor, and ended by looking down on the deck. He maintained

[20]In *Redburn* Melville pleaded passionately for improving conditions aboard emigrant ships, on which the "friendless emigrants" were "stowed away like bales of cotton, and packed like slaves in a slave-ship" (Chaps. 47, 58).

this posture so long, that Captain Delano, almost equally disconcerted, and involuntarily almost as rude, turned suddenly from him, walking forward to accost one of the Spanish seamen for the desired information. But he had hardly gone five paces, when with a sort of eagerness Don Benito invited him back, regretting his momentary absence of mind, and professing readiness to gratify him.

While most part of the story was being given, the two captains stood on the after part of the main-deck, a privileged spot, no one being near but the servant.

"It is now a hundred and ninety days," began the Spaniard, in his husky whisper, "that this ship, well officered and well manned, with several cabin passengers—some fifty Spaniards in all—sailed from Buenos Ayres bound to Lima, with a general cargo, hardware, Paraguay tea and the like—and," pointing forward, "that parcel of negroes, now not more than a hundred and fifty, as you see, but then numbering over three hundred souls. Off Cape Horn we had heavy gales. In one moment, by night, three of my best officers, with fifteen sailors, were lost, with the main-yard; the spar snapping under them in the slings, as they sought, with heavers,[21] to beat down the icy sail. To lighten the hull, the heavier sacks of mate[22] were thrown into the sea, with most of the water-pipes lashed on deck at the time. And this last necessity it was, combined with the prolonged detentions afterwards experienced, which eventually brought about our chief causes of suffering. When—"

Here there was a sudden fainting attack of his cough, brought on, no doubt, by his mental distress. His servant sustained him, and drawing a cordial from his pocket placed it to his lips. He a little revived. But unwilling to leave him unsupported while yet imperfectly restored, the black with one arm still encircled his master, at the same time keeping his eye fixed on his face, as if to watch for the first sign of complete restoration, or relapse, as the event might prove.

The Spaniard proceeded, but brokenly and obscurely, as one in a dream.

—"Oh, my God! rather than pass through what I have, with joy I would have hailed the most terrible gales; but—"

His cough returned and with increased violence; this subsiding, with reddened lips and closed eyes he fell heavily against his supporter.

"His mind wanders. He was thinking of the plague that followed the gales," plaintively sighed the servant; "my poor, poor master!" wringing one hand, and with the other wiping the mouth. "But be patient, Señor," again turning to Captain Delano, "these fits do not last long; master will soon be himself."

Don Benito reviving, went on; but as this portion of the story was very brokenly delivered, the substance only will here be set down.

It appeared that after the ship had been many days tossed in storms off the Cape, the scurvy broke out, carrying off numbers of the whites and blacks. When at last they had worked round into the Pacific, their spars and sails were so damaged, and so inadequately handled by the surviving mariners, most of whom were become invalids, that, unable to lay her northerly course by the wind, which was powerful, the unmanageable ship for successive days and nights was blown northwestward, where the breeze suddenly deserted her, in unknown waters, to sultry calms. The absence of the water-pipes now proved as fatal to life as before their presence had menaced

[21]Bars used as levers.

[22]Mate: Paraguay tea; water-pipes: water casks.

it. Induced, or at least aggravated, by the more than scanty allowance of water, a malignant fever followed the scurvy; with the excessive heat of the lengthened calm, making such short work of it as to sweep away, as by billows, whole families of the Africans, and a yet larger number, proportionably, of the Spaniards, including, by a luckless fatality, every remaining officer on board. Consequently, in the smart west winds eventually following the calm, the already rent sails having to be simply dropped, not furled, at need, had been gradually reduced to the beggar's rags they were now. To procure substitutes for his lost sailors, as well as supplies of water and sails, the captain at the earliest opportunity had made for Baldivia, the southermost civilized port of Chili and South America; but upon nearing the coast the thick weather had prevented him from so much as sighting that harbor. Since which period, almost without a crew, and almost without canvas and almost without water, and at intervals giving its added dead to the sea, the San Dominick had been battledored about by contrary winds, inveigled by currents, or grown weedy in calms. Like a man lost in woods, more than once she had doubled upon her own track.

"But throughout these calamities," huskily continued Don Benito, painfully turning in the half embrace of his servant, "I have to thank those negroes you see, who, though to your inexperienced eyes appearing unruly, have, indeed, conducted themselves with less of restlessness than even their owner could have thought possible under such circumstances."

Here he again fell faintly back. Again his mind wandered: but he rallied, and less obscurely proceeded.

"Yes, their owner was quite right in assuring me that no fetters would be needed with his blacks; so that while, as is wont in this transportation, those negroes have always remained upon deck—not thrust below, as in the Guinea-men[23]—they have, also, from the beginning, been freely permitted to range within given bounds at their pleasure."

Once more the faintness returned—his mind roved—but, recovering, he resumed:

"But it is Babo here to whom, under God, I owe not only my own preservation, but likewise to him, chiefly, the merit is due, of pacifying his more ignorant brethren, when at intervals tempted to murmurings."

"Ah, master," sighed the black, bowing his face, "don't speak of me; Babo is nothing; what Babo has done was but duty."

"Faithful fellow!" cried Capt. Delano. "Don Benito, I envy you such a friend; slave I cannot call him."

As master and man stood before him, the black upholding the white, Captain Delano could not but bethink him of the beauty of that relationship which could present such a spectacle of fidelity on the one hand and confidence on the other. The scene was heightened by the contrast in dress, denoting their relative positions. The Spaniard wore a loose Chili jacket of dark velvet; white small clothes and stockings, with silver buckles at the knee and instep; a high-crowned sombrero, of fine grass; a slender sword, silver mounted, hung from a knot in his sash; the last being an almost invariable adjunct, more for utility than ornament, of a South American gentleman's

[23]Ships engaged in the African slave trade, of which the Guinea coast in West Africa was a center. Like American slaveholders, Don Benito considers the slave trade between ports of his own region less inhumane than the trade between Africa and the Americas.

dress to this hour. Excepting when his occasional nervous contortions brought about disarray, there was a certain precision in his attire, curiously at variance with the unsightly disorder around; especially in the belittered Ghetto, forward of the mainmast, wholly occupied by the blacks.

The servant wore nothing but wide trowsers, apparently, from their coarseness and patches, made out of some old topsail; they were clean, and confined at the waist by a bit of unstranded rope, which, with his composed, deprecatory air at times, made him look something like a begging friar of St. Francis.

However unsuitable for the time and place, at least in the blunt-thinking American's eyes, and however strangely surviving in the midst of all his afflictions, the toilette of Don Benito might not, in fashion at least, have gone beyond the style of the day among South Americans of his class. Though on the present voyage sailing from Buenos Ayres, he had avowed himself a native and resident of Chili, whose inhabitants had not so generally adopted the plain coat and once plebeian pantaloons; but, with a becoming modification, adhered to their provincial costume, picturesque as any in the world. Still, relatively to the pale history of the voyage, and his own pale face, there seemed something so incongruous in the Spaniard's apparel, as almost to suggest the image of an invalid courtier tottering about London streets in the time of the plague.

The portion of the narrative which, perhaps, most excited interest, as well as some surprise, considering the latitudes in question, was the long calms spoken of, and more particularly the ship's so long drifting about. Without communicating the opinion, of course, the American could not but impute at least part of the detentions both to clumsy seamanship and faulty navigation. Eying Don Benito's small, yellow hands, he easily inferred that the young captain had not got into command at the hawse-hole,[24] but the cabin-window; and if so, why wonder at incompetence, in youth, sickness, and gentility united?

But drowning criticism in compassion, after a fresh repetition of his sympathies, Captain Delano having heard out his story, not only engaged, as in the first place, to see Don Benito and his people supplied in their immediate bodily needs, but, also, now further promised to assist him in procuring a large permanent supply of water, as well as some sails and rigging; and, though it would involve no small embarrassment to himself, yet he would spare three of his best seamen for temporary deck officers; so that without delay the ship might proceed to Conception, there fully to refit for Lima, her destined port.

Such generosity was not without its effect, even upon the invalid. His face lighted up; eager and hectic, he met the honest glance of his visitor. With gratitude he seemed overcome.

"This excitement is bad for master," whispered the servant, taking his arm, and with soothing words gently drawing him aside.

When Don Benito returned, the American was pained to observe that his hopefulness, like the sudden kindling in his cheek, was but febrile and transient.

[24]Metal-lined hole in the bow of a ship through which cables pass. Don Benito's hands show that he has never worked among common sailors and has won his captaincy through social influence, not experience.

Ere long, with a joyless mien, looking up towards the poop, the host invited his guest to accompany him there, for the benefit of what little breath of wind might be stirring.

As during the telling of the story, Captain Delano had once or twice started at the occasional cymballing of the hatchet-polishers, wondering why such an interruption should be allowed, especially in that part of the ship, and in the ears of an invalid; and moreover, as the hatchets had anything but an attractive look, and the handlers of them still less so, it was, therefore, to tell the truth, not without some lurking reluctance, or even shrinking, it may be, that Captain Delano, with apparent complaisance, acquiesced in his host's invitation. The more so, since with an untimely caprice of punctilio, rendered distressing by his cadaverous aspect, Don Benito, with Castilian bows, solemnly insisted upon his guest's preceding him up the ladder leading to the elevation; where, one on each side of the last step, sat for armorial supporters and sentries two of the ominous file. Gingerly enough stepped good Captain Delano between them, and in the instant of leaving them behind, like one running the gauntlet, he felt an apprehensive twitch in the calves of his legs.

But when, facing about, he saw the whole file, like so many organ-grinders, still stupidly intent on their work, unmindful of everything beside, he could not but smile at his late fidgeting panic.

Presently, while standing with his host, looking forward upon the decks below, he was struck by one of those instances of insubordination previously alluded to. Three black boys, with two Spanish boys, were sitting together on the hatches, scraping a rude wooden platter, in which some scanty mess had recently been cooked. Suddenly, one of the black boys, enraged at a word dropped by one of his white companions, seized a knife, and though called to forbear by one of the oakum-pickers, struck the lad over the head, inflicting a gash from which blood flowed.

In amazement, Captain Delano inquired what this meant. To which the pale Don Benito dully muttered, that it was merely the sport of the lad.

"Pretty serious sport, truly," rejoined Captain Delano. "Had such a thing happened on board the Bachelor's Delight, instant punishment would have followed."

At these words the Spaniard turned upon the American one of his sudden, staring, half-lunatic looks; then relapsing into his torpor, answered, "Doubtless, doubtless, Señor."

Is it, thought Captain Delano, that this hapless man is one of those paper captains I've known, who by policy wink at what by power they cannot put down? I know no sadder sight than a commander who has little of command but the name.

"I should think, Don Benito," he now said, glancing towards the oakum-picker who had sought to interfere with the boys, "that you would find it advantageous to keep all your blacks employed, especially the younger ones, no matter at what useless task, and no matter what happens to the ship. Why, even with my little band, I find such a course indispensable. I once kept a crew on my quarter-deck thrumming mats[25] for my cabin, when, for three days, I had given up my ship—mats, men, and

[25]Inserting short pieces of rope yarn into a piece of canvas, thus making a rough surface or mat which can be wrapped about rigging to prevent chafing or to stop a leak.

all—for a speedy loss, owing to the violence of a gale, in which we could do nothing but helplessly drive before it."

"Doubtless, doubtless," muttered Don Benito.

"But," continued Captain Delano, again glancing upon the oakum-pickers and then at the hatchet-polishers, near by, "I see you keep some at least of your host employed."

"Yes," was again the vacant response.

"Those old men there, shaking their pows[26] from their pulpits," continued Captain Delano, pointing to the oakum-pickers, "seem to act the part of old dominies to the rest, little heeded as their admonitions are at times. Is this voluntary on their part, Don Benito, or have you appointed them shepherds to your flock of black sheep?"

"What posts they fill, I appointed them," rejoined the Spaniard, in an acrid tone, as if resenting some supposed satiric reflection.

"And these others, these Ashantee[27] conjurors here," continued Captain Delano, rather uneasily eying the brandished steel of the hatchet-polishers, where in spots it had been brought to a shine, "this seems a curious business they are at, Don Benito?"

"In the gales we met," answered the Spaniard, "what of our general cargo was not thrown overboard was much damaged by the brine. Since coming into calm weather, I have had several cases of knives and hatchets daily brought up for overhauling and cleaning."

"A prudent idea, Don Benito. You are part owner of ship and cargo, I presume; but not of the slaves, perhaps?"

"I am owner of all you see," impatiently returned Don Benito, "except the main company of blacks, who belonged to my late friend, Alexandro Aranda."

As he mentioned this name, his air was heart-broken; his knees shook: his servant supported him.

Thinking he divined the cause of such unusual emotion, to confirm his surmise, Captain Delano, after a pause, said, "And may I ask, Don Benito, whether—since awhile ago you spoke of some cabin passengers—the friend, whose loss so afflicts you at the outset of the voyage accompanied his blacks?"

"Yes."

"But died of the fever?"

"Died of the fever.—Oh, could I but——"

Again quivering, the Spaniard paused.

"Pardon me," said Captain Delano lowly, "but I think that, by a sympathetic experience, I conjecture, Don Benito, what it is that gives the keener edge to your grief. It was once my hard fortune to lose at sea a dear friend, my own brother, then supercargo.[28] Assured of the welfare of his spirit, its departure I could have borne

[26]Heads. Dominies: pedagogues, schoolmasters, ministers.

[27]A West African people in what is now Ghana. They formed a powerful kingdom in the 17th and 18th centuries after acquiring a regular supply of firearms. In the 19th century they fiercely resisted British conquest, beginning in 1824.

[28]Officer in a merchant ship whose duty is to manage the commercial concerns of the voyage.

like a man; but that honest eye, that honest hand—both of which had so often met mine—and that warm heart; all, all—like scraps to the dogs—to throw all to the sharks! It was then I vowed never to have for fellow-voyager a man I loved, unless, unbeknown to him, I had provided every requisite, in case of a fatality, for embalming his mortal part for interment on shore. Were your friend's remains now on board this ship, Don Benito, not thus strangely would the mention of his name affect you."

"On board this ship?" echoed the Spaniard. Then, with horrified gestures, as directed against some specter, he unconsciously fell into the ready arms of his attendant, who, with a silent appeal toward Captain Delano, seemed beseeching him not again to broach a theme so unspeakably distressing to his master.

This poor fellow now, thought the pained American, is the victim of that sad superstition which associates goblins with the deserted body of man, as ghosts with an abandoned house. How unlike are we made! What to me, in like case, would have been a solemn satisfaction, the bare suggestion, even, terrifies the Spaniard into this trance. Poor Alexandro Aranda! what would you say could you here see your friend—who, on former voyages, when you for months were left behind, has, I dare say, often longed, and longed, for one peep at you—now transported with terror at the least thought of having you anyway nigh him.

At this moment, with a dreary grave-yard toll, betokening a flaw,[29] the ship's forecastle bell, smote by one of the grizzled oakum-pickers, proclaimed ten o'clock through the leaden calm; when Captain Delano's attention was caught by the moving figure of a gigantic black, emerging from the general crowd below, and slowly advancing towards the elevated poop. An iron collar was about his neck, from which depended a chain, thrice wound round his body; the terminating links padlocked together at a broad band of iron, his girdle.

"How like a mute Atufal moves," murmured the servant.

The black mounted the steps of the poop, and, like a brave prisoner, brought up to receive sentence, stood in unquailing muteness before Don Benito, now recovered from his attack.

At the first glimpse of his approach, Don Benito had started, a resentful shadow swept over his face; and, as with the sudden memory of bootless rage, his white lips glued together.

This is some mulish mutineer, thought Captain Delano, surveying, not without a mixture of admiration, the colossal form of the negro.

"See, he waits your question, master," said the servant.

Thus reminded, Don Benito, nervously averting his glance, as if shunning, by anticipation, some rebellious response, in a disconcerted voice, thus spoke:—

"Atufal, will you ask my pardon now?"

The black was silent.

[29]Probably an allusion to the Liberty Bell famous for the irreparable flaw that had made it crack repeatedly. Like many abolitionists, Melville interpreted the flaw as a symbol of America's failure to obey the Biblical command inscribed on the bell, which enjoined the Israelites to free their slaves on the Jubilee: "Proclaim liberty throughout all the land unto all the inhabitants thereof" (Leviticus 25:10).

"Again, master," murmured the servant, with bitter upbraiding eying his countryman, "Again, master; he will bend to master yet."

"Answer," said Don Benito, still averting his glance, "say but the one word *pardon,* and your chains shall be off."

Upon this, the black, slowly raising both arms, let them lifelessly fall, his links clanking, his head bowed; as much as to say, "no, I am content."

"Go," said Don Benito, with inkept and unknown emotion.

Deliberately as he had come, the black obeyed.

"Excuse me, Don Benito," said Captain Delano, "but this scene surprises me; what means it, pray?"

"It means that that negro alone, of all the band, has given me peculiar cause of offense. I have put him in chains; I—"

Here he paused; his hand to his head, as if there were a swimming there, or a sudden bewilderment of memory had come over him; but meeting his servant's kindly glance seemed reassured, and proceeded:—

"I could not scourge such a form. But I told him he must ask my pardon. As yet he has not. At my command, every two hours he stands before me."

"And how long has this been?"

"Some sixty days."

"And obedient in all else? And respectful?"

"Yes."

"Upon my conscience, then," exclaimed Captain Delano, impulsively, "he has a royal spirit in him, this fellow."

"He may have some right to it," bitterly returned Don Benito, "he says he was king in his own land."

"Yes," said the servant, entering a word, "those slits in Atufal's ears once held wedges of gold; but poor Babo here, in his own land, was only a poor slave; a black man's slave was Babo, who now is the white's."

Somewhat annoyed by these conversational familiarities, Captain Delano turned curiously upon the attendant, then glanced inquiringly at his master; but, as if long wonted to these little informalities, neither master nor man seemed to understand him.

"What, pray, was Atufal's offense, Don Benito?" asked Captain Delano; "if it was not something very serious, take a fool's advice, and, in view of his general docility, as well as in some natural respect for his spirit, remit him his penalty."

"No, no, master never will do that," here murmured the servant to himself, "proud Atufal must first ask master's pardon. The slave there carries the padlock, but master here carries the key."

His attention thus directed, Captain Delano now noticed for the first time that, suspended by a slender silken cord, from Don Benito's neck hung a key. At once, from the servant's muttered syllables divining the key's purpose, he smiled and said:—"So, Don Benito—padlock and key—significant symbols, truly."

Biting his lip, Don Benito faltered.

Though the remark of Captain Delano, a man of such native simplicity as to be incapable of satire or irony, had been dropped in playful allusion to the Spaniard's singularly evidenced lordship over the black; yet the hypochondriac seemed in some way to have taken it as a malicious reflection upon his confessed inability thus far to break down, at least, on a verbal summons, the entrenched will of the slave. Deploring this supposed misconception, yet despairing of correcting it, Captain Delano shifted the subject; but finding his companion more than ever withdrawn, as if still sourly digesting the lees of the presumed affront above-mentioned, by-and-by Captain Delano likewise became less talkative, oppressed, against his own will, by what seemed the secret vindictiveness of the morbidly sensitive Spaniard. But the good sailor himself, of a quite contrary disposition, refrained, on his part, alike from the appearance as from the feeling of resentment, and if silent, was only so from contagion.

Presently the Spaniard, assisted by his servant, somewhat discourteously crossed over from his guest; a procedure which, sensibly enough, might have been allowed to pass for idle caprice of ill-humor, had not master and man, lingering round the corner of the elevated skylight, began whispering together in low voices. This was unpleasing. And more: the moody air of the Spaniard, which at times had not been without a sort of valetudinarian[30] stateliness, now seemed anything but dignified; while the menial familiarity of the servant lost its original charm of simple-hearted attachment.

In his embarrassment, the visitor turned his face to the other side of the ship. By so doing, his glance accidentally fell on a young Spanish sailor, a coil of rope in his hand, just stepped from the deck to the first round of the mizzen-rigging. Perhaps the man would not have been particularly noticed, were it not that, during his ascent to one of the yards, he, with a sort of covert intentness, kept his eye fixed on Captain Delano, from whom, presently, it passed, as if by a natural sequence, to the two whisperers.

His own attention thus redirected to that quarter, Captain Delano gave a slight start. From something in Don Benito's manner just then, it seemed as if the visitor had, at least partly, been the subject of the withdrawn consultation going on—a conjecture as little agreeable to the guest as it was little flattering to the host.

The singular alternations of courtesy and ill-breeding in the Spanish captain were unaccountable, except on one of two suppositions—innocent lunacy, or wicked imposture.

But the first idea, though it might naturally have occurred to an indifferent observer, and, in some respect, had not hitherto been wholly a stranger to Captain Delano's mind, yet, now that, in an incipient way, he began to regard the stranger's conduct something in the light of an intentional affront, of course the idea of lunacy was virtually vacated. But if not a lunatic, what then? Under the circumstances, would a gentleman, nay, any honest boor, act the part now acted by his host? The man was an impostor. Some low-born adventurer, masquerading as an oceanic grandee; yet so ignorant of the first requisites of mere gentlemanhood as to be betrayed into the present remarkable indecorum. That strange ceremoniousness, too, at other times evinced, seemed not uncharacteristic of one playing a part above his real level. Benito Cereno—Don Benito Cereno—a sounding name. One, too, at that period, not unknown, in the surname, to supercargoes and sea captains trading along

[30]Sickly, infirm.

the Spanish Main, as belonging to one of the most enterprising and extensive mercantile families in all those provinces; several members of it having titles; a sort of Castilian Rothschild,[31] with a noble brother, or cousin, in every great trading town of South America. The alleged Don Benito was in early manhood, about twenty-nine or thirty. To assume a sort of roving cadetship in the maritime affairs of such a house, what more likely scheme for a young knave of talent and spirit? But the Spaniard was a pale invalid. Never mind. For even to the degree of simulating mortal disease, the craft of some tricksters had been known to attain. To think that, under the aspect of infantile weakness, the most savage energies might be couched—those velvets of the Spaniard but the silky paw to his fangs.

From no train of thought did these fancies come; not from within, but from without; suddenly, too, and in one throng, like hoar frost; yet as soon to vanish as the mild sun of Captain Delano's good-nature regained its meridian.

Glancing over once more towards his host—whose side-face, revealed above the skylight, was now turned towards him—he was struck by the profile, whose clearness of cut was refined by the thinness incident to ill-health, as well as ennobled about the chin by the beard. Away with suspicion. He was a true off-shoot of a true hidalgo Cereno.

Relieved by these and other better thoughts, the visitor, lightly humming a tune, now began indifferently pacing the poop, so as not to betray to Don Benito that he had at all mistrusted incivility, much less duplicity; for such mistrust would yet be proved illusory, and by the event; though, for the present, the circumstance which had provoked that distrust remained unexplained. But when that little mystery should have been cleared up, Captain Delano thought he might extremely regret it, did he allow Don Benito to become aware that he had indulged in ungenerous surmises. In short, to the Spaniard's black-letter text, it was best, for awhile, to leave open margin.[32]

Presently, his pale face twitching and overcast, the Spaniard, still supported by his attendant, moved over towards his guest, when, with even more than his usual embarrassment, and a strange sort of intriguing intonation in his husky whisper, the following conversation began:—

"Señor, may I ask how long you have lain at this isle?"

"Oh, but a day or two, Don Benito."

"And from what port are you last?"

"Canton."

"And there, Señor, you exchanged your seal-skins for teas and silks, I think you said?"

"Yes. Silks, mostly."

"And the balance you took in specie, perhaps?"

Captain Delano, fidgeting a little, answered—

"Yes; some silver; not a very great deal, though."

"Ah—well. May I ask how many men have you, Señor?"

Captain Delano slightly started, but answered—

[31]Wealthy German Jewish banking family with noble relatives in many European countries.

[32]Black-letter was an early typeface imitating medieval manuscript lettering and hence difficult to read. Delano has decided to leave this text without explanatory notes in the margin—that is, to reserve judgment.

"About five-and-twenty, all told."

"And at present, Señor, all on board, I suppose?"

"All on board, Don Benito," replied the Captain, now with satisfaction.

"And will be to-night, Señor?"

At this last question, following so many pertinacious ones, for the soul of him Captain Delano could not but look very earnestly at the questioner, who, instead of meeting the glance, with every token of craven discomposure dropped his eyes to the deck; presenting an unworthy contrast to his servant, who, just then, was kneeling at his feet, adjusting a loose shoe-buckle; his disengaged face meantime, with humble curiosity, turned openly up into his master's downcast one.

The Spaniard, still with a guilty shuffle, repeated his question:—

"And—and will be to-night, Señor?"

"Yes, for aught I know," returned Captain Delano,—"but nay," rallying himself into fearless truth, "some of them talked of going off on another fishing party about midnight."

"Your ships generally go—go more or less armed, I believe, Señor?"

"Oh, a six-pounder or two, in case of emergency," was the intrepidly indifferent reply, "with a small stock of muskets, sealing-spears, and cutlasses, you know."

As he thus responded, Captain Delano again glanced at Don Benito, but the latter's eyes were averted; while abruptly and awkwardly shifting the subject, he made some peevish allusion to the calm, and then, without apology, once more, with his attendant, withdrew to the opposite bulwarks, where the whispering was resumed.

At this moment, and ere Captain Delano could cast a cool thought upon what had just passed, the young Spanish sailor before mentioned was seen descending from the rigging. In act of stooping over to spring inboard to the deck, his voluminous, unconfined frock, or shirt, of coarse woollen, much spotted with tar, opened out far down the chest, revealing a soiled under garment of what seemed the finest linen, edged, about the neck, with a narrow blue ribbon, sadly faded and worn. At this moment the young sailor's eye was again fixed on the whisperers, and Captain Delano thought he observed a lurking significance in it, as if silent signs of some Freemason[33] sort had that instant been interchanged.

This once more impelled his own glance in the direction of Don Benito, and, as before, he could not but infer that himself formed the subject of the conference. He paused. The sound of the hatchet-polishing fell on his ears. He cast another swift side-look at the two. They had the air of conspirators. In connection with the late questionings and the incident of the young sailor, these things now begat such return of involuntary suspicion, that the singular guilelessness of the American could not endure it. Plucking up a gay and humorous expression, he crossed over to the two rapidly, saying:—"Ha, Don Benito, your black here seems high in your trust; a sort of privy-counselor, in fact."

Upon this, the servant looked up with a good-natured grin, but the master started as from a venomous bite. It was a moment or two before the Spaniard

[33] A worldwide secret society of men united for fraternal purposes, whose members used coded signs as means of communicating. Organized churches viewed freemasons as heretical, irreligious, and dangerous. A strong Anti-Mason movement influenced American politics in the 1820s and 1830s.

sufficiently recovered himself to reply; which he did, at last, with cold restraint:—"Yes, Señor, I have trust in Babo."

Here Babo, changing his previous grin of mere animal humor into an intelligent smile, not ungratefully eyed his master.

Finding that the Spaniard now stood silent and reserved, as if involuntarily, or purposely giving hint that his guest's proximity was inconvenient just then, Captain Delano, unwilling to appear uncivil even to incivility itself, made some trivial remark and moved off; again and again turning over in his mind the mysterious demeanor of Don Benito Cereno.

He had descended from the poop, and, wrapped in thought, was passing near a dark hatchway, leading down into the steerage, when, perceiving motion there, he looked to see what moved. The same instant there was a sparkle in the shadowy hatchway, and he saw one of the Spanish sailors prowling there hurriedly placing his hand in the bosom of his frock, as if hiding something. Before the man could have been certain who it was that was passing, he slunk below out of sight. But enough was seen of him to make it sure that he was the same young sailor before noticed in the rigging.

What was that which so sparkled? thought Captain Delano. It was no lamp—no match—no live coal. Could it have been a jewel? But how come sailors with jewels?—or with silk-trimmed under-shirts either? Has he been robbing the trunks of the dead cabin passengers? But if so, he would hardly wear one of the stolen articles on board ship here. Ah, ah—if now that was, indeed, a secret sign I saw passing between this suspicious fellow and his captain awhile since; if I could only be certain that in my uneasiness my senses did not deceive me, then——

Here, passing from one suspicious thing to another, his mind revolved the point of the strange questions put to him concerning his ship.

By a curious coincidence, as each point was recalled, the black wizards of Ashantee would strike up with their hatchets, as in ominous comment on the white stranger's thoughts. Pressed by such enigmas and portents, it would have been almost against nature, had not, even into the least distrustful heart, some ugly misgivings obtruded.

Observing the ship now helplessly fallen into a current, with enchanted sails, drifting with increased rapidity seaward; and noting that, from a lately intercepted projection of the land, the sealer was hidden, the stout mariner began to quake at thoughts which he barely durst confess to himself. Above all, he began to feel a ghostly dread of Don Benito. And yet when he roused himself, dilated his chest, felt himself strong on his legs, and coolly considered it—what did all these phantoms amount to?

Had the Spaniard any sinister scheme, it must have reference not so much to him (Captain Delano) as to his ship (the Bachelor's Delight).[34] Hence the present

[34]The name of a famous pirate ship belonging to William Cowley and William Dampier, who captured it from Danish slavers off the coast of Sierra Leone, sold the slaves found on board, and sailed it to South America and the Pacific, where they raided Spanish ports and shipping. Note the references to piracy that immediately follow. Melville mentions the "Buccaneers" Cowley and Dampier in Sketches Fifth and Sixth of "The Encantadas." The name of the historical Delano's ship was the *Perseverance.* The substitution offers a fascinating glimpse into the workings of Melville's imagination, showing how the activities Delano reports in his narrative remind Melville of earlier narratives by the pirates and slave-traders who plied the same waters.

drifting away of the one ship from the other, instead of favoring any such possible scheme, was, for the time at least, opposed to it. Clearly any suspicion, combining such contradictions, must need be delusive. Beside, was it not absurd to think of a vessel in distress—a vessel by sickness almost dismanned of her crew—a vessel whose inmates were parched for water—was it not a thousand times absurd that such a craft should, at present, be of a piratical character; or her commander, either for himself or those under him, cherish any desire but for speedy relief and refreshment? But then, might not general distress, and thirst in particular, be affected? And might not that same undiminished Spanish crew, alleged to have perished off to a remnant, be at that very moment lurking in the hold? On heart-broken pretense of entreating a cup of cold water, fiends in human form had got into lonely dwellings, nor retired until a dark deed had been done. And among the Malay pirates, it was no unusual thing to lure ships after them into their treacherous harbors, or entice boarders from a declared enemy at sea, by the spectacle of thinly manned or vacant decks, beneath which prowled a hundred spears with yellow arms ready to upthrust them through the mats. Not that Captain Delano had entirely credited such things. He had heard of them—and now, as stories, they recurred. The present destination of the ship was the anchorage. There she would be near his own vessel. Upon gaining that vicinity, might not the San Dominick, like a slumbering volcano, suddenly let loose energies now hid?

He recalled the Spaniard's manner while telling his story. There was a gloomy hesitancy and subterfuge about it. It was just the manner of one making up his tale for evil purposes, as he goes. But if that story was not true, what was the truth? That the ship had unlawfully come into the Spaniard's possession? But in many of its details, especially in reference to the more calamitous parts, such as the fatalities among the seamen, the consequent prolonged beating about, the past sufferings from obstinate calms, and still continued suffering from thirst; in all these points, as well as others, Don Benito's story had been corroborated not only by the wailing ejaculations of the indiscriminate multitude, white and black, but likewise—what seemed impossible to be counterfeit—by the very expression and play of every human feature, which Captain Delano saw. If Don Benito's story was throughout an invention, then every soul on board, down to the youngest negress, was his carefully drilled recruit in the plot: an incredible inference. And yet, if there was ground for mistrusting his veracity, that inference was a legitimate one.

But those questions of the Spaniard. There, indeed, one might pause. Did they not seem put with much the same object with which the burglar or assassin, by daytime, reconnoitres the walls of a house? But, with ill purposes, to solicit such information openly of the chief person endangered, and so, in effect, setting him on his guard; how unlikely a procedure was that? Absurd, then, to suppose that those questions had been prompted by evil designs. Thus, the same conduct, which, in this instance, had raised the alarm, served to dispel it. In short, scarce any suspicion or uneasiness, however apparently reasonable at the time, which was not now, with equal apparent reason, dismissed.

At last he began to laugh at his former forebodings; and laugh at the strange ship for, in its aspect someway siding with them, as it were; and laugh, too, at the odd-looking blacks, particularly those old scissors-grinders, the Ashantees; and those bed-ridden old knitting-women, the oakum-pickers; and almost at the dark Spaniard himself, the central hobgoblin of all.

For the rest, whatever in a serious way seemed enigmatical, was now good-naturedly explained away by the thought that, for the most part, the poor invalid scarcely knew what he was about; either sulking in black vapors, or putting idle questions without sense or object. Evidently, for the present, the man was not fit to be entrusted with the ship. On some benevolent plea withdrawing the command from him, Captain Delano would yet have to send her to Conception, in charge of his second mate, a worthy person and good navigator—a plan not more convenient for the San Dominick than for Don Benito; for, relieved from all anxiety, keeping wholly to his cabin, the sick man, under the good nursing of his servant, would probably, by the end of the passage, be in a measure restored to health, and with that he should also be restored to authority.

Such were the American's thoughts. They were tranquilizing. There was a difference between the idea of Don Benito's darkly pre-ordaining Captain Delano's fate, and Captain Delano's lightly arranging Don Benito's. Nevertheless, it was not without something of relief that the good seaman presently perceived his whale-boat in the distance. Its absence had been prolonged by unexpected detention at the sealer's side, as well as its returning trip lengthened by the continual recession of the goal.

The advancing speck was observed by the blacks. Their shouts attracted the attention of Don Benito, who, with a return of courtesy, approaching Captain Delano, expressed satisfaction at the coming of some supplies, slight and temporary as they must necessarily prove.

Captain Delano responded; but while doing so, his attention was drawn to something passing on the deck below: among the crowd climbing the landward bulwarks, anxiously watching the coming boat, two blacks, to all appearances accidentally incommoded by one of the sailors, flew out against him with horrible curses, which the sailor someway resenting, the two blacks dashed him to the deck and jumped upon him, despite the earnest cries of the oakum-pickers.

"Don Benito," said Captain Delano quickly, "do you see what is going on there? Look!"

But, seized by his cough, the Spaniard staggered, with both hands to his face, on the point of falling. Captain Delano would have supported him, but the servant was more alert, who, with one hand sustaining his master, with the other applied the cordial. Don Benito restored, the black withdrew his support, slipping aside a little, but dutifully remaining within call of a whisper. Such discretion was here evinced as quite wiped away, in the visitor's eyes, any blemish of impropriety which might have attached to the attendant, from the indecorous conferences before mentioned; showing, too, that if the servant were to blame, it might be more the master's fault than his own, since when left to himself he could conduct thus well.

His glance thus called away from the spectacle of disorder to the more pleasing one before him, Captain Delano could not avoid again congratulating his host upon possessing such a servant, who, though perhaps a little too forward now and then, must upon the whole be invaluable to one in the invalid's situation.

"Tell me, Don Benito," he added, with a smile—"I should like to have your man here myself—what will you take for him? Would fifty doubloons be any object?"

"Master wouldn't part with Babo for a thousand doubloons," murmured the black, overhearing the offer, and taking it in earnest, and, with the strange vanity of a faithful slave appreciated by his master, scorning to hear so paltry a valuation put upon him by a stranger. But Don Benito, apparently hardly yet completely restored, and again interrupted by his cough, made but some broken reply.

Soon his physical distress became so great, affecting his mind, too, apparently, that, as if to screen the sad spectacle, the servant gently conducted his master below.

Left to himself, the American, to while away the time till his boat should arrive, would have pleasantly accosted some one of the few Spanish seamen he saw; but recalling something that Don Benito had said touching their ill conduct, he refrained, as a ship-master indisposed to countenance cowardice or unfaithfulness in seamen.

While, with these thoughts, standing with eye directed forward towards that handful of sailors, suddenly he thought that one or two of them returned the glance and with a sort of meaning. He rubbed his eyes, and looked again; but again seemed to see the same thing. Under a new form, but more obscure than any previous one, the old suspicions recurred, but, in the absence of Don Benito, with less of panic than before. Despite the bad account given of the sailors, Captain Delano resolved forthwith to accost one of them. Descending the poop, he made his way through the blacks, his movement drawing a queer cry from the oakum-pickers, prompted by whom, the negroes, twitching each other aside, divided before him; but, as if curious to see what was the object of this deliberate visit to their Ghetto, closing in behind, in tolerable order, followed the white stranger up. His progress thus proclaimed as by mounted kings-at-arms, and escorted as by a Caffre[35] guard of honor, Captain Delano, assuming a good humored, off-handed air, continued to advance; now and then saying a blithe word to the negroes, and his eye curiously surveying the white faces, here and there sparsely mixed in with the blacks, like stray white pawns venturously involved in the ranks of the chess-men opposed.

While thinking which of them to select for his purpose, he chanced to observe a sailor seated on the deck engaged in tarring the strap of a large block, with a circle of blacks squatted round him inquisitively eying the process.

The mean employment of the man was in contrast with something superior in his figure. His hand, black with continually thrusting it into the tar-pot held for him by a negro, seemed not naturally allied to his face, a face which would have been a very fine one but for its haggardness. Whether this haggardness had aught to do with criminality, could not be determined; since, as intense heat and cold, though unlike, produce like sensations, so innocence and guilt, when, through casual association with mental pain, stamping any visible impress, use one seal—a hacked one.

Not again that this reflection occurred to Captain Delano at the time, charitable man as he was. Rather another idea. Because observing so singular a haggardness combined with a dark eye, averted as in trouble and shame, and then again recalling Don Benito's confessed ill opinion of his crew, insensibly he was operated upon by certain general notions, which, while disconnecting pain and abashment from virtue, invariably link them with vice.

If, indeed, there be any wickedness on board this ship, thought Captain Delano, be sure that man there has fouled his hand in it, even as now he fouls it in the pitch. I don't like to accost him. I will speak to this other, this old Jack here on the windlass.

[35]Kaffir (derived from the Arabic word for infidel), a Bantu people in Southern Africa; often applied to Africans in general.

He advanced to an old Barcelona tar, in ragged red breeches and dirty night-cap, cheeks trenched and bronzed, whiskers dense as thorn hedges. Seated between two sleepy-looking Africans, this mariner, like his younger shipmate, was employed upon some rigging—splicing a cable—the sleepy-looking blacks performing the inferior function of holding the outer parts of the ropes for him.

Upon Captain Delano's approach, the man at once hung his head below its previous level; the one necessary for business. It appeared as if he desired to be thought absorbed, with more than common fidelity, in his task. Being addressed, he glanced up, but with what seemed a furtive, diffident air, which sat strangely enough on his weather-beaten visage, much as if a grizzly bear, instead of growling and biting, should simper and cast sheep's eyes. He was asked several questions concerning the voyage, questions purposely referring to several particulars in Don Benito's narrative, not previously corroborated by those impulsive cries greeting the visitor on first coming on board. The questions were briefly answered, confirming all that remained to be confirmed of the story. The negroes about the windlass joined in with the old sailor, but, as they became talkative, he by degrees became mute, and at length quite glum, seemed morosely unwilling to answer more questions, and yet, all the while, this ursine air was somehow mixed with his sheepish one.

Despairing of getting into unembarrassed talk with such a centaur, Captain Delano, after glancing round for a more promising countenance, but seeing none, spoke pleasantly to the blacks to make way for him; and so, amid various grins and grimaces, returned to the poop, feeling a little strange at first, he could hardly tell why, but upon the whole with regained confidence in Benito Cereno.

How plainly, thought he, did that old whiskerando yonder betray a consciousness of ill-desert. No doubt, when he saw me coming, he dreaded lest I, apprised by his Captain of the crew's general misbehavior, came with sharp words for him, and so down with his head. And yet—and yet, now that I think of it, that very old fellow, if I err not, was one of those who seemed so earnestly eying me here awhile since. Ah, these currents spin one's head round almost as much as they do the ship. Ha, there now's a pleasant sort of sunny sight; quite sociable, too.

His attention had been drawn to a slumbering negress, partly disclosed through the lace-work of some rigging, lying, with youthful limbs carelessly disposed, under the lee of the bulwarks, like a doe in the shade of a woodland rock. Sprawling at her lapped breasts was her wide-awake fawn, stark naked, its black little body half lifted from the deck, crosswise with its dam's; its hands, like two paws, clambering upon her; its mouth and nose ineffectually rooting to get at the mark; and meantime giving a vexatious half-grunt, blending with the composed snore of the negress.

The uncommon vigor of the child at length roused the mother. She started up, at distance facing Captain Delano. But as if not at all concerned at the attitude in which she had been caught, delightedly she caught the child up, with maternal transports, covering it with kisses.

There's naked nature, now; pure tenderness and love, thought Captain Delano, well pleased.

This incident prompted him to remark the other negresses more particularly than before. He was gratified with their manners; like most uncivilized women, they seemed at once tender of heart and tough of constitution; equally ready to die for their infants or fight for them. Unsophisticated as leopardesses; loving as doves. Ah!

thought Captain Delano, these perhaps are some of the very women whom Mungo Park[36] saw in Africa, and gave such a noble account of.

These natural sights somehow insensibly deepened his confidence and ease. At last he looked to see how his boat was getting on; but it was still pretty remote. He turned to see if Don Benito had returned; but he had not.

To change the scene, as well as to please himself with a leisurely observation of the coming boat, stepping over into the mizzen-chains he clambered his way into the starboard quarter-gallery; one of those abandoned Venetian-looking water-balconies previously mentioned; retreats cut off from the deck. As his foot pressed the half-damp, half-dry sea-mosses matting the place, and a chance phantom cats-paw—an islet of breeze, unheralded, unfollowed—as this ghostly cats-paw came fanning his cheek, as his glance fell upon the row of small, round dead-lights, all closed like coppered eyes of the coffined, and the state-cabin door, once connecting with the gallery, even as the dead-lights had once looked out upon it, but now calked fast like a sarcophagus lid, to a purple-black, tarred-over panel, threshold, and post; and he bethought him of the time, when that state-cabin and this state-balcony had heard the voices of the Spanish king's officers, and the forms of the Lima viceroy's daughters had perhaps leaned where he stood—as these and other images flitted through his mind, as the cats-paw through the calm, gradually he felt rising a dreamy inquietude, like that of one who alone on the prairie feels unrest from the repose of the noon.

He leaned against the carved balustrade, again looking off toward his boat; but found his eye falling upon the ribbon grass, trailing along the ship's water-line, straight as a border of green box; and parterres[37] of sea-weed, broad ovals and crescents, floating nigh and far, with what seemed long formal alleys between, crossing the terraces of swells, and sweeping round as if leading to the grottoes below. And overhanging all was the balustrade by his arm, which, partly stained with pitch and partly embossed with moss, seemed the charred ruin of some summer-house in a grand garden long running to waste.

Trying to break one charm, he was but becharmed anew. Though upon the wide sea, he seemed in some far inland country; prisoner in some deserted château, left to stare at empty grounds, and peer out at vague roads, where never wagon or wayfarer passed.

But these enchantments were a little disenchanted as his eye fell on the corroded main-chains. Of an ancient style, massy and rusty in link, shackle and bolt, they seemed even more fit for the ship's present business than the one for which probably she had been built.

[36]Scottish explorer (1771–1806), whose *Travels in the Interior of Africa* (1799) was one of the nineteenth century's main sources of information on African culture. Melville is probably referring to Park's tribute in Chapter 20 to the "disinterested charity, and tender solicitude" he received from "many of these poor heathens," especially the women, of whom he wrote: "I do not recollect a single instance of hardheartedness towards me in the women. In all my wanderings and wretchedness, I found them uniformly kind and compassionate." Park proceeds to quote an equally warm tribute by his predecessor, the American traveler John Ledyard (1751–1789). Thus in *The Piazza Tales* edition of "Benito Cereno," Melville or his editor substituted Ledyard's name for Mungo Park's.

[37]Gardens having ornamental and diversified arrangements of flower beds separated by paths.

Presently he thought something moved nigh the chains. He rubbed his eyes, and looked hard. Groves of rigging were about the chains; and there, peering from behind a great stay, like an Indian from behind a hemlock, a Spanish sailor, a marlingspike in his hand, was seen, who made what seemed an imperfect gesture towards the balcony, but immediately, as if alarmed by some advancing step along the deck within, vanished into the recesses of the hempen forest, like a poacher.

What meant this? Something the man had sought to communicate, unbeknown to any one, even to his captain. Did the secret involve aught unfavorable to his captain? Were those previous misgivings of Captain Delano's about to be verified? Or, in his haunted mood at the moment, had some random, unintentional motion of the man, while busy with the stay, as if repairing it, been mistaken for a significant beckoning?

Not unbewildered, again he gazed off for his boat. But it was temporarily hidden by a rocky spur of the isle. As with some eagerness he bent forward, watching for the first shooting view of its beak, the balustrade gave way before him like charcoal. Had he not clutched an outreaching rope he would have fallen into the sea. The crash, though feeble, and the fall, though hollow, of the rotten fragments, must have been overheard. He glanced up. With sober curiosity peering down upon him was one of the old oakum-pickers, slipped from his perch to an outside boom; while below the old negro, and, invisible to him, reconnoitering from a port-hole like a fox from the mouth of its den, crouched the Spanish sailor again. From something suddenly suggested by the man's air, the mad idea now darted into Captain Delano's mind, that Don Benito's plea of indisposition, in withdrawing below, was but a pretense: that he was engaged there maturing some plot, of which the sailor, by some means gaining an inkling, had a mind to warn the stranger against; incited, it may be, by gratitude for a kind word on first boarding the ship. Was it from foreseeing some possible interference like this, that Don Benito had, beforehand, given such a bad character of his sailors, while praising the negroes; though, indeed, the former seemed as docile as the latter the contrary? The whites, too, by nature, were the shrewder race. A man with some evil design, would he not be likely to speak well of that stupidity which was blind to his depravity, and malign that intelligence from which it might not be hidden? Not unlikely, perhaps. But if the whites had dark secrets concerning Don Benito, could then Don Benito be any way in complicity with the blacks? But they were too stupid. Besides, who ever heard of a white so far a renegade as to apostatize from his very species almost, by leaguing in against it with negroes?[38] These difficulties recalled former ones. Lost in their mazes, Captain Delano, who had now regained the deck, was uneasily advancing along it, when he observed a new face; an aged sailor seated cross-legged near the main hatchway. His skin was shrunk up with wrinkles like a pelican's empty pouch; his hair frosted; his countenance grave and composed. His hands were full of ropes, which he was working into a large knot. Some blacks were about him obligingly dipping the strands for him, here and there, as the exigencies of the operation demanded.

[38]Delano considers it both unnatural (like the crossbreeding of species) and irreligious (like the renunciation of one's inherited religious faith) for whites to side with blacks. He is echoing the racist theory that the human races are distinct species. Melville probably encountered this theory through a review in *Putnam's* of Josiah C. Nott's and George R. Gliddon's *Types of Mankind* (1854). He satirized scientific racism in "The 'Gees" (1856).

Captain Delano crossed over to him, and stood in silence surveying the knot; his mind, by a not uncongenial transition, passing from its own entanglements to those of the hemp. For intricacy such a knot he had never seen in an American ship, or indeed any other. The old man looked like an Egyptian priest, making gordian knots for the temple of Ammon.[39] The knot seemed a combination of double-bowline-knot, treble-crown-knot, back-handed-well-knot, knot-in-and-out-knot, and jamming-knot.

At last, puzzled to comprehend the meaning of such a knot, Captain Delano addressed the knotter:—

"What are you knotting there, my man?"

"The knot," was the brief reply, without looking up.

"So it seems; but what is it for?"

"For some one else to undo," muttered back the old man, plying his fingers harder than ever, the knot being now nearly completed.

While Captain Delano stood watching him, suddenly the old man threw the knot towards him, saying in broken English,—the first heard in the ship,—something to this effect—"Undo it, cut it, quick." It was said lowly, but with such condensation of rapidity, that the long, slow words in Spanish, which had preceded and followed, almost operated as covers to the brief English between.

For a moment, knot in hand, and knot in head, Captain Delano stood mute; while, without further heeding him, the old man was now intent upon other ropes. Presently there was a slight stir behind Captain Delano. Turning, he saw the chained negro, Atufal, standing quietly there. The next moment the old sailor rose, muttering, and, followed by his subordinate negroes, removed to the forward part of the ship, where in the crowd he disappeared.

An elderly negro, in a clout like an infant's, and with a pepper and salt head, and a kind of attorney air, now approached Captain Delano. In tolerable Spanish, and with a good-natured, knowing wink, he informed him that the old knotter was simple-witted, but harmless; often playing his old tricks. The negro concluded by begging the knot, for of course the stranger would not care to be troubled with it. Unconsciously, it was handed to him. With a sort of congé,[40] the negro received it, and turning his back, ferreted into it like a detective Custom House officer after smuggled laces. Soon, with some African word, equivalent to pshaw, he tossed the knot overboard.

All this is very queer now, thought Captain Delano, with a qualmish sort of emotion; but as one feeling incipient sea-sickness, he strove, by ignoring the symptoms,

[39]Melville is compressing two episodes in the career of Alexander the Great. In 333 B.C. Alexander entered the ancient Phrygian city of Gordium (near present-day Ankara, Turkey). According to prophecy, whoever untied the intricate knot that bound the chariot of Gordius, the city's founder, to a pole, would rule Asia. Alexander cut the Gordian knot with his sword and went on to defeat the Persian army. The following year, on capturing Egypt from the Persians, he consulted the oracle of the Egyptian god Amon on the prospects of his conquest schemes and was supposedly hailed as a son of Amon. Unlike Alexander, Delano cannot cut this Gordian knot; like Alexander, however, who was initially welcomed by the Egyptians as a liberator, he is merely stepping into the place of the previous ruler. Also relevant here is the status of Amon as an African deity, worshipped both by the Egyptians and the Black Cushites of Nubia, and especially revered for his impartiality by the poor and oppressed.

[40]Ceremonious bow.

to get rid of the malady. Once more he looked off for his boat. To his delight, it was now again in view, leaving the rocky spur astern.

The sensation here experienced, after at first relieving his uneasiness, with unforeseen efficacy, soon began to remove it. The less distant sight of that well-known boat—showing it, not as before, half blended with the haze, but with outline defined, so that its individuality, like a man's, was manifest; that boat, Rover[41] by name, which, though now in strange seas, had often pressed the beach of Captain Delano's home, and, brought to its threshold for repairs, had familiarly lain there, as a Newfoundland dog; the sight of that household boat evoked a thousand trustful associations, which, contrasted with previous suspicions, filled him not only with lightsome confidence, but somehow with half humorous self-reproaches at his former lack of it.

"What, I, Amasa Delano—Jack of the Beach, as they called me when a lad—I, Amasa; the same that, duck-satchel in hand, used to paddle along the waterside to the school-house made from the old hulk;—I, little Jack of the Beach, that used to go berrying with cousin Nat and the rest; I to be murdered here at the ends of the earth, on board a haunted pirate-ship by a horrible Spaniard?—Too nonsensical to think of! Who would murder Amasa Delano? His conscience is clean. There is some one above. Fie, fie, Jack of the Beach! you are a child indeed; a child of the second childhood, old boy; you are beginning to dote and drule, I'm afraid."

Light of heart and foot, he stepped aft, and there was met by Don Benito's servant, who, with a pleasing expression, responsive to his own present feelings, informed him that his master had recovered from the effects of his coughing fit, and had just ordered him to go present his compliments to his good guest, Don Amasa, and say that he (Don Benito) would soon have the happiness to rejoin him.

There now, do you mark that? again thought Captain Delano, walking the poop. What a donkey I was. This kind gentleman who here sends me his kind compliments, he, but ten minutes ago, dark-lantern in hand, was dodging round some old grindstone in the hold, sharpening a hatchet for me, I thought. Well, well; these long calms have a morbid effect on the mind, I've often heard, though I never believed it before. Ha! glancing towards the boat; there's Rover; good dog; a white bone in her mouth. A pretty big bone though, seems to me.—What? Yes, she has fallen afoul of the bubbling tide-rip there. It sets her the other way, too, for the time. Patience.

It was now about noon, though, from the grayness of everything, it seemed to be getting towards dusk.

The calm was confirmed. In the far distance, away from the influence of land, the leaden ocean seemed laid out and leaded up, its course finished, soul gone, defunct. But the current from landward, where the ship was, increased; silently sweeping her further and further towards the tranced waters beyond.

Still, from his knowledge of those latitudes, cherishing hopes of a breeze, and a fair and fresh one, at any moment, Captain Delano, despite present prospects, buoyantly counted upon bringing the San Dominick safely to anchor ere night. The distance swept over was nothing; since, with a good wind, ten minutes' sailing would

[41]Michael Rogin has suggested that the name is an allusion to the pirate ship disguised as a slave-trading vessel that gives its name to James Fenimore Cooper's novel, *The Red Rover* (1827), reviewed by Melville in 1850.

retrace more than sixty minutes' drifting. Meantime, one moment turning to mark "Rover" fighting the tide-rip, and the next to see Don Benito approaching, he continued walking the poop.

Gradually he felt a vexation arising from the delay of his boat; this soon merged into uneasiness; and at last, his eye falling continually, as from a stage-box into the pit, upon the strange crowd before and below him, and by and by recognising there the face—now composed to indifference—of the Spanish sailor who had seemed to beckon from the main chains, something of his old trepidations returned.

Ah, thought he—gravely enough—this is like the ague: because it went off, it follows not that it won't come back.

Though ashamed of the relapse, he could not altogether subdue it; and so, exerting his good nature to the utmost, insensibly he came to a compromise.

Yes, this is a strange craft; a strange history, too, and strange folks on board. But—nothing more.

By way of keeping his mind out of mischief till the boat should arrive, he tried to occupy it with turning over and over, in a purely speculative sort of way, some lesser peculiarities of the captain and crew. Among others, four curious points recurred.

First, the affair of the Spanish lad assailed with a knife by the slave boy; an act winked at by Don Benito. Second, the tyranny in Don Benito's treatment of Atufal, the black; as if a child should lead a bull of the Nile by the ring in his nose. Third, the trampling of the sailor by the two negroes; a piece of insolence passed over without so much as a reprimand. Fourth, the cringing submission to their master of all the ship's underlings, mostly blacks; as if by the least inadvertence they feared to draw down his despotic displeasure.

Coupling these points, they seemed somewhat contradictory. But what then, thought Captain Delano, glancing towards his now nearing boat,—what then? Why, Don Benito is a very capricious commander. But he is not the first of the sort I have seen; though it's true he rather exceeds any other. But as a nation—continued he in his reveries—these Spaniards are all an odd set; the very word Spaniard has a curious, conspirator, Guy-Fawkish[42] twang to it. And yet, I dare say, Spaniards in the main are as good folks as any in Duxbury, Massachusetts. Ah good! At last "Rover" has come.

As, with its welcome freight, the boat touched the side, the oakum-pickers, with venerable gestures, sought to restrain the blacks, who, at the sight of three gurried[43] water-casks in its bottom, and a pile of wilted pumpkins in its bow, hung over the bulwarks in disorderly raptures.

Don Benito with his servant now appeared; his coming, perhaps, hastened by hearing the noise. Of him Captain Delano sought permission to serve out the water, so that all might share alike, and none injure themselves by unfair excess. But sensible, and, on Don Benito's account, kind as this offer was, it was received with

[42]Guy Fawkes (1570–1606), Catholic conspirator, participated in the Gunpowder Plot, aimed at blowing up the Parliament building while King James I and his chief ministers were meeting inside on November 5, 1605. Fawkes's name became a byword for Catholic villainy, and the annual celebration of Guy Fawkes Day regularly fanned anti-Catholic sentiment.

[43]Slimy from whale and fish refuse.

what seemed impatience; as if aware that he lacked energy as a commander, Don Benito, with the true jealousy of weakness, resented as an affront any interference. So, at least, Captain Delano inferred.

In another moment the casks were being hoisted in, when some of the eager negroes accidentally jostled Captain Delano, where he stood by the gangway; so that, unmindful of Don Benito, yielding to the impulse of the moment, with good-natured authority he bade the blacks stand back; to enforce his words making use of a half-mirthful, half-menacing gesture. Instantly the blacks paused, just where they were, each negro and negress suspended in his or her posture, exactly as the word had found them—for a few seconds continuing so—while, as between the responsive posts of a telegraph, an unknown syllable ran from man to man among the perched oakum-pickers. While the visitor's attention was fixed by this scene, suddenly the hatchet-polishers half rose, and a rapid cry came from Don Benito.

Thinking that at the signal of the Spaniard he was about to be massacred, Captain Delano would have sprung for his boat, but paused, as the oakum-pickers, dropping down into the crowd with earnest exclamations, forced every white and every negro back, at the same moment, with gestures friendly and familiar, almost jocose, bidding him, in substance, not be a fool. Simultaneously the hatchet-polishers resumed their seats, quietly as so many tailors, and at once, as if nothing had happened, the work of hoisting in the casks was resumed, whites and blacks singing at the tackle.

Captain Delano glanced towards Don Benito. As he saw his meager form in the act of recovering itself from reclining in the servant's arms, into which the agitated invalid had fallen, he could not but marvel at the panic by which himself had been surprised on the darting supposition that such a commander, who upon a legitimate occasion, so trivial, too, as it now appeared, could lose all self-command, was, with energetic iniquity, going to bring about his murder.

The casks being on deck, Captain Delano was handed a number of jars and cups by one of the steward's aids, who, in the name of his captain, entreated him to do as he had proposed: dole out the water. He complied, with republican impartiality as to this republican element, which always seeks one level, serving the oldest white no better than the youngest black; excepting, indeed, poor Don Benito, whose condition, if not rank, demanded an extra allowance. To him, in the first place, Captain Delano presented a fair pitcher of the fluid; but, thirsting as he was for it, the Spaniard quaffed not a drop until after several grave bows and salutes. A reciprocation of courtesies which the sight-loving Africans hailed with clapping of hands.

Two of the less wilted pumpkins being reserved for the cabin table, the residue were minced up on the spot for the general regalement. But the soft bread, sugar, and bottled cider, Captain Delano would have given the whites alone, and in chief Don Benito; but the latter objected; which disinterestedness, on his part, not a little pleased the American; and so mouthfuls all around were given alike to whites and blacks; excepting one bottle of cider, which Babo insisted upon setting aside for his master.

Here it may be observed that as, on the first visit of the boat, the American had not permitted his men to board the ship, neither did he now; being unwilling to add to the confusion of the decks.

Not uninfluenced by the peculiar good humor at present prevailing, and for the time oblivious of any but benevolent thoughts, Captain Delano, who from recent indications counted upon a breeze within an hour or two at furthest, dispatched the boat back to the sealer with orders for all the hands that could be spared immediately to set about rafting casks to the watering-place and filling them. Likewise he bade word be carried to his chief officer, that if against present expectation the ship was not brought to anchor by sunset, he need be under no concern, for as there was to be a full moon that night, he (Captain Delano) would remain on board ready to play the pilot, come the wind soon or late.

As the two Captains stood together, observing the departing boat—the servant as it happened having just spied a spot on his master's velvet sleeve, and silently engaged rubbing it out—the American expressed his regrets that the San Dominick had no boats; none, at least, but the unseaworthy old hulk of the long-boat, which, warped as a camel's skeleton in the desert, and almost as bleached, lay pot-wise inverted amidships, one side a little tipped, furnishing a subterraneous sort of den for family groups of the blacks, mostly women and small children; who, squatting on old mats below, or perched above in the dark dome, on the elevated seats, were descried, some distance within, like a social circle of bats, sheltering in some friendly cave; at intervals, ebon flights of naked boys and girls, three or four years old, darting in and out of the den's mouth.

"Had you three or four boats now, Don Benito," said Captain Delano, "I think that, by tugging at the oars, your negroes here might help along matters some.—Did you sail from port without boats, Don Benito?"

"They were stove in the gales, Señor."

"That was bad. Many men, too, you lost then. Boats and men.—Those must have been hard gales, Don Benito."

"Past all speech," cringed the Spaniard.

"Tell me, Don Benito," continued his companion with increased interest, "tell me, were these gales immediately off the pitch of Cape Horn?"

"Cape Horn?—who spoke of Cape Horn?"

"Yourself did, when giving me an account of your voyage," answered Captain Delano with almost equal astonishment at this eating of his own words, even as he ever seemed eating his own heart, on the part of the Spaniard. "You yourself, Don Benito, spoke of Cape Horn," he emphatically repeated.

The Spaniard turned, in a sort of stooping posture, pausing an instant, as one about to make a plunging exchange of elements, as from air to water.

At this moment a messenger-boy, a white, hurried by, in the regular performance of his function carrying the last expired half hour forward to the forecastle, from the cabin time-piece, to have it struck at the ship's large bell.

"Master," said the servant, discontinuing his work on the coat sleeve, and addressing the rapt Spaniard with a sort of timid apprehensiveness, as one charged with a duty, the discharge of which, it was foreseen, would prove irksome to the very person who had imposed it, and for whose benefit it was intended, "master told me never mind where he was, or how engaged, always to remind him, to a minute, when shaving-time comes. Miguel has gone to strike the half-hour afternoon. It is *now,* master. Will master go into the cuddy?"

"Ah—yes," answered the Spaniard, starting, somewhat as from dreams into realities; then turning upon Captain Delano, he said that ere long he would resume the conversation.

"Then if master means to talk more to Don Amasa," said the servant, "why not let Don Amasa sit by master in the cuddy, and master can talk, and Don Amasa can listen, while Babo here lathers and strops."

"Yes," said Captain Delano, not unpleased with this sociable plan, "yes, Don Benito, unless you had rather not, I will go with you."

"Be it so, Señor."

As the three passed aft, the American could not but think it another strange instance of his host's capriciousness, this being shaved with such uncommon punctuality in the middle of the day. But he deemed it more than likely that the servant's anxious fidelity had something to do with the matter; inasmuch as the timely interruption served to rally his master from the mood which had evidently been coming upon him.

The place called the cuddy was a light deck-cabin formed by the poop, a sort of attic to the large cabin below. Part of it had formerly been the quarters of the officers; but since their death all the partitionings had been thrown down, and the whole interior converted into one spacious and airy marine hall; for absence of fine furniture and picturesque disarray, of odd appurtenances, somewhat answering to the wide, cluttered hall of some eccentric bachelor-squire in the country, who hangs his shooting-jacket and tobacco-pouch on deer antlers, and keeps his fishing-rod, tongs, and walking-stick in the same corner.

The similitude was heightened, if not originally suggested, by glimpses of the surrounding sea; since, in one aspect, the country and the ocean seem cousins-german.

The floor of the cuddy was matted. Overhead, four or five old muskets were stuck into horizontal holes along the beams. On one side was a claw-footed old table lashed to the deck; a thumbed missal on it, and over it a small, meager crucifix attached to the bulk-head. Under the table lay a dented cutlass or two, with a hacked harpoon, among some melancholy old rigging, like a heap of poor friar's girdles. There were also two long, sharp-ribbed settees of malacca cane, black with age, and uncomfortable to look at as inquisitors' racks,[44] with a large, misshapen armchair, which, furnished with a rude barber's crutch at the back, working with a screw, seemed some grotesque, middle-age engine of torment. A flag locker was in one corner, open, exposing various colored bunting, some rolled up, others half unrolled, still others tumbled. Opposite was a cumbrous washstand, of black mahogany, all of one block, with a pedestal, like a font, and over it a railed shelf, containing combs, brushes, and other implements of the toilet. A torn hammock of stained grass swung near; the sheets tossed, and the pillow wrinkled up like a brow, as if whoever slept here slept but illy, with alternate visitations of sad thoughts and bad dreams.

The further extremity of the cuddy, overhanging the ship's stern, was pierced with three openings, windows or port holes, according as men or cannon might peer,

[44]As John Bernstein has pointed out, references to the Spanish Inquisition, which reached its height under Charles V, structure the story.

socially or unsocially, out of them. At present neither men nor cannon were seen, though huge ring-bolts and other rusty iron fixtures of the wood-work hinted of twenty-four-pounders.

Glancing towards the hammock as he entered, Captain Delano said, "You sleep here, Don Benito?"

"Yes, Señor, since we got into mild weather."

"This seems a sort of dormitory, sitting-room, sail-loft, chapel, armory, and private closet all together, Don Benito," added Captain Delano, looking round.

"Yes, Señor; events have not been favorable to much order in my arrangements."

Here the servant, napkin on arm, made a motion as if waiting his master's good pleasure. Don Benito signified his readiness, when, seating him in the malacca arm-chair, and for the guest's convenience drawing opposite it one of the settees, the servant commenced operations by throwing back his master's collar and loosening his cravat.

There is something in the negro which, in a peculiar way, fits him for avocations about one's person. Most negroes are natural valets and hair-dressers; taking to the comb and brush congenially as to the castinets, and flourishing them apparently with almost equal satisfaction. There is, too, a smooth tact about them in this employment, with a marvelous, noiseless, gliding briskness, not ungraceful in its way, singularly pleasing to behold, and still more so to be the manipulated subject of. And above all is the great gift of good humor. Not the mere grin or laugh is here meant. Those were unsuitable. But a certain easy cheerfulness, harmonious in every glance and gesture; as though God had set the whole negro to some pleasant tune.

When to all this is added the docility arising from the unaspiring contentment of a limited mind, and that susceptibility of blind attachment sometimes inhering in indisputable inferiors, one readily perceives why those hypochondriacs, Johnson and Byron—it may be something like the hypochondriac, Benito Cereno—took to their hearts, almost to the exclusion of the entire white race, their serving men, the negroes, Barber and Fletcher.[45] But if there be that in the negro which exempts him from the inflicted sourness of the morbid or cynical mind, how, in his most prepossessing aspects, must he appear to a benevolent one? When at ease with respect to exterior things, Captain Delano's nature was not only benign, but familiarly and humorously so. At home, he had often taken rare satisfaction in sitting in his door, watching some free man of color at his work or play. If on a voyage he chanced to have a black sailor, invariably he was on chatty, and half-gamesome terms with him. In fact, like most men of a good, blithe heart, Captain Delano took to negroes, not philanthropically, but genially, just as other men to Newfoundland dogs.

Hitherto the circumstances in which he found the San Dominick had repressed the tendency. But in the cuddy, relieved from his former uneasiness, and, for various reasons, more sociably inclined than at any previous period of the day, and seeing

[45]Francis Barber, the faithful black servant of Samuel Johnson (1709–1784), is mentioned frequently in James Boswell's *Life of Samuel Johnson,* which comments on the warm relationship between the two men. William Fletcher was the white English valet of Lord Byron (1788–1824). Melville apparently confused him with the black servant of Byron's companion Edward Trelawny.

the colored servant, napkin on arm, so debonair about his master, in a business so familiar as that of shaving, too, all his old weakness for negroes returned.

Among other things, he was amused with an odd instance of the African love of bright colors and fine shows, in the black's informally taking from the flag-locker a great piece of bunting of all hues, and lavishly tucking it under his master's chin for an apron.

The mode of shaving among the Spaniards is a little different from what it is with other nations. They have a basin, specifically called a barber's basin, which on one side is scooped out, so as accurately to receive the chin, against which it is closely held in lathering; which is done, not with a brush, but with soap dipped in the water of the basin and rubbed on the face.

In the present instance salt-water was used for lack of better; and the parts lathered were only the upper lip, and low down under the throat, all the rest being cultivated beard.

The preliminaries being somewhat novel to Captain Delano, he sat curiously eying them, so that no conversation took place, nor for the present did Don Benito appear disposed to renew any.

Setting down his basin, the negro searched among the razors, as for the sharpest, and having found it, gave it an additional edge by expertly strapping it on the firm, smooth, oily skin of his open palm; he then made a gesture as if to begin, but midway stood suspended for an instant, one hand elevating the razor, the other professionally dabbling among the bubbling suds on the Spaniard's lank neck. Not unaffected by the close sight of the gleaming steel, Don Benito nervously shuddered; his usual ghastliness was heightened by the lather, which lather, again, was intensified in its hue by the contrasting sootiness of the negro's body. Altogether the scene was somewhat peculiar, at least to Captain Delano, nor, as he saw the two thus postured, could he resist the vagary, that in the black he saw a headsman, and in the white, a man at the block. But this was one of those antic conceits, appearing and vanishing in a breath, from which, perhaps, the best regulated mind is not always free.

Meantime the agitation of the Spaniard had a little loosened the bunting from around him, so that one broad fold swept curtain-like over the chair-arm to the floor, revealing, amid a profusion of armorial bars and ground-colors—black, blue, and yellow—a closed castle in a blood-red field diagonal with a lion rampant in a white.

"The castle and the lion," exclaimed Captain Delano—"why, Don Benito, this is the flag of Spain you use here.[46] It's well it's only I, and not the King, that sees this," he added with a smile, "but"—turning towards the black,—"it's all one, I suppose, so the colors be gay;" which playful remark did not fail somewhat to tickle the negro.

"Now, master," he said, readjusting the flag, and pressing the head gently further back into the crotch of the chair; "now master," and the steel glanced nigh the throat.

Again Don Benito faintly shuddered.

[46]Bernstein points out the resemblance of the Spanish flag to the *sanbenito,* a garment worn by accused heretics in the Inquisition. Penitents wore a yellow sanbenito with a red cross, and the impenitent wore a black one ornamented with flames and devils, signifying that they were condemned to death at the stake.

"You must not shake so, master.—See, Don Amasa, master always shakes when I shave him. And yet master knows I never yet have drawn blood, though it's true, if master will shake so, I may some of these times. Now master," he continued. "And now, Don Amasa, please go on with your talk about the gale, and all that, master can hear, and between times master can answer."

"Ah yes, these gales," said Captain Delano; "but the more I think of your voyage, Don Benito, the more I wonder, not at the gales, terrible as they must have been, but at the disastrous interval following them. For here, by your account, have you been these two months and more getting from Cape Horn to St. Maria, a distance which I myself, with a good wind, have sailed in a few days. True, you had calms, and long ones, but to be becalmed for two months, that is, at least, unusual. Why, Don Benito, had almost any other gentleman told me such a story, I should have been half disposed to a little incredulity."

Here an involuntary expression came over the Spaniard, similar to that just before on the deck, and whether it was the start he gave, or a sudden gawky roll of the hull in the calm, or a momentary unsteadiness of the servant's hand; however it was, just then the razor drew blood, spots of which stained the creamy lather under the throat; immediately the black barber drew back his steel, and remaining in his professional attitude, back to Captain Delano, and face to Don Benito, held up the trickling razor, saying, with a sort of half humorous sorrow, "See, master,—you shook so—here's Babo's first blood."

No sword drawn before James the First of England, no assassination in that timid King's presence,[47] could have produced a more terrified aspect than was now presented by Don Benito.

Poor fellow, thought Captain Delano, so nervous he can't even bear the sight of barber's blood; and this unstrung, sick man, is it credible that I should have imagined he meant to spill all my blood, who can't endure the sight of one little drop of his own? Surely, Amasa Delano, you have been beside yourself this day. Tell it not when you get home, sappy Amasa. Well, well, he looks like a murderer, doesn't he? More like as if himself were to be done for. Well, well, this day's experience shall be a good lesson.

Meantime, while these things were running through the honest seaman's mind, the servant had taken the napkin from his arm, and to Don Benito had said—"But answer Don Amasa, please, master, while I wipe this ugly stuff off the razor, and strop it again."

As he said the words, his face was turned half round, so as to be alike visible to the Spaniard and the American, and seemed by its expression to hint, that he was desirous, by getting his master to go on with the conversation, considerately to withdraw his attention from the recent annoying accident. As if glad to snatch the offered relief, Don Benito resumed, rehearsing to Captain Delano, that not only were the calms of unusual duration, but the ship had fallen in with obstinate currents; and other things he added, some of which were but repetitions of former statements, to explain how it came to pass that the passage from Cape Horn to St. Maria had been so exceedingly long, now and then mingling with his words, incidental praises, less qualified than before, to the blacks, for their general good conduct.

[47] Proverbially timid, James I (1566–1625) was haunted by fears of assassination at Catholic hands, especially after the Gunpowder Plot of 1605.

These particulars were not given consecutively, the servant, at convenient times, using his razor, and so, between the intervals of shaving, the story and panegyric went on with more than usual huskiness.

To Captain Delano's imagination, now again not wholly at rest, there was something so hollow in the Spaniard's manner, with apparently some reciprocal hollowness in the servant's dusky comment of silence, that the idea flashed across him, that possibly master and man, for some unknown purpose, were acting out, both in word and deed, nay, to the very tremor of Don Benito's limbs, some juggling play before him. Neither did the suspicion of collusion lack apparent support, from the fact of those whispered conferences before mentioned. But then, what could be the object of enacting this play of the barber before him? At last, regarding the notion as a whimsy, insensibly suggested, perhaps, by the theatrical aspect of Don Benito in his harlequin ensign, Captain Delano speedily banished it.

The shaving over, the servant bestirred himself with a small bottle of scented waters, pouring a few drops on the head, and then diligently rubbing; the vehemence of the exercise causing the muscles of his face to twitch rather strangely.

His next operation was with comb, scissors and brush; going round and round, smoothing a curl here, clipping an unruly whisker-hair there, giving a graceful sweep to the temple-lock, with other impromptu touches evincing the hand of a master; while, like any resigned gentleman in barber's hands, Don Benito bore all, much less uneasily, at least, than he had done the razoring; indeed, he sat so pale and rigid now, that the negro seemed a Nubian[48] sculptor finishing off a white statue-head.

All being over at last, the standard of Spain removed, tumbled up, and tossed back into the flag-locker, the negro's warm breath blowing away any stray hair which might have lodged down his master's neck; collar and cravat readjusted; a speck of lint whisked off the velvet lapel; all this being done; backing off a little space, and pausing with an expression of subdued self-complacency, the servant for a moment surveyed his master, as, in toilet at least, the creature of his own tasteful hands.

Captain Delano playfully complimented him upon his achievement; at the same time congratulating Don Benito.

But neither sweet waters, nor shampooing, nor fidelity, nor sociality, delighted the Spaniard. Seeing him relapsing into forbidding gloom, and still remaining seated, Captain Delano, thinking that his presence was undesired just then, withdrew, on pretense of seeing whether, as he had prophecied, any signs of a breeze were visible.

Walking forward to the mainmast, he stood awhile thinking over the scene, and not without some undefined misgivings, when he heard a noise near the cuddy, and turning, saw the negro, his hand to his cheek. Advancing, Captain Delano perceived that the cheek was bleeding. He was about to ask the cause, when the negro's wailing soliloquy enlightened him.

"Ah, when will master get better from his sickness; only the sour heart that sour sickness breeds made him serve Babo so; cutting Babo with the razor, because, only by accident, Babo had given master one little scratch; and for the first time in so many a day, too. Ah, ah, ah," holding his hand to his face.

[48]Nubia, an ancient black kingdom in what is now Sudan, was cited by abolitionists along with Egypt as evidence that Africans had a heritage of civilization, not savagery. A Nubian dynasty ruled Egypt in the eighth and seventh centuries B.C., as Egyptian dynasties had earlier ruled Nubia, and a high degree of crossfertilization enriched the two cultures.

Is it possible, thought Captain Delano; was it to wreak in private his Spanish spite against this poor friend of his, that Don Benito, by his sullen manner, impelled me to withdraw? Ah, this slavery breeds ugly passions in man.—Poor fellow!

He was about to speak in sympathy to the negro, but with a timid reluctance he now reëntered the cuddy.

Presently master and man came forth; Don Benito leaning on his servant as if nothing had happened.

But a sort of love-quarrel, after all, thought Captain Delano.

He accosted Don Benito, and they slowly walked together. They had gone but a few paces, when the steward—a tall, rajah-looking mulatto, orientally set off with a pagoda turban formed by three or four Madras handkerchiefs wound about his head, tier on tier—approaching with a salaam, announced lunch in the cabin.

On their way thither, the two Captains were preceded by the mulatto, who, turning round as he advanced, with continual smiles and bows, ushered them on, a display of elegance which quite completed the insignificance of the small bareheaded Babo, who, as if not unconscious of inferiority, eyed askance the graceful steward. But in part, Captain Delano imputed his jealous watchfulness to that peculiar feeling which the full-blooded African entertains for the adulterated one. As for the steward, his manner, if not bespeaking much dignity of self-respect, yet evidenced his extreme desire to please; which is doubly meritorious, as at once Christian and Chesterfieldian.[49]

Captain Delano observed with interest that while the complexion of the mulatto was hybrid, his physiognomy was European; classically so.

"Don Benito," whispered he, "I am glad to see this usher-of-the-golden-rod[50] of yours; the sight refutes an ugly remark once made to me by a Barbadoes planter; that when a mulatto has a regular European face, look out for him; he is a devil. But see, your steward here has features more regular than King George's of England; and yet there he nods, and bows, and smiles; a king, indeed—the king of kind hearts and polite fellows. What a pleasant voice he has, too!"

"He has, Señor."

"But, tell me, has he not, so far as you have known him, always proved a good, worthy fellow?" said Captain Delano, pausing, while with a final genuflexion the steward disappeared into the cabin; "come, for the reason just mentioned, I am curious to know."

"Francesco is a good man," a sort of sluggishly responded Don Benito, like a phlegmatic appreciator, who would neither find fault nor flatter.

"Ah, I thought so. For it were strange indeed, and not very creditable to us white-skins, if a little of our blood mixed with the African's, should, far from improving the latter's quality, have the sad effect of pouring vitriolic acid into black broth; improving the hue, perhaps, but not the wholesomeness."

[49]Philip Dormer Stanhope, fourth Earl of Chesterfield (1694–1773), was famous for the worldly advice on policy and manners that he conveyed in letters to his illegitimate son. Melville often contrasts Chesterfield's code of morality with Christ's.

[50]Melville is punning on the Usher-of-the-Black-Rod who attended the English King. Ushers were officers at court whose duty was to walk before dignitaries of high rank, bearing a rod. In the ensuing discussion, Delano once again echoes racist theories.

"Doubtless, doubtless, Señor, but"—glancing at Babo—"not to speak of negroes, your planter's remark I have heard applied to the Spanish and Indian intermixtures in our provinces. But I know nothing about the matter," he listlessly added.

And here they entered the cabin.

The lunch was a frugal one. Some of Captain Delano's fresh fish and pumpkins, biscuit and salt beef, the reserved bottle of cider, and the San Dominick's last bottle of Canary.

As they entered, Francesco, with two or three colored aids, was hovering over the table giving the last adjustments. Upon perceiving their master they withdrew, Francesco making a smiling congé, and the Spaniard, without condescending to notice it, fastidiously remarking to his companion that he relished not superfluous attendance.

Without companions, host and guest sat down, like a childless married couple, at opposite ends of the table, Don Benito waving Captain Delano to his place, and, weak as he was, insisting upon that gentleman being seated before himself.

The negro placed a rug under Don Benito's feet, and a cushion behind his back, and then stood behind, not his master's chair, but Captain Delano's. At first, this a little surprised the latter. But it was soon evident that, in taking his position, the black was still true to his master; since by facing him he could the more readily anticipate his slightest want.

"This is an uncommonly intelligent fellow of yours, Don Benito," whispered Captain Delano across the table.

"You say true, Señor."

During the repast, the guest again reverted to parts of Don Benito's story, begging further particulars here and there. He inquired how it was that the scurvy and fever should have committed such wholesale havoc upon the whites, while destroying less than half of the blacks. As if this question reproduced the whole scene of plague before the Spaniard's eyes, miserably reminding him of his solitude in a cabin where before he had had so many friends and officers round him, his hand shook, his face became hueless, broken words escaped; but directly the sane memory of the past seemed replaced by insane terrors of the present. With starting eyes he stared before him at vacancy. For nothing was to be seen but the hand of his servant pushing the Canary over towards him. At length a few sips served partially to restore him. He made random reference to the different constitution of races, enabling one to offer more resistance to certain maladies than another. The thought was new to his companion.

Presently Captain Delano, intending to say something to his host concerning the pecuniary part of the business he had undertaken for him, especially—since he was strictly accountable to his owners—with reference to the new suit of sails, and other things of that sort; and naturally preferring to conduct such affairs in private, was desirous that the servant should withdraw; imagining that Don Benito for a few minutes could dispense with his attendance. He, however, waited awhile; thinking that, as the conversation proceeded, Don Benito, without being prompted, would perceive the propriety of the step.

But it was otherwise. At last catching his host's eye, Captain Delano, with a slight backward gesture of his thumb, whispered, "Don Benito, pardon me, but there is an interference with the full expression of what I have to say to you."

Upon this the Spaniard changed countenance; which was imputed to his resenting the hint, as in some way a reflection upon his servant. After a moment's pause, he assured his guest that the black's remaining with them could be of no disservice; because since losing his officers he had made Babo (whose original office, it now appeared, had been captain of the slaves) not only his constant attendant and companion, but in all things his confidant.

After this, nothing more could be said; though, indeed, Captain Delano could hardly avoid some little tinge of irritation upon being left ungratified in so inconsiderable a wish, by one, too, for whom he intended such solid services. But it is only his querulousness, thought he; and so filling his glass he proceeded to business.

The price of the sails and other matters was fixed upon. But while this was being done, the American observed that, though his original offer of assistance had been hailed with hectic animation, yet now when it was reduced to a business transaction, indifference and apathy were betrayed. Don Benito, in fact, appeared to submit to hearing the details more out of regard to common propriety, than from any impression that weighty benefit to himself and his voyage was involved.

Soon, this manner became still more reserved. The effort was vain to seek to draw him into social talk. Gnawed by his splenetic mood, he sat twitching his beard, while to little purpose the hand of his servant, mute as that on the wall,[51] slowly pushed over the Canary.

Lunch being over, they sat down on the cushioned transom; the servant placing a pillow behind his master. The long continuance of the calm had now affected the atmosphere. Don Benito sighed heavily, as if for breath.

"Why not adjourn to the cuddy," said Captain Delano; "there is more air there." But the host sat silent and motionless.

Meantime his servant knelt before him, with a large fan of feathers. And Francesco coming in on tiptoes, handed the negro a little cup of aromatic waters, with which at intervals he chafed his master's brow; smoothing the hair along the temples as a nurse does a child's. He spoke no word. He only rested his eye on his master's, as if, amid all Don Benito's distress, a little to refresh his spirit by the silent sight of fidelity.

Presently the ship's bell sounded two o'clock; and through the cabin-windows a slight rippling of the sea was discerned; and from the desired direction.

"There," exclaimed Captain Delano, "I told you so, Don Benito, look!"

He had risen to his feet, speaking in a very animated tone, with a view the more to rouse his companion. But though the crimson curtain of the stern-window near him that moment fluttered against his pale cheek, Don Benito seemed to have even less welcome for the breeze than the calm.

[51]In Daniel 5, in the midst of a great feast given by King Belshazzar of Babylon, the "fingers of a man's hand" mysteriously appear and begin writing on the palace wall. Like Cereno, Belshazzar blanches and trembles in terror. The Hebrew prophet Daniel interprets the handwriting on the wall to mean that the days of Belshazzar's kingdom are numbered, that Belshazzar has been "weighed in the balances, and . . . found wanting," and that his kingdom is to be divided and given to the Medes and the Persians. The Biblical allusion suggests that the days of the slave empires over which Spain and the United States preside are likewise numbered. By implication, it also identifies Babo's hand with "that on the wall."

Poor fellow, thought Captain Delano, bitter experience has taught him that one ripple does not make a wind, any more than one swallow a summer. But he is mistaken for once. I will get his ship in for him, and prove it.

Briefly alluding to his weak condition, he urged his host to remain quietly where he was, since he (Captain Delano) would with pleasure take upon himself the responsibility of making the best use of the wind.

Upon gaining the deck, Captain Delano started at the unexpected figure of Atufal, monumentally fixed at the threshold, like one of those sculptured porters of black marble guarding the porches of Egyptian tombs.

But this time the start was, perhaps, purely physical. Atufal's presence, singularly attesting docility even in sullenness, was contrasted with that of the hatchet-polishers, who in patience evinced their industry; while both spectacles showed, that lax as Don Benito's general authority might be, still, whenever he chose to exert it, no man so savage or colossal but must, more or less, bow.

Snatching a trumpet which hung from the bulwarks, with a free step Captain Delano advanced to the forward edge of the poop, issuing his orders in his best Spanish. The few sailors and many negroes, all equally pleased, obediently set about heading the ship towards the harbor.

While giving some directions about setting a lower stu'n'-sail, suddenly Captain Delano heard a voice faithfully repeating his orders. Turning, he saw Babo, now for the time acting, under the pilot, his original part of captain of the slaves. This assistance proved valuable. Tattered sails and warped yards were soon brought into some trim. And no brace or halyard was pulled but to the blithe songs of the inspirited negroes.

Good fellows, thought Captain Delano, a little training would make fine sailors of them. Why see, the very women pull and sing too. These must be some of those Ashantee negresses that make such capital soldiers, I've heard. But who's at the helm. I must have a good hand there.

He went to see.

The San Dominick steered with a cumbrous tiller, with large horizontal pullies attached. At each pully-end stood a subordinate black, and between them, at the tiller-head, the responsible post, a Spanish seaman, whose countenance evinced his due share in the general hopefulness and confidence at the coming of the breeze.

He proved the same man who had behaved with so shame-faced an air on the windlass.

"Ah,—it is you, my man," exclaimed Captain Delano—"well, no more sheep's-eyes now;—look straight forward and keep the ship so. Good hand, I trust? And want to get into the harbor, don't you?"

The man assented with an inward chuckle, grasping the tiller-head firmly. Upon this, unperceived by the American, the two blacks eyed the sailor intently.

Finding all right at the helm, the pilot went forward to the forecastle, to see how matters stood there.

The ship now had way enough to breast the current. With the approach of evening, the breeze would be sure to freshen.

Having done all that was needed for the present, Captain Delano, giving his last orders to the sailors, turned aft to report affairs to Don Benito in the cabin; perhaps additionally incited to rejoin him by the hope of snatching a moment's private chat while his servant was engaged upon deck.

From opposite sides, there were, beneath the poop, two approaches to the cabin; one further forward than the other, and consequently communicating with a longer passage. Marking the servant still above, Captain Delano, taking the nighest entrance—the one last named, and at whose porch Atufal still stood—hurried on his way, till, arrived at the cabin threshold, he paused an instant, a little to recover from his eagerness. Then, with the words of his intended business upon his lips, he entered. As he advanced toward the seated Spaniard, he heard another footstep, keeping time with his. From the opposite door, a salver in hand, the servant was likewise advancing.

"Confound the faithful fellow," thought Captain Delano; "what a vexatious coincidence."

Possibly, the vexation might have been something different, were it not for the brisk confidence inspired by the breeze. But even as it was, he felt a slight twinge, from a sudden indefinite association in his mind of Babo with Atufal.

"Don Benito," said he, "I give you joy; the breeze will hold, and will increase. By the way, your tall man and time-piece, Atufal, stands without. By your order, of course?"

Don Benito recoiled, as if at some bland satirical touch, delivered with such adroit garnish of apparent good-breeding as to present no handle for retort.

He is like one flayed alive, thought Captain Delano; where may one touch him without causing a shrink?

The servant moved before his master, adjusting a cushion; recalled to civility, the Spaniard stiffly replied: "you are right. The slave appears where you saw him, according to my command; which is, that if at the given hour I am below, he must take his stand and abide my coming."

"Ah now, pardon me, but that is treating the poor fellow like an ex-king indeed. Ah, Don Benito," smiling, "for all the license you permit in some things, I fear lest, at bottom, you are a bitter hard master."

Again Don Benito shrank; and this time, as the good sailor thought, from a genuine twinge of his conscience.

Again conversation became constrained. In vain Captain Delano called attention to the now perceptible motion of the keel gently cleaving the sea; with lack-lustre eye, Don Benito returned words few and reserved.

By-and-by, the wind having steadily risen, and still blowing right into the harbor, bore the San Dominick swiftly on. Rounding a point of land, the sealer at distance came into open view.

Meantime Captain Delano had again repaired to the deck, remaining there some time. Having at last altered the ship's course, so as to give the reef a wide berth, he returned for a few moments below.

I will cheer up my poor friend, this time, thought he.

"Better and better, Don Benito," he cried as he blithely reëntered; "there will soon be an end to your cares, at least for awhile. For when, after a long, sad voyage, you know, the anchor drops into the haven, all its vast weight seems lifted from the captain's heart. We are getting on famously, Don Benito. My ship is in sight. Look through this side-light here; there she is; all a-taunt-o! The Bachelor's Delight, my good friend. Ah, how this wind braces one up. Come, you must take a cup of coffee with me this evening. My old steward will give you as fine a cup as ever any sultan tasted. What say you, Don Benito, will you?"

At first, the Spaniard glanced feverishly up, casting a longing look towards the sealer, while with mute concern his servant gazed into his face. Suddenly the old ague of coldness returned, and dropping back to his cushions he was silent.

"You do not answer. Come, all day you have been my host; would you have hospitality all on one side?"

"I cannot go," was the response.

"What? it will not fatigue you. The ships will lie together as near as they can, without swinging foul. It will be little more than stepping from deck to deck; which is but as from room to room. Come, come, you must not refuse me."

"I cannot go," decisively and repulsively repeated Don Benito.

Renouncing all but the last appearance of courtesy, with a sort of cadaverous sullenness, and biting his thin nails to the quick, he glanced, almost glared, at his guest; as if impatient that a stranger's presence should interfere with the full indulgence of his morbid hour. Meantime the sound of the parted waters came more and more gurglingly and merrily in at the windows; as reproaching him for his dark spleen; as telling him that, sulk as he might, and go mad with it, nature cared not a jot; since, whose fault was it, pray?

But the foul mood was now at its depth, as the fair wind at its height.

There was something in the man so far beyond any mere unsociality or sourness previously evinced, that even the forbearing good-nature of his guest could no longer endure it. Wholly at a loss to account for such demeanor, and deeming sickness with eccentricity, however extreme, no adequate excuse, well satisfied, too, that nothing in his own conduct could justify it, Captain Delano's pride began to be roused. Himself became reserved. But all seemed one to the Spaniard. Quitting him, therefore, Captain Delano once more went to the deck.

The ship was now within less than two miles of the sealer. The whale-boat was seen darting over the interval.

To be brief, the two vessels, thanks to the pilot's skill, ere long in neighborly style lay anchored together.

Before returning to his own vessel, Captain Delano had intended communicating to Don Benito the smaller details of the proposed services to be rendered. But, as it was, unwilling anew to subject himself to rebuffs, he resolved, now that he had seen the San Dominick safely moored, immediately to quit her, without further allusion to hospitality or business. Indefinitely postponing his ulterior plans, he would regulate his future actions according to future circumstances. His boat was ready to receive him; but his host still tarried below. Well, thought Captain Delano, if he has little breeding, the more need to show mine. He descended to the cabin to bid a ceremonious, and, it may be, tacitly rebukeful adieu. But to his great satisfaction, Don Benito, as if he began to feel the weight of that treatment with which his slighted guest had, not indecorously, retaliated upon him, now supported by his servant, rose to his feet, and grasping Captain Delano's hand, stood tremulous; too much agitated to speak. But the good augury hence drawn was suddenly dashed, by his resuming all his previous reserve, with augmented gloom, as, with half-averted eyes, he silently reseated himself on his cushions. With a corresponding return of his own chilled feelings, Captain Delano bowed and withdrew.

He was hardly midway in the narrow corridor, dim as a tunnel, leading from the cabin to the stairs, when a sound, as of the tolling for execution in some jail-yard, fell on his ears. It was the echo of the ship's flawed bell, striking the hour, drearily reverberated in this subterranean vault. Instantly, by a fatality not to be withstood, his mind, responsive to the portent, swarmed with superstitious suspicions. He paused. In images far swifter than these sentences, the minutest details of all his former distrusts swept through him.

Hitherto, credulous good-nature had been too ready to furnish excuses for reasonable fears. Why was the Spaniard, so superfluously punctilious at times, now heedless of common propriety in not accompanying to the side his departing guest? Did indisposition forbid? Indisposition had not forbidden more irksome exertion that day. His last equivocal demeanor recurred. He had risen to his feet, grasped his guest's hand, motioned toward his hat; then, in an instant, all was eclipsed in sinister muteness and gloom. Did this imply one brief, repentent relenting at the final moment, from some iniquitous plot, followed by remorseless return to it? His last glance seemed to express a calamitous, yet acquiescent farewell to Captain Delano forever. Why decline the invitation to visit the sealer that evening? Or was the Spaniard less hardened than the Jew, who refrained not from supping at the board of him whom the same night he meant to betray?[52] What imported all those day-long enigmas and contradictions, except they were intended to mystify, preliminary to some stealthy blow? Atufal, the pretended rebel, but punctual shadow, that moment lurked by the threshold without. He seemed a sentry, and more. Who, by his own confession, had stationed him there? Was the negro now lying in wait?

The Spaniard behind—his creature before: to rush from darkness to light was the involuntary choice.

The next moment, with clenched jaw and hand, he passed Atufal, and stood unharmed in the light. As he saw his trim ship lying peacefully at her anchor, and almost within ordinary call; as he saw his household boat, with familiar faces in it, patiently rising and falling on the short waves by the San Dominick's side; and then, glancing about the decks where he stood, saw the oakum-pickers still gravely plying their fingers; and heard the low, buzzing whistle and industrious hum of the hatchet-polishers, still bestirring themselves over their endless occupation; and more than all, as he saw the benign aspect of nature, taking her innocent repose in the evening; the screened sun in the quiet camp of the west shining out like the mild light from Abraham's tent; as charmed eye and ear took in all these, with the chained figure of the black, clenched jaw and hand relaxed. Once again he smiled at the phantoms which had mocked him, and felt something like a tinge of remorse, that, by harboring them even for a moment, he should, by implication, have betrayed an almost atheist doubt of the ever-watchful Providence above.[53]

There was a few minutes' delay, while, in obedience to his orders, the boat was being hooked along to the gangway. During this interval, a sort of saddened satisfaction stole over Captain Delano, at thinking of the kindly offices he had that day discharged for a stranger. Ah, thought he, after good actions one's conscience is never ungrateful, however much so the benefited party may be.

Presently, his foot, in the first act of descent into the boat, pressed the first round of the side-ladder, his face presented inward upon the deck. In the same moment, he

[52]Judas, who sat with Jesus at the Last Supper before betraying him (Matthew 26:20–25).

[53]In contrast to Delano, who considers it atheistic to doubt that Providence benevolently keeps the black man in chains, Melville in the prose Supplement to his volume of Civil War poetry, *Battle-Pieces,* calls slavery an "atheistical iniquity."

heard his name courteously sounded; and, to his pleased surprise, saw Don Benito advancing—an unwonted energy in his air, as if, at the last moment, intent upon making amends for his recent discourtesy. With instinctive good feeling, Captain Delano, withdrawing his foot, turned and reciprocally advanced. As he did so, the Spaniard's nervous eagerness increased, but his vital energy failed; so that, the better to support him, the servant, placing his master's hand on his naked shoulder, and gently holding it there, formed himself into a sort of crutch.

When the two captains met, the Spaniard again fervently took the hand of the American, at the same time casting an earnest glance into his eyes, but, as before, too much overcome to speak.

I have done him wrong, self-reproachfully thought Captain Delano; his apparent coldness has deceived me; in no instance has he meant to offend.

Meantime, as if fearful that the continuance of the scene might too much unstring his master, the servant seemed anxious to terminate it. And so, still presenting himself as a crutch, and walking between the two captains, he advanced with them towards the gangway; while still, as if full of kindly contrition, Don Benito would not let go the hand of Captain Delano, but retained it in his, across the black's body.

Soon they were standing by the side, looking over into the boat, whose crew turned up their curious eyes. Waiting a moment for the Spaniard to relinquish his hold, the now embarrassed Captain Delano lifted his foot, to overstep the threshold of the open gangway; but still Don Benito would not let go his hand. And yet, with an agitated tone, he said, "I can go no further; here I must bid you adieu. Adieu, my dear, dear Don Amasa. Go—go!" suddenly tearing his hand loose, "go, and God guard you better than me, my best friend."

Not unaffected, Captain Delano would now have lingered; but catching the meekly admonitory eye of the servant, with a hasty farewell he descended into his boat, followed by the continual adieus of Don Benito, standing rooted in the gangway.

Seating himself in the stern, Captain Delano, making a last salute, ordered the boat shoved off. The crew had their oars on end. The bowsman pushed the boat a sufficient distance for the oars to be lengthwise dropped. The instant that was done, Don Benito sprang over the bulwarks, falling at the feet of Captain Delano; at the same time, calling towards his ship, but in tones so frenzied, that none in the boat could understand him. But, as if not equally obtuse, three sailors, from three different and distant parts of the ship, splashed into the sea, swimming after their captain, as if intent upon his rescue.

The dismayed officer of the boat eagerly asked what this meant. To which, Captain Delano, turning a disdainful smile upon the unaccountable Spaniard, answered that, for his part, he neither knew nor cared; but it seemed as if Don Benito had taken it into his head to produce the impression among his people that the boat wanted to kidnap him. "Or else—give way for your lives," he wildly added, starting at a clattering hubbub in the ship, above which rang the tocsin[54] of the hatchet-polishers; and seizing Don Benito by the throat he added, "this plotting pirate means murder!" Here, in apparent verification of the words, the servant, a dagger in his hand, was seen on the rail overhead, poised, in the act of leaping, as if

[54]Alarm bell.

with desperate fidelity to befriend his master to the last; while, seemingly to aid the black, the three white sailors were trying to clamber into the hampered bow. Meantime, the whole host of negroes, as if inflamed at the sight of their jeopardized captain, impended in one sooty avalanche over the bulwarks.

All this, with what preceded, and what followed, occurred with such involutions of rapidity, that past, present, and future seemed one.

Seeing the negro coming, Captain Delano had flung the Spaniard aside, almost in the very act of clutching him, and, by the unconscious recoil, shifting his place, with arms thrown up, so promptly grappled the servant in his descent, that with dagger presented at Captain Delano's heart, the black seemed of purpose to have leaped there as to his mark. But the weapon was wrenched away, and the assailant dashed down into the bottom of the boat, which now, with disentangled oars, began to speed through the sea.

At this juncture, the left hand of Captain Delano, on one side, again clutched the half-reclined Don Benito, heedless that he was in a speechless faint, while his right foot, on the other side, ground the prostrate negro;[55] and his right arm pressed for added speed on the after oar, his eye bent forward, encouraging his men to their utmost.

But here, the officer of the boat, who had at last succeeded in beating off the towing sailors, and was now, with face turned aft, assisting the bowsman at his oar, suddenly called to Captain Delano, to see what the black was about; while a Portuguese oarsman shouted to him to give heed to what the Spaniard was saying.

Glancing down at his feet, Captain Delano saw the freed hand of the servant aiming with a second dagger—a small one, before concealed in his wool—with this he was snakishly writhing up from the boat's bottom, at the heart of his master, his countenance lividly vindictive, expressing the centred purpose of his soul; while the Spaniard, half-choked, was vainly shrinking away, with husky words, incoherent to all but the Portuguese.

That moment, across the long-benighted mind of Captain Delano, a flash of revelation swept, illuminating in unanticipated clearness his host's whole mysterious demeanor, with every enigmatic event of the day, as well as the entire past voyage of the San Dominick. He smote Babo's hand down, but his own heart smote him harder. With infinite pity he withdrew his hold from Don Benito. Not Captain Delano, but Don Benito, the black, in leaping into the boat, had intended to stab.

Both the black's hands were held, as, glancing up towards the San Dominick, Captain Delano, now with the scales dropped from his eyes, saw the negroes, not in misrule, not in tumult, not as if frantically concerned for Don Benito, but with mask torn away, flourishing hatchets and knives, in ferocious piratical revolt. Like delirious black dervishes, the six Ashantees danced on the poop. Prevented by their foes from springing into the water, the Spanish boys were hurrying up to the topmost spars, while such of the few Spanish sailors, not already in the sea, less alert, were descried, helplessly mixed in, on deck, with the blacks.

Meantime Captain Delano hailed his own vessel, ordering the ports up and the guns run out. But by this time the cable of the San Dominick had been cut; and the

[55]Compare with the description of the "symbolical devices" on the *San Dominick*'s "shield-like stern-piece," p. 2500.

fag-end, in lashing out, whipped away the canvas shroud about the beak, suddenly revealing, as the bleached hull swung round towards the open ocean, death for the figure-head, in a human skeleton; chalky comment on the chalked words below, *"Follow your leader."*

At the sight, Don Benito, covering his face, wailed out: "'Tis he, Aranda! my murdered, unburied friend!"

Upon reaching the sealer, calling for ropes, Captain Delano bound the negro, who made no resistance, and had him hoisted to the deck. He would then have assisted the now almost helpless Don Benito up the side; but Don Benito, wan as he was, refused to move, or be moved, until the negro should have been first put below out of view. When, presently assured that it was done, he no more shrank from the ascent.

The boat was immediately dispatched back to pick up the three swimming sailors. Meantime, the guns were in readiness, though, owing to the San Dominick having glided somewhat astern of the sealer, only the aftermost one could be brought to bear. With this, they fired six times; thinking to cripple the fugitive ship by bringing down her spars. But only a few inconsiderable ropes were shot away. Soon the ship was beyond the gun's range, steering broad out of the bay; the blacks thickly clustering round the bowsprit, one moment with taunting cries towards the whites, the next with upthrown gestures hailing the now dusky moors of ocean—cawing crows escaped from the hand of the fowler.

The first impulse was to slip the cables and give chase. But, upon second thoughts, to pursue with whale-boat and yawl seemed more promising.

Upon inquiring of Don Benito what fire arms they had on board the San Dominick, Captain Delano was answered that they had none that could be used; because, in the earlier stages of the mutiny, a cabin-passenger, since dead, had secretly put out of order the locks of what few muskets there were. But with all his remaining strength, Don Benito entreated the American not to give chase, either with ship or boat; for the negroes had already proved themselves such desperadoes, that, in case of a present assault, nothing but a total massacre of the whites could be looked for. But, regarding this warning as coming from one whose spirit had been crushed by misery, the American did not give up his design.

The boats were got ready and armed. Captain Delano ordered his men into them. He was going himself when Don Benito grasped his arm.

"What! have you saved my life, señor, and are you now going to throw away your own?"

The officers also, for reasons connected with their interests and those of the voyage, and a duty owing to the owners, strongly objected against their commander's going. Weighing their remonstrances a moment, Captain Delano felt bound to remain; appointing his chief mate—an athletic and resolute man, who had been a privateer's-man,[56] and, as his enemies whispered, a pirate—to head the party. The more to encourage the sailors, they were told, that the Spanish captain considered his ship as good as lost; that she and her cargo, including some gold and silver, were

[56]A privateer was a pirate commissioned by a government to prey on foreign shipping, like the British pirates who preyed on Spanish shipping in the sixteenth and seventeenth centuries. In *The Piazza Tales* version, Melville omitted the phrase "and, as his enemies whispered, a pirate," perhaps to eliminate the distinction between privateering and piracy. He added this detail to his source.

worth more than a thousand doubloons. Take her, and no small part should be theirs. The sailors replied with a shout.

The fugitives had now almost gained an offing. It was nearly night; but the moon was rising. After hard, prolonged pulling, the boats came up on the ship's quarters, at a suitable distance laying upon their oars to discharge their muskets. Having no bullets to return, the negroes sent their yells. But, upon the second volley, Indian-like, they hurtled their hatchets. One took off a sailor's fingers. Another struck the whale-boat's bow, cutting off the rope there, and remaining stuck in the gunwale like a woodman's axe. Snatching it, quivering from its lodgment, the mate hurled it back. The returned gauntlet now stuck in the ship's broken quarter-gallery, and so remained.

The negroes giving too hot a reception, the whites kept a more respectful distance. Hovering now just out of reach of the hurtling hatchets, they, with a view to the close encounter which must soon come, sought to decoy the blacks into entirely disarming themselves of their most murderous weapons in a hand-to-hand fight, by foolishly flinging them, as missiles, short of the mark, into the sea. But ere long perceiving the stratagem, the negroes desisted, though not before many of them had to replace their lost hatchets with handspikes; an exchange which, as counted upon, proved in the end favorable to the assailants.

Meantime, with a strong wind, the ship still clove the water; the boats alternately falling behind, and pulling up, to discharge fresh volleys.

The fire was mostly directed towards the stern, since there, chiefly, the negroes, at present, were clustering. But to kill or maim the negroes was not the object. To take them, with the ship, was the object. To do it, the ship must be boarded; which could not be done by boats while she was sailing so fast.

A thought now struck the mate. Observing the Spanish boys still aloft, high as they could get, he called to them to descend to the yards, and cut adrift the sails. It was done. About this time, owing to causes hereafter to be shown, two Spaniards, in the dress of sailors and conspicuously showing themselves, were killed; not by volleys, but by deliberate marksman's shots; while, as it afterwards appeared, by one of the general discharges, Atufal, the black, and the Spaniard at the helm likewise were killed. What now, with the loss of the sails, and loss of leaders, the ship became unmanageable to the negroes.

With creaking masts, she came heavily round to the wind; the prow slowly swinging, into view of the boats, its skeleton gleaming in the horizontal moonlight, and casting a gigantic ribbed shadow upon the water. One extended arm of the ghost seemed beckoning the whites to avenge it.

"Follow your leader!" cried the mate; and, one on each bow, the boats boarded. Sealing-spears and cutlasses crossed hatchets and hand-spikes. Huddled upon the long-boat amidships, the negresses raised a wailing chant, whose chorus was the clash of the steel.

For a time, the attack wavered; the negroes wedging themselves to beat it back; the half-repelled sailors, as yet unable to gain a footing, fighting as troopers in the saddle, one leg sideways flung over the bulwarks, and one without, plying their cutlasses like carters' whips. But in vain. They were almost overborne, when, rallying themselves into a squad as one man, with a huzza, they sprang inboard; where, entangled, they involuntarily separated again. For a few breaths' space, there was a vague, muffled, inner sound, as of submerged sword-fish rushing hither and thither through shoals of black-fish. Soon, in a reunited band, and joined by the Spanish seamen, the whites came to the surface, irresistibly driving the negroes toward the stern. But a barricade of casks and sacks, from side to side, had been thrown up by the mainmast. Here the negroes faced about, and though scorning peace or truce, yet fain would have had a respite. But, without pause, overleaping the barrier, the unflagging sailors again closed. Exhausted, the blacks now fought in despair. Their red tongues lolled, wolf-like, from their black mouths. But the pale sailors' teeth were set; not a word was spoken; and, in five minutes more, the ship was won.

Nearly a score of the negroes were killed. Exclusive of those by the balls, many were mangled; their wounds—mostly inflicted by the long-edged sealing-spears—resembling those shaven ones of the English at Preston Pans, made by the poled scythes of the Highlanders.[57] On the other side, none were killed, though several were wounded; some severely, including the mate. The surviving negroes were temporarily secured, and the ship, towed back into the harbor at midnight, once more lay anchored.

Omitting the incidents and arrangements ensuing, suffice it that, after two days spent in refitting, the two ships sailed in company for Conception, in Chili, and thence for Lima, in Peru; where, before the vice-regal courts, the whole affair, from the beginning, underwent investigation.

Though, midway on the passage, the ill-fated Spaniard, relaxed from constraint, showed some signs of regaining health with free-will; yet, agreeably to his own foreboding, shortly before arriving at Lima, he relapsed, finally becoming so reduced as to be carried ashore in arms. Hearing of his story and plight, one of the many religious institutions of the City of Kings opened an hospitable refuge to him, where both physician and priest were his nurses, and a member of the order volunteered to be his one special guardian and consoler, by night and by day.

The following extracts, translated from one of the official Spanish documents, will it is hoped, shed light on the preceding narrative, as well as, in the first place, reveal the true port of departure and true history of the San Dominick's voyage, down to the time of her touching at the island of St. Maria.[58]

But, ere the extracts come, it may be well to preface them with a remark.

The document selected, from among many others, for partial translation, con-

[57]At the battle of Prestonpans in 1745, Scottish Highlanders under Charles Edward Stuart, armed mainly with scythes, axes, and swords, routed and butchered British forces.

[58]Melville substantially rewrote the Deposition found in Delano's *Narrative.* One effect of his revisions is to emphasize the biased, self-serving point of view from which the "official" version of events is being presented, by accentuating the ferocity of the slaves and whitewashing Don Benito, the author of the Deposition. At the same time, the many embellishments Melville introduces have the effect of highlighting the brilliance of Babo's plot and the subtlety of his mind. For example, Melville invents and credits to Babo the devices of the oakum-pickers, the hatchet-polishers, and the chains worn by Atufal; the use of the Spanish flag as a bib and sanbenito; and the preparation of the skeleton substituted for the figurehead of Columbus.

As mentioned above, Melville also changed the date of the events from 1805 to 1799. H. Bruce Franklin has pointed out that the revised date and name link the slave revolt on board the *San Dominick* with the most famous slave revolt in history, the Santo Domingo uprising of 1791–1804, led by Toussaint L'Ouverture, who began extending his rule over the entire island in 1799.

Also relevant to the story, as Sidney Kaplan has shown, are the revolts on board the Spanish slave-trading schooner *Amistad* in 1839 and the American domestic slave-trading brig *Creole* in tains the deposition of Benito Cereno; the first taken in the case. Some disclosures therein were, at the time, held dubious for both learned and natural reasons. The tribunal inclined to the opinion that the deponent, not undisturbed in his mind by recent events, raved of some things which could never have happened. But subsequent depositions of the surviving sailors, bearing out the revelations of their captain in several of the strangest particulars, gave credence to the rest. So that the tribunal, in its final decision, rested its capital sentences upon statements which, had they lacked confirmation, it would have deemed it but duty to reject.

I, DON JOSE DE ABOS AND PADILLA, His Majesty's Notary for the Royal Revenue, and Register of this Province, and Notary Public of the Holy Crusade of this Bishopric, etc.

Do certify and declare, as much as is requisite in law, that, in the criminal cause commenced the twenty-fourth of the month of September, in the year seventeen hundred and ninety-nine, against the negroes of the ship San Dominick, the following declaration before me was made.

Declaration of the first witness, DON BENITO CERENO.

The same day, and month, and year, His Honor, Doctor Juan Martinez de Rozas, Councilor of the Royal Audience of this Kingdom, and learned in the law of this Intendency, ordered the captain of the ship San Dominick, Don Benito Cereno, to appear; which he did in his litter, attended by the monk Infelez; of whom he received the oath, which he took by God, our Lord, and a sign of the Cross; under which he promised to tell the truth of whatever he should know and should be asked;—and being interrogated agreeably to the tenor of the act commencing the process, he said, that on the twentieth of May last, he set sail with his ship from the port of Valparaiso, bound to that of Callao; loaded with the produce of the country beside thirty cases of hardware and one hundred and sixty blacks, of both sexes, mostly belonging to Don Alexandro Aranda, gentleman, of the city of Mendoza; that the crew of the ship consisted of thirty-six men, beside the persons who went as passengers; that the negroes were in part as follows:

1841. The *Amistad* case in particular seems to have furnished Melville with additional details, as Jean Fagan Yellin has shown. Led by a West African captive named Cinque or Singbe, the *Amistad*'s fifty-three recently kidnaped Africans mutinied near Cuba, killed the captain and two crew members, and demanded that their Spanish owner, a former sea captain, navigate them back to Africa, threatening him with death if he betrayed them. He adopted the ruse of shifting the vessel's course at night, sailing north instead of east. After a voyage of two months, during which supplies gave out, barnacles accumulated, the sails disintegrated, and two American ships tried to take the *Amistad* in tow, but were frightened off when the Africans tried to board, the *Amistad* finally landed on Long Island. The American brig of war *Washington,* whose officers hoped to claim the *Amistad*'s cargo as salvage, took the rebels into custody, and the Africans remained in jail for two years until the Supreme Court freed them in 1841. Charges of piracy were central to the trial. The press had repeatedly described the *Amistad* as a pirate ship when it was sighted off the East coast, but the Africans' abolitionist defense team, headed by former President John Quincy Adams, succeeded in casting the onus of piracy on the ship's captain and owner by proving that the *Amistad* rebels had been illegally kidnapped from Africa in violation of international laws branding the slave trade as piracy.

[Here, in the original, follows a list of some fifty names, descriptions, and ages, compiled from certain recovered documents of Aranda's, and also from recollections of the deponent, from which portions only are extracted.]

—One, from about eighteen to nineteen years, named José, and this was the man that waited upon his master, Don Alexandro, and who speaks well the Spanish, having served him four or five years; * * * a mulatto, named Francesco, the cabin steward, of a good person and voice, having sung in the Valparaiso churches, native of the province of Buenos Ayres, aged about thirty-five years. * * * A smart negro, named Dago, who had been for many years a grave-digger among the Spaniards, aged forty-six years. * * * Four old negroes, born in Africa, from sixty to seventy, but sound, calkers by trade, whose names are as follows:—the first was named Mure, and he was killed (as was also his son named Diamelo); the second, Natu; the third, Yola, likewise killed; the fourth, Ghofan; and six full-grown negroes, aged from thirty to forty-five, all raw, and born among the Ashantees—Matiluqui, Yau, Lecbe, Mapenda, Yambaio, Akim; four of whom were killed; * * * a powerful negro named Atufal, who, being supposed to have been a chief in Africa, his owners set great store by him. * * * And a small negro of Senegal, but some years among the Spaniards, aged about thirty, which negro's name was Babo; * * * that he does not remember the names of the others, but that still expecting the residue of Don Alexandro's papers will be found, will then take due account of them all, and remit to the court; * * * and thirty-nine women and children of all ages.

[The catalogue over, the deposition goes on:]

* * * That all the negroes slept upon deck, as is customary in this navigation, and none wore fetters, because the owner, his friend Aranda, told him that they were all tractable; * * * that on the seventh day after leaving port, at three o'clock in the morning, all the Spaniards being asleep except the two officers on the watch, who were the boatswain, Juan Robles, and the carpenter, Juan Bautista Gayete, and the helmsman and his boy, the negroes revolted suddenly, wounded dangerously the boatswain and the carpenter, and successively killed eighteen men of those who were sleeping upon deck, some with hand-spikes and hatchets, and others by throwing them alive overboard, after tying them; that of the Spaniards upon deck, they left about seven, as he thinks, alive and tied, to manoeuvre the ship, and three or four more who hid themselves, remained also alive. Although in the act of revolt the negroes made themselves masters of the hatchway, six or seven wounded went through it to the cockpit, without any hindrance on their part; that during the act of revolt, the mate and another person, whose name he does not recollect, attempted to come up through the hatchway, but being quickly wounded, they were obliged to return to the cabin; that the deponent resolved at break of day to come up the companion-way, where the negro Babo was, being the ringleader, and Atufal, who assisted him, and having spoken to them, exhorted them to cease committing such atrocities, asking them, at the same time, what they wanted and intended to do, offering, himself, to obey their commands; that, notwithstanding this, they threw, in his presence, three men, alive and tied, overboard; that they told the deponent to come up, and that they would not kill him; which having done, the negro Babo asked him whether there were in those seas any negro countries where they might be carried, and he answered them, No; that the negro Babo afterwards told him to carry them to Senegal, or to

the neighboring islands of St. Nicolas; and he answered, that this was impossible, on account of the great distance, the necessity involved of rounding Cape Horn, the bad condition of the vessel, the want of provisions, sails, and water; but that the negro Babo replied to him he must carry them in any way; that they would do and conform themselves to everything the deponent should require as to eating and drinking; that after a long conference, being absolutely compelled to please them, for they threatened him to kill all the whites if they were not, at all events, carried to Senegal, he told them that what was most wanting for the voyage was water; that they would go near the coast to take it, and thence they would proceed on their course; that the negro Babo agreed to it; and the deponent steered towards the intermediate ports, hoping to meet some Spanish or foreign vessel that would save them; that within ten or eleven days they saw the land, and continued their course by it in the vicinity of Nasca; that the deponent observed that the negroes were now restless and mutinous, because he did not effect the taking in of water, the negro Babo having required, with threats, that it should be done, without fail, the following day; he told him they saw plainly that the coast was steep, and the rivers designated in the maps were not to be found, with other reasons suitable to the circumstances; that the best way would be to go to the island of Santa Maria, where they might water and victual easily, it being a solitary island, as the foreigners did; that the deponent did not go to Pisco, that was near, nor make any other port of the coast, because the negro Babo had intimated to him several times, that he would kill all the whites the very moment he should perceive any city, town, or settlement of any kind on the shores to which they should be carried: that having determined to go to the island of Santa Maria, as the deponent had planned, for the purpose of trying whether, on the passage or near the island itself, they could find any vessel that should favor them, or whether he could escape from it in a boat to the neighboring coast of Arauco; to adopt the necessary means he immediately changed his course, steering for the island; that the negroes Babo and Atufal held daily conferences, in which they discussed what was necessary for their design of returning to Senegal, whether they were to kill all the Spaniards, and particularly the deponent; that eight days after parting from the coast of Nasca, the deponent being on the watch a little after day-break, and soon after the negroes had their meeting, the negro Babo came to the place where the deponent was, and told him that he had determined to kill his master, Don Alexandro Aranda, both because he and his companions could not otherwise be sure of their liberty, and that, to keep the seamen in subjection, he wanted to prepare a warning of what road they should be made to take did they or any of them oppose him; and that, by means of the death of Don Alexandro, that warning would best be given; but, that what this last meant, the deponent did not at the time comprehend, nor could not, further than that the death of Don Alexandro was intended; and moreover, the negro Babo proposed to the deponent to call the mate Raneds, who was sleeping in the cabin, before the thing was done, for fear, as the deponent understood it, that the mate, who was a good navigator, should be killed with Don Alexandro and the rest; that the deponent, who was the friend, from youth, of Don Alexandro, prayed and conjured, but all was useless; for the negro Babo answered him that the thing could not be prevented, and that all the Spaniards risked their death if they should attempt to frustrate his will in this matter, or any other; that, in this conflict, the deponent called the mate, Raneds, who was forced to go apart, and immediately the negro Babo commanded the Ashantee Matiluqui and the Ashantee Lecbe to go and commit the murder; that those two went down with hatchets to the berth of Don Alexandro; that, yet half alive and mangled, they dragged him on deck; that they were going to throw him overboard in that state, but the negro Babo stopped them bidding the murder be completed on the deck before him, which was done, when, by his orders, the body was carried below, forward; that nothing more was seen of it by the deponent for three days; * * * that Don Alonzo Sidonia, an old man, long resident at Valparaiso, and lately appointed to a civil office in Peru, whither he had taken passage, was at the time sleeping in the berth opposite Don Alexandro's; that, awakening at his cries, surprised by them, and at the sight of the negroes with their bloody hatchets in their hands, he threw himself into the sea through a window which was near him, and was drowned, without it being in the power of the deponent to assist or take him up; * * * that, a short time after killing Aranda, they brought upon deck his german-cousin, of middle-age, Don Francisco Masa, of Mendoza, and the young Don Joaquin, Marques de Arambaolaza, then lately from Spain, with his Spanish servant Ponce, and the three young clerks of Aranda, José Morairi, Lorenzo Bargas, and Hermenegildo Gandix, all of Cadiz; that Don Joaquin and Hermenegildo Gandix, the negro Babo for purposes hereafter to appear, preserved alive; but Don Francisco Masa, José Morairi, and Lorenzo Bargas, with Ponce the servant, beside the boatswain, Juan Robles, the boatswain's mates, Manuel Viscaya and Roderigo Hurta, and four of the sailors, the negro Babo ordered to be thrown alive into the sea, although they made no resistance, nor begged for anything else but mercy; that the boatswain, Juan Robles, who knew how to swim, kept the longest above water, making acts of contrition, and, in the last words he uttered, charged this deponent to cause mass to be said for his soul to our Lady of Succor; * * * that, during the three days which followed, the deponent, uncertain what fate had befallen the remains of Don Alexandro, frequently asked the negro Babo where they were, and, if still on board, whether they were to be preserved for interment ashore, entreating him so to order it; that the negro Babo answered nothing till the fourth day, when at sunrise, the deponent coming on deck, the negro Babo showed him a skeleton, which had been substituted for the ship's proper figure-head, the image of Christopher Colon, the discoverer of the New World; that the negro Babo asked him whose skeleton that was, and whether, from its whiteness, he should not think it a white's; that, upon his covering his face, the negro Babo, coming close, said words to this effect: "Keep faith with the blacks from here to Senegal, or you shall in spirit, as now in body, follow your leader," pointing to the prow; * * * that the same morning the negro Babo took by succession each Spaniard forward, and asked him whose skeleton that was, and whether, from its whiteness, he should not think it a white's; that each Spaniard covered his face; that then to each the negro Babo repeated the words in the first place said to the deponent; * * * that they (the Spaniards), being then assembled aft, the negro Babo harangued them, saying that he had now done all; that the deponent (as navigator for the negroes) might pursue his course, warning him and all of them that they should, soul and body, go the way of Don Alexandro if he saw them (the Spaniards) speak or plot anything against them (the negroes)—a threat which was repeated every day; that, before the events last mentioned, they had tied the cook to throw him overboard, for it is not known what thing they heard him speak, but finally the negro Babo spared his life, at the request of the deponent; that a few days after, the deponent, endeavoring not to omit any means to preserve the lives of the remaining whites, spoke to the negroes peace and tranquillity, and agreed to draw up a paper, signed by the deponent and the sailors who could write, as also by the negro Babo, for himself and all the blacks, in which the deponent obliged himself to carry them to Senegal, and they not to kill any more, and he formally to make over to them the ship, with the cargo, with which they were for that time satisfied and quieted. * * * But the next day, the more surely to guard against the sailors' escape, the negro Babo commanded all the boats to be destroyed but the long-boat, which was unseaworthy, and another, a cutter in good condition, which, knowing it would yet be wanted for towing the water casks, he had it lowered down into the hold.

[Various particulars of the prolonged and perplexed navigation ensuing here follow, with incidents of a calamitous calm, from which portion one passage is extracted, to wit:]

—That on the fifth day of the calm, all on board suffering much from the heat, and want of water, and five having died in fits, and mad, the negroes became irritable, and for a chance gesture, which they deemed suspicious—though it was harmless—made by the mate, Raneds, to the deponent, in the act of handing a quadrant, they killed him; but that for this they afterwards were sorry, the mate being the only remaining navigator on board, except the deponent.

—That omitting other events, which daily happened, and which can only serve uselessly to recall past misfortunes and conflicts, after seventy-three days' navigation, reckoned from the time they sailed from Nasca, during which they navigated under a scanty allowance of water, and were afflicted with the calms before mentioned, they at last arrived at the island of Santa Maria, on the seventeenth of the month of August, at about six o'clock in the afternoon, at which hour they cast anchor very near the American ship, Bachelor's Delight, which lay in the same bay, commanded by the generous Captain Amasa Delano; but at six o'clock in the morning, they had already descried the port, and the negroes became uneasy, as soon as at distance they saw the ship, not having expected to see one there; that the negro Babo pacified them, assuring them that no fear need be had; that straightway he ordered the figure on the bow to be covered with canvas, as for repairs, and had the decks a little set in order; that for a time the negro Babo and the negro Atufal conferred; that the negro Atufal was for sailing away, but the negro Babo would not, and, by himself, cast about what to do; that at last he came to the deponent, proposing to him to say and do all that the deponent declares to have said and done to the American captain; * * * * * * that the negro Babo warned him that if he varied in the least, or uttered any word, or gave any look that should give the least intimation of the past events or present state, he would instantly kill him, with all his companions, showing a dagger, which he carried hid, saying something which, as he understood it, meant that that dagger would be alert as his eye; that the negro Babo then announced the plan to all his companions, which pleased them; that he then, the better to disguise the truth, devised many expedients, in some of them uniting deceit and defense; that of this sort was the device of the six Ashantees before named, who were his bravoes;[59] that them he stationed on the break of the poop, as if to clean certain hatchets (in cases,

[59]Hired soldiers or assassins.

which were part of the cargo), but in reality to use them, and distribute them at need, and at a given word he told them; that, among other devices, was the device of presenting Atufal, his right-hand man, as chained, though in a moment the chains could be dropped; that in every particular he informed the deponent what part he was expected to enact in every device, and what story he was to tell on every occasion, always threatening him with instant death if he varied in the least: that, conscious that many of the negroes would be turbulent, the negro Babo appointed the four aged negroes, who were calkers, to keep what domestic order they could on the decks; that again and again he harangued the Spaniards and his companions, informing them of his intent, and of his devices, and of the invented story that this deponent was to tell, charging them lest any of them varied from that story; that these arrangements were made and matured during the interval of two or three hours, between their first sighting the ship and the arrival on board of Captain Amasa Delano; that this happened about half-past seven o'clock in the morning, Captain Amasa Delano coming in his boat, and all gladly receiving him; that the deponent, as well as he could force himself, acting then the part of principal owner, and a free captain of the ship, told Captain Amasa Delano, when called upon, that he came from Buenos Ayres, bound to Lima, with three hundred negroes; that off Cape Horn, and in a subsequent fever, many negroes had died; that also, by similar casualties, all the sea officers and the greatest part of the crew had died.

* * * * *

[And so the deposition goes on, circumstantially recounting the fictitious story dictated to the deponent by Babo, and through the deponent imposed upon Captain Delano; and also recounting the friendly offers of Captain Delano, with other things, but all of which is here omitted. After the fictitious, strange story, etc., the deposition proceeds:]

—that the generous Captain Amasa Delano remained on board all the day, till he left the ship anchored at six o'clock in the evening, deponent speaking to him always of his pretended misfortunes, under the fore-mentioned principles, without having had it in his power to tell a single word, or give him the least hint, that he might know the truth and state of things; because the negro Babo, performing the office of an officious servant with all the appearance of submission of the humble slave, did not leave the deponent one moment; that this was in order to observe the deponent's actions and words, for the negro Babo understands well the Spanish; and besides, there were thereabout some others who were constantly on the watch, and likewise understood the Spanish; * * * that upon one occasion, while deponent was standing on the deck conversing with Amasa Delano, by a secret sign the negro Babo drew him (the deponent) aside, the act appearing as if originating with the deponent; that then, he being drawn aside, the negro Babo proposed to him to gain from Amasa Delano full particulars about his ship, and crew, and arms; that the deponent asked "For what?" that the negro Babo answered he might conceive; that, grieved at the prospect of what might overtake the generous Captain Amasa Delano, the deponent at first refused to ask the desired questions, and used every argument to induce the negro Babo to give up this new design; that the negro Babo showed the point of his dagger; that, after the information had been obtained, the negro Babo again drew him aside, telling him that that very night he (the deponent) would be captain of two ships, instead of one, for that, great part of the American's ship's crew being to be absent fishing, the six Ashantees, without any one else, would easily take it; that at this time he said other things to the same purpose; that no entreaties availed; that, before Amasa Delano's coming on board, no hint had been given touching the capture of the American ship: that to prevent this project the deponent was powerless; * * *—that in some things his memory is confused, he cannot distinctly recall every event; * * *—that as soon as they had cast anchor at six of the clock in the evening, as has before been stated, the American Captain took leave to return to his vessel; that upon a sudden impulse, which the deponent believes to have come from God and his angels, he, after the farewell had been said, followed the generous Captain Amasa Delano as far as the gunwale, where he stayed, under pretense of taking leave, until Amasa Delano should have been seated in his boat; that on shoving off, the deponent sprang from the gunwale into the boat, and fell into it, he knows not how, God guarding him; that—

[Here, in the original, follows the account of what further happened at the escape, and how the San Dominick was retaken, and of the passage to the coast; including in the recital many expressions of "eternal gratitude" to the "generous Captain Amasa Delano." The deposition then proceeds with recapitulatory remarks, and a partial renumeration of the negroes, making record of their individual part in the past events, with a view to furnishing, according to command of the court, the data whereon to found the criminal sentences to be pronounced. From this portion is the following:]

—That he believes that all the negroes, though not in the first place knowing to the design of revolt, when it was accomplished, approved it. * * * That the negro, José, eighteen years old, and in the personal service of Don Alexandro, was the one who communicated the information to the negro Babo, about the state of things in the cabin, before the revolt; that this is known, because, in the preceding midnights, he used to come from his berth, which was under his master's, in the cabin, to the deck where the ringleader and his associates were, and had secret conversations with the negro Babo, in which he was several times seen by the mate; that, one night, the mate drove him away twice; * * that this same negro José, was the one who, without being commanded to do so by the negro Babo, as Lecbe and Matiluqui were, stabbed his master, Don Alexandro, after he had been dragged half-lifeless to the deck; * * that the mulatto steward, Francesco, was of the first band of revolters, that he was, in all things, the creature and tool of the negro Babo; that, to make his court, he, just before a repast in the cabin, proposed, to the negro Babo, poisoning a dish for the generous Captain Amasa Delano; this is known and believed, because the negroes have said it; but that the negro Babo, having another design, forbade Francesco; * * that the Ashantee Lecbe was one of the worst of them; for that, on the day the ship was retaken, he assisted in the defense of her, with a hatchet in each hand, with one of which he wounded, in the breast, the chief mate of Amasa Delano, in the first act of boarding; this all knew; that, in sight of the deponent, Lecbe struck, with a hatchet, Don Francisco Masa when, by the negro Babo's orders, he was carrying him to throw him overboard, alive; beside participating in the murder, before mentioned, of Don Alexandro Aranda, and others of the cabin-passengers; that, owing to the fury with which the Ashantees fought in the engagement with the boats, but this Lecbe and Yau survived; that Yau was bad as Lecbe; that Yau was the man who, by Babo's command, willingly prepared the skeleton of Don Alexandro, in a way the negroes afterwards told the deponent, but which he, so long as reason is left him, can never divulge; that Yau and Lecbe were the two who, in a calm by night, riveted the skeleton to the bow; this also the negroes told him; that the negro Babo was he who traced the inscription below it; that the negro Babo was the plotter from first to last; he ordered every murder, and was the helm and keel of the revolt; that Atufal was his lieutenant in all; but Atufal, with his own hand, committed no murder; nor did the negro Babo; * * that Atufal was shot, being killed in the fight with the boats, ere boarding; * * that the negresses, of age, were knowing to the revolt, and testified themselves satisfied at the death of their master, Don Alexandro; that, had the negroes not restrained them, they would have tortured to death, instead of simply killing, the Spaniards slain by command of the negro Babo; that the negresses used their utmost influence to have the deponent made away with; that, in the various acts of murder, they sang songs and danced—not gaily, but solemnly; and before the engagement with the boats, as well as during the action, they sang melancholy songs to the negroes, and that this melancholy tone was more inflaming than a different one would have been, and was so intended; that all this is believed, because the negroes have said it.—that of the thirty-six men of the crew exclusive of the passengers, (all of whom are now dead), which the deponent had knowledge of, six only remained alive, with four cabin-boys and ship-boys, not included with the crew; * *—that the negroes broke an arm of one of the cabin-boys and gave him strokes with hatchets.

[Then follow various random disclosures referring to various periods of time. The following are extracted:]

—That during the presence of Captain Amasa Delano on board, some attempts were made by the sailors, and one by Hermenegildo Gandix, to convey hints to him of the true state of affairs; but that these attempts were ineffectual, owing to fear of incurring death, and furthermore owing to the devices which offered contradictions to the true state of affairs; as well as owing to the generosity and piety of Amasa Delano incapable of sounding such wickedness; * * * that Luys Galgo, a sailor about sixty years of age, and formerly of the king's navy, was one of those who sought to convey tokens to Captain Amasa Delano; but his intent, though undiscovered, being suspected, he was, on a pretense, made to retire out of sight, and at last into the hold, and there was made away with. This the negroes have since said; * * * that one of the ship-boys feeling, from Captain Amasa Delano's presence, some hopes of release, and not having enough prudence, dropped some chance-word respecting his expectations, which being overheard and understood by a slave-boy with whom he was eating at the time, the latter struck him on the head with a knife, inflicting a bad wound, but of which the boy is now healing; that likewise, not long before the ship was brought to anchor, one of the seamen, steering at the time, endangered himself by letting the blacks remark some expression in his countenance, arising from a cause similar to the above; but this sailor, by his heedful after conduct, escaped; * * * that these statements are made to show the court that from the beginning to the end of the revolt, it was impossible for the deponent and his men to act otherwise than they did; * * *—that the third clerk, Hermenegildo Gandix, who before had been forced to live among the seamen, wearing a seaman's habit, and in all respects appearing to be one for the time; he, Gandix, was killed by a musket-ball fired through a mistake from the American boats before boarding; having in his fright ran up the mizzen-rigging, calling to the boats—"don't board," lest upon their boarding the negroes should kill him; that this inducing the Americans to believe he some way favored the cause of the negroes, they fired two balls at him, so that he fell wounded from the rigging, and was drowned in the sea; * * *—that the young Don Joaquin, Marques de Arambaolaza, like Hermenegildo Gandix, the third clerk, was degraded to the office and appearance of a common seaman; that upon one occasion when Don Joaquin shrank, the negro Babo commanded the Ashantee Lecbe to take tar and heat it, and pour it upon Don Joaquin's hands; * * *—that Don Joaquin was killed owing to another mistake of the Americans, but one impossible to be avoided, as upon the approach of the boats, Don Joaquin, with a hatchet tied edge out and upright to his hand, was made by the negroes to appear on the bulwarks; whereupon, seen with arms in his hands and in a questionable attitude, he was shot for a renegade seaman; * * *—that on the person of Don Joaquin was found secreted a jewel, which, by papers that were discovered, proved to have been meant for the shrine of our Lady of Mercy in Lima; a votive offering, beforehand prepared and guarded, to attest his gratitude, when he should have landed in Peru, his last destination, for the safe conclusion of his entire voyage from Spain; * * *—that the jewel, with the other effects of the late Don Joaquin, is in the custody of the brethren of the Hospital de Sacerdotes, awaiting the disposition of the honorable court; * * *—that, owing to the condition of the deponent, as well as the haste in which the boats departed for the attack, the Americans were not forewarned that there were, among the apparent crew, a passenger and one of the clerks disguised by the negro Babo; * * *—that, beside the negroes killed in the action, some were killed after the capture and re-anchoring at night, when shackled to the ring-bolts on deck; that these deaths were committed by the sailors, ere they could be prevented. That so soon as informed of it, Captain Amasa Delano used all his authority, and, in particular with his own hand, struck down Martinez Gola, who, having found a razor in the pocket of an old jacket of his, which one of the shackled negroes had on, was aiming it at the negro's throat; that the noble Captain Amasa Delano also wrenched from the hand of Bartholomew Barlo, a dagger secreted at the time of the massacre of the whites, with which he was in the act of stabbing a shackled negro, who, the same day, with another negro, had thrown him down and jumped upon him; * * *—that, for all the events, befalling through so long a time, during which the ship was in the hands of the negro Babo, he cannot here give account; but that, what he has said is the most substantial of what occurs to him at present, and is the truth under the oath which he has taken; which declaration he affirmed and ratified, after hearing it read to him.

He said that he is twenty-nine years of age, and broken in body and mind; that when finally dismissed by the court, he shall not return home to Chili; but betake himself to the monastery on Mount Agonia without; and signed with his honor, and crossed himself, and, for the time, departed as he came, in his litter, with the monk Infelez, to the Hospital de Sacerdotes.

Benito Cereno.

Doctor Rozas.

If the Deposition have served as the key to fit into the lock of the complications which precede it, then, as a vault whose door has been flung back, the San Dominick's hull lies open to-day.[60]

Hitherto the nature of this narrative, besides rendering the intricacies in the beginning unavoidable, has more or less required that many things, instead of being set down in the order of occurrence, should be retrospectively, or irregularly given; this last is the case with the following passages, which will conclude the account:

During the long, mild voyage to Lima, there was, as before hinted, a period during which the sufferer a little recovered his health, or, at least in some degree, his tranquillity. Ere the decided relapse which came, the two captains had many cordial conversations—their fraternal unreserve in singular contrast with former withdrawments.

Again and again, it was repeated, how hard it had been to enact the part forced on the Spaniard by Babo.

"Ah, my dear friend," Don Benito once said, "at those very times when you thought me so morose and ungrateful, nay, when, as you now admit, you half thought me plotting your murder, at those very times my heart was frozen; I could not look at you, thinking of what, both on board this ship and your own, hung, from other hands, over my kind benefactor. And as God lives, Don Amasa, I know not whether desire for my own safety alone could have nerved me to that leap into your boat, had it not been for the thought that, did you, unenlightened, return to your ship, you, my best friend, with all who might be with you, stolen upon, that night, in your hammocks, would never in this world have wakened again. Do but think how you walked this deck, how you sat in this cabin, every inch of ground mined into honey-combs under you. Had I dropped the least hint, made the least advance towards an understanding between us, death, explosive death—yours as mine—would have ended the scene."

"True, true," cried Captain Delano, starting, "you have saved my life, Don Benito, more than I yours; saved it, too, against my knowledge and will."

"Nay, my friend," rejoined the Spaniard, courteous even to the point of religion, "God charmed your life, but you saved mine. To think of some things you did—those smilings and chattings, rash pointings and gesturings. For less than these, they slew my mate, Raneds; but you had the Prince of Heaven's safe conduct through all ambuscades."

"Yes, all is owing to Providence, I know; but the temper of my mind that morning was more than commonly pleasant, while the sight of so much suffering, more apparent than real, added to my good nature, compassion, and charity, happily interweaving the three. Had it been otherwise, doubtless, as you hint, some of my interferences might have ended unhappily enough. Besides that, those feelings I spoke of enabled me to get the better of momentary distrust, at times when acuteness might have cost me my life, without saving another's. Only at the end did my suspicions get the better of me, and you know how wide of the mark they then proved."

[60]Note the parallel to the key worn by Don Benito, which fits the padlock holding Atufal in chains. We readers are now standing in Don Benito's and Delano's shoes, as Melville offers us a key and invites us to unlock the problem symbolizing slavery.

"Wide, indeed," said Don Benito, sadly; "you were with me all day; stood with me, sat with me, talked with me, looked at me, ate with me, drank with me; and yet, your last act was to clutch for a monster, not only an innocent man, but the most pitiable of all men. To such degree may malign machinations and deceptions impose. So far may even the best man err, in judging the conduct of one with the recesses of whose condition he is not acquainted. But you were forced to it; and you were in time undeceived. Would that, in both respects, it was so ever, and with all men."

"You generalize, Don Benito; and mournfully enough. But the past is passed; why moralize upon it? Forget it. See, yon bright sun has forgotten it all, and the blue sea, and the blue sky; these have turned over new leaves."

"Because they have no memory," he dejectedly replied; "because they are not human."

"But these mild trades that now fan your cheek, do they not come with a human-like healing to you? Warm friends, steadfast friends are the trades."

"With their steadfastness they but waft me to my tomb, Señor," was the foreboding response.

"You are saved," cried Captain Delano, more and more astonished and pained; "you are saved; what has cast such a shadow upon you?"

"The negro."

There was silence, while the moody man sat, slowly and unconsciously gathering his mantle about him, as if it were a pall.

There was no more conversation that day.

But if the Spaniard's melancholy sometimes ended in muteness upon topics like the above, there were others upon which he never spoke at all; on which, indeed, all his old reserves were piled. Pass over the worst, and, only to elucidate, let an item or two of these be cited. The dress so precise and costly, worn by him on the day whose events have been narrated, had not willingly been put on. And that silver-mounted sword, apparent symbol of despotic command, was not, indeed, a sword, but the ghost of one. The scabbard, artificially stiffened, was empty.

As for the black—whose brain, not body, had schemed and led the revolt, with the plot—his slight frame, inadequate to that which it held, had at once yielded to the superior muscular strength of his captor, in the boat. Seeing all was over, he uttered no sound, and could not be forced to. His aspect seemed to say, since I cannot do deeds, I will not speak words. Put in irons in the hold, with the rest, he was carried to Lima. During the passage Don Benito did not visit him. Nor then, nor at any time after, would he look at him. Before the tribunal he refused. When pressed by the judges he fainted. On the testimony of the sailors alone rested the legal identity of Babo.

Some months after, dragged to the gibbet at the tail of a mule, the black met his voiceless end. The body was burned to ashes; but for many days, the head, that hive of subtlety, fixed on a pole in the Plaza, met, unabashed, the gaze of the whites; and across the Plaza looked towards St. Bartholomew's church, in whose vaults slept then, as now, the recovered bones of Aranda; and across the Rimac bridge looked towards the monastery, on Mount Agonia without; where, three months after being dismissed by the court, Benito Cereno, borne on the bier, did, indeed, follow his leader.

1855

Billy Budd, Sailor

(An inside narrative)[1]

Dedicated
to
JACK CHASE
Englishman
Wherever that great heart may now be
Here on Earth or harbored in Paradise
Captain of the Maintop
in the year 1843
in the U.S. Frigate
United States[2]

1

In the time before steamships, or then more frequently than now, a stroller along the docks of any considerable seaport would occasionally have his attention arrested by a group of bronzed mariners, man-of-war's men or merchant sailors in holiday attire, ashore on liberty. In certain instances they would flank, or like a bodyguard, quite surround, some superior figure of their own class, moving along with them like Aldebaran[3] among the lesser lights of his constellation. That signal object was the "Handsome Sailor" of the less prosaic time alike of the military and merchant navies. With no perceptible trace of the vainglorious about him, rather with the offhand unaffectedness of natural regality, he seemed to accept the spontaneous homage of his shipmates.

A somewhat remarkable instance recurs to me. In Liverpool, now half a century ago, I saw under the shadow of the great dingy street-wall of Prince's Dock (an obstruction long since removed) a common sailor so intensely black that he must needs have been a native African of the unadulterate blood of Ham—a symmetric figure much above the average height. The two ends of a gay silk handkerchief thrown

[1]Melville probably began working on Billy Budd after his retirement from the New York Custom House in December 1885. He was still revising it when he died in 1891. The story was first published by Raymond Weaver in 1924. The present text follows the edition of Harrison Hayford and Merton M. Sealts, Jr., the most reliable transcription to date, and draws throughout on their indispensable notes. According to Hayford and Sealts, the story began as a prose headnote to a ballad about a sailor condemned to hanging for having fomented mutiny. In later stages of composition, Melville successively changed Billy from a mutineer into an innocent, introduced the character of Claggart, and developed Vere from a minor into a major character.

[2]In *White-Jacket,* echoed throughout *Billy Budd,* Melville describes his shipmate Jack Chase as a "stickler for the Rights of Man, and the liberties of the world," who deserts temporarily from the *Neversink* to "befriend, heart and soul, what he deemed the cause of the Right" in Peru's war against Bolivian domination (Chap. 5).

[3]The "eye" and brightest star in the constellation Taurus, the Bull.

loose about the neck danced upon the displayed ebony of his chest, in his ears were big hoops of gold, and a Highland bonnet with a tartan band set off his shapely head. It was a hot noon in July; and his face, lustrous with perspiration, beamed with barbaric good humor. In jovial sallies right and left, his white teeth flashing into view, he rollicked along, the center of a company of his shipmates. These were made up of such an assortment of tribes and complexions as would have well fitted them to be marched up by Anacharsis Cloots[4] before the bar of the first French Assembly as Representatives of the Human Race. At each spontaneous tribute rendered by the wayfarers to this black pagod of a fellow—the tribute of a pause and stare, and less frequently an exclamation—the motley retinue showed that they took that sort of pride in the evoker of it which the Assyrian priests doubtless showed for their grand sculptured Bull when the faithful prostrated themselves.

To return. If in some cases a bit of a nautical Murat[5] in setting forth his person ashore, the Handsome Sailor of the period in question evinced nothing of the dandified Billy-be-Dam, an amusing character all but extinct now, but occasionally to be encountered, and in a form yet more amusing than the original, at the tiller of the boats on the tempestuous Erie Canal or, more likely, vaporing in the groggeries along the towpath.[6] Invariably a proficient in his perilous calling, he was also more or less of a mighty boxer or wrestler. It was strength and beauty. Tales of his prowess were recited. Ashore he was the champion; afloat the spokesman; on every suitable occasion always foremost. Close-reefing topsails in a gale, there he was, astride the weather yardarm-end, foot in the Flemish horse as stirrup, both hands tugging at the earing as at a bridle, in very much the attitude of young Alexander curbing the fiery Bucephalus.[7] A superb figure, tossed up as by the horns of Taurus against the thunderous sky, cheerily hallooing to the strenuous file along the spar.

The moral nature was seldom out of keeping with the physical make. Indeed, except as toned by the former, the comeliness and power, always attractive in masculine conjunction, hardly could have drawn the sort of honest homage the Handsome Sailor in some examples received from his less gifted associates.

Such a cynosure, at least in aspect, and something such too in nature, though with important variations made apparent as the story proceeds, was welkin-eyed[8] Billy Budd—or Baby Budd, as more familiarly, under circumstances hereafter to be given, he at last came to be called—aged twenty-one, a foretopman of the British

[4]Described in Thomas Carlyle's *The French Revolution,* Part II, Book I, Chapter 10, the procession of the Human Species that the Prussian-born revolutionary, Jean Baptiste du Val de Grâce, Baron de Cloots (1755–1794), led before the French Assembly in 1790 as "mute representatives of their tongue-tied, befettered, heavy-laden Nations," became one of Melville's favorite metaphors for the brotherhood of humankind's diverse races. He calls the crew of the *Pequod* in *Moby-Dick* an "Anacharsis Clootz deputation" and the passengers of the *Fidele* in *The Confidence-Man* an "Anacharsis Cloots congress," and he echoes Carlyle's description of Cloots' procession in *Redburn* while hymning America as a multiracial nation (Chaps. 27, 2, and 33 respectively).

[5]Joachim Murat (1767?–1815), who owed his throne to Napoleon, was known as the "Dandy King" of Naples.

[6]A joke, since tempests do not occur on canals. Unlike the Handsome Sailor, the Billy-be-Dam is fit only to steer canal boats, or more likely, to boast in barrooms.

[7]Alexander the Great (356–323 B.C.) tamed the fiery war horse Bucephalus, whose head resembled a bull's (hence his name).

[8]Blue-eyed, like the welkin (sky).

fleet toward the close of the last decade of the eighteenth century. It was not very long prior to the time of the narration that follows that he had entered the King's service, having been impressed on the Narrow Seas from a homeward-bound English merchantman into a seventy-four[9] outward bound, H.M.S. *Bellipotent;* which ship, as was not unusual in those hurried days, having been obliged to put to sea short of her proper complement of men. Plump upon Billy at first sight in the gangway the boarding officer, Lieutenant Ratcliffe, pounced, even before the merchantman's crew was formally mustered on the quarter-deck for his deliberate inspection. And him only he elected. For whether it was because the other men when ranged before him showed to ill advantage after Billy, or whether he had some scruples in view of the merchantman's being rather short-handed, however it might be, the officer contented himself with his first spontaneous choice. To the surprise of the ship's company, though much to the lieutenant's satisfaction, Billy made no demur. But, indeed, any demur would have been as idle as the protest of a goldfinch popped into a cage.

Noting this uncomplaining acquiescence, all but cheerful, one might say, the shipmaster turned a surprised glance of silent reproach at the sailor. The shipmaster[10] was one of those worthy mortals found in every vocation, even the humbler ones—the sort of person whom everybody agrees in calling "a respectable man." And—nor so strange to report as it may appear to be—though a ploughman of the troubled waters, lifelong contending with the intractable elements, there was nothing this honest soul at heart loved better than simple peace and quiet. For the rest, he was fifty or thereabouts, a little inclined to corpulence, a prepossessing face, unwhiskered, and of an agreeable color—a rather full face, humanely intelligent in expression. On a fair day with a fair wind and all going well, a certain musical chime in his voice seemed to be the veritable unobstructed outcome of the innermost man. He had much prudence, much conscientiousness, and there were occasions when these virtues were the cause of overmuch disquietude in him. On a passage, so long as his craft was in any proximity to land, no sleep for Captain Graveling. He took to heart those serious responsibilities not so heavily borne by some shipmasters.

Now while Billy Budd was down in the forecastle getting his kit together, the *Bellipotent*'s lieutenant, burly and bluff, nowise disconcerted by Captain Graveling's omitting to proffer the customary hospitalities on an occasion so unwelcome to him, an omission simply caused by preoccupation of thought, unceremoniously invited himself into the cabin, and also to a flask from the spirit locker, a receptacle which his experienced eye instantly discovered. In fact he was one of those sea dogs in whom all the hardship and peril of naval life in the great prolonged wars of his time never impaired the natural instinct for sensuous enjoyment. His duty he always faithfully did; but duty is sometimes a dry obligation, and he was for irrigating its aridity,

[9]Seized from the crew of a merchant ship on the channels separating England from the Continent and Ireland and forced to serve on a seventy-four gun warship. British impressment of American sailors had helped provoke the War of 1812. Melville discusses impressment in *White-Jacket,* where he explains that in navies the world over, the low pay and brutal discipline, epitomized by the practice of flogging, deterred all but the most desperate men from enlisting voluntarily (Chap. 90). Melville at first called this seventy-four the *Indomitable,* which connotes bravery, but later changed the name to the *Bellipotent,* which suggests mere brute force (potency in war).

[10]Captain.

whensoever possible, with a fertilizing decoction of strong waters. For the cabin's proprietor there was nothing left but to play the part of the enforced host with whatever grace and alacrity were practicable. As necessary adjuncts to the flask, he silently placed tumbler and water jug before the irrepressible guest. But excusing himself from partaking just then, he dismally watched the unembarrassed officer deliberately diluting his grog a little, then tossing it off in three swallows, pushing the empty tumbler away, yet not so far as to be beyond easy reach, at the same time settling himself in his seat and smacking his lips with high satisfaction, looking straight at the host.

These proceedings over, the master broke the silence; and there lurked a rueful reproach in the tone of his voice: "Lieutenant, you are going to take my best man from me, the jewel of 'em."

"Yes, I know," rejoined the other, immediately drawing back the tumbler preliminary to a replenishing. "Yes, I know. Sorry."

"Beg pardon, but you don't understand, Lieutenant. See here, now. Before I shipped that young fellow, my forecastle was a rat-pit of quarrels. It was black times, I tell you, aboard the *Rights* here. I was worried to that degree my pipe had no comfort for me. But Billy came; and it was like a Catholic priest striking peace in an Irish shindy.[11] Not that he preached to them or said or did anything in particular; but a virtue went out of him, sugaring the sour ones. They took to him like hornets to treacle; all but the buffer of the gang, the big shaggy chap with the fire-red whiskers. He indeed, out of envy, perhaps, of the newcomer, and thinking such a "sweet and pleasant fellow," as he mockingly designated him to the others, could hardly have the spirit of a gamecock, must needs bestir himself in trying to get up an ugly row with him. Billy forebore with him and reasoned with him in a pleasant way—he is something like myself, Lieutenant, to whom aught like a quarrel is hateful—but nothing served. So, in the second dogwatch one day, the Red Whiskers in presence of the others, under pretense of showing Billy just whence a sirloin steak was cut—for the fellow had once been a butcher—insultingly gave him a dig under the ribs. Quick as lightning Billy let fly his arm. I dare say he never meant to do quite as much as he did, but anyhow he gave the burly fool a terrible drubbing. It took about half a minute, I should think. And, lord bless you, the lubber was astonished at the celerity. And will you believe it, Lieutenant, the Red Whiskers now really loves Billy—loves him, or is the biggest hypocrite that ever I heard of. But they all love him. Some of 'em do his washing, darn his old trousers for him; the carpenter is at odd times making a pretty little chest of drawers for him. Anybody will do anything for Billy Budd; and it's the happy family here. But now, Lieutenant, if that young fellow goes—I know how it will be aboard the *Rights.* Not again very soon shall I, coming up from dinner, lean over the capstan smoking a quiet pipe—no, not very soon again, I think. Ay, Lieutenant, you are going to take away the jewel of 'em; you are going to take away my peacemaker!" And with that the good soul had really some ado in checking a rising sob.

"Well," said the lieutenant, who had listened with amused interest to all this and now was waxing merry with his tipple; "well, blessed are the peacemakers, especially the fighting peacemakers. And such are the seventy-four beauties some of which you see poking their noses out of the portholes of yonder warship lying to for me," point-

[11]Brawl.

ing through the cabin window at the *Bellipotent*. "But courage! Don't look so downhearted, man. Why, I pledge you in advance the royal approbation. Rest assured that His Majesty will be delighted to know that in a time when his hardtack is not sought for by sailors with such avidity as should be, a time also when some shipmasters privily resent the borrowing from them a tar or two for the service; His Majesty, I say, will be delighted to learn that *one* shipmaster at least cheerfully surrenders to the King the flower of his flock, a sailor who with equal loyalty makes no dissent.—But where's my beauty? Ah," looking through the cabin's open door, "here he comes; and, by Jove, lugging along his chest—Apollo with his portmanteau!—My man," stepping out to him, "you can't take that big box aboard a warship. The boxes there are mostly shot boxes. Put your duds in a bag, lad. Boot and saddle for the cavalryman, bag and hammock for the man-of-war's man."

The transfer from chest to bag was made. And, after seeing his man into the cutter and then following him down, the lieutenant pushed off from the *Rights-of-Man*. That was the merchant ship's name, though by her master and crew abbreviated in sailor fashion into the *Rights*. The hardheaded Dundee owner was a staunch admirer of Thomas Paine, whose book in rejoinder to Burke's arraignment of the French Revolution had then been published for some time and had gone everywhere.[12] In christening his vessel after the title of Paine's volume the man of Dundee was something like his contemporary shipowner, Stephen Girard of Philadelphia, whose sympathies, alike with his native land and its liberal philosophers, he evinced by naming his ships after Voltaire, Diderot,[13] and so forth.

But now, when the boat swept under the merchantman's stern, and officer and oarsmen were noting—some bitterly and others with a grin—the name emblazoned there; just then it was that the new recruit jumped up from the bow where the coxswain[14] had directed him to sit, and waving hat to his silent shipmates sorrowfully looking over at him from the taffrail, bade the lads a genial good-bye. Then, making a salutation as to the ship herself, "And good-bye to you too, old *Rights-of-Man*."

"Down, sir!" roared the lieutenant, instantly assuming all the rigor of his rank, though with difficulty repressing a smile.

To be sure, Billy's action was a terrible breach of naval decorum. But in that decorum he had never been instructed; in consideration of which the lieutenant would hardly have been so energetic in reproof but for the concluding farewell to the ship. This he rather took as meant to convey a covert sally on the new recruit's part, a sly slur at impressment in general, and that of himself in especial. And yet, more likely, if satire it was in effect, it was hardly so by intention, for Billy, though happily endowed with the gaiety of high health, youth, and a free heart, was yet by no means of a satirical turn. The will to it and the sinister dexterity were alike wanting. To deal in double meanings and insinuations of any sort was quite foreign to his nature.

[12]Thomas Paine wrote *The Rights of Man* (1791–1792) as a rejoinder to Edmund Burke's *Reflections on the Revolution in France* (1790). As Hayford and Sealts point out, the opposing positions the two authors take on the issue of natural rights "lie behind the dialectic of *Billy Budd*."

[13]The French-born merchant, banker, and philanthropist Stephen Girard of Philadelphia (1750–1831) named his ships for various French philosophes whose ideas laid the groundwork for the Revolution, such as Voltaire (1694–1778) and Denis Diderot (1713–1784).

[14]Boat steersman.

As to his enforced enlistment, that he seemed to take pretty much as he was wont to take any vicissitude of weather. Like the animals, though no philosopher, he was, without knowing it, practically a fatalist. And it may be that he rather liked this adventurous turn in his affairs, which promised an opening into novel scenes and martial excitements.

Aboard the *Bellipotent* our merchant sailor was forthwith rated as an able seaman and assigned to the starboard watch of the foretop.[15] He was soon at home in the service, not at all disliked for his unpretentious good looks and a sort of genial happy-go-lucky air. No merrier man in his mess: in marked contrast to certain other individuals included like himself among the impressed portion of the ship's company; for these when not actively employed were sometimes, and more particularly in the last dogwatch[16] when the drawing near of twilight induced revery, apt to fall into a saddish mood which in some partook of sullenness. But they were not so young as our foretopman, and no few of them must have known a hearth of some sort, others may have had wives and children left, too probably, in uncertain circumstances, and hardly any but must have had acknowledged kith and kin, while for Billy, as will shortly be seen, his entire family was practically invested in himself.

2

Though our new-made foretopman was well received in the top and on the gun decks, hardly here was he that cynosure he had previously been among those minor ship's companies of the merchant marine, with which companies only had he hitherto consorted.

He was young; and despite his all but fully developed frame, in aspect looked even younger than he really was, owing to a lingering adolescent expression in the as yet smooth face all but feminine in purity of natural complexion but where, thanks to his seagoing, the lily was quite suppressed and the rose had some ado visibly to flush through the tan.

To one essentially such a novice in the complexities of factitious life, the abrupt transition from his former and simpler sphere to the ampler and more knowing world of a great warship; this might well have abashed him had there been any conceit or vanity in his composition. Among her miscellaneous multitude, the *Bellipotent* mustered several individuals who however inferior in grade were of no common natural stamp, sailors more signally susceptive of that air which continuous martial discipline and repeated presence in battle can in some degree impart even to the average man. As the Handsome Sailor, Billy Budd's position aboard the seventy-four was something analogous to that of a rustic beauty transplanted from the provinces and brought into competition with the highborn dames of the court. But this change of circumstances he scarce noted. As little did he observe that something about him provoked an ambiguous smile in one or two harder faces among the bluejackets. Nor less unaware was he of the peculiar favorable effect his person and

[15]Melville himself served as a maintopman on the *United States.* Crews were traditionally divided into two "watches," on duty for alternate periods at opposite sides of the ship, starboard (right) and port (left).

[16]From 6–8 P.M.

demeanor had upon the more intelligent gentlemen of the quarter-deck. Nor could this well have been otherwise. Cast in a mold peculiar to the finest physical examples of those Englishmen in whom the Saxon strain would seem not at all to partake of any Norman or other admixture, he showed in face that humane look of reposeful good nature which the Greek sculptor in some instances gave to his heroic strong man, Hercules. But this again was subtly modified by another and pervasive quality. The ear, small and shapely, the arch of the foot, the curve in mouth and nostril, even the indurated hand dyed to the orange-tawny of the toucan's[17] bill, a hand telling alike of the halyards[18] and tar bucket; but, above all, something in the mobile expression, and every chance attitude and movement, something suggestive of a mother eminently favored by Love and the Graces; all this strangely indicated a lineage in direct contradiction to his lot. The mysteriousness here became less mysterious through a matter of fact elicited when Billy at the capstan was being formally mustered into the service. Asked by the officer, a small, brisk little gentleman as it chanced, among other questions, his place of birth, he replied, "Please, sir, I don't know."

"Don't know where you were born? Who was your father?"

"God knows, sir."

Struck by the straightforward simplicity of these replies, the officer next asked, "Do you know anything about your beginning?"

"No, sir. But I have heard that I was found in a pretty silk-lined basket hanging one morning from the knocker of a good man's door in Bristol."

"*Found,* say you? Well," throwing back his head and looking up and down the new recruit; "well, it turns out to have been a pretty good find. Hope they'll find some more like you, my man; the fleet sadly needs them."

Yes, Billy Budd was a foundling, a presumable by-blow,[19] and, evidently, no ignoble one. Noble descent was as evident in him as in a blood horse.

For the rest, with little or no sharpness of faculty or any trace of the wisdom of the serpent, nor yet quite a dove,[20] he possessed that kind and degree of intelligence going along with the unconventional rectitude of a sound human creature, one to whom not yet has been proffered the questionable apple of knowledge. He was illiterate; he could not read, but he could sing, and like the illiterate nightingale was sometimes the composer of his own song.

Of self-consciousness he seemed to have little or none, or about as much as we may reasonably impute to a dog of Saint Bernard's breed.

Habitually living with the elements and knowing little more of the land than as a beach, or, rather, that portion of the terraqueous globe providentially set apart for dance-houses, doxies, and tapsters,[21] in short what sailors call a "fiddler's green,"[22] his simple nature remained unsophisticated by those moral obliquities which are not in every case incompatible with that manufacturable thing known as respectability. But are sailors, frequenters of fiddlers' greens, without vices? No; but less often than

[17]Tropical bird native to Brazil, with brightcolored plumage and a broad orange beak.

[18]Ropes for hoisting sails and spars.

[19]Bastard child.

[20]"Behold, I send you forth as sheep in the midst of wolves: be ye therefore wise as serpents, and harmless as doves," Christ instructs his disciples (Matthew 10:16).

[21]Whores and bartenders.

[22]Traditional sailor's paradise, with unlimited fiddling, dancing, and liquor.

with landsmen do their vices, so called, partake of crookedness of heart, seeming less to proceed from viciousness than exuberance of vitality after long constraint: frank manifestations in accordance with natural law. By his original constitution aided by the co-operating influences of his lot, Billy in many respects was little more than a sort of upright barbarian, much such perhaps as Adam presumably might have been ere the urbane Serpent wriggled himself into his company.

And here be it submitted that apparently going to corroborate the doctrine of man's Fall, a doctrine now popularly ignored, it is observable that where certain virtues pristine and unadulterate peculiarly characterize anybody in the external uniform of civilization, they will upon scrutiny seem not to be derived from custom or convention, but rather to be out of keeping with these, as if indeed exceptionally transmitted from a period prior to Cain's city[23] and citified man. The character marked by such qualities has to an unvitiated taste an untampered-with flavor like that of berries, while the man thoroughly civilized, even in a fair specimen of the breed, has to the same moral palate a questionable smack as of a compounded wine. To any stray inheritor of these primitive qualities found, like Caspar Hauser,[24] wandering dazed in any Christian capital of our time, the good-natured poet's famous invocation, near two thousand years ago, of the good rustic out of his latitude in the Rome of the Caesars, still appropriately holds:

> Honest and poor, faithful in word and thought,
> What hath thee, Fabian, to the city brought?[25]

Though our Handsome Sailor had as much of masculine beauty as one can expect anywhere to see; nevertheless, like the beautiful woman in one of Hawthorne's minor tales,[26] there was just one thing amiss in him. No visible blemish indeed, as with the lady; no, but an occasional liability to a vocal defect. Though in the hour of elemental uproar or peril he was everything that a sailor should be, yet under sudden provocation of strong heart-feeling his voice, otherwise singularly musical, as if expressive of the harmony within, was apt to develop an organic hesitancy, in fact more or less of a stutter or even worse. In this particular Billy was a striking instance that the arch interferer, the envious marplot of Eden, still has more or less to do with every human consignment to this planet of Earth. In every case, one way or another he is sure to slip in his little card, as much as to remind us—I too have a hand here.

The avowal of such an imperfection in the Handsome Sailor should be evidence not alone that he is not presented as a conventional hero, but also that the story in which he is the main figure is no romance.

[23]In Genesis 4:8–17, after Cain kills his brother Abel, God tells him that henceforth the earth he tills will no longer yield fruit. "And Cain went out from the presence of the LORD . . . and he builded a city."

[24]A mysterious foundling (1812?–1833) who turned up in Nuremberg in 1828, bewildered and incoherent, after having allegedly been confined in a dark space all his life. In 1833 he was stabbed to death by a man believed to have promised him information on his origins. He was thought to be of noble blood and to exemplify the innocence of human beings in a state of nature.

[25]Martial, *Epigrams* I.iv.1–2.

[26]"The Birthmark," whose heroine dies when her scientist husband tries to remove the blemish from her cheek symbolizing "the fatal flaw of humanity which Nature, in one shape or another, stamps ineffaceably on all her productions. . . ."

3

At the time of Billy Budd's arbitrary enlistment into the *Bellipotent* that ship was on her way to join the Mediterranean fleet. No long time elapsed before the junction was effected. As one of that fleet the seventy-four participated in its movements, though at times on account of her superior sailing qualities, in the absence of frigates, dispatched on separate duty as a scout and at times on less temporary service. But with all this the story has little concernment, restricted as it is to the inner life of one particular ship and the career of an individual sailor.

It was the summer of 1797. In the April of that year had occurred the commotion at Spithead followed in May by a second and yet more serious outbreak in the fleet at the Nore.[27] The latter is known, and without exaggeration in the epithet, as "the Great Mutiny." It was indeed a demonstration more menacing to England than the contemporary manifestoes and conquering and proselyting armies of the French Directory.[28] To the British Empire the Nore Mutiny was what a strike in the fire brigade would be to London threatened by general arson. In a crisis when the kingdom might well have anticipated the famous signal that some years later published along the naval line of battle what it was that upon occasion England expected of Englishmen;[29] *that* was the time when at the mastheads of the three-deckers and seventy-fours moored in her own roadstead—a fleet the right arm of a Power then all but the sole free conservative one of the Old World—the bluejackets, to be numbered by thousands, ran up with huzzas the British colors with the union and cross wiped out; by that cancellation transmuting the flag of founded law and freedom defined, into the enemy's red meteor of unbridled and unbounded revolt. Reasonable discontent growing out of practical grievances in the fleet had been ignited into irrational combustion as by live cinders blown across the Channel from France in flames.

The event converted into irony for a time those spirited strains of Dibdin[30]—as a song-writer no mean auxiliary to the English government at that European conjuncture—strains celebrating, among other things, the patriotic devotion of the British tar: "And as for my life, 'tis the King's!"

Such an episode in the Island's grand naval story her naval historians naturally abridge, one of them (William James)[31] candidly acknowledging that fain would he

[27]According to Hayford and Sealts, Melville noted the exact dates of the Spithead and Nore uprisings (April 15 and May 20, 1797, respectively) on two library call-slips attached to Leaf 364 of the *Billy Budd* manuscript. Spithead is a roadstead (protected anchorage) in the English Channel, between Portsmouth and the Isle of Wight, and the Nore is a sandbank at the mouth of the Thames.

[28]Five-member executive body that governed France from 1795 to 1799, after the Revolution.

[29]Nelson's famous signal to his fleet at the Battle of Trafalgar (1805): "England expects every man to do his duty!"

[30]Charles Dibdin (1745–1814), English dramatist and songwriter. In *White-Jacket* Melville wrote that Dibdin's songs—"which would lead one to think that man-of-war's-men are the most carefree, contented, virtuous, and patriotic of mankind—were composed at a time when the English Navy was principally manned by felons and paupers. . . . Still more, these songs are pervaded by . . . a reckless acquiescence in fate, and an implicit, unquestioning, dog-like devotion to whoever may be lord and master. Dibdin was a man of genius; but no wonder Dibdin was a government pensioner at £200 per annum" (Chap. 90).

[31]British historian, whose *Naval History of Great Britain* (6 vols., 1860) Melville is quoting somewhat inaccurately.

pass it over did not "impartiality forbid fastidiousness." And yet his mention is less a narration than a reference, having to do hardly at all with details. Nor are these readily to be found in the libraries. Like some other events in every age befalling states everywhere, including America, the Great Mutiny was of such character that national pride along with views of policy would fain shade it off into the historical background. Such events cannot be ignored, but there is a considerate way of historically treating them. If a well-constituted individual refrains from blazoning aught amiss or calamitous in his family, a nation in the like circumstance may without reproach be equally discreet.

Though after parleyings between government and the ringleaders, and concessions by the former as to some glaring abuses, the first uprising—that at Spithead—with difficulty was put down, or matters for the time pacified; yet at the Nore the unforeseen renewal of insurrection on a yet larger scale, and emphasized in the conferences that ensued by demands deemed by the authorities not only inadmissible but aggressively insolent, indicated—if the Red Flag did not sufficiently do so—what was the spirit animating the men. Final suppression, however, there was; but only made possible perhaps by the unswerving loyalty of the marine corps[32] and a voluntary resumption of loyalty among influential sections of the crews.

To some extent the Nore Mutiny may be regarded as analogous to the distempering irruption of contagious fever in a frame constitutionally sound, and which anon throws it off.

At all events, of these thousands of mutineers were some of the tars who not so very long afterwards—whether wholly prompted thereto by patriotism, or pugnacious instinct, or by both—helped to win a coronet for Nelson at the Nile, and the naval crown of crowns for him at Trafalgar. To the mutineers, those battles and especially Trafalgar were a plenary absolution and a grand one. For all that goes to make up scenic naval display and heroic magnificence in arms, those battles, especially Trafalgar, stand unmatched in human annals.[33]

4

In this matter of writing, resolve as one may to keep to the main road, some bypaths have an enticement not readily to be withstood. I am going to err into such a bypath. If the reader will keep me company I shall be glad. At the least, we can promise ourselves that pleasure which is wickedly said to be in sinning, for a literary sin the divergence will be.

Very likely it is no new remark that the inventions of our time have at last brought about a change in sea warfare in degree corresponding to the revolution in all warfare effected by the original introduction from China into Europe of gunpowder. The first European firearm, a clumsy contrivance, was, as is well known, scouted by no few of the knights as a base implement, good enough peradventure

[32]Melville discusses the "antagonism between the marine and the sailor" in *White-Jacket* and notes that officers habitually play the two groups against each other (Chap. 89).

[33]Nelson won a baron's coronet for defeating the French fleet at the Battle of the Nile (1798). The "naval crown of crowns" was his hero's death at the Battle of Trafalgar (1805), which gave Britain undisputed mastery of the seas.

for weavers too craven to stand up crossing steel with steel in frank fight. But as ashore knightly valor, though shorn of its blazonry, did not cease with the knights, neither on the seas—though nowadays in encounters there a certain kind of displayed gallantry be fallen out of date as hardly applicable under changed circumstances—did the nobler qualities of such naval magnates as Don John of Austria, Doria, Van Tromp, Jean Bart, the long line of British admirals, and the American Decaturs of 1812 become obsolete with their wooden walls.[34]

Nevertheless, to anybody who can hold the Present at its worth without being inappreciative of the Past, it may be forgiven, if to such an one the solitary old hulk at Portsmouth, Nelson's *Victory,* seems to float there, not alone as the decaying monument of a fame incorruptible, but also as a poetic reproach, softened by its picturesqueness, to the *Monitors*[35] and yet mightier hulls of the European ironclads. And this not altogether because such craft are unsightly, unavoidably lacking the symmetry and grand lines of the old battleships, but equally for other reasons.

There are some, perhaps, who while not altogether inaccessible to that poetic reproach just alluded to, may yet on behalf of the new order be disposed to parry it; and this to the extent of iconoclasm, if need be. For example, prompted by the sight of the star inserted in the *Victory*'s quarter-deck designating the spot where the Great Sailor fell, these martial utilitarians may suggest considerations implying that Nelson's ornate publication of his person in battle was not only unnecessary, but not military, nay, savored of foolhardiness and vanity. They may add, too, that at Trafalgar it was in effect nothing less than a challenge to death; and death came; and that but for his bravado the victorious admiral might possibly have survived the battle, and so, instead of having his sagacious dying injunctions overruled by his immediate successor in command, he himself when the contest was decided might have brought his shattered fleet to anchor, a proceeding which might have averted the deplorable loss of life by shipwreck in the elemental tempest that followed the martial one.

Well, should we set aside the more than disputable point whether for various reasons it was possible to anchor the fleet, then plausibly enough the Benthamites[36] of war may urge the above. But the *might-have-been* is but boggy ground to build on. And, certainly, in foresight as to the larger issue of an encounter, and anxious preparations for it—buoying the deadly way and mapping it out, as at Copenhagen[37]—few commanders have been so painstakingly circumspect as this same reckless declarer of his person in fight.

Personal prudence, even when dictated by quite other than selfish considerations, surely is no special virtue in a military man; while an excessive love of glory,

[34]Don John of Austria (1547–1578) commanded the fleet of the Holy League that defeated the Turks at Lepanto in 1571; Andrea Doria (1468?–1560) freed Genoa from the Turks; Maarten Tromp (1597–1653) commanded Dutch fleets against Spain, Portugal, and Britain; Jean Bart (1651?–1702), a French privateer, fought against the Dutch; Stephen Decatur (1779–1820) led American naval forces against the Tripoli pirates in 1803–1804 and against the British in 1812.

[35]See Melville's poem "A Utilitarian View of the Monitor's Fight," reprinted in the present anthology.

[36]Disciples of Jeremy Bentham (1748–1832), English philosopher who originated the concept of utilitarianism, or usefulness, as a guide to action.

[37]Prior to the Battle of Copenhagen (1801), the Danes had removed the buoys marking the intricate channel leading to the port, but Nelson took soundings and replaced the buoys, thus literally preparing the way to victory.

impassioning a less burning impulse, the honest sense of duty, is the first. If the name *Wellington* is not so much of a trumpet to the blood as the simpler name *Nelson,* the reason for this may perhaps be inferred from the above. Alfred in his funeral ode on the victor of Waterloo ventures not to call him the greatest soldier of all time, though in the same ode he invokes Nelson as "the greatest sailor since our world began."[38]

At Trafalgar Nelson on the brink of opening the fight sat down and wrote his last brief will and testament. If under the presentiment of the most magnificent of all victories to be crowned by his own glorious death, a sort of priestly motive led him to dress his person in the jewelled vouchers of his own shining deeds; if thus to have adorned himself for the altar and the sacrifice were indeed vainglory, then affectation and fustian is each more heroic line in the great epics and dramas, since in such lines the poet but embodies in verse those exaltations of sentiment that a nature like Nelson, the opportunity being given, vitalizes into acts.

5

Yes, the outbreak at the Nore was put down. But not every grievance was redressed. If the contractors, for example, were no longer permitted to ply some practices peculiar to their tribe everywhere, such as providing shoddy cloth, rations not sound, or false in the measure; not the less impressment, for one thing, went on. By custom sanctioned for centuries, and judicially maintained by a Lord Chancellor as late as Mansfield,[39] that mode of manning the fleet, a mode now fallen into a sort of abeyance but never formally renounced, it was not practicable to give up in those years. Its abrogation would have crippled the indispensable fleet, one wholly under canvas, no steam power, its innumerable sails and thousands of cannon, everything in short, worked by muscle alone; a fleet the more insatiate in demand for men, because then multiplying its ships of all grades against contingencies present and to come of the convulsed Continent.

Discontent foreran the Two Mutinies, and more or less it lurkingly survived them. Hence it was not unreasonable to apprehend some return of trouble sporadic or general. One instance of such apprehensions: In the same year with this story, Nelson, then Rear Admiral Sir Horatio, being with the fleet off the Spanish coast, was directed by the admiral in command to shift his pennant from the *Captain* to the *Theseus;* and for this reason: that the latter ship having newly arrived on the station from home, where it had taken part in the Great Mutiny, danger was apprehended from the temper of the men; and it was thought that an officer like Nelson was the one, not indeed to terrorize the crew into base subjection, but to win them, by force of his mere presence and heroic personality, back to an allegiance if not as enthusiastic as his own yet as true.

So it was that for a time, on more than one quarter-deck, anxiety did exist. At sea, precautionary vigilance was strained against relapse. At short notice an

[38]Alfred Lord Tennyson (1809–1892), in his *Ode on the Death of the Duke of Wellington,* from which Melville is quoting, pays tribute to the general who defeated Napoleon at Waterloo in 1815, but praises Nelson even more warmly.

[39]William Murray, Earl of Mansfield (1705–1793) became Lord Chief Justice of Britain in 1756.

engagement might come on. When it did, the lieutenants assigned to batteries felt it incumbent on them, in some instances, to stand with drawn swords behind the men working the guns.

6

But on board the seventy-four in which Billy now swung his hammock, very little in the manner of the men and nothing obvious in the demeanor of the officers would have suggested to an ordinary observer that the Great Mutiny was a recent event. In their general bearing and conduct the commissioned officers of a warship naturally take their tone from the commander, that is if he have that ascendancy of character that ought to be his.

Captain the Honorable Edward Fairfax Vere, to give his full title, was a bachelor of forty or thereabouts, a sailor of distinction even in a time prolific of renowned seamen. Though allied to the higher nobility, his advancement had not been altogether owing to influences connected with that circumstance. He had seen much service, been in various engagements, always acquitting himself as an officer mindful of the welfare of his men, but never tolerating an infraction of discipline; thoroughly versed in the science of his profession, and intrepid to the verge of temerity, though never injudiciously so. For his gallantry in the West Indian waters as flag lieutenant under Rodney in that admiral's crowning victory over De Grasse,[40] he was made a post captain.

Ashore, in the garb of a civilian, scarce anyone would have taken him for a sailor, more especially that he never garnished unprofessional talk with nautical terms, and grave in his bearing, evinced little appreciation of mere humor. It was not out of keeping with these traits that on a passage when nothing demanded his paramount action, he was the most undemonstrative of men. Any landsman observing this gentleman not conspicuous by his stature and wearing no pronounced insignia, emerging from his cabin to the open deck, and noting the silent deference of the officers retiring to leeward, might have taken him for the King's guest, a civilian aboard the King's ship, some highly honorable discreet envoy on his way to an important post. But in fact this unobtrusiveness of demeanor may have proceeded from a certain unaffected modesty of manhood sometimes accompanying a resolute nature, a modesty evinced at all times not calling for pronounced action, which shown in any rank of life suggests a virtue aristocratic in kind. As with some others engaged in various departments of the world's more heroic activities, Captain Vere though practical enough upon occasion would at times betray a certain dreaminess of mood. Standing alone on the weather side of the quarter-deck, one hand holding by the rigging, he would absently gaze off at the blank sea. At the presentation to him then of some minor matter interrupting the current of his thoughts, he would show more or less irascibility; but instantly he would control it.

[40]The British admiral George Brydges, Baron Rodney (1719–1792) defeated the French admiral François de Grasse (1723–1788) off the West Indian island of Dominica in 1782. As Stanton Garner points out, De Grasse had just helped the Americans to defeat the British by keeping the English fleet in the Chesapeake from aiding Cornwallis at Yorktown in 1781. Charles Anderson suggests that Melville may be basing his account of Vere's career on that of Sir William George Fairfax, a hero of the Rodney de Grasse engagement.

In the navy he was popularly known by the appellation "Starry Vere." How such a designation happened to fall upon one who whatever his sterling qualities was without any brilliant ones, was in this wise: A favorite kinsman, Lord Denton, a free-hearted fellow, had been the first to meet and congratulate him upon his return to England from his West Indian cruise; and but the day previous turning over a copy of Andrew Marvell's poems had lighted, not for the first time, however, upon the lines entitled "Appleton House," the name of one of the seats of their common ancestor, a hero in the German wars of the seventeenth century, in which poem occur the lines:

This 'tis to have been from the first
In a domestic heaven nursed,
Under the discipline severe
Of Fairfax and the starry Vere.[41]

And so, upon embracing his cousin fresh from Rodney's great victory wherein he had played so gallant a part, brimming over with just family pride in the sailor of their house, he exuberantly exclaimed, "Give ye joy, Ed; give ye joy, my starry Vere!" This got currency, and the novel prefix serving in familiar parlance readily to distinguish the *Bellipotent*'s captain from another Vere his senior, a distant relative, an officer of like rank in the navy, it remained permanently attached to the surname.

7

In view of the part that the commander of the *Bellipotent* plays in scenes shortly to follow, it may be well to fill out that sketch of him outlined in the previous chapter.

Aside from his qualities as a sea officer Captain Vere was an exceptional character. Unlike no few of England's renowned sailors, long and arduous service with signal devotion to it had not resulted in absorbing and *salting* the entire man. He had a marked leaning toward everything intellectual. He loved books, never going to sea without a newly replenished library, compact but of the best. The isolated leisure, in some cases so wearisome, falling at intervals to commanders even during a war cruise, never was tedious to Captain Vere. With nothing of that literary taste which less heeds the thing conveyed than the vehicle, his bias was toward those books to which every serious mind of superior order occupying any active post of authority in the world naturally inclines: books treating of actual men and events no matter of what era—history, biography, and unconventional writers like Montaigne, who, free from cant and convention, honestly and in the spirit of common sense philosophize upon realities. In this line of reading he found confirmation of his own more reserved thoughts—confirmation which he had vainly sought in social converse, so that as touching most fundamental topics, there had got to be established in him some positive convictions which he forefelt would abide in him essentially unmodified so long as his intelligent part remained unimpaired. In view of the troubled period in which his lot was cast, this was well for him. His settled convictions were as a dike against

[41]English poet (1621–1678), whose "Upon Appleton House, to my Lord Fairfax" also refers to the Fairfax estate of Denton, from which Melville draws his "Lord Denton."

those invading waters of novel opinion social, political, and otherwise, which carried away as in a torrent no few minds in those days, minds by nature not inferior to his own. While other members of that aristocracy to which by birth he belonged were incensed at the innovators mainly because their theories were inimical to the privileged classes, Captain Vere disinterestedly opposed them not alone because they seemed to him insusceptible of embodiment in lasting institutions, but at war with the peace of the world and the true welfare of mankind.

With minds less stored than his and less earnest, some officers of his rank, with whom at times he would necessarily consort, found him lacking in the companionable quality, a dry and bookish gentleman, as they deemed. Upon any chance withdrawal from their company one would be apt to say to another something like this: "Vere is a noble fellow, Starry Vere. 'Spite the gazettes,[42] Sir Horatio" (meaning him who became Lord Nelson) "is at bottom scarce a better seaman or fighter. But between you and me now, don't you think there is a queer streak of the pedantic running through him? Yes, like the King's yarn in a coil of navy rope?"

Some apparent ground there was for this sort of confidential criticism; since not only did the captain's discourse never fall into the jocosely familiar, but in illustrating of any point touching the stirring personages and events of the time he would be as apt to cite some historic character or incident of antiquity as he would be to cite from the moderns. He seemed unmindful of the circumstance that to his bluff company such remote allusions, however pertinent they might really be, were altogether alien to men whose reading was mainly confined to the journals. But considerateness in such matters is not easy to natures constituted like Captain Vere's. Their honesty prescribes to them directness, sometimes far-reaching like that of a migratory fowl that in its flight never heeds when it crosses a frontier.

8

The lieutenants and other commissioned gentlemen forming Captain Vere's staff it is not necessary here to particularize, nor needs it to make any mention of any of the warrant officers. But among the petty officers was one who, having much to do with the story, may as well be forthwith introduced. His portrait I essay, but shall never hit it. This was John Claggart, the master-at-arms.[43] But that sea title may to landsmen seem somewhat equivocal. Originally, doubtless, that petty officer's function was the instruction of the men in the use of arms, sword or cutlass. But very long ago, owing to the advance in gunnery making hand-to-hand encounters less frequent and giving to niter and sulphur the pre-eminence over steel, that function ceased; the master-at-arms of a great warship becoming a sort of chief of police charged among other matters with the duty of preserving order on the populous lower gun decks.

Claggart was a man about five-and-thirty, somewhat spare and tall, yet of no ill figure upon the whole. His hand was too small and shapely to have been accustomed to hard toil. The face was a notable one, the features all except the chin cleanly cut

[42] Whatever the newspapers say.

[43] In *White-Jacket* Melville described the master-at-arms as an officer "whom all sailors hate . . . a universal informer and hunter-up of delinquents" (Chap. 6). The *Neversink*'s master-at-arms Bland is an early version of Claggart.

as those on a Greek medallion; yet the chin, beardless as Tecumseh's,[44] had something of strange protuberant broadness in its make that recalled the prints of the Reverend Dr. Titus Oates, the historic deponent with the clerical drawl in the time of Charles II and the fraud of the alleged Popish Plot.[45] It served Claggart in his office that his eye could cast a tutoring glance. His brow was of the sort phrenologically associated with more than average intellect; silken jet curls partly clustering over it, making a foil to the pallor below, a pallor tinged with a faint shade of amber akin to the hue of time-tinted marbles of old. This complexion, singularly contrasting with the red or deeply bronzed visages of the sailors, and in part the result of his official seclusion from the sunlight, though it was not exactly displeasing, nevertheless seemed to hint of something defective or abnormal in the constitution and blood. But his general aspect and manner were so suggestive of an education and career incongruous with his naval function that when not actively engaged in it he looked like a man of high quality, social and moral, who for reasons of his own was keeping incog. Nothing was known of his former life. It might be that he was an Englishman; and yet there lurked a bit of accent in his speech suggesting that possibly he was not such by birth, but through naturalization in early childhood. Among certain grizzled sea gossips of the gun decks and forecastle went a rumor perdue that the master-at-arms was a *chevalier*[46] who had volunteered into the King's navy by way of compounding for some mysterious swindle whereof he had been arraigned at the King's Bench.[47] The fact that nobody could substantiate this report was, of course, nothing against its secret currency. Such a rumor once started on the gun decks in reference to almost anyone below the rank of a commissioned officer would, during the period assigned to this narrative, have seemed not altogether wanting in credibility to the tarry old wiseacres of a man-of-war crew. And indeed a man of Claggart's accomplishments, without prior nautical experience entering the navy at mature life, as he did, and necessarily allotted at the start to the lowest grade in it; a man too who never made allusion to his previous life ashore; these were circumstances which in the dearth of exact knowledge as to his true antecedents opened to the invidious a vague field for unfavorable surmise.

But the sailors' dogwatch gossip concerning him derived a vague plausibility from the fact that now for some period the British navy could so little afford to be squeamish in the matter of keeping up the muster rolls, that not only were press gangs[48] notoriously abroad both afloat and ashore, but there was little or no secret about another matter, namely, that the London police were at liberty to capture any able-bodied suspect, any questionable fellow at large, and summarily ship him to the dockyard or fleet. Furthermore, even among voluntary enlistments there were instances where the motive thereto partook neither of patriotic impulse nor yet of a random desire to experience a bit of sea life and martial adventure. Insolvent debtors of minor grade, together with the promiscuous lame ducks of morality, found in the

[44]Shawnee chief (1768?–1813) who tried to unite Indian tribes from Florida to the head of the Missouri against whites and sided with the British in the War of 1812.

[45]In 1678 Titus Oates (1649–1705) fabricated evidence of an alleged Catholic plot to massacre English Protestants, burn London, and assassinate King Charles II. His unfounded accusations sent many people to their deaths before Oates's perjury was exposed in 1685.

[46]Swindler, sharper.

[47]Court of law.

[48]Impressment gangs serving to draft or kidnap men for the navy.

navy a convenient and secure refuge, secure because, once enlisted aboard a King's ship, they were as much in sanctuary as the transgressor of the Middle Ages harboring himself under the shadow of the altar. Such sanctioned irregularities, which for obvious reasons the government would hardly think to parade at the time and which consequently, and as affecting the least influential class of mankind, have all but dropped into oblivion, lend color to something for the truth whereof I do not vouch, and hence have some scruple in stating; something I remember having seen in print though the book I cannot recall; but the same thing was personally communicated to me now more than forty years ago by an old pensioner in a cocked hat with whom I had a most interesting talk on the terrace at Greenwich, a Baltimore Negro, a Trafalgar man.[49] It was to this effect: In the case of a warship short of hands whose speedy sailing was imperative, the deficient quota, in lack of any other way of making it good, would be eked out by drafts culled direct from the jails. For reasons previously suggested it would not perhaps be easy at the present day directly to prove or disprove the allegation. But allowed as a verity, how significant would it be of England's straits at the time confronted by those wars which like a flight of harpies rose shrieking from the din and dust of the fallen Bastille.[50] That era appears measurably clear to us who look back at it, and but read of it. But to the grandfathers of us graybeards, the more thoughtful of them, the genius of it presented an aspect like that of Camoëns' Spirit of the Cape,[51] an eclipsing menace mysterious and prodigious. Not America was exempt from apprehension. At the height of Napoleon's unexampled conquests, there were Americans who had fought at Bunker Hill who looked forward to the possibility that the Atlantic might prove no barrier against the ultimate schemes of this French portentous upstart from the revolutionary chaos who seemed in act of fulfilling judgment prefigured in the Apocalypse.[52]

But the less credence was to be given to the gun-deck talk touching Claggart, seeing that no man holding his office in a man-of-war can ever hope to be popular with the crew. Besides, in derogatory comments upon anyone against whom they have a grudge, or for any reason or no reason mislike, sailors are much like landsmen: they are apt to exaggerate or romance it.

About as much was really known to the *Bellipotent*'s tars of the master-at-arms' career before entering the service as an astronomer knows about a comet's travels prior to its first observable appearance in the sky. The verdict of the sea quidnuncs[53] has been cited only by way of showing what sort of moral impression the man made

[49]Veteran of Trafalgar. An entry for November 21, 1849 in Melville's *Journal of a Visit to London and the Continent* contains the following telegraphic notes of an excursion to Greenwich Hospital near London: "The negro. . . . Pensioners in palaces! . . . Walked in Greenwich Park . . . talk with an old pensioner there."

[50]Infamous prison stormed by the citizens of Paris on July 14, 1789, at the outbreak of the French Revolution. The Harpies were fierce, filthy monsters with the faces of women and the bodies and claws of vultures, who served as ministers of divine vengeance and punished criminals.

[51]In *The Lusiads,* an epic on Vasco Da Gama's voyage to India by the Portuguese poet Luis de Camoëns (1524–1580), the Spirit embodies the natural forces that threaten to destroy Da Gama and his crew at the Cape of Good Hope. Melville acquired his love of Camoëns from his friend Jack Chase.

[52]Contemporary Christians who applied the prophecies in the book of Revelation to their own time often identified Napoleon with one of the blasphemous beasts given power to rule over all nations and to make war on the saints. They also equated the defeat of Napoleonic France with the fall of Babylon (Revelation 13–14).

[53]Literally "what now?" Hence busybodies, gossips.

upon rude uncultivated natures whose conceptions of human wickedness were necessarily of the narrowest, limited to ideas of vulgar rascality—a thief among the swinging hammocks during a night watch, or the man-brokers and land-sharks[54] of the seaports.

It was no gossip, however, but fact that though, as before hinted, Claggart upon his entrance into the navy was, as a novice, assigned to the least honorable section[55] of a man-of-war's crew, embracing the drudgery, he did not long remain there. The superior capacity he immediately evinced, his constitutional sobriety, an ingratiating deference to superiors, together with a peculiar ferreting genius manifested on a singular occasion; all this, capped by a certain austere patriotism, abruptly advanced him to the position of master-at-arms.

Of this maritime chief of police the ship's corporals, so called, were the immediate subordinates, and compliant ones; and this, as is to be noted in some business departments ashore, almost to a degree inconsistent with entire moral volition. His place put various converging wires of underground influence under the chief's control, capable when astutely worked through his understrappers of operating to the mysterious discomfort, if nothing worse, of any of the sea commonalty.

9

Life in the foretop well agreed with Billy Budd. There, when not actually engaged on the yards yet higher aloft, the topmen, who as such had been picked out for youth and activity, constituted an aerial club lounging at ease against the smaller stun'sails rolled up into cushions, spinning yarns like the lazy gods, and frequently amused with what was going on in the busy world of the decks below. No wonder then that a young fellow of Billy's disposition was well content in such society. Giving no cause of offense to anybody, he was always alert at a call. So in the merchant service it had been with him. But now such a punctiliousness in duty was shown that his topmates would sometimes good-naturedly laugh at him for it. This heightened alacrity had its cause, namely, the impression made upon him by the first formal gangway-punishment he had ever witnessed, which befell the day following his impressment. It had been incurred by a little fellow, young, a novice after-guardsman absent from his assigned post when the ship was being put about;[56] a dereliction resulting in a rather serious hitch to that maneuver, one demanding instantaneous promptitude in letting go and making fast. When Billy saw the culprit's naked back under the scourge, gridironed with red welts and worse, when he marked the dire expression in the liberated man's face as with his woolen shirt flung over him by the executioner he rushed forward from the spot to bury himself in the crowd, Billy was horrified. He resolved that never through remissness would he make himself liable to such a visitation or do or omit aught that might merit even verbal reproof. What then was

[54]Man-brokers, or crimps, made money by impressing or shanghaiing sailors. Land-sharks swindled sailors ashore.

[55]The waisters, who, as Melville explains in *White-Jacket,* attended to "the drainage and sewerage below hatches" (Chap. 3).

[56]Melville's persona White-Jacket narrowly escapes a flogging for the same offense and is saved by the intervention of Jack Chase and the corporal of marines. According to *White-Jacket,* novices often found their way into the After-Guard, which demanded "little seamanship" (Chaps. 3, 67).

his surprise and concern when ultimately he found himself getting into petty trouble occasionally about such matters as the stowage of his bag or something amiss in his hammock, matters under the police oversight of the ship's corporals of the lower decks, and which brought down on him a vague threat from one of them.

So heedful in all things as he was, how could this be? He could not understand it, and it more than vexed him. When he spoke to his young topmates about it they were either lightly incredulous or found something comical in his unconcealed anxiety. "Is it your bag, Billy?" said one. "Well, sew yourself up in it, bully boy, and then you'll be sure to know if anybody meddles with it."

Now there was a veteran aboard who because his years began to disqualify him for more active work had been recently assigned duty as mainmastman in his watch, looking to the gear belayed at the rail roundabout that great spar near the deck. At off-times the foretopman had picked up some acquaintance with him, and now in his trouble it occurred to him that he might be the sort of person to go to for wise counsel. He was an old Dansker[57] long anglicized in the service, of few words, many wrinkles, and some honorable scars. His wizened face, time-tinted and weather-stained to the complexion of an antique parchment, was here and there peppered blue by the chance explosion of a gun cartridge in action.

He was an *Agamemnon* man, some two years prior to the time of this story having served under Nelson when still captain in that ship immortal in naval memory, which dismantled and in part broken up to her bare ribs is seen a grand skeleton in Haden's etching.[58] As one of a boarding party from the *Agamemnon* he had received a cut slantwise along one temple and cheek leaving a long pale scar like a streak of dawn's light falling athwart the dark visage. It was on account of that scar and the affair in which it was known that he had received it, as well as from his blue-peppered complexion, that the Dansker went among the *Bellipotent*'s crew by the name of "Board-Her-in-the-Smoke."

Now the first time that his small weasel eyes happened to light on Billy Budd, a certain grim internal merriment set all his ancient wrinkles into antic play. Was it that his eccentric unsentimental old sapience, primitive in its kind, saw or thought it saw something which in contrast with the warship's environment looked oddly incongruous in the Handsome Sailor? But after slyly studying him at intervals, the old Merlin's[59] equivocal merriment was modified; for now when the twain would meet, it would start in his face a quizzing sort of look, but it would be but momentary and sometimes replaced by an expression of speculative query as to what might eventually befall a nature like that, dropped into a world not without some mantraps and against whose subtleties simple courage lacking experience and address, and without any touch of defensive ugliness, is of little avail; and where such innocence as man is capable of does yet in a moral emergency not always sharpen the faculties or enlighten the will.

However it was, the Dansker in his ascetic way rather took to Billy. Nor was this only because of a certain philosophic interest in such a character. There was another cause. While the old man's eccentricities, sometimes bordering on the ursine,

[57]Dane.

[58]"The Breaking Up of the *Agamemnon,*" famous etching by Sir Francis Seymour Haden (1818–1910).

[59]The magician in the legends of King Arthur; hence a sage.

repelled the juniors, Billy, undeterred thereby, revering him as a salt hero, would make advances, never passing the old *Agamemnon* man without a salutation marked by that respect which is seldom lost on the aged, however crabbed at times or whatever their station in life.

There was a vein of dry humor, or what not, in the mastman; and, whether in freak of patriarchal irony touching Billy's youth and athletic frame, or for some other and more recondite reason, from the first in addressing him he always substituted *Baby* for Billy, the Dansker in fact being the originator of the name by which the foretopman eventually became known aboard ship.

Well then, in his mysterious little difficulty going in quest of the wrinkled one, Billy found him off duty in a dogwatch ruminating by himself, seated on a shot box of the upper gun deck, now and then surveying with a somewhat cynical regard certain of the more swaggering promenaders there. Billy recounted his trouble, again wondering how it all happened. The salt seer attentively listened, accompanying the foretopman's recital with queer twitchings of his wrinkles and problematical little sparkles of his small ferret eyes. Making an end of his story, the foretopman asked, "And now, Dansker, do tell me what you think of it."

The old man, shoving up the front of his tarpaulin and deliberately rubbing the long slant scar at the point where it entered the thin hair, laconically said, "Baby Budd, *Jemmy Legs*" (meaning the master-at-arms) "is down on you."

"*Jemmy Legs!*" ejaculated Billy, his welkin eyes expanding. "What for? Why, he calls me 'the sweet and pleasant young fellow,' they tell me."

"Does he so?" grinned the grizzled one; then said, "Ay, Baby lad, a sweet voice has Jemmy Legs."

"No, not always. But to me he has. I seldom pass him but there comes a pleasant word."

"And that's because he's down upon you, Baby Budd."

Such reiteration, along with the manner of it, incomprehensible to a novice, disturbed Billy almost as much as the mystery for which he had sought explanation. Something less unpleasingly oracular he tried to extract; but the old sea Chiron, thinking perhaps that for the nonce he had sufficiently instructed his young Achilles,[60] pursed his lips, gathered all his wrinkles together, and would commit himself to nothing further.

Years, and those experiences which befall certain shrewder men subordinated lifelong to the will of superiors, all this had developed in the Dansker the pithy guarded cynicism that was his leading characteristic.

10

The next day an incident served to confirm Billy Budd in his incredulity as to the Dansker's strange summing up of the case submitted. The ship at noon, going large before the wind, was rolling on her course, and he below at dinner and engaged in some sportful talk with the members of his mess, chanced in a sudden lurch to spill

[60]In Greek myth, the wise centaur Chiron tutored the warrior Achilles.

the entire contents of his soup pan upon the new-scrubbed deck. Claggart, the master-at-arms, official rattan[61] in hand, happened to be passing along the battery in a bay of which the mess was lodged, and the greasy liquid streamed just across his path. Stepping over it, he was proceeding on his way without comment, since the matter was nothing to take notice of under the circumstances, when he happened to observe who it was that had done the spilling. His countenance changed. Pausing, he was about to ejaculate something hasty at the sailor, but checked himself, and pointing down to the streaming soup, playfully tapped him from behind with his rattan, saying in a low musical voice peculiar to him at times, "Handsomely done, my lad! And handsome is as handsome did it, too!" And with that passed on. Not noted by Billy as not coming within his view was the involuntary smile, or rather grimace, that accompanied Claggart's equivocal words. Aridly it drew down the thin corners of his shapely mouth. But everybody taking his remark as meant for humorous, and at which therefore as coming from a superior they were bound to laugh "with counterfeited glee,"[62] acted accordingly; and Billy, tickled, it may be, by the allusion to his being the Handsome Sailor, merrily joined in; then addressing his messmates exclaimed, "There now, who says that Jemmy Legs is down on me!"

"And who said he was, Beauty?" demanded one Donald with some surprise. Whereat the foretopman looked a little foolish, recalling that it was only one person, Board-Her-in-the-Smoke, who had suggested what to him was the smoky idea that this master-at-arms was in any peculiar way hostile to him. Meantime that functionary, resuming his path, must have momentarily worn some expression less guarded than that of the bitter smile, usurping the face from the heart—some distorting expression perhaps, for a drummer-boy heedlessly frolicking along from the opposite direction and chancing to come into light collision with his person was strangely disconcerted by his aspect. Nor was the impression lessened when the official, impetuously giving him a sharp cut with the rattan, vehemently exclaimed, "Look where you go!"

11

What was the matter with the master-at-arms? And, be the matter what it might, how could it have direct relation to Billy Budd, with whom prior to the affair of the spilled soup he had never come into any special contact official or otherwise? What indeed could the trouble have to do with one so little inclined to give offense as the merchant-ship's "peacemaker," even him who in Claggart's own phrase was "the sweet and pleasant young fellow"? Yes, why should Jemmy Legs, to borrow the Dansker's expression, be "down" on the Handsome Sailor? But, at heart and not for nothing, as the late chance encounter may indicate to the discerning, down on him, secretly down on him, he assuredly was.

Now to invent something touching the more private career of Claggart, something involving Billy Budd, of which something the latter should be wholly ignorant,

[61]Cane.

[62]Like the schoolboys in Oliver Goldsmith's "The Deserted Village" (1770), who laugh "with counterfeited glee" at their harsh schoolmaster's jokes.

some romantic incident implying that Claggart's knowledge of the young blue-jacket began at some period anterior to catching sight of him on board the seventy-four—all this, not so difficult to do, might avail in a way more or less interesting to account for whatever of enigma may appear to lurk in the case. But in fact there was nothing of the sort. And yet the cause necessarily to be assumed as the sole one assignable is in its very realism as much charged with that prime element of Radcliffian romance, the mysterious, as any that the ingenuity of the author of *The Mysteries of Udolpho* could devise.[63] For what can more partake of the mysterious than an antipathy spontaneous and profound such as is evoked in certain exceptional mortals by the mere aspect of some other mortal, however harmless he may be, if not called forth by this very harmlessness itself?

Now there can exist no irritating juxtaposition of dissimilar personalities comparable to that which is possible aboard a great warship fully manned and at sea. There, every day among all ranks, almost every man comes into more or less of contact with almost every other man. Wholly there to avoid even the sight of an aggravating object one must needs give it Jonah's toss[64] or jump overboard himself. Imagine how all this might eventually operate on some peculiar human creature the direct reverse of a saint!

But for the adequate comprehending of Claggart by a normal nature these hints are insufficient. To pass from a normal nature to him one must cross "the deadly space between." And this is best done by indirection.

Long ago an honest scholar, my senior, said to me in reference to one who like himself is now no more, a man so unimpeachably respectable that against him nothing was ever openly said though among the few something was whispered, "Yes, X——is a nut not to be cracked by the tap of a lady's fan. You are aware that I am the adherent of no organized religion, much less of any philosophy built into a system. Well, for all that, I think that to try and get into X——, enter his labyrinth and get out again, without a clue derived from some source other that what is known as 'knowledge of the world'—that were hardly possible, at least for me."

"Why," said I, "X——, however singular a study to some, is yet human, and knowledge of the world assuredly implies the knowledge of human nature, and in most of its varieties."

"Yes, but a superficial knowledge of it, serving ordinary purposes. But for anything deeper, I am not certain whether to know the world and to know human nature be not two distinct branches of knowledge, which while they may coexist in the same heart, yet either may exist with little or nothing of the other. Nay, in an average man of the world, his constant rubbing with it blunts that finer spiritual

[63] Ann Radcliffe (1764–1823), popular British author of Gothic novels, best known for *The Mysteries of Udolpho* (1794), in which all mysteries are ultimately explained away. In *The Confidence-Man* Melville disparages the "sallies of ingenuity" displayed by "certain psychological novelists" who "challenge astonishment at the tangled web of some character, and then raise admiration still greater at their satisfactory unraveling of it; in this way throwing open, sometimes to the understanding even of school misses, the last complications of that spirit which is affirmed by its Creator to be fearfully and wonderfully made" (Chap. 14).

[64] When Jonah's disobedience provoked God to raise a storm at sea that endangered the ship, the sailors "took up Jonah, and cast him forth into the sea" (Jonah 1:15).

insight indispensable to the understanding of the essential in certain exceptional characters, whether evil ones or good. In a matter of some importance I have seen a girl wind an old lawyer about her little finger. Nor was it the dotage of senile love. Nothing of the sort. But he knew law better than he knew the girl's heart. Coke and Blackstone[65] hardly shed so much light into obscure spiritual places as the Hebrew prophets. And who were they? Mostly recluses."

At the time, my inexperience was such that I did not quite see the drift of all this. It may be that I see it now. And, indeed, if that lexicon which is based on Holy Writ were any longer popular, one might with less difficulty define and denominate certain phenomenal men. As it is, one must turn to some authority not liable to the charge of being tinctured with the biblical element.

In a list of definitions included in the authentic translation of Plato, a list attributed to him, occurs this: "Natural Depravity: a depravity according to nature,"[66] a definition which, though savoring of Calvinism, by no means involves Calvin's dogma as to total mankind. Evidently its intent makes it applicable but to individuals. Not many are the examples of this depravity which the gallows and jail supply. At any rate, for notable instances, since these have no vulgar alloy of the brute in them, but invariably are dominated by intellectuality, one must go elsewhere. Civilization, especially if of the austerer sort, is auspicious to it. It folds itself in the mantle of respectability. It has its certain negative virtues serving as silent auxiliaries. It never allows wine to get within its guard. It is not going too far to say that it is without vices or small sins. There is a phenomenal pride in it that excludes them. It is never mercenary or avaricious. In short, the depravity here meant partakes nothing of the sordid or sensual. It is serious, but free from acerbity. Though no flatterer of mankind it never speaks ill of it.

But the thing which in eminent instances signalizes so exceptional a nature is this: Though the man's even temper and discreet bearing would seem to intimate a mind peculiarly subject to the law of reason, not the less in heart he would seem to riot in complete exemption from that law, having apparently little to do with reason further than to employ it as an ambidexter implement for effecting the irrational. That is to say: Toward the accomplishment of an aim which in wantonness of atrocity would seem to partake of the insane, he will direct a cool judgment sagacious and sound. These men are madmen, and of the most dangerous sort, for their lunacy is not continuous, but occasional, evoked by some special object; it is protectively secretive, which is as much as to say it is self-contained, so that when, moreover, most active it is to the average mind not distinguishable from sanity, and for the reason above suggested: that whatever its aims may be—and the aim is never declared—the method and the outward proceeding are always perfectly rational.

Now something such an one was Claggart, in whom was the mania of an evil nature, not engendered by vicious training or corrupting books or licentious living, but born with him and innate, in short "a depravity according to nature."

Dark sayings are these, some will say. But why? Is it because they somewhat

[65]Sir Edward Coke (1552–1634) and Sir William Blackstone (1723–1780), who laid the foundations of British jurisprudence.

[66]According to Hayford and Sealts, Melville found this definition in the Bohn edition of Plato's works, Vol. 6 (1854). He distinguishes it from the Calvinist doctrine of *total* depravity, which applies not merely to individuals, but to the entire human race.

savor of Holy Writ in its phrase "mystery of iniquity"?[67] If they do, such savor was far enough from being intended, for little will it commend these pages to many a reader of today.

The point of the present story turning on the hidden nature of the master-at-arms has necessitated this chapter. With an added hint or two in connection with the incident at the mess, the resumed narrative must be left to vindicate, as it may, its own credibility.

12

That Claggart's figure was not amiss, and his face, save the chin, well molded, has already been said. Of these favorable points he seemed not insensible, for he was not only neat but careful in his dress. But the form of Billy Budd was heroic; and if his face was without the intellectual look of the pallid Claggart's, not the less was it lit, like his, from within, though from a different source. The bonfire in his heart made luminous the rose-tan in his cheek.

In view of the marked contrast between the persons of the twain, it is more than probable that when the master-at-arms in the scene last given applied to the sailor the proverb "Handsome is as handsome does," he there let escape an ironic inkling, not caught by the young sailors who heard it, as to what it was that had first moved him against Billy, namely, his significant personal beauty.

Now envy and antipathy, passions irreconcilable in reason, nevertheless in fact may spring conjoined like Chang and Eng[68] in one birth. Is Envy then such a monster? Well, though many an arraigned mortal has in hopes of mitigated penalty pleaded guilty to horrible actions, did ever anybody seriously confess to envy? Something there is in it universally felt to be more shameful than even felonious crime. And not only does everybody disown it, but the better sort are inclined to incredulity when it is in earnest imputed to an intelligent man. But since its lodgment is in the heart not the brain, no degree of intellect supplies a guarantee against it. But Claggart's was no vulgar form of the passion. Nor, as directed toward Billy Budd, did it partake of that streak of apprehensive jealousy that marred Saul's visage perturbedly brooding on the comely young David.[69] Claggart's envy struck deeper. If askance he eyed the good looks, cheery health, and frank enjoyment of young life in Billy Budd, it was because these went along with a nature that, as Claggart magnetically felt, had in its simplicity never willed malice or experienced the reactionary bite of that serpent. To him, the spirit lodged within Billy, and looking out from his welkin eyes as from windows, that ineffability it was which made the dimple in his dyed cheek, suppled his joints, and dancing in his yellow curls made him pre-eminently the Handsome Sailor. One person excepted, the master-at-arms was perhaps the only man in the ship intellectually capable of adequately appreciating

[67]II Thessalonians 2:7 warns believers against the "man of sin," or Antichrist, temporarily allowed by God to deceive the world: "For the mystery of iniquity doth already work."

[68]The original Siamese twins (1811–1874), exhibited as freaks in P.T. Barnum's American Museum.

[69]I Samuel 16:14–23 and 18:6–12 tell of the relationship between King Saul and the "comely" David he adopts as his armourbearer. Saul's envy arises when David becomes a favorite with the people, who praise his military prowess more than Saul's.

the moral phenomenon presented in Billy Budd. And the insight but intensified his passion, which assuming various secret forms within him, at times assumed that of cynic disdain, disdain of innocence—to be nothing more than innocent! Yet in an aesthetic way he saw the charm of it, the courageous free-and-easy temper of it, and fain would have shared it, but he despaired of it.

With no power to annul the elemental evil in him, though readily enough he could hide it; apprehending the good, but powerless to be it; a nature like Claggart's, surcharged with energy as such natures almost invariably are, what recourse is left to it but to recoil upon itself and, like the scorpion for which the Creator alone is responsible, act out to the end the part allotted it.

13

Passion, and passion in its profoundest, is not a thing demanding a palatial stage whereon to play its part. Down among the groundlings, among the beggars and rakers of the garbage, profound passion is enacted. And the circumstances that provoke it, however trivial or mean, are no measure of its power. In the present instance the stage is a scrubbed gun deck, and one of the external provocations a man-of-war's man's spilled soup.

Now when the master-at-arms noticed whence came that greasy fluid streaming before his feet, he must have taken it—to some extent wilfully, perhaps—not for the mere accident it assuredly was, but for the sly escape of a spontaneous feeling on Billy's part more or less answering to the antipathy on his own. In effect a foolish demonstration, he must have thought, and very harmless, like the futile kick of a heifer, which yet were the heifer a shod stallion would not be so harmless. Even so was it that into the gall of Claggart's envy he infused the vitriol of his contempt. But the incident confirmed to him certain telltale reports purveyed to his ear by "Squeak," one of his more cunning corporals, a grizzled little man, so nicknamed by the sailors on account of his squeaky voice and sharp visage ferreting about the dark corners of the lower decks after interlopers, satirically suggesting to them the idea of a rat in a cellar.

From his chief's employing him as an implicit tool in laying little traps for the worriment of the foretopman—for it was from the master-at-arms that the petty persecutions heretofore adverted to had proceeded—the corporal, having naturally enough concluded that his master could have no love for the sailor, made it his business, faithful understrapper that he was, to foment the ill blood by perverting to his chief certain innocent frolics of the good-natured foretopman, besides inventing for his mouth sundry contumelious epithets he claimed to have overheard him let fall. The master-at-arms never suspected the veracity of these reports, more especially as to the epithets, for he well knew how secretly unpopular may become a master-at-arms, at least a master-at-arms of those days, zealous in his function, and how the bluejackets shoot at him in private their raillery and wit; the nickname by which he goes among them (Jemmy Legs) implying under the form of merriment their cherished disrespect and dislike. But in view of the greediness of hate for pabulum[70] it hardly needed a purveyor to feed Claggart's passion.

[70]Nourishment.

An uncommon prudence is habitual with the subtler depravity, for it has everything to hide. And in case of an injury but suspected, its secretiveness voluntarily cuts it off from enlightenment or disillusion; and, not unreluctantly, action is taken upon surmise as upon certainty. And the retaliation is apt to be in monstrous disproportion to the supposed offense; for when in anybody was revenge in its exactions aught else but an inordinate usurer? But how with Claggart's conscience? For though consciences are unlike as foreheads, every intelligence, not excluding the scriptural devils who "believe and tremble,"[71] has one. But Claggart's conscience being but the lawyer to his will, made ogres of trifles, probably arguing that the motive imputed to Billy in spilling the soup just when he did, together with the epithets alleged, these, if nothing more, made a strong case against him; nay, justified animosity into a sort of retributive righteousness. The Pharisee is the Guy Fawkes[72] prowling in the hid chambers underlying some natures like Claggart's. And they can really form no conception of an unreciprocated malice. Probably the master-at-arms' clandestine persecution of Billy was started to try the temper of the man; but it had not developed any quality in him that enmity could make official use of or even pervert into plausible self-justification; so that the occurrence at the mess, petty if it were, was a welcome one to that peculiar conscience assigned to be the private mentor of Claggart; and, for the rest, not improbably it put him upon new experiments.

14

Not many days after the last incident narrated, something befell Billy Budd that more graveled[73] him than aught that had previously occurred.

It was a warm night for the latitude; and the foretopman, whose watch at the time was properly below, was dozing on the uppermost deck whither he had ascended from his hot hammock, one of hundreds suspended so closely wedged together over a lower gun deck that there was little or no swing to them. He lay as in the shadow of a hillside, stretched under the lee[74] of the booms, a piled ridge of spare spars amidships between foremast and mainmast among which the ship's largest boat, the launch, was stowed. Alongside of three other slumberers from below, he lay near that end of the booms which approaches the foremast; his station aloft on duty as a foretopman being just over the deck-station of the forecastlemen, entitling him according to usage to make himself more or less at home in that neighborhood.

Presently he was stirred into semiconsciousness by somebody, who must have previously sounded the sleep of the others, touching his shoulder, and then, as the foretopman raised his head, breathing into his ear in a quick whisper, "Slip into the lee forechains, Billy; there is something in the wind. Don't speak. Quick, I will meet you there," and disappearing.

[71]James 2:19: "Thou believest that there is one God; . . . the devils also believe, and tremble."

[72]In Matthew 22 and 23, the Pharisees try to entrap Jesus, who denounces them as hypocrites for splitting hairs over the letter of the law while neglecting "the weightier matters of the law, judgment, mercy, and faith." The Catholic conspirator Guy Fawkes, a participant in the Gunpowder Plot of 1605, was caught in the cellar of the Parliament building, which he was trying to blow up.

[73]Perplexed, bothered.

[74]Shelter (from the wind).

Now Billy, like sundry other essentially good-natured ones, had some of the weaknesses inseparable from essential good nature; and among these was a reluctance, almost an incapacity of plumply saying *no* to an abrupt proposition not obviously absurd on the face of it, nor obviously unfriendly, nor iniquitous. And being of warm blood, he had not the phlegm tacitly to negative any proposition by unresponsive inaction. Like his sense of fear, his apprehension as to aught outside of the honest and natural was seldom very quick. Besides, upon the present occasion, the drowse from his sleep still hung upon him.

However it was, he mechanically rose and, sleepily wondering what could be in the wind, betook himself to the designated place, a narrow platform, one of six, outside of the high bulwarks and screened by the great deadeyes and multiple columned lanyards of the shrouds and backstays;[75] and, in a great warship of that time, of dimensions commensurate to the hull's magnitude; a tarry balcony in short, overhanging the sea, and so secluded that one mariner of the *Bellipotent,* a Nonconformist old tar of a serious turn, made it even in daytime his private oratory.[76]

In this retired nook the stranger soon joined Billy Budd. There was no moon as yet; a haze obscured the starlight. He could not distinctly see the stranger's face. Yet from something in the outline and carriage, Billy took him, and correctly, for one of the afterguard.

"Hist! Billy," said the man, in the same quick cautionary whisper as before. "You were impressed, weren't you? Well, so was I"; and he paused, as to mark the effect. But Billy, not knowing exactly what to make of this, said nothing. Then the other: "We are not the only impressed ones, Billy. There's a gang of us.—Couldn't you—help—at a pinch?"

"What do you mean?" demanded Billy, here thoroughly shaking off his drowse.

"Hist, hist!" the hurried whisper now growing husky. "See here," and the man held up two small objects faintly twinkling in the night-light; "see, they are yours, Billy, if you'll only——"

But Billy broke in, and in his resentful eagerness to deliver himself his vocal infirmity somewhat intruded. "D—d—damme, I don't know what you are d—d—driving at, or what you mean, but you had better g—g—go where you belong!" For the moment the fellow, as confounded, did not stir; and Billy, springing to his feet, said, "If you d—don't start, I'll t—t—toss you back over the r—rail!" There was no mistaking this, and the mysterious emissary decamped, disappearing in the direction of the mainmast in the shadow of the booms.

"Hallo, what's the matter?" here came growling from a forecastleman awakened from his deck-doze by Billy's raised voice. And as the foretopman reappeared and was recognized by him: "Ah, Beauty, is it you? Well, something must have been the matter, for you st—st—stuttered."

"Oh," rejoined Billy, now mastering the impediment, "I found an afterguardsman in our part of the ship here, and I bid him be off where he belongs."

"And is that all you did about it, Foretopman?" gruffly demanded another, an irascible old fellow of brick-colored visage and hair who was known to his associate

[75]Deadeyes are flat, round wooden blocks with holes for lanyards, short ropes which fasten the shrouds. Shrouds and backstays are sets of ropes extending sideways and back from the masts, to give them support.

[76]Place of prayer.

forecastlemen as "Red Pepper." "Such sneaks I should like to marry to the gunner's daughter!"—by that expression meaning that he would like to subject them to disciplinary castigation over a gun.

However, Billy's rendering of the matter satisfactorily accounted to these inquirers for the brief commotion, since of all the sections of a ship's company the forecastlemen, veterans for the most part and bigoted in their sea prejudices, are the most jealous in resenting territorial encroachments, especially on the part of any of the afterguard, of whom they have but a sorry opinion—chiefly landsmen, never going aloft except to reef or furl the mainsail, and in no wise competent to handle a marlinspike or turn in a deadeye, say.

15

This incident sorely puzzled Billy Budd. It was an entirely new experience, the first time in his life that he had ever been personally approached in underhand intriguing fashion. Prior to this encounter he had known nothing of the afterguardsman, the two men being stationed wide apart, one forward and aloft during his watch, the other on deck and aft.

What could it mean? And could they really be guineas, those two glittering objects the interloper had held up to his (Billy's) eyes? Where could the fellow get guineas? Why, even spare buttons are not so plentiful at sea. The more he turned the matter over, the more he was nonplussed, and made uneasy and discomfited. In his disgustful recoil from an overture which, though he but ill comprehended, he instinctively knew must involve evil of some sort, Billy Budd was like a young horse fresh from the pasture suddenly inhaling a vile whiff from some chemical factory, and by repeated snortings trying to get it out of his nostrils and lungs. This frame of mind barred all desire of holding further parley with the fellow, even were it but for the purpose of gaining some enlightenment as to his design in approaching him. And yet he was not without natural curiosity to see how such a visitor in the dark would look in broad day.

He espied him the following afternoon in his first dogwatch below, one of the smokers on that forward part of the upper gun deck allotted to the pipe. He recognized him by his general cut and build more than by his round freckled face and glassy eyes of pale blue, veiled with lashes all but white. And yet Billy was a bit uncertain whether indeed it were he—yonder chap about his own age chatting and laughing in freehearted way, leaning against a gun; a genial young fellow enough to look at, and something of a rattlebrain, to all appearance. Rather chubby too for a sailor, even an afterguardsman. In short, the last man in the world, one would think, to be overburdened with thoughts, especially those perilous thoughts that must needs belong to a conspirator in any serious project, or even to the underling of such a conspirator.

Although Billy was not aware of it, the fellow, with a sidelong watchful glance, had perceived Billy first, and then noting that Billy was looking at him, thereupon nodded a familiar sort of friendly recognition as to an old acquaintance, without interrupting the talk he was engaged in with the group of smokers. A day or two afterwards, chancing in the evening promenade on a gun deck to pass Billy, he offered a flying word of good-fellowship, as it were, which by its unexpectedness, and equivocalness under the circumstances, so embarrassed Billy that he knew not how to respond to it, and let it go unnoticed.

Billy was now left more at a loss than before. The ineffectual speculations into which he was led were so disturbingly alien to him that he did his best to smother them. It never entered his mind that here was a matter which, from its extreme questionableness, it was his duty as a loyal bluejacket to report in the proper quarter. And, probably, had such a step been suggested to him, he would have been deterred from taking it by the thought, one of novice magnanimity, that it would savor overmuch of the dirty work of a telltale. He kept the thing to himself. Yet upon one occasion he could not forbear a little disburdening himself to the old Dansker, tempted thereto perhaps by the influence of a balmy night when the ship lay becalmed; the twain, silent for the most part, sitting together on deck, their heads propped against the bulwarks. But it was only a partial and anonymous account that Billy gave, the unfounded scruples above referred to preventing full disclosure to anybody. Upon hearing Billy's version, the sage Dansker seemed to divine more than he was told; and after a little meditation, during which his wrinkles were pursed as into a point, quite effacing for the time that quizzing expression his face sometimes wore: "Didn't I say so, Baby Budd?"

"Say what?" demanded Billy.

"Why, *Jemmy Legs* is *down* on you."

"And what," rejoined Billy in amazement, "has *Jemmy Legs* to do with that cracked afterguardsman?"

"Ho, it was an afterguardsman, then. A cat's-paw, a cat's-paw!"[77] And with that exclamation, whether it had reference to a light puff of air just then coming over the calm sea, or a subtler relation to the afterguardsman, there is no telling, the old Merlin gave a twisting wrench with his black teeth at his plug of tobacco, vouchsafing no reply to Billy's impetuous question, though now repeated, for it was his wont to relapse into grim silence when interrogated in skeptical sort as to any of his sententious oracles, not always very clear ones, rather partaking of that obscurity which invests most Delphic[78] deliverances from any quarter.

Long experience had very likely brought this old man to that bitter prudence which never interferes in aught and never gives advice.

16

Yes, despite the Dansker's pithy insistence as to the master-at-arms being at the bottom of these strange experiences of Billy on board the *Bellipotent,* the young sailor was ready to ascribe them to almost anybody but the man who, to use Billy's own expression, "always had a pleasant word for him." This is to be wondered at. Yet not so much to be wondered at. In certain matters, some sailors even in mature life

[77]Hayford and Sealts point out that Melville is punning on the double meaning of the word as a light puff of air that barely ruffles the surface of the water, and as a "good-looking seaman employed to entice volunteers."

[78]The oracle of Delphi issued ambiguous and obscure prophecies.

remain unsophisticated enough. But a young seafarer of the disposition of our athletic foretopman is much of a child-man. And yet a child's utter innocence is but its blank ignorance, and the innocence more or less wanes as intelligence waxes. But in Billy Budd intelligence, such as it was, had advanced while yet his simple-mindedness remained for the most part unaffected. Experience is a teacher indeed; yet did Billy's years make his experience small. Besides, he had none of that intuitive knowledge of the bad which in natures not good or incompletely so foreruns experience, and therefore may pertain, as in some instances it too clearly does pertain, even to youth.

And what could Billy know of man except of man as a mere sailor? And the old-fashioned sailor, the veritable man before the mast, the sailor from boyhood up, he, though indeed of the same species as a landsman, is in some respects singularly distinct from him. The sailor is frankness, the landsman is finesse. Life is not a game with the sailor, demanding the long head—no intricate game of chess where few moves are made in straightforwardness and ends are attained by indirection, an oblique, tedious, barren game hardly worth that poor candle burnt out in playing it.

Yes, as a class, sailors are in character a juvenile race. Even their deviations are marked by juvenility, this more especially holding true with the sailors of Billy's time. Then too, certain things which apply to all sailors do more pointedly operate here and there upon the junior one. Every sailor, too, is accustomed to obey orders without debating them; his life afloat is externally ruled for him; he is not brought into that promiscuous commerce with mankind where unobstructed free agency on equal terms—equal superficially, at least—soon teaches one that unless upon occasion he exercise a distrust keen in proportion to the fairness of the appearance, some foul turn may be served him. A ruled undemonstrative distrustfulness is so habitual, not with businessmen so much as with men who know their kind in less shallow relations than business, namely, certain men of the world, that they come at last to employ it all but unconsciously; and some of them would very likely feel real surprise at being charged with it as one of their general characteristics.

17

But after the little matter at the mess Billy Budd no more found himself in strange trouble at times about his hammock or his clothes bag or what not. As to that smile that occasionally sunned him, and the pleasant passing word, these were, if not more frequent, yet if anything more pronounced than before.

But for all that, there were certain other demonstrations now. When Claggart's unobserved glance happened to light on belted Billy rolling along the upper gun deck in the leisure of the second dogwatch, exchanging passing broadsides of fun with other young promenaders in the crowd, that glance would follow the cheerful sea Hyperion[79] with a settled meditative and melancholy expression, his eyes strangely suffused with incipient feverish tears. Then would Claggart look like the man of sorrows. Yes, and sometimes the melancholy expression would have in it a

[79]A Titan and sun god, later identified with Apollo, and similarly depicted as an epitome of youthful, manly beauty.

touch of soft yearning, as if Claggart could even have loved Billy but for fate and ban. But this was an evanescence, and quickly repented of, as it were, by an immitigable look, pinching and shriveling the visage into the momentary semblance of a wrinkled walnut. But sometimes catching sight in advance of the foretopman coming in his direction, he would, upon their nearing, step aside a little to let him pass, dwelling upon Billy for the moment with the glittering dental satire of a Guise.[80] But upon any abrupt unforeseen encounter a red light would flash forth from his eye like a spark from an anvil in a dusk smithy. That quick, fierce light was a strange one, darted from orbs which in repose were of a color nearest approaching a deeper violet, the softest of shades.

Though some of these caprices of the pit could not but be observed by their object, yet were they beyond the construing of such a nature. And the thews of Billy were hardly compatible with that sort of sensitive spiritual organization which in some cases instinctively conveys to ignorant innocence an admonition of the proximity of the malign. He thought the master-at-arms acted in a manner rather queer at times. That was all. But the occasional frank air and pleasant word went for what they purported to be, the young sailor never having heard as yet of the "too fair-spoken man."

Had the foretopman been conscious of having done or said anything to provoke the ill will of the official, it would have been different with him, and his sight might have been purged if not sharpened. As it was, innocence was his blinder.

So was it with him in yet another matter. Two minor officers, the armorer and captain of the hold, with whom he had never exchanged a word, his position in the ship not bringing him into contact with them, these men now for the first began to cast upon Billy, when they chanced to encounter him, that peculiar glance which evidences that the man from whom it comes has been some way tampered with, and to the prejudice of him upon whom the glance lights. Never did it occur to Billy as a thing to be noted or a thing suspicious, though he well knew the fact, that the armorer and captain of the hold, with the ship's yeoman, apothecary, and others of that grade, were by naval usage messmates of the master-at-arms, men with ears convenient to his confidential tongue.

But the general popularity that came from our Handsome Sailor's manly forwardness upon occasion and irresistible good nature, indicating no mental superiority tending to excite an invidious feeling, this good will on the part of most of his shipmates made him the less to concern himself about such mute aspects toward him as those whereto allusion has just been made, aspects he could not so fathom as to infer their whole import.

As to the afterguardsman, though Billy for reasons already given necessarily saw little of him, yet when the two did happen to meet, invariably came the fellow's offhand cheerful recognition, sometimes accompanied by a passing pleasant word or two. Whatever that equivocal young person's original design may really have

[80]French ducal family notorious for anti-Protestant intrigues. Henri de Guise (1550–1588) helped mastermind the massacre of the Huguenots on St. Bartholomew's Day, 1572. "Glittering dental satire" is Melville's version of "one may smile, and smile, and be a villain" (*Hamlet* I.v.108).

been, or the design of which he might have been the deputy, certain it was from his manner upon these occasions that he had wholly dropped it.

It was as if his precocity of crookedness (and every vulgar villain is precocious) had for once deceived him, and the man he had sought to entrap as a simpleton had through his very simplicity ignominiously baffled him.

But shrewd ones may opine that it was hardly possible for Billy to refrain from going up to the afterguardsman and bluntly demanding to know his purpose in the initial interview so abruptly closed in the forechains. Shrewd ones may also think it but natural in Billy to set about sounding some of the other impressed men of the ship in order to discover what basis, if any, there was for the emissary's obscure suggestions as to plotting disaffection aboard. Yes, shrewd ones may so think. But something more, or rather something else than mere shrewdness is perhaps needful for the due understanding of such a character as Billy Budd's.

As to Claggart, the monomania in the man—if that indeed it were—as involuntarily disclosed by starts in the manifestations detailed, yet in general covered over by his self-contained and rational demeanor; this, like a subterranean fire, was eating its way deeper and deeper in him. Something decisive must come of it.

18

After the mysterious interview in the forechains, the one so abruptly ended there by Billy, nothing especially germane to the story occurred until the events now about to be narrated.

Elsewhere it has been said that in the lack of frigates (of course better sailers than line-of-battle ships) in the English squadron up the Straits at that period, the *Bellipotent 74* was occasionally employed not only as an available substitute for a scout, but at times on detached service of more important kind. This was not alone because of her sailing qualities, not common in a ship of her rate, but quite as much, probably, that the character of her commander, it was thought, specially adapted him for any duty where under unforeseen difficulties a prompt initiative might have to be taken in some matter demanding knowledge and ability in addition to those qualities implied in good seamanship. It was on an expedition of the latter sort, a somewhat distant one, and when the *Bellipotent* was almost at her furthest remove from the fleet, that in the latter part of an afternoon watch she unexpectedly came in sight of a ship of the enemy. It proved to be a frigate. The latter, perceiving through the glass that the weight of men and metal would be heavily against her, invoking her light heels crowded sail to get away. After a chase urged almost against hope and lasting until about the middle of the first dogwatch, she signally succeeded in effecting her escape.

Not long after the pursuit had been given up, and ere the excitement incident thereto had altogether waned away, the master-at-arms, ascending from his cavernous sphere, made his appearance cap in hand by the mainmast respectfully waiting the notice of Captain Vere, then solitary walking the weather side of the quarter-deck, doubtless somewhat chafed at the failure of the pursuit. The spot where Claggart stood was the place allotted to men of lesser grades seeking some more particular interview either with the officer of the deck or the captain himself. But from the latter it was not often that a sailor or petty officer of those days would seek a hearing; only some exceptional cause would, according to established custom, have warranted that.

Presently, just as the commander, absorbed in his reflections, was on the point of turning aft in his promenade, he became sensible of Claggart's presence, and saw the doffed cap held in deferential expectancy. Here be it said that Captain Vere's personal knowledge of this petty officer had only begun at the time of the ship's last sailing from home, Claggart then for the first, in transfer from a ship detained for repairs, supplying on board the *Bellipotent* the place of a previous master-at-arms disabled and ashore.

No sooner did the commander observe who it was that now deferentially stood awaiting his notice than a peculiar expression came over him. It was not unlike that which uncontrollably will flit across the countenance of one at unawares encountering a person who, though known to him indeed, has hardly been long enough known for thorough knowledge, but something in whose aspect nevertheless now for the first provokes a vaguely repellent distaste. But coming to a stand and resuming much of his wonted official manner, save that a sort of impatience lurked in the intonation of the opening word, he said "Well? What is it, Master-at-arms?"

With the air of a subordinate grieved at the necessity of being a messenger of ill tidings, and while conscientiously determined to be frank yet equally resolved upon shunning overstatement, Claggart at this invitation, or rather summons to disburden, spoke up. What he said, conveyed in the language of no uneducated man, was to the effect following, if not altogether in these words, namely, that during the chase and preparations for the possible encounter he had seen enough to convince him that at least one sailor aboard was a dangerous character in a ship mustering some who not only had taken a guilty part in the late serious troubles, but others also who, like the man in question, had entered His Majesty's service under another form than enlistment.

At this point Captain Vere with some impatience interrupted him: "Be direct, man; say *impressed men.*"

Claggart made a gesture of subservience, and proceeded. Quite lately he (Claggart) had begun to suspect that on the gun decks some sort of movement prompted by the sailor in question was covertly going on, but he had not thought himself warranted in reporting the suspicion so long as it remained indistinct. But from what he had that afternoon observed in the man referred to, the suspicion of something clandestine going on had advanced to a point less removed from certainty. He deeply felt, he added, the serious responsibility assumed in making a report involving such possible consequences to the individual mainly concerned, besides tending to augment those natural anxieties which every naval commander must feel in view of extraordinary outbreaks so recent as those which, he sorrowfully said it, it needed not to name.

Now at the first broaching of the matter Captain Vere, taken by surprise, could not wholly dissemble his disquietude. But as Claggart went on, the former's aspect changed into restiveness under something in the testifier's manner in giving his testimony. However, he refrained from interrupting him. And Claggart, continuing, concluded with this: "God forbid, your honor, that the *Bellipotent*'s should be the experience of the ——"

"Never mind that!" here peremptorily broke in the superior, his face altering with anger, instinctively divining the ship that the other was about to name, one in which the Nore Mutiny had assumed a singularly tragical character that for a time jeopardized the life of its commander. Under the circumstances he was indignant at the purposed allusion. When the commissioned officers themselves were on all occasions very heedful how they referred to the recent events in the fleet, for a petty officer unnecessarily to allude to them in the presence of his captain, this struck him as a most immodest presumption. Besides, to his quick sense of self-respect it even looked under the circumstances something like an attempt to alarm him. Nor at first was he without some surprise that one who so far as he had hitherto come under his notice had shown considerable tact in his function should in this particular evince such lack of it.

But these thoughts and kindred dubious ones flitting across his mind were suddenly replaced by an intuitional surmise which, though as yet obscure in form, served practically to affect his reception of the ill tidings. Certain it is that, long versed in everything pertaining to the complicated gun-deck life, which like every other form of life has its secret mines and dubious side, the side popularly disclaimed, Captain Vere did not permit himself to be unduly disturbed by the general tenor of his subordinate's report.

Furthermore, if in view of recent events prompt action should be taken at the first palpable sign of recurring insubordination, for all that, not judicious would it be, he thought, to keep the idea of lingering disaffection alive by undue forwardness in crediting an informer, even if his own subordinate and charged among other things with police surveillance of the crew. This feeling would not perhaps have so prevailed with him were it not that upon a prior occasion the patriotic zeal officially evinced by Claggart had somewhat irritated him as appearing rather supersensible and strained. Furthermore, something even in the official's self-possessed and somewhat ostentatious manner in making his specifications strangely reminded him of a bandsman, a perjurous witness in a capital case before a court-martial ashore of which when a lieutenant he (Captain Vere) had been a member.

Now the peremptory check given to Claggart in the matter of the arrested allusion was quickly followed up by this: "You say that there is at least one dangerous man aboard. Name him."

"William Budd, a foretopman, your honor."

"William Budd!" repeated Captain Vere with unfeigned astonishment. "And mean you the man that Lieutenant Ratcliffe took from the merchantman not very long ago, the young fellow who seems to be so popular with the men—Billy, the Handsome Sailor, as they call him?"

"The same, your honor; but for all his youth and good looks, a deep one. Not for nothing does he insinuate himself into the good will of his shipmates, since at the least they will at a pinch say—all hands will—a good word for him, and at all hazards. Did Lieutenant Ratcliffe happen to tell your honor of that adroit fling of Budd's, jumping up in the cutter's bow under the merchantman's stern when he was being taken off? It is even masked by that sort of good-humored air that at heart he resents his impressment. You have but noted his fair cheek. A mantrap may be under the ruddy-tipped daisies."

Now the Handsome Sailor as a signal figure among the crew had naturally enough attracted the captain's attention from the first. Though in general not very demonstrative to his officers, he had congratulated Lieutenant Ratcliffe upon his good fortune in lighting on such a fine specimen of the *genus homo,* who in the nude might have posed for a statue of young Adam before the Fall. As to Billy's adieu to the ship *Rights-of-Man,* which the boarding lieutenant had indeed reported to him, but, in a deferential way, more as a good story than aught else, Captain Vere, though mistakenly understanding it as a satiric sally, had but thought so much the better of the impressed man for it; as a military sailor, admiring the spirit that could take an arbitrary enlistment so merrily and sensibly. The foretopman's conduct, too, so far as it had fallen under the captain's notice, had confirmed the first happy augury, while the new recruit's qualities as a "sailor-man" seemed to be such that he had thought of recommending him to the executive officer for promotion to a place that would more frequently bring him under his own observation, namely, the captaincy of the mizzentop, replacing there in the starboard watch a man not so young whom partly for that reason he deemed less fitted for the post. Be it parenthesized here that since the mizzentopmen have not to handle such breadths of heavy canvas as the lower sails on the mainmast and foremast, a young man if of the right stuff not only seems best adapted to duty there, but in fact is generally selected for the captaincy of that top, and the company under him are light hands and often but striplings. In sum, Captain Vere had from the beginning deemed Billy Budd to be what in the naval parlance of the time was called a "King's bargain": that is to say, for His Britannic Majesty's navy a capital investment at small outlay or none at all.

After a brief pause, during which the reminiscences above mentioned passed vividly through his mind and he weighed the import of Claggart's last suggestion conveyed in the phrase "mantrap under the daisies," and the more he weighed it the less reliance he felt in the informer's good faith, suddenly he turned upon him and in a low voice demanded: "Do you come to me, Master-at-arms, with so foggy a tale? As to Budd, cite me an act or spoken word of his confirmatory of what you in general charge against him. Stay," drawing nearer to him; "heed what you speak. Just now, and in a case like this, there is a yardarm-end[81] for the false witness."

"Ah, your honor!" sighed Claggart, mildly shaking his shapely head as in sad deprecation of such unmerited severity of tone. Then, bridling—erecting himself as in virtuous self-assertion—he circumstantially alleged certain words and acts which collectively, if credited, led to presumptions mortally inculpating Budd. And for some of these averments, he added, substantiating proof was not far.

With gray eyes impatient and distrustful essaying to fathom to the bottom Claggart's calm violet ones, Captain Vere again heard him out; then for the moment stood ruminating. The mood he evinced, Claggart—himself for the time liberated from the other's scrutiny—steadily regarded with a look difficult to render: a look curious of the operation of his tactics, a look such as might have been that of the spokesman of the envious children of Jacob deceptively imposing upon the troubled patriarch the blood-dyed coat of young Joseph.[82]

[81]Used for hangings. Hayford and Sealts compare the scene to the one in which Shakespeare's Othello insists on "ocular proof" in response to Iago's accusations against Desdemona (III.iii).

[82]After selling Joseph into slavery, his jealous brothers dipped his coat in blood to convince their father Jacob that Joseph had been killed by a wild beast (Genesis 37:31–33).

Though something exceptional in the moral quality of Captain Vere made him, in earnest encounter with a fellow man, a veritable touchstone of that man's essential nature, yet now as to Claggart and what was really going on in him his feeling partook less of intuitional conviction than of strong suspicion clogged by strange dubieties. The perplexity he evinced proceeded less from aught touching the man informed against—as Claggart doubtless opined—than from considerations how best to act in regard to the informer. At first, indeed, he was naturally for summoning that substantiation of his allegations which Claggart said was at hand. But such a proceeding would result in the matter at once getting abroad, which in the present stage of it, he thought, might undesirably affect the ship's company. If Claggart was a false witness—that closed the affair. And therefore, before trying the accusation, he would first practically test the accuser; and he thought this could be done in a quiet, undemonstrative way.

The measure he determined upon involved a shifting of the scene, a transfer to a place less exposed to observation than the broad quarter-deck. For although the few gun-room officers there at the time had, in due observance of naval etiquette, withdrawn to leeward the moment Captain Vere had begun his promenade on the deck's weather side; and though during the colloquy with Claggart they of course ventured not to diminish the distance; and though throughout the interview Captain Vere's voice was far from high, and Claggart's silvery and low; and the wind in the cordage and the wash of the sea helped the more to put them beyond earshot; nevertheless, the interview's continuance already had attracted observation from some topmen aloft and other sailors in the waist or further forward.

Having determined upon his measures, Captain Vere forthwith took action. Abruptly turning to Claggart, he asked, "Master-at-arms, is it now Budd's watch aloft?"

"No, your honor."

Whereupon, "Mr. Wilkes!" summoning the nearest midshipman. "Tell Albert to come to me." Albert was the captain's hammock-boy, a sort of sea valet in whose discretion and fidelity his master had much confidence. The lad appeared.

"You know Budd, the foretopman?"

"I do, sir."

"Go find him. It is his watch off. Manage to tell him out of earshot that he is wanted aft. Contrive it that he speaks to nobody. Keep him in talk yourself. And not till you get well aft here, not till then let him know that the place where he is wanted is my cabin. You understand. Go.—Master-at-arms, show yourself on the decks below, and when you think it time for Albert to be coming with his man, stand by quietly to follow the sailor in."

19

Now when the foretopman found himself in the cabin, closeted there, as it were, with the captain and Claggart, he was surprised enough. But it was a surprise unaccompanied by apprehension or distrust. To an immature nature essentially honest and humane, forewarning intimations of subtler danger from one's kind come tardily if at all. The only thing that took shape in the young sailor's mind was this: Yes, the captain, I have always thought, looks kindly upon me. Wonder if he's going to make me his coxswain. I should like that. And may be now he is going to ask the master-at-arms about me.

"Shut the door there, sentry," said the commander; "stand without, and let nobody come in.—Now, Master-at-arms, tell this man to his face what you told of him to me," and stood prepared to scrutinize the mutually confronting visages.

With the measured step and calm collected air of an asylum physician approaching in the public hall some patient beginning to show indications of a coming paroxysm, Claggart deliberately advanced within short range of Billy and, mesmerically looking him in the eye, briefly recapitulated the accusation.

Not at first did Billy take it in. When he did, the rose-tan of his cheek looked struck as by white leprosy. He stood like one impaled and gagged. Meanwhile the accuser's eyes, removing not as yet from the blue dilated ones, underwent a phenomenal change, their wonted rich violet color blurring into a muddy purple. Those lights of human intelligence, losing human expression, were gelidly protruding like the alien eyes of certain uncatalogued creatures of the deep. The first mesmeristic glance was one of serpent fascination; the last was as the paralyzing lurch of the torpedo fish.[83]

"Speak, man!" said Captain Vere to the transfixed one, struck by his aspect even more than by Claggart's. "Speak! Defend yourself!" Which appeal caused but a strange dumb gesturing and gurgling in Billy; amazement at such an accusation so suddenly sprung on inexperienced nonage;[84] this, and, it may be, horror of the accuser's eyes, serving to bring out his lurking defect and in this instance for the time intensifying it into a convulsed tongue-tie; while the intent head and entire form straining forward in an agony of ineffectual eagerness to obey the injunction to speak and defend himself, gave an expression to the face like that of a condemned vestal priestess in the moment of being buried alive, and in the first struggle against suffocation.[85]

Though at the time Captain Vere was quite ignorant of Billy's liability to vocal impediment, he now immediately divined it, since vividly Billy's aspect recalled to him that of a bright young schoolmate of his whom he had once seen struck by much the same startling impotence in the act of eagerly rising in the class to be foremost in response to a testing question put to it by the master. Going close up to the young sailor, and laying a soothing hand on his shoulder, he said, "There is no hurry, my boy. Take your time, take your time." Contrary to the effect intended, these words so fatherly in tone, doubtless touching Billy's heart to the quick, prompted yet more violent efforts at utterance—efforts soon ending for the time in confirming the paralysis, and bringing to his face an expression which was as a crucifixion to behold. The next instant, quick as the flame from a discharged cannon at night, his right arm shot out, and Claggart dropped to the deck. Whether intentionally or but owing to the young athlete's superior height, the blow had taken effect full upon the forehead, so shapely and intellectual-looking a feature in the master-at-arms; so that the body fell

[83]Also known as the electric ray, a flat fish with a tapering tail, which paralyzes its victims with electricity.

[84]Youth.

[85]The vestal virgins, priestesses of the Roman goddess Vesta, were buried alive for violating their vows of chastity.

over lengthwise, like a heavy plank tilted from erectness. A gasp or two, and he lay motionless.

"Fated boy," breathed Captain Vere in tone so low as to be almost a whisper, "what have you done! But here, help me."

The twain raised the felled one from the loins up into a sitting position. The spare form flexibly acquiesced, but inertly. It was like handling a dead snake. They lowered it back. Regaining erectness, Captain Vere with one hand covering his face stood to all appearance as impassive as the object at his feet. Was he absorbed in taking in all the bearings of the event and what was best not only now at once to be done, but also in the sequel? Slowly he uncovered his face; and the effect was as if the moon emerging from eclipse should reappear with quite another aspect than that which had gone into hiding. The father in him, manifested towards Billy thus far in the scene, was replaced by the military disciplinarian. In his official tone he bade the foretopman retire to a stateroom aft (pointing it out), and there remain till thence summoned. This order Billy in silence mechanically obeyed. Then going to the cabin door where it opened on the quarter-deck, Captain Vere said to the sentry without, "Tell somebody to send Albert here." When the lad appeared, his master so contrived it that he should not catch sight of the prone one. "Albert," he said to him, "tell the surgeon I wish to see him. You need not come back till called."

When the surgeon entered—a self-poised character of that grave sense and experience that hardly anything could take him aback—Captain Vere advanced to meet him, thus unconsciously intercepting his view of Claggart, and, interrupting the other's wonted ceremonious salutation, said, "Nay. Tell me how it is with yonder man," directing his attention to the prostrate one.

The surgeon looked, and for all his self-command somewhat started at the abrupt revelation. On Claggart's always pallid complexion, thick black blood was now oozing from nostril and ear. To the gazer's professional eye it was unmistakably no living man that he saw.

"Is it so, then?" said Captain Vere, intently watching him. "I thought it. But verify it." Whereupon the customary tests confirmed the surgeon's first glance, who now, looking up in unfeigned concern, cast a look of intense inquisitiveness upon his superior. But Captain Vere, with one hand to his brow, was standing motionless. Suddenly, catching the surgeon's arm convulsively, he exclaimed, pointing down to the body, "It is the divine judgment on Ananias![86] Look!"

Disturbed by the excited manner he had never before observed in the *Bellipotent*'s captain, and as yet wholly ignorant of the affair, the prudent surgeon nevertheless held his peace, only again looking an earnest interrogatory as to what it was that had resulted in such a tragedy.

But Captain Vere was now again motionless, standing absorbed in thought. Again starting, he vehemently exclaimed, "Struck dead by an angel of God! Yet the angel must hang!"

At these passionate interjections, mere incoherences to the listener as yet unapprised of the antecedents, the surgeon was profoundly discomposed. But now, as recollecting himself, Captain Vere in less passionate tone briefly related the

[86]In Acts 5:3–5, the Apostle Peter tells the false Christian Ananias, "thou hast not lied unto men, but unto God," whereupon Ananias falls dead.

circumstances leading up to the event. "But come; we must dispatch," he added. "Help me to remove him" (meaning the body) "to yonder compartment," designating one opposite that where the foretopman remained immured. Anew disturbed by a request that, as implying a desire for secrecy, seemed unaccountably strange to him, there was nothing for the subordinate to do but comply.

"Go now," said Captain Vere with something of his wonted manner. "Go now. I presently shall call a drumhead court.[87] Tell the lieutenants what has happened, and tell Mr. Mordant" (meaning the captain of marines), "and charge them to keep the matter to themselves."

20

Full of disquietude and misgiving, the surgeon left the cabin. Was Captain Vere suddenly affected in his mind, or was it but a transient excitement, brought about by so strange and extraordinary a tragedy? As to the drumhead court, it struck the surgeon as impolitic, if nothing more. The thing to do, he thought, was to place Billy Budd in confinement, and in a way dictated by usage, and postpone further action in so extraordinary a case to such time as they should rejoin the squadron, and then refer it to the admiral. He recalled the unwonted agitation of Captain Vere and his excited exclamations, so at variance with his normal manner. Was he unhinged?

But assuming that he is, it is not so susceptible of proof. What then can the surgeon do? No more trying situation is conceivable than that of an officer subordinate under a captain whom he suspects to be not mad, indeed, but yet not quite unaffected in his intellects. To argue his order to him would be insolence. To resist him would be mutiny.

In obedience to Captain Vere, he communicated what had happened to the lieutenants and captain of marines, saying nothing as to the captain's state. They fully shared his own surprise and concern. Like him too, they seemed to think that such a matter should be referred to the admiral.

21

Who in the rainbow can draw the line where the violet tint ends and the orange tint begins? Distinctly we see the difference of the colors, but where exactly does the one first blendingly enter into the other? So with sanity and insanity. In pronounced cases there is no question about them. But in some supposed cases, in various degrees supposedly less pronounced, to draw the exact line of demarcation few will undertake, though for a fee becoming considerate some professional experts will. There is nothing namable but that some men will, or undertake to, do it for pay.

Whether Captain Vere, as the surgeon professionally and privately surmised, was really the sudden victim of any degree of aberration, every one must determine for himself by such light as this narrative may afford.

[87] A court-martial held on the spot to try offenses committed during military operations (from the upturned drum used as a table).

That the unhappy event which has been narrated could not have happened at a worse juncture was but too true. For it was close on the heel of the suppressed insurrections, an aftertime very critical to naval authority, demanding from every English sea commander two qualities not readily interfusable—prudence and rigor. Moreover, there was something crucial in the case.

In the jugglery of circumstances preceding and attending the event on board the *Bellipotent,* and in the light of that martial code whereby it was formally to be judged, innocence and guilt personified in Claggart and Budd in effect changed places. In a legal view the apparent victim of the tragedy was he who had sought to victimize a man blameless; and the indisputable deed of the latter, navally regarded, constituted the most heinous of military crimes. Yet more. The essential right and wrong involved in the matter, the clearer that might be, so much the worse for the responsibility of a loyal sea commander, inasmuch as he was not authorized to determine the matter on that primitive basis.

Small wonder then that the *Bellipotent*'s captain, though in general a man of rapid decision, felt that circumspectness not less than promptitude was necessary. Until he could decide upon his course, and in each detail; and not only so, but until the concluding measure was upon the point of being enacted, he deemed it advisable, in view of all the circumstances, to guard as much as possible against publicity. Here he may or may not have erred. Certain it is, however, that subsequently in the confidential talk of more than one or two gun rooms and cabins he was not a little criticized by some officers, a fact imputed by his friends and vehemently by his cousin Jack Denton to professional jealousy of Starry Vere. Some imaginative ground for invidious comment there was. The maintenance of secrecy in the matter, the confining all knowledge of it for a time to the place where the homicide occurred, the quarter-deck cabin; in these particulars lurked some resemblance to the policy adopted in those tragedies of the palace which have occurred more than once in the capital founded by Peter the Barbarian.[88]

The case indeed was such that fain would the *Bellipotent*'s captain have deferred taking any action whatever respecting it further than to keep the foretopman a close prisoner till the ship rejoined the squadron and then submitting the matter to the judgment of his admiral.

But a true military officer is in one particular like a true monk. Not with more of self-abnegation will the latter keep his vows of monastic obedience than the former his vows of allegiance to martial duty.

Feeling that unless quick action was taken on it, the deed of the foretopman, so soon as it should be known on the gun decks, would tend to awaken any slumbering embers of the Nore among the crew, a sense of the urgency of the case overruled in Captain Vere every other consideration. But though a conscientious disciplinarian, he was no lover of authority for mere authority's sake. Very far was he from embracing opportunities for monopolizing to himself the perils of moral responsibility, none at least that could properly be referred to an official superior or shared with him by his official equals or even subordinates. So thinking, he was glad it would not be at variance with usage to turn the matter over to a summary court of his own officers, reserving to himself, as the one on whom the ultimate accountability would rest, the

[88]Russian Czar Peter the Great (1672–1725).

right of maintaining a supervision of it, or formally or informally interposing at need. Accordingly a drumhead court was summarily convened, he electing the individuals composing it: the first lieutenant, the captain of marines, and the sailing master.[89]

In associating an officer of marines with the sea lieutenant and the sailing master in a case having to do with a sailor, the commander perhaps deviated from general custom. He was prompted thereto by the circumstance that he took that soldier to be a judicious person, thoughtful, and not altogether incapable of grappling with a difficult case unprecedented in his prior experience. Yet even as to him he was not without some latent misgiving, for withal he was an extremely good-natured man, an enjoyer of his dinner, a sound sleeper, and inclined to obesity—a man who though he would always maintain his manhood in battle might not prove altogether reliable in a moral dilemma involving aught of the tragic. As to the first lieutenant and the sailing master, Captain Vere could not but be aware that though honest natures, of approved gallantry upon occasion, their intelligence was mostly confined to the matter of active seamanship and the fighting demands of their profession.

The court was held in the same cabin where the unfortunate affair had taken place. This cabin, the commander's, embraced the entire area under the poop deck. Aft, and on either side, was a small stateroom, the one now temporarily a jail and the other a dead-house, and a yet smaller compartment, leaving a space between expanding forward into a goodly oblong of length coinciding with the ship's beam. A skylight of moderate dimension was overhead, and at each end of the oblong space were two sashed porthole windows easily convertible back into embrasures for short carronades.[90]

All being quickly in readiness, Billy Budd was arraigned, Captain Vere necessarily appearing as the sole witness in the case, and as such temporarily sinking his rank, though singularly maintaining it in a matter apparently trivial, namely, that he testified from the ship's weather side,[91] with that object having caused the court to sit on the lee side. Concisely he narrated all that had led up to the catastrophe, omitting nothing in Claggart's accusation and deposing as to the manner in which the prisoner had received it. At this testimony the three officers glanced with no little surprise at Billy Budd, the last man they would have suspected either of the mutinous design alleged by Claggart or the undeniable deed he himself had done. The first lieutenant, taking judicial primacy and turning toward the prisoner, said, "Captain Vere has spoken. Is it or is it not as Captain Vere says?"

In response came syllables not so much impeded in the utterance as might have been anticipated. They were these: "Captain Vere tells the truth. It is just as Captain Vere says, but it is not as the master-at-arms said. I have eaten the King's bread and I am true to the King."

[89]In *White-Jacket* Melville notes that officers habitually played marines against sailors, but the corporal of marines is also one of the two men who speak up for White-Jacket when he is arraigned at the mast to be flogged (Chaps. 67, 89). As Hayford and Sealts point out, the inclusion of these two officers in a drumhead court is "doubly a deviation 'from general custom.'" In fact British naval statutes provided that a captain refer court-martial cases to his Chief Commander, or admiral (as Vere's subordinate officers think he should have done). Critics are divided, however, as to whether Melville was familiar with those statutes.

[90]Openings for light iron cannons.

[91]The side from which the wind is blowing, hence the higher side, raising Vere above the level of the court.

"I believe you, my man," said the witness, his voice indicating a suppressed emotion not otherwise betrayed.

"God will bless you for that, your honor!" not without stammering said Billy, and all but broke down. But immediately he was recalled to self-control by another question, to which with the same emotional difficulty of utterance he said, "No, there was no malice between us. I never bore malice against the master-at-arms. I am sorry that he is dead. I did not mean to kill him. Could I have used my tongue I would not have struck him. But he foully lied to my face and in presence of my captain, and I had to say something, and I could only say it with a blow, God help me!"

In the impulsive aboveboard manner of the frank one the court saw confirmed all that was implied in words that just previously had perplexed them, coming as they did from the testifier to the tragedy and promptly following Billy's impassioned disclaimer of mutinous intent—Captain Vere's words, "I believe you, my man."

Next it was asked of him whether he knew of or suspected aught savoring of incipient trouble (meaning mutiny, though the explicit term was avoided) going on in any section of the ship's company.

The reply lingered. This was naturally imputed by the court to the same vocal embarrassment which had retarded or obstructed previous answers. But in main it was otherwise here, the question immediately recalling to Billy's mind the interview with the afterguardsman in the forechains. But an innate repugnance to playing a part at all approaching that of an informer against one's own shipmates—the same erring sense of uninstructed honor which had stood in the way of his reporting the matter at the time, though as a loyal man-of-war's man it was incumbent on him, and failure so to do, if charged against him and proven, would have subjected him to the heaviest of penalties; this, with the blind feeling now his that nothing really was being hatched, prevailed with him. When the answer came it was a negative.

"One question more," said the officer of marines, now first speaking and with a troubled earnestness. "You tell us that what the master-at-arms said against you was a lie. Now why should he have so lied, so maliciously lied, since you declare there was no malice between you?"

At that question, unintentionally touching on a spiritual sphere wholly obscure to Billy's thoughts, he was nonplussed, evincing a confusion indeed that some observers, such as can readily be imagined, would have construed into involuntary evidence of hidden guilt. Nevertheless, he strove some way to answer, but all at once relinquished the vain endeavor, at the same time turning an appealing glance towards Captain Vere as deeming him his best helper and friend. Captain Vere, who had been seated for a time, rose to his feet, addressing the interrogator. "The question you put to him comes naturally enough. But how can he rightly answer it?—or anybody else, unless indeed it be he who lies within there," designating the compartment where lay the corpse. "But the prone one there will not rise to our summons. In effect, though, as it seems to me, the point you make is hardly material. Quite aside from any conceivable motive actuating the master-at-arms, and irrespective of the provocation to the blow, a martial court must needs in the present case confine its attention to the blow's consequence, which consequence justly is to be deemed not otherwise than as the striker's deed."

This utterance, the full significance of which it was not at all likely that Billy took in, nevertheless caused him to turn a wistful interrogative look toward the speaker, a look in its dumb expressiveness not unlike that which a dog of generous breed might turn upon his master, seeking in his face some elucidation of a previous gesture ambiguous to the canine intelligence.[92] Nor was the same utterance without marked effect upon the three officers, more especially the soldier. Couched in it seemed to them a meaning unanticipated, involving a prejudgment on the speaker's part. It served to augment a mental disturbance previously evident enough.

The soldier once more spoke, in a tone of suggestive dubiety addressing at once his associates and Captain Vere: "Nobody is present—none of the ship's company, I mean—who might shed lateral light, if any is to be had, upon what remains mysterious in this matter."

"That is thoughtfully put," said Captain Vere; "I see your drift. Ay, there is a mystery; but, to use a scriptural phrase, it is a 'mystery of iniquity,' a matter for psychologic theologians to discuss. But what has a military court to do with it? Not to add that for us any possible investigation of it is cut off by the lasting tongue-tie of—him—in yonder," again designating the mortuary stateroom. "The prisoner's deed—with that alone we have to do."

To this, and particularly the closing reiteration, the marine soldier, knowing not how aptly to reply, sadly abstained from saying aught. The first lieutenant, who at the outset had not unnaturally assumed primacy in the court, now overrulingly instructed by a glance from Captain Vere, a glance more effective than words, resumed that primacy. Turning to the prisoner, "Budd," he said, and scarce in equable tones, "Budd, if you have aught further to say for yourself, say it now."

Upon this the young sailor turned another quick glance toward Captain Vere; then, as taking a hint from that aspect, a hint confirming his own instinct that silence was now best, replied to the lieutenant, "I have said all, sir."

The marine—the same who had been the sentinel without the cabin door at the time that the foretopman, followed by the master-at-arms, entered it—he, standing by the sailor throughout these judicial proceedings, was now directed to take him back to the after compartment originally assigned to the prisoner and his custodian. As the twain disappeared from view, the three officers, as partially liberated from some inward constraint associated with Billy's mere presence, simultaneously stirred in their seats. They exchanged looks of troubled indecision, yet feeling that decide they must and without long delay. For Captain Vere, he for the time stood—unconsciously with his back toward them, apparently in one of his absent fits—gazing out from a sashed porthole to windward upon the monotonous blank of the twilight sea. But the court's silence continuing, broken only at moments by brief consultations, in low earnest tones, this served to arouse him and energize him. Turning, he to-and-fro paced the cabin athwart; in the returning ascent to windward climbing the slant deck in the ship's lee roll, without knowing it symbolizing thus in his action a mind resolute to surmount difficulties even if against primitive instincts strong as the wind and the sea. Presently he came to a stand before the three. After scanning their faces he stood less as mustering his thoughts for expression than as one inly deliberating how best to put them to well-meaning men not intellectually mature, men with whom it was necessary to demonstrate certain principles that were axioms to

[92]In *White-Jacket* Melville objects to the "implicit, unquestioning, dog-like devotion to whoever may be lord and master" that Dibdin's songs inculcate in sailors (Chapter 90).

himself. Similar impatience as to talking is perhaps one reason that deters some minds from addressing any popular assemblies.

When speak he did, something, both in the substance of what he said and his manner of saying it, showed the influence of unshared studies modifying and tempering the practical training of an active career. This, along with his phraseology, now and then was suggestive of the grounds whereon rested that imputation of a certain pedantry socially alleged against him by certain naval men of wholly practical cast, captains who nevertheless would frankly concede that His Majesty's navy mustered no more efficient officer of their grade than Starry Vere.

What he said was to this effect: "Hitherto I have been but the witness, little more; and I should hardly think now to take another tone, that of your coadjutor for the time, did I not perceive in you—at the crisis too—a troubled hesitancy, proceeding, I doubt not, from the clash of military duty with moral scruple—scruple vitalized by compassion. For the compassion, how can I otherwise than share it? But, mindful of paramount obligations, I strive against scruples that may tend to enervate decision. Not, gentlemen, that I hide from myself that the case is an exceptional one. Speculatively regarded, it well might be referred to a jury of casuists.[93] But for us here, acting not as casuists or moralists, it is a case practical, and under martial law practically to be dealt with.

"But your scruples: do they move as in a dusk? Challenge them. Make them advance and declare themselves. Come now; do they import something like this: If, mindless of palliating circumstances, we are bound to regard the death of the master-at-arms as the prisoner's deed, then does that deed constitute a capital crime whereof the penalty is a mortal one. But in natural justice is nothing but the prisoner's overt act to be considered? How can we adjudge to summary and shameful death a fellow creature innocent before God, and whom we feel to be so?—Does that state it aright? You sign sad assent. Well, I too feel that, the full force of that. It is Nature. But do these buttons that we wear attest that our allegiance is to Nature? No, to the King.[94] Though the ocean, which is inviolate Nature primeval, though this be the element where we move and have our being as sailors, yet as the King's officers lies our duty in a sphere correspondingly natural? So little is that true, that

[93]Those who seek to resolve difficult cases of conscience through close reading of scriptural rules or legal statutes (usually with connotations of twisting rules to suit their purposes).

[94]George III (1738–1820), against whom the American colonies had just successfully revolted. As Stanton Garner has pointed out, George III, whose mental instability was an open secret, was frequently caricatured in the press as "The Button-Maker" (an allusion to his hobby of making buttons on a lathe). See Thomas Wright's *England Under the House of Hanover . . . Illustrated from the Caricatures and Satires of the Day,* 2 vols. (London: Bentley, 1848), Chapter 9, for examples. One such caricature pictures the King "as he shews his buttons to two noblemen in attendance," saying, "I cannot attend to your remonstrance! Do not you see that I have been employed in business of much more consequence?" "Not a prince in Europe can make such buttons!" exclaims one of the noblemen in response. Wright also mentions a political satire that accuses the King of indulging his taste for making buttons while neglecting the needs of his subjects, and particularly of the sailors in his navy. Even more relevant are a pair of caricatures mocking the prostitution of Justice. In one, a partially blindfolded secretary of state insists: "Somebody must be hanged for this, right or wrong, to quiet the mob and save our credit." In the other, Britannia is depicted being hanged from the gallows.

in receiving our commissions we in the most important regards ceased to be natural free agents. When war is declared are we the commissioned fighters previously consulted? We fight at command. If our judgments approve the war, that is but coincidence. So in other particulars. So now. For suppose condemnation to follow these present proceedings. Would it be so much we ourselves that would condemn as it would be martial law operating through us? For that law and the rigor of it, we are not responsible. Our vowed responsibility is in this: That however pitilessly that law may operate in any instances, we nevertheless adhere to it and administer it.

"But the exceptional in the matter moves the hearts within you. Even so too is mine moved. But let not warm hearts betray heads that should be cool. Ashore in a criminal case, will an upright judge allow himself off the bench to be waylaid by some tender kinswoman of the accused seeking to touch him with her tearful plea? Well, the heart here, sometimes the feminine in man, is as that piteous woman, and hard though it be, she must here be ruled out."

He paused, earnestly studying them for a moment; then resumed.

"But something in your aspect seems to urge that it is not solely the heart that moves in you, but also the conscience, the private conscience. But tell me whether or not, occupying the position we do, private conscience should not yield to that imperial one formulated in the code under which alone we officially proceed?"

Here the three men moved in their seats, less convinced than agitated by the course of an argument troubling but the more the spontaneous conflict within.

Perceiving which, the speaker paused for a moment; then abruptly changing his tone, went on.

"To steady us a bit, let us recur to the facts.—In wartime at sea a man-of-war's man strikes his superior in grade, and the blow kills. Apart from its effect the blow itself is, according to the Articles of War, a capital crime. Furthermore—"

"Ay, sir," emotionally broke in the officer of marines, "in one sense it was. But surely Budd purposed neither mutiny nor homicide."

"Surely not, my good man. And before a court less arbitrary and more merciful than a martial one, that plea would largely extenuate. At the Last Assizes[95] it shall acquit. But how here? We proceed under the law of the Mutiny Act. In feature no child can resemble his father more than that Act resembles in spirit the thing from which it derives—War. In His Majesty's service—in this ship, indeed—there are Englishmen forced to fight for the King against their will. Against their conscience, for aught we know. Though as their fellow creatures some of us may appreciate their position, yet as navy officers what reck we of it? Still less recks the enemy. Our impressed men he would fain cut down in the same swath with our volunteers. As regards the enemy's naval conscripts, some of whom may even share our own abhorrence of the regicidal French Directory, it is the same on our side. War looks but to the frontage, the appearance. And the Mutiny Act, War's child, takes after the father. Budd's intent or non-intent is nothing to the purpose.

"But while, put to it by those anxieties in you which I cannot but respect, I only repeat myself—while thus strangely we prolong proceedings that should be summary—the enemy may be sighted and an engagement result. We must do; and one of two things must we do—condemn or let go."

[95]The Last Judgment.

"Can we not convict and yet mitigate the penalty?" asked the sailing master, here speaking, and falteringly, for the first.

"Gentlemen, were that clearly lawful for us under the circumstances, consider the consequences of such clemency. The people" (meaning the ship's company) "have native sense; most of them are familiar with our naval usage and tradition; and how would they take it? Even could you explain to them—which our official position forbids—they, long molded by arbitrary discipline, have not that kind of intelligent responsiveness that might qualify them to comprehend and discriminate. No, to the people the foretopman's deed, however it be worded in the announcement, will be plain homicide committed in a flagrant act of mutiny. What penalty for that should follow, they know. But it does not follow. *Why?* they will ruminate. You know what sailors are. Will they not revert to the recent outbreak at the Nore? Ay. They know the well-founded alarm—the panic it struck throughout England. Your clement sentence they would account pusillanimous. They would think that we flinch, that we are afraid of them—afraid of practicing a lawful rigor singularly demanded at this juncture, lest it should provoke new troubles. What shame to us such a conjecture on their part, and how deadly to discipline. You see then, whither, prompted by duty and the law, I steadfastly drive. But I beseech you, my friends, do not take me amiss. I feel as you do for this unfortunate boy. But did he know our hearts, I take him to be of that generous nature that he would feel even for us on whom in this military necessity so heavy a compulsion is laid."

With that, crossing the deck he resumed his place by the sashed porthole, tacitly leaving the three to come to a decision. On the cabin's opposite side the troubled court sat silent. Loyal lieges, plain and practical, though at bottom they dissented from some points Captain Vere had put to them, they were without the faculty, hardly had the inclination, to gainsay one whom they felt to be an earnest man, one too not less their superior in mind than in naval rank. But it is not improbable that even such of his words as were not without influence over them, less came home to them than his closing appeal to their instinct as sea officers: in the forethought he threw out as to the practical consequences to discipline, considering the unconfirmed tone of the fleet at the time, should a man-of-war's man's violent killing at sea of a superior in grade be allowed to pass for aught else than a capital crime demanding prompt infliction of the penalty.

Not unlikely they were brought to something more or less akin to that harassed frame of mind which in the year 1842 actuated the commander of the U.S. brig-of-war *Somers* to resolve, under the so-called Articles of War, Articles modeled upon the English Mutiny Act, to resolve upon the execution at sea of a midshipman and two sailors as mutineers designing the seizure of the brig.[96] Which resolution was carried out though in a time of peace and within not many days' sail of home. An act vindicated by a naval court of inquiry subsequently convened ashore. History, and here cited without comment. True, the circumstances on board the *Somers* were different from those on board the *Bellipotent.* But the urgency felt, well-warranted or otherwise, was much the same.

[96] *White-Jacket* cites the *Somers* case to illustrate the arbitrary tyranny under which sailors live and the harshness of the naval code embodied in the Articles of War (Chap. 72). Melville's cousin Guert Gansevoort, First Lieutenant of the *Somers,* was implicated in the decision to hang the three alleged mutineers.

Says a writer whom few know, "Forty years after a battle it is easy for a noncombatant to reason about how it ought to have been fought. It is another thing personally and under fire to have to direct the fighting while involved in the obscuring smoke of it. Much so with respect to other emergencies involving considerations both practical and moral, and when it is imperative promptly to act. The greater the fog the more it imperils the steamer, and speed is put on though at the hazard of running somebody down.[97] Little ween the snug card players in the cabin of the responsibilities of the sleepless man on the bridge."

In brief, Billy Budd was formally convicted and sentenced to be hung at the yardarm in the early morning watch, it being now night. Otherwise, as is customary in such cases, the sentence would forthwith have been carried out. In wartime on the field or in the fleet, a mortal punishment decreed by a drumhead court—on the field sometimes decreed by but a nod from the general—follows without delay on the heel of conviction, without appeal.

22

It was Captain Vere himself who of his own motion communicated the finding of the court to the prisoner, for that purpose going to the compartment where he was in custody and bidding the marine there to withdraw for the time.

Beyond the communication of the sentence, what took place at this interview was never known. But in view of the character of the twain briefly closeted in that stateroom, each radically sharing in the rarer qualities of our nature—so rare indeed as to be all but incredible to average minds however much cultivated—some conjectures may be ventured.

It would have been in consonance with the spirit of Captain Vere should he on this occasion have concealed nothing from the condemned one—should he indeed have frankly disclosed to him the part he himself had played in bringing about the decision, at the same time revealing his actuating motives. On Billy's side it is not improbable that such a confession would have been received in much the same spirit that prompted it. Not without a sort of joy, indeed, he might have appreciated the brave opinion of him implied in his captain's making such a confidant of him. Nor, as to the sentence itself, could he have been insensible that it was imparted to him as to one not afraid to die. Even more may have been. Captain Vere in end may have developed the passion sometimes latent under an exterior stoical or indifferent. He was old enough to have been Billy's father. The austere devotee of military duty, letting himself melt back into what remains primeval in our formalized humanity, may in end have caught Billy to his heart, even as Abraham may have caught young Isaac on the brink of resolutely offering him up in obedience to the exacting behest.[98] But there is no telling the sacrament, seldom if in any case revealed to the

[97]Stanton Garner points out that in *Redburn* (Chap. 20), Melville describes the opposite practice of shortening sail to reduce speed in a fog, and that the practices of reducing speed and sounding warnings in a fog were "codified into international law" in 1889, while Melville was writing *Billy Budd.*

[98]In Genesis 22:1–13, God tries Abraham's faith by commanding him to sacrifice his only son Isaac, but as Abraham is standing over Isaac with upraised knife, an angel intervenes with the words: "Lay not thine hand upon the lad . . . for now I know that thou fearest God, seeing thou has not withheld thy son. . . ."

gadding world, wherever under circumstances at all akin to those here attempted to be set forth two of great Nature's nobler order embrace. There is privacy at the time, inviolable to the survivor; and holy oblivion, the sequel to each diviner magnanimity, providentially covers all at last.

The first to encounter Captain Vere in act of leaving the compartment was the senior lieutenant. The face he beheld, for the moment one expressive of the agony of the strong, was to that officer, though a man of fifty, a startling revelation. That the condemned one suffered less than he who mainly had effected the condemnation was apparently indicated by the former's exclamation in the scene soon perforce to be touched upon.

23

Of a series of incidents within a brief term rapidly following each other, the adequate narration may take up a term less brief, especially if explanation or comment here and there seem requisite to the better understanding of such incidents. Between the entrance into the cabin of him who never left it alive, and him who when he did leave it left it as one condemned to die; between this and the closeted interview just given, less than an hour and a half had elapsed. It was an interval long enough, however, to awaken speculations among no few of the ship's company as to what it was that could be detaining in the cabin the master-at-arms and the sailor; for a rumor that both of them had been seen to enter it and neither of them had been seen to emerge, this rumor had got abroad upon the gun decks and in the tops, the people of a great warship being in one respect like villagers, taking microscopic note of every outward movement or non-movement going on. When therefore, in weather not at all tempestuous, all hands were called in the second dogwatch, a summons under such circumstances not usual in those hours, the crew were not wholly unprepared for some announcement extraordinary, one having connection too with the continued absence of the two men from their wonted haunts.

There was a moderate sea at the time; and the moon, newly risen and near to being at its full, silvered the white spar deck wherever not blotted by the clear-cut shadows horizontally thrown of fixtures and moving men. On either side the quarter-deck the marine guard under arms was drawn up; and Captain Vere, standing in his place surrounded by all the wardroom officers, addressed his men. In so doing, his manner showed neither more nor less than that properly pertaining to his supreme position aboard his own ship. In clear terms and concise he told them what had taken place in the cabin: that the master-at-arms was dead, that he who had killed him had been already tried by a summary court and condemned to death, and that the execution would take place in the early morning watch. The word *mutiny* was not named in what he said. He refrained too from making the occasion an opportunity for any preachment as to the maintenance of discipline, thinking perhaps that under existing circumstances in the navy the consequence of violating discipline should be made to speak for itself.

Their captain's announcement was listened to by the throng of standing sailors in a dumbness like that of a seated congregation of believers in hell listening to the clergyman's announcement of his Calvinistic text.

At the close, however, a confused murmur went up. It began to wax. All but instantly, then, at a sign, it was pierced and suppressed by shrill whistles of the boatswain and his mates. The word was given to about ship.

To be prepared for burial Claggart's body was delivered to certain petty officers of his mess. And here, not to clog the sequel with lateral matters, it may be added that at a suitable hour, the master-at-arms was committed to the sea with every funeral honor properly belonging to his naval grade.

In this proceeding as in every public one growing out of the tragedy strict adherence to usage was observed. Nor in any point could it have been at all deviated from, either with respect to Claggart or Billy Budd, without begetting undesirable speculations in the ship's company, sailors, and more particularly men-of-war's men, being of all men the greatest sticklers for usage. For similar cause, all communication between Captain Vere and the condemned one ended with the closeted interview already given, the latter being now surrendered to the ordinary routine preliminary to the end. His transfer under guard from the captain's quarters was effected without unusual precautions—at least no visible ones. If possible, not to let the men so much as surmise that their officers anticipate aught amiss from them is the tacit rule in a military ship. And the more that some sort of trouble should really be apprehended, the more do the officers keep that apprehension to themselves, though not the less unostentatious vigilance may be augmented. In the present instance, the sentry placed over the prisoner had strict orders to let no one have communication with him but the chaplain. And certain unobtrusive measures were taken absolutely to insure this point.

24

In a seventy-four of the old order the deck known as the upper gun deck was the one covered over by the spar deck, which last, though not without its armament, was for the most part exposed to the weather. In general it was at all hours free from hammocks; those of the crew swinging on the lower gun deck and berth deck, the latter being not only a dormitory but also the place for the stowing of the sailors' bags, and on both sides lined with the large chests or movable pantries of the many messes of the men.

On the starboard side of the *Bellipotent*'s upper gun deck, behold Billy Budd under sentry lying prone in irons in one of the bays formed by the regular spacing of the guns comprising the batteries on either side. All these pieces were of the heavier caliber of that period. Mounted on lumbering wooden carriages, they were hampered with cumbersome harness of breeching and strong side-tackles for running them out. Guns and carriages, together with the long rammers and shorter linstocks[99] lodged in loops overhead—all these, as customary, were painted black; and the heavy hempen breechings, tarred to the same tint, wore the like livery of the undertakers. In contrast with the funereal hue of these surroundings, the prone sailor's exterior apparel, white jumper and white duck trousers, each more or less soiled, dimly glimmered in the obscure light of the bay like a patch of discolored snow in

[99]Sticks with pointed feet and forked tips, used to hold lighted matches when firing cannons.

early April lingering at some upland cave's black mouth. In effect he is already in his shroud, or the garments that shall serve him in lieu of one. Over him but scarce illuminating him, two battle lanterns swing from two massive beams of the deck above. Fed with the oil supplied by the war contractors (whose gains, honest or otherwise, are in every land an anticipated portion of the harvest of death), with flickering splashes of dirty yellow light they pollute the pale moonshine all but ineffectually struggling in obstructed flecks through the open ports from which the tampioned[100] cannon protrude. Other lanterns at intervals serve but to bring out somewhat the obscurer bays which, like small confessionals or side-chapels in a cathedral, branch from the long dim-vistaed broad aisle between the two batteries of that covered tier.

Such was the deck where now lay the Handsome Sailor. Through the rose-tan of his complexion no pallor could have shown. It would have taken days of sequestration from the winds and the sun to have brought about the effacement of that. But the skeleton in the cheekbone at the point of its angle was just beginning delicately to be defined under the warm-tinted skin. In fervid hearts self-contained, some brief experiences devour our human tissue as secret fire in a ship's hold consumes cotton in the bale.

But now lying between the two guns, as nipped in the vice of fate, Billy's agony, mainly proceeding from a generous young heart's virgin experience of the diabolical incarnate and effective in some men—the tension of that agony was over now. It survived not the something healing in the closeted interview with Captain Vere. Without movement, he lay as in a trance, that adolescent expression previously noted as his taking on something akin to the look of a slumbering child in the cradle when the warm hearth-glow of the still chamber at night plays on the dimples that at whiles mysteriously form in the cheek, silently coming and going there. For now and then in the gyved[101] one's trance a serene happy light born of some wandering reminiscence or dream would diffuse itself over his face, and then wane away only anew to return.

The chaplain, coming to see him and finding him thus, and perceiving no sign that he was conscious of his presence, attentively regarded him for a space, then slipping aside, withdrew for the time, peradventure feeling that even he, the minister of Christ though receiving his stipend from Mars, had no consolation to proffer which could result in a peace transcending that which he beheld. But in the small hours he came again. And the prisoner, now awake to his surroundings, noticed his approach, and civilly, all but cheerfully, welcomed him. But it was to little purpose that in the interview following, the good man sought to bring Billy Budd to some godly understanding that he must die, and at dawn. True, Billy himself freely referred to his death as a thing close at hand; but it was something in the way that children will refer to death in general, who yet among their other sports will play a funeral with hearse and mourners.

Not that like children Billy was incapable of conceiving what death really is. No, but he was wholly without irrational fear of it, a fear more prevalent in highly civilized communities than those so-called barbarous ones which in all respects stand nearer to unadulterate Nature. And, as elsewhere said, a barbarian Billy radically

[100]Plugged, muzzled.
[101]Fettered, shackled.

was—as much so, for all the costume, as his countrymen the British captives, living trophies, made to march in the Roman triumph of Germanicus.[102] Quite as much so as those later barbarians, young men probably, and picked specimens among the earlier British converts to Christianity, at least nominally such, taken to Rome (as today converts from lesser isles of the sea may be taken to London), of whom the Pope of that time, admiring the strangeness of their personal beauty so unlike the Italian stamp, their clear ruddy complexion and curled flaxen locks, exclaimed, "Angles" (meaning *English,* the modern derivative), "Angles, do you call them? And is it because they look so like angels?"[103] Had it been later in time, one would think that the Pope had in mind Fra Angelico's seraphs, some of whom, plucking apples in gardens of the Hesperides,[104] have the faint rosebud complexion of the more beautiful English girls.

If in vain the good chaplain sought to impress the young barbarian with ideas of death akin to those conveyed in the skull, dial, and crossbones on old tombstones, equally futile to all appearance were his efforts to bring home to him the thought of salvation and a Savior. Billy listened, but less out of awe or reverence, perhaps, than from a certain natural politeness, doubtless at bottom regarding all that in much the same way that most mariners of his class take any discourse abstract or out of the common tone of the workaday world. And this sailor way of taking clerical discourse is not wholly unlike the way in which the primer of Christianity, full of transcendent miracles, was received long ago on tropic isles by any superior *savage,* so called—a Tahitian, say, of Captain Cook's[105] time or shortly after that time. Out of natural courtesy he received, but did not appropriate. It was like a gift placed in the palm of an outreached hand upon which the fingers do not close.

But the *Bellipotent*'s chaplain was a discreet man possessing the good sense of a good heart. So he insisted not in his vocation here. At the instance of Captain Vere, a lieutenant had apprised him of pretty much everything as to Billy; and since he felt that innocence was even a better thing than religion wherewith to go to Judgment, he reluctantly withdrew; but in his emotion not without first performing an act strange enough in an Englishman, and under the circumstances yet more so in any regular priest. Stooping over, he kissed on the fair cheek his fellow man,[106] a felon in martial law, one whom though on the confines of death he felt he could never convert to a dogma; nor for all that did he fear for his future.

[102]Germanicus Caesar (15 B.C.–A.D. 19), fought German tribes and received a hero's triumph in Rome in A.D. 17, described in the *Annals* of Tacitus, 2.41. The captives displayed were German, not British, however. Melville may be thinking of a later passage in the *Annals,* 12.33–37, describing the capture of the British hero Caractacus, displayed in Rome with his family in A.D. 50.

[103]Pope Gregory the Great (540?–604). This episode occurred before Gregory became Pope, however, and the Angles were not converts, but slaves being exposed for sale in the market.

[104]The Florentine painter Fra Angelico (1387–1455) was famous for his angels (hence his name). In Greek mythology, the Hesperides were daughters of Atlas in whose garden grew a tree with golden apples, guarded by a dragon.

[105]James Cook (1728–1779), English navigator, who first visited Tahiti in 1769. Melville discusses the attitude of the Tahitians toward Christian missionaries in *Omoo,* Chap. 45.

[106]Perhaps an allusion to the kiss with which Judas betrays Christ (Matthew 26:47–49).

Marvel not that having been made acquainted with the young sailor's essential innocence the worthy man lifted not a finger to avert the doom of such a martyr to martial discipline. So to do would not only have been as idle as invoking the desert, but would also have been an audacious transgression of the bounds of his function, one as exactly prescribed to him by military law as that of the boatswain or any other naval officer. Bluntly put, a chaplain is the minister of the Prince of Peace serving in the host of the God of War—Mars. As such, he is as incongruous as a musket would be on the altar at Christmas. Why, then, is he there? Because he indirectly subserves the purpose attested by the cannon; because too he lends the sanction of the religion of the meek to that which practically is the abrogation of everything but brute Force.

25

The night so luminous on the spar deck, but otherwise on the cavernous ones below, levels so like the tiered galleries in a coal mine—the luminous night passed away. But like the prophet in the chariot disappearing in heaven and dropping his mantle to Elisha,[107] the withdrawing night transferred its pale robe to the breaking day. A meek, shy light appeared in the East, where stretched a diaphanous fleece of white furrowed vapor. That light slowly waxed. Suddenly *eight bells* was struck aft, responded to by one louder metallic stroke from forward. It was four o'clock in the morning. Instantly the silver whistles were heard summoning all hands to witness punishment. Up through the great hatchways rimmed with racks of heavy shot the watch below came pouring, overspreading with the watch already on deck the space between the mainmast and foremast including that occupied by the capacious launch and the black booms tiered on either side of it, boat and booms making a summit of observation for the powder-boys and younger tars. A different group comprising one watch of topmen leaned over the rail of that sea balcony, no small one in a seventy-four, looking down on the crowd below. Man or boy, none spake but in whisper, and few spake at all. Captain Vere—as before, the central figure among the assembled commissioned officers—stood nigh the break of the poop deck facing forward. Just below him on the quarter-deck the marines in full equipment were drawn up much as at the scene of the promulgated sentence.

At sea in the old time, the execution by halter of a military sailor was generally from the foreyard. In the present instance, for special reasons the mainyard was assigned. Under an arm of that yard the prisoner was presently brought up, the chaplain attending him. It was noted at the time, and remarked upon afterwards, that in this final scene the good man evinced little or nothing of the perfunctory. Brief speech indeed he had with the condemned one, but the genuine Gospel was less on his tongue than in his aspect and manner towards him. The final preparations personal to the latter being speedily brought to an end by two boatswain's mates, the consummation impended. Billy stood facing aft. At the penultimate moment, his words, his only ones, words wholly unobstructed in the utterance, were these: "God

[107] In II Kings 2:9–15, as the prophet Elijah is being carried to heaven in a chariot of fire, he drops his mantle to his disciple Elisha.

bless Captain Vere!" Syllables so unanticipated coming from one with the ignominious hemp about his neck—a conventional felon's benediction directed aft towards the quarters of honor; syllables too delivered in the clear melody of a singing bird on the point of launching from the twig—had a phenomenal effect, not unenhanced by the rare personal beauty of the young sailor, spiritualized now through late experiences so poignantly profound.

Without volition, as it were, as if indeed the ship's populace were but the vehicles of some vocal current electric, with one voice from alow and aloft came a resonant sympathetic echo: "God bless Captain Vere!" And yet at that instant Billy alone must have been in their hearts, even as in their eyes.

At the pronounced words and the spontaneous echo that voluminously rebounded them, Captain Vere, either through stoic self-control or a sort of momentary paralysis induced by emotional shock, stood erectly rigid as a musket in the ship-armorer's rack.

The hull, deliberately recovering from the periodic roll to leeward, was just regaining an even keel when the last signal, a preconcerted dumb one, was given. At the same moment it chanced that the vapory fleece hanging low in the East was shot through with a soft glory as of the fleece of the Lamb of God seen in mystical vision,[108] and simultaneously therewith, watched by the wedged mass of upturned faces, Billy ascended; and, ascending, took the full rose of the dawn.

In the pinioned figure arrived at the yard-end, to the wonder of all no motion was apparent, none save that created by the slow roll of the hull in moderate weather, so majestic in a great ship ponderously cannoned.

26

When some days afterwards, in reference to the singularity just mentioned, the purser,[109] a rather ruddy, rotund person more accurate as an accountant than profound as a philosopher, said at mess to the surgeon, "What testimony to the force lodged in will power," the latter, saturnine, spare, and tall, one in whom a discreet causticity went along with a manner less genial than polite, replied, "Your pardon, Mr. Purser. In a hanging scientifically conducted—and under special orders I myself directed how Budd's was to be effected—any movement following the completed suspension and originating in the body suspended, such movement indicates mechanical spasm in the muscular system. Hence the absence of that is no more attributable to will power, as you call it, than to horsepower—begging your pardon."

"But this muscular spasm you speak of, is not that in a degree more or less invariable in these cases?"

"Assuredly so, Mr. Purser."

"How then, my good sir, do you account for its absence in this instance?"

"Mr. Purser, it is clear that your sense of the singularity in this matter equals not mine. You account for it by what you call will power—a term not yet included in the

[108]In Revelation 1:10–16, St. John describes his vision of "one like unto the Son of man," whose "head and his hairs were white like wool," and whose "eyes were as a flame of fire."

[109]Paymaster.

lexicon of science. For me, I do not, with my present knowledge, pretend to account for it at all. Even should we assume the hypothesis that at the first touch of the halyards the action of Budd's heart, intensified by extraordinary emotion at its climax, abruptly stopped—much like a watch when in carelessly winding it up you strain at the finish, thus snapping the chain—even under that hypothesis how account for the phenomenon that followed?"

"You admit, then, that the absence of spasmodic movement was phenomenal."

"It was phenomenal, Mr. Purser, in the sense that it was an appearance the cause of which is not immediately to be assigned."

"But tell me, my dear sir," pertinaciously continued the other, "was the man's death effected by the halter, or was it a species of euthanasia?"[110]

"*Euthanasia,* Mr. Purser, is something like your *will power:* I doubt its authenticity as a scientific term—begging your pardon again. It is at once imaginative and metaphysical—in short, Greek.—But," abruptly changing his tone, "there is a case in the sick bay that I do not care to leave to my assistants. Beg your pardon, but excuse me." And rising from the mess he formally withdrew.

27

The silence at the moment of execution and for a moment or two continuing thereafter, a silence but emphasized by the regular wash of the sea against the hull or the flutter of a sail caused by the helmsman's eyes being tempted astray, this emphasized silence was gradually disturbed by a sound not easily to be verbally rendered. Whoever has heard the freshet-wave of a torrent suddenly swelled by pouring showers in tropical mountains, showers not shared by the plain; whoever has heard the first muffled murmur of its sloping advance through precipitous woods may form some conception of the sound now heard. The seeming remoteness of its source was because of its murmurous indistinctness, since it came from close by, even from the men massed on the ship's open deck. Being inarticulate, it was dubious in significance further than it seemed to indicate some capricious revulsion of thought or feeling such as mobs ashore are liable to, in the present instance possibly implying a sullen revocation on the men's part of their involuntary echoing of Billy's benediction. But ere the murmur had time to wax into clamor it was met by a strategic command, the more telling that it came with abrupt unexpectedness: "Pipe down the starboard watch, Boatswain, and see that they go."

Shrill as the shriek of the sea hawk, the silver whistles of the boatswain and his mates pierced that ominous low sound, dissipating it; and yielding to the mechanism of discipline the throng was thinned by one-half. For the remainder, most of them were set to temporary employments connected with trimming the yards and so forth, business readily to be got up to serve occasion by any officer of the deck.

Now each proceeding that follows a mortal sentence pronounced at sea by a drumhead court is characterized by promptitude not perceptibly merging into hurry,

[110]Critics have suggested that Melville may be using the word either in the Greek sense of "patriotic self-sacrifice" or in the sense he found in Schopenhauer: "an easy death, not ushered in by disease, and free from all pain and struggle."

though bordering that. The hammock, the one which had been Billy's bed when alive, having already been ballasted with shot and otherwise prepared to serve for his canvas coffin, the last offices of the sea undertakers, the sailmaker's mates, were now speedily completed. When everything was in readiness a second call for all hands, made necessary by the strategic movement before mentioned, was sounded, now to witness burial.

The details of this closing formality it needs not to give. But when the tilted plank let slide its freight into the sea, a second strange human murmur was heard, blended now with another inarticulate sound proceeding from certain larger seafowl who, their attention having been attracted by the peculiar commotion in the water resulting from the heavy sloped dive of the shotted hammock into the sea, flew screaming to the spot. So near the hull did they come, that the stridor or bony creak of their gaunt double-jointed pinions was audible. As the ship under light airs passed on, leaving the burial spot astern, they still kept circling it low down with the moving shadow of their outstretched wings and the croaked requiem of their cries.

Upon sailors as superstitious as those of the age preceding ours, men-of-war's men too who had just beheld the prodigy of repose in the form suspended in air, and now foundering in the deeps; to such mariners the action of the seafowl, though dictated by mere animal greed for prey, was big with no prosaic significance. An uncertain movement began among them, in which some encroachment was made. It was tolerated but for a moment. For suddenly the drum beat to quarters, which familiar sound happening at least twice every day, had upon the present occasion a signal peremptoriness in it. True martial discipline long continued superinduces in average man a sort of impulse whose operation at the official word of command much resembles in its promptitude the effect of an instinct.

The drumbeat dissolved the multitude, distributing most of them along the batteries of the two covered gun decks. There, as wonted, the guns' crews stood by their respective cannon erect and silent. In due course the first officer, sword under arm and standing in his place on the quarter-deck, formally received the successive reports of the sworded lieutenants commanding the sections of batteries below; the last of which reports being made, the summed report he delivered with the customary salute to the commander. All this occupied time, which in the present case was the object in beating to quarters at an hour prior to the customary one. That such variance from usage was authorized by an officer like Captain Vere, a martinet as some deemed him, was evidence of the necessity for unusual action implied in what he deemed to be temporarily the mood of his men. "With mankind," he would say, "forms, measured forms, are everything; and that is the import couched in the story of Orpheus[111] with his lyre spellbinding the wild denizens of the wood." And this he once applied to the disruption of forms going on across the Channel and the consequences thereof.

At this unwonted muster at quarters, all proceeded as at the regular hour. The band on the quarter-deck played a sacred air, after which the chaplain went through the customary morning service. That done, the drum beat the retreat; and toned by

[111]In Greek mythology the music of Orpheus, son of Apollo and the Muse Calliope, had the power to charm wild beasts, overcome destructive forces of nature, and even sway the relentless gods of the underworld.

music and religious rites subserving the discipline and purposes of war, the men in their wonted orderly manner dispersed to the places allotted them when not at the guns.

And now it was full day. The fleece of low-hanging vapor had vanished, licked up by the sun that late had so glorified it. And the circumambient air in the clearness of its serenity was like smooth white marble in the polished block not yet removed from the marble-dealer's yard.

28

The symmetry of form attainable in pure fiction cannot so readily be achieved in a narration essentially having less to do with fable than with fact. Truth uncompromisingly told will always have its ragged edges; hence the conclusion of such a narration is apt to be less finished than an architectural finial.[112]

How it fared with the Handsome Sailor during the year of the Great Mutiny has been faithfully given. But though properly the story ends with his life, something in way of sequel will not be amiss. Three brief chapters will suffice.

In the general rechristening under the Directory of the craft originally forming the navy of the French monarchy, the *St. Louis* line-of-battle ship was named the *Athée* (the *Atheist*). Such a name, like some other substituted ones in the Revolutionary fleet, while proclaiming the infidel audacity of the ruling power, was yet, though not so intended to be, the aptest name, if one consider it, ever given to a warship; far more so indeed than the *Devastation,* the *Erebus* (the *Hell*), and similar names bestowed upon fighting ships.

On the return passage to the English fleet from the detached cruise during which occurred the events already recorded, the *Bellipotent* fell in with the *Athée.* An engagement ensued, during which Captain Vere, in the act of putting his ship alongside the enemy with a view of throwing his boarders across her bulwarks, was hit by a musket ball from a porthole of the enemy's main cabin. More than disabled, he dropped to the deck and was carried below to the same cockpit where some of his men already lay. The senior lieutenant took command. Under him the enemy was finally captured, and though much crippled was by rare good fortune successfully taken into Gibraltar, an English port not very distant from the scene of the fight. There, Captain Vere with the rest of the wounded was put ashore. He lingered for some days, but the end came. Unhappily he was cut off too early for the Nile and Trafalgar. The spirit that 'spite its philosophic austerity may yet have indulged in the most secret of all passions, ambition, never attained to the fulness of fame.

Not long before death, while lying under the influence of that magical drug which, soothing the physical frame, mysteriously operates on the subtler element in man, he was heard to murmur words inexplicable to his attendant: "Billy Budd, Billy Budd." That these were not the accents of remorse would seem clear from what the attendant said to the *Bellipotent*'s senior officer of marines, who, as the most reluctant to condemn of the members of the drumhead court, too well knew, though here he kept the knowledge to himself, who Billy Budd was.

[112] An ornament terminating or capping an architectural monument. Many critics have noted the contrast between this view of art and the "measured forms" Vere prefers.

29

Some few weeks after the execution, among other matters under the head of "News from the Mediterranean," there appeared in a naval chronicle of the time, an authorized weekly publication, an account of the affair. It was doubtless for the most part written in good faith, though the medium, partly rumor, through which the facts must have reached the writer served to deflect and in part falsify them. The account was as follows:

"On the tenth of the last month a deplorable occurrence took place on board H.M.S. *Bellipotent.* John Claggart, the ship's master-at-arms, discovering that some sort of plot was incipient among an inferior section of the ship's company, and that the ringleader was one William Budd; he, Claggart, in the act of arraigning the man before the captain, was vindictively stabbed to the heart by the suddenly drawn sheath knife of Budd.

"The deed and the implement employed sufficiently suggest that though mustered into the service under an English name the assassin was no Englishman, but one of those aliens adopting English cognomens whom the present extraordinary necessities of the service have caused to be admitted into it in considerable numbers.

"The enormity of the crime and the extreme depravity of the criminal appear the greater in view of the character of the victim, a middle-aged man respectable and discreet, belonging to that minor official grade, the petty officers, upon whom, as none know better than the commissioned gentlemen, the efficiency of His Majesty's navy so largely depends. His function was a responsible one, at once onerous and thankless; and his fidelity in it the greater because of his strong patriotic impulse. In this instance as in so many other instances in these days, the character of this unfortunate man signally refutes, if refutation were needed, that peevish saying attributed to the late Dr. Johnson, that patriotism is the last refuge of a scoundrel.[113]

"The criminal paid the penalty of his crime. The promptitude of the punishment has proved salutary. Nothing amiss is now apprehended aboard H.M.S. *Bellipotent.*"

The above, appearing in a publication now long ago superannuated and forgotten, is all that hitherto has stood in human record to attest what manner of men respectively were John Claggart and Billy Budd.

30

Everything is for a term venerated in navies. Any tangible object associated with some striking incident of the service is converted into a monument. The spar from which the foretopman was suspended was for some few years kept trace of by the bluejackets. Their knowledges followed it from ship to dockyard and again from dockyard to ship, still pursuing it even when at last reduced to a mere dockyard boom. To them a chip of it was as a piece of the Cross. Ignorant though they were of the secret facts of the tragedy, and not thinking but that the penalty was somehow

[113]As Hayford and Sealts note, James Boswell's *Life of Samuel Johnson* (1791) records this phrase under the date April 7, 1775, and explains that it refers to "pretended patriotism" used as "a cloak for self-interest."

unavoidably inflicted from the naval point of view, for all that, they instinctively felt that Billy was a sort of man as incapable of mutiny as of wilful murder. They recalled the fresh young image of the Handsome Sailor, that face never deformed by a sneer or subtler vile freak of the heart within. This impression of him was doubtless deepened by the fact that he was gone, and in a measure mysteriously gone. On the gun decks of the *Bellipotent* the general estimate of his nature and its unconscious simplicity eventually found rude utterance from another foretopman, one of his own watch, gifted, as some sailors are, with an artless *poetic* temperament. The tarry hand made some lines which, after circulating among the shipboard crews for a while, finally got rudely printed at Portsmouth as a ballad. The title given to it was the sailor's.

Billy in the Darbies[114]

Good of the chaplain to enter Lone Bay
And down on his marrowbones here and pray
For the likes just o' me, Billy Budd.—But. look:
Through the port comes the moonshine astray!
It tips the guard's cutlass and silvers this nook;
But 'twill die in the dawning of Billy's last day.
A jewel-block[115] they'll make of me tomorrow,
Pendant pearl from the yardarm-end
Like the eardrop I gave to Bristol Molly—
O, 'tis me, not the sentence they'll suspend.
Ay, ay, all is up; and I must up too,
Early in the morning, aloft from alow.
On an empty stomach now never it would do.
They'll give me a nibble—bit o' biscuit ere I go.
Sure, a messmate will reach me the last parting cup;
But, turning heads away from the hoist and the belay,[116]
Heaven knows who will have the running of me up!
No pipe to those halyards.[117]—But aren't it all sham?
A blur's in my eyes; it is dreaming that I am.

[114]Handcuffs.

[115]A block at the yardarm end through which the halyard of the studding-sail passes. Hayford and Sealts explain that the poet is punning on Billy's reputation as the "jewel" of the crew.

[116]Apparatus that will be used to hoist and secure Billy's body.

[117]Melville's comments in *White-Jacket* on the sailor's recourse to "the bottle to seek relief from the intolerable ennui" of man-of-war life perhaps shed light on this obscure line: "His ordinary government allowance of spirits . . . is not enough . . . he craves a more vigorous *nip at the cable,* a more sturdy *swig at the halyards;* and if opium were to be had, many would steep themselves a thousand fathoms down in the densest fumes of that oblivious drug" (Chap. 43). Melville may be punning on several slang and nautical meanings of pipe: the opium pipe; the large measure of wine containing two hogsheads (a meaning reflected in the expression "piped up," signifying drunk); and the boatswain's whistle that pipes the men to duty. The second meaning would fit the references to the "last parting cup" and the "drum roll to grog." Milton Stern suggests that Melville is using the word pipe in the sense of "pipe dream" (also derived from the opium pipe) and offers the interpretation: "The halyard from which he'll hang is very real and not his mere dream of it."

A hatchet to my hawser?[118] All adrift to go?
The drum roll to grog, and Billy never know?
But Donald he has promised to stand by the plank;
So I'll shake a friendly hand ere I sink.
But—no! It is dead then I'll be, come to think.
I remember Taff the Welshman when he sank.
And his cheek it was like the budding pink.
But me they'll lash in hammock, drop me deep.
Fathoms down, fathoms down, how I'll dream fast asleep.
I feel it stealing now. Sentry, are you there?
Just ease these darbies at the wrist,
And roll me over fair!
I am sleepy, and the oozy weeds about me twist.

1924

Hawthorne and His Mosses

By a Virginian Spending July in Vermont[1]

A papered chamber in a fine old farm-house—a mile from any other dwelling, and dipped to the eaves in foliage—surrounded by mountains, old woods, and Indian ponds,—this, surely, is the place to write of Hawthorne. Some charm is in this

[118] Rope for towing a ship or securing it at a dock.

[1] The most substantial of five book reviews Melville published in the *Literary World,* edited by his friend Evert A. Duyckinck, this essay appeared in the issues of 17 and 24 August 1850. The present text is from the standard Northwestern-Newberry edition of *The Piazza Tales and Other Prose Pieces, 1839–1860* and draws on the editors' textual and historical notes. In it Merton M. Sealts, Jr. has restored a number of passages from the manuscript, which were deleted or diluted by Duyckinck in the original published text, to avoid offending contemporary authors. According to Sealts, the manuscript indicates that Melville's "Virginian" persona was an afterthought, to conceal his identity. Scholars disagree on whether Melville began the essay before meeting Hawthorne at an August 5 "literary outing" in the Berkshires, or wrote the entire essay after the encounter. Through his praise of Hawthorne and Shakespeare as explorers of "blackness" and "masters of the great Art of Telling the Truth," Melville indirectly comments on his own aims and strategies as a writer covertly conveying dangerous truths to an unsympathetic public. A bold expression of literary nationalism, "Hawthorne and His Mosses" invites comparison with Emerson's "The American Scholar" and Whitman's 1855 Preface to *Leaves of Grass* and "Democratic Vistas." Melville calls on Americans to promote the creation of an art in keeping with their "unshackled, democratic" creed by giving their own writers "priority of appreciation," instead of worshiping at the shrines of British writers. This stance aligns him with critics who argue against "universal" and "timeless" standards of literary merit. At the same time, read in the light of Lawrence W. Levine's *Highbrow/Lowbrow: The Emergence of Cultural Hierarchy in America* (1988), Melville's essay reveals a tension between "two Shakespeares: the humble, everyday poet who sprang from the people and found his strength and inspiration among them, and the towering genius" whose deepest meanings could only be discerned by a few sophisticated readers—the first a product of the early nineteenth century's democratic culture, the second of the late nineteenth century's elitist bifurcation between "serious" and "popular" culture (Levine p. 69).

northern air, for love and duty seem both impelling to the task. A man of a deep and noble nature has seized me in this seclusion. His wild, witch voice rings through me; or, in softer cadences, I seem to hear it in the songs of the hill-side birds, that sing in the larch trees at my window.

Would that all excellent books were foundlings, without father or mother, that so it might be, we could glorify them, without including their ostensible authors. Nor would any true man take exception to this;—least of all, he who writes,—"When the Artist rises high enough to achieve the Beautiful, the symbol by which he makes it perceptible to mortal senses becomes of little value in his eyes, while his spirit possesses itself in the enjoyment of the reality."[2]

But more than this. I know not what would be the right name to put on the title-page of an excellent book, but this I feel, that the names of all fine authors are fictitious ones, far more so than that of Junius,[3]—simply standing, as they do, for the mystical, ever-eluding Spirit of all Beauty, which ubiquitously possesses men of genius. Purely imaginative as this fancy may appear, it nevertheless seems to receive some warranty from the fact, that on a personal interview no great author has ever come up to the idea of his reader. But that dust of which our bodies are composed, how can it fitly express the nobler intelligences among us? With reverence be it spoken, that not even in the case of one deemed more than man, not even in our Saviour, did his visible frame betoken anything of the augustness of the nature within. Else, how could those Jewish eyewitnesses fail to see heaven in his glance.

It is curious, how a man may travel along a country road, and yet miss the grandest, or sweetest of prospects, by reason of an intervening hedge, so like all other hedges, as in no way to hint of the wide landscape beyond. So has it been with me concerning the enchanting landscape in the soul of this Hawthorne, this most excellent Man of Mosses. His "Old Manse" has been written now four years, but I never read it till a day or two since. I had seen it in the book-stores—heard of it often—even had it recommended to me by a tasteful friend, as a rare, quiet book, perhaps too deserving of popularity to be popular. But there are so many books called "excellent", and so much unpopular merit, that amid the thick stir of other things, the hint of my tasteful friend was disregarded; and for four years the Mosses on the old Manse never refreshed me with their perennial green. It may be, however, that all this while, the book, like wine, was only improving in flavor and body. At any rate, it so chanced that this long procrastination eventuated in a happy result. At breakfast the other day, a mountain girl, a cousin of mine,[4] who for the last two weeks has every morning helped me to strawberries and raspberries,—which, like the roses and pearls in the fairy-tale, seemed to fall into the saucer from those strawberry-beds her cheeks,—this delightful creature, this charming Cherry says to me—"I see you spend your mornings in the hay-mow; and yesterday I found there 'Dwight's Travels in

[2]The concluding words of Hawthorne's "The Artist of the Beautiful," slightly modified by Melville.

[3]Unidentified pseudonymous author of the *Letters of Junius* (London, 1770, Philadelphia 1791), which went through many editions and exerted a strong influence on American polemicists of the Revolutionary era as well as on the debates over ratification of the Federal Constitution. "Junius" was best known for defending liberty of the press as the guardian of "all the civil, political, and religious rights of an Englishman."

[4]Melville's notation in his copy of *Mosses from an Old Manse* (1846) in fact indicates that he received the book from his Aunt Mary, widow of his Uncle Thomas Melvill in Pittsfield, on July 18, 1850.

New England'.[5] Now I have something far better than that,—something more congenial to our summer on these hills. Take these raspberries, and then I will give you some moss."—"Moss!" said I.—"Yes, and you must take it to the barn with you, and good-bye to 'Dwight' ".

With that she left me, and soon returned with a volume, verdantly bound, and garnished with a curious frontispiece in green,—nothing less, than a fragment of real moss cunningly pressed to a fly-leaf.—"Why this," said I spilling my raspberries, "this is the 'Mosses from an Old Manse' ". "Yes" said cousin Cherry "yes, it is that flowery Hawthorne."—"Hawthorne and Mosses" said I "no more: it is morning: it is July in the country: and I am off for the barn".

Stretched on that new mown clover, the hill-side breeze blowing over me through the wide barn door, and soothed by the hum of the bees in the meadows around, how magically stole over me this Mossy Man! and how amply, how bountifully, did he redeem that delicious promise to his guests in the Old Manse, of whom it is written—"Others could give them pleasure, or amusement, or instruction—these could be picked up anywhere—but it was for me to give them rest. Rest, in a life of trouble! What better could be done for weary and world-worn spirits? what better could be done for anybody, who came within our magic circle, than to throw the spell of a magic spirit over him?"—So all that day, half-buried in the new clover, I watched this Hawthorne's "Assyrian dawn, and Paphian sunset and moonrise, from the summit of our Eastern Hill."[6]

The soft ravishments of the man spun me round about in a web of dreams, and when the book was closed, when the spell was over, this wizard "dismissed me with but misty reminiscences, as if I had been dreaming of him".

What a mild moonlight of contemplative humor bathes that Old Manse!—the rich and rare distilment of a spicy and slowly-oozing heart. No rollicking rudeness, no gross fun fed on fat dinners, and bred in the lees of wine,—but a humor so spiritually gentle, so high, so deep, and yet so richly relishable, that it were hardly inappropriate in an angel. It is the very religion of mirth; for nothing so human but it may be advanced to that. The orchard of the Old Manse seems the visible type of the fine mind that has described it. Those twisted, and contorted old trees, "that stretch out their crooked branches, and take such hold of the imagination, that we remember them as humorists, and odd-fellows." And then, as surrounded by these grotesque forms, and hushed in the noon-day repose of this Hawthorne's spell, how aptly might the still fall of his ruddy thoughts into your soul be symbolized by "the thump of a great apple, in the stillest afternoon, falling without a breath of wind, from the mere necessity of perfect ripeness"! For no less ripe than ruddy are the apples of the thoughts and fancies in this sweet Man of Mosses.

"Buds and Bird-voices"—What a delicious thing is that!—"Will the world ever be so decayed, that Spring may not renew its greenness?"—And the "Fire-Worship". Was ever the hearth so glorified into an altar before? The mere title of that piece is better than any common work in fifty folio volumes. How exquisite is this:—"Nor did it lessen the charm of his soft, familiar courtesy and helpfulness, that the mighty

[5]Timothy Dwight's *Travels in New-England and New-York* (1821–1822).

[6]Adapted from "The Old Manse," the prefatory sketch of *Mosses from an Old Manse.* The story titles and quotations that follow are all from *Mosses,* but Melville frequently introduces slight alterations, a typical nineteenth-century practice.

spirit, were opportunity offered him, would run riot through the peaceful house, wrap its inmates in his terrible embrace, and leave nothing of them save their whitened bones. This possibility of mad destruction only made his domestic kindness the more beautiful and touching. It was so sweet of him, being endowed with such power, to dwell, day after day, and one long, lonesome night after another, on the dusky hearth, only now and then betraying his wild nature, by thrusting his red tongue out of the chimney-top! True, he had done much mischief in the world, and was pretty certain to do more, but his warm heart atoned for all. He was kindly to the race of man."

But he has still other apples, not quite so ruddy, though full as ripe;—apples, that have been left to wither on the tree, after the pleasant autumn gathering is past. The sketch of "The Old Apple Dealer" is conceived in the subtlest spirit of sadness; he whose "subdued and nerveless boyhood prefigured his abortive prime, which, likewise, contained within itself the prophecy and image of his lean and torpid age". Such touches as are in this piece can not proceed from any common heart. They argue such a depth of tenderness, such a boundless sympathy with all forms of being, such an omnipresent love, that we must needs say, that this Hawthorne is here almost alone in his generation,—at least, in the artistic manifestation of these things. Still more. Such touches as these,—and many, very many similar ones, all through his chapters—furnish clews, whereby we enter a little way into the intricate, profound heart where they originated. And we see, that suffering, some time or other and in some shape or other,—this only can enable any man to depict it in others. All over him, Hawthorne's melancholy rests like an Indian Summer, which though bathing a whole country in one softness, still reveals the distinctive hue of every towering hill, and each far-winding vale.

But it is the least part of genius that attracts admiration. Where Hawthorne is known, he seems to be deemed a pleasant writer, with a pleasant style,—a sequestered, harmless man, from whom any deep and weighty thing would hardly be anticipated:—a man who means no meanings. But there is no man, in whom humor and love, like mountain peaks, soar to such a rapt height, as to receive the irradiations of the upper skies;—there is no man in whom humor and love are developed in that high form called genius; no such man can exist without also possessing, as the indispensable complement of these, a great, deep intellect, which drops down into the universe like a plummet. Or, love and humor are only the eyes, through which such an intellect views this world. The great beauty in such a mind is but the product of its strength. What, to all readers, can be more charming than the piece entitled "Monsieur du Miroir"; and to a reader at all capable of fully fathoming it, what, at the same time, can possess more mystical depth of meaning?—Yes, there he sits, and looks at me,—this "shape of mystery", this "identical Monsieur du Miroir".—"Methinks I should tremble now, were his wizard power of gliding through all impediments in search of me, to place him suddenly before my eyes".

How profound, nay appalling, is the moral evolved by the "Earth's Holocaust"; where—beginning with the hollow follies and affectations of the world,—all vanities and empty theories and forms, are, one after another, and by an admirably graduated, growing comprehensiveness, thrown into the allegorical fire, till, at length, nothing is left but the all-engendering heart of man; which remaining still unconsumed, the great conflagration is nought.

Of a piece with this, is the "Intelligence Office", a wondrous symbolizing of the secret workings in men's souls. There are other sketches, still more charged with ponderous import.

"The Christmas Banquet", and "The Bosom Serpent" would be fine subjects for a curious and elaborate analysis, touching the conjectural parts of the mind that produced them. For spite of all the Indian-summer sunlight on the hither side of Hawthorne's soul, the other side—like the dark half of the physical sphere—is shrouded in a blackness, ten times black. But this darkness but gives more effect to the ever-moving dawn, that forever advances through it, and circumnavigates his world. Whether Hawthorne has simply availed himself of this mystical blackness as a means to the wondrous effects he makes it to produce in his lights and shades; or whether there really lurks in him, perhaps unknown to himself, a touch of Puritanic gloom,—this, I cannot altogether tell. Certain it is, however, that this great power of blackness in him derives its force from its appeals to that Calvinistic sense of Innate Depravity and Original Sin, from whose visitations, in some shape or other, no deeply thinking mind is always and wholly free. For, in certain moods, no man can weigh this world, without throwing in something, somehow like Original Sin, to strike the uneven balance. At all events, perhaps no writer has ever wielded this terrific thought with greater terror than this same harmless Hawthorne. Still more: this black conceit pervades him, through and through. You may be witched by his sunlight,—transported by the bright gildings in the skies he builds over you;—but there is the blackness of darkness beyond; and even his bright gildings but fringe, and play upon the edges of thunder-clouds.—In one word, the world is mistaken in this Nathaniel Hawthorne. He himself must often have smiled at its absurd misconception of him. He is immeasurably deeper than the plummet of the mere critic. For it is not the brain that can test such a man; it is only the heart. You cannot come to know greatness by inspecting it; there is no glimpse to be caught of it, except by intuition; you need not ring it, you but touch it, and you find it is gold.

Now it is that blackness in Hawthorne, of which I have spoken, that so fixes and fascinates me. It may be, nevertheless, that it is too largely developed in him. Perhaps he does not give us a ray of his light for every shade of his dark. But however this may be, this blackness it is that furnishes the infinite obscure of his back-ground,—that back-ground, against which Shakespeare plays his grandest conceits, the things that have made for Shakespeare his loftiest, but most circumscribed renown, as the profoundest of thinkers. For by philosophers Shakespeare is not adored as the great man of tragedy and comedy.—"Off with his head! so much for Buckingham!"[7] this sort of rant, interlined by another hand, brings down the house,—those mistaken souls, who dream of Shakespeare as a mere man of Richard-the-Third humps, and Macbeth daggers. But it is those deep far-away things in him; those occasional flashings-forth of the intuitive Truth in him; those short, quick probings at the very axis of reality;—these are the things that make Shakespeare, Shakespeare. Through the mouths of the dark characters of Hamlet, Timon, Lear, and Iago, he craftily says, or sometimes insinuates the things, which we feel to be so terrifically true, that it were all but madness for any good man, in his own proper character, to utter, or even hint

[7]One of many lines interpolated into Shakespeare's *Richard III* (IV. iv) by the British actor and dramatist Colley Cibber (1671–1757), whose popular revision of the play dominated the American stage until the late nineteenth century.

of them. Tormented into desperation, Lear the frantic King tears off the mask, and speaks the sane madness of vital truth. But, as I before said, it is the least part of genius that attracts admiration. And so, much of the blind, unbridled admiration that has been heaped upon Shakespeare, has been lavished upon the least part of him. And few of his endless commentators and critics seem to have remembered, or even perceived, that the immediate products of a great mind are not so great, as that undeveloped, (and sometimes undevelopable) yet dimly-discernable greatness, to which these immediate products are but the infallible indices. In Shakespeare's tomb lies infinitely more than Shakspeare ever wrote. And if I magnify Shakespeare, it is not so much for what he did do, as for what he did not do, or refrained from doing. For in this world of lies, Truth is forced to fly like a scared white doe in the woodlands; and only by cunning glimpses will she reveal herself, as in Shakespeare and other masters of the great Art of Telling the Truth,—even though it be covertly, and by snatches.

But if this view of the all-popular Shakespeare be seldom taken by his readers, and if very few who extol him, have ever read him deeply, or, perhaps, only have seen him on the tricky stage, (which alone made, and is still making him his mere mob renown)—if few men have time, or patience, or palate, for the spiritual truth as it is in that great genius;—it is, then, no matter of surprise that in a contemporaneous age, Nathaniel Hawthorne is a man, as yet, almost utterly mistaken among men. Here and there, in some quiet arm-chair in the noisy town, or some deep nook among the noiseless mountains, he may be appreciated for something of what he is. But unlike Shakespeare, who was forced to the contrary course by circumstances, Hawthorne (either from simple disinclination, or else from inaptitude) refrains from all the popularizing noise and show of broad farce, and blood-besmeared tragedy; content with the still, rich utterances of a great intellect in repose, and which sends few thoughts into circulation, except they be arterialized at his large warm lungs, and expanded in his honest heart.

Nor need you fix upon that blackness in him, if it suit you not. Nor, indeed, will all readers discern it, for it is, mostly, insinuated to those who may best understand it, and account for it; it is not obtruded upon every one alike.

Some may start to read of Shakespeare and Hawthorne on the same page. They may say, that if an illustration were needed, a lesser light might have sufficed to elucidate this Hawthorne, this small man of yesterday. But I am not, willingly, one of those, who, as touching Shakespeare at least, exemplify the maxim of Rochefoucault,[8] that "we exalt the reputation of some, in order to depress that of others";—who, to teach all noble-souled aspirants that there is no hope for them, pronounce Shakespeare absolutely unapproachable. But Shakespeare has been approached. There are minds that have gone as far as Shakespeare into the universe. And hardly a mortal man, who, at some time or other, has not felt as great thoughts in him as any you will find in Hamlet. We must not inferentially malign mankind for the sake of any one man, whoever he may be. This is too cheap a purchase of contentment for conscious mediocrity to make. Besides, this absolute and unconditional adoration of Shakespeare has grown to be a part of our Anglo Saxon superstitions. The Thirty

[8]François de la Rochefoucauld (1613–1680), French writer of moral maxims. The exact source for Melville's wording has not been identified.

Nine articles[9] are now Forty. Intolerance has come to exist in this matter. You must believe in Shakespeare's unapproachability, or quit the country. But what sort of a belief is this for an American, a man who is bound to carry republican progressiveness into Literature, as well as into Life? Believe me, my friends, that Shakespeares are this day being born on the banks of the Ohio. And the day will come, when you shall say who reads a book by an Englishman that is a modern?[10] The great mistake seems to be, that even with those Americans who look forward to the coming of a great literary genius among us, they somehow fancy he will come in the costume of Queen Elizabeth's day,—be a writer of dramas founded upon old English history, or the tales of Boccaccio.[11] Whereas, great geniuses are parts of the times; they themselves are the times; and possess a correspondent coloring. It is of a piece with the Jews, who while their Shiloh[12] was meekly walking in their streets, were still praying for his magnificent coming; looking for him in a chariot, who was already among them on an ass. Nor must we forget, that, in his own life-time, Shakespeare was not Shakespeare, but only Master William Shakespeare of the shrewd, thriving, business firm of Condell, Shakespeare & Co., proprietors of the Globe Theatre in London; and by a courtly author, of the name of Greene, was hooted at, as an "upstart crow" beautified "with other birds' feathers".[13] For, mark it well, imitation is often the first charge brought against real originality. Why this is so, there is not space to set forth here. You must have plenty of sea-room to tell the Truth in; especially, when it seems to have an aspect of newness, as America did in 1492, though it was then just as old, and perhaps older than Asia, only those sagacious philosophers, the common sailors, had never seen it before; swearing it was all water and moonshine there.

Now, I do not say that Nathaniel of Salem is a greater than William of Avon, or as great. But the difference between the two men is by no means immeasurable. Not a very great deal more, and Nathaniel were verily William.

This, too, I mean, that if Shakespeare has not been equalled, he is sure to be surpassed, and surpassed by an American born now or yet to be born. For it will never do for us who in most other things out-do as well as out-brag the world, it will not do for us to fold our hands and say, In the highest department advance there is none. Nor will it at all do to say, that the world is getting grey and grizzled now, and has lost that fresh charm which she wore of old, and by virtue of which the great poets of past times made themselves what we esteem them to be. Not so. The world is as young today, as when it was created; and this Vermont morning dew is as wet to my feet, as Eden's dew to Adam's. Nor has Nature been all over ransacked by our

[9]Tenets of the Anglican creed, metaphorically referring to the ironic worship of things English by a people whose ancestors threw off the yoke of the Anglican church and the British king.

[10]Melville is reversing the famous insult by the British critic Sydney Smith (1771–1845): "In the four quarters of the globe, who reads an American book?" (*Edinburgh Review* 1820).

[11]Giovanni Boccaccio (1313–1375), Italian author of the *Decameron.*

[12]The name of the city and the sanctuary where the Ark of the Covenant was first kept after the entry into Canaan (Joshua 18:1), and the site of the early Israelites' great yearly sacrifice; hence used by Melville as a synonym for Messiah.

[13]An altered quotation from Robert Greene's *A Groatsworth of Wit* (1592). In both the manuscript and the original published text, Melville misattributed the quotation to Greene's publisher, Henry Chettle, but the Northwestern-Newberry editors have emended his error.

progenitors, so that no new charms and mysteries remain for this latter generation to find. Far from it. The trillionth part has not yet been said; and all that has been said, but multiplies the avenues to what remains to be said. It is not so much paucity, as superabundance of material that seems to incapacitate modern authors.

Let America then prize and cherish her writers; yea, let her glorify them. They are not so many in number, as to exhaust her good-will. And while she has good kith and kin of her own, to take to her bosom, let her not lavish her embraces upon the household of an alien. For believe it or not England, after all, is, in many things, an alien to us. China has more bowels of real love for us than she. But even were there no Hawthorne, no Emerson, no Whittier, no Irving, no Bryant, no Dana, no Cooper, no Willis (not the author of the "Dashes", but the author of the "Belfry Pigeon")[14]—were there none of these, and others of like calibre among us, nevertheless, let America first praise mediocrity even, in her own children, before she praises (for everywhere, merit demands acknowledgment from every one) the best excellence in the children of any other land. Let her own authors, I say, have the priority of appreciation. I was much pleased with a hot-headed Carolina cousin of mine, who once said,—"If there were no other American to stand by, in Literature,—why, then, I would stand by Pop Emmons and his 'Fredoniad,'[15] and till a better epic came along, swear it was not very far behind the Iliad." Take away the words, and in spirit he was sound.

Not that American genius needs patronage in order to expand. For that explosive sort of stuff will expand though screwed up in a vice, and burst it, though it were triple steel. It is for the nation's sake, and not for her authors' sake, that I would have America be heedful of the increasing greatness among her writers. For how great the shame, if other nations should be before her, in crowning her heroes of the pen. But this is almost the case now. American authors have received more just and discriminating praise (however loftily and ridiculously given, in certain cases) even from some Englishmen, than from their own countrymen. There are hardly five critics in America; and several of them are asleep. As for patronage, it is the American author who now patronizes his country, and not his country him. And if at times some among them appeal to the people for more recognition, it is not always with selfish motives, but patriotic ones.

It is true, that but few of them as yet have evinced that decided originality which merits great praise. But that graceful writer, who perhaps of all Americans has received the most plaudits from his own country for his productions,—that very popular and amiable writer, however good, and self-reliant in many things, perhaps owes his chief reputation to the self-acknowledged imitation of a foreign model,

[14]In the original published text, Duyckinck deleted these names and substituted: "But even were there no strong literary individualities among us, as there are some dozens at least. . . ." Richard Henry Dana, Jr. (1815–1882) was the author of *Two Years Before the Mast* (1840), which Melville hailed as a model for his own sea fiction. Nathaniel Parker Willis (1806–1867) was a dandified author and editor (and the employer of the escaped slave Harriet Jacobs, whose *Incidents in the Life of a Slave Girl* is reprinted in this volume). Melville is referring to Willis's volume of short fiction, *Dashes at Life with a Free Pencil* (1845) and to his poem, "The Belfry Pigeon" (1831). Willis, Irving, and Bryant were late additions to Melville's list.

[15]Identified by the Northwestern-Newberry editors as "the jocular nickname for Richard Emmons, author of the blatantly nationalistic and bathetic four-volume epic on the War of 1812, *The Fredoniad*" (1827).

and to the studied avoidance of all topics but smooth ones.[16] But it is better to fail in originality, than to succeed in imitation. He who has never failed somewhere, that man can not be great. Failure is the true test of greatness. And if it be said, that continual success is a proof that a man wisely knows his powers,—it is only to be added, that, in that case, he knows them to be small. Let us believe it, then, once for all, that there is no hope for us in these smooth pleasing writers that know their powers. Without malice, but to speak the plain fact, they but furnish an appendix to Goldsmith, and other English authors. And we want no American Goldsmiths; nay, we want no American Miltons. It were the vilest thing you could say of a true American author, that he were an American Tompkins.[17] Call him an American, and have done; for you can not say a nobler thing of him.—But it is not meant that all American writers should studiously cleave to nationality in their writings; only this, no American writer should write like an Englishman, or a Frenchman; let him write like a man, for then he will be sure to write like an American. Let us away with this Bostonian leaven of literary flunkeyism towards England. If either must play the flunkey in this thing, let England do it, not us. And the time is not far off when circumstances may force her to it. While we are rapidly preparing for that political supremacy among the nations, which prophetically awaits us at the close of the present century; in a literary point of view, we are deplorably unprepared for it; and we seem studious to remain so. Hitherto, reasons might have existed why this should be; but no good reason exists now. And all that is requisite to amendment in this matter, is simply this: that, while freely acknowledging all excellence, everywhere, we should refrain from unduly lauding foreign writers and, at the same time, duly recognize the meritorious writers that are our own;—those writers, who breathe that unshackled, democratic spirit of Christianity in all things, which now takes the practical lead in this world, though at the same time led by ourselves—us Americans. Let us boldly contemn all imitation, though it comes to us graceful and fragrant as the morning; and foster all originality, though, at first, it be crabbed and ugly as our own pine knots. And if any of our authors fail, or seem to fail, then, in the words of my enthusiastic Carolina cousin, let us clap him on the shoulder, and back him against all Europe for his second round. The truth is, that in our point of view, this matter of a national literature has come to such a pass with us, that in some sense we must turn bullies, else the day is lost, or superiority so far beyond us, that we can hardly say it will ever be ours.

And now, my countrymen, as an excellent author, of your own flesh and blood,—an unimitating, and, perhaps, in his way, an inimitable man—whom better can I commend to you, in the first place, than Nathaniel Hawthorne. He is one of the new, and far better generation of your writers. The smell of your beeches and hemlocks is upon him; your own broad praries are in his soul; and if you travel away inland into his deep and noble nature, you will hear the far roar of his

[16]Washington Irving. Melville may be alluding either to the German sources of "Rip Van Winkle" and "The Legend of Sleepy Hollow" or to Irving's imitation of the British writer Oliver Goldsmith (1728–1774). See his reference later in this paragraph to Irving's reputation as the "American Goldsmith."

[17]Tompkins has not been identified, but some annotators have suggested that the name was commonly associated with liveried servants ("flunkeys")—hence Melville's references below to "literary flunkeyism" and "play[ing] the flunkey."

Niagara. Give not over to future generations the glad duty of acknowledging him for what he is. Take that joy to your self, in your own generation; and so shall he feel those grateful impulses in him, that may possibly prompt him to the full flower of some still greater achievement in your eyes. And by confessing him, you thereby confess others; you embrace the whole brotherhood. For genius, all over the world, stands hand in hand, and one shock of recognition runs the whole circle round.

In treating of Hawthorne, or rather of Hawthorne in his writings (for I never saw the man; and in the chances of a quiet plantation life, remote from his haunts, perhaps never shall) in treating of his works, I say, I have thus far omitted all mention of his "Twice Told Tales", and "Scarlet Letter". Both are excellent; but full of such manifold, strange and diffusive beauties, that time would all but fail me, to point the half of them out. But there are things in those two books, which, had they been written in England a century ago, Nathaniel Hawthorne had utterly displaced many of the bright names we now revere on authority. But I am content to leave Hawthorne to himself, and to the infallible finding of posterity; and however great may be the praise I have bestowed upon him, I feel, that in so doing, I have more served and honored myself, than him. For, at bottom, great excellence is praise enough to itself; but the feeling of a sincere and appreciative love and admiration towards it, this is relieved by utterance; and warm, honest praise ever leaves a pleasant flavor in the mouth; and it is an honorable thing to confess to what is honorable in others.

But I cannot leave my subject yet. No man can read a fine author, and relish him to his very bones, while he reads, without subsequently fancying to himself some ideal image of the man and his mind. And if you rightly look for it, you will almost always find that the author himself has somewhere furnished you with his own picture.—For poets (whether in prose or verse), being painters of Nature, are like their brethren of the pencil, the true portrait-painters, who, in the multitude of likenesses to be sketched, do not invariably omit their own; and in all high instances, they paint them without any vanity, though, at times, with a lurking something, that would take several pages to properly define.

I submit it, then, to those best acquainted with the man personally, whether the following is not Nathaniel Hawthorne;—and to himself, whether something involved in it does not express the temper of his mind,—that lasting temper of all true, candid men—a seeker, not a finder yet:—

> *"A man now entered, in neglected attire, with the aspect of a thinker, but somewhat too rough-hewn and brawny for a scholar. His face was full of sturdy vigor, with some finer and keener attribute beneath; though harsh at first, it was tempered with the glow of a large, warm heart, which had force enough to heat his powerful intellect through and through. He advanced to the Intelligencer, and looked at him with a glance of such stern sincerity, that perhaps few secrets were beyond its scope.*
>
> *"'I seek for Truth', said he."*[18]

* * *

[18]Quoted from Hawthorne's "The Intelligence Office" in *Mosses.*

Twenty four hours have elapsed since writing the foregoing. I have just returned from the hay mow, charged more and more with love and admiration of Hawthorne. For I have just been gleaning through the Mosses, picking up many things here and there that had previously escaped me. And I found that but to glean after this man, is better than to be in at the harvest of others. To be frank (though, perhaps, rather foolish) notwithstanding what I wrote yesterday of these Mosses, I had not then culled them all; but had, nevertheless, been sufficiently sensible of the subtle essence, in them, as to write as I did. To what infinite height of loving wonder and admiration I may yet be borne, when by repeatedly banquetting on these Mosses, I shall have thoroughly incorporated their whole stuff into my being,—that, I can not tell. But already I feel that this Hawthorne has dropped germinous seeds into my soul. He expands and deepens down, the more I contemplate him; and further, and further, shoots his strong New-England roots into the hot soil of my Southern soul.

By careful reference to the "Table of Contents", I now find, that I have gone through all the sketches; but that when I yesterday wrote, I had not at all read two particular pieces, to which I now desire to call special attention,—"A Select Party", and "Young Goodman Brown". Here, be it said to all those whom this poor fugitive scrawl of mine may tempt to the perusal of the "Mosses," that they must on no account suffer themselves to be trifled with, disappointed, or deceived by the triviality of many of the titles to these Sketches. For in more than one instance, the title utterly belies the piece. It is as if rustic demijohns containing the very best and costliest of Falernian and Tokay, were labelled "Cider", "Perry," and "Elderberry wine".[19] The truth seems to be, that like many other geniuses, this Man of Mosses takes great delight in hoodwinking the world,—at least, with respect to himself. Personally, I doubt not, that he rather prefers to be generally esteemed but a so-so sort of author; being willing to reserve the thorough and acute appreciation of what he is, to that party most qualified to judge—that is, to himself. Besides, at the bottom of their natures, men like Hawthorne, in many things, deem the plaudits of the public such strong presumptive evidence of mediocrity in the object of them, that it would in some degree render them doubtful of their own powers, did they hear much and vociferous braying concerning them in the public pastures. True, I have been braying myself (if you please to be witty enough, to have it so) but then I claim to be the first that has so brayed in this particular matter; and therefore, while pleading guilty to the charge still claim all the merit due to originality.

But with whatever motive, playful or profound, Nathaniel Hawthorne has chosen to entitle his pieces in the manner he has, it is certain, that some of them are directly calculated to deceive—egregiously deceive, the superficial skimmer of pages. To be downright and candid once more, let me cheerfully say, that two of these titles did dolefully dupe no less an eagle-eyed reader than myself; and that, too, after I had been impressed with a sense of the great depth and breadth of this American man. "Who in the name of thunder" (as the country-people say in this neighborhood) "who in the name of thunder", would anticipate any marvel in a piece entitled "Young Goodman Brown"? You would of course suppose that it was a simple little tale, intended as a supplement to "Goody Two Shoes". Whereas, it is deep as Dante; nor can you finish it, without addressing the author in his own words—"It is yours

[19]Falernian and Tokay were famous wines from Italy and Hungary, while apple cider, perry (pear cider), and elderberry wine were common home-fermented drinks.

to penetrate, in every bosom, the deep mystery of sin". And with Young Goodman, too, in allegorical pursuit of his Puritan wife, you cry out in your anguish,—

> *"'Faith!' shouted Goodman Brown, in a voice of agony and desperation; and the echoes of the forest mocked him, crying—'Faith! Faith!' as if bewildered wretches were seeking her all through the wilderness."*

Now this same piece, entitled "Young Goodman Brown", is one of the two that I had not all read yesterday; and I allude to it now, because it is, in itself, such a strong positive illustration of that blackness in Hawthorne, which I had assumed from the mere occasional shadows of it, as revealed in several of the other sketches. But had I previously perused "Young Goodman Brown", I should have been at no pains to draw the conclusion, which I came to, at a time, when I was ignorant that the book contained one such direct and unqualified manifestation of it.

The other piece of the two referred to, is entitled "A Select Party", which, in my first simplicity upon originally taking hold of the book, I fancied must treat of some pumpkin-pie party in Old Salem, or some chowder party on Cape Cod. Whereas, by all the gods of Peedee![20] it is the sweetest and sublimest thing that has been written since Spencer wrote. Nay, there is nothing in Spencer that surpasses it, perhaps, nothing that equals it. And the test is this: read any canto in "The Faery Queen", and then read "A Select Party", and decide which pleases you the most,—that is, if you are qualified to judge. Do not be frightened at this; for when Spencer was alive, he was thought of very much as Hawthorne is now,—was generally accounted just such a "gentle" harmless man. It may be, that to common eyes, the sublimity of Hawthorne seems lost in his sweetness,—as perhaps in this same "Select Party" of his; for whom, he has builded so august a dome of sunset clouds, and served them on richer plate, than Belshazzar's when he banquetted his lords in Babylon.[21]

But my chief business now, is to point out a particular page in this piece, having reference to an honored guest, who under the name of "The Master Genius" but in the guise of "a young man of poor attire, with no insignia of rank or acknowledged eminence", is introduced to the Man of Fancy, who is the giver of the feast. Now the page having reference to this "Master Genius", so happily expresses much of what I yesterday wrote, touching the coming of the literary Shiloh of America, that I cannot but be charmed by the coincidence; especially, when it shows such a parity of ideas, at least in this one point, between a man like Hawthorne and a man like me.

And here, let me throw out another conceit of mine touching this American Shiloh, or "Master Genius", as Hawthorne calls him. May it not be, that this commanding mind has not been, is not, and never will be, individually developed in any one man? And would it, indeed, appear so unreasonable to suppose, that this great fullness and overflowing may be, or may be destined to be, shared by a plurality of men of genius? Surely, to take the very greatest example on record, Shakespeare cannot be regarded as in himself the concretion of all the genius of his time; nor as so immeasurably beyond Marlow, Webster, Ford, Beaumont, Jonson,[22] that those great

[20]River in the Carolinas (in keeping with Melville's Southern persona).

[21]Daniel 5:1 tells of how the Babylonian king Belshazzar "made a great feast to a thousand of his lords, and drank wine before the thousand."

[22]Christopher Marlowe (1564–1593), John Webster (c. 1580–c. 1625), John Ford (c. 1586–c. 1640), Francis Beaumont (c. 1584–1616), and Ben Jonson (1572–1637) were dramatists contemporary with Shakespeare.

men can be said to share none of his power? For one, I conceive that there were dramatists in Elizabeth's day, between whom and Shakespeare the distance was by no means great. Let anyone, hitherto little acquainted with those neglected old authors, for the first time read them thoroughly, or even read Charles Lamb's Specimens[23] of them, and he will be amazed at the wondrous ability of those Anaks[24] of men, and shocked at this renewed example of the fact, that Fortune has more to do with fame than merit,—though, without merit, lasting fame there can be none.

Nevertheless, it would argue too illy of my country were this maxim to hold good concerning Nathaniel Hawthorne, a man, who already, in some few minds, has shed "such a light, as never illuminates the earth, save when a great heart burns as the household fire of a grand intellect."

The words are his,—in the "Select Party"; and they are a magnificent setting to a coincident sentiment of my own, but ramblingly expressed yesterday, in reference to himself. Gainsay it who will, as I now write, I am Posterity speaking by proxy—and after times will make it more than good, when I declare—that the American, who up to the present day, has evinced, in Literature, the largest brain with the largest heart, that man is Nathaniel Hawthorne. Moreover, that whatever Nathaniel Hawthorne may hereafter write, "The Mosses from an Old Manse" will be ultimately accounted his masterpiece. For there is a sure, though a secret sign in some works which prove the culmination of the powers (only the developable ones, however) that produced them. But I am by no means desirous of the glory of a prophet. I pray Heaven that Hawthorne may *yet* prove me an impostor in this prediction. Especially, as I somehow cling to the strange fancy, that, in all men, hiddenly reside certain wondrous, occult properties—as in some plants and minerals—which by some happy but very rare accident (as bronze was discovered by the melting of the iron and brass in the burning of Corinth) may chance to be called forth here on earth; not entirely waiting for their better discovery in the more congenial, blessed atmosphere of heaven.

Once more—for it is hard to be finite upon an infinite subject, and all subjects are infinite. By some people, this entire scrawl of mine may be esteemed altogether unnecessary, inasmuch, "as years ago" (they may say) "we found out the rich and rare stuff in this Hawthorne, whom you now parade forth, as if only *yourself* were the discoverer of this Portuguese diamond in our Literature".—But even granting all this; and adding to it, the assumption that the books of Hawthorne have sold by the five-thousand,—what does that signify?—They should be sold by the hundred-thousand; and read by the million; and admired by every one who is capable of admiration.

1850

[23]The English essayist Charles Lamb (1775–1834) helped promote a revival of Elizabethan literature through his *Specimens of English Dramatic Poets, Who Lived about the Time of Shakespeare* (1808), which featured selections from most of the writers mentioned above.

[24]A race of reputedly unconquerable giants destroyed by Joshua. See Moses Book 4 (Numbers) 13:33 and Joshua 11:21.

from Battle-Pieces and Aspects of the War

The Portent[1] *(1859)*

Hanging from the beam,
  Slowly swaying (such the law),
Gaunt the shadow on your green,
  Shenandoah!
The cut is on the crown
(Lo, John Brown),
And the stabs shall heal no more.

Hidden in the cap
  Is the anguish none can draw;
So your future veils its face,
  Shenandoah!
But the streaming beard is shown
(Weird John Brown),
The meteor of the war.

1866

A Utilitarian View of the Monitor's Fight[1]

Plain be the phrase, yet apt the verse,
  More ponderous than nimble;
For since grimed War here laid aside
His Orient pomp, 'twould ill befit
    Overmuch to ply

  The rhyme's barbaric cymbal.
Hail to victory without the gaud
  Of glory; zeal that needs no fans
Of banners; plain mechanic power
Plied cogently in War now placed—

[1] "The Portent" is the opening poem in *Battle-Pieces and Aspects of the War* (1866), the source of the present texts. Set in italics in the original, it commemorates the hanging of John Brown after his unsuccessful raid on the Federal arsenal at Harpers Ferry, Virginia, in October, 1859, and portrays Brown as a portent of the ensuing Civil War. The imagery suggests both an Old Testament prophet and a Christlike martyr—analogies common among antislavery sympathizers. Compare the poem with Thoreau's "A Plea for Captain John Brown" and the hanging of Brown with that of Billy Budd.

[1] Adopting a verse style in keeping with the new technology of warfare, the poem commemorates the battle of the first American ironclad battleships, the Union *Monitor* and the Confederate *Merrimack,* on May 9, 1862, at Hampton Roads, Virginia.

Where War belongs—
Among the trades and artisans.

Yet this was battle, and intense—
Beyond the strife of fleets heroic;
Deadlier, closer, calm 'mid storm;
No passion; all went on by crank,
Pivot, and screw,

And calculations of caloric.
Needless to dwell; the story's known.
The ringing of those plates on plates
Still ringeth round the world—
The clangor of that blacksmiths' fray.
The anvil-din
Resounds this message from the Fates:

War shall yet be, and to the end;
But war-paint shows the streaks of weather;
War yet shall be, but warriors
Are now but operatives;[2] War's made
Less grand than Peace,
And a singe runs through lace and feather.

1866

from Timoleon[1]

Monody

To have known him, to have loved him
After loneness long;
And then to be estranged in life,
And neither in the wrong;
And now for death to set his seal—
Ease me, a little ease, my song!

By wintry hills his hermit-mound
The sheeted snow-drifts drape,
And houseless there the snow-bird flits

[2]Factory workers.

[1]Melville had this volume of poems privately published in 1891. He seems to have composed "Monody" in response to Hawthorne's death in May, 1864. A reclusive character named Vine, whom most critics identify as a portrait of Hawthorne, appears in *Clarel* (1876).

Beneath the fir-trees' crape:
Glazed now with ice the cloistral vine
That hid the shyest grape.

1891

Art

In placid hours well-pleased we dream
Of many a brave unbodied scheme.
But form to lend, pulsed life create,
What unlike things must meet and mate:
A flame to melt—a wind to freeze;
Sad patience—joyous energies;
Humility—yet pride and scorn;
Instinct and study; love and hate;
Audacity—reverence. These must mate,
And fuse with Jacob's mystic heart,
To wrestle with the angel[1]—Art.

1891

[1]In Genesis 32:24–29, Jacob wrestles all night long with an angel. The struggle ends with the angel's blessing Jacob and renaming him Israel.

William Wells Brown 1815–1884

William Wells Brown has been criticized as an early proponent of the assimilationist policies of Booker T. Washington and hailed as black America's first professional man of letters. Despite being an advocate of economic aspirations similar to those of Washington, Brown demonstrated through his outspoken anti-slavery activity the militance and political shrewdness of Washington's opponent, W.E.B. Du Bois. He published the first African-American novel, drama, travel book, and military histories of blacks in the American Revolution, the War of 1812, and the Civil War. And while his writing reflects the sentimental standards of popular midcentury taste, his allegiance to the slave narratives' trope of the flight to freedom, his "worrying" again and again with the figure of the person of mixed blood, his concern with the concept of identity—both in his most famous character, Clotel(le), and in his own life—mark him as the ancestor not only of later writers like Charles Chesnutt, but of contemporary black artists.

One way of understanding Brown's contribution to African-American tradition is to read his pioneering literary efforts and his work for abolition, temperance, and black education as responses to what was at once a personal and racial imperative. Throughout his life he was devoted to improving the condition of his people and also, emblematically and materially, to creating a self and a world of possibility for a former slave who never forgot how that "peculiar institution" had operated to limit and dehumanize him. Once released, Brown's Protean energies could not be contained by one literary genre, any more than by one professional career.

William Wells Brown was born the child of a slaveholding father and a slave mother in Kentucky in 1815. His first master, a Dr. Young, for whom he worked as both a house servant and, later, a part-time assistant, hired him out to a Major Freeland when he was around fourteen or fifteen. Freeland treated him so cruelly that, at this early age, Brown made his first escape attempt but was captured with the help of bloodhounds. In 1832, hired out again to James Walker, a slave trader, Brown witnessed many slave auctions, memories of which he drew upon in his subsequent writing.

In 1833, Brown made another escape attempt, this time with his mother, but they were captured after eleven days. His mother was sold down to New Orleans, and he was sold to Samuel Willi, a merchant tailor in Saint Louis. Willi sold Brown to Enoch Price, a Saint Louis commission merchant and steamboat owner, facilitating the young slave's final "leap to freedom," for on New Year's Day, 1834, Brown escaped in Cincinnati, Ohio. Quickly moving to Cleveland, the nineteen-year-old became a steamboat worker and a barber in the off season. There, the same year, he met and married Elizabeth Schooner and, two years later, settled with his family in Buffalo, New York, a center of anti-slavery activity. In Buffalo, Brown began the political involvement that was to make him well known among activists in America and abroad. He welcomed anti-slavery agents into his home and made his house a station on the Underground Railroad. Another social cause attracted him: temperance. He organized one of the first temperance societies in western New York, aiming his efforts particularly at blacks. At the same time, recognizing his need to catch up educationally, he was studying English grammar, mathematics, history, and literature.

After an 1840 trip to Haiti and Cuba, he himself became professionally active in the anti-slavery cause. Brown was chosen as a delegate to the convention of "colored citizens" held in 1843 in Buffalo and spoke at one of the sessions. That fall, he became a lecturer for the Western New York Anti-Slavery Society.

In 1847, he launched what was to prove an extraordinarily prolific writing career by publishing the *Narrative* of his own escape from slavery, an autobiography that was to go through at least eight editions at home and abroad. He followed this piece in 1848 with a compilation, *The Antislavery Harp,* of interest not only historically, but also for its inclusion of "Jefferson's Daughter," based upon the well-known rumor of the sale of Thomas Jefferson's mulatto daughter at a New Orleans slave auction, the apparent inspiration for Brown's subsequent novel.

In 1848, Brown separated from his wife and moved with their two daughters to Boston. The next year found him in Europe as a delegate from the American Peace Society to the Peace Congress in Paris. He moved to London, becoming a journalist on several newspapers, and there, in 1850, commissioned the painting of a series of scenes representative of American slavery.

Because of the passage of the Fugitive Slave Law in 1850, Brown stayed in England longer than he had originally intended. In 1852, he published *Three Years in Europe,* a travel book consisting primarily of letters the author had written friends and newspapers in America. In 1853, the first version of *Clotel, or The President's Daughter,* was published in London. Brown's British friends purchased his freedom in 1854, and he returned home the same year.

In 1860, he was married to Annie Elizabeth Gray, with whom he was to have two children, both of whom were to die as infants. He continued his journalistic endeavors and, in August 1861, traveled to Canada as a field agent for Haitian immigration. This trip afforded him the opportunity to observe the Canadian blacks and resulted in articles about their lives and about those in New York. His historical study, *The Black Man, His Antecedants, His Genius, and His Achievements,* appeared in 1862.

By 1864, his career took another professional turn, and he began practicing medicine and opened a doctor's office in Boston. A second historical work, but the first of its kind, *The Negro in the American Rebellion,* appeared in 1867. An 1871 trip to Kentucky on behalf of temperance and black education resulted in Brown's hair-breadth escape from the Ku Klux Klan. His last historical work, which includes a sketch of Frances Harper, *The Rising Son,* was published in 1873; his final book, *My Southern Home,* which appeared in 1880, contains an account of Brown's trip to the South in the winter of 1879–80 and is notable for its generous inclusion of slave songs and black folk songs of the Reconstruction period.

In addition to producing these works, Brown spent his last years energetically engaged in his multiple careers: practicing medicine, doing temperance work, lecturing, and writing. William Wells Brown died in Chelsea, a suburb of Boston, on November 6, 1884.

Brown's *Clotel* was until recently accepted as the first novel written by an American black; it is certainly among the earliest-known attempts at a fictional representation of American life from a black viewpoint. First published in London in 1853, the novel, which fiercely attacks slavery, attracted no special attention. When Brown returned to America, perhaps hoping to reach a larger audience, he changed the names of the major characters and made a number of other revisions in the narrative. For example, in *Clotel* the light-skinned heroine's beloved is near-white in appearance, whereas in the revision he is quite dark; thus Brown raises the issue of color preference, a theme frequently encountered in later African-American texts. The revised novel, with essentially the same story line, was published as "Miralda; or, the Beautiful Quadroon: A Romance of American Slavery, Founded on Fact," in sixteen front-page installments in the December 1, 1860–March 16, 1861 *Weekly Anglo-African.* Brown later shortened the novel, no doubt to fit the format of works in the Campfire Series, published by abolitionist James Redpath primarily for sale at ten cents a copy to Union soldiers. With the names of the characters again changed, the third revision, *Clotelle: A Tale of the Southern States,* was brought out by Redpath in 1864 and, simultaneously, in New York by Dexter, Hamilton, and Company. The final version of the story, *Clotelle; or, The Colored Heroine—A Tale of the Southern States,* appeared in 1867, it contains four new chapters in which Brown brought the action up to date, carrying it forward to two years after the Civil War.

Arlene Elder
University of Cincinnati

PRIMARY WORKS

William Wells Brown, *The Travels of William Wells Brown: The Narrative of William Wells Brown, a fugitive slave, and The American Fugitive in Europe, sketches of places and people abroad,* 1847, 1852, ed. Paul Jefferson, 1991; *Clotel, or The President's Daughter,* 1853, 1969; *Clotelle, or The Colored Heroine,* 1857, 1969.

SECONDARY WORKS

William Edward Farrison, *William Wells Brown,* 1969; J. Noel Heermance, *William Wells Brown and Clotelle,* 1969; Jean Fagan Yellin, *The Intricate Knot,* 1972; Curtis William Ellison, *William Wells Brown and Martin R. Delany: A Reference Guide,* 1978; Richard Orlando Lewis, *Irony in the Fiction of William Wells Brown and Charles Chesnutt,* 1978; Josephine Brown, "Biography of an American Bondman," *Two Biographies by African-American Women,* 1991.

from Clotelle; or, The Colored Heroine

[At this sale, eighteen-year-old Isabella, who will become Clotelle's mother, and her mother and sister are to be sold. Isabella, "admitted by all who knew her to be the handsomest girl, colored or white" in Richmond, will be bought by Henry Linwood who has become attracted to her at one of the city's "negro balls," "usually made up of quadroon women, a few negro men, and any number of white gentlemen."]

Chapter II The Negro Sale

As might have been expected, the day of sale brought an unusually large number together to compete for the property to be sold. Farmers, who make a business of raising slaves for the market, were there, and slave-traders, who make a business of buying human beings in the slave-raising States and taking them to the far South, were also in attendance. Men and women, too, who wished to purchase for their own use, had found their way to the slave sale.

In the midst of the throng was one who felt a deeper interest in the result of the sale than any other of the bystanders. This was young Linwood. True to his promise, he was there with a blank bank-check in his pocket, awaiting with impatience to enter the list as a bidder for the beautiful slave.

It was indeed a heart-rending scene to witness the lamentations of these slaves, all of whom had grown up together on the old homestead of Mr. Graves, and who had been treated with great kindness by that gentleman, during his life. Now they were to be separated, and form new relations and companions. Such is the precarious condition of the slave. Even when with a good master, there is no certainty of his happiness in the future.

The less valuable slaves were first placed upon the auction-block, one after another, and sold to the highest bidder. Husbands and wives were separated with a degree of indifference that is unknown in any other relation in life. Brothers and sisters were torn from each other, and mothers saw their children for the last time on earth.

It was late in the day, and when the greatest number of persons were thought to be present, when Agnes and her daughters were brought out to the place of sale. The mother was first put upon the auction-block, and sold to a noted negro trader named Jennings. Marion was next ordered to ascend the stand, which she did with a trembling step, and was sold for $1200.

All eyes were now turned on Isabella, as she was led forward by the auctioneer. The appearance of the handsome quadroon caused a deep sensation among the crowd. There she stood, with a skin as fair as most white women, her features as beautifully regular as any of her sex of pure Anglo-Saxon blood, her long black hair done up in the neatest manner, her form tall and graceful, and her whole appearance indicating one superior to her condition.

The auctioneer commenced by saying that Miss Isabella was fit to deck the drawing-room of the finest mansion in Virginia.

"How much, gentlemen, for this real Albino!—fit fancy-girl for any one! She enjoys good health, and has a sweet temper. How much do you say?"

"Five hundred dollars."

"Only five hundred for such a girl as this? Gentlemen, she is worth a deal more than that sum. You certainly do not know the value of the article you are bidding on. Here, gentlemen, I hold in my hand a paper certifying that she has a good moral character."

"Seven hundred."

"Ah, gentlemen, that is something like. This paper also states that she is very intelligent."

"Eight hundred."

"She was first sprinkled, then immersed, and is now warranted to be a devoted Christian, and perfectly trustworthy."

"Nine hundred dollars."

"Nine hundred and fifty."

"One thousand."

"Eleven hundred."

Here the bidding came to a dead stand. The auctioneer stopped, looked around, and began in a rough manner to relate some anecdote connected with the sale of slaves, which he said had come under his own observation.

At this juncture the scene was indeed a most striking one. The laughing, joking, swearing, smoking, spitting, and talking, kept up a continual hum and confusion among the crowd, while the slave-girl stood with tearful eyes, looking alternately at her mother and sister and toward the young man whom she hoped would become her purchaser.

"The chastity of this girl," now continued the auctioneer, "is pure. She has never been from under her mother's care. She is virtuous, and as gentle as a dove."

The bids here took a fresh start, and went on until $1800 was reached. The auctioneer once more resorted to his jokes, and concluded by assuring the company that Isabella was not only pious, but that she could make an excellent prayer.

"Nineteen hundred dollars."

"Two thousand."

This was the last bid, and the quadroon girl was struck off, and became the property of Henry Linwood.

This was a Virginia slave-auction, at which the bones, sinews, blood, and nerves of a young girl of eighteen were sold for $500; her moral character for $200; her superior intellect for $100; the benefits supposed to accrue from her having been sprinkled and immersed, together with a warranty of her devoted Christianity, for $300; her ability to make a good prayer for $200; and her chastity for $700 more. This, too, in a city thronged with churches, whose tall spires look like so many signals pointing to heaven, but whose ministers preach that slavery is a God-ordained institution!

The slaves were speedily separated, and taken along by their respective masters. Jennings, the slave-speculator, who had purchased Agnes and her daughter Marion, with several of the other slaves, took them to the county prison, where he usually kept his human cattle after purchasing them, previous to starting for the New Orleans market.

Linwood had already provided a place for Isabella, to which she was taken. The most trying moment for her was when she took leave of her mother and sister. The "Good-by" of the slave is unlike that of any other class in the community. It is indeed a farewell forever. With tears streaming down their cheeks, they embraced and commended each other to God, who is no respector of persons, and before whom master and slave must one day appear.

Chapter X The Quadroon's Home

[Isabella's sister, Marion, aged sixteen, is bought from her original owner by Adolphus Morton, a northerner, opposed to slavery, who marries her and moves to another part of the city, where Marion passes for white. Morton attempts to purchase Isabella's and Marion's mother, Agnes, but she has died of a fever.]

A few miles out of Richmond is a pleasant place, with here and there a beautiful cottage surrounded by trees so as scarcely to be seen. Among these was one far retired from the public roads, and almost hidden among the trees. This was the spot that Henry Linwood had selected for Isabella, the eldest daughter of Agnes. The young man hired the house, furnished it, and placed his mistress there, and for many months no one in his father's family knew where he spent his leisure hours.

When Henry was not with her, Isabella employed herself in looking after her little garden and the flowers that grew in front of her cottage. The passion-flower, peony, dahlia, laburnum, and other plants, so abundant in warm climates, under the tasteful hand of Isabella, lavished their beauty upon this retired sport, and miniature paradise.

Although Isabella had been assured by Henry that she should be free and that he would always consider her as his wife, she nevertheless felt that she ought to be married and acknowledged by him. But this was an impossibility under the State laws, even had the young man been disposed to do what was right in the matter. Related as he was, however, to one of the first families in Virginia, he would not have dared to marry a woman of so low an origin, even had the laws been favorable.

Here, in this secluded grove, unvisited by any other except her lover, Isabella lived for years. She had become the mother of a lovely daughter, which its father named Clotelle. The complexion of the child was still fairer than that of its mother. Indeed, she was not darker than other white children, and as she grew older she more and more resembled her father.

As time passed away, Henry became negligent of Isabella and his child, so much so, that days and even weeks passed without their seeing him, or knowing where he was. Becoming more acquainted with the world, and moving continually in the society of young women of his own station, the young man felt that Isabella was a burden to him, and having as some would say, "outgrown his love," he longed to free himself of the responsibility; yet every time he saw the child, he felt that he owed it his fatherly care.

Henry had now entered into political life, and been elected to a seat in the legislature of his native State; and in his intercourse with his friends had become acquainted with Gertrude Miller, the daughter of a wealthy gentleman living near Richmond. Both Henry and Gertrude were very good-looking, and a mutual attachment sprang up between them.

Instead of finding fault with the unfrequent visits of Henry, Isabella always met him with a smile, and tried to make both him and herself believe that business was the cause of his negligence. When he was with her, she devoted every moment of her time to him, and never failed to speak of the growth and increasing intelligence of Clotelle.

The child had grown so large as to be able to follow its father on his departure out to the road. But the impression made on Henry's feelings by the devoted woman and her child was momentary. His heart had grown hard, and his acts were guided by no fixed principle. Henry and Gertrude had been married nearly two years before Isabella knew anything of the event, and it was merely by accident that she became acquainted with the facts.

One beautiful afternoon, when Isabella and Clotelle were picking wild strawberries some two miles from their home, and near the road-side, they observed a one-horse chaise driving past. The mother turned her face from the carriage not wishing to be seen by strangers, little dreaming that the chaise contained Henry and his wife. The child, however, watched the chaise, and startled her mother by screaming out at the top of her voice, "Papa! papa!" and clapped her little hands for joy. The mother turned in haste to look at the strangers, and her eyes encountered those of Henry's pale and dejected countenance. Gertrude's eyes were on the child. The swiftness with which Henry drove by could not hide from his wife the striking resemblance of the child to himself. The young wife had heard the child exclaim "Papa! papa!" and she immediately saw by the quivering of his lips and the agitation depicted in his countenance, that all was not right.

"Who is that woman? and why did that child call you papa?" she inquired, with a trembling voice.

Henry was silent; he knew not what to say, and without another word passing between them, they drove home.

On reaching her room, Gertrude buried her face in her handkerchief and wept. She loved Henry, and when she had heard from the lips of her companions how their husbands had proved false, she felt that he was an exception, and fervently thanked God that she had been so blessed.

When Gertrude retired to her bed that night, the sad scene of the day followed her The beauty of Isabella, with her flowing curls, and the look of the child, so much resembling the man whom she so dearly loved, could not be forgotten; and little Clotelle's exclamation of "Papa! papa!" rang in her ears during the whole night.

The return of Henry at twelve o'clock did not increase her happiness. Feeling his guilt, he had absented himself from the house since his return from the ride.

Chapter XI To-Day a Mistress, To-Morrow a Slave

The night was dark, the rain descended in torrents from the black and overhanging clouds, and the thunder, accompanied with vivid flashes of lightning, resounded fearfully, as Henry Linwood stepped from his chaise and entered Isabella's cottage.

More than a fortnight had elapsed since the accidental meeting, and Isabella was in doubt as to who the lady was that Henry was with in the carriage. Little, however, did she think that it was his wife. With a smile, Isabella met the young man as he entered her little dwelling. Clotelle had already gone to bed, but her father's voice aroused her from her sleep, and she was soon sitting on his knee.

The pale and agitated countenance of Henry betrayed his uneasiness, but Isabella's mild and laughing allusion to the incident of their meeting him on the day of his pleasure-drive, and her saying, "I presume, dear Henry, that the lady was one of your relatives," led him to believe that she was still in ignorance of his marriage. She was, in fact, ignorant who the lady was who accompanied the man she loved on that eventful day. He, aware of this, now acted more like himself, and passed the thing off as a joke. At heart, however, Isabella felt uneasy, and this uneasiness would at times show itself to the young man. At last, and with a great effort, she said,—

"Now, dear Henry, if I am in the way of your future happiness, say so, and I will release you from any promises that you have made me. I know there is no law by which I can hold you, and if there was, I would not resort to it. You are as dear to me as ever, and my thoughts shall always be devoted to you. It would be a great sacrifice for me to give you up to another, but if it be your desire, as great as the sacrifice is, I will make it. Send me and your child into a Free State if we are in your way."

Again and again Linwood assured her that no woman possessed his love but her. Oh, what falsehood and deceit man can put on when dealing with woman's love!

The unabated storm kept Henry from returning home until after the clock had struck two, and as he drew near his residence he saw his wife standing at the window. Giving his horse in charge of the servant who was waiting, he entered the house, and found his wife in tears. Although he had never satisfied Gertrude as to who the quadroon woman and child were, he had kept her comparatively easy by his close attention to her, and by telling her that she was mistaken in regard to the child's calling him "papa." His absence that night, however, without any apparent cause, had again aroused the jealousy of Gertrude; but Henry told her that he had been caught in the rain while out, which prevented his sooner returning, and she, anxious to believe him, received the story as satisfactory.

Somewhat heated with brandy, and wearied with much loss of sleep, Linwood fell into a sound slumber as soon as he retired. Not so with Gertrude. That faithfulness which has ever distinguished her sex, and the anxiety with which she watched all his movements, kept the wife awake while the husband slept. His sleep, though apparently sound, was nevertheless uneasy. Again and again she heard him pronounce the name of Isabella, and more than once she heard him say, "I am not married; I will never marry while you live." Then he would speak the name of Clotelle and say, "My dear child, how I love you!"

After a sleepless night, Gertrude arose from her couch, resolved that she would reveal the whole matter to her mother. Mrs. Miller was a woman of little or no feeling, proud, peevish, and passionate, thus making everybody miserable that came near her; and when she disliked any one, her hatred knew no bounds. This Gertrude knew; and had she not considered it her duty, she would have kept the secret locked in her own heart.

During the day, Mrs. Linwood visited her mother and told her all that had happened. The mother scolded the daughter for not having informed her sooner, and immediately determined to find out who the woman and child were that Gertrude had met on the day of her ride. Three days were spent by Mrs. Miller in this endeavor, but without success.

Four weeks had elapsed, and the storm of the old lady's temper had somewhat subsided, when, one evening, as she was approaching her daughter's residence, she saw Henry walking in the direction of where the quadroon was supposed to reside. Being satisfied that the young man had not seen her, the old woman at once resolved to follow him. Linwood's boots squeaked so loudly that Mrs. Miller had no difficulty in following him without being herself observed.

After a walk of about two miles, the young man turned into a narrow and unfrequented road, and soon entered the cottage occupied by Isabella. It was a fine starlight night, and the moon was just rising when they got to their journey's end. As usual, Isabella met Henry with a smile, and expressed her fears regarding his health.

Hours passed, and still old Mrs. Miller remained near the house, determined to know who lived there. When she undertook to ferret out anything, she bent her whole energies to it. As Michael Angelo, who subjected all things to his pursuit and the idea he had formed of it, painted the crucifixion by the side of a writhing slave and would have broken up the true cross for pencils, so Mrs. Miller would have entered the sepulchre, if she could have done it, in search of an object she wished to find.

The full moon had risen, and was pouring its beams upon surrounding objects as Henry stepped from Isabella's door, and looking at his watch, said,—

"I must go, dear; it is now half-past ten."

Had little Clotelle been awake, she too would have been at the door. As Henry walked to the gate, Isabella followed with her left hand locked in his. Again he looked at his watch, and said,—

"I must go."

"It is more than a year since you staid all night," murmured Isabella, as he folded her convulsively in his arms, and pressed upon her beautiful lips a parting kiss.

He was nearly out of sight when, with bitter sobs, the quadroon retraced her steps to the door of the cottage. Clotelle had in the mean time awoke, and now inquired of her mother how long her father had been gone. At that instant, a knock was heard at the door, and supposing that it was Henry returning for something he had forgotten, as he frequently did, Isabella flew to let him in. To her amazement, however, a strange woman stood in the door.

"Who are you that comes here at this late hour?" demanded the half-frightened Isabella.

Without making any reply, Mrs. Miller pushed the quadroon aside, and entered the house.

"What do you want here?" again demanded Isabella.

"I am in search of you," thundered the maddened Mrs. Miller; but thinking that her object would be better served by seeming to be kind, she assumed a different tone of voice, and began talking in a pleasing manner.

In this way, she succeeded in finding out the connection existing between Linwood and Isabella, and after getting all she could out of the unsuspecting woman, she informed her that the man she so fondly loved had been married for more than two years. Seized with dizziness, the poor, heart-broken woman fainted and fell upon the floor. How long she remained there she could not tell; but when she returned to consciousness, the strange woman was gone, and her child was standing by her side. When she was so far recovered as to regain her feet, Isabella went to the door, and even into the yard, to see if the old woman was not somewhere about.

As she stood there, the full moon cast its bright rays over her whole person, giving her an angelic appearance and imparting to her flowing hair a still more golden hue. Suddenly another change came over her features, and her full red lips trembled as with suppressed emotion. The muscles around her faultless mouth became convulsed, she gasped for breath, and exclaiming, "Is it possible that man can be so false!" again fainted.

Clotelle stood and bathed her mother's temples with cold water until she once more revived.

Although the laws of Virginia forbid the education of slaves, Agnes had nevertheless employed an old free negro to teach her two daughters to read and write. After being separated from her mother and sister, Isabella turned her attention to the subject of Christianity, and received that consolation from the Bible which is never denied to the children of God. This was now her last hope, for her heart was torn with grief and filled with all the bitterness of disappointment.

The night passed away, but without sleep to poor Isabella. At the dawn of day, she tried to make herself believe that the whole of the past night was a dream, and determined to be satisfied with the explanation which Henry should give on his next visit.

Chapter XVIII A Slave-Hunting Parson

It was a delightful evening after a cloudless day, with the setting sun reflecting his golden rays on the surrounding hills which were covered with a beautiful greensward, and the luxuriant verdure that forms the constant garb of the tropics, that the steamer Columbia ran into the dock at Natchez, and began unloading the cargo, taking in passengers and making ready to proceed on her voyage to New Orleans. The plank connecting the boat with the shore had scarcely been secured in its place, when a good-looking man about fifty years of age, with a white neck-tie, and a pair of gold-rimmed glasses on, was seen hurrying on board the vessel. Just at that moment could be seen a stout man with his face pitted with the small-pox, making his way up to the above-mentioned gentleman.

"How do you do, my dear sir? this is Mr. Wilson, I believe," said the short man, at the same time taking from his mouth a large chew of tobacco, and throwing it down on the ship's deck.

"You have the advantage of me, sir," replied the tall man.

"Why, don't you know me? My name is Jennings; I sold you a splendid negro woman some years ago."

"Yes, yes," answered the Natchez man. "I remember you now, for the woman died in a few months, and I never got the worth of my money out of her."

"I could not help that," returned the slave-trader; "she was as sound as a roach when I sold her to you."

"Oh, yes," replied the parson, "I know she was; but now I want a young girl, fit for house use,—one that will do to wait on a lady."

"I am your man," said Jennings, "just follow me," continued he, "and I will show you the fairest little critter you ever saw." And the two passed to the stern of the boat to where the trader had between fifty and sixty slaves, the greater portion being women.

"There," said Jennings, as a beautiful young woman shrunk back with modesty. "There, sir, is the very gal that was made for you. If she had been made to your order, she could not have suited you better."

"Indeed, sir, is not that young woman white?" inquired the parson.

"Oh, no, sir; she is no whiter than you see!"

"But is she a slave?" asked the preacher.

"Yes," said the trader, "I bought her in Richmond, and she comes from an excellent family. She was raised by Squire Miller, and her mistress was one of the most pious ladies in that city, I may say; she was the salt of the earth, as the ministers say."

"But she resembles in some respect Agnes, the woman I bought from you," said Mr. Wilson. As he said the name of Agnes, the young woman started as if she had been struck. Her pulse seemed to quicken, but her face alternately flushed and turned pale, and tears trembled upon her eyelids. It was a name she had heard her mother mention, and it brought to her memory those days,—those happy days, when she was so loved and caressed. This young woman was Clotelle, the granddaughter of Agnes. The preacher, on learning the fact, purchased her, and took her home, feeling that his daughter Georgiana would prize her very highly. Clotelle found in Georgiana more a sister than a mistress, who, unknown to her father, taught the slave-girl how to read, and did much toward improving and refining Clotelle's manners, for her own sake. Like her mother fond of flowers, the "Virginia Maid," as she was sometimes called, spent many of her leisure hours in the garden. Beside the flowers which sprang up from the fertility of soil unplanted and unattended, there was the heliotrope, sweet-pea, and cup-rose, transplanted from the island of Cuba. In her new home Clotelle found herself saluted on all sides by the fragrance of the magnolia. When she went with her young mistress to the Poplar Farm, as she sometimes did, nature's wild luxuriance greeted her, wherever she cast her eyes.

The rustling citron, lime, and orange, shady mango with its fruits of gold, and the palmetto's umbrageous beauty, all welcomed the child of sorrow. When at the farm, Huckelby, the overseer, kept his eye on Clotelle if within sight of her, for he knew she was a slave, and no doubt hoped that she might some day fall into his hands. But she shrank from his looks as she would have done from the charm of the rattlesnake. The negro-driver always tried to insinuate himself into the good opinion of Georgiana and the company that she brought. Knowing that Miss Wilson at heart hated slavery, he was ever trying to show that the slaves under his charge were happy and contented. One day, when Georgiana and some of her Connecticut friends were there, the overseer called all the slaves up to the "great house," and set some of the young ones to dancing. After awhile whiskey was brought in and a dram given to each slave, in return for which they were expected to give a toast, or sing a short piece of his own composition; when it came to Jack's turn he said,—

"The big bee flies high, the little bee makes the honey: the black folks make the cotton, and the white folks gets the money."

Of course, the overseer was not at all elated with the sentiment contained in Jack's toast. Mr. Wilson had lately purchased a young man to assist about the house and to act as coachman. This slave, whose name was Jerome, was of pure African origin, was perfectly black, very fine-looking, tall, slim, and erect as any one could possibly be. His features were not bad, lips thin, nose prominent, hands and feet small. His brilliant black eyes lighted up his whole countenance. His hair which was nearly straight, hung in curls upon his lofty brow. George Combe or Fowler would have selected his head for a model. He was brave and daring, strong in person, fiery in spirit, yet kind and true in his affections, earnest in his doctrines. Clotelle had been at the parson's but a few weeks when it was observed that a mutual feeling had grown up between her and Jerome. As time rolled on, they became more and more attached to each other. After satisfying herself that these two really loved, Georgiana advised their marriage. But Jerome contemplated his escape at some future day, and therefore feared that if married it might militate against it. He hoped, also, to be able to get Clotelle away too, and it was this hope that kept him from trying to escape by himself. Dante did not more love his Beatrice, Swift his Stella, Waller his Saccharissa, Goldsmith his Jessamy bride, or Burns his Mary, than did Jerome his Clotelle. Unknown to her father, Miss Wilson could permit these two slaves to enjoy more privileges than any of the other servants. The young mistress taught Clotelle, and the latter imparted her instructions to her lover, until both could read so as to be well understood. Jerome felt his superiority, and always declared that no master should ever flog him. Aware of his high spirit and determination, Clotelle was in constant fear lest some difficulty might arise between her lover and his master.

One day Mr. Wilson, being somewhat out of temper and irritated at what he was pleased to call Jerome's insolence, ordered him to follow him to the barn to be flogged. The young slave obeyed his master, but those who saw him at the moment felt that he would not submit to be whipped.

"No, sir," replied Jerome, as his master told him to take off his coat: "I will serve you, Master Wilson, I will labor for you day and night, if you demand it, but I will not be whipped."

This was too much for a white man to stand from a negro, and the preacher seized his slave by the throat, intending to choke him. But for once he found his match. Jerome knocked him down, and then escaped through the back-yard to the street, and from thence to the woods.

Recovering somewhat from the effect of his fall, the parson regained his feet and started in pursuit of the fugitive. Finding, however, that the slave was beyond his reach, he at once resolved to put the dogs on his track. Tabor, the negro-catcher, was sent for, and in less than an hour, eight or ten men, including the parson, were in the woods with hounds, trying the trails. These dogs will attack a negro at their master's bidding; and cling to him as the bull-dog will cling to a beast. Many are the speculations as to whether the negro will be secured alive or dead, when these dogs once get on his track. Whenever there is to be a negro hunt, there is no lack of participants. Many go to enjoy the fun which it is said they derive from these scenes.

The company had been in the woods but a short time ere they got on the track of two fugitives, one of whom was Jerome. The slaves immediately bent their steps toward the swamp, with the hope that the dogs, when put upon their scent would be unable to follow them through the water.

The slaves then took a straight course for the Baton Rouge and Bayou Sara road, about four miles distant. Nearer and nearer the whimpering pack pressed on; their delusion begins to dispel. All at once the truth flashes upon the minds of the fugitives like a glare of light,—'tis Tabor with his dogs!

The scent becomes warmer and warmer, and what was at first an irregular cry now deepens into one ceaseless roar, as the relentless pack presses on after its human prey.

They at last reach the river, and in the negroes plunge, followed by the catch-dog. Jerome is caught and is once more in the hands of his master, while the other poor fellow finds a watery grave. They return, and the preacher sends his slave to jail.

1867

Alice Cary 1820–1871

Alice Cary was born on a farm in Hamilton County, Ohio, eight miles north of Cincinnati. The village nearest this farm was called Mt. Healthy and it is this village with its surrounding farms and houses that became the Clovernook memorialized in her short fiction. Cary's father, Robert Cary, had an American ancestry that could be traced back to the Plymouth Colony of 1630. Cary's mother, Elizabeth Jessup Cary, was of Irish descent and, according to Cary herself, "a woman of superior intellect and of a good, well-ordered life. In my memory she stands apart from all others, wiser and purer, doing more and loving better than any other woman" (*Ladies' Repository,* August, 1855). Cary's fiction, however, does not support this vision of a loving mother; it records instead a motherless universe in which parents provide neither physical affection nor emotional support for their children and are often overtly hostile to them.

While she was growing up, Cary chose as her particular companion Rhoda, a sister two years older than herself, and, according to Cary, the most gifted member of the family. On the way to and from school Rhoda would tell stories, and "when we saw the house in sight, we would often sit down under a tree, that she might have more time to finish the story" (Ames, p. 17). Cary never fully recovered from the death in 1833 of this sister who not only taught her the art and fascination of storytelling but also encouraged her first attempts at poetry.

Though both Cary parents were literate, apparently formal education for their children mattered little to them. In an early letter to Rufus Griswold, Cary described her formal education as "limited to the meagre and infrequent advantages of an obscure district school." Whether from lack of money or lack of interest the Cary household contained few books. As Universalists, however, the Carys subscribed to the *Trumpet,* a Boston Universalist periodical, whose poet's corner, according to Phoebe Cary (1824–1871), Alice's lifelong companion and fellow writer, served as Cary's major model and source of inspiration.

Evidently, Alice Cary began writing poetry at an early age. In 1838, Cincinnati's Universalist paper, the *Sentinel,* printed "The Child of Sorrow." For roughly a decade thereafter Cary continued to publish in local newspapers and periodicals. In 1847, however, she began to write fiction for the *National Era* (1847–1860), an abolitionist paper whose editor, Gamaliel Bailey, had recently moved from Cincinnati to Washington, D.C. The *Era,* best known perhaps for its serialization of *Uncle Tom's Cabin,* brought Cary a national audience; it also brought her the attention of John Greenleaf Whittier, notable for his support of nineteenth-century American women writers. In 1848, Rufus W. Griswold, editor of two anthologies of American poetry and prose, wrote to Alice and Phoebe Cary requesting material for inclusion in his latest project, *The Female Poets of America.* As a result of Griswold's often vexed but often amicable relations with Edgar Allan Poe, Poe wrote a review of this anthology for the *Southern Literary Messenger* (February, 1849) and singled out the work of Alice Cary, declaring her "Pictures of Memory" to be *"decidedly the noblest poem in the collection."* In 1849, Griswold arranged for the publication of *Poems of Alice and Phoebe Cary.*

By 1850 Alice Cary was well on her way to becoming a writer with a national reputation. In the summer of this year, she made her first trip east, visiting New York, Boston, and Amesbury, Massachusetts, where Whittier lived. Shortly thereafter, Cary determined to make New York her home. In November of 1850 she left Ohio; in the spring of 1851 Phoebe joined her in New York. Cary eventually purchased a house on East Twentieth Street, where she lived until her death. Here she set up a household that became famous for its Sunday evening receptions. Cary herself was the financial and executive center of this household, managing both its external and internal affairs. Though the events of her life tell a story of achievement against the odds of being poor, female, uneducated and unsupported, Cary evidently paid a high price for her success. Her biographer presents her as working to live and living to work, finding pleasure only in labor and permanently destroying her health by refusing to rest. Alice Cary died on February 12, 1871, at her home in New York, and was buried two days later in Brooklyn's Greenwood cemetery.

Cary thought of herself primarily as a poet and it was as a poet that she achieved her popular success. During her lifetime she published four volumes of poetry, two collections of poetry and prose for children, and three novels. Cary deserves a place in American literary history, however, not for her poetry or her novels, but for her short fiction. There she was able to use her art to explore her consciousness. In so doing, Cary worked against the grain of a culture that labelled such privileging of the self in women as negatively egocentric or even pathologically narcissistic. This consciousness, located in the narrative "I" of her sketches, experiences human life primarily as a mystery, a fragment of some larger and essentially unknowable whole. For Cary consciousness determined form. The sketch permitted her to accept and express the fragmentary nature of reality in fiction as she perceived it in life. Cary's interest lies not in plot but in character; action for her is rarely complete or completed. The strength of Cary's fiction lies in her insistence on specificity and her resistance to closure; her gift is recollections and sketches, by definition partial, personal, and incomplete, of one particular neighborhood in the West.

Cary shares with her female contemporaries a commitment to realism. With her male contemporaries she shares an understanding of fiction as psychic exploration and dream work. "My Grandfather" is, in a sense, a story about the birth of a poet, for it tells readers how the narrator developed the consciousness capable of telling her stories. Like "Uncle Christopher's," too, the story reflects Cary's characteristic misgivings about the relations of younger and older people. "Uncle Christopher's" demonstrates Cary's dual interest in realism and romance. It combines detailed descriptions of the contents of Uncle Christopher's attic with the portrait of seven women, exactly alike, knitting the same stocking in the same way at the same time. Indeed, the story contains much that we tend to associate with fairy tale and myth and might be taken for a bad dream, were it not from start to finish so chillingly realistic. Recording a world in which children don't matter and in which the death of a child transforms no one, Cary's fiction offers a harsh antidote to those child-centered works so popular with other 19th-century American writers.

Judith Fetterley
State University of New York at Albany

PRIMARY WORKS

Clovernook; or, Recollections of Our Neighborhood in the West, 1852; *Clovernook, Second Series,* 1853; *Pictures of Country Life,* 1859.

SECONDARY WORKS

Mary Clemmer Ames, *A Memorial of Alice and Phoeby Cary, with Some of Their Later Poems,* 1873; W. H. Venable, *Beginnings of Literary Culture in the Ohio Valley,* 1891; Janice G. Pulsifer, "Alice and Phoebe Cary, Whittier's Sweet Singers of the West," *Essex Institute Historical Collections,* 109 (January, 1973): 9–59; Annette Kolodny, *The Land Before Her,* 1984; Judith Fetterley and Marjorie Pryse, eds., *American Women Regionalists, 1850–1910,* 1992.

from Clovernook, or, Recollections of Our Neighborhood in the West

My Grandfather

Change is the order of nature; the old makes way for the new; over the perished growth of the last year brighten the blossoms of this. What changes are to be counted, even in a little noiseless life like mine! How many graves have grown green; how many locks have grown gray; how many, lately young, and strong in hope and courage, are faltering and fainting; how many hands that reached eagerly for the roses are drawn back bleeding and full of thorns; and, saddest of all, how many hearts are broken! I remember when I had no sad memory, when I first made room in my bosom for the consciousness of death. How—like striking out from a wilderness of dew-wet blossoms where the shimmer of the light is lovely as the wings of a thousand bees, into an open plain where the clear day strips things to their natural truth—we go from young visions to the realities of life!

I remember the twilight, as though it were yesterday—gray, and dim, and cold, for it was late in October, when the shadow first came over my heart, that no subsequent sunshine has ever swept entirely away. From the window of our cottage home streamed a column of light, in which I sat stringing the red berries of the brier-rose.

I had heard of death, but regarced it only with that vague apprehension which I felt for the demons and witches that gather poison herbs under the new moon, in fairy forests, or strange harmless travellers with wands of the willow, or with vines of the wild grape or ivy. I did not much like to think about them, and yet I felt safe from their influence.

There might be people, somewhere, that would die some time; I didn't know, but it would not be myself, or any one I knew. They were so well and so strong, so full of joyous hopes, how could their feet falter, and their eyes grow dim, and their fainting hands lay away their work, and fold themselves together! No, no—it was not a thing to be believed.

Drifts of sunshine from that season of blissful ignorance often come back, as lightly

> As the winds of the May-time flow,
> And lift up the shadows brightly
> As the daffodil lifts the snow—

the shadows that have gathered with the years! It is pleasant to have them thus swept off—to find myself a child again—the crown of pale pain and sorrow that presses heavily now, unfelt, and the graves that lie lonesomely along my way, covered up with flowers—to feel my mother's dark locks falling on my cheek, as she teaches me the lesson or the prayer—to see my father, now a sorrowful old man whose hair has thinned and whitened almost to the limit of three score years and ten, fresh and vigorous, strong for the race—and to see myself a little child, happy with a new hat and a pink ribbon, or even with the string of brier-buds that I called coral. Now I tie it about my neck, and now around my forehead, and now twist it among my hair, as I have somewhere read great ladies do their pearls. The winds are blowing the last yellow leaves from the cherry tree—I know not why, but it makes me sad. I draw closer to the light of the window, and slyly peep within: all is quiet and cheerful; the logs on the hearth are ablaze; my father is mending a bridle-rein, which "Traveller," the favorite riding horse, snapt in two yesterday, when frightened at the elephant that (covered with a great white cloth) went by to be exhibited at the coming show,—my mother is hemming a ruffle, perhaps for me to wear to school next quarter—my brother is reading in a newspaper, I know not what, but I see, on one side, the picture of a bear: let me listen—and flattening my cheek against the pane, I catch his words distinctly, for he reads loud and very clearly—it is an improbable story of a wild man who has recently been discovered in the woods of some far-away island—he seems to have been there a long time, for his nails are grown like claws, and his hair, in rough and matted strings, hangs to his knees; he makes a noise like something between the howl of a beast and a human cry, and, when pursued, runs with a nimbleness and swiftness that baffle the pursuers, though mounted on the fleetest of steeds, urged through brake and bush to their utmost speed. When first seen, he was sitting on the ground and cracking nuts with his teeth; his arms are corded with sinews that make it probable his strength is sufficient to strangle a dozen men; and yet on seeing human beings, he runs into the thick woods, lifting such a hideous scream, the while, as make his discoverers clasp their hands to their ears. It is suggested that this is not a solitary individual, become wild by isolation, but that a race exists, many of which are perhaps larger and of more terrible aspects; but whether they have any intelligible language, and whether they live in caverns of rocks or in trunks of hollow trees, remains for discovery by some future and more daring explorers.

My brother puts down the paper and looks at the picture of the bear. "I would not read such foolish stories," says my father, as he holds the bridle up to the light, to see that it is neatly mended; my mother breaks the thread which gathers the ruffle; she is gentle and loving, and does not like to hear even implied reproof, but she says nothing; little Harry, who is playing on the floor, upsets his block-house, and my father, clapping his hands together, exclaims, "This is the house that Jack built!" and adds, patting Harry on the head, "Where is my little boy? this is not he, this is a little carpenter; you must make your houses stronger, little carpenter!" But Harry insists that he is the veritable little Harry, and no carpenter, and hides his tearful eyes in the lap of my mother, who assures him that he is her own little boy, and soothes his childish grief by buttoning on his neck the ruffle she has just completed; and off he scampers again, building a new house, the roof of which he makes very steep, and calls it grandfather's house, at which all laugh heartily.

While listening to the story of the wild man I am half afraid, but now, as the joyous laughter rings out, I am ashamed of my fears, and skipping forth, I sit down on a green ridge which cuts the door-yard diagonally, and where, I am told, there was once a fence. Did the rose-bushes and lilacs and flags that are in the garden, ever grow here? I think so—no, it must have been a long while ago, if indeed the fence were ever here, for I can't conceive the possibility of such change, and then I fall to arranging my string of brier-buds into letters that will spell some name, now my own, and now that of some one I love. A dull strip of cloud, from which the hues of pink and red and gold have but lately faded out, hangs low in the west; below is a long reach of withering woods—the gray sprays of the beech clinging thickly still, and the gorgeous maples shooting up here and there like sparks of fire among the darkly magnificent oaks and silvery columned sycamores—the gray and murmurous twilight gives way to darker shadows and a deeper hush.

I hear, far away, the beating of quick hoof-strokes on the pavement; the horseman, I think to myself, is just coming down the hill through the thick woods beyond the bridges. I listen close, and presently a hollow rumbling sound indicates that I was right; and now I hear the strokes more faintly—he is climbing the hill that slopes directly away from me; but now again I hear distinctly—he has almost reached the hollow below me—the hollow that in summer is starry with dandelions and now is full of brown nettles and withered weeds—he will presently have passed—where can he be going, and what is his errand? I will rise up and watch. The cloud passes from the face of the moon, and the light streams full and broad on the horseman—he tightens his rein, and looks eagerly toward the house—surely I know him, the long red curls, streaming down his neck, and the straw hat, are not to be mistaken—it is Oliver Hillhouse, the miller, whom my grandfather, who lives in the steep-roofed house, has employed three years—longer than I can remember! He calls to me, and I laughingly bound forward, with an exclamation of delight, and put my arms about the slender neck of his horse, that is champing the bit and pawing the pavement, and I say, "Why do you not come in?"

He smiles, but there is something ominous in his smile, as he hands me a folded paper, saying "Give this to your mother," and, gathering up his reins, he rides hurriedly forward. In a moment I am in the house, for my errand, "Here, mother, is a paper which Oliver Hillhouse gave me for you." Her hand trembles as she receives it, and waiting timidly near, I watch her as she reads; the tears come, and without speaking a word she hands it to my father.

That night there came upon my soul the shadow of an awful fear; sorrowful moans and plaints disturbed my dreams that have never since been wholly forgot. How cold and spectral-like the moonlight streamed across my pillow; how dismal the chirping of the cricket in the hearth; and how more than dismal the winds among the naked boughs that creaked against my window. For the first time in my life I could not sleep, and I longed for the light of the morning. At last it came, whitening up the East, and the stars faded away, and there came a flush of crimson and purple fire, which was presently pushed aside by the golden disk of the sun. Daylight without, but within there was thick darkness still.

I kept close about my mother, for in her presence I felt a shelter and protection that I found no where else.

"Be a good girl till I come back," she said, stooping and kissing my forehead; "mother is going away to-day, your poor grandfather is very sick."

"Let me go too," I said, clinging to her hand. We were soon ready; little Harry pouted his lips and reached out his hands, and my father gave him his pocket-knife to play with; and the wind blowing the yellow curls over his eyes and forehead, he stood on the porch looking eagerly while my mother turned to see him again and again. We had before us a walk of perhaps two miles—northwardly along the turnpike nearly a mile, next, striking into a grass-grown road that crossed it, in an easternly direction nearly another mile, and then turning northwardly again, a narrow land bordered on each side by old and decaying cherry-trees, led us to the house, ancient fashioned, with high steep gables, narrow windows, and low, heavy chimneys of stone. In the rear was an old mill, with a plank sloping from the door-sill to the ground, by way of step, and a square open window in the gable, through which, with ropes and pulleys, the grain was drawn up.

This mill was an especial object of terror to me, and it was only when my aunt Carry led me by the hand, and the cheerful smile of Oliver Hillhouse lighted up the dusky interior, that I could be persuaded to enter it. In truth it was a lonesome sort of place, with dark lofts and curious binns, and ladders leading from place to place; and there were cats creeping stealthily along the beams in wait for mice or shallows, if, as sometimes happened, the clay nest should be loosened from the rafter, and the whole tumble ruinously down. I used to wonder that aunt Carry was not afraid in the old place, with its eternal rumble, and its great dusty wheel moving slowly round and round, beneath the steady tread of the two sober horses that never gained a hair's breadth for their pains; but on the contrary, she seemed to like the mill, and never failed to show me through all its intricacies, on my visits. I have unravelled the mystery now, or rather, from the recollections I still retain, have apprehended what must have been clear to older eyes at the time.

A forest of oak and walnut stretched along this extremity of the farm, and on either side of the improvements (as the house and barn and mill were called) shot out two dark forks, completely cutting off the view, save toward the unfrequented road to the south, which was traversed mostly by persons coming to the mill, for my grandfather made the flour for all the neighborhood round about, besides making corn-meal for Johnny-cakes, and "chops" for the cows.

He was an old man now, with a tall, athletic frame, slightly bent, thin locks white as the snow, and deep blue eyes full of fire and intelligence, and after long years of uninterrupted health and useful labor, he was suddenly stricken down, with no prospect of recovery.

"I hope he is better," said my mother, hearing the rumbling of the mill-wheel. She might have known my grandfather would permit no interruption of the usual business on account of his illness—the neighbors, he said, could not do without bread because he was sick, nor need they all be idle, waiting for him to die. When the time drew near, he would call them to take his farewell and his blessing, but till then let them sew and spin, and do all things just as usual, so they would please him best. He was a stern man—even his kindness was uncompromising and unbending, and I remember of his making toward me no manifestation of fondness, such as grandchildren usually receive, save one, when he gave me a bright red apple, without speaking a word till my timid thanks brought out his "Save your thanks for something better." The apple gave me no pleasure, and I even slipt into the mill to escape from his cold forbidding presence.

Nevertheless, he was a good man, strictly honest, and upright in all his dealings, and respected, almost reverenced, by everybody. I remember once, when young Winters, the tenant of Deacon Granger's farm, who paid a great deal too much for his ground, as I have heard my father say, came to mill with some withered wheat, my grandfather filled up the sacks out of his own flour, while Tommy was in the house at dinner. That was a good deed, but Tommy Winters never suspected how his wheat happened to turn out so well.

As we drew near the house, it seemed to me more lonesome and desolate than it ever looked before. I wished I had staid at home with little Harry. So eagerly I noted every thing, that I remember to this day, that near a trough of water, in the lane, stood a little surly looking cow, of a red color, and with a white line running along her back. I had gone with aunt Carry often when she went to milk her, but to-day she seemed not to have been milked. Near her was a black and white heifer, with sharp short horns, and a square board tied over her eyes; two horses, one of them gray, and the other sorrel, with a short tail, were reaching their long necks into the garden, and browsing from the currant bushes. As we approached they trotted forward a little, and one of them, half playfully, half angrily, bit the other on the shoulder, after which they returned quietly to their cropping of the bushes, heedless of the voice that from across the field was calling to them.

A flock of turkeys were sunning themselves about the door, for no one came to scare them away; some were black, and some speckled, some with heads erect and tails spread, and some nibbling the grass; and with a gabbling noise, and a staid and dignified march, they made way for us. The smoke arose from the chimney in blue, graceful curls, and drifted away to the woods; the dead morning-glory vines had partly fallen from the windows, but the hands that tended them were grown careless, and they were suffered to remain blackened and void of beauty, as they were. Under these, the white curtain was partly put aside, and my grandmother, with the speckled handkerchief pinned across her bosom, and her pale face, a shade paler than usual, was looking out, and seeing us she came forth, and in answer to my mother's look of inquiry, shook her head, and silently led the way in. The room we entered had some home-made carpet, about the size of a large table-cloth, spread in the middle of the floor, the remainder of which was scoured very white; the ceiling was of walnut wood, and the side walls were white-washed—a table, an old-fashioned desk, and some wooden chairs, comprised the furniture. On one of the chairs was a leather cushion; this was set to one side, my grandmother neither offering it to my mother, nor sitting in it herself, while, by way of composing herself, I suppose, she took off the black ribbon with which her cap was trimmed. This was a more simple process than the reader may fancy, the trimming, consisting merely of a ribbon, always black, which she tied around her head after the cap was on, forming a bow and two ends just above the forehead. Aunt Carry, who was of what is termed an even disposition, received us with her usual cheerful demeanor, and then, re-seating herself comfortably near the fire, resumed her work, the netting of some white fringe.

I liked aunt Carry, for that she always took especial pains to entertain me, showing me her patchwork, taking me with her to the cow-yard and dairy, as also to the mill, though in this last I fear she was a little selfish; however, that made no difference to me at the time, and I have always been sincerely grateful to her: children know more, and want more, and feel more, than people are apt to imagine.

On this occasion she called me to her, and tried to teach me the mysteries of her netting, telling me I must get my father to buy me a little bureau, and then I could net fringe and make a nice cover for it. For a little time I thought I could, and arranged in my mind where it should be placed, and what should be put into it, and even went so far as to inquire how much fringe she thought would be necessary. I never attained to much proficiency in the netting of fringe, nor did I ever get the little bureau, and now it is quite reasonable to suppose I never shall.

Presently my father and mother were shown into an adjoining room, the interior of which I felt an irrepressible desire to see, and by stealth I obtained a glimpse of it before the door closed behind them. There was a dull brown and yellow carpet on the floor, and near the bed, on which was a blue and white coverlid, stood a high-backed wooden chair, over which hung a towel, and on the bottom of which stood a pitcher, of an unique pattern. I know not how I saw this, but I did, and perfectly remember it, notwithstanding my attention was in a moment completely absorbed by the sick man's face, which was turned towards the opening door, pale, livid, and ghastly. I trembled and was transfixed; the rings beneath the eyes, which had always been deeply marked, were now almost black, and the blue eyes within looked glassy and cold, and terrible. The expression of agony on the lips (for his disease was one of a most painful nature) gave place to a sort of smile, and the hand, twisted among the gray locks, was withdrawn and extended to welcome my parents, as the door closed. That was a fearful moment; I was near the dark steep edges of the grave; I felt, for the first time, that I was mortal too, and I was afraid.

Aunt Carry put away her work, and taking from a nail in the window-frame a brown muslin sun-bonnet, which seemed to me of half a yard in depth, she tied it on my head, and then clapt her hands as she looked into my face, saying, "bo-peep!" at which I half laughed and half cried, and making provision for herself in grandmother's bonnet, which hung on the opposite side of the window, and was similar to mine, except that it was perhaps a little larger, she took my hand and we proceeded to the mill. Oliver, who was very busy on our entrance, came forward, as aunt Carry said, by way of introduction, "A little visiter I've brought you," and arranged a seat on a bag of meal for us, and taking off his straw hat, pushed the red curls from his low white forehead, and looked bewildered and anxious.

"It's quite warm for the season," said aunt Carry, by way of breaking silence, I suppose. The young man said "yes," abstractedly, and then asked if the rumble of the mill were not a disturbance to the sick room, to which aunt Carry answered, "No, my father says it is his music."

"A good old man," said Oliver, "he will not hear it much longer," and then, even more sadly, "every thing will be changed." Aunt Carry was silent, and he added, "I have been here a long time, and it will make me very sorry to go away, especially when such trouble is about you all."

"Oh, Oliver," said aunt Carry, "you don't mean to go away?" "I see no alternative," he replied; "I shall have nothing to do; if I had gone a year ago it would have been better." "Why?" asked aunt Carry; but I think she understood why, and Oliver did not answer directly, but said, "Almost the last thing your father said to me was, that you should never marry any man who had not a house and twenty acres of land; if he has not, he will exact that promise of you, and I cannot ask you not to make it, nor would you refuse him if I did; I might have owned that long ago, but for my sister (she had lost her reason) and my lame brother, whom I must educate to be a schoolmaster, because he never can work, and my blind mother; but God forgive me! I must not and do not complain; you will forget me, before long, Carry, and some body who is richer and better, will be to you all I once hoped to be, and perhaps more."

I did not understand the meaning of the conversation at the time, but I felt out of place some way, and so, going to another part of the mill, I watched the sifting of the flour through the snowy bolter, listening to the rumbling of the wheel. When I looked around I perceived that Oliver had taken my place on the meal-bag, and that he had put his arm around the waist of aunt Carry in a way I did not much like.

Great sorrow, like a storm, sweeps us aside from ordinary feelings, and we give our hearts into kindly hands—so cold and hollow and meaningless seem the formulae of the world. They had probably never spoken of love before, and now talked of it as calmly as they would have talked of any thing else; but they felt that hope was hopeless; at best, any union was deferred, perhaps, for long years; the future was full of uncertainties. At last their tones became very low, so low I could not hear what they said; but I saw that they looked very sorrowful, and that aunt Carry's hand lay in that of Oliver as though he were her brother.

"Why don't the flour come through?" I said, for the sifting had become thinner and lighter, and at length quite ceased. Oliver smiled, faintly, as he arose, and saying, "This will never buy the child a frock," poured a sack of wheat into the hopper, so that it nearly run over. Seeing no child but myself, I supposed he meant to buy me a new frock, and at once resolved to put it in my little bureau, if he did.

"We have bothered Mr. Hillhouse long enough," said aunt Carry, taking my hand, "and will go to the house, shall we not?"

I wondered why she said "Mr. Hillhouse," for I had never heard her say so before; and Oliver seemed to wonder, too, for he said reproachfully, laying particular stress on his own name, "You don't bother Mr. Hillhouse, I am sure, but I must not insist on your remaining if you wish to go."

"I don't want you to insist on my staying," said aunt Carry, "if you don't want to, and I see you don't" and lifting me out to the sloping plank, that bent beneath us, we descended.

"Carry," called a voice behind us; but she neither answered nor looked back, but seemed to feel a sudden and expressive fondness for me, took me up in her arms, though I was almost too heavy for her to lift, and kissing me over and over, said I was light as a feather, at which she laughed as though neither sorrowful nor lacking for employment.

This little passage I could never precisely explain, aside from the ground that "the course of true love never did run smooth." Half an hour after we returned to the house, Oliver presented himself at the door, saying, "Miss Caroline, shall I trouble you for a cup, to get a drink of water?" Carry accompanied him to the well, where they lingered some time, and when she returned her face was sunshiny and cheerful as usual.

The day went slowly by, dinner was prepared, and removed, scarcely tasted; aunt Carry wrought at her fringe, and grandmother moved softly about, preparing teas and cordials.

Towards sunset the sick man became easy, and expressed a wish that the door of his chamber might be opened, that he might watch our occupations and hear our talk. It was done accordingly, and he was left alone. My mother smiled, saying she hoped he might yet get well, but my father shook his head mournfully, and answered, "He wishes to go without our knowledge." He made amplest provision for his family always, and I believe had a kind nature, but he manifested no little fondnesses, nor did he wish caresses for himself. Contrary to the general tenor of his character, was a love of quiet jests, that remained to the last. Once, as Carry gave him some drink, he said, "You know my wishes about your future, I expect you to be mindful."

I stole to the door of his room in the hope that he would say something to me, but he did not, and I went nearer, close to the bed, and timidly took his hand in mine; how damp and cold it felt! yet he spoke not, and climbing upon the chair, I put back his thin locks, and kissed his forehead. "Child, you trouble me," he said, and these were the last words he ever spoke to me.

The sun sunk lower and lower, throwing a beam of light through the little window, quite across the carpet, and now it reached the sick man's room, climbed over the bed and up the wall; he turned his face away, and seemed to watch its glimmer upon the ceiling. The atmosphere grew dense and dusky, but without clouds, and the orange light changed to a dull lurid red, and the dying and dead leaves dropt silently to the ground, for there was no wind, and the fowls flew into the trees, and the gray moths came from beneath the bushes and fluttered in the waning light. From the hollow tree by the mill came the bat, wheeling and flitting blindly about, and once or twice its wings struck the window of the sick man's chamber. The last sunlight faded off at length, and the rumbling of the mill-wheel was still: he had fallen asleep in listening to its music.

The next day came the funeral. What a desolate time it was! All down the lane were wagons and carriages and horses, for every body that knew my grandfather would pay him the last honors he could receive in the world. "We can do him no further good," they said, "but it seemed right that we should come." Close by the gate waited the little brown wagon to bear the coffin to the grave, the wagon in which he was used to ride while living. The heads of the horses were drooping, and I thought they looked consciously sad.

The day was mild, and the doors and windows of the old house stood all open, so that the people without could hear the words of the preacher. I remember nothing he said: I remember of hearing my mother sob, and of seeing my grandmother with her face buried in her hands, and of seeing aunt Carry sitting erect, her face pale but tearless, and Oliver near her, with his hands folded across his breast save once or twice, when he lifted them to brush away tears.

I did not cry, save from a frightened and strange feeling, but kept wishing that we were not so near the dead, and that it were another day. I tried to push the reality away with thoughts of pleasant things—in vain. I remember the hymn, and the very air in which it was sung.

"Ye fearful souls fresh courage take
The clouds ye so much dread,
Are big with mercy, and shall break
In blessings on your head.
Blind unbelief is sure to err,

And scan his works in vain;
God is his own interpreter,
And he will make it plain."

Near the door blue flagstones were laid, bordered with a row of shrubberies and trees, with lilacs, and roses, and pears, and peach-trees, which my grandfather had planted long ago, and here, in the open air, the coffin was placed, and the white cloth removed, and folded over the lid. I remember how it shook and trembled as the gust came moaning from the woods, and died off over the next hill, and that two or three withered leaves fell on the face of the dead, which Oliver gently removed, and brushed aside a yellow-winged butterfly that hovered near.

The friends hung over the unsmiling corpse till they were led weeping and one by one away; the hand of some one rested for a moment on the forehead, and then the white cloth was replaced, and the lid screwed down. The coffin was placed in the brown wagon, with a sheet folded about it, and the long train moved slowly to the burial-ground woods, where the words "dust to dust" were followed by the rattling of the earth, and the sunset light fell there a moment, and the dead leaves blew across the smoothly shapen mound.

When the will was read, Oliver found himself heir to a fortune—the mill and the homestead and half the farm—provided he married Carry, which he must have done, for though I do not remember the wedding, I have had an aunt Caroline Hillhouse almost as long as I can remember. The lunatic sister was sent to an asylum, where she sung songs about a faithless lover till death took her up and opened her eyes in heaven. The mother was brought home, and she and my grandmother lived at their ease, and sat in the corner, and told stories of ghosts, and witches, and marriages, and deaths, for long years. Peace to their memories! for they have both gone home; and the lame brother is teaching school, in his leisure playing the flute, and reading Shakespeare—all the book he reads.

Years have come and swept me away from my childhood, from its innocence and blessed unconsciousness of the dark, but often comes back the memory of its first sorrow!

Death is less terrible to me now.

1852

from Clovernook, SECOND SERIES

Uncle Christopher's

I

The night was intensely cold, but not dismal, for all the hills and meadows, all the steep roofs of the farm-houses, and the black roofs of the barns, were white as snow could make them. The haystacks looked like high, smooth heaps of snow, and the fences, in their zigzag course across the fields, seemed made of snow too, and half the trees had their limbs encrusted with the pure white.

Through the middle of the road, and between banks out of which it seemed to have been cut, ran a path, hard and blue and icy, and so narrow that only two horses could move in it abreast; and almost all the while I could hear the merry music of bells, or the clear and joyous voices of sleigh riders, exultant in the frosty and sparkling air.

With his head pushed under the curtain of the window next the road, so that his face touched the glass, stood my father, watching with as much interest, the things without, as I the pictures in the fire. His hands were thrust deep in his pockets; both his vest and coat hung loosely open; and so for a half hour he had stood, dividing my musings with joyous exclamations as the gay riders went by, singly, or in companies. Now it was a sled running over with children that he told me of; now an old man and woman wrapt in a coverlid and driving one poor horse; and now a bright sleigh with fine horses, jingling bells, and a troop of merry young folks. Then again he called out, "There goes a spider-legged thing that I wouldn't ride in," and this remark I knew referred to one of those contrivances which are gotten up on the spur of a moment, and generally after the snow begins to fall, consisting of two limber saplings on which a seat is fixed, and which serve for runners, fills, and all.

It was not often we had such a deep snow as this, and it carried the thoughts of my father away back to his boyhood, for he had lived among the mountains then, and been used to the hardy winters which keep their empire nearly half the year. Turning from the window, he remarked, at length, "This is a nice time to go to Uncle Christopher's, or some where."

"Yes," I said, "it would be a nice time;" but I did not think so, all the while, for the snow and I were never good friends. I knew, however, that my father would like above all things to visit Uncle Christopher, and that, better still, though he did not like to own it, he would enjoy the sleighing.

"I want to see Uncle Christopher directly," he continued, "about getting some spring wheat to sow."

"It is very cold," I said, "isn't it?" I really couldn't help the question.

"Just comfortably so," he answered, moving back from the fire.

Two or three times I tried to say, "Suppose we go," but the words were difficult, and not till he had said, "Nobody ever wants to go with me to Uncle Christopher's, nor anywhere," did I respond, heartily, "Oh, yes, father, I want to go."

In a minute afterwards, I heard him giving directions about the sleigh and horses.

"I am afraid, sir, you'll find it pretty cold," replied Billy, as he rose to obey.

"I don't care about going myself," continued my father apologetically, "but my daughter has taken a fancy to a ride, and so I must oblige her."

A few minutes, and a pair of handsome, well-kept horses were champing the bit, and pawing the snow at the door, while shawls, mittens, &c., were warmed at the fire. It was hard to see the bright coals smothered under the ashes, and the chairs set away; but I forced a smile to my lips, and as my father said "Ready?" I answered "Ready," and the door closed on the genial atmosphere—the horses stepped forward and backward, flung their heads up and down, curved their necks to the tightening rein, and we were off. The fates be praised, it is not to do again. All the shawls and muffs in Christendom could not avail against such a night—so still, clear, and intensely cold. The very stars seemed sharpened against the ice, and the white moonbeams slanted earthward, and pierced our faces like thorns—I think they had substance that night, and were stiff; and the thickest veil, doubled twice or thrice, was less than gossamer, and yet the wind did not blow, even so much as to stir one flake of snow from the bent boughs.

At first we talked with some attempts at mirth, but sobered presently and said little, as we glided almost noiselessly along the hard and smooth road. We had gone, perhaps, five miles to the northward, when we turned from the paved and level way into a narrow lane, or neighborhood road, as it was called, seeming to me hilly and winding and wild, for I had never been there before. The track was not so well worn, but my father pronounced it better than that we had left, and among the stumps and logs, and between hills and over hills, now through thick woods, and now through openings, we went crushing along. We passed a few cabins and old-fashioned houses, but not many, and the distances between them grew greater and greater, and there were many fields and many dark patches of woods between the lights. Every successive habitation I hoped would terminate our journey—our pleasure, I should have said—yet still we went on, and on.

"Is it much farther?" I asked, at length.

"Oh, no—only four or five miles," replied my father; and he added, "Why, are you getting cold?"

"Not much," I said, putting my hand to my face to ascertain that it was not frozen.

At last we turned into a lane, narrower, darker, and more lonesome still—edged with woods on either side, and leading up and up farther than I could see. No path had been previously broken, and the horses sunk knee deep at every step, their harness tightening as they strained forward, and their steamy breath drifting back, and freezing stiff my veil. At the summit the way was interrupted by a cross fence, and a gate was to be opened—a heavy thing, painted red, and fastened with a chain. It had been well secured, for after half an hour's attempts to open it, we found ourselves defied.

"I guess we'll have to leave the horses and walk to the house," said my father; "it's only a little step."

I felt terrible misgivings; the gate opened into an orchard; I could see no house, and the deep snow lay all unbroken; but there was no help; I must go forward as best I could, or remain and freeze. It was difficult to choose, but I decided to go on. In some places the snow was blown aside, and we walked a few steps on ground almost bare, but in the end high drifts met us, through which we could scarcely press our way. In a little while we began to descend, and soon, abruptly, in a nook sheltered by trees, and higher hills, I saw a curious combination of houses—brick, wood, and stone—and a great gray barn, looking desolate enough in the moonlight, though about it stood half a dozen of inferior size. But another and a more cheerful indication of humanity attracted me. On the brink of the hill stood two persons with a small hand-sled between them, which they seemed to have just drawn up; in the imperfect light, they appeared to be mere youths, the youngest not more than ten or twelve years of age. Their laughter rang on the cold air, and our approach, instead of checking, seemed to increase their mirth.

"Laugh, Mark, laugh," said the taller of the two, as we drew near, "so they will see our path—they're going right through the deep snow."

But instead, the little fellow stepped manfully forward, and directed us into the track broken by their sleds.

At the foot of the hill we came upon the medley of buildings, so incongruous that they might have been blown together by chance. Light appeared in the windows of that portion which was built of stone, but we heard no sound, and the snow about the door had not been disturbed since its fall. "And this," said I, "is where Uncle Christopher Wright lives?"

A black dog, with yellow spots under his eyes, stood suddenly before us, and growled so forbiddingly that we drew back.

"He will not bite," said the little boy; for the merry makers had landed on their sled at the foot of the hill, and followed us to the door; and in a moment the larger youth dashed past us, seized the dog by the fore paws, and dragged him violently aside, snarling and whimpering all the time. "Haven't you got no more sense," he exclaimed, "than to bark so at a gentleman and ladies?"

II

In answer to our quick rap, the door opened at once, and the circle about the great blazing log fire was broken by a general rising. The group consisted of eight persons—one man and seven women; the women so closely resembling each other, that one could not tell them apart; not even the mother from the daughters—for she appeared as young as the oldest of them—except by her cap and spectacles. All the seven were very slender, very straight, and very tall; all had dark complexions, black eyes, low foreheads, straight noses, and projecting teeth; and all were dressed precisely alike, in gowns of brown flannel, and coarse leather boots, with blue woollen stockings, and small capes, of red and yellow calico. The six daughters were all marriageable; at least the youngest of them was. They had staid, almost severe, expressions of countenances, and scarcely spoke during the evening. By one corner of the great fireplace they huddled together, each busy with knitting, and all occupied with long blue stockings, advanced in nearly similar degrees toward completion. Now and then they said "Yes, ma'm," or "No ma'm," when I spoke to them, but never or very rarely any thing more. As I said, Mrs. Wright differed from her daughters in appearance, only in that she wore a cap and spectacles; but she was neither silent nor ill at ease as they were; on the contrary, she industriously filled up all the little spaces unoccupied by her good man in the conversation; she set off his excellencies, as a frame does a picture; and before we were even seated, she expressed her delight that we had come when "Christopher" was at home, as, owing to his *gift,* he was much abroad.

Uncle Christopher was a tall muscular man of sixty or thereabouts, dressed in what might be termed stylish homespun coat, trowsers and waistcoat, of snuff-colored cloth. His cravat was of red-and-white-checked gingham, but it was quite hidden under his long grizzly beard, which he wore in full, this peculiarity being a part of his religion. His hair was of the same color, combed straight from his forehead, and turned over in one even curl on the back of the neck. Heavy gray eyebrows met over a hooked nose, and deep in his head twinkled two little blue eyes, which seemed to say, "I am delighted with myself, and, of course, you are with me." Between his knees he held a stout hickory stick, on which, occasionally, when he had settled something beyond the shadow of doubt, he rested his chin for a moment, and enjoyed the triumph. He rose on our entrance, for he had been seated beside a small table, where he monopolized a good portion of the light, and all the warmth, and having shaken hands with my father and welcomed him in a long and pompous speech, during which the good wife bowed her head, and listened as to an oracle, he greeted me in the same way, saying, "This, I suppose, is the virgin who abideth still in the house with you. She is not given, I hope, to gadding overmuch, nor to vain and foolish decorations of her person with ear-rings and finger-rings, and crisping-pins: for such are unprofitable, yea, abominable. My daughter, consider it well, and look upon it, and receive instruction." I was about replying, I don't know what, when he checked me by saying, "Much speech in a woman is as the crackling of thorns under a pot. Open rebuke," he continued, "is better than secret love." Then pointing with his cane in the direction of the six girls, he said, "Rise, maidens, and salute your kinswoman;" and as they stood up, pointing to each with his stick, he called their names, beginning with Abagail, eldest of the daughters of Rachael Wright and Christopher Wright, and ending with Lucinda, youngest born of Rachael Wright and Christopher Wright. Each, as she was referred to, made a quick ungraceful curtsy, and resumed her seat and her knitting.

A half hour afterward, seeing that we remained silent, the father said, by way of a gracious permission of conversation, I suppose, "A little talk of flax and wool, and of household diligence, would not ill become the daughters of our house." Upon hearing this, Lucinda, who, her mother remarked, had the "liveliest turn" of any of the girls, asked me if I liked to knit; to which I answered, "Yes," and added, "Is it a favorite occupation with you?" she replied, "Yes ma'm," and after a long silence, inquired how many cows we milked, and at the end of another pause, whether we had colored our flannel brown or blue; if we had gathered many hickory nuts; if our apples were keeping well, etc.

The room in which we sat was large, with a low ceiling, and bare floor, and so open about the windows and doors, that the slightest movement of the air without would keep the candle flame in motion, and chill those who were not sitting nearest the fire, which blazed and crackled and roared in the chimney. Uncle Christopher, as my father had always called him (though he was uncle so many degrees removed that I never exactly knew the relationship), laid aside the old volume from which he had been reading, removed the two pairs of spectacles he had previously worn, and hung them, by leather strings connecting their bows, on a nail in the stone jamb by which he sat, and talked, and talked; and talked, and I soon discovered by his conversation, aided by the occasional explanatory whispers of his wife, that he was one of those infatuated men who fancy themselves "called" to be teachers of religion, though he had neither talents, education, nor anything else to warrant such a notion, except a faculty for joining pompous and half scriptural phrases, from January to December.

That inward purity must be manifested by a public washing of the feet, that it was a sin to shave the beard, and an abomination for a man to be hired to preach, were his doctrines, I believe, and much time and some money he spent in their vindication. From neighborhood to neighborhood he traveled, now entering a blacksmith's shop and delivering a homily, now debating with the boys in the cornfield, and now obtruding into some church, where peaceable worshippers were assembled, with intimations that they had "broken teeth, and feet out of joint," that they were "like cold and snow in the time of harvest, yea, worse, even as pot-sheds covered with silver dross." And such exhortations he often concluded by quoting the passage: "Though thou shouldst bray a fool in a mortar among wheat, with a postle, yet will not his foolishness depart from him."

More than half an hour elapsed before the youths whose sliding down the hill had been interrupted by us, entered the house. Their hands and faces were red and stiffened with the cold, yet they kept shyly away from the fire, and no one noticed or made room for them. Both interested me at once, and partly, perhaps, that they seemed to interest nobody else. The taller was not so young as I at first imagined; he was ungraceful, shambling, awkward, and possessed one of those clean, pinky complexions which look so youthful; his hair was yellow, his eyes small and blue, with an unquiet expression, and his hands and feet inordinately large; and when he spoke, it was to the boy who sat on a low stool beside him, in a whisper, which he evidently meant to be inaudible to others, but which was, nevertheless, quite distinct to me. He seemed to exercise a kind of brotherly care over the boy, but he did not speak, nor move, nor look up, nor look down, nor turn aside, nor sit still, without an air of the most wretched embarrassment. I should not have written "sit still," for he changed his position continually, and each time his face grew crimson, and, to cover his confusion, as it were, he drew from his pocket a large silk handkerchief, rubbed his lips, and replaced it, at the same time moving and screwing and twisting the toe of his boot in every direction.

I felt glad of his attention to the boy, for he seemed silent and thoughtful beyond his years; perhaps he was lonesome, I thought; certainly he was not happy, for he leaned his chin on his hand, which was cracked and bleeding, and now and then when his companion ceased to speak, the tears gathered to his eyes; but he seemed willing to be pleased, and brushed the tears off his face and smiled, when the young man laid his great hand on his head, and, shaking it roughly, said, "Mark, Mark, Marky!"

"I can't help thinking about the money," said the boy, at last, "and how many new things it would have bought: just think of it, Andrew!"

"How Towser did bark at them people, didn't he, Mark?" said Andrew, not heeding what had been said to him.

"All new things!" murmured the boy, sorrowfully, glancing at his patched trowsers and ragged shoes.

"In three days it will be New-Year's; and then, Mark, won't we have fun!" and Andrew rubbed his huge hands together, in glee, at the prospect.

"It won't be no fun as I know of," replied the boy.

"May be the girls will bake some cakes," said Andrew, turning red, and looking sideways at the young women.

Mark laughed, and, looking up, he recognized the interested look with which I regarded him, and from that moment we were friends.

At the sound of laughter, Uncle Christopher struck his cane on the floor, and looking sternly toward the offenders, said, "A whip for the horse, a bridle for the ass, and a rod for the fool's back!" leaving to them the application, which they made, I suppose, for they became silent—the younger dropping his chin in his hands again, and the elder twisting the toe of his boot, and using his handkerchief very freely.

I thought we should never go home, for I soon tired of Uncle Christopher's conversation, and of Aunt Rachael's continual allusions to his "gift;" he was evidently regarded by her as not only the man of the house, but also as the man of all the world. The six young women had knitted their six blue stockings from the heel to the toe, and had begun precisely at the same time to taper them off, with six little white balls of yarn.

The clock struck eleven, and I ventured, timidly, to suggest my wish to return home. Mark, who sat drowsily in his chair, looked at me beseechingly, and when Aunt Rachael said, "Tut, tut! you are not going home to-night!" he laughed again, despite the late admonition. All the six young women also said, "You can stay just as well as not;" and I felt as if I were to be imprisoned, and began urging the impossibility of doing so, when Uncle Christopher put an end to remonstrance by exclaiming, "It is better to dwell in the corner of the housetop, than with a brawling woman, and in a wide house." It was soon determined that I should remain, not only for the night, but till the weather grew warmer; and I can feel now something of the pang I experienced when I heard the horses snorting on their homeward way, after the door had closed upon me.

"I am glad you didn't get to go!" whispered Mark, close to me, favored by a slight confusion induced by the climbing of the six young ladies upon six chairs, to hang over six lines, attached to the rafters, the six stockings.

There was no variableness in the order of things at Uncle Christopher's, but all went regularly forward without even a casual observation, and to see one day, was to see the entire experience in the family.

"He has a great gift in prayer," said Aunt Rachael, pulling my sleeve, as the hour for worship arrived.

I did not then, nor can I to this day, agree with her. I would not treat such matters with levity, and will not repeat the formula which this "gifted man" went over morning and evening, but he did not fail on each occasion to make known to the All-Wise the condition in which matters stood, and to assure him, that he himself was doing a great deal for their better management in the future. It was not so much a prayer as an announcement of the latest intelligence, even to "the visit of his kinswoman who was still detained by the severity of the elements."

It was through the exercise of his wonderful gift, that I first learned the histories of Andrew and Mark; that the former was a relation from the interior of Indiana, who, for feeding and milking Uncle Christopher's cows morning and evening, and the general oversight of affairs, when the great man was abroad, enjoyed the privilege of attending the district school in the neighborhood; and that the latter was the "son of his son," a "wicked and troublesome boy, for the present subjected to the chastening influences of a righteous discipline."

As a mere matter of form, Uncle Christopher always said, I will do so or so, "Providence permitting;" but he felt competent to do anything and everything on his own account, to "the drawing out of the Leviathan with an hook, or his tongue with a cord—to the putting a hook into his nose, or the boring his jaw through with a thorn."

"I believe it's getting colder," said Andrew, as he opened the door of the stairway, darkly winding over the great oven, to a low chamber; and, chuckling, he disappeared. He was pleased, as a child would be, with the novelty of a visitor, and perhaps half believed it was colder, because he hoped it was so. Mark gave me a smile as he sidled past his grandfather, and disappeared within the smoky avenue. We had scarcely spoken together, but somehow he had recognized the kindly disposition I felt toward him.

As I lay awake, among bags of meal and flour, boxes of hickory nuts and apples, with heaps of seed, wheat, oats, and barley, that filled the chamber into which I had been shown—cold, despite the twenty coverlids heaped over me—I kept thinking of little Mark, and wondering what was the story of the money he had referred to. I could not reconcile myself to the assumption of Uncle Christopher that he was a wicked boy; and, falling asleep at last, I dreamed the hard old man was beating him with his walking-stick, because the child was not big enough to fill his own snuff-colored coat and trowsers. And certainly this would have been little more absurd than his real effort to change the boy into a man.

There was yet no sign of daylight, when the stir of the family awoke me, and, knowing they would think very badly of me should I further indulge my disposition for sleep, I began to feel in the darkness for the various articles of my dress. At length, half awake, I made my way through and over the obstructions in the chamber, to the room below, which the blazing logs filled with light. The table was spread, and in the genial warmth sat Uncle Christopher, doing nothing. He turned his blue eyes upon me as I entered, and said, "Let a bear robbed of her whelps meet a man, rather than she who crieth, A little more sleep, and a little more slumber."

"Did he say anything to you?" asked Aunt Rachael, as I entered the kitchen in search of a wash-bowl. "It must have been just to the purpose," she continued; "Christopher always says something to the purpose."

There was no bowl, no accommodations, for one's toilet: Uncle Christopher did not approve of useless expenditures. I was advised to make an application of snow to my hands and face, and while I was doing so, I saw a light moving about the stables, and heard Andrew say, in a chuckling, pleased tone, "B'lieve it's colder, Mark—she can't go home to-day; and if she is only here till New-Years, maybe they will kill the big turkey." I felt, while melting on my cheeks the snow, that it was no warmer, and, perhaps, a little flattered with the evident liking of the young man and the boy, I resolved to make the best of my detention. I could see nothing to do, for seven women were already moving about by the light of a single tallow candle; the pork was frying, and the coffee boiling; the bread and butter were on the table, and there was nothing more, apparently, to be accomplished. I dared not sit down, however, and so remained in the comfortless kitchen, as some atonement for my involuntary idleness. At length the tin-horn was sounded, and shortly after Andrew and Mark came in, and breakfast was announced; in other words, Aunt Rachael placed her hand on her good man's chair, and said, "Come."

To the coarse fare before us we all helped ourselves in silence, except of the bread, and that was placed under the management of Uncle Christopher, and with the same knife he used in eating, slices were cut as they were required. The little courage I summoned while alone in the snow—thinking I might make myself useful, and do something to occupy my time, and oblige the family—flagged and failed during that comfortless meal. My poor attempts at cheerfulness fell like moonbeams on ice, except, indeed, that Andrew and Mark looked grateful.

Several times, before we left the table, I noticed the cry of a kitten, seeming to come from the kitchen, and that when Uncle Christopher turned his ear in that direction, Mark looked at Andrew, who rubbed his lips more earnestly than I had seen him before.

When the breakfast, at last, was ended, the old man proceeded to search out the harmless offender, with the instincts of some animal hungry for blood. I knew its doom, when it was discovered, clinging so tightly to the old hat, in which Mark had hidden it, dry and warm, by the kitchen fire; it had been better left in the cold snow, for I saw that the sharp little eyes which looked on it grew hard as stone.

"Mark," said Uncle Christopher, "into your hands I deliver this unclean beast: there is an old well digged by my father, and which lieth easterly a rod or more from the great barn—uncover the mouth thereof, and when you have borne the creature thither, cast it down!"

Mark looked as if he were suffering torture, and when, with the victim, he had reached the door, he turned, as if constrained by pity, and said, "Can't it stay in the barn?"

"No," answered Uncle Christopher, bringing down his great stick on the floor; "but you can stay in the barn, till you learn better than to gainsay my judgment." Rising, he pointed in the direction of the well, and followed, as I inferred, to see that his order was executed, deigning to offer neither reason nor explanation.

Andrew looked wistfully after, but dared not follow, and, taking from the mantle-shelf Walker's Dictionary, he began to study a column of definitions, in a whisper sufficiently loud for every one in the house to hear.

I inquired if that were one of his studies at school; but so painful was the embarrassment occasioned by the question, though he simply answered, "B'lieve it is," that I repented, and perhaps the more, as it failed of its purpose of inducing a somewhat lower whisper, in his mechanical repetitions of the words, which he resumed with the same annoying distinctness.

With the first appearance of daylight the single candle was snuffed out, and it now stood filling the room with smoke from its long limber wick, while the seven women removed the dishes, and I changed from place to place that I might seem to have some employment; and Andrew, his head and face heated in the blaze from the fireplace, studied the Dictionary. In half an hour Uncle Christopher returned, with stern satisfaction depicted in his face: the kitten was in the well, and Mark was in the barn; I felt that, and was miserable.

I asked for something to do, as the old man, resuming his seat, and, folding his hands over his staff, began a homily on the beauty of industry, and was given some patch-work; "There are fifty blocks in the quilt," said Aunt Rachael, "and each of them contains three hundred pieces."

I wrought diligently all the day, though I failed to see the use or beauty of the work on which I was engaged.

At last Andrew, putting his Dictionary in his pocket, saying, "I b'lieve I have my lesson by heart," and, a piece of bread and butter in the top of his hat, tucked the ends of his green woolen trowsers in his cowhide boots, and, without a word of kindness or encouragement, left the house for the school.

By this time the seven women had untwisted seven skeins of blue yarn, which they wound into seven blue balls, and each at the same time began the knitting of seven blue stockings.

That was a very long day to me, and as the hours went by I grew restless, and then wretched. Was little Mark all this time in the cold barn? Scratching the frost from the window pane, I looked in the direction from which I expected him to come, but he was nowhere to be seen.

The quick clicking of the knitting-needles grew hateful, the shut mouths and narrow foreheads of the seven women grew hateful, and hatefulest of all grew the small blue shining eyes of Uncle Christopher, as they bent on the yellow worm-eaten page of the old book he read. He was warm and comfortable, and had forgotten the existence of the little boy he had driven out into the cold.

I put down my work at last, and cold as it was, ventured out. There were narrow paths leading to the many barns and cribs, and entering one after another, I called to Mark, but in vain. Calves started up, and, placing their fore feet in the troughs from which they usually fed, looked at me, half in wonder and half in fear; the horses—and there seemed to be dozens of them—stamped, and whinnied, and, thrusting their noses through their mangers, pressed them into a thousand wrinkles, snuffing the air instead of expected oats. It was so intensely cold I began to fear the boy was dead, and turned over bundles of hay and straw, half expecting to find his stiffened corpse beneath them, but I did not, and was about leaving the green walls of hay that rose smoothly on each side of me, the great dusty beams and black cobwebs swaying here and there in the wind, when a thought struck me: the well—he might have fallen in! Having gone "a rod or more, easterly from the barn," directed by great footprints and little footprints, I discovered the place, and to my joy, the boy also. There was no curb about the well, and, with his hands resting on a decayed strip of plank that lay across its mouth, the boy was kneeling beside it, and looking in. He had not heard my approach, and, stooping, I drew him carefully back, showed him how the plank was decayed, and warned him against such fearful hazards.

"But," he said, half laughing, and half crying, "just see!" and he pulled me toward the well. The opening was small and dark, and seemed very deep, and as I looked more intently my vision gradually penetrated to the bottom; I could see the still pool there, and a little above it, crouching on a loose stone or other projection of the wall, the kitten, turning her shining eyes upward now and then, and mewing piteously.

"Do you think she will get any of it?" said Mark, the tears coming into his eyes; "and if she does, how long will she live there?" The kind-hearted child had been dropping down bits of bread for the prisoner.

He was afraid to go to the house, but when I told him Uncle Christopher might scold me if he scolded any one, and that I would tell him so, he was prevailed upon to accompany me. The hard man was evidently ashamed when he saw the child hiding behind my skirts for fear, and at first said nothing. But directly Mark began to cry—there was such an aching and stinging in his fingers and toes, he could not help it.

"Boo, hoo, hoo!" said the old man, making three times as much noise as the boy—"what's the matter now?"

"I suppose his hands and feet are frozen," said I, as though I knew it, and would maintain it in spite of him, and I confess I felt a secret satisfaction in showing him his cruelty.

"Oh, I guess not," Aunt Rachael said, quickly, alarmed for my cool assertion as well as for the child: "only a leetle frosted, I reckon. Whereabouts does it hurt you, my son?" she continued, stooping over him with a human sympathy and fondness I had not previously seen in any of the family.

"Frosted a leetle—that's all, Christopher," she said, by way of soothing her lord's compunction, and, at the same time, taking in her hands the feet of the boy, which he flung about for pain, crying bitterly. "Hush, little honey," she said, kissing him, and afraid the good man would be vexed at the crying; and as she sat there holding his feet, and tenderly soothing him, I at first could not believe she was the same dark and sedate matron who had been knitting the blue stocking.

"Woman, fret not thy gizzard!" said Christopher, slapping his book on the table, and hanging his spectacles on the jamb. The transient beauty all dropt away, the old expression of obsequious servility was back, and she resumed her seat and her knitting.

"There, let me doctor you," he continued, drawing the child's stocking off. The feet were covered with blisters, and presented the appearance of having been scalded. "Why, boy alive," said he, as he saw the blisters, "these are nothing—they will make you grow." He was forgetting his old pomposity, and, as if aware of it, resumed, "Thou hast been chastised according to thy deserts—go forth in the face of the wind, even the north wind, and, as the ox treadeth the mortar, tread thou the snow."

"You see, Markey," interposed Mrs. Wright, whose heart was really kind,—"you see your feet are a leetle frosted, and that will make them well."

The little fellow wiped his tears with his hand, which was cracked and bleeding from the cold; and, between laughing and crying, ran manfully out into the snow.

It was almost night, and the red clouds about the sunset began to cast their shadows along the hills. The seven women went into the kitchen for the preparation of dinner, (we ate but two meals in the day) and I went to the window to watch Mark as he trod the snow "even as an ox treadeth the mortar." There he was, running hither and thither, and up and down, but, to my surprise, not alone. Andrew, who had returned from school, and found his little friend in such a sorry plight, had, for the sake of giving him courage, bared his own feet, and was chasing after him in generously well-feigned enjoyment. Towser, too, had come forth from his kennel of straw, and a gay frolic they made of it, all together.

I need not describe the dinner—it differed only from the breakfast, in that it had potatoes added to the bread and pork.

I remember never days so long, before nor since; and that night, as the women resumed their knitting, and Uncle Christopher his old book, I could hardly keep from crying like a child, I was so lonesome and homesick. The wind roared in the neighboring woods, the frozen branches rattled against the stone wall, and sometimes the blaze was blown quite out of the fire-place. I could not see to make my patch-work, for Uncle Christopher monopolized the one candle, and no one questioned his right to do so; and, at last, conscious of the displeasure that would follow me, I put by the patches, and joined Mark and Andrew, who were shelling corn in the kitchen. They were not permitted to burn a candle, but the great fire-place was full of blazing logs, and, on seeing me, their faces kindled into smiles, which helped to light the room, I thought. The floor was covered with red and white cobs, and there were sacks of ripe corn, and tubs of shelled corn, about the floor, and, taking a stool, I joined them at their work. At first, Andrew was so much confused, and rubbed his mouth so much with his handkerchief, that he shelled but little; gradually, however, he overcame his diffidence, and seemed to enjoy the privilege of conversation, which he did not often have, poor fellow. Little Mark made slow progress; his tender hands shrank from contact with the rough ears, and when I took his place, and asked him where he lived, and how old he was, his heart was quite won, and he found delight in communicating to me his little joys and sorrows. He was not pretty, certainly—his eyes were gray and large, his hair red, his expression surly, his voice querulous, and his manner unamiable, except, indeed, when talking with Andrew or myself.

I have been mistaken, I thought; he is really amiable and sweet-tempered; and, as I observed him very closely, his more habitual expression came to his face, and he said, abruptly, "I don't like grandfather!" "Why?" I said, smoothing back his hair, for I liked him better for saying so. "Because," he replied, "he don't like me;" and, in a moment, he continued, while his eyes moistened, "nobody likes me—everybody says I'm bad and ugly." "Oh, Mark!" exclaimed Andrew, "I like you, but I know somebody I don't like—somebody that wears spectaclesses, and a long beard—I don't say it's Uncle Christopher, and I don't say it ain't." Mark laughed, partly at the peculiar manner in which Andrew expressed himself; and when I told him I liked him too, and didn't think him either bad or ugly, he pulled at the hem of my apron as he remarked, that he should like to live with Andrew and me, always.

I answered that I would very gladly take him with me when I went home, and his face shone with pleasure, as he told me he had never yet ridden in a sleigh. But the pleasure lasted only a moment, and, with an altered and pained expression, he said, "I can't go—these things are all I have got," and he pointed to his homely and ill-conditioned clothes.

"Never mind, I will mend them," I said; and, wiping his eyes, he told me that once he had enough money to buy ever so many clothes, that he earned it by doing errands, sawing wood, and other services, for the man who lived next door to his father in the city, and that one Saturday night, when he had done something that pleased his employer, he paid him all he owed, and a little more, for being a good boy. "As I was running home," said he, "I met two boys that I knew; so I stopped to show them how much money I had, and when they told me to put it on the pavement in three little heaps, so we could see how much it made, I did so, and they, each one of them, seized a heap and ran away, and that," said Mark, "is just the truth."

"And what did you do then?" I asked.

"I told father," he answered, "and he said I was a simpleton, and it was good enough for me—that he would send me out here, and grandfather would straighten me."

"Never mind, Markey," said Andrew, "it will be New-Year's, day after tomorrow."

And so, sitting in the light of the cob-fire, and guessing what they would get in their stockings, I left them for the night.

I did not dampen their expectations of a good time, but I saw little cause to believe any pleasant dreams of their's would be realized, as I had seen no indications of preparation for the holidays, even to the degree of a plumb cake, or mince-pie. But I was certain of one thing—whatever Mark was, they would not make him any better. As he said, nobody loved him, nobody spoke to him, from morning till night, unless to correct or order him, in some way; and so, perhaps, he sometimes did things he ought not to do, merely to amuse his idleness. In all ways he was expected to have the wisdom of a man—to rise as early, and sit up as late, endure the heat and cold as well, and perform nearly as much labor. So, to say the truth, he was, for the most part, sulky and sullen, and did reluctantly that which he had to do, and no more, except, indeed, at the suggestion of Andrew, or while I was at the house, because it was at my request, and then work seemed only play to him.

The following morning was precisely like the morning that preceded it; the family rose before the daylight, and moved about by the tallow candle, and prepared breakfast, while Uncle Christopher sat in the great arm-chair, and Mark and Andrew fed the cattle by the light of a lantern.

"To-morrow will be New-Year's," said Mark, when breakfast was concluded, and Andrew took down the old Dictionary. No one noticed him, and he presently repeated it.

"Well, and what of it?" replied the old man, giving him a severe look.

"Nothing of it, as I know of," said the boy; "only I thought, maybe we would have something nice."

"Something nice!" echoed the grandfather; "don't we have something nice every day?"

"Well, but I want to do something," urged Mark, sure that he wished to have the dull routine broken in some way.

"Boys will be boys," said Aunt Rachael, in her most conciliatory tone, and addressing nobody in particular; and presently she asked Mark what had become of the potatoes he gleaned. He replied that they were in a barrel in the cellar.

"Eaten up by the rats," added Uncle Christopher.

"No, sir," said Mark, "they are as good as ever—may I sell them?"

"It's a great wonder you didn't let the rats eat them; but, I suppose, it's from no oversight of yours," Uncle Christopher said.

"Yes, sir, I covered them," replied the boy; "and now, may I sell them?—you said I might."

"Sell them—yes, you may sell them," replied the grandfather, in a mocking tone; "why don't you run along and sell them?"

Of course, the boy did not feel that he could sell his little crop, nor did the grandfather intend to grant any such permission.

"Uncle Christopher," said Andrew, looking up from his Dictionary, "do them ere potatoes belong to you, or do they belong to Markey?"

The old man did not reply directly, but said something about busy bodies and meddlers, which caused Andrew to study very earnestly, while Mark withdrew to the kitchen and cried, alone. Toward noon, however, his grandfather asked him if he could ride the old sorrel horse to the blacksmith's, three miles away, and get new shoes set on him, "because," said he, "if you can, you can carry a bag of the potatoes, and sell them."

Mark forgot how cold it was, forgot his ragged trowsers, forgot everything, except that the next day was New-Year's, and that he should have some money; and, mounting the old horse, with a bag of potatoes for a saddle, he was soon facing the north wind. He had no warm cap to turn against his ears, and no mittens for his hands, but he had something pleasant to think about, and so did not feel the cold so much.

When Andrew came from school, and found that Mark was gone to sell his potatoes, he was greatly pleased, and went out early to feed the cattle, first carrying the bundles of oats over the hill to the sheep—a portion of the work belonging to Mark; and he also made a blazing fire, and watched his coming at the window; but no one else seemed to think of him—the supper was served and removed, and not even the tea was kept by the fire for him. It was long after dark when he came, cold and hungry—but nobody made room at the hearth, and nobody inquired the result of his speculation, or what he had seen or heard during the day.

"You will find bread and butter in the cupboard," said Aunt Rachael, after a while, and that was all.

But he had received a dollar for the potatoes; that was fortune enough for one day, and he was careless and thoughtless of their indifference.

There was not light for my patch-work, and Aunt Rachael gave me instead a fine linen sheet to hem. "Isn't it fine and pretty?" said Mark, coming close to me before he went to bed; "I wish I could have it over me."

"Thoughtless child," said the grandfather, "you will have it over you soon enough, and nothing else about you, but your coffin-boards." And, with this benediction, he was dismissed for the night.

I awoke in the morning early, and heard the laughter of Andrew and Mark—it was New-Year's—and, in defiance of the gloomy prospect, they were merry; but when I descended the grandson looked grave—he had found nothing in his stockings.

"Put your feet in them," said Uncle Christopher, "and that will be something."

Fresh snow had fallen in the night, and the weather was milder than it had been, but within the house, the day began as usual.

"Grandfather," said Mark, "shall we not have the fat turkey-hen for dinner, today? I could run her down in the snow so easy!"

"So could I run you down in the snow, if I tried," he responded, with a surly quickness.

"New-Year's day," said Aunt Rachael, "is no better than any other, that I know of; and if you get very hungry, you can eat good bread and milk."

So, as in other mornings, Andrew whispered over the Dictionary, the old man sat in the corner, and the seven women began to knit.

Toward the noon, the happy thought came into the mind of Uncle Christopher: there would be wine-bibbers and mirthmakers at the village, three miles away—he would ride thither, and discourse to them of righteousness, temperance, and judgment to come. Mark was directed to bring his horse to the door, and, having combed his long beard with great care, and slipped over his head a knitted woollen cap, he departed on his errand, but not without having taken from little Mark the dollar he had received for his potatoes. "It may save a soul," he said, "and shall a wayward boy have his will, and a soul be lost?"

The child, however, was not likely in this way to be infused with religious feeling, whatever Uncle Christopher might think of the subject, and it was easy to see that a sense of the injustice he suffered had induced a change in his heart that no good angel would have joy to see. I tried to appease his anger, but he recounted, with the exactest particularity, all the history of the wrong he had suffered, and would not believe there was the slightest justification possible for robbing him of what was his own, instead of making him, as his grandfather should have done, a handsome present. About the middle of the afternoon Andrew came home from school, having been dismissed at so early an hour because it was a holiday, and to prepare for a spelling match to be held at the school-house in the evening. The chores were done long before sundown, and Andrew was in high spirits, partly in anticipation of the night's triumphs, and partly at the prospect of bringing some happiness to the heart of Mark, with whom he several times read over the lesson, impressing on his memory with all the skill he had the harder words which might come to him. Andrew went early, having in charge the school-house fire, and Mark did not accompany him, but I supposed he would follow presently, and so was not uneasy about him.

As the twilight darkened, Uncle Christopher came in, and, recounting his pious labors, with a conceited cant that was now become disgusting to me, he inquired for Mark, that the "brand" might hear and rejoice at the good accomplished with the money thus applied for the regeneration of the gentiles; but Mark was not to be found, and Aunt Rachael meekly hinted that from what she had overheard, she suspected he had gone with Andrew to the spelling match.

"Gone to the spelling match—and without asking me!" said the good man; "the rod has been spared too long." And taking from his pocket his knife, he opened it with deliberate satisfaction, and left the house.

I thought of the words of Mark, "I don't like my grandfather;" and I felt that he was not to blame. All the long evening the lithe sapling lay over the mantel, while Uncle Christopher knitted his brows, and the seven women knitted their seven stockings. I could not use my needle, nor think of what was being done about me; all the family practised their monotonous tasks in gloomy silence; the wind shrieked in the trees, whose branches were flung violently sometimes against the windows; Towser came scratching and whining at the door, without attracting the notice of any one; and Uncle Christopher sat in his easy-chair, in the most comfortable corner, seeming almost as if he were in an ecstasy with intense self-satisfaction, or, once in a while, looking joyously grim and stern as his eye rested on the instrument of torture he had prepared for poor Mark, for whose protection I found myself praying silently, as I half dreamed that he was in the hands of a pitiless monster.

The old clock struck eleven, from a distant part of the house, and we all counted the strokes, it was so still; the sheet I had finished lay on the settee beneath the window, where the rosevine creaked, and the mice peered out of the gnawed holes, and the rats ran through the mouldy cellar. There was a stamping at the door, in the moist snow; I listened, but could hear no voices; the door opened, and Andrew came in alone.

"Where is Mark?" asked the stern voice of the disciplinarian.

"I don't know," replied Andrew; "isn't he here?"

"No," said Aunt Rachael, throwing down her knitting, "nor hasn't been these many hours. Mercy on us, where can he be?"

"Fallen asleep somewhere about the house, likely," replied the old man; and taking up the candle, he began the search.

"And he hasn't been with you, Andrew?" asked Aunt Rachael again, in the faint hope that he would contradict his previous assertion.

"No ma'm, as true as I live and breathe," he replied, with childish simplicity and earnestness.

"Mercy on us!" she exclaimed again.

We could hear doors opening and shutting, and floors creaking in distant parts of the house; but nothing more.

"It's very strange," said the old man. "Don't be afraid, girls;" but he was evidently alarmed, and his hand shook as he lighted the lantern, saying, "he must be in the barn!"

Aunt Rachael would go, and I would go, too—I could not stay away. Andrew climbed along the scaffolds, stooping and reaching the lantern before him, and now and then we called to know if he had found him, as if he would not tell it when he did. So all the places we could think of had been searched, and we had began to call and listen, and call again.

"Hark," said Andrew, "I heard something."

We were all so still that it seemed as if we might hear the falling of flakes of snow.

"Only the howl of a dog," said Uncle Christopher.

"It's Towser's," suggested Andrew, fearfully; and with an anxious look he lowered the lantern to see what indications were in the way. Going toward the well were seen small footprints, and there were none returning. Even Uncle Christopher was evidently disturbed. Seeing the light, the dog began to yelp and whine, looking earnestly at us, and then suddenly down in the well, and when we came to the place every one felt a sinking of the heart, and no one dared to speak. The plank, on which I had seen him resting, was broken, and a part of it had fallen in. Towser whined, and his eyes shone as if he were in agony for words, and trying to throw all his intelligence into each piteous look he gave us.

"Get a rope, and lower the light," said one of the sisters; but the loose stones of the well were already rattling to the touch of Andrew, who, planting hands and feet on either side, was rapidly but cautiously descending. In a moment he was out of sight, but still we heard him, and soon there was a pause, then the sound of a hand, plashing the water, then a groan, sounding hollow and awful through the damp, dark opening, and a dragging, soughing movement, as if something were drawn up from the water. Presently we heard hands and feet once more against the sides of the well, and then, shining through the blackness into the light, two fiery eyes, and quickly after, as the bent head and shoulders of Andrew came nearer the surface, the kitten leaped from them, and dashed blindly past the old man, who was kneeling and looking down, pale with remorseful fear. Approaching the top, Andrew said, "I've got him!" and the grandfather reached down and lifted the lifeless form of the boy into his arms, where he had never reposed before. He was laid on the settee, by the window; the fine white sheet that I had hemmed, was placed over him; the stern and hard master walked backward and forward in the room, softened and contrite, though silent, except when occasional irrepressible groans disclosed the terrible action of his conscience; and Towser, who had been Mark's dearest playmate, nearly all the while kept his face, from without, against the window pane.

"Oh, if it were yesterday!" murmured Uncle Christopher, when the morning came; "Andrew," he said, and his voice faltered, as the young man took from the mantel the long, limber rod, and measured the shrouded form from the head to the feet, "get the coffin as good as you can—I don't care what it costs—get the best."

The Dictionary was not opened that day; Andrew was digging through the snow, on a lonesome hill-side, pausing now and then to wipe his eyes on his sleeve. Upright on the grave's edge, his only companion, sat the black dog.

Poor little Mark!—we dressed him very carefully, more prettily, too, than he had ever been in his life, and as he lay on the white pillow, all who saw him said, "How beautiful he is!" The day after the funeral, I saw Andrew, previously to his setting out for school, cutting from the sweet-brier such of the limbs as were reddest with berries, and he placed them over the heaped earth, as the best offering he could bring to beautify the last home of his companion. In the afternoon I went home, and have never seen him since, but, ignorant and graceless as he was, he had a heart full of sympathy and love, and Mark had owed to him the happiest hours of his life.

Perhaps, meditating of the injustice he himself was suffering, the unhappy boy, whose terrible death had brought sadness and perhaps repentance to the house of Uncle Christopher, had thought of the victim consigned by the same harsh master to the well, and determined, before starting for the schoolhouse, to go out and drop some food for it over the decayed plank on which I had seen him resting, and by its breaking had been precipitated down its uneven sides to the bottom, and so killed. But whether the result was by such accident, or by voluntary violence, his story is equally instructive to those straight and ungenial natures which see no beauty in childhood, and would drive before its time all childishness from life.

1853

Elizabeth Stoddard 1823–1902

Elizabeth Stoddard's writings present women strongly moved by passion, struggling for self-realization, and rejecting conventional piety with its emphasis on female self-sacrifice. Writing in an era which endorsed "the cult of true womanhood," Stoddard failed to find an audience, not only because of her unconventional characterization of women, but also because of her cryptic narrative strategies. Nevertheless, during her lifetime, Stoddard managed to publish three novels, approximately 75 newspaper columns, 40 or so poems, and more than 80 prose works.

Stoddard was born and raised in Mattapoisett, Massachusetts, a fishing village on the northwest shore of Buzzard's Bay. The bleak, seacoast landscape of Stoddard's youth, a landscape which seemingly gave rise to intense, fixated, and often bizarre passions, provided the setting and the characters found in her best work, including all three of her novels. Almost pathologically close to her family, particularly to her brother Wilson Barstow, Stoddard left Mattapoisett only briefly until her marriage; she attended Wheaton Female Seminary for one term in 1837 and again in 1840–1841; she traveled in New England and to New York City where, in 1851, she met Richard Stoddard, an aspiring poet.

During this era, the official ideology emphasized that the female virtues were piety, passionlessness, submissiveness, and domesticity. Stoddard struggled to find her own identity both as a woman and as a writer. In letters written to a friend in the early 1850s, Stoddard expresses her sense of being different from other women, sexually passionate, intellectual, indomitably self-possessed, seeing marriage as a battle for mastery rather than a peaceful state, and estimating future motherhood as a distraction from her true purposes. Not surprisingly, the heroines of Stoddard's fiction display these attributes rather than those glorified in the cult of true womanhood.

Despite Stoddard's doubts, she and Richard were married in 1852. The couple lived in New York City always on the edge of poverty. Elizabeth bore three children, only one of whom lived to adulthood. The couple sporadically held a salon for aspiring artists, actors, and writers, members of what literary historians have called "the genteel circle." Although Richard encouraged Elizabeth's writings and recognized her originality and her genius, most of the other writers of their circle feared her power as a woman and her daring as a writer; they called her "The Pythoness" and wrote that she was mentally and morally diseased.

During the 1850s Stoddard began publishing poetry, sketches, and short fiction. Most important among these apprentice efforts was a bi-monthly column Stoddard wrote between 1854–1858 for the *Daily Alta California,* San Francisco's oldest daily newspaper. With great wit, Stoddard's "letters" regularly reported on the New York cultural scene, the newest books, fashions, scandals, opera stars, painters. These columns reveal Stoddard's iconoclasm about the received pieties of the day—manifest destiny, established religion, the confinement of women to the domestic sphere. In particular, Stoddard's columns mocked the values of the sentimental novel with its "eternal preachment about self-denial"; Stoddard asks "Is goodness, then, incompatible with the enjoyment of the senses?" Stoddard looked to the Brontës rather than to American women writers as models for her own literary efforts.

All three of Stoddard's novels were written during the 1860s. Although her work questions many of the cherished assumptions of the sentimental tradition, she uses the structure of the sentimental novel to mock its domestic feminism and to demonstrate that the romantic quest for total empowerment is inevitably defeated by the institutions of society. In her first novel, *The Morgesons* (1862), Stoddard's heroine, Cassandra Morgeson, evolves into a mature, passionate woman, who has accepted her essential isolation in a world in which social institutions are decaying, Nature is indifferent, and the existence of God problematical. Buell and Zagarell, in their excellent critical introduction to the novel, aptly compare Stoddard's conception of Cassandra with Margaret Fuller's feminist insistence on self-realization.

Stoddard's other two novels, *Two Men* (1865) and *Temple House* (1867), present the New England family as the locus of power struggles, incestuous impulses, hatred, and guilt rather than as a domestic sanctuary. When Thomas Wentworth Higginson first visited Emily Dickinson's household in Amherst, he wrote his wife that he was reminded of the families in Stoddard's novels. Indeed, Stoddard's

New England, as the critic Mary Moss noted, is "A country of hereditary taints, of families divided against themselves, of violence, of excess."

During the 1860s Stoddard also published the best of her short prose, often set in the New England of her childhood, utilizing popular stereotypes and plot conventions to question the values associated with those stereotypes. Her last major achievement was her collection of children's tales called *Lolly Dinks' Doings* (1874), a perplexing mixture of the whimsical and the bizarre. Increasingly, however, the poverty of her life with Richard forced her to become a hack writer; she became a bitter, often tiresome woman, who doubted her own gifts and alienated many of the couple's friends.

Despite the failure of Stoddard's three novels to sell, they impressed critics, including Nathaniel Hawthorne, William Dean Howells, and E.C. Stedman. The novels were reprinted twice in her lifetime, in 1888–1889 and in 1901, but again failed to capture the interest of the public although the critical reception was favorable. After her death in 1902, Stoddard was forgotten until 1971 when her three novels were reprinted; once again, her novels failed to sell but this time the critics as well as the public ignored her work. The 1984 Buell and Zagarell edition of her writings began a revival of interest in Stoddard; there is no doubt that both in content and in fictional technique she is our contemporary and speaks to us.

Sybil Weir
San Jose State University

PRIMARY WORKS

The Morgesons, 1862; *Two Men,* 1865; *Temple House,* 1867; *Lolly Dinks' Doings,* 1874; *Poems,* 1895; Lawrence Buell and Sandra A. Zagarell, eds., *The Morgesons & Other Writings, Published and Unpublished, by Elizabeth Stoddard,* 1984.

SECONDARY WORKS

Lawrence Buell and Sandra A. Zagarell, "Biographical and Critical Introduction," *The Morgesons and Other Writings, Published and Unpublished, by Elizabeth Stoddard,* 1984; Sandra A. Zagarell, "The Repossession of a Heritage; Elizabeth Stoddard's *The Morgesons,*" *Studies in American Fiction* 13 (1985); Susan Harris, *19th-Century American Women's Novels: Interpretive Strategies,* 1990; Stacy Alaimo, "Elizabeth Stoddard's *The Morgesons:* A Feminist Dialogics of Bildung and Descent," *Legacy* 8 (1991).

Lemorne *Versus* Huell[1]

The two months I spent at Newport[2] with Aunt Eliza Huell, who had been ordered to the sea-side for the benefit of her health, were the months that created all that is dramatic in my destiny. My aunt was troublesome, for she was not only out of health, but in a lawsuit. She wrote to me, for we lived apart, asking me to accompany her—

[1]The text is that which originally appeared in *Harper's* 26 (1863).

[2]Newport, Rhode Island, was an extremely fashionable seaport resort during the nineteenth century.

not because she was fond of me, or wished to give me pleasure, but because I was useful in various ways. Mother insisted upon my accepting her invitation, not because she loved her late husband's sister, but because she thought it wise to cotton to her in every particular, for Aunt Eliza was rich, and we—two lone women—were poor.

I gave my music-pupils a longer and earlier vacation than usual, took a week to arrange my wardrobe—for I made my own dresses—and then started for New York, with the five dollars which Aunt Eliza had sent for my fare thither. I arrived at her house in Bond Street at 7 a.m., and found her man James in conversation with the milkman. He informed me that Miss Huell was very bad, and that the housekeeper was still in bed. I supposed that Aunt Eliza was in bed also, but I had hardly entered the house when I heard her bell ring as she only could ring it—with an impatient jerk.

"She wants hot milk," said James, "and the man has just come."

I laid my bonnet down, and went to the kitchen. Saluting the cook, who was an old acquaintance, and who told me that the "divil" had been in the range that morning, I took a pan, into which I poured some milk, and held it over the gaslight till it was hot; then I carried it up to Aunt Eliza.

"Here is your milk, Aunt Eliza. You have sent for me to help you, and I begin with the earliest opportunity."

"I looked for you an hour ago. Ring the bell."

I rang it.

"Your mother is well, I suppose. She would have sent you, though, had she been sick in bed."

"She has done so. She thinks better of my coming than I do."

The housekeeper, Mrs. Roll, came in, and Aunt Eliza politely requested her to have breakfast for her niece as soon as possible.

"I do not go down of mornings yet," said Aunt Eliza, "but Mrs. Roll presides. See that the coffee is good, Roll."

"It is good generally, Miss Huell."

"You see that Margaret brought me my milk."

"Ahem!" said Mrs. Roll, marching out.

At the beginning of each visit to Aunt Eliza I was in the habit of dwelling on the contrast between her way of living and ours. We lived from "hand to mouth." Every thing about her wore a hereditary air; for she lived in my grandfather's house, and it was the same as in his day. If I was at home when these contrasts occurred to me I should have felt angry; as it was, I felt them as in a dream—the china, the silver, the old furniture, and the excellent fare soothed me.

In the middle of the day Aunt Eliza came down stairs, and after she had received a visit from her doctor, decided to go to Newport on Saturday. It was Wednesday; and I could, if I chose, make any addition to my wardrobe. I had none to make, I informed her. What were my dresses?—had I a black silk? she asked. I had no black silk, and thought one would be unnecessary for hot weather.

"Who ever heard of a girl of twenty-four having no black silk! You have slimsy muslins, I dare say?"

"Yes."

"And you like them?"

"For present wear."

That afternoon she sent Mrs. Roll out, who returned with a splendid heavy silk for me, which Aunt Eliza said should be made before Saturday, and it was. I went to a fashionable dress-maker of her recommending, and on Friday it came home, beautifully made and trimmed with real lace.

"Even the Pushers could find no fault with this," said Aunt Eliza, turning over the sleeves and smoothing the lace. Somehow she smuggled into the house a white straw-bonnet, with white roses; also a handsome mantilla. She held the bonnet before me with a nod, and deposited it again in the box, which made a part of the luggage for Newport.

On Sunday morning we arrived in Newport, and went to a quiet hotel in the town. James was with us, but Mrs. Roll was left in Bond Street, in charge of the household. Monday was spent in an endeavor to make an arrangement regarding the hire of a coach and coachman. Several livery-stable keepers were in attendance, but nothing was settled, till I suggested that Aunt Eliza should send for her own carriage. James was sent back the next day, and returned on Thursday with coach, horses, and William her coachman. That matter being finished, and the trunks being unpacked, she decided to take her first bath in the sea, expecting me to support her through the trying ordeal of the surf. As we were returning from the beach we met a carriage containing a number of persons with a family resemblance.

When Aunt Eliza saw them she angrily exclaimed, "Am I to see those Uxbridges every day?"

Of the Uxbridges this much I knew—that the two brothers Uxbridge were the lawyers of her opponents in the lawsuit which had existed three or four years. I had never felt any interest in it, though I knew that it was concerning a tract of ground in the city which had belonged to my grandfather, and which had, since his day, become very valuable. Litigation was a habit of the Huell family. So the sight of the Uxbridge family did not agitate me as it did Aunt Eliza.

"The sly, methodical dogs! but I shall beat Lemorne yet!"

"How will you amuse yourself then, aunt?"

"I'll adopt some boys to inherit what I shall save from his clutches."

The bath fatigued her so she remained in her room for the rest of the day; but she kept me busy with a hundred trifles. I wrote for her, computed interest, studied out bills of fare, till four o'clock came, and with it a fog. Nevertheless I must ride on the Avenue, and the carriage was ordered.

"Wear your silk, Margaret; it will just about last your visit through—the fog will use it up."

"I am glad of it," I answered.

"You will ride every day. Wear the bonnet I bought for you also."

"Certainly; but won't that go quicker in the fog than the dress?"

"Maybe; but wear it."

I rode every day afterward, from four to six, in the black silk, the mantilla, and the white straw. When Aunt Eliza went she was so on the alert for the Uxbridge family carriage that she could have had little enjoyment of the ride. Rocks never were a passion with her, she said, nor promontories, chasms, or sand. She came to Newport to be washed with salt-water; when she had washed up to the doctor's prescription she should leave, as ignorant of the peculiar pleasures of Newport as when she arrived. She had no fancy for its conglomerate societies, its literary cottages, its parvenue suits of rooms, its saloon habits, and its bathing herds.

I considered the rides a part of the contract of what was expected in my two months' performance. I did not dream that I was enjoying them, any more than I supposed myself to be enjoying a sea-bath while pulling Aunt Eliza to and fro in the surf. Nothing in the life around me stirred me, nothing in nature attracted me. I liked the fog; somehow it seemed to emanate from me instead of rolling up from the ocean, and to represent me. Whether I went alone or not, the coachman was ordered to drive a certain round; after that I could extend the ride in whatever direction I pleased, but I always said, "Any where, William." One afternoon, which happened to be a bright one, I was riding on the road which led to the glen, when I heard the screaming of a flock of geese which were waddling across the path in front of the horses. I started, for I was asleep probably, and, looking forward, saw the Uxbridge carriage, filled with ladies and children, coming toward me; and by it rode a gentleman on horseback. His horse was rearing among the hissing geese, but neither horse nor geese appeared to engage him; his eyes were fixed upon me. The horse swerved so near that its long mane almost brushed against me. By an irresistible impulse I laid my ungloved hand upon it, but did not look at the rider. Carriage and horseman passed on, and William resumed his pace. A vague idea took possession of me that I had seen the horseman before on my various drives. I had a vision of a man galloping on a black horse out of the fog, and into it again. I was very sure, however, that I had never seen him on so pleasant a day as this! William did not bring his horses to time; it was after six when I went into Aunt Eliza's parlor, and found her impatient for her tea and toast. She was crosser than the occasion warranted; but I understood it when she gave me the outlines of a letter she desired me to write to her lawyer in New York. Something had turned up, he had written her; the Uxbridges believed that they had ferreted out what would go against her. I told her that I had met the Uxbridge carriage.

"One of them is in New York; how else could they be giving me trouble just now?"

"There was a gentleman on horseback beside the carriage."

"Did he look mean and cunning?"

"He did not wear his legal beaver up, I think; but he rode a fine horse and sat it well."

"A lawyer on horseback should, like the beggar of the adage, ride to the devil."

"Your business now is the 'Lemorne?' "

"You know it is."

"I did not know but that you had found something besides to litigate."

"It must have been Edward Uxbridge that you saw. He is the brain of the firm."

"You expect Mr. Van Horn?"

"Oh, he must come; I can not be writing letters."

We had been in Newport two weeks when Mr. Van Horn, Aunt Eliza's lawyer, came. He said that he would see Mr. Edward Uxbridge. Between them they might delay a term, which he thought would be best. "Would Miss Huell ever be ready for a compromise?" he jestingly asked.

"Are you suspicious?" she inquired.

"No; but the Uxbridge chaps are clever."

He dined with us; and at four o'clock Aunt Eliza graciously asked him to take a seat in the carriage with me, making some excuse for not going herself.

"Hullo!" said Mr. Van Horn when we had reached the country road; "there's Uxbridge now." And he waved his hand to him.

It was indeed the black horse and the same rider that I had met. He reined up beside us, and shook hands with Mr. Van Horn.

"We are required to answer this new complaint?" said Mr. Van Horn.

Mr. Uxbridge nodded.

"And after that the judgment?"

Mr. Uxbridge laughed.

"I wish that certain gore of land had been sunk instead of being mapped in 1835."

"The surveyor did his business well enough, I am sure."

They talked together in a low voice for a few minutes, and then Mr. Van Horn leaned back in his seat again. "Allow me," he said, "to introduce you, Uxbridge, to Miss Margaret Huell, Miss Huell's niece. Huell *vs.* Brown, you know," he added, in an explanatory tone; for I was Huell *vs.* Brown's daughter.

"Oh!" said Mr. Uxbridge bowing, and looking at me gravely. I looked at him also; he was a pale, stern-looking man, and forty years old certainly. I derived the impression at once that he had a domineering disposition, perhaps from the way in which he controlled his horse.

"Nice beast that," said Mr. Van Horn.

"Yes," he answered, laying his hand on its mane, so that the action brought immediately to my mind the recollection that I had done so too. I would not meet his eye again, however.

"How long shall you remain, Uxbridge?"

"I don't know. You are not interested in the lawsuit, Miss Huell?" he said, putting on his hat.

"Not in the least; nothing of mine is involved."

"We'll gain it for your portion yet, Miss Margaret," said Mr. Van Horn, nodding to Mr. Uxbridge, and bidding William drive on. He returned the next day, and we settled into the routine of hotel life. A few mornings after, she sent me to a matinée, which was given by some of the Opera people, who were in Newport strengthening the larynx with applications of brine. When the concert was half over, and the audience were making the usual hum and stir, I saw Mr. Uxbridge against a pillar, with his hands incased in pearl-colored gloves, and holding a shiny hat. He turned half away when he caught my eye, and then darted toward me.

"You have not been much more interested in the music than you are in the lawsuit," he said, seating himself beside me.

"The *tutoyer*[3] of the Italian voice is agreeable, however."

"It makes one dreamy."

"A child."

"Yes, a child; not a man nor a woman."

"I teach music. I can not dream over 'one, two, three.' "

"*You*—a music teacher!"

"For six years."

[3]*Tutoyer* means "to speak familiarly to" (to use the French *tu* form). Here its use also registers the singer's tone of voice.

I was aware that he looked at me from head to foot, and I picked at the lace of my invariable black silk; but what did it matter whether I owned that I was a genteel pauper, representing my aunt's position for two months, or not?

"Where?"

"In Waterbury."

"Waterbury differs from Newport."

"I suppose so."

"You suppose!"

A young gentleman sauntered by us, and Mr. Uxbridge called to him to look up the Misses Uxbridge, his nieces, on the other side of the hall.

"Paterfamilias Uxbridge has left his brood in my charge," he said. "I try to do my duty," and he held out a twisted pearl-colored glove, which he pulled off while talking. What white nervous fingers he had! I thought they might pinch like steel.

"You suppose," he repeated.

"I do not look at Newport."

"Have you observed Waterbury?"

"I observe what is in my sphere."

"Oh!"

He was silent then. The second part of the concert began; but I could not compose myself to appreciation. Either the music or I grew chaotic. So many tumultuous sounds I heard—of hope, doubt, inquiry, melancholy, and desire; or did I feel the emotions which these words express? Or was there magnetism stealing into me from the quiet man beside me? He left me with a bow before the concert was over, and I saw him making his way out of the hall when it was finished.

I had been sent in the carriage, of course; but several carriages were in advance of it before the walk, and I waited there for William to drive up. When he did so, I saw by the oscillatory motion of his head, though his arms and whiphand were perfectly correct, that he was inebriated. It was his first occasion of meeting fellow-coachmen in full dress, and the occasion had proved too much for him. My hand, however, was on the coach door, when I heard Mr. Uxbridge say, at my elbow.

"It is not safe for you."

"Oh, Sir, it is in the programme that I ride home from the concert." And I prepared to step in.

"I shall sit on the box, then."

"But your nieces?"

"They are walking home, squired by a younger knight."

Aunt Eliza would say, I thought, "Needs must when a lawyer drives"; and I concluded to allow him to have his way, telling him that he was taking a great deal of trouble. He thought it would be less if he were allowed to sit inside; both ways were unsafe.

Nothing happened. William drove well from habit; but James was obliged to assist him to dismount. Mr. Uxbridge waited a moment at the door, and so there was quite a little sensation, which spread its ripples till Aunt Eliza was reached. She sent for William, whose only excuse was "dampness."

"Uxbridge knew my carriage, of course," she said, with a complacent voice.

"He knew me," I replied.

"You do not look like the Huells."

"I look precisely like the young woman to whom he was introduced by Mr. Van Horn."

"Oh ho!"

"He thought it unsafe for me to come alone under William's charge."

"Ah ha!"

No more was said on the subject of his coming home with me. Aunt Eliza had several fits of musing in the course of the evening while I read aloud to her, which had no connection with the subject of the book. As I put it down she said that it would be well for me to go to church the next day. I acquiesced, but remarked that my piety would not require the carriage, and that I preferred to walk. Besides, it would be well for William and James to attend divine service. She could not spare James, and thought William had better clean the harness, by way of penance.

The morning proved to be warm and sunny. I donned a muslin dress of home manufacture and my own bonnet, and started for church. I had walked but a few paces when the consciousness of being *free* and *alone* struck me. I halted, looked about me, and concluded that I would not go to church, but walk into the fields. I had no knowledge of the whereabouts of the fields; but I walked straight forward, and after a while came upon some barren fields, cropping with coarse rocks, along which ran a narrow road. I turned into it, and soon saw beyond the rough coast the blue ring of the ocean—vast, silent, and splendid in the sunshine. I found a seat on the ruins of an old stone-wall, among some tangled bushes and briers. There being no Aunt Eliza to pull through the surf, and no animated bathers near, I discovered the beauty of the sea, and that I loved it.

Presently I heard the steps of a horse, and, to my astonishment, Mr. Uxbridge rode past. I was glad he did not know me. I watched him as he rode slowly down the road, deep in thought. He let drop the bridle, and the horse stopped, as if accustomed to the circumstance, and pawed the ground gently, or yawed his neck for pastime. Mr. Uxbridge folded his arms and raised his head to look seaward. It seemed to me as if he were about to address the jury. I had dropped so entirely from my observance of the landscape that I jumped when he resumed the bridle and turned his horse to come back. I slipped from my seat to look among the bushes, determined that he should not recognize me; but my attempt was a failure—he did not ride by the second time.

"Miss Huell!" And he jumped from his saddle, slipping his arm through the bridle.

"I am a runaway. What do you think of the Fugitive Slave Bill?"[4]

"I approve of returning property to its owners."

"The sea must have been God's temple first, instead of the groves."[5]

"I believe the Saurians were an Orthodox tribe."

"Did you stop yonder to ponder the sea?"

"I was pondering 'Lemorne vs. Huell.'"

[4]Reference to the Fugitive Slave Law, whose mandate that slaves who had escaped to the North must be returned to their owners was honored by conservative Northerners like Uxbridge.

[5]Adaptation of the first line of William Cullen Bryant's "A Forest Hymn" (1825).

He looked at me earnestly, and then gave a tug at the bridle, for his steed was inclined to make a crude repast from the bushes.

"How was it that I did not detect you at once?" he continued.

"My apparel is Waterbury apparel."

"Ah!"

We walked up the road slowly till we came to the end of it; then I stopped for him to understand that I thought it time for him to leave me. He sprang into the saddle.

"Give us good-by!" he said, bringing his horse close to me.

"We are not on equal terms; I feel too humble afoot to salute you."

"Put your foot on the stirrup then."

A leaf stuck in the horse's forelock, and I pulled it off and waved it in token of farewell. A powerful light shot into his eyes when he saw my hand close on the leaf. "May I come and see you?" he asked, abruptly. "I will."

"I shall say neither 'No' nor 'Yes.' "

He rode on at a quick pace, and I walked homeward forgetting the sense of liberty I had started with, and proceeded straightway to Aunt Eliza.

"I have not been to church, aunt, but to walk beyond the town; it was not so nominated in the bond, but I went. The taste of freedom was so pleasant that I warn you there is danger of my 'striking.' When will you have done with Newport?"

"I am pleased with Newport now," she answered, with a curious intonation. "I like it."

"I do also."

Her keen eyes sparkled.

"Did you ever like anything when you were with me before?"

"Never. I will tell you why I like it: because I have met, and shall probably meet, Mr. Uxbridge. I saw him to-day. He asked permission to visit me."

"Let him come."

"He will come."

But we did not see him either at the hotel or when we went abroad. Aunt Eliza rode with me each afternoon, and each morning we went to the beach. She engaged me every moment when at home, and I faithfully performed all my tasks. I clapped to the door on self-investigation—locked it against any analysis or reasoning upon any circumstance connected with Mr. Uxbridge. The only piece of treachery to my code that I was guilty of was the putting of the leaf which I brought home on Sunday between the leaves of that poem whose motto is,

"Mariana in the moated grange."[6]

On Saturday morning, nearly a week after I saw him on my walk, Aunt Eliza proposed that we should go to Turo Street on a shopping excursion; she wanted a cap, and various articles besides. As we went into a large shop I saw Mr. Uxbridge at a counter buying gloves; her quick eye caught sight of him, and she edged away,

[6]"Mariana" (1830), by Alfred Lord Tennyson. The motto is from Shakespeare's "Measure for Measure," III, i.

saying she would look at some goods on the other side; I might wait where I was. As he turned to go out he saw me and stopped.

"I have been in New York since I saw you," he said. "Mr. Lemorne sent for me."

"There is my aunt," I said.

He shrugged his shoulders.

"I shall not go away soon again," he remarked. "I missed Newport greatly."

I made some foolish reply, and kept my eyes on Aunt Eliza, who dawdled unaccountably. He appeared amused, and after a little talk went away.

Aunt Eliza's purchase was a rose-colored moire antique, which she said was to be made for me; for Mrs. Bliss, one of our hotel acquaintances, had offered to chaperon me to the great ball which would come off in a few days, and she had accepted the offer for me.

"There will be no chance for you to take a walk instead," she finished with.

"I can not dance, you know."

"But you will be *there*."

I was sent to a dress-maker of Mrs. Bliss's recommending; but I ordered the dress to be made after my own design, long plain sleeves, and high plain corsage, and requested that it should not be sent home till the evening of the ball. Before it came off Mr. Uxbridge called, and was graciously received by Aunt Eliza, who could be gracious to all except her relatives. I could not but perceive, however, that they watched each other in spite of their lively conversation. To me he was deferential, but went over the ground of our acquaintance as if it had been the most natural thing in the world. But for my life-long habit of never calling in question the behavior of those I came in contact with, and of never expecting any thing different from that I received, I might have wondered over his visit. Every person's individuality was sacred to me, from the fact, perhaps, that my own individuality had never been respected by any person with whom I had any relation—not even by my own mother.

After Mr. Uxbridge went, I asked Aunt Eliza if she thought he looked mean and cunning? She laughed, and replied that she was bound to think that Mr. Lemorne's lawyer could not look otherwise.

When, on the night of the ball, I presented myself in the rose-colored moire antique for her inspection, she raised her eyebrows, but said nothing about it.

"I need not be careful of it, I suppose, aunt?"

"Spill as much wine and ice-cream on it as you like."

In the dressing room Mrs. Bliss surveyed me.

"I think I like this mass of rose-color," she said. "Your hair comes out in contrast so brilliantly. Why, you have not a single ornament on!"

"It is so easy to dress without."

This was all the conversation we had together during the evening, except when she introduced some acquaintance to fulfill her matronizing duties. As I was no dancer I was left alone most of the time, and amused myself by gliding from window to window along the wall, that it might not be observed that I was a fixed flower. Still I suffered the annoyance of being stared at by wandering squads of young gentlemen, the "curled darlings" of the ballroom. I borrowed Mrs. Bliss's fan in one of her visits for a protection. With that, and the embrasure of a remote window where I finally stationed myself, I hoped to escape further notice. The music of the celebrated band which played between the dances recalled the chorus of spirits which charmed Faust:

"And the fluttering
Ribbons of drapery
Cover the plains,
Cover the bowers,
Where lovers,
Deep in thought,
Give themselves for life."[7]

The voice of Mrs. Bliss broke its spell.

"I bring an old friend, Miss Huell, and he tells me an acquaintance of yours."

It was Mr. Uxbridge.

"I had no thought of meeting you, Miss Huell."

And he coolly took the seat beside me in the window, leaving to Mrs. Bliss the alternative of standing or of going away; she chose the latter.

"I saw you as soon as I came in," he said, "gliding from window to window, like a vessel hugging the shore in a storm."

"With colors at half-mast; I have no dancing partner."

"How many have observed you?"

"Several young gentlemen."

"Moths."

"Oh no, butterflies."

"They must keep away now."

"Are you Rhadamanthus?"

"And Charon, too. I would have you row in the same boat with me."

"Now you are fishing."

"Won't you compliment me. Did I ever look better?"

His evening costume *was* becoming, but he looked pale, and weary, and disturbed. But if we were engaged for a tournament, as his behavior indicated, I must do my best at telling. So I told him that he never looked better, and asked him how I looked. He would look at me presently, he said, and decide. Mrs. Bliss skimmed by us with nods and smiles; as she vanished our eyes followed her, and we talked vaguely on various matters, sounding ourselves and each other. When a furious redowa set in which cut our conversation into rhythm he pushed up the window and said, "Look out."

I turned my face to him to do so, and saw the moon at the full, riding through the strip of sky which our vision commanded. From the moon our eyes fell on each other. After a moment's silence, during which I returned his steadfast gaze, for I could not help it, he said:

"If we understand the impression we make upon each other, what must be said?"

[7]Johann Wolfgang von Goethe, *Faust,* Part I (1808), II, l. 1463–69. Gretchen, Faust's beloved and victim, is also called Margaret. *Faust* and "Lemorne vs. Huell" both feature illicit or illegal pacts and the theme of enchantment.

I made no reply, but fanned myself, neither looking at the moon, nor upon the redowa, nor upon any thing.

He took the fan from me.

"Speak of yourself," he said.

"Speak you."

"I am what I seem, a man within your sphere. By all the accidents of position and circumstance suited to it. Have you not learned it?"

"I am not what I seem. I never wore so splendid a dress as this till tonight, and shall not again."

He gave the fan such a twirl that its slender sticks snapped, and it dropped like the broken wing of a bird.

"Mr. Uxbridge, that fan belongs to Mrs. Bliss."

He threw it out of the window.

"You have courage, fidelity, and patience—this character with a passionate soul. I am sure that you have such a soul?"

"I do not know."

"I have fallen in love with you. It happened on the very day when I passed you on the way to the Glen. I never got away from the remembrance of seeing your hand on the mane of my horse."

He waited for me to speak, but I could not; the balance of my mind was gone. Why should this have happened to me—a slave? As it had happened, why did I not feel exultant in the sense of power which the chance for freedom with him should give?

"What is it, Margaret? your face is as sad as death."

"How do you call me 'Margaret?' "

"As I would call my wife—Margaret."

He rose and stood before me to screen my face from observation. I supposed so, and endeavored to stifle my agitation.

"You are better," he said, presently. "Come go with me and get some refreshment." And he beckoned to Mrs. Bliss, who was down the hall with an unwieldly gentleman.

"Will you go to supper now?" she asked.

"We are only waiting for you," Mr. Uxbridge answered, offering me his arm.

When we emerged into the blaze and glitter of the supper-room I sought refuge in the shadow of Mrs. Bliss's companion, for it seemed to me that I had lost my own.

"Drink this Champagne," said Mr. Uxbridge. "Pay no attention to the Colonel on your left; he won't expect it."

"Neither must you."

"Drink."

The Champagne did not prevent me from reflecting on the fact that he had not yet asked whether I loved him.

The spirit chorus again floated through my mind:

"Where lovers,
Deep in thought,
Give themselves for life."

I was not allowed to give myself—I was *taken.*

"No heel-taps," he whispered, "to the bottom quaff."

"Take me home, will you?"

"Mrs. Bliss is not ready."

"Tell her that I must go."

He went behind her chair and whispered something, and she nodded to me to go without her.

When her carriage came up, I think he gave the coachman an order to drive home in a round-about way, for we were a long time reaching it. I kept my face to the window, and he made no effort to divert my attention. When we came to a street whose thick rows of trees shut out the moonlight my eager soul longed to leap out into the dark and demand of him his heart, soul, life, for me.

I struck him lightly on the shoulder; he seized my hand.

"Oh, I know you, Margaret; you are mine!"

"We are at the hotel."

He sent the carriage back, and said that he would leave me at my aunt's door. He wished that he could see her then. Was it magic that made her open the door before I reached it?

"Have you come on legal business?" she asked him.

"You have divined what I come for."

"Step in, step in; it's very late. I should have been in bed but for neuralgia. Did Mr. Uxbridge come home with you, Margaret?"

"Yes, in Mrs. Bliss's carriage; I wished to come before she was ready to leave."

"Well, Mr. Uxbridge is old enough for your protector, certainly."

"I *am* forty, ma'am."

"Do you want Margaret?"

"I do."

"You know exactly how much is involved in your client's suit?"

"Exactly."

"You also know that his claim is an unjust one."

"Do I?"

"I shall not be poor if I lose; if I gain, Margaret will be rich."

" 'Margaret will be rich,' " he repeated, absently.

"What! have you changed your mind respecting the orphans, aunt?"

"She has, and is—nothing," she went on, not heeding my remark. "Her father married below his station; when he died his wife fell back to her place—for he spent his fortune—and there she and Margaret must remain, unless Lemorne is defeated."

"Aunt, for your succinct biography of my position many thanks."

"Sixty thousand dollars," she continued. "Van Horn tells me that, as yet, the firm of Uxbridge Brothers have only an income—no capital."

"It is true," he answered, musingly.

The clock on the mantle struck two.

"A thousand dollars for every year of my life," she said. "You and I, Uxbridge, know the value and beauty of money."

"Yes, there is beauty in money, and"—looking at me—"beauty without it."

"The striking of the clock," I soliloquized, "proves that this scene is not a phantasm."

"Margaret is fatigued," he said, rising. "May I come to-morrow?"

"It is my part only," replied Aunt Eliza, "to see that she is, or is not, Cinderella."

"If you have ever thought of me, aunt, as an individual, you must have seen that I am not averse to ashes."

He held my hand a moment, and then kissed me with a kiss of appropriation.

"He is in love with you," she said, after he had gone. "I think I know him. He has found beauty ignorant of itself; he will teach you to develop it."

The next morning Mr. Uxbridge had an interview with Aunt Eliza before he saw me.

When we were alone I asked him how her eccentricities affected him; he could not but consider her violent, prejudiced, warped, and whimsical. I told him that I had been taught to accept all that she did on this basis. Would this explain to him my silence in regard to her?

"Can you endure to live with her in Bond Street for the present, or would you rather return to Waterbury?"

"She desires my company while she is in Newport only. I have never been with her so long before."

"I understand her. Law is a game, in her estimation, in which cheating can as easily be carried on as at cards."

"Her soul is in this case."

"Her soul is not too large for it. Will you ride this afternoon?"

I promised, of course. From that time till he left Newport we saw each other every day, and though I found little opportunity to express my own peculiar feelings, he comprehended many of my wishes, and all my tastes. I grew fond of him hourly. Had I not reason? Never was friend so considerate, never was lover more devoted.

When he had been gone a few days, Aunt Eliza declared that she was ready to depart from Newport. The rose-colored days were ended! In two days we were on the Sound, coach, horses, servants, and ourselves.

It was the 1st of September when we arrived in Bond Street. A week from that date Samuel Uxbridge, the senior partner of Uxbridge Brothers, went to Europe with his family, and I went to Waterbury, accompanied by Mr. Uxbridge. He consulted mother in regard to our marriage, and appointed it in November. In October Aunt Eliza sent for me to come back to Bond Street and spend a week. She had some fine marking to do, she wrote. While there I noticed a restlessness in her which I had never before observed, and conferred with Mrs. Roll on the matter. "She do be awake nights a deal, and that's the reason," Mrs. Roll said. Her manner was the same in other respects. She said she would not give me any thing for my wedding outfit, but she paid my fare from Waterbury and back.

She could not spare me to go out, she told Mr. Uxbridge, and in consequence I saw little of him while there.

In November we were married. Aunt Eliza was not at the wedding, which was a quiet one. Mr. Uxbridge desired me to remain in Waterbury till spring. He would not decide about taking a house in New York till then; by that time his brother might return, and if possible we would go to Europe for a few months. I acquiesced in all his plans. Indeed I was not consulted; but I was happy—happy in him, and happy in every thing.

The winter passed in waiting for him to come to Waterbury every Saturday; and in the enjoyment of the two days he passed with me. In March Aunt Eliza wrote me that Lemorne was beaten! Van Horn had taken up the whole contents of his snuff-box in her house the evening before in amazement at the turn things had taken.

That night I dreamed of the scene in the hotel at Newport. I heard Aunt Eliza saying, "If I gain, Margaret will be rich." And I heard also the clock strike two. As it struck I said, *"My husband is a scoundrel,"* and woke with a start.

1863

Harriet E. Wilson 1827?–1863?

For many decades, *Our Nig; Or, Sketches From The Life of A Free Black, In A Two-Story White House, North. Showing That Slavery's Shadows Fall Even There. By "Our Nig.",* by Mrs. H.E. Wilson, was a book consigned to a literary limbo. Known to researchers and bibliographers in African-American literature, it was generally thought to be the work of a white author, perhaps even a male writer. The virtually complete lack of any contemporary reference to its publication or its existence remains a continuing mystery.

In an act of extraordinary literary sleuthing, however, the critics Henry Louis Gates, Jr., and David Ames Curtis were able to painstakingly construct a somewhat sketchy history of the author and her work based essentially on records of her 1851 marriage, the subsequent birth of her son, and his death in 1860. Gates's introduction and notes to the 1983 facsimile edition of *Our Nig,* establishing it as the work of a black author, are an engaging and informative mix of scholarly analysis and imaginative detective work. Further work by Barbara White uncovered a variety of details about Wilson's life and the possible identity of the family she represented in her book as the Bellmonts.

Our Nig, probably a work of fiction, is certainly the thinly disguised autobiographical account of a young girl of mixed race growing to womanhood as an indentured servant in pre-Civil War New England. Her black father dead, Alfrado, called Frado, is abandoned by her mother to the care of the large and well-to-do Bellmont family. The Bellmonts are ruled by a brutal matriarch, Frado's constant antagonist, whose violent physical and emotional assaults against her young charge succeed in breaking her body but not her spirit. The racist Mrs. Bellmont is not Frado's only problem, however; even the sympathetic and occasionally anti-slavery characters are of little help to her.

Still, consoled and nurtured by certain sympathetic members of the household, Frado at last serves out her time and at age eighteen is thrown upon her own limited resources to make her way in the larger world. An unfortunate marriage, the birth of a child she must support essentially on her own, and early widowhood leave Frado as narrator/protagonist to appeal to her readers to aid her cause by forwarding the sale of her account. "Refuse not," she entreats her audience, "Enough has been unrolled to demand your sympathy and aid."

An intriguing mix of certain nineteenth-century literary modes and techniques, *Our Nig* incorporates aspects of abolitionist protest writing, sentimental fiction, and introspective autobiography. Most important, identified as the work of Harriet E. Adams Wilson, it stands as the earliest known novel published in the United States by a black writer; it has, since its reprinting, received the recognition and scholarly attention it was due as a founding and powerful text of African-American literature.

There is no other known work by Wilson. As an appendix to *Our Nig* she included letters from friends and supporters, a common gesture by black writers of that era designed to dispel any skepticism about the genuineness of the book's black authorship. One letter quotes from a letter by Wilson herself and includes a five stanza poem composed of hymn-like quatrains expressing her faith in divine providence and protection.

Marilyn Richardson

PRIMARY WORKS:

Our Nig; Or, Sketches From The Life of A Free Black, 1859. Rpt., Henry Louis Gates, Jr., ed., 1983.

SECONDARY WORKS

Henry Louis Gates, Jr., "Introduction" to 1983 edition of *Our Nig;* Barbara A. White, "'Our Nig' and the She-Devil: New Information About Harriet Wilson and the 'Bellmont' Family," *American Literature,* 1993.

from Our Nig; Or, Sketches from the Life of a Free Black

Chapter IV A Friend for Nig

"Hours of my youth! when nurtured in my breast,
To love a stranger, friendship made me blest;—
Friendship, the dear peculiar bond of youth,
When every artless bosom throbs with truth;
Untaught by worldly wisdom how to feign;
And check each impulse with prudential reign;
When all we feel our honest souls disclose—
In love to friends, in open hate to foes;
No varnished tales the lips of youth repeat,
No dear-bought knowledge purchased by deceit."

BYRON

With what differing emotions have the denizens of earth awaited the approach of today. Some sufferer has counted the vibrations of the pendulum impatient for its dawn, who, now that it has arrived, is anxious for its close. The votary of pleasure, conscious of yesterday's void, wishes for power to arrest time's haste till a few more hours of mirth shall be enjoyed. The unfortunate are yet gazing in vain for golden-edged clouds they fancied would appear in their horizon. The good man feels that he has accomplished too little for the Master, and sighs that another day must so soon close. Innocent childhood, weary of its stay, longs for another morrow; busy manhood cries, hold! hold! and pursues it to another's dawn. All are dissatisfied. All crave some good not yet possessed, which time is expected to bring with all its morrows.

Was it strange that, to a disconsolate child, three years should seem a long, long time? During school time she had rest from Mrs. Bellmont's tyranny. She was now nine years old; time, her mistress said, such privileges should cease.

She could now read and spell, and knew the elementary steps in grammar, arithmetic, and writing. Her education completed, as *she* said, Mrs. Bellmont felt that her time and person belonged solely to her. She was under her in every sense of the word. What an opportunity to indulge her vixen nature! No matter what occurred to ruffle her, or from what source provocation came, real or fancied, a few blows on Nig seemed to relieve her of a portion of ill-will.

These were days when Fido was the entire confidant of Frado. She told him her griefs as though he were human; and he sat so still, and listened so attentively, she really believed he knew her sorrows. All the leisure moments she could gain were used in teaching him some feat of dog-agility, so that Jack pronounced him very knowing, and was truly gratified to know he had furnished her with a gift answering his intentions.

Fido was the constant attendant of Frado, when sent from the house on errands, going and returning with the cows, out in the fields, to the village. If ever she forgot her hardships it was in his company.

Spring was now retiring. James, one of the absent sons, was expected home on a visit. He had never seen the last acquisition to the family. Jack had written faithfully of all the merits of his colored *protegé,* and hinted plainly that mother did not always treat her just right. Many were the preparations to make the visit pleasant, and as the day approached when he was to arrive, great exertions were made to cook the favorite viands, to prepare the choicest table-fare.

The morning of the arrival day was a busy one. Frado knew not who would be of so much importance; her feet were speeding hither and thither so unsparingly. Mrs. Bellmont seemed a trifle fatigued, and her shoes which had, early in the morning, a methodic squeak, altered to an irregular, peevish snap.

"Get some little wood to make the fire burn," said Mrs. Bellmont, in a sharp tone. Frado obeyed, bringing the smallest she could find.

Mrs. Bellmont approached her, and, giving her a box on her ear, reiterated the command.

The first the child brought was the smallest to be found; of course, the second must be a trifle larger. She well knew it was, as she threw it into a box on the hearth. To Mrs. Bellmont it was a greater affront, as well as larger wood, so she "taught her" with the raw-hide, and sent her the third time for "little wood."

Nig, weeping, knew not what to do. She had carried the smallest; none left would suit her mistress; of course further punishment awaited her; so she gathered up whatever came first, and threw it down on the hearth. As she expected, Mrs. Bellmont, enraged, approached her, and kicked her so forcibly as to throw her upon the floor. Before she could rise, another foiled the attempt, and then followed kick after kick in quick succession and power, till she reached the door. Mr. Bellmont and Aunt

Abby, hearing the noise, rushed in, just in time to see the last of the performance. Nig jumped up, and rushed from the house, out of sight.

Aunt Abby returned to her apartment, followed by John, who was muttering to himself.

"What were you saying?" asked Aunt Abby.

"I said I hoped the child never would come into the house again."

"What would become of her? You cannot mean *that,*" continued his sister.

"I do mean it. The child does as much work as a woman ought to; and just see how she is kicked about!"

"Why do you have it so, John?" asked his sister.

"How am I to help it? Women rule the earth, and all in it."

"I think I should rule my own house, John,"—

"And live in hell meantime," added Mr. Bellmont.

John now sauntered out to the barn to await the quieting of the storm.

Aunt Abby had a glimpse of Nig as she passed out of the yard; but to arrest her, or shew her that *she* would shelter her, in Mrs. Bellmont's presence, would only bring reserved wrath on her defenceless head. Her sister-in-law had great prejudices against her. One cause of the alienation was that she did not give her right in the homestead to John, and leave it forever; another was that she was a professor of religion, (so was Mrs. Bellmont;) but Nab, as she called her, did not live according to her profession; another, that she *would* sometimes give Nig cake and pie, which she was never allowed to have at home. Mary had often noticed and spoken of her inconsistencies.

The dinner hour passed. Frado had not appeared. Mrs. B. made no inquiry or search. Aunt Abby looked long, and found her concealed in an outbuilding. "Come into the house with me," implored Aunt Abby.

"I ain't going in any more," sobbed the child.

"What will you do?" asked Aunt Abby.

"I've got to stay out here and die. I ha'n't got no mother, no home. I wish I was dead."

"Poor thing," muttered Aunt Abby; and slyly providing her with some dinner, left her to her grief.

Jane went to confer with her Aunt about the affair; and learned from her the retreat. She would gladly have concealed her in her own chamber, and ministered to her wants; but she was dependent on Mary and her mother for care, and any displeasure caused by attention to Nig, was seriously felt.

Toward night the coach brought James. A time of general greeting, inquiries for absent members of the family, a visit to Aunt Abby's room, undoing a few delicacies for Jane, brought them to the tea hour.

"Where's Frado?" asked Mr. Bellmont, observing she was not in her usual place, behind her mistress' chair.

"I don't know, and I don't care. If she makes her appearance again, I'll take the skin from her body," replied his wife.

James, a fine looking young man, with a pleasant countenance, placid, and yet decidedly serious, yet not stern, looked up confounded. He was no stranger to his mother's nature; but years of absence had erased the occurrences once so familiar, and he asked, "Is this that pretty little Nig, Jack writes to me about, that you are so severe upon, mother?"

"I'll not leave much of her beauty to be seen, if she comes in sight; and now, John," said Mrs. B., turning to her husband, "you need not think you are going to learn her to treat me in this way; just see how saucy she was this morning. She shall learn her place."

Mr. Bellmont raised his calm, determined eye full upon her, and said, in a decisive manner: "You shall not strike, or scald, or skin her, as you call it, if she comes back again. Remember!" and he brought his hand down upon the table. "I have searched an hour for her now, and she is not to be found on the premises. Do *you* know where she is? Is she *your* prisoner?"

"No! I have just told you I did not know where she was. Nab has her hid somewhere, I suppose. Oh, dear! I did not think it would come to this; that my own husband would treat me so." Then came fast flowing tears, which no one but Mary seemed to notice. Jane crept into Aunt Abby's room; Mr. Bellmont and James went out of doors, and Mary remained to condole with her parent.

"Do you know where Frado is?" asked Jane of her aunt.

"No," she replied. "I have hunted everywhere. She has left her first hiding-place. I cannot think what has become of her. There comes Jack and Fido; perhaps he knows;" and she walked to a window near, where James and his father were conversing together.

The two brothers exchanged a hearty greeting, and then Mr. Bellmont told Jack to eat his supper; afterward he wished to send him away. He immediately went in. Accustomed to all the phases of indoor storms, from a whine to thunder and lightning, he saw at a glance marks of disturbance. He had been absent through the day, with the hired men.

"What's the fuss?" asked he, rushing into Aunt Abby's.

"Eat your supper," said Jane; "go home, Jack."

Back again through the dining-room, and out to his father.

"What's the fuss?" again inquired he of his father.

"Eat your supper, Jack, and see if you can find Frado. She's not been seen since morning, and then she was kicked out of the house."

"I shan't eat my supper till I find her," said Jack, indignantly. "Come, James, and see the little creature mother treats so."

They started, calling, searching, coaxing, all their way along. No Frado. They returned to the house to consult. James and Jack declared they would not sleep till she was found.

Mrs. Bellmont attempted to dissuade them from the search. "It was a shame a little *nigger* should make so much trouble."

Just then Fido came running up, and Jack exclaimed, "Fido knows where she is, I'll bet."

"So I believe," said his father; "but we shall not be wiser unless we can outwit him. He will not do what his mistress forbids him."

"I know how to fix him," said Jack. Taking a plate from the table, which was still waiting, he called, "Fido! Fido! Frado wants some supper. Come!" Jack started, the dog followed, and soon capered on before, far, far into the fields, over walls and through fences, into a piece of swampy land. Jack followed close, and soon appeared to James, who was quite in the rear, coaxing and forcing Frado along with him.

A frail child, driven from shelter by the cruelty of his mother, was an object of interest to James. They persuaded her to go home with them, warmed her by the kitchen fire, gave her a good supper, and took her with them into the sitting-room.

"Take that nigger out of my sight," was Mrs. Bellmont's command, before they could be seated.

James led her into Aunt Abby's, where he knew they were welcome. They chatted awhile until Frado seemed cheerful; then James led her to her room, and waited until she retired.

"Are you glad I've come home?" asked James.

"Yes; if you won't let me be whipped to-morrow."

"You won't be whipped. You must try to be a good girl," counselled James.

"If I do, I get whipped;" sobbed the child. "They won't believe what I say. Oh, I wish I had my mother back; then I should not be kicked and whipped so. Who made me so?"

"God;" answered James.

"Did God make you?"

"Yes."

"Who made Aunt Abby?"

"God."

"Who made your mother?"

"God."

"Did the same God that made her make me?"

"Yes."

"Well, then, I don't like him."

"Why not?"

"Because he made her white, and me black. Why didn't he make us *both* white?"

"I don't know; try to go to sleep, and you will feel better in the morning," was all the reply he could make to her knotty queries. It was a long time before she fell asleep; and a number of days before James felt in a mood to visit and entertain old associates and friends.

Chapter X Perplexities—Another Death

Neath the billows of the ocean,
Hidden treasures wait the hand,
That again to light shall raise them
With the diver's magic wand.

G.W. COOK

The family, gathered by James' decease, returned to their homes. Susan and Charles returned to Baltimore. Letters were received from the absent, expressing their sympathy and grief. The father bowed like a "bruised reed," under the loss of his beloved son. He felt desirous to die the death of the righteous; also, conscious that he was unprepared, he resolved to start on the narrow way, and some time solicit entrance through the gate which leads to the celestial city. He acknowledged his too ready acquiescence with Mrs. B., in permitting Frado to be deprived of her only religious privileges for weeks together. He accordingly asked his sister to take her to meeting once more, which she was ready at once to do.

The first opportunity they once more attended meeting together. The minister conversed faithfully with every person present. He was surprised to find the little colored girl so solicitous, and kindly directed her to the flowing fountain where she might wash and be clean. He inquired of the origin of her anxiety, of her progress up to this time, and endeavored to make Christ, instead of James, the attraction of Heaven. He invited her to come to his house, to speak freely her mind to him, to pray much, to read her Bible often.

The neighbors, who were at meeting,—among them Mrs. Reed,—discussed the opinions Mrs. Bellmont would express on the subject. Mrs. Reed called and informed Mrs. B. that her colored girl "related her experience the other night at the meeting."

"What experience?" asked she, quickly, as if she expected to hear the number of times she had whipped Frado, and the number of lashes set forth in plain Arabic numbers.

"Why, you know she is serious, don't you? She told the minister about it."

Mrs. B. made no reply, but changed the subject adroitly. Next morning she told Frado she "should not go out of the house for one while, except on errands; and if she did not stop trying to be religious, she would whip her to death."

Frado pondered; her mistress was a professor of religion; was *she* going to heaven? then she did not wish to go. If she should be near James, even, she could not be happy with those fiery eyes watching her ascending path. She resolved to give over all thought of the future world, and strove daily to put her anxiety far from her.

Mr. Bellmont found himself unable to do what James or Jack could accomplish for her. He talked with her seriously, told her he had seen her many times punished undeservedly; he did not wish to have her saucy or disrespectful, but when she was *sure* she did not deserve a whipping, to avoid it if she could. "You are looking sick," he added, "you cannot endure beating as you once could."

It was not long before an opportunity offered of profiting by his advice. She was sent for wood, and not returning as soon as Mrs. B. calculated, she followed her, and, snatching from the pile a stick, raised it over her.

"Stop!" shouted Frado, "strike me, and I'll never work a mite more for you;" and throwing down what she had gathered, stood like one who feels the stirring of free and independent thoughts.

By this unexpected demonstration, her mistress, in amazement, dropped her weapon, desisting from her purpose of chastisement. Frado walked towards the house, her mistress following with the wood she herself was sent after. She did not know, before, that she had a power to ward off assaults. Her triumph in seeing her enter the door with *her* burden, repaid her for much of her former suffering.

It was characteristic of Mrs. B. never to rise in her majesty, unless she was sure she should be victorious.

This affair never met with an "after clap," like many others.

Thus passed a year. The usual amount of scoldings, but fewer whippings. Mrs. B. longed once more for Mary's return, who had been absent over a year; and she wrote imperatively for her to come quickly to her. A letter came in reply, announcing that she would comply as soon as she was sufficiently recovered from an illness which detained her.

No serious apprehensions were cherished by either parent, who constantly looked for notice of her arrival, by mail. Another letter brought tidings that Mary was seriously ill; her mother's presence was solicited.

She started without delay. Before she reached her destination, a letter came to the parents announcing her death.

No sooner was the astounding news received, than Frado rushed into Aunt Abby's, exclaiming:—

"She's dead, Aunt Abby!"

"Who?" she asked, terrified by the unprefaced announcement.

"Mary; they've just had a letter."

As Mrs. B. was away, the brother and sister could freely sympathize, and she sought him in this fresh sorrow, to communicate such solace as she could, and to learn particulars of Mary's untimely death, and assist him in his journey thither.

It seemed a thanksgiving to Frado. Every hour or two she would pop in into Aunt Abby's room with some strange query:

"She got into the *river* again, Aunt Abby, didn't she; the Jordan is a big one to tumble into, any how. S'posen she goes to hell, she'll be as black as I am. Wouldn't mistress be mad to see her a nigger!" and others of a similar stamp, not at all acceptable to the pious, sympathetic dame; but she could not evade them.

The family returned from their sorrowful journey, leaving the dead behind. Nig looked for a change in her tyrant; what could subdue her, if the loss of her idol could not?

Never was Mrs. B. known to shed tears so profusely, as when she reiterated to one and another the sad particulars of her darling's sickness and death. There was, indeed, a season of quiet grief; it was the lull of the fiery elements. A few weeks revived the former tempests, and so at variance did they seem with chastisement sanctified, that Frado felt them to be unbearable. She determined to flee. But where? Who would take her? Mrs. B. had always represented her ugly. Perhaps every one thought her so. Then no one would take her. She was black, no one would love her. She might have to return, and then she would be more in her mistress' power than ever.

She remembered her victory at the wood-pile. She decided to remain to do as well as she could; to assert her rights when they were trampled on; to return once more to her meeting in the evening, which had been prohibited. She had learned how to conquer; she would not abuse the power while Mr. Bellmont was at home.

But had she not better run away? Where? She had never been from the place far enough to decide what course to take. She resolved to speak to Aunt Abby. *She* mapped the dangers of her course, her liability to fail in finding so good friends as John and herself. Frado's mind was busy for days and nights. She contemplated administering poison to her mistress, to rid herself and the house of so detestable a plague.

But she was restrained by an overruling Providence; and finally decided to stay contentedly through her period of service, which would expire when she was eighteen years of age.

In a few months Jane returned home with her family, to relieve her parents, upon whom years and affliction had left the marks of age. The years intervening since she had left her home, had, in some degree, softened the opposition to her unsanctioned marriage with George. The more Mrs. B. had about her, the more energetic seemed her directing capabilities, and her fault-finding propensities. Her own, she had full power over; and Jane after vain endeavors, became disgusted, weary, and perplexed, and decided that, though her mother might suffer, she could not endure her home. They followed Jack to the West. Thus vanished all hopes of sympathy or relief from this source to Frado. There seemed no one capable of enduring the oppressions of the house but her. She turned to the darkness of the future with the determination previously formed, to remain until she should be eighteen. Jane begged her to follow her so soon as she should be released; but so wearied out was she by her mistress, she felt disposed to flee from any and every one having her similitude of name or feature.

Chapter XII The Winding Up of the Matter

Nothing new under the sun.
SOLOMON

A few years ago, within the compass of my narrative, there appeared often in some of our New England villages, professed fugitives from slavery, who recounted their personal experience in homely phrase, and awakened the indignation of non-slaveholders against brother Pro. Such a one appeared in the new home of Frado; and as people of color were rare there, was it strange she should attract her dark brother; that he should inquire her out; succeed in seeing her; feel a strange sensation in his heart towards her; that he should toy with her shining curls, feel proud to provoke her to smile and expose the ivory concealed by thin, ruby lips; that her sparkling eyes should fascinate; that he should propose; that they should marry? A short acquaintance was indeed an objection, but she saw him often, and thought she knew him. He never spoke of his enslavement to her when alone, but she felt that, like her own oppression, it was painful to disturb oftener than was needful.

He was a fine, straight negro, whose back showed no marks of the lash, erect as if it never crouched beneath a burden. There was a silent sympathy which Frado felt attracted her, and she opened her heart to the presence of love—that arbitrary and inexorable tyrant.

She removed to Singleton, her former residence, and there was married. Here were Frado's first feelings of trust and repose on human arm. She realized, for the first time, the relief of looking to another for comfortable support. Occasionally he would leave her to "lecture."

Those tours were prolonged often to weeks. Of course he had little spare money. Frado was again feeling her self-dependence, and was at last compelled to resort alone to that. Samuel was kind to her when at home, but made no provision for his absence, which was at last unprecedented.

He left her to her fate—embarked at sea, with the disclosure that he had never seen the South, and that his illiterate harangues were humbugs for hungry abolitionists. Once more alone! Yet not alone. A still newer companionship would soon force itself upon her. No one wanted her with such prospects. Herself was burden enough; who would have an additional one?

The horrors of her condition nearly prostrated her, and she was again thrown upon the public for sustenance. Then followed the birth of her child. The long absent Samuel unexpectedly returned, and rescued her from charity. Recovering from her expected illness, she once more commenced toil for herself and child, in a room obtained of a poor woman, but with better fortune. One so well known would not be wholly neglected. Kind friends watched her when Samuel was from home, prevented her from suffering, and when the cold weather pinched the warmly clad, a kind friend took them in, and thus preserved them. At last Samuel's business became very engrossing, and after long desertion, news reached his family that he had become a victim of yellow fever, in New Orleans.

So much toil as was necessary to sustain Frado, was more than she could endure. As soon as her babe could be nourished without his mother, she left him in charge of a Mrs. Capon, and procured an agency, hoping to recruit her health, and gain an easier livelihood for herself and child. This afforded her better maintenance than she had yet found. She passed into the various towns of the State she lived in, then into Massachusetts. Strange were some of her adventures. Watched by kidnappers, maltreated by professed abolitionists, who didn't want slaves at the South, nor niggers in their own houses, North. Faugh! to lodge one; to eat with one; to admit one through the front door; to sit next one; awful!

Traps slyly laid by the vicious to ensnare her, she resolutely avoided. In one of her tours, Providence favored her with a friend who, pitying her cheerless lot, kindly provided her with a valuable recipe, from which she might herself manufacture a useful article for her maintenance. This proved a more agreeable, and an easier way of sustenance.

And thus, to the present time, may you see her busily employed in preparing her merchandise; then sallying forth to encounter many frowns, but some kind friends and purchasers. Nothing turns her from her steadfast purpose of elevating herself. Reposing on God, she has thus far journeyed securely. Still an invalid, she asks your sympathy, gentle reader. Refuse not, because some part of her history is unknown, save by the Omniscient God. Enough has been unrolled to demand your sympathy and aid.

Do you ask the destiny of those connected with her *early* history? A few years only have elapsed since Mr. and Mrs. B. passed into another world. As age increased, Mrs. B. became more irritable, so that no one, even her own children, could remain with her; and she was accompanied by her husband to the home of Lewis, where, after an agony in death unspeakable, she passed away. Only a few months since, Aunt Abby entered heaven. Jack and his wife rest in heaven, disturbed by no intruders; and Susan and her child are yet with the living. Jane has silver locks in place of auburn tresses, but she has the early love of Henry still, and has never regretted her exchange of lovers. Frado has passed from their memories, as Joseph from the butler's, but she will never cease to track them till beyond mortal vision.

1859

The Emergence of American Poetic Voices

There was a time not so very long ago when virtually every student who went through the American educational system would have read, or at least heard, lines like these:

> Listen, my children, and you shall hear
> Of the midnight ride of Paul Revere,
> On the eighteenth of April, in Seventy-
> five;
> Hardly a man is now alive
> Who remembers that famous day or
> year.

If students remembered nothing else about this poem—apart from the innumerable parodies which drifted around most junior high schools—they were likely to recollect its famous warning signals against the British: "One, if by land, and two, if by sea."

They would almost certainly have read, as well, lines like the following:

> By the shore of Gitche Gumee,
> By the shining Big-Sea-Water,
> At the doorway of his wigwam,
> In the pleasant Summer morning,
> Hiawatha stood and waited.
> All the air was full of freshness,
> All the earth was bright and joyous,
> And before him, through the sunshine,
> Westward toward the neighboring forest
> Passed in golden swarms the Ahmo,
> Passed the bees, the honey-makers,
> Burning, singing in the sunshine.

Or they might have been taught to recite with patriotic fervor the whole of this poem:

> Ay, tear her tattered ensign down!
> Long has it waved on high,
> And many an eye has danced to see
> That banner in the sky;
> Beneath it rung the battle shout,
> And burst the cannon's roar;—
> The meteor of the ocean air
> Shall sweep the clouds no more!
>
> Her deck, once red with heroes' blood
> Where knelt the vanquished foe,
> When winds were hurrying o'er the
> flood
> And waves were white below,
> No more shall feel the victor's tread,
> Or know the conquered knee;—
> The harpies of the shore shall pluck
> The eagle of the sea!
>
> O better that her shattered hulk
> Should sink beneath the wave;
> Her thunders shook the mighty deep
> And there should be her grave;
> Nail to the mast her holy flag,
> Set every thread-bare sail,
> And give her to the god of storms,—
> The lightning and the gale!

The first two selections, as today's readers may or may not know, were written by Henry Wadsworth Longfellow; they are from "Paul Revere's Ride" (*Tales of a Wayside Inn,* 1860), and the beginning of a section of "The Song of Hiawatha" (1855). The full poem is Oliver Wendell Holmes's "Old Ironsides," which he wrote in 1830 in a successful effort to prevent the frigate Constitution from being dismantled.

For the better part of a century, such verse constituted the poetic mainstream of American literature. The "Schoolroom Poets" who wrote it, Cambridge gentlemen and Harvard professors like Longfellow, Holmes, and James Russell Lowell, embodied what many saw as the ideal of an American man of letters. The metrical regularity and linguistic simplicity of such verse recommended it for classroom recitation and study. Its unconflicted, ingenuous views of American history and of nature, its sentimental portraits of noble Indians and magnanimous Puritans, its elevated and highminded tone—all these appealed to generations of readers wishing to sustain an idealized view of the past.

To be sure, "Schoolroom" poetry did not constitute the full range of American verse in the first half of the nineteenth century. As this section indicates, a variety of distinctive folk traditions emerged in the early years of this republic. Black slaves in the South created from African and western European sources an altogether new genre, the "sorrow songs" or spirituals, as well as secular work songs to pace, and in a measure to complain against, their heavy labors. In many other areas people used the work, conflicts, and loves attendant on building a new society to create what are generally described as "folk" songs and poems.

Among the more formal poets, William Cullen Bryant was the first American successfully to adapt the innovations in style and subject of British romantics like Wordsworth, Keats, and Shelley, and to win the reputation of poet on both sides of the Atlantic. In these respects he set a pattern not only for the "Schoolroom" poets but for others, including Emerson, who found in nature both inspiration and symbol. Read, perhaps, as widely as Bryant and Longfellow in her day, but not since, Lydia Sigourney's work illustrates another dimension of nineteenth-century poetry, what has been demeaned—and therefore often misunderstood—as "sentimental." The popular reception—and large sales—of the work of these poets suggests a public function to their work unfamiliar to most twentieth-century readers of poetry.

Of the contemporaries of Emerson and Longfellow, however, it was Poe (represented elsewhere in this volume) whose work most influenced other poets. Not so much in the United States, though works like "The Raven" and "The Bells" won wide attention and also lent themselves to the popular forms of oral recitation. Still, it was in France, through the responsive passion of writers like Baudelaire and Rimbaud, that Poe's reputation flourished and his approach to invoking the mysterious states of mind was developed.

In the United States, as the nineteenth century drew to a close, as the men and women who wrote the best-known poetry themselves died (Holmes, the last, in 1894), and as the first volumes of Emily Dickinson's poems began to be published, conceptions of poetic excellence were undergoing rapid change. Within a quarter century, and certainly into our own day, very different kinds of poetry came to be seen as the major achievements of American writers in the nineteenth century. Thinking about why helps us understand the changes from nineteenth-century ideas and tastes to those of our own day. Compare these lines, for example:

> Each heart has its haunted chamber,
> Where the silent moonlight falls!
> On the floor are mysterious footsteps,
> There are whispers along the walls!
>
> And mine at times is haunted
> By phantoms of the Past,
> As motionless as shadows,
> By the silent moonlight cast. . . .

Longfellow, *from* "The Haunted Chamber"

And now consider these:

> One need not be a Chamber—to be
> Haunted—
> One need not be a House—
> The Brain has Corridors—surpassing
> Material Place—

Far safer, of a Midnight Meeting
External Ghost
Than its interior Confronting—
That Cooler Host. . . .

Emily Dickinson, poem #670

In certain respects, the very regularity of Longfellow's lines works against the mood he is trying to create, and the abstractness and generality of his language makes it far less startling or memorable than Dickinson's internal ghost. The jaggedness, the tension, the unusual concreteness of Dickinson's lines also came to appeal to twentieth-century sensibility far more; they came to be seen, in fact, as embodying many of the spasmodic, discordant qualities of contemporary life, even though the poem was written around 1863.

Or consider a further comparison, the octave of a sonnet by Longfellow:

The sea awoke at midnight from its sleep,
And round the pebbly beaches far and wide
I heard the first wave of the rising tide
Rush onward with uninterrupted sweep;
A voice out of the silence of the deep,
A sound mysteriously multiplied
As of a cataract from the mountain's side,
Or roar of winds upon a wooded steep.

"The Sound of the Sea"

And here is the opening of a poem from Walt Whitman's "Sea-Drift":

Out of the cradle endlessly rocking,
Out of the mocking-bird's throat, the musical shuttle,
Out of the Ninth-month midnight,
Over the sterile sands and the fields beyond, where the child leaving his bed wander'd alone, bareheaded, barefoot,
Down from the shower'd halo,
Up from the mystic play of shadows twining and twisting as if they were alive,
Out from the patches of briers and blackberries,
From the memories of the bird that chanted to me,
From your memories sad brother, from the fitful risings and fallings I heard,
From under that yellow half-moon late-risen and swollen as if with tears,
From those beginning notes of yearning and love there in the mist,
From the thousand responses of my heart never to cease. . .

"Out of the cradle endlessly rocking"

The point of this comparison is not to demean Longfellow; on the contrary, we have included him in this anthology because some of his poetry continues to live and to move us. Besides, precisely because he was by far this country's most popular and respected poet, not only in the United States but in Europe, reading him tells us a great deal about the sensibility of mid-nineteenth-century America.

By contrast, Whitman's "barbaric yawp" initially shocked many of his contemporaries. But his effort to create something new under the sun, a distinctively American poetic style, drawing from platform rhetoric, Quaker terminology, and youthful romantic yearnings, has come to appear a more vital voice in American literary history. The shift in valuation from Longfellow to Whitman can be used to mark the changes in critical standards from a century ago to our own day. And if we can perceive why most of their contemporaries much preferred Longfellow to Whitman, we can understand a great deal about the taste, the style, the concerns of American poets during the first part of the nineteenth century.

Paul Lauter
Trinity College

Songs and Ballads

Songs do not really exist on the printed page. Indeed, certain kinds of songs, notably those like spirituals given expression in congregational singing, do not exist even through music printed with their texts. For they live only in the process of their fresh creation each time they are sung. Thus, printing the texts of some representative songs being sung in the first part of the nineteenth century in a sense falsifies them, as well as the cultural history of the time. And yet, it would be equally false to omit them. For the United States had a vigorous popular culture—or, more accurately, cultures—in which songs constituted a major element.

Determining which songs to include in such a selection is equally problematic. While the composition of some songs can be dated with reasonable accuracy, many will have been sung for decades before they are noted by collectors. Furthermore, new versions are always appearing: an old tune may be resurrected with fresh lyrics; simpler texts can be set to differing melodies. In some degree, therefore, placing certain of these songs in this particular time frame is arbitrary—some may well have been around since the previous century, and the printed versions may reflect late nineteenth- or even twentieth-century variations. In addition, no selection can fully reflect the range of the American people's cultures, even of the early nineteenth century. Here we have included a somewhat larger selection of African-American songs of the time, in part because they represent the most characteristically "American," as distinct from imported compositions, in part because of the enormous influence African-American folk styles have had in the development of American culture generally.

Most of the songs in this section were not sung by performers observed and listened to by a silent audience. Singing was among the more vital activities people did together. In certain respects, as Bernice Reagon has put it, "the song is only a vehicle to get to the singing." For the *singing*—in church, in the fields, at a quilting bee or a party, around a campfire or a piano—is what unifies, inspires, moves people to hope and to act. The singing defines the nature of the gathering, predominantly for those engaged in it. Some of these verses were sung in meetings, for worship or for politics; some, like "John Brown's Body," were chanted by soldiers marching to battle; some were set out to pace or perhaps to ease work. One needs to imagine the circumstances in which they were created and re-created to gain a real sense of most of these songs.

Like other kinds of poetry, these songs convey a broad range of human emotions—affection, aspiration, complaint—but they are often more explicit about the roles they play in the lives of the people who sing them. Some songs were designed to support political parties, others, like "Paper of Pins," to give form to courting rituals. Some served multiple purposes: a spiritual like "Steal Away" could in some situations express the desire of slaves for a salvation beyond the oppression of daily life; in other circumstances, the song could serve as a signal for some to prepare to "steal away" literally on the underground railway. Often the songs voiced the common experiences and beliefs of particular groups of people—black slaves, Irish immigrants, Forty-niners—as well as embodying images, rhythms, and harmonies characteristic of their cultures. In that sense, songs functioned to preserve and sustain important elements of group culture against the homogenizing tendencies of the developing nation.

Groups did borrow language and music from each other, but many songs bear the distinctive marks of particular historical cultures. Most African-American congregational songs, for example, display a call-and-response pattern, in which the song leader sets out a line or phrase and the group responds by repeating or working variations on it. In one of the more famous examples, the leader cries out "Swing low, sweet chariot" and the congregation responds "Comin' for to carry me home"; or again, "When Israel was in Egypt land," and the response, "Let my people go." But the pattern of call-andresponse is not limited to such fully structured lines; in fact, the essence of such African-American congregational music depends upon many individuals extemporaneously singing out words or phrases—like "hallelujah" or "yes, Lord"—or even appropriate new lines. Many Anglo-American songs are marked by refrains whose "nonsense" syllables—e.g., "hoodle dang fol di dye yo, hoodle dang fol di day" in "Sweet Betsy from Pike"—vary according to the area of the country or the original nationality of the singers. In general, the language of these songs reflects the language of the people who sang them, just as the music significantly emerged from the European or African origins of the singers.

Most of the texts printed below are those of "folk songs," though a few are the compositions of specific writers. That is, the authors of most are unknown, the language of the songs colloquial, their images drawn from the common stock available to everyone in the group. They are designed to be *sung,* and thus their words may differ from versions a reader might know. The texts of such songs often changed, in fact, sometimes by accident as a song was recreated by people who might not have remembered all of the version they had once heard. Sometimes, however, songs were consciously changed to reflect new circumstances or to broaden their appeal. "Bury Me Not on the Lone Prairie" began as a sailor's lament about burial at sea. Songs like "Sweet Betsy from Pike" and "Pat Works on the Railway" probably had dozens of verses added or subtracted at one or another time. "The Battle Hymn of the Republic" was composed by Julia Ward Howe after she had sung "John Brown's Body" with a troop of Union soldiers and had been asked by her minister to set new words to that "stirring tune." In still other cases, as with the version of "Go Down, Moses" included here, a song originally sung in dialect was later redone in more "standard" English when it began to be presented to a white audience. In the singing, then, the precise texts are less important than the process of reshaping the language to fit the inclinations of the singers.

In this respect, these texts represent snapshots of songs, freezing them into uncharacteristically stationary, historical forms. In fact, as readers will know, many of these songs have reemerged over the years as their sentiments or their phrases have come to echo the needs of new times and new singers.

Paul Lauter
Trinity College

Songs of the Slaves[1]

Lay Dis Body Down

I know moon-rise, I know star-rise
  I lay dis body down.
I walk in de moonlight, I walk in de starlight,
  To lay dis body down.
I walk in de graveyard, I walk troo de graveyard,
  To lay dis body down.
I lie in de grave an' stretch out my arms,
  I lay dis body down.
I go to de jedgment in de evenin' of de day
  When I lay dis body down,
An' my soul an' your soul will meet in de day
  When I lay dis body down.

Nobody Knows the Trouble I've Had

Nobody knows de trouble I've had [or, I've seen],
  Nobody knows but Jesus
Nobody knows de trouble I've had
  Glory hallelu.

One morning I was a-walking down,
  O yes, Lord!
I saw some berries a-hanging down,
  O yes, Lord!
    (Refrain)
I pick de berry and I suck de juice,
  O yes, Lord!
Just as sweet as the honey in de comb,
  O yes, Lord!
    (Refrain)
Sometimes I'm up, sometimes I'm down,
Sometimes I'm almost on de groun'.
    (Refrain)

[1]The texts of the following "spirituals" or "sorrow songs" are derived primarily from William Francis Allen, Charles Pickard Ware, and Lucy McKim Garrison, *Slave Songs of the United States,* 1867 (reprinted: New York: Peter Smith, 1951) and James Weldon Johnson and J. Rosamond Johnson, *The Books of American Negro Spirituals,* 1925, 1926 (reprinted: New York: Da Capo Press, 1977). Other sources, like Thomas Wentworth Higginson's *Army Life in a Black Regiment,* have also been consulted. The spellings are those of the volume from which the text is taken.

What make ole Satan hate me so?
Cause he got me once and he let me go.
(Refrain)

Deep River

Deep river, my home is over Jordan, Deep river,
Lord, I want to cross over into campground,
Lord, I want to cross over into campground,
Lord, I want to cross over into campground.
Oh, chillun, Oh, don't you want to go to that gospel feast,
That promised land, that land, where all is peace?
Walk into heaven, and take my seat,
And cast my crown at Jesus feet,
Lord, I want to cross over into campground,
Lord, I want to cross over into campground,
Lord, I want to cross over into campground.
Deep river, my home is over Jordan, Deep river
Lord, I want to cross over into campground,
Lord, I want to cross over into campground,
Lord, I want to cross over into campground, Lord!

Roll, Jordan, Roll

My brudder [sister, or a name] sittin' on de tree of life,
An' he yearde when Jordan roll;
Roll, Jordan, Roll, Jordan, Roll, Jordan, roll!
O march de angel march, O march de angel march;
O my soul arise in Heaven, Lord,
For to year when Jordan roll.
Little chil'en, learn to fear de Lord,
And let your days be long;
Roll, Jordan, &c.
O, let no false nor spiteful word,
Be found upon your tongue;
Roll, Jordan, &c.

Michael Row the Boat Ashore

1. Michael row the boat ashore, Hallelujah! (repeat)
2. Michael boat a gospel boat, Hallelujah!
3. I wonder where my mudder deh [there].
4. See my mudder on de rock gwine home.
5. On de rock gwine home in Jesus' name.

6. Michael boat a music boat.
7. Gabriel blow de trumpet horn.
8. O you mind your boastin' talk.
9. Boastin' talk will sink your soul.
10. Brudder, lend a helpin' hand.
11. Sister, help for trim dat boat.
12. Jordan stream is wide and deep.
13. Jesus stand on t' oder side.
14. I wonder if my maussa der.
15. My fader gone to unknown land.
16. O de Lord he plant his garden deh.
17. He raise de fruit for you to eat.
18. He dat eat shall neber die.
19. When de riber overflow.
20. O poor sinner, how you land?
21. Riber run and darkness comin'.
22. Sinner row to save your soul.

Steal Away to Jesus

Steal away, steal away, steal away to Jesus!
Steal away, steal away home, I ain't got long to stay here.
Steal away, steal away, steal away to Jesus!
Steal away, steal away home, I ain't got long to stay here.
My Lord, He calls me, He calls me by the thunder,
The trumpet sounds within-a my soul, I ain't got long to stay here.
Steal away, steal away, steal away to Jesus!
Steal away, steal away home, I ain't got long to stay here.
Steal away, steal away, steal away to Jesus!
Steal away, steal away home, I ain't got long to stay here.
Green trees a-bending, po' sinner stand a-tembling,
The trumpet sounds within-a my soul.
I ain't got long to stay here, Oh, Lord, I ain't got long to stay
here.

There's a Meeting Here To-Night

I take my text in Matthew, and by de Revelation,
I know you by your garment,
Dere's a meeting here to-night.
Dere's a meeting here to-night (Brudder Tony),
Dere's a meeting here to-night (Sister Rina),
Dere's a meeting here to-night,
I hope to meet again.

Brudder John was a writer, he write de laws of God;
Sister Mary say to brudder John, "Brudder John, don't write no
more."
(Refrain)

Many Thousand Go[1]

1. No more peck o' corn for me,
   No more, no more;
   No more peck o' corn for me,
   Many thousand go.
2. No more driver's lash for me.
3. No more pint o' salt for me.
4. No more hundred lash for me.
5. No more mistress' call for me.

Go Down, Moses

When Israel was in Egypt's land,
Let my people go;
Oppressed so hard they could not stand,
Let my people go.

Chorus:
Go down, Moses, way down in Egypt's land;
Tell old Pharoah, to let my people go.

Thus saith the Lord, bold Moses said,
Let my people go;
If not I'll smite your first born dead,
Let my people go.

No more shall they in bondage toil,
Let my people go;
Let them come out with Egypt's spoil,
Let my people go.

O 'twas a dark and dismal night,
Let my people go;

[1]A song "to which the Rebellion had actually given rise. This was composed by nobody knows whom—though it was the most recent doubtless of all these 'spirituals,'—and had been sung in secret to avoid detection. It is certainly plaintive enough. The peck of corn and pint of salt were slavery's rations."—Thomas Wentworth Higginson. Lt. Col. Trowbridge learned that it was first sung when Beauregard took the slaves of the islands to build fortifications at Hilton Head and Bay Point. [Note of Allen, Ware, and Garrison]

When Moses led the Israelites,
  Let my people go.

The Lord told Moses what to do,
  Let my people go;
To lead the children of Israel through,
  Let my people go.

O come along, Moses, you won't get lost,
  Let my people go;
Stretch our your rod and come across,
  Let my people go.

As Israel stood by the water side,
  Let my people go;
At the command of God it did divide,
  Let my people go.

And when they reached the other side,
  Let my people go;
They sang a song of triumph o'er,
  Let my people go.

You won't get lost in the wilderness,
  Let my people go;
With a lighted candle in your breast,
  Let my people go.

O let us all from bondage flee,
  Let my people go;
And let us all in Christ be free,
  Let my people go.

We need not always weep and moan,
  Let my people go;
And wear these slavery chains forlorn,
  Let my people go.

What a beautiful morning that will be,
  Let my people go;
When time breaks up in eternity,
Let my people go.

Didn't My Lord Deliver Daniel

Didn't my Lord deliver Daniel, deliver Daniel, deliver Daniel,
Didn't my Lord deliver Daniel,

An' why not every man.
He delivered Daniel from de lion's den,
Jonah from de belly of de whale,
An' de Hebrew chillun from de fiery furnace,
An' why not every man.
Didn't my Lord deliver Daniel, deliver Daniel, deliver Daniel,
Didn't my Lord deliver Daniel,
An' why not every man.
De moon run down in a purple stream,
De sun forbear to shine,
An' every star disappear,
King Jesus shall-a be mine.
(Refrain)
De win' blows eas' an' de win' blows wes',
It blows like de judgament day,
An' every po' soul dat never did pray
'll be glad to pray dat day.
(Refrain)
I set my foot on de Gospel ship,
An de ship begin to sail,
It landed me over on Canaan's shore,
An' I'll never come back no mo'.
(Refrain)

Songs of White Communities

John Brown's Body

John Brown's body lies a-moldering in the grave,
John Brown's body lies a-moldering in the grave,
John Brown's body lies a-moldering in the grave,
But his soul goes marching on.

Chorus:
Glory, glory, hallelujah!
Glory, glory, hallelujah!
Glory, glory, hallelujah!
His soul goes marching on!

John Brown died that the slaves might be free,
John Brown died that the slaves might be free,
John Brown died that the slaves might be free,
But his soul goes marching on.

He's gone to be a soldier in the army of the Lord,
He's gone to be a soldier in the army of the Lord,
He's gone to be a soldier in the army of the Lord,
    And his soul is marching on.

The stars of heaven are looking kindly down,
The stars of heaven are looking kindly down,
The stars of heaven are looking kindly down,
    On the grave of old John Brown.

The Battle Hymn of the Republic

by Julia Ward Howe[1]

Mine eyes have seen the glory of the coming of the Lord;
He is trampling out the vintage where the grapes of wrath are stored;
He hath loosed the fateful lightning of His terrible swift sword;
  His truth is marching on.
    Chorus:
    Glory, glory, hallelujah,
    Glory, glory, hallelujah,
    Glory, glory, hallelujah,
      His truth is marching on.

I have seen Him in the watch-fires of a hundred circling camps;
They have builded Him an altar in the evening dews and damps;
I can read His righteous sentence by the dim and flaring lamps;
  His day is marching on.

I have read a fiery gospel writ in burnished rows of steel:
"As ye deal with My contemners, so with you My grace shall deal;
Let the Hero, born of woman, crush the serpent with His heel,
  Since God is marching on."

[1]In her *Reminiscences* (1899), Julia Ward Howe recounts how she came to write "The Battle Hymn of the Republic." She had visited an army camp near Washington in the company of her minister, a Mr. Clarke. Returning with a band of soldiers, they had joined in singing "John Brown's Body." Clarke asked why she did not "write some good words for that stirring tune," but she felt as yet uninspired, though she wished to do so. That night, as she later wrote, "as I lay waiting for the dawn, the long lines of the desired poem began to twine themselves in my mind." She quickly arose, lest she "fall asleep and forget them . . . and scrawled the verses almost without looking at the paper." The poem was published in *The Atlantic Monthly* of February 1862, from which this text is taken.

The poem represents a striking instance of the adaptation by a self-conscious poet of the music and rhythms of an already-popular, if simpler, song.

He has sounded forth the trumpet that shall never call retreat;
He is sifting out the hearts of men before His judgment seat:
Oh! be swift, my soul, to answer Him! be jubilant, my feet!
Our God is marching on.

In the beauty of the lilies Christ was born across the sea,
With a glory in His bosom that transfigures you and me:
As He died to make men holy, let us die to make men free,
While God is marching on.

1862

Pat Works on the Railway

In eighteen hundred and forty-one
I put my corduroy breeches on.
I put my corduroy breeches on
To work upon the railway.
Chorus:
Fill-i-me-oo-ree-i-ree-ay (three times)
To work upon the railway.

In eighteen hundred and forty-two
I left the Old World for the New.
Bad cess to the luck that brought me through
To work upon the railway.

In eighteen hundred and forty-three
'Twas then that I met sweet Molly McGee.
An elegant wife she's been to me
While working on the railway.

In eighteen hundred and forty-four
I traveled the land from shore to shore,
I traveled the land from shore to shore
To work upon the railway.

In eighteen hundred and forty-five
I found myself more dead than alive.
I found myself more dead than alive
From working on the railway.

It's "Pat do this" and "Pat do that,"
Without a stocking or cravat,
Nothing but an old straw hat
While I worked on the railway.

In eighteen hundred and forty-seven
Sweet Biddy McGee she went to heaven;
If she left one kid she left eleven,
To work upon the railway.

Sweet Betsy from Pike[1]

Oh don't you remember sweet Betsy from Pike,
Who crossed the big mountains with her lover Ike,
With two yoke of oxen, a big yellow dog,
A tall Shanghai rooster, and one spotted hog?

Chorus:
Singing dang fol dee dido,
Singing dang fol dee day.

One evening quite early they camped on the Platte.
'Twas near by the road on a green shady flat,
Where Betsy, sore-footed, lay down to repose—
With wonder Ike gazed on that Pike County rose.

The Shanghai ran off, and their cattle all died;
That morning the last piece of bacon was fried;
Poor Ike was discouraged and Betsy got mad,
The dog drooped his tail and looked wondrously sad.

They stopped at Salt Lake to inquire of the way,
Where Brigham declared that sweet Betsy should stay;
But Betsy got frightened and ran like a deer,
While Brigham stood pawing the ground like a steer.

They soon reached the desert where Betsy gave out,
And down in the sand she lay rolling about;
While Ike, half distracted, looked on with surprise,
Saying, "Betsy, get up, you'll get sand in your eyes."

Sweet Betsy got up in a great deal of pain,
Declared she'd go back to Pike County again;

[1]To illustrate how traditional songs emerge in many variants, consider an alternative opening verse and chorus of "Sweet Betsy":
Did you ever hear of Sweet Betsy from Pike,
Who crossed the wide prairies with her lover Ike,
With two yoke of oxen and one spotted hog,
A tall Shanghai rooster and one yaller dog.
Saying "Good-bye Pike county, farewell for a while,
We'll come back again when we panned out our pile."
Other versions of the chorus take their character from groups supposed to have sung the song; an Irish-like chorus reads "Sing too ra li oo ra li oo ra li aye."

But Ike gave a sigh, and they fondly embraced,
And they traveled along with his arm round her waist.

The Injuns came down in a wild yelling horde,
And Betsy was scared they would scalp her adored;
Behind the front wagon wheel Betsy did crawl,
And there fought the Injuns with musket and ball.

They suddenly stopped on a very high hill,
With wonder looked down upon old Placerville;
Ike sighed when he said, and he cast his eyes down,
"Sweet Betsy, my darling, we've got to Hangtown."

Long Ike and sweet Betsy attended a dance;
Ike wore a pair of his Pike County pants;
Sweet Betsy was dressed up in ribbons and rings;
Says Ike, "You're an angel, but where are your wings?"

[Following are additional or alternative verses to "Sweet Betsy." Some portray Betsy in rather a stronger light.]

'Twas out on the prairie one bright starry night,
They broke out the whiskey and Betsy got tight,
She sang and she howled and she danced o'er the plain,
And showed her bare legs to the whole wagon train.

The terrible desert was burning and bare,
And Isaac he shrank from the death lurkin' there,
"Dear old Pike County, I'll come back to you."
Says Betsy, "You'll go by yourself if you do."

They swam wild rivers and climbed the tall peaks,
And camped on the prairies for weeks upon weeks,
Starvation and cholera, hard work and slaughter,
They reached Californy, spite of hell and high water.

A miner said, "Betsy, will you dance with me?"
"I will, you old hoss, if you don't make too free.
But don't dance me hard, do you want to know why?
Doggone ye, I'm chock full of strong alkali.

Long Ike and sweet Betsy got married, of course,
But Ike, getting jealous, obtained a divorce,
While Betsy, well satisfied, said with a shout,
"Goodbye, you big lummox, I'm glad you backed out!"

Bury Me Not On the Lone Prairie[1]

"O bury me not on the lone prairie."
These words came low and mournfully,
From the pallid lips of a youth who lay
On his dying bed at the close of day.

He had wasted and pined till o'er his brow
Death's shades were slowly gathering now.
He thought of home and loved ones nigh,
As the cowboys gathered to see him die.

"O bury me not on the lone prairie,
Where the coyotes howl and the wind blows free.
In a narrow grave just six by three—
O bury me not on the lone prairie."

"It matters not, I've oft been told,
Where the body lies when the heart grows cold.
Yet grant, o grant, this wish to me,
O bury me not on the lone prairie."

"I've always wished to be laid when I died
In a little churchyard on the green hillside.
By my father's grave there let me be,
O bury me not on the lone prairie."

"I wish to lie where a mother's prayer
And a sister's tear will mingle there.
Where friends can come and weep o'er me.
O bury me not on the lone prairie."

"For there's another whose tears will shed
For the one who lies in a prairie bed.
It breaks my heart to think of her now,
She has curled these locks; she has kissed this brow"

"O bury me not . . ." And his voice failed there.
But they took no heed to his dying prayer.
In a narrow grave, just six by three,
They buried him there on the lone prairie.

[1]This song probably originated as one among a number of ballads of the 1840s concerned with burial *at sea*. It appears to have migrated in some fashion to the western range, where it became the most popular of early cowboy songs.

And the cowboys now as they roam the plain,
For they marked the spot where his bones were lain,
Fling a handful of roses o'er his grave
With a prayer to God, his soul to save.

Shenandoah[1]

Oh, Shenandoah, I long to hear you—
Away, you rolling river;
Oh, Shenandoah, I long to hear you—
Away, I'm bound away
'Cross the wide Missouri.

Oh, Shenandoah, I love your daughter—
Away, you rolling river;
I'll take her 'cross that rolling water—
Away, I'm bound away
'Cross the wide Missouri.

This white man loves your Indian maiden—
Away, you rolling river;
In my canoe with notions laden—
Away, I'm bound away
'Cross the wide Missouri.

Farewell, goodbye, I shall not grieve you—
Away, you rolling river;
Oh, Shenandoah, I'll not deceive you—
Away, I'm bound away
'Cross the wide Missouri.

The ship sails free, a gale is blowing—
Away, you rolling river;
The braces taut, the sheets aflowing—
Away, I'm bound away
'Cross the wide Missouri.

Clementine[1]

In a cavern, in a canyon, excavating for a mine,
Lived a miner, forty-niner, and his daughter Clementine.

[1]This song of a white trader who fell in love with the daughter of an Indian chieftan appears to have originated in the Missouri River valley in the early nineteenth century. Later, reversing the course of "Bury Me Not," it migrated east to the ocean, where in a slightly different version it emerged as a capstan chantey.

[1]Both this and the following song, "Acres of Clams," were popular among the gold-miners of California, the Forty-niners.

Oh my darlin', oh my darlin', oh my darlin' Clementine,
You are lost and gone forever, dreadful sorry Clementine.

Light she was and like a fairy, And her
shoes were number nine;
Herring boxes without topses, Sandals
were for Clementine.
(Chorus)

Drove she duckling to the water, Every
morning just at nine,
Hit her foot against a splinter, Fell into
the foaming brine.
(Chorus)

Ruby lips above the water, Blowing
bubbles soft and fine,
Alas for me, I was no swimmer, So I
lost my Clementine.
(Chorus)

In a churchyard near the canyon,
Where the myrtle doth entwine,
There grow roses and other posies,
Fertilized by Clementine.
(Chorus)

In my dreams she oft doth haunt me,
With her garments soaked in brine;
Though in life I used to hug her, Now
she's dead I draw the line.
(Chorus)

Then the miner, forty-niner, Soon
began to peak and pine;
Thought he 'oughter jin'e his daughter,
Now he's with his Clementine.
(Chorus)

Acres of Clams

I've wandered all over this country,
Prospecting and digging for gold;
I've tunneled, hydraulicked, and cradled,
And I have been frequently sold.

And I have been frequently sold,
And I have been frequently sold.

I've tunneled, hydraulicked, and cradled,
And I have been frequently sold!

For one who got rich by mining,
I saw there were hundreds grew poor;
I made up my mind to try farming,
The only pursuit that is sure.

I rolled up my grub in my blanket,
I left all my tools on the ground,
I started one morning to shank it
For the country they call Puget Sound.

No longer the slave of ambition,
I laugh at the world and its shams,
And think of my happy condition,
Surrounded by acres of clams.

Surrounded by acres of clams,
Surrounded by acres of clams.
And think of my happy condition,
Surrounded by acres of clams!

Cindy[1]

You ought to see my Cindy,
She lives way down south;
She's so sweet the honey bees
Swarm around her mouth.

Chorus:
Get-a-long home, Cindy, Cindy,
Get-a-long home, Cindy, Cindy,
Get-a-long home, Cindy, Cindy,
I'll marry you some day.

The first time I saw Cindy,
She was standing in the door,
Her shoes and stockings in her hand,
Her feet all over the floor.

She took me to her parlor,
She cooled me with her fan;

[1]"Cindy" is but one of a large group of ditties called "Play-Party Songs." They were generally sung and danced to without instrumental accompaniment, since many people viewed fiddle-playing as the work of the Devil. Verses were often improvised about local people and events as the song went along.

She said I was the prettiest thing
  In the shape of mortal man.

She kissed me and she hugged me,
  She called me sugar plum;
She throwed her arms around me,
  I thought my time had come.

Oh, Cindy is a pretty girl,
  Cindy is a peach;
She throwed her arms around my neck,
  And hung on like a leech.

And if I was a sugar tree
  Standing in the town,
Every time my Cindy passed
  I'd shake some sugar down.

And if I had a needle and thread
  Fine as I could sew,
I'd sew that girl to my coat tails
  And down the road I'd go.

Paper of Pins[1]

I'll give to you a paper of pins,
If you will tell me how our love begins,
If you marry, if you marry,
If you marry me.

I'll not accept a paper of pins,
To tell you how our love begins,
Nor I'll not marry, marry, marry,
Nor I'll not marry you.

I'll give to you a pink silk gown,
With golden laces hanging round,
If you marry, if you marry,
If you marry me.

I'll not accept the pink silk gown,
With golden laces hanging round,

[1] "Paper of Pins" could also be danced to or sung as an "answering-back" song between boys and girls. There are many variations; for example, the first answer back might be sung:

No, I'll not accept your paper of pins
If that's the way your love a-gins.
And I'll not marry you, you, you,
And I'll not marry you.

Nor I'll not marry, marry, marry,
Nor I'll not marry you.

I'll give to you a dress of green,
That you may be my fairy Queen,
If you marry, if you marry,
If you marry me.

I'll not accept your dress of green,
That I may be your fairy queen,
Nor I'll not marry, marry, marry,
Nor I'll not marry you.

I'll give to you a little lap dog,
To take with you when you go abroad,
If you marry, if you marry,
If you marry me.

I'll not accept your little lap dog,
To take with me when I go abroad,
Nor I'll not marry, marry, marry,
Nor I'll not marry you.

I'll give to you the key of my heart,
That we may love and never part,
If you marry, if you marry,
If you marry me.

I'll not accept the key of your heart,
That we may love and never part,
Nor I'll not marry, marry, marry,
Nor I'll not marry you.

I'll give to you the key of my chest,
That you may have money at your request,
If you marry, if you marry,
If you marry me.

Yes! I'll accept the key of your chest,
That I'll have money at my request;
I will marry, I will marry,
I will marry you.

Ha! ha! ha! money is all,
Woman's love is none at all;
And I'll not marry, marry, marry,
And I'll not marry you.

Come Home, Father

by Henry Clay Work[1]

Father, dear father, come home with me now!
The clock in the steeple strikes one.
You said you were coming right home from the shop,
As soon as your day's work was done.
Our fire has gone out, our house is all dark,
And mother's been watching since tea,
With poor brother Benny so sick in her arms,
And no one to help her but me.
Come home! come home! come home!
Please, father, dear father, come home.

Chorus:
Hear the sweet voice of the child
Which the night winds repeat as they roam!
Oh, who could resist this most plaintive of prayers?
"Please, father, dear father, come home!
Come home! come home! come home!
Please, father, dear father, come home."

Father, dear father, come home with me now!
The clock in the steeple strikes two.
The night has grown colder and Benny is worse,
But he has been calling for you.
Indeed he is worse, Ma says he will die,
Perhaps before morning shall dawn;
And this is the message she sent me to bring:
"Come quickly, or he will be gone."
Come home! come home! come home!
Please, father, dear father, come home.

Father, dear father, come home with me now!
The clock in the steeple strikes three.
The house is so lonely, the hours are so long,
For poor weeping mother and me.
Yes, we are alone, poor Benny is dead,
And gone with the angels of light;
And these were the very last words that he said:
"I want to kiss Papa good night."

[1]Work, an active abolitionist and temperance supporter, composed this song in 1864. For many years it was sung in what was probably the most popular temperance drama, "Ten Nights in a Barroom."

Come home! come home! come home!
Please, father, dear father, come home.

Life Is a Toil

One day as I wandered, I heard a complaining,
And saw an old woman, the picture of gloom;
She gazed at the mud on her doorstep ('twas raining),
And this was her song as she wielded her broom:
Chorus:
"Oh, life is a toil and love is a trouble,
And beauty will fade and riches will flee;
Oh, pleasures they dwindle and prices they double,
And nothing is as I would wish it to be.

"It's sweeping at six and it's dusting at seven,
It's victuals at eight and it's dishes at nine;
It's potting and panning from ten to eleven—
We scarce break our fast till we plan how to dine.

"There's too much of worriment goes in a bonnet,
There's too much of ironing goes in a shirt;
There's nothing that pays for the time you waste on it,
There's nothing that lasts us but trouble and dirt.

"In March it is mud, it is snow in December,
The mid-summer breezes are loaded with dust;
In fall the leaves litter; in rainy September
The wallpaper rots and the candlesticks rust.

"Last night in my dreams I was stationed forever
On a far little isle in the midst of the sea;
My one chance for life was a ceaseless endeavor
To sweep off the waves ere they swept over me.

"Alas, 'twas no dream, for ahead I behold it;
I know I am helpless my fate to avert."
She put down her broom and her apron she folded,
Then lay down and died, and was buried in dirt.

William Cullen Bryant 1794–1878

Born in Cummington, Massachusetts, William Cullen Bryant was the son of a country doctor who served several terms in the Massachusetts State Legislature and was both a stern Calvinist and a strict disciplinarian. Dr. Bryant's library, which contained at least seven hundred books, provided Bryant with a formidable basis for his copious early reading, reading which apparently began when he was sixteen months old. At thirteen, Bryant was sent to live with an uncle so that he might begin to study Latin and Greek and he learned so rapidly that at sixteen he entered Williams College as a sophomore. Despite his wish to continue working towards a classical education, Bryant was compelled by family financial circumstances to leave college during his first year and he reluctantly turned to the law, reading for the bar in Worthington and entering practice in Plainfield, Massachusetts, at the age of twenty-one.

Bryant's precocity was evident also in his early poetry. At thirteen, he wrote an anti-Jeffersonian poem called "The Embargo" after the manner of the seventeenth- and eighteenth-century satires of Dryden and Pope. Even though the political sentiments of the poem probably owed more to his father's opinions than to any political views young Cullen might claim, the poem so impressed Dr. Bryant that he had it printed in the *Hampshire Gazette*. Other early compositions which in their subject matter and manner prefigure the later poetry included a pair of odes in praise of the Connecticut River and patriotic stanzas called "The Genius of Columbia." In these, Bryant's style was influenced by his reading of English poets of the preceding generation, such as Thomas Gray, William Cowper, Henry Kirke White, Robert Southey, and Robert Blair. Their subjects, which tended to be pastoral and philosophical, helped to form Bryant's conception of what a poem should be: grave, somber, dignified, meditative, and above all, regular.

His most famous poem, "Thanatopsis," was composed when he was eighteen. His father, having discovered it, recopied the poem and submitted it to *The North American Review,* where it was published in September, 1817. Although "Thanatopsis" means a "meditation on death," the poem is also a meditation on nature, and in its implicit pantheism the poem looks at once backward to William Wordsworth's *Lyrical Ballads* (1798;1800) and forward to the Transcendentalists. Of "Thanatopsis," Richard Henry Dana remarked that "no one on this side of the Atlantic is capable of writing such verses." Steeped as he was in English poetry, Bryant was able to manufacture American verses altogether as satisfactory as those produced abroad. Although poems such as "The Yellow Violet" and "To a Fringed Gentian" could as easily refer to English settings as American, the nationality of the author gave them a domestic stamp, and in poems such as "The Prairies" and "To Cole, the Painter, Departing for Europe," Bryant attempted to capture the spirit and landscape of the New World.

In 1821, the year of his marriage to Frances Fairchild, Bryant published a small book entitled simply *Poems.* The connection established with Richard Henry Dana and Willard Philips at the *North American Review* had led to an invitation from the Phi Beta Kappa Society of Harvard College to present a "poetical address" at the 1821 commencement, and his poem for that occasion, "The Ages," together with seven others, was published in a forty-four page pamphlet which was warmly reviewed by the *North American Review* and promptly reprinted in a British anthology of American poetry. Bryant's literary career was now launched.

Moving to New York in 1825, Bryant happily abandoned his job as justice of the peace in Berkshire County to become an editor of *The New York Review and Athenaeum,* but when the publication folded in 1827 he renewed his license to practice law in New York. Yet his return to the legal profession was brief, for he was offered a job as assistant editor of the New York *Evening Post* and in 1829 became its editor-in-chief, a position he held until his death in 1878 at the age of eighty-four. During his years at the *Post,* he published a dozen volumes of his poetry to great acclaim. Although his poetic production fell off in his middle years, new collections of his poetry continued to be published and republished and he achieved the sort of fame ordinarily reserved for traditional public figures, such as actors and politicians. Seemingly indefatigable, later in his life he undertook translations of both *The Iliad* and *The Odyssey.*

As editor of the *Evening Post* he was first in the vanguard of the Free Soil movement and later a founder of the Republican party. Although relatively little of his published poetry even hints at the existence of politics, his editorials in the *Post* were influential in shaping public opinion and he was a staunch supporter of Abraham Lincoln in 1860. Yet, even when he wrote on subjects which had some currency, Bryant was careful to keep his distance. In his poem "Civil War" (1861), for example, he drew on Horace's Epode VII and was ultimately ambiguous about the war, except to deplore its fraternal bloodshed. Thus, Bryant's phenomenal career existed in two carefully separated spheres: the political journalist and the philosophical poet were never confounded. Yet, he was lionized chiefly for his poetry and his extraordinary popularity owed greatly to his ability to select subjects with which no one could disagree and then to cast them in forms recognizable and understandable to all.

Allison Heisch
San Jose State University

PRIMARY WORK

The Poetical Works of William Cullen Bryant, ed. Henry C. Sturges, 1903. AMS 1969, 1972.

SECONDARY WORK

Charles H. Brown, *William Cullen Bryant,* 1971; *William Cullen Bryant and his America: Centennial Conference Proceedings, 1878–1978,* 1983; Albert F. McLean, *William Cullen Bryant,* 1989.

Thanatopsis[1]

To him who in the love of Nature holds
Communion with her visible forms, she speaks
A various language; for his gayer hours
She has a voice of gladness, and a smile
And eloquence of beauty, and she glides
Into his darker musings, with a mild
And healing sympathy, that steals away
Their sharpness, ere he is aware. When thoughts
Of the last bitter hour come like a blight
Over thy spirit, and sad images
Of the stern agony, and shroud, and pall.
And breathless darkness, and the narrow house,
Make thee to shudder, and grow sick at heart;—
Go forth, under the open sky, and list

[1]Greek for meditation on death.

To Nature's teachings, while from all around—
Earth and her waters, and the depths of air—
Comes a still voice.—
Yet a few days, and thee
The all-beholding sun shall see no more
In all his course; nor yet in the cold ground,
Where thy pale form was laid, with many tears,
Nor in the embrace of ocean, shall exist
Thy image. Earth, that nourished thee, shall claim
Thy growth, to be resolved to earth again,
And, lost each human trace, surrendering up
Thine individual being, shalt thou go
To mix for ever with the elements,
To be a brother to the insensible rock
And to the sluggish clod, which the rude swain
Turns with his share,[2] and treads upon. The oak
Shall send his roots abroad, and pierce thy mould.

Yet not to thine eternal resting-place
Shalt thou retire alone, nor couldst thou wish
Couch more magnificent. Thou shalt lie down
With patriarchs of the infant world—with kings,
The powerful of the earth—the wise, the good,
Fair forms, and hoary seers of ages past,
All in one mighty sepulchre. The hills
Rock-ribbed and ancient as the sun,—the vales
Stretching in pensive quietness between;
The venerable woods—rivers that move
In majesty, and the complaining brooks
That make the meadows green; and, poured round all,
Old Ocean's gray and melancholy waste,—
Are but the solemn decorations all
Of the great tomb of man. The golden sun,
The planets, all the infinite host of heaven,
Are shining on the sad abodes of death,
Through the still lapse of ages. All that tread
The globe are but a handful to the tribes
That slumber in its bosom.—Take the wings
Of morning, pierce the Barcan wilderness,[3]
Or lose thyself in the continuous woods
Where rolls the Oregon, and hears no sound,
Save his own dashings—yet the dead are there:
And millions in those solitudes, since first
The flight of years began, have laid them down

[2]Plowshare. [3]A desert area of Libya.

In their last sleep—the dead reign there alone.
So shalt thou rest, and what if thou withdraw
In silence from the living, and no friend
Take note of thy departure? All that breathe
Will share thy destiny. The gay will laugh
When thou art gone, the solemn brood of care
Plod on, and each one as before will chase
His favorite phantom; yet all these shall leave
Their mirth and their employments, and shall come
And make their bed with thee. As the long train
Of ages glides away, the sons of men,
The youth in life's fresh spring, and he who goes
In the full strength of years, matron and maid,
The speechless babe and the gray-headed man—
Shall one by one be gathered to thy side,
By those, who in their turn shall follow them.
So live, that when thy summons comes to join
The innumerable caravan, which moves
To that mysterious realm, where each shall take
His chamber in the silent halls of death,
Thou go not like the quarry-slave at night,
Scourged to his dungeon, but, sustained and soothed
By an unfaltering trust, approach thy grave,
Like one who wraps the drapery of his couch
About him, and lies down to pleasant dreams.

1817

The Yellow Violet

When beechen buds begin to swell,
And woods the blue-bird's warble know,
The yellow violet's modest bell
Peeps from the last year's leaves below.

Ere russet fields their green resume,
Sweet flower, I love, in forest bare,
To meet thee, when thy faint perfume
Alone is in the virgin air.

Of all her train, the hands of Spring
First plant thee in the watery mould,
And I have seen thee blossoming
Beside the snow-bank's edges cold.

They parent sun, who bade thee view
Pale skies, and chilling moisture sip,

Has bathed thee in his own bright hue,
And streaked with jet thy glowing lip.

Yet slight thy form, and low thy seat,
And earthward bent thy gentle eye,
Unapt the passing view to meet,
When loftier flowers are flaunting nigh.

Oft, in the sunless April day,
Thy early smile has stayed my walk;
But midst the gorgeous blooms of May,
I passed thee on thy humble stalk.

So they, who climb to wealth, forget
The friends in darker fortunes tried.
I copied them—but I regret
That I should ape the ways of pride.

And when again the genial hour
Awakes the painted tribes of light.
I'll not o'erlook the modest flower
That made the woods of April bright.

1814

To a Waterfowl

Whither, midst falling dew,
While glow the heavens with the last steps of day,
Far, through their rosy depths, dost thou pursue
Thy solitary way?

Vainly the fowler's eye
Might mark thy distant flight to do thee wrong,
As, darkly painted on the crimson sky,
Thy figure floats along.

Seek'st thou the plashy brink
Of weedy lake, or marge of river wide,
Or where the rocking billows rise and sink
On the chafed ocean-side?

There is a Power whose care
Teaches thy way along that pathless coast—

The desert and illimitable air—
Lone wandering, but not lost.

All day thy wings have fanned,
At that far height, the cold, thin atmosphere,
Yet stoop not, weary, to the welcome land,
Though the dark night is near.

And soon that toil shall end;
Soon shalt thou find a summer home, and rest,
And scream among thy fellows; reeds shall bend,
Soon, o'er thy sheltered nest.

Thou'rt gone, the abyss of heaven
Hath swallowed up thy form; yet, on my heart
Deeply has sunk the lesson thou hast given,
And shall not soon depart.

He who, from zone to zone,
Guides through the boundless sky thy certain flight,
In the long way that I must tread alone,
Will lead my steps aright.

1815

To Cole, the Painter, Departing for Europe[1]

Thine eyes shall see the light of distant skies;
Yet, COLE! thy heart shall bear to Europe's strand
A living image of our own bright land,
Such as upon thy glorious canvas lies;
Lone lakes—savannas where the bison roves—
Rocks rich with summer garlands—solemn streams—
Skies, where the desert eagle wheels and screams—
Spring bloom and autumn blaze of boundless groves.
Fair scenes shall greet thee where thou goest—fair,
But different—everywhere the trace of men,
Paths, homes, graves, ruins, from the lowest glen
To where life shrinks from the fierce Alpine air.
Gaze on them, till the tears shall dim thy sight,
But keep that earlier, wilder image bright.

1829

[1]Thomas Cole, one of the "Hudson River School" of painters who, like his friend Bryant, was interested in presenting and preserving the beauties of the American landscape.

To the Fringed Gentian

Thou blossom bright with autumn dew,
And colored with the heaven's own blue,
That openest when the quiet light
Succeeds the keen and frosty night.

Thou comest not when violets lean
O'er wandering brooks and springs unseen,
Or columbines, in purple dressed,
Nod o'er the ground-bird's hidden nest.

Thou waitest late and com'st alone,
When woods are bare and birds are flown,
And frosts and shortening days portend
The aged year is near his end.

Then doth thy sweet and quiet eye
Look through its fringes to the sky,
Blue—blue—as if that sky let fall
A flower from its cerulean wall.

I would that thus, when I shall see
The hour of death draw near to me,
Hope, blossoming within my heart,
May look to heaven as I depart.

1829

The Prairies

These are the gardens of the Desert, these
The unshorn fields, boundless and beautiful,
For which the speech of England has no name—[1]
The Prairies. I behold them for the first,
And my heart swells, while the dilated sight
Takes in the encircling vastness. Lo! they stretch,
In airy undulations, far away,
As if the ocean, in his gentlest swell,
Stood still, with all his rounded billows fixed,

[1]The term "prairie" is derived from the French for meadow.

And motionless forever.—Motionless?—
No—they are all unchained again. The clouds
Sweep over with their shadows, and, beneath,
The surface rolls and fluctuates to the eye;
Dark hollows seem to glide along and chase
The sunny ridges. Breezes of the South!
Who toss the golden and the flame-like flowers,
And pass the prairie-hawk that, poised on high,
Flaps his broad wings, yet moves not—ye have played
Among the palms of Mexico and vines
Of Texas, and have crisped the limpid brooks
That from the fountains of Sonora[2] glide
Into the calm Pacific—have ye fanned
A nobler or a lovelier scene than this?
Man hath no power in all this glorious work:
The hand that built the firmament hath heaved
And smoothed these verdant swells, and sown their slopes
With herbage, planted them with island groves,
And hedged them round with forests. Fitting floor
For this magnificent temple of the sky—
With flowers whose glory and whose multitude
Rival the constellations! The great heavens
Seem to stoop down upon the scene in love,—
A nearer vault, and of a tendered blue,
Than that which bends above our eastern hills.

As o'er the verdant waste I guide my steed,
Among the high rank grass that sweeps his sides
The hollow beating of his footstep seems
A sacrilegious sound. I think of those
Upon whose rest he tramples. Are they here—
The dead of other days?—and did the dust
Of these fair solitudes once stir with life
And burn with passion? Let the mighty mounds
That overlook the rivers, or that rise
In the dim forest crowded with old oaks,
Answer. A race, that long has passed away,
Built them;[3]—a disciplined and populous race
Heaped, with long toil, the earth, while yet the Greek
Was hewing the Pentelicus[4] to forms
Of symmetry, and rearing on its rock
The glittering Parthenon. These ample fields

[2]A state in northern Mexico.

[3]Such mounds, common to much of the midwest, were erected for ceremonial or burial purposes. Bryant ascribes them to a race predating the Indians of the area.

[4]The mountain from which the Greeks quarried marble for structures like the Parthenon, the temple of the goddess Athena.

Nourished their harvests, here their herds were fed,
When haply by their stalls the bison lowed,
And bowed his maned shoulder to the yoke.
All day this desert murmured with their toils,
Till twilight blushed, and lovers walked, and wooed
In a forgotten language, and old tunes,
From instruments of unremembered form,
Gave the soft winds a voice. The red man came—
The roaming hunter tribes, warlike and fierce,
And the mound-builders vanished from the earth.
The solitude of centuries untold
Has settled where they dwelt. The prairie-wolf
Hunts in their meadows, and his fresh-dug den
Yawns by my path. The gopher mines the ground
Where stood their swarming cities. All is gone;
All—save the piles of earth that hold their bones,
The platforms where they worshipped unknown gods,
The barriers which they builded from the soil
To keep the foe at bay—till o'er the walls
The wild beleaguerers broke, and, one by one,
The strongholds of the plain were forced, and heaped
With corpses. The brown vultures of the wood
Flocked to those vast uncovered sepulchres,
And sat unscared and silent at their feast.
Haply some solitary fugitive,
Lurking in marsh and forest, till the sense
Of desolation and of fear became
Bitterer than death, yielded himself to die.
Man's better nature triumphed then. Kind words
Welcomed and soothed him; the rude conquerors
Seated the captive with their chiefs; he chose
A bride among their maidens, and at length
Seemed to forget—yet ne'er forgot—the wife
Of his first love, and her sweet little ones,
Butchered, amid their shrieks, with all his race.

Thus change the forms of being. Thus arise
Races of living things, glorious in strength,
And perish, as the quickening breath of God
Fills them, or is withdrawn. The red man, too,
Has left the blooming wilds he ranged so long,
And, nearer to the Rocky Mountains, sought
A wilder hunting-ground. The beaver builds
No longer by these streams, but far away,
On waters whose blue surface ne'er gave back
The white man's face—among Missouri's springs,
And pools whose issues swell the Oregon—

He rears his little Venice. In these plains
The bison feeds no more. Twice twenty leagues
Beyond remotest smoke of hunter's camp,
Roams the majestic brute, in herds that shake
The earth with thundering steps—yet here I meet
His ancient footprints stamped beside the pool.

Still this great solitude is quick with life.
Myriads of insects, gaudy as the flowers
They flutter over, gentle quadrupeds,
And birds, that scarce have learned the fear of man,
Are here, and sliding reptiles of the ground,
Startlingly beautiful. The graceful deer
Bounds to the wood at my approach. The bee,
A more adventurous colonist than man,
With whom he came across the eastern deep,
Fills the savannas with his murmurings,
And hides his sweets, as in the golden age,
Within the hollow oak. I listen long
To his domestic hum, and think I hear
The sound of that advancing multitude
Which soon shall fill these deserts. From the ground
Comes up the laugh of children, the soft voice
Of maidens, and the sweet and solemn hymn
Of Sabbath worshippers. The low of herds
Blends with the rustling of the heavy grain
Over the dark brown furrows. All at once
A fresher wind sweeps by, and breaks my dream,
And I am in the wilderness alone.

1832

Abraham Lincoln

Oh, slow to smite and swift to spare,
  Gentle and merciful and just!
Who, in the fear of God, didst bear
  The sword of power, a nation's trust!

In sorrow by thy bier we stand,
  Amid the awe that hushes all,
And speak the anguish of a land
  That shook with horror at thy fall.

Thy task is done; the bond are free:
  We bear thee to an honored grave,

Whose proudest monument shall be
  The broken fetters of the slave.

Pure was thy life; its bloody close
  Hath placed thee with the sons of light,
Among the noble host of those
  Who perished in the cause of Right.

1865

Lydia Howard Huntley Sigourney 1791–1865

When Lafayette, the French hero of the American Revolutionary War, visited the United States in the 1820s, a procession of schoolchildren with wreathes proclaiming "NOUS AIMONS LA FAYETTE" greeted him in the city of Hartford, Connecticut. The phrase was the refrain of a poem in his honor by Lydia Howard Huntley Sigourney. This event illuminates Sigourney's position as a writer. Her poetry, like her prose, was about public subjects—history, slavery, missionary work as well as current events—or treated personal matters, especially loss and death, as experiences common to all. In contrast to a Dickinson or an Emerson, she wrote for popular consumption and her work expressed a communal ethic based on compassionate Christianity and on orthodox republicanism.

Sigourney succeeded in being enormously popular. In 1848 the respected publishers Cary and Hart issued her selected poems as the fourth volume in their series of works by American poets, the preceding ones having been devoted to three highly regarded male writers, Bryant, Longfellow, and N. P. Willis. She was also enormously productive: at her death in 1865 she had published over fifty books. Their range attests to the variety of forms in which antebellum writers could undertake to guide the public. She wrote communitarian narratives, educational volumes, advice manuals, travel literature, temperance pieces, meditative prose and exemplary memoirs as well as a vast and varied quantity of poetry.

Sigourney's personal history was testimony to women's possibilities for self-betterment in America. Born in Norwich, Connecticut, in 1791, she was the only child of a gardener-handyman and his wife. As a child she was the protege of her father's employer, Mrs. Lathrop, and when Mrs. Lathrop died, her aristocratic family in Hartford assumed the position of patron to the talented girl. Lydia's commitments to education, writing, and charity were formed early. As a child she wrote poetry and essays and kept a journal. When her formal schooling ended she was tutored in Latin and Hebrew and conducted classes for impoverished children, among them African-Americans (something quite uncommon at the time). In 1811 she and a friend established a girl's school in Hartford. In 1814 Mrs. Lathrop's wealthy relative Daniel Wadsworth established a school for her whose pupils he gathered from among members of his circle in Hartford. Here she pursued a progressive educational policy, dispensing with the ornamental aspects of girls' education like needlework and concentrating instead on comprehension and moral development. In 1815 Wadsworth published pedagogical materials Sigourney had written as *Moral Pieces in Prose and Verse*.

Despite her success, she gave up teaching upon her engagement to Charles

Sigourney, a prominent Hartford widower whom she married in 1819 (only two of their five children lived to adulthood). Though she continued to write, her stern, conservative husband objected to public authorship and the matter was long a source of conflict in a marriage which remained unhappy. Her wish to publish prevailed, though she usually did so anonymously until her authorship of an advice book became publicly known in 1833. Henceforth she published under her name, her output soaring: in her first two years of acknowledged authorship she produced nine volumes as well as many ephemeral pieces for newspapers and magazines. Charles Sigourney's deteriorating economic circumstances probably contributed to this rate. They may also have sharpened her entrepreneurial skills. She was adroit at negotiating contracts and obtaining remunerative terms for her work, taking advantage of the substantial royalties she received for *The Girl's Reading Book* (1838) and *The Boy's Reading Book* (1839), for instance, by arranging for their adoption in numerous schools.

However assertive Sigourney was, her activities always remained within the boundaries of feminine propriety of her era. Her work was not solely for personal gain. She supported her parents and family and devoted at least ten percent of her annual income to charity. Her writing itself conformed to the idea of ladyhood to which she had paid homage in her portrait of Mrs. Lathrop in *Sketch of Connecticut* (1824): that of a conservative benevolence dedicated to the public good. Written with great skill, it was accessible to the broad readership it sought to influence. Unlike Romantic poetry, her poems are not about the subjective ego of poetic persona, nor do they appeal to readers' subjective states. They use familiar language, often language associated with hymns and the Bible, to present events like the death of an infant or spouse as painful instances of humanity's common fate. They also encourage readers' compassion for others and urge them to draw religious conclusions from the contemplation of natural processes and historical events.

Her work also asserts a notion of the American polity which, while it embraces class hierarchy, stresses cross-class obligations and represents Americans as a diverse people. In *Sketch of Connecticut* she grants voices to members of different groups in the community of Norwich—African-Americans, Native Americans, the poor, members of various religions, as well as a "Yankee" farmer. In *Lucy Howard's Journal* (1858) she advances a vision of the American West as an interdependent, though stratified, community. Sigourney's beliefs also fueled her concern about white treatment of Native Americans, which was quite unusual in her day. In her many works on Native Americans' history and circumstances she treats whites' conduct as a violation of Christian principles. As Nina Baym has noted, she did not condemn settlers' appropriation of land, but she felt they failed in Christian and republican virtues by not Christianizing Native Americans and granting them citizenship and she tried to represent Native American perspectives.

While Sigourney's professional conduct was sometimes questionable—presenting literary notables as friends when they were mere acquaintances, publishing papers intended to remain private, including, after his death, her son's personal journals—she was always true to her sense of writing as public service. She distributed many copies of her books *gratis* and published at least one at her own expense so that she could give copies away. In her memoir, *Letters of Life,* she estimates responding to two thousand letters annually and lists some of the curious requests she received from complete strangers, including one for an ode to a dead canary. Numerous letters from readers attest to the consolation and sustenance her work provided her contemporaries. The low esteem in which public literature—and most women writers—have long been held has allowed twentieth-century commentators to repeat with contempt her antebellum sobriquet "the Sweet Singer of Hartford." Yet her great success and the seriousness with which she pursued her vocation make it worth our while to explore both the nature of her appeal and the potential, as well as the limits, of popular antebellum writing.

Sandra A. Zagarell
Oberlin College

PRIMARY WORKS

Traits of the Aborigines of America, 1822; *Sketch of Connecticut, Forty Years Since,* 1824; *Poems,* 1827; *Zinzendorff and Other Poems,* 1835; *Illustrated Poems,* 1848; *Past Meridian,* 1854; *Lucy Howard's Journal,* 1858; *Letters of Life,* 1866.

SECONDARY WORKS

Gordon Haight, *The Sweet Singer of Hartford,* 1931; Sandra A. Zagarell, "Expanding 'America': Lydia Sigourney's *Sketch of Connecticut,* Catharine Sedgwick's *Hope Leslie,*" *Tulsa Studies in Women's Literature* 6 (1987); May G. DeJong, "Profile: Lydia Howard Huntley Sigourney," *Legacy* 5 (1988); Annie Finch, "The Sentimental Poetess in the World: Metaphor and Subjectivity in Lydia Sigourney's Nature Poetry," *Legacy* 5 (1988); Nina Baym, "Reinventing Lydia Sigourney," *American Literature* 62 (1990); Sharon Harris, ed., *Redefining the Political Novel: American Women Writers, 1797–1901,* 1995.

The Suttee[1]

She sat upon the pile by her dead lord,
And in her full, dark eye, and shining hair
Youth revell'd.—The glad murmur of the crowd
Applauding her consent to the dread doom,
And the hoarse chanting of infuriate priests
She heeded not, for her quick ear had caught
An infant's wail.—Feeble and low that moan,
Yet it was answer'd in her heaving heart,
For the Mimosa in its shrinking fold
From the rude pressure, is not half so true,
So tremulous, as is a mother's soul
Unto her wailing babe.—There was such wo
In her imploring aspect,—in her tones
Such thrilling agony, that even the hearts
Of the flame-kindlers soften'd, and they laid
The famish'd infant on her yearning breast.
There with his tear-wet cheek he lay and drew
Plentiful nourishment from that full fount
Of infant happiness,—and long he prest

[1]From *Poems by the author of Moral pieces in prose and verse* (1827). "Suttee" was an Indian (that is, from India) practice in which a widow was immolated along with her husband's corpse. Suttee was supposed to be voluntary.

With eager lip the chalice of his joy.—
And then his little hands he stretch'd to grasp
His mother's flower-wove tresses, and with smile
And gay caress embraced his bloated sire,—
As if kind Nature taught that innocent one
With fond delay to cheat the hour which seal'd
His hopeless orphanage.—But those were near
Who mock'd such dalliance, as that Spirit malign
Who twined his serpent length mid Eden's bowers
Frown'd on our parents' bliss.—The victim mark'd
Their harsh intent, and clasp'd the unconscious babe
With such convulsive force, that when they tore
His writhing form away, the very nerves
Whose deep-sown fibres rack the inmost soul
Uprooted seem'd.—
With voice of high command
Tossing her arms, she bade them bring her son,—
And then in maniac rashness sought to leap
Among the astonish'd throng.—But the rough cord
Compress'd her slender limbs, and bound her fast
Down to her loathsome partner.—Quick the fire
In showers was hurl'd upon the reeking pile;—
But yet amid the wild, demoniac shout
Of priest and people, mid the thundering yell
Of the infernal gong,—was heard to rise
Thrice a dire death-shriek.—And the men who stood
Near the red pile and heard that fearful cry,
Call'd on their idol-gods, and stopp'd their ears,
And oft amid their nightly dream would start
As frighted Fancy echoed in her cell
That burning mother's scream.

1827

Death of an Infant[1]

Death found strange beauty on that polish'd brow,
And dash'd it out. There was a tint of rose

[1]From *Select Poems,* sixth ed., revised and corrected, 1848. Sigourney's most widely anthologized poem. Sigourney notes, "This little poem has been inserted by mistake, in one of the American editions of the late Mrs. Hemans. Though this is accounted by the real author, as an honor, it is still proper to state, that it was originally composed at Hartford, in the winter of 1824, and comprised in a volume of poems, published in Boston, by S. G. Goodrich, Esq., in 1827. Should other testimony be necessary, it may be mentioned that a letter from Mrs. Hemans, to a friend in this country, pointing out some poems in that volume which pleased her, designated, among others, this "Death of an Infant."

On cheek and lip. He touched the veins with ice,
And the rose faded.
Forth from those blue eyes
There spake a wishful tenderness, a doubt
Whether to grieve or sleep, which innocence
Alone may wear. With ruthless haste he bound
The silken fringes of those curtaining lids
For ever.
There had been a murmuring sound,
With which the babe would claim its mother's ear,
Charming her even to tears. The spoiler set
The seal of silence.
But there beam'd a smile,
So fix'd, so holy, from that cherub brow,
Death gazed, and left it there. He dar'd not steal
The signet-ring of Heaven.

1827

The Father[1]

"Yes,—I am he,—who look'd and saw decay
Steal o'er the lov'd of earth,—the ador'd too much.—
It is a fearful thing, to love what Death may touch."
—MRS. HEMANS[2]

I was in the full tide of a laborious and absorbing profession,—of one which imposes on intellect an unsparing discipline, but ultimately opens the avenues to wealth and fame. I pursued it, as one determined on distinction,—as one convinced that *mind* may assume a degree of omnipotence over matter and circumstance, and popular opinion. Ambition's promptings were strong within me, nor was its career unprosperous.—I had no reason to complain that its promises were deceptive, or its harvest tardy.

Yet as my path was among the competitions and asperities of men, a character combining strong elements might have been in danger of becoming indurated, had it not been softened and refined by the domestic charities. Conjugal love, early fixing on an object most amiable and beautiful, was as a fountain of living water, springing up to allay thirst, and to renovate weariness. I was anxious that my home should be the centre of intellectual and polished society, where the buddings of thought should expand unchilled, and those social feelings which are the life-blood of existence, flow forth, unfettered by heartless ceremony.—And it was so.

[1]From *Sketches* (1834).
[2]Felicia Dorothea (Brown) Hemans (1793–1835), English poet.

But my present purpose is to delineate a single, and simple principle of our nature,—the most deep-rooted and holy,—*the love of a father for a daughter.* My province has led me to analyze mankind; and in doing this, I have sometimes thrown their affections into the crucible. And the one of which I speak, has come forth most pure, most free from drossy admixture. Even the earth that combines with it, is not like other earth. It is what the foot of a seraph might rest upon, and contract no pollution. With the love of our sons, ambition mixes its spirit, till it becomes a fiery essence. We anticipate great things for them,—we covet honors,—we goad them on in the race of glory;—if they are victors, we too proudly exult,—if vanquished, we are prostrate and in bitterness. Perhaps we detect in them the same latent perverseness, with which we have waged warfare in our own breasts, or some imbecility of purpose with which we have no affinity; and then, from the very nature of our love, an impatience is generated, which they have no power to soothe, or we to control. A father loves his son, as he loves himself,—and in all selfishness, there is a bias to disorder and pain. But his love for his daughter is different and more disinterested; possibly he believes that it is called forth by a being of a higher and better order. It is based on the integral and immutable principles of his nature. It recognizes the sex in hearts, and from the very gentleness and mystery of womanhood, takes that coloring and zest which romance gathers from remote antiquity. It draws nutriment from circumstances which he may not fully comprehend, from the power which she possesses to awaken his sympathies, to soften his irritability, to sublimate his aspirations;—while the support and protection which she claims in return, elevate him with a consciousness of assimilation to the ministry of those benevolent and powerful spirits, who ever "bear us up in their hands, lest we dash our foot against a stone."

I should delight longer to dwell on this development of affection, for who can have known it more perfectly in its length and breadth, in its depth and height? I had a daughter, beautiful in infancy, to whom every year added some new charm to awaken admiration, or to rivet love. To me, it was of no slight import, that she resembled her mother, and that in grace and accomplishment, she early surpassed her contemporaries. I was desirous that her mind should be worthy of the splendid temple allotted for its habitation. I decided to render it familiar with the whole circle of the arts and sciences. I was not satisfied with the commendation of her teachers. I determined to take my seat in the sacred pavilion of intellect, and superintend what entered there. But how should one buried beneath the ponderous tomes and Sysiphean toils of jurisprudence, gain freedom, or undivided thought, for such minute supervision? A father's love can conquer, if it cannot create. I deprived myself of sleep: I sat till the day dawned, gathering materials for the lectures that I gave her. I explored the annals of architecture and sculpture, the recesses of literature and poetry, the labyrinthine and colossal treasure-houses of history,—I entered the ancient catacombs of the illustrious dead, traversed the regions of the dim and shadowy past, with no coward step,—ransacked earth and heaven, to add one gem to her casket. At stated periods, I required her to condense, to illustrate, to combine, what I had brought her. I listened, with wonder, to her intuitive eloquence: I gazed with intense delight upon the intellect that I thus embellished,—upon the Corinthian capital[3] that I had erected and

[3]An elaborately graceful pillar in Greek architecture.

adorned. Not a single acanthus-leaf started forth, but I cherished and fostered it with the dews of a father's blessing.

Yet while the outpoured riches of a masculine understanding were thus incorporating themselves with her softer structure, I should not have been content, unless she had also borne the palm of female grace and loveliness. Was it therefore nothing to me, that she evinced in her bloom of youth, a dignity surpassing her sex, that in symmetry she restored the image of the Medicean Venus,[4] that amid the circles of rank and fashion, she was the model—the cynosure? Still was she saved from that vanity which would have been the destroyer of all these charms, by the hallowed prevalence of her filial piety. It was *for my sake,* that she strove to render herself the most graceful among women,—*for my sake,* that she rejoiced in the effect of her attainments. Her gentle and just nature felt that the "husbandman who had labored, should be first partaker of the fruits." Returning from those scenes of splendor, where she was the object of every eye, the theme of every tongue, when the youthful bosom might be forgiven for inflation from the clouds of incense that had breathed upon it, to the inquiry of her mother, if she had been happy, the tender and sweet reply was, "Yes,—because I saw that my dear father was so."

Sometimes, I was conscious of gathering roughness from the continual conflict with passion and prejudice, and that the fine edge of the feelings could not ever be utterly proof against the corrosions of such an atmosphere. Then I sought my home, and called my bird of song, and listened to the warbling of her high, heaven-toned voice. The melody of that music fell upon my soul, like oil upon the troubled billows,—and all was tranquil. I wondered where my perturbations had fled, but still more, that I had ever indulged them. Sometimes, the turmoil and fluctuation of the world, threw a shade of dejection over me: then it was her pride to smooth my brow, and to restore its smile. Once, a sorrow of no common order had fallen upon me; it rankled in my breast, like a dagger's point; I came to my house, but I shunned all its inmates. I threw myself down, in solitude, that I might wrestle alone with my fate, and subdue it; a light footstep approached, but I heeded it not. A form of beauty was on the sofa, by my side, but I regarded it not. Then my hand was softly clasped, breathed upon,—pressed to ruby lips. It was enough. I took my daughter in my arms, and my sorrow vanished. Had she essayed the hackneyed expressions of sympathy, or even the usual epithets of endearment, I might have desired her to leave my presence. Had she uttered only a single word, it would have been too much, so wounded was my spirit within me. But the deed, the very poetry of tenderness, breathing, not speaking, melted "the winter of my discontent." Ever was she endued with that most exquisite of woman's perfections, a knowledge both *when* to be silent, and *where* to speak,—and *so* to speak, that the frosts might dissolve from around the heart she loved, and its discords be tuned to harmony.

Thus was she my comforter, and in every hour of our intercourse, was my devotion to her happiness richly repaid. Was it strange that I should gaze on the work of my own hands with ineffable delight? At twilight I quickened my homeward step, with the thought of that countenance, which was both my evening and morning star; as the bird nerves her wearied wing, when she hears from the still-distant forest, the chirpings of her own nest.

[4]A well-known statue of the goddess, now in the Uffizi museum.

I sat in the house of God, in the silence of sabbath meditation, and tears of thrilling exultation moistened my eyes. I gazed upon my glorious creature, in the stainless blossom of unfolding youth, and my whole soul overflowed with a father's pride. I said, *What more can man desire?* I challenged the whole earth to add another drop to my cup of felicity. Did I forget to give glory to the Almighty, that his decree even then went forth, to smite down my idol?

I came from engrossing toil, and found her restless, with strange fire upon her cheek. Fever had lain rankling in her veins, and they had concealed it from me. I raved. I filled my house with physicians. I charged them wildly to restore her to health and to me. It was in vain. I saw that God claimed her. His will was written upon her brow. The paleness and damps of the tomb settled upon her.

I knelt by the bed of death, and gave her back to her Creator. Amid the tears and groans of mourners, I lifted up a firm voice. A fearful courage entered into me. I seemed to rush even upon the buckler of the Eternal. I likened myself unto him who, on Mount Moria, "stretched forth his hand, and took the knife to slay his son."[5] The whole energy of my nature armed itself for the awful conflict. I gloried in my strength to suffer. With terrible sublimity, I stood forth, as the High Priest of my smitten and astonished household. I gave the lamb in sacrifice, with an unshrinking hand, though it was my own heart's blood, that steeped, and streamed over the altar.

It was over. She had gone. She stayed not for my embraces. She was permitted to give me no parting-token. The mind that I had adored, shrouded itself and fled. I knew that the seal upon those eyes must not be broken, till the trump of the Archangel.

Three days and nights, I sat by the dead. Beauty lingered there, in deep, and solemn, and sacred repose. I laid my head upon her pillow. I pressed my lips to hers, and their ice entered into my soul. I spoke to her of the angels, her companions. I talked long to the beautiful spirit, and methought, it answered me. Then I listened breathlessly, but "there was no voice, nor any that regarded." And still, I wept not.

The fatal day came, in which even that clay was to be no longer mine. The funeral knell, with its heavy, yet suppressed summons, came over me like the dividing of soul and body. There was a flood of weeping, when that form, once so replete with every youthful charm, so instinct with the joyous movement of the mysterious principle of life, was borne in marble stillness from its paternal halls. The eye of the mother that bore her, of the friend that had but casually beheld her, even of the poor menial that waited upon her, knew the luxury of tears. All were wet with that balm of sorrow, to overflowing—*all save mine.*

The open grave had a revolting aspect. I could not bear that the form which I had worshipped, should be left to its cold and hideous guardianship. At the hollow sound of the first falling clod, I would fain have leaped into the pit, and demanded her. But I ruled myself. I committed her to the frozen earth, without a tear. There was a tremendous majesty in such grief. I was a wonder to myself.

I returned to my desolated abode. The silence that reigned there was appalling. My spirit sank beneath it, as a stone goes down into the depths of ocean, bearing the everlasting burden of its fathomless tide. I sought the room where I had last seen her,

[5]That is, the Old Testament patriarch Abraham. See Genesis 22:10.

arrayed in the vestments of the tomb. There lay the books which we had read together. Their pages bore the marks of her pencil. I covered my eyes from them, and turned away. I bowed down to inhale the fragrance of her flowers, and felt that they had no right to bloom so fair, when she, their culturer and their queen, was blighted. I pressed my fingers upon the keys of her piano, and started back at the mournful sound they made. I wandered to her own apartment. I threw myself on the couch where from infancy she had slumbered. I trusted to have wept there. But my grief was too mighty, to be thus unchained. It disdained the relief of tears. I seemed to rush as upon a drawn sword, and still it refused to pierce me.

Yet all this was when no eye saw me. In the presence of others, I was like Mount Atlas,[6] bearing unmoved the stormy heavens upon his shoulders.

I went forth, amid the jarring competitions and perpetual strifes of men. I adjusted their opposing interests, while I despised them and their concerns. I unravelled their perplexities. I penetrated their subterfuges. I exposed their duplicity. I cut the Gordian knots of their self-conceit. I made the "crooked straight, and the rough places plain,"—with an energy that amazed them and myself. It was like that of a spirit, which has nothing to do with the flesh. I suffered the tumult of my soul to breathe itself out in bursts of stormy declamation. I exerted the strength of a giant, when it was not required. I scorned to balance power with necessity. The calculations of prudence, and the devices of cunning, seemed equally pitiful, and despicable. I put forth the same effort to crush an emmet, as to uproot the oak of a thousand centuries. It was sufficient for me always to triumph. While men marvelled at the zeal with which I served them, I was loathing them in my heart. I was sick of their chicanery, and their sabbathless rush after empty honors and perishable dross. The whole world seemed to me, "less than nothing, and vanity." Still, I was sensible of neither toil, nor fatigue, nor physical exhaustion. I was like one, who in his troubled dream of midnight, treads on air, and finds it strangely sustaining him.

But every night, I went to my daughter's grave. I laid me down there, in unutterable bitterness. While the stars looked coldly on me, I spoke to her fondly and earnestly, as one who could not be denied. I said,—"Angel! who art mine no longer, listen to me. Thou, who art raised above all tears, cause *one tear* to moisten my burning brow. Give it to me, as a token that thou hearest me, that thou hast not forgotten me." And the blasts of Winter, through the leafless boughs, mocking replied,—"*Give it to me,—Give it to me.*" But I wept not. Ten days and nights passed over me,—and still I wept not.

My brain was heated to agony. The visual nerves were scorched and withered. My heart was parched and arid, as the Libyan desert. Then I knew that the throne of Grief was in *the heart:* that though her sceptre may reach the remotest nerve, and touch the minutest cell where the brain slumbers, and perplex every ethereal ambassador from spirit to sense,—yet the pavilion where her darkest dregs are wrung out, the laboratory where her consuming fires are compounded, is *the heart,—the heart.*

I have implied that my intellect faltered. Yet every morning I went to the scene of my labors. I put my shoulder to the wheel, caring not though it crushed me. I

[6]In Greek mythology, the defeated Titan Atlas was condemned to hold up the earth and the sky.

looked at men fixedly and haughtily with my red eye-balls. But I spoke no word to betray the flame feeding at my vitals. The heartstrings shrivelled and broke before it, yet the martyrdom was in silence.

Again, Night drew her sable curtain, and I sought my daughter's grave. Methought, its turf-covering was discomposed, and some half-rooted shrubs that shuddered and drooped when placed in that drear assemblage of the dead, had been trampled and broken. A horrible suspicion took possession of my mind. I rushed to the house of the sexton.—"Has any one troubled my daughter's grave?" Alarmed at my vehemence, he remained speechless and irresolute.

"Tell me," I exclaimed, in a voice of terror, "who has disturbed my daughter's grave." He evaded my adjuration, and murmured something about an injunction to secrecy. With the grasp of a maniac, I bore him to an inner apartment, and bade him satisfy my question. Trembling at my violence, he confessed that the grave had been watched for ten nights.

"Who has watched my daughter's grave?" Reluctantly he gave me the names of those friends,—names for ever graven upon my soul.

And so, for those ten long, wintry nights, so dreary and interminable, which I had cast away amid the tossings of profitless, delirious, despairing sorrow, they had been watching, that the repose of that unsullied clay might remain unbroken.

A new tide of emotion was awakened. I threw myself down, as powerless as the weaned infant. Torrents of tears flowed. The tenderness of man wrought what the severity of Heaven had failed to produce. It was not the earthquake, nor the thunder, nor the tempest, that subdued me. It was the still, small voice. I wept until the fountains of tears failed. The relief of that hour of weeping, can never be shadowed forth in language. The prison-house of passionate agony was unlocked. I said to God that he was merciful, and I loved him because my angel lived in his presence. Since then, it would seem, that my heart has been made better. Its aspirations are upward, whither she has ascended, and as I tread the devious path of my pilgrimage, both the sunbeam and the thorn point me as a suppliant to the Redeemer of Man, that I may be at last fitted to dwell with her for ever.

1833

The Indian's Welcome to the Pilgrim Fathers[1]

"On Friday, March 16th, 1622, while the colonists were busied in their usual labors, they were much surprised to see a savage walk boldly towards them, and salute them with, 'much welcome, English, much welcome, Englishmen.'"

Above them spread a stranger sky
　Around, the sterile plain,

[1]From *Zinzendorff and Other Poems* (1835).

The rock-bound coast rose frowning nigh,
  Beyond,—the wrathful main:
Chill remnants of the wintry snow
  Still chok'd the encumber'd soil,
Yet forth these Pilgrim Fathers go,
  To mark their future toil.

'Mid yonder vale their corn must rise
  In Summer's ripening pride,
And there the church-spire woo the skies
  Its sister-school beside.
Perchance 'mid England's velvet green
  Some tender thought repos'd,—
Though nought upon their stoic mien.
  Such soft regret disclos'd.

When sudden from the forest wide
  A red-brow'd chieftain came,
With towering form, and haughty stride,
  And eye like kindling flame:
No wrath he breath'd, no conflict sought,
  To no dark ambush drew,
But simply *to the Old World brought,*
  The welcome of the New.

That *welcome* was a blast and ban
  Upon thy race unborn.
Was there no seer, thou fated Man!
  Thy lavish zeal to warn?
Thou in thy fearless faith didst hail
  A weak, invading band,
But who shall heed thy children's wail,
  Swept from their native land?

Thou gav'st the riches of thy streams,
  The lordship o'er thy waves,
The region of thine infant dreams,
  And of thy fathers' graves,
But who to yon proud mansions pil'd
  With wealth of earth and sea,
Poor outcast from thy forest wild,
  Say, who shall welcome thee?

1835

Indian Names[1]

"How can the Red men be forgotten, while so many of our states and territories, bays, lakes and rivers, are indelibly stamped by names of their giving?"

Ye say, they all have passed away,
That noble race and brave,
That their light canoes have vanished
From off the crested wave;
That 'mid the forests where they roamed
There rings no hunter's shout;
But their name is on your waters,
Ye may not wash it out.

'Tis where Ontario's billow
Like Ocean's surge is curl'd,
Where strong Niagara's thunders wake
The echo of the world,
Where red Missouri bringeth
Rich tributes from the west,
And Rappahannock sweetly sleeps
On green Virginia's breast.

Ye say, their cone-like cabins,
That clustered o'er the vale,
Have fled away like withered leaves
Before the autumn gale:
But their memory liveth on your hills,
Their baptism on your shore,
Your everlasting rivers speak
Their dialect of yore.

Old Massachusetts wears it
Within her lordly crown,
And broad Ohio bears it
Amid her young renown;
Connecticut hath wreathed it
Where her quiet foliage waves,
And bold Kentucky breathes it hoarse
Through all her ancient caves.

[1]From *Select Poems,* sixth edition, revised and corrected (1848).

Wachuset hides its lingering voice
  Within his rocky heart,
And Alleghany graves its tone
  Throughout his lofty chart;
Monadnock on his forehead hoar
  Doth seal the sacred trust,
Your mountains build their monument,
  Though ye destroy their dust.

1838

The Needle, Pen, and Sword[1]

What hast thou seen, with thy shining eye,
  Thou Needle, so subtle and keen?—
"I have been in Paradise, stainless and fair.
And fitted the apron of fig-leaves there,
  To the form of its fallen queen.

"The mantles and wimples, the hoods and veils,
  That the belles of Judah wore,
When their haughty mien and their glance of fire
Enkindled the eloquent prophet's ire,
  I help'd to fashion of yore.

"The beaded belt of the Indian maid
  I have deck'd with as true a zeal
As the gorgeous ruff of the knight of old,
Or the monarch's mantle of purple and gold,
  Or the satrap's broider'd heel.

"I have lent to Beauty new power to reign,
  At bridal and courtly hall,
Or wedded to Fashion, have help'd to bind
Those gossamer links, that the strongest mind
  Have sometimes held in thrall.

"I have drawn a blood-drop, round and red,
  From the finger small and white
Of the startled child, as she strove with care
Her doll to deck with some gewgaw rare,
  But wept at my puncture bright.

[1]From *Illustrated Poems* (1849).

"I have gazed on the mother's patient brow,
As my utmost speed she plied,
To shield from winter her children dear,
And the knell of midnight smote her ear,
While they slumber'd at her side.

"I have heard in the hut of the pining poor
The shivering inmate's sigh,
When faded the warmth of her last, faint brand,
As slow from her cold and clammy hand
She let me drop,—*to die!*"

* * *

What dost thou know, thou gray goose-quill?—
And methought, with a spasm of pride,
It sprang from the inkstand, and flutter'd in vain,
Its nib to free from the ebon stain,
As it fervently replied:

"*What do I know!*—Let the lover tell
When into his secret scroll
He poureth the breath of a magic lyre,
And traceth those mystical lines of fire
That move the maiden's soul.

"*What do I know!*—The wife can say,
As the leaden seasons move,
And over the ocean's wildest sway,
A blessed missive doth wend its way,
Inspired by a husband's love.

"Do ye doubt my power? Of the statesman ask,
Who buffets ambition's blast,—
Of the convict, who shrinks in his cell of care,
A flourish of mine hath sent him there,
And lock'd his fetters fast;

"And a flourish of mine can his prison ope,
From the gallows its victim save,
Break off the treaty that kings have bound,
Make the oath of a nation an empty sound,
And to liberty lead the slave.

"Say, what were History, so wise and old,
And Science that reads the sky?
Or how could Music its sweetness store,

Or Fancy and Fiction their treasures pour,
Or what were Poesy's heaven-taught lore,
Should the pen its aid deny?

"Oh, doubt if ye will, that the rose is fair,
That the planets pursue their way,
Go, question the fires of the noontide sun,
Or the countless streams that to ocean run,
But ask no more what the Pen hath done."
And it scornfully turn'd away.

* * *

What are thy deeds, thou fearful thing
By the lordly warrior's side?
And the Sword answer'd, stern and slow,
"The hearth-stone lone and the orphan know,
And the pale and widow'd bride.

"The shriek and the shroud of the battle-cloud,
And the field that doth reek below,
The wolf that laps where the gash is red,
And the vulture that tears ere the life hath fled,
And the prowling robber that strips the dead,
And the foul hyena know.

"The rusted plough, and the seed unsown,
And the grass that doth rankly grow
O'er the rotting limb, and the blood-pool dark,
Gaunt Famine that quenches life's lingering spark,
And the black-wing'd Pestilence know.

"Death with the rush of his harpy-brood,
Sad Earth in her pang and throe,
Demons that riot in slaughter and crime,
And the throng of the souls sent, before their time,
To the bar of the judgment—know."

Then the terrible Sword to its sheath return'd,
While the Needle sped on in peace,
But the Pen traced out from a Book sublime
The promise and pledge of that better time
When the warfare of earth shall cease.

1849

Niagara[1]

Flow on for ever, in thy glorious robe
Of terror and of beauty. Yea, flow on
Unfathom'd and resistless. God hath set
His rainbow on thy forehead, and the cloud
Mantled around thy feet. And he doth give
Thy voice of thunder power to speak of Him
Eternally—bidding the lip of man
Keep silence—and upon thine altar pour
Incense of awe-struck praise.
Earth fears to lift
The insect-trump that tells her trifling joys
Or fleeting triumphs, mid the peal sublime
Of thy tremendous hymn. Proud Ocean shrinks
Back from thy brotherhood, and all his waves
Retire abash'd. For he hath need to sleep,
Sometimes, like a spent labourer, calling home
His boisterous billows, from their vexing play,
To a long dreary calm: but thy strong tide
Faints not, nor e'er with failing heart forgets
Its everlasting lesson, night nor day.
The morning stars, that hail'd creation's birth,
Heard thy hoarse anthem mixing with their song
Jehovah's name; and the dissolving fires,
That wait the mandate of the day of doom
To wreck the earth, shall find it deep inscribed
Upon thy rocky scroll.
The lofty trees
That list thy teachings, scorn the lighter lore
Of the too fitful winds; while their young leaves
Gather fresh greenness from thy living spray,
Yet tremble at the baptism. Lo! yon birds,
How bold they venture near, dipping their wing
In all thy mist and foam. Perchance 'tis meet
For them to touch thy garment's hem, or stir
Thy diamond wreath, who sport upon the cloud
Unblamed, or warble at the gate of heaven
Without reproof. But, as for us, it seems
Scarce lawful with our erring lips to talk
Familiarly of thee. Methinks, to trace
Thine awful features with our pencil's point
Were but to press on Sinai.

[1]From *Illustrated Poems* (1849). Mrs. Sigourney's best-known nature poem.

Thou dost speak
Alone of God, who pour'd thee as a drop
From his right-hand,—bidding the soul that looks
Upon thy fearful majesty be still,
Be humbly wrapp'd in its own nothingness,
And lose itself in Him.

1849

To a Shred of Linen[1]

Would they swept cleaner!
Here's a littering shred
Of linen left behind—a vile reproach
To all good housewifery. Right glad am I
That no neat lady, train'd in ancient times
Of pudding-making, and of sampler-work,
And speckless sanctity of household care,
Hath happen'd here to spy thee. She, no doubt,
Keen looking through her spectacles, would say,
"This comes of reading books." Or some spruce beau,
Essenced and lily-handed, had he chanced
To scan thy slight superfices, 'twould be,
"This comes of writing poetry."—Well, well,
Come forth, offender!—hast thou aught to say?
Canst thou, by merry thought or quaint conceit,
Repay this risk that I have run for thee?
——Begin at alpha, and resolve thyself
Into thine elements. I see the stalk
And bright blue flower of flax, which erst o'erspread
That fertile land, where mighty Moses stretch'd
His rod miraculous. I see thy bloom
Tinging, too scantly, these New England vales.
But, lo! the sturdy farmer lifts his flail
To crush thy bones unpitying, and his wife,
With kerchief'd head and eye brimfull of dust,
Thy fibrous nerves with hatchel-tooth divides.
——I hear a voice of music—and behold!
The ruddy damsel singeth at her wheel,[2]
While by her side the rustic lover sits.
Perchance, his shrewd eye secretly doth count
The mass of skeins, which, hanging on the wall,

[1]From *Illustrated Poems* (1849).
[2]Spinning.

Increaseth day by day. Perchance his thought
(For men have deeper minds than women—sure!)
Is calculating what a thrifty wife
The maid will make; and how his dairy shelves
Shall groan beneath the weight of golden cheese,
Made by her dexterous hand, while many a keg
And pot of butter to the market borne,
May, transmigrated, on his back appear
In new thanksgiving coats.
Fain would I ask,
Mine own New England, for thy once loved wheel,
By sofa and piano quite displaced.
Why dost thou banish from thy parlour hearth
That old Hygeian[3] harp, whose magic ruled
Dyspepsia, as the minstrel-shepherd's skill
Exorcised Saul's ennui? There was no need,
In those good times of callisthenics, sure;
And there was less of gadding, and far more
Of home-born, heart-felt comfort, rooted strong
In industry, and bearing such rare fruit
As wealth might never purchase.
But come back,
Thou shred of linen. I did let thee drop
In my harangue, as wiser ones have lost
The thread of their discourse. What was thy lot
When the rough battery of the loom had stretch'd
And knit thy sinews, and the chemist sun
Thy brown complexion bleach'd?
Methinks I scan
Some idiosyncrasy that marks thee out
A defunct pillow-case. Did the trim guest,
To the best chamber usher'd, e'er admire
The snowy whiteness of thy freshen'd youth,
Feeding thy vanity? or some sweet babe
Pour its pure dream of innocence on thee?
Say, hast thou listen'd to the sick one's moan,
When there was none to comfort?—or shrunk back
From the dire tossings of the proud man's brow?
Or gather'd from young beauty's restless sigh
A tale of untold love?
Still close and mute!—
Wilt tell no secrets, ha?—Well then, go down,
With all thy churl-kept hoard of curious lore,
In majesty and mystery, go down
Into the paper-mill, and from its jaws,

[3]Hygeia was the Greek goddess of health.

Stainless and smooth, emerge. Happy shall be
The renovation, if on thy fair page
Wisdom and truth their hallow'd lineaments
Trace for posterity. So shall thine end
Be better than thy birth, and worthier bard
Thine apotheosis immortalize.

1849

Henry Wadsworth Longfellow 1807–1882

Henry Wadsworth Longfellow was born in Portland, Maine, when it was still part of the Commonwealth of Massachusetts. He was educated at Portland Academy and along with his older brother Stephen entered Bowdoin College in Brunswick, Maine, in 1822, at the age of fifteen. He graduated in 1825, in the same class as Nathaniel Hawthorne, and resisting his father's wishes that he follow in his footsteps and take up the law, Longfellow persuaded his father to underwrite informal postgraduate study in Europe. He had been offered a newly created professorship in modern languages at Bowdoin, but the position was contingent upon his undertaking further study of French and Spanish. For the next three years, Longfellow lived and studied in France, Germany, Spain, and Italy, returning to take up his post as professor (and part-time college librarian) in September 1829. During his six years at Bowdoin, Longfellow turned out French, Italian, and Spanish textbooks, published translations and a travel book, *Outre-Mer: A Pilgrimage Beyond the Sea,* written in the fashion of Washington Irving's popular *Sketch Book.*

In 1834, when Harvard College offered him the Smith Professorship of French and Spanish, it was once more conditional upon further study, this time of German. So in April 1835, with his wife, Mary Storer Potter, he sailed once more to Europe. But Mary, after suffering a miscarriage, died in Rotterdam, and Longfellow took himself off to Heidelberg, trying to immerse himself in books to overcome his grief.

The following spring, when Longfellow's passport difficulties forced him to go to the Tyrol, in Switzerland, rather than to Italy, he chanced to meet Fanny Appleton, the daughter of a prominent Beacon Hill family. Seven years later Fanny, who was initially reluctant and ten years younger than he, finally agreed to marry him, and her family made them a present of Craigie House, a few blocks down Brattle Street from Harvard Yard. Now called the Longfellow Historic Site, the house still stands. Longfellow remained at Harvard until 1854, when he resigned in order to devote himself completely to poetry. He was succeeded in his post by James Russell Lowell.

By all accounts his marriage was a happy one; yet Longfellow's domestic life was to be the source of profound sorrow. They had six children, but two of them did not live much more than a year, and their son Charles was persistently troubled. But most tragically, in July 1861, in the eighteenth year of their marriage, Fanny's dress caught fire in a freak accident and she died of her injuries, Longfellow having been unable to quench the flames in time to save her life. Left to raise the children himself, Longfellow now grew the full beard with which he is always pictured, quite possibly to cover the scars from his badly burned face, and for the next twenty-one years he lived as a widower in Craigie House, becoming increasingly famous with the passing years.

During his first years at Harvard, Longfellow was able to publish several volumes of poetry, including *Voices of the Night* (1839), *Ballads and Other Poems* (1841), and a collection of abolitionist ballads called *Poems on Slavery* (1842), but it was not until 1845 that he began to publish the dramatic compositions for which he earned a great part of his popular reputation. The idyllic *Evangeline,* published in 1847, tells the tragic story of the heroine's search for her lover. Longfellow set his story in America. Indeed, Evangeline wanders through a great deal of America before finding her lover in a Philadelphia almshouse just before his death. The poem is written in unrhymed hexameter lines modelled on the Greek and Latin lines of the epic poems of Homer and Virgil.

Longfellow used the same hexameter line for *The Courtship of Miles Standish* (1856), another dramatic rendering of American legend. As with *The Song of Hiawatha* (1855), for which Longfellow contrived an accentual, unrhymed stanza to imitate the sound of oral folk narrative, *Evangeline* and *The Courtship of Miles Standish* are poems rooted in a scholar's understanding of poetic history and form. In choosing domestic legends and casting them in classical forms, Longfellow was attempting to create an American epic poetry. Unfortunately, poems so easily memorised are sitting targets for parody, and the fact that these three great poems were recited by generations of school children has inevitably distorted both their importance and Longfellow's achievement.

Always accessible, Longfellow's poems reflect his wide reading and cultural breadth—so much so, in fact, that Poe accused him of poaching. And although the sentiments of old favorites such as "A Psalm of Life" may seem to our somewhat cynical, late-twentieth-century ears to be simplistic, Longfellow's uplifting moral verses, like his memorable narrative poems, added inestimably to a growing American literary voice. His seventy-fifth birthday was an occasion for national celebration, and his reputation in England, where he was acknowledged the equal of poets such as Wordsworth and Tennyson, earned him a bust in the poet's corner at Westminster Abbey.

Allison Heisch
San Jose State University

PRIMARY WORKS

Poems, 1886; 1891; *The Poems of Henry Wadsworth Longfellow,* ed. Louis Untermeyer, 1961.

SECONDARY WORKS

Edward Wagenknecht, *Henry Wadsworth Longfellow: Portrait of an American Humanist,* 1966; Kenneth W. Cameron, *Longfellow Among His Contemporaries,* 1978; Edward Wagenknecht, *Henry Wadsworth Longfellow, His Poetry and Prose,* 1986.

A Psalm of Life

What the Heart of the Young Man Said to the Psalmist

Tell me not, in mournful numbers,[1]
　　Life is but an empty dream!—

[1]Poetic rhythms.

For the soul is dead that slumbers,
And things are not what they seem.

Life is real! Life is earnest!
And the grave is not its goal;
Dust thou art, to dust returnest,
Was not spoken of the soul.

Not enjoyment, and not sorrow,
Is our destined end or way;
But to act, that each to-morrow
Find us farther than to-day.

Art is long, and Time is fleeting,
And our hearts, though stout and brave,
Still, like muffled drums, are beating
Funeral marches to the grave.

In the world's broad field of battle,
In the bivouac[2] of Life,
Be not like dumb, driven cattle!
Be a hero in the strife!

Trust no Future, howe'er pleasant!
Let the dead Past bury its dead!
Act,—act in the living Present!
Heart within, and God o'erhead!

Lives of great men all remind us
We can make our lives sublime,
And, departing, leave behind us
Footprints on the sands of time;

Footprints, that perhaps another,
Sailing o'er life's solemn main,
A forlorn and shipwrecked brother,
Seeing, shall take heart again.

Let us, then, be up and doing,
With a heart for any fate;
Still achieving, still pursuing,
Learn to labor and to wait.

1838

[2]Temporary battle shelter.

The Warning[1]

Beware! The Israelite of old, who tore
The lion in his path,—when, poor and blind,
He saw the blessed light of heaven no more,
Shorn of his noble strength and forced to grind
In prison, and at last led forth to be
A pander to Philistine revelry,—

Upon the pillars of the temple laid
His desperate hands, and in its overthrow
Destroyed himself, and with him those who made
A cruel mockery of his sightless woe;
The poor, blind Slave, the scoff and jest of all,
Expired, and thousands perished in the fall!

There is a poor, blind Samson in this land,
Shorn of his strength and bound in bonds of steel,
Who may, in some grim revel, raise his hand,
And shake the pillars of this Commonweal,
Till the vast Temple of our liberties
A shapeless mass of wreck and rubbish lies.

1842

The Jewish Cemetery at Newport

How strange it seems! These Hebrews in their graves,
Close by the street of this fair seaport town,
Silent beside the never-silent waves,
At rest in all this moving up and down!

The trees are white with dust, that o'er their sleep
Wave their broad curtains in the south-wind's breath,
While underneath these leafy tents they keep
The long, mysterious Exodus of Death.

And these sepulchral stones, so old and brown,
That pave with level flags their burial-place,
Seem like the tablets of the Law, thrown down
And broken by Moses at the mountain's base.

[1]Samson, an Israelite who had been captured and blinded, single-handedly destroyed the temple of the licentious Philistines and brought them to ruin.

The very names recorded here are strange,
Of foreign accent, and of different climes;
Alvares and Rivera interchange
With Abraham and Jacob of old times.

"Blessed be God! for he created Death!"
The mourners said, "and Death is rest and peace;"
Then added, in the certainty of faith,
"And giveth Life that nevermore shall cease."

Closed are the portals of their Synagogue,
No Psalms of David now the silence break,
No Rabbi reads the ancient Decalogue
In the grand dialect the Prophets spake.

Gone are the living, but the dead remain,
And not neglected; for a hand unseen,
Scattering its bounty, like a summer rain,
Still keeps their graves and their remembrance green.

How came they here? What burst of Christian hate,
What persecution, merciless and blind,
Drove o'er the sea—that desert desolate—
These Ishmaels and Hagars of mankind?

They lived in narrow streets and lanes obscure,
Ghetto and Judenstrass, in mirk and mire;
Taught in the school of patience to endure
The life of anguish and the death of fire.

All their lives long, with the unleavened bread
And bitter herbs of exile and its fears,
The wasting famine of the heart they fed,
And slaked its thirst with marah of their tears.

Anathema maranatha![1] was the cry
That rang from town to town, from street to street;
At every gate the accursed Mordecai
Was mocked and jeered, and spurned by Christian feet.

Pride and humiliation hand in hand
Walked with them through the world where'er they went;

[1]A curse applied by Christians to non-believers, especially Jews.

Trampled and beaten were they as the sand,
And yet unshaken as the continent.

For in the background figures vague and vast
Of patriarchs and of prophets rose sublime,
And all the great traditions of the Past
They saw reflected in the coming time.

And thus forever with reverted look
The mystic volume of the world they read,
Spelling it backward, like a Hebrew book,
Till life became a Legend of the Dead.

But ah! what once has been shall be no more!
The groaning earth in travail and in pain
Brings forth its races, but does not restore,
And the dead nations never rise again.

1852

Aftermath

When the summer fields are mown,
When the birds are fledged and flown,
And the dry leaves strew the path;
With the falling of the snow,
With the cawing of the crow,
Once again the fields we mow
And gather in the aftermath.

Not the sweet, new grass with flowers
Is this harvesting of ours;
Not the upland clover bloom;
But the rowen mixed with weeds,
Tangled tufts from marsh and meads,
Where the poppy drops its seeds
In the silence and the gloom.

1873

Chaucer

An old man in a lodge within a park;
The chamber walls depicted all around
With portraitures of huntsman, hawk, and hound,
And the hurt deer. He listeneth to the lark,
Whose song comes with the sunshine through the dark
Of painted glass in leaden lattice bound;
He listeneth and he laugheth at the sound,
Then writeth in a book like any clerk.
He is the poet of the dawn, who wrote
The Canterbury Tales, and his old age
Made beautiful with song; and as I read
I hear the crowing cock, I hear the note
Of lark and linnet, and from every page
Rise odors of ploughed field or flowery mead.

1873

The Harvest Moon

It is the Harvest Moon! On gilded vanes
And roofs of villages, on woodland crests
And their aerial neighborhoods of nests
Deserted, on the curtained window-panes
Of rooms where children sleep, on country lanes
And harvest-fields, its mystic splendor rests!
Gone are the birds that were our summer guests;
With the last sheaves return the laboring wains!
All things are symbols: the external shows
Of Nature have their image in the mind,
As flowers and fruits and falling of the leaves;
The song-birds leave us at the summer's close,
Only the empty nests are left behind,
And pipings of the quail among the sheaves.

1876

Frances Sargent Locke Osgood 1811–1850

Frances Sargent Locke Osgood was a popular and versatile poet who wrote both in the high sentimental mode and in a mode of sheer mischief. A focus on children, flowers, and death earns her the designation of sentimental (and that in no reductive sense), but she was also a New York City sophisticate, welcome in the most exalted literary circles, and adept—as Edgar Allan Poe said of her—at literary *espièglerie* (roguishness). In Osgood's published poetry she deals quite seriously with sentimental themes, issues of motherhood and of romantic love, writing about these central human concerns with both personal insight and poetic skill. On the other hand, in a group of "salon poems"—deliberately unpublished verses composed for social occasions—she wittily destabilizes the underlying premises of the sentimental ethos. In her poetry of relations between the sexes, both published poems and manuscript salon verses, Osgood presents an urbane and sophisticated voice, quite unlike anything our traditional constructs of American literature have led us to expect from either women's or men's writing of the era. A contemporary reviewer claimed Osgood was Elizabeth Barrett Browning's equal as a poet but far superior in "grace and tenderness." Dying of tuberculosis at age thirty-nine, Osgood did not have the opportunity to realize the full promise of that comparison.

Frances Sargent Locke was born in Boston in 1811 to a prosperous mercantile family with a literary bent, including an older sister, Anna Maria Wells, who was also a published poet. The young Fanny Locke's school notebooks show evidence of considerable poetic talent, and she was "discovered" in her youth by writer and editor Lydia Maria Child, who published many of Fanny's verses under the pen name of Florence, the first of many Osgood noms de plume, in her "Juvenile Miscellany." Frances met the widely traveled, and self-romanticizing, portrait artist Samuel Stillman Osgood in 1834, and he invited her to sit for her portrait. Married in 1834, the couple spent the next five years in England while Samuel pursued his career among the aristocracy there.

The sophistication of Fanny Osgood's poetic voice was fostered by this cosmopolitan experience. During the years in which they lived in London, Fanny and Samuel circulated among the social and intellectual elite; in 1838, she published *A Wreath of Wild Flowers from New England* there. As Poe, Osgood's friend during the New York years, tells us, "the fair American authoress grew . . . into high favor with the fashionable literati and the literary fashionables of England." Returning to American shores in 1840, Osgood seems to have imported into New York literary high life the wit and sparkle of the London intelligentsia. At the literary salons of Anne Lynch and Emma Embury, she became acquainted with well-known American writers and editors, among them Poe, Margaret Fuller, N. P. Willis, Grace Greenwood, and Horace Greeley.

By the time the Osgoods settled in New York, they had two daughters, Ellen and May. Osgood's third child, Fanny Fay, was born in 1846, at a time when the marriage seems to have been less than stable. Some writers have speculated that during this period Osgood had a love affair with Poe, but convincing evidence does not, at this time, exist to prove such a claim. Osgood met Poe in 1845, and they quickly became friends. She socialized with Poe at literary salons, visited him and his wife, Virginia, at their home, and published a number of poems in the *Broadway Journal,* of which he was editor. In the pages of the *Journal* they conducted an open literary flirtation, but, as critic Mary DeJong has said, "For Osgood, writing itself was a kind of performance, and she reveled in drama as much as Poe did." Their flirtatious poems, DeJong speculates, "define their roles as patron and protégé, artist and admirer—not the quality or depth of their emotions."

During the 1840s Osgood was a much-revered popular poet. She thought of herself as a professional writer rather than as a literary artist and took full advantage of the many opportunities presented by a burgeoning print culture. Her work and circumstances embody both the opportunities and the constraints of the contemporary literary marketplace. Osgood published in every venue available to her—books, magazines, pamphlets, anthologies, newspapers. Her poems, including beautiful and poignant expressions of maternal love and impassioned articulations of heterosexual love and enthrallment, were widely sought after by magazines such as *Godey's Lady's Book* and *Sartain's Union Magazine.* Although Osgood does not ever seem to have suffered the kind of dire economic hardship faced by some of her female literary contemporaries, she nonetheless depended on her literary income to support herself and her family; proceeds from her husband's society portraits were evidently insufficient to maintain an affluent and comfortable New York City society life. Osgood lived with her children in rooms at the Astor Hotel, an elite address, but she claimed poverty; "I am poor," she wrote in a published letter to Grace Greenwood in 1847, "and have others dependant upon my talents." This regrettable circumstance, she says, forces her to "measure 'thoughts that breathe and words that burn,' like a rose-colored ribbon, by the yard-stick of a publisher!" And, indeed, while many of her published poems are idiosyncratic, moving, and skillful, a number of others do exhibit the hallmarks of having been written in haste and composed to meet editorial specifications and audience expectations.

At their best, Osgood's published poems are either witty or powerfully emotional, skillfully employing, and bringing to vivid life, common literary conventions. With masterful versification, impressive range of subject matter, and compelling imaginative power, Osgood addresses a variety of issues. In her delightful "A Flight of Fancy," she takes on the nature of imagination itself. In "Woman" and in her *New York Tribune* poem on the Married Women's Property Act of 1848, she addresses gender politics, not from a strictly feminist perspective. "Oh! Hasten to My Side," surprisingly for its time, inscribes the dilemma of sexual temptation. In "To a Slandered Poetess," Osgood investigates dynamics of celebrity and reputation. "The Indian Maid's Reply to the Missionary" exhibits an understanding of the short-sighted nature of religious imperialism. As her literary executor Rufus Griswold says of Osgood, "[s]he was . . . of the first rank of female poets." Then he goes on to specify that "in her special domain, of the Poetry of the Affections, she had scarcely a rival among women or men. . . ." And nowhere is her work as enduring or as rewarding to a modern reader as it is in her poems about children. In "Ellen Learning to Walk," "Ashes of Roses," and "A Mother's Prayer in Illness," she explores both the joys and griefs of motherhood with an intensity that Griswold calls an "almost wild tenderness," presenting compelling and poignant representations of maternal love and loss.

Osgood seems to have seen no contradiction between her published—public—verse and a group of more worldly verses she wrote to be shared solely with an intimate circle of friends—most likely at the salons she attended regularly. This *vers de société,* as Griswold calls it, includes satires, Valentines, billets-doux, and commentary on contemporary current events. In particular, Osgood's "coterie" verses wittily investigate the play of eroticism and social forms, a subject seldom addressed by other writers of the era. Osgood's salon poetry was, according to an obituary writer, produced for the "temporary gratification of her friends, and then thrown aside and forgotten." Treasured in manuscript by friends and kept in draft form by Osgood herself, these poems reveal a far more complex nineteenth-century literary milieu, in terms of class and gender representations, than American literary history has commonly acknowledged.

The complex mechanics of literary reputation have been delineated by many scholars, and Frances Osgood, for any number of reasons, both personal and critical, has been obscured in the scholarly record. Until recently she has had no advocate. As DeJong has pointed out, Osgood lacks a book-length biography, a complete collection of her poems, and a published bibliography. In addition, Griswold, her editor, tells us that even the most complete compilation of Osgood's poetry, the 1850 edition, contains less than half her acknowledged pieces. Much work remains to be done in order to recover this poet more fully, whose life and poetry significantly enrich our literary record and problematize several major literary historical paradigms, particularly those of gender and class. Osgood testifies to us, for instance, that a mid-nineteenth-century woman was capable of recognizing and dealing with sexual temptation and writing about it as well. She brings a new kind of critical respectability to sentimental poetry, treating its range of domestic, affectional topics with passion and skill. She reveals that the boundaries between British and American writing of the era were not as impermeable as has often been suggested. And, finally, she sketches a portrait of an upper-class, sophisticated, urban society seldom acknowledged in a literary history of the era long dominated by New England literati. The genuine wit and charm of this poet's vision were summed up in a published tribute by Grace Greenwood: "She charms *lions* to sleep with her silver lute, and then throws around them the delicate net-work of her exquisite fancy." Osgood can work a similar, and no less "charming," poetic enchantment on the readers of today.

Joanne Dobson
Fordham University

PRIMARY WORKS

A Wreath of Wild Flowers from New England, 1838; *Poems,* 1846; *Poems,* 1850.

SECONDARY WORKS

Cheryl Walker, *The Nightingale's Burden: Women Poets and American Culture Before 1900,* 1982; Mary G. DeJong, "Her Fair Fame: The Reputation of Frances Sargent Osgood, Woman Poet," *Studies in the American Renaissance,* 1987; idem, "Lines from a Partly Published Drama: The Romance of Frances Sargent Osgood and Edgar Allan Poe," in *Patrons and Protégées,* ed. Shirley Marchalonis, 1988; Joanne Dobson, "Sex, Wit, and Sentiment: Frances Osgood and the Poetry of Love," *American Literature,* 1993.

Ellen Learning to Walk

My beautiful trembler! how wildly she shrinks!
  And how wistful she looks while she lingers!
Papa is extremely uncivil, she thinks,—
  She but pleaded for one of his fingers!

What eloquent pleading! the hand reaching out,
As if doubting so strange a refusal;
While her blue eyes say plainly, "What is he about
That he does not assist me as usual?"

Come on, my pet Ellen! we won't let you slip,—
Unclasp those soft arms from his knee, love;
I see a faint smile round that exquisite lip,
A smile half reproach and half glee, love.

So! that's my brave baby! one foot falters forward,
Half doubtful the other steals by it!
What, shrinking again! why, you shy little coward!
'Twon't kill you to walk a bit!—try it!

There! steady, my darling! huzza! I have caught her!
I clasp her, caress'd and caressing!
And she hides her bright face, as if what we had taught her
Were something to blush for—the blessing!

Now back again! Bravo! that shout of delight,
How it thrills to the hearts that adore her!
Joy, joy for her mother! and blest be the night
When her little light feet first upbore her!

1838

The Little Hand

We wandered sadly round the room,—
We missed the voice's play,
That warbled through our hours of gloom,
And charmed the cloud away;—

We missed the footstep, loved and light,—
The tiny, twining hand,—
The quick, arch smile, so wildly bright,—
The brow, with beauty bland!

We wandered sadly round the room,—
No relic could we find,
No toy of hers, to soothe our gloom,—
She left not one behind!

But look! there is a misty trace,
Faint, undefined and broken,
Of fingers, on the mirror's face,—
A dear, though simple token!

A cherub hand!—the child we loved
Had left its impress there,
When first, by young Ambition moved,
She climbed the easy-chair;—

She saw her own sweet self, and tried
To touch what seemed to be
So near, so beautiful! and cried,—
"Why! there's another me!"

Dear hand! though from the mirror's face
Thy form did soon depart,
I wore its welcome, tender trace,
Long after, in my heart!

1838

Oh! Hasten to My Side

Oh! hasten to my side, I pray!
I dare not be alone!
The smile that tempts, when thou'rt away,
Is fonder than thine own.

The voice that oftenest charms mine ear
Hath such beguiling tone,
'Twill steal my very *soul,* I fear;
Ah! leave me not alone!

It speaks in accents low and deep,
It murmurs praise too dear,
It makes me passionately weep,
Then gently soothes my fear;

It calls me sweet, endearing names,
With Love's own childlike art;
My tears, my doubts, it softly blames—
'Tis *music* to my heart!

And dark, deep, eloquent, soul-fill'd eyes
  Speak tenderly to mine;
Beneath that gaze what feelings rise!
  It is more kind than thine!

A hand, even pride can scarce repel,
  Too fondly seeks mine own;
It is not safe!—it is not well!
  Ah! leave me not alone!

I try to calm, in cold repose,
  Beneath his earnest eye,
The heart that thrills, the cheek that glows—
  Alas! *in vain* I try!

Oh trust me not—a woman frail—
  To brave the snares of life!
Lest—lonely, sad, unloved—I *fail,*
  And shame the name of wife!

Come back! though cold and harsh to me,
  There's *honour* by thy side!
Better unblest, yet safe to be,
  Than lost to truth, to pride.

Alas! my peril hourly grows,
  In every thought and dream;
Not—not to *thee* my spirit goes,
  But still—yes! I still to *him!*

Return with those cold eyes to me,
  And chill my soul once more
Back to the loveless apathy
  It learn'd so well before!

1843

A Flight of Fancy

At the bar of Judge Conscience stood Reason arraign'd,
The jury impannell'd—the prisoner chain'd.
The judge was facetious at times, though severe,
Now waking a smile, and now drawing a tear;
An old-fashion'd, fidgety, queer-looking wight,
With a clerical air, and an eye quick as light.

"Here, Reason, you vagabond! look in my face;
I'm told you're becoming an idle scapegrace.
They say that young Fancy, that airy coquette,
Has dared to fling round you her luminous net;
That she ran away with you, in spite of yourself,
For pure love of frolic—the mischievous elf.

"The scandal is whisper'd by friends and by foes,
And darkly they hint, too, that when they propose
Any question to *your* ear, so lightly you're led,
At once to gay Fancy you turn your wild head:
And *she* leads you off in some dangerous dance,
As wild as the Polka that gallop'd from France.

"Now up to the stars with you, laughing, she springs,
With a whirl and a whisk of her changeable wings;
Now dips in some fountain her sun-painted plume,
That gleams through the spray, like a rainbow in bloom;
Now floats in a cloud, while her tresses of light
Shine through the frail boat and illumine its flight;
Now glides through the woodland to gather its flowers;
Now darts like a flash to the sea's coral bowers;
In short—cuts such capers, that with her, I ween,
It's a wonder you are not ashamed to be seen!

"Then she talks such a language!—melodious enough,
To be sure, but a strange sort of outlandish stuff!
I'm told that it licenses many a whapper,
And when once she commences, no frowning can stop her;
Since it's new, I've no doubt it is very improper!
They say that she cares not for order or law;
That of you, you great dunce! she but makes a cat's-paw.
I've no sort of objection to fun in its season,
But it's plain that this Fancy is *fooling* you, Reason!"

Just then into court flew a strange little sprite,
With wings of all colours and ringlets of light!
She frolick'd round Reason, till Reason grew wild,
Defying the court and caressing the child.
The judge and the jury, the clerk and recorder,
In vain call'd this exquisite creature to order:—
"Unheard of intrusion!"—They bustled about,
To seize her, but, wild with delight, at the rout,
She flew from their touch like a bird from a spray,
And went waltzing and whirling and singing away!

Now up to the ceiling, now down to the floor!
Were never such antics in courthouse before!
But a lawyer, well versed in the tricks of his trade,
A trap for the gay little innocent laid:
He held up a *mirror,* and Fancy was caught
By her image within it,—so lovely, she thought.
What could the fair creature be!—bending its eyes
On her own with so wistful a look of surprise!
She flew to embrace it. The lawyer was ready:
He closed round the spirit a grasp cool and steady,
And she sigh'd, while he tied her two luminous wings,
"Ah! Fancy and Falsehood are different things!"

The witnesses—maidens of uncertain age,
With a critic, a publisher, lawyer, and sage—
All scandalized greatly at what they had heard
Of this poor little Fancy, (who flew like a bird!)
Were call'd to the stand, and their evidence gave.
The judge charged the jury, with countenance grave:
Their verdict was "Guilty," and Reason look'd down,
As his honour exhorted her thus, with a frown:—

"This Fancy, this vagrant, for life shall be chain'd
In your own little cell, where *you* should have remain'd;
And you—for *your* punishment—jailer shall be:
Don't let your accomplice come coaxing to me!
I'll none of her nonsense—the little wild witch!
Nor her bribes—although rumour does say she is rich.

"I've heard that all treasures and luxuries rare
Gather round at her bidding, from earth, sea, and air;
And some go so far as to hint, that the powers
Of darkness attend her more sorrowful hours.
But go!" and Judge Conscience, who never was bought,
Just bow'd the pale prisoner out of the court.

'Tis said, that poor Reason next morning was found,
At the door of her cell, fast asleep on the ground,
And nothing within but one plume rich and rare,
Just to show that young Fancy's wing once had been there.
She had dropp'd it, no doubt, while she strove to get through
The hole in the lock, which she could not undo.

A Reply

To One Who Said, Write from Your Heart.

Ah! woman still
Must veil the shrine,
Where feeling feeds the fire divine,
Nor sing at will,
Untaught by art,
The music prison'd in her heart!

Still gay the note
And light the day,
The woodbird warbles on the spray,
Afar to float;
But homeward flown,
Within his nest, how changed the tone!

Oh! none can know,
Who have not heard
The music-soul that thrills the bird,
The carol low,
As coo of dove
He warbles to his woodland love!

The world would say
'Twas vain and wild,
Th'impassion'd lay of Nature's child;
And Feeling, so
Should veil the shrine,
Where softly glows her fires divine!

1846

Lines

Suggested by the announcement that "A Bill for the Protection of the Property of Married Women has passed both Houses" of our State Legislature

[For *The New-York Tribune*]

Oh, ye who in those Houses hold
 The sceptre of command!
Thought's sceptre, sunlit, in the soul,
 Not golden, in the hand!

Was there not one among ye all,
 No heart, that Love could thrill,
To move some slight amendment there,
 Before you passed the bill?

Ye make our gold and lands secure;
 Maybe you do not know,
That we have other property,
 We'd *rather* not forego.

There *are* such things in woman's heart,
 As fancies, tastes, affections;—
Are no encroachments made on these?
 Do *they* need no "protections"?

Do we not daily sacrifice,
 To our lords—and Creation's
Some darling wish—some petted whim,
 Ah, me! in vain oblations!

These "cold realities" of life,—
 These men, with their intrusions;
Do they not rob us, one by one,
 Of all our "warm illusions"?

These highway robbers, prowling round,
 Our "young affections" stealing,
Do they not take our richest store
 Of Truth and Faith and Feeling!

Our "better judgment," "finer sense,"
We yield with souls that falter,—
A costly, dainty holocaust,
Upon a tyrant's altar;

We waste on them our "golden" hours,
Our "real estate" of Beauty,
The bloom of Life's young passion-flowers—
And still they talk of "Duty."

Alas for those, whose all of wealth
Is in their souls and faces,
Whose only "rents" are rents in heart,
Whose only tenants—graces.

How must that poor protection bill
Provoke their bitter laughter,
Since they themselves are leased for life,
And no *pay-day* till after!

By all the rest you fondly hope,
When ends this lengthened session,
That household peace, which Woman holds
Thank Heaven! at *her* discretion.

If a light of generous chivalry,
This wild appeal arouses,
Present a truer, nobler bill!
And let it pass—*all houses!*

1848

Woman

A Fragment from an Unpublished Manuscript

Within a frame, more glorious than the gem
To which Titania could her sylph condemn,
Fair woman's spirit dreams the hours away,
Content at times in that bright home to stay,
So that you let her deck her beauty still,
And waltz and warble at her own sweet will.
Taught to restrain, in cold Decorum's school,

The step, the smile, to glance and dance by rule;
To smooth alike her words and waving trees,
And her pure *heart's* impetuous play repress;
Each airy impulse—every frolic thought
Forbidden, if by Fashion's law untaught,
The graceful houri of your heavenlier hours
Forgets, in gay saloons, her native bowers,
Forgets her glorious home—her angel-birth—
Content to share the passing joys of earth;
Save when, at intervals, a ray of love
Pleads to her spirit from the realms above,
Plays on her pinions shut, and softly sings
In low Æolian tones of heavenly things.
  Ah! *then* dim memories dawn upon the soul
Of that celestial home from which she stole;
She feels its fragrant airs around her blow;
She sees the immortal bowers of beauty glow;
And faint and far, but how divinely sweet!
She hears the music where its angels meet.
  Then wave her starry wings in hope and shame,
Their fire illumes the fair, transparent frame,
Fills the dark eyes with passionate thought the while,
Blooms in the blush and lightens in the smile:
No longer then the toy, the doll, the slave,
But frank, heroic, beautiful, and brave,
She rises, radiant in immortal youth,
And wildly pleads for Freedom and for Truth!
  These captive Peris all around you smile,
And one I've met who might a god beguile.
She's stolen from Nature all her loveliest spells:
Upon her cheek morn's blushing splendour dwells,
The starry midnight kindles in her eyes,
The gold of sunset on her ringlets lies,
And to the ripple of a rill, 'tis said,
She tuned her voice and timed her airy tread!
  No rule restrains *her* thrilling laugh, or moulds
Her flowing robe to tyrant Fashion's folds;
No custom chains the grace in that fair girl,
That sways her willowy form or waves her careless curl.
I plead not that she share each sterner task;
The cold reformers know not what they ask;
I only seek for our transplanted fay,
That she may have—in all *fair ways*—*her way!*
  I would not see the aerial creature trip,
A blooming sailor, up some giant ship,
Some man-of-war—to reef the topsail high—
Ah! reef your *curls*—and let the *canvas* fly!

Nor would I bid her quit her 'broidery frame,
A fairy blacksmith by the forge's flame:
No! be the fires *she* kindles only those
With which man's iron nature wildly glows.
"Strike while the iron's hot," with all your art,
But strike *Love's* anvil in his yielding heart!
Nor should our sylph her tone's low music strain,
A listening senate with her wit to chain,
To rival Choate in rich and graceful lore,
Or challenge awful Webster to the floor,
Like that rash wight who raised the casket's lid,
And set a genius free the stars that hid.
Not thus forego the poetry of life,
The sacred names of mother, sister, wife!
Rob not the household hearth of all its glory,
Lose not those tones of musical delight,
All man has left, to tell him the sweet story
Of his remember'd home—beyond the night.
Yet men too proudly use their tyrant power;
They chill the soft bloom of the fairy flower;
They bind the wing, that would but soar above
In search of purer air and holier love;
They hush the heart, that fondly pleads its wrong
In plaintive prayer or in impassion'd song.
Smile on, sweet flower! soar on, enchanted wing!
Since she ne'er asks but for *one trifling thing*,
Since but *one* want disturbs the graceful fay,
Why *let* the docile darling *have—her way!*

1848

Alone

Once more alone—and desolate now for ever,
In truth, the heart whose home was once in thine;
Once more alone on Life's terrific river,
All human help exulting I resign.

Alone I brave the tempest and the terror,
Alone I guide my being's fragile bark,
And bless the Past with all its grief and error,
Since heaven still bends above my pathway dark.

At last, I taste the joy of self-reliance;
At last I reverence, calmly, my own soul;

At last, I glory in serene defiance
Of all the wrong that would my fate control.

Elastic bounds above the waves of sorrow
The bark, wo's lightest breath could once o'erwhelm;
It turns triumphant to the radiant morrow—
Faith at the mast and Courage at the helm.

Away! away! its pure sail softly swelling
With the glad gale, that springs to speed its flight,
The beauteous sunset of the Past foretelling
How rich shall be the Future's morning light.

Too long it trusted Love, the treacherous pilot,
Who, lingering, lured it toward the whirlpool wild,
And, idly moor'd to many a flowery islet,
Forgot the glorious shore afar that smiled.

But now untrammell'd, buoyant as a bird,
Without one coward fear, one poor regret,
By heaven's melodious breath to rapture stirr'd,
It springs, inspired, with all its white sails set.

And rosy bowers may woo it from its duty,
Where Joy supine sits weaving garlands frail,
And other barks, freighted with love and beauty,
May tempt,—but it glides onward with the gale.

True to its destined port, through storm and shine,
Though sails be rent and waves in fury rise,
Its beacon light a burning hope divine,
For ever bright, though tempests sweep the skies!

1849

Little Children

"Of such is the kingdom of heaven."

And yet we check and chide
The airy angels as they float about us,
With rules of so-call'd wisdom, till they grow
The same tame slaves to custom and the world.
And day by day the fresh frank soul that looked

Out of those wistful eyes, and smiling play'd
With the wild roses of that changing cheek,
And modulated all those earnest tones,
And danced in those light foot-falls to a tune
Heart-heard by them, inaudible to us,
Folds closer its pure wings, whereon the hues
They caught in heaven already pale and pine,
And shrinks amazed and scared back from our gaze.
And so the evil grows. The graceful flower
May have its own sweet way in bud and bloom—
May drink, and dare with upturn'd gaze the light,
Or nestle 'neath the guardian leaf, or wave
Its fragrant bells to ever-roving breeze,
Or wreathe with blushing grace the fragile spray
In bashful loveliness. The wild wood-bird
May plume at will his wings, and soar or sing;
The mountain brook may wind where'er it would,
Dash in wild music down the deep ravine,
Or, rippling drowsily in forest haunts,
Dream of the floating cloud, the waving flower,
And murmur to itself sweet lulling words
In broken tones so like the faltering speech
Of early childhood: but our human flowers,
Our soul-birds, caged and pining—they must sing
And grow, not as their own but our caprice
Suggests, and so the blossom and the lay
Are but half bloom and music at the best.
And if by chance some brave and buoyant soul,
More bold or less forgetful of the lessons
God taught them first, disdain the rule—the bar—
And, wildly beautiful, rebellious rise,
How the hard world, half startled from itself,
Frowns the bright wanderer down, or turns away,
And leaves her lonely in her upward path.
Thank God! to such His smile is not denied.

1849

To a Slandered Poetess

My brilliant Blue-bell! droop no more;
  But let them mock, and mew and mutter!

I marvel, though a whirlwind roar,
Your eagle soul should deign to flutter!

So low the pigmies aimed the dart,
(Ah, yes! your looks of scorn reveal it.)
You must have *stooped* your haughty heart,
Oh, wilful, wayward child!—to feel it.

My dark-eyed darling! don't you know,
If you were homely, cold, and stupid,
Unbent for you were Slander's bow?
Her shafts but follow those of Cupid.

'Tis but the penalty you pay,
For wit so rare, and grace so peerless:
So let the snarlers say their say,
And smile to hear them, free and fearless.

Nay! hear them *not!* Oh! you should listen
To spheral tunes! the angels love you!
The stars with kindred beauty glisten:—
No "evil eye" can lower *above* you!

Dear child of Genius! strike the lyre,
And drown with melody delicious,
Soft answering to your touch of fire,
The envious hint—the sneer malicious.

Remember is it Music's law,
Each *pure, true* note, though low you sound it,
Is heard through Discord's wildest war
Of rage and madness, storming round it.

You smile!—Nay, raise your queenly head;
Braid up your hair, lest I upbraid it;
Be that last coward tear unshed.
Or in this dancing dimple shed it!

Serenely go your glorious way,
Secure that every footstep onward,
Will lead you from *their* haunts away,
Since you go *up,* and they go—*down*ward.

Yet from your love-lit, heavenly flight,
Some pity dole to those who blame you,
You only can forgive them quite.
You only, smile, while they defame you.

Oh! think how poor in all the wealth,
  That makes *your* frame a fairy palace—
The mind's pure light,—the heart's sweet health,—
  Are they whose dearest joy is malice.

1849

The Indian Maid's Reply to the Missionary[1]

Half earnest, half sportive, yet listening, she stood,
That queenly young creature, the child of the wood;
Her curving lips parted—her dark eyes downcast—
Her hands lock'd before her—her heart beating fast;
And around her the forest's majestic arcade,
With the pure sunset burning like fire through the shade:
He spake of the goodness, the glory of Him
Whose smile lit the heavens—whose frown made them dim.
And with one flashing glance of the eyes she upraised
Full of rapture impassion'd, her Maker she praised.
He spake of the Saviour, his sorrow, his truth,
His pity celestial, the wrong and the ruth;
And quick gushing tears dimm'd the gaze that she turn'd
To his face, while her *soul* on her sunny cheek burn'd.
Then he thought in his fond zeal to wile her within
The pale of the church; but as well might he win
Yon cloud that floats changefully on in the light,
A fawn of the forest, a star-ray of light,
As tame to his purpose, or lure from her race
That wild child of freedom, all impulse and grace.
She listens in sad, unbelieving surprise;
Then shakes back her dark, glossy locks from her eyes,
And with eloquent gesture points up to the skies.
At last, to awaken her fears he essays;
He threatens God's wrath if thus freely she strays.
Wild, sweet, and incredulous rang through the wood
The laugh of the maiden, as proudly she stood.
Soft, thrilling, and glad woke the echo around;
True nature's harmonious reply to that sound.
Then lowly and reverent answer'd the maid:—
"God speaketh afar in the forest," she said,
"And he sayeth—'Behold in the woodland so wild,
With its heaven-arch'd aisle, the true church of my child.'"

1850

[1]The friend who related to me this incident was, I believe, himself an eye-witness to the scene. [Author's note.]

The Hand That Swept the Sounding Lyre

The hand that swept the sounding lyre
With more than mortal skill,
The lightning eye, the heart of fire,
The fervent lip are still!
No more, in rapture or in wo,
With melody to thrill,
Ah! nevermore!

Oh! bring the flowers he cherish'd so,
With eager childlike care;
For o'er his grave they'll love to grow,
And sigh their sorrow there:
Ah me! no more their balmy glow
May soothe his heart's despair,
No! nevermore!

But angel hands shall bring him balm
For every grief he knew,
And Heaven's soft harps his soul shall calm
With music sweet and true,
And teach to him the holy charm
Of Israfel anew,
For evermore!

Love's silver lyre he play'd so well
Lies shatter'd on his tomb;
But still in air its music-spell
Floats on through light and gloom,
And in the hearts where soft they fell,
His words of beauty bloom
For evermore!

1850

The Lady's Mistake

That his eyebrows were false—that his hair
Was assumed I was fully aware!
I knew his moustache of a barber was bought
And that Cartwright provided his teeth—but I thought
That his *heart* was at least true & fair

I saw that the exquisite glow
Spreading over the cheek of my beau
From a carmine shell came and I often was told
That his elegant calf by his tailor was sold
I dreamed not that his *love* was but show

I was sure—I could easily tell
That the form which deluded each belle
Was made over his own—but I could not believe
That his flattering tongue too was made to deceive
That his *fortune* was humbug as well

I had made up my mind to dispense
With a figure, hair, teeth, heart & sense
The calf I'd o'erlook were it ever so small
But to think that he is not a *count* after all
That's a not to be pardoned offence!

The Wraith of the Rose

An impromptu written on a visiting card

The magic of that name is fled,
The music of that dream is dead,
Long since Love's rose, its perfume, shed,
And what art *thou* to me?
If you have come to clasp again,
The fetter of that fairy chain,
You'd better far at home remain,
And save your time—and *knee!*
And yet that dream was strangely dear,
And yet that name awakes a tear,
The *wraith* of Love's sweet Rose is here,
It haunts me everywhere!
I wish the chain were still unbroken,
I wish those words again were spoken,
I wish I'd kept that last fond token,
And had not burned your hair!
I wish your voice still sounded sweet,
I wish you dared Love's vow repeat,
I wish you were not all deceit,
And I so fickle-hearted!

I wish we might go back again,
I wish you *could* reclasp the chain!
I wish—*you hadn't drank champagne,*
So freely since we parted!
Alas! While Flattery baits your line,
You fish in shallower hearts than mine!
You'll never find a pearl divine
Like that *my* spirit wasted!
But should you catch a seeming prise,
A *flying* fish you'll see it rise,
Away—beyond your wicked eyes,
Before the treasure's tasted!
Oh! *if* those eyes were splendid now,
As when they spoke the silent vow!
Oh! *if* the locks that wreath your brow,
Were not—but this is idle!
My wish shall be with kindness rife,
I'll wish you all the joys of life,
A pleasant home—a peerless wife,
Whose wishes, Sense shall bridle!

Walt Whitman 1819–1892

The publication of *Leaves of Grass* on or about July 4, 1855, represented a revolutionary departure in American literature. Printed at Whitman's expense, the green, quarto-sized volume bore no author's name. Opposite the title page appeared a daguerreotype engraving of the poet, dressed in workingman's trowsers, a shirt unbuttoned to reveal his undershirt, and a hat cocked casually upon his head. In a rousing Preface, the poet declared America's literary independence, and in verse that rolled freely and dithyrambically across the page, he presented himself as "Walt Whitman, an American, one of the roughs, a kosmos,/Disorderly fleshy and sensual . . . . eating drinking and breeding." Like his poet as common man, Whitman's act of self-naming represented an assault on literary decorum and the Puritan pieties of the New England literary establishment. "It is as if the beasts spoke," wrote the otherwise sympathetic Thoreau.

In the six editions of *Leaves of Grass* that were published between 1855 and 1881, Whitman opened the field of American and ultimately of modern poetry. His subject was not "the smooth walks, trimm'd hedges, poseys and nightingales of the English poets, but the whole orb, with its geologic history, the Kosmos, carrying fire and snow." He was the poet not only of Darwinian evolution, but of the city and the crowd, science and the machine. Presenting himself as a model Democrat who spoke as and for rather than apart from the people, Whitman's poet was a breaker of bounds: he was female and male, farmer and factory worker, prostitute and slave, citizen of America and citizen of the world; shuttling between past, present, and future, he was "an acme of things accomplished" and an "encloser of things to be." His songs were songs not only of occupations but of sex and the body. He sang of masturbation, the sexual organs, and the sexual act; he was one of the first poets to write of the "body electric," of female eroticism, homosexual love, and the anguish of repressed desire.

Puzzled by Whitman's sudden emergence at age 36 in 1855 as the American bard, critics have proposed several explanations: a reading of Emerson, a love affair, a mystic experience, an Oedipal crisis. Considered within the context of his time, however, Whitman's emergence seems neither mystifying nor particularly disconnected from his family background and his early life as radical Democrat, political journalist, and sometime dandy. His mother was an ardent follower of the mystical doctrines of the Quaker preacher Elias Hicks, whom Whitman later described as "the democrat in religion as Jefferson was the democrat in politics." His father was a carpenter who embraced the radical political philosophy of Tom Paine and subscribed to the *Free Enquirer,* edited by Frances Wright and Robert Dale Owen, which sought through the rhetoric of class warfare to unite the grievances of New York City workers in an anticapitalist and anticlerical platform. Raised among eight brothers and sisters whose very names—Andrew Jackson, George Washington, and Thomas Jefferson—bore the inscription of the democratic ideals of his family, Whitman early began to develop a sense of self that was inextricably bound up with the political identity of America.

Although Whitman attended school between 1825 and 1830, he was largely self-educated. During the thirties he served as a printer's apprentice, engaged in local politics, and taught for a few years in Long Island schools. He read voraciously but erratically, attended the theater and the opera, and poked about the antiquities at Dr. Abbott's Egyptian Museum. As editor of the *Aurora* in 1842 and later of the Brooklyn *Daily Eagle* (1846–1847), Whitman placed himself at the very center of the political battles over slavery, territorial expansion, the Mexican War, sectionalism, free trade, states' rights, worker strife, and the new market economy. His support for David Wilmot's proposal to forbid the extension of slavery into the new territory led to his being fired as editor of the *Eagle.* Perhaps disillusioned by party politics, he began to experiment with the idea of using poetry as a form of political action. When in his earliest notebook, dated 1847, Whitman breaks for the first time into lines approximating the free verse of *Leaves of Grass,* the lines bear the impress of the slavery issue:

I am the poet of slaves, and of the
    masters of slaves
I am the poet of the body
And I am

Similarly, Whitman's first free verse poems, "Blood Money," "House of Friends," and "Resurgemus," which were published in 1850, emerged out of the political passions aroused by slavery, free soil, and the European revolutions of 1848.

Although Whitman continued to support the cause of Free Soil, in the early fifties he withdrew from party politics. Working part-time as a house builder in Brooklyn, he completed his 1855 edition of *Leaves of Grass.* The poems are propelled by the desire to enlighten and regenerate the people in the ideals of the democratic republic. The drama of identity in the initially untitled "Song of Myself," the first and longest poem in the 1855 *Leaves,* is rooted in the political drama of a nation in crisis. The poet's conflict between separate person and en masse, between pride and sympathy, individualism and equality, nature and the city, the body and the soul, symbolically enacts the larger political conflicts in the nation, which grew out of the controversies over industrialization, wage labor, women's rights, finance, immigration, slavery, territorial expansion, technological progress, and the whole question of the relation of individual and state, state and nation.

Whitman sent a copy of the 1855 *Leaves of Grass* to Ralph Waldo Emerson, whose response was immediate and generous: "I find it the most extraordinary piece of wit and wisdom that America has yet contributed." Spurred by Emerson's words of praise, Whitman published a second edition of *Leaves of Grass* with several new poems in 1856. While he was planning a third edition of *Leaves* as a kind of "New Bible" of democracy, Whitman had an unhappy love affair with a man. This tale of love and loss is the subject of a small sheaf of twelve poems, initially titled "Live Oak with Moss," which was later incorporated into the "Calamus" cluster in the 1860 *Leaves of Grass.* Whitman's homosexual love crisis along with the impending dissolution of the Union caused him to become increasingly doubtful about the future of America and his own future as the bard of democracy.

This doubt is evident in the 1860 edition of *Leaves of Grass,* particularly in the "Chants Democratic" and "Calamus" groupings, and in such individual poems as "Out of the Cradle Endlessly Rocking" and "As I Ebb'd with the Ocean of Life." In the poems of "Calamus," Whitman draws upon the language of democracy and phrenology to name his erotic feeling for men as both comradeship and "adhesiveness" (the phrenological term which Whitman defined as "the personal attachment of man to man"). The love poems of "Calamus" are paired with the procreation poems of "Children of Adam," which focus upon "amative" love, the phrenological term for the love between men and women. Although the press and the literary establishment immediately focused upon the "sex" poems of "Children of Adam" as Whitman's most provocative grouping, the love poems of "Calamus" were in fact his most radical sequence sexually and politically. Whitman infused the abstractions of democracy with the intensity of erotic passion, giving literature some of its first and most potent images of democratic comradeship; and by linking homoeroticism with a democratic breaking of bounds, he presents one of the most tender and moving accounts of homosexual love in Western literature.

For Whitman, as for the nation, the Civil War was a period of major crisis. Uncertain of the role of a national poet during a time of fratricidal war, Whitman published little during the war years. In 1862, when he went to the front in search of his brother George, he found the role he would play: he would become a kind of spiritual "wound-dresser" by visiting the sick and dying soldiers in the hospital wards of Washington. Like Lincoln's "Gettysburg Address," the poems of *Drum-Taps and Sequel* (1865–1866) and the prose of *Memoranda During the War* (1875–1876) were attempts to come to terms with the massive carnage of the war by placing its waste and apparent unreason within some larger providential design. In these volumes Whitman turns from romance to realism, vision to history, anticipating the naturalistic war writings of Stephen Crane, Ernest Hemingway, and Norman Mailer.

Whitman remained in Washington during and after the war, working first as a clerk in the Indian Bureau and then, after being dismissed in 1865 for moral turpitude by Secretary of the Interior James Harlan, in the Attorney General's office. For all Whitman's effort to (re)present the war as testing ground for democracy, the Civil War unleashed a hoard of psychic and socio-economic demons that would continue to haunt his dream of America in the postwar period.

In his incisive political essay *Democratic Vistas* (1871), which was initially composed as a response to Carlyle's attack on the "democratic rabble" in "Shooting Niagara," Whitman seeks to come to terms with the gilded monsters of post-Civil War America. Even before the worst scandals of the Grant administration were exposed, he presents an image of America saturated in corruption and greed from the national to the local level. In "reconstructing, democratizing society" Whitman argues, the true "revolution" would be of the "interior life"; and in bringing about this democratic revolution, the poet would play the leading role by overhauling the "Culture theory" of the past and by providing the language, commonality, and myths by which America named itself. Like *Leaves of Grass, Democratic Vistas* works dialectically, as Whitman seeks to reconcile self and other, state and nation, North and South, country and city, labor and capital, money and soul. He arrives at no final synthesis of the values he seeks to juggle. Amid the modernizing, standardizing, and capitalizing whirl of America, where "with steam-engine speed" generations of humanity are turned out "like uniform iron castings," Whitman recognizes that the road to the future might be the road of the "fabled damned."

Whereas Whitman's war poems were merely tagged onto the end of the fourth edition of *Leaves,* which was published in 1867, in the 1871 *Leaves* these poems were incorporated into the main body of his work. By 1872, Whitman came to regard *Leaves of Grass* as essentially complete. In his 1872 "Preface" to "As a Strong Bird on Pinions Free," he announced his intention of turning away from his former emphasis on "a great composite *democratic individual,* male or female" toward an increased emphasis on "an aggregated, inseparable, unprecedented, vast, composite, electric *democratic nationality.*" His plan was cut short by a paralytic stroke which he suffered at the beginning of 1873. The seizure left him bedridden for several weeks and paralyzed for the rest of his life.

Whitman made a trip to Camden, New Jersey, a few days before his mother's death in May 1873, and never returned to Washington. He spent the remainder of his life in Camden, first at his brother George's house and finally, beginning in 1884, in his own home at 328 Mickle Street. Struggling with occasional spells of dizziness and a prematurely aging body, Whitman mustered enough strength to publish a dual volume of poetry and prose on the occasion of the American centennial in 1876. Invigorated by the visits to the New Jersey farm of Susan and George Stafford that he began making in 1876, by the economic recovery of the nation under the new political regime of Rutherford B. Hayes (1877–1881), and by the attention his work was beginning to receive in England and abroad, Whitman revised, reintegrated, and reordered all of his poems into the final 1881 edition of *Leaves of Grass.* In 1882, he published a prose companion to his poems titled *Specimen Days,* in which he refigures the events of his life and times as a narrative of personal, national, and cosmic restoration.

The poems that Whitman wrote in the last two decades of his life, such as "Passage to India" and "Prayer of Columbus," are characterized by a leap away from the physical landscape of America toward a more traditionally religious vision of God's providence and spiritual grace. Despite his apparent disillusionment with the material conditions of America, however, Whitman continued to name the possibility of an *other* America. Figuring himself in the image of a new-world Columbus, he continued to imagine the possibility of a democratic golden world which, like the dream of a passage to India and a world in round, might bloom in some future transformation of vision into history.

Betsy Erkkila
Northwestern University

PRIMARY WORKS

Malcolm Cowley, ed., *Leaves of Grass: The First (1855) Edition*, 1959; F. De Wolfe Miller, ed., *Drum-Taps and Sequel (1865–66): A Facsimile Reproduction*, 1959; Edwin H. Miller, ed., *The Correspondence (1842–1892)*, 1961–69; Roy Harvey Pearce, ed., *Leaves of Grass: Facsimile of the 1860 Text*, 1961; *Memoranda During the War (1876): Facsimile*, 1962; Gay Wilson Allen and Sculley Bradley, eds., *The Collected Writings of Walt Whitman*, includes: Floyd Stovall, ed., *Prose Works (1892): Specimen Days, Collect, and Other Prose*, 1963; Thomas L. Brasher, ed., *The Early Poems and the Fiction*, 1963; Sculley Bradley and Harold Blodgett, eds., *Leaves of Grass: A Norton Critical Edition*, 1973; William White, ed., *Daybooks and Notebooks*, 1978; Justin Kaplan, ed., *Whitman Poetry and Prose*, 1982; Edward Grier, ed., *Notebooks and Unpublished Prose Manuscripts*, 1984.

SECONDARY WORKS

F.O. Matthiessen, *The American Renaissance*, 1941; Gay Wilson Allen, *The Solitary Singer*, 1955; Richard Chase, *Walt Whitman Reconsidered*, 1955; Joseph Jay Rubin, *The Historic Whitman*, 1973; *The New Walt Whitman Handbook*, 1975; Jeanetta Boswell, ed., *Walt Whitman and the Critics: A Checklist of Criticism, (1900–1978)*, 1980; Justin Kaplan, *Walt Whitman: A Life*, 1980; Charley Shively, ed., *Calamus Lovers: Walt Whitman's Working-Class Cameradoes*, 1987; M. Wynn Thomas, *The Lunar Light of Whitman's Poetry*, 1987; Betsy Erkkila, *Whitman the Political Poet*, 1989; Michael Moon, *Disseminating Whitman*, 1991; Betsy Erkkila and Jay Grossman, eds., *Breaking Bounds: Whitman and American Cultural Studies*, 1994; *The Cambridge Companion to Walt Whitman*, 1995; David S. Reynolds, *Walt Whitman's America: A Cultural Biography*, 1995.

from Leaves of Grass

1855 Preface

America does not repel the past or what it has produced under its forms or amid other politics or the idea of castes or the old religions . . . . accepts the lesson with calmness . . . is not so impatient as has been supposed that the slough still sticks to opinions and manners and literature while the life which served its requirements has passed into the new life of the new forms . . . perceives that the corpse is slowly borne from the eating and sleeping rooms of the house . . . perceives that it waits a little while in the door . . . that it was fittest for its days . . . that its action has descended to the stalwart and wellshaped heir who approaches . . . and that he shall be fittest for his days.

The Americans of all nations at any time upon the earth have probably the fullest poetical nature. The United States themselves are essentially the greatest poem. In the history of the earth hitherto the largest and most stirring appear tame and orderly to their ampler largeness and stir. Here at last is something in the doings of man that corresponds with the broadcast doings of the day and night. Here is not merely a nation but a teeming nation of nations. Here is action untied from strings necessarily blind to particulars and details magnificently moving in vast masses. Here is the hospitality which forever indicates heroes. . . . Here are the roughs and beards and space and ruggedness and nonchalance that the soul loves. Here the performance disdaining the trivial unapproached in the tremendous audacity of its crowds and groupings and the push of its perspective spreads with crampless and flowing breadth and showers its prolific and splendid extravagance. One sees it must indeed own the riches of the summer and winter, and need never be bankrupt while corn grows from the ground or the orchards drop apples or the bays contain fish or men beget children upon women.

Other states indicate themselves in their deputies . . . . but the genius of the United States is not best or most in its executives or legislatures, nor in its ambassadors or authors or colleges or churches or parlors, nor even in its newspapers or inventors . . . but always most in the common people. Their manners speech dress friendships—the freshness and candor of their physiognomy—the picturesque looseness of their carriage . . . their deathless attachment to freedom—their aversion to anything indecorous or soft or mean—the practical acknowledgment of the citizens of one state by the citizens of all other states—the fierceness of their roused resentment—their curiosity and welcome of novelty—their self-esteem and wonderful sympathy—their susceptibility to a slight—the air they have of persons who never knew how it felt to stand in the presence of superiors—the fluency of their speech—their delight in music, the sure symptom of manly tenderness and native elegance of soul . . . their good temper and openhandedness—the terrible significance of their elections—the President's taking off his hat to them not they to him—these too are unrhymed poetry. It awaits the gigantic and generous treatment worthy of it.

The largeness of nature or the nation were monstrous without a corresponding largeness and generosity of the spirit of the citizen. Not nature nor swarming states nor streets and steamships nor prosperous business nor farms nor capital nor learning may suffice for the ideal of man . . . nor suffice the poet. No reminiscences may suffice either. A live nation can always cut a deep mark and can have the best authority the cheapest . . . namely from its own soul. This is the sum of the profitable uses of individuals or states and of present action and grandeur and of the subjects of poets.—As if it were necessary to trot back generation after generation to the eastern records! As if the beauty and sacredness of the demonstrable must fall behind that of the mythical! As if men do not make their mark out of any times! As if the opening of the western continent by discovery and what has transpired since in North and South America were less than the small theatre of the antique or the aimless sleepwalking of the middle ages! The pride of the United States leaves the wealth and finesse of the cities and all returns of commerce and agriculture and all the magnitude of geography or shows of exterior victory to enjoy the breed of fullsized men or one fullsized man unconquerable and simple.

The American poets are to enclose old and new for America is the race of races. Of them a bard is to be commensurate with a people. To him the other continents arrive as contributions . . . he gives them reception for their sake and his own sake. His spirit responds to his country's spirit . . . . he incarnates its geography and natural life and rivers and lakes. Mississippi with annual freshets and changing chutes, Missouri and Columbia and Ohio and Saint Lawrence with the falls and beautiful masculine Hudson, do not embouchure where they spend themselves more than they embouchure into him. The blue breadth over the inland sea of Virginia and

Maryland and the sea off Massachusetts and Maine and over Manhattan bay and over Champlain and Erie and over Ontario and Huron and Michigan and Superior, and over the Texan and Mexican and Floridian and Cuban seas and over the seas off California and Oregon, is not tallied by the blue breadth of the waters below more than the breadth of above and below is tallied by him. When the long Atlantic coast stretches longer and the Pacific coast stretches longer he easily stretches with them north or south. He spans between them also from east to west and reflects what is between them. On him rise solid growths that offset the growths of pine and cedar and hemlock and liveoak and locust and chestnut and cypress and hickory and limetree and cottonwood and tuliptree and cactus and wildvine and tamarind and persimmon . . . . and tangles as tangled as any canebrake or swamp . . . . and forests coated with transparent ice and icicles hanging from the boughs and crackling in the wind . . . . and sides and peaks of mountains . . . . and pasturage sweet and free as savannah or upland or prairie . . . . with flights and songs and screams that answer those of the wildpigeon and highhold and orchard-oriole and coot and surf-duck and red-shouldered-hawk and fish-hawk and white-ibis and indian-hen and cat-owl and water-pheasant and qua-bird and pied-sheldrake and blackbird and mockingbird and buzzard and condor and night-heron and eagle. To him the hereditary countenance descends both mother's and father's. To him enter the essences of the real things and past and present events—of the enormous diversity of temperature and agriculture and mines—the tribes of red aborigines—the weather-beaten vessels entering new ports or making landings on rocky coasts—the first settlements north or south—the rapid stature and muscle—the haughty defiance of '76, and the war and peace and formation of the constitution . . . . the union always surrounded by blatherers and always calm and impregnable—the perpetual coming of immigrants—the wharfhem'd cities and superior marine—the unsurveyed interior—the loghouses and clearings and wild animals and hunters and trappers . . . . the free commerce—the fisheries and whaling and gold-digging—the endless gestation of new states—the convening of Congress every December, the members duly coming up from all climates and the uttermost parts . . . . the noble character of the young mechanics and of all free American workmen and workwomen . . . . the general ardor and friendliness and enterprise—the perfect equality of the female with the male . . . . the large amativeness—the fluid movement of the population—the factories and mercantile life and laborsaving machinery—the Yankee swap—the New-York firemen and the target excursion—the southern plantation life—the character of the northeast and of the northwest and southwest—slavery and the tremulous spreading of hands to protect it, and the stern opposition to it which shall never cease till it ceases or the speaking of tongues and the moving of lips cease. For such the expression of the American poet is to be transcendant and new. It is to be indirect and not direct or descriptive or epic. Its quality goes through these to much more. Let the age and wars of other nations be chanted and their eras and characters be illustrated and that finish the verse. Not so the great psalm of the republic. Here the theme is creative and has vista. Here comes one among the wellbeloved stonecutters and plans with decision and science and sees the solid and beautiful forms of the future where there are now no solid forms.

Of all nations the United States with veins full of poetical stuff most need poets and will doubtless have the greatest and use them the greatest. Their Presidents shall not be their common referee so much as their poets shall. Of all mankind the great poet is the equable man. Not in him but off from him things are grotesque or eccentric or fail of their sanity. Nothing out of its place is good and nothing in its place is bad. He bestows on every object or quality its fit proportions neither more nor less. He is the arbiter of the diverse and he is the key. He is the equalizer of his age and land . . . . he supplies what wants supplying and checks what wants checking. If peace is the routine out of him speaks the spirit of peace, large, rich, thrifty, building vast and populous cities, encouraging agriculture and the arts and commerce—lighting the study of man, the soul, immortality—federal, state or municipal government, marriage, health, freetrade, intertravel by land and sea . . . . nothing too close, nothing too far off . . . the stars not too far off. In war he is the most deadly force of the war. Who recruits him recruits horse and foot . . . he fetches parks of artillery the best that engineer ever knew. If the time becomes slothful and heavy he knows how to arouse it . . . he can make every word he speaks draw blood. Whatever stagnates in the flat of custom or obedience or legislation he never stagnates. Obedience does not master him, he masters it. High up out of reach he stands turning a concentrated light . . . he turns the pivot with his finger . . . he baffles the swiftest runners as he stands and easily overtakes and envelops them. The time straying toward infidelity and confections and persiflage he withholds by his steady faith . . . he spreads out his dishes . . . he offers the sweet firmfibred meat that grows men and women. His brain is the ultimate brain. He is no arguer . . . he is judgment. He judges not as the judge judges but as the sun falling around a helpless thing. As he sees the farthest he has the most faith. His thoughts are the hymns of the praise of things. In the talk on the soul and eternity and God off of his equal plane he is silent. He sees eternity less like a play with a prologue and denouement . . . . he sees eternity in men and women . . . he does not see men and women as dreams or dots. Faith is the antiseptic of the soul . . . it pervades the common people and preserves them . . . they never give up believing and expecting and trusting. There is that indescribable freshness and unconsciousness about an illiterate person that humbles and mocks the power of the noblest expressive genius. The poet sees for a certainty how one not a great artist may be just as sacred and perfect as the greatest artist. . . . The power to destroy or remould is freely used by him but never the power of attack. What is past is past. If he does not expose superior models and prove himself by every step he takes he is not what is wanted. The presence of the greatest poet conquers . . . not parleying or struggling or any prepared attempts. Now he has passed that way see after him! there is not left any vestige of despair or misanthropy or cunning or exclusiveness or the ignominy of a nativity or color or delusion of hell or the necessity of hell . . . . and no man thenceforward shall be degraded for ignorance or weakness or sin.

The greatest poet hardly knows pettiness or triviality. If he breathes into any thing that was before thought small it dilates with the grandeur and life of the universe. He is a seer . . . . he is individual . . . he is complete in himself . . . . the others are as good as he, only he sees it and they do not. He is not one of the chorus . . . . he does not stop for any regulation . . . he is the president of regulation. What the eyesight does to the rest he does to the rest. Who knows the curious mystery of the eyesight? The other senses corroborate themselves, but this is removed from any proof but its own and foreruns the identities of the spiritual world. A single glance of it mocks all the investigations of man and all the instruments and books of the earth and all reasoning. What is marvellous? what is unlikely? what is impossible or baseless or vague? after you have once just opened the space of a peachpit and given audience to far and near and to the sunset and had all things enter with electric swiftness softly and duly without confusion or jostling or jam.

The land and sea, the animals fishes and birds, the sky of heaven and the orbs, the forests mountains and rivers, are not small themes . . . but folks expect of the poet to indicate more than the beauty and dignity which always attach to dumb real objects . . . . they expect him to indicate the path between reality and their souls. Men and women perceive the beauty well enough . . probably as well as he. The passionate tenacity of hunters, woodmen, early risers, cultivators of gardens and orchards and fields, the love of healthy women for the manly form, seafaring persons, drivers of horses, the passion for light and the open air, all is an old varied sign of the unfailing perception of beauty and of a residence of the poetic in outdoor people. They can never be assisted by poets to perceive . . . some may but they never can. The poetic quality is not marshalled in rhyme or uniformity or abstract addresses to things nor in melancholy complaints or good precepts, but is the life of these and much else and is in the soul. The profit of rhyme is that it drops seeds of a sweeter and more luxuriant rhyme, and of uniformity that it conveys itself into its own roots in the ground out of sight. The rhyme and uniformity of perfect poems show the free growth of metrical laws and bud from them as unerringly and loosely as lilacs or roses on a bush, and take shapes as compact as the shapes of chestnuts and oranges and melons and pears, and shed the perfume impalpable to form. The fluency and ornaments of the finest poems or music or orations or recitations are not independent but dependent. All beauty comes from beautiful blood and a beautiful brain. If the greatnesses are in conjunction in a man or woman it is enough . . . . the fact will prevail through the universe . . . . but the gaggery and gilt of a million years will not prevail. Who troubles himself about his ornaments or fluency is lost. This is what you shall do: Love the earth and sun and the animals, despise riches, give alms to every one that asks, stand up for the stupid and crazy, devote your income and labor to others, hate tyrants, argue not concerning God, have patience and indulgence toward the people, take off your hat to nothing known or unknown or to any man or number of men, go greely with powerful uneducated persons and with the young and with the mothers of families, read these leaves in the open air every season of every year of your life, re-examine all you have been told at school or church or in any book, dismiss whatever insults you own soul, and your very flesh shall be a great poem and have the richest fluency not only in its words but in the silent lines of its lips and face and between the lashes of your eyes and in every motion and joint of your body . . . . The poet shall not spend his time in unneeded work. He shall know that the ground is always ready ploughed and manured . . . . others may not know it but he shall. He shall go directly to the creation. His trust shall master the trust of everything he touches . . . . and shall master all attachment.

The known universe has one complete lover and that is the greatest poet. He consumes an eternal passion and is indifferent which chance happens and which possible contingency of fortune or misfortune and persuades daily and hourly his delicious pay. What balks or breaks others is fuel for his burning progress to contact and amorous joy. Other proportions of the reception of pleasure dwindle to nothing to his proportions. All expected from heaven or from the highest he is rapport with in the sight of the daybreak or a scene of the winter woods or the presence of children playing or with his arm round the neck of a man or woman. His love above all love has leisure and expanse . . . . he leaves room ahead of himself. He is no irresolute or suspicious lover . . . he is sure . . . he scorns intervals. His experience and the showers and thrills are not for nothing. Nothing can jar him . . . . suffering and darkness cannot—death and fear cannot. To him complaint and jealousy and envy are corpses buried and rotten in the earth . . . . he saw them buried. The sea is not surer of the shore or the shore of the sea than he is of the fruition of his love and of all perfection and beauty.

The fruition of beauty is no chance of hit or miss . . . it is inevitable as life . . . . it is exact and plumb as gravitation. From the eyesight proceeds another eyesight and from the hearing proceeds another hearing and from the voice proceeds another voice eternally curious of the harmony of things with man. To these respond perfections not only in the committees that were supposed to stand for the rest but in the rest themselves just the same. These understand the law of perfection in masses and floods . . . that its finish is to each for itself and onward from itself . . . that it is profuse and impartial . . . that there is not a minute of the light or dark nor an acre of the earth or sea without it—nor any direction of the sky nor any trade or employment nor any turn of events. This is the reason that about the proper expression of beauty there is precision and balance . . . one part does not need to be thrust above another. The best singer is not the one who has the most lithe and powerful organ . . . the pleasure of poems is not in them that take the handsomest measure and similes and sound.

Without effort and without exposing in the least how it is done the greatest poet brings the spirit of any or all events and passions and scenes and persons some more and some less to bear on your individual character as you hear or read. To do this well is to compete with the laws that pursue and follow time. What is the purpose must surely be there and the clue of it must be there . . . . and the faintest indication is the indication of the best and then becomes the clearest indication. Past and present and future are not disjoined but joined. The greatest poet forms the consistence of what is to be from what has been and is. He drags the dead out of their coffins and stands them again on their feet . . . . he says to the past, Rise and walk before me that I may realize you. He learns the lesson . . . . he places himself where the future becomes present. The greatest poet does not only dazzle his rays over character and scenes and passions . . . he finally ascends and finishes all . . . he exhibits the pinnacles that no man can tell what they are for or what is beyond . . . . he glows a moment on the extremest verge. He is most wonderful in his last half-hidden smile or frown . . . by that flash of the moment of parting the one that sees it shall be encouraged or terrified afterward for many years. The greatest poet does not moralize or make applications of morals . . . he knows the soul. The soul has that measureless pride which consists in never acknowledging any lessons but its own. But it has sympathy as measurless as its pride and the one balances the other and neither can stretch too far while it stretches in company with the other. The inmost secrets of art sleep with the twain. The greatest poet has lain close betwixt both and they are vital in his style and thoughts.

The art of art, the glory of expression and the sunshine of the light of letters is simplicity. Nothing is better than simplicity . . . . nothing can make up for excess or for the lack of definiteness. To carry on the heave of impulse and pierce intellectual depths and give all subjects their articulations are powers neither common nor very uncommon. But to speak in literature with the perfect rectitude and insousiance of the movements of animals and the unimpeachableness of the sentiment of trees in the woods and grass by the roadside is the flawless triumph of art. If you have looked on him who has achieved it you have looked on one of the masters of the artists of all nations and times. You shall not contemplate the flight of the graygull over the bay or the mettlesome action of the blood horse or the tall leaning of sunflowers on their stalk or the appearance of the sun journeying through heaven or the appearance of the moon afterward with any more satisfaction than you shall contemplate him. The greatest poet has less a marked style and is more the channel of thoughts and things without increase or diminution, and is the free channel of himself. He swears to his art, I will not be meddlesome, I will not have in my writing any elegance or effect or originality to hang in the way between me and the rest like curtains. I will have nothing hang in the way, not the richest curtains. What I tell I tell for precisely what it is. Let who may exalt or startle or fascinate or soothe I will have purposes as health or heat or snow has and be as regardless of observation. What I experience or portray shall go from my composition without a shred of my composition. You shall stand by my side and look in the mirror with me.

The old red blood and stainless gentility of great poets will be proved by their unconstraint. A heroic person walks at his ease through and out of that custom or precedent or authority that suits him not. Of the traits of the brotherhood of writers savans[1] musicians inventors and artists nothing is finer than silent defiance advancing from new free forms. In the need of poems philosophy politics mechanism science behaviour, the craft of art, an appropriate native grand-opera, ship-craft, or any craft, he is greatest forever and forever who contributes the greatest original practical example. The cleanest expression is that which finds no sphere worthy of itself and makes one.

The messages of great poets to each man and women are, Come to us on equal terms, Only then can you understand us, We are no better than you, What we enclose you enclose, What we enjoy you may enjoy. Did you suppose there could be only one Supreme? We affirm there can be unnumbered Supremes, and that one does not countervail another any more than one eyesight countervails another . . and that men can be good or grand only of the consciousness of their supremacy within them. What do you think is the grandeur of storms and dismemberments and the deadliest battles and wrecks and the wildest fury of the elements and the power of the sea and the motion of nature and of the throes of human desires and dignity and hate and love? It is that something in the soul which says, Rage on, Whirl on, I tread master here and everywhere, Master of the spasms of the sky and of the shatter of the sea, Master of nature and passion and death, And of all terror and all pain.

The American bards shall be marked for generosity and affection and for encouraging competitors . . They shall be kosmos . . without monopoly or secrecy . . glad to pass any thing to any one . . hungry for equals night and day. They shall not be careful of riches and privilege . . . . they shall be riches and privilege . . . . they shall perceive who the most affluent man is. The most affluent man is he that confronts all the shows he sees by equivalents out of the stronger wealth of himself. The American bard shall delineate no class of persons nor one or two out of the strata of inter-

[1]Scientists.

ests nor love most nor truth most nor the soul most nor the body most . . . . and not be for the eastern states more than the western or the northern states more than the southern.

Exact science and its practical movements are no checks on the greatest poet but always his encouragement and support. The outset and remembrance are there . . there the arms that lifted him first and brace him best . . . . there he returns after all his goings and comings. The sailor and traveler . . the anatomist chemist astronomer geologist phrenologist spiritualist mathematician historian and lexicographer are not poets, but they are the lawgivers of poets and their construction underlies the structure of every perfect poem. No matter what rises or is uttered they sent the seed of the conception of it . . . of them and by them stand the visible proofs of souls . . . . . always of their fatherstuff must be begotten the sinewy races of bards. If there shall be love and content between the father and the son and if the greatness of the son is the exuding of the greatness of the father there shall be love between the poet and the man of demonstrable science. In the beauty of poems are the tuft and final applause of science.

Great is the faith of the flush of knowledge and of the investigation of the depths of qualities and things. Cleaving and circling here swells the soul of the poet yet is president of itself always. The depths are fathomless and therefore calm. The innocence and nakedness are resumed . . . they are neither modest nor immodest. The whole theory of the special and supernatural and all that was twined with it or educed out of it departs as a dream. What has ever happened . . . . what happens and whatever may or shall happen, the vital laws enclose all . . . . they are sufficient for any case and for all cases . . . none to be hurried or retarded . . . . any miracle of affairs or persons inadmissible in the vast clear scheme where every motion and every spear of grass and the frames and spirits of men and women and all that concerns them are unspeakably perfect miracles all referring to all and each distinct and in its place. It is also not consistent with the reality of the soul to admit that there is anything in the known universe more divine than men and women.

Men and women and the earth and all upon it are simply to be taken as they are, and the investigation of their past and present and future shall be unintermitted and shall be done with perfect candor. Upon this basis philosophy speculates ever looking toward the poet, ever regarding the eternal tendencies of all toward happiness never inconsistent with what is clear to the senses and to the soul. For the eternal tendencies of all toward happiness make the only point of sane philosophy. Whatever comprehends less than that . . . whatever is less than the laws of light and of astronomical motion . . . or less than the laws that follow the thief the liar the glutton and the drunkard through this life and doubtless afterward . . . . . . or less than vast stretches of time or the slow formation of density or the patient upheaving of strata—is of no account. Whatever would put God in a poem or system of philosophy as contending against some being or influence is also of no account. Sanity and ensemble characterise the great master . . . spoilt in one principle all is spoilt. The great master has nothing to do with miracles. He sees health for himself in being one of the mass . . . . he sees the hiatus in singular eminence. To the perfect shape comes common ground. To be under the general law is great for that is to correspond with it. The master knows that he is unspeakably great and that all are unspeakably great . . . . that nothing for instance is greater than to conceive children and bring them up well . . . that to be is just as great as to perceive or tell.

In the make of the great masters the idea of political liberty is indispensible. Liberty takes the adherence of heroes wherever men and women exist . . . . but never takes any adherence or welcome from the rest more than from poets. They are the voice and exposition of liberty. They out of ages are worthy the grand idea . . . . to them it is confided and they must sustain it. Nothing has precedence of it and nothing can warp or degrade it. The attitude of great poets is to cheer up slaves and horrify despots. The turn of their necks, the sound of their feet, the motions of their wrists, are full of hazard to the one and hope to the other. Come nigh them awhile and though they neither speak or advise you shall learn the faithful American lesson. Liberty is poorly served by men whose good intent is quelled from one failure or two failures or any number of failures, or from the casual indifference or ingratitude of the people, or from the sharp show of the tushes of power, or the bringing to bear soldiers and cannon or any penal statutes. Liberty relies upon itself, invites no one, promises nothing, sits in calmness and light, is positive and composed, and knows no discouragement. The battle rages with many a loud alarm and frequent advance and retreat . . . . the enemy triumphs . . . . the prison, the handcuffs, the iron necklace and anklet, the scaffold, garrote and leadballs do their work . . . . the cause is asleep . . . . the strong throats are choked with their own blood . . . . the young men drop their eyelashes toward the ground when they pass each other . . . . and is liberty gone out of that place? No never. When liberty goes it is not the first to go nor the second or third to go . . it waits for all the rest to go . . it is the last. . . When the memories of the old martyrs are faded utterly away . . . . when the large names of patriots are laughed at in the public halls from the lips of the orators . . . . when the boys are no more christened after the same but christened after tyrants and traitors instead . . . . when the laws of the free are grudgingly permitted and laws for informers and blood-money are sweet to the taste of the people . . . . when I and you walk abroad upon the earth stung with compassion at the sight of numberless brothers answering our equal friendship and calling no man master—and when we are elated with noble joy at the sight of slaves . . . . when the soul retires in the cool communion of the night and surveys its experience and has much extasy over the word and deed that put back a helpless innocent person into the gripe of the gripers or into any cruel inferiority . . . . when those in all parts of these states who could easier realize the true American character but do not yet—when the swarms of cringers, suckers, dough-faces, lice of politics, planners of sly involutions for their own preferment to city offices or state legislatures or the judiciary or congress or the presidency, obtain a response of love and natural deference from the people whether they get the offices or no . . . . when it is better to be a bound booby and rogue in office at a high salary than the poorest free mechanic or farmer with his hat unmoved from his head and firm eyes and a candid and generous heart . . . . and when servility by town or state or the federal government or any oppression on a large scale or small scale can be tried on without its own punishment following duly after in exact proportion against the smallest chance of escape . . . . or rather when all life and all the souls of men and women are discharged from that part of the earth.

As the attributes of the poets of the kosmos concentre in the real body and soul and in the pleasure of things they possess the superiority of genuineness over all fiction and romance. As they emit themselves facts are showered over with light . . . . the daylight is lit with more volatile light . . . . also the deep between the setting and rising sun goes deeper many fold. Each precise object or condition or combination or process exhibits a beauty . . . . the multiplication table its—old age its—the carpenter's trade its—the grand-opera its . . . . the hugehulled clean-shaped New-York clipper at sea under steam or full sail gleams with unmatched beauty . . . . the American circles and large harmonies of government gleam with theirs . . . . and the commonest definite intentions and actions with theirs. The poets of the kosmos advance through all interpositions and coverings and turmoils and stratagems to first principles. They are of use . . . . they dissolve poverty from its need and riches from its conceit. You large proprietor they say shall not realize or perceive more than any one else. The owner of the library is not he who holds a legal title to it having bought and paid for it. Any one and every one is owner of the library who can read the same through all the varieties of tongues and subjects and styles, and in whom they enter with ease and take residence and force toward paternity and maternity, and make supple and powerful and rich and large. . . . . These American states strong and healthy and accomplished shall receive no pleasure from violations of natural models and must not permit them. In paintings or mouldings or carvings in mineral or wood, or in the illustrations of books or newspapers, or in any comic or tragic prints, or in the patterns of woven stuffs or any thing to beautify rooms or furniture or costumes, or to put upon cornices or monuments or on the prows or sterns of ships, or to put anywhere before the human eye indoors or out, that which distorts honest shapes or which creates unearthly beings or places or contingencies is a nuisance and revolt. Of the human form especially it is so great it must never be made ridiculous. Of ornaments to a work nothing outre[2] can be allowed . . but those ornaments can be allowed that conform to the perfect facts of the open air and that flow out of the nature of the work and come irrepressibly from it and are necessary to the completion of the work. Most works are most beautiful without ornament. . . Exaggerations will be revenged in human physiology. Clean and vigorous children are jetted and conceived only in those communities where the models of natural forms are public every day. . . . . Great genius and the people of these states must never be demeaned to romances. As soon as histories are properly told there is no more need of romances.

The great poets are also to be known by the absence in them of tricks and by the justification of perfect personal candor. Then folks echo a new cheap joy and a divine voice leaping from their brains: How beautiful is candor! All faults may be forgiven of him who has perfect candor. Henceforth let no man of us lie, for we have seen that openness wins the inner and outer world and that there is no single exception, and that never since our earth gathered itself in a mass have deceit or subterfuge or prevarication attracted its smallest particle or the faintest tinge of a shade—and that through the enveloping wealth and rank of a state or the whole republic of states a sneak or sly person shall be discovered and despised . . . . and that the soul has never been once fooled and never can be fooled . . . . and thrift without the loving nod of the soul is only a fœtid puff . . . . and there never grew up in any of the continents of the globe nor upon any planet or satellite or star, nor upon the asteroids, nor in any part of ethereal space, nor in the midst of density, nor under the fluid wet of the sea, nor in that condition which precedes the birth of babes, nor at any time during the changes of life, nor in that condition that follows what we term death, nor in

[2]Excessive, extravagant. An example of Whitman's many "borrowings" from the French language.

any stretch of abeyance or action afterward of vitality, nor in any process of formation or reformation anywhere, a being whose instinct hated the truth.

Extreme caution or prudence, the soundest organic health, large hope and comparison and fondness for women and children, large alimentiveness and destructiveness and causality, with a perfect sense of the oneness of nature and the propriety of the same spirit applied to human affairs . . these are called up of the float of the brain of the world to be parts of the greatest poet from his birth out of his mother's womb and from her birth out of her mother's. Caution seldom goes far enough. It has been thought that the prudent citizen was the citizen who applied himself to solid gains and did well for himself and his family and completed a lawful life without debt or crime. The greatest poet sees and admist these economies as he sees the economies of food and sleep, but has higher notions of prudcence than to think he gives much when he gives a few slight attentions at the latch of the gate. The premises of the prudence of life are not the hospitality of it or the ripeness and harvest of it. Beyond the independence of a little sum laid aside for burial-money, and of a few clap-boards around and shingles overhead on a lot of American soil owned, and the easy dollars that supply the year's plain clothing and meals, the melancholy prudence of the abandonment of such a great being as a man is to the toss and pallor of years of money-making with all their scorching days and icy nights and all their stifling deceits and underhanded dodgings, or infinitessimals of parlors, or shameless stuffing while others starve . . and all the loss of the bloom and odor of the earth and of the flowers and atmosphere and of the sea and of the true taste of the women and men you pass or have to do with in youth or middle age, and the issuing sickness and desperate revolt at the close of a life without elevation or naivete, and the ghastly chatter of a death without serenity or majesty, is the great fraud upon modern civilization and forethought, blotching the surface and system which civilization undeniably drafts, and moistening with tears the immense features it spreads and spreads with such velocity before the reached kisses of the soul. . . Still the right explanation remains to be made about prudence. The prudence of the mere wealth and respectability of the most esteemed life appears too faint for the eye to observe at all when little and large alike drop quietly aside at the thought of the prudence suitable for immortality. What is wisdom that fills the thinness of a year or seventy or eighty years to wisdom spaced out by ages and coming back at a certain time with strong reinforcements and rich presents and the clear faces of wedding-guests as far as you can look in every direction running gaily toward you? Only the soul is of itself . . . . all else has reference to what ensues. All that a person does or thinks is of consequence. Not a move can a man or woman make that affects him or her in a day or a month or any part of the direct lifetime or the hour of death but the same affects him or her onward afterward through the indirect lifetime. The indirect is always as great and real as the direct. The spirit receives from the body just as much as it gives to the body. Not one name of word or deed . . not of venereal sores or discolorations . . not the privacy of the onanist . . not of the putrid veins of gluttons or rumdrinkers . . . not peculation or cunning or betrayal or murder . . no serpentine poision of those that seduce women . . not the foolish yielding of women . . not prostitution . . not of any depravity of young men . . not of the attainment of gain by discreditable means . . not any nastiness of appetite . . not any harshness of officers to men or judges to prisoners or fathers to sons or sons to fathers or of husbands to wives or bosses to their boys . . not of greedy looks or malignant wishes . . . nor any of the wiles practised by people upon themselves . . . ever is or ever can be stamped on the programme but it is duly realized and returned, and that returned in further performances . . . and they returned again. Nor can the push of charity or personal force ever be any thing else than the profoundest reason, whether it bring arguments to hand or no. No specification is necessary . . to add or subtract or divide is in vain. Little or big, learned or unlearned, white or black, legal or illegal, sick or well, from the first inspiration down the windpipe to the last expiration out of it, all that a male or female does that is vigorous and benevolent and clean is so much sure profit to him or her in the unshakable order of the universe and through the whole scope of it forever. If the savage or felon is wise it is well . . . . if the greatest poet or savan is wise it is simply the same . . if the President or chief justice is wise it is the same . . . if the young mechanic or farmer is wise it is no more or less . . if the prositute is wise it is no more nor less. The interest will come round . . all will come round. All the best actions of war and peace . . . all help given to relatives and strangers and the poor and old and sorrowful and young children and widows and the sick, and to all shunned persons . . all furtherance of fugitives and of the escape of slaves . . all the self-denial that stood steady and aloof on wrecks and saw others take the seats of the boats . . . all offering of substance or life for the good old cause, or for a friend's sake or opinion's sake . . . all pains of enthusiasts scoffed at by their neighbors . . all the vast sweet love and precious suffering of mothers . . . all honest men baffled in strifes recorded or unrecorded . . . . all the grandeur and good of the few ancient nations whose fragments of annals we inherit . . and all the good of the hundreds of far mightier and more ancient nations unknown to us by name or date or location . . . . all that was ever manfully begun, whether it succeeded or no . . . . all that has at any time been well suggested out of the divine heart of man or by the divinity of his mouth or by the shaping of his great hands . . and all that is well thought or done this day on any part of the surface of the globe . . or on any of the wandering stars or fixed stars by those there as we are here . . or that is henceforth to be well thought or done by you whoever you are, or by any one—these singly and wholly inured at their time and inure now and will inure always to the identities from which they sprung or shall spring. . . Did you guess any of them lived only its moment? The world does not so exist . . no parts palpable or impalpable so exist . . . no result exists now without being from its long antecedent result, and that from its antecdent, and so backward without the farthest mentionable spot coming a bit nearer the beginning than any other spot. . . . . Whatever satisfies the soul is truth. The prudence of the greatest poet answers at last the craving and glut of the soul, is not contemptuous of less ways of prudence if they conform to its ways, puts off nothing, permits no let-up for its own case or any case, has no particular sabbath or judgment-day, divides not the living from the dead or the righteous from the unrighteous, is satisfied with the present, matches every thought or act by its correlative, knows no possible forgiveness or deputed atonement . . knows that the young man who composedly periled his life and lost it has done exceeding well for himself, while the man who has not periled his life and retains it to old age in riches and ease has perhaps achieved nothing for himself worth mentioning . . and that only that person has no great prudence to learn who has learnt to prefer real longlived things, and favors body and soul the same, and perceives the indirect assuredly following the direct, and what evil or good he does leaping onward and waiting to meet him again—and who in his spirit in any emergency whatever neither hurries or avoids death.

The direct trial of him who would be the greatest poet is today. If he does not flood himself with the immediate age as with vast oceanic tides . . . . . and if he does not attract his own land body and soul to himself and hang on its neck with incomparable love and plunge his semitic[3] muscle into its merits and demerits . . . . and if he be not himself the age transfigured . . . . and if to him is not opened the eternity which gives similitude to all periods and locations and processes and animate and inanimate forms, and which is the bond of time, and rises up from its inconceivable vagueness and infiniteness in the swimming shape of today, and is held by the ductile anchors of life, and makes the present spot the passage from what was to what shall be, and commits itself to the representation of this wave of an hour and this one of the sixty beautiful children of the wave—let him merge in the general run and wait his development. . . . . Still the final test of poems or any character or work remains. The prescient poet projects himself centuries ahead and judges performer or performance after the changes of time. Does it live through them? Does it still hold on untired? Will the same style and the direction of genius to similar points be satisfactory now? Has no new discovery in science or arrival at superior planes of thought and judgment and behaviour fixed him or his so that either can be looked down upon? Have the marches of tens and hundreds and thousands of years made willing detours to the right hand and the left hand for his sake? Is he beloved long and long after he is buried? Does the young man think often of him? and the young woman think often of him? and do the middleaged and the old think of him?

A great poem is for ages and ages in common and for all degrees and complexions and all departments and sects and for a woman as much as a man and a man as much as a woman. A great poem is no finish to a man or woman but rather a beginning. Has any one fancied he could sit at last under some due authority and rest satisfied with explanations and realize and be content and full? To no such terminus does the greatest poet bring . . . he brings neither cessation or sheltered fatness and ease. The touch of him tells in action. Whom he takes he takes with firm sure grasp into live regions previously unattained . . . . thenceforward is no rest . . . . they see the space and ineffable sheen that turn the old spots and lights into dead vacuums. The companion of him beholds the birth and progress of stars and learns one of the meanings. Now there shall be a man cohered out of tumult and chaos . . . . the elder encourages the younger and shows him how . . . they two shall launch off fearlessly together till the new world fits an orbit for itself and looks unabashed on the lesser orbits of the stars and sweeps through the ceaseless rings and shall never be quiet again.

There will soon be no more priests. Their work is done. They may wait awhile . . perhaps a generation or two . . dropping off by degrees. A superior breed shall take their place . . . . the gangs of kosmos and prophets en masse shall take their place. A new order shall arise and they shall be the priests of man, and every man shall be his own priest. The churches built under their umbrage shall be the churches of men and women. Through the divinity of themselves shall the kosmos and the new breed of poets be interpreters of men and women and of all events and things. They shall find their inspiration in real objects today, symptoms of the past and future . . . . They shall

[3]Whitman's own rather awkward coinage, suggesting the sexual organ through which semen passes.

not deign to defend immortality or God or the perfection of things or liberty or the exquisite beauty and reality of the soul. They shall arise in America and be responded to from the remainder of the earth.

The English language befriends the grand American expression . . . . it is brawny enough and limber and full enough. On the tough stock of a race who through all change of circumstance was never without the idea of political liberty, which is the animus of all liberty, it has attracted the terms of daintier and gayer and subtler and more elegant tongues. It is the powerful language of resistance . . . it is the dialect of common sense. It is the speech of the proud and melancholy races and of all who aspire. It is the chosen tongue to express growth faith self-esteem freedom justice equality friendliness amplitude prudence decision and courage. It is the medium that shall well nigh express the inexpressible.

No great literature nor any like style of behaviour or oratory or social intercourse or household arrangements or public institutions or the treatment by bosses of employed people, nor executive detail or detail of the army or navy, nor spirit of legislation or courts or police or tuition or architecture or songs or amusements or the costumes of young men, can long elude the jealous and passionate instinct of American standards. Whether or no the sign appears from the mouths of the people, it throbs a live interrogation in every freeman's and freewoman's heart after that which passes by or this built to remain. Is it uniform with my country? Are its disposals without ignominious distinctions? Is it for the evergrowing communes of brothers and lovers, large, well-united, proud beyond the old models, generous beyond all models? Is it something grown fresh out of the fields or drawn from the sea for use to me today here? I know that what answers for me an American must answer for any individual or nation that serves for a part of my materials. Does this answer? or is it without reference to universal needs? or sprung of the needs of the less developed society of special ranks? or old needs of pleasure overlaid by modern science and forms? Does this acknowledge liberty with audible and absolute acknowledgement, and set slavery at nought for life and death? Will it help breed one goodshaped and wellhung man, and a woman to be his perfect and independent mate? Does it improve manners? Is it for the nursing of the young of the republic? Does it solve readily with the sweet milk of the nipples of the breasts of the mother of many children? Has it too the old ever-fresh forbearance and impartiality? Does it look with the same love on the last born and on those hardening toward stature, and on the errant, and on those who disdain all strength of assault outside of their own?

The poems distilled from other poems will probably pass away. The coward will surely pass away. The expectation of the vital and great can only be satisfied by the demeanor of the vital and great. The swarms of the polished deprecating and reflectors and the polite float off and leave no remembrance. America prepares with composure and goodwill for the visitors that have sent word. It is not intellect that is to be their warrant and welcome. The talented, the artist, the ingenious, the editor, the statesman, the erudite . . . they are not unappreciated . . . they fall in their place and do their work. The soul of the nation also does its work. No disguise can pass on it . . . no disguise can conceal from it. It rejects none, it permits all. Only toward as good as itself and toward the like of itself will it advance half-way. An individual is as superb as a nation when he has the qualities which make a superb nation. The soul of the largest and wealthiest and proudest nation may well go half-way to meet that of its poets. The signs are effectual. There is no fear of mistake. If the one is true the other is true. The proof of a poet is that his country absorbs him as affectionately as he has absorbed it.

Song of Myself[1]

[1] I celebrate myself,
And what I assume you shall assume,
For every atom belonging to me as good belongs to you.

I loafe and invite my soul,
I lean and loafe at my ease . . . . observing a spear of summer grass.

[2] Houses and rooms are full of perfumes . . . . the shelves are crowded with perfumes,
I breathe the fragrance myself, and know it and like it,
The distillation would intoxicate me also, but I shall not let it.

The atmosphere is not a perfume . . . . it has no taste of the distillation . . . . it is odorless,
It is for my mouth forever . . . . I am in love with it,
I will go to the bank by the wood and become undisguised and naked,
I am mad for it to be in contact with me.

The smoke of my own breath,
Echos, ripples, and buzzed whispers . . . . loveroot, silkthread, crotch and vine,
My respiration and inspiration . . . . the beating of my heart . . . . the passing of blood and air through my lungs,
The sniff of green leaves and dry leaves, and of the shore and darkcolored sea-rocks, and of hay in the barn,
The sound of the belched words of my voice . . . . words loosed to the eddies of the wind,

[1]"Song of Myself" was the first of the twelve untitled poems that followed the Preface in the first edition of *Leaves of Grass* (1855). In the 1856 *Leaves* it was titled "Poem of Walt Whitman, An American." It was not until the final edition of *Leaves of Grass* in 1881 that the poem was titled "Song of Myself." We have used the 1855 versions of "Song of Myself," "The Sleepers," and "There Was a Child Went Forth" because in later editions of the poems, Whitman toned down some of the more radical stylistic, linguistic, and thematic features of the original edition of *Leaves of Grass* For the convenience of readers familiar with the later version of "Song of Myself," which is divided into fifty-two sections, we have provided the section numbers in marginal brackets at the point at which each section begins in the 1881 edition. The line numbers will not, of course, correspond to those of later versions of the poem, since Whitman added and, less frequently, deleted lines from the text.

A few light kisses . . . . a few embraces . . . . a reaching around of arms,
The play of shine and shade on the trees as the supple boughs wag,
The delight alone or in the rush of the streets, or along the fields and hillsides,
The feeling of health . . . . the full-noon trill . . . . the song of me rising from bed and meeting the sun.

Have you reckoned a thousand acres much? Have you reckoned the earth much?
Have you practiced so long to learn to read?
Have you felt so proud to get at the meaning of poems?

Stop this day and night with me and you shall possess the origin of all poems,
You shall possess the good of the earth and sun . . . . there are millions of suns left,
You shall no longer take things at second or third hand . . . . nor look through the eyes of the dead . . . . nor feed on the spectres in books,
You shall not look through my eyes either, nor take things from me,
You shall listen to all sides and filter them from yourself.

[3] I have heard what the talkers were talking . . . . the talk of the beginning and the end,
But I do not talk of the beginning or the end.

There was never any more inception than there is now,
Nor any more youth or age than there is now;
And will never be any more perfection than there is now,
Nor any more heaven or hell than there is now.

Urge and urge and urge,
Always the procreant urge of the world.

Out of the dimness opposite equals advance . . . . Always substance and increase,
Always a knit of identity . . . . always distinction . . . . always a breed of life.
To elaborate is no avail . . . . Learned and unlearned feel that it is so.

Sure as the most certain sure . . . . plumb in the uprights, well entretied, braced in the beams,
Stout as a horse, affectionate, haughty, electrical,
I and this mystery here we stand.

Clear and sweet is my soul . . . . and clear and sweet is all that is
not my soul.

Lack one lacks both . . . . and the unseen is proved by the seen,
Till that becomes unseen and receives proof in its turn.

Showing the best and dividing it from the worst, age vexes age,
Knowing the perfect fitness and equanimity of things, while they
discuss I am silent, and go bathe and admire myself.

Welcome is every organ and attribute of me, and of any man
hearty and clean,
Not an inch nor a particle of an inch is vile, and none shall be less
familiar than the rest.

I am satisfied . . . . I see, dance, laugh, sing;
As God comes a loving bedfellow and sleeps at my side all night
and close on the peep of the day,
And leaves for me baskets covered with white towels bulging the
house with their plenty,
Shall I postpone my acceptation and realization and scream at my
eyes,
That they turn from gazing after and down the road,
And forthwith cipher and show me to a cent,
Exactly the contents of one, and exactly the contents of two, and
which is ahead?

[4] Trippers and askers surround me,
People I meet . . . . the effect upon me of my early life . . . . of
the ward and city I live in . . . . of the nation,
The latest news . . . . discoveries, inventions, societies . . . .
authors old and new,
My dinner, dress, associates, looks, business, compliments, dues,
The real or fancied indifference of some man or woman I love,
The sickness of one of my folks—or of myself . . . . or illdoing
. . . . or loss or lack of money . . . . or depressions or
exaltations,
They come to me days and nights and go from me again,
But they are not the Me myself.

Apart from the pulling and hauling stands what I am,
Stands amused, complacent, compassionating, idle, unitary,
Looks down, is erect, bends an arm on an impalpable certain rest,
Looks with its sidecurved head curious what will come next,
Both in and out of the game, and watching and wondering at it.

Backward I see in my own days where I sweated through fog with linguists and contenders,
I have no mockings or arguments . . . . I witness and wait.

[5] I believe in you my soul . . . . the other I am must not abase itself to you,
And you must not be abased to the other.

Loafe with me on the grass . . . . loose the stop from your throat,
Not words, not music or rhyme I want . . . . not custom or lecture, not even the best,
Only the lull I like, the hum of your valved voice.

I mind how we lay in June, such a transparent summer morning;
You settled your head athwart my hips and gently turned over upon me,
And parted the shirt from my bosom-bone, and plunged your tongue to my barestript heart,
And reached till you felt my beard, and reached till you held my feet.

Swiftly arose and spread around me the peace and joy and knowledge that pass all the art and argument of the earth;
And I know that the hand of God is the elderhand of my own,
And I know that the spirit of God is the eldest brother of my own,
And that all the men ever born are also my brothers . . . . and the women my sisters and lovers,
And that a kelson[2] of the creation is love;
And limitless are leaves stiff or drooping in the fields,
And brown ants in the little wells beneath them,
And mossy scabs of the wormfence, and heaped stones, and elder and mullen and pokeweed.

[6] A child said, What is the grass? fetching it to me with full hands;

How could I answer the child? . . . . I do not know what it is any more than he.

I guess it must be the flag of my disposition, out of hopeful green stuff woven.

[2]A structural unit that connects or reinforces, like the keelson that braces the keel of a ship.

Or I guess it is the handkerchief of the Lord,
A scented gift and remembrancer designedly dropped,
Bearing the owner's name someway in the corners, that we may see
and remark, and say Whose?

Or I guess the grass is itself a child . . . . the produced babe of
the vegetation.

Or I guess it is a uniform hieroglyphic,
And it means, Sprouting alike in broad zones and narrow zones,
Growing among black folks as among white,
Kanuck, Tuckahoe, Congressman, Cuff,[3] I give them the same, I
receive them the same.

And now it seems to me the beautiful uncut hair of graves.

Tenderly will I use you curling grass,
It may be you transpire from the breasts of young men,
It may be if I had known them I would have loved them;
It may be you are from old people and from women, and from
offspring taken soon out of their mothers' laps,
And here you are the mothers' laps.

This grass is very dark to be from the white heads of old mothers,
Darker than the colorless beards of old men,
Dark to come from under the faint red roofs of mouths.

O I perceive after all so many uttering tongues!
And I perceive they do not come from the roofs of mouths for
nothing.

I wish I could translate the hints about the dead young men and
women,
And the hints about old men and mothers, and the offspring taken
soon out of their laps.

What do you think has become of the young and old men?
And what do you think has become of the women and children?

They are alive and well somewhere;
The smallest sprout shows there is really no death,
And if ever there was it led forward life, and does not wait at the
end to arrest it,
And ceased the moment life appeared.

[3]Kanuck, a French Canadian; Tuckahoe, a Virginian; Cuff, a black person.

All goes onward and outward . . . . and nothing collapses,
And to die is different from what any one supposed, and luckier.

[7] Has any one supposed it lucky to be born?
I hasten to inform him or her it is just as lucky to die, and I know it.

I pass death with the dying, and birth with the new-washed babe . . . . and am not contained between my hat and boots,
And peruse manifold objects, no two alike, and every one good,
The earth good, and the stars good, and their adjuncts all good.
I am not an earth nor an adjunct of an earth,
I am the mate and companion of people, all just as immortal and fathomless as myself;
They do not know how immortal, but I know.

Every kind for itself and its own . . . . for me mine male and female,
For me all that have been boys and that love women,
For me the man that is proud and feels how it stings to be slighted,
For me the sweetheart and the old maid . . . . for me mothers and the mothers of mothers,
For me lips that have smiled, eyes that have shed tears,
For me children and the begetters of children.

Who need be afraid of the merge?
Undrape . . . . you are not guilty to me, nor stale nor discarded,
I see through the broadcloth and gingham whether or no,
And am around, tenacious, acquisitive, tireless . . . . and can never be shaken away.

[8] The little one sleeps in its cradle,
I lift the gauze and look a long time, and silently brush away flies with my hand.

The youngster and the redfaced girl turn aside up the bushy hill,
I peeringly view them from the top.

The suicide sprawls on the bloody floor of the bedroom.
It is so . . . . I witnessed the corpse . . . . there the pistol had fallen.

The blab of the pave . . . . the tires of carts and sluff of bootsoles and talk of the promenaders,
The heavy omnibus, the driver with his interrogating thumb, the clank of the shod horses on the granite floor,

The carnival of sleighs, the clinking and shouted jokes and pelts of
snowballs;
The hurrahs for popular favorites . . . . the fury of roused mobs,
The flap of the curtained litter—the sick man inside, borne to the
hospital,
The meeting of enemies, the sudden oath, the blows and fall,
The excited crowd—the policeman with his star quickly working
his passage to the centre of the crowd;
The impassive stones that receive and return so many echoes,
The souls moving along . . . . are they invisible while the least
atom of the stones is visible?
What groans of overfed or half-starved who fall on the flags[4]
sunstruck or in fits,
What exclamations of women taken suddenly, who hurry home
and give birth to babes,
What living and buried speech is always vibrating here . . . . what
howls restrained by decorum,
Arrests of criminals, slights, adulterous offers made, acceptances,
rejections with convex lips,
I mind them or the resonance of them . . . . I come again and
again.

[9] The big doors of the country-barn stand open and ready,
The dried grass of the harvest-time loads the slow-drawn
wagon,
The clear light plays on the brown gray and green intertinged,
The armfuls are packed to the sagging mow:
I am there . . . . I help . . . . I came stretched atop of the load,
I felt its soft jolts . . . . one leg reclined on the other,
I jump from the crossbeams, and seize the clover and timothy,
And roll head over heels, and tangle my hair full of wisps.

[10] Alone far in the wilds and mountains I hunt,
Wandering amazed at my own lightness and glee,
In the late afternoon choosing a safe spot to pass the night,
Kindling a fire and broiling the freshkilled game,
Soundly falling asleep on the gathered leaves, my dog and gun by
my side.

The Yankee clipper is under her three skysails . . . . she cuts the
sparkle and scud,
My eyes settle the land . . . . I bend at her prow or shout joyously
from the deck.

[4]Slabs of flagstone used for paving.

The boatmen and clamdiggers arose early and stopped for me,
I tucked my trowser-ends in my boots and went and had a good time,
You should have been with us that day round the chowder-kettle.

I saw the marriage of the trapper in the open air in the farwest .... the bride was a red girl,
Her father and his friends sat near by crosslegged and dumbly smoking .... they had moccasins to their feet and large thick blankets hanging from their shoulders;
On a bank lounged the trapper .... he was dressed mostly in skins .... his luxuriant beard and curls protected his neck,
One hand rested on his rifle .... the other hand held firmly the wrist of the red girl,
She had long eyelashes .... her head was bare .... her coarse straight locks descended upon her voluptuous limbs and reached to her feet.

The runaway slave[5] came to my house and stopped outside,
I heard his motions crackling the twigs of the woodpile,
Through the swung half-door of the kitchen I saw him limpsey and weak,
And went where he sat on a log, and led him in and assured him,
And brought water and filled a tub for his sweated body and bruised feet,
And gave him a room that entered from my own, and gave him some coarse clean clothes,
And remember perfectly well his revolving eyes and his awkwardness,
And remember putting plasters on the galls of his neck and ankles;
He staid with me a week before he was recuperated and passed north,
I had him sit next me at table .... my firelock leaned in the corner.

[11] Twenty-eight young men bathe by the shore,
Twenty-eight young men, and all so friendly,
Twenty-eight years of womanly life, and all so lonesome.

She owns the fine house by the rise of the bank,
She hides handsome and richly drest aft the blinds of the window.

Which of the young men does she like the best?
Ah the homeliest of them is beautiful to her.

[5]A new and more rigorous Fugitive Slave Act, which required that inhabitants of the free states assist in the capture and return of runaway slaves, was adopted as part of the politically controversial Compromise of 1850.

Where are you off to, lady? for I see you,
You splash in the water there, yet stay stock still in your room.

Dancing and laughing along the beach came the twenty-ninth bather,
The rest did not see her, but she saw them and loved them.

The beards of the young men glistened with wet, it ran from their long hair,
Little streams passed all over their bodies.

An unseen hand also passed over their bodies,
It descended tremblingly from their temples and ribs.

The young men float on their backs, their white bellies swell to the sun . . . . they do not ask who seizes fast to them,
They do not know who puffs and declines with pendant and bending arch,
They do not think whom they souse with spray.

[12]

The butcher-boy puts off his killing-clothes, or sharpens his knife at the stall in the market,
I loiter enjoying his repartee and his shuffle and breakdown.[6]
Blacksmiths with grimed and hairy chests environ the anvil,
Each has his main-sledge . . . . they are all out . . . . there is a great heat in the fire.

From the cinder-strewed threshold I follow their movements,
The lithe sheer of their waists plays even with their massive arms,
Overhand the hammers roll—overhand so slow—overhand so sure,
They do not hasten, each man hits in his place.

[13]

The negro holds firmly the reins of his four horses . . . . the block swags underneath on its tied-over chain,
The negro that drives the huge dray of the stoneyard . . . . steady and tall he stands poised on one leg on the stringpiece,
His blue shirt exposes his ample neck and breast and loosens over his hipband,
His glance is calm and commanding . . . . he tosses the slouch of his hat away from his forehead,
The sun falls on his crispy hair and moustache . . . . falls on the black of his polish'd and perfect limbs.

I behold the picturesque giant and love him . . . . and I do not stop there,
I go with the team also.

[6] Dances popularized by minstrel shows.

In me the caresser of life wherever moving . . . . backward as well as forward slueing,
To niches aside and junior bending.

Oxen that rattle the yoke or halt in the shade, what is that you express in your eyes?
It seems to me more than all the print I have read in my life.

My tread scares the wood-drake and wood-duck on my distant and daylong ramble,
They rise together, they slowly circle around.
. . . . I believe in those winged purposes,
And acknowledge the red yellow and white playing within me,
And consider the green and violet and the tufted crown intentional;
And do not call the tortoise unworthy because she is not something else,
And the mockingbird in the swamp never studied the gamut, yet trills pretty well to me,
And the look of the bay mare shames silliness out of me.

[14] The wild gander leads his flock through the cool night,
Ya-honk! he says, and sounds it down to me like an invitation;
The pert may suppose it meaningless, but I listen closer,
I find its purpose and place up there toward the November sky.

The sharphoofed moose of the north, the cat on the housesill, the chickadee, the prairie-dog,
The litter of the grunting sow as they tug at her teats,
The brood of the turkeyhen, and she with her halfspread wings,
I see in them and myself the same old law.

The press of my foot to the earth springs a hundred affections,
They scorn the best I can do to relate them.

I am enamoured of growing outdoors,
Of men that live among cattle or taste of the ocean or woods,
Of the builders and steerers of ships, of the wielders of axes and mauls, of the drivers of horses,
I can eat and sleep with them week in and week out.

What is commonest and cheapest and nearest and easiest is Me,
Me going in for my chances, spending for vast returns,
Adorning myself to bestow myself on the first that will take me,
Not asking the sky to come down to my goodwill,
Scattering it freely forever.

[15] The pure contralto sings in the organloft,
The carpenter dresses his plank . . . . the tongue of his foreplane whistles its wild ascending lisp,
The married and unmarried children ride home to their thanksgiving dinner,
The pilot seizes the king-pin, he heaves down with a strong arm,
The mate stands braced in the whaleboat, lance and harpoon are ready,
The duck-shooter walks by silent and cautious stretches,
The deacons are ordained with crossed hands at the altar,
The spinning-girl retreats and advances to the hum of the big wheel,
The farmer stops by the bars of a Sunday and looks at the oats and rye,
The lunatic is carried at last to the asylum a confirmed case,
He will never sleep any more as he did in the cot in his mother's bedroom;
The jour printer with gray head and gaunt jaws works at his case,
He turns his quid of tobacco, his eyes get blurred with the manuscript;
The malformed limbs are tied to the anatomist's table,
What is removed drops horribly in a pail;
The quadroon girl is sold at the stand . . . . the drunkard nods by the barroom stove,
The machinist rolls up his sleeves . . . . the policeman travels his beat . . . . the gate-keeper marks who pass,
The young fellow drives the express-wagon . . . . I love him though I do not know him;
The half-breed straps on his light boots to compete in the race,
The western turkey-shooting draws old and young . . . . some lean on their rifles, some sit on logs,
Out from the crowd steps the marksman and takes his position and levels his piece;
The groups of newly-come immigrants cover the wharf or levee,
The woollypates hoe in the sugarfield, the overseer views them from his saddle;
The bugle calls in the ballroom, the gentlemen run for their partners, the dancers bow to each other;
The youth lies awake in the cedar-roofed garret and harks to the musical rain,
The Wolverine[7] sets traps on the creek that helps fill the Huron,
The reformer ascends the platform, he spouts with his mouth and nose,
The company returns from its excursion, the darkey brings up the rear and bears the well-riddled target,

[7]Inhabitant of Michigan.

The squaw wrapt in her yellow-hemmed cloth is offering moccasins and beadbags for sale,
The connoisseur peers along the exhibition-gallery with halfshut eyes bent sideways,
The deckhands make fast the steamboat, the plank is thrown for the shoregoing passengers,
The young sister holds out the skein, the elder sister winds it off in a ball and stops now and then for the knots,
The one-year wife is recovering and happy, a week ago she bore her first child,
The cleanhaired Yankee girl works with her sewing-machine or in the factory or mill,
The nine months' gone is in the parturition chamber, her faintness and pains are advancing;
The pavingman leans on his twohanded rammer—the reporter's lead flies swiftly over the notebook—the signpainter is lettering with red and gold,
The canal-boy trots on the towpath—the bookkeeper counts at his desk—the shoemaker waxes his thread,
The conductor beats time for the band and all the performers follow him,
The child is baptised—the convert is making the first professions,
The regatta is spread on the bay . . . . how the white sails sparkle!
The drover watches his drove, he sings out to them that would stray,
The pedlar sweats with his pack on his back—the purchaser higgles about the odd cent,
The camera and plate are prepared, the lady must sit for her daguerreotype,
The bride unrumples her white dress, the minutehand of the clock moves slowly,
The opium eater reclines with rigid head and just-opened lips,
The prostitute draggles her shawl, her bonnet bobs on her tipsy and pimpled neck,
The crowd laugh at her blackguard oaths, the men jeer and wink to each other,
(Miserable! I do not laugh at your oaths nor jeer you,)
The President holds a cabinet council, he is surrounded by the great secretaries,
On the piazza walk five friendly matrons with twined arms;
The crew of the fish-smack pack repeated layers of halibut in the hold,
The Missourian crosses the plains toting his wares and his cattle,
The fare-collector goes through the train—he gives notice by the jingling of loose change,
The floormen are laying the floor—the tinners are tinning the roof—the masons are calling for mortar,
In single file each shouldering his hod pass onward the laborers;

Seasons pursuing each other the indescribable crowd is gathered . . . . it is the Fourth of July . . . . what salutes of cannon and small arms!
Seasons pursuing each other the plougher ploughs and the mower mows and the wintergrain falls in the ground;
Off on the lakes the pikefisher watches and waits by the hole in the frozen surface,
The stumps stand thick round the clearing, the squatter strikes deep with his axe,
The flatboatmen make fast toward dusk near the cottonwood or pekantrees,
The coon-seekers go now through the regions of the Red river, or through those drained by the Tennessee, or through those of the Arkansas,
The torches shine in the dark that hangs on the Chattahoochee or Altamahaw;
Patriarchs sit at supper with sons and grandsons and great grandsons around them,
In walls of adobe, in canvass tents, rest hunters and trappers after their day's sport.
The city sleeps and the country sleeps,
The living sleep for their time . . . . the dead sleep for their time,
The old husband sleeps by his wife and the young husband sleeps by his wife;
And these one and all tend inward to me, and I tend outward to them,
And such as it is to be of these more or less I am.

[16] I am of old and young, of the foolish as much as the wise,
Regardless of others, ever regardful of others,
Maternal as well as paternal, a child as well as a man,
Stuffed with the stuff that is coarse, and stuffed with the stuff that is fine,
One of the great nation, the nation of many nations—the smallest the same and the largest the same,
A southerner soon as a northerner, a planter nonchalant and hospitable,
A Yankee bound my own way . . . . ready for trade . . . . my joints the limberest joints on earth and the sternest joints on earth,
A Kentuckian walking the vale of the Elkhorn in my deerskin leggings,
A boatman over the lakes or bays or along coasts . . . . a Hoosier, a Badger, a Buckeye,[8]

[8]Inhabitants of Indiana, Wisconsin, and Ohio respectively.

A Louisianian or Georgian, a poke-easy from sandhills and pines,
At home on Canadian snowshoes or up in the bush, or with fishermen off Newfoundland,
At home in the fleet of iceboats, sailing with the rest and tacking,
At home on the hills of Vermont or in the woods of Maine or the Texan ranch,
Comrade of Californians .... comrade of free northwesterners, loving their big proportions,
Comrade of raftsmen and coalmen—comrade of all who shake hands and welcome to drink and meat;
A learner with the simplest, a teacher of the thoughtfulest,
A novice beginning experient of myriads of seasons,
Of every hue and trade and rank, of every caste and religion,
Not merely of the New World but of Africa Europe or Asia .... a wandering savage,
A farmer, mechanic, or artist .... a gentleman, sailor, lover or quaker,
A prisoner, fancy-man, rowdy, lawyer, physician or priest.

I resist anything better than my own diversity,
And breathe the air and leave plenty after me,
And am not stuck up, and am in my place.

The moth and the fisheggs are in their place,
The suns I see and the suns I cannot see are in their place,
The palpable is in its place and the impalpable is in its place.

[17] These are the thoughts of all men in all ages and lands, they are not original with me,
If they are not yours as much as mine they are nothing or next to nothing,
If they do not enclose everything they are next to nothing,
If they are not the riddle and the untying of the riddle they are nothing,
If they are not just as close as they are distant they are nothing.

This is the grass that grows wherever the land is and the water is,
This is the common air that bathes the globe.

This is the breath of laws and songs and behaviour,
This is the tasteless water of souls .... this is the true sustenance,
It is for the illiterate .... it is for the judges of the supreme court .... it is for the federal capitol and the state capitols,
It is for the admirable communes of literary men and composers and singers and lecturers and engineers and savans,
It is for the endless races of working people and farmers and seamen.

This is the trill of a thousand clear cornets and scream of the octave flute and strike of triangles.

[18] I play not a march for victors only . . . . I play great marches for conquered and slain persons.

Have you heard that it was good to gain the day?
I also say it is good to fall . . . . battles are lost in the same spirit in which they are won.

I sound triumphal drums for the dead . . . . I fling through my embouchures[9] the loudest and gayest music to them,
Vivas to those who have failed, and to those whose war-vessels sank in the sea, and those themselves who sank in the sea,
And to all generals that lost engagements, and all overcome heroes, and the numberless unknown heroes equal to the greatest heroes known.

[19] This is the meal pleasantly set . . . . this is the meat and drink for natural hunger,
It is for the wicked just the same as the righteous . . . . I make appointments with all,
I will not have a single person slighted or left away,
The keptwoman and sponger and thief are hereby invited . . . . the heavy-lipped slave is invited. . . . the venerealee is invited,
There shall be no difference between them and the rest.

This is the press of a bashful hand . . . . this is the float and odor of hair,
This is the touch of my lips to yours . . . . this is the murmur of yearning,
This is the far-off depth and height reflecting my own face,
This is the thoughtful merge of myself and the outlet again.
Do you guess I have some intricate purpose?
Well I have . . . . for the April rain has, and the mica on the side of a rock has.

Do you take it I would astonish?
Does the daylight astonish? or the early redstart twittering through the woods?
Do I astonish more than they?

[9] Another borrowing from the French, suggesting an opening, or a mouthpiece of a musical instrument.

This hour I tell things in confidence,
I might not tell everybody but I will tell you.

[20] Who goes there! hankering, gross, mystical, nude?
How is it I extract strength from the beef I eat?

What is a man anyhow? What am I? and what are you?
All I mark as my own you shall offset it with your own,
Else it were time lost listening to me.

I do not snivel that snivel the world over,
That months are vacuums and the ground but wallow and filth,
That life is a suck and a sell, and nothing remains at the end but threadbare crape and tears.

Whimpering and truckling fold with powders for invalids . . . . conformity goes to the fourth-removed,
I cock my hat as I please indoors or out.

Shall I pray? Shall I venerate and be ceremonious?

I have pried through the strata and analyzed to a hair,
And counselled with doctors and calculated close and found no sweeter fat than sticks to my own bones.

In all people I see myself, none more and not one a barleycorn less,
And the good or bad I say of myself I say of them.

And I know I am solid and sound,
To me the converging objects of the universe perpetually flow,
All are written to me, and I must get what the writing means.

And I know I am deathless,
I know this orbit of mine cannot be swept by a carpenter's compass,
I know I shall not pass like a child's carlacue cut with a burnt stick at night.

I know I am august,
I do not trouble my spirit to vindicate itself or be understood,
I see that the elementary laws never apologize,
I reckon I behave no prouder than the level I plant my house by after all.

I exist as I am, that is enough,

If no other in the world be aware I sit content,
And if each and all be aware I sit content.

One world is aware, and by far the largest to me, and that is myself,
And whether I come to my own today or in ten thousand or ten million years,
I can cheerfully take it now, or with equal cheerfulness I can wait.

My foothold is tenoned and mortised in granite,
I laugh at what you call dissolution,
And I know the amplitude of time.

[21] I am the poet of the body,
And I am the poet of the soul.

The pleasures of heaven are with me, and the pains of hell are with me,
The first I graft and increase upon myself . . . . the latter I translate into a new tongue.

I am the poet of the woman the same as the man,
And I say it is as great to be a woman as to be a man,
And I say there is nothing greater than the mother of men.
I chant a new chant of dilation or pride,
We have had ducking and deprecating about enough,
I show that size is only development.

Have you outstript the rest? Are you the President?
It is a trifle . . . . they will more than arrive there every one, and still pass on.

I am he that walks with the tender and growing night;
I call to the earth and sea half-held by the night.

Press close barebosomed night! Press close magnetic nourishing night!
Night of south winds! Night of the large few stars!
Still nodding night! Mad naked summer night!

Smile O voluptuous coolbreathed earth!
Earth of the slumbering and liquid trees!
Earth of departed sunset! Earth of the mountains misty-topt!
Earth of the vitreous pour of the full moon just tinged with blue!
Earth of shine and dark mottling the tide of the river!
Earth of the limpid gray of clouds brighter and clearer for my sake!

Far-swooping elbowed earth! Rich apple-blossomed earth!
Smile, for your lover comes!

Prodigal! you have given me love! . . . . therefore I to you give love!
O unspeakable passionate love!

Thruster holding me tight and that I hold tight!
We hurt each other as the bridegroom and the bride hurt each other.

[22] You sea! I resign myself to you also . . . . I guess what you mean,
I behold from the beach your crooked inviting fingers,
I believe you refuse to go back without feeling of me;
We must have a turn together . . . . I undress . . . . hurry me out of sight of the land,
Cushion me soft . . . . rock me in billowy drowse,
Dash me with amorous wet . . . . I can repay you.

Sea of stretched ground-swells!
Sea breathing broad and convulsive breaths!
Sea of the brine of life! Sea of unshovelled and always-ready graves!
Howler and scooper of storms! Capricious and dainty sea!
I am integral with you . . . . I too am of one phase and of all phases.

Partaker of influx and efflux . . . . extoler of hate and conciliation,
Extoler of amies[10] and those that sleep in each others' arms.

I am he attesting sympathy;
Shall I make my list of things in the house and skip the house that supports them?

I am the poet of commonsense and of the demonstrable and of immortality;
And am not the poet of goodness only . . . . I do not decline to be the poet of wickedness also.

Washes and razors for foofoos . . . . for me freckles and a bristling beard.

What blurt is it about virtue and about vice?

[10]French for girlfriend; Whitman probably intended to suggest comrades and lovers of either sex.

Evil propels me, and reform of evil propels me . . . . I stand indifferent,
My gait is no faultfinder's or rejecter's gait,
I moisten the roots of all that has grown.

Did you fear some scrofula out of the unflagging pregnancy?
Did you guess the celestial laws are yet to be worked over and rectified?

I step up to say that what we do is right and what we affirm is right . . . . and some is only the ore of right,
Witnesses of us . . . . one side a balance and the antipodal side a balance,
Soft doctrine as steady help as stable doctrine,
Thoughts and deeds of the present our rouse and early start.

This minute that comes to me over the past decillions,
There is no better than it and now.

What behaved well in the past or behaves well today is not such a wonder,
The wonder is always and always how there can be a mean man or an infidel.

[23] Endless unfolding of words of ages!
And mine a word of the modern . . . . a word en masse.

A word of the faith that never balks,
One time as good as another time . . . . here or henceforward it is all the same to me.

A word of reality . . . . materialism first and last imbueing.

Hurrah for positive science! Long live exact demonstration!
Fetch stonecrop and mix it with cedar and branches of lilac;
This is the lexicographer or chemist . . . . this made a grammar of the old cartouches,[11]
These mariners put the ship through dangerous unknown seas,
This is the geologist, and this works with the scalpel, and this is a mathematician.

Gentlemen I receive you, and attach and clasp hands with you,
The facts are useful and real . . . . they are not my dwelling . . . . I enter by them to an area of the dwelling.

[11]Scroll-like tablets used for the inscription of Egyptian hieroglyphics.

I am less the reminder of property or qualities, and more the reminder of life,
And go on the square for my own sake and for others' sakes,
And make short account of neuters and geldings, and favor men and women fully equipped,
And beat the gong of revolt, and stop with fugitives and them that plot and conspire.

[24] Walt Whitman, an American, one of the roughs, a kosmos,
Disorderly fleshy and sensual . . . . eating drinking and breeding,
No sentimentalist . . . . no stander above men and women or apart from them . . . . no more modest than immodest.

Unscrew the locks from the doors!
Unscrew the doors themselves from their jambs!

Whoever degrades another degrades me . . . . and whatever is done or said returns at last to me,
And whatever I do or say I also return.

Through me the afflatus[12] surging and surging . . . . through me the current and index.

I speak the password primeval . . . . I give the sign of democracy;
By God! I will accept nothing which all cannot have their counterpart of on the same terms.

Through me many long dumb voices,
Voices of the interminable generations of slaves,
Voices of prostitutes and of deformed persons,
Voices of the diseased and despairing, and of thieves and dwarfs,
Voices of cycles of preparation and accretion,
And of the threads that connect the stars—and of wombs, and of the fatherstuff,
And of the rights of them the others are down upon,
Of the trivial and flat and foolish and despised,
Of fog in the air and beetles rolling balls of dung.

Through me forbidden voices,
Voices of sexes and lusts . . . . voices veiled, and I remove the veil,
Voices indecent by me clarified and transfigured.
I do not press my finger across my mouth,
I keep as delicate around the bowels as around the head and heart,
Copulation is no more rank to me than death is.

[12]Creative spirit or divine breath.

I believe in the flesh and the appetites,
Seeing hearing and feeling are miracles, and each part and tag of me is a miracle.

Divine am I inside and out, and I make holy whatever I touch or am touched from;
The scent of these arm-pits is aroma finer than prayer,
This head is more than churches or bibles or creeds.

If I worship any particular thing it shall be some of the spread of my body;
Translucent mould of me it shall be you,
Shaded ledges and rests, firm masculine coulter,[13] it shall be you,
Whatever goes to the tilth of me it shall be you,
You my rich blood, your milky stream pale strippings of my life;
Breast that presses against other breasts it shall be you,
My brain it shall be your occult convolutions,
Root of washed sweet-flag, timorous pond-snipe, nest of guarded duplicate eggs, it shall be you,
Mixed tussled hay of head and beard and brawn it shall be you,
Trickling sap of maple, fibre of manly wheat, it shall be you;
Sun so generous it shall be you,
Vapors lighting and shading my face it shall be you,
You sweaty brooks and dews it shall be you,
Winds whose soft-tickling genitals rub against me it shall be you,
Broad muscular fields, branches of liveoak, loving lounger in my winding paths, it shall be you,
Hands I have taken, face I have kissed, mortal I have ever touched, it shall be you.

I dote on myself . . . . there is that lot of me, and all so luscious,
Each moment and whatever happens thrills me with joy.
I cannot tell how my ankles bend . . . . nor whence the cause of my faintest wish,
Nor the cause of the friendship I emit . . . . nor the cause of the friendship I take again.

To walk up my stoop is unaccountable . . . . I pause to consider if it really be,
That I eat and drink is spectacle enough for the great authors and schools,
A morning-glory at my window satisfies me more than the metaphysics of books.

[13]The iron blade of a plow.

To behold the daybreak!
The little light fades the immense and diaphanous shadows,
The air tastes good to my palate.

Hefts of the moving world at innocent gambols, silently rising, freshly exuding,
Scooting obliquely high and low.

Something I cannot see puts upward libidinous[14] prongs,
Seas of bright juice suffuse heaven.

The earth by the sky staid with . . . . the daily close of their junction,
The heaved challenge from the east that moment over my head,
The mocking taunt, See then whether you shall be master!

[25]

Dazzling and tremendous how quick the sunrise would kill me,
If I could not now and always send sunrise out of me.

We also ascend dazzling and tremendous as the sun,
We found our own my soul in the calm and cool of the daybreak.

My voice goes after what my eyes cannot reach,
With the twirl of my tongue I encompass worlds and volumes of worlds.
Speech is the twin of my vision . . . . it is unequal to measure itself.

It provokes me forever,
It says sarcastically, Walt, you understand enough . . . . why don't you let it out then?

Come now I will not be tantalized . . . . you conceive too much of articulation.

Do you not know how the buds beneath are folded?
Waiting in gloom protected by frost,
The dirt receding before my prophetical screams,
I underlying causes to balance them at last,
My knowledge my live parts . . . . it keeping tally with the meaning of things,
Happiness . . . . which whoever hears me let him or her set out in search of this day.

My final merit I refuse you . . . . I refuse putting from me the best I am.

[14]Full of sexual energy, desire.

Encompass worlds but never try to encompass me,
I crowd your noisiest talk by looking toward you.

Writing and talk do not prove me,
I carry the plenum of proof and every thing else in my face,
With the hush of my lips I confound the topmost skeptic.

[26] I think I will do nothing for a long time but listen,
And accrue what I hear into myself . . . . and let sounds
contribute toward me.

I hear the bravuras of birds . . . . the bustle of growing wheat
. . . . gossip of flames . . . . clack of sticks cooking my meals.

I hear the sound of the human voice . . . . a sound I love,
I hear all sounds as they are tuned to their uses . . . . sounds of
the city and sounds out of the city . . . . sounds of the day
and night;
Talkative young ones to those that like them . . . . the recitative of
fish-pedlars and fruit-pedlars . . . . the loud laugh of
workpeople at their meals,
The angry base of disjointed friendship . . . . the faint tones of the
sick,
The judge with hands tight to the desk, his shaky lips pronouncing
a death-sentence,
The heave'e'yo of stevedores unlading ships by the wharves . . . .
the refrain of the anchor-lifters;
The ring of alarm-bells . . . . the cry of fire . . . . the whirr of
swift-streaking engines and hose-carts with premonitory tinkles
and colored lights,
The steam-whistle . . . . the solid roll of the train of approaching
cars;
The slow-march played at night at the head of the association,
They go to guard some corpse . . . . the flag-tops are draped with
black muslin.

I hear the violincello or man's heart's complaint,
And hear the keyed cornet or else the echo of sunset.

I hear the chorus . . . . it is a grand-opera . . . . this indeed is
music!

A tenor large and fresh as the creation fills me,
The orbic flex of his mouth is pouring and filling me full.

I hear the trained soprano . . . . she convulses me like the climax
of my love-grip;

The orchestra whirls me wider than Uranus flies,
It wrenches unnamable ardors from my breast,
It throbs me to gulps of the farthest down horror,
It sails me . . . . I dab with bare feet . . . . they are licked by the indolent waves,
I am exposed . . . . cut by bitter and poisoned hail,
Steeped amid honeyed morphine . . . . my windpipe squeezed in the fakes[15] of death,
Let up again to feel the puzzle of puzzles,
And that we call Being.

[27] To be in any form, what is that?
If nothing lay more developed the quahaug and its callous shell were enough.

Mine is no callous shell,
I have instant conductors all over me whether I pass or stop,
They seize every object and lead it harmlessly through me.

I merely stir, press, feel with my fingers, and am happy,
To touch my person to some one else's is about as much as I can stand.

[28] Is this then a touch? . . . . quivering me to a new identity,
Flames and ether making a rush for my veins,
Treacherous tip of me reaching and crowding to help them,
My flesh and blood playing out lightning, to strike what is hardly different from myself,
On all sides prurient provokers stiffening my limbs,
Straining the udder of my heart for its withheld drip,
Behaving licentious toward me, taking no denial,
Depriving me of my best as for a purpose,
Unbuttoning my clothes and holding me by the bare waist,
Deluding my confusion with the calm of the sunlight and pasture fields,
Immodestly sliding the fellow-senses away,
They bribed to swap off with touch, and go and graze at the edges of me,
No consideration, no regard for my draining strength or my anger,
Fetching the rest of the herd around to enjoy them awhile,
Then all uniting to stand on a headland and worry me.

The sentries desert every other part of me,
They have left me helpless to a red marauder,
They all come to the headland to witness and assist against me.

[15]Coils of a rope.

I am given up by traitors;
I talk wildly . . . . I have lost my wits . . . . I and nobody else am the greatest traitor.
I went myself first to the headland . . . . my own hands carried me there.

You villain touch! what are you doing? . . . . my breath is tight in its throat;
Unclench your floodgates! you are too much for me.

[29]

Blind loving wrestling touch! Sheathed hooded sharptoothed touch!
Did it make you ache so leaving me?

Parting tracked by arriving . . . . perpetual payment of the perpetual loan,
Rich showering rain, and recompense richer afterward.

Sprouts take and accumulate . . . . stand by the curb prolific and vital,
Landscapes projected masculine full-sized and golden.

[30]

All truths wait in all things,
They neither hasten their own delivery nor resist it,
They do not need the obstetric forceps of the surgeon,
The insignificant is as big to me as any,
What is less or more than a touch?

Logic and sermons never convince,
The damp of the night drives deeper into my soul.

Only what proves itself to every man and woman is so,
Only what nobody denies is so.

A minute and a drop of me settle my brain;
I believe the soggy clods shall become lovers and lamps,
And a compend of compends is the meat of a man or woman,
And a summit and flower there is the feeling they have for each other,
And they are to branch boundlessly out of that lesson until it becomes omnific,
And until every one shall delight us, and we them.

[31]

I believe a leaf of grass is no less than the journeywork of the stars,
And the pismire is equally perfect, and a grain of sand, and the egg of the wren,

And the tree-toad is a chef-d'ouvre[16] for the highest,
And the running blackberry would adorn the parlors of heaven,
And the narrowest hinge in my hand puts to scorn all machinery,
And the cow crunching with depressed head surpasses any statue,
And a mouse is miracle enough to stagger sextillions of infidels,
And I could come every afternoon of my life to look at the farmer's girl boiling her iron tea-kettle and baking shortcake.

I find I incorporate gneiss and coal and long-threaded moss and fruits and grains and esculent roots,
And am stucco'd with quadrupeds and birds all over,
And have distanced what is behind me for good reasons,
And call any thing close again when I desire it.

In vain the speeding or shyness,
In vain the plutonic rocks send their old heat against my approach,
In vain the mastadon retreats beneath its own powdered bones,
In vain objects stand leagues off and assume manifold shapes,
In vain the ocean settling in hollows and the great monsters lying low,
In vain the buzzard houses herself with the sky,
In vain the snake slides through the creepers and logs,
In vain the elk takes to the inner passes of the woods,
In vain the razorbilled auk sails far north to Labrador,
I follow quickly . . . . I ascend to the nest in the fissure of the cliff.

[32] I think I could turn and live awhile with the animals . . . . they are so placid and self-contained,
I stand and look at them sometimes half the day long.

They do not sweat and whine about their condition,
They do not lie awake in the dark and weep for their sins,
They do not make me sick discussing their duty to God,
Not one is dissatisfied . . . . not one is demented with the mania of owning things,
Not one kneels to another nor to his kind that lived thousands of years ago,
Not one is respectable or industrious over the whole earth.

So they show their relations to me and I accept them;
They bring me tokens of myself . . . . they evince them plainly in their possession.

I do not know where they got those tokens,

[16]Masterpiece.

I must have passed that way untold times ago and negligently
dropt them,
Myself moving forward then and now and forever,
Gathering and showing more always and with velocity,
Infinite and omnigenous and the like of these among them;
Not too exclusive toward the reachers of my remembrancers,
Picking out here one that shall be my amie,
Choosing to go with him on brotherly terms.

A gigantic beauty of a stallion, fresh and responsive to my caresses,
Head high in the forehead and wide between the ears,
Limbs glossy and supple, tail dusting the ground,
Eyes well apart and full of sparkling wickedness . . . . ears finely
cut and flexibly moving.

His nostrils dilate . . . . my heels embrace him . . . . his well built
limbs tremble with pleasure . . . . we speed around and
return.
I but use you a moment and then I resign you stallion . . . . and
do not need your paces, and outgallop them,
And myself as I stand or sit pass faster than you.

[33] Swift wind! Space! My Soul! Now I know it is true what I guessed
at;
What I guessed when I loafed on the grass,
What I guessed while I lay alone in my bed . . . . and again as I
walked the beach under the paling stars of the morning.

My ties and ballasts[17] leave me . . . . I travel . . . . I sail . . . . my
elbows rest in the sea-gaps,
I skirt the sierras . . . . my palms cover continents,
I am afoot with my vision.

By the city's quadrangular houses . . . . in log-huts, or camping
with lumbermen,
Along the ruts of the turnpike . . . . along the dry gulch and
rivulet bed,
Hoeing my onion-patch, and rows of carrots and parsnips . . . .
crossing savannas . . . trailing in forests,
Prospecting . . . . gold-digging . . . . girdling the trees of a new
purchase,
Scorched ankle-deep by the hot sand . . . . hauling my boat down
the shallow river;
Where the panther walks to and fro on a limb overhead . . . .
where the buck turns furiously at the hunter,

[17]As of a hot air balloon.

Where the rattlesnake suns his flabby length on a rock . . . . where the otter is feeding on fish,
Where the alligator in his tough pimples sleeps by the bayou,
Where the black bear is searching for roots or honey . . . . where the beaver pats the mud with his paddle-tail;
Over the growing sugar . . . . over the cottonplant . . . . over the rice in its low moist field;
Over the sharp-peaked farmhouse with its scalloped scum and slender shoots from the gutters;
Over the western persimmon . . . . over the longleaved corn and the delicate blueflowered flax;
Over the white and brown buckwheat, a hummer and a buzzer there with the rest,
Over the dusky green of the rye as it ripples and shades in the breeze;
Scaling mountains . . . . pulling myself cautiously up . . . . holding on by low scragged limbs,
Walking the path worn in the grass and beat through the leaves of the brush;
Where the quail is whistling betwixt the woods and the wheatlot,
Where the bat flies in the July eve . . . . where the great goldbug drops through the dark;
Where the flails keep time on the barn floor,
Where the brook puts out of the roots of the old tree and flows to the meadow,
Where cattle stand and shake away flies with the tremulous shuddering of their hides,
Where the cheese-cloth hangs in the kitchen, and andirons straddle the hearth-slab, and cobwebs fall in festoons from the rafters;
Where triphammers crash . . . . where the press is whirling its cylinders;
Wherever the human heart beats with terrible throes out of its ribs:
Where the pear-shaped balloon is floating aloft . . . . floating in it myself and looking composedly down:
Where the life-car[18] is drawn on the slipnoose . . . . where the heat hatches pale-green eggs in the dented sand,
Where the she-whale swims with her calves and never forsakes them,
Where the steamship trails hindways its long pennant of smoke,
Where the ground-shark's fin cuts like a black chip out of the water,
Where the half-burned brig is riding on unknown currents,

[18]A water-tight rescue vessel used to save passengers at sea.

Where shells grow to her slimy deck, and the dead are corrupting
below;
Where the striped and starred flag is borne at the head of the
regiments;
Approaching Manhattan, up by the long-stretching island,
Under Niagara, the cataract falling like a veil over my
countenance;
Upon a door-step . . . . upon the horse-block of hard wood
outside,
Upon the race-course, or enjoying pic-nics or jigs or a good game
of base-ball,
At he-festivals with blackguard jibes and ironical license and bull-
dances and drinking and laughter,
At the cider-mill, tasting the sweet of the brown sqush[19] . . . .
sucking the juice through a straw,
At apple-pealings, wanting kisses for all the red fruit I find,
At musters[20] and beach-parties and friendly bees and huskings and
house-raisings;
Where the mockingbird sounds his delicious gurgles, and cackles
and screams and weeps,
Where the hay-rick stands in the barnyard, and the dry-stalks are
scattered, and the brood cow waits in the hovel,
Where the bull advances to do his masculine work, and the stud
to the mare, and the cock is treading the hen,
Where the heifers browse, and the geese nip their food with short
jerks;
Where the sundown shadows lengthen over the limitless and
lonesome prairie,
Where the herds of buffalo make a crawling spread of the square
miles far and near;
Where the hummingbird shimmers . . . . where the neck of the
longlived swan is curving and winding;
Where the laughing-gull scoots by the slappy shore and laughs her
near-human laugh;
Where beehives range on a gray bench in the garden half-hid by
the high weeds;
Where the band-necked partridges roost in a ring on the ground
with their heads out;
Where burial coaches enter the arched gates of a cemetery;
Where winter wolves bark amid wastes of snow and icicled trees;
Where the yellow-crowned heron comes to the edge of the marsh
at night and feeds upon small crabs;
Where the splash of swimmers and divers cools the warm noon;

[19]Mush.
[20]Gatherings of people.

Where the katydid works her chromatic reed on the walnut-tree over the well;
Through patches of citrons and cucumbers with silver-wired leaves,
Through the salt-lick or orange glade . . . . or under conical firs;
Through the gymnasium . . . . through the curtained saloon . . . . through the office or public hall;
Pleased with the native and pleased with the foreign . . . . pleased with the new and old,
Pleased with women, the homely as well as the handsome,
Pleased with the quakeress as she puts off her bonnet and talks melodiously,
Pleased with the primitive tunes of the choir of the whitewashed church,
Pleased with the earnest words of the sweating Methodist preacher, or any preacher . . . . looking seriously at the camp-meeting;
Looking in at the shop-windows in Broadway the whole forenoon . . . . pressing the flesh of my nose to the thick plate-glass,
Wandering the same afternoon with my face turned up to the clouds;
My right and left arms round the sides of two friends and I in the middle;
Coming home with the bearded and dark-cheeked bush-boy . . . . riding behind him at the drape of the day;
Far from the settlements studying the print of animals' feet, or the moccasin print;
By the cot in the hospital reaching lemonade to a feverish patient,
By the coffined corpse when all is still, examining with a candle;
Voyaging to every port to dicker and adventure;
Hurrying with the modern crowd, as eager and fickle as any,
Hot toward one I hate, ready in my madness to knife him;
Solitary at midnight in my back yard, my thoughts gone from me a long while,
Walking the old hills of Judea with the beautiful gentle god by my side;
Speeding through space . . . . speeding through heaven and the stars,
Speeding amid the seven satellites and the broad ring and the diameter of eighty thousand miles,
Speeding with tailed meteors . . . . throwing fire-balls like the rest,
Carrying the crescent child that carries its own full mother in its belly;
Storming enjoying planning loving cautioning,
Backing and filling, appearing and disappearing,
I tread day and night such roads.

I visit the orchards of God and look at the spheric product,
And look at quintillions ripened, and look at quintillions green.

I fly the flight of the fluid and swallowing soul,
My course runs below the soundings of plummets.

I help myself to material and immaterial,
No guard can shut me off, no law can prevent me.

I anchor my ship for a little while only,
My messengers continually cruise away or bring their returns to me.

I go hunting polar furs and the seal . . . . leaping chasms with a pike-pointed staff . . . . clinging to topples[21] of brittle and blue.

I ascend to the foretruck . . . . I take my place late at night in the crow's nest . . . . we sail through the arctic sea . . . . it is plenty light enough,
Through the clear atmosphere I stretch around on the wonderful beauty,
The enormous masses of ice pass me and I pass them . . . . the scenery is plain in all directions,
The white-topped mountains point up in the distance . . . . I fling out my fancies toward them;
We are about approaching some great battlefield in which we are soon to be engaged,
We pass the colossal outposts of the encampments . . . . we pass with still feet and caution;
Or we are entering by the suburbs some vast and ruined city . . . . the blocks and fallen architecture more than all the living cities of the globe.

I am a free companion . . . . I bivouac by invading watchfires.

I turn the bridegroom out of bed and stay with the bride myself,
And tighten her all night to my thighs and lips.

My voice is the wife's voice, the screech by the rail of the stairs,
They fetch my man's body up dripping and drowned.

I understand the large hearts of heroes,
The courage of present times and all times;
How the skipper[22] saw the crowded and rudderless wreck of the steamship, and death chasing it up and down the storm,

[21]Pieces of ice.
[22]Whitman describes the shipwreck of the *San Francisco,* which was reported in the New York *Weekly Tribune* on January 21, 1854; he kept a copy of this article among his belongings.

How he knuckled tight and gave not back one inch, and was faithful of days and faithful of nights,
And chalked in large letters on a board, Be of good cheer, We will not desert you;
How he saved the drifting company at last,
How the lank loose-gowned women looked when boated from the side of their prepared graves,
How the silent old-faced infants, and the lifted sick, and the sharp-lipped unshaved men;
All this I swallow and it tastes good . . . . I like it well, and it becomes mine,
I am the man . . . . I suffered . . . . I was there.

The disdain and calmness of martyrs,
The mother condemned for a witch and burnt with dry wood, and her children gazing on;
The hounded slave that flags in the race and leans by the fence, blowing and covered with sweat,
The twinges that sting like needles his legs and neck,
The murderous buckshot and the bullets,
All these I feel or am.

I am the hounded slave . . . . I wince at the bite of the dogs,
Hell and despair are upon me . . . . crack and again crack the marksmen,
I clutch the rails of the fence . . . . my gore dribs[23] thinned with the ooze of my skin,
I fall on the weeds and stones,
The riders spur their unwilling horses and haul close,
They taunt my dizzy ears . . . . they beat me violently over the head with their whip-stocks.

Agonies are one of my changes of garments;
I do not ask the wounded person how he feels . . . . I myself become the wounded person,
My hurt turns livid upon me as I lean on a cane and observe.

I am the mashed fireman with breastbone broken . . . . tumbling walls buried me in their debris,
Heat and smoke I inspired . . . . I heard the yelling shouts of my comrades,
I heard the distant click of their picks and shovels;
They have cleared the beams away . . . . they tenderly lift me forth.

[23]Short for dribbles.

I lie in the night air in my red shirt . . . . the pervading hush is for my sake,
Painless after all I lie, exhausted but not so unhappy,
White and beautiful are the faces around me . . . . the heads are bared of their fire-caps,
The kneeling crowd fades with the light of the torches.

Distant and dead resuscitate,
They show as the dial or move as the hands of me . . . . and I am the clock myself.
I am an old artillerist, and tell of some fort's bombardment . . . . and am there again.

Again the reveille of drummers . . . . again the attacking cannon and mortars and howitzers,
Again the attacked send their cannon responsive.

I take part . . . . I see and hear the whole,
The cries and curses and roar . . . . the plaudits for well aimed shots,
The ambulanza slowly passing and trailing its red drip,
Workmen searching after damages and to make indispensible repairs,
The fall of grenades through the rent roof . . . . the fan-shaped explosion,
The whizz of limbs heads stone wood and iron high in the air.

Again gurgles the mouth of my dying general . . . . he furiously waves with his hand,
He gasps through the clot . . . . Mind not me . . . . mind . . . . the entrenchments.

[34]

I tell not the fall of Alamo . . . . not one escaped to tell the fall of Alamo,
The hundred and fifty are dumb yet at Alamo.

Hear now the tale of a jetblack sunrise,
Hear of the murder in cold blood of four hundred and twelve young men.[24]

Retreating they had formed in a hollow square with their baggage for breastworks,

[24]Whitman tells the story of the death of Captain Fannin and his company of 371 Texans at the hands of the Mexicans after their surrender at Goliad on March 27, 1836; unlike Emerson and Thoreau, Whitman supported the Mexican War (1846–1848).

Nine hundred lives out of the surrounding enemy's nine times their number was the price they took in advance,
Their colonel was wounded and their ammunition gone,
They treated for an honorable capitulation, received writing and seal, gave up their arms, and marched back prisoners of war.
They were the glory of the race of rangers,
Matchless with a horse, a rifle, a song, a supper, or a courtship,
Large, turbulent, brave, handsome, generous, proud and affectionate,
Bearded, sunburnt, dressed in the free costume of hunters,
Not a single one over thirty years of age.

The second Sunday morning they were brought out in squads and massacred . . . . it was beautiful early summer,
The work commenced about five o'clock and was over by eight.

None obeyed the command to kneel,
Some made a mad and helpless rush . . . . some stood stark and straight,
A few fell at once, shot in the temple or heart . . . . the living and dead lay together,
The maimed and mangled dug in the dirt . . . . the new-comers saw them there;
Some half-killed attempted to crawl away,
These were dispatched with bayonets or battered with the blunts of muskets;
A youth not seventeen years old seized his assassin till two more came to release him,
The three were all torn, and covered with the boy's blood.

At eleven o'clock began the burning of the bodies;
And that is the tale of the murder of the four hundred and twelve young men,
And that was a jetblack sunrise.

[35] Did you read in the seabooks of the oldfashioned frigate-fight?[25]
Did you learn who won by the light of the moon and stars?

Our foe was no skulk in his ship, I tell you,
His was the English pluck, and there is no tougher or truer, and never was, and never will be;
Along the lowered eve he came, horribly raking us.
We closed with him . . . . the yards entangled . . . . the cannon touched,
My captain lashed fast with his own hands.

[25]Whitman tells the story of the Revolutionary sea battle on September 23, 1779, between the *Bonhomme Richard,* commanded by John Paul Jones, and the British *Serapis.*

We had received some eighteen-pound shots under the water,
On our lower-gun-deck two large pieces had burst at the first fire, killing all around and blowing up overhead.

Ten o'clock at night, and the full moon shining and the leaks on the gain, and five feet of water reported,
The master-at-arms loosing the prisoners confined in the after-hold to give them a chance for themselves.

The transit to and from the magazine was now stopped by the sentinels,
They saw so many strange faces they did not know whom to trust.

Our frigate was afire . . . . the other asked if we demanded quarters? if our colors were struck and the fighting done?

I laughed content when I heard the voice of my little captain,
We have not struck, he composedly cried, We have just begun our part of the fighting.

Only three guns were in use,
One was directed by the captain himself against the enemy's mainmast,
Two well-served with grape and canister silenced his musketry and cleared his decks.

The tops alone seconded the fire of this little battery, especially the maintop,
They all held out bravely during the whole of the action.

Not a moment's cease,
The leaks gained fast on the pumps . . . . the fire eat toward the powder-magazine,
One of the pumps was shot away . . . . it was generally thought we were sinking.
Serene stood the little captain,
He was not hurried . . . . his voice was neither high nor low,
His eyes gave more light to us than our battle-lanterns.

Toward twelve at night, there in the beams of the moon they surrendered to us.

[36] Stretched and still lay the midnight,
Two great hulls motionless on the breast of the darkness,
Our vessel riddled and slowly sinking . . . . preparations to pass to the one we had conquered,
The captain on the quarter deck coldly giving his orders through a countenance white as a sheet,

Near by the corpse of the child that served in the cabin,
The dead face of an old salt with long white hair and carefully curled whiskers,
The flames spite of all that could be done flickering aloft and below,
The husky voices of the two or three officers yet fit for duty,
Formless stacks of bodies and bodies by themselves . . . . dabs of flesh upon the masts and spars,
The cut of cordage and dangle of rigging . . . . the slight shock of the soothe of waves,
Black and impassive guns, and litter of powder-parcels, and the strong scent,
Delicate sniffs of the seabreeze . . . . smells of sedgy grass and fields by the shore . . . death-messages given in charge to survivors,
The hiss of the surgeon's knife and the gnawing teeth of his saw,
The wheeze, the cluck, the swash of falling blood . . . . the short wild scream, the long dull tapering groan,
These so . . . . these irretrievable.

[37] O Christ! My fit is mastering me!
What the rebel said gaily adjusting his throat to the rope-noose,
What the savage at the stump, his eye-sockets empty, his mouth spirting whoops and defiance,
What stills the traveler come to the vault at Mount Vernon,
What sobers the Brooklyn boy as he looks down the shores of the Wallabout and remembers the prison ships,[26]
What burnt the gums of the redcoat at Saratoga[27] when he surrendered his brigades,
These become mine and me every one, and they are but little,
I become as much more as I like.

I become any presence or truth of humanity here,
And see myself in prison shaped like another man,
And feel the dull unintermitted pain.

For me the keepers of convicts shoulder their carbines and keep watch,
It is I let out in the morning and barred at night.

Not a mutineer walks handcuffed to the jail, but I am handcuffed to him and walk by his side,

[26]British prison ships along Wallabout Bay, where American rebels were held captive during the Revolutionary War.

[27]On October 17, 1777, the British General Burgoyne surrendered to American forces at Saratoga; the battle was a turning point because it enlisted French assistance for the American cause.

I am less the jolly one there, and more the silent one with sweat on my twitching lips.
Not a youngster is taken for larceny, but I go up too and am tried and sentenced.

Not a cholera patient lies at the last gasp, but I also lie at the last gasp,
My face is ash-colored, my sinews gnarl . . . . away from me people retreat.

Askers embody themselves in me, and I am embodied in them,
I project my hat and sit shamefaced and beg.

I rise extatic through all, and sweep with the true gravitation,
The whirling and whirling is elemental within me.

[38]

Somehow I have been stunned. Stand back!
Give me a little time beyond my cuffed head and slumbers and dreams and gaping,
I discover myself on a verge of the usual mistake.

That I could forget the mockers and insults!
That I could forget the trickling tears and the blows of the bludgeons and hammers!
That I could look with a separate look on my own crucifixion and bloody crowning!

I remember . . . . I resume the overstaid fraction,[28]
The grave of rock multiplies what has been confided to it . . . . or to any graves,
The corpses rise . . . . the gashes heal . . . . the fastenings roll away.

I troop forth replenished with supreme power, one of an average unending procession,
We walk the roads of Ohio and Massachusetts and Virginia and Wisconsin and New York and New Orleans and Texas and Montreal and San Francisco and Charleston and Savannah and Mexico,
Inland and by the seacoast and boundary lines . . . . and we pass the boundary lines.

[28]Whitman's meaning is unclear. The reference may be temporal, alluding to the poet's having stayed too long among scenes of suffering and pain. But the words may also allude to Christ as the "overstaid fraction" that the poet "resumes" as a living power within himself.

Our swift ordinances are on their way over the whole earth,
The blossoms we wear in our hats are the growth of two thousand years.

Eleves[29] I salute you,
I see the approach of your numberless gangs . . . . I see you understand yourselves and me,
And know that they who have eyes are divine, and the blind and lame are equally divine,
And that my steps drag behind yours yet go before them,
And are aware how I am with you no more than I am with everybody.

[39] The friendly and flowing savage . . . . Who is he?
Is he waiting for civilization or past it and mastering it?

Is he some southwesterner raised outdoors? Is he Canadian?
Is he from the Mississippi country? or from Iowa, Oregon or California? or from the mountains? or prairie life or bush-life? or from the sea?
Wherever he goes men and women accept and desire him,
They desire he should like them and touch them and speak to them and stay with them.

Behaviour lawless as snow-flakes . . . . words simple as grass . . . . uncombed head and laughter and naivete;
Slowstepping feet and the common features, and the common modes and emanations,
They descend in new forms from the tips of his fingers,
They are wafted with the odor of his body or breath . . . . they fly out of the glance of his eyes.

[40] Flaunt of the sunshine I need not your bask . . . . lie over,
You light surfaces only . . . . I force the surfaces and the depths also.

Earth! you seem to look for something at my hands,
Say old topknot! what do you want?

Man or woman! I might tell how I like you, but cannot,
And might tell what it is in me and what it is in you, but cannot,
And might tell the pinings I have . . . . the pulse of my nights and days.

[29] French for students.

Behold I do not give lectures or a little charity,
What I give I give out of myself.

You there, impotent, loose in the knees, open your scarfed chops till I blow grit within you,
Spread your palms and lift the flaps of your pockets,
I am not to be denied . . . . I compel . . . . I have stores plenty and to spare,
And any thing I have I bestow.

I do not ask who you are . . . . that is not important to me,
You can do nothing and be nothing but what I will infold you.

To a drudge of the cottonfields or emptier of privies I lean . . . . on his right cheek I put the family kiss,
And in my soul I swear I never will deny him.
On women fit for conception I start bigger and nimbler babes,
This day I am jetting the stuff of far more arrogant republics.

To any one dying . . . . thither I speed and twist the knob of the door,
Turn the bedclothes toward the foot of the bed,
Let the physician and the priest go home.

I seize the descending man . . . . I raise him with resistless will.

O despairer, here is my neck,
By God! you shall not go down! Hang your whole weight upon me.

I dilate you with tremendous breath . . . . I buoy you up;
Every room of the house do I fill with an armed force . . . . lovers of me, bafflers of graves:
Sleep! I and they keep guard all night;
Not doubt, not decease shall dare to lay finger upon you,
I have embraced you, and henceforth possess you to myself,
And when you rise in the morning you will find what I tell you is so.

[41] I am he bringing help for the sick as they pant on their backs,
And for strong upright men I bring yet more needed help.

I heard what was said of the universe,
Heard it and heard of several thousand years;
It is middling well as far as it goes . . . . but is that all?

Magnifying and applying come I,
Outbidding at the start the old cautious hucksters,

The most they offer for mankind and eternity less than a spirt of my own seminal wet,
Taking myself the exact dimensions of Jehovah and laying them away,
Lithographing Kronos and Zeus his son, and Hercules his grandson,
Buying drafts of Osiris and Isis and Belus and Brahma and Adonai,
In my portfolio placing Manito loose, and Allah on a leaf, and the crucifix engraved,
With Odin, and the hideous-faced Mexitli, and all idols and images,[30]
Honestly taking them all for what they are worth, and not a cent more,
Admitting they were alive and did the work of their day,
Admitting they bore mites as for unfledged birds who have now to rise and fly and sing for themselves,
Accepting the rough deific sketches to fill out better in myself . . . . bestowing them freely on each man and woman I see,
Discovering as much or more in a framer framing a house,
Putting higher claims for him there with his rolled-up sleeves, driving the mallet and chisel;
Not objecting to special revelations . . . . considering a curl of smoke or a hair on the back of my hand as curious as any revelation;
Those ahold of fire-engines and hook-and-ladder ropes more to me than the gods of the antique wars,
Minding their voices peal through the crash of destruction,
Their brawny limbs passing safe over charred laths . . . . their white foreheads whole and unhurt out of the flames;
By the mechanic's wife with her babe at her nipple interceding for every person born;
Three scythes at harvest whizzing in a row from three lusty angels with shirts bagged out at their waists;
The snag-toothed hostler with red hair redeeming sins past and to come,
Selling all he possesses and traveling on foot to fee lawyers for his brother and sit by him while he is tried for forgery:
What was strewn in the amplest strewing the square rod about me, and not filling the square rod then;
The bull and the bug never worshipped half enough,
Dung and dirt more admirable than was dreamed,

[30]Whitman's list of gods includes sacred figures from several different religions: Jehovah (the Jewish and Christian God); Kronos, Zeus, and Hercules (Greek gods); Osiris and Isis (Egyptian fertility gods); Belus (a legendary Assyrian king); Brahma (the supreme Hindu spirit); Adonai (Lord, in Judaism); Manito (an Algonquian Indian spirit); Allah (Moslem god); Odin (a Norwegian god of war); Mexitli (an Aztec Indian god of war).

The supernatural of no account . . . . myself waiting my time to be one of the supremes,
The day getting ready for me when I shall do as much good as the best, and be as prodigious,
Guessing when I am it will not tickle me much to receive puffs out of pulpit or print;
By my life-lumps! becoming already a creator!
Putting myself here and now to the ambushed womb of the shadows!

[42] . . . . A call in the midst of the crowd,
My own voice, orotund sweeping and final.

Come my children,
Come my boys and girls, and my women and household and intimates,
Now the performer launches his nerve . . . . he has passed his prelude on the reeds within.

Easily written loosefingered chords! I feel the thrum of their climax and close.

My head evolves on my neck,
Music rolls, but not from the organ . . . . folks are around me, but they are no household of mine.

Ever the hard and unsunk ground,
Ever the eaters and drinkers . . . . ever the upward and downward sun . . . . ever the air and the ceaseless tides,
Ever myself and my neighbors, refreshing and wicked and real,
Ever the old inexplicable query . . . . ever that thorned thumb—that breath of itches and thirsts,
Ever the vexer's hoot! hoot! till we find where the sly one hides and bring him forth;
Ever love . . . . ever the sobbing liquid of life,
Ever the bandage under the chin . . . . ever the tressels of death.

Here and there with dimes on the eyes walking,
To feed the greed of the belly the brains liberally spooning,
Tickets buying or taking or selling, but in to the feast never once going;
Many sweating and ploughing and thrashing, and then the chaff for payment receiving,
A few idly owning, and they the wheat continually claiming.

This is the city . . . . and I am one of the citizens;
Whatever interests the rest interests me . . . . politics, churches, newspapers, schools,
Benevolent societies, improvements, banks, tariffs, steamships, factories, markets,

Stocks and stores and real estate and personal estate.

They who piddle and patter here in collars and tailed coats . . . . I am aware who they are . . . . and that they are not worms or fleas,
I acknowledge the duplicates of myself under all the scrape-lipped and pipe-legged concealments.

The weakest and shallowest is deathless with me,
What I do and say the same waits for them,
Every thought that flounders in me the same flounders in them.

I know perfectly well my own egotism,
And know my omniverous words, and cannot say any less,
And would fetch you whoever you are flush with myself.

My words are words of a questioning, and to indicate reality;
This printed and bound book . . . . but the printer and the printing-office boy?
The marriage estate and settlement . . . . but the body and mind of the bridegroom? also those of the bride?
The panorama of the sea . . . . but the sea itself?
The well-taken photographs . . . . but your wife or friend close and solid in your arms?
The fleet of ships of the line and all the modern improvements . . . . but the craft and pluck of the admiral?
The dishes and fare and furniture . . . . but the host and hostess, and the look out of their eyes?
The sky up there . . . . yet here or next door or across the way?
The saints and sages in history . . . . but you yourself?
Sermons and creeds and theology . . . . but the human brain, and what is called reason, and what is called love and what is called life?

[43] I do not despise you priests;
My faith is the greatest of faiths and the least of faiths,
Enclosing all worship ancient and modern, and all between ancient and modern,
Believing I shall come again upon the earth after five thousand years,
Waiting responses from oracles . . . . honoring the gods . . . . saluting the sun,
Making a fetish of the first rock or stump . . . . powowing with sticks in the circle of obis,[31]

[31]Sorcery, of African origin, practiced by blacks in the British West Indies and in the American south.

Helping the lama[32] or brahmin as he trims the lamps of the idols,
Dancing yet through the streets in a phallic procession . . . . rapt and austere in the woods, a gymnosophist,[33]
Drinking mead from the skull-cup . . . . to shasta and vedas admirant . . . . minding the koran,[34]
Walking the teokallis,[35] spotted with gore from the stone and knife—beating the serpent-skin drum;
Accepting the gospels, accepting him that was crucified, knowing assuredly that he is divine,
To the mass kneeling—to the puritan's prayer rising—sitting patiently in a pew,
Ranting and frothing in my insane crisis—waiting dead-like till my spirit arouses me;
Looking forth on pavement and land, and outside of pavement and land,
Belonging to the winders of the circuit of circuits.

One of that centripetal and centrifugal gang,
I turn and talk like a man leaving charges before a journey.
Down-hearted doubters, dull and excluded,
Frivolous sullen moping angry affected disheartened atheistical,
I know every one of you, and know the unspoken interrogatories,
By experience I know them.

How the flukes splash!
How they contort rapid as lightning, with spasms and spouts of blood!

Be at peace bloody flukes of doubters and sullen mopers,
I take my place among you as much as among any;
The past is the push of you and me and all precisely the same,
And the night is for you and me and all,
And what is yet untried and afterward is for you and me and all.

I do not know what is untried and afterward,
But I know it is sure and alive, and sufficient.

Each who passes is considered, and each who stops is considered, and not a single one can it fail.

It cannot fail the young man who died and was buried,
Nor the young woman who died and was put by his side,
Nor the little child that peeped in at the door and then drew back and was never seen again,

[32]Tibetan high priest; brahmin, Hindu high priest.
[33]Member of an ancient sect of naked Hindu ascetics.
[34]*Shasta* and *vedas,* Hindu sacred texts; the *Koran,* the sacred text of Islam.
[35]An Aztec temple.

Nor the old man who has lived without purpose, and feels it with bitterness worse than gall,
Nor him in the poorhouse tubercled by rum and the bad disorder,
Nor the numberless slaughtered and wrecked . . . . nor the brutish koboo,[36] called the ordure of humanity,
Nor the sacs merely floating with open mouths for food to slip in,
Nor any thing in the earth, or down in the oldest graves of the earth,
Nor any thing in the myriads of spheres, nor one of the myriads of myriads that inhabit them,
Nor the present, nor the least wisp that is known.

[44] It is time to explain myself . . . . let us stand up.

What is known I strip away . . . . I launch all men and women forward with me into the unknown.
The clock indicates the moment . . . but what does eternity indicate?

Eternity lies in bottomless reservoirs . . . . its buckets are rising forever and ever,
They pour and they pour and they exhale away.

We have thus far exhausted trillions of winters and summers;
There are trillions ahead, and trillions ahead of them.

Births have brought us richness and variety,
And other births will bring us richness and variety.

I do not call one greater and one smaller,
That which fills its period and place is equal to any.

Were mankind murderous or jealous upon you my brother or my sister?
I am sorry for you . . . . they are not murderous or jealous upon me;
All has been gentle with me . . . . I keep no account with lamentation;
What have I to do with lamentation?

I am an acme of things accomplished, and I am encloser of things to be.

[36]Native of Sumatra.

My feet strike an apex of the apices of the stairs,
On every step bunches of ages, and larger bunches between the steps,
All below duly traveled—and still I mount and mount.

Rise after rise bow the phantoms behind me,
Afar down I see the huge first Nothing, the vapor from the nostrils of death,
I know I was even there . . . . I waited unseen and always,
And slept while God carried me through the lethargic mist,
And took my time . . . . and took no hurt from the foetid carbon.

Long I was hugged close . . . . long and long.

Immense have been the preparations for me,
Faithful and friendly the arms that have helped me.

Cycles ferried my cradle, rowing and rowing like cheerful boatmen;
For room to me stars kept aside in their own rings,
They sent influences to look after what was to hold me.

Before I was born out of my mother generations guided me,
My embryo has never been torpid . . . . nothing could overlay it;
For it the nebula cohered to an orb . . . . the long slow strata piled to rest it on . . . . vast vegetables gave it sustenance,
Monstrous sauroids[37] transported it in their mouths and deposited it with care.

All forces have been steadily employed to complete and delight me,
Now I stand on this spot with my soul.

[45] Span of youth! Ever-pushed elasticity! Manhood balanced and florid and full!

My lovers suffocate me!
Crowding my lips, and thick in the pores of my skin,
Jostling me through streets and public halls . . . . coming naked to me at night,
Crying by day Ahoy from the rocks of the river . . . . swinging and chirping over my head,
Calling my name from flowerbeds or vines or tangled underbrush,
Or while I swim in the bath . . . . or drink from the pump at the corner . . . . or the curtain is down at the opera . . . . or I glimpse at a woman's face in the railroad car;

[37]Prehistoric reptiles.

Lighting on every moment of my life,
Bussing[38] my body with soft and balsamic busses,
Noiselessly passing handfuls out of their hearts and giving them to be mine.

Old age superbly rising! Ineffable grace of dying days!

Every condition promulges not only itself . . . . it promulges what grows after and out of itself,
And the dark hush promulges as much as any.

I open my scuttle at night and see the far-sprinkled systems,
And all I see, multiplied as high as I can cipher, edge but the rim of the farther systems.

Wider and wider they spread, expanding and always expanding,
Outward and outward and forever outward.

My sun has his sun, and round him obediently wheels,
He joins with his partners a group of superior circuit,
And greater sets follow, making specks of the greatest inside them.

There is no stoppage, and never can be stoppage;
If I and you and the worlds and all beneath or upon their surfaces, and all the palpable life, were this moment reduced back to a pallid float, it would not avail in the long run,
We should surely bring up again where we now stand,
And as surely go as much farther, and then farther and farther.

A few quadrillions of eras, a few octillions of cubic leagues, do not hazard the span, or make it impatient,
They are but parts . . . . any thing is but a part.

See ever so far . . . . there is limitless space outside of that,
Count ever so much . . . . there is limitless time around that.
Our rendezvous is fitly appointed . . . . God will be there and wait till we come.

[46] I know I have the best of time and space—and that I was never measured, and never will be measured.

I tramp a perpetual journey,
My signs are a rain-proof coat and good shoes and a staff cut from the woods;

[38]Kissing.

No friend of mine takes his ease in my chair,
I have no chair, nor church nor philosophy;
I lead no man to a dinner-table or library or exchange,
But each man and each woman of you I lead upon a knoll,
My left hand hooks you round the waist,
My right hand points to landscapes of continents, and a plain public road.

Not I, not any one else can travel that road for you,
You must travel it for yourself.

It is not far . . . . it is within reach,
Perhaps you have been on it since you were born, and did not know,
Perhaps it is every where on water and on land.

Shoulder your duds, and I will mine, and let us hasten forth;
Wonderful cities and free nations we shall fetch as we go.

If you tire, give me both burdens, and rest the chuff of your hand on my hip,
And in due time you shall repay the same service to me;
For after we start we never lie by again.

This day before dawn I ascended a hill and looked at the crowded heaven,
And I said to my spirit, When we become the enfolders of those orbs and the pleasure and knowledge of every thing in them, shall we be filled and satisfied then?
And my spirit said No, we level that lift to pass and continue beyond.
You are also asking me questions, and I hear you;
I answer that I cannot answer . . . . you must find out for yourself.

Sit awhile wayfarer,
Here are biscuits to eat and here is milk to drink,
But as soon as you sleep and renew yourself in sweet clothes I will certainly kiss you with my goodbye kiss and open the gate for your egress hence.

Long enough have you dreamed contemptible dreams,
Now I wash the gum from your eyes,
You must habit yourself to the dazzle of the light and of every moment of your life.

Long have you timidly waded, holding a plank by the shore,
Now I will you to be a bold swimmer,

To jump off in the midst of the sea, and rise again and nod to me and shout, and laughingly dash with your hair.

[47]

I am the teacher of athletes,
He that by me spreads a wider breast than my own proves the width of my own,
He most honors my style who learns under it to destroy the teacher.

The boy I love, the same becomes a man not through derived power but in his own right,
Wicked, rather than virtuous out of conformity or fear,
Fond of his sweetheart, relishing well his steak,
Unrequited love or a slight cutting him worse than a wound cuts,
First rate to ride, to fight, to hit the bull's eye, to sail a skiff, to sing a song or play on the banjo,
Preferring scars and faces pitted with smallpox over all latherers and those that keep out of the sun.

I teach straying from me, yet who can stray from me?
I follow you whoever you are from the present hour;
My words itch at your ears till you understand them.
I do not say these things for a dollar, or to fill up the time while I wait for a boat;
It is you talking just as much myself . . . . I act as the tongue of you,
It was tied in your mouth . . . . in mine it begins to be loosened.

I swear I will never mention love or death inside a house,
And I swear I never will translate myself at all, only to him or her who privately stays with me in the open air.

If you would understand me go to the heights or water-shore,
The nearest gnat is an explanation and a drop or the motion of waves a key,
The maul the oar and the handsaw second my words.

No shuttered room or school can commune with me,
But roughs and little children better than they.

The young mechanic is closest to me . . . . he knows me pretty well,
The woodman that takes his axe and jug with him shall take me with him all day,
The farmboy ploughing in the field feels good at the sound of my voice,
In vessels that sail my words must sail . . . . I go with fishermen and seamen, and love them,

My face rubs to the hunter's face when he lies down alone in his blanket,
The driver thinking of me does not mind the jolt of his wagon,
The young mother and old mother shall comprehend me,
The girl and the wife rest the needle a moment and forget where they are,
They and all would resume what I have told them.

[48] I have said that the soul is not more than the body,
And I have said that the body is not more than the soul,
And nothing, not God, is greater to one than one's-self is,
And whoever walks a furlong without sympathy walks to his own funeral, dressed in his shroud,
And I or you pocketless of a dime may purchase the pick of the earth,
And to glance with an eye or show a bean in its pod confounds the learning of all times,
And there is no trade or employment but the young man following it may become a hero,
And there is no object so soft but it makes a hub for the wheeled universe,
And any man or woman shall stand cool and supercilious before a million universes.

And I call to mankind, Be not curious about God,
For I who am curious about each am not curious about God,
No array of terms can say how much I am at peace about God and about death.

I hear and behold God in every object, yet I understand God not in the least,
Nor do I understand who there can be more wonderful than myself.

Why should I wish to see God better than this day?
I see something of God each hour of the twenty-four, and each moment then,
In the faces of men and women I see God, and in my own face in the glass;
I find letters from God dropped in the street, and every one is signed by God's name,
And I leave them where they are, for I know that others will punctually come forever and ever.

[49] And as to you death, and you bitter hug of mortality . . . . it is idle to try to alarm me.

To his work without flinching the accoucheur[39] comes,
I see the elderhand pressing receiving supporting,
I recline by the sills of the exquisite flexible doors . . . . and mark the outlet, and mark the relief and escape.
And as to you corpse I think you are good manure, but that does not offend me,
I smell the white roses sweetscented and growing,
I reach to the leafy lips . . . . I reach to the polished breasts of melons.

And as to you life, I reckon you are the leavings of many deaths,
No doubt I have died myself ten thousand times before.

I hear you whispering there O stars of heaven,
O suns . . . . O grass of graves . . . . O perpetual transfers and promotions . . . . if you do not say anything how can I say anything?

Of the turbid pool that lies in the autumn forest,
Of the moon that descends the steeps of the soughing twilight,
Toss, sparkles of day and dusk . . . . toss on the black stems that decay in the muck,
Toss to the moaning gibberish of the dry limbs.

I ascend from the moon . . . . I ascend from the night,
And perceive of the ghastly glitter the sunbeams reflected,
And debouch[40] to the steady and central from the offspring great or small.

[50] There is that in me . . . . I do not know what it is . . . . but I know it is in me.

Wrenched and sweaty . . . . calm and cool then my body becomes;
I sleep . . . . I sleep long.

I do not know it . . . . it is without name . . . . it is a word unsaid,
It is not in any dictionary or utterance or symbol.

Something it swings on more than the earth I swing on,
To it the creation is the friend whose embracing awakes me.
Perhaps I might tell more . . . . Outlines! I plead for my brothers and sisters.

[39]French for midwife.

[40]From the French word *deboucher,* to issue forth.

Do you see O my brothers and sisters?
It is not chaos or death . . . . it is form and union and plan . . . . it is eternal life . . . . it is happiness.

[51] The past and present wilt . . . . I have filled them and emptied them,
And proceed to fill my next fold of the future.

Listener up there! Here you . . . . what have you to confide to me?
Look in my face while I snuff the sidle of evening,
Talk honestly, for no one else hears you, and I stay only a minute longer.

Do I contradict myself?
Very well then . . . . I contradict myself;
I am large . . . . I contain multitudes.

I concentrate toward them that are nigh . . . . I wait on the door-slab.

Who has done his day's work and will soonest be through with his supper?
Who wishes to walk with me?

Will you speak before I am gone? Will you prove already too late?

[52] The spotted hawk swoops by and accuses me . . . . he complains of my gab and my loitering.

I too am not a bit tamed . . . . I too am untranslatable,

I sound my barbaric yawp over the roofs of the world.
The last scud of day holds back for me,
It flings my likeness after the rest and true as any on the shadowed wilds,
It coaxes me to the vapor and the dusk.

I depart as air . . . . I shake my white locks at the runaway sun,
I effuse my flesh in eddies and drift it in lacy jags.

I bequeath myself to the dirt to grow from the grass I love,
If you want me again look for me under your bootsoles.

You will hardly know who I am or what I mean,
But I shall be good health to you nevertheless,
And filter and fibre your blood.

Failing to fetch me at first keep encouraged,
Missing me one place search another,
I stop some where waiting for you[41]

1855

The Sleepers

[1] I wander all night in my vision,
Stepping with light feet .... swiftly and noiselessly stepping and stopping,
Bending with open eyes over the shut eyes of sleepers;
Wandering and confused .... lost to myself .... ill-assorted .... contradictory,
Pausing and gazing and bending and stopping.

How solemn they look there, stretched and still;
How quiet they breathe, the little children in their cradles.

The wretched features of ennuyees, the white features of corpses, the livid faces of drunkards, the sick-gray faces of onanists,[1]
The gashed bodies on battlefields, the insane in their strong-doored rooms, the sacred idiots,
The newborn emerging from gates and the dying emerging from gates,
The night pervades them and enfolds them.

The married couple sleep calmly in their bed, he with his palm on the hip of the wife, and she with her palm on the hip of the husband,
The sisters sleep lovingly side by side in their bed,
The men sleep lovingly side by side in theirs,
And the mother sleeps with her little child carefully wrapped.

The blind sleep, and the deaf and dumb sleep,
The prisoner sleeps well in the prison .... the runaway son sleeps,
The murderer that is to be hung next day .... how does he sleep?
And the murdered person .... how does he sleep?
The female that loves unrequited sleeps,
And the male that loves unrequited sleeps;

[41]There is no period at the end of the original version of "Song of Myself."

[1]Ennuyees, French for bored people; onanists, persons who masturbate.

The head of the moneymaker that plotted all day sleeps,
And the enraged and treacherous dispositions sleep.

I stand with drooping eyes by the worstsuffering and restless,
I pass my hands soothingly to and fro a few inches from them;
The restless sink in their beds . . . . they fitfully sleep.

The earth recedes from me into the night,
I saw that it was beautiful . . . . and I see that what is not the
earth is beautiful.

I go from bedside to bedside . . . . I sleep close with the other
sleepers, each in turn;
I dream in my dream all the dreams of the other dreamers,
And I become the other dreamers.

I am a dance . . . . Play up there! the fit is whirling me fast.

I am the everlaughing . . . . it is new moon and twilight,
I see the hiding of douceurs[2] . . . . I see nimble ghosts whichever
way I look,
Cache and cache[3] again deep in the ground and sea, and where it
is neither ground or sea.

Well do they do their jobs, those journeymen divine,
Only from me can they hide nothing and would not if they
could;
I reckon I am their boss, and they make me a pet besides,
And surround me, and lead me and run ahead when I walk,
And lift their cunning covers and signify me with stretched arms,
and resume the way;
Onward we move, a gay gang of blackguards with mirthshouting
music and wildflapping pennants of joy.

I am the actor and the actress . . . . the voter . . the politician,
The emigrant and the exile . . the criminal that stood in the box,
He who has been famous, and he who shall be famous after today,
The stammerer . . . . the wellformed person . . the wasted or
feeble person.

I am she who adorned herself and folded her hair expectantly,
My truant lover has come and it is dark.

[2]French for sweetness, delight, pleasure.
[3]French for hide.

Double yourself and receive me darkness,
Receive me and my lover too . . . . he will not let me go without him.

I roll myself upon you as upon a bed . . . . I resign myself to the dusk.

He whom I call answers me and takes the place of my lover,
He rises with me silently from the bed.

Darkness you are gentler than my lover . . . . his flesh was sweaty and panting,
I feel the hot moisture yet that he left me.

My hands are spread forth . . I pass them in all directions,
I would sound up the shadowy shore to which you are journeying.

Be careful, darkness . . . . already, what was it touched me?
I thought my lover had gone . . . . else darkness and he are one,
I hear the heart-beat . . . . I follow . . I fade away.

O hotcheeked and blushing! O foolish hectic!
O for pity's sake, no one must see me now! . . . . my clothes were stolen while I was abed,
Now I am thrust forth, where shall I run?

Pier that I saw dimly last night when I looked from the windows,
Pier out from the main, let me catch myself with you and stay . . . . I will not chafe you;
I feel ashamed to go naked about the world,
And am curious to know where my feet stand . . . . and what is this flooding me, childhood or manhood . . . . and the hunger that crosses the bridge between.

The cloth laps a first sweet eating and drinking,
Laps life-swelling yolks . . . . laps ear of rose-corn, milky and just ripened:
The white teeth stay, and the boss-tooth advances in darkness,
And liquor is spilled on lips and bosoms by touching glasses, and the best liquor afterward.

[2] I descend my western course . . . . my sinews are flaccid,
Perfume and youth course through me, and I am their wake.

It is my face yellow and wrinkled instead of the old woman's,
I sit low in a strawbottom chair and carefully darn my grandson's stockings.

It is I too . . . . the sleepless widow looking out on the winter midnight,
I see the sparkles of starshine on the icy and pallid earth.

A shroud I see—and I am the shroud . . . . I wrap a body and lie in the coffin;
It is dark here underground . . . . it is not evil or pain here . . . . it is blank here, for reasons.

It seems to me that everything in the light and air ought to be happy;
Whoever is not in his coffin and the dark grave, let him know he has enough.

[3] I see a beautiful gigantic swimmer swimming naked through the eddies of the sea,
His brown hair lies close and even to his head . . . . he strikes out with courageous arms . . . . he urges himself with his legs.
I see his white body . . . . I see his undaunted eyes;
I hate the swift-running eddies that would dash him headforemost on the rocks.

What are you doing you ruffianly red-trickled waves?
Will you kill the courageous giant? Will you kill him in the prime of his middle age?

Steady and long he struggles;
He is baffled and banged and bruised . . . . he holds out while his strength holds out.
The slapping eddies are spotted with his blood . . . . they bear him away . . . . they roll him and swing him and turn him:
His beautiful body is borne in the circling eddies . . . . it is continually bruised on rocks,
Swiftly and out of sight is borne the brave corpse.

[4] I turn but do not extricate myself;
Confused . . . . a pastreading . . . . another, but with darkness yet.

The beach is cut by the razory ice-wind . . . . the wreck-guns sound,
The tempest lulls and the moon comes floundering through the drifts.

I look where the ship helplessly heads end on . . . . I hear the burst as she strikes . . . . I hear the howls of dismay . . . . they grow fainter and fainter.

I cannot aid with my wringing fingers;
I can but rush to the surf and let it drench me and freeze upon me.

I search with the crowd . . . . not one of the company is washed to us alive;
In the morning I help pick up the dead and lay them in rows in a barn.

[5] Now of the old war-days . . the defeat at Brooklyn;[4]
Washington stands inside the lines . . he stands on the entrenched hills amid a crowd of officers,
His face is cold and damp . . . . he cannot repress the weeping drops . . . . he lifts the glass perpetually to his eyes . . . . the color is blanched from his cheeks,
He sees the slaughter of the southern braves confided to him by their parents.

The same at last and at last when peace is declared,[5]
He stands in the room of the old tavern . . . . the wellbeloved soldiers all pass through,
The officers speechless and slow draw near in their turns,
The chief encircles their necks with his arm and kisses them on the cheek,
He kisses lightly the wet cheeks one after another . . . . he shakes hands and bids goodbye to the army.

[6] Now I tell what my mother told me today as we sat at dinner together,
Of when she was a nearly grown girl living home with her parents on the old homestead.

A red squaw came one breakfasttime to the old homestead,
On her back she carried a bundle of rushes for rushbottoming chairs;
Her hair straight shiny coarse black and profuse halfenveloped her face,
Her step was free and elastic . . . . her voice sounded exquisitely as she spoke.

My mother looked in delight and amazement at the stranger,
She looked at the beauty of her tallborne face and full and pliant limbs,
The more she looked upon her she loved her,

[4]Whitman describes Washington's reaction to the American defeat at the Battle of Brooklyn Heights at the outset of the Revolutionary War.

[5]Washington bid farewell to his troops in 1783 at Fraunce's Tavern in New York City.

Never before had she seen such wonderful beauty and purity;
She made her sit on a bench by the jamb of the fireplace . . . . she cooked food for her,
She had no work to give her but she gave her remembrance and fondness.

The red squaw staid all the forenoon, and toward the middle of the afternoon she went away;
O my mother was loth to have her go away,
All the week she thought of her . . . . she watched for her many a month,
She remembered her many a winter and many a summer,
But the red squaw never came nor was heard of there again.

Now Lucifer was not dead . . . . or if he was I am his sorrowful terrible heir;[6]
I have been wronged . . . . I am oppressed . . . . I hate him that oppresses me,
I will either destroy him, or he shall release me.

Damn him! how he does defile me,
How he informs against my brother and sister and takes pay for their blood,
How he laughs when I look down the bend after the steamboat that carries away my woman.

Now the vast dusk bulk that is the whale's bulk . . . . it seems mine,
Warily, sportsman! though I lie so sleepy and sluggish, my tap is death.

[7] A show of the summer softness . . . . a contact of something unseen . . . . an amour of the light and air;
I am jealous and overwhelmed with friendliness,
And will go gallivant with the light and the air myself,
And have an unseen something to be in contact with them also.

O love and summer! you are in the dreams and in me,
Autumn and winter are in the dreams . . . . the farmer goes with his thrift,
The droves and crops increase . . . . the barns are wellfilled.
Elements merge in the night . . . . ships make tacks in the dreams . . . . the sailor sails . . . . the exile returns home,
The fugitive returns unharmed . . . . the immigrant is back beyond months and years;

[6]A slave is speaking these words.

The poor Irishman lives in the simple house of his childhood, with the wellknown neighbors and faces,
They warmly welcome him . . . . he is barefoot again . . . . he forgets he is welloff;
The Dutchman voyages home, and the Scotchman and Welchman voyage home . . . . and the native of the Mediterranean voyages home;
To every port of England and France and Spain enter wellfilled ships;
The Swiss foots it toward his hills . . . . the Prussian goes his way, and the Hungarian his way, and the Pole goes his way,
The Swede returns, and the Dane and Norwegian return.

The homeward bound and the outward bound,
The beautiful lost swimmer, the ennuyee, the onanist, the female that loves unrequited, the moneymaker,
The actor and actress . . those through with their parts and those waiting to commence,
The affectionate boy, the husband and wife, the voter, the nominee that is chosen and the nominee that has failed,
The great already known, and the great anytime after to day,
The stammerer, the sick, the perfectformed, the homely,
The criminal that stood in the box, the judge that sat and sentenced him, the fluent lawyers, the jury, the audience,
The laugher and weeper, the dancer, the midnight widow, the red squaw,
The consumptive, the erysipalite,[7] the idiot, he that is wronged,
The antipodes, and every one between this and them in the dark,
I swear they are averaged now . . . one is no better than the other,
The night and sleep have likened them and restored them.
I swear they are all beautiful,
Every one that sleeps is beautiful . . . . every thing in the dim night is beautiful,
The wildest and bloodiest is over and all is peace.

Peace is always beautiful,
The myth of heaven indicates peace and night.

The myth of heaven indicates the soul;
The soul is always beautiful . . . . it appears more or it appears less . . . . it comes or lags behind,
It comes from its embowered garden and looks pleasantly on itself and encloses the world;

[7]Someone suffering from erysipelas, a skin disease.

Perfect and clean the genitals previously jetting, and perfect and clean the womb cohering,
The head wellgrown and proportioned and plumb, and the bowels and joints proportioned and plumb.

The soul is always beautiful,
The universe is duly in order . . . . every thing is in its place,
What is arrived is in its place, and what waits is in its place;
The twisted skull waits . . . . the watery or rotten blood waits,
The child of the glutton or venerealee waits long, and the child of the drunkard waits long, and the drunkard himself waits long,
The sleepers that lived and died wait . . . . the far advanced are to go on in their turns, and the far behind are to go on in their turns,
The diverse shall be no less diverse, but they shall flow and unite . . . . they unite now.

The sleepers are very beautiful as they lie unclothed,
They flow hand in hand over the whole earth from east to west as they lie unclothed;
The Asiatic and African are hand in hand . . . . the European and American are hand in hand,
Learned and unlearned are hand in hand . . and male and female are hand in hand;
The bare arm of the girl crosses the bare breast of her lover . . . . they press close without lust . . . . his lips press her neck,
The father holds his grown or ungrown son in his arms with measureless love . . . . and the son holds the father in his arms with measureless love,
The white hair of the mother shines on the white wrist of the daughter,
The breath of the boy goes with the breath of the man . . . . friend is inarmed by friend,
The scholar kisses the teacher and the teacher kisses the scholar . . . . the wronged is made right,
The call of the slave is one with the master's call . . . . and the master salutes the slave,
The felon steps forth from the prison . . . . the insane becomes sane . . . . the suffering of sick persons is relieved,
The sweatings and fevers stop . . the throat that was unsound is sound . . the lungs of the consumptive are resumed . . the poor distressed head is free,
The joints of the rheumatic move as smoothly as ever, and smoother than ever,
Stiflings and passages open . . . . the paralysed become supple,
The swelled and convulsed and congested awake to themselves in condition,

They pass the invigoration of the night and the chemistry of the night and awake.

I too pass from the night;
I stay awhile away O night, but I return to you again and love you;
Why should I be afraid to trust myself to you?
I am not afraid . . . . I have been well brought forward by you;
I love the rich running day, but I do not desert her in whom I lay so long;
I know not how I came of you, and I know not where I go with you . . . . but I know I came well and shall go well.
I will stop only a time with the night . . . . and rise betimes.

I will duly pass the day O my mother and duly return to you;
Not you will yield forth the dawn again more surely than you will yield forth me again,
Not the womb yields the babe in its time more surely than I shall be yielded from you in my time.

1855

There Was a Child Went Forth

There was a child went forth every day,
And the first object he looked upon and received with wonder or pity or love or dread, that object he became,
And that object became part of him for the day or a certain part of the day . . . . or for many years or stretching cycles of years.

The early lilacs became part of this child,
And grass, and white and red morning-glories, and white and red clover, and the song of the phoebe-bird,
And the March-born lambs, and the sow's pink-faint litter, and the mare's foal, and the cow's calf, and the noisy brood of the barnyard or by the mire of the pond-side . . and the fish suspending themselves so curiously below there . . and the beautiful curious liquid . . and the water-plants with their graceful flat heads . . all became part of him.

And the field-sprouts of April and May became part of him . . . . wintergrain sprouts, and those of the light-yellow corn, and of the esculent roots of the garden,

And the appletrees covered with blossoms, and the fruit afterward .... and woodberries .. and the commonest weeds by the road;
And the old drunkard staggering home from the outhouse of the tavern whence he had lately risen,
And the schoolmistress that passed on her way to the school .. and the friendly boys that passed .. and the quarrelsome boys .. and the tidy and freshcheeked girls .. and the barefoot negro boy and girl,
And all the changes of city and country wherever he went.

His own parents .. he that had propelled the fatherstuff at night, and fathered him .. and she that conceived him in her womb and birthed him .... they gave this child more of themselves than that,
They gave him afterward every day .... they and of them became part of him.
The mother at home quietly placing the dishes on the suppertable,
The mother with mild words .... clean her cap and gown .... a wholesome odor falling off her person and clothes as she walks by:
The father, strong, selfsufficient, manly, mean, angered, unjust,
The blow, the quick loud word, the tight bargain, the crafty lure,
The family usages, the language, the company, the furniture .... the yearning and swelling heart,
Affection that will not be gainsayed .... The sense of what is real .... the thought if after all it should prove unreal,
The doubts of daytime and the doubts of nighttime .... the curious whether and how,
Whether that which appears so is so .... Or is it all flashes and specks?
Men and women crowding fast in the streets .. if they are not flashes and specks what are they?
The streets themselves, and the facades of houses .... the goods in the windows,
Vehicles .. teams .. the tiered wharves, and the huge crossing at the ferries;
The village on the highland seen from afar at sunset .... the river between,
Shadows .. aureola and mist .. light falling on roofs and gables of white or brown, three miles off,
The schooner near by sleepily dropping down the tide .. the little boat slacktowed astern,
The hurrying tumbling waves and quickbroken crests and slapping;
The strata of colored clouds .... the long bar of maroontint away solitary by itself .... the spread of purity it lies motionless in,

The horizon's edge, the flying seacrow, the fragrance of saltmarsh and shoremud;
These became part of that child who went forth every day, and who now goes and will always go forth every day,
And these become of him or her that peruses them now.

1855

from Inscriptions[1]

One's-Self I Sing

One's-Self I sing, a simple separate person,
Yet utter the word Democratic, the word En-Masse.

Of physiology from top to toe I sing,
Not physiognomy alone nor brain alone is worthy for the Muse, I say the Form complete is worthier far,
The Female equally with the Male I sing.

Of Life immense in passion, pulse, and power,
Cheerful, for freest action form'd under the laws divine,
The Modern Man I sing.

1867

from Children of Adam[1]

To the Garden the World

To the garden the world anew ascending,
Potent mates, daughters, sons, preluding,
The love, the life of their bodies, meaning and being,

[1] *Inscriptions* first appeared as the opening grouping in the 1871 edition of *Leaves of Grass.* Beginning in 1867, "One's-Self I Sing" appeared as the opening poem of all future editions of *Leaves of Grass.*

[1] *Children of Adam* and its companion cluster *Calamus,* which first appeared in the 1860 edition of *Leaves of Grass,* are Whitman's most controversial poetic sequences. In *Children of Adam* he focuses on what he calls "amative love," the phrenological term for the love between men and women. In *Calamus* he focuses on "adhesive love," the phrenological term for the love between men.

Curious here behold my resurrection after slumber,
The revolving cycles in their wide sweep having brought me again,
Amorous, mature, all beautiful to me, all wondrous,
My limbs and the quivering fire that ever plays through them, for reasons, most wondrous,
Existing I peer and penetrate still,
Content with the present, content with the past,
By my side or back of me Eve following,
Or in front, and I following her just the same.

1860

A Woman Waits for Me

A woman waits for me, she contains all, nothing is lacking,
Yet all were lacking if sex were lacking, or if the moisture of the right man were lacking.

Sex contains all, bodies, souls,
Meanings, proofs, purities, delicacies, results, promulgations
Songs, commands, health, pride, the maternal mystery, the seminal milk,
All hopes, benefactions, bestowals, all the passions, loves, beauties, delights of the earth,
All the governments, judges, gods, follow'd persons of the earth,
These are contain'd in sex as parts of itself and justifications of itself.

Without shame the man I like knows and avows the deliciousness of his sex,
Without shame the woman I like knows and avows hers.

Now I will dismiss myself from impassive women,
I will go stay with her who waits for me, and with those women that are warm-blooded and sufficient for me,
I see that they understand me and do not deny me,
I see that they are worthy of me, I will be the robust husband of those women.

They are not one jot less than I am,
They are tann'd in the face by shining suns and blowing winds,
Their flesh has the old divine suppleness and strength,
They know how to swim, row, ride, wrestle, shoot, run, strike, retreat, advance, resist, defend themselves,
They are ultimate in their own right—they are calm, clear, well-possess'd of themselves.

I draw you close to me, you women,
I cannot let you go, I would do you good,
I am for you, and you are for me, not only for our own sake, but
for others' sakes,
Envelop'd in you sleep greater heroes and bards,
They refuse to awake at the touch of any man but me.

It is I, you women, I make my way,
I am stern, acrid, large, undissuadable, but I love you,
I do not hurt you any more than is necessary for you,
I pour the stuff to start sons and daughters fit for these States, I
press with slow rude muscle,
I brace myself effectually, I listen to no entreaties,
I dare not withdraw till I deposit what has so long accumulated
within me.

Through you I drain the pent-up rivers of myself,
In you I wrap a thousand onward years,
On you I graft the grafts of the best-beloved of me and America,
The drops I distil upon you shall grow fierce and athletic girls,
new artists, musicians, and singers,
The babes I beget upon you are to beget babes in their turn,
I shall demand perfect men and women out of my love-spendings,
I shall expect them to interpenetrate with others, as I and you
interpenetrate now,
I shall count on the fruits of the gushing showers of them, as I
count on the fruits of the gushing showers I give now,
I shall look for loving crops from the birth, life, death,
immortality, I plant so lovingly now.

1856

from Calamus[1]

In Paths Untrodden

In paths untrodden,
In the growth by margins of pond-waters,
Escaped from the life that exhibits itself,

[1]Calamus is another word for sweet flag, a hardy, aromatic grass that grows near ponds and swamps.

From all the standards hitherto publish'd, from the pleasures, profits, conformities,
Which too long I was offering to feed my soul,
Clear to me now standards not yet publish'd, clear to me that my soul,
That the soul of the man I speak for rejoices in comrades,
Here by myself away from the clank of the world,
Tallying and talk'd to here by tongues aromatic,
No longer abash'd, (for in this secluded spot I can respond as I would not dare elsewhere,)
Strong upon me the life that does not exhibit itself, yet contains all the rest,
Resolv'd to sing no songs to-day but those of manly attachment,
Projecting them along that substantial life,
Bequeathing hence types of athletic love,
Afternoon this delicious Ninth-month[2] in my forty-first year,
I proceed for all who are or have been young men,
To tell the secret of my nights and days,
To celebrate the need of comrades.

1860

Recorders Ages Hence

Recorders ages hence,
Come, I will take you down underneath this impassive exterior, I will tell you what to say of me,
Publish my name and hang up my picture as that of the tenderest lover,
The friend the lover's portrait, of whom his friend his lover was fondest,
Who was not proud of his songs, but of the measureless ocean of love within him, and freely pour'd it forth,
Who often walk'd lonesome walks thinking of his dear friends, his lovers,
Who pensive away from one he lov'd often lay sleepless and dissatisfied at night,
Who knew too well the sick, sick dread lest the one he lov'd might secretly be indifferent to him,

[2]Quaker term for September, the 9th month of the year. Whitman associated the pagan names of the days and the months with the feudal past; his substitution of Quaker names was part of his attempt to invent a specifically American idiom expressive of the beliefs and values of the American people.

Whose happiest days were far away through fields, in woods, on hills, he and another wandering hand in hand, they twain apart from other men,
Who oft as he saunter'd the streets curv'd with his arm the shoulder of his friend, while the arm of his friend rested upon him also.

1860

When I Heard at the Close of the Day

When I heard at the close of the day how my name had been receiv'd with plaudits in the capitol, still it was not a happy night for me that follow'd,
And else when I carous'd, or when my plans were accomplish'd, still I was not happy,
But the day when I rose at dawn from the bed of perfect health, refresh'd, singing, inhaling the ripe breath of autumn,
When I saw the full moon in the west grow pale and disappear in the morning light,
When I wander'd alone over the beach, and undressing bathed, laughing with the cool waters, and saw the sun rise,
And when I thought how my dear friend my lover was on his way coming, O then I was happy,
O then each breath tasted sweeter, and all that day my food nourish'd me more, and the beautiful day pass'd well,
And the next came with equal joy, and with the next at evening came my friend,
And that night while all was still I heard the waters roll slowly continually up the shores,
I heard the hissing rustle of the liquid and sands as directed to me whispering to congratulate me,
For the one I love most lay sleeping by me under the same cover in the cool night,
In the stillness in the autumn moonbeams his face was inclined toward me,
And his arm lay lightly around my breast—and that night I was happy.

1860

Here the Frailest Leaves of Me

Here the frailest leaves of me and yet my strongest lasting,
Here I shade and hide my thoughts, I myself do not expose them,
And yet they expose me more than all my other poems.

1860

I Dream'd in a Dream

I dream'd in a dream I saw a city invincible to the attacks of the whole of the rest of the earth,
I dream'd that was the new city of Friends,
Nothing was greater there than the quality of robust love, it led the rest,
It was seen every hour in the actions of the men of that city,
And in all their looks and words.

1860

from Sea-Drift

Out of the Cradle Endlessly Rocking

Out of the cradle endlessly rocking,
Out of the mocking-bird's throat, the musical shuttle,
Out of the Ninth-month midnight,
Over the sterile sands and the fields beyond, where the child leaving his bed wander'd alone, bareheaded, barefoot,
Down from the shower'd halo,
Up from the mystic play of shadows twining and twisting as if they were alive,
Out from the patches of briers and blackberries,
From the memories of the bird that chanted to me,
From your memories sad brother, from the fitful risings and fallings I heard,
From under that yellow half-moon late-risen and swollen as if with tears,
From those beginning notes of yearning and love there in the mist,
From the thousand responses of my heart never to cease,
From the myriad thence-arous'd words,
From the word stronger and more delicious than any,
From such as now they start the scene revisiting,
As a flock, twittering, rising, or overhead passing,
Borne hither, ere all eludes me, hurriedly,
A man, yet by these tears a little boy again,
Throwing myself on the sand, confronting the waves,
I, chanter of pains and joys, uniter of here and hereafter,
Taking all hints to use them, but swiftly leaping beyond them,
A reminiscence sing.

Once Paumanok,[1]
When the lilac-scent was in the air and Fifth-month grass was growing,
Up this seashore in some briers,
Two feather'd guests from Alabama, two together,
And their nest, and four light-green eggs spotted with brown.
And every day the he-bird to and fro near at hand.
And every day the she-bird crouch'd on her nest, silent, with bright eyes,
And every day I, a curious boy, never too close, never disturbing them,
Cautiously peering, absorbing, translating.

Shine! shine! shine!
Pour down your warmth, great sun!
While we bask, we two together.

Two together!
Winds blow south, or winds blow north,
Day come white, or night come black,
Home, or rivers and mountains from home,
Singing all time, minding no time,
While we two keep together.

Till of a sudden,
May-be kill'd, unknown to her mate,
One forenoon the she-bird crouch'd not on the nest,
Nor return'd that afternoon, nor the next,
Nor ever appear'd again.

And thenceforward all summer in the sound of the sea,
And at night under the full of the moon in calmer weather,
Over the hoarse surging of the sea,
Or flitting from brier to brier by day,
I saw, I heard at intervals the remaining one, the he-bird,
The solitary guest from Alabama.

Blow! blow! blow!
Blow up sea-winds along Paumanok's shore;
I wait and I wait till you blow my mate to me.

Yes, when the stars glisten'd,
All night long on the prong of a moss-scallop'd stake,

[1]Native American Indian name for Long Island.

Down almost amid the slapping waves,
Sat the lone singer wonderful causing tears.

He call'd on his mate,
He pour'd forth the meanings which I of all men know.

Yes my brother I know,
The rest might not, but I have treasur'd every note,
For more than once dimly down to the beach gliding,
Silent, avoiding the moonbeams, blending myself with the shadows,
Recalling now the obscure shapes, the echoes, the sounds and
sights after their sorts,
The white arms out in the breakers tirelessly tossing,
I, with bare feet, a child, the wind wafting my hair,
Listen'd long and long.

Listen'd to keep, to sing, now translating the notes,
Following you my brother.

Soothe! soothe! soothe!
Close on its wave soothes the wave behind,
And again another behind embracing and lapping, every one
close,
But my love soothes not me, not me.

Low hangs the moon, it rose late,
It is lagging—O I think it is heavy with love, with love.

O madly the sea pushes upon the land,
With love, with love.

O night! do I not see my love fluttering out among the breakers?
What is that little black thing I see there in the white?

Loud! loud! loud!
Loud I call to you, my love!

High and clear I shoot my voice over the waves,
Surely you must know who is here, is here,
You must know who I am, my love.

Low-hanging moon!
What is that dusky spot in your brown yellow?
O it is the shape, the shape of my mate!
O moon do not keep her from me any longer.

Land! land! O land!
Whichever way I turn, O I think you could give me my mate back again if you only would,
For I am almost sure I see her dimly whichever way I look.

O rising stars!
Perhaps the one I want so much will rise, will rise with some of you.

O throat! O trembling throat!
Sound clearer through the atmosphere!
Pierce the woods, the earth,
Somewhere listening to catch you must be the one I want.

Shake out carols!
Solitary here, the night's carols!
Carols of lonesome love! death's carols!
Carols under that lagging, yellow, waning moon!
O under that moon where she droops almost down into the sea!
O reckless despairing carols.

But soft! sink low!
Soft! let me just murmur,
And do you wait a moment you husky-nois'd sea,
For somewhere I believe I heard my mate responding to me,
So faint, I must be still, be still to listen,
But not altogether still, for then she might not come immediately to me.

Hither my love!
Here I am! here!
With this just-sustain'd note I announce myself to you,
This gentle call is for you my love, for you.

Do not be decoy'd elsewhere,
That is the whistle of the wind, it is not my voice,
That is the fluttering, the fluttering of the spray,
Those are the shadows of leaves.

O darkness! O in vain!
O I am very sick and sorrowful.

O brown halo in the sky near the moon, drooping upon the sea!
O troubled reflection in the sea!
O throat! O throbbing heart!
And I singing uselessly, uselessly all the night.

O past! O happy life! O songs of joy!
In the air, in the woods, over fields,

Loved! loved! loved! loved! loved!
But my mate no more, no more with me!
We two together no more.

The aria sinking,
All else continuing, the stars shining,
The winds blowing, the notes of the bird continuous echoing,
With angry moans the fierce old mother incessantly moaning,
On the sands of Paumanok's shore gray and rustling,
The yellow half-moon enlarged, sagging down, drooping, the face of the sea almost touching,
The boy ecstatic, with his bare feet the waves, with his hair the atmosphere dallying,
The love in the heart long pent, now loose, now at last tumultuously bursting,
The aria's meaning, the ears, the soul, swiftly depositing,
The strange tears down the cheeks coursing,
The colloquy there, the trio, each uttering,
The undertone, the savage old mother incessantly crying,
To the boy's soul's questions sullenly timing, some drown'd secret hissing,
To the outsetting bard.

Demon or bird! (said the boy's soul,)
Is it indeed toward your mate you sing? or is it really to me?
For I, that was a child, my tongue's use sleeping, now I have heard you,
Now in a moment I know what I am for, I awake,
And already a thousand singers, a thousand songs, clearer, louder and more sorrowful than yours,
A thousand warbling echoes have started to life within me, never to die.
O you singer solitary, singing by yourself, projecting me,
O solitary me listening, never more shall I cease perpetuating you,
Never more shall I escape, never more the reverberations,
Never more the cries of unsatisfied love be absent from me,
Never again leave me to be the peaceful child I was before what there in the night,
By the sea under the yellow and sagging moon,
The messenger there arous'd, the fire, the sweet hell within,
The unknown want, the destiny of me.

O give me the clew! (it lurks in the night here somewhere,)
O if I am to have so much, let me have more!

A word then, (for I will conquer it,)
The word final, superior to all,
Subtle, sent up—what is it?—I listen;

Are you whispering it, and have been all the time, you sea-waves?
Is that it from your liquid rims and wet sands?

Whereto answering, the sea,
Delaying not, hurrying not,
Whisper'd me through the night, and very plainly before daybreak,
Lisp'd to me the low and delicious word death,
And again death, death, death, death,
Hissing melodious, neither like the bird nor like my arous'd child's heart,
But edging near as privately for me rustling at my feet,
Creeping thence steadily up to my ears and laving me softly all over,
Death, death, death, death, death.

Which I do not forget,
But fuse the song of my dusky demon and brother,
That he sang to me in the moonlight on Paumanok's gray beach,
With the thousand responsive songs at random,
My own songs awaked from that hour,
And with them the key, the word up from the waves,
The word of the sweetest song and all songs,
That strong and delicious word which, creeping to my feet,
(Or like some old crone rocking the cradle, swathed in sweet garments, bending aside,)
The sea whisper'd me.

1859

As I Ebb'd with the Ocean of Life

1

As I ebb'd with the ocean of life,
As I wended the shores I know,
As I walk'd where the ripples continually wash you Paumanok,
Where they rustle up hoarse and sibilant,
Where the fierce old mother endlessly cries for her castaways,
I musing late in the autumn day, gazing off southward,
Held by this electric self out of the pride of which I utter poems,
Was seiz'd by the spirit that trails in the lines underfoot,
The rim, the sediment that stands for all the water and all the land of the globe.

Fascinated, my eyes reverting from the south, dropt, to follow those slender windrows,

Chaff, straw, splinters of wood, weeds, and the sea-gluten,
Scum, scales from shining rocks, leaves of salt-lettuce, left by the tide,
Miles walking, the sound of breaking waves the other side of me,
Paumanok there and then as I thought the old thought of likenesses,
These you presented to me you fish-shaped island,
As I wended the shores I know,
As I walk'd with that electric self seeking types.

2

As I wend to the shores I know not,
As I list to the dirge, the voices of men and women wreck'd,
As I inhale the impalpable breezes that set in upon me,
As the ocean so mysterious rolls toward me closer and closer,
I too but signify at the utmost a little wash'd-up drift,
A few sands and dead leaves to gather,
Gather, and merge myself as part of the sands and drift.

O baffled, balk'd, bent to the very earth,
Oppress'd with myself that I have dared to open my mouth,
Aware now that amid all that blab whose echoes recoil upon me I have not once had the least idea who or what I am,
But that before all my arrogant poems the real Me stands yet untouch'd, untold, altogether unreach'd,
Withdrawn far, mocking me with mock-congratulatory signs and bows,
With peals of distant ironical laughter at every word I have written,
Pointing in silence to these songs, and then to the sand beneath.

I perceive I have not really understood any thing, not a single object, and that no man ever can,
Nature here in sight of the sea taking advantage of me to dart upon me and sting me,
Because I have dared to open my mouth to sing at all.

3

You oceans both, I close with you,
We murmur alike reproachfully rolling sands and drift, knowing not why,
These little shreds indeed standing for you and me and all.

You friable[1] shore with trials of debris,
You fish-shaped island, I take what is underfoot,

[1]Crumbling.

What is yours is mine my father.

I too Paumanok,
I too have bubbled up, floated the measureless float, and been wash'd on your shores,
I too am but a trail of drift and debris,
I too leave little wrecks upon you, you fish-shaped island.
I throw myself upon your breast my father,
I cling to you so that you cannot unloose me,
I hold you so firm till you answer me something.

Kiss me my father,
Touch me with your lips as I touch those I love,
Breathe to me while I hold you close the secret of the murmuring I envy.

4

Ebb, ocean of life, (the flow will return,)
Cease not your moaning you fierce old mother,
Endlessly cry for your castaways, but fear not, deny not me,
Rustle not up so hoarse and angry against my feet as I touch you or gather from you.

I mean tenderly by you and all,
I gather for myself and for this phantom looking down where we lead, and following me and mine.

Me and mine, loose windrows, little corpses,
Froth, snowy white, and bubbles,
(See, from my dead lips the ooze exuding at last,
See, the prismatic colors glistening and rolling,)
Tufts of straw, sands, fragments,
Buoy'd hither from many moods, one contradicting another,
From the storm, the long calm, the darkness, the swell,
Musing, pondering, a breath, a briny tear, a dab of liquid or soil,
Up just as much out of fathomless workings fermented and thrown,
A limp blossom or two, torn, just as much over waves floating, drifted at random,
Just as much for us that sobbing dirge of Nature,
Just as much whence we come that blare of the cloud-trumpets,
We, capricious, brought hither we know not whence, spread out before you,
You up there walking or sitting,
Whoever you are, we too lie in drifts at your feet.

1860

from By the Roadside

Europe[1]

The 72d and 73d Years of These States

Suddenly out of its stale and drowsy lair, the lair of slaves,
Like lightning it le'pt forth half startled at itself,
Its feet upon the ashes and the rags, its hands tight to the throats of kings.

O hope and faith!
O aching close of exiled patriots' lives!
O many a sicken'd heart!
Turn back unto this day and make yourselves afresh.

And you, paid to defile the People—you liars, mark!
Not for numberless agonies, murders, lusts,
For court thieving in its manifold mean forms, worming from his simplicity the poor man's wages,
For many a promise sworn by royal lips and broken and laugh'd at in the breaking,
Then in their power not for all these did the blows strike revenge, or the heads of the nobles fall;
The People scorn'd the ferocity of kings.

But the sweetness of mercy brew'd bitter destruction, and the frighten'd monarchs come back,
Each comes in state with his train, hangman, priest, tax-gatherer,
Soldier, lawyer, lord, jailer, and sycophant.

Yet behind all lowering stealing, lo, a shape,
Vague as the night, draped interminably, head, front and form, in scarlet folds,
Whose face and eyes none may see,
Out of its robes only this, the red robes lifted by the arm,
One finger crook'd pointed high over the top, like the head of a snake appears.

Meanwhile corpses lie in new-made graves, bloody corpses of young men,

[1]This poem, which was first published in the New York *Daily Tribune* on June 21, 1850, was included among the initial twelve poems of *Leaves of Grass* in 1855. It was inspired by the 1848 revolutions throughout Europe.

The rope of the gibbet hangs heavily, the bullets of princes are
flying, the creatures of power laugh aloud,
And all these things bear fruits, and they are good.

Those corpses of young men,
Those martyrs that hang from the gibbets, those hearts pierc'd by
the gray lead,
Cold and motionless as they seem live elsewhere with unslaughter'd
vitality.

They live in other young men O kings!
They live in brothers again ready to defy you,
They were purified by death, they were taught and exalted.

Not a grave of the murder'd for freedom but grows seed for
freedom, in its turn to bear seed,
Which the winds carry afar and re-sow, and the rains and the
snows nourish.

Not a disembodied spirit can the weapons of tyrants let loose,
But it stalks invisibly over the earth, whispering, counseling,
cautioning.

Liberty, let others despair of you—I never despair of you.

Is the house shut? is the master away?
Nevertheless, be ready, be not weary of watching,
He will soon return, his messengers come anon.

1850

When I Heard the Learn'd Astronomer

When I heard the learn'd astronomer,
When the proofs, the figures, were ranged in columns before me,
When I was shown the charts and diagrams, to add, divide, and
measure them,
When I sitting heard the astronomer where he lectured with much
applause in the lecture-room,
How soon unaccountable I became tired and sick,
Till rising and gliding out I wander'd off by myself,
In the mystical moist night-air, and from time to time,
Look'd up in perfect silence at the stars.

1865

To a President[1]

All you are doing and saying is to America dangled mirages,
You have not learn'd of Nature—of the politics of Nature you have not learn'd the great amplitude, rectitude, impartiality,
You have not seen that only such as they are for these States,
And that what is less than they must sooner or later lift off from these States.

1860

The Dalliance of the Eagles

Skirting the river road, (my forenoon walk, my rest,)
Skyward in air a sudden muffled sound, the dalliance of the eagles,
The rushing amorous contact high in space together,
The clinching interlocking claws, a living, fierce, gyrating wheel,
Four beating wings, two beaks, a swirling mass tight grappling,
In tumbling turning clustering loops, straight downward falling,
Till o'er the river pois'd, the twain yet one, a moment's lull,
A motionless still balance in the air, then parting, talons loosing,
Upward again on slow-firm pinions slanting, their separate diverse flight,
She hers, he his, pursuing.

1880

To the States

To Identify the 16th, 17th, or 18th Presidentiad.[1]

Why reclining, interrogating? why myself and all drowsing?
What deepening twilight—scum floating atop of the waters,
Who are they as bats and night-dogs askant in the capitol?
What a filthy Presidentiad! (O South, your torrid suns! O North, your arctic freezings!)

[1]The poem was initially addressed to James Buchanan, the Democratic president whose support for slavery expansion and other controversial policies seemed, in Whitman's view, to undermine the fundamental values of the American republic.

[1]The 16th, 17th, and 18th Presidentiad refers to the presidencies of Millard Fillmore, Franklin Pierce, and James Buchanan, all of whom pursued a policy of compromise on the issue of slavery in order to avoid armed conflict between North and South. The poem, which was included in the 1860 edition of *Leaves of Grass*, appears to predict the imminent outbreak of the Civil War.

Are those really Congressmen? are those the great Judges?[2] is that the President?
Then I will sleep awhile yet, for I see that these States sleep, for reasons;
(With gathering murk, with muttering thunder and lambent shoots we all duly awake,
South, North, East, West, inland and seaboard, we will surely awake.)

1860

from Drum-Taps[1]

Beat! Beat! Drums!

Beat! beat! drums!—blow! bugles! blow!
Through the windows—through doors—burst like a ruthless force,
Into the solemn church, and scatter the congregation,
Into the school where the scholar is studying;
Leave not the bridegroom quiet—no happiness must he have now with his bride,
Nor the peaceful farmer any peace, ploughing his field or gathering his grain,
So fierce you whirr and pound you drums—so shrill you bugles blow.

Beat! beat! drums!—blow! bugles! blow!
Over the traffic of cities—over the rumble of wheels in the streets;
Are beds prepared for sleepers at night in the houses? no sleepers must sleep in those beds,
No bargainers' bargains by day—no brokers or speculators—would they continue?
Would the talkers be talking? would the singer attempt to sing?
Would the lawyer rise in the court to state his case before the judge?
Then rattle quicker, heavier drums—you bugles wilder blow.

Beat! beat! drums!—blow! bugles! blow!
Make no parley—stop for no expostulation,

[2]Whitman may be referring to Chief Justice Taney's 1857 Dred Scott Decision, which denied blacks citizenship under the Constitution of the United States.

[1]*Drum-Taps* was initially published as a separate volume in 1865. It was added to *Leaves of Grass* in 1867.

Mind not the timid—mind not the weeper or prayer,
Mind not the old man beseeching the young man,
Let not the child's voice be heard, nor the mother's entreaties,
Make even the trestles to shake the dead where they lie awaiting the hearses,
So strong you thump O terrible drums—so loud you bugles blow.

1861

Cavalry Crossing a Ford

A line in long array where they wind betwixt green islands,
They take a serpentine course, their arms flash in the sun—hark to the musical clank,
Behold the silvery river, in it the splashing horses loitering stop to drink,
Behold the brown-faced men, each group, each person a picture, the negligent rest on the saddles,
Some emerge on the opposite bank, others are just entering the ford—while,
Scarlet and blue and snowy white,
The guidon flags flutter gayly in the wind.

1865

Vigil Strange I Kept on the Field One Night

Vigil strange I kept on the field one night;
When you my son and my comrade dropt at my side that day,
One look I but gave which your dear eyes return'd with a look I shall never forget,
One touch of your hand to mine O boy, reach'd up as you lay on the ground,
Then onward I sped in the battle, the even-contested battle,
Till late in the night reliev'd to the place at last again I made my way,
Found you in death so cold dear comrade, found your body son of responding kisses, (never again on earth responding,)
Bared your face in the starlight, curious the scene, cool blew the moderate night-wind,
Long there and then in vigil I stood, dimly around me the battle-field spreading,
Vigil wondrous and vigil sweet there in the fragrant silent night,
But not a tear fell, not even a long-drawn sigh, long, long I gazed,
Then on the earth partially reclining sat by your side leaning my chin in my hands,

Passing sweet hours, immortal and mystic hours with you dearest comrade—not a tear, not a word,
Vigil of silence, love and death, vigil for you my son and my soldier,
As onward silently stars aloft, eastward new ones upward stole,
Vigil final for you brave boy, (I could not save you, swift was your death,
I faithfully loved you and cared for you living, I think we shall surely meet again,)
Till at latest lingering of the night, indeed just as the dawn appear'd,
My comrade I wrapt in his blanket, envelop'd well his form,
Folded the blanket well, tucking it carefully over head and carefully under feet,
And there and then and bathed by the rising sun, my son in his grave, in his rude-dug grave I deposited,
Ending my vigil strange with that, vigil of night and battle-field dim,
Vigil for boy of responding kisses, (never again on earth responding,)
Vigil for comrade swiftly slain, vigil I never forget, how as day brighten'd,
I rose from the chill ground and folded my soldier well in his blanket,
And buried him where he fell.

1865

A March in the Ranks Hard-Prest, and the Road Unknown

A march in the ranks hard-prest, and the road unknown,
A route through a heavy wood with muffled steps in the darkness,
Our army foil'd with loss severe, and the sullen remnant retreating,
Till after midnight glimmer upon us the lights of a dim-lighted building,
We come to an open space in the woods, and halt by the dim-lighted building,
'Tis a large old church at the crossing roads, now an impromptu hospital,
Entering but for a minute I see a sight beyond all the pictures and poems ever made,
Shadows of deepest, deepest black, just lit by moving candles and lamps,
And by one great pitchy torch stationary with wild red flame and clouds of smoke,

By these, crowds, groups of forms vaguely I see on the floor, some in the pews laid down,
At my feet more distinctly a soldier, a mere lad, in danger of bleeding to death, (he is shot in the abdomen,)
I stanch the blood temporarily, (the youngster's face is white as a lily,)
Then before I depart I sweep my eyes o'er the scene fain to absorb it all,
Faces, varieties, postures beyond description, most in obscurity, some of them dead,
Surgeons operating, attendants holding lights, the smell of ether, the odor of blood,
The crowd, O the crowd of the bloody forms, the yard outside also fill'd,
Some on the bare ground, some on planks or stretchers, some in the death-spasm sweating,
An occasional scream or cry, the doctor's shouted orders or calls,
The glisten of the little steel instruments catching the glint of the torches,
These I resume as I chant, I see again the forms, I smell the odor,
Then hear outside the orders given, *Fall in, my men, fall in;*
But first I bend to the dying lad, his eyes open, a half-smile gives he me,
Then the eyes close, calmly close, and I speed forth to the darkness,
Resuming, marching, ever in darkness marching, on in the ranks,
The unknown road still marching.

1865

Year That Trembled and Reel'd Beneath Me[1]

Year that trembled and reel'd beneath me!
Your summer wind was warm enough, yet the air I breathed froze me,
A thick gloom fell through the sunshine and darken'd me,
Must I change my triumphant songs? said I to myself,
Must I indeed learn to chant the cold dirges of the baffled?
And sullen hymns of defeat?

1865

[1]The year is probably the crisis year 1863–1864 when the outcome of the Civil War was not at all certain.

The Artilleryman's Vision

While my wife at my side lies slumbering, and the wars are over long,
And my head on the pillow rests at home, and the vacant midnight passes,
And through the stillness, through the dark, I hear, just hear, the breath of my infant,
There in the room as I wake from sleep this vision presses upon me;
The engagement opens there and then in fantasy unreal,
The skirmishers begin, they crawl cautiously ahead, I hear the irregular snap! snap!
I hear the sounds of the different missiles, the short *t-h-t! t-h-t!* of the rifle-balls,
I see the shells exploding leaving small white clouds, I hear the great shells shrieking as they pass,
The grape like the hum and whirr of wind through the trees, (tumultuous now the contest rages,)
All the scenes at the batteries rise in detail before me again,
The crashing and smoking, the pride of the men in their pieces,
The chief-gunner ranges and sights his piece and selects a fuse of the right time,
After firing I see him lean aside and look eagerly off to note the effect;
Elsewhere I hear the cry of a regiment charging, (the young colonel leads himself this time with brandish'd sword,)
I see the gaps cut by the enemy's volleys, (quickly fill'd up, no delay,)
I breathe the suffocating smoke, then the flat clouds hover low concealing all;
Now a strange lull for a few seconds, not a shot fired on either side,
Then resumed the chaos louder than ever, with eager calls and orders of officers,
While from some distant part of the field the wind wafts to my ears a shout of applause, (some special success,)
And ever the sound of the cannon far or near, (rousing even in dreams a devilish exultation and all the old mad joy in the depths of my soul,)
And ever the hastening of infantry shifting positions, batteries, cavalry, moving hither and thither,
(The falling, dying, I heed not, the wounded dripping and red I heed not, some to the rear are hobbling,)
Grime, heat, rush, aide-de-camps galloping by or on a full run,

With the patter of small arms, the warning *s-s-t* of the rifles, (these
in my vision I hear or see,)
And bombs bursting in air, and at night the vari-color'd rockets.

1865

Ethiopia Saluting the Colors[1]

Who are you dusky woman, so ancient hardly human,
With your woolly-white and turban'd head, and bare bony feet?
Why rising by the roadside here, do you the colors greet?

('Tis while our army lines Carolina's sands and pines,
Forth from thy hovel door thou Ethiopia com'st to me,
As under doughty Sherman[2] I march toward the sea.)

Me master years a hundred since from my parents sunder'd,
A little child, they caught me as the savage beast is caught,
Then hither me across the sea the cruel slaver brought.

No further does she say, but lingering all the day,
Her high-borne turban'd head she wags, and rolls her darkling eye,
And courtesies to the regiments, the guidons moving by.

What is it fateful woman, so blear, hardly human?
Why wag your head with turban bound, yellow, red and green?
Are the things so strange and marvelous you see or have seen?

1870

Reconciliation

Word over all, beautiful as the sky,
Beautiful that war and all its deeds or carnage must in time be
utterly lost,
That the hands of the sisters Death and Night incessantly softly
wash again, and ever again, this soil'd world;
For my enemy is dead, a man divine as myself is dead,
I look where he lies white-faced and still in the coffin—I draw
near,
Bend down and touch lightly with my lips the white face in the
coffin.

1865–66

[1]Whitman uses Ethiopia as a generic name for Africa or the black race.

[2]Whitman is referring to General William Sherman's famous march from Atlanta to Savannah in 1864; his army was followed by many black refugees seeking freedom.

As I Lay with My Head in Your Lap Camerado[1]

As I lay with my head in your lap camerado,
The confession I made I resume, what I said to you and the open air I resume,
I know I am restless and make others so,
I know my words are weapons full of danger, full of death,
For I confront peace, security, and all the settled laws, to unsettle them,
I am more resolute because all have denied me than I could ever have been had all accepted me,
I heed not and have never heeded either experience, cautions, majorities, nor ridicule,
And the threat of what is call'd hell is little or nothing to me,
And the lure of what is call'd heaven is little or nothing to me;
Dear camerado! I confess I have urged you onward with me, and still urge you, without the least idea what is our destination,
Or whether we shall be victorious, or utterly quell'd and defeated.

1865–66

from Memories of President Lincoln[1]

When Lilacs Last in the Dooryard Bloom'd[2]

1

When lilacs last in the dooryard bloom'd,
And the great star early droop'd in the western sky in the night,[3]
I mourn'd, and yet shall mourn with ever-returning spring.

Ever-returning spring, trinity sure to me you bring,
Lilac blooming perennial and drooping star in the west,
And thought of him I love.

2

O powerful western fallen star!
O shades of night—O moody, tearful night!
O great star disappear'd—O the black murk that hides the star!

[1]Spanish for comrade.

[1]This is the only place that Lincoln is specifically named as the subject of these poems.

[2]"Lilacs" was written immediately following Lincoln's death. He was shot on Good Friday, April 14, 1865, by John Wilkes Booth; he died the next morning. In a long procession through various American cities, his body was carried by train back to Springfield, Illinois, where he was buried on May 4, 1865.

[3]The "great star" is the Western star, Venus.

O cruel hands that hold me powerless—O helpless soul of me!
O harsh surrounding cloud that will not free my soul.

3

In the dooryard fronting an old farm-house near the white-wash'd palings,
Stands the lilac-bush tall-growing with heart-shaped leaves of rich green,
With many a pointed blossom rising delicate, with the perfume strong I love,
With every leaf a miracle—and from this bush in the dooryard,
With delicate-color'd blossoms and heart-shaped leaves of rich green,
A sprig with its flower I break.

4

In the swamp in secluded recesses,
A shy and hidden bird is warbling a song.

Solitary the thrush,
The hermit withdrawn to himself, avoiding the settlements,
Sings by himself a song.

Song of the bleeding throat,
Death's outlet song of life, (for well dear brother I know,
If thou wast not granted to sing thou would'st surely die.)

5

Over the breast of the spring, the land, amid cities,
Amid lanes and through old woods, where lately the violets peep'd from the ground, spotting the gray debris,
Amid the grass in the fields each side of the lanes, passing the endless grass,
Passing the yellow-spear'd wheat, every grain from its shroud in the dark-brown fields uprisen,
Passing the apple-tree blows of white and pink in the orchards,
Carrying a corpse to where it shall rest in the grave,
Night and day journeys a coffin.

6

Coffin that passes through lanes and streets,
Through day and night with the great cloud darkening the land,
With the pomp of the inloop'd flags with the cities draped in black,
With the show of the States themselves as of crape-veil'd women standing,

With processions long and winding and the flambeaus[4] of the night,
With the countless torches lit, with the silent sea of faces and the unbared heads,
With the waiting depot, the arriving coffin, and the sombre faces,
With dirges through the night, with the thousand voices rising strong and solemn,
With all the mournful voices of the dirges pour'd around the coffin,
The dim-lit churches and the shuddering organs—where amid these you journey,
With the tolling tolling bells' perpetual clang,
Here, coffin that slowly passes,
I give you my sprig of lilac.

7

(Nor for you, for one alone,
Blossoms and branches green to coffins all I bring,
For fresh as the morning, thus would I chant a song for you O sane and sacred death.

All over bouquets of roses,
O death, I cover you over with roses and early lilies,
But mostly and now the lilac that blooms the first,
Copious I break, I break the sprigs from the bushes,
With loaded arms I come, pouring for you,
For you and the coffins all of you O death.)

8

O western orb sailing the heaven,
Now I know what you must have meant as a month since I walk'd,
As I walk'd in silence the transparent shadowy night,
As I saw you had something to tell as you bent to me night after night,
As you droop'd from the sky low down as if to my side, (while the other stars all look'd on,)
As we wander'd together the solemn night, (for something I know not what kept me from sleep,)
As the night advanced, and I saw on the rim of the west how full you were of woe,
As I stood on the rising ground in the breeze in the cool transparent night,
As I watch'd where you pass'd and was lost in the netherward black of the night,

[4]Large candlesticks.

As my soul in its trouble dissatisfied sank, as where you sad orb,
Concluded, dropt in the night, and was gone.

9

Sing on there in the swamp,
O singer bashful and tender, I hear your notes, I hear your call,
I hear, I come presently, I understand you,
But a moment I linger, for the lustrous star has detain'd me,
The star my departing comrade holds and detains me.

10

O how shall I warble myself for the dead one there I loved?
And how shall I deck my song for the large sweet soul that has
gone?
And what shall my perfume be for the grave of him I love?

Sea-winds blown from east and west,
Blown from the Eastern sea and blown from the Western sea, till
there on the prairies meeting,
These and with these and the breath of my chant,
I'll perfume the grave of him I love.

11

O what shall I hang on the chamber walls?
And what shall the pictures be that I hang on the walls,
To adorn the burial-house of him I love?

Pictures of growing spring and farms and homes,
With the Fourth-month eve at sundown, and the gray smoke lucid
and bright,
With floods of the yellow gold of the gorgeous, indolent, sinking
sun, burning, expanding the air,
With the fresh sweet herbage under foot, and the pale green leaves
of the trees prolific,
In the distance the flowing glaze, the breast of the river, with a
wind-dapple here and there,
With ranging hills on the banks, with many a line against the sky,
and shadows,
And the city at hand with dwellings so dense, and stacks of
chimneys,
And all the scenes of life and the workshops, and the workmen
homeward returning.

12

Lo, body and soul—this land,
My own Manhattan with spires, and the sparkling and hurrying
tides, and the ships,

The varied and ample land, the South and the North in the light,
Ohio's shores and flashing Missouri,
And ever the far-spreading prairies cover'd with grass and corn.

Lo, the most excellent sun so calm and haughty,
The violet and purple morn with just-felt breezes,
The gentle soft-born measureless light,
The miracle spreading bathing all, the fulfill'd noon,
The coming eve delicious, the welcome night and the stars,
Over my cities shining all, enveloping man and land.

13

Sing on, sing on you gray-brown bird,
Sing from the swamps, the recesses, pour your chant from the bushes,
Limitless out of the dusk, out of the cedars and pines.

Sing on dearest brother, warble your reedy song,
Loud human song, with voice of uttermost woe.

O liquid and free and tender!
O wild and loose to my soul—O wondrous singer!
You only I hear—yet the star holds me, (but will soon depart,)
Yet the lilac with mastering odor holds me.

14

Now while I sat in the day and look'd forth,
In the close of the day with its light and the fields of spring, and the farmers preparing their crops,
In the large unconscious scenery of my land with its lakes and forests,
In the heavenly aerial beauty, (after the perturb'd winds and the storms,)
Under the arching heavens of the afternoon swift passing, and the voices of children and women,
The many-moving sea-tides, and I saw the ships how they sail'd,
And the summer approaching with richness, and the fields all busy with labor,
And the infinite separate houses, how they all went on, each with its meals and minutia of daily usages,
And the streets how their throbbings throbb'd, and the cities pent—lo, then and there,
Falling upon them all and among them all, enveloping me with the rest,
Appear'd the cloud, appear'd the long black trail,
And I knew death, its thought, and the sacred knowledge of death.

Then with the knowledge of death as walking one side of me,
And the thought of death close-walking the other side of me,
And I in the middle as with companions, and as holding the hands of companions,
I fled forth to the hiding receiving night that talks not,
Down to the shores of the water, the path by the swamp in the dimness,
To the solemn shadowy cedars and ghostly pines so still.

And the singer so shy to the rest receiv'd me,
The gray-brown bird I know receiv'd us comrades three,
And he sang the carol of death, and a verse for him I love.

From deep secluded recesses,
From the fragrant cedars and the ghostly pines so still,
Came the carol of the bird.

And the charm of the carol rapt me,
As I held as if by their hands my comrades in the night,
And the voice of my spirit tallied the song of the bird.

Come lovely and soothing death,
Undulate round the world, serenely arriving, arriving,
In the day, in the night, to all, to each,
Sooner or later delicate death.

Prais'd be the fathomless universe,
For life and joy, and for objects and knowledge curious,
And for love, sweet love—but praise! praise! praise!
For the sure-enwinding arms of cool-enfolding death.

Dark mother always gliding near with soft feet,
Have none chanted for thee a chant of fullest welcome?
Then I chant it for thee, I glorify thee above all,
I bring thee a song that when thou must indeed come, come unfalteringly.

Approach strong deliveress,
When it is so, when thou hast taken them I joyously sing the dead,
Lost in the loving floating ocean of thee,
Laved in the flood of thy bliss O death.

From me to thee glad serenades,
Dances for thee I propose saluting thee, adornments and feastings for thee,
And the sights of the open landscape and the high-spread sky are fitting,

And life and the fields, and the huge and thoughtful night.
The night in silence under many a star,
The ocean shore and the husky whispering wave whose voice I know,
And the soul turning to thee O vast and well-veil'd death,
And the body gratefully nestling close to thee.

Over the tree-tops I float thee a song,
Over the rising and sinking waves, over the myriad fields and the prairies wide,
Over the dense-pack'd cities all and the teeming wharves and ways,
I float this carol with joy, with joy to thee O death.

15

To the tally of my soul,
Loud and strong kept up the gray-brown bird,
With pure deliberate notes spreading filling the night.

Loud in the pines and cedars dim,
Clear in the freshness moist and the swamp-perfume,
And I with my comrades there in the night.

While my sight that was bound in my eyes unclosed,
As to long panoramas of visions.

And I saw askant the armies,
I saw as in noiseless dreams hundreds of battle-flags,
Borne through the smoke of the battles and pierc'd with missiles I saw them,
And carried hither and yon through the smoke, and torn and bloody,
And at last but a few shreds left on the staffs, (and all in silence,)
And the staffs all splinter'd and broken.

I saw battle-corpses, myriads of them,
And the white skeletons of young men, I saw them,
I saw the debris and debris of all the slain soldiers of the war,
But I saw they were not as was thought,
They themselves were fully at rest, they suffer'd not,
The living remain'd and suffer'd, the mother suffer'd,
And the wife and the child and the musing comrade suffer'd,
And the armies that remain'd suffer'd.

16

Passing the visions, passing the night,
Passing, unloosing the hold of my comrades' hands,

Passing the song of the hermit bird and the tallying song of my soul,
Victorious song, death's outlet song, yet varying ever-altering song,
As low and wailing, yet clear the notes, rising and falling, flooding the night,
Sadly sinking and fainting, as warning and warning, and yet again bursting with joy,
Covering the earth and filling the spread of the heaven,
As that powerful psalm in the night I heard from recesses,
Passing, I leave thee lilac with heart-shaped leaves,
I leave thee there in the door-yard, blooming, returning with spring.

I cease from my song for thee,
From my gaze on thee in the west, fronting the west, communing with thee,
O comrade lustrous with silver face in the night.
Yet each to keep and all, retrievements out of the night,
The song, the wondrous chant of the gray-brown bird,
And the tallying chant, the echo arous'd in my soul,
With the lustrous and drooping star with the countenance full of woe,
With the holders holding my hand nearing the call of the bird,
Comrades mine and I in the midst, and their memory ever to keep, for the dead I loved so well,
For the sweetest, wisest soul of all my days and lands—and this for his dear sake,
Lilac and star and bird twined with the chant of my soul,
There in the fragrant pines and the cedars dusk and dim.

1865–66

from Autumn Rivulets

Sparkles from the Wheel

Where the city's ceaseless crowd moves on the livelong day,
Withdrawn I join a group of children watching, I pause aside with them.

By the curb toward the edge of the flagging,
A knife-grinder works at his wheel sharpening a great knife,

Bending over he carefully holds it to the stone, by foot and knee,
With measur'd tread he turns rapidly, as he presses with light but firm hand,
Forth issue then in copious golden jets,
Sparkles from the wheel.

The scene and all its belongings, how they seize and affect me,
The sad sharp-chinn'd old man with worn clothes and broad shoulder-band of leather,
Myself effusing and fluid, a phantom curiously floating, now here absorb'd and arrested,
The group, (an unminded point set in a vast surrounding,)
The attentive, quiet children, the loud, proud, restive base of the streets,
The low hoarse purr of the whirling stone, the light-press'd blade,
Diffusing, dropping, sideways-darting, in tiny showers of gold,
Sparkles from the wheel.

1871

Prayer of Columbus[1]

A batter'd, wreck'd old man,
Thrown on this savage shore, far, far from home,
Pent by the sea and dark rebellious brows, twelve dreary months,
Sore, stiff with many toils, sicken'd and nigh to death,
I take my way along the island's edge,
Venting a heavy heart.

I am too full of woe!
Haply I may not live another day;
I cannot rest O God, I cannot eat or drink or sleep,
Till I put forth myself, my prayer, once more to Thee,
Breathe, bathe myself once more in Thee, commune with Thee,
Report myself once more to Thee.

Thou knowest my years entire, my life,
My long and crowded life of active work, not adoration merely;
Thou knowest the prayers and vigils of my youth,
Thou knowest my manhood's solemn and visionary meditations,
Thou knowest how before I commenced I devoted all to come to Thee,
Thou knowest I have in age ratified all those vows and strictly kept them,

[1]Whitman describes the hardships of Columbus on the island of Jamaica, where he was ship-wrecked in his attempt to sail around the world.

Thou knowest I have not once lost nor faith nor ecstasy in Thee,
In shackles, prison'd, in disgrace, repining not,
Accepting all from Thee, as duly come from Thee.

All my emprises[2] have been fill'd with Thee,
My speculations, plans, begun and carried on in thoughts of Thee,
Sailing the deep or journeying the land for Thee;
Intentions, purports, aspirations mine, leaving results to Thee.

O I am sure they really came from Thee,
The urge, the ardor, the unconquerable will,
The potent, felt, interior command, stronger than words,
A message from the Heavens whispering to me even in sleep,
These sped me on.

By me and these the work so far accomplish'd,
By me earth's elder cloy'd and stifled lands uncloy'd, unloos'd,
By me the hemispheres rounded and tied, the unknown to the known.

The end I know not, it is all in Thee,
Or small or great I know not—haply what broad fields, what lands,
Haply the brutish measureless human undergrowth I know,
Transplanted there may rise to stature, knowledge worthy Thee,
Haply the swords I know may there indeed be turn'd to reaping-tools,
Haply the lifeless cross I know, Europe's dead cross, may bud and blossom there.

One effort more, my altar this bleak sand;
That Thou O God my life hast lighted,
With ray of light, steady, ineffable, vouchsafed of Thee,
Light rare untellable, lighting the very light,
Beyond all signs, descriptions, languages;
For that O God, be it my latest word, here on my knees,
Old, poor, and paralyzed, I thank Thee.

My terminus near,
The clouds already closing in upon me,
The voyage balk'd, the course disputed, lost,
I yield my ships to Thee.
My hands, my limbs grow nerveless,

[2]Daring adventures.

My brain feels rack'd, bewilder'd,
Let the old timbers part, I will not part,
I will cling fast to Thee, O God, though the waves buffet me,
Thee, Thee at least I know.

Is it the prophet's thought I speak, or am I raving?
What do I know of life? what of myself?
I know not even my own work past or present,
Dim ever-shifting guesses of it spread before me,
Of newer better worlds, their mighty parturition,
Mocking, perplexing me.

And these things I see suddenly, what mean they?
As if some miracle, some hand divine unseal'd my eyes,
Shadowy vast shapes smile through the air and sky,
And on the distant waves sail countless ships,
And anthems in new tongues I hear saluting me.

1874

from Whispers of Heavenly Death

Quicksand Years[1]

Quicksand years that whirl me I know not whither,
Your schemes, politics, fail, lines give way, substances mock and elude me,
Only the theme I sing, the great and strong-possess'd soul, eludes not,
One's-self must never give way—that is the final substance—that out of all is sure,
Out of politics, triumphs, battles, life, what at last finally remains?
When shows break up what but One's-Self is sure?

1865

[1]The poem was drafted in 1862–1863.

from From Noon to Starry Night

To a Locomotive in Winter

Thee for my recitative,
Thee in the driving storm even as now, the snow, the winter-day declining,
Thee in thy panoply, thy measur'd dual throbbing and thy beat convulsive,
Thy black cylindric body, golden brass and silvery steel,
Thy ponderous side-bars, parallel and connecting rods, gyrating, shuttling at thy sides,
Thy metrical, now swelling pant and roar, now tapering in the distance,
Thy great protruding head-light fix'd in front,
Thy long, pale, floating vapor-pennants, tinged with delicate purple,
The dense and murky clouds out-belching from thy smoke-stack,
Thy knitted frame, thy springs and valves, the tremulous twinkle of thy wheels,
Thy train of cars behind, obedient, merrily following,
Through gale or calm, now swift, now slack, yet steadily careering;
Type of the modern—emblem of motion and power—pulse of the continent,
For once come serve the Muse and merge in verse, even as here I see thee,
With storm and buffeting gusts of wind and falling snow,
By day thy warning ringing bell to sound its notes,
By night thy silent signal lamps to swing.

Fierce-throated beauty!
Roll through my chant with all thy lawless music, thy swinging lamps at night,
Thy madly-whistled laughter, echoing, rumbling like an earth-quake, rousing all,
Law of thyself complete, thine own track firmly holding,
(No sweetness debonair of tearful harp or glib piano thine,)
Thy trills of shrieks by rocks and hills return'd,
Launch'd o'er the prairies wide, across the lakes,
To the free skies unpent and glad and strong.

1876

from Songs of Parting

So Long![1]

To conclude, I announce what comes after me.

I remember I said before my leaves sprang at all,
I would raise my voice jocund and strong with reference to consummations.

When America does what was promis'd,
When through these States walk a hundred millions of superb persons,
When the rest part away for superb persons and contribute to them,
When breeds of the most perfect mothers denote America,
Then to me and mine our due fruition.

I have press'd through in my own right,
I have sung the body and the soul, war and peace have I sung, and the songs of life and death,
And the songs of birth, and shown that there are many births.

I have offer'd my style to every one, I have journey'd with confident step;
While my pleasure is yet at the full I whisper *So long!*
And take the young woman's hand and the young man's hand for the last time.

I announce natural persons to arise,
I announce justice triumphant,
I announce uncompromising liberty and equality,
I announce the justification of candor and the justification of pride.
I announce that the identity of these States is a single identity only,
I announce the Union more and more compact, indissoluble,
I announce splendors and majesties to make all the previous politics of the earth insignificant.

I announce adhesiveness,[2] I say it shall be limitless, unloosen'd,

[1]In the mid-nineteenth century, "So Long" was an idiomatic expression much used among sailors and street people. This poem concluded *Leaves of Grass* in 1860 and in all subsequent editions.

[2]A term Whitman borrowed from phrenology meaning, he said, the "passion of friendship for man."

I say you shall yet find the friend you were looking for.

I announce a man or woman coming, perhaps you are the one, (*So long!*)
I announce the great individual, fluid as Nature, chaste, affectionate, compassionate, fully arm'd.

I announce a life that shall be copious, vehement, spiritual, bold,
I announce an end that shall lightly and joyfully meet its translation.

I announce myriads of youths, beautiful, gigantic, sweet-blooded,
I announce a race of splendid and savage old men.

O thicker and faster—(*So long!*)
O crowding too close upon me,
I foresee too much, it means more than I thought,
It appears to me I am dying.

Hasten throat and sound your last,
Salute me—salute the days once more. Peal the old cry once more.

Screaming electric, the atmosphere using,
At random glancing, each as I notice absorbing,
Swiftly on, but a little while alighting,
Curious envelop'd messages delivering,
Sparkles hot, seed ethereal down in the dirt dropping,
Myself unknowing, my commission obeying, to question it never daring,
To ages and ages yet the growth of the seed leaving,
To troops out of the war arising, they the tasks I have set promulging,
To women certain whispers of myself bequeathing, their affection me more clearly explaining,
To young men my problems offering—no dallier I—I the muscle of their brains trying,
So I pass, a little time vocal, visible, contrary,
Afterward a melodious echo, passionately bent for, (death making me really undying,)
The best of me then when no longer visible, for toward that I have been incessantly preparing.

What is there more, that I lag and pause and crouch extended with unshut mouth?
Is there a single final farewell?

My songs cease, I abandon them,
From behind the screen where I hid I advance personally solely to you.

Camerado, this is no book,
Who touches this touches a man,
(Is it night? are we here together alone?)
It is I you hold and who holds you,
I spring from the pages into your arms—decease calls me forth.

O how your fingers drowse me,
Your breath falls around me like dew, your pulse lulls the tympans of my ears,
I feel immerged from head to foot,
Delicious, enough.

Enough O deed impromptu and secret,
Enough O gliding present—enough O summ'd-up past.

Dear friend whoever you are take this kiss,
I give it especially to you, do not forget me,
I feel like one who has done work for the day to retire awhile,
I receive now again of my many translations, from my avataras ascending, while others doubtless await me,
An unknown sphere more real than I dream'd, more direct, darts awakening rays about me, *So long!*
Remember my words, I may again return,
I love you, I depart from materials,
I am as one disembodied, triumphant, dead.

1860

from Sands at Seventy (First Annex)

Yonnondio

[The sense of the word is lament for the aborigines. *It is an Iroquois term; and has been used for a personal name.]*

A song, a poem of itself—the word itself a dirge,
Amid the wilds, the rocks, the storm and wintry night,
To me such misty, strange tableaux the syllables calling up;
Yonnondio—I see, far in the west or north, a limitless ravine, with plains and mountains dark,
I see swarms of stalwart chieftains, medicine-men, and warriors,
As flitting by like clouds of ghosts, they pass and are gone in the twilight,

(Race of the woods, the landscapes free, and the falls!
No picture, poem, statement, passing them to the future:)
Yonnondio! Yonnondio!—unlimn'd they disappear;
To-day gives place, and fades—the cities, farms, factories fade;
A muffled sonorous sound, a wailing word is borne through the air for a moment,
Then blank and gone and still, and utterly lost.

1887

from Good-bye My Fancy (Second Annex)

Good-bye My Fancy!

Good-bye my Fancy!
Farewell dear mate, dear love!
I'm going away, I know not where,
Or to what fortune, or whether I may ever see you again,
So Good-bye my Fancy.

Now for my last—let me look back a moment;
The slower fainter ticking of the clock is in me,
Exit, nightfall, and soon the heart-thud stopping.

Long have we lived, joy'd, caress'd together;
Delightful!—now separation—Good-bye my Fancy.

Yet let me not be too hasty,
Long indeed have we lived, slept, filter'd, become really blended into one;
Then if we die we die together, (yes, we'll remain one,)
If we go anywhere we'll go together to meet what happens,
May-be we'll be better off and blither, and learn something,
May-be it is yourself now really ushering me to the true songs, (who knows?)
May-be it is you the mortal knob really undoing, turning—so now finally,
Good-bye—and hail! my Fancy.

1891

Poem Deleted from *Leaves of Grass*

Respondez![1]

Respondez! Respondez!
(The war is completed—the price is paid—the title is settled beyond recall;)
Let every one answer! let those who sleep be waked! let none evade!
Must we still go on with our affectations and sneaking?
Let me bring this to a close—I pronounce openly for a new distribution of roles;
Let that which stood in front go behind! and let that which was behind advance to the front and speak;
Let murderers, bigots, fools, unclean persons, offer new propositions!
Let the old propositions be postponed!
Let faces and theories be turn'd inside out! let meanings be freely criminal, as well as results!
Let there be no suggestion above the suggestion of drudgery!
Let none be pointed toward his destination! (Say! do you know your destination?)
Let men and women be mock'd with bodies and mock'd with Souls!
Let the love that waits in them, wait! let it die, or pass still-born to other spheres!
Let the sympathy that waits in every man, wait! or let it also pass, a dwarf, to other spheres!
Let contradictions prevail! let one thing contradict another! and let one line of my poems contradict another!
Let the people sprawl with yearning, aimless hands! let their tongues be broken! let their eyes be discouraged! let none descend into their hearts with the fresh lusciousness of love!
(Stifled, O days! O lands! in every public and private corruption!
Smother'd in thievery, impotence, shamelessness, mountain-high;
Brazen effrontery, scheming, rolling like ocean's waves around and upon you, O my days! my lands!
For not even those thunderstorms, nor fiercest lightnings of the war, have purified the atmosphere;)
—Let the theory of America still be management, caste, comparison! (Say! what other theory would you?)

[1]Initially entitled "Poem of the Propositions of Nakedness," this poem first appeared in the 1856 edition of *Leaves of Grass.* Later entitled "Respondez," it was deleted from *Leaves of Grass* in 1881.

Let them that distrust birth and death still lead the rest! (Say! why shall they not lead you?)
Let the crust of hell be neared and trod on! let the days be darker than the nights! let slumber bring less slumber than waking time brings!
Let the world never appear to him or her for whom it was all made!
Let the heart of the young man still exile itself from the heart of the old man! and let the heart of the old man be exiled from that of the young man!
Let the sun and moon go! let scenery take the applause of the audience! let there be apathy under the stars!
Let freedom prove no man's inalienable right! every one who can tyrannize, let him tyrannize to his satisfaction!
Let none but infidels be countenanced!
Let the eminence of meanness, treachery, sarcasm, hate, greed, indecency, impotence, lust, be taken for granted above all! let writers, judges, governments, households, religions, philosophies, take such for granted above all!
Let the worst men beget children out of the worst women!
Let the priest still play at immortality!
Let death be inaugurated!
Let nothing remain but the ashes of teachers, artists, moralists, lawyers, and learn'd and polite persons!
Let him who is without my poems be assassinated!
Let the cow, the horse, the camel, the garden-bee—let the mud-fish, the lobster, the mussel, eel, the sting-ray, and the grunting pig-fish—let these, and the like of these, be put on a perfect equality with man and woman!
Let churches accommodate serpents, vermin, and the corpses of those who have died of the most filthy of diseases!
Let marriage slip down among fools, and be for none but fools!
Let men among themselves talk and think forever obscenely of women! and let women among themselves talk and think obscenely of men!
Let us all, without missing one, be exposed in public, naked, monthly, at the peril of our lives! let our bodies be freely handled and examined by whoever chooses!
Let nothing but copies at second hand be permitted to exist upon the earth!
Let the earth desert God, nor let there ever henceforth be mention'd the name of God!
Let there be no God!
Let there be money, business, imports, exports, custom, authority, precedents, pallor, dyspepsia, smut, ignorance, unbelief!
Let judges and criminals be transposed! let the prison-keepers be put in prison! let those that were prisoners take the keys! (Say! why might they not just as well be transposed?)

Let the slaves be masters! let the masters become slaves!
Let the reformers descend from the stands where they are forever bawling! let an idiot or insane person appear on each of the stands!
Let the Asiatic, the African, the European, the American, and the Australian, go armed against the murderous stealthiness of each other! let them sleep armed! let none believe in good will!
Let there be no unfashionable wisdom! let such be scorn'd and derided off from the earth!
Let a floating cloud in the sky—let a wave of the sea—let growing mint, spinach, onions, tomatoes—let these be exhibited as shows, at a great price for admission!
Let all the men of These States stand aside for a few smouchers! let the few seize on what they choose! let the rest gawk, giggle, starve, obey!
Let shadows be furnish'd with genitals! let substances be deprived of their genitals!
Let there be wealthy and immense cities—but still through any of them, not a single poet, savior, knower, lover!
Let the infidels of These States laugh all faith away!
If one man be found who has faith, let the rest set upon him!
Let them affright faith! let them destroy the power of breeding faith!
Let the she-harlots and the he-harlots be prudent! let them dance on, while seeming lasts! (O seeming! seeming! seeming!)
Let the preachers recite creeds! let them still teach only what they have been taught!
Let insanity still have charge of sanity!
Let books take the place of trees, animals, rivers, clouds!
Let the daub'd portraits of heroes supersede heroes!
Let the manhood of man never take steps after itself!
Let it take steps after eunuchs, and after consumptive and genteel persons!
Let the white person again tread the black person under his heel! (Say! which is trodden under heel, after all?)
Let the reflections of the things of the world be studied in mirrors! let the things themselves still continue unstudied!
Let a man seek pleasure everywhere except in himself!
Let a woman seek happiness everywhere except in herself!
(What real happiness have you had one single hour through your whole life?)
Let the limited years of life do nothing for the limitless years of death! (What do you suppose death will do, then?)

1856

from Democratic Vistas (1871)[1]

As the greatest lessons of Nature through the universe are perhaps the lessons of variety and freedom, the same present the greatest lessons also in New World politics and progress. If a man were ask'd, for instance, the distinctive points contrasting modern European and American political and other life with the old Asiatic cultus, as lingering-bequeath'd yet in China and Turkey, he might find the amount of them in John Stuart Mill's profound essay on Liberty in the future, where he demands two main constituents, or sub-strata, for a truly grand nationality—1st, a large variety of character—and 2d, full play for human nature to expand itself in numberless and even conflicting directions—(seems to be for general humanity much like the influences that make up, in their limitless field, that perennial health-action of the air we call the weather—an infinite number of currents and forces, and contributions, and temperatures, and cross purposes, whose ceaseless play of counterpart upon counterpart brings constant restoration and vitality.) With this thought—and not for itself alone, but all it necessitates, and draws after it—let me begin my speculations.

America, filling the present with greatest deeds and problems, cheerfully accepting the past, including feudalism, (as, indeed, the present is but the legitimate birth of the past, including feudalism,) counts, as I reckon, for her justification and success, (for who, as yet, dare claim success?) almost entirely on the future. Nor is that hope unwarranted. To-day, ahead, though dimly yet, we see, in vistas, a copious, sane, gigantic offspring. For our New World I consider far less important for what it has done, or what it is, than for results to come. Sole among nationalities, these States have assumed the task to put in forms of lasting power and practicality, on areas of amplitude rivaling the operations of the physical kosmos, the moral political speculations of ages, long, long deferr'd, the democratic republican principle, and the theory of development and perfection by voluntary standards, and self-reliance. Who else, indeed, except the United States, in history, so far, have accepted in unwitting faith, and, as we now see, stand, act upon, and go security for, these things?

But preluding no longer, let me strike the key-note of the following strain. First premising that, though the passages of it have been written at widely different times, (it is, in fact, a collection of memoranda, perhaps for future designers, comprehenders,) and though it may be open to the charge of one part contradicting another—for there are opposite sides to the great question of democracy, as to every great question—I feel the parts harmoniously blended in my own realization and convictions, and present them to be read only in such oneness, each page and each claim and assertion modified and temper'd by the others. Bear in mind, too, that they are not the result of studying up in political economy, but of the ordinary sense, observing,

[1] *Democratic Vistas* was written in response to Thomas Carlyle's critique of democracy in "Shooting Niagara" (1867). In this essay, Carlyle described democratic enfranchisement as an unchaining of the devil—or a suicidal leap over Niagara Falls. Sections of this essay, originally entitled "Democracy" and "Personalism," appeared in the New York *Galaxy* in 1867–1868. *Democratic Vistas* was published as a pamphlet in 1871.

wandering among men, these States, these stirring years of war and peace. I will not gloss over the appalling dangers of universal suffrage in the United States. In fact, it is to admit and face these dangers I am writing. To him or her within whose thought rages the battle, advancing, retreating, between democracy's convictions, aspirations, and the people's crudeness, vice, caprices, I mainly write this essay. I shall use the words America and democracy as convertible terms. Not an ordinary one is the issue. The United States are destined either to surmount the gorgeous history of feudalism, or else prove the most tremendous failure of time. Not the least doubtful am I on any prospects of their material success. The triumphant future of their business, geographic and productive departments, on larger scales and in more varieties than ever, is certain. In those respects the republic must soon (if she does not already) outstrip all examples hitherto afforded, and dominate the world. . . .

For my part, I would alarm and caution even the political and business reader, and to the utmost extent, against the prevailing delusion that the establishment of free political institutions, and plentiful intellectual smartness, with general good order, physical plenty, industry, &c., (desirable and precious advantages as they all are,) do, of themselves, determine and yield to our experiment of democracy the fruitage of success. With such advantages at present fully, or almost fully, possess'd—the Union just issued, victorious, from the struggle with the only foes it need ever fear, (namely, those within itself, the interior ones,) and with unprecedented materialistic advancement—society, in these States, is canker'd, crude, superstitious, and rotten. Political, or law-made society is, and private, or voluntary society, is also. In any vigor, the element of the moral conscience, the most important, the verteber to State or man, seems to me either entirely lacking, or seriously enfeebled or ungrown.

I say we had best look our times and lands searchingly in the face, like a physician diagnosing some deep disease. Never was there, perhaps, more hollowness at heart than at present, and here in the United States. Genuine belief seems to have left us. The underlying principles of the States are not honestly believ'd in, (for all this hectic glow, and these melo-dramatic screamings,) nor is humanity itself believ'd in. What penetrating eye does not everywhere see through the mask? The spectacle is appalling. We live in an atmosphere of hypocrisy throughout. The men believe not in the women, nor the women in the men. A scornful superciliousness rules in literature. The aim of all the *littérateurs* is to find something to make fun of. A lot of churches, sects, &c., the most dismal phantasms I know, usurp the name of religion. Conversation is a mass of badinage. From deceit in the spirit, the mother of all false deeds, the offspring is already incalculable. An acute and candid person, in the revenue department in Washington, who is led by the course of his employment to regularly visit the cities, north, south and west, to investigate frauds, has talk'd much with me about his discoveries. The depravity of the business classes of our country is not less than has been supposed, but infinitely greater. The official services of America, national, state, and municipal, in all their branches and departments, except the judiciary, are saturated in corruption, bribery, falsehood, mal-administration; and the judiciary is tainted. The great cities reek with respectable as much as non-respectable robbery and scoundrelism. In fashionable life, flippancy, tepid amours, weak infidelism, small aims, or no aims at all, only to kill time. In business, (this all-devouring modern word, business,) the one sole object is, by any means, pecuniary gain. The magician's serpent in the fable ate up all the other serpents; and money-making is our magician's serpent, remaining to-day sole master of the field. The best class we show, is but a mob of fashionably dress'd speculators and vulgarians. True, indeed, behind this fantastic farce, enacted on the visible stage of society, solid things and stupendous labors are to be discover'd, existing crudely and going on in the background, to advance and tell themselves in time. Yet the truths are none the less terrible. I say that our New World democracy, however great a success in uplifting the masses out of their sloughs, in materialistic development, products, and in a certain highly-deceptive superficial popular intellectuality, is, so far, an almost complete failure in its social aspects, and in really grand religious, moral, literary, and esthetic results. In vain do we march with unprecedented strides to empire so colossal, outvying the antique, beyond Alexander's, beyond the proudest sway of Rome. In vain have we annex'd Texas, California, Alaska, and reach north for Canada and south for Cuba. It is as if we were somehow being endow'd with a vast and more and more thoroughly-appointed body, and then left with little or no soul. . . .

Confess that to severe eyes, using the moral microscrope upon humanity, a sort of dry and flat Sahara appears, these cities, crowded with petty grotesques, malformations, phantoms, playing meaningless antics. Confess that everywhere, in shop, street, church, theatre, bar-room, official chair, are pervading flippancy and vulgarity, low cunning, infidelity—everywhere the youth puny, impudent, foppish, prematurely ripe—everywhere an abnormal libidinousness, unhealthy forms, male, female, painted, padded, dyed, chignon'd, muddy complexions, bad blood, the capacity for good motherhood deceasing or deceas'd, shallow notions of beauty, with a range of manners, or rather lack of manners, (considering the advantages enjoy'd,) probably the meanest to be seen in the world.[2]

Of all this, and these lamentable conditions, to breathe into them the breath recuperative of sane and heroic life, I say a new founded literature, not merely to copy and reflect existing surfaces, or pander to what is called taste—not only to amuse, pass away time, celebrate the beautiful, the refined, the past, or exhibit technical, rhythmic, or grammatical dexterity—but a literature underlying life, religious, consistent with science, handling the elements and forces with competent power, teaching and training men—and, as perhaps the most precious of its results, achieving the entire redemption of woman out of these incredible holds and webs of silliness,

[2]Of these rapidly-sketch'd hiatuses, the two which seem to me most serious are, for one, the condition, absence, or perhaps the singular abeyance, of moral conscientious fibre all through American society; and, for another, the appalling depletion of women in their powers of sane athletic maternity, their crowning attribute, and ever making the woman, in loftiest spheres, superior to the man.

I have sometimes thought, indeed, that the sole avenue and means of a reconstructed sociology depended, primarily, on a new birth, elevation, expansion, invigoration of woman, affording, for races to come, (as the conditions that antedate birth are indispensable,) a perfect motherhood. Great, great, indeed, far greater than they know, is the sphere of women. But doubtless the question of such new sociology all goes together, includes many varied and complex influences and premises, and the man as well as the woman, and the woman as well as the man. [Whitman's note] millinery, and every kind of dyspeptic depletion—and thus insuring to the States a strong and sweet Female Race, a race of perfect Mothers—is what is needed.

And now, in the full conception of these facts and points, and all that they infer, pro and con—with yet unshaken faith in the elements of the American masses, the composites, of both sexes, and even consider'd as individuals—and ever recognizing in them the broadest bases of the best literary and esthetic appreciation—I proceed with my speculations, Vistas. . . .

I say the mission of government, henceforth, in civilized lands, is not repression alone, and not authority alone, not even of law, nor by that favorite standard of the eminent writer, the rule of the best men, the born heroes and captains of the race, (as if such ever, or one time out of a hundred, get into the big places, elective or dynastic)—but higher than the highest arbitrary rule, to train communities through all their grades, beginning with individuals and ending there again, to rule themselves. What Christ appear'd for in the moral-spiritual field for human-kind, namely, that in respect to the absolute soul, there is in the possession of such by each single individual, something so transcendent, so incapable of gradations, (like life,) that, to that extent, it places all beings on a common level, utterly regardless of the distinctions of intellect, virtue, station, or any height or lowliness whatever—is tallied in like manner, in this other field, by democracy's rule that men, the nation, as a common aggregate of living identities, affording in each a separate and complete subject for freedom, worldly thrift and happiness, and for a fair chance for growth, and for protection in citizenship, &c., must, to the political extent of the suffrage or vote, if no further, be placed, in each and in the whole, on one broad, primary, universal, common platform. . . .

Democracy too is law, and of the strictest, amplest kind. Many suppose, (and often in its own ranks the error,) that it means a throwing aside of law, and running riot. But, briefly, it is the superior law, not alone that of physical force, the body, which, adding to, it supersedes with that of the spirit. Law is the unshakable order of the universe forever; and the law over all, and law of laws, is the law of successions; that of the superior law, in time, gradually supplanting and overwhelming the inferior one. (While, for myself, I would cheerfully agree—first covenanting that the formative tendencies shall be administer'd in favor, or at least not against it, and that this reservation be closely construed—that until the individual or community show due signs, or be so minor and fractional as not to endanger the State, the condition of authoritative tutelage may continue, and self-government must abide its time.) Nor is the esthetic point, always an important one, without fascination for highest aiming souls. The common ambition strains for elevations, to become some privileged exclusive. The master sees greatness and health in being part of the mass; nothing will do as well as common ground. Would you have in yourself the divine, vast, general law? Then merge yourself in it.

And, topping democracy, this most alluring record, that it alone can bind, and ever seeks to bind, all nations, all men, of however various and distant lands, into a brotherhood, a family. It is the old, yet ever-modern dream of earth, out of her eldest and her youngest, her fond philosophers and poets. Not that half only, individualism, which isolates. There is another half, which is adhesiveness or love, that fuses, ties and aggregates, making the races comrades, and fraternizing all. Both are to be vitalized by religion, (sole worthiest elevator of man or State,) breathing into the proud, material tissues, the breath of life. For I say at the core of democracy, finally, is the religious element. All the religions, old and new, are there. Nor may the scheme step forth, clothed in resplendent beauty and command, till these, bearing the best, the latest fruit, the spiritual, shall fully appear.

A portion of our pages we might indite with reference toward Europe, especially the British part of it, more than our own land, perhaps not absolutely needed for the home reader. But the whole question hangs together, and fastens and links all peoples. The liberalist of to-day has this advantage over antique or medieval times, that his doctrine seeks not only to individualize but to universalize. The great word Solidarity has arisen. Of all dangers to a nation, as things exist in our day, there can be no greater one than having certain portions of the people set off from the rest by a line drawn—they not privileged as others, but degraded, humiliated, made of no account. Much quackery teems, of course, even on democracy's side, yet does not really affect the orbic quality of the matter. To work in, if we may so term it, and justify God, his divine aggregate, the People, (or, the veritable horn'd and sharp-tail'd Devil, *his* aggregate, if there be who convulsively insist upon it)—this, I say, is what democracy is for; and this is what our America means, and is doing—may I not say, has done? If not, she means nothing more, and does nothing more, than any other land. And as, by virtue of its kosmical, antiseptic power, Nature's stomach is fully strong enough not only to digest the morbific matter always presented, not to be turn'd aside, and perhaps, indeed, intuitively gravitating thither—but even to change such contributions into nutriment for highest use and life—so American democracy's. That is the lesson we, these days, send over to European lands by every western breeze.

And, truly, whatever may be said in the way of abstract argument, for or against the theory of a wider democratizing of institutions in any civilized country, much trouble might well be saved to all European lands by recognizing this palpable fact, (for a palpable fact it is,) that some form of such democratizing is about the only resource now left. *That,* or chronic dissatisfaction continued, mutterings which grow annually louder and louder, till, in due course, and pretty swiftly in most cases, the inevitable crisis, crash, dynastic ruin. Anything worthy to be call'd statesmanship in the Old World, I should say, among the advanced students, adepts, or men of any brains, does not debate to-day whether to hold on, attempting to lean back and monarchize, or to look forward and democratize—but *how,* and in what degree and part, most prudently to democratize. . . .

The true gravitation-hold of liberalism in the United States will be a more universal ownership of property, general homesteads, general comfort—a vast, intertwining reticulation of wealth. As the human frame, or, indeed, any object in this manifold universe, is best kept together by the simple miracle of its own cohesion, and the necessity, exercise and profit thereof, so a great and varied nationality, occupying millions of square miles, were firmest held and knit by the principle of the safety and endurance of the aggregate of its middling property owners. So that, from another point of view, ungracious as it may sound, and a paradox after what we have been saying, democracy looks with suspicious, ill-satisfied eye upon the very poor, the ignorant, and on those out of business. She asks for men and women with occupations, well-off, owners of houses and acres, and with cash in the bank—and with some cravings for literature, too; and must have them, and hastens to make them. Luckily, the seed is already well-sown, and has taken ineradicable root.[3] . . .

America has yet morally and artistically originated nothing. She seems singularly unaware that the models of persons, books, manners, &c., appropriate for former conditions and for European lands, are but exiles and exotics here. No current of her life, as shown on the surfaces of what is authoritatively called her society, accepts or runs into social or esthetic democracy; but all the currents set squarely against it. Never, in the Old World, was thoroughly upholster'd exterior appearance and show, mental and other, built entirely on the idea of caste, and on the sufficiency of mere outside acquisition—never were glibness, verbal intellect, more the test, the emulation—more loftily elevated as head and sample—than they are on the surface of our republican States this day. The writers of a time hint the mottoes of its gods. The word of the modern, say these voices, is the word Culture.

We find ourselves abruptly in close quarters with the enemy. This word Culture, or what it has come to represent, involves, by contrast, our whole theme, and has been, indeed, the spur, urging us to engagement. Certain questions arise. As now taught, accepted and carried out, are not the processes of culture rapidly creating a class of supercilious infidels, who believe in nothing? Shall a man lose himself in countless masses of adjustments, and be so shaped with reference to this, that, and the other, that the simply good and healthy and brave parts of him are reduced and clipp'd away, like the bordering of box in a garden? You can cultivate corn and roses and orchards—but who shall cultivate the mountain peaks, the ocean, and the tumbling gorgeousness of the clouds? Lastly—is the readily-given reply that culture only seeks to help, systematize, and put in attitude, the elements of fertility and power, a conclusive reply?

I do not so much object to the name, or word, but I should certainly insist, for the purposes of these States, on a radical change of category, in the distribution of precedence. I should demand a programme of culture, drawn out, not for a single class alone, or for the parlors or lecture-rooms, but with an eye to practical life, the west, the working-men, the facts of farms and jack-planes and engineers, and of the broad range of the women also of the middle and working strata, and with reference to the perfect equality of women, and of a grand and powerful motherhood. I should demand of this programme or theory a scope generous enough to include the widest human area. It must have for its spinal meaning the formation of a typical personality of character, eligible to the uses of the high average of men—and *not* restricted by

[3]For fear of mistake, I may as well distinctly specify, as cheerfully included in the model and standard of these Vistas, a practical, stirring, worldly, money-making, even materialistic character. It is undeniable that our farms, stores, offices, dry-goods, coal and groceries, enginery, cash-accounts, trades, earnings, markets, &c., should be attended to in earnest, and actively pursued, just as if they had a real and permanent existence. I perceive clearly that the extreme business energy, and this almost maniacal appetite for wealth prevalent in the United States, are parts of amelioration and progress, indispensably needed to prepare the very results I demand. My theory includes riches, and the getting of riches, and the amplest products, power, activity, inventions, movements, &c. Upon them, as upon substrata, I raise the edifice design'd in these Vistas. [Whitman's note]

conditions ineligible to the masses. The best culture will always be that of the manly and courageous instincts, and loving perceptions, and of self-respect—aiming to form, over this continent, an idiocrasy of universalism, which, true child of America, will bring joy to its mother, returning to her in her own spirit, recruiting myriads of offspring, able, natural, perceptive, tolerant, devout believers in her, America, and with some definite instinct why and for what she has arisen, most vast, most formidable of historic births, and is, now and here, with wonderful step, journeying through Time. . . .

Of course, in these States, for both man and woman, we must entirely recast the types of highest personality from what the oriental, feudal, ecclesiastical worlds bequeath us, and which yet possess the imaginative and esthetic fields of the United States, pictorial and melodramatic, not without use as studies, but making sad work, and forming a strange anachronism upon the scenes and exigencies around us. Of course, the old undying elements remain. The task is, to successfully adjust them to new combinations, our own days. Nor is this so incredible. I can conceive a community, to-day and here, in which, on a sufficient scale, the perfect personalities, without noise meet; say in some pleasant western settlement or town, where a couple of hundred best men and women, of ordinary worldly status, have by luck been drawn together, with nothing extra of genius or wealth, but virtuous, chaste, industrious, cheerful, resolute, friendly and devout. I can conceive such a community organized in running order, powers judiciously delegated—farming, building, trade, courts, mails, schools, elections, all attended to; and then the rest of life, the main thing, freely branching and blossoming in each individual, and bearing golden fruit. I can see there, in every young and old man, after his kind, and in every woman after hers, a true personality, develop'd, exercised proportionately in body, mind, and spirit. I can imagine this case as one not necessarily rare or difficult, but in buoyant accordance with the municipal and general requirements of our times. And I can realize in it the culmination of something better than any stereotyped *éclat* of history or poems. Perhaps, unsung, undramatized, unput in essays or biographies—perhaps even some such community already exists, in Ohio, Illinois, Missouri, or somewhere, practically fulfilling itself, and thus outvying, in cheapest vulgar life, all that has been hitherto shown in best ideal pictures. . . .

There are still other standards, suggestions, for products of high literatuses. That which really balances and conserves the social and political world is not so much legislation, police, treaties, and dread of punishment, as the latent eternal intuitional sense, in humanity, of fairness, manliness, decorum, &c. Indeed, this perennial regulation, control, and oversight, by self-suppliance, is *sine qua non* to democracy; and a highest widest aim of democratic literature may well be to bring forth, cultivate, brace, and strengthen this sense, in individuals and society. A strong mastership of the general inferior self by the superior self, is to be aided, secured, indirectly, but surely, by the literatus, in his works, shaping, for individual or aggregate democracy, a great passionate body, in and along with which goes a great masterful spirit.

And still, providing for contingencies, I fain confront the fact, the need of powerful native philosophs and orators and bards, these States, as rallying points to come, in times of danger, and to fend off ruin and defection. For history is long, long, long. Shift and turn the combinations of the statement as we may, the problem of the future of America is in certain respects as dark as it is vast. Pride, competition, segregation, vicious wilfulness, and license beyond example, brood already upon us. Unwieldy and immense, who shall hold in behemoth? who bridle leviathan? Flaunt it as we choose, athwart and over the roads of our progress loom huge uncertainty, and dreadful, threatening gloom. It is useless to deny it: Democracy grows rankly up the thickest, noxious, deadliest plants and fruits of all—brings worse and worse invaders—needs newer, larger, stronger, keener compensations and compellers.

Our lands, embracing so much, (embracing indeed the whole, rejecting none,) hold in their breast that flame also, capable of consuming themselves, consuming us all. Short as the span of our national life has been, already have death and downfall crowded close upon us—and will again crowd close, no doubt, even if warded off. Ages to come may never know, but I know, how narrowly during the late secession war—and more than once, and more than twice or thrice—our Nationality, (wherein bound up, as in a ship in a storm, depended, and yet depend, all our best life, all hope, all value,) just grazed, just by a hair escaped destruction. Alas! to think of them! the agony and bloody sweat of certain of those hours! those cruel, sharp, suspended crises!

Even to-day, amid these whirls, incredible flippancy, and blind fury of parties, infidelity, entire lack of first-class captains and leaders, added to the plentiful meanness and vulgarity of the ostensible masses—that problem, the labor question, beginning to open like a yawning gulf, rapidly widening every year—what prospect have we? We sail a dangerous sea of seething currents, cross and under-currents, vortices—all so dark, untried—and whither shall we turn? It seems as if the Almighty had spread before this nation charts of imperial destinies, dazzling as the sun, yet with many a deep intestine difficulty, and human aggregate of cankerous imperfection,—saying, lo! the roads, the only plans of development, long and varied with all terrible balks and ebullitions. You said in your soul, I will be empire of empires, overshadowing all else, past and present, putting the history of old-world dynasties, conquests behind me, as of no account—making a new history, a history of democracy, making old history a dwarf—I alone inaugurating largeness, culminating time. If these, O lands of America, are indeed the prizes, the determinations of your soul, be it so. But behold the cost, and already specimens of the cost. Thought you greatness was to ripen for you like a pear? If you would have greatness, know that you must conquer it through ages, centuries—must pay for it with a proportionate price. For you too, as for all lands, the struggle, the traitor, the wily person in office, scrofulous wealth, the surfeit of prosperity, the demonism of greed, the hell of passion, the decay of faith, the long postponement, the fossil-like lethargy, the ceaseless need of revolutions, prophets, thunderstorms, deaths, births, new projections and invigorations of ideas and men.

Yet I have dream'd, merged in that hidden-tangled problem of our fate, whose long unraveling stretches mysteriously through time—dream'd out, portray'd, hinted already—a little or a larger band—a band of brave and true, unprecedented yet—arm'd and equipt at every point—the members separated, it may be, by different dates and States, or south, or north, or east, or west—Pacific, Atlantic, Southern, Canadian—a year, a century here, and other centuries there—but always one, compact in soul, conscience-conserving, God-inculcating, inspired achievers, not only in literature, the greatest art, but achievers in all art—a new, undying order, dynasty, from age to age transmitted—a band, a class, at least as fit to cope with current years, our dangers, needs, as those who, for their times, so long, so well, in armor or in cowl, upheld and made illustrious, that far-back feudal, priestly world. To offset chivalry, indeed, those vanish'd countless knights, old altars, abbeys, priests, ages and strings of ages, a knightlier and more sacred cause to-day demands, and shall supply, in a New World, to larger, grander work, more than the counterpart and tally of them.

Arrived now, definitely, at an apex for these Vistas, I confess that the promulgation and belief in such a class or institution—a new and greater literatus order—its possibility, (nay certainty,) underlies these entire speculations—and that the rest, the other parts, as superstructures, are all founded upon it. It really seems to me the condition, not only of our future national and democratic development, but of our perpetuation. In the highly artificial and materialistic bases of modern civilization, with the corresponding arrangements and methods of living, the force-infusion of intellect alone, the depraving influences of riches just as much as poverty, the absence of all high ideals in character—with the long series of tendencies, shapings, which few are strong enough to resist, and which now seem, with steam-engine speed, to be everywhere turning out the generations of humanity like uniform iron castings—all of which, as compared with the feudal ages, we can yet do nothing better than accept, make the best of, and even welcome, upon the whole, for their oceanic practical grandeur, and their restless wholesale kneading of the masses—I say of all this tremendous and dominant play of solely materialistic bearings upon current life in the United States, with the results as already seen, accumulating, and reaching far into the future, that they must either be confronted and met by at least an equally subtle and tremendous force-infusion for purposes of spiritualization, for the pure conscience, for genuine esthetics, and for absolute and primal manliness and womanliness—or else our modern civilization, with all its improvements, is in vain, and we are on the road to a destiny, a status, equivalent, in its real world, to that of the fabled damned.

Prospecting thus the coming unsped days, and that new order in them—marking the endless train of exercise, development, unwind, in nation as in man, which life is for—we see, fore-indicated, amid these prospects and hopes, new law-forces of spoken and written language—not merely the pedagogue-forms, correct, regular, familiar with precedents, made for matters of outside propriety, fine words, thoughts definitely told out—but a language fann'd by the breath of Nature, which leaps overhead, cares mostly for impetus and effects, and for what it plants and invigorates to grow—tallies life and character, and seldomer tells a thing than suggests or necessitates it. In fact, a new theory of literary composition for imaginative works of the very first class, and especially for highest poems, is the sole course open to these States. Books are to be call'd for, and supplied, on the assumption that the process of reading is not a halfsleep, but, in highest sense, an exercise, a gymnast's struggle; that the reader is to do something for himself, must be on the alert, must himself or herself construct indeed the poem, argument, history, metaphysical essay—the text furnishing the hints, the clue, the start or frame-work. Not the book needs so much to be the complete thing, but the reader of the book does. That were to make a nation of supple and athletic minds, well-train'd, intuitive, used to depend on themselves, and not on a few coteries of writers.

Investigating here, we see, not that it is a little thing we have, in having the bequeath'd libraries, countless shelves of volumes, records, &c.; yet how serious the danger, depending entirely on them, of the bloodless vein, the nerveless arm, the false application, at second or third hand. We see that the real interest of this people of ours in the theology, history, poetry, politics, and personal models of the past, (the British islands, for instance, and indeed all the past,) is not necessarily to mould ourselves or our literature upon them, but to attain fuller, more definite comparisons, warnings, and the insight to ourselves, our own present, and our own far grander, different, future history, religion, social customs, &c. We see that almost everything that has been written, sung, or stated, of old, with reference to humanity under the feudal and oriental institutes, religions, and for other lands, needs to be re-written, re-sung, re-stated, in terms consistent with the institution of these States, and to come in range and obedient uniformity with them.

We see, as in the universes of the material kosmos, after meteorological, vegetable, and animal cycles, man at last arises, born through them, to prove them, concentrate them, to turn upon them with wonder and love—to command them, adorn them, and carry them upward into superior realms—so, out of the series of the preceding social and political universes, now arise these States. We see that while many were supposing things established and completed, really the grandest things always remain; and discover that the work of the New World is not ended, but only fairly begun.

We see our land, America, her literature, esthetics, &c., as, substantially, the getting in form, or effusement and statement, of deepest basic elements and loftiest final meanings, of history and man—and the portrayal, (under the eternal laws and conditions of beauty,) of our own physiognomy, the subjective tie and expression of the objective, as from our own combination, continuation, and points of view—and the deposit and record of the national mentality, character, appeals, heroism, wars, and even liberties—where these, and all, culminate in native literary and artistic formulation, to be perpetuated; and not having which native, first-class formulation, she will flounder about, and her other, however imposing, eminent greatness, prove merely a passing gleam; but truly having which, she will understand herself, live nobly, nobly contribute, emanate, and, swinging, poised safely on herself, illumin'd and illuming, become a full-form'd world, and divine Mother not only of material but spiritual worlds, in ceaseless succession through time—the main thing being the average, the bodily, the concrete, the democratic, the popular, on which all the superstructures of the future are to permanently rest.

1871

Emily Dickinson 1830–1886

For Emily Dickinson, the immeasurable, unrecorded life was far more real than the verifiable one; the intersections of visible and invisible worlds far more electric than facts recognized by biographers. A sketch of her known dates and places cannot capture or account for Dickinson's extraordinary sensibility or originality, which brought fresh currents into American thought and literature and expanded the possibilities of poetry.

Dickinson lived in Amherst, Massachusetts, where she was born in 1830 and died in 1886. She shared her family's household with her younger sister Lavinia, her mother, Emily Norcross Dickinson, and her father, Edward Dickinson, a lawyer, Congressman, and Treasurer of Amherst College. Her brother Austin, one year older, a lawyer like his father, lived for most of his life in the house next door, after marrying Dickinson's friend Susan Huntington Gilbert. We know very little about Dickinson's mother, although recently uncovered evidence shows that she had a year of higher education, which for a woman in the early decades of the nineteenth century was unusual. Emily Norcross Dickinson seems to have been a remote and reclusive woman largely dependent on her husband and children. We know that the Dickinson daughters were expected to take considerable domestic responsibility for the family and the family's servants, and that much of the household management seems to have fallen to Lavinia. Dickinson's attitude toward her mother was ambivalent: "Mother does not care for thought," she wrote. A friend quoted her as having said, "I never had a mother. I suppose a mother is one to whom you hurry when you are troubled."

Squire Edward Dickinson emerges as a dominant and domineering figure in the family, whom Emily Dickinson seems to have both honored and humored. To her brother Austin, away at law school, she wrote:

> *We dont* have *many jokes tho'* now, *it is pretty much all sobriety, and we do not have much poetry, father having made up his mind that its pretty much all* real life. *Fathers real life and* mine *sometimes come into collision, but as yet, escape unhurt!* . . .

About ten years later she wrote to a friend: "He buys me many Books—but begs me not to read them—because he fears they joggle the Mind." Dickinson implied that her parents neither comprehended nor aided her development, but we know that their quiet style of living, their secure economic class, and perhaps even their emotional remoteness allowed her the privacy in which to develop her writing. Lavinia protected that privacy, and said after Dickinson's death that Emily was the one of the family who had *thinking* to do.

By the age of twelve, Dickinson was a fluent and prolific writer of letters. Austin described the dramatic effect of her talent at Amherst Academy and Mount Holyoke Female Seminary (now Mount Holyoke College), where she spent one year. "Her compositions were unlike anything ever heard—and always produced a sensation—both with the scholars and Teachers—her imagination sparkled—and she gave it free rein. She was full of courage—but always had a peculiar personal sensitiveness. She saw things directly and just as they were. She abhorred sham. . . ."

Dickinson's early letters reveal a witty, startling, irreverent imagination, and a passion for situations which combined friendship, honesty, secrecy, private jokes, and talk about books and ideas. Though her childhood was a time of mass evangelistic conversions, or revivals, in the churches of western Massachusetts, when all souls were urged to commit themselves to Christ, Dickinson refused to think badly of "the world," or believe that greater pleasures could be found in heaven than on earth. Of her family's habits of traditional prayer and churchgoing she wrote, "[They] are religious—except me—and address an Eclipse, every morning—whom they call 'Father.'" Her letters indicate that she found life exhilarating and sufficient, if only it would last, and that for her, heaven was embodied in familiar surroundings, in nature, in love, and in the power of thought.

Why Dickinson spent only one year at Mount Holyoke, we do not know. Her father seems to have wanted her at home. Religious pressure may also have contributed to her departure. Mary Lyon, founder of the Seminary, ranked incoming students on the basis of their spiritual condition, and her staff made separate lists of those who "*had* a hope" (of receiving God's grace), or had "indulged" a hope, or had no hope. Dickinson's name remained on the final list, despite intense public pressure to attend religious meetings and re-examine her soul. Her letters suggest that she refused to profess a sense of sin; such a refusal required an astonishing degree of originality and courage. Her poems and letters indicate that throughout her life she felt she had a direct route to the Infinite, especially through the world of the mind, and that churches, sermons, preachers, revival meetings, and theological vocabulary did not express her sense of eternity, tremendousness, awe, or spiritual center, which she also named Circumference. Attention to her own experience was her great route to the Infinite.

After one year of college, Dickinson made only five or six trips away from Amherst, traveling in her twenty-fifth year with her father to Philadelphia and Washington, and spending time in Boston in her early thirties when she developed an acute eye problem. Explaining her decision to remain at home, Austin wrote, "As she saw more and more of society—in Boston, where she visited often—in Washington, where she spent some time with her father when he was a member of Congress—and in other places . . . she could not resist the feeling that it was painfully hollow. It was to her so thin and unsatisfying in the face of the Great Realities of Life. . . ."

For women of Dickinson's class, the appropriate social institutions were the family and the church; with those came many societal obligations. Women of her day were not expected to be intellectuals, leaders, thinkers, philosophers, or creators. But Dickinson rebelled, and Adrienne Rich's phrase "disloyal to civilization" describes her in that rebellion. She was a woman who created her own avenues of thought, refusing those offered by church, society, and existing language. She provides a striking example of an alternative sensibility, a dissenting imagination, a re-creating mind.

Attenuated doses of society were enough for Dickinson. She found the electricity between two individuals in a room quite overpowering, when it wasn't stifling, and she needed much time for solitude.

Dickinson rarely, if ever, left her family's house and grounds during the last twenty years of her life, but we should not imagine her disconnected from life. The Dickinson family was prominent in the town and the state, and many visitors came to visit at the two Dickinson houses. Susan, Austin, and their children lived next door. The family holdings included gardens, lawns, a meadow, a stream, an oak grove, a barn, and a conservatory. At all times there were servants in the household. Dickinson's bedroom overlooked the main road from Boston to Amherst, on which there was constant traffic. She could look from the windows of that room, where she wrote most of her poetry, toward the house of her sister-in-law and brother, and toward Amherst College and the town's center with its churches, shops, and citizens coming and going. She could also look back toward the gardens she tended and the fields beyond—the natural world in which she found mirrors of her own process of creation.

We also know that Dickinson was a cosmopolitan and eclectic reader. Her letters indicate that she read newspapers and periodicals, following closely local and national events, and reading contemporary poetry and fiction as soon as it came into print. Many of her letters contain requests to borrow books or offers to loan them. She seems to have learned much of the Bible and Shakespeare by heart; her letters are filled with scriptural and literary allusion. She read women writers with particular passion, including Elizabeth Barrett Browning, George Eliot, the Brontës, Harriet Beecher Stowe, and her own friend, Helen Hunt Jackson, who urged her vehemently, and in vain, to publish her poems.

Dickinson was immensely responsive to friendship with those she found interesting, and loved both women and men with a passionate intensity expressed in both letters and poems. "My friends are my estate," she once wrote. Throughout her life she referred to those she loved as "treasures" and "possessions." For her, friendship was like Heaven, and she resented the Calvinistic God, both "burglar" and "banker," who would jealously take those she loved from her. At the same time, she hoped, and believed with "uncertain certainty," that, after death, God would "refund" her "confiscated Gods." "Unable are the Loved to die," she wrote. "For Love is Immortality/Nay, it is Deity."

One whom Dickinson loved was her sister-in-law Susan, a woman with whom she was closely connected from her late teens until her death. As far as we know, Susan received more of Dickinson's writing than any other correspondent. The letters and poems sent across the lawn to Susan are evidence of the intimacy and constancy as well as the tensions of this friendship. Those inclined to view Dickinson as emotionally impoverished might think instead of her living for three decades next door to the woman to whom she wrote: "With the exception of Shakespeare, you have told me of more knowledge than any one living—To say that sincerely is strange praise."

From the time that Dickinson's writing was first published, numerous attempts have been made to suppress the evidence of this relationship, and during our time, anthologies and selections from Dickinson's work have omitted love poems and letters to Susan. Apparently Austin Dickinson, with the knowledge of his mistress, Mabel Loomis Todd, who was editing the poems for publication, mutilated manuscripts, erasing his wife's name and scissoring out references to her. One poem sent to Susan, "One Sister have I in our house," included in our selection, was completely scratched out, line by line. It seems that Susan, too, withheld information. Only after her death in 1913 did she allow her daughter Martha Dickinson Bianchi to publish poems and letters she had received from Dickinson, and it is possible that this writing to be shared with the world was carefully chosen, while other work was destroyed.

It is important to understand the role in Dickinson studies played by homophobia, which is the fear and hatred of love between people of the same sex. Increasingly, feminist scholarship is revealing close same-sex attachments that have been covered up, denied, and effaced, and such is the case with this poet. We do not know to what extent Dickinson expressed her sexual desires physically, but we do have clear evidence that her affinities were both lesbian and heterosexual. Bonding between women in the 19th-century United States was far more accepted than it is today; even so, Susan and Emily's relatives went to unusual lengths to mutilate and destroy evidence of the women's relationship. Perhaps Austin, bitterly estranged from Susan in his last years, also wanted to clear his sister of identification with his wife.

It is significant that it was Susan's daughter, Martha Dickinson Bianchi, who, perhaps in attempts to protect images of both her aunt and her mother, began to construct one of the most enduring legends in Dickinson studies, the story that the love poems were written to the man Dickinson addressed in several passionate letters as "Master." (It is unclear whether these letters were ever actually sent.) Bianchi argued that "Master" could be identified as the Reverend Charles Wadsworth of Philadelphia, and claimed that it was Wadsworth who "broke the poet's heart." Her biography set off the search for "the one true [male] love" of Dickinson's life, which has extended into many contemporary readings of Dickinson.

In the end, though we cannot define the exact nature of Dickinson's bonds with the women and men of her "estate," it is important to realize that she counted each a "treasure." Among them were Benjamin Newton, her early friend; *Springfield Daily Republican* editor Samuel Bowles, his wife Mary, and his cousin Maria Whitney; Judge Otis Lord, a family friend in love with her and she with him late in her life; Mrs. Holland, whom she addressed as "Little Sister"; the writer and reformer Thomas Wentworth Higginson, whom she called her "Mentor." Each to her was a rare object of love and desire, as well as a source of intellectual stimulation, and an audience for aspects of her writing.

At the age of 31, Dickinson sent several poems to Higginson, responding to his "Letter to a Young Contributor" in *The Atlantic Monthly.* She asked, "Are you too deeply occupied to say if my Verse is alive?" Higginson's response gave "deep pleasure," and the correspondence developed into a lasting friendship. The Higginson selection in this anthology includes a letter to his wife describing his first visit to Dickinson eight years after their correspondence began. "I never was with a person who drained my nerve power so much," he wrote. At her funeral he said that she had put on immortality, though she seemed never in her lifetime to have put it off. Even though Higginson stood in awe of the poet, he apparently commented that the poetry was "spasmodic" and "uncontrolled," and despite Dickinson's admiration for her "teacher," she seems never to have taken any of his advice. The only documentation we have of Dickinson ever having taken anyone's suggestions concerning her poems is an exchange of letters in which she sent Susan a requested revision.

Although a dozen poems by Emily Dickinson were published during her lifetime, we have no evidence that she sought, desired, or welcomed their publication, and considerable evidence that she did not. She wrote to Higginson: "I smile when you suggest that I delay 'to publish'—that being foreign to my thought, as Firmament to Fin." One poem begins: "Publication is the Auction of the Mind of Man." She enclosed many poems in letters, but no member of the family guessed how seriously she took herself as a poet until after she died, when it was realized that over a period of years, she had engaged in what is probably the most remarkable instance of private publication in American letters.

Dickinson's mode of writing was informal, at the start. She began a draft of a poem on ordinary writing paper, or perhaps on the back of a previously used envelope or a torn scrap. Then she copied the poems onto folded sheets of white, unlined stationery, marking with a small "x" certain words and phrases she considered revising. She listed possible alternative word choices at the bottom of the page. She then stacked several folded sheets on top of one another, punched two holes, and tied each packet together along one edge with cotton string. Each of the "packets," also now called "booklets" or "fascicles" (we have no way of knowing what name Dickinson had for them), contains 16–24 pages and an average of 20 poems. Dickinson's use of and intentions for these packets are unknown. They may have constituted a storage and filing system that allowed her to locate a poem if she wanted to revise it or send it to a friend. Some scholars think that the packets have thematic coherence. Ralph Franklin, in *The Manuscript Books of Emily Dickinson* (1981) prints the fascicles in their original arrangements, making photostatic representations of these poems available to readers for the first time.

The manuscript books allow us to follow Dickinson's exact use of punctuation. She used dashes in the place of more traditional marks, such as periods, commas, colons, and semi-colons, and some see it as significant that the dashes vary in length and that some slope upward, some downward. One supposition is that Dickinson may have used the dash to direct a reader to stress certain words and phrases. With the dash, Dickinson could avoid what she may have considered the spurious finality of the period. Photostats of the poems also show us Dickinson's original line breaks, which have become a subject of debate among editors and critics. The poems continue to invite research and intense discussion of their appearance and their meaning more than one hundred years after their discovery.

When she died, Dickinson left Lavinia and Maggie, a woman who worked in the household, specific instructions to destroy her papers, that is, the letters she had received and saved. She made no mention of the cherry-wood box Lavinia found in the bottom drawer of her bedroom bureau, which held 814 poems bound into 40 packets, as well as 333 poems ready for binding, and numerous worksheet drafts. When Lavinia discovered the poems, she was determined to get them into print. She took them first to Susan, who kept them for two years, and may have begun to select poems, but made no move toward publication. Lavinia then took them back, and persuaded Higginson and Mabel Loomis Todd to edit them. Todd and Higginson published volumes of selected poems in 1890 and 1891; in 1896 Todd edited a third volume. The poems were received with great excitement; the 1890 volume went through seven printings in a year, the 1891 volume five printings in two years. Because of complex family feuds which separated the manuscripts, Dickinson's complete poems and all known variant readings were not published until 1955 when Thomas Johnson produced a three-volume variorum edition. He and Theodora Ward also published three volumes of letters in 1958. These three volumes are thought to constitute only a small fraction of the letters she actually wrote. The majority of existing manuscripts of Dickinson's letters and poems can be found in the libraries of Amherst College and Harvard University.

In reading Dickinson's poetry, it is best not to look for creeds or statements of belief. Though she reflects her community's Protestant and Calvinistic frames of reference, religious terminology in her poetry does not indicate that she held orthodox religious beliefs. She is by turn satirical, skeptical, awed, reverent, speculative, outraged, tantalized, ironic, or God-like herself. She scorns theological portraits of "God" but aligns herself personally with divinity, sometimes as Jesus and sometimes as co-creator. Dickinson wrote a remarkable number of poems on pain, a taboo subject in her time and place. She refused to accept the Calvinistic teaching that she had earned pain, through original sin, or the Transcendentalist habit of transcending it, through denial or euphemism. She felt appalling losses, which in some cases also brought compensations of knowledge or spiritual insight, but she insisted on recording her perception of pain in language which was unflinching: "I like a look of Agony,/Because I know it's true—"

As far as she was concerned, the church had lied about God's righteousness and justice, and had equivocated about death, and the society would make her lie about herself if she followed its customs and adopted its terms. Tracking her experience led her to fearful and dire states of insight, often bordering on madness and despair, which she chose to describe fearlessly. In the end, she chose to withdraw from routine human interchange in order to concentrate intensely, to fashion language which rang true to her. Imagining her, Adrienne Rich wrote, ". . . the air buzzing with spoiled language/sang in your ears/of Perjury/. . . you chose/silence for entertainment,/chose to have it out at last/on your own premises."

Like Walt Whitman, another rejecter of custom and received wisdom, Dickinson experimented radically with poetic style. Unlike Whitman, she condensed; where he was discursive and celebratory, she was taut, terse, suggestive, oblique. The words she chose live vividly on the page, and invite readers to fill the poems with their own sense of connection. Her tone is often both intimate and stark, especially in the many first lines beginning with "I": "I felt a funeral in my brain . . . ," "I dwell in possibility . . . ," "I measure every grief I meet. . . ." She rearranged word order, ignored rules of punctuation, evaded rhyme schemes even while suggesting them, and in general tried to ventilate and open up language to the point where it approximated her own sense of the layered complexity of matter, spirit, and consciousness. The English sentence as she inherited it must have seemed to her like a blunt instrument. Her meter suggests not certainty or regularity, but mobility, unfinished business, life in motion. Because she rarely rhymed exactly, one critic has suggested that for her, life did not rhyme. But it seems to have come tantalizingly, agonizingly close before it refused. Many of the poems trace a thought or an image, carrying it in many directions, opening from a startling first line into an exploration of connections between seen and unseen worlds, and indicating finally that human beings in our arrangements of life seldom attain what we need, desire, and are capable of understanding.

Dickinson's growing fame in the twentieth century, and the fact that she speaks so clearly to our time, has been a subject of increasing comment. Critical notions about her may become obsolete, but she does not. Books which analyze her poems as though they dealt with "subjects" or "topics" like Life, Death, Nature, and Love have missed the phenomenon of interconnected processes which give life to the poetry. Certainly Dickinson's explorations of consciousness, and the strategies she used to free language from traditional structures and expectations continue to challenge, reward, and astonish readers year after year. Dickinson was a poet who had the courage to resist many authorities, even at the price of being misunderstood. Wresting language back to the service of her own experience, she gives us glimpses of a person too startling to be acceptable to her community, with a mind too exacting to use language as she had learned it, a heart of unacceptable desires and unanswerable demands, and a sensibility embodying in life and language an early and genuine example of the sometimes illusory American trait of self-reliance.

Peggy McIntosh
Wellesley College, Center for Research on Women

Ellen Louise Hart
University of California at Santa Cruz, Cowell College

PRIMARY WORKS

The Poems of Emily Dickinson, ed. Thomas H. Johnson, 3 vols., 1951, 1955; *The Letters of Emily Dickinson,* ed. Thomas H. Johnson and Theodora Ward, 3 vols., 1958; Ralph W. Franklin, ed., *The Manuscript Books of Emily Dickinson,* 2 vols., 1981.

SECONDARY WORKS

Richard Wilbur, "Sumptuous Destitution," in *Emily Dickinson: Three Views,* 1960; Richard B. Sewall, *The Life of Emily Dickinson.* 2 vols., 1974; Suzanne Juhasz, ed., *Feminist Critics Read Emily Dickinson,* 1983; Paul J. Ferlazzo, ed., *Critical Essays on Emily Dickinson,* 1984; Vivian Pollak, *Dickinson: The Anxiety of Gender,* 1984; Shira Wolosky, *Emily Dickinson: A Voice of War,* 1984; Susan Howe, *My Emily Dickinson,* 1985; Cristanne Miller, *Emily Dickinson: A Poet's Grammar,* 1987; Ellen Louise Hart, "The Encoding of Homoerotic Desire: Emily Dickinson's Letters and Poems to Susan Dickinson, 1850–1886," in *Tulsa Studies in Women's Literature,* Fall 1990; Edwin H. Cady and Louis J. Budd, eds., *On Dickinson: The Best from American Literature,* 1990; Susan Howe, "These Flames and Generosities of the Heart: Emily Dickinson and the Illogic of Sumptuary Values," in *Sulfur* (28), 1991; Judith Farr, *The Passion of Emily Dickinson,* 1992; Martha Nell Smith, *Rowing in Eden: Rereading Emily Dickinson,* 1992.

Poems

14[1]

One Sister have I in our house,
And one, a hedge away.
There's only one recorded,
But both belong to me.

One came the road that I came—
And wore my last year's gown—
The other, as a bird her nest,
Builded our hearts among.

She did not sing as we did—
It was a different tune—
Herself to her a music
As Bumble bee of June.

Today is far from Childhood—
But up and down the hills
I held her hand the tighter—
Which shortened all the miles—

And still her hum
The years among,
Deceives the Butterfly;
Still in her Eye
The Violets lie
Mouldered this many May.

[1]This poem was in Fascicle 2, which originally contained 24 poems. Sometime in 1891, it was cancelled out, probably by Austin Dickinson and Mabel Loomis Todd. We have the complete text in a copy sent by Dickinson to Sue Gilbert in 1858.

I spilt the dew—
But took the morn—
I chose this single star
From out the wide night's numbers—
Sue—forevermore!

1858 1914[2]

21

We lose—because we win—
Gamblers—recollecting which
Toss their dice again!

c. 1858 1945

49

I never lost as much but twice,
And that was in the sod.[1]
Twice have I stood a beggar
Before the door of God!

Angels—twice descending
Reimbursed my store—
Burglar! Banker—Father!
I am poor once more!

c. 1858 1890

67

Success is counted sweetest
By those who ne'er succeed.
To comprehend a nectar[1]
Requires sorest need.

Not one of all the purple Host
Who took the Flag[2] today
Can tell the definition
So clear of Victory

[2]The year on the left is the date the poem was written; if "c." precedes the year, the date is approximate. The year on the right is the earliest date of publication.

[1]The sod: *i.e.,* burial.

[1]Drink of Greek and Roman gods.

[2]Vanquished the enemy.

As he defeated—dying—
On whose forbidden ear
The distant strains of triumph
Burst agonized and clear!

c. 1859 1878

84

Her breast is fit for pearls,
But I was not a "Diver"—
Her brow is fit for thrones
But I have not a crest.
Her heart is fit for *home*—
I—a Sparrow—build there
Sweet of twigs and twine
My perennial nest.

c. 1859 1894

106

The Daisy follows soft the Sun—
And when his golden walk is done—
Sits shily at his feet—
He—waking—finds the flower there—
Wherefore—Marauder—art thou here?
Because, Sir, love is sweet!

We are the Flower—Thou the Sun!
Forgive us, if as days decline—
We nearer steal to Thee!
Enamored of the parting West—
The peace—the flight—the Amethyst—
Night's possibility!

c. 1859 1890

130

These are the days when Birds come back—
A very few—a Bird or two—
To take a backward look.

These are the days when skies resume
The old—old sophistries[1] of June—
A blue and gold mistake.

Oh fraud that cannot cheat the Bee—
Almost thy plausibility
Induces my belief.

Till ranks of seeds their witness bear—
And softly thro' the altered air
Hurries a timid leaf.

Oh Sacrament of summer days,
Oh Last Communion in the Haze—
Permit a child to join,

Thy sacred emblems to partake—
Thy consecrated bread to take
And thine immortal wine![2]

c. 1859 1890

211

Come slowly—Eden!
Lips unused to Thee—
Bashful—sip thy Jessamines—[1]
As the fainting Bee—

Reaching late his flower,
Round her chamber hums—
Counts his nectars—
Enters—and is lost in Balms.[2]

c. 1860 1890

213

Did the Harebell loose her girdle[1]
To the lover Bee
Would the Bee the Harebell *hallow*
Much as formerly?

[1]Deceptive arguments.
[2]Dickinson compares the end of summer to the last supper of Christ, celebrated in some churches as the Sacrament of Communion.

[1]Jasmines; fragrant flowers.
[2]Healing ointments.
[1]Loosen her sash.

Did the "Paradise"—persuaded—
Yield her moat of pearl—
Would the Eden *be* an Eden,
Or the Earl—an *Earl?*

c. 1860 1891

219

She sweeps with many-colored Brooms—
And leaves the Shreds behind—
Oh Housewife in the Evening West—
Come back, and dust the Pond!

You dropped a Purple Ravelling in—
You dropped an Amber thread—
And now you've littered all the East
With Duds[1] of Emerald!

And still, she plies her spotted Brooms,
And still the Aprons fly,
Till Brooms fade softly into stars—
And then I come away—

c. 1861 1891

241

I like a look of Agony,
Because I know it's true—
Men do not sham Convulsion,
Nor simulate, a Throe—

The Eyes glaze once—and that is Death—
Impossible to feign
The Beads upon the Forehead
By homely Anguish strung.

c. 1861 1890

249

Wild Nights—Wild Nights!
Were I with thee

[1]Ragged or tattered clothes.

Wild Nights should be
Our luxury!

Futile—the Winds—
To a Heart in port—
Done with the Compass—
Done with the Chart!

Rowing in Eden—
Ah, the Sea!
Might I but moor—Tonight—
In Thee![1]

c. 1861 1891

252

I can wade Grief—
Whole Pools of it—
I'm used to that—
But the least push of Joy
Breaks up my feet—
And I tip—drunken—
Let no Pebble—smile—
'Twas the New Liquor—
That was all!

Power is only Pain—
Stranded, thro' Discipline,
Till Weights—will hang—
Give Balm—to Giants—
And they'll wilt, like Men—
Give Himmaleh—[1]
They'll Carry—Him!

c. 1861 1891

258

There's a certain Slant of light,
Winter Afternoons—
That oppresses, like the Heft[1]
Of Cathedral Tunes—

[1]Dickinson juxtaposes stormy nights with lovers' sheltered ports and moorings.

[1]A personification of the Himalayan mountains.

[1]Weight or bulk.

Heavenly Hurt, it gives us—
We can find no scar,
But internal difference,
Where the Meanings, are—

None may teach it—Any—
'Tis the Seal Despair—
An imperial affliction
Sent us of the Air—

When it comes, the Landscape listens—
Shadows—hold their breath—
When it goes, 'tis like the Distance
On the look of Death—

c. 1861 1890

271

A solemn thing—it was—I said—
A Woman—white—to be—
And wear—if God should count me fit—
Her blameless mystery—

A timid thing—to drop a life
Into the mystic well—
Too plummetless[1]—that it come back—
Eternity—until—

I pondered how the bliss would look—
And would it feel as big—
When I could take it in my hand—
As hovering—seen—through fog—

And then—the size of this "small" life—
The Sages—call it small—
Swelled—like Horizons—in my breast—
And I sneered—softly—"small"!

c. 1861 1896

280

I felt a Funeral, in my Brain,
And Mourners to and fro

[1]Unfathomable.

Kept treading—treading—till it seemed
That Sense was breaking through—[1]

And when they all were seated,
A Service, like a Drum—
Kept beating—beating—till I thought
My Mind was going numb—

And then I heard them lift a Box
And creak across my Soul
With those same Boots of Lead, again,
Then Space—began to toll,

As[2] all the Heavens were a Bell,
And Being, but an Ear,
And I, and Silence, some strange Race
Wrecked, solitary, here—

And then a Plank in Reason, broke,
And I dropped down, and down—
And hit a World, at every plunge,
And Finished knowing—then—

c. 1861 1896

285

The Robin's my Criterion for Tune—
Because I grow—where Robins do—
But, were I Cuckoo[1] born—
I'd swear by him—
The ode familiar—rules the Noon—
The Buttercup's, my Whim for Bloom—
Because, we're Orchard sprung—
But, were I Britain born,
I'd Daisies spurn—
None but the Nut—October fit—
Because, through dropping it,
The Seasons flit—I'm taught—
Without the Snow's Tableau
Winter, were lie—to me—
Because I see—New Englandly—

[1] *I.e.*, sense was giving way.
[2] As if. Dickinson often uses "as" in this way.

[1] A bird preferring a more temperate climate than that of New England.

The Queen, discerns like me—
Provincially—

c. 1861 1929

288

I'm Nobody! Who are you?
Are you—Nobody—too?
Then there's a pair of us!
Dont tell! they'd banish us—you know!

How dreary—to be—Somebody!
How public—like a Frog—
To tell your name—the livelong June—
To an admiring Bog!

c. 1861 1891

292

If your Nerve, deny you—
Go above your Nerve—
He can lean against the Grave,
If he fear to swerve—

That's a steady posture—
Never any bend
Held of those Brass arms—
Best Giant made—

If your Soul seesaw—
Lift the Flesh door—
The Poltroon[1] wants Oxygen—
Nothing more—

c. 1861 1935

293

I got so I could hear his name—
Without—Tremendous gain—

[1]Coward.

That Stop-sensation—on my Soul—
And Thunder—in the Room—

I got so I could walk across
That Angle in the floor,
Where he turned so, and I turned—how—
And all our Sinew tore—

I got so I could stir the Box—
In which his letters grew
Without that forcing, in my breath—
As Staples—driven through—

Could dimly recollect a Grace—
I think, they call it "God"—
Renowned to ease Extremity—
When Formula, had failed—

And shape my Hands—
Petition's way,
Tho' ignorant of a word
That Ordination[1]—utters—

My Business, with the Cloud,
If any Power behind it, be,
Not subject to Despair—
It care, in some remoter way,
For so minute affair
As Misery—
Itself, too great, for interrupting—more—

c. 1861 1929

299

Your Riches—taught me—Poverty.
Myself—a Millionaire
In little Wealths, as Girls could boast
Till broad as Buenos Ayre—[1]

You drifted your Dominions—
A Different Peru—
And I esteemed All Poverty
For Life's Estate with you—

[1]The ministry.
[1]Buenos Aires, Argentina.

Of Mines, I little know—myself—
But just the names, of Gems—
The Colors of the Commonest—
And scarce of Diadems—

So much, that did I meet the Queen—
Her Glory I should know—
But this, must be a different Wealth—
To miss it—beggars so—

I'm sure 'tis India—all Day—
To those who look on You—
Without a stint—without a blame,
Might I—but be the Jew—

I'm sure it is Golconda—[2]
Beyond my power to deem—
To have a smile for Mine—each Day,
How better, than a Gem!

At least, it solaces to know
That there exists—a Gold—
Altho' I prove it, just in time
It's distance—to behold—

It's far—far Treasure to surmise—
And estimate the Pearl—
That slipped my simple fingers through—
While just a Girl at School.

1862 1891

301

I reason, Earth is short—
And Anguish—absolute—
And many hurt,
But, what of that?

I reason, we could die—
The best Vitality
Cannot excel Decay,
But, what of that?

[2]Dickinson associates Latin countries and the ruined city of Golconda in India with gems, gold, and pearls.

I reason, that in Heaven—
Somehow, it will be even—
Some new Equation, given—
But, what of that?

c. 1862 1890

303

The Soul selects her own Society—
Then—shuts the Door—
To her divine Majority—
Present no more—

Unmoved—she notes the Chariots—pausing—
At her low Gate—
Unmoved—an Emperor be kneeling
Upon her Mat—

I've known her—from an ample nation—
Choose One—
Then—close the Valves of her attention—
Like Stone—

c. 1862 1890

306

The Soul's Superior instants
Occur to Her—alone—
When friend—and Earth's occasion
Have infinite withdrawn—

Or She—Herself—ascended
To too remote a Hight
For lower Recognition
Than Her Omnipotent—

This Mortal Abolition[1]
Is seldom—but as fair

[1]Dismissal or rejection of the time-bound.

As Apparition[2]—subject
To Autocratic Air—

Eternity's disclosure
To favorites—a few—
Of the Colossal substance
Of Immortality

c. 1862 1914

308

I send Two Sunsets—
Day and I—in competition ran—
I finished Two—and several Stars—
While He—was making One—

His own was ampler—but as I
Was saying to a friend—
Mine—is the more convenient
To Carry in the Hand—

c. 1862 1914

311

It sifts from Leaden Sieves—
It powders all the Wood.
It fills with Alabaster Wool
The Wrinkles of the Road—

It makes an Even Face
Of Mountain, and of Plain—
Unbroken Forehead from the East
Unto the East again—

It reaches to the Fence—
It wraps it Rail by Rail
Till it is lost in Fleeces—
It deals Celestial Vail

To Stump, and Stack—and Stem—
A Summer's empty Room—

[2]Vision of an unearthly being.

Acres of Joints, where Harvests were,
Recordless, but for them—

It Ruffles Wrists of Posts
As Ankles of a Queen—
Then stills it's Artisans—like Ghosts—
Denying they have been—

c. 1862 1891

315

He fumbles at your Soul
As Players at the Keys
Before they drop full Music on—
He stuns you by degrees—
Prepares your brittle Nature
For the Etherial Blow
By fainter Hammers—further heard—
Then nearer—Then so slow
Your Breath has time to straighten—
Your Brain—to bubble Cool—
Deals—One—imperial—Thunderbolt—
That scalps your naked Soul—

When Winds take Forests in their Paws—
The Universe—is still—

c. 1862 1896

322

There came a Day at Summer's full,
Entirely for me—
I thought that such were for the Saints,
Where Resurrections—be—

The Sun, as common, went abroad,
The flowers, accustomed, blew,
As if no soul the solstice passed
That maketh all things new—

The time was scarce profaned, by speech—
The symbol of a word
Was needless, as at Sacrament,
The Wardrobe—of our Lord—

Each was to each The Sealed Church,
Permitted to commune this—time—
Lest we too awkward show
At Supper of the Lamb.[1]

The Hours slid fast—as Hours will,
Clutched tight, by greedy hands—
So faces on two Decks, look back,
Bound to opposing lands—

And so when all the time had leaked,
Without external sound
Each bound the Other's Crucifix—
We gave no other Bond—

Sufficient troth, that we shall rise—
Deposed—at length, the Grave—
To that new Marriage,
Justified—through Calvaries[2] of Love—

c. 1861 1890

324

Some keep the Sabbath going to Church—
I keep it, staying at Home—
With a Bobolink for a Chorister—
And an Orchard, for a Dome—

Some keep the Sabbath in Surplice[1]—
I just wear my Wings—
And instead of tolling the Bell, for Church,
Our little Sexton[2]—sings.

God preaches, a noted Clergyman—
And the sermon is never long,
So instead of getting to Heaven, at last—
I'm going, all along.

c. 1860 1864

[1]The Last Supper or Lord's Supper.
[2]Calvary was the hill outside Jerusalem on which Jesus was crucified.

[1]A white gown-like vestment with open sleeves worn by clergymen at services.
[2]Church custodian and keeper of property.

327

Before I got my eye put out
I liked as well to see—
As other Creatures, that have Eyes
And know no other way—

But were it told to me—Today—
That I might have the sky
For mine—I tell you that my Heart
Would split, for size of me—

The Meadows—mine—
The Mountains—mine—
All Forests—Stintless[1] Stars—
As much of Noon as I could take
Between my finite eyes—

The Motions of The Dipping Birds—
The Morning's Amber Road—
For mine—to look at when I liked—
The News would strike me dead—

So safer Guess—with just my soul
Upon the Window pane—
Where other Creatures put their eyes—
Incautious—of the Sun—

c. 1862 1891

328

A Bird came down the Walk—
He did not know I saw—
He bit an Angleworm in halves
And ate the fellow, raw,

And then he drank a Dew
From a convenient Grass—
And then hopped sidewise to the Wall
To let a Beetle pass—

He glanced with rapid eyes
That hurried all around—

[1]Unending.

They looked like frightened Beads, I thought—
He stirred his Velvet Head

Like one in danger, Cautious,
I offered him a Crumb
And he unrolled his feathers
And rowed him softer home—

Than Oars divide the Ocean,
Too silver for a seam—
Or Butterflies, off Banks of Noon
Leap, plashless[1] as they swim.

c. 1862 1891

338

I know that He exists.
Somewhere—in Silence—
He has hid his rare life
From our gross eyes.

'Tis an instant's play.
'Tis a fond Ambush—
Just to make Bliss
Earn her own surprise!

But—should the play
Prove piercing earnest—
Should the glee—glaze—
In Death's—stiff—stare—

Would not the fun
Look too expensive!
Would not the jest—
Have crawled too far!

c. 1862 1891

341

After great pain, a formal feeling comes—
The Nerves sit ceremonious, like Tombs—

[1]Splashless.

The stiff Heart questions was it He, that bore,
And Yesterday, or Centuries before?

The Feet, mechanical, go round—
Of Ground, or Air, or Ought—[1]
A Wooden way
Regardless grown,[2]
A Quartz contentment, like a stone—

This is the Hour of Lead—
Remembered, if outlived,
As Freezing persons, recollect the Snow—
First—Chill—then Stupor—then the letting go—

c. 1862 1929

348

I dreaded that first Robin, so,
But He is mastered, now,
I'm some accustomed to Him grown,
He hurts a little, though—

I thought if I could only live
Till that first Shout got by—
Not all Pianos in the Woods
Had power to mangle me—

I dared not meet the Daffodils—
For fear their Yellow Gown
Would pierce me with a fashion
So foreign to my own—

I wished the Grass would hurry—
So—when 'twas time to see—
He'd be too tall, the tallest one
Could stretch—to look at me—

I could not bear the Bees should come,
I wished they'd stay away
In those dim countries where they go,
What word had they, for me?

[1]Dickinson's spelling of Aught; anything.
[2]Having stopped noticing.

They're here, though; not a creature failed—
No Blossom stayed away
In gentle deference to me—
The Queen of Calvary—[1]

Each one salutes me, as he goes,
And I, my childish Plumes,
Lift, in bereaved acknowledgement
Of their unthinking Drums—

c. 1862 1891

357

God is a distant—stately Lover—
Woos, as He states us—by His Son—
Verily, a Vicarious Courtship—
"Miles", and "Priscilla", were such an One—

But, lest the Soul—like fair "Priscilla"
Choose the Envoy—and spurn the Groom—
Vouches, with hyperbolic archness—
"Miles", and "John Alden" were Synonyme—[1]

c. 1862 1891

365

Dare you see a Soul *at the White Heat?*
Then crouch within the door—
Red—is the Fire's common tint—
But when the vivid Ore
Has vanquished Flame's conditions,
It quivers from the Forge
Without a color, but the light
Of unannointed Blaze.
Least[1] Village has it's Blacksmith
Whose Anvil's even ring
Stands symbol for the finer Forge
That soundless tugs—within—
Refining these impatient Ores

[1]See note 2 in poem 322.

[1]"Miles": the New England puritan Miles Standish is said to have sent a younger man, John Alden, to propose to Priscilla Mullen for him. Priscilla answered, "Speak for yourself, John," and married the younger man.

[1]The smallest.

With Hammer, and with Blaze
Until the Designated Light
Repudiate[2] the Forge—

c. 1862 1891

381

A Secret told—
Ceases to be a Secret—then—
A Secret—kept—
That—can appal but One—

Better of it—continual be afraid—
Than it—
And Whom you told it to—beside—

c. 1862 1929

401

What Soft—Cherubic Creatures—
These Gentlewomen are—
One would as soon assault a Plush—[1]
Or violate[2] a Star—

Such Dimity[3] Convictions—
A Horror so refined
Of freckled Human Nature—
Of Deity—ashamed—

It's such a common—Glory—
A Fisherman's—Degree—[4]
Redemption—Brittle Lady—
Be so—ashamed of Thee—

c. 1862 1896

435

Much Madness is divinest Sense—
To a discerning Eye—

[2]Leave behind, disown.

[1]Piece of upholstery material or upholstered furniture.

[2]Rape; desecrate.

[3]Delicate cotton fabric.

[4]*I.e.,* merely having the status of Christ, who was associated with fishing and later symbolized by a fish.

Much Sense—the starkest Madness—
'Tis the Majority
In this, as All, prevail—
Assent—and you are sane—
Demur[1]—you're straightway dangerous—
And handled with a Chain—

c. 1862 1890

441

This is my letter to the World
That never wrote to Me—
The simple News that Nature told—
With tender Majesty

Her Message is committed
To Hands I cannot see—
For love of Her—Sweet—countrymen—
Judge tenderly—of Me[1]

c. 1862 1890

443

I tie my Hat—I crease my Shawl—
Life's little duties do—precisely—
As[1] the very least
Were infinite—to me—

I put new Blossoms in the Glass—
And throw the old—away—
I push a petal from my Gown
That anchored there—I weigh
The time 'twill be till six o'clock
I have so much to do—
And yet—Existence—some way back—
Stopped—struck—my ticking—through—
We cannot put Ourself away
As a completed Man
Or Woman—When the Errand's done

[1]Disagree.

[1]This poem was placed by Higginson and Todd just after the table of contents and before the first page of selections in the first edition of Dickinson's poetry, published in 1890. There is no indication that she intended it as an introduction to all of the fascicles; it is lodged in fascicle 24 where it shares a page with part of another poem.

[1]As if.

We came to Flesh—upon—
There may be—Miles on Miles of Nought—
Of Action—sicker far—
To simulate—is stinging work—
To cover what we are
From Science—and from Surgery—
Too Telescopic Eyes
To bear on us unshaded—
For their—sake—not for Our's—
'Twould start them—
We—could tremble—
But since we got a Bomb—
And held it in our Bosom—
Nay—Hold it—it is calm—

_______________[2]

Therefore—we do life's labor—
Though life's Reward—be done—
With scrupulous exactness—
To hold our Senses—on—

c. 1862 1929

446

I showed her Hights she never saw—
"Would'st Climb," I said?
She said—"Not so"—
"With *me*—" I said—With *me*?
I showed her Secrets—Morning's Nest—
The Rope the Nights were put across—
And *now*—"Would'st have me for a Guest?"
She could not find her Yes—
And then, I brake my life—And Lo,
A Light, for her, did solemn glow,
The larger, as her face withdrew—
And *could* she, further, "No"?[1]

c. 1862 1896

[2]It was unusual for Dickinson to draw a line, as she did here, between parts of a poem.

[1]This copy of the poem was sent to Sue in 1862. In the same year, Dickinson copied the poem into a fascicle, with different pronouns:

He showed me Hights I never saw
"Would'st Climb," He said?
I said, "Not so."
"With me—" He said—"With me?" . . .

For further notes, see the Johnson variorum edition.

448

This was a Poet—It is That
Distills amazing sense
From Ordinary Meanings—
And Attar[1] so immense

From the familiar species
That perished by the Door—
We wonder it was not Ourselves
Arrested it—before—

Of Pictures, the Discloser—
The Poet—it is He—
Entitles Us—by Contrast—
To ceaseless Poverty—

Of Portion—so unconscious—
The Robbing—could not harm—[2]
Himself—to Him—a Fortune—
Exterior—to Time—

c. 1862 1929

458

Like Eyes that looked on Wastes—
Incredulous of Ought[1]
But Blank—and steady Wilderness—
Diversified by Night—

Just Infinites of Nought—
As far as it could see—
So looked the face I looked upon—
So looked itself—on Me—

I offered it no Help—
Because the Cause was Mine—
The Misery a Compact
As hopeless—as divine—

Neither—would be absolved—[2]
Neither would be a Queen

[1]Perfume obtained by crushing flower petals.
[2]So unaware of his treasure that stealing could not hurt him.

[1]Aught; anything.
[2]Set free from an obligation, agreement, or consequences of guilt.

Without the Other—Therefore—
We perish—tho' We reign—

c. 1862 1945

465

I heard a Fly buzz—when I died—
The Stillness in the Room
Was like the Stillness in the Air—
Between the Heaves of Storm—

The Eyes around—had wrung them dry—
And Breaths were gathering firm
For that last Onset—when the King
Be witnessed—in the Room—

I willed my Keepsakes—Signed away
What portion of me be
Assignable—and then it was
There interposed a Fly—

With Blue—uncertain—stumbling Buzz—
Between the light—and me—
And then the Windows failed—and then
I could not see to see—

c. 1862 1896

501

This World is not Conclusion.
A Species stands beyond—
Invisible, as Music—
But positive, as Sound—
It beckons, and it baffles—
Philosophy—dont know—
And through a Riddle, at the last—
Sagacity,[1] must go—
To guess it, puzzles scholars—
To gain it, Men have borne
Contempt of Generations
And Crucifixion, shown—
Faith slips—and laughs, and rallies—

[1]Keenness of sense perception.

Blushes, if any see—
Plucks at a twig of Evidence—
And asks a Vane,[2] the way—
Much Gesture, from the Pulpit—
Strong Hallelujahs roll—
Narcotics cannot still the Tooth
That nibbles at the soul—

c. 1862 1896

502

At least—to pray—is left—is left—
Oh Jesus—in the Air—
I know not which thy chamber is—
I'm knocking—everywhere—

Thou settest Earthquake in the South—
And Maelstrom,[1] in the Sea—
Say, Jesus Christ of Nazareth—
Hast thou no Arm for Me?

c. 1862 1891

508

I'm ceded—I've stopped being Their's—
The name They dropped upon my face
With water, in the country church
Is finished using, now,
And They can put it with my Dolls,
My childhood, and the string of spools,
I've finished threading—too—

Baptized, before, without the choice,
But this time, consciously, of Grace—
Unto supremest name—
Called to my Full—The Crescent[1] dropped—
Existence's whole Arc, filled up,
With one small Diadem.

My second Rank—too small the first—
Crowned—Crowing—on my Father's breast—[2]

[2]Weathervane.
[1]Very turbulent and violent whirlpool.
[1]Incomplete state, as in crescent moon.
[2]Perhaps a reference to being held, as an infant, at her "first" baptism.

A half unconscious Queen—
But this time—Adequate—Erect,
With Will to choose, or to reject,
And I choose, just a Crown—

c. 1862 1890

512

The Soul has Bandaged moments—
When too appalled to stir—
She feels some ghastly Fright come up
And stop to look at her—

Salute her—with long fingers—
Caress her freezing hair—
Sip, Goblin, from the very lips
The Lover—hovered—o'er—
Unworthy, that a thought so mean
Accost a Theme—so—fair—

The soul has moments of Escape—
When bursting all the doors—
She dances like a Bomb, abroad,
And swings upon the Hours,

As do the Bee—delirious borne—
Long Dungeoned from his Rose—
Touch Liberty—then know no more,
But Noon, and Paradise—

The Soul's retaken moments—
When, Felon led along,
With shackles[1] on the plumed feet,
And staples,[2] in the Song,

The Horror welcomes her, again,
These, are not brayed of Tongue—

c. 1862 1945

[1]A variant reading in the manuscript is "irons—" for "shackles."

[2]A variant reading in the manuscript is "rivets—" for "staples."

518

Her sweet Weight on my Heart a Night
Had scarcely deigned to lie—
When, stirring, for Belief's delight,
My Bride had slipped away—

If 'twas a Dream—made solid—just
The Heaven to confirm—
Or if Myself were dreamed of Her—
The power to presume—

With Him remain—who unto Me—
Gave—even as to All—
A Fiction superseding Faith—
By so much—as 'twas real—

c. 1862 1945

520

I started Early—Took my Dog—
And visited the Sea—
The Mermaids in the Basement
Came out to look at me—

And Frigates—in the Upper Floor
Extended Hempen Hands—[1]
Presuming Me to be a Mouse—
Aground—upon the Sands—

But no Man moved Me—till the Tide
Went past my simple Shoe—
And past my Apron—and my Belt
And past my Boddice[2]—too—

And made as He would eat me up—
As wholly as a Dew
Upon a Dandelion's Sleeve—
And then—I started—too—

And He—He followed—close behind—
I felt His Silver Heel

[1]Ropes.
[2]An article of women's clothing laced and worn like a vest over a blouse.

Upon my Ancle—Then my Shoes
Would overflow with Pearl—

Until We met the Solid Town—
No One He seemed to know—
And bowing—with a Mighty look—
At me—The Sea withdrew—

c. 1862 1891

553

One Crucifixion is recorded—only—
How many be
Is not affirmed of Mathematics—
Or History—

One Calvary[1]—exhibited to Stranger—
As many be
As Persons—or Peninsulas—
Gethsemane—[2]

Is but a Province—in the Being's Centre—
Judea—[3]
For Journey—or Crusade's Achieving—
Too near—

Our Lord—indeed—made Compound Witness—[4]
And yet—
There's newer—nearer Crucifixion
Than That—

c. 1862 1945

556

The Brain, within it's Groove
Runs evenly—and true—
But let a Splinter swerve—
'Twere easier for You—

[1]Hill of Jesus' crucifixion.
[2]Garden in which Jesus was arrested before his death.
[3]The Holy Land.
[4]Had many witnesses.

To put a Current back—
When Floods have slit the Hills—
And scooped a Turnpike for Themselves—
And trodden out the Mills—

c. 1862 1890

564

My period had come for Prayer—
No other Art—would do—
My Tactics missed a rudiment—
Creator—Was it you?

God grows above—so those who pray
Horizons—must ascend—
And so I stepped upon the North
To see this Curious Friend—

His House was not—no sign had He—
By Chimney—nor by Door—
Could I infer his Residence—
Vast Prairies of Air

Unbroken by a Settler—
Were all that I could see—
Infinitude—Had'st Thou no Face
That I might look on Thee?

The Silence condescended—
Creation stopped—for Me—
But awed beyond my errand—
I worshipped—did not "pray"—

c. 1862 1929

569

I reckon—when I count at all—
First—Poets—Then the Sun—
Then Summer—Then the Heaven of God—
And then—the List is done—

But, looking back—the First so seems
To Comprehend the Whole—
The Others look a needless Show—
So I write—Poets—All—

Their Summer—lasts a Solid Year—
They can afford a Sun
The East—would deem extravagant—
And if the Further Heaven—

Be Beautiful as they prepare
For Those who worship Them—
It is too difficult a Grace—
To justify the Dream—

c. 1862 1929

579

I had been hungry, all the Years—
My Noon had Come—to dine—
I trembling drew the Table near—
And touched the Curious Wine—

'Twas this on Tables I had seen—
When turning, hungry, Home
I looked in Windows, for the Wealth
I could not hope—for Mine—

I did not know the ample Bread—
'Twas so unlike the Crumb
The Birds and I, had often shared
In Nature's—Dining Room—

The Plenty hurt me—'twas so new—
Myself felt ill—and odd—
As Berry—of a Mountain Bush—
Transplanted—to the Road—

Nor was I hungry—so I found
That Hunger—was a way
Of Persons outside Windows—
The Entering—takes away—

c. 1862 1891

587

Empty my Heart, of Thee—
It's single Artery—
Begin, and leave Thee out—
Simply Extinction's Date—

Much Billow hath the Sea—
One Baltic—They—[1]
Subtract Thyself, in play,
And not enough of me
Is left—to put away—
"Myself" meant Thee—

Erase the Root—no Tree—
Thee—then—no me—
The Heavens stripped—
Eternity's vast pocket, picked—

c. 1862 1929

593

I think I was enchanted
When first a sombre Girl—
I read that Foreign Lady—[1]
The Dark—felt beautiful—

And whether it was noon at night—
Or only Heaven—at Noon—
For very Lunacy of Light
I had not power to tell—

The Bees—became as Butterflies—
The Butterflies—as Swans—
Approached—and spurned the narrow Grass—
And just the meanest Tunes

That Nature murmured to herself
To keep herself in Cheer—
I took for Giants—practising
Titanic Opera—[2]

The Days—to Mighty Metres stept—
The Homeliest—adorned
As if unto a Jubilee
'Twere suddenly confirmed—

I could not have defined the change—
Conversion of the Mind

[1]The waves (billows) make one [Baltic] sea.
[1]The English poet Elizabeth Barrett Browning.
[2]Of heroic proportions.

Like Sanctifying in the Soul—
Is witnessed—not explained—

'Twas a Divine Insanity—
The Danger to be Sane
Should I again experience—
'Tis Antidote to turn—

To Tomes of solid Witchcraft—
Magicians be asleep—
But Magic—hath an Element
Like Deity—to keep—

c. 1862 1935

599

There is a pain—so utter—
It swallows substance up—
Then covers the Abyss with Trance—
So Memory can step
Around—across—upon it—
As One within a Swoon—
Goes safely—where an open eye—
Would drop Him—Bone by Bone.

c. 1862 1929

612

It would have starved a Gnat—
To live so small as I—
And yet I was a living Child—
With Food's necessity

Upon me—like a Claw—
I could no more remove
Than I could coax a Leech away—
Or make a Dragon—move—

Nor like the Gnat—had I—
The privilege to fly
And seek a Dinner for myself—
How mightier He—than I—

Nor like Himself—the Art
Upon the Window Pane

To gad my little Being out—
And not begin—again—

c. 1862 1945

613

They shut me up in Prose—
As when a little Girl
They put me in the Closet—
Because they liked me "still"—

Still! Could themself have peeped—
And seen my Brain—go round—
They might as wise have lodged a Bird
For Treason—in the Pound—[1]

Himself has but to will
And easy as a Star
Look down upon Captivity—
And laugh—No more have I—[2]

c. 1862 1935

631

Ourselves were wed one summer—dear—
Your Vision—was in June—
And when Your little Lifetime failed,
I wearied—too—of mine—

And overtaken in the Dark—
Where You had put me down—
By Some one carrying a Light—
I—too—received the Sign.

'Tis true—Our Futures different lay—
Your Cottage—faced the sun—
While Oceans—and the North must be—
On every side of mine

'Tis true, Your Garden led the Bloom,
For mine—in Frosts—was sown—

[1]An enclosure without a roof for livestock or other animals.

[2]*I.e.,* I need do no more than the bird to escape my captivity.

And yet, one Summer, we were Queens—
But You—were crowned in June—

c. 1862 1945

632

The Brain—is wider than the Sky—
For—put them side by side—
The one the other will contain
With ease—and You—beside—

The Brain is deeper than the sea—
For—hold them—Blue to Blue—
The one the other will absorb—
As Sponges—Buckets—do—

The Brain is just the weight of God—
For—Heft them—Pound for Pound—
And they will differ—if they do—
As Syllable from Sound—

c. 1862 1896

640

I cannot live with You—
It would be Life—
And Life is over there—
Behind the Shelf

The Sexton[1] keeps the Key to—
Putting up
Our Life—His Porcelain—
Like a Cup—

Discarded of the Housewife—
Quaint—or Broke—
A newer Sevres[2] pleases—
Old Ones crack—

[1]Custodian of church property; bellringer; grave-digger.
[2]Fine French porcelain china.

I could not die—with You—
For One must wait
To shut the Other's Gaze down—
You—could not—

And I—Could I stand by
And see You—freeze—
Without my Right of Frost—
Death's privilege?

Nor could I rise—with You—
Because Your Face
Would put out Jesus'—
That New Grace

Glow plain—and foreign
On my homesick Eye—
Except that You than He
Shone closer by—

They'd judge Us—How—
For You—served Heaven—You know,
Or sought to—
I could not—

Because You saturated Sight—
And I had no more Eyes
For sordid excellence
As Paradise

And were You lost, I would be—
Though My Name
Rang loudest
On the Heavenly fame—

And were You—saved—
And I—condemned to be
Where You were not—
That self—were Hell to Me—

So We must meet apart—
You there—I—here—
With just the Door ajar
That Oceans are—and Prayer—
And that White Sustenance—
Despair—

c. 1862 1890

657

I dwell in Possibility—
A fairer House than Prose—
More numerous of Windows—
Superior—for Doors—

Of Chambers as the Cedars—
Impregnable of Eye—[1]
And for an Everlasting Roof
The Gambrels[2] of the Sky—

Of Visiters—the fairest—
For Occupation—This—
The spreading wide my narrow Hands
To gather Paradise—

c. 1862 1929

664

Of all the Souls that stand create—
I have elected—One—
When Sense from Spirit—files away—
And Subterfuge—is done—
When that which is—and that which was—
Apart—intrinsic—stand—
And this brief Tragedy of Flesh—
Is shifted—like a Sand—
When Figures show their royal Front—
And Mists—are carved away,
Behold the Atom—I preferred—
To all the lists[1] of Clay!

c. 1862 1891

668

"Nature" is what we see—
The Hill—the Afternoon—
Squirrel—Eclipse—the Bumble bee—
Nay—Nature is Heaven—

[1]Impenetrable, impossible to see through, like some dense cedar trees.
[2]Ridged roofs with two slopes on each side, the lower slope having the steeper pitch.

[1]Probably in the archaic sense of limits, boundaries, borders.

Nature is what we hear—
The Bobolink—the Sea—

Thunder—the Cricket—
Nay—Nature is Harmony—
Nature is what we know—
Yet have no art to say—
So impotent Our Wisdom is
To her Simplicity

c. 1863 1914

669

No Romance sold unto[1]
Could so enthrall a Man
As the perusal of
His Individual One—
'Tis Fiction's—to dilute to Plausibility
Our Novel—When 'tis small enough
To Credit—'Tis'nt true!

c. 1863 1891

670

One need not be a Chamber—to be Haunted—
One need not be a House—
The Brain has Corridors—surpassing
Material Place—
Far safer, of a Midnight Meeting
External Ghost
Than it's interior Confronting—
That Cooler Host.

Far safer, through an Abbey gallop,
The Stones a' chase—
Than Unarmed, one's a'self encounter—
In lonesome Place—

Ourself behind ourself, concealed—
Should startle most—

[1]*I.e.,* no fictional tale sold to [a Man].

Assassin hid in our Apartment
Be Horror's least.[1]

The Body—borrows a Revolver—
He bolts the Door—
O'erlooking a superior spectre—[2]
Or More—

c. 1863 1891

673

The Love a Life can show Below
Is but a filament, I know,
Of that diviner thing
That faints upon the face of Noon—
And smites the Tinder in the Sun—
And hinders Gabriel's Wing—[1]
'Tis this—in Music—hints and sways—
And far abroad on Summer days—
Distils uncertain pain—
'Tis this enamors in the East—
And tints the Transit in the West[2]
With harrowing Iodine—

'Tis this—invites—appalls—endows—
Flits—glimmers—proves—dissolves—
Returns—suggests—convicts—enchants—
Then—flings in Paradise—

c. 1863 1929

675

Essential Oils—are wrung—
The Attar[1] from the Rose
Be not expressed[2] by Suns—alone—
It is the gift of Screws—

[1] *I.e.,* should be the least horrifying of the things we fear.
[2] Not seeing that there is a greater ghost within.
[1] Gabriel, according to the *Bible,* was an angel who acted as God's messenger. There may also be a reference here to Icarus, in Greek mythology, who made himself a pair of wax wings which melted when he flew too close to the sun.
[2] A reference to the setting of the sun.
[1] Perfume derived from crushing flower petals.
[2] Pressed out, or brought out.

The General Rose—decay—
But this—in Lady's Drawer
Make Summer—When the Lady lie
In Ceaseless Rosemary—[3]

c. 1863 1891

686

They say that "Time assuages"—[1]
Time never did assuage—
An actual suffering strengthens
As Sinews do, with age—

Time is a Test of Trouble—
But not a Remedy—
If such it prove, it prove too
There was no Malady—

c. 1863 1896

696

Their Hight in Heaven comforts not—
Their Glory—nought to me—
'Twas best imperfect—as it was—
I'm finite—I cant see—

The House of Supposition—
The Glimmering Frontier that
skirts the Acres of Perhaps—
To Me—shows insecure—

The Wealth I had—contented me—
If 'twas a meaner size—
Then I had counted it until
It pleased my narrow Eyes—

Better than larger values—
That show however true—
This timid life of Evidence
Keeps pleading—"I dont know."

c. 1863 1891

[3]Herb associated with remembrance, or memory.

[1]Eases or reduces a hurt.

704

No matter—now—Sweet—
But when I'm Earl—
Wont you wish you'd spoken
To that dull Girl?

Trivial a Word—just—
Trivial—a Smile—
But wont you wish you'd spared one
When I'm Earl?

I shant need it—then—
Crests—will do—
Eagles on my Buckles—
On my Belt—too—

Ermine—my familiar Gown—
Say—Sweet—then
Wont you wish you'd smiled—just—
Me upon?

c. 1863 1945

709

Publication—is the Auction
Of the Mind of Man—
Poverty—be justifying
For so foul a thing

Possibly[1]—but We—would rather
From Our Garret go
White—Unto the White Creator—
Than invest—Our Snow—

Thought belong to Him who gave it—
Then—to Him Who bear
It's Corporeal illustration—Sell
The Royal Air—

In the Parcel—Be the Merchant
Of the Heavenly Grace—

[1] *I.e.,* possibly the alternative of poverty would justify publication.

But reduce no Human Spirit
To Disgrace of Price—

c. 1863 1929

712

Because I could not stop for Death—
He kindly stopped for me—
The Carriage held but just Ourselves—
And Immortality.

We slowly drove—He knew no haste
And I had put away
My labor and my leisure too,
For His Civility—

We passed the School, where Children strove
At Recess—in the Ring—
We passed the Fields of Gazing Grain—
We passed the Setting Sun—

Or rather—He passed Us—
The Dews drew quivering and chill—
For only Gossamer,[1] my Gown—
My Tippet[2]—only Tulle—[3]

We paused before a House that seemed
A Swelling of the Ground—
The Roof was scarcely visible—
The Cornice[4]—in the Ground—

Since then—'tis Centuries—and yet
Feels shorter than the Day
I first surmised the Horses Heads
Were toward Eternity—

c. 1863 1890

721

Behind Me—dips Eternity—
Before Me—Immortality—

[1]Very fine fabric.
[2]Shoulder cape.
[3]Thin silk netting.
[4]Molding, often decorative, below the roof of a building.

Myself—the Term between—
Death but the Drift of Eastern Gray,
Dissolving into Dawn away,
Before the West begin—

'Tis Kingdoms—afterward—they say—
In perfect—pauseless Monarchy—
Whose Prince—is Son of None—
Himself—His Dateless Dynasty—
Himself—Himself diversity—
In Duplicate divine—

'Tis Miracle before Me—then—
'Tis Miracle behind—between—
A Crescent in the Sea—
With Midnight to the North of Her—
And Midnight to the South of Her—
And Maelstrom[1]—in the Sky—

c. 1863 1929

732

She rose to His Requirement—dropt
The Playthings of Her Life
To take the honorable Work
Of Woman, and of Wife—

If ought[1] She missed in Her new Day,
Of Amplitude, or Awe—
Or first Prospective—Or the Gold
In using, wear away,

It lay unmentioned—as the Sea
Develope Pearl, and Weed,
But only to Himself—be known
The Fathoms[2] they abide—

c. 1863 1890

742

Four Trees—upon a solitary Acre—
Without Design

[1]A whirlpool of extraordinary size or violence.
[1]Aught; anything.
[2]*I.e.,* how deep they lie and in what surroundings. The fathom measures water depth.

Or Order, or Apparent Action—[1]
Maintain—[2]

The Sun—upon a Morning meets them—
The Wind—
No nearer Neighbor—have they—
But God—

The Acre gives them—Place—
They—Him—Attention of Passer by—
Of Shadow, or of Squirrel, haply—
Or Boy—

What Deed is Their's[3] unto the General Nature—
What Plan
They severally—retard—or further—[4]
Unknown—

c. 1863 1945

747

It dropped so low—in my Regard—
I heard it hit the Ground—
And go to pieces on the Stones
At bottom of my Mind—

Yet blamed the Fate that fractured—*less*
Than I reviled Myself,
For entertaining Plated Wares[1]
Upon my Silver Shelf—

c. 1863 1896

754

My Life had stood—a Loaded Gun—
In Corners—till a Day
The Owner passed—identified—
And carried Me away—

[1]A variant reading in the manuscript is "signal—/notice" for "Action."

[2]A variant reading in the manuscript is "Do reign—" for "Maintain."

[3]A variant reading in the manuscript is "they bear" for "is Their's."

[4]A variant reading in the manuscript is "promote—or hinder—" for "retard—or further."

[1]China coated with metallic paint.

And now We roam in Sovreign Woods—
And now We hunt the Doe—
And every time I speak for Him—
The Mountains straight reply—

And do I smile, such cordial light
Upon the Valley glow—
It is as a Vesuvian[1] face
Had let it's pleasure through—

And when at Night—Our good Day done—
I guard My Master's Head—
'Tis better than the Eider-Duck's[2]
Deep Pillow—to have shared—

To foe of His—I'm deadly foe—
None stir the second time—
On whom I lay a Yellow Eye—
Or an Emphatic Thumb—

Though I than He—may longer live
He longer must—than I—
For I have but the power to kill,
Without—the power to die—

c. 1863 1929

764

Presentiment—is that long Shadow—on the Lawn—
Indicative that Suns go down—

The Notice to the startled Grass
That Darkness—is about to pass—

c. 1863 1890

812

A Light exists in Spring
Not present on the Year
At any other period—
When March is scarcely here

[1]Volcanic, like Mt. Vesuvius in Italy; capable of breathing fire, light, and destruction.
[2]*I.e.,* downy (with duck down).

A Color stands abroad
On Solitary Fields
That Science cannot overtake
But Human Nature feels.

It waits upon the Lawn,
It shows the furthest Tree
Upon the furthest Slope you know
It almost speaks to you.

Then as Horizons step
Or Noons report away
Without the Formula of sound
It passes and we stay—

A quality of loss
Affecting our Content
As Trade had suddenly encroached
Upon a Sacrament.

c. 1864 1896

822

This Consciousness that is aware
Of Neighbors and the Sun
Will be the one aware of Death
And that itself alone

Is traversing the interval
Experience between
And most profound experiment
Appointed unto Men—

How adequate unto itself
It's properties shall be
Itself unto itself and none
Shall make discovery.

Adventure most unto itself
The Soul condemned to be—
Attended by a single Hound
It's own identity.

c. 1864 1945

883

The Poets light but Lamps—
Themselves—go out—
The Wicks they stimulate—
If vital Light

Inhere as do the Suns—
Each Age a Lens
Disseminating their
Circumference—

c. 1864 1945

959

A loss of something ever felt I—
The first that I could recollect
Bereft I was—of what I knew not
Too young that any should suspect

A Mourner walked among the children
I notwithstanding went about
As one bemoaning a Dominion
Itself the only Prince cast out—

Elder, Today, a session wiser
And fainter, too, as Wiseness is—
I find myself still softly searching
For my Delinquent Palaces—

And a Suspicion, like a Finger
Touches my Forehead now and then
That I am looking oppositely[1]
For the site of the Kingdom of Heaven—

c. 1864 1945

974

The Soul's distinct connection
With immortality
Is best disclosed by Danger
Or quick Calamity—

[1]In the wrong direction, or manner.

As Lightning on a Landscape
Exhibits Sheets of Place—
Not yet suspected—but for Flash—
And Click—and Suddenness.

c. 1864 1929

985

The Missing All, prevented Me
From missing minor Things.
If nothing larger than a World's
Departure from a Hinge

Or Sun's extinction, be observed
'Twas not so large that I
Could lift my Forehead from my work
For Curiosity.

c. 1865 1914

986

A narrow Fellow in the Grass
Occasionally rides—
You may have met Him—did you not
His notice sudden is—

The Grass divides as with a Comb—
A spotted Shaft is seen—
And then it closes at your feet
And opens further on—

He likes a Boggy Acre
A Floor too cool for Corn—
Yet when a Boy, and Barefoot—
I more than once at Noon
Have passed, I thought, a Whip lash
Unbraiding in the Sun
When stooping to secure it
It wrinkled, and was gone—

Several of Nature's People
I know, and they know me—
I feel for them a transport
Of Cordiality—

But never met this Fellow
Attended, or alone
Without a tighter breathing
And Zero at the Bone—

c. 1865 1866

1071

Perception of an object costs
Precise the Object's loss—
Perception in itself a Gain
Replying to it's Price—

The Object Absolute—is nought—
Perception sets it fair
And then upbraids[1] a Perfectness
That situates so far—

c. 1866 1914

1072

Title divine—is mine!
The Wife—without the Sign!
Acute Degree—conferred on me—
Empress of Calvary!
Royal—all but the Crown!
Betrothed—without the swoon
God sends us Women—
When you—hold—Garnet to Garnet—
Gold—to Gold—
Born—Bridalled—Shrouded—
In a Day—
"My Husband"—women say—
Stroking the Melody—
Is *this*—the way?

c. 1862 1924

1078

The Bustle in a House
The Morning after Death

[1]Reproaches.

Is solemnest of industries
Enacted upon Earth—

The Sweeping up the Heart
And putting Love away
We shall not want to use again
Until Eternity.

c. 1866 1890

1082

Revolution is the Pod
Systems rattle from
When the Winds of Will are stirred
Excellent is Bloom

But except[1] it's Russet[2] Base
Every Summer be
The Entomber of itself,
So of Liberty—

Left inactive on the Stalk
All it's Purple fled
Revolution shakes it for
Test if it be dead.

c. 1866 1929

1100

The last Night that She lived
It was a Common Night
Except the Dying—this to Us
Made Nature different

We noticed smallest things—
Things overlooked before
By this great light upon our Minds
Italicized—as 'twere.

As We went out and in
Between Her final Room

[1]But for, *i.e.,* if it were not for.
[2]Reddish brown associated with leaves, pods, stalks in autumn.

And Rooms where Those to be alive
Tomorrow were, a Blame

That Others could exist
While She must finish quite
A Jealousy for Her arose
So nearly infinite—

We waited while She passed—
It was a narrow time—
Too jostled were Our Souls to speak
At length the notice came.

She mentioned, and forgot—
Then lightly as a Reed
Bent to the Water, struggled scarce—
Consented, and was dead—

And We—We placed the Hair—
And drew the Head erect—
And then an awful leisure was
Belief to regulate—

c. 1866 1890

1129

Tell all the Truth but tell it slant—
Success in Circuit lies
Too bright for our infirm Delight
The Truth's superb surprise
As Lightning to the Children eased
With explanation kind
The Truth must dazzle gradually
Or every man be blind—

c. 1868 1945

1207

He preached upon "Breadth" till it argued him narrow—
The Broad are too broad to define
And of "Truth" until it proclaimed him a Liar—
The Truth never flaunted a Sign—

Simplicity fled from his counterfeit presence
As Gold the Pyrites[1] would shun—
What confusion would cover the innocent Jesus
To meet so enabled a Man!

c. 1872 1891

[A worksheet draft of this poem printed below reveals some of Dickinson's characteristic ways of working. For other examples of variant readings, see poems 512 and 742, as well as the three-volume Johnson edition and the manuscript books edited by Franklin.]

He preached about Breadth till ~~we~~ knew ~~he was~~ narrow
upon *it argued him*
The Broad are too broad to define
And of Truth until it proclaimed him a Liar
The Truth never ~~hoisted~~ a sign—
flaunted
Simplicity fled from his counterfeit presence
As Gold the Pyrites would shun
a
What confusion would cover the innocent Jesus
To meet so ~~learned~~ a man—
at meeting *Religious*
enabled
so accomplished
discerning
accoutred
established
conclusive

1304

Not with a Club, the Heart is broken
Nor with a Stone—
A Whip so small you could not see it
I've known

To lash the Magic Creature
Till it fell,
Yet that Whip's Name
Too noble then to tell.

[1]A bright, brassy metal known as Fool's Gold.

Magnanimous as Bird
By Boy descried—[1]
Singing unto the Stone[2]
Of which it died—

Shame need not crouch
In such an Earth as Our's—
Shame—stand erect—
The Universe is your's.

c. 1874 1896

1355

The Mind lives on the Heart
Like any Parasite—
If that is full of Meat
The Mind is fat.

But if the Heart omit
Emaciate the Wit—[1]
The Aliment[2] of it
So absolute.

c. 1876 1932

1400

What mystery pervades a well!
The water lives so far—
A neighbor from another world
Residing in a jar

Whose limit none have ever seen,
But just his lid of glass—
Like looking every time you please
In an abyss's face!

The grass does not appear afraid,
I often wonder he
Can stand so close and look so bold
At what is awe to me.

[1]Sought out, found.
[2]*I.e.,* stone fired from a slingshot.

[1]*I.e.,* the wit is emaciated.
[2]Nourishment.

Related somehow they may be,
The sedge stands next the sea—
Where he is floorless
And does no timidity betray

But nature is a stranger yet;
The ones that cite her most[1]
Have never passed her haunted house.
Nor simplified her ghost.[2]

To pity those that know her not
Is helped by the regret
That those who know her, know her less
The nearer her they get.[3]

c. 1877 1896

1453

A Counterfeit—a Plated Person—
I would not be—
Whatever strata of Iniquity
My Nature underlie—
Truth is good Health—and Safety, and the Sky.
How meagre, what an Exile—is a Lie,
And Vocal—when we die—

c. 1879 1924

1461

"Heavenly Father"—take to thee
The supreme iniquity[1]
Fashioned by thy candid Hand
In a moment contraband—[2]

[1]Refer to her most often as an authority, example, or proof.
[2]Spirit.
[3]ED sent Sue a variant of the last two stanzas. It is signed "Emily—"and was written about 1877.

But Susan is a Stranger yet—
The Ones who cite her most
Have never scaled her Haunted House
Nor compromised her Ghost—
To pity those who know her not
Is helped by the regret
That those who know her know her less
The nearer her they get—

[1]Wickedness; sinfulness.
[2]Forbidden moment.

Though to trust us—seem to us
More respectful—"We are Dust"—
We apologize to thee
For thine own Duplicity—[3]

c. 1879 1914

1463

A Route of Evanescence
With a revolving Wheel—
A Resonance of Emerald—
A Rush of Cochineal—[1]
And every Blossom on the Bush
Adjusts it's tumbled Head—
The mail from Tunis,[2] probably,
An easy Morning's Ride—[3]

c. 1879 1891

1545

The Bible is an antique Volume—
Written by faded Men
At the suggestion of Holy Spectres—
Subjects—Bethlehem—
Eden—the ancient Homestead—
Satan—the Brigadier—
Judas—the Great Defaulter—
David—the Troubadour—
Sin—a distinguished Precipice
Others must resist—
Boys that "believe" are very lonesome—
Other Boys are "lost"—
Had but the Tale a warbling Teller—
All the Boys would come—
Orpheus' Sermon captivated—
It did not condemn—[1]

c. 1882 1924

[3] *I.e.,* your doubleness, in creating something and then holding it accountable for the wicked nature you gave it. The quotation marks around "Heavenly Father" and "We are Dust" call attention to the ironic tone of this apology.

[1] Brilliant red dye.

[2] An African city in Tunisia, near the ancient site of Carthage.

[3] Dickinson sent copies of this poem in several letters to friends and referred to it as "A Humming Bird."

[1] Dickinson sent this poem to her nephew Ned Gilbert when he was 21. She entitled an earlier version of the poem "Diagnosis of the Bible, by a Boy—." In Dickinson's view, the Bible's didactic tone alienates many readers.

1583

Witchcraft was hung, in History,
But History and I
Find all the Witchcraft that we need
Around us, every Day—

c. 1883 1945

1624

Apparently with no surprise
To any happy Flower
The Frost beheads it at it's play—
In accidental power—
The blonde Assassin passes on—
The Sun proceeds unmoved
To measure off another Day
For an Approving God.

c. 1884 1890

1651

A Word made Flesh[1] is seldom
And tremblingly partook
Nor then perhaps reported
But have I not mistook
Each one of us has tasted
With ecstasies of stealth
The very food debated
To our specific strength—

A Word that breathes distinctly
Has not the power to die
Cohesive as the Spirit
It may expire if He—
"Made Flesh and dwelt among us[2]
Could condescension be
Like this consent of Language
This loved Philology[3]

? 1955

[1]This phrase alludes to God as the Word and to Christ as the incarnation of God in man.
[2]Dickinson did not close the quote.
[3]Dickinson appears to be using this word in the sense of its Greek roots, to mean love of learning and language.

1670

In Winter in my Room
I came upon a Worm
Pink lank and warm
But as he was a worm
And worms presume
Not quite with him at home
Secured him by a string
To something neighboring
And went along.

A Trifle afterward[1]
A thing occurred
I'd not believe it if I heard
But state with creeping blood
A snake with mottles rare
Surveyed my chamber floor
In feature as the worm before
But ringed with power
The very string with which
I tied him—too
When he was mean[2] and new
That string was there—

I shrank—"How fair you are"!
Propitiation's claw—[3]
"Afraid he hissed
Of me"?
"No cordiality"—
He fathomed me—
Then to a Rhythm *Slim*
Secreted in his Form
As Patterns swim
Projected him.[4]

That time I flew
Both eyes his way
Lest he pursue
Nor ever ceased to run
Till in a distant Town

[1]Soon after.
[2]Small.
[3]*I.e.,* this was a brave attempt to appease the snake.
[4]Advanced toward me.

Towns on from mine
I set me down
This was a dream—

? 1914

1695

There is a solitude of space
A solitude of sea
A solitude of death, but these
Society shall be
Compared with that profounder site
That polar privacy
A soul admitted to itself—
Finite Infinity.

? 1914

1705

Volcanoes be in Sicily
And South America
I judge from my Geography
Volcanoes nearer here
A Lava step at any time
Am I inclined to climb
A Crater I may contemplate
Vesuvius[1] at Home

? 1914

1719

God is indeed a jealous God—
He cannot bear to see
That we had rather not with Him
But with each other play.

? 1945

[1]Mt. Vesuvius, a powerful and active volcano in Italy.

1737

Rearrange a "Wife's" affection!
When they dislocate my Brain!
Amputate my freckled Bosom!
Make me bearded like a man!

Blush, my spirit, in thy Fastness—
Blush, my unacknowledged clay—
Seven years of troth have taught thee
More than Wifehood ever may!

Love that never leaped its socket—
Trust entrenched in narrow pain—
Constancy thro' fire—awarded—
Anguish—bare of anodyne![1]

Burden—borne so far triumphant—
None suspect me of the crown,
For I wear the "Thorns"[2] till *Sunset*—
Then—my Diadem[3] put on.

Big my Secret but it's *bandaged*—
It will never get away
Till the Day its Weary Keeper
Leads it through the Grave to thee.[4]

c. 1861 1945

1755

To make a prairie it takes a clover and one bee,
One clover, and a bee,
And revery.
The revery alone will do,
If bees are few.

? 1896

[1]Pain-killing medicine.

[2]A reference to the crown of thorns which Christ was forced to wear before the crucifixion.

[3]Crown or headband, often of jewels, worn by royalty.

[4]This poem was originally copied into fascicle 11 by Dickinson around 1861. Seven years earlier would have been 1854, a year after Sue became engaged to Austin. The poem was removed from fascicle 11 by someone after Dickinson's death.

Letters

To Abiah Root

29 January 1850

Very dear Abiah.[1]

The folks have all gone away—they thought that they left me alone, and contrived things to amuse me should they stay long, and *I* be lonely. Lonely indeed—they did'nt look, and they could'nt have seen if they had, who should bear me company. *Three* here instead of *one*—would'nt it scare them? A curious trio, part earthly and part spiritual two of us—the other all heaven, and no earth. *God* is sitting here, looking into my very soul to see if I think right tho'ts. Yet I am not afraid, for I try to be right and good, and he knows every one of my struggles. He looks very gloriously, and everything bright seems dull beside him, and I dont dare to look directly at him for fear I shall die. Then *you* are here—dressed in that quiet black gown and cap—that funny little cap I used to laugh at you about, and you dont appear to be thinking about anything in particular, not in one of your *breaking dish* moods I take it, you seem aware that I'm writing you, and are amused I should think at any such friendly manifestation when you are already present. *Success* however even in making a fool of one's-self is'nt to be despised, so I shall persist in writing, and you may in laughing at me, if you are fully aware of the value of time as regards your immortal spirit. I cant say that I advise you to laugh, but if you are punished, and I warned you, that can be no business of mine. So I fold up my arms, and leave you to fate—may it deal very kindly with you! The trinity winds up with me, as you may have surmised, and I certainly would'nt be at the fag end but for civility to you. This selfsacrificing spirit will be the ruin of me! I am occupied principally with a cold just now, and the dear creature *will* have so much attention that my time slips away amazingly. It has heard *so* much of New Englanders, of their kind attentions to strangers, that it's come all the way from the Alps to determine the truth of the tale—it says the half was'nt told it, and I begin to be afraid it was'nt. Only think, came all the way from that distant Switzerland to find what was the truth! Neither husband—protector—nor friend accompanied it, and so utter a state of loneliness gives friends if nothing else. You are dying of curiosity, let me arrange that pillow to make your exit easier! I stayed at home all Saturday afternoon, and treated some disagreable people who insisted upon calling here as tolerably as I could—when evening shades began to fall, I turned upon my heel, and walked. Attracted by the gaiety visible in the street I still kept walking till a little creature pounced upon a thin shawl I wore, and commenced riding—I stopped, and begged the creature to alight, as I was fatigued already, and quite unable to assist others. It would'nt get down, and commenced talking to itself—"cant be New England—must have made some mistake, disappointed in my reception, dont agree with accounts, Oh what a world of deception, and fraud—Marm, will [you]

[1]Abiah Root was among Dickinson's early circle of friends. Letters to Abiah are intimate and affectionate. No correspondence remains after 1854, the year Abiah Root married.

tell me the name of this country—it's Asia Minor, is'nt it. I intended to stop in New England." By this time I was so completely exhausted that I made no farther effort to rid me of my load, and travelled home at a moderate jog, paying no attention whatever to it, got into the house, threw off both bonnet, and shawl, and out flew my tormentor, and putting both arms around my neck began to kiss me immoderately, and express so much love, it completely bewildered me. Since then it has slept in my bed, eaten from my plate, lived with me everywhere, and will tag me through life for all I know. I think I'll wake first, and get out of bed, and leave it, but early, or late, it is dressed before me, and sits on the side of the bed looking right in my face with such a comical expression it almost makes me laugh in spite of myself. I cant call it interesting, but it certainly *is* curious—has two peculiarities which would quite win your heart, a huge pocket-handkerchief, and a very red nose. The first seems so very *abundant,* it gives you the idea of independence, and prosperity in business. The last brings up the "jovial bowl,[2] my boys," and such an association's worth the having. If it *ever* gets tired of *me,* I will forward it to *you*—you would love it for *my* sake, if not for it's own, it will tell you some queer stories about me—how I sneezed so loud one night that the family thought the last trump[3] was sounding, and climbed into the currant-bushes to get out of the way—how the rest of the people arrayed in long night-gowns folded their arms, and were waiting—but this is a wicked story, it can tell some *better* ones. Now my dear friend, let me tell you that these last thoughts are fictions—vain imaginations to lead astray foolish young women. They are flowers of speech, they both *make,* and *tell* deliberate falsehoods, avoid them as the snake, and turn aside as from the *Bottle* snake, and I dont *think* you will be harmed. Honestly tho', a snake bite is a serious matter, and there cant be too much said, or done about it. The big serpent bites the deepest, and we get so accustomed to it's bites that we dont mind about them. "Verily I say unto you fear *him.*" . . .

Your very sincere, and *wicked* friend,
Emily E Dickinson.

Letter 31

To Austin Dickinson

17 October 1851

. . . How glad I am you are well—you must try hard to be careful and not get sick again. I hope you will be better than ever you were in your life when you come home *this time,* for it never seemed so long since we have seen you. I thank you for such a long letter, and yet if I might choose, *the next* should be a longer. I think a letter just about *three days* long would make me happier than any other kind of one—if you please, dated at Boston, but thanks be to our Father, you may conclude it *here.* Everything has changed since my other letter—the doors are shut this morning, and all the kitchen wall is covered with chilly flies who are trying to warm themselves—poor things, they do not understand that there are no summer mornings

[2]A bowl of alcoholic punch.
[3]Trumpet.

remaining to them and me and they have a bewildered air which is really very droll, did'nt one feel *sorry* for them. You would say t'was a gloomy morning if you were sitting here—the frost has been severe and the few lingering leaves seem anxious to be going and wrap their faded cloaks more closely about them as if to shield them from the chilly northeast wind. The earth looks like some poor old lady who by dint of pains has bloomed e'en till *now,* yet in a forgetful moment a few silver hairs from out her cap come stealing, and she tucks them back so hastily and thinks nobody *sees.* The cows are going to pasture and little boys with their hands in their pockets are whistling to try to keep warm. Dont think that the sky will frown so the day when you come home! She will smile and look happy, and be full of sunshine *then*—and even *should* she frown upon her child returning, there is *another* sky ever serene and fair, and there is *another* sunshine, tho' it be darkness there—never mind faded forests, Austin, never mind silent fields—*here* is a little forest whose leaf is ever green, here is a *brighter* garden, where not a frost has been, in its unfading flowers I hear the bright bee hum, prithee, my Brother, into *my* garden come![1]

Your very aff
Sister.

Letter 58

To Susan Gilbert (Dickinson)

late April 1852

So sweet and still, and Thee, Oh Susie, what need I more, to make my heaven whole?

Sweet Hour, blessed Hour, to carry me to you, and to bring you back to me, long enough to snatch one kiss, and whisper Good bye, again.

I have thought of it all day, Susie, and I fear of but little else, and when I was gone to meeting it filled my mind so full, I could not find a *chink* to put the worthy pastor; when he said "Our Heavenly Father," I said "Oh Darling Sue"; when he read the 100th Psalm, I kept saying your precious letter all over to myself, and Susie, when they sang—it would have made you laugh to hear one little voice, piping to the departed. I made up words and kept singing how I loved you, and you had gone, while all the rest of the choir were singing Hallelujahs. I presume nobody heard me, because I sang *so small,* but it was a kind of a comfort to think I might put them out, singing of you. I a'nt there this afternoon, tho', because I am here, writing a little letter to my dear Sue, and I am very happy. I think of ten weeks—Dear One, and I think of love, and you, and my heart grows full and warm, and my breath stands still. The sun does'nt shine at all, but I can feel a sunshine stealing into my soul and making it all summer, and every thorn, a *rose.* And I pray that such summer's sun shine on my Absent One, and cause her bird to sing!

You have been happy, Susie, and now are sad—and the whole world seems lone; but it wont be so always, "some days *must* be dark and dreary"! You wont cry any more, will you, Susie, for my father will be your father, and my home will be your home, and where you go, I will go, and we will lie side by side in the kirkyard.

[1]Note the poem embedded in this letter.

I have parents on earth, dear Susie, but your's are in the skies, and I have an earthly fireside, but you have one above, and you have a "Father in Heaven," where I have *none*—and *sister* in heaven, and I know they love you dearly, and think of you every day.

Oh I wish I had half so many dear friends as you in heaven—I could'nt spare them now—but to know they had got there safely, and should suffer nevermore—Dear Susie! . . .

Emilie—

Letter 88

To Susan Gilbert (Dickinson)

27 June 1852

. . . Susie, will you indeed come home next Saturday, and be my own again, and kiss me as you used to? Shall I indeed behold you, not "darkly, but face to face" or am I *fancying* so, and dreaming blessed dreams from which the day will wake me? I hope for you so much, and feel so eager for you, feel that I *cannot* wait, feel that *now* I must have you—that the expectation once more to see your face again, makes me feel hot and feverish, and my heart beats so fast—I go to sleep at night, and the first thing I know, I am sitting there wide awake, and clasping my hands tightly, and thinking of next Saturday, and "never a bit" of you.

Sometimes I must have Saturday before tomorrow comes, and I wonder if it w'd make any difference with God, to give it to me *today,* and I'd let him have Monday, to make him a Saturday; and then I feel so funnily, and wish the precious day would'nt come quite so soon, till I could know how to feel, and get my thoughts ready for it.

Why, Susie, it seems to me as if my absent Lover was coming home so soon—and my heart must be so busy, making ready for him.

While the minister this morning was giving an account of the Roman Catholic system, and announcing several facts which were usually startling, I was trying to make up my mind wh' of the two was prettiest to go and welcome *you* in, my fawn colored dress, or my blue dress. Just as I had decided by all means to wear the blue, down came the minister's fist with a terrible rap on the counter, and Susie, it scared me so, I hav'nt got over it yet, but I'm glad I reached a conclusion! I walked home from meeting with Mattie, and *incidentally* quite, something was said of you, and I think one of us remarked that you would be here next Sunday; well—Susie—what it was *I* dont presume to know, but my gaiters seemed to leave me, and I seemed to move on wings—and I move on wings now, Susie, on wings as white as snow, and as bright as the summer sunshine—because I am with you, and so few short days, you are with me at home. Be patient then, my Sister, for the hours will haste away, and Oh *so* soon! Susie, I write most hastily, and very carelessly too, for it is time for me to get the supper, and my mother is gone and besides, my darling, so near I seem to you, that I *disdain* this pen, and wait for a *warmer* language. With Vinnie's love, and my love, I am once more

Your Emilie—

Letter 96

To Susan Gilbert (Dickinson)

late August 1854

Susie—

I have been very busy since you went away, but that is'nt the reason I've not written to you, and we've had a great deal of company too, but *that* is not the reason—I was foolish eno' to be vexed at a little thing, and I hope God will forgive me, as he'll have to many times, if he lives long enough.

Thro' Austin, I've known of you, and nobody in this world except Vinnie and Austin, know that in all the while, I have not heard from you. Many have asked me for you, and I have answered promptly that you had reached there safely, and were better every day, and Susie, do you think, H. Hinsdale came to our house several days ago; came just to ask for you, and went away supposing I'd heard from you quite often. Not that I told her so, but spoke of you so naturally, in such a daily way, she never guessed the fact that I'd not written to you, nor had you thus to me.

Never think of it, Susie—never mention it—I trust your truth for that, but when you meet, and I meet—we'll try and forgive each other. There has not been a day, Child, that I've not thought of you, nor have I shut my eyes upon a summer night, without your sweet remembrance, and tho' full much of sorrow has gathered at your name, that ought but peace was 'tween us, yet I remembered on, and bye and bye the day came. I do not miss you Susie—of course I do not miss you—I only sit and stare at nothing from my window, and know that all is gone—Dont *feel* it—no—any more than the stone feels, that it is very cold, or the block, that it is silent, where once 'twas warm and green, and birds danced in it's branches.

I rise, because the sun shines, and sleep has done with me, and I brush my hair, and dress me, and wonder what I am and who has made me so, and then I wash the dishes, and anon, wash them again, and then 'tis afternoon, and Ladies call, and evening, and some members of another sex come in to spend the hour, and then that day is done. And, prithee, what is Life? There was much that was sweet Commencement week—much too that was dusty, but my bee gathered many drops of the sweetest and purest honey—

I had many talks with Emmons,[1] which I will not forget, and a charming farewell ride, before he went away—he stayed more than a week after Commencement was done, and came to see me often—He brought his Hadley friend to pass the day with me, and we passed it very sweetly—*Her* name is Susie too, and that endeared me to her.

I shall miss Emmons very much. Father and mother were gone last week, upon a little journey—and we rested somewhat, like most ungodly children—John came down twice from Sunderland, to pass a day with us. Susie, I wished for you— . . . It's of no use to write to you—Far better bring dew in my thimble to quench the endless fire—My love for those I love—not many—not very many, but dont I love them so?—and Vinnie's love and Mother's for Martha[2] and for you. Write if you love, to

Emilie—

Letter 172

[1]Henry Vaughn Emmons attended Amherst College where he was a friend of Dickinson's cousin, John Graves, another Amherst student, who is also mentioned as having visited the Dickinson home during this time.

[2]Martha was one of Susan's sisters.

To Mrs. J. G. Holland

early August 1856?

Don't tell, dear Mrs. Holland,[1] but wicked as I am, I read my Bible sometimes, and in it as I read today, I found a verse like this, where friends should "go no more out"; and there were "no tears," and I wished as I sat down to-night that we were *there*—not *here*—and that wonderful world had commenced, which makes such promises, and rather than to write you, I were by your side, and the "hundred and forty and four thousand" were chatting pleasantly, yet not disturbing us. And I'm half tempted to take my seat in that Paradise of which the good man writes, and begin forever and ever *now,* so wondrous does it seem. My only sketch, profile, of Heaven is a large, blue sky, bluer and larger than the *biggest* I have seen in June, and in it are my friends—all of them—every one of them—those who are with me now, and those who were "parted" as we walked, and "snatched up to Heaven."[2]

If roses had not faded, and frosts had never come, and one had not fallen here and there whom I could not waken, there were no need of other Heaven than the one below—and if God had been here this summer, and seen the things that *I* have seen—I guess that He would think His Paradise superfluous. Don't tell Him, for the world, though, for after all He's said about it, I should like to see what He *was* building for us, with no hammer, and no stone, and no journeyman either. Dear Mrs. Holland, I love, to-night—love you and Dr. Holland, and "time and sense"—and fading things, and things that do *not* fade.

I'm so glad you are not a blossom, for those in my garden fade, and then a "reaper whose name is Death"[3] has come to get a few to help him make a bouquet for himself, so I'm glad you are not a rose—and I'm glad you are not a bee, for where they go when summer's done, only the thyme knows, and even were you a robin, when the west winds came, you would coolly wink at me, and away, some morning!

As "little Mrs. Holland," then, I think I love you most, and trust that tiny lady will dwell below while we dwell, and when with many a wonder we seek the new Land, *her* wistful face, *with* ours, shall look the last upon the hills, and first upon—well, *Home!*

Pardon my sanity, Mrs. Holland, in a world *insane,* and love me if you will, for I had rather *be* loved than to be called a king in earth, or a lord in Heaven. . . .

Dearly,
Emilie

Letter 185

[1]Mrs. Holland and her husband Dr. Holland were among Dickinson's closest friends. The friendship lasted a lifetime and Dickinson often addressed Mrs. Holland as "Sister."

[2]In her letters Dickinson often quotes or paraphrases lines from the Bible. The "hundred and forty and four thousand" here are those who will be saved after the Second Coming of Christ, according to the Book of Revelation. Biblical references in this paragraph are to Revelation 3:12, 21:4, 14:3, and Luke 24:51.

[3]This is the opening line of a poem by Henry Wadsworth Longfellow.

To Samuel Bowles

about February 1861

Dear friend.[1]

You remember the little "Meeting"—we held for you—last spring? We met again—Saturday—'Twas May—when we "adjourned"—but then Adjourns—are all—The meetings wore alike—Mr Bowles—The Topic—did not tire us—so we chose no new—We voted to remember you—so long as both should live—including Immortality. To count you as ourselves—except sometimes more tenderly—as now—when you are ill—and we—the haler of the two—and so I bring the Bond—we sign so many times—for you to read, when Chaos comes—or Treason—or Decay—still witnessing for Morning.

We hope—it is a tri-Hope—composed of Vinnie's—Sue's—and mine—that you took no more pain—riding in the sleigh.

We hope our joy to see you—gave of it's own degree—to you—We pray for your new health—the prayer that goes not down—when they shut the church—We offer you our cups—stintless—as to the Bee—the Lily, her new Liquors—

Would you like summer? Taste of our's.
Spices? Buy here!
Ill! We have berries, for the parching!
Weary! Furloughs of down!
Perplexed! Estates of violet trouble ne'er looked on!
Captive! We bring reprieve of roses!
Fainting! Flasks of air!
Even for Death, a fairy medicine—
But, which is it, sir?

Emily

Letter 229

To recipient unknown

about 1861

Master.[1]

If you saw a bullet hit a Bird—and he told you he was'nt shot—you might weep at his courtesy, but you would certainly doubt his word.

One drop more from the gash that stains your Daisy's bosom—then would you *believe?* Thomas' faith in Anatomy, was stronger than his faith in faith.[2] God made me—[Sir] Master—I did'nt be—myself. I dont know how it was done. He built

[1]Samuel Bowles was the editor of the *Springfield Daily Republican,* Amherst's local daily, a politically liberal and nationally influential newspaper. Bowles and his wife were lifelong friends of Dickinson's. Some scholars argue that Dickinson was in love with Bowles, and for some he is a likely candidate for the "Master" whose identity has never been revealed.

[1]Drafts of three letters to "Master" were among Dickinson's papers when she died. It is not known if final copies were ever made and sent. She refers to herself as "Daisy" in two of the letters.

[2]Doubting Thomas (John 20:25) required physical proof of Christ's resurrection.

the heart in me—Bye and bye it outgrew me—and like the little mother—with the big child—I got tired holding him. I heard of a thing called "Redemption"—which rested men and women. You remember I asked you for it—you gave me something else. I forgot the Redemption [in the Redeemed—I did'nt tell you for a long time, but I knew you had altered me—I] and was tired—no more—[so dear did this stranger become that were it, or my breath—the Alternative—I had tossed the fellow away with a smile.] I am older—tonight, Master—but the love is the same—so are the moon and the crescent. If it had been God's will that I might breathe where you breathed—and find the place—myself—at night—if I (can) never forget that I am not with you—and that sorrow and frost are nearer than I—if I wish with a might I cannot repress—that mine were the Queen's place—the love of the Plantagenet[3] is my only apology—To come nearer than presbyteries[4]—and nearer than the new Coat—that the Tailor made—the prank of the Heart at play on the Heart—in holy Holiday—is forbidden me—You make me say it over—I fear you laugh—when I do not see—[but] "Chillon"[5] is not funny. Have you the Heart in your breast—Sir—is it set like mine—a little to the left—has it the misgiving—if it wake in the night—perchance—itself to it—a timbrel is it—itself to it a tune?

These things are [reverent] holy, Sir, I touch them [reverently] hallowed, but persons who pray—dare remark [our] "Father"! You say I do not tell you all—Daisy confessed—and denied not.

Vesuvius dont talk—Etna—dont—[Thy] one of them—said a syllable—a thousand years ago, and Pompeii heard it, and hid forever—[6] She could'nt look the world in the face, afterward—I suppose—Bashfull Pompeii! "Tell you of the want"—you know what a leech is, dont you—and [remember that] Daisy's arm is small—and you have felt the horizon hav'nt you—and did the sea—never come so close as to make you dance?

I dont know what you can do for it—thank you—Master—but if I had the Beard on my cheek—like you—and you—had Daisy's petals—and you cared so for me—what would become of you? Could you forget me in fight, or flight—or the foreign land? Could'nt Carlo,[7] and you and I walk in the meadows an hour—and nobody care but the Bobolink—and *his*—a *silver* scruple? I used to think when I died—I could see you—so I died as fast as I could—but the "Corporation"[8] are going Heaven too so [Eternity] wont be sequestered—now [at all]—Say I may wait for you—say I need go with no stranger to the to me—untried [country] fold—I waited a long time—Master—but I can wait more—wait till my hazel hair is dappled—and you carry the cane—then I can look at my watch—and if the Day is too far declined—we can take the chances [of] for Heaven—What would you do with me if I came "in white?"[9] Have you the little chest to put the Alive—in?

[3]The family name of a line of English sovereigns is used here perhaps as a generic term for royalty.

[4]Priests or ruling elders of a church.

[5]A castle prison in a poem by Lord Byron.

[6]Vesuvius and Etna are volcanoes in Italy and Sicily. Vesuvius, erupting, destroyed the town of Pompeii in the first century A.D.

[7]Dickinson's dog.

[8]Ruling elders, perhaps of a church.

[9]This may mean dressed in white, a color Dickinson associated with immortality. Late in her life she is said to have dressed exclusively in white. Or here she may be associating white with the paper on which she presented herself in letters and poems.

I want to see you more—Sir—than all I wish for in this world—and the wish—altered a little—will be my only one—for the skies.

Could you come to New England—[this summer—could] would you come to Amherst—Would you like to come—Master?

[Would it do harm—yet we both fear God—] Would Daisy disappoint you—no—she would'nt—Sir—it were comfort forever—just to look in your face, while you looked in mine—then I could play in the woods till Dark—till you take me where Sundown cannot find us—and the true keep coming—till the town is full. [Will you tell me if you will?]

I did'nt think to tell you, you did'nt come to me "in white," nor ever told me why,

No Rose, yet felt myself a'bloom,
No Bird—yet rode in Ether.

Letter 233

To Susan Gilbert Dickinson

date uncertain

Dear Sue—[1]

Your praise is good—to me—because I *know* it *knows*—and *suppose*—it *means*—

Could I make you and Austin—proud—sometime—a great way off—'twould give me taller feet—

Here is a crumb—for the "Ring dove"—and a spray for *his Nest,*[2] a little while ago—*just—"Sue."*

Emily.

Letter 238

To T.W. Higginson

15 April 1862

Mr Higginson,[1]

Are you too deeply occupied to say if my Verse is alive?

The Mind is so near itself—it cannot see, distinctly—and I have none to ask—

Should you think it breathed—and had you the leisure to tell me, I should feel quick gratitude—

[1]This note is part of an exchange of remarks about "Safe in their Alabaster Chambers," Poem 238. Susan seems to have suggested changes in the original version of the poem. After Dickinson sent the next version, Susan praised the first verse but wrote that she was still not suited with the second. So Dickinson sent a third version along with this note. The exchange reveals how exacting a critic Susan could be and how willing Dickinson was to please her.

[2]"Ring dove" was the term Susan had used for her new baby. Dickinson probably sent a "crumb" from her kitchen and a "spray" from her garden with the note.

[1]Dickinson wrote this unsigned letter to Higginson after reading his "Letter to a Young Contributor" in the *Atlantic Monthly,* April, 1862. She enclosed a card with her signature and four poems. The correspondence developed into a friendship which lasted a lifetime.

If I make the mistake—that you dared to tell me—would give me sincerer honor—toward you—

I enclose my name—asking you, if you please—Sir—to tell me what is true?

That you will not betray me—it is needless to ask—since Honor is it's own pawn—

Letter 260

To T.W. Higginson

25 April 1862

Mr Higginson,

Your kindness claimed earlier gratitude—but I was ill—and write today, from my pillow.

Thank you for the surgery[1]—it was not so painful as I supposed. I bring you others[2]—as you ask—though they might not differ—

While my thought is undressed—I can make the distinction, but when I put them in the Gown—they look alike, and numb.[3]

You asked how old I was? I made no verse—but one or two—until this winter—Sir—

I had a terror—since September—I could tell to none—and so I sing, as the Boy does by the Burying Ground—because I am afraid—[4]You inquire my Books—For Poets—I have Keats—and Mr and Mrs Browning. For Prose—Mr Ruskin—Sir Thomas Browne—and the Revelations.[5] I went to school—but in your manner of the phrase—had no education. When a little Girl, I had a friend, who taught me Immortality—but venturing too near, himself—he never returned—Soon after, my Tutor, died—and for several years, my Lexicon—was my only companion—Then I found one more—but he was not contented I be his scholar—so he left the Land.[6]

You ask of my Companions Hills—Sir—and the Sundown—and a Dog—large as myself, that my Father bought me—They are better than Beings—because they know—but do not tell—and the noise in the Pool, at Noon—excels my Piano. I have a Brother and Sister—My Mother does not care for thought—and Father, too busy with his Briefs[7]—to notice what we do—He buys me many Books—but begs me not to read them—because he fears they joggle the Mind. They are religious—except me—and address an Eclipse, every morning—whom they call their "Father."

[1]Perhaps cuts in poems suggested by Higginson.

[2]More poems.

[3]The imagery of "thought" "undressed" and "in the Gown" is unclear, but probably refers to Higginson's previous letter or to his "Letter to a Young Contributor."

[4]There has been much critical speculation on "the terror since September." Biographers have suggested a spiritual crisis, fear of blindness due to an acute eye problem, an emotional breakdown the result of abandonment by someone Dickinson loved. The exact nature of the "terror" cannot be determined.

[5]Dickinson lists five English writers: three nineteenth-century poets, a nineteenth-century art critic, a seventeenth-century prose writer; and the last book of the Bible.

[6]None of these—the "friend," the "Tutor," the one who "left the Land"—can be positively identified.

[7]Legal documents.

But I fear my story fatigues you—I would like to learn—Could you tell me how to grow—or is it unconveyed—like Melody—or Witchcraft?

You speak of Mr Whitman—I never read his Book—but was told that he was disgraceful—[8]

I read Miss Prescott's "Circumstance," but it followed me, in the Dark—so I avoided her—[9]

Two Editors of Journals came to my Father's House, this winter—and asked me for my Mind—and when I asked them "Why," they said I was penurious—and they, would use it for the World—[10]

I could not weigh myself—Myself—

My size felt small—to me—I read your Chapters in the Atlantic—and experienced honor for you—I was sure you would not reject a confiding question—

Is this—Sir—what you asked me to tell you?

Your friend,
E—Dickinson.

Letter 261

To T.W. Higginson

7 June 1862

Dear friend.

Your letter gave no Drunkenness, because I tasted Rum before—Domingo comes but once[1]—yet I have had few pleasures so deep as your opinion, and if I tried to thank you, my tears would block my tongue—

My dying Tutor told me that he would like to live till I had been a poet, but Death was much of Mob as I could master—then—And when far afterward—a sudden light on Orchards, or a new fashion in the wind troubled my attention—I felt a palsy, here—the Verses just relieve—

Your second letter surprised me, and for a moment, swung—I had not supposed it. Your first—gave no dishonor, because the True—are not ashamed—I thanked you for your justice—but could not drop the Bells whose jingling cooled my Tramp—Perhaps the Balm, seemed better, because you bled me, first.

I smile when you suggest that I delay "to publish"—that being foreign to my thought, as Firmament to Fin—

[8]Walt Whitman's *Leaves of Grass* was first published in 1855. Readers were shocked by the poet's descriptions of his passions and appetites. The innovative appearance of the poetry with its unconventional punctuation may have prompted Higginson to ask if Dickinson had read Whitman. He seems to be looking for stylistic influences.

[9]Harriet Prescott Spofford's "Circumstance," published in the *Atlantic Monthly* in May, 1860, is a terrifying story of a woman held hostage ". . . in a tree by a beast which is pacified only when she sings to him." See Volume 2 of this anthology.

[10]Dr. Holland and Samuel Bowles, both of the *Springfield Daily Republican,* appear to have urged Dickinson to publish. By this time, Bowles had published one of her poems, probably without her permission.

[1]Santo Domingo is the capital of the rum-producing Dominican Republic. Dickinson is saying that she had tasted praise before, and that the first taste is like no other.

If fame belonged to me, I could not escape her—if she did not, the longest day would pass me on the chase—and the approbation of my Dog, would forsake me—then—My Barefoot-Rank is better—

You think my gait "spasmodic"—I am in danger—Sir—

You think me "uncontrolled"[2]—I have no Tribunal.[3]

Would you have time to be the "friend" you should think I need? I have a little shape—it would not crowd your Desk—nor make much Racket as the Mouse, that dents your Galleries—

If I might bring you what I do—not so frequent to trouble you—and ask you if I told it clear—'twould be control, to me—

The Sailor cannot see the North—but knows the Needle[4] can—

The "hand you stretch me in the Dark," I put mine in, and turn away—I have no Saxon,[5] now—

As if I asked a common Alms,
And in my wondering hand
A Stranger pressed a Kingdom,
And I, bewildered, stand—
As if I asked the Orient[6]
Had it for me a Morn—
And it should lift it's purple Dikes,
And shatter me with Dawn!

But, will you be my Preceptor, Mr Higginson?

Your friend
E Dickinson—

Letter 265

To Samuel Bowles

early summer 1862

Dear friend—

You go away—and where you go, we cannot come[1]—but then the Months have names—and each one comes but once a year—and though it seems they never could, they sometimes do—go by.

We hope you are more well, than when you lived in America—and that those Foreign people are kind, and true, to you. We hope you recollect each life you left behind, even our's, the least—

[2]Dickinson is quoting Higginson who apparently was describing rhythms and phrasing in the poems.

[3]A position from which to judge herself and pronounce her own sentence. It is likely that Dickinson is being ironic. There is no indication that she ever adopted any of Higginson's suggested changes.

[4]Needle of a compass.

[5]The English language. Dickinson is saying that she has no words.

[6]The East.

[1]Samuel Bowles was travelling in Europe.

We wish we knew how Amherst looked, in your memory. Smaller than it did, maybe—and yet things swell, by leaving—if big in themselves—We hope you will not alter, but be the same we grieved for, when the "China" sailed.[2] If you should like to hear the news, we did not die—here—We did not change. We have the Guests we did, except yourself—and the Roses hang on the same stems—as before you went. Vinnie trains the Honeysuckle—and the Robins steal the string for Nests—quite, quite as they used to—I have the errand from my heart—I might forget to tell it. Would you please to come Home? The long life's years are scant, and fly away, the Bible says, like a told story—and sparing is a solemn thing, somehow, it seems to me—and I grope fast, with my fingers, for all out of my sight I own—to get it nearer—

I had one letter from Mary[3]—I think she tries to be patient—but you would'nt want her to succeed, would you, Mr Bowles?

It's fragrant news, to know they pine, when we are out of sight. . . .

Should anybody where you go, talk of Mrs. Browning,[4] you must hear for us—and if you touch her Grave, put one hand on the Head, for me—her unmentioned Mourner—

Father and Mother, and Vinnie, and Carlo, send their love to you, and warm wish for your health—and I am taking lessons in prayer, so to coax God to keep you safe—Good night—dear friend. You sleep so far, how can I know you hear?

Emily.

Letter 266

To T.W. Higginson

July 1862

Could you believe me—without? I had no portrait, now,[1] but am small, like the Wren, and my Hair is bold, like the Chestnut Bur—and my eyes, like the Sherry in the Glass, that the Guest leaves—Would this do just as well?

It often alarms Father—He says Death might occur, and he has Molds of all the rest—but has no Mold of me, but I noticed the Quick wore off those things, in a few days, and forestall the dishonor—You will think no caprice of me—

You said "Dark." I know the Butterfly—and the Lizard—and the Orchis—

Are not those *your* Countrymen?

I am happy to be your scholar, and will deserve the kindness, I cannot repay.

If you truly consent, I recite, now—

Will you tell me my fault, frankly as to yourself, for I had rather wince, than die. Men do not call the surgeon, to commend—the Bone, but to set it, Sir, and

[2]The name of the ship Bowles sailed on.

[3]Mary was Bowles's wife and a friend of Dickinson's.

[4]The poet Elizabeth Barrett Browning.

[1]Here, and in the following paragraph, she explains that she has no photograph of herself to send to Higginson. At age ten a portrait had been painted of the three Dickinson children, and when she was about sixteen, her daguerrotype was made, but, as she tells Higginson, she had never had a photograph taken. This appears to have been the case throughout her life since there are no verified photographs or portraits of Dickinson as an adult.

fracture within, is more critical. And for this, Preceptor, I shall bring you—Obedience—the Blossom from my Garden, and every gratitude I know. Perhaps you smile at me. I could not stop for that—My Business is Circumference—An ignorance, not of Customs, but if caught with the Dawn—or the Sunset see me—Myself the only Kangaroo among the Beauty, Sir, if you please, it afflicts me, and I thought that instruction would take it away.

Because you have much business, beside the growth of me—you will appoint, yourself, how often I shall come—without your inconvenience. And if at any time—you regret you received me, or I prove a different fabric to that you supposed—you must banish me—

When I state myself, as the Representative of the Verse—it does not mean—me—but a supposed person. . . .

To thank you, baffles me. Are you perfectly powerful? Had I a pleasure you had not, I could delight to bring it.

Your Scholar

Letter 268

To Mrs. J.G. Holland

early May 1866

Dear Sister,

After you went, a low wind warbled through the house like a spacious bird, making it high but lonely. When you had gone the love came. I supposed it would. The supper of the heart is when the guest has gone.

Shame is so intrinsic in a strong affection we must all experience Adam's reticence. I suppose the street that the lover travels is thenceforth divine, incapable of turnpike aims.

That you be with me annuls fear and I await Commencement[1] with merry resignation. Smaller than David you clothe me with extreme Goliath.

Friday I tasted life. It was a vast morsel. A circus passed the house—still I feel the red in my mind though the drums are out.

The book you mention, I have not met. Thank you for tenderness.

The lawn is full of south and the odors tangle, and I hear today for the first the river in the tree.

You mentioned spring's delaying—I blamed her for the opposite. I would eat evanescence slowly.

Vinnie is deeply afflicted in the death of her dappled cat, though I convince her it is immortal which assists her some. Mother resumes lettuce, involving my transgression—suggestive of yourself, however, which endears disgrace.

"House" is being "cleaned." I prefer pestilence. That is more classic and less fell. . . .

Emily.

Letter 318

[1]Commencement exercises at Amherst College.

To Susan Gilbert Dickinson

about 1870

Oh Matchless Earth—We underrate the chance to dwell in Thee

Letter 347

To Susan Gilbert Dickinson

about 1870

We meet no Stranger but Ourself.

Letter 348

To T.W. Higginson

1876

Nature is a Haunted House—but Art—a House that tries to be haunted.

Letter 459A

To Otis P. Lord [rough draft]

about 1878

My lovely Salem smiles at me I seek his Face so often—but I am past disguises (have dropped—) (have done with guises—)[1]

I confess that I love him—I rejoice that I love him—I thank the maker of Heaven and Earth that gave him me to love—the exultation floods me—I can not find my channel—The Creek turned Sea at thoughts of thee—will you punish it—[turn I] involuntary Bankruptcy as the Debtors say. Could that be a Crime—How could that be crime—Incarcerate me in yourself—that will punish me—Threading with you this lovely maze which is not Life or Death tho it has the intangibleness of one and the flush of the other waking for your sake on Day made magical with [before] you before I went to sleep—What pretty phrase—we went to sleep as if it were a country—let us make it one—we could (will) make it one, my native Land—my Darling come oh *be* a patriot now—Love is a patriot now Gave her life for its (its) country Has it meaning now—Oh nation of the soul thou hast thy freedom now

Letter 559

[1]Dickinson drafted letters as she did poems—writing several words or versions of a line or phrase, and then making a choice. This is a rough copy of a piece of a letter to Judge Otis Lord, a friend of the Dickinson family. Dickinson corresponded with Lord, who lived in Salem, Massachusetts, from about 1878 to his death in 1884. Her letters indicate that the two were in love with each other.

To Susan Gilbert Dickinson

about 1878

I must wait a few Days before seeing you—You are too momentous. But remember it is idolatry, not indifference.

Emily.

Letter 581

To Mrs. J. Howard Sweetser

November 1882

Dear Nellie,[1]

I cannot resist your sweet appeal, though the departure of our Mother is so bleak a surprise, we are both benumbed—for the Doctor assured us she was recovering and only the night before she died, she was happy and hungry and ate a little Supper I made her with such enthusiasm, I laughed with delight, and told her she was as hungry as Dick.[2]

Wondering with sorrow, how we could spare our lost Neighbors, our first Neighbor, our Mother, quietly stole away.

So unobtrusive was it, so utterly unexpected, that she almost died with Vinnie alone before one could be called. Amid these foreign Days the thought of you is homelike, for you were peculiarly gentle to her for whom service has ceased.

The last Token but one, on which her dear Eyes looked, was the Grapes from you. The very last, a little Bird, from thoughtful Mrs Hills.

Grapes and Birds, how typic, for was she not on her sweet way to a frostless Land?

Plundered of her dear face, we scarcely know each other, and feel as if wrestling with a Dream, waking would dispel.

Thank you for every sweetness to her and to us and please to thank your Husband for the lovely desire to honor her for the last time, and Alice and Nettie[3] too, for many a little Banquet she was indebted to them. Thank them with a Kiss.

I hope you are stronger than you were, and that all is safe in your unspeakable Home.

Oh, Vision of Language!

Emily.

Letter 782

[1]Nellie Sweetser was a friend to whom Dickinson often wrote in the later years of her life.

[2]Richard Matthews worked for the Dickinson family caring for the house, grounds, and stables.

[3]The Sweetser daughters.

To Otis P. Lord

3 December 1882

What if you are writing! Oh, for the power to look, yet were I there, I would not, except you invited me—reverence for each other being the sweet aim. I have written you, Dear, so many Notes since receiving one, it seems like writing a Note to the Sky—yearning and replyless—but Prayer has not an answer and yet how many pray! While others go to Church, I go to mine, for are not you my Church, and have we not a Hymn that no one knows but us?

I hope your "Thanksgiving" was not too lonely, though if it were *a little,* Affection must not be displeased.

Sue [? *name altered*][1] sent me a lovely Banquet of Fruit, which I sent to a dying Irish Girl in our neighborhood—That was my Thanksgiving. Those that die seem near me because I lose my own.

Not *all* my own, thank God, a darling "own" remains—more darling than I name.

The Month in which our Mother died, closed it's Drama Thursday, and I cannot conjecture a form of space without her timid face. Speaking to you as I feel, Dear, without that Dress of Spirit must be worn for most, Courage is quite changed.

Your Sorrow was in Winter—one of our's in June and the other, November, and my Clergyman passed from Earth in spring, but sorrow brings it's own chill. Seasons do not warm it. You said with loved timidity in asking me to your dear Home, you would "try not to make it unpleasant." So delicate a diffidence, how beautiful to see! I do not think a Girl extant has so divine a modesty.

You even call me to your Breast with apology! Of what must my poor Heart be made?

That the one for whom Modesty is felt, himself should feel it sweetest and ask his own with such a grace, is beloved reproach. The tender Priest of Hope need not allure his Offering—'tis on his Altar ere he asks. I hope you wear your Furs today. Those and the love of me, will keep you sweetly warm, though the Day is bitter. The love I feel for you, I mean, your own for me a treasure I still keep . . .[2]

Letter 790

To Susan Gilbert Dickinson

early October 1883

Dear Sue—

The Vision of Immortal Life has been fulfilled—[1]

How simply at the last the Fathom comes! The Passenger and not the Sea, we find surprises us—

[1]Members of Dickinson's family may have mutilated this letter in order to disguise a reference to Susan Dickinson.

[2]This letter, which breaks off here, was found among Dickinson's papers. It is unclear whether it was ever sent.

[1]Gilbert, Susan and Austin's youngest child, died of typhoid fever on October 5, 1883.

Gilbert rejoiced in Secrets—

His Life was panting with them—With what menace of Light he cried "Dont tell, Aunt Emily"! Now my ascended Playmate must instruct *me.* Show us, prattling Preceptor, but the way to thee!

He knew no niggard movement—His Life was full of Boon—The Playthings of the Dervish were not so wild as his—

No crescent was this Creature—He traveled from the Full—

Such soar, but never set—

I see him in the Star, and meet his sweet velocity in everything that flies—His Life was like the Bugle, which winds itself away, his Elegy an echo—his Requiem ecstasy—

Dawn and Meridian in one.

Wherefore would he wait, wronged only of Night, which he left for us—

Without a speculation, our little Ajax[2] spans the whole—

Pass to thy Rendezvous of Light,
Pangless except for us—
Who slowly ford the Mystery
Which thou hast leaped across!

Emily.

Letter 868

To Susan Gilbert Dickinson

about 1884

Morning[1]
might come
by Accident—
Sister—
Night comes
by Event—
To believe the
final line of
the Card[2] would
foreclose Faith—
Faith is *Doubt*—

Sister—
Show me

[2]A hero of Greek mythology known for his size and his courage.

[1]Because Thomas Johnson inaccurately represents margins, line breaks, and spaces between apparent stanzas, we reprint here an exact copy of the original manuscript of what can be seen as a letter-poem.

[2]"The final line of the Card" may refer to a standard Victorian greeting card or to a message written on a card. Or the card may be a playing card or a fortune-telling card. By metaphorical extension the "Card" may refer to the Bible.

Eternity—and
I will show
you Memory—
Both in one
package lain
And lifted
back again—

Be Sue—while
I am Emily—
Be next—what
you have ever
been—Infinity—

Letter 912

To T.W. Higginson

spring 1886

. . . Thank you for "the Sonnet"[1]—I have lain it at her loved feet.

Not knowing when Herself may come
I open every Door,
Or has she Feathers, like a Bird,
Or Billows, like a Shore—

I think she would rather have stayed with us, but perhaps she will learn the Customs of Heaven, as the Prisoner of Chillon[2] of Captivity.

You asked had I read "the Notices."[3]

. . . I have been very ill, Dear friend, since November, bereft of Book and Thought, by the Doctor's reproof, but begin to roam in my Room now—

I think of you with absent Affection, and the Wife and Child I never have seen, Legend and Love in one—

Audacity of Bliss, said Jacob to the Angel "I will not let thee go except I bless thee"—[4]Pugilist and Poet, Jacob was correct—

Your Scholar—

Letter 1042

[1]Dickinson is referring to a sonnet written by Higginson on the occasion of the death of a mutual friend, the writer Helen Hunt Jackson. Of Jackson's novel *Ramona,* Dickinson once wrote "Pity me . . . I have finished Ramona." The poem that follows, like Higginson's sonnet, honors Jackson.

[2]A reference to a poem by Lord Byron.

[3]She means the "notices" in the newspapers announcing Jackson's death. Here she is letting Higginson know that she has not only known of the death, but has felt it deeply.

[4]This line is an inversion of Jacob's words while wrestling with the angel: "I will not let thee go, except thou bless me" (Genesis 32:26). Here Dickinson blesses Higginson before she closes the letter.

Permissions Acknowledgments

John Adams. Pages 321–323, 419 from Vol. III and pages 36–37 from Vol. IV of *Diary and Autobiography of John Adams,* L. H. Butterfield, ed., Cambridge, Mass.: Harvard University Press, Copyright © 1961 by the Massachusetts Historical Society. Pages 121–123, 218 from *The Book of Abigail and John: Selected Letters of the Adams Family 1762–1784,* L. H. Butterfield, ed., Cambridge, Mass.: Harvard University Press, Copyright © 1975 by the Massachusetts Historical Society. Text from *The Spur of Fame: Dialogues of John Adams and Benjamin Rush, 1805–1813,* ed. John A. Schutz and Douglas Adair, 1966. Reprinted with the permission of the Henry E. Huntington Library.

Anti-Federalist Paper from *The Complete Anti-Federalist,* ed. Herbert J. Storing, 1981. Reprinted by permission of University of Chicago Press.

Elizabeth Ashbridge. Shea, Daniel B., ed. "Some Account of the Fore Part of the Life of Elizabeth Ashbridge" from Andrews, William L. *Journeys in New Worlds: Early American Women's Narrative.* Copyright 1990. Reprinted by permission of the University of Wisconsin Press.

Aztec "Two Songs" from *Grammatical Examples, Exercises, and Review, for Use with "Rules of the Aztec Language,"* Salt Lake City: University of Utah, 1973, translated by Arthur J. O. Anderson. Permission granted by University of Utah Press.

William Bradford. From *Of Plymouth Plantation 1620–1647,* edited by Samuel Eliot Morison. Copyright 1952 by Samuel Eliot Morison & renewed 1980 by Emily M. Beck. Reprinted by permission of Alfred A. Knopf, Inc.

Mary Boykin Chesnut. From *Mary Chesnut's Civil War* edited by C. Vann Woodward, copyright © by Yale University Press. Reprinted by permission of the publisher.

Chief Seattle. "Speech" (1855) from *Indian Oratory: Famous Speeches by Noted Indian Chieftans,* ed. W. C. Vanderwerth. Copyright © 1971 by the University of Oklahoma Press.

Columbus. From *The Four Voyages of Christopher Columbus* edited and translated by J. M. Cohen (Penguin Classics, 1969) copyright © J. M. Cohen, 1969. Reprinted by permission of Penguin Books Ltd.

Emily Dickinson. From *The Complete Poems of Emily Dickinson* by T. H. Johnson. Copyright 1929, 1935 by Martha Dickinson Bianchi; copyright © renewed 1957, 1963 by Mary L. Hampson. By permission of Little, Brown and Company. Poems are reprinted by permission of the publishers and the Trustees of Amherst College from *The Poems of Emily Dickinson,* Thomas H. Johnson, ed., Cambridge, Mass: The Belknap Press of Harvard University Press. Copyright 1951, © 1955, 1979, 1983 by the President and Fellows of Harvard College. Additional poems are from *The Complete Poems of Emily Dickinson,* edited by Thomas H. Johnson, Copyright 1914, 1929, 1935, 1942 by Martha Dickinson Bianchi; © renewed 1957, 1963 by Mary L. Hampson. Letters are reprinted by permission of the publishers from *The Letters of Emily Dickinson,* edited by Thomas H. Johnson, Cambridge, Mass. The Belknap Press of Harvard University Press, Copyright © 1958, 1986 by the President and Fellows of Harvard College. Poem #1072, from *Life and Letters of Emily Dickinson,* edited by Martha Dickinson Bianchi. Copyright 1924 by Martha Dickinson Bianchi, © renewed 1952 by Alfred Leete Hampson. Reprinted by permission of Houghton Mifflin Company. All rights reserved.

Eskimo Poems. Reprinted from *Eskimo Poems from Canada and Greenland,* translated by Tom Lowenstein. Copyright © 1973 by Tom Lowenstein. Reprinted by permission of the translator.

Federalist Papers. No. 6 and No. 10, copyright © 1961 by Wesleyan University. Reprinted from *The Federalist* edited by Jacob E. Cooke by permission of University of New England Press.

Fanny Fern. From *Ruth Hall and Other Writings by Fanny Fern,* ed. Joyce W. Warren. Copyright © 1986 by Rutgers, The State University. Reprinted by permission of Rutgers University Press.

Benjamin Franklin. Text from *The Papers of Benjamin Franklin* are copyright © 1959, 1961, 1963, 1964, 1967, 1976, 1988 by the American Philosophical Society and Yale University. All rights reserved.

Lemuel Haynes. From *Black Preacher to White America: The Collected Writings of Lemuel Haynes, 1774–1833*, ed. Richard Newman, 1990. Reprinted by permission of the Carlson Publishing Company.

Herman Melville. *Billy Budd, Sailor*, edited by Harrison Hayford and Merton M. Sealts, Jr. Copyright © 1962. Reprinted by permission of the University of Chicago Press and the editors.

Mexican-American Oral Tale. "The Devil Woman" told by Flo Sais in Artell Dorman, "Speak of the Devil" in *And Horns on the Toads*, Publications of the Texas Folklore Society Number XXIX, 1959. Reprinted by permission.

Francisco Palou. Text from *Palou's Life of Junípero Serra*, translated and edited by Maynard J. Geiger, 1955. Used with permission of the Academy of American Franciscan History.

Parker Papers. "Iroquois, or the Confederacy of the Five Nations" (Seneca, Ely S. Parker). Reprinted by permission of the Buffalo and Erie County Historical Society.

Gaspar Pérez de Villagrá. From *Historia de la Nueva Mexico* by Gaspar Pérez de Villagrá, edited and translated by Miguel Encinias, Alfred Rodriguez, and Joseph P. Sanchez. Copyright © 1992. Reprinted by permission of The University of New Mexico Press.

Mary Rowlandson. From *Held Captive by Indians: Selected Narratives, 1642–1836*, edited by Richard VanDerBeets. Copyright © 1973 by The University of Tennessee Press. Reprinted by permission of The University of Tennessee Press.

Samuel Sewall. Excerpts from *The Diary of Samuel Sewall: 1674–1729* edited by M. Halsey Thomas. Copyright © 1973 by Farrar, Straus & Giroux, Inc. Reprinted by permission of Farrar, Straus & Giroux, Inc.

Anna Young Smith. "A Song," reprinted by permission of Dickinson College Library.

Tales. From *Cuentos: Tales from the Hispanic Southwest* selected by Jose Griego y Maestas, retold in English by Rudolfo A. Anaya, Copyright © 1980 Museum of New Mexico Press. Reprinted with permission.

Edward Taylor. Poems from *The Poems of Edward Taylor*, edited by Donald E. Stanford, Yale University Press, 1960. Copyright © 1960, 1988 by Donald E. Stanford. Reprinted by permission.

Edward Taylor. Reprinted with permission of Twayne Publishers, an imprint of Simon & Schuster Macmillan, from *Edward Taylor's Minor Poetry*, edited by Thomas M. Davis and Virginia L. Davis. Copyright © 1981 by G. K. Hall & Co.

Henry David Thoreau. "Resistance to Civil Government" and "A Plea for Captain John Brown" from *The Writings of Henry D. Thoreau: Reform Papers*, edited by Wendell Glick. Copyright © 1973 by Princeton University Press. Excerpts, pp. 63–90 and pp. 111–138. *Walden: The Writings of Henry D. Thoreau*, edited by J. Lyndon Shanley. Copyright © 1971 by Princeton University Press. Excerpts, pp. 81–98, 210–222, 299–319, 320–333. Reprinted with permission of Princeton University Press.

David Walker. Excerpts from *One Continual Cry: David Walker's Appeal to the Colored Citizens of the World*, 1965. Reprinted by permission of Dr. Herbert Aptheker.

James R. Walker. Reprinted from *Lakota Belief and Ritual*, by James R. Walker, edited by Raymond J. DeMallie and Elaine A. Jahner, by permission of the University of Nebraska Press. Copyright © 1980, 1991, by the University of Nebraska Press.

Mercy Otis Warren. "A Thought on the Inestimable Blessing of Reason . . ." poem reprinted Courtesy Massachusetts Historical Society.

Michael Wigglesworth. From *The Poems of Michael Wigglesworth*, edited by Ronald A. Bosco, 1989, and published by the University Press of America.

Roger Williams. Text reprinted with the permission of Scribner, a Division of Simon & Schuster from *The Complete Writings of Roger Williams* by Roger Williams, edited by Perry Miller (Russell & Russell, NY, 1963). Text reprinted with the permission of Scribner, a Division of Simon & Schuster from *A Key into the Language of America* by Roger Williams, edited with Preface and Notes by J. Hammond Trumbell, edited with introduction by Howard M. Chapin (Russell & Russell, NY,

1973). From *The Complete Writings of Roger Williams* from *A Key into the Language of America*. Reprinted by permission of Russell and Russell Publishers. Reprinted from *The Correspondence of Roger Williams, Vol. II, 1654–1682*, edited by Glenn LaFantasie by permission of the University Press of New England. Copyright © 1988 by the Rhode Island Historical Society.

John Winthrop. Text from *A Modell of Christian Charity*, and "Winthrop's Christian Experience," entries from *The Journal of John Winthrop*, Courtesy Massachusetts Historical Society.

John Woolman. Text from *The Journal and Major Essays of John Woolman,* edited by Phillips P. Moulton, copyright holder, published 1971 by Oxford University Press. Reprinted by permission.

Index of Authors, Titles, and First Lines of Poems